Readers' Guide to
Periodical Literature®
2017

READERS' GUIDE TO
PERIODICAL LITERATURE®

Cumulated Volumes

READERS' GUIDE TO PERIODICAL LITERATURE®

2017

An Author and Subject Index

Volume 77

H. W. Wilson
A Division of EBSCO Information Services
Ipswich, Massachusetts
2017
GREY HOUSE PUBLISHING
PRINTED IN CANADA

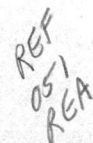

Readers' Guide to Periodical Literature, 2017, published by Grey House Publishing, Inc., Amenia, NY, under exclusive license from EBSCO Information Services, Inc.

International Standard Serial Number 0034-0464

International Standard Book Number
978-1-68217-465-4

Library of Congress Catalog Card Number 6-8232

PRINTED IN CANADA

PREFATORY NOTE

The READERS' GUIDE TO PERIODICAL LITERATURE® is a cumulative author-subject index to English language periodicals of general interest.

The main body of the Index consists of subject and author entries to periodical articles arranged in one alphabet. In addition there is a listing of citations to book reviews following the main body of the Index.

Suggestions for addition or deletion of titles should be brought to the attention of H. W. Wilson, 10 Estes Street, Ipswich, MA 01938.

This volume includes indexing from October 8, 2016— October 20, 2017. It supersedes the paper issues of Readers' Guide for March 2017 (Vol. 117 No. 1) through September 2017 (Vol. 117 No. 3).

SUGGESTIONS FOR THE USE OF THE READERS' GUIDE TO PERIODICAL LITERATURE®

Arrangement

Authors and subjects are arranged in one alphabet. Subjects beginning with numbers appear before those beginning with letter A. Under authors and subjects, titles are arranged in alphabetical order by the first word, initial articles being disregarded. Subjects with subdivisions are captured as new subject headings in alphabetical order.

Author entries

Articles are indexed under the last name of the author, with the exception that author entries may be omitted for staff writers. The author's name always appears as part of the citation under the subject entry.

Book reviews

For citations to reviews of individual books, see book review section following the main body of the Index.

Choreographic Works

Choreographic works (ballet and modern dance) are indexed under the title of the work. Entries may also be made for the choreographer, the dance type (e.g. Ballet), the individual dancers and the dance company, as appropriate.

Cross-References

See references are made from variant forms of subject headings and personal names to the form used in READERS' GUIDE. *See also* references are made from a subject to related subjects under which additional material may be found.

Fiction

Fiction is indexed under the heading "Fiction." Specific titles are indexed using the author's name and the title of the work.

Movies

Movies are indexed under the title of the film. They may be indexed with a topical heading such as "Motion pictures—Reviews" or a narrower term such as "Documentary films—Reviews." Entries may also be made for the director and actors, as appropriate.

Operas and Operettas

Operas and operettas are indexed under the title of the work. Entries may also be made for topical headings (e.g. "Opera"), composers, singers, performers and for the opera company, as appropriate.

Performances

Articles about live musicals, musical performances, revues or theatrical performances that do not belong to other defined categories may be indexed under the composer, performer, or performing group, as appropriate.. Additional topical headings may include "Concerts," "Entertainment events," "Music—Performance," or the type of music, such as "Jazz —Reviews."

Poems

Poems are indexed under the topical heading "Poems," the title of the poem, and the author. Poetry criticisms are indexed under the headings "Poetry (Literary form)—History & criticism," the title of the poem, and the author.

Product Reviews

Product reviews are indexed under the subject headings that describes the product followed by the subdivision "Evaluation," e.g. "Automobiles—Evaluation." Additional headings may include the brand of the product followed by the subdivision "Evaluation," e.g. "Honda Civic automobile —Evaluation, the name of the manufacturer, or the heading "Commercial products—Evaluation."

Radio Programs

Radio programs are indexed under the the topical heading "Radio programs." Entries may also be made for the title of the program, or the subject of the program.

Sound Recordings

Sound (music) recordings are generally indexed under the title of the music, the name of the performer, and the type of music followed by the subdivision "Review" (e.g. Jazz— Reviews.)

Television Programs

Television programs are indexed under the title of the program, as well as the heading "Television programs— Reviews" or a narrower term such as "Reality television programs—Reviews." Entries may also include actor names, as appropriate.

Theater

EP creates headings for Broadway-level/professional theatrical productions. Performances of plays are indexed under "Theater—Reviews." Entries may be made for actors, dramatists, directors, or the theater company, as appropriate.

Video Recording Reviews

Reviews of video recordings or DVD recordings of movies, TV shows, or concerts are indexed under the title of the recording and appropriate headings such as "DVD-Video discs —Reviews," "Video recordings—Reviews," or "Blu-ray discs—Reviews."

SAMPLE ENTRIES

Periodical entry: **Social behavior in animals**
Male Bonding [Cover story] C. O'Connell-Rodwell
il *Smithsonian* v41 no7 p50-9 N 2010

Explanation: An article on the subject "Social behavior in animals" entitled "Male Bonding", and written by C. O'Connell-Rodwell. The phrase "Cover story" has been added by the indexer. Square brackets are used to indicate these editorial interpolations. The article is illustrated. It appears in *Smithsonian*, volume 41, issue number 7 on pages 50 through 59 of the November 2010 issue.

Full forms of authors' names will be found in the author entry.

Book review: **Harris, R.** Dreyfus. 2010
The Nation v291 no12 p33 S 20 2010 J. Palattella

Explanation: A review of a book by R. Harris entitled "Dreyfus", and published in 2010. The review appears in *The Nation*, volume 291, issue number 12 on page 33 of the September 20 2010 issue. The author of the review is J. Palattella.

ABBREVIATIONS

+	continued on later pages of same issue	Ltd	Limited
		m	monthly
Ag	August	Mr	March
ann	annual	My	May
Ap	April		
Assn	Association	N	November
Aut	Autumn	no	number
Ave	Avenue		
		O	October
bi-m	bimonthly		
bi-w	biweekly	p	page
bibl	bibliography	por	portrait
bibl f	bibliographical footnotes	pt	part
bldg	building		
		q	quarterly
Co	Company		
cont	continued	rev	revised
Corp	Corporation		
		S	September
D	December	semi-m	semimonthly
Dept	Department	Spr	Spring
		Sr	Senior
ed	edited, edition, editor	St	Street
		Summ	Summer
F	February	supp	supplement
f	footnotes		
		tab	table
il	illustration,-s	tr	translated, translation, translator
Inc	Incorporated		
introd	introduction, introductory		
		v	volume
Ja	January		
Je	June	w	weekly
Jl	July	Wint	Winter
Jr	Junior		
jt auth	joint author	yr	year

PERIODICALS INDEXED

A

AARP The Magazine. bi-m ISSN (1548-2014) American Association of Retired Persons, 601 E St. NW, Washington, DC 20049
> Merger of AARP Modern Maturity (1538-5981) and My Generation with v. 46, no. 2 (March-April 2003)

Ad Astra. q ISSN (1041-102X) National Space Society, 600 Pennsylvania Ave., SE, Washington, DC 20003-4316

Advocate (Los Angeles, Calif.). m ISSN (0001-8996) Regent Media, 10960 Wilshire Blvd., Suite 1050 Los Angeles, CA 90024

AJR. See American Journalism Review

Alternatives Journal. bi-m ISSN (1205-7398) Alternatives Inc., University of Waterloo, Waterloo, Ontario N2L 3G1, Canada

Amazing Wellness. 6 times a yr Active Interest Media, 300 Continental Boulevard, Suite 650, El Segundo, CA 90245

Amber Waves. q ISSN (1545-8741) U.S. Department of Agriculture, Economic Research Service, 5285 Port Royal Road, Springfield, VA 22161

America. w (except occasional bi-w issues) ISSN (0002-7049) America Press Inc., 106 W. 56th St., New York, NY 10019

American Artist. m ISSN (0002-7375) Aspire Media, Interweave Press, Inc., 201 E. Fourth Street, Loveland, CO 80537

The American Conservative. m ISSN (1540-966X) American Conservative LLC, 1300 Wilson Blvd., Ste. 120, Arlington, VA 22209 US

American Cowboy. bi-m ISSN (1079-3690) Active Interest Media, 300 Continental Boulevard, Suite 650, El Segundo, CA 90245

American Craft. bi-m ISSN (0194-8008) American Craft Council, Dept. AC, P.O. Box 3000, Denville, NJ 07834

American Forests. q ISSN (0002-8541) American Forestry Association, P.O. Box 2000, Washington, DC 20013

The American Geographical Society's Focus on Geography. q ISSN (1549-4934) American Geographical Society, 120 Wall St., Ste. 100, New York, NY 10005-3904
> Formerly Focus (New York, N.Y.: 1950); name changed with Vol. 46, No. 3 (Summer 2001)

American Heritage. q ISSN (0002-8738) American Heritage Publishing, 416 Hungerford Drive, Suite 216, Rockville, MD 20850-4127
> Temporarily ceased publication with Vol. 58, No. 2 (April/May 2007); resumed publication with Vol. 58, No. 3 (Winter 2008).

American History. bi-m ISSN (1076-8866) American History, P.O. Box 8200, Harrisburg, PA 17105-8200

American Journalism Review. 5 times a yr ISSN (1067-8654) American Journalism Review, Subscription Dept., P.O. Box 561, Mount Morris, IL 61054

The American Scholar. q ISSN (0003-0937) The American Scholar, Editorial and Circulation Offices, 1606 New Hampshire Ave., NW, Washington, DC 20009

The American Spectator. m ISSN (0148-8414) American Spectator, 2020 N. 14th St., Ste. 750, Arlington, VA 22201

Américas. 6 times a yr ISSN (0379-0940) Americas, P.O. Box 3000, Denville, NJ 07834-3000

Antiques. See The Magazine Antiques (1971)

Antiques & Collecting Magazine. m ISSN (1084-0818) Antiques & Collecting Magazine, Circulation Dept., 1006 S. Michigan Ave., Chicago, IL 60605
> Formerly Antiques & Collecting Hobbies; name changed with October 1993. Name changed to Treasures with Vol. 1, No. 1 (July 2011).

Arabian Horse World. m ISSN (0003-7494) Active Interest Media, 300 Continental Boulevard, Suite 650, El Segundo, CA 90245

Archaeology. bi-m ISSN (0003-8113) Archaeology Subscription Service, P.O. Box 469025, Escondido, CA 92046-9025

Architectural Digest. m ISSN (0003-8520) Architectural Digest, P.O. Box 59061, Boulder, CO 80322-9061

Architectural Record. m ISSN (0003-858X) Architectural Record, P.O. Box 566, Hightstown, NJ 08520

Arizona Highways. m ISSN (0004-1521) Arizona Highways, 2039 W. Lewis Ave., Phoenix, AZ 85009

Art in America. m ISSN (0004-3214) Art in America, P.O. Box 37003, Boone, IA 50037-0003

Art News. See ARTnews

Arthur Frommer's Budget Travel. m (bi-m D/Ja, Jl/Ag) ISSN (1521-5210) Newsweek Budget Travel Inc.

ARTnews. m (except Ag) ISSN (0004-3273) ARTnews Associates, Subscription Service, P.O. Box 56590, Boulder, CO 80322-6590

Arts & Crafts Homes and the Revival. q ISSN (1559-6117) Active Interest Media, 300 Continental Boulevard, Suite 650, El Segundo, CA 90245

Arts Education Policy Review. q ISSN (1063-2913) Taylor & Francis Group, LLC, 325 Chestnut St, Ste 800, Philadelphia, PA 19106

Astronomy. m ISSN (0091-6358) Astronomy, 21027 Crossroads Circle, P.O. Box 1612, Waukesha, WI 53187-9950

Atlanta Magazine. m ISSN (0004-6701) Emmis Broadcasting Corp., 1330 W. Peachtree St, Ste. 400, Atlanta, GA 30309

Atlantic Monthly (1993). m (bi-m Ja/F and Jl/Ag) ISSN (1072-7825) Atlantic Subscription Processing Center, Box 52661, Boulder, CO 80322

Audubon. 6 times a yr ISSN (0097-7136) National Audubon Society, Membership Data Center, P.O. Box 52529, Boulder, CO 80322
> Formerly Audubon Magazine; name changed with v. 63, no. 4 (July/August 1961)

B

Baby Talk. 10 times a yr ISSN (1092-1869) Bonnier Corporation, 460 N. Orlando Ave., Suite 200, Winter Park, FL 32789

BabyTalk. See Baby Talk

Backpacker. 9 times a yr ISSN (0277-867X) Active Interest Media, 300 Continental Boulevard, Suite 650, El Segundo, CA 90245

Better Homes and Gardens. m ISSN (0006-0151) Better Homes and Gardens, Customer Service, P.O. Box 37449, Boone, IA 50037-0449

Better Nutrition – 12/yr (monthly) ISSN: (0405-668X) Active Interest Media, Inc. 2520 55th Street Suite 210 Boulder CO 80301-5736 http://www.aimmedia.com/

Bicycling. 11 times a yr ISSN (0006-2073) Rodale Inc., 33 E. Minor St., Emmaus, PA 18098 Absorbed Mountain Bike with Vol. 52, No. 1 (January/February 2011).

Bike Magazine. 8 times a yr ISSN (1072-4869) Source Interlink Magazines, LLC, 831 S. Douglas Street, El Segundo, CA 90245

BioScience. m ISSN (0006-3568) University of California Press, 2000 Ctr St, Ste 303, Berkeley, CA 94704

Black Belt. m ISSN (0277-3066) Active Interest Media, 300 Continental Boulevard, Suite 650, El Segundo, CA 90245

Black Enterprise. m ISSN (0006-4165) Black Enterprise, Circulation Service Center, P.O. Box 3009, Harlan, IA 51537-4100

Bloomberg Business Week. See Business Week

Bloomberg Businessweek. See Business Week

Boating World. 8 times a yr ISSN (1059-5155) Duncan McIntosh Company, Inc., 17782 Cowan, Ste. A, Irvine, CA 92614 Absorbed Go Boating with November/December 2008.

Bon Appétit. m ISSN (0006-6990) Bon Appetit, P.O. Box 59191, Boulder, CO 80322

Bridges. q Community Affairs, Federal Reserve Bank of St. Louis, P.O. Box 442, St. Louis, MO 63166-0442

The Bulletin of the Atomic Scientists. bi-m ISSN (0096-3402) Sage Publications, Inc., 2455 Teller Rd., Thousand Oaks, CA 91320
> Ceased publication in print with Vol. 65, No. 1 (January/February 2009). Electronic resource

Business Week. w ISSN (0007-7135) Business Week, P.O. Box 430, Hightstown, NJ 08520

BusinessWeek. See Business Week

C

Canadian Geographic. bi-m ISSN (0706-2168) Royal Canadian Geographic Society, 39 McArthur Ave., Vanier, Ont. K1L 8L7, Canada

Canadian Wildlife. 6 times a yr ISSN (1201-673X) Canadian Wildlife Federation, 350 Michael Cowpland Drive, Kanata, ON K2M 2W1

Canoe & Kayak. bi-m ISSN (1077-3258) Source Interlink Magazines, LLC, 831 S. Douglas Street, El Segundo, CA 90245

Car and Driver. m ISSN (0008-6002) Car and Driver, P.O. Box

52906, Boulder, CO 80322-2906

Catnip. m ISSN (1069-6687) Tufts Media, 196 Boston Avenue, Suite 2100, Medford, MA 02155

Change. bi-m ISSN (0009-1383) Taylor & Francis Group, LLC, Mortimer House, 37-41 Mortimer Street, London, W1T 3JH.

Chicago (1975). m ISSN (0362-4595) PRIMEDIA Consumer Media and Magazine Group, 500 N. Dearborn St., Chicago, IL 60610-4901

Chicago Magazine. See Chicago (1975)

The Christian Century. 14 times a yr ISSN (0009-5281) Christian Century Subscription Service, 407 S. Dearborn St., Chicago, IL 60605-1150

Christianity Today. m (semi-m Ap, O) ISSN (0009-5753) Christianity Today Subscription Services, P.O. Box 37059, Boone, IA 50037-0059

Cincinnati Magazine. m ISSN (0746-8210) Emmis Broadcasting Corp., 705 Central Ave., Ste. 370, Cincinnati, OH 45202

Claremont Review of Books. q ISSN (1554-0839) Claremont Institute for the Study of Statesmanship and Political Philosophy, 937 West Foothill Boulevard, Suite E, Claremont, CA 91711

Climbing. 10 times a yr ISSN (0045-7159) Active Interest Media, 300 Continental Boulevard, Suite 650, El Segundo, CA 90245

Columbia Journalism Review. bi-m ISSN (0010-194X) Columbia Journalism Review, Subscription Service Dept., P.O. Box 578, Mt. Morris, IL 61054

Commentary. m ISSN (0010-2601) Commentary, Inc., 165 East 56th Street, New York, N.Y. 10022

Common Ground (Washington, D.C.). q ISSN (1087-9889) National Park Service, U.S. Department of the Interior, National Center for Cultural Resources, 1849 C Street NW (2251), Washington, DC 20240-0001

Commonweal. bi-w (except Christmas/New Year's; m in Jl, Ag) ISSN (0010-3330) Commonweal Foundation, 475 Riverside Dr., Room 405, New York, NY 10115

Condé Nast Traveler. m ISSN (0893-9683) Conde Nast Traveler, Box 57018, Boulder, CO 80322-7018

Congressional Digest. m (except Jl, Ag) ISSN (0010-5899) Congressional Digest Corp., 3231 P St., N.W., Washington, DC 20007

Consumer Reports. m ISSN (0010-7174) Subscription Director, Consumer Reports, P.O. Box 53029, Boulder, CO 80322

Country's Best Cabins. bi-m ISSN (2157-0183) Active Interest Media, 300 Continental Boulevard, Suite 650, El Segundo, CA 90245 Preceding Title: Country's Best Log Homes, 1089-3466

Crisis (Baltimore, Md.: 2003). q ISSN (1559-1573) Crisis Publishing Co., 4805 Mt Hope Dr, Baltimore, MD 21215 US
     Formerly The New Crisis; name changed with Vol. 110, No. 3 (May/June 2003).

Current Biography. m (except D) ISSN (0011-3344) The H.W. Wilson Co., 950 University Ave., Bronx, NY 10452

Current Events. 23 times per sch yr ISSN (0011-3492) The Weekly Reader, 3001 Cindel Drive, Delran, NJ 08075

Current Health Teens. 8 times a yr Weekly Reader Corporation, 3001 Cindel Dr, PO Box 8037, Delran, NJ 08075
     Formerly Current Health 2; name changed with Vol. 37, No. 1 (September 2010).

Current History (New York, N.Y.: 1941). m (except Je, Jl, Ag) ISSN (0011-3530) Current History, 4225 Main St., Philadelphia, PA 19127

Current Science. bi-w (except Je, Jl, Ag, & Christmas) ISSN (0011-3905) Weekly Reader Corporation, Secondary Periodicals, 3001 Cindel Dr., Delran, NJ 08075

Current (Washington, D.C.). m (bi-m Mr/Ap, Jl/Ag) ISSN (0011-3131) Taylor & Francis Group, LLC, Routledge, 325 Chestnut St, Ste 800, Philadelphia, PA 19106

Cycle World. m ISSN (0011-4286) Cycle World, P.O. Box 53170, Boulder, CO 80323-1222

D

D. m ISSN (0164-8292) Magazine Limited Partners LP, 4311 Oak Lawn Avenue, Suite 100, Dallas, TX 75219

Daedalus. q ISSN (0011-5266) MIT Press Journals, 55 Hayward St, Cambridge, MA 02142 US

Dallas Fort Worth. See D

Dance Magazine. m ISSN (0011-6009) Dance Magazine, 333 7th Avenue, 11th Floor, New York, NY

Dirt Sports. See Dirtsports

Dirtsports. m ISSN (1553-7633) Ryan Communications Group

Discover. m ISSN (0274-7529) Discover, P.O. Box 420105, Palm Coast, FL 32142-0105

Discover Horses. ann ISSN (1558-1837) Active Interest Media, 300 Continental Boulevard, Suite 650, El Segundo, CA 90245

Down Beat. m ISSN (0012-5768) Down Beat, P.O. Box 906, Elmhurst, IL 60126-0906

Dressage Today. m ISSN (1079-1167) Active Interest Media, 300 Continental Boulevard, Suite 650, El Segundo, CA 90245

E

E Magazine. See E: the Environmental Magazine

E: the Environmental Magazine. bi-m ISSN (1046-8021) E Magazine, Subscription Dept., P.O. Box 2047, Marion, OH 43306

Ebony. m ISSN (0012-9011) Ebony, 820 S. Michigan Ave., Chicago, IL 60605

Economic Indicators. m ISSN (0013-0125) U.S. Government Printing Office, For sale by the Superintendent of Documents, Washington, D.C. 20402

EconSouth. q ISSN (0899-6571) Federal Reserve Bank of Atlanta, 1000 Peachtree St NE, Atlanta, GA 30309

The Education Digest. m (S-My) ISSN (0013-127X) Prakken Publications, Inc., 3970 Varsity Dr., P.O. Box 8623, Ann Arbor, MI 48107-8623

Entertainment Weekly. w ISSN (1049-0434) Entertainment Weekly Inc., 1675 Broadway, 29th floor, New York, NY 10019

Environment. bi-m ISSN (0013-9157) Taylor & Francis Inc., 325 Chestnut St, Ste 800, Philadelphia, PA 19106

Equus. m ISSN (0149-0672) Active Interest Media, 300 Continental Boulevard, Suite 650, El Segundo, CA 90245

Esquire. m ISSN (0194-9535) Esquire Subscriptions, P.O. Box 7146, Red Oak, IA 51591

Essence. m ISSN (0014-0880) Essence, P.O. Box 53400, Boulder, CO 80322-3400

Extra! m ISSN (0895-2310) FAIR (Fairness & Accuracy in Reporting, Inc.), 112 West 27th Street, New York, NY 10001-6240

F

The Family Handyman. m (bi-m Jl/Ag, D/Ja) ISSN (0014-7230) Family Handyman, Subscription Service Dept., Box 5232, Harlan, IA 51593-0732

Field & Stream (2002). m ISSN (8755-8599) Bonnier Corporation, 460 N. Orlando Ave., Suite 200, Winter Park, FL 32789
     Formerly Field & Stream (Northeast ed.); name changed with v. 106, no. 12 (April 2002)

Film Comment. bi-m ISSN (0015-119X) Film Comment, P.O. Box 3000, Denville, NJ 07834-9925

Film Quarterly. q ISSN (0015-1386) University of California Press, 2120 Berkeley Way, Berkeley, CA 94720

Flying. m ISSN (0015-4806) Bonnier Corporation, 460 N. Orlando Ave., Suite 200, Winter Park, FL 32789

Focus on Geography. See The American Geographical Society's Focus on Geography

Forbes. bi-w (except semi-m in Je, Jl and 2 weeks in O) ISSN (0015-6914) Forbes Subscriber Service, P.O. Box 5471, Harlan, IA 51593-0971

Foreign Affairs. bi-m ISSN (0015-7120) Foreign Affairs, P.O. Box 420235, Palm Coast, FL 32142-0235

Foreign Policy. bi-m ISSN (0015-7228) Foreign Policy, 1779 Massachusetts Ave., NW, Washington, DC 20036

Fortune. bi-w (combined issues in Ag, S, & at year-end) ISSN (0015-8259) Fortune, P.O. Box 30604, Tampa, FL 33630-0604

The Futurist. bi-m ISSN (0016-3317) World Future Society, 7910 Woodmont Ave., Ste. 450, Bethesda, MD 20897-1405

G

Gentlemen's Quarterly. m ISSN (0016-6979) Gentlemen's Quarterly, Box 53816, Boulder, CO 80322

Glamour. m ISSN (0017-0747) Glamour, P.O. Box 37690, Boone, IA 50037-0690 Incorporating: Mademoiselle

Golf Magazine. m ISSN (1056-5493) Golf Magazine, P.O. Box 53733, Boulder, CO 80322-3733

Good Housekeeping. m ISSN (0017-209X) Good Housekeeping, P.O. Box 7186, Red Oak, IA 51591-0186

S

Sail. m ISSN (0036-2700) Source Interlink Magazines, LLC, 831 S. Douglas Street, El Segundo, CA 90245

The Saturday Evening Post. bi-m ISSN (0048-9239) Saturday Evening Post Subscription Offices, P.O. Box 420235, Palm Coast, FL 32142-1235

Scholastic Choices. m (S-My, bi-m N/D) ISSN (0883-475X) Scholastic Inc., 555 Broadway, New York, NY 10012-3999

Science. w (except last week in D) ISSN (0036-8075) American Association for the Advancement of Science, P.O. Box 1811, Danbury, CT 06813-1811

Science & Technology Review. 8 times a yr ISSN (1092-3055) University of California, Lawrence Livermore National Security LLC, 7000 East Ave, PO Box 808, Livermore, CA 94551-0808

Science News. bi-w ISSN (0036-8423) Science News, Subscription Dept., P.O. Box 1925, Marion, OH 43305

Scientific American. m ISSN (0036-8733) Scientific American, 75 Varick Street, NY, NY 10013-1917

Sea. m ISSN (0746-8601) Duncan McIntosh Company, Inc., 17782 Cowan, Ste. A, Irvine, CA 92614

Seventeen. m ISSN (0037-301X) Seventeen Subscription Dept., Box 55195, Boulder, CO 80322-5195

Sierra. bi-m ISSN (0161-7362) Sierra Club, 85 Second St., San Francisco, CA 94105

Skateboarder. 6 times a yr ISSN (1535-2889) Source Interlink Magazines, LLC, 831 S. Douglas Street, El Segundo, CA 90245

Skeptical Inquirer. bi-m ISSN (0194-6730) Skeptical Inquirer, Box 703, Amherst, NY 14226-0703

Sky and Telescope. m ISSN (0037-6604) Sky Publishing Corp., 49 Bay State Rd., Cambridge, MA 02138

Smart Computing. m ISSN (1093-4170) Sandhills Publishing, 120 W. Harvest Dr., P.O. Box 85380, Lincoln, NE 68501

Smithsonian. m ISSN (0037-7333) Smithsonian, P.O. Box 420311, Palm Coast, FL 32142-0311

Snow Boarder. 8 times a yr ISSN (1046-0403) Source Interlink Magazines, LLC, 831 S. Douglas Street, El Segundo, CA 90245

Society. bi-m ISSN (0147-2011) Springer SMB B.V, van Godewijckstraat 30, 3311GX Dordrecht, The Netherlands

Sound & Vision. 10 times a yr ISSN (1537-5838) Bonnier Corporation, 460 N. Orlando Ave., Suite 200, Winter Park, FL 32789
     Formerly Stereo Review's Sound & Vision; name changed with February/March 2001

South Dakota Magazine. bi-m ISSN (0886-2680) South Dakota Magazine, 410 E Third St, Yankton, SD 57078-0175

Southern Living. m ISSN (0038-4305) Southern Living, P.O. Box 523, Birmingham, AL 35201 Southeast edition indexed

Spin to Win Rodeo. m ISSN (1096-9772) Active Interest Media, 300 Continental Boulevard, Suite 650, El Segundo, CA 90245

Successful Farming. m (semi-m F, Mr, bi-m My/Je, Jl/Ag) ISSN (0039-4432) Successful Farming, Customer Service, P.O. Box 55165, Boulder, CO 80322-5165

Sunset. m ISSN (0039-5404) Sunset Magazine, Box 2040, Harlan, IA 51593-0003

Surfer. m ISSN (0039-6036) Source Interlink Magazines, LLC, 831 S. Douglas Street, El Segundo, CA 90245

Surfing. m ISSN (0194-9314) Source Interlink Magazines, LLC, 831 S. Douglas Street, El Segundo, CA 90245

T

Technology Review (Cambridge, Mass.: 1998). 6 times a yr ISSN (1099-274X) Technology Review, MIT Building W59, 201 Vassar St., Cambridge, MA 02139

Tennis. m (bi-m Jl/Ag, D/Ja) ISSN (0040-3423) Tennis, P.O. Box 2039, Harlan, IA 51537

Texas Monthly. m ISSN (0148-7736) Texas Monthly, Subscription Service Center, P.O. Box 7090, Red Oak, IA 51591-0090

Timber Home Living. bi-m ISSN (1073-6654) Active Interest Media, 300 Continental Boulevard, Suite 650, El Segundo, CA 90245

Time. w ISSN (0040-781X) Time, P.O. Box 30601, Tampa, FL 33630-0601

Trail Rider. m ISSN (1530-9657) Active Interest Media, 300 Continental Boulevard, Suite 650, El Segundo, CA 90245

Tricycle. q ISSN (1055-484X) The Buddhist Ray, Inc., 92 Vandam St., New York, NY 10013

Tufts University Health & Nutrition Letter. m ISSN (1526-0143) Tufts Media, 196 Boston Avenue, Suite 2100, Medford, MA 02155

TV Guide. w ISSN (0039-8543) TV Guide, Box 400, Radnor, PA 19088

U

U.S. Catholic. m ISSN (0041-7548) U.S. Catholic, 205 W. Monroe St., Chicago, IL 60606

UN Chronicle. q ISSN (0251-7329) United Nations Publications, Room DC2-0853, Dept. 502, United Nations, New York, NY 10017

Urban Climber Magazine. 8 times a yr ISSN (1943-8370) Active Interest Media, 300 Continental Boulevard, Suite 650, El Segundo, CA 90245

USA Today (Periodical). m ISSN (0161-7389) The Society for the Advancement of Education, 99 W. Hawthorne Ave., Valley Stream, NY 11580

Utne. bi-m ISSN (1544-2225) Utne, P.O. Box 7460, Red Oak, IA 51591-0460
     Formerly Utne Reader; name changed with no. 114 (November-December 2002)

Utne Reader. See Utne

V

Vanity Fair. m ISSN (0733-8899) Vanity Fair, Box 53516, Boulder, CO 80322

Vegetarian Journal. q ISSN (0885-7636) Vegetarian Resource Group, PO Box 1463, Baltimore, MD 21203

Vegetarian Times. m ISSN (0164-8497) Active Interest Media, 300 Continental Boulevard, Suite 650, El Segundo, CA 90245

Virginia Living. bi-m ISSN (1534-9984) Cape Fear Publishing, 109 East Cary Street, Richmond, VA 23219

Vital Speeches of the Day. m ISSN (0042-742X) City News Publishing Co., 389 Jonnie Dodd Blvd., Ste. C, Box 1247, Mount Pleasant, SC 29465

Vogue. m ISSN (0042-8000) Vogue, Box 55980, Boulder, CO 80322

Volleyball. m ISSN (1058-4668) Madavor Media, LLC, 420 Boylston Street, Boston, MA 02116

W

The Walrus. 10 times a yr ISSN (1708-4032) The Walrus Foundation, 19 Duncan St., Suite 101, Toronto, ON M5H 3H1, Canada

The Washington Monthly. m (bi-m Ja/F, Jl/Ag) ISSN (0043-0633) Washington Monthly, 1611 Connecticut Ave. NW, Washington, DC 20009

Washingtonian. m ISSN (0043-0897) Washingtonian Subscription Service, P.O. Box 58897, Boulder, CO 80322-8897

Weatherwise. bi-m ISSN (0043-1672) Heldref Publications, Taylor & Francis Group, 325 Chestnut Street, Suite 800, Philadelphia, PA

Weekly Standard. w ISSN (1083-3013) Weekly Standard, 1150 17th St. N.W., Suite 505, Washington, DC 20036-4617

The Wilson Quarterly. q ISSN (0363-3276) The Wilson Quarterly, P.O. Box 420406, Palm Coast, FL 32142-0406

Wired. m ISSN (1059-1028) Conde Nast Publications Inc., 520 Third St., 4th Floor, San Francisco, CA 94107-1815

Women's Basketball. bi-m ISSN (1524-9204) Goldman Publishing, 4125 Gunn Hwy., Suite B1, Tampa, FL 33618 Publication temporarily suspended after Vol. 9, No. 1 (January/February 2009).

Women's Health. m ISSN (0884-7355) Rodale Inc., 33 East Minor Street, Emmaus, PA 18098-0099

Working Mother. m (bi-m D/Ja, Jl/Ag) ISSN (0278-193X) Working Mother Media Inc., 60 E 42nd St., 27th Fl, New York, NY 10165 US

The Writer. m ISSN (0043-9517) The Writer, Inc., 120 Boylston St., Boston, MA 02116-4615

Y

Yankee. 6 times a yr ISSN (0044-0191) Yankee, P.O. Box 37017, Boone, IA 50037-0017

Yoga Journal. 7 times a yr ISSN (0191-0965) Active Interest Media, 300 Continental Boulevard, Suite 650, El Segundo, CA 90245

Your Dog. m ISSN (1078-0343) Tufts Media, 196 Boston Avenue, Suite 2100, Medford, MA 02155

READERS' GUIDE

2017

Je 23 2017

Corey Hawkins Takes the Lead in 24: Legacy L. CROSS color *Ebony* v72 no4 p39 F 2017

Racing the Clock In the ISIS Era D. D'addario color *Time* v188 no27-28 p108 D 26 2016

Sufficient unto the Day J. LILEKS *National Review* v69 no4 p33 Mr 6 2017

Tick... Tick... BOOM! [Cover story] M. ROFFMAN *TV Guide* v65 no6 p20 Ja 30 2017

What to Watch R. Rahman, J. Jensen et al color *Entertainment Weekly* no1462 p57 Ap 21 2017

24k Magic (Music)

Bruno Mars N. Feeney color *Entertainment Weekly* no1441 p55 N 25 2016

The Must List color *Entertainment Weekly* no1441 p2 N 25 2016

2XU Pty. Ltd.

Leggings for Days G. Porcaro color *Women's Health* v14 no2 p72 Mr 2017

3-D computer games

Quern - Undying Thoughts: The closest we may ever come to a Riven sequel H. DINGMAN color *PCWorld* p120 Mr 2017

3-D printers

GEARHEAD: STEAM POWER L. STINSON color *Wired* v25 no9 p46 S 2017

3-D television

3D TV Is Dead K. C. POHLMANN *Sound & Vision* v82 no5 p21 Je 2017

3 Percent (TV program)

BINGE C. Agard color *Entertainment Weekly* no1449 p51 Ja 20 2017

301/302 (Film)

FINDING MOONLIGHT J. McGovern color *Entertainment Weekly* no1436/1437 p83 O 21 2016

360-degree feedback (Rating of employees)

Responding to Feedback You Disagree With S. Heen and D. Goldstein *Harvard Business Review Digital Articles* p2 Ap 14 2017

We Like Leaders Who Underrate Themselves J. Zenger and J. Folkman *Harvard Business Review Digital Articles* p2 N 10 2015

360fly Inc.

Power Play: Amplify your next adventure with these cutting-edge outdoor gadgets R. HORJUS color *Backpacker* p45 S 2017

3G Capital Inc.—Officials & employees

BUY. SQUEEZE. REPEAT [Cover story] G. Colvin chart color *Fortune* v175 no2 p74 F 1 2017

3M Co.

HOLI DAY STAIN Guide [Cover story] C. FORTÉ color *Good Housekeeping* v263 no6 p89 D 2016

WHEN 3M BOUGHT INTO THE ANKLE MONITOR BUSINESS, IT ACQUIRED TROUBLE L. ETTER bw color diag graph *Bloomberg Businessweek* no4518 p44 Ap 10 2017

3rd Battle of Ypres, Ieper, Belgium, 1917

FORLORN VICTORY [Cover story] R. Soodalter bw color map *Military History* v34 no4 p38 N 2017

SAVING LIVES ON THE FRONT LINE C. E. Hallett *History Today* v67 no7 p24 Jl 2017

3WW (Music)

The Playlist color *Rolling Stone* no1284 p10 Ap 6 2017

3x1 NYC LLC

The Thousand-Dollar Pair of Jeans J. MOORE color *GQ: Gentlemen's Quarterly* v87 no1 p9 Ja 2017

401(k) plan administrative fees

Low-Fee 401(k) Choices Are Hiding in Plain Sight E. O'Brien color diag *Money* v46 no6 p25 Jl 2017

401(k) plans

401(k) Interrupted A. EBELING color *Forbes* v199 no1 p58 Ja 24 2017

5 WAYS YOUR 401(K) IS HELPING YOU SAVE BETTER P. Wang color diag *Money* v46 no1 p78 Ja/F 2017

Blueprint for Retirement *Forbes* v199 no2 p89 F 28 2017

Break the Cycle of Recurring Fees M. CROSS cartoon *Kiplinger's Personal Finance* v71 no1 p31 Ja 2017

How to Get Good Advice J. Bodnar *Kiplinger's Personal Finance* v71 no5 p6 My 2017

How to Save If You Don't Have a 401(k) S. BLOCK chart color *Kiplinger's Personal Finance* v71 no1 p24 Ja 2017

The New Retirement [Cover story] T. Stanger color *Consumer Reports* v82 no1 p22 Ja 2017

Private Equity Is Eyeing Your Nest Egg M. Mittelman *Bloomberg Businessweek* no4519 p47 Ap 24 2017

Roll Your Money Into an IRA? S. BLOCK color *Kiplinger's Personal Finance* v71 no5 p38 My 2017

Turning Pennsylvania N. BENEFIELD and G. ALEXANDER color *Weekly Standard* v22 no13 p22 D 5 2016

You're Retiring. Should Your Savings Move On Too? E. O'Brien color diag *Money* v46 no4 p23 My 2017

401(k) plans—Charts, diagrams, etc.

401(k) Nation: Who's Left Out B. Steverman color *Bloomberg Businessweek* no4540 p49 O 2 2017

4:44 (Music)

BEY AND JAY'S DOUBLE DEBUT M. Vain chart color *Entertainment Weekly* no1472 p12 Je 30 2017

47 Meters Down (Film)

47 METERS DOWN C. Holub color *Entertainment Weekly* no1463/1464 p57 Ap/My 2017

47 Ronin, The (Film)

Site Lines R. Brody color *New Yorker* v92 no39 p17 N 28 2016

50 (Music)

In the Rick of Time C. Collis color *Entertainment Weekly* no1435 p36 O 14 2016

50 North Yachts (Company)

Fairline Squadron 48 *Sea Magazine* v108 no12 p52 D 2016

Jeanneau NC795 *Sea Magazine* v108 no12 p53 D 2016

Monte Carlo Yachts MCY70 *Sea Magazine* v108 no12 p50 D 2016

50 Shades Darker (Music)

Fifty Shades' Top 40 Freakfest N. Feeney color *Entertainment Weekly* no1453 p56 F 17 2017

If There's Pain In Fifty Shades, There's Pleasure In Its Soundtrack S. Lansky color *Time* v189 no6 p52 F 20 2017

508 Software LLC

DISK DRILL 3: MAC UTILITY NOW RECOVERS DATA FROM iOS DEVICES, TOO J. R. BOOKWALTER cartoon color *Macworld - Digital Edition* p26 D 2016

529 plans

EMPLOYERS HELP WITH COLLEGE SAVING K. PITSKER color *Kiplinger's Personal Finance* v71 no5 p13 My 2017

53rd Street (Music)

53rd Street J. Hale color *Downbeat* v84 no2 p79 F 2017

53T Courier (Company)

RIDE ALONG A. BRANDT *Cincinnati Magazine* v50 no7 p25 Ap 2017

57th & Ninth (Music)

Sting Makes a Surprise Return to Rock & Roll J. DOLAN color *Rolling Stone* no1274 p58 N 17 2016

Sting's Rock & Roll Salvation S. RODRICK bw color *Rolling Stone* no1276 p48 D 15 2016

5G (Telecommunication)

The Greatest Generation Is Around the Corner O. Kharif and S. Moritz chart color *Bloomberg Businessweek* no4512 p41 F 20 2017

The Inelegant Beginnings of a Dazzling New Wireless Technology E. Woyke bw color *MIT Technology Review* v120 no3 p94 My/Je 2017

REMEMBER NOKIA? D. Bennett and K. Pohjanpalo color *Bloomberg Businessweek* no4529 p66 Jl 3 2017

5G (Telecommunication)—Equipment & supplies

The Inelegant Beginnings of a Dazzling New Wireless Technology E. Woyke bw color *MIT Technology Review* v120 no3 p94 My/Je 2017

5K races (Running)

SECOND CHANCE [Cover story] J. Galloway cartoon *Runner's World* v52 no5 p24 Je 2017

YOU CAN FLY! C. KUZMA chart color *Runner's World* v52 no5 p18 Je 2017

60 Minutes (TV program)

America's Most Watched 25 TOP SHOWS *TV Guide* v65 no39 p16 S 18 2017

SALUTE THE OLD GUARD D. Bianculli *TV Guide* v65 no31 p10 Jl 24 2017

THEIR FINEST HOURS J. FAGER bw color *Vanity Fair* v59 no10 p192 O 2017

History v125 no5 p30 My 2017

Abbey Road Studios (London, England)

That Magic Feeling J. ROSEN bw *National Review* v69 no17 p19 S 11 2017

Abbeys—Scotland

Take a Few Days in the Scottish Borders color *British Heritage Travel* v38 no5 p20 S/O 2017

Abbington, Amanda, 1974-

Sherlock Shocker: Her Last Bow J. Hibberd color *Entertainment Weekly* no1448 p13 Ja 13 2017

Abbink, Peter

Rapid development of a DNA vaccine for Zika virus bibl graph *Science* v354 no6309 p237 O 14 2016

ABBONDANZA, KATIE

City Bountiful *Sierra* v102 no2 p60 Mr/Ap 2017

Abbott, Alina

COMMENT color *Canadian Geographic* v137 no1 p72 F 2017

Abbott, Alysia

LOVE BEYOND GENDER *Psychology Today* v49 no5 p72 S/O 2016

The Nonconformists *New York Times Book Review* p14 O 16 2016

Abbott, Betty

NEBRASKA Female Pioneers bw color *Nebraska Life* v20 no6 p19 N/D 2016

Abbott, Carl

The next New York bibl color *Science* v355 no6330 p1135 Mr 17 2017

Abbott, Carrie

Eat Praline Love *Indianapolis Monthly* v40 no5 p35 Ja 2017

Abbott, Christmas

The Badass Life: 30 Amazing Days to a Lifetime of Great Habits—Body, Mind, and Spirit *Publishers Weekly* v264 no16 p63 Ap 17 2017

ABBOTT, CLIFTON

MOUNT LEMMON *Arizona Highways* v93 no6 p42 Je 2017

Abbott, Greg, 1957-

THE PLEASE *Texas Monthly* v45 no2 p88 F 2017

Putting the Constitution Up for Sale J. HIGHTOWER cartoon *Progressive* v81 no2 p46 F 2017

Taken for a Ride M. HEMINGWAY color *Weekly Standard* v22 no41 p14 Jl 3 2017

Abbott, Jack Henry, 1944-2002

Killer Celebrities P. TERZIAN bw *Weekly Standard* v23 no6 p19 O 16 2017

Abbott, Jeff

Keep Out! How the U.S. Is Militarizing Mexico's Southern Border color *Progressive* v81 no7 p40 O/N 2017

Mexico's Uprising Against Education 'Reform' color *Progressive* v81 no2 p24 F 2017

Abbott, Karen

PRESENTERS *South Dakota Magazine* p14 S/O 2017 Supplement

ABBOTT, MEGAN

BULLISH ON BOOKS L. Martin *Virginia Living* v15 no3 p27 Ap 2017

Dreamers and Schemers: In Colin Harrison's thriller, noir has a complicated relationship with nostalgia *New York Times Book Review* p17 Je 18 2017

Abbott, Monica, 1985-

The Case for ... Monica Abbott K. Mckinney and T. Keith color *Sports Illustrated* v126 no18 p22 Je 26 2017

Abbott Healthcare (Company)

100 BEST COMPANIES 2017 chart color graph *Working Mother* v40 no4 p30 O/N 2017

Abbott Nutrition Manufacturing Inc.

Pedialyte D. Brooks color *New York Times Magazine* p22 Ja 29 2017

Abboud, Dennis

Readerlink Rules J. Milliot *Publishers Weekly* v263 no40 p5 O 3 2016

Abboud, Joseph

TRUE-BLUE WINNERS E. Moody, M. Ozawa et al color *Martha Stewart Living* no271 p76 Ja/F 2017

AbbVie Inc.

Guarding Big Pharma's Crown Jewel C. Koons *Bloomberg Businessweek* no4537 p17 S 11 2017

Abby Lee Dance Co.

Dance Moms *TV Guide* v65 no43 p33 O 16 2017

ABC Carpet & Home (Company)

Resources color *House Beautiful* v159 no9 p110 N 2017

Abdallah, Jad

Guanine glycation repair by DJ-1/Park7 and its bacterial homologs chart color diag graph *Science* v357 no6347 p208 Jl 14 2017

ABDELKADER, ENGY

Islamophobia in Focus *Islamic Horizons* v46 no1 p32 Ja/F 2017

The Way to Hope and Guidance: Muslims have the Quran to lead them toward success *Islamic Horizons* v46 no4 p30 Jl/Ag 2017

Abdel-Samed, Noor

How Consumer Brands Can Connect with Customers in a Changing Retail Landscape *Harvard Business Review Digital Articles* p2 Ag 4 2017

Abdo, Geneive

The New Sectarianism: The Arab Uprisings and the Rebirth of the Shi'a-Sunni Divide J. Waterbury *Foreign Affairs* v95 no6 p189 N/D 2016

Understanding Middle Eastern Tumult *South Dakota Magazine* p11 S/O 2017 Supplement

Abdo, Hind

miR-183 cluster scales mechanical pain sensitivity by regulating basal and neuropathic pain genes diag graph *Science* v356 no6343 p1168 Je 16 2017

Multipotent peripheral glial cells generate neuroendocrine cells of the adrenal medulla color *Science* v357 no6346 p46 Jl 7 2017

Abdominal abnormalities

EASE GAS WITH HERBS K. P. S. Khalsa color *Amazing Wellness* v9 no6 p40 EarlyWint 2017

Abdominal exercises

Abs Made Easy A. COSGROVE color *Men's Health* v32 no5 p50 Je 2017

CARRIE'S FLAT-BELLY SECRET color *Health* v31 no5 p13 Je 2017

CRAWL FOR A KILLER CORE color *Health* v31 no4 p12 My 2017

FINALLY, FLAT ABS! color *Health* v30 no10 p16 D 2016

A New Way to Attack Your Six-Pack L. SCHULER cartoon color *Men's Health* v32 no5 p47 Je 2017

POWER UP YOUR CORE R. S. Frazier color *Health* v31 no7 p128 S 2017

Tone up while watching TV color *Redbook* p70 Jl/Ag 2017

Your Ab Flab Challenges, Solved! M. Masters color *Health* v31 no4 p41 My 2017

Abdominal muscles

AB-SOLUTELY CENTERED A. Forrest color *Yoga Journal* p50 2017 Special Issue

FINALLY, FLAT ABS! color *Health* v30 no10 p16 D 2016

HARD CORE J. Crandell color *Yoga Journal* p48 2017 Special Issue

IN THIS SECTION color *Yoga Journal* p40 2017 Special Issue

JIFFY MOVES S. ROUNTREE color *Runner's World* v52 no8 p22 S 2017

Poses of the month [Cover story] J. Schumacher color *Yoga Journal* no289 p37 F 2017

TAP YOUR CORE POWER SOURCE C. Brown and H. Dowdle color *Yoga Journal* p42 2017 Special Issue

Your Ab Flab Challenges, Solved! M. Masters color *Health* v31 no4 p41 My 2017

Abdominal pain

See also

Colic

EAT, DRINK, AND BE SPEEDY A. MACMILLAN and J. GALLOWAY color *Runner's World* v52 no9 p16 O 2017

IS YOUR CHILD SICK OR JUST FAKING IT? D. L. Hill color *Parents* v92 no9 p34 S 2017

Tough or Stupid? M. REMY color *Runner's World* v52 no9 p52 O 2017

Abdominal pain—Patients

A college student experienced stomach pain and vomiting that quickly devolved into something much worse. No one could figure out the problem - until it was too late L. Sanders *New York Times Magazine* p24 Ap 30 2017

Abdominal pain—Prevention

Heal Your Gut [Cover story] L. Turner color *Better Nutrition* v79 no11 p68 N 2017

Abdominal pain—Treatment
Hot-Water Bottles C. Tattoli *New York Times Magazine* p20 Ja 22 2017

Abdominal physiology
POWER UP YOUR CORE R. S. Frazier color *Health* v31 no7 p128 S 2017

Abdoolcarim, Zoher
Leaders color *Time* v189 no16/17 p64 My 1-8 2017
The Negotiator color *Time* v189 no18 p40 My 15 2017

Abdool Karim, Quarraisha
Vaginal bacteria modify HIV tenofovir microbicide efficacy in African women chart graph *Science* v356 no6341 p938 Je 1 2017

Abdool Karim, Salim S.
Vaginal bacteria modify HIV tenofovir microbicide efficacy in African women chart graph *Science* v356 no6341 p938 Je 1 2017

Abduction
> *See also*
> Child abduction

Stopping A Kidnapper A. JUNG color *Reader's Digest* v189 no1131 p8 Je 2017

Abduction From the Seraglio, The (Theatrical production)
CLASSICAL MUSIC *New Yorker* v93 no22 p8 Jl 31 2017

Abduction—Law & legislation
Another Abduction by North Korea? D. P. HALPIN *Weekly Standard* v22 no6 p12 O 17 2016

Abdulhamid II, Sultan of the Turks, 1842-1918
From Abdulhamid II to Ataturk: Change or Continuity in Turkey's History M. GÖKÇEK *Islamic Horizons* v46 no3 p54 My/Je 2017

ABDUL-JABBAR, KAREEM
Matters of Faith *New York Times Book Review* p10 Ja 15 2017
The Year in Reading [Cover story] *New York Times Book Review* p8 D 25 2016

Abdul-Jabbar, Kareem, 1947-—Awards
The Activist Minds W. Lowery color *Sports Illustrated* v125 no20 p52 D 19 2016

Abdul-Jabbar, Kareem, 1947-—Interviews
Kareem Abdul-Jabbar: The basketball star and author of 'Coach Wooden and Me' says he looks forward to anything written by Walter Mosley: 'I'd be very happy if he wrote a novel every week' *New York Times Book Review* p11 Je 4 2017

ABDULLAH, MOHAMMAD
Halal from Farm to Fork: To build trust, the halal meat certification system needs a tune-up *Islamic Horizons* v46 no3 p32 My/Je 2017

ABDULLAH, UMBERINE
Allies All Around Us *Islamic Horizons* v46 no2 p38 Mr/Ap 2017
In Arms Sales We Trust *Islamic Horizons* v46 no1 p58 Ja/F 2017
Muslim Women March with the Mainstream *Islamic Horizons* v46 no2 p45 Mr/Ap 2017

Abdulmajid, Iman
I Am Iman bw color *Vogue* v207 no9 p302 S 2017

ABDUL-SALAAM, OSAMA
Hope & Guidance through the Quran: The ISNA convention will show attendees how to apply the Quran's lessons today *Islamic Horizons* v46 no4 p26 Jl/Ag 2017

Abdurraqib, Hanif
They Can't Kill Us Until They Kill Us: Essays *Publishers Weekly* v264 no33 p62 Ag 14 2017

Abe, Junichi
Junichi ABE C. KELSEY *Interview* v47 no1 p32 F 2017

Abe, Shinzō, 1954-
Abe Tries To Polish His Tarnished Image I. Reynolds color *Bloomberg Businessweek* no4534 p30 Ag 14 2017
America Last M. JANCER *Car & Driver* v62 no11 p94 My 2017
NEW OPPORTUNITY UNDER THE ABE ADMINISTRATION M. Foster and D. W. Russell color *Forbes* v199 no1 p(Sp)1 Ja 24 2017
Sorry, Brits: Abe and Trump Have the Real 'Special Relationship' I. Bremmer *Time* v189 no7/8 p18 F 27 2017
WE MUST NEVER REPEAT THE HORRORS OF WAR AGAIN *Vital Speeches of the Day* v83 no2 p47 F 2017
What's Behind Shinzo Abe's Plummeting Popularity C. Campbell color *Time* v190 no6 p9 Ag 7 2017

Abebe, Nitsuh
Apocalypse Now *New York Times Magazine* p11 O 8 2017
Elvis, outside of Flagstaff/Driving a camper van/Looking for meaning in a cloud mass/Sees the face of Joseph Stalin/And is disheartened *New York Times Magazine* p15 Jl 23 2017
THE MUSIC ISSUE color *New York Times Magazine* p16 Mr 12 2017
New Sentences *New York Times Magazine* p16 My 21 2017
Panic Attack *New York Times Magazine* p13 Ap 23 2017
Power Games *New York Times Magazine* p11 Je 25 2017
QUIET PLACES *New York Times Magazine* p36 D 25 2016

Abedi, Salman
The Known Wolf D. GREEN color *Weekly Standard* v22 no38 p20 Je 12 2017

Abegg, Jenny
The Givers color *Climbing* no355 p52 Ag 2017

Abel, Allen
Admission is free. Exit is not bw color *Maclean's* v129 no40 p36 O 10 2016
America's loss color *Maclean's* v129 no40 p32 O 10 2016
Are you a spy? color *Maclean's* v130 no7 p46 Ag 2017
A border runs through it color *Maclean's* v130 no7 p15 Ag 2017
The Cassini-Huygens space probe [Cover story] color *Maclean's* v129 no51/52 p74 D 26 2016
Commander in confusion [Cover story] color *Maclean's* v129 no51/52 p40 D 26 2016
COULD THIS GET ANY WORSE? color *Maclean's* v129 no41 p30 O 17 2016
Dreams of Canada [Cover story] color *Maclean's* v130 no6 p28 Jl 2017
FATHER ISSUES color *Maclean's* p40 Je 2017
THE FORGOTTEN HABS bw color *Maclean's* v130 no10 p122 N 2017
It ain't over for Trump color *Maclean's* v129 no42 p41 O 24 2016
Mourning in America color *Maclean's* v129 no47 p37 N 28 2016
Obama's broken legacy color *Maclean's* no1 p36 F 17 2017
The people for Donald Trump color *Maclean's* v129 no46 p42 N 21 2016
PLOT OF GOLD color *Maclean's* v130 no10 p40 N 2017
THE RETURN OF THE CZAR [Cover story] bw color *Maclean's* v130 no3 p40 Ap 2017
The swamp creatures color *Maclean's* v129 no48/49 p24 D 5 2016
THERE'S ONLY ONE PRESIDENT CLINTON color *Maclean's* v129 no45 p36 N 14 2016
The victory lap color *Maclean's* v129 no43 p37 O 31 2016
WHO REALLY KILLED JFK? bw color *Maclean's* v129 no51/52 p42 D 26 2016
World War What? color *Maclean's* v130 no4 p44 My 2017

ABEL, ANN
A Fresh Slice of Orange County color *Forbes* v198 no8 p106 D 20 2016
The Haute Bungalow color *Forbes* v199 no5 p118 My 16 2017
THE SPIRIT OF '17 color *Forbes* v199 no2 p66 F 28 2017

ABEL, JANICE A.
The Perfect Tree *Idaho Magazine* v16 no3 p20 D 2016

Abel, Jessica
DIY Self-Help R. SALKOWITZ color *Publishers Weekly* v264 no31 p38 Jl 31 2017

Abel, Jon
How America Lost Its Mind color *Atlantic* v320 no4 p12 N 2017

Abel, Martin G.
TOP DENTISTS *Washingtonian Magazine* v52 no6 p106 Mr 2017

Abell, George O.
George Abell's Ethereal Bubbles S. Gottlieb *Sky & Telescope* v134 no1 p34 Jl 2017

Abelson, Max
'Chairman Cohn' Has a Nice Ring to It color graph *Bloomberg Businessweek* no4533 p32 Ag 7 2017
FINANCE graph *Bloomberg Businessweek* no4532 p25 Jl 31 2017
Five Stages of Trump Grief *Bloomberg Businessweek* no4501 p32 N 28 2016
Long Shots That May Pay Off Big bw *Bloomberg Businessweek* no4499 p23 N 14 2016
MAN OF THE (VERY RICH) PEOPLE [Cover story] color *Bloomberg Businessweek* no4509 p38 Ja 30 2017
Obama Goes From the White House To Wall Street *Bloomberg*

STREET SCENES J. ACOCELLA cartoon *New Yorker* v92 no43 p74 Ja 2 2017

Abraham, Magid

Augmented Reality Is Already Improving Worker Performance *Harvard Business Review Digital Articles* p2 Mr 13 2017

ABRAHAMIAN, ATOSSA ARAXIA

BEFORE THE BAN bw color *New Republic* v248 no4 p26 Ap 2017

COSMOPOLITAN POP color *Nation* v33 no21 p20 N 21 2016

DEBT IS NOT THE END color *Nation* v304 no16 p12 My 22 2017

INTERNATIONAL TERRITORY color *Nation* v305 no11 p48 O 30 2017

Abraham.In.Motion (Company)

A COMPANY IN MOTION K. SCHWAB *Dance Magazine* v91 no8 p26 Ag 2017

Abrahams, Robin

How to Survive a Company Scandal You Had Nothing to Do With *Harvard Business Review Digital Articles* p2 Ag 31 2016

ABRAHAMSON, JAKE

Yellowstone 2.0 *Sierra* v101 no4 p36 Jl/Ag 2016

Abrahms, Max

Why People Keep Saying, "That's What the Terrorists Want" *Harvard Business Review Digital Articles* p2 N 20 2015

ABRAMCYK, NADINE

42 new ALL-STAR PRODUCTS of the year [Cover story] color *Redbook* p27 Jl/Ag 2017

Abramczyk, Dariusz

Deep functional analysis of synII, a 770-kilobase synthetic yeast chromosome diag *Science* v355 no6329 p1047 Mr 10 2017

Abramović, Marina, 1946-

All of Her R. SYME *New Republic* v247 no11 p56 N 2016

ART IN THE EXTREME F. PROSE color *New York Times Book Review* p72 D 4 2016

Marina ABRAMOVIĆ A. LENNOX color *Vanity Fair* v58 no11 p154 N 2016

Marina Abramovic at 70 C. Swanson img *New York* v49 no21 p99 O 17 2016

My LIST 24 hours with Marina Abramović S. Cristobal color *Harper's Bazaar* no3648 p120 N 2016

Abramović, Marina, 1946—Interviews

Life's Work: An Interview with Marina Abramović A. Beard color img *Harvard Business Review* v94 no11 p116 N 2016

Marina Abramovic B. Luscombe color *Time* v188 no21 p74 N 21 2016

Abrams (Company)

Around the Booths bw *Publishers Weekly* v264 no20 p(Sp)55 My 15 2017

Abrams, Abigail

The Age of Bannon color *Time* v189 no5 p26 F 13 2017

American Hate, a History color *Time* v190 no8 p36 Ag 28 2017

Kid Sports Inc [Cover story] color diag *Time* v190 no9 p42 S 4 2017

New Ways to Become Happier—and Healthier color *Time* v190 no13 p30 O 2 2017

Trump's Gilded Team color diag *Time* v189 no3 p37 Ja 30 2017

ABRAMS, BURTON

FROM THE ARCHIVES bw *Reason* v49 no1 p70 My 2017

Abrams, Elliott

A Big Deal? color *Weekly Standard* v22 no24 p9 F 27 2017

The Harm in Trying color *Weekly Standard* v22 no41 p8 Jl 3 2017

History Will Not Absolve Him bw color *Weekly Standard* v22 no14 p19 D 12 2016

The Nation-Building Straw Man cartoon color *Weekly Standard* v22 no48 p11 S 4 2017

Secretary of Genocide E. Alterman bw *Nation* v304 no5 p6 F 20 2017

Stop Supporting Palestinian Terror *National Review* v69 no7 p20 Ap 17 2017

Trump the Traditionalist color *Foreign Affairs* v96 no4 p10 Jl/Ag 2017

Abrams, Floyd

IN FREE-SPEECH TERRITORY G. LAMARCHE color *Nation* v305 no8 p34 O 9 2017

Is free speech under threat IN THE UNITED STATES? WE RECEIVED TWENTY-SEVEN RESPONSES. WE PUBLISH THEM HERE, IN ALPHABETICAL ORDER *Commentary* v144 no1 p13 Jl/Ag 2017

The Soul of the First Amendment: Why Freedom of Speech Matters *Publishers Weekly* v264 no7 p66 F 13 2017

Abrams, Floyd—Interviews

3 Questions: on Free speech J. Wolf *Saturday Evening Post* v289 no4 p27 Jl/Ag 2017

Abrams, J. J. (Jeffrey Jacob), 1966-

ANTON YELCHIN color *Entertainment Weekly* no1446/1447 p89 D 2016/Ja 2017

STAR TREK INTO DARKNESS T. J. Norton color *Sound & Vision* v81 no9 p67 N 2016

Abrams, Natalie

9JKL color *Entertainment Weekly* no1482/1483 p49 S 22 2017

After the Verdict color *Entertainment Weekly* no1482/1483 p62 S 22 2017

ALL IN THE FAMILY [Cover story] color *Entertainment Weekly* no1440 p20 N 18 2016

American Housewife *Entertainment Weekly* no1482/1483 p79 S 22 2017

ARROW color *Entertainment Weekly* no1474/1475 p73 Jl 21-28 2017

Better Things color *Entertainment Weekly* no1482/1483 p91 S 22 2017

black-ish *Entertainment Weekly* no1482/1483 p63 S 22 2017

BLACK LIGHTNING color *Entertainment Weekly* no1474/1475 p73 Jl 21-28 2017

The Blacklist color *Entertainment Weekly* no1482/1483 p74 S 22 2017

The Blacklist's Big Reveal color *Entertainment Weekly* no1467 p14 My 26 2017

Blindspot color *Entertainment Weekly* no1482/1483 p95 S 22 2017

Blue Bloods color *Entertainment Weekly* no1482/1483 p99 S 22 2017

The Brave color *Entertainment Weekly* no1482/1483 p55 S 22 2017

Breaking Big BRANDON MICHEAL HALL color *Entertainment Weekly* no1482/1483 p65 S 22 2017

Breaking Big EMMA DUMONT color *Entertainment Weekly* no1482/1483 p51 S 22 2017

Broad City color *Entertainment Weekly* no1482/1483 p79 S 22 2017

Bull color *Entertainment Weekly* no1482/1483 p66 S 22 2017

Chicago Fire *Entertainment Weekly* no1482/1483 p91 S 22 2017

Chicago P.D *Entertainment Weekly* no1482/1483 p79 S 22 2017

COMING SOON TO A TV NEAR YOU color *Entertainment Weekly* no1477 p16 Ag 11 2017

Crazy Ex-Girlfriend color *Entertainment Weekly* no1482/1483 p98 S 22 2017

Criminal Minds color *Entertainment Weekly* no1482/1483 p79 S 22 2017

Dancing With the Stars *Entertainment Weekly* no1482/1483 p48 S 22 2017

DC's Legends of Tomorrow color *Entertainment Weekly* no1482/1483 p66 S 22 2017

DEMI MOORE OF Empire color *Entertainment Weekly* no1482/1483 p78 S 22 2017

Designated Survivor color *Entertainment Weekly* no1482/1483 p74 S 22 2017

DIVE INTO Brooklyn Nine-Nine color *Entertainment Weekly* no1482/1483 p67 S 22 2017

Dynasty color *Entertainment Weekly* no1482/1483 p76 S 22 2017

The Exorcist color *Entertainment Weekly* no1482/1483 p92 S 22 2017

The Flash color *Entertainment Weekly* no1482/1483 p66 S 22 2017

FREDDIE HIGHMORE OF The Good Doctor color *Entertainment Weekly* no1482/1483 p54 S 22 2017

Fresh Off the Boat color *Entertainment Weekly* no1482/1483 p63 S 22 2017

The Gifted color *Entertainment Weekly* no1482/1483 p50 S 22 2017

GOING OUT WITH A BANG color *Entertainment Weekly* no1463/1464 p10 Ap/My 2017

The Goldbergs color *Entertainment Weekly* no1482/1483 p74 S

Abrams, Samuel E.

When Public Goes Private, as Trump Wants: What Happens? D. Ravitch color *New York Review of Books* v63 no19 p58 D 8 2016

Abrams, Zara

Scholars re-create the sounds of worship at an ancient Greek church color *Christian Century* v134 no10 p20 My 10 2017

ABRAMSKY, SASHA

CARAVAN AGAINST FEAR color *Nation* v305 no3 p14 Jl 31 2017

EUROPE'S NEW CLOSED-DOOR POLICY bw *Nation* v303 no16 p16 O 17 2016

Our Bigot in Chief *Nation* v305 no6 p3 S 11 2017

TRUMP AND THE TRIUMPH OF FEAR IN AMERICAN POLITICS bw color *Nation* v305 no8 p18 O 9 2017

The West Coast Fights Back Against Trump color il *Nation* v304 no6 p16 F 27 2017

WHEN VIOLENCE COMES color *Nation* v305 no10 p16 O 23 2017

ABRAMSON, JILL

Enduring Trump: Katy Tur describes life on the front lines during the Trump presidential campaign *New York Times Book Review* p10 S 17 2017

When all the news that fits is Trump color *Columbia Journalism Review* v56 no2 p18 Fall 2017

ABRAMSON, LEIGH McMULLAN

mothering with a migraine color *Parents* v92 no4 p94 Ap 2017

Abrash, Emily

Mobile MUTE specifies subsidiary cells to build physiologically improved grass stomata bibl diag *Science* v355 no6330 p1215 Mr 17 2017

Abrasion (Engineering)
Oh No! Your Car Got Scratched! E. DYER color *Popular Mechanics* v193 no7 p52 S 2016

Abreu, Alê
BOY & THE WORLD T. J. Norton color *Sound & Vision* v81 no10 p69 D 2016

abreu, manuel arturo
EMBODYING SURVIVANCE color *Art in America* p92 O 2017

Abreu, P.
Observation of a large-scale anisotropy in the arrival directions of cosmic rays above 8 × 1018 eV *Science* v357 no6357 p1266 S 22 2017

Abrikosov, Alexei A., 1928-2017
Alexei Alexeyevich Abrikosov M. R. Norman and A. A. Varlamov *Physics Today* v70 no10 p73 O 2017

Abritis, Alison
Cash incentives for papers go global graph *Science* v357 no6351 p541 Ag 11 2017

Abruzzo, Emily
Abruzzo Bodziak Architects D. Sokol bw color *Architectural Record* v204 no12 p44 D 2016

Abscesses
ask the experts G. DeMone and L. Borzynski color *Dressage Today* v23 no4 p67 D 2016
My Soft Spot J. Paulson *Horse & Rider* v56 no2 p6 F 2017

Abscesses—Prevention
INVESTIGATING REPEAT HOOF ABSCESSES C. Barakat and M. Freckleton color *Equus* no470 p22 N 2016

Absence of Sound, The (Short story)
THE ABSENCE OF SOUND N. W. MOSS *Saturday Evening Post* v289 no4 p62 Jl/Ag 2017

Absentee voting
We Need More Voters P. B. Denison *Humanist* v77 no1 p47 Ja/F 2017

Absenteeism (Labor)
See also
Sick leave
My coworkers are making me sick E. Karageorge *Monthly Labor Review* p1 N 2016

Absenteeism (Labor)—Prevention
"We were heading for a perfect storm": How a housing association tackled high absence rates by overhauling its culture *People Management* p25 Jl 2017

Absenteeism (School)
Many Parents Underestimate the Harm of School Absences *Education Digest* v82 no4 p62 D 2016
No Time Off M. LINDBERG *Education Digest* v82 no5 p36 Ja 2017

Absolute Kitchens (Company)
KITCHEN HELP: Resources for creating your own dream kitchen *Washingtonian Magazine* v53 no1 p166 O 2017

Absolute pitch
Acquiring "Perfect" Pitch Now Possible *USA Today Magazine* v145 no2865 p8 Je 2017

Absolute sea level change
Darkness Falls in the Arctic J. T. Mathis color *Wilson Quarterly* p1 Summ 2017
WHAT SEA RISE? C. Solomon color *National Geographic* v231 no5 p158 My 2017

Absolute Yachts (Company)
Absolute 50 Fly color *Power & Motoryacht* v32 no12 p32 D 2016

Absorption
Angular momentum can slow down photoemission V. S. Yakovlev and N. Karpowicz color *Science* v357 no6357 p1239 S 22 2017
Frequency combs enable rapid and high-resolution multidimensional coherent spectroscopy B. Lomsadze and S. T. Cundiff diag graph *Science* v357 no6358 p1389 S 29 2017
Restored iron transport by a small molecule promotes absorption and hemoglobinization in animals A. S. Grillo, A. M. SantaMaria et al color graph *Science* v356 no6338 p608 My 12 2017

Abstract algebra
The Universe According to Emmy Noether S. NADIS color diag *Discover* v38 no5 p48 Je 2017

Abstract art
See also
Abstract painting

Studio Bedfellows L. Lou color *Art in America* v105 no1 p35 Ja 2017

Abstract art—Exhibitions
RIOT ON THE CANVAS H. ADJEI-KONTOH *In These Times* v41 no3 p41 Mr 2017

Abstract expressionism—Exhibitions
Opposites Attract D. GREEN bw color *Weekly Standard* v22 no11 p34 N 21 2016

Abstract painting
Editor's Letter L. POLLOCK bw *Art in America* v105 no1 p14 Ja 2017

Abstract painting—Exhibitions
"The Figurative Pollock" H. Ghorashi *ARTnews* v115 no3 p32 Fall 2016

Abstract painting—United States
Line Drive color *ARTnews* v115 no4 p9 Wint 2016/2017

Absurd (Philosophy)
That's Outrageous! cartoon *Reader's Digest* v190 no1134 p117 O 2017

Abt Electronics (Company)
Top Shops for Tech chart *Consumer Reports* v81 no12 p33 D 2016

ABT Studio Co.
Living That #BalletLife M. Fuhrer *Dance Spirit* v21 no7 p88 S 2017

Abu, Nur
Seagrass ecosystems reduce exposure to bacterial pathogens of humans, fishes, and invertebrates bibl graph *Science* v355 no6326 p731 F 17 2017

Abu-Alhayyat, Maya
The Blue Pool of Questions *Publishers Weekly* v264 no30 p57 Jl 24 2017

Abu-Assad, Hany, 1961-
THE MOUNTAIN BETWEEN US S. Li color *Entertainment Weekly* no1478 / 1479 p56 Ag 18-25 2017

ABUC (Music)
ABUC J. Hale color *Downbeat* v83 no12 p79 D 2016
Different Perspective B. Reed color *Downbeat* v84 no4 p8 Ap 2017
Fonseca Explores Cuban Styles J. Murph color *Downbeat* v84 no4 p14 Ap 2017

Abudayyeh, Omar O.
Nucleic acid detection with CRISPR-Cas13a/C2c2 color diag *Science* v356 no6336 p438 Ap 28 2017

Abugattas, Alonso
A Globally Rare eco system *Parks & Recreation* v52 no4 p38 Ap 2017

Abu Hassan, Yahya
AMERICAN JIHADI G. Wood cartoon color *Atlantic* v319 no2 p74 Mr 2017

Abulafia, David
REDBEARD IN ITALY *History Today* v67 no5 p92 My 2017

Abulafia, Lew
BIKE BLUR S. Cravatts color *Popular Photography* v80 no11 p24 D 2016

Abul-Husn, Noura S.
Distribution and clinical impact of functional variants in 50,726 whole-exome sequences from the DiscovEHR study chart graph *Science* v354 no6319 paaf6814-1 D 23 2016
Genetic identification of familial hypercholesterolemia within a single U.S. health care system chart graph *Science* v354 no6319 paaf7000-1 D 23 2016

Abu-Nasr, Donna
After the Bombs Have Fallen color *Bloomberg Businessweek* no4531 p34 Jl 24 2017
The Hand of Iran In Nigeria color *Bloomberg Businessweek* no4514 p17 Mr 13 2017
A Mideast Rivalry Leads to a Split color map *Bloomberg Businessweek* no4526 p23 Je 12 2017
Royal Visionary Meets Popular Pushback *Bloomberg Businessweek* no4528 p35 Je 26 2017

Abundant Robotics Inc.
A BUMPER CROP OF FRUIT-PICKING BOTS A. VLASITS diag *Wired* v25 no9 p38 S 2017

Abunnassr, Muhammad
The Waiting Room color *Commonweal* v144 no5 p39 Mr 10 2017

Abuse of administrative power

Presidential Power G. SCHMITT color *Weekly Standard* v22 no21 p18 F 6 2017

Abuse of African American women
ONE OF THE LUCKY ONES Z. BRITTON bw *Ebony* v72/73 no12/1 p20 O/N 2017

Abuse of employees
Research: Shifting the Power Balance with an Abusive Boss Hui Liao, E. Wee et al *Harvard Business Review Digital Articles* p2 O 9 2017

Abuse of indigenous women
The Place Where Happiness Dwelled C. CARSWELL *Sierra* v102 no5 p24 St/O 2017

Abuse of women
ABUSES OF POWER R. FARROW bw color *New Yorker* v93 no33 p42 O 23 2017
CAUSE & EFFECT D. Gluck color *InStyle* v24 no2 p52 F 2017
Don't Stop Believin' M. DEAN il *New Republic* v247 no12 p14 D 2016
My Country: Liz Meriweather img *New York* v49 no22 p15 O 31 2016

Abused women
Domestic Abuse and Protecting Pets C. Lindner *Catnip* v24 no10 p7 O 2016

Abusive relationships
EDITOR'S LETTER T. M. FERGUSON color *Ebony* v72/73 no12/1 p12 O/N 2017
ONE OF THE LUCKY ONES Z. BRITTON bw *Ebony* v72/73 no12/1 p20 O/N 2017

Abusive supervision (Work environment)
What Research Shows About Talking Back to a Jerk Boss W. Frick *Harvard Business Review Digital Articles* p2 Ap 9 2015

Abutilon
A FLORAL AFFAIR J. Silver color *Sunset* v238 no6 p39 Je 2017

Abyzov, Alexej
Intersection of diverse neuronal genomes and neuropsychiatric disease: The Brain Somatic Mosaicism Network color *Science* v356 no6336 p395 Ap 28 2017

Abzalimov, Rinat R.
Polymeric peptide pigments with sequence-encoded properties color graph *Science* v356 no6342 p1064 Je 9 2017

Academic achievement
See also
    Achievement gap
    Graduation (Education)
    Motivation in education
avoid the homework trap E. ZAMMETT RUDDY *Parents* v91 no9 p96 S 2016
CHASING A MOVING TARGET D. R. WILSON cartoon *New Orleans Magazine* v51 no1 p34 N 2016
Critical consciousness A key to student achievement A. El-Amin, S. Seider et al bw il *Phi Delta Kappan* v98 no5 p18 F 2017
High Marks For Fair Praise K. GOLDYNIA *Psychology Today* v50 no3 p21 My/Je 2017
An Invisible Edge M. HUSTON *Psychology Today* v49 no6 p22 N/D 2016
New tools for measuring academic performance C. Tachibana color *Science* v355 no6325 p651 F 10 2017
Promoting Student Academic Achievement Through Faculty Development about Inclusive Teaching M. E. Schmid, D. L. Gillian-Daniel et al *Change* v48 no5 p16 S/O 2016
School Bullying Linked to Lower Academic Achievement cartoon *Education Digest* v82 no8 p53 Ap 2017
school support L. GARISTO PFAFF *Parents* v91 no11 p148 N 2016
Seize the Private School Advantage J. Southerst color *Maclean's* v130 no9 p50 O 2017
Teachers Underrate Girls' Math Skills *USA Today Magazine* v145 no2859 p4 D 2016
THE WAY TO SURVIVE IT WAS TO MAKE A's M. SECRET *New York Times Magazine* p56 S 10 2017
WHO ASKED YOU? (WE DID!) *Parents* v91 no9 p24 S 2016

Academic achievement research
REFRAMING STUDENT SUCCESS IN COLLEGE: Advancing Know-What and Know-How J. Kinzie and G. Kuh *Change* v49 no3 p19 My/Je 2017

Academic achievement—Canada
In praise of teenagers (really) *Maclean's* v130 no7 p4 Ag 2017

Academic achievement—Singapore
Educational and STM Publishing in SINGAPORE T. TAN *Publishers Weekly* v263 no41 p31 O 10 2016

Academic achievement—United States
Looking race in the face D. Mitchell, J. Hinueber et al bw *Phi Delta Kappan* v98 no5 p24 F 2017
SETTING THE EXAMPLE M. C. Ciccarelli color *Literacy Today (2411-7862)* v34 no5 p8 Mr/Ap 2017
Spending dollars to make a difference J. P. STARR color *Phi Delta Kappan* v98 no5 p72 F 2017

Academic degrees
See also
    Bachelor's degree
    College majors
    Master's degree
Decline in Diplomas: Students aren't seeking public service careers the way they used to M. Maciag *Governing* v30 no8 p56 My 2017
get into GEAR: Your four-year college-prep timeline M. BENJAMIN *Dance Magazine* p28 2016/2017
The Institute for American Musical Theatre *Dance Magazine* v90 p75 2016/2017 Supplement College Guide
STATE-BY-STATE GUIDE *Dance Magazine* p123 2016/2017

Academic degrees—Great Britain
Is a degree losing its value at work? *People Management* p11 O 2016

Academic discourse
Paper writing gone Hollywood J. J. McDonnell cartoon *Science* v355 no6320 p102 Ja 6 2017

Academic dissertations
Creating a culture of ethics in Iran M. S. Rezaee-Zavareh, Z. Naji et al bibl *Science* v354 no6310 p296 O 21 2016
The Doctor Is In J. COST color *Weekly Standard* v22 no20 p5 Ja 30 2017
The problem with 'alternative' M. Zaringhalam color *Science* v354 no6313 p798 N 11 2016

Academic-industrial collaboration
Bridging Health Care's Innovation-Education Gap R. Herzlinger, V. K. Ramaswamy et al *Harvard Business Review Digital Articles* p2 N 11 2014
Industry-Academic Partnerships Can Solve Bigger Problems A. Tanikella *Harvard Business Review Digital Articles* p2 My 2 2016
Innovative Companies Get Their Best Ideas from Academic Research—Here's How They Do It G. Satell *Harvard Business Review Digital Articles* p2 Ap 19 2016
Why Higher Ed and Business Need to Work Together M. D. King *Harvard Business Review Digital Articles* p2 Jl 17 2015

Academic language
Understanding Academic Language and Its Connection to School Success C. FRIEDBERG, A. MITCHELL et al *Education Digest* v82 no6 p58 F 2017

Academic libraries
An Original River Town C. KENZY *South Dakota Magazine* v32 no4 p20 N/D 2016

Academic libraries—Virginia
21st Century Know-How: WOODBERRY FOREST CREATES NEW LEARNING COMMONS *Virginia Living* v15 no6 p97 O 2017

Academic underachievement
Is Design to Blame When a School Underperforms? A. FIXSEN color *Architectural Record* v205 no5 p30 My 2017

Academic achievement—Cross-cultural studies
Closing global achievement gaps in MOOCs R. F. Kizilcec, A. J. Saltarelli et al bibl graph *Science* v355 no6322 p251 Ja 20 2017

Academic achievement—United States—Charts, diagrams, etc.
PUMPING IT UP? graph *Phi Kappa Phi Forum* v97 no2 p5 Summ 2017

Academies (British public schools)
The One Type of Leader Who Can Turn Around a Failing School A. Hill, L. Mellon et al bw color *Harvard Business Review Digital Articles* p2 O 20 2016

Academy Awards (Motion pictures)
AND THE OSCAR COMES FROM... R. KEEGAN color *Vanity Fair* v59 no11 p79 N 2017

BALLOT color *Entertainment Weekly* no1451/1452 p77 F 3-10 2017

BEST ACTOR S. Vilkomerson, K. P. Sullivan et al color diag *Entertainment Weekly* no1451/1452 p54 F 3-10 2017

BEST ACTRESS J. McGovern, D. Coggan et al color diag *Entertainment Weekly* no1451/1452 p44 F 3-10 2017

BEST DIRECTOR J. McGovern, S. Vilkomerson et al color diag *Entertainment Weekly* no1451/1452 p66 F 3-10 2017

BEST SUPPORTING ACTOR S. Li, D. Franich et al color diag *Entertainment Weekly* no1451/1452 p50 F 3-10 2017

BEST SUPPORTING ACTRESS N. Sperling, J. McGovern et al color diag *Entertainment Weekly* no1451/1452 p62 F 3-10 2017

BEYOND BLACK AND WHITE C. M. Smith and D. Lawrence *Entertainment Weekly* no1451/1452 p43 F 3-10 2017

Charlize Theron A. Synnott color *InStyle* v24 no1 p60 Ja 2017

Could Deadpool Get a Best Picture Nod? N. Sperling color *Entertainment Weekly* no1450 p16 Ja 27 2017

Cue the Walking Music bw *Weekly Standard* v22 no19 p2 Ja 23 2017

DANCING IN THE MOONLIGHT D. GILMORE color *Vanity Fair* v59 no5 p61 Ap 2017

Diversity at the Oscars Is More than a Numbers Game K. H. Banks *Harvard Business Review Digital Articles* p2 F 24 2016

Fairground color *Vanity Fair* v59 no6 p57 My 2017

Glittering Prizes R. DOUTHAT color *National Review* v69 no6 p47 Ap 3 2017

Gold Rush K. Peiffer color *InStyle* v24 no5 p84 My 2017

The Hidden Figures of the Oscars Ad Blitz T. J. Huddleston color *Fortune* v175 no2 p14 F 1 2017

LEAD ACTOR CONTENDER ANDREW GARFIELD N. Sperling color *Entertainment Weekly* no1439 p46 N 11 2016

Mel BROOKS *Interview* v47 no5 p24 Je/Jl 2017

Oscar Ballot *TV Guide* v65 no7 p14 F 13 2017

OSCAR DEAREST M. SCHULMAN cartoon *New Yorker* v93 no2 p26 F 27 2017

The Oscar Race Is On! N. Sperling color *Entertainment Weekly* no1436/1437 p24 O 21 2016

OSCAR RACE TAKES SHAPE S. Vilkomerson color *Entertainment Weekly* no1484 p38 S 29 2017

Oscar Shows Its Colors P. Travers color *Rolling Stone* no1281/1282 p54 F 23 2017

OSCARS SO RIGHT? [Cover story] N. Sperling color *Entertainment Weekly* no1451/1452 p40 F 3-10 2017

OSCARS TURNED UPSIDE DOWN N. Sperling color *Entertainment Weekly* no1453 p13 F 17 2017

The OTHER RACES N. Sperling color *Entertainment Weekly* no1454/1455 p50 F 24 2017

Out of Step with Movie History S. ERICKSON *Los Angeles Magazine* p66 F 2017

REPRESENTATION S. Marikar cartoon *New Yorker* v93 no4 p30 Mr 13 2017

SHOCK of MOONLIGHT N. Sperling, D. Coggan et al color *Entertainment Weekly* no1456 p42 Mr 10 2017

THE STATE OF THE OSCAR RACE N. Sperling color *Entertainment Weekly* no1446/1447 p23 D 2016/Ja 2017

To Do J. SALTZ, M. Z. SEITZ et al img *New York* p78 F 20 2017

Who Should Really Win *Los Angeles Magazine* p68 F 2017

WHO WILL WIN N. Sperling color *Entertainment Weekly* no1454/1455 p44 F 24 2017

The WRONG ENVELOPE: HOW IT HAPPENED N. Sperling color *Entertainment Weekly* no1456 p46 Mr 10 2017

Academy Awards (Motion pictures)—History

The Definitive Guide to Random Oscar Facts E. Berman color *Time* v189 no7/8 p112 F 27 2017

Academy Awards (Motion pictures)—News briefs

Pop Chart color *Time* v189 no9 p57 Mr 13 2017

Academy of Motion Picture Arts & Sciences

AND THE OSCAR COMES FROM... R. KEEGAN color *Vanity Fair* v59 no11 p79 N 2017

Academy of Nutrition & Dietetics

WATER, BABY! color *Women's Health* v14 no5 p140 Je 2017

Academy Awards (Motion pictures)—Charts, diagrams, etc.

OSCAR SECRET BALLOT N. Sperling color *Entertainment Weekly* no1454/1455 p52 F 24 2017

Acadia National Park (Me.)

A Celebration of Acadia color *Martha Stewart Living* p19 Jl/Ag 2017

A Storied Isle S. Turrentine color *Climbing* no351 p34 F/Mr 2017

Acadia sport utility vehicle—Evaluation

GMC Acadia All Terrain chart color *Motor Trend* v69 no1 p65 Ja 2017

Accarrino, Matthew

THE LONG ROUTE P. Flax color *Sunset* v238 no6 p17 Je 2017

Acceleration (Mechanics)

RACING KEEPS GETTING FASTER, DESPITE ALL EFFORTS K. C. Colwell graph *Car & Driver* v63 no2 p26 Ag 2017

Acceleration principle (Economics)

Startup Accelerators Have Become More Popular in Emerging Markets—and They're Working P. Roberts and R. Kempner *Harvard Business Review Digital Articles* p2 O 2 2017

Accelerator physicists

African Arrow sees hints of structure in the fabric of space P. Kornilovich *Physics Today* v69 no12 p49 D 2016

Accents & accentuation—Social aspects

Voice of America K. D. WILLIAMSON *National Review* v69 no3 p31 F 20 2017

Accenture (Company)

Company Profiles color *Working Mother* v40 no2 p38 Je/Jl 2017

Paying It Forward E. LEE color *Working Mother* v40 no2 p44 Je/Jl 2017

The Winners chart *Working Mother* v40 no2 p26 Je/Jl 2017

Accenture (Company)—Officials & employees

It Might Be Time to Spill Your Corporate Secrets S. G. Carmichael *Harvard Business Review Digital Articles* p2 Ap 13 2015

"We want to be the most diverse organisation on the planet": Why networks and targets aren't enough to meet the incredible ambition at Accenture *People Management* p20 Ap 2017

Access to information—Psychological aspects

Data Deliver in the Clutch S. Mirsky color *Scientific American* v316 no1 p70 Ja 2017

Accessible design

ADA Accessibility Rules for Alterations to Existing Facilities J. C. Kozlowski *Parks & Recreation* v52 no8 p24 Ag 2017

Finding the Right Fit: Designing trails using automatic counters in Sioux Falls *Parks & Recreation* v52 no5 p48 My 2017

Accident prevention

MAKING EVERY HOME A SAFER PLACE A. JACOBSON *Parents* v91 no6 p30 Je 2016

uphill battle T. REECE *Parents* v91 no6 p140 Je 2016

Accident victims

Experiment to raise dead blocked *Science* v354 no6314 p808 N 18 2016

Accidents

    See also

    Drowning

    Explosions

    Falls (Accidents)

    Medical emergencies

    Mountaineering accidents

    Work-related injuries

Cliff-Hanger A. SIMMONS *Reader's Digest* v189 no1128 p12 Mr 2017

Falling off a Bridge S. Arrasmith cartoon *Men's Health* v32 no3 p80 Ap 2017

Overcome any setback A. Sweeney color *Redbook* p27 O 2017

What loss taught me about life M. Celeste Beall color *Redbook* p115 O 2017

Accidents in buildings

Flames of Contempt: The Grenfell Tower fire wasn't just a tragedy--it was the physical manifestation of political neglect J. DAVIDSON img *New York* v50 no13 p80 Je 26 2017

Accipitridae

    See also

    Hawks

When Birds Become Bird Food M. A. Barker color *National Wildlife (World Edition)* v54 no6 p12 O/N 2016

Accommodation (Hermeneutics)

Sadness: A Love Story J. Klausner color *InStyle* v24 no9 p218 S 2017

Accommodation rigs (Offshore structures)

Rigged for Success P. Nielsen *Sail* v48 no1 p6 Ja 2017

Accountable care organizations (Medical care)

3 Keys to Shifting How We Pay for Health Care T. Rothenhaus and J. Fox *Harvard Business Review Digital Articles* p2 S 25 2015

How to Make Health Care Accountable When We Don't Know What Works B. Richman *Harvard Business Review Digital Articles* p2 N 25 2014

Accountant, The (Film)

THE ACCOUNTANT C. Chiarella color *Sound & Vision* v82 no5 p66 Je 2017

The Accountant L. Greenblatt color *Entertainment Weekly* no1436/1437 p83 O 21 2016

The Accountant Pays Small Dividends on Its Star S. Zacharek color *Time* v188 no16/17 p87 O 24 2016

Kind of a Drag J. PODHORETZ *Weekly Standard* v22 no8 p43 O 31 2016

A Strange Superman R. DOUTHAT color *National Review* v68 no21 p47 N 21 2016

Accounting

See also

Earnings management

A Refresher on Marketing ROI A. Gallo *Harvard Business Review Digital Articles* p1 Jl 25 2017

Accounting fraud

Brokerage Account Fraud Protection K. LANKFORD *Kiplinger's Personal Finance* v71 no1 p40 Ja 2017

Acculturation

All-American Angst G. DREVITCH *Psychology Today* v50 no1 p27 Ja/F 2017

Acculturation—Social aspects

A Case for Acculturation J. Paterson *Education Digest* v83 no1 p29 S 2017

Accuracy in journalism

BOTS BITE MAN A. WEBB color *Mother Jones* v42 no2 p51 Mr/Ap 2017

Fake News *Change* v82 no3 p19 Mr 2017

Gawkermania *Commentary* v142 no1 p1 Jl/Ag 2016

Google combats fake news with 'Fact Check' results in search and news I. PAUL color *PCWorld* v35 no5 p57 My 2017

How to Stamp Out Fake News D. Pogue color *Scientific American* v316 no2 p24 F 2017

How We Honor The First Amendment L. D'VORKIN *Forbes* v199 no2 p14 F 28 2017

Just the Facts color *Weekly Standard* v22 no15 p3 D 19 2016

Just the Facts D. COURTNEY *Texas Monthly* v45 no6 p288 Je 2017

The Rapture or a Rupture? S. CARR *Idaho Magazine* v17 no1 p54 Ja 2017

Accuracy of information

See also

Accuracy in journalism

WE MUST #PRESS ON V. K. De Luca color *Essence* v47 no12 p10 Ap 2017

Accurail Inc.

Accurail HO scale 36-foot double-sheathed boxcar kit D. Kawala color *Model Railroader* v84 no8 p62 Ag 2017

Acer computers

Acer Predator 21 X: The most insane laptop ever built [Cover story] G. MAH UNG color graph *PCWorld* v35 no10 p48 O 2017

Acer's Switch 7 could overpower the Surface Pro and MacBook Pro G. MAH UNG color *PCWorld* v35 no10 p12 O 2017

Acer Swift 7: The world's thinnest laptop is starving for power A. YEE color graph *PCWorld* v35 no1 p90 Ja 2017

Acetic acid

See also

Vinegar

DRINKING VINEGARS: HEALTHY OR HYPE? color *Health* v31 no5 p16 Je 2017

HAVE YOU HEARD C. DOW *Nutrition Action Health Letter* v44 no2 p6 Mr 2017

Quick & Healthy Homemade Sausage J. BOWDEN and J. BESSINGER color *Better Nutrition* v79 no10 p78 O 2017

Acetylation

Microtubules acquire resistance from mechanical breakage through intralumenal acetylation Z. Xu, L. Schaedel et al diag graph *Science* v356 no6335 p328 Ap 21 2017

Acetylene

Molecular imaging at 1-femtosecond resolution Chong-Yu Ruan bibl diag *Science* v354 no6310 p283 O 21 2016

Acetylene—Molecular structure

Ultrafast electron diffraction imaging of bond breaking in di-ionized acetylene B. Wolter, M. G. Pullen et al bibl graph *Science* v354 no6310 p308 O 21 2016

Aceved, Nathalia

French Twist E. Wilson color *InStyle* v23 no12 p260 N 2016

Acevedo, Art

The point of sanctuary cities *Christian Century* v134 no11 p7 My 24 2017

Acevedo, Chantel

Storm Surge color *Vogue* v207 no11 p84 N 2017

Acevedo, Manuel—Exhibitions

DOWN THESE MEAN STREETS *USA Today Magazine* v146 no2866 p52 Jl 2017

Acevedo, Sylvia

THE FUTURE FOR GIRL SCOUTS IN AMERICA AND ABROAD *Vital Speeches of the Day* v82 no10 p312 O 2016

ACEVES, ANA V.

FIRST LIGHT ı MeerKAT Online *Sky & Telescope* v132 no6 p15 D 2016

GALAXIES ı Giant "Frankenstein" Spiral *Sky & Telescope* v132 no6 p14 D 2016

Aceves, Fred

The Closest I've Come *Publishers Weekly* v264 no41 p69 O 9 2017

Ach Brito & CA SA

DREAM CREAM color *Esquire* v166 no4 p68 N 2016

ACHARA, ESTHER ADAMS

Bringing Up Bébé color *Vogue* v206 no11 p164 N 2016

Acharya, Lavanya

Dynamics of cortical dendritic membrane potential and spikes in freely behaving rats diag *Science* v355 no6331 p1281 Mr 24 2017

Achatz, Grant

My Dinner Party with GRANT C. Schedler color *Chicago* v66 no10 p98 O 2017

Achebe, Chinua, 1930-2013

Portrait of the Author as a Historian A. Lee *History Today* v66 no12 p54 D 2016

Achenbach, Joel

Mars chart color *National Geographic* v230 no5 p31 N 2016

Achidi, Eric

Resistance to malaria through structural variation of red blood cell invasion receptors diag *Science* v356 no6343 p1139 Je 16 2017

Achievement

See also

Academic achievement

Occupational achievement

Winning & losing (Contests & competitions)

Radetzky's march into obscurity G. Darby *History Today* v66 no12 p28 D 2016

Achievement gap

Learning from schools that close opportunity gaps S. E. LaCour, A. York et al *Phi Delta Kappan* v99 no1 p8 S 2017

Learning from the other achievement gap T. L. Pittinsky *Phi Delta Kappan* v98 no5 p80 F 2017

The revitalized tutoring center J. koselak chart color graph *Phi Delta Kappan* v98 no5 p61 F 2017

Achievement in science

U.S. science test shows gains *Science* v354 no6312 p530 N 4 2016

ACHILLEOS, ANTONIS

THE SINISTER SCIENCE OF IRRESISTIBLE JUNK FOOD *Scholastic Choices* v32 no4 p6 Ja 2017

Achilles Inflatable Craft Corp.

Tender Touch-Up [Cover story] P. Nielsen color *Sail* v48 no8 p58 Ag 2017

Achison, Geoff

Places To Go, People To See HADLEY color *Downbeat* v84 no6 p70 Je 2017

Achor, Shawn

Are the People Who Take Vacations the Ones Who Get Promoted? *Harvard Business Review Digital Articles* p2 Je 12 2015

The Benefits of Peer-to-Peer Praise at Work *Harvard Business Review Digital Articles* p2 F 19 2016

Tap Masters bw *New Yorker* v93 no20 p14 Jl 10 2017

Time Flies cartoon *New Yorker* v92 no38 p10 N 21 2016

Well Tempered bw *New Yorker* v93 no29 p22 S 25 2017

When Worlds Collide bw *New Yorker* v92 no48 p11 F 6 2017

Acolytes

Highbrow Eyebrows M. GUNCH color *New Orleans Magazine* v52 no1 p52 S 2017

Aconite

Hardy Harbingers color *Canadian Wildlife* v23 no1 p38 Mr/Ap 2017

Acorn squash

EASY WEEKNIGHTS color *Good Housekeeping* v264 no2 p125 F 2017

THE SPICE IS RIGHT L. L. Sercarz and M. GLISAN color *Better Homes & Gardens* v95 no9 p94 S 2017

YOUR PANTRY chart color *Good Housekeeping* v263 no5 p191 N 2016

Acorns

BARREN OAKS G. Almy color *Field & Stream* v121 no6 pW4 N 2016

ACOSTA, DARIO

Diva CALIENTE *Opera News* v81 no5 p36 N 2016

Acosta, Hipolita—Interviews

THE SECRET Agent J. N. LOMAX *Texas Monthly* v45 no5 p60 My 2017

Acosta, Jim

The Acosta of Freedom M. CONTINETTI *Commentary* v144 no2 p56 S 2017

Acosta, Rina Mae

The Happiest Kids in the World: A Stress-Free Approach to Parenting—the Dutch Way color *Publishers Weekly* v264 no3 p55 Ja 16 2017

Acoustic imaging

Imaging cancer with PHOTOACOUSTIC RADAR A. Mandelis *Physics Today* v70 no5 p42 My 2017

Acoustic receivers

Solidly Serious D. Kumin chart color graph *Sound & Vision* v82 no7 p58 S 2017

YOU CAN'T BURY IT IF IT 'S NOT DEAD R. SABIN *Sound & Vision* v81 no9 p8 N 2016

Acoustical materials

The Art Of Noise K. L. Beamon color *Architectural Record* v205 no8 p69 Ag 2017

Acoustical materials—Evaluation

Staging Concepts - Elevate Your Experience *Stage Directions* v30 no3 p36 Mr 2017

Surface Value R. C. Orrell *Architectural Record* v205 no6 p57 Je 2017

Acox, Clarence

THE MAGIC TOUCH P. de Barros color *Downbeat* v84 no6 p126 Je 2017

Acquino, Maureen

'In Tune' with the Community *Parks & Recreation* v52 no8 p80 Ag 2017

The Outdoor Alliance for Kids Holds Capitol Hill Briefing *Parks & Recreation* v52 no8 p66 Ag 2017

Parks for Inclusion Launches During Annual Conference *Parks & Recreation* v52 no10 p48 O 2017

Summer Camp on Capitol Hill: Play On to Protect Programming at Parks *Parks & Recreation* v52 no8 p60 Ag 2017

Acquisition of data

Microsoft finally reveals what data Windows 10 collects from your PC I. PAUL color *PCWorld* v35 no5 p54 My 2017

Needed: better labor market data C. PEÑA *Issues in Science & Technology* v33 no2 p5 Wint 2017

What Cancer Researchers Can Learn from Direct-to-Consumer Companies K. Giusti and R. G. Hamermesh color *Harvard Business Review Digital Articles* p2 Ja 12 2017

You Don't Have to Be an Expert: As cities become inundated with data, they're turning to citizens for help T. Newcombe color *Governing* v30 no11 p60 Ag 2017

Acquisition of data—Moral & ethical aspects

NOW TRENDING: #ethicalproblems J. J. Roberts color *Fortune* v174 no8 p42 D 15 2016

Acquisition of property—Methodology

A SHORE THING J. BREWSTER color *Cabin Living* p38 Ap 2017

Acquisition of territory

Imperial Designs: Cromwell's move on Jamaica transformed Britain's early empire C. G. Pestana *History Today* v67 no6 p8 Je 2016

Acriche, Yoni

How to Make Better Predictions When You Don't Have Enough Data *Harvard Business Review Digital Articles* p2 D 29 2016

Acrobatics

POSING OUTSIDE THE BOX cartoon chart color *AARP: The Magazine* v60 no3A p40 Ap/My 2017

Acrobatics—Study & teaching

Balancing Act: Morocco's circus school takes women to new heights--though many in the country may not approve S. CASTELIER and P. MASSY *Ms.* v27 no3 p18 Fall 2017

Acropolis Museum (Athens, Greece)

World Wonders Under Wraps K. Samuelson color *Time* v190 no9 p14 S 4 2017

Across the River (Film)

20 DISCS TO WATCH *Film Comment* v52 no6 p91 N/D 2016

Acrylamide

ACRYLAMIDE: Avoiding a likely carcinogen *Nutrition Action Health Letter* v44 no8 p10 O 2017

Acrylic coatings

ALL ABOUT YVES H. MARTIN color *Architectural Digest* v73 no12 p34 D 2016

How to Make a... CONCRETE FRAME B. LOSLEBEN chart color *Popular Mechanics* p82 S 2017

Acrylic painting

ART IS LIFE: AND LACK OF IT ALMOST KILLED ME J. TOOKEY *Idaho Magazine* v16 no9 p12 Je 2017

Fin color *Art in America* v105 no1 p11 Ja 2017

Acrylic painting equipment & supplies

PAINTING TIPS, TRICKS: HERE ARE FOUR HOMEMADE IDEAS THAT CAN STREAMLINE YOUR PAINTING CHORES D. Mowitz *Successful Farming* v115 no9 p36 Ag 2017

Acrylic painting—Exhibitions

Benoit DELHOMME M. MULLEN *Interview* v47 no2 p70 Mr 2017

HOLDING ON T. MALONE *Atlanta* v57 no2 p30 Je 2017

SELF-PORTRAIT A. KARNES *Texas Monthly* v44 no11 p101 N 2016

Acsády, László

Synaptic scaling in sleep bibl color *Science* v355 no6324 p457 F 3 2017

ACT (Company)

ACT CELEBRATES 25 J. Hale color *Downbeat* v84 no6 p59 Je 2017

Act Now To Stop War & End Racism (Organization)

Inaugural Parade Regulations Constitutional Challenge J. C. Kozlowski *Parks & Recreation* v52 no1 p20 Ja 2017

Act UP (Organization)

ART, ACTIVISM & AIDS: THESE DECADES WERE FILLED WITH LGBT CHANGE, BUT THE IMPACT OF AIDS WAS THE BIGGEST D. ARTAVIA and D. ANDERSON-MINSHALL bw *Advocate* no1091 p87 Je/Jl 2017

Actelion Pharmaceuticals Ltd.

J&J Plays the Spurned Suitor J. Koch, A. Torsoli et al cartoon *Bloomberg Businessweek* no4503 p20 D 12 2016

Actev Motors (Company)

The Kid-Proof Go-Kart color *Popular Mechanics* p52 D 2016/Ja 2017

Actin

    See also

      F-actin

Actin divides to conquer H. Maiato and C. Ferrás color diag *Science* v357 no6353 p756 Ag 25 2017

Actin protects mammalian eggs against chromosome segregation errors B. Mogessie and M. Schuh color *Science* v357 no6353 p772 Ag 25 2017

Acting

16 ACTORS W. MORRIS and A. O. SCOTT color *New York Times Magazine* p52 D 11 2016

Bulletproof! J. Roth color *Esquire* p66 Ag 2017

FEEL THE Dern L. Hill color *InStyle* v24 no4 p200 Ap 2017

Taraji P. Henson K. B. Brown color *InStyle* v24 no7 p91 Jl 2017

Acting career counseling

THE CAREER MAKEOVER ISSUE WITH Billy Eichner [Cover story] K. Bahler color *Money* v46 no7 p38 Ag 2017

Acting—Study & teaching

Refine Your Talent *Stage Directions* v30 no3 p71 Mr 2017

Action & adventure films

    See also

      James Bond films

      Martial arts in motion pictures

THE BEST, BADDEST ACTION HERO NAMES K. P. Sullivan color *Entertainment Weekly* no1449 p44 Ja 20 2017

THE SECRET LIFE OF PETS T. J. Norton color *Sound & Vision* v82 no4 p68 My 2017

UNFORGIVEN B. A. DuHamel color *Sound & Vision* v82 no8 p67 O 2017

Action & adventure television programs—Reviews

Mac Attack! I. Rudolph color *TV Guide* v64 no42 p11 O 10 2016

Action in motion pictures

Don Wilson Is Playing a Hit Man? D. J. Moore color *Black Belt* v55 no6 p24 O/N 2017

Action photography

Freeze the Moment color *Backpacker* v45 no2 p33 Mr 2017

Actions & defenses (Law)

    See also

      Equity

      Whistleblowing—Lawsuits & claims

BATTLE FOR THE BAY A. DOUGLAS color *Surfer* v58 no5 p62 S 2017

Can Trump Clean Up His Messy World of Conflicts? M. Calabresi color *Time* v188 no24 p13 D 12 2016

FLORISTS LOSE ON FREE EXPRESSION S. SHACKFORD color *Reason* v49 no2 p6 Je 2017

FOR THE DEFENSE A. French color *Esquire* p130 S 2017

If you've ever owned a PC with a DVD drive, you may get a $10 settlement M. HACHMAN color *PCWorld* p38 Mr 2017

The Kids Are Not All Right M. BENNET *Audubon* v118 no6 p12 Wint 2016

Pride of Place—Sort of color *Weekly Standard* v22 no26 p4 Mr 13 2017

Root of the Problem J. Servaas *Saturday Evening Post* v288 no6 p27 N/D 2016

Should bank customers be allowed to file class-action suits? K. KIPLINGER *Kiplinger's Personal Finance* v70 no12 p16 D 2016

Venus, Exonerated D. ZIRIN *Nation* v305 no3 p8 Jl 31 2017

Actions & defenses (Law)—United States

Censorship Tale B. KAUFFMAN *American Conservative* v16 no3 p43 My/Je 2017

Four Decades of Court Battles and Counting T. J. DONOHUE *Weekly Standard* v22 no28 p9 Mr 27 2017

Will the GOP Finally Crush Class Actions? P. M. Barrett *Bloomberg Businessweek* no4514 p28 Mr 13 2017

Actions & defenses (Law)—United States—History—21st century

A Lawyer Stalks Wall Street Banks M. Robinson color *Bloomberg Businessweek* no4528 p24 Je 26 2017

Activated carbon

PAINT IT BLACK C. Jones color *Bloomberg Businessweek* no4497 p67 O 31 2016

Activated carbon—Evaluation

THIS IS CLEAN COAL S. Chodosh color *Popular Science* v289 no2 p24 Mr/Ap 2017

Activated carbon—Therapeutic use

BLACK MAGIC L. Turner color *Amazing Wellness* v9 no4 p66 Summ 2017

Active biological transport

From chaos to order in active fluids A. Morozov bibl color *Science* v355 no6331 p1262 Mr 24 2017

Active galactic nuclei

A CLOSER LOOK AT A SUPERMASSIVE BLACK HOLE diag *Astronomy* v45 no8 p18 Ag 2017

Active galaxies

The Perseus Galaxy Cluster T. Forte *Sky & Telescope* v133 no1 p57 Ja 2017

Active Interest Media Inc.

Operations cont. USTRC & WSTR *Spin to Win Rodeo* v21 no6 p10 Ag 2017

USTRC CHANGES OWNERSHIP color *Spin to Win Rodeo* v21 no6 p8 Ag 2017

Active learning

Room for Debate M. Rubino *Indianapolis Monthly* v40 no5 p8 Ja 2017

Activision Blizzard Inc.

A GIANT ENTERS A NEW ARENA M. Lev-ram chart color *Fortune* v175 no8 p192 Je 15 2017

Activism

    See also

      Civil disobedience

      Environmental activism

      Shareholder activism

Apocalypse Hound J. LILEKS *National Review* v69 no16 p37 Ag 28 2017

As American as Refusing to Stand for the National Anthem R. Wiedeman img *New York* p34 F 20 2017

THE CAMERA MAN: Duane Cramer is on a mission to change the narrative around black men in popular culture D. ANDERSON-MINSHALL *Advocate* no1093 p14 O/N 2017

CIVIL UNREST C. P. Pierce and T. Keith color *Sports Illustrated* v127 no8 p16 S 18 2017

Don't forget the kids S. Butler *U.S. Catholic* v82 no11 p4 N 2017

HOW CONSUMERS REACT WHEN CEOS TAKE CONTROVERSIAL STANDS *Harvard Business Review* v94 no11 p26 N 2016

In Praise of Women Who Speak Their Minds C. Leive color *Glamour* v115 no3 p28 Mr 2017

Is It Safe for CEOs to Voice Strong Political Opinions? L. Gaines-Ross *Harvard Business Review Digital Articles* p2 Je 23 2016

MEDEA BENJAMIN AND THE POLITICS OF DISRUPTION R. Conniff color *Progressive* p58 D 2016/Ja 2017

PROGRESSIVE 2016 Honor Role J. Nichols color *Nation* v304 no2 p20 Ja 16 2017

Starbucks' "Race Together" Campaign and the Upside of CEO Activism A. Chatterji and M. Toffel *Harvard Business Review Digital Articles* p2 Mr 24 2015

What CEO Activism Looks Like in the Trump Era L. Gaines-Ross *Harvard Business Review Digital Articles* p2 O 2 2017

YOU: THE INSTANT EXPERT ACTIVISM color *Women's Health* v14 no3 p161 Ap 2017

Activism—Social aspects

CENTURY marks *Christian Century* v134 no14 p8 Jl 5 2017

Activists

    See also

      Environmentalists

      Radicals

      Women political activists

4 Types of Activist Investors and How to Spot Them D. Romito *Harvard Business Review Digital Articles* p2 O 7 2015

ALICIA RIVERA: THE COMMUNITY ORGANIZER DETAILS HER QUEST FOR ENVIRONMENTAL JUSTICE IN WILMINGTON, WHERE RESIDENTS LIVE IN THE SHADOW OF AN OIL FACILITY J. HERBST *Los Angeles Magazine* v62 no9 p97 S 2017

CONSTITUENTS AT THE GATES L. PENZ *In These Times* v41 no4 p11 Ap 2017

Hipsters Go Home cartoon color *Weekly Standard* v22 no44 p3 Jl 31 2017

Jamie Green-Fergerson *Atlanta* v57 no2 p109 Je 2017

Malala Yousafzai R. Collard color *Time* v190 no4 p56 Jl 24 2017

Not in Her Name color *Weekly Standard* v22 no39 p2 Je 19 2017

THEY'VE CREATED HEIR OWN MEDIA ECOSYSTEM N. RICHARDSON img *New York* v50 no9 p46 My 1 2017

THE TROUBLE WITH "ACTIVIST": A case for dropping the A-word J. M. SMUCKER *In These Times* v41 no6 p28 Je 2017

Youth Voices Are Powerful Z. LOFTUS-FARREN color *Earth Island Journal* v32 no1 p47 Spr 2017

Activists—Attitudes

THE WAR IN SYRIA CANNOT BE WON. BUT IT CAN BE ENDED P. BENNIS color *Nation* v303 no22 p12 N 28 2016

Activists—China

Liu Xiaobo C. Campbell color *Time* v190 no5 p17 Jl 31 2017

Activists—Interviews

Billie Jean King Understands Colin Kaepernick A. M. Cox *New York Times Magazine* p70 S 17 2017

'Great Things Come Out of Discomfort': An Interview with Our Revolution's Nina Turner N. Stockwell color *Progressive* v81 no7 p60 O/N 2017

Life's Work: An Interview with Alice Waters A. Beard color *Harvard Business Review* v95 no3 p176 My/Je 2017

Activists—United States

Charlene Carruthers D. HOLLIDAY color *Chicago* v66 no6 p93 Je 2017

ON MARTIN LUTHER KING D. Halberstam *Harper's Magazine* v334 no2001 p39 F 2017

RISE OF THE GRASSROOTS T. Dickinson color *Rolling Stone* no1295 p31 S 7 2017

SIRDEANER WALKER S. DOMINUS *New York Times Magazine* p47 D 25 2016

Tubman Time S. Richardson bw *American History* v52 no2 p6 Je 2017

UNDERMINED E. GRISWOLD cartoon color *New Yorker* v93 no19 p48 Jl 3 2017

Activists—United States—Social conditions—21st century

The Rise of the Violent Left P. Beinart color *Atlantic* v320 no2 p13 S 2017

Activities of daily living

17 HAPPY, HEALTHY CHOICES for 2017 [Cover story] B. BURKE color *Redbook* p13 F 2017

day tripping A. BURROUGHS *Psychology Today* v49 no5 p96 S/O 2016

How to Stop Overplanning (Even If You're a Perfectionist) E. G. Saunders *Harvard Business Review Digital Articles* p2 Ag 24 2015

My LIST: 24 hours with Cindy Crawford N. Silva-Jelly color *Harper's Bazaar* no3657 p126 O 2017

Would You Rather... color *Seventeen* v76 no5 p110 S 2017

Your Perfect Day S. KLEIN cartoon color *Prevention* v68 no11 p50 N 2016

Activity programs in education

How Can I Rock a... Group Project? *Scholastic Choices* v32 no3 p24 N/D 2016

Actman, Jani

BORN TO BE WILD color *National Geographic* v232 no4 p22 O 2017

Acton, Peter

Is the Era of Mass Manufacturing Coming to an End? *Harvard Business Review Digital Articles* p2 D 5 2014

Actors

    See also

    Actresses

    African American actors

    Child actors

    Drag queens

    Male actors

    Motion picture actors & actresses

    Photography of actors

    Stunt performers

    Television actors & actresses

The 10 Best Performances S. Zacharek color *Time* v188 no25-26 p134 D 19 2016 Double Issue

16 ACTORS W. MORRIS and A. O. SCOTT color *New York Times Magazine* p52 D 11 2016

5 JUICY QUESTIONS with... SCOTT SPEEDMAN C. Keller color *Women's Health* v14 no4 p128 My 2017

Adam DRIVER N. BAUMBACH *Interview* v46 no10 p74 D 2016/Ja 2017

Adam West (1928-2017) M. Roush *TV Guide* v65 no27 p3 Je 26 2017

Adam West S. Zacharek color *Time* v189 no24 p11 Je 26 2017

Alan Thicke: 1947-2016 M. Roush *TV Guide* v65 no2 p10 Ja 2 2017

Alan Thicke D. D'addario color *Time* v188 no27-28 p17 D 26 2016

Alden EHRENREICH M. MARTIN *Interview* v46 no9 p86 N 2016

ALMOST FAMOUS N. PARSI color *Chicago* v66 no11 p37 N 2017

Armie Hammer Has Two Turkeys D. WALTERS color *Bon Ap-*

petit no11 p24 N 2017

Ben SCHNETZER M. MARTIN *Interview* v46 no8 p30 O 2016

The Big Chill color *GQ: Gentlemen's Quarterly* v97 no11 p142 N 2017

Dustin Hoffman on Playing Fathers E. Berman color *Time* v190 no16/17 p105 O 23 2017

ELBA'S EASE [Cover story] M. POTTER bw color *Esquire* p50 Ag 2017

Everything Old Is New Again L. Mulcahy *Stage Directions* v30 no1 p20 Ja 2017

Fit to be KING P. SYKES color *Vogue* v206 no11 p174 N 2016

From thirtysomething to This Is Us: My Pop Culture Milestones K. OLIN and J. Halterman *TV Guide* v65 no43 p12 O 16 2017

Genius I. Rudolph *TV Guide* v65 no13 p32 Mr 20 2017

GOSLING'S FIRST LAW OF STYLE bw *GQ: Gentlemen's Quarterly* v87 no1 p100 Ja 2017

HIS OWN VERSION J. DUBOFF color *Vanity Fair* v59 no7 p107 Summ 2017

HOLLYWOOD GRABS BACK *Interview* v47 no5 p40 Je/Jl 2017

HOW I GOT MY STYLE J. Roth color *Esquire* p44 O 2017

HOW TED DANSON FOUND HIS Balance D. HOCHMAN color *AARP: The Magazine* v30 no6A p54 O/N 2017

Jack LOWDEN G. BANKS *Interview* v47 no3 p20 Ap 2017

Jeremy Irons M. Rochlin color *AARP: The Magazine* v59 no2A p14 F/Mr 2016

JON GLASER N. Weldon color *Runner's World* v52 no1 p112 Ja/F 2017

Keir GILCHRIST J. ORTVED *Interview* v47 no6 p10 Ag 2017

Keith Stanfield D. Kiper color *Current Biography* v78 no8 p73 Ag 2017

Kyle MACLACHLAN B. Handy bw *Esquire* p124 My 2017

Laurence Lightens Up color *AARP: The Magazine* v30 no6A p11 O/N 2017

Lighten Your Workload B. CARLEY color *GQ: Gentlemen's Quarterly* v97 no7 p84 Jl 2017

THE LOOK BOOK A. SWERDLOFF img *New York* v50 no15 p43 Jl 24 2017

Lucas HEDGES M. MARTIN *Interview* v46 no10 p30 D 2016/ Ja 2017

MAKING THE COVER color *Ebony* v72/73 no12/1 p14 O/N 2017

Miguel Ferrer L. Rice color *Entertainment Weekly* no1451/1452 p20 F 3-10 2017

Mike Judge R. MCCAMMON color *GQ: Gentlemen's Quarterly* v97 no6 p128 Je 2017

MOTY DUDE FINALLY MADE IT [Cover story] A. Peele color *GQ: Gentlemen's Quarterly* v86 no12 p172 D 2016

Nelsan Ellis: 1977-2017 K. Hahn *TV Guide* v65 no31 p9 Jl 24 2017

Nelsan Ellis T. Stack color *Entertainment Weekly* no1474/1475 p20 Jl 21-28 2017

New Wave N. HELLER and C. SCHAMA color *Vogue* v207 no9 p614 S 2017

"People Need a Villain": T. J. Miller knows you think he's crazy for leaving HBO's Silicon Valley, and he cares not in the least D. Marchese img *New York* v50 no15 p57 Jl 24 2017

Pierce BROSNAN S. HAYEK *Interview* v47 no3 p34 My 2017

PLAY ANYTHING A. Bilmes color *Esquire* p27 O 2017

POWERS BOOTHE A. Breznican color *Entertainment Weekly* no1467 p17 My 26 2017

Robert Vaughn, 1932-2016 cartoon color *Weekly Standard* v22 no12 p3 N 28 2016

School of LIFE A. Green bw *Vogue* v206 no11 p222 N 2016

The Self-Made Screenwriter: Taylor Sheridan has a two-step approach to becoming an Oscar-nominated writer. One: Read lots of bad scripts. Two: Do better D. Marchese img *New York* v50 no15 p62 Jl 24 2017

Shabby Chic J. EPSTEIN color *Weekly Standard* v23 no1 p5 S 11 2017

SPIRITED AWAY J. Powers color *Vogue* v206 no12 p254 D 2016

SPOTLIGHT ON: BILLY BROWN A. TINUBU color *Ebony* v72 no11 p76 S 2017

STARCATION: WASHINGTON, D.C K. CHANEY color *Ebony* v72 no8 p56 Je 2017

To Life! [Cover story] D. HOCHMAN color *AARP: The Magazine* v59 no2A p56 F/Mr 2016

Tom Hanks *New York Times Book Review* p8 O 15 2017

Tom Selleck J. STOWE color *Men's Health* v32 no9 p124 N 2017

Trevante RHODES R. JUZWIAK *Interview* v46 no9 p22 N 2016

Twilight Cowboy or (Why Michael Keaton Would Rather Be a Dog) B. Luscombe color *Time* v188 no24 p56 D 12 2016

VOTE tHE ROCK [Cover story] C. WEAVER bw color *GQ: Gentlemen's Quarterly* v97 no6 p84 Je 2017

WHEN LIFE GOES BOOM T. DASWICK and P. Kita cartoon color *Men's Health* v32 no2 p20 Mr 2017

A WOMAN OF INFLUENCE E. POENISCH bw color *Esquire* p120 O 2017

THE WORLD ACCORDING TO GOLDBLUM A. PEELE color *GQ: Gentlemen's Quarterly* v97 no11 p134 N 2017

YES, CAMERON DALLAS WOULD DATE YOU! K. Williams color *Seventeen* v76 no3 p74 My 2017

Actors as motion picture producers & directors

A MAN FOR ALL REASONS [Cover story] C. Nashawaty color *Entertainment Weekly* no1486 p26 O 13 2017

Actors Theatre of Louisville

Props *Stage Directions* v30 no7 p48 Jl 1 2017

Actors—Attitudes

ALAN THICKE J. Kerns and D. Snierson color *Entertainment Weekly* no1446/1447 p84 D 2016/Ja 2017

PARTY LINES img *New York* v49 no24 p152 N 28 2016

Actors—Australia—Biography

Ben Mendelsohn J. Crelin color *Current Biography* v78 no2 p48 F 2017

Actors—Awards

BEST ACTOR S. Vilkomerson, K. P. Sullivan et al color diag *Entertainment Weekly* no1451/1452 p54 F 3-10 2017

BEST SUPPORTING ACTOR S. Li, D. Franich et al color diag *Entertainment Weekly* no1451/1452 p50 F 3-10 2017

Oscar Shows Its Colors P. Travers color *Rolling Stone* no1281/1282 p54 F 23 2017

Should Awards Shows Be Gender-Neutral? N. Sperling color *Entertainment Weekly* no1466 p16 My 19 2017

Actors—Biography

Alexander Skarsgård R. Means color *Current Biography* v78 no1 p78 Ja 2017

Actors—Congresses

Fairground color *Vanity Fair* v59 no1 p102 Holiday 2017

Actors—Employment

But Seriously, Folks M. Snetiker color *Entertainment Weekly* no1434 p62 O 7 2016

What's Next for Hamilton's Breakout Stars? I. Biedenharn, J. Derschowitz et al color *Entertainment Weekly* no1454/1455 p104 F 24 2017

Actors—Great Britain

Hot Actor Joe Alwyn D. FEAR color *Rolling Stone* no1274 p41 N 17 2016

No Rest for the Wicked M. Z. SEITZ img *New York* p76 Ja 9 2017

ROGER MOORE C. Nashawaty color *Entertainment Weekly* no1468/1469 p80 Je 2-9 2017

Actors—Great Britain—Biography

Alex Sharp D. Kiper color *Current Biography* v78 no2 p74 F 2017

Actors—Health

The 7.5 Rules of Awesome [Cover story] M. ZIMMERMAN and R. REYNOLDS color *Men's Health* v32 no7 p27 S 2017

LIFE ON THE BIG SCREEN WITH TYPE 1 DIABETES A. Yu color *Maclean's* v129 no48/49 p38 D 5 2016

Actors—Interviews

12 Questions for Kumail Nanjiani A. RAPOPORT bw *Bon Appetit* v62 no7 p24 Jl 2017

Andrew Rannells A. ROSEN color *Bon Appetit* v61 no11 p28 N 2016

And Then God Gave Us... Sam Heughan color *Glamour* v115 no10 p46 O 2017

Beat Shazam M. Roffman *TV Guide* v65 no21 p38 My 15 2017

Blindspot D. Holbrook color *TV Guide* v64 no42 p35 O 10 2016

BOYFRIEND MATERIAL C. Murray color *Essence* v47 no7 p48 N 2016

David HYDE PIERCE cartoon *Vanity Fair* v59 no5 p166 Ap 2017

DAYTIME M. LOGAN *TV Guide* v65 no37 p54 S 4 2017

Ellar COLTRANE T. E. SHULTS *Interview* v47 no1 p102 F 2017

GROUNDHOG Deus D. MARTINEZ *Texas Monthly* v45 no4 p74 Ap 2017

Guess who's in the new LEMONY SNICKET? C. KOPACZEWSKI color *Good Housekeeping* v264 no2 p140 F 2017

I Love Dick D. Holbrook *TV Guide* v65 no13 p38 Mr 20 2017

THE NATURAL [Cover story] M. Hainey bw color *Esquire* p92 O 2017

NO MORE MR. NICE GUY: On HBO's Ballers, good egg Steve Guttenberg breaks bad--and puts Dwayne Johnson between a rock and a hard place M. LOGAN *TV Guide* v65 no31 p22 Jl 24 2017

Open to Possibilities B. Levine bw *Publishers Weekly* v263 no44 p(Sp)18 O 31 2016

Supernatural color *TV Guide* v64 no42 p41 O 10 2016

THE THINKING MAN: MIKE COLTER M. Khidekel color *Women's Health* v14 no8 p118 O 2017

Actors—Italy—Biography

ISABELLA ROSSELLINI D. KAMP bw *Vanity Fair* v59 no1 p106 Holiday 2017

Actors—Salaries, wages, etc.

Big Exits on Hawaii Five-0: The drama says "aloha" to actors Daniel Dae Kim and Grace Park J. Halterman *TV Guide* v65 no31 p3 Jl 24 2017

Actors—United States

See also

African American actors

1926-2017 Harry Dean Stanton D. Franich color *Entertainment Weekly* no1484 p17 S 29 2017

The 3-Minute Interview J. Kantor and J. Harman bw *Glamour* no8 p40 Ag 2017

58 MINUTES WITH...: Alec Baldwin: Swanning through the Hamptons with the presidential impersonator J. PRESSLER *New York* v50 no16 p24 Ag 7 2017

Actors bw cartoon color *American Cowboy* p24 LEGENDS OF TEXAS Special Issue 2017

Adam West J. McGovern color *Entertainment Weekly* no1471 p20 Je 23 2017

Bill Paxton J. Cameron color *Time* v189 no9 p14 Mr 13 2017

CALL TO STARDOM R. COHEN color *Vanity Fair* v59 no2 p62 F 2017

CANDID Cameraman: JASON LEE EXPLAINS WHY HE LEFT LOS ANGELES FOR DENTON AND WHY, RIGHT NOW, HE PREFERS TAKING PHOTOGRAPHS TO ACTING M. J. MOONEY *Texas Monthly* v45 no7 p52 Jl 2017

CHADWICK BOSEMAN UPS HIS GAME [Cover story] B. SCHMIDT and C. Saunders color *Ebony* v72/73 no12/1 p70 O/N 2017

CLEAR WEATHERLY [Cover story] A. D'ARMINIO color *TV Guide* v64 no42 p20 O 10 2016

Droll Model M. WAKIM color *Los Angeles Magazine* v62 no10 p84 O 2017

GETTING ON WITH IT E. HYNES color *Film Comment* v53 no3 p31 My/Je 2017

HIT AND RUN J. ANDERSON-MINSHALL color *Advocate* no1090 p38 Ap 2017

John Heard J. McGovern color *Entertainment Weekly* no1476 p49 Ag 4 2017

KURT RUSSELL E. SPITZNAGEL bw *Men's Health* v32 no3 p128 Ap 2017

Lakeith Stanfield, Contemporary Chameleon E. Berman color *Time* v190 no8 p47 Ag 28 2017

LIFE'S WORK: An Interview with ALAN ALDA ACTOR bw *Harvard Business Review* v95 no4 p152 Jl/Ag 2017

A MAN APART M. HASKELL bw color *Film Comment* v53 no3 p26 My/Je 2017

Mike Colter C. Mari color *Current Biography* v78 no6 p30 Je 2017

REAL WORK I. Parker cartoon *New Yorker* v93 no18 p19 Je 26 2017

A SHARED REALITY P. BERG bw *Vanity Fair* v59 no1 p156 Holiday 2017

SHOWTIME'S FORAY INTO GENDERLESS TV D. ARTAVIA color *Advocate* no1090 p36 Ap 2017

St. Midas' Prep M. S. Thomas bw *Commonweal* v114 no14 p9 S 8 2017

STYLE YOUR GUY A. Dorsey color *Essence* v48 no6 p36 O 2017

A True Texas Gentleman D. Franich, C. Collis et al color *Enter-*

tainment Weekly no1456 p12 Mr 10 2017
TURN IT UP TO 11 J. YUAN img *New York* v49 no24 p114 N 28 2016
Tyrese Gibson P. G. Cooper *Current Biography* v78 no6 p47 Je 2017

Actors—United States—Attitudes
TRAVOLTA HOLDS COURT C. WEAVER color *GQ: Gentlemen's Quarterly* v86 no12 p182 D 2016

Actors—United States—Biography
Daveed Diggs J. Johnson color *Current Biography* v78 no2 p26 F 2017
The Lightness of Errol Flynn B. DOYLE *American Scholar* v86 no1 p100 Wint 2017

Actors—United States—Economic conditions
DEPP FINANCING M. SEAL color *Vanity Fair* v59 no8 p110 Ag 2017

Actors—United States—Economic conditions—21st century
Dwayne Johnson ALMIGHTY BALLER [Cover story] A. Shipnuck color *Sports Illustrated* v125 no18 p28 D 5 2016

Actors—United States—Interviews
Bob Odenkirk C. HOARD bw *Rolling Stone* no1285 p58 Ap 20 2017

Actors—United States—Political activity
Lena Dunham B. HIATT color *Rolling Stone* no1281/1282 p21 F 23 2017

Actresses
See also
Women stunt performers
1917-2016 Zsa Zsa Gabor D. Coggan color *Entertainment Weekly* no1446/1447 p26 D 2016/Ja 2017
36 MINUTES WITH ... Isabelle Huppert A. LAROCCA img *New York* p20 Ja 9 2017
The 3-Minute Interview color *Glamour* v115 no5 p28 My 2017
ACCORDING TO: Kaitlin Olson J. DUBOFF bw *Vanity Fair* v59 no11 p72 N 2017
AMAZING GRACE N. Silva-Jelly color *Harper's Bazaar* no3657 p244 O 2017
Anna Kendrick color *New York Times Book Review* p10 D 4 2016
Babe RUTH M. HOLGATE and M. GUIDUCCI color *Vogue* v207 no3 p348 Mr 2017
BEAT STREET color *Essence* v47 no7 p84 N 2016
BEHIND THE SCENES WITH Ariel Winter color *Seventeen* v75 no11 p10 N 2016
BEST DRESS E. Wilson color *InStyle* v24 no6 p41 Je 2017
Big5-Oh C. Ianzito color *AARP: The Magazine* v30 no6A p76 O/N 2017
Big 5-Oh C. Ianzito color *AARP: The Magazine* v60 no5A p72 Ag/S 2017
BLONDE Ambition G. WILLIAMS color *Vogue* v207 no7 p53 Jl 2017
THE Boss [Cover story] color *Glamour* v115 no10 p156 O 2017
Brie Spirit [Cover story] K. SMITH color *Vanity Fair* v59 no6 p76 My 2017
Brit MARLING [Cover story] M. GLADWELL *Interview* v47 no2 p118 Mr 2017
Cate Blanchett HER BEST EVER E. Wilson color *InStyle* v24 no11 p78 N 2017
Claire Foy C. Mari color *Current Biography* v78 no5 p30 My 2017
Cynthia Erivo B. Muteba color *Current Biography* v77 no11 p40 N 2016
Daisy Ridley J. Crelin color *Current Biography* v77 no11 p73 N 2016
Danai Gurira B. Muteba color *Current Biography* v77 no10 p44 O 2017
DAYS OF OUR LIVES M. LOGAN *TV Guide* v65 no41 p42 O 2 2017
DAYTIME M. LOGAN *TV Guide* v65 no43 p44 O 16 2017
Debra Winger B. Luscombe color *Time* v189 no18 p54 My 15 2017
A DIFFERENT DIRECTION T. A. Christian color *Essence* v48 no3 p51 Jl 2017
Edie Falco As an Attorney Ripped from the Headlines D. D'addario color *Time* v190 no10/11 p108 S 18 2017
EDIE FALCO I. Rudolph *TV Guide* v65 no37 p28 S 4 2017
EVA [Cover story] L. BERGER color *Redbook* p102 D 2016

Eva Green J. Crelin color *Current Biography* v77 no10 p39 O 2016
Felicity Goes Rogue K. Valby color *Glamour* v115 no1 p88 Ja 2017
THE FEMALE VOICE OF NJÁLL V. HAFSTAÐ *Iceland Review* v54 no5 p14 S-O 2016
FEROCIOUS SUSAN HAYWARD *Saturday Evening Post* v289 no2 p93 Mr/Ap 2017
Florence Henderson 1934-2016 D. D'Addario color *Time* v188 no24 p70 D 12 2016
FRESH FACE: RUTH NEGGA color *Essence* v47 no8 p58 D 2016
THE Fresh Faces A. Rambharose color *Glamour* v115 no10 p178 O 2017
FROM HEAVEN TO HELL A. D'ARMINIO *TV Guide* v65 no31 p16 Jl 24 2017
FROM THE ARCHIVE J. Nilsson *Saturday Evening Post* v289 no2 p94 Mr/Ap 2017
GET SCULPTED LIKE YOUR GIRL CRUSH T. E. Hopkins color *Essence* v48 no3 p115 Jl 2017
getting ready with SALMA HAYEK D. GLUCK color *Better Homes & Gardens* v95 no4 p16 Ap 2017
GHOUL TALK C. Collis color *Entertainment Weekly* no1436/1437 p104 O 21 2016
THE GOOD WIFE: She has our vote! Sela Ward makes a power play in the dramatic new season of Graves J. HALTERMAN *TV Guide* v65 no43 p16 O 16 2017
A GOOD YEAR FOR BAD WOMEN D. Coggan color *Entertainment Weekly* no1444/1445 p54 D 16 2016
GROWING UP NICELY C. Murray color *Essence* v48 no3 p52 Jl 2017
Gugu Mbatha-Raw J. Crelin color *Current Biography* v78 no5 p58 My 2017
Gus BIRNEY C. KELSEY *Interview* v46 no10 p28 D 2016/Ja 2017
Hannah GROSS *Interview* v47 no5 p67 Je/Jl 2017
HARD AS NAILS T. S. Young color *Essence* v48 no3 p52 Jl 2017
Herizen GUARDIOLA S. LACAVA *Interview* v46 no9 p20 N 2016
I Love My Dining Room M. HARDIN color *House Beautiful* v159 no5 p104 Je 2017
I Was a Child Star--and Lived to Tell About It A. JOHNSON and D. Holbrook *TV Guide* v65 no19 p13 My 1 2017
A Jersey Girl Dreams Big S. Zacharek color *Time* v190 no8 p50 Ag 28 2017
Jessica HENWICK S. LACAVA *Interview* v47 no1 p12 F 2017
Jodie COMER K. AFTAB *Interview* v47 no2 p64 Mr 2017
JUDE DEMOREST K. SMITH color *Vanity Fair* v59 no1 p65 Holiday 2017
Jurnee toward justice M. CHARLES color *Ebony* v72 no5 p76 Mr 2017
Kate Mara J. ZAMBRANO color *O, The Oprah Magazine* p23 Je 2017
KATHY BATES *Interview* v47 no6 p16 Ag 2017
Kathy Bates M. WAKIM *Los Angeles Magazine* p78 D 2016
KRISTEN SCHAAL N. Weldon color *Runner's World* v52 no5 p96 Je 2017
Looking Sharp J. POWERS and C. SCHAMA color *Vogue* v207 no9 p611 S 2017
Loretta Devine P. G. Cooper color *Current Biography* v78 no5 p23 My 2017
LUCKY IN LOVE: Actress Diora Baird discovered her family's missing piece D. ANDERSON-MINSHALL *Advocate* no1093 p26 O/N 2017
Mandy Moore M. Gajanan color *Time* v189 no24 p50 Je 26 2017
MATILDA LUTZ K. SMITH color *Vanity Fair* v59 no2 p29 F 2017
Melissa LEO color *O, The Oprah Magazine* p32 N 2017
MILLIE BOBBY BROWN M. ZIEGLER *Interview* v46 no9 p56 N 2016
My LIST L. Christensen color *Harper's Bazaar* no3655 p66 Ag 2017
My Obsessions... *TV Guide* v65 no13 p8 Mr 20 2017
My Sister's Keeper K. Kyles *Ebony* v72 no5 p14 Mr 2017
Nice to See You color *Glamour* v115 no7 p110 Jl 2017
On the Bright Side A. GREEN and V. STEIKER color *Vogue* v207

no3 p384 Mr 2017

Phillipa Soo M. Hagan color *Current Biography* v77 no11 p77 N 2016

Pom KLEMENTIEFF A. LEDGERWOOD *Interview* v47 no3 p18 My 2017

Rachel KELLER S. LACAVA *Interview* v46 no8 p28 O 2016

Real Talk L. REGENSDORF color *Vogue* v207 no4 p167 Ap 2017

Ruth Negga M. Rich color *Current Biography* v78 no5 p63 My 2017

Sarah Jessica PARKER *Interview* v46 no9 p128 N 2016

Sasha LANE M. GUIDUCCI color *Vogue* v206 no12 p138 D 2016

THE Sex Bomb K. Hahn bw *Glamour* v115 no10 p170 O 2017

SOFIA Boutella L. RAMZI color *Vogue* v207 no7 p48 Jl 2017

Sophie Turner M. Hagan color *Current Biography* v77 no10 p92 O 2016

Still Standing P. Williams *Indianapolis Monthly* v12 no40 p86 Ag 2017

SYLVIA HOEKS K. SMITH color *Vanity Fair* v59 no9 p113 S 2017

That GIRL J. POWERS color *Vogue* v206 no11 p178 N 2016

We Are Family A. Teran color *Glamour* v115 no5 p180 My 2017

A WEEK OF Awesome Outfits L. BELL color *Good Housekeeping* v265 no3 p36 S 2017

A Wellspring of Comfort M. Mccormick color *Time* v188 no24 p70 D 12 2016

WHAT'S IN THE CARDS FOR '17? color *Esquire* v167 no1 p5 F 2017

THE Z FACTOR [Cover story] A. Aguirre color *Vogue* v207 no7 p74 Jl 2017

Zoe Saldana, Actor E. Dockterman color *Time* v189 no3 p60 Ja 16 2017

Actresses—Attitudes

APOLOGIZER T. Friend cartoon *New Yorker* v92 no36 p17 N 7 2016

Emma Stone's Hollywood Ending [Cover story] J. Weiner color *Rolling Stone* no1278/1279 p34 Ja 12 2017

NICOLE KIDMAN'S BAD WOMEN K. BUCHANAN img *New York* v49 no24 p130 N 28 2016

Actresses—Awards

BALLOT color *Entertainment Weekly* no1451/1452 p77 F 3-10 2017

BEST ACTRESS J. McGovern, D. Coggan et al color diag *Entertainment Weekly* no1451/1452 p44 F 3-10 2017

BEST SUPPORTING ACTRESS N. Sperling, J. McGovern et al color diag *Entertainment Weekly* no1451/1452 p62 F 3-10 2017

THE ORIGINAL S. Li color *Entertainment Weekly* no1474/1475 p76 Jl 21-28 2017

Actresses—Biography

Allison Tolman C. Mari color *Current Biography* v78 no3 p82 Mr 2017

Jessie Mueller D. Kiper color *Current Biography* v78 no1 p41 Ja 2017

Maisie Williams J. Crelin color *Current Biography* v78 no3 p91 Mr 2017

Margot Robbie M. Rich color *Current Biography* v78 no1 p69 Ja 2017

Pamela Adlon J. Crelin color *Current Biography* v78 no1 p3 Ja 2017

Tracee Ellis Ross J. Crelin color *Current Biography* v78 no1 p74 Ja 2017

Actresses—Great Britain

LUCY BOYNTON K. SMITH color *Vanity Fair* v59 no11 p59 N 2017

Mystery Woman H. Als cartoon *New Yorker* v92 no33 p10 O 17 2016

Actresses—Great Britain—Biography

WALKING TALL J. LAHR bw cartoon *New Yorker* v92 no34 p34 O 24 2016

Actresses—Interviews

AMERICA [Cover story] A. SPENCER color *Redbook* p94 Mr 2017

Being Bardot L. CAMHI bw *Vogue* v206 no11 p100 N 2016

Carrie Fisher A. GREENE bw *Rolling Stone* no1276 p70 D 15 2016

Christine BARANSKI Z. POSEN *Interview* v47 no1 p21 F 2017

Dark Angel Star Joanne Froggatt on Playing England's First Se-

rial Killer S. GUTIERREZ *British Heritage Travel* v38 no3 p58 My/Je 2017

Downward Dog I. Ratledge *TV Guide* v65 no21 p35 My 15 2017

Goldie HAWN: AFTER A 15-YEAR HIATUS, THE GREAT, GLASS-CEILING-SHATTERING GOLDIE HAWN IS BACK IN THE PICTURE, AND HAVING A LAUGH WITH THE LADIES FOR WHOM SHE PAVED THE WAY K. HUDSON *Interview* v47 no3 p88 My 2017

Heroine Chic B. VOSS color *Advocate* no1089 p64 F/Mr 2017

Mackenzie DAVIS N. Haramis *Interview* v47 no5 p45 Je/Jl 2017

REESE'S SOUTHERN CHARM J. Reed color *Southern Living* v52 no9 p74 S 2017

RENAISSANCE Woman A. Grant color *Esquire* p56 O 2017

Ruth WILSON J. C. MITCHELL *Interview* v46 no9 p34 N 2016

Sigourney Weaver E. Berman color *Time* v189 no3 p57 Ja 16 2017

Somebody to Love B. VOSS *Advocate* no1088 p64 D 2016/Ja 2017

Somewhere Between J. Halterman *TV Guide* v65 no31 p30 Jl 24 2017

With The Band M. WAKIM *Los Angeles Magazine* p84 Ap 2017

Actresses—Political activity

Anne Hathaway E. Dockterman color *Time* v189 no10 p60 Mr 20 2017

Actresses—Social conditions—21st century

Kerry's Got This [Cover story] P. Mendoza color *Glamour* v115 no5 p156 My 2017

Actresses—United States

1932 - 2016 DEBBIE REYNOLDS C. Nashawaty color *Entertainment Weekly* no1448 p24 Ja 13 2017

ACCORDING TO: Anna Kendrick J. DUBOFF bw *Vanity Fair* v59 no1 p100 Holiday 2017

BEHIND THE SCENES WITH Maddie Ziegler color *Seventeen* v76 no4 p6 Jl/Ag 2017

Carol Burnett *Saturday Evening Post* v289 no1 p29 Ja/F 2017

DeWanda Wise D. L. D'oyley color *Essence* v47 no11 p42 Mr 2017

DOUBLE-SIDED M. Schulman cartoon *New Yorker* v93 no9 p22 Ap 17 2017

Elle Fanning J. Crelin color *Current Biography* v78 no8 p33 Ag 2017

Everything You Think You Know About Kathryn Hahn Is Wrong *New York* v50 no8 p126 Ap 17 2017

GILLIAN'S RAINBOW H. PORTER cartoon *Vanity Fair* v59 no1 p115 Holiday 2017

GRITTY WOMAN M. LOGAN *TV Guide* v64 no40 p46 O 3 2016

Hot Actress Haley Bennett A. MORRIS color *Rolling Stone* no1274 p40 N 17 2016

Impossible Dream K. Onstad img *New York* p55 Ja 23 2017

Insecure A. D'Arminio *TV Guide* v64 no40 p58 O 3 2016

Julia Garner M. Rich color *Current Biography* v78 no6 p43 Je 2017

Kate McKinnon D. Kiper color *Current Biography* v77 no11 p54 N 2016

KELLY ROHRBACH K. SMITH color *Vanity Fair* v59 no6 p49 My 2017

A Life in Bold [Cover story] E. PERETZ bw color *Vanity Fair* v59 no9 p182 S 2017

Lily Collins J. Johnson color *Current Biography* v78 no8 p22 Ag 2017

The MARY MARY MARY MARY MARY MARY MARY I Knew E. Asner and D. Snierson color *Entertainment Weekly* no1453 p34 F 17 2017

Mary Tyler Moore M. Roush color *TV Guide* v65 no7 p6 F 13 2017

Melissa Benoist J. Johnson color *Current Biography* v78 no6 p15 Je 2017

ME...SLOW DOWN? HELL, NO! R. R. Robertson color *Essence* v47 no11 p59 Mr 2017

Natalie Portman D. D'Addario color *Time* v188 no22-23 p112 N/D 2016

The Natural: Frances McDormand has built a career, and a passionate fan base, playing supporting roles; now, at 60, she has become an unconventional star J. Kisner *New York Times Magazine* p44 O 8 2017

NO BONES ABOUT IT D. ANDERSON-MINSHALL color *Advocate* no1090 p32 Ap 2017

Queen Sugar M. Logan color *TV Guide* v64 no42 p40 O 10 2016

Rashida Jones Changed Her Mind About Porn A. M. Cox *New York Times Magazine* p54 Jl 30 2017

Riley Keough R. SULLIVAN, M. HOLGATE et al color *Vogue* v207 no9 p372 S 2017

Star Without a Script J. MILLER bw color *Vanity Fair* v59 no1 p136 Holiday 2017

Susan Sarandon Is Ready to Rumble img *New York* p112 Mr 6 2017

TALL TALES? D. ANDERSON-MINSHALL color *Advocate* no1090 p34 Ap 2017

WHAT SHE SAID D. Owen cartoon *New Yorker* v92 no43 p21 Ja 2 2017

Actresses—United States—Employment

HALEY'S COMET I. Biedenharn color *Entertainment Weekly* no1435 p26 O 14 2016

Actresses—United States—Interviews

Michelle PFEIFFER: AFTER A BRIEF HIATUS, THE ONE-TIME SO-CAL SURFER GIRL TURNED SCREEN SIREN, THE THREE-TIME OSCAR NOMINEE—AND STILL SOMEHOW WOEFULLY UNDERRATED—MICHELLE PFEIFFER IS BACK IN A BIG WAY, WITH A BEVY OF FILMS TO ADD TO HER ALREADY... D. ARONOFSKY *Interview* v47 no3 p64 Ap 2017

STATE OF THE UNION [Cover story] C. Murray color *Essence* v47 no7 p76 N 2016

Acuff, Jon

A Tourist's Guide to Changing Careers *Harvard Business Review Digital Articles* p2 Ap 13 2015

ACUÑA-SOTO, RODOLFO

The Mystery of Cocoliztli bw color *Natural History* v125 no9 p21 S 2017

Acupressure

See also

Reflexotherapy

Acupuncture

Acupuncture for Colicky Babies?! Yes, It's a Thing! K. Rockwood color *Parents* v92 no7 p26 Jl 2017

Acupuncture *Mayo Clinic Health Letter* v35 no7 p4 Jl 2017

Alternative Medicine for Your Pet L. Oster color *Health* v31 no4 p70 My 2017

EMBRACE YOUR NATURAL BEAUTY M. Rabbitt and D. MACY color *Yoga Journal* no294 p27 S 2017

The ENERGY for HEALING [Cover story] B. ANDREWS color *Prevention* v69 no1 p64 Ja 2017

PULSE *Prevention* v69 no8 p8 Ag 2017

A SHARP APPROACH D. Bruno *Washingtonian Magazine* v52 no3 p181 D 2016

Acupuncture—Physiological aspects

ACUPUNCTURE A HOLISTIC TOOL FOR OPTIMUM HEALTH M. DEPAOLO *Arabian Horse World* v57 no4 p182 Ja 2017

Acupuncture—Therapeutic use

ACUPUNCTURE AS HEADACHE REMEDY *Saturday Evening Post* v289 no3 p69 My/Je 2017

Moving THE Needle N. Loeffler-Gladstone *Dance Spirit* v21 no7 p58 S 2017

Acupuncture—Therapeutic use—Research

This Just In J. Zorthian *Time* v189 no4 p21 F 6 2017

Acura automobile

See also

Acura MDX sport utility vehicle

2018 Acura TLX E. DYER color *Popular Mechanics* p43 S 2017

NEW CARS 2018-2019 [Cover story] M. Cantu, Z. Gale et al chart color *Motor Trend* v69 no9 p34 S 2017

ONCE MORE, INTO THE GREAT WIDE OPEN P. EGAN color *Road & Track* v68 no10 p88 Jl 2017

Acura automobile—Evaluation

New Car Profiles color diag *Consumer Reports* v82 no4 p52 Ap 2017

Acura Inc.

2018 Acura TLX E. DYER color *Popular Mechanics* p43 S 2017

Halo Bender B. Halvorson color *Car & Driver* v63 no1 p108 Jl 2017

LABOR PAINS D. ZENLEA color *Road & Track* v68 no5 p76 D 2016/Ja 2017

ONCE MORE, INTO THE GREAT WIDE OPEN P. EGAN color *Road & Track* v68 no10 p88 Jl 2017

ROAD TEST SUMMARY chart *Road & Track* v68 no5 p118 D 2016/Ja 2017

TITLE FIGHT J. BARUTH cartoon chart color diag graph *Road & Track* v68 no5 p42 D 2016/Ja 2017

Acura MDX sport utility vehicle

EVERYBODY'S EVERYTHING C. Walton color *Motor Trend* v69 no1 p38 Ja 2017

Halo Bender B. Halvorson color *Car & Driver* v63 no1 p108 Jl 2017

NEW SUVS & TRUCKS 2018-2019 [Cover story] M. Cantu, Z. Gale et al color *Motor Trend* v69 no10 p32 O 2017

Acura MDX sport utility vehicle—Evaluation

Acura MDX chart color *Motor Trend* v69 no1 p42 Ja 2017

Acura NSX automobile

Borrowed Time S. SMITH bw color *Road & Track* v69 no2 p24 S 2017

ROAD TEST SUMMARY chart *Road & Track* v68 no10 p106 Jl 2017

Acura NSX automobile—Evaluation

LABOR PAINS D. ZENLEA color *Road & Track* v68 no5 p76 D 2016/Ja 2017

ROAD TEST SUMMARY chart *Road & Track* v68 no5 p118 D 2016/Ja 2017

SUPERCAR SLAYER SEEKS WORTHY OPPONENT J. Cammisa chart color *Motor Trend* v68 no12 p52 D 2016

TITLE FIGHT J. BARUTH cartoon chart color diag graph *Road & Track* v68 no5 p42 D 2016/Ja 2017

Acushnet Co.

First Look STEALTH BOMBERS R. Sauerhaft and R. Sauerhaft color *Golf Magazine* v58 no11 p78 N 2016

Weapons of Choice M. Chwasky color *Golf Magazine* v59 no10 p94 O 2017

Acute diseases

The End M. Fischetti graph *Scientific American* v317 no3 p96 S 2017

Acyclovir

Why was the 3-year-old so irritable, and what was wrong with her eye? L. Sanders *New York Times Magazine* p20 F 19 2017

Ad Astra Rocket Co.

Here Comes the Space Cleanup Crew J. Bachman bw color diag *Bloomberg Businessweek* no4525 p32 Je 5 2017

Ad blockers (Computer software)

Ad Blockers and the Next Chapter of the Internet D. Searls *Harvard Business Review Digital Articles* p2 N 6 2015

Adair, Amy

An environment-dependent transcriptional network specifies human microglia identity color *Science* v356 no6344 p1248 Je 23 2017

Adair, Randy

THE COP WHO BECAME A ROBBER J. MAYSH *Los Angeles Magazine* v62 no9 p100 S 2017

Adalimumab

Guarding Big Pharma's Crown Jewel C. Koons *Bloomberg Businessweek* no4537 p17 S 11 2017

Adam (Biblical figure)

THE BIG QUESTION L. Grunwald, J. Eugenides et al cartoon *Atlantic* v320 no4 p124 N 2017

Adam, Bradley

COMMUNITY M. HOYER *Cycle World* v55 no10 p6 N 2016

Adamczyk, Alicia

3 Great Podcasts About Money color *Money* v46 no7 p15 Ag 2017

The BEST BANK FOR YOU color diag map *Money* v45 no10 p86 N 2016

Escape Gym Fees! color *Money* v46 no6 p21 Jl 2017

Paid Parent Leave: Rare color *Money* v46 no1 p21 Ja/F 2017

STRESSING OUT ABOUT MONEY WILL MAKE YOU LOOK OLDER color *Money* v45 no11 p15 D 2016

The War on Pre-Existing Conditions color *Money* v46 no8 p56 S 2017

What to Do If You Get Medical Bills You Can't Pay Off Promptly color *Money* v46 no8 p18 S 2017

What Young Adults Need to Know About Buying Health Insurance color *Money* v46 no7 p17 Ag 2017

Adameyko, Igor

Multipotent peripheral glial cells generate neuroendocrine cells of the adrenal medulla color *Science* v357 no6346 p46 Jl 7 2017

Neural circuitry gets rewired bibl color *Science* v354 no6314 p833 N 18 2016

Adamov, Alexey

Global atmospheric particle formation from CERN CLOUD measurements bibl graph map *Science* v354 no6316 p1119 D 2 2016

ADAMOVIC, MICHAEL

Woodland Wildflowers on the Edge *American Forests* v123 no2 p32 Summ 2017

Adams, Abigail, 1744-1818

1800: Washington, DC A. S. Adams *Lapham's Quarterly* v10 no1 p64 Wint 2017

Social Science and the Public Interest *Society* v54 no2 p93 Ap 2017

Adams, Amy, 1974-

HER 10 BEST EVER! Amy Adams E. Wilson color *InStyle* v23 no12 p74 N 2016

In Arrival, Amy Adams Takes a Listening Tour of the Universe S. Lansky color *Time* v188 no21 p65 N 21 2016

Only Connect R. DOUTHAT color *National Review* v68 no23 p42 D 19 2016

THOSE WONDROUS POWERS S. KLAWANS *Nation* v303 no23/24 p35 D 5 2016

ADAMS, BIBA

Rap Radar Podcast Shines as Voice of Hip-Hop Culture color *Ebony* v72 no8 p22 Je 2017

Adams, Bradley

2017 DUCATI SCRAMBLER DESERT SLED bw color *Cycle World* v56 no1 p24 Ja/F 2017

2017 DUCATI SCRAMBLER DESERT SLED color *Cycle World* v56 no3 p34 Ap 2017

2017 KTM 1090 ADVENTURE R color *Cycle World* v56 no5 p44 Je 2017

2017 MOTO GUZZI MGX-21 FLYING FORTRESS color *Cycle World* v55 no10 p10 N 2016

2017 SUZUKI GSX-R1000R [Cover story] color *Cycle World* v56 no4 p36 My 2017

ALPINESTARS' ALL-NEW SUPERTECH GLOVE color *Cycle World* v56 no1 p16 Ja/F 2017

ALPINESTARS TRACK VEST 2 color *Cycle World* v56 no4 p28 My 2017

THE BEAST 2.0 color *Cycle World* v56 no2 p52 Mr 2017

BELL PRO STAR HELMET color *Cycle World* v56 no3 p22 Ap 2017

DT-07 STREET TRACKER [Cover story] color *Cycle World* v56 no2 p30 Mr 2017

HEAD TRAUMA HITS HOME color *Cycle World* v56 no3 p18 Ap 2017

HITTING A MARK chart color *Cycle World* v56 no6 p56 Jl 2017

HONDA PUTS ONE FOOT IN THE MOTOAMERICA DOOR color *Cycle World* v56 no4 p24 My 2017

THE LITTLE ADVENTURE color *Cycle World* v56 no3 p38 Ap 2017

OSCAR BY ALPINESTARS MONTY RIDING SHOE color *Cycle World* v56 no1 p18 Ja/F 2017

STUDYING ABROAD color *Cycle World* v56 no1 p14 Ja/F 2017

THREE OF A KIND chart color *Cycle World* v56 no4 p42 My 2017

Totally Committed color *Cycle World* v55 no11 p54 D 2016

THE WAITING GAME chart color diag graph *Cycle World* v56 no7 p32 Ag 2017

ZAETA 530 SE color *Cycle World* v56 no2 p34 Mr 2017

Adams, Brooks

A BECKONING ANGST color *Art in America* v105 no5 p102 My 2017

DITHYRAMBS AND CENTAURS color *Art in America* v105 no8 p82 S 2017

ADAMS, BYRON

The Impact of a Large-Scale Climate Event on Antarctic Ecosystem Processes chart graph *BioScience* v66 no10 p848 O 1 2016

Adams, Carolyn

CAROLYN ADAMS R. Berman *Dance Magazine* v90 no12 p50 D 2016

ADAMS, CHARLES R., JR.

In Spite of Education ... *American Scholar* v86 no1 p3 Wint 2017

Adams, Danny

CAR TALK J. UHL *Indianapolis Monthly* p18 My 2017

Adams, Derrick

Interview *Interview* v46 no10 p67 D 2016/Ja 2017

Snowballs and Flags color *Art in America* v105 no3 p54 Mr 2017

The Society PAGE *Interview* v47 no1 p38 F 2017

Adams, Ed

log cabin tranquility N. E. OATES color diag *Cabin Living* p32 S 2017

Adams, Elizabeth J.

SOX2 promotes lineage plasticity and antiandrogen resistance in TP53- and RB1-deficient prostate cancer bibl graph *Science* v355 no6320 p1 Ja 6 2017

Adams, Eric

NEW HAMPSHIRE HAS THE SECOND-HIGHEST RATE OF DRUG OVERDOSES IN THE COUNTRY. A POLICE OFFICER IN LACONIA (POPULATION 16,000) HAS BEEN ASSIGNED ONE TASK: TO STOP THEM B. RACHLIN *New York Times Magazine* p22 Jl 16 2017

Adams, Gina

OUT SIDE THE BOX: THESE NINE TRENDSETTERS ARE STEPPING UP WASHINGTON STYLE WITH UNEXPECTED PAIRINGS, BOLD PRINTS, AND PERFECT TAILORING A. MOELLER *Washingtonian Magazine* v52 no12 p78 S 2017

Adams, Guy B.

The Evil That Institutions Do: Preventing it is a dilemma for managers, but it can be done M. Funkhouser *Governing* v30 no8 p59 My 2017

Adams, Henry, 1838-1918

SHOT OF COURAGE A. GOPNIK cartoon *New Yorker* v93 no30 p64 O 2 2017

Adams, Jamal

SAFETY First A. Benoit color *Sports Illustrated* v126 no12 p38 My 1 2017

Adams, James

Valor The Fighting Parson F. Jastrzembski color *Military History* v34 no4 p16 N 2017

Adams, Jane A.

The Murder Book: A Henry Johnstone Mystery color *Publishers Weekly* v263 no42 p52 O 17 2016

ADAMS, JENNY

Siam Revival color *Conde Nast Traveler* v52 no6 p38 Je/Jl 2017

Adams, Jill

Pretty farmhouse in Bennington bw color *Nebraska Life* v21 no5 p19 S/O 2017

Adams, John

THE QUEEN WHO BECAME A WENCH D. A. WOOD color *Missouri Life* v44 no5 p10 Ag 2017

Adams, Karen

DEVELOPING COLLECTION WITHOUT RESISTANCE color *Practical Horseman* v45 no9 p46 S 2017

Adams, Karla

YOU LIKE H&R! color *Horse & Rider* v56 no10 p22 O 2017

Adams, Kate

Why Leaders Are Easier to Coach than Followers *Harvard Business Review Digital Articles* p2 Mr 5 2015

Adams, Katrina, 1965-

Equal Measures N. Pantic color *Tennis* v53 no2 p6 Mr/Ap 2017

Adams, Kristin

CAR TALK J. UHL *Indianapolis Monthly* p18 My 2017

Adams, Kristina K.—Interviews

Member Spotlight: Kristina K. Adams S. Myrick *Parks & Recreation* v51 no11 p54 N 2016

Adams, Lance J.

Distribution and clinical impact of functional variants in 50,726 whole-exome sequences from the DiscovEHR study chart graph *Science* v354 no6319 paaf6814-1 D 23 2016

ADAMS, LORRAINE

For the Cause: Mary Gordon's novel looks back on a woman's idealistic days in the Spanish Civil War *New York Times Book Review* p12 Jl 23 2017

Adams, Lucy

HR Disrupted *People Management* p52 F 2017

Adams, Lucy—Interviews

"I'M A RECOVERING HR DIRECTOR": Lucy Adams has recast herself as a tough-talking consultant asking difficult questions about the future of HR. We posed a few of our own - on the BBC, the tabloids and the death of the HR manual R. JEFFERY *People Management* p42 Mr 2017

ADAMS, LYNN

Your True Stories *Reader's Digest* v188 no1126 p30 D 2016/Ja 2017

Adams, Marla

DAYTIME M. LOGAN *TV Guide* v65 no43 p44 O 16 2017

Adams, Michael, 1961-

Dirty Words K. CURRIE-KNIGHT cartoon color *Reason* v48 no8 p56 Ja 2017

Adams, Mike

Find Your Personal Power Move color *Golf Magazine* v59 no7 p54 Jl 2017

Adams, Nick

Parks and Rec and BMX: Alternative programming for today's youth *Parks & Recreation* v52 no8 p16 Ag 2017

Adams, Patrick

NIGHT LIFE cartoon *New Yorker* v93 no13 p25 My 15 2017

Adams, Paul

The Proxima Trail cartoon color *Popular Science* p69 Ja/F 2017

Adams, Richard, 1920-2016

Milestones *Time* v189 no3 p11 Ja 16 2017

Adams, Ryan, 1974-

RYAN ADAMS L. Greenblatt color *Entertainment Weekly* no1454/1455 p94 F 24 2017

Ryan Adams Offers His Opus of Despair I. Guzmán color *Time* v189 no6 p51 F 20 2017

Ryan Adams Relives His Wonder Years J. DOLAN color *Rolling Stone* no1281/1282 p52 F 23 2017

Adams, Ryan, 1974—Interviews

Hot Tracks: RYAN ADAMS L. ROBINSON color *Vanity Fair* v59 no9 p140 S 2017

ADAMS, SAMUEL

"A JOSEPH BEUYS" color *ARTnews* v115 no4 p138 Wint 2016/2017

AROUND BOSTON cartoon color *ARTnews* v115 no3 p147 Fall 2016

Adams, Sandra

JOHN MUIR SOCIETY *Sierra* v101 no4 p56 Jl/Ag 2016

Adams, Scott

COMIC TRIP C. WINTER color *Bloomberg Businessweek* no4516 p58 Mr 27 2017

Lost star may be failed supernova C. CROCKETT *Science News* v190 no8 p8 O 15 2016

Potential "Failed Supernova" Discovered M. YOUNG *Sky & Telescope* v134 no3 p10 S 2017

Adams, Stephanie

Echoes *National Parks* v91 no1 p8 Wint 2017

ADAMS, SUSAN

Driven color *Forbes* v199 no5 p46 My 16 2017

FREE MARKET PHILANTHROPY color *Forbes* v198 no6 p92 N 8 2016

Growing Pains color *Forbes* v200 no1 p35 Jl 27 2017

LESSONS AND IDEAS BY THE 100 GREATEST LIVING BUSINESS MINDS bw color *Forbes* v200 no3 p115 S 28 2017

Oh, the Places You'll Go! color *Forbes* v198 no7 p52 N 29 2016

Pet Smarter color *Forbes* v199 no1 p42 Ja 24 2017

The Point of All Returns color *Forbes* v200 no4 p75 O 24 2017

Shark Tank's Toothless Deals color graph *Forbes* v198 no7 p24 N 29 2016

THE WORLD'S BILLIONAIRES bw color diag graph map *Forbes* v199 no3 p84 Mr 28 2017

Adams, Timothy

A gift from the czar, and a puzzle solved color *Magazine Antiques* v184 no4 p46 Jl/Ag 2017

Adams, William D.

If Odysseus Started a Book Club *Humanities* v37 no4 p1 Fall 2016

Oh, the Humanities! color *Weekly Standard* v22 no41 p2 Jl 3 2017

Adams County (Ohio)

AU NATUREL: Eighty miles east of downtown, Edge of Appalachia Nature Preserve is expanding, and late summer is peak time to visit its prairie lands A. KONERMANN *Cincinnati Magazine* v50 no11 p26 Ag 2017

Adams Morgan (Washington, D.C.)

Take Us to Church R. MISNER color *Conde Nast Traveler* v52

no1 p46 Ja 2017

Adamson, Brent

Avoid These Common B2B Content Marketing Mistakes *Harvard Business Review Digital Articles* p2 F 10 2016

THE NEW SALES IMPERATIVE color diag il img *Harvard Business Review* v95 no2 p118 Mr/Ap 2017

Why Self Image Matters in B2B Sales *Harvard Business Review Digital Articles* p2 Ap 2 2015

ADAMSON, FIONA B.

The Growing Importance of Diaspora Politics *Current History* v115 no784 p291 N 2016

Adamson, Glenn

And that's the way it isn't bw cartoon color *Magazine Antiques* v184 no2 p24 Mr/Ap 2017

ANNABETH ROSEN color *Art in America* v105 no5 p122 My 2017

A fighting chance color *Magazine Antiques* v184 no3 p20 My/Je 2017

HEAVEN SENT cartoon color *Art in America* v105 no4 p90 Ap 2017

How we see refugees, yesterday and today color *Magazine Antiques* v183 no6 p22 N/D 2016

Knocking It Off color *Magazine Antiques* v184 no4 p22 Jl/Ag 2017

Make Americana great again: The Wunsch family has a plan color *Magazine Antiques* v183 no6 p42 N/D 2016

Matters of taste color *Magazine Antiques* v184 no1 p24 Ja/F 2017

MICHELLE GRABNER color *Art in America* v105 no3 p127 Mr 2017

Seeking asylum bw color *Magazine Antiques* v184 no5 p22 S/O 2017

Adamson, Göran

Was National Socialism Anti-Sex? On Left-Wing Fantasies and Sex as the Dark Matter of Politics *Society* v54 no1 p23 F 2017

Adamson, Matthew

The secret search for URANIUM IN COLD WAR MOROCCO *Physics Today* v70 no6 p54 Je 2017

Adansonia digitata

HELPING THE PLANET V. Tweed color *Amazing Wellness* v9 no1 p12 Wint 2017

Adaptability (Psychology)

See also

Resistance to change

The 3 Ways People React to Career Disasters P. Mirvis, M. Marks et al *Harvard Business Review Digital Articles* p2 Je 18 2015

Bumblebees show cognitive flexibility by improving on an observed complex behavior O. J. Loukola, C. J. Perry et al bibl diag *Science* v355 no6327 p833 F 24 2017

FIND A DEEPER HAPPINESS G. Graves color *Health* v31 no5 p100 Je 2017

Freeing Up J. SHERMAN *Psychology Today* v50 no1 p36 Ja/F 2017

life lessons J. LYTHCOTT-HAIMS *Parents* v91 no10 p48 O 2016

Things Are Looking Down A. MARKMAN *Psychology Today* v50 no3 p18 My/Je 2017

WE ARE DIFFERENT WE ARE FRIENDS J. BANIN and S. Booth color *Parents* v92 no11 p30 N 2017

When the Body Speaks S. O'Sullivan *Psychology Today* v50 no1 p72 Ja/F 2017

Adaptation (Biology)

See also

Adaptive radiation (Biology)

Stress (Physiology)

EVOLUTION AT THE LIMITS R. Riesch and M. Plath color diag map *Scientific American* v316 no4 p54 Ap 2017

FORECAST: UNCERTAIN K. Pierre-Louis color *Earth Island Journal* v32 no2 p48 Summ 2017

moisture misers P. Hess cartoon *Popular Science* v289 no2 p10 Mr/Ap 2017

Adaptation (Physiology)

Detection of human adaptation during the past 2000 years Y. Field, E. A. Boyle et al bibl graph *Science* v354 no6313 p760 N 11 2016

Palate and Possibility H. ESTROFF MARANO *Psychology Today* v50 no1 p34 Ja/F 2017

Adapters (Telecommunication)

GLIF TRIPOD ADAPTER FOR iPHONE G. FLEISHMAN color *Macworld - Digital Edition* v34 no8 p48 Ag 2017

Adapters (Telecommunication)—Evaluation

AUTOMATIC PRO: BE A BETTER DRIVER WITH THIS DRIVING DATA TRACKER IN YOUR CAR G. FLEISHMAN color map *Macworld - Digital Edition* v33 no11 p85 N 2016

BELKIN LIGHTNING AUDIO + CHARGE ROCKSTAR ADAPTER L. YAMSHON color *Macworld - Digital Edition* v33 no11 p53 N 2016

NONDA HUB+ MINI G. FLEISHMAN color *Macworld - Digital Edition* p43 D 2016

SATECHI SLIM ALUMINUM TYPE-C MULTIPORT ADAPTER: PORTABLE MACBOOK DOCK MAKES NO COMPROMISES G. FLEISHMAN color *Macworld - Digital Edition* p23 D 2016

Adaptive natural resource management

Bridging the Gaps between Science and Policy for the Sustainable Management of Rangeland Resources in the Developing World SHIKUI DONG, S. A. WOLF et al *BioScience* v67 no7 p656 Jl 2017

Adaptive radiation (Biology)

Pitcher Plants Shape Up L. GAUME, V. BAZILE et al color diag *Natural History* v125 no5 p12 My 2017

Adaptive reuse of buildings

Gathering Place color *Timber Home Living* v27 no5 p46 O 2017

A New Angle B. KAMIN color diag *Architectural Record* v205 no2 p74 F 2017

RENOVATION, RESTORATION, ADAPTATION color *Architectural Record* v205 no2 p61 F 2017

Where Credit Is Due bw color *Architectural Record* v205 no2 p16 F 2017

Adashi, Eli Y.

Influence, integrity, and the FDA: An ethical framework color *Science* v357 no6354 p876 S 1 2017

Aday (Company)

MEG HE J. Chen color *Bloomberg Businessweek* no4518 p79 Ap 10 2017

Addario, Lynsey

DO YOU (STILL) NEED A REAL CAMERA? color *Popular Mechanics* p10 Jl 2017

When the Call Comes color map *Time* v189 no6 p32 F 20 2017

Addicoat, Matthew A.

Two-dimensional sp2 carbon–conjugated covalent organic frameworks diag graph *Science* v357 no6352 p673 Ag 18 2017

Addictions

2017 TOP DOCTORS *Indianapolis Monthly* p69 N 2017

3 Ways to Control Your Phone Addiction on Vacation R. Walsh *Harvard Business Review Digital Articles* p2 Jl 31 2017

Art therapy J. R. Brownstein cartoon *Magazine Antiques* v184 no1 p54 Ja/F 2017

Brains, environments, and policy responses to addiction K. Humphreys, R. C. Malenka et al color *Science* v356 no6344 p1237 Je 23 2017

How to Dispose of Drugs Safely E. BAZAR color *Kiplinger's Personal Finance* v70 no12 p69 D 2016

NEW INSIGHTS INTO ADDICTION S. Goldberg color *National Geographic* v232 no3 p6 S 2017

THE SINISTER SCIENCE OF IRRESISTIBLE JUNK FOOD M. CROUCH and A. ACHILLEOS *Scholastic Choices* v32 no4 p6 Ja 2017

Addictions—Prevention

Unsweetened N. Buhayar and P. Clark bw color *Bloomberg Businessweek* no4516 p27 Mr 27 2017

Addictions—Social aspects

Why We're Addicted to Email-and How to Fix It J. K. Glei *Time* v188 no14 p23 O 10 2016

Addictions—Treatment

FOUR ASPECTS of RECOVERY [Cover story] M. LOFTUS cartoon *Christianity Today* v60 no10 p40 D 2016

Lights, Camera, Therapy A. KRAFT color *Discover* v38 no5 p24 Je 2017

Addington, Catherine

"Jane the Virgin" offers a refreshing look at Christian sexuality color *America* v216 no6 p38 Mr 20 2017

Addington, Lori A.

Crafted with a Purpose color *Missouri Life* v44 no4 p16 Je 2017

CULINARY SURPRISES color *Missouri Life* v44 no2 p92 Ap 2017

Dark in the Parks chart color map *Missouri Life* v44 no3 p28 My 2017

Rawhide and Java color *Missouri Life* v44 no2 p18 Ap 2017

Sawmill to Showroom color *Missouri Life* v44 no6 p22 S 2017

Sweet Fun St. Louis color *Missouri Life* v44 no5 p18 Ag 2017

What to Expect During the Eclipse color map *Missouri Life* v44 no4 p26 Je 2017

ADDINGTON, LORIS

ACROSS THE DEVILS BACK IN 1973 *Idaho Magazine* v16 no10 p12 Jl 2017

No Business Down There: A Canyon and Its Lore *Idaho Magazine* v16 no11 p28 Ag 2017

ADDIS, FERDIE

6 Surprising Times You Are Quoting the Bible *Reader's Digest* v188 no1126 p124 D 2016/Ja 2017

Addison, Bill

BEST OF ATLANTA *Atlanta* v56 no8 p106 D 2016

ADDISON, GRANT

Classes of Kindergarteners il *National Review* v69 no19 p36 O 16 2017

Addison, Laura M.

Who are you calling a tramp? color *Magazine Antiques* v184 no1 p140 Ja/F 2017

ADDISON, LYNN

Hang In There color *AARP: The Magazine* v59 no3A p83 Ap/My 2016

Tall Tales on the High Seas color *AARP: The Magazine* v59 no2A p42 F/Mr 2016

ADDISON, PRUE F. E.

Society Is Ready for a New Kind of Science--Is Academia? *BioScience* v67 no7 p591 Jl 2017

Additives—Evaluation

PARTS & STUFF color *Hot Rod* v70 no1 p108 Ja 2017

Address books (Blank-books)

The Joys of Keeping An Address Book P. GOULD color *Reader's Digest* v190 no1133 p40 S 2017

Addy, Kevin—Interviews

SECRETS OF A SCOUTMASTER N. KREBS color *Outdoor Life* v224 no7 pW6 S 2017

Ade, Maren

Candid CAMERA color *Vogue* v206 no12 p210 D 2016

Don't Let Your Babies Grow Up to Be Consultants M. ATKINSON *In These Times* v40 no12 p38 D 2016

The End color *Film Comment* v53 no1 p44 Ja/F 2017

TONI ERDMANN R. R. Cooper color *Commonweal* v144 no5 p26 Mr 10 2017

Ade, Maren—Interviews

TONI ERDMANN, FAUX PA: INTERVIEW WITH MAREN ADE M. Ratner *Film Quarterly* v70 no3 p43 Spr 2017

Adebesin, Funmilayo

Emission of volatile organic compounds from petunia flowers is facilitated by an ABC transporter diag *Science* v356 no6345 p1386 Je 30 2017

Adebowale, Akin—Interviews

ONE-CLICK WONDERS J. Amay and M. BOBO color *Ebony* v72 no5 p42 Mr 2017

ADEL, DANIEL

CALIFORNIA STUDENT SUSTAIN ABILITY COALITION: Complacency Is Not an Option color *Earth Island Journal* v32 no1 p16 Spr 2017

Adelberg, Ashley

Party SWIRL color *Seventeen* v76 no12 p27 D 2016/Ja 2017

Adele, 1988-

2016 BY THE NUMBERS *TV Guide* p14 D 19 2016

NIGHT LIFE *New Yorker* v92 no30 p7 S 26 2016

Queen of Hearts L. ROBINSON bw color *Vanity Fair* v58 no12 p122 D 2016

'Send My Love (to Your New Lover)' W. MORRIS color *New York Times Magazine* p18 Mr 12 2017

Sound Bites color *Entertainment Weekly* no1454/1455 p11 F 24 2017

THEY SAID WHAT? color *Maclean's* v129 no48/49 p74 D 5 2016

Adele, 1988-—Awards

For the Record color *Time* v189 no7/8 p6 F 27 2017

Adelmann, Marlene

HERBAL SUPPORT for Wintertime Blues *Mother Earth News* no280 p56 F/Mr 2017

Adelphi University

DEGREE DANCE PROGRAMS *Dance Magazine* p39 2016/2017

Adelson, Sheldon, 1934-

The Mogul Empire E. Alterman bw diag *Nation* v304 no7 p6 Mr 6 2017

Sheldon Adelson's Not-So-Winning Year C. Palmeri, B. Allison et al bw *Bloomberg Businessweek* no4530 p40 Jl 17 2017

Aden, Halima

CENTURY marks cartoon graph *Christian Century* v134 no1 p8 Ja 4 2017

MODESTY BLAZES! L. Camhi color *Vogue* v207 no7 p90 Jl 2017

Adenoid cystic carcinoma—Diagnosis

ATHLETE GETS CANCER. ATHLETE FIGHTS CANCER. RE-PEAT, AGAIN & AGAIN ... T. Layden color *Sports Illustrated* v127 no2 p54 Jl 17 2017

Adenosine triphosphatase

The methanogenic CO2 reducing-and-fixing enzyme is bifunctional and contains 46 [4Fe-4S] clusters T. Wagner, U. Ermler et al bibl diag *Science* v354 no6308 p114 O 7 2016

Adenosine triphosphate

ATP as a biological hydrotrope A. Patel, L. Malinovska et al color graph *Science* v356 no6339 p753 My 19 2017

ATP controls the crowd A. M. Rice and M. K. Rosen color *Science* v356 no6339 p701 My 19 2017

RNA polymerase motions during promoter melting A. Feklistov, B. Bae et al color diag graph *Science* v356 no6340 p863 My 26 2017

Adenosine—Physiological effect

How Caffeine Works J. COVERT cartoon color *Men's Health* v32 no4 p72 My 2017

Adenuga, Julie

HEY, MISS DJ C. Murray color *Essence* v48 no2 p58 Je 2017

Adenylate kinase

Evolutionary drivers of thermoadaptation in enzyme catalysis [Cover story] V. Nguyen, C. Wilson et al bibl color graph *Science* v355 no6322 p289 Ja 20 2017

Adenylic acid

Targeting an energy sensor to treat diabetes D. Grahame Hardie color *Science* v357 no6350 p455 Ag 4 2017

Adepoju, Florence—Interviews

BEAUTY & THE BEAT J. AMAY and A. LUCAS color *Ebony* v72 no6 p44 Ap/My 2017

Ader, János, 1959-

Academia under fire in Hungary Barabási color *Science* v356 no6338 p563 My 12 2017

Adès, Thomas, 1971-

Salzburg A. J. Goldmann *Opera News* v81 no5 p48 N 2016

Adesina, Akinwumi A., 1960-

Africa's Unique Opportunity to Promote Inclusive Growth J. Berman *Harvard Business Review Digital Articles* p2 Jl 9 2015

Adey, Andrew

Comprehensive single-cell transcriptional profiling of a multicellular organism diag *Science* v357 no6352 p661 Ag 18 2017

Adeyemi, Kunle

Kunlé Adeyemi color *Architectural Digest* v74 no10 p104 O 1 2017

Adeyemo, Kolade—Interviews

ONE-CLICK WONDERS J. Amay and M. BOBO color *Ebony* v72 no5 p42 Mr 2017

Adgate, Brad

The Future of Fox News I. RUDOLPH *TV Guide* v65 no19 p16 My 1 2017

Adger, W. Neil

Social norms as solutions bibl color *Science* v354 no6308 p42 O 7 2016

Adhan

Is it religious freedom or noise disturbance? Israelis debate call to prayer J. Greenberg color *Christian Century* v134 no10 p17 My 10 2017

Adhesion

Preventing mussel adhesion using lubricant-infused materials S.

Amini, S. Kolle et al color diag graph *Science* v357 no6352 p668 Ag 18 2017

Adhesive research

RESEARCH color *Science* v357 no6349 p366 Jl 28 2017

Tough adhesives for diverse wet surfaces J. Li, A. D. Celiz et al diag *Science* v357 no6349 p378 Jl 28 2017

Adhesive tape

See also

Duct tape

SCOTCH MAGIC TAPE C. LEU color *Wired* v24 no12 p36 D 2016

Adhesive tape—Evaluation

A Lego-Like Tape J. Zorthian color *Time* v189 no12 p25 Ap 3 2017

Adhesives

The Gratitude Meter Z. Donaldson color *O, The Oprah Magazine* p26 N 2017

Adhesives in surgery

Designing a better glue from slug goo L. HAMERS color *Science News* v192 no5 p14 S 30 2017

Adhesives—Evaluation

Focus on materials, semiconductors, vacuum, and cryogenics A. Mandelis *Physics Today* v69 no10 p62 O 2016

Smartest. Cooker. Ever [Cover story] S. Bushwick and H. Murphy color diag *Popular Science* v289 no6 p60 N/D 2017

Adhvaryu, Achyuta

An Experiment in India Shows How Much Companies Have to Gain by Investing in Their Employees *Harvard Business Review Digital Articles* p1 Jl 25 2017

Adi, Lubana

The Trump Touch color *Commonweal* v144 no9 p11 My 19 2017

Adichie, Chimamanda Ngozi, 1977-

We Should All Be Feminists *Publishers Weekly* v264 no9 p97 F 27 2017

Adichie, Chimamanda Ngozi, 1977-—Interviews

Chimamanda Ngozi Adichie S. Begley color *Time* v189 no9 p60 Mr 13 2017

adidas AG

Adidas Automates to Make Shoes Faster R. Weiss bw color *Bloomberg Businessweek* no4541 p17 O 9 2017

the buzz color *InStyle* v24 no8 p122 Ag 2017

JUST DO IT REDO IT TRY NOT TO UNDO IT DON'T LOSE TO ADIDAS I. Boudway, K. Stock et al color *Bloomberg Businessweek* no4523 p42 My 22 2017

THE PERFECT FIT B. HANSEN-BUNDY color *GQ: Gentlemen's Quarterly* v87 no1 p68 Ja 2017

WATCH OUT, NIKE, THE GERMANS ARE COMING J. Kell color *Fortune* v175 no8 p46 Je 15 2017

adidas AG—Finance

How a 70-Year-Old in Nerdy Shoes Got Cool R. Weiss color *Bloomberg Businessweek* no4521 p20 My 8 2017

How Adidas Got Back In the Game A. Ricadela color graph *Bloomberg Businessweek* no4493 p32 O 3 2016

SHOESTORM [Cover story] A. Staples color *Sports Illustrated* v127 no11 p22 O 9 2017

Adiga, Aravind

Pitch of Dreams M. THEROUX color *New York Times Book Review* p10 Ja 29 2017

Selection Day color *Publishers Weekly* v263 no44 p2 O 31 2016

Adiga, Vivekananda P.

Single-particle mapping of nonequilibrium nanocrystal transformations bibl bw graph *Science* v354 no6314 p874 N 18 2016

Adil, Karim

Hydrolytically stable fluorinated metal-organic frameworks for energy-efficient dehydration diag *Science* v356 no6339 p731 My 19 2017

Adipose Boatworks (Company)

ULTIMATE DRIFT BOAT J. B. SNOW diag *Outdoor Life* v224 no1 p104 D 2016/Ja 2017

Adipose tissue physiology

Our Doc Will See You Now R. Rajapaksa color *Health* v31 no7 p92 S 2017

Adipose tissues

See also

Fat cells

Mastering Appetite Control *Tufts University Health & Nutrition*

Letter v35 no2 p4 2017

OVERFAT *Health* v31 no4 p12 My 2017

Slim Your Middle with HIIT color *Health* v30 no9 p18 N 2016

Adirondack chairs

THE Adirondack CHAIR D. Howland color *Cabin Living* p7 Ag 2017

THE NATURE OF ALL Things [Cover story] J. BREWSTER color *Cabin Living* p44 Ag 2017

Adirondack Mountains (N.Y.)

Oh, Crap! O. DWYER color *Backpacker* p21 Ag 2017

Adirondack Mountains (N.Y.)—Description & travel

Panther Gorge A. Wechsler color *Climbing* no357 p18 N 2017

Adityanath, Yogi

Modi's Turbulent Priest Signals Change In Approach N. Kumar color *Time* v189 no13 p9 Ap 10 2017

Adjaye, David, 1966-

The Avant-Garde color *Architectural Digest* v74 no1 p94 Ja 2017

David Adjaye J. Crelin color *Current Biography* v78 no5 p3 My 2017

GUEST LIST *Washingtonian Magazine* v52 no1 p26 O 2016

ADJEI-KONTOH, HUBERT

RIOT ON THE CANVAS *In These Times* v41 no3 p41 Mr 2017

Adjustment (Psychology)

Can you, should you, have medically tailored food delivered to your home? *Harvard Health Letter* v42 no10 pCover Ag 2017

Cat Calm and Carry On J. HOFVE color *Better Nutrition* v78 no11 p42 N 2016

cope with the crazy J. KING LINDLEY color *Parents* v92 no5 p76 My 2017

COPING SKILLS K. Peek graph map *Scientific American* v315 no3 p38 S 2016

A DIAGNOSTIC DILEMMA H. ESTROFF MARANO *Psychology Today* v50 no2 p22 Mr/Ap 2017

The Fertility Problem No One Talks About L. Kaufman color *Health* v31 no1 p72 Ja 2017

FIND A DEEPER HAPPINESS G. Graves color *Health* v31 no5 p100 Je 2017

get through your child's hospital stay V. SOLE-SMITH color *Parents* v92 no4 p34 Ap 2017

Get Your Mojo Back B. Avila and J. Paulson color *Horse & Rider* v55 no11 p30 N 2016

Holiday Happiness: Will You Fake It or Make It? S. T. BROWN color *Ebony* v72 no3 p98 D 2016/Ja 2017

How Can Families Develop Resilience Against Patient Relapse Behaviors? M. Powers *Psychology Today* v50 no1 p14 Ja/F 2017

How to Respond When You're Left Out of Important Meetings M. Raffoni *Harvard Business Review Digital Articles* p2 N 17 2016

perspective, please! K. CICERO *Parents* v91 no6 p146 Je 2016

RAISE A TOUGH COOKIE C. Newman color *Parents* v92 no9 p48 S 2017

Rough Day? Hit Reset M. HUTSON *Psychology Today* v50 no1 p16 Ja/F 2017

An Unlikely Bond A. ACKERMAN *Psychology Today* v49 no6 p41 N/D 2016

Adjustment disorders

STUDY CONFIRMS EFFECTIVENESS OF THE "SQUEEZE TECHNIQUE" C. Barakat and M. McCluskey color *Equus* no482 p13 N 2017

Adjuvant treatment of mental depression

DEATH BY TECH HAS GONE VIRAL RENE CHUN color *Los Angeles Magazine* v62 no7 p76 Jl 2017

Adkins, Amy

What Great Managers Do to Engage Employees *Harvard Business Review Digital Articles* p2 Ap 2 2015

What Millennials Want from a New Job *Harvard Business Review Digital Articles* p2 My 11 2016

Adkins, Mim

'My New England' PHOTO CONTEST bw color *Yankee* p100 Mr 2017

Adkins, Terry, 1953-2014

ART color *New Yorker* v93 no28 p6 S 18 2017

ADKISSON, GID

Your True Stories *Reader's Digest* v189 no1127 p28 F 2017

ADLER, BEN

The Next Standing Rock color *New Republic* v248 no10 p10 O

2017

NYC Releases First Climate Resiliency Design Guidelines *Architectural Record* v205 no6 p25 Je 2017

Why Lying Is So Easy for Trump color *New Republic* v248 no4 p10 Ap 2017

ADLER, DOUGLAS G.

A Gutsy Call color *Discover* v38 no2 p20 Mr 2017

A Master of Evasion color *Discover* v38 no4 p70 My 2017

Adler, H. G., 1910-1988

A Gruesome Ghost Dance T. Nagel bw *New York Review of Books* v64 no14 p50 S 28 2017

Adler, Henry J.

Community network for deaf scientists color *Science* v356 no6336 p386 Ap 28 2017

Adler, Jennifer

FRESHWATER AT THE SOURCE D. Stone color *National Geographic* v231 no4 p18 Ap 2017

Adler, Jerry

Mighty Mouse *Smithsonian* v47 no8 p54 D 2016

ADLER, JONATHAN

I Love My Dressing Room color *House Beautiful* v159 no2 p128 Mr 2017

ADLER, JONATHAN H.

Pangloss And the Bureaucrats color *National Review* v69 no2 p35 F 6 2017

Adler, Laure

DESTROYER OF WORDS *Harper's Magazine* v334 no2000 p24 Ja 2017

Adler, Nancy J.

Want to Be an Outstanding Leader? Keep a Journal *Harvard Business Review Digital Articles* p2 Ja 13 2016

Adler, Renata

WHISTLING IN THE DARK *Lapham's Quarterly* v10 no1 p191 Wint 2017

Adler, Seymour

Should Your Voice Determine Whether You Get Hired? *Harvard Business Review Digital Articles* p2 Ap 20 2015

What Science Says About Identifying High-Potential Employees *Harvard Business Review Digital Articles* p2 O 3 2017

Adler, Tamar

Accounting for TASTE color *Vogue* v207 no7 p32 Jl 2017

CHANGING COURSE color *Vogue* v207 no9 p724 S 2017

GENOA bw color *Conde Nast Traveler* v52 no6 p70 Je/Jl 2017

MASTER OF CEREMONIES bw color *Vogue* v207 no6 p140 Je 2017

Adler-Bell, Sam

Not Like Us color *Commonweal* v144 no4 p22 F 24 2017

Adler-Olsen, Jussi

The Scarred Woman: A Department Q Novel *Publishers Weekly* v264 no28 p64 Jl 10 2017

Adlon, Pamela, 1966-

All Happy Families, Alike D. D'addario color *Time* v190 no14 p48 O 9 2017

The GREAT Debate S. Simon color *InStyle* v24 no11 p92 N 2017

Mom, Interrupted R. SYME il *New Republic* v248 no11 p58 N 2017

Pamela Adlon J. Crelin color *Current Biography* v78 no1 p3 Ja 2017

Administration of drugs

See also

Dosage of drugs

Injections

STRESSED OUT? *New York Times Upfront* v149 no8 p20 Ja 30 2017

Administrative & political divisions

See also

Gerrymandering

IN MATH WE TRUST HOW DATA CAN SAVE DEMOCRACY C. THOMPSON cartoon *Wired* v25 no5 p40 My 2017

Is the Gerrymander on Its Way Out? New court action may threaten a 200-year-old practice T. Helfman *Commentary* v143 no1 p34 Ja 2017

Administrative assistants—Interviews

What Executive Assistants Know About Managing Up N. Torres *Harvard Business Review Digital Articles* p2 D 23 2014

Administrative fees

See also

User charges

Escape Gym Fees! A. Adamczyk color *Money* v46 no6 p21 Jl 2017

Highlighted & Underlined color graph *Phi Delta Kappan* v98 no4 p6 D 2016/Ja 2017

Administrative law—United States

Regulatory Relief Is on the Way T. J. DONOHUE *Weekly Standard* v22 no25 p9 Mr 6 2017

Administrative procedure—United States

UMBRAGE COURT: Our highly subjective adjudication of recent skirmishes, kerfuffles, and brouhahas J. SIDMAN *Washingtonian Magazine* v52 no8 p25 My 2017

Administrative reform

Banks? E. Robinson and S. Sirletti cartoon *Bloomberg Businessweek* no4503 p32 D 12 2016

Administrative reform—History—21st century

THE FED NEEDS A NEW HEAD—AND POLICY *Forbes* v198 no8 p15 D 20 2016

Adnan, Etel

ETEL ADNAN E. Fullerton color *Art in America* v104 no10 p161 N 2016

Adner, Ron

Many Companies Still Don't Know How to Compete in the Digital Age *Harvard Business Review Digital Articles* p2 Mr 28 2016

Right Tech, Wrong Time color img *Harvard Business Review* v94 no11 p60 N 2016

Adobe Flash (Computer software)

Adobe Flash will die by 2020, Adobe and browser makers say M. HACHMAN color *PCWorld* v35 no9 p23 S 2017

Adobe Photoshop (Computer software)

Adobe Photoshop Elements 15 review: Image editor boosts its photo-manipulation features J. DOVE color *Macworld - Digital Edition* p111 D 2016

How to use Photoshop Elements to combine images like a pro L. SNIDER color *Macworld - Digital Edition* p122 D 2016

Ne Retouche Pas color *Weekly Standard* v23 no6 p3 O 16 2017

RAW TO GO T. Nikitas color *Popular Photography* v80 no11 p40 D 2016

THE YEAR IN MEMES M. MALONE KIRCHER, B. FELDMAN et al img *New York* v49 no26 p38 D 26 2016

Adobe Systems Inc.

100 BEST COMPANIES 2017 chart color graph *Working Mother* v40 no4 p30 O/N 2017

ADOBE AUDITION CC (2015.2). AUDIO EDITING BECOMES MORE USER-FRIENDLY J. R. BOOKWALTER color *Macworld - Digital Edition* p37 D 2016

FACE FACTS D. Grossman color *Popular Photography* v81 no1 p46 Ja/F 2017

How Adobe Got Its Customers Hooked R. Walker color graph *Bloomberg Businessweek* no4526 p37 Je 12 2017

How to create powerful presentations with Adobe Spark Video J. DOVE color *Macworld - Digital Edition* p99 F 2017

Inside Adobe's Innovation Kit D. Burkus *Harvard Business Review Digital Articles* p2 F 23 2015

Adolescence

Child of Mine color *Vogue* v207 no10 p136 O 2017

The Long View R. LONG il *National Review* v69 no2 p34 F 6 2017

Adolescent psychology

Oh Zit! K. Castañon cartoon color *Seventeen* v76 no12 p84 D 2016/Ja 2017

RAGING BRAIN A. BARTZ *Scholastic Choices* v32 no3 p20 N/D 2017

Adolph, Anthony

Are you related to Charlemagne? G. Tindall *History Today* v66 no10 p56 O 2016

Adolph, Gerald

Growth Needs to Come from the Entire Company *Harvard Business Review Digital Articles* p2 Je 17 2016

Adolphe, Julia

Voice of the Viola A. Ross cartoon *New Yorker* v92 no38 p20 N 21 2016

Adomaitis, Chelsea

FOREIGN FOODS J. A. MCELIECE *Dance Magazine* v91 no4 p50 Ap 2017

Adomian, James, 1980-

The Little Comedy Fest That Could J. HERBST *Los Angeles Magazine* p57 Ja 2017

Adopted children

'Who's My Tummy Mommy?' S. SILVERMAN color *Reader's Digest* v190 no1135 p102 N 2017

Adoption

Love at First Touch T. Roberts color *Parents* v92 no6 p20 Je 2017

We are one C. Gorrell color *Yoga Journal* no291 p16 My 2017

Adoption of ideas

Influence People by Leveraging the Brain's Laziness A. Markman *Harvard Business Review Digital Articles* p2 My 29 2015

Adoptive parents

She Adopts Babies Who Are Dying Alone [Cover story] L. ULATOWSKI *Reader's Digest* v188 no1125 p88 N 2016

Adoration of the Christ Child (Poem)

Adoration of the Christ Child G. D. CLARK color *America* v215 no19 p30 D 19 2016

Adoration of the Magi (Motif)

Adoration of the Magi H. J. Hornik and M. C. Parsons *Christian Century* v133 no25 p47 D 7 2016

Adorno, Theodor W., 1903-1969

1951: Frankfurt T. Adorno *Lapham's Quarterly* v10 no1 p51 Wint 2017

Adoyo, Priscilla

Why Africa Needed Its Own Study Bible M. LEE map *Christianity Today* v60 no9 p22 N 2016

Adrenaline

Why We Fight M. Bean *Men's Health* v32 no8 p6 O 2017

Adrenaline Dance Inc.

ADRENALINE *Dance Spirit* v20 no10 p10 D 2016

Adrenaline—Research

Multipotent peripheral glial cells generate neuroendocrine cells of the adrenal medulla A. Furlan, V. Dyachuk et al color *Science* v357 no6346 p46 Jl 7 2017

Adrenaline—Therapeutic use

mom vs. food allergy [Cover story] N. RONES color *Parents* v92 no3 p24 Mr 2017

Adrenocortical hormones

Giant cell arteritis: New treatment for inflammation *Mayo Clinic Health Letter* v35 no11 p6 N 2017

GLOSSARY *Equus* no480 p79 S 2017

Adrenocortical hormones—Therapeutic use

Dr. Weil [Cover story] cartoon color *Prevention* v68 no11 p22 N 2016

Skin fold rashes *Mayo Clinic Health Letter* v35 no3 p6 Mr 2017

Adrenogenital syndrome—Patients

Which Way to Go? L. FLEMING *USA Today Magazine* v146 no2868 p19 S 2017

Adrenogenital syndrome—Treatment

Which Way to Go? L. FLEMING *USA Today Magazine* v146 no2868 p19 S 2017

Adrian, Jeff

TINTYPE TRICK? *Popular Photography* v81 no2 p27 Mr/Ap 2017

ADRIAN, KIM

Let it go! [Cover story] color *O, The Oprah Magazine* p92 Ag 2017

Adrian, Nathan

LOCAL HERO D. Greene color *Sports Illustrated* v126 no9 p39 Mr 27 2017

Adrian, Susan

Nutcracked *Publishers Weekly* v264 no36 p102 S 4 2017

Adriani, A.

Jupiter's interior and deep atmosphere: The initial pole-to-pole passes with the Juno spacecraft [Cover story] color graph *Science* v356 no6340 p821 My 26 2017

Jupiter's magnetosphere and aurorae observed by the Juno spacecraft during its first polar orbits diag graph *Science* v356 no6340 p826 My 26 2017

Adron Harris, R.

Interacting amino acid replacements allow poison frogs to evolve epibatidine resistance chart diag graph *Science* v357 no6357 p1261 S 22 2017

ADS-B (Automatic dependent surveillance-broadcast)

THE ADS-B MANDATE: WHY YOU NEED A PLAN S. Pope

Flying v143 no12 p8 D 2016

INSIDE ADS-B B. Whitfield color *Flying* v143 no12 p16 D 2016

SAFETY NET IN THE SKY C. Dillow color *Fortune* v174 no6 p24 N 1 2016

ADS-B (Automatic dependent surveillance-broadcast)—Equipment & supplies

EASY, AND FREE color *Flying* v144 no10 p18 O 2017

Adsay, Volkan

Sustained virologic control in SIV+ macaques after antiretroviral and α4β7 antibody therapy bibl graph *Science* v354 no6309 p197 O 14 2016

Adua, Eric

Glycomics and its application potential in precision medicine bibl diag *Science* v354 no6319 p36 D 23 2016

Aduba, Uzo, 1981-

All the Feels A. E. Walker color *Glamour* v115 no6 p142 Je 2017

UZO ADUBA PAYS IT FORWARD M. L. Lenker color *Entertainment Weekly* no1472 p15 Je 30 2017

Adult child abuse victims—Psychology

Together we rise C. Gorrell color *Yoga Journal* no287 p10 N 2016

Adult child sexual abuse victims

SNAP leader resigns while group faces suit on legal practices D. Gibson color *Christian Century* v134 no5 p15 Mr 1 2017

Adult children

The Bank of Mom and Dad S. PERRINE color *AARP; The Magazine* v60 no1A p20 D 2016/Ja 2017

BOYS TO MEN V. K. De Luca color *Essence* v48 no2 p8 Je 2017

Fatima's Freedom L. VACCARIELO *Reader's Digest* v188 no1124 p32 O 2016

HAVING "THE TALK ": How seniors can have a serious conversation with their adult children Rin-rin Yu *Washingtonian Magazine* v52 no8 p154 My 2017

Adult film actors & actresses

Amateur Hour: Three stars of Pornhub Community, the site's user-contributed channel img *New York* v50 no12 p38 Je 12 2017

"Sexual power is valuing yourself enough to say what you want." *Glamour* v115 no7 p92 Jl 2017

Adult learning

Empowering Older Adults to Age Out Loud! C. Gilchrist and L. Spencer-Brown *Parks & Recreation* v52 no5 p38 My 2017

Lifelong Learning Is Good for Your Health, Your Wallet, and Your Social Life J. Coleman color *Harvard Business Review Digital Articles* p2 F 7 2017

Adult students

2016 College Guide and Rankings *Washington Monthly* p1 S/O 2016

BEST 2-YEAR COLLEGES FOR ADULT LEARNERS chart *Washington Monthly* v49 no9/10 p32 S/O 2017

BEST 4-YEAR COLLEGES FOR ADULT LEARNERS chart *Washington Monthly* v49 no9/10 p28 S/O 2017

A NOTE ON METHODOLOGY: BEST COLLEGES FOR ADULT LEARNERS *Washington Monthly* v49 no9/10 p36 S/O 2017

THE TWELVE MOST INNOVATIVE COLLEGES FOR ADULT LEARNERS J. Alvarez color *Washington Monthly* v49 no9/10 p38 S/O 2017

WONDER WOMEN S. KLAWANS color *Nation* v305 no1 p44 Jl 3 2017

Adult students—Services for

A Note on Methodology: Best Colleges For Adult Learners *Washington Monthly* p1 S/O 2016

Adultery

UNLOCKING THE VAULT [Cover story] C. FLORA *Psychology Today* v50 no2 p46 Mr/Ap 2017

Why Happy People Cheat E. Perel color *Atlantic* v320 no3 p44 O 2017

Adults

   See also

     Older people

     Young adults

BREAKING UP WITH YOUR PARENTS C. FRAZIER cartoon *New Yorker* v92 no37 p43 N 14 2016

Down, Girl! M. BECK color *O, The Oprah Magazine* p42 S 2017

Not Your Kid's ADHD T. BURRELL cartoon *Discover* v38 no1 p65 Ja/F 2017

Pathways to Adulthood J. KNOLL *Education Digest* v82 no4 p13

D 2016

Poverty vs. Professional Fighting in Southeast Asia A. Graceffo color *Black Belt* v55 no6 p22 O/N 2017

Adults—Attitudes

Science for life B. Alberts color *Science* v355 no6332 p1353 Mr 31 2017

Adults—Psychology

How Thinking Like a Kid Can Spur Creativity P. Himmelman *Time* v188 no16/17 p15 O 24 2016

Adumitroaie, V.

Jupiter's interior and deep atmosphere: The initial pole-to-pole passes with the Juno spacecraft [Cover story] color graph *Science* v356 no6340 p821 My 26 2017

Advanced Micro Devices Inc.

AMD busts Ryzen performance myths, clearing Windows 10 from blame G. M. UNG color graph *PCWorld* v35 no4 p9 Ap 2017

AMD, Nvidia coin-mining cards appear as gaming GPU shortage intensifies B. CHACOS color *PCWorld* v35 no8 p21 Ag 2017

AMD Ryzen Threadripper: Everything we know so far about this monster CPU [Cover story] G. MAH UNG color *PCWorld* v35 no6 p9 Je 2017

AMD shows how Zen—now renamed Ryzen—is its best chip family in a decade [Cover story] M. HACHMAN color *PCWorld* v35 no1 p9 Ja 2017

AMD's Ryzen 3 lineup brings competitive quad-core CPUs to the masses B. CHACOS color *PCWorld* v35 no8 p14 Ag 2017

AMD Threadripper prices undercut Intel's Core i9 by as much as $1,000 M. HACHMAN chart color *PCWorld* v35 no8 p9 Ag 2017

BETTING IT ALL, WITH BRAND-NEW CHIPS A. Pressman color diag *Fortune* v176 no1 p90 Jl 1 2017

Hands-on: AMD's Radeon Vega Frontier Edition vs Nvidia Titan Xp G. MAH UNG color *PCWorld* v35 no8 p105 Ag 2017

Ryzen 51600X: Building a versatile work-and-play PC with AMD's 6-core CPU champion B. CHACOS color graph *PCWorld* v35 no5 p175 My 2017

Ryzen 5 vs. Core i5: Ryzen 5 1600X wins for best mainstream power CPU G. MAH UNG chart color graph *PCWorld* v35 no5 p107 My 2017

Ryzen review: AMD is back [Cover story] G. M. UNG chart color diag graph map *PCWorld* v35 no4 p49 Ap 2017

Advanced placement programs (Education)

THE A.P. CALCULUS A. TUGEND *New York Times Magazine* p66 S 10 2017

Leadership J. P. Starr il *Phi Delta Kappan* v99 no2 p72 O 2017

Advanced Publications Inc.

THE T-P AND THE ADVOCATE cartoon *New Orleans Magazine* v51 no1 p22 N 2016

Advanced Television Systems Committee Inc.

ATSC 3.0: TV's Next Generation B. Ankosko color *Sound & Vision* v82 no7 p18 S 2017

Advent

Faith MATTERS S. Paulsell *Christian Century* v133 no26 p35 D 21 2016

LIVING BY The Word *Christian Century* v133 no23 p20 N 9 2016

Reflections on the lectionary C. Chinn *Christian Century* v133 no23 p21 N 9 2016

Waiting by the Jesse Tree M. Wilson O'Reilly color *Commonweal* v143 no20 p7 D 16 2016

Advent calendars

Cutest Advent Calendar color *Good Housekeeping* v263 no6 p163 D 2016

Deck the halls in a hurry color *Redbook* p123 D 2016

Adventure & adventurers

   See also

     Explorers

     Frontier & pioneer life

     Shipwrecks

18 GREAT SUMMER ESCAPES *Cincinnati Magazine* p50 Je 2017

ABSENCE MAKES THE HEART GROW FONDER S. Weigel bw color *Flying* v144 no6 p38 Je 2017

THE ADVENTURE ISSUE color *Men's Health* v32 no6 p99 Ag 2017

BALANCING ACT K. Vaughn *Arizona Highways* v93 no2 p30

Why were electric cars of the early 1900s advertised as "ladies' cars"? C. Jones and K. Nodjimbadem *Smithsonian* v47 no9 p140 Ja/F 2017

Advertising—Beer—History

Before Prohibition, Breweries Made Advertising an Art E. Machulak *Humanities* v37 no4 p1 Fall 2016

Advertising—Books

Archive Dive *Publishers Weekly* v263 no39 p4 S 26 2016

Advertising—Brazil

In Brazil, It's Now Beer—Without the Babes F. Moura and J. Brice color *Bloomberg Businessweek* no4508 p20 Ja 23 2017

Advertising—Drugs—Social aspects

DRUG ADVERTISING J. PEARSON, E. CRONQUIST et al color *Scientific American* v315 no3 p5 S 2016

Advertising—Economic aspects

Augmenting Snap's Financial Reality S. Frier color *Bloomberg Businessweek* no4523 p33 My 22 2017

Advertising—Humor

Lost in Translation color *Consumer Reports* v82 no2 p59 F 2017

Advertising—Restaurants

DINING GUIDE *Cincinnati Magazine* v50 no3 p139 D 2016

Advertising—Social aspects

See also

Internet advertising—Social aspects

Advertising—United States

Fact: J. Tanz diag *Wired* v25 no3 p48 Mr 2017

Our Boys in Blue color *Weekly Standard* v22 no42 p2 Jl 17 2017

Advertising—United States—Social aspects

Why Every Ad Today Feels Political (Even If It Isn't) C. Graves color *Harvard Business Review Digital Articles* p2 F 7 2017

Advice

Boiling it down G. Gundersen color *Bloomberg Businessweek* no4526 p76 Je 12 2017

Want My Advice? M. REMY color *Runner's World* v52 no7 p49 Ag 2017

Advice columnists

ASK AMY ABOUT HERSELF ALREADY C. ZULKEY color *Chicago* v66 no3 p30 Mr 2017

THE QUOTABLE CURMUDGEON cartoon *Outdoor Life* v224 no1 p14 D 2016/Ja 2017

Advice columns

advice for dancers L. HAMILTON *Dance Magazine* v91 no8 p24 Ag 2017

Advice—Congresses

The White House Survival Guide M. Scherer, Z. J. Miller et al color *Time* v189 no4 p30 Ja 23 2017

Advisement of Ladies c. 1226 (Poem)

CONVERSATIONS *Lapham's Quarterly* v10 no1 p209 Wint 2017

Advisory boards

See also

Citizen participation in police administration

Whose kids are these? M. CAMPBELL *Maclean's* p15 Je 2017

Advocate, The (Newspaper)

A New Home for The Advocate bw *New Orleans Magazine* v51 no5 p20 Mr 2017

Advocate Healthcare Network v. Stapleton (Supreme Court case)

Hospitals with church ties win Supreme Court case on employee pensions L. Markoe *Christian Century* v134 no14 p17 Jl 5 2017

Aebersold, Carol V.

Character Builders C. Kopaczewski cartoon color *Good Housekeeping* v263 no6 p75 D 2016

Aebi, A.

A worldwide survey of neonicotinoids in honey graph *Science* v357 no6359 p109 O 6 2017

Aedes aegypti

BITE FRIGHT color *Missouri Life* v44 no3 p70 My 2017

Copepods Against Aedes Mosquitoes: A Very Risky Strategy P. N. COELHO and R. HENRY *BioScience* v67 no6 p489 Je 2017

De novo assembly of the Aedes aegypti genome using Hi-C yields chromosome-length scaffolds O. Dudchenko, S. S. Batra et al chart color diag *Science* v356 no6333 p92 Ap 7 2017

Mosquitoes on the move J. R. Powell bibl color map *Science* v354 no6315 p971 N 25 2016

A Thirst For Blood M. SEGAL bw *Los Angeles Magazine* v62

no10 p14 O 2017

To fight skeeters, disrupt their sex lives S. MILIUS color *Science News* v191 no11 p10 Je 10 2017

Aedes albopictus

They're Taking Our Tires! K. N. SMITH color *Discover* v38 no9 p12 N 2017

AEGEAN SEA

AEGEAN ODYSSEY I. Drogin color map *Sail* v48 no3 p44 Mr 2017

OUR OWN ODYSSEY M. BREEN bw color *Advocate* no1089 p48 F/Mr 2017

Aeneid

Lost and Founder S. KRISTOL color *Weekly Standard* v23 no2 p38 S 18 2017

The Quiz T. BALAZO color *Maclean's* no1 p64 F 17 2017

Aerial bombing

AT LAST *Harper's Magazine* no2007 p59 Ag 2017

A Catastrophic Error In Nigeria Kills Scores color *Time* v189 no3 p9 Ja 30 2017

Moments A. Katz color *Time* v188 no25-26 p18 D 19 2016 Double Issue

Mother of All Bombers J. WILSON il *New Republic* v248 no11 p10 N 2017

Aerial bombing—Iraq

President Trump Continues Obama's War From Above *America* v216 no8 p8 Ap 17 2017

Aerial bombing—Syria

President Trump Continues Obama's War From Above *America* v216 no8 p8 Ap 17 2017

Soundbites *Extra!* v30 no5 p2 Je 2017

Syrian Airstrikes Rekindle Media's Love Affair With US Violence [Cover story] J. Jackson *Extra!* v30 no4 p1 My 2017

Aerial dance

WHERE ARE YOU GOING? A. Rudolph color *O, The Oprah Magazine* p116 O 2017

Aerial photography

The Earth From Above color *Entertainment Weekly* no1462 p66 Ap 21 2017

EDITOR'S LETTER T. TALIAFERRO *Texas Monthly* v45 no5 p14 My 2017

Sky Cycle: Aerial images of water in all of its forms color *Orion Magazine* v36 no2 p28 Mr/Ap 2017

Aerial propellers

COOL inventions C. M. TOMLIN cartoon color *National Geographic Kids* no470 p11 My 2017

FLYING JETS: WHAT'S THE BIG DEAL? J. King color *Flying* v144 no1 p28 Ja 2017

VTOL RIDES AGAIN P. Garrison color *Flying* v144 no11 p80 N 2017

Aerialists

Girl Runs Away, Joins Circus K. Finley and M. Mertens color *Glamour* v114 no12 p180 D 2016

Aerin LLC

AERIN LAUDER K. MOLVAR color *Conde Nast Traveler* v52 no7 p22 Ag 2017

Aerion Corp.

How to Go Sonic Without a Boom R. F. MANDELBAUM color *Popular Science* v288 no6 p56 N/D 2016

Aero Studios Ltd.

American Beauties color *Architectural Digest* v74 no1 p110 Ja 2017

sources *Architectural Digest* v74 no1 p230 Ja 2017

Aerobic exercises

See also

Cycling

Interval training

Rebounding (Exercise)

Running

Swimming

Walking

18-MINUTE MIRACLE WORKOUT E. SAMUEL bw color *Men's Health* v32 no7 p96 S 2017

The 4 most important types of exercise color *Harvard Health Letter* v42 no4 p4 F 2017

Aerobic vs. Anaerobic Exercise L. BOYCE color *Muscle & Performance* v9 no11 p22 N 2017

Aesthetics
> See also
> Feminine beauty (Aesthetics)
> Light & darkness (Aesthetics)
> Spectacular, The
> Values (Ethics)

The Beauty Complex G. DOYLE color *O, The Oprah Magazine* p39 N 2017

BREATHE F. KAFKA color *Prevention* v69 no6 p38 Je 2017

The Guide to Car Options E. DYER color *Popular Mechanics* p44 F 2017

Aesthetics in the Bible
Prayer that echoes God L. F. Winner *Christian Century* v134 no18 p26 Ag 30 2017

Afanador, Ruven
All the Way Back img *New York* v50 no10 p81 My 15 2017

Affair, The (TV program)
The Must List color *Entertainment Weekly* no1443 p3 D 9 2016

STATE OF THE AFFAIR J. RUSSELL *TV Guide* v64 no48 p26 N 21 2016

Affect (Psychology)
CAN NUTRITION CHANGE YOUR PERSONALITY? K. James color *Better Nutrition* v79 no6 p46 Je 2017

The Happiness Effect M. D. SMITH color *Better Nutrition* v79 no1 p62 Ja 2017

hotBUYS. We Love It! color *Better Nutrition* v78 no12 p16 D 2016

Sip Before You Sweat color *Health* v31 no2 p12 Mr 2017

Sugar Swings [Cover story] E. A. Kane color *Better Nutrition* v79 no11 p30 N 2017

Affectional orientation
WHAT YOU NEED IS LOVE C. Lee color *O, The Oprah Magazine* p24 Je 2017

Affective disorders
> See also
> Anhedonia
> Mental depression
> Seasonal affective disorder

"I had no idea I had an illness" C. Enlow and S. G. Levy color *Glamour* v115 no4 p120 Ap 2017

Our Mental Health Now S. G. Levy color *Glamour* v115 no4 p119 Ap 2017

THE THINKING MAN RYAN PHILLIPPE M. Khidekel color *Women's Health* v14 no7 p128 S 2017

AFFELT, STACIA
FASHION UNDER $100 color *Redbook* p60 N 2017

Affidavits
GROUND CONTROL *Harper's Magazine* v334 no2000 p22 Ja 2017

Affiliation need
AJAHN BUDDHADASA color *Tricycle: The Buddhist Review* v26 no4 p18 Summ 2017

Mismatched needs and wants cause burnout *People Management* p61 O 2016

Affirmations
Think It, Speak It, Live It J. CHAPMAN *USA Today Magazine* v145 no2860 p69 Ja 2017

When Saying Something Nice Is the Only Way to Change Someone's Mind C. Graves color *Harvard Business Review Digital Articles* p2 O 10 2016

Affirmative action programs
Beyond Affirmative Action B. COVERT and M. KONCZAL *Nation* v305 no6 p5 S 11 2017

How CEOs Can Put Gender Balance on the Agenda at Their Companies A. Wittenberg-Cox *Harvard Business Review Digital Articles* p2 N 30 2016

In the Land of the Blind Hire E. Huet cartoon color *Bloomberg Businessweek* no4508 p27 Ja 23 2017

What Board Directors Really Think of Gender Quotas M. Wiersema and M. L. Mors *Harvard Business Review Digital Articles* p2 N 14 2016

Affirmative action programs in education
Campus Chaos M. S. GOLDMAN *Commentary* v142 no1 p14 Jl/Ag 2016

Affleck, Ben, 1972-
BEN AFFLECK'S LIVE BY NIGHT N. Sperling color *Entertain-*

ment Weekly no1439 p42 N 11 2016

Live by Night L. Greenblatt color *Entertainment Weekly* no1446/1447 p101 D 2016/Ja 2017

A Strange Superman R. DOUTHAT color *National Review* v68 no21 p47 N 21 2016

A TALE OF TWO BATMANS J. Hibberd color *Entertainment Weekly* no1454/1455 p18 F 24 2017

Affleck, Ben, 1972—Interviews
Ben Affleck S. Vilkomerson color *Entertainment Weekly* no1444/1445 p20 D 16 2016

Affleck, Casey, 1975-
Dark Journey R. DOUTHAT color *National Review* v68 no24 p43 D 31 2016

A Ghost of a Storyline M. ATKINSON *In These Times* v41 no7 p37 Jl 2017

Afghan refugees
My time at a refugee camp in Greece: Waiting in Malakasa A. Zwartjes color *Christian Century* v134 no2 p30 Ja 18 2017

Afghanistan
PEDALING A REVOLUTION S. GALPIN *UN Chronicle* v53 no2 p25 2016

Afghanistan—Foreign relations—Pakistan
Pakistan's Deadly Grip on Afghanistan C. C. FAIR *Current History* v116 no789 p136 Ap 2017

THE PATIENT WAR May Jeong *Harper's Magazine* v334 no2001 p51 F 2017

Afghanistan—Foreign relations—United States
Fox in the White House E. Alterman color il *Nation* v305 no5 p6 Ag 28 2017

Afghanistan—History
Transnational Jihadism & Civil Wars M. CRENSHAW *Daedalus* v146 no4 p59 Fall 2017

Afghanistan—History—2001-
Poster Boys of Afghan History D. Loyn *History Today* v67 no1 p39 Ja 2017

Afghanistan—History—20th century
Poster Boys of Afghan History D. Loyn *History Today* v67 no1 p39 Ja 2017

Afghanistan—Military relations
Afghanistan and Its Neighbors K. J. Torrance color *Weekly Standard* v22 no48 p6 S 4 2017

Afghanistan—Social conditions
The Improbable Life and Stunning Death of a Child Warrior J. Hammer color *GQ: Gentlemen's Quarterly* v87 no1 p34 Ja 2017

Afghanistan—Social conditions—21st century
ON THE EDGE OF AFGHANISTAN S. E. RASMUSSEN color *Foreign Policy* no226 p50 S/O 2017

Afghans
Afghanistan's Romeo & Juliet: The true story of two young Afghans who risked death by defying their families and their culture to be together R. NORDLAND *New York Times Upfront* v150 no1 p14 S 4 2017

Afghan War, 2001-
America's Longest War: U.S. troops have been fighting in Afghanistan for the past 16 years. And there's no end in sight P. Smith *New York Times Upfront* v150 no1 p16 S 4 2017

ON THE EDGE OF AFGHANISTAN S. E. RASMUSSEN color *Foreign Policy* no226 p50 S/O 2017

OUR WARLORDS IN AFGHANISTAN M. JEONG *In These Times* v41 no10 p28 O 2017

Staying the Course in Afghanistan K. Sadat and S. McChrystal color *Foreign Affairs* v96 no6 p2 N/D 2017

Afia, Nura—Interviews
Nura Afia S. Pulia color *InStyle* v24 no3 p174 Mr 2017

Afink, Gijs B.
ELABELA deficiency promotes preeclampsia and cardiovascular malformations in mice color diag graph *Science* v357 no6352 p707 Ag 18 2017

Aflac Inc.
50 BEST COMPANIES FOR DIVERSITY [Cover story] D. T. Dingle, L. Fraser et al color *Black Enterprise* v47 no3 p52 O 2016

Aflalo, Yael, 1978-
Bricks and Clicks K. CHAYKOWSKI and G. PUTNAM color *Forbes* v200 no4 p40 O 24 2017

Aflatoxins

The Peanut Plague J. LEWIS color *Discover* v38 no10 p50 D 2017

Afonso, Swansy

How India Tripped Itself Up graph *Bloomberg Businessweek* no4538 p30 S 18 2017

Afonso V, King of Portugal, 1432-1481

ARTISTS: THREADS OF HISTORY P. D. Toler color *MHQ: Quarterly Journal of Military History* v30 no1 p84 Aut 2017

Africa

Uber's Africa Push Hits Roadblocks T. Jackson color *Fortune* v175 no6 p14 My 1 2017

Africa, Sub-Saharan—Economic conditions—21st century

Sub-Saharan Africa's Most and Least Resilient Economies A. Rosenberg *Harvard Business Review Digital Articles* p2 F 5 2016

Africa, West

My Wrench D. BRANCACCIO cartoon *Popular Mechanics* p54 D 2016/Ja 2017

Africa—Description & travel

DAKAR A. MERRILL and D. JEFFERYS color *Conde Nast Traveler* v52 no4 p30 Ap 2017

THE LAST WORD *Conde Nast Traveler* v52 no4 p46 Ap 2017

New Comfort Zones P. Guzmán bw *Conde Nast Traveler* v52 no4 p12 Ap 2017

RWANDA + UGANDA A. WHITTLE color *Conde Nast Traveler* v52 no4 p32 Ap 2017

Time for africa color *Conde Nast Traveler* v52 no4 p28 Ap 2017

Africa—Economic conditions—21st century

AFRICA'S NEW GENERATION OF INNOVATORS C. M. CHRISTENSEN, E. OJOMO et al color il img *Harvard Business Review* v95 no1 p128 Ja/F 2017

Africa—Economic conditions—1960-

Why African Entrepreneurship Is Booming N. Ekekwe *Harvard Business Review Digital Articles* p2 Jl 11 2016

Africa—Emigration & immigration

WE HAVE NO CHOICE B. TAUB cartoon color map *New Yorker* v93 no8 p36 Ap 10 2017

African American actors

The Breakout Star of 'Atlanta' D. FEAR color *Rolling Stone* no1293 p22 Ag 10 2017

LEADERS of the NEW SCHOOL C. Coleman and T. Lewis color *Essence* v47 no11 p100 Mr 2017

SPOTLIGHT ON: STERLING K. BROWN J. BENNETT color *Ebony* v72/73 no12/1 p82 O/N 2017

Stanfield's Hot Streak color *Rolling Stone* no1293 p22 Ag 10 2017

African American actors—History—20th century

I NEED A (BLACK) HERO W. K. BELL bw *Wired* v25 no6 p15 Je 2017

African American actresses

10 YEARS TEN STORIES C. Murray color *Essence* v47 no11 p96 Mr 2017

ACT OF GRACE J. LAHR cartoon color *New Yorker* v92 no42 p52 D 19 2016

LEADERS of the NEW SCHOOL C. Coleman and T. Lewis color *Essence* v47 no11 p100 Mr 2017

African American architects

Paul Revere Williams, Unsung Hero A. FIXSEN *Architectural Record* v205 no1 p21 Ja 2017

African American artists

See also

   African American women artists

Door Project artists from The Learning Tree, Derek Tuder and Astoshia Young L. Copan color *Christian Century* v134 no10 p63 My 10 2017

African American athletes

See also

   African American basketball players

BLACK ATHLETES MATTER M. A. Green bw *GQ: Gentlemen's Quarterly* v86 no12 p184 D 2016

African American attitudes

TRIGGER WARNING M. J. GRAY color *Ebony* v72 no8 p86 Je 2017

African American automobile dealers

IN THE CHAMPION'S CIRCLE R. W. Goode color graph *Black Enterprise* v47 no7 p64 My/Je 2017

African American bankers

FINANCE M. Abelson and J. Holman graph *Bloomberg Business-week* no4532 p25 Jl 31 2017

African American baseball players

History's Greatest Hits K. BOATNER *National Geographic Kids* no469 p11 Ap 2017

African American basketball players

Allen IVERSON [Cover story] L. Jenkins color *Sports Illustrated* v127 no1 p32 Jl 3 2017

CONNIE HAWKINS J. McCallum and S. Kwak color *Sports Illustrated* v127 no12 p18 O 16 2017

African American basketball players—Awards

HE'S THE ONE DURANT [Cover story] L. Jenkins color *Sports Illustrated* v126 no17 p32 Je 19 2017

African American boys

DADDY'S HOME W. KETCHUM color *Ebony* v72 no8 p64 Je 2017

African American boys—Education

PDK Connection *Phi Delta Kappan* v98 no3 p79 N 2016

African American business enterprises

THE BE 100s FOR A NEW GENERATION E. G. Graves Jr. color *Black Enterprise* v47 no7 p8 My/Je 2017

BE 100s MILESTONES D. T. Dingle bw color *Black Enterprise* v47 no7 p76 My/Je 2017

B.E. AUTO 50 *Black Enterprise* v47 no7 p60 My/Je 2017

The Decline of Black Business B. S. Feldman bw color *Washington Monthly* v49 no3-5 p31 Mr-My 2017

EVOLUTION D. T. Dingle, J. McKinney et al color diag graph *Black Enterprise* v47 no7 p46 My/Je 2017

Executive Memo color *Black Enterprise* v47 no3 p8 O 2016

FINANCIAL 45 LISTS *Black Enterprise* v47 no7 p68 My/Je 2017

Join Us in Houston: America's Next Great Black Business Mecca *Black Enterprise* v47 no3 p6 O 2016

THE NATION'S LARGEST BLACK BUSINESSES *Black Enterprise* v47 no7 p51 My/Je 2017

The New #BankBlack Movement T. E. Holmes color *Essence* v47 no11 p73 Mr 2017

RISE OF THE NEW BLACK WALL STREET M. S. Hopkins color *Ebony* v72 no9 p72 Jl/Ag 2017

African American businesspeople

5 Black-Owned Startups to Watch [Cover story] S. Blodgett, S. Lynn cartoon color *Black Enterprise* v47 no3 p29 O 2016

How Juicing Changed My Life K. Wilder and A. GUMBS color *Black Enterprise* v47 no4 p46 N/D 2016

WOMEN UP G. JEFFERS and S. T. BROWN color *Ebony* v72 no5 p70 Mr 2017

African American businesspeople—Congresses

4 CAREER GEMS FROM BLACK BUSINESS MASTERMINDS C. RHINEHART and N. K. Webb color *Black Enterprise* v47 no7 p25 My/Je 2017

BLACK MEN XCEL: CHANGING THE NARRATIVE OF MEN OF COLOR E. G. S. Graves color *Black Enterprise* v47 no7 p6 My/Je 2017

Join Us in Houston: America's Next Great Black Business Mecca *Black Enterprise* v47 no3 p6 O 2016

African American capitalists & financiers

MOLDING HBCU STUDENTS INTO TECH INVESTORS J. McKinney color *Black Enterprise* v47 no7 p20 My/Je 2017

African American Catholics

A Crossroads in Oakland K. OAKES color *America* v215 no16 p14 N 21 2016

African American Catholics—Congresses

'Act justly, love goodness': Black Catholics in America A. Marchese color *America* v217 no3 p14 Ag 7 2017

African American celebrities

THE EBONY POWER 100 bw color *Ebony* v72 no3 p110 D 2016/Ja 2017

African American children—Education

Education For Us, By Us B. Packnett color *Essence* v47 no12 p132 Ap 2017

African American choreographers

Dance in the Age of Black Lives Matter B. SCHAEFER *Dance Magazine* v90 no12 p38 D 2016

African American comedians—Interviews

MINING COMEDY GOLD E. Griffith, A. Vandermey et al color *Fortune* v176 no3 p70 S 1 2017

African American composers

GUERRILLA MINIMALISM A. ROSS bw *New Yorker* v92 no46

p78 Ja 23 2017

African American cooking

Food for Thought N. H. REEDER and D. POINTDUJOUR color *Ebony* v72 no6 p50 Ap/My 2017

GRANDMA USED TO MAKE P. MALKUS *Atlanta* v56 no9 p76 Ja 2017

African American cooks

Culinary Queens N. HEMPHILL and D. POINTDUJOUR color *Ebony* v72 no5 p56 Mr 2017

African American couples

#RelationshipGoals Z. HUGHES and S. TIABROWN color *Ebony* v72 no4 p78 F 2017

African American dancers

Dance in the Age of Black Lives Matter B. SCHAEFER *Dance Magazine* v90 no12 p38 D 2016

African American dramatists

WORKED H. ALS cartoon *New Yorker* v92 no39 p94 N 28 2016

African American executives

13 POWER PLAYERS R. R. Robertson color *Essence* v47 no11 p104 Mr 2017

Designing Women C. M. BROWN color *Black Enterprise* v47 no5 p40 Ja/F 2017

Qualified Black Women Are Being Held Back from Management S. A. Hewlett and T. Wingfield *Harvard Business Review Digital Articles* p2 Je 11 2015

Track Stars T. ANDERSON color *Ebony* v72 no8 p68 Je 2017

African American families

CLOSING THE FAMILIAL DIVIDE T. Lewis Ellison color *Literacy Today (2411-7862)* v34 no3 p16 N/D 2016

Making Room at the Table T. D. Jakes and D. POINTDUJOUR color *Ebony* v72 no4 p73 F 2017

MAKING THE COVER K. NELSON bw color *Ebony* v72 no4 p20 F 2017

thank you, god, for this food. amen R. Browne color *Bon Appetit* no11 p68 N 2017

African American fathers

Father's Day: The Real Stories of Black Single Dads G. JEFFERS color *Ebony* v72 no8 p58 Je 2017

African American football players

THE GRIDIRON AND SOCIAL JUSTICE A. EMMANUEL bw color *Ebony* v72 no4 p100 F 2017

African American gay men

WRITING OUR OWN STORIES: Reality star Karamo Brown says it's time for LGBT people to "take the pen out of Hollywood's hands." J. ANDERSON-MINSHALL *Advocate* no1093 p30 O/N 2017

African American girls—Education

Highlighted & Underlined J. Richardson color diag *Phi Delta Kappan* v99 no1 p6 S 2017

African American golfers

GLORY ON THE GREEN G. BLACK color *Ebony* v72 no4 p106 F 2017

African American guitarists

Chuck Berry C. Richard color *Time* v189 no12 p19 Ap 3 2017

African American historians

A People's Historian: Talking about the past and the future with the Park Service's new chief historian J. SCHARPER *National Parks* v91 no3 p10 Summ 2017

African American history

AN AMERICAN PLACE R. Smith bw color *American History* v52 no3 p72 Ag 2017

Discussion P. Werner, K. MK et al *Smithsonian* v48 no2 p8 My 2017

African American History Month

Don't Worry, Be Happy R. CONNIFF cartoon *Progressive* v81 no4 p6 Ap/My 2017

February! T. PAYNE and L. CROSS cartoon color *Ebony* v72 no4 p24 F 2017

African American journalists

YAMICHE ALCINDOR L. N. Williams color map *Essence* v47 no11 p70 Mr 2017

African American lawyers

THE POWER BROKER D. T. Dingle *Black Enterprise* v47 no8 p50 Jl/Ag 2017

African American male singers

Khalid's Teen Spirit J. Weiner color *Rolling Stone* no1293 p32

Ag 10 2017

African American mayors

Hot Do-Gooder Svante Myrick R. WIEDEMAN color *Rolling Stone* no1274 p46 N 17 2016

African American men—Attitudes

BOYS TO MEN V. K. De Luca color *Essence* v48 no2 p8 Je 2017

African American migrations

See also

Great Migration, 1910-1970

The Great Migration R. K. ELDER img *New York Times Upfront* v149 no4 p16 O 31 2016

African American military personnel

UNKNOWN: LOST LEADER P. Brecher bw *MHQ: Quarterly Journal of Military History* v30 no1 p87 Aut 2017

African American models

5 BIG fall LOOKS color *Ebony* v72 no11 p34 S 2017

GUCCI, do better M. HARRIS color *Ebony* v72 no11 p27 S 2017

African American motion picture actors & actresses—Awards

Halle Berry C. Ianzito color *AARP: The Magazine* v59 no5A p80 Ag/S 2016

African American motion picture producers & directors

Why Black Gay Filmmaker Marlon Riggs Matters Now C. STEPHENS bw *Advocate* no1090 p63 Ap 2017

African American motion picture producers & directors—Interviews

Barry Jenkins E. Berman color *Time* v189 no5 p56 F 13 2017

African American motion pictures

INTO THE SPOTLIGHT S. HENRY *Atlanta* v56 no8 p38 D 2016

African American music

See also

Funk music

Jazz

Rap music

Strings in Jazz: Learning To Swing & Articulate in Style A. DIXON bw color *Downbeat* v84 no10 p186 O 2017

African American neighborhoods

RISE OF THE NEW BLACK WALL STREET M. S. Hopkins color *Ebony* v72 no9 p72 Jl/Ag 2017

African American painting—Exhibitions

COLOR AS CODE B. SCHWABSKY *Nation* v304 no4 p31 F 6 2017

NO ORDINARY LIFE K. S. SMITH color *America* v215 p30 N 28 2016

African American political activists

Meet Eritha Akilè Cainion, Millennial of Change S. E. Jamison color *Ebony* v72 no9 p25 Jl/Ag 2017

African American presidents

BLACK LIKE WHO? C. Baker *Harper's Magazine* v334 no2002 p49 Mr 2017

The Judgment K. NODJIMBADEM *Smithsonian* v47 no9 p12 Ja/F 2017

My President Was Black [Cover story] Coates bw color *Atlantic* v319 no1 p46 Ja/F 2017

African American professional employees

Research: Black Employees Are More Likely to Be Promoted When They Were Referred by Another Employee J. Merluzzi and A. Sterling color *Harvard Business Review Digital Articles* p2 F 28 2017

African American scientists

Prejudgment call Han Lin color *Science* v355 no6320 p22 Ja 6 2017

African American singers

NO LONGER SILENT R. R. Robertson color *Essence* v47 no7 p82 N 2016

African American social conditions

THE FIRST WHITE PRESIDENT COATES bw *Atlantic* v320 no3 p74 O 2017

African American students

The burden of inequity — AND WHAT SCHOOLS CAN DO ABOUT IT V. Mayfield color *Phi Delta Kappan* v98 no5 p8 F 2017

African American students—Education

Critical consciousness A key to student achievement A. El-Amin, S. Seider et al bw il *Phi Delta Kappan* v98 no5 p18 F 2017

Looking race in the face D. Mitchell, J. Hinueber et al bw *Phi Delta Kappan* v98 no5 p24 F 2017

Through our eyes Perspectives from black teachers A. Griffin and H. Tackie color *Phi Delta Kappan* v98 no5 p36 F 2017

African American teachers
Through our eyes Perspectives from black teachers A. Griffin and H. Tackie color *Phi Delta Kappan* v98 no5 p36 F 2017

African American teachers—History
Learning from our elders R. Moore bw *Phi Delta Kappan* v98 no5 p45 F 2017

African American teenage boys—Crimes against
A BLACK AND WHITE CASE J. Edgar Wideman bw color *Esquire* v166 no4 p100 N 2016

African American television producers & directors
"My beauty standard is me" A. Gardner color *Glamour* v115 no10 p92 O 2017

African American women
10 THINGS WE'RE TALKING ABOUT T. A. Christian color *Essence* v47 no9 p46 Ja 2017
Black Girl Magic Works in Tech Too B. Lee color *Essence* v48 no5 p124 S 2017
Face Forward J. Wilson color *Essence* v48 no3 p29 Jl 2017
Interstates E. BERNARD *American Scholar* v86 no2 p43 Spr 2017
Support Black Businesses J. Harris color *Essence* v47 no8 p83 D 2016

African American women artists
KARA WALKER, AFTER SUBTLETY [Cover story] D. ST. FÉLIX img *New York* v50 no8 p34 Ap 17 2017

African American women authors
L.A.'s Black Renaissance E. J. HOLLEY color *Publishers Weekly* v264 no17 p36 Ap 24 2017

African American women college teachers
ACTS OF FAITH R. Graham *New York Times Magazine* p48 O 16 2016

African American women executives
THE BLACK CEILING E. McGirt, K. Bellstrom et al color *Fortune* v176 no5 p94 O 1 2017
Getting More Black Women into the C-Suite M. Marshall and T. Wingfield *Harvard Business Review Digital Articles* p2 Jl 1 2016

African American women librarians
PW TALKS WITH LIBRARIAN OF CONGRESS CARLA HAYDEN S. MAUGHAN color *Publishers Weekly* v263 no52 p54 D 19 2016

African American women mathematicians
SHOOT FOR THE STARS V. K. De Luca color *Essence* v47 no10 p14 F 2017

African American women tennis players—Attitudes
VENUS VENERATED S. I. Price, T. Keith et al color *Sports Illustrated* v127 no7 p17 S 4 2017

African American women—Employment
Getting More Black Women into the C-Suite M. Marshall and T. Wingfield *Harvard Business Review Digital Articles* p2 Jl 1 2016
Qualified Black Women Are Being Held Back from Management S. A. Hewlett and T. Wingfield *Harvard Business Review Digital Articles* p2 Je 11 2015

African American women—Political activity
THE YEAR OF THE BLACK WOMAN MAYOR D. M. Owens color *Essence* v47 no12 p78 Ap 2017

African American women—Psychology
BLACK WOMEN SOUND OFF D. M. Owens color *Essence* v47 no7 p64 N 2016

African American women—Social life & customs
Race & Dating: It's Complicated V. Carter color *Glamour* v115 no6 p91 Je 2017

African American youth—Education
Wanted: Soft skills for today's jobs B. J. Hirsch il *Phi Delta Kappan* v98 no5 p12 F 2017

African Americans
2016: A LOOK BACK AT THE YEAR IN BLACK CULTURE D. Henderson color *Essence* v47 no8 p100 D 2016
African-Americans and the Diamond M. CAMPBELL color *Ebony* v72 no6 p88 Ap/My 2017
ASH CASH'S LAWS FOR FINANCIAL SUCCESS J. MCKINNEY color *Black Enterprise* v47 no8 p24 Jl/Ag 2017
Black History, Black Future K. Kyles *Ebony* v72 no4 p16 F 2017

BLACK LOVE THROUGH THE AGES C. K. Jackson color *Essence* v47 no10 p97 F 2017
Conscientious Consumerism: Making Black Dollars Matter E. G. Graves color *Black Enterprise* v47 no2 p6 S 2016
The Decline of Black Business B. S. Feldman bw color *Washington Monthly* v49 no3-5 p31 Mr-My 2017
Discussion D. Montgomery Kovacs, C. J. WOODRING et al *Smithsonian* v47 no7 p10 N 2016
Emmett Till Revisited V. MAJEROL, A. Blinder et al img *New York Times Upfront* v149 no11 p16 Ap 3 2017
THE HOUSING MARKET & BLACK AMERICA M. HOBSON color *Black Enterprise* v47 no8 p22 Jl/Ag 2017
HOW BLACK WOMEN ATHLETES AT THE OLYMPICS HELPED RESTORE MY PATRIOTISM C. Coleman color *Essence* v47 no8 p102 D 2016
HOW LIFE INSURANCE CAN BUILD WEALTH FOR BLACKS J. McKinney color *Black Enterprise* v47 no8 p19 Jl/Ag 2017
INNOCENCE Is IRRELEVANT E. Yoffe bw *Atlantic* v320 no2 p66 S 2017
In Our Cities K. H. TAYLOR and L. CROSS bw color *Ebony* v72 no6 p32 Ap/My 2017
IN THE MIDST OF A NATIONAL CRISIS OF POLICE VIOLENCE, SHE GAMBLED THAT PROSECUTING SIX OFFICERS WOULD HELP HEAL HER CITY. SHE LOST MUCH MORE THAN JUST THE CASE W. S. Hylton *New York Times Magazine* p42 O 2 2016
JESSE WHITE B. Zehme color *Chicago* v66 no5 p148 My 2017
Keep Your Hands Off Our Collards T. R. TOWNSEND and D. POINTDUJOUR color *Ebony* v72 no4 p60 F 2017
Little Coffee Shop of Horrors color *Weekly Standard* v22 no43 p2 Jl 24 2017
The National Interest: Jonathan Chait img *New York* v50 no7 p12 Ap 3 2017
The Question E. SY, M. VELA-WILLIAMSON et al *O, The Oprah Magazine* p16 My 2017
Resistance In These Times J. BLEIFUSS *In These Times* v40 no12 p5 D 2016
STRENGTH IN OUR STORY V. K. De Luca color *Essence* v47 no9 p8 Ja 2017
Walks of Life M. ALLEN bw color *Yankee* p12 Mr 2017
WE LOVE HEARING FROM YOU! color diag *Essence* v47 no8 p16 D 2016
WHEN THE GIVING IS GOOD J. Thompson color *Essence* v47 no8 p114 D 2016
When We Were Very Young L. VACCARIELLO bw color *Cincinnati Magazine* v51 no1 p58 O 2017
Where have all the black digital publishers gone? G. H. Burkins color *Columbia Journalism Review* v56 no1 p23 Spr 2017
WHO OWNS BLACK PAIN? ON RACE AND RISK IN AMERICAN CULTURE Z. SMITH *Harper's Magazine* v335 no2006 p83 Jl 2017
WITH BOARD SERVICE COMES RESPONSIBILITY E. G. S. Graves bw color *Black Enterprise* v47 no8 p6 Jl/Ag 2017
With Intent to Suppress diag *Commonweal* v144 no11 p5 Je 16 2017

African Americans—Conduct of life
Keeping Your Mind Right While Fighting the Good Fight A. HARDY and D. POINTDUJOUR color *Ebony* v72 no3 p84 D 2016/Ja 2017

African Americans—Congresses
THE FIRST EVER BLACK MEN A. A. Edmond Jr. bw color *Black Enterprise* v47 no7 p40 My/Je 2017

African Americans—Crimes against
Keeping Your Mind Right While Fighting the Good Fight A. HARDY and D. POINTDUJOUR color *Ebony* v72 no3 p84 D 2016/Ja 2017
The Mind of Dylann Roof E. Ball color *New York Review of Books* v64 no5 p12 Mr 23 2017
THE PREACHER AND THE SHERIFF N. RICH color *New York Times Magazine* p28 F 12 2017

African Americans—Diseases
Tracking the Monster L. HUNTER and D. POINTDUJOUR color *Ebony* v72 no3 p86 D 2016/Ja 2017
When the Sugar Ain't Sweet D. POINTDUJOUR color *Ebony* v72 no3 p88 D 2016/Ja 2017

African Americans—Economic conditions

How America's Wealthiest Black Families Invest Money S. G. Carmichael *Harvard Business Review Digital Articles* p2 F 10 2015

The New #BankBlack Movement T. E. Holmes color *Essence* v47 no11 p73 Mr 2017

African Americans—Education

See also

Segregation in education—United States

For-Profit Trade Schools Prove Costly for Disadvantaged Black Youth *Education Digest* v82 no6 p63 F 2017

African Americans—Employment

See also

African American businesspeople

The Talk About Racial Bias Companies Should Be Having M. Gee *Harvard Business Review Digital Articles* p2 Ag 23 2016

African Americans—Finance

Your Guide to Recycling Black Dollars G. JEFFERS cartoon color *Ebony* v72 no3 p100 D 2016/Ja 2017

African Americans—Florida—History—19th century

Whose War Was It? C. S. MONACO *American Indian Quarterly* v41 no1 p31 Wint 2017

African Americans—Georgia—History

In Our Cities M. D. SIMON color *Ebony* v72 no8 p32 Je 2017

African Americans—History

Architecture and the History of Race C. McGuigan *Architectural Record* v204 no10 p21 O 2016

Full CIRCLE D. M. Owens color *Essence* v47 no10 p92 F 2017

In Our Cities A. V. WATSON, K. Kyles et al bw color *Ebony* v72 no4 p42 F 2017

Portrait of the Author as a Historian A. Lee *History Today* v67 no2 p54 F 2017

African Americans—Housing

Public Housing and Racial Reality A. Ehrenhalt *Governing* v30 no7 p14 Ap 2017

African Americans—Michigan—Detroit

THE FIRE LAST TIME M. BINELLI bw *New Republic* v248 no5 p28 My 2017

African Americans—News briefs

10 THINGS WE'RE TALKING ABOUT T. A. Christian color *Essence* v47 no10 p63 F 2017

African Americans—Periodicals

MY YEAR-END MESSAGE TO YOU V. K. De Luca color *Essence* v47 no8 p10 D 2016

African Americans—Political activity

Black churches in North Carolina have responded to cutbacks in early voting by the Republican legislature by organizing "Souls to the Polls" marches after services J. Kelso color *Bloomberg Businessweek* no4498 p37 N 7 2016

From the Ground Up: Black Voters in a Florida City Become a Potent Political Force C. Persaud color *Progressive* v81 no6 p28 Ag/S 2017

African Americans—Psychology

FINDINGS *Harper's Magazine* p104 Ap 2017

African Americans—Segregation

See also

Segregation in education—United States

THE WAY FORWARD K. W. SAVALI, G. JEFFERS et al bw color *Ebony* v72 no4 p84 F 2017

African Americans—Social conditions

Architecture and the History of Race C. McGuigan *Architectural Record* v204 no10 p21 O 2016

A COLONY IN A NATION C. HAYES color *Vanity Fair* v59 no4 p128 Mr 2017

O SAY CAN YOU SEE A. CLARK bw *Film Comment* v53 no1 p57 Ja/F 2017

African Americans—South Carolina

In black Charleston, a struggle to find both justice and mercy P. Jonsson color *Christian Century* v134 no4 p13 F 15 2017

African armyworm

New crop pest takes Africa at lightning speed E. Stokstad color map *Science* v356 no6337 p473 My 5 2017

African Development Bank (Company)

Africa's Unique Opportunity to Promote Inclusive Growth J. Berman *Harvard Business Review Digital Articles* p2 Jl 9 2015

African elephant—Behavior

Elephants may set new sleep record S. MILIUS color *Science News* v191 no6 p10 Ap 1 2017

African horse sickness

African Horse Sickness—Could It Be Our Next West Nile? C. Reich *Arabian Horse World* v57 no8 p155 My 2017

A survivor's story S. Baker color map *Equus* no476 p29 My 2017

African migrations

Great Migrations *Lapham's Quarterly* v10 no2 p10 Spr 2017

African National Congress

Patience Is Running Out in South Africa bw *Bloomberg Businessweek* no4518 p10 Ap 10 2017

South Africa's Graft Scandal Grows color *Time* v189 no23 p12 Je 19 2017

African students—Foreign countries

Out of India P. RAINA color *Foreign Policy* no225 p62 Jl/Ag 2017

African violets

THE GRUMPY GARDENER S. Bender color *Southern Living* v52 no6 p39 Je 2017

African Americans—Legal status, laws, etc.

Reparations' Best Chance Since 1865 S. MUWAKKIL *In These Times* v41 no5 p17 My 2017

African City, An (TV program)

5 BINGE-WORTHY SHOWS WE LOVE color *Essence* v47 no8 p70 D 2016

Africa—News briefs

Africa img *New York Times Upfront* v149 no6 p20 D 12 2016

Africans—Migrations

One Africa exodus populated globe T. H. SAEY color *Science News* v190 no8 p6 O 15 2016

A single wave of migration from Africa peopled the globe E. Culotta color *Science* v354 no6319 p1522 D 23 2016

Africans—Religion

Why were electric cars of the early 1900s advertised as "ladies' cars"? C. Jones and K. Nodjimbadem *Smithsonian* v47 no9 p140 Ja/F 2017

Africa—Social conditions

TEAMWORK CITY OF HOPE C. MURPHY color *Vanity Fair* v59 no8 p83 Ag 2017

Afrikaners

THE LAST WHITE AFRICANS E. FAIRBANKS color *Foreign Policy* no222 p48 Ja/F 2017

AFSCME—Trials, litigation, etc.

The Public Sector on Trial N. WALKER *In These Times* v41 no6 p15 Je 2017

Afshar, Yasmin

Affordability Is the Hardest Shade of Green color *Alternatives Journal (AJ) - Canada's Environmental Voice* v42 no2 p40 2016

AFTAB, KALEEM

Jodie COMER *Interview* v47 no2 p64 Mr 2017

After Callimachus (Poem)

After Callimachus S. Burt *American Scholar* v86 no2 p59 Spr 2017

Shorter Means Sweeter L. HAMMER *American Scholar* v86 no2 p58 Spr 2017

After Laughter (Music)

PARAMORE'S HAYLEY WILLIAMS A. Bacle color *Entertainment Weekly* no1466 p56 My 19 2017

After school programs

Building a Culture of Literacy: Ideas for making literacy the foundation in your school [Cover story] L. Jacobson *Literacy Today* (2411-7862) v35 no1 p20 Jl/Ag 2017

FIREWALL P. Williams cartoon *New Yorker* v93 no7 p35 Ap 3 2017

After Simeon (Poem)

After Simeon D. CRAIG *America* v216 no1 p39 Ja 2 2017

After the Blast (Theatrical production)

I Am Not Interchangeable A. Sternbergh img *New York* v50 no11 p109 My 29 2017

THE THEATRE *New Yorker* v93 no33 p22 O 23 2017

Aftermarkets

SMOKE AND MIRRORS S. RICHARDS color *Dirt Sports + Off-Road* v51 no9 p26 S 2017

'Sold Out' Is for Suckers E. Novy-Williams cartoon *Bloomberg Businessweek* no4495 p70 O 17 2016

Aftermath (Film)

MEN ON MISSIONS A. LANE cartoon *New Yorker* v93 no9 p78 Ap 17 2017

Afternoon

SAN FRANCISCO color *Surfer* v57 no13 p94 Mr 2017

Afternoon teas

Lonely Places Jor Ajternoon Tea *British Heritage Travel* v38 no1 p71 Ja/F 2017

Tea's Noble Afternoon Ritual M. Kaufman color *British Heritage Travel* v38 no5 p76 S/O 2017

Afterplay (Theatrical production)

To Do img *New York* v49 no19 p100 S 19 2016

Aftershave

NOT YOUR DAD'S AFTER-SHAVE A. Mangum color *Bloomberg Businessweek* no4523 p62 My 22 2017

Aftershave—Evaluation

SCIENCE OF SMOOTH J. Roth cartoon color *Men's Health* v32 no2 p71 Mr 2017

Agafonov, Roman V.

Evolutionary drivers of thermoadaptation in enzyme catalysis [Cover story] bibl color graph *Science* v355 no6322 p289 Ja 20 2017

Against Democracy (Book : Brennan)

BLAMING THE PEOPLE MÜLLER color *Nation* v305 no8 p31 O 9 2017

Aga Khan Museum (Toronto, Ont.)

SHOWCASING CAN GEO'S PHOTO CLUB color *Canadian Geographic* v137 no3 p14 My 2017

AGANG, SUNDAY BOBAI

RADICAL ISLAM IS NOT THE NIGERIAN CHURCH'S GREATEST THREAT color *Christianity Today* v61 no4 p54 My 2017

Agard, Chancellor

1908 IN REVIEW color *Entertainment Weekly* no1440 p17 N 18 2016

24: Legacy color *Entertainment Weekly* no1448 p44 Ja 13 2017

5 MORE SHOWS YOU NEED TO SEE color *Entertainment Weekly* no1435 p24 O 14 2016

ADAN CANTO color *Entertainment Weekly* no1440 p49 N 18 2016

BEST COMIC BOOKS color *Entertainment Weekly* no1444/1445 p110 D 16 2016

The Best Small-Screen Soundtracks color *Entertainment Weekly* no1439 p53 N 11 2016

BILLY TAKES A STAND color *Entertainment Weekly* no1470 p50 Je 16 2017

BINGE color *Entertainment Weekly* no1449 p51 Ja 20 2017

Calling the Shots, Making an Impact color *Entertainment Weekly* no1457/1458 p80 Mr 17 2017

DAYTIME DIVAS color *Entertainment Weekly* no1439 p12 N 11 2016

DEAR IN THE SPOTLIGHT color *Entertainment Weekly* no1472 p52 Je 30 2017

DIFFICULT PEOPLE color *Entertainment Weekly* no1468/1469 p40 Je 2-9 2017

Fake Lives, Real Paydays color *Entertainment Weekly* no1485 p48 O 6 2017

THE GREATEST DISNEY SONGS OF ALL TIME color *Entertainment Weekly* no1454/1455 p36 F 24 2017

GREAT EXPECTATIONS color *Entertainment Weekly* no1463/1464 p18 Ap/My 2017

How to Make an American Pie! color *Entertainment Weekly* no1460/1461 p66 Ap 7-17 2017

INTRODUCING TROLLHUNTERS color *Entertainment Weekly* no1434 p16 O 7 2016

Leonard Cohen 1934-2016 color *Entertainment Weekly* no1441 p12 N 25 2016

A Life in Parts color *Entertainment Weekly* no1436/1437 p106 O 21 2016

MARSHALL color *Entertainment Weekly* no1478 / 1479 p55 Ag 18-25 2017

THE (MS. AND CAPTAIN) MARVEL UNIVERSE color *Entertainment Weekly* no1436/1437 p65 O 21 2016

NO. 27 CAPTAIN MARVEL color *Entertainment Weekly* no1436/1437 p64 O 21 2016

NO. 41 Mr. Fant astic color *Entertainment Weekly* no1436/1437 p74 O 21 2016

NO. 42 BLADE color *Entertainment Weekly* no1436/1437 p75 O 21 2016

PATTI CAKE$ color *Entertainment Weekly* no1463/1464 p70 Ap/My 2017

A Podcast for Every Season color *Entertainment Weekly* no1477 p47 Ag 11 2017

A POP CULTURE LEXICON color *Entertainment Weekly* no1468/1469 p41 Je 2-9 2017

PROFESSOR MARSTON & THE WONDER WOMEN color *Entertainment Weekly* no1478 / 1479 p51 Ag 18-25 2017

THE PROS OF CON color *Entertainment Weekly* no1476 p32 Ag 4 2017

PSYCH: THE MOVIE color *Entertainment Weekly* no1474/1475 p74 Jl 21-28 2017

REBUILDING THE VATICAN color *Entertainment Weekly* no1449 p49 Ja 20 2017

Ripped From the History Books? color *Entertainment Weekly* no1473 p51 Jl 7 2017

Sorkin's West Wing Swan Song color *Entertainment Weekly* no1460/1461 p95 Ap 7-17 2017

STREAM THESE OTHER FOREIGN-LANGUAGE SHOWS ON NETFLIX NOW color *Entertainment Weekly* no1449 p51 Ja 20 2017

TAKEN color *Entertainment Weekly* no1448 p43 Ja 13 2017

TV chart color *Entertainment Weekly* no1444/1445 p66 D 16 2016

TV'S NEW AWARDS SHOW DARLINGS color *Entertainment Weekly* no1446/1447 p24 D 2016/Ja 2017

What to Watch color *Entertainment Weekly* no1434 p50 O 7 2016

What to Watch color *Entertainment Weekly* no1462 p57 Ap 21 2017

What to Watch color *Entertainment Weekly* no1466 p53 My 19 2017

What to Watch color *Entertainment Weekly* no1474/1475 p108 Jl 21-28 2017

Your LGBTQ Pop Preview color *Entertainment Weekly* no1471 p44 Je 23 2017

YOUR NEXT TRUE-CRIME OBSESSION IS HERE color *Entertainment Weekly* no1466 p48 My 19 2017

Agard, David A.

Assembly of a nucleus-like structure during viral replication in bacteria bibl color graph *Science* v355 no6321 p1 Ja 13 2017

Agarwal, J.

Rosetta's comet 67P/Churyumov-Gerasimenko sheds its dusty mantle to reveal its icy nature bibl graph *Science* v354 no6319 p1566 D 23 2016

AGARWAL, SABRINA C.

Reading the Bones bw color *Natural History* v125 no5 p26 My 2017

Agassi, Andre, 1970-

Class Act S. TIGNOR *Tennis* v52 no6 p57 N/D 2016

THOUGHTS ON Treating Others Well bw color *Forbes* v198 no8 p112 D 20 2016

Agathosma

BLADDER CONTROL K. P. S. Khalsa color *Amazing Wellness* v9 no4 p36 Summ 2017

Agdal, Nina

The End color *Sports Illustrated* v126 no6 p170 F 20 2017

Age

See also

Age distribution (Demography)

Longevity

socially speaking color *Horse & Rider* v56 no8 p24 Ag 2017

Who's the Richest Person Your Age? T. Tepper color *Money* v46 no7 p12 Ag 2017

Age & sports

The Case for ... LOWERING THE NBA AGE MINIMUM J. Woo and S. Kwak color *Sports Illustrated* v127 no12 p24 O 16 2017

THIS IS 40 G. Bishop color *Sports Illustrated* v127 no3 p76 Jl 24 2017

Age discrimination

How Ageism Is Robbing Seniors of Their Independence S. MacGregor color *Maclean's* v129 no40 p62 O 10 2016

Age discrimination in employment

Is our redundancy process ageist? *People Management* p53 F 2017

JOB HUNTING? ERASE YOUR PAST D. Lyons color *Fortune*

v175 no2 p46 F 1 2017

Age discrimination in employment—Law & legislation

Age Discrimination Claim by Beach Patrol Chief J. C. Kozlowski *Parks & Recreation* v51 no11 p26 N 2016

Age discrimination in employment—United States

Is there age discrimination in hiring? E. S. Baker *Monthly Labor Review* p1 Ap 2017

Age discrimination—United States

Age discrimination and reform of the U.S. Social Security System S. Hyde *Monthly Labor Review* p1 Ag 2017

Age distribution (Demography)

BIRTH CONTROL UPDATE: A USER'S MANUAL H. Levine color *Health* v31 no6 p95 Jl 2017

Have the time of your life N. Isaacs color *Yoga Journal* p69 2017 Special Issue

Poses to last a lifetime [Cover story] M. Bolster color *Yoga Journal* p14 2017 Special Issue

Stretching: The new mobility protection *Harvard Health Letter* v42 no2 p4 D 2016

you REALLY can wear GLITTER after 30 L. Desantis color *Health* v31 no9 p88 N 2017

Age groups

See also

Adults

Age distribution (Demography)

Children

Generations

Older people

Youth

Family-Style B. Welch bw *Horse & Rider* v56 no8 p17 Ag 2017

Agee, James, 1909-1955

Beyond the Kael *Commentary* v142 no2 p1 S 2016

Agee, Jon

Watch Your Language! In these frisky new picture books, the spotlight is on the power of words *New York Times Book Review* p16 Jl 16 2017

Ageism

DON'T PATRONIZE ME! K. W. Reyes *Saturday Evening Post* v288 no6 p30 N/D 2016

How Ageism Is Robbing Seniors of Their Independence S. MacGregor color *Maclean's* v129 no40 p62 O 10 2016

Agence Charles Zana (Company)

French Connection color *Architectural Digest* v74 no1 p124 Ja 2017

Agent (Philosophy)

The Error at the Heart of Corporate Leadership J. L. BOWER and L. S. PAINE chart img *Harvard Business Review* v95 no3 p50 My/Je 2017

EXECUTIVE SUMMARIES MAY–JUNE 2017 color *Harvard Business Review* v95 no3 p170 My/Je 2017

Agents of S.H.I.E.L.D. (TV program)

MARVEL'S AGENTS OF S.H.I.E.L.D M. Roffman *TV Guide* v64 no15 p46 Ap 4 2016

Age of Consequences, The (Film)

The Age of Consequences D. Chevlen *Science* v356 no6337 p481 My 5 2017

Age of Spin, The (TV program)

Dave Chappelle's Stand-up Comedy Specials R. Rahman color *Entertainment Weekly* no1459 p53 Mr 31 2017

Ager, Susan

The Perils of Pale bw color diag *National Geographic* v231 no6 p70 Je 2017

Age & sports—Charts, diagrams, etc.

Outside the Box T. Keith chart *Sports Illustrated* v127 no2 p20 Jl 17 2017

AgFunder (Company)

10 UP & COMERS: ROB LECLERC G. Johnston *Successful Farming* v115 no8 p38 Je/Jl 2017

Aggarwal, Shweta

A switch from canonical to noncanonical autophagy shapes B cell responses bibl graph *Science* v355 no6325 p641 F 10 2017

Aggarwal, Varinder K.

Photoinduced decarboxylative borylation of carboxylic acids diag *Science* v357 no6348 p283 Jl 21 2017

Aggarwal, Vikram

DIY Solar: Build Your Own System *Mother Earth News* no282

p91 Je/Jl 2017

How to Cut the Costs of Going Solar *Mother Earth News* no280 p77 F/Mr 2017

AGGEN, JANEEN

Travel Like Truman *Missouri Life* v43 no6 p54 O/N 2016

Aggression (Psychology)

See also

Bullying

Alpha Male vs. Alpha Female T. RICHTER *USA Today Magazine* v145 no2862 p66 Mr 2017

A Double-Edged Hormone M. HUSTON *Psychology Today* v50 no1 p22 Ja/F 2017

HIP-HOP AND HYPERMASCULINITY A. EMMANUEL color *Ebony* v72 no8 p67 Je 2017

is he just acting his age? J. BENJAMIN *Parents* v91 no10 p54 O 2016

Krewesin' for a Brewsin' C. Rose color *New Orleans Magazine* v51 no4 p42 F 2017

MY KIND of PEOPLE color *Good Housekeeping* v265 no2 p8 Ag 2017

Warped Reality A. ROSENBLUM *Psychology Today* v49 no5 p35 S/O 2016

Aggressive behavior in animals

Fear Aggression Usually Kicks In During Canine Adolescence *Your Dog (10780343)* v22 no10 p4 O 2016

What Causes Hostile Behavior? L. I. HAUG *Horse & Rider* v55 no12 p12 D 2016

Aggressive behavior in reptiles

Turtle Tussle *New York State Conservationist* v71 no5 p31 Ap 2017

Aghai-Khozani, Hossein

Buffer-gas cooling of antiprotonic helium to 1.5 to 1.7 K, and antiproton-to-electron mass ratio bibl chart diag graph *Science* v354 no6312 p610 N 4 2016

AGHair Care (Company)

"No, I won't color my hair" J. M. Hickman color *Glamour* no8 p82 Ag 2017

AghaKouchak, Amir

Lessons from the Oroville dam bibl *Science* v355 no6330 p1139 Mr 17 2017

Making SDGs Work for Climate Change Hotspots bibl *Environment* v58 no6 p24 N/D 2016

Agile software development

How HR Can Become Agile (and Why It Needs To) J. Gothelf *Harvard Business Review Digital Articles* p2 Je 19 2017

The Secret History of Agile Innovation D. K. Rigby, J. Sutherland et al *Harvard Business Review Digital Articles* p2 Ap 20 2016

AgileCraft (Company)

THE BEST SMALL AND MEDIUM-SIZE COMPANIES TO WORK FOR J. Alsever color map *Fortune* v174 no6 p51 N 1 2016

Agilent Technologies Inc.

NEW PRODUCTS bw *Science* v354 no6314 p913 N 18 2016

Aging

4 tricks to rev up your memory color *Harvard Health Letter* v42 no9 p1 Jl 2017

50 Reasons to Love Being 50+ color *AARP: The Magazine* v59 no6A p63 O/N 2016

5 Myths About Aging [Cover story] J. McCAFFERY cartoon *Prevention* v69 no4 p34 Ap 2017

AGE BEFORE BEAUTY G. Sheehy color *Harper's Bazaar* no3652 p155 Ap 2017

AGING gracefully V. Tweed color *Amazing Wellness* p58 Fall 2017

ALL ABOUT MUSCLES: A USER'S MANUAL H. Levine color *Health* v31 no5 p77 Je 2017

Anti-aging by the numbers M. ABERMAN *Redbook* p50 O 2017

An Anti-Aging Diet? [Cover story] B. LIEBMAN *Nutrition Action Health Letter* v44 no4 p3 My 2017

Anti-Aging Nutrition for Eyes *Tufts University Health & Nutrition Letter* v35 no5 p4 Jl 2017

Can relationships boost longevity and well-being? *Harvard Health Letter* v42 no8 p5 Je 2017

CRAZY ABOUT COLLAGEN J. BOWDEN color *Better Nutrition* v78 no12 p40 D 2016

Eat Your Fruits and Vegetables to Help Fight Frailty *Tufts Univer-*

sity Health & Nutrition Letter v34 no8 p7 O 2016

EMBRACE YOUR NATURAL BEAUTY M. Rabbitt and D. MACY color *Yoga Journal* no294 p27 S 2017

Getting Over Gray W. KIRN *Reader's Digest* v188 no1125 p98 N 2016

THE GOD PILL T. FRIEND cartoon color *New Yorker* v93 no7 p54 Ap 3 2017

HERE'S LOOKING AT YOU, 2050 P. TAYLOR cartoon graph map *Foreign Policy* no222 p30 Ja/F 2017

Hitting Eighty J. EPSTEIN cartoon *Weekly Standard* v22 no17 p18 Ja 2 2017

In With the New color *Better Nutrition* v79 no1 p20 Ja 2017

"I wasn't over the hill, I was on top of the mountain, and I liked being there." J. A. Jenkins color *AARP: The Magazine* v59 no2A p26 F/Mr 2016

Keeping Your Arteries Young: Help your arteries age gracefully with a healthy diet and lifestyle [Cover story] *Tufts University Health & Nutrition Letter* v35 no8 p1 O 2017

LIFE WITHOUT END E. KEEP *Smithsonian* v48 no3 p43 Je 2017

The Link Between Your Walking Pace and Aging Well: As you age, your normal walking speed can provide a peek into your overall health. Regular physical activity is important to help keep up your pace *Tufts University Health & Nutrition Letter* v35 no8 p4 O 2017

Longevity Dietary Pattern: Fruits, Vegetables, Fish *Tufts University Health & Nutrition Letter* v34 no9 p7 N 2016

Looking for Life's MIDUS Touch *USA Today Magazine* v145 no2863 p14 Ap 2017

Lovely BONES C. Krucoff color *Yoga Journal* p60 2017 Special Issue

News and our views *Mayo Clinic Health Letter* v35 no6 p4 Je 2017

NEWS BITES [Cover story] *Tufts University Health & Nutrition Letter* v35 no2 p1 2017

OVER 50 AND FABULOUS G. Roberts-Grey color *Essence* v47 no8 p140 D 2016

Potential new benefits from an old drug *Mayo Clinic Health Letter* v35 no4 p7 Ap 2017

Product Spotlights color *Better Nutrition* v79 no7 p63 Jl 2017

The Stress Problems No One Talks About G. Saltz color *Health* v31 no3 p72 Ap 2017

Ways to stay sharp behind the wheel *Harvard Health Letter* v42 no11 p1 S 2017

What Price for a Plain Pony? K. Pando color *Horse & Rider* v56 no1 p10 Ja 2017

What's your sleep IQ? color *Harvard Health Letter* v42 no9 p6 Jl 2017

What to Do About Getting Old K. FRANCE, C. GALLOP et al img *New York* p32 Ja 23 2017

When the Water Ran Cold K. DOUNGLOMCHAN *Reader's Digest* v189 no1128 p20 Mr 2017

Aging in place

Mom, Dad: Your House Isn't Safe K. Clark and P. Wang color *Money* v46 no5 p22 Je 2017

Aging parents

LES BELLES iMAGES P. Bagieu *New York Times Book Review* p27 Ap 30 2017

Aging—Genetic aspects

Aging increases cell-to-cell transcriptional variability upon immune stimulation C. Pilar Martinez-Jimenez, N. Eling et al color diag graph *Science* v355 no6332 p1433 Mr 31 2017

Old moms say, no Sir A. D. Gitler and D. F. Jarosz bibl diag *Science* v355 no6330 p1126 Mr 17 2017

Aging—Molecular aspects

Aging increases cell-to-cell transcriptional variability upon immune stimulation C. Pilar Martinez-Jimenez, N. Eling et al color diag graph *Science* v355 no6332 p1433 Mr 31 2017

Aging—Physiological aspects

FROM LOSS TO ABILITY J. Barratt color *Maclean's* v129 no42 p35 O 24 2016

Proteins turn back aging clock T. HESMAN SAEY color graph *Science News* v191 no1 p6 Ja 21 2017

Aging—Prevention

ANTI-AGING SUPPLEMENTS THAT WORK K. Asp color *Harper's Bazaar* no3651 p326 Mr 2017

BEAT THE CLOCK color *O, The Oprah Magazine* p128 F 2017

LIVING TO 120 B. Gifford color *Scientific American* v315 no3 p62 S 2016

PROVEN ANTI-AGERS color *Good Housekeeping* v263 no5 p30 N 2016

What are the best ANTI-AGING TRICKS? A. FRANZINO cartoon color *Good Housekeeping* v264 no2 p23 F 2017

Younger Next Year C. Crowley and H. S. Lodge cartoon color *AARP: The Magazine* v59 no6A p32 O/N 2016

Aging—Prevention—Equipment & supplies

Skin Care Atlas C. Martin color *Essence* v47 no10 p31 F 2017

Aging—Research

Google's Long Strange Life Span Trip A. Regalado color *MIT Technology Review* v120 no1 p52 Ja/F 2017

Aging—United States

Can Crowdfunding Help Solve Our Health Issues? J. Englis *AARP: The Magazine* v59 no2A p81 F/Mr 2016

Agius, Dion

Lining Up color *Surfer* v58 no3 p16 Je 2017

Aglietta, M.

Observation of a large-scale anisotropy in the arrival directions of cosmic rays above 8 × 1018 eV *Science* v357 no6357 p1266 S 22 2017

AGLIO, JUSTIN

Three Ways the Flipped Classroom Leads to Better Subject Mastery *Education Digest* v82 no5 p52 Ja 2017

AGNESE, BRAULIO

perspective interiors *Architectural Record* v205 no4 p45 Ap 2017

Whitman-Walker Health *Architectural Record* v205 no4 p190 Ap 2017

Agnew, Spiro T., 1918-1996

Pioneering Press Critic P. Terzian bw *Weekly Standard* v22 no26 p14 Mr 13 2017

Agnon, Jean-Paul—Interviews

MANAGING L'ORÉAL'S 'ORGANIZED CHAOS' E. Griffith color *Fortune* v175 no4 p26 Mr 15 2017

Agnon, Shmuel Yosef, 1888-1970

The Great Genius of Jewish Literature R. Alter bw *New York Review of Books* v64 no6 p35 Ap 6 2017

THE PROMISED LAND A. KIRSCH cartoon *New Yorker* v92 no38 p87 N 21 2016

AGOSTA, SALVATORE J.

Transformational Principles for NEON Sampling of Mammalian Parasites and Pathogens: A Response to Springer and Colleagues *BioScience* v66 no11 p917 N 1 2016

Agostino, Bob

BOMBARDIER SAFETY STANDDOWN R. MARK bw color *Flying* v144 no3 p70 Mr 2017

Agrarian societies

Wild emmer genome architecture and diversity elucidate wheat evolution and domestication R. Avni, M. Nave et al color *Science* v357 no6346 p93 Jl 7 2017

Agrawal, Ajay

How AI Will Change Strategy: A Thought Experiment *Harvard Business Review Digital Articles* p2 O 3 2017

How AI Will Change the Way We Make Decisions *Harvard Business Review Digital Articles* p2 Jl 26 2017

The Obama Administration's Roadmap for AI Policy *Harvard Business Review Digital Articles* p2 D 21 2016

The Simple Economics of Machine Intelligence *Harvard Business Review Digital Articles* p2 N 17 2016

The Trade-Off Every AI Company Will Face *Harvard Business Review Digital Articles* p2 Mr 28 2017

Agrawal, Ankur

Who's Better at Strategy: CFOs or CSOs? *Harvard Business Review Digital Articles* p2 Ja 11 2016

Agrawal, Anurag

Monarchs and Milkweed: A Migrating Butterfly, A Poisonous Plant, and Their Remarkable Story of Coevolution L. A. MARSCHALL color *Natural History* v125 no4 p46 Ap 2017

Agrawal, Avinash

Which U.S. Companies Are Doing the Most R&D in China and India? *Harvard Business Review Digital Articles* p2 Mr 26 2015

Agrawal, Neha

Drosophila insulin release is triggered by adipose Stunted ligand to brain Methuselah receptor bibl graph *Science* v353 no6307

p1553 S 30 2016

AGRBA, LIZA

CLASSROOM CHEMISTRY color *Maclean's* v130 no2 p63 Mr 2017

The digital classroom color *Maclean's* v130 no10 p81 N 2017

Agre, Peter

Driving mosquito refractoriness to Plasmodium falciparum with engineered symbiotic bacteria color graph *Science* v357 no6358 p1399 S 29 2017

AGRESTA, JEN

awes8me EXTREME SPORTS *National Geographic Kids* no467 p9 F 2017

awes8me FUNKY FOSSILS *National Geographic Kids* no466 p8 D 2016/Ja 2017

awes8me Wicked Weapons color *National Geographic Kids* no465 p11 N 2016

Awesome 8 color *National Geographic Kids* no475 p8 N 2017

Agresta, Maria

April/2017 M. MAZZARO *Opera News* v81 no10 p8 Ap 2017

AGRESTA, MICHAEL

Bonnie and Clyde at 50 *Texas Monthly* v45 no9 p50 S 2017

A Brooklyn Bridge Too Far *Texas Monthly* v45 no3 p66 Mr 2017

REVENGE OF THE FILM NERDS *Texas Monthly* v45 no7 p70 Jl 2017

A Serious Writer *Texas Monthly* v45 no4 p58 Ap 2017

The Steve Jobs OF WEST TEXAS *Texas Monthly* v45 no2 p43 F 2017

Wards Matter *Texas Monthly* v44 no12 p84 D 2016

The Wonderful World of Bluth *Texas Monthly* v45 no8 p40 Ag 2017

Agricultural antibiotics

    See also

      Antibiotics in animal nutrition

Q AND A WITH MARYN MCKENNA S. Fennessy *Atlanta* v57 no5 p100 S 2017

Agricultural chemicals industry—Mergers

Mergers and Competition in Seed and Agricultural Chemical Markets J. M. MacDonald *Amber Waves: The Economics of Food, Farming, Natural Resources, & Rural America* p1 Ap 2017

Unsavory Alliance *Earth Island Journal* v32 no4 p12 Wint 2017

Agricultural credit

MICROLOANS D. Keller *Successful Farming* v114 no10 p61 O 2016

Agricultural credit—United States

HOW STRONG IS YOUR BANK? EVEN WITH LOW COMMODITY PRICES, BANKS THAT LEND TO AGRICULTURE CONTIUNE TO STRENGTHEN D. LOOKER *Successful Farming* v115 no12 p24 O 2017

STAYING AFLOAT: MANAGING FINANCIAL UNCERTAINTY IS KEY D. Looker *Successful Farming* v115 no12 p14 O 2017

Agricultural development

AG FORECAST: GLUM BUT SUNNY AT THE SAME TIME *Successful Farming* v115 no4 p16 Mr 2017

Agricultural development—Congresses

FARMER UP! AT THE 2017 COMMODITY CLASSIC M. Jennett *Successful Farming* v115 no3 p48 Mid-F 2017

Agricultural diversification

    See also

      Crop diversification

10 UP & COMERS: TYLER SCHNAITHMAN J. Davey *Successful Farming* v115 no8 p34 Je/Jl 2017

GAIN FROM CROP DIVERSITY: INCREASE VARIETY IN CROP ROTATION TO BOOST THE OVERALL HEALTH OF YOUR FIELD K. Birchmier *Successful Farming* v115 no9 p53 Ag 2017

Agricultural economics

    See also

      Agricultural industries

      Agricultural prices

      Agricultural productivity

      Farm management

Gathering Experimental Evidence To Improve the Design of Agricultural Programs L. Lynch, D. Hellerstein et al *Amber Waves: The Economics of Food, Farming, Natural Resources, & Rural America* p1 Ag 2017

Agricultural education

Abiodun Henderson J. BAINBRIDGE *Atlanta* v57 no2 p54 Je 2017

Agricultural equipment

    See also

      Harvesting machinery

      Planters (Agricultural machinery)

      Threshing machines

      Tillage

ALL AROUND THE FARM N. Lehman, C. Geiger et al *Successful Farming* v115 no2 p79 F 2017

CONTEST WINNERS SELECTED L. Bedord *Successful Farming* v115 no1 p55 Ja 2017

DEALER DEALS FOR LARGE FWDs D. Mawitz *Successful Farming* v114 no13 p38 D 2016

DUALS ON DIESELS R. Bohacz *Successful Farming* v115 no5 p24 Mid-Mr 2017

THE FARM D. Gephart, G. Gunn et al *Successful Farming* v115 no11 p75 S 2017

FLEX-WING ROTARY CUTTERS: TACKLE TALL WEEDS WITH THESE VERSATILE MACHINES B. Freese *Successful Farming* v115 no11 p34 S 2017

IDEA OF THE MONTH P. Barbour *Successful Farming* v114 no13 p90 D 2016

IDEA OF THE MONTH P. Barbour *Successful Farming* v115 no11 p76 S 2017

IDEA OF THE MONTH P. Barbour *Successful Farming* v115 no5 p76 Mid-Mr 2017

IT ALL STARTS NOW D. KURNS *Successful Farming* v115 no4 p4 Mr 2017

LET'S MAKE A DEAL D. Mowitz *Successful Farming* v114 no13 p32 D 2016

MOTHER's Product Picks *Mother Earth News* no281 p14 Ap/My 2017

A NEW DAY DAWNS IN AGRICULTURE D. KURNS *Successful Farming* v115 no1 p6 Ja 2017

SKID STEER PRICES SLIP D. Mowitz *Successful Farming* v115 no2 p26 F 2017

WINTER WORK GLOVES J. Scott *Successful Farming* v114 no11 p58 N 2016

Agricultural equipment auctions

HOPPER-BOTTOM BUYING: SOFTNESS IN LATE-MODEL HOPPER-BOTTOM TRAILER VALUES OFFERS BUYING OPPORTUNITY D. Mowitz *Successful Farming* v115 no11 p21 S 2017

Agricultural equipment laws

TECH FIGHT ON THE FARM J. J. Roberts color *Fortune* v176 no1 p24 Jl 1 2017

Agricultural equipment—Design & construction

IDEA OF THE MONTH P. Barbour *Successful Farming* v115 no3 p72 Mid-F 2017

Agricultural equipment—Evaluation

AHEAD OF THE CURVE L. Bedord *Successful Farming* v115 no2 p54 F 2017

INNOVATION IN IRRIGATION T. Gaines *Successful Farming* v115 no2 p58 F 2017

ONE MASSIVE MACHINE A. McConnell and L. Bedord *Successful Farming* v115 no2 p32 F 2017

POCKET PRICE GUIDE: Asking Prices for Precision Ag Displays *Successful Farming* v115 no1 p29 Ja 2017

POCKET PRICE GUIDE: Late-Model 16/31 Planters *Successful Farming* v115 no4 p31 Mr 2017

POST DRIVERS K. Birchmier *Successful Farming* v115 no3 p44 Mid-F 2017

SEED FIRMERS, COVERS G. Gullickson *Successful Farming* v114 no13 p51 D 2016

SIDEDRESS AND SEED COVER CROPS A. McConnell and L. Bedord *Successful Farming* v115 no1 p32 Ja 2017

TAGGED A. McConnell and L. Bedord *Successful Farming* v115 no2 p32 F 2017

TILLERS R. BERENDSOHN color *Popular Mechanics* p28 Ap 2017

Agricultural equipment—Maintenance & repair

LONG WINTER LAYOFF L. Bedord *Successful Farming* v114 no13 p46 D 2016

MECHANIC MAKE-DOs D. Mowitz *Successful Farming* v114

Life v21 no5 p20 S/O 2017

A RECIPE FOR TOMORROW H. Rosner color *Wired* v24 no11 p104 N 2016

THINK OF YOUR CROPS LIKE MONEY, BECAUSE THEY ARE D. KURNS *Successful Farming* v114 no10 p4 O 2016

TOP PICKS J. BALL, S. DUGGER et al *Indianapolis Monthly* v12 no40 p62 Ag 2017

Agricultural productivity—Management

Managing Agricultural Risk Under Different Scenarios: Selected 2014 Farm Act Programs A. Hungerford, M. Motamed et al *Amber Waves: The Economics of Food, Farming, Natural Resources, & Rural America* p22 F 2017

Agricultural productivity—United States

Examining Farm Sector and Farm Household Income D. Prager, C. Burns et al *Amber Waves: The Economics of Food, Farming, Natural Resources, & Rural America* p23 Ag 2017

Farm Households Experience High Levels of Income Volatility N. Key, D. Prager et al *Amber Waves: The Economics of Food, Farming, Natural Resources, & Rural America* p43 F 2017

Managing Agricultural Risk Under Different Scenarios: Selected 2014 Farm Act Programs A. Hungerford, M. Motamed et al *Amber Waves: The Economics of Food, Farming, Natural Resources, & Rural America* p22 F 2017

Productivity Growth Is Still the Major Driver in Growing U.S. Agricultural Output Sun Ling Wang, E. Ball et al *Amber Waves: The Economics of Food, Farming, Natural Resources, & Rural America* p5 S 2016

Pulses Production Expanding as Consumers Cultivate a Taste for U.S. Lentils and Chickpeas J. Bond *Amber Waves: The Economics of Food, Farming, Natural Resources, & Rural America* p35 F 2017

U.S. Agricultural R&D in an Era of Falling Public Funding M. Clancy, K. Fuglie et al *Amber Waves: The Economics of Food, Farming, Natural Resources, & Rural America* p1 N 2016

Agricultural risk assessment

FINE-TUNE YOUR 2017 MARKETING PLAN A. Kluis *Successful Farming* v115 no4 p22 Mr 2017

Growing Organic Demand Provides High-Value Opportunities for Many Types of Producers C. Greene, G. Ferreira et al *Amber Waves: The Economics of Food, Farming, Natural Resources, & Rural America* p51 F 2017

WHAT'S THE BIG IDEA? *Successful Farming* v114 no10 p12 O 2016

Agricultural safety—Congresses

PUTTING FARM SAFETY INTO PRACTICE: THAT'S THE THEME OF THIS YEAR'S NATIONAL FARM SAFETY AND HEALTH WEEK J. Scott *Successful Farming* v115 no11 p54 S 2017

Agricultural sociology

PLANTING PEACE N. Strochlic color *National Geographic* v232 no5 p22 N 2017

WE OWE A LOT TO OUR VETERANS D. KURNS *Successful Farming* v114 no11 p6 N 2016

Agricultural systems

PUT DRAIN TILING UNDER THE FINANCIAL MICROSCOPE *Successful Farming* v114 no13 p18 D 2016

Agricultural technology

   See also

   Irrigation

AFTER The Next Big Thing B. D. JOHNSON *Successful Farming* v114 no12 p78 Mid-N 2016

cut+paste B. Freese *Successful Farming* v114 no12 p58 Mid-N 2016

Elsie Will Text You When She's in Heat M. Scaturro color *Bloomberg Businessweek* no4498 p52 N 7 2016

How Digital Technology Is Changing Farming in Africa N. Ekekwe *Harvard Business Review Digital Articles* p2 My 18 2017

IDEA OF THE MONTH P. Barbour *Successful Farming* v114 no11 p76 N 2016

MAKING OUR PLANET SUSTAINABLE AGAIN *Vital Speeches of the Day* v83 no6 p174 Je 2017

PICTURE THIS: THE QUESTIONS THAT IMAGERY CAN HELP ANSWER ARE SIMPLE YET IMPORTANT L. Bedord *Successful Farming* v115 no11 p50 S 2017

THIRSTY CROPS RUN A TEMP D. Mowitz *Successful Farming* v114 no10 p48 O 2016

Agricultural technology—Economic aspects

Precision Agriculture Technologies and Factors Affecting Their Adoption D. Schimmelpfennig color graph *Amber Waves: The Economics of Food, Farming, Natural Resources, & Rural America* p32 D 2016

Agricultural laborers—Societies, etc.

CERCLE D'ART DES TRAVAILLEURS DE PLANTATION CONGOLAISE M. Heddaya color *Art in America* v105 no5 p129 My 2017

Agriculture

   See also

   Agricultural antibiotics

   Agricultural diversification

   Corn farming

   Crop science

   Farm produce

   Farms

   Forests & forestry

   Gardening

   Pastures

   Plant protection

   Planting (Plant culture)

   Ranching

   Tillage

   Vertical farming

10 SUCCESSFUL FARMERS: ANNE WHITMAN ONGSTAD A. McConnell *Successful Farming* v115 no8 p20 Je/Jl 2017

10 SUCCESSFUL FARMERS: DOUG MARTIN M. McGinnis *Successful Farming* v115 no8 p18 Je/Jl 2017

10 SUCCESSFUL FARMERS: JOE BREKER G. Johnson *Successful Farming* v115 no8 p14 Je/Jl 2017

10 SUCCESSFUL FARMERS: PEOPLE TO WATCH IN AGRICULTURE D. Mawita *Successful Farming* v115 no8 p12 Je/Jl 2017

8 RULES FOR YOUNG FARMERS: YOU CAN BE A SUCCESS IN AGRICULTURE, EVEN IN HARD TIMES, IF YOU LIVE BY THESE GUIDELINES *Successful Farming* v115 no6 p14 Ap 2017

Ask Our Experts J. Walljasper, C. Conner et al *Mother Earth News* no281 p91 Ap/My 2017

CARBON FARMING WILL (HELP) SAVE THE PLANET J. MCDOUGALL color *Rodale's Organic Life* v3 no1 p68 Ja 2017

editor's LETTER R. STIEVE *Arizona Highways* v93 no6 p2 Je 2017

Fishes M. FINELLI *Vegetarian Journal* v36 no2 p26 2017

GLEANINGS A. Luety *Successful Farming* v115 no2 p8 F 2017

GROW YOUR TRIBE J. Scott *Successful Farming* v115 no5 p16 Mid-Mr 2017

THE GUARDIAN E. S. ARNARSDÓTTIR *Iceland Review* v55 no3 p40 My/Je 2017

The Hidden Story of Tasteless Chicken V. TWEED color *Better Nutrition* v79 no10 p10 O 2017

Hydroponic Farming: Organic or Not? L. Noyes *Mother Earth News* no282 p8 Je/Jl 2017

IS THIS THE YEAR? *Successful Farming* v115 no1 p68 Ja 2017

IT ALL STARTS NOW D. KURNS *Successful Farming* v115 no4 p4 Mr 2017

kids * health news *Parents* v92 no2 p28 F 2017

Moringa: How One Plant Is Changing Lives N. Zevnik color *Better Nutrition* v79 no6 p16 Je 2017

A NEW DAY DAWNS IN AGRICULTURE D. KURNS *Successful Farming* v115 no1 p6 Ja 2017

THE NEW FOOD FRONTIER color *Better Nutrition* v79 no9 p46 S 2017

Organic and Non-GMO, Simplified! M. D. SMITH color *Better Nutrition* v79 no10 p72 O 2017

Paradise Unwound T. Gibson color map *National Wildlife (World Edition)* v55 no2 p32 F/Mr 2017

THE PLANTING SQUAD L. BEDORD *Successful Farming* v115 no4 p41 Mr 2017

A SIDE BUSINESS COMES FULL CIRCLE D. KURNS *Successful Farming* v114 no13 p4 D 2016

SMART APP TELLS WHEN TO IRRIGATE: INTERNET PROGRAM TAPS INTO NATIONAL WEATHER SERVICE AND OTHER DATA TO GUIDE IRRIGATION SCHEDULING FOR MISSOURI FARMERS G. Johnston *Successful Farming*

v115 no9 p56 Ag 2017
STARTING A PODCAST J. SCOTT *Successful Farming* v115 no6 p16 Ap 2017
THE SUCCESSFUL INTERVIEW A. McConnell *Successful Farming* v115 no4 p12 Mr 2017
Targeting TRACTORS T. Nephew *Mother Earth News* no284 p18 O/N 2017
THROWBACK: FARMING 100 YEARS AGO *Successful Farming* v115 no1 p8 Ja 2017
UPGRADING SHOP LIGHTS D. Mowitz *Successful Farming* v114 no10 p55 O 2016
Vegetarian Action. Scott Nash: Founder and CEO of MOM's Organic Market S. Gendler *Vegetarian Journal* v35 no4 p35 2016
WE CAN FEED 9 BILLION: HOW DOES AMERICAN AGRICULTURE HELP FEED THE POPULATION? LET'S DO THE MATH D. Kurns *Successful Farming* v115 no6 p2 Ap 2017
WHAT MAKES A FARMER SUCCESSFUL? D. KURNS *Successful Farming* v115 no8 p3 Je/Jl 2017
What's the Beef? Do the Math E. Malter and J. Mark *Sierra* v102 no2 p38 Mr/Ap 2017
What's Your Dietary "Food-Print"? *Tufts University Health & Nutrition Letter* v34 no10 p3 D 2016
WORDS MATTER D. KURNS *Successful Farming* v115 no5 p4 Mid-Mr 2017
a yard-to-table family *Parents* v91 no6 p124 Je 2016
ZERO TO 140 L. BEDORD *Successful Farming* v115 no1 p44 Ja 2017

Agriculture & state—China
CHINA'S $43 BILLION BID FOR FOOD SECURITY G. Colvin color diag *Fortune* v175 no6 p78 My 1 2017
China's Troubles Down on the Farm E. O'Brien, B. Nhamire et al color *Bloomberg Businessweek* no4525 p16 Je 5 2017
China Unleashes Its Farmers K. Hamlin, D. Roberts et al color *Bloomberg Businessweek* no4540 p36 O 2 2017

Agriculture & state—Environmental aspects
Beyond Politics A. Kolton color *National Wildlife (World Edition)* v54 no6 p40 O/N 2016

Agriculture & state—United States
Conservation Compliance in the Crop Insurance Era R. Claassen and M. Bowman *Amber Waves: The Economics of Food, Farming, Natural Resources, & Rural America* p29 Jl 2017
FILLING IN THE BLANKS: SEARCHING FOR FARM POLICY DETAILS IN TRUMP'S WORDS AND ACTIONS *Successful Farming* v115 no7 p8 My 2017

Agriculture & the environment
BUILDING A SMALL-SCALE FARMING REVOLUTION J. W. J. BOYD *Nation* v305 no11 p17 O 30 2017

Agriculture—Africa
How to Help Africa Feed Itself A. Bjerga and S. Gebre *Bloomberg Businessweek* no4520 p20 My 1 2017

Agriculture—Argentina
Climate Change Could Dampen Argentina's Recovery J. Gilbert map *Bloomberg Businessweek* no4539 p35 S 25 2017

Agriculture—Arizona
Dwight B. Heard: Although his legacy lives on in a world-renowned museum that bears his name, Dwight Bancroft Heard made a name for himself as a newspaper publisher, cattle baron and political ally of Teddy Roosevelt R. SANTISTEVAN *Arizona Highways* v93 no10 p8 O 2017
Yuma Agriculture N. AUSTIN *Arizona Highways* v93 no10 p7 O 2017

Agriculture—Canada
Crops and Robbers M. HAYES cartoon *Walrus* v13 no10 p19 D 2016
FOOD R. GIBSON *Alternatives Journal (AJ) - Canada's Environmental Voice* v42 no2 p80 2016

Agriculture—China
China aims to sow a revolution with GM seed takeover M. Hvistendahl color *Science* v356 no6333 p16 Ap 7 2017

Agriculture—Computer network resources
FINDING THE RIGHT PARTNER *Successful Farming* v114 no10 p16 O 2016

Agriculture—Congresses
BEHIND THE SCENES AT TOP SFIELD FAIR: IT MAY TURN 200 NEXT YEAR, BUT ITS APPEAL NEVER GETS OLD

Yankee v81 no5 p128 S/O 2017
Grassroots Movements Invigorate Communities *Mother Earth News* no280 p5 F/Mr 2017
IT HAPPENED AT THE FAIR *Mother Earth News* no283 p56 Ag/S 2017

Agriculture—Export & import trade
Increased Demand for U.S. Agricultural Exports Would Likely Lead to More U.S. Jobs S. Zahniser, T. Hertz et al *Amber Waves: The Economics of Food, Farming, Natural Resources, & Rural America* p1 Je 2017

Agriculture—Forecasting
SUPERFORECASTING FOR THE FARM J. WALTER *Successful Farming* v115 no1 p38 Ja 2017
WINDS OF CHANGE? *Successful Farming* v115 no2 p12 F 2017

Agriculture—Hawaii
POI POWER J. MILLER *Sierra* v102 no2 p42 Mr/Ap 2017

Agriculture—Indiana
BEHIND THE NUMBERS: WHAT YOU CAN GLEAN FROM YIELD CONTESTS G. GULLICKSON *Successful Farming* v115 no9 p48 Ag 2017

Agriculture—Kansas
'I Need More Mexicans' M. Jamrisko map *Bloomberg Businessweek* no4528 p26 Je 26 2017

Agriculture—Management
FEEDING THE BEAST J. Scott *Successful Farming* v114 no11 p20 N 2016
LONG-TERM FARM PROFIT ANALYSIS A. Kluis *Successful Farming* v115 no2 p20 F 2017
ORGANIZING PARTS R. Bohacz *Successful Farming* v114 no11 p28 N 2016

Agriculture—Michigan
Urban Farming *Congressional Digest* v95 no9 p13 N 2016

Agriculture—Missouri
CHASING THE AMERICAN Dream R. HANSEN color *Missouri Life* v44 no4 p38 Je 2017

Agriculture—Montana
Amber Waves OF GRAINS C. Nelson color *Vegetarian Times* v43 no2 p38 N/D 2017

Agriculture—Nebraska
Heritage Highway J. HARDIN color map *Nebraska Life* v21 no5 p22 S/O 2017
Nebraska at 150: RETROSPECTIVE - PART V OF VI 1967-1992 A. J. BARTELS bw color map *Nebraska Life* v21 no5 p62 S/O 2017
Nebraska raises the steaks on ag C. SHORT bw color *Nebraska Life* v21 no5 p20 S/O 2017

Agriculture—Netherlands
A tiny country feeds the world F. Viviano color graph map *National Geographic* v232 no3 p82 S 2017

Agriculture—New Zealand
In a first, natural selection defeats a biocontrol insect E. Pennisi color *Science* v356 no6338 p570 My 12 2017

Agriculture—Nigeria
PLANTING PEACE N. Strochlic color *National Geographic* v232 no5 p22 N 2017

Agriculture—North Dakota
Boom and Bust *American Scholar* v86 no2 p12 Spr 2017

Agriculture—Research—China
BIG SHIFT IN RESEARCH *Successful Farming* v115 no4 p14 Mr 2017

Agriculture—Research—Finance
U.S. Agricultural R&D in an Era of Falling Public Funding M. Clancy, K. Fuglie et al *Amber Waves: The Economics of Food, Farming, Natural Resources, & Rural America* p1 N 2016

Agriculture—Software—Evaluation
AHEAD OF THE CURVE L. Bedord *Successful Farming* v115 no2 p54 F 2017
There's An Ag App For That J. WALTER *Successful Farming* v114 no12 p70 Mid-N 2016

Agriculture—Study & teaching
EDUCATE YOURSELF M. McGinnis *Successful Farming* v114 no13 p30 D 2016

Agriculture—Ukraine
BOOM That You Hear Is Ukraine's Agriculture A. Bjerga and V. Verbyany color *Bloomberg Businessweek* no4495 p12 O 17 2016

Agriculture—United States

ANOTHER 4-BILLION-BUSHEL SOYBEAN CROP? *Successful Farming* v115 no1 p14 Ja 2017

BLUE SKY IN AGRICULTURE M. McGinnis, T. Dreibus et al *Successful Farming* v115 no1 p34 Ja 2017

CHANGE OF COURSE *Successful Farming* v115 no1 p12 Ja 2017

Farmers Employ Strategies To Reduce Risk of Drought Damages S. Wallander, E. Marshall et al *Amber Waves: The Economics of Food, Farming, Natural Resources, & Rural America* p57 Je 2017

The Insider's Guide to FARMERS' MARKETS [Cover story] J. R. Fuller and C. Schedler color *Chicago* v66 no6 p72 Je 2017

LARGE SPLIT-ROW PLANTER PRICES ARE UP D. Mowitz *Successful Farming* v115 no4 p28 Mr 2017

Organic for Everyone Z. SCHAEFFER color *Rodale's Organic Life* v3 no1 p33 Ja 2017

PASSION FOR FARM AND COUNTRY: VIETNAM WAR VETERAN STEVE CONRAD HAS A DEEP LOVE FOR HIS EIGHTH-GENERATION FARM AND THE COUNTRY HE FOUGHT FOR J. Scott *Successful Farming* v115 no12 p60 O 2017

THE PROBLEM: EVERYTHING SEEMS TO BE ROLLING ALONG PERFECTLY RIGHT NOW. I HEAR ABOUT ALL THESE PROBLEMS, BUT WE DON'T SEEM TO HAVE ANY. AM I MISSING SOMETHING? M. Friesen *Successful Farming* v115 no9 p68 Ag 2017

TERRY BRANSTAND A. McConnell *Successful Farming* v115 no8 p8 Je/Jl 2017

Understanding Irrigated Agriculture G. Schaible *Amber Waves: The Economics of Food, Farming, Natural Resources, & Rural America* p9 Je 2017

AN UPHILL BATTLE *Successful Farming* v114 no13 p14 D 2016

U.S. Agricultural Trade in 2016: Major Commodities and Trends B. Cooke, A. Melton et al *Amber Waves: The Economics of Food, Farming, Natural Resources, & Rural America* p1 My 2017

Agriculture—United States—Research

Changes in Farmers' Financial Status May Affect Crop Insurance Demand K. Farrin *Amber Waves: The Economics of Food, Farming, Natural Resources, & Rural America* p45 N 2016

Agriculturists

See also

Farmers

Plant pathologists

BUILDING A BETTER HARVEST M. Broadfoot color *Scientific American* v317 no2 p66 Ag 2017

Agritourism

The 10TH Annual Scottsdale Farm Tours K. HOPP *Arabian Horse World* v57 no5 p202 F 2017

Bay Watch E. J. CURRAN *Virginia Living* p11 2017 Smoke & Salt

New Crop: As the nation's largest agritourism site, Northwest Indiana'... J. VRABEL color *Indianapolis Monthly* v41 no2 p53 S 2017

Agroforestry—Missouri

EAT YOUR HART OUT S. COTHRAN color *Missouri Life* v44 no4 p66 Je 2017

Agrokor d.d.—Finance

From Russia, With Debt L. Casiraghi, J. Kuzmanovic et al color *Bloomberg Businessweek* no4517 p42 Ap 3 2017

Agropastoral systems

The Consequences of Internal Migration in Sub-Saharan Africa: A Case Study J. SALERNO, J. MWALYOYO et al *BioScience* v67 no7 p664 Jl 2017

Agualusa, José Eduardo, 1960-

José Eduardo Agualusa C. Cullen color *Current Biography* v77 no11 p3 N 2016

Aguayo, Sergio

The Scotosis in the U.S.-Mexico Relationship *Wilson Quarterly* p3 Spr 2017

Agudelo, Leandro Z.

Kynurenines: Tryptophan's metabolites in exercise, inflammation, and mental health color *Science* v357 no6349 p369 Jl 28 2017

Aguilar, Andrea

Microtubules acquire resistance from mechanical breakage through intralumenal acetylation diag graph *Science* v356 no6335 p328 Ap 21 2017

AGUILAR, GARY L.

Dallas Revisited *American Scholar* v86 no1 p4 Wint 2017

Aguilera, Roberto F.

The future of oil prices: a break with the past? Y. Ivanchev *Monthly Labor Review* p1 Jl 2017

Aguillard, Anna

An Azalea Affair color *Southern Living* v52 no3 p11 Mr 2017

The Essence of Spring color *Southern Living* v52 no5 p68 My 2017

French Court color *Southern Living* v52 no5 p15 My 2017

My Mom, the Beauty Icon color *Southern Living* v52 no6 p54 Je 2017

Skin Guards color *Southern Living* v52 no6 p50 Je 2017

Aguirre, Abby

THE Z FACTOR [Cover story] color *Vogue* v207 no7 p74 Jl 2017

AGUIRRE, DESIRÉ

Don't Call Him Goofy *Idaho Magazine* v16 no2 p43 N 2016

Mixed Blessings: In the Month of May *Idaho Magazine* v16 no11 p24 Ag 2017

Aguirre, Jorge

'THE BRIEF WONDROUS LIFE OF OSCAR WAO' *New York Times Book Review* p30 Ja 8 2017

Aguirre, Sergio

FASTER AND BETTER: A LOOK AT THE NEXT-GENERATION NETWORK POWERING IN-FLIGHT ENTERTAINMENT T. VELOCCI color *Forbes* v200 no3 p72 S 28 2017

Aguirre-Muñoz, Alfonso

Mexico's invasive species plan in context bw *Science* v356 no6336 p386 Ap 28 2017

Agus, David B.

Fortune Brainstorm HEALTH color *Fortune* v175 no7 p20 Je 1 2017

Taking Health Into Your Own Hands *AARP: The Magazine* v59 no1A p24 D 2015/Ja 2016

What doctors tell their friends about energy [Cover story] L. MULCAHY color *Redbook* p66 Jl/Ag 2017

Agus, Sydney

100 FASTEST-GROWING COMPANIES chart color diag map *Fortune* v176 no4 p157 S 15 2017

CHANGE THE WORLD !!!! color diag map *Fortune* v176 no4 p74 S 15 2017

RISING STARS color *Fortune* v176 no4 p89 S 15 2017

Ágústdóttir, Ragnhildur

IMAGINATION TAKES FLIGHT A. ELLIOTT *Iceland Review* v54 no6 p8 N/D 2016

Ágústsson, Sigurður

TIME CAPSULE P. STEFÁNSSON *Iceland Review* v55 no2 p68 Mr/Ap 2017

Aguzzi, J.

An ecosystem-based deep-ocean strategy bibl color map *Science* v355 no6324 p452 F 3 2017

Ahalt, Ryan

FOOT SOLDIERS R. AHALT and A. ASSILI *Washingtonian Magazine* v52 no1 p126 O 2016

Ahamed, Liaquat

OFF THE MARKET! *Washingtonian Magazine* v52 no4 p195 Ja 2017

Ahanotu, Onyemaechi

Preventing mussel adhesion using lubricant-infused materials color diag graph *Science* v357 no6352 p668 Ag 18 2017

Ahdieh, Renée

Flame in the Mist *Publishers Weekly* v264 no11 p84 Mr 13 2017

A'Hearn, M.

Rosetta's comet 67P/Churyumov-Gerasimenko sheds its dusty mantle to reveal its icy nature bibl graph *Science* v354 no6319 p1566 D 23 2016

Surface changes on comet 67P/Churyumov-Gerasimenko suggest a more active past bw graph *Science* v355 no6332 p1392 Mr 31 2017

Ahern, Philip P.

Lactobacillus reuteri induces gut intraepithelial CD4+CD8αα+ T cells diag graph *Science* v357 no6353 p806 Ag 25 2017

Ahern-Dodson, Jennifer

Teach the Moment *Change* v48 no6 p24 N/D 2016

Ahlberg, Per E.
A Silurian maxillate placoderm illuminates jaw evolution bibl color *Science* v354 no6310 p334 O 21 2016

Ahmad, Irfan
Religion as Critique: Islamic Critical Thinking from Mecca to the Marketplace *Publishers Weekly* v264 no41 p62 O 9 2017

Ahmad, Komal
Feeding Our App-etite D. CHEN *Reader's Digest* v188 no1125 p8 N 2016

Ahmad, Komal—Interviews
Using Tech to Feed Hungry People P. M. ESSWEIN color *Kiplinger's Personal Finance* v71 no1 p22 Ja 2017

Ahmad, Muhammad A.
TALKING TO THE DEAD *Saturday Evening Post* v289 no2 p10 Mr/Ap 2017

Ahmad, Wasil
The Improbable Life and Stunning Death of a Child Warrior J. Hammer color *GQ: Gentlemen's Quarterly* v87 no1 p34 Ja 2017

Ahmad, Zainab
A RIGHTEOUS CASE W. FINNEGAN cartoon color *New Yorker* v93 no13 p66 My 15 2017

Ahmadiah Group (Company)
AHMADIAH: Setting The Standards In Construction Excellence A. A. Al-Thuwainy *Foreign Affairs* v95 no6 p120f N/D 2016

Ahmadiyya members
People M. W. Qureshi and M. I. Pinsky color *Christian Century* v134 no18 p17 Ag 30 2017

Ahmad Khan, Sayyid, Sir, 1817-1898
A Few Movie Stars Don't Make Happy Muslim Indians A. HAMEED *Islamic Horizons* v46 no2 p52 Mr/Ap 2017

Ahmadpoor, Mohammad
The dual frontier: Patented inventions and prior scientific advance graph *Science* v357 no6351 p583 Ag 11 2017

Ahmari, Sohrab
Can Europe Be Saved? *Commentary* v144 no2 p42 S 2017
Christianity's Russian Temptation color *America* v216 no7 p26 Ap 3 2017
Defending the State M. Wolfish and J. Blankfort *Commentary* v140 no2 p11 S 2015
Every Picture Tells M. M. Rosen color *Weekly Standard* v22 no23 p34 F 20 2017
The Identitarians A. ROBERTS *Commentary* v142 no4 p51 N 2016
ILLIBERALISM: THE WORLDWIDE CRISIS *Commentary* v142 no1 p17 Jl/Ag 2016
The terrible American turn toward illiberalism *Commentary* v144 no3 p13 O 2017

AHMED, AMAL
VITAL SIGNS *Texas Monthly* v45 no9 p62 S 2017

Ahmed, Azam
HAITI IN CRISIS *New York Times Upfront* v149 no6 p8 D 12 2016

AHMED, BEENISH
VODOU AND THE RAINBOW *Advocate* no1088 p56 D 2016/Ja 2017

AHMED, M. BASHEER
Childlessness Should Lead to Exploring Options: Are Muslim American communities geared to supporting childless couples? *Islamic Horizons* v46 no3 p40 My/Je 2017

Ahmed, Majid
Promoting human rights through science color *Science* v357 no6359 p34 O 6 2017

Ahmed, Nabila
Payless Flops, But the Owners Get a Payday graph *Bloomberg Businessweek* no4516 p35 Mr 27 2017

Ahmed, Rafi
IgG antibodies to dengue enhanced for FcγRIIIA binding determine disease severity bibl graph *Science* v355 no6323 p395 Ja 27 2017
Rescue of exhausted CD8 T cells by PD-1–targeted therapies is CD28-dependent bw diag graph *Science* v355 no6332 p1423 Mr 31 2017

Ahmed, Riz
THE BREAK-OUTS 2016 S. Ball, Z. Baron et al color *GQ: Gentlemen's Quarterly* v86 no12 p198 D 2016

Episodes in hell B. F. Jones color *Christian Century* v133 no23 p43 N 9 2016
Pioneers [Cover story] Miranda, L. DiCaprio et al color *Time* v189 no16/17 p14 My 1-8 2017
Power Tools: Leaders C. Alter color *Time* v189 no16/17 p90 My 1-8 2017
Rebel With a Cause A. Breznican color *Entertainment Weekly* no1443 p22 D 9 2016
Riz Ahmed J. Crelin color *Current Biography* v78 no4 p3 Ap 2017
RIZ AHMED: THE NEW BOY ON GIRLS S. Li and R. Rahman color *Entertainment Weekly* no1453 p52 F 17 2017
ROGUE ONE A. Breznican color *Entertainment Weekly* no1460/1461 p93 Ap 7-17 2017

Ahmed, Riz—Interviews
The 3-Minute Interview K. Branch and J. Harman color *Glamour* v115 no1 p18 Ja 2017
5 JUICY QUESTIONS with... Riz Ahmed C. Keller color *Women's Health* v13 no10 p108 D 2016

Ahmed, Rizwan
the artists bw color *Foreign Policy* no221 p67 N/D 2016

Ahmed, Sara
IDENTITY, EMPATHY, AND INQUIRY color *Literacy Today (2411-7862)* v34 no5 p44 Mr/Ap 2017

Ahmetoglu, Gorkan
The Pros and Cons of Robot Managers *Harvard Business Review Digital Articles* p2 D 12 2016

Ahn, Kwangwon
Wall Street Rewards CEOs Who Talk About Their Strategies *Harvard Business Review Digital Articles* p2 D 28 2015

Ahn, Natalie G.
Structure of histone-based chromatin in Archaea diag *Science* v357 no6351 p609 Ag 11 2017

AHN, THOMAS
The Problem with Measuring Effects of Delinquent Peers in Education—and How to Get Around It *Education Digest* v82 no9 p18 My 2017

ahrens & grabenhorst architekten stadtplaner BDA (Company)
Second Coming M. PEPCHINSKI color diag *Architectural Record* v205 no2 p70 F 2017

Ahrman, Jim
You Never Forget Your First Time diag il *Backpacker* v45 no2 p64 Mr 2017

AHSAN, AZIZ M.
Becoming An American *Islamic Horizons* v45 no6 p42 N/D 2016

Ahuile, Leylha
30 Years of Jorge Ramos bw *Publishers Weekly* v263 no44 p(Sp)20 O 31 2016
Andrew Wylie Makes First FIL Appearance color *Publishers Weekly* v263 no50 p25 D 5 2016
Distributors and Wholesalers Meet the Growing Demand For Books in Spanish color *Publishers Weekly* v263 no46 p6 N 14 2016
Diversity on Display color *Publishers Weekly* v263 no50 p24 D 5 2016
Examining the Mexican-American Book Connection color *Publishers Weekly* v264 no32 p16 Ag 7 2017
Fall Changes *Publishers Weekly* v263 no40 p19 O 3 2016
Ismael Cala: CNN Host Turned Life Strategist color *Publishers Weekly* v264 no18 p18 My 1 2017
María Paulina Camejo color *Publishers Weekly* v264 no14 p18 Ap 3 2017
New Publishers Give Readers More Choices *Publishers Weekly* v264 no6 p18 F 6 2017
Nicolás Kanellos Wins Tejano Association for Historical Preservation Award color *Publishers Weekly* v264 no23 p16 Je 5 2017
Olé! Spanish Language Programs at the Fair bw color *Publishers Weekly* v263 no44 p(Sp)21 O 31 2016
PW Talks with Sara Galindo color *Publishers Weekly* v264 no23 p15 Je 5 2017
Select June and July Spanish-Language Titles color *Publishers Weekly* v264 no27 p17 Jl 3 2017
Thirty Years of Telling Great Stories *Publishers Weekly* v263 no46 p4 N 14 2016

Ahuja, Akshay
AS GOOD AS IT GETS *Cincinnati Magazine* v50 no4 p144 Ja 2017

CHAIN GANG *Cincinnati Magazine* v50 no5 p156 F 2017
CLUB MED *Cincinnati Magazine* p108 Je 2017
COW PALACE *Cincinnati Magazine* v50 no2 p118 N 2016
GOING DUTCH *Cincinnati Magazine* v50 no3 p126 D 2016
LOCAL WONDER *Cincinnati Magazine* v50 no7 p150 Ap 2017
PLEASE ADVISE *Cincinnati Magazine* v50 no8 p99 My 2017
ROOM SERVICE: COPPIN'S built a regional menu. Will locavores come? *Cincinnati Magazine* v50 no10 p118 Jl 2017
WURST BEHAVIOR *Cincinnati Magazine* v50 no12 p100 S 2017

Ahuja, Jasvinder S.
Control of meiotic pairing and recombination by chromosomally tethered 26S proteasome bibl graph *Science* v355 no6323 p408 Ja 27 2017

Ahuja, Simone
How Intuit Built a Better Support System for Intrapreneurs *Harvard Business Review Digital Articles* p2 Ap 5 2016
The Innovative Mindset Your Company Can't Afford to Lose *Harvard Business Review Digital Articles* p2 O 13 2015
What It Takes to Innovate Within Large Corporations *Harvard Business Review Digital Articles* p2 Je 15 2016
What Stitch Fix Figured Out About Mass Customization *Harvard Business Review Digital Articles* p2 My 26 2015

AIAZZI, TONY
How to Make... JERKY color *Popular Mechanics* p80 S 2017
How to Make... JERKY color *Popular Mechanics* v193 no7 p80 S 2016

Aiche, Jacquie
Hot Links *Los Angeles Magazine* p32 Ap 2017

Aida, Makoto
MAKOTO AIDA R. Holmberg *Art in America* v104 no9 p165 O 2016

Aidelsburger, Monika
Cold atoms twisting spin and momentum bibl diag *Science* v354 no6308 p35 O 7 2016

Aiden, Erez Lieberman
De novo assembly of the Aedes aegypti genome using Hi-C yields chromosome-length scaffolds chart color diag *Science* v356 no6333 p92 Ap 7 2017

AIDS (Disease)
Geek Love K. PATTERSON cartoon *Walrus* v13 no10 p54 D 2016
HIV/AIDS—A History K. M. DE COCK color *Natural History* v125 no9 p36 S 2017
Pinpointing HIV spread in Africa poses risks J. Cohen color *Science* v356 no6338 p568 My 12 2017
Surviving the '80s D. DUDLEY, M. GRANT et al color *AARP: The Magazine* v59 no5A p47 Ag/S 2016

AIDS (Disease)—Prevention
AIDS epidemic nears control in three African countries J. Cohen color *Science* v354 no6317 p1213 D 9 2016
HIV REMAINS A PREVALENT ISSUE IN CANADA R. Druzin *Maclean's* v129 no50 p52 D 19 2016

AIDS (Disease)—Social aspects
ART, ACTIVISM & AIDS: THESE DECADES WERE FILLED WITH LGBT CHANGE, BUT THE IMPACT OF AIDS WAS THE BIGGEST D. ARTAVIA and D. ANDERSON-MINSHALL bw *Advocate* no1091 p87 Je/Jl 2017

AIDS (Disease)—Treatment
AIDS epidemic nears control in three African countries J. Cohen color *Science* v354 no6317 p1213 D 9 2016
Surprising treatment 'cures' monkey HIV infection J. Cohen color *Science* v354 no6309 p157 O 14 2016

AIDS (Disease)—Vaccination
Controversial HIV vaccine strategy gets a second chance J. Cohen color *Science* v354 no6312 p535 N 4 2016
Developing an HIV vaccine B. F. Haynes and D. R. Burton bibl diag *Science* v355 no6330 p1129 Mr 17 2017

AIDS (Disease)—Vaccination—Research
HIV's ACHILLES' HEEL R. W. Sanders, I. A. Wilson et al color diag *Scientific American* v315 no6 p50 D 2016

Aids to air navigation
THE SYNTHETIC AND THE REAL P. Garrison color *Flying* v144 no7 p80 Jl 2017

Aids to navigation
See also
Nautical charts

C-MAP Genesis Edge Premium Marine-Mapping Service J. Y. WOOD color *Power & Motoryacht* v34 no10 p58 O 2017
Five Essential Questions for Your Chart Briefing Z. Prochazka color *Sail* v47 no12 p55 D 2016

AIDS (Disease)—Societies, etc.
THE C.E.O. OF H.I.V. C. GLAZEK *New York Times Magazine* p44 Ap 30 2017
Of Scorched Earth and Skyscrapers G. KAHN *Los Angeles Magazine* v61 no11 p26 N 2016

AIDS (Disease)—Sub-Saharan Africa
AIDS in Africa: Progress and Obstacles S. A. MOJOLA *Current History* v116 no790 p170 My 2017

Aiduss, Michael
INSTANT ROOM: A DAPPER FAMILY SALON color *House Beautiful* v159 no9 p46 N 2017

Aikas, Timo
WHAT LIES BENEATH A. CURRY color *Atlantic* v320 no3 p52 O 2017

AIKAWA, TATSU
Our Ramen Changed Texas... ...and Texas Changed Our Ramen color *Bon Appetit* v62 no2 p66 Mr 2017

Aiken (S.C.)—Description & travel
SPRINGTIME IN HORSE COUNTRY V. F. Luesse color *Southern Living* v52 no3 p100 Mr 2017

Aiken, Joan, 1924-2004
In sequels, prequels and spinoffs, Joan Aiken took up some of the stories Austen never intended to tell L. Skurnick *New York Times Book Review* p12 Jl 16 2017

Aikin, Taylor
Record Products 2016 L. Lentz, R. Orrell et al color *Architectural Record* v204 no12 p113 D 2016

Aikman, Becky
How Thelma & Louise Changed Hollywood S. Begley color *Time* v190 no4 p18 Jl 24 2017

Aikman, Rebecca
Suspense *New York Times Book Review* p26 S 3 2017

AIKMAN, TROY
Why Everyone Loves the Big Game *TV Guide* v65 no6 p16 Ja 30 2017

Ailes, Roger, 1940-2017
How Unusual Is the Roger Ailes Sexual Harassment Case? D. L. Rhode *Harvard Business Review Digital Articles* p2 Ag 10 2016
The Loudest Voice in 'New York' C. Bonanos img *New York* v49 no15 p10 Jl 25 2016
Pulling the Strings F. Barnes *New Republic* v247 no11 p4 N 2016
Roger Ailes J. Dickey color *Time* v189 no21 p14 Je 5 2017
ROGER, OVER AND OUT! S. ELLISON cartoon *Vanity Fair* v58 no11 p104 N 2016
THE STRATEGY OF TRUTH J. Lepore cartoon *New Yorker* v93 no16 p37 Je 5 2017
TRIBUTES I. Rudolph *TV Guide* v65 no23 p11 My 29 2017
The Witch Is Dead E. Alterman diag *Nation* v304 no18 p6 Je 19 2017
The Ziegfeld of Political Theater A. FERGUSON color *Weekly Standard* v22 no36 p12 My 29 2017

Ailes, Roger, 1940-—Trials, litigation, etc.
Comments img *New York* v49 no19 p10 S 19 2016

Aillery, Marcel
Farmers Employ Strategies To Reduce Risk of Drought Damages *Amber Waves: The Economics of Food, Farming, Natural Resources, & Rural America* p57 Je 2017

Ailworth, Erin
MY HOMETOWN PAPER: Erin Ailworth color *Columbia Journalism Review* v56 no1 p81 Spr 2017

Aima, Rahel
Art Without America color map *Art in America* v105 no4 p37 Ap 2017
Consumed Culture color *Art in America* v105 no1 p29 Ja 2017
Lawrie Shabibi bw *Art in America* v105 no6 p149 Je/Jl 2017
Mitchell-Innes & Nash color *Art in America* v105 no1 p83 Ja 2017
Residents and Residencies *Art in America* v104 no9 p55 O 2016

Aime, Federico
10 Years of Data on Baseball Teams Shows When Pay Transparency Backfires *Harvard Business Review Digital Articles* p2 My 9 2017

Aimless Bullet (Film)

Hello, Cruel World G. HENDRIX bw color *Film Comment* v53 no2 p74 Mr/Ap 2017

Aims & objectives of education
   See also
   Educational equalization
SOMETHING TO rely on: Through changing times, ILA, and its dedicated network of educators, remains the constant J. F. Savage *Literacy Today (2411-7862)* v35 no1 p44 Jl/Ag 2017

Aims & objectives of education—United States
Backtalk B. Sevier *Phi Delta Kappan* v99 no1 p48 S 2017

Ain, Sanford
WASHINGTON'S TOP DIVORCE LAWYERS *Washingtonian Magazine* v52 no3 p124 D 2016

Aina, Oluwaseun
BEYOND NATIONAL borders color *Literacy Today (2411-7862)* v34 no5 p52 Mr/Ap 2017

Ainger, John
Spread Your Wings and Fly, Penguin color graph *Bloomberg Businessweek* no4509 p17 Ja 30 2017

Ainley, David G.
Science-based management in decline in the Southern Ocean bibl map *Science* v354 no6309 p185 O 14 2016

Ainsworth, Grover
Community and Economic Development: Around the Globe and Back to the Mississippi Delta Region *Bridges (Federal Reserve Bank of St. Louis)* p7 Wint 2016/2017

Ainsworth, Kat
A BACKUP PLAN color map *Outdoor Life* v223 no9 pH7 N 2016

Ainsworth, Lydia
NIGHT LIFE *New Yorker* v93 no10 p29 Ap 24 2017

Alpert, Alice
Coral - Current Connections color *Oceanus* v51 no2 p48 Wint 2016

Air
clear THE AIR M. RABBITT color *Yoga Journal* no290 p17 Mr 2017
Feng Shui Beauty S. STRAUSFOGEL color *Better Nutrition* v79 no1 p54 Ja 2017
It's all ELEMENTAL [Cover story] T. EICHENSEHER color *Yoga Journal* no290 p64 Mr 2017

Air bag restraint systems
Deal Snapshot: Takata Corp Ma Jie chart *Bloomberg Businessweek* no4529 p21 Jl 3 2017

Air bases
Into the Wild Blue Yonder with the Air National Guard S. W. KANSTEINER color *Nebraska Life* v21 no4 p20 Jl/Ag 2017

Air compressors
   See also
   Compressed air
COLD-AIR CARBS J. Smith color graph *Hot Rod* v70 no11 p86 N 2017

Air conditioning
Happy Campers R. DeBruhl color *AARP: The Magazine* v60 no4A p11 Je/Jl 2017
Sterling K. Brown J. ZAMBRANO color *O, The Oprah Magazine* p30 S 2017

Air conditioning equipment
AIR CONDITIONER K. Dupzyk color *Popular Mechanics* p18 Je 2017
The refrigerant is also the pump Q. M. Zhang and T. Zhang diag *Science* v357 no6356 p1094 S 15 2017

Air conditioning—Evaluation
DOCK BOX: GEAR, TOOLS AND TOYS *Sea Magazine* v109 no4 p32 Ap 2017

Air-cooled condensers—Evaluation
NEW PRODUCTS color *Science* v354 no6318 p1445 D 16 2016
new products color *Science* v357 no6349 p418 Jl 28 2017

Air Force One (Presidential aircraft)
TRUMP FORCE ONE G. M. Graff bw color *Bloomberg Businessweek* no4515 p48 Mr 20 2017

Air forces
AIR WAR: DAY 4 color *AARP: The Magazine* v59 no3A p68 Ap/My 2016

Air masses
   See also
   Heat waves (Meteorology)

   Lows (Meteorology)
one crazy month in Montana S. Chodosh color *Popular Science* v289 no4 p18 Jl/Ag 2017

Air mattresses—Evaluation
Odd Couples Can Find Happiness, Too color *Consumer Reports* v82 no2 p26 F 2017

Air pilot certification
BELONGING M. Lunken *Flying* v144 no11 p66 N 2017
A Fast-Track Promotion—With a Catch J. Johnsson and M. Schlangenstein diag *Bloomberg Businessweek* no4536 p19 S 4 2017

Air pilots
   See also
   Astronauts
   Women air pilots
ATMOSPHERIC ELECTRICAL PHENOMENA: A Pilot's View G. J. Mulvey, J. F. Miller et al il *Weatherwise* v70 no5 p32 S/O 2017
AVIATION CAREERS S. Pope color *Flying* v144 no9 p58 S 2017
BLAME IT ON THE BRUSSELS SPROUTS L. Abend color *Flying* v144 no3 p82 Mr 2017
BRAVE NEW WORLD S. Weigel color *Flying* v144 no11 p36 N 2017
Corey Michael Mijac A. HUTCHINS color *Maclean's* v129 no47 p66 N 28 2016
DREAMING VERSUS DOING S. Weigel bw color *Flying* v144 no8 p38 Ag 2017
THE GREATEST AIRPORT PARTY EVER M. King color *Flying* v144 no11 p32 N 2017
High-Pressure Jobs and Mental Illness D. Coutu *Harvard Business Review Digital Articles* p2 Ap 2 2015
The Iditarod Air Force J. BENNETT color map *Popular Mechanics* p15 Mr 2017
IN THE HOT SEAT S. Weigel color *Flying* v144 no7 p40 Jl 2017
LOST SOUL OR GUARDIAN ANGEL? T. TEXTOR color *Flying* v144 no4 p30 Ap 2017
A NEAR MISS D. FRANCIS color map *Flying* v144 no10 p28 O 2017
NEVER A DULL MOMENT L. Abend color *Flying* v144 no10 p74 O 2017
PILOTS OF THE CARIBBEAN R. MARK color *Flying* v144 no11 p58 N 2017
PILOTS WANTED color *Flying* v144 no8 p82 Ag 2017
A QUESTION OF JUDGMENT P. Garrison *Flying* v144 no3 p36 Mr 2017
The Risk Taker G. DREVITCH *Psychology Today* v50 no3 p27 My/Je 2017
Runyon Canyon 911 C. KAZDIN color *Los Angeles Magazine* v62 no10 p15 O 2017
SPEED SECRETS P. BERGQVIST color *Flying* v144 no8 p52 Ag 2017
Thunderbird Field N. AUSTIN *Arizona Highways* v93 no9 p8 S 2017
THUNDERSTORM AVOIDANCE, PENETRATION AND SURVIVAL R. Lengel color *Flying* v144 no6 p28 Je 2017
TWO BOBS P. Garrison bw *Flying* v144 no9 p80 S 2017
UNDER THE HOOD S. Weigel bw *Flying* v144 no3 p46 Mr 2017
WHAT PILOT SHORTAGE? PART TWO S. Weigel color *Flying* v144 no9 p38 S 2017
WHERE ARE YOU GOING? A. DARRISAW color *O, The Oprah Magazine* p126 N 2017
WHY BE AN AIRLINE PILOT? L. Abend color *Flying* v144 no9 p74 S 2017
WORKING EVERY DAY AT 35,000 FEET M. VANHOENACKER color *Reader's Digest* v189 no1130 p114 My 2017

Air pilots—Attitudes
THE TYRANNY OF EFFICIENCY J. Zimmerman color *Flying* v144 no6 p30 Je 2017
Virgin Atlantic Tested 3 Ways to Change Employee Behavior R. Metcalfe, G. Gosnell et al *Harvard Business Review Digital Articles* p2 Ag 1 2016

Air pilots—Certification
ACS MAKES MY HEAD ACHE M. Lunken chart graph *Flying* v144 no4 p74 Ap 2017

Air pilots—Congresses
PETER PAN AND WENDY M. Lunken *Flying* v143 no12 p64 D 2016

WE'D JUST LIKE TO ASK YOU A FEW QUESTIONS P. Garrison color *Flying* v144 no3 p88 Mr 2017

Airhart, Kathleen M.
Microcredentials color il *Phi Delta Kappan* v98 no3 p34 N 2016

AIRHART, MARC
Stay Sharp this Semester *USA Today Magazine* v146 no2868 p45 S 2017

Airhead (Company)
name the boat color *Boating World* v38 no7 p64 Jl 2017

Airline boarding procedures
FLOOD AIRLINES A. BEATTIE cartoon *New Yorker* v93 no12 p27 My 8 2017

Airline industry
Case Study: Can an Airline Cut "Turn Times" Without Adding Staff? E. Bernstein and R. Buell *Harvard Business Review Digital Articles* p2 Ja 27 2016
CONSIDERING A CAREER IN THE CHARTER WORLD D. Karl color *Flying* v144 no9 p70 S 2017
Curbing Aviation Emissions *Congressional Digest* v95 no10 p13 D 2016
InDepth D. Pimentel color *Flying* v144 no3 p41 Mr 2017
IN THE HOT SEAT S. Weigel color *Flying* v144 no7 p40 Jl 2017
The Iranian Express E. OTTOLENGHI color map *Weekly Standard* v22 no44 p22 Jl 31 2017
NONSTOP TRAVEL A. RODERIQUE-JONES color *Louisiana Life* v37 no4 p100 Mr/Ap 2017
The Reason Air Travel Is Terrible and So Few Airlines Are Profitable J. P. Vazquez Sampere *Harvard Business Review Digital Articles* p2 My 27 2016
Season to Stopover *New York* v50 no17 p148 Ag 21 2017

Airline industry customer services
TRIP OF A LIFETIME [Cover story] N. Saporita color *Good Housekeeping* v265 no3 p146 S 2017

Airline industry employees
THE WORLD IS NOT ENOUGH [Cover story] M. Campbell and D. Kamel color *Bloomberg Businessweek* no4506 p34 Ja 9 2017

Airline industry—China
China Challenges the Giants With Low Fares A. Whitley, K. Park et al color graph *Bloomberg Businessweek* no4504 p22 D 19 2016

Airline industry—Cost of operation
Save on Airline Costs E. AMBROSE color *AARP: The Magazine* v60 no3A p21 Ap/My 2017

Airline industry—Europe
Europe's Big Airlines Struggle for Altitude R. Weiss color graph *Bloomberg Businessweek* no4503 p19 D 12 2016

Airline industry—Mergers
Europe's Big Airlines Struggle for Altitude R. Weiss color graph *Bloomberg Businessweek* no4503 p19 D 12 2016

Airline industry—North America
THE PILOT PIPELINE D. PIMENTEL color *Flying* v144 no2 p48 F 2017

Airline industry—Rates
Airlines' New Basic Economy Fares Show the Power of No-Frills Pricing R. Mohammed color *Harvard Business Review Digital Articles* p2 Mr 3 2017
THE BEST ROUTE TO BARGAIN AIRFARES R. ERMEY color *Kiplinger's Personal Finance* v71 no4 p10 Ap 2017
China Challenges the Giants With Low Fares A. Whitley, K. Park et al color graph *Bloomberg Businessweek* no4504 p22 D 19 2016
FROM USA TO EUR [Cover story] B. Tuttle color *Money* v46 no5 p42 Je 2017
HOW TO FIND 2017'S CHEAPEST FLIGHTS B. Tuttle color *Money* v46 no2 p21 Mr 2017

Airline industry—Tickets
The Dark Art of How (and When) to Buy an Airline Ticket A. HALPERN img *New York* v50 no10 p70 My 15 2017
Ombudsman: A Mega-Pricey Missed Flight R. Marnell color *Conde Nast Traveler* v52 no2 p109 F 2017
On the House C. BONANOS color *Conde Nast Traveler* v52 no7 p98 Ag 2017

Airline industry—United States
AIRLINES' STOCK RALLY SHOWS IT'S BETTER TO BE GOOD THAN NICE A. Vandermey diag *Fortune* v175 no7 p16 Je 1 2017

THE MUNOZ WAY J. CROWN cartoon color *Chicago* v65 no11 p19 N 2016
AN ODE TO AUGUST color *Flying* v144 no8 p8 Ag 2017
Warren Buffett Is Betting the Airline Oligopoly Is Here to Stay M. Schmalz *Harvard Business Review Digital Articles* p2 N 17 2016
YOUR FLIGHT IS DELAYED R. W. J. POOLE color *Reason* v49 no6 p16 N 2017

Airline industry—United States—Finance
AVOIDING A STEEP DESCENT R. Derousseau color diag *Fortune* v175 no4 p44 Mr 15 2017

Airline tickets—Law & legislation
Your Rights on Flights K. PITSKER cartoon *Kiplinger's Personal Finance* v71 no7 p42 Jl 2017

AIROLDI, LAURA
The Resilience of Marine Ecosystems to Climatic Disturbances *BioScience* v67 no3 p208 Mr 2017

Airplane! (Film : 1980)
50 Things Black Mirror Is Made Of J. SINGAL img *New York* v49 no21 p106 O 17 2016

Airplane cockpits
AUTO-THROTTLES R. Mark color *Flying* v144 no9 p20 S 2017
"NEVER LOOK LIKE A TOURIST. ACT LIKE YOU KNOW WHERE YOU ARE." A. WHITTLE color *Conde Nast Traveler* v52 no3 p32 Mr 2017
POLISHING OFF THE RUST J. King color *Flying* v144 no9 p30 S 2017

Airplane control systems
COMMUNICATION BREAKDOWN S. DUNN cartoon *Flying* v144 no3 p26 Mr 2017
CONSIDER THE OPERATING ENVIRONMENT AROUND AN ILS APPROACH R. MARK and J. BLAIR color *Flying* v144 no10 p27 O 2017
EVERYTHING ABOUT V SPEEDS EXPLAINED: PART ONE R. Lengel color *Flying* v144 no8 p28 Ag 2017
STICK SHAKER/PUSHER R. Mark diag *Flying* v144 no8 p20 Ag 2017
TRAINING & TECHNIQUE cartoon *Flying* v144 no3 p25 Mr 2017

Airplane crash survival
THE FAIRY TALE AND THE NIGHTMARE S. I. Price and K. Steiker-ginzberg color *Sports Illustrated* v127 no3 p104 Jl 24 2017

Airplane design & construction
FREE BIRD: Anne Morrow Lindbergh's first plane could be hanging in a museum. Instead, it's still flying over Maryland A. Beaujon *Washingtonian Magazine* v52 no12 p54 S 2017
GAMEBIRD FAA CERTIFIED bw color *Flying* v144 no11 p20 N 2017
WHAT WORKED AND WHAT DIDN'T P. Garrison color *Flying* v144 no6 p80 Je 2017

Airplane equipment
PORTABLE WEATHER color *Flying* v144 no11 p16 N 2017

Airplane motors
COOL inventions C. M. TOMLIN cartoon color *National Geographic Kids* no470 p11 My 2017
PILATUS PC-24 ENGINE CERTIFIED color *Flying* v144 no10 p22 O 2017
VTOL RIDES AGAIN P. Garrison color *Flying* v144 no11 p80 N 2017

Airplane piloting
3,600 Miles and a Dream B. URMSTON color *Popular Mechanics* p50 Jl 2017
EVEN AN ILS APPROACH DEMANDS ATTENTION R. MARK and J. BLAIR bw *Flying* v144 no7 p25 Jl 2017

Airplane racing
THE ART OF AIR RACING P. BERGQVIST color diag *Flying* v144 no9 p50 S 2017
SPEED SECRETS P. BERGQVIST color *Flying* v144 no8 p52 Ag 2017

Airplane seats
9 Secrets to Scoring First-Class Upgrades on the Cheap J. Calfas color *Money* v46 no9 p30 O 2017

Airplane sounds
Sounds In the Night E. Laborde bw *New Orleans Magazine* v51 no5 p152 Mr 2017

Airplane wings—Maintenance & repair
DAMAGE HISTORY L. Abend color *Flying* v144 no4 p82 Ap 2017

Airplanes
See also
    Airplane cockpits
    Business airplanes
    Cessna aircraft
    Gliders (Aeronautics)
    Jet planes
    Light aircraft
    Photography of airplanes
    Turboprop airplanes
3,600 Miles and a Dream B. URMSTON color *Popular Mechanics* p50 Jl 2017
AVIATION SIGHTS D. Karl color *Flying* v144 no6 p70 Je 2017
BACK IN THE SADDLE J. BERLIN color *Flying* v144 no6 p60 Je 2017
COOL inventions C. M. TOMLIN cartoon color *National Geographic Kids* no470 p11 My 2017
DAMAGE HISTORY: PART II L. Abend color *Flying* v144 no8 p74 Ag 2017
EVERYTHING ABOUT V SPEEDS EXPLAINED: PART TWO R. Lengel color *Flying* v144 no9 p28 S 2017
FLYING THE HONDAJET color *Flying* v144 no5 p82 My 2017
LET'S MEET IN NEW YORK color *Flying* v144 no11 p82 N 2017
NICKNAMES, DESERVED OR NOT! M. Lunken *Flying* v144 no9 p67 S 2017
OSHKOSH OR BUST C. GREGOIRE color *Flying* v144 no11 p50 N 2017
PARTY LINES J. Vineyard img *New York* v49 no19 p99 S 19 2016
THE PILOTS WHO CRASHED INTO THE SEA N. HUNE-BROWN color map *Reader's Digest* v189 no1129 p84 Ap 2017
ROTARY RISING P. Garrison diag *Flying* v144 no8 p80 Ag 2017
STRANGE WINGS P. Garrison bw color *Flying* v144 no5 p80 My 2017

Airplanes—Awards
2016 FLYING EDITORS' CHOICE AWARDS color *Flying* v144 no1 p46 Ja 2017
CONGRATULATIONS, HONDAJET color *Flying* v144 no10 p14 O 2017

Airplanes—Defects
THE END OF A LOVE AFFAIR D. Karl color *Flying* v143 no12 p70 D 2016

Airplanes—Design & construction
PERKS FOR THE 99% A. MARSHALL cartoon chart *Wired* v24 no12 p86 D 2016

Airplanes—Equipment & supplies
HEAD-UP DISPLAY R. Mark color *Flying* v144 no4 p26 Ap 2017

Airplanes—Equipment & supplies—Evaluation
2016 HOLIDAY GIFTS color *Flying* v143 no12 p48 D 2016
TCAS II S. Pope color *Flying* v144 no2 p20 F 2017

Airplanes—Evaluation
BEST USED SIX SEATERS S. POPE chart color *Flying* v144 no6 p42 Je 2017
CIRRUS SR22 G6 S. POPE bw chart color *Flying* v144 no3 p52 Mr 2017
DIAMOND LAUNCHES A FAMILY OF DA50 MODELS color *Flying* v144 no6 p17 Je 2017
FIRST CLASS L. STRAUSS bw color *Vanity Fair* v58 no12 p84 D 2016
GIANTS OF THE SKY K. ATHERTON color *Popular Science* p54 Ja/F 2017
Trailer Queen A. Robinson color *Car & Driver* v62 no6 p102 D 2016

Airplanes—Exhibitions
SPORTING FUN color *Flying* v144 no4 p90 Ap 2017

Airplanes—Ferrying
FERRY FLIGHT L. Abend color *Flying* v143 no12 p74 D 2016
In Depth D. PIMENTEL color *Flying* v143 no12 p66 D 2016

Airplanes—Fuel
See also
    Jet planes—Fuel
DIGITAL FUEL SENDERS color *Flying* v144 no1 p13 Ja 2017

Airplanes—Landing gear
COMMUNICATION BREAKDOWN S. DUNN cartoon *Flying* v144 no3 p26 Mr 2017
DROP TEST P. Garrison color *Flying* v143 no12 p80 D 2016

Airplanes—Landing gear—Evaluation
TRAILING-LINK LANDING GEAR R. Mark color *Flying* v144 no3 p20 Mr 2017

Airplanes—Maintenance & repair
DAMAGE HISTORY L. Abend color *Flying* v144 no4 p82 Ap 2017
THE END OF A LOVE AFFAIR D. Karl color *Flying* v143 no12 p70 D 2016

Airplanes—Painting
IMMACULATE PROTECTION P. BERGQVIST color *Flying* v144 no4 p60 Ap 2017

Airplanes—Piloting
See also
    Landing of airplanes
FERRY FLIGHT L. Abend color *Flying* v143 no12 p74 D 2016
MY LONGEST TRIP TO VEGAS P. TEIRSTEIN color *Flying* v143 no12 p20 D 2016
UNDER THE HOOD S. Weigel bw *Flying* v144 no3 p46 Mr 2017
WHY LEFT? P. Garrison color *Flying* v144 no4 p88 Ap 2017

Airplanes—Piloting—Research
WASN'T THAT A TIME M. Lunken color *Flying* v144 no3 p76 Mr 2017

Airplanes—Purchasing
THERE, I SAID IT D. Karl bw color *Flying* v144 no3 p78 Mr 2017

Airplanes—Sales & prices
SHE'S GONE: A 17-YEAR LOVE AFFAIR COMES TO AN ABRUPT END D. Karl color *Flying* v144 no10 p70 O 2017

Airplanes—Tail surfaces
WE'D JUST LIKE TO ASK YOU A FEW QUESTIONS P. Garrison color *Flying* v144 no3 p88 Mr 2017

Airplanes—Weight
WEIGHT & BALANCE R. Lengel diag *Flying* v144 no3 p30 Mr 2017

Air pollution—United States—Charts, diagrams, etc.
Top Air Polluters M. Fischetti map *Scientific American* v316 no1 p72 Ja 2017

Airport associations
Airport Passenger Fees *Congressional Digest* v96 no5 p31 My 2017

Airport communication systems
STANDARD CLASS B AIRPORT R. Lengel color *Flying* v144 no7 p30 Jl 2017

Airport fees—Law & legislation
Airport Passenger Fees *Congressional Digest* v96 no5 p31 My 2017

Airport remodeling
I LOVE LAGUARDIA C. Suddath color *Bloomberg Businessweek* no4514 p72 Mr 13 2017

Airport runway accidents
A COMPLICATED SIMPLE REQUEST L. Abend *Flying* v144 no7 p72 Jl 2017

Airport specifications
STANDARD CLASS B AIRPORT R. Lengel color *Flying* v144 no7 p30 Jl 2017

Airports
See also
    Runways (Aeronautics)
AIRLINES AND PORTS color *Conde Nast Traveler* v52 no10 p98 N 2017
Brave Hearts T. BROOKS, D. LANGFORD et al color *O, The Oprah Magazine* p14 Mr 2017
CLASS D AIRSPACE R. Lengel map *Flying* v144 no11 p30 N 2017
EARLY BIRD BEATS THE CROWD: Providing the best service possible *Iceland Review* v55 no4 p60 Jl/Ag 2017
VIRTUAL AIRPORTS OF MY DIGITAL DREAMS S. Weigel color *Flying* v144 no4 p44 Ap 2017

Airports Council International (Organization)
EUROPE'S BEST AIRPORT *Iceland Review* v54 no6 p62 N/D 2016

Airports—Access roads

THE ULTIMATE AIRPORT OF TOMORROW J. BIEN-KAHN cartoon *Wired* v24 no12 p88 D 2016

Airports—Awards

EUROPE'S BEST AIRPORT *Iceland Review* v55 no3 p56 My/Je 2017

Airports—China

Everything Is Fine at Cathay Pacific K. Park and D. Lyu cartoon graph *Bloomberg Businessweek* no4516 p17 Mr 27 2017

Airports—Design & construction

Achtung, Berlin: Your Flight Is Five Years Late S. Nicola, R. Weiss et al color *Bloomberg Businessweek* no4517 p18 Ap 3 2017

Airports—History

BELOW AND ABOVE G. Westrup and R. Wright bw *MHQ: Quarterly Journal of Military History* v29 no4 p10 Summ 2017

Airports—Lighting

RUNWAY STATUS LIGHTS R. Lengel color *Flying* v144 no4 p34 Ap 2017

Airports—Maintenance & repair

Project Runway D. C. Vock *Governing* v30 no3 p48 D 2016

The Universally Acknowledged Dump That Is La Guardia Airport Is Finally Getting an Upgrade C. BONANOS img *New York* v49 no25 p72 D 12 2016

Airports—Repair & reconstruction

Makeover in Queens *Governing* v30 no3 p53 D 2016

Airports—United States

THE GREATEST AIRPORT PARTY EVER M. King color *Flying* v144 no11 p32 N 2017

Airports—Washington (D.C.)

Destination: The Airports C. Cunningham, M. J. Gaynor et al *Washingtonian Magazine* v52 no2 p80 N 2016

Airship design & construction

Google's Other Founder Wants to Fly, Too A. Vance color *Bloomberg Businessweek* no4521 p32 My 8 2017

Airships

ANTI-ZEPPELIN DART C. McNab color *MHQ: Quarterly Journal of Military History* v29 no4 p27 Summ 2017

AirSoft Inc.

Earplugs R. Berendsohn color *Popular Mechanics* v193 no7 p35 S 2016

Airspace (International law)

What's Wrong with the FAA's New Drone Rules L. Downes *Harvard Business Review Digital Articles* p2 Mr 2 2015

Airspace Systems Inc.

Innovation O. Kharif bw color *Bloomberg Businessweek* no4506 p28 Ja 9 2017

Air That I Breathe, The (Music)

Taylor Hawkins color *Rolling Stone* no1283 p8 Mr 23 2017

Airturn (Company)

GEAR BOX color *Downbeat* v84 no8 p92 Ag 2017

Airwair International Ltd.

"We don't like to talk about our values": How Dr Martens kick-started a new phase of global growth with 'rebellious self-expression' at its heart *People Management* p18 Ag 2017

Airways (Aeronautics)

A NEW GPS PROCEDURE DEMANDS SOME STUDY R. MARK and J. BLAIR map *Flying* v144 no9 p23 S 2017

Aisenbrey, Jessica

What Health Care Leaders Need to Do to Improve Value for Patients *Harvard Business Review Digital Articles* p2 D 3 2015

Aistleitner, Karin

In situ architecture, function, and evolution of a contractile injection system color diag *Science* v357 no6352 p713 Ag 18 2017

Ait Blal, Hammou

A subcellular map of the human proteome color *Science* v356 no6340 p820 My 26 2017

Aite Group LLC

Collaboration Can Help Merchants and Issuers *USA Today Magazine* v145 no2859 p8 D 2016

Aitken, Doug, 1968——Exhibitions

The Multimedia Artwork of Doug Aitken D. AITKEN bw color *Issues in Science & Technology* v33 no2 p73 Wint 2017

Ai Weiwei, 1957-

Ai Weiwei B. Luscombe color *Time* v190 no16/17 p112 O 23 2017

THE LENS OF A DISSIDENT J. FOUMBERG bw *Chicago* v66 no4 p37 Ap 2017

Roots and Branches color *Art in America* v104 no10 p9 N 2016

What It Means to be Modern C. McGuigan *Architectural Record* v205 no7 p24 Jl 2017

Ai Weiwei, 1957——Exhibitions

All Seeing, If Not All Knowing P. PLAGENS *Architectural Record* v205 no7 p51 Jl 2017

Left Behind J. SALTZ img *New York* v49 no23 p76 N 14 2016

Aizenberg, Joanna

Controlled growth and form of precipitating microsculptures bw color diag graph *Science* v355 no6332 p1395 Mr 31 2017

Preventing mussel adhesion using lubricant-infused materials color diag graph *Science* v357 no6352 p668 Ag 18 2017

Aizpurua, Javier

Single-molecule optomechanics in "picocavities" bibl graph *Science* v354 no6313 p726 N 11 2016

Ajanta Caves (India)

Amanda Giacomini W. J. Biddlecombe color *Tricycle: The Buddhist Review* v27 no1 p26 Fall 2017

Ajayan, P. M.

Extremely efficient internal exciton dissociation through edge states in layered 2D perovskites bibl graph *Science* v355 no6331 p1288 Mr 24 2017

Ajkun Ballet Theatre (Performer)

DANCE SPIRIT Auditions Guide 2017 C. Dutton and J. Roit *Dance Spirit* v21 no2 p60 F 2017

AJUDUA, CHRISTINE

All Roads Lead to Dubai color *Conde Nast Traveler* v51 no10 p52 N 2016

Ajunwa, Ifeoma

Workplace Wellness Programs Could Be Putting Your Health Data at Risk color *Harvard Business Review Digital Articles* p2 Ja 19 2017

AJW Surfboards (Company)

2017 SURFBOARD GUIDE bw cartoon color *Surfing Magazine* v53 no3 p85 Mr 2017

Ak Parti (Political party : Turkey)

An Islamist Power Grab Derails Democracy in Turkey K. ÖKTEM *Current History* v115 no785 p331 D 2016

Turkey's president builds an Islamic nationalism while amassing power S. Peterson *Christian Century* v134 no8 p1 Ap 12 2017

AKAM, SIMON

'For £750,000 Per Dear, I'll Call Anyone Sir' color *Bloomberg Businessweek* no4524 p48 My 29 2017

Rat On Me, Father *New York Times Book Review* p11 Je 25 2017

Akashi, Satoko

Crystal structure of the overlapping dinucleosome composed of hexasome and octasome graph *Science* v356 no6334 p205 Ap 14 2017

Akatsuki (Space probe)

Akatsuki Spies Massive Wave on Venus D. DICKINSON *Sky & Telescope* v133 no5 p8 My 2017

Akbalik, Güney

Activity-dependent spatially localized miRNA maturation in neuronal dendrites bibl graph *Science* v355 no6325 p634 F 10 2017

AKBAR, KAVEH

Pilgrim Bell *Nation* v305 no8 p30 O 9 2017

Akbari, Anna

Startup Your Life: Hustle and Hack Your Way to Happiness *Publishers Weekly* v263 no42 p61 O 17 2016

Akbarian, Schahram

Intersection of diverse neuronal genomes and neuropsychiatric disease: The Brain Somatic Mosaicism Network color *Science* v356 no6336 p395 Ap 28 2017

Akbulatov, Sergey

Experimentally realized mechanochemistry distinct from force-accelerated scission of loaded bonds diag graph *Science* v357 no6348 p299 Jl 21 2017

Akcigit, Ufuk

When America Was Most Innovative, and Why bw graph *Harvard Business Review Digital Articles* p2 Mr 6 2017

AKENSON, HOLLY

Building a Hay Barn: The Old Way in New Idaho *Idaho Magazine* v16 no9 p24 Je 2017

AKENSON, JIM

Building a Hay Barn: The Old Way in New Idaho *Idaho Magazine* v16 no9 p24 Je 2017

Akerlof, George A., 1940-
SOMETHING SMELLS PHISHY G. L. Priest *Claremont Review of Books* v16 no4 p57 Fall 2016

Akerman, Christina
Better Value in Health Care Requires Focusing on Outcomes *Harvard Business Review Digital Articles* p2 S 17 2015

Akerman, Malin
MALIN AKERMAN FIGHTS GLOBAL POVERTY R. Kinane color *Entertainment Weekly* no1465 p16 My 12 2017

Akers, Beth
Beth Akers and Matthew M. Chingos, Game of Loans: The Rhetoric and Reality of Student Debt J. Best and E. Best *Society* v54 no4 p372 Ag 2017

Akesson, Lovisa
A subcellular map of the human proteome color *Science* v356 no6340 p820 My 26 2017

Akhavan, Payam, 1965-
THE INTERVIEW B. BETHUNE color *Maclean's* v130 no9 p22 O 2017

Akhenaton, King of Egypt, d. 1336 B.C.
Akhenaten: EGYPT'S FIRST REVOLUTIONARY P. Hessler bw color diag map *National Geographic* v231 no5 p120 My 2017
Akhenaten P. Hessler bw color diag map *National Geographic* v231 no5 p120 My 2017

Akhmerov, A. R.
Demonstration of an ac Josephson junction laser bibl diag *Science* v355 no6328 p939 Mr 3 2017

Akhnaten (Theatrical production)
PYRAMIDS AND WIKILEAKS A. ROSS cartoon *New Yorker* v92 no41 p86 D 12 2016

Akhtar, Rabia
Managing nuclear risk in South Asia bibl *Bulletin of the Atomic Scientists* v73 no1 p62 Ja 2017

Akhunov, Eduard D.
Wild emmer genome architecture and diversity elucidate wheat evolution and domestication color *Science* v357 no6346 p93 Jl 7 2017

Akihiro Fujimoto
Mutational signatures associated with tobacco smoking in human cancer bibl graph *Science* v354 no6312 p618 N 4 2016

Akihito, Emperor of Japan, 1933-
A changing of the guard P. TREBLE color *Maclean's* v129 no48/49 p62 D 5 2016

Akimov, D.
Observation of coherent elastic neutrino-nucleus scattering diag *Science* v357 no6356 p1123 S 15 2017

Akin, Bradley
Examining price transmission across labor compensation costs, consumer prices, and finished-goods prices bibl *Monthly Labor Review* p1 Ap 2017

AKIN, HEATHER
Mapping the Landscape of Public Attitudes on Synthetic Biology *BioScience* v67 no3 p290 Mr 2017

Akin, Jeremiah
MOSCOW, IDAHO color *Runner's World* v52 no1 p10 Ja/F 2017

Akin, Wendy
DAILY BREADS *Mother Earth News* no279 p30 D/Ja 2017

Akinmusire, Ambrose—Interviews
AMBROSE AKINMUSIRE: THE THINKER [Cover story] Y. Kato color *Downbeat* v84 no9 p28 S 2017

Akinobu Suzuki
Overlapping memory trace indispensable for linking, but not recalling, individual memories bibl graph *Science* v355 no6323 p398 Ja 27 2017

Akinola, Modupe
To Be More Creative, Schedule Your Breaks *Harvard Business Review Digital Articles* p2 My 10 2017

AKINTOYE, DOTUN
One Day It Shall Please Us to REMEMBER THIS color *O, The Oprah Magazine* p69 Ja 2017
OUR TOWN cartoon color *O, The Oprah Magazine* p109 My 2017
Story HOUR color *O, The Oprah Magazine* p103 F 2017

Akiyama, Benjamin M.
Zika virus produces noncoding RNAs using a multi-pseudoknot structure that confounds a cellular exonuclease bibl color graph *Science* v354 no6316 p1148 D 2 2016

Akkadian cuneiform inscriptions
Bangs and Whimpers *Lapham's Quarterly* v10 no3 p194 Summ 2017

Akkaynak, Derya
Avian egg shape: Form, function, and evolution color diag *Science* v356 no6344 p1249 Je 23 2017
Epiphany Among the Manta Rays color *Oceanus* v51 no2 p98 Wint 2016

Akkerhuis, Bart
Studio Akkerhuis J. Krichels bw color *Architectural Record* v204 no12 p42 D 2016

Akkuratova, Natalia
Multipotent peripheral glial cells generate neuroendocrine cells of the adrenal medulla color *Science* v357 no6346 p46 Jl 7 2017

AKLER, HOWARD
AM I ALONE HERE? color *Maclean's* v129 no47 p61 N 28 2016
TRANSIT color *Maclean's* no1 p61 F 17 2017

Akron Brass Co.
IDEA OF THE MONTH P. Barbour *Successful Farming* v115 no5 p76 Mid-Mr 2017

AKSYONOV, YURI
THE WORLD'S BILLIONAIRES bw color diag graph map *Forbes* v199 no3 p84 Mr 28 2017

Akufo-Addo, Nana Addo Dankwa
The Commencement of the Free Senior High School Policy *Vital Speeches of the Day* v83 no10 p283 O 2017

Akunin, Boris, 1956-
FROM RUSSIA WITH LOVE? E. NORTON color *Publishers Weekly* v264 no13 p25 Mr 27 2017
The State Counsellor: A Fandorin Mystery *Publishers Weekly* v264 no15 p51 Ap 10 2017

Akuno, Kali
Don't Just Fight, Build! color *Progressive* v81 no4 p30 Ap/My 2017

Akyol, Mustafa
A Muslim journalist sets out to investigate Jesus Christ T. P. Rausch color *America* v216 no6 p42 Mr 20 2017

Al-Aqsa Mosque (Jerusalem)
Lightbox color *Time* v190 no6 p18 Ag 7 2017
No hate, no fear W. Massey color *U.S. Catholic* v82 no4 p12 Ap 2017

Alabama. Supreme Court
NO MOORE: ALABAMA IS FINALLY RID OF THE WORST JUDGE IN AMERICA R. BOSTON *Humanist* v76 no6 p38 N/D 2016

Alabama—Description & travel
ALABAMA COASTING C. Coen color *Louisiana Life* v37 no6 p48 Jl/Ag 2017
ETC M. Cameran color *New Orleans Magazine* v51 no10 p215 Ag 2017
TRAVEL DESTINATIONS color *New Orleans Magazine* v51 no5 p108 Mr 2017

Aladdin (Film)
Disney's Renaissance Revival E. Berman color *Time* v189 no11 p58 Mr 27 2017

Aladdin (Theatrical production)
MUSICAL MAESTRO M. Lassell *Cincinnati Magazine* v50 no8 p20 My 2017

Alaedini, Armin
THE TOOLS THEY USE color *Popular Mechanics* p104 My 2017

Alagem, Amanda
IN THE PINK color *Harper's Bazaar* no3654 p78 Je/Jl 2017
RED-HOT color *Harper's Bazaar* no3654 p126 Je/Jl 2017
TIMELESS TAN color *Harper's Bazaar* no3654 p80 Je/Jl 2017

Alaïa, Azzedine
ALAÏA'S RETURN color *Harper's Bazaar* no3656 p319 S 2017

Alain Saint-Joanis (Company)
for 2018 [Cover story] C. SWANSON and K. RENDA color *House Beautiful* v159 no9 p29 N 2017

Alam, Iftekhar
Emission of volatile organic compounds from petunia flowers is facilitated by an ABC transporter diag *Science* v356 no6345 p1386 Je 30 2017

ALAM, RUMAAN

Blackish color *O, The Oprah Magazine* p91 S 2017

The Pages' Turn *New York Times Book Review* p30 N 13 2016

Alameda (Calif.)

THE NEXT GREAT PLACE I. Edwards color *Sunset* v238 no2 p4 F 2017

Alameda Shade Shop (Company)

FROM REAL TO FAUX bw color *Old House Journal* v45 no2 p88 Ap 2017

Alamo (San Antonio, Tex.)—History

KEYS TO THE ALAMO B. SHACKELFORD *Texas Monthly* v44 no11 p98 N 2016

Alamo (San Antonio, Tex.)—Siege, 1836

The Alamo Remembered G. R. Schiavino bw *American Cowboy* p38 LEGENDS OF TEXAS Special Issue 2017

Alamrani, Danielle

A Muslim police officer sues the NYPD, citing religious harassment G. Kauffman *Christian Century* v134 no6 p15 Mr 15 2017

Alamwar Textiles (Company)

Summer Covers color *House Beautiful* v159 no5 p46 Je 2017

ALAN, DAVID

COCK TAIL OF THE MONTH *Texas Monthly* v45 no1 p36 Ja 2017

COOKTAIL OF THE MONTH *Texas Monthly* v44 no11 p48 N 2016

THE TIPSY TEXAN'S COCKTAIL OF THE MONTH *Texas Monthly* v45 no3 p48 Mr 2017

THE TIPSY TEXAN'S COOK TAIL OF THE MONTH *Texas Monthly* v45 no2 p40 F 2017

Alargan International Real Estate Co.

ALARGAN : Aim To Lead K. K. Al-Mashaan *Foreign Affairs* v95 no6 p120g N/D 2016

Alarm clocks—Evaluation

THE BEST BET img *New York* v50 no18 p55 S 4 2017

GIFT GUIDE 2016 S. Zlotnick, C. Cunningham et al *Washingtonian Magazine* v52 no3 p84 D 2016

Alarms

50 Everyday Mistakes And How to Fix Them [Cover story] B. SPECKTOR color *Reader's Digest* v189 no1129 p62 Ap 2017

Alaska

ALASKA CROSSING M. HAGE color *Canoe & Kayak Magazine* v45 no1 p56 Wint 2017

save on bucket-list trips K. CICERO *Parents* v91 no9 p64 S 2016

Alaska Peninsula (Alaska)—History

Months Past MARCH *History Today* v67 no3 p8 Mr 2017

Alaska—Description & travel

ADVENTURES IN ALASKA R. ROBERTS *Sea Magazine* v109 no2 p18 F 2017

The Big Wild color map *Backpacker* p52 Je 2017

PHOTOGRAPHS OF ALASKA K. LAWRENCE *Prologue* v49 no2 p28 Summ 2017

SIERRA CLUB OUTINGS *Sierra* v101 no6 p52 N/D 2016

Wild Alaska S. Slon and L. Grier *Saturday Evening Post* v289 no2 p54 Mr/Ap 2017

Alaska—Discovery & exploration

The Great White Hope B. Braverman *Smithsonian* v47 no10 p11 Mr 2017

Alaska—Economic conditions—21st century

Biting the Hand That Feeds You C. HELMAN color map *Forbes* v198 no7 p48 N 29 2016

There's Oil Up There, But Is It Worth Getting? A. Nussbaum color *Bloomberg Businessweek* no4515 p36 Mr 20 2017

Alaska—Environmental conditions

Alaska's Big Problem With Warmer Winters C. Flavelle color *Bloomberg Businessweek* no4514 p26 Mr 13 2017

Alaska's Close-Up N. KIRSCHNER *American Scholar* v86 no2 p16 Spr 2017

Celebrating America's "Great Land" [Cover story] M. Wexler color *National Wildlife (World Edition)* v55 no6 p22 O/N 2017

Hot Alaska: As the Climate Warms, Alaska Experiences Record High Temperatures R. Thoman and B. Brettschneider color graph map *Weatherwise* v69 no6 p12 N-D 2016

Alaska Purchase, 1867

Celebrating America's "Great Land" [Cover story] M. Wexler color *National Wildlife (World Edition)* v55 no6 p22 O/N 2017

DOCUMENTS ON Loan *Prologue* v48 no4 p48 Wint 2016

Making the Case for Conservation C. O'MARA color *National*

Wildlife (World Edition) v55 no6 p6 O/N 2017

Alassimone, Julien

Root diffusion barrier control by a vasculature-derived peptide binding to the SGN3 receptor color *Science* v355 no6322 p280 Ja 20 2017

Alava, Juan José

Pipelines imperil Canada's ecosystem *Science* v355 no6321 p140 Ja 13 2017

Al-Ayat, Rokaya

Laboratory Investments Drive Computational Advances *Science & Technology Review* p3 S 2016

ALBA, DAVEY

NEXT LIST 2017 bw graph *Wired* v25 no5 p63 My 2017

Alba, Jessica

Why I Love MY DAUGHTERS' ARTWORK color *InStyle* v24 no8 p176 Ag 2017

Albacore

FALSE TRUTHS S. SAUTNER color *Outdoor Life* v224 no7 p60 S 2017

Albadawi, Abeer

Children of No Nation [Cover story] color map *Time* v188 no27-28 p38 D 26 2016

Promised Land color *Time* v190 no14 p40 O 9 2017

Al-Baghdadi, Abu Bakr, 1971-

Greetings from ISIS M. D. Silber *Commentary* v140 no2 p33 S 2015

Al-Bakr, Jaber

Bad Syrian, Good Syrians *Weekly Standard* v22 no7 p2 O 24 2016

Albanese, Andrew

The Big Deal at the Frankfurt Book Fair: Free Speech color *Publishers Weekly* v263 no43 p4 O 24 2016

Carla Hayden: U.S. Librarian of Congress *Publishers Weekly* v263 no52 p27 D 19 2016

Changes Coming To the Copyright Office? color *Publishers Weekly* v263 no44 p6 O 31 2016

For Librarians, 2017 Is Off To a Rough Start color *Publishers Weekly* v264 no5 p2 Ja 30 2017

The Pallante Era Begins at AAP color *Publishers Weekly* v264 no3 p5 Ja 16 2017

Publishers Keep Calm And Carry On color *Publishers Weekly* v264 no12 p5 Mr 20 2017

PW Talks with Thomas L. Friedman color *Publishers Weekly* v263 no45 p12 N 7 2016

See You in London *Publishers Weekly* v264 no9 p20 F 27 2017

Albanese, Andrew Richard

The Carnegie Medals Turn Six color *Publishers Weekly* v264 no25 p38 Je 19 2017

Copyright Reform Is Never Happening *Publishers Weekly* v264 no16 p21 Ap 17 2017

Discovery Happens Here color *Publishers Weekly* v264 no38 p40 S 18 2017

Four Questions with Skip Prichard color *Publishers Weekly* v264 no25 p58 Je 19 2017

THE FRANKFURT BOOK FAIR IS TRENDING UP color *Publishers Weekly* v264 no39 p32 S 25 2017

Hope and Change color *Publishers Weekly* v264 no25 p47 Je 19 2017

In Chicago, Librarians Get Their Mojo Back color *Publishers Weekly* v264 no27 p4 Jl 3 2017

Librarians, Check This Out color *Publishers Weekly* v264 no20 p(Sp)28 My 15 2017

Librarians Take Capitol Hill color *Publishers Weekly* v264 no19 p4 My 8 2017

Making ALA Great Again color *Publishers Weekly* v264 no8 p21 F 20 2017

The Next Chapter for Library E-books color *Publishers Weekly* v264 no25 p54 Je 19 2017

Politics & Current Events bw color *Publishers Weekly* v263 no51 p94 D 12 2016

Politics & Current Events color *Publishers Weekly* v264 no26 p103 Je 26 2017

Small Stories, Big Picture color *Publishers Weekly* v263 no47 p19 N 21 2016

"The Challenge of a Lifetime" color *Publishers Weekly* v264 no25 p29 Je 19 2017

"THE POLITICAL EQUIVALENT OF ENRICHED URANI-

UM" color *Publishers Weekly* v263 no52 p50 D 19 2016

TIME TO BE A TEXAN *Publishers Weekly* v264 no14 p22 Ap 3 2017

THE TOP 10 LIBRARY STORIES OF 2016 color *Publishers Weekly* v263 no52 p34 D 19 2016

TRANSITION color *Publishers Weekly* v263 no52 p31 D 19 2016

Trump Budget Renews Call to Eliminate Arts, Library Funding *Publishers Weekly* v264 no22 p14 My 29 2017

WORLDVIEWS *Publishers Weekly* v263 no39 p32 S 26 2016

Albanese, Chiara

A Sun-Dappled Tuscan Banking Mess color *Bloomberg Businessweek* no4511 p36 F 13 2017

An Uber-Tinder Mashup Hits the Spanish Steps color *Bloomberg Businessweek* no4502 p42 D 5 2016

When Coders Become Stickup Artists color *Bloomberg Businessweek* no4517 p35 Ap 3 2017

ALBANESE, LOUISA

Get the Shot color *Backpacker* p61 Je 2017

Leaf Swirls color *Backpacker* p35 O 2017

Albarn, Damon, 1968—Interviews

Gorillaz in Our Midst L. Greenblatt color *Entertainment Weekly* no1463/1464 p107 Ap/My 2017

Albarq, Dawood

Harvesting electrical energy from carbon nanotube yarn twist diag graph *Science* v357 no6353 p773 Ag 25 2017

Albarracin-Caballero, Jonatan D.

Dynamic multinuclear sites formed by mobilized copper ions in NOx selective catalytic reduction bw color diag graph *Science* v357 no6354 p898 S 1 2017

Albatrosses

ENGINEERING A BETTER MOUSETRAP B. BOREL *Audubon* v119 no2 p48 Summ 2017

Albedo

Next L. KRATOCHWILL color *Popular Science* v288 no6 p24 N/D 2016

Albee, Edward, 1928-2016

EDWARD ALBEE M. Ruehl and C. Nashawaty color *Entertainment Weekly* no1446/1447 p96 D 2016/Ja 2017

Alberdi, M. T.

Decoupled ecomorphological evolution and diversification in Neogene-Quaternary horses bibl graph *Science* v355 no6325 p627 F 10 2017

Albers, Anni

When the Bauhaus came to Monte Albán J. Reynolds-Kaye cartoon *Magazine Antiques* v184 no1 p166 Ja/F 2017

Albers, Josef, 1888-1976

When the Bauhaus came to Monte Albán J. Reynolds-Kaye cartoon *Magazine Antiques* v184 no1 p166 Ja/F 2017

Albers, Sarah

i did it! K. SELZER color *Better Homes & Gardens* v95 no9 p64 S 2017

Albers, Susan

MEDITATE ON THE MANDARIN color *Prevention* v68 no12 p8 D 2016

ALBERT, CHRISTIAN

National Ecosystem Assessments in Europe: A Review chart *BioScience* v66 no10 p813 O 1 2016

Albert, Gary

Of troughs and trophies color *Magazine Antiques* v184 no3 p110 My/Je 2017

Albert, J. B.

Observation of coherent elastic neutrino-nucleus scattering diag *Science* v357 no6356 p1123 S 15 2017

Albert, Julie

FEAST WITH BENEFITS [Cover story] color *O, The Oprah Magazine* p128 N 2017

Albert, Stacy Durr

In a League of Its Own color map *Timber Home Living* v27 no3 p42 Je 2017

Making History color diag *Log Home Living* v34 no2 p58 Mr 2017

Perfect Harmony cartoon color *Log Home Living* v33 no9 p64 D 2016

What Lies Beneath [Cover story] color *Log Home Living* v33 no7 p56 S 2016

Albert-László Barabási

Quantifying the evolution of individual scientific impact graph

Science v354 no6312 p596 N 4 2016

Albert Schweitzer Organ (Music)

ALBERT SCHWEITZER ORGAN VS. THE MIGHTY MO T. REHAGEN *Atlanta* v57 no1 p30 My 2017

ALBERTA, TIM

The Blue Wave color *National Review* v68 no20 p26 N 7 2016

The Education Gap color *National Review* v68 no19 p14 O 24 2016

Alberta—Description & travel

Alberta's Hidden Gem color *Horse & Rider* v56 no8 p28 Ag 2017

Moraine Lake, Banff National Park, Alberta diag *Backpacker* p96 Je 2017

Alberta—Politics & government—1971-

The right path J. MARKUSOFF color *Maclean's* v129 no48/49 p23 D 5 2016

ALBERT-DEITCH, CAMERON

COMMON GROUND *Atlanta* v56 no11 p96 Mr 2017

Alberti, Giorgio

Positive biodiversity-productivity relationship predominant in global forests bibl chart graph map *Science* v354 no6309 paaf8957-1 O 14 2016

Alberti, Leon Battista, 1404-1472

1435: Florence *Lapham's Quarterly* v10 no2 p149 Spr 2017

Albert I, Prince of Monaco, 1848-1922

Prince Albert II J. GEIGER color *Canadian Geographic* v137 no5 p17 S/O 2017

Alberti, Simon

ATP as a biological hydrotrope color graph *Science* v356 no6339 p753 My 19 2017

Albert II, Prince of Monaco, 1958-

Prince Albert II J. GEIGER color *Canadian Geographic* v137 no5 p17 S/O 2017

Alberts, Bruce

Science for life color *Science* v355 no6332 p1353 Mr 31 2017

Alberts, Elizabeth Claire

bush beat color *Earth Island Journal* v32 no4 p36 Wint 2017

Wolves, Lies & Logging color *Alternatives Journal (AJ) - Canada's Environmental Voice* v42 no2 p66 2016

Albinos & albinism

The Perils of Pale S. Ager bw color diag *National Geographic* v231 no6 p70 Je 2017

Al-Biruni, ca. 973-1048

THE INVENTION OF WORLD HISTORY S. F. Starr *History Today* v67 no7 p36 Jl 2017

Albom, Mitch, 1958—Interviews

Mitch Albom *New York Times Book Review* p8 Ap 9 2017

Albrecht, Cheryl

SILVERTON, COLORADO color *Runner's World* v51 no11 p14 D 2016

Albrecht, Fredrick C.

IN MEMORIAM *Phi Kappa Phi Forum* v96 no4 p33 Wint 2016

ALBRECHT, LAURA

Your True Stories IN 100 WORDS color *Reader's Digest* v189 no1129 p25 Ap 2017

Albrechtsen, Anders

Ancient genomic changes associated with domestication of the horse color diag *Science* v356 no6336 p442 Ap 28 2017

Albright, Amanda

Another Way to Tap the 1 Percent color *Bloomberg Businessweek* no4493 p39 O 3 2016

Raising Private Money For Public Projects *Bloomberg Businessweek* no4513 p46 Mr 6 2017

Albright, Madeleine Korbel, 1937-

Happy Birthday, Marie Jana Korbelova E. TAMKIN *Foreign Policy* no225 p25 Jl/Ag 2017

Albumins

GLOSSARY *Equus* no478 p79 Jl 2017

Albuquerque (N.M.)—Description & travel

THE WELLTHIEST CITIES IN AMERICA K. DOLD and J. MOYE bw color *Women's Health* v14 no6 p120 Jl 2017

Albuquerque, I. F. M.

Observation of a large-scale anisotropy in the arrival directions of cosmic rays above 8×10^{18} eV *Science* v357 no6357 p1266 S 22 2017

Alburt, Lev, 1945-

Game of Kings J. Tarmy color *Bloomberg Businessweek* no4539

p67 S 25 2017

ALCALA, NATALIE

Maternity Clothes *Los Angeles Magazine* p38 Ap 2017

Alcaly, Roger

The Man Who Knew Better bw cartoon *New York Review of Books* v64 no3 p24 F 23 2017

Alcazar, Noelia

Tissue damage and senescence provide critical signals for cellular reprogramming in vivo bibl chart graph *Science* v354 no6315 paaf4445-1 N 25 2016

Alchemist, The (Poem)

1908: Paris R. M. Rilke *Lapham's Quarterly* v10 no2 p148 Spr 2017

Alchemist, The (Theatrical production)

BUBBLING UNDER D. STEWART color *America* v215 no15 p30 N 14 2016

Alchemy Supply Co.

Broad Ripple Avenue A. LYNCH *Indianapolis Monthly* p32 My 2017

Alcindor, Yamiche

YAMICHE ALCINDOR L. N. Williams color map *Essence* v47 no11 p70 Mr 2017

Alcock, George

The Bright One That Got Away: Fifty years ago this month, the author, then 16, came a hair's breadth from making a huge discovery S. P. Cook *Sky & Telescope* v134 no1 p84 Jl 2017

ALCOCK, JAMES E.

The Scientist and the Philosopher *Skeptical Inquirer* v41 no2 p58 Mr/Ap 2017

Alcohol

ARDENT SPRITS M. W. Spencer color *Louisiana Life* v37 no6 p8 Jl/Ag 2017

The Drinking Game, Ladies Who Lunch, Mother's Day L. KOGAN color *O, The Oprah Magazine* p35 Jl 2017

Alcohol industry—Government policy

GOVERNMENT ALMOST KILLED THE COCKTAIL P. Suderman color *Reason* v49 no5 p54 O 2017

Alcoholic beverage industry

GOING GREEN (AND YELLOW) A. Spiegel *Washingtonian Magazine* v52 no6 p151 Mr 2017

Alcoholic beverages

See also

    Beer

    Cocktails

    Drinking of alcoholic beverages

    Liquors

    Wine & wine making

American Wine? Whine Not! J. STEIN *Los Angeles Magazine* p44 F 2017

Day-Drinking Essentials color *Glamour* v115 no5 p24 My 2017

Fancy Cocktails? A Breeze! K. O'Shea-Evans and C. SWANSON color *House Beautiful* v159 no4 p65 My 2017

Good Blood R. Schaap *New York Times Magazine* p32 O 30 2016

HIT ME WITH YOUR BEST SHOTS M. Reyes color *Bloomberg Businessweek* no4506 p63 Ja 9 2017

Hold the Liquor R. Schaap *New York Times Magazine* p22 Ja 1 2017

How to Be a Holiday Boozetender R. McCAMMON color *GQ: Gentlemen's Quarterly* v97 no11 p50 N 2017

ICED E. Laborde *New Orleans Magazine* v51 no3 p12 Ja 2017

Is It Cocktailing Season Yet? color *Glamour* v115 no5 p23 My 2017

IT'S COME TO THIS *Parents* v91 no11 p15 N 2016

Martini, Please, No BS J. GORDINIER color *Esquire* v166 no5 p46 D 2016/Ja 2017

Not-So-Sweet Heart J. MIGALA cartoon color *AARP: The Magazine* v60 no2A p23 F/Mr 2017

PRAISE (JUST) JACK—WILL & GRACE IS BACK! R. Kinane color *Entertainment Weekly* no1484 p50 S 29 2017

Props Still Has a Drinking Problem J. Duckworth *Stage Directions* v30 no5 p28 My 2017

SHOT IN A BEER T. Willey color *Bon Appetit* v62 no6 p86 Je 2017

The wise woman's guide to booze D. VILIBERT color *Redbook* p89 D 2016

Alcoholic beverages—Evaluation

BEYOND BASIC BREWS S. MEINBERG *Cincinnati Magazine* v50 no6 p143 Mr 2017

A Cooler Wine Cooler A. Erace color *Bloomberg Businessweek* no4515 p62 Mr 20 2017

Drink map *Rodale's Organic Life* v2 no7 p42 D 2016/Ja 2017

The MH Low-Calorie Beer Awards color *Men's Health* v32 no5 p68 Je 2017

That's the Spirit L. J. Solmonson *Sierra* v102 no3 p8 My/Je 2017

Alcoholic beverages—Religious aspects

They Will Know We Are Christians by Our Drinks J. CASPER *Christianity Today* p20 Ap 2017

Alcoholic beverages—Sales & prices

See also

    Beer—Sales & prices

Milestones *Time* v189 no6 p13 F 20 2017

Alcoholic intoxication

One Deadly Night M. CROUCH *Scholastic Choices* v32 no7 p10 Ap 2017

Under the Influence T. John color *Time* v188 no16/17 p8 O 24 2016

Alcoholics

200,000 ALCOHOLICS CAN'T BE WRONG P. BAGGE cartoon *Reason* v48 no10 p32 Mr 2017

Alcoholics Anonymous

and the survey says *U.S. Catholic* v82 no11 p29 N 2017

YOU DON'T DO GOD ALONE B. McGARVEY bw *America* v215 no12 p32 O 24 2016

Alcoholism

"8 things I learned in my first year of being sober" K. Coulter *Glamour* v115 no1 p50 Ja 2017

ANXIETY, CALMED color *Health* v30 no9 p18 N 2016

College Students Experience High Rates of Alcohol Abuse, Mental Health issues D. Gilbert *Psychology Today* v50 no5 p25 S/O 2017

Sanity and Grace B. Hasselbring color *AARP: The Magazine* v59 no1A p54 D 2015/Ja 2016

Alcoholism—Religious aspects

A Curable Disease H. SIDDIQUI *Islamic Horizons* v46 no2 p58 Mr/Ap 2017

Alcohol—Physiological effect

See also

    Alcoholic intoxication

A Curable Disease H. SIDDIQUI *Islamic Horizons* v46 no2 p58 Mr/Ap 2017

Jogging the Brain G. Reynolds color *New York Times Magazine* p28 N 27 2016

Libation Situation K. Massicot color *New Orleans Magazine* v51 no4 p34 F 2017

One Deadly Night M. CROUCH *Scholastic Choices* v32 no7 p10 Ap 2017

Alcohols (Chemical class)

See also

    Glycols

Nice Cream St. Louis A. Burger color *Missouri Life* v44 no3 p16 My 2017

Alcohol—Taxation

Raise Alcohol Taxes, Reduce Violence K. Sobowale color *Scientific American* v317 no1 p10 Jl 2017

Alcorn, Brandon

Who's Benefiting from MOOCs, and Why *Harvard Business Review Digital Articles* p2 S 22 2015

Alda, Alan, 1936-

If I Understood You, Would I Have This Look on My Face? A. Marks color *Scientific American* v316 no6 p74 Je 2017

If I Understood You, Would I Have This Look on My Face? My Adventures in the Art and Science color *Publishers Weekly* v264 no31 p81 Jl 31 2017

Alda, Alan, 1936—Interviews

LIFE'S WORK: An Interview with ALAN ALDA ACTOR bw *Harvard Business Review* v95 no4 p152 Jl/Ag 2017

Al Dabbagh, May

Research: When Men Have Lower Status at Work, They're Less Likely to Negotiate *Harvard Business Review Digital Articles* p2 S 8 2017

Aldana, Gerardo

Early and Modern Views on Celestial Events *Physics Today* v70

no9 p61 S 2017

Aldebaran

Celestial Calendar *Sky & Telescope* v134 no3 p50 S 2017

Moon Again Occults Aldebaran *Sky & Telescope* v132 no6 p50 D 2016

Occultations of Aldebaran and Regulus chart color *Sky & Telescope* v134 no5 p51 N 2017

Aldehydes

A Surprising Danger in Your Wineglass color *Health* v31 no3 p13 Ap 2017

Alden, Christopher

SWeeNey ToDD R. Minetor *Stage Directions* v29 no11 p40 N 2016

Alden, Normandy

PICKLE RECIPES for the Picking: Ferment or quick-pickle your harvest with this assortment of ideas from Mother Earth News bloggers *Mother Earth News* no282 p56 Je/Jl 2017

Aldenderfer, M. S.

Permanent human occupation of the central Tibetan Plateau in the early Holocene bibl bw color diag *Science* v355 no6320 p1 Ja 6 2017

Alderman, Brandon

The Undepressing News About Depression C. Flora color *O, The Oprah Magazine* p80 Ap 2017

ALDERMAN, NATHAN

RAPIDWEAVER 7: GREAT NEW FEATURES BUT NE-GLECTS EXISTING GAPS color *Macworld - Digital Edition* v33 no11 p38 N 2016

TACOMA: THE MAKERS OF GONE HOME UNSPOOL A MESMERIZING SCIENCE FICTION STORY color *Macworld - Digital Edition* v34 no10 p31 O 2017

Aldersey-Williams, Hugh

Time and Tides *History Today* v67 no3 p37 Mr 2017

ALDO Group Inc.

The Accessories Face-Off color *Seventeen* v75 no11 p28 N 2016

GREAT BUYS UNDER $100: GRAPHIC CONTENT color *O, The Oprah Magazine* p48 Jl 2017

Aldous, Richard

THE POWER HISTORIAN D. MARCUS bw *Nation* v305 no11 p43 O 30 2017

The Two Winstons: A dual biography of two independent thinkers *New York Times Book Review* p9 Je 11 2017

The White House Mythmaker S. TANENHAUS color *Atlantic* v320 no4 p46 N 2017

Aldrich, Ian

A Gift for All *Yankee* p99 Mr 2017

Into the Woods: The Patten Lumbermen's Museum takes visitors into the rugged and essential lives of those who felled the trees that helped build a nation *Yankee* v81 no5 p80 S/O 2017

THE ISLAND DOCTOR bw color *Yankee* p98 My/Je 2017

LEAF PEQPLE: A WEEK ON A GUIDED FOLIAGE TOUR SHOWS OFF NOT ONLY NEW ENGLAND BUT A BIT OF HUMAN NATURE, TOO *Yankee* v81 no5 p110 S/O 2017

OUR 11TH ANNUAL APPRECIATION OF Angels AMONG US color *Yankee* v80 no6 p130 N/D 2016

The Picture-Perfect Stroll color *Yankee* p94 Mr 2017

Aldrich, Richard J., 1961-

Intelligence Matters A. Lycett *History Today* v67 no4 p64 Ap 2017

ALDRIDGE, JOHN

A Speck In the Sea bw color *Power & Motoryacht* v34 no7 p48 Jl 2017

Aldridge, Lily, 1985-

Lily Aldridge A. Syrett color *InStyle* v24 no3 p172 Mr 2017

Aldrin, Buzz, 1930-

Buzz Aldrin: What That Apollo 11 'UFO' Really Was, and Why He Punched That Moon-Landing Denier K. FRAZIER *Skeptical Inquirer* v41 no1 p5 Ja/F 2017

The Summer Job I'll Never Forget color *Time* v190 no2/3 p55 Jl 10-17 2017

Titans color *Time* v189 no16/17 p94 My 1-8 2017

Ale—Evaluation

Drink the Beer, Lose the Gut color *Men's Health* v31 no10 p70 D 2016

HOMEGROWN HOPS J. CARRUTHERS color *Chicago* v66 no8 p54 Ag 2017

ALEJANDRO, HANNAH

Not OK *Ms.* v26 no4 p38 Wint 2016

ALEKSANDER, IRINA

The Empire Knocks One Back cartoon color diag *GQ: Gentlemen's Quarterly* v97 no7 p40 Jl 2017

Aleksievich, Svetlana, 1948-

Anguished Echoes of Empire J. LUSTIG *Current History* v115 no783 p284 O 2016

Women on the Battlefield: Conversations with female combatants in Russia's war against Hitler R. REICH *New York Times Book Review* p11 Ag 20 2017

Alemany, Anna

Experimental measurement of binding energy, selectivity, and allostery using fluctuation theorems bibl graph *Science* v355 no6323 p412 Ja 27 2017

Alen Yachts (Company)

Alen 45 C. Sisson color *Power & Motoryacht* v34 no11 p78 N 2017

ALEN 55 D. Harding Jr. color *Power & Motoryacht* v33 no1 p46 Ja 2017

Aleppo (Syria)

Superheroes and the Sacking of Cities G. NORMAN color *Weekly Standard* v22 no17 p15 Ja 2 2017

Aleppo (Syria)—Military history—21st century

In Aleppo, finding God among the ruins J. Martin color *America* v216 no7 p15 Ap 3 2017

Aleppo (Syria)—Social conditions—21st century

In Aleppo, finding God among the ruins J. Martin color *America* v216 no7 p15 Ap 3 2017

People D. Martens and M. I. Pinsky color *Christian Century* v134 no3 p17 F 2017

Alerion Yachts (Company)

Alerion Sport 30 Z. Prochazka color *Sail* v48 no3 p26 Mr 2017

Alessi SpA

How to Really Do Cocktails at 35,000 Feet color *Conde Nast Traveler* v52 no4 p100 Ap 2017

ALESSIO, CAROLYN

A Missing Memorial bw color *America* v215 no19 p21 D 19 2016

Aleutian Islands (Alaska)

Northern Lights K. Laird color *Sail* v48 no1 p12 Ja 2017

Aleutian Islands (Alaska)—History

Unfinished Business R. Rowland *MHQ: Quarterly Journal of Military History* v30 no1 p12 Aut 2017

Alex & Ani Inc.

Alex and Ani E. Wilson color *InStyle* v23 no12 p102 N 2016

Bangle Billionaire [Cover story] C. O'CONNOR bw color *Forbes* v199 no6 p70 Je 13 2017

ALEX, BRIDGET

Ancient DNA color diag map *Discover* v38 no6 p52 Jl/Ag 2017

Birds Sleep During Flights, Too color *Discover* v38 no1 p49 Ja/F 2017

A BONE TO PICK ABOUT PHILISTINES color *Discover* v38 no1 p36 Ja/F 2017

Finding China's Great Flood color map *Discover* v38 no1 p31 Ja/F 2017

Flossing — What Is It Good For? bw color *Discover* v27 no10 p12 D 2016

Greenland Sharks Can Live 500 Years and Counting color *Discover* v38 no1 p79 Ja/F 2017

Meet the Denisovans color map *Discover* v27 no10 p64 D 2016

Oldest Human DNA Revises Our Family Tree color map *Discover* v38 no1 p14 Ja/F 2017

Our First Date Out of Africa? color *Discover* v38 no1 p70 Ja/F 2017

Skin-Deep Evolutionary Link color *Discover* v38 no1 p58 Ja/F 2017

Stone Cold Science bw color *Discover* v38 no9 p64 N 2017

UNRAVELING A SECRET bw color map *Discover* v38 no8 p40 O 2017

We Are All Africans color *Discover* v38 no1 p26 Ja/F 2017

Alex, Brittany

Q: If you had an extra hour in your day, what would you do with it? color *O, The Oprah Magazine* p18 O 2017

Alex, Ken

Merging paleobiology with conservation biology to guide the future of terrestrial ecosystems color *Science* v355 no6325 p594 F 10 2017

Alex Papachristidis Interiors (Company)
The New Traditionalists color *Architectural Digest* v74 no1 p128 Ja 2017

Alexander, Amy
Posthole color *Powder* v45 no4 p146 D 2016

Alexander, B. M.
How economics can shape precision medicines bibl color *Science* v355 no6330 p1131 Mr 17 2017

Alexander, Brian
Shattered Illusions in Lancaster, Ohio R. Conniff color *Progressive* v81 no5 p63 Je/Jl 2017

Alexander, Caroline
THE DREAD GORGON *Lapham's Quarterly* v10 no3 p186 Summ 2017
Russia's Deadly Mideast Game *Bloomberg Businessweek* no4505 p16 D 26 2016

Alexander, Charles Stuart
A Walrus Tribute G. Lazare and B. R. Bennett color *Walrus* v14 no2 p56 Mr 2017

Alexander, Chinae
BEING MY OWN CHEERLEADER color *Women's Health* v14 no9 p36 N 2017

Alexander, Chris—Interviews
THE INTERVIEW J. GEDDES color *Maclean's* v129 no43 p12 O 31 2016

ALEXANDER, DAN
"Everybody Gets Billed" [Cover story] color *Forbes* v199 no7 p104 Je 29 2017
Fake Trump Tower color map *Forbes* v200 no2 p94 S 5 2017
HOW MUCH IS PRESIDENT TRUMP WORTH NOW? color *Forbes* v199 no3 p82 Mr 28 2017
IN TRUMP THEY TRUST color map *Forbes* v199 no3 p42 Mr 28 2017
LESSONS AND IDEAS BY THE 100 GREATEST LIVING BUSINESS MINDS bw color *Forbes* v200 no3 p115 S 28 2017
LOCKED IN bw color *Forbes* v199 no3 p76 Mr 28 2017
POORER PRESIDENT color *Forbes* v200 no5 p62 N 14 2017
THE PRESIDENT'S GAMBLING BUDDY color *Forbes* v199 no3 p66 Mr 28 2017
SHELDON YELLEN'S BIG SECRET bw color map *Forbes* v199 no2 p80 F 28 2017
SOUTH OF THE WALL bw *Forbes* v199 no3 p74 Mr 28 2017
TRUMP: THE ART OF THE SPIEL bw color *Forbes* v200 no3 p98 S 28 2017
TRUMP: THE EARLY TWEETS (1982-2000) color *Forbes* v200 no3 p94 S 28 2017
WHAT'S ROSS WORTH? color *Forbes* v200 no5 p42 N 14 2017
THE WORLD'S BILLIONAIRES bw color diag graph map *Forbes* v199 no3 p84 Mr 28 2017

Alexander, Dave
Super Sonic C. MARTINS color *Los Angeles Magazine* v62 no10 p82 O 2017

Alexander, David L.
Patriotism in the pews color *U.S. Catholic* v82 no11 p5 N 2017

ALEXANDER, DON
LITTLE BEAN, FAIRLY BIG IMPACT color *Alternatives Journal (AJ) - Canada's Environmental Voice* v42 no2 p77 2016

Alexander, Ellie
Death on Tap *Publishers Weekly* v264 no32 p52 Ag 7 2017

ALEXANDER, GERARD
Apathy in the Executive color *Weekly Standard* v22 no14 p24 D 12 2016
Turning Pennsylvania color *Weekly Standard* v22 no13 p22 D 5 2016

Alexander, Jaimie
Blindspot N. Abrams, S. Highfill et al color *Entertainment Weekly* no1482/1483 p95 S 22 2017

Alexander, Jason, 1959-
Hit the Road N. Abrams, A. Bacle et al *Entertainment Weekly* no1482/1483 p60 S 22 2017
Serenity Now! M. Schulman color *New Yorker* v93 no33 p22 O 23 2017

Alexander, Julia
HACKER CRACK-UP color *Wired* v25 no6 p10 Je 2017

Alexander, Kirk
When Pizza Saved a Life B. SPECKTOR *Reader's Digest* v188

no1124 p12 O 2016

Alexander, Kwame, 1968-
Booked color *Publishers Weekly* v263 no49 p71 D 7 2016
Kwame Alexander J. Johnson color *Current Biography* v78 no1 p8 Ja 2017
Surf's Up *Publishers Weekly* v263 no49 p17 D 7 2016

Alexander, Kwame, 1968—Interviews
SCHOOL OF ROCK M. Mechanic color *Mother Jones* v42 no4 p58 Jl/Ag 2017

Alexander, Lamar, 1940—Interviews
Making the Grade? A. G. Kingo color *Working Mother* v40 no3 p44 Ag/S 2017

Alexander, Lexi
THE UNBREAKABLE LEXI ALEXANDER B. RAFTERY color *Wired* v25 no8 p80 Ag 2017

Alexander, Max
EXPLORE THE IMPACT that killed the dinosaurs color map *Astronomy* v44 no12 p26 D 2016

Alexander, Meena
Letter to My Son *America* v216 no3 p41 F 6 2017

Alexander, Thomas
Time & Again L. CUTRONE *New Orleans Homes & Lifestyles* v20 no1 p42 Wint 2016

Alexander, Thomas Theron
Finding Jesus in Japan J. R. Shelton color *Christianity Today* v60 no10 p79 D 2016

Alexander, Ty
Missing Mama S. HUBBARD and D. POINTDUJOUR color *Ebony* v72 no6 p65 Ap/My 2017

Alexander, William
Give Ghosts a Chance: Banishing the spirits of the dead has put a town on the path to destruction B. A. SÁENZ *New York Times Book Review* p17 O 8 2017

Alexander Gorlin Architects (Company)
Boston Road Supportive Housing A. Klimoski *Architectural Record* v205 no4 p193 Ap 2017

Alexander McQueen Trading Ltd.
Strip It Down M. MARDEN color *Esquire* v167 no1 p32 F 2017

Alexander String Quartet (Performer)
A Sense of the In-Between color *Idaho Magazine* v16 no1 p51 O 2016

Alexander Wang Inc.
Alexander Wang T. Patterson color *Bloomberg Businessweek* no4535 p72 Ag 28 2017
STYLE CRUSH Bella Heathcote S. Simon color *InStyle* v24 no5 p96 My 2017

Alexandria (La.)
RENAISSANCE RAMBLE P. F. STAHLS JR. color *Louisiana Life* v37 no2 p36 N/D 2016

Alexandria (Va.)
FRESH PICKINGS J. Benson color *Louisiana Life* v38 no1 p50 S/O 2017
ONE SIZE FITS ALL A. Brandy *Cincinnati Magazine* v50 no12 p36 S 2017
QUICK TAKES A. Limpert *Washingtonian Magazine* v52 no2 p258 N 2016

Alexandria (Va.)—Description & travel
ALEXANDRIA: Where to eat, shop, and explore K. Olsen *Washingtonian Magazine* v53 no1 p176 O 2017

Alexandrov, Ludmil B.
Mutational signatures associated with tobacco smoking in human cancer bibl graph *Science* v354 no6312 p618 N 4 2016

Alexiades, M. N.
Persistent effects of pre-Columbian plant domestication on Amazonian forest composition bibl chart graph map *Science* v355 no6328 p925 Mr 3 2017

ALEXIADES, MACRENE
42 new ALL-STAR PRODUCTS of the year [Cover story] color *Redbook* p27 Jl/Ag 2017

Alexie, Sherman, 1966-
CLEAN, CLEANER, CLEANEST S. ALEXIE bw *New Yorker* v93 no16 p48 Je 5 2017
A patchwork quilt K. Weber *America* v217 no5 p48 S 4 2017
SHERMAN ALEXIE color *Entertainment Weekly* no1468/1469 p108 Je 2-9 2017
The Summer Job I'll Never Forget color *Time* v190 no2/3 p55 Jl

10-17 2017

Alexiévich, Svetlana
Hot Type S. CROSLEY color *Vanity Fair* v59 no8 p48 Ag 2017

Alexion Pharmaceuticals Inc.
How do you maximize the profits of a drug that treats a very rare disease? [Cover story] B. Elgin, D. Bloomfield et al color *Bloomberg Businessweek* no4524 p42 My 29 2017

Alexiou, Joseph
Over the River: A man known for his engineering legacy endured hardships throughout his life *New York Times Book Review* p9 Ag 13 2017

Alexis, Lentine
Sugar High! A. C. Shilton color *Bicycling* v58 no6 p36 Jl 2017

Alexy, Oliver
How Investors React When Companies Announce They're Moving to a SaaS Business Model color *Harvard Business Review Digital Articles* p2 Ja 12 2017

Alfa Romeo automobile
FUTURE CARS [Cover story] bw color *Motor Trend* v69 no7 p36 Jl 2017
ROAD TEST SUMMARY chart *Road & Track* v68 no10 p106 Jl 2017
SPECIAL COMES STANDARD J. BARUTH color *Road & Track* v69 no2 p88 S 2017
TWISTY SISTER J. Gall color graph *Car & Driver* v62 no8 p13 F 2017
VELOCEE BELLA M. Rechtin chart color *Motor Trend* v69 no10 p82 O 2017

Alfa Romeo automobile—Evaluation
1965 ALFA ROMEO GIULIA SPRINT SPECIALE C. Comer color *Road & Track* v68 no8 p95 My 2017
Inside Out D. North Dillwyn color *Architectural Digest* no5 p36 My 2017
RISING TIDE M. PRINCE cartoon chart color graph *Road & Track* v68 no7 p38 Mr/Ap 2017
ROAD TEST SUMMARY cartoon chart *Road & Track* v68 no7 p100 Mr/Ap 2017

Alfa Romeo Automobiles SpA
1965 ALFA ROMEO GIULIA SPRINT SPECIALE C. Comer color *Road & Track* v68 no8 p95 My 2017
ROAD TEST SUMMARY cartoon chart *Road & Track* v68 no7 p100 Mr/Ap 2017

Alfa Romeo Giulia automobile
EDITOR'S LETTER K. WOLFKILL *Road & Track* v68 no7 p22 Mr/Ap 2017
WHAT LIES BENEATH D. N. Dillwyn color *Wired* v25 no5 p78 My 2017

Alfa Romeo Giulia automobile—Evaluation
Alfa Bits T. Quiroga bw color *Car & Driver* v62 no8 p78 F 2017
ANTICIPAZIONE M. PRINCE color *Road & Track* v68 no6 p66 F 2017
INSIDE OUT D. N. DILLWYN bw color *Conde Nast Traveler* v52 no5 p44 My 2017
O TRESPASS SWEETLY URGED! S. Evans chart color *Motor Trend* v69 no3 p60 Mr 2017

Alfa Romeo Inc.
Alfa Bits T. Quiroga bw color *Car & Driver* v62 no8 p78 F 2017
ANTICIPAZIONE M. PRINCE color *Road & Track* v68 no6 p66 F 2017
O TRESPASS SWEETLY URGED! S. Evans chart color *Motor Trend* v69 no3 p60 Mr 2017
WHAT LIES BENEATH D. N. Dillwyn color *GQ: Gentlemen's Quarterly* v97 no5 p38 My 2017

Alfalfa
Genetically Modified Alfalfa Production in the United States S. J. Wechsler and D. Milkove *Amber Waves: The Economics of Food, Farming, Natural Resources, & Rural America* p1 My 2017
Mineral-Rich Herbs K. P. SINGH KHALSA color *Better Nutrition* v78 no12 p20 D 2016

Alfalfa growing
RATIONING H2O TO ALFALFA D. Mowitz *Successful Farming* v114 no11 p60 N 2016

Al-Falih, Khalid
TO MAKE PETROLEUM USE MORE ACCEPTABLE AND MORE SUSTAINABLE *Vital Speeches of the Day* v83 no5 p158 My 2017

Alfarhan, Ahmed H.
Ancient genomic changes associated with domestication of the horse color diag *Science* v356 no6336 p442 Ap 28 2017

Alfonso, Alberto
Museum Breaks New Ground color *Arts & Crafts Homes & the Revival* v12 no3 p16 Summ 2017

Alford, Henry
COOKIE MONSTER ON THE DOLE cartoon *New Yorker* v93 no9 p29 Ap 17 2017
Travels of a Lifetime *New York Times Book Review* p1 Jl 30 2017

Alford, Stephen
London's Triumph: Merchants, Adventurers, and Money in Shakespeare's City *Publishers Weekly* v264 no41 p57 O 9 2017

Alfredson, Tomas
THE SNOWMAN S. Vilkomerson color *Entertainment Weekly* no1478 / 1479 p55 Ag 18-25 2017

Algae
Beauty's More than Skin Deep L. TURNER color *Better Nutrition* v79 no4 p62 Ap 2017
Please Pass the Algae H. ESTROFF MARANO *Psychology Today* v50 no2 p34 Mr/Ap 2017

Algae & the environment
Algae speed up melting of glacial snow L. HAMERS color *Science News* v192 no6 p10 O 14 2017
An algal photoenzyme converts fatty acids to hydrocarbons D. Sorigué, B. Légeret et al color graph *Science* v357 no6354 p903 S 1 2017

Algae—Therapeutic use
Can Algae Fight Ulcers? S. D. Wenholz color *Practical Horseman* v45 no7 p68 Jl 2017

Algal blooms
Our Ailing Oceans map *Earth Island Journal* v32 no3 p10 Aut 2017
Physiological and ecological drivers of early spring blooms of a coastal phytoplankter K. R. Hunter-Cevera, M. G. Neubert et al bibl graph *Science* v354 no6310 p326 O 21 2016

Algebra
See also
Algorithms
Mathematicians Find the Answers J. REHMEYER diag *Discover* v38 no1 p41 Ja/F 2017

Algebra—Study & teaching
Why Didn't I Think of That?! A. SIMMONS *Reader's Digest* v189 no1128 p88 Mr 2017

Algethami, Sarah
A Building Collapse in the Desert color *Bloomberg Businessweek* no4538 p32 S 18 2017

Algonquian literature
Early Algonquian Tomes Displayed S. Richardson color *American History* v52 no2 p8 Je 2017

Algonquin Books (Company)
Deals R. DEAHL bw color *Publishers Weekly* v264 no16 p12 Ap 17 2017

Algonquin Provincial Park (Ont.)
THE CALL OF Algonquin R. MACGREGOR color map *Canadian Geographic* v137 no1 p64 F 2017

Algorithms
See also
Computer algorithms
DeepStack: Expert-level artificial intelligence in heads-up no-limit poker [Cover story] M. Moravčík, M. Schmid et al chart diag *Science* v356 no6337 p508 My 5 2017
FAIR-MINDED MACHINES M. Temming color graph map *Science News* v192 no4 p26 S 16 2017
Here's Why People Trust Human Judgment Over Algorithms W. Frick *Harvard Business Review Digital Articles* p2 F 27 2015
Hollywood's Search for a Blockbuster Algorithm T. J. Huddleston color *Fortune* v175 no6 p12 My 1 2017
How to Make Better Predictions When You Don't Have Enough Data K. Radinsky and Y. Acriche *Harvard Business Review Digital Articles* p2 D 29 2016
The Perils of Algorithm- Based Marketing U. M. Dholakia *Harvard Business Review Digital Articles* p2 Je 17 2015
Using Algorithms to Predict the Next Outbreak K. Radinsky *Harvard Business Review Digital Articles* p2 N 5 2014

Using an Algorithm to Figure Out What Luxury Customers Really Want A. Brant *Harvard Business Review Digital Articles* p2 Jl 18 2016

What's Driving the Machine Learning Explosion? E. Brynjolfsson and A. McAfee *Harvard Business Review Digital Articles* p2 Jl 18 2017

You Need an Algorithm, Not a Data Scientist K. Radinsky *Harvard Business Review Digital Articles* p2 D 15 2014

ALHASSAN, BAAKO

BREAKING CAMP: HUMANIST SERVICE CORPS ASSISTS GHANAIANS ACCUSED OF WITCHCRAFT *Humanist* v77 no5 p32 S/O 2017

Al-Hussein, Hamzeh

The Refugee Puppeteer Hamzeh al-Hussein A. SU color *Foreign Policy* no223 p18 Mr/Ap 2017

Al Hussein, Zeid Ra'ad

The Evolving Role of the United Nations in Securing Human Rights *UN Chronicle* v53 no4 p1 2016

The Evolving Role of the United Nations in Securing Human Rights *UN Chronicle* v54 no4 p6 2017

Ali, Amjad

HALF A CENTURY OF CARE [Cover story] *Islamic Horizons* v46 no3 p22 My/Je 2017

ALI, AYAAN HIRSI

Is free speech under threat IN THE UNITED STATES? WE RECEIVED TWENTY-SEVEN RESPONSES. WE PUBLISH THEM HERE, IN ALPHABETICAL ORDER *Commentary* v144 no1 p13 Jl/Ag 2017

March for Every Woman: Far too many feminists in the West prove reluctant to condemn practices that harm their sisters in the developing world *Hoover Digest: Research & Opinion on Public Policy* no3 p128 Summ 2017

ALI, KAZIM

Text Cloud Anthology *New Republic* v248 no7 p63 Jl 2017

Ali, Mahershala, 1974-

Limelight [Cover story] C. Wallace color *GQ: Gentlemen's Quarterly* v97 no7 p48 Jl 2017

A Night They'll Remember color *Vanity Fair* v59 no5 p72 Ap 2017

MARVELOUS MAHERSHALA S. Li color *Entertainment Weekly* no1434 p30 O 7 2016

Ali, Mohamad

Backdoor Government Decryption Hurts My Business and Yours *Harvard Business Review Digital Articles* p2 S 15 2016

Immigration Is at the Heart of U.S. Competitiveness *Harvard Business Review Digital Articles* p2 My 15 2017

Ali, Monica

The Midas Touch: Salman Rushdie's new novel, set in New York, follows the story of an enigmatic family from abroad during the Obama years *New York Times Book Review* p14 S 17 2017

A Room Of Her Own [Cover story] color *New York Times Book Review* p1 Ja 29 2017

Ali, Muhammad, 1942-2016

Farewell M. Bechtel color *Sports Illustrated* v125 no21 p52 D 26 2016

The Greatest and Me D. Miller color *AARP: The Magazine* v59 no1A p56 D 2015/Ja 2016

THE GREATEST PRICE J. Eig color *Sports Illustrated* v127 no10 p54 O 2 2017

MUHAMMAD ALI L. Gast and J. Labrecque color *Entertainment Weekly* no1446/1447 p90 D 2016/Ja 2017

REEXAMINING ALI R. LINN bw *Chicago* v66 no10 p26 O 2017

WHAT IF? ... MUHAMMAD ALI HAD NEVER MET MALCOLM X? R. O'Brien and J. Feldman color *Sports Illustrated* v126 no11 p61 Ap 17-24 2017

Ali, Mustafa

"We're All in the Same Boat" Z. LOFTUS-FARREN color *Earth Island Journal* v32 no3 p46 Aut 2017

ALI, NOOR

Guiding the Youth Amidst Islamophobia *Islamic Horizons* v45 no6 p40 N/D 2016

Ali, Robleh

The Blockchain Will Do to the Financial System What the Internet Did to Media color *Harvard Business Review Digital Articles* p2 Mr 8 2017

Ali, Rozina

HINDUS FOR TRUMP cartoon *New Yorker* v92 no36 p16 N 7 2016

Ali, Wajahat—Interviews

After the Shock R. CONNIFF *Progressive* p5 D 2016/Ja 2017

'This Is like My 9/11 All Over Again' N. Stockwell color *Progressive* p37 D 2016/Ja 2017

Alia, Eanas

Without inclusion, diversity initiatives may not be enough color *Science* v357 no6356 p1101 S 15 2017

Alias (TV program)

The Rest of the ATX Fest N. Abrams color *Entertainment Weekly* no1471 p15 Je 23 2017

Alias Grace (TV program)

ALSO COMING… I. Ratledge *TV Guide* v65 no37 p44 S 4 2017

Alibaba Group Holding Ltd.

10 JACK MA S. Cendrowski color *Fortune* v174 no7 p85 D 1 2016

Alibaba Tries To Get in the Game J. D. Bateman *Bloomberg Businessweek* no4531 p20 Jl 24 2017

What 7 Top Pros Are Doing Now D. FONDA color *Kiplinger's Personal Finance* v71 no8 p42 Ag 2017

Alice Through the Looking Glass (Film)

The 18th Annual Alternative Oscars color *Esquire* v167 no1 p15 F 2017

Alidad Ltd.

British Invasion color *Architectural Digest* v74 no1 p120 Ja 2017

Alien (Film)

ALIEN S. Vilkomerson color *Entertainment Weekly* no1460/1461 p28 Ap 7-17 2017

Alien: Covenant (Film)

ALIEN AWAKENS K. P. Sullivan color *Entertainment Weekly* no1467 p44 My 26 2017

ALIEN: COVENANT S. Vilkomerson color *Entertainment Weekly* no1446/1447 p53 D 2016/Ja 2017

ALIEN: COVENANT S. Vilkomerson color *Entertainment Weekly* no1463/1464 p42 Ap/My 2017

CHOOSE YOUR OWN SPACE ADVENTURE SAVING THE GALAXY ... AGAIN M. YARM cartoon *Wired* v25 no5 p37 My 2017

DANNY McBRIDE S. Vilkomerson color *Entertainment Weekly* no1467 p45 My 26 2017

HORROR SHOW T. Friend cartoon *New Yorker* v93 no16 p40 Je 5 2017

Monster Mash R. DOUTHAT color *National Review* v69 no11 p42 Je 12 2017

MONSTERS' BALL A. LANE cartoon *New Yorker* v93 no15 p74 My 29 2017

The Must List color *Entertainment Weekly* no1467 p2 My 26 2017

NOW PLAYING color *Entertainment Weekly* no1471 p53 Je 23 2017

Summer Movie Preview: May S. Begley, E. Berman et al color *Time* v189 no20 p48 My 29 2017

Where Do Xenomorphs Come From? Alien: Covenant traces the origin of species D. EDELSTEIN img *New York* v50 no10 p96 My 15 2017

Alien plants

WEBB DESIGN E. MASTROIANNI color *Discover* v38 no6 p83 Jl/Ag 2017

Alienation (Philosophy)

See also

Isolation (Philosophy)

Thoreau for the Ages B. T. MAURER *American Scholar* v86 no4 p3 Aut 2017

Alienation (Social psychology)

CARTOONS *In These Times* v40 no12 p34 D 2016

Conservatives in Cruise Wear P. NORMAN cartoon *Walrus* v14 no3 p26 Ap 2017

Revenge of the Trolls J. M. COLÓN *In These Times* v41 no8 p34 Ag 2017

Aliens (Film : 1986)

The Essential Paxton D. Franich color *Entertainment Weekly* no1456 p14 Mr 10 2017

Alienware Corp.

Alienware 17 R4: Worth its weight in gold H. DINGMAN color graph *PCWorld* v35 no9 p49 S 2017

How Alienware's 20-year history with PC gaming can help drive the future of VR A. SHAH color *PCWorld* v35 no11 p21 N 2016

Alifano, Aurora
Committing to socially responsible seafood color *Science* v356 no6341 p912 Je 1 2017

Aligarh movement
A Few Movie Stars Don't Make Happy Muslim Indians A. HA-MEED *Islamic Horizons* v46 no2 p52 Mr/Ap 2017

Aligica, Paul
Alternative Interpretations of Economic Theory and its Limits *Society* v54 no1 p70 F 2017

Alike, Yet Not Quite (Poem)
Alike, Yet Not Quite J. XIE *New Republic* v248 no8/9 p62 Ag/S 2017

Ali-Khan, Sofia—Interviews
Dialogue Across Difference A. Cooper color *Tricycle: The Buddhist Review* v26 no4 p48 Summ 2017

ALINI, ERICA
Bathroom wars 2.0 color *Maclean's* v129 no43 p48 O 31 2016

Ali Oshaghi, Mohammad
Driving mosquito refractoriness to Plasmodium falciparum with engineered symbiotic bacteria color graph *Science* v357 no6358 p1399 S 29 2017

AliphCom Inc.
DATA WON'T MAKE YOU FIT L. Entis color *Fortune* v176 no2 p33 Ag 1 2017

Alisport (Company)
Alibaba Tries To Get in the Game J. D. Bateman *Bloomberg Businessweek* no4531 p20 Jl 24 2017

Alivisatos, A. Paul
Single-particle mapping of nonequilibrium nanocrystal transformations bibl bw graph *Science* v354 no6314 p874 N 18 2016

Aljabooli, Ghazweh
The Syrians Next Door R. Shulman color *Time* v188 no20 p40 N 14 2016

Aljasem, Lamis
Promised Land color *Time* v190 no14 p40 O 9 2017
When Home Isn't Where the Heart Is color map *Time* v189 no21 p40 Je 5 2017

Alkalay, Loretta—Interviews
Ask a Drone Lawyer L. Amico *Harvard Business Review Digital Articles* p2 My 18 2017

Alkalimat, Abdul
The Wall of Respect: Public Art and Black Liberation in 1960s Chicago *Publishers Weekly* v264 no35 p123 Ag 28 2017

Alkaloids
See also
Neonicotinoids
GLOSSARY *Equus* no477 p87 Je 2017

Alkama, Ramdane
Satellites reveal contrasting responses of regional climate to the widespread greening of Earth diag *Science* v356 no6343 p1180 Je 16 2017

Alkemade, R.
The impact of hunting on tropical mammal and bird populations graph map *Science* v356 no6334 p180 Ap 14 2017

Alkenes
See also
Ethylene
Catalytic intermolecular hydroaminations of unactivated olefins with secondary alkyl amines A. J. Musacchio; B. C. Lainhart et al bibl diag *Science* v355 no6326 p727 F 17 2017
Metal-catalyzed electrochemical diazidation of alkenes N. Fu, G. S. Sauer et al diag *Science* v357 no6351 p575 Ag 11 2017
RESEARCH color *Science* v357 no6351 p560 Ag 11 2017

Al-Khalili, Jim
ALIENS: THE WORLD'S LEADING SCIENTISTS ON THE SEARCH FOR EXTRATERRESTRIAL LIFE C. Smallwood *Harper's Magazine* v334 no2004 p81 My 2017
Why Aliens Would (Probably) Come In Peace S. Begley color *Time* v189 no18 p21 My 15 2017

Al-Khatahtbeh, Amani
They'll Blame Us R. ZAKARIA *New York Times Book Review* p9 N 13 2016

Alkhateeb, Nasreen
Space careers: A universe of options D. Angeles and D. Vilorio chart color *Career Outlook* p1 N 2016

Alkire, Matthew B.
Greater role for Atlantic inflows on sea-ice loss in the Eurasian Basin of the Arctic Ocean chart diag graph *Science* v356 no6335 p285 Ap 21 2017

Alkyer, Frank
DownBeat Celebrates 40 Years of SMAs color *Downbeat* v84 no6 p97 Je 2017
JEN Grows Up color *Downbeat* v84 no4 p19 Ap 2017

Alkyl group
Transition metal-catalyzed alkyl-alkyl bond formation: Another dimension in cross-coupling chemistry J. Choi and G. C. Fu diag *Science* v356 no6334 p152 Ap 14 2017

All Along the Watchtower (Music)
ST. VINCENT E. R. Brown color *Entertainment Weekly* no1462 p63 Ap 21 2017

All-Clad MetalCrafters LLC
The All-Clad Prep & Cook color *Bloomberg Businessweek* no4528 p75 Je 26 2017

All Disco (Music)
THE ULTIMATE WINTER SINGLES SWAP color *Entertainment Weekly* no1451/1452 p104 F 3-10 2017

All Eyez on Me (Film)
ALL EYEZ ON ME C. Holub color *Entertainment Weekly* no1463/1464 p50 Ap/My 2017
CALIFORNIA LOVE B. WESTHOFF *Los Angeles Magazine* v61 no11 p78 N 2016
DEAR TUPAC W. L. Wilson color *Essence* v48 no2 p58 Je 2017
Diversity Waits on a Green Light S. Zacharek color *Time* v188 no27-28 p114 D 26 2016

All-Star Baseball Game—History—21st century
All-Star Struck M. Rosenberg color *Sports Illustrated* v125 no19 p122 D 12 2016

All terrain vehicles
See also
Mountain bikes
EATON COUNTY, MI T. Hansen color *Outdoor Life* v224 no7 p7 S 2017

All terrain vehicles—Design & construction
GREAT UNKNOWNS cartoon color *Popular Mechanics* p22 Ap 2017

All terrain vehicles—Evaluation
ATV AND UTV TEST 2017 T. HANSEN chart color *Outdoor Life* v224 no7 p14 S 2017
THE MECHANICS OF FUN E. DYER chart color *Popular Mechanics* p84 Mr 2017

All the Dreams (Music)
All The Dreams/Dream In The Blue A. Morrison color *Downbeat* v83 no11 p60 N 2016

All the Money in the World (Film)
ALL THE MONEY IN THE WORLD S. Li color *Entertainment Weekly* no1478 / 1479 p75 Ag 18-25 2017

All the Things You Are (Music)
Improvising Freely Over Complex Left-Hand Keyboard Figures V. NESELOVSKYI color *Downbeat* v84 no9 p92 S 2017

All These Hands (Music)
All These Hands J. Macnie color *Downbeat* v84 no3 p53 Mr 2017

All U Do Is Kill (Music)
Ghost Wave B. Flemister color *Surfing Magazine* v53 no2 p26 F 2017

Allam, Rodney
Green Gas C. HELMAN and W. BALDWIN color *Forbes* v199 no2 p50 F 28 2017

Allan, Jonathan
Mitigating coastal landslide damage color *Science* v357 no6355 p981 S 8 2017

ALLAN, MARC D.
Vonnegut Fest *Indianapolis Monthly* v40 no5 p12 Ja 2017

Allan, Mica
THE BIG CHEESE *Iceland Review* v55 no4 p54 Jl/Ag 2017
DAFT ABOUT DILL *Iceland Review* v55 no3 p46 My/Je 2017
GRANDI'S GREATEST HITS *Iceland Review* v55 no1 p58 Ja/F 2017

Allan, Samantha
For the Love of the Horse color *Practical Horseman* v45 no2 p72 F 2017

Allarà, Marco

Activity-based protein profiling reveals off-target proteins of the FAAH inhibitor BIA 10-2474 chart color graph *Science* v356 no6342 p1084 Je 9 2017

Allard, Linda

The Prettiest VEGETABLE GARDEN IN NEW ENGLAND: WHEN FASHION DESIGNER LINDA ALLARD MOVED TO LITCHFIELD COUNTY, EVERYONE FIGURED THERE'D BE A GORGEOUS GARDEN IN HER FUTURE. THEY DIDN'T SUSPECT VEGETABLES, THOUGH... T. MARTIN color *Yankee* p28 Jl 2017

Allcard, Edward

A Cruising Family Reunion C. J. Doane color *Sail* v47 no12 p80 D 2016

Allegiance

See also

Dual nationality

Allegiant (Film)

ALLEGIANT D. Vaughn color *Sound & Vision* v81 no9 p67 N 2016

Allegory

Elusive Illusions H. Sherman *Stage Directions* v30 no8 p16 Ag 2017

May the Force Be With Us K. ARONOFF *In These Times* v41 no2 p36 F 2017

Allegrini, F.

Jupiter's magnetosphere and aurorae observed by the Juno spacecraft during its first polar orbits diag graph *Science* v356 no6340 p826 My 26 2017

Allekotte, I.

Observation of a large-scale anisotropy in the arrival directions of cosmic rays above 8 × 1018 eV *Science* v357 no6357 p1266 S 22 2017

Alleles

See also

Single nucleotide polymorphisms

Glycophorin alleles link to malaria protection E. A. Winzeler diag *Science* v356 no6343 p1122 Je 16 2017

Resistance to malaria through structural variation of red blood cell invasion receptors E. M. Leffler, G. Band et al diag *Science* v356 no6343 p1139 Je 16 2017

Allen, Ben—Interviews

design masters l. cutrone *New Orleans Homes & Lifestyles* v20 no4 p70 Aut 2017

Allen, Bob

New Jersey case tests whether historic churches can get state grants *Christian Century* v134 no17 p16 Ag 16 2017

People color *Christian Century* v134 no11 p18 My 24 2017

ALLEN, BRAD

FIND YOUR CALLING color *Field & Stream* v122 no5 p50 O 2017

Allen, Brooke

Goodbye, Palmyra color *Weekly Standard* v22 no33 p38 My 8 2017

Allen, Bruce Ware

DISASTER AT DJERBA: During a period of European peace, Spain sought to establish control of the Mediterranean. Yet a disastrous attempt to oust the Ottomans from North Africa threatened to accelerate the westward advance of Islam *History Today* v67 no6 p24 Je 2016

ALLEN, CHARLOTTE

The Church Militant *Weekly Standard* v22 no8 p34 O 31 2016

Circus at Sunset color *Weekly Standard* v22 no35 p36 My 22 2017

Journalists in the Dock color *Weekly Standard* v22 no31 p14 Ap 17 2017

Seeing Pink color *Weekly Standard* v22 no21 p8 F 6 2017

The Whole World Was Watching [Cover story] color *Weekly Standard* v22 no39 p26 Je 19 2017

ALLEN, CONRAD

SURVIVE ANYWHERE bw cartoon color diag *Outdoor Life* v224 no3 p33 Ap 2017

Allen, Danielle

A Failed War: A Harvard professor mourns her cousin's short life, much of it spent behind bars G. HOWARD *New York Times Book Review* p10 O 15 2017

Allen, Debbie

Grey's Anatomy M. Logan *TV Guide* v65 no19 p29 My 1 2017

Allen, Emma

BULL'S-EYE cartoon *New Yorker* v92 no47 p19 Ja 30 2017

CUP COUNT cartoon *New Yorker* v92 no30 p23 S 26 2016

LUXURY ELVES cartoon *New Yorker* v92 no43 p19 Ja 2 2017

MOM-AND-POP SHOP cartoon color *New Yorker* v93 no5 p72 Mr 20 2017

Pith color *New Yorker* v93 no14 p23 My 22 2017

Allen, Eric

Vanguard in the Spotlight T. Panken color *Downbeat* v84 no6 p23 Je 2017

Allen, Frederick

Excuse Me, Sir, How Much Do You Make? C. Bonanos img *New York* v50 no10 p14 My 15 2017

A Love Supreme color *AARP: The Magazine* v59 no1A p53 D 2015/Ja 2016

ALLEN, GREG

HOW TO GET FORGOTTEN bw color *ARTnews* v116 no1 p90 Spr 2017

Allen, Gwen

SUZANNE BLANK REDSTONE color *Art in America* v104 no11 p126 D 2016

Allen, James

The 3 Things That Keep Companies Growing *Harvard Business Review Digital Articles* p2 Je 1 2016

The Curious Downside of an Owner's Mindset *Harvard Business Review Digital Articles* p2 Je 7 2016

Great Companies Stay True to the Spirit of Their Founders *Harvard Business Review Digital Articles* p2 Mr 14 2016

How the Best CEOs Get the Important Work Done *Harvard Business Review Digital Articles* p2 S 27 2016

How to Stop People Who Bog Things Down with Bureaucracy *Harvard Business Review Digital Articles* p2 Jl 12 2016

Keeping the Zeal of a Startup as You Scale *Harvard Business Review Digital Articles* p2 Jl 5 2016

Professionalize a Startup Without Stifling It *Harvard Business Review Digital Articles* p2 Jl 29 2016

Why CEOs Should Commit to Many Small Battles Instead of a Single Big One *Harvard Business Review Digital Articles* p2 D 14 2016

Allen, Jeff

2017 HONDA CRF250L RALLY bw color *Cycle World* v56 no6 p16 Jl 2017

Allen, Jonathan, 1957-

The Anatomy of Defeat D. HALPER *Commentary* v143 no6 p50 Je 2017

Allen, Joseph G.

Research: Stale Office Air Is Making You Less Productive *Harvard Business Review Digital Articles* p2 Mr 21 2017

Allen, Josh

NO ONE TO NO. 1 A. Staples color *Sports Illustrated* v126 no14 p96 My 15-22 2017

WHO'S NO. 1? THESE PLAYERS COULD CHALLENGE JOSH ALLEN FOR THE TOP SPOT C. Becht color *Sports Illustrated* v126 no14 p101 My 15-22 2017

Allen, Judith E.

Local amplifiers of IL-4Rα-mediated macrophage activation promote repair in lung and liver diag *Science* v356 no6342 p1076 Je 9 2017

Allen, Justin

PE Firms Are Creating a New Role: Leadership Capital Partner *Harvard Business Review Digital Articles* p2 Ag 11 2017

Private Equity's New Phase *Harvard Business Review Digital Articles* p2 Ag 9 2016

Allen, Kelly Brook

Around the Campfire color *Trail Rider* v29 no1 p6 Ja/F 2017

Allen, Laura

PRAIRIE PORTAL *National Parks* v91 no1 p44 Wint 2017

Allen, Lila

Teachers Village *Architectural Record* v205 no4 p198 Ap 2017

Allen, Lisa

Health Care Providers Can Use Design Thinking to Improve Patient Experiences *Harvard Business Review Digital Articles* p2 Ag 31 2017

Allen, Mel

THE AUDACITY OF LIZ PUTNAM bw color *Yankee* p86 My/Je 2017

The Best Walk in Newport *Yankee* p91 Mr 2017

Getting Out the Vote bw *Yankee* v80 no6 p168 N/D 2016

Gifts of the Sea *Yankee* v81 no1 p12 Ja/F 2017

THE HOUSE AT ALLEN COVE *Yankee* v81 no5 p40 S/O 2017

Photographer of a Lost Valley *Yankee* v81 no1 p140 Ja/F 2017

slow boat on a big lake bw color map *Yankee* p70 My/Je 2017

Spirits color *Yankee* v80 no6 p12 N/D 2016

A Traveler's Best Friend color *Yankee* p12 My/Je 2017

Unexpected Encounters *Yankee* v81 no5 p12 S/O 2017

THE VIETNAM WAR: How the film story of the most divisive event in America since the Civil War came to life in a small New Hampshire town *Yankee* v81 no5 p136 S/O 2017

Walks of Life bw color *Yankee* p12 Mr 2017

ALLEN, PAUL GOAT

Baseball Bat to the Head color *Publishers Weekly* v264 no6 p46 F 6 2017

Allen, Paul, 1953-

Billionaire's gift pushes ocean sensors deeper P. Voosen color diag *Science* v357 no6355 p956 S 8 2017

Allen, Peggy

GREENER PASTURES J. Seaton color *O, The Oprah Magazine* p28 O 2017

Allen, Ray, 1975——Interviews

JUST MY TYPE D. Patrick and T. Keith color *Sports Illustrated* v125 no17 p29 N 21 2016 Double Issue

Allen, Raymond

Ask the Expert *Atlanta* v56 no7 p220 N 2016

Allen, Rik

ROCKET MAN B. Haugen color *American Craft* v76 no6 p50 D 2016-Ja 2017

Allen, Terry

Caring for Aging Loved Ones color *Consumer Reports* v82 no12 p6 D 2017

Allen, Terry, 1943-

THERE AND BACK AGAIN J. COHEN *Texas Monthly* v45 no2 p94 F 2017

Allen, Todd M.

The epigenetic landscape of T cell exhaustion bibl graph *Science* v354 no6316 p1165 D 2 2016

Allen, Trudy

THE BRITISH HERITAGE TRAVEL PUZZLER color *British Heritage Travel* v38 no5 p78 S/O 2017

Allen, Whitney

Horsemanship, Front and Center *In Stride* v12 no5 p36 S 2017

Allen, William E.

Thirst-associated preoptic neurons encode an aversive motivational drive diag *Science* v357 no6356 p1149 S 15 2017

Allen, William L.

The biology of color color *Science* v357 no6350 p470 Ag 4 2017

Allen, Woody, 1935-

CAFÉ SOCIETY J. Krebs color *Sound & Vision* v82 no5 p67 Je 2017

Her Little Black Book [Cover story] *New York Times Book Review* p1 Ja 1 2017

Reader's Digest COMPLETE GUIDE TO witticisms Quips RETORTS Rejoinders AND PITHY REPLIES FOR EVERY OCCASION [Cover story] *Reader's Digest* v188 no1124 p76 O 2016

The Remarkable Laziness of Woody Allen C. ORR cartoon *Atlantic* v320 no3 p34 O 2017

WONDER WHEEL J. Derschowitz and S. Li color *Entertainment Weekly* no1478 / 1479 p76 Ag 18-25 2017

Allen, Zel

Come Meet the Grand Dames of the Brassica Family! *Vegetarian Journal* v36 no1 p14 2017

VEGGIE BURGERS ROCK! From B.C.E to OMG! *Vegetarian Journal* v35 no2 p10 2016

Allenby, Brad

Here be dragons: DARPA in the age of hybrid war bibl color *Bulletin of the Atomic Scientists* v73 no3 p188 My 2017

Soft law: New tools for governing emerging technologies bibl *Bulletin of the Atomic Scientists* v73 no2 p108 Mr 2017

Allenby, Braden R.

The Age of Weaponized Narrative or, Where Have You Gone, Walter Cronkite? *Issues in Science & Technology* v33 no4 p65 Summ 2017

Can Science End War? color *Issues in Science & Technology* v33 no1 p91 Fall 2016

Allende, Barbara

"WHY I GIVE BACK" color *Good Housekeeping* v263 no5 p95 N 2016

Allende, Isabel, 1942-

Beads, Books and Bijoux I. Allende color *AARP: The Magazine* v59 no1A p52 D 2015/Ja 2016

In the Midst of Winter *Publishers Weekly* v264 no35 p99 Ag 28 2017

WELCOME, MS. PARTNERS AND LIFETIME MEMBERS! *Ms.* v26 no4 p34 Wint 2016

Allende Gossens, Salvador, 1908-1973

When Allende TOLD US HAPPINESS IS A HUMAN RIGHT L. SEPÚLVEDA bw *Nation* v305 no6 p16 S 11 2017

ALLENDORF, FRED W.

Evolution in a Toxic World *BioScience* v67 no6 p476 Je 2017

Allen-Ebrahimian, Bethany

Religion vs. Culture color *Foreign Policy* no225 p112 Jl/Ag 2017

What a Just Immigration Policy Looks Like cartoon *Foreign Policy* no226 p80 S/O 2017

Allergens

Heaves flare-up L. Bonner color *Equus* no472 p18 Ja 2017

How Clean Is Your Pet? A. Levi color *Health* v31 no7 p104 S 2017

This Cupcake Could Kill Me...But This One Won't! K. SCHUG and J. PRESS *Scholastic Choices* v32 no5 p20 F 2017

Allergy

> *See also*
>
> Allergy in animals
>
> Food allergy

Chronic cough: Finding the cause *Mayo Clinic Health Letter* v35 no11 p7 N 2017

MISERABLE? HERE'S WHY R. Laliberte cartoon chart color *Men's Health* v32 no3 p73 Ap 2017

Most penicillin allergies are off base E. DeMarco color *Science News* v190 no13 p5 D 24 2016

The rash formed rings around the young boy's ankles, and his joints hurt. Was it an allergy? L. Sanders *New York Times Magazine* p18 Jl 9 2017

the Sting R. K. JOHNSON cartoon *New Yorker* v93 no7 p40 Ap 3 2017

UNSTOPPABLE ENERGY: A USER'S MANUAL H. Levine color *Health* v31 no4 p75 My 2017

Why So Itchy? L. Murray color *Health* v31 no2 p94 Mr 2017

Allergy in animals

NERVE'S ROLE IN HEADSHAKING INVESTIGATED C. Barakat and M. McCluskey color *Equus* no481 p12 O 2017

SUSCEPTIBILITY TO SWEET ITCH INVESTIGATED C. Barakat and M. McCluskey color *Equus* no478 p18 Jl 2017

Allergy prevention

Ah-CHOO! color *Missouri Life* v44 no2 p66 Ap 2017

allergy SURVIVAL GUIDE L. TURNER color *Better Nutrition* v79 no4 p56 Ap 2017

FEED-BASED ALLERGY TREATMENT SHOWS PROMISE C. Barakat and M. McCluskey color *Equus* no475 p28 Ap 2017

a lawn that loves you back V. SOLE-SMITH bw color *Parents* v92 no4 p114 Ap 2017

Nothing to Sneeze At J. SZABO color *Better Nutrition* v79 no4 p32 Ap 2017

the pet & pollen connection S. SEA GOLD color *Parents* v92 no4 p23 Ap 2017

Problem Solved! [Cover story] R. LALIBERTE cartoon *Prevention* v69 no5 p18 My 2017

Surprisingly Ordinary Allergy Triggers A. NUÑEZ and L. GELMAN color *Reader's Digest* v189 no1129 p54 Ap 2017

Allergy treatment

Eat these to fight allergies M. TAYLOR cartoon *Redbook* p88 My 2017

Alleva, Richard

An American Spartacus bw *Commonweal* v143 no18 p28 N 11 2016

Blockbusting color *Commonweal* v144 no13 p21 Ag 11 2017

Character Studies color *Commonweal* v144 no3 p21 F 10 2017

Grounded color *Commonweal* v144 no6 p23 Mr 24 2017

How to Dramatize Heroism—and How Not To color *Common-*

weal v143 no17 p27 O 21 2016

Missions Accomplished color *Commonweal* v144 no4 p20 F 24 2017

No Refuge color *Commonweal* v143 no20 p18 D 16 2016

Stay-at-Home Heroes color *Commonweal* v144 no1 p26 Ja 6 2017

Timely Provocations color *Commonweal* v144 no7 p24 Ap 14 2017

Two Beauties and Some Beasts color *Commonweal* v144 no9 p26 My 19 2017

Waving & Drowning color *Commonweal* v144 no11 p29 Je 16 2017

Alley, Richard B.

How high will the seas rise? bibl color graph *Science* v354 no6318 p1375 D 16 2016

Alleys

ALLEYS ARE BACK D. Reed *Washingtonian Magazine* v52 no6 p51 Mr 2017

ALLFREY, DAVID

Thunder Thighs color *Climbing* no354 p27 Jl 2017

Allgaier-Lamberti, Donna

AGING GRACEFULLY on the Homestead *Mother Earth News* no280 p34 F/Mr 2017

Alliance Builders LLC

Custom Home Builders Directory *Washingtonian Magazine* v52 no6 p162 Mr 2017

Custom Home Builders Directory *Washingtonian Magazine* v52 no8 p186 My 2017

Alliance Consumer Growth (Company)

Brand Boys A. FELDMAN and J. BUCKINGHAM color *Forbes* v199 no2 p58 F 28 2017

Alliances (International relations)

Allies First, Mr. President M. A. McFaul *Hoover Digest: Research & Opinion on Public Policy* no1 p77 Wint 2017

Pipe Dreams of a Normal Iran T. Donnelly *Hoover Digest: Research & Opinion on Public Policy* no1 p131 Wint 2017

Reviving Spheres of Interest W. S. LIND *American Conservative* v16 no2 p8 Mr/Ap 2017

Science without Walls color *Scientific American* v316 no6 p7 Je 2017

Alliances (International relations)—History—21st century

The Trouble With Russia M. Calabresi, S. Shuster et al color map *Time* v189 no7/8 p44 F 27 2017

The U.S. Should Form a Closer Military Alliance With Israel A. J. Stavridis color *Time* v189 no3 p20 Ja 16 2017

Alliance Theater (Atlanta, Ga.)

A BRILLIANT PAIRING R. L. ELDREDGE *Atlanta* v56 no9 p78 Ja 2017

Allibhoy, Omar

Spanish Made Simple: Foolproof Spanish Recipes for Every Day color *Publishers Weekly* v264 no12 p68 Mr 20 2017

Allied (Film)

ALLIED C. Chiarella color *Sound & Vision* v82 no6 p69 Jl/Ag 2017

Allied C. Nashawaty color *Entertainment Weekly* no1442 p40 D 2 2016 Rebellious Special Issue

CAN ALLIED SURVIVE THE BREAKUP? N. Sperling and L. Rice color *Entertainment Weekly* no1434 p13 O 7 2016

CASABLANCA REVISITED D. Coggan color *Entertainment Weekly* no1441 p38 N 25 2016

WIVES AND HUSBANDS A. LANE cartoon *New Yorker* v92 no40 p86 D 5 2016

Allied Window Inc.

FROM REAL TO FAUX bw color *Old House Journal* v45 no2 p88 Ap 2017

Allied Works Architecture Inc.

High Note J. MINUTILLO and J. BITTERMANN color diag *Architectural Record* v204 no12 p96 D 2016

Allied Forces. Supreme Headquarters. Monuments, Fine Arts & Archives Section

OKINAWA *AARP: The Magazine* v59 no3A p65 Ap/My 2016

Allied Powers (1919-)

Hardware R621 Gruppenstand J. Guttman color *Military History* v34 no5 p20 Ja 2018

Nebraska AND THE GREAT WAR M. MASICH bw color *Nebraska Life* v21 no6 p22 N/D 2017

Alligator gar

Cheers & Jeers M. James, S. Brown et al color *Field & Stream* v121 no6 p12 N 2016

Alligator hunting

FOR THE RECORD H. Ribons color *Field & Stream* v121 no7 p17 D 2016/Ja 2017

Alligators—Behavior

Desert Gator: The life and times of Clem of Grand Canyon-Parashant N. BRULLIARD *National Parks* v91 no3 p58 Summ 2017

Allin, Dana H.

Trump and the Holy Land color *Foreign Affairs* v96 no2 p37 Mr/Ap 2017

Allina, Johnny

The Dryden Arms *Publishers Weekly* v263 no43 p55 O 24 2016

Allison, Bill

A Georgia Election Is a TV Ad Bonanza bw *Bloomberg Businessweek* no4527 p50 Je 19 2017

How to Lobby But Not Be a Lobbyist *Bloomberg Businessweek* no4511 p25 F 13 2017

The Quiet Official Who's Trump Enemy No. 1 color *Bloomberg Businessweek* no4508 p24 Ja 23 2017

Sheldon Adelson's Not-So-Winning Year bw *Bloomberg Businessweek* no4530 p40 Jl 17 2017

Until Donald Trump, U.S. presidents and vice presidents went to extremes to avoid conflicts of interest... real or apparent bw color *Bloomberg Businessweek* no4503 p22 D 12 2016

Allison, Edward H.

Committing to socially responsible seafood color *Science* v356 no6341 p912 Je 1 2017

Allison, Graham

DANCE WITH THE DRAGON I. BURUMA cartoon color *New Yorker* v93 no17 p61 Je 19 2017

High Stakes: Can Trump and Xi Avoid War and Strike a North Korea Deal? color *Time* v189 no14 p12 Ap 17 2017

Past Is Prologue *Hoover Digest: Research & Opinion on Public Policy* no1 p175 Wint 2017

Pondering Prospects for a U.S.-China War N. MILLMAN *American Conservative* v16 no4 p60 Jl/Ag 2017

The Thucydides Trap color *Foreign Policy* no224 p80 My/Je 2017

Allison, Hannah R.

Mobile MUTE specifies subsidiary cells to build physiologically improved grass stomata bibl diag *Science* v355 no6330 p1215 Mr 17 2017

Allison, J. R.

Molecular gas in the halo fuels the growth of a massive cluster galaxy at high redshift bibl graph *Science* v354 no6316 p1128 D 2 2016

Allison, James

James Allison Has Unfinished Business with Cancer [Cover story] A. Piore bw color il *MIT Technology Review* v120 no3 p78 My/Je 2017

Allison, James P.

THE ICON OCLAST E. BENSON *Texas Monthly* v44 no11 p92 N 2016

ALLISON, JOHN

Born to Sing *Opera News* v81 no6 p18 D 2016

Allison, M.

Jupiter's interior and deep atmosphere: The initial pole-to-pole passes with the Juno spacecraft [Cover story] color graph *Science* v356 no6340 p821 My 26 2017

ALLISON, SIMON

Harare, Zimbabwe color *Foreign Policy* no225 p18 Jl/Ag 2017

Allison, Wes

SHREDDING ON THE SANDS OF TIME color diag *Hot Rod* v70 no12 p38 D 2017

Allison engines

HOT ROD's Sea Monster T. Taylor bw color *Hot Rod* v69 no12 p52 D 2016

Allison Stegner, M.

Merging paleobiology with conservation biology to guide the future of terrestrial ecosystems color *Science* v355 no6325 p594 F 10 2017

ALLITT, PATRICK

Looking Outward bw *Weekly Standard* v22 no13 p39 D 5 2016

Allium

See also

Garlic
Wild leek

BLACK GOLD W. Sheppard *Virginia Living* v15 no3 p27 Ap 2017

The Elegance of Alliums Z. Gowen color *Southern Living* v52 no5 p48 My 2017

Nodding Onion M. WALWYN color *Canadian Wildlife* v23 no1 p37 Mr/Ap 2017

Allium fistulosum

THAT SWEET CHAR A. RAPOPORT color *Bon Appetit* no11 p128 N 2017

Allman, Devon

SON'S RISE A. BURGER color *Missouri Life* v44 no2 p24 Ap 2017

Allman, Gregg, 1947-2017

Essential Allman D. Fricke *Rolling Stone* no1290 p49 Je 29 2017

Gregg Allman S. Lansky color *Time* v189 no22 p11 Je 12 2017

Gregg Allman's Last Ride D. BROWNE color *Rolling Stone* no1294 p18 Ag 24 2017

The Last Brother: Gregg Allman 1947-2017 M. Gilmore color *Rolling Stone* no1290 p44 Je 29 2017

Allman Brothers Band (Performer)

The Heart of the Allmans D. TRUCKS and D. FRICKE bw *Rolling Stone* no1281/1282 p19 F 23 2017

The Last Brother: Gregg Allman 1947-2017 M. Gilmore color *Rolling Stone* no1290 p44 Je 29 2017

Allmax Nutrition Inc.

AllMax Nutrition TestoFX color *Muscle & Performance* v9 no10 p64 O 2017

Allotropy

Allotropy by design—Carbon nanohoops J. S. Siegel diag *Science* v356 no6334 p135 Ap 14 2017

Alloys

Transformation of bulk alloys to oxide nanowires D. Lei, J. Benson et al bibl color graph *Science* v355 no6322 p267 Ja 20 2017

Allsop, Chris

Hallowed Ground Bosworth Field, England [Cover story] color *Military History* v34 no4 p76 N 2017

Allstate Corp.

AS BUSINESSES, WE HAVE TO DEFINE OUR ROLE MORE BROADLY *Vital Speeches of the Day* v83 no5 p138 My 2017

Allstate Insurance Co.

BY THE NUMBERS chart *Working Mother* p26 F/Mr 2017

Alluri, Hari

The Flayed City *Publishers Weekly* v264 no8 p62 F 20 2017

Alluvial plains

Hallowed Ground Fort Necessity National Battlefield W. J. Shepherd *Military History* v33 no5 p76 Ja 2017

Allwood, Abigail

X-RAY VISIONARY L. PARKER color *Wired* v25 no10 p20 O 2017

Allworth, James

3 Questions to Get the Most Out of Your Company's Data *Harvard Business Review Digital Articles* p2 Ja 29 2015

How the Apple/FBI Fight Risks the Whole U.S. Tech Industry *Harvard Business Review Digital Articles* p2 F 24 2016

Is OpenAI Solving the Wrong Problem? *Harvard Business Review Digital Articles* p2 D 15 2015

Old Management Systems Stifle New Business Models *Harvard Business Review Digital Articles* p2 Ap 28 2015

Ally Bank (Company)

Best Bets: Online Banks T. Cettina cartoon color *Working Mother* p56 F/Mr 2017

ALLYN, MATT

99 BOTTLES OF IPA ON THE WALL chart color *Popular Mechanics* p71 Ap 2017

Alm, Tove

A subcellular map of the human proteome color *Science* v356 no6340 p820 My 26 2017

Almada, Amalia Aruda

Journey Into the Ocean's Microbiomes color *Oceanus* v51 no2 p68 Wint 2016

Almadoz, Juan

When Having Too Many Experts on the Board Backfires *Harvard Business Review Digital Articles* p2 Ag 29 2016

Al Marzouq, Mohammed—Interviews

A CONVERSATION WITH MOHAMMED AL MARZOUQ *Arabian Horse World* v57 no8 p10 My 2017

Almas, Ingvild

Is It OK to Get Paid More for Being Lucky? color graph *Harvard Business Review Digital Articles* p2 Mr 9 2017

Al-Mashaan, Khaled K.

ALARGAN : Aim To Lead *Foreign Affairs* v95 no6 p120g N/D 2016

Almeida, João

Global atmospheric particle formation from CERN CLOUD measurements bibl graph map *Science* v354 no6316 p1119 D 2 2016

Almeida, Mafalda

PCGF3/5–PRC1 initiates Polycomb recruitment in X chromosome inactivation color *Science* v356 no6342 p1081 Je 9 2017

Almela, A.

Observation of a large-scale anisotropy in the arrival directions of cosmic rays above 8×1018 eV *Science* v357 no6357 p1266 S 22 2017

ALMENDRAL, AURORA

A State of Grief color *National Geographic* v231 no6 p106 Je 2017

Almereyda, Michael

Marjorie Prime E. Taylor color *Film Comment* v53 no4 p72 Jl/Ag 2017

Almodóvar, Pedro, 1949-

Julieta A. Lane *New Yorker* v92 no44 p12 Ja 9 2017

PEDRO ALMODÓVAR color *Vanity Fair* v58 no12 p80 D 2016

Pedro Almodóvar Grows Up J. THOMAS *Advocate* no1088 p60 D 2016/Ja 2017

SOMBRE COLORS D. T. MAX cartoon color *New Yorker* v92 no40 p42 D 5 2016

Almond

ACHE BREAKER [Cover story] color *Prevention* v69 no1 p15 Ja 2017

ASK TUFTS EXPERTS A. H. Lichtenstein *Tufts University Health & Nutrition Letter* v34 no10 p8 D 2016

Beauty's More than Skin Deep L. TURNER color *Better Nutrition* v79 no4 p62 Ap 2017

Dr. Low Dog [Cover story] cartoon color *Prevention* v68 no11 p24 N 2016

THE REAL MOST IMPORTANT MEAL OF THE DAY J. Dean color *Bloomberg Businessweek* no4493 p82 O 3 2016

Weird But True! M. HARRIS color *National Geographic Kids* no474 p4 O 2017

Almond, Ann

LETTER TO THE WORLD *Arabian Horse World* v56 no12 p245 S 2016

Almond milk—Evaluation

MOM ON A MISSION color *Martha Stewart Living* p40 My 2017

Almond—Therapeutic use

Dairy-Free Do's and Don'ts color *Health* v31 no6 p16 Jl 2017

ALMONTE, PAUL

HOW THE WORLD WILL END *America* v215 p32 N 28 2016

Almost Christmas (Film)

Almost Christmas D. Coggan color *Entertainment Weekly* no1440 p43 N 18 2016

Almost Like Praying (Music)

Salvation Song M. Snetiker color *Entertainment Weekly* no1486 p23 O 13 2017

Almquist, Eric

The 30 Things Customers Really Value *Harvard Business Review Digital Articles* p2 Ag 11 2016

Almy, Gerald

Acorn Alternatives color *Field & Stream* v122 no3 pW6 Ag 2017

BARREN OAKS color *Field & Stream* v121 no6 pW4 N 2016

Busted! color *Field & Stream* v122 no4 pW11 S 2017

Extreme Success color *Field & Stream* v121 no6 pW1 N 2016

FOOD-PLOT Rx NOCTURNAL BUCKS color *Field & Stream* v122 no4 pW8 S 2017

Gobblers When It Blows color *Field & Stream* v121 no9 pT4 Ap 2017

Hot Spots color *Field & Stream* v122 no3 pB1 Ag 2017

Stunted Growth color *Field & Stream* v122 no5 pW5 O 2017

Tornado Watch color *Field & Stream* v122 no3 pW11 Ag 2017

Woods Rx: Overexposure color *Field & Stream* v122 no3 pW9 Ag 2017

Al Nahyan, Khalifah ibn Zayid, 1948-
March Racing in Abu Dhabi Featuring Five Stakes Races S. Andersen color *Arabian Horse World* v57 no7 p100 Ap 2017

Aloe
7 WAYS TO LOWER BLOOD SUGAR V. TWEED cartoon graph *Better Nutrition* v78 no11 p62 N 2016
Fall Favorites color *Better Nutrition* v79 no10 p24 O 2017

Aloe (Poem)
Aloe M. J. Salter *American Scholar* v86 no3 p59 Summ 2017

Aloe vera
ALOE AGAIN, NATURALLY color *Prevention* v69 no1 p8 Ja 2017
Aloe M. J. Salter *American Scholar* v86 no3 p59 Summ 2017
Sound and Sense L. HAMMER *American Scholar* v86 no3 p54 Summ 2017

Aloe vera—Therapeutic use
Soothe a Sunburn T. L. Dog color *Prevention* v69 no7 p24 Jl 2017
SOOTHE YOURSELF C. ZULKEY color *Runner's World* v52 no7 p28 Ag 2017

Alomar, Osama
The Teeth of the Comb color *Publishers Weekly* v264 no7 p47 F 13 2017

Alonso, A.
Persistent effects of pre-Columbian plant domestication on Amazonian forest composition bibl chart graph map *Science* v355 no6328 p925 Mr 3 2017

ALONSO, ALEXANDRA DÉLANO
Mexicans in the United States: In Pursuit of Inclusion *Current History* v115 no784 p305 N 2016

Alonso, Alfonso
Plant diversity increases with the strength of negative density dependence at the global scale diag *Science* v356 no6345 p1389 Je 30 2017

Alonso, Axel
MEET MARVEL'S CHIEF MYTHMAKER R. Hackett color *Fortune* v175 no3 p24 Mr 1 2017

Alonso, Jose
Edward Joseph Lofgren *Physics Today* v70 no2 p69 F 2017

Alonso, Laz
STARCATION: WASHINGTON, D.C K. CHANEY color *Ebony* v72 no8 p56 Je 2017

Alonso, Pablo González
Doing Business in a Post-Fidel Cuba *Harvard Business Review Digital Articles* p2 D 19 2016
The Potential and Pitfalls of Doing Business in Cuba *Harvard Business Review Digital Articles* p2 Mr 16 2016
Strategies for Succeeding in Today's Brazil *Harvard Business Review Digital Articles* p2 N 19 2015

Alonso, Shantha Ready—Interviews
Creation stories S. R. Alonso bw color *U.S. Catholic* v82 no11 p32 N 2017

ALONSO-ALVAREZ, CARLOS
The Oxidative Cost of Reproduction: Theoretical Questions and Alternative Mechanisms *BioScience* v67 no3 p258 Mr 2017

Alonso-González, Pablo
Tuning quantum nonlocal effects in graphene plasmonics bw diag *Science* v357 no6347 p187 Jl 14 2017

Alonso-Mori, Roberto
Metalloprotein entatic control of ligand-metal bonds quantified by ultrafast x-ray spectroscopy diag *Science* v356 no6344 p1276 Je 23 2017

Alonzo King LINES Ballet (Performer)
Alonzo King LINES Ballet Gets Musical color *Dance Spirit* v20 no9 p23 N 2016
DancesSPiRiT 2017 Summer Study GUIDE *Dance Spirit* v21 no1 p60 Ja 2017
SUMMER STUDY GUIDE 2017 *Dance Magazine* v91 no1 p140 Ja 2017
why i dance A. Cissoko *Dance Magazine* v91 no4 p72 Ap 2017

Alopecia areata—Patients
Bald Is Beautiful! A. SIMMONS color *Reader's Digest* v190 no1133 p11 S 2017

Alorwoyie, Gideon
Drumming J. DAVIDSON *New York* v49 no24 p154 N 28 2016

Aloui, Kamel
The extent of forest in dryland biomes [Cover story] chart map *Science* v356 no6338 p635 My 12 2017

ALOUSH, ABEER
French Muslims and a Changed Scenario: What does the future hold for France's Muslims after Marine Le Pen's defeat? *Islamic Horizons* v46 no4 p56 Jl/Ag 2017

Aloy, Patrick
Exploring genetic suppression interactions on a global scale diag *Science* v354 no6312 p599 N 4 2016

Alozainah, Salim—Interviews
CITRA: The ICT sector role on boosting Kuwait's economy S. Alozainah color *Foreign Affairs* v95 no6 p120e N/D 2016

Alpenfels, Eric
A GOLF MAGAZINE STUDY IT'S TIME TO CHANGE YOUR AIM color *Golf Magazine* v59 no11 p76 N 2017
HOW MUCH CAN YOU BITE OFF? color *Golf Magazine* v59 no5 p67 My 2017

Alper, E. H.
An unusual white dwarf star may be a surviving remnant of a subluminous Type Ia supernova chart diag *Science* v357 no6352 p680 Ag 18 2017

Alpers, Michael P.
A Neolithic expansion, but strong genetic structure, in the independent history of New Guinea diag *Science* v357 no6356 p1160 S 15 2017

Alpert, Alice
Not Just Another Lovely Summer Day on the Water K. Madin *Oceanus* v52 no1 p30 Summ 2016

Alpert, Herb, 1935-
Alpert Shines Spotlight on Community College Programs B. Zimmerman color *Downbeat* v84 no1 p96 Ja 2017

Alpert, Yelena Moroz
Healing stones color *Yoga Journal* no295 p24 O 2017
Jessamyn Stanley color *Yoga Journal* no287 p78 N 2016
Orange you pretty color *Yoga Journal* no292 p26 Je 2017

Alpeyev, Pavel
At Work With Rent-a-Dad color *Bloomberg Businessweek* no4535 p41 Ag 28 2017
Cashing In on The Fear Factor color *Bloomberg Businessweek* no4495 p35 O 17 2016
How to Lose $6 Billion color graph *Bloomberg Businessweek* no4512 p19 F 20 2017
Japan's Priests Turn to Property Development color *Bloomberg Businessweek* no4521 p38 My 8 2017
A Real Mr. Fusion Feeds on Used Clothing *Bloomberg Businessweek* no4509 p29 Ja 30 2017
Why Japan's Idemitsu Isn't Feeling Blue color *Bloomberg Businessweek* no4520 p34 My 1 2017

Alpha Centauri
75, 50 & 25 YEARS AGO R. W. Sinnott color *Sky & Telescope* v134 no5 p7 N 2017
Breakthrough to the Stars S. NADIS chart color *Discover* v38 no1 p92 Ja/F 2017
EXOPLANETS 1 World Found Around Proxima Centauri C. M. CARLISLE *Sky & Telescope* v132 no6 p10 D 2016
NEAR-LIGHT-SPEED MISSION TO ALPHA CENTAURI [Cover story] A. Finkbeiner color *Scientific American* v316 no3 p30 Mr 2017
Proxima Centauri b Likely a Desert World C. M. CARLISLE *Sky & Telescope* v133 no5 p10 My 2017
To Boldly Go M. DiChristina color *Scientific American* v316 no3 p4 Mr 2017

Alpha Natural Resources Inc.
Footing the Bill D. Slater *Sierra* v101 no6 p22 N/D 2016

Alpha Orthopedics & Sports Medicine (Company)
BEST DOCTORS IN DALLAS [Cover story] *D: The Magazine of Dallas* v43 no10 p174 O 2016

Alpha Sound & Lighting Co.
Audio Design, Service & Rentals *Stage Directions* v30 no7 p5 Jl 1 2017

Alpha-synuclein
Parkinson's may provoke T cells A. CUNNINGHAM *Science News* v192 no1 p14 Ag 5 2017

Alphabet Inc.
4 LARRY PAGE L. Rao color *Fortune* v174 no7 p75 D 1 2016
Alphabet Isn't a Typical Conglomerate N. V. Venkatraman *Harvard Business Review Digital Articles* p2 Ag 18 2015

Alphabet T. Simonite color il *MIT Technology Review* v120 no4 p58 Jl/Ag 2017

THE COMPANIES OF THE YEAR C. Austin color diag *Fortune* v174 no8 p62 D 15 2016

G IS FOR GRAVEYARD R. Hackett color *Fortune* v175 no4 p40 Mr 15 2017

Google's Alphabet Move Is Reorganizing 101 S. Cliffe *Harvard Business Review Digital Articles* p2 Ag 13 2015

Alphabet Inc.—Trials, litigation, etc.

FURY ROAD M. CHAFKIN, M. BERGEN et al color *Bloomberg Businessweek* no4515 p54 Mr 20 2017

WHAT COULD TAKE DOWN UBER? A. Lashinsky color *Fortune* v175 no7 p40 Je 1 2017

Alphabets

A Brief, Alphabetical Love Affair L. MERIWETHER *New York* v49 no15 p16 Jl 25 2016

Oldest alphabet identified as Hebrew B. BOWER color *Science News* v190 no13 p8 D 24 2016

Alphaland (Short story)

Alphaland R. LOMBREGLIA *American Scholar* v86 no3 p91 Summ 2017

Alpine (Ariz.)

Alpine Inn Bed & Breakfast K. MONTGOMERY *Arizona Highways* v93 no8 p14 Ag 2017

Alpinestars SpA

ALPINESTARS TRACK VEST 2 B. Adams color *Cycle World* v56 no4 p28 My 2017

OSCAR BY ALPINESTARS MONTY RIDING SHOE B. Adams color *Cycle World* v56 no1 p18 Ja/F 2017

RIDING GLOVES D. Canet color *Cycle World* v56 no4 p26 My 2017

Alps, French (France)

Chamonix J. Ellison color *Climbing* no355 p34 Ag 2017

The Ultimate Winter Adventure Guide color *Wired* v24 no12 p93 D 2016

Alquraishi, Saleh

Ancient genomic changes associated with domestication of the horse color diag *Science* v356 no6336 p442 Ap 28 2017

Al-Rasheid, Khaled

Ancient genomic changes associated with domestication of the horse color diag *Science* v356 no6336 p442 Ap 28 2017

Al-Razi, Abu Hatim, d. 933

c. 930: Rayy A. H. al-Razi *Lapham's Quarterly* v10 no2 p101 Spr 2017

Al-Rodhan, Nayef

Tomorrow's arsenal color *Science* v354 no6319 p1538 D 23 2016

Alrubail, Rusul

DISRUPTION IN THE CLASSROOM *Literacy Today (2411-7862)* v34 no5 p36 Mr/Ap 2017

ALS, HILTON

ALLIES cartoon *New Yorker* v92 no47 p74 Ja 30 2017

The Art of Difference [Cover story] bw *New York Review of Books* v64 no10 p31 Je 8 2017

BLACK POWER color *New Yorker* v92 no34 p70 O 24 2016

Body Politics color *New Yorker* v93 no10 p26 Ap 24 2017

BULLIES cartoon *New Yorker* v92 no42 p128 D 19 2016

Cinema Scope cartoon *New Yorker* v93 no2 p16 F 27 2017

Club King cartoon *New Yorker* v92 no48 p6 F 6 2017

DEAR HEART color *New Yorker* v92 no40 p84 D 5 2016

FADE TO BLACK bw cartoon *New Yorker* v92 no49 p84 F 13 2017

THE FALL GUYS color *New Yorker* v93 no8 p74 Ap 10 2017

First Star to the Right cartoon *New Yorker* v93 no27 p14 S 11 2017

A GIRL LIKE I cartoon *New Yorker* v92 no32 p106 O 10 2016

GOD ONLY KNOWS cartoon *New Yorker* v93 no3 p80 Mr 6 2017

GOLDEN BOY cartoon *New Yorker* v93 no27 p76 S 11 2017

Let the Sunshine In color *New Yorker* v92 no46 p8 Ja 23 2017

MAD ABOUT THE BOY cartoon *New Yorker* v93 no2 p76 F 27 2017

MOTHER! cartoon *New Yorker* v93 no30 p76 O 2 2017

Mystery Woman cartoon *New Yorker* v92 no33 p10 O 17 2016

Odd Man In color *New Yorker* v93 no32 p8 O 16 2017

Paging Geraldine cartoon *New Yorker* v92 no49 p23 F 13 2017

PARTNERS color *New Yorker* v93 no4 p82 Mr 13 2017

Primal Edge cartoon *New Yorker* v93 no6 p6 Mr 27 2017

REWIND cartoon *New Yorker* v93 no12 p74 My 8 2017

SHOWOFFS cartoon *New Yorker* v92 no36 p80 N 7 2016

THE SICK ROOM color *New Yorker* v93 no20 p90 Jl 10 2017

THE STAR color *New Yorker* v93 no11 p60 My 1 2017

Stoking the Fire cartoon *New Yorker* v92 no40 p13 D 5 2016

Time Flies cartoon *New Yorker* v92 no42 p20 D 19 2016

WORKED cartoon *New Yorker* v92 no39 p94 N 28 2016

Al Sabah, Meshaal Jaber Al Ahmad a.—Interviews

KDIPA: Changing the business landscape in Kuwait M. J. Al Ahmad A. Al Sabah *Foreign Affairs* v95 no6 p120d N/D 2016

ALSADIR, NUAR

ALTER EGO color *O, The Oprah Magazine* p72 Ja 2017

Alsaeed, N.

Mars' atmospheric history derived from upper-atmosphere measurements of 38 Ar/36Ar diag *Science* v355 no6332 p1408 Mr 31 2017

Alsaid, Adi

North of Happy *Publishers Weekly* v264 no6 p70 F 6 2017

Alsaleh, Ahmad

Q: Who Is the Worst Leader of All Time? color *Atlantic* v319 no1 p100 Ja/F 2017

Al Saleh, Raed

the healers bw *Foreign Policy* no221 p89 N/D 2016

Al Samarai, I.

Observation of a large-scale anisotropy in the arrival directions of cosmic rays above 8×1018 eV *Science* v357 no6357 p1266 S 22 2017

Al Saud, Mohammad bin Salman, ca. 1985-

Saudi Women In the Driver's Seat T. John color *Time* v190 no14 p10 O 9 2017

The Startling Rise of the Brash Young Man Who Would Be King of Saudi Arabia I. Bremmer color *Time* v190 no2/3 p10 Jl 10-17 2017

Al Saʿūd, Salmān ibn ʿAbd al-ʾAzīz, King of Saudi Arabia, 1935-

'Principled Realism' R. M. GERECHT color *Weekly Standard* v22 no38 p24 Je 12 2017

Alsever, Jennifer

THE BEST SMALL AND MEDIUM-SIZE COMPANIES TO WORK FOR color map *Fortune* v174 no6 p51 N 1 2016

Big Food Swallows the Meal-Kit Hype color *Fortune* v176 no4 p27 S 15 2017

Cannabiz Hype Is About to Go Up in Smoke color *Fortune* v174 no8 p15 D 15 2016

FOR THOSE TIRED OF TRUMP NEWS, THERE'S A PLUG-IN FOR THAT color *Fortune* v176 no1 p10 Jl 1 2017

IS THIS ROBOT A FRIEND—OR A FOE? color diag *Fortune* v175 no4 p22 Mr 15 2017

THE KINDLE EFFECT chart color *Fortune* v75 no1 p32 Ja 1 2017

THE RISE OF SYNTHETIC DNA color *Fortune* v175 no2 p19 F 1 2017

ROCKET BOOM IN THE DESERT color *Fortune* v175 no3 p20 Mr 1 2017

TOTAL ECLIPSE OF HOTEL AVAILABILITY color *Fortune* v176 no1 p11 Jl 1 2017

TURNING WASTE INTO GOLD (OR COPPER) color *Fortune* v175 no8 p66 Je 15 2017

WANTED: FRESH SOLUTIONS FOR AGE-OLD PROBLEMS color diag *Fortune* v175 no6 p68 My 1 2017

WHERE DOES THE ALGORITHM SEE YOU IN 10 YEARS? color *Fortune* v175 no7 p74 Je 1 2017

AL-SHAMMARI, KHALAF F.

An Ecoregion-Based Approach to Protecting Half the Terrestrial Realm *BioScience* v67 no6 p534 Je 2017

Al Shaqab, Marwan

Wortex Kalliste J. Wintersteen color *Arabian Horse World* v57 no7 p116 Ap 2017

Al-Sharif, Manal, 1980-

Driving While Female P. KARIM *Ms.* v27 no2 p43 Summ 2017

ALSPAUGH, LEANN DAVIS

A Rebel's Faith bw *Weekly Standard* v22 no34 p45 My 15 2017

Surface Depth cartoon *Weekly Standard* v22 no17 p37 Ja 2 2017

ALSUP, WENDY

RE-COVERING GOD'S PROTECTION FOR WOMEN color *Christianity Today* v61 no7 p60 S 2017

SAVED THROUGH CHILD-BEARING color *Christianity Today*

v60 no10 p54 D 2016

Alt, Clemens

Self-renewal of a purified Tie2+ hematopoietic stem cell population relies on mitochondrial clearance bibl graph *Science* v354 no6316 p1156 D 2 2016

Alt, Jeremiah

The Prescription color *Men's Health* v31 no10 p12 D 2016

Alt-J (Performer)

Alt-J color *Rolling Stone* no1289 p58 Je 15 2017

Alt-Right (Political science)

THE BIRTH OF A NOTION S. RATHOD *Mother Jones* v42 no1 p28 Ja/F 2017

THE MOVEMENT HAS A REAL PROBLEM WITH WOMEN img *New York* v50 no9 p44 My 1 2017

POPPING THE RED PILL E. G. ELLIS color graph *Wired* v25 no10 p28 O 2017

THEY'VE CREATED HEIR OWN MEDIA ECOSYSTEM N. RICHARDSON img *New York* v50 no9 p46 My 1 2017

TO UNDERSTAND THIS NEW RIGHT, IT HELPS TO SEE IT NOT AS A FRINGE MOVEMENT, BUT A POWERFUL COUNTERCULTURE N. MALONE, M. Read et al img *New York* v50 no9 p24 My 1 2017

WHAT ARE THE ROOTS OF THIS RAGE?: A few theories, not all of them having to do entirely with race *New York* v50 no9 p42 My 1 2017

When Hate Goes Mainstream T. KHANDAKER color *Walrus* v14 no9 p14 N 2017

WHICH IS WHY THE MOVEMENT EXPRESSES ITSELF IS WAY: Memes of the alt-right img *New York* v50 no9 p36 My 1 2017

WHY TRUMP CAN'T QUIT THE ALT-RIGHT M. Taibbi color *Rolling Stone* no1295 p28 S 7 2017

WITH STRANGE TOTEMS ... img *New York* v50 no9 p38 My 1 2017

Alta Motors (Company)

AT PLAY M. Hoyer color *Cycle World* v56 no3 p52 Ap 2017

UNPLUG + PLAY S. Anderson color *Cycle World* v56 no3 p46 Ap 2017

Altar de Sacrificios site (Guatemala)

DISPATCHES FROM THE AIA color *Archaeology* v70 no3 p65 My/Je 2017

Altchek, Chris

CHRIS ALTCHEK J. Chen color *Bloomberg Businessweek* no4517 p75 Ap 3 2017

Altebrando, Tara

The Possible color *Publishers Weekly* v264 no18 p60 My 1 2017

Altehenger, Jennifer

CHAPTERS IN CHINA'S LONG HISTORY *History Today* v67 no5 p104 My 2017

Alter, Adam

IRRESISTIBLE: The business of technology is the business of addiction *Saturday Evening Post* v289 no4 p12 Jl/Ag 2017

Alter, Allan

5 Ways Product Design Needs to Evolve for the Internet of Things *Harvard Business Review Digital Articles* p2 N 14 2014

Business Processes Are Learning to Hack Themselves *Harvard Business Review Digital Articles* p2 Je 27 2016

Companies Are Reimagining Business Processes with Algorithms *Harvard Business Review Digital Articles* p2 F 8 2016

How Companies Are Using Machine Learning to Get Faster and More Efficient *Harvard Business Review Digital Articles* p2 My 3 2016

Alter, Cathy

HOW TO SELL A $12 MILLION HOUSE color *Washingtonian Magazine* v52 no7 p52 Ap 2017

my night in the doghouse *Washingtonian Magazine* v52 no11 p60 Ag 2017

Alter, Charlotte

After the Massacre [Cover story] color diag *Time* v190 no15 p22 O 16 2017

The Angels of Irma [Cover story] color map *Time* v190 no12 p34 S 25 2017

An Attack on Girlhood color *Time* v189 no21 p37 Je 5 2017

Bottom Lines [Cover story] color *Time* v188 no20 p28 N 14 2016

The Campus Culture Wars color *Time* v190 no16/17 p48 O 23 2017

Emotional Divide color diag *Time* v189 no7/8 p38 F 27 2017

Hate Incidents Sow Fear Across U.S color *Time* v189 no9 p13 Mr 13 2017

Hillary Clinton color *Time* v188 no25-26 p92 D 19 2016 Double Issue

Houston After Harvey color *Time* v190 no10/11 p38 S 18 2017

How She Lost color *Time* v188 no21 p58 N 21 2016

Lightbox color *Time* v190 no16/17 p24 O 23 2017

A New Abortion Landscape color *Time* v188 no22-23 p29 N/D 2016

New Friends, Common Foe color *Time* v189 no3 p40 Ja 30 2017

The New Scarlet Letter color *Time* v190 no2/3 p60 Jl 10-17 2017

Next Generation Leaders color *Time* v188 no15 p41 O 17 2016

Next Generation Leaders color *Time* v189 no9 p38 Mr 13 2017

Now What? color *Time* v188 no21 p42 N 21 2016

The Other Side [Cover story] color diag *Time* v189 no4 p24 F 6 2017

Power Tools: Artists color *Time* v189 no16/17 p62 My 1-8 2017

Power Tools: Icons color *Time* v189 no16/17 p150 My 1-8 2017

Power Tools: Leaders color *Time* v189 no16/17 p90 My 1-8 2017

Power Tools: Pioneers color *Time* v189 no16/17 p36 My 1-8 2017

Power Tools: Titans color *Time* v189 no16/17 p118 My 1-8 2017

Trump Goes to War [Cover story] color *Time* v188 no16/17 p20 O 24 2016

Trump's Immigration Crackdown Seems Designed to Spread Fear color *Time* v189 no7/8 p15 F 27 2017

The Truth Is Out There color *Time* v188 no15 p28 O 17 2016

The United Patients of America color *Time* v190 no4 p28 Jl 24 2017

When Millennials Rule color *Time* v190 no16/17 p88 O 23 2017

Why It's Still Legal for Underage Girls to Marry in the U.S color *Time* v189 no22 p15 Je 12 2017

ALTER, ELINA

The Fiction of Everyday Life color *Publishers Weekly* v264 no8 p52 F 20 2017

LOST IN TRANSLATION bw color *Publishers Weekly* v264 no1 p31 Ja 2 2017

Whose Reality Is It? color *Publishers Weekly* v264 no35 p101 Ag 28 2017

Alter, Jonathan

I WISH TO HELL I'D JUST KEPT SAYING THE EXACT SAME THING *New York Times Magazine* p40 Ja 22 2017

Trans-Atlantic Populism *New York Times Book Review* p24 O 9 2016

War Paint: The unexpected power of George W. Bush's book of paintings color *New York Times Book Review* p17 Ap 23 2017

Alter, Robert

The Diaspora of Jewish Thought *New York Times Book Review* p13 N 20 2016

The Great Genius of Jewish Literature bw *New York Review of Books* v64 no6 p35 Ap 6 2017

Alterg Inc.

TECH RX *Cincinnati Magazine* v50 no4 p77 Ja 2017

Alterman, Eddie

Editor's Letter *Car & Driver* v62 no11 p12 My 2017

Editor's Letter *Car & Driver* v62 no6 p15 D 2016

Editor's Letter *Car & Driver* v62 no8 p8 F 2017

Editor's Letter *Car & Driver* v63 no1 p12 Jl 2017

The Smart Appliance color graph *Car & Driver* v62 no7 p76 Ja 2017

Alterman, Eric

Bromance News il *Nation* v303 no20 p6 N 14 2016

A Climate of Denial color il *Nation* v305 no1 p6 Jl 3 2017

The Crime of Obama's Cool il *Nation* v304 no1 p10 Ja 2 2017 The Obama Years

Fox in the White House color il *Nation* v305 no5 p6 Ag 28 2017

Game, Set, Match *Nation* v304 no13 p6 Ap 17 2017

The Hatreds They Share *Nation* v305 no6 p10 S 11 2017

Hot Air il *Nation* v303 no18 p8 O 31 2016

Kafka Wouldn't Dare il *Nation* v304 no11 p6 Ap 3 2017

Liar and Lunatic *Nation* v305 no11 p8 O 30 2017

The Mogul Empire bw diag *Nation* v304 no7 p6 Mr 6 2017

The Real Big Lie il *Nation* v305 no7 p6 S 25 2017

Secretary of Genocide bw *Nation* v304 no5 p6 F 20 2017

The Serfdom of the Press il *Nation* v304 no3 p10 Ja 30 2017

Speak for Yourselves il *Nation* v303 no16 p6 O 17 2016

MCCABE & MRS. MILLER F. Kaplan color *Sound & Vision* v82 no5 p67 Je 2017

Altman, Sam

ADDING A ZERO T. FRIEND cartoon *New Yorker* v92 no32 p68 O 10 2016

Sam Altman J. Crelin color *Current Biography* v78 no4 p7 Ap 2017

Altmann, Karl-Heinz

RNA polymerase motions during promoter melting color diag graph *Science* v356 no6340 p863 My 26 2017

ALTOBELLO, BRIAN

World War I CENTENNIAL bw *New Orleans Magazine* v51 no12 p92 O 2017

Altobello, Craig

Pictures Hidden in Wood A. GRAVES and M. FLEMING color *Yankee* p40 Mr 2017

Altopp-Miller, Shelli

Our Bodies. No Shame color *Glamour* v115 no9 p32 S 2017

Altra Footwear (Company)

FEED YOUR LUST FOR ADVENTURE color *Men's Health* v31 no10 p(Sp)4 D 2016

Altrichter, Mariana

Forest conservation: Remember Gran Chaco bibl color *Science* v355 no6324 p465 F 3 2017

Altruism

Bridge Builder A. JUNG color *Reader's Digest* v190 no1133 p8 S 2017

DOWN WITH EXTREMES! HEALTH, WELL-BEING, AND SUCCESS REST ON ONE PRINCIPLE: IN ALL THINGS MODERATION C. FLORA *Psychology Today* v50 no4 p80 Ag 2017

STATES OF ALARM M. HUSTON *Psychology Today* v50 no5 p14 S/O 2017

Altschuler, Max

When You Have to Fire Good People color *Harvard Business Review Digital Articles* p2 Mr 3 2017

Altschwager, Kelly

Fit for Your Ride [Cover story] color *Horse & Rider* v56 no5 p60 My 2017

ALTSHUL, SARA

Walk This Way color *AARP: The Magazine* v60 no4A p17 Je/Jl 2017

Altstedter, Ari

Limiting a Drug's Use To Maintain Its Efficacy *Bloomberg Businessweek* no4507 p20 Ja 16 2017

Medical Journals Have a Problem color *Bloomberg Businessweek* no4536 p52 S 4 2017

A Miracle Drug Big Pharma Doesn't Want color graph *Bloomberg Businessweek* no4517 p22 Ap 3 2017

Opening the Door For Future Drug Sales color *Bloomberg Businessweek* no4533 p15 Ag 7 2017

Altucher, James

Stop Believing That You Have to Be Perfect D. Clark *Harvard Business Review Digital Articles* p2 O 8 2014

Altug, H.

Breaking Lorentz reciprocity to overcome the time-bandwidth limit in physics and engineering bw diag graph *Science* v356 no6344 p1260 Je 23 2017

Altuzarra (Company)

THE HERO N. FRITTON color *Harper's Bazaar* no3648 p74 N 2016

Altwegg, K.

Xenon isotopes in 67P/Churyumov-Gerasimenko show that comets contributed to Earth's atmosphere diag *Science* v356 no6342 p1069 Je 9 2017

Aluko, Eniola, 1987-

Eniola Aluko J. Crelin color *Current Biography* v77 no10 p3 O 2016

Aluminum

See also

Aluminum foil

HOW TO CHOOSE THE BEST COOKWARE color *Good Housekeeping* v265 no4 p64f O 2017

Installing Clapboards R. Tschoepe diag *Old House Journal* v45 no4 p58 Je 2017

Aluminum foil

Aluminum Foil T. BROWN JR. color *Backpacker* p40 O 2017

Low-Tech Eclipse Viewing: What to do if you're caught without optics on eclipse day J. Oltion color *Sky & Telescope* v134 no2 p66 Ag 2017

Aluminum industry—China

Will Trump Crush China Over Aluminum? J. Deaux color *Bloomberg Businessweek* no4510 p22 F 6 2017

Aluminum sculpture

Liquid Lens color *Art in America* v105 no1 p18 Ja 2017

Alumni associations

Hostile Takeover High V. SILVER color *Bloomberg Businessweek* no4541 p46 O 9 2017

ALVAR, MIA

Aftershocks *New York Times Book Review* p13 F 19 2017

Alvaré, Helen

Answering Our Daughters *America* v215 no15 p14 N 14 2016

Francis' Heavy Lift color *America* v216 no7 p54 Ap 3 2017

Alvarez, Adriana

The Fast-Food Worker B. Austen *New York Times Magazine* p40 F 26 2017

Alvarez, Ana M.

Preserving a Marsh for People and Wildlife: The Dotson Family Marsh *Parks & Recreation* v52 no2 p28 F 2017

Alvarez, Candida

CANDIDA'S COLORING BOOK J. FOUMBERG color *Chicago* v66 no5 p43 My 2017

Alvarez, Canelo

Keys to a Canelo upset ... B. Baskin color *Sports Illustrated* v127 no6 p56 Ag 28 2017

PICK A FIGHT T. Keith chart color *Sports Illustrated* v127 no8 p18 S 18 2017

Alvarez, Diego D.

A disynaptic feedback network activated by experience promotes the integration of new granule cells bibl graph *Science* v354 no6311 p459 O 28 2016

Alvarez, Joshua

Battle of the Banned color *Washington Monthly* v49 no6-8 p7 Je-Ag 2017

CONTRACTOR CEOS SHOULDN'T MAKE TEN TIMES MORE THAN THE POTUS *Washington Monthly* v49 no6-8 p33 Je-Ag 2017

REWRITING THE RULES OF BEDTIME *Psychology Today* v50 no2 p20 Mr/Ap 2017

THE TWELVE MOST INNOVATIVE COLLEGES FOR ADULT LEARNERS color *Washington Monthly* v49 no9/10 p38 S/O 2017

Alvarez, Julia

American Dreams, 1963 *America* v216 no5 p38 Mr 6 2017

Alvarez, Ted

Come Out and Play color *Backpacker* p84 Je 2017

Day DREAMING: The best dayhike in every state color *Backpacker* p52 S 2017

Make Hiking Great Again color il *Backpacker* p18 Je 2017

PIPE DREAM color *Backpacker* v45 no1 p77 Ja 2017

SECRETS OF THE GUIDES color il *Backpacker* p75 Ag 2017

WHERE NOBODY KNOWS YOUR TRAIL NAME color *Backpacker* v45 no1 p80 Ja 2017

Alvarez, Walter

4.5 billion years of human history E. Underwood color *Science News* v190 no10 p28 N 12 2016

Against all odds J. S. Schneiderinan bibl color *Science* v354 no6312 p559 N 4 2016

Alvarez family

Great Dynasties of Science *Discover* v38 no4 p48 My 2017

Alvarez-Buylla, Arturo

Extensive migration of young neurons into the infant human frontal lobe color diag graph *Science* v354 no6308 paaf7073-1 O 7 2016

Alvarez-Castelao, Beatriz

Activity-dependent spatially localized miRNA maturation in neuronal dendrites bibl graph *Science* v355 no6325 p634 F 10 2017

Alvarez Castillo, J.

Observation of a large-scale anisotropy in the arrival directions of cosmic rays above 8×10^{18} eV *Science* v357 no6357 p1266 S 22 2017

Alvarez-Loayza, Patricia

Positive biodiversity-productivity relationship predominant in global forests bibl chart graph map *Science* v354 no6309 paaf8957-1 O 14 2016

Alvarez-Muniz, J.

Observation of a large-scale anisotropy in the arrival directions of cosmic rays above 8 × 1018 eV *Science* v357 no6357 p1266 S 22 2017

Alver, Bonnie

Deep functional analysis of synII, a 770-kilobase synthetic yeast chromosome diag *Science* v355 no6329 p1047 Mr 10 2017

Alverson, Bridget

BookWalker Offers Digital Manga And Light Novels in English *Publishers Weekly* v263 no46 p12 N 14 2016

Alverson, Brigid

Pioneering NBM Marks 40 Years of Graphic Novels color *Publishers Weekly* v264 no21 p12 My 22 2017

VISUALIZING THE THIRD REICH color *Publishers Weekly* v264 no39 p55 S 25 2017

Alves, Jorge

Pipe Dream A. Prewitt and T. Keith color *Sports Illustrated* v126 no1 p14 Ja 9 2017

ALVES, JOSÉ A.

From Agricultural Benefits to Aviation Safety: Realizing the Potential of Continent-Wide Radar Networks *BioScience* v67 no10 p912 O 2017

ALVI, TALIA

Making Emotional and Spiritual Hijrah in the Post-Election Era *Islamic Horizons* v46 no1 p30 Ja/F 2017

Alvin Ailey American Dance Theater

Dancer with Alvin Ailey American Dance Theater R. McLaren *Dance Magazine* v91 no9 p72 S 2017

GOINGS ON ABOUT TOWN color *New Yorker* v92 no40 p9 D 5 2016

Alward, Donna

Someone to Love: Darling, Vt., Book 2 *Publishers Weekly* v264 no6 p52 F 6 2017

Always This Way (Music)

Singles Swap K. O'Donnell color *Entertainment Weekly* no1459 p61 Mr 31 2017

Alwyn, Joe

Hot Actor Joe Alwyn D. FEAR color *Rolling Stone* no1274 p41 N 17 2016

INTO THE COUNTRY J. BLACK color *Esquire* v166 no5 p122 D 2016/Ja 2017

Alÿs, Francis

FRANCIS ALŸS E. Fullerton color *Art in America* v104 no10 p160 N 2016

ALYSSA, CALEY

Turn Your Practice UPSIDE DOWN [Cover story] color *Yoga Journal* no293 p82 Ag 2017

Alzheimer's disease

Alzheimer's and the 15-Year Window M. Cohen color *Prevention* v69 no8 p80 Ag 2017

Big Data May Lead to Earlier Alzheimer's Diagnosis L. MARSA color graph *Discover* v38 no1 p23 Ja/F 2017

Brain health should be top of mind M. Wadman color *Science* v354 no6310 p277 O 21 2016

Deciphering microglial diversity in Alzheimer's disease G. C. Brown and P. H. St George-Hyslop color *Science* v356 no6343 p1123 Je 16 2017

Dissecting the effects of APOE *Science* v355 no6326 p707 F 17 2017

DOING GOOD S. Pulia color *InStyle* v24 no11 p66 N 2017

Elderly chimps may get Alzheimer's disease R. Cross color *Science* v357 no6350 p440 Ag 4 2017

"I THOUGHT I HAD ALZHEIMER'S" M. COHEN color *Prevention* v69 no11 p54 N 2017

Ladies, Check Your BRAINS M. SHRIVER color *O, The Oprah Magazine* p68 Je 2017

MOTHERS DAUGHTERS STRANGERS A. ROSS color *Women's Health* v14 no2 p152 Mr 2017

POWER [Cover story] C. J. Rottman, W. H. Camp II et al color *Christian Century* v134 no1 p22 Ja 4 2017

Site-specific phosphorylation of tau inhibits amyloid-β toxicity in Alzheimer's mice A. Ittner, Sook Wern Chua et al bibl graph *Science* v354 no6314 p904 N 18 2016

TRIAL JUDGMENT J. CHRISTIAN JENSENIUS and N. S. CAPLAN *Scientific American* v317 no2 p5 Ag 2017

THE UNBLINDING A. WREN *Indianapolis Monthly* v40 no3 p100 N 2016

What can you do to avoid Alzheimer's disease? *Harvard Health Letter* v42 no4 p3 F 2017

Alzheimer's disease prevention

CAN ALZHEIMER'S DISEASE BE PREVENTED? E. A. Kane color *Amazing Wellness* v9 no3 p30 EarlySumm 2017

DEFEATING ALZHEIMER'S J. Bowden color *Better Nutrition* v79 no11 p54 N 2017

Keeping the Future in Mind M. DiChristina *Scientific American* v316 no4 p4 Ap 2017

Mind Games *Prevention* v69 no5 p3 My 2017

Minor Memory Lapse... or Something More? V. TWEED *Better Nutrition* v79 no9 p72 S 2017

Remember When? E. A. KANE color *Better Nutrition* v79 no1 p32 Ja 2017

What can you do to avoid Alzheimer's disease? *Harvard Health Letter* v42 no4 p3 F 2017

Alzheimer's disease risk factors

Alzheimer's-linked gene is triple threat T. H. SAEY color *Science News* v192 no6 p13 O 14 2017

Better Diet and Sleep Might Help Protect Your Brain [Cover story] *Tufts University Health & Nutrition Letter* v34 no9 p1 N 2016

DEFEATING ALZHEIMER'S J. Bowden color *Better Nutrition* v79 no11 p54 N 2017

The Fight for Women's Minds color *Prevention* v69 no6 p20 Je 2017

Will Limiting Red Meat Help Stave Off Alzheimer's? *Tufts University Health & Nutrition Letter* v34 no11 p6 Ja 2017

Alzheimer's disease treatment

Brain waves fight Alzheimer's protein L. SANDERS color *Science News* v191 no1 p13 Ja 21 2017

Can immunotherapy treat neurodegeneration? M. Schwartz color *Science* v357 no6348 p254 Jl 21 2017

Promising Alzheimer's drug will test amyloid hypothesis L. Sanders color *Science News* v190 no13 p27 D 24 2016

Alzheimer's disease—Diagnosis

My Lab Is Studying an Alzheimer's Treatment. Can I Try It on Myself? K. A. Appiah *New York Times Magazine* p18 F 12 2017

Alzheimer's disease—Economic aspects

Bearing the Financial Burden of Alzheimer's L. Braham *Bloomberg Businessweek* no4493 p54 O 3 2016

Alzheimer's disease—Physiological aspects

RESEARCH color *Science* v357 no6347 p159 Jl 14 2017

Alzheimer's disease—Research

My Lab Is Studying an Alzheimer's Treatment. Can I Try It on Myself? K. A. Appiah *New York Times Magazine* p18 F 12 2017

New citizen science project turns Alzheimer's research into a game L. Sanders *Science News* v190 no11 p28 N 26 2016

Alzheimer's patients

Discoveries From the Deepest Sleep J. Ingram color *Canadian Wildlife* v22 no5 p13 N/D 2016

SECRETS OF THE DEAD B. Reilly *Saturday Evening Post* v289 no3 p56 My/Je 2017

Alzheimer's patients—Care

Two Ways to Better Care for Patients with Dementia S. H. Jain and J. Pratty *Harvard Business Review Digital Articles* p2 Ag 11 2015

Alzheimer's patients—Family relationships

Love in an Age of Alzheimer's J. Ruck color *America* v216 no6 p32 Mr 20 2017

Alzheimer's patients—Research

Bearing the Financial Burden of Alzheimer's L. Braham *Bloomberg Businessweek* no4493 p54 O 3 2016

Alzheimer's patients—Services for

ANTHONY ANDERSON'S MISSION M. L. Lenker color *Entertainment Weekly* no1471 p18 Je 23 2017

A&M Truck Center Corp.

Country REVIVAL: HOW THE STRAIGHT-TALKING, COYOTE-SHOOTING, TOBACCO CHEWING JOHN SHARP HAS LED A BONANZA AT TEXAS A&M M. HARDY *Texas Monthly* v45 no8 p78 Ag 2017

Amado, Jorge

MISCELLANY *Lapham's Quarterly* v10 no2 p208 Spr 2017

STORM WARNING *Lapham's Quarterly* v10 no3 p107 Summ 2017

Aman, M. Javad

A "Trojan horse" bispecific-antibody strategy for broad protection against ebolaviruses bibl graph *Science* v354 no6310 p350 O 21 2016

Amancha, Praveen K.

Sustained virologic control in SIV+ macaques after antiretroviral and α4β7 antibody therapy bibl graph *Science* v354 no6309 p197 O 14 2016

Amanda Knox (Film)

Amanda Knox K. P. Sullivan color *Entertainment Weekly* no1434 p42 O 7 2016

NOW PLAYING color *Entertainment Weekly* no1435 p45 O 14 2016

Amann, M.

A climate policy pathway for near- and long-term benefits color *Science* v356 no6337 p493 My 5 2017

Amano, Takashi

How to Lose $6 Billion color graph *Bloomberg Businessweek* no4512 p19 F 20 2017

Amanpour, Christiane

Bono color *Glamour* v114 no12 p212 D 2016

CRISIS OF THE HEART color *Vanity Fair* v59 no9 p217 S 2017

How Did I Get Here? CHRISTIANE AMANPOUR bw color *Bloomberg Businessweek* no4520 p76 My 1 2017

Amanullah, R.

iPTF16geu: A multiply imaged, gravitationally lensed type Ia supernova color diag graph *Science* v356 no6335 p291 Ap 21 2017

Amar, Akhil Reed

Frank Exchange T. HELFMAN color *Weekly Standard* v22 no9 p32 N 7 2016

Our Timeless, Timely Constitution J. Waldron bw cartoon *New York Review of Books* v64 no7 p50 Ap 20 2017

Amaranthus palmeri

Palmer amaranth is bedeviling farmers like no other weed. Ultimately, though, tools exist to defeat it G. Gullickson *Successful Farming* v115 no5 p32 Mid-Mr 2017

PALMER PLAGUES CRP ACRES K. Birchmier *Successful Farming* v115 no5 p40 Mid-Mr 2017

Amaryllis (Genus)

AROUND THE GARDEN S. Bender color map *Southern Living* v51 no12 p62 D 2016

Your CHECKLIST E. Jardina color *Sunset* v237 no5 p48 N 2016

Amate-Fortes, Ignacio

Determinants of Child Health Inequalities in Developing Countries: a New Perspective chart diag *Society* v53 no6 p641 D 2016

Amateur astronomy

Double star marathon redux G. CHAPLE color *Astronomy* v45 no3 p64 Mr 2017

Going for gold B. BERMAN color *Astronomy* v45 no3 p10 Mr 2017

The need for dark skies map *Astronomy* v45 no9 p6 S 2017

The Real Origins of Amateur Telescope Making K. Venables *Sky & Telescope* v133 no5 p22 My 2017

Restoring an Ellison Reflector *Sky & Telescope* v133 no5 p26 My 2017

Seek Exoplanets From Your Backyard D. CONTI color diag *Discover* v38 no2 p64 Mr 2017

Amateur athletes

The Biggest Mistakes Nonpro Riders Make B. Avila and J. Paulson color *Horse & Rider* v56 no4 p35 Ap 2017

FACES IN THE CROWD T. Keith color *Sports Illustrated* v126 no16 p32 Je 5 2017

FACES IN THE CROWD T. Keith color *Sports Illustrated* v126 no9 p26 Mr 27 2017

Amateur plays

See also

College & school drama

HIGH SCHOOL THEATRE HONORS PROGRAM L. Mulcahy *Stage Directions* v29 no11 p24 N 2016

Amateurs

See also

Amateur athletes

Kavar Kerr's Legacy of Service T. Booker *In Stride* v12 no3 p45

My 2017

Amay, Joane

BEAUTY & THE BEAT color *Ebony* v72 no6 p44 Ap/My 2017

COUNTRY ROOTS color *Ebony* v72 no9 p46 Jl/Ag 2017

CULTURAL WAVES color *Ebony* v72 no9 p40 Jl/Ag 2017

Divine Locs color *Ebony* v72 no9 p42 Jl/Ag 2017

FALL'S TOP NOTES bw color *Ebony* v72/73 no12/1 p50 O/N 2017

Forever Young color *Ebony* v72 no9 p92 Jl/Ag 2017

glowed UP color *Ebony* v72/73 no12/1 p48 O/N 2017

Great Innovators color *Ebony* v72 no5 p44 Mr 2017

HOLIDAY GIFT GUIDE color *Ebony* v72 no3 p51 D 2016/Ja 2017

JANET JACKSON color *Ebony* v72/73 no12/1 p56 O/N 2017

MANE MATTERS color *Ebony* v72/73 no12/1 p52 O/N 2017

ONE-CLICK WONDERS color *Ebony* v72 no5 p42 Mr 2017

STILL SLAYED color *Ebony* v72/73 no12/1 p42 O/N 2017

Amazing Horse Woman LLC

WELCOME TO THE AUCTION AND FUTURITY PROGRAM *Arabian Horse World* v57 no4 p10 Ja 2017

Amazing Spider-Man 2, The (Film)

Spider-Man, Ranked E. Dockterman color *Time* v190 no5 p59 Jl 31 2017

Amazon Content Services LLC

AMAZON BECOMES A PUBLISHING FORCE *Publishers Weekly* v263 no47 p34 N 21 2016

Amazon Echo (Smart speaker)

Alexa Takes the Stand: Listening Devices Raise Privacy Issues H. S. Edwards color *Time* v189 no18 p28 My 15 2017

HOME SMART HOME K. PITSKER bw color *Kiplinger's Personal Finance* v71 no10 p64 O 2017

STILL the BEST [Cover story] bw color *Popular Science* v289 no6 p70 N/D 2017

Talk to Your Home D. Pogue cartoon *AARP: The Magazine* v60 no2A p16 F/Mr 2017

Your Echo Is Listening D. Pogue color *Scientific American* v316 no3 p28 Mr 2017

Amazon River Valley

Amazon Atlantis A. Posada-Swafford color map *Scientific American* v317 no1 p12 Jl 2017

Lab tests aren't the answer for every science question E. Quill *Science News* v191 no6 p2 Ap 1 2017

Amazon River Watershed

By the Numbers RAIN FOREST J. BEER and M. HARRIS *National Geographic Kids* no468 p8 Mr 2017

Amazon.com Inc.

2 JEFF BEZOS L. Rao color *Fortune* v174 no7 p74 D 1 2016

50 MOST ENGAGED COMPANIES *Forbes* v200 no5 p76 N 14 2017

5 Ways to Save Money on Amazon B. Tuttle color *Money* v46 no8 p21 S 2017

Alexa, at Your Command K. PITSKER color *Kiplinger's Personal Finance* v71 no1 p37 Ja 2017

Alexa: Is There a Safer Way to Bet on the Amazon Economy? J. Waggoner diag *Money* v46 no8 p38 S 2017

Alexa, please define knowledge E. Sundrup color *America* v216 no4 p51 F 20 2017

"Alexa, Understand Me" G. Anders *MIT Technology Review* v120 no5 p26 S/O 2017

AMAZON BOOKS LOCATIONS, MARCH 2017 map *Publishers Weekly* v264 no13 p4 Mr 27 2017

Amazon Books Spreads Out J. Milliot *Publishers Weekly* v264 no13 p4 Mr 27 2017

Amazon Buy-Button Change Raises Alarms, Questions J. Milliot *Publishers Weekly* v264 no20 p4 My 15 2017

Amazon Echo Dot: This is the Echo most people should buy M. BROWN color *PCWorld* v35 no1 p101 Ja 2017

Amazon Goes After The Walmart Shopper S. Soper and C. Giammona *Bloomberg Businessweek* no4508 p19 Ja 23 2017

Amazon Is Right That Disagreement Results in Better Decisions C. R. Sunstein *Harvard Business Review Digital Articles* p2 Ag 18 2015

Amazon Is the Big First-Quarter Winner J. Milliot chart *Publishers Weekly* v264 no15 p16 Ap 10 2017

Amazon's acquisition of Whole Foods is not only a clash between online and brick-and-mortar retail—it is also one between vastly different visions for the future of service work J. Herrman *New York Times Magazine* p16 Jl 23 2017

Amazon's Brick-and-Mortar Store Shouldn't Come as a Surprise A. Bernstein *Harvard Business Review Digital Articles* p2 O 10 2014

Amazon, Whole Foods, and the Future of the (Old) New Economy B. Taylor *Harvard Business Review Digital Articles* p2 Je 16 2017

THE BEST BET img *New York* p49 F 20 2017

Big-screen blowout S. HORACZEK color *Popular Science* v289 no6 p22 N/D 2017

Colorblock Cubbies color *Good Housekeeping* v265 no3 p47 S 2017

Companies Like Amazon Need to Run More Tests on Workplace Practices F. Gino *Harvard Business Review Digital Articles* p2 Ag 20 2015

The Deal That Made an Industry Shudder B. Kowitt color diag *Fortune* v176 no1 p7 Jl 1 2017

Don't Let Your Data Sleep With the Enemy S. McBride bw color *Bloomberg Businessweek* no4498 p55 N 7 2016

Everything We Know About Platforms We Learned from Medieval France R. Fisman and T. Sullivan *Harvard Business Review Digital Articles* p2 Mr 24 2016

Hello? Alexa? K. C. POHLMANN *Sound & Vision* v82 no2 p28 F/Mr 2017

How Amazon Adapted Its Business Model to India V. Govindarajan and A. Warren *Harvard Business Review Digital Articles* p2 Jl 20 2016

It's All About SKUs L. DAWSON *Publishers Weekly* v264 no26 p19 Je 26 2017

Jeff Bezos Goes Grocery Shopping S. Soper and O. Zaleski color *Bloomberg Businessweek* no4517 p21 Ap 3 2017

The Logic Behind Amazon's Prime Day R. Mohammed *Harvard Business Review Digital Articles* p2 Jl 13 2015

MAKE YOUR HOME WORK color *Men's Health* v31 no10 p(Sp)19 D 2016

MERRY AND MOD L. HOWARD *Better Homes & Gardens* v94 no12 p56 D 2016

On Technology J. Wortham color *New York Times Magazine* p16 Ja 29 2017

OUT OF THE BOX L. Rao color *Fortune* v174 no7 p22 D 1 2016

PERSON OF INTEREST L. Rao color *Fortune* v174 no6 p23 N 1 2016

PUNCH list K. SELZER *Better Homes & Gardens* v94 no12 p64 D 2016

Real books, fake store A. Frykholm *Christian Century* v133 no21 p10 O 12 2016

SMART SPEAKER K. Dupzyk color *Popular Mechanics* p24 Mr 2017

Stock X-Ray: Costco Wholesale T. Tepper color diag *Money* v46 no8 p40 S 2017

Streaming on a Shoestring L. Eadicicco color *Money* v46 no4 p15 My 2017

The Truth About Cheap Turbos [Cover story] E. Perkins color graph *Hot Rod* v69 no12 p64 D 2016

Walmart Won't Stay on Top If Its Strategy Is "Copy Amazon" D. L. Yohn *Harvard Business Review Digital Articles* p2 Mr 21 2017

'We Are as Gods and Might as Well Get Good at It' K. D. WILLIAMSON color *National Review* v69 no19 p29 O 16 2017

What Amazon Risks by Eliminating List Prices R. Mohammed *Harvard Business Review Digital Articles* p2 Jl 13 2016

What Does Whole Foods Get from Amazon? Alexa, for Starters B. Gomes-Casseres *Harvard Business Review Digital Articles* p2 Je 19 2017

Why Amazon Bought Whole Foods L. Eadicicco color *Time* v190 no1 p11 Jl 3 2017

Would Amazon's 30-Hour-Week Experiment Work in Your Company? S. Behson *Harvard Business Review Digital Articles* p2 S 26 2016

Amazon.com Inc.—Finance

Amazon's Next Big Move: Take Over the Mall N. Carr il *MIT Technology Review* v120 no1 p96 Ja/F 2017

At Amazon, It's All About Cash Flow J. Fox *Harvard Business Review Digital Articles* p2 O 20 2014

Amazon.com Inc.—Officials & employees

Alexis DePree color *Working Mother* v40 no3 p12 Ag/S 2017

ROY PRICE bw color *Bloomberg Businessweek* no4511 p68 F 13 2017

Ambar, Saladin

American Cicero: Mario Cuomo and the Defense of American Liberalism color *Publishers Weekly* v264 no32 p59 Ag 7 2017

Ambassadors

See also

American ambassadors

GARDEN VARIETY K. RANDALL *Washingtonian Magazine* v52 no9 p28 Je 2017

The Power of Speaking Out M. Sorvino color *Time* v190 no16/17 p33 O 23 2017

THE RISE AND RISE OF AHMED HUSSEN S. PROUDFOOT bw *Maclean's* v130 no3 p28 Ap 2017

State Department to keep anti-Semitism envoy but scrap many others M. A. Kellner *Christian Century* v134 no20 p15 S 27 2017

Amber, David

Rookie Sensation B. POPPLEWELL bw *Walrus* v13 no9 p16 N 2016

Amber, Jeannine

OUR FATHERS IN THEIR OWN WORDS color *Essence* v48 no2 p94 Je 2017

TRUMPED color *Essence* v48 no5 p100 S 2017

Ambient conditions (Electronics)

Maintaining a stable phase P. D. S *Science* v354 no6308 p77 O 7 2016

Ambiguity

Whose Reality Is It? E. ALTER color *Publishers Weekly* v264 no35 p101 Ag 28 2017

Ambiguity in art

THE ART OF THE CON M. KONNIKOVA *Saturday Evening Post* v289 no1 p34 Ja/F 2017

Ambition

THE Boss [Cover story] color *Glamour* v115 no10 p156 O 2017

OFFICE POLITICS D. K. GOODWIN bw color *Vanity Fair* v58 no11 p156 N 2016

Should You Give Up on Your New Dream? W. Johnson *Harvard Business Review Digital Articles* p2 Ja 28 2016

Ambler, Brett R.

Ruthenium-catalyzed insertion of adjacent diol carbon atoms into C-C bonds: Entry to type II polyketides diag *Science* v357 no6353 p779 Ag 25 2017

AMBROSE, EILEEN

Bring Your Smartphone Shopping color *AARP: The Magazine* v59 no6A p23 O/N 2016

Deals on Wheels color *AARP: The Magazine* v59 no5A p27 Ag/S 2016

GET INCOME FOR LIFE [Cover story] chart color *Kiplinger's Personal Finance* v71 no10 p26 O 2017

Money Help for Aging Parents color *Kiplinger's Personal Finance* v71 no11 p34 N 2017

Q: My alma mater is offering a charitable gift annuity. Is that a good way to generate income? color *Kiplinger's Personal Finance* v71 no11 p46 N 2017

Riding the Highs and Lows of a Fickle Market color *AARP: The Magazine* v59 no4A p24 Je/Jl 2016

Save on Airline Costs color *AARP: The Magazine* v60 no3A p21 Ap/My 2017

When You Need Cash Quick color *AARP: The Magazine* v60 no4A p21 Je/Jl 2017

AMBROSE, JUNE

SHE'S GOT THE LOOK *O, The Oprah Magazine* p121 Mr 2017

Ambrose, Monique

Maternal antibodies' role in immunity bibl color *Science* v355 no6326 p704 F 17 2017

Potent protection against H5N1 and H7N9 influenza via childhood hemagglutinin imprinting bibl chart graph *Science* v354 no6313 p722 N 11 2016

Ambrose, Rona

HARDEST WORKING S. PROUDFOOT color *Maclean's* v129 no47 p20 N 28 2016

Ambrose, Shelley

FEATURED FELLOW: SHELLEY AMBROSE S. Doyle color *Canadian Geographic* v137 no1 p78 F 2017

AAAS urges Trump team to value science and its benefits M. Jarvis color *Science* v355 no6323 p359 Ja 27 2017

Don't Pass the Weed or Say "Guns" S. Mirsky color *Scientific American* v316 no5 p78 My 2017

FROM THE HILL chart *Issues in Science & Technology* v33 no1 p22 Fall 2016

Invention Ambassadors take on society's challenge color *Science* v357 no6353 p766 Ag 25 2017

New AAAS president emphasizes making the case for science M. Jarvis color *Science* v355 no6327 p807 F 24 2017

Over 150 Scientific Organizations, Sixty-Two Nobel Laureates Urge Repeal of Controversial Immigration Ban K. FRAZIER *Skeptical Inquirer* v41 no3 p5 My/Je 2017

American Association for the Advancement of Science—Congresses

AAAS 2017 ANNUAL MEETING PROGRAM chart color *Science* v354 no6310 p363 O 21 2016

AAAS seeks to uphold science's role in policy-making B. Ham color *Science* v355 no6332 p1383 Mr 31 2017

Bridges, not walls? M. Jarvis color *Science* v356 no6336 p388 Ap 28 2017

S&T Policy Forum examines evolving opioid epidemic K. O'Neil color *Science* v356 no6336 p390 Ap 28 2017

American Association for the Advancement of Science—Officials & employees

Results of the 2016 election of AAAS officers M. Jarvis *Science* v355 no6323 p360 Ja 27 2017

American Association of Retired Persons

AARP Is Good for Your Brain Health E. J. Schneidewind *AARP: The Magazine* v59 no5A p75 Ag/S 2016

Videos Showcase Diverse Caregiving color *AARP: The Magazine* v59 no5A p74 Ag/S 2016

American Association of School Librarians

ALA Annual 2017: Picks for Advocacy Panels *Publishers Weekly* v264 no25 p72 Je 19 2017

American Astronomical Society

The eclipse of a generation A. Speck *Physics Today* v70 no8 p10 Ag 2017

American attitudes

AMERICA IS BETTER THAN THIS E. G. J. Graves color *Black Enterprise* v47 no8 p8 Jl/Ag 2017

HOW AMERICA LOST ITS MIND [Cover story] K. Andersen color *Atlantic* v320 no2 p76 S 2017

HOW AMERICANS LEARNED TO STOP WORRYING AND LOVE THE ACA S. Mukherjee diag *Fortune* v175 no8 p46 Je 15 2017

Me, My Liberal Wife and What Happened When We Went to a Gun Range J. Stein color *Time* v190 no9 p62 S 4 2017

Scientists can't be silent C. Coons color *Science* v357 no6350 p431 Ag 4 2017

Washington View M. Ferguson color *Phi Delta Kappan* v99 no2 p74 O 2017

American authors

DAN WEEKEND NEEDS A RIDE E. WEST *Indianapolis Monthly* v40 no5 p60 Ja 2017

A ferocious attention J. Hiskes *Christian Century* v134 no14 p10 Jl 5 2017

Grace R. WILSON *American Scholar* v86 no2 p2 Spr 2017

John Green R. Means *Current Biography* v78 no8 p38 Ag 2017

A Museum for the People Behind the Volumes *American Scholar* v86 no1 p16 Wint 2017

Vacances J. von Sothen color *Esquire* p62 Ag 2017

American authors—21st century—Biography

Chris Bachelder C. Mari color *Current Biography* v78 no2 p8 F 2017

Ottessa Moshfegh J. Johnson color *Current Biography* v78 no2 p53 F 2017

American authors—Interviews

Hidden HISTORY *Interview* v47 no3 p37 Ap 2017

American Ballet Theatre

DANCE *New Yorker* v93 no14 p6 My 22 2017

DancesSPiRiT 2017 Summer Study GUIDE *Dance Spirit* v21 no1 p60 Ja 2017

editor's letter color *Architectural Digest* v74 no7 p10 Jl 2017

A group effort—led by AD100 designer Dan Fink—transforms the dancers' lounge for American Ballet Theatre into a trium-

phant tour de force S. COCHRAN bw color *Architectural Digest* v74 no7 p76 Jl 2017

In Character M. HARSS *Dance Magazine* v91 no1 p128 Ja 2017

American Bar Association

A New Look For New York J. MILLIOT color *Publishers Weekly* v264 no20 p(Sp)6 My 15 2017

Wednesday's Focus L. HARTMAN *Publishers Weekly* v264 no20 p(Sp)16 My 15 2017

American Basketball Association

Game Changers: The spectacular play you see today owes a mighty debt to the revolutionary, slam-dunking ABA F. Lidz *Smithsonian* v48 no6 p26 O 2017

American beaver

Natural Hydrologists K. Spence *Natural History* v125 no1 p22 D 2016/Ja 2017

American bison

American Bison K. Vaughn *Arizona Highways* v93 no4 p13 Ap 2017

Up to Speed: Two Months, One Page P. Rauber *Sierra* v101 no5 p19 S/O 2016

American bison—Social aspects

Home at Last [Cover story] J. Kohler color *National Wildlife (World Edition)* v55 no5 p22 Ag/S 2017

American Booksellers Association (Company)—Congresses

Chilling Out in Minneapolis J. ROSEN color *Publishers Weekly* v264 no3 p3 Ja 16 2017

American Broadcasting Co.

13 MUST-SEE EVENTS R. A. BERENZ *TV Guide* v65 no23 p44 My 29 2017

AMERICAN IDOL IS BACK! M. L. Lenker color *Entertainment Weekly* no1466 p16 My 19 2017

American Building Restoration Products Inc.

Resources color *Old House Journal* v45 no3 p87 My 2017

American Cancer Society Inc.

ALL ABOUT EVE L. Rodriguez color *Los Angeles Magazine* v62 no10 p156 O 2017

FIFTH HARMONY'S NORMANI KORDEI HELPS FIGHT CANCER M. L. Lenker color *Entertainment Weekly* no1484 p59 S 29 2017

FIGHTING BACK: HOW LOCAL TEAMS ARE TREATING A CHALLENGING DISEASE J. H. REDMOND color *Cincinnati Magazine* v51 no1 p91 O 2017

American chestnut

RETURN OF THE GIANTS: The once and future mighty American chestnut C. KETTLEWELL *Virginia Living* v15 no6 p17 O 2017

American Civil Liberties Union

The ACLU Is Ready to Rumble A. RICE img *New York* v49 no25 p59 D 12 2016

ACLU V CATHOLIC HEALTH CARE [Cover story] S. Slade color il *America* v216 no13 p18 Je 12 2017

Can the ACLU Stop Trump? G. Edelman color *Washington Monthly* v49 no3-5 p16 Mr-My 2017

The D.C. Subway System Banned These Ads C. J. CIARAMELLA color *Reason* v49 no6 p54 N 2017

ENCYCLOPEDIA CINCINNATI A. BROWNLEE, B. COLEMAN et al bw cartoon color *Cincinnati Magazine* v51 no1 p42 O 2017

When the Nazis Came to Skokie *America* v217 no6 p40 S 18 2017

American Civil Liberties Union—Officials & employees

FAMILY BUSINESS E. T. Kim cartoon *New Yorker* v92 no49 p33 F 13 2017

American collage

LIGHT OF THE WORLD color *ARTnews* v115 no4 p141 Wint 2016/2017

American College of Sports Medicine

HIIT PLAN [Cover story] J. Metzl color *Runner's World* v52 no1 p58 Ja/F 2017

American Composers Orchestra (Performer)

CLASSICAL MUSIC *New Yorker* v93 no6 p8 Mr 27 2017

American Conservative (Periodical)

Why I Read The American Conservative R. C. Young color *American Conservative* v16 no1 p2 Ja/F 2017

American Corporate Partners (Company)

OPERATION MENTORSHIP M. Roney color *Forbes* v198 no7 p100 N 29 2016

American Council of Trustees & Alumni (Organization)

Too Many Voters Lost in a Land of Clueless *USA Today Magazine* v145 no2859 p1 D 2016

American Council on Exercise

COMPOSITION Class G. GRAVES and C. ELLENBERG color *Vogue* v207 no3 p382 Mr 2017

American Cowboy (Periodical)

CELEBRATING COWBOYS color *American Cowboy* v24 no1 p26 Je/Jl 2017

American craftsman style (Architecture)

AFFORDABLE CRAFTSMAN color *Arts & Crafts Homes & the Revival* v12 no2 p18 Spr 2017

FOR THE Love of SHIPLAP D. Howland color *Cabin Living* p9 Ap 2017

Gentle Stewards for a 1908 house D. PIZZI color *Arts & Crafts Homes & the Revival* v12 no2 p40 Spr 2017

Satisfying Nonconformity P. Poore *Arts & Crafts Homes & the Revival* v12 no2 p8 Spr 2017

SPLENDID CRAFTSMAN on the East Coast P. Poore color diag *Arts & Crafts Homes & the Revival* v12 no2 p24 Spr 2017

wright ON THE RIVER R. COLE color *Arts & Crafts Homes & the Revival* v12 no2 p50 Spr 2017

American Crime (TV program)

American Crime J. Jensen and A. Wilkinson color *Entertainment Weekly* no1456 p58 Mr 10 2017

AMERICAN CRIME T. Stack color *Entertainment Weekly* no1446/1447 p61 D 2016/Ja 2017

CHEERS & JEERS D. HOLBROOK *TV Guide* v65 no14 p80 Ap 3 2017

FIELD NOTES E. NUSSBAUM color *New Yorker* v93 no11 p76 My 1 2017

American Crime Story: Assassination of Gianni Versace (TV program)

CRIME OF Fashion [Cover story] T. Stack color *Entertainment Weekly* no1472 p22 Je 30 2017

ENTERTAINMENT WEEKLY'S PARTNERS IN CRIME H. Goldblatt color *Entertainment Weekly* no1472 p10 Je 30 2017

American Dance Awards Inc.

AMERICAN DANCE AWARDS *Dance Spirit* v20 no10 p12 D 2016

American Dance Machine for the 21st Century (Performer)

Dynamic Duo S. Fnscia *Dance Magazine* v90 no12 p28 D 2016

American Dream

THE AMERICAN DREAM IS ALIVE AND WELL...ON THE FORBES 400 M. BURKE, S. Sharf et al color graph map *Forbes* v198 no5 p58 O 25 2016

CHASING A DREAM M. O. SIMINGTON color *Phi Kappa Phi Forum* v96 no4 p11 Wint 2016

THE NEW KIDS B. LARMER *New York Times Magazine* p40 F 5 2017

American Dream (Music)

A Disco-Punk Epic for the Age of Trump R. SHEFFIELD color *Rolling Stone* no1295 p53 S 7 2017

LCD Soundsystem L. Greenblatt color *Entertainment Weekly* no1480 p53 S 1 2017

American eel

Ottawa's slimiest problem M. CAMPBELL color *Maclean's* v130 no9 p18 O 2017

WHERE THE WILD THINGS ARE R. Annis, S. Bahr et al color *Indianapolis Monthly* v41 no2 p62 S 2017

American exceptionalism

Make America Exceptional Again: The rule of law, the centerpiece of American exceptionalism, is under assault. How to halt the predations of the regulatory state J. H. Cochrane *Hoover Digest: Research & Opinion on Public Policy* no2 p32 Spr 2017

American Express Co.

PLAYING YOUR CARDS RIGHT M. CROSS color *Kiplinger's Personal Finance* v71 no2 p46 F 2017

American folk art—Exhibitions

BLACK FOLK ART, REVISITED A. KENT *In These Times* v40 no12 p41 D 2016

Folk fun in Williamsburg color *Magazine Antiques* v184 no4 p28 Jl/Ag 2017

American folk music

Trading Banjos for Balalaikas bw *Weekly Standard* v22 no42 p3 Jl 17 2017

American Football (Music)

Play All B. RATLIFF color *Esquire* v166 no4 p28 N 2016

American Football Conference—History—21st century

AFC + EAST color *Sports Illustrated* v126 no5 p44 F 13 2017

AFC + NORTH color *Sports Illustrated* v126 no5 p45 F 13 2017

AFC + SOUTH color *Sports Illustrated* v126 no5 p46 F 13 2017

AFC + WEST color *Sports Illustrated* v126 no5 p47 F 13 2017

American Forests (Association)

Christopher Horn, Director of Communications *American Forests* v123 no1 p8 Wint/Spr 2017

Coast live oak *American Forests* v122 no3 p11 Fall 2016

DISH Network *American Forests* v123 no1 p10 Wint/Spr 2017

Doubling Down on Urban Forests D. Irvin *American Forests* v123 no2 p7 Summ 2017

How Panamanians and Trees Are Saving Each Other Suah Cheong *American Forests* v123 no2 p6 Summ 2017

Ian Leahy, Director of Urban Forests Programs *American Forests* v122 no3 p8 Fall 2016

Joan and Mike Diggs *American Forests* v123 no2 p8 Summ 2017

New Administration and New Congress Provide Opportunities and Challenges *American Forests* v123 no1 p14 Wint/Spr 2017

NEW ONLINE *American Forests* v123 no1 p12 Wint/Spr 2017

Our Best Idea S. STEEN *American Forests* v122 no3 p2 Fall 2016

The Path Ahead S. STEEN *American Forests* v123 no1 p2 Wint/Spr 2017

Rebuilding the Home of the "People of the Forest" L. Seventko *American Forests* v122 no3 p7 Fall 2016

A Thousand Acres and Counting *American Forests* v123 no2 p8 Summ 2017

American Forests (Association)—Officials & employees

Pioneer in American Forests' Boardroom L. SLOAN *American Forests* v123 no1 p46 Wint/Spr 2017

American Geophysical Union

Society labels harassment as research misconduct M. Kuo color *Science* v356 no6335 p233 Ap 21 2017

American Gods (TV program)

American Gods J. Halterman *TV Guide* v65 no13 p34 Mr 20 2017

American Gods J. Halterman *TV Guide* v65 no25 p34 Je 2017

AMERICAN GODS M. Snetiker color *Entertainment Weekly* no1446/1447 p62 D 2016/Ja 2017

Are You There God? It's Me Television J. Jensen color *Entertainment Weekly* no1463/1464 p92 Ap/My 2017

Everything You Think You Know About Neil Gaiman Is Wrong *New York* v50 no9 p83 My 1 2017

GODS GONE WILD M. Snetiker color *Entertainment Weekly* no1462 p26 Ap 21 2017

Is American Gods the Most Outrageous Show on TV? M. Snetiker color *Entertainment Weekly* no1467 p53 My 26 2017

American Grit (TV program)

ALSO COMING... A. D'Arminio and J. Russell *TV Guide* v65 no23 p19 My 29 2017

The New American Gladiators E. Aslanian *TV Guide* v65 no25 p9 Je 2017

TRUE GRIT: WWE phenom John Cena transforms average Joes into G.I. Joes on Season 2 of Fox's reality competition American Grit I. RATLEDGE *TV Guide* v65 no27 p22 Je 26 2017

American Heart Association

JUST DO IT C. KETTLEWELL *Virginia Living* v15 no3 p13 Ap 2017

This Just In J. Zorthian *Time* v190 no15 p19 O 16 2017

Watch This Weight-Loss Saboteur *Health* v31 no6 p12 Jl 2017

American Honda Motor Co. Inc.

2017 HONDA CRF450R B. Lutes color *Cycle World* v56 no1 p12 Ja/F 2017

Acura MDX chart color *Motor Trend* v69 no1 p42 Ja 2017

HONDA PUTS ONE FOOT IN THE MOTOAMERICA DOOR B. Adams color *Cycle World* v56 no4 p24 My 2017

American Honey (Film)

American Honey L. Greenblatt color *Entertainment Weekly* no1434 p44 O 7 2016

IN DEEP A. LANE cartoon *New Yorker* v92 no32 p108 O 10 2016

The Kids of American Honey Hit the Road With a Sweet-and-Sour Hustle S. Zacharek color *Time* v188 no14 p55 O 10 2016

NOW PLAYING color *Entertainment Weekly* no1436/1437 p87 O 21 2016

Sasha Lane N. Sperling color *Entertainment Weekly* no1434 p44

O 7 2016

American Horror Story (TV program)
Ask Matt M. Roush *TV Guide* v64 no40 p4 O 3 2016

American Horror Story: Cult (TV program)
Art's Latest Inspiration? TRUMP C. Holub color *Entertainment Weekly* no1476 p16 Ag 4 2017

American Horror Story: Hotel (TV program)
STREAMING A. D'ARMINIO *TV Guide* v64 no40 p64 O 3 2016

American Horror Story: My Roanoke Nightmare (TV program)
American Horror Story Is Frightfully Good With Secrets D. D'Addario color *Time* v188 no19 p55 N 7 2016

American Horticultural Society
ABOUT TOWN *Virginia Living* v15 no4 p41 Je 2017

American Housewife (TV program)
American Housewife N. Abrams, B. L. Heldman et al *Entertainment Weekly* no1482/1483 p79 S 22 2017
KATY MIXON M. Snetiker color *Entertainment Weekly* no1434 p47 O 7 2016
PRIME-TIME HUNGER GAMES R. KEEGAN color *Vanity Fair* v59 no7 p61 Summ 2017
TV'S WINNERS AND LOSERS BY THE NUMBERS *TV Guide* v64 no48 p13 N 21 2016
What to Watch R. Rahman, S. Li et al color *Entertainment Weekly* no1435 p51 O 14 2016

American Humanist Association
EDITOR'S NOTE J. BARDI *Humanist* v76 no6 p3 N/D 2016
HUMANIST PROFILE C. Lamont *Humanist* v77 no1 p2 Ja/F 2017

American Humanist Association—Congresses
ACTIVE DUTY: My Dedication to Liberty, Justice, and an End to Wars M. Benjamin *Humanist* v76 no6 p17 N/D 2016
A BRIDGE SUPREME: Connecting Humanism to a Liberal, Loving Christianity J. Shelby Spong *Humanist* v76 no6 p21 N/D 2016
I AM WHAT I AM AND OTHER TRUTHS E. Chambers *Humanist* v76 no6 p25 N/D 2016
INSPIRATION, SCI-FI, and the IMPORTANCE of Driving Your Own Bus J. de Lancie *Humanist* v76 no6 p33 N/D 2016
TO ENHANCE JUSTICE: The Risk and Reward of Studying Memory E. F. Loftus *Humanist* v76 no6 p29 N/D 2016

American hunting stories
HOT CHOCOLATE J. Arterburn cartoon *Outdoor Life* v223 no9 p86 N 2016
THE ONES THAT GOT AWAY cartoon color *Outdoor Life* v223 no9 p54 N 2016

American Idol (TV program)
AMERICAN IDOL IS BACK! M. L. Lenker color *Entertainment Weekly* no1466 p16 My 19 2017
Farewell Idol R. MOYNIHAN *TV Guide* v64 no15 p35 Ap 4 2016
IDOL'S RETURN: ARE WE READY? J. Hibberd color *Entertainment Weekly* no1467 p16 My 26 2017

American Institute of Biological Sciences
Advancing Team Research for Science and Society R. E. GROPP *BioScience* v67 no2 p103 F 2017
AIBS Photo Contest Brings Biology into Focus J. PALAKOVICH CARR *BioScience* v67 no4 p323 Ap 2017

American investments
Misdirected Investment C. R. Morris color *Commonweal* v143 no18 p6 N 11 2016
Which U.S. Companies Are Doing the Most R&D in China and India? V. Govindarajan, G. Bagla et al *Harvard Business Review Digital Articles* p2 Mr 26 2015

American Jewish identity
Drifting Backward: The world feels more dangerous than the one I used to know D. Paul *Indianapolis Monthly* v40 no11 p128 Jl 2017

American Jews
American Jews campaign to change Israeli minds about Judaism's diversity M. Chabin *Christian Century* v134 no17 p15 Ag 16 2017
#King Of The Mitzvahs J. Ruby bw color *Chicago* v66 no8 p80 Ag 2017

American Jews—Exhibitions
Chicken Soup and Other Remedies P. Wasley *Humanities* v37 no4 p1 Fall 2016

American Jews—Social life & customs

Cecil B. DeMille Was Right *Commentary* v143 no4 p8 Ap 2017

American Journal of Public Health (Periodical)
Stalled Numbers Do Not Bode Well *USA Today Magazine* v145 no2863 p6 Ap 2017
STRENGTH IN NUMBERS E. Klinenberg color *Wired* v24 no11 p106 N 2016

American League of Professional Baseball Clubs
THE MISFITS OF SUMMER F. J. FROMMER *Washingtonian Magazine* v52 no8 p70 My 2017

American legends
See also
Stagolee (Legendary character)
THAT BAD MAN STAGGER LEE R. SOODALTER bw *Missouri Life* v44 no2 p52 Ap 2017

American Legislative Exchange Council
ALEC's War on Local Control J. HIGHTOWER color *Progressive* v81 no7 p70 O/N 2017

American Library Association
Hope and Change A. RICHARD ALBANESE color *Publishers Weekly* v264 no25 p47 Je 19 2017
Librarians Take Capitol Hill A. Albanese color *Publishers Weekly* v264 no19 p4 My 8 2017
Library Advocacy Efforts Gaining Steam S. MAUGHAN color *Publishers Weekly* v264 no25 p64 Je 19 2017
Making ALA Great Again A. Richard Albanese color *Publishers Weekly* v264 no8 p21 F 20 2017
The Next Chapter for Library E-books A. RICHARD ALBANESE color *Publishers Weekly* v264 no25 p54 Je 19 2017

American Library Association. Digital Content & Libraries Working Group
The Next Chapter for Library E-books A. RICHARD ALBANESE color *Publishers Weekly* v264 no25 p54 Je 19 2017

American Library Association. Office for Intellectual Freedom
THE TOP 10: MOST CHALLENGED BOOKS OF 2016 S. MAUGHAN color *Publishers Weekly* v264 no25 p60 Je 19 2017

American Library Association—Congresses
ALA, Chicago Style B. KENNEY *Publishers Weekly* v264 no25 p40 Je 19 2017
For Librarians, 2017 Is Off To a Rough Start A. Albanese color *Publishers Weekly* v264 no5 p2 Ja 30 2017
How to Maximize ALA Midwinter S. MAUGHAN color *Publishers Weekly* v263 no52 p62 D 19 2016
In Chicago, Librarians Get Their Mojo Back A. Albanese color *Publishers Weekly* v264 no27 p4 Jl 3 2017
SHARJAH INTERNATIONAL BOOK FAIR/AMERICAN LIBRARY ASSOCIATION LIBRARY CONFERENCE NOW IN ITS THIRD YEAR M. MACKAY and M. DOWLING color *Publishers Weekly* v263 no43 p(Sp)6 O 24 2016
"The Challenge of a Lifetime" A. RICHARD ALBANESE color *Publishers Weekly* v264 no25 p29 Je 19 2017
A Time to Lead B. Kenney *Publishers Weekly* v264 no3 p21 Ja 16 2017
TRANSITION A. RICHARD ALBANESE color *Publishers Weekly* v263 no52 p31 D 19 2016

American Library Association—Political activity
Nonpartisan Nonprofits Fight for Free Expression, Part 2 J. Maher *Publishers Weekly* v264 no14 p5 Ap 3. 2017

American literature
Your Writing Tools Aren't Mine V. T. NGUYEN *New York Times Book Review* p13 Ap 30 2017

American literature—Hispanic American authors
Invisible Latinos N. A. DENIS *Publishers Weekly* v264 no4 p84 Ja 23 2017

American Made (Film)
American Made C. Nashawaty color *Entertainment Weekly* no1485 p38 O 6 2017
Cruise, the Smuggest of Drug Smugglers S. Zacharek color *Time* v190 no14 p50 O 9 2017
MOVIES A. Lane *New Yorker* v93 no33 p18 O 23 2017
UNRELIABLE HISTORIES A. LANE cartoon *New Yorker* v93 no30 p78 O 2 2017

American male authors
Jimmy Breslin G. Troy color *Time* v189 no12 p18 Ap 3 2017

American marble sculpture
A William Henry Rinehart Leander comes to the surface S. P. Feld

bw color *Magazine Antiques* v184 no5 p54 S/O 2017

American Medical Association—Congresses

"Right" You Aren't A. ECK *USA Today Magazine* v146 no2868 p17 S 2017

American military assistance

Why Military Assistance Programs Disappoint M. Karlin color *Foreign Affairs* v96 no6 p111 N/D 2017

American Motorcyclist Association

INDIAN THROWS DOWN THE GLOVE K. Cameron color *Cycle World* v55 no11 p26 D 2016

MAN. VAN. PLAN M. Hoyer color *Cycle World* v55 no11 p60 D 2016

American Motors Corp.

The Unbelievable Story of How AMC Won a Trans-Am Championship T. Taylor bw color *Hot Rod* v69 no12 p42 D 2016

American mural painting & decoration

All About Edie A. Brownlee *Cincinnati Magazine* v50 no12 p112 S 2017

American Museum of Natural History

One Cartoonist's Rather Particular Guide to Manhattan R. Chast cartoon *Conde Nast Traveler* v52 no9 p110 O 2017

American national characteristics

Commonplace Book A. Matthews *American Scholar* v86 no2 p126 Spr 2017

Is America great? M. Schubert, V. Gaglione et al graph *America* v216 no5 p6 Mr 6 2017

The. American. People A. Ferguson *Commentary* v143 no3 p12 Mr 2017

American Negro Academy

THE RETURN OF JAMES BALDWIN R. A. Schroth bw color *America* v216 no9 p8 Ap 24 2017

American Ninja Warrior (TV program)

COWBOY NINJA: THE RANCHER AS OBSTACLE RACER T. T. MURRISON *Idaho Magazine* v16 no10 p6 Jl 2017

Do You Even Code, Bro? T. CONFOY cartoon color *Esquire* v166 no5 p48 D 2016/Ja 2017

The New American Gladiators E. Aslanian *TV Guide* v65 no25 p9 Je 2017

The Rise of the Ninja Gym D. Eng color *Fortune* v75 no1 p24 Ja 1 2017

STRONG FOR LIFE A. Heffernan color diag *Men's Health* v31 no10 p98 D 2016

Swing Shift J. Gorant and T. Keith color *Sports Illustrated* v126 no15 p22 My 29 2017

What to Watch R. Rahman, C. Agard et al color *Entertainment Weekly* no1477 p50 Ag 11 2017

American novelists

The Summit of Life P. BAUER bw color *Weekly Standard* v22 no11 p40 N 21 2016

The Untameable Nell Zink B. Kachka img *New York* v49 no20 p120 O 3 2016

American paint horse

Conformation Correction color *Horse & Rider* v56 no3 p11 Mr 2017

you should know color *Horse & Rider* v56 no8 p21 Ag 2017

American painting

AMERICAN PLACES *American Scholar* v86 no1 p128 Wint 2017

ARTISTIC LIBERTY AT THE TABLE N. Stroehlic color *National Geographic* v231 no2 p16 F 2017

American painting—Exhibitions

See also

American watercolor painting—Exhibitions

100th birthday tributes to Andrew Wyeth color *Magazine Antiques* v184 no3 p34 My/Je 2017

Arts and letters: A new exhibition explores the affinities between the work of Henry James and the American painting of his time E. Pochoda color *Magazine Antiques* v184 no4 p68 Jl/Ag 2017

"My native continent" D. M. Cassidy, E. Finch et al cartoon *Magazine Antiques* v184 no2 p100 Mr/Ap 2017

Reality Principle P. Schjeldahl cartoon *New Yorker* v92 no30 p8 S 26 2016

American Pastoral (Film)

Adapting the unadaptable J. J. WEINMAN color *Maclean's* v129 no42 p56 O 24 2016

American penmanship

Why the Left Curses Cursive J. W. EMORD *USA Today Magazine* v146 no2868 p40 S 2017

American Pharoah (Race horse)

Let us now praise famous horses E. McGraw bw color *Equus* no472 p72 Ja 2017

A role model G. Schramm color *Equus* no482 p72 N 2017

American Physical Society

PARODY *Weekly Standard* v22 no40 p40 Je 26 2017

American Planning Association—Congresses

Activate Your Parks and Your People B. Tulipane *Parks & Recreation* v52 no6 p8 Je 2017

American Playboy: The Hugh Hefner Story (TV program)

HEF AS CHANGE AGENT T. WALDEN color *Chicago* v66 no4 p44 Ap 2017

A New View of Playboy E. Aslanian *TV Guide* v65 no11 p14 Mr 6 2017

American poetry—Women authors

OUT OF PRINT D. CHIASSON color *New Yorker* v92 no40 p77 D 5 2016

American political satire

How satire failed F. DEAN color *Maclean's* v129 no47 p56 N 28 2016

The Long View R. LONG *National Review* v68 no21 p38 N 21 2016

TRUMP'S AMERICAN GIRL DOLLS M. AMRAM cartoon *New Yorker* v92 no36 p27 N 7 2016

Varieties of Ridiculous Experience D. FOSTER *National Review* v69 no1 p44 Ja 23 2017

American Political Science Association—Congresses

Academic Gabfest M. HEMINGWAY color *Weekly Standard* v23 no2 p20 S 18 2017

American Psychological Association

Chicken Acceleration? APA Puts Imprimatur on Credulous Psi Book D. M. STOKES *Skeptical Inquirer* v41 no3 p6 My/Je 2017

A Scientist Pushes Psychology Journals toward Open Data T. Witkowski *Skeptical Inquirer* v41 no4 p6 Jl/Ag 2017

American public sculpture

Girl, Misplaced J. NORDLINGER color *National Review* v69 no8 p18 My 2017

American Quarter Horse Association (Organization)

AQHA Executive Council Introduces Jerk-Down Rule *Spin to Win Rodeo* v21 no5 p16 Jl 2017

Senior Quarter Horse Geldings M. KAPUSHION color *Horse & Rider* v56 no10 p53 O 2017

American Recreation Products Inc.

Tents H. B. ROCHFORT color diag graph il *Backpacker* v45 no3 p57 Ap 2017

American Society of Civil Engineers

INFRASTRUCTURE RUPTURE B. Preston graph *Car & Driver* v63 no4 p26 O 2017

American Society of Clinical Oncology

THE INVASION EQUATION S. MUKHERJEE cartoon color *New Yorker* v93 no27 p40 S 11 2017

American Teen (Music)

Khalid's Teenage Dream N. Feeney color *Entertainment Weekly* no1456 p65 Mr 10 2017

Khalid's Teen Spirit J. Weiner color *Rolling Stone* no1293 p32 Ag 10 2017

R&B's New Wave Is Embracing Creative Destruction J. Cox color *Time* v189 no14 p49 Ap 17 2017

American television plays

Can Pitch Be a Major League Success? J. HALTERMAN color *TV Guide* v64 no42 p8 O 10 2016

American Tin Ceiling Co.

Resources color *Old House Journal* v45 no3 p87 My 2017

American watercolor painting—Exhibitions

Water and Light D. GREEN color *Weekly Standard* v23 no5 p44 O 9 2017

American wit & humor

LAUGHING MATTERS C. BUCKLEY *Forbes* v200 no3 p90 S 28 2017

American women authors

A FEMALE ANTIHERO E. BLAIR cartoon color *New Yorker* v92 no38 p42 N 21 2016

IRENE POLLIN P. O'Donnell *Washingtonian Magazine* v52 no2

Most of the unaffiliated just "stopped believing," according to new study K. Winston graph *Christian Century* v133 no22 p16 O 26 2016

Americans—Sexual behavior
This Just In J. Zorthian *Time* v189 no10 p21 Mr 20 2017

Americans—South America
Importing Business Lessons From El Norte C. Elton diag *Bloomberg Businessweek* no4495 p38 O 17 2016

Americans—Travel
Americans Are Traveling More E. Fry map *Fortune* v75 no1 p15 Ja 1 2017

American University (Washington, D.C.)
QUAD GOALS: A political insider takes on a new challenge: running American University P. O'Donnell *Washingtonian Magazine* v53 no1 p41 O 2017

America's Cup
America's Cup S. Gregory color *Time* v190 no2/3 p11 Jl 10-17 2017
Back to Monohulls for the Cup A. Cort color *Sail* v48 no11 p17 N 2017
Cup Half Empty A. PHILLIPS bw color *Weekly Standard* v22 no42 p37 Jl 17 2017
A Dramatic Pause color *Sail* v48 no3 p17 Mr 2017
FLIGHT C. JONES color *Popular Mechanics* p90 Je 2017
In Defense of Larry Ellison C. J. DOANE color *Sail* v48 no10 p120 O 2017
Lionheart Wins Worlds A. Cort color *Sail* v48 no11 p16 N 2017
Revenge of the Monomarans C. J. DOANE color *Sail* v48 no11 p80 N 2017
Setting Sail for the Cup A. Cort color *Sail* v48 no4 p18 Ap 2017

America's Got Talent (TV program)
AMERICA NEEDS TALENT M. KINSLEY color *Vanity Fair* v59 no11 p82 N 2017
America's Most Watched 25 TOP SHOWS *TV Guide* v65 no35 p11 Ag 21 2017
America's Most Watched 25 TOP SHOWS *TV Guide* v65 no39 p16 S 18 2017
BEST OF SUMMER 2017 *TV Guide* v65 no23 p15 My 29 2017

America's National Parks (Music)
JAZZ ALBUM OF THE YEAR color *Downbeat* v84 no8 p30 Ag 2017

America's Next Top Model (TV program)
America's Next Top Model I. Ratledge *TV Guide* p44 D 5 2016
America's Next Top Model Struts Again T. Stack color *Entertainment Weekly* no1443 p52 D 9 2016

America's Promise—The Alliance for Youth
Colin Powell C. Howorth color *Time* v189 no15 p8 Ap 24 2017

Amerland, David
The Sniper Mind: Eliminate Fear, Deal with Uncertainty, and Make Better Decisions *Publishers Weekly* v264 no39 p102 S 25 2017

Amfitheatrof, Francesca
Francesca Amfitheatrof E. Wilson color *InStyle* v23 no13 p124 D 2016

Amherst College
BEST BANG FOR THE BUCK NORTHEAST COLLEGES chart *Washington Monthly* v49 no9/10 p50 S/O 2017
Education *Stage Directions* v30 no7 p26 Jl 1 2017

AMI (Company)
Sickest Collaborations of the Year, Part 1 > Gap x GQ bw color *GQ: Gentlemen's Quarterly* v97 no6 p34 Je 2017

AMI Paris SAS
WHERE TO BUY color *Essence* v48 no2 p114 Je 2017

Amico, Laura
Ask a Drone Lawyer *Harvard Business Review Digital Articles* p2 My 18 2017
Loneliness and the Digital Workplace *Harvard Business Review Digital Articles* p2 S 29 2017

Amico, Richard
How Artificial Intelligence Will Redefine Management *Harvard Business Review Digital Articles* p2 N 2 2016

Amidon, Sam
NIGHT LIFE *New Yorker* v92 no44 p15 Ja 9 2017

Amiel, Geraldine
The Duck That Clipped Fillon's Wings color *Bloomberg Businessweek* no4518 p17 Ap 10 2017

Amine synthesis
Illuminating amination T. L. Buchanan and K. L. Hull bibl diag *Science* v355 no6326 p690 F 17 2017

Amines
A general catalytic β-C–H carbonylation of aliphatic amines to β-lactams D. Willcox, B. G. N. Chappell et al bibl diag *Science* v354 no6314 p851 N 18 2016
Illuminating amination T. L. Buchanan and K. L. Hull bibl diag *Science* v355 no6326 p690 F 17 2017

Amines—Derivatives
Catalytic intermolecular hydroaminations of unactivated olefins with secondary alkyl amines A. J. Musacchio, B. C. Lainhart et al bibl diag *Science* v355 no6326 p727 F 17 2017

Amini, Shahrouz
Preventing mussel adhesion using lubricant-infused materials color diag graph *Science* v357 no6352 p668 Ag 18 2017

Aminian, Manuchehr
How boundaries shape chemical delivery in microfluidics bibl diag graph *Science* v354 no6317 p1252 D 9 2016

Amino acid supplements
AMAZING AMINOS V. Tweed color *Amazing Wellness* v8 no2 p28 Spr 2016

Amino acids
See also
Branched chain amino acids
Leucine
Tryptophan
An Alternative to the RNA World C. W. CARTER, JR. *Natural History* v125 no1 p28 D 2016/Ja 2017
AMAZING AMINOS V. Tweed color *Amazing Wellness* v8 no2 p28 Spr 2016
Interacting amino acid replacements allow poison frogs to evolve epibatidine resistance R. D. Tarvin, C. M. Borghese et al chart diag graph *Science* v357 no6357 p1261 S 22 2017
Kynurenines: Tryptophan's metabolites in exercise, inflammation, and mental health I. Cervenka, L. Z. Agudelo et al color *Science* v357 no6349 p369 Jl 28 2017
Sleep Tight with CASEIN J. WUEBBEN color *Muscle & Performance* v9 no4 p9 Ap 2017
What Is Nitric Oxide? V. TWEED color *Better Nutrition* v79 no7 p22 Jl 2017

Amino acids—Evaluation
AMINOS: ATHLETIC ASSETS D. N. JACKSON color diag *Muscle & Performance* v9 no11 p58 N 2017
Maximize Your Postworkout Recovery A. ATKINSON color *Muscle & Performance* v9 no11 p64 N 2017

AMIRA, DAN
HOW YOUR: COMEDY GETS MADE cartoon color *Wired* v25 no4 p70 Ap 2017

Amiri, Masoud Talebi
Formaldehyde stabilization facilitates lignin monomer production during biomass depolymerization bibl diag graph *Science* v354 no6310 p329 O 21 2016

Amirpour, Ana Lily
The Bad Batch F. ZAMAN color *Film Comment* v53 no3 p70 My/Je 2017

Amis, Martin
POX AMERICANA bw color *Esquire* p110 N 2017

Amish
POST-APOCALYPTIC NOW E. Palmer *Christian Century* v134 no16 p27 Ag 2 2017

Amish farmers
WHEAT MONTANA NOODLES *South Dakota Magazine* v33 no3 p31 S/O 2017

Amistad (Company)
At 30, Amistad Press Looks Ahead D. Patrick *Publishers Weekly* v263 no41 p11 O 10 2016

Amitai, Gil
Intracellular signaling in CRISPR-Cas defense color *Science* v357 no6351 p550 Ag 11 2017

Amitay, Morrie
How Israel Wins *Commentary* v143 no3 p6 Mr 2017

Ammann, Brigitta
The fourth dimension of vegetation bibl color graph *Science* v354 no6311 p412 O 28 2016

Ammannito, E.

Extensive water ice within Ceres' aqueously altered regolith: Evidence from nuclear spectroscopy bibl graph *Science* v355 no6320 p1 Ja 6 2017

Localized aliphatic organic material on the surface of Ceres bibl graph *Science* v355 no6326 p719 F 17 2017

Seasonal exposure of carbon dioxide ice on the nucleus of comet 67P/Churyumov-Gerasimenko bibl bw graph *Science* v354 no6319 p1563 D 23 2016

Ammer, Christian

Positive biodiversity-productivity relationship predominant in global forests bibl chart graph map *Science* v354 no6309 paaf8957-1 O 14 2016

Ammidown, Margot

My President Was Black *Atlantic* v319 no2 p8 Mr 2017

AMMIRATI, RACHEL

Superstition Masquerading as Science *Skeptical Inquirer* v40 no6 p14 N/D 2016

Ammonia

Ammonia activation at a metal J. Hoover bibl diag *Science* v354 no6313 p707 N 11 2016

Coordination-induced weakening of ammonia,water, and hydrazine X–H bonds in a molybdenum complex M. J. Bezdek, Sheng Guo et al bibl diag *Science* v354 no6313 p730 N 11 2016

Ammonia as fertilizer

THE DOs & DON'Ts OF APPLICATIONS K. BIRCHMIER *Successful Farming* v114 no11 p34 N 2016

Ammonia—Therapeutic use

Top 10 Natural Pain Relievers E. A. KANE color *Better Nutrition* v79 no3 p28 Mr 2017

Ammonium bicarbonate

CHRISTMAS COOKIES WITH A TWIST L. J. ANDREWS *South Dakota Magazine* v32 no4 p38 N/D 2016

Ammons, A. R., 1926-2001

AMERICAN EXPANSION H. Vendler *Harper's Magazine* no2007 p68 Ag 2017

DELIGHT A. R. Ammons *Harper's Magazine* no2007 p75 Ag 2017

Ammunition

Non-lead Ammunition--a safer alternative T. Salo *New York State Conservationist* v72 no2 p8 O 2017

Ammunition—Evaluation

A 20 FOR TOM P. Bourjaily cartoon color *Field & Stream* v121 no9 p28 Ap 2017

Ammunition—Law & legislation

HEAVY METAL J. Yuskavitch color *Earth Island Journal* v32 no3 p41 Aut 2017

Amniotic liquid—Physiology

signs it's almost time M. COHEN *Parents* v92 no4 p124 Ap 2017

Amodei, Joe

POETRY IN MOTION M. Leuchter color *Popular Photography* v81 no1 p28 Ja/F 2017

AMODIO, JOSEPH V.

THE RISE OF ACTIVE STYLE color *Men's Health* v32 no7 p(Sp)4 S 2017

Amoeba—Research

Amoeba gives clues to animal origins L. HAMERS *Science News* v190 no10 p7 N 12 2016

Amon, Angelika

Not just Salk color *Science* v357 no6356 p1105 S 15 2017

Amorim Reis-Filho, José

Fringe on the brink: Intertidal reefs at risk color *Science* v357 no6348 p261 Jl 21 2017

Amoroso, Vince G.

Fructose-driven glycolysis supports anoxia resistance in the naked mole-rat diag graph *Science* v356 no6335 p307 Ap 21 2017

Amorth, Gabriele, 1925-2016

Battling the Devil color *Vanity Fair* v58 no12 p140 D 2016

This EXORCIST Is Real W. FRIEDKIN bw color *Reader's Digest* v190 no1134 p118 O 2017

Amoruso, Sophia, 1984-

Starting Over color *InStyle* v24 no5 p101 My 2017

Amos, Victoria

LIP SERVICE color *Ebony* v72 no4 p54 F 2017

Amour Vert (Company)

Amour Vert *American Forests* v122 no3 p10 Fall 2016

Amphetamines

Put the Kids First N. S. RILEY color *Weekly Standard* v22 no41 p18 Jl 3 2017

Amphibian conservation

Amphibians on the brink D. S. Bower, K. R. Lips et al color map *Science* v357 no6350 p454 Ag 4 2017

Amphibian eggs

Reproductive Decisions in Anurans: A Review of How Predation and Competition Affects the Deposition of Eggs And Tadpoles V. L. BUXTON and J. H. SPERRY *BioScience* v67 no1 p26 Ja 2017

Amphibians

Frogs K. KUBE cartoon color *Discover* v27 no10 p74 D 2016

SMACKDOWN! G. TARLACH cartoon *Discover* v38 no1 p50 Ja/F 2017

Amphibians—Conservation

Overcoming Challenges to the Recovery of Declining Amphibian Populations in the United States S. C. WALLS, L. C. BALL et al *BioScience* v67 no2 p156 F 2017

Amphibians—Physiology

Anesthesia and Euthanasia of Amphibians and Reptiles Used in Scientific Research: Should Hypothermia and Freezing Be Prohibited? H. B. LILLYWHITE, R. SHINE et al *BioScience* v67 no1 p53 Ja 2017

Amphitheaters

Last Look D. Kidd color *Governing* v30 no11 p64 Ag 2017

Amphitheaters—Evaluation

John Anson Ford Amphitheatre Sparkles in LA *Stage Directions* v30 no9 p4 S 2017

Ampleman, Lisa

Finding the Catholic Voices In Social Justice Poetry color *America* v216 no10 p42 My 1 2017

Amplifier Technologies Inc.

ATI AT527NC and AT524NC Amplifiers D. Vaughn chart color graph *Sound & Vision* v82 no3 p48 Ap 2017

Ampuero, J. P.

The hidden simplicity of subduction megathrust earthquakes graph *Science* v357 no6357 p1277 S 22 2017

Ampuero, Jean Paul

Localized seismic deformation in the upper mantle revealed by dense seismic arrays bibl graph *Science* v354 no6308 p88 O 7 2016

AMRAM, MEGAN

JARED KUSHNER'S HARVARD ADMISSIONS ESSAY cartoon *New Yorker* v93 no27 p33 S 11 2017

TRUMP'S AMERICAN GIRL DOLLS cartoon *New Yorker* v92 no36 p27 N 7 2016

Amrein-Beardsley, Audrey

All sizzle and no steak color graph il *Phi Delta Kappan* v99 no2 p53 O 2017

AMSOIL Inc.

850HP LS FORMULA B. Gillogly color *Hot Rod* v70 no4 p78 Ap 2017

Joe Carroll Pulls Spec Puzzle Pieces Together at Engine Masters Challenge P. Thomas color *Hot Rod* v70 no4 p72 Ap 2017

STREETABLE 469CI BIG-BLOCK CHEVY B. Gillogly color *Hot Rod* v70 no4 p74 Ap 2017

Amsterdam, Anthony

TWO POEMS *Harper's Magazine* no2007 p67 Ag 2017

Amstutz, Mark R.

WELCOMING THE STRANGER ... AND UPHOLDING THE LAW S. D. JAMES color *Christianity Today* v61 no4 p59 My 2017

AMSTUTZ, VALERIE

Q: What was the greatest summer read of your life? color *O, The Oprah Magazine* p16 Jl 2017

Amtrak (Company)

For Love and Trains K. MCKINNEY *National Parks* v91 no4 p16 Fall 2017

High-Speed Waste E. Boehm *Reason* v48 no7 p8 D 2016

Leaving On That Late- Night Train A. KONERMANN *Cincinnati Magazine* p59 Je 2017

Amundsen, David S.

HAT-P-26b: A Neptune-mass exoplanet with a well-constrained heavy element abundance chart diag graph *Science* v356 no6338 p628 My 12 2017

Amundsen, Roald, 1872-1928

THE GJØA DIARIES COME TO CANADA N. Walker bw *Canadian Geographic* v137 no3 p74 My 2017

Amundson, Christopher

1867 - The Time of our Birth *Nebraska Life* v21 no1 p9 Ja/F 2017

Back Again: Our Migrating Contributors *Nebraska Life* v21 no2 p9 Mr/Ap 2017

Border, beach, buried wonders, Old Baldy & Bells color *Nebraska Life* v21 no6 p56 N/D 2017

George Goes to the Trenches of France bw *Nebraska Life* v21 no6 p8 N/D 2017

Politics and murder *Nebraska Life* v21 no5 p11 S/O 2017

Taking Nebraska Life Doorstep to Doorstep *Nebraska Life* v20 no6 p9 N/D 2016

Under the shade of a thirsty cottonwood *Nebraska Life* v21 no4 p9 Jl/Ag 2017

Amunts, Alexey

The structure of the yeast mitochondrial ribosome bibl color *Science* v355 no6324 p528 F 3 2017

Amunts, Katrin

Microstructural proliferation in human cortex is coupled with the development of face processing bibl graph *Science* v355 no6320 p1 Ja 6 2017

Amusement parks

See also

Water parks

Of Course Disney Should Use Surge Pricing at Its Theme Parks R. Mohammed *Harvard Business Review Digital Articles* p2 Je 4 2015

SEASON TICKETS R. Cooper *Washingtonian Magazine* v52 no3 p96 D 2016

A Short Ride C. ZEIGLER *Indianapolis Monthly* p20 My 2017

Staying Ahead of the Curve K. Hobson and K. Stokke *Parks & Recreation* v52 no3 p18 Mr 2017

WATER PARK ADVENTURE [Cover story] color *Good Housekeeping* v265 no2 p138 Ag 2017

Amusement parks—California

SEASIDE AMUSEMENT AND MORE!: SANTA CRUZ IS A SLEEPY BEACH TOWN WITH A RICH AND UNIQUE HISTORY *Sea Magazine* v109 no5 pCA-1 My 2017

Amusement parks—Denmark

Denmark's Treetop Walkway J. Zorthian color *Time* v190 no2/3 p23 Jl 10-17 2017

Amusement parks—Design & construction

Los Angeles's New Circus Act N. Piper color *Bloomberg Businessweek* no4517 p44 Ap 3 2017

Amusement parks—Economic aspects

Fish Story cartoon color *Weekly Standard* v22 no26 p3 Mr 13 2017

Amusement parks—Georgia

See also

Six Flags Over Georgia (Ga.)

EASY Rider *Atlanta* v57 no2 p132 Je 2017

Amusement parks—Humor

ALL IN A Day's Work color *Reader's Digest* v190 no1133 p64 S 2017

Amusement parks—Marketing

Media Engagement C. Seward and M. Denison *Parks & Recreation* p12 Aquatics Guide 2017

Amusement parks—Ohio

Magnificent Thrill Machines C. C. W. COOKE color *National Review* v69 no15 p24 Ag 14 2017

Amusement rides

See also

Roller coasters

STRIP TEASE N. Padova chart color *Sunset* v238 no2 p20 F 2017

Amusement parks—Charts, diagrams, etc.

50 YEARS OF SIX FLAGS J. GREEN *Atlanta* v57 no2 p32 Je 2017

Amusements

See also

Amusement parks

Circus

Concerts

Dance

Entertainment events

Family recreation

Haunted houses (Amusements)

Hobbies

Internet entertainment

Nightclubs

Nightlife

Puzzles

Break Out! S. HOLLAND MURPHY D: *The Magazine of Dallas* v43 no10 p56 O 2016

PANIC ROOMS Z. MATTHEW color *Los Angeles Magazine* v62 no10 p90 O 2017

Rock & Roll Can Never Die *USA Today Magazine* v145 no2858 p56 N 2016

True Blood J. KENT-DOOLAN bw color *Indianapolis Monthly* v42 no2 p13 O 2017

weekend getaways: family *Washingtonian Magazine* v52 no11 p89 Ag 2017

Amusements industry

See also

Amusement parks

Amusements industry—Economic aspects

DISNEY'S GALACTIC GAMBIT D. LEONARD and C. PALMERI color diag *Bloomberg Businessweek* no4519 p56 Ap 24 2017

Amygdaloid body

STATES OF ALARM M. HUSTON *Psychology Today* v50 no5 p14 S/O 2017

Two brain circuits help mice hunt L. HAMERS *Science News* v191 no3 p8 F 18 2017

Amyloid

De novo design of a biologically active amyloid R. Gallardo, M. Ramakers et al bibl graph *Science* v354 no6313 paah4949-1 N 11 2016

Site-specific phosphorylation of tau inhibits amyloid-β toxicity in Alzheimer's mice A. Ittner, Sook Wern Chua et al bibl graph *Science* v354 no6314 p904 N 18 2016

Amyloid plaque

The molecular basis of Alzheimer's plaques S. Pospich and S. Raunser color *Science* v357 no6359 p45 O 6 2017

Amyloid beta-protein

See also

Amyloid plaque

Fibril structure of amyloid-β(1–42) by cryo–electron microscopy L. Gremer, D. Schölzel et al color diag *Science* v357 no6359 p116 O 6 2017

The molecular basis of Alzheimer's plaques S. Pospich and S. Raunser color *Science* v357 no6359 p45 O 6 2017

Amyloid beta-protein—Physiological aspects

RESEARCH color *Science* v357 no6347 p159 Jl 14 2017

Amyotrophic lateral sclerosis

UNLOCKING THE MYSTERY OF ALS L. Petrucelli and A. D. Gitler color *Scientific American* v316 no6 p46 Je 2017

What Once Was Lost L. MARSA color *Discover* v38 no8 p32 O 2017

An, Kirkland

More congregations become sanctuaries for immigrants under threat of deportation *Christian Century* v133 no26 p18 D 21 2016

An, P.

Observation of coherent elastic neutrino-nucleus scattering diag *Science* v357 no6356 p1123 S 15 2017

An, Yu

An adipo-biliary-uridine axis that regulates energy homeostasis diag *Science* v355 no6330 p1173 Mr 17 2017

An-12 (Transport plane)

LAST DANCE S. Weigel color *Flying* v144 no2 p36 F 2017

Anabolic steroids

See also

Anabolic steroids in sports

HOW WASHINGTON LOST THE WAR ON MUSCLE M. RIGGS color *Reason* v49 no2 p54 Je 2017

Anabolic steroids in sports

PUMP IT UP T. Layden and J. Feldman color *Sports Illustrated* v126 no11 p58 Ap 17-24 2017

Anabolic steroids—Evaluation

PREMIER PRODUCTS color *Muscle & Performance* v8 no12 p64 D 2016

Anachronistic art

Map Quest color map *Publishers Weekly* v264 no35 p40 Ag 28 2017

Anacostia (Washington, D.C.)

THAT TOWN A. Wiener color *Mother Jones* v42 no4 p6 Jl/Ag 2017

Anaerobic exercises

Aerobic vs. Anaerobic Exercise L. BOYCE color *Muscle & Performance* v9 no11 p22 N 2017

Anal sex

HOW TO BE A BETTER BOTTOM D. E. GOLDSTEIN color *Advocate* no1090 p40 Ap 2017

Analgesia

Conquer Aches Without Drugs D. Watkins *AARP: The Magazine* v30 no6A p32 O/N 2017

FEEL YOUR BEST C. Guthrie color *Yoga Journal* p12 2017 Special Issue

Pain promoter also acts to relieve it R. EHRENBERG *Science News* v191 no2 p6 F 4 2017

UNDER PRESSURE A. SHAFFER cartoon color *Better Homes & Gardens* v95 no4 p158 Ap 2017

Analgesics

See also

Capsaicin

Codeine

Fentanyl

Ask anything [Cover story] H. Cullen, K. Glassman et al color *Women's Health* v14 no1 p24 Ja/F 2017

What should doctors and drugmakers do to stop painkiller addiction? K. KIPLINGER color *Kiplinger's Personal Finance* v71 no5 p14 My 2017

Analogy

Why Sports Are a Terrible Metaphor for Business B. Taylor bw *Harvard Business Review Digital Articles* p2 F 3 2017

Analysis of DNA

See also

DNA sequencing

China's policies regarding next-generation sequencing diagnostic tests Rui Zhang and Jinming Li *Science* v354 no6319 p9 D 23 2016

DNA EVIDENCE FREES THE INNOCENT R. J. NORRIS color *Reason* v49 no4 p34 Ag/S 2017

DNA tests inflate species counts T. H. SAEY color *Science News* v191 no4 p6 Mr 4 2017

Genetic stability found in Russia M. ROSEN map *Science News* v191 no4 p10 Mr 4 2017

ORIGINS OF AMBLING HORSES TRACED C. Barakat and M. McCluskey bw color *Equus* no471 p13 D 2016

Pocket-sized sequencers start to pay off big E. Pennisi color *Science* v356 no6338 p572 My 12 2017

A ROGUES' GALLERY OF BAD FORENSICS LABS C. J. CIARAMELLA *Reason* v49 no4 p38 Ag/S 2017

Sometimes failure is the springboard to success E. Emerson *Science News* v190 no8 p2 O 15 2016

WORTH OF MOUTH: One doctor uses a DNA swab to put the chill on opioid pills T. REHAGEN *Indianapolis Monthly* p73 N 2017

Analysis of DNA—Equipment & supplies—Evaluation

NEW PRODUCTS: DNA/RNA ANALYSIS color *Science* v354 no6317 p1309 D 9 2016

new products: dna/rna analysis color *Science* v355 no6326 p761 F 17 2017

Analysts (Finance)

What to Do When People Draw Different Conclusions From the Same Data W. Frick *Harvard Business Review Digital Articles* p2 Mr 31 2015

YOUR HANDY EARNINGS-CALL DRINKING GAME color *Fortune* v175 no7 p14 Je 1 2017

Analytical mechanics

See also

Many-body problem

Controlled growth and form of precipitating microsculptures C. Nadir Kaplan, W. L. Noorduin et al bw color diag graph *Science* v355 no6332 p1395 Mr 31 2017

Analytical skills

See also

Problem solving

Why Technologists Should Think Like Biologists S. Arbesman *Harvard Business Review Digital Articles* p2 Jl 20 2016

Ananat, Elizabeth O.

Linking job loss, inequality, mental health, and education color *Science* v356 no6343 p1127 Je 16 2017

Anand, Bharat N.

The U.S. Media's Problems Are Much Bigger than Fake News and Filter Bubbles color *Harvard Business Review Digital Articles* p2 Ja 5 2017

What Harvard Business School Has Learned About Online Collaboration From HBX *Harvard Business Review Digital Articles* p2 Ap 14 2015

Anand, Priyanka

An analysis of private long-term disability insurance access, cost, and trends bibl chart color *Monthly Labor Review* p1 Mr 2017

Anantara Hotels Resorts & Spa (Company)

A Haven for The Hunted N. Ekstein color *Bloomberg Businessweek* no4532 p59 Jl 31 2017

Anaphylaxis—Prevention

mom vs. food allergy [Cover story] N. RONES color *Parents* v92 no3 p24 Mr 2017

Anastas, Benjamin

Dad Drops In *New York Times Book Review* p17 Ap 9 2017

Martha Gellhorn's Choice Words *New York Times Book Review* p17 My 28 2017

Anastasi, G. A.

Observation of a large-scale anisotropy in the arrival directions of cosmic rays above 8×10^{18} eV *Science* v357 no6357 p1266 S 22 2017

ANASTASI, JOAN

THE SECRET LIFE OF ANIMALS cartoon *Reader's Digest* v190 no1134 p38 O 2017

Anastasia (Theatrical production)

THE THEATRE *New Yorker* v93 no6 p6 Mr 27 2017

THE THEATRE *New Yorker* v93 no8 p5 Ap 10 2017

ANASTASIA, GEORGE

OldFellas color *AARP: The Magazine* v59 no1A p44 D 2015/Ja 2016

ANASTASIA, LAURA

the bye-bye blues *Parents* p132 2015

From Farm to Trash: Every year, billions of pounds of food end up in U.S. landfills. Can reducing the amount we throw away help end hunger—and protect the environment? *New York Times Upfront* v149 no12 p14 Ap 24 2017

Introduce Team Sports *Parents* v92 no9 p168 S 2017

The Real Cost of CHEAP FASHION: Many of our trendy, inexpensive clothes are made in places like Bangladesh, where workers--including children--toil under conditions that may shock you *New York Times Upfront* v150 no1 p8 S 4 2017

Think About Pacifiers *Parents* v92 no9 p163 S 2017

Anastasio, Trey, 1964-

Phish's New Harmony P. DOYLE bw color *Rolling Stone* no1273 p40 N 3 2016

Anat, Berna

How Can I Survive...Public Speaking? *Scholastic Choices* v32 no5 p24 F 2017

Anatomy education

HOLO BONES N. Strochlic color *National Geographic* v231 no6 p4 Je 2017

SEEING TOMORROW C. Leaf color *Fortune* v175 no6 p4 My 1 2017

Anatomy of Melancholy (Poem)

HARM DONE R. Burton *Lapham's Quarterly* v10 no3 p85 Summ 2017

Anavation (Company)

50 GREAT PLACES TO WORK S. DALPHONSE *Washingtonian Magazine* v52 no6 p84 Mr 2017

Anaya, Rudolfo Alfonso, 1937-

Rudolfo Anaya R. González *Humanities* v37 no4 p1 Fall 2016

Anbang Insurance Group Co. Ltd.

It's Insurance. It's an Investment. It's Trouble *Bloomberg Businessweek* no4528 p25 Je 26 2017

Anbinder, Tyler

Where America Begins K. HYMOWITZ *New York Times Book Review* p12 N 6 2016

Anbuhl, Kelsey L.

Community network for deaf scientists color *Science* v356 no6336 p386 Ap 28 2017

Ancarani, Yuri

The Challenge V. LUCCA color *Film Comment* v53 no5 p71 S/O 2017

Ancestors

Newest member of human family is surprisingly young A. Gibbons color *Science* v356 no6338 p571 My 12 2017

Anchor Audio Inc.

Products *Parks & Recreation* v52 no8 p74 Ag 2017

Anchor stones

Fast, Safe, and Easy Anchoring R. COPPOLILLO and M. CHAUVIN color *Climbing* no355 p50 Ag 2017

Anchorage

Ground Rules [Cover story] J. Neeves color *Sail* v48 no8 p52 Ag 2017

Star Struck P. Nielsen *Sail* v48 no9 p4 S 2017

WHAT'S OLD IS NEW M. YOUNGBLOOD *Sea Magazine* v108 no10 p22 O 2016

Anchorage (Alaska)—Description & travel

America's Most Adventurous Cities J. MESSIMER color *Men's Health* v32 no6 p42 Ag 2017

WONDERLAND J. Brown bw color *Powder* v45 no3 p82 N 2016

Anchordoqui, L.

Observation of a large-scale anisotropy in the arrival directions of cosmic rays above 8×1018 eV *Science* v357 no6357 p1266 S 22 2017

Anchorman: The Legend of Ron Burgundy (Film)

ANCHORMAN: An ambitious newsreader's career is being held back by rampant sexism *People Management* p62 Jl 2017

I'M WITH STUPID J. Gordinier color *Esquire* p15 Je/Jl 2017

Anchors

See also

Windlasses

ANCHORING 201: SOMETIMES, SIMPLY FIGURING OUT SCOPE AND DROPPING THE HOOK ISN'T ENOUGH F. LANIER color *Sea Magazine* v109 no6 p52 Je 2017

Anchor Locker Arrangement D. Everitt cartoon *Sail* v48 no6 p56 Je 2017

Non-traditional Anchoring *Boating World* v38 no4 p57 Ap 2017

Stay Put F. LANIER *Boating World* v38 no4 p54 Ap 2017

Anchors—Maintenance & repair

Stay Grounded (In a Good Way) M. SMITH *Power & Motoryacht* v32 no11 p150 N 2016

Ancient architecture—Conservation & restoration

Tug of the familiar P. Poore bw cartoon *Old House Journal* v45 no1 p8 F 2017

Ancient armor

METAL OF HONOR color *MHQ: Quarterly Journal of Military History* v30 no1 p58 Aut 2017

Ancient boats

A PHARAOH'S LAST FLEET J. URBANUS color *Archaeology* v70 no1 p13 Ja/F 2017

The Untold Truth D. Harding Jr. color *Power & Motoryacht* v34 no8 p12 Ag 2017

Ancient cities & towns—Greece

A SURPRISE CITY IN THESSALY J. URBANUS color *Archaeology* v70 no2 p16 Mr/Ap 2017

Ancient philosophy

See also

Neoplatonism

Skeptics (Greek philosophy)

Stoicism

What Aristotle Can Teach Firms About CSR R. Chun *Harvard Business Review Digital Articles* p2 S 12 2016

Ancient tapestry

ARTISTS: THREADS OF HISTORY P. D. Toler color *MHQ: Quarterly Journal of Military History* v30 no1 p84 Aut 2017

Ancient weapons

King Tut's dagger J. HESTER color *Astronomy* v45 no8 p82 Ag 2017

Ancrile, Joyce

KITCHEN-TESTED TIPS color *Vegetarian Today* no2 p4 Ap 2017

And I Still Speak of It (Poem)

And I Still Speak of It R. ZUCKER *Nation* v304 no8 p34 Mr 13

2017

And Soon the Darkness (Film)

TO WATCH *Film Comment* v53 no3 p75 My/Je 2017

And What Of (Poem)

And What Of E. MOURE *Walrus* v14 no2 p40 Mr 2017

Andalusian horse

The 2017 Baroque Annual Gallery bw color *Dressage Today* v23 no11 p58 Ag 2017

Andé, Philippe

ART THERAPY C. Zuckerman cartoon color *National Geographic* v231 no4 p154 Ap 2017

Andela, N.

A human-driven decline in global burned area chart graph map *Science* v356 no6345 p1356 Je 30 2017

Anderer, Paul

'RASHOMON' REDUX P. LOPATE *New York Times Book Review* p30 D 4 2016

Anderies, John M.

Social norms as solutions bibl color *Science* v354 no6308 p42 O 7 2016

ANDERS, CHARLIE JANE

STOCHASTIC FANCY cartoon *Wired* v25 no1 p34 Ja 2017

Anders, George

"Alexa, Understand Me" *MIT Technology Review* v120 no5 p26 S/O 2017

For Wind Power, Bigger Is Better graph il *MIT Technology Review* v120 no5 p24 S/O 2017

LESSONS AND IDEAS BY THE 100 GREATEST LIVING BUSINESS MINDS bw color *Forbes* v200 no3 p115 S 28 2017

THE LOOMING RETAIL BAILOUT color graph map *Forbes* v199 no6 p94 Je 13 2017

Major Decisions T. AUBRY *New York Times Book Review* p20 Ag 27 2017

Anders, Greg

The Lost Cadet L. SHINER *Smithsonian* v47 no7 p20 N 2016

Anders, Helen

TEXAS WELCOME bw color *Louisiana Life* v38 no1 p48 S/O 2017

ANDERS, MARK

8 Beach-Body Secrets from the Life of Kai color *Men's Health* v32 no6 p47 Ag 2017

Anders, Robert A.

Mismatch repair deficiency predicts response of solid tumors to PD-1 blockade chart graph *Science* v357 no6349 p409 Jl 28 2017

Anders Berensson Architects (Company)

Revenge of the Trees J. DAVIDSON img *New York* v49 no26 p80 D 26 2016

Andersen, Alex Hogh

VIKINGS D. Franich color *Entertainment Weekly* p24 Jl 24 2017

Andersen, Arild

Kaiser Dives into Intriguing Waters J. Ephland color *Downbeat* v84 no3 p17 Mr 2017

ANDERSEN, B. J.

Q: What did you let go of that changed your life? color *O, The Oprah Magazine* p16 Ag 2017

Andersen, B. M.

Discovery of orbital-selective Cooper pairing in FeSe diag *Science* v357 no6346 p75 Jl 7 2017

ANDERSEN, CHARLOTTE HILTON

13 Things Savvy Shoppers Look for in Online Reviews *Reader's Digest* v188 no1126 p120 D 2016/Ja 2017

Empty Promises color *Reader's Digest* v190 no1133 p52 S 2017

ANDERSEN, ERIK

MADRID UNCLASSIFIED color *Conde Nast Traveler* v51 no10 p144 N 2016

Andersen, Erika

Admitting You Don't Know, When You're the CEO *Harvard Business Review Digital Articles* p2 Ag 17 2015

How to Decide What Skill to Work On Next *Harvard Business Review Digital Articles* p2 Ja 25 2016

Andersen, Hanne

Rapid development of a DNA vaccine for Zika virus bibl graph *Science* v354 no6309 p237 O 14 2016

Andersen, Holly S.

5 supersmart moves for your heart color *Redbook* p97 F 2017

Be good to your heart and head color *Redbook* p77 S 2017

Andersen, Kurt
Fantasia on a Theme J. BOWMAN color *Weekly Standard* v23 no2 p45 S 18 2017
A FIVE-MINUTE GUIDE TO FIVE MILLENNIA OF HUMAN HISTORY cartoon *Esquire* p123 S 2017
HOW AMERICA LOST ITS MIND [Cover story] color *Atlantic* v320 no2 p76 S 2017
National Delusions H. Rosin *New York Times Book Review* p1 S 10 2017
Rolls Of the Dice [Cover story] *New York Times Book Review* p1 O 16 2016

Andersen, Lisa
Lisa Andersen A. DOUGLAS color *Surfer* v58 no3 p28 Je 2017

Andersen, Morten B.
Ocean mixing and ice-sheet control of seawater 234U/238U during the last deglaciation bibl graph *Science* v354 no6312 p626 N 4 2016

Andersen, Richard—Interviews
MEET RICHARD ANDERSEN *Sea Magazine* v108 no8 pPNW-8 Ag 2016

Andersen, Ross
2014: Los Angeles *Lapham's Quarterly* v10 no2 p23 Spr 2017
Pleistocene Park color *Atlantic* v319 no3 p74 Ap 2017

Andersen, Steve
The $100,000 Darley Awards Stake *Arabian Horse World* v57 no8 p114 My 2017
Abu Dhabi Racing *Arabian Horse World* v57 no6 p141 Mr 2017
Arabian Stakes at Deauville, France *Arabian Horse World* v56 no12 p196 S 2016
A CONVERSATION with Jean-Pierre Deroubaix of The Royal Cavalry of Oman *Arabian Horse World* v57 no6 p66 Mr 2017
A CONVERSATION with Jon and Krista Henningsgard *Arabian Horse World* v57 no6 p70 Mr 2017
A CONVRSATION with Thomas Fourcy Al Shaqab Racing-Ecurie Haras Bouquetot Sas *Arabian Horse World* v57 no6 p56 Mr 2017
The Cre Run Oaks and Bob Magness Derby at Delaware Park *Arabian Horse World* v57 no12 p184 S 2017
Darley Awards *Arabian Horse World* v57 no8 p106 My 2017
DARLEY PREVIEW *Arabian Horse World* v57 no6 p16 Mr 2017
European Racing Report *Arabian Horse World* v57 no1 p150 O 2016
French Racing *Arabian Horse World* v57 no11 p152 Ag 2017
HH Sheikh Mansoor Festival Races at Sam Houston Race Park color *Arabian Horse World* v57 no7 p98 Ap 2017
Major Stakes for Arabians in Qatar and the U.A.E. January Racing *Arabian Horse World* v57 no5 p226 F 2017
Major Summer Stakes Races in England *Arabian Horse World* v56 no12 p190 S 2016
March Racing in Abu Dhabi Featuring Five Stakes Races color *Arabian Horse World* v57 no7 p100 Ap 2017
October Arabian Stakes in Texas *Arabian Horse World* v57 no2 p102 N 2016
Paddys Day Tours America *Arabian Horse World* v57 no1 p147 O 2016
The President of the UAE Cup at Deauville *Arabian Horse World* v57 no9 p146 Je 2017
Qatar World Cup Weekend in Paris *Arabian Horse World* v57 no2 p96 N 2016
Racing Arabians Khataab and Joudh Make Statements in France *Arabian Horse World* v57 no12 p176 S 2017
RANKINGS Top International Racehorses *Arabian Horse World* v57 no6 p60 Mr 2017
Sheikh Zayed bin sultan Al Nahyan Jewel Crown *Arabian Horse World* v57 no4 p156 Ja 2017
SPRING RACING IN THE GULF Kahayla Classic and Qatar Gold Sword *Arabian Horse World* v57 no8 p117 My 2017
Summer Racing in England—Tayf Claims England's Richest Arabian Race *Arabian Horse World* v57 no12 p178 S 2017
U.S. Racing at Delaware Park *Arabian Horse World* v56 no12 p194 S 2016
U.S. Summer Racing *Arabian Horse World* v57 no11 p150 Ag 2017

Andersen, T. I.
Magnetic resonance spectroscopy of an atomically thin material using a single-spin qubit bibl color diag graph *Science* v355 no6324 p503 F 3 2017

Anderson, Alex
#Honnolding color *Climbing* no350 p17 D 2016/Ja 2017

Anderson, Alexander H.
This Coalition of 20 Companies Thinks It Can Change U.S. Health Care *Harvard Business Review Digital Articles* p2 F 24 2016
The Value of Teaching Patients to Administer Their Own Care color *Harvard Business Review Digital Articles* p1 Je 2 2017

Anderson, Anthony, 1970-
ANTHONY ANDERSON'S MISSION M. L. Lenker color *Entertainment Weekly* no1471 p18 Je 23 2017
BLACK-ISH L. Ratledge *TV Guide* v65 no43 p26 O 16 2017
The Honor Guard B. MOCKENHAUPT color *Atlantic* v318 no5 p20 D 2016
MAKING THE COVER: September color *Ebony* v72 no11 p14 S 2017

Anderson, Anthony, 1970-—Interviews
BLACK-ISH STARS ACT LIKE REAL-LIFE HUSBAND & WIFE [Cover story] B. VIERA color *Ebony* v72 no11 p68 S 2017

Anderson, B. J.
Structure, force balance, and topology of Earth's magnetopause diag graph *Science* v356 no6341 p960 Je 1 2017

ANDERSON, BRADLEY
Taking on the PC Crowd: A Canadian professor gains fame and followers *American Conservative* v16 no4 p41 Jl/Ag 2017

Anderson, Brenda S.
Chain of Mercy *Publishers Weekly* v264 no4 p50a Ja 23 2017

ANDERSON, BRIAN C.
Dark Intellect color *National Review* v69 no2 p38 F 6 2017
THE LIVING CITY *Claremont Review of Books* v17 no3 p80 Summ 2017
Zombie Lenin *National Review* v69 no18 p38 O 2 2017

Anderson, C. B.
Airborne laser-guided imaging spectroscopy to map forest trait diversity and guide conservation bibl chart graph *Science* v355 no6323 p385 Ja 27 2017

Anderson, Cameron
Powerful People Underperform When They Work Together *Harvard Business Review Digital Articles* p2 F 24 2016

ANDERSON, CAROL
American Apartheid *New York Times Book Review* p12 O 2 2016
Carol Anderson M. Rich color *Current Biography* v78 no2 p3 F 2017
What HR Needs to Do to Get a Seat at the Table *Harvard Business Review Digital Articles* p2 N 27 2014

Anderson, Catherine
Step Up to a Breakthrough color *Women's Health* v14 no9 p88 N 2017

Anderson, Clinton
Curing a Stumbler color *Horse & Rider* v56 no4 p64 Ap 2017
Master Log (& Other) Obstacles color *Horse & Rider* v56 no11 p96 N 2017
REFORMING A Jigger [Cover story] color *Horse & Rider* v56 no1 p52 Ja 2017

ANDERSON, CONNIE
mt. hood obsession color map *Cabin Living* p18 Ja/F 2017

Anderson, Craig E.
ENEMY color *Christian Century* v134 no5 p20 Mr 1 2017

ANDERSON, CYNTHIA
CITY OF HOPE color *Yankee* p118 Mr 2017

Anderson, Darran
Imaginary Cities: A Tour of Dream Cities, Nightmare Cities, and Everywhere in Between *Publishers Weekly* v264 no4 p70 Ja 23 2017

ANDERSON, DIANE
happy days color *Yoga Journal* p44 2017 Special Issue

Anderson, Ever—Interviews
Ever ANDERSON SOKO *Interview* v46 no10 p48 D 2016/Ja 2017

Anderson, Gary, 1959-
WHAT IF? ... THESE FIVE FAILED FIELD GOAL ATTEMPTS HAD BEEN GOOD? J. Feldman color *Sports Illustrated* v126 no11 p67 Ap 17-24 2017

ANDERSON, GIEVES

DINING IN STYLE WITH SARA STORY color *Harper's Bazaar* no3654 p98 Je/Jl 2017

Anderson, Gillian, 1968-

GILLIAN'S RAINBOW H. PORTER cartoon *Vanity Fair* v59 no1 p115 Holiday 2017

Gillian's Valentine Advice color *AARP: The Magazine* v60 no2A p11 F/Mr 2017

We: A Manifesto for Women Everywhere T. Jordan color *Entertainment Weekly* no1459 p63 Mr 31 2017

Anderson, Hannah

Giving Gifted Women a Chance in the Church color *Christianity Today* v61 no6 p88 Jl/Ag 2017

Why God Won't Answer Right Away H. Roots color *Christianity Today* v60 no8 p81 O 2016

Anderson, Heather

Heather Anderson A. A. DAVIS color *Maclean's* v130 no3 p74 Ap 2017

Anderson, J.

Jupiter's interior and deep atmosphere: The initial pole-to-pole passes with the Juno spacecraft [Cover story] color graph *Science* v356 no6340 p821 My 26 2017

Anderson, Jacob B.

Restored iron transport by a small molecule promotes absorption and hemoglobinization in animals color graph *Science* v356 no6338 p608 My 12 2017

Anderson, James R.

Save the world's primates in peril bibl color *Science* v354 no6311 p425 O 28 2016

Anderson, Jay

Relativistic deflection of background starlight measures the mass of a nearby white dwarf star chart color graph *Science* v356 no6342 p1046 Je 9 2017

What weather should you expect? color graph map *Astronomy* v45 no8 p32 Ag 2017

Anderson, Jed

NEW YORK CITY, NY O. Gagnon bw cartoon color *Snowboarder* v29 no5 p82 Ja 2017

SEQUENCE DESTROY color *Snowboarder* v29 no4 p46 D 2016

ANDERSON, JEFFREY H.

Bill Clinton Was Right *Weekly Standard* v22 no6 p8 O 17 2016

Electoral Mapmaking *Weekly Standard* v22 no4 p11 O 3 2016

Electoral Masterpiece map *Weekly Standard* v22 no17 p10 Ja 2 2017

Anderson, Jeremy

APPARATUS J. V. BOND *Interview* v46 no9 p30 N 2016

ANDERSON, JILL

DANCE THAT ADAPTS TO DISABILITIES *USA Today Magazine* v145 no2864 p60 My 2017

Anderson, John

Between heaven and hell, a half-lit existence color *America* v216 no9 p58 Ap 24 2017

French-Canadian nuns face modernity in 'The Passion of Augustine' color *America* v217 no6 p56 S 18 2017

LEAK, PAY, LOVE color *America* v215 no10 p43 O 10 2016

A political life of Pope Francis, from Argentina to the Vatican color *America* v216 no8 p48 Ap 17 2017

PORTRAITS OF AMERICA color *America* v215 no16 p29 N 21 2016

A Swedish curmudgeon, redeemed by children and cats color *America* v216 no4 p50 F 20 2017

'Will' explores the genesis of genius and Shakespeare's Catholic roots color *America* v217 no3 p48 Ag 7 2017

ANDERSON, JON LEE

BOUNDARY ISSUES cartoon color *New Yorker* v93 no31 p24 O 9 2017

OUT OF THE JUNGLE cartoon color *New Yorker* v93 no11 p28 My 1 2017

Anderson, Jonathan William, 1984-

HOME RUN H. MARTIN color *Architectural Digest* v74 no7 p62 Jl 2017

The Loewe* Way E. Wilson color *InStyle* v24 no2 p142 F 2017

Anderson, Kare

Create a "Mastermind Group" to Help Your Career D. Clark *Harvard Business Review Digital Articles* p2 Ag 13 2015

ANDERSON, KAREN

Doses of Neighborhood Nature: The Benefits for Mental Health of

Living with Nature *BioScience* v67 no2 p147 F 2017

Anderson, Kate

INTeRNATiONAL PHOTOgrAPHY CONTeST 2016 FOR KiDS Winners! K. JAZYNKA color *National Geographic Kids* no470 p14 My 2017

Anderson, Kevin

The promise of negative emissions bibl *Science* v354 no6313 p714 N 11 2016

The trouble with negative emissions bibl graph *Science* v354 no6309 p182 O 14 2016

Anderson, Laurie Halse, 1961-

Ashes color *Publishers Weekly* v263 no49 p80 D 7 2016

Dangerous Journey L. BAYARD *New York Times Book Review* p32 N 13 2016

Anderson, Laurie, 1947-

Fairground bw color *Vanity Fair* v58 no12 p95 D 2016

Anderson, Lindsey

The 4 Things It Takes to Succeed in the Digital Economy *Harvard Business Review Digital Articles* p2 Mr 24 2016

Anderson, Louie

louie Anderson A. Wallace color *GQ: Gentlemen's Quarterly* v97 no6 p132 Je 2017

Anderson, M. T., 1968-

Epic Quests: A graphic novel with a wandering hero raises questions about honor and social codes in medieval society M. MELOY *New York Times Book Review* p23 My 14 2017

Yvain: The Knight of the Lion *Publishers Weekly* v263 no51 p150 D 12 2016

Anderson, Mally

THE IMPOSSIBLE LIST bw cartoon color *Esquire* v167 no1 p70 F 2017

ANDERSON, MARCUS

PRADAL SEREY bw color *Black Belt* v55 no5 p48 Ag/S 2017

Anderson, Marian, 1897-1993

Marian Anderson: Let Freedom Ring I. Siff *Opera News* v81 no9 p55 Mr 2017

ANDERSON, MARY

Hit the Playground! color *Parents* v92 no9 p104 S 2017

We've Got Your Back! color *Parents* v92 no11 p84 N 2017

ANDERSON, MATTHEW LEE

THE CALLING OF THE INFERTILE WHO HOPE color *Christianity Today* v61 no4 p48 My 2017

Anderson, Meaghan

10 UP & COMERS: MEAGHAN ANDERSON G. Gullickson *Successful Farming* v115 no8 p36 Je/Jl 2017

Anderson, Mel

The Klan and Other Cowboy Stories *South Dakota Magazine* v32 no4 p66 N/D 2016

Anderson, Michael

How to beat the traffic color *Science* v357 no6346 p36 Jl 7 2017

Anderson, Michael L.

Research: How Leadership Experience Affects Students *Harvard Business Review Digital Articles* p2 F 21 2017

ANDERSON, MICHELLE

Highlines & Picket Lines color *Trail Rider* v29 no3 p34 Ap 2017

ANDERSON, N. JOHN

The Arctic in the Twenty-First Century: Changing Biogeochemical Linkages across a Paraglacial Landscape of Greenland *BioScience* v67 no2 p118 F 2017

Anderson, Nancy K.

SUMMIT CIRCLE *Sierra* v101 no4 p55 Jl/Ag 2016

Anderson, Natalie C.

City of Saints & Thieves *Publishers Weekly* v263 no45 p62 N 7 2016

Anderson, Nicole

Current and coming bw color *Magazine Antiques* v184 no5 p26 S/O 2017

GUIDE TO Hudson NEW YORK and nearby points of interest color map *Magazine Antiques* v184 no3 p49 My/Je 2017

Anderson, Osborne Perry

Escape from Harpers Ferry T. Huntingto *American History* v52 no1 p42 Ap 2017

Anderson, Paul Thomas

GILLIAN JACOBS L. M. M. BLUME bw *Vanity Fair* v59 no4 p124 Mr 2017

PUNCH-DRUNK LOVE F. Kaplan color *Sound & Vision* v82 no3

p69 Ap 2017

Anderson, Ray

The Sun Rises Again B. Henley *Tennis* v52 no6 p12 N/D 2016

Anderson, Richard A.

Keeping in touch with the ER network color *Science* v356 no6338 p584 My 12 2017

ANDERSON, ROBERT P.

Transformational Principles for NEON Sampling of Mammalian Parasites and Pathogens: A Response to Springer and Colleagues *BioScience* v66 no11 p917 N 1 2016

ANDERSON, RYAN T.

The Continuing Threat to Religious Liberty color *National Review* v69 no15 p32 Ag 14 2017

Anderson, Sam

THE ANGLER: John McPhee's radical structures *New York Times Magazine* p28 O 1 2017

THE MYSTERiES OF AN EVERYTHiNG MAN *New York Times Magazine* p32 F 5 2017

New Sentences *New York Times Magazine* p13 Jl 30 2017

Sales is kind of like the Grand Canyon *New York Times Magazine* p14 S 10 2017

VOYAGES *New York Times Magazine* p37 Mr 26 2017

When is silence a lie *New York Times Magazine* p15 Ap 30 2017

WHITE GOLD *New York Times Magazine* p34 Jl 30 2017

You're so quiet you're almost tomorrow *New York Times Magazine* p13 Ap 2 2017

Anderson, Samuel

home & help img *New York* p96 Mr 6 2017

ANDERSON, SCOTT

And Then She Was Gone: An undercover journalist searches for her guide, an Iraqi refugee who was living in Syria *New York Times Book Review* p20 S 10 2017

Anderson, Scott D.

LIVING BY The Word *Christian Century* v133 no22 p23 O 26 2016

Anderson, Sherwood, 1876-1941

On My Obsession with Sherwood Anderson: Revisiting Winesburg, Ohio again and again B. Falconer *Humanities* v38 no4 p1 Fall 2017

Anderson, Steve

The Emir's Sword *Arabian Horse World* v57 no6 p138 Mr 2017

UNPLUG + PLAY color *Cycle World* v56 no3 p46 Ap 2017

Anderson, Sulome

Terrorism's Child N. BURLEIGH *New York Times Book Review* p20 N 27 2016

Anderson, Susan

SOCAL SO COOL C. Hong color *Martha Stewart Living* p88 Mr 2017

Anderson, T. Denise

Reflections on the lectionary *Christian Century* v134 no1 p21 Ja 4 2017

Anderson, Terry L.

Freedom for Indian Country: The federal government has long been proven unworthy of Indians' trust. How the new administration can do better *Hoover Digest: Research & Opinion on Public Policy* no2 p136 Spr 2017

Warning: Semantic Traps Ahead: Environmental politics are littered with language that obscures meaning and hinders good policy *Hoover Digest: Research & Opinion on Public Policy* no3 p77 Summ 2017

Anderson, Tharon

Island Girl color *House Beautiful* v159 no4 p43 My 2017

ANDERSON, THEO

The Century That Could Have Been *In These Times* v41 no2 p40 F 2017

CITIES GO ROGUE *In These Times* v41 no3 p24 Mr 2017

The high Priest of the Church of Trump *In These Times* v41 no1 p44 Ja 2017

RAGE AGAINST - THE - DEMOCRATIC MACHINE: A grassroots revolt from the left is wresting control of the party away from the corporate establishment, one state at a time *In These Times* v41 no7 p18 Jl 2017

THE RIGHT-WING MACHINE BEHIND THE CURTAIN *In These Times* v41 no4 p14 Ap 2017

Two Paths Diverged in the Midwest. Here's Where They Led *In These Times* v41 no8 p20 Ag 2017

Where Trump Voters and Socialists Agree: Single-payer healthcare is picking up unexpected steam *In These Times* v41 no6 p24 Je 2017

Anderson, Theresa

Finding my way color *Equus* no473 p63 F 2017

Anderson, Tim

CROWDSOURCING *Kiplinger's Personal Finance* v71 no12 p20 D 2017

ANDERSON, TOM

Easy Rider color *Road & Track* v68 no8 p108 My 2017

ANDERSON, TOMIKA

The Gift That Keeps on Giving color *Ebony* v72 no6 p62 Ap/My 2017

Helping Kids Cope color *Ebony* v72 no4 p70 F 2017

REALITY TV color *Ebony* v72 no5 p65 Mr 2017

A Silent War: The Battle Between Black Women and Fibroids bw color *Ebony* v72 no5 p62 Mr 2017

Track Stars color *Ebony* v72 no8 p68 Je 2017

THE WAY FORWARD bw color *Ebony* v72 no4 p84 F 2017

Anderson, Tracy

5 Moves to Reinvent Your Rear color *Health* v30 no10 p42 D 2016

Beach Body Boot Camp color *Health* v31 no6 p46 Jl 2017

Build a Body Like J.Lo color *Health* v30 no9 p59 N 2016

Help Me Transform My Thighs! color *Health* v31 no3 p52 Ap 2017

Look better in the buff color *Health* v31 no8 p37 O 2017

New Year, New Arms color *Health* v31 no1 p58 Ja 2017

Sculpt your body like a celeb color *Health* v31 no9 p48 N 2017

Tighten Up with a Towel color *Health* v31 no2 p51 Mr 2017

Anderson, Truman

FRENCH RESISTANCE *Claremont Review of Books* v17 no1 p16 Wint 2016/2017

Anderson localization

Observation of Anderson localization in disordered nanophotonic structures H. Herzig Sheinfux, Y. Lumer et al diag graph *Science* v356 no6341 p953 Je 1 2017

ANDERSON-MINSHALL, DIANE

ART, ACTIVISM & AIDS: THESE DECADES WERE FILLED WITH LGBT CHANGE, BUT THE IMPACT OF AIDS WAS THE BIGGEST bw *Advocate* no1091 p87 Je/Jl 2017

ASIAN AWAKENING color *Advocate* no1090 p11 Ap 2017

THE CAMERA MAN: Duane Cramer is on a mission to change the narrative around black men in popular culture *Advocate* no1093 p14 O/N 2017

COMING OUT-OF THE COFFIN: Born on Halloween, actor MASSIMO DOBROVIC was destined to play the king of vampires, but "happily married gay man" may be his favorite role yet *Advocate* no1093 p61 O/N 2017

EDITOR'S LETTER *Advocate* no1093 p7 O/N 2017

EDITOR'S LETTER bw color *Advocate* no1090 p8 Ap 2017

EDITOR'S LETTER bw color *Advocate* no1091 p8 Je/Jl 2017

FINDING FAMILY, FINDING FREEDOM color *Advocate* no1091 p94 Je/Jl 2017

GRACE AND FRANKIES SAN DIEGO: The artsy burg of La Jolla, California, deserves all the attention it gets *Advocate* no1093 p52 O/N 2017

HOLLYWOOD LESBIANS ARE SLOWLY COMING OUT: Boze Hedleigh opened the closet to some of Hollywood's most famous lesbians. 23 years later, he's doing it again color *Advocate* no1091 p37 Je/Jl 2017

LUCKY IN LOVE: Actress Diora Baird discovered her family's missing piece *Advocate* no1093 p26 O/N 2017

Murder Most Foul color *Advocate* no1090 p57 Ap 2017

NO BONES ABOUT IT color *Advocate* no1090 p32 Ap 2017

THE POWER OF POP CULTURE: ELLEN DEGENERES CHANGED EVERYTHING, BUT SHE DIDN'T DO IT ALONE color *Advocate* no1091 p83 Je/Jl 2017

QUESTIONS FOR MEGAN MULLALLY color *Advocate* no1090 p58 Ap 2017

REVEALING THE "THROUPLE" BEHIND WONDER WOMAN: Did you know the world's hottest superhero was inspired by a polyamorous relationship? *Advocate* no1093 p27 O/N 2017

RISING TIDES LIFT ALL BOATS color *Advocate* no1090 p22 Ap 2017

So Good It's Criminal *Advocate* no1088 p62 D 2016/Ja 2017

Somebody to Love bw color *Advocate* no1089 p60 F/Mr 2017

TALL TALES? color *Advocate* no1090 p34 Ap 2017

THAT SONG IS NOT ABOUT HIM: Carly Simon's ex-husband talks coming out, Hillary's loss, and how truth sets us free color *Advocate* no1091 p34 Je/Jl 2017

WHY AMERICA LOVES NEIL PATRICK HARRIS: THIS FORMER CHILD ACTOR IS AMONG OUR MOST BELOVED GAY ACTORS, BUT TO HIS KIDS HE'S JUST DAD color *Advocate* no1091 p85 Je/Jl 2017

ANDERSON-MINSHALL, JACOB

COURT'S IN SESSION: THE COUNTRY'S FIRST TRANSGENDER JUDGE WAS ALWAYS A RABBLE ROUSER bw *Advocate* no1091 p96 Je/Jl 2017

THE EMPATHY MACHINE color *Advocate* no1090 p57 Ap 2017

ESCAPE TO KEY WEST color *Advocate* no1090 p50 Ap 2017

FORGET ME NOT: TRANS FOLKS ARE AMONG THE COUNTRY'S GREATEST REVOLUTIONARIES. SO WHY DO AMERICANS KEEP FORGETTING WE EXIST? bw color *Advocate* no1091 p74 Je/Jl 2017

HIT AND RUN color *Advocate* no1090 p38 Ap 2017

Judges Rule Queers Have Civil Rights color *Advocate* no1091 p21 Je/Jl 2017

Know Thyself (And Try to Understand Everyone Else): Our 101 guide to gender identities and sexual orientations *Advocate* no1093 p17 O/N 2017

LET'S STOP SHAMING BLACK MEN color *Advocate* no1090 p16 Ap 2017

LOST ON U.S.? LP is a bonafide star with a #1 hit single—in Europe. When will America catch on? bw *Advocate* no1091 p32 Je/Jl 2017

MAINTAINING BISEXUAL SEXUAL HEALTH AND WELLNESS bw *Advocate* no1090 p46 Ap 2017

MARRIAGE EQUALITY WAS WON BY WIDOWERS: THE LOVE STORIES BEHIND THE LANDMARK COURT CASES BOTH ENDED TRAGICALLY bw color *Advocate* no1091 p80 Je/Jl 2017

MORE THAN 40% OF GAY AND BI MEN ARE HAVING CONDOMLESS SEX *Advocate* no1088 p27 D 2016/Ja 2017

MYSTERIOUS SKIN *Advocate* no1088 p32 D 2016/Ja 2017

THE NEW GAY SEXUAL REVOLUTION: PrEP, TasP, and fearless sex remind us we can't advance social justice without including sex in the equation color *Advocate* no1091 p115 Je/Jl 2017

POP ROCKS: Meet rock's next big thing: middle-aged, but still nerdy, trans girl Cait Brennan *Advocate* no1093 p24 O/N 2017

RETHINKING MASCULINITY: A new study shows that gay porn is even driving how straight guys see themselves—and that's a good thing *Advocate* no1093 p59 O/N 2017

THIS WASN'T HIS FIRST RODEO: LONE STAR STATE ACTIVISTS LIKE RAY HILL HAD A GREATER IMPACT THAN MANY KNOW color *Advocate* no1091 p97 Je/Jl 2017

TRUMPOCALYPSE NOW *Advocate* no1090 p9 Ap 2017

VIVA PRIDE! Celebrate LGBT Life at World Pride in Gay Madrid color *Advocate* no1091 p116 Je/Jl 2017

Why You Probably Need an Anal Pap Smear color *Advocate* no1090 p47 Ap 2017

WRITING OUR OWN STORIES: Reality star Karamo Brown says it's time for LGBT people to "take the pen out of Hollywood's hands." *Advocate* no1093 p30 O/N 2017

Anderson-Morrison, Michelle

HOW I'M THRIVING WITH HIV G. Roberts-Grey color *Essence* v47 no8 p144 D 2016

Anderson .Paak, 1986-

Anderson .Paak M. Hagan color *Current Biography* v78 no6 p88 Je 2017

Anderson .Paak, 1986—Interviews

ANDERSON Paak F. LOTUS *Interview* v47 no2 p68 Mr 2017

Andersson, Anna M. C.

Biased partitioning of the multidrug efflux pump AcrAB-TolC underlies long-lived phenotypic heterogeneity diag *Science* v356 no6335 p311 Ap 21 2017

Andersson, Ellen

ELLEN ANDERSSON Leaving Spaces J. Ephland color *Downbeat* v84 no2 p23 F 2017

Andersson, Rebecka

A three-dimensional movie of structural changes in bacteriorho-

dopsin bibl diag graph *Science* v354 no6319 p1552 D 23 2016

Andes, Elizabeth

COLD CASE J. WILLIAMS *Cincinnati Magazine* v50 no3 p30 D 2016

Andes, Scott

Robots Seem to Be Improving Productivity, Not Costing Jobs *Harvard Business Review Digital Articles* p2 Je 16 2015

Why Today's Corporate Research Centers Need to Be in Cities *Harvard Business Review Digital Articles* p2 Mr 1 2016

Andes Region

GROWN AT HOME L. M. Roberts color *National Geographic* v232 no5 p18 N 2017

And Even the Black Guy's Profile Reads Sorry, No Black Guys (Poem)

& even the black guy's profile reads sorry, no black guys D. Smith *New York Times Magazine* p21 Ag 27 2017

Andl, Thomas

Regeneration of fat cells from myofibroblasts during wound healing bibl color graph *Science* v355 no6326 p748 F 17 2017

Andō, Tadao, 1941-

Haute Concrete B. BOSKER color *Atlantic* v319 no3 p28 Ap 2017

Andrabi, Shaida A.

A nuclease that mediates cell death induced by DNA damage and poly(ADP-ribose) polymerase-1 bw graph *Science* v354 no6308 paad6872-1 O 7 2016

Pathological α-synuclein transmission initiated by binding lymphocyte-activation gene 3 bibl graph *Science* v353 no6307 paah3374-1 S 30 2016

Andrada, B.

Observation of a large-scale anisotropy in the arrival directions of cosmic rays above 8×1018 eV *Science* v357 no6357 p1266 S 22 2017

Andrade, A.

Persistent effects of pre-Columbian plant domestication on Amazonian forest composition bibl chart graph map *Science* v355 no6328 p925 Mr 3 2017

Andrades, Ryan

Fringe on the brink: Intertidal reefs at risk color *Science* v357 no6348 p261 Jl 21 2017

Andre (Seal)

Seal of Honor J. Johnson color *Yankee* p24 My/Je 2017

Andreas, Peter

Rebel Mother: My Childhood Chasing the Revolution R. Feinberg *Foreign Affairs* v96 no3 p165 My/Je 2017

Andreas Stihl AG & Co. KG

Reno Gains a Powerful Sponsor color *Flying* v143 no12 p82 D 2016

Andreassen, K.

Massive blow-out craters formed by hydrate-controlled methane expulsion from the Arctic seafloor graph map *Science* v356 no6341 p948 Je 1 2017

Andreatta, Jolie

Meet the crew... D. Holbrook *TV Guide* v65 no35 p7 Ag 21 2017

Andreesen, Marc

On The Forbes 400 bw color *Forbes* v198 no5 p220 O 25 2016

Andreo, Rogelio Bernal

MEET THE MASTER OF Stellar Vistas color *Astronomy* v44 no12 p52 D 2016

Andrés, Aida M.

Chimpanzee genomic diversity reveals ancient admixture with bonobos bibl diag graph map *Science* v354 no6311 p477 O 28 2016

Andrés, José, 1969-

HOW DONALD TRUMP LOST HIS DC RESTAURANTS J. Sidman *Washingtonian Magazine* v52 no2 p68 N 2016

José Andrés M. Ruhlman *Humanities* v37 no4 p1 Fall 2016

My Dad Is a Clown/Mi papá es un payaso *Publishers Weekly* v263 no47 p107 N 21 2016

Andrés, Vicente

Clonal hematopoiesis associated with TET2 deficiency accelerates atherosclerosis development in mice bibl diag *Science* v355 no6327 p842 F 24 2017

Andrésdóttir, Valgerdur

A supramolecular assembly mediates lentiviral DNA integration bibl color *Science* v355 no6320 p1 Ja 6 2017

Andresen, Scott

Scott Andresen L. Cutrone *New Orleans Homes & Lifestyles* v20 no2 p20 Spr 2017

Andrésson, Gunnar V.
CAPTURED BY CURIOSITY G. V. Andrésson *Iceland Review* v55 no1 p52 Ja/F 2017

Andretti, Mario
DRIVING LESSON S. Slon *Saturday Evening Post* v289 no3 p4 My/Je 2017
MARIO ANDRETTI S. Slon *Saturday Evening Post* v289 no3 p48 My/Je 2017
MARIO IS FEELING FINE J. Skow *Saturday Evening Post* v289 no3 p52 My/Je 2017
The Wrecked, Rebuilt Life OF ALDO ANDRETTI D. S. COMISKEY *Indianapolis Monthly* p72 My 2017

Andrew, David
How to Cut in Line J. Stewart color *Atlantic* v320 no2 p22 S 2017

Andrew, Doug
Prioritize Your Opportunities with This Checklist *Harvard Business Review Digital Articles* p2 S 22 2017

Andrew, Nigel R.
Higher predation risk for insect prey at low latitudes and elevations graph *Science* v356 no6339 p742 My 19 2017

Andrew, Paul
FLORENCE in Abundance M. HOLGATE color *Vogue* v207 no4 p150 Ap 2017
Kindred SOLES R. WALDMAN color *Vogue* v206 no12 p158 D 2016

Andrew, Prince, Duke of York, 1960-
Tech's Royal Kingmaker P. OLSON *Forbes* v199 no4 p42 Ap 25 2017

Andrew Cyrille Quartet (Performer)
The Declaration Of Musical Independence/Proximity C. Wolff color *Downbeat* v83 no12 p70 D 2016

Andrewes, Ian—Interviews
MEET IAN ANDREWES *Sea Magazine* v108 no10 pPNW-8 O 2016

Andrew Martin, J.
Synthesis, debugging, and effects of synthetic chromosome consolidation: synVI and beyond color *Science* v355 no6329 p1045 Mr 10 2017

ANDREWS, ALICE
Clean It Like You Mean It color *Martha Stewart Living* no271 p30 Ja/F 2017

Andrews, Avital
THE 10 COOLEST SCHOOL 10 YEARS ON *Sierra* v101 no5 p39 S/O 2016
The Majestic Ahwahnee Hotel *Sierra* v101 no4 p17 Jl/Ag 2016
A Natural Start *Sierra* v102 no1 p9 Ja/F 2017
THE TOP 10 *Sierra* v101 no5 p40 S/O 2016

Andrews, Barbara McClatchie
Barbara McClatchie Andrews A. HUTCHINS color *Maclean's* v129 no43 p66 O 31 2016

Andrews, Becca
"WE JUST FEEL LIKE WE DON'T BELONG HERE ANYMORE" color *Mother Jones* v42 no6 p14 N/D 2017

Andrews, Benedict
Una L. Greenblatt color *Entertainment Weekly* no1486 p43 O 13 2017

Andrews, Benny
Benny Andrews: The Bicentennial Series color *Art in America* v104 no10 p169 N 2016

Andrews, Betsy
BIRD CRAZY color *Prevention* v69 no6 p64 Je 2017
The ENERGY for HEALING [Cover story] color *Prevention* v69 no1 p64 Ja 2017
Nature's Medicine color *Prevention* v69 no8 p54 Ag 2017
new orleAns' new Groove color *Rodale's Organic Life* v2 no7 p66 D 2016/Ja 2017
ORANGES color *Rodale's Organic Life* v2 no7 p45 D 2016/Ja 2017
TINY BUT MIGHTY color *Rodale's Organic Life* v2 no7 p92 D 2016/Ja 2017

ANDREWS, BILL
How Juno Met Jupiter color *Discover* v38 no1 p73 Ja/F 2017
Isaac Newton color *Discover* v38 no4 p40 My 2017

Andrews, Brandon

BRINGING ART TO THE PUBLIC cartoon color *Black Enterprise* v47 no8 p102 Jl/Ag 2017

Andrews, Brenda J.
Exploring genetic suppression interactions on a global scale diag *Science* v354 no6312 p599 N 4 2016

Andrews, Dianne
ENEMY color *Christian Century* v134 no5 p20 Mr 1 2017

Andrews, Donna
Gone Gull: A Meg Langslow Mystery *Publishers Weekly* v264 no25 p94 Je 19 2017
How the Finch Stole Christmas! A Meg Langslow Mystery *Publishers Weekly* v264 no34 p91 Ag 21 2017

Andrews, Erin, 1978-
Reporting Dates T. Keith chart color *Sports Illustrated* v125 no20 p24 D 19 2016

Andrews, Erin, 1978-—Trials, litigation, etc.
THE PAIN YOU CAN'T SEE E. Kaplan color *Sports Illustrated* v126 no4 p40 Ja 30 2017

ANDREWS, FRANK
Frank ANDREWS *Interview* v46 no10 p46 D 2016/Ja 2017

ANDREWS, HELEN
Laugh Fiercely color *Weekly Standard* v22 no13 p28 D 5 2016

Andrews, John
Disciple for Dakota: Joseph Ward came to Yankton to spread Congregationalism, but he also built schools and helped create a state *South Dakota Magazine* v33 no2 p32 Jl/Ag 2017
THE DUSTY TRAIL: The Fort Meade National Backcountry Byway might be our most historic gravel road *South Dakota Magazine* v33 no3 p74 S/O 2017
Life Among the Monks: As archivists at Augustana University sift through Blue Cloud Abbey's treasured photo collection, we learn more about how the Benedictines lived and worked *South Dakota Magazine* v33 no2 p56 Jl/Ag 2017
Meeting Place *South Dakota Magazine* v32 no6 p36 Mr/Ap 2017
WHO LIES IN THE CUSTER GRAVES? *South Dakota Magazine* v32 no4 p40 N/D 2016

Andrews, Josh
A Fighter Pilot's New Career Takes Off K. LANKFORD color *Kiplinger's Personal Finance* v71 no4 p72 Ap 2017

Andrews, Julie, 1935-
LUCKY M. Schulman cartoon *New Yorker* v93 no2 p25 F 27 2017
WHAT DOES JULIE THINK? M. Snetiker color *Entertainment Weekly* no1470 p23 Je 16 2017

Andrews, Julie, 1935-—Interviews
Julie Andrews S. Begley color *Time* v189 no12 p54 Ap 3 2017

Andrews, Kate
All in the Family *Virginia Living* v15 no3 p72 Ap 2017

Andrews, Kathryn
LOOK AGAIN S. COCHRAN color *Architectural Digest* v73 no12 p64 D 2016

ANDREWS, LAURA JOHNSON
CHRISTMAS COOKIES WITH A TWIST *South Dakota Magazine* v32 no4 p38 N/D 2016

ANDREWS, LEON T. JR.
Starting My Journey as NRPA's Chair *Parks & Recreation* v52 no10 p8 O 2017

Andrews, Lisa
SUNDRY SAMARITANS J. DRILLING *Cincinnati Magazine* v50 no8 p106 My 2017

ANDREWS, SANDEE
The Rise of EVEREST *Arabian Horse World* v57 no12 p140 S 2017

Andrews, Sean M.
Spiral density waves in a young protoplanetary disk bibl graph *Science* v353 no6307 p1519 S 30 2016

ANDREWS, SUZANNA
THE WHITE HOUSE INC color *Vanity Fair* v59 no4 p132 Mr 2017

Andrews, Taylor
How I Solved My Horse's Problem cartoon *Horse & Rider* v56 no1 p72 Ja 2017

Andrews, Tom
Artifact exposure J. BENNETT color *Canadian Geographic* v137 no1 p31 F 2017

Andrews, Troy, 1986-
TROMBONE SHORTY SPIRITUAL CONNECTION J. ODELL

color *Downbeat* v84 no6 p48 Je 2017

Andrews-Hanna, Jeffrey C.

Formation of the Orientale lunar multiring basin bibl graph *Science* v354 no6311 p441 O 28 2016

Gravity field of the Orientale basin from the Gravity Recovery and Interior Laboratory Mission bibl graph *Science* v354 no6311 p438 O 28 2016

Andriakos, Jacqueline

17 Eat-Clean Secrets from Top Chefs color *Health* v31 no3 p42 Ap 2017

6 burning workout questions—answered! color *Health* v31 no9 p41 N 2017

BETH BEHRS "Healthy Doesn't Have to Be So Stressful" color *Health* v31 no6 p21 Jl 2017

Be your own personal trainer color *Health* v31 no8 p21 O 2017

CAN FASTING BE GOOD FOR YOU? color *Health* v31 no7 p86 S 2017

CHRISTIE BRINKLEY "Feeling Good Is Looking Good" color *Health* v31 no5 p19 Je 2017

Do a Digital Detox color *Health* v31 no5 p22 Je 2017

Get Your Best Rest Ever color *Health* v31 no4 p24 My 2017

Get Zen in a Hurry color *Health* v31 no7 p28 S 2017

KELLY ROWLAND "You Have to Treat Yourself" color *Health* v31 no2 p22 Mr 2017

Let Go of Guilt color *Health* v30 no10 p26 D 2016

No More Party Pounds color *Health* v30 no10 p37 D 2016

RACHEL BRATHEN "Life Takes You Where You're Supposed to Go" color *Health* v31 no3 p22 Ap 2017

The right (and wrong) ways to get a hot Hollywood bod color *Health* v31 no8 p43 O 2017

SKYLAR DIGGINS "Everything Happens for a Reason" color *Health* v31 no1 p20 Ja 2017

Slash Refined Carbs All Day color *Health* v31 no4 p114 My 2017

Squeeze More Joy Out of Life color *Health* v31 no3 p24 Ap 2017

Start a Gratitude Habit color *Health* v30 no9 p26 N 2016

Stay-Slim Moves That Will Make You Smile color *Health* v31 no1 p37 Ja 2017

Stop the Fat Talk color *Health* v31 no2 p24 Mr 2017

Stop the Weekend Weight Gain color *Health* v31 no2 p45 Mr 2017

This Quiz Will Save Your Waist color *Health* v31 no7 p63 S 2017

Turn up your burn color *Health* v31 no9 p26 N 2017

Which Cooking Methods Are Healthiest? color *Health* v31 no6 p128 Jl 2017

Your A to Z Summer Shape-Up color *Health* v31 no6 p39 Jl 2017

Andringa, S.

Observation of a large-scale anisotropy in the arrival directions of cosmic rays above 8 × 1018 eV *Science* v357 no6357 p1266 S 22 2017

Androgyny (Psychology)

DAVID BOWIE J. C. Mitchell and L. Greenblatt color *Entertainment Weekly* no1446/1447 p88 D 2016/Ja 2017

editor's note. ON BECOMING A LEADER K. Perina *Psychology Today* v50 no1 p3 Ja/F 2017

UNLABELED: Ari Fitz doesn't care if you think she's a boy or a girl—just don't put her in a box *Advocate* no1093 p14 O/N 2017

Android (Operating system)

4 ways to keep from sleeping through your Android alarm B. PATTERSON color *PCWorld* v35 no2 p193 F 2017

6 quick ways to clear space on an overstuffed Android device B. PATTERSON color *PCWorld* v35 no9 p101 S 2017

6 settings to make your Android phone anticipate your needs B. PATTERSON color *PCWorld* p168 D 2016

8 Android gestures that speed up everyday tasks B. PATTERSON color *PCWorld* v35 no1 p192 Ja 2017

ANDROID 8 OREO M. SIMON color *PCWorld* v35 no10 p95 O 2017

THE ESSENTIAL PHONE IS A BEAUTIFUL EXAMPLE OF EVERYTHING THAT'S WRONG WITH ANDROID [Cover story] M. SIMON color *PCWorld* v35 no7 p161 Jl 2017

GOOGLE ASSISTANT: 5 KILLER NEW FEATURES YOU SHOULD BE USING R. WHITWAM color *PCWorld* v35 no8 p121 Ag 2017

HTC U11 : A powerful Android phone that knows how to have fun M. SIMON color graph *PCWorld* v35 no7 p116 Jl 2017

Transfer everything from your old Android phone to your new one M. SIMON and D. WALTER bw color *PCWorld* v35 no8 p134

Ag 2017

With the Galaxy Note7 dead, here are 7 other Android phablets to consider I. PAUL color *PCWorld* v35 no11 p31 N 2016

Android (Operating system)—Evaluation

Hands-on: Running Android apps on a Chromebook could be the best of both worlds M. RIOFRIO color *PCWorld* p112 Mr 2017

Android (Operating system)—Security measures

5 alternative (and easier) ways to unlock your Android phone B. PATTERSON color *PCWorld* v35 no4 p136 Ap 2017

6 easy ways to keep your Android phone secure B. PATTERSON color *PCWorld* v35 no6 p39 Je 2017

Andromeda (Constellation)

Priceless royalty G. CHAPLE color *Astronomy* v45 no11 p14 N 2017

Andromeda Galaxy

Going deep for Andromeda P. HARRINGTON color *Astronomy* v44 no12 p68 D 2016

Priceless royalty G. CHAPLE color *Astronomy* v45 no11 p14 N 2017

Andrus, Jerry

an introduction to JERRY ANDRUS R. Worth, J. Collver et al *Skeptical Inquirer* v41 no1 p65 Ja/F 2017

Andrus, Joel

Boards Aren't the Right Way to Monitor Companies *Harvard Business Review Digital Articles* p2 My 10 2016

Andrusiak, Kerry

Exploring genetic suppression interactions on a global scale diag *Science* v354 no6312 p599 N 4 2016

And When I Die, I Won't Stay Dead (Film)

DIGGING AND BLUING WITH BILLY WOODBERRY J. Luckett *Film Quarterly* v70 no4 p67 Summ 2017

Anecdotes

A Day's Work M. BEST, J. BOEHM et al *Reader's Digest* v188 no1126 p64 D 2016/Ja 2017

Humor in Uniform color *Reader's Digest* v190 no1135 p135 N 2017

Humor in Uniform *Reader's Digest* v188 no1124 p141 O 2016

IN THE RED *Reader's Digest* v188 no1126 p81 D 2016/Ja 2017

Laughter *Reader's Digest* v188 no1126 p80 D 2016/Ja 2017

Life S. BUZEK, R. BLOUNT JR. et al *Reader's Digest* v188 no1126 p36 D 2016/Ja 2017

Anemia

GLOSSARY *Equus* no476 p95 My 2017

Stay Sharp J. TEITELBAUM color *Better Nutrition* v78 no11 p34 N 2016

Anemia in pregnancy

second-trimester surprises L. SINGER MORAN *Parents* v92 no8 p128 Ag 2017

Anemia—Prevention

Lucky Iron Fish to Add Iron to Food [Cover story] color *Prevention* p13 Mr 2017

Anemones

Dividing the Spoils K. Moore color *Natural History* v125 no5 p7 My 2017

Aneuploidy

Tumor aneuploidy correlates with markers of immune evasion and with reduced response to immunotherapy T. Davoli, H. Uno et al diag *Science* v355 no6322 p261 Ja 20 2017

Aneurysms—Treatment

Targeting nitric oxide to treat aneurysm *Science* v355 no6324 p492 F 3 2017

Ang, Andrew

Faceless Returns N. VARDI color *Forbes* v199 no7 p148 Je 29 2017

ANG, KRISTIANO

Being Salinger cartoon color *Esquire* v167 no1 p21 F 2017

Angconeb, Ahmoo

Ahmoo Angeconeb A. A. DAVIS color *Maclean's* v130 no8 p66 S 2017

Angedakin, Samuel

Chimpanzee genomic diversity reveals ancient admixture with bonobos bibl diag graph map *Science* v354 no6311 p477 O 28 2016

Angel, Karen

The Soft Edge That's Landing Solid Sales color *Bloomberg Businessweek* no4535 p39 Ag 28 2017

This Land Ain't My Land color *Bloomberg Businessweek* no4503 p38 D 12 2016

ANGEL, TRACI

DANCING WITH ART bw color *Missouri Life* v44 no3 p24 My 2017

Angeles, Domingo

Interview with a ... Character actor *Career Outlook* p1 F 2017

Interview with a ... Professor of aerospace engineering *Career Outlook* p1 Mr 2017

Putting your liberal arts degree to work *Career Outlook* p1 Ag 2017

Space careers: A universe of options chart color *Career Outlook* p1 N 2016

Summer employment: A snapshot of teen workers *Career Outlook* p2 Je 2017

ANGELI, MICHAEL

MISS VAL color *Los Angeles Magazine* v62 no10 p142 O 2017

Angelico, fra, ca. 1400-1455

Transfiguration H. J. Hornik and M. C. Parsons color *Christian Century* v134 no3 p39 F 2017

Angelidakis, Andreas

ATHENS Chorus of Complaint color *Art in America* v105 no8 p45 S 2017

Angelini, Marcello

Start Smart J. Stahl color *Dance Magazine* v91 no3 p10 Mr 2017

Angell, Marcia

The Abortion Battlefield bw color *New York Review of Books* v64 no11 p8 Je 22 2017

Why Be a Parent? bw color *New York Review of Books* v63 no17 p8 N 10 2016

Angell, Rob

Leicester City FC and the Benefits of an Underdog Brand *Harvard Business Review Digital Articles* p2 Ag 12 2016

Angelo, Bonnie

Bonnie Angelo J. Schecter color *Time* v190 no13 p17 O 2 2017

Milestones *Time* v190 no13 p17 O 2 2017

Angelo, C. Mark

Teaching Hospitals Are the Best Place to Test Health Innovation *Harvard Business Review Digital Articles* p2 N 21 2014

Angelo State University

Education *Stage Directions* v30 no7 p26 Jl 1 2017

Angeloni, Lisa

Noise pollution is pervasive in U.S. protected areas graph map *Science* v356 no6337 p531 My 5 2017

ANGELOS, JAMES

THE FRENCH DEFECTION bw color *New York Times Magazine* p44 Ja 29 2017

Angelou, Maya, 1928-2014

Use Your Gift [Cover story] K. Drew bw color *Glamour* v115 no3 p174 Mr 2017

What I Know for Sure Oprah color *O, The Oprah Magazine* p174 My 2017

What I Know for Sure O. Winfrey color *O, The Oprah Magazine* p140 S 2017

Angels (Investors)

What Angel Investors Value Most When Choosing What to Fund N. Torres *Harvard Business Review Digital Articles* p2 Ag 6 2015

Angels in America (Theatrical production)

GOINGS ON ABOUT TOWN color *New Yorker* v93 no16 p9 Je 5 2017

To Do: Twenty-five things to see, hear, watch, and read img *New York* v50 no11 p128 My 29 2017

Angels in America: A Gay Fantasia on National Themes (Theatrical production)

ANGELS AND DEMONS O. EUSTIS color *Vanity Fair* v59 no5 p120 Ap 2017

Angels in art

Angels Speaking Hebrew L. Copan color *Christian Century* v133 no22 p47 O 26 2016

ON ART P. Solovyev color *Christian Century* v133 no26 p47 D 21 2016

Angels in the Bible

The Right Word M. R. SIMONE il *America* v215 no19 p38 D 19 2016

Angels—Christianity

Encounters With Angels M. R. SIMONE *America* v215 no18 p42 D 5 2016

Anger

5 Signs Your Job is Completely Stressing You Out S. Floyd and A. GUMBS color *Black Enterprise* v47 no4 p29 N/D 2016

BEAUTIFUL ORTHODOXY [Cover story] M. GALLI bw color *Christianity Today* v60 no8 p34 O 2016

Don't Let Emotions Screw Up Your Decisions F. Gino *Harvard Business Review Digital Articles* p2 My 6 2015

LET IT GO! color *Good Housekeeping* v265 no3 p110 S 2017

OVERCOMING ILL WILL B. GUNARATANA color *Tricycle: The Buddhist Review* v26 no3 p38 Spr 2017

Viral Anger Spreads Like a Disease—and It's Making the Country Sick S. Schrobsdorff color *Time* v190 no2/3 p19 Jl 10-17 2017

What I Know for Sure Oprah color *O, The Oprah Magazine* p124 Ag 2017

Anger in the workplace

What to Do Before You Lose Your Cool at Work N. M. Williams color *Black Enterprise* v47 no3 p38 O 2016

Anger management

All the Rage L. Featherstone color *Nation* v305 no5 p5 Ag 28 2017

CALM THE F#©% DOWN bw chart color *GQ: Gentlemen's Quarterly* v97 no10 p94 O 2017

Angie Tribeca (TV program)

Angie Tribeca J. Russell *TV Guide* v65 no14 p37 Ap 3 2017

JAGGER THE DOG N. Serrao color *Entertainment Weekly* no1466 p50 My 19 2017

Angiosperms

Woodland Wildflowers on the Edge M. ADAMOVIC *American Forests* v123 no2 p32 Summ 2017

Angkor (Extinct city)

NATIONAL GALLERY CAMBODIA R. Griffiths *History Today* v67 no5 p78 My 2017

Anglada-Escude, Guillem

Earth's Surprise Neighbor Hints at Exoplanet Abundance E. BETZ color diag *Discover* v38 no1 p10 Ja/F 2017

Angle, Alexandra—Interviews

A New Americana D. BRENNER color *House Beautiful* v159 no9 p94 N 2017

Angle, Jared

OUT LATE: Jared Angle Talks Opera F. P. DRISCOLL *Opera News* v81 no10 p16 Ap 2017

Variety Artist F. P. DRISCOLL *Opera News* v81 no10 p6 Ap 2017

Angle, Karen

Another Conch Regatta on Tap color *Sail* v48 no1 p19 Ja 2017

Angle of attack (Aerodynamics)

ANGLE OF ATTACK INDICATOR diag *Flying* v144 no6 p20 Je 2017

Angleberger, Tom

Deals R. DEAHL *Publishers Weekly* v263 no40 p9 O 3 2016

Anglerfishes

ROMANTIC ATTACHMENT P. Edmonds color *National Geographic* v230 no6 p25 D 2016

Anglers Journal Television (TV program)

A Fishing Life J. Brownlee color *Power & Motoryacht* v34 no8 p20 Ag 2017

Angles (Geometry)—Measurement

POINT-SIZED UNIVERSE? D. Hooper, M. E. Bakich et al color *Astronomy* v45 no2 p34 F 2017

Anglican chants

Aren't Anglicans Protestant? T. C. MORGAN *Christianity Today* p19 Mr 2017

Anglicans—History

The Maori: separate and equal? P. Jenkins *Christian Century* v133 no22 p45 O 26 2016

Anglo-Saxon chronicle

CHRONICLES OF THE CONQUERED C. Konshuh and R. Lavelle *History Today* v66 no10 p15 O 2016

Out of the Margins E. Parker *History Today* v67 no1 p25 Ja 2017

Anglo-Saxon civilization—History

Revolt in Madagascar, 70 Years On R. T. Howard *History Today* v67 no4 p4 Ap 2017

ANGRIST, MISHA

Inherited Conditions: Two books about living with rare genetic diseases—the science, the suffering, the hope *New York Times*

Book Review p20 Ap 30 2017

Angry Birds Movie, The (Film)

THE ANGRY BIRDS MOVIE T. J. Norton cartoon *Sound & Vision* v82 no1 p69 Ja 2017

Anguilla—Description & travel

TRAVEL Body Paint color *Sports Illustrated* v126 no6 p148 F 20 2017

Angular momentum (Nuclear physics)

See also

Proton spin

Revealing the subfemtosecond dynamics of orbital angular momentum in nanoplasmonic vortices G. Spektor, D. Kilbane et al bibl diag *Science* v355 no6330 p1187 Mr 17 2017

Angus, martha—Interviews

luxe be a lady K. RENDA color *House Beautiful* v159 no7 p88 S 2017

untamed chic A. PREISER color *House Beautiful* v159 no7 p96 S 2017

Angwin, Julia

A World Apart color *Consumer Reports* v82 no7 p52 Jl 2017

Anh, Vu L.

Evolution of the wheat blast fungus through functional losses in a host specificity determinant diag map *Science* v357 no6346 p80 Jl 7 2017

Anhalt, Emily Katz

Wrath in the Time of Choler: What the Greek myths teach us about anger in troubled times M. BEARD *New York Times Book Review* p18 S 10 2017

Anhedonia

From Food to Mood: The bugs in your gut have hidden ways of helping you master your emotions H. ESTROFF MARANO *Psychology Today* v50 no5 p31 S/O 2017

Anheuser-Busch InBev SA/NV

Better, Bigger, Beerier color *Weekly Standard* v22 no45 p2 Ag 7 2017

BY THE NUMBERS *TV Guide* v65 no6 p12 Ja 30 2017

COUTURE SHOCK G. BLACK bw *Ebony* v72 no6 p98 Ap/My 2017

A Simple Graph Explains the Complex Logic of the Big Beer Merger N. Dawar and C. K. Bagga *Harvard Business Review Digital Articles* p2 O 20 2015

Why More M&As Is a Sign That Scale Is No Longer an Advantage N. Mele *Harvard Business Review Digital Articles* p2 O 26 2015

Anheuser-Busch InBev SA/NV—Finance

CHINA'S NEW CRAFT-BEER BULLY S. Cendrowski color diag *Fortune* v175 no4 p152 Mr 15 2017

Anh Pham, Tuan

Enhanced water permeability and tunable ion selectivity in subnanometer carbon nanotube porins chart color *Science* v357 no6353 p792 Ag 25 2017

ANICH, BOB SOROK

JAMBOREE color *Road & Track* v69 no4 p80 N 2017

Anichkina, Tatiana

The future of US–Russian nuclear deterrence and arms control bibl *Bulletin of the Atomic Scientists* v73 no4 p271 Jl 2017

Anicich, Eric M.

How Powerful, Low-Status Jobs Lead to Conflict *Harvard Business Review Digital Articles* p2 F 11 2016

Why Being a Middle Manager Is So Exhausting *Harvard Business Review Digital Articles* p2 Mr 22 2017

Anicka Yi—Interviews

ANICKA YI IN THE STUDIO R. Simonini color *Art in America* v105 no4 p100 Ap 2017

Aniello, Lucia

Rough Night L. Greenblatt color *Entertainment Weekly* no1471 p51 Je 23 2017

Animal attacks

A BAD DAY IN BEAR COUNTRY T. ORR cartoon color *Outdoor Life* v224 no8 p49 O 2017

WILL IT KILL YOU? E. HILDEBRANDT, C. Jones et al bw color *Popular Mechanics* p88 Jl 2017

Animal behavior

See also

Animal communication

Animal migration

Bird behavior

Feeding behavior in animals

Grooming behavior in animals

Herding behavior in animals

Horse behavior

Nocturnal animals

Play behavior in animals

Seasonal effects on wildlife

Sexual behavior in animals

Social behavior in animals

Animal Valentines *National Geographic Kids* no467 p28 F 2017

Decode Your Pet's Body Language L. Murray color *Health* v31 no3 p71 Ap 2017

Epic Animal Fake Outs J. KIFFEL-ALCHIEH *National Geographic Kids* no469 p14 Ap 2017

Find the HIDDEN ANIMALS *National Geographic Kids* no468 p31 Mr 2017

Find Your Spirit Animal color *Powder* v46 no2 p96 O 2017

Kitty Myths — Busted! S. Bower color *Good Housekeeping* v265 no2 p136 Ag 2017

Moose Amour J. WARBURTON *Idaho Magazine* v17 no1 p24 Ja 2017

PET THERAPY J. Szabo color *Amazing Wellness* v8 no6 p46 Early Winter2016

The PLAY'S the THING M. ZARASKA color diag *Discover* v38 no5 p54 Je 2017

RAISING A RACKET T. HANSEN color *Outdoor Life* v224 no9 p31 N 2017

Reveal Your Animal Instincts! *National Geographic Kids* no466 p32 D 2016/Ja 2017

Using Animals to Predict the Future A. Popescu color *Bloomberg Businessweek* no4533 p19 Ag 7 2017

Animal breeding

See also

Artificial insemination (Animals)

Dog breeding

Horse breeding

Siberia yields earliest evidence for dog breeding D. Grimm color *Science* v356 no6341 p896 Je 1 2017

What it takes to breed horses S. Steuck color *Equus* no475 p15 Ap 2017

Animal breeds

See also

Dog breeds

Aged Arabian Geldings color *Horse & Rider* v56 no9 p59 S 2017

Animal carcasses

See also

Fish carcasses

MORTALITY COMPOSTING J. Henke *Successful Farming* v115 no2 p32 F 2017

Animal classification

See also

Animal species

CELEBRITY STATUS C. Zuckerman color *National Geographic* v232 no4 p29 O 2017

Collections Matter C. KEMP color *Natural History* v125 no10 p38 O 2017

Animal clutches

Cardinal Rules A. Hadhazy color *Natural History* v125 no4 p6 Ap 2017

Animal coloration

See also

Melanism

The biology of color I. C. Cuthill, W. L. Allen et al color *Science* v357 no6350 p470 Ag 4 2017

IN SCIENCE JOURNALS color *Science* v355 no6331 p1277 Mr 24 2017

POP QUIZ C. Barakat and M. Freckleton color *Equus* no475 p30 Ap 2017

Animal communication

Critter Chat A. SHAW color *National Geographic Kids* no473 p37 S 2017

Animal communication—Humor

CRiTTER CHAT A. SHAW color *National Geographic Kids* no470 p31 My 2017

Animal culture

See also
Deer farming
Ranching
The Bad Modern History of Farming W. Berry bw *Progressive* v81 no5 p46 Je/Jl 2017
DON'T HAVE A COW: It seemed like a bright idea to raise cattle, but the average cow is a disaster waiting to happen P. Gulley *Saturday Evening Post* v289 no5 p16 S/O 2017

Animal defenses
See also
Camouflage (Biology)
AN EYE FOR CAMOUFLAGE E. MASTROIANNI color *Discover* v38 no5 p9 Je 2017
Secrets of the Houdini-like hagfish color *Science* v355 no6321 p112 Ja 13 2017
Unusually loose skin protects hagfish S. MILIUS color *Science News* v191 no2 p13 F 4 2017

Animal diseases
See also
Avian influenza
Baldness in animals
Chronic wasting disease
First Aid for Your Pet L. Murray color *Health* v30 no9 p106 N 2016
GLOSSARY *Equus* no471 p71 D 2016

Animal diseases—Norway
Norway seeks to stamp out prion disease E. Stokstad color map *Science* v356 no6333 p12 Ap 7 2017

Animal diseases—Prevention
Beat the Heat A. Levi color *Health* v31 no5 p72 Je 2017

Animal diversity
More Training in Animal Ethics Needed for European Biologists M. A. ZEMANOVA *BioScience* v67 no3 p301 Mr 2017
Stone Forest K. B. RATTINI color map *National Geographic Kids* no473 p20 S 2017

Animal diversity conservation
Shadow Cats C. Dell'Amore color diag map *National Geographic* v231 no2 p104 F 2017

Animal ecology
See also
Animal defenses
Animals—Population biology
Wildlife habitat improvement
Celebrating Canada's Natural Heritage R. J. Bates *Canadian Wildlife* v23 no2 p5 My/Je 2017
The Moral Urgency of Action to Protect the World's Megafauna M. P. NELSON and K. D. MOORE *BioScience* v66 no12 p1009 D 1 2016
More Training in Animal Ethics Needed for European Biologists M. A. ZEMANOVA *BioScience* v67 no3 p301 Mr 2017
SAN JUAN ISLANDS GEMS D. HISLOP *Sea Magazine* v109 no4 p1 Ap 2017
Up to Speed: Two Months, One Page P. Rauber *Sierra* v102 no4 p22 Jl/Ag 2017

Animal epigenetics
Clonal hematopoiesis associated with TET2 deficiency accelerates atherosclerosis development in mice J. J. Fuster, S. MacLauchlan et al bibl diag *Science* v355 no6327 p842 F 24 2017

Animal experimentation
Sloppy reporting on animal studies proves hard to change M. Enserink color *Science* v357 no6358 p1337 S 29 2017

Animal experimentation & ethics
A trans-Atlantic transparency gap on animal experiments M. Wadman color graph *Science* v357 no6347 p119 Jl 14 2017

Animal experimentation—Moral & ethical aspects
To Treat Primates More Humanely: Transparency M. Brouillette color *Scientific American* v316 no2 p14 F 2017

Animal experimentation—United States
To Treat Primates More Humanely: Transparency M. Brouillette color *Scientific American* v316 no2 p14 F 2017

Animal feeding
See also
Grazing
FOOD FOR THOUGHT: Five tasty trivia tidbits color *Yankee* p98 Jl 2017
HEAD OFF HAY SHORTAGES C. Barakat and M. Freckleton

Equus no474 p14 Mr 2017
MANAGE GRAZING BEHAVIOR: INFLUENCING THE GRAZING HABITS OF CATTLE CAN LEAD TO MORE UNIFORM FORAGE USE R. Nickel *Successful Farming* v115 no9 p58 Ag 2017
SAFEGUARDS FOR GRAZING ALFALFA: MANAGE THE RISK OF BLOAT WHEN HARVESTING ALFALFA BY GRAZING R. Nickel *Successful Farming* v115 no9 p62 Ag 2017

Animal fibers
UNRAVELING A SECRET B. ALEX bw color map *Discover* v38 no8 p40 O 2017
Wool Gathering M. ENGELHARD *Sierra* v101 no6 p64 N/D 2016

Animal flight
A genetic signature of the evolution of loss of flight in the Galapagos cormorant A. Burga, W. Wang et al color diag *Science* v356 no6341 p921 Je 1 2017

Animal flight—Evolution
Ancient birds could achieve liftoff M. ROSEN *Science News* v190 no11 p9 N 26 2016

Animal flight—Research
Ancient birds could achieve liftoff M. ROSEN *Science News* v190 no11 p9 N 26 2016

Animal genetics
Charting genetic diversity around the world K. Travis map *Science News* v190 no9 p32 O 29 2016

Animal grooming
How Can I Maximize Rides When I Have Minimal Time? J. Susser *Dressage Today* v23 no6 p16 F 2017
SADDLE CHAT J. Sheldon, J. Bagot et al bw color graph *Horse & Rider* v56 no9 p21 S 2017

Animal habitations
Ghost Cat [Cover story] J. KIFFEL-ALCHEH color map *National Geographic Kids* no475 p12 N 2017

Animal handling
AQHA Executive Council Introduces Jerk-Down Rule *Spin to Win Rodeo* v21 no5 p16 Jl 2017
Hind-End 'L' [Cover story] L. Place and J. Paulson color *Horse & Rider* v56 no5 p31 My 2017
Na'mous Al Shahania J. Wintersteen color *Arabian Horse World* v57 no7 p114 Ap 2017

Animal health
Beyond basic care L. Bonner color *Equus* no476 p62 My 2017

Animal health technicians
Healing Hands J. SULLIVAN color *Trail Rider* v29 no4 p26 My 2017

Animal herds
Changes in Herd Composition a Key to Indian Dairy Production M. Landes and J. Cessna *Amber Waves: The Economics of Food, Farming, Natural Resources, & Rural America* p5 Je 2017
Coping with a "macho" gelding K. A. Houpt color *Equus* no476 p89 My 2017
Dividends of Diversity N. Wilson color *Natural History* v125 no6 p8 Je 2017
Family Flock E. Conant bw color *National Geographic* v230 no5 p140 N 2016
HERD REPLACEMENTS: RAISE OR BUY? THAT QUESTION IS BACK ON THE RADAR WITH MUCH LOWER PRICES G. Johnston *Successful Farming* v115 no6 p59 Ap 2017
Turkey color *National Geographic* v230 no5 p7 N 2016

Animal herds—Management
Lost Skills of the cattle drive L. Miller bw *American Cowboy* p66 LEGENDS OF TEXAS Special Issue 2017

Animal industry
See also
Livestock
Meat industry
Swine industry

Animal industry—United States
Learning Lessons from Lambing Season *Mother Earth News* no281 p5 Ap/My 2017

Animal jumping
See also
Jumping (Horsemanship)
Bet You Didn't Know V. C. CLARK color *National Geographic*

Kids no471 p11 Je/Jl 2017

Animal Kingdom (TV program)

Animal Kingdom J. Halterman *TV Guide* v65 no35 p35 Ag 21 2017

ANIMAL KINGDOM S. Highfill color *Entertainment Weekly* no1468/1469 p65 Je 2-9 2017

ANIMAL KINGDOM: The Cody clan at the center of the California-set crime drama often get into hot water. But on set, they know how to keep it cool J. HALTERMAN *TV Guide* v65 no27 p20 Je 26 2017

More Family Drama on Animal Kingdom *TV Guide* v65 no19 p11 My 1 2017

Animal life spans

See also

Animals—Longevity

Dating a Greenland Shark J. NIELSEN *Natural History* v125 no2 p10 F 2017

Animal locomotion

See also

Horse paces, gaits, etc.

Running

Walking

Active Perception N. Wilson *Natural History* v125 no2 p6 F 2017

The emergent physics of animal locomotion: Many physiological systems must work together to enable movement in animals and other organisms. Neuromechanics explores how those systems interact with each other and the environment S. Sponberg *Physics Today* v70 no9 p34 S 2017

Animal mechanics

See also

Animal locomotion

Making Moves J. H. TIBBETTS *BioScience* v67 no1 p7 Ja 2017

Animal migration

See also

Bird migration

Drowned wildebeest provide ecological feast E. Pennisi color diag *Science* v356 no6344 p1217 Je 23 2017

From Agricultural Benefits to Aviation Safety: Realizing the Potential of Continent-Wide Radar Networks S. BAUER, J. W. CHAPMAN et al *BioScience* v67 no10 p912 O 2017

Join the herd diag *Backpacker* v45 no1 p14 Ja 2017

Mass seasonal bioflows of high-flying insect migrants Gao Hu, K. S. Lim et al bibl graph *Science* v354 no6319 p1584 D 23 2016

Animal models in research

THE MOODS OF ANIMALS C. Console *Harper's Magazine* v334 no2001 p11 F 2017

Animal models in research—Moral & ethical aspects

A trans-Atlantic transparency gap on animal experiments M. Wadman color graph *Science* v357 no6347 p119 Jl 14 2017

Animal morphology

See also

Body size

Embryology

Early body layout depends on brain L. SANDERS *Science News* v192 no7 p12 O 28 2017

Why midsize animals have the most zip H. Thompson graph *Science News* v192 no2 p32 Ag 19 2017

Animal nutrition

See also

Cattle—Pregnancy—Nutritional aspects

Egg yolk

GENETICS Going gray D. P. Sponenberg color *Equus* no470 p68 N 2016

GET YOUR HORSE'S SHINE ON C. Barakat and M. Freckleton color *Equus* no478 p24 Jl 2017

IN THE SHADOW OF DEATH E. Freedman color *Earth Island Journal* v32 no1 p42 Spr 2017

Animal owners

See also

Horse owners

Pet owners

Meow or Never: Was I up to pet parenthood one more time? D. Paul color *Indianapolis Monthly* v41 no2 p168 S 2017

Animal pigments

The biology of color I. C. Cuthill, W. L. Allen et al color *Science* v357 no6350 p470 Ag 4 2017

Animal-plant relationships

See also

Insect-plant relationships

Using Plant-Animal Interactions to Inform Tree Selection in Tree-Based Agroecosystems for Enhanced Biodiversity V. E. PETERS, T. A. CARLO et al *BioScience* v66 no12 p1046 D 1 2016

Animal population density

The Pollinator BLAME GAME K. Birchmier *Successful Farming* v114 no10 p36 O 2016

Animal population estimates

Counting Whales in the Seas, Trees in the Forests, and Mountain Lions on the Ridges C. L. DYBAS *BioScience* v66 no12 p1013 D 1 2016

Animal populations

See also

Animal herds

Bird populations

Fish populations

Mammal populations

RISE of the SYNANTHROPES K. BANKS color *Canadian Geographic* v137 no3 p56 My 2017

Animal prints (Decoration & ornament)

ANIMAL KINGDOM O. J. WILLIAMS color *Ebony* v72/73 no12/1 p38 O/N 2017

Animal products

See also

Meat

U.S. Per Capita Availability of Red Meat, Poultry, and Fish Lowest Since 1983 J. Bentley *Amber Waves: The Economics of Food, Farming, Natural Resources, & Rural America* p18 F 2017

Animal psychology—Research

The Future of Zoos J. Worland color *Time* v189 no7/8 p54 F 27 2017

Animal radio tracking

MINIATURIZED GPS COLLARS, SOPHISTICATED DNA MAPPING, AND CROWDSOURCED DATA ARE CHANGING THE WAY WE MANAGE OUR WILDLIFE D. KRAMER cartoon color *Outdoor Life* v224 no2 p50 F/Mr 2017

Remote Sensors Bring Wildlife Tracking to New Level J. H. TIBBETTS *BioScience* v67 no5 p411 My 2017

Animal rescue

See also

First aid for animals

Wildlife rescue

Agony and hope in the ashes N. MACDONALD color *Maclean's* v130 no8 p11 S 2017

Badger S. ELDER color *National Geographic Kids* no472 p26 Ag 2017

COMMUNING WITH NATURE *Cincinnati Magazine* v50 no8 p46 My 2017

ELEPHANT "ASKS" FOR HELP R. Davidson *National Geographic Kids* no467 p13 F 2017

KATHERINE HEIGL GUARDS DOGS (AND CATS) C. M. Smith color *Entertainment Weekly* no1462 p16 Ap 21 2017

NOT-FOREVER FAMILIES D. Bruno color *Washingtonian Magazine* v52 no7 p161 Ap 2017

PADEMELON A. KLEPEIS *National Geographic Kids* no466 p20 D 2016/Ja 2017

Animal research

Early animal fossils at risk K. McLaughlin color *Science* v356 no6335 p230 Ap 21 2017

FANCY FOOTWORK S. MORROW color *Discover* v38 no9 p9 N 2017

Sloppy reporting on animal studies proves hard to change M. Enserink color *Science* v357 no6358 p1337 S 29 2017

WILDLIFE color *Canadian Geographic* v137 no5 p20 S/O 2017

Animal rights—United States

Captive Royals & Meat MACHINES ANIMALS in AMERICA TODAY G. Sager *Vegetarian Journal* v35 no2 p18 2016

Animal sanctuaries

See also

Wildlife refuges

CHIMPS IN WAITING D. Grimm color *Science* v356 no6343 p1114 Je 16 2017

Save the world's primates in peril Bin Yang, J. R. Anderson et al bibl color *Science* v354 no6311 p425 O 28 2016

TURTLES, EAGLES, AND BEAVERS, OH MY: Tucked among development and woods, the Chattahoochee Nature Center saves animals' lives C. DYER *Atlanta* v57 no4 p52 Ag 2017

The Wolves of Winter L. M. MILLER *Yankee* v81 no1 p20 Ja/F 2017

Animal sculpture

ANIMAL ATTRACTION F. VIGNA color *Martha Stewart Living* p116 My 2017

DRESSAGE SNAPSHOTS color *Dressage Today* v23 no4 p13 D 2016

Animal sedation

SAFE RECOVERY FROM SEDATION C. Barakat and M. Freckleton *Equus* no482 p16 N 2017

Animal shelters

Homeward Bound E. BATTAGLIA color *Martha Stewart Living* p74 O 2017

"No-Kill" Versus "Kill" Shelters *Your Dog (10780343)* v22 no10 p10 O 2016

Animal sounds—Recording & reproducing

Call of the Wild color *O, The Oprah Magazine* p26 F 2017

Animal specialists

See also

Horsemen & horsewomen

Veterinarians

Animal species

The Challenge of Invasives R. J. Bates *Canadian Wildlife* v23 no4 p5 S/O 2017

Collections Matter C. KEMP color *Natural History* v125 no10 p38 O 2017

The First Art: The Earliest Hominin Engraving C. KEMP bw color diag *Natural History* v125 no10 p34 O 2017

Going... Going...? P. Tolmé color *National Wildlife (World Edition)* v55 no2 p22 F/Mr 2017

In the Wild color *Canadian Wildlife* v23 no4 p10 S/O 2017

Research color *Canadian Wildlife* v23 no2 p10 My/Je 2017

SMACKDOWN! G. TARLACH cartoon *Discover* v38 no1 p50 Ja/F 2017

Animal tagging

See also

Animal radio tracking

Bird banding

Fish tagging

Nooner Booner D. Draper color *Field & Stream* v121 no6 pW5 N 2016

Shark Tales G. Schanker *Oceanus* v52 no1 p32 Summ 2016

Animal tracks

THE FAST TRACK R. STUART color *Outdoor Life* v224 no1 p46 D 2016/Ja 2017

FRESH TRACKS IN THE BIG WOODS R. STUART bw *Outdoor Life* v224 no1 p40 D 2016/Ja 2017

Home Is Where They Make It J. R. Platt color diag *Scientific American* v315 no5 p20 N 2016

The Track Attack R. Flannery color *Field & Stream* v121 no7 p47 D 2016/Ja 2017

Animal training

See also

Horse training

Stay Positive V. Green-Gott color *Practical Horseman* v45 no11 p72 N 2017

Animal waste

See also

Manures

FECAL SAMPLE 101 C. Barakat and M. Freckleton color *Equus* no475 p30 Ap 2017

What to do about Enteroliths H. S. Thomas color *Equus* no481 p36 O 2017

Animal welfare

See also

Animal rescue

Animal sanctuaries

Animal shelters

2017 STALLION Directory II *Arabian Horse World* v57 no6 p160 Mr 2017

Abuse: Several Faces, All Ugly J. Wofford color *Practical Horseman* v45 no5 p16 My 2017

Animal House A. SIMMONS color *Reader's Digest* v189 no1130 p8 My 2017

Animal Killers Busted K. B. RATTINI color *National Geographic Kids* no471 p24 Je/Jl 2017

Benkelman hero PLUGGED INTO HIS DESTINY K. LONG color *Nebraska Life* v20 no6 p45 N/D 2016

THE GOOD WITH THE BAAAD: Not tempted by traditional yoga? Perhaps you'd enjoy trying it with goats C. CUNNINGHAM *Washingtonian Magazine* v52 no11 p17 Ag 2017

THE MOODS OF ANIMALS C. Console *Harper's Magazine* v334 no2001 p11 F 2017

Rescue from the Meat Farm: Flying Dogs to Safety P. RORK *Idaho Magazine* v16 no11 p6 Ag 2017

Some Animals Are More Equal than Others: Wild Animal Welfare in the Media R. E. FEBER, E. M. RAEBEL et al *BioScience* v67 no1 p62 Ja 2017

TRAVEL TACTICS M. DEPAOLO *Arabian Horse World* v57 no6 p156 Mr 2017

TURTLES, EAGLES, AND BEAVERS, OH MY: Tucked among development and woods, the Chattahoochee Nature Center saves animals' lives C. DYER *Atlanta* v57 no4 p52 Ag 2017

USDA sued on animal data *Science* v355 no6326 p670 F 17 2017

Animal welfare & ethics

Is It Best To Get a Pet From a No-Kill Shelter? K. A. Appiah *New York Times Magazine* p22 Ap 30 2017

Animal welfare associations

Courts ponder how public animal reports must be M. Wadman color *Science* v356 no6340 p790 My 26 2017

Animal welfare—Government policy

RENSSELAER COUNTY, NEW YORK L. Davis *Harper's Magazine* p26 O 2017

Animal Wisdom (Theatrical production)

THE THEATRE *New Yorker* v93 no32 p8 O 16 2017

Animal young—Weaning

STUD FARM DIARIES C. Reich *Arabian Horse World* v56 no12 p246 S 2016

Animal rights activists—Trials, litigation, etc.

A Case of Compassion M. SCULLY color *National Review* v68 no20 p22 N 7 2016

Animals

See also

Animal diversity

Bloodsucking animals

Endangered species

Invertebrates

Migratory animals

Pets

Photography of animals

6 New Attractions for Summer K. Cicero *Parents* v91 no6 p16 Je 2016

8 totally wild facts about animals E. WHITMER *National Geographic Kids* no469 p10 Ap 2017

Amazing Animals K. JAZYNKA color map *National Geographic Kids* no470 p12 My 2017

awesome 8 S. W. FLYNN color *National Geographic Kids* no470 p6 My 2017

Awesome Animals! R. A. MUSGRAVE color *National Geographic Kids* no471 p35A Je/Jl 2017

Awesome Animals! R. A. MUSGRAVE *National Geographic Kids* no466 p42 D 2016/Ja 2017

A DEEPER BOOM G. FERGUSON *Orion Magazine* v35 no4/5 p14 Jl-O 2016

Escape to Alaska *American Forests* v122 no3 p40 Fall 2016

Find the HIDDEN ANIMALS *National Geographic Kids* no468 p31 Mr 2017

Funny Fill-in color *National Geographic Kids* no475 p30 N 2017

Increase your vocabulary R. ZURER *Backpacker* p14 S 2017

Incredible Animal Friends K. GALLAGHER color *National Geographic Kids* no471 p9 Je/Jl 2017

Jungle Jam color *National Geographic Kids* no473 p32 S 2017

Laugh Out Loud *National Geographic Kids* no468 p32 Mr 2017

LIFE at River Bottom A. G. Landis color *Earth Island Journal* v32 no1 p49 Spr 2017

My Shot *National Geographic Kids* no467 p34 F 2017

Nature's treasure hunt S. Boyer *Science* v356 no6336 p387 Ap 28 2017

Rearview Sharer C. P. Pierce and T. Keith color *Sports Illustrated*

v125 no21 p20 D 26 2016

Reveal Your Animal Instincts! *National Geographic Kids* no466 p32 D 2016/Ja 2017

The Secret Language Of Dolphins C. BOYER color *National Geographic Kids* no471 p14 Je/Jl 2017

SIGNS OF THE TIMES *National Geographic Kids* no468 p33 Mr 2017

Sleeping with Oil T. HAINES *Orion Magazine* v35 no4/5 p8 Jl-O 2016

Students *Oceanus* v52 no2 p21 Spr 2017

STUMP YOUR PARENTS *National Geographic Kids* no466 p38 D 2016/Ja 2017

What in the World? *National Geographic Kids* no468 p29 Mr 2017

Animals as aids for people with disabilities
See also
Horses as aids for people with disabilities
Psychiatric service dogs
Service dogs

LETTER FROM THE EDITOR J. STOWE *Cincinnati Magazine* v50 no4 p16 Ja 2017

Animals as carriers of disease
See also
Bats as carriers of disease

As the bat flies D. T. S. Hayman bibl color *Science* v354 no6316 p1099 D 2 2016

Animals in art
See also
Animal sculpture
Horses in art

CONCRETE JUNGLES color *Mother Jones* v42 no2 p10 Mr/Ap 2017

Survival of The Cutest E. GAUKEL *Treasures* v6 no2 p26 O/N 2016

Tree of Life *Archaeology* v69 no6 pCover N/D 2016

Animals—Africa
DISPLACED C. Cox *Orion Magazine* v35 no3 p18 My/Je 2016

Animals—Arizona
Bobcats N. Austin *Arizona Highways* v93 no8 p13 Ag 2017

Animals—Canada
A welcome invasion *Maclean's* v130 no8 p4 S 2017
WILDLIFE color *Canadian Geographic* v137 no1 p22 F 2017

Animals—Longevity
Dating a Greenland Shark J. NIELSEN *Natural History* v125 no2 p10 F 2017

Animals—Ohio
JUNGLE LOVE: A brief history of Cincinnati's love affair with animals, from fat-rendered soap to Fiona the hippo J. GILBERT *Cincinnati Magazine* v50 no10 p23 Jl 2017

Animals—Population biology
See also
Animal clutches
Animal herds

As Mass Extinction Threatens, Are Catholics Listening to 'Laudato Si'? K. CLARKE color *America* v215 no15 p9 N 14 2016

The Resurrection Zoo Z. BARON and C. SKIPPER bw color *GQ: Gentlemen's Quarterly* v86 no11 p96 N 2016

Vanishing Life *Change* v82 no3 p9 Mr 2017

Animals—Services for
Animal House A. SIMMONS color *Reader's Digest* v189 no1130 p8 My 2017

Animals—Societies, etc.
Amazing Animals K. JAZYNKA color map *National Geographic Kids* no470 p12 My 2017

Animals—South Africa
bush beat E. C. Alberts color *Earth Island Journal* v32 no4 p36 Wint 2017

Animals—Symbolic aspects
Extinction Risk and Conservation of the Earth's National Animal Symbols N. HAMMERSCHLAG and A. J. GALLAGHER *BioScience* v67 no8 p744 Ag 2017

Animals—United States
How Do You Save a Species? Save Its Habitat C. O'MARA *National Wildlife (World Edition)* v55 no4 p6 Je/Jl 2017

Animals—Wounds & injuries
WHEN WOUNDS DON'T HEAL [Cover story] C. Barakat and

D. Knottenbelt color *Equus* no471 p24 D 2016

Animas River (Colo. & N.M.)
Animas River Spill Spawns Conspiracy Theories B. RADFORD *Skeptical Inquirer* v40 no6 p11 N/D 2016

Animated films
See also
Live action/animation films

The Truth Behind 3 AWESOME MOVIES J. RIZZO *National Geographic Kids* no466 p22 D 2016/Ja 2017

Animated films—Production & direction
Around the Country *Natural History* v125 no2 p38 F 2017

Animated television programs
BIGGER, RISKIER & STILL 100% UNCOUTH D. Franich color *Entertainment Weekly* no1435 p30 O 14 2016

Extradimensional: Rick and Morty is as affecting as it is loopy M. Z. SEITZ img *New York* v50 no16 p107 Ag 7 2017

MICKEY AND THE ROADSTER RACERS M. LOGAN *TV Guide* v65 no2 p44 Ja 2 2017

Animated television programs—History
The Great Pumpkin Turns 50! D. Holbrook cartoon *TV Guide* v64 no42 p10 O 10 2016

Animated television programs—Reviews
600 AND COUNTING... M. LOGAN cartoon *TV Guide* v64 no42 p30 O 10 2016

Animation (Cinematography)—Congresses
ABOVE & BEYOND bw *New Yorker* v93 no22 p14 Jl 31 2017

Animators
A Funny Direction *USA Today Magazine* v145 no2858 p62 N 2016

Animatronics
The World's First RoboCop *New York Times Upfront* v150 no1 p2 S 4 2017

Anions
See also
Radical anions

Radical-polar crossover reactions of vinylboron ate complexes M. Kischkewitz, K. Okamoto et al bibl diag *Science* v355 no6328 p936 Mr 3 2017

Synthesis and characterization of the pentazolate anion cyclo-N5⁻ in (N5)6(H3O)3(NH4)4Cl Chong Zhang, Chengguo Sun et al bibl diag graph *Science* v355 no6323 p374 Ja 27 2017

Anisotropic crystals
Growing anisotropic crystals at the nanoscale L. M. Liz-Marzán and M. Grzelczak color diag *Science* v356 no6343 p1120 Je 16 2017

Anisotropy
New angle on cosmic rays J. S. I. Gallagher and F. Halzen color *Science* v357 no6357 p1240 S 22 2017

Observation of a large-scale anisotropy in the arrival directions of cosmic rays above 8 × 1018 eV P. Ristori, V. Rizi et al *Science* v357 no6357 p1266 S 22 2017

Strong peak in Tc of Sr2RuO4 under uniaxial pressure Lishan Zhao, M. E. Barber et al bibl color graph *Science* v355 no6321 p1 Ja 13 2017

Aniston, Jennifer
The A-LIST bw color *Harper's Bazaar* no3657 p118 O 2017

THE BOMBER SQUAD E. Sullivan bw color *Esquire* p86 My 2017

Feeling Social color *InStyle* v23 no12 p18 N 2016

The Quiz T. BALAZO color *Maclean's* v129 no42 p64 O 24 2016

Sound Bites color *Entertainment Weekly* no1467 p8 My 26 2017

Aniston, Jennifer, 1969-—Interviews
HAVE YOURSELF A FILTHY LITTLE CHRISTMAS [Cover story] D. Snierson color diag *Entertainment Weekly* no1443 p28 D 9 2016

NOW AND JEN A. Sedaris color *Harper's Bazaar* no3657 p205 O 2017

Aniston, John—Interviews
DAYS OF OUR LIVES M. LOGAN *TV Guide* p44 Ap 17 2017

ANKENY, MATTHEW
STRONGER FOR LONGER color *Bicycling* v58 no10 p28 N/D 2017

Anker, Heinrich
Why Leadership Training Fails—and What to Do About It: Interaction *Harvard Business Review* v94 no12 p19 D 2016

Anki Inc.

Artificial Intelligence Invades the Home ... In Toys L. Eadicicco color *Time* v188 no24 p20 D 12 2016

Ankle

Ankle arthritis [Cover story] *Mayo Clinic Health Letter* v358 no8 p1 Ag 2017

The ankle joint [Cover story] J. Miller color *Yoga Journal* no293 p60 Ag 2017

I wish I didn't feel so swell color *AARP: The Magazine* v30 no6A p12 O/N 2017

Ankle wounds—Risk factors

Unassailable Ankles L. Boyce color *Muscle & Performance* v9 no8 p53 Ag 2017

Ankle—Anatomy

The ankle joint [Cover story] J. Miller color *Yoga Journal* no293 p60 Ag 2017

Anklets (Jewelry)—Evaluation

Shake A Leg *Los Angeles Magazine* p34 Ap 2017

Ankonina, Guy

Observation of Anderson localization in disordered nanophotonic structures diag graph *Science* v356 no6341 p953 Je 1 2017

Ankosko, Bob

Apple Revisits Home Audio color *Sound & Vision* v82 no8 p18 O 2017

ATSC 3.0: TV's Next Generation color *Sound & Vision* v82 no7 p18 S 2017

Circle of Sound color *Sound & Vision* v82 no4 p20 My 2017

Come Fly With Me color *Sound & Vision* v82 no2 p74 F/Mr 2017

Conversation Starter color *Sound & Vision* v82 no5 p74 Je 2017

Dynamic Duo color *Sound & Vision* v82 no3 p20 Ap 2017

Finding Sonic Paradise color *Sound & Vision* v82 no4 p74 My 2017

Holiday Tech Guide color *Sound & Vision* v81 no10 p34 D 2016

LET'S TAKE IT OUTSIDE color *Sound & Vision* v82 no6 p28 Jl/Ag 2017

Naim Mu-so Qb Wireless Music System color graph *Sound & Vision* v82 no5 p60 Je 2017

Oswalds Mill AC1 Speaker color *Sound & Vision* v81 no10 p74 D 2016

Party Animal color *Sound & Vision* v82 no1 p18 Ja 2017

Petite and Discreet color *Sound & Vision* v82 no8 p74 O 2017

Play Me a Tune color *Sound & Vision* v82 no1 p74 Ja 2017

Retro Elegance color *Sound & Vision* v82 no5 p20 Je 2017

Sonic Boom color *Sound & Vision* v81 no10 p2 D 2016

Spinning with Style color *Sound & Vision* v82 no3 p74 Ap 2017

Taking HDMI to the Next Level color *Sound & Vision* v82 no4 p16 My 2017

Teac AI-503 USB DAC/Integrated Amplifier color *Sound & Vision* v82 no7 p74 S 2017

Ultra Style color *Sound & Vision* v81 no9 p74 N 2016

Wrensilva Loft Record Console color *Sound & Vision* v82 no6 p74 Jl/Ag 2017

Ankylosaurus

Who you gonna call? L. Hamers color *Science News* v191 no12 p4 Je 24 2017

Anleu Gil, M. Ximena

Mobile MUTE specifies subsidiary cells to build physiologically improved grass stomata bibl diag *Science* v355 no6330 p1215 Mr 17 2017

Ann, Debra—Interviews

Moved By Color E. GAUKEL *Treasures* v6 no2 p56 O/N 2016

Anna (Film)

Exile on Main Street N. DAVIS color *Film Comment* v52 no6 p18 N/D 2016

Anna Sui Corp.

PAT McGRATH'S Golden Touch G. Macnicol color *InStyle* v24 no2 p110 F 2017

Annabelle: Creation (Film)

ANNABELLE: CREATION D. Coggan color *Entertainment Weekly* no1474/1475 p48 Jl 21-28 2017

Annas, George J.

The mythology of CRISPR bibl color *Science* v354 no6309 p189 O 14 2016

Anne of Green Gables (TV program)

Anne of Green Gables J. Russell *TV Guide* v64 no48 p36 N 21 2016

Anne With an E (TV program)

In the new adaptation of Anne of Green Gables, hope is replaced by horror H. Stewart color *America* v216 no13 p56 Je 12 2017

Reimagining Anne A. Wilkinson color *Entertainment Weekly* no1465 p47 My 12 2017

Annealing of metals

IT PAYS TO INCREASE YOUR Word Power E. COX and H. RATHVON *Reader's Digest* v189 no1129 p133 Ap 2017

Annett, Anthony

'This Economy Kills' color *Commonweal* v144 no11 p21 Je 16 2017

Annie Hall (Film)

ANNIE HALL'S TICKET LINE TELL-OFF A. Breznican color *Entertainment Weekly* no1460/1461 p29 Ap 7-17 2017

Happy Birthday, Annie Hall J. Ferrise color *InStyle* v24 no4 p186 Ap 2017

Annis, Robert

AHEAD OF THE CURRENT color *Indianapolis Monthly* v41 no2 p68 S 2017

BEST NEW Breweries *Indianapolis Monthly* v40 no11 p57 Jl 2017

Broad RIPPLE color map *Indianapolis Monthly* v41 no2 p66 S 2017

CAN YOU DIG IT? diag *Indianapolis Monthly* v41 no2 p72 S 2017

A DAM SHAME *Indianapolis Monthly* v41 no2 p64 S 2017

Downtown color map *Indianapolis Monthly* v41 no2 p73 S 2017

Farther Downstream color map *Indianapolis Monthly* v41 no2 p77 S 2017

GM STAMPING PLANT color map *Indianapolis Monthly* v41 no2 p75 S 2017

Hamilton COUNTY color map *Indianapolis Monthly* v41 no2 p63 S 2017

Hot on the TRAILS: A ROAD-FREE GUIDE TO EXPLORING CENTRAL INDIANA *Indianapolis Monthly* v40 no10 p59 Je 2017

MAKING A SPLASH color *Indianapolis Monthly* v41 no2 p76 S 2017

Mounds STATE PARK color map *Indianapolis Monthly* v41 no2 p60 S 2017

Off the Chain *Indianapolis Monthly* p30 My 2017

Riverside PARK color map *Indianapolis Monthly* v41 no2 p68 S 2017

Speed Read color *Indianapolis Monthly* p15 Ap 2017

STAR TREK: Prime viewing of a rare celestial phenomenon puts a different kind of spotlight on Nashville *Indianapolis Monthly* v12 no40 p40 Ag 2017

TOUR OF DOODY diag *Indianapolis Monthly* v41 no2 p65 S 2017

The Vogue *Indianapolis Monthly* v40 no7 p18 Mr 2017

WHERE THE WILD THINGS ARE color *Indianapolis Monthly* v41 no2 p62 S 2017

THE White RIVER diag *Indianapolis Monthly* v41 no2 p59 S 2017

Anniston Star (Newspaper)

Fishing for the Moon R. Bragg color *Southern Living* v52 no3 p140 Mr 2017

Anniversaries

See also

Centennials

2017 Milestones L. Rothman color *Time* v188 no27-28 p118 D 26 2016

50 Years of Black Literature and Politics at Third World Press C. Reid bw chart *Publishers Weekly* v264 no40 p8 O 2 2017

50 YEARS OF JAZZ CAMPS AT SHELL LAKE T. PERKINS color *Downbeat* v84 no3 p88 Mr 2017

ACT CELEBRATES 25 J. Hale color *Downbeat* v84 no6 p59 Je 2017

Anniversary Celebration F. P. DRISCOLL *Opera News* v81 no6 p4 D 2016

A Battle for Fair Rates M. KONCZAL *Nation* v305 no4 p5 Ag 14 2017

Ben Nye Makeup Celebrates 50th Anniversary *Stage Directions* v30 no3 p59 Mr 2017

BY THE NUMBERS P. Treble bw color *Maclean's* v129 no51/52 p52 D 26 2016

CHAPTER 7 THE 70TH ANNIVERSARY OF THE COUNCIL

OF ECONOMIC ADVISERS *Economic Indicators* p291 O 2016

CH-CH-CH-CH-CHANGES B. CROWDER *Virginia Living* v15 no3 p29 Ap 2017

The Cold War's Pivot A. R. Johnson *Hoover Digest: Research & Opinion on Public Policy* no4 p199 Fall 2016

Confederation smackdown! M. CAMPBELL *Maclean's* v130 no3 p17 Ap 2017

The Corvette at 65 M. SOLOMON bw color *Forbes* v199 no6 p26 Je 13 2017

EASTER ANNIVERSARY: IT'S A TIME OF NEW BEGIN-NINGS AND A TIME TO REFLECT AND REMEMBER L. F. Prater *Successful Farming* v115 no6 p63 Ap 2017

Edgefest Now Bigger Than Ever A. Drouot color *Downbeat* v83 no11 p95 N 2016

EDITOR'S LETTER G. Bailey color *Harper's Bazaar* no3655 p50 Ag 2017

Evolution of Dance: Choreography's constantly shifting role on the Great White Way S. GOLD *Dance Magazine* v91 no7 p20 Jl 2017

Fasching Fosters Creativity J. Ephland color *Downbeat* v84 no2 p60 F 2017

For More than 100 Years, D.C. Has Drawn People to Protest A. Stern *Humanities* v37 no4 p1 Fall 2016

A HALF CENTURY OF PENSKE M. PRINCE color *Road & Track* v68 no5 p14 D 2016/Ja 2017

Happy Birthday, Annie Hall J. Ferrise color *InStyle* v24 no4 p186 Ap 2017

HAPPY BIRTHDAY TO US! color *Vogue* v207 no9 p464 S 2017

Hockey year in Canada J. GATEHOUSE color *Maclean's* v129 no51/52 p57 D 26 2016

KARATE COLLEGE TRAINING CAMP BEGINS ITS THIRD DECADE J. William McNeil bw color *Black Belt* v55 no6 p12 O/N 2017

Life IN THESE UNITED STATES M. WEBSTER, A. BARRETT et al *Reader's Digest* v189 no1127 p38 F 2017

Macy's Thanksgiving Day Parade 90th Celebration *TV Guide* v64 no48 p34 N 21 2016

Nebraska at 150: RETROSPECTIVE - PART V OF VI 1967-1992 A. J. BARTELS bw color map *Nebraska Life* v21 no5 p62 S/O 2017

NEEDLE'S EYE MINISTRIES *Virginia Living* v15 no6 p43 O 2017

NEW NEXT *Texas Monthly* v45 no3 p187 Mr 2017

The NEWS bw color *Harper's Bazaar* no3655 p80 Ag 2017

Passport to Fun! S. Myrick *Parks & Recreation* v51 no12 p56 D 2016

Pioneering NBM Marks 40 Years of Graphic Novels B. Alverson color *Publishers Weekly* v264 no21 p12 My 22 2017

PRETTY IN PLATINUM C. D. MIRANDA *Sea Magazine* v108 no10 pCA-4 O 2016

RATIFYING the BILL of RIGHTS... in 1939 *Prologue* v48 no4 p72 Wint 2016

SHINE ON: George Balanchine's Jewels celeb rates its 50th anniversary this year. But what is it that makes this plotless fulllength so timeless? P. BOAL *Dance Magazine* v91 no7 p35 Jl 2017

A SHORT HISTORY OF THE RNCFR B. Welch map *Spin to Win Rodeo* v21 no4 p88 Je 2017

Smart Cookie S. SHELLEY *Virginia Living* v15 no3 p49 Ap 2017

STATES OF CHANGE *Vogue* v207 no9 p629 S 2017

A Year of Celebration M. L. Tellado *Consumer Reports* v81 no12 p5 D 2016

YOUTH CULTURE S. Slon *Saturday Evening Post* v289 no4 p6 Jl/Ag 2017

Anniversaries—Political aspects

THE 70TH ANNIVERSARY OF THE COUNCIL OF ECONOM-IC ADVISERS *Economic Indicators* p291 S 2016

Ann-Margret, 1941-

Yes, for You, Ann-Margret color *AARP: The Magazine* v60 no3A p7 Ap/My 2017

AnnTaylor Stores Corp.

Collared! color *Women's Health* v13 no10 p59 D 2016

Annunziata, Marco

Augmented Reality Is Already Improving Worker Performance *Harvard Business Review Digital Articles* p2 Mr 13 2017

ANOLIK, LILI

The Critic AND THE STAR bw cartoon *Vanity Fair* p180 Hollywood 2017 Supplement

DAVID LYNCH'S DARK ART color *Vanity Fair* p118 Hollywood 2017 Supplement

THE McKinnon Report color *Vanity Fair* v59 no11 p112 N 2017

A SEASON IN PURGATORY color *Vanity Fair* v59 no7 p66 Summ 2017

Anolon Bakeware (Company)

THE NONSTICK PAN cartoon color *Men's Health* v32 no8 p82 O 2017

Anomalous Hall effect

Chiral Majorana fermion modes in a quantum anomalous Hall insulator–superconductor structure Q. Lin He, L. Pan et al diag *Science* v357 no6348 p294 Jl 21 2017

Anonymity—Social aspects

Virtual Trolls M. Mossey il *MIT Technology Review* v120 no4 p10 Jl/Ag 2017

Anonymous persons

Gnawing Anonymice M. Hemingway *Weekly Standard* v22 no24 p14 F 27 2017

Anopheles

Driving mosquito refractoriness to Plasmodium falciparum with engineered symbiotic bacteria S. Wang, A. L. A. Dos-Santos et al color graph *Science* v357 no6358 p1399 S 29 2017

Anopheles gambiae

A key malaria metabolite modulates vector blood seeking, feeding, and susceptibility to infection S. N. Emami, B. G. Lindberg et al bibl chart diag *Science* v355 no6329 p1076 Mr 10 2017

Anorexia nervosa

Eating Disorder S. M. FERNANDEZ *Scholastic Choices* v32 no6 p10 Mr 2017

Another Country (Company)

All-Star Pitchers color *Treasures* v5 no5 p8 Ap/My 2016

Another Mile, Another Minute (Music)

Places To Go, People To See HADLEY color *Downbeat* v84 no6 p70 Je 2017

Anoxemia

Fructose-driven glycolysis supports anoxia resistance in the naked mole-rat T. J. Park, J. Reznick et al diag graph *Science* v356 no6335 p307 Ap 21 2017

Rewiring metabolism under oxygen deprivation J. F. Storz and G. B. McClelland color *Science* v356 no6335 p248 Ap 21 2017

Anoxia (Water)

Oceans on the edge of anoxia A. J. Watson bibl diag *Science* v354 no6319 p1529 D 23 2016

Anoxic zones

Can Animals Live Without Oxygen? K. Madin *Oceanus* v52 no1 p4 Summ 2016

Oceans on the edge of anoxia A. J. Watson bibl diag *Science* v354 no6319 p1529 D 23 2016

Anquetil, Patrick

Innovation: Needle-Free Injections M. Belfiore color *Bloomberg Businessweek* no4494 p37 O 10 2016

ANSALDO, MICHAEL

3 tools that easily unsubscribe you from emails color *PCWorld* v35 no6 p44 Je 2017

Best password managers of 2017: Reviews of the top products color *PCWorld* v35 no10 p79 O 2017

D-Link DCS-8200LH HD 180-Degree Wi-Fi Camera: An all-seeing eye for large spaces color *PCWorld* p125 Mr 2017

It's football season! These second-screen apps make NFL games even more fun color *PCWorld* p34 O 2016

LOGITECH CIRCLE 2 HOME SECURITY CAMERA color *Macworld - Digital Edition* v34 no10 p37 O 2017

Ansari, Aftab A.

Sustained virologic control in SIV+ macaques after antiretroviral and α4β7 antibody therapy bibl graph *Science* v354 no6309 p197 O 14 2016

Ansari, Aziz, 1983-

Aziz Ansari's Masterpiece R. Rahman color *Entertainment Weekly* no1466 p36 My 19 2017

Comments img *New York* v50 no10 p12 My 15 2017

Master of None: A delicious new season of the slice-of-life comedy M. ROUSH *TV Guide* v65 no21 p16 My 15 2017

Master of None J. Jensen color *Entertainment Weekly* no1465 p46

My 12 2017
MODERN ROMANTIC J. PRESSLER *Smithsonian* v47 no8 p42
D 2016
PARTY LINES K. V. Syckle, S. Huver et al img *New York* v50
no11 p127 My 29 2017
Sound Bites color *Entertainment Weekly* no1451/1452 p2 F 3-10
2017
The Triumph of Aziz Ansari R. SHEFFIELD color *Rolling Stone*
no1288 p19 Je 1 2017

Anschuetz, Eric R.
Atom-by-atom assembly of defect-free one-dimensional cold
atom arrays bibl diag graph *Science* v354 no6315 p1024 N 25
2016

Anschutz, Philip, 1939——Finance
A VIEW FROM THE TOP C. HELMAN color *Forbes* v198 no5
p112 O 25 2016

Anseel, Frederik
How Entrepreneurs Can Keep Their Passion from Fading *Harvard
Business Review Digital Articles* p2 Je 16 2016

Ansel, Dominique
the life C. Stern color *InStyle* v24 no6 p159 Je 2017

Ansel, Karen
CUT IT OUT color *Women's Health* v14 no3 p108 Ap 2017
love your BELLY color *Yoga Journal* p102 2017 SpecialIssue
SWEET (AND SALTY) DREAMS [Cover story] color *Women's
Health* v14 no7 p108 S 2017

ANSELMI, ELAINE
The Inuit Whale Hunter Emmanuel Adam color *Foreign Policy*
no224 p24 My/Je 2017

Anselmo, Aaron C.
Fabrication of fillable microparticles and other complex 3D microstructures color diag *Science* v357 no6356 p1138 S 15 2017

Anson, Weston
Why Is the NFL's Brand More Valuable than Ever? *Harvard Business Review Digital Articles* p2 N 26 2015

Ant, Onur
Erdogan's Empire State of Mind color *Bloomberg Businessweek*
no4511 p14 F 13 2017
The Purge That's Paralyzed Turkey *Bloomberg Businessweek*
no4506 p15 Ja 9 2017
A Putin Fixer Claims Success With Turkey color *Bloomberg Businessweek* no4512 p15 F 20 2017

Antacids
See also
Proton pump inhibitors
FEELING THE BURN? J. Teitelbaum color *Amazing Wellness* v8
no6 p28 Early Winter2016

Antagonism (Ecology)
See also
Predation (Biology)
Racial Justice A. R. RANSBY-SPORN *In These Times* v41 no1
p27 Ja 2017

Antarctic environmental conditions
How Antarctica Is Being Invaded T. John color *Time* v190 no1
p10 Jl 3 2017

Antarctic glaciers
The Doomsday Glacier J. GOODELL color *Rolling Stone* no1287
p44 My 18 2017

Antarctic Ocean—Environmental conditions
How deep water surfaces around Antarctica E. DeMarco color
graph *Science News* v192 no4 p36 S 16 2017
Science-based management in decline in the Southern Ocean C.
M. Brooks, L. B. Crowder et al bibl map *Science* v354 no6309
p185 O 14 2016

Antarctic Peninsula (Antarctica)
INTERNATIONAL MARCHES *Ms.* v27 no1 p27 Spr 2017

Antarctic research stations
Science suffers in cold war over polar base M. Enserink color *Science* v355 no6322 p231 Ja 20 2017

Antarctica
Lifetime experience #25 J. Jerabek color *Canadian Geographic*
v137 no1 p27 F 2017
that time i bombed antarctica N. HOLSCHUH and S. Bushwick
cartoon *Popular Science* v289 no2 p75 Mr/Ap 2017
Where is the South Pole? E. LEANE *Natural History* v124 no10
p48 N 2016

Antarctica—Environmental conditions
The Impact of a Large-Scale Climate Event on Antarctic Ecosystem Processes A. G. FOUNTAIN, R. A. VIRGINIA et al chart
graph *BioScience* v66 no10 p848 O 1 2016
Unraveling Ecosystem Responses to Climate Change on the Antarctic Continent through Long-Term Ecological Research J. C.
PRISCU *BioScience* v66 no10 p799 O 1 2016

Antcliff, Brad
TALK TO US color graph *Chicago* v66 no11 p16 N 2017

Antelman, Alison
To The Editor color *American Craft* v77 no3 p10 Je/Jl 2017

Antelman, Maria—Exhibitions
MARIA ANTELMAN R. Rhee color *Art in America* v105 no4
p119 Ap 2017

Antelope hunting
THE SCRODE-HOLE MYSTERY J. ARTERBURN *Outdoor
Life* v224 no2 p98 F/Mr 2017

Antelopes
See also
Gnus
Pronghorn
American Pronghorns N. Austin *Arizona Highways* v92 no11 p13
N 2016
The Purest Type S. BUTCHER *Texas Monthly* v45 no7 p60 Jl
2017

Antenna design & construction
Tiny antennas read signals in new way M. TEMMING *Science
News* v192 no4 p17 S 16 2017

Antennas (Electronics)—Evaluation
For the BOAT *Sea Magazine* v108 no12 p45 D 2016
WATCHAIR SMART ANTENNA M. BROWN color *Macworld -
Digital Edition* p40 F 2017

Antepli, Abdullah—Interviews
When Muslims talk to Jews D. Heim color *Christian Century*
v134 no4 p41 F 15 2017

Anterea, Claire
A MATTER OF FAITH M. IVES *Sierra* v101 no6 p40 N/D 2016

Anterior cruciate ligament injury treatment
Olympic Recovery J. Fuchs and T. Keith color *Sports Illustrated*
v127 no3 p18 Jl 24 2017

Antetokounmpo, Giannis
FREAK UNLEASHED L. Jenkins chart color *Sports Illustrated*
v126 no1 p40 Ja 9 2017
Giannis Antetokounmpo M. Hagan color *Current Biography* v78
no6 p3 Je 2017

Anthem (Company)
Anthem AVM 60 A/V Processor D. Kumin color graph *Sound &
Vision* v82 no1 p56 Ja 2017
Anthem MRX 1120 A/V Receiver D. Vaughn chart color graph
Sound & Vision v81 no9 p36 N 2016

Anthes, Emily
THE HOUSE-CAT MYSTERY color *New York Times Magazine*
p54 My 21 2017
WHAT DO WE HAVE TO DO TO GET THE MALE PILL? color
Bloomberg Businessweek no4533 p44 Ag 7 2017

Anthocyanins
new ways with RED CABBAGE M. XERAKIA *Better Homes &
Gardens* v95 no1 p70 Ja 2017

Anthofer, Derek
ALL AROUND THE FARM® *Successful Farming* v114 no13
p88 D 2016

Anthologies
At 30, the Writers Studio Gets an Anthology J. Maher chart *Publishers Weekly* v264 no19 p7 My 8 2017

Anthony, Carmelo, 1984-
BLACK ATHLETES MATTER M. A. Green bw *GQ: Gentle-
men's Quarterly* v86 no12 p184 D 2016
No Exit C. P. Pierce, T. Keith et al color *Sports Illustrated* v126
no7 p30 Mr 6 2017
WHAT IF? ... THESE FOUR PIVOTAL DRAFT MOMENTS
HAD HAPPENED DIFFERENTLY? J. Feldman color *Sports
Illustrated* v126 no11 p51 Ap 17-24 2017

Anthony, Dave
GOING IRL C. Everett color *Entertainment Weekly* no1465 p57
My 12 2017

ANTHONY, LESLIE

515" color *Powder* p66 S 2017

Biodiversity Apocalypse color *Canadian Geographic* v137 no5 p52 S/O 2017

CANADA'S NATIONAL BIRD THE GRAY JAY [Cover story] color map *Canadian Geographic* v136 no6 p36 D 2016

KOMO MAI E AI color map *Canadian Geographic* v137 p24 2017 Travel

SHALE GAME color map *Canadian Geographic* v137 no1 p50 F 2017

'We know that insect species are being lost across the planet ... but no one is really looking.' color *Canadian Geographic* v135 no6 p50 D 2015

Anthony, Scott

4 Assumptions About Risk You Shouldn't Be Making *Harvard Business Review Digital Articles* p2 Ag 15 2016

The 6 Most Common Innovation Mistakes Companies Make *Harvard Business Review Digital Articles* p2 Je 23 2015

Calculate How Much Your Company Should Invest in Innovation *Harvard Business Review Digital Articles* p2 D 17 2014

How Singapore Became an Entrepreneurial Hub *Harvard Business Review Digital Articles* p2 F 25 2015

How to Break Up with an Innovation Project *Harvard Business Review Digital Articles* p2 Ag 7 2015

How to Tell If a Company Is Good at Innovating or Just Good at PR *Harvard Business Review Digital Articles* p2 D 18 2015

How Understanding Disruption Helps Strategists *Harvard Business Review Digital Articles* p2 N 18 2015

Innovation Isn't the Answer to All Your Problems *Harvard Business Review Digital Articles* p2 Je 2 2015

Innovation Leadership Lessons from the Marshmallow Challenge *Harvard Business Review Digital Articles* p2 D 9 2014

Leading a Digital Transformation? Learn to Code *Harvard Business Review Digital Articles* p2 S 2 2015

What Do You Really Mean by Business "Transformation"? *Harvard Business Review Digital Articles* p2 F 29 2016

What the Best Transformational Leaders Do *Harvard Business Review Digital Articles* p2 My 8 2017

What the Media Industry Can Teach Us About Digital Business Models *Harvard Business Review Digital Articles* p2 Je 10 2015

When It Comes to Digital Innovation, Less Action, More Thought *Harvard Business Review Digital Articles* p2 Ja 21 2015

Zombie Projects: How to Find Them and Kill Them *Harvard Business Review Digital Articles* p2 Mr 4 2015

Anthony, Susan B. (Susan Brownell), 1820-1906

THE GRIEF OF SUSAN B. ANTHONY A. KINGSTON and S. GILMORE color *Maclean's* v129 no46 p39 N 21 2016

Anthrax

BEST OF BRICKBATS: THE OBAMA YEARS, 2009-2016 C. OLIVER cartoon *Reason* v48 no9 p72 F 2017

Anthrax toxin

TIME TO WORRY ABOUT ANTHRAX AGAIN P. S. Keim, D. H. Walker et al color diag *Scientific American* v316 no4 p70 Ap 2017

Anthropocene Epoch

Anthropocene has begun, group says T. SUMNER color graph *Science News* v190 no8 p14 O 15 2016

An Anthropocene map of genetic diversity A. Miraldo, Sen Li et al bibl graph map *Science* v353 no6307 p1532 S 30 2016

Biodiversity losses and conservation responses in the Anthropocene C. N. Johnson, A. Balmford et al color diag graph map *Science* v356 no6335 p270 Ap 21 2017

DEEP TIME, DEEP SURVIVAL D. Grinspoon color *Scientific American* v315 no3 p76 S 2016

A HISTORY IN LAYERS [Cover story] J. Zalasiewicz and K. Peek color graph *Scientific American* v315 no3 p30 S 2016

Looking Forward M. DiChristina color *Scientific American* v315 no3 p4 S 2016

Paleoecology--Looking to the Past to Inform the Future: Researchers uncover the buried history of lakes and estuaries S. LEVY *BioScience* v67 no9 p791 S 2017

WELCOME TO THE ANTHROPOCENE N. SCHARPING color *Discover* v38 no1 p89 Ja/F 2017

Anthropogenic effects on nature

See also

Environmental degradation

Habitat (Ecology)

Nitrogen pollution knows no bounds E. Boyle color *Science* v356 no6339 p700 My 19 2017

Only Human W. Yang *New York Times Magazine* p9 F 19 2017

Shipbuilding Docks as Experimental Systems for Realistic Assessments of Anthropogenic Stressors on Marine Organisms R. BRUINTJES, H. R. HARDING et al *BioScience* v67 no9 p853 S 2017

Anthropologie Inc.

CREATE A HAPPY SUMMER SPACE [Cover story] color *Redbook* p110 Je 2017

Anthropologists

See also

Archaeologists

Ancient DNA B. ALEX color diag map *Discover* v38 no6 p52 Jl/Ag 2017

Social Science and the Public Interest *Society* v54 no4 p313 Ag 2017

Anthropology

See also

Archaeology

Social structure

KIM FICARO M. B. EYERS color *Better Homes & Gardens* v95 no9 p22 S 2017

Traces of the Future color map *National Geographic* v230 no6 p122 D 2016

Anti (Music)

Chaos Reigns B. RATLIFF cartoon *Esquire* v166 no5 p40 D 2016/Ja 2017

Anti-aging

Aging? What's That? T. FERRISS bw cartoon color *Men's Health* v32 no5 p34 Je 2017

David Colbert A. Serrano color *InStyle* v24 no7 p94 Jl 2017

I WISH SOMEONE WOULD INVENT... A. Nathan, C. Maldarelli et al cartoon *Popular Science* v289 no5 p98 S/O 2017

Lab Fab L. Weil and C. ELLENBERG color *Vogue* v207 no9 p446 S 2017

Old Money A. Hess *New York Times Magazine* p13 S 17 2017

THE SEARCH FOR IMMORTALITY H. JAFFE color *Men's Health* v32 no5 p132 Je 2017

Anti-American propaganda

For North Koreans, the War Never Ended J. H. Lee *Wilson Quarterly* p1 Spr 2017

Anti-Christianity movements

From 'Enemy of the People' to Friend K. A. ELLIS *Christianity Today* v60 no9 p30 N 2016

Anti-fascist movements

A Beating in Berkeley [Cover story] M. LABASH color *Weekly Standard* v23 no1 p18 S 11 2017

The Joy of Destruction J. BOTTUM color *Weekly Standard* v23 no3 p21 S 25 2017

The Rise of the Violent Left P. Beinart color *Atlantic* v320 no2 p13 S 2017

Anti-globalization movement

Business: Localization Can Help America Win Around the World J. Immelt color *Time* v188 no27-28 p32 D 26 2016

People Are Angry About Globalization. Here's What to Do About It P. Ghemawat *Harvard Business Review Digital Articles* p2 N 4 2016

Anti-HIV agents

Cows make powerful HIV antibodies A. CUNNINGHAM color graph *Science News* v192 no2 p7 Ag 19 2017

Anti-infective agents

See also

Antibacterial agents

Antibiotics

IT'S NOT A WASH J. CASPERMEYER *USA Today Magazine* v145 no2862 p54 Mr 2017

Reducing antimicrobial use in food animals T. P. Van Boeckel, E. E. Glennon et al color graph *Science* v357 no6358 p1350 S 29 2017

Anti-inflammatory agents

See also

Nonsteroidal anti-inflammatory agents

Anti-inflammatory prevents heart attacks J. Couzin-Frankel color *Science* v357 no6354 p855 S 1 2017

WATCH OUT FOR WASPS C. Barakat and M. Freckleton color

Equus no481 p20 O 2017

Anti-intellectualism

Duke Divinity professor disciplined amid complaint over antiracism event C. Kennel-Shank *Christian Century* v134 no12 p16 Je 7 2017

Anti-racism

Antiracist without sacrifice T. M. Ott bw *Christian Century* v134 no11 p10 My 24 2017

A beloved community: Christian churches can address racism through spiritual formation color *U.S. Catholic* v82 no10 p18 O 2017

Change the conversation *U.S. Catholic* v82 no10 p20 O 2017

Duke Divinity professor disciplined amid complaint over antiracism event C. Kennel-Shank *Christian Century* v134 no12 p16 Je 7 2017

Anti-war art

AN EXHIBIT TO END ALL EXHIBITS J. BULLINGTON *In These Times* v41 no5 p39 My 2017

Antibacterial agents

See also

Penicillin

fall WELLNESS GUIDE [Cover story] chart color *Amazing Wellness* p40 Fall 2017

LUCKY BREAK P. A. Smith *Smithsonian* v48 no3 p30 Je 2017

Moving Back to Stay Ahead: Phage Research Comes Out of Storage M. STONE *BioScience* v67 no2 p188 F 2017

OIL Boom J. BUNTIN color *Vogue* v207 no6 p78 Je 2017

Antibiotics

4 small health tweaks with huge rewards color *Redbook* p89 Mr 2017

A Bug in the System H. ESTROFF MARANO *Psychology Today* v50 no3 p31 My/Je 2017

COULD THE ANSWER TO OUR MOST URGENT HEALTH CRISIS BE FOUND ON A TOILET SEAT? M. McKENNA color *Atlantic* v320 no1 p88 Jl/Ag 2017

THE EXCHANGE bw cartoon *Men's Health* v32 no4 p14 My 2017

feed your child's gut E. SONNENBURG *Parents* v91 no10 p42 O 2016

Fighting the enemy within E. Tacconelli, I. B. Autenrieth et al bibl diag *Science* v355 no6326 p689 F 17 2017

Gut Check A. Hadhazy color *Natural History* v125 no6 p8 Je 2017

It takes a village D. SCHARDT *Nutrition Action Health Letter* v43 no10 p9 D 2016

Microbiota-activated PPAR-γ signaling inhibits dysbiotic Enterobacteriaceae expansion M. X. Byndloss, E. E. Olsan et al graph *Science* v357 no6351 p570 Ag 11 2017

A modular and enantioselective synthesis of the pleuromutilin antibiotics S. K. Murphy, M. Zeng et al diag graph *Science* v356 no6341 p956 Je 1 2017

New 'rules' for finding antibiotics A. CUNNINGHAM *Science News* v191 no11 p8 Je 10 2017

The Superbug Crisis M. NISBET *Skeptical Inquirer* v41 no1 p27 Ja/F 2017

What To Ask About Antibiotics Before You Start A Course M. LAUBERTE *Reader's Digest* v188 no1124 p64 O 2016

Antibiotics in animal nutrition

FREE BIRD *Atlanta* v57 no5 p96 S 2017

Antibiotics in aquaculture

ON CHINESE AQUACULTURE FARMS, THE FISH ARE PUMPED WITH ANTIBIOTICS, AS ARE THE PIGS, WHOSE WASTE FEEDS THE FISH. SO LET'S TALK ABOUT THAT SEAFOOD PLATTER [Cover story] J. GALE, L. MULVANY et al color graph *Bloomberg Businessweek* no4504 p38 D 19 2016

Antibiotics in veterinary medicine

THE LOOMING THREAT OF FACTORY — FARM SUPERBUGS M. Wenner Moyer color diag *Scientific American* v315 no6 p70 D 2016

Antibiotics—Physiological effect

My home insurer is offering identity-theft coverage. Is it worth buying? color *Consumer Reports* v82 no2 p15 F 2017

Antibiotics—Therapeutic use

Common causes of eye redness [Cover story] *Mayo Clinic Health Letter* v35 no5 p1 My 2017

Preventing painful attacks *Mayo Clinic Health Letter* v35 no4 p4

Ap 2017

Antibody-dependent enhancement

Dengue may bring out the worst in Zika J. Cohen color *Science* v355 no6332 p1362 Mr 31 2017

Anticoagulants (Medicine)—Therapeutic use

ASK THE DOCTOR A. L. KOMAROFF *Harvard Health Letter* v42 no6 p2 Ap 2017

Antidepressants

See also

Fluoxetine

Hope from a Strange Source [Cover story] M. Oaklander color *Time* v190 no6 p38 Ag 7 2017

Jagged Little Pills P. PEARSON color *Walrus* v14 no8 p42 O 2017

What to do when medication makes you constipated *Harvard Health Letter* v42 no10 p7 Ag 2017

Antidepressants—Therapeutic use

Is your antidepressant making life a little too blah? *Harvard Health Letter* v42 no2 p3 D 2016

No autism link to antidepressants A. CUNNINGHAM graph *Science News* v191 no9 p9 My 13 2017

Antidote

In Focus color *Publishers Weekly* v264 no35 p34 Ag 28 2017

Antidote (Music)

The Hot Box J. Murph, J. Macnie et al *Downbeat* v84 no8 p69 Ag 2017

Antidotes

Carbon monoxide, the silent killer, may have met its match Wudan Yan *Science* v354 no6317 p1215 D 9 2016

Antiferromagnetic materials

All-oxide–based synthetic antiferromagnets exhibiting layer-resolved magnetization reversal B. Chen, H. Xu et al diag *Science* v357 no6347 p191 Jl 14 2017

Revealing hidden antiferromagnetic correlations in doped Hubbard chains via string correlators T. A. Hilker, G. Salomon et al bw diag graph *Science* v357 no6350 p484 Ag 4 2017

Antiferromagnetism

See also

Antiferromagnetic materials

Quantum gases cooled to long-range antiferromagnetic order: The observation of a checkerboard pattern in a lattice of ultracold atoms is a sign of even more exciting experiments to come J. Miller *Physics Today* v70 no8 p17 Ag 2017

Antifouling paint—Environmental aspects

The Bottom Line J. Seidel color *Sail* v48 no4 p60 Ap 2017

Antigen presenting cells

See also

Dendritic cells

Macrophages

Mapping the human DC lineage through the integration of high-dimensional techniques P. See, Dutertre et al diag *Science* v356 no6342 p1044 Je 9 2017

Antigen receptors

CAR T-cell–based therapeutic modality in solid tumors: How to achieve precision Yang Liu, Hanren Dai et al bibl color *Science* v354 no6319 p27 D 23 2016

Antigens

See also

Toxins

Reovirus infection triggers inflammatory responses to dietary antigens and development of celiac disease R. Bouziat, R. Hinterleitner et al color diag *Science* v356 no6333 p44 Ap 7 2017

Antigua

take OM HOME M. Rabbitt color *Yoga Journal* no290 p96 Mr 2017

Antigua Winds Inc.

Antigua 'Model 25' PowerBell Saxophone E. Enright color *Downbeat* v84 no5 p85 My 2017

Antigua—Description & travel

ISLAND Fling E. VOHR color map *Sail* v48 no9 p40 S 2017

Antiheroes

EXAMINING THE ALLURE OF THE ANTIHERO *USA Today Magazine* v146 no2867 p10 Ag 2017

Antihistamines

Antihistamine Alternatives E. A. KANE color *Better Nutrition* p24 My 2017

Antihistamines—Therapeutic use

FIRST AID BASICS color *Women's Health* v14 no1 p188 Ja/F 2017

Antihydrogen
Antihydrogen gives way to spectroscopic study J. Miller *Physics Today* v70 no2 p16 F 2017

Antimatter hydrogen passes test E. Conover diag *Science News* v191 no1 p16 Ja 21 2017

Anti-ISIL intervention, Iraq, 2014-
The Battle for Mosul: A Humanitarian Disaster B. SMITH color *Progressive* v81 no7 p12 O/N 2017

Anti-ISIL intervention, Syria, 2014-
WHAT IS THE RECIPE FOR HOME? D. MORTADA color *Nation* v305 no11 p24 O 30 2017

Antikythēra Island (Greece)
Treasures Beneath the Ancient Sands M. BARNA color map *Discover* v38 no5 p70 Je 2017

Antimatter
Antihydrogen gives way to spectroscopic study J. Miller *Physics Today* v70 no2 p16 F 2017

Antineoplastic agents
See also
Interferons

Anticancer sulfonamides target splicing by inducing RBM39 degradation via recruitment to DCAF15 T. Han, M. Goralski et al color diag *Science* v356 no6336 p397 Ap 28 2017

RESCUING THE GUARDIAN OF THE GENOME R. F. Service color diag *Science* v354 no6308 p26 O 7 2016

RESEARCH color *Science* v356 no6345 p1346 Je 30 2017

Antioxidants
17 Healthy Hacks the Food Pros Use C. Sass color *Health* v31 no2 p63 Mr 2017

8 SERVINGS OF FRUITS AND VEGETABLES *Better Homes & Gardens* v95 no1 p115 Ja 2017

ASK TUFTS EXPERTS A. H. Lichtenstein *Tufts University Health & Nutrition Letter* v34 no12 p8 F 2017

DIY MATCHA color *Women's Health* v14 no9 p144 N 2017

E-ssential! Vitamin E is as necessary as oxygen, but just how much we need is still up in the air H. ESTROFF MARANO *Psychology Today* v50 no2 p31 Mr/Ap 2017

Good Food eat to Beat inflammation P. O. BLUMBERG color *Prevention* v69 no9 p20 O 2017

haute COCOA M. RABBITT color *Yoga Journal* no289 p67 F 2017

Hello antioxidants. Goodbye free radicals *Psychology Today* v50 no3 p7 My/Je 2017

LOOK YOUNGER WITHOUT TRYING K. D. HODES color *Redbook* p30 Mr 2017

PURPLE POWER color *Vegetarian Today* no2 p20 Ap 2017

RADIANT SKIN Guarnieri color *Harper's Bazaar* no3651 p314 Mr 2017

A Sip of Summer M. BURKLAND and H. GRAY color *Better Nutrition* v79 no7 p28 Jl 2017

SKIN SAVER color *Prevention* v69 no9 p13 O 2017

Up Your Nut Butter Game color *Health* v31 no2 p18 Mr 2017

What to Eat Now: Cranberries J. PIOTROWSKI color *Better Nutrition* v78 no12 p58 D 2016

Antioxidants—Physiological effect
Free Radicals & Antioxidants D. N. JACKSON chart color *Muscle & Performance* v9 no5 p58 My 2017

Antiparticles
Signs of Majorana fermion detected E. CONOVER color *Science News* v192 no2 p8 Ag 19 2017

Antipodes, The (Theatrical production)
THE THEATRE *New Yorker* v93 no10 p27 Ap 24 2017

Antiprotons
Antimatter hydrogen passes test E. Conover diag *Science News* v191 no1 p16 Ja 21 2017

Buffer-gas cooling of antiprotonic helium to 1.5 to 1.7 K, and antiproton-to-electron mass ratio Masaki Hori, H. Aghai-Khozani et al bibl chart diag graph *Science* v354 no6312 p610 N 4 2016

A testing time for antimatter W. Ubachs bibl color diag *Science* v354 no6312 p546 N 4 2016

Antique & classic aircraft
Vintage Weekend in Key Largo color *Flying* v144 no2 p82 F 2017

Antique & classic car sales & prices
Old Cars in New Time D. Freiburger color *Hot Rod* v70 no12 p114

D 2017

Surviving a Classic Car Slump E. Behrmann and B. Katz color *Bloomberg Businessweek* no4530 p64 Jl 17 2017

Antique & classic cars
1976 Ferrari Dino 208 GT4 B. Price color *Popular Mechanics* p56 S 2017

1991 Nissan Skyline GTS-t Type M color *Popular Mechanics* p40 N 2017

AMERICAN BEAUTIES color *Road & Track* v68 no8 p10 My 2017

Automotive Archaeology: Junkyard Jewels R. Brutt color *Hot Rod* v70 no8 p22 Ag 2017

Automotive Archaeology: Mopars in the Trees R. Brutt color *Hot Rod* v70 no11 p16 N 2017

Automotive Archaeology: The Bee in the Garage R. Brutt color *Hot Rod* v70 no12 p14 D 2017

Bob Reisner's "Invader" Twin-Everything Roadster T. Taylor bw *Hot Rod* v70 no8 p10 Ag 2017

CAPTURING THE LIFE AT SPEED OLD CARS, CHANGING TIMES color *Road & Track* v68 no8 p8 My 2017

Every Year (Almost) of "Ohio" George Montgomery's Iconic Willys Gasser T. Taylor bw *Hot Rod* v70 no8 p94 Ag 2017

Antique & classic cars—Competitions
Chasing the Dream: Speed is always in style when vintage sports-cars hit the track at Virginia International Raceway in Danville T. PILKINGTON *Virginia Living* v15 no4 p49 Je 2017

Antique & classic cars—Conservation & restoration
Birds in the Barn—and a Charger! R. Brutt color *Hot Rod* v70 no7 p20 Jl 2017

Chasing the Dream: Speed is always in style when vintage sports-cars hit the track at Virginia International Raceway in Danville T. PILKINGTON *Virginia Living* v15 no4 p49 Je 2017

Running Cars are More Fun E. Perkins color *Hot Rod* v70 no1 p12 Ja 2017

Antique & classic cars—Maintenance & repair
Old Cars in New Time D. Freiburger color *Hot Rod* v70 no12 p114 D 2017

Antique & classic cars—Sales & prices
HOW TO BUY CLASSIC CARS D. Bentley and K. Korosec color *Fortune* v175 no4 p53 Mr 15 2017

Antique & classic motorcycles
SLIPSTREAM color *Cycle World* v55 no11 p70 D 2016

SLIPSTREAM color *Cycle World* v56 no10 p70 N 2017

Antique & classic motorcycles—Exhibitions
IN IT FOR THE MONEY P. D'ORLÉANS *Cycle World* v56 no3 p26 Ap 2017

Antique auctions
$1 million Day V. Kagan and J. Dubuffet *Treasures* v6 no2 p8 O/N 2016

Bar Carts We Love *Treasures* v6 no4 p10 F/Mr 2017

Cultural Pop *Treasures* v6 no4 p8 F/Mr 2017

Pay to Play *Treasures* v6 no5 p8 Ap/My 2017

Rack Your magazines *Treasures* v6 no5 p10 Ap/My 2017

Antique dealers
All About Color E. GAUKEL *Treasures* v6 no3 p14 D 2016/Ja 2017

CALENDAR *Treasures* v6 no6 p14 Je/Jl 2017

Get Ready - It's Show Time! E. Gaukel *Treasures* v6 no6 p4 Je/Jl 2017

Kindred Spirits color *Magazine Antiques* v184 no2 p108 Mr/Ap 2017

THE LOOK BOOK A. SWERDLOFF img *New York* v50 no9 p61 My 1 2017

Pyrex and Pickle Jars E. GAUKEL *Treasures* v6 no2 p6 O/N 2016

Antique dealers—Evaluation
DIVINE UNDERSTATEMENT J. Withers color *Vogue* v207 no3 p466 Mr 2017

Antique fairs
10 Tips: for scoring the best finds and prices at summer and fall outdoor antique markets E. GAUKEL *Treasures* v6 no6 p11 Je/Jl 2017

CALENDAR OF SHOWS color *Magazine Antiques* v184 no4 p124 Jl/Ag 2017

CALENDAR *Treasures* v6 no6 p14 Je/Jl 2017

Get Ready - It's Show Time! E. Gaukel *Treasures* v6 no6 p4 Je/Jl 2017

Antique toys

At Play: Antique toys add history and whimsy to any room L. Claverie *New Orleans Homes & Lifestyles* v20 no3 p28 Summ 2017

Antiques

10 Tips: for scoring the best finds and prices at summer and fall outdoor antique markets E. GAUKEL *Treasures* v6 no6 p11 Je/Jl 2017

The Accidental Collector E. YOUNG *Los Angeles Magazine* p52 D 2016

A "Circa '70" Pattern Silver Tea & Coffee Service color *Magazine Antiques* v184 no3 p11 My/Je 2017

DESTINATION CAMBRIDGE CITY ANTIQUES color *Indianapolis Monthly* v42 no2 p62 O 2017

DESTINATION KIRKLIN ANTIQUES color *Indianapolis Monthly* v42 no2 p71 O 2017

DESTINATION KOKOMO ANTIQUES color *Indianapolis Monthly* v42 no2 p65 O 2017

DESTINATION ROANOKE ANTIQUES color *Indianapolis Monthly* v42 no2 p66 O 2017

Early American Glass: A recent Norman C. Heckler auction featured several 18th- and 19th-century glass pieces with decidedly modern lines *Treasures* v6 no6 p8 Je/Jl 2017

EDITOR'S LETTER G. Cerio *Magazine Antiques* v184 no5 p14 S/O 2017

THE GOLDEN AGE OF BRONZE JOHNSON *Treasures* v6 no6 p24 Je/Jl 2017

Gorham Sterling 'Japanese' Tea & Coffee Service color *Magazine Antiques* v184 no3 p137 My/Je 2017

HERE COME THE BRIDE'S BASKETS! JOHNSON *Treasures* v6 no6 p30 Je/Jl 2017

The Historic New Orleans Collection: Teresa Devlin P. Marquis *New Orleans Homes & Lifestyles* v20 no3 p98 Summ 2017

Kirklin T. KIRTS *Indianapolis Monthly* v40 no3 p40 N 2016

Mario Buccellati Large Seafood Basket color *Magazine Antiques* v184 no3 p36 My/Je 2017

MIDCENTURY-MODERN POTTERY color *Indianapolis Monthly* v42 no2 p64 O 2017

Monobloc: A Chair for the World *Treasures* v6 no6 p5 Je/Jl 2017

Monumental Scottish Terrestrial Globe color *Magazine Antiques* v184 no3 p7 My/Je 2017

My Collection T. Johnson color *Horse & Rider* v56 no11 p136 N 2017

The New Crew J. K. Hanus color *American Craft* v77 no2 p74 Ap/My 2017

Of troughs and trophies G. Albert color *Magazine Antiques* v184 no3 p110 My/Je 2017

Presidential appointments chart color *Magazine Antiques* v184 no2 p74 Mr/Ap 2017

Queen Anne figured maple high chest with stylized lobster tail scrolled apron color *Magazine Antiques* v184 no3 p13 My/Je 2017

RESOURCES *New Orleans Homes & Lifestyles* v20 no3 p110 Summ 2017

ROAD TRIP color *Indianapolis Monthly* v42 no2 p58 O 2017

South MEETS Southwest: Atlantans discover Texas's mammoth Round Top Antiques Week B. RILEY *Atlanta* v57 no3 p87 Jl 2017

TRUE GRIT bw color *Esquire* p80 2017 BigBlackBook

welcome P. POORE *Design Center Sourcebook* p9 2017

Antiques business

Kindred Spirits color *Magazine Antiques* v184 no2 p108 Mr/Ap 2017

Moved By Color E. GAUKEL *Treasures* v6 no2 p56 O/N 2016

Antiques Roadshow (TV program)

IN IT FOR THE MONEY P. D'ORLÉANS *Cycle World* v56 no3 p26 Ap 2017

Antiques—Bibliographies

Resources *Old House Journal* v45 no7 p87 O 2017

Antiques—Collection & preservation

SUBURBAN GLORY E. HIMMELSBACH-WEINSTEIN *Los Angeles Magazine* p126 Ap 2017

Antiques—Evaluation

DIVINE UNDERSTATEMENT J. Withers color *Vogue* v207 no3 p466 Mr 2017

Antiques—Exhibitions

See also

Antique fairs

Around and about at the Biennale des Antiquaires in Paris M. Bartolucci color *Magazine Antiques* v183 no6 p56 N/D 2016

CALENDAR OF SHOWS color *Magazine Antiques* v184 no3 p132 My/Je 2017

EDITOR'S LETTER G. Cerio *Magazine Antiques* v184 no1 p20 Ja/F 2017

Metal of honor B. Laurence Scherer color *Magazine Antiques* v184 no3 p42 My/Je 2017

Antiquities

See also

Antiques

Celtic antiquities

Phoenician antiquities

Prehistoric antiquities

ARTIFACT J. A. LOBELL color *Archaeology* v70 no4 p68 Je-Ag 2017

DOCUMENTS ON Loan *Prologue* v49 no1 p30 Spr 2017

DOCUMENTS ON Loan *Prologue* v49 no2 p54 Summ 2017

HANDFORMS color *Indianapolis Monthly* v42 no2 p61 O 2017

It Just Never Stops ... J. RANDI *Skeptical Inquirer* v41 no3 p18 My/Je 2017

One-Off S. Moyer *Humanities* v37 no4 p1 Fall 2016

PONDERING THE PAST E. MASTROIANNI color *Discover* v38 no3 p9 Ap 2017

ROAD TRIP color *Indianapolis Monthly* v42 no2 p58 O 2017

Antiquities sales & prices

Hobby Lobby purchase shows ethical problems in the antiquities trade M. Chabin color *Christian Century* v134 no19 p15 S 13 2017

Antiquities—Collectors & collecting

HEY, BIG SPENDERS J. FOUMBERG bw color *Chicago* v65 no12 p50 D 2016

Antiquities—Exhibitions

Editor's Letter L. POLLOCK bw *Art in America* v105 no4 p14 Ap 2017

Antiquities—Forgeries—England

See also

Piltdown forgery

Piltdown's Lone Forger S. S. PATEL bw color *Archaeology* v69 no6 p9 N/D 2016

Antiquities—Law & legislation

Establishment of National Monuments: Controversies Surrounding the Antiquities Act *Congressional Digest* v96 no6 p6 Je 2017

Antireflective coatings

The Perils of Smartphones R. BACHER *AARP: The Magazine* v59 no5A p19 Ag/S 2016

Antiretroviral agents

See also

Anti-HIV agents

Drugs now reach millions more with HIV color *Science* v357 no6349 p336 Jl 28 2017

A microbiome variable in the HIV-prevention equation S. Tuddenham and K. G. Ghanem color *Science* v356 no6341 p907 Je 1 2017

Sustained virologic control in SIV+ macaques after antiretroviral and α4β7 antibody therapy S. N. Byrareddy, J. Arthos et al bibl graph *Science* v354 no6309 p197 O 14 2016

Antisemitism

BDS Beat Down D. DANON *USA Today Magazine* v145 no2860 p53 Ja 2017

Grave Matter: The desecration of Jewish cemeteries has a long history—one that has nothing to do with the election of Donald Trump S. Mandel *Commentary* v143 no4 p27 Ap 2017

Is the Pope 'Anti-Jewish'? P. A. Cunningham color *Commonweal* v144 no9 p19 My 19 2017

Leo Strauss's Forgotten Letter S. B. Smith *Commentary* v142 no3 p17 O 2016

Sex and the Single Girl, Puppy Love, Oy Vey L. KOGAN color *O, The Oprah Magazine* p38 Ag 2017

State Department to keep anti-Semitism envoy but scrap many others M. A. Kellner *Christian Century* v134 no20 p15 S 27 2017

Antisemitism—Europe—History

Synagogues, Cemeteries, and Frontiers: Anti-Semitism in Switzerland L. Tartakoff *Society* v54 no1 p56 F 2017

Antisemitism—Germany

A toy figure of Luther sparked accusations of anti-Semitism T. Heneghan color *Christian Century* v134 no3 p14 F 2017

Antisemitism—United States

Election tensions lead to rise in anti-Semitic incidents color *America* v216 no11 p17 My 15 2017

Jews and Muslims partner in efforts to defend religious minorities J. Mendoza *Christian Century* v134 no2 p17 Ja 18 2017

Standing With Our Jewish Brothers and Sisters *America* v216 no6 p8 Mr 20 2017

Trump's Anti-Semites J. Kirchick *Commentary* v142 no2 p7 S 2016

Antiseptics

TRUSTED BRAND *Reader's Digest* v188 no1124 p50 O 2016

Antisocial personality disorders

The Antisocial Network M. Mariani *Psychology Today* v49 no5 p80 S/O 2016

When Your Child Is a Psychopath B. B. HAGERTY color *Atlantic* v319 no5 p78 Je 2017

Anti-Trump protest movements, 2015-

See also

Women's March on Washington, 2017

Cassandra smiling J. HESTER color *Astronomy* v45 no9 p16 S 2017

First She Marched, Then She Ran: Alexis Frank, a 26-year-old political novice, never considered vying for Congress--until she saw Hillary Clinton lose M. COGAN img *New York* v50 no11 p42 My 29 2017

Resistance Is Not Enough [Cover story] J. WALSH color *Nation* v304 no17 p16 Je 5 2017

THEY PERSISTED E. J. GRAFF color *Mother Jones* v42 no4 p34 Jl/Ag 2017

Visible and Indivisible: The Birth of a Resistance Movement K. Aronoff color *Progressive* v81 no6 p15 Ag/S 2017

Antitrust investigations

Google's $2.7 Billion Antitrust Fine T. John color *Time* v190 no2/3 p9 Jl 10-17 2017

Antitrust law

Google vs. the EU Explains the Digital Economy B. Iyer and U. S. Rangan *Harvard Business Review Digital Articles* p2 D 12 2016

The Next Battle in Antitrust Will Be About Whether One Company Knows Everything About You B. Iyer, M. Subramaniam et al *Harvard Business Review Digital Articles* p2 Jl 6 2017

Should Antitrust Regulators Stop Companies from Collecting So Much Data? J. Kennedy *Harvard Business Review Digital Articles* p2 Ap 17 2017

Antitrust law—United States

What We Can Learn from Merger Deals That Never Happened B. Gomes-Casseres *Harvard Business Review Digital Articles* p2 Je 21 2016

Antitussive agents

See also

Codeine

Purple Drank, Corpotate Bank T. Bella color *Bloomberg Businessweek* no4514 p60 Mr 13 2017

Antiviral agents—Therapeutic use

Before You Take It S. KLEIN color *Prevention* v69 no1 p22 Ja 2017

Antivirus software

Meet Windows Defender Security Center, your PC's safety belt in the Creators Update I. PAUL color *PCWorld* v35 no6 p29 Je 2017

Antivirus software—Awards

The best consumer antivirus products of 2016 are Avira and Norton M. HACHMAN chart color *PCWorld* p33 Mr 2017

ANTLE, W. JAMES III

Sanctuaries of Defiance: The latest battle in the immigration wars *American Conservative* v16 no4 p24 Jl/Ag 2017

Antler Chandeliers & Lighting Co.

LIGHTING color *Timber Home Living* p64 2017 SpecialIssue

Antlers

Hard Times S. Bestul color *Field & Stream* v122 no4 pW1 S 2017

Horn Hunting H. Fuge *New York State Conservationist* v71 no4 p17 F 2017

MAKE IT LAST T. HANSEN color *Outdoor Life* v224 no7 p28 S 2017

RACK ATTACK K. EVANS cartoon color *Outdoor Life* v224 no6 p14 Ag 2017

SECRETS OF THE SHED MASTERS T. CARPENTER and A. McKEAN color *Outdoor Life* v224 no2 p80 F/Mr 2017

TINES UP *South Dakota Magazine* v32 no6 p94 Mr/Ap 2017

Antlers in art

BOUNTIES FOR BUCKS B. Fitzpatrick color *Outdoor Life* v223 no9 p36 N 2016

Antlers—Equipment & supplies

BOUNTIES FOR BUCKS B. Fitzpatrick color *Outdoor Life* v223 no9 p36 N 2016

Antoine, Romy

GET FIT THE 2017 WAY color *Black Enterprise* v47 no5 p70 Ja/F 2017

Antoine, Rudy

Reversion of antibiotic resistance in Mycobacterium tuberculosis by spiroisoxazoline SMARt-420 bibl diag *Science* v355 no6330 p1206 Mr 17 2017

Anton, Carrie

THE OTHER BIG C *Women's Health* v14 no4 p86 My 2017

Anton, Joshua

GUEST LIST *Washingtonian Magazine* v52 no3 p20 D 2016

Anton, Michael

'Decius' Comes in from the Cold M. WARREN *Weekly Standard* v22 no22 p11 F 13 2017

Antonakis, John

About face color *Science* v357 no6348 p259 Jl 21 2017

Antonarakis, Stylianos E.

Genomic databases: A WHO affair *Science* v356 no6340 p812 My 26 2017

Antonelli, Paola

THE DIGITIZED MUSEUM B. Droitcour and W. S. Smith *Art in America* v104 no9 p77 O 2016

LOOK AGAIN color *New York Times Magazine* p50 N 13 2016

Antonine Wall (Scotland)

THE OTHER WALL color *Archaeology* v70 no3 p32 My/Je 2017

Antonio, José

THE STRONGMAN'S MIDDLEMAN A. BROWN color *Forbes* v199 no3 p60 Mr 28 2017

Antonio, Robbie

THE STRONGMAN'S MIDDLEMAN A. BROWN color *Forbes* v199 no3 p60 Mr 28 2017

Antonio Lopez 1970: Sex Fashion & Disco (Film)

Antonio LOPEZ *Interview* v47 no2 p84 Mr 2017

Antonius, Gabriel

More details on Israel's water story S. R. Cohen *Physics Today* v70 no6 p11 Je 2017

Antonius, Marcus, ca. 83 B.C.-30 B.C.

HIS OWN WORST ENEMY R. A. Gabriel color *Military History* v34 no2 p30 Jl 2017

Antonoff, Jack, 1984-

INSIDE JACK ANTONOFF'S POP LABORATORY K. O'Donnell color *Entertainment Weekly* no1470 p56 Je 16 2017

Jack Antonoff Shines a Light In the Dark S. Lansky color *Time* v189 no22 p56 Je 12 2017

Jack Antonoff's Therapy Rock P. DOYLE color *Rolling Stone* no1290 p22 Je 29 2017

ANTONOFF, MICHAEL

Bingeing on CBS Assets color *Sound & Vision* v82 no6 p25 Jl/Ag 2017

The Download on Netflix color *Sound & Vision* v82 no4 p25 My 2017

The Golden Age of Podcasting color *Sound & Vision* v82 no5 p26 Je 2017

Outfitting Robo Car color graph *Sound & Vision* v82 no7 p21 S 2017

Outta Obsolescence color *Sound & Vision* v82 no3 p19 Ap 2017

Running with Apps color *Sound & Vision* v82 no1 p24 Ja 2017

Shopping with Apps color *Sound & Vision* v82 no2 p24 F/Mr 2017

Sleeping with Apps color *Sound & Vision* v82 no8 p22 O 2017

Streamin' in the Shower cartoon color *Sound & Vision* v81 no10 p28 D 2016

Watching Your DVR From Anywhere color *Sound & Vision* v81 no9 p24 N 2016

Witness to suffering J. G. Phelan *America* v217 no7 p49 O 2 2017

A.O. Smith Corp.

WATER HEATER K. Dupzyk color *Popular Mechanics* p30 D 2016/Ja 2017

Ao Zhang

Precision medicine for nasopharyngeal carcinoma bibl diag *Science* v354 no6319 p24 D 23 2016

Aoi, Yuki

PAF1 regulation of promoter-proximal pause release via enhancer activation color *Science* v357 no6357 p1294 S 22 2017

AOKI, DEB

NINE REASONS MANGA PUBLISHERS CAN SMILE IN 2017 color *Publishers Weekly* v264 no25 p80 Je 19 2017

AOL Inc.

Why Mega-Mergers Are Back in Vogue for Internet Companies Moatti *Harvard Business Review Digital Articles* p2 Je 1 2015

Aorta abnormalities

Innovation: Tiny Blood Pump M. Belfiore color *Bloomberg Businessweek* no4540 p29 O 2 2017

Aortic dissection—Case studies

Under Pressure C. TEDESCHI color *Discover* v38 no6 p18 Jl/Ag 2017

Aoun, Joseph E.

Hybrid Jobs Call for Hybrid Education *Harvard Business Review Digital Articles* p2 Ap 12 2016

Aoun, Michel, 1935-

Lebanon's New Leader Aims to Keep 'Regional Fires' at Bay J. Malsin color *Time* v188 no20 p9 N 14 2016

Presiding over Chaos L. SMITH color *Weekly Standard* v22 no10 p10 N 14 2016

Apa, K. J.

Archie and Betty and Veronica and Zombies A. Riesman img *New York* p62 Ja 23 2017

Archie and the Gang Come Back to a Much Darker World D. D'Addario color *Time* v189 no4 p47 F 6 2017

The New Boy Next Door D. Coggan color *Entertainment Weekly* no1450 p44 Ja 27 2017

Riverdale J. Jensen color *Entertainment Weekly* no1450 p50 Ja 27 2017

Riverdale T. Stack color *Entertainment Weekly* no1448 p42 Ja 13 2017

Apache County (Ariz.)

LIKE A MOUNTAIN K. VAUGHN *Arizona Highways* v96 no7 p30 Jl 2017

Apai, D.

Zones, spots, and planetary-scale waves beating in brown dwarf atmospheres color graph *Science* v357 no6352 p683 Ag 18 2017

Apalachicola Bay (Fla.)

The Water Keeper's Dilemma L. POPPICK *Audubon* v119 no3 p10 Fall 2017

Aparium Hotel Group (Company)

SLEEP ON IT A. KONERMANN *Cincinnati Magazine* v50 no2 p36 N 2016

Apartheid

See also

Townships (South Africa)

56 MILES OF FREEDOM R. Lenora Brown color *Runner's World* v52 no9 p84 O 2017

backstory color *New Republic* v248 no3 p72 Mr 2017

Apartment building design & construction

See also

High-rise apartment buildings—Design & construction

Double Vision in South Park: RISING UP OUT OF NOWHERE NEAR STAPLES CENTER, THE TWIN CIRCA TOWERS HAVE ALREADY ALTERED HOW WE SEE DOWNTOWN C. NICHOLS *Los Angeles Magazine* v62 no9 p24 S 2017

Farewell, Lebanon's First Brewery D. KENNER color *Foreign Policy* no225 p21 Jl/Ag 2017

K-Pop C. A. PEARSON *Architectural Record* v205 no10 p108 O 2017

MULTIFAMILY HOUSING *Architectural Record* v205 no10 p83 O 2017

snapshot A. Klimoski *Architectural Record* v205 no10 p172 O 2017

Triple Play D. MADSEN *Architectural Record* v205 no10 p114 O 2017

Apartment buildings

See also

Apartments

High-rise apartment buildings

DOMAIN IN THE SKYLINE K. FINN color *New Orleans Magazine* v51 no1 p32 N 2016

home base: THE BEST TRAILS ARE NEVER FAR AWAY n. formosa bw *Bike Magazine* v24 no8 p19 N 2017

Life Before and After All the High-Rises *New York* v50 no18 p68 S 4 2017

Shelter from the Storm: Architects must continue to explore new forms for urban living C. McGuigan *Architectural Record* v205 no10 p14 O 2017

STILL NIGHT P. STEFÁNSSON *Iceland Review* v55 no2 p58 Mr/Ap 2017

Apartment buildings—Maintenance & repair

Urban Symphony R. BROOKHISER il *National Review* v69 no19 p59 O 16 2017

Apartment buildings—New York (State)—New York

When the President Is Your Landlord N. TABOR img *New York* p52 F 20 2017

Apartment design & construction

Color Theory A. MARTINS *Architectural Record* v205 no9 p98 S 2017

interiors M. PEPCHINSKI *Architectural Record* v205 no6 p33 Je 2017

Wonder Brothers: The Goethe-, Tolstoy-, and Melnikov-inspired Carroll Gardens apartment of two young siblings and business partners W. GOODMAN img *New York* v50 no12 p78 Je 12 2017

Apartments

City of Sand S. THOMAS bw *Orion Magazine* v35 no6 p9 N/D 2016

He's Funny That Way: THE LIFE, TIMES, AND PICKLED GARLIC OF ALAN KIGER K. LAUR *Cincinnati Magazine* v50 no11 p40 Ag 2017

Movin' on Up D. Paul *Indianapolis Monthly* p136 F 2017

My Studio J. KENT-DOOLAN *Indianapolis Monthly* v40 no4 p44 D 2016

Rent Control D. Frolovskiy *New York Times Magazine* p38 O 30 2016

Apartments—Design & construction

LESS IS MORE M. COHEN MARILL *Atlanta* v56 no8 p32 D 2016

Apartments—Evaluation

THINKING INSIDE THE BOX *Washingtonian Magazine* v52 no3 p166 D 2016

Apartments—Interior decoration

#4: In a New York apartment, Bachman Brown Clem performs an about-face: The moldings and trim—not walls—are in gleaming blue, framing a neutral backdrop filled with antiques and treasures T. McKEOUGH color *House Beautiful* v159 no2 p108 Mr 2017

Old Hollywood Haunt A. HEROLD *Los Angeles Magazine* p38 Ja 2017

Perfect Harmony D. SHAW color *Architectural Digest* v73 no12 p112 D 2016

SECRET HISTORY D. COLMAN color *Architectural Digest* v73 no12 p120 D 2016

SMALL SPACE, BIG STYLE A. LONGOBUCCO color diag *Good Housekeeping* v264 no5 p64 My 2017

Apatow, Judd, 1967-

DAVID COPPERFIELD *Interview* v47 no1 p84 F 2017

Judd APATOW color *Esquire* v167 no2 p160 Mr 2017

The Year in Reading [Cover story] *New York Times Book Review* p8 D 25 2016

Apatow, Judd, 1967-—Interviews

Bromantic Comedy *Los Angeles Magazine* p56 F 2017

Is This Guy Making the Next Girls? R. Rahman color *Entertainment Weekly* no1454/1455 p86 F 24 2017

Judd Apatow P. DOYLE bw *Rolling Stone* no1288 p58 Je 1 2017

APB (TV program)

APB K. Freeze *TV Guide* v65 no6 p39 Ja 30 2017

The Best Police Money Can Buy K. Williams *In These Times* v41 no4 p54 Ap 2017

Apel, Ashley

Committing to socially responsible seafood color *Science* v356 no6341 p912 Je 1 2017

Aperion Audio Inc.

Aperion Audio Verus II Grand Speaker System T. J. Norton color graph *Sound & Vision* v82 no3 p54 Ap 2017

Apes—Behavior

Apes recognize others' false beliefs B. BOWER *Science News* v190 no10 p8 N 12 2016

Mind the Monkey Business E. UNDERWOOD *Smithsonian* v47 no8 p21 D 2016

Apex Ski Boots (Company)

COMFY CARVING M. BEHAR color *Bloomberg Businessweek* no4506 p59 Ja 9 2017

Apfel, Iris

Friends for the Ages A. J. BAIME and G. M. GARRETT color *AARP: The Magazine* v60 no4A p42 Je/Jl 2017

Apfelbaum, Evan

Why Your Diversity Program May Be Helping Women but Not Minorities (or Vice Versa) *Harvard Business Review Digital Articles* p2 Ag 8 2016

Apgar, Virginia, 1909-1974

The Test That Can Save a Newborn's Life R. Beach bw color *Glamour* v115 no11 p26 N 2017

Apgar score

Speeding Up Baby's First Test M. Quinn *Governing* v30 no2 p18 N 2016

The Test That Can Save a Newborn's Life R. Beach bw color *Glamour* v115 no11 p26 N 2017

Aphorisms & apothegms

Laugh Lines MY FUNNY VALENTINE *Reader's Digest* v189 no1127 p103 F 2017

Portal_Ranch.txt I. Cheng color *Art in America* v105 no4 p42 Ap 2017

Apichatpong Weerasethakul, 1970-

Cemetery of Splendor D. Lim *Film Comment* v53 no1 p46 Ja/F 2017

Apinjoh, Tobias O.

Resistance to malaria through structural variation of red blood cell invasion receptors diag *Science* v356 no6343 p1139 Je 16 2017

Apitherapy

THE NEW BUZZ S. Cristobal color *Harper's Bazaar* no3648 p266 N 2016

APLET, GREGORY H.

Mapping Conservation Strategies under a Changing Climate *BioScience* v67 no6 p494 Je 2017

Apocalypse

Over It P. GULLEY color *Indianapolis Monthly* p52 Ap 2017

Apocryphal Gospels

LIVING BY The Word *Christian Century* v134 no19 p18 S 13 2017

Reflections on the lectionary D. Thomas *Christian Century* v134 no20 p21 S 27 2017

Apodaca, Rose

Ladies' Night color *InStyle* v24 no4 p82 Ap 2017

Apolipoprotein E

Dissecting the effects of APOE *Science* v355 no6326 p707 F 17 2017

Apolipoprotein E4

How ApoE4 endangers brains E. Underwood color *Science* v357 no6357 p1224 S 22 2017

Apologies

Guilt Free W. Morris *New York Times Magazine* p11 Jl 30 2017

The Hardest Word? Is it ahistorical for public figures to say sorry for events that took place before they were born? The issue cuts to the heart of the relationship between the living and the dead S. Lipscomb *History Today* v67 no6 p106 Je 2016

Research: For a Corporate Apology to Work, the CEO Should Look Sad S. G. Carmichael *Harvard Business Review Digital Articles* p2 Ag 24 2015

Apologizing

The 4 Types of Ineffective Apologies A. Molinsky *Harvard Business Review Digital Articles* p2 N 15 2016

A Letter of Apology to a Son Graduating from College K. Van Ogtrop color *Time* v189 no15 p55 Ap 24 2017

REALLY I'M SORRY cartoon *Seventeen* v76 no2 p96 Mr 2017

Sorry Not Sorry M. Ruiz *Women's Health* v14 no2 p128 Mr 2017

When a Public Mistake Requires an Old-Fashioned Apology R. Ashkenas *Harvard Business Review Digital Articles* p2 Ja 7 2015

Apology of Patroclus, The (Poem)

The Apology of Patroclus T. Lindberg *Commentary* v142 no3 p20 O 2016

Apoptosis

Stupid Stuff Guys Do to Lose Weight E. Spitznagel cartoon *Men's Health* v32 no2 p66 Mr 2017

Apostles, The (Theatrical production)

CLASSICAL MUSIC *New Yorker* v93 no13 p8 My 15 2017

Apostolic exhortations (Papal letters)

Can Catholics dissent from Pope Francis' teaching on the family? Wrong question P. Folan color *America* v216 no8 p36 Ap 17 2017

Apostolides, Pierre F.

Deconstructing behavioral neuropharmacology with cellular specificity color *Science* v356 no6333 p42 Ap 7 2017

Apostolou, Andrew

A Proto-Zion *Commentary* v143 no1 p56 Ja 2017

Apovian, Caroline

The Snacking Diaries color *Women's Health* v14 no2 p106 Mr 2017

Appalachian Antique Hardwoods LLC

BEST OUTDOOR SPACE color *Timber Home Living* p24 2017 SpecialIssue

History Repeats color *Log Home Living* v34 no2 p16 Mr 2017

Appalachian Region—Economic conditions

THE WAR ON HILLBILLIES S. JONES color *New Republic* v248 no6 p42 Je 2017

Appalachian Trail

Find your Stride: Hiking in the Zone L. ". Thomas color *Backpacker* v45 no1 p16 Ja 2017

Golden Rules color *Backpacker* v45 no1 p51 Ja 2017

LONG DRIVE, SHORT HIKE J. Davis color *Backpacker* v45 no1 p79 Ja 2017

MIND THE GAPS W. ". Kemsley Jr. *Backpacker* v45 no1 p75 Ja 2017

out alive: lost & blind C. Webber color *Backpacker* p43 My 2017

Raise a Kid Who Loves Hiking D. WORCESTER il *Backpacker* v45 no2 p34 Mr 2017

Appalachian Trail—Description & travel

The Dayhiker's Triple Crown J. MONTALVO color *Backpacker* v45 no1 p14 Ja 2017

Hike your own hike color *Backpacker* v45 no1 p12 Ja 2017

Appalachians (People)

APPALACHIAN SLY: Unfortunate characters suffer multiple miseries before attempting to turn calamity into good fortune B. GLOSE *Virginia Living* v15 no6 p27 O 2017

Appaloosa horse

HOW NOT TO BUY A HORSE D. McVicker cartoon color *Equus* no474 p40 Mr 2017

Apparition, M.—Interviews

THE LOOK BOOK A. SWERDLOFF img *New York* v49 no20 p99 O 3 2016

Appavoo, K.

Extremely efficient internal exciton dissociation through edge states in layered 2D perovskites bibl graph *Science* v355 no6331 p1288 Mr 24 2017

Appel, Allen

Golden Eyes *Publishers Weekly* v264 no23 p31 Je 5 2017

Ordinary Soldiers in Extraordinary Circumstances color *Publishers Weekly* v264 no13 p34 Mr 27 2017

Standing Literary Watch color *Publishers Weekly* v263 no44 p53 O 31 2016

Appel, Ian

Research: Index Funds Are Improving Corporate Governance *Harvard Business Review Digital Articles* p2 My 9 2016

Appel, Marty

Casey Stengel: Baseball's Greatest Character *Publishers Weekly* v263 no51 p134 D 12 2016

Appelbaum, Binyamin

On Money color *New York Times Magazine* p20 O 9 2016

POPULAR IDEAS ABOUT THE WORKING CLASS ARE WOEFULLY OUT OF DATE. HERE ARE NINE PEOPLE WHO TELL A TRUER STORY OF WHAT THE AMERICAN

WORK FORCE DOES TODAY—AND WILL DO TOMOR-ROW *New York Times Magazine* p36 F 26 2017

APPELBAUM, YONI

Is the American Idea Over? color *Atlantic* v320 no4 p17 N 2017

Appelfeld, Aharon

The Man Who Never Stopped Sleeping: A Novel R. M. Stone *Christian Century* v134 no13 p40 Je 21 2017

Sleep and Dreams G. BROOKS *New York Times Book Review* p7 F 5 2017

Appellate courts

The Saga of Kenya's Disputed Election Is a Good-News Story I. Bremmer *Time* v190 no12 p14 S 25 2017

Appelo, Tim

Back on the Train color *AARP: The Magazine* v30 no6A p14 O/N 2017

Primetime Combat color *AARP: The Magazine* v30 no6A p15 O/N 2017

Appelt, Kathi, 1954-

Maybe a Fox *Publishers Weekly* v263 no49 p68 D 7 2016

Appendicitis

CUT IT OUT! cartoon *Canoe & Kayak Magazine* v45 no1 p42 Wint 2017

Appenzeller, Tim

THE SCIENTISTS' APPRENTICE [Cover story] color *Science* v357 no6346 p16 Jl 7 2017

An unprecedented march for science color *Science* v356 no6336 p356 Ap 28 2017

Appetite

Haute Cuisine C. J. Doane color *Sail* v48 no6 p80 Je 2017

Mastering Appetite Control *Tufts University Health & Nutrition Letter* v35 no2 p4 2017

Appetite (Poem)

Appetite S. Golden *Orion Magazine* v36 no2 p44 Mr/Ap 2017

Appetite depressants

See also

    Amphetamines

QUICK FIXES J. Rice color *Amazing Wellness* v8 no2 p40 Spr 2016

Appetite for Destruction (Music)

GUNS N' ROSES' APPETITE FOR DESTRUCTION L. Greenblatt color *Entertainment Weekly* no1474/1475 p116 Jl 21-28 2017

Appetite—Research

This Just In J. Zorthian *Time* v189 no4 p23 Ja 23 2017

Appetizers

See also

    Dips (Appetizers)

    Salads

February 2017 cartoon color *O, The Oprah Magazine* p113 F 2017

Give Peas a Chance color *House Beautiful* v159 no1 p44 F 2017

GOd bLeSS ReD SAUCe AMeRiCA N. RICHARDSON color *Bon Appetit* p126 S 2017

IN THE KITCHEN: VENETIAN BITES M. HENNESSY color *Chicago* v66 no9 p68 S 2017

Take It Slow R. Schaap *New York Times Magazine* p23 F 26 2017

there's an app for that C. Saffitz bw color *Bon Appetit* v61 no11 p76 N 2016

Appetizers—Psychological aspects

Take It Slow R. Schaap *New York Times Magazine* p23 F 26 2017

Appiah, Kwame Anthony

Am I Obliged To Support My Elderly Mother? *New York Times Magazine* p30 N 20 2016

Can a Therapist Fake His Online Reviews? *New York Times Magazine* p20 F 26 2017

Can Dad Bring His Second Wife to Mom's Funeral? *New York Times Magazine* p24 My 14 2017

Can I Keep A Baby My Boyfriend Doesn't Want? cartoon *New York Times Magazine* p22 Ag 6 2017

Can I Out My Ex-Husband To His Girlfriend? *New York Times Magazine* p20 Ja 8 2017

Can I Pretend to Be A Lesbian to Get a Couples Discount? *New York Times Magazine* p26 O 16 2016

Can I Spread The Word About an Unvaccinated Child? *New York Times Magazine* p18 O 1 2017

Does Confining Deplorable Remarks to Your Home Make Them All Right? *New York Times Magazine* p28 Ap 23 2017

Does My Ex Owe Anything To Our Grown Kids? *New York Times Magazine* p24 Je 11 2017

Do I Get Involved When A Parent Treats a Child Badly? color *New York Times Magazine* p38 D 11 2016

Do I Have To Tell My Family I'm No Longer Religious? *New York Times Magazine* p24 O 2 2016

Do I Report A Teacher's Racist Facebook Post? *New York Times Magazine* p18 Jl 2 2017

The Ethicist *New York Times Magazine* p22 S 3 2017

The Ethicist *New York Times Magazine* p26 N 6 2016

How Do I Deal With a Gun At a Relative's Home? *New York Times Magazine* p16 Ag 13 2017

I Accidentally Killed a Child. May I Contact The Family? *New York Times Magazine* p26 My 21 2017

Is It Best To Get a Pet From a No-Kill Shelter? *New York Times Magazine* p22 Ap 30 2017

Is It O.K. to Fire a Muslim Driver for Refusing to Carry Wine? *New York Times Magazine* p20 Jl 23 2017

Is It O.K. to Give Cigarettes To a Homeless Person? *New York Times Magazine* p18 O 8 2017

Is It O.K. to Have Another Man Satisfy Me Sexually, Since My Husband Can't? *New York Times Magazine* p26 O 9 2016

Is It O.K. To Protest Trump by Withholding Taxes? *New York Times Magazine* p18 Jl 30 2017

Is Sex With A Brain-Damaged Man Assault? *New York Times Magazine* p22 S 10 2017

A Man I Know Faked His Academic Credentials. Should I Tell His Fiancée? *New York Times Magazine* p20 O 23 2016

Mom Left Me the House. What Do I Owe My Brothers? *New York Times Magazine* p20 Ag 20 2017

Must I Tell My Therapist About My Other Therapist? *New York Times Magazine* p28 S 17 2017

My Ex Is Advertising For Sugar Daddies. Can I Tell Her Mother? *New York Times Magazine* p18 O 30 2016

My Friend Is Bankrupting Herself. Should I Speak Up? *New York Times Magazine* p18 Ap 2 2017

My Lab Is Studying an Alzheimer's Treatment. Can I Try It on Myself? *New York Times Magazine* p18 F 12 2017

My Sister Won't Vaccinate Her Son. Can I Help Him? *New York Times Magazine* p18 Ja 1 2017

My Teenage Patient's Mom Is Slipping Her Prozac. What Should I Do? *New York Times Magazine* p16 Jl 16 2017

My Wife Is a Trump Zealot. What's a Liberal to Do? *New York Times Magazine* p16 F 19 2017

Should I Help an Unjustly Fired Co-Worker? *New York Times Magazine* p22 Je 25 2017

Should I Out My Friend's 'Service Dog' Scam? *New York Times Magazine* p22 D 4 2016

Should I Speak Up About a Green-Card Marriage? *New York Times Magazine* p24 Ja 29 2017

Should I Tell Someone That His Father-in-Law Is a Child Molester? *New York Times Magazine* p22 Jl 9 2017

Should I Tell Uber My Driver Was High? *New York Times Magazine* p20 Mr 5 2017

Should I Turn In My Tax-Cheating Relative? *New York Times Magazine* p24 Ag 27 2017

Should Parents Be Expected To Donate To a Public School? *New York Times Magazine* p34 N 27 2016

What Should I Do About A Co-Worker Who Drinks On the Job? *New York Times Magazine* p18 F 5 2017

What Should I Do About A Physician Who May Be a Quack? *New York Times Magazine* p26 Ja 15 2017

What Should I Do With My Father's Nazi Keepsake? *New York Times Magazine* p28 Mr 26 2017

What Should We Have Told A Betrayed Wife? *New York Times Magazine* p22 Ja 22 2017

Appignanesi, Lisa

Freud's Clay Feet color *New York Review of Books* v64 no16 p36 O 26 2017

Apple, Anne H. K.

LIVING BY The Word *Christian Century* v134 no10 p25 My 10 2017

Apple cider

Apple cider is amazing C. Hall color *Redbook* p28 N 2017

Hot Toddy Mocktail color *Good Housekeeping* v265 no5 p81 N 2017

IN BRIEF color graph *Bloomberg Businessweek* no4533 p6 Ag 7 2017

Movers K. Stock bw cartoon color *Bloomberg Businessweek* no4497 p15 O 31 2016

Apple Inc.—History

News: Apple's latest product is a £249 book C. McGarry color *Macworld - Digital Edition* p6 Ja 2017

Apple Inc.—Officials & employees

News: Apple to support automation in Sierra R. Loyola color *Macworld - Digital Edition* p16 Ja 2017

Tim Cook CEO, Apple: "I am so excited about it, I just want to yell out and scream" [Cover story] M. Murphy color *Bloomberg Businessweek* no4527 p52 Je 19 2017

Apple Music (Company)

HEY, MISS DJ C. Murray color *Essence* v48 no2 p58 Je 2017

A Star Is Born L. Shaw and A. Webb color graph *Bloomberg Businessweek* no4520 p22 My 1 2017

Apple operating systems

iOS Accessories J. MATHIS color *Macworld - Digital Edition* p74 D 2016

macOS HIGH SIERRA: FEATURES, SYSTEM REQUIREMENTS, RELEASE DATE, AND MORE M. Simon and R. Loyola color *Macworld - Digital Edition* p72 Je 13 2017

Apple TV (Digital media receiver)—Software

The new Apple TV update is no friend to cord cutters J. NEWMAN color *PCWorld* v35 no1 p35 Ja 2017

Applebaum, Anne

DESTRUCTION MYTH *Harper's Magazine* v333 no1999 p89 D 2016

Is the Liberal Order in Peril? color graph *Foreign Affairs* v96 no3 p178 My/Je 2017

A New European Narrative? [Cover story] color *New York Review of Books* v64 no15 p44 O 12 2017

Soundbites *Extra!* v29 no8 p2 O 2016

Applebaum, Michael—Trials, litigation, etc.

BAD NEWS color *Maclean's* v129 no47 p11 N 28 2016

Applebroog, Ida

GENTLEMEN, AMERICA IS IN TROUBLE J. Shaw bw color *Art in America* v104 no10 p66 N 2016

Appleby, R. Scott

America First? color *Commonweal* v143 no17 p11 O 21 2016

Appleford, Steve

Chester's Last Days color *Rolling Stone* no1294 p13 Ag 24 2017

Applegate, Christina, 1971-

CHRISTINA APPLEGATE FIGHTS FOR WOMEN'S HEALTH CARE M. L. Lenker color *Entertainment Weekly* no1486 p45 O 13 2017

Applegate, Daniel T.

Fructose-driven glycolysis supports anoxia resistance in the naked mole-rat diag graph *Science* v356 no6335 p307 Ap 21 2017

Applegate, Katherine

If This Tree Could Talk: Katherine Applegate's new novel channels the natural world to take on prejudice against immigrants D. BROWNING *New York Times Book Review* p25 S 10 2017

APPLEGATE, LIZ

BEST BITES color *Runner's World* v51 no10 p50 N 2016

EAT TO REMEMBER color *Runner's World* v52 no2 p41 Mr 2017

FEAST FIRST color *Runner's World* v52 no1 p56 Ja/F 2017

WARM UP YOUR COOLDOWN color *Runner's World* v51 no11 p50 D 2016

Applegate, MaryAnne

BREEDERS PROFILES *Arabian Horse World* v57 no3 p120 D 2016

Apple Inc.—Trials, litigation, etc.

Apple Tries the Full-Court Press I. King and A. Webb color graph *Bloomberg Businessweek* no4509 p28 Ja 30 2017

Appleman, Nate

GLASS ACT color *Runner's World* v52 no2 p42 Mr 2017

Apples

Apple Eaters A. WELDON *Orion Magazine* v35 no6 p12 N/D 2016

As American as Apple Pie? S. SETHI color *Reader's Digest* v190 no1132 p40 Jl/Ag 2017

Heart Benefit Seen from Compound in Tea, Cocoa, Apples *Tufts University Health & Nutrition Letter* v34 no8 p6 O 2016

Hot Toddy Mocktail color *Good Housekeeping* v265 no5 p81 N 2017

MAKE-AHEAD holiday meal J. Silverman Hough color *Yoga Journal* no296 p25 N 2017

MELT WITH ME [Cover story] M. Kadey cartoon color *Runner's World* v51 no11 p48 D 2016

Photos from the Field *Mother Earth News* no283 p96 Ag/S 2017

Quick & Healthy Homemade Sausage J. BOWDEN and J. BESSINGER color *Better Nutrition* v79 no10 p78 O 2017

Soup's On J. BOWDEN and J. BESSINGER color *Better Nutrition* v78 no11 p86 N 2016

Weird Things from the Blue K. Samuelson color *Time* v190 no6 p16 Ag 7 2017

Apples & Sand (Poem)

APPLES AND SAND A. HOFFMAN *Phi Kappa Phi Forum* v96 no4 p30 Wint 2016

Applesauce

SWEET TO THE CORE S. COLLINS color *Martha Stewart Living* p96 O 2017

Apples—Physiology

Perfect Pare F. VALDESOLO and C. ELLENBERG color *Vogue* v207 no9 p450 S 2017

APPLETON, MARC

AN ARCHITECT'S GARDEN color *Architectural Digest* v74 no4 p164 Ap 2017

Application program interfaces (Computer software)

Are You Using APIs to Gain Competitive Advantage? B. Iyer and M. Subramaniam *Harvard Business Review Digital Articles* p2 Ap 13 2015

The Strategic Value of APIs B. Iyer and M. Subramaniam *Harvard Business Review Digital Articles* p2 Ja 7 2015

The Untapped Potential of Health Care APIs R. Huckman and M. Uppaluru *Harvard Business Review Digital Articles* p2 D 23 2015

Why We Ask Every New Employee to Code an App Their First Week on the Job M. Nowack *Harvard Business Review Digital Articles* p2 D 23 2016

Application software

See also

Computer games

Mobile apps

Adobe Photoshop Elements 15 review: Image editor boosts its photo-manipulation features J. DOVE color *Macworld - Digital Edition* p111 D 2016

Apps That Make You Happy color *Health* v31 no4 p10 My 2017

The Best Apps for Pet Lovers L. Murray color *Health* v30 no10 p91 D 2016

Cessna Flights For the Masses P. Robison *Bloomberg Businessweek* no4524 p35 My 29 2017

COOKED DATA A. Kleeman cartoon *New Yorker* v92 no39 p76 N 28 2016

D.C. Is Building an Uber-Fighting Test Lab J. Brustein color *Bloomberg Businessweek* no4524 p34 My 29 2017

Google Maps tips color *PCWorld* v35 no9 p112 S 2017

How to set up the Calendar Service in macOS Sierra Server J. BATTERSBY color *Macworld - Digital Edition* p97 D 2016

Imagining Productivity Apps for the Apple Watch H. J. Wilson *Harvard Business Review Digital Articles* p2 O 30 2014

I STINK AT EMAIL A. GEORGE *Popular Mechanics* p26 S 2017

Our Doc Will See You Now R. Rajapaksa color *Health* v31 no4 p67 My 2017

REELGOOD: ONE APP, SO MANY STREAMING OR THEATRICAL MOVIES TO DISCOVER J. R. BOOKWALTER color *Macworld - Digital Edition* p69 D 2016

Sunrise calendar is dead, and only some features live on in Outlook M. HACHMAN color *PCWorld* p26 O 2016

TripMode 2 review: Utility manages, blocks, and caps macOS Internet use K. MCELHEARN color *Macworld - Digital Edition* v34 no8 p106 Ag 2017

The Untapped Potential of Health Care APIs R. Huckman and M. Uppaluru *Harvard Business Review Digital Articles* p2 D 23 2015

USING CROSSOVER ANDROID TO RUN WINDOWS APPS ON A CHROME-BOOK J. NEWMAN color *PCWorld* p148 D 2016

Application software evaluation

3.15 P.M. ON PERISCOPE color *Popular Mechanics* p50 O 2017

Apple's new Swift Playgrounds 1.5 includes controls for robots R. LOYOLA color *Macworld - Digital Edition* p16 Je 13 2017

BlueRail Trains App upgrade D. Kawala *Model Railroader* v84 no9 p63 S 2017

Can You "UBERIZE" Wellness? R. Hilmantel color *Women's Health* v13 no10 p86 D 2016

A Different Kind of Apple a Day A. Webb color *Bloomberg Businessweek* no4493 p44 O 3 2016

GAME FINDERS T. HANSEN chart color *Outdoor Life* v224 no2 p15 F/Mr 2017

The Gratitude Meter Z. Donaldson color *O, The Oprah Magazine* p24 Ag 2017

Hands on with Setapp: Getting started with the Netflix of Mac apps J. DOVE color *Macworld - Digital Edition* p7 Mr 2017

It's football season! These second-screen apps make NFL games even more fun M. ANSALDO color *PCWorld* p34 O 2016

LIP SYNC BATTLE J. MATHIS color *Macworld - Digital Edition* p73 D 2016

Narrowband Color in Pixlnsight W. A. Keller *Sky & Telescope* v133 no4 p36 Ap 2017

new products color *Science* v357 no6350 p516 Ag 4 2017

NEW PRODUCTS *Physics Today* v70 no6 p68 Je 2017

Siri vs. Google Assistant: Which is better for iPhone users? O. RAYMUNDO and M. SIMON color *Macworld - Digital Edition* p37 Je 13 2017

THINGS 3 color *Macworld - Digital Edition* p57 Je 13 2017

Application stores—Evaluation

What's new at the App Store J. MATHIS cartoon *Macworld - Digital Edition* v33 no11 p95 N 2016

Applied ecology

    See also

        Environmental monitoring

The Effort-Outcomes Relationship in Applied Ecology: Evaluation and Implications J. HONE, V. A. DRAKE et al *BioScience* v67 no9 p845 S 2017

Applied psychology

    See also

        Behavior modification

        Negotiation

        Personal coaching

        Self-efficacy

        Self-help techniques

The Two Conversations You're Having When You Negotiate A. Molinsky *Harvard Business Review Digital Articles* p2 Ap 5 2016

You're a what? Life coach K. Green *Career Outlook* p1 Ja 2017

Applied Underwriters Inc.

A Buffett Company With Angry Customers N. Buhayar color *Bloomberg Businessweek* no4499 p53 N 14 2016

Appointed counsel

BETTER CALL DON [Cover story] A. KROLL color *Mother Jones* v42 no3 p24 My/Je 2017

Appointees

People and posts *People Management* p55 D 2016/Ja 2017

Predators' Ball color *Nation* v304 no3 p3 Ja 30 2017

Appointment to public office

How Trump Is Restocking the Washington Swamp Z. J. Miller color *Time* v188 no27-28 p14 D 26 2016

Normalizing Deceit W. STEPHENSON *Nation* v304 no2 p4 Ja 16 2017

Apportionment (Election law)

THE BATHROOM AND THE BALLOT BOX M. McCLELLAND color *Mother Jones* v41 no6 p38 N/D 2016

Apportionment (Election law)—Lawsuits & claims

The Future of the Gerrymander M. Kokai *Commentary* v143 no3 p8 Mr 2017

Apprentice, The (Film)

UNHOLY FOOLS AND BEAUTIFUL LOSERS A. NAYMAN color *Film Comment* v53 no3 p62 My/Je 2017

Apprentice, The (TV program)

TRUMP, BETWEEN TAKES N. BILTON color *Vanity Fair* v59 no2 p52 F 2017

Apprentices

ARAN BELL *Dance Spirit* v21 no3 p37 Mr 2017

Apprenticeship laws

READY OR NOT, HERE THEY COME: It could be the biggest shift in the way young people are trained for decades. But how businesses plan to put the upcoming payroll tax to use has yet to be seen G. GSYTON *People Management* p34 Ap 2017

Apprenticeship programs

Apprenticeship pressure piles on *People Management* p6 Ag 2017

Get ready for #HRmegamonth: From gender pay reporting to the minimum wage, People Management rounds up key legal and practical changes coming to the UK in April M. CALNAN *People Management* p8 Ap 2017

How Self-Managed Companies Help People Learn on the Job E. Bernstein, N. Canner et al *Harvard Business Review Digital Articles* p2 Ag 3 2017

A More Practical Model for Law Schools A. Armitage and R. Feldman *Harvard Business Review Digital Articles* p2 D 24 2015

READY OR NOT, HERE THEY COME: It could be the biggest shift in the way young people are trained for decades. But how businesses plan to put the upcoming payroll tax to use has yet to be seen G. GSYTON *People Management* p34 Ap 2017

The Right Way to Off-Board a Departing Employee R. Knight *Harvard Business Review Digital Articles* p2 Ja 15 2016

Apprenticeship programs—Government policy

"THIS ISN'T A STEALTH TAX": Skills minister Robert Halfon explains the thinking behind the apprenticeship levy R. Halfon *People Management* p37 Ap 2017

Apprenticeship of Duddy Kravitz, The (Film)

UNHOLY FOOLS AND BEAUTIFUL LOSERS A. NAYMAN color *Film Comment* v53 no3 p62 My/Je 2017

Appriss Inc.

Making Opioid Addiction Searchable J. Green *Bloomberg Businessweek* no4535 p22 Ag 28 2017

Aprea AB

RESCUING THE GUARDIAN OF THE GENOME R. F. Service color diag *Science* v354 no6308 p26 O 7 2016

April (Month)

The MONEY Do List color *Money* v46 no3 p15 Ap 2017

April Fools' Day

Notice Anything Unusual? J. Nilsson *Saturday Evening Post* v289 no2 p102 Mr/Ap 2017

PRANK YOU VERY MUCH K. Ellison color *O, The Oprah Magazine* p30 Ap 2017

Aprilia SpA

THE WAITING GAME B. Adams chart color diag graph *Cycle World* v56 no7 p32 Ag 2017

Aprons—Evaluation

In the SUNSET KITCHEN color *Sunset* v237 no5 p96 N 2016

Apstein, Stephanie

11 UP CLOSE AND PERSONAL color *Sports Illustrated* v126 no9 p57 Mr 27 2017

14 HANDY MEN color diag *Sports Illustrated* v126 no9 p67 Mr 27 2017

1 THE NEW TESTAMENT color *Sports Illustrated* v126 no9 p40 Mr 27 2017

5 FIREMEN IN THE HOLE color *Sports Illustrated* v126 no9 p47 Mr 27 2017

8 BRAVE NEW WORLD color *Sports Illustrated* v126 no9 p50 Mr 27 2017

ALL RISE [Cover story] chart color *Sports Illustrated* v126 no14 p76 My 15-22 2017

American Voices J.J. Barea color *Sports Illustrated* v126 no10 p34 Ap 10 2017

BLUE BLAZES chart color *Sports Illustrated* v127 no6 p24 Ag 28 2017

Gamer Shape color *Sports Illustrated* v127 no6 p18 Ag 28 2017

Gimme Shelter color *Sports Illustrated* v126 no5 p22 F 13 2017

Lifting Off color *Sports Illustrated* v126 no1 p16 Ja 9 2017

MACKENZIE GORE color *Sports Illustrated* v127 no2 p32 Jl 17 2017

Money for Something color *Sports Illustrated* v126 no9 p24 Mr 27 2017

Nobody Home chart color *Sports Illustrated* v125 no12 p18 O 10 2016

NO PIPE DREAM color *Sports Illustrated* v126 no3 p40 Ja 23 2017

PAIR OF ACES color *Sports Illustrated* v127 no11 p28 O 9 2017

SIX PLAYOFF QUESTIONS color *Sports Illustrated* v127 no10 p42 O 2 2017

Sports and Autism color *Sports Illustrated* v125 no16 p52 N 14 2016

Taking HER SHOT color *Sports Illustrated* v126 no8 p62 Mr 20 2017

APT, JAY

Climate engineering *Issues in Science & Technology* v33 no4 p5 Summ 2017

Apt, Marla

Chart Your Depths color *Yoga Journal* p60 2017 Special Issue

Peace Process color *Yoga Journal* p78 2017 Special Issue

The Right Angle color *Yoga Journal* p40 2017 Special Issue

Apter, Terri

Passing Judgment: The Power of Praise and Blame in Everyday Life *Publishers Weekly* v264 no39 p96 S 25 2017

Aquaculture

See also

Antibiotics in aquaculture

Fish culture

Calling for kelp J. RICHLER color *Maclean's* no1 p63 F 17 2017

Aquaculture—China

ON CHINESE AQUACULTURE FARMS, THE FISH ARE PUMPED WITH ANTIBIOTICS, AS ARE THE PIGS, WHOSE WASTE FEEDS THE FISH. SO LET'S TALK ABOUT THAT SEAFOOD PLATTER [Cover story] J. GALE, L. MULVANY et al color graph *Bloomberg Businessweek* no4504 p38 D 19 2016

Aquaman (Fictitious character)

NO. 30 Aquaman S. Vilkomerson color *Entertainment Weekly* no1436/1437 p68 O 21 2016

Aquaporins

Improving on aquaporins Z. Siwy and F. Fornasiero diag *Science* v357 no6353 p753 Ag 25 2017

Aquarian Soul (Company)

BODY AND SOUL... SKIN LIKE THIS I. VALDESOLO bw color *Women's Health* v13 no10 p126 D 2016

Aquariums

CHALLENGE #NGMH2O bw *National Geographic* v231 no4 p12 Ap 2017

COMMUNING WITH NATURE *Cincinnati Magazine* v50 no8 p46 My 2017

How to Make a... BAIT BARREL C. J. CHIVERS bw *Popular Mechanics* v193 no7 p77 S 2016

Researchers parse ecosystems fueled by chemistry, not light E. Pennisi color *Science* v357 no6357 p1223 S 22 2017

Aquarius Ltd.

Slosh, Slosh, Zzzzz: The hot (if you turned on the heater) mattress craze of 1970 C. Bonanos img *New York* v50 no9 p10 My 1 2017

Aquatic animal behavior

Envisioning the Future of Aquatic Animal Tracking: Technology, Science, and Application R. J. LENNOX, K. AARESTRUP et al *BioScience* v67 no10 p884 O 2017

Aquatic animals

See also

Fishes

Keep Your Distance S. O'DONNELL color *Natural History* v125 no6 p48 Je 2017

Aquatic biodiversity

See also

Freshwater biodiversity

Marine biodiversity

Freshwater Megafauna: Flagships for Freshwater Biodiversity under Threat S. F. CARRIZO, S. C. JÄHNIG et al *BioScience* v67 no10 p919 O 2017

Aquatic exercises

H20, GO! J. Ator color *Women's Health* v14 no6 p(Sp)28 Jl 2017

Liquid Crunch B. Marston and T. Keith color *Sports Illustrated* v127 no1 p20 Jl 3 2017

Aquatic exercises—Therapeutic use

Modern Aquatic Therapy and a New Clientele S. Lynch and T. Sawyer *Parks & Recreation* v51 no11 p58 N 2016

Aquatic organisms

See also

Marine organisms

Shipbuilding Docks as Experimental Systems for Realistic Assessments of Anthropogenic Stressors on Marine Organisms R. BRUINTJES, H. R. HARDING et al *BioScience* v67 no9 p853 S 2017

Aquatic parks & reserves

See also

Marine parks & reserves

Aquatics Trends G. Deines *Parks & Recreation* v51 no12 p50 D 2016

Now is the time to protect the Arctic N. E. Hussey, R. G. Harcourt et al bibl color *Science* v354 no6317 p1243 D 9 2016

Providing Equal Access to Aquatic Facility Locker Rooms for People Who are Transgender L. P. Richmond *Parks & Recreation* v51 no10 p88 O 2016

Aquatic parks & reserves—Conservation & restoration

NRPA Aquatics Update M. Cowan *Parks & Recreation* p6 Aquatics Guide 2017

Aquatic plants

FLOATING IN PLAIN SIGHT: Invasive Aquatic Garden Plants C. McGlynn *New York State Conservationist* v71 no5 p32 Ap 2017

NATIVE AQUATIC PLANT ALTERNATIVES *New York State Conservationist* v71 no5 p35 Ap 2017

Safe Harbour? color *Canadian Wildlife* v22 no5 p12 N/D 2016

Saharan Dust Has Big Impact on Caribbean *USA Today Magazine* v145 no2865 p10 Je 2017

Aquatic sports

See also

Canoes & canoeing

Deep diving

Diving

Fishing

Kneeboarding

Paddleboarding

Rafting (Sports)

Sailing

Surfing

Swimming

Water skiing

10 Tips for Kneeboarding Success: Minimize wipeouts by following a few simple suggestions T. KOHL *Boating World* v38 no8 p16 S/O 2017

8 Beach-Body Secrets from the Life of Kai M. ANDERS color *Men's Health* v32 no6 p47 Ag 2017

"All decisions, even those of a traveler roaming the world, require a compromise." A. GOGGANS color *Surfer* v58 no2 p38 My 2017

Another Vendée War of Attrition A. Cort color *Sail* v48 no2 p20 F 2017

ANOTHER YEAR, ANOTHER ARC D. KENT color diag *Sail* v48 no2 p44 F 2017

THE ART OF ORGANIC COASTING D. BUCKMAN color *Sail* v48 no6 p44 Je 2017

AT LEISURE *Sea Magazine* v109 no4 p1 Ap 2017

The Beauty of Baja J. BROWNLEE color *Power & Motoryacht* v33 no2 p38 F 2017

Better With Two J. Fiedler color *Parents* v92 no7 p13 Jl 2017

CRUISING TIPS T. Cunliffe color *Sail* v48 no6 p48 Je 2017

Don't Call It "Alternative" Z. MORTON color *Surfer* v58 no3 p32 Je 2017

DOUBLE JEOPARDY M. SHANKLIN and N. KREBS cartoon color *Outdoor Life* v224 no3 p12 Ap 2017

Driving the Boat *Boating World* v38 no2 p16 F 2017

Exploring Parts Unknown J. Y. Wood color *Power & Motoryacht* v33 no4 p24 Ap 2017

A Fiasco by Any Standard color *Sail* v48 no4 p10 Ap 2017

Fishing for Kids J. BROWNLEE color *Power & Motoryacht* v33 no4 p30 Ap 2017

Frankenboat S. SHIBATA and A. Jones *Boating World* v38 no4 p6 Ap 2017

Kid Power A. JONES *Boating World* v38 no6 p4 Je 2017

Lining Up D. Agius color *Surfer* v58 no3 p16 Je 2017

Move Over, Gilligan! B. PIKE bw *Power & Motoryacht* v33 no4 p184 Ap 2017

name the boat *Boating World* v38 no3 p64 Mr 2017

PARODY color *Weekly Standard* v22 no23 p40 F 20 2017

Row bots Boucher, R. Labbé et al *Physics Today* v70 no6 p82 Je 2017

...the water's fine *Atlanta* v57 no2 p38 Je 2017

Volvo Race Renews its U.S. Roots color *Sail* v48 no6 p17 Je 2017

WHERE DO ALL THE BOATS GO? J. Cornell color map *Sail* v48 no2 p36 F 2017

Aquatic sports competitions
> *See also*
>> Sailing competitions
>> Surfing competitions

The Thrill of Letting Go A. DAWSON color *Men's Health* v32 no6 p12 Ag 2017

When the Oyster is Your World... color *Sail* v47 no12 p10 D 2016

Aquatic sports injuries—Prevention

SAFE ON THE water J. TIGER color *Cabin Living* p56 Ap 2017

Aquatic sports injuries—Risk factors

Dump the Slump: If midseason finds you stuck in a rut instead of excelling, we have nine tips to break you out S. O'BRIEN color *Boating World* v38 no7 p16 Jl 2017

Aquatic sports safety measures

SAFE ON THE water J. TIGER color *Cabin Living* p56 Ap 2017

Start Strong: Make sure the first session of the season goes well T. MIKACICH *Boating World* v38 no5 p16 My 2017

Aquatic sports—Equipment & supplies

PRODUCT PREVIEW *Parks & Recreation* v52 no9 p92 S 2017

Aquatic weeds—Control

CONTROLLING LAKE WEEDS J. Tiger color *Cabin Living* p67 Ap 2017

Aqueducts—Washington (D.C.)

WATER GATE: Could Trump once again make the Washington Aqueduct a center of political intrigue? E. SLOAN *Washingtonian Magazine* v52 no12 p20 S 2017

Aquion Energy Inc.

Why Bad Things Happen to Clean-Energy Startups J. Temple il *MIT Technology Review* v120 no4 p92 Jl/Ag 2017

AR-15 rifle

ALL-AMERICAN KILLER T. DICKINSON color *Rolling Stone* no1275 p50 D 1 2016

Arab American men

PRISON BREAK'S GAY MUSLIM BAD GUY IS A FORCE FOR GOOD: As an out Arab-American actor, Amin El Gamal is shaking up Hollywood D. REYNOLDS color *Advocate* no1091 p30 Je/Jl 2017

Arab American sexual minorities

PRISON BREAK'S GAY MUSLIM BAD GUY IS A FORCE FOR GOOD: As an out Arab-American actor, Amin El Gamal is shaking up Hollywood D. REYNOLDS color *Advocate* no1091 p30 Je/Jl 2017

Arab Americans

CITIZENS IN TRAINING L. Widdicombe cartoon *New Yorker* v92 no49 p32 F 13 2017

Arab countries—Economic conditions

A Different Story from the Middle East: Entrepreneurs Building an Arab Tech Economy C. M. Schroeder bw *MIT Technology Review* v120 no5 p64 S/O 2017

Arab countries—History
> *See also*
>> Arab-Israeli conflict

Stop the Settlements diag *Commonweal* v144 no2 p5 Ja 27 2017

Arab-Israeli conflict

Cartoons *New York Times Upfront* v149 no12 p24 Ap 24 2017

How Israel Wins M. Amitay *Commentary* v143 no3 p6 Mr 2017

Lightbox color *Time* v190 no6 p18 Ag 7 2017

THE MONTH IN REVIEW *Current History* v116 no789 p160 Ap 2017

READY TO REACH FOR PEACE D. TRUMP *Vital Speeches of the Day* v83 no7 p194 Jl 2017

SETTLEMENTS ARE NOT THE CAUSE OF THE CONFLICT, BUT NO ONE CAN IGNORE THE THREAT THEY POSE TO PEACE *Vital Speeches of the Day* v83 no2 p30 F 2017

The Six-Day War, THEN & NOW: Fifty years after the 1967 war that redrew the Middle East map, here's what you need to know about the ongoing Israeli-Palestinian conflict J. BERGER *New York Times Upfront* v149 no12 p18 Ap 24 2017

Stop the Settlements diag *Commonweal* v144 no2 p5 Ja 27 2017

Arab-Israeli conflict—Peace

How to Build Middle East Peace M. Yaalon color *Foreign Affairs* v96 no1 p73 Ja/F 2017

Interfaith women's group marches for peace in Israel N. Darom *Christian Century* v133 no25 p16 D 7 2016

Arab women—Social conditions

MUSLIM SISTERHOOD L. Widdicombe cartoon *New Yorker* v92 no38 p30 N 21 2016

ARABADJIS, HEATHER

THE COMMON CORE CONUNDRUM *USA Today Magazine* v145 no2864 p54 My 2017

POLITICS MATTER *USA Today Magazine* v146 no2866 p26 Jl 2017

Arabadjis, Sophia

How One California Medical Group Is Decreasing Physician Burnout color *Harvard Business Review Digital Articles* p2 Je 7 2017

Arab countries—History—Arab Spring Uprisings, 2011-
> *See also*
>> Syria—History—Civil War, 2011-

Labor's Role in the Arab Uprisings and Beyond I. M. HARTS-HORN *Current History* v115 no785 p349 D 2016

Women and the Arab Spring T. Karman *UN Chronicle* v53 no4 p1 2016

Arabia Mountain National Heritage Area (Ga.)

SCOUT ABOUT TOWN L. SCHOLZ *Atlanta* v56 no12 p44 Ap 2017

THAT'S A STRETCH T. WHEATLEY *Atlanta* v57 no2 p26 Je 2017

Arabian English pleasure horses

ALL THE RIGHT PARTS G. Dearth *Arabian Horse World* v57 no5 p2 F 2017

AWPA Board of Directors *Arabian Horse World* v57 no5 p32 F 2017

AWPA Innovations, Rules, and Regulations *Arabian Horse World* v57 no5 p76 F 2017

AWPA Leading Sires of National Western Pleasure Winners *Arabian Horse World* v57 no5 p52 F 2017

Where Are They Now? Haji Rabba's Second Career K. Youngberg *Arabian Horse World* v57 no2 p10 N 2016

Arabian horse

The 10TH Annual Scottsdale Farm Tours K. HOPP *Arabian Horse World* v57 no5 p202 F 2017

2016 bruges international arabian horse event *Arabian Horse World* v56 no12 p218 S 2016

2016 egyption event europe B. Finke *Arabian Horse World* v57 no1 p140 O 2016

2016 elran cup F. Aragno *Arabian Horse World* v56 no12 p214 S 2016

2017 Egyptian BREEDER PROFILES *Arabian Horse World* v57 no11 p68 Ag 2017

2017 Egyptian Event LEADING SIRES *Arabian Horse World* v57 no11 p52 Ag 2017

2017 Egyptian Event RESULT *Arabian Horse World* v57 no11 p50 Ag 2017

2017 Las Vegas Arabian Breeders World Cup J. Winlersteen *Arabian Horse World* v57 no9 p20 Je 2017

2017 ströhen european c-show and international b-show B. Finke *Arabian Horse World* v57 no11 p132 Ag 2017

26th Qatar International Arabian Horse Show C. Reid *Arabian Horse World* v57 no9 p86 Je 2017

the 27th ukiahs a-show C. Reid *Arabian Horse World* v57 no2 p122 N 2016

all nations cup festival B. Finke *Arabian Horse World* v57 no3 p244 D 2016

Al Rashediah Stud [Cover story] J. Winsteen *Arabian Horse World* v57 no1 p105 O 2016

ANSATA HEJAZI *Arabian Horse World* v57 no8 p3 My 2017

ANSATA HEJAZI—BORN TO RULE J. Forbis *Arabian Horse World* v57 no8 p5 My 2017

ARABIAN HORSE DAYS POLAND 2016 A. MATTSSON *Arabian Horse World* v57 no2 p108 N 2016

Arabian MEADOWS J. WINTERSTEEN *Arabian Horse World* v57 no8 p1 My 2017

Arabian National BREEDER FINALS K. Hopp *Arabian Horse World* v57 no2 p78 N 2016

Arabian Stakes at Deauville, France S. Andersen *Arabian Horse*

Small Breeders BIG RESULTS M. J. Parkinson *Arabian Horse World* v57 no9 p82 Je 2017

SYLVIA ZERBINI AND RAJALI KA—a conversation E. K. McCall *Arabian Horse World* v57 no9 p34 Je 2017

Twisted TALES: How Not to Electrolyte Your Horse D. WHYTE *Arabian Horse World* v57 no11 p90 Ag 2017

UPCOMING ISSUES *Arabian Horse World* v57 no3 p293 D 2016

Up to the Challenge *Arabian Horse World* v57 no3 p284 D 2016

U.S. Racing at Delaware Park S. Andersen *Arabian Horse World* v56 no12 p194 S 2016

Varian Arabians Summer Jubilee & CELEBRATION OF LIFE K. Youngberg *Arabian Horse World* v56 no12 p108 S 2016

The Varian Way Weekend C. Maupin *Arabian Horse World* v57 no12 p60 S 2017

VERACITY KSB k. S. Buford *Arabian Horse World* v56 no12 p62 S 2016

WADEE AL SHAQAB D. Hearst *Arabian Horse World* v57 no9 p1 Je 2017

WARRIOR HORSE C. REICH *Arabian Horse World* v57 no9 p38 Je 2017

the WAY WE WERE B. Fauls *Arabian Horse World* v57 no8 p61 My 2017

WC CIAO PSYCHE *Arabian Horse World* v57 no9 p33 Je 2017

We love Scottsdale... *Arabian Horse World* v57 no4 p4 Ja 2017

Wit and Wisdom from Our Early Breeders M. J. PARKINSON *Arabian Horse World* v57 no1 p100 O 2016

Wit and Wisdom From our Early Breeders M. J. PARKINSON *Arabian Horse World* v57 no4 p36 Ja 2017

Arabian horse division (Horse shows)
    See also
        Arabian English pleasure horse class

2016 Canadian Nationals G. Dearth *Arabian Horse World* v57 no2 p50 N 2016

the 27th ukiahs a-show C. Reid *Arabian Horse World* v57 no2 p122 N 2016

ARABIAN HORSE DAYS POLAND 2016 A. MATTSSON *Arabian Horse World* v57 no2 p108 N 2016

Arabian Horse World presents the AWPA Western Pleasure Futurity *Arabian Horse World* v57 no5 p31 F 2017

Arabian National BREEDER FINALS K. Hopp *Arabian Horse World* v57 no2 p78 N 2016

Arabian U.S. Open central park show J. Wintersteen *Arabian Horse World* v57 no2 p90 N 2016

ARAB YEAR *Arabian Horse World* v57 no2 p144 N 2016

AWPA 2016 Futurity Winners *Arabian Horse World* v57 no5 p62 F 2017

AWPA Nominated Stallions *Arabian Horse World* v57 no5 p82 F 2017

Beating the Odds D. Hearst color *Arabian Horse World* v57 no7 p111 Ap 2017

LEADING DAMS OF 2015 U.S. NATIONAL WINNERS *Arabian Horse World* v56 no12 p158 S 2016

MARQUISE INVITATIONAL AUCTION color *Arabian Horse World* v57 no7 p130 Ap 2017

MARWAN AL SHAQAB B. FINKE *Arabian Horse World* v57 no2 p72 N 2016

My Most Amazing 24 Hours N. Sheridan color *Horse & Rider* v55 no12 p10 D 2016

A Prized Commodity M. Byatt color *Arabian Horse World* v57 no7 p112 Ap 2017

SCOTTSDALE 2017: The View from Center Ring G. Dearth color *Arabian Horse World* v57 no7 p104 Ap 2017

THIRTY-THIRD PUNTA DEL ESTE: ARABIAN HORSE SHOW G. Labadie color *Arabian Horse World* v57 no7 p94 Ap 2017

WHAT IN THE WORLD G. Knowles *Arabian Horse World* v57 no5 p10 F 2017

Arabian horse in art
MEMORIES OF Carle Vernet J. WICH-WENNING *Arabian Horse World* v57 no9 p148 Je 2017

Arabian horse—Awards
WESTERN DIVISION STATISTICS *Arabian Horse World* v57 no10 p46 Jl 2017

Arabian horse—Competitions
2016 european championships *Arabian Horse World* v57 no3 p266 D 2016

2016 U. S. NATIONAL RESULTS *Arabian Horse World* v57 no4 p144 Ja 2017

2016 U.S. NATIONALS HALTER DIVISION C. Reich *Arabian Horse World* v57 no4 p130 Ja 2017

2017 Egyptian Event Preview *Arabian Horse World* v57 no8 p30 My 2017

Dr. Karlan Downing's Trail Stars M. Moore *Arabian Horse World* v57 no3 p68 D 2016

GUEST EDITORIAL: MAKE HALTER GREAT AGAIN? C. Reich *Arabian Horse World* v57 no4 p142 Ja 2017

A Prized Commodity M. Byatt color *Arabian Horse World* v57 no7 p112 Ap 2017

Summer Racing in England—Tayf Claims England's Richest Arabian Race S. Andersen *Arabian Horse World* v57 no12 p178 S 2017

WESTERN DIVISION STATISTICS *Arabian Horse World* v57 no10 p46 Jl 2017

A WORLDWIDE LEGACY B. Finke *Arabian Horse World* v57 no8 p8 My 2017

Arabian horse—Congresses
ARAB YEAR *Arabian Horse World* v57 no12 p191 S 2017

ARAB YEAR *Arabian Horse World* v57 no2 p144 N 2016

Arabian horse—Diseases
The Arabian Horse Foundation Continues Funding of Research Projects to Protect the Arabian Horse *Arabian Horse World* v57 no5 p237 F 2017

ULGERS PART TWO M. DEPAOLO *Arabian Horse World* v57 no3 p286 D 2016

Arabian horse—Sales & prices
Cal Poly Pomona Auction Grosses $126,950 C. Reich *Arabian Horse World* v57 no11 p162 Ag 2017

Wit & Wisdom from Our Early Breeders: The Dr. Joseph L. Doyle Family M. J. Parkinson *Arabian Horse World* v57 no10 p54 Jl 2017

Arabians International LLC
WELCOME TO THE AUCTION AND FUTURITY PROGRAM *Arabian Horse World* v57 no4 p10 Ja 2017

Arabians Ltd.
ARABIANS LTD J. WINTERSTEEN *Arabian Horse World* v57 no3 p1 D 2016

Arabic language—Dialects—Egypt
TALK LIKE AN EGYPTIAN P. HESSLER cartoon color *New Yorker* v93 no9 p48 Ap 17 2017

Arabic language—Study & teaching
    See also
        Arabic language—Study & teaching—Foreign speakers
Teaching Arabic to Non-Native Speakers [Cover story] N. ZAKI *Islamic Horizons* v46 no2 p32 Mr/Ap 2017

Arabic language—Study & teaching—Foreign speakers
TALK LIKE AN EGYPTIAN P. HESSLER cartoon color *New Yorker* v93 no9 p48 Ap 17 2017

Arabidopsis
    See also
        Arabidopsis thaliana
A peptide hormone required for Casparian strip diffusion barrier formation in Arabidopsis roots T. Nakayama, H. Shinohara et al bibl color graph *Science* v355 no6322 p284 Ja 20 2017

Phytochromes function as thermosensors in Arabidopsis Jae-Hoon Jung, M. Domijan et al bibl graph *Science* v354 no6314 p886 N 18 2016

The receptor kinase FER is a RALF-regulated scaffold controlling plant immune signaling M. Stegmann, J. Monaghan et al bibl graph *Science* v355 no6322 p287 Ja 20 2017

Regulation of sugar transporter activity for antibacterial defense in Arabidopsis K. Yamada, Yusuke Saijo et al bibl diag graph *Science* v354 no6318 p1427 D 16 2016

RETINOBLASTOMA RELATED1 mediates germline entry in Arabidopsis X. Zhao, J. Bramsiepe et al color diag *Science* v356 no6336 p396 Ap 28 2017

Arabidopsis thaliana
Avoiding Overreaction N. Wilson color *Natural History* v125 no4 p7 Ap 2017

Dry Plants? Add Vinegar A. Braun color *Natural History* v125 no10 p8 O 2017

Arabidopsis thaliana—Genetics
FROM PLEBE WEED TO FAMOUS FLORA E. MASTROIAN-

NI color *Discover* v38 no2 p11 Mr 2017

Arabidopsis—Physiology

Distinct phases of Polycomb silencing to hold epigenetic memory of cold in Arabidopsis H. Yang, S. Berry et al diag *Science* v357 no6356 p1142 S 15 2017

Arab Spring Uprisings, 2011-

See also

Syrian Civil War, 2011-

Tunisian Revolution, 2010-2011

WOMEN AND THE ARAB SPRING T. KARMAN *UN Chronicle* v54 no4 p21 2017

Arabs—Travel

Occupational Hazards F. G. MOHAMED *American Scholar* v86 no4 p6 Aut 2017

Arabs—United States

See also

Arab Americans

Research: Arab Inventors Make the U.S. More Innovative S. Mahroum, G. Zahradnik et al *Harvard Business Review Digital Articles* p2 F 23 2017

Arachidonic acid

MUTANT VEGETARIANS? R. Racicot *Vegetarian Journal* v36 no1 p26 2017

Arachnida

See also

Scorpions

Spiders

Second opinion *Mayo Clinic Health Letter* v34 no12 p8 D 2016

Aragno, Francesca

2016 elran cup *Arabian Horse World* v56 no12 p214 S 2016

A Handler's Life—David Pujalt Martinez *Arabian Horse World* v56 no12 p226 S 2016

Aragón, Salvador

To Foster Innovation, Connect Coworkers Who Share Aspirations *Harvard Business Review Digital Articles* p2 Jl 14 2016

ARAGONCILLO, MIGUEL

Welcome to the Jungle Gym color *Men's Health* v32 no6 p50 Ag 2017

Arai Americas Inc.

ARAI QUANTUM-X AND SIGNET-X HELMETS S. MacDonald cartoon color *Cycle World* v55 no11 p14 D 2016

Araki, Eiichiro

Recurring and triggered slow-slip events near the trench at the Nankai Trough subduction megathrust diag graph *Science* v356 no6343 p1157 Je 16 2017

Araki, Koichi

Rescue of exhausted CD8 T cells by PD-1–targeted therapies is CD28-dependent bw diag graph *Science* v355 no6332 p1423 Mr 31 2017

Araks (Company)

SET IT and FORGET IT *Interview* v47 no5 p36 Je/Jl 2017

ARAL, BIRNUR

3 experts on... SMILE LINES color *Good Housekeeping* v265 no5 p22 N 2017

GH BEAUTY LAB color *Good Housekeeping* v265 no4 p30 O 2017

inside the GH BEAUTY LAB color *Good Housekeeping* v265 no3 p34 S 2017

Aramo, C.

Observation of a large-scale anisotropy in the arrival directions of cosmic rays above 8×10^{18} eV *Science* v357 no6357 p1266 S 22 2017

Arandjelovic, Mimi

Chimpanzee genomic diversity reveals ancient admixture with bonobos bibl diag graph map *Science* v354 no6311 p477 O 28 2016

Aransas National Wildlife Refuge (Tex.)

Where Whooping Cranes Winter R. H. MOHLENBROCK color *Natural History* v125 no10 p42 O 2017

Arapaima

Monster Splash color *Field & Stream* v122 no2 p12 Je/Jl 2017

Araújo, Miguel B.

Biodiversity redistribution under climate change: Impacts on ecosystems and human well-being color *Science* v355 no6332 p1389 Mr 31 2017

Araújo Gonçalves, Rafaella

Pathological α-synuclein transmission initiated by binding lymphocyte-activation gene 3 bibl graph *Science* v353 no6307 paah3374-1 S 30 2016

Araujo-Murakami, A.

Persistent effects of pre-Columbian plant domestication on Amazonian forest composition bibl chart graph map *Science* v355 no6328 p925 Mr 3 2017

Aravamudhan, Pavithra

Reovirus infection triggers inflammatory responses to dietary antigens and development of celiac disease color diag *Science* v356 no6333 p44 Ap 7 2017

Aravind, L.

A conserved NAD+ binding pocket that regulates protein-protein interactions during aging bibl graph *Science* v355 no6331 p1312 Mr 24 2017

Aravind Eye Care System (Company)

Build a Company Where Everyone's Looking for New Ideas K. Ramdas *Harvard Business Review Digital Articles* p2 D 11 2014

ARB Corp. Ltd.

GEAR BOX color *Dirt Sports + Off-Road* v51 no5 p68 My 2017

Arbes, Ross

FONTGATE cartoon *New Yorker* v93 no22 p20 Jl 31 2017

Arbesman, Samuel

Why Technologists Should Think Like Biologists *Harvard Business Review Digital Articles* p2 Jl 20 2016

Arbib, Allison

Committing to socially responsible seafood color *Science* v356 no6341 p912 Je 1 2017

ARBICO Organics (Company)

Why I Use Beneficial Insects For My Fly Control S. R. H. de Frey *Equus* no475 p17 Ap 2017

ARBITER, DICKIE

REMEMBERING DIANA color *AARP: The Magazine* v60 no5A p50 Ag/S 2017

Arbitration & award

'No Suits for You!' B. Lueders color *Progressive* p19 D 2016/Ja 2017

Arbitration & award—Government policy

How to Make Lawsuits Work for Consumers *Bloomberg Businessweek* no4532 p10 Jl 31 2017

Arbitration clauses (Contracts)

'No Suits for You!' B. Lueders color *Progressive* p19 D 2016/Ja 2017

ARBOGAST, BRIAN S.

Transformational Principles for NEON Sampling of Mammalian Parasites and Pathogens: A Response to Springer and Colleagues *BioScience* v66 no11 p917 N 1 2016

Arbogast, Meghan

Western States Master M. HAMILTON bw color *Runner's World* v52 no5 p58 Je 2017

Arboleda, N. C.

Persistent effects of pre-Columbian plant domestication on Amazonian forest composition bibl chart graph map *Science* v355 no6328 p925 Mr 3 2017

Arbona, Fred

THE IMPOSSIBLE LIST bw cartoon color *Esquire* v167 no1 p70 F 2017

Arbor Day

STATEWIDE N. BUCK color *Nebraska Life* v21 no2 p63 Mr/Ap 2017

Arbuckle, Kevin

The biology of color color *Science* v357 no6350 p470 Ag 4 2017

Arbus, Diane, 1923-1971—Exhibitions

The Art of Difference [Cover story] H. Als bw *New York Review of Books* v64 no10 p31 Je 8 2017

Arca (Performer)

Summer Preview M. Trammell cartoon *New Yorker* v93 no14 p18 My 22 2017

Arcade Fire (Performer)

Arcade Fire E. R. Brown color *Entertainment Weekly* no1476 p59 Ag 4 2017

Arcade Fire Go Dancing in the Dark W. HERMES color *Rolling Stone* no1293 p53 Ag 10 2017

Arcade Fire looks for God in a material world T. Kroenert color *America* v217 no5 p50 S 4 2017

So...Rock Is Dead? F. Guan img *New York* v50 no10 p91 My 15

sand castle M. RUS color *Architectural Digest* v74 no4 p158 Ap 2017

SCHOOLS OF THE 21ST CENTURY *Architectural Record* v205 no1 p69 Ja 2017

Social Infrastructure C. McGuigan *Architectural Record* v205 no1 p16 Ja 2017

Spruce Street Residence San Francisco L. Lee *Architectural Record* v204 no10 p132 O 2016

Architecture—Africa

Francis Kéré Envisions House of Parliament for Burkina Faso J. M. MCKNIGHT *Architectural Record* v204 no11 p25 N 2016

Architecture—Alabama

Out of the Woods A. FIXSEN *Architectural Record* v205 no1 p84 Ja 2017

Architecture—Argentina

horse country D. BLASBERG color *Architectural Digest* no5 p102 My 2017

Architecture—Arkansas

The Big Idea M. COCKRAM *Architectural Record* v205 no1 p70 Ja 2017

Architecture—Australia

30 Adelaide Street Sydney S. Davies *Architectural Record* v204 no10 p138 O 2016

Architecture—Awards

See also

Architectural designs—Awards

Aga Khan Bestows Architecture Awards in Dubai C. MCGUIGAN color *Architectural Record* v204 no12 p20 D 2016

Everyone's a Winner! C. McGuigan color *Architectural Record* v205 no3 p18 Mr 2017

Jenny Sabin to Design PS1 Pavilion A. Klimoski color *Architectural Record* v205 no3 p23 Mr 2017

Architecture—Belgium—21st century

Star Ship H. PEARMAN *Architectural Record* v204 no11 p78 N 2016

Architecture—British Columbia

JACK POOLE PLAZA *Sea Magazine* v108 no8 pPNW-13 Ag 2016

Architecture—California

Day in Court C. MCGUIGAN color diag *Architectural Record* v205 no3 p92 Mr 2017

house of the month L. LEE *Architectural Record* v204 no10 p31 O 2016

Light Touch P. SLATIN *Architectural Record* v204 no10 p41 O 2016

The Midcentury As Muse A. HEROLD *Los Angeles Magazine* p40 Ap 2017

Nancy & Stephen Grand Family House J. Zara *Architectural Record* v205 no4 p192 Ap 2017

Architecture—Canada

High Note J. MINUTILLO and J. BITTERMANN color diag *Architectural Record* v204 no12 p96 D 2016

interiors A. KLIMOSKI color *Architectural Record* v204 no12 p29 D 2016

Ramped Up J. MINUTILLO color diag *Architectural Record* v205 no3 p100 Mr 2017

Architecture—China

interiors C. A. PEARSON *Architectural Record* v205 no1 p31 Ja 2017

Architecture—Congresses

See also

Architectural design—Congresses

Norman Foster Foundation Hosts Inaugural Forum, Dedicates Building D. COHN *Architectural Record* v205 no7 p29 Jl 2017

Record Hosts 19th Innovation Conference, in San Francisco B. BROOME and J. GONCHAR *Architectural Record* v205 no7 p34 Jl 2017

Record's Innovation Conference Explores Craft F. A. BERNSTEIN color *Architectural Record* v204 no12 p17 D 2016

Record's Innovation Conference in NYC Considers the Public Realm E. K. HUDSON *Architectural Record* v205 no10 p26 O 2017

Women in Architecture Forum & Awards 2016 A. Klimoski color *Architectural Record* v204 no12 p17 D 2016

Architecture—Conservation & restoration

See also

Adaptive reuse of buildings

Church architecture—Conservation & restoration

Dwellings—Conservation & restoration

Historic buildings—Conservation & restoration

Victorian architecture—Conservation & restoration

Windmills—Conservation & restoration

The Beauty of Imperfection R. Ashwell color *AARP: The Magazine* v59 no5A p72 Ag/S 2016

BEING PRESENT C. Moss color *House Beautiful* v159 no2 p57 Mr 2017

Bumped Off C. CALDWELL cartoon *Weekly Standard* v22 no27 p9 Mr 20 2017

"LANDLORD" T. Chiarella color *Popular Mechanics* p78 Mr 2017

RENOVATION, RESTORATION, ADAPTATION color *Architectural Record* v205 no2 p61 F 2017

SPECIFIC OBJECTIVES Z. LESCAZE bw color *ARTnews* v115 no3 p110 Fall 2016

Architecture—Conservation & restoration—History—20th century

The Lovers of Shanxi T. PERROTTET *Smithsonian* v47 no9 p110 Ja/F 2017

Architecture—England

See also

Tudor architecture

Design Museum Redux C. FOGES *Architectural Record* v205 no1 p44 Ja 2017

York Theatre Royal C. Foges *Architectural Record* v204 no11 p150 N 2016

Architecture—England—London

Newport Street Art Gallery Wins 2016 RIBA Stirling Prize A. KLIMOSKI *Architectural Record* v204 no11 p29 N 2016

Architecture—Environmental aspects

The Architectural Experience S. W. Goldhagen *Architectural Record* v205 no4 p67 Ap 2017

Architecture—Equipment & supplies—Evaluation

Bright Ideas J. Taraska *Architectural Record* v204 no11 p159 N 2016

Facades color *Architectural Record* v204 no12 p114 D 2016

Finishes & Surfacing color *Architectural Record* v204 no12 p116 D 2016

Furnishings color *Architectural Record* v204 no12 p120 D 2016

Hardware, Software & Control Systems color *Architectural Record* v204 no12 p122 D 2016

HVAC color *Architectural Record* v204 no12 p124 D 2016

Kitchen & Bath color *Architectural Record* v204 no12 p126 D 2016

Lighting & Electrical color *Architectural Record* v204 no12 p128 D 2016

Open and Shut J. Taraska *Architectural Record* v204 no10 p57 O 2016

Openings color *Architectural Record* v204 no12 p132 D 2016

Record Products 2016 L. Lentz, R. Orrell et al color *Architectural Record* v204 no12 p113 D 2016

Architecture—Evaluation

See also

Interior architecture—Evaluation

Landscape architecture—Evaluation

BATON ROUGE AND THE VISUAL ARTS J. R. KEMP cartoon color *Louisiana Life* v37 no4 p32 Mr/Ap 2017

The Full-Time Getaway color diag *Log Home Living* v34 no1 p50 F 2017

LANDFORMS *Architectural Record* v205 no4 p133 Ap 2017

LANDMARKS *Architectural Record* v204 no11 p69 N 2016

Movable Feasts J. Gonchar *Architectural Record* v204 no10 p119 O 2016

MUSIC IN THE AIR F. A. BERNSTEIN color *Architectural Digest* v74 no2 p72 F 2017

Out of the Ordinary J. GIOVANNINI color *Architectural Digest* v74 no2 p36 F 2017

QUIET TIMES AT THE CAPITOL P. F. STAHLS JR. cartoon color *Louisiana Life* v37 no4 p36 Mr/Ap 2017

RETAIL & RESTAURANTS *Architectural Record* v205 no4 p151 Ap 2017

SNMAAHC in the Middle of the Mall G. TATE color *ARTnews* v115 no4 p30 Wint 2016/2017

tification for Existing Buildings M. SITZ *Architectural Record* v204 no11 p27 N 2016

Social Infrastructure C. McGuigan *Architectural Record* v205 no1 p16 Ja 2017

Architecture—Wisconsin

house of the month M. SITZ color diag *Architectural Record* v205 no3 p33 Mr 2017

Architecture—Wyoming

peak performance D. BRADBURY color *Architectural Digest* no11 p114 N 1 2017

Archival materials

Documented: What some of the world's most historic documents tell us about the documents of the future J. Janes color *Publishers Weekly* v264 no29 p15 Jl 17 2017

Dylan's Secret Archives A. GREENE bw color *Rolling Stone* no1291/1292 p11 Jl 13 2017

Archival materials—Conservation & restoration

Preserving Family Recipes M. L. Ritzenthaler *Prologue* v48 no3 p31 Fall 2016

Archives

> See also
>
> Church records & registers
>
> Periodical archives

FROM THE ARCHIVES B. DOHERTY, M. WELCH et al cartoon *Reason* v49 no2 p70 Je 2017

The HOT ROD Archives D. Wallace color *Hot Rod* v70 no8 p14 Ag 2017

Overdue Notice R. J. Smith *Cincinnati Magazine* v50 no5 p68 F 2017

Archives—Congresses

ARCHIVES Events *Prologue* v49 no2 p66 Summ 2017

Archives—Exhibitions

Noteworthy & Now F. P. Driscoll *Opera News* v81 no12 p13 Je 2017

Archives—United States

DOCUMENTS ON Loan *Prologue* v49 no1 p30 Spr 2017

DOCUMENTS ON Loan *Prologue* v49 no2 p54 Summ 2017

Searching for Captain Blye A. J. Begley *Prologue* v49 no1 p58 Spr 2017

Archives—United States—Exhibitions

NATIONAL ARCHIVES FOUNDATION A. Bundles *Prologue* v49 no1 p70 Spr 2017

Archivists

The First Shock Jock K. Cook *Smithsonian* v48 no3 p16 Je 2017

Archosauromorpha

Ancient marine reptile gave live birth E. S. EATON color *Science News* v191 no5 p9 Mr 18 2017

Arcia, Orlando

Leading Off color *Sports Illustrated* v126 no13 p6 My 8 2017

Arc'teryx Equipment Inc.

Floaties C. Sagan color *Powder* v45 no5 p42 Ja 2017

Arctic Cat Inc.

2017 SXS/UTV BUYER'S GUIDE [Cover story] E. MADERO color *Dirt Sports + Off-Road* v51 no1 p30 Ja 2017

Arctic climate

Climate change in the Arctic accelerates: Improved models, new icebreakers, and more observations are needed to gauge global effects of the polar region's diminishing ice cover D. Kramer *Physics Today* v70 no9 p24 S 2017

Arctic Council

The Arctic, from Romance to Reality M. Sfraga bw color *Wilson Quarterly* p1 Summ 2017

The Challenge of Arctic Governance D. C. Nord color *Wilson Quarterly* p1 Summ 2017

Arctic exploration

POLAR EXPRESSED K. SCHULZ cartoon color *New Yorker* v93 no10 p88 Ap 24 2017

A Year on Ice R. MEYER bw color map *Atlantic* v320 no3 p28 O 2017

Arctic fox

Awesome Animals! R. A. MUSGRAVE *National Geographic Kids* no466 p42 D 2016/Ja 2017

in a snap color *Canadian Geographic* v137 no2 p14 Mr/Ap 2017

Arctic National Wildlife Refuge (Alaska)

The Big Wild color map *Backpacker* p52 Je 2017

STALKING AN ELUSIVE PRIZE IN ALASKA B. Reiss color

diag map *Fortune* v176 no4 p144 S 15 2017

Arctic National Wildlife Refuge (Alaska)—Environmental conditions

Time to Debate Arctic Drilling Again A. Nussbaum color map *Bloomberg Businessweek* no4509 p36 Ja 30 2017

Arctic Ocean

Greater role for Atlantic inflows on sea-ice loss in the Eurasian Basin of the Arctic Ocean I. V. Polyakov, A. V. Pnyushkov et al chart diag graph *Science* v356 no6335 p285 Ap 21 2017

Arctic Ocean—Environmental conditions

Climate change in the Arctic accelerates: Improved models, new icebreakers, and more observations are needed to gauge global effects of the polar region's diminishing ice cover D. Kramer *Physics Today* v70 no9 p24 S 2017

Arctic regions

> See also
>
> Northeast Passage
>
> Northwest Passage

Alone Across the Arctic S. DOYLE map *Canadian Geographic* v137 no2 p30 Mr/Ap 2017

The Arctic, from Romance to Reality M. Sfraga bw color *Wilson Quarterly* p1 Summ 2017

The Elusive Northwest Passage K. Peek color graph *Scientific American* v316 no5 p80 My 2017

Ice-free in the Arctic M. Rosano color map *Canadian Geographic* v135 no6 p30 D 2015

Michael Byers A. POPE color *Canadian Geographic* v137 no2 p17 Mr/Ap 2017

Arctic regions—Climate

Art at the edge B. A. Jordan color map *Canadian Geographic* v137 no2 p24 Mr/Ap 2017

Signs of Big Changes in the Arctic L. Lippsett *Oceanus* v52 no1 p14 Summ 2016

Arctic regions—Economic aspects

An Investment Model for the Arctic T. Vauraste color *Wilson Quarterly* p1 Summ 2017

Arctic regions—Environmental conditions

How to Produce Translational Research to Guide Arctic Policy A. H. FLEMING and N. D. PYENSON *BioScience* v67 no6 p490 Je 2017

A view of the Arctic in high relief bw *Science* v353 no6307 p1474 S 30 2016

A Year on Ice R. MEYER bw color map *Atlantic* v320 no3 p28 O 2017

Arctic regions—Foreign relations

Changing Climates for Arctic Security S. Goodman bw color *Wilson Quarterly* p1 Summ 2017

Arctic regions—Politics & government

The Challenge of Arctic Governance D. C. Nord color *Wilson Quarterly* p1 Summ 2017

Arctic regions—Strategic aspects

Is Russia Going Hard or Soft in the Arctic? A. Sergunin color map *Wilson Quarterly* p1 Summ 2017

Arctic research stations

'It's been raining! In the High Arctic!' C. WILKINS color map *Canadian Geographic* v137 no4 p62 Jl/Ag 2017

Arctostaphylos

THE CHIRICAHUA IS A STUDY IN ROCKS AND HISTORY N. N. DODGE *Arizona Highways* v93 no9 p36 S 2017

ARD, KERRY

Modernization, Risk, and Conservation of the World's Largest Carnivores *BioScience* v67 no7 p646 Jl 2017

Ardasheva, Angelica

Top of the LINE color *Vogue* v206 no12 p140 D 2016

Arden, Katherine

Deals R. DEAHL bw color *Publishers Weekly* v264 no23 p9 Je 5 2017

The Girl in the Tower *Publishers Weekly* v264 no34 p93 Ag 21 2017

ARDEN, ROSALIND

Taking the IQ Test: ONE OF THE HARDEST TRICKS IS COMING UP WITH A WAY TO MEASURE DOG INTELLIGENCE *Psychology Today* v50 no5 p74 S/O 2017

Ardennes, Battle of the, 1944-1945

THE BULGE *AARP: The Magazine* v59 no3A p64 Ap/My 2016

Ardennes, The (Film)

FAMILY PACKS A. LANE cartoon *New Yorker* v92 no45 p86 Ja 16 2017

Ardern, Jacinda, 1980-
New Zealand's Rising Star Puts Election In Play T. John color *Time* v190 no10/11 p13 S 18 2017

AreaBFE LLC
NEW MANAGEMENT, POSITIVE CHANGES AHEAD FOR AREA BFE color *Dirt Sports + Off-Road* v51 no4 p8 Ap 2017

Areaware (Company)
Open Season color *Bon Appetit* no8 p19 Ag 2017

Arecibo Observatory
Arecibo Under the Gun J. T. Schmelz and G. L. Verschuur *Sky & Telescope* v133 no5 p84 My 2017
Fates of two big radio dishes hang in the balance T. Feder *Physics Today* v70 no2 p26 F 2017
Hurricane damage threatens Arecibo's future D. Clery color *Science* v357 no6358 p1336 S 29 2017
TO WHOM IT MAY CONCERN S. Johnson *New York Times Magazine* p32 Jl 2 2017
upside-down lightning C. Maldarelli color *Popular Science* v289 no4 p90 Jl/Ag 2017

Arefaine, Samson
THE AWAY TEAM A. OKEOWO cartoon color *New Yorker* v92 no41 p42 D 12 2016

Arena, Bruce, 1951-
BRUCE ALMIGHTY: PART 2 G. Wahl color *Sports Illustrated* v126 no5 p94 F 13 2017

Arenas
The Name Game P. Bodo color *Tennis* v53 no5 p6 S/O 2017
The Ol' Ballgame J. Williams *Cincinnati Magazine* v50 no5 p63 F 2017

Arenas, Reinaldo, 1943-1990
The Verdict on Castro L. SMITH bw *Weekly Standard* v22 no14 p12 D 12 2016

Arendt, Hannah, 1906-1975
Designed to Unsettle R. L. Kehoe Iii *Commonweal* v143 no19 p36 D 2 2016
Resisting the spell *Christian Century* v133 no26 p7 D 21 2016

Arequipa (Peru)
The Cloistered Books of Peru H. HAZEN *American Scholar* v86 no2 p64 Spr 2017

Ares Capital Corp.
A Takeover Boosts My Portfolio K. KRISTOF *Kiplinger's Personal Finance* v71 no4 p58 Ap 2017

Areshidze, Giorgi
MAKING CHRISTIANITY SAFE FOR DEMOCRACY S. Yenor *Claremont Review of Books* v17 no1 p44 Wint 2016/2017

Arevalo, Chuchi
A Is for Arbitrage [Cover story] P. Robison color *Bloomberg Businessweek* no4502 p52 D 5 2016

Arevalo, F. R.
Persistent effects of pre-Columbian plant domestication on Amazonian forest composition bibl chart graph map *Science* v355 no6328 p925 Mr 3 2017

AREWA, OLUFUNMILAYO B.
LOVE, HATE, AND CULTURE WARS color il *Phi Kappa Phi Forum* v97 no1 p26 Spr 2017

Argali hunting
THE MOST UNUSUAL GAME N. Krebs bw color *Outdoor Life* v223 no9 p14 N 2016

Argenti, L.
Attosecond dynamics through a Fano resonance: Monitoring the birth of a photoelectron bibl graph *Science* v354 no6313 p734 N 11 2016

Argenti, Paul A.
Stop Letting Email Control Your Work Day *Harvard Business Review Digital Articles* p2 S 7 2017

Argentina
Where the Dogs Are *Your Dog (10780343)* v22 no10 p14 O 2016

Argentina—Antiquities
ANDEAN COPPER AGE E. A. POWELL color *Archaeology* v70 no5 p20 S/O 2017

Argentina—Description & travel
Free Range M. Hranek color map *Conde Nast Traveler* v51 no11 p108 D 2016
Hitting BA Just Right K. LAGRAVE color *Conde Nast Traveler* v52 no3 p18 Mr 2017
Viva Los Vino Pioneers N. M. WULFHART color map *Conde Nast Traveler* v51 no10 p56 N 2016

Argentina—Economic conditions—21st century
Argentina Finds Free Trade Is Hard to Do C. Devereux cartoon color graph *Bloomberg Businessweek* no4499 p40 N 14 2016
Argentina's Mauricio Macri on the Challenge of Change I. Bremmer color *Time* v188 no18 p12 O 31 2016

Argentina—Politics & government—2002-
Argentina Finds Free Trade Is Hard to Do C. Devereux cartoon color graph *Bloomberg Businessweek* no4499 p40 N 14 2016

Arginine
ANTI-AGING SUPPLEMENTS THAT WORK K. Asp color *Harper's Bazaar* no3651 p326 Mr 2017

Arginteanu, Judy
Light Fantastic color *American Craft* v77 no2 p52 Ap/My 2017

Argonne National Laboratory
THE DOOMSDAY SQUAD B. Smith color *Chicago* v66 no2 p84 F 2017

Argument
3 Ways to Stay Calm When Conversations Get Intense A. J. Su *Harvard Business Review Digital Articles* p2 Je 9 2016
How to De-Escalate an Argument with a Coworker L. Davey *Harvard Business Review Digital Articles* p2 Je 27 2017

Argyris, Chris, 1923-
Double-Loop Government: It's a learning strategy that produces conflict--and innovation M. Funkhouser *Governing* v30 no9 p59 Je 2017

Arheimer, Berit
Changing climate shifts timing of European floods color graph *Science* v357 no6351 p588 Ag 11 2017

ARIAD Pharmaceuticals Inc.
Wielding Weapons Against Cancer T. PETRUNO color *Kiplinger's Personal Finance* v71 no6 p68 Je 2017

Ariane (Music)
Martinů: Ariane/Martinů Julietta *Opera News* v81 no7 p47 Ja 2017

Arianespace SA
Make Progress Exciting Again P. J. O'ROURKE color *Weekly Standard* v22 no41 p20 Jl 3 2017

ARIAS, ELISA FELICITAS
WATCHING THE CLOCKS *Popular Science* v289 no5 p45 S/O 2017

ARIAS, JIMMY
US Open Special bw color *Tennis* v53 no5 p30 S/O 2017

Arias, Jimmy—Interviews
THE TENNIS CONVERSATION: Wimbledon A. FRIEDMAN *Tennis* v53 no4 p38 Jl/Ag 2017

ARIAS, SALVADOR
The Role of Botanical Gardens in the Conservation of Cactaceae *BioScience* v66 no12 p1057 D 1 2016

Arias From Verdi & Puccini (Music)
Diva Playlist F. P. DRISCOLL *Opera News* v81 no5 p18 N 2016

Arias-Rotondo, Daniela M.
Photosensitized, energy transfer-mediated organometallic catalysis through electronically excited nickel(II) bibl diag graph *Science* v355 no6323 p380 Ja 27 2017

Arid regions
See also
Deserts
The Desert's Living Skin K. MAST color *Discover* v38 no6 p22 Jl/Ag 2017

Ariel Motor Co.
APOCALYPSE NOW B. SOROKANICH color *Road & Track* v68 no9 p38 Je 2017

Ariel Lieberman, Jenna
ZATT (ZNF451)–mediated resolution of topoisomerase 2 DNA-protein cross-links diag *Science* v357 no6358 p1412 S 29 2017

Ariely, Dan
Dollars and Sense: How We Misthink Money and How to Spend Smarter *Publishers Weekly* v264 no38 p62 S 18 2017

Arif, Muhammad
A pathology atlas of the human cancer transcriptome diag *Science* v357 no6352 p660 Ag 18 2017

Ariker, Matt
How Marketers Can Personalize at Scale *Harvard Business Re-*

view *Digital Articles* p2 N 23 2015

Quantifying the Impact of Marketing Analytics *Harvard Business Review Digital Articles* p2 N 5 2015

ARIKHA, NOGA

FRENCH EVOLUTION color *Architectural Digest* no11 p126 N 1 2017

Arimah, Lesley Nneka

Otherworldly Ties M. WARNER *New York Times Book Review* p10 My 7 2017

Arimura, Yasuhiro

Crystal structure of the overlapping dinucleosome composed of hexasome and octasome graph *Science* v356 no6334 p205 Ap 14 2017

Arington, Hannah

A greater good color *Equus* no480 p27 S 2017

Arinze Okonkwo, Charles

READER COMMENTS *America* v216 no6 p7 Mr 20 2017

Aristocracy (Political science)

HOMELAND SECURITY M. Robespierre *Lapham's Quarterly* v10 no3 p159 Summ 2017

Aristotle, 384-322 B.C.

BREATHE color *Prevention* v69 no4 p38 Ap 2017

EXPECTATION MANAGEMENT Aristotle *Lapham's Quarterly* v10 no3 p90 Summ 2017

Arizona

arizona is GORGES N. AUSTIN *Arizona Highways* v92 no12 p2 D 2016

Bobby D's BBQ K. VAUGHN color *Arizona Highways* v93 no5 p12 My 2017

Coyotes K. Vaughn *Arizona Highways* v93 no2 p13 F 2017

The Downtown Clifton N. B. TRULSSON *Arizona Highways* v93 no2 p14 F 2017

Paradise Point Café: Known as "Old Town's sweet retreat," Paradise Point Café has built a loyal following with its baked goods, including a signature carrot cake and salted caramel apple pie that's made with house-made caramel. Mmmm ... K. MONTGOMERY *Arizona Highways* v96 no7 p12 Jl 2017

Ring a Bell? *Arizona Highways* v93 no4 p56 Ap 2017

The Tucson Tornado N. AUSTIN *Arizona Highways* v93 no1 p8 Ja 2017

Arizona (Battleship)

Inside the Sunken USS Arizona *Oceanus* v52 no2 p9 Spr 2017

Uncovering the secrets of the USS Arizona in Pearl Harbor color *PCWorld* p192 D 2016

Arizona Beverages (Company)

THE MAN, THE CAN & THE PLAN C. PETERSON-WITHORN color graph *Forbes* v200 no5 p68 N 14 2017

Arizona Cardinals (Football team)

2 Arizona Cardinals color *Sports Illustrated* v127 no7 p101 S 4 2017

Arizona Diamondbacks (Baseball team)

4 DIAMONDBACKS color *Sports Illustrated* v126 no9 p112 Mr 27 2017

Arizona Highways (Periodical)

editor's LETTER R. STIEVE *Arizona Highways* v93 no10 p2 O 2017

from our archives [May 1967] *Arizona Highways* v93 no8 p10 Ag 2017

Arizona State University

Dissent with Modification R. Lloyd diag *Scientific American* v316 no5 p14 My 2017

THE EMPTY "CHOICE" ARGUMENT B. SHUCART *Advocate* no1088 p18 D 2016/Ja 2017

JAMMING UP SEX TRAFFIC E. BARTON *USA Today Magazine* v145 no2864 p68 My 2017

Arizona Trail (Ariz.)

The View Is Made by Walking J. Mark *Sierra* v102 no2 p14 Mr/Ap 2017

Arizona Trail (Ariz.)—Description & travel

Take the scenic route color *Backpacker* v45 no1 p22 Ja 2017

Arizona—Description & travel

Arizona A to Z H. Wilson color *Canadian Geographic* v135 no6 p14 D 2015

Arizona Paradise J. DROWN color *Trail Rider* v29 no3 p54 Ap 2017

The Big Pictures: LAKE POWELL J. KIDA color *Arizona High-*

ways v93 no5 p16 My 2017

Crescent Moon Ranch A. McGIVNEY color *Arizona Highways* v93 no5 p14 My 2017

EXPLORERS, GUNFIGHTERS & SMUGGLERS [Cover story] J. KOPYCINSKI color *Dirt Sports + Off-Road* v51 no10 p30 O 2017

EXPLORE THE WILD WEST ON THE ROAD LESS TRAVELED *Los Angeles Magazine* p130 Mr 2017

HOPE CAMP TRAIL R. STIEVE *Arizona Highways* v93 no2 p54 F 2017

IT'S TIME TO BOARD E. BALLI color *Arizona Highways* v93 no5 p38 My 2017

A Place in the Sun bw color *Arizona Highways* v93 no5 p56 My 2017

PRESCOTT *Los Angeles Magazine* p134 Mr 2017

A RIM COUNTRY ALMANAC E. LIERLE *Arizona Highways* v92 no7 p28 Jl 2016

SPRING VALLEY LOOP: Historic Route 66, the National Old Trails Road, the Beale Wagon Road ... some of the state's most iconic routes can be experienced along the Spring Valley Loop in Northern Arizona A. McGIVNEY *Arizona Highways* v96 no7 p52 Jl 2017

WHY ARE PEOPLE TALKING ABOUT TUCSON? *Los Angeles Magazine* p132 Mr 2017

Arizona—Politics & government

BACK TO BASICS A. GREENBLATT *Governing* v30 no6 p26 Mr 2017

CLASS DISMISSED: When a state divests from public education A. Neason *Harper's Magazine* p35 S 2017

Arjona, Adria

Emerald City J. Jensen color *Entertainment Weekly* no1446/1447 p108 D 2016/Ja 2017

Arkansas

Scary (and true) tales from a crag near you M. Parker and J. Lucas *Climbing* no350 p19 D 2016/Ja 2017

THERE'S ONLY ONE PRESIDENT CLINTON A. ABEL color *Maclean's* v129 no45 p36 N 14 2016

Arkansas State University

10 UP & COMERS: CASEY HOOK G. Gullickson *Successful Farming* v115 no8 p46 Je/Jl 2017

Arkansas—Antiquities

I See Your Cahokia and Raise You My Quivira S. Richardson color *American History* v52 no4 p8 O 2017

Arkansas—Description & travel

Ozark Magic J. Jennings color *Southern Living* v52 no9 p63 S 2017

Travel *D: The Magazine of Dallas* v43 no10 p100 O 2016

Arkell, Simon

Create a Strategy That Anticipates and Learns *Harvard Business Review Digital Articles* p2 O 6 2014

Arkhipov, Ilya

Does Putin Still Favor His Sidekick? color graph *Bloomberg Businessweek* no4520 p28 My 1 2017

The Fight for Syria's Future Has Only Begun map *Bloomberg Businessweek* no4525 p28 Je 5 2017

Moscow Confidential: Private Jets for Dogs bw color *Bloomberg Businessweek* no4498 p24 N 7 2016

Putin Isn't So Sure Trump's a Pal color *Bloomberg Businessweek* no4509 p13 Ja 30 2017

Putin's Rival Targets Provincial Russians color *Bloomberg Businessweek* no4517 p28 Ap 3 2017

Russia, Japan, and China Fill the Trade Gap *Bloomberg Businessweek* no4502 p22 D 5 2016

Will Beijing Also Have A Friend at State? bw *Bloomberg Businessweek* no4504 p26 D 19 2016

ArkivMusic LLC

ArkivMusic Launches ArkivJazz K. Micallef color *Downbeat* v84 no10 p19 O 2017

Arky, David

High Concepts P. Kolonia bw color *Popular Photography* v81 no2 p68 Mr/Ap 2017

Arlen, Tessa

A Death by Any Other Name *Publishers Weekly* v264 no1 p37 Ja 2 2017

Arlidge, M. J.

Hide and Seek: A Detective Helen Grace Thriller *Publishers*

Weekly v264 no34 p89 Ag 21 2017

Arlington (Music)

Pen: Arlington A. McKinnon *Opera News* v81 no7 p48 Ja 2017

Arlington (Theatrical production)

THE THEATRE cartoon *New Yorker* v93 no13 p22 My 15 2017

Arm

See also

Arm muscles

ARM YOURSELF J. Crandell color *Yoga Journal* p26 2017 Special Issue

Score A-List Arms color *Health* v31 no4 p10 My 2017

Arm muscles

TONE YOUR TRICEPS V. Tweed color *Amazing Wellness* v9 no3 p74 EarlySumm 2017

Armacost, Barbara

The Organizational Reasons Police Departments Don't Change *Harvard Business Review Digital Articles* p2 Ag 19 2016

Armadillos

Movin' On Up E. BETZ map *Discover* v38 no3 p13 Ap 2017

Armand Hammer Museum of Art & Cultural Center

"MADE IN L.A. 2016" E. RAPPAPORT bw color *ARTnews* v115 no4 p128 Wint 2016/2017

Masterful mixing at the Hammer E. H. Gustafson color *Magazine Antiques* v184 no3 p136 My/Je 2017

Armani, Georgio

INTERVIEW WITH THE MAESTRO J. Picardie color *Harper's Bazaar* no3657 p236 O 2017

My LIST N. Vinson color *Harper's Bazaar* no3649 p144 D 2016/Ja 2017

ARMANTROUT, RAE

Return *Nation* v303 no25/26 p30 D 19 2016

ARMARSÓTTIR, EYGLÓ SVALA

MARCH OF THE DESIGNERS *Iceland Review* v55 no2 p10 Mr/Ap 2017

Armbrust, Doyle

MUSICAL MARATHON G. MEYER cartoon *Chicago* v66 no3 p54 Mr 2017

Armchairs

Art + Craft color *Arts & Crafts Homes & the Revival* v12 no5 p11 Wint 2018

GET OUTSIDE! S. JEAN SHELTON color *Good Housekeeping* v265 no1 p35 Jl 2017

Armchairs—Evaluation

BHG throwback 1976 VELVET L. HEDRICK *Better Homes & Gardens* v95 no1 p124 Ja 2017

Armed Forces

See also

Air forces

Marines

Military personnel

Military reform

Military reserve forces

Militia

Paramilitary forces

Sailors

Special forces (Military science)

Veterans

FOR THOSE LEFT BEHIND M. GRIMM *USA Today Magazine* v145 no2858 p38 N 2016

From the Director's Chair S. Bartram *Parks & Recreation* v51 no11 p20 N 2016

Humor in Uniform *Reader's Digest* v188 no1124 p141 O 2016

The Long View R. LONG *National Review* v69 no12 p34 Je 26 2017

PATRIOT GAMES S. Rathod bw cartoon color *Mother Jones* v41 no6 p21 N/D 2016

Still Resonating a Half-Century Later F. KREBSBACH *USA Today Magazine* v145 no2864 p40 My 2017

What Is Russia's Military Up To? B. Bender *Hoover Digest: Research & Opinion on Public Policy* no4 p119 Fall 2016

Armed Forces—Appropriations & expenditures

Trump's Fake Defense Buildup T. Donnelly and G. Schmitt color *Weekly Standard* v22 no26 p9 Mr 13 2017

Armed Forces—Humor

Humor in Uniform M. GARVEY, P. TRUSH et al *Reader's Digest* v189 no1128 p134 Mr 2017

Armed Forces—Vocational guidance

Cheating Death D. Sears *American History* v51 no6 p60 F 2017

United We Serve G. MULLINS-COHEN *Parks & Recreation* v51 no11 p8 N 2016

Armendariz, Saúl

Mexican and U.S. scientists: Partners bibl color *Science* v355 no6330 p1139 Mr 17 2017

Armenian history

75, 50 & 25 YEARS AGO R. W. Sinnott color *Sky & Telescope* v134 no5 p7 N 2017

ARMENTERAS, DOLORS

Deforestation and Coca Cultivation Rooted in Twentieth-Century Development Projects *BioScience* v66 no11 p974 N 1 2016

Armfield, Neil

Die Zauberflöte M. T. Ketterson *Opera News* v81 no9 p38 Mr 2017

Armide (Theatrical production)

Armide A. J. Goldmann *Opera News* v81 no7 p42 Ja 2017

Armies

FROM OUR READERS D. Phillips, H. E. Came et al *Archaeology* v70 no4 p8 Je-Ag 2017

Hallowed Ground Bosworth Field, England [Cover story] C. Allsop color *Military History* v34 no4 p76 N 2017

MILITARY-GRADE AVIANS color *Reason* v49 no1 p8 My 2017

Armington, Susan

AFTER THE SKY FELL color *Progressive* v81 no5 p22 Je/Jl 2017

Armisen, Fred, 1966-—Interviews

Fred Armisen A. GREENE color *Rolling Stone* no1272 p28 O 20 2016

Portlandia's "Put a Bird on It!" D. Snierson color *Entertainment Weekly* no1454/1455 p89 F 24 2017

Armistices—International cooperation

The U.S. Has a Weak Hand In Syria-and Russia Knows It I. Bremmer *Time* v188 no14 p10 O 10 2016

Armitage, Alice

A More Practical Model for Law Schools *Harvard Business Review Digital Articles* p2 D 24 2015

ARMITAGE, DAN

my amish-built cabin color *Cabin Living* p28 Mr 2017

Paddlecraft Racks color *Cabin Living* p59 Ap 2017

PADDLING + fishing A WINNING COMBO color *Cabin Living* p62 Mr 2017

Armitage, David

The green art of the deathtrap ambush S. Milius color *Science News* v191 no1 p4 Ja 21 2017

Talkin' 'bout a revolution *History Today* v67 no2 p72 F 2017

What Gets Called 'Civil War'? L. Colley color *New York Review of Books* v64 no10 p42 Je 8 2017

Armitage, Iain

A Tale of Two Sheldons D. Franich, N. Abrams et al color *Entertainment Weekly* no1482/1483 p44 S 22 2017

YOUNG SHELDON J. Halterman *TV Guide* v65 no37 p25 S 4 2017

Armitage, N. P.

Quantized Faraday and Kerr rotation and axion electrodynamics of a 3D topological insulator bibl graph *Science* v354 no6316 p1124 D 2 2016

Armitron (Company)

Bright Now color *Good Housekeeping* v264 no1 p15 Ja 1 2017

ARMON, CHARA

Beyond Words color *O, The Oprah Magazine* p17 Ap 2017

Armor

THE THREAT REPORT color *Popular Mechanics* p70 Mr 2017

Armored military vehicles

FLASHBACK *MHQ: Quarterly Journal of Military History* v29 no2 p4 Wint 2017

Armour Home Electronics Ltd.

Retro 5.1 Done Right M. Fleischmann color graph *Sound & Vision* v82 no7 p62 S 2017

Arms control

See also

Nuclear arms control

Europe's nuclear woes: Mitigating the challenges of the next years U. Kühn, S. Shetty et al bibl *Bulletin of the Atomic Scientists* v73 no4 p245 Jl 2017

Arms control—Russia

The future of US–Russian nuclear deterrence and arms control T. Anichkina, A. Péczeli et al bibl *Bulletin of the Atomic Scientists* v73 no4 p271 Jl 2017

Arms dealers

In Arms Sales We Trust U. ABDULLAH *Islamic Horizons* v46 no1 p58 Ja/F 2017

Arms race

'It All Looks As If the World Is Preparing for War' M. Gorbachev color *Time* v189 no5 p22 F 13 2017

Armstead, Jessie

IN THE CHAMPION'S CIRCLE R. W. Goode color graph *Black Enterprise* v47 no7 p64 My/Je 2017

Armstrong, Andra

College Promise: Pathway to the 21 Century *Change* v48 no6 p6 N/D 2016

Armstrong, Beverly

Raising the Bar color *O, The Oprah Magazine* p28 S 2017

Armstrong, Billie Joe, 1972-

BILLIE JOE ARMSTRONG E. R. Brown color *Entertainment Weekly* no1435 p54 O 14 2016

What Not to Wear Flying T. John color *Time* v189 no13 p10 Ap 10 2017

Armstrong, Charlotte

Northern Bounty color *Alternatives Journal (AJ) - Canada's Environmental Voice* v42 no2 p14 2016

OMG NASA! color *Alternatives Journal (AJ) - Canada's Environmental Voice* v42 no2 p11 2016

Armstrong, Deborah K.

Mismatch repair deficiency predicts response of solid tumors to PD-1 blockade chart graph *Science* v357 no6349 p409 Jl 28 2017

Armstrong, Devon—Interviews

Blackmagic Design Helps Theatres Capture the Magic *Stage Directions* v29 no11 p22 N 2016

Armstrong, Guy

Emptiness: A Practical Introduction for Meditators *Publishers Weekly* v264 no11 p78 Mr 13 2017

Armstrong, Josephine Bonavia

Popular piety color *U.S. Catholic* v82 no2 p5 F 2017

Armstrong, Kelley, 1968-

A Darkness Absolute *Publishers Weekly* v263 no50 p51 D 5 2016

Lost Souls *Publishers Weekly* v264 no6 p50 F 6 2017

ARMSTRONG, KEN

SALVATION *Smithsonian* v47 no9 p70 Ja/F 2017

Armstrong, Lance, 1971—Substance use

LIVE STRONGISH A. Murphy and J. Feldman color *Sports Illustrated* v126 no11 p54 Ap 17-24 2017

Armstrong, Lance, 1971—Trials, litigation, etc.

Wheels of Justice M. McCann and T. Keith color *Sports Illustrated* v126 no15 p13 My 29 2017

Armstrong, Lisa

THE BEST OF WHAT'S NEW color *Harper's Bazaar* no3656 p302 S 2017

CHIC easy PIECES bw color *Harper's Bazaar* no3651 p420 Mr 2017

VICTORIA BECKHAM color *Vogue* v207 no3 p422 Mr 2017

Armstrong, Lou

SOLUTIONS color *Horse & Rider* v56 no2 p18 F 2017

Armstrong, Louis, 1901-1971

Seventh Inning Stretch K. SILSBEE color *Downbeat* v84 no6 p76 Je 2017

Armstrong, Neil, 1930-2012

SPACE CONSERVATION K. RANDALL *Washingtonian Magazine* v52 no12 p24 S 2017

Armstrong, Robert

The Art of Seeing Things Invisible *History Today* v67 no4 p56 Ap 2017

Armstrong, Scott A.

PI3K pathway regulates ER-dependent transcription in breast cancer through the epigenetic regulator KMT2D bibl graph *Science* v355 no6331 p1324 Mr 24 2017

Armstrong, Tibby

Surrender the Dark *Publishers Weekly* v264 no18 p45 My 1 2017

Armstrong, Zan

The Baby Spike diag *Scientific American* v317 no1 p76 Jl 2017

ARMSWORTH, PAUL R.

When, Where, and How Nature Matters for Ecosystem Services: Challenges for the Next Generation of Ecosystem Service Models *BioScience* v67 no9 p820 S 2017

ARN, LARRY P.

Trump's Triumph Should Show the Way *USA Today Magazine* v145 no2862 p12 Mr 2017

Arnadottir, Arngunnur

From the Editor P. Stefánsson *Iceland Review* v55 no1 p4 Ja/F 2017

Árnadóttir, Arngunnur—Interviews

MUSIC IN HER WORDS A. M. I. Grímsson *Iceland Review* v55 no1 p14 Ja/F 2017

Árnadóttir, Kristín Linda—Interviews

FROSTY WELCOME Z. Robert color *Iceland Review* v54 no5 p72 S-O 2016

ARNARSDÓTTIR, EYGLÓ SVALA

AUTUMN AMUSEMENTS color *Iceland Review* v54 no5 p8 S-O 2016

BELOVED BACKWARDNESS *Iceland Review* v55 no1 p38 Ja/F 2017

COMING AROUND THE MOUNTAIN color *Iceland Review* v54 no5 p82 S-O 2016

FORCE OF CREATION *Iceland Review* v55 no3 p18 My/Je 2017

THE GUARDIAN *Iceland Review* v55 no3 p40 My/Je 2017

HEROINES OF THE SEA color *Iceland Review* v54 no5 p78 S-O 2016

IN HARMONY WITH HORSES *Iceland Review* v55 no1 p48 Ja/F 2017

ISLAND OF OPPORTUNITY color *Iceland Review* v54 no5 p52 S-O 2016

News Roundup color *Iceland Review* v54 no5 p18 S-O 2016

A NEW TOMORROW *Iceland Review* v54 no6 p80 N/D 2016

OFF THE LAND color *Iceland Review* v54 no5 p92 S-O 2016

OF LOVE AND MURDER *Iceland Review* v54 no5 p42 S-O 2016

REDUCED TO ASHES *Iceland Review* v54 no6 p64 N/D 2016

RESTAURANTS color *Iceland Review* v54 no5 p113 S-O 2016

SLAUGHTER SEASON color *Iceland Review* v54 no6 p86 N/D 2016

TAKING COMMAND *Iceland Review* v55 no2 p52 Mr/Ap 2017

THERMAL BLISS *Iceland Review* v55 no3 p106 My/Je 2017

THE TURKISH RAID *Iceland Review* v55 no2 p48 Mr/Ap 2017

VISIONS OF VIĐEY *Iceland Review* v54 no6 p45 N/D 2016

Arnaud, Claude

The High Wire of Jean Cocteau E. White cartoon color *New York Review of Books* v63 no18 p67 N 24 2016

Arndt, Ingo

The Grass Menagerie J. Chen color *Popular Photography* v81 no2 p42 Mr/Ap 2017

Arnett, Autumn A.

Partnerships Between Schools and Communities Promote Reading Success *Education Digest* v83 no2 p57 O 2017

To Develop Teachers, Look to Other Teachers *Education Digest* v83 no1 p50 S 2017

Arnett, Jeffrey

What Really Motivates Workers in Their 20s *Harvard Business Review Digital Articles* p2 Ag 25 2015

Arnett, Lisa

BIKE AND BOOZE color *Chicago* v66 no7 p56 Jl 2017

Thirsty? color diag *Chicago* v66 no2 p57 F 2017

Arnett, Will, 1970-

Lego Batman Finds the Funny In Existential Angst S. Zacharek color *Time* v189 no6 p50 F 20 2017

Arnn, Larry P.

Churchill Challenged A. ROBERTS *Commentary* v143 no4 p47 Ap 2017

Arnold & Porter Kaye Scholer (Company)

Best Law Firms for Women 2017 *Working Mother* v40 no3 p30 Ag/S 2017

Arnold, Alexandria

Seattle Breaks New Ground on Opioids color graph *Bloomberg Businessweek* no4494 p28 O 10 2016

Arnold, Amy L.

Industrial Evolution W. Moonan color *Architectural Record* v205 no3 p53 Mr 2017

Arnold, Andrea, 1961-

American Honey L. Greenblatt color *Entertainment Weekly* no1434 p44 O 7 2016

Arnold, Benedict, 1741-1801
Tracks of a Traitor N. Goldstein bw color map *American History* v52 no4 p56 O 2017

ARNOLD, CARRIE
women struggling... "smiling depression" bw color *Women's Health* v14 no4 p144 My 2017

Arnold, Chuck
LOVING LIFE color *Essence* v48 no6 p70 O 2017
SOUL GATHERING color *Essence* v47 no12 p68 Ap 2017
TLC STORIES BEHIND THE SONGS color *Entertainment Weekly* no1472 p28 Je 30 2017

ARNOLD, DANIEL
FREE AT LAST *Sierra* v102 no3 p52 My/Je 2017

Arnold, Frances H.
Directed evolution of cytochrome c for carbon–silicon bond formation: Bringing silicon to life bibl diag graph *Science* v354 no6315 p1048 N 25 2016

Arnold, G.
Seasonal exposure of carbon dioxide ice on the nucleus of comet 67P/Churyumov-Gerasimenko bibl bw graph *Science* v354 no6319 p1563 D 23 2016

Arnold, Janice
Janice Arnold A. Ranallo color *American Craft* v77 no3 p44 Je/Jl 2017

Arnold, John
THE MOST HATED MAN IN PENSIONLAND L. Farmer *Governing* v30 no7 p38 Ap 2017
Older Workers Need to Stop Believing Stereotypes About Themselves *Harvard Business Review Digital Articles* p2 Je 20 2016
The Pension Hammer M. Funkhouser *Governing* v30 no7 p4 Ap 2017

ARNOLD, KATHRYN
Hanging It Up color *Runner's World* v52 no5 p56 Je 2017
THE RUNNING DEAD cartoon *Runner's World* v52 no1 p30 Ja/F 2017
A RUN TO FORGET cartoon *Runner's World* v51 no11 p24 D 2016
THAT MAGIC MOMENT cartoon *Runner's World* v52 no3 p22 Ap 2017

Arnold, Kelly B.
Sustained virologic control in SIV+ macaques after antiretroviral and α4β7 antibody therapy bibl graph *Science* v354 no6309 p197 O 14 2016

Arnold, Lindsay
THE DIRT with Lindsay Arnold *Dance Spirit* v21 no7 p42 S 2017

Arnold, Matthew, 1822-1888
The Cultured Life J. EPSTEIN bw color *Weekly Standard* v22 no27 p26 Mr 20 2017

Arnold, Michael
Sheldon Adelson's Not-So-Winning Year bw *Bloomberg Businessweek* no4530 p40 Jl 17 2017

Arnold, Michael L.
The Web of Life, the Tangled Bank, and the Frequency of Genetic Exchange S. P. EGAN *BioScience* v67 no1 p91 Ja 2017

Arnold, Michael S.
THE MAYOR IS IN color *Bloomberg Businessweek* no4534 p66 Ag 14 2017

ARNOLD, SCOTT
Chords & Discords color *Downbeat* v84 no9 p10 S 2017

Arnold, Scotty
SCOTTY ARNOLD B. Merrill color *Snowboarder* v29 no3 p38 N 2016

Arnold, Susan
REIMAGINE THE TRADITIONAL A. GRAVES *Yankee* v81 no1 p45 Ja/F 2017

Arnold, Tichina
ME...SLOW DOWN? HELL, NO! R. R. Robertson color *Essence* v47 no11 p59 Mr 2017
NOW STREAMING! B. GARWOOD color *Ebony* v72/73 no12/1 p88 O/N 2017

Arnold Palmer Enterprises Inc.
PITCH HITTER M. Chwasky color *Golf Magazine* v58 no12 p65 D 2016

ARNOLD-RATLIFF, KATIE
Boldly Going! color *O, The Oprah Magazine* p84 Ja 2017
Let it go! [Cover story] color *O, The Oprah Magazine* p92 Ag 2017
WHAT A BOOK CAN DO [Cover story] color *O, The Oprah Magazine* p76 Jl 2017

Arnoldson, Erick
SPACE-AGE LURES THAT LOOK, SOUND, ACT—AND EVEN SMELL—LIKE LIVE BAIT J. BRANDT color *Outdoor Life* v224 no2 p44 F/Mr 2017

Arnoux, Pascal
An algal photoenzyme converts fatty acids to hydrocarbons color graph *Science* v357 no6354 p903 S 1 2017

Arnswald, Stefan
FIT TO PRINT bw color *Wired* v25 no5 p14 My 2017

Arnulf, Adrien F.
Seismic constraints on caldera dynamics from the 2015 Axial Seamount eruption bibl color graph *Science* v354 no6318 p1395 D 16 2016

Arocena, Daymé
DAYMÉ AROCENA J. Murph color *Downbeat* v84 no4 p26 Ap 2017

Aroh, Ben
A Maker's Guide to... LOUISVILLE F. MAROUKIAN color map *Popular Mechanics* p22 S 2017

Aroma of food
SHRINK YOUR GUT WITH GASTROPHYSICS S. Subramanian color *Men's Health* v32 no2 p63 Mr 2017

Aromatherapy
7 SURPRISING USES FOR COCONUT OIL color *Prevention* v69 no4 p12 Ap 2017
AROMATHERAPY TRAVEL KIT C. Cromer color *Amazing Wellness* v9 no4 p70 Summ 2017
DETOXIFY WITH AROMATHERAPY C. Cromer color *Amazing Wellness* v9 no2 p68 Spr 2017
Fun Gift Ideas N. Brechka *Better Nutrition* v78 no12 p6 D 2016
A Healthier & Happier 2017 N. Brechka *Better Nutrition* v79 no1 p6 Ja 2017
the health nut A. Brightfield cartoon *Better Homes & Gardens* v95 no4 p150 Ap 2017
HIT REFRESH! A. Nix *Amazing Wellness* v9 no2 p8 Spr 2017
THE NOSE KNOWS [Cover story] color *Prevention* v69 no5 p6 My 2017
SCENTS THAT SLIM K. Keniston-Pond color *Amazing Wellness* v8 no2 p70 Spr 2016

Aromatic fluorine compounds
Hydrogenation of fluoroarenes: Direct access to all-cis-(multi)fluorinated cycloalkanes M. P. Wiesenfeldt, Z. Nairoukh et al diag *Science* v357 no6354 p908 S 1 2017

Aron, Gerri
KITCHEN-TESTED TIPS color *Vegetarian Today* no1 p4 F 2017

Aron, Jules
Vegan Cheese: Simple, Delicious, Plant-Based Recipes color *Publishers Weekly* v264 no20 p51 My 15 2017

Aron, Leon
The Eurasian Judo Master: Vladimir Putin uses martial-arts tactics to undergird his dangerous view of the clash of civilizations *Commentary* v143 no1 p38 Ja 2017

Aronia
ARONIA JUICE *South Dakota Magazine* v33 no3 p40 S/O 2017

Aronica, Giuseppe T.
Changing climate shifts timing of European floods color graph *Science* v357 no6351 p588 Ag 11 2017

Aronoff, Kate
Blue Collar, Green Future *Progressive* v81 no4 p28 Ap/My 2017
Campuses Without Borders *In These Times* v41 no1 p8 Ja 2017
THE FIGHT OF OUR LIFETIME *In These Times* v41 no3 p20 Mr 2017
From Movement to Mayor *In These Times* v41 no6 p30 Je 2017
How to Resist, in 6 Books *In These Times* v41 no5 p34 My 2017
How To Win Fights and Influence Congresspeople *In These Times* v41 no3 p8 Mr 2017
May the Force Be With Us *In These Times* v41 no2 p36 F 2017
PIPELINE POPULISM: Out on the prairie, unlikely alliances may hold the key to transforming the Democratic Party *In These Times* v41 no10 p18 O 2017
Privateers on the Jersey Shore *In These Times* v41 no7 p10 Jl 2017

Socialism's Trump Bump *In These Times* v41 no2 p10 F 2017

Visible and Indivisible: The Birth of a Resistance Movement color *Progressive* v81 no6 p15 Ag/S 2017

We Need a Plan, Not a Brand *In These Times* v41 no8 p28 Ag 2017

Aronofsky, Darren, 1969-

Michelle PFEIFFER: AFTER A BRIEF HIATUS, THE ONE-TIME SO-CAL SURFER GIRL TURNED SCREEN SIREN, THE THREE-TIME OSCAR NOMINEE—AND STILL SOMEHOW WOEFULLY UNDERRATED—MICHELLE PFEIFFER IS BACK IN A BIG WAY, WITH A BEVY OF FILMS TO ADD TO HER ALREADY... *Interview* v47 no3 p64 Ap 2017

MOTHER! S. Vilkomerson color *Entertainment Weekly* no1478 / 1479 p40 Ag 18-25 2017

Oh, mother! J. Nolfi and S. Vilkomerson color *Entertainment Weekly* no1484 p16 S 29 2017

Sight Unseen A. RIESMAN img *New York* v50 no17 p102 Ag 21 2017

Aronofsky, Darren, 1969——Interviews

Darren Aronofsky E. Dockterman color *Time* v190 no13 p72 O 2 2017

Aronow, Don

Don Aronow: The Legend in My Corner M. PETERS color *Power & Motoryacht* v33 no2 p36 F 2017

ARONOWITZ, ALFRED G.

Hail! Hail! rock 'n' roll! *Saturday Evening Post* v289 no4 p40 Jl/Ag 2017

Arons, Steven

Paris and Frankfurt Vie For Brexit's Spoils *Bloomberg Businessweek* no4530 p30 Jl 17 2017

Aronsohn, Lee

THE LOVE BOAT: LIFE ON THE (VERY) HIGH SEAS color *Entertainment Weekly* no1460/1461 p21 Ap 7-17 2017

ARONSON, ELLIOT

Why We Believe--Long After We Shouldn't *Skeptical Inquirer* v41 no2 p51 Mr/Ap 2017

ARONSON, MYLA F. J.

Biodiversity in the City: Fundamental Questions for Understanding the Ecology of Urban Green Spaces for Biodiversity Conservation *BioScience* v67 no9 p799 S 2017

Planning for the Future of Urban Biodiversity: A Global Review of City-Scale Initiatives *BioScience* v67 no4 p332 Ap 2017

Aronson, Robert D.

Robert D. Aronson H. MARTIN color *Architectural Digest* v74 no3 p30 Mr 2017

Arora, Akash

Thermal processing of diblock copolymer melts mimics metallurgy diag graph *Science* v356 no6337 p520 My 5 2017

Arora, Arjun Dev

A Manager's Job Is Making Sure Employees Have a Life Outside Work *Harvard Business Review Digital Articles* p2 Mr 25 2016

Arora, Gabo

The Future of Humanitarianism [Cover story] M. J. MOONEY bw color *Popular Mechanics* p13 S 2017

The Future of Humanitarianism [Cover story] M. J. MOONEY bw color *Popular Mechanics* v193 no7 p13 S 2016

Arora, Jason

A Blueprint for Measuring Health Care Outcomes *Harvard Business Review Digital Articles* p2 D 12 2016

Arora, Radha

What I Wear to Work J. Chen color *Bloomberg Businessweek* no4523 p67 My 22 2017

Arp, Halton C.

A Whale of a Galaxy Cluster: Reel in the denizens of Abell 194 — if those autumn skies ever clear K. Hewitt-White color *Sky & Telescope* v134 no5 p58 N 2017

Arp, Jean, 1887-1966——Exhibitions

ARTISTIC AFFINITIES C. Bauer color *Magazine Antiques* v183 no6 p98 N/D 2016

Arpaio, Joe, 1932-

The Law Is King color *Weekly Standard* v23 no1 p6 S 11 2017

Arquebus

CASE FOR THE REVOLVER B. M. TOWSLEY color *Outdoor Life* v224 no4 pP15 My 2017

Arqueros, F.

Observation of a large-scale anisotropy in the arrival directions of cosmic rays above 8×1018 eV *Science* v357 no6357 p1266 S 22 2017

Arraf, Jane

In Iraq, mercurial cleric redefines himself as a nationalist patriot *Christian Century* v134 no13 p14 Je 21 2017

Arran, Island of (Scotland)

And the Winning Photos Are... *British Heritage Travel* v38 no2 p80 Mr/Ap 2017

Arrangement, The (TV program)

The Arrangement K. Freeze *TV Guide* v65 no8 p34 F 27 2017

CHRISTINE EVANGELISTA S. Highfill and A. Wilkinson color *Entertainment Weekly* no1456 p59 Mr 10 2017

Arras, Nathan

You Never Forget Your First Time diag il *Backpacker* v45 no2 p64 Mr 2017

Arrasmith, Steven

Falling off a Bridge cartoon *Men's Health* v32 no3 p80 Ap 2017

Arrest

Duterte's Fiercest Critic Finds Herself In Jail N. Jenkins color *Time* v189 no9 p11 Mr 13 2017

GLEANINGS *Christianity Today* v61 no6 p16 Jl/Ag 2017

PHOTO color *Reason* v49 no3 p7 Jl 2017

The Scary New Normal for Immigrants A. Gupta color *Progressive* v81 no5 p55 Je/Jl 2017

WINNERS AND LOSERS A. Robinson color *Car & Driver* v62 no7 p18 Ja 2017

Arrest (Police methods)

The Grave Hunter, Hunted J. NORDLINGER color *National Review* v69 no19 p24 O 16 2017

Arrested Development (TV program)

Parental Guidance M. Rubino *Indianapolis Monthly* v40 no4 p12 D 2016

Arrest—United States

A Judge's DWI Arrest A. Johnson color *New Orleans Magazine* v51 no8 p38 Je 2017

Arrhenius, Svante, 1859-1927

Is Global Warming Good, or Was Arrhenius Erroneous? S. D. Gedzelman *Weatherwise* v70 no1 p30 Ja/F 2017

Arrington, Alanna

STYLE CRUSH Alanna Arrington S. Simon color *InStyle* v24 no8 p80 Ag 2017

ARRINGTON, BOB

Drill Instructor color *Power & Motoryacht* v34 no9 p34 S 2017

Situational Awareness color *Power & Motoryacht* v34 no11 p54 N 2017

Arrivabene, Vera

The Merchants of Venice H. Bowles color *Vogue* v207 no11 p130 N 2017

Arrivabene, Viola

The Merchants of Venice H. Bowles color *Vogue* v207 no11 p130 N 2017

Arrival (Film)

Arrival C. Chiarella chart color *Sound & Vision* v82 no5 p64 Je 2017

ARRIVAL S. Vilkomerson color *Entertainment Weekly* no1438 p40 N 4 2016

The Bullseye M. Snetiker color *Entertainment Weekly* no1440 p64 N 18 2016

GIRL POWER: BACK TO THE FUTURE OF FEMINIST SCIENCE FICTION WITH INTO THE FOREST AND ARRIVAL S. Mayer *Film Quarterly* v70 no3 p32 Spr 2017

In Arrival, Amy Adams Takes a Listening Tour of the Universe S. Lansky color *Time* v188 no21 p65 N 21 2016

The Must List color *Entertainment Weekly* no1440 p3 N 18 2016

NOW PLAYING color *Entertainment Weekly* no1443 p48 D 9 2016

Only Connect R. DOUTHAT color *National Review* v68 no23 p42 D 19 2016

TALK TO THEM A. LANE cartoon *New Yorker* v92 no37 p78 N 14 2016

THOSE WONDROUS POWERS S. KLAWANS *Nation* v303 no23/24 p35 D 5 2016

Universal Translator D. EDELSTEIN img *New York* v49 no22 p104 O 31 2016

When They Came from Another World J. Gleick color diag *New York Review of Books* v64 no1 p28 Ja 19 2017

Worlds in Collision J. PODHORETZ color *Weekly Standard* v22 no12 p39 N 28 2016

Arrow (TV program)

Arrow D. Holbrook *TV Guide* v64 no40 p57 O 3 2016

ARROW N. Abrams color *Entertainment Weekly* no1474/1475 p73 Jl 21-28 2017

The Must List color *Entertainment Weekly* no1467 p2 My 26 2017

Arrow, Kenneth J.

Social norms as solutions bibl color *Science* v354 no6308 p42 O 7 2016

Arrowsmith, Cheryl H.

Global analysis of protein folding using massively parallel design, synthesis, and testing color diag *Science* v357 no6347 p168 Jl 14 2017

Arroyo, L.

Persistent effects of pre-Columbian plant domestication on Amazonian forest composition bibl chart graph map *Science* v355 no6328 p925 Mr 3 2017

Arroyo-Cabrales, Joaquín

Mexico's ambiguous invasive species plan bibl *Science* v355 no6329 p1033 Mr 10 2017

Arroyos

Arroyos N. G. Shannon *New York Times Magazine* p18 Mr 5 2017

Arscott, Christie Hunter

Pay Fairness Isn't Just About Teaching Employees to Negotiate *Harvard Business Review Digital Articles* p2 My 4 2016

Arscott, Simon

One Tough MUDDER N. Sullivan bw color *Esquire* p48 Big-BlackBook

Arsenals

See also

Nuclear weapons plants

Worldwide deployments of nuclear weapons, 2017. H. M. Kristensen and R. S. Norris bibl *Bulletin of the Atomic Scientists* v73 no5 p289 2017

Arsenault, Peter J.

Designing with Concrete in the 21st Century color *Architectural Record* v204 no12 p174 D 2016

The Evolving Workplace Environment color graph *Architectural Record* v205 no8 p138 Ag 2017

Exploring Resilient Building Design: Past experience with disasters inform current design decisions *Architectural Record* v205 no7 p134 Jl 2017

Lifelong Housing color *Architectural Record* v204 no12 p183 D 2016

A Look at What's New in Retail and Hospitality Design color graph *Architectural Record* v205 no8 p128 Ag 2017

Meeting New Water Quality Mandates in Health-Care Settings *Architectural Record* v205 no9 p170 S 2017

Mitigating Water Leaks around Windows in Wood-Framed Walls color diag *Architectural Record* v204 no12 p178 D 2016

The Modernization of Multifamily Housing: Providing luxury living without sacrificing affordability color graph *Architectural Record* v205 no5 p140 My 2017

State-of-the-Art Design in Higher Education *Architectural Record* v205 no9 p156 S 2017

System Solutions for Stadiums: More sophisticated structures call for high design with durable and safe performance color graph *Architectural Record* v205 no5 p152 My 2017

What's New in Fenestration? color diag *Architectural Record* v205 no2 p128 F 2017

Arsene, N.

Observation of a large-scale anisotropy in the arrival directions of cosmic rays above 8×10^{18} eV *Science* v357 no6357 p1266 S 22 2017

Arsenic content in groundwater

RESEARCH color *Science* v357 no6353 p768 Ag 25 2017

Arsenic in soils

Enzymes aid rice's arsenic defenses L. HAMERS color *Science News* v191 no5 p14 Mr 18 2017

Arsenic poisoning

Global Arsenic Contamination: Living With the Poison Nectar S. K. Singh and E. A. Stern bibl color map *Environment* v59 no2 p24 Mr/Ap 2017

Arsham, Daniel, 1980-

ULTRA VIOLET J. R. MARQUEZ *Atlanta* v57 no1 p29 My 2017

Arson

SAN FRANCISCO BURNING J. Ronson color *GQ: Gentlemen's Quarterly* v97 no7 p92 Jl 2017

Art

See also

Anachronistic art

Antiques

Architecture

Art & culture

Art & society

Art movements

Ceramics

Collectors & collecting

Commercial art

Decorative arts

Drawing

Folk art

Gender in art

Glass art

Hindu art & symbolism

Interior decoration

Mexican art

Mochica art

Outsider art

Palette (Color range)

Photography

Portraits

Public art

Rock art (Archaeology)

Sculpture

63-F-5 color *Art in America* v104 no10 p38 N 2016

All-American Angst G. DREVITCH *Psychology Today* v50 no1 p27 Ja/F 2017

ALL MY RIVERS ARE GONE: The Prologue K. LEE color *Arizona Highways* v93 no5 p48 My 2017

Benny Andrews: The Bicentennial Series color *Art in America* v104 no10 p169 N 2016

bless the mess K. M. REILLY *Parents* v92 no5 p118 My 2017

build bigger skills R. SAGIV RIEBLING *Parents* v92 no4 p128 Ap 2017

Dark Palette color *Art in America* v104 no10 p1 N 2016

EBONY color *Art in America* v104 no10 p7 N 2016

ELEMENTS OF CHANCE color *Art in America* v104 no10 p45 N 2016

ENGINEERED TO DECEIVE J. HALPERIN bw color diag *Wired* v25 no5 p92 My 2017

ENJOY A NATURAL CRAFTERNOON A. KINGLOFF color *Parents* v92 no11 p108 N 2017

HEADS UP JOHNSON *Treasures* v6 no5 p38 Ap/My 2017

A HOUSE TO SAVOR L. Christensen color *Harper's Bazaar* no3652 p171 Ap 2017

Indeterminate cartoon *Art in America* v104 no11 p47 D 2016

intention INSPIRATION [Cover story] M. RABBITT color *Yoga Journal* no290 p45 Mr 2017

Interlochen Center for the Arts focuses on performance and design and production *Stage Directions* v30 no3 p74 Mr 2017

Media Market color *Art in America* v104 no10 p170 N 2016

MEET ROBERT LEBSACK & KIMBERLY F. DAVIS: PROPRIETORS OF CHANCE ARTWORKS *Sea Magazine* v109 no4 p6 Ap 2017

ON Art L. Copan *Christian Century* v134 no16 p39 Ag 2 2017

PERMANENT COLLECTION G. MONTES color *Architectural Digest* v73 no12 p66 D 2016

PORTFOLIO color *Art in America* v104 no10 p114 N 2016

power by design T. EICHENSEHER color *Yoga Journal* no294 p17 S 2017

RAZZLE DOWN (SALVAGE) color *Art in America* v104 no10 p11 N 2016

Roots and Branches color *Art in America* v104 no10 p9 N 2016

Self-Portrait (Fright Wig) bw *Art in America* v104 no10 p47 N 2016

(sm)art idea C. Harris *Parents* v91 no11 p109 N 2016

sources *Architectural Digest* v74 no3 p144 Mr 2017

space to create L. FENTON color *Parents* v92 no5 p94 My 2017

Study of Hands color *Art in America* v104 no10 p28 N 2016

Tear Down This Wall M. Huston *Psychology Today* v49 no6 p9

N/D 2016

that's so cool! S. R. MURPHY *Parents* v92 no1 p32 Ja 2017

think inside the box *Parents* v91 no10 p68 O 2016

To The Editor A. Mason, M. Carney et al color *American Craft* v76 no6 p10 D 2016-Ja 2017

TribuT color *Art in America* v104 no10 p167 N 2016

Tula Telfair: Invented Landscapes color *Art in America* v104 no10 p55 N 2016

WHAT'S THE DEAL WITH ADULT COLORING BOOKS? E. SILBER *Psychology Today* v49 no5 p20 S/O 2016

Art & architecture

Trudie Styler's Tuscany color *AARP: The Magazine* v60 no3A p68 Ap/My 2017

Art & culture

California Dreaming: A contemporary visual journey color *Orion Magazine* v36 no1 p46 Ja/F 2017

Art & literature

In Praise of the Coffee Table Book B. W. PAYNE *Publishers Weekly* v264 no16 p72 Ap 17 2017

Art & photography

The Eyes of The World Are Watching Now M. DERY bw color *Publishers Weekly* v264 no15 p28 Ap 10 2017

Art & politics

Healthy Through History J. STAHL *Dance Magazine* v91 no7 p46 Jl 2017

Art & politics—United States

The Eyes of The World Are Watching Now M. DERY bw color *Publishers Weekly* v264 no15 p28 Ap 10 2017

Art & religion

#24 Freud's Last Words: Dreams Follow the Mouth L. Copan *Christian Century* v134 no12 p47 Je 7 2017

Churches see benefits in sponsoring art shows G. J. MacDonald *Christian Century* v134 no13 p16 Je 21 2017

Art & religion—Exhibitions

Landmark Luther exhibits explore his technological and theological legacy D. Gibson color *Christian Century* v133 no23 p16 N 9 2016

Art & science

Plot Lines D. Bishop color diag *American Craft* v77 no3 p34 Je/Jl 2017

Art & science—Exhibitions

Flim-flam and chicanery exposed at Winterthur color *Magazine Antiques* v184 no3 p35 My/Je 2017

Art & society

Common Good J. Lovelace color *American Craft* v77 no3 p26 Je/Jl 2017

In Praise of the Coffee Table Book B. W. PAYNE *Publishers Weekly* v264 no16 p72 Ap 17 2017

Next Gen Arts D. MICHAUD *Atlanta* v57 no6 p73 O 2017

Art & spirituality

#24 Freud's Last Words: Dreams Follow the Mouth L. Copan *Christian Century* v134 no12 p47 Je 7 2017

Art & war—Exhibitions

See also

World War I in art—Exhibitions

FLOWERS of DEATH E. Pochoda bw color *Magazine Antiques* v184 no3 p118 My/Je 2017

The moral blindness of war R. A. Schroth color *America* v217 no2 p49 Jl 24 2017

Art advocacy

BANNER YEAR A. CAMPBELL bw color *ARTnews* v115 no4 p110 Wint 2016/2017

Art appreciation

Art for App's Sake *Commentary* v142 no1 p1 Jl/Ag 2016

Art as an investment

Managing the Boss's Art Collection K. Kazakina color *Bloomberg Businessweek* no4520 p38 My 1 2017

Art auctions

ABOVE & BEYOND cartoon *New Yorker* v92 no35 p28 O 31 2016

ABOVE & BEYOND cartoon *New Yorker* v93 no31 p14 O 9 2017

ABOVE & BEYOND cartoon *New Yorker* v93 no5 p26 Mr 20 2017

Editor's Letter *ARTnews* v115 no3 p18 Fall 2016

HOUSE ARRE$T N. FREEMAN bw cartoon *ARTnews* v115 no3 p92 Fall 2016

Mackintosh Debris Turned to Art A. FIXSEN color *Architectural Record* v205 no3 p24 Mr 2017

Pablo's Pots A. BROWN color *Forbes* v198 no6 p32 N 8 2016

Sound and Vision J. SLATE bw color *Esquire* v166 no4 p27 N 2016

Art auctions—Moral & ethical aspects

To the Tipsy Guy on the Lido Deck! V. SILVER color *Bloomberg Businessweek* no4504 p50 D 19 2016

Art auctions—New York (State)

ABOVE & BEYOND cartoon *New Yorker* v92 no37 p28 N 14 2016

Art awards

Amara Hark-Weber A. Ranallo color *American Craft* v77 no3 p40 Je/Jl 2017

Art center design & construction

GRAND (I) PALACE K. MURRAY-BERGQUIST *Iceland Review* v55 no3 p52 My/Je 2017

Art centers

AUTHENTIC for the festival J. Coakley *Stage Directions* v29 no10 p22 O 2016

KENWOOD J. REESE color map *Chicago* v66 no1 p32 Ja 2017

'We were here first' K. PINCHIN color map *Canadian Geographic* v137 no3 p34 My 2017

Art centers—Design & construction

Back on Track C. ROUX color diag *Architectural Record* v205 no2 p80 F 2017

Art centers—Management

One for All: The Woodruff Arts Center's new CEO aims to boost arts groups citywide S. HENRY *Atlanta* v57 no6 p75 O 2017

Art centers—Ohio

POOL PARTY A. KONERMANN *Cincinnati Magazine* v50 no4 p21 Ja 2017

Art collecting

See also

Pottery collecting

Art criticism

EDITOR'S LETTER S. DOUGLAS color *ARTnews* v115 no4 p12 Wint 2016/2017

Art criticism—21st century

Some Perspective, Please L. PERRY *American Scholar* v86 no2 p105 Spr 2017

Art critics

John Ruskin Taught Victorian Readers and Travelers the Art of Cultivation D. Heitman *Humanities* v38 no1 p1 Wint 2017

MY LIFE AS A FAILED ARTIST J. SALTZ img *New York* v50 no8 p28 Ap 17 2017

Art dealers

See also

Antique dealers

David Hadjer H. MARTIN cartoon *Architectural Digest* v74 no4 p38 Ap 2017

Art Deco

DECO delight D. Pizzi color *Old House Journal* v45 no2 p14 Ap 2017

My favorite girl P. Poore color *Old House Journal* v45 no2 p8 Ap 2017

Art education

See also

Photography education

Defining quality in visual art education for young children: Building on the position statement of the Early Childhood Art Educators M. McClure, P. Tarr et al bibl *Arts Education Policy Review* v118 no3 p154 2017

Early childhood arts education in the United States: A special issue of Arts Education Policy Review A. M. Reynolds and W. H. Valerio bibl *Arts Education Policy Review* v118 no3 p133 2017

Language policy, language ideology, and visual art education for emergent bilingual students B. A. Thomas bibl *Arts Education Policy Review* v118 no4 p228 2017

Art education advocacy

A Blueprint for Successful Arts Education L. PERILLE *Education Digest* v82 no7 p26 Mr 2017

Art education in universities & colleges

Western Oregon University *Dance Magazine* v90 p109 2016/2017 Supplement College Guide

Art exhibitions

Lightly on the Land A. WEDER color diag *Architectural Record* v204 no12 p84 D 2016

The Lucas Museum of Lucas Arts Invites You to Appreciate George Lucas D. Leonard color *Bloomberg Businessweek* no4506 p42 Ja 9 2017

Private Practices H. GHORASHI and A. GREENBERGER bw cartoon chart color *ARTnews* v115 no3 p84 Fall 2016

Art museums—Evaluation

Beyond George Washington C. Ward bw cartoon color *Magazine Antiques* v184 no1 p188 Ja/F 2017

The Corona Rising C. J. Martin color *Art in America* v105 no3 p45 Mr 2017

The Middle Ages meets the Digital Age in Chicago color *Magazine Antiques* v184 no3 p26 My/Je 2017

NEWPORT M. SULLIVAN *Cincinnati Magazine* v50 no7 p33 Ap 2017

THE PUBLIC AS PRODUCER D. Gonzalez *Art in America* v104 no9 p82 O 2016

Summer School *Atlanta* v57 no2 p148 Je 2017

WATER WORKS J. FOUMBERG cartoon *Chicago* v66 no8 p40 Ag 2017

Art museums—Germany

Noble Spirit S. WALLIS color *Architectural Digest* no11 p62 N 1 2017

Art museums—History

A Legacy in Ruins: What now for Iraq's Mosul Museum, recently liberated from ISIS? C. OTTEN *American Scholar* v86 no3 p99 Summ 2017

Art museums—Humor

HONEST MUSEUM AUDIO TOUR R. CLEGG cartoon *New Yorker* v92 no40 p32 D 5 2016

Art museums—Maintenance & repair

Flat Broke P. SIMEK *D: The Magazine of Dallas* v43 no10 p88 O 2016

Art museums—New York (State)

"INVISIBLE ADVERSARIES" A. GREENBERGER color *ARTnews* v115 no4 p134 Wint 2016/2017

THE PUBLIC AS PRODUCER D. Gonzalez *Art in America* v104 no9 p82 O 2016

Art museums—New York (State)—New York

SILICON VALUES M. Pepi *Art in America* v104 no9 p90 O 2016

Art museums—Remodeling

Rafa Esparza E. Lyle color *Art in America* v105 no4 p23 Ap 2017

Art museums—United States

ART, HISTORY AND FUN D. HISLOP *Sea Magazine* v109 no1 pPNW-8 Ja 2017

SUMMERING M. P. Spencer color *Louisiana Life* v37 no5 p48 My/Je 2017

Art objects

GROWING INTERESTS S. F. Hood, K. S. Ivey et al cartoon *Magazine Antiques* v184 no1 p118 Ja/F 2017

When Life Imitates Artifacts C. CHOCANO img *New York* p75 Ja 9 2017

Who are you calling a tramp? L. M. Addison color *Magazine Antiques* v184 no1 p140 Ja/F 2017

Art previews

Art img *New York* v50 no17 p120 Ag 21 2017

Object Lessons D. Green color *Weekly Standard* v22 no37 p37 Je 5 2017

Art publishing

Sources *Lapham's Quarterly* v10 no3 p220 Summ 2017

Art reproduction

UNKNOWN MAKERS A. Provan *Art in America* v104 no9 p138 O 2016

Art sales & prices

See also

Comic books, strips, etc.—Sales & prices

Folk art sales & prices

Hating on Canadian art M. CAMPBELL *Maclean's* v130 no4 p12 My 2017

Art schools

ART SCHOOLS *Art in America* v105 no1 p94 Ja 2017

Art teachers

An interview with Olivia Gude about connecting school and community arts practice J. Berglin *Arts Education Policy Review* v118 no1 p60 2017

Art thefts—Recovery

THE PURLOINED LETTER B. Freed *Washingtonian Magazine* v52 no6 p18 Mr 2017

Art thefts—Recovery—History

Stolen Art That Made a Return T. John color *Time* v188 no15 p8 O 17 2016

Art therapy

Connect the Dots N. HORVATH cartoon color *Prevention* p96 Mr 2017

Art treasures in war

FLASHBACK *MHQ: Quarterly Journal of Military History* v29 no2 p4 Wint 2017

Art woodwork

ESSENTIAL TRUTH S. SARGENT *Virginia Living* v15 no1 p31 D 2016

Art workshops (Adult education)

Small Ant Workshop B. MARTIN color *American Craft* v76 no6 p14 D 2016-Ja 2017

Art—21st century—Exhibitions

BANK SHOT M. Singer cartoon *New Yorker* v92 no30 p22 S 26 2016

National Treasure S. COCHRAN color *Architectural Digest* no5 p62 My 2017

Shows to See color *American Craft* v77 no2 p18 Ap/My 2017

snapshot A. Klimoski *Architectural Record* v204 no11 p216 N 2016

Artan, Abdul Razak Ali

The Not-Talking Cure S. SCHULMAN color *Weekly Standard* v22 no15 p11 D 19 2016

ARTAVIA, DAVID

50 FOR 50: EVERY STATE HAS ITS OWN LGBT LEADERS AND HEROES. 50 CURRENT LGBT LEADERS SHARE THEIR STATE'S HEROES map *Advocate* no1091 p98 Je/Jl 2017

8 MILLION FOLLOWERS CANT BE WRONG: Why Tyler Oakley has an army of YouTube fans *Advocate* no1093 p25 O/N 2017

ART, ACTIVISM & AIDS: THESE DECADES WERE FILLED WITH LGBT CHANGE, BUT THE IMPACT OF AIDS WAS THE BIGGEST bw *Advocate* no1091 p87 Je/Jl 2017

THE BIGGEST HOMOPHOBES: THE LGBT RIGHTS MOVEMENT HAS HAD ITS SHARE OF VILLAINS color *Advocate* no1091 p102 Je/Jl 2017

FUN HOUSE color *Advocate* no1090 p20 Ap 2017

GINGER SNAPS: The Walking Dead's bi star on being the change he wants to see in Hollywood *Advocate* no1093 p28 O/N 2017

GOODBYE, BOMBSHELL: Aleshia Brevard was one of the first trans actresses on the silver screen *Advocate* no1093 p13 O/N 2017

MAKING THAT KITTY PURR color *Advocate* no1090 p44 Ap 2017

SHOWTIME'S FORAY INTO GENDERLESS TV color *Advocate* no1090 p36 Ap 2017

SOMEBODY TO LOVE color *Advocate* no1091 p34 Je/Jl 2017

TALKING ABOUT MY GENERATION: CONNOR FRANTA MADE MILLIONS OFF BEING HIMSELF, AND IT'S ONLY THE BEGINNING color *Advocate* no1091 p78 Je/Jl 2017

WICKED GOOD TIME: New Orleans a decadent location to spend Halloween *Advocate* no1093 p62 O/N 2017

Art—Canada

Hating on Canadian art M. CAMPBELL *Maclean's* v130 no4 p12 My 2017

Art—Collectors & collecting

See also

Women art collectors

FROM PALACE TO TANK B. POLLACK color diag *ARTnews* v115 no3 p128 Fall 2016

HEY, BIG SPENDERS J. FOUMBERG bw color *Chicago* v65 no12 p50 D 2016

Lone star D. B. Warren bw cartoon *Magazine Antiques* v184 no1 p160 Ja/F 2017

What do you collect and why? G. HUBERMAN, H. H. TIDWELL et al color *American Craft* v77 no2 p20 Ap/My 2017

The World's Top 200 COLLECTORS bw cartoon chart color *ARTnews* v115 no3 p76 Fall 2016

Art—Congresses

EVENTS color *Magazine Antiques* v184 no5 p114 S/O 2017

Art—Conservation & restoration

Editor's Letter *ARTnews* v115 no3 p18 Fall 2016

Where science meets art R. Ploeger and A. Shugar bibl bw color *Science* v354 no6314 p826 N 18 2016

XAVIER GONZALEZ J. R. KEMP cartoon *Louisiana Life* v37 no2 p32 N/D 2016

Art—Digitization

MARK LECKEY S. Sandhu color *Art in America* v104 no11 p88 D 2016

Arte Publico Press (Company)

Nicolás Kanellos Wins Tejano Association for Historical Preservation Award L. Ahuile color *Publishers Weekly* v264 no23 p16 Je 5 2017

Artemisinin

The 'Super-Malaria' on the Rise In Southeast Asia T. John color *Time* v190 no14 p11 O 9 2017

ARTERBURN, JOE

A CHRISTMAS RIFLE cartoon *Outdoor Life* v224 no1 p114 D 2016/Ja 2017

CODE'S KNIFE cartoon *Outdoor Life* v224 no6 p82 Ag 2017

THE DISTANCE cartoon *Outdoor Life* v224 no8 p78 O 2017

EEB AND SCOOB *Outdoor Life* v224 no3 p78 Ap 2017

HOT CHOCOLATE cartoon *Outdoor Life* v223 no9 p86 N 2016

IRREGULAR JOE cartoon *Outdoor Life* v224 no4 p78 My 2017

NEXT-LEVEL TURKEY CALLS color *Outdoor Life* v224 no3 p50 Ap 2017

THE SCRODE-HOLE MYSTERY *Outdoor Life* v224 no2 p98 F/Mr 2017

SHOOTING MAGIC cartoon *Outdoor Life* v224 no7 p78 S 2017

TARNISHED TROPHIES *Outdoor Life* v224 no5 p102 Je/Jl 2017

TICKLE TUMMY HILL *Outdoor Life* v224 no9 p78 N 2017

Arterial physiology

Keeping Your Arteries Young: Help your arteries age gracefully with a healthy diet and lifestyle [Cover story] *Tufts University Health & Nutrition Letter* v35 no8 p1 O 2017

Arteries

FOR BRAIN HEALTH chart color *AARP: The Magazine* v59 no3A p39 Ap/My 2016

Arteta, Miguel

Beatriz at Dinner Means Well but Flags Before the Last Course S. Zacharek color *Time* v189 no23 p50 Je 19 2017

Beatriz at Dinner V. LUCCA color *Film Comment* v53 no3 p68 My/Je 2017

A Masseuse in Newport Beach M. Rochlin color *AARP: The Magazine* v60 no4A p13 Je/Jl 2017

Art—Exhibitions—Abstracts

ART cartoon *New Yorker* v92 no43 p8 Ja 2 2017

Art—Exhibitions—California

"MADE IN L.A. 2016" E. RAPPAPORT bw color *ARTnews* v115 no4 p128 Wint 2016/2017

Arthos, James

Sustained virologic control in SIV+ macaques after antiretroviral and α4β7 antibody therapy bibl graph *Science* v354 no6309 p197 O 14 2016

Arthritis

See also

 Gout

 Osteoarthritis

The Agenda color *Men's Health* v31 no10 p8 D 2016

Diagnosis L. Sanders *New York Times Magazine* p18 S 3 2017

EASE ARTHRITIS IN PETS J. Szabo color *Amazing Wellness* p82 Fall 2017

LIVING BETTER WITH ARTHRITIS J. HOGAN REDMOND *Cincinnati Magazine* v50 no7 p90 Ap 2017

LOOKING FOR HELP B. LUT color *New Orleans Magazine* v51 no3 p30 Ja 2017

My BIG Foot D. Garner color *Esquire* p68 Ap 2017

SELF-HEALTH M. Bryan cartoon *O, The Oprah Magazine* p97 My 2017

Arthritis Foundation

JINGLE ALL THE WAY K. Massicot cartoon *New Orleans Magazine* v51 no1 p38 N 2016

Arthritis in animals

7 Arthritis risk factors [Cover story] C. Barakat color *Equus* no478 p42 Jl 2017

HEALING HANDS L. F. Prater *Successful Farming* v115 no4 p63 Mr 2017

Keep Them Moving! J. McCAFFERY color *Prevention* v69 no4 p92 Ap 2017

Arthritis prevention

Are Your Joints Healthy? V. TWEED color *Better Nutrition* v79 no10 p80 O 2017

Arthritis—Risk factors

Are Your Joints Healthy? V. TWEED color *Better Nutrition* v79 no10 p80 O 2017

Arthritis—Treatment

A RESPONSE TO PAIN J. YALE color *Maclean's* v130 no3 p48 Ap 2017

Arthropoda

See also

 Insects

Overlooked mass migration spotted S. MILIUS cartoon color *Science News* v191 no2 p12 F 4 2017

Arthropoda ecology

The importance of being modular M. Sales-Pardo diag *Science* v357 no6347 p128 Jl 14 2017

Arthroscopy

advice for dancers L. HAMILTON *Dance Magazine* v91 no9 p28 S 2017

Arthur, James

In a Rented Cabin in the Haliburton Highlands, Oriented toward Algonquin Park J. ARTHUR *Walrus* v14 no9 p38 N 2017

Arthur, King

In Search of King Arthur's Roots G. TARLACH color *Discover* v38 no1 p86 Ja/F 2017

Arthur, King, in motion pictures

50 YEARS OF ARTHUR K. P. Sullivan color *Entertainment Weekly* no1450 p37 Ja 27 2017

Arthur, Lake (Pa.)

PECKING ORDER color *Louisiana Life* v38 no1 p8 S/O 2017

Arthur, Patrick Kobina

Adaptation *Science* v356 no6335 p243 Ap 21 2017

Arthur, Sarah

The Year of Small Things: Radical Faith for the Rest of Us G. Williams *Christian Century* v134 no15 p42 Jl 19 2017

Arthur, Wallace

The origins of intelligent life M. Huerta color *Science* v357 no6351 p556 Ag 11 2017

Arthur M. Sackler Gallery (Smithsonian Institution)

Lights. Camera. Peacocks: A unique Smithsonian museum devoted to Asian arts reopens with an innovative new film that turns the building inside out A. Diamond *Smithsonian* v48 no6 p22 O 2017

Artichokes

soul FOOD L. Ladoceour and R. Rinaldi color *Yoga Journal* no288 p75 D 2016

Artificial Christmas trees

Artificial Intelligence J. BOTTUM color *Weekly Standard* v22 no16 p5 D 26 2016

Artificial chromosomes

Design of a synthetic yeast genome S. M. Richardson, L. A. Mitchell et al bibl chart color graph *Science* v355 no6329 p1040 Mr 10 2017

Artificial chromosomes—Research

3D organization of synthetic and scrambled chromosomes G. Mercy, J. Mozziconacci et al diag *Science* v355 no6329 p1050 Mr 10 2017

BUILDING ON NATURE'S DESIGN [Cover story] L. M. Zahn and G. Riddihough color *Science* v355 no6329 p1038 Mr 10 2017

Deep functional analysis of synII, a 770-kilobase synthetic yeast chromosome Y. Shen, Y. Wang et al diag *Science* v355 no6329 p1047 Mr 10 2017

Engineering the ribosomal DNA in a megabase synthetic chromosome W. Zhang, G. Zhao et al diag *Science* v355 no6329 p1049 Mr 10 2017

Synthesis, debugging, and effects of synthetic chromosome consolidation: synVI and beyond L. A. Mitchell, A. Wang et al color *Science* v355 no6329 p1045 Mr 10 2017

Artificial flies

SPEED BUGS J. Cermele color *Field & Stream* v121 no7 p26 D

2016/Ja 2017

THE TIE THAT BINDS J. BRANDT color *Outdoor Life* v224 no8 p66 O 2017

Artificial fur

FIND YOUR PERFECT Skirt Suit & Faux-Fur Collar color *InStyle* v23 no12 p113 N 2016

Artificial habitats

Preamble *Orion Magazine* v36 no2 p1 Mr/Ap 2017

Small Victories M. Moses bw color *American Craft* v77 no3 p24 Je/Jl 2017

Artificial hibernation

nap your way to Mars J. Lederman cartoon *Popular Science* v289 no5 p18 S/O 2017

Artificial implant complications

IMPLANTS color *Prevention* v69 no9 p10 O 2017

Artificial implants

Chip Implants Make It Impossible to Forget Your Keys C. Britschgi bw *Reason* v48 no7 p64 D 2016

COULD NEW TECH (FINALLY) DESTROY THE PILLBOX? E. Fry color *Fortune* v176 no1 p12 Jl 1 2017

The future of bionic dynamos C. Dagdeviren bibl color *Science* v354 no6316 p1109-A D 2 2016

Innovation Synthetic Cartilage M. Belfiore bw color diag *Bloomberg Businessweek* no4518 p37 Ap 10 2017

REVERSING Paralysis A. REGALADO color *MIT Technology Review* v120 no2 p82 Mr/Ap 2017

Stellar storyteller color *Science News* v191 no6 p31 Ap 1 2017

Artificial implants—Evaluation

NEW CARDIOVASCULAR PROCEDURE V. Prevish *Cincinnati Magazine* v50 no12 p80 S 2017

Artificial implants—Research

Bypassing Paralysis Altogether J. KEATS color *Discover* v38 no1 p81 Ja/F 2017

Artificial insemination (Animals)

February Madness C. Reich *Arabian Horse World* v57 no5 p232 F 2017

THE HYBRID FACTOR B. Bower color map *Science News* v190 no8 p22 O 15 2016

Artificial intelligence

See also
> Machine learning
> Neural networks (Computer science)

3 Ways Companies Are Building a Business Around AI Q. Hardy *Harvard Business Review Digital Articles* p2 2017

AD SENSES: THE NEW BODY LANGUAGE A. POWELL cartoon *Wired* v25 no8 p22 Ag 2017

AI Apparently Is for Real J. M. LAING and T. ATWOOD *USA Today Magazine* v145 no2862 p35 Mr 2017

AI Can Be a Troublesome Teammate K. Gray *Harvard Business Review Digital Articles* p2 Jl 20 2017

THE AI DETECTIVES P. Voosen color diag *Science* v357 no6346 p22 Jl 7 2017

AI Is Going to Change the 80/20 Rule M. Schrage color *Harvard Business Review Digital Articles* p2 F 28 2017

AI Is the Future of Cybersecurity, for Better and for Worse R. V. Yampolskiy *Harvard Business Review Digital Articles* p2 My 8 2017

AI's early proving ground: the hunt for new particles A. Cho color *Science* v357 no6346 p20 Jl 7 2017

AI'S KILLER APP? DUH ... MARKETING D. Lyons color *Fortune* v175 no5 p40 Ap 1 2017

AI's Real Risk M. Schrage *Harvard Business Review Digital Articles* p2 D 16 2015

An AI stereotype catcher A. G. Greenwald color *Science* v356 no6334 p133 Ap 14 2017

AI WILL FIND ET C. DILLOW *Popular Science* v288 no6 p30 N/D 2016

AlphaGo and the Declining Advantage of Big Companies H. Yu *Harvard Business Review Digital Articles* p2 Mr 24 2016

Artificial Intelligence Can't Replace Hard-Earned Knowledge - Yet W. Swap and D. Leonard *Harvard Business Review Digital Articles* p2 N 17 2014

Artificial intelligence, in so many words M. Hutson *Science* v357 no6346 p19 Jl 7 2017

Artificial Intelligence Is Almost Ready for Business B. Power *Harvard Business Review Digital Articles* p2 Mr 19 2015

ARTIFICIAL INTELLIGENCE, REAL FOOD *Harvard Business Review Digital Articles* p30 Jl 1 2017

Artificial intelligence ups its game J. Bohannon color *Science* v354 no6319 p1518 D 23 2016

(Automated) planning for tomorrow: Will artificial intelligence get smarter? E. M. Geist bibl *Bulletin of the Atomic Scientists* v73 no2 p80 Mr 2017

BETTING ON AI B. O'Keefe diag *Fortune* v175 no3 p144 Mr 1 2017

Betting the futureon artificial intelligence F. Markus color *Motor Trend* v69 no5 p22 My 2017

The Bot That Bluffed Me J. Brustein color *Bloomberg Businessweek* no4511 p29 F 13 2017

Can AI Ever Be as Curious as Humans? T. Chamorro-Premuzic and B. Taylor color *Harvard Business Review Digital Articles* p2 Ap 5 2017

Caring Computers [Cover story] J. KEATS color *Discover* v38 no4 p10 My 2017

Combing the genome for the roots of autism E. Pennisi color *Science* v357 no6346 p25 Jl 7 2017

The Competitive Landscape for Machine Intelligence S. Zilis and J. Cham *Harvard Business Review Digital Articles* p2 N 2 2016

THE CYBERSCIENTIST J. Bohannon color diag *Science* v357 no6346 p18 Jl 7 2017

Data Scientists Don't Scale S. Frankel *Harvard Business Review Digital Articles* p2 My 22 2015

Deep Learning Will Radically Change the Ways We Interact with Technology A. Singh bw color diag *Harvard Business Review Digital Articles* p2 Ja 30 2017

DeepStack: Expert-level artificial intelligence in heads-up no-limit poker [Cover story] M. Moravčík, M. Schmid et al chart diag *Science* v356 no6337 p508 My 5 2017

Elon Musk's FUTURE SHOCK M. DOWD bw color *Vanity Fair* v59 no5 p116 Ap 2017

Emergent consciousness decoded J. LaSala *Physics Today* v69 no12 p52 D 2016

features cartoon *Foreign Policy* no222 p29 Ja/F 2017

From the Editor *MIT Technology Review* v120 no2 p2 Mr/Ap 2017

The Future of Humanitarianism [Cover story] M. J. MOONEY bw color *Popular Mechanics* p13 S 2017

Go, Go AlphaGo C. ENGELKING color *Discover* v38 no1 p37 Ja/F 2017

Hackathons Aren't Just for Coders E. Spaulding and G. Caimi *Harvard Business Review Digital Articles* p2 Ap 1 2016

Hiring Your First Chief AI Officer A. Ng *Harvard Business Review Digital Articles* p2 N 11 2016

How AI Is Getting More Human L. Eadicicco color *Time* v188 no27-28 p96 D 26 2016

How AI Will Change the Way We Make Decisions A. Agrawal, J. Gans et al *Harvard Business Review Digital Articles* p2 Jl 26 2017

How algorithms can analyze the mood of the masses M. Hutson *Science* v357 no6346 p23 Jl 7 2017

How Artificial Intelligence Will Redefine Management V. Kolbjørnsrud, R. Amico et al *Harvard Business Review Digital Articles* p2 N 2 2016

How Companies Are Already Using AI S. Ramaswamy *Harvard Business Review Digital Articles* p2 Ap 14 2017

How Harley-Davidson Used Artificial Intelligence to Increase New York Sales Leads by 2,930% *Harvard Business Review Digital Articles* p2 My 30 2017

How One Clothing Company Blends AI and Human Expertise H. J. Wilson, P. Daugherty et al *Harvard Business Review Digital Articles* p2 N 21 2016

How P&G and American Express Are Approaching AI T. H. Davenport and R. Bean *Harvard Business Review Digital Articles* p2 Mr 31 2017

How to Prepare the Next Generation for Jobs in the AI Economy D. Kosbie, A. W. Moore et al color *Harvard Business Review Digital Articles* p2 Je 5 2017

How to Win with Automation (Hint: It's Not Chasing Efficiency) G. Satell color *Harvard Business Review Digital Articles* p2 Mr 30 2017

The Humans Working Behind the AI Curtain M. L. Gray and S. Suri bw *Harvard Business Review Digital Articles* p2 Ja 9 2017

If Your Company Isn't Good at Analytics, It's Not Ready for AI N.

Artificial intelligence in business

Artificial intelligence in engineering

Artificial intelligence in industry

Artificial intelligence in medicine

See also
Diagnostic expert systems
The AI Doctor Orders More Tests M. Bergen cartoon *Bloomberg Businessweek* no4526 p39 Je 12 2017
To Get Consumers to Trust AI, Show Them Its Benefits E. Enkel *Harvard Business Review Digital Articles* p2 Ap 17 2017

Artificial intelligence in the military
Should Artificial Intelligence Be Regulated? A. ETZIONI and O. ETZIONI *Issues in Science & Technology* v33 no4 p32 Summ 2017

Artificial intelligence research
Artificial intelligence needs smart senses to be useful *Science News* v190 no10 p2 N 12 2016
CULTIVATING COMMON SENSE C. ENGELKING cartoon color graph *Discover* v38 no3 p32 Ap 2017
The Dark Secret at the Heart of AI [Cover story] W. KNIGHT bw color *MIT Technology Review* v120 no3 p54 My/Je 2017
General Electric E. Woyke bw color il *MIT Technology Review* v120 no4 p78 Jl/Ag 2017
Life, Or Something Like It A. Vance color *Bloomberg Businessweek* no4537 p42 S 11 2017
Who Is Winning the AI Race? chart graph *MIT Technology Review* v120 no4 p20 Jl/Ag 2017

Artificial intelligence tests
See also
Turing test
THE NEW TURING TESTS J. Pavlus color *Scientific American* v316 no3 p61 Mr 2017

Artificial intelligence—Business applications
The age of the cyborg J. Stray color *Columbia Journalism Review* p70 Fall/Wint 2016
AI Is Getting Good Enough to Delegate the Work It Can't Do K. Barr *Harvard Business Review Digital Articles* p2 My 12 2015
AlphaGo and the Limits of Machine Intuition Dae Ryun Chang *Harvard Business Review Digital Articles* p2 Mr 18 2016
How Companies Are Benefiting from "Lite" Artificial Intelligence S. Earley *Harvard Business Review Digital Articles* p2 Jl 19 2016
Machine Intelligence Will Let Us All Work Like CEOs S. Zilis *Harvard Business Review Digital Articles* p2 Je 13 2016
Reimagining the Boardroom for an Age of Virtual Reality and AI D. Lancefield and C. Gagliardi *Harvard Business Review Digital Articles* p2 Ap 3 2015
WHAT SKILLS WILL KEEP YOU AHEAD OF AI? graph img *Harvard Business Review* v95 no2 p36 Mr/Ap 2017

Artificial intelligence—Economic aspects
Artificial Intelligence Goes Microbial L. BRODY bw chart color *Forbes* v199 no5 p82 My 16 2017

Artificial intelligence—Equipment & supplies
Artificial Intelligence: Not Your Father's Toolbox: Some new artificial intelligence business tools to help park and rec agencies J. Dysart *Parks & Recreation* v52 no8 p72 Ag 2017

Artificial intelligence—Finance
ANNUAL ARTIFICIAL INTELLIGENCE DEALS diag *Fortune* v175 no2 p11 F 1 2017

Artificial intelligence—Government policy
The Obama Administration's Roadmap for AI Policy A. Agrawal, J. Gans et al *Harvard Business Review Digital Articles* p2 D 21 2016
"The Relentless Pace of Automation" D. Rotman color graph *MIT Technology Review* v120 no2 p92 Mr/Ap 2017

Artificial intelligence—History
50, 100 & 150 YEARS AGO bw color *Scientific American* v315 no3 p91 S 2016

Artificial intelligence—Industrial applications
4 Models for Using AI to Make Decisions M. Schrage color *Harvard Business Review Digital Articles* p2 Ja 27 2017
How People Will Use AI to Do Their Jobs Better H. J. Wilson and C. Bataller *Harvard Business Review Digital Articles* p2 My 27 2015
What Artificial Intelligence Can and Can't Do Right Now A. Ng *Harvard Business Review Digital Articles* p2 N 9 2016

Artificial intelligence—Moral & ethical aspects
Teaching an Algorithm to Understand Right and Wrong G. Satell *Harvard Business Review Digital Articles* p2 N 15 2016

Artificial intelligence—Social aspects

See also
Human-artificial intelligence interaction
AI That Dreams Up Drugs T. Simonite il *MIT Technology Review* v120 no1 p18 Ja/F 2017
The great equalizer P. NOWAK color *Maclean's* v130 no4 p60 My 2017
Making AI Smarter, Faster W. Knight *MIT Technology Review* v120 no1 p22 Ja/F 2017
The Smartest Machines Are Playing Games J. Kahn color *Bloomberg Businessweek* no4517 p34 Ap 3 2017

Artificial intelligence—Software
The $200 All-Seeing Line Judge A. Vance color *Bloomberg Businessweek* no4513 p37 Mr 6 2017
AI Speed-Reading For the Masses A. Vance cartoon *Bloomberg Businessweek* no4512 p33 F 20 2017
AI With Chinese Characteristics D. Ramli and A. Webb color diag *Bloomberg Businessweek* no4515 p38 Mr 20 2017
Artificial intelligence bests poker pros E. CONOVER color *Science News* v191 no6 p12 Ap 1 2017
Will AI Companies Make Any Money? T. H. Davenport *Harvard Business Review Digital Articles* p2 Jl 12 2016

Artificial islands
Cool Inventions C. M. TOMLIN color *National Geographic Kids* no472 p7 Ag 2017

Artificial livers
Mini-livers reveal fine details of organ development E. Pennisi color *Science* v356 no6343 p1109 Je 16 2017

Artificial pancreases
The Artificial Pancreas Gets Real E. Sheng bw *Scientific American* v315 no5 p14 N 2016
A Body Computer to Manage Insulin L. PANDELL color *AARP: The Magazine* v30 no6A p32 O/N 2017

Artificial photosynthesis
Biology leads the race to turn sunlight into fuels D. Kramer *Physics Today* v70 no4 p30 Ap 2017
Photosynthesis reinvented L. Hamers color diag *Science News* v192 no6 p20 O 14 2017

Artificial plant growing media
HOME HYDROPONICS D. KLUKO color diag *Popular Mechanics* p85 F 2017

Artificial satellite launching
The Developing Space Race T. John color *Time* v188 no14 p8 O 10 2016

Artificial satellites
See also
Artificial satellites in telecommunication
Explorer 1 (Artificial satellite)
Low earth orbit satellites
Japan reboots x-ray probe— and mission management D. Normile color diag *Science* v354 no6314 p814 N 18 2016
Quantum entanglement reaches new heights: The satellite-based distribution of entangled photons to cities 1200 km apart bolsters prospects for a global quantum communication network A. G. Smart *Physics Today* v70 no8 p14 Ag 2017
A 'Teleportation' to Outer Space J. Kluger color *Time* v190 no4 p13 Jl 24 2017
The View From Above: What do we lose when a research satellite goes dark? J. Gertner *New York Times Magazine* p54 S 17 2017
Weather Front M. Branom *Weatherwise* v70 no2 p6 Mr/Ap 2017

Artificial satellites in navigation
See also
Global Positioning System
A BRIEF HISTORY OF GPS G. Barber and A. Sammon cartoon color *Mother Jones* v41 no6 p54 N/D 2016

Artificial satellites in remote sensing
THEY CAME FOR OUTER SPACE A. Vance color graph map *Bloomberg Businessweek* no4529 p40 Jl 3 2017

Artificial satellites in telecommunication
Skymate Mazu App and mSeries Satellite Communications System J. Y. WOOD color *Power & Motoryacht* v34 no10 p56 O 2017

Artificial satellites in telecommunication—Equipment & supplies—Evaluation
Garmin InReach SE+ and Explorer+ Satellite Communication Devices J. Y. WOOD color *Power & Motoryacht* v33 no3 p48 Mr 2017

The University of Southern Mississippi *Dance Magazine* v90 p100 2016/2017 Supplement College Guide

University of South Florida *Dance Magazine* v90 p99 2016/2017 Supplement College Guide

The University of Texas at Austin *Dance Magazine* v90 p102 2016/2017 Supplement College Guide

Arts fund raising

Arts, Culture & Entertainment *Virginia Living* p27 2017 Best 20of Virginia

Arts in education

The art of partnerships D. H. Bowen and B. Kisida color graph il *Phi Delta Kappan* v98 no7 p8 Ap 2017

A districtwide commitment to arts integration E. Mackin, R. Mackin et al color il *Phi Delta Kappan* v98 no7 p29 Ap 2017

Arts in social service

Power of Art L. Judge cartoon *Alternatives Journal (AJ) - Canada's Environmental Voice* v42 no3 p68 2016

Arts—Congresses

The Conference Skinny B. D. Coleman bw color *Arts & Crafts Homes & the Revival* v12 no5 p20 Wint 2018

Arts—Evaluation

The QUEEN of COOL L. S. FORD *Texas Monthly* v45 no8 p66 Ag 2017

Arts—Exhibitions

See also

Art exhibitions

Ai Weiwei B. Luscombe color *Time* v190 no16/17 p112 O 23 2017

The Art of Repetition M. WAKIM color *Los Angeles Magazine* v62 no10 p86 O 2017

Arts, Culture & Entertainment *Virginia Living* p27 2017 Best 20of Virginia

Fall Preview A. K. Scott color *New Yorker* v93 no25 p10 Ag 28 2017

LA SOCIAL *Los Angeles Magazine* v62 no9 p117 S 2017

Moses in Mexico [Cover story] J. Fenton color *New York Review of Books* v64 no15 p12 O 12 2017

RAINBOW SHOWERS: An exhibition exceptionally rich in color our attention at the National Gallery of Iceland P. STEFÁNSSON *Iceland Review* v55 no4 p12 Jl/Ag 2017

SOUTH BEACH IN SOUTHWEST B. L. Smith *Washingtonian Magazine* v52 no1 p47 O 2016

Viva Tropicália! L. Rohter color *New York Review of Books* v64 no14 p28 S 28 2017

Arts—Exhibitions—Reviews

Acquisitions & mergers: A new exhibition at the Craft and Folk Art Museum in Los Angeles is the latest showcase for the powerful work of assemblage artist Betye Saar M. Slenske bw color *Magazine Antiques* v184 no4 p84 Jl/Ag 2017

ZERO GRAVITY B. SCHWABSKY color *Nation* v305 no6 p32 S 11 2017

Arts—Finance

Bill de Blasio, Culture-meister B. SWAIM color *Weekly Standard* v22 no46 p14 Ag 14 2017

Save the Arts, Save America L. Lalami *Nation* v304 no13 p10 Ap 17 2017

Art—Societies, etc.

RACING MAGPIE *South Dakota Magazine* v32 no6 p77 Mr/Ap 2017

Arts—Political aspects

See also

Music—Political aspects

Creative Reconstruction M. ATWOOD il *Nation* v304 no4 p15 F 6 2017

Art—Study & teaching

Adding Value to Learning [Cover story] K. JAMIL *Islamic Horizons* v46 no2 p28 Mr/Ap 2017

A Blueprint for Successful Arts Education L. PERILLE *Education Digest* v82 no7 p26 Mr 2017

Community arts: (Re)contextualizing the narrative of teaching and learning R. H. Schlemmer bibl *Arts Education Policy Review* v118 no1 p27 2017

Creating community from the inside out: A concentric perspective on collective artmaking C. Blatt-Gross bibl *Arts Education Policy Review* v118 no1 p51 2017

A districtwide commitment to arts integration E. Mackin, R. Mackin et al color il *Phi Delta Kappan* v98 no7 p29 Ap 2017

The eugenics movement and its impact on art education in the United States T. Hunter-Doniger bibl *Arts Education Policy Review* v118 no2 p83 2017

Let's get rid of art education in schools D. Gregory color *Phi Delta Kappan* v98 no7 p21 Ap 2017

MODEL BEHAVIOR T. McCarthy cartoon *New Yorker* v92 no32 p72 O 10 2016

On the goals and outcomes of arts education R. Heller color *Phi Delta Kappan* v98 no7 p15 Ap 2017

Research, practice, and policy connections: The ArtPlay case study R. Brown and N. Jeanneret bibl chart diag *Arts Education Policy Review* v118 no1 p37 2017

The rise of creative youth development D. Montgomery bibl *Arts Education Policy Review* v118 no1 p1 2017

A Way of Knowing bw *American Craft* v76 no6 p8 D 2016-Ja 2017

Where Making Matters J. Lovelace and M. R. Leach color *American Craft* v76 no6 p66 D 2016-Ja 2017

See also

Painting—Study & teaching

Music—Instruction & study

Arts—United States

DISOWNING IVANKA N. FREEMAN cartoon color *ARTnews* v116 no1 p98 Spr 2017

To All Tomorrow's Parties A. RUSSETH bw cartoon *ARTnews* v116 no1 p26 Spr 2017

Trump Can Thank the Arts for His Wealth K. Finley *Time* v189 no4 p29 F 6 2017

Wait-What Was That?! A. Greenberger and A. Russeth bw color *ARTnews* v116 no1 p96 Spr 2017

YOU'VE GOTTA SEE THIS! B. POLLACK cartoon color *ARTnews* v116 no1 p72 Spr 2017

Art—Themes, motives

See also

Animals in art

Food in art

Painting—Themes, motives

Sculpture—Themes, motives

Works of art in art

Consumed Culture R. Aima color *Art in America* v105 no1 p29 Ja 2017

Artun, Omer

What Lilly Pulitzer Learned About Marketing to Millennials *Harvard Business Review Digital Articles* p2 Mr 31 2016

Artyomov, Maxim N.

The microbial metabolite desaminotyrosine protects from influenza through type I interferon graph *Science* v357 no6350 p498 Ag 4 2017

Artz, Benjamin

If Your Boss Could Do Your Job, You're More Likely to Be Happy at Work *Harvard Business Review Digital Articles* p2 D 29 2016

Arudpragasam, Anuk

A Day in the Life of a Refugee R. FREEMAN *New York Times Book Review* p15 O 9 2016

Arulanantham, Ahilan—Interviews

Civil Rights And Trump G. KAHN *Los Angeles Magazine* p98 Ap 2017

Arundel (England)

Arunded - In the Shadow of the Castle *British Heritage Travel* v37 no6 p74 N/D 2016

Arundel Castle (Arundel, England)

Arunded - In the Shadow of the Castle *British Heritage Travel* v37 no6 p74 N/D 2016

Arussy, Lior

When and Why to Part Ways with a Customer *Harvard Business Review Digital Articles* p2 F 13 2015

ARVANITIS, JIM

The Pankration Flow bw color *Black Belt* v55 no3 p54 Ap/My 2017

Arvidsson, Nils

SOUTH OF THE BOARDERS M. Georges cartoon color *Snowboarder* v29 no5 p64 Ja 2017

Arylation

Arylation of hydrocarbons enabled by organosilicon reagents and weakly coordinating anions B. Shao, A. L. Bagdasarian et al diag *Science* v355 no6332 p1403 Mr 31 2017

Palladium-catalyzed carbon-sulfur or carbon-phosphorus bond metathesis by reversible arylation Z. Lian, B. N. Bhawal et al diag *Science* v356 no6342 p1059 Je 9 2017

Arzon, Robin

A Thing for Bling D. ZICKL color *Runner's World* v52 no7 p46 Ag 2017

As We Grow (Company)

CLOTHING A GENERATION I. R. BJÖRNSDÓTTIR *Iceland Review* v54 no6 p12 N/D 2016

As You Like It (Theatrical production)

THE THEATRE *New Yorker* v93 no28 p10 S 18 2017

As You Were (Music)

FALL ALBUM PREVIEW P. Doyle, A. Greene et al *Rolling Stone* no1297 p12 O 5 2017

Liam Gallagher's Sweet Revenge B. HIATT color *Rolling Stone* no1298 p16 O 19 2017

As You Would Have Told It to Me (Sort Of) If We Had Know Each Other Before You Died (Short story)

As You Would Have Told It to Me (Sort Of) If We Had Know Each Other Before You Died J. H. Khemiri cartoon color *New Yorker* v93 no29 p86 S 25 2017

Asada, Mizue

Two-dimensional sp2 carbon–conjugated covalent organic frameworks diag graph *Science* v357 no6352 p673 Ag 18 2017

Asai, David

Not just Salk color *Science* v357 no6356 p1105 S 15 2017

Asana Inc.

New Tools for Working Smarter K. PALMER cartoon *AARP: The Magazine* v59 no6A p24 O/N 2016

Asano, Hokuto

Evolution of the wheat blast fungus through functional losses in a host specificity determinant diag map *Science* v357 no6346 p80 Jl 7 2017

Asante, Amma

ON A ROLE M. M. Lewis color *Essence* v47 no10 p55 F 2017

A United Kingdom L. Greenblatt color *Entertainment Weekly* no1453 p48 F 17 2017

ASAP Ferg (Performer)

GOINGS ON ABOUT TOWN color *New Yorker* v92 no39 p9 N 28 2016

Asare, Amma

Coupling organelle inheritance with mitosis to balance growth and differentiation diag *Science* v355 no6324 p493 F 3 2017

Asaro, Catherine

THE MATH POLYMATH B. Peterson *Washingtonian Magazine* v52 no4 p45 Ja 2017

Asawa, Ruth, 1926-2013

Woman on Wire A. K. Scott color *New Yorker* v93 no31 p8 O 9 2017

Asbaty, Diandra

BOWLED OVER R. O'CONNOR cartoon *Chicago* v66 no4 p34 Ap 2017

Asbell, Robin

baked GOOD color *Yoga Journal* no288 p85 D 2016

Ascencio, Diana I.

Gene duplication can impart fragility, not robustness, in the yeast protein interaction network bibl color graph *Science* v355 no6325 p630 F 10 2017

Ascent Energy Inc.

Ascent Protein color *Muscle & Performance* v9 no10 p36 O 2017

Asch, David A.

Use Behavioral Economics to Achieve Wellness Goals *Harvard Business Review Digital Articles* p2 D 1 2014

Ascher, David B.

DNA-PKcs structure suggests an allosteric mechanism modulating DNA double-strand break repair bibl graph *Science* v355 no6324 p520 F 3 2017

Ascher, Saul

An Inconvenient Maverick P. Schröder *History Today* v67 no2 p4 F 2017

Ascherson, Neal

Corrective Affinities bw *New York Review of Books* v64 no16 p55 O 26 2017

Ascites

Understanding Ascites in Cats A. Plotnick *Catnip* v24 no10 p5 O 2016

ASEAN

ASEAN – Turning Vision into Reality *Foreign Affairs* v95 no6 p(Sp)2 N/D 2016

Aselton, Katie

Legion J. Jensen color *Entertainment Weekly* no1451/1452 p96 F 3-10 2017

Asen, Daniel

CSI: CHINA: The 19th and 20th centuries saw a revolution in Chinese forensic science, when traditional techniques were replaced by new methods from the West. Today, the world confronts another moment of transformation in forensic science *History Today* v67 no7 p54 Jl 2017

Asexual reproduction

See also

Cloning

All Moms, No Dads P. Edmonds color *National Geographic* v230 no5 p30 N 2016

Asgari, Reza

Tuning quantum nonlocal effects in graphene plasmonics bw diag *Science* v357 no6347 p187 Jl 14 2017

Ash (Music)

Soul Sisters C. NNADI color *Vogue* v207 no10 p226 O 2017

WHAT TO STREAM color *Entertainment Weekly* no1485 p57 O 6 2017

Ash, Alison—Interviews

MAKING THAT KITTY PURR D. ARTAVIA color *Advocate* no1090 p44 Ap 2017

Ash, Caroline

Grow! Raise! Catch! color *Science* v354 no6317 p1222 D 9 2016

OUTBREAK [Cover story] color *Science* v357 no6347 p144 Jl 14 2017

Ash, Chris

"Look What We Did!" *Stage Directions* v30 no10 p19 O 2017

Ash, Mary Kay, 1918-2001

Business Tycoons bw cartoon color *American Cowboy* p32 LEGENDS OF TEXAS Special Issue 2017

Ash, Summer

Magnetic Bridge Found Between Magellanic Clouds color *Sky & Telescope* v134 no2 p13 Ag 2017

Ash Hollow State Historical Park (Neb.)

History in a rut at Ash Hollow State Historical Park color *Nebraska Life* v21 no5 p60 S/O 2017

Ash scattering (Human remains)

Marvin's Ashes K. STEINBERG *Idaho Magazine* v16 no3 p28 D 2016

Ash vs. Evil Dead (TV program)

HOMECOMING SCREAM D. HOLBROOK *TV Guide* v64 no40 p52 O 3 2016

That's One Hell of an Evil Keg Party! D. Holbrook *TV Guide* v64 no15 p10 Ap 4 2016

ASHBACH, HEATHER

Home Alone *USA Today Magazine* v145 no2864 p29 My 2017

Ashbery, John, 1927-

Cracks in Language M. MATTIX bw *Weekly Standard* v23 no2 p44 S 18 2017

John Ashbery (1927–2017) [Cover story] L. Sante bw *New York Review of Books* v64 no15 p4 O 12 2017

Milestones color *Time* v190 no10/11 p16 S 18 2017

ASHBY, AIMEE

Your True Stories IN 100 WORDS color *Reader's Digest* v189 no1131 p32 Je 2017

Ashe, Erin

U.S. seafood import restriction presents opportunity and risk bibl color map *Science* v354 no6318 p1372 D 16 2016

Ashe + Leandro (Company)

AD100 *Architectural Digest* v74 no1 p91 Ja 2017

Young Guns color *Architectural Digest* v74 no1 p138 Ja 2017

Ashenden, Jackie

Make It Hurt *Publishers Weekly* v263 no45 p47 N 7 2016

Asher, Diana Harmon

Running for Their Lives T. RINALDI *New York Times Book Review* p26 Ag 27 2017

Asher, Jay

Things to Do! J. Abidor color *Seventeen* v76 no2 p17 Mr 2017

What Light S. Vilkomerson color *Entertainment Weekly* no1438 p63 N 4 2016

ASHER, SALLY

Last Days Of Storyville bw color *New Orleans Magazine* v51 no12 p78 O 2017

Asheville (N.C.)

SOUTH'S BEST BREWERY K. Purvis color *Southern Living* v52 no4 p72 Ap 2017

SOUTH'S BEST HOTEL V. F. Luesse color *Southern Living* v52 no4 p78 Ap 2017

Asheville (N.C.)—Description & travel

Asheville, North Carolina A. BRANDT *Cincinnati Magazine* p60 Je 2017

ASHEVILLE T. MALONE *Atlanta* v56 no7 p56 N 2016

DESTINATIONS *Atlanta* v57 no2 p145 Je 2017

Ashford, Doug

GWANGJU BIENNALE M. Heddaya color *Art in America* v104 no10 p164 N 2016

ASHFORD, KATE

win your flextime fight color *Parents* v92 no7 p90 Jl 2017

Ashford, Susan J.

Good Leaders Are Good Learners *Harvard Business Review Digital Articles* p2 Ag 10 2017

Your Boss Won't Say Yes If Emotions Are Running High *Harvard Business Review Digital Articles* p2 D 19 2014

Ashik, Igor M.

Greater role for Atlantic inflows on sea-ice loss in the Eurasian Basin of the Arctic Ocean chart diag graph *Science* v356 no6335 p285 Ap 21 2017

Ashkenas, Ron

The 3 Ways People React to Career Disasters *Harvard Business Review Digital Articles* p2 Je 18 2015

A Consultant's Guide to Difficult Client Feedback *Harvard Business Review Digital Articles* p2 Ag 21 2015

Don't Ask for New Ideas If You're Not Ready to Act on Them *Harvard Business Review Digital Articles* p2 F 2 2015

Even Experienced Executives Avoid Conflict *Harvard Business Review Digital Articles* p2 Mr 8 2016

First-Time Managers, Don't Do Your Team's Work for Them *Harvard Business Review Digital Articles* p2 S 21 2015

The Go-to-Market Approach Startups Need to Adopt *Harvard Business Review Digital Articles* p2 Je 10 2016

Help Your Team Spend Time on the Right Things *Harvard Business Review Digital Articles* p2 O 23 2014

How Thomson Reuters Is Creating a Culture of Innovation *Harvard Business Review Digital Articles* p2 O 2 2014

How to Be an Effective Executive Sponsor *Harvard Business Review Digital Articles* p2 My 18 2015

How to Handle Underperformers on a Team You Inherit *Harvard Business Review Digital Articles* p2 Je 15 2017

How to Overcome Executive Isolation color *Harvard Business Review Digital Articles* p2 F 2 2017

If Your Boss Tells You to Get a Coach, Don't Panic *Harvard Business Review Digital Articles* p2 F 26 2015

Jack Welch's Approach to Breaking Down Silos Still Works *Harvard Business Review Digital Articles* p2 S 9 2015

Keeping Meetings on Track When You're Not in Charge *Harvard Business Review Digital Articles* p2 Ap 22 2016

Leadership Development Should Focus on Experiments *Harvard Business Review Digital Articles* p2 Ap 12 2016

Navigating the Emotional Side of a Career Transition *Harvard Business Review Digital Articles* p2 Ap 5 2016

Stop Trying to Please Everyone *Harvard Business Review Digital Articles* p2 Jl 29 2015

A Successful M&A Considers the Human Element *Harvard Business Review Digital Articles* p2 N 18 2014

SURVIVING M&A color il *Harvard Business Review* v95 no2 p145 Mr/Ap 2017

There's a Difference Between Cooperation and Collaboration *Harvard Business Review Digital Articles* p2 Ap 20 2015

To Lead Change, Explain the Context *Harvard Business Review Digital Articles* p2 N 24 2015

We Still Don't Know the Difference Between Change and Transformation *Harvard Business Review Digital Articles* p2 Ja 15 2015

When a Public Mistake Requires an Old-Fashioned Apology *Harvard Business Review Digital Articles* p2 Ja 7 2015

When Not to Celebrate Failure *Harvard Business Review Digital Articles* p2 D 11 2014

Win Over Executives by Proving Customers Support Your Idea *Harvard Business Review Digital Articles* p2 Jl 14 2015

You Can't Delegate Talent Management to the HR Department *Harvard Business Review Digital Articles* p2 S 23 2016

Your Innovation Team Shouldn't Run Like a Well-Oiled Machine *Harvard Business Review Digital Articles* p2 O 28 2015

Ashker, Valerie

Coast to Coast for a Cause L. Threlkeld color *Practical Horseman* v45 no3 p72 Mr 2017

Ashley, Amanda

Understanding What You're Part Of color *Climbing* no353 p24 My/Je 2017

Ashley, Christopher

A 9/11 Musical With Heart and Nostalgia R. Zoglin color *Time* v189 no11 p62 Mr 27 2017

Canadian Nice: The Musical J. GREEN *New York* v50 no6 p86 Mr 20 2017

Ashley, Mike

THERE ARE LOTS OF MIKE ASHLEYS OUT THERE R. JEFFERY *People Management* p46 O 2016

Ashley, Mike—Finance

Spare any change, Mike? *People Management* p6 O 2016

Ashley Stewart Inc.

How I Brought Ashley Stewart Back from Bankruptcy J. Rhee *Harvard Business Review Digital Articles* p2 Jl 31 2015

Ash-Milby, Kathleen

ART WARRIORS AND WOODEN INDIANS bw color *Art in America* p58 O 2017

Ashton, Deborah

What HR Can Do to Fix the Gender Pay Gap *Harvard Business Review Digital Articles* p2 D 2 2014

ASHTON, JACKIE

travel smartly *Parents* v91 no12 p118 D 2016

Ashton, John M.

Tudor-SN–mediated endonucleolytic decay of human cell microRNAs promotes G1/S phase transition graph *Science* v356 no6340 p859 My 26 2017

Ashtrays

Why There's Still an Ashtray on Your Airplane J. Hincks *Time* v190 no14 p23 O 9 2017

Ashville (N.C.)

KIND OF BLUE K. West color *Conde Nast Traveler* v51 no10 p148 N 2016

Ashwell, Rachel

The Beauty of Imperfection color *AARP: The Magazine* v59 no5A p72 Ag/S 2016

Ashworth, Alan

PARP inhibitors: Synthetic lethality in the clinic bibl diag *Science* v355 no6330 p1152 Mr 17 2017

Ashworth, John

THE WINNING LOOK Linksoul and C. Barrett color *Golf Magazine* v59 no8 p38 Ag 2017

Ashworth, William J.

A CAST IRON LEGACY *History Today* v67 no8 p100 Ag 2017

Asia

ASIAN AWAKENING D. ANDERSON-MINSHALL color *Advocate* no1090 p11 Ap 2017

Asia, Central—History

The Soviet Legacy and Women's Rights in Central Asia M. KAMP *Current History* v115 no783 p270 O 2016

Asia—Foreign economic relations—United States

Geopolitics: Trump's Top Priority Must Be a Strong China Strategy A. J. Stavridis *Time* v188 no27-28 p30 D 26 2016

How Singapore Sees Asia-and America I. Bremmer *Time* v188 no19 p10 N 7 2016

Asia—Foreign relations—United States

Asia: Trump's Shock Doctrine Will Make China Even Stronger Y. Funabashi color *Time* v188 no27-28 p26 D 26 2016

Danger in Asia M. AUSLIN *National Review* v69 no2 p28 F 6 2017

The Rebalance and Asia-Pacific Security A. Carter color *Foreign Affairs* v95 no6 p65 N/D 2016

Why America Is Losing Asia H. Beech color *Time* v188 no27-28 p66 D 26 2016

Asian American actors

Breaking the Other Color Line S. Li color *Entertainment Weekly* no1439 p10 N 11 2016

Asian American executives

Why Aren't There More Asian Americans in Leadership Positions? S. K. Johnson and T. Sy *Harvard Business Review Digital Articles* p2 D 19 2016

Asian Americans—Education

Learning from the other achievement gap T. L. Pittinsky *Phi Delta Kappan* v98 no5 p80 F 2017

Asian cooking

See also

Chinese cooking

5 More Asian-Style Starts *Los Angeles Magazine* p110 Ap 2017

BAO WOW J. WALKER and D. LI color *Bon Appetit* v61 no11 p118 N 2016

Pacific Heights J. GORDINIER color *Esquire* v166 no4 p32 N 2016

Asian Infrastructure Investment Bank

China's New Development Bank Is a Wake-Up Call for Washington B. Chakravorti *Harvard Business Review Digital Articles* p2 Ap 20 2015

Asia—News briefs

Asia K. Stock color *Bloomberg Businessweek* no4535 p8 Ag 28 2017

Asia K. Stock color graph *Bloomberg Businessweek* no4529 p9 Jl 3 2017

Asia & Oceania *New York Times Upfront* v149 no7 p28 Ja 9 2017

Asians

See also

Japanese

are asian kids really better at math? M. THIAGARAJAN *Parents* v91 no9 p58 S 2016

Asians in motion pictures

Breaking the Other Color Line S. Li color *Entertainment Weekly* no1439 p10 N 11 2016

The Invisible Minority S. Li *Entertainment Weekly* no1439 p11 N 11 2016

Asians—United States

See also

East Asians—United States

The Invisible Minority S. Li *Entertainment Weekly* no1439 p11 N 11 2016

Asiatic elephant

Getting Out of One's Own Way A. Braun color *Natural History* v125 no7 p6 Jl/Ag 2017

ASICS America Corp.

RUNNING LIST J. WUEBBEN color *Muscle & Performance* v9 no4 p12 Ap 2017

ASICS Corp.

POWER SNEAKS color *Women's Health* v14 no8 p160 O 2017

ASIM, JABARI

Black Lives Didn't Matter *New York Times Book Review* p28 N 13 2016

Asimov, Isaac, 1920-1992

AI, people, and society E. Horvitz *Science* v357 no6346 p7 Jl 7 2017

Our Personal Favorites C. ENGELKING, E. NECKAR et al bw *Discover* v38 no4 p44 My 2017

Asimow, Paul D.

A measure of mantle melting bibl graph *Science* v355 no6328 p908 Mr 3 2017

Asinof, Lynn

Retirement Plans for Going It Alone color *Money* v46 no8 p28 S 2017

A Social Security Perk for Some Older Parents diag *Money* v46 no5 p29 Je 2017

Asl, Z. Mohammadi

Coseismic rupturing stopped by Aso volcano during the 2016 Mw 7.1 Kumamoto earthquake, Japan bibl color graph *Science* v354 no6314 p869 N 18 2016

Aslam, Nabeel

Nanoscale nuclear magnetic resonance with chemical resolution diag *Science* v357 no6346 p67 Jl 7 2017

Aslam, Nadeem

Powder Keg: Violence drives Muslims and Christians from a city of despots and collateral damage F. Prose *New York Times Book Review* p10 My 21 2017

Aslan, Reza, 1972-

The Great Pretender cartoon *Weekly Standard* v22 no30 p2 Ap 10 2017

Religion vs. Culture color *Foreign Policy* no225 p112 Jl/Ag 2017

Aslan, Reza, 1972-—Interviews

Reza Aslan Thinks TV Can End Bigotry A. M. Cox *New York Times Magazine* p94 Mr 26 2017

Aslani, Lauleh

real style color *InStyle* v24 no4 p28 Ap 2017

ASLANIAN, ARTOUR

A Case Study of Descriptive Representation: The Experience of Native American Elected Officials in South Dakota *American Indian Quarterly* v41 no3 p250 Summ 2017

Aslanian, Emily

13 Reasons Why *TV Guide* v65 no19 p38 My 1 2017

Betty White Gets Crazy on Young & Hungry *TV Guide* v65 no8 p11 F 27 2017

Dancing With the Stars THE COUPLES TO WATCH *TV Guide* v65 no14 p6 Ap 3 2017

The Foster' Family Crisis *TV Guide* v65 no2 p12 Ja 2 2017

LATE NIGHT *TV Guide* v65 no23 p43 My 29 2017

The Librarians *TV Guide* v64 no46 p37 N 7 2016

Meet the crew... *TV Guide* v65 no43 p8 O 16 2017

The New American Gladiators *TV Guide* v65 no25 p9 Je 2017

A New View of Playboy *TV Guide* v65 no11 p14 Mr 6 2017

SVU STAR POWER *TV Guide* v65 no4 p21 Ja 16 2017

Today's Most Memorable Moments bw color *TV Guide* v65 no7 p24 F 13 2017

Asma, Stephen T.

Imagine this M. Merritt color *Science* v356 no6344 p1240 Je 23 2017

Asmar, Sami W.

Gravity field of the Orientale basin from the Gravity Recovery and Interior Laboratory Mission bibl graph *Science* v354 no6311 p438 O 28 2016

Asmis, Knut R.

Spectroscopic snapshots of the proton-transfer mechanism in water bibl diag graph *Science* v354 no6316 p1131 D 2 2016

Asmus, Ashley

Higher predation risk for insect prey at low latitudes and elevations graph *Science* v356 no6339 p742 My 19 2017

Asner, Ed

The MARY MARY MARY MARY MARY MARY MARY I Knew color *Entertainment Weekly* no1453 p34 F 17 2017

Asner, G. P.

Airborne laser-guided imaging spectroscopy to map forest trait diversity and guide conservation bibl chart graph *Science* v355 no6323 p385 Ja 27 2017

Asokan, Mangaiarkarasi

Trispecific broadly neutralizing HIV antibodies mediate potent SHIV protection in macaques color graph *Science* v357 no6359 p85 O 6 2017

Asomugha, Caleb—Interviews

Special Ed Teacher Puts His Background to Work in the Classroom C. Veiga bw *Education Digest* v83 no2 p21 O 2017

Asorey, H.

Observation of a large-scale anisotropy in the arrival directions of cosmic rays above 8×10^{18} eV *Science* v357 no6357 p1266 S 22 2017

Asp, Karen

ANTI-AGING SUPPLEMENTS THAT WORK color *Harper's Bazaar* no3651 p326 Mr 2017

ARE YOU A SAVVY HOLIDAY EATER? color *O, The Oprah Magazine* p124 D 2016

Boost Your Immunity color *Martha Stewart Living* p68 O 2017

KNOW YOUR RISKS color *Better Homes & Gardens* v95 no10 p180 O 2017

Step Up to a Breakthrough color *Women's Health* v14 no9 p88 N 2017

Strong BONES, Flat BELLY color *Prevention* v69 no8 p70 Ag 2017

your Healthiest you AN ANY AGE [Cover story] color *Prevention* v69 no7 p36 Jl 2017

Your Pooch Is Becoming A PIZZA ADDICT color *O, The Oprah Magazine* p76 Ag 2017

Asparagus

23 and Pee S. Mirsky color *Scientific American* v316 no3 p78 Mr 2017

ASK SUSAN S. WESTMORELAND color *Good Housekeeping* v264 no5 p112 My 2017

Seasonal Salads color *Amazing Wellness* v9 no2 p82 Spr 2017

SPRING-CLEAN Your Kitchen M. OZ cartoon *O, The Oprah Magazine* p99 Mr 2017

Asparagus growers

A SIDE BUSINESS COMES FULL CIRCLE D. KURNS *Successful Farming* v114 no13 p4 D 2016

ASPDEN, RACHEL

Freedom of The Press is Not a Given *Publishers Weekly* v264 no9 p104 F 27 2017

Youth Was Not Enough T. CAMBANIS *New York Times Book Review* p12 F 12 2017

Aspelmeyer, M.

Direct frequency comb measurement of OD + CO→DOCO kinetics bibl graph *Science* v354 no6311 p444 O 28 2016

Aspen (Colo.)—Description & travel

Aspen K. BASTONE *Los Angeles Magazine* v61 no11 p86 N 2016

Aspen (Trees)

The Big Pictures: THE SAN FRANCISCO PEAKS *Arizona Highways* v93 no8 p16 Ag 2017

The Life and Death of Pando C. KETCHAM color graph map *Discover* v38 no10 p24 D 2017

Aspen Power Catamarans (Company)

CROSSOVER CAT S. SHIBATA *Boating World* v38 no3 p8 Mr 2017

A Different Breed of Cat R. THIEL chart color *Power & Motoryacht* v33 no4 p78 Ap 2017

Asperger's syndrome patients

Recruiters urged to rethink testing after tribunal win: EAT agrees multiple-choice test discriminated against applicant with Asperger's syndrome *People Management* p16 Je 2017

Aspergillus fumigatus

In the lungs, mold cells self-destruct L. HAMERS color *Science News* v192 no5 p16 S 30 2017

Asphalt Jungle, The (Film)

20 DISCS TO WATCH *Film Comment* v52 no6 p91 N/D 2016

Asphyxia

See also

Anoxemia

Drowning

Strangling

If crib bumpers are so dangerous for babies, why are they still sold? *Parents* v91 no6 p22 Je 2016

Asphyxia—Prevention

New Baby-Sleep Rules *Parents* v92 no1 p18 Ja 2017

protection plan V. BEISER *Parents* v91 no10 p136 O 2016

Aspirin

Aspirin to Prevent Heart Attacks S. KLEIN *Prevention* v69 no4 p22 Ap 2017

Secrets of a Southern Salon A. Roderique-jones color *Southern Living* v52 no9 p37 S 2017

Vacation Items You'll Almost Always Regret Packing J. LABIANCA *Reader's Digest* v188 no1126 p52 D 2016/Ja 2017

Aspirin—Therapeutic use

ASK THE DOCTOR A. L. KOMAROFF *Harvard Health Letter* v42 no3 p2 Ja 2017

Aspirin vs. Cancer V. Callier color *Scientific American* v316 no5 p24 My 2017

FIVE FACTS: STROKE F. Esker *Louisiana Life* v37 no5 p12 My/Je 2017

Asplund, Anna

A subcellular map of the human proteome color *Science* v356 no6340 p820 My 26 2017

Asplund, Jim

Developing Employees' Strengths Boosts Sales, Profit, and Engagement *Harvard Business Review Digital Articles* p2 S 1 2016

Asplund, Peter

PETER ASPLUND J. Ephland color *Downbeat* v84 no4 p20 Ap 2017

Aspuru-Guzik, Alan

Taking six-dimensional spectra in finite time diag *Science* v356

no6345 p1333 Je 30 2017

ASQUITH, CHRISTINA

TURKISH WOMEN RISING *Ms.* v27 no1 p34 Spr 2017

Assad, Bashar, 1965-

How Assad Is Winning C. Glass color map *New York Review of Books* v64 no3 p15 F 23 2017

Lament for Aleppo *Christian Century* v134 no2 p7 Ja 18 2017

No-Win War in Syria P. J. BUCHANAN *American Conservative* v15 no6 p11 N/D 2016

TOP SECRET: CONFIDENTIAL B. FEIRSTEIN color *Vanity Fair* v59 no9 p136 S 2017

Assadi, Hannah Lillith

Sonora *Publishers Weekly* v264 no3 p33 Ja 16 2017

Assadipour, Farah

TOP DENTISTS *Washingtonian Magazine* v52 no6 p106 Mr 2017

Assange, Julian, 1971-

Can a lonely man in a tiny bedroom deliver a real October surprise? M. Chafkin and V. Silver color *Bloomberg Businessweek* no4495 p62 O 17 2016

MAN WITHOUT A COUNTRY R. KHATCHADOURIAN cartoon color *New Yorker* v93 no24 p36 Ag 21 2017

SANTA'S SURVEILLANCE R. MARR *Missouri Life* v43 no7 p65 D 2016/Ja 2017

Assassin, The (Film)

Wealth Management Y. TALU bw color *Film Comment* v53 no3 p77 My/Je 2017

Assassination

An Outlaw State E. Epstein color *Weekly Standard* v22 no25 p9 Mr 6 2017

The UNTOLD STORY of the ACCIDENTAL ASSASSINS of NORTH KOREA D. Bock Clark color *GQ: Gentlemen's Quarterly* v97 no10 p168 O 2017

Assassination Nation (Film)

Odessa YOUNG *Interview* v47 no5 p65 Je/Jl 2017

Assassins

Becoming a Christian Almost Got Me Killed V. Prodan bw *Christianity Today* v60 no8 p111 O 2016

Tilting at Windmills T. Noah *Washington Monthly* p1 S/O 2016

Assassins (Ismailites)

HULEGU THE MONGOL: Unlike his grandfather Chinggis Khan, the Mongol ruler Hulegu Khan is little known in the West. But his destruction of two Islamic empires, as well as a failed attempt to forge an alliance with Christendom, gave him a notoriety... N. Kinloch *History Today* v67 no6 p52 Je 2016

Assassins (Theatrical production)

American Carnage M. Schulman color *New Yorker* v93 no20 p12 Jl 10 2017

Assassin's Creed (Film)

ASSASSIN'S CREED C. Gunnestad color *Sound & Vision* v82 no7 p68 S 2017

Assassins in literature

What Next? G. HURWITZ *Publishers Weekly* v263 no47 p93 N 21 2016

Assassins—United States—Biography

A Stalwart of Stalwarts J. Bellamy *Prologue* v48 no3 p36 Fall 2016

Assault & battery

See also

Acid throwing

Sexual assault

Stabbings (Crime)

Avoid Rather Than Fight K. McCann color *Black Belt* v55 no6 p18 O/N 2017

Charles Murray's Attackers *Commentary* v143 no4 p10 Ap 2017

People L. Markoe color *Christian Century* v134 no15 p19 Jl 19 2017

Assault & battery lawsuits

The Handshake M. Wolfe color *New Republic* v248 no8/9 p36 Ag/S 2017

The Joy of Destruction J. BOTTUM color *Weekly Standard* v23 no3 p21 S 25 2017

Assault & battery—Great Britain

Acid Attacks Have Become a Brutal New Trend In the U.K T. John *Time* v190 no5 p16 Jl 31 2017

Assault & battery—Lawsuits & claims

She had tried so hard to be Gouda A. Gadag *Texas Monthly* v45

no1 p91 Ja 2017

Assaut Sur L'univers (Short story)

ASSAUT SUR L'UNIVERS G. D. GOLD cartoon *Wired* v25 no1 p87 Ja 2017

Assayas, Olivier, 1955-

Personal Shopper L. Greenblatt color *Entertainment Weekly* no1457/1458 p73 Mr 17 2017

Assayas, Olivier, 1955—Interviews

THE MATERIAL WORLD J. ROMNEY color *Film Comment* v53 no2 p36 Mr/Ap 2017

Asseily, Anna Gavazzi

"FLYING ALONE FOR WORK IS LIKE A VACATION. FLYING WITH MY SON IS DEFINITELY WORK." A. WHITTLE color *Conde Nast Traveler* v52 no6 p30 Je/Jl 2017

Asselta, Ryan

Bucking the Trend color *Golf Magazine* v59 no11 p21 N 2017

Playing It Cool color *Golf Magazine* v59 no8 p27 Ag 2017

playing with fire color *Golf Magazine* v59 no8 p76 Ag 2017

Still Going Strong color *Golf Magazine* v59 no9 p25 S 2017

Assemblage (Art)

Collage As an Act of Defiance SU WU *Los Angeles Magazine* p56 My 2017

Assembly line methods

There Are Two Types of Performance—but Most Organizations Only Focus on One L. McGregor and N. Doshi *Harvard Business Review Digital Articles* p2 O 10 2017

Assenova, Valentina

Expand innovation finance via crowdfunding bibl color graph map *Science* v354 no6319 p1526 D 23 2016

Assertiveness (Psychology)

A Simple Way to Be More Assertive (Without Being Pushy) A. Molinsky *Harvard Business Review Digital Articles* p2 Ag 31 2017

social influence T. REECE *Parents* v92 no5 p119 My 2017

Asset acquisitions

BUYING YOUR WAY INTO ENTREPRENEURSHIP R. S. RUBACK and R. YUDKOFF color il *Harvard Business Review* v95 no1 p149 Ja/F 2017

Asset allocation

How to Navigate a Digital Transformation B. Libert, M. Beck et al *Harvard Business Review Digital Articles* p2 Je 22 2016

PERSONALITY QUIZ: WHAT IS YOUR MONEY PERSONALITY? *Scholastic Choices* p8 O 2017 Supplement

A Simple Habit With a Big Payoff W. Updegrave diag *Money* v46 no9 p41 O 2017

Asset management

See also

Return on assets

FINDING THAT Special Someone F. TORABI color *O, The Oprah Magazine* p41 Je 2017

The Retirement of Baby Boomers [Cover story] M. Hobson color *Black Enterprise* v47 no3 p26 O 2016

Asset management accounts

3 Reality Checks You Must Face To Fix Your Finances A. Edmond Jr. color *Black Enterprise* v47 no4 p14 N/D 2016

Assets (Accounting)

See also

Liquid assets

Investors Today Prefer Companies with Fewer Physical As sets B. Libert, M. Beck et al *Harvard Business Review Digital Articles* p2 S 29 2016

Joint Ventures Reduce the Risk of Major Capital Investments H. Vantrappen and D. Deneffe *Harvard Business Review Digital Articles* p2 Ap 6 2016

Assets (Accounting)—Management

Inflation-Proof Your Assets A. K. SMITH cartoon chart *Kiplinger's Personal Finance* v71 no4 p59 Ap 2017

Assignment, The (Film)

The Assignment N. LEE color *Film Comment* v53 no2 p70 Mr/Ap 2017

CRITICS' CHOICE chart color *Film Comment* v53 no3 p12 My/Je 2017

Assignment: China (Film)

Assignment: China A. J. Nathan *Foreign Affairs* v96 no6 p170 N/D 2017

ASSIL, REEM

FEW THINGS BRING PEOPLE TOGETHER LIKE MAN'OUSHE color *Bon Appetit* v62 no2 p61 Mr 2017

ASSILI, AMIR

FOOT SOLDIERS *Washingtonian Magazine* v52 no1 p126 O 2016

Assis, P.

Observation of a large-scale anisotropy in the arrival directions of cosmic rays above 8×1018 eV *Science* v357 no6357 p1266 S 22 2017

Assisted suicide

COMPLICATED CARE W. RYAN *Commonweal* v114 no14 p2 S 8 2017

QUESTIONS AT THE END H. W. BAILLIE and G. MEILAENDER color *Commonweal* v144 no15 p2 S 22 2017

Assisted suicide—Canada

The doctor who took on death S. PROUDFOOT color *Maclean's* v130 no8 p52 S 2017

Assisted suicide—Law & legislation

D.C. Affirms Assisted Suicide color *America* v215 no16 p9 N 21 2016

'THIS IS NO WAY TO LIVE' S. PROUDFOOT color *Maclean's* v129 no47 p14 N 28 2016

Assistive listening systems

PSST...WANNA TRY A PSAP? [Cover story] *Nutrition Action Health Letter* v43 no10 p4 D 2016

Associate degree education

Anne Arundel Community College *Dance Magazine* v90 p42 2016/2017 Supplement College Guide

Associated Press

ASSOCIATED PRESS ADMITS WARTIME DEAL WITH NAZIS B. Manley bw *Military History* v34 no4 p8 N 2017

PARODY *Weekly Standard* v22 no13 p44 D 5 2016

Association management

Embracing the Hack Attack M. Brubaker *Parks & Recreation* v52 no5 p70 My 2017

Association of American Physicians & Surgeons

Are the Liberal Democrats Serious?—Is Everyone (read, Republicans) Really Racist? *USA Today Magazine* v145 no2863 p4 Ap 2017

Association of American Publishers

The Pallante Era Begins at AAP A. Albanese color *Publishers Weekly* v264 no3 p5 Ja 16 2017

Association of American University Presses

University Presses: More Relevant than Ever E. Nawotka color *Publishers Weekly* v264 no25 p12 Je 19 2017

Association of Tennis Professionals

SOCK IT TO HIM E. KONIGSBERG color *Esquire* p74 Ag 2017

Tour Guide: An inside look at upcoming ATP and WTA tournaments color *Tennis* v53 no5 p27 S/O 2017

Tour Guide: ATP color *Tennis* v53 no2 p14 Mr/Ap 2017

Tour Guide *Tennis* v53 no4 p34 Jl/Ag 2017

Association of Theological Schools in the United States & Canada

People C. Kennel-Shank color *Christian Century* v134 no5 p17 Mr 1 2017

Association of Writers & Writing Programs—Congresses

Politics Was Front and Center At This Year's AWP Conference C. Teicher, C. Kirch et al color *Publishers Weekly* v264 no8 p4 F 20 2017

Associations, institutions, etc.

See also

Boards of directors

Charities

Clubs

Community organization

Dance companies

Nonprofit organizations

Opera companies

Societies

Theatrical companies

Don't Waste Your Time on Networking Events D. Coburn *Harvard Business Review Digital Articles* p2 S 26 2016

Help Your Team Stop Overcommitting by Empowering Them to Say No D. Kander color *Harvard Business Review Digital Articles* p2 Je 6 2017

A National Muslim Indian Presence M. A. RAHMAN *Islamic Ho-*

rizons v46 no2 p54 Mr/Ap 2017

Talon Show L. VACCARIELLO *Cincinnati Magazine* v50 no3 p160 D 2016

Thumbs Up on Dakota K's Recovery K. Santos *Spin to Win Rodeo* v20 no10 p32 D 2016

THE WHITE CITY REMAKE: HOW BOISE'S COLUMBIAN CLUB RECREATED THE 1893 WORLD'S FAIR J. S. DALE *Idaho Magazine* v16 no7 p8 Ap 2017

Whose idea was it? D. Kilgannon *History Today* v66 no11 p7 N 2016

Associations, institutions, etc.—Computer network resources

An Amazing Year! S. ECKELBERRY *Parks & Recreation* v52 no8 p8 Ag 2017

Associations, institutions, etc.—Management

Using Technology to Enhance Our Community D. Barone *Literacy Today (2411-7862)* v34 no3 p6 N/D 2016

Associations, institutions, etc.—Membership

Build a Fan Base *Practical Horseman* v45 no4 p59 Ap 2017

Get Involved With ILA D. Fisher *Literacy Today (2411-7862)* v34 no4 p6 Ja/F 2017

LIFE MEMBERS *Arabian Horse World* v57 no3 p63 D 2016

Thank You for the Honor B. Moroney *In Stride* v11 no6 p8 N 2016

USEF Reveals New Vision color *Practical Horseman* v45 no4 p58 Ap 2017

Associations, institutions, etc.—Mergers

Taking a Positive View of the IDPF-W3C Merger L. Dawson *Publishers Weekly* v264 no9 p19 F 27 2017

Associations, institutions, etc.—Taxation

SHOULD YOUR MINISTRY BE A 'CHURCH'? T. TOWNSEND color *Christianity Today* v60 no10 p19 D 2016

Associations, institutions, etc.—United States

HOW COMMUNISTS AND CATHOLICS BUILT A COMMON-WEALTH N. Schneider color *America* v217 no6 p18 S 18 2017

Associative learning

The limits of Negative Reinforcement [Cover story] J. L. Jones bw color *Equus* no480 p40 S 2017

Associative memory (Psychology)

There are places I'll remember E. Bence color *U.S. Catholic* v82 no7 p23 Jl 2017

Assoulin, Rosie

Rosie Assoulin A. Syrett color *InStyle* v24 no5 p98 My 2017

Assu, Sonny—Exhibitions

Art Attack *Smithsonian* v47 no8 p12 D 2016

Assyrians

Freed Iraqi Christians tell of life under the IS K. Chick color *Christian Century* v134 no1 p12 Ja 4 2017

Assyro-Babylonian astrology

Babylonian Tablets Tracked Jupiter J. KEATS color diag *Discover* v38 no1 p54 Ja/F 2017

Astakhova, Alla

Paolo Macchiarini's academic afterlife in Russia ends color *Science* v356 no6339 p672 My 19 2017

Astana (Kazakhstan)

Astana, Kazakhstan J. LILLIS color *Foreign Policy* no223 p70 Mr/Ap 2017

Astānga yoga

YOGAWARS! color *Women's Health* v14 no5 p32 Je 2017

Aster, Paul

FORK YOU L. MILLER cartoon *New Yorker* v92 no47 p68 Ja 30 2017

Astereognosis (Poem)

Astereognosis A. Majmudar *America* v216 no12 p47 My 29 2017

Asterisms (Astronomy)

FINDING PATTERNS IN THE SKY P. Harrington chart color *Astronomy* v45 no1 p60 Ja 2017

GALLERY *Sky & Telescope* v134 no1 p74 Jl 2017

Asteroid belt

Amateurs Find Asteroid's Moon J. K. BEATTY color *Sky & Telescope* v134 no5 p8 N 2017

Original asteroids came only in size XL M. TEMMING *Science News* v192 no3 p8 S 2 2017

Asteroid detection

Effort in asteroid defense under way despite funding constraints D. Kramer *Physics Today* v70 no2 p31 F 2017

Track an asteroid pair G. CHAPLE color *Astronomy* v45 no10 p18 O 2017

Asteroid orbits

Effort in asteroid defense under way despite funding constraints D. Kramer *Physics Today* v70 no2 p31 F 2017

Asteroids

See also

Itokawa (Asteroid)

Kleopatra (Asteroid)

Pallas (Asteroid)

3122 Florence Flies By, Reveals Two Moons J. K. BEATTY and B. KING *Sky & Telescope* v134 no6 p10 D 2017

Asteroids N. SCHARPING diag graph map *Discover* v38 no6 p50 Jl/Ag 2017

Cooling Element H. Leifert color *Natural History* v125 no5 p8 My 2017

Identification of a primordial asteroid family constrains the original planetesimal population M. Delbo, K. Walsh et al diag graph *Science* v357 no6355 p1026 S 8 2017

Impostors in the asteroid belt N. T. Redd bw color diag *Astronomy* v45 no4 p28 Ap 2017

Localized aliphatic organic material on the surface of Ceres M. C. De Sanctis, E. Ammannito et al bibl graph *Science* v355 no6326 p719 F 17 2017

Lunar Landscaping K. J. P. Smith diag *Scientific American* v315 no5 p16 N 2016

MAKING AN IMPACT ON ASTEROID DEFLECTION H. Auten *Science & Technology Review* p16 D 2016

Meet the primordial asteroid family F. DeMeo color diag *Science* v357 no6355 p972 S 8 2017

Our Rocks, Ourselves D. FOX color *Discover* v38 no5 p60 Je 2017

Recent Briny Eruptions on Ceres? J. K. BEATTY *Sky & Telescope* v134 no1 p10 Jl 2017

Space Prospecting J. Dunietz color *Scientific American* v317 no4 p14 O 2017

What Would Happen? C. BOYER *National Geographic Kids* no469 p5 Ap 2017

Asteroids—Research

ASTEROID MISSION S. MURPHY and LAURETTA *Scientific American* v315 no6 p8 D 2016

EXPLORE THE IMPACT that killed the dinosaurs M. Alexander color map *Astronomy* v44 no12 p26 D 2016

PROGRAMMING FOR ALL J. BATTERSON, D. L. STREINER et al color *Scientific American* v315 no6 p8 D 2016

Asthagiri, Aravind

Low-temperature activation of methane on the IrO2(110) surface bw diag graph *Science* v356 no6335 p299 Ap 21 2017

Asthma

Dancing with Asthma K. SCHWAB *Dance Magazine* v90 no12 p90 D 2016

It takes a village D. SCHARDT *Nutrition Action Health Letter* v43 no10 p9 D 2016

What's That Cough? A. Macmillan color *Health* v30 no9 p86 N 2016

YOU ON A CHIP N. Daly color diag *National Geographic* v232 no3 p136 S 2017

Asthma in children—Risk factors

Common fungus may raise asthma risk R. EHRENBERG *Science News* v191 no5 p16 Mr 18 2017

Asthma prevention

Attack Asthma *Parents* v91 no9 p32 S 2016

kids * health news *Parents* v91 no11 p30 N 2016

the night shift K. ROCKWOOD *Parents* v92 no1 p20 Ja 2017

The Perks of PDA *Parents* v91 no10 p34 O 2016

Asthma risk factors

Stick With Your Doctor color *Prevention* v69 no6 p8 Je 2017

Asthma treatment

Finding a new purpose for old drugs E. Y. Snyder color *Science* v357 no6354 p869 S 1 2017

Astill, Gregory

Applications for the Noninsured Crop Disaster Program Increased After the Agricultural Act of 2014 *Amber Waves: The Economics of Food, Farming, Natural Resources, & Rural America* p5 Jl 2017

Astin, Sean, 1971-

Things Get Stranger T. Stack color *Entertainment Weekly* no1440 p13 N 18 2016

ASTLEY, AMY

editor's letter color *Architectural Digest* no5 p24 My 2017

Editor's Letter color *Architectural Digest* v73 no11 p48 N 2016

editor's letter color *Architectural Digest* v74 no10 p28 O 1 2017

Editor's note color *Architectural Digest* v73 no12 p32 D 2016

Fashion Moments color *Architectural Digest* v74 no9 p28 S 2017

Astley, Rick

GREAT MOMENTS IN RICKROLLING C. Collis *Entertainment Weekly* no1435 p38 O 14 2016

In the Rick of Time C. Collis color *Entertainment Weekly* no1435 p36 O 14 2016

RETURN ENGAGEMENT M. Schulman cartoon *New Yorker* v92 no30 p24 S 26 2016

ASTM International (Company)

Application of Current Standards to Natural Playgrounds J. Barber *Parks & Recreation* p9 2017 Supplement Field Guide - Supplier and Resource Directory

Aston, Louise

How to spot the warning signs of suicide *People Management* p48 Jl 2017

Aston Martin automobile

DIVINE DRIVES [Cover story] C. Seabaugh and S. Evans color diag graph map *Motor Trend* v69 no11 p34 N 2017

A Hypercar Made to Measure B. Berk color *Bloomberg Businessweek* no4539 p70 S 25 2017

WHEELS OF DESIRE J. Lieberman chart color *Motor Trend* v69 no7 p80 Jl 2017

Aston Martin Lagonda Ltd.

DIVINE DRIVES [Cover story] C. Seabaugh and S. Evans color diag graph map *Motor Trend* v69 no11 p34 N 2017

A Hypercar Made to Measure B. Berk color *Bloomberg Businessweek* no4539 p70 S 25 2017

WHEELS OF DESIRE J. Lieberman chart color *Motor Trend* v69 no7 p80 Jl 2017

Astor Place (New York, N.Y.)

The Next New Astor Place J. DAVIDSON img *New York* p83 Ja 9 2017

Astrachan, Joseph

Study: Customers Really Do Trust Family Businesses More *Harvard Business Review Digital Articles* p2 Ap 27 2015

Astro (Company)

The $60 A10 headset is Astro's first budget-priced audio gear H. DINGMAN color *PCWorld* v35 no7 p29 Jl 2017

Astro-Physics Inc.

The Astro-Physics 1100GTO: This powerful German equatorial mount offers many features for astrophotographers J. Lodriguss *Sky & Telescope* v134 no1 p60 Jl 2017

Astrocytes

Three-dimensional Ca2+ imaging advances understanding of astrocyte biology E. Bindocci, I. Savtchouk et al diag *Science* v356 no6339 p715 My 19 2017

Astrodon (Company)

MEET THE filter guy D. Goldman color *Astronomy* v45 no11 p52 N 2017

Astrolabes

GLOSSARY *Lapham's Quarterly* v10 no2 p220 Spr 2017

Astrology

See also

Horoscopes

Zodiac

Astrology's Bait of a Caring Cosmos J. Szimhart *Skeptical Inquirer* v40 no6 p62 N/D 2016

Astronautics

See also

Outer space

Rocketry

Space exploration

Galaxy Quest K. Tingley color *New York Times Magazine* p28 Ag 6 2017

Astronautics & state

Future of space J. JOHNSON-FREESE and C. BOARDMAN color *Issues in Science & Technology* v33 no1 p15 Fall 2016

Astronautics & state—United States

Let NASA Take Flight color *Scientific American* v316 no1 p7 Ja 2017

U.S. OUT OF SPACE K. MANGU-WARD color *Reason* v48 no9 p4 F 2017

Astronauts

10 THINGS WE'RE TALKING ABOUT T. A. Christian color *Essence* v47 no8 p75 D 2016

Bed and Beyond color *O, The Oprah Magazine* p22 Mr 2017

Eugene Cernan J. Kluger color *Time* v189 no3 p11 Ja 30 2017

going for boeing S. Chodosh color *Popular Science* v289 no6 p80 N/D 2017

THE LAST LAUGH B. RADFORD *Skeptical Inquirer* v41 no4 p66 Jl/Ag 2017

THE LAST SOVIET CITIZEN E. BETZ bw cartoon color *Discover* v27 no10 p40 D 2016

MISSION to MARS S. W. DRIMMER bw color *National Geographic Kids* no465 p14 N 2016

More Than Exploration color *National Geographic* v232 no2 p65 Ag 2017

'ROID RAGE G. PENDLE cartoon color *Esquire* p100 Ap 2017

SPACESHIP EARTH W. LAWRENCE color map *Phi Kappa Phi Forum* v97 no1 p18 Spr 2017

WHAT I LEARNED IN SPACE S. Kelly color *AARP: The Magazine* v30 no6A p41 O/N 2017

Astronauts—Interviews

OUT OF THIS WORLD: SCOTT KELLY'S YEAR IN SPACE N. STOCKTON bw color *Wired* v25 no9 p15 S 2017

Astronauts—Physiology

COSMIC CAN-DO J. KELLY *Scientific American* v316 no6 p6 Je 2017

Astronauts—Safety measures

WELL SUITED FOR SPACE WORK J. Berlin color *National Geographic* v232 no2 p18 Ag 2017

Astronauts—United States

EDGAR MITCHELL C. HOMANS *New York Times Magazine* p16 D 25 2016

Glenn the Good [Cover story] J. GELERNTER bw *National Review* v68 no24 p22 D 31 2016

John Glenn J. Kluger color *Time* v188 no27-28 p17 D 26 2016

The Man Who Fell to Earth: America's longest-orbiting astronaut describes his rocky return home in this adaptation from his book Endurance S. KELLY *Smithsonian* v48 no5 p29 S 2017

ROCKET MAN E. NAWOTKA color *Publishers Weekly* v264 no32 p44 Ag 7 2017

Shannon Walker B. Lightner *Current Biography* v77 no11 p93 N 2016

Astronomers

See also

Women astronomers

1615: Florence *Lapham's Quarterly* v10 no2 p29 Spr 2017

ASK ASTRO C. Trujillo, M. E. Bakich et al color diag *Astronomy* v45 no3 p34 Mr 2017

Astroimaging without a telescope M. Reynolds color *Astronomy* v45 no5 p52 My 2017

Astronomy Tools Actions Set E. RIX color *Astronomy* v44 no12 p66 D 2016

Comet viewing the whole night through M. RATCLIFFE and A. LING color *Astronomy* v45 no5 p42 My 2017

CONFESSIONS OF A master sketcher C. R. James bw color *Astronomy* v45 no2 p58 F 2017

Designers squabble over giant Chinese scope D. Normile color *Science* v356 no6343 p1107 Je 16 2017

Eyepieces for Planetary Observing T. A. Dobbins *Sky & Telescope* v134 no1 p52 Jl 2017

The Father of Southern Astronomy B. Ventrudo *Sky & Telescope* v134 no4 p34 O 2017

Following my lucky star N. G. Roman color *Science* v354 no6317 p1346 D 9 2016

GALAXIES ι Giant "Frankenstein" Spiral A. V. ACEVES *Sky & Telescope* v132 no6 p14 D 2016

How Astronomers Measure Brightness M. E. BAKICH color *Discover* v38 no8 p64 O 2017

THE MAP THE MOON, 1647 K. Wiles *History Today* v67 no7 p4 Jl 2017

Missing Matter Found L. KRUESI color *Discover* v38 no7 p70 S 2017

The Next Horizon E. BETZ color *Discover* v38 no10 p44 D 2017

The obsessive comet hunter R. Jakiel bw color *Astronomy* v45 no2 p54 F 2017

PERCIVAL LOWELL A life in astronomy K. Schindler bw color map *Astronomy* v45 no4 p44 Ap 2017

A perfect circle B. BERMAN color *Astronomy* v45 no5 p10 My 2017

Phantom planets cartoon color *Astronomy* v45 no9 p46 S 2017

A Simple Observing Stool, Plus: Build the Swiss Army Knife of observing stools J. Oltion *Sky & Telescope* v134 no3 p70 S 2017

Story of a supernova D. J. EICHER *Astronomy* v45 no3 p6 Mr 2017

Telescope design spat heats up *Science* v357 no6352 p628 Ag 18 2017

A Thrilling Trio F. Schaaf *Sky & Telescope* v134 no5 p45 N 2017

VASTER THAN THE ANCIENTS IMAGINED C. MEEKS color *Christianity Today* v60 no8 p70 O 2016

Vera Cooper Rubin N. A. Bahcall *Physics Today* v70 no3 p73 Mr 2017

Vera Rubin was a pioneer in dark matter research bw *Astronomy* v45 no4 p19 Ap 2017

World Weary? The Best Is Yet to Come S. SCOLES color *Discover* v38 no3 p40 Ap 2017

Astronomers—Attitudes

Night Train F. Schaaf *Sky & Telescope* v133 no6 p45 Je 2017

Astronomical catalogs

Celebrate with Charles G. CHAPLE color *Astronomy* v45 no2 p20 F 2017

Astronomical clocks—Evaluation

BREITLING AEROSPACE EVO CIRRUS AIRCRAFT WATCH color *Flying* v144 no2 p15 F 2017

Astronomical errors

Deep Space Network glitches worry scientists P. Voosen color *Science* v353 no6307 p1477 S 30 2016

Astronomical instruments

See also

Spectrographs
Telescopes

A Gentleman's Observatory T. Wetherell *Sky & Telescope* v134 no4 p30 O 2017

Great telescopes of the past M. Reynolds bw color *Astronomy* v45 no5 p58 My 2017

Mount Wilson's famous telescope celebrates a century R. L. Voller bw color *Astronomy* v45 no5 p28 My 2017

State of the Art — 63 Years Ago: How amateur telescope making was done in the early days J. Oltion *Sky & Telescope* v134 no4 p70 O 2017

Astronomical instruments—Evaluation

Get started in VIDEO ASTRONOMY J. Thompson color *Astronomy* v45 no11 p62 N 2017

MallinCarrVs SkyRaider DS2.3 Plus: This device promises to be three cameras in one convenient package R. Mollise *Sky & Telescope* v134 no4 p58 O 2017

NEW PRODUCTS color *Astronomy* v45 no10 p69 O 2017

New Product Showcase *Sky & Telescope* v132 no6 p64 D 2016

The Other 130-mm Tabletops *Sky & Telescope* v132 no6 p62 D 2016

A quick guide to scopes for kids T. Trusock color *Astronomy* v45 no11 p60 N 2017

The Star Adventurer Mini Tracker: Sky-Watcher's newest Star Adventurer merges an astronomical tracker with a time-lapse motion controller A. Dyer *Sky & Telescope* v134 no6 p58 D 2017

Astronomical observations

See also

Asteroid detection
Observations of the Moon
Planetary observations
Star observations

Against the Wall of Night M. Wedel *Sky & Telescope* v134 no1 p42 Jl 2017

Aim High F. Schaaf *Sky & Telescope* v133 no6 p46 Je 2017

Brilliant Venus Owns the Evening Sky F. Schaaf *Sky & Telescope* v133 no2 p46 F 2017

A Cornucopia of Celestial Curiosities: The year's end prompts reminiscences of stellar things past F. SCHAAF *Sky & Telescope* v134 no6 p45 D 2017

December Delights: The Moon occults Aldebaran, and Mars and Jupiter dance with a star F. Schaaf *Sky & Telescope* v134 no6 p46 D 2017

A Deep Penumbral Lunar Eclipse A. MacRobert *Sky & Telescope* v133 no2 p48 F 2017

Doodles in the Sky S. French *Sky & Telescope* v133 no6 p54 Je 2017

Eclipse Day's Big Unknown P. Tyson color *Sky & Telescope* v134 no2 p4 Ag 2017

Enter the Summer Citadel: The sights and scents of the season encourage a visit to an old friend F. Schaaf *Sky & Telescope* v134 no1 p45 Jl 2017

The Evening Star Reigns Supreme F. Schaaf *Sky & Telescope* v133 no1 p46 Ja 2017

Event Calendar color *Sky & Telescope* v134 no5 p83 N 2017

Event Calendar *Sky & Telescope* v134 no3 p83 S 2017

A Foolproof Analemma Box: This project practically guarantees good results J. Oltion *Sky & Telescope* v134 no6 p68 D 2017

Four Out of Five: Whether you're a night owl or an early riser, you can observe a bright planet this month F. Schaaf *Sky & Telescope* v134 no1 p46 Jl 2017

Four Planets for Tau Ceti M. YOUNG *Sky & Telescope* v134 no6 p11 D 2017

Hail to the King M. Wedel *Sky & Telescope* v133 no5 p41 My 2017

Historical Observations Reveal an Ancient Explosion J. BARBUZANO *Sky & Telescope* v134 no6 p12 D 2017

How Are Crater Rims Made? C. A. Wood *Sky & Telescope* v133 no2 p52 F 2017

It's All About the Ears S. French *Sky & Telescope* v133 no2 p54 F 2017

The Jewel in the Sword: An observer captures on a sketchpad the stunning details of one of the most wondrous objects in the night sky H. Banich *Sky & Telescope* v134 no6 p32 D 2017

Join me in Costa Rica D. J. EICHER color *Astronomy* v45 no8 p6 Ag 2017

JUNE NIGHTS OUT *Natural History* v125 no6 p45 Je 2017

Jupiter Enters the Evening Sky A. MacRobert *Sky & Telescope* v133 no4 p48 Ap 2017

Jupiter High at Dawn *Sky & Telescope* v133 no2 p50 F 2017

Jupiter Rediscovered F. Bagenal *Sky & Telescope* v134 no6 p14 D 2017

KEEPING TRACK OF THE NIGHT: An experienced observer describes the benefits and pleasures of keeping an astrojournal B. King *Sky & Telescope* v134 no3 p33 S 2017

Keep your eyes on the eclipse G. CHAPLE color *Astronomy* v45 no8 p84 Ag 2017

Lost star may be failed supernova C. CROCKETT *Science News* v190 no8 p8 O 15 2016

Lunar Almanac Northern Hemisphere Sky Chart *Sky & Telescope* v134 no3 p42 S 2017

Machines Learning Astronomy: The new era of artificial intelligence & Big Data is changing how we do astronomy M. Young *Sky & Telescope* v134 no6 p20 D 2017

Navigating the sky M. E. Bakich color *Astronomy* v45 no8 p52 Ag 2017

New haul of distant worlds casts doubt on Planet Nine J. Sokol *Science* v356 no6344 p1221 Je 23 2017

NOVEMBER 2017 OBSERVING color *Sky & Telescope* v134 no5 p41 N 2017

OBSERVING August 2017 color *Sky & Telescope* v134 no2 p41 Ag 2017

OBSERVING December 2017 M. WEDEL *Sky & Telescope* v134 no6 p41 D 2017

OBSERVING July 2017 *Sky & Telescope* v134 no1 p41 Jl 2017

Observing on the edge R. Pommier color *Astronomy* v45 no3 p50 Mr 2017

OBSERVING *Sky & Telescope* v133 no2 p41 F 2017

Oklahoma skies J. HESTER color *Astronomy* v45 no3 p18 Mr 2017

An Outburst At Last? *Sky & Telescope* v134 no6 p50 D 2017

Overlooked Wonders of Summer: Take some time to explore these lesser-known deep-sky sights S. French chart color *Sky & Telescope* v134 no2 p54 Ag 2017

The past, present, and future of ASTRONOMY IN JAPAN I. Loomis color *Astronomy* v45 no3 p44 Mr 2017

PATH OF THE PLANETS chart color diag graph map *Astronomy* v45 no3 p40 Mr 2017

Peaks of "Eternal" Light C. Wood *Sky & Telescope* v133 no6 p52 Je 2017

Pluto's slushy heart contains a large ocean bw *Astronomy* v45 no3 p13 Mr 2017

Proxima Centauri b Likely a Desert World C. M. CARLISLE *Sky & Telescope* v133 no5 p10 My 2017

A Rainbow in the Velvet of the Night L. E. Jasinski *Sky & Telescope* v133 no2 p84 F 2017

The Silver Coin M. Wedel chart color *Sky & Telescope* v134 no5 p42 N 2017

The Star Adventurer Mini Tracker: Sky-Watcher's newest Star Adventurer merges an astronomical tracker with a time-lapse motion controller A. Dyer *Sky & Telescope* v134 no6 p58 D 2017

STAR DOME chart map *Astronomy* v45 no3 p38 Mr 2017

STRANGE NEWS FROM Another Star K. Cartier and J. T. Wright color diag graph *Scientific American* v316 no5 p36 My 2017

The strange star discovered by Planet Hunters B. E. Schaefer *Physics Today* v70 no3 p82 Mr 2017

TRAPPIST-1 Star Is Old C. M. CARLISLE *Sky & Telescope* v134 no6 p10 D 2017

Twelve Steps to Infinity M. Wedel *Sky & Telescope* v132 no6 p24 D 2016

Understanding Surface Brightness J. Oltion *Sky & Telescope* v134 no6 p28 D 2017

A universe with 10 times more galaxies D. J. Eicher color *Astronomy* v45 no3 p8 Mr 2017

Whatever you do, just look D. J. Eicher color *Astronomy* v45 no8 p8 Ag 2017

What's in the sky tonight? *Sky & Telescope* v133 no1 p84 Ja 2017

The White Dwarf That Survived The Blast J. BARBUZANO *Sky & Telescope* v134 no6 p11 D 2017

Wonders of the Year-Start Sky F. Schaaf *Sky & Telescope* v133 no1 p45 Ja 2017

Astronomical observations—International cooperation

Amateurs Find Asteroid's Moon J. K. BEATTY color *Sky & Telescope* v134 no5 p8 N 2017

Astronomical observatories

75, 50 & 25 YEARS AGO R. W. Sinnott *Sky & Telescope* v133 no1 p7 Ja 2017

HOUSE OF THE SUN I. Loomis color map *Science* v357 no6350 p444 Ag 4 2017

Prepping for the Really Big Show M. W. SCHWARTZ chart color diag *Missouri Life* v44 no2 p28 Ap 2017

The Square KILOMETRE ARRAY G. Schilling *Sky & Telescope* v133 no6 p24 Je 2017

A Star Wars-Inspired Observatory J. Zorthian color *Time* v190 no12 p23 S 25 2017

Triplet of high-energy neutrinos detected from unknown source E. Conover *Science News* v191 no6 p16 Ap 1 2017

Astronomical observatories—California

Peering into the FUTURE of LICK OBSERVATORY L. L. Rivera *Science & Technology Review* p16 S 2016

Astronomical observatories—Chile

The Stellar Storyteller C. Crockett color *Science News* v191 no3 p20 F 18 2017

Astronomical observatories—Management

U.S. observers seek a more perfect union D. Clery chart color *Science* v355 no6324 p442 F 3 2017

Astronomical observatories—United States

Hilo, Hawaii color *National Geographic* v231 no3 p12 Mr 2017

Astronomical photography

    See also
    Lunar photography
    Space photography
    Spectrographs

ASK ASTRO C. Trujillo, M. E. Bakich et al color diag *Astronomy* v45 no3 p34 Mr 2017

CLUSTERS IN CONTRAST R. Brecher *Sky & Telescope* v133 no6 p74 Je 2017

Galaxy with a twist color *Astronomy* v45 no7 p74 Jl 2017

GALLERY color *Sky & Telescope* v134 no5 p74 N 2017

Gallery J. K. Beatty *Sky & Telescope* v132 no6 p73 D 2016

Going for gold B. BERMAN color *Astronomy* v45 no3 p10 Mr 2017

Imaging Adventure: Dry Tortugas R. S. Wright Jr. *Sky & Telescope* v133 no2 p32 F 2017

MEET THE MASTER OF Stellar Vistas R. B. Andreo color *Astronomy* v44 no12 p52 D 2016

My Stars! *Arizona Highways* v93 no4 p5 Ap 2017

MYSTERY SPOT J. O. Johnson *Sky & Telescope* v133 no6 p76 Je 2017

Oklahoma skies J. HESTER color *Astronomy* v45 no3 p18 Mr 2017

Orion with a twist color *Astronomy* v44 no12 p74 D 2016

Phantoms of the Deep Sky R. Jakiel *Sky & Telescope* v133 no6 p70 Je 2017

READER GALLERY color *Astronomy* v45 no3 p70 Mr 2017

A smartphone lunar atlas G. CHAPLE color *Astronomy* v45 no6 p62 Je 2017

Snap the Night Sky on a Phone S. BUSHWICK cartoon *Popular Science* p78 Ja/F 2017

The stellar shreds of supernovas C. Crockett color *Science News* v191 no3 p32 F 18 2017

TAKE A SWIM IN THE LAGOON C. Manges *Sky & Telescope* v133 no6 p74 Je 2017

Astronomical photography—Congresses

Event Calendar color *Sky & Telescope* v134 no5 p83 N 2017

Astronomical photography—Equipment & supplies

Turn your smartphone into an astro-camera T. Trusock color *Astronomy* v45 no3 p58 Mr 2017

Astronomical photometry

    See also
    Galactic magnitudes

How Astronomers Measure Brightness M. E. BAKICH color *Discover* v38 no8 p64 O 2017

Astronomical research

KEEPING TRACK OF THE NIGHT: An experienced observer describes the benefits and pleasures of keeping an astrojournal B. King *Sky & Telescope* v134 no3 p33 S 2017

When Galaxies Become Cannibals M. WEST color *Discover* v38 no8 p70 O 2017

Astronomical software

WHAT'S NEW AT THE APP STORE J. MATHIS color *Macworld - Digital Edition* v34 no6 p75 Je 2017

Astronomical transits

Get ready for the next generation planet hunter J. Wenz color *Astronomy* v45 no7 p44 Jl 2017

Nebraska's magical moment in the shade 2017 ECLIPSE A. J. BARTELS color *Nebraska Life* v21 no6 p14 N/D 2017

Astronomical observations—Charts, diagrams, etc.

A COSMIC CONTROVERSY J. You, C. Bickel et al diag *Science* v355 no6329 p1013 Mr 10 2017

Planetary Almanac *Sky & Telescope* v133 no6 p44 Je 2017

Astronomy

    See also
    Astronomical instruments
    Astronomical observations
    Astronomical observatories
    Astronomical photometry
    Astronomical transits
    Astrophysics
    Calendar
    Cosmology
    Galaxies
    Meteors
    Outer space
    Seasons
    Spherical astronomy
    Statistical astronomy
    Stellar density (Stellar population)
    Zenith distance

3 Cosmic Chirps & Counting V. Kalogera *Sky & Telescope* v134 no3 p24 S 2017

The amazing William Herschel D. J. Eicher color *Astronomy* v45 no6 p8 Je 2017

BLACK AND BLUE MOON K. Haynes, J. Fuller et al color *Astronomy* v44 no12 p44 D 2016

DO YOU SPEAK "ECLIPSE"? M. E. Bakich color *Astronomy* v45 no8 p76 Ag 2017

Event Calendar *Sky & Telescope* v134 no3 p83 S 2017

EXPLORE CENTAURUS' DEEP-SKY TREASURES M. E. Bakich color *Astronomy* v45 no6 p44 Je 2017

Exploring Capricornus P. HARRINGTON bw color *Astronomy* v45 no10 p68 O 2017

The Fast Pulse of the RR Lyraes A. MacRobert *Sky & Telescope* v133 no6 p48 Je 2017

I'll have a Cosmo L. Kruesi cartoon color *Astronomy* v44 no12 p58 D 2016

Is telescope making a lost art? M. Reynolds color *Astronomy* v45 no1 p46 Ja 2017

June 2017: Peak for the ringed planet M. RATCLIFFE and A. LING color *Astronomy* v45 no6 p36 Je 2017

Let's hear it for abiogenesis D. J. Eicher color *Astronomy* v45 no9 p8 S 2017

Making sense of the exoplanetary zoo R. Naeye color *Astronomy* v45 no6 p24 Je 2017

Mapping the galaxy one star at a time K. Haynes color diag *Astronomy* v45 no6 p31 Je 2017

Memory hooks E. RIX bw *Astronomy* v45 no2 p68 F 2017

Moonwalkers and women scientists highlighted at STARMUS IV D. J. Eicher color *Astronomy* v45 no6 p50 Je 2017

NEW BOOKS *Physics Today* v70 no3 p63 Mr 2017

The past, present, and future of ASTRONOMY IN JAPAN I. Loomis color *Astronomy* v45 no3 p44 Mr 2017

PATH OF THE PLANETS chart diag graph map *Astronomy* v45 no1 p40 Ja 2017

POINT-SIZED UNIVERSE? D. Hooper, M. E. Bakich et al color *Astronomy* v45 no2 p34 F 2017

READER GALLERY color *Astronomy* v45 no10 p70 O 2017

Sandpaper blocks E. RIX color *Astronomy* v45 no5 p64 My 2017

A smartphone lunar atlas G. CHAPLE color *Astronomy* v45 no6 p62 Je 2017

A spinning, star-eating black hole color *Science* v354 no6318 p1358 D 16 2016

STAR DOME chart map *Astronomy* v45 no1 p38 Ja 2017

STAR DOME/PATH OF THE PLANETS R. TALCOTT color diag *Astronomy* v45 no6 p38 Je 2017

STAR DOME R. TALCOTT color *Astronomy* v45 no11 p38 N 2017

TALK ASTRONOMY with your un-cosmic friends M. E. Bakich bw color diag *Astronomy* v45 no10 p58 O 2017

Uncommon bino galaxies S. J. O'MEARA color *Astronomy* v45 no5 p20 My 2017

Astronomy charts & diagrams
>   *See also*
>   Star maps (Astronomy)

Charting the dark side of the universe E. Conover color map *Science News* v192 no3 p32 S 2 2017

Astronomy conferences

FUN AT AMERICA'S DARKEST SKY STAR PARTY color map *Astronomy* v45 no9 p60 S 2017

Astronomy education in universities & colleges

Student Aid A. Fraknoi color *Sky & Telescope* v134 no2 p84 Ag 2017

Astronomy in art

CONFESSIONS OF A master sketcher C. R. James bw color *Astronomy* v45 no2 p58 F 2017

MERGING TIME E. MASTROIANNI color *Discover* v38 no2 p9 Mr 2017

Astronomy in literature

The Comets of Edgar Allan Poe D. W. Olson and S. B. Ford *Sky & Telescope* v132 no6 p30 D 2016

Astronomy projects

A Mars Colony Near Dubai J. Zorthian color *Time* v190 no15 p19 O 16 2017

Astronomy—Bibliographies

BOOKS REVIEWED *Physics Today* v69 no12 p86 D 2016

NEW BOOKS *Physics Today* v69 no11 p61 N 2016

Astronomy—Competitions

Scientists, visionaries, evangelists, dreamers color *National Geographic* v232 no2 p30 Ag 2017

Astronomy—Congresses

Event Calendar *Sky & Telescope* v133 no1 p83 Ja 2017

Astronomy—Equipment & supplies

NEW PRODUCTS bw color *Astronomy* v45 no9 p69 S 2017

Astronomy—Humor

THE IRISH CONSTELLATION C. TRILLIN color *New Yorker* v93 no11 p27 My 1 2017

Astronomy—Periodicals

An astronomical workhorse D. J. EICHER *Astronomy* v45 no5 p6 My 2017

A Herculean enigma color *Astronomy* v45 no1 p74 Ja 2017

Our New Look *Sky & Telescope* v133 no1 p4 Ja 2017

TWO IMAGERS are better than one C. Temple and T. Temple color *Astronomy* v45 no1 p50 Ja 2017

Astronomy—Pictorial works

GALLERY *Sky & Telescope* v133 no4 p74 Ap 2017

Astronomy—Societies, etc.

Event Calendar *Sky & Telescope* v134 no1 p83 Jl 2017

Huge "Gancedo" Found in Argentina D. DICKINSON *Sky & Telescope* v133 no1 p18 Ja 2017

Astronomy—United States

America's observatory D. J. Eicher color *Astronomy* v45 no4 p6 Ap 2017

Astrophysical radiation
>   *See also*
>   Albedo
>   Cosmic background radiation
>   Cosmic rays

Figuring Out FRBs Y. CENDES color *Discover* v38 no1 p71 Ja/F 2017

Astrophysicists

LATE NIGHT L. ACKEN *TV Guide* p45 D 19 2016

Meg Urry J. Crelin color *Current Biography* v78 no5 p87 My 2017

Supernovae, supercomputers, and galactic evolution P. F. Hopkins *Physics Today* v70 no4 p70 Ap 2017

Astrophysicists—Interviews

Neil DeGRASSE TYSON L. WILMORE *Interview* v46 no9 p25 N 2016

Astrophysics
>   *See also*
>   Celestial mechanics
>   Collisions (Astrophysics)
>   Dark energy (Astronomy)
>   Solar evolution

Astrophysics missions vie for NASA money D. Clery color *Science* v357 no6352 p634 Ag 18 2017

Measurement of the small-scale structure of the intergalactic medium using close quasar pairs A. Rorai, J. F. Hennawi et al diag graph *Science* v356 no6336 p418 Ap 28 2017

NEW BOOKS *Physics Today* v70 no10 p64 O 2017

Astrophysics—History

POP goes the universe A. Ijjas, P. J. Steinhardt et al color graph *Scientific American* v316 no2 p32 F 2017

AstroTwins (Company)

What I Wear to Work: TALI EDUT J. Chen color *Bloomberg Businessweek* no4515 p67 Mr 20 2017

ASTRUE, MICHAEL

A Disaster That Will Tar the GOP color *Weekly Standard* v22 no32 p12 My 1 2017

Not Racing for the Cure *Weekly Standard* v23 no3 p18 S 25 2017

Putting Obamacare Out of Its Misery color *Weekly Standard* v22 no11 p26 N 21 2016

Asuka Hirai-Yuki

MAVS-dependent host species range and pathogenicity of human hepatitis A virus bibl graph *Science* v353 no6307 p1541 S 30 2016

Asuke, Soichiro

Evolution of the wheat blast fungus through functional losses in a host specificity determinant diag map *Science* v357 no6346 p80 Jl 7 2017

ASW Distillery (Company)

Rye Revival W. BROCK *Atlanta* v56 no11 p55 Mr 2017

Asylums (Institutions)

Buffalo's Fall and Rise: An inspiring case history of an urban turnaround B. KAUFFMAN *American Conservative* v16 no5 p20 S/O 2017

Seeking asylum G. Adamson bw color *Magazine Antiques* v184 no5 p22 S/O 2017

Asymmetric warfare

The Age of Weaponized Narative or, Where Have You Gone, Walter Cronkite? B. R. ALLENBY *Issues in Science & Technology* v33 no4 p65 Summ 2017

Asymmetry (Chemistry)

Mirror asymmetry in life and in space B. A. McGuire and P. B. Carroll *Physics Today* v69 no11 p86 N 2016

Asymptote Ltd.

new products: cell/tissue culture color *Science* v355 no6329 p1085 Mr 10 2017

Async (Music)

Classical Confluence Y. KATO color *Downbeat* v84 no10 p68 O 2017

At Home With Amy Sedaris (TV program)

At Home With Amy Sedaris D. Holbrook *TV Guide* v65 no43 p37 O 16 2017

Every Home Needs a Wig Wall A. Sternbergh img *New York* v50 no18 p74 S 4 2017

At-risk youth

Arts Unleashed: Creating Successful, Lasting Arts Programs P. Jacoby-Garrett *Parks & Recreation* v52 no8 p38 Ag 2017

Changing the Praxis of Retention in Higher Education: A Plan to TEACH All Learners A. M. Eitzen, M. A. Kinney et al *Change* v48 no6 p58 N/D 2016

State Street's CEO on Creating Employment for At-Risk Youths J. Hooley color graph img *Harvard Business Review* v95 no3 p41 My/Je 2017

At the Fork (Film)

BIRD FRIENDLY S. Stonebrook *Mother Earth News* no281 p10 Ap/My 2017

At the Hawk's Well (Theatrical production)

Otherworldly J. Acocella cartoon *New Yorker* v92 no35 p20 O 31 2016

At the Supermax: For Vernon (Poem)

At the Supermax: For Vernon S. M. Babbs color *U.S. Catholic* v82 no9 p11 S 2017

At Winter (Poem)

AT WINTER C. D'ESTE *Humanist* v77 no1 p46 Ja/F 2017

Atacama Large Millimeter Array (Project)

Identifying the hosts of quasar absorbers color *Science* v355 no6331 p1277 Mr 24 2017

Spiral arms detected around an infant star A. G. Smart *Physics Today* v69 no12 p22 D 2016

Atala, Anthony

MIRACLE MAKER M. SHAER *Smithsonian* v47 no8 p40 D 2016

Atallah, Bassam V.

Midbrain dopamine neurons control judgment of time bibl graph *Science* v354 no6317 p1273 D 9 2016

Atamian, Christopher

Dancing in Space color *Weekly Standard* v22 no29 p37 Ap 3 2017

On Their Feet color *Weekly Standard* v22 no15 p35 D 19 2016

Perchance to Dream color *Weekly Standard* v22 no31 p43 Ap 17 2017

ATANMO, GLORIA

Balling on a Budget color *Ebony* v72 no8 p54 Je 2017

Atatürk, Kemal, 1881-1938

Measured Terror S. Ihrig *History Today* v67 no2 p38 F 2017

Atcherson, Samuel R.

Community network for deaf scientists color *Science* v356 no6336 p386 Ap 28 2017

ATEN, JAMIE

A WALKING DISASTER color *Christianity Today* v61 no5 p44 Je 2017

Atencio, Peter

KEANU C. Gunnestad color *Sound & Vision* v81 no10 p70 D 2016

Atesoglu, Ayhan

The extent of forest in dryland biomes [Cover story] chart map *Science* v356 no6338 p635 My 12 2017

Athalia

GYNOPHOBIA *Lapham's Quarterly* v10 no3 p73 Summ 2017

ATHAR, SHAHID

Mysteries of the Self: The poet-philosopher Mohammad Iqbal stressed discovering and valuing the self for ever-lasting success *Islamic Horizons* v46 no4 p58 Jl/Ag 2017

A Supportive Advisor: The IMANA Medical Ethics Committee reaches out to physicians, patients and all those who want Islam-

ic answers to crucial life issues [Cover story] *Islamic Horizons* v46 no3 p28 My/Je 2017

Atheists

THE NEW SECULAR MOMENT T. KRATTENMAKER *Humanist* v77 no2 p16 Mr/Ap 2017

Atheists—Legal status, laws, etc.

Religious Freedom Act also protects atheists K. Winston *Christian Century* v134 no2 p15 Ja 18 2017

Atheists—Social aspects

HUMANIST PROFILE K. Winston *Humanist* v77 no5 p2 S/O 2017

Athena (Poem)

ATHENA F. Seidel *New York Review of Books* v64 no11 p55 Je 22 2017

Athens (Greece)—History

Athens as Analogy J. Borini color *Atlantic* v319 no5 p12 Je 2017

Athens, Paul

The SAILING SCENE color *Sail* v48 no10 p8 O 2017

Atherosclerosis

Senescent intimal foam cells are deleterious at all stages of atherosclerosis B. G. Childs, D. J. Baker et al bibl *Science* v354 no6311 p472 O 28 2016

Atherosclerosis—Genetic aspects

Hematopoietic stem cells gone rogue Y. Peipei Zhu, C. C. Hedrick et al bibl color diag *Science* v355 no6327 p798 F 24 2017

Atherosclerosis—Risk factors

Clonal hematopoiesis associated with TET2 deficiency accelerates atherosclerosis development in mice J. J. Fuster, S. MacLauchlan et al bibl diag *Science* v355 no6327 p842 F 24 2017

Atherton, Kelsey

AERO-SPACE color *Popular Science* v288 no6 p52 N/D 2016

A botnet vaccine [Cover story] color *Popular Science* v289 no6 p49 N/D 2017

a brief history of time(keeping) bw color *Popular Science* v289 no5 p14 S/O 2017

The Drone Catcher color *Popular Science* v288 no6 p64 N/D 2016

GIANTS OF THE SKY color *Popular Science* p54 Ja/F 2017

i catch clouds for a living cartoon *Popular Science* v289 no4 p86 Jl/Ag 2017

I flew combat drones... and I'm not a pilot color *Popular Science* v289 no6 p82 N/D 2017

MACHINES OF THE ABYSS diag *Popular Science* p26 Ja/F 2017

Rocket to the Red Planet color diag *Popular Science* v289 no6 p54 N/D 2017

WATER *Popular Science* v289 no2 p64 Mr/Ap 2017

WHERE THEY TAME THE UNDRINKABLE OCEAN color *Popular Science* v289 no2 p66 Mr/Ap 2017

Athey, Susan

Beyond prediction: Using big data for policy problems bibl color *Science* v355 no6324 p483 F 3 2017

Athie, Mamoudou

Mamoudou ATHIE *Interview* v47 no5 p63 Je/Jl 2017

Athitakis, Mark

SURVEY SAYS C. FEHRMAN *Cincinnati Magazine* v50 no5 p20 F 2017

Athlete awards

GATORADE Players Of the Year J. Fuchs color diag *Sports Illustrated* v127 no1 p72 Jl 3 2017

Athletes

See also

Baseball players
Basketball players
Bodybuilders
Canoeists
Child athletes
Cyclists
Football players
Golfers
Hockey players
Martial artists
Mexican athletes
Mountaineers
Older athletes
Rugby football players
Runners (Sports)

See also
Sneakers
Back in Style: White Kicks color *Health* v31 no5 p9 Je 2017
GOINGS ON ABOUT TOWN color *New Yorker* v93 no29 p11 S 25 2017
Knit to Be Tied R. S. Frazier color *Health* v31 no7 p77 S 2017
LIFT AIR BOSS color *Flying* v144 no6 p12 Je 2017
WORKING GIRL *Interview* v47 no6 p27 Ag 2017

Athletic shoes—Evaluation
And the Techy Goes To... M. Chwasky color *Golf Magazine* v58 no11 p66 N 2016
Best in Shoe: 2017 T. NEWCOMB *Tennis* v53 no3 p16 My/Je 2017
DUTY FREE: MAKE EXTRA ROOM FOR THE SEASON'S MUST-HAVE ACCESSORIES *Interview* v47 no3 p48 Ap 2017
Field Notes color *Climbing* no357 p26 N 2017
GROUND BREAKERS J. Dengate and M. Shorten color *Runner's World* v52 no9 p71 O 2017
I Wanna Wear Sneakers! color *Glamour* v114 no7 p58 Jl 2016
The Sneaker Selector D. MICHEL cartoon color *Men's Health* v32 no4 p60 My 2017
Spring SHOE GUIDE J. DENGATE and M. SHORTEN cartoon chart color diag *Runner's World* v52 no2 p71 Mr 2017
Sweatshirt + Dress = Yes! color *Glamour* v114 no7 p54 Jl 2016
Women's Health 2017 SHOE GUIDE M. Gainsburg color *Women's Health* v14 no3 p62 Ap 2017

Athletic tape
Let's Talk TAPE N. Chirico color *Horse & Rider* v56 no1 p58 Ja 2017

Athletic trainers
See also
Personal trainers
ACTIVATE YOUR HORSE'S MOTOR J. M. V. Torrão and A. Morris color *Dressage Today* v23 no7 p22 Mr 2017
The Trainer Certification Program Moves From Tortoise to Hare S. Campf *In Stride* v12 no3 p8 My 2017

Athletic leagues—Charts, diagrams, etc.
Developing Story T. Keith chart color *Sports Illustrated* v126 no3 p16 Ja 23 2017

Athletics
See also
Boxing
Fencing
Gymnastics
Mixed martial arts
Swimming
Triathlon
Walking
Wrestling
COMMON GROUND T. KOCH bw color *Black Belt* v55 no5 p54 Ag/S 2017
Country REVIVAL: HOW THE STRAIGHT-TALKING, COYOTE-SHOOTING, TOBACCO CHEWING JOHN SHARP HAS LED A BONANZA AT TEXAS A&M M. HARDY *Texas Monthly* v45 no8 p78 Ag 2017
A Family Reunion with a Twist [Cover story] S. KELLY bw color *Cabin Living* p46 Ag 2017
POWER PLAY M. BERG color *Muscle & Performance* v9 no1 p18 Ja 2017
TAI CHI VS. MMA MATCH ANGERS CHINA *Black Belt* v55 no5 p8 Ag/S 2017

Athyntiq (Company)
Inspired by Athena and Aided by Facebook R. SCHABAUER and K. INCHINGALO *USA Today Magazine* v145 no2862 p74 Mr 2017

Atikian, H. A.
An integrated diamond nanophotonics platform for quantum-optical networks bibl graph *Science* v354 no6314 p847 N 18 2016

Atiyeh, Clifford
auto no mo' us bw color diag graph *Car & Driver* v63 no5 p58 N 2017
AXLES TO GRIND color graph *Car & Driver* v62 no6 p28 D 2016
FINE PRINT color *Car & Driver* v63 no1 p22 Jl 2017
HAULIN' JUICE color *Car & Driver* v62 no11 p24 My 2017
HOT CARS chart graph *Car & Driver* v63 no5 p22 N 2017

New Life for the Gas Engine color *Popular Science* v288 no6 p42 N/D 2016

Atkeson, Christopher G.
Human-in-the-loop optimization of exoskeleton assistance during walking diag *Science* v356 no6344 p1280 Je 23 2017

Atkins, Ace
Southern Discomfort L. PICKER color *Publishers Weekly* v264 no26 p129 Je 26 2017

Atkins, Andrea
The Good FIGHT cartoon *O, The Oprah Magazine* p92 F 2017
YOU BETTER WATCH OUT cartoon *O, The Oprah Magazine* p121 D 2016

Atkins, Finn
Behind the Scenes J. POWERS and V. STEIKER color *Vogue* v207 no3 p386 Mr 2017

Atkins, Juan
NIGHT LIFE *New Yorker* v93 no24 p5 Ag 21 2017

Atkins, Ken
Publish openly but responsibly color *Science* v357 no6347 p141 Jl 14 2017

Atkins, Robert
Our Kind of Memoir color *Art in America* v105 no5 p55 My 2017

Atkins v. Virginia (Supreme Court case)
Should the Death Penalty Be Abolished? D. RUST-TIERNEY and J. MARQUIS *New York Times Upfront* v149 no9 p22 F 20 2017

ATKINSON, ASHLEIGH
Maximize Your Postworkout Recovery color *Muscle & Performance* v9 no11 p64 N 2017

Atkinson, Caitlin
BEST OF THE WEST J. Chamberlain and M. Mccrea color *Sunset* v237 no5 p11 N 2016
URBAN JUNGLE color *Sunset* v238 no2 p42 F 2017

Atkinson, Cale
Where Oliver Fits In *Publishers Weekly* v264 no27 p72 Jl 3 2017

Atkinson, Geoff
THE MOST CONTROVERSIAL TV SHOW EVER S. Li color *Entertainment Weekly* no1460/1461 p80 Ap 7-17 2017

Atkinson, Gordon
Trading in my narrative *Christian Century* v134 no7 p30 Mr 29 2017

ATKINSON, JO
COLOUR confident bw color *House Beautiful* p78 Ag 2017

ATKINSON, MICHAEL
All the World's Their Stage *In These Times* v41 no10 p44 O 2017
Don't Let Your Babies Grow Up to Be Consultants *In These Times* v40 no12 p38 D 2016
The Elusive Emily Dickinson *In These Times* v41 no5 p36 My 2017
The Filmmaker Banned By Trump *In These Times* v41 no3 p39 Mr 2017
A Ghost of a Storyline *In These Times* v41 no7 p37 Jl 2017
Girl, You'll Be a Cannibal Soon *In These Times* v41 no4 p52 Ap 2017
A Love Poem to Neruda *In These Times* v41 no1 p37 Ja 2017
Okja, Super-Pig in the City *In These Times* v41 no8 p36 Ag 2017
The Real Best Pictures of 2016 *In These Times* v41 no2 p38 F 2017
The Return of Nunsploitation *In These Times* v41 no6 p36 Je 2017

Atkinson, Niall
U.S. Pavilion to Explore Citizenship at 2018 Venice Architecture Biennale M. SITZ *Architectural Record* v205 no10 p28 O 2017

ATKINSON, ROBERT D.
In Defense Of Robots *National Review* v69 no7 p35 Ap 17 2017
Industrial Policy by Tweet color *National Review* v69 no4 p20 Mr 6 2017
Manufacturing's loss, Trump's gain color *Issues in Science & Technology* v33 no1 p5 Fall 2016
The Neo-Brandeisian Attack on Big Business bw color *National Review* v69 no18 p18 O 2 2017
Our Approach to Economic Growth Isn't Working *Harvard Business Review Digital Articles* p2 F 16 2016
Toward a National Productivity Strategy [Cover story] il *National Review* v68 no24 p24 D 31 2016

Atlanta (Ga.)
50 Best, Refreshed C. KUMMER, C. LAUTERBACH et al *Atlanta* v56 no11 p2 Mr 2017

Barbershop Bonanza *Atlanta* v57 no3 p39 Jl 2017

BEST FOOT FORWARD *Atlanta* v57 no5 p103 S 2017

COMMON GROUND C. ALBERT-DEITCH *Atlanta* v56 no11 p96 Mr 2017

DINING GUIDE *Atlanta* v56 no9 p163 Ja 2017

Dinner with the Youngs: Our new column looks at how Atlantans dine--at home. This month politician Andrew Young, his son, and his grandchildren are "Home for Dinner" *Atlanta* v57 no3 p49 Jl 2017

EMPIRE BUILDING, MARIETTA & BROAD 1900 T. Wheatley *Atlanta* v57 no5 p160 S 2017

FEEL-GOOD DISHES [Cover story] M. FORD *Atlanta* v56 no9 p70 Ja 2017

FRESH ON THE SCENE C. LAUTERBACH *Atlanta* v56 no9 p62 Ja 2017

A LEAGUE OF YOUR OWN L. BELLOWS *Atlanta* v56 no11 p102 Mr 2017

LOVING SPOONFUL C. KUMMER *Atlanta* v56 no9 p73 Ja 2017

Paletas, Not Pops *Atlanta* v57 no2 p56 Je 2017

A PARK FOR VINE CITY S. HENRY *Atlanta* v56 no9 p24 Ja 2017

PAST LIFE J. RAINEY MARQUEZ *Atlanta* v56 no9 p38 Ja 2017

THE PATTERSON PAPERS H. KLIBANOFF *Atlanta* v56 no10 p90 F 2017

PLAY STATION C. PENDLEY *Atlanta* v56 no11 p95 Mr 2017

SAVING PLACE J. GREEN *Atlanta* v56 no11 p35 Mr 2017

THE SECOND BURNING OF ATLANTA R. Burns *Atlanta* v56 no10 p84 F 2017

SOCCER CITY! *Atlanta* v56 no11 p90 Mr 2017

A SOCCER TOWN... W. PARKER *Atlanta* v56 no11 p94 Mr 2017

Spring J. ZYMAN *Atlanta* v56 no9 p60 Ja 2017

TO-GO M. FORD *Atlanta* v56 no9 p75 Ja 2017

TRANSITION A. RICHARD ALBANESE color *Publishers Weekly* v263 no52 p31 D 19 2016

Atlanta (Ga.)—Description & travel

EAST ATLANTA VILLAGE G. CHAPMAN *Atlanta* v56 no10 p50 F 2017

In Search of MLK's Atlanta N. SHAVIN *Smithsonian* v47 no9 p18 Ja/F 2017

Starcation: Atlanta O. RAYMOND and D. POINTDUJOUR color *Ebony* v72 no5 p59 Mr 2017

UPPER WESTSIDE M. BLAU *Atlanta* v56 no12 p52 Ap 2017

Atlanta (Ga.)—Economic conditions

THE TWO ATLANTAS: Things are looking up right now in the city. Well, at least part of it A. Greenblatt *Governing* v31 no1 p36 O 2017

Atlanta (Ga.)—Politics & government

Atlanta Blues B. SEITZ color *National Review* v69 no12 p29 Je 26 2017

Atlanta (Ga.)—Social conditions

GIVE ATLANTA S. MCGINNIS *Atlanta* v57 no6 p20 O 2017

Atlanta (TV program)

5 MORE SHOWS YOU NEED TO SEE L. Rice, C. Agard et al color *Entertainment Weekly* no1435 p24 O 14 2016

CHEERS & JEERS D. HOLBROOK *TV Guide* v65 no6 p88 Ja 30 2017

The Culturati Caucus img *New York* v49 no25 p124 D 12 2016

Off to the Races! M. Roush *TV Guide* v65 no31 p4 Jl 24 2017

TELEVISION OF THE YEAR R. SHEFFIELD color *Rolling Stone* no1276 p22 D 15 2016

Atlanta Ballet

DIY Ballet: Five former Atlanta Ballet dancers have taken their careers into their own hands C. Thompson *Dance Magazine* v91 no10 p14 O 2017

TURNING POINTE C. BOND PERRY *Atlanta* v56 no8 p48 D 2016

Atlanta Braves (Baseball team)

3 BRAVES color *Sports Illustrated* v126 no9 p97 Mr 27 2017

8 BRAVE NEW WORLD S. Apstein color *Sports Illustrated* v126 no9 p50 Mr 27 2017

The BRAVES' NEW WORLD J. GREEN *Atlanta* v56 no12 p84 Ap 2017

COUNTERPOINTS S. FENNESSY *Atlanta* v56 no12 p16 Ap 2017

Atlanta Falcons (Football team)

1 Atlanta Falcons color *Sports Illustrated* v127 no7 p96 S 4 2017

THE FOX FOCUS color *Sports Illustrated* v126 no4 p29 Ja 30 2017

NFL PREVIEW TOP 10 CONTENDERS R. A. BERENZ *TV Guide* v65 no37 p55 S 4 2017

OUR CIVIC DNA S. FENNESSY *Atlanta* v56 no11 p16 Mr 2017

OUR TIME? NOT THIS TIME J. KOVAC JR. *Atlanta* v56 no11 p19 Mr 2017

Atlanta Falcons (Football team)—History

RUN THIS TOWN [Cover story] J. Jones color *Sports Illustrated* v126 no4 p24 Ja 30 2017

Atlanta Falcons (Football team)—Management

Atlanta's Patriot Way S. Gregory color *Time* v189 no4 p55 F 6 2017

Atlanta Hawks (Basketball team)

12 HAWKS color *Sports Illustrated* v127 no12 p71 O 16 2017

6 Hawks R. Mahoney, B. Golliver et al color *Sports Illustrated* v125 no14 p80 O 24-31 2016

Atlanta Hawks (Basketball team)—Officials & employees

SI NOW M. Gray color *Sports Illustrated* v125 no14 p6 O 24-31 2016

Atlanta Meal Prep (Company)

Sliced, Sealed, Delivered J. ZYMAN *Atlanta* v56 no9 p53 Ja 2017

Atlanta Opera (Performer)

IN PERFECT HARMONY T. MALONE *Atlanta* v56 no12 p40 Ap 2017

Atlanta Public Schools

Camille Russell Love *Atlanta* v57 no2 p94 Je 2017

DIVERSE BY DESIGN T. Wheatley *Atlanta* v57 no5 p23 S 2017

Atlanta Symphony Orchestra (Performer)

HOME GROWN J. R. MARQUEZ *Atlanta* v56 no12 p33 Ap 2017

Atlantic Coast (N.J.)

New Jersey Builds Walls Against a Rising Tide C. Flavelle color *Bloomberg Businessweek* no4521 p25 My 8 2017

Atlantic multidecadal oscillation

How an ocean climate cycle favored Harvey J. Rosen color graph *Science* v357 no6354 p853 S 1 2017

Atlantic Ocean

Greater role for Atlantic inflows on sea-ice loss in the Eurasian Basin of the Arctic Ocean I. V. Polyakov, A. V. Pnyushkov et al chart diag graph *Science* v356 no6335 p285 Ap 21 2017

Atlantic Provinces

Least Coast R. MCNUTT color *Walrus* v14 no8 p17 O 2017

Atlantic salmon

Born to be wild A. Pope cartoon map *Canadian Geographic* v137 no1 p28 F 2017

Atlantis (Legendary place)

'Atlantis at its Prime', 1896 K. Wiles *History Today* v66 no12 p18 D 2016

ATLAS, JAMES

Headed for the Graveyard of Books *New York Times Book Review* p21 F 12 2017

Atlas, Scott W.

Mythbusting Health Care: How health insurance should work *Hoover Digest: Research & Opinion on Public Policy* no3 p38 Summ 2017

Atlas Model Railroad Co. Inc.

Atlas HO scale FMC 5347 boxcar C. Grivno color *Model Railroader* v84 no9 p62 S 2017

Atlas HO scale NJ Transit commuter train [Cover story] D. Kawala color *Model Railroader* v84 no7 p60 Jl 2017

Atlas N Dry-Flo covered hopper C. Grivno *Model Railroader* v84 no6 p68 Je 2017

Atlas N scale FMC boxcar color *Model Railroader* v84 no2 p75 F 2017

Atlas N scale Norfolk Southern gondola C. Grivno color *Model Railroader* v84 no4 p99 Ap 2017

FREELANCED PAINT SCHEMES from factory-painted models B. Kingsnorth color *Model Railroader* v84 no2 p42 F 2017

New paint schemes for smooth-running Atlas N scale General Electric B36-7 E. White bw color *Model Railroader* v83 no12 p68 D 2016

Atlas O LLC

Atlas O Maxi-IV well cars pack a heavy punch E. White color

Model Railroader v84 no3 p68 Mr 2017
Atlas O Pullman troop sleeper S. Otte Model Railroader v84 no10 p63 O 2017

Atlases
Knowledge keepers J. BENNETT color Canadian Geographic v137 no5 p29 S/O 2017

Atlases—Computer network resources
An interactive three-dimensional digital atlas and quantitative database of human development B. S. de Bakker, K. H. de Jong et al bibl color graph Science v354 no6315 paag0053-1 N 25 2016

Atli, Kristján—Interviews
FINE PRINT L. KYZER Iceland Review v55 no2 p62 Mr/Ap 2017

Atmosphere
See also
Sky
ECLIPSE your fears T. EICHENSEHER color Yoga Journal no293 p51 Ag 2017

Atmosphere of Jupiter
See also
Jupiter's Great Red Spot
Juno's early results reveal a mysterious Jupiter color Astronomy v45 no10 p17 O 2017

Atmospheres of extrasolar planets
Exoplanet's skies hint at origin story A. YEAGER color Science News v191 no11 p11 Je 10 2017

Atmospheric carbon dioxide
What Carbon Really Costs E. BETZ color Discover v38 no6 p10 Jl/Ag 2017

Atmospheric carbon dioxide—Environmental aspects
Sea ice shrinks in step with carbon emissions W. Cornwall color map Science v354 no6312 p533 N 4 2016

Atmospheric chemistry
Global atmospheric particle formation from CERN CLOUD measurements E. M. Dunne, H. Gordon et al bibl graph map Science v354 no6316 p1119 D 2 2016

Atmospheric methane
Mystery over methane rise deepens T. SUMNER Science News v191 no9 p14 My 13 2017

Atmospheric models
Climate scientists open up their black boxes to scrutiny P. Voosen color Science v354 no6311 p401 O 28 2016
Using climate models to estimate the quality of global observational data sets F. Massonnet, O. Bellprat et al bibl graph Science v354 no6311 p452 O 28 2016

Atmospheric nucleation
Active sites in heterogeneous ice nucleation—the example of K-rich feldspars A. Kiselev, F. Bachmann et al bibl bw diag Science v355 no6323 p367 Ja 27 2017
Cracking the problem of ice nucleation B. J. Murray bibl color diag Science v355 no6323 p346 Ja 27 2017

Atmospheric physics
See also
Atmospheric pressure
Atmospheric structure
Auroras
Precipitation (Meteorology)
Rainbow Detectives: When Art Gets Meteorology Wrong R. C. Balling, R. Cerveny et al Weatherwise v70 no2 p24 Mr/Ap 2017

Atmospheric pressure
Aching In The Rain K. Massicot color New Orleans Magazine v51 no8 p36 Je 2017
ALTIMETRY AROUND THE WORLD R. Lengel color Flying v144 no10 p32 O 2017
Weather Queries T. W. Schlatter Weatherwise v70 no2 p32 Mr/Ap 2017

Atmospheric pressure measurement
Weather Queries T. W. Schlatter diag graph map Weatherwise v69 no6 p42 N-D 2016
WHAT IS THE FOUR-STROKE CYCLE? K. Cameron color Cycle World v56 no5 p30 Je 2017

Atmospheric rivers
California rains put spotlight on atmospheric rivers J. Rosen color Science v355 no6327 p787 F 24 2017

Atmospheric structure
Mars' atmospheric history derived from upper-atmosphere measurements of 38 Ar/36Ar B. M. Jakosky, M. Slipski et al diag Science v355 no6332 p1408 Mr 31 2017

Atmospheric temperature
Cooling Effect of an Eclipse H. Leifert Natural History v125 no1 p7 D 2016/Ja 2017
Data show no sign of methane boost T. SUMNER Science News v191 no1 p15 Ja 21 2017

Atmospheric temperature measurements
2016 shattered Earth's heat record T. SUMNER map Science News v191 no3 p9 F 18 2017

Atmospheric temperature—Environmental aspects
EARTH'S REVERINE BLOODSTREAM J. Hemingway color Oceanus v51 no2 p12 Wint 2016

Atmospheric waves
See also
Radio waves
Fast Radio Burst Has Surprising Source S. HALL Sky & Telescope v133 no4 p10 Ap 2017
Fast radio burst's home identified C. CROCKETT color Science News v191 no2 p10 F 4 2017

Atom-probe tomography
Atoms on the move—finding the hydrogen J. Cairney bibl diag Science v355 no6330 p1128 Mr 17 2017

Atomic (Company)
The Best Boots of 2018 A. Buecking, C. Sagan et al color Powder p95 S 2017

Atomic Blonde (Film)
Atomic Blonde C. Nashawaty color Entertainment Weekly no1476 p48 Ag 4 2017
Atomic Blonde Kicks You Where It Hurts S. Zacharek color Time v190 no6 p54 Ag 7 2017
ATOMIC BLONDE N. Sperling color Entertainment Weekly no1463/1464 p60 Ap/My 2017
BLONDE AMBITION: FILMING A KILLER ACTION SEQUENCE M. YARM bw color Wired v25 no8 p16 Ag 2017
BLONDE, SWEAT & TEARS [Cover story] S. Vilkomerson color Entertainment Weekly p12 Jl 24 2017
Charlize Theron in Atomic Blonde N. Sperling color Entertainment Weekly no1457/1458 p76 Mr 17 2017
A Fierce Role Model S. ERICKSON Los Angeles Magazine v62 no9 p72 S 2017
GAME PLAN M. Zimmerman color diag map Men's Health v32 no6 p10 Ag 2017
GENTLEMEN BEWARE BLONDES S. Vilkomerson color Entertainment Weekly no1474/1475 p50 Jl 21-28 2017
Going Theronuclear J. Podhoretz color Weekly Standard v22 no47 p47 Ag 21 2017
Lethally Blonde E. Dockterman color Time v190 no6 p46 Ag 7 2017
Summer Movie Preview: July S. Begley, E. Berman et al color Time v189 no20 p56 My 29 2017

Atomic bomb—History—20th century
Hiroshima, His Amour Commentary v142 no1 p1 Jl/Ag 2016

Atomic bomb—Social aspects
Confronting the Heart of Darkness R. Patti Nakai bw Tricycle: The Buddhist Review v26 no4 p28 Summ 2017

Atomic frequency standards
Storing light in a tiny box E. Waks and E. A. Goldschmidt diag Science v357 no6358 p1354 S 29 2017

Atomic models
Life in Picoseconds Issues in Science & Technology v33 no3 p6 Spr 2017

Atomic nucleus
Neutrinos caught bouncing off nuclei E. CONOVER color Science News v192 no3 p7 S 2 2017

Atomic number
GETTING TO THE END OF THE MATTER Science & Technology Review p12 D 2016

Atomic structure
See also
Electronic structure
Physicists discover 'bubble nucleus' E. CONOVER color Science News v190 no11 p11 N 26 2016

Atomics (Performer)
FAMILY Style J. Abidor color Seventeen v76 no4 p68 Jl/Ag 2017

Atoms

See also

Electrons

An atom-by-atom assembler of defect-free arbitrary two-dimensional atomic arrays D. Barredo, S. de Léséleuc et al bibl bw diag graph *Science* v354 no6315 p1021 N 25 2016

Atom-by-atom assembly of defect-free one-dimensional cold atom arrays M. Endres, H. Bernien et al bibl diag graph *Science* v354 no6315 p1024 N 25 2016

Bringing order to neutral atom arrays C. Regal bibl diag *Science* v354 no6315 p972 N 25 2016

Cold molecules: Progress in quantum engineering of chemistry and quantum matter J. L. Bohn, A. Maria Rey et al bw color *Science* v357 no6355 p1002 S 8 2017

Entangled atoms break record E. CONOVER *Science News* v191 no8 p8 Ap 29 2017

Atoms—Research

Nothin' But Neutrons S. PALUS color *Discover* v38 no1 p52 Ja/F 2017

Ator, Jen

H20, GO! color *Women's Health* v14 no6 p(Sp)28 Jl 2017

KICKING ASPHALT color *Women's Health* v14 no6 p(Sp)16 Jl 2017

Wrap. Me. Up [Cover story] color *Women's Health* v13 no10 p110 D 2016

YES, YOU CAN! CLIMB A MOUNTAIN color *Women's Health* v14 no8 p69 O 2017

Atos SE

How One Company Reduced Email by 64% A. Shipilov and R. J. Crawford *Harvard Business Review Digital Articles* p2 Je 18 2015

Atran, Scott

Challenges in researching terrorism from the field bibl color *Science* v355 no6323 p352 Ja 27 2017

Atreya, S.

Jupiter's interior and deep atmosphere: The initial pole-to-pole passes with the Juno spacecraft [Cover story] color graph *Science* v356 no6340 p821 My 26 2017

Atrial fibrillation

Poor sleep tied to heart rhythm issue L. BEIL *Science News* v190 no12 p7 D 10 2016

Atrial fibrillation—Prevention

News and our views *Mayo Clinic Health Letter* v35 no3 p4 Mr 2017

Atrius Health (Company)

How Atrius Health Is Making the Shift from Volume to Value T. Toussaint, K. DaSilva et al *Harvard Business Review Digital Articles* p2 D 13 2016

AT&T Inc.

Is AT&T Buying a Big Dog to Get a Fancy Tail? O. Kharif *Bloomberg Businessweek* no4498 p30 N 7 2016

AT&T Inc.—Finance

THE AT&T-TIME WARNER MERGER (UNLESS ...) A. Pressman diag *Fortune* v174 no8 p20 D 15 2016

Milestones *Time* v188 no19 p11 N 7 2016

Where the Future's AT(&T) G. Smith cartoon *Bloomberg Businessweek* no4497 p22 O 31 2016

Attachment behavior

Getting Close [Cover story] L. A. PHILLIPS *Psychology Today* v50 no1 p44 Ja/F 2017

gotta have it! J. BENJAMIN *Parents* p134 2015

Which One Is Mom Again? J. G. Goldman color *Scientific American* v316 no4 p18 Ap 2017

See also

Imprinting (Psychology)

Attack (Poem)

ATTACK S. Sassoon *Lapham's Quarterly* v10 no3 p57 Summ 2017

Attack helicopters—Evaluation

Hardware AH-64D Apachen Longbow J. Guttman *Military History* v33 no6 p16 Mr 2017

Attack on Pearl Harbor (Hawaii), 1941

CAMP DHARMA M. Scarles bw color *Tricycle: The Buddhist Review* v26 no4 p54 Summ 2017

The Day America Went Global G. NORMAN bw *Weekly Standard* v22 no15 p19 D 19 2016

The Day of INFAMY *Prologue* v48 no4 p30 Wint 2016

THE DAY WASHINGTON WOKE UP J. Lacey *MHQ: Quarterly Journal of Military History* v29 no3 p46 Spr 2017

SHOWDOWN IN THE ALEUTIANS D. Hammett *MHQ: Quarterly Journal of Military History* v29 no3 p54 Spr 2017

VETERANS MARK 75 YEARS SINCE PEARL HARBOR STRIKE B. Manley color *Military History* v34 no1 p8 My 2017

WE MUST NEVER REPEAT THE HORRORS OF WAR AGAIN *Vital Speeches of the Day* v83 no2 p47 F 2017

Attar, Andrew R.

Femtosecond x-ray spectroscopy of an electrocyclic ring-opening reaction diag graph *Science* v356 no6333 p54 Ap 7 2017

'Attār, Farīd al-Dīn, d. ca. 1230

The Seal of the Poets R. Creswell color *New York Review of Books* v64 no16 p24 O 26 2017

Attar, Samer—Awards

CHICAGOANS OF THE YEAR [Cover story] R. Babcock, A. Samuels Gibbs et al color *Chicago* v65 no12 p74 D 2016

Attara, Gail

Is 40 Years of Progress Enough? cartoon *Maclean's* v129 no48/49 p76 D 5 2016

ATTEBERRY, MEG

Walk on Snow il *Backpacker* p28 N 2017

Attenberg, Jami

FANCY FREE color *O, The Oprah Magazine* p118 Mr 2017

It's My Fiction, Not My Life! *New York Times Book Review* p13 Mr 26 2017

Turn On, Burn Out: A memoir recalls a tumultuous journey of self-discovery *New York Times Book Review* p21 Ag 13 2017

Winging Single H. SCHULMAN *New York Times Book Review* p18 Mr 19 2017

Attenborough, David, 1926-

DAVID ATTENBOROUGH T. Obreht cartoon *New Yorker* v92 no42 p104 D 19 2016

A Trestles Taxonomy T. PRODANOVICH color *Surfer* v58 no5 p32 S 2017

A View to a Kill C. DICKEY color *New Republic* v248 no3 p54 Mr 2017

Attenborough, David, 1926—Awards

ATTENBOROUGH AWARDED RCGS GOLD A. Pope color *Canadian Geographic* v137 no3 p73 My 2017

Attenborough, Robert

A Neolithic expansion, but strong genetic structure, in the independent history of New Guinea diag *Science* v357 no6356 p1160 S 15 2017

Attenello, Frank J.

CRISPRi-based genome-scale identification of functional long noncoding RNA loci in human cells bibl graph *Science* v355 no6320 p1 Ja 6 2017

Attention

See also

Boredom

Mindfulness (Psychology)

Vigilance (Psychology)

4 Signs That Your Focus Is Holding You Back at Work S. Pillay *Harvard Business Review Digital Articles* p1 Ag 30 2017

5 Tips to Improve MENTAL FOCUS A. Brock and E. S. Romm color *Dressage Today* v24 no1 p36 O 2017

7 Ways to Capture Someone's Attention B. Parr *Harvard Business Review Digital Articles* p2 Mr 3 2015

Adoration Economy N. Schneider color *America* v216 no7 p37 Ap 3 2017

BOOST YOUR BRAIN POWER [Cover story] S. Klein color *Prevention* v69 no9 p68 O 2017

Confessions of a Short Attention Span Man: Boredom is the enemy, and fear of boredom the spur J. Epstein *Commentary* v144 no3 p41 O 2017

Everything You Need to Know About Becoming a Better Listener S. G. Carmichael *Harvard Business Review Digital Articles* p2 F 6 2015

Examining Attention I. MCGILCHRIST cartoon *Tricycle: The Buddhist Review* v26 no3 p24 Spr 2017

FOCUS, FOOL! J. L. Stein color *Cycle World* v56 no6 p22 Jl 2017

Get Zen in a Hurry J. Andriakos color *Health* v31 no7 p28 S 2017

Gimme a Break C. HEITGER-EWING color *Cabin Living* p16 S 2017

Keep Calm and Shine On *O, The Oprah Magazine* p89 Mr 2017

A Mental Trick to Help with Challenging Conversations L. Davey *Harvard Business Review Digital Articles* p2 D 16 2015

MISSION: POSSIBLE! D. Phillips chart color *Golf Magazine* v59 no9 p76 S 2017

The Power of Focus A. Fox *Tennis* v53 no4 p12 Jl/Ag 2017

Stop the Negative Self-Talk *Dressage Today* v24 no1 p12 O 2017

Taking a broader view T. Koester color *Model Railroader* v84 no1 p90 Ja 2017

To Improve Your Focus, Notice How You Lose It M. Lipson *Harvard Business Review Digital Articles* p2 N 4 2015

Attention control

Manage Your Team's Attention J. Birkinshaw *Harvard Business Review Digital Articles* p2 Ja 29 2015

To Stay Focused, Manage Your Emotions E. Batista *Harvard Business Review Digital Articles* p2 F 2 2015

Attention-deficit disorder in adolescence

Focusing on ADHD V. Tweed color *Amazing Wellness* p16 Fall 2017

Attention-deficit disorder in adults

4 Signs That Your Focus Is Holding You Back at Work S. Pillay *Harvard Business Review Digital Articles* p1 Ag 30 2017

Attention-deficit hyperactivity disorder

    See also

      Attention-deficit disorder in adolescence

      Attention-deficit disorder in adults

BOOKSHOP *Psychology Today* v49 no6 p93 N/D 2016

Degrees of Separation L. SCHLEY *Discover* v38 no8 p14 O 2017

HOW ADHD MADE ME A BETTER CEO B. Fiske bw color *Men's Health* v31 no10 p83 D 2016

"I wouldn't put 'I have mental illnesses' in my Tinder profile" M. Yagoda and S. G. Levy color *Glamour* v115 no4 p124 Ap 2017

Attention-deficit hyperactivity disorder—Research

Not Your Kid's ADHD T. BURRELL cartoon *Discover* v38 no1 p65 Ja/F 2017

Attention-deficit hyperactivity disorder—Treatment

a game changer for ADHD V. SOLE-SMITH color *Parents* v92 no5 p30 My 2017

Attention span

Short attention spans, short news cycles and short form Gospels M. Malone and S. Sawyer *America* v216 no7 p3 Ap 3 2017

Attia, Kader, 1970-

KADER ATTIA L. DeLand color *Art in America* v105 no5 p134 My 2017

Attia, Mohamed ben

the chroniclers bw color *Foreign Policy* no221 p79 N/D 2016

Attias, Michaël

MICHAËL ATTIAS B. Milkowski color *Downbeat* v84 no4 p22 Ap 2017

Attic maintenance & repair

From Attic to the Basement L. Elliott color *Old House Journal* v45 no7 p46 O 2017

Attics

Ventilating an Attic M. E. Polson color diag *Old House Journal* v45 no4 p52 Je 2017

Attics—Remodeling

RAISE THE ROOF C. Lamers color *Sunset* v238 no1 p33 Ja 2017

Attitude (Psychology)

    See also

      American attitudes

      Attitudes toward entitlement

      Attitudes toward sex

      Attitudes toward technology

      Attitudes toward work

      Confidence

      Empathy

      Employee attitudes

      Executives' attitudes

      Men's attitudes

      Prejudices

      Rejection (Psychology)

      Scientists' attitudes

      Sexism

      Student attitudes

      Tourists—Attitudes

      Trust

      Women—Attitudes

Youths' attitudes

16 LIFE LESSONS J. I. Krueger, P. Kramer et al *Psychology Today* v49 no5 p62 S/O 2016

ADJUST YOUR ATTITUDE AND LOSE BIG color *Health* v31 no1 p14 Ja 2017

The Bard of Self-Awareness G. DREVITCH *Psychology Today* v50 no4 p24 Ag 2017

BET ON FRIENDSHIP M. BRADY *Psychology Today* v50 no4 p10 Ag 2017

Boomerang Wisdom... Steven Poole E. SILBER *Psychology Today* v49 no6 p16 N/D 2016

CELEB CHAT M. Bykofsky *Parents* p20 2015

editor's note. WHAT DOES IT MEAN TO BE ON THE RIGHT SIDE OF THE FUTURE? K. Perina *Psychology Today* v49 no6 p3 N/D 2016

Gabrielle Union IS OUR... glrL CruSH [Cover story] A. Prato color *Health* v31 no7 p116 S 2017

GABRIELLE UNION What I Love color *Health* v31 no7 p31 S 2017

Grief Is a Genesis. Not a Finale S. SABBAGE *Psychology Today* v50 no3 p44 My/Je 2017

How to Bounce Back from Anything J. Dunn color *Health* v31 no7 p96 S 2017

how to raise an optimist V. GLEMBOCKI color *Parents* v92 no4 p50 Ap 2017

if you ask me... S. JAMES color *Parents* v92 no6 p100 Je 2017

ISKRA LAWRENCE "BODY POSITIVE IS A CHOICE" J. Naftulin color *Health* v31 no7 p26 S 2017

Jillian Gets You Strong [Cover story] A. Spencer color *Health* v30 no9 p116 N 2016

The Kids Are All Right S. James *Parents* v92 no2 p13 F 2017

Me, Minus 108 Pounds A. Levi color *Health* v31 no3 p44 Ap 2017

MILD LOVE A. BEN-ZEÉV *Psychology Today* v50 no3 p76 My/Je 2017

MISTY COPELAND "It is so amazing to be unique" R. S. Frazier color *Health* v31 no8 p16 O 2017

OPENING UP C. PARK *Psychology Today* v50 no4 p18 Ag 2017

THE PROBING PROVOCATEUR *Psychology Today* v49 no6 p9 N/D 2016

SCIENTIFIC UPDATE R. Mangels *Vegetarian Journal* v36 no1 p12 2017

SKYLAR DIGGINS "Everything Happens for a Reason" J. Andriakos color *Health* v31 no1 p20 Ja 2017

Solutions For the Solitary: Loneliness requires courage and altered perception to escape, but it is possible G. WINCH *Psychology Today* v50 no4 p32 Ag 2017

THE STARGAZING STORYTELLER E. Silber *Psychology Today* v49 no6 p10 N/D 2016

Start a Gratitude Habit J. Andriakos color *Health* v30 no9 p26 N 2016

Stay-Slim Moves That Will Make You Smile J. Andriakos color *Health* v31 no1 p37 Ja 2017

STOP BEATING YOURSELF UP ABOUT FOOD V. Sole-smith color *Health* v31 no8 p112 O 2017

Things Are Looking Down A. MARKMAN *Psychology Today* v50 no3 p18 My/Je 2017

To Recover Faster from Rejection, Shift Your Mindset N. Torres *Harvard Business Review Digital Articles* p2 Ap 6 2016

UNDENIABLY EVA [Cover story] A. Prato color *Health* v31 no5 p84 Je 2017

An undivided life P. W. Marty *Christian Century* v134 no16 p3 Ag 2 2017

Vision Quest... Isaac Lidsky J. BLEYER *Psychology Today* v50 no3 p96 My/Je 2017

Attitude-behavior consistency

The Best Strategic Leaders Balance Agility and Consistency J. Coleman bw color *Harvard Business Review Digital Articles* p2 Ja 4 2017

Attitude change (Psychology)

WHY WE HATE TO CHANGE OUR MINDS il *Harvard Business Review* v95 no5 p28 S/O 2017

Attitudes of mothers

'Happy Little Wives and Mothers' K. M. Byrne *America* v216 no11 p42 My 15 2017

Parent Trap *Commentary* v142 no1 p1 Jl/Ag 2016

Attitudes toward abortion

Core Dogma J. BOTTUM color *Weekly Standard* v22 no34 p16 My 15 2017

Attitudes toward death

Dispatches From the End of Life M. HUSTON *Psychology Today* v50 no1 p18 Ja/F 2017

Mourning Becomes Her K. BOLONIK color *Prevention* v68 no11 p34 N 2016

Attitudes toward entitlement

How to Mentor a Narcissist W. B. Johnson and D. G. Smith *Harvard Business Review Digital Articles* p2 S 19 2017

Attitudes toward health

For a Fabulous 2016, One Tip: Take It Slow T. SPIKER color *AARP: The Magazine* v59 no1A p22 D 2015/Ja 2016

Help Create a Veggie World *Vegetarian Journal* v35 no1 p32 2016

A Premier Path Toward Health *Psychology Today* v49 no5 p24 S/O 2016

Rules Smart Gynos Break M. Masters color *Health* v31 no5 p57 Je 2017

The Truth About Twins A. MENCEL color *Parents* v92 no8 p26 Ag 2017

Attitudes toward sex

CARNAL KNOWLEDGE A. Orr color *Louisiana Life* v38 no1 p16 S/O 2017

Attitudes toward technology

AI CAN BE A TROUBLESOME TEAMMATE: AI is a focused intelligence, groomed for maximum perfection. That's why, research shows, most people don't trust it K. Gray *Harvard Business Review Digital Articles* p20 Jl 1 2017

Here, Kitty Kitty! H. KRISCHER *Reader's Digest* v190 no1134 p41 O 2017

MODERN PROBLEMS R. MARR color *Missouri Life* v44 no4 p60 Je 2017

When early adopters don't adopt C. Catalini and C. Tucker graph *Science* v357 no6347 p135 Jl 14 2017

Attitudes toward technology—History

How GPS Learns to Speak Your Language A. Rogers *Smithsonian* v48 no4 p20 Jl/Ag 2017

Attitudes toward work

BARN PROBLEMS *Successful Farming* v114 no11 p64 N 2016

Differing Work Styles Can Help Team Performance C. Tate *Harvard Business Review Digital Articles* p2 Ap 3 2015

Does Doing the Same Work Over and Over Again Make You Less Ethical? R. Derfler-Rozin, C. Moore et al *Harvard Business Review Digital Articles* p2 Mr 28 2017

Every Generation Wants Meaningful Work—but Thinks Other Age Groups Are in It for the Money K. P. Weeks *Harvard Business Review Digital Articles* p2 Jl 31 2017

Our Assumptions About Old and Young Workers Are Wrong A. Scott and L. Gratton *Harvard Business Review Digital Articles* p2 N 14 2016

Reduce Passive-Aggressive Behavior on Your Team L. Davey *Harvard Business Review Digital Articles* p2 Ja 25 2016

Research: Sleep Deprivation Can Make It Harder to Stay Calm at Work C. Guarana and C. M. Barnes *Harvard Business Review Digital Articles* p2 2017

To Get More Feedback, Act More Coachable Manzoni *Harvard Business Review Digital Articles* p2 S 22 2016

What Everyone Needs to Know to Be More Productive D. Rousmaniere *Harvard Business Review Digital Articles* p2 Ap 7 2015

What to Do If You're Smarter than Your Boss A. Gallo *Harvard Business Review Digital Articles* p2 D 12 2014

Why a Messy Workspace Undermines Your Persistence B. (. Chae *Harvard Business Review Digital Articles* p2 Ja 22 2015

Attlee, C. R. (Clement Richard), 1883-1967

Cold War Clem: Fiercely anti-Communist, Clement Attlee found Britain's intelligence agencies to be invaluable tools D. W. B. Lomas *History Today* v67 no9 p16 S 2017

The Party of Left-Wing Anti-Semitism: The shocking decline and fall of Labour D. Murray *Commentary* v142 no4 p29 N 2016

Attore, Fabio

The extent of forest in dryland biomes [Cover story] chart map *Science* v356 no6338 p635 My 12 2017

Attorney Street (Theatrical production)

Odd Man In H. Als color *New Yorker* v93 no32 p8 O 16 2017

Attorneys general

See also

Women attorneys general

THE TELEVANGELISM OF KEN PAXTON R. G. RATCLIFFE *Texas Monthly* v44 no12 p118 D 2016

Attorneys general—United States

The Democrats' Last Hope F. LUCAS cartoon *Weekly Standard* v22 no25 p21 Mr 6 2017

Attorneys general—United States—States

Blue State AGs: The Dems' New Resistance E. Larson, E. E. Deprez et al bw *Bloomberg Businessweek* no4516 p25 Mr 27 2017

Attosecond pulses

Attosecond dynamics through a Fano resonance: Monitoring the birth of a photoelectron V. Gruson, L. Barreau et al bibl graph *Science* v354 no6313 p734 N 11 2016

Coherent imaging of an attosecond electron wave packet D. M. Villeneuve, P. Hockett et al bw chart diag *Science* v356 no6343 p1150 Je 16 2017

Tracking the dynamics of electron expulsion C. Vozzi diag *Science* v356 no6343 p1126 Je 16 2017

Attribution of news

JUST THE NEWS, PLEASE color *Vanity Fair* v59 no6 p46 My 2017

Attwell, William

3 Things Multinationals Don't Understand About Africa's Middle Class *Harvard Business Review Digital Articles* p2 2017

Atufunwa, Benice

the Best Beaches for Black Women color *Essence* v48 no3 p94 Jl 2017

Atun, Rifat

Fixing the Recruiting and Retention Problems in Britain's NHS *Harvard Business Review Digital Articles* p2 2017

Atuyambe, Lyn

Applying Deliberative Democracy in Africa: Uganda's First Deliberative Polls *Daedalus* v146 no3 p140 Summ 2017

ATWAN, HELENE

But Is It Reading? *Publishers Weekly* v263 no47 p112 N 21 2016

Atwell, Esther—Interviews

SELF-RELIANCE Is a Family Affair K. C. Compton *Mother Earth News* no281 p12 Ap/My 2017

Atwell, Hayley, 1982-

Conviction D. Franich color *Entertainment Weekly* no1434 p48 O 7 2016

Atwell, John

PICKLE RECIPES for the Picking: Ferment or quick-pickle your harvest with this assortment of ideas from Mother Earth News bloggers *Mother Earth News* no282 p56 Je/Jl 2017

Atwell, John—Interviews

SELF-RELIANCE Is a Family Affair K. C. Compton *Mother Earth News* no281 p12 Ap/My 2017

ATWOOD, LESLEY W.

Agriculture in 2050: Recalibrating Targets for Sustainable Intensification *BioScience* v67 no4 p386 Ap 2017

Atwood, Margaret, 1939-

Brave New World E. ST. JOHN MANDEL *New York Times Book Review* p9 O 30 2016

Creative Reconstruction il *Nation* v304 no4 p15 F 6 2017

Faith, Feminism and 'The Handmaid's Tale' [Cover story] E. Blondiau color *America* v216 no11 p46 My 15 2017

Handmaids Rising *New York Times Book Review* p1 Mr 19 2017

HARSH REALM E. NUSSBAUM cartoon *New Yorker* v93 no14 p78 My 22 2017

Newly Resonant Nonsense color *Weekly Standard* v22 no33 p2 My 8 2017

Power Tools: Icons C. Alter color *Time* v189 no16/17 p150 My 1-8 2017

THE PROPHET OF DYSTOPIA R. MEAD cartoon color *New Yorker* v93 no9 p38 Ap 17 2017

Resistance on the inside K. Reklis *Christian Century* v134 no13 p42 Je 21 2017

Second chances and Shakespeare B. BETHUNE color *Maclean's* v129 no41 p54 O 17 2016

SEEN & HEARD *Humanist* v77 no3 p7 My/Je 2017

Viva Margaret Atwood! B. J. BIRZER il *American Conservative* v15 no6 p38 N/D 2016

The Writing on the Wall *Ms.* v27 no2 p39 Summ 2017

The Year in Reading [Cover story] *New York Times Book Review*

p8 D 25 2016

Atwood, Margaret, 1939——Awards

THE 2015 RCGS HONOUREES color *Canadian Geographic* v135 no6 p79 D 2015

Louise Erdrich, Matthew Desmond Win 2017 NBCC Awards C. Reid color *Publishers Weekly* v264 no12 p14 Mr 20 2017

Atwood, Margaret, 1939——Interviews

BEAUTY & THE HANDMAID'S TELLER color *Entertainment Weekly* no1474/1475 p118 Jl 21-28 2017

Atwood, Rebecca

MIX MASTER *Martha Stewart Living* no268 p66 O 2016

ATWOOD, ROGER

CONNECTING TWO REALMS color *Archaeology* v70 no4 p55 Je-Ag 2017

EGYPT'S FINAL REDOUBT IN CANAAN [Cover story] color *Archaeology* v70 no4 p26 Je-Ag 2017

TOP 10 DISCOVERIES OF 2016 bw cartoon color *Archaeology* v70 no1 p26 Ja/F 2017

ATWOOD, THOMAS

AI Apparently Is for Real *USA Today Magazine* v145 no2862 p35 Mr 2017

Atwood, Tom——Interviews

FUN HOUSE D. ARTAVIA color *Advocate* no1090 p20 Ap 2017

Atxabal, Ainhoa

A molecular spin-photovoltaic device color diag *Science* v357 no6352 p677 Ag 18 2017

Atypical (TV program)

A Family Story With a Son on the Spectrum D. D'addario color *Time* v190 no7 p52 Ag 21 2017

Au Sable River (Mich.)

THE WISHING TREE K. McCafferty color *Field & Stream* v122 no2 p56 Je/Jl 2017

Aubert, Nathalie

MUSING ON THE SEA OF BRITTANY *History Today* v67 no5 p100 My 2017

Aublin, J.

Observation of a large-scale anisotropy in the arrival directions of cosmic rays above 8 × 1018 eV *Science* v357 no6357 p1266 S 22 2017

Aubrey, G.

STAYING FOCUSED AFTER 40 color *Maclean's* v129 no42 p34 O 24 2016

AUBRY, TIMOTHY

Major Decisions *New York Times Book Review* p20 Ag 27 2017

Auburn University

Southern Revival B. BROOME *Architectural Record* v205 no7 p80 Jl 2017

Auburn University. Dept. of Architecture. Rural Studio

Fertile Imaginations F. A. BERNSTEIN color *Architectural Digest* v74 no10 p60 O 1 2017

Auburn University——Sports

10 Auburn color *Sports Illustrated* v127 no5 p98 Ag 14 2017

Auckland, Kathryn

A Neolithic expansion, but strong genetic structure, in the independent history of New Guinea diag *Science* v357 no6356 p1160 S 15 2017

Aucoin, Christy

Country Lore *Mother Earth News* no280 p85 F/Mr 2017

Aucoin, Kevyn

Boy on Film L. M. M. BLUME and C. ELLENBERG bw color *Vogue* v207 no9 p458 S 2017

Auction fees

John Phillips J. Phillips color *Car & Driver* v63 no4 p32 O 2017

Auctions

See also

Agricultural equipment auctions
Art auctions
Automobile auctions
Book auctions
Internet auctions
Publishing rights auctions

ABOVE & BEYOND bw *New Yorker* v93 no11 p14 My 1 2017

ABOVE & BEYOND cartoon *New Yorker* v92 no32 p30 O 10 2016

ABOVE & BEYOND cartoon *New Yorker* v93 no7 p26 Ap 3 2017

APROPOS OF NOTHING *Saturday Evening Post* v289 no4 p30

Jl/Ag 2017

At Christie's M. Willoughby color *Magazine Antiques* v184 no1 p84 Ja/F 2017

Early American Glass: A recent Norman C. Heckler auction featured several 18th- and 19th-century glass pieces with decidedly modern lines *Treasures* v6 no6 p8 Je/Jl 2017

IntArah Dream Embryo Auction *Arabian Horse World* v57 no9 p32 Je 2017

Magnate School R. L. BOFFERDING color *Architectural Digest* v74 no4 p69 Ap 2017

Modern Traditions B. LIBBY *Treasures* v6 no4 p22 F/Mr 2017

SKID STEER PRICES SLIP D. Mowitz *Successful Farming* v115 no2 p26 F 2017

Auctions——New York (State)

ABOVE & BEYOND cartoon *New Yorker* v92 no41 p20 D 12 2016

Auctions——Social aspects

ABOUT TOWN color *Virginia Living* v15 no5 p35 Ag 2017

Audeze LLC

The Shock of the New S. Guttenberg color *Sound & Vision* v82 no4 p18 My 2017

Audi A4 automobile——Evaluation

Audi A4 chart color *Motor Trend* v69 no1 p136 Ja 2017

THE CHALLENGERS T. QUIROGA color *Car & Driver* v62 no7 p54 Ja 2017

Four Play J. Jacquot color diag *Car & Driver* v62 no11 p102 My 2017

New Car Profiles color diag *Consumer Reports* v82 no4 p52 Ap 2017

VS cartoon *Car & Driver* v62 no7 p44 Ja 2017

WAGONS, HO! S. Evans, A. MacKenzie et al color *Motor Trend* v69 no2 p62 F 2017

Audi AG

And the Beat Goes On J. Capparella color *Car & Driver* v63 no2 p96 Ag 2017

Audi A4 chart color *Motor Trend* v69 no1 p136 Ja 2017

Audi Q7 chart color *Motor Trend* v69 no1 p64 Ja 2017

Cars That Go the Distance P. Olsen chart color diag *Consumer Reports* v82 no12 p52 D 2017

Four Play J. Jacquot color diag *Car & Driver* v62 no11 p102 My 2017

RAISING ARIZONA J. Jacquot chart color graph map *Car & Driver* v63 no1 p56 Jl 2017

THE RIGHT STUFF J. H. HARPER color *Road & Track* v68 no7 p58 Mr/Ap 2017

SLEEPER STREAKER K. KINARD color *Road & Track* v68 no5 p102 D 2016/Ja 2017

SMARTER NOT HARDER B. BARRY bw color *Road & Track* v69 no3 p90 O 2017

The Stoic Beast E. Johnson color *Car & Driver* v63 no4 p100 O 2017

STRANGER THINGS A. Stoklosa color *Car & Driver* v62 no10 p13 Ap 2017

TAKE THE WHEEL: SELF-DRIVING CARS MUST CONNECT WITH HUMANS A. DAVIES color *Wired* v25 no7 p13 Jl 2017

WAGONS, HO! S. Evans, A. MacKenzie et al color *Motor Trend* v69 no2 p62 F 2017

YOUNG LOVE C. Seabaugh chart color *Motor Trend* v69 no8 p72 Ag 2017

Audi AG——Awards

Who's Gonna Buy All These Audis in China? color graph *Bloomberg Businessweek* no4506 p16 Ja 9 2017

Audi automobile——Evaluation

And the Beat Goes On J. Capparella color *Car & Driver* v63 no2 p96 Ag 2017

eins, zwei, drei, quattros! C. Walton chart color *Motor Trend* v69 no8 p76 Ag 2017

NEW CARS 2018-2019 [Cover story] M. Cantu, Z. Gale et al chart color *Motor Trend* v69 no9 p34 S 2017

RAISING ARIZONA J. Jacquot chart color graph map *Car & Driver* v63 no1 p56 Jl 2017

Redemption Songs A. Robinson color graph *Car & Driver* v62 no7 p110 Ja 2017

THE RETREADS J. SABATINI color *Car & Driver* v62 no7 p50 Ja 2017

RINGERS M. PRINCE color diag graph *Road & Track* v69 no4 p26 N 2017

RS KICKER M. Duff color *Car & Driver* v62 no6 p21 D 2016

SAME SWAGGER R. PINTO color *Road & Track* v68 no9 p82 Je 2017

SMARTER NOT HARDER B. BARRY bw color *Road & Track* v69 no3 p90 O 2017

The Stoic Beast E. Johnson color *Car & Driver* v63 no4 p100 O 2017

STRANGER THINGS A. Stoklosa color *Car & Driver* v62 no10 p13 Ap 2017

Taller AND STRONGER E. Ayapana chart color *Motor Trend* v69 no3 p80 Mr 2017

YOUNG LOVE C. Seabaugh chart color *Motor Trend* v69 no8 p72 Ag 2017

Audi Q7 automobile

The Finalists... color *Motor Trend* v69 no1 p62 Ja 2017

Audi Q7 automobile—Evaluation

Audi Q7 chart color *Motor Trend* v69 no1 p64 Ja 2017

Ratings chart *Consumer Reports* v82 no1 p60 Ja 2017

Audi R8 automobile

DESIGNATED RIDES C. J. WASHINGTON color *Ebony* v72 no11 p91 S 2017

Audi S8 automobile—Evaluation

SLEEPER STREAKER K. KINARD color *Road & Track* v68 no5 p102 D 2016/Ja 2017

Audi TT automobile—Evaluation

THE RIGHT STUFF J. H. HARPER color *Road & Track* v68 no7 p58 Mr/Ap 2017

Audia, Pino G.

When Public Opinion Shifts, How Should Your Company Respond? *Harvard Business Review Digital Articles* p2 S 29 2015

Audible Inc.

More Originals from Audible S. MAUGHAN *Publishers Weekly* v263 no41 p21 O 10 2016

Audio acoustics

See also

  Audio equipment

  Sound recording & reproducing

  Video recording

Will Your Video Go Viral? color *Popular Mechanics* p100 O 2017

Audio amplifiers

Hi-Res Streams A. L. GRIFFIN color *Sound & Vision* v82 no5 p19 Je 2017

Audio amplifiers—Design & construction

REVIVING THE PAST, DEFINING THE FUTURE K. Baumann color *Downbeat* v84 no7 p68 Jl 2017

Audio amplifiers—Evaluation

ATI AT527NC and AT524NC Amplifiers D. Vaughn chart color graph *Sound & Vision* v82 no3 p48 Ap 2017

AudioQuest DragonFly Red and DragonFly Black Amp/DACs M. Fleischmann color *Sound & Vision* v81 no10 p66 D 2016

Elac Element EA101EQ-G Integrated Amplifier/DAC D. Kumin chart color graph *Sound & Vision* v82 no3 p58 Ap 2017

Finding Sonic Paradise B. Ankosko color *Sound & Vision* v82 no4 p74 My 2017

GEAR BOX color *Downbeat* v84 no7 p84 Jl 2017

Rotel A12 Integrated Amplifier M. Fleischmann chart color graph *Sound & Vision* v82 no3 p42 Ap 2017

STUFF YOU WANT *Boating World* v38 no8 p28 S/O 2017

Teac AI-503 USB DAC/Integrated Amplifier B. Ankosko color *Sound & Vision* v82 no7 p74 S 2017

Vintage 47's VA-185G Amplifier K. Baumann color *Downbeat* v84 no7 p80 Jl 2017

Yamaha MusicCast WXA-50 Amplifier and WX-010 Speaker M. Fleischmann chart color graph *Sound & Vision* v82 no5 p56 Je 2017

Audio Design Experts Inc.

LET'S TAKE IT OUTSIDE B. Ankosko color *Sound & Vision* v82 no6 p28 Jl/Ag 2017

Audio Engineering Society

Associations & Conferences *Stage Directions* v30 no7 p4 Jl 1 2017

Audio equipment

Analog Video Bites the Dust K. C. POHLMANN color *Sound & Vision* v82 no1 p28 Ja 2017

Audio Equipment, Manufacturers & Distributors *Stage Directions* v30 no7 p6 Jl 1 2017

HEAD-TO-HEAD: FINE TUNERS R. CHUN color *Wired* v25 no8 p44 Ag 2017

Audio equipment in automobiles

HOW TO BLUETOOTH AN OLD CAR E. DYER color *Popular Mechanics* p44 Jl 2017

Passing the Screen Test M. Monticello chart color graph il *Consumer Reports* v82 no10 p54 O 2017

Audio equipment in automobiles—Evaluation

Passing the Screen Test M. Monticello chart color graph il *Consumer Reports* v82 no10 p54 O 2017

Audio equipment—Evaluation

HiFiMan SuperMini Music Player M. Fleischmann color *Sound & Vision* v82 no1 p54 Ja 2017

Looking Good S. Guttenberg color *Sound & Vision* v82 no7 p22 S 2017

Meridian Audio Explorer2 USB DAC review: An inexpensive path to high-resolution audio M. BROWN color *Macworld - Digital Edition* p97 Je 13 2017

New Gear C. Crowley color *Sound & Vision* v82 no2 p30 F/Mr 2017

PreSonus Studio 192 Mobile M. Kern color *Downbeat* v84 no2 p98 F 2017

Russound MCA-88X Streaming Housewide Audio Controller J. Sciacca color *Sound & Vision* v82 no2 p60 F/Mr 2017

Tools: Heard at InfoComm 2017 *Stage Directions* v30 no8 p6 Ag 2017

Wrensilva Loft Record Console B. Ankosko color *Sound & Vision* v82 no6 p74 Jl/Ag 2017

Audio equipment—Sales & prices

Worshipping at the Altar of Brick and Mortar K. C. POHLMANN color *Sound & Vision* v82 no3 p30 Ap 2017

Audio frequency

What's the Frequency? A. GRIFFIN color *Sound & Vision* v82 no3 p23 Ap 2017

Audio Publishers Association (Organization)

All Ears on APAC S. MAUGHAN color *Publishers Weekly* v264 no20 p(Sp)22 My 15 2017

Audio-Technica US Inc.

Bedazzled S. Guttenberg color *Sound & Vision* v82 no4 p22 My 2017

Audio tours

HONEST MUSEUM AUDIO TOUR R. CLEGG cartoon *New Yorker* v92 no40 p32 D 5 2016

Audiobook awards

'Hamilton' Named Audiobook Of the Year A. Coreno color *Publishers Weekly* v264 no24 p24 Je 12 2017

Audiobook industry

Publishers See More Good Times Ahead for Audiobooks S. Maughan color *Publishers Weekly* v264 no3 p6 Ja 16 2017

Audiobook publishing

Inside the Audio Department S. MAUGHAN color *Publishers Weekly* v264 no19 p18 My 8 2017

Audiobooks

AUDIO BESTSELLERS C. JURIS chart *Publishers Weekly* v264 no24 p16 Je 12 2017

Audiobook Publishing And Sales Take Off Up North E. NAWOTKA color *Publishers Weekly* v264 no41 p18 O 9 2017

Beyond Inspiration S. BALIN color *Publishers Weekly* v264 no27 p80 Jl 3 2017

But Is It Reading? H. ATWAN *Publishers Weekly* v263 no47 p112 N 21 2016

Hear Here! S. PHILLIPS *Smithsonian* v47 no8 p17 D 2016

In the Studio *Publishers Weekly* v263 no41 p22 O 10 2016

IN THE STUDIO WITH ZACHARY QUINTO I. Biedenharn color *Entertainment Weekly* no1435 p60 O 14 2016

'Mason & Dixon' and Me: A personal foray into the long-lost Pynchon tapes A. Nazaryan *New York Times Book Review* p18 My 21 2017

More Originals from Audible S. MAUGHAN *Publishers Weekly* v263 no41 p21 O 10 2016

NICK OFFERMAN I. Biedenharn color *Entertainment Weekly* no1486 p61 O 13 2017

SPRING 2017 AUDIO ANNOUNCEMENTS S. Maughan color *Publishers Weekly* v264 no6 p20 F 6 2017

Audiobooks—Charts, diagrams, etc.

AUDIO BESTSELLERS chart *Publishers Weekly* v263 no46 p19 N 14 2016

AUDIO BESTSELLERS C. JURIS chart *Publishers Weekly* v264 no28 p16 Jl 10 2017

AUDIO BESTSELLERS C. JURIS chart *Publishers Weekly* v264 no7 p15 F 13 2017

AUDIO BESTSELLERS J. Maher and C. JURIS chart color *Publishers Weekly* v264 no41 p16 O 9 2017

iBOOKS AUDIO TOP 10 J. Maher and C. JURIS chart color *Publishers Weekly* v264 no28 p16 Jl 10 2017

ROYAL RECEPTION J. Maher chart graph *Publishers Weekly* v264 no2 p14 Ja 9 2017

Audiobooks.com (Company)

The Evolution Of RBmedia S. Maughan *Publishers Weekly* v264 no22 p11 My 29 2017

Fiction Most Popular Category on Audiobooks.com J. Milliot graph *Publishers Weekly* v264 no11 p20 Mr 13 2017

Audiobooks—News briefs

In the Studio S. Maughan bw color *Publishers Weekly* v264 no11 p19 Mr 13 2017

In The Studio S. Maughan bw color *Publishers Weekly* v264 no15 p25 Ap 10 2017

Audiobooks—Sales & prices

FALL 2017 AUDIO ANNOUNCEMENTS S. MAUGHAN color *Publishers Weekly* v264 no27 p21 Jl 3 2017

Fiction Most Popular Category on Audiobooks.com J. Milliot graph *Publishers Weekly* v264 no11 p20 Mr 13 2017

Getting the Measure of Downloadable Audio J. Milliot chart *Publishers Weekly* v264 no38 p5 S 18 2017

iBOOKS AUDIO TOP 10 J. Maher and C. JURIS chart color *Publishers Weekly* v264 no24 p16 Je 12 2017

Audiobooks—Sales & prices—Charts, diagrams, etc.

AUDIO BESTSELLERS chart *Publishers Weekly* v264 no11 p15 Mr 13 2017

iBOOKS AUDIO TOP 10 J. Maher and C. JURIS chart color *Publishers Weekly* v264 no19 p17 My 8 2017

Audiocassette reproduction & distribution

TALE OF THE TAPE D. Sax color *Bloomberg Businessweek* no4517 p70 Ap 3 2017

Audiocassettes—Sales & prices

TALE OF THE TAPE D. Sax color *Bloomberg Businessweek* no4517 p70 Ap 3 2017

Audioengine Corp.

Audioengine HD3 Loudspeaker M. Fleischmann color graph *Sound & Vision* v82 no6 p64 Jl/Ag 2017

Audiofly (Company)

Come Fly With Me S. Guttenberg color *Sound & Vision* v82 no3 p22 Ap 2017

Audiology instruments

See also

Hearing aids

Audiometry

More Bang for Your Membership Buck color *AARP: The Magazine* v30 no6A p72 O/N 2017

Audiovisual equipment

See also

Sound recording & reproducing—Equipment & supplies

AVR Advice A. L. GRIFFIN color *Sound & Vision* v82 no1 p26 Ja 2017

Top Four System Install Mistakes J. SCIACCA color *Sound & Vision* v82 no7 p28 S 2017

Audiovisual equipment—Evaluation

Anthem AVM 60 A/V Processor D. Kumin color graph *Sound & Vision* v82 no1 p56 Ja 2017

New Gear color *Sound & Vision* v82 no7 p32 S 2017

Ultra-Short-Throw Projectors color *Popular Mechanics* p28 F 2017

Yamaha Aventage RX-A3060 A/V Receiver M. Fleischmann chart color graph *Sound & Vision* v82 no1 p50 Ja 2017

Audiovisual presentations—Reviews

Pop Tech A. Popescu color *Bloomberg Businessweek* no4502 p41 D 5 2016

Audited financial statements

Bogus Audited Statements Are Holding Africa Back N. Ekekwe *Harvard Business Review Digital Articles* p2 Ag 22 2016

Auditing—Government policy

Watchdog, Undone: Will budget cuts and political ire endanger performance audits? K. Barrett and R. Greene *Governing* v30 no12 p60 S 2017

Auditing—United States

Advising on Tax Moves And Auditing Them, Too D. Kocieniewski *Bloomberg Businessweek* no4497 p42 O 31 2016

Auditions

See also

Dance—Auditions

Auditoriums

See also

Theaters

Purple Pose S. CARR *Idaho Magazine* v16 no6 p54 Mr 2017

Auditory cortex

Intonational speech prosody encoding in the human auditory cortex C. Tang, L. S. Hamilton et al diag *Science* v357 no6353 p797 Ag 25 2017

Auditory cortex—Anatomy

Restoring auditory cortex plasticity in adult mice by restricting thalamic adenosine signaling J. A. Blundon, N. C. Roy et al graph *Science* v356 no6345 p1352 Je 30 2017

Audran, Stéphane

Brideshead Reunited M. LINDSAY-HOGG color *Vanity Fair* v58 no12 p148 D 2016

Audrie & Daisy (Film)

Redemption Time L. BARCA *Ms.* v26 no4 p37 Wint 2016

Audubon, John James, 1785-1851

AMERICAN FLAMINGO BY DAN WINTERS J. Leibach *Audubon* v119 no2 p60 Summ 2017

Audubon, John James, 1785-1851—Exhibitions

APRIL'S COOLEST EVENTS color *Indianapolis Monthly* p22 Ap 2017

Audubon Aquarium of the Americas (New Orleans, La.)

OTTER THIS WORLD K. MASSICOT color *New Orleans Magazine* v51 no2 p151 D 2016

Audubon Park (New Orleans, La.)

NEW ORLEANS N. Weldon bw color map *Runner's World* v52 no1 p76 Ja/F 2017

Audy, Robin

Cash for carbon: A randomized trial of payments for ecosystem services to reduce deforestation bw chart *Science* v357 no6348 p267 Jl 21 2017

Auel, Jean M.

Quest for Fire M. MELTZER color *Walrus* v14 no4 p63 My 2017

Auerbach, Anna—Interviews

Want Your Boss to Say Yes to Flextime? W. Naugle color *Glamour* no8 p112 Ag 2017

Auerbach, Dan

Auerbach's Cheat Sheet P. DOYLE bw color *Rolling Stone* no1290 p16 Je 29 2017

Dan Auerbach's Nashville Love Letter J. HUDAK color *Rolling Stone* no1278/1279 p22 Ja 12 2017

Auerbach, David

A Coming of (Information) Age Story: The Cybernetics Moment: Or Why We Call Our Age the Information Age *Issues in Science & Technology* v33 no4 p89 Summ 2017

If Only AI Could Save Us from Ourselves color diag *MIT Technology Review* v120 no1 p104 Ja/F 2017

Auerswald, Philip E.

The Code Economy: A Forty-Thousand-Year History *Publishers Weekly* v263 no43 p65 O 24 2016

Aufderheide, Patricia

Cuban Documentary Retrospective at DocLisboa 2016 *Film Quarterly* v70 no3 p80 Spr 2017

Auger, A.-T.

Surface changes on comet 67P/Churyumov-Gerasimenko suggest a more active past bw graph *Science* v355 no6332 p1392 Mr 31 2017

Auger effect

ALL AROUND THE FARM® J. Glanzer, B. Broering et al *Successful Farming* v115 no6 p77 Ap 2017

Observing the ultrafast buildup of a Fano resonance in the time domain A. Kaldun, A. Blättermann et al bibl graph *Science* v354 no6313 p738 N 11 2016

Auger-Méthé, Marie

Now is the time to protect the Arctic bibl color *Science* v354 no6317 p1243 D 9 2016

Augmentation mammaplasty

Bigger Breasts Without Implants? *USA Today Magazine* v146 no2869 p5 O 2017

Top Countries for Plastic Surgery *USA Today Magazine* v146 no2869 p4 O 2017

Augmented reality

Apple's Alternative to Virtual Reality M. Gurman, A. Webb et al color *Bloomberg Businessweek* no4516 p29 Mr 27 2017

Beyond the Nickel Ride N. PINKERTON color *Film Comment* v53 no2 p20 Mr/Ap 2017

BRINGING LESSONS TO LIFE M. Baird color diag *Literacy Today (2411-7862)* v34 no3 p24 N/D 2016

CHANGING THE WORLD KIDS SEE N. Strochlic color *National Geographic* v231 no3 p24 Mr 2017

Moving Beyond E-books L. Dawson *Publishers Weekly* v264 no38 p24 S 18 2017

My Pokémon Addiction T. ROGERS *D: The Magazine of Dallas* v43 no10 p94 O 2016

Opinion: Why Apple is smart to pursue AR D. Moren color *Macworld - Digital Edition* p111 Ja 2017

TECH QUIZ P. McCartney *Popular Mechanics* p72 O 2017

Virtual and Augmented Reality Will Reshape Retail D. McKone, R. Haslehurst et al *Harvard Business Review Digital Articles* p2 S 9 2016

What Marketers Need to Understand About Augmented Reality A. Javornik *Harvard Business Review Digital Articles* p2 Ap 18 2016

Augmented reality—Equipment & supplies

Meet SwapBots, an augmented-reality toy that pairs with the iPad L. YAMSHON color *Macworld - Digital Edition* v34 no4 p51 My 2017

Augmented reality—Software—Evaluation

LOOKING GLASS K. SHEIKH cartoon *Popular Science* p14 Ja/F 2017

Windows 10 Creators Update could ship March 31, and we're already worried about bugs M. HACHMAN and M. Riofrio color *PCWorld* p14 Mr 2017

August (Company)

GET SMART C. Lamers and N. Farrell color *Sunset* v239 no3 p46 S 2017

Augustin, Hellmut G.

Organotypic vasculature: From descriptive heterogeneity to functional pathophysiology color *Science* v357 no6353 p771 Ag 25 2017

Augustin, Sally

Rules for Designing an Engaging Workplace *Harvard Business Review Digital Articles* p2 O 28 2014

Augustine, Blessy

KOCHI-MUZIRIS BIENNALE color *Art in America* v105 no3 p140 Mr 2017

Lehmann Maupin *Art in America* v105 no1 p80 Ja 2017

Augustine, Kate E.

Precipitation drives global variation in natural selection bibl chart diag map *Science* v355 no6328 p959 Mr 3 2017

Augustine, Peter

To Love Another T. MARKATOS *Weekly Standard* v22 no46 p36 Ag 14 2017

Augustine, Saint, Bishop of Hippo, 354-430

Augustine gets a makeover E. Bruenig color *America* v217 no4 p44 Ag 21 2017

Dialogue With God P. Brown color *New York Review of Books* v64 no16 p45 O 26 2017

THE INVENTION OF SEX S. GREENBLATT cartoon color *New Yorker* v93 no17 p24 Je 19 2017

Auh, Seigyoung

Does Your Company Have What It Takes to Go Global? *Harvard Business Review Digital Articles* p2 Ap 11 2016

AUKEMA, JULIANN E.

Skills and Knowledge for Data-Intensive Environmental Research *BioScience* v67 no6 p546 Je 2017

Aukey (Company)

AUKEY MULTIPORT USB-C HUB G. FLEISHMAN color *Macworld - Digital Edition* v34 no6 p47 Je 2017

Aulakh, Laveet K.

Mismatch repair deficiency predicts response of solid tumors to PD-1 blockade chart graph *Science* v357 no6349 p409 Jl 28 2017

AU LEVITT, ANDREA

SOUP UP YOUR RECALL color *Reader's Digest* v190 no1133 p106 S 2017

Words To Live (Longer & Better) By [Cover story] color *Reader's Digest* v189 no1130 p70 My 2017

AUMEN, ADRIAN

Technology to the Rescue? *USA Today Magazine* v146 no2868 p34 S 2017

Aung San Suu Kyi, 1945-

FALLEN IDOL H. BEECH bw cartoon *New Yorker* v93 no30 p22 O 2 2017

Spires in the Sky Myanmar lifts the curtain on the Golden Land of Burma T. PEARSALL *Virginia Living* v15 no6 p52 O 2017

Aung San Suu Kyi, 1945——Political & social views

The world is watching K. Clarke *U.S. Catholic* v82 no10 p42 O 2017

Aura (Parapsychology)

THE EMOTIONAL WAKE A. Calhoun color *Women's Health* v14 no7 p122 S 2017

Aurignacian culture—France

AURIGNACIAN SCHOOL OF ART Z. ZORICH color *Archaeology* v70 no3 p16 My/Je 2017

Aurik, Johan

Why Your Employees' Suggestions Aren't Going Anywhere *Harvard Business Review Digital Articles* p2 Ag 31 2015

Aurora Theatre Co.

Play by Play: Lawrenceville's Aurora Theatre finds inspiration in the diversity of its audience T. MALONE *Atlanta* v57 no6 p82 O 2017

Auroras

All of the lights M. HEMMADI color *Maclean's* v130 no4 p18 My 2017

Auroras E. BETZ color diag *Discover* v38 no6 p30 Jl/Ag 2017

BASKING IN THE GLOW *Iceland Review* v54 no6 p130 N/D 2016

big picture color *Canadian Geographic* v137 no2 p10 Mr/Ap 2017

DANCING QUEEN *Iceland Review* v54 no6 p126 N/D 2016

Johnny Canuck R. Fawkes color *Canadian Geographic* v137 no4 p82 Jl/Ag 2017

PRESERVING THE VIEW E. MASTROIANNI color *Discover* v38 no4 p59 My 2017

Protecting America's Last Dark Skies E. BETZ cartoon color map *Discover* v38 no4 p60 My 2017

UP ALL NIGHT E. Ehmsen color *Sunset* v237 no5 p25 N 2016

Aurthur, Kate

Gaines and Losses *Weekly Standard* v22 no14 p2 D 12 2016

Auschwitz (Poland : Concentration camp)

How evils wins S. Wells *Christian Century* v134 no7 p35 Mr 29 2017

Ausikaitis, Melina

THE CITY'S NEW ART HUB J. FOUMBERG color *Chicago* v66 no1 p42 Ja 2017

AUSLIN, MICHAEL

A Different Kind of Crisis color *National Review* v69 no9 p19 My 15 2017

WHEN THE SUN NEVER SET *Claremont Review of Books* v17 no2 p84 Spr 2017

Auslin, Michael R.

After the Miracle *Commentary* v143 no4 p1 Ap 2017

ASIA WHOLE AND FREE? C. Horner *Claremont Review of Books* v17 no1 p61 Wint 2016/2017

Clouds over The Pacific J. HOLMES color *National Review* v69 no3 p45 F 20 2017

Danger in Asia *National Review* v69 no2 p28 F 6 2017

Tigers at Bay J. Psaropoulos color *Weekly Standard* v22 no37 p30 Je 5 2017

Aussignargues, Clement

Assembly principles and structure of a 6.5-MDa bacterial microcompartment shell color diag *Science* v356 no6344 p1293 Je 23 2017

Austen, Ashleigh

Editors Tell All! bw color *Women's Health* v14 no2 p60 Mr 2017

Austen, Ben

The Fast-Food Worker *New York Times Magazine* p40 F 26 2017

MIRACLE MAN *New York Times Magazine* p44 Ag 27 2017

RUNNING ON HOPE color *New Republic* v248 no10 p18 O 2017

Austen, Jane, 1775-1817

1813: Longbourn J. Austen *Lapham's Quarterly* v10 no1 p45 Wint 2017

And the Winning Photo Is... color *British Heritage Travel* v38 no5 p80 S/O 2017

Austen at the Theater L. BUTTS color *Publishers Weekly* v264 no22 p53 My 29 2017

Celebrating Jane Austen 2017 S. Lawrence color *British Heritage Travel* v38 no5 p28 S/O 2017

The Comforts of Jane S. CHIRA *New York Times Book Review* p25 D 25 2016

Death and the Maiden R. Jones *New York Times Book Review* p14 Jl 16 2017

Did she hide radical messages in her books? M. FORBES *Weekly Standard* v22 no42 p28 Jl 17 2017

FUTURE AUSTEN ADAPTATIONS B. ROBERSON cartoon *New Yorker* v93 no23 p29 Ag 7 2017

Have You Met Miss Jane?: Test your Austen I.Q.—from family scandals to a wet-shirted Colin Firth J. Schuessler and M. J. Murphy *New York Times Book Review* p15 Jl 16 2017

In sequels, prequels and spinoffs, Joan Aiken took up some of the stories Austen never intended to tell L. Skurnick *New York Times Book Review* p12 Jl 16 2017

Jane Austen Is Everything N. Dames color *Atlantic* v320 no2 p92 S 2017

A Jane Austen Kind of Guy: I GET IT THAT WOMEN FIND MY AFFINITY FOR THEIR WRITER INTRUSIVE, BUT HER WORLD HAS MUCH TO OFFER MEN, TOO W. DERESIEWICZ *American Scholar* v86 no4 p84 Aut 2017

LAST LAUGH A. LANE cartoon *New Yorker* v93 no4 p77 Mr 13 2017

Reading her novels on the bicentennial of her death A. VALIUNAS color *Weekly Standard* v22 no42 p28 Jl 17 2017

Style and Substance: Can genius be graphed? The word choices that explain why Jane Austen's work survives and thrives K. A. Flynn and J. Katz *New York Times Book Review* p13 Jl 16 2017

Auster, Paul, 1947-

Four Roads Diverge In a Wood S. Begley color *Time* v189 no4 p54 F 6 2017

LIFE CHOICES S. Sacks *Harper's Magazine* v334 no2001 p88 F 2017

Mixed-Up Kids N. Rich bw color *New York Review of Books* v64 no6 p14 Ap 6 2017

Parallel Lives T. PERROTTA *New York Times Book Review* p8 F 5 2017

Paul AUSTER W. WENDERS *Interview* v47 no1 p26 F 2017

What Happened to Paul Auster? A decade ago, he was a Nobel contender C. LORENTZEN img *New York* p68 Ja 23 2017

WHAT IF? W. SMITH bw color *Publishers Weekly* v263 no48 p26 N 28 2016

Auster, Paul, 1947-—Interviews

Paul Auster *New York Times Book Review* p8 Ja 15 2017

Austerity (Economics)—Social aspects

Rocking the Cradle of Democracy J. PSAROPOULOS *American Scholar* v86 no2 p6 Spr 2017

Austin (Tex.)

AUSTIN POWERED N. VARDI color *Forbes* v200 no1 p98 Jl 27 2017

Cheers for Speer P. SHARPE *Texas Monthly* v45 no6 p30 Je 2017

COCK TAIL OF THE MONTH D. ALAN *Texas Monthly* v44 no12 p52 D 2016

Hot New Wave Austin Synth Rock C. R. WEINGARTEN bw color *Rolling Stone* no1274 p39 N 17 2016

Austin (Tex.)—Description & travel

AUSTIN, TEXAS A. FLANGO *Cincinnati Magazine* v50 no6 p46 Mr 2017

THE GIRLFRIEND GETAWAY GUIDE K. VALENTINI and S. Humphreys Collins color *Redbook* p118 O 2017

SOUTH'S BEST CITY J. Mischner color *Southern Living* v52 no4 p74 Ap 2017

Austin, Angela

MOST OUTSTANDING WOMEN *Washingtonian Magazine* v53

no1 p64 O 2017

AUSTIN, CHARLOTTE

BEAR NECESSITIES color *Outdoor Life* v224 no7 p30 S 2017

Austin, Christina

100 FASTEST-GROWING COMPANIES chart color diag map *Fortune* v176 no4 p157 S 15 2017

The 10 Best Workplaces for Millennials color *Fortune* v176 no2 p20 Ag 1 2017

The 10 Best Workplaces for Women color *Fortune* v176 no5 p20 O 1 2017

THE 2017 Fortune Crystal Ball color diag *Fortune* v174 no7 p11 D 1 2016

CHANGE THE WORLD !!!! color diag map *Fortune* v176 no4 p74 S 15 2017

THE COMPANIES OF THE YEAR color diag *Fortune* v174 no8 p62 D 15 2016

DREAM WEAVER color *Fortune* v176 no3 p74 S 1 2017

FORTY UNDER FORTY 2017 color *Fortune* v176 no3 p62 S 1 2017

MINING COMEDY GOLD color *Fortune* v176 no3 p70 S 1 2017

MOST POWERFUL WOMEN INTERNATIONAL color *Fortune* v176 no5 p111 O 1 2017

YOUTH REVOLT color *Fortune* v176 no3 p64 S 1 2017

Austin, Denise

Denise Austin Shows How to Keep Fit color *AARP: The Magazine* v60 no4A p64 Je/Jl 2017

Austin, Greg

Class A. D'Arminio *TV Guide* v65 no14 p38 Ap 3 2017

Austin, Isaiah—Health

Austin Power D. Gardner and T. Keith color *Sports Illustrated* v125 no19 p22 D 12 2016

AUSTIN, LISA

The Question *O, The Oprah Magazine* p16 Ap 2017

Austin, Maggie

Maggie Austin Cake: Artistry and Technique *Publishers Weekly* v264 no3 p53 Ja 16 2017

Austin, Manila

The Brands That Make Customers Feel Respected *Harvard Business Review Digital Articles* p2 N 1 2016

Austin, Mary Chellis

Top Shelf: Celeb chef Ed Lee has a new burgers-and-bourbon spot. Let's go eat in Louisville *Indianapolis Monthly* v40 no10 p36 Je 2017

Austin, Noah

American Pronghorns *Arizona Highways* v92 no11 p13 N 2016

arizona is GORGES *Arizona Highways* v92 no12 p2 D 2016

Bee Line Dragway *Arizona Highways* v93 no8 p8 Ag 2017

Black-Tailed Rattlesnakes *Arizona Highways* v93 no1 p13 Ja 2017

BLUE RANGE LOOP *Arizona Highways* v92 no7 p52 Jl 2016

Bobcats *Arizona Highways* v93 no8 p13 Ag 2017

CAPE ROYAL ROAD Cape Royal offers one of the best overlooks in Grand Canyon National Park. It's impressive, and so is the narrow, winding road that takes you there *Arizona Highways* v93 no6 p52 Je 2017

Chapel of the Holy Dove *Arizona Highways* v93 no9 p6 S 2017

CHEVELON CANYON LAKE: The Mogoiion Rim gets busy this time of year, especially at Woods Canyon Lake. However, not far from there, along a scenic road lined with giant ponderosas, is an isolated lake that's every bit as beautiful *Arizona Highways* v93 no8 p52 Ag 2017

Cooper's Hawks *Arizona Highways* v93 no10 p13 O 2017

Copper Queen Mine: Over the course of nearly 100 years, the Copper Queen Mine produced billions of pounds of copper. The mining operation closed in 1975, but the mine itself is still open to tourists who aren't afraid to take a train 1,500 feet into... *Arizona Highways* v93 no6 p8 Je 2017

The Cubs *Arizona Highways* v93 no3 p8 Mr 2017

Flagstaff Train Station *Arizona Highways* v93 no1 p6 Ja 2017

Fort Apache Historic Park *Arizona Highways* v93 no4 p6 Ap 2017

Governor's Mansion *Arizona Highways* v93 no11 p6 N 2017

GRAVE SITUATION *Arizona Highways* v93 no3 p50 Mr 2017

HARQUAHALA MOUNTAIN *Arizona Highways* v92 no11 p52 N 2016

IRONWOOD FOREST *Arizona Highways* v93 no1 p52 Ja 2017

Jacob Lake Ranger Station *Arizona Highways* v96 no7 p6 Jl 2017

Javelinas *Arizona Highways* v93 no11 p13 N 2017

Little Italy: Authentic Italian cuisine is among the last things you'd expect to find in Gila Bend, but Little Italy is the real deal. Even Prince Harry says it serves "the best pizza in the world" *Arizona Highways* v93 no6 p12 Je 2017

MIDDLEMARCH ROAD *Arizona Highways* v93 no11 p52 N 2017

Navajo Nation Council Chamber *Arizona Highways* v93 no6 p6 Je 2017

Perrin Ranch Wind Farm *Arizona Highways* v93 no3 p6 Mr 2017

PRONGHORN DRIVE *Arizona Highways* v93 no3 p52 Mr 2017

Prophet Elias' Chapel color *Arizona Highways* v93 no5 p6 My 2017

ROUTE 66: SELIGMAN TO KINGMAN *Arizona Highways* v93 no2 p52 F 2017

RUNE with a VIEW *Arizona Highways* v93 no4 p50 Ap 2017

School House Inn *Arizona Highways* v93 no4 p14 Ap 2017

St. Luke's Sanatorium *Arizona Highways* v93 no11 p8 N 2017

Tavern Hotel *Arizona Highways* v92 no11 p14 N 2016

Thunderbird Field *Arizona Highways* v93 no9 p8 S 2017

TRIPP CANYON ROAD *Arizona Highways* v93 no9 p52 S 2017

Tuba City Water Tower *Arizona Highways* v92 no11 p6 N 2016

The Tucson Tornado *Arizona Highways* v93 no1 p8 Ja 2017

Up the Creek B&B *Arizona Highways* v93 no7 p14 Jl 2016

Willcox Playa *Arizona Highways* v93 no8 p6 Ag 2017

Yuma Agriculture *Arizona Highways* v93 no10 p7 O 2017

Austin, Robert

Megatelescope releases its first image *Physics Today* v69 no12 p42 D 2016

Austin, Robert D.

Leading in a World Without Secrets *Harvard Business Review Digital Articles* p2 D 2 2016

Neurodiversity as a Competitive Advantage color *Harvard Business Review* v95 no3 p96 My/Je 2017

Austin, Steve

a perfect marriage D. PIZZA color *Arts & Crafts Homes & the Revival* v12 no3 p40 Summ 2017

Austin-Tse, Christina A.

Distribution and clinical impact of functional variants in 50,726 whole-exome sequences from the DiscovEHR study chart graph *Science* v354 no6319 paaf6814-1 D 23 2016

Austra (Performer)

AN EAR FOR THE MOMENT E. VANDERHOOF color *Nation* v304 no7 p35 Mr 6 2017

Australia

Australia's Storied Ghosts J. NICKELL *Skeptical Inquirer* v41 no5 p12 S/O 2017

Giant radio telescope faces downsizing E. Cartlidge color *Science* v356 no6334 p124 Ap 14 2017

Significant Other J. SERRAO *Natural History* v125 no1 p48 D 2016/Ja 2017

Australia. Australian Army

OZ IN 'NAM R. Willis bw color map *Military History* v34 no5 p54 Ja 2018

Australia—Antiquities

STATE OF PRESERVATION J. C. Weber and N. Spooner *Archaeology* v70 no5 p8 S/O 2017

Australia—Description & travel

FAR OUT D. Prior color map *Conde Nast Traveler* v52 no2 p74 F 2017

Australia—Economic conditions—21st century

The Price of Australia's Complacency M. Heath and K. Painter color *Bloomberg Businessweek* no4541 p33 O 9 2017

Australian authors—Interviews

What to Do When the World Goes Crazy H. BAKER color *Christianity Today* v61 no5 p68 Je 2017

Australian magpie

Thank God for That Crazy Little Bird C. BLOOM and B. T. GREIVE *Audubon* v119 no1 p20 Spr 2017

Australian Open (Tennis tournament)

Man Out of Time S. Gregory color diag *Time* v189 no5 p42 F 13 2017

PEAK FEDERER [Cover story] R. BALDWIN bw color *GQ: Gentlemen's Quarterly* v97 no4 p82 Ap 2017

Second Chances C. Evert *Tennis* v53 no3 p4 My/Je 2017

Australians—United States

FACES IN THE CROWD T. Keith color *Sports Illustrated* v125

no18 p24 D 5 2016

Austria

Drainage Pipe Lodge R. DAVIDSON color *National Geographic Kids* no475 p7 N 2017

Austrian Alps (Austria)

MEDIEVAL TRACTION CONTROL color *Cycle World* v56 no3 p74 Ap 2017

Austrian novelists

Stefan Zweig's Ordeal J. P. O'MALLEY bw *American Conservative* v16 no3 p39 My/Je 2017

AUSUBEL, RAMONA

Bear Hugs *New York Times Book Review* p11 N 27 2016

Autarchy

THE NEW SELF-SUFFICIENCY R. D'AGOSTINO *Popular Mechanics* p4 F 2017

Auten, Holly

Detonation Science Blasts into a New Frontier *Science & Technology Review* p12 Jl/Ag 2017

Forcing Failure in Granular Materials *Science & Technology Review* p20 Mr 2017

LOOKING for TROUBLE on Optical Surfaces *Science & Technology Review* p17 Ap/My 2017

MAKING AN IMPACT ON ASTEROID DEFLECTION *Science & Technology Review* p16 D 2016

Ready, Set, Innovate! ENTREPRENEURSHIP FLOURISHES AT THE LABORATORY *Science & Technology Review* p4 Je 2017

Autenrieth, Ingo B.

Fighting the enemy within bibl diag *Science* v355 no6326 p689 F 17 2017

Auteur theory (Motion pictures)

A Six-Letter Word K. Jones bw color *Film Comment* v53 no4 p58 Jl/Ag 2017

Words of Past Images W. D. GEHRING *USA Today Magazine* v146 no2868 p49 S 2017

Authentic assessment

Big Progress in Authentic Assessment, But by Itself Not Enough D. F. Sullivan and K. D. McConnell *Change* v49 no1 p14 Ja/F 2017

Authentic Brands Group LLC

Where Dead Celebrities Go to Live L. Coleman-Lochner cartoon color *Bloomberg Businessweek* no4530 p16 Jl 17 2017

Authenticity (Philosophy)

By Being Authentic, You May Just Be Conforming H. Ibarra *Harvard Business Review Digital Articles* p2 Ja 19 2015

Our Biases Undermine Our Colleagues' Attempts to Be Authentic T. R. Opie and R. E. Freeman *Harvard Business Review Digital Articles* p2 Jl 5 2017

Authoritarian personality

This Isn't Normal color *Commonweal* v144 no4 p5 F 24 2017

Authoritarianism

Authoritarian Deliberation in China Baogang He and M. E. Warren *Daedalus* v146 no3 p155 Summ 2017

Baby, Behave! C. De Robertis bw color *Weekly Standard* v22 no32 p3 My 1 2017

Don't Mourn. Fight C. JEFFERY cartoon *Mother Jones* v42 no1 p6 Ja/F 2017

THE GOP'S AGE OF AUTHORITARIANISM HAS ONLY JUST BEGUN AND IT WILL NOT END WITH A CLINTON PRESIDENCY J. CHAIT img *New York* v49 no22 p52 O 31 2016

HOW TO BUILD AN AUTOCRACY D. FRUM cartoon color *Atlantic* v319 no2 p48 Mr 2017

Return Of the Strongman J. Kurlantzick color *Bloomberg Businessweek* no4522 p8 My 15 2017

Authoritarianism—History

Learn From History S. Benhabib *New Republic* v248 no3 p33 Mr 2017

Authoritarianism—History—20th century

The Tightening Authoritarian Grip on Thailand C. SOPRANZETTI *Current History* v116 no791 p230 S 2017

Authority

A NEW MAN A. GOPNIK cartoon color *New Yorker* v93 no19 p61 Jl 3 2017

Authors

See also

Authors & critics

Crime and Power J. FOSTER color *Publishers Weekly* v264 no8 p65 F 20 2017

David Sedaris Wants You to Read His Diary A. M. Cox *New York Times Magazine* p54 Jl 2 2017

Empathizing with the Villain M. BARSON color *Publishers Weekly* v263 no50 p50 D 5 2016

Family Lore B. Kachka img *New York* v49 no23 p78 N 14 2016

THE GHOSTS OF GEORGE SAUNDERS T. Murphy bw *Mother Jones* v42 no2 p53 Mr/Ap 2017

Golden Eyes A. APPEL *Publishers Weekly* v264 no23 p31 Je 5 2017

The Good Wife P. H. Bass color *Essence* v47 no7 p90 N 2016

Gretchen Rubin D. HANDLER *New York Times Book Review* p11 O 23 2016

Imagining Hollywood from the Outside In: A Conversation with Celestino Deleyto on From Tinseltown to Bordertown: Los Angeles on Film R. Longo *Film Quarterly* v70 no4 p118 Summ 2017

Is There a Connection Between Entrepreneurship and Mental Health Conditions? D. McGinn *Harvard Business Review Digital Articles* p2 F 22 2016

Jesmyn Ward *New York Times Book Review* p7 S 3 2017

Kenneth LONERGAN T. GEVINSON *Interview* v46 no9 p40 N 2016

Lives: A Reading from Three Novels L. Hartman bw *Publishers Weekly* v263 no44 p(Sp)10 O 31 2016

Michael Eric Dyson Believes In Individual Reparations A. M. Cox *New York Times Magazine* p50 Ja 8 2017

A MOTHER'S LOVE A. Orr color *Louisiana Life* v37 no6 p12 Jl/Ag 2017

Murderous Storms L. PICKER color *Publishers Weekly* v264 no13 p77 Mr 27 2017

My Home Has 'Murder' in Its Name M. LEE bw color *Christianity Today* v60 no10 p68 D 2016

Naoki Higashida N. Hopper color *Time* v190 no6 p60 Ag 7 2017

N.Y.C.: Tales of the City— A Reading from Three Novels L. Hartman bw *Publishers Weekly* v263 no44 p(Sp)24 O 31 2016

"Only Tell the Best Stories" G. M. KRAMER color *Publishers Weekly* v264 no31 p72 Jl 31 2017

THE PERFECT HORSE: A Conversation with Author Elizabeth Letts G. DEARTH *Arabian Horse World* v57 no11 p154 Ag 2017

PW talks with Nina Lindsay S. MAUGHAN color *Publishers Weekly* v264 no14 p28 Ap 3 2017

PW Talks with Thomas L. Friedman A. Albanese color *Publishers Weekly* v263 no45 p12 N 7 2016

Rain of Terror L. PICKER color *Publishers Weekly* v264 no39 p86 S 25 2017

A Refresher on Randomized Controlled Experiments A. Gallo *Harvard Business Review Digital Articles* p2 Mr 30 2016

Remembering Emmett Till E. Holley Jr. color *Publishers Weekly* v264 no2 p52 Ja 9 2017

Savoring Life in the Slow Lane B. HAHN color *Publishers Weekly* v264 no24 p40 Je 12 2017

The Strange Happy Life of a Scholar Gipsy H. Vynkier *Society* v53 no6 p581 D 2016

A Thousand Religions Bloom Again R. MOLL bw color *Christianity Today* p70 Ap 2017

What Do Animals Think of the Greek Financial Crisis? In a new adult picture book, Ungrateful Mammals, the ever-inventive Dave Eggers pairs his whimsical drawings with quirky quotations K. Frischkorn *Smithsonian* v48 no6 p28 O 2017

When Eugenics Was Progressive: Improve society by improving human stock? A century ago, the Progressive movement cheered that disturbing idea. Historian Thomas Leonard, author of Illiberal Reformers, explains R. Roberts *Hoover Digest: Research & Opinion on Public Policy* no3 p175 Summ 2017

"YOUR EMPLOYEES ARE THE PEOPLE WHO MAKE YOU WIN": Organisations are too focused on great players, says HR guru Dave Ulrich - it's time to start playing a team game G. GYTON *People Management* p40 Ap 2017

Authors—Salaries, etc.

BOOKING IT H. CUCCINELLO, N. ROBEHMED et al color *Forbes* v200 no2 p22 S 5 2017

Authors—Social conditions

Bookends: Do grants, professorships and other forms of insti-

tutional support help writers but hurt writing? S. Deb and B. Moser *New York Times Book Review* p23 Jl 9 2017

Authors—Travel

THE ESCAPE ARTIST: Nicole Krauss and her precursors R. Franklin *Harper's Magazine* p90 S 2017

Autism

AAAS Members Stand Up for Science M. Jarvis color *Science* v357 no6349 p365 Jl 28 2017

Baby Teeth Link Autism and Heavy Metals *USA Today Magazine* v146 no2869 p11 O 2017

Businesses With Heart S. SEA GOLD color *Parents* v92 no4 p28 Ap 2017

The Dangerous Delusion about Vaccines and Autism J. RANDI *Skeptical Inquirer* v41 no2 p29 Mr/Ap 2017

The Domesticated Human C. BADCOCK *Psychology Today* v50 no1 p41 Ja/F 2017

THE MAD GENIUS MYSTERY K. Perina *Psychology Today* v50 no4 p70 Ag 2017

treating depression J. MONINGER *Parents* v91 no11 p137 N 2016

The Way Forward J. BAUER, A. RIEGLER et al color *O, The Oprah Magazine* p18 My 2017

Why Debunking Myths About Vaccines Hasn't Convinced Dubious Parents C. Graves *Harvard Business Review Digital Articles* p2 F 20 2015

Autism in children—Diagnosis

Scientists seek early signs of autism L. SANDERS color graph *Science News* v191 no8 p10 Ap 29 2017

Autism in children—Risk factors

No autism link to antidepressants A. CUNNINGHAM graph *Science News* v191 no9 p9 My 13 2017

Autism in children—Treatment

Scientists seek early signs of autism L. SANDERS color graph *Science News* v191 no8 p10 Ap 29 2017

Autism spectrum disorders

    See also

    Autism

Data in public health color *Science* v355 no6326 p669 F 17 2017

The Farce Known as 'FC' J. RANDI *Skeptical Inquirer* v41 no4 p14 Jl/Ag 2017

Gut Reaction: Bacteria to Autism in Four (Not-So-) Easy Steps M. STONE *BioScience* v66 no11 p1004 N 1 2016

Recent progress in autism spectrum disorder research in China Jinchen Li, Lin Wang et al bibl chart diag *Science* v354 no6319 p48 D 23 2016

Autism spectrum disorders—Risk factors

Autism Spectrum Disorder M. BARNA color diag *Discover* v38 no6 p62 Jl/Ag 2017

Autistic athletes

Sports and Autism L. J. Wertheim and S. Apstein color *Sports Illustrated* v125 no16 p52 N 14 2016

Autistic children

THE HELP REFLEX R. D'AGOSTINO color *Popular Mechanics* p6 Mr 2017

Autistic children—Social conditions

OPENING DOORS FOR MY AUTISTIC SON J. NEWMAN color *Reader's Digest* v190 no1134 p78 O 2017

Autistic people

    See also

    Autistic children

REALITY TV T. ANDERSON and D. POINTDUJOUR color *Ebony* v72 no5 p65 Mr 2017

SOCIAL STUDIES G. Hardy color *America* v216 no5 p30 Mr 6 2017

Autistic people—Employment

How to support autistic employees *People Management* p48 My 2017

Autistic people—Psychology

An Auditory Component to Autism A. Pycha color *Scientific American* v315 no3 p16 S 2016

Autistic youth—Psychology

A Friend Indeed C. Eyster color *Money* v46 no4 p76 My 2017

Auto body repair

Oh No! Your Car Got Scratched! E. DYER color *Popular Mechanics* v193 no7 p52 S 2016

Autobiographical fiction

Automation & economics

The Asian Jobs Ladder Is Broken K. Hamlin, D. Roberts et al *Bloomberg Businessweek* no4528 p58 Je 26 2017

Robot Anxiety: Fears are spreading that automation will be a massive job-killer. Some of that is hype. Some is not M. Maciag *Governing* v30 no11 p56 Ag 2017

Automation in automobile factories

Remodeling a Sedan Plant for the SUV Era J. Lippert and K. Buckland bw *Bloomberg Businessweek* no4529 p18 Jl 3 2017

Automation in ships

Who's Driving? J. MOSER color *Power & Motoryacht* v34 no8 p24 Ag 2017

Automation in steel mills

500,000 Tons of Steel. 14 Jobs T. Biesheuvel color *Bloomberg Businessweek* no4528 p16 Je 26 2017

Automation in the petroleum industry

Can Oil Sands Pay Off At $50 a Barrel? K. Orland and N. O. Pearson graph *Bloomberg Businessweek* no4535 p33 Ag 28 2017

Automation—Charts, diagrams, etc.

AUTOMATION AHEAD B. O'keefe diag *Fortune* v176 no3 p96 S 1 2017

How Screwed Is Your Job? M. Whitehouse and D. Gambrell diag *Bloomberg Businessweek* no4528 p50 Je 26 2017

Automation—Economic aspects

25% of CEOs' Time Is Spent on Tasks Machines Could Do J. Manyika, M. Chui et al color *Harvard Business Review Digital Articles* p2 F 3 2017

IS THIS ROBOT A FRIEND—OR A FOE? J. Alsever color diag *Fortune* v175 no4 p22 Mr 15 2017

When robots steal your job S. GILMORE color *Maclean's* no1 p8 F 17 2017

Automation—Economic aspects—United States

Automation Makes Things Cheaper, So Why Doesn't It Feel That Way? W. H. Davidow color *Harvard Business Review Digital Articles* p2 Ap 3 2017

Automation—Equipment & supplies

What Comes After Smart Products B. Iyer and N. V. Venkatraman *Harvard Business Review Digital Articles* p2 Jl 1 2015

Automation—Forecasting

Robot Anxiety: Fears are spreading that automation will be a massive job-killer. Some of that is hype. Some is not M. Maciag *Governing* v30 no11 p56 Ag 2017

Automation—Government policy

"The Relentless Pace of Automation" D. Rotman color graph *MIT Technology Review* v120 no2 p92 Mr/Ap 2017

Automation—Management

Touring with Stage Automation S. Cox *Stage Directions* v29 no11 p18 N 2016

Automation—Social aspects

How to Win with Automation (Hint: It's Not Chasing Efficiency) G. Satell color *Harvard Business Review Digital Articles* p2 Mr 30 2017

Automobile auctions

Regal Rides M. SOLOMON color *Forbes* v198 no7 p30 N 29 2016

Surviving a Classic Car Slump E. Behrmann and B. Katz color *Bloomberg Businessweek* no4530 p64 Jl 17 2017

Automobile batteries

How Do You Check Battery Health? M. Davis color *Hot Rod* v70 no3 p86 Mr 2017

Automobile brake maintenance & repair

FIXING TRAIL FAILURESL J. KOPYCINSKI color *Dirt Sports + Off-Road* v51 no9 p66 S 2017

Automobile brakes

New & Used Car Reliability chart diag *Consumer Reports* v82 no4 p86 Ap 2017

PIT STOP M. Davis color diag *Hot Rod* v70 no10 p96 O 2017

What Is the Proper Brake System Pressure Range, and How Should it Be Checked? M. Davis color *Hot Rod* v69 no12 p86 D 2016

Automobile clutches

Inside a Fuel Car's 3,700-Degree Slider Clutch P. Thomas color *Hot Rod* v70 no12 p76 D 2017

Automobile collecting

HOW DJ KHALED ROLLS Z. O. GREENBURG color *Forbes* v200 no4 p58 O 24 2017

Automobile conversion

Kitbashing an early B&O wagontop boxcar D. Kawala color *Model Railroader* v84 no9 p22 S 2017

Automobile corrosion prevention

How Do You Keep Grounds From Corroding? M. Davis chart color *Hot Rod* v70 no8 p96 Ag 2017

Automobile cylinder blocks

Msgt. Mike Yates, USAF (Ret.), Asks... Why Won't a 454 Big-Block Properly Fit in Place of My 1974 GMC Sprint's Original Small-Block? M. Davis bw color *Hot Rod* v70 no7 p112 Jl 2017

Automobile dealers

Aaron Robinson A. Robinson color *Car & Driver* v62 no11 p30 My 2017

Dealer vs. Mechanic Showdown E. DYER color *Popular Mechanics* p40 F 2017

Drive Home a Better Deal D. Bortz color diag *Money* v45 no11 p23 D 2016

Help Keep Cincinnati Safe S. HARRISON *Cincinnati Magazine* v50 no5 p118 F 2017

Shopping *Virginia Living* p47 2017 Best 20of Virginia

Automobile detailing

Detail a boxcar interior L. Sassi color *Model Railroader* v84 no11 p26 N 2017

Automobile driver education

SLOW LEARNERS K. KINARD cartoon *Road & Track* v68 no7 p96 Mr/Ap 2017

Automobile driver education teachers

IN THE RIGHT J. BARUTH color *Road & Track* v69 no1 p98 Ag 2017

Automobile drivers

See also

    Automobile racing drivers
    Older automobile drivers
    Women automobile drivers

AMERICANS' $2 BILLION GAS MISTAKE M. C. White color *Money* v45 no10 p20 N 2016 ANATOMY OF A DRIFT CAR P. Thomas color *Hot Rod* v70 no8 p60 Ag 2017

AT THE WHEEL OVER 65: Driving Safer, Driving Longer [Cover story] M. Tortorello chart color graph *Consumer Reports* v82 no7 p18 Jl 2017

Is It O.K. to Fire a Muslim Driver for Refusing to Carry Wine? K. A. Appiah *New York Times Magazine* p20 Jl 23 2017

John Phillips J. Phillips color *Car & Driver* v63 no2 p30 Ag 2017

READERS' THOUGHTS ON PAST ISSUES P. CARAVELLA, B. ROBESON et al color *Motor Trend* v69 no2 p26 F 2017

Road Tunes D. Freiburger color *Hot Rod* v70 no8 p122 Ag 2017

Uber's Campsites O. Zaleski and E. Newcomer color *Bloomberg Businessweek* no4510 p24 F 6 2017

Automobile driving

See also

    Automobile racing
    Fully autonomous automobile driving

6 DRIVES TO TAKE YOUR BREATH AWAY G. HERBERT color *House Beautiful* p158 Ag 2017

The Car and Driver Guide to Automotive Bullsh!t J. Gall color *Car & Driver* v63 no1 p76 Jl 2017

COMFORTABLY DUMB J. P. Huffman cartoon *Car & Driver* v62 no11 p22 My 2017

DIFFERENTIAL DIFFERENCES J. JONES chart color *Dirt Sports + Off-Road* v51 no11 p32 N 2017

DRIVE TIME I. FRAZIER cartoon color *New Yorker* v93 no25 p34 Ag 28 2017

Dumb and Dumber America's driver education is failing us all M. Rechtin color *Motor Trend* v69 no8 p28 Ag 2017

Easy Rider G. WISHARD cartoon *Weekly Standard* v23 no4 p5 O 2 2017

I'VE GOT SOMETHING TO CONFESS... A. KELLER LAIRD color *Women's Health* v14 no2 p8 Mr 2017

Nonstandardized Testing J. Sabatini chart color *Car & Driver* v62 no8 p66 F 2017

No Picnic: Nothing is as good in real life as it is in theory P. Gulley *Indianapolis Monthly* v40 no10 p50 Je 2017

The Power of Just Driving Around D. Freiburger color *Hot Rod* v70 no1 p114 Ja 2017

The Price of Fear M. Gunch cartoon *New Orleans Magazine* v51 no8 p46 Je 2017

Road Trip, Bad Romance, Future Fashionista L. KOGAN cartoon *O, The Oprah Magazine* p44 F 2017

TICKLE TUMMY HILL J. ARTERBURN *Outdoor Life* v224 no9 p78 N 2017

WHAT HAPPENS TO AMERICAN MYTH WHEN YOU TAKE THE DRIVER OUT OF IT? R. MOOR *New York* v49 no21 p36 O 17 2016

WHERE WE'RE GOING, WE WON'T NEED ROADS J. BROWN color *Popular Science* v289 no6 p42 N/D 2017

Automobile driving at night
See also
  Headlight glare
AM I NORMAL? S. Yeager color *AARP: The Magazine* v60 no2A p18 F/Mr 2017

Automobile driving in winter
Winter Driving: Your Survival Guide M. Monticello chart color *Consumer Reports* v82 no11 p52 N 2017

Automobile driving laws
How to beat the traffic M. Anderson color *Science* v357 no6346 p36 Jl 7 2017

Automobile driving on mountain roads
NEW PERSPECTIVE ON THE ROAD R. HOWELL color *Car & Driver* v62 no6 p15 D 2016

Automobile driving schools
Christmas at 120 MPH bw color map *GQ: Gentlemen's Quarterly* v86 no12 p112 D 2016

Automobile driving—Equipment & supplies
NEW WAYS TO LOVE YOUR VEHICLE color *Popular Mechanics* p44 Ap 2017

Automobile driving—Evaluation
Ways to stay sharp behind the wheel *Harvard Health Letter* v42 no11 p1 S 2017

Automobile driving—Germany
Dumb and Dumber America's driver education is failing us all M. Rechtin color *Motor Trend* v69 no8 p28 Ag 2017

Automobile driving—Social aspects
Coolness: A Moving Target D. Freiburger color *Hot Rod* v70 no10 p106 O 2017

Automobile driving—Software
AUTOMATIC PRO: BE A BETTER DRIVER WITH THIS DRIVING DATA TRACKER IN YOUR CAR G. FLEISHMAN color map *Macworld - Digital Edition* v33 no11 p85 N 2016

Automobile driving—Steering
Editor's Letter E. Alterman *Car & Driver* v62 no10 p8 Ap 2017

Automobile emissions
California vs. Trump Over Car Emissions bw *Bloomberg Businessweek* no4517 p10 Ap 3 2017
Is VW's Fraud the End of Large-Scale Corporate Deception? M. Schrage *Harvard Business Review Digital Articles* p2 S 29 2015
VERY CLOSE VANES color *Road & Track* v68 no5 p116 D 2016/Ja 2017

Automobile emissions—Law & legislation
Vehicle Emissions Standards *Congressional Digest* v95 no9 p13 N 2016

Automobile engine cylinder fluid dynamics
Will More Cylinder-Head Flow Always Make More Power? M. Davis bw color *Hot Rod* v70 no7 p98 Jl 2017

Automobile engine design & construction
BARK + BITE M. Gearhart color *Hot Rod* v70 no8 p68 Ag 2017
Take 5 With KENNY DUTTWEILER J. P. Huffman color *Hot Rod* v70 no12 p12 D 2017

Automobile engine equipment
Mike Davis Asks... What Distributor Gear, Break-In Procedure, and Lifter-Adjustment Method Works on a Small-Block Chevy Hydraulic-Roller Cam? M. Davis color *Hot Rod* v70 no12 p104 D 2017

Automobile engine performance
How Does Header Primary-Tube Length Affect Performance? M. Davis graph *Hot Rod* v70 no11 p6 N 2017

Automobile engineers
IDENTITY CRISIS A. MacKenzie color *Motor Trend* v69 no10 p117 O 2017

Automobile engineers—Interviews
What I'd Do Differently Marcello Gandini, 78 J. PEARLEY HUFFMAN color *Car & Driver* v62 no6 p108 D 2016

Automobile engines

See also
  Fuel pumps
200-MPH TRICKLE-DOWN J. F. MUSIAL color *Road & Track* v69 no4 p66 N 2017
2.5 HORSEPOWER PER CUBIC INCH! B. Gillogly color *Hot Rod* v70 no4 p76 Ap 2017
The 350 Crate Engine in Carl Arentz's 1964 Chevelle Has Severe Driveability Issues. We're Gonna Fix It M. Davis chart color *Hot Rod* v70 no9 p94 S 2017
850HP LS FORMULA B. Gillogly color *Hot Rod* v70 no4 p78 Ap 2017
CAPTURING THE LIFE AT SPEED color *Road & Track* v69 no4 p6 N 2017
FINDING FORGOTTEN HORSEPOWER B. Gillogly color *Hot Rod* v70 no3 p64 Mr 2017
Give the Kid a Chance E. Perkins color *Hot Rod* v70 no4 p8 Ap 2017
HOT ROD TO THE RESCUE chart color graph *Hot Rod* v69 no12 p92 D 2016
How Do I Bolt a T5 Trans to a 1960s Small-Block Ford Bellhousing? M. Davis color *Hot Rod* v70 no11 p120 N 2017
IRON SUPPLEMENT M. Gearhart color *Hot Rod* v70 no6 p86 Je 2017
It's a Hellcat Thing J. GALL color *Car & Driver* v63 no5 p100 N 2017
John Phillips J. Phillips color *Car & Driver* v62 no11 p28 My 2017
New Classes, New Winners, and New Recipes for Horsepower B. Gillogly color *Hot Rod* v70 no3 p56 Mr 2017
ONE MAN, ONE ENGINE bw *Road & Track* v69 no4 p8 N 2017
Pam Jacoby's 700-R4 Trans Won't Lock Up the Torque Converter. We're Gonna Fix It M. Davis chart color diag *Hot Rod* v70 no11 p110 N 2017
Program Your Camshafts? E. Perkins color *Hot Rod* v70 no2 p8 F 2017
STREETABLE 469CI BIG-BLOCK CHEVY B. Gillogly color *Hot Rod* v70 no4 p74 Ap 2017
A WEDGED BLUE OVAL J. Machaqueiro color *Hot Rod* v70 no4 p46 Ap 2017

Automobile engines—Accidents
THE YEAR THAT WAS M. Emery *Dirt Sports + Off-Road* v51 no4 p6 Ap 2017

Automobile engines—Camshafts
Degrees of Separation E. Perkins chart color graph *Hot Rod* v70 no6 p72 Je 2017
What's the Crossover Point Between a "Torque" Cam Versus One Ground to Maximize Top-End Power? M. Davis color *Hot Rod* v70 no1 p92 Ja 2017
Why Is a Cam's Intake Closing Point So Important? M. Davis color *Hot Rod* v70 no6 p100 Je 2017

Automobile engines—Carburetors
FORCE FED E. Perkins color graph *Hot Rod* v69 no12 p74 D 2016

Automobile engines—Evaluation
ENGINES J. Jacquot color *Car & Driver* v62 no7 p26 Ja 2017
The Future of Fueling J. Smith color *Hot Rod* v70 no2 p78 F 2017
New Life for the Gas Engine C. ATIYEH color *Popular Science* v288 no6 p42 N/D 2016
Old Engine, New Tricks E. DYER cartoon color *Popular Mechanics* p38 Je 2017
PARTS & STUFF color *Hot Rod* v70 no4 p100 Ap 2017

Automobile engines—Fuel injection systems
2016 Pro Stock Problems, Solutions, and the Future T. Taylor color *Hot Rod* v70 no6 p60 Je 2017

Automobile engines—Maintenance & repair
(Don't) DIY E. DYER color *Popular Mechanics* p62 D 2016/Ja 2017

Automobile engines—Modification
RAM RUNNER [Cover story] M. EMERY color *Dirt Sports + Off-Road* v51 no1 p24 Ja 2017

Automobile engines—Parts
FORCE FED E. Perkins color graph *Hot Rod* v69 no12 p74 D 2016

Automobile engines—Specifications
ENGINES J. Jacquot color *Car & Driver* v62 no7 p26 Ja 2017

Automobile engines—Superchargers

FORCING THE ISSUE D. SCANLON color graph *Dirt Sports + Off-Road* v51 no7 p38 Jl 2017

ONE STEP BEYOND C. Shelton color *Hot Rod* v70 no3 p68 Mr 2017

Automobile engines—Timing belts

Is a Timing Cover Change Needed When Going From a Reverse-to a Standard-Rotation Water Pump on a Small-Block Ford? M. Davis color *Hot Rod* v70 no5 p104 My 2017

Automobile engines—Valves

Boost-Ready M. Gearhart color *Hot Rod* v70 no5 p20 My 2017

Automobile equipment

See also

Automobile safety appliances

Automotive electronics

Beyond the Iron Curtain J. Bryant color *Hot Rod* v70 no10 p74 O 2017

CAR SMARTIFIER color *Good Housekeeping* v264 no6 p77 Je 2017

HEAD-TO-HEAD: BABY DRIVERS C. NULL color *Wired* v25 no9 p48 S 2017

How Does Header Primary-Tube Diameter Affect Performance? M. Davis graph *Hot Rod* v70 no12 p94 D 2017

PARTS & STUFF color *Hot Rod* v70 no10 p100 O 2017

Progress R. D'AGOSTINO *Popular Mechanics* p6 S 2017

Small Wonders Two promising boosters for our ever-shrinking engines F. Markus bw *Motor Trend* v69 no8 p30 Ag 2017

U-JOINT SURVIVAL J. KOPYCINSKI color *Dirt Sports + Off-Road* v51 no11 p66 N 2017

WEEKEND EFI E. Perkins color *Hot Rod* v70 no10 p46 O 2017

Automobile equipment—Evaluation

THE BUYER'S GUIDE color *Hot Rod* v70 no7 p84 Jl 2017

DIRTY TALK color *Road & Track* v68 no9 p94 Je 2017

Automobile exhaust systems

Are Exhaust Headers a Waste of Money on the Street? M. Davis chart color graph *Hot Rod* v70 no9 p104 S 2017

IMPERFECT PIPES P. LERNER color *Road & Track* v69 no3 p98 O 2017

Automobile exhibitions

The First HOT ROD Power Tour T. Taylor color *Hot Rod* v70 no9 p10 S 2017

So Much Love D. Freiburger color *Hot Rod* v70 no4 p106 Ap 2017

Automobile factory shutdowns

THE END OF LABOR A. GOLDSTEIN bw color *Nation* v305 no6 p22 S 11 2017

Automobile fuel systems

See also

Fuel injection systems in automobiles

Buy the Gas Your Car Deserves D. MUHLBAUM *Kiplinger's Personal Finance* v71 no11 p71 N 2017

Automobile ignition

ALL IN THE TIMING J. Smith chart color graph *Hot Rod* v70 no9 p70 S 2017

COOL MOVE [Cover story] B. W. SMITH color *Dirt Sports + Off-Road* v51 no12 p62 D 2017

We Finally Fixed It! J.B. Bracken's Blown Rat Rod Now Burns Out, But It Took Ignition and Cooling Fixes to Perfect M. Davis color graph *Hot Rod* v70 no12 p96 D 2017

Automobile industry

See also

Service stations

Aaron Robinson A. Robinson color *Car & Driver* v62 no10 p24 Ap 2017

Aaron Robinson A. Robinson color *Car & Driver* v63 no1 p32 Jl 2017

Automotive Archaeology A Junkyard That No Longer Is R. Brutt color *Hot Rod* v70 no3 p14 Mr 2017

Bona Fides Does a car company need a car guy for a CEO? M. Rechtin color *Motor Trend* v69 no9 p26 S 2017

Brand Report Card J. S. Bartlett chart *Consumer Reports* v82 no4 p36 Ap 2017

END OF THE ROAD B. Coleman *Cincinnati Magazine* v50 no5 p66 F 2017

The Existential Question Facing the Auto Industry M. L. Tushman *Harvard Business Review Digital Articles* p2 Ap 12 2016

FINDING FORGOTTEN HORSEPOWER B. Gillogly color *Hot Rod* v70 no3 p64 Mr 2017

GLOBAL MOTORS A. MacKenzie color *Motor Trend* v69 no4 p98 Ap 2017

Hands of Time J. BARUTH bw color *Road & Track* v69 no2 p26 S 2017

Hot Rod Anything! Clearing Snow With 4,000 HP P. Thomas bw color *Hot Rod* v70 no3 p10 Mr 2017

It's in Our Blood E. Perkins color *Hot Rod* v70 no9 p8 S 2017

Just Don't Ask B. LUTZ *Road & Track* v69 no4 p100 N 2017

The Miracle Material E. DYER color *Popular Mechanics* p51 Mr 2017

MOST PROMISING TECHNOLOGY E. Tingwall and D. Beard cartoon color diag *Car & Driver* v62 no7 p28 Ja 2017

MOTOR CITY MADE B. Boyé bw color *Men's Health* v32 no2 p(Sp)20 Mr 2017

Mustang Mutability B. LUTZ color *Road & Track* v69 no1 p108 Ag 2017

Program Your Camshafts? E. Perkins color *Hot Rod* v70 no2 p8 F 2017

TRUE NORTH A. MacKenzie color *Motor Trend* v69 no6 p117 Je 2017

THE VALUE OF NOTHING A. MacKenzie color *Motor Trend* v68 no12 p118 D 2016

What Happens If Apple Starts Making Cars M. Schrage *Harvard Business Review Digital Articles* p2 F 19 2015

What the Trump presidency may mean for the future of the auto industry M. Rechtin cartoon *Motor Trend* v69 no2 p20 F 2017

Automobile industry executives

What I'd Do Differently Johan de Nysschen, 57 J. PEARLEY HUFFMAN *Car & Driver* v63 no4 p108 O 2017

Automobile industry personnel—Attitudes

Globalism Is Alive and Well: Just Ask Carlos Ghosn M. Reel, K. Inoue et al color *Bloomberg Businessweek* no4531 p50 Jl 24 2017

Automobile industry personnel—Training of

BMW to Staff: Be Afraid, Be Very Afraid E. Behrmann graph *Bloomberg Businessweek* no4520 p25 My 1 2017

Automobile industry—China

Cheap's No Longer Chic For China's Carmakers color graph *Bloomberg Businessweek* no4502 p29 D 5 2016

Chinese Cars May Lose Their Learner's Permits *Bloomberg Businessweek* no4519 p28 Ap 24 2017

TESLA MAKES A U-TURN IN CHINA S. Cendrowski chart color diag *Fortune* v175 no8 p128 Je 15 2017

Who's Gonna Buy All These Audis in China? color graph *Bloomberg Businessweek* no4506 p16 Ja 9 2017

Automobile industry—Corrupt practices

The Moral Cost of Dieselgate E. Loh color *Motor Trend* v69 no4 p14 Ap 2017

What 100,000 Tweets About the Volkswagen Scandal Tell Us About Angry Customers V. Swaminathan and S. Mah *Harvard Business Review Digital Articles* p2 S 2 2016

Automobile industry—Economic aspects

Let's Cancel B. LUTZ *Road & Track* v69 no3 p108 O 2017

Automobile industry—Germany

AXLES OF EVIL? A. MacKenzie color *Motor Trend* v69 no9 p118 S 2017

Automobile industry—Government policy—United States

Assessing the Sins of Volkswagen, Toyota, and General Motors J. Liker *Harvard Business Review Digital Articles* p2 S 24 2015

Automobile industry—Japan

Art and Seoul B. LUTZ color *Road & Track* v68 no6 p92 F 2017

Automobile industry—Korea (South)

Art and Seoul B. LUTZ color *Road & Track* v68 no6 p92 F 2017

Automobile industry—Mexico

Carmakers Could Hit That Wall, Too C. Trudell, K. Naughton et al chart color graph *Bloomberg Businessweek* no4500 p20 N 21 2016

Automobile industry—News briefs

THE GRID: AUTO INNOVATIONS *Saturday Evening Post* v289 no3 p24 My/Je 2017

WINNERS AND LOSERS A. Robinson color *Car & Driver* v62 no7 p18 Ja 2017

Automobile industry—North America

Trump Threatens to Undo Nafta's Auto Alley B. Greeley, D. Welch et al bw graph *Bloomberg Businessweek* no4509 p25 Ja

30 2017

Automobile industry—Officials & employees—Awards

Elon Musk CEO TESLA MOTORS cartoon *Motor Trend* v69 no1 p108 Ja 2017

POWER LIST A. MacKenzie and A. Priddle cartoon *Motor Trend* v69 no1 p100 Ja 2017

Automobile industry—Southern States

DON'T LET THE MONSTER EAT YOU UP' P. WALDMAN color *Bloomberg Businessweek* no4516 p46 Mr 27 2017

Automobile industry—United States

America Last M. JANCER *Car & Driver* v62 no11 p94 My 2017

AXLES OF EVIL? A. MacKenzie color *Motor Trend* v69 no9 p118 S 2017

BAD NEWS: THE GOVERNMENT WANTS TO 'HELP' DRIVERLESS CAR COMPANIES R. BAILEY bw *Reason* v48 no10 p13 Mr 2017

B.E. AUTO 50 *Black Enterprise* v47 no7 p60 My/Je 2017

Changing Tides B. LUTZ *Road & Track* v68 no9 p100 Je 2017

Come for the Treadmill Desk, Stay for the ... K. Naughton, D. Welch et al color *Bloomberg Businessweek* no4522 p40 My 15 2017

Count Our Blessings B. LUTZ color *Road & Track* v68 no10 p112 Jl 2017

Dieter Zetsche A. MacKenzie color *Motor Trend* v69 no6 p30 Je 2017

The Real Cause of the U.S. Car Slide: SUVs D. Welch, J. Butters et al diag *Bloomberg Businessweek* no4518 p24 Ap 10 2017

Rolling Back the Year color *Consumer Reports* v82 no4 p6 Ap 2017

Smashing NAFTA Apart Is Harder Than It Seems, Especially When You're Blindfolded J. SABATINI color graph *Car & Driver* v62 no11 p90 My 2017

Sorry to Disappoint You, Mr. President R. BURR color *Weekly Standard* v22 no31 p26 Ap 17 2017

Automobile industry—United States—Officials & employees

GREAT UNKNOWNS bw *Popular Mechanics* p108 Jl 2017

Automobile insurance

See also

Medical payments insurance

Exposing Unfair Pricing in Auto Insurance Rates R. Root, R. Fischer et al color *Consumer Reports* v82 no5 p6 My 2017

Hey Mr. Green! Is it better to scoop or to bury dog poop? Trudi, Janet et al *Sierra* v102 no3 p12 My/Je 2017

How to Save on Car Insurance T. Stanger chart diag graph *Consumer Reports* v82 no3 p42 Mr 2017

Automobile insurance companies

Can Insurance Companies Incentivize Their Customers to Be Healthier? A. Gore, P. Harmer et al *Harvard Business Review Digital Articles* p2 Je 23 2017

Insurers Ding Innocent Drivers After Accidents M. Leonhardt color *Money* v46 no3 p18 Ap 2017

Automobile insurance premiums

Estimate Your Social Security Benefit K. LANKFORD *Kiplinger's Personal Finance* v71 no2 p50 F 2017

A World Apart J. Angwin, J. Larson et al color *Consumer Reports* v82 no7 p52 Jl 2017

Automobile insurance—United States

Cut Car Insurance Rates M. CROSS color *Kiplinger's Personal Finance* v71 no5 p43 My 2017

How to Find a Home's Claims History K. LANKFORD color *Kiplinger's Personal Finance* v71 no10 p42 O 2017

A World Apart J. Angwin, J. Larson et al color *Consumer Reports* v82 no7 p52 Jl 2017

Automobile internet connections

Building a Better World, Together color *Consumer Reports* v82 no7 p5 Jl 2017

Automobile keys

Progress R. D'AGOSTINO *Popular Mechanics* p6 S 2017

Automobile leasing & renting

ALL IN A Day's Work color graph *Reader's Digest* v189 no1131 p58 Je 2017

Alt Boating A. JONES *Boating World* v38 no3 p4 Mr 2017

Baby, You Can Rent My Car N. Leiber *Bloomberg Businessweek* no4494 p36 O 10 2016

Flip Your Ride: Jaguar on Wednesday, Lexus on Thursday, Porsche on Friday--welcome to Clutch! S. FENNESSY *Atlanta*

v57 no3 p44 Jl 2017

John Phillips J. Phillips color *Car & Driver* v62 no8 p24 F 2017

Rental Cars to The Rescue J. Butters, J. Lippert et al cartoon graph *Bloomberg Businessweek* no4526 p18 Je 12 2017

ROAD WARRIORS E. Malter color *Sunset* v239 no1 p24 Jl 2017

Why the SUV boom is great news for sedan drivers M. Rechtin color *Motor Trend* v69 no10 p22 O 2017

The Worry-Free Way to Rent a Car M. CROSS color *Kiplinger's Personal Finance* v71 no8 p69 Ag 2017

Automobile license plate laws

LICENSE-PLATE MARRIAGES B. Carlson color *Atlantic* v320 no3 p22 O 2017

Automobile license plates

See also

Specialty license plates

VEHICULAR VANITY RUN AMUCK R. NELSON *Virginia Living* v15 no1 p112 D 2016

Automobile lighting

See also

Headlight glare

Automobile lighting—Evaluation

WHELEN LEDS color *Flying* v144 no7 p16 Jl 2017

Automobile loans

See also

Subprime automobile loans

How to Get a Great Deal on a New Car D. MUHLBAUM color *Kiplinger's Personal Finance* v71 no5 p48 My 2017

Warning Signs from the showroom floor M. Rechtin cartoon *Motor Trend* v69 no3 p30 Mr 2017

Why a Lower Car Payment Can Be a Costly Mistake C. Fried color graph *Consumer Reports* v82 no12 p60 D 2017

Automobile museums—Evaluation

BEAULIEU *British Heritage Travel* v38 no2 p20 Mr/Ap 2017

TAKE TEN *British Heritage Travel* v38 no2 p12 Mr/Ap 2017

Automobile ownership

GREAT UNKNOWNS bw *Popular Mechanics* p108 Jl 2017

Staying Power M. Naranjo chart color diag *Consumer Reports* v81 no12 p66 D 2016

Automobile ownership—Surveys

Cars That Owners Love and Hate M. Monticello chart color *Consumer Reports* v82 no2 p46 F 2017

Automobile parking

THE FALLACY OF THE SELF-PARKING CAR E. DYER color *Popular Mechanics* p73 My 2017

Automobile parking—United States

IS THIS SPACE FREE? D. Reed color *Washingtonian Magazine* v52 no7 p49 Ap 2017

PARK AND SIGH A. WHITING *Washingtonian Magazine* v52 no8 p12 My 2017

Automobile part design & construction

HANDY ADJUSTABILITY M. KAUSCH color *Dirt Sports + Off-Road* v51 no9 p62 S 2017

Automobile parts

Ezra Dyer E. Dyer color *Car & Driver* v63 no1 p34 Jl 2017

Frame-Draggin' Brat Rod P. Thomas color *Hot Rod* v70 no9 p12 S 2017

GEARBOX color *Dirt Sports + Off-Road* v51 no12 p70 D 2017

How Do You Keep Grounds From Corroding? M. Davis chart color *Hot Rod* v70 no8 p96 Ag 2017

Inside a Fuel Car's 3,700-Degree Slider Clutch P. Thomas color *Hot Rod* v70 no12 p76 D 2017

PARTS & STUFF color *Hot Rod* v70 no8 p116 Ag 2017

Scott Sortor From Sebring, Florida, Asks... Does a TH350 Need a Kickdown Cable? M. Davis color diag *Hot Rod* v70 no4 p96 Ap 2017

Step by Step: Solid Foundations J. Bryant color *Hot Rod* v70 no12 p84 D 2017

Automobile parts—Evaluation

PARTS & STUFF color *Hot Rod* v70 no4 p100 Ap 2017

Automobile periodicals

2.5 HORSEPOWER PER CUBIC INCH! B. Gillogly color *Hot Rod* v70 no4 p76 Ap 2017

The HOT ROD Archives D. Wallace color *Hot Rod* v70 no11 p12 N 2017

Joe Carroll Pulls Spec Puzzle Pieces Together at Engine Masters Challenge P. Thomas color *Hot Rod* v70 no4 p72 Ap 2017

Automobile piston & piston rings

Jake Jacobs Asks... Can Pistons Be Changed on a Rotating Assembly Without Upsetting Its Balance? M. Davis color *Hot Rod* v70 no8 p112 Ag 2017

Automobile power trains

See also

Automobile engines

Does More Boost Always Make More Power? M. Davis color *Hot Rod* v70 no9 p92 S 2017

Automobile purchasing

BUYING A NEW CAR? CHECK THE RESALE VALUE M. CROSS color *Kiplinger's Personal Finance* v71 no10 p13 O 2017

SUMMER MOTORING M. MCCARTHY and V. CROWE color *House Beautiful* p156 Ag 2017

Automobile racing

See also

Automobile rallies

Drag racing

Karting

NASCAR (Association)

2017 UTV WORLD CHAMPIONSHIPS M. EMERY color *Dirt Sports + Off-Road* v51 no9 p10 S 2017

90-DEGREE DREAMS & QUARTER-MILE SIDESHOW T. Taylor bw color *Hot Rod* v70 no9 p46 S 2017

BEST DRIVER'S LAP K. Reynolds bw color diag *Motor Trend* v69 no11 p80 N 2017

CARS AND SAKI color *Road & Track* v69 no2 p14 S 2017

Color Schemes S. SMITH cartoon *Road & Track* v68 no6 p20 F 2017

COMPETITION color *Road & Track* v69 no2 p12 S 2017

Coolness: A Moving Target D. Freiburger color *Hot Rod* v70 no10 p106 O 2017

The Corvette Curse T. Taylor bw *Hot Rod* v70 no11 p8 N 2017

CURRENT AFFAIRS A. Lindberg color *Car & Driver* v63 no5 p24 N 2017

Drivers Not Wanted: An Oral History of the Darpa Grand Challenge A. DAVIES bw color diag *Wired* v25 no8 p49 Ag 2017

DROP THE HAMMER T. L. Byrd color *Hot Rod* v70 no12 p32 D 2017

EDITOR'S LETTER K. WOLFKILL color *Road & Track* v68 no8 p20 My 2017

EDITOR'S LETTER K. WOLFKILL *Road & Track* v69 no4 p20 N 2017

Ezra Dyer E. Dyer color *Car & Driver* v63 no5 p32 N 2017

FAST CORNERS AND FLYING HIGH S. RICHARDS color *Dirt Sports + Off-Road* v51 no11 p36 N 2017

FINISH LINE D. Freiburger color *Hot Rod* v70 no6 p122 Je 2017

GMZ UTV WINTER NATIONALS/BITD PARKER 250 M. EMERY color *Dirt Sports + Off-Road* v51 no5 p28 My 2017

Go color *Road & Track* v68 no10 p9 Jl 2017

JURASSIC WORLD S. SMITH color *Road & Track* v68 no6 p34 F 2017

LEGEND OF THE FALL J. H. HARPER color *Road & Track* v68 no6 p24 F 2017

Live from Pebble Beach E. Loh color *Motor Trend* v68 no12 p12 D 2016

LS All the Things! T. L. Byrd color *Hot Rod* v70 no2 p68 F 2017

McQueen for a Day R. LANE color *Forbes* v199 no4 p108 Ap 25 2017

PUT UP OR SHUT UP E. Loh color *Motor Trend* v69 no10 p12 O 2017

Race to the Bottom S. SMITH color *Road & Track* v68 no9 p22 Je 2017

RACING color *Road & Track* v69 no4 p10 N 2017

ROADKILL DAYS LEAD TO ROADKILL NIGHTS E. Scherr, E. Rood et al color *Hot Rod* v70 no1 p84 Ja 2017

SHREDDING ON THE SANDS OF TIME S. Lachenauer and W. Allison color diag *Hot Rod* v70 no12 p38 D 2017

THE (SOGGY) RACE OF GENTLEMEN D. Hardin bw color *Hot Rod* v70 no3 p48 Mr 2017

So Much Love D. Freiburger color *Hot Rod* v70 no4 p106 Ap 2017

What's On Demand This Month? E. Loh *Motor Trend* v69 no11 p14 N 2017

Automobile racing competitions

Churn and Burn B. Marks and T. Keith color *Sports Illustrated* v127 no2 p20 Jl 17 2017

FAST CORNERS AND FLYING HIGH S. RICHARDS color *Dirt Sports + Off-Road* v51 no11 p36 N 2017

LEGACY LEGITIMIZATION S. RICHARDS color *Dirt Sports + Off-Road* v51 no11 p10 N 2017

MOUNTAIN HAVOC 2017 J. JONES color *Dirt Sports + Off-Road* v51 no11 p48 N 2017

A NATION'S DATEBOOK *Dirt Sports + Off-Road* v51 no9 p72 S 2017

Time MACHINES A. Shuler *Indianapolis Monthly* v40 no10 p78 Je 2017

What's On Demand This Month? *Motor Trend* v69 no10 p12 O 2017

A WINNING FORMULA color *Road & Track* v68 no6 p14 F 2017

World's Greatest Drag Race E. Loh color graph *Motor Trend* v69 no11 p84 N 2017

Automobile racing drivers

See also

Drag racers

Women automobile racing drivers

1987 MINI-METAL CHAMPIONSHIP J. OBER bw *Dirt Sports + Off-Road* v51 no11 p74 N 2017

BOB "WEATHERMAN" STEINBERGER DIES color *Dirt Sports + Off-Road* v51 no11 p8 N 2017

CASEY FOLKS: RACER, BEST IN THE DESERT FOUNDER, AND DRIVING FORCE DIES color *Dirt Sports + Off-Road* v51 no6 p6 Je 2017

DRIVING LESSON S. Slon *Saturday Evening Post* v289 no3 p4 My/Je 2017

EDITOR'S LETTER K. WOLFKILL color *Road & Track* v68 no5 p31 D 2016/Ja 2017

ENOUGH? D. TREMAYNE bw color *Road & Track* v68 no7 p68 Mr/Ap 2017

The Fastest Man on Wheels S. Gregory color *Time* v188 no27-28 p74 D 26 2016

FORWARD MOMENTUM M. PRINCE bw *Road & Track* v69 no4 p64 N 2017

HEADSTRONG M. PRINCE *Road & Track* v68 no8 p98 My 2017

MARIO ANDRETTI S. Slon *Saturday Evening Post* v289 no3 p48 My/Je 2017

MARIO IS FEELING FINE J. Skow *Saturday Evening Post* v289 no3 p52 My/Je 2017

MASTER'S PROGRAM J. BARUTH color *Road & Track* v69 no3 p68 O 2017

Petersen's Toast to "THE KING" P. Thomas color *Hot Rod* v70 no10 p60 O 2017

Pomona Fairgrounds Dragstrip, May 1958 T. Taylor bw *Hot Rod* v70 no10 p10 O 2017

THE SPECIALISTS M. SCHIRMER color *Road & Track* v68 no6 p48 F 2017

STAR POWER P. LERNER color *Road & Track* v68 no9 p66 Je 2017

Take 5 With DALE EARNHARDT JR J. P. Huffman color *Hot Rod* v70 no11 p14 N 2017

What I'd Do Differently A.J. Foyt, 82 J. P. HUFFMAN cartoon *Car & Driver* v62 no8 p92 F 2017

What I'd Do Differently Kyle Petty, 57 J. PEARLEY HUFFMAN color *Car & Driver* v63 no5 p128 N 2017

The Wrecked, Rebuilt Life OF ALDO ANDRETTI D. S. COMISKEY *Indianapolis Monthly* p72 My 2017

Automobile racing drivers—United States

AMERICAN PRIDE color *Road & Track* v68 no6 p12 F 2017

YOUTH BE KNOWN S. Kwak color *Sports Illustrated* v127 no10 p20 O 2 2017

Automobile racing fans

GO bw color *Road & Track* v69 no3 p8 O 2017

Automobile racing training

IN THE RIGHT J. BARUTH color *Road & Track* v69 no1 p98 Ag 2017

Automobile racing—Congresses

2017 SCHEDULE *Dirt Sports + Off-Road* v51 no11 p72 N 2017

Automobile racing—History

GO bw color *Road & Track* v69 no3 p8 O 2017

See also

Four-wheel drive vehicles

How Do I Bolt a T5 Trans to a 1960s Small-Block Ford Bellhousing? M. Davis color *Hot Rod* v70 no11 p120 N 2017

Automobile travel

The Road More Traveled M. Hornung color *Money* v46 no3 p80 Ap 2017

ROAD SHOWS: FOUR SCENIC DRIVES WHERE YOU CAN TAKE IN FALL LEAVES, SAMPLE WINES, EXPLORE HISTORY, AND GET A TASTE OF THE VALLEY L. Ward *Washingtonian Magazine* v53 no1 p94 O 2017

SUMMER MOTORING M. MCCARTHY and V. CROWE color *House Beautiful* p156 Ag 2017

Automobile travel in literature

EIGHT GREAT ROAD-TRIP BOOKS E. Staff color *Entertainment Weekly* no1476 p64 Ag 4 2017

Automobile travel—Texas

The North Texas Loop G. R. SCHIAVINO map *American Cowboy* v23 no6 p35 Ap/My 2017

Automobile turbochargers

Upped Ante M. Gearhart color diag graph *Hot Rod* v70 no7 p54 Jl 2017

Automobile wiring

DIY POWER MANAGEMENT [Cover story] J. KOPYCINSKI color *Dirt Sports + Off-Road* v51 no12 p66 D 2017

Automobile industry personnel—Salaries, wages, etc.

Why Mexico's Autoworkers Aren't Prospering D. Welch, N. Cattan et al color graph *Bloomberg Businessweek* no4521 p12 My 8 2017

Automobile racing—Charts, diagrams, etc.

The HOT ROD Archives D. Wallace color *Hot Rod* v70 no10 p16 O 2017

Automobiles

See also

Alfa Romeo automobile

Antique & classic cars

Aston Martin automobile

Automobile parts

BMW automobiles

Bugatti automobile

Electric automobiles

Ferrari automobile

Ford automobile

Hydrogen cars

Lamborghini automobile

Maybach automobile

Nissan automobiles

Racing automobiles

Remodeled automobiles

Rolls-Royce automobile

Station wagons

Toyota automobiles

Used cars

Volkswagen automobiles

the 10 best new family cars [Cover story] L. ULRICH cartoon color *Parents* v92 no7 p100 Jl 2017

Automotive Archaeology A Junkyard That No Longer Is R. Brutt color *Hot Rod* v70 no3 p14 Mr 2017

Cars That Go the Distance P. Olsen chart color diag *Consumer Reports* v82 no12 p52 D 2017

Citywide effects of high-occupancy vehicle restrictions: Evidence from "three-in-one" in Jakarta R. Hanna, G. Kreindler et al chart graph map *Science* v357 no6346 p89 Jl 7 2017

CREATE A WORKSHOP ON WHEELS R. BERENDSOHN color *Popular Mechanics* p16 Je 2017

Daniel Pund D. Pund color *Car & Driver* v63 no5 p30 N 2017

DIG IN, DIG OUT P. STEFÁNSSON *Iceland Review* v55 no3 p82 My/Je 2017

THE DREAMERS color *Road & Track* v69 no4 p56 N 2017

Editor's Letter E. Alterman *Car & Driver* v62 no8 p8 F 2017

The Future of Cars L. Hamers color *Science News* v190 no13 p34 D 24 2016

Gone Gassers T. Taylor bw *Hot Rod* v70 no3 p8 Mr 2017

The Guide to Car Options E. DYER color *Popular Mechanics* p44 F 2017

Have a Safer Ride *Parents* v91 no6 p28 Je 2016

HOT ROD Power Tour 2017 color *Hot Rod* v70 no11 p18 N 2017

How to Stick New Tech on an Old Car E. DYER color *Popular Mechanics* p56 Mr 2017

The Industry Bottom Line A. JONES *Boating World* v38 no2 p4 F 2017

MADE in the USA F. Maroukian and K. Dupzyk color *Popular Mechanics* p64 Jl 2017

MOUNTAIN HAVOC 2017 J. JONES color *Dirt Sports + Off-Road* v51 no11 p48 N 2017

On-the-road organization J. Jones color *Redbook* p24 S 2017

Pier Review color *Los Angeles Magazine* v62 no10 p16 O 2017

Power Tour's ROAD TO RECOVERY P. Thomas color *Hot Rod* v70 no11 p38 N 2017

Power Tour's TOP 5 FREAKS T. Taylor color *Hot Rod* v70 no11 p54 N 2017

Road Tunes D. Freiburger color *Hot Rod* v70 no8 p122 Ag 2017

SACRE BLEU! A. MacKenzie color *Motor Trend* v69 no2 p102 F 2017

STRIPES AND STICKERS color *Road & Track* v68 no8 p12 My 2017

Thom On Design Aero Ugly T. Taylor color *Hot Rod* v70 no11 p104 N 2017

TOM MEDLEY T. Taylor bw cartoon color *Hot Rod* v70 no3 p74 Mr 2017

Two of a Kind E. Perkins color *Hot Rod* v70 no3 p6 Mr 2017

Automobiles—Automatic systems

See also

Fully autonomous automobile driving

Automobiles—Awards

GALA OF THE YEAR! E. Loh color *Motor Trend* v69 no2 p10 F 2017

Kaizen Of The Year E. Loh color *Motor Trend* v69 no1 p12 Ja 2017

MOTOR TREND AWARDS color *Motor Trend* v69 no1 p36 Ja 2017

WHEN DODGE WON THE MTEG GRAND NATIONAL SPORT TRUCK CHAMPIONSHIP J. OBER bw *Dirt Sports + Off-Road* v51 no4 p74 Ap 2017

Automobiles—Chassis

THE VOLVO WAGON B. Berk bw color *Car & Driver* v62 no8 p20 F 2017

Automobiles—Cleaning

Robert Stgrym From Royal Oak, Michigan, Asks... Why are the Driver-Side Lifters Noisy on My Buick 350? M. Davis color *Hot Rod* v70 no3 p98 Mr 2017

Automobiles—Collectors & collecting

The Hoarding Problem D. Freiburger color *Hot Rod* v69 no12 p113 D 2016

Automobiles—Congresses

2017 SCHEDULE: A NATION'S DATEBOOK *Dirt Sports + Off-Road* v51 no2 p72 F 2017

Automobiles—Conservation & restoration

1966 CHAPARRAL 2E D. Kimble bw color *Hot Rod* v70 no1 p60 Ja 2017

Automotive Archaeology This Olds 442 Is Waiting to be Saved R. Brutt color *Hot Rod* v70 no1 p26 Ja 2017

Batanides Asks... Why Is White Smoke Coming Out My Exhaust Pipes? M. Davis color *Hot Rod* v70 no6 p112 Je 2017

THE FALCONER DODICI B. Gillogly color *Hot Rod* v70 no1 p76 Ja 2017

Greg Zoetmulder's Supercharged Small-Block Jeep Runs 8s With Ease J. Reiss color *Hot Rod* v70 no1 p50 Ja 2017

Restoring the Beauty in the Beast D. TOHT *Treasures* v6 no5 p22 Ap/My 2017

Automobiles—Crash tests

BACK ON THE HORSE M. PRINCE cartoon *Road & Track* v68 no6 p88 F 2017

Automobiles—Customizing

The 50 Quickest Cars of Drag Week 2016 —and Then Some B. Gillogly chart color *Hot Rod* v70 no2 p18 F 2017

BLACK BULLION S. Lachenaur color *Hot Rod* v70 no2 p60 F 2017

Black Ops T. Taylor color *Hot Rod* v69 no12 p34 D 2016

Comparing Customs From 1956 T. Taylor bw *Hot Rod* v70 no5 p88 My 2017

THE GALLOPING GHOST M. EMERY color *Dirt Sports + Off-

Road v51 no6 p42 Je 2017

THE INDY OFFY LAND-SPEED MASH-UP T. Taylor bw color *Hot Rod* v70 no3 p30 Mr 2017

JEFF OPPENHEIM WINS SPIRIT OF DRAG WEEK P. Thomas color *Hot Rod* v70 no2 p48 F 2017

MCKILLER M. EMERY color *Dirt Sports + Off-Road* v51 no4 p38 Ap 2017

MPG HEADS CHAMPION SMALL-BLOCK FORD B. Gillogly color *Hot Rod* v70 no3 p58 Mr 2017

The New Café Racer Paradigm P. d 'Orléans color *Cycle World* v55 no11 p42 D 2016

NOT YOUR FATHER'S SHOEBOX P. Thomas color *Hot Rod* v70 no5 p46 My 2017

ONE STEP BEYOND C. Shelton color *Hot Rod* v70 no3 p68 Mr 2017

PURPLE MAJESTY S. Lacheanauer color *Hot Rod* v70 no5 p38 My 2017

PUT AWAY WET S. Lachenauer bw color *Hot Rod* v70 no3 p40 Mr 2017

A RACER'S SENDOFF E. Perkins color *Hot Rod* v70 no2 p46 F 2017

RED BALL EXPRES B. W. SMITH color *Dirt Sports + Off-Road* v51 no2 p14 F 2017

RESPECT YOUR ELDERS E. Perkins color *Hot Rod* v70 no3 p62 Mr 2017

Roadster Shop's Widebody 1970 Camaro Track Weapoon RAMPAGE B. Gillogly color *Hot Rod* v69 no12 p18 D 2016

SALT CHARGER B. Gillogly color *Hot Rod* v70 no2 p52 F 2017

THE SAMURAI CODE P. d 'Orléans color *Cycle World* v55 no11 p36 D 2016

Sean Price's 1965 Nova 350 Nose-Dives Over 4,500 RPM. We Fixed the Cam; Now We're Gonna Fix the Heads and Valvetrain M. Davis color *Hot Rod* v69 no12 p90 D 2016

SPARE CHANGE J. Jacquot chart color *Car & Driver* v62 no8 p22 F 2017

STREET MACHINE ELIMINATOR'S ELITE EIGHT B. Gillogly color *Hot Rod* v70 no3 p80 Mr 2017

SUCKER PUNCH E. Perkins color *Hot Rod* v70 no3 p60 Mr 2017

Thom On Design T. Taylor bw *Hot Rod* v70 no2 p84 F 2017

TRAIL-READY TRUNK M. EMERY color *Dirt Sports + Off-Road* v51 no6 p50 Je 2017

TWO YEARS, TWO TURBOS: THE AUSSIE CHEVELLE RETURNS! P. Thomas color *Hot Rod* v70 no2 p38 F 2017

ZR71 B. Gillogly color *Hot Rod* v70 no5 p26 My 2017

Automobiles—Customizing—Equipment & supplies—Evaluation

PARTS & STUFF color *Hot Rod* v69 no12 p106 D 2016

Automobiles—Differentials—Evaluation

LOW DOWN AND DIRTY D. SCANLON color *Dirt Sports + Off-Road* v51 no2 p34 F 2017

Automobiles—Disc brakes

BRAKE DOWN E. Perkins color *Hot Rod* v70 no5 p78 My 2017

Running Cars are More Fun E. Perkins color *Hot Rod* v70 no1 p12 Ja 2017

Automobiles—Doors

More Doors, More Fun E. Perkins, B. Gillogly et al color *Hot Rod* v70 no5 p8 My 2017

Automobiles—Economic aspects

YEA BOXY BRONCOS, NAY BEATNIK BOLSHEVIKS W. CARINI, A. BRENNER et al bw color *Forbes* v200 no2 p31 S 5 2017

Automobiles—Engine mounts—Evaluation

PARTS & STUFF color *Hot Rod* v70 no5 p108 My 2017

Automobiles—Equipment & supplies

See also

   Automobiles—Safety appliances

Ask Martha color *Martha Stewart Living* no271 p52 Ja/F 2017

COIL SCIENCE J. KOPYCINSKI color *Dirt Sports + Off-Road* v51 no6 p64 Je 2017

GEARBOX color *Dirt Sports + Off-Road* v51 no4 p68 Ap 2017

Ken Zimmer Swapped a Modern Ford AOD Trans into His 1967 Mustang. Now it Has a Shift-Timing Problem. We're Gonna Fix It M. Davis chart color *Hot Rod* v70 no1 p94 Ja 2017

Larry Musto Ask... Which Edelbrock Head Yields 9.5:1 Compression on a Stock 1971 402? M. Davis color *Hot Rod* v70 no1 p104 Ja 2017

Automobiles—Equipment & supplies—Evaluation

GEAR BOX color *Dirt Sports + Off-Road* v51 no5 p68 My 2017

GEARBOX color *Dirt Sports + Off-Road* v51 no6 p68 Je 2017

GEARHEAD A. DAVIES color *Wired* v25 no3 p34 Mr 2017

NEW WAYS TO LOVE YOUR VEHICLE color *Popular Mechanics* p44 Ap 2017

PARTS & STUFF color *Hot Rod* v70 no2 p100 F 2017

PARTS & STUFF color *Hot Rod* v70 no5 p108 My 2017

PROTECTION PLUS M. EMERY color *Dirt Sports + Off-Road* v51 no4 p58 Ap 2017

When Are Titanium Retainers Needed? M. Davis chart color *Hot Rod* v70 no2 p86 F 2017

Automobiles—Evaluation

2018 Chevrolet Camaro ZL1 1LE A. Nishimoto color *Motor Trend* v69 no6 p20 Je 2017

THE $399 LEASE-DEAL SPECIAL [Cover story] chart color *Motor Trend* v69 no6 p34 Je 2017

4-DOORS, 6-WHEELERS, AND GULLWINGS color *Road & Track* v69 no4 p12 N 2017

5 CARS THAT PUT AMG AT THE HEAD OF THE PACK C. PERKINS color *Esquire* p52 2017 BigBlackBook

Attack of the Cute Utes A. Nishimoto color *Motor Trend* v69 no2 p14 F 2017

THE BEST OF DETROIT AND CES S. Evans color *Motor Trend* v69 no4 p20 Ap 2017

A BIGGER HAMMER J. Lieberman chart color *Motor Trend* v69 no5 p62 My 2017

THE BRITISH BRUISER A. GEORGE color *Popular Mechanics* p41 Ap 2017

Cars Your Way *Consumer Reports* v82 no4 p39 Ap 2017

CHEMISTRY LESSON K. KINARD color *Road & Track* v68 no6 p80 F 2017

CROSSING OVER S. SMITH color diag *Road & Track* v68 no10 p54 Jl 2017

Enemy of the Estate J. Sabatini bw chart color diag *Car & Driver* v63 no4 p74 O 2017

Esquire's 2016 CAR AWARDS color *Esquire* v166 no4 p73 N 2016

Fast and Flawed *Consumer Reports* v82 no1 p59 Ja 2017

Feel Lucky, Punk? [Cover story] J. Jacquot, A. Robinson et al color *Car & Driver* v63 no1 p36 Jl 2017

FIVE-SEAT FURY J. Cammisa color *Motor Trend* v69 no6 p54 Je 2017

FROM THE ROAD & TRACK ARCHIVES color *Road & Track* v69 no4 p90 N 2017

THE FULL KIT K. KINARD color *Road & Track* v69 no2 p86 S 2017

GARAGE cartoon chart color *Motor Trend* v69 no4 p86 Ap 2017

GARAGE C. Clonts, J. Lieberman et al chart color diag *Motor Trend* v69 no10 p102 O 2017

GARAGE chart color diag *Motor Trend* v69 no2 p90 F 2017

GARRAGE bw chart color *Motor Trend* v69 no6 p104 Je 2017

GARRAGE S. Evans, A. Nishimoto et al cartoon chart color *Motor Trend* v69 no3 p86 Mr 2017

Genesis G90 chart color *Motor Trend* v69 no1 p139 Ja 2017

Geneva's Greatest Hits S. Evans color *Motor Trend* v69 no6 p12 Je 2017

Inside Out D. North Dillwyn color *Architectural Digest* no5 p36 My 2017

IN THE BELLY OF THE BRAZEN BULL D. Bentley color *Fortune* v176 no3 p37 S 1 2017

the leftovers... [Cover story] J. Lieberman, C. Seabaugh et al chart color *Motor Trend* v69 no4 p36 Ap 2017

LEXUS RISING J. H. HARPER color *Road & Track* v68 no7 p32 Mr/Ap 2017

Lynk & Co 01 A. MacKenzie color *Motor Trend* v69 no2 p16 F 2017

maximum mini A. MacKenzie chart color *Motor Trend* v69 no6 p92 Je 2017

MEET THE NEW E43 E. Ayapana chart color *Motor Trend* v69 no5 p66 My 2017

ON THE WAGON K. Sintumuang color *Esquire* p18 Je/Jl 2017

POWER RISING M. DE PAULA color *Road & Track* v69 no4 p84 N 2017

The Real Cars of Geneva color *Motor Trend* v69 no6 p16 Je 2017

RINGERS M. PRINCE color diag graph *Road & Track* v69 no4

p26 N 2017

RISING TIDE M. PRINCE cartoon chart color graph *Road & Track* v68 no7 p38 Mr/Ap 2017

Road Test chart color *Consumer Reports* v82 no2 p54 F 2017

Road Test chart color *Consumer Reports* v82 no5 p58 My 2017

Road Test chart *Consumer Reports* v82 no11 p62 N 2017

ROAD TESTED E. DYER color *Popular Mechanics* p36 Ap 2017

ROAD TEST SUMMARY cartoon chart *Road & Track* v69 no4 p94 N 2017

ROAD TEST SUMMARY chart *Road & Track* v69 no2 p98 S 2017

SIZE MATTERS C. Seabaugh chart color *Motor Trend* v69 no2 p72 F 2017

SPECIAL COMES STANDARD J. BARUTH color *Road & Track* v69 no2 p88 S 2017

SUPERFREAK M. PRINCE color *Road & Track* v69 no4 p74 N 2017

Taller AND STRONGER E. Ayapana chart color *Motor Trend* v69 no3 p80 Mr 2017

TECH TO THE FUTURE J. GORZELANY color *Forbes* v198 no6 p74 N 8 2016

Tesla Model S 60/75 chart color *Motor Trend* v69 no1 p144 Ja 2017

UNSPOILED B. MCALEER color *Road & Track* v69 no2 p76 S 2017

VERSION 3.0 B. Gillogly color *Hot Rod* v70 no8 p54 Ag 2017

Why Our Car Testing Is Unique color *Consumer Reports* v82 no4 p4 Ap 2017

Automobiles—Exhibitions
See also
North American International Auto Show (Detroit, Mich.)

2017 SCHEDULE chart *Dirt Sports + Off-Road* v51 no4 p73 Ap 2017

58 GREAT THINGS TO DO THIS MONTH J. FOUMBERG, J. HARDBERGER et al color *Chicago* v66 no2 p101 F 2017

Aaron Robinson A. Robinson color *Car & Driver* v62 no6 p32 D 2016

On behalf of the Greater Cincinnati Automobile Dealers Association, it is my pleasure to welcome you to the Cincinnati Auto Expo 2017! T. R. Fiehrer *Cincinnati Magazine* v50 no5 p116 F 2017

WARM WHEELS G. FREKING *Cincinnati Magazine* v50 no6 p30 Mr 2017

Automobiles—Fuel systems—Evaluation
PARTS & STUFF bw color *Hot Rod* v70 no3 p100 Mr 2017

Automobiles—Government policy
Driverless Cars *Congressional Digest* v95 no9 p12 N 2016

Automobiles—Instrument panels
John Phillips J. Phillips color *Car & Driver* v62 no10 p22 Ap 2017

Automobiles—Off-road operation
5TH ANNUAL RAPTOR WINTER WONDERLAND M. KAUSCH color *Dirt Sports + Off-Road* v51 no6 p58 Je 2017

THE OTHER SIDE OF DEATH VALLEY K. CLARK color *Dirt Sports + Off-Road* v51 no6 p36 Je 2017

TO EVERYTHING—TURN, TURN, TURN M. Emery *Dirt Sports + Off-Road* v51 no6 p4 Je 2017

Automobiles—Parts
Ezra Dyer E. Dyer *Car & Driver* v62 no8 p28 F 2017

How Do You Check Battery Health? M. Davis color *Hot Rod* v70 no3 p86 Mr 2017

TAILGATE PARTY B. W. SMITH color *Dirt Sports + Off-Road* v51 no3 p52 Mr 2017

The Truth About Cheap Turbos [Cover story] E. Perkins color graph *Hot Rod* v69 no12 p64 D 2016

UTV PROTECTION J. HEADLEE color *Dirt Sports + Off-Road* v51 no6 p24 Je 2017

Automobiles—Parts—Evaluation
PARTS & STUFF bw color *Hot Rod* v70 no3 p100 Mr 2017

PARTS & STUFF color *Hot Rod* v70 no6 p116 Je 2017

Automobiles—Performance
EDITOR'S LETTER K. WOLFKILL color *Road & Track* v68 no5 p31 D 2016/Ja 2017

Automobiles—Pollution control devices
Why Is a Cam's Intake Closing Point So Important? M. Davis color *Hot Rod* v70 no6 p100 Je 2017

Automobiles—Power trains

See also
Automobile engines

How Do the Chrysler Gen III Hemi's Physical Dimensions Compare to Other Mopar Engines? M. Davis chart color diag *Hot Rod* v69 no12 p100 D 2016

Automobiles—Power trains—Evaluation
GEOGRAPHY LESSONS J. DEMATIO color *Road & Track* v68 no5 p108 D 2016/Ja 2017

Automobiles—Purchasing
Buicks K. Pandolfi *New York Times Magazine* p28 O 30 2016

How to Get a Great Deal on a New Car D. MUHLBAUM color *Kiplinger's Personal Finance* v71 no5 p48 My 2017

The Wheel Deal B. HEWITT *Yankee* v81 no1 p16 Ja/F 2017

Why Our Car Testing Is Unique color *Consumer Reports* v82 no4 p4 Ap 2017

Automobiles—Reliability
Cars Your Way *Consumer Reports* v82 no4 p39 Ap 2017

A Right to Keep and Drive Cars? J. GELERNTER cartoon *Weekly Standard* v22 no7 p16 O 24 2016

Automobiles—Reliability—Charts, diagrams, etc.
New & Used Car Reliability chart diag *Consumer Reports* v82 no4 p86 Ap 2017

Automobiles—Safety appliances
Coming to a Dashboard Near You M. Naranjo chart color *Consumer Reports* v82 no3 p58 Mr 2017

March Madness color *Consumer Reports* v82 no3 p67 Mr 2017

ONE-HOUR WONDER BURN OUT M. EMERY color *Dirt Sports + Off-Road* v51 no4 p46 Ap 2017

preemie primer M. BEHEN *Parents* v92 no2 p100 F 2017

Automobiles—Sales & prices
See also
Used cars—Sales & prices

Drive Home a Better Deal D. Bortz color diag *Money* v45 no11 p23 D 2016

Go Lutz Yourself B. LUTZ color *Road & Track* v68 no5 p126 D 2016/Ja 2017

John Phillips color *Car & Driver* v62 no6 p30 D 2016

Warning Signs from the showroom floor M. Rechtin cartoon *Motor Trend* v69 no3 p30 Mr 2017

Automobiles—Sales & prices—Charts, diagrams, etc.
DATA CENTRAL K. C. Colwell cartoon diag graph *Car & Driver* v62 no7 p20 Ja 2017

Automobiles—Springs & suspension
AFFORDABLE OFF-ROADING D. SCANLON color *Dirt Sports + Off-Road* v51 no5 p58 My 2017

HAPPY WANDERERS UNITE IN FLAGSTAFF M. EMERY color *Dirt Sports + Off-Road* v51 no2 p42 F 2017

PRACTICE HOW YOU PLAY [Cover story] M. EMERY color *Dirt Sports + Off-Road* v51 no2 p36 F 2017

TUN OF FUN D. SCANLON color diag *Dirt Sports + Off-Road* v51 no3 p30 Mr 2017

Automobiles—Testing
See also
Automobiles—Crash tests

Danger and deliberation in the desert color *Motor Trend* v69 no1 p120 Ja 2017

The finalist round F. Markus color *Motor Trend* v69 no1 p136 Ja 2017

Noblesse Oblique Privileged with fed resources, NHTSA upgrades NCAP F. Markus color *Motor Trend* v68 no12 p32 D 2016

THE NUMBER GAME K. Reynolds color *Motor Trend* v69 no1 p116 Ja 2017

PROVING A POINT A. MacKenzie color *Motor Trend* v69 no1 p177 Ja 2017

Sand and Deliver Three contests, six weeks, and a river of Gatorade M. Rechtin color *Motor Trend* v69 no1 p24 Ja 2017

Automobiles—United States
Staying Power M. Naranjo chart color diag *Consumer Reports* v81 no12 p66 D 2016

Automobiles—United States—Sales & prices
Is China's Trumpchi Coming to America? color *Bloomberg Businessweek* no4509 p19 Ja 30 2017

Automobiles—Windows & windshields
PROTECTION PLUS M. EMERY color *Dirt Sports + Off-Road* v51 no4 p58 Ap 2017

STAY WELL ON THE WAY L. Goldman color *Good Housekeeping* v264 no5 p101 My 2017

Automobili Lamborghini SpA

Aging Bull M. Duff color *Car & Driver* v63 no5 p120 N 2017

Bullet with Butterfly Wings C. Csere color *Car & Driver* v63 no2 p90 Ag 2017

Ezra Dyer E. Dyer color *Car & Driver* v62 no10 p26 Ap 2017

Maurizio Reggiani H. Elliott color *Bloomberg Businessweek* no4541 p68 O 9 2017

A NEW FORCE J. Lieberman chart color *Motor Trend* v69 no4 p76 Ap 2017

RENAISSANCE J. H. HARPER bw color *Road & Track* v69 no4 p46 N 2017

Ringing the Bull A. Robinson color diag *Car & Driver* v62 no6 p52 D 2016

SHOW STEALER C. CHILTON color *Road & Track* v68 no8 p86 My 2017

Viva La RIVOLUZIONE S. Evans chart color *Motor Trend* v69 no5 p46 My 2017

Automotive drafting

Thom On Design BDR T. Taylor bw color *Hot Rod* v70 no7 p96 Jl 2017

Automotive electronics

See also

Automatic systems in automobiles

Electronic fuel injection systems in automobiles

EFI FUEL PUMP PRIME STRATEGY: EVERYTHING GAS IS NOW RUNING ON EFI SYSTEMS R. Bohacz *Successful Farming* v115 no9 p32 Ag 2017

Automotive engineering

See also

Customizing of automobiles

3-D Classes Showing the industry a new way to design and build cars F. Markus bw *Motor Trend* v69 no3 p32 Mr 2017

Arresting Development bw *Car & Driver* v62 no6 p41 D 2016

DIY STEEL SHEET FAB J. KOPYCINSKI color *Dirt Sports + Off-Road* v51 no3 p64 Mr 2017

Driving Into the Future J. Plungis color map *Consumer Reports* v82 no4 p10 Ap 2017

EDITOR'S LETTER K. WOLFKILL *Road & Track* v69 no2 p20 S 2017

GROUNDBREAKING PERFORMANCE E. Loh color *Motor Trend* v69 no9 p12 S 2017

Hands of Time J. BARUTH bw color *Road & Track* v69 no2 p26 S 2017

HIGH RANGE A. MacKenzie color *Motor Trend* v69 no5 p102 My 2017

Hot Rod Anything! Medieval One P. Thomas bw color *Hot Rod* v70 no8 p12 Ag 2017

IDENTITY CRISIS A. MacKenzie color *Motor Trend* v69 no10 p117 O 2017

IFS ARM UPGRADES J. KOPYCINSKI color *Dirt Sports + Off-Road* v51 no8 p66 Ag 2017

Mint Jelly D. Pund color diag map *Car & Driver* v62 no8 p30 F 2017

Msgt. Mike Yates, USAF (Ret.), Asks... Why Won't a 454 Big-Block Properly Fit in Place of My 1974 GMC Sprint's Original Small-Block? M. Davis bw color *Hot Rod* v70 no7 p112 Jl 2017

Peter Schreyer, 63 M. DUFF cartoon *Car & Driver* v62 no10 p92 Ap 2017

Peter Schreyer A. Priddle bw color *Motor Trend* v69 no1 p30 Ja 2017

Ray Evernham R. Evernham color *Car & Driver* v62 no6 p38 D 2016

Rolling Back the Year color *Consumer Reports* v82 no4 p6 Ap 2017

TECH TO THE FUTURE J. GORZELANY color *Forbes* v198 no6 p74 N 8 2016

Thom On Design Oddity Allure T. Taylor *Hot Rod* v70 no6 p98 Je 2017

TWISTY SISTER J. Gall color graph *Car & Driver* v62 no8 p13 F 2017

What I'd Do Differently Ed Welburn, 66 J. P. HUFFMAN color *Car & Driver* v62 no11 p120 My 2017

Who Needs TV? E. Perkins color *Hot Rod* v70 no8 p8 Ag 2017

Automotive fuel consumption—Standards—United States

High-Octane The key to efficiency? F. Markus cartoon *Motor Trend* v69 no2 p22 F 2017

Rolling Back Fuel Efficiency Is a Bad Deal for Everyone—Including U.S. Carmakers A. Winston *Harvard Business Review Digital Articles* p2 Mr 17 2017

TRUE NORTH A. MacKenzie color *Motor Trend* v69 no6 p117 Je 2017

Vehicle Emissions Standards *Congressional Digest* v95 no9 p13 N 2016

Automotive journalists

Editor's Letter E. Alterman *Car & Driver* v63 no1 p12 Jl 2017

Automotive painting & paint shops

Oh No! Your Car Got Scratched! E. DYER color *Popular Mechanics* p52 S 2017

Thom On Design The Most Notorious Custom Paint Job Ever Sprayed T. Taylor bw *Hot Rod* v70 no1 p90 Ja 2017

Automotive telematics

The Internet-Connected Engine Will Change Trucking G. Westerman *Harvard Business Review Digital Articles* p2 N 4 2014

Automotive engineering—Charts, diagrams, etc.

AUTO TECH GETS SOME GAS color diag *Fortune* v175 no7 p11 Je 1 2017

Auton, G. H.

High-temperature quantum oscillations caused by recurring Bloch states in graphene superlattices color *Science* v357 no6347 p181 Jl 14 2017

Autonomic nervous system

See also

Enteric nervous system

Neural circuitry gets rewired I. Adameyko bibl color *Science* v354 no6314 p833 N 18 2016

Autonomous robots

See also

Roomba vacuum cleaner

The Age of Smart, Safe, Cheap Robots Is Already Here M. Miremadi, S. Narayanan et al *Harvard Business Review Digital Articles* p2 Je 15 2015

THE SOFTER SIDE OF ROBOTICS N. Daly diag *National Geographic* v231 no5 p18 My 2017

Autonomous underwater vehicles

Expanding the Scientific Arsenal L. Lippsett *Oceanus* v52 no2 p60 Spr 2017

Autonomous vehicles

See also

Automated guided vehicle systems

Drone aircraft

Fully autonomous automobile driving

8 drones that delighted us in 2016 color *PCWorld* v35 no1 p214 Ja 2017

As Machines Take Jobs, Companies Need to Get Creative About Making New Ones D. Damm *Harvard Business Review Digital Articles* p2 My 22 2017

auto no mo' us M. Gladwell, T. Vanderbilt et al bw color diag graph *Car & Driver* v63 no5 p58 N 2017

BABY BOOMERS *Harper's Magazine* v334 no2004 p16 My 2017

COMFORTABLY DUMB J. P. Huffman cartoon *Car & Driver* v62 no11 p22 My 2017

Drivers Wanted J. P. Hoffa *MIT Technology Review* v120 no2 p10 Mr/Ap 2017

Editor's Letter: E. Alterman *Car & Driver* v62 no6 p15 D 2016

ENTREPRENEURS W. Knight, A. Regalado et al color il *MIT Technology Review* v120 no5 p48 S/O 2017

The Future of Cars L. Hamers color *Science News* v190 no13 p34 D 24 2016

GAME THEORY A. MacKenzie color *Motor Trend* v69 no3 p98 Mr 2017

Innovation A. Popescu color *Bloomberg Businessweek* no4525 p34 Je 5 2017

ROBOTS, TAKE THE WHEEL!: Driverless cars are coming to Atlanta. Are we ready? S. HENRY *Atlanta* v57 no4 p15 Ag 2017

Startups Are Laser-Focused on Helping Self-Driving Cars See K. Steinmetz color *Time* v190 no9 p26 S 4 2017

What Should an Apple Car Be? E. Yoon *Harvard Business Review Digital Articles* p2 Jl 4 2017

When Driving Is Obsolete D. HARSANYI *National Review* v68

no23 p44 D 19 2016

Autonomous vehicles—Economic aspects

THE END OF PARKING TICKETS M. Maciag chart color *Governing* v30 no11 p44 Ag 2017

Autonomous vehicles—Evaluation

The 'Roboat' J. Zorthian color *Time* v188 no15 p15 O 17 2016

TOP THREE: ENJOY THE RIDE A. DAVIES color *Wired* v25 no10 p48 O 2017

Autonomous vehicles—Law & legislation

The Right and Wrong Ways to Regulate Self-Driving Cars L. Downes *Harvard Business Review Digital Articles* p2 D 6 2016

Autonomous vehicles—Safety measures

Laser Vision J. Condliffe color *MIT Technology Review* v120 no5 p88 S/O 2017

Autonomous vehicles—Software

Report: Apple slams the brakes on electric Apple Car to focus on auto software I. PAUL color *PCWorld* v35 no11 p17 N 2016

Autonomy & independence movements

America's 'Real' Independence Day Is Not July 4 O. B. Waxman *Time* v190 no2/3 p23 Jl 10-17 2017

Anatomy of a Bad Marriage P. Coy, C. Penty et al color *Bloomberg Businessweek* no4541 p10 O 9 2017

Crisis In Catalonia L. Abend color *Time* v190 no16/17 p62 O 23 2017

No, California [Cover story] K. D. WILLIAMSON color *National Review* v69 no7 p27 Ap 17 2017

Autonomy & independence movements—History—21st century

Where National Breakups Are In the Cards T. John color *Time* v189 no7/8 p18 F 27 2017

Autonomy (Political science)

Catalanguish C. CALDWELL color *Weekly Standard* v23 no6 p17 O 16 2017

Crisis In Catalonia L. Abend color *Time* v190 no16/17 p62 O 23 2017

The Referendum Vote That Could Fracture Iraq J. Malsin map *Time* v190 no12 p13 S 25 2017

Autonomy (Psychology)

new power struggles T. REECE *Parents* v92 no6 p136 Je 2017

Autophagic vacuoles

The ATG conjugation systems are important for degradation of the inner autophagosomal membrane Kotaro Tsuboyama, Ikuko Koyama-Honda et al bibl graph *Science* v354 no6315 p1036 N 25 2016

A switch from canonical to noncanonical autophagy shapes B cell responses N. Martinez-Martin, P. Maldonado et al bibl graph *Science* v355 no6325 p641 F 10 2017

Autopsy: The Last Hours of Prince (TV program)

Autopsy: The Last Hours of Prince M. Roffman *TV Guide* v65 no21 p33 My 15 2017

Autopsy—Moral & ethical aspects

SECRETS OF THE DEAD B. Reilly *Saturday Evening Post* v289 no3 p56 My/Je 2017

Autore, Marta

Tuning quantum nonlocal effects in graphene plasmonics bw diag *Science* v357 no6347 p187 Jl 14 2017

Autry, Jenni

FULL CIRCLE color *Practical Horseman* v45 no5 p44 My 2017

A LEAP OF FAITH color *Practical Horseman* v45 no5 p30 My 2017

Autumn

Autumn Spectacle W. Jones *New York State Conservationist* v72 no2 p2 O 2017

FALL INTO AUTUMN GALAXIES S. James O'Meara color *Astronomy* v45 no11 p46 N 2017

The Joys of autumn color *New York State Conservationist* v71 no2 p2 O 2016

Making light of galaxies D. J. EICHER color *Astronomy* v45 no11 p6 N 2017

On our radar color *Canadian Geographic* v137 p18 2017 Travel

ORIENT EPITHALAMION J. Galassi *New Yorker* v92 no43 p40 Ja 2 2017

Plant Now for Winter (Really!) E. Millard color *Log Home Living* v33 no7 p38 S 2016

Autumn festivals

AUTUMN AMUSEMENTS E. S. ARNARSDÓTTIR color *Iceland Review* v54 no5 p8 S-O 2016

DON'T MISS LIST NOVEMBER 2016 *Sea Magazine* v108 no10 pCA-11 O 2016

Autzen, Bengt

Leveling up bibl color *Science* v353 no6307 p1505 S 30 2016

Auxier, Jonathan

New Worlds and Old: Two books for middle-grade readers evoke both the past and the future of fantasy novels *New York Times Book Review* p17 Jl 16 2017

Auxin

Directional Signals L. E. Ogden *Natural History* v125 no2 p6 F 2017

Auxin—Physiological effect

The source of plants' spiral symmetry *Physics Today* v69 no12 p92 D 2016

AU-YEUNG, ANGEL

THE APPLE CORPS color *Forbes* v200 no1 p26 Jl 27 2017

DOCTORATE, DEGREE OR DROPOUT? diag graph *Forbes* v200 no5 p24 N 14 2017

AV Homes Inc.

I'm Still Cheering for GM and Gilead K. KRISTOF color *Kiplinger's Personal Finance* v71 no2 p61 F 2017

A.V. Max (Company)

GREAT GIFTS under $50 color *Redbook* p40 D 2016

Avakian, Brad

A Culture War Casualty M. Hemingway *Weekly Standard* v22 no12 p7 N 28 2016

Avalanches

Bet you didn't know E. WHITMER *National Geographic Kids* no466 p10 D 2016/Ja 2017

Ice, Wind & Fury M. Oltmanns color *Oceanus* v51 no2 p24 Wint 2016

Avalon Peninsula (N.L.)

LIFE ON THE EDGE T. Monmaney *Smithsonian* v48 no1 p56 Ap 2017

Avan, Michelle

the STRATEGIC BOSS J. Thompson color *Essence* v48 no3 p80 Jl 2017

Avanzi, Charlotte

Red squirrels in the British Isles are infected with leprosy bacilli bibl color diag map *Science* v354 no6313 p744 N 11 2016

Avarice—Humor

Laughter THE BEST MEDICINE J. GAFFIGAN *Reader's Digest* v189 no1128 p78 Mr 2017

Avatar 2 (Film)

Meet the New Faces of Avatar 2 J. Hibberd color *Entertainment Weekly* no1485 p40 O 6 2017

Avatars (Virtual reality)

The Lady Teaching Brazilians How to Shop Online F. Moura and P. Sambo *Bloomberg Businessweek* no4536 p21 S 4 2017

Avaya Inc.

How Avaya Turned Around Its Customer Ratings U. Neren *Harvard Business Review Digital Articles* p2 O 25 2016

Avdellidou, Chrysa

Identification of a primordial asteroid family constrains the original planetesimal population diag graph *Science* v357 no6355 p1026 S 8 2017

Avdic, Asa

The Dying Game *Publishers Weekly* v264 no23 p31 Je 5 2017

Avedon, Gregg

BUILD COVER GUY MUSCLE [Cover story] J. KITA bw cartoon chart color *Men's Health* v32 no1 p98 Ja/F 2017

Avedon, Richard

BAZAAR: THE DEFINITION OF FASHION S. Mooallem bw *Harper's Bazaar* no3653 p268 My 2017

Avena, Erica Wimber

POWER [Cover story] color *Christian Century* v134 no1 p22 Ja 4 2017

Aveni, Anthony

In the Shadow of the Moon: The Science, Magic, and Mystery of Solar Eclipses L. A. MARSCHALL color *Natural History* v125 no7 p47 Jl/Ag 2017

Avenue Strategies (Company)

Trump's K Street Office J. Green color *Bloomberg Businessweek* no4508 p22 Ja 23 2017

AVERICK, MOSHE

Science's Confusion Concerning the Origin of Life *USA Today*

Magazine v145 no2862 p46 Mr 2017

averill, graham

ARE YOU A BELIEVER IN SUFFERING? BELIEVING YOU AREN'T ALLOWED TO HAVE FUN UNTIL YOU'VE PUT IN SOME SOLID WORK? bw color *Bike Magazine* v24 no4 p76 Je 2017

Day DREAMING: The best dayhike in every state color *Backpacker* p52 S 2017

EARNED EQUITY bw color *Bike Magazine* v23 no9 p58 D 2016

outer edge bw color *Bike Magazine* v23 no9 p32 D 2016

ROAD TO RYCHLEBY bw color map *Bike Magazine* v24 no8 p48 N 2017

Avero Inc.

INDUSTRY INSIDER A. Orr color *Louisiana Life* v37 no5 p14 My/Je 2017

Aversa, Paolo

Sometimes, Less Innovation Is Better S. Berinato *Harvard Business Review* v95 no3 p38 My/Je 2017

Aversion

THE CASE AGAINST THE MEDIA BY THE MEDIA *New York* v49 no15 p40 Jl 25 2016

Food Fright D. Paul *Indianapolis Monthly* v40 no5 p132 Ja 2017

Urbanities: Justin Davidson J. Davidson img *New York* v50 no8 p21 Ap 17 2017

Avery, Andrea

Sonata: A Memoir of Pain and the Piano *Publishers Weekly* v264 no11 p75 Mr 13 2017

Avery, Anne

A Passion for Teaching J. Caplin color *Money* v45 no10 p26 N 2016

Avery, Jill

Case Study: How Do You Compete with a Goliath? *Harvard Business Review Digital Articles* p2 Jl 7 2016

Avery, Jill—Interviews

A Refresher on Breakeven Quantity A. Gallo *Harvard Business Review Digital Articles* p2 Je 22 2015

A Refresher on Economic Value to the Customer A. Gallo *Harvard Business Review Digital Articles* p2 My 7 2015

A Refresher on Marketing ROI A. Gallo *Harvard Business Review Digital Articles* p1 Jl 25 2017

A Refresher on Price Elasticity A. Gallo *Harvard Business Review Digital Articles* p2 Ag 21 2015

The Value of Keeping the Right Customers A. Gallo *Harvard Business Review Digital Articles* p2 O 29 2014

Avery, Ron

Publish openly but responsibly color *Science* v357 no6347 p141 Jl 14 2017

Avian anatomy

See also
   Feathers

Emergent cellular self-organization and mechanosensation initiate follicle pattern in the avian skin A. E. Shyer, A. R. Rodrigues et al color *Science* v357 no6353 p811 Ag 25 2017

Tuning up their vocal cords color *National Wildlife (World Edition)* v55 no4 p10 Je/Jl 2017

Avian influenza

New bird flu strain takes human toll color *Science* v355 no6327 p778 F 24 2017

Avian influenza A virus

In Flew Enza N. J. COX color *Natural History* v125 no9 p16 S 2017

New bird flu strain brings death and questions K. Kupferschmidt color diag *Science* v354 no6318 p1363 D 16 2016

Role for migratory wild birds in the global spread of avian influenza H5N8 S. J. Lycett, R. Bodewes et al bibl graph map *Science* v354 no6309 p213 O 14 2016

Sick birds don't fly...or do they? C. A. Russell bibl color map *Science* v354 no6309 p174 O 14 2016

Avian influenza—Prevention

Ask Our Experts *Mother Earth News* no279 p77 D/Ja 2017

Aviation law

See also
   Commercial aeronautics laws

GETTING TO YES color *Flying* v144 no6 p8 Je 2017

A TALE OF TWO FAAS P. STRICKLAND color *Flying* v144 no7 p56 Jl 2017

Avicii, 1989—Interviews

Q&A: Avicii S. VOZICK-LEVINSON *Rolling Stone* no1295 p23 S 7 2017

Avidyne Corp.

AVIDYNE CERTIFIES NEW IFDS AND SOFTWARE color *Flying* v144 no5 p18 My 2017

Avila, Bob

The Biggest Mistakes Nonpro Riders Make color *Horse & Rider* v56 no4 p35 Ap 2017

Body Control color *Horse & Rider* v56 no11 p44 N 2017

Broaden Your Horizons color *Horse & Rider* v56 no3 p26 Mr 2017

The Finer Points of Fencing *Horse & Rider* v56 no6 p40 Je 2017

Get Out of the Way color *Horse & Rider* v56 no10 p46 O 2017

Get Ready to Win color *Horse & Rider* v55 no12 p28 D 2016

Get Your Mojo Back color *Horse & Rider* v55 no11 p30 N 2016

Is It You? Or Your Horse? color *Horse & Rider* v56 no8 p44 Ag 2017

Lead-Change Precision color *Horse & Rider* v56 no2 p26 F 2017

Road-Ready Tips color *Horse & Rider* v56 no7 p47 Jl 2017

School With Class color *Horse & Rider* v56 no1 p28 Ja 2017

Show-Horse Care at Home color *Horse & Rider* v56 no5 p35 My 2017

Youth Riders Should Know... color *Horse & Rider* v56 no9 p47 S 2017

Avila, Dana

Save a Shoe color *Horse & Rider* v56 no1 p50 Ja 2017

Avila, G.

Observation of a large-scale anisotropy in the arrival directions of cosmic rays above 8 × 1018 eV *Science* v357 no6357 p1266 S 22 2017

AVILA, WES

HERE'S HOW YOU MAKE AN "AUTHENTIC" AMERICAN TACO color *Bon Appetit* v62 no2 p68 Mr 2017

Avildsen, John G., 1935-2017

Milestones *Time* v190 no1 p13 Jl 3 2017

Avionics software

FLIGHT MANAGEMENT SYSTEMS R. Mark color *Flying* v144 no11 p22 N 2017

Avionics—Equipment & supplies

DYNON'S UPWARD PUSH color *Flying* v144 no10 p23 O 2017

Aviv, Jonathan

The Acid Watcher Diet: A 28-day Reflux Prevention and Healing Program *Publishers Weekly* v263 no47 p102 N 21 2016

AVIV, RACHEL

THE APATHETIC cartoon color *New Yorker* v93 no7 p68 Ap 3 2017

MEMORIES OF A MURDER bw cartoon *New Yorker* v93 no17 p36 Je 19 2017

A MUSLIM COP'S TRIAL bw cartoon *New Yorker* v93 no27 p50 S 11 2017

SURVIVING SOLITARY cartoon color *New Yorker* v92 no45 p54 Ja 16 2017

THE TAKEOVER cartoon color *New Yorker* v93 no31 p48 O 9 2017

Avizia Inc.

50 GREAT PLACES TO WORK S. DALPHONSE *Washingtonian Magazine* v52 no6 p84 Mr 2017

Avlon, John

Timely counsel from America's first commander in chief W. Lanouette color *America* v216 no7 p44 Ap 3 2017

Washington's Farewell: The Founding Father's Warning to Future Generations W. Russell Mead *Foreign Affairs* v96 no3 p161 My/Je 2017

Avni, Raz

Wild emmer genome architecture and diversity elucidate wheat evolution and domestication color *Science* v357 no6346 p93 Jl 7 2017

Avocado

Avocados, Unleashed color *Health* v31 no3 p107 Ap 2017

Dj Cavem H. Nordhaus bw *Rodale's Organic Life* v3 no1 p76 Ja 2017

Eat-The-Bowl Summer Salad [Cover story] J. BOWDEN and J. BESSINGER color *Better Nutrition* v79 no6 p62 Je 2017

Fitness Fashion *Parents* v91 no9 p124 S 2016

For the Record color *Time* v190 no1 p6 Jl 3 2017

Lily Aldridge A. Syrett color *InStyle* v24 no3 p172 Mr 2017

NUTRITION HOTLINE R. MANGELS *Vegetarian Journal* v35 no1 p2 2016

Salad DAYS [Cover story] K. Caldesi and G. Caldesi color *Yoga Journal* no292 p28 Je 2017

Vegan Cooking Tips. Quick and Easy Taco Fillings N. Berkoff *Vegetarian Journal* v35 no1 p34 2016

A Winning Hand *Los Angeles Magazine* v62 no6 p8 Je 2017

Your A to Z Summer Shape-Up J. Andriakos color *Health* v31 no6 p39 Jl 2017

Avocado industry

Hass Avocado S. Maki color graph *Bloomberg Businessweek* no4533 p31 Ag 7 2017

Avocado—Export & import trade

Hass Avocado S. Maki color graph *Bloomberg Businessweek* no4533 p31 Ag 7 2017

Avocado—Therapeutic use

NATURAL GLOW color *Better Homes & Gardens* v95 no7 p20 Jl 2017

Avon Products Inc.

Why I Love L. Dern color *InStyle* v24 no2 p164 F 2017

Avraham, Roi

Potential role of intratumor bacteria in mediating tumor resistance to the chemotherapeutic drug gemcitabine diag *Science* v357 no6356 p1156 S 15 2017

AVUTU, AMANDA

OUT of the RUBBLE *Atlanta* v57 no1 p100 My 2017

Awaken, My Love! (Music)

THE DONALD GLOVER EXPERIMENT M. J. MOORE color *Nation* v304 no3 p37 Ja 30 2017

New Music Containing Multitudes R. Bruner color *Time* v189 no14 p50 Ap 17 2017

WEIRD WAR C. BATTAN cartoon *New Yorker* v92 no41 p70 D 12 2016

What to Stream color *Entertainment Weekly* no1443 p59 D 9 2016

Awan, Imran

Cyber-Extremism: Isis and the Power of Social Media chart color *Society* v54 no2 p138 Ap 2017

Awan, Nate

The Pipe Fitter C. Rotella *New York Times Magazine* p47 F 26 2017

Award presentations

ART OF CREATIVITY CELEBRATES ITS INAUGURAL AWARDS SHOW *Interview* v46 no10 p73 D 2016/Ja 2017

DAN ABOUT TOWN *Washingtonian Magazine* v52 no2 p30 N 2016

DARLEY PREVIEW S. Andersen *Arabian Horse World* v57 no6 p16 Mr 2017

WEST RIVER EVENTS *South Dakota Magazine* v33 no3 p87 S/O 2017

Award presentations (Motion pictures)

DANCING IN THE MOONLIGHT D. GILMORE color *Vanity Fair* v59 no5 p61 Ap 2017

Award presentations (Television programs)

2017 Rock and Roll Hall of Fame Induction Ceremony A. D'Arminio *TV Guide* p40 Ap 17 2017

Award winners

See also

Nobel Prize winners

INCLUSION S. Marikar cartoon *New Yorker* v93 no31 p22 O 9 2017

Nobel by the Numbers L. SCHLEY color graph *Discover* v38 no9 p16 N 2017

WRITING YOURSELF INTO EXISTENCE C. Patrice Clark color *Literacy Today (2411-7862)* v34 no5 p20 Mr/Ap 2017

Awards

See also

Incentive awards

Nobel Prizes

Scholarships

2015 Essay Contest Winner *Vegetarian Journal* v35 no2 p20 2016

2016 NATURAL BEAUTY AWARDS color *Yoga Journal* no287 p17 N 2016

2016 SCHOLARSHIP winners *Vegetarian Journal* v35 no4 p20 2016

2017 AUDUBON PHOTOGRAPHY AWARDS IN ASSOCIA-

TION WITH NATURE'S BEST PHOTOGRAPHY *Audubon* v119 no2 p30 Summ 2017

2017 betternutrition: BEST OF SUPPLEMENTS AWARD WINNERS [Cover story] color *Better Nutrition* v79 no11 p43 N 2017

And the Winner Is... *Parks & Recreation* v52 no2 p46 F 2017

BEAUTY'S NEXT BIG THINGS L. Desantis color *Health* v31 no7 p35 S 2017

I ♥ SUPPLEMENTS color *Better Nutrition* v78 no11 p49 N 2016

Knit to Be Tied R. S. Frazier color *Health* v31 no7 p77 S 2017

Master the Brown Bag Lunch C. McHugh color *Health* v31 no7 p12 S 2017

Purple Pose S. CARR *Idaho Magazine* v16 no6 p54 Mr 2017

SCHOLARSHIP *Vegetarian Journal* v35 no1 p23 2016

Stiff Competition N. Brechka *Better Nutrition* v79 no11 p6 N 2017

THIS IS WHAT SEVA LOOKS LIKE [Cover story] M. Rabbitt color *Yoga Journal* no295 p40 O 2017

Winner's CIRCLE color *Practical Horseman* v45 no11 p64 N 2017

Awards for authors

Latino Authors Celebrated At Annual Book Awards A. Bardales *Publishers Weekly* v264 no40 p18 O 2 2017

Awards—Canada

Award Kremlinology B. BETHUNE color *Maclean's* v129 no44 p108 N 7 2016

Award winners—Charts, diagrams, etc.

GATORADE Players Of the Year J. Fuchs color diag *Sports Illustrated* v127 no1 p72 Jl 3 2017

Awareness

See also

Mindfulness (Psychology)

Self-perception

Situational awareness

Awareness Is Good. Attention Is Better M. Loftus *Christianity Today* v60 no8 p31 O 2016

DIABETES AWARENESS F. ESKER color *Louisiana Life* v37 no2 p12 N/D 2016

EQUUS Film Festival K. Brittle bw color *Dressage Today* v23 no7 p54 Mr 2017

'Good' Times in Pennsylvania T. Herd *Parks & Recreation* v52 no2 p18 F 2017

Improve Body Awareness for a Better Seat D. Thind and A. Morris color *Dressage Today* v23 no8 p24 Ap 2017

Mindfulness Can Literally Change Your Brain C. Congleton, B. K. Hölzel et al *Harvard Business Review Digital Articles* p2 Ja 8 2015

Sport Can Transform Children's Lives and the World Y. KIM *UN Chronicle* v53 no2 p42 2016

Awareness advertising

mommy & me *Atlanta* v56 no7 p220 N 2016

New Deal on Pollutants Caps Good Year for Climate Action J. Worland color *Time* v188 no18 p11 O 31 2016

Awazu, Kiyoshi

KIYOSHI AWAZU bw color *Film Comment* v53 no5 p80 S/O 2017

Awe, C.

Observation of coherent elastic neutrino-nucleus scattering diag *Science* v357 no6356 p1123 S 15 2017

Awe, Stephan

Blocking promiscuous activation at cryptic promoters directs cell type–specific gene expression diag *Science* v356 no6339 p717 My 19 2017

Awe Inspired (Poem)

1862: Amherst, MA E. Dickinson *Lapham's Quarterly* v10 no2 p100 Spr 2017

Awe—Religious aspects

Awesomeness Is Everything M. HUTSON color *Atlantic* v319 no1 p15 Ja/F 2017

Awkard, Tiffany

The power of reflective action to build teacher efficacy color *Phi Delta Kappan* v98 no6 p53 Mr 2017

Awuah, Patrick

Patrick Awuah E. Turner *Current Biography* v78 no6 p8 Je 2017

Ax, Emanuel, 1949-

Deep Freeze R. Platt color *New Yorker* v93 no23 p14 Ag 7 2017

Axe, Josh
PROBIOTICS AND PREBIOTICS V. Tweed color *Amazing Wellness* v9 no2 p24 Spr 2017

Axelrad, Daniel A.
Estimating the health benefits of environmental regulations color *Science* v357 no6350 p457 Ag 4 2017

AXELROD, DAVID
OBAMA'S AMERICA img *New York* v49 no20 p12 O 3 2016

Axelrod, Maura
GOINGS ON ABOUT TOWN bw *New Yorker* v93 no9 p5 Ap 17 2017

Axelrod, Robert
Challenges in researching terrorism from the field bibl color *Science* v355 no6323 p352 Ja 27 2017

Axes—Evaluation
Cooler Gear, Hotter Deals C. Carter and P. Kita color *Men's Health* v32 no2 p24 Mr 2017
Invest in American Steel color *Men's Health* v32 no9 p33 N 2017

Axial R/C Inc.
Hot Rod Anything!: The Bomber R/C D. Glad color *Hot Rod* v70 no4 p12 Ap 2017

Axial Seamount
Seismic constraints on caldera dynamics from the 2015 Axial Seamount eruption W. S. D. Wilcock, M. Tolstoy et al bibl color graph *Science* v354 no6318 p1395 D 16 2016

Axial stresses
Putting the squeeze on superconductivity K. M. Shen bibl diag *Science* v355 no6321 p133 Ja 13 2017

Aximu-Petri, Ayinuer
Neandertal and Denisovan DNA from Pleistocene sediments bw color *Science* v356 no6338 p605 My 12 2017

Axions
Brain's physical structure aids wiring L. SANDERS color *Science News* v190 no8 p12 O 15 2016

Axis Architecture (Company)
Our Tech Office H. COX color *Indianapolis Monthly* v42 no2 p34 O 2017

Axis Dance Co. (Oakland, Calif.)
AXIS Dance Company Turns 30! color *Dance Spirit* v21 no8 p36 O 2017

Axles
DIFFERENTIAL DIFFERENCES J. JONES chart color *Dirt Sports + Off-Road* v51 no11 p32 N 2017
IDEA OF THE MONTH P. Barbour *Successful Farming* v115 no1 p80 Ja 2017

Axles—Evaluation
NINE-INCH STRONG M. Davis color *Hot Rod* v70 no2 p88 F 2017
PARTS & STUFF color *Hot Rod* v70 no6 p116 Je 2017

Axmann, Ilka M.
Structures of the cyanobacterial circadian oscillator frozen in a fully assembled state bibl diag *Science* v355 no6330 p1181 Mr 17 2017

AXON, SAMUEL
How I deleted Google from my life color diag *PCWorld* v35 no7 p179 Jl 2017

Axopar Boats Oy
Axopar 37 Sport Cabin D. J. Harding color *Power & Motoryacht* v33 no4 p42 Ap 2017
Cutting Corners D. J. HARDING bw chart color *Power & Motoryacht* v34 no11 p124 N 2017

Axtell, Paul
6 Reasons to Get Better at Leading Meetings *Harvard Business Review Digital Articles* p2 D 8 2016
The Condensed Guide to Running Meetings A. Gallo *Harvard Business Review Digital Articles* p2 Jl 6 2015
How to Design Meetings Your Team Will Want to Attend color *Harvard Business Review Digital Articles* p2 Ap 5 2017
How to Get Your Team to Follow Through After a Meeting color *Harvard Business Review Digital Articles* p2 Mr 30 2017
Just Because You're in Charge Doesn't Mean You Should Run Every Meeting *Harvard Business Review Digital Articles* p2 D 23 2016
The Right Way to End a Meeting *Harvard Business Review Digital Articles* p2 Mr 11 2015
Two Things to Do After Every Meeting *Harvard Business Review*
Digital Articles p2 N 26 2015
What Everyone Should Know About Running Virtual Meetings *Harvard Business Review Digital Articles* p2 Ap 14 2016
When Your Boss Is Terrible at Leading Meetings *Harvard Business Review Digital Articles* p2 My 16 2016

Ayahuasca
Trip Adviser L. W. Shapiro and C. ELLENBERG color *Vogue* v207 no9 p460 S 2017

Ayako M. Watabe
Overlapping memory trace indispensable for linking, but not recalling, individual memories bibl graph *Science* v355 no6323 p398 Ja 27 2017

Ayala, Paola
Turmoil imperils research university in Andes E. Rodríguez Mega color *Science* v357 no6349 p340 Jl 28 2017

Ayanian, John Z.
The Costs of Racial Disparities in Health Care *Harvard Business Review Digital Articles* p2 O 1 2015
How to Stop the Overconsumption of Health Care *Harvard Business Review Digital Articles* p2 D 11 2014

Ayano Kanazawa
Depleting dietary valine permits nonmyeloablative mouse hematopoietic stem cell transplantation bibl graph *Science* v354 no6316 p1152 D 2 2016

Ayapana, Erick
GARAGE chart color diag *Motor Trend* v69 no10 p102 O 2017
GARRAGE cartoon chart color *Motor Trend* v69 no3 p86 Mr 2017
GET USED TO THIS MUG chart color *Motor Trend* v69 no6 p82 Je 2017
MEET THE NEW E43 chart color *Motor Trend* v69 no5 p66 My 2017
Taller AND STRONGER chart color *Motor Trend* v69 no3 p80 Mr 2017

Ayduk, Ozlem
Pronouns Matter when Psyching Yourself Up *Harvard Business Review Digital Articles* p2 F 6 2015

Ayer, David
BRIGHT D. Franich color *Entertainment Weekly* no1478 / 1479 p78 Ag 18-25 2017
SUICIDE SQUAD D. Vaughn color *Sound & Vision* v82 no4 p67 My 2017

AYERS, DANA
THE ZEN OF HUFFING AND PUFFING *USA Today Magazine* v146 no2868 p66 S 2017

Ayers, Edward L., 1953-
The Thin Light of Freedom: Civil War and Emancipation in the Heart of America bw color *Publishers Weekly* v264 no31 p71 Jl 31 2017

Ayers, Mike
Beck's Colors Finds Joy In Its Time color *Time* v190 no16/17 p107 O 23 2017
A Match Made in Florida color *Money* v46 no9 p92 O 2017
Three Alt-Country Stars Align With New Albums color *Time* v189 no24 p51 Je 26 2017

Ayers, Nick
A Republican Crackup? W. Kristol *Weekly Standard* v23 no6 p10 O 16 2017

Ayesha's Homemade (TV program)
AYESHA AND STEPH CURRY P. MARTIN color *Bon Appetit* no1 p108 F 2017

Aymara (South American people)
NATIONAL GALLERY BOLIVIA R. Griffiths *History Today* v67 no8 p76 Ag 2017

Aymard C., G. A.
Persistent effects of pre-Columbian plant domestication on Amazonian forest composition bibl chart graph map *Science* v355 no6328 p925 Mr 3 2017

Ayoub, Mohammad
PROTECTING YOUR SON FROM ISLAMAPHOBIA color *Men's Health* v32 no5 p118 Je 2017

Ayoub, Salah
Loss of a mammalian circular RNA locus causes miRNA deregulation and affects brain function color *Science* v357 no6357 p1254 S 22 2017

Ayres, Alyssa

Will India Start Acting Like a Global Power? cartoon *Foreign Affairs* v96 no6 p83 N/D 2017

Ayris, Art A.

The Kingstone Bible F. EDWORDS *Humanist* v77 no2 p44 Mr/Ap 2017

Ayscue, Jennifer B.

When choice fosters inequality chart color graph il *Phi Delta Kappan* v98 no4 p49 D 2016/Ja 2017

Ayumi Yamashita

A three-dimensional movie of structural changes in bacteriorhodopsin bibl diag graph *Science* v354 no6319 p1552 D 23 2016

Ayurvedic medicine

Ayurvedic TRANSFORMATION [Cover story] T. EICHENSEHER color *Yoga Journal* no287 p52 N 2016

Be kind to body and mind V. LATONA color *Yoga Journal* p14 2016 Special Issue

EAT LIKE A YOGI D. Macy color *Yoga Journal* p100 2017 Special Issue

gather ROUND S. Sexton and K. O'Donnell chart color *Yoga Journal* no287 p68 N 2016

Ayurvedic medicine—India

"I Traveled 19 Hours to Chill Out" color *Glamour* v115 no11 p80 N 2017

Azad, Arezou

Islam's forgotten scholars *History Today* v66 no10 p24 O 2016

Azad, Nilofer S.

Mismatch repair deficiency predicts response of solid tumors to PD-1 blockade chart graph *Science* v357 no6349 p409 Jl 28 2017

Azaleas

An Azalea Affair A. Aguillard color *Southern Living* v52 no3 p11 Mr 2017

Azam, Shyema

EVERY WHICH WAY BUT LOOSE color *Vogue* v207 no7 p93 Jl 2017

Azaransky, Sarah

Until There Is Justice: The Life of Anna Arnold Hedgeman/Black Women's Christian Activism: Seeking Social Justice in a Northern Suburb *Christian Century* v134 no4 p49 F 15 2017

Azaria, Hank

HANK AZARIA D. KAMP bw *Vanity Fair* v59 no5 p58 Ap 2017

Azaria, Hank—Interviews

Broadcast Muse T. Keith color *Sports Illustrated* v126 no12 p17 My 1 2017

Azaria, Katie Wright

HANK AZARIA D. KAMP bw *Vanity Fair* v59 no5 p58 Ap 2017

Azaria, Rachel

People M. Jaffe-Hoffman *Christian Century* v133 no24 p21 N 23 2016

Azeez, Azhar, 1971-

ISNA ELECTS 2016-18 MAJLIS ASH-SHURA *Islamic Horizons* v45 no6 p8 N/D 2016

Azerrad, David

CON-FUSION *Claremont Review of Books* v17 no3 p28 Summ 2017

TIES THAT BIND *Claremont Review of Books* v16 no4 p18 Fall 2016

AZEVEDO, ANN

EXERCISING RESTRAINT color *Scientific American* v316 no6 p5 Je 2017

AZEVEDO, INÊS L.

Rethinking the Social Cost of Carbon Dioxide: The standard benefit-cost methodology that is used to calculate marginal costs of environmental regulations should not be used for long-lasting greenhouse gases *Issues in Science & Technology* v33 no4 p43 Summ 2017

AZEVEDO-SANTOS, VALTER M.

Nonnative Fish to Control Aedes Mosquitoes: A Controversial, Harmful Tool *BioScience* v67 no1 p84 Ja 2017

Azidation

Metal-catalyzed electrochemical diazidation of alkenes N. Fu, G. S. Sauer et al diag *Science* v357 no6351 p575 Ag 11 2017

Azilian culture

LATE PALEOLITHIC MASTERPIECES E. A. POWELL color *Archaeology* v70 no4 p20 Je-Ag 2017

AZIMI, NEGAR

THE GULF ART WAR cartoon color *New Yorker* v92 no42 p74 D 19 2016

On the Edge of Something bw *New York Times Book Review* p13 Ap 23 2017

Azimut-Benetti SpA

AZIMUT 50 FLYBRIDGE: A NEW ITALIAN 50-FOOTER IS MAKING WAVES ON THE WEST COAST Z. PROCHAZKA color *Sea Magazine* v109 no8 p38 Ag 2017

AZIMUT 60 Z. PROCHAZKA *Sea Magazine* v108 no9 p36 S 2016

Azimut Grande 35 Metri J. Y. Wood color *Power & Motoryacht* v34 no11 p74 N 2017

Azimut S7 J. Y. Wood color *Power & Motoryacht* v34 no6 p34 Je 2017

YOU GOT A LOTTA VERVE S. SHIBATA *Sea Magazine* v109 no2 p6 F 2017

Aziz, Navaid

Peace Be upon You N. ROBERTS color *Walrus* p24 Ja\F 2017

Aziz, Sahar F.

Opposing the Rise of State-Sponsored Islamophobia *Progressive* v81 no4 p24 Ap/My 2017

AZMAT, SUFIA

Teaching Social Justice at Islamic Schools [Cover story] *Islamic Horizons* v46 no2 p30 Mr/Ap 2017

Aznauryan, Erik

Xist recruits the X chromosome to the nuclear lamina to enable chromosome-wide silencing bibl graph *Science* v354 no6311 p468 O 28 2016

Azoulay, Pierre

The applied value of public investments in biomedical research diag graph *Science* v356 no6333 p78 Ap 7 2017

Azria, Jacqueline

Ask anything [Cover story] cartoon color *Women's Health* v13 no10 p22 D 2016

AZT (Drug)—Therapeutic use

Simple Drugs Stopped This Child from Getting HIV from Her Mother. Yet 400 Babies Are Born Every Day With the Disease. What Will It Take to Protect Them All? A. Park color diag map *Time* v189 no11 p40 Mr 27 2017

Aztec cartography

Tenochtitlan, 1524 K. Wiles *History Today* v66 no10 p22 O 2016

AZZARO, MARIA M.

Dec/2016 *Opera News* v81 no6 p6 D 2016

Azzi, Stephen

THE BIG QUESTION cartoon *Atlantic* v320 no4 p124 N 2017

King among PMs bw chart color *Maclean's* v129 no41 p19 O 17 2016

B

B & W Group Ltd.

The Joy of Sound S. Guttenberg color *Sound & Vision* v82 no3 p18 Ap 2017

B cells

A switch from canonical to noncanonical autophagy shapes B cell responses N. Martinez-Martin, P. Maldonado et al bibl graph *Science* v355 no6325 p641 F 10 2017

B Lab (Organization)

Why Companies Are Becoming B Corporations S. Kim, M. J. Karlesky et al *Harvard Business Review Digital Articles* p2 Je 17 2016

Baahubali 2: The Conclusion (Film)

India's Movie Industry Gets a New Script S. Philip and J. Thorpe color graph *Bloomberg Businessweek* no4525 p20 Je 5 2017

Baak, Ilse L.

Activity-based protein profiling reveals off-target proteins of the FAAH inhibitor BIA 10-2474 chart color graph *Science* v356 no6342 p1084 Je 9 2017

Baatz, Simon

The Girl on the Velvet Swing: Sex, Murder, and Madness at the Dawn of the Twentieth Century *Publishers Weekly* v264 no41 p54 O 9 2017

Bałazy, Radomir

Positive biodiversity-productivity relationship predominant in global forests bibl chart graph map *Science* v354 no6309 paaf8957-1 O 14 2016

Baba, Koki

A peptide hormone required for Casparian strip diffusion barrier formation in Arabidopsis roots bibl color graph *Science* v355 no6322 p284 Ja 20 2017

Babayigit, Aslihan

Perovskite-perovskite tandem photovoltaics with optimized band gaps bibl chart graph *Science* v354 no6314 p861 N 18 2016

Babbitt, Arthur

Picket Lines in Paradise J. S. Friedman bw color *American History* v52 no2 p40 Je 2017

Babbitt, Mark

The 7 Attributes of CEOs Who Get Social Media *Harvard Business Review Digital Articles* p2 D 3 2014

Babbitt metal

BABBITT BEARINGS S. SMITH color *Road & Track* v69 no1 p94 Ag 2017

Babbs, Sarah Margaret

At the Supermax: For Vernon color *U.S. Catholic* v82 no9 p11 S 2017

Babcock, Bill

Variable Frequency Drives in the Aquatics Industry *Parks & Recreation* p2 Aquatics Guide 2017

Babcock, Linda

10 Myths About Negotiating Your First Salary *Harvard Business Review Digital Articles* p2 Jl 3 2017

Babcock, Richard

CHICAGOANS OF THE YEAR [Cover story] color *Chicago* v65 no12 p74 D 2016

Babcock International Group PLC

You can't succeed if you don't know your colleagues *People Management* p20 N 2016

Babesiosis

Tick bites *Mayo Clinic Health Letter* v35 no6 p6 Je 2017

Babesiosis in horses—Treatment

STUD FARM DIARIES C. Reich *Arabian Horse World* v57 no1 p153 O 2016

Babick, Mary

Look, Ma—No Hands! *In Stride* v12 no1 p8 Ja 2017

Mary Babick Arrives for the 'Formative Years' T. Booker *In Stride* v11 no6 p32 N 2016

News BITS color *Practical Horseman* v44 no12 p67 D 2016

Remember to Sport Your Integrity *In Stride* v12 no4 p34 Jl 2017

Where Do You Stand? *In Stride* v12 no2 p8 Mr 2017

Babincsak, Jarrett

ALONE TOGETHER color *Outdoor Life* v224 no5 p82 Je/Jl 2017

Babine, Karen

The Vegetarian's Guide to Eating Meat color *Orion Magazine* v36 no2 p59 Mr/Ap 2017

Babineau, Alex

Q&A: Beyond Boarding School color *Maclean's* v130 no9 p66 O 2017

Babiš, Andrej, 1954-

Gaining From the EU But Hating It Anyway L. Bauerova and D. Rocks bw *Bloomberg Businessweek* no4537 p38 S 11 2017

BABIS, KASIA

COMICS *In These Times* v41 no10 p46 O 2017

Babi Yar Massacre, Ukraine, 1941

The Many Lives of Babi Yar N. M. Naimark *Hoover Digest: Research & Opinion on Public Policy* no2 p176 Spr 2017

Babka (Cake)

A BETTER BABKA A. BROWNLEE *Cincinnati Magazine* v50 no3 p134 D 2016

Babo, A.

'Civilization' and 'Mission' *Society* v54 no2 p124 Ap 2017

Babolat Corp.

Best in Shoe: 2017 T. NEWCOMB *Tennis* v53 no3 p16 My/Je 2017

Baboon behavior

FINDINGS *Harper's Magazine* p96 O 2017

Baby boom generation

Celebrating the 50th Anniversary of the SUMMER OF LOVE 1967-2017 R. LOVE *AARP: The Magazine* v60 no5A p29 Ag/S 2017

Q: IS SLOW WAGE GROWTH BOOMERS' FAULT? J. Porter *Fortune* v176 no4 p28 S 15 2017

SEPARATED AT BIRTH D. A. Rose *Harper's Magazine* v333 no1999 p33 D 2016

Baby boom generation—Attitudes

What Millennials Want from a New Job B. Rigoni and A. Adkins *Harvard Business Review Digital Articles* p2 My 11 2016

Baby boom generation—Employment

Companies Have Always Struggled to Engage Young People A. Ovans *Harvard Business Review Digital Articles* p2 N 18 2014

Baby boom generation—Political activity

Institutional Decay G. HOFFMAN *Commentary* v143 no2 p7 F 2017

Baby boom generation—Retirement

Design a Retirement That Excites You J. Giesea *Harvard Business Review Digital Articles* p2 N 17 2015

Baby boom generation—Retirement—United States

The Retirement of Baby Boomers [Cover story] M. Hobson color *Black Enterprise* v47 no3 p26 O 2016

Baby boom generation—United States

Generation Trump? W. Kristol *Weekly Standard* v22 no37 p8 Je 5 2017

THE MARIJUANA REVIVAL: A LOOK AT WEED'S CHANGING DEMOGRAPHIC S. E. JAMISON color *Ebony* v72/73 no12/1 p66 O/N 2017

Baby boomer retirement

PILOTS WANTED color *Flying* v144 no8 p82 Ag 2017

Baby boomers as consumers

HEY BIG SPENDERS cartoon color *Bloomberg Businessweek* no4496 p64 O 24 2016

Baby carriages—Evaluation

TEST DRIVE: DOONA INFANT CAR SEAT/STROLLER bw *Conde Nast Traveler* v51 no10 p175 N 2016

Baby cribs

Country Lore S. Stith, S. M. Furl et al *Mother Earth News* no281 p84 Ap/My 2017

If crib bumpers are so dangerous for babies, why are they still sold? *Parents* v91 no6 p22 Je 2016

our cradle: it's ugly, but it rocks! M. DICKS color *Parents* v92 no8 p52 Ag 2017

Baby cribs—Evaluation

The Reader Page B. Shanley, J. Petkiewicz et al color *Popular Mechanics* p5 F 2017

Baby Daddy (TV program)

Baby Daddy Marks 100 Episodes D. Lawrence color *Entertainment Weekly* no1454/1455 p21 F 24 2017

Baby dolls—Design & construction

THIS ROBOTIC BABY MIGHT NEED CHANGING E. E. DEPREZ color *Bloomberg Businessweek* no4505 p64 D 26 2016

Baby Driver (Film)

THE Anticipation Index *New York* v50 no6 p77 Mr 20 2017

THE Anticipation Index: What we're excited about right now *New York* v50 no9 p81 My 1 2017

Baby Driver Is Fast, Furious and Full of Heart S. Zacharek color *Time* v190 no2/3 p89 Jl 10-17 2017

Baby on Board C. Collis color *Entertainment Weekly* no1471 p50 Je 23 2017

CRITICS' CHOICE bw chart color *Film Comment* v53 no5 p14 S/O 2017

Dead Or Alive S. ERICKSON *Los Angeles Magazine* v62 no7 p54 Jl 2017

Eiza GONZÁLEZ *Interview* v47 no5 p68 Je/Jl 2017

Joyride of Summer! P. Travers color *Rolling Stone* no1291/1292 p67 Jl 13 2017

Meek but Mighty J. PODHORETZ color *Weekly Standard* v22 no42 p39 Jl 17 2017

The Must List color *Entertainment Weekly* no1473 p1 Jl 7 2017

NOW PLAYING color *Entertainment Weekly* no1473 p49 Jl 7 2017

NOW PLAYING color *Entertainment Weekly* no1476 p48 Ag 4 2017

PURSUIT OF PERFECTION M. PRINCE color *Road & Track* v69 no1 p74 Ag 2017

STYLE AND SUBSTANCE A. LANE color *New Yorker* v93 no19 p74 Jl 3 2017

Baby foods

See also

Infant formulas

BABY ON BOARD I. CORTES *USA Today Magazine* v145 no2858 p68 N 2016

not picky [Cover story] S. KUZEMCHAK color *Parents* v92 no7 p44 Jl 2017

Baby foods—Evaluation

Meals for Munchkins J. Laird color *Working Mother* v40 no3 p18 Ag/S 2017

Baby2Baby (Organization)

Julie Bowen C. M. Smith color *Entertainment Weekly* no1454/1455 p20 F 24 2017

Babylon Line, The (Theatrical production)

THE THEATRE *New Yorker* v92 no37 p27 N 14 2016

Babysitting

Sitters in a Snap J. Laird color *Working Mother* v40 no4 p18 O/N 2017

Baca, Judith Francisca, 1946-

CONCRETE History [Cover story] M. DURÓN bw cartoon color *ARTnews* v116 no1 p78 Spr 2017

Editor's Letter cartoon *ARTnews* v116 no1 p12 Spr 2017

Bacal, Norman

Case Study J. KAY cartoon *Walrus* v14 no2 p63 Mr 2017

Bacall, Lauren, 1924-2014

THE 1940S S. Mooallem bw color *Harper's Bazaar* no3652 p228 Ap 2017

Bacevice, Peter

7 Factors of Great Office Design *Harvard Business Review Digital Articles* p2 My 20 2016

Bacevich, Andrew J., 1947-

Andrew Bacevich M. Rich color *Current Biography* v77 no11 p12 N 2016

Behold, the Jihad of Freedom bw *Commonweal* v144 no9 p36 My 19 2017

Debunking America's 'Good' Occupation *American Conservative* v16 no1 p46 Ja/F 2017

An Education in Statecraft bw color *Nation* v304 no1 p28 Ja 2 2017 The Obama Years

Election 2016 [Cover story] color *Commonweal* v144 no1 p14 Ja 6 2017

The 'Global Order' Myth *American Conservative* v16 no3 p19 My/Je 2017

Grappling with the Gordian knot *America* v216 no7 p46 Ap 3 2017

MANIFEST QUAGMIRE C. Lord *Claremont Review of Books* v16 no4 p59 Fall 2016

The New Normal color *Commonweal* v144 no12 p8 Jl 7 2017

Now Shut Up and Shop color *Commonweal* v143 no17 p33 O 21 2016

The Odds Against Antiwar Warriors *American Conservative* v16 no2 p46 Mr/Ap 2017

The Tragedy of Foreign Policy: Walter McDougall produces another gem of a book *American Conservative* v16 no4 p10 Jl/Ag 2017

Bacevich, Andrew J., 1947-—Interviews

Disaster Area: U.S. Policy in the Middle East N. Stockwell color *Progressive* v81 no2 p37 F 2017

Bach, Matthew S.

Is the Oil and Gas Industry Serious About Climate Action? bibl chart color graph *Environment* v59 no2 p4 Mr/Ap 2017

Bach, Peter B.

A New Way to Define Value in Drug Pricing *Harvard Business Review Digital Articles* p2 O 6 2015

BACH, THOMAS

THE OLYMPIC MOVEMENT THE UNITED NATIONS AND THE PURSUIT OF COMMON IDEALS *UN Chronicle* v53 no2 p14 2016

Bach, Trevor

Genital cutting case in Michigan will test limits of religious liberty *Christian Century* v134 no18 p14 Ag 30 2017

Michigan's Iraqi Christians fear deportation color *Christian Century* v134 no15 p12 Jl 19 2017

Bachan, A.

The geologic history of seawater pH bibl diag *Science* v355 no6329 p1069 Mr 10 2017

Bachanalia (Music)

KEYBOARD SCHOOL: THE MELDING OF CLASSICAL

PIANO & BIG BAND JAZZ B. Cunliffe bw color *Downbeat* v84 no9 p82 S 2017

Bacharach, Elizabeth

BETTER BOARDWALK BITES color *Women's Health* v14 no5 p141 Je 2017

Bacharach, Jacob

The Doorposts of Your House and On Your Gates *Publishers Weekly* v264 no4 p54 Ja 23 2017

Schemes for Living: An Isaac and Abraham reboot looks at a shady side of real estate S. DEEN *New York Times Book Review* p14 Jl 9 2017

Bachata

FAKE I.D S. JIMENEZ bw *O, The Oprah Magazine* p138 My 2017

Bachelard, Gaston, 1884-1962

1957: Paris G. Bachelard *Lapham's Quarterly* v10 no1 p147 Wint 2017

Bachelder, Chris

All About Eve *New York Times Book Review* p1 Ag 13 2017

Chris Bachelder C. Mari color *Current Biography* v78 no2 p8 F 2017

Bachelet, D.

A human-driven decline in global burned area chart graph map *Science* v356 no6345 p1356 Je 30 2017

Bachelet, Michelle, 1951-

Chile's President on Her Country's Fitful Progress and Future Challenges I. Bremmer color *Time* v189 no22 p10 Je 12 2017

Bachelor, The (TV program)

Ask Matt M. Roush *TV Guide* v65 no11 p4 Mr 6 2017

The Bullseye M. Snetiker color *Entertainment Weekly* no1448 p64 Ja 13 2017

DRAFTING THE BACHELOR FANTASY LEAGUE R. Desantis color *Entertainment Weekly* no1446/1447 p26 D 2016/ Ja 2017

The Must List color *Entertainment Weekly* no1448 p2 Ja 13 2017

What to Watch R. Rahman, D. Franich et al color *Entertainment Weekly* no1457/1458 p88 Mr 17 2017

Bachelor in Paradise (TV program)

Bachelor in Paradise Halts Production L. Rice color *Entertainment Weekly* no1471 p16 Je 23 2017

CHEERS & JEERS D. HOLBROOK *TV Guide* v65 no37 p96 S 4 2017

Next on Bachelor in Paradise S. Highfill and R. Ross color *Entertainment Weekly* no1473 p14 Jl 7 2017

What to Watch R. Rahman, J. Jensen et al color *Entertainment Weekly* no1478 / 1479 p97 Ag 18-25 2017

Bachelor of arts degree

Bard College *Dance Magazine* v90 p44 2016/2017 Supplement College Guide

Barnard College Columbia University *Dance Magazine* v90 p45 2016/2017 Supplement College Guide

Bates College *Dance Magazine* v90 p45 2016/2017 Supplement College Guide

Bennington College *Dance Magazine* v90 p46 2016/2017 Supplement College Guide

Brenau University *Dance Magazine* v90 p47 2016/2017 Supplement College Guide

Butler University Jordan College of the Arts *Dance Magazine* v90 p49 2016/2017 Supplement College Guide

California Institute of the Arts *Dance Magazine* v90 p50 2016/2017 Supplement College Guide

California State University—Fullerton *Dance Magazine* v90 p51 2016/2017 Supplement College Guide

California State University—Long Beach *Dance Magazine* v90 p52 2016/2017 Supplement College Guide

Canada's National Ballet School *Dance Magazine* v90 p52 2016/2017 Supplement College Guide

Case Western Reserve University *Dance Magazine* v90 p53 2016/2017 Supplement College Guide

Chapman University *Dance Magazine* v90 p53 2016/2017 Supplement College Guide

College at Brockport State University of New York *Dance Magazine* v90 p48 2016/2017 Supplement College Guide

Cornish College of the Arts Focuses on the Technical Side *Stage Directions* v30 no3 p52 Mr 2017

Friends University *Dance Magazine* v90 p64 2016/2017 Supple-

no4538 p64 S 18 2017

Bachman, Justin

Here Comes the Space Cleanup Crew bw color diag *Bloomberg Businessweek* no4525 p32 Je 5 2017

Innovation color *Bloomberg Businessweek* no4517 p37 Ap 3 2017

Bachmann, Felix

Active sites in heterogeneous ice nucleation—the example of K-rich feldspars bibl bw diag *Science* v355 no6323 p367 Ja 27 2017

Bachmann, John, fl. 1849-1885

SHATTERING EFFECT J. Gardner bw cartoon color *Magazine Antiques* v184 no2 p126 Mr/Ap 2017

Bachmann Industries Inc.

Bachmann HO scale lighted passenger cars E. White *Model Railroader* v84 no10 p62 O 2017

Bachmann HO SoundValue USRA light 4-6-2 D. Kawala chart color *Model Railroader* v84 no4 p92 Ap 2017

Bachmann SoundValue HO scale EMD E7A D. Kawala chart color diag *Model Railroader* v84 no5 p60 My 2017

Bachmann Sound Value HO scale GS-4 [Cover story] D. Kawala color *Model Railroader* v84 no10 p58 O 2017

Bachmann Sound Value HO scale PCC trolley E. White chart color diag *Model Railroader* v84 no8 p60 Ag 2017

Bachor, Kenneth

The No-Frills, Full-Fun Snapshot Is Back color *Time* v190 no4 p52 Jl 24 2017

Bachrach, Judy

The Class Act bw *Weekly Standard* v22 no18 p34 Ja 16 2017

Fascists in Love color *Weekly Standard* v22 no31 p39 Ap 17 2017

A Soldier's Word *Weekly Standard* v22 no37 p32 Je 5 2017

What Rinka Wrought bw *Weekly Standard* v22 no12 p30 N 28 2016

Bächtiger, André

Deliberative Citizens, (Non)Deliberative Politicians: A Rejoinder *Daedalus* v146 no3 p106 Summ 2017

Baciadonna, Luigi

Unexpected rewards induce dopamine-dependent positive emotion–like state changes in bumblebees bibl graph *Science* v353 no6307 p1529 S 30 2016

BACICH, MICK

ACTING A LITTLE DINGHY *Sea Magazine* v109 no1 p26 Ja 2017

BACICH, PAM

ACTING A LITTLE DINGHY *Sea Magazine* v109 no1 p26 Ja 2017

Bacillus (Bacteria)

See also

Bacillus cereus

EVERYDAY COMPANIONS E. MASTROIANNI color *Discover* v38 no8 p12 O 2017

Bacillus cereus

Anthrax cousin wreaks havoc in the rainforest K. Kupferschmidt color *Science* v357 no6350 p438 Ag 4 2017

Bacillus subtilis

Chromosome stitch-up? D. J. Sherratt bibl color *Science* v355 no6324 p460 F 3 2017

Command of active matter by topological defects and patterns Chenhui Peng, T. Turiv et al bibl graph *Science* v354 no6314 p882 N 18 2016

Bacillus subtilis—Genetics

Bacillus subtilis SMC complexes juxtapose chromosome arms as they travel from origin to terminus X. Wang, H. B. Brandão et al bibl graph *Science* v355 no6324 p524 F 3 2017

Bacillus thuringiensis

A selective insecticidal protein from Pseudomonas for controlling corn rootworms U. Schellenberger, J. Oral et al bibl chart graph *Science* v354 no6312 p634 N 4 2016

Bacitracin

LUCKY BREAK P. A. Smith *Smithsonian* v48 no3 p30 Je 2017

Back

BACK IN ACTION R. Yee color *Yoga Journal* p88 2017 Special Issue

A home practice to build a strong back J. Elmer color *Yoga Journal* no287 p45 N 2016

A home practice to build a strong back J. Elmer color *Yoga Journal* p57 2017 SpecialIssue

How to move from High Lunge to Dhanurasana J. Blumstein color *Yoga Journal* no294 p55 S 2017

IN THIS SECTION color *Yoga Journal* p70 2017 Special Issue

LOWER-BACK LOVE R. Rosen color *Yoga Journal* p80 2017 Special Issue

THE LUMBAR LOWDOWN A. Bauman color *Yoga Journal* p84 2017 Special Issue

reinvent your wheel A. Ferretti and J. Crandell color *Yoga Journal* p20 2017 Special Issue

REVOLVE TO EVOLVE P. Sterios color *Yoga Journal* p90 2017 Special Issue

shoulder saver J. Crandell color *Yoga Journal* p28 2017 Special Issue

BACK, LAUREN

ON-THE-GO GEAR color *Trail Rider* v29 no1 p52 Ja/F 2017

ON-THE-GO GEAR color *Trail Rider* v29 no2 p56 Mr 2017

ON-THE-GO GEAR color *Trail Rider* v29 no3 p22 Ap 2017

PRACTICAL PRODUCTS color *Trail Rider* v29 no1 p53 Ja/F 2017

PRACTICAL PRODUCTS color *Trail Rider* v29 no2 p57 Mr 2017

PRACTICAL PRODUCTS color *Trail Rider* v29 no4 p52 My 2017

Trailer Updates 2017 bw color *Trail Rider* v29 no3 p8 Ap 2017

Back care

See also

Back exercises

Back to Life T. Narula color *O, The Oprah Magazine* p71 Ag 2017

Back Cove Yachts (Company)

The Future Faces of Boatbuilding D. HARDING JR. color *Power & Motoryacht* v33 no1 p32 Ja 2017

You Can Go Home Again P. A. JANSSEN chart color *Power & Motoryacht* v33 no1 p54 Ja 2017

Back exercises

2 Exercises to Prevent "Dowager's Hump" cartoon *Prevention* v69 no1 p17 Ja 2017

CRAWL FOR A KILLER CORE color *Health* v31 no4 p12 My 2017

GET BACK AT IT! M. Gainsburg color *Women's Health* v14 no4 p84 My 2017

play leads the way E. WINTER color *Yoga Journal* p36 2017 Special Issue

Back in the Game (TV program)

Ask the Host T. Keith color *Sports Illustrated* v126 no4 p19 Ja 30 2017

Back injuries

See also

Backache

All About the Deadlift L. BOYCE color *Muscle & Performance* v9 no8 p22 Ag 2017

Back issues (Periodicals)

From the Archives color *Black Belt* v55 no4 p82 Je/Jl 2017

Back the Way You Went (Short story)

Back the Way You Went A. Carson cartoon *New Yorker* v92 no35 p80 O 31 2016

Back up systems

Back up all your data—and we mean all of it—to your NAS box without installing any software J. L. JACOBI color *Macworld - Digital Edition* v34 no4 p86 My 2017

Back up systems software

ARQ: OFFERS AN ARCHIVING ALTERNATIVE TO TIME MACHINE AND HOSTED CLOUD BACKUP SERVICES G. FLEISHMAN color *Macworld - Digital Edition* v34 no4 p27 My 2017

Back up via a network without using Time Machine G. Fleishman color *Macworld - Digital Edition* p119 Ap 2017

How to move from CrashPlan for Home to another backup solution G. FLEISHMAN color *Macworld - Digital Edition* v34 no10 p12 O 2017

If we show you how to back up your PC for free, will you finally do it? M. CHIAPPETTA and L. SPECTOR color *PCWorld* p155 Mr 2017

Back up systems—Evaluation

The difference between backing up an iPhone to iCloud and iTunes J. BATTERSBY cartoon color *Macworld - Digital Edition* v33 no11 p123 N 2016

PICTURE KEEPER CONNECT: SIMPLE PHOTO BACKUP FOR THE ENTIRE FAMILY J. R. BOOKWALTER color *Macworld - Digital Edition* v33 no11 p92 N 2016

Backache

21 HEALTH REASONS TO DO YOGA K. DiNardo cartoon color *AARP: The Magazine* v60 no3A p38 Ap/My 2017

35 All-Time Favorite Natural Remedies J. McCAFFERY color *Prevention* v69 no8 p38 Ag 2017

5 Surprising Reasons Your Back Is Killing You T. SPIKER color *AARP: The Magazine* v59 no2A p16 F/Mr 2016

Back to Basics D. Yuhas color *Scientific American* v317 no4 p28 O 2017

Back to Life T. Narula color *O, The Oprah Magazine* p71 Ag 2017

Don't Blame the Rain color *Prevention* v69 no5 p10 My 2017

Empty Promises C. HILTON ANDERSEN color *Reader's Digest* v190 no1133 p52 S 2017

Fit for Life B. Howard color *AARP: The Magazine* v59 no3A p44 Ap/My 2016

The Strength Secret Most Men Ignore K. Dold bw color *Men's Health* v31 no10 p56 D 2016

Backache exercise therapy

LOW BACK ON TRACK L. McGLASHAN color *Muscle & Performance* v9 no4 p22 Ap 2017

Oh, My Aching Back H. VanEs and R. Harvey *USA Today Magazine* v146 no2868 p23 S 2017

Backache prevention

5 Surprising Reasons Your Back Is Killing You T. SPIKER color *AARP: The Magazine* v59 no2A p16 F/Mr 2016

Back pain color *Yoga Journal* p53 2017 SpecialIssue

Banish Back Pain the Natural Way K. ALEISHA FETTERS color *Men's Health* v32 no7 p75 S 2017

Getting Zen: THE NEW CURE-ALL color *Health* v30 no9 p16 N 2016

Get to know ... Your thoracic spine J. Miller color *Yoga Journal* no296 p64 N 2017

A home practice to build a strong back J. Elmer color *Yoga Journal* p57 2017 SpecialIssue

LOW BACK ON TRACK L. McGLASHAN color *Muscle & Performance* v9 no4 p22 Ap 2017

Stretching: The new mobility protection *Harvard Health Letter* v42 no2 p4 D 2016

Yoga vs. Back Pain K. McGee color *Health* v31 no4 p49 My 2017

Your Back Pain Prescription B. J. Gaddour bw color *Men's Health* v32 no1 p137 Ja/F 2017

Backache—Treatment

The Body's Repair Kit at Work K. RIDDERBUSCH *Atlanta* v56 no7 p212 N 2016

Dr. Weil [Cover story] cartoon color *Prevention* v68 no11 p22 N 2016

Back—Anatomy

Body of knowledge [Cover story] R. Long color *Yoga Journal* no290 p54 Mr 2017

Backcountry skiing

GRAVITY IN MIDDLE EARTH B. Fredlund color *Skiing* p66 D 2016

Toni: Gora Mamay, Russia J. CLARY DAVIES color *Powder* v46 no2 p9 O 2017

Backdrops Beautiful (Company)

Backdrops Beautiful® Custom-Designed Backdrops that Set the Stage *Stage Directions* v30 no3 p46 Mr 2017

Backdrops Fantastic (Company)

The Difference Is in the Details *Stage Directions* v30 no3 p32 Mr 2017

BACKER, KYM ALLISON

Celebrate Good Times color *Ebony* v72 no3 p74 D 2016/Ja 2017

Backes, Claudia

All-printed thin-film transistors from networks of liquid-exfoliated nanosheets diag *Science* v356 no6333 p69 Ap 7 2017

Sensitive electromechanical sensors using viscoelastic graphene-polymer nanocomposites bibl graph *Science* v354 no6317 p1257 D 9 2016

Backes, David

Gimme Shelter S. Apstein and T. Keith color *Sports Illustrated* v126 no5 p22 F 13 2017

Backfield play (Football)

See also

Quarterbacking (Football)

INSIDE THE TEXAS QUARTERBACK FACTORY E. BENSON *Texas Monthly* v45 no9 p56 S 2017

Background checks

See also

Refugee screening

Refugee Security Screening Process *Congressional Digest* v96 no3 p8 Mr 2017

Backhauling (Trucking)

Road-Ready Tips B. Avila and J. Paulson color *Horse & Rider* v56 no7 p47 Jl 2017

Backhoes

Bad Hair Daze W. DURST cartoon *Progressive* v81 no5 p66 Je/Jl 2017

Backhouse, Stephen

Kierkegaard: A Single Life E. Palmer color *Christian Century* v134 no11 p30 My 24 2017

KIERKEGAARD J. Green color *Christianity Today* v61 no1 p54 Ja/F 2017

Backlist (Publishing)

Why Backlist Matters J. Rosen color *Publishers Weekly* v264 no7 p4 F 13 2017

Backlog (Music)

6-String Sidestream B. MILKOWSKI color *Downbeat* v84 no8 p73 Ag 2017

Backlund, J. R.

Among the Dead: A Rachel Carver Novel color *Publishers Weekly* v264 no24 p43 Je 12 2017

Backman, Fredrik, 1981-

Fredrik Backman *Publishers Weekly* v263 no40 p95 O 3 2016

MISCELLANEOUS BEST SELLERS *New York Times Book Review* p80 D 4 2016

Backman, Jan

Release of mineral-bound water prior to subduction tied to shallow seismogenic slip off Sumatra graph *Science* v356 no6340 p841 My 26 2017

Backpackers

A Legend in the Making E. BARKER *Idaho Magazine* v16 no6 p16 Mr 2017

Picture Perfect color *Backpacker* v45 no2 p88 Mr 2017

SEARCHING FOR POPS R. Woodie color *Backpacker* p71 O 2017

Backpackers—Attitudes

Find the Perfect Partner C. GERARD color *Backpacker* v45 no2 p31 Mr 2017

Backpacking

BACKPACKER FESTIVAL EXPERIENCE *Backpacker* p70 O 2017

BACKPACK *Sierra* v102 no1 p58 Ja/F 2017

Choose Your Adventure A. Opar *Audubon* v119 no2 p54 Summ 2017

Cold Comfort M. HORJUS color *Backpacker* v45 no2 p24 Mr 2017

den mother: Man Overboard il *Backpacker* p43 S 2017

Girls Gone Wild E. TAYLOR color *Indianapolis Monthly* v42 no2 p36 O 2017

The Hiker and the Sexologist M. NORDSTROM *Sierra* v101 no6 p18 N/D 2016

A Legend in the Making E. BARKER *Idaho Magazine* v16 no6 p16 Mr 2017

Lost and Found D. LEWON color *Backpacker* p4 O 2017

Make Hiking Great Again T. ALVAREZ and T. VANDERMOLEN color il *Backpacker* p18 Je 2017

A MOUNTAIN OF TROUBLE K. MILLER *Reader's Digest* v188 no1124 p108 O 2016

On Two Wheels N. YORK *Idaho Magazine* v16 no6 p24 Mr 2017

OPEN TRIPS FOR 2017 *Sierra* v102 no3 p59 My/Je 2017

QUEST: BACKPACKING ACROSS WESTERN NEW YORK M. Foley *New York State Conservationist* v71 no5 p14 Ap 2017

Southern Charm E. KWAK-HEFFERAN color map *Backpacker* p12 O 2017

Spring into action color *Backpacker* p10 My 2017

Stay dry in a downpour color *Backpacker* p25 O 2017

THIS COULD BE YOU *Sierra* v102 no3 p64 My/Je 2017

Tour de California C. GRAHAM color *Backpacker* p12 My 2017

#trailchat J. Kay, D. O'Dell et al color *Backpacker* p8 My 2017

Two Kinds of Wilderness: On foot through an ecological experiment J. MILLER bw *Orion Magazine* v36 no2 p34 Mr/Ap 2017

YOUNGER PARTICIPANTS *Sierra* v102 no1 p76 Ja/F 2017

Backpacking equipment

Back in Style K. O'Reilly *Sierra* v102 no3 p18 My/Je 2017

Backpacking—Equipment & supplies

Plan a Big Trip D. LEWON diag *Backpacker* v45 no2 p32 Mr 2017

Backpacking—Equipment & supplies—Evaluation

Bikepacking A. H. BIBLE color *Backpacker* p52 My 2017

Hall of Fame E. KWAK-HEFFERAN and S. YORKO color *Backpacker* v45 no2 p45 Mr 2017

Backpacking—Idaho

Packing the Tot C. BONK *Idaho Magazine* v16 no5 p23 F 2017

Backpacking—Social aspects

Find the Perfect Partner C. GERARD color *Backpacker* v45 no2 p31 Mr 2017

Backpacks

A BACKPACK WITH A COOLER K. Dupzyk color *Popular Mechanics* p83 D 2016/Ja 2017

DOOMSDAY IN IGLOO R. Holtzmann *South Dakota Magazine* v33 no3 p52 S/O 2017

GH CLEANING LAB C. FORTÉ bw color *Good Housekeeping* v265 no4 p62 O 2017

Making a Splash N. BOUCHARD color *Backpacker* p43 O 2017

The O List: PET EDITION color *O, The Oprah Magazine* p53 O 2017

Toughen Up L. ". THOMAS color *Backpacker* v45 no1 p31 Ja 2017

Yara Shahidi color *Seventeen* v76 no5 p30 S 2017

Backpacks—Evaluation

2017 Women's Gear Guide color *Climbing* no356 p34 S/O 2017

All-Star Stashes! K. FOSTER color *Seventeen* v76 no3 p41 My 2017

Back in Style K. O'Reilly *Sierra* v102 no3 p18 My/Je 2017

Best in Class color *Martha Stewart Living* p26 S 2017

EQUIPMENT N. BOUCHARD, W. M. ROCHFORT et al color *Backpacker* p73 N 2017

ESSENTIAL GEAR color *Black Belt* v55 no3 p60 Ap/My 2017

Field Notes color *Climbing* no355 p44 Ag 2017

gear color *Climbing* no352 p18 Ap 2017

Girly Girl cartoon color *Seventeen* v76 no12 p42 D 2016/Ja 2017

HOLIDAY GIFT GUIDE M. BOBO and J. AMAY color *Ebony* v72 no3 p51 D 2016/Ja 2017

JOSHUA BLAKE CARTER J. BERG color *Chicago* v66 no5 p54 My 2017

Labels We Love: The Three Kings of Streetwear N. Marino color *GQ: Gentlemen's Quarterly* v97 no9 p66 S 2017

The latest word from our testers color *Backpacker* p56 Ag 2017

Little Big Packs N. BOUCHARD color diag *Backpacker* p49 My 2017

Next: The Backpack color *Glamour* v114 no7 p48 Jl 2016

on demand color *InStyle* v24 no4 p49 Ap 2017

A Pack Perfected M. GOULET cartoon *Popular Mechanics* p24 D 2016/Ja 2017

PACKS D. Pogge and K. Beekman color *Skiing* p82 D 2016

Packs N. BOUCHARD bw color diag graph il *Backpacker* v45 no3 p29 Ap 2017

PICKING THE RIGHT PACK S. MacDonald color *Cycle World* v56 no2 p16 Mr 2017

POCKET CHANGE *Los Angeles Magazine* p28 My 2017

Seven Great Ways to Blow a Grand—Serious Enthusiasm Required color *GQ: Gentlemen's Quarterly* v87 no1 p16 Ja 2017

SHOULDER ON color *Esquire* v167 no2 p68 Mr 2017

STRAPPED A. McKEAN color *Outdoor Life* v224 no9 p19 N 2017

TIMBUK2 AUTHORITY PACK O. RAYMUNDO color *Macworld - Digital Edition* v34 no9 p36 S 2017

When Two Labels Love Each Other Very Much... color *GQ: Gentlemen's Quarterly* v97 no10 p64 O 2017

Backpage.com LLC—Trials, litigation, etc.

The Right To Run Sex Ads D. Lawrence *Bloomberg Businessweek* no4493 p14 O 3 2016

Backrests

Comfort in the Cockpit D. Everitt cartoon *Sail* v48 no4 p58 Ap 2017

Backstreet Boys (Performer)

When Florida Georgia Line Met the Backstreet Boys M. Vain color *Entertainment Weekly* no1453 p12 F 17 2017

Backstroke (Swimming)

swim your way stronger [Cover story] J. A. DEDIC and J. Kageleiyr chart color *Redbook* p77 Je 2017

Bäckström, Anna

A subcellular map of the human proteome color *Science* v356 no6340 p820 My 26 2017

BACKSTROM, DOUGLAS

BEGINNER'S GUIDELINES TO MEAL PREP color *Ebony* v72 no11 p64 S 2017

SHAUN T LETS NOTHING STOP HIM color *Ebony* v72 no11 p65 S 2017

STEP OUT OF YOUR COMFORT ZONE color *Ebony* v72/73 no12/1 p65 O/N 2017

Back—Wounds & injuries—Prevention

Lighten Their Load *Parents* v91 no9 p27 S 2016

Bacle, Ariana

3 ROUNDS WITH HANSON color *Entertainment Weekly* no1467 p40 My 26 2017

ADAM SCOTT AND CRAIG ROBINSON color *Entertainment Weekly* no1482/1483 p42 S 22 2017

After the Verdict color *Entertainment Weekly* no1482/1483 p62 S 22 2017

THE BEST ALBUMS OF 2017 (SO FAR) color *Entertainment Weekly* no1468/1469 p98 Je 2-9 2017

The Best Small-Screen Soundtracks color *Entertainment Weekly* no1439 p53 N 11 2016

black-ish *Entertainment Weekly* no1482/1483 p63 S 22 2017

Bob's Burgers *Entertainment Weekly* no1482/1483 p34 S 22 2017

Breaking Big BRANDON MICHEAL HALL color *Entertainment Weekly* no1482/1483 p65 S 22 2017

Bull color *Entertainment Weekly* no1482/1483 p66 S 22 2017

CLAUDIA O'DOHERTY: LOVES OF MY LIFE color *Entertainment Weekly* no1457/1458 p81 Mr 17 2017

Curb Your Enthusiasm color *Entertainment Weekly* no1482/1483 p40 S 22 2017

DC's Legends of Tomorrow color *Entertainment Weekly* no1482/1483 p66 S 22 2017

The Deuce color *Entertainment Weekly* no1482/1483 p29 S 22 2017

DIVE INTO Brooklyn Nine-Nine color *Entertainment Weekly* no1482/1483 p67 S 22 2017

Family Guy *Entertainment Weekly* no1482/1483 p34 S 22 2017

The Flash color *Entertainment Weekly* no1482/1483 p66 S 22 2017

Fresh Off the Boat color *Entertainment Weekly* no1482/1483 p63 S 22 2017

Fuller House *Entertainment Weekly* no1482/1483 p106 S 22 2017

Future Man *Entertainment Weekly* no1482/1483 p106 S 22 2017

The Girlfriend Experience color *Entertainment Weekly* no1482/1483 p38 S 22 2017

THE GOLDEN AGE OF HAIM color *Entertainment Weekly* no1467 p32 My 26 2017

Good Behavior *Entertainment Weekly* no1482/1483 p39 S 22 2017

Hit the Road *Entertainment Weekly* no1482/1483 p60 S 22 2017

JASON RITTER OF Kevin (Probably) Saves the World color *Entertainment Weekly* no1482/1483 p61 S 22 2017

Kathryn Hahn's Awkward Artistry color *Entertainment Weekly* no1465 p48 My 12 2017

Katy Perry Talks (and Talks...) color *Entertainment Weekly* no1471 p61 Je 23 2017

THE KIDS OF STRANGER THINGS color *Entertainment Weekly* no1444/1445 p32 D 16 2016

Law & Order True Crime: The Menendez Murders color *Entertainment Weekly* no1482/1483 p62 S 22 2017

Lethal Weapon color *Entertainment Weekly* no1482/1483 p60 S 22 2017

Madam Secretary color *Entertainment Weekly* no1482/1483 p39 S 22 2017

Major Crimes *Entertainment Weekly* no1482/1483 p66 S 22 2017

MANCHESTER UNITED color *Entertainment Weekly* no1470 p11 Je 16 2017

Marvel's The Punisher color *Entertainment Weekly* no1482/1483

p106 S 22 2017

The Mick color *Entertainment Weekly* no1482/1483 p67 S 22 2017

The Middle color *Entertainment Weekly* no1482/1483 p60 S 22 2017

Mindhunter color *Entertainment Weekly* no1482/1483 p107 S 22 2017

THE MINDY PROJECT color *Entertainment Weekly* no1477 p32 Ag 11 2017

NCIS *Entertainment Weekly* no1482/1483 p60 S 22 2017

NCIS: Los Angeles *Entertainment Weekly* no1482/1483 p38 S 22 2017

NCIS: New Orleans *Entertainment Weekly* no1482/1483 p67 S 22 2017

One Direction? Try 5 Directions color *Entertainment Weekly* no1477 p58 Ag 11 2017

Outlander color *Entertainment Weekly* no1482/1483 p26 S 22 2017

PARAMORE'S HAYLEY WILLIAMS color *Entertainment Weekly* no1466 p56 My 19 2017

Paula Abdul's Greatest Hits color *Entertainment Weekly* no1465 p55 My 12 2017

PHOENIX color *Entertainment Weekly* no1470 p55 Je 16 2017

Poldark *Entertainment Weekly* no1482/1483 p38 S 22 2017

Riviera color *Entertainment Weekly* no1482/1483 p106 S 22 2017

Ryan Hansen Solves Crimes on Television* *Entertainment Weekly* no1482/1483 p109 S 22 2017

SARAH SILVERMAN I Love You, America color *Entertainment Weekly* no1482/1483 p108 S 22 2017

Shameless color *Entertainment Weekly* no1482/1483 p30 S 22 2017

The Simpsons color *Entertainment Weekly* no1482/1483 p34 S 22 2017

SMILF *Entertainment Weekly* no1482/1483 p43 S 22 2017

Star Trek Discovery color *Entertainment Weekly* no1482/1483 p104 S 22 2017

StartUp *Entertainment Weekly* no1482/1483 p109 S 22 2017

Stranger Things 2 color *Entertainment Weekly* no1482/1483 p100 S 22 2017

Ten Days in the Valley color *Entertainment Weekly* no1482/1483 p43 S 22 2017

This Is Us color *Entertainment Weekly* no1482/1483 p56 S 22 2017

THROWING SHADE LIKE A PRO color *Entertainment Weekly* no1450 p52 Ja 27 2017

Tin Star *Entertainment Weekly* no1482/1483 p109 S 22 2017

THE TRANSFORMATION OF KATY PERRY color *Entertainment Weekly* no1467 p28 My 26 2017

Transparent color *Entertainment Weekly* no1482/1483 p109 S 22 2017

The Walking Dead color *Entertainment Weekly* no1482/1483 p38 S 22 2017

What to Watch color *Entertainment Weekly* no1436/1437 p94 O 21 2016

What to Watch color *Entertainment Weekly* no1456 p62 Mr 10 2017

What to Watch color *Entertainment Weekly* no1463/1464 p99 Ap/My 2017

What to Watch color *Entertainment Weekly* no1478 / 1479 p97 Ag 18-25 2017

White Famous color *Entertainment Weekly* no1482/1483 p36 S 22 2017

Wisdom of the Crowd color *Entertainment Weekly* no1482/1483 p34 S 22 2017

The Workaholics' Finest Work color *Entertainment Weekly* no1449 p52 Ja 20 2017

Your LGBTQ Pop Preview color *Entertainment Weekly* no1471 p44 Je 23 2017

Bacon, Amanda Chantal

103 MINUTES WITH ... Amanda Chantal Bacon J. PRESSLER img *New York* v49 no25 p24 D 12 2016

Your New Beauty Meal Plan color *Glamour* v114 no11 p108 N 2016

BACON, DAVID

The Changing Face of Work and Poverty in Yakima color *Progressive* v81 no6 p12 Ag/S 2017

Five Years of Vigils and Protests at the West County Detention Center color *Progressive* v81 no2 p12 F 2017

Bacon, Francis, 1561-1626

1620: London F. Bacon *Lapham's Quarterly* v10 no2 p97 Spr 2017

Bacon, Kevin, 1958-

KEVIN BACON IS NOT A DICK E. Lepucki bw color *Esquire* p21 My 2017

Bacon, Kevin, 1958—Interviews

I Love Dick D. Holbrook *TV Guide* v65 no13 p38 Mr 20 2017

Bacon, Roger, ca. 1214-1294

1267: Paris R. Bacon *Lapham's Quarterly* v10 no2 p153 Spr 2017

BACON, ROXANA

The ICE-Men Cometh *Ms.* v27 no1 p43 Spr 2017

My Own Words *Ms.* v26 no4 p39 Wint 2016

Nevertheless, She Persisted *Ms.* v27 no2 p45 Summ 2017

WOMEN ON THE RUN *Ms.* v27 no2 p18 Summ 2017

Bacon, Steve

COME ONE, COME ALL C. Gerard color *Backpacker* v45 no1 p64 Ja 2017

Bacteria

Assembly of a nucleus-like structure during viral replication in bacteria V. Chaikeeratisak, K. Nguyen et al bibl color graph *Science* v355 no6321 p1 Ja 13 2017

Bacteria Beef Up New Tree of Life J. KEATS diag *Discover* v38 no1 p90 Ja/F 2017

Command of active matter by topological defects and patterns Chenhui Peng, T. Turiv et al bibl graph *Science* v354 no6314 p882 N 18 2016

do bacteria make it rain? V. Greenwood color *Popular Science* v289 no4 p22 Jl/Ag 2017

Enzyme links up carbon and silicon L. HAMERS color *Science News* v190 no13 p11 D 24 2016

EVERYDAY COMPANIONS E. MASTROIANNI color *Discover* v38 no8 p12 O 2017

Swimming with Bacteria B. Lutz color *New Orleans Magazine* v51 no8 p34 Je 2017

Zero Tolerance H. Levine bw color graph *Consumer Reports* v82 no1 p32 Ja 2017

Bacteria behavior

Bacteria's physical playbook T. H. Saey color *Science News* v192 no6 p17 O 14 2017

Bacteria morphology

Microbes reveal their inner selves T. HESMAN SAEY color *Science News* v192 no1 p12 Ag 5 2017

Bacterial cell walls

New 'rules' for finding antibiotics A. CUNNINGHAM *Science News* v191 no11 p8 Je 10 2017

Bacterial cells

Mechanisms of bacterial persistence during stress and antibiotic exposure A. Harms, E. Maisonneuve et al bibl diag graph *Science* v354 no6318 paaf4268-1 D 16 2016

Viral Decisions K. Moore color *Natural History* v125 no4 p8 Ap 2017

Bacterial colonies

Coupling and sharing when life is hard V. Gordon color *Science* v356 no6338 p583 My 12 2017

Bacterial cultures

Biased inheritance protects older bacteria from harm T. C. Barrett, W. W. K. Mok et al diag *Science* v356 no6335 p247 Ap 21 2017

A WHIFF OF CULTURE A. TITTIGER color *Wired* v25 no4 p28 Ap 2017

Bacterial diseases

Quick Hits L. Nemo map *Scientific American* v317 no2 p18 Ag 2017

TRUST YOUR GUT [Cover story] R. EBERSOLE cartoon *Prevention* v69 no9 p60 O 2017

Bacterial evolution

Evolution promises unpleasant surprises E. Pennisi color *Science* v354 no6310 p274 O 21 2016

Bacterial flagella

Nanoscale-length control of the flagellar driveshaft requires hitting the tethered outer membrane E. J. Cohen, J. L. Ferreira et al color diag graph *Science* v356 no6334 p197 Ap 14 2017

Bacterial pigments

See also

Bacteriorhodopsin

Hidden dynamics in the unfolding of individual bacteriorhodopsin proteins H. Yu, M. G. W. Siewny et al bibl diag *Science* v355 no6328 p945 Mr 3 2017

Bacterial proteins

See also

Bacteriorhodopsin

Tips for battling billion-dollar beetles B. E. Tabashnik bibl color graph *Science* v354 no6312 p552 N 4 2016

Bacterial vaginitis—Prevention

Probiotics: What's in a name? C. DOW and D. SCHARDT *Nutrition Action Health Letter* v44 no6 p8 Jl/Ag 2017

Bacteria—Research

Digging Deep for New Bacteria E. BETZ color *Discover* v38 no1 p85 Ja/F 2017

Bacteriophage lambda

Ecological speciation of bacteriophage lambda in allopatry and sympatry J. R. Meyer, D. T. Dobias et al bibl graph *Science* v354 no6317 p1301 D 9 2016

Bacteriophages

Inflammation boosts bacteriophage transfer between Salmonella spp M. Diard, E. Bakkeren et al bibl diag *Science* v355 no6330 p1211 Mr 17 2017

Bacteriophages—Therapeutic use

Moving Back to Stay Ahead: Phage Research Comes Out of Storage M. STONE *BioScience* v67 no2 p188 F 2017

Bacteriophages—Virulence

Viral Decisions K. Moore color *Natural History* v125 no4 p8 Ap 2017

Bacteriorhodopsin

Hidden dynamics in the unfolding of individual bacteriorhodopsin proteins H. Yu, M. G. W. Siewny et al bibl diag *Science* v355 no6328 p945 Mr 3 2017

A three-dimensional movie of structural changes in bacteriorhodopsin Eriko Nango, A. Royant et al bibl diag graph *Science* v354 no6319 p1552 D 23 2016

Baculard, Laurent-Pierre

To Lead a Digital Transformation, CEOs Must Prioritize color *Harvard Business Review Digital Articles* p2 Ja 2 2017

WhatsApp Grew to One Billion Users by Focusing on Product, Not Technology *Harvard Business Review Digital Articles* p2 Jl 1 2016

Bad & Boujee (Music)

'Bad and Boujee' N. ZEICHNER *New York Times Magazine* p65 Mr 12 2017

Bad Bad Hats (Performer)

GOINGS ON ABOUT TOWN color *New Yorker* v92 no49 p11 F 13 2017

NIGHT LIFE *New Yorker* v93 no22 p12 Jl 31 2017

Bad Brains (Performer)

Bad Mind M. Trammell color *New Yorker* v92 no43 p10 Ja 2 2017

Bad Moms (Film)

Chill lessons from Kristen Bell [Cover story] J. PRESSLER color *Redbook* p104 O 2017

Bad news

You Can Deliver Bad News to Your Team Without Crushing Them M. Gielan *Harvard Business Review Digital Articles* p2 Mr 21 2016

Bad Santa 2 (Film)

BROUGHT UP BAD C. Collis color *Entertainment Weekly* no1441 p35 N 25 2016

The Bullseye M. Snetiker color *Entertainment Weekly* no1442 p64 D 2 2016 Rebellious Special Issue

NAUGHTY BY NATURE C. Collis color *Entertainment Weekly* no1441 p32 N 25 2016

Badaki, Yetide

American Gods J. Halterman *TV Guide* v65 no25 p34 Je 2017

Badal, Kelly Phillips

California dreamy color *Sunset* v238 no6 p46 Je 2017

COMING CLEAN color *Sunset* v239 no1 p43 Jl 2017

ESCAPE FROM L.A color *Sunset* v239 no3 p72 S 2017

Badar, Jeanmarie

It's instruction over place — not the other way around! color diag il *Phi Delta Kappan* v98 no4 p55 D 2016/Ja 2017

Badaracco, Joseph L.

Before You Make a Tough Decision, Imagine How You'll Have to Sell It *Harvard Business Review Digital Articles* p2 Ag 29 2016

Timeless Advice for Making a Hard Choice *Harvard Business Review Digital Articles* p2 Ag 25 2016

When You Feel Pressured to Do the Wrong Thing at Work *Harvard Business Review Digital Articles* p2 N 2 2016

Badau, Flavius

U.S. Beef and Pork Consumption Projected To Rebound *Amber Waves: The Economics of Food, Farming, Natural Resources, & Rural America* p1 S 2016

U.S. Upland Cotton Exports and Mill Use Projected To Improve *Amber Waves: The Economics of Food, Farming, Natural Resources, & Rural America* p34 Ag 2017

Bad Batch, The (Film)

The Bad Batch F. ZAMAN color *Film Comment* v53 no3 p70 My/Je 2017

CRITICS' CHOICE chart color *Film Comment* v53 no3 p12 My/Je 2017

BADCOCK, CHRISTOPHER

The Domesticated Human *Psychology Today* v50 no1 p41 Ja/F 2017

Tend and Defend *Psychology Today* v50 no2 p38 Mr/Ap 2017

BADENHAUSEN, KURT

America's Richest Celebrities color *Forbes* v198 no9 p18 D 30 2016

The Best Countries For Business color *Forbes* v199 no2 p22 F 28 2017

INSIDE THE HUDDLE color *Forbes* v200 no4 p15 O 24 2017

The Most Valuable Baseball Teams chart color *Forbes* v199 no5 p28 My 16 2017

The Most Valuable NBA Teams chart color *Forbes* v199 no2 p30 F 28 2017

The Most Valuable NFL Teams color graph *Forbes* v198 no5 p32 O 25 2016

THE WORLD'S BILLIONAIRES bw color diag graph map *Forbes* v199 no3 p84 Mr 28 2017

Bader, Harrison

Bader Up T. Keith and S. Kwak color *Sports Illustrated* v127 no5 p30 Ag 14 2017

Bader, Joel S.

3D organization of synthetic and scrambled chromosomes diag *Science* v355 no6329 p1050 Mr 10 2017

Bug mapping and fitness testing of chemically synthesized chromosome X diag *Science* v355 no6329 p1048 Mr 10 2017

Deep functional analysis of synII, a 770-kilobase synthetic yeast chromosome diag *Science* v355 no6329 p1047 Mr 10 2017

Design of a synthetic yeast genome bibl chart color graph *Science* v355 no6329 p1040 Mr 10 2017

Engineering the ribosomal DNA in a megabase synthetic chromosome diag *Science* v355 no6329 p1049 Mr 10 2017

"Perfect" designer chromosome V and behavior of a ring derivative diag *Science* v355 no6329 p1046 Mr 10 2017

Synthesis, debugging, and effects of synthetic chromosome consolidation: synVI and beyond color *Science* v355 no6329 p1045 Mr 10 2017

Bader, Sam

Arthur J. Freeman *Physics Today* v69 no11 p69 N 2016

Badescu, A. M.

Observation of a large-scale anisotropy in the arrival directions of cosmic rays above 8×10^{18} eV *Science* v357 no6357 p1266 S 22 2017

BADGER, DONNA

r.s.v.p bw color *Bon Appetit* v62 no7 p12 Jl 2017

Badgers

Badger S. ELDER color *National Geographic Kids* no472 p26 Ag 2017

Badgley, Grayson

Mobile MUTE specifies subsidiary cells to build physiologically improved grass stomata bibl diag *Science* v355 no6330 p1215 Mr 17 2017

Badgley Mischka (Company)

Tailor Made M. OWENS color *Architectural Digest* v74 no7 p18 Jl 2017

Badila, Milandou

YOUNG PARIS T. Payne color *Ebony* v72 no5 p28 Mr 2017

Badlands

Theodore Roosevelt National Park R. H. MOHLENBROCK color map *Natural History* v125 no3 p42 Mr 2017

Badlands National Park (S.D.)
Colorful Wilderness *South Dakota Magazine* v33 no3 p91 S/O 2017
Where the Heart Is G. Schafel color *AARP: The Magazine* v59 no3A p86 Ap/My 2016

Bad Moms Christmas, A (Film)
ALSO PLAYING color *Entertainment Weekly* no1478 / 1479 p65 Ag 18-25 2017

Badoo (Company)
A Reputation for Badoo Behavior G. Turner, A. Satariano et al color *Bloomberg Businessweek* no4526 p30 Je 12 2017

Badu, Erykah, 1971-
ESSENCE'S GLAM GRAMMY WARM-UP R. Kinane color *Entertainment Weekly* no1454/1455 p14 F 24 2017
Sound Bites color *Entertainment Weekly* no1443 p6 D 9 2016
STILL ON & ON C. Murray color *Essence* v47 no11 p60 Mr 2017

Baduizm (Music)
STILL ON & ON C. Murray color *Essence* v47 no11 p60 Mr 2017

Bae, Brian
RNA polymerase motions during promoter melting color diag graph *Science* v356 no6340 p863 My 26 2017

Bae, Taejeong
Intersection of diverse neuronal genomes and neuropsychiatric disease: The Brain Somatic Mosaicism Network color *Science* v356 no6336 p395 Ap 28 2017

Bae, Wooli
Molecular force spectroscopy with a DNA origami–based nanoscopic force clamp bibl diag graph *Science* v354 no6310 p305 O 21 2016

Baecque, Antoine de, 1962-
Parsimonious Eye J. LEAF color *Weekly Standard* v22 no19 p38 Ja 23 2017

Baehr, Evan
7 Ways to Thank People in Your Network *Harvard Business Review Digital Articles* p2 D 1 2015
Startups Need Relationships Before They Ask for Money *Harvard Business Review Digital Articles* p2 Mr 3 2016

Baek, Jieun
The Opening of the North Korean Mind cartoon *Foreign Affairs* v96 no1 p104 Ja/F 2017

Baena, Jeff
The Little Hours D. Coggan color *Entertainment Weekly* no1473 p48 Jl 7 2017
Medieval Laughs for the Modern Day S. Zacharek color *Time* v190 no2/3 p90 Jl 10-17 2017
The Return of Nunsploitation M. ATKINSON *In These Times* v41 no6 p36 Je 2017
UNICORN ROOM A. Russell cartoon *New Yorker* v93 no19 p19 Jl 3 2017

BAER, ADAM J.
GETTING IT RIGHT *Washingtonian Magazine* v52 no4 p216 Ja 2017

Baer, Merritt
MAKING IT ON BROAD-WAY T. J. Huddleston color *Fortune* v174 no8 p75 D 15 2016

Baer, Robert B., 1952-
MINDING THE MIDDLE EAST E. PEPPERS *USA Today Magazine* v146 no2866 p32 Jl 2017

Baesens, Bart
What to Do Before You Fire a Pivotal Employee *Harvard Business Review Digital Articles* p2 Ja 29 2016

BAE Systems Maritime-Naval Ships (Company)
People tell us this is the best thing we've ever done G. NEWBERY *People Management* p22 O 2016

BAETEN, LANDER
Combining Biodiversity Resurveys across Regions to Advance Global Change Research *BioScience* v67 no1 p73 Ja 2017

Baetzel, Karen
She Helps Launch Future Leaders P. M. ESSWEIN color *Kiplinger's Personal Finance* v71 no12 p18 D 2017

BAEV, PAVEL K.
What Drives Moscow's Military Adventurism? *Current History* v115 no783 p251 O 2016

Baez, Javier
HOT | NOT T. Keith color *Sports Illustrated* v125 no14 p24 O 24-31 2016

Baez, Joan, 1941-
The Fighting Side of Joan D. BROWNE bw color *Rolling Stone* no1285 p38 Ap 20 2017
Random Notes color *Rolling Stone* no1284 p26 Ap 6 2017

Baeza, Jo
AT HOME IN THE WOODS *Arizona Highways* v96 no7 p48 Jl 2017

BAFAQUIH, A. A.
By the $ & £ We Live *Islamic Horizons* v46 no2 p47 Mr/Ap 2017
Undo the Chains *Islamic Horizons* v46 no1 p36 Ja/F 2017

Baffin Island (Nunavut)
THE BIG EMPTY A. FRANKEL color *Bike Magazine* v24 no3 p70 My 2017
ᑉᑉᕐᑢᒡ N. WALKER color map *Canadian Geographic* v137 no2 p52 Mr/Ap 2017

Bag design
Rawhide and Java L. A. Addington color *Missouri Life* v44 no2 p18 Ap 2017

Bagasao, Maria Fides F.
Why Organized Grassroots Women Matter in the Sustainable Development of Rural Communities *UN Chronicle* v53 no3 p25 2016

Bagasra, Omar
The business of doing good color *Science* v354 no6310 p294 O 21 2016

BAGBY, IHSAN
Healthy Mosques Hold the Future: ISNA teams up with ISPU to help make mosques welcoming, inclusive and dynamic *Islamic Horizons* v46 no3 p36 My/Je 2017
Our Model Mosque: Muslims have a model for shaping their institutions: the way that the Prophet nurtured his Mosque *Islamic Horizons* v46 no4 p46 Jl/Ag 2017
The Science of Giving *Islamic Horizons* v46 no2 p44 Mr/Ap 2017

Bagdasarian, Alex L.
Arylation of hydrocarbons enabled by organosilicon reagents and weakly coordinating anions diag *Science* v355 no6332 p1403 Mr 31 2017

Bagels
New Year's Bagel Fest color *Good Housekeeping* v264 no1 p113 Ja 1 2017
What'll it be FOR THE NEW YORK DINER? A. Platt and A. Schonbek img *New York* v50 no13 p30 Je 26 2017

Bagenal, Fran
Jupiter's magnetosphere and aurorae observed by the Juno spacecraft during its first polar orbits diag graph *Science* v356 no6340 p826 My 26 2017
Jupiter Rediscovered *Sky & Telescope* v134 no6 p14 D 2017

Bagg, Robert
Celebration of the World W. H. Pritchard bw *Commonweal* v114 no14 p33 S 8 2017

Bagga, Charan K.
A Simple Graph Explains the Complex Logic of the Big Beer Merger *Harvard Business Review Digital Articles* p2 O 20 2015

Baggage handling in airports
THE ULTIMATE AIRPORT OF TOMORROW J. BIEN-KAHN cartoon *Wired* v24 no12 p88 D 2016

Bagge, Peter
200,000 ALCOHOLICS CAN'T BE WRONG cartoon *Reason* v48 no10 p32 Mr 2017
FIRE!!: THE ZORA NEALE HURSTON STORY B. DOHERTY color *Reason* v49 no3 p68 Jl 2017
The Fleeting Glory of Trump Magazine color *Reason* v49 no3 p64 Jl 2017

Baggelaar, Marc P.
Activity-based protein profiling reveals off-target proteins of the FAAH inhibitor BIA 10-2474 chart color graph *Science* v356 no6342 p1084 Je 9 2017

BAGGETT, JAMES A.
COLOR crescendo color *Better Homes & Gardens* v95 no10 p95 O 2017
CUTTING EDGE color *Better Homes & Gardens* v95 no9 p84 S 2017
ENLIGHTENED LAWNS color *Better Homes & Gardens* v95 no7 p91 Jl 2017
everyday getaway color *Better Homes & Gardens* v95 no6 p77 Je 2017

garden SMART color *Better Homes & Gardens* v95 no8 p92 Ag 2017

kinder gardening color *Better Homes & Gardens* v95 no8 p98 Ag 2017

Bagieu, Pénélope

LES BELLES iMAGES *New York Times Magazine* p27 Ap 30 2017

BAGKEY, JANE

Aged Quarter Horse Geldings color *Horse & Rider* v56 no8 p51 Ag 2017

Bagla, Gunjan

3 Myths about Engineering Talent in China and India *Harvard Business Review Digital Articles* p2 D 9 2014

Doing Business in India Requires a Mobile-First Strategy *Harvard Business Review Digital Articles* p2 D 23 2016

How the U.S. and India Can Strengthen Their Business Ties *Harvard Business Review Digital Articles* p2 Ja 22 2015

How U.S. Businesses Can Succeed in India in 2015 *Harvard Business Review Digital Articles* p2 D 22 2014

Understanding the Rise of Manufacturing in India *Harvard Business Review Digital Articles* p2 S 18 2015

What U.S. CEOs Can Learn from GM's India Failure *Harvard Business Review Digital Articles* p2 Je 15 2017

Which U.S. Companies Are Doing the Most R&D in China and India? *Harvard Business Review Digital Articles* p2 Mr 26 2015

Bagley, Christopher

Above AND Crillon color *Conde Nast Traveler* v52 no8 p96 S 2017

BLOND AMBITION [Cover story] color *InStyle* v24 no2 p120 F 2017

Eye of the Teigen [Cover story] color *InStyle* v24 no11 p172 N 2017

Man of the People color *InStyle* v24 no1 p88 Ja 2017

This Year's GIRL [Cover story] color *InStyle* v24 no3 p300 Mr 2017

Bagley, Constance E.

A Board Member's Guide to Corporate Political Spending *Harvard Business Review Digital Articles* p2 O 30 2015

Bagley, Fred

Manitoulin Island color *Sail* v48 no6 p43 Je 2017

Bagley, William

READER COMMENTS *America* v216 no7 p7 Ap 3 2017

Baglione, Lisa A.

Music key to a Cold War thaw color il *America* v216 no9 p46 Ap 24 2017

Bagot, Jan

SADDLE CHAT bw color graph *Horse & Rider* v56 no9 p21 S 2017

Bagot, P. A. J.

Direct observation of individual hydrogen atoms at trapping sites in a ferritic steel bibl diag *Science* v355 no6330 p1196 Mr 17 2017

Bagot, Rosemary C.

Early life stress confers lifelong stress susceptibility in mice via ventral tegmental area OTX2 diag *Science* v356 no6343 p1185 Je 16 2017

Bagpipe

James Rivers and the 'Pipes E. Laborde *New Orleans Magazine* v51 no8 p16 Je 2017

Bagpipers

ALBERT SCHWEITZER ORGAN VS. THE MIGHTY MO T. REHAGEN *Atlanta* v57 no1 p30 My 2017

Bags

See also
   Handbags
   Plastic bags
   Pouches (Containers)

ANIMAL KINGDOM O. J. WILLIAMS color *Ebony* v72/73 no12/1 p38 O/N 2017

GEAR A. Opar *Audubon* v118 no6 p47 Wint 2016

KENDALL REYNOLDS J. BERG color *Chicago* v66 no7 p34 Jl 2017

Last Look V. SMITH color *Vogue* v207 no7 p132 Jl 2017

The LIST color *Harper's Bazaar* no3651 p197 Mr 2017

Treasure ISLAND E. ELWICK-BATES color *Vogue* v207 no7 p126 Jl 2017

WAKE-UP Call *Interview* v46 no10 p61 D 2016/Ja 2017

Bags—Evaluation

25 DAYS of Gift-mas H. Rolfe *Dance Spirit* v20 no10 p48 D 2016

BETTER THAN BESPOKE J. LLOYD and J. PARKIN color *House Beautiful* p139 Ag 2017

BLOCK PARTY color *Harper's Bazaar* no3653 p128 My 2017

The Bucket List E. Velluto color *Glamour* v115 no3 p72 Mr 2017

Bulgari/Nicholas Kirkwood Bags E. ELWICK-BATES, M. HOLGATE et al color *Vogue* v207 no9 p368 S 2017

BUSH PILOT BAG color *Flying* v144 no11 p15 N 2017

The BUY Fashion color *Harper's Bazaar* no3648 p86 N 2016

CANDYLAND color *Harper's Bazaar* no3651 p278 Mr 2017

Case closed L. BIRCH color *House Beautiful* p76 Ag 2017

A Case For Travel color *Conde Nast Traveler* v51 no10 p33 N 2016

CHAIN REACTION color *Harper's Bazaar* no3651 p277 Mr 2017

Changing the Game color *Glamour* v115 no2 p110 F 2017

code RED *Interview* v47 no5 p38 Je/Jl 2017

DINING IN STYLE WITH SARA STORY B. Mazurek and G. ANDERSON color *Harper's Bazaar* no3654 p98 Je/Jl 2017

DREAM WEAVER color *Conde Nast Traveler* v52 no6 p24 Je/Jl 2017

Dual Threats J. LEVEY *Tennis* v53 no4 p18 Jl/Ag 2017

DUTY FREE: MAKE EXTRA ROOM FOR THE SEASON'S MUST-HAVE ACCESSORIES *Interview* v47 no3 p48 Ap 2017

Emma WATSON: THE FUTURE IS TERRIFYING. THE FUTURE IS UNCERTAIN. THE FUTURE IS ... HERE. AND IF EMMA WATSON HAS ANYTHING TO SAY ABOUT IT, THE FUTURE IS GOING TO BE MAGICAL J. CHASTAIN *Interview* v47 no3 p46 My 2017

EQUIP THE KIDS K. Bastone color *Backpacker* p71 Je 2017

The Essential: Workbag J. TUNG *Martha Stewart Living* no267 p36 S 2016

EYE CANDY color *Harper's Bazaar* no3653 p127 My 2017

FABULOUS at Every Age color *Harper's Bazaar* no3648 p201 N 2016

FABULOUS at Every Age color *Harper's Bazaar* no3657 p185 O 2017

FACE-LIFT color *Harper's Bazaar* no3651 p400 Mr 2017

Fashion Masterpiece color *Glamour* v115 no7 p34 Jl 2017

FASHION UNDER $100 color *Redbook* p69 S 2017

Fendi Mini Peekaboo bag color *Vogue* v206 no12 p296 D 2016

Floaties C. Sagan color *Powder* v45 no5 p42 Ja 2017

The Get color *InStyle* v23 no12 p43 N 2016

Get the LOOK SPRINGS MUST-HAVES color *Harper's Bazaar* no3651 p271 Mr 2017

Gift Guide color *Vanity Fair* v59 no1 p68 Holiday 2017

GOLD STANDARD color *Harper's Bazaar* no3655 p70 Ag 2017

GRACE VAN PATTEN K. SMITH color *Vanity Fair* v59 no10 p89 O 2017

THE HERO N. FRITTON color *Harper's Bazaar* no3648 p74 N 2016

HIGH SCORE *Interview* v46 no8 p52 O 2016

Hip Service color *Los Angeles Magazine* v62 no10 p26 O 2017

Hood Game Strong [Cover story] color *Glamour* v114 no11 p56 N 2016

The In/Out List color *Harper's Bazaar* no3648 p116 N 2016

The In/Out LIST color *Harper's Bazaar* no3655 p62 Ag 2017

instant style color *InStyle* v24 no5 p105 My 2017

IN THE PINK A. ALAGEM color *Harper's Bazaar* no3654 p78 Je/Jl 2017

It's a Small World L. IMMEDIATO *Los Angeles Magazine* p31 Ap 2017

IT'S IN THE BAG J. Dengate color *Runner's World* v52 no2 p48 Mr 2017

THE LADY Robin Wright E. Wilson color *InStyle* v23 no13 p112 D 2016

Last Look V. SMITH color *Vogue* v207 no9 p753 S 2017

The latest word from our testers color *Backpacker* p48 Je 2017

La Vie en Rose color *Conde Nast Traveler* v52 no2 p21 F 2017

LEATHER HEADS *Cincinnati Magazine* v50 no7 p30 Ap 2017

Little Big Packs N. BOUCHARD color diag *Backpacker* p49 My 2017

Mary-Kate & Ashley Olsen E. Wilson color *InStyle* v24 no9 p187 S 2017

MAXIMUM GLAMOUR color *Harper's Bazaar* no3653 p191 My 2017

Michael Kors Collection messenger bag V. SMITH color *Vogue* v207 no3 p512 Mr 2017

Money Bags color *GQ: Gentlemen's Quarterly* v86 no11 p122 N 2016

My Style color *InStyle* v23 no13 p158 D 2016

NEW WEAVE color *Harper's Bazaar* no3653 p129 My 2017

Nothing but Bags color *Glamour* v115 no6 p130 Je 2017

Not Your Basic Bag, Man N. Silverstein color *Glamour* v115 no4 p48 Ap 2017

On Demand color *InStyle* v23 no13 p51 D 2016

on demand color *InStyle* v24 no10 p63 O 2017

on demand color *InStyle* v24 no8 p49 Ag 2017

ON-THE-GO GEAR L. BACK color *Trail Rider* v29 no3 p22 Ap 2017

Ornot Bar Bag T. Rojek color *Bicycling* v58 no4 p79 My 2017

Pack Your Bags color *Horse & Rider* v56 no11 p34 N 2017

Pack Your Bags F. Kane, S. P. Nadella et al color *Glamour* v115 no3 p206 Mr 2017

PARTY IN PINK A. B. RAYA color *Chicago* v65 no12 p54 D 2016

PEARL JAM color *Harper's Bazaar* no3655 p75 Ag 2017

PETAL PUSHERS color *Harper's Bazaar* no3655 p71 Ag 2017

PUT YOUR GEAR IN HERE color *Men's Health* v32 no2 p(Sp)11 Mr 2017

RAF SIMONS'S BRAVE NEW WORLD N. Silva-Jelly color *Harper's Bazaar* no3654 p96 Je/Jl 2017

ROOM TO MOVE color *Esquire* p56 Ap 2017

THE SCENE MAKER H. BEACHLER color *Martha Stewart Living* p54 S 2017

The SCORE color *InStyle* v23 no13 p153 D 2016

THE SEASON'S MOST DARING LOOKS color *Harper's Bazaar* no3648 p60 N 2016

SEEING GREEN M. BOBO color *Ebony* v72 no5 p40 Mr 2017

SEEING RED color *Harper's Bazaar* no3648 p252 N 2016

Shop Guide cartoon color *O, The Oprah Magazine* p138 Ap 2017

SHOP THE ISSUE bw color *Harper's Bazaar* no3648 p70 N 2016

SILVER STREAK color *Harper's Bazaar* no3655 p74 Ag 2017

Skins Game color *Esquire* v166 no5 p62 D 2016/Ja 2017

Sky's the LIMIT color *InStyle* v24 no9 p305 S 2017

Snow Business color *Log Home Living* v34 no1 p26 F 2017

SOLUTIONS A. White chart color *Horse & Rider* v56 no6 p28 Je 2017

SPEED RACER color *Harper's Bazaar* no3648 p129 N 2016

TOWN AND COUNTRY C. Dash color *Sunset* v239 no3 p32 S 2017

Treasure Hunting E. ELWICK-BATES color *Vogue* v207 no11 p120 N 2017

TROPICAL THUNDER color *Harper's Bazaar* no3648 p132 N 2016

Two Words: No. Plastic R. Spinks *Sierra* v101 no5 p12 S/O 2016

Wait LIST color *Harper's Bazaar* no3650 p74 F 2017

Wait LIST color *Harper's Bazaar* no3651 p216 Mr 2017

Wait LIST color *Harper's Bazaar* no3655 p60 Ag 2017

WATER WORLD: WHETHER YOU'RE LOUNGING POOLSIDE OR WITH THE SAND BETWEEN YOUR TOES, COME PREPARED *Cincinnati Magazine* v50 no10 p36 Jl 2017

WELCOME TO MIAMI color *Harper's Bazaar* no3654 p102 Je/Jl 2017

THE WELL-SPENT $ DOLLAR color *Harper's Bazaar* no3648 p136 N 2016

western PROMISES E. STUART *Virginia Living* v15 no2 p29 F 2017

WHAT WE LOVE color *Harper's Bazaar* no3653 p34 My 2017

WHAT WE LOVE color *Harper's Bazaar* no3655 p30 Ag 2017

WHO'S THAT GIRL? E. CIUFO bw color *Harper's Bazaar* no3648 p124 N 2016

WISH YOU WERE HERE color *Conde Nast Traveler* v52 no6 p21 Je/Jl 2017

THE WOMAN Chrissy Teigen E. Wilson color *InStyle* v23 no12 p80 N 2016

WOWZA! color *Bicycling* v58 no8 p68 S 2017

YOUR AIRPORT SECURITY UPGRADE color *Esquire* v167 no2 p148 Mr 2017

BAGSHAW, ELIZABETH A.

The Arctic in the Twenty-First Century: Changing Biogeochemical Linkages across a Paraglacial Landscape of Greenland *BioScience* v67 no2 p118 F 2017

BAHADUR, GAIUTRA

Instruments of Memory *New York Times Book Review* p10 My 28 2017

Bahai Faith

Yemen's Bahá'is keep faith amid conflict, crackdown B. Pellot color *Christian Century* v134 no1 p15 Ja 4 2017

Bahais—Persecutions

Yemen's Bahá'is keep faith amid conflict, crackdown B. Pellot color *Christian Century* v134 no1 p15 Ja 4 2017

Bahamas

16 BEST YOGA ESCAPES [Cover story] M. Rabbitt color *Yoga Journal* no290 p19 Mr 2017

Bahamas—Description & travel

island time T. DeBacco and K. Payne color *Power & Motoryacht* v34 no10 p84 O 2017

Bahbout, Scialom

Chief rabbi of Venice works for return of Jewish community J. McKenna *Christian Century* v134 no7 p15 Mr 29 2017

Bahcall, Neta A.

Vera Cooper Rubin *Physics Today* v70 no3 p73 Mr 2017

Bahl, Nikhil

3 Strategies for Flocks *Audubon* v119 no3 p49 Fall 2017

BAHLER, BRENT

BUZZWORTHY *Indianapolis Monthly* p14 N 2017

Bahler, Kristen

ASK THE EXPERT diag *Money* v46 no2 p31 Mr 2017

THE BEST PLACES FOR WORKING PARENTS color *Money* v45 no10 p21 N 2016

THE CAREER MAKEOVER ISSUE WITH Billy Eichner [Cover story] color *Money* v46 no7 p38 Ag 2017

Classes for All Classes color *Money* v46 no3 p19 Ap 2017

GET A BETTER JOB NOW color diag *Money* v46 no2 p76 Mr 2017

HOW THEY DID IT color *Money* v46 no8 p52 S 2017

How This 29-Year-Old Makes a Living as a Professional Bridesmaid color *Money* v46 no6 p10 Jl 2017

How to Be a Stealthy Job Seeker When You Know It's Time to Go color *Money* v46 no4 p17 My 2017

How to Get Back in the Game *Money* v46 no1 p31 Ja/F 2017

LinkedIn Makes It Easier to Sneak In a Job Hunt color *Money* v45 no11 p14 D 2016

SOLUTIONS TO END YOUR JOB DROUGHT *Money* v46 no6 p75 Jl 2017

UNEMPLOYMENT IS REALLY LOW color map *Money* v46 no6 p70 Jl 2017

YOUR 20 BEST MONEY MOVES FOR 2017 color diag *Money* v45 no11 p60 D 2016

BAHNSEN, DAVID

Unjust Prosecution color *National Review* v69 no17 p38 S 11 2017

Bahnson, Fred

THE PRIEST IN THE TREES *Harper's Magazine* v333 no1999 p45 D 2016

Bahr, Sarah

AHEAD OF THE CURRENT color *Indianapolis Monthly* v41 no2 p68 S 2017

Broad RIPPLE color map *Indianapolis Monthly* v41 no2 p66 S 2017

CAN YOU DIG IT? diag *Indianapolis Monthly* v41 no2 p72 S 2017

A DAM SHAME *Indianapolis Monthly* v41 no2 p64 S 2017

Delicate Subject: Bust a move to Carmel's new lingerie boutique *Indianapolis Monthly* p36 N 2017

Downtown color map *Indianapolis Monthly* v41 no2 p73 S 2017

Farther Downstream color map *Indianapolis Monthly* v41 no2 p77 S 2017

Flex Appeal: The city's newest athleisure shop pushes style to the edge *Indianapolis Monthly* v12 no40 p34 Ag 2017

GM STAMPING PLANT color map *Indianapolis Monthly* v41 no2 p75 S 2017

Hamilton COUNTY color map *Indianapolis Monthly* v41 no2 p63 S 2017

MAKING A SPLASH color *Indianapolis Monthly* v41 no2 p76

S 2017

Martin Kuntz Sculptor color *Indianapolis Monthly* v42 no2 p49 O 2017

Mounds STATE PARK color map *Indianapolis Monthly* v41 no2 p60 S 2017

New Wave color *Indianapolis Monthly* v42 no2 p31 O 2017

RACING WIENER DOGS color *Indianapolis Monthly* v42 no2 p16 O 2017

Riverside PARK color map *Indianapolis Monthly* v41 no2 p68 S 2017

SCENE STEALERS bw color *Indianapolis Monthly* v41 no2 p78 S 2017

Sprouted Corn Cavatelli color *Indianapolis Monthly* v41 no2 p46 S 2017

TOUR OF DOODY diag *Indianapolis Monthly* v41 no2 p65 S 2017

WHERE THE WILD THINGS ARE color *Indianapolis Monthly* v41 no2 p62 S 2017

THE White RIVER diag *Indianapolis Monthly* v41 no2 p59 S 2017

Bai, Li

THE LONG WAR *MHQ: Quarterly Journal of Military History* v29 no4 p89 Summ 2017

BAI, MATT

Drumbeats *New York Times Book Review* p18 N 20 2016

Bai, Xue

Bug mapping and fitness testing of chemically synthesized chromosome X diag *Science* v355 no6329 p1048 Mr 10 2017

"Perfect" designer chromosome V and behavior of a ring derivative diag *Science* v355 no6329 p1046 Mr 10 2017

Bai, Xue-Ning

Lifetime of the solar nebula constrained by meteorite paleomagnetism bibl graph *Science* v355 no6325 p623 F 10 2017

Bai Bing

Jieli Publishing House color *Publishers Weekly* v264 no12 p20 Mr 20 2017

BAIANO, ENN

ALL THAT GLITTERS... color *Dance Spirit* v20 no9 p59 N 2016

Baider, C.

Persistent effects of pre-Columbian plant domestication on Amazonian forest composition bibl chart graph map *Science* v355 no6328 p925 Mr 3 2017

Baidu Inc.

AI With Chinese Characteristics D. Ramli and A. Webb color diag *Bloomberg Businessweek* no4515 p38 Mr 20 2017

The President of Search Giant Baidu Has Global Plans T. Simonite color *MIT Technology Review* v120 no4 p52 Jl/Ag 2017

BAIER, BRET

In Some Ways, He's a Bit Like Ike bw *Weekly Standard* v22 no20 p10 Ja 30 2017

Baier, Bret—Interviews

Bret Baier J. Marksbury and C. Barrett color *Golf Magazine* v58 no11 p37 N 2016

BAIERL, KAREN

Q: Who's your trusty sidekick for summer adventures, and why? color *O, The Oprah Magazine* p14 Je 2017

Baigorri, Manuel

THE TALKING CAT AND THE PEROXIDE CORPORATION color *Bloomberg Businessweek* no4523 p54 My 22 2017

Baikal Yachts Group (Company)

Baikal 16 Cat D. HARDING JR. color *Power & Motoryacht* v33 no1 p50 Ja 2017

Bail

See also

Bail bond agents

BAIL MEANS JAIL: DEBTOR'S PRISON FOR THE UNCONVICTED Y. GUNASEKERA color *Progressive* v81 no6 p56 Ag/S 2017

BAIL OUT J. J. CLAYTON *USA Today Magazine* v145 no2858 p22 N 2016

A DOWN PAYMENT ON ENDING MASS INCARCERATION A. RICHARDS *In These Times* v41 no1 p11 Ja 2017

Time to Abolish Cash Bail A. Kim *Washington Monthly* p15 Ja/F 2017

Bail bond agents

Our Bail-Bond System Is Predatory and Destroys Families S.

Carter color *Time* v190 no2/3 p28 Jl 10-17 2017

Time to Abolish Cash Bail A. Kim *Washington Monthly* p15 Ja/F 2017

Bailer, Robert T.

Trispecific broadly neutralizing HIV antibodies mediate potent SHIV protection in macaques color graph *Science* v357 no6359 p85 O 6 2017

Bailes, Luke

NATURE LOVER J. Lovell bw color *Conde Nast Traveler* v52 no4 p54 Ap 2017

Bailes, M.

The magnetic field and turbulence of the cosmic web measured using a brilliant fast radio burst bibl chart graph *Science* v354 no6317 p1249 D 9 2016

Bailey, Anthony D.

VIRGINIA'S TOP DENTISTS *Virginia Living* v15 no5 p81 Ag 2017

Bailey, Beryl Irene

FEEDING TWO BIRDS WITH ONE WORM color *Literacy Today (2411-7862)* v34 no4 p26 Ja/F 2017

BAILEY, BLAKE

Chicago's Other Writer *New York Times Book Review* p15 N 13 2016

Lost and Found *New York Times Book Review* p22 Je 4 2017

BAILEY, BOB

Cops I've Known: A Salesmans Story *Idaho Magazine* v16 no8 p26 My 2017

Bailey, Chloe

CHLOE AND HALLE S. Cristobal color *InStyle* v24 no6 p128 Je 2017

STYLE CRUSHES Chloe & Halle S. Simon color *InStyle* v23 no12 p76 N 2016

Bailey, Chris

5 Research-Based Strategies for Overcoming Procrastination *Harvard Business Review Digital Articles* p2 O 4 2017

Bailey, Chuck

High Forest Hideout C. Johnson color *Cabin Living* p46 S 2017

High Forest Hideout C. Johnson color *Log Home Living* v34 no1 p60 F 2017

Bailey, Colin B.

Fragonard: The Heights of Drawing cartoon *New York Review of Books* v64 no2 p19 F 9 2017

Bailey, David H.

Enhancing reproducibility for computational methods bibl color *Science* v354 no6317 p1240 D 9 2016

Bailey, David J.

Value-Based Care Alone Won't Reduce Health Spending and Improve Patient Outcomes *Harvard Business Review Digital Articles* p2 Je 16 2017

Bailey, Elizabeth

Global drainage patterns and the origins of topographic relief on Earth, Mars, and Titan diag graph *Science* v356 no6339 p727 My 19 2017

Bailey, Forest

GARAGE BRANDS T. Bird color *Snowboarder* v29 no5 p28 Ja 2017

Bailey, Glenda

EDITOR'S LETTER color *Harper's Bazaar* no3648 p94 N 2016

EDITOR'S LETTER color *Harper's Bazaar* no3649 p118 D 2016/Ja 2017

EDITOR'S LETTER color *Harper's Bazaar* no3653 p78 My 2017

EDITOR'S LETTER color *Harper's Bazaar* no3655 p50 Ag 2017

EDITOR'S LETTER color *Harper's Bazaar* no3656 p182 S 2017

EDITOR'S LETTER *Harper's Bazaar* no3657 p114 O 2017

Glenda Bailey on the past and the future of Harper's Bazaar color *Harper's Bazaar* no3651 p180 Mr 2017

Packing LIST color *Harper's Bazaar* no3653 p90 My 2017

Bailey, Halle

CHLOE AND HALLE S. Cristobal color *InStyle* v24 no6 p128 Je 2017

STYLE CRUSHES Chloe & Halle S. Simon color *InStyle* v23 no12 p76 N 2016

Bailey, James R.

The Difference Between Good Leaders and Great Ones *Harvard Business Review Digital Articles* p2 S 22 2016

We Know Female CEOs Get Paid More, But We Don't Know

Why *Harvard Business Review Digital Articles* p2 Mr 13 2017
Why Leaders Don't Brag About Successfully Managing Stress *Harvard Business Review Digital Articles* p2 O 29 2014

Bailey, Jerry
   Hitting the Road color *Team Roping Journal* p75 O 2017

BAILEY, JOHN
   AMAZING GRACE bw color *Film Comment* v52 no6 p24 N/D 2016

Bailey, Justin
   CABIN art color *Cabin Living* p11 Mr 2017

Bailey, Katie
   THE PATH TO EXEMPLARY color *Literacy Today (2411-7862)* v34 no4 p34 Ja/F 2017

Bailey, Kyle
   DAN ABOUT TOWN: Party photographer Dan Swartz's monthly roundup of bashes, balls, and benefits *Washingtonian Magazine* v52 no11 p26 Ag 2017
   THE SALT LINE: Chef Kyle Bailey makes a splash right next door to Nats Park A. Limpert *Washingtonian Magazine* v52 no11 p130 Ag 2017

BAILEY, LESLIE
   Bear Necessity *Indianapolis Monthly* v40 no4 p33 D 2016
   Best New Restaurants *Indianapolis Monthly* p58 My 2017
   best of Indy *Indianapolis Monthly* v40 no4 p73 D 2016
   CHANGE the CITY *Indianapolis Monthly* p55 Ap 2017
   CUTE REBOOT *Indianapolis Monthly* p26 F 2017
   Encounter *Indianapolis Monthly* v40 no3 p24 N 2016
   A GAME TO RELISH: Pickleball finds a home at a new racquet club *Indianapolis Monthly* v40 no11 p32 Jl 2017
   Gold Standard *Indianapolis Monthly* v40 no3 p38 N 2016
   Little Bit Country *Indianapolis Monthly* p27 F 2017
   Little Darlings: A Fishers-based shop for children's clothing rental offers storybook styles at fairytale prices *Indianapolis Monthly* v40 no11 p27 Jl 2017
   THE MERINGUE GANG *Indianapolis Monthly* v40 no7 p41 Mr 2017
   My Living Room *Indianapolis Monthly* v40 no7 p33 Mr 2017
   My Studio *Indianapolis Monthly* v40 no3 p46 N 2016
   My Tiny House *Indianapolis Monthly* v40 no11 p34 Jl 2017
   NAP TOWN *Indianapolis Monthly* v40 no5 p24 Ja 2017
   Off the Wall *Indianapolis Monthly* v40 no7 p29 Mr 2017
   ON A FIRST DATE *Indianapolis Monthly* p65 F 2017
   Rock Star *Indianapolis Monthly* v40 no3 p36 N 2016
   Safe Bet *Indianapolis Monthly* v40 no10 p27 Je 2017
   SEW CUTE *Indianapolis Monthly* p28 My 2017
   SOCK IT TO ME *Indianapolis Monthly* v40 no3 p34 N 2016
   Wanted *Indianapolis Monthly* v40 no3 p33 N 2016
   Wheels Up *Indianapolis Monthly* v40 no11 p25 Jl 2017

Bailey, Linda
   Under-the-Bed Fred color *Publishers Weekly* v264 no39 p106 S 25 2017

Bailey, Lisa Powell
   All Decked Out color *Southern Living* v51 no12 p34 D 2016

Bailey, Logan R. J.
   A SUMO-ubiquitin relay recruits proteasomes to chromosome axes to regulate meiotic recombination bibl graph *Science* v355 no6323 p403 Ja 27 2017

Bailey, Nancy J.
   Learning life's lessons together color *Equus* no471 p64 D 2016

Bailey, Rick
   American English, Italian Chocolate: Small Subjects of Great Importance *Publishers Weekly* v264 no17 p77 Ap 24 2017

BAILEY, RONALD
   23ANDME.COM *Reason* v48 no8 p60 Ja 2017
   Are ROBOTS Going to Steal Our Jobs? [Cover story] bw color *Reason* v49 no3 p24 Jl 2017
   BAD NEWS: THE GOVERNMENT WANTS TO 'HELP' DRIVERLESS CAR COMPANIES bw *Reason* v48 no10 p13 Mr 2017
   Cancer Moonshot Misses the Mark color *Reason* v48 no9 p6 F 2017
   An Epidemic of Bad Epidemiology color *Reason* v49 no1 p62 My 2017
   GO AHEAD, PUT SALT ON YOUR FOOD color *Reason* v49 no4 p6 Ag/S 2017
   IT'S OK TO EDIT YOUR KIDS' GENES color *Reason* v49 no6

p6 N 2017
   THE RISE OF ATOMIC HUMANISM color *Reason* v49 no5 p6 O 2017
   STUCK bw color *Reason* v48 no8 p18 Ja 2017
   Transhumanism Is Inevitable *Reason* v48 no7 p18 D 2016
   WILL FLORIDA BAN FRACKING? color *Reason* v49 no2 p8 Je 2017

Bailey, Sarah
   The Dark Lake color *Publishers Weekly* v264 no32 p50 Ag 7 2017

Bailey, Tammy
   Dream Buddy on a Trail Ride cartoon *Horse & Rider* v56 no3 p72 Mr 2017

Bailey, Tom
   ROADKILL DAYS LEAD TO ROADKILL NIGHTS E. Scherr, E. Rood et al color *Hot Rod* v70 no1 p84 Ja 2017

Bailey, Wil
   Trapped! cartoon *Sail* v47 no12 p20 D 2016

Bailey, Xenobia
   SITElines J. Griffin color *Art in America* v104 no10 p157 N 2016

BAILLIE, HAROLD W.
   QUESTIONS AT THE END color *Commonweal* v144 no15 p2 S 22 2017

BAILLIE, JONATHAN E. M.
   An Ecoregion-Based Approach to Protecting Half the Terrestrial Realm *BioScience* v67 no6 p534 Je 2017

Baillio, Maddie
   MADDIE BAILLIO M. Snetiker color *Entertainment Weekly* no1442 p51 D 2 2016 Rebellious Special Issue

Bailouts (Finance)
   Diagnosis: Heartburn J. Cost color *Weekly Standard* v22 no47 p17 Ag 21 2017
   It's Time to Worry About Italian Debt G. Smith diag *Fortune* v176 no2 p17 Ag 1 2017

Bail—United States
   Bailing OUT: Everyone agrees that America's bail system is broken. So why is it so hard to get anything done? J. Buntin *Governing* v31 no1 p30 O 2017

BAIME, A. J.
   Friends for the Ages color *AARP: The Magazine* v60 no4A p42 Je/Jl 2017

Bain & Co. Inc.
   How to Manage a Team of All-Stars M. Mankins bw *Harvard Business Review Digital Articles* p2 Je 6 2017

Bain, Ben
   A Gold Rush in Mexico's Deadly South color *Bloomberg Businessweek* no4497 p20 O 31 2016
   SEC's Acting Chair Acts Like He Runs the Place bw *Bloomberg Businessweek* no4512 p29 F 20 2017

BAIN, ROBERT
   I CAN MAKE LEOPARDS CHANGE THEIR SPOTS *People Management* p26 O 2016

Bainbridge, Julia
   BEST NEW RESTAURANTS *Atlanta* v57 no5 p78 S 2017
   50 Best, Refreshed *Atlanta* v56 no11 p2 Mr 2017
   Abiodun Henderson *Atlanta* v57 no2 p54 Je 2017
   ALL ABOUT ANNIE *Atlanta* v57 no2 p78 Je 2017
   Andrew Young: Politician, activist, national treasure *Atlanta* v57 no3 p60 Jl 2017
   CHILL-GIVING color *Bon Appetit* v61 no11 p116 N 2016
   A Cut Above color *Bon Appetit* v61 no11 p38 N 2016
   DOG DAYS *Atlanta* v57 no1 p58 My 2017
   EL FLORIDITA #2 AT 8ARM *Atlanta* v57 no4 p38 Ag 2017
   Ford Fry: Chef and mega-restaurateur *Atlanta* v57 no5 p66 S 2017
   FRIDAY NIGHT AT THE COLONNADE *Atlanta* v57 no6 p94 O 2017
   it's not all gravy color *Bon Appetit* v61 no11 p58 N 2016
   JOE REYNOLDS *Atlanta* v57 no5 p62 S 2017
   Joseph Guay & Tara Lee *Atlanta* v57 no6 p62 O 2017
   starters color *Bon Appetit* p25 S 2017
   That Fizzy Feeling *Atlanta* v57 no6 p54 O 2017
   THE POTLIKKER PAPERS *Atlanta* v57 no1 p62 My 2017
   starters bw color diag *Bon Appetit* v62 no2 p19 Mr 2017
   Victoria Camblin *Atlanta* v57 no4 p46 Ag 2017
   What is American food? *Atlanta* v57 no6 p56 O 2017
   WORLD SALSA CHAMPIONSHIP *Atlanta* v56 no10 p26 F 2017

Bainbridge Island (Wash.)
STROLL THROUGH BAINBRIDGE D. HISLOP *Sea Magazine* v109 no4 p6 Ap 2017

Baio, Angelo
THE DISAPPEARING BACK FORTY--and Long Island's rising deer population *New York State Conservationist* v72 no2 p17 O 2017

BAIOCCHI, TALIA
On the Bubble color *Bon Appetit* v61 no12 p53 D 2016 /Jan2017

BAIR, AMY
RIGHT UNDER YOUR NOSE *USA Today Magazine* v145 no2860 p32 Ja 2017

Bair, Deirdre
SCARFACE J. A. MORONE *New York Times Book Review* p36 D 4 2016

Baird, Barbara
FIELD TEST color *Field & Stream* v122 no2 p99 Je/Jl 2017

Baird, Chad
UNSOLICITED BETA color *Climbing* no353 p18 My/Je 2017

Baird, Diora
LUCKY IN LOVE: Actress Diora Baird discovered her family's missing piece D. ANDERSON-MINSHALL *Advocate* no1093 p26 O/N 2017

Baird, Julia
When Your Paycheck Is Bigger Than His color *Glamour* v114 no12 p165 D 2016

Baird, Julia---Interviews
Victoria: The Queen S. Gutierrez *British Heritage Travel* v37 no6 p12 N/D 2016

Baird, Maria
BRINGING LESSONS TO LIFE color diag *Literacy Today (2411-7862)* v34 no3 p24 N/D 2016

Baird, Robert P.
DIFFICULT MEN color *Esquire* p38 O 2017

Baird-Daniel, Eliza
Dopamine neurons encode performance error in singing birds bibl graph *Science* v354 no6317 p1278 D 9 2016

Bairlein, Franz
Migratory birds under threat bibl diag *Science* v354 no6312 p547 N 4 2016

Bais, Babette
An interactive three-dimensional digital atlas and quantitative database of human development bibl color graph *Science* v354 no6315 paag0053-1 N 25 2016

Bait fishing
Autumn isn't just the end of summertime, it's bonus time L. Whiteley color *Cabin Living* p13 S 2017
SEASON'S EATINGS M. Modoski bw color *Field & Stream* v122 no5 p20 O 2017

Baitman, Frank
3 Health Care Trends That Don't Hinge on the ACA *Harvard Business Review Digital Articles* p2 My 25 2017

Baja California (Mexico : Peninsula)
THE CIRCUS COMES TO TOWN J. OBER color *Dirt Sports + Off-Road* v51 no7 p74 Jl 2017
TOYOTAS GO FULL MOON IN BAJA S. OCHSNER color *Dirt Sports + Off-Road* v51 no3 p58 Mr 2017

Baja California (Mexico : Peninsula)---Description & travel
Fish Tacos Were Just the Beginning K. SOLLER color map *Bon Appetit* v62 no6 p52 Je 2017
HOW TO PLAN A BETTER BASH: WHILE THE CONDITIONS FOR THE BAJA BASH ARE INEVITABLE, FACING THEM DOESN'T HAVE TO BE *Sea Magazine* v109 no5 p14 My 2017

BAJAJ, VIKAS
India Personified *New York Times Book Review* p24 N 20 2016

BAJWA, NIDA
MAD SCIENTISTS GET EVEN *In These Times* v41 no3 p11 Mr 2017

Baked products
See also
Biscuits
Bread
Cake
Crackers
Muffins

Pastry
HEART-HEALTHY CHOCOLATE CAKE L. F. Prater *Successful Farming* v115 no2 p65 F 2017
A MERRY SOUTHERN CELEBRATION color *Southern Living* v51 no12 p141 D 2016
Morning Glories J. DEMELO color diag *Bon Appetit* v61 no11 p30 N 2016
Pastries Galore J. RITZ *Los Angeles Magazine* v61 no11 p126 N 2016
Pound Cake Perfection L. Cericola color *Southern Living* v52 no5 p146 My 2017
Toffee Date Cake img *New York* p64 F 9 2017

Baked products---Evaluation
Bread WINNERS T. MALONE *Atlanta* v56 no7 p85 N 2016

Baker, Agnes
Why The Best Hospitals Are Managed by Doctors *Harvard Business Review Digital Articles* p2 D 27 2016

Baker, Annie, 1981-—Interviews
Annie BAKER: ON THE STAGE, THE PULITZER PRIZE--WINNING PLAYWRIGHT BUILDS DIORAMA-LIKE REALITIES. IN HER OWN LIFE, THINGS ARE MUCH MORE MYSTERIOUS G. GERWIG *Interview* v47 no3 p24 Ap 2017

Baker, Aryn
Boko Haram's Other Victims color *Time* v190 no2/3 p40 Jl 10-17 2017
Children of No Nation [Cover story] color map *Time* v188 no27-28 p38 D 26 2016
Icons color *Time* v189 no16/17 p122 My 1-8 2017
Next Generation Leaders color *Time* v188 no15 p41 O 17 2016
Next Generation Leaders color *Time* v190 no16/17 p74 O 23 2017
No Way Home color *Time* v189 no14 p34 Ap 17 2017
Promised Land color *Time* v190 no14 p40 O 9 2017
Salome Karwah color *Time* v189 no9 p14 Mr 13 2017
TIME's Foreign Correspondents on How the World Sees the U.S. Election *Time* v188 no16/17 p34 O 24 2016
What Man, and Climate Change, Has Wrought color *Time* v189 no11 p15 Mr 27 2017
When Home Isn't Where the Heart Is color map *Time* v189 no21 p40 Je 5 2017
When the Call Comes color map *Time* v189 no6 p32 F 20 2017

BAKER, BETH
Big Data Opens Promising Career Paths for Biologists *BioScience* v67 no1 p100 Ja 2017
Can Modern Agriculture Be Sustainable? *BioScience* v67 no4 p325 Ap 2017
Frontiers of Citizen Science *BioScience* v66 no11 p921 N 1 2016
Synthetic Biology and the Marketplace *BioScience* v67 no10 p877 O 2017

Baker, Bishard
Budda's DELIGHT L. Schnell color *Sports Illustrated* v125 no18 p50 D 5 2016

Baker, Brian
Mr. Comeback *Tennis* v52 no6 p72 N/D 2016

Baker, Brian I.
Water and food security in a changing world *Monthly Labor Review* p1 Mr 2017

Baker, Calvin
BLACK LIKE WHO? *Harper's Magazine* v334 no2002 p49 Mr 2017
Driver's Seat *New York Times Magazine* p58 O 8 2017

Baker, Cannonball, 1882-1960
CANNONBALLS DEEP P. D'ORLÉANS *Cycle World* v56 no1 p21 Ja/F 2017
Speed King: The first commissioner of NASCAR, "Cannon Ball" Baker, was already a legend in his own time C. ZEIGLER *Indianapolis Monthly* v40 no11 p19 Jl 2017

BAKER, CARRIE N.
CIVIL RIGHTS WRONGED *Ms.* v27 no3 p20 Fall 2017
Nevada Says ERA Yes!: Propelled by a record number of women lawmakers, the state becomes the 36th to ratify the Equal Rights Amendment--and the first in 40 years *Ms.* v27 no2 p8 Summ 2017

Baker, Darren J.
Cyclin A2 is an RNA binding protein that controls Mre11 mRNA translation bibl graph *Science* v353 no6307 p1549 S 30 2016
Senescent intimal foam cells are deleterious at all stages of athero-

sclerosis bibl *Science* v354 no6311 p472 O 28 2016

Baker, David
THE BIG QUESTION cartoon *Atlantic* v319 no2 p100 Mr 2017
Global analysis of protein folding using massively parallel design, synthesis, and testing color diag *Science* v357 no6347 p168 Jl 14 2017
Principles for designing proteins with cavities formed by curved β sheets bibl color graph *Science* v355 no6321 p1 Ja 13 2017
Protein structure determination using metagenome sequence data color graph *Science* v355 no6322 p294 Ja 20 2017

Baker, David J.
2020 VISION [Cover story] *Opera News* v81 no9 p22 Mr 2017
Gluck: Iphigénie en Tauride *Opera News* v81 no7 p49 Ja 2017
Meyerbeer: Dinorah *Opera News* v81 no5 p58 N 2016
Mussorgsky: Boris Godunov *Opera News* v81 no7 p46 Ja 2017
Pesacov: The Edge of Forever *Opera News* v81 no5 p55 N 2016

Baker, Deren
Getting More-Granular Data on Customer Journeys *Harvard Business Review Digital Articles* p2 Je 8 2016

Baker, Edith S.
Analyzing OMB classification of regions: three case studies *Monthly Labor Review* p1 N 2016
Is there age discrimination in hiring? *Monthly Labor Review* p1 Ap 2017

Baker, Emily G.
How do miniproteins fold? diag *Science* v357 no6347 p133 Jl 14 2017

Baker, Frank
Fire on the Water: A newly discovered account of the biggest explosion of the pre-nuclear era surfaces after 100 years M. Wortman *Smithsonian* v48 no5 p15 S 2017

Baker, Gilbert
Gilbert Baker M. Vella color *Time* v189 no14 p15 Ap 17 2017

Baker, Grant, 1973-
SOUTH AFRICA color *Surfer* v57 no12 p94 Ja/F 2017

Baker, Holly
Setting the Table for a Successful Summer at South Burlington Recreation and Parks *Parks & Recreation* v51 no12 p28 D 2016

BAKER, HUNTER
What to Do When the World Goes Crazy color *Christianity Today* v61 no5 p68 Je 2017

Baker, Jeff
USUALLY color *Snowboarder* v29 no5 p12 Ja 2017

Baker, Jennifer L.
NATIVE ROSES ARE FOR THE BIRDS color *Cabin Living* p9 Ag 2017

Baker, Jessica
WHERE ARE YOU GOING? color *O, The Oprah Magazine* p126 F 2017

Baker, Josephine, 1906-1975
FKA twigs L. Robinson color *Vanity Fair* v58 no12 p88 D 2016

Baker, Joy
PORTRAIT OF A Country Doctor J. R. MARQUEZ *Atlanta* v57 no3 p80 Jl 2017

Baker, Julien, 1995-
Julien Baker M. Rich color *Current Biography* v77 no11 p17 N 2016

Baker, Kenny
KENNY BAKER A. Daniels color *Entertainment Weekly* no1446/1447 p91 D 2016/Ja 2017

BAKER, KEVIN
BLUEXIT il *New Republic* v248 no4 p18 Ap 2017
The Plot in America: Two brothers fleeing their Irish captivities get embroiled in a wild assassination plot at the 1939 World's Fair in New York *New York Times Book Review* p15 S 17 2017
THANKS TRUMP! [Cover story] color *New Republic* v247 no12 p16 D 2016
TRAIL OF FEARS color *New Republic* v248 no7 p18 Jl 2017

Baker, Mairead
A placental growth factor is silenced in mouse embryos by the zinc finger protein ZFP568 color graph *Science* v356 no6339 p757 My 19 2017

Baker, Mount (Wash.)
There's Something in the Snow at Mount Baker H. Hansman color *Powder* v46 no2 p33 O 2017

Baker, Nicholson, 1957-

EVERYTHING IS INTERESTING E. KINDLEY color il *Nation* v303 no16 p27 O 17 2016
Mr. Nick Baker Teaches Today—Listen W. Finnegan color *New York Review of Books* v64 no5 p31 Mr 23 2017
Pedagogy of the Distracted M. S. Thomas bw *Commonweal* v144 no7 p32 Ap 14 2017

Baker, Nick
A China Moonshot for Chicago's Exchange *Bloomberg Businessweek* no4514 p40 Mr 13 2017

Baker, Noelle A.
Mary Moody Emerson Was a Scholar, a Thinker, and an Inspiration *Humanities* v38 no1 p1 Wint 2017

Baker, Peter
NYT, Reviewing Trump's '100 Days,' Shows Folly of 'Both Sides' Journalism A. Johnson *Extra!* v30 no5 p1 Je 2017
Yes He Did *New York Times Book Review* p9 Ja 22 2017

Baker, Peter C.
CPR Training *New York Times Magazine* p26 S 10 2017

Baker, Regan
In the Western HOME color *Sunset* v237 no6 p44 D 2016

Baker, Robert
Around the Campfire color *Trail Rider* v29 no1 p6 Ja/F 2017

BAKER, ROBERT J.
Transformational Principles for NEON Sampling of Mammalian Parasites and Pathogens: A Response to Springer and Colleagues *BioScience* v66 no11 p917 N 1 2016

Baker, Roberta
A meal for many color *U.S. Catholic* v82 no6 p5 Je 2017

BAKER, SANDRA E.
Some Animals Are More Equal than Others: Wild Animal Welfare in the Media *BioScience* v67 no1 p62 Ja 2017

Baker, Sean
The Florida Project C. DA COSTA color *Film Comment* v53 no5 p72 S/O 2017
A Slice of Childhood Heaven In the Sunshine State S. Zacharek color *Time* v190 no15 p56 O 16 2017

Baker, Sophie
A survivor's story color map *Equus* no476 p29 My 2017

Baker, Stephanie
THE BEST YARD SALE color *Bloomberg Businessweek* no4501 p22 N 28 2016
Bring on the lawyers color *Bloomberg Businessweek* no4496 p16 O 24 2016
Cambridge Analytica's Low-Tech Fisticuffs color *Bloomberg Businessweek* no4516 p23 Mr 27 2017
The Loophole Under The Mountain color *Bloomberg Businessweek* no4493 p48 O 3 2016
SECRET FORMULA cartoon color graph *Bloomberg Businessweek* no4501 p18 N 28 2016
Until Donald Trump, U.S. presidents and vice presidents went to extremes to avoid conflicts of interest... real or apparent bw color *Bloomberg Businessweek* no4503 p22 D 12 2016
Who'll Pay to Protect Trump's Towers? *Bloomberg Businessweek* no4503 p35 D 12 2016

BAKER, SUSAN C.
Assessing National Biodiversity Trends for Rocky and Coral Reefs through the Integration of Citizen Science and Scientific Monitoring Programs *BioScience* v67 no2 p134 F 2017

Baker, T. R.
Persistent effects of pre-Columbian plant domestication on Amazonian forest composition bibl chart graph map *Science* v355 no6328 p925 Mr 3 2017

Baker, Terry
Boxed in B. DAVIES bw *Walrus* p16 Ja\F 2017

Baker, Thomas
An Ordinary Sunday [Cover story] color *Commonweal* v144 no15 p11 S 22 2017
The Perils of Apartness color *Commonweal* v144 no3 p23 F 10 2017

Baker, Virginia Gordy
REMEMBERING PEARL HARBOR *Saturday Evening Post* v288 no6 p6 N/D 2016

Baker, Wayne
5 Ways to Get Better at Asking for Help *Harvard Business Review Digital Articles* p2 D 18 2014

Baker, Yolanda

Baking powder
  LOVE AT FIRST BITE S. CAREY color *Martha Stewart Living* p76 S 2017

Baking—Equipment & supplies
  Baker's Choice A. MASON color *Bon Appetit* v61 no11 p23 N 2016
  SL cooking school K. Hammonds color *Southern Living* v51 no12 p230 D 2016

Baking—Study & teaching
  Eleven Things You're Likely to Do Poorly (But Love Anyway) L. SCHWARTZBERG img *New York* v49 no23 p66 N 14 2016

Bakken, Russell R.
  A "Trojan horse" bispecific-antibody strategy for broad protection against ebolaviruses bibl graph *Science* v354 no6310 p350 O 21 2016

Bakker, Gary
  Fate *Skeptical Inquirer* v41 no1 p62 Ja/F 2017

Bakker, Michiel
  How Google Optimized Healthy Office Snacks *Harvard Business Review Digital Articles* p2 Mr 3 2016

Bakkeren, Erik
  Inflammation boosts bacteriophage transfer between Salmonella spp bibl diag *Science* v355 no6330 p1211 Mr 17 2017

Bakopoulos, Dean
  The Ancient Minstrel *Orion Magazine* v35 no4/5 p109 Jl-O 2016

Bakr, Osman M.
  Powering up perovskite photoresponse bibl color *Science* v355 no6331 p1260 Mr 24 2017

Bakr, Waseem S.
  Spin-imbalance in a 2D Fermi-Hubbard system diag graph *Science* v357 no6358 p1385 S 29 2017

BAKSHIAN, ARAM, JR.
  The Builder's Art *Weekly Standard* v22 no6 p36 O 17 2016
  The 'Golden Age' Myth of Spain's Muslim Era il *American Conservative* v16 no4 p57 Jl/Ag 2017
  Honor and Glory color *Weekly Standard* v22 no16 p33 D 26 2016

Bakula, Scott
  NCIS: NEW ORLEANS *TV Guide* v65 no39 p41 S 18 2017

Balaban, Nathalie Q.
  Antibiotic tolerance facilitates the evolution of resistance bibl bw chart diag graph *Science* v355 no6327 p826 F 24 2017

Balaceanu, A.
  Observation of a large-scale anisotropy in the arrival directions of cosmic rays above 8 × 1018 eV *Science* v357 no6357 p1266 S 22 2017

Balagov, Kantemir
  Blood Ties N. Rapold color *Film Comment* v53 no4 p8 Jl/Ag 2017

Balaji, V.
  Eutrophication will increase during the 21st century as a result of precipitation changes map *Science* v357 no6349 p405 Jl 28 2017

Balance of power
  The China Challenge Z. KHALILZAD *American Conservative* v16 no3 p32 My/Je 2017
  The Rebalance and Asia-Pacific Security A. Carter color *Foreign Affairs* v95 no6 p65 N/D 2016
  Should America Retrench? H. Brands and P. Feaver *Foreign Affairs* v95 no6 p164 N/D 2016
  World Elections: Races to Watch T. John color *Time* v188 no27-28 p63 D 26 2016
  YOU SAY SLOVAKIA L. Mirani cartoon *New Yorker* v93 no15 p16 My 29 2017

Balance of power—History
  Mearsheimer and Walt Reply *Foreign Affairs* v95 no6 p169 N/D 2016

Balanchine, George, 1904-1983
  Lost and Found J. Acocella bw *New Yorker* v93 no13 p14 My 15 2017

Balancing machines
  To activate your core and maintain your balance.... J. Rentz color *Dressage Today* v24 no1 p72 O 2017

Balandin, Taras
  Mechanism of transmembrane signaling by sensor histidine kinases color *Science* v356 no6342 p1043 Je 9 2017

Balani, Neil
  Party Animals F. SUN *Atlanta* v56 no7 p47 N 2016

Balassa, Gisela
  keeping it local *Better Homes & Gardens* v94 no11 p20 N 2016

Balasubramanian, Suganthi
  Distribution and clinical impact of functional variants in 50,726 whole-exome sequences from the DiscovEHR study chart graph *Science* v354 no6319 paaf6814-1 D 23 2016

BALAZO, TERRANCE
  The Quiz color *Maclean's* v129 no51/52 p72 D 26 2016
  The Quiz color *Maclean's* v130 no3 p71 Ap 2017
  The Quiz *Maclean's* v130 no10 p126 N 2017
  The Quiz *Maclean's* v130 no4 p72 My 2017

Balch, Stephen
  The Anti-Axial Age *Society* v54 no4 p346 Ag 2017
  For a Concert of Powers *American Conservative* v15 no6 p23 N/D 2016

Balconies
  BALCONY POLITICS B. Freed *Washingtonian Magazine* v52 no9 p51 Je 2017
  RACCON SCALES BUILDING S. Schwartz *National Geographic Kids* no467 p12 F 2017
  ROOM WITH A VIEW A. TAMBURRINI color *Conde Nast Traveler* v52 no10 p142 N 2017

Bald eagle
  do you know your eagles? M. Furtman color *Cabin Living* p9 D 2016
  Ospreys E. Balli *Arizona Highways* v96 no7 p13 Jl 2017

Bald eagle—Behavior
  THE BALD EAGLES OF BESNARD LAKE N. WALKER color *Canadian Geographic* v137 no5 p63 S/O 2017

Balda, Kyle
  DESPICABLE ME 3 M. Snetiker color *Entertainment Weekly* no1463/1464 p44 Ap/My 2017

Baldacci, David
  DAVID BALDACCI color *Entertainment Weekly* no1442 p61 D 2 2016 Rebellious Special Issue

Baldassarre, Leonardo
  GE's Real-Time Performance Development *Harvard Business Review Digital Articles* p2 Ag 12 2015

Baldet, Amber
  Amber Baldet M. Leising color *Bloomberg Businessweek* no4536 p72 S 4 2017

Baldi, Germán
  Forest conservation: Remember Gran Chaco bibl color *Science* v355 no6324 p465 F 3 2017

BALDINI, ELLYN
  RISK MANAGEMENT *Psychology Today* v50 no4 p6 Ag 2017

Baldness
  Bald Is Beautiful! A. SIMMONS color *Reader's Digest* v190 no1133 p11 S 2017
  My Hair, Lost & Found Again D. Pai color *Glamour* v115 no9 p104 S 2017

Baldness in animals
  What Causes a Thin Mane and Tail? [Cover story] K. DELPH *Horse & Rider* v56 no1 p14 Ja 2017

Baldness—Diagnosis
  My Immune System Attacked My Hair M. Kita and R. McCall color *Health* v31 no2 p91 Mr 2017

Baldness—Genetic aspects
  Baldness: The Final Frontier L. SOROKANICH color *Popular Mechanics* p26 Ap 2017
  My Immune System Attacked My Hair M. Kita and R. McCall color *Health* v31 no2 p91 Mr 2017

Baldness—Prevention
  Problem Solved! R. LALIBERTE color *Prevention* v68 no12 p22 D 2016

Baldness—Psychological aspects
  LOSING IT P. Rao color *Women's Health* v14 no2 p43 Mr 2017

Baldness—Treatment
  Baldness: The Final Frontier L. SOROKANICH color *Popular Mechanics* p26 Ap 2017

Baldoli, Claudia
  Europe at war and between the wars *History Today* v66 no10 p62 O 2016

Baldoni, Daniel
  Branch-specific plasticity of a bifunctional dopamine circuit encodes protein hunger graph *Science* v356 no6337 p534 My 5

2017
Baldoni, Justin
My Obsessions... *TV Guide* v65 no4 p8 Ja 16 2017
Baldridge, Mark—Interviews
Light Fantastic J. Arginteanu color *American Craft* v77 no2 p52 Ap/My 2017
BALDWIN, ALEC
Prince of the City color *Vanity Fair* v59 no5 p104 Ap 2017
Baldwin, Alec, 1958-
58 MINUTES WITH...: Alec Baldwin: Swanning through the Hamptons with the presidential impersonator J. PRESSLER *New York* v50 no16 p24 Ag 7 2017
Alec BALDWIN: "I WANTED TO BECOME PRESIDENT OF THE UNITED STATES. I REALLY DID. THE OLDER I GET, THE LESS PREPOSTEROUS THE IDEA SEEMS" *Interview* v47 no3 p112 Ap 2017
Sound Bites color *Entertainment Weekly* no1435 p6 O 14 2016
Baldwin, Andrew J.
Posttranslational mutagenesis: A chemical strategy for exploring protein side-chain diversity diag *Science* v354 no6312 p597 N 4 2016
Baldwin, Doug
Leading Off color *Sports Illustrated* v126 no2 p6 Ja 16 2017
Baldwin, Doug—Interviews
Beyond Words L. J. Wertheim and T. Keith color *Sports Illustrated* v125 no12 p16 O 10 2016
Baldwin, Doug—Political & social views
... And Now What? G. Bishop and B. Baskin color *Sports Illustrated* v125 no20 p64 D 19 2016
Baldwin, Frank
HEARTS AND MINDS IN MINDANAO [Cover story] P. Maggioni bw color map *Military History* v34 no4 p48 N 2017
Baldwin, Hailey, 1996-
In Check E. Wilson color *InStyle* v24 no9 p178 S 2017
So What Do You Do, HAILEY BALDWIN? color *InStyle* v24 no6 p90 Je 2017
With the BAND color *Vogue* v207 no7 p48 Jl 2017
Baldwin, Hilaria
NON-STOP Hilaria F. Penn color *InStyle* v24 no1 p58 Ja 2017
Baldwin, James, 1924-1987
1959: Paris J. Baldwin *Lapham's Quarterly* v10 no1 p136 Wint 2017
HEDGE OF ALLEGIANCE J. Baldwin *Lapham's Quarterly* v10 no3 p161 Summ 2017
HUMANIST PROFILE *Humanist* v77 no2 p1 Mr/Ap 2017
More Notes of a Native Son S. Zacharek color *Time* v189 no7/8 p109 F 27 2017
THE RETURN OF JAMES BALDWIN R. A. Schroth bw color *America* v216 no9 p8 Ap 24 2017
White moral infantilism and some help avoiding it color *Christian Century* v134 no8 p1 Ap 12 2017
BALDWIN, JOAQUIN
Guardian of the Blood Moon *American Forests* v123 no3 p48 Fall 2017
Baldwin, Kate
The Paradox of Traditional Chiefs in Democratic Africa N. van de Walle *Foreign Affairs* v96 no1 p179 Ja/F 2017
Baldwin, Melinda
IN REFEREES WE TRUST? *Physics Today* v70 no2 p44 F 2017
In the digital age, physics students and professors prefer paper textbooks: Whether electronic textbooks become more popular may depend on making them more interactive and user-friendly *Physics Today* v70 no8 p30 Ag 2017
Peer review as conflict P. T. Williams *Physics Today* v70 no10 p17 O 2017
Baldwin, Richard
SENDING JOBS OVERSEAS C. Caldwell *Claremont Review of Books* v17 no2 p20 Spr 2017
BALDWIN, ROSECRANS
PEAK FEDERER [Cover story] bw color *GQ: Gentlemen's Quarterly* v97 no4 p82 Ap 2017
Baldwin, Ryan
Creating Custom Furniture from SALVAGED WOOD: Bootstrap business Baldwin Custom Woodworking transforms diseased trees into nandmade heirloom woodworks K. Roberts *Mother Earth News* no282 p66 Je/Jl 2017

Baldwin, Stephen
DREAM WEAVER color *Fortune* v176 no3 p74 S 1 2017
FORTY UNDER FORTY 2017 color *Fortune* v176 no3 p62 S 1 2017
THE INVISIBLE SELLING MACHINE color *Fortune* v175 no4 p162 Mr 15 2017
MINING COMEDY GOLD color *Fortune* v176 no3 p70 S 1 2017
YOUTH REVOLT color *Fortune* v176 no3 p64 S 1 2017
BALDWIN, WILLIAM
Amazon Woman color *Forbes* v200 no4 p52 O 24 2017
Are You Betting Too Big on Trump? chart color graph *Forbes* v199 no2 p90 F 28 2017
DON'T MESS WITH TAXES color *Forbes* v200 no3 p74 S 28 2017
AN ETF TAX HUSTLE color *Forbes* v198 no6 p67 N 8 2016
Game of Porcelain Thrones color *Forbes* v200 no2 p37 S 5 2017
Gold Is for Cranks? Not So Fast chart color *Forbes* v199 no7 p128 Je 29 2017
Green Gas color *Forbes* v199 no2 p50 F 28 2017
Hide Cash From the IRS—Legally diag *Forbes* v199 no2 p94 F 28 2017
How the West Was Won color *Forbes* v199 no6 p44 Je 13 2017
INFLATION PLAY chart color graph *Forbes* v198 no9 p88 D 30 2016
Make Poughkeepsie Great Again color *Forbes* v199 no5 p40 My 16 2017
Protect Yourself From Ugly Currencies chart color graph *Forbes* v199 no1 p62 Ja 24 2017
This Man Will Purify Your Portfolio chart color *Forbes* v199 no4 p62 Ap 25 2017
TRUMP THE IRS [Cover story] color graph *Forbes* v198 no9 p90 D 30 2016
When Paper Beats Cash color *Forbes* v199 no7 p142 Je 29 2017
YOUR ETF, YOUR LIBERATOR *Forbes* v198 no8 p65 D 20 2016
Baldwinsville (N.Y.)
Delayed Gratification J. Berube and D. Berube color *Arts & Crafts Homes & the Revival* v12 no5 p18 Wint 2018
Baldy, Mount (Ariz.)
MOUNT BALDY CROSSOVER TRAIL Although it's overshadowed by its celebrated neighbors, the Mount Baldy Crossover Trail is the epitome of a gorgeous walk in the woods R. STIEVE *Arizona Highways* v93 no6 p54 Je 2017
Bale, Christian, 1974-
Is This Thing On? C. Collis color *Entertainment Weekly* no1436/1437 p15 O 21 2016
BALE, MIRIAM
Mad as Hell il *New Republic* v247 no11 p48 N 2016
BALE, RACHAEL
A SEA'S FADING BOUNTY color map *National Geographic* v231 no3 p74 Mr 2017
Baleen whales
Fossil whale hints at baleen makeover L. HAMERS color *Science News* v191 no11 p12 Je 10 2017
Origin of Baleen N. Wilson color *Natural History* v125 no10 p6 O 2017
Balenciaga, Cristóbal, 1895-1972
CRISTOBAL CRAZE bw *Harper's Bazaar* no3653 p82 My 2017
Balenciaga SA
Cameos on the Catwalk K. Samuelson color *Time* v190 no15 p12 O 16 2017
Last Look V. SMITH color *Vogue* v207 no7 p132 Jl 2017
STRATEGIST img *New York* v50 no16 p87 Ag 7 2017
Bales, Roger
Making SDGs Work for Climate Change Hotspots bibl *Environment* v58 no6 p24 N/D 2016
Balestier, Courtney
The Other Charleston color *Southern Living* v52 no10 p67 O 2017
Balestrini, Nanni—Interviews
NANNI BALESTRINI il *Nation* v303 no23/24 p5 D 5 2016
Balf, Todd
THE WAY BACK color *Yankee* v80 no6 p124 N/D 2016
Balfe, Caitriona, 1979-
OUTLANDER L. Rice color *Entertainment Weekly* p22 Jl 24 2017
Outlander's Claire Moves On K. Hahn color *TV Guide* v65 no7

p13 F 13 2017

Balfe, Caitriona, 1979——Interviews

Out of the Highlands: Outlander stars Sam Heughan and Caitriona Balfe and writer Matthew B. Roberts on season three, post-Culloden Scotland and the resilient, far-reaching Scots culture S. Gutierrez color *British Heritage Travel* v38 no5 p42 S/O 2017

Balfour, Amy C.

Kindness of Strangers *Sierra* v101 no4 p15 Jl/Ag 2016

BALIN, SUSANNAH

Beyond Inspiration color *Publishers Weekly* v264 no27 p80 Jl 3 2017

Balis, Janet

3 Strategic Questions the Media Industry's Future Depends On *Harvard Business Review Digital Articles* p2 O 5 2015

What an OTT Future Means for Brands *Harvard Business Review Digital Articles* p2 My 13 2015

What Sesame Street's Move to HBO Says About the Media Business *Harvard Business Review Digital Articles* p2 Ag 20 2015

Balistidae

Color Coded cartoon *National Geographic Kids* no470 p28 My 2017

Balk, Steven P.

Reprogramming to resist bibl diag *Science* v355 no6320 p29 Ja 6 2017

Balkan Peninsula—Economic conditions—21st century

All Quiet on the Balkan Front? N. M. Naimark and A. Matovski *Hoover Digest: Research & Opinion on Public Policy* no1 p120 Wint 2017

Balke, Jon

JON BALKE J. Ephland bw *Downbeat* v84 no4 p24 Ap 2017

Ball, Bethany

What to Do About the Solomons *Publishers Weekly* v264 no6 p40 F 6 2017

BALL, DAVE

HOW TO MAKE ANYTHING [Cover story] color diag *Popular Mechanics* p56 S 2017

Ball, Don

Build: DISPATCHER AND OPERATOR DESKS [Cover story] color diag *Model Railroader* v84 no10 p45 O 2017

Ball, Edward

At Last, a Black History Museum bw color *New York Review of Books* v63 no18 p14 N 24 2016

The Mind of Dylann Roof color *New York Review of Books* v64 no5 p12 Mr 23 2017

United States v. Dylann Roof color *New York Review of Books* v64 no4 p4 Mr 9 2017

Ball, Eldon

Productivity Growth Is Still the Major Driver in Growing U.S. Agricultural Output *Amber Waves: The Economics of Food, Farming, Natural Resources, & Rural America* p5 S 2016

Ball, George

Points to Ponder color *Reader's Digest* v189 no1130 p31 My 2017

Ball, Hugo

1916: Zurich H. Ball *Lapham's Quarterly* v10 no2 p110 Spr 2017

Ball, Jeffrey

THE BEST ENERGY REVOLUTION MONEY CAN BUY color diag map *Fortune* v175 no4 p172 Mr 15 2017

Trump and Tillerson: Conflict Ahead? color *Fortune* v75 no1 p20 Ja 1 2017

BALL, JOSEPH

CALL OF THE WILD: No need for camo. Catch these beasts at your local butcher shop *Indianapolis Monthly* v12 no40 p75 Ag 2017

HERB APPEAL *Indianapolis Monthly* v12 no40 p66 Ag 2017

The HOOSIER KITCHEN *Indianapolis Monthly* v12 no40 p60 Ag 2017

Q+A *Indianapolis Monthly* p46 My 2017

Speed Read *Indianapolis Monthly* p18 N 2017

TOP PICKS *Indianapolis Monthly* v12 no40 p62 Ag 2017

TUDOR 101 color *Indianapolis Monthly* v42 no2 p32 O 2017

Ball, Krystal

Is It Safe to Talk Politics Yet? bw color *Glamour* v115 no2 p77 F 2017

Ball, LaVar

The Ballsiest Father in America Z. BARON bw color *GQ: Gentle-*

men's Quarterly v97 no7 p24 Jl 2017

Flashback D. Kahn and T. Keith color *Sports Illustrated* v126 no18 p12 Je 26 2017

BALL, LIANNE C.

Overcoming Challenges to the Recovery of Declining Amphibian Populations in the United States *BioScience* v67 no2 p156 F 2017

Ball, Lonzo

Fun & Gun L. Jenkins color *Sports Illustrated* v126 no3 p44 Ja 23 2017

HERE WE GO, 'ZO B. Hamilton color *Sports Illustrated* v125 no13 p42 O 17 2016

One-Man Shoe M. Rosenberg color *Sports Illustrated* v126 no14 p112 My 15-22 2017

Ball, Lucille, 1911-1989

Lily at Large H. HALTERMAN *TV Guide* v65 no4 p6 Ja 16 2017

Ball, Margo

CONFORMATION CLINIC color *Horse & Rider* v55 no12 p33 D 2016

BALL, MOLLY

The Doomsayer cartoon *Atlantic* v318 no4 p24 N 2016

KELLYANNE'S ALTERNATIVE UNIVERSE color *Atlantic* v319 no3 p44 Ap 2017

Save It for the Car: To succeed as a senator, Al Franken had to suppress his sense of humor. Until now *New York Times Book Review* p10 Je 11 2017

Ball, Sarah

BECKHAM THE YOUNGER color *GQ: Gentlemen's Quarterly* v97 no9 p160 S 2017

THE BREAK-OUTS 2016 color *GQ: Gentlemen's Quarterly* v86 no12 p198 D 2016

the LOONY TUNES of FATHER JOHN MISTY color *GQ: Gentlemen's Quarterly* v97 no6 p136 Je 2017

OFF the BEATEN PATH color *GQ: Gentlemen's Quarterly* v97 no9 p154 S 2017

Ball bearings

Bearings, blocks, and more D. Everitt color *Sail* v48 no8 p62 Ag 2017

Ball games

See also

Football

Golf

Hurling (Game)

Quidditch (Game)

Table tennis

Volleyball

How to Play Like You Practice A. Fox *Tennis* v53 no3 p10 My/Je 2017

Pickleballed L. TANNER *Idaho Magazine* v16 no5 p6 F 2017

Quidditch for Muggles R. Kinane color *Entertainment Weekly* no1476 p20 Ag 4 2017

Whole New Ballgame T. PERROTTA color *Weekly Standard* v23 no6 p44 O 16 2017

BALLA, LESLEY

Cookie Town *Los Angeles Magazine* v61 no11 p130 N 2016

Meet Me in Vegas color *Bon Appetit* v62 no4 p24 Ap 2017

Stirring The Pot *Los Angeles Magazine* p62 Mr 2017

Ballabio, Andrea

Transcriptional activation of RagD GTPase controls mTORC1 and promotes cancer growth diag *Science* v356 no6343 p1188 Je 16 2017

Ballad of the Landlord (Poem : Hughes)

1933: Harlem L. Hughes *Lapham's Quarterly* v10 no1 p168 Wint 2017

Ballandras-Colas, Allison

A supramolecular assembly mediates lentiviral DNA integration bibl color *Science* v355 no6320 p1 Ja 6 2017

Ballard, Chris

AFTER THE PROCESS chart color *Sports Illustrated* v125 no18 p54 D 5 2016

BRING US TOGETHER color *Sports Illustrated* v127 no10 p28 O 2 2017

IN THE MIDDLE color *Sports Illustrated* v126 no5 p100 F 13 2017

NO COACH, NO PROBLEM color *Sports Illustrated* v126 no15 p28 My 29 2017

THE PLIGHT OF PUERTO RICO color *Sports Illustrated* v127 no11 p56 O 9 2017

Seven for The Road color *Sports Illustrated* v125 no20 p122 D 19 2016

WILD MAN OF A CERTAIN AGE color *Sports Illustrated* v127 no10 p48 O 2 2017

YOU CAN'T GIVE IN color *Sports Illustrated* v126 no10 p70 Ap 10 2017

Ballard, David W.

Navigating Political Talk at Work color graph *Harvard Business Review Digital Articles* p2 Mr 2 2017

Ballard, Izzy

Alaska Virgin Air *Publishers Weekly* v264 no6 p44 F 6 2017

Ballard, Robert D., 1942-

Robert Ballard M. B. GRIGGS cartoon *Popular Science* p50 Ja/F 2017

Ballard, Thea

Bridget Donahue color *Art in America* v105 no6 p137 Je/Jl 2017

KEN OKIISHI color *Art in America* v105 no4 p113 Ap 2017

ROSEMARY MAYER color *Art in America* v105 no3 p130 Mr 2017

Ballast (Ships)—Maintenance & repair

Finish the Job D. Thompson *Boating World* v37 no9 p14 N/D 2016

Ballatore, C. K.

America's First Nation *History Today* v67 no4 p51 Ap 2017

BALLEN, CISSY J.

Longitudinal Analysis of a Diversity Support Program in Biology: A National Call for Further Assessment *BioScience* v67 no4 p367 Ap 2017

Ballentine, Claire

The Everyman Ride For the Upper Half bw *Bloomberg Businessweek* no4533 p14 Ag 7 2017

Ballentine, Ella

Anne of Green Gables J. Russell *TV Guide* v64 no48 p36 N 21 2016

Ballerinas

advice for dancers L. HAMILTON *Dance Magazine* v91 no6 p24 Je 2017

Carla Körbes G. BERARDI *Dance Magazine* v91 no1 p44 Ja 2017

Coached by Gelsey A. BRANDT *Dance Magazine* v91 no1 p134 Ja 2017

THE DIRT with Nicole Ciapponi C. Bowers *Dance Spirit* v20 no10 p20 D 2016

Greta HODGKINSON C. Bowers color *Dance Spirit* v21 no1 p28 Ja 2017

Living That #BalletLife M. Fuhrer *Dance Spirit* v21 no7 p88 S 2017

ON POINTE *Los Angeles Magazine* p148 Ap 2017

Paloma Herrera M. HARSS *Dance Magazine* v91 no6 p20 Je 2017

THE REBIRTH OF DAVID HALLBERG C. THOMPSON *Dance Magazine* v91 no6 p26 Je 2017

Shelby Colona G. M. GARRETT *Dance Magazine* v91 no10 p22 O 2017

Tate TALK M. McNamara color *Dance Spirit* v21 no4 p30 Ap 2017

TILER PECK M. Harss *Dance Magazine* v90 no12 p47 D 2016

Ballerinas—Interviews

PEG + CAT M. LOGAN cartoon color *TV Guide* v64 no42 p46 O 10 2016

This Is What a Beauty Icon Looks Like Y. Chu color *Glamour* v115 no10 p87 O 2017

Ballerinas—Training of

Isabella LaFreniere G. KOURLAS *Dance Magazine* v91 no6 p22 Je 2017

Ballerini, Kelsea

Kelsea Ballerini J. Johnson color *Current Biography* v78 no5 p8 My 2017

KELSEA BALLERINI M. Vain *Entertainment Weekly* no1446/1447 p76 D 2016/Ja 2017

Ballerini, Laura

Nanomaterials for stimulating nerve growth color *Science* v356 no6342 p1010 Je 9 2017

Ballers (TV program)

Steve Guttenberg Joins Ballers I. Ratledge *TV Guide* v65 no25 p8 Je 2017

BALLESTA, LAURENT

THE BEAUTY BELOW THE ICE color *National Geographic* v232 no1 p50 Jl 2017

Ballesteros, Carlos

First, Sheriff Joe. Next, President Trump *In These Times* v41 no3 p32 Mr 2017

THE NEW SANCTUARY MOVEMENT [Cover story] *In These Times* v41 no6 p16 Je 2017

Ballesteros, Mithra

Finder Not Keeper D. DANIEL color *American Craft* v77 no2 p14 Ap/My 2017

Ballet

2017 Dance Annual Directory *Dance Magazine* v91 no6 p54 Je 2017

AFTER THE BARRE J. KINDELA chart color *Muscle & Performance* v8 no12 p32 D 2016

Annabelle LOPEZ OCHOA N. Loeffler-Gladstone color *Dance Spirit* v20 no10 p28 D 2016

BARRE ESSENTIALS J. VRABEL *Indianapolis Monthly* v40 no3 p29 N 2016

DANCE *New Yorker* v92 no42 p38 D 19 2016

He's Back J. STAHL *Dance Magazine* v91 no1 p108 Ja 2017

How to Choose the Right Summer Program: A Checklist C. THOMPSON *Dance Magazine* v91 no1 p132 Ja 2017

"I'm sold on Harlequin Floors D. Roberts *Dance Magazine* v91 no10 p5 O 2017

Kylling It *Dance Magazine* v90 no12 p24 D 2016

LET'S HEAR IT for the Boys *Dance Spirit* v21 no3 p10 Mr 2017

LIVING BY The Word *Christian Century* v134 no17 p20 Ag 16 2017

QUICK CHANGE H. Rolte and L. Chilezuk color *Dance Spirit* v21 no2 p48 F 2017

WHERE & WHEN M. J. Gaynor, A. Beaujon et al color *Washingtonian Magazine* v52 no7 p31 Ap 2017

Ballet companies

A CAREER & LEARNING RESOURCE GUIDE *Dance Magazine* v91 no9 p60 S 2017

Dynamic Duo S. Fnscia *Dance Magazine* v90 no12 p28 D 2016

Price Pointe J. CARMAN *Dance Magazine* v91 no6 p37 Je 2017

Raising Revenues: Ballet companies today are proving that building new audiences for dance is possible A. RIVERS *Dance Magazine* v91 no9 p54 S 2017

Trouble in Paradise L. HAMILTON *Dance Magazine* v91 no1 p48 Ja 2017

Ballet competitions

OCTOBER'S COOLEST EVENTS bw color *Indianapolis Monthly* v42 no2 p22 O 2017

Ballet costume

See also

Ballet slippers

Pointe shoes

ALL THAT GLITTERS... A. MARKS, H. ROLFE et al color *Dance Spirit* v20 no9 p59 N 2016

THE Dance Spirit 2016 COSTUME GUIDE C. Dutton and L. Renck *Dance Spirit* v20 no9 p76 N 2016

MINIMALIST MAGIC H. Rolfe *Dance Spirit* v21 no7 p90 S 2017

Ballet costume—Evaluation

Dare to Stand Out S. FRISCIA *Dance Magazine* v91 no4 p45 Ap 2017

From Catlike to Classical S. Friscia color *Dance Magazine* v91 no3 p38 Mr 2017

POINTES ON PARADE S. FRISCIA *Dance Magazine* v91 no4 p43 Ap 2017

Ballet dancers

See also

Ballerinas

advice for dancers L. HAMILTON *Dance Magazine* v91 no4 p24 Ap 2017

Alfa Romeo J. Acocella bw *New Yorker* v93 no17 p12 Je 19 2017

ALL THAT GLITTERS... A. MARKS, H. ROLFE et al color *Dance Spirit* v20 no9 p59 N 2016

All the Way Back R. Milzoff and R. Afanador img *New York* v50 no10 p81 My 15 2017

Becoming an Artist E. Villella *Dance Magazine* v90 no11 p31 N 2016

Take Corrections, Correctly J. DIANA *Dance Magazine* v91 no4 p52 Ap 2017

Balleza, Enrique

Biased partitioning of the multidrug efflux pump AcrAB-TolC underlies long-lived phenotypic heterogeneity diag *Science* v356 no6335 p311 Ap 21 2017

BALLÍ, CECILIA

WHAT WALL? *Texas Monthly* v45 no5 p101 My 2017

Balli, Emily

Chiricahua Leopard Frogs color *Arizona Highways* v93 no5 p13 My 2017

Greater Roadrunners *Arizona Highways* v93 no9 p15 S 2017

IT'S TIME TO BOARD color *Arizona Highways* v93 no5 p38 My 2017

Ospreys *Arizona Highways* v96 no7 p13 Jl 2017

Western Patch-Nosed Snakes *Arizona Highways* v93 no6 p13 Je 2017

Balling, Robert C.

Rainbow Detectives: When Art Gets Meteorology Wrong *Weatherwise* v70 no2 p24 Mr/Ap 2017

Ballinger, Colleen

Haters Back Off Takes a Star from YouTube to TV D. D'Addario color *Time* v188 no16/17 p92 O 24 2016

Ballinger, Rachel

THE VIEW MASTERS E. G. ELLIS color graph *Wired* v25 no4 p18 Ap 2017

Ballistic instruments—Evaluation

MEET THE TECH THAT MAKES BALLISTIC COEFFICIENTS OBSOLETE J. B. SNOW color diag *Outdoor Life* v224 no2 p40 F/Mr 2017

Ballistic missile defenses

The future of US–Russian nuclear deterrence and arms control T. Anichkina, A. Péczeli et al bibl *Bulletin of the Atomic Scientists* v73 no4 p271 Jl 2017

Now More Than Ever [Cover story] P. J. BOYER color *Weekly Standard* v23 no5 p21 O 9 2017

Ballistic missile defenses—United States

Beijing Is Mad About Thaad B. Einhorn, Sohee Kim et al color *Bloomberg Businessweek* no4514 p16 Mr 13 2017

Ballistic missile testing

Pressuring North Korea E. Epstein color *Weekly Standard* v22 no42 p7 Jl 17 2017

PREVENTIVE STRIKES ON NORTH KOREA FAIL JUST WAR CRITERIA K. Clarke color *America* v217 no3 p12 Ag 7 2017

Ballistic missiles

See also

Intercontinental ballistic missiles

FLASHBACK bw color *MHQ: Quarterly Journal of Military History* v30 no1 p6 Aut 2017

Indian nuclear forces, 2017 H. M. Kristensen and R. S. Norris bibl chart *Bulletin of the Atomic Scientists* v73 no4 p205 Jl 2017

Kim Jong Un Isn't the Only Wild Card In the North Korea Crisis P. Elliott, C. Campbell et al color *Time* v190 no10/11 p11 S 18 2017

Korean War Drums B. CUMINGS *Nation* v304 no12 p5 Ap 10 2017

The Long View R. LONG *National Review* v69 no12 p34 Je 26 2017

Russian nuclear forces, 2017 H. M. Kristensen and R. S. Norris bibl chart *Bulletin of the Atomic Scientists* v73 no2 p115 Mr 2017

Seeking a path toward missile nonproliferation M. Ikegami bibl *Bulletin of the Atomic Scientists* v72 no6 p365 N 2016

Ballmer, Steve

I Crunched the Numbers on the U.S. Government. Here's What I Learned color *Time* v190 no5 p30 Jl 31 2017

Ballooning

Albuquerque International Balloon Fiesta *Saturday Evening Post* v289 no4 p29 Jl/Ag 2017

Balloons in astronomy

All eyes on the eclipse L. Grossman color *Science News* v192 no1 p4 Ag 5 2017

Balloons—Models

Kamifusen, the self-inflating Japanese paper balloon Ichiro Fukumori *Physics Today* v70 no1 p78 Ja 2017

Balloons—Research

Kamifusen, the self-inflating Japanese paper balloon Ichiro Fukumori *Physics Today* v70 no1 p78 Ja 2017

Ballot

See also

Preferential ballot

Voting machines

Other Big Issues on the Ballot K. Reilly *Time* v188 no20 p39 N 14 2016

Should 'Ballot Box Selfies' Be Banned? W. GARDNER and G. BISSONNETTE *New York Times Upfront* v149 no4 p22 O 31 2016

Ballou, Jec A.

Modifying Muscle Patterns to Build A Better Athlete color diag *Dressage Today* v23 no6 p34 F 2017

Ballouli, Khalid

American Dreamer color *Sports Illustrated* v126 no5 p16 F 13 2017

Ballroom dancers—Interviews

THE DIRT with Lindsay Arnold *Dance Spirit* v21 no7 p42 S 2017

Ballroom dancing

The War Before the Waltz R. Hughes *History Today* v66 no12 p40 D 2016

Ballroom dancing—Study & teaching

FOLLOW Like a Boss C. Bohen *Dance Spirit* v21 no7 p100 S 2017

Balls (Parties)

See also

Proms

2017 WASHINGTONIAN INAUGURAL BALL color *Washingtonian Magazine* v52 no7 p28 Ap 2017

ABOVE & BEYOND cartoon *New Yorker* v92 no49 p26 F 13 2017

PANDAS WILL FIX EVERYTHING C. SWANSON img *New York* p54 Mr 6 2017

Balls (Sporting goods)—Design & construction

Whole New Ball Game S. Rushin color *Sports Illustrated* v127 no3 p116 Jl 24 2017

Balls (Sporting goods)—Evaluation

MORE PRESSURE, LESS PAIN M. Reinold color *Men's Health* v32 no5 p56 Je 2017

The O List color *O, The Oprah Magazine* p47 Ap 2017

BALL-TUFFORD, JENNIFER

The Gift of Food *Reader's Digest* v188 no1126 p50 D 2016/Ja 2017

Bally (Company)

CHAIN REACTION color *Harper's Bazaar* no3651 p277 Mr 2017

THE STEP UP color *Esquire* v167 no2 p34 Mr 2017

Balmer, Randall

Faith in the New Millennium: The Future of Religion and American Politics *Christian Century* v133 no22 p41 O 26 2016

Balmford, Andrew

Biodiversity losses and conservation responses in the Anthropocene color diag graph map *Science* v356 no6335 p270 Ap 21 2017

Why Earth Optimism? color *Science* v356 no6335 p225 Ap 21 2017

Balmori, Diana, 1932-2016

Blurring the Boundaries J. SANDERS *Architectural Record* v205 no1 p34 Ja 2017

Balogh, Mary

Someone to Hold: Westcott, Book 2 *Publishers Weekly* v264 no1 p43 Ja 2 2017

Balogun, Damisola

FABULOUS AT EVERY AGE CELEBRATION color *Harper's Bazaar* no3648 p206 N 2016

Balotelli, Mario, 1990-

Mario Balotelli J. Pritchard *Current Biography* v77 no10 p7 O 2016

Balsam, Martin

The Little Guy S. Mears color *Film Comment* v53 no4 p18 Jl/Ag 2017

Balsam Hill LLC

UP YOUR TREE GAME B. THORKELSON *Better Homes & Gardens* v94 no12 p48 D 2016

BALSAMO, LAUREN
For best results, wait... how long? color *Redbook* p38 Jl/Ag 2017
join the charcoal party! color *Seventeen* v76 no3 p100 My 2017
Not Your Basic Braids color *Seventeen* v76 no4 p29 Jl/Ag 2017
The Secret to... KNOCKOUT SKIN color *Seventeen* v76 no4 p74 Jl/Ag 2017
Sun's Out Buns Out color *Seventeen* v76 no3 p92 My 2017
TEMPTED TO TAN? Read This First! color *Seventeen* v76 no2 p80 Mr 2017

Balshaw, Maria
PEOPLE *Art in America* v105 no3 p152 Mr 2017

Balsiger, H.
Xenon isotopes in 67P/Churyumov-Gerasimenko show that comets contributed to Earth's atmosphere diag *Science* v356 no6342 p1069 Je 9 2017

Balskus, Emily P.
Chemical transformation of xenobiotics by the human gut microbiota diag *Science* v356 no6344 p1246 Je 23 2017
A prominent glycyl radical enzyme in human gut microbiomes metabolizes trans-4-hydroxy-L-proline diag *Science* v355 no6325 p595 F 10 2017

Balslev, H.
Persistent effects of pre-Columbian plant domestication on Amazonian forest composition bibl chart graph map *Science* v355 no6328 p925 Mr 3 2017

Baltensperger, Urs
Global atmospheric particle formation from CERN CLOUD measurements bibl graph map *Science* v354 no6316 p1119 D 2 2016

Balter, Margie
Go From Sucking to 60 K. SCHAEFER and L. SCHWARTZ-BERG img *New York* v49 no23 p68 N 14 2016

BALTER, MICHAEL
SCHIZOPHRENIA'S UNYIELDING MYSTERIES color diag *Scientific American* v316 no5 p54 My 2017

Balti, Bianca
ROOKIES color *Sports Illustrated* v126 no6 p21 F 20 2017

Baltic States—Military policy
Tensions With Russia Rise In the Baltics map *Time* v189 no10 p8 Mr 20 2017

Baltic States—Foreign relations—1991-
Smaller Countries, Far Away J. NORDLINGER *National Review* v68 no19 p27 O 24 2016

Baltimore (Md.)—Description & travel
Come Out and Play T. ALVAREZ color *Backpacker* p84 Je 2017
MAKER CITY: BALTIMORE F. MAROUKIAN color *Popular Mechanics* p28 S 2017
TAKE A DRIVE: FELLS POINT: Even if you love our town, it's nice to get away. This month-new reasons to visit a historic waterfront neighborhood in Baltimore J. Sugarman *Washingtonian Magazine* v52 no12 p106 S 2017

Baltimore, David
The boldness of philanthropists color *Science* v353 no6307 p1473 S 30 2016

Baltimore Orioles (Baseball team)
5 ORIOLES color *Sports Illustrated* v126 no9 p81 Mr 27 2017
Sports Funnies K. MILLER color *National Geographic Kids* no472 p9 Ag 2017

Baltimore Ravens (Football team)
2 Baltimore Ravens color *Sports Illustrated* v127 no7 p71 S 4 2017

Balzac, Honoré de, 1799-1850
1838: Paris H. de Balzac *Lapham's Quarterly* v10 no1 p97 Wint 2017

Balzarotti, Francisco
Nanometer resolution imaging and tracking of fluorescent molecules with minimal photon fluxes bibl graph *Science* v355 no6325 p606 F 10 2017

Bambarger, Bradley
Bells For The South Side color *Downbeat* v84 no10 p65 O 2017
Center of the Storm bw *Downbeat* v84 no10 p32 O 2017
Dialectrical/Port Bou color *Downbeat* v84 no3 p59 Mr 2017
DRIVEN & DETERMINED color *Downbeat* v84 no9 p54 S 2017
KRIS DAVIS: 'Open To Surprise' color *Downbeat* v84 no8 p51 Ag 2017
Speak Low/Speak Low Renditions bw *Downbeat* v84 no6 p71 Je 2017

Bamber, Greg J.
Navigating national regulations and global changes: international and comparative employment J. Wheeler *Monthly Labor Review* p1 Je 2017

Bamberger, Michael
Air Palmer color *Golf Magazine* v58 no12 p104 D 2016
THE BALLAD OF A BIG CAT AND A GATOR color *Sports Illustrated* v126 no11 p64 Ap 17-24 2017
The Case for ... The Career Slam color *Sports Illustrated* v127 no4 p24 Ag 7 2017
CHASING 62 color diag *Sports Illustrated* v126 no10 p54 Ap 10 2017
The Education of Samantha Els color *Golf Magazine* v59 no10 p116 O 2017
Erin Go Par color *Sports Illustrated* v126 no17 p15 Je 19 2017
Fairways to Heaven color *Golf Magazine* v59 no9 p112 S 2017
FIRST GOLFER color *Sports Illustrated* v127 no4 p48 Ag 7 2017
Major problem? Major solution! color *Golf Magazine* v59 no8 p112 Ag 2017
The Other Player of the Year color *Golf Magazine* v59 no1 p108 Ja 2017
Paging Tiger color *Sports Illustrated* v126 no9 p19 Mr 27 2017
Paradise Island color *Golf Magazine* v59 no11 p112 N 2017
A Perfect Read color *Golf Magazine* v58 no11 p114 N 2016
Rules Aren't Made to Be Broken color *Golf Magazine* v59 no6 p124 Je 2017
School's Out for... the Masters?! color *Golf Magazine* v59 no4 p140 Ap 2017
See Jane Thrive color *Golf Magazine* v59 no7 p112 Jl 2017
The Tao of Sam color *Golf Magazine* v59 no5 p120 My 2017
What About Bob? color *Golf Magazine* v59 no2 p104 F 2017
Why Marcus? color *Golf Magazine* v59 no3 p128 Mr 2017
Winner-in-Chief color *Sports Illustrated* v126 no4 p16 Ja 30 2017

Bambola, Sylvia
Mercy at Midnight color *Publishers Weekly* v263 no47 p76b N 21 2016

BAMBURAK, PATRICK
SELF-TAUGHT MMA THUGS, PART 1 bw *Black Belt* v55 no3 p40 Ap/My 2017

BAMFORD, JAMES
Bigly Brother cartoon *Foreign Policy* no222 p68 Ja/F 2017
Helicopter President color *Foreign Policy* no223 p66 Mr/Ap 2017
The Ministry of Preemption color *Foreign Policy* no224 p78 My/Je 2017
Spooks in Space color *Foreign Policy* no221 p96 N/D 2016

BamTech (Company)
HOT | NOT T. Keith color *Sports Illustrated* v125 no21 p24 D 26 2016

Ban, Shigeru, 1957-
Finding the Right Angle N. R. POLLOCK *Architectural Record* v205 no6 p80 Je 2017

Banakis, Kat
Reset the Heart: Unlearning Violence, Relearning Hope *Christian Century* v134 no20 p38 S 27 2017

Banana trade
THE PROBLEMS WITH FAIR TRADE R. PATEL *Nation* v305 no11 p16 O 30 2017

Bananaglue GmbH
How to manage your network with iNet Network Scanner J. BATTERSBY color *Macworld - Digital Edition* p108 F 2017

Bananas
EAT LIKE A MONKEY! J. London color *Good Housekeeping* v264 no6 p81 Je 2017
Fresh Smoothie Bowls B. Lipton color *Health* v31 no6 p121 Jl 2017
SMOOTHIE MOVE D. DeNunzio color *Golf Magazine* v59 no4 p64 Ap 2017
STREET SMARTS L. Haney color *Runner's World* v51 no10 p40 N 2016
THE WORLD ACCORDING TO Gayle color *O, The Oprah Magazine* p30 Mr 2017

Banavar, Guru
What It Will Take for Us to Trust AI *Harvard Business Review Digital Articles* p2 N 29 2016

Banc One Corp.
What's In a Name? K. Finn color *New Orleans Magazine* v51 no4

p30 F 2017

Banca Monte dei Paschi di Siena SpA

A Sun-Dappled Tuscan Banking Mess L. Casiraghi and C. Albanese color *Bloomberg Businessweek* no4511 p36 F 13 2017

Bancroft, Ruth

THE PLANT PIONEER J. Silver color *Sunset* v237 no5 p64 N 2016

Band, Gavin

Resistance to malaria through structural variation of red blood cell invasion receptors diag *Science* v356 no6343 p1139 Je 16 2017

Band, The (Performer)

THE BIRTH OF THE BAND R. ROBERTSON bw *Rolling Stone* no1274 p48 N 17 2016

We Were the Band R. ROBERTSON bw color *Vanity Fair* v58 no11 p176 N 2016

Band directors

JAMES MORRISON THE ADVENTURER M. Jackson color *Downbeat* v84 no10 p176 O 2017

Bandannas

A Bandana C. LYONS color *Backpacker* p38 Je 2017

Banda-R, Karina

Forest conservation: Humans' handprints bibl color *Science* v355 no6324 p466 F 3 2017

Forest conservation: Remember Gran Chaco bibl color *Science* v355 no6324 p465 F 3 2017

Bandi

DYSTOPIAS AND ARTY DOGS B. J. GRUBISIC color *Maclean's* v130 no3 p68 Ap 2017

Bandi, M. M.

Mind the gap: Neural coding of species identity in birdsong prosody bibl graph *Science* v354 no6317 p1282 D 9 2016

Bandiera, Oriana

A Survey of How 1,000 CEOs Spend Their Day Reveals What Makes Leaders Successful *Harvard Business Review Digital Articles* p2 O 12 2017

BANDOW, DOUG

THE ASIA PIVOT: PROBLEMS, PROBLEMS, PROBLEMS *USA Today Magazine* v145 no2862 p32 Mr 2017

Rasmussen's Refrain: Let Uncle Sam Do It *American Conservative* v16 no2 p50 Mr/Ap 2017

Bandow, Grace

O's 2017 HEALTH HEROES J. THOMPSON, E. MOODY et al color *O, The Oprah Magazine* p57 Ja 2017

Bands (Musical groups)

BIG PHAT PRODUCTION VALUES G. Goodwin color *Downbeat* v84 no2 p88 F 2017

Chords & Discords S. COMINGS, G. MILLIKEN et al bw color *Downbeat* v84 no2 p10 F 2017

Confessions of a Total Poseur D. SKINNER color *Weekly Standard* v23 no5 p5 O 9 2017

Front porch music sessions take center stage in Hastings E. CASE color *Nebraska Life* v21 no5 p76 S/O 2017

JAM SESH J. WILLIAMS bw *Cincinnati Magazine* v51 no1 p22 O 2017

Lovano, Valdés Explore Common Language B. Milkowski color *Downbeat* v84 no3 p16 Mr 2017

THE MAGIC TOUCH P. de Barros color *Downbeat* v84 no6 p126 Je 2017

MIDWEST color *Downbeat* v84 no3 p92 Mr 2017

My Blond D. Harry and L. B. Ray color *InStyle* v24 no5 p216 My 2017

Neil Young color *AARP: The Magazine* v59 no2A p12 F/Mr 2016

Opening Doors Z. CRAIN *D: The Magazine of Dallas* v43 no10 p60 O 2016

Sights and Sounds color *National Geographic* v230 no5 p14 N 2016

Speed Read J. BALL *Indianapolis Monthly* p18 N 2017

WEST color *Downbeat* v84 no3 p98 Mr 2017

What Happened When Linkin Park Asked Harvard for Help with Its Business Model K. Berry *Harvard Business Review Digital Articles* p2 Je 23 2015

Bands (Musical groups)—Awards

FOSTERING A WINNING TEAM T. Perkins color *Downbeat* v84 no6 p118 Je 2017

Bandstand (Theatrical production)

THE THEATRE *New Yorker* v93 no11 p8 My 1 2017

Band's Visit, The (Theatrical production)

Dancing in a Chair and in the Air: in the Air Katrina Lenk's Broadway gigs are wildly diverse. Her latest is The Bands visit S. GOLD *Dance Magazine* v91 no10 p20 O 2017

Fall Preview M. Schulman color *New Yorker* v93 no25 p6 Ag 28 2017

A Little Night Music A. GREEN bw *Vogue* v207 no11 p165 N 2017

THE THEATRE *New Yorker* v92 no43 p7 Ja 2 2017

THE THEATRE *New Yorker* v93 no33 p22 O 23 2017

Bandurin, D. A.

High-temperature quantum oscillations caused by recurring Bloch states in graphene superlattices color *Science* v357 no6347 p181 Jl 14 2017

Bandwidth allocation (Networks)

Comcast's 1TB data cap starts rolling out across the U.S I. PAUL color diag *PCWorld* v35 no11 p39 N 2016

Bandwidths

Breaking Lorentz reciprocity to overcome the time-bandwidth limit in physics and engineering K. L. Tsakmakidis, L. Shen et al bw diag graph *Science* v356 no6344 p1260 Je 23 2017

BANDY, ALAN

OF AGE and innocence color *Christianity Today* v61 no5 p60 Je 2017

Banerjee, Abhijit V.

The impact of training informal health care providers in India: A randomized controlled trial chart diag *Science* v354 no6308 paaf7384-1 O 7 2016

Banerjee, Arnab

Neutron scattering in the proximate quantum spin liquid a-RuCl3 bw diag *Science* v356 no6342 p1055 Je 9 2017

Banerjee, Prith

5 Ways Product Design Needs to Evolve for the Internet of Things *Harvard Business Review Digital Articles* p2 N 14 2014

Banff National Park (Alta.)

CELEBRATING CANADA'S GRANDEUR color *Canadian Geographic* v137 no3 p12 My 2017

Moraine Lake, Banff National Park, Alberta diag *Backpacker* p96 Je 2017

Why are grizzlies dying on Canada's railway tracks? C. Derworiz color *Science* v355 no6325 p561 F 10 2017

Banff National Park (Alta.)—History

First among equals H. Wilson map *Canadian Geographic* v137 no1 p24 F 2017

Bang & Olufsen A/S

The Art of Sound S. Guttenberg and C. Crowley color *Sound & Vision* v81 no9 p20 N 2016

FETISH: EAR CANDY H. GENDREAU color *Wired* v25 no8 p39 Ag 2017

Sophistication From Above D. Wilkinson color *Sound & Vision* v82 no8 p58 O 2017

Bang, Mary Jo

'PORTRAIT AS SELF-PORTRAIT' bw *New York Times Book Review* p17 Ag 6 2017

Bang, Mikkel

METHOD OF THE MONTH cartoon color *Snowboarder* v29 no4 p134 D 2016

MIKKEL BANG BURTON color *Snowboarder* v29 no4 p2 D 2016

Banga, Ajay

What CEOs Think of Trump R. T. Beckwith color *Time* v189 no6 p10 F 20 2017

Bangladesh Rural Advancement Committee (Organization)

An Approach to Ending Poverty That Works S. Davis *Harvard Business Review Digital Articles* p2 Ja 22 2015

Bangs & Works: A Chicago Footwork Compilation (Music)

MOOD MUSIC HUA HSU color *New Yorker* v93 no14 p92 My 22 2017

Banich, Howard

16 Pisces, Arp 284 & the Unexpected Quasar: A Story of Time and Distance *Sky & Telescope* v134 no4 p62 O 2017

The Jewel in the Sword: An observer captures on a sketchpad the stunning details of one of the most wondrous objects in the night sky *Sky & Telescope* v134 no6 p32 D 2017

Ml7: The Nebula With Too Many Names: Follow this observers guide to find one of the best H II regions in the night sky *Sky &*

Doing Business in India Requires a Mobile-First Strategy V. Govindarajan and G. Bagla *Harvard Business Review Digital Articles* p2 D 23 2016

Banking industry—Risk management

Research: Hiring Chief Risk Officers Led Banks to Take on Even More Risk K. Pernell, J. Jung et al *Harvard Business Review Digital Articles* p2 Jl 13 2017

Banking industry—Switzerland

Data Mining to Find Tax Cheaters D. Voreacos and C. Berthelsen color *Bloomberg Businessweek* no4524 p41 My 29 2017

Banking industry—United States

BANKING ON RESISTANCE J. TOBIAS color *Nation* v304 no16 p24 My 22 2017

The BEST BANK FOR YOU M. Leonhardt, A. Adamczyk et al color diag map *Money* v45 no10 p86 N 2016

The Infrastructure Bank We Need S. R. STALEY *National Review* v68 no24 p18 D 31 2016

Taking Socialism to the Bank D. DAYEN *In These Times* v41 no5 p27 My 2017

We Pick the Best Banks *Kiplinger's Personal Finance* v71 no7 p8 Jl 2017

Banking industry—United States—Government policy

Banking Regulation Y. Onaran color *Bloomberg Businessweek* no4502 p47 D 5 2016

Banking industry—United States—Officials & employees

FINANCE M. Abelson and J. Holman graph *Bloomberg Businessweek* no4532 p25 Jl 31 2017

Banking law & legislation—United States

If Not Dodd-Frank, Then ... What? P. Coy color graph *Bloomberg Businessweek* no4513 p40 Mr 6 2017

Banking research

One Very Important Footnote S. H. e. Costa bw *Bloomberg Businessweek* no4493 p51 O 3 2016

Banking industry—Charts, diagrams, etc.

MONEY, CREDIT, AND SECURITY MARKETS *Economic Indicators* p26 Ja 2017

Banking industry—Trials, litigation, etc.

Legalio Password? G. Farrell and K. Geiger color *Bloomberg Businessweek* no4495 p30 O 17 2016

Bank loans—Charts, diagrams, etc.

MONEY, CREDIT, AND SECURITY MARKETS *Economic Indicators* p26 Ja 2017

Bank loans—United States—Charts, diagrams, etc.

MONEY, CREDIT, AND SECURITY MARKETS *Economic Indicators* p26 N 2016

Bankruptcy

Companies Can't Be Great Unless They've Almost Failed B. Taylor *Harvard Business Review Digital Articles* p2 Mr 21 2016

Does bankruptcy hurt an individual's ability to be hired or borrow money? Y. Ivanchev *Monthly Labor Review* p1 My 2017

GOING IN STYLE J. OBER bw *Dirt Sports + Off-Road* v51 no5 p74 My 2017

My Friend Is Bankrupting Herself. Should I Speak Up? K. A. Appiah *New York Times Magazine* p18 Ap 2 2017

THE SINKING OF SEARS T. C. FISHMAN color *Chicago* v66 no4 p28 Ap 2017

Bankruptcy costs

Last Rites: Leaders at St. Joseph's College allowed its finances to get so bad for so long, the situation became impossible to fix. If the historic Catholic school ever returns now, it will be a miracle C. KENLEY *Indianapolis Monthly* v12 no40 p54 Ag 2017

Bankruptcy prevention

Back in Black: Cities that once faced bankruptcy have made remarkable recoveries F. Shafroth *Governing* v30 no10 p62 Jl 2017

Don't Treat Innovation as a Cure-All W. McKinley, S. Latham et al *Harvard Business Review Digital Articles* p2 D 8 2014

Bankruptcy—Statistics

THE SCARY TRUTH ABOUT CORPORATE SURVIVAL il *Harvard Business Review* v94 no12 p24 D 2016

Banks, Adelle M.

Army now allows soldiers to wear turbans, beards, and headscarves color *Christian Century* v134 no4 p14 F 15 2017

Baptist ethicist and commentator dies at age 63 *Christian Century* v134 no8 p1 Ap 12 2017

CLERGY MARCH ON WASHINGTON color *Christian Century* v134 no20 p18 S 27 2017

Georgetown University apologizes for its role in historical slave trade color *Christian Century* v134 no11 p16 My 24 2017

Iconography classes draw non-Orthodox in search of spiritual images color *Christian Century* v134 no4 p16 F 15 2017

Life in a fishbowl: Survey reveals stresses and joys of pastors' spouses color *Christian Century* v134 no22 p18 O 25 2017

People *Christian Century* v134 no16 p16 Ag 2 2017

People color *Christian Century* v134 no2 p19 Ja 18 2017

Religious groups rally around issues after election color *Christian Century* v133 no25 p12 D 7 2016

Smithsonian exhibit shows religious diversity in early American life *Christian Century* v134 no18 p16 Ag 30 2017

Southern Baptists condemn white supremacy, call for 'moral character' in officials color *Christian Century* v134 no15 p15 Jl 19 2017

Unitarian Universalist head resigns amid controversy about staff diversity color *Christian Century* v134 no9 p15 Ap 26 2017

Banks, Bernard

To Develop Cultural Dexterity, Seek It Out *Harvard Business Review Digital Articles* p2 Je 24 2016

Banks, Brian

Capital considerations map *Canadian Geographic* v137 no3 p32 My 2017

CITY WIDE map *Canadian Geographic* v137 no3 p62 My 2017

ENDANGERED! color *Canadian Wildlife* v23 no1 p26 Mr/Ap 2017

The Mystery of Our Disappearing Moose color *Canadian Wildlife* v23 no4 p18 S/O 2017

BANKS, ELIZABETH

The Year in Reading [Cover story] *New York Times Book Review* p8 D 25 2016

Banks, Elizabeth, 1974-

PARTY LINES img *New York* v50 no13 p84 Je 26 2017

BANKS, GRACE

Jack LOWDEN *Interview* v47 no3 p20 Ap 2017

Banks, Jill

Role for migratory wild birds in the global spread of avian influenza H5N8 bibl graph map *Science* v354 no6309 p213 O 14 2016

Banks, Jillian Rose—Interviews

BANKS *Interview* v46 no10 p32 D 2016/Ja 2017

Banks, Jim

Introducing Jim Banks J. J. MILLER color *National Review* v68 no23 p24 D 19 2016

BANKS, KERRY

RISE of the SYNANTHROPES color *Canadian Geographic* v137 no3 p56 My 2017

Banks, Kira Hudson

Diversity at the Oscars Is More than a Numbers Game *Harvard Business Review Digital Articles* p2 F 24 2016

How Managers Can Promote Healthy Discussions About Race *Harvard Business Review Digital Articles* p2 Ja 7 2016

Banks, Nikita

THERAPY SAVED ME G. Roberts-grey color *Essence* v47 no7 p107 N 2016

Banks, Tyra

Icons color *Time* v189 no16/17 p122 My 1-8 2017

Banksy, 1974-

I WAS MARRIED TO BANKSY D. Dernavich cartoon *Esquire* p130 N 2017

BANNER, JAMES M. JR.

Finding the Founder color *Weekly Standard* v22 no32 p37 My 1 2017

Mutiny and Identity color *Weekly Standard* v23 no1 p35 S 11 2017

Renaissance Hal cartoon *Weekly Standard* v22 no13 p34 D 5 2016

This Is the Place color *Weekly Standard* v22 no28 p37 Mr 27 2017

Westward, Oh cartoon *Weekly Standard* v22 no12 p37 N 28 2016

Banner Road Baking Co.

No Grains, No Glory *Missouri Life* v43 no7 p21 D 2016/Ja 2017

Banner stones

SET IN STONE E. A. POWELL color *Archaeology* v70 no4 p44 Je-Ag 2017

Banners

BALCONY POLITICS B. Freed *Washingtonian Magazine* v52 no9 p51 Je 2017

WHAT MAKES PROTEST ART GOOD? R. CORBETT img *New*

York v50 no8 p66 Ap 17 2017

BANNISTER, DAVID JR.

OBAMA'S AMERICA img *New York* v49 no20 p12 O 3 2016

Bannister, Jo

Other Countries color *Publishers Weekly* v264 no17 p70 Ap 24 2017

Bannister, K.

The magnetic field and turbulence of the cosmic web measured using a brilliant fast radio burst bibl chart graph *Science* v354 no6317 p1249 D 9 2016

Bannister, Stephen

Complex multifault rupture during the 2016 Mw 7.8 Kaikōura earthquake, New Zealand color map *Science* v356 no6334 p154 Ap 14 2017

Bannon, Shawn

THE NIGHT I FOUND MYSELF IN THE BASEMENT AT 3 A.M S. BANNON *Vital Speeches of the Day* v82 no11 p350 N 2016

Bannon, Stephen K., 1954-

AFTER BANNON J. Cobb cartoon *New Yorker* v93 no26 p19 S 4 2017

The Age of Bannon A. Abrams color *Time* v189 no5 p26 F 13 2017

BALANCING ACT A. Marantz cartoon *New Yorker* v92 no41 p26 D 12 2016

BIG PLANS SMALL MINDS J. REICHERT color *Film Comment* v53 no1 p78 Ja/F 2017

DEPARTMENT OF JUSTIFICATION E. Bazelon *New York Times Magazine* p36 Mr 5 2017

Enter the Bannon [Cover story] J. Green color *Bloomberg Businessweek* no4540 p40 O 2 2017

The high Priest of the Church of Trump T. ANDERSON *In These Times* v41 no1 p44 Ja 2017

A HOLLYWOOD STORY C. BRUCK cartoon *New Yorker* v93 no11 p34 My 1 2017

I Told Steve Bannon: 'We Are Not At War With Islam.' He Disagreed F. Rose *NPQ: New Perspectives Quarterly* v34 no2 p17 My 2017

Of Popes & Trumpists cartoon *Commonweal* v144 no5 p5 Mr 10 2017

The Palace Intrigue Obsession A. FERGUSON *Commentary* v143 no6 p11 Je 2017

PRESIDENT BANNON'S BANNON A. Marantz color *New Yorker* v92 no49 p30 F 13 2017

The Second Most Powerful Man In the World? [Cover story] D. Von Drehle, A. Altman et al color *Time* v189 no5 p24 F 13 2017

Steve Bannon, Trump's Right-Hand Batterer B. LUEDERS cartoon *Progressive* v81 no2 p14 F 2017

Terrifying Trump E. Drew color *New York Review of Books* v64 no4 p37 Mr 9 2017

TRUMP VS. CONGRESS R. DRAPER *New York Times Magazine* p30 Ap 2 2017

Trump Will Always Be Trump R. Ponnuru *Bloomberg Businessweek* no4535 p12 Ag 28 2017

Trump's Brain M. PHELAN color *New Republic* v248 no4 p14 Ap 2017

THE WAR IN THE WHITE HOUSE M. Taibbi color *Rolling Stone* no1287 p24 My 18 2017

What Bannon Wrought R. L. BOROSAGE *Nation* v305 no6 p6 S 11 2017

What You Said About ... color *Time* v189 no6 p6 F 20 2017

Bans, Lauren

GOLDIE Hawn color *GQ: Gentlemen's Quarterly* v97 no6 p124 Je 2017

LAND OF THE LEAF EATERS color *Bon Appetit* no1 p80 F 2017

Bansak, Kirk

How economic, humanitarian, and religious concerns shape European attitudes toward asylum seekers bibl graph map *Science* v354 no6309 p217 O 14 2016

Bansal, Charlotte

SCARY (AND TRUE) TALES FROM A CRAG NEAR YOU *Climbing* no351 p21 F/Mr 2017

Bansal, Pritpal

Exploring genetic suppression interactions on a global scale diag *Science* v354 no6312 p599 N 4 2016

Banta, Ken

Great Strategy Begins with a CEO on the Frontlines *Harvard Business Review Digital Articles* p2 O 7 2014

How CEOs Can Work with an Active Board *Harvard Business Review Digital Articles* p2 Ag 8 2017

This Pharma Company Stays Innovative by Doing Two Things *Harvard Business Review Digital Articles* p2 Mr 14 2017

Bantu languages

Dispersals and genetic adaptation of Bantu-speaking populations in Africa and North America E. Patin, M. Lopez et al diag *Science* v356 no6337 p543 My 5 2017

Bantu-speaking peoples

See also

Nguni (African people)

THE RIVER RAN RED K. Bell bw color map *Military History* v34 no5 p62 Ja 2018

Bantu-speaking peoples—History

Dispersals and genetic adaptation of Bantu-speaking populations in Africa and North America E. Patin, M. Lopez et al diag *Science* v356 no6337 p543 My 5 2017

Bantum, Brian

Bodies in the vernacular color *Christian Century* v134 no7 p26 Mr 29 2017

Diversity and disability . . B. Gaventa *Christian Century* v134 no10 p6 My 10 2017

Banville, John

1595: Graz *Lapham's Quarterly* v10 no2 p49 Spr 2017

Philip Marlowe's Revolution bw *New York Review of Books* v63 no16 p38 O 27 2016

The Strange Genius of the Master bw *New York Review of Books* v64 no2 p14 F 9 2017

Tender Is the Fall bw *New York Review of Books* v64 no17 p40 N 9 2017

Banwart, Steve

Microbial mass movements color *Science* v357 no6356 p1099 S 15 2017

Bányai, Krisztián

Role for migratory wild birds in the global spread of avian influenza H5N8 bibl graph map *Science* v354 no6309 p213 O 14 2016

Banyan tree

THE FIG AND THE WASP B. Crair *Smithsonian* v48 no1 p63 Ap 2017

Why the Lowly Dandelion Is a Better Metaphor for Leaders than the Mighty Banyan V. Bapat *Harvard Business Review Digital Articles* p2 Mr 23 2017

BANYASZ, MALIN GRUNBERG

OFF THE GRID color *Archaeology* v69 no6 p10 N/D 2016

OFF THE GRID color *Archaeology* v70 no1 p12 Ja/F 2017

OFF THE GRID color *Archaeology* v70 no3 p10 My/Je 2017

Bao-Zong Wang

Realization of two-dimensional spin-orbit coupling for Bose-Einstein condensates bibl graph *Science* v354 no6308 p83 O 7 2016

Baogang He

Authoritarian Deliberation in China *Daedalus* v146 no3 p155 Summ 2017

Baoguo Li

Save the world's primates in peril bibl color *Science* v354 no6311 p425 O 28 2016

Baorong Gao

Gene expression profiling–guided clinical precision treatment for patients with endometrial carcinoma bibl color diag *Science* v354 no6319 p33 D 23 2016

Bapat, Vivek

Why the Lowly Dandelion Is a Better Metaphor for Leaders than the Mighty Banyan *Harvard Business Review Digital Articles* p2 Mr 23 2017

Bapst, Ellen

Still worried *U.S. Catholic* v82 no10 p5 O 2017

Baptism

Love becomes fruitful S. Wells *Christian Century* v134 no19 p35 S 13 2017

Rites of Passage color *Chicago* v65 no12 p104 D 2016

Baptism—Biblical teaching

LIVING BY The Word N. L. Parish *Christian Century* v134 no4 p23 F 15 2017

BAPTIST, EDWARD E.

p12 N 2017

A LONG-LASTING EFFECT OF PREMATURITY color *Equus* no480 p14 S 2017

MAINTAIN FITNESS THROUGH CANTERING color *Equus* no477 p16 Je 2017

MORE EVIDENCE THAT HELMETS PROTECT AGAINST BRAIN TRAUMA color *Equus* no478 p16 Jl 2017

MUD TROUBLES *Equus* no472 p14 Ja 2017

NAHMS SNAPSHOT: HOW WE FIGHT FLIES chart color *Equus* no478 p20 Jl 2017

NAHMS SNAPSHOT: HOW WE MANAGE MANURE chart color *Equus* no477 p20 Je 2017

NAHMS SNAPSHOT: WHERE THE BREEDS ARE chart color *Equus* no476 p22 My 2017

NERVE'S ROLE IN HEADSHAKING INVESTIGATED color *Equus* no481 p12 O 2017

NEW DEWORMING AGENT SHOWS PROMISE color *Equus* no473 p11 F 2017

NEW FLY REPELLENT IN THE WORKS color *Equus* no471 p10 D 2016

NEW LIFESTYLE FOR PRZEWALSKI'S HORSES color *Equus* no481 p14 O 2017

NEW TEST FOR TAPEWORMS color *Equus* no481 p14 O 2017

NEW WAY TO ASSESS PAIN color *Equus* no473 p12 F 2017

NIACIN DEFICIENCY RULED OUT AS GRASS SICKNESS CAUSE *Equus* no470 p20 N 2016

NOTHING BORING ABOUT YAWNING color *Equus* no470 p21 N 2016

ORGAN ID *Equus* no478 p22 Jl 2017

ORIGINS OF AMBLING HORSES TRACED bw color *Equus* no471 p13 D 2016

OUTCOMES FOR ESOPHAGEAL SURGERY REVIEWED *Equus* no475 p25 Ap 2017

PASS THE SALT color *Equus* no478 p22 Jl 2017

POP QUIZ: ALL EARS color *Equus* no480 p20 S 2017

POP QUIZ: ANATOMY color *Equus* no473 p16 F 2017

POP QUIZ color *Equus* no470 p22 N 2016

POP QUIZ? color *Equus* no474 p14 Mr 2017

POP QUIZ color *Equus* no475 p30 Ap 2017

POP QUIZ color *Equus* no482 p16 N 2017

A POSITIVE FOR PEER PRESSURE color *Equus* no471 p12 D 2016

PREVENT WINTER WEIGHT LOSS color *Equus* no471 p14 D 2016

Rabies color *Equus* no477 p29 Je 2017

REASSURING FINDINGS ABOUT PREDNISOLONE color *Equus* no476 p18 My 2017

REASSURING STUDY OF CARRIAGE HORSES color *Equus* no475 p25 Ap 2017

REMOVING GRASS STAINS *Equus* no475 p32 Ap 2017

SAFE RECOVERY FROM SEDATION *Equus* no482 p16 N 2017

SIGNS OF A HOOF ABSCESS *Equus* no481 p22 O 2017

SLEEP LIKE A BABY? color *Equus* no477 p22 Je 2017

SOME SMALL SARCOIDS GO AWAY ON THEIR OWN color *Equus* no473 p11 F 2017

STEM CELLS MAY HELP HEAL SOFT-TISSUE INJURIES AND ARTHRITIS color *Equus* no477 p16 Je 2017

STRAP SAFETY color *Equus* no472 p14 Ja 2017

STUDY CONFIRMS EFFECTIVENESS OF THE "SQUEEZE TECHNIQUE" color *Equus* no482 p13 N 2017

STUDY: GAS IS IMPORTANT SIGN IN SAND COLIC CASES *Equus* no481 p12 O 2017

SUSCEPTIBILITY TO SWEET ITCH INVESTIGATED color *Equus* no478 p18 Jl 2017

TAKING STOCK color *Equus* no473 p16 F 2017

THE TOLL TRAVEL TAKES color *Equus* no477 p22 Je 2017

TRAINING TECHNIQUE HELPS HORSES "TALK" color *Equus* no472 p10 Ja 2017

TWO WAYS TO SOAK HAY *Equus* no476 p24 My 2017

WATCH OUT FOR WASPS color *Equus* no481 p20 O 2017

WATCH WINTER WATER INTAKE *Equus* no473 p18 F 2017

A WAY TO GET MORE FROM HOCK INJECTIONS color *Equus* no472 p12 Ja 2017

WHAT INFECTION LOOKS LIKE color *Equus* no482 p16 N 2017

WHAT'S YOUR SUPPLEMENT IQ? color *Equus* no472 p36 Ja 2017

What to expect as your horse grows old [Cover story] color *Equus* no473 p24 F 2017

WHEN WOUNDS DON'T HEAL [Cover story] color *Equus* no471 p24 D 2016

WHEN YOUR HORSE IS COLICKY *Equus* no480 p20 S 2017

WHICH BEDDING HARBORS MORE BACTERIA? color *Equus* no471 p11 D 2016

WHIRLS AND HAIR WHORLS color *Equus* no470 p18 N 2016

WINTER BARN VENTILATION color *Equus* no470 p24 N 2016

WINTER PREP TO-DO LIST color *Equus* no482 p22 N 2017

Barakat, Ibtisam

Balcony on the Moon: Coming of Age in Palestine *Publishers Weekly* v263 no49 p121 D 7 2016

Baraloto, C.

Persistent effects of pre-Columbian plant domestication on Amazonian forest composition bibl chart graph map *Science* v355 no6328 p925 Mr 3 2017

Baraloto, Christopher

Positive biodiversity-productivity relationship predominant in global forests bibl chart graph map *Science* v354 no6309 paaf8957-1 O 14 2016

Baram, Nir

Facts on the ground E. Webb *America* v217 no7 p48 O 2 2017

Baran, Madeleine

4 — IN THE DARK A. Sadlier *Entertainment Weekly* no1444/1445 p114 D 16 2016

Baran, Phil S.

Decarboxylative borylation color *Science* v356 no6342 p1045 Je 9 2017

Barandun, Jonas

Architecture of the yeast small subunit processome bibl color *Science* v355 no6321 p1 Ja 13 2017

Baranski, Christine

The Good Fight J. Jensen color *Entertainment Weekly* no1454/1455 p85 F 24 2017

GOOD NEWS L. Rice color *Entertainment Weekly* no1453 p28 F 17 2017

Packing Even More Punch Into The Good Fight L. Rice color *Entertainment Weekly* no1463/1464 p14 Ap/My 2017

Baranski, Christine—Interviews

Christine BARANSKI Z. POSEN *Interview* v47 no1 p21 F 2017

The GOOD LIFE I. Rudolph color *TV Guide* v65 no7 p30 F 13 2017

Bara-Popa, Adrian

Discussion *Smithsonian* v48 no1 p10 Ap 2017

Baras, Aris

Distribution and clinical impact of functional variants in 50,726 whole-exome sequences from the DiscovEHR study chart graph *Science* v354 no6319 paaf6814-1 D 23 2016

Genetic identification of familial hypercholesterolemia within a single U.S. health care system chart graph *Science* v354 no6319 paaf7000-1 D 23 2016

Baras, Yevgeniya

YEVGENIYA BARAS N. Griffin cartoon *Art in America* v104 no11 p121 D 2016

Barash, David

Tele-Mentoring Is Creating Global Communities of Practice in Health Care *Harvard Business Review Digital Articles* p2 N 22 2016

Baratta, Anthony

NEXT WAVE: Bright Young Thing E. Espinoza color *House Beautiful* v159 no9 p39 N 2017

Baratta, Anthony—Interviews

Call of the Wild D. BRENNER color *House Beautiful* p76 Jl 2017

Barau, Joan

The DNA methyltransferase DNMT3C protects male germ cells from transposon activity bibl diag graph *Science* v354 no6314 p909 N 18 2016

Barba, Lorena A.

The hard road to reproducibility cartoon *Science* v354 no6308 p142 O 7 2016

Barbados—Description & travel

BACK TO Barbados H. Silva color diag *Conde Nast Traveler* v52 no1 p82 Ja 2017

The new Barbados T. HALL color map *Canadian Geographic*

v135 no6 p9 D 2015

Barbara, Chris

MICKEY THOMPSON TIRES & WHEELS UNVEILS RE-FRESHED BRAND IDENTITY *Dirt Sports + Off-Road* v51 no3 p8 Mr 2017

Barbarin, Paul

Best of Brass J. Berry bw *New Orleans Magazine* v51 no5 p54 Mr 2017

Barbary sheep—Behavior

GOING LONG S. Reese color *Outdoor Life* v223 no9 p40 N 2016

Barbash, Mark

Profiles in Courage *Sierra* v102 no4 p4 Jl/Ag 2017

Barbato, F.

Observation of a large-scale anisotropy in the arrival directions of cosmic rays above 8×1018 eV *Science* v357 no6357 p1266 S 22 2017

Barbato, Randy

Revisiting the Menendez Murders A. D'Arminio *TV Guide* v65 no23 p9 My 29 2017

Barbeau, Jeffrey W.

Selected Poems of Edna St. Vincent Millay: An Annotated Edition *Christian Century* v133 no24 p41 N 23 2016

Barbeau, P. S.

Observation of coherent elastic neutrino-nucleus scattering diag *Science* v357 no6356 p1123 S 15 2017

Barbecue cooking

15 QUESTIONS ABOUT BARBEQUE ANSWERED M. Diffee and P. Noth cartoon map *Esquire* p110 S 2017

4 small steps to a cheerier household color *Redbook* p130 Je 2017

Barbecue Italian Style D. VAUGHN *Texas Monthly* v45 no4 p34 Ap 2017

EDITOR'S LETTER E. PARKHURST *Virginia Living* p9 2017 Smoke & Salt

EDITOR'S LETTER T. TALIAFERRO *Texas Monthly* v45 no6 p20 Je 2017

EVENTS *Virginia Living* p15 2017 Smoke & Salt

FIRE UP YOUR WEEK C. Morocco color diag *Bon Appetit* v62 no6 p64 Je 2017

Let's Eat Pig's Feet R. Bragg color *Southern Living* v52 no4 p150 Ap 2017

MISCELLANY *Texas Monthly* v45 no6 p8 Je 2017

THE PERFECT BITE *Texas Monthly* v45 no6 p106 Je 2017

Smoke Over the Water D. VAUGHN *Texas Monthly* v45 no8 p26 Ag 2017

Barbecue cooking—Economic aspects

SAVED BY BARBECUE CHICKEN PIZZA D. Eng color *Fortune* v174 no8 p58 D 15 2016

Barbecue cooking—Evaluation

SMOKE RING: The litmus test for good barbecue, tender, no-nonsense beef brisket represents low, slow food at its best J. SPALDING *Indianapolis Monthly* v12 no40 p45 Ag 2017

Barbecue pits—Evaluation

IRVING PARK J. REESE cartoon color *Chicago* v66 no2 p20 F 2017

Barbecue restaurants

The Best BBQ Awards 2017 *Virginia Living* p31 2017 Smoke & Salt

DIM SUM AT BEST BBQ J. ZYMAN *Atlanta* v57 no3 p54 Jl 2017

EDITOR'S LETTER T. TALIAFERRO *Texas Monthly* v45 no6 p20 Je 2017

MISCELLANY *Texas Monthly* v45 no6 p8 Je 2017

The South's Best Butts M. Moore color *Southern Living* v52 no4 p134 Ap 2017

Where There's SmoQue: Nigerian-born chef Seni Alabi-Isama is about to open a sous-vide barbecue restaurant called the SmoQue Pit in Statesboro. Yes, Statesboro C. BETHEA *Atlanta* v57 no3 p50 Jl 2017

Barbecue restaurants—Evaluation

Bar Excellence J. K. WOLFE *Cincinnati Magazine* v50 no3 p128 D 2016

Cheers to the South's Best S. Evans color *Southern Living* v52 no4 p12 Ap 2017

DISH OF THE MONTH J. SIDMAN *Washingtonian Magazine* v52 no6 p149 Mr 2017

EAT. DRINK. ENJOY J. Forman, T. Mcnally et al color *New Or-*

leans Magazine v51 no9 p56 Jl 2017

Food & Drink *Virginia Living* p39 2017 Best 20of Virginia

THE GOLDEN AGE OF BBQ D. VAUGHN *Texas Monthly* v45 no6 p94 Je 2017

LINK TO THE PAST J. C. REID *Texas Monthly* v45 no6 p117 Je 2017

PARLEZ-VOUS BBQ? J. SALAMON *Texas Monthly* v45 no6 p111 Je 2017

THE REST *Texas Monthly* v45 no6 p104 Je 2017

Rib Crib J. K. WOLFE *Cincinnati Magazine* v50 no4 p147 Ja 2017

SECRETS IN THE SAUCE L. COLLINS cartoon *New Yorker* v93 no10 p66 Ap 24 2017

Smoke Signal J. K. WOLFE *Cincinnati Magazine* v50 no8 p105 My 2017

SOUTH'S BEST BARBECUE R. Moss color *Southern Living* v52 no4 p70 Ap 2017

TYLER TWO-STEP M. HALL *Texas Monthly* v45 no6 p118 Je 2017

Where to Eat Now *Texas Monthly* v44 no11 p122 N 2016

Barbecue sauce

SECRETS IN THE SAUCE L. COLLINS cartoon *New Yorker* v93 no10 p66 Ap 24 2017

When Burgers Go Bad *Atlanta* v56 no10 p58 F 2017

Barbells

the (next) 10 BEST BACK exercises M. BERG color *Muscle & Performance* v9 no6 p36 Je 2017

[RE]BALANCING ACT M. BERG chart color *Muscle & Performance* v9 no1 p20 Ja 2017

BARBER, BENJAMIN

Think Globally, Resist Locally color *Nation* v304 no4 p17 F 6 2017

BARBER, CHARLES VICTOR

An Ecoregion-Based Approach to Protecting Half the Terrestrial Realm *BioScience* v67 no6 p534 Je 2017

Barber, Dan

How Sweet It Isn't *New York Times Book Review* p1 Ja 8 2017

Barber, Daniel L.

Rescue of exhausted CD8 T cells by PD-1–targeted therapies is CD28-dependent bw diag graph *Science* v355 no6332 p1423 Mr 31 2017

Barber, David

Just Saying *American Scholar* v86 no1 p52 Wint 2017

The Lion's Bride *American Scholar* v86 no1 p58 Wint 2017

Mamihlapinatapai D. Barber *American Scholar* v86 no1 p53 Wint 2017

On a Shaker Admonition *American Scholar* v86 no1 p54 Wint 2017

Saying *American Scholar* v86 no1 p56 Wint 2017

Barber, Diane E.

Bringing the Dream Horse Home color *Dressage Today* v23 no4 p48 D 2016

REMEMBERING A LEGEND color *Dressage Today* v23 no11 p54 Ag 2017

Barber, Felix

Many CEOs Aren't Breakthrough Innovators (and That's OK) *Harvard Business Review Digital Articles* p2 S 4 2015

Barber, Gregory

A BRIEF HISTORY OF GPS cartoon color *Mother Jones* v41 no6 p54 N/D 2016

THE BRIGHT STUFF color *Wired* v24 no11 p90 N 2016

Barber, Jeff

Application of Current Standards to Natural Playgrounds *Parks & Recreation* p9 2017 Supplement Field Guide - Supplier and Resource Directory

Barber, Mark E.

Strong peak in Tc of Sr2RuO4 under uniaxial pressure bibl color graph *Science* v355 no6321 p1 Ja 13 2017

Barber, Samuel, 1910-1981

Shchedrin: The Left-Hander W. R. Braun *Opera News* v81 no6 p50 D 2016

Barber, William

CENTURY marks cartoon *Christian Century* v134 no11 p8 My 24 2017

Barberio, Joseph

career coach color *Working Mother* v40 no3 p6 Ag/S 2017

Career Coach color *Working Mother* v40 no4 p8 O/N 2017
family matters color *Working Mother* v40 no3 p38 Ag/S 2017
No Sweat color *Working Mother* v40 no2 p58 Je/Jl 2017
Zen Master color *Working Mother* v40 no3 p47 Ag/S 2017

Barberis, George
LIGHT REPAST P. Kolonia color *Popular Photography* v81 no2 p40 Mr/Ap 2017

BARBER-MEYER, SHANNON
An Unparalleled Opportunity for an Important Ecological Study *BioScience* v67 no10 p875 O 2017

Barberon, Marie
Root diffusion barrier control by a vasculature-derived peptide binding to the SGN3 receptor bibl color *Science* v355 no6322 p280 Ja 20 2017

Barbers
BLUNT *Interview* v47 no1 p80 F 2017
Force of Nature M. Carlos color *Essence* v48 no3 p43 Jl 2017
Hung Vanngo S. Zuckerman color *InStyle* v24 no9 p342 S 2017
Stan's Barber Shop B. COSSAVELLA *Arizona Highways* v93 no2 p6 F 2017

Barbers—Attitudes
The Storybook Barber A. SIMMONS *Reader's Digest* v188 no1126 p8 D 2016/Ja 2017

Barbershops
See also
Barbers
Barbershop Bonanza *Atlanta* v57 no3 p39 Jl 2017
BLADE RUNNERS [Cover story] C. PRICE color *New Orleans Magazine* v51 no10 p70 Ag 2017

Barbershops—Evaluation
BARBERSHOP QUARTET *Atlanta* v57 no3 p40 Jl 2017

Barbey, Jacques—Interviews
Q&A: Jacques Barbey *Arizona Highways* v92 no7 p9 Jl 2016

Barbie dolls
Make-Believe D. D'Addario color *Time* v188 no25-26 p36 D 19 2016 Double Issue

BARBIER, JULES
Roméo et Juliette *Opera News* v81 no7 p56 Ja 2017

Barbieri, C.
Rosetta's comet 67P/Churyumov-Gerasimenko sheds its dusty mantle to reveal its icy nature bibl graph *Science* v354 no6319 p1566 D 23 2016
Surface changes on comet 67P/Churyumov-Gerasimenko suggest a more active past bw graph *Science* v355 no6332 p1392 Mr 31 2017

Barbieri, Elisa
Reticulon 3–dependent ER-PM contact sites control EGFR non-clathrin endocytosis color diag graph *Science* v356 no6338 p617 My 12 2017

BARBIERI, PIERPAOLO
The Agony of Venezuela color *National Review* v69 no16 p30 Ag 28 2017

Barbizon Lighting Co.
Barbizon Lighting Company Your Trusted Partner in Production *Stage Directions* v30 no3 p62 Mr 2017

Barbosa, E. M.
Persistent effects of pre-Columbian plant domestication on Amazonian forest composition bibl chart graph map *Science* v355 no6328 p925 Mr 3 2017

Barbot, Sylvain
Imaging the distribution of transient viscosity after the 2016 Mw 7.1 Kumamoto earthquake map *Science* v356 no6334 p163 Ap 14 2017

BARBOUR, CELIA
Flight of Fancy color *House Beautiful* v159 no5 p68 Je 2017
in the pink color *House Beautiful* v159 no7 p104 S 2017
MAKE IT HUM color *House Beautiful* v159 no1 p76 F 2017
MOUNTAINS' MAJESTY color *House Beautiful* v158 no10 p64 D 2016/Ja 2017
New House, Old Soul color *House Beautiful* v159 no9 p100 N 2017
YOTAM OTTOLENGHI color *Architectural Digest* v73 no11 p112 N 2016

Barbour, Paula
ALL AROUND: THE FARM® *Successful Farming* v115 no12 p77 O 2017

ALL AROUND THE FARM *Successful Farming* v115 no8 p62 Je/Jl 2017
IDEA OF THE MONTH: CANS AND JUGS DISAPPEAR IN ROLLING WORKBENCH DOOR THAT ADDS STORAGE SPACE *Successful Farming* v115 no9 p80 Ag 2017
IDEA OF THE MONTH: CATTLE HANDLING CAN BE A ONE-PERSON JOB color *Successful Farming* v115 no7 p68 My 2017
IDEA OF THE MONTH: SHOP-BUILT SIDEDRESSER CONVERTED FROM SPRAYER ALLOWS SPLIT APPLICATIONS *Successful Farming* v115 no6 p78 Ap 2017
IDEA OF THE MONTH *Successful Farming* v114 no13 p90 D 2016
IDEA OF THE MONTH *Successful Farming* v115 no11 p76 S 2017
IDEA OF THE MONTH *Successful Farming* v115 no2 p80 F 2017
WORK AT THE PERFECT HEIGHT *Successful Farming* v115 no4 p80 Mr 2017

Barbujani, Guido
Chimpanzee genomic diversity reveals ancient admixture with bonobos bibl diag graph map *Science* v354 no6311 p477 O 28 2016

BARBUZANO, JAVIER
Historical Observations Reveal an Ancient Explosion *Sky & Telescope* v134 no6 p12 D 2017
The White Dwarf That Survived The Blast *Sky & Telescope* v134 no6 p11 D 2017

BARCA, LISA
One Tough (Rebel, Activist, Feminist) Mother: The documentary Dolores shines a light on an overlooked hero of farmworkers' and women's rights *Ms.* v27 no3 p46 Fall 2017
Redemption Time *Ms.* v26 no4 p37 Wint 2016

Barceló, Miquel, 1957-
Larvaire color *Art in America* v104 no10 p39 N 2016

Barcelona (Spain)—Buildings, structures, etc.
Cloud Nine D. COHN *Architectural Record* v205 no9 p92 S 2017

Barclay, Linwood
Revenge of the Internet E. NORTON color *Publishers Weekly* v264 no33 p48 Ag 14 2017
The Twenty-Three *Publishers Weekly* v263 no39 p64 S 26 2016

BARCLAY, MICHAEL
A farewell for the ages color *Maclean's* v129 no48/49 p70 D 5 2016
Goodnight, grocer of despair color *Maclean's* v129 no47 p52 N 28 2016
Howlin' at the Moondog bw *Maclean's* v129 no48/49 p36 D 5 2016
THE INTERVIEW color *Maclean's* v129 no46 p10 N 21 2016
TRAGICALLY HIP ADDED TO THE SYLLABUS color *Maclean's* v129 no44 p50 N 7 2016

Barclays PLC
IN BRIEF K. Stock color *Bloomberg Businessweek* no4528 p6 Je 26 2017

BARCZI, NATHAN
IN THE IMAGE OF OUR CHOOSING diag *Christianity Today* p48 Mr 2017

Bard, Nolan
DeepStack: Expert-level artificial intelligence in heads-up no-limit poker [Cover story] chart diag *Science* v356 no6337 p508 My 5 2017

BARDAJÍ, RAFAEL L.
Spain Is Different color *Weekly Standard* v22 no48 p15 S 4 2017

Bardales, Aída
Latino Authors Celebrated At Annual Book Awards *Publishers Weekly* v264 no40 p18 O 2 2017

BARDE, JOEL
Second Coming [Cover story] color *Walrus* v14 no9 p22 N 2017

Barde, Yves-Alain
Scaling pain threshold with microRNAs diag *Science* v356 no6343 p1124 Je 16 2017

Bardem, Javier, 1969-
MaD MaN J. Pressler bw color *Esquire* p70 My 2017

Barden, Christine Rew
KEEPING YOUR CABIN IN THE FAMILY [Cover story] *Cabin Living* p12 Ag 2017

Barder, Brian

How Bad Was Tony Blair? bw *New York Review of Books* v64 no1 p64 Ja 19 2017

Bardhi, Fleura

The Sharing Economy Isn't About Sharing at All *Harvard Business Review Digital Articles* p2 Ja 28 2015

BARDI, JENNIFER

EDITOR'S NOTE *Humanist* v77 no1 p3 Ja/F 2017

EDITOR'S NOTE *Humanist* v77 no2 p3 Mr/Ap 2017

EDITOR'S NOTE *Humanist* v77 no4 p3 Jl/Ag 2017

EDITOR'S NOTE *Humanist* v77 no5 p3 S/O 2017

GAMM ON: The Humanist Interview with Philanthropist Gordon Gamm *Humanist* v77 no5 p20 S/O 2017

Bardi, Lina Bo—Exhibitions

CLEAR VISION B. BERGDOLL color *Architectural Digest* v73 no12 p106 D 2016

Bardina, Susana V.

Enhancement of Zika virus pathogenesis by preexisting antiflavivirus immunity graph *Science* v356 no6334 p175 Ap 14 2017

Bardot, Brigitte, 1934-—Interviews

Being Bardot L. CAMHI bw *Vogue* v206 no11 p100 N 2016

Bards & bardism

Laughter THE BEST MEDICINE *Reader's Digest* v189 no1127 p74 F 2017

Bardzell, Ashton

Catching Trout J. Fuchs and T. Keith color *Sports Illustrated* v127 no1 p26 Jl 3 2017

Bare, Stacy

STACY BARE J. Foersterling color *Skiing* p28 Wint 2017

Barea, J.j.

THE PLIGHT OF PUERTO RICO color *Sports Illustrated* v127 no11 p56 O 9 2017

Bareilles, Sara, 1979-

Sugar, Butter, Flour M. Schulman cartoon *New Yorker* v93 no7 p14 Ap 3 2017

Bareilles, Sara, 1979-—Interviews

SARA BAREILLES ON "SOULFUL STORYTELLING" *Cincinnati Magazine* v50 no8 p12 My 2017

Barenboim, Daniel, 1942-

NO CIGAR A. Gopnik cartoon *New Yorker* v92 no47 p20 Ja 30 2017

Bargaining power

10 Myths About Negotiating Your First Salary L. Babcock and J. Bear *Harvard Business Review Digital Articles* p2 Jl 3 2017

Barger, Jennifer

MAKE MINE NEAT *Washingtonian Magazine* v52 no3 p119 D 2016

OLD TOWN, NEW VIBE: One of the area's most interesting fashion hubs these days? Try Alexandria, with its delightful mix of independent boutiques *Washingtonian Magazine* v52 no8 p115 My 2017

PROFESSIONAL GRADE: Curious how the experts live? Take a look inside four kitchens belonging to people who design or work in them for a living *Washingtonian Magazine* v53 no1 p161 O 2017

Think You Can Flip a House? color *Washingtonian Magazine* v52 no7 p95 Ap 2017

Barger, Joe

NOT FADE AWAY [Cover story] T. Hamilton bw color *Runner's World* v52 no5 p80 Je 2017

Bargh, John

How Hidden Factors Drive What We Think S. Begley color *Time* v190 no15 p18 O 16 2017

Bar-Gill, Nir

Observing chemical shifts from nanosamples diag graph *Science* v357 no6346 p38 Jl 7 2017

BARGLOW, RAYMOND

STEM CELL RESEARCH *Skeptical Inquirer* v41 no1 p34 Ja/F 2017

Barham, Bradford L.

Cellulosic biofuel contributions to a sustainable energy future: Choices and outcomes color *Science* v356 no6345 p1349 Je 30 2017

Baribault, Beverly

The 2016 Magnolia Designer Show House *Atlanta* v56 no7 p2 N 2016

DESIGNER PROFILES *Atlanta* v56 no7 p38 N 2016

EVENT CHAIRS *Atlanta* v56 no7 p12 N 2016

BARICHIVICH, WILLIAM J.

Overcoming Challenges to the Recovery of Declining Amphibian Populations in the United States *BioScience* v67 no2 p156 F 2017

Baril, Karen Elizabeth

On guard against EYE INJURIES [Cover story] color *Equus* no476 p42 My 2017

Barinka, Alex

Dropbox Gets Ready For the Road bw *Bloomberg Businessweek* no4534 p22 Ag 14 2017

Snapchat Can't Keep It Private color *Bloomberg Businessweek* no4509 p27 Ja 30 2017

Tech IPOs Want to Get Ahead of Trump *Bloomberg Businessweek* no4500 p33 N 21 2016

Barish, Barry

Will Nobel Prize overlook LIGO's master builder? A. Cho color *Science* v353 no6307 p1478 S 30 2016

Baritones (Singers)

ROAD SHOW: Paulo Szot in Marseilles M. R. MERCADO *Opera News* v81 no9 p18 Mr 2017

Sean Michael Plumb H. STEWART *Opera News* v81 no10 p12 Ap 2017

Bar-Joseph, Ziv

A transcription factor hierarchy defines an environmental stress response network diag *Science* v354 no6312 p598 N 4 2016

Barkemeyer, Brad

Transition Turmoil color *Horse & Rider* v55 no12 p66 D 2016

BARKENBUS, JACK

Electric Vehicles Climate Saviors, or Not? chart color *Issues in Science & Technology* v33 no2 p55 Wint 2017

Barker, Calli

MAKING TIME FOR FUN: Retirement is a great time to take up new interests and activities *Washingtonian Magazine* v52 no8 p145 My 2017

Barker, Danny

BOOK AND BANJO J. BERRY color *New Orleans Magazine* v51 no3 p50 Ja 2017

Barker, David G.

Ancestral alliances: Plant mutualistic symbioses with fungi and bacteria color *Science* v356 no6340 p819 My 26 2017

BARKER, ELISE

A Legend in the Making *Idaho Magazine* v16 no6 p16 Mr 2017

ON THE CUSP OF CHANGE *Idaho Magazine* v16 no9 p32 Je 2017

BARKER, JAN

WELL-SEASONED *Atlanta* v56 no7 p72 N 2016

Barker, Margaret A.

When Birds Become Bird Food color *National Wildlife (World Edition)* v54 no6 p12 O/N 2016

Barker, Patricia

On the Move: Two American artistic directors are taking over major international troupes S. Sucato *Dance Magazine* v91 no9 p20 S 2017

Barker, Terry

Faith and Science at a Crossroad *Sky & Telescope* v134 no3 p6 S 2017

Barker, Tim

TERMS OF ENGAGEMENT *Harper's Magazine* v334 no2001 p28 F 2017

Barker, Travis

TRAVIS BARKER D. M. Zepeda color *Runner's World* v52 no6 p96 Jl 2017

Barker, Trey R.

East of the Sun: A Jace Salome Novel *Publishers Weekly* v263 no42 p54 O 17 2016

Barkho, Gabriela

Boxed In color graph *Bloomberg Businessweek* no4535 p23 Ag 28 2017

Barkin, Ellen, 1954-

ANIMAL KINGDOM S. Highfill color *Entertainment Weekly* no1468/1469 p65 Je 2-9 2017

More Family Drama on Animal Kingdom *TV Guide* v65 no19 p11 My 1 2017

Barkley, Hannah

Coral Crusader color *Oceanus* v51 no2 p28 Wint 2016

Barkley, Jim

TRUE GRITS S. Castle and M. C. Cairns color *Southern Living* v52 no10 p78 O 2017

Barkley, Saquon

Leading Off color *Sports Illustrated* v125 no19 p12 D 12 2016

A LION IN SUMMER P. Thamel color *Sports Illustrated* v127 no3 p92 Jl 24 2017

SAQUON BARKLEY'S TOUGHEST COMPETITION IN THE HEISMAN RACE B. Feldman color *Sports Illustrated* v127 no3 p97 Jl 24 2017

Barletta, William

Edward Joseph Lofgren *Physics Today* v70 no2 p69 F 2017

Bar-Lev, Amir

THE FOUR-HOUR GRATEFUL DEAD FILM... REVIEWED BY A DEADHEAD E. R. Brown color *Entertainment Weekly* no1468/1469 p89 Je 2-9 2017

Barley

Eat these to hit your perfect weight M. TAYLOR color *Redbook* p82 N 2017

Barley, Rebecca

Essential Framework for Adaptive Aquatics *Parks & Recreation* v52 no10 p54 O 2017

Barley, Sarah Dotts

Deals R. DEAHL color *Publishers Weekly* v263 no43 p7 O 24 2016

Barliant, Claire

FUTUREFARMERS color *Art in America* v105 no5 p131 My 2017

"THE ARTIST'S MUSEUM" color *Art in America* v105 no3 p133 Mr 2017

Barlow, Dade

Show Up. Be You color *Glamour* v115 no5 p18 My 2017

Barlow, Liddy

Reflections on the lectionary *Christian Century* v134 no12 p21 Je 7 2017

Barlow, Nathan

Community network for deaf scientists color *Science* v356 no6336 p386 Ap 28 2017

Barlow, Phyllida, 1944-

Kunsthalle Zurich A. Rosenmeyer color *Art in America* v105 no1 p91 Ja 2017

Barlow, Steve

Memphis Fights Blight: Collaborating to Win the Battle Against Vacant and Abandoned Property *Bridges (Federal Reserve Bank of St. Louis)* p8 Fall 2016

Barmak, Sarah

Pleasure Principal color *Walrus* v14 no5 p38 Je 2017

Barman, Bill

A hard knot to untie: It's difficult to ensure parishioners from different cultures all feel welcome color *U.S. Catholic* v82 no8 p31 Ag 2017

Barmet, Peter

Global atmospheric particle formation from CERN CLOUD measurements bibl graph map *Science* v354 no6316 p1119 D 2 2016

Barn design & construction

American Beauty S. BROWN color *Timber Home Living* v27 no5 p10 O 2017

The Back Story G. WOOD color *Missouri Life* v44 no3 p98 My 2017

Building a Hay Barn: The Old Way in New Idaho J. AKENSON and H. AKENSON *Idaho Magazine* v16 no9 p24 Je 2017

POSITIVE FILTRATION: IOWA SELECT FARMS IS BUILDING HIGH-TECH SOW BARNS DESIGNED TO KEEP DISEASE OUT B. Freese color *Successful Farming* v115 no7 p45 My 2017

Barn owl

Tricks For Treats A. SHAW color *National Geographic Kids* no474 p12 O 2017

Barn remodeling

barn style color *Timber Home Living* v27 no5 p54 O 2017

Nature's Course bw color *Log Home Living* v34 no7 p16 S 2017

Barna, Daniel

Buffer-gas cooling of antiprotonic helium to 1.5 to 1.7 K, and antiproton-to-electron mass ratio bibl chart diag graph *Science* v354 no6312 p610 N 4 2016

BARNA, MARK

Albert Einstein color *Discover* v38 no4 p36 My 2017

Autism Spectrum Disorder color diag *Discover* v38 no6 p62 Jl/Ag 2017

Dawning of the Planet of the Apes color map *Discover* v38 no1 p67 Ja/F 2017

History Unwrapped color *Discover* v38 no5 p12 Je 2017

Human Activity Shakes Up Geological Hazard Map color map *Discover* v38 no1 p64 Ja/F 2017

The Lava Catcher color *Discover* v38 no7 p16 S 2017

Researchers Finally ID Poison Ivy Suspect color *Discover* v38 no1 p88 Ja/F 2017

Superbug Arrives in the U.S color *Discover* v38 no1 p41 Ja/F 2017

Treasures Beneath the Ancient Sands color map *Discover* v38 no5 p70 Je 2017

TRENDING chart color map *Discover* v38 no4 p12 My 2017

Barnabas, Apostle, Saint

Composition notes: The New Testament letters give us a window into the early church A. Camille color *U.S. Catholic* v82 no10 p47 O 2017

Barnaby, Hannah

Bad Guy *Publishers Weekly* v264 no13 p98 Mr 27 2017

Some of the Parts *Publishers Weekly* v263 no49 p102 D 7 2016

Barnard, Alan

What's next for the Ju/'hoansi? color *Science* v356 no6345 p1340 Je 30 2017

Barnard, Kathy

Through the Looking Glass Z. Glasgow bw *Missouri Life* v44 no6 p23 S 2017

Barnard, Matt

The Future Of Farming Is Looking Up Selina Wang color *Bloomberg Businessweek* no4537 p62 S 11 2017

Barnard, Neal

GUEST LIST color *Washingtonian Magazine* v52 no7 p20 Ap 2017

Barnard College

Education Directory *Stage Directions* v29 no10 p36 O 2016

The St. Augustine Prize cartoon *Weekly Standard* v22 no28 p3 Mr 27 2017

BARNER, ALLISON K.

Long-Term Studies Contribute Disproportionately to Ecology and Policy *BioScience* v67 no3 p271 Mr 2017

Barnes & Noble Education Inc.

News Briefs *Publishers Weekly* v264 no33 p9 Ag 14 2017

Barnes & Noble Inc.

The Big Stories of 2016 J. Milliot color *Publishers Weekly* v263 no52 p6 D 19 2016

B&N Keeps Its Focus On Revenue Growth J. Milliot chart *Publishers Weekly* v264 no26 p2 Je 26 2017

Parneros Charged with Reversing B&N Sales Slide J. Milliot chart *Publishers Weekly* v264 no18 p5 My 1 2017

Barnes & Noble Inc.—Finance

B&N Looking for a Sales Rebound J. Milliot chart color *Publishers Weekly* v263 no48 p4 N 28 2016

Barnes, Christopher M.

The Ideal Work Schedule, as Determined by Circadian Rhythms *Harvard Business Review Digital Articles* p2 Ja 28 2015

Jet Lag Doesn't Have to Ruin Your Business Trip *Harvard Business Review Digital Articles* p2 N 4 2015

Research: Sleep Deprivation Can Make It Harder to Stay Calm at Work *Harvard Business Review Digital Articles* p2 2017

Research: Sleep-Deprived Leaders Are Less Inspiring *Harvard Business Review Digital Articles* p2 Je 15 2016

Research: Your Abusive Boss Is Probably an Insomniac *Harvard Business Review Digital Articles* p2 N 7 2014

Sleep-Deprived Judges Dole Out Harsher Punishments *Harvard Business Review Digital Articles* p2 F 15 2017

Barnes, Eleanor J.

Immunology taught by rats graph *Science* v357 no6347 p129 Jl 14 2017

BARNES, FRED

All Hands on Deck color *Weekly Standard* v22 no7 p8 O 24 2016

Angling for a Supreme Pick *Weekly Standard* v22 no22 p10 F 13 2017

Are Republicans Mid-Terminal? [Cover story] color *Weekly Stan-*

dard v22 no36 p10 My 29 2017

As Joe Heck Goes... *Weekly Standard* v22 no8 p8 O 31 2016

Better Luck Next Time *Weekly Standard* v22 no5 p10 O 10 2016

The Big 4 color *Weekly Standard* v23 no2 p14 S 18 2017

Can This Relationship Survive? cartoon *Weekly Standard* v22 no28 p10 Mr 27 2017

The Counterpuncher cartoon *Weekly Standard* v22 no19 p9 Ja 23 2017

The Courting of Pro-life Leaders color *Weekly Standard* v22 no16 p10 D 26 2016

Cozying Up to the Dictator bw *Weekly Standard* v22 no14 p11 D 12 2016

Details, Details cartoon *Weekly Standard* v23 no3 p11 S 25 2017

Disappointed Dems color *Weekly Standard* v22 no41 p9 Jl 3 2017

Evangelist to the Press Corps color *Weekly Standard* v23 no1 p13 S 11 2017

Fine-Tuned Chaos color *Weekly Standard* v22 no24 p12 F 27 2017

Gunning for Hillary color *Weekly Standard* v22 no25 p14 Mr 6 2017

He Liked Ike *Weekly Standard* v22 no5 p30 O 10 2016

He Was One of a Kind, Alas *Weekly Standard* v22 no10 p9 N 14 2016

His Favorite Punching Bag *Weekly Standard* v22 no9 p9 N 7 2016

Impatient for Impeachment color *Weekly Standard* v22 no40 p11 Je 26 2017

Incurable Obamacare cartoon *Weekly Standard* v22 no18 p6 Ja 16 2017

Learn from His Mistakes color *Weekly Standard* v22 no15 p8 D 19 2016

The Little Guy and the Billionaire color *Weekly Standard* v22 no11 p10 N 21 2016

Make America Gipper Again color *Weekly Standard* v23 no5 p10 O 9 2017

Missouri's Political Phenom cartoon color *Weekly Standard* v22 no42 p16 Jl 17 2017

Mucking Out the Justice Department cartoon *Weekly Standard* v22 no17 p9 Ja 2 2017

Price Takes a Beating color *Weekly Standard* v22 no21 p7 F 6 2017

Pulling the Strings *New Republic* v247 no11 p4 N 2016

Repeal, Replace, Resist color *Weekly Standard* v22 no12 p13 N 28 2016

The Republican To-Do List color *Weekly Standard* v22 no37 p10 Je 5 2017

The Road to Victory in Virginia cartoon *Weekly Standard* v22 no38 p10 Je 12 2017

Rules of Disorder color *Weekly Standard* v22 no39 p11 Je 19 2017

Sand in the Gears color *Weekly Standard* v22 no29 p10 Ap 3 2017

Schumer's Losing This One color *Weekly Standard* v22 no47 p14 Ag 21 2017

Senator on the Rise color *Weekly Standard* v22 no31 p12 Ap 17 2017

Simplify, Simplify, Simplify color *Weekly Standard* v22 no30 p9 Ap 10 2017

Situation Normal, All Trumped Up color *Weekly Standard* v22 no45 p10 Ag 7 2017

The Swamp Suburb color *Weekly Standard* v22 no34 p14 My 15 2017

A Tale of Two Speeches color *Weekly Standard* v22 no26 p11 Mr 13 2017

Tax Reform First color *Weekly Standard* v22 no23 p9 F 20 2017

The Trump Era Begins color *Weekly Standard* v22 no20 p9 Ja 30 2017

Trump Gets Himself in Hot Water—Again color *Weekly Standard* v22 no35 p12 My 22 2017

Trump Goes Bigly on Tax Reform color *Weekly Standard* v22 no33 p9 My 8 2017

Trump Unbound color *Weekly Standard* v22 no32 p18 My 1 2017

Tweeter in Chief cartoon *Weekly Standard* v22 no13 p11 D 5 2016

Virginia Slim: The Race Tightens *Weekly Standard* v22 no4 p9 O 3 2016

When You've Lost the Bushes . . *Weekly Standard* v22 no6 p9 O 17 2016

Why So Expensive? color *Weekly Standard* v22 no46 p16 Ag 14 2017

Barnes, Greg

THE SECRETS TO Floor Plan Perfection diag *Log Home Living* v34 no1 p44 F 2017

Barnes, Heather

SOCIAL MEDIA SOUND OFF L. F. Prater *Successful Farming* v114 no10 p63 O 2016

Barnes, Jake, 1959-

FALL FIGHT to the finish color *Team Roping Journal* p48 O 2017

GAME PLAN for Gaining Success color *Team Roping Journal* p54 S 2017

GETTING STARTED ON THE RIGHT (ROPING) FOOT color *Spin to Win Rodeo* v21 no2 p38 Ap 2017 LEGENDARY CONNECTION color *Team Roping Journal* p12 O 2017

Barnes, Julian

The Flash of the Blade J. Bell color *New York Review of Books* v64 no11 p4 Je 22 2017

A Marvelous Moment for French Writers and Artists color *New York Review of Books* v64 no6 p25 Ap 6 2017

BARNES, KATHY

color theory color *Better Homes & Gardens* v95 no4 p56 Ap 2017

DRY by DESIGN *Better Homes & Gardens* v95 no1 pZ1 Ja 2017

FACE VALUE color *Better Homes & Gardens* v95 no5 p66 My 2017

GRAND TOUR *Better Homes & Gardens* v94 no12 pZ1 D 2016

grow a GARDEN RUG color *Better Homes & Gardens* v95 no3 p84 Mr 2017

HIGH and DRY color *Better Homes & Gardens* v95 no3 p71 Mr 2017

OPEN invitation color *Better Homes & Gardens* v95 no6 p57 Je 2017

PERFECT FIT color *Better Homes & Gardens* v95 no6 p35 Je 2017

room to grow *Better Homes & Gardens* v94 no12 pN1 D 2016

ship shape *Better Homes & Gardens* v94 no12 pN8 D 2016

Barnes, M. Craig

Faith MATTERS *Christian Century* v133 no23 p35 N 9 2016

Faith Matters *Christian Century* v134 no12 p40 Je 7 2017

Finding God at the bottom *Christian Century* v134 no9 p31 Ap 26 2017

Glimpses of the beloved community *Christian Century* v134 no5 p35 Mr 1 2017

Lessons from the Keller controversy *Christian Century* v134 no17 p35 Ag 16 2017

The pastors I worry about *Christian Century* v134 no1 p35 Ja 4 2017

The temporary gift of marriage *Christian Century* v134 no13 p33 Je 21 2017

Barnes, Megan

FIGHTING SPIRITS *Nation* v305 no11 p41 O 30 2017

BARNES, NANCY OWENS

Imagining Imogene *Idaho Magazine* v17 no1 p6 Ja 2017

Barnes, Peter

EXIT LEFT bw color *Nation* v304 no16 p16 My 22 2017

Barnes, Philip

Complex multifault rupture during the 2016 Mw 7.8 Kaikōura earthquake, New Zealand color map *Science* v356 no6334 p154 Ap 14 2017

Barneson, Jake

DEAR ROPER B. Welch color *Spin to Win Rodeo* v20 no9 p10 N 2016

Barnett, Amy DuBois

"Be your whole self" color *Glamour* v115 no9 p130 S 2017

What I Wish I'd Known bw color *Glamour* v115 no11 p138 N 2017

Barnett, Courtney, 1987-

Kurt and Courtney: Indie Rock's Superduo S. VOZICK-LEVINSON bw *Rolling Stone* no1295 p18 S 7 2017

Barnett, Cynthia

The Brothers Vonnegut *Orion Magazine* v35 no3 p54 My/Je 2016

SAVING THE SEAS color map *National Geographic* v231 no2 p54 F 2017

Barnett, Gregory

Eugene Onegin *Opera News* v81 no7 p34 Ja 2017

It's a Wonderful Life *Opera News* v81 no9 p38 Mr 2017

Nixon in China *Opera News* v81 no10 p50 Ap 2017

Barnett, Mac

Places to Be color *Publishers Weekly* v264 no8 p82 F 20 2017

Barnett, Mary
    SURPRISE *Christian Century* v134 no12 p22 Je 7 2017
Barnett, Michael A.
    Microstructural proliferation in human cortex is coupled with the development of face processing bibl graph *Science* v355 no6320 p1 Ja 6 2017
Barnett, Randy E.
    LIBERTY OR DEATH J. Rabkin *Claremont Review of Books* v16 no4 p35 Fall 2016
    Me the People J. ROZANSKY *Commentary* v142 no1 p46 Jl/Ag 2016
Barnett, Sam—Interviews
    BOX-OFFICE MIND READERS C. ZULKEY color *Chicago* v66 no6 p24 Je 2017
Barnett, Steve
    Building community for deaf scientists bibl color *Science* v355 no6322 p255 Ja 20 2017
Barney, Matthew, 1967-—Awards
    Matthew Barney's Universe img *New York* v49 no21 p111 O 17 2016
Barnhill, Kelly
    Moon Maiden D. WAGMAN *New York Times Book Review* p20 O 9 2016
Barnitz, R. Anthony
    The epigenetic landscape of T cell exhaustion bibl graph *Science* v354 no6316 p1165 D 2 2016
    Epigenetic stability of exhausted T cells limits durability of reinvigoration by PD-1 blockade bibl graph *Science* v354 no6316 p1160 D 2 2016
Barnosky, Anthony D.
    Merging paleobiology with conservation biology to guide the future of terrestrial ecosystems color *Science* v355 no6325 p594 F 10 2017
Barns
    Airplane Mode T. Johnston color *Practical Horseman* v45 no11 p16 N 2017
    BEAUTY IN WILD PLACES—NAMBIA, AFRICA: AT CHARLOTTENBERG ARABIANS C. REICH *Arabian Horse World* v57 no8 p102 My 2017
    December Duties C. Reich *Arabian Horse World* v57 no3 p212 D 2016
    Fancy Barns J. Paulson *Horse & Rider* v56 no4 p11 Ap 2017
    Free Yourself from Feelings Of Guilt Over Barn Time J. Susser *Dressage Today* v24 no2 p16 N 2017
    Heritage Highway J. HARDIN color map *Nebraska Life* v21 no5 p22 S/O 2017
    Photographer shoots for lofty goal of rustic barn book A. J. Bartels cartoon color *Nebraska Life* v20 no6 p14 N/D 2016
    Q&A: Feed-Through Fly Control color *Horse & Rider* v56 no6 p30 Je 2017
    Settling In B. HEWITT and P. HEWITT color *Yankee* v80 no6 p16 N/D 2016
    Take a friend to the barn cartoon *Equus* no474 p72 Mr 2017
    Where's My Barn Find? E. Perkins color *Hot Rod* v70 no6 p8 Je 2017
    WINTER PREP TO-DO LIST C. Barakat color *Equus* no482 p22 N 2017
Barns—Design & construction
    THE BARN JOB R. BERENDSOHN color *Popular Mechanics* p46 Ap 2017
Barns—Heating & ventilation
    WINTER BARN VENTILATION C. Barakat and M. Freckleton color *Equus* no470 p24 N 2016
Barns—Maintenance & repair
    Nature's Course bw color *Log Home Living* v34 no7 p16 S 2017
Barnstable (Mass.)
    Retro Summer-Fun Spots: Where a vintage vibe and timeless appeal keep the generations coming back K. K. BECKIUS color *Yankee* p66 Jl 2017
Barnstone, Howard
    The Rothko Chapel J. Shine *New York Times Magazine* p26 Ag 27 2017
Barns—United States
    My little barn T. Mitman color *Equus* no475 p77 Ap 2017
Barnum, P. T. (Phineas Taylor), 1810-1891
    Becoming Barnum P. Carlson *American History* v51 no6 p26 F

2017
    CIRCUS MAXIMUS H. BOWLES color *Vogue* v207 no9 p718 S 2017
    DEAD WEIGHT J. LEPORE cartoon *New Yorker* v93 no32 p83 O 16 2017
Bar-Nun, A.
    Xenon isotopes in 67P/Churyumov-Gerasimenko show that comets contributed to Earth's atmosphere diag *Science* v356 no6342 p1069 Je 9 2017
Barocas, Solon
    What Customer Data Collection Could Mean for Workers *Harvard Business Review Digital Articles* p2 Ag 31 2016
BAROFSKY, NEIL
    OBAMA'S AMERICA img *New York* v49 no20 p12 O 3 2016
Barok Main (Music)
    'BAROK MAIN' R. BRADLEY color *New York Times Magazine* p36 Mr 12 2017
BARON, ALEX
    THE LAST DAYS OF THE NAM OU RIVER *Orion Magazine* v35 no3 p36 My/Je 2016
Baron, Alexandre
    Anti-coalescence of bosons on a lossy beam splitter bw chart diag graph *Science* v356 no6345 p1373 Je 30 2017
Baron, David
    The Agony of 'Old Probabilities' bw color *Natural History* v125 no5 p30 My 2017
    The Sun spotters J. Carson color *Science* v357 no6347 p137 Jl 14 2017
Baron, David—Interviews
    Have Sun, Will Travel J. R. Gritz *Smithsonian* v48 no4 p28 Jl/Ag 2017
BARON, JILL S.
    Synthesis Centers as Critical Research Infrastructure *BioScience* v67 no8 p750 Ag 2017
Baron, Jonathan
    Contingent valuation: Flawed logic? color *Science* v357 no6349 p363 Jl 28 2017
Baron, Josh
    The 5 Models of Family Business Ownership *Harvard Business Review Digital Articles* p2 S 20 2016
    Dealing with the Unique Work-Life Challenges of Family Businesses *Harvard Business Review Digital Articles* p2 Mr 19 2015
    Family Businesses Need One Person to Conquer and Another to Rule *Harvard Business Review Digital Articles* p2 D 3 2014
    Making Better Decisions in Your Family Business *Harvard Business Review Digital Articles* p2 S 8 2015
    Signs You're Losing Control of Your Family Business *Harvard Business Review Digital Articles* p2 Ap 7 2017
    Surviving in a Family Business When You're Not Part of the Family *Harvard Business Review Digital Articles* p2 Ja 15 2015
    Warren Buffett's Risky Final Bet *Harvard Business Review Digital Articles* p2 Ap 21 2016
    What to Do If a Feud Threatens Your Family Business *Harvard Business Review Digital Articles* p2 Ap 15 2015
    When You've Made Enough Money to Cause Family Tension *Harvard Business Review Digital Articles* p2 Ja 8 2016
    Why the 21st Century Will Belong to Family Businesses *Harvard Business Review Digital Articles* p2 Mr 28 2016
Baron, Naomi S.
    Reading in a digital age graph il *Phi Delta Kappan* v99 no2 p15 O 2017
BARON, ZACH
    The Ballsiest Father in America bw color *GQ: Gentlemen's Quarterly* v97 no7 p24 Jl 2017
    THE BREAK-OUTS 2016 color *GQ: Gentlemen's Quarterly* v86 no12 p198 D 2016
    CAN YOU CHANGE YOUR LIFE BY CHANGING YOUR PANTS? color *GQ: Gentlemen's Quarterly* v97 no4 p70 Ap 2017
    The Fifty Greatest Living Athletes bw color *GQ: Gentlemen's Quarterly* v97 no11 p96 N 2017
    GUCCI'S MAIN MAN color *GQ: Gentlemen's Quarterly* v86 no12 p216 D 2016
    JOEL EDGERTON bw color *GQ: Gentlemen's Quarterly* v86 no12 p218 D 2016
    The Man Who Escaped Hollywood color *GQ: Gentlemen's Quar-*

terly v97 no9 p104 S 2017

The Resurrection Zoo bw color *GQ: Gentlemen's Quarterly* v86 no11 p96 N 2016

The Ten Who'll Be Next color *GQ: Gentlemen's Quarterly* v97 no11 p114 N 2017

Tracy Morgan color *GQ: Gentlemen's Quarterly* v97 no6 p127 Je 2017

Upside Down All Over Again color *GQ: Gentlemen's Quarterly* v97 no11 p68 N 2017

Viva los Migos color *GQ: Gentlemen's Quarterly* v97 no5 p104 My 2017

Baroncini, Massimo

Gearing up molecular rotary motors color *Science* v356 no6341 p906 Je 1 2017

BARON-COHEN, SIMON

The Danger of Empathy *New York Times Book Review* p12 Ja 1 2017

Barone, Daniel A.

Let's Talk About Sleep: A Guide to Understanding and Improving Your Slumber color *Publishers Weekly* v264 no40 p131 O 2 2017

Barone, Diane

Ready for a New Year *Literacy Today (2411-7862)* v35 no1 p6 Jl/Ag 2017

Using Technology to Enhance Our Community *Literacy Today (2411-7862)* v34 no3 p6 N/D 2016

Barone, Emily

Bridge to the Future color *Time* v189 no13 p42 Ap 10 2017

Computers Made Gerrymandering Worse. Can They Fix It? diag map *Time* v190 no14 p14 O 9 2017

Crossing the Border color diag map *Time* v188 no16/17 p66 O 24 2016

The Digital Cloud Is Underwater-and Vulnerable color diag map *Time* v188 no15 p16 O 17 2016

The Dirtiest Election Ever? color *Time* v188 no21 p18 N 21 2016

The Great American Eclipse color diag map *Time* v190 no2/3 p14 Jl 10-17 2017

One Nation, Up In Arms color diag map *Time* v188 no16/17 p64 O 24 2016

Rebuilding Our Foundations color diag map *Time* v188 no16/17 p46 O 24 2016

The Results: Congress color diag map *Time* v188 no21 p14 N 21 2016

The Results: President color diag map *Time* v188 no21 p12 N 21 2016

A Tale of Two Tax Plans color diag *Time* v188 no16/17 p37 O 24 2016

What Happens to Gun Laws After a Mass Shooting color diag *Time* v190 no16/17 p23 O 23 2017

What It Takes to Win It All color diag *Time* v188 no14 p24 O 10 2016

Why Political Predictions Still Contain So Much Uncertainty color *Time* v188 no19 p18 N 7 2016

Barone, Michael

Was Ronald Reagan an FDR Republican? *American Conservative* v16 no5 p60 S/O 2017

WHEN THE GOING WAS GOOD *Claremont Review of Books* v17 no1 p85 Wint 2016/2017

Baroness Von Sketch Show (TV program)

HOW TO: Assemble a Sketch-Comedy Troupe From Scratch S. LISS img *New York* v50 no15 p63 Jl 24 2017

Baroque painting—Exhibitions

A New World Old Master: The Met rescues a seventeenth-century Mexican artist from obscurity J. Gardner color *Magazine Antiques* v184 no5 p102 S/O 2017

Barouch, Dan H.

Rapid development of a DNA vaccine for Zika virus bibl graph *Science* v354 no6309 p237 O 14 2016

Trispecific broadly neutralizing HIV antibodies mediate potent SHIV protection in macaques color graph *Science* v357 no6359 p85 O 6 2017

BARR, CHARLES

FROM THE ARCHIVES cartoon *Reason* v48 no10 p66 Mr 2017

Barr, Francis

Organelle inheritance—what players have skin in the game? bibl color *Science* v355 no6324 p459 F 3 2017

Barr, G.

Particle Physics in the LHC Era M. Cirelli *Physics Today* v70 no6 p62 Je 2017

Barr, Glenn—Interviews

Fix It Up B. LOI *Alternatives Journal (AJ) - Canada's Environmental Voice* v42 no2 p52 2016

Barr, Katherine

AI Is Getting Good Enough to Delegate the Work It Can't Do *Harvard Business Review Digital Articles* p2 My 12 2015

Barr, Marci L.

Genetic identification of familial hypercholesterolemia within a single U.S. health care system chart graph *Science* v354 no6319 paaf7000-1 D 23 2016

Barr, Matt

VALOR D. Holbrook *TV Guide* v65 no37 p26 S 4 2017

Barr, Mick

NIGHT LIFE *New Yorker* v92 no37 p12 N 14 2016

BARR, NAOMI

THE ORAL REPORT color *Martha Stewart Living* p42 My 2017

BARRA, ALLEN

FOUNDERS' DAY *American History* v52 no1 p22 Ap 2017

MAGIC ON THE MOUND *American History* v51 no6 p22 F 2017

MAKING IT UP AS WE GO ALONG *American History* v51 no6 p70 F 2017

Barra, Mary T., 1961-

12 MARY BARRA N. Varchaver color *Fortune* v174 no7 p86 D 1 2016

Barrack, Thomas J., 1948-—Interviews

'He knew how to get things done, but he managed by chaos' M. Murphy color *Bloomberg Businessweek* no4526 p42 Je 12 2017

Barracuda automobile

EXTRA FINS FOR THIS FISH R. C. Johnson color *Hot Rod* v70 no12 p58 D 2017

MENACE B. Gillogly color *Hot Rod* v70 no7 p44 Jl 2017

Mopar Sacrifice R. Brutt color *Hot Rod* v70 no5 p14 My 2017

Barrada, Yto

Secession K. Bellmann *Art in America* v105 no1 p92 Ja 2017

Barragàn, Luis, 1902-1988—Exhibitions

ART *New Yorker* v92 no37 p25 N 14 2016

Barral, Yves

Aggregation of the Whi3 protein, not loss of heterochromatin, causes sterility in old yeast cells bibl diag *Science* v355 no6330 p1184 Mr 17 2017

Barras, Claude

Oscar Nominee My Life As a Zucchini Is a Stop-Motion Marvel S. Zacharek color *Time* v189 no7/8 p110 F 27 2017

Barratt, Jane

FROM LOSS TO ABILITY color *Maclean's* v129 no42 p35 O 24 2016

Barratt, Michael J.

Food and microbiota in the FDA regulatory framework color *Science* v357 no6346 p39 Jl 7 2017

Barre, Martin

63-F-5 color *Art in America* v104 no10 p38 N 2016

Barreau, L.

Attosecond dynamics through a Fano resonance: Monitoring the birth of a photoelectron bibl graph *Science* v354 no6313 p734 N 11 2016

Barreca, Regina

16 LIFE LESSONS *Psychology Today* v49 no5 p62 S/O 2016

Barredo, Daniel

An atom-by-atom assembler of defect-free arbitrary two-dimensional atomic arrays bibl bw diag graph *Science* v354 no6315 p1021 N 25 2016

Barreira Luz, R. J.

Observation of a large-scale anisotropy in the arrival directions of cosmic rays above 8×10^{18} eV *Science* v357 no6357 p1266 S 22 2017

Barreiro, Luis B.

Dispersals and genetic adaptation of Bantu-speaking populations in Africa and North America diag *Science* v356 no6337 p543 My 5 2017

Reovirus infection triggers inflammatory responses to dietary antigens and development of celiac disease color diag *Science* v356 no6333 p44 Ap 7 2017

Social status alters immune regulation and response to infection in macaques bibl graph *Science* v354 no6315 p1041 N 25 2016

Barrell, David J. A.

Complex multifault rupture during the 2016 Mw 7.8 Kaikōura earthquake, New Zealand color map *Science* v356 no6334 p154 Ap 14 2017

Barrels

How to Make a... BAIT BARREL C. J. CHIVERS cartoon *Popular Mechanics* v193 no7 p77 S 2016

BARRENECHE, RAUL

NORTHERN LIGHT color *Architectural Digest* v74 no2 p78 F 2017

Barres, Ben

Not just Salk color *Science* v357 no6356 p1105 S 15 2017

Barreto, Raimundo

A coalition to impeach *Christian Century* v133 no23 p11 N 9 2016

Barrett (Company)

BARRETT FIELDCRAFT J. B. SNOW color *Outdoor Life* v224 no6 p72 Ag 2017

Barrett, Amy

Bad Faith? *Commonweal* v144 no16 p5 O 6 2017

Seventh-Circuit Shakedown C. Kaveny color *Commonweal* v144 no16 p8 O 6 2017

Barrett, Andrea

1920: Philadelphia A. Barrett *Lapham's Quarterly* v10 no2 p119 Spr 2017

Chasing Henrietta *American Scholar* v86 no3 p14 Summ 2017

BARRETT, ANN

Life IN THESE UNITED STATES *Reader's Digest* v189 no1127 p38 F 2017

Barrett, Austin G.

Local Officials' Opinions About Local Park and Recreation Services *Parks & Recreation* v52 no8 p48 Ag 2017

Barrett, Brian

FETISH color *Wired* v25 no3 p33 Mr 2017

OK, HOUSE. GET SMART chart color *Wired* v25 no6 p39 Je 2017

WISH LIST 2016 color *Wired* v24 no12 p45 D 2016

Barrett, Casey

Under Water *Publishers Weekly* v264 no40 p116 O 2 2017

Barrett, Christopher B.

Forest value: More than commercial *Science* v354 no6319 p1541 D 23 2016

Positive biodiversity-productivity relationship predominant in global forests bibl chart graph map *Science* v354 no6309 paaf8957-1 O 14 2016

Barrett, Claire

REJECTED! color *MHQ: Quarterly Journal of Military History* v29 no4 p17 Summ 2017

Barrett, Connell

The 43% Solution chart color *Golf Magazine* v59 no6 p32 Je 2017

The 6th Annual Travelin' Joe AWARDS color *Golf Magazine* v59 no2 p38 F 2017

ASK THE RULES GUY color *Golf Magazine* v58 no11 p28 N 2016

ASK THE RULES GUY color *Golf Magazine* v59 no5 p34 My 2017

Bank On Him color *Golf Magazine* v59 no3 p25 Mr 2017

The Big Breakthrough color *Golf Magazine* v59 no1 p35 Ja 2017

Brendan Steele color *Golf Magazine* v59 no6 p23 Je 2017

Bret Baier color *Golf Magazine* v58 no11 p37 N 2016

Brutish Empire color *Golf Magazine* v59 no3 p36 Mr 2017

Cheyenne Woods color *Golf Magazine* v59 no6 p34 Je 2017

A "Dear Jay" Letter color *Golf Magazine* v59 no1 p24 Ja 2017

Designated Drivers color *Golf Magazine* v59 no3 p28 Mr 2017

DJ's Secret Sauce color *Golf Magazine* v59 no6 p28 Je 2017

A Few of My Favorite Things color *Golf Magazine* v58 no11 p26 N 2016

Fly It High, Land It Softly color *Golf Magazine* v59 no5 p40 My 2017

Game of Thrones color *Golf Magazine* v59 no5 p30 My 2017

A Ghost of a Chance color *Golf Magazine* v59 no6 p22 Je 2017

Go the Distance color *Golf Magazine* v58 no11 p32 N 2016

Grains & Beauty color *Golf Magazine* v59 no5 p42 My 2017

Grin to Win color *Golf Magazine* v58 no11 p23 N 2016

Hats Off to Ollie color *Golf Magazine* v59 no5 p27 My 2017

Have No Fear! color *Golf Magazine* v59 no3 p38 Mr 2017

Henrik Stenson color *Golf Magazine* v59 no8 p31 Ag 2017

"I Need to Win" color *Golf Magazine* v59 no4 p29 Ap 2017

IN HIS OWN WORDS color *Golf Magazine* v58 no12 p20 D 2016

It's All Fun and Gains color *Golf Magazine* v59 no6 p30 Je 2017

It's a One-derful Life color *Golf Magazine* v59 no1 p28 Ja 2017

It's Tome for a Change color *Golf Magazine* v58 no11 p34 N 2016

Jason Connery color *Golf Magazine* v59 no4 p44 Ap 2017

J.B. Holmes color *Golf Magazine* v59 no5 p31 My 2017

Jeff Sluman color *Golf Magazine* v59 no8 p39 Ag 2017

Jon Rahm color *Golf Magazine* v59 no7 p29 Jl 2017

Justin Thomas color *Golf Magazine* v59 no4 p33 Ap 2017

King of Clubs color *Golf Magazine* v59 no7 p36 Jl 2017

Kira Kazantsev color *Golf Magazine* v59 no2 p41 F 2017

Let the Gains Begin color *Golf Magazine* v59 no2 p36 F 2017

Long-Distance Service color *Golf Magazine* v59 no4 p40 Ap 2017

Luke Donald color *Golf Magazine* v59 no2 p29 F 2017

A Man in Full color *Golf Magazine* v59 no7 p28 Jl 2017

MAN on a MISSION [Cover story] color *Golf Magazine* v59 no8 p62 Ag 2017

Mississippi Queen color *Golf Magazine* v59 no1 p36 Ja 2017

Missouri Tiger color *Golf Magazine* v59 no8 p36 Ag 2017

Modern Love color *Golf Magazine* v58 no11 p36 N 2016

Morgan Hoffmann color *Golf Magazine* v59 no1 p37 Ja 2017

The New Kids are All Right color *Golf Magazine* v59 no2 p28 F 2017

No Gust, No Glory color *Golf Magazine* v59 no1 p34 Ja 2017

North Star color *Golf Magazine* v59 no2 p40 F 2017

One for the Money color *Golf Magazine* v59 no4 p38 Ap 2017

Patrick Reed color *Golf Magazine* v59 no1 p25 Ja 2017

Paul Goydos color *Golf Magazine* v59 no5 p45 My 2017

Peter's Parting Shot color *Golf Magazine* v59 no1 p32 Ja 2017

Playing It Cool color *Golf Magazine* v59 no8 p27 Ag 2017

Public Defender color *Golf Magazine* v59 no6 p19 Je 2017

Pulling Out All the Flops color *Golf Magazine* v59 no7 p35 Jl 2017

Ryan Moore color *Golf Magazine* v59 no3 p29 Mr 2017

Scott Piercy color *Golf Magazine* v59 no7 p38 Jl 2017

Small Wonder color *Golf Magazine* v59 no4 p42 Ap 2017

Spanish Class color *Golf Magazine* v59 no2 p25 F 2017

Tee, Ball chart color *Golf Magazine* v59 no3 p40 Mr 2017

That Hits the Spot color *Golf Magazine* v59 no2 p32 F 2017

Title Fight color *Golf Magazine* v59 no8 p30 Ag 2017

Turn In, Plug Out color *Golf Magazine* v59 no8 p33 Ag 2017

Under Pressure color *Golf Magazine* v59 no7 p25 Jl 2017

Watch + Learn color *Golf Magazine* v58 no11 p30 N 2016

Watch + Learn color *Golf Magazine* v59 no3 p32 Mr 2017

Watch + Learn color *Golf Magazine* v59 no8 p34 Ag 2017

What A Girl Wants color *Golf Magazine* v59 no4 p32 Ap 2017

What a Journey, Man! color *Golf Magazine* v59 no1 p21 Ja 2017

What in the World? color *Golf Magazine* v59 no5 p38 My 2017

William McGirt color *Golf Magazine* v58 no11 p27 N 2016

THE WINNING LOOK color *Golf Magazine* v59 no5 p32 My 2017

THE WINNING LOOK color *Golf Magazine* v59 no8 p38 Ag 2017

Your Lucky Number: 13 color *Golf Magazine* v59 no7 p34 Jl 2017

Barrett, Curtis

GOOD NEWS color *Maclean's* v129 no44 p8 N 7 2016

Barrett, Hadley

DEAR ROPER B. Welch *Spin to Win Rodeo* v21 no3 p8 My 2017

Hadley Barrett: Sept. 18, 1929-March 2, 2017 color *Spin to Win Rodeo* v21 no3 p18 My 2017

In Memory... color *American Cowboy* v24 no1 p25 Je/Jl 2017

Barrett, Jordan

Jordan Barrett L. SCHWARTZBERG img *New York* v49 no19 p18 S 19 2016

Barrett, Katherine

Big Little Lies: Ten ways public officials fool some of the people most of the time *Governing* v30 no8 p58 My 2017

Collective Edge *Governing* v30 no3 p58 D 2016

Did We Say That? *Governing* v30 no4 p58 Ja 2017

Does Business Know Best? You can't run a public agency like a private company, but you can borrow ideas *Governing* v30 no10 p58 Jl 2017

Flipping the Safety Switch *Governing* v30 no5 p60 F 2017

Hickenlooper's Fellows *Governing* v30 no2 p58 N 2016

Informally Grading the States *Governing* v30 no7 p58 Ap 2017

Keeping It In-House *Governing* v30 no1 p60 O 2016

Managing Expectations for 2047: Here are the five trends we predict will unfold over the next three decades *Governing* v31 no1 p58 O 2017

Open Wide: Why can't legislative websites be less opaque? color *Governing* v30 no11 p58 Ag 2017

Operating Room *Governing* v30 no6 p58 Mr 2017

Shopper's Guide: Purchasing managers are pushing to have critical thinking lead the buying process *Governing* v30 no9 p58 Je 2017

Watchdog, Undone: Will budget cuts and political ire endanger performance audits? *Governing* v30 no12 p60 S 2017

BARRETT, LIA

HOG HELL *Sierra* v102 no2 p28 Mr/Ap 2017

BARRETT, LOUISE

ESTABLISHING PRIMATE SCIENCE *BioScience* v67 no3 p309 Mr 2017

Uniting the (Social) Sciences? *BioScience* v67 no10 p937 O 2017

Barrett, Malcolm

Timeless I. Rudolph *TV Guide* p40 D 5 2016

BARRETT, MATTHEW

The Evolution of Sunday color *Christianity Today* v61 no5 p70 Je 2017

Barrett, Michael

The Campus Sex-Crime Tribunals Are Losing: How the courts are intervening to block some of the most unjust punishments of our time K. C. Johnson *Commentary* v144 no3 p20 O 2017

Barrett, Neil

ANDY'S CANDY *Interview* v46 no8 p46 O 2016

BARRETT, NEVILLE S.

Assessing National Biodiversity Trends for Rocky and Coral Reefs through the Integration of Citizen Science and Scientific Monitoring Programs *BioScience* v67 no2 p134 F 2017

Barrett, Paul M.

Amid Chaos, Trump Needs a Strong Lawyer color *Bloomberg Businessweek* no4512 p26 F 20 2017

Another Dispute Over The Sept. 11 Lawsuit Bill color *Bloomberg Businessweek* no4495 p22 O 17 2016

The Big Case: 'Pharma Bro' on Trial color *Bloomberg Businessweek* no4527 p29 Je 19 2017

Cleaning Up Leaks Is a Messy Business *Bloomberg Businessweek* no4533 p35 Ag 7 2017

The Crazy Math Behind Drug Prices graph *Bloomberg Businessweek* no4529 p14 Jl 3 2017

DANGER ZONE color diag *Bloomberg Businessweek* no4518 p50 Ap 10 2017

Donald Trump's Favorite Law Firm color *Bloomberg Businessweek* no4515 p25 Mr 20 2017

Do You Love It Now? color *Bloomberg Businessweek* no4530 p36 Jl 17 2017

HELL IS OTHER LAWYERS color *Bloomberg Businessweek* no4499 p72 N 14 2016

How to Remove A President 101 color *Bloomberg Businessweek* no4523 p26 My 22 2017

The Judiciary: Realigning the Courts graph *Bloomberg Businessweek* no4530 p41 Jl 17 2017

The Ninth Justice color *Bloomberg Businessweek* no4499 p33 N 14 2016

Saving Coal Country color graph *Bloomberg Businessweek* no4507 p46 Ja 16 2017

SMOKE'EM OUT [Cover story] bw color *Bloomberg Businessweek* no4541 p40 O 9 2017

States Are the Nuclear Industry's Best Hope color map *Bloomberg Businessweek* no4505 p28 D 26 2016

TO INFINITY AND BEYOND cartoon *Bloomberg Businessweek* no4499 p86 N 14 2016

THE TROLLS ARE COMING color *Bloomberg Businessweek* no4501 p27 N 28 2016

When Spotting a Hack Doesn't Help You *Bloomberg Businessweek* no4497 p36 O 31 2016

When the President's A Billionaire cartoon *Bloomberg Businessweek* no4499 p24 N 14 2016

Will the GOP Finally Crush Class Actions? *Bloomberg Business-*

week no4514 p28 Mr 13 2017

Barrett, Scott

Social norms as solutions bibl color *Science* v354 no6308 p42 O 7 2016

BARRETT, STEPHEN

The Fakery of Electrodermal Screening: Souped-up galvanometers are being used to assess people's health and determine what they supposedly need. Tests expose them as preposterous, and government agencies should stop their use *Skeptical Inquirer* v41 no5 p40 S/O 2017

Barrett, Theresa C.

Biased inheritance protects older bacteria from harm diag *Science* v356 no6335 p247 Ap 21 2017

BARRETT, WAYNE M.

SF SANTA SAYS IT'S BATTER UP *USA Today Magazine* v145 no2858 p76 N 2016

BARRETT, WILLIAM P.

America's Largest Charities color *Forbes* v198 no9 p24 D 30 2016

No Car, No Problem color *Forbes* v199 no2 p99 F 28 2017

WHERE SHOULD YOU RETIRE? color *Forbes* v200 no1 p20 Jl 27 2017

Barrett family

DREAM WEAVER J. TESAURO color *Better Homes & Gardens* v95 no9 p120 S 2017

BARRIA, CARLOS

At a Loss color *Nation* v303 no22 p11 N 28 2016

Barrick, Murray

Should You Chat Informally Before an Interview? *Harvard Business Review Digital Articles* p2 S 14 2016

Barrier islands

Crossing Scales: The Complexity of Barrier-Island Processes for Predicting Future Change J. C. ZINNERT, J. A. STALLINS et al *BioScience* v67 no1 p39 Ja 2017

Barrio, Isabel C.

Higher predation risk for insect prey at low latitudes and elevations graph *Science* v356 no6339 p742 My 19 2017

Barris, Chuck, 1929-2017

Chuck Barris 1929-2017 M. Roush *TV Guide* v65 no14 p13 Ap 3 2017

Milestones color *Time* v189 no12 p18 Ap 3 2017

THOUGHTS ON Property *Forbes* v199 no5 p124 My 16 2017

Barris, Michael

Deelee Dubé Wins Sarah Vaughan Jazz Vocal Competition color *Downbeat* v84 no2 p13 F 2017

Barro, Robert J.

Non-explanation for Non-recovery *Hoover Digest: Research & Opinion on Public Policy* no1 p53 Wint 2017

Barrodale, Amie

Coming Out Buddhist color *Tricycle: The Buddhist Review* v26 no4 p88 Summ 2017

THE NIGHT REPORT color *Tricycle: The Buddhist Review* v26 no2 p60 Wint 2016

Barron, Andrew B.

Epigenetics and the evolution of instincts color diag *Science* v356 no6333 p26 Ap 7 2017

Barron, David J.

The Battle for War Powers J. WALDRON *New York Times Book Review* p25 N 20 2016

CONFLICTED OVER COMBAT R. Culyer *American History* v52 no1 p66 Ap 2017

Waging War: The Clash Between Presidents and Congress, 1776 to ISIS W. J. Shepherd *Military History* v33 no6 p72 Mr 2017

Barron, James

Keyboard Diplomacy bw *New York Times Book Review* p23 S 25 2016

The One-Cent Magenta: Inside the Quest to Own the Most Valuable Stamp in the World *Publishers Weekly* v263 no52 p112 D 19 2016

Postage Paid S. LASKOW *New York Times Book Review* p17 Mr 26 2017

Barron, Jesse

The Girl from Plainville bw color *Esquire* p100 O 2017

THE VIGILANTE OF WALL STREET-ANDREW LEFT HUNTS FOR CORPORATE FRAUD--AND GETS RICH DOING IT *New York Times Magazine* p30 Je 11 2017

BARRON, ROBERT

Grace stet OR Grace ALONE? bw *Christianity Today* p42 Ap 2017

Barronian, Abigail

597" bw *Powder* p62 S 2017

THE BOYS' CLUB cartoon *Powder* v45 no4 p50 D 2016

The Free Spirit color *Powder* v45 no3 p42 N 2016

NEW YORK STATE OF MIND color *Powder* v46 no2 p42 O 2017

BARROS, NATHAN

Greenhouse Gas Emissions from Reservoir Water Surfaces: A New Global Synthesis *BioScience* v66 no11 p949 N 1 2016

Barroso, Mark

The Core Principles color *Men's Health* v32 no2 p50 Mr 2017

Barrow, Adama, 1965-——Interviews

Adama Barrow T. John color *Time* v189 no4 p12 F 6 2017

Barrow, Bill

Firebrand Moore wins GOP primary runoff color *Christian Century* v134 no22 p15 O 25 2017

BARRY, BEN

EASY E color *Road & Track* v68 no5 p104 D 2016/Ja 2017

SMARTER NOT HARDER bw color *Road & Track* v69 no3 p90 O 2017

What Happens When Men Don't Conform to Masculine Clothing Norms at Work? *Harvard Business Review Digital Articles* p2 Ag 31 2017

BARRY, BILLY

An American in Tel Aviv *Dance Magazine* v91 no1 p101 Ja 2017

Barry, Brunonia

The Fifth Petal color *Publishers Weekly* v263 no48 p40 N 28 2016

Barry, Canyon

THE COMMON TOUCH D. Gardner color *Sports Illustrated* v126 no7 p60 Mr 6 2017

BARRY, CHRISTOPHER D.

The Arctic in the Twenty-First Century: Changing Biogeochemical Linkages across a Paraglacial Landscape of Greenland *BioScience* v67 no2 p118 F 2017

Barry, Cora Masters

Congratulations to the 2017 National Award, Fellowship and Scholarship Recipients *Parks & Recreation* v52 no8 p63 Ag 2017

BARRY, DAN

JACK T. CHICK *New York Times Magazine* p20 D 25 2016

Barry, Dave, 1947-——Interviews

Best. Interview. Ever H. S. Kayle bw *Publishers Weekly* v263 no44 p(Sp)8 O 31 2016

Barry, Devin M.

Molecular and neural basis of contagious itch behavior in mice bibl diag *Science* v355 no6329 p1072 Mr 10 2017

Barry, Kevin

DEER SEASON cartoon *New Yorker* v92 no32 p84 O 10 2016

Barry, Marion Christopher

The TRAGEDY of CHRISTOPHER BARRY H. JAFFE *Washingtonian Magazine* v52 no4 p62 Ja 2017

Barry, Michele

Civil War & the Global Threat of Pandemics *Daedalus* v146 no4 p71 Fall 2017

BARRY, MONIQUE

Let it go! [Cover story] color *O, The Oprah Magazine* p92 Ag 2017

Barry, Ramona

The Handmade Life: A Companion to Modern Crafting J. K. HANUS color *American Craft* v76 no6 p18 D 2016-Ja 2017

Barry, Sebastian, 1955-

Days Without End *Publishers Weekly* v263 no44 p50 O 31 2016

A Lover and a Fighter K. S. SMITH *New York Times Book Review* p18 F 5 2017

The Silver Linings of Big Sky S. Begley color *Time* v189 no3 p57 Ja 30 2017

Barry, Subha

Coming Around on Cannabis [Cover story] color *Working Mother* v40 no3 p24 Ag/S 2017

Immigrants Make America Great color *Working Mother* v40 no2 p50 Je/Jl 2017

A New Chapter *Working Mother* p5 F/Mr 2017

Remote Chance color *Working Mother* v40 no4 p83 O/N 2017

Step Up and Lead cartoon *Working Mother* p49 F/Mr 2017

Barry Harmon, R.

SHOT ACROSS THE BOW, KUK SOOL STYLE [Cover story] color *Black Belt* v55 no6 p32 O/N 2017

Barrymore, Drew, 1975-

Drew Barrymore's Brilliant Zombie Return R. SHEFFIELD color *Rolling Stone* no1281/1282 p22 F 23 2017

Streaming's New Stars J. Halterman *TV Guide* v65 no2 p14 Ja 2 2017

UNDEAD AND LOVING IT A. D'ARMINIO *TV Guide* v65 no6 p24 Ja 30 2017

Barrymore, Drew, 1975-——Interviews

Drew Barrymore K. B. Brown color *InStyle* v24 no11 p145 N 2017

DREW BARRYMORE R. Rahman color *Entertainment Weekly* no1451/1452 p98 F 3-10 2017

Barry's Bootcamp (Company)

What I Wear to Work J. Chen color *Bloomberg Businessweek* no4504 p67 D 19 2016

Bars (Desserts)

RISE. EAT. SHINE color *Better Homes & Gardens* v95 no9 p164 S 2017

THE SOUTHERN LIVING COOKIE COOKBOOK L. Cericola, K. Hammonds et al color *Southern Living* v51 no12 p190 D 2016

Bars (Drinking establishments)

See also

Gay bars

48 hours in VANCOUVER S. Walter color *Good Housekeeping* v264 no2 p35 F 2017

BATON ROUGE T. DAY color *Louisiana Life* v37 no4 p54 Mr/Ap 2017

BEST OF THE WEST J. Chamberlain, C. Dash et al color *Sunset* v238 no6 p9 Je 2017

BIKE AND BOOZE L. ARNETT color *Chicago* v66 no7 p56 Jl 2017

DINING GUIDE color *New Orleans Magazine* v51 no3 p120 Ja 2017

DOWN TO THE ATP K. Pandolfi *Cincinnati Magazine* p64 Je 2017

Everything I Know About Bartending I Learned from My Korean Mother E. MARSZEWSKI color *Bon Appetit* v62 no2 p73 Mr 2017

Florida's Unsung Beach Towns V. F. Luesse color map *Southern Living* v52 no6 p63 Je 2017

From Miami Department Stores to Handheld Lasagna img *New York* v50 no17 p71 Ag 21 2017

FUN AND GAMES *Cincinnati Magazine* v50 no8 p42 My 2017

How Dixie Got Its 45 E. LABORDE color *New Orleans Magazine* v52 no1 p168 S 2017

i did it! J. GARLOCK color *Better Homes & Gardens* v95 no4 p50 Ap 2017

It Happened Here: Pinos Altos, N.M G. R. Schiavino color *American Cowboy* v23 no5 p43 F/Mr 2017

JULIA STREET | WITH POYDRAS THE PARROT J. STREET bw *New Orleans Magazine* v51 no6 p22 Ap 2017

LALO'S SPORTSMAN CLUB *Texas Monthly* v45 no1 p103 Ja 2017

A Little Slice Of Havana D. ROTHBART *Los Angeles Magazine* p55 F 2017

A Maker's Guide to... LOUISVILLE F. MAROUKIAN color map *Popular Mechanics* v193 no7 p22 S 2016

MIDWEST color *Downbeat* v84 no2 p55 F 2017

My Place color *Vanity Fair* v59 no4 p107 Mr 2017

Pure Bar J. DRILLING *Cincinnati Magazine* p114 Je 2017

Rabbit at Rest P. SHARPE *Texas Monthly* v45 no3 p46 Mr 2017

Second Coming C. RAINEY and P. BRADY color *Conde Nast Traveler* v52 no5 p56 My 2017

SOCCER FANS AT CHATHAM TAP K. RAMMEL *Indianapolis Monthly* v40 no5 p14 Ja 2017

SOMETHING TO SIP ON N. H. REEDER and D. POINTDUJOUR color *Ebony* v72 no6 p54 Ap/My 2017

SOUTH color *Downbeat* v84 no2 p52 F 2017

The South's Best color *Southern Living* v52 no4 p67 Ap 2017

The Well-Stocked Wet Bar D. Wondrich chart color *Esquire* p140 BigBlackBook

WINNER'S CIRCLE A. Spiegel *Washingtonian Magazine* v52

no3 p150 D 2016

WITH POYDRAS THE PARROT J. Street bw *New Orleans Magazine* v51 no9 p22 Jl 2017

Bars (Drinking establishments)—Awards

Raising The Bar K. Tablang color *Forbes* v198 no9 p51 D 30 2016

Bars (Drinking establishments)—California

BRITISH (RE)INVASION color *Esquire* p30 My 2017

Cheers! K. Hansen color *Cabin Living* p13 Ap 2017

Dr. Strange Brew C. MARTINS color *Los Angeles Magazine* v62 no10 p42 O 2017

Hot Biscuits P. KUH *Los Angeles Magazine* p50 Ja 2017

How Koreatown Became the Cool Center of L.A S. SCHUBE color *GQ: Gentlemen's Quarterly* v97 no11 p54 N 2017

Bars (Drinking establishments)—Canada

Drinks for the House S. PROUDFOOT color *Maclean's* v130 no2 p12 Mr 2017

THE FRASERHOOD SHORT LIST color *Conde Nast Traveler* v52 no5 p60 My 2017

There Goes The Neighborhood H. WALLACE color *Conde Nast Traveler* v52 no5 p60 My 2017

Bars (Drinking establishments)—Customer services

Where Everybody J. N. LOMAX *Texas Monthly* v45 no1 p97 Ja 2017

Bars (Drinking establishments)—Design & construction

RAISING THE BAR J. TUNG *Martha Stewart Living* no269 p38 N 2016

snapshot N. R. Pollock *Architectural Record* v205 no6 p168 Je 2017

Bars (Drinking establishments)—England—History

Pubs and Politics in Stuart England M. Hailwood *History Today* v67 no1 p3 Ja 2017

Bars (Drinking establishments)—Equipment & supplies

LIQUID ASSETS A. Shaffer color *Wired* v24 no12 p78 D 2016

Raise The Bar L. IMMEDIATO *Los Angeles Magazine* p38 My 2017

Bars (Drinking establishments)—Evaluation

49th & Penn A. LYNCH color *Indianapolis Monthly* v42 no2 p38 O 2017

AFTER HOURS J. Sidman *Washingtonian Magazine* v52 no2 p261 N 2016

BARS J. WILLIAMS *Cincinnati Magazine* v50 no8 p52 My 2017

BARTENDERS' CHOICE J. Sidman *Washingtonian Magazine* v52 no2 p260 N 2016

The Best BARS IN AMERICA, 2017 bw color *Esquire* p57 Je/Jl 2017

BEST NEW RESTAURANTS J. RUBY color *Chicago* v66 no5 p80 My 2017

BETTY'S BATTALION *Texas Monthly* v45 no1 p100 Ja 2017

THE BOOZE SLEUTH S. FREEMAN color *Chicago* v66 no1 p60 Ja 2017

BRITISH (RE)INVASION color *Esquire* p30 My 2017

CENTRAL J. FROIS color map *Louisiana Life* v37 no4 p95 Mr/Ap 2017

Cheers! K. Hansen color *Cabin Living* p13 Ap 2017

CHICAGO'S COZIEST BARS M. HENNESSY color *Chicago* v66 no10 p47 O 2017

Chucktown Fresh M. ROTHSTEIN and N. Richardson color *Bon Appetit* no8 p48 Ag 2017

CITIZEN CANE: Chris Coy gets a little tiki behind the bar at The Inferno Room, opening this fall S. KROWIAK *Indianapolis Monthly* v12 no40 p46 Ag 2017

COCK TAIL OF THE MONTH D. ALAN *Texas Monthly* v44 no12 p52 D 2016

COOKTAIL OF THE MONTH D. ALAN *Texas Monthly* v44 no11 p48 N 2016

Corpus Christi *Texas Monthly* v45 no3 p132 Mr 2017

Dallas *Texas Monthly* v45 no3 p134 Mr 2017

DINING GUIDE color *New Orleans Magazine* v51 no7 p90 My 2017

DIVE BARS *Indianapolis Monthly* p66 F 2017

Do *Los Angeles Magazine* p51 Ag 2017

DRINKS and DANCE HALLS *Texas Monthly* v45 no3 p106 Mr 2017

Dr. Strange Brew C. MARTINS color *Los Angeles Magazine* v62 no10 p42 O 2017

THE DUDE ABIDES *Iceland Review* v54 no6 p132 N/D 2016

D&W LOUNGE *Texas Monthly* v45 no1 p101 Ja 2017

EAST *Indianapolis Monthly* v42 no2 p120 O 2017

EL FLORIDITA #2 AT 8ARM J. BAINBRIDGE *Atlanta* v57 no4 p38 Ag 2017

The Fat Monk Jiayang Fan color *New Yorker* v93 no17 p17 Je 19 2017

Food & Drink *Virginia Living* p95 2017 Best 20of Virginia

Fort North *Texas Monthly* v45 no3 p136 Mr 2017

FRESH ON THE SCENE C. LAUTERBACH *Atlanta* v56 no7 p66 N 2016

fun img *New York* p78 Mr 6 2017

GENIE IN A BOTTLE J. Gordinier cartoon color *Esquire* p42 S 2017

GO NATUREL IN PARIS J. Gordinier color *Esquire* p100 My 2017

HAVE A BALL WITH BOCCE C. SCHEDLER color *Chicago* v66 no7 p51 Jl 2017

HEY, SHORTY B. MCKIBBEN *Atlanta* v56 no12 p79 Ap 2017

Hot Biscuits P. KUH *Los Angeles Magazine* p50 Ja 2017

The Hot List P. POLLACK color *Chicago* v66 no2 p48a F 2017

The Hot List P. POLLACK color *Chicago* v66 no6 p51 Je 2017

The Hot List P. POLLACK color *Chicago* v66 no8 p53 Ag 2017

Houston *Texas Monthly* v45 no3 p138 Mr 2017

Italian Flair in Sheridan Square img *New York* v50 no17 p74 Ag 21 2017

KING ARTHUR'S PUB *Texas Monthly* v45 no1 p101 Ja 2017

LALO'S SPORTSMAN CLUB *Texas Monthly* v45 no1 p103 Ja 2017

LATE PLATES *Indianapolis Monthly* p63 F 2017

More than Meets the Izakaya G. SNYDER *Los Angeles Magazine* v62 no9 p114 S 2017

MOVE OVER, HARD CIDER C. BOERS color *Chicago* v66 no5 p70 My 2017

Nebraska Wineries and Breweries color *Nebraska Life* v21 no2 p64 Mr/Ap 2017

New Bars for Everyone M. J. WEEDMAN img *New York* v50 no17 p84 Ag 21 2017

Noble Parentage D. Breshears color *Missouri Life* v44 no2 p98 Ap 2017

NORTHEAST *Indianapolis Monthly* v42 no2 p123 O 2017

NORTH SUBURBAN *Indianapolis Monthly* v42 no2 p120 O 2017

OFF the BEATEN PATH N. MARINO, J. NELSON et al color *GQ: Gentlemen's Quarterly* v97 no9 p154 S 2017

ON A FIRST DATE L. Bailey, D. Dark et al *Indianapolis Monthly* p65 F 2017

On Tapa His Game P. SHARPE *Texas Monthly* v45 no1 p34 Ja 2017

Out of The Box L. IMMEDIATO *Los Angeles Magazine* p43 D 2016

PAST PERFECTED C. SCHEDLER color *Chicago* v65 no11 p56 N 2016

P.I.Y.: POUR-IT-YOURSELF J. B. Patton color *Missouri Life* v44 no6 p21 S 2017

Prix Fixe Banchan, New Nordic à la Carte R. RAISFELD and R. PATRONITE img *New York* v49 no25 p110 D 12 2016

Raising the Bar: Cocktails and small plates create a stir at Bar One Fourteen, the Patachou family's sexy black sheep J. SPALDING color *Indianapolis Monthly* v42 no2 p46 O 2017

Restaurant GUIDE *Indianapolis Monthly* p119 F 2017

RESTAURANTS E. S. ARNARSDÓTTIR color *Iceland Review* v54 no5 p113 S-O 2016

SANDWICHES! E. MAH *Atlanta* v56 no7 p78 N 2016

Sexy Taco/Dirty Cash N. Niarchos color *New Yorker* v92 no48 p13 F 6 2017

Small Plates, Big Ambition A. PLATT img *New York* p62 Ja 9 2017

SOUND ADVICE *Indianapolis Monthly* p68 F 2017

SOUTH'S BEST BAR H. Hayes color *Southern Living* v52 no4 p68 Ap 2017

SOUTH SUBURBAN *Indianapolis Monthly* v42 no2 p126 O 2017

TABLES FOR TWO: The Aviary S. Lyon color *New Yorker* v93 no33 p31 O 23 2017

Tchoup Yard J. Forman color *New Orleans Magazine* v51 no2 p74 D 2016

THESE DIVES HAVE RAISED THE BAR S. SHIBATA *Sea Magazine* v108 no10 pCA-1 O 2016

Thirsty? L. Arnett, C. Boers et al color diag *Chicago* v66 no2 p57 F 2017

This Month in Beer N. RICHARDSON, A. DELANY et al color *Bon Appetit* no8 p24 Ag 2017

THE TIPSY TEXAN'S COCKTAIL OF THE MONTH D. ALAN *Texas Monthly* v45 no3 p48 Mr 2017

TRIVIAL PURSUITS *Indianapolis Monthly* p69 F 2017

THE URBANIST: Lisbon: Why the European expats are coming by the EasyJet-ful Z. NIEMTUS img *New York* v50 no9 p62 My 1 2017

VINTAGE STOCK J. DRILLING *Cincinnati Magazine* v50 no5 p160 F 2017

WEST COASTERS M. Ferreira color *Sunset* v239 no4 p26 O 2017

Where to Eat Now *Texas Monthly* v45 no3 p128 Mr 2017

Where to Eat Now *Texas Monthly* v45 no5 p114 My 2017

WINTER WARMERS P. GIANOPULOS color *Chicago* v66 no2 p45 F 2017

WITH OUT-OF-TOWNERS *Indianapolis Monthly* p64 F 2017

THE WIZZARD *Texas Monthly* v45 no1 p103 Ja 2017

Bars (Drinking establishments)—Great Britain

Fancy a Call at the Pub? *British Heritage Travel* v38 no4 p9 Jl/Ag 2017

Bars (Drinking establishments)—Management

Where Everybody J. N. LOMAX *Texas Monthly* v45 no1 p97 Ja 2017

Bars (Drinking establishments)—New York (State)—New York

The Fat Monk Jiayang Fan color *New Yorker* v93 no17 p17 Je 19 2017

New Bars for Everyone M. J. WEEDMAN img *New York* v50 no17 p84 Ag 21 2017

Bars (Drinking establishments)—United States

BARS J. WILLIAMS *Cincinnati Magazine* v50 no8 p52 My 2017

The Best BARS IN AMERICA, 2017 bw color *Esquire* p57 Je/Jl 2017

Bourbon, Brews, BBQ & Blues D. BRESHEARS color *Missouri Life* v44 no4 p44 Je 2017

MURDER IN THE HEARTLAND L. SMILEY bw color map *Wired* v25 no7 p72 Jl 2017

PAST PERFECTED C. SCHEDLER color *Chicago* v65 no11 p56 N 2016

Pop the corks! T. McNally color *New Orleans Magazine* v51 no8 p106 Je 2017

Swim-up Bar *Los Angeles Magazine* p22 Ap 2017

WEST COASTERS M. Ferreira color *Sunset* v239 no4 p26 O 2017

Bars (Furniture)

Tambour Home Bar color *Bloomberg Businessweek* no4539 p75 S 25 2017

Barsade, Sigal

Quantifying Your Company's Emotional Culture *Harvard Business Review Digital Articles* p2 Ja 6 2017

Barshack, Iris

Potential role of intratumor bacteria in mediating tumor resistance to the chemotherapeutic drug gemcitabine diag *Science* v357 no6356 p1156 S 15 2017

BARSHAD, AMOS

'MASK OFF' color *New York Times Magazine* p21 Mr 12 2017

Barsky, Jack—Interviews

PUTIN'S LONG GAME A. Dejean, H. Levintova et al color *Mother Jones* v42 no4 p26 Jl/Ag 2017

Barslund, Charlotte

The Lake *Publishers Weekly* v264 no21 p70 My 22 2017

BARSON, MICHAEL

Empathizing with the Villain color *Publishers Weekly* v263 no50 p50 D 5 2016

Barsoux, Jean-Louis

3 Situations Where Cross-Cultural Communication Breaks Down *Harvard Business Review Digital Articles* p2 Je 8 2016

Bartal, Guy

Observation of Anderson localization in disordered nanophotonic structures diag graph *Science* v356 no6341 p953 Je 1 2017

Bartel, Caroline A.

Research: Insecure Managers Don't Want Your Suggestions *Har-*

vard Business Review Digital Articles p2 N 24 2014

Bartell, Tonya

To engage students, give them meaningful choices in the classroom il *Phi Delta Kappan* v99 no2 p37 O 2017

Bartelloni, John

Popular piety color *U.S. Catholic* v82 no2 p5 F 2017

BARTELS, ALAN J.

Big rig rolls statewide to celebrate Nebraska's big birthday cartoon color *Nebraska Life* v21 no4 p82 Jl/Ag 2017

Border, beach, buried wonders, Old Baldy & Bells color *Nebraska Life* v21 no6 p56 N/D 2017

BORDER to BORDER I-80 Adventure bw color *Nebraska Life* v21 no1 p18 Ja/F 2017

Broken Bow bricks hide buried treasure color *Nebraska Life* v21 no4 p15 Jl/Ag 2017

Case NOT closed color *Nebraska Life* v21 no5 p41 S/O 2017

Columbus artist paints farm-fresh art color *Nebraska Life* v21 no5 p74 S/O 2017

Dark Skies Over Nebraska cartoon color *Nebraska Life* v21 no4 p80 Jl/Ag 2017

Documentary reveals Osborne in his own words bw color *Nebraska Life* v21 no4 p14 Jl/Ag 2017

DUNDY COUNTY Road Trip color *Nebraska Life* v20 no6 p40 N/D 2016

Grand Island Painter color *Nebraska Life* v21 no1 p60 Ja/F 2017

The Inside Track color *Nebraska Life* v21 no2 p20 Mr/Ap 2017

Mini church replica looms large in Elgin color *Nebraska Life* v21 no6 p44 N/D 2017

Nebraska at 150 bw color map *Nebraska Life* v21 no2 p50 Mr/Ap 2017

Nebraska at 150 bw color map *Nebraska Life* v21 no6 p50 N/D 2017

Nebraska at 150 bw color *Nebraska Life* v21 no1 p50 Ja/F 2017

Nebraska at 150 bw color *Nebraska Life* v21 no4 p56 Jl/Ag 2017

Nebraska at 150: RETROSPECTIVE - PART V OF VI 1967-1992 bw color map *Nebraska Life* v21 no5 p62 S/O 2017

Nebraska's magical moment in the shade 2017 ECLIPSE color *Nebraska Life* v21 no6 p14 N/D 2017

Oshkosh: Heart of Garden County color *Nebraska Life* v21 no5 p52 S/O 2017

Outlaw Trail Byway becomes a 'Quiltway' color *Nebraska Life* v21 no5 p88 S/O 2017

Photographer shoots for lofty goal of rustic barn book cartoon color *Nebraska Life* v20 no6 p14 N/D 2016

Platte River REUNION cartoon color *Nebraska Life* v21 no2 p70 Mr/Ap 2017

Sandhills murders solved after 80 years bw color *Nebraska Life* v21 no6 p18 N/D 2017

Singing seldom-told Sandhills stories color *Nebraska Life* v21 no1 p63 Ja/F 2017

"Terrible Terry" CARPENTER color *Nebraska Life* v21 no4 p62 Jl/Ag 2017

Waiting on Winter color *Nebraska Life* v20 no6 p20 N/D 2016

Winter HARVEST color *Nebraska Life* v20 no6 p72 N/D 2016

Bartels, Meghan

Flamingo Road *Audubon* v119 no2 p20 Summ 2017

Master Carver color *Audubon* v119 no3 p15 Fall 2017

A Photographer on the Dance Floor *Audubon* v119 no1 p49 Spr 2017

Swamp Steward color *Audubon* v119 no3 p49 Fall 2017

Take It Up a Notch color *Audubon* v119 no3 p47 Fall 2017

Bartels, Mel

Herschel's Ghosts *Sky & Telescope* v133 no4 p30 Ap 2017

Bartels, Tim

β2-Adrenoreceptor is a regulator of the a-synuclein gene driving risk of Parkinson's disease cartoon chart graph *Science* v357 no6354 p891 S 1 2017

Bartenders

More (or Less) Core Division J. HOUSMAN color *Surfer* v58 no4 p34 Ag 2017

Paul Gustings T. McNally color *New Orleans Magazine* v51 no2 p76 D 2016

Bartenstein, Ben

THE BEST YARD SALE color *Bloomberg Businessweek* no4501 p22 N 28 2016

Hyperinflation graph *Bloomberg Businessweek* no4505 p19 D 26

2016

Meet Venezuela's New Iron-Fisted No. 2 color *Bloomberg Businessweek* no4511 p16 F 13 2017

Under new management color *Bloomberg Businessweek* no4496 p18 O 24 2016

Barter

See also

Trading posts

To Stretch a Shoestring color *Yankee* p26 My/Je 2017

TRAIL HERO WORKS WITH UPLA TO SAVE SAND MOUNTAIN OHV ACCESS color *Dirt Sports + Off-Road* v51 no2 p6 F 2017

Barter—Exhibitions

ONE OF THOSE THINGS M. EMERY color *Dirt Sports + Off-Road* v51 no2 p60 F 2017

Bartering services

THE LAST TRADING POSTS M. JAFFE *Arizona Highways* v92 no11 p16 N 2016

BARTH, AMY

THE FIGHT OVER FRACKING *New York Times Upfront* v149 no9 p10 F 20 2017

Barth, Erling

The Average Mid-Forties Male College Graduate Earns 55% More Than His Female Counterparts *Harvard Business Review Digital Articles* p2 Je 12 2017

Barthelat, Francois

Growing a synthetic mollusk shell bibl color diag *Science* v354 no6308 p32 O 7 2016

Barthelemy, Jerome

Does It Pay to Hire Consultants? Evidence from the Bordeaux Wine Industry *Harvard Business Review Digital Articles* p2 My 19 2017

BARTHOLOMEW, ANITA

The Mudslide color *Reader's Digest* v190 no1134 p8 O 2017

BARTHOLOMEW, BRETT

ASK RW color *Runner's World* v52 no4 p35 My 2017

Bartholomew, James

High Horses J. Coaston *New York Times Magazine* p9 Ag 13 2017

Bartholomew, John G.

Nanophotonic rare-earth quantum memory with optically controlled retrieval diag graph *Science* v357 no6358 p1392 S 29 2017

Bartholomew, Sarah

Flight of Fancy C. BARBOUR color *House Beautiful* v159 no5 p68 Je 2017

Bartiromo, Maria, 1967-

MARIA BARTIROMO: GLOBAL MARKETS EDITOR, FOX BUSINESS NETWORK bw color *Harvard Business Review* v95 no4 p144 Jl/Ag 2017

Bartkus, Viva Ona

How Anxiety Affects CEO Decision Making *Harvard Business Review Digital Articles* p2 Jl 19 2016

Bartlett, Bjarne R.

Mismatch repair deficiency predicts response of solid tumors to PD-1 blockade chart graph *Science* v357 no6349 p409 Jl 28 2017

BARTLETT, BRUCE

FROM THE ARCHIVES bw cartoon *Reason* v48 no11 p70 Ap 2017

Bartlett, Gail J.

How do miniproteins fold? diag *Science* v357 no6347 p133 Jl 14 2017

Bartlett, Jeff S.

10 Top Picks color *Consumer Reports* v82 no4 p22 Ap 2017

Brand Report Card chart *Consumer Reports* v82 no4 p36 Ap 2017

Bartlett, Robert C.

DARE TO BE WISE? K. Whitaker *Claremont Review of Books* v17 no3 p68 Summ 2017

BARTLEY, JESSIY

POSTHOLE color *Powder* v46 no2 p94 O 2017

BARTLOW, DIANNE

SENATOR-ELECT KAMALA HARRIS *Ms.* v26 no3 p6 Fall 2016

Bartlow, Jeremy

The Forecasting Sweet Spot Between Micro and Macro *Harvard Business Review Digital Articles* p2 Ag 26 2016

Bartman, Caroline

Epigenetic stability of exhausted T cells limits durability of reinvigoration by PD-1 blockade bibl graph *Science* v354 no6316 p1160 D 2 2016

Bartman, Steve

HOT | NOT T. Keith color *Sports Illustrated* v127 no4 p22 Ag 7 2017

Bartman, Thomas

The Future of Electric Vehicles Is Golf Carts, Not Tesla *Harvard Business Review Digital Articles* p2 My 14 2015

Start-ups Should Sell to Small Businesses, Not Big Enterprises *Harvard Business Review Digital Articles* p2 Ja 27 2015

When Start-ups Should (and Shouldn't) Partner with Industry Leaders *Harvard Business Review Digital Articles* p2 O 9 2014

Why Tesla Won't Be Able to Scale *Harvard Business Review Digital Articles* p2 Ap 23 2015

BARTO, LINDA "ILHAM"

Teaching Rape Prevention *Islamic Horizons* v46 no1 p49 Ja/F 2017

Bartocci, Cristina

TZAP: A telomere-associated protein involved in telomere length control bibl diag graph *Science* v355 no6325 p638 F 10 2017

Bartol, Kathryn M.

Why Certain Managers Thrive in Tough New Jobs While Others Get Fed Up *Harvard Business Review Digital Articles* p2 Ap 22 2015

Bartoli, Cecilia, 1966-

Frederica von Stade: The Complete Columbia Recital Albums D. Shengold *Opera News* v81 no6 p55 D 2016

BARTOLOMEO, JOEY

FRESHMAN YEAR VS. SENIOR YEAR color *Seventeen* v76 no3 p102 My 2017

Bartolucci, Marisa

Around and about at the Biennale des Antiquaires in Paris color *Magazine Antiques* v183 no6 p56 N/D 2016

Polished Performances: Classic and contemporary silver in dialogue at the Museum of the City of New York color *Magazine Antiques* v184 no5 p78 S/O 2017

TEFAF color *Magazine Antiques* v184 no3 p38 My/Je 2017

BARTON, BENJAMIN H.

Simplify The Law color *National Review* v69 no15 p20 Ag 14 2017

Barton, Dominic

The Data: Where Long-Termism Pays Off graph img *Harvard Business Review* v95 no3 p67 My/Je 2017

Finally, Proof That Managing for the Long Term Pays Off color graph *Harvard Business Review Digital Articles* p2 F 7 2017

Priorities for Jumpstarting the U.S. Industrial Economy *Harvard Business Review Digital Articles* p2 F 2 2015

BARTON, EMILY

Judas, Jesus and Politics *New York Times Book Review* p26 D 11 2016

Pirate Love *New York Times Book Review* p13 My 7 2017

Barton, Eric

NO HILLS, NO PROBLEM! color *Bicycling* v58 no7 p42 Ag 2017

BARTON, ERIN

JAMMING UP SEX TRAFFIC *USA Today Magazine* v145 no2864 p68 My 2017

Living Lab for Sustainable Cities *USA Today Magazine* v146 no2868 p69 S 2017

Barton, Fiona

The Child L. Greenblatt color *Entertainment Weekly* no1471 p66 Je 23 2017

Do You Want to Know a Secret? F. BARTON color *Publishers Weekly* v264 no17 p67 Ap 24 2017

Barton, Gavin

What's Lost When Experts Retire *Harvard Business Review Digital Articles* p2 D 2 2014

Barton, Jacqueline K.

The [4Fe4S] cluster of human DNA primase functions as a redox switch using DNA charge transport color *Science* v355 no6327 p813 F 24 2017

Barton, Jamie

ALL NATURAL W. R. BRAUN and F. FOX *Opera News* v81 no7 p22 Ja 2017

Viewpoint: As Thousands Cheer *Opera News* v81 no12 p69 Je 2017

Barton, Lisa M.

Decarboxylative borylation color *Science* v356 no6342 p1045 Je 9 2017

Barton, Mischa, 1986-—Interviews

Some Like It Aught J. Harman color *Glamour* v114 no12 p84 D 2016

Barton, Penny

Revealing the dynamics of a large impact bibl color *Science* v354 no6314 p836 N 18 2016

Barton, Susanne

Gold Gets Its Own Flash Crash graph *Bloomberg Businessweek* no4529 p26 Jl 3 2017

Why Trump Is Making Bond Markets Nervous *Bloomberg Businessweek* no4500 p39 N 21 2016

Barton, Teghan

Proactive Intervention diag graph *Alternatives Journal (AJ) - Canada's Environmental Voice* v42 no3 p40 2016

State of Belonging color diag *Alternatives Journal (AJ) - Canada's Environmental Voice* v42 no3 p42 2016

BARTON-FUMO, MARGARET

By Your Side color *Film Comment* v53 no1 p22 Ja/F 2017

Home Invasion color *Film Comment* v52 no6 p93 N/D 2016

PLEASURES OF THE FLESH color *Film Comment* v53 no2 p42 Mr/Ap 2017

Barton-Yerrington, Kristy

WHAT'S YOUR NUMBER? A. Gentry color *Spin to Win Rodeo* v21 no4 p26 Je 2017

Bartos, Alma—Interviews

Alma Bartos A. BRANDT *Cincinnati Magazine* v50 no4 p40 Ja 2017

Bartos, Aneta

The Photographs I Can't Stop Thinking About J. SALTZ img *New York* v50 no6 p74 Mr 20 2017

Bartoszek, Pawel

A NEW TOMORROW E. S. ARNARSDÓTTIR *Iceland Review* v54 no6 p80 N/D 2016

Bartram, Samantha

From the Director's Chair *Parks & Recreation* v51 no10 p30 O 2016

Member Spotlight. Carolyn McKnight *Parks & Recreation* v51 no10 p84 O 2016

The Preservation of a Naturalist *Parks & Recreation* v52 no5 p20 My 2017

Restorative Healing at Youth Visions Relection Park *Parks & Recreation* v51 no10 p58 O 2016

Bartumeus, Frederic

Visualizing dynamic microvillar search and stabilization during ligand detection by T cells color *Science* v356 no6338 p598 My 12 2017

BARTUSIAK, MARCIA

The Cheshire Cat *Natural History* v124 no10 p10 N 2016

In Good Company color *Natural History* v125 no10 p10 O 2017

Like This World of Ours color *Natural History* v125 no5 p10 My 2017

Bartyzel, Dorota

Christ, King, and Corporate Savior bw *Bloomberg Businessweek* no4531 p33 Jl 24 2017

BARTZ, ANDREA

FEEL YOUR BEST INSIDE AND OUT chart color *Redbook* p89 O 2017

MAKE SOME AMAZING MEMORIES color *Redbook* p88 Jl/Ag 2017

RAGING BRAIN *Scholastic Choices* v32 no3 p20 N/D 2016

TINY TREATS color *Women's Health* v14 no8 p84 O 2017

Bartz, Peter

Angular momentum–induced delays in solid-state photoemission enhanced by intra-atomic interactions chart color graph *Science* v357 no6357 p1274 S 22 2017

Barucci, M. A.

Rosetta's comet 67P/Churyumov-Gerasimenko sheds its dusty mantle to reveal its icy nature bibl graph *Science* v354 no6319 p1566 D 23 2016

Seasonal exposure of carbon dioxide ice on the nucleus of comet 67P/Churyumov-Gerasimenko bibl bw graph *Science* v354 no6319 p1563 D 23 2016

Surface changes on comet 67P/Churyumov-Gerasimenko suggest a more active past bw graph *Science* v355 no6332 p1392 Mr 31 2017

Baruch, Kobi

Wild emmer genome architecture and diversity elucidate wheat evolution and domestication color *Science* v357 no6346 p93 Jl 7 2017

BARUTH, JACK

AMERICAN GLADIATOR color *Road & Track* v69 no4 p88 N 2017

THE GREAT ESCAPE [Cover story] chart color diag graph *Road & Track* v69 no3 p30 O 2017

Hands of Time bw color *Road & Track* v69 no2 p26 S 2017

IN THE RIGHT color *Road & Track* v69 no1 p98 Ag 2017

MASTER'S PROGRAM color *Road & Track* v69 no3 p68 O 2017

RETURN FLIGHT color *Road & Track* v68 no6 p76 F 2017

A SHEEP IN WOLF'S CLOTHING color *Road & Track* v68 no8 p30 My 2017

SPECIAL COMES STANDARD color *Road & Track* v69 no2 p88 S 2017

TITLE FIGHT cartoon chart color diag graph *Road & Track* v68 no5 p42 D 2016/Ja 2017

Baruth, Philip

Senator Leahy: A Life in Scenes color *Publishers Weekly* v264 no10 p52 Mr 6 2017

Barwich, Sebastian

Sensitive electromechanical sensors using viscoelastic graphene-polymer nanocomposites bibl graph *Science* v354 no6317 p1257 D 9 2016

Barwin, Gary

'Be true to the parrot' B. BETHUNE color *Maclean's* v129 no42 p46 O 24 2016

Baryshnikova, Anastasia

Exploring genetic suppression interactions on a global scale diag *Science* v354 no6312 p599 N 4 2016

Barzani, Massoud, 1946-

The Kurds Get Under Way D. DEVOSS color *Weekly Standard* v23 no5 p19 O 9 2017

Barzenji, Alend

Their Goal: A Place on the Team J. GREEN *Atlanta* v56 no11 p101 Mr 2017

Barzilai, Nir

THE LIFE EXPANDERS chart color *Men's Health* v32 no7 p116 S 2017

Barzily-Rokni, Michal

Potential role of intratumor bacteria in mediating tumor resistance to the chemotherapeutic drug gemcitabine diag *Science* v357 no6356 p1156 S 15 2017

Barzini, Chiara

La-La Land R. LEE color *O, The Oprah Magazine* p89 S 2017

MIUCCIA PRADA color *Vogue* v207 no3 p406 Mr 2017

Under the California Sun L. ERMELINO color *Publishers Weekly* v264 no23 p24 Je 5 2017

Basak, Sonali

The Fading Financial Magic Of Reinsurance cartoon *Bloomberg Businessweek* no4496 p52 O 24 2016

The Pension Hole color graph *Bloomberg Businessweek* no4533 p27 Ag 7 2017

Basal metabolism

ALL ABOUT MUSCLES: A USER'S MANUAL H. Levine color *Health* v31 no5 p77 Je 2017

YOUR METABOLISM: A USER'S MANUAL H. Levine color *Health* v30 no9 p109 N 2016

Basalt

Tungsten-182 heterogeneity in modern ocean island basalts A. Mundl, M. Touboul et al chart diag *Science* v356 no6333 p66 Ap 7 2017

Basanta, Benjamin

Principles for designing proteins with cavities formed by curved β sheets bibl color graph *Science* v355 no6321 p1 Ja 13 2017

Basch, Amy

Dream Buddy on a Trail Ride cartoon *Horse & Rider* v56 no3 p72 Mr 2017

Basch, Peter

TIME EXPOSURE H. Martin bw color *Popular Photography* v81 no2 p87 Mr/Ap 2017

Baschieri, Francesco

Tubular clathrin/AP-2 lattices pinch collagen fibers to support 3D cell migration color *Science* v356 no6343 p1138 Je 16 2017

Bascomb, Neal—Interviews

Interview Living History With Neal Bascomb bw cartoon *Military History* v34 no2 p14 Jl 2017

Bascompte, Jordi

Effects of network modularity on the spread of perturbation impact in experimental metapopulations diag graph *Science* v357 no6347 p199 Jl 14 2017

Basden, James

How Utilities Are Using Blockchain to Modernize the Grid *Harvard Business Review Digital Articles* p2 Mr 23 2017

BASE jumping

THE SPORT THAT SOARS—AND KILLS N. Strochlic color *National Geographic* v232 no1 p18 Jl 2017

Base stealing (Baseball)

CAN TREA TURNER SAVE THE STEAL? J. Tayler color diag *Sports Illustrated* v126 no14 p82 My 15-22 2017

Baseball

> *See also*
> Baseball competitions
> Baseball playoffs
> Minor league baseball
> Professional baseball

50 Reasons to Love Being 50+ color *AARP: The Magazine* v60 no3A p61 Ap/My 2017

For those of you just tuning in color *Christian Century* v134 no8 p1 Ap 12 2017

FROM THE ARCHIVES J. RAUCH, C. M. COLLINS et al color *Reason* v49 no4 p78 Ag/S 2017

Jake's John Hancock G. PROFITT *Idaho Magazine* v16 no6 p27 Mr 2017

The Old Brawl Game L. SMITH color *Weekly Standard* v22 no40 p5 Je 26 2017

Play Ball-Everywhere! D. M. SOMMERVILLE *USA Today Magazine* v145 no2858 p48 N 2016

RED-LETTER DAYS C. DOTSON *Cincinnati Magazine* v50 no8 p22 My 2017

TAKE ME OUT TO THE "SONG" PARK *USA Today Magazine* v145 no2862 p42 Mr 2017

Together at the Seams: Baseball meets art in Sioux Falls *South Dakota Magazine* v33 no2 p68 Jl/Ag 2017

Baseball announcers

Look Who's Talking S. Rushin color *Sports Illustrated* v126 no12 p60 My 1 2017

Made for TV B. Reiter color *Sports Illustrated* v125 no15 p35 N 7 2016

Baseball attendance

SEAT FILLER T. Horka and T. Keith color *Sports Illustrated* v127 no9 p14 S 25 2017

Baseball bats

You know you're in America when ... map *Reader's Digest* v190 no1132 p28 Jl/Ag 2017

Baseball caps

The O List: PET EDITION color *O, The Oprah Magazine* p53 O 2017

PUT THE BASEBALL CAP BACK IN YOUR ROTATION color *Esquire* p52 O 2017

Baseball coaches

BatLike a Lumberjack color *Popular Science* v288 no6 p62 N/D 2016

On the Team: College Baseball As a Rite of Passage D. WINKEL-MAIER *Idaho Magazine* v16 no9 p45 Je 2017

The Week color *National Review* v69 no18 p4 O 2 2017

Baseball competitions

The Cubs N. AUSTIN *Arizona Highways* v93 no3 p8 Mr 2017

Fair-Weather Fandom J. Gordon *New York Times Magazine* p28 Ja 15 2017

Laugh Lines K. WHITEHORN, K. HALL et al color *Reader's Digest* v189 no1130 p107 My 2017

MAGIC ON THE MOUND A. BARRA *American History* v51 no6 p22 F 2017

MLB PLAYOFFS K. ROSEN *TV Guide* v64 no40 p66 O 3 2016

OCTOBER MAGIC R. A. BERENZ *TV Guide* v65 no41 p43 O 2 2017

Play Ball L. SMITH color *Weekly Standard* v22 no31 p5 Ap 17 2017

STANDSTILL T. Verducci color *Sports Illustrated* v126 no18 p36 Je 26 2017

Baseball draft—History—20th century

WHAT IF? ... THESE FOUR PIVOTAL DRAFT MOMENTS HAD HAPPENED DIFFERENTLY? J. Feldman color *Sports Illustrated* v126 no11 p51 Ap 17-24 2017

Baseball fans

11 UP CLOSE AND PERSONAL S. Apstein color *Sports Illustrated* v126 no9 p57 Mr 27 2017

Baseball fans—Wounds & injuries

PLAYING IT SAFER B. Reiter color *Sports Illustrated* v127 no10 p60 O 2 2017

Baseball fields

2017'S COOLEST DEVELOPMENTS M. M. Kashino *Washingtonian Magazine* v52 no4 p188 Ja 2017

38,000 CUTS (GIVE OR TAKE) M. McKnight color *Sports Illustrated* v126 no16 p50 Je 5 2017

The BRAVES' NEW WORLD J. GREEN *Atlanta* v56 no12 p84 Ap 2017

Home-Field Advantages J. VRABEL *Indianapolis Monthly* v40 no11 p13 Jl 2017

Out of Left Field M. Malamut color *Rodale's Organic Life* v3 no1 p84 Ja 2017

Who Would Vote Against This? E. CELESTE *D: The Magazine of Dallas* v43 no10 p82 O 2016

Baseball fields—Design & construction

Stadium Shutout: Localities are no longer so willing to take on the risky business of building a ballpark F. Shafroth *Governing* v30 no12 p63 S 2017

Baseball fields—Finance

Stadium Shutout: Localities are no longer so willing to take on the risky business of building a ballpark F. Shafroth *Governing* v30 no12 p63 S 2017

Baseball fields—Safety measures

PLAYING IT SAFER B. Reiter color *Sports Illustrated* v127 no10 p60 O 2 2017

Baseball for children—Training

Kid Sports Inc [Cover story] S. Gregory, A. Abrams et al color diag *Time* v190 no9 p42 S 4 2017

Baseball injuries

Games: Will Leitch B. Doherty img *New York* v50 no10 p30 My 15 2017

Baseball managers

BASEBALL BLOOD C. Jones *New York Times Magazine* p38 S 17 2017

Baseball managers—Attitudes

17 MACRO MANAGING T. Verducci color *Sports Illustrated* v126 no9 p70 Mr 27 2017

Baseball managers—United States

Bruce Bochy J. Crelin color *Current Biography* v77 no10 p10 O 2016

Baseball players

> *See also*
> Pitchers (Baseball)
> Women baseball players

12 ETA: RIGHT NOW J. Tayler color *Sports Illustrated* v126 no9 p60 Mr 27 2017

15 HOME SWEET HOMERS T. Verducci color *Sports Illustrated* v126 no9 p68 Mr 27 2017

9 BORN TO WIN [Cover story] T. Verducci color diag *Sports Illustrated* v126 no9 p52 Mr 27 2017

Ben Zobrist J. Crelin color *Current Biography* v78 no8 p91 Ag 2017

CAN THE EMERGENCE OF A HIGH-TECH TOOL BRING BASE BALL'S STATISTICAL REVOLUTION TO FIELDING? B. SCHOENFELD *New York Times Magazine* p48 O 2 2016

GRAND SLAM ENTREPRENEUR D. T. Dingle bw color *Black Enterprise* v47 no8 p48 Jl/Ag 2017

Homegrown Nebraskans hit early baseball home run J. Boschen color *Nebraska Life* v21 no2 p17 Mr/Ap 2017

Ichiro SUZUKI A. Belth bw *Esquire* p70 Ap 2017

NEW YORK GIANT A. Belth color *Esquire* p30 O 2017

RED-LETTER DAYS C. DOTSON *Cincinnati Magazine* v50 no8 p22 My 2017

Baseball players—Abuse of

The Case for ... Banishing Beanballs J. Dickey and T. Keith color *Sports Illustrated* v126 no15 p26 My 29 2017

Baseball players—Health

IN THE RIGHT FIELD M. MURPHY color *Muscle & Performance* v9 no8 p36 Ag 2017

Baseball players—History—21st century

The Class Of 2016 B. Reiter *Sports Illustrated* v125 no15 p36 N 7 2016

IT'S ALIVE! THE SLASHER COULD BE MAKING A Comeback B. Reiter color *Sports Illustrated* v126 no12 p29 My 1 2017

Baseball players—Psychology

HOT | NOT T. Keith color *Sports Illustrated* v126 no10 p28 Ap 10 2017

Baseball players—Travel

International Harvest Z. Pereles and T. Keith chart color *Sports Illustrated* v126 no15 p16 My 29 2017

Baseball players—United States

Michael Fulmer M. Hagan color *Current Biography* v78 no6 p39 Je 2017

Paul Goldschmidt C. Cullen color *Current Biography* v77 no10 p30 O 2016

Baseball playoffs

Leading Off B. Reiter color *Sports Illustrated* v125 no13 p6 O 17 2016

SF SANTA SAYS IT'S BATTER UP W. M. BARRETT *USA Today Magazine* v145 no2858 p76 N 2016

SIX PLAYOFF QUESTIONS S. Apstein color *Sports Illustrated* v127 no10 p42 O 2 2017

Baseball statistics

16 PITCH WHISPERERS T. Verducci color *Sports Illustrated* v126 no9 p69 Mr 27 2017

Why are some stats—like baseball's 'exit velocity' this year—embraced more than others? J. Caspian Kang *New York Times Magazine* p14 S 3 2017

Baseball teams

Baseball is flirting with new rules. But if it really wants to embrace change - and speed things up - it should look to its ancient, woolier past J. C. Kang *New York Times Magazine* p14 Ap 2 2017

COUNTERPOINTS S. FENNESSY *Atlanta* v56 no12 p16 Ap 2017

A father's dilemma: Which baseball team will my baby daughter root for? J. C. Kang *New York Times Magazine* p14 Jl 2 2017

GO TEAM! L. MYERS color *Missouri Life* v44 no4 p62 Je 2017

IT WAS NOT AN INSTINCT, IT WAS A CHOICE T. EPSTEIN *Vital Speeches of the Day* v83 no8 p222 Ag 2017

The Quiz T. BALAZO *Maclean's* v130 no9 p80 O 2017

SF SANTA SAYS IT'S BATTER UP W. M. BARRETT *USA Today Magazine* v145 no2858 p76 N 2016

Baseball teams—Finance

The Most Valuable Baseball Teams M. K. OZANIAN, K. BADENHAUSEN et al chart color *Forbes* v199 no5 p28 My 16 2017

Baseball techniques

See also

Batting (Baseball)

Pitching (Baseball)

Philosopher Up to Bat M. KINGWELL cartoon *Walrus* v14 no2 p59 Mr 2017

Baseball Tonight (TV program)

MAJOR LEAGUE BASEBALL K. Rosen *TV Guide* v64 no15 p47 Ap 4 2016

Baseball tournaments

GO TEAM! L. MYERS color *Missouri Life* v44 no4 p62 Je 2017

WHEN ALL WAS LOST: A team of outmatched kids--and a bigger surprise than a win M. R. Fisher *Washingtonian Magazine* v52 no9 p208 Je 2017

Baseball umpires

CENTURY marks *Christian Century* v134 no16 p8 Ag 2 2017

THE LAST COWBOY M. Rosenberg color *Sports Illustrated* v127 no3 p84 Jl 24 2017

Baseball—Anecdotes

HARD BALL R. NELSON *Virginia Living* v15 no3 p100 Ap 2017

Baseball—China

Baseball Wants A Home Run in China color *Bloomberg Businessweek* no4498 p31 N 7 2016

Baseball—Cuba

Purpose Pitch S. L. Price and T. Keith color *Sports Illustrated* v125 no18 p17 D 5 2016

Baseball—History

ABOVE & BEYOND cartoon *New Yorker* v92 no34 p16 O 24 2016

Baseball—Humor

Embrace The Crazy S. Rushin color *Sports Illustrated* v126 no15 p60 My 29 2017

Finally, All Is Revealed S. Rushin color *Sports Illustrated* v126 no2 p64 Ja 16 2017

Baseball—Japan

HAVE IT BOTH WAYS L. J. Wertheim color *Sports Illustrated* v126 no11 p92 Ap 17-24 2017

Baseball players—Charts, diagrams, etc.

14 HANDY MEN S. Apstein color diag *Sports Illustrated* v126 no9 p67 Mr 27 2017

Baseball players—Salaries, wages, etc.

10 Years of Data on Baseball Teams Shows When Pay Transparency Backfires A. D. Hill, F. Aime et al *Harvard Business Review Digital Articles* p2 My 9 2017

Should Minor-League Ballplayers Get a Big Pay Raise? color *Kiplinger's Personal Finance* v71 no7 p16 Jl 2017

Baseball—Rules

Baseball is flirting with new rules. But if it really wants to embrace change - and speed things up - it should look to its ancient, woolier past J. C. Kang *New York Times Magazine* p14 Ap 2 2017

Baseball—Statistics—Charts, diagrams, etc.

TROUT'S POND K. Ducey chart *Sports Illustrated* v126 no9 p45 Mr 27 2017

Baseball—United States

Home-Field Advantages J. VRABEL *Indianapolis Monthly* v40 no11 p13 Jl 2017

Whole New Ballgame T. PERROTTA color *Weekly Standard* v23 no6 p44 O 16 2017

Baseball—United States—History

REAL MEN HAVE CURVES [Cover story] T. Verducci color *Sports Illustrated* v126 no15 p36 My 29 2017

Baseball—United States—History—20th century

WHAT IF? ... MICHAEL JORDAN HAD NEVER BAGGED IT? T. Keith and J. Feldman color *Sports Illustrated* v126 no11 p60 Ap 17-24 2017

Basel (Switzerland)

SWITZERLAND D. Heimburger color *Christianity Today* v61 no4 p24 My 2017

Baselga, José

PI3K pathway regulates ER-dependent transcription in breast cancer through the epigenetic regulator KMT2D bibl graph *Science* v355 no6331 p1324 Mr 24 2017

Basements

A CLEAN, WELL-LIGHTED WORKROOM R. D'AGOSTINO cartoon color *Popular Mechanics* p103 D 2016/Ja 2017

HOME R. D'AGOSTINO color *Popular Mechanics* p6 D 2016/Ja 2017

Basford, Johanna

queen of COLORING K. K. CONDON color *Better Homes & Gardens* v95 no11 p20 N 2017

BASH, BRUCE

Hell's Half Acre: Strolling the Lava Trails *Idaho Magazine* v16 no11 p15 Ag 2017

Bash, Jeremy

The Former Head of the CIA on Managing the Hunt for Bin Laden *Harvard Business Review Digital Articles* p2 My 2 2016

Bashi, Kishi

POP RULES M. GRIFFITH color *New Orleans Magazine* v51 no1 p52 N 2016

Bashinsky, Robin

Back to Your Roots color *Health* v30 no9 p122 N 2016

TOO HOT TO COOK? color *Health* v31 no6 p106 Jl 2017

Veggie Steaks color *Health* v31 no4 p88 My 2017

Bashir, Naheed

URBAN JUNGLE C. Atkinson color *Sunset* v238 no2 p42 F 2017

Bashir, Ruzwana

THE VALLEY'S FAVORITE BRITISH IMPORT L. Rao color *Fortune* v174 no6 p46 N 1 2016

Basil

Can't-Say-No Risotto K. SHERWOOD *Nutrition Action Health Letter* v44 no3 p13 Ap 2017

BASILE, STEVE

What do you collect and why? color *American Craft* v77 no2 p20 Ap/My 2017

BASINGER, JEANINE

Dancin' in the Rain *New York Times Book Review* p46 Je 4 2017

Basins (Containers)

SHOP NOTES cartoon color *Popular Mechanics* p40 Mr 2017

Basins (Geology)

Conifer Cruising T. WILLIAM *American Forests* v122 no3 p24 Fall 2016

Baskaron, John—Interviews

EVANGELISM Is Alive in Portland M. BINDER color *Christianity Today* p36 Ap 2017

Baskerville-Burrows, Jennifer

People *Christian Century* v133 no24 p20 N 23 2016

Basket making

The great plastic basket makeover J. Jones color *Redbook* p20 Mr 2017

Basketball

See also

Basketball—Competitions

Basketball for women

Basketball playoffs

BASKETBALL CATAPULT! chart color diag *Popular Mechanics* p96 My 2017

THE LAKERS' DIET V. TWEED color *Better Nutrition* v79 no3 p55 Mr 2017

The Pickup Artist I. Eger *Los Angeles Magazine* v62 no6 p76 Je 2017

SKYLAR DIGGINS "Everything Happens for a Reason" J. Andriakos color *Health* v31 no1 p20 Ja 2017

Basketball arenas—Design & construction

This Old House E. Laase and T. Keith color *Sports Illustrated* v127 no6 p16 Ag 28 2017

Basketball coaches

Brad Stevens J. Crelin color *Current Biography* v77 no11 p82 N 2016

Home Court C. FEHRMAN *Indianapolis Monthly* p60 N 2017

Basketball coaches—Interviews

Life's Work: An Interview with Mike Krzyzewski A. Beard bw *Harvard Business Review* v95 no2 p164 Mr/Ap 2017

Basketball coaches—United States

TAKE THAT! R. Nadkarni color *Sports Illustrated* v126 no12 p35 My 1 2017

Basketball courts

Alley-Oop S. COCHRAN color *Architectural Digest* v74 no9 p184 S 2017

Paris' Technicolor Basketball Court J. Zorthian color *Time* v190 no4 p19 Jl 24 2017

Basketball defense

Defense Mechanisms M. Rosenberg color *Sports Illustrated* v126 no18 p64 Je 26 2017

DIFFERENCE MAKER R. Nadkarni color *Sports Illustrated* v126 no12 p34 My 1 2017

THE HUSTLE L. Jenkins color *Sports Illustrated* v126 no14 p32 My 15-22 2017

Basketball draft

FOX ON THE RUN A. Sharp color *Sports Illustrated* v126 no18 p30 Je 26 2017

HOT | NOT T. Keith color *Sports Illustrated* v126 no18 p16 Je 26 2017

Leading Off color *Sports Illustrated* v127 no1 p6 Jl 3 2017

LOTTERY TICKETS color *Sports Illustrated* v126 no18 p33 Je 26 2017

Basketball draft—Humor

Defense Mechanisms M. Rosenberg color *Sports Illustrated* v126 no18 p64 Je 26 2017

Basketball fans

The Ballsiest Father in America Z. BARON bw color *GQ: Gentlemen's Quarterly* v97 no7 p24 Jl 2017

BEST (AND WORST) CITIES TO GOTO THE HOOP *USA Today Magazine* v146 no2868 p8 S 2017

Basketball for children

Hoop Dreams A. R. Fleming color *Good Housekeeping* v264 no3 p71 Mr 2017

Basketball for women

HUSKIES GET STAR ROLES R. A. BERENZ *TV Guide* v65 no8 p40 F 27 2017

Basketball for women—Records

Breaking Points J. Stiles color *Sports Illustrated* v126 no7 p80 Mr 6 2017

Basketball on television

COLLEGE HOOPS TIP-OFF MARATHON K. ROSEN *TV Guide* v64 no46 p46 N 7 2016

COMPLETE MADNESS R. A. BERENZ *TV Guide* v65 no11 p50 Mr 6 2017

Sports Highlights *TV Guide* v64 no15 p51 Ap 4 2016

Basketball players

See also

Rookie basketball players

Women basketball players

April/May T. PAYNE color *Ebony* v72 no6 p18 Ap/My 2017

Giannis Antetokounmpo M. Hagan color *Current Biography* v78 no6 p3 Je 2017

"I'M A POET." B. SMITH color *Chicago* v65 no12 p98 D 2016

Isaiah Thomas M. Hagan color *Current Biography* v78 no8 p82 Ag 2017

Kareem Abdul-Jabbar: The basketball star and author of 'Coach Wooden and Me' says he looks forward to anything written by Walter Mosley: 'I'd be very happy if he wrote a novel every week' *New York Times Book Review* p11 Je 4 2017

Leap Year [Cover story] color *GQ: Gentlemen's Quarterly* v86 no11 p106 N 2016

The Revenge of the Happy Warrior A. CORSELLO color *GQ: Gentlemen's Quarterly* v97 no5 p80 My 2017

STAR ROCKET IN FLIGHT C. O'CONNELL *Texas Monthly* v45 no4 p90 Ap 2017

TAKING A SHOT IN "TERROR" A. BLUE *USA Today Magazine* v145 no2860 p66 Ja 2017

UNEVEN PLAYING FIELD M. CAMPBELL color *Ebony* v72 no5 p92 Mr 2017

Basketball players—Attitudes

The Liberation of Kevin Durant [Cover story] P. Solotaroff color *Rolling Stone* no1273 p34 N 3 2016

Starring The King [Cover story] M. Anthony Green color *GQ: Gentlemen's Quarterly* v97 no11 p86 N 2017

Basketball players—Awards

WHOSE TROPHY IS IT? R. Nadkarni color *Sports Illustrated* v126 no5 p56 F 13 2017

Basketball players—Biography

Al Horford J. Crelin color *Current Biography* v78 no9 p37 S 2017

THE MYSTERiES OF AN EVERYTHiNG MAN S. ANDERSON *New York Times Magazine* p32 F 5 2017

Basketball players—Finance

Arrival Instincts J. Lisanti and T. Keith color *Sports Illustrated* v125 no14 p24 O 24-31 2016

Basketball players—History—21st century

OPENING ACT B. G. R. Mahoney and R. Nadkarni color *Sports Illustrated* v126 no13 p52 My 8 2017

SI's Top 100 B. Golliver, R. Mahoney et al color *Sports Illustrated* v125 no14 p94 O 24-31 2016

Basketball players—Interviews

Cinnaticin kid: justin doellman J. COHEN *Cincinnati Magazine* v50 no6 p86 Mr 2017

SI NOW M. Gray color *Sports Illustrated* v126 no9 p4 Mr 27 2017

Basketball players—Trading of

WHAT IF? ... THESE FOUR ENTIRELY REALISTIC TRADES HAD GONE DOWN? J. Feldman color *Sports Illustrated* v126 no11 p68 Ap 17-24 2017

Basketball players—United States

See also

African American basketball players

American Voices J.J. Barea S. Apstein and T. Keith color *Sports Illustrated* v126 no10 p34 Ap 10 2017

Damian Lillard C. Cullen color *Current Biography* v77 no11 p49

N 2016

THE FIFTH QUARTER D. Bry color *Esquire* p24 Je/Jl 2017

IN THE MIDDLE C. Ballard color *Sports Illustrated* v126 no5 p100 F 13 2017

Kyle Lowry C. Cullen color *Current Biography* v77 no10 p77 O 2016

Missouri Compromise J. Fuchs and T. Keith color *Sports Illustrated* v126 no10 p32 Ap 10 2017

Basketball playoffs

February Events F. Esker color *New Orleans Magazine* v51 no4 p26 F 2017

FO' BETTER OR FO' WORSE? [Cover story] L. Jenkins color *Sports Illustrated* v126 no16 p34 Je 5 2017

NBA JUMPSTART R. A. BERENZ *TV Guide* v65 no43 p45 O 16 2017

Run It Back W. Leitch and T. Keith color *Sports Illustrated* v126 no11 p17 Ap 17-24 2017

Basketball playoffs—History

HOT | NOT T. Keith color *Sports Illustrated* v126 no12 p17 My 1 2017

Basketball playoffs—History—21st century

L.A. Story B. Golliver color *Sports Illustrated* v125 no19 p106 D 12 2016

OPENING ACT B. G. R. Mahoney and R. Nadkarni color *Sports Illustrated* v126 no13 p52 My 8 2017

TAKE THAT! R. Nadkarni color *Sports Illustrated* v126 no12 p35 My 1 2017

VIEW SOME TWOSOME R. Deitsch and S. Kwak color *Sports Illustrated* v127 no11 p18 O 9 2017

WONDER WALL L. Jenkins color *Sports Illustrated* v126 no12 p30 My 1 2017

Basketball rules

HOT | NOT T. Keith color *Sports Illustrated* v127 no9 p15 S 25 2017

Basketball team owners

BILLIONAIRES PLAY BALL color *Fortune* v175 no7 p14 Je 1 2017

CUBAN REVOLUTION S. HOLLANDSWORTH *Texas Monthly* v45 no4 p110 Ap 2017

Basketball teams

See also

College basketball teams

10 Bucks A. Sharp, B. Golliver et al color *Sports Illustrated* v125 no14 p84 O 24-31 2016

10 Mavericks R. Nadkarni, B. Golliver et al color *Sports Illustrated* v125 no14 p110 O 24-31 2016

11 Bulls A. Sharp, B. Golliver et al color *Sports Illustrated* v125 no14 p86 O 24-31 2016

11 Pelicans R. Nadkarni, B. Golliver et al color *Sports Illustrated* v125 no14 p111 O 24-31 2016

12 Heat R. Mahoney, B. Golliver et al color *Sports Illustrated* v125 no14 p88 O 24-31 2016

12 Suns B. Golliver, R. Mahoney et al color *Sports Illustrated* v125 no14 p112 O 24-31 2016

13 Magic R. Mahoney, B. Golliver et al color *Sports Illustrated* v125 no14 p89 O 24-31 2016

14 76ers R. Nadkarni, B. Golliver et al color *Sports Illustrated* v125 no14 p90 O 24-31 2016

14 Kings B. Golliver, R. Mahoney et al color *Sports Illustrated* v125 no14 p114 O 24-31 2016

15 Lakers B. Golliver, R. Mahoney et al color *Sports Illustrated* v125 no14 p116 O 24-31 2016

1 Cavaliers A. Sharp, B. Golliver et al color *Sports Illustrated* v125 no14 p72 O 24-31 2016

2 Celtics R. Nadkarni, B. Golliver et al *Sports Illustrated* v125 no14 p74 O 24-31 2016

2 Spurs R. Nadkarni, B. Golliver et al color *Sports Illustrated* v125 no14 p98 O 24-31 2016

3 Clippers B. Golliver, R. Nadkarni et al color *Sports Illustrated* v125 no14 p99 O 24-31 2016

3 Raptors R. Nadkarni, B. Golliver et al color *Sports Illustrated* v125 no14 p75 O 24-31 2016

4 Pistons A. Sharp, B. Golliver et al color *Sports Illustrated* v125 no14 p84 O 24-31 2016

5 Hornets R. Mahoney, B. Golliver et al color *Sports Illustrated* v125 no14 p78 O 24-31 2016

5 Thunder R. Nadkarni, B. Golliver et al color *Sports Illustrated* v125 no14 p102 O 24-31 2016

6 Hawks R. Mahoney, B. Golliver et al color *Sports Illustrated* v125 no14 p80 O 24-31 2016

6 Jazz R. Nadkarni, B. Golliver et al color *Sports Illustrated* v125 no14 p103 O 24-31 2016

7 Grizzlies R. Nadkarni, B. Golliver et al color *Sports Illustrated* v125 no14 p104 O 24-31 2016

7 Pacers A. Sharp, B. Golliver et al color *Sports Illustrated* v125 no14 p81 O 24-31 2016

8 Rockets R. Nadkarni, B. Golliver et al color *Sports Illustrated* v125 no14 p106 O 24-31 2016

8 Wizards R. Mahoney, B. Golliver et al color *Sports Illustrated* v125 no14 p82 O 24-31 2016

9 Knicks R. Nadkarni, B. Golliver et al color *Sports Illustrated* v125 no14 p83 O 24-31 2016

9 Timberwolves R. Nadkarni, B. Golliver et al color *Sports Illustrated* v125 no14 p108 O 24-31 2016

Scouting Reports B. Golliver, R. Mahoney et al color *Sports Illustrated* v125 no14 p70 O 24-31 2016

Basketball teams—Finance

13 Nuggets R. Nadkarni, B. Golliver et al color *Sports Illustrated* v125 no14 p113 O 24-31 2016

15 Nets R. Nadkarni, B. Golliver et al color *Sports Illustrated* v125 no14 p92 O 24-31 2016

4 Trail Blazers R. Nadkarni, B. Golliver et al color *Sports Illustrated* v125 no14 p100 O 24-31 2016

Basketball teams—History

1 Warriors B. Golliver, R. Nadkarni et al color *Sports Illustrated* v125 no14 p96 O 24-31 2016

Basketball teams—History—21st century

The Most Valuable NBA Teams K. BADENHAUSEN, M. K. OZANIAN et al chart color *Forbes* v199 no2 p30 F 28 2017

Basketball teams—Social aspects

2016-17 Viewers' Guide B. Golliver and A. Mirchandani color *Sports Illustrated* v125 no14 p118 O 24-31 2016

Basketball techniques

See also

Basketball defense

Dribbling (Basketball)

Basketball tournaments

See also

Basketball playoffs

THROWING IN THE CHAIR J. WERTHEIM *Indianapolis Monthly* v40 no7 p80 Mr 2017

Basketball training

Pistol Pete's Homework Basketball B. Swanson *New York Times Magazine* p20 Ap 30 2017

Basketball—Competitions

Double-Loop Government: It's a learning strategy that produces conflict--and innovation M. Funkhouser *Governing* v30 no9 p59 Je 2017

EAST RIVER EVENTS *South Dakota Magazine* v32 no6 p82 Mr/Ap 2017

When League Pass Takes You Courtside I. Boudway color *Bloomberg Businessweek* no4498 p42 N 7 2016

Basketball—Computer network resources

Hoop for Thought C. Stone color *Sports Illustrated* v125 no14 p16 O 24-31 2016

Basketball Hall of Fame (Springfield, Mass.)

AT HOME IN THE HALL S. Rushin color *Sports Illustrated* v127 no8 p68 S 18 2017

Basketball—History

Game Changers: The spectacular play you see today owes a mighty debt to the revolutionary, slam-dunking ABA F. Lidz *Smithsonian* v48 no6 p26 O 2017

Basketball—History—21st century

2017-18 ENTERTAINMENT VALUE GUIDE B. Golliver color *Sports Illustrated* v127 no12 p76 O 16 2017

Basketball—Offense

See also

Free throw (Basketball)

FEELING THE CRUNGH B. Golliver color *Sports Illustrated* v126 no3 p36 Ja 23 2017

Basketball—Offense—Charts, diagrams, etc.

Triple Double Bubble A. Ross and T. Keith color diag *Sports Il-*

lustrated v126 no3 p16 Ja 23 2017

Basketball—Offense—Universities & colleges

Inside LOOK L. Winn color diag *Sports Illustrated* v126 no8 p42 Mr 20 2017

In with a Bang L. Winn color *Sports Illustrated* v125 no20 p132 D 19 2016

Basketball players—Charts, diagrams, etc.

NBA or BBC? T. Keith chart color *Sports Illustrated* v126 no18 p16 Je 26 2017

Basketball players—United States—Salaries, wages, etc.

BASKETBALL SALARIES GET SOME AIR M. Heimer color diag *Fortune* v75 no1 p24 Ja 1 2017

Basketball—Rebound—Charts, diagrams, etc.

Triple Double Bubble A. Ross and T. Keith color diag *Sports Illustrated* v126 no3 p16 Ja 23 2017

Basketball—Records—United States

For the Record color *Time* v189 no15 p6 Ap 24 2017

KEENESANITY D. Greene color *Sports Illustrated* v126 no4 p52 Ja 30 2017

Basketballs

A Baller's Guide to Abs B. J. Gaddour cartoon color *Men's Health* v32 no2 p8 Mr 2017

Basketball—Shooting

LITTLE MAN, BIG SHOTS T. Layden color *Sports Illustrated* v126 no5 p52 F 13 2017

Basketball—United States—History

GOLDEN DAYS J. McCallum color *Sports Illustrated* v127 no12 p98 O 16 2017

Baskets

organize your DROP ZONE A. MAZE color *Better Homes & Gardens* v95 no11 p62 N 2017

Baskets—Evaluation

Dreamy Headboard color *Good Housekeeping* v265 no5 p39 N 2017

Here comes the sun color *House Beautiful* p88 Ag 2017

PACK A PRETTY PICNIC: No yard? No problem. Turn one of Washington's beautiful parks into your own outdoor dining room H. Kelly *Washingtonian Magazine* v52 no8 p169 My 2017

TOAST THE HOST color *Martha Stewart Living* p68 Jl/Ag 2017

TO HAVE AND TO HOLD color *Martha Stewart Living* p38 S 2017

Baskin, Ben

... And Now What? color *Sports Illustrated* v125 no20 p64 D 19 2016

The Case for ... Exercising Caution color *Sports Illustrated* v126 no8 p29 Mr 20 2017

DEEP PURPLE color *Sports Illustrated* v125 no13 p30 O 17 2016

THE DEVIL GETS HIS DUE color *Sports Illustrated* v125 no18 p42 D 5 2016

FIRST GOLFER color *Sports Illustrated* v127 no4 p48 Ag 7 2017

Ground Effect chart color *Sports Illustrated* v127 no6 p16 Ag 28 2017

Keys to a Canelo upset ... color *Sports Illustrated* v127 no6 p56 Ag 28 2017

Keys to a McGregor upset ... color *Sports Illustrated* v127 no6 p54 Ag 28 2017

Leading Off color *Sports Illustrated* v127 no7 p6 S 4 2017

OVER-THE-TOP DOGS color *Sports Illustrated* v127 no1 p108 Jl 3 2017

SUSPENDED DISBELIEF [Cover story] color *Sports Illustrated* v126 no5 p26 F 13 2017

This is 40 color *Sports Illustrated* v126 no7 p79 Mr 6 2017

Baskin, Jake A.

Code.org: A Resource for Computer Science in Your District *Education Digest* v83 no2 p31 O 2017

BASKIN, JON

IN THE SICK-BOX color *Nation* v304 no16 p35 My 22 2017

Baskin, Nora Raleigh, 1961-

Nine, Ten: A September 11 Story color *Publishers Weekly* v263 no49 p74 D 7 2016

Bason, Christian

Look to Government—Yes, Government—for New Social Innovations *Harvard Business Review Digital Articles* p2 N 20 2014

Basov, D. N.

Plasmonic imaging is gaining momentum graph *Science* v357 no6347 p132 Jl 14 2017

Polaritons in van der Waals materials bibl chart color diag graph *Science* v354 no6309 paag1992-1 O 14 2016

Basquiat, Jean-Michel, 1960-1988

PROPHET MOTIVE: Decades later, Jean-Michel Basquiat's complex works are increasingly prescient--and valuable A. Crawford *Smithsonian* v48 no5 p12 S 2017

Basquiat, Jean-Michel, 1960-1988—Exhibitions

Pop Chart R. Bruner, C. Lang et al color *Time* v190 no13 p69 O 2 2017

Bass, Brenda

Not just Salk color *Science* v357 no6356 p1105 S 15 2017

Bass, Clarence

79 IS THE NEW 29 N. HEIL bw color *Men's Health* v32 no5 p126 Je 2017

Bass, Debbie

Truman Named Hunter of the Year color *Practical Horseman* v45 no5 p70 My 2017

Bass, Dina

Dropbox Gets Ready For the Road bw *Bloomberg Businessweek* no4534 p22 Ag 14 2017

Dropbox's Drew Houston color *Bloomberg Businessweek* no4526 p40 Je 12 2017

Get Your Own Broadband cartoon map *Bloomberg Businessweek* no4496 p38 O 24 2016

Home Is Where The Data Is graph *Bloomberg Businessweek* no4498 p54 N 7 2016

Microsoft Surfaces color graph *Bloomberg Businessweek* no4521 p31 My 8 2017

Bass, Ellen

INDIGO *New Yorker* v93 no32 p60 O 16 2017

BASS, FLORA GONZALES

The Question *O, The Oprah Magazine* p18 S 2017

BASS, GITA

42 new ALL-STAR PRODUCTS of the year [Cover story] color *Redbook* p27 Jl/Ag 2017

Bass, Holly

Brown Girls Dreaming *New York Times Book Review* p1 N 13 2016

Bass, Ian

MIRACLE in the MARCHES *History Today* v67 no3 p40 Mr 2017

Bass, Joseph

Circadian time signatures of fitness and disease bibl diag map *Science* v354 no6315 p994 N 25 2016

Bass, Patrik Henry

THE BEST BOOKS OF 2016 color *Essence* v47 no8 p72 D 2016

Call Her Madame color *Essence* v47 no12 p73 Ap 2017

THE CRITIC'S CHOICE color *Essence* v48 no2 p62 Je 2017

DEAR WHITE PEOPLE color *Essence* v47 no11 p62 Mr 2017

EVERY LITTLE THING SHE DOES IS MAGIC color *Essence* v47 no7 p54 N 2016

Fall's FINEST color *Essence* v48 no6 p74 O 2017

The Good Wife color *Essence* v47 no7 p90 N 2016

HARLEM ON HIS MIND color *Essence* v47 no7 p55 N 2016

HISTORY, HER STORIES & FUTURE THINKERS color *Essence* v47 no10 p58 F 2017

HOUSEWIVES AND HEROINES color *Essence* v47 no12 p70 Ap 2017

I, TINA color *Essence* v47 no8 p104 D 2016

LOVE AND LUST color *Essence* v48 no6 p76 O 2017

Michelle, Our Belle color *Essence* v47 no10 p60 F 2017

Our Ms. Brooks color *Essence* v48 no2 p63 Je 2017

PLAYING IN THE DARK color *Essence* v48 no5 p68 S 2017

Season of GOOD READS color *Essence* v48 no5 p66 S 2017

Summer's BEST BOOKS color *Essence* v48 no3 p56 Jl 2017

BASS, RICK

Culling the Herd: A widow and her brother-in-law hunt buffalo in the 1870s *New York Times Book Review* p18 O 15 2017

For a Little While: New and Selected Stories H. K. Bush *Christian Century* v134 no1 p41 Ja 4 2017

FOR THE LOVE OF THE GAME *Texas Monthly* v45 no9 p68 S 2017

LIFE ON THE EDGE 3,822 MILES *Texas Monthly* v45 no5 p73 My 2017

They Do Declare *New York Times Book Review* p16 Ap 2 2017

Bass, S. Jonathan

Justice In Slow Motion T. B. Tyson *New York Times Book Review*
p1 My 21 2017

Bass, Sam
EDITORS' 100 bw color *Skiing* p36 Wint 2017

Bass fishing
10! P. ROBBINS, L. VICK et al cartoon color *Field & Stream*
v122 no1 p30 My 2017
FEEDING THE COWS J. Cermele color *Field & Stream* v122
no6 p22 N 2017
Flipping Genius B. Duchesney color *Field & Stream* v122 no1
pF1 My 2017
THE RUN N. HONACHEFSKY color *Outdoor Life* v224 no8 p65
O 2017
SUMMER SURFACE BASS D. A. BROWN and G. BETHGE
color *Outdoor Life* v224 no5 p31 Je/Jl 2017
THE TIE THAT BINDS J. BRANDT color *Outdoor Life* v224
no8 p66 O 2017

Bass guitar
Establishing the Perfect Groove M. JONES color diag *Downbeat*
v84 no7 p74 Jl 2017

Bass guitarists
ERIC REVIS: Endless Possibilities J. WOODARD color *Down-
beat* v84 no10 p50 O 2017
THE SLANTS M. BRAGG color *Reason* v48 no11 p36 Ap 2017

Bass guitarists—Interviews
Gene Simmons A. GREENE bw *Rolling Stone* no1297 p58 O 5
2017

Bass Pro Shops Inc.
Living & Recreation *Virginia Living* p64 2017 Best 20of Virginia

Bass trombone with band
The Exposed Melodic Use OF BASS TROMBONE IN A BIG
BAND B. Wallarab color *Downbeat* v84 no4 p82 Ap 2017

Bassard, Jean-Etienne
Characterization of a dynamic metabolon producing the defense
compound dhurrin in sorghum bibl graph *Science* v354 no6314
p890 N 18 2016

Bassel-Duby, Rhonda
Control of muscle formation by the fusogenic micropeptide myomixer diag *Science* v356 no6335 p323 Ap 21 2017

Basset, Yves
Higher predation risk for insect prey at low latitudes and elevations graph *Science* v356 no6339 p742 My 19 2017

Bassett, Abigail
SPLITTING THE HAIRS OF LUXURY chart color *Motor Trend*
v68 no12 p74 D 2016

Bassett, Joe
JOE BASSETT J. Scott *Successful Farming* v115 no5 p8 Mid-
Mr 2017

Bassett, Win
The Sport of Kings: A Novel *Christian Century* v134 no7 p41 Mr
29 2017

Bassi, Joseph P.
How did a scientific Siberia turn into AstroBoulder? *Physics Today* v70 no2 p36 F 2017

Basskin, David A.
The Thread *New York Times Magazine* p8 Mr 26 2017

Bassler, Bonnie
Not just Salk color *Science* v357 no6356 p1105 S 15 2017

Bassos, Stephanie
CONVERGENCE E. Fishman color *Chicago* v65 no11 p92 N
2016

Bassuk, Alicia
7 Tricky Work Situations, and How to Respond to Them *Harvard
Business Review Digital Articles* p2 O 11 2017
The Antidote to Office Gossip *Harvard Business Review Digital
Articles* p2 N 11 2016
Divorce Doesn't Have to Derail Your Career *Harvard Business
Review Digital Articles* p2 Ap 15 2015
How to Deal with an Office Soapboxer *Harvard Business Review
Digital Articles* p2 Ag 30 2016
Interview Techniques That Get Beyond Canned Responses *Har-
vard Business Review Digital Articles* p2 F 19 2016
When Should You Fire a "Good Enough" Employee? *Harvard
Business Review Digital Articles* p2 My 25 2015

Bassüllü, Çağlar
The extent of forest in dryland biomes [Cover story] chart map

Science v356 no6338 p635 My 12 2017

Bastards (Film)
ALSO PLAYING D. Heching color *Entertainment Weekly* no1478
/ 1479 p78 Ag 18-25 2017

Bastian, Boris C.
Mutations in the promoter of the telomerase gene TERT contribute
to tumorigenesis by a two-step mechanism diag *Science* v357
no6358 p1416 S 29 2017

Bastianich, Lidia
The Joy of Gardening J. Newman color *AARP: The Magazine* v59
no4A p63 Je/Jl 2016

Bastidas, Grace
The Power of Language *Parents* v91 no10 p16 O 2016

Bastien, Laurent
How local is the local news at Gannett? diag *Columbia Journalism
Review* v56 no1 p69 Spr 2017

Bastille Day
ABOVE & BEYOND bw *New Yorker* v93 no20 p20 Jl 10 2017
DAN ABOUT TOWN: Party photographer Dan Swartz's monthly
roundup of bashes, balls, and benefits *Washingtonian Magazine*
v52 no12 p26 S 2017
The Surprisingly Peaceful Origins of Bastille Day M. Fabry *Time*
v190 no4 p19 Jl 24 2017

Bastin, Jean-François
The extent of forest in dryland biomes [Cover story] chart map
Science v356 no6338 p635 My 12 2017

Bastir, Markus
The growth pattern of Neandertals, reconstructed from a juvenile skeleton from El Sidrón (Spain) color graph *Science* v357
no6357 p1282 S 22 2017

BASTONE, KELLY
Aspen *Los Angeles Magazine* v61 no11 p86 N 2016
cabins For Snow play color *Cabin Living* p52 D 2016
Color Country color *Backpacker* v45 no2 p16 Mr 2017
EQUIP THE KIDS color *Backpacker* p71 Je 2017
EXPIRES NEVER cartoon color *Runner's World* v51 no10 p48
N 2016
FIND YOUR SPARK [Cover story] color *Runner's World* v51
no11 p34 D 2016
Sea World map *Backpacker* p20 Ag 2017
SHOW of SUPPORT color *Runner's World* v52 no7 p78 Ag 2017
Start Where You Are [Cover story] color *Runner's World* v52 no1
p66 Ja/F 2017
Women SUPPORTING Women bw color *Runner's World* v52 no7
p86 Ag 2017

BASTOS, ELIZABETH
Where the Wild Things Are In the Suburbs color *Reader's Digest*
v189 no1130 p56 My 2017

Basu, Diksha
The Windfall *Publishers Weekly* v264 no17 p59 Ap 24 2017

Basu, Shankha
To Make Better Choices, Look at All Your Options Together *Harvard Business Review Digital Articles* p2 Je 28 2017

Basu, Shrabani
The Raj Duet: An account of Queen Victoria's late-life bond with
an Indian Muslim J. MORRIS *New York Times Book Review*
p26 O 8 2017

Bat behavior
Amazing Animals G. S. Hennessey and S. Schwartz color map
National Geographic Kids no473 p12 S 2017

Bat diseases
Give Bats a Break M. D. TUTTLE *Issues in Science & Technology*
v33 no3 p41 Spr 2017

Bataller, Cyrille
How People Will Use AI to Do Their Jobs Better *Harvard Business Review Digital Articles* p2 My 27 2015

Batay-Csorba Architects (Company)
house of the month J. MINUTILLO color diag *Architectural Record* v205 no2 p31 F 2017

BATCHELOR, STEPHEN
A BUDDHIST BREXIT color *Tricycle: The Buddhist Review* v26
no3 p68 Spr 2017

Batchelor, Stephen—Interviews
Understand, Realize, Give Up, Develop D. Brazier color *Tricycle:
The Buddhist Review* v27 no1 p44 Fall 2017

BATCHELOR, THOMAS

Humor in Uniform *Reader's Digest* v189 no1127 p135 F 2017

Bateman, Hallie

CLOSE ENCOUNTERS color *New York Times Magazine* p48 My 21 2017

Bateman, Jason, 1969-

Bateman's Stab at High Drama D. D'addario color *Time* v190 no5 p61 Jl 31 2017

Ozark: A gripping thriller of money, murder and family M. ROUSH *TV Guide* v65 no31 p14 Jl 24 2017

Bateman, Joshua D.

Alibaba Tries To Get in the Game *Bloomberg Businessweek* no4531 p20 Jl 24 2017

BATEMAN, LINDEN B.

The Spirit of Ollokot *Idaho Magazine* v16 no6 p42 Mr 2017

Bateman, Rocky

REBUILDING A FARM R. Nickel *Successful Farming* v115 no3 p42 Mid-F 2017

Bateman, Thomas

Motivate Me C. NEWMAN *USA Today Magazine* v145 no2864 p63 My 2017

BATES, AMANDA E.

Assessing National Biodiversity Trends for Rocky and Coral Reefs through the Integration of Citizen Science and Scientific Monitoring Programs *BioScience* v67 no2 p134 F 2017

Bates, Callie

The Waking Land *Publishers Weekly* v264 no12 p59 Mr 20 2017

Bates, Carolyn

Morrisbow bw color *Old House Journal* v44 no8 p38 D 2016

Bates, David Westfall

Getting Buy-In for Predictive Analytics in Health Care *Harvard Business Review Digital Articles* p2 Je 20 2017

Making Predictive Analytics a Routine Part of Patient Care *Harvard Business Review Digital Articles* p2 Ap 21 2016

Bates, Desiree M.

Enantioselective photochemistry through Lewis acid–catalyzed triplet energy transfer bibl chart diag graph *Science* v354 no6318 p1391 D 16 2016

BATES, ERIC

Bernie Looks Ahead bw color *New Republic* v247 no11 p24 N 2016

BEYOND HOPE [Cover story] color il *New Republic* v248 no1/2 p20 Ja/F 2017

Bates, Frank S.

Combining polyethylene and polypropylene: Enhanced performance with PE/iPP multiblock polymers bibl chart graph *Science* v355 no6327 p814 F 24 2017

Thermal processing of diblock copolymer melts mimics metallurgy diag graph *Science* v356 no6337 p520 My 5 2017

Bates, Kathy, 1948-

KATHY BATES L. Rice color *Entertainment Weekly* no1478 / 1479 p92 Ag 18-25 2017

Bates, Kathy, 1948—Interviews

High Times: Kathy Bates lights up talking about her new comedy, Disjointed I. RUDOLPH *TV Guide* v65 no35 p3 Ag 21 2017

KATHY BATES *Interview* v47 no6 p16 Ag 2017

Bates, Mason

THE GRAND iOPERA: STEVE JOBS, ULTIMATE DIVA L. MURROW color *Wired* v25 no7 p22 Jl 2017

Bates, Matthew W.

Do We Need a New Word for 'Faith'? K. M. Kapic color *Christianity Today* v61 no6 p90 Jl/Ag 2017

Bates, Paul A.

Opposing effects of Elk-1 multisite phosphorylation shape its response to ERK activation bibl graph *Science* v354 no6309 p233 O 14 2016

Bates, Rick

A Call to Action *Canadian Wildlife* v23 no1 p5 Mr/Ap 2017

Celebrating Canada's Natural Heritage *Canadian Wildlife* v23 no2 p5 My/Je 2017

The Challenge of Invasives *Canadian Wildlife* v23 no4 p5 S/O 2017

Let's Show a Little Love *Canadian Wildlife* v22 no5 p5 N/D 2016

Bates, Rick—Interviews

FIVE QUESTIONS ON THE IUCN WORLD CONGRESS WITH Rick Bates color *Canadian Wildlife* v22 no5 p42 N/D 2016

Bates, Stephen

Reinhold Niebuhr's Trump Prophecy *Society* v54 no1 p4 F 2017

Bates Masi + Architects LLC

Amagansett Residence D. Sokol *Architectural Record* v205 no9 p146 S 2017

The Sum of Its Parts M. SITZ *Architectural Record* v205 no6 p86 Je 2017

Bates Motel (TV program)

Bates Motel I. Rudolph color *TV Guide* v65 no7 p40 F 13 2017

Becoming Psycho F. HIGHMORE *TV Guide* v65 no14 p16 Ap 3 2017

RIHANNA CHECKS INTO BATES MOTEL N. Abrams and R. Rahman color *Entertainment Weekly* no1453 p51 F 17 2017

What's the Most Bingeworthy Show? S. Highfill, K. P. Sullivan et al color *Entertainment Weekly* no1443 p21 D 9 2016

What to Watch R. Rahman, J. Jensen et al color *Entertainment Weekly* no1454/1455 p90 F 24 2017

What to Watch R. Rahman, L. Greenblatt et al color *Entertainment Weekly* no1463/1464 p99 Ap/My 2017

Batgirl (Fictitious character)

NO. 18 Batgirl/Oracle D. Franich color *Entertainment Weekly* no1436/1437 p59 O 21 2016

Bath (England)

And the Winning Photo Is... color *British Heritage Travel* v38 no5 p80 S/O 2017

Båth, Petra

A three-dimensional movie of structural changes in bacteriorhodopsin bibl diag graph *Science* v354 no6319 p1552 D 23 2016

Bath towels

WAR STORIES color *Los Angeles Magazine* v62 no10 p123 O 2017

Bathgate, Jackson

ALL OR NOTHING S. Davis color *Powder* v45 no5 p106 Ja 2017

Bathhouses—Design & construction

BATHING, ANCIENT ROMAN STYLE J. A. LOBELL color *Archaeology* v70 no2 p20 Mr/Ap 2017

Bathing accessories—Evaluation

BEAUTY BUYS UNDER $25 color *Good Housekeeping* v264 no3 p22 Mr 2017

SOAK IT ALL IN A. Mangum color *Bloomberg Businessweek* no4498 p84 N 7 2016

Bathing suit design & construction

CULTURAL WAVES J. Amay color *Ebony* v72 no9 p40 Jl/Ag 2017

Bathing suits

Enjoy your downtime more *Redbook* p128 Jl/Ag 2017

Feminine Touches color *Glamour* v115 no5 p34 My 2017

Grown-up Florals color *Glamour* v115 no5 p42 My 2017

MARCH OF THE DESIGNERS E. S. ARMARSÓTTIR *Iceland Review* v55 no2 p10 Mr/Ap 2017

New Neutrals color *Glamour* v115 no5 p39 My 2017

Oh Hey, Thongs: Welcome Back! A. Edwards Walker color *Glamour* v114 no7 p40 Jl 2016

The Season's Best Swimsuits color *Glamour* v115 no5 p33 My 2017

True Blues color *Glamour* v115 no5 p40 My 2017

Bathing suits—Evaluation

$50 & UNDER SUMMER STYLE color *Seventeen* v76 no4 p14 Jl/Ag 2017

Away You Go! color *Glamour* v115 no7 p38 Jl 2017

The BUY Fashion color *Harper's Bazaar* no3654 p52 Je/Jl 2017

The End color *Sports Illustrated* v126 no6 p170 F 20 2017

Eye of the Teigen [Cover story] C. Bagley color *InStyle* v24 no11 p172 N 2017

find your BEST BATHING SUIT color *Good Housekeeping* v264 no6 p16 Je 2017

GEAR UP FOR SUMMER A. Wisch color *Sail* v48 no7 p28 Jl 2017

Heat WAVE *Interview* v47 no2 p104 Mr 2017

Home CHIC Home bw color *Vogue* v207 no3 p450 Mr 2017

JANE BIRKIN bw color *Harper's Bazaar* no3654 p82 Je/Jl 2017

LINES IN THE SAND color *Harper's Bazaar* no3652 p234 Ap 2017

LOVE SWIMSUIT SEASON! [Cover story] color *Redbook* p52 Je 2017

MORE DREAM SUITS! color *Redbook* p60 Je 2017

p17 N 2016

All Systems Go M. MILRAD GOLDSTEIN color *Martha Stewart Living* p46 S 2017

bath bombs J. SMALL color *Parents* v92 no3 p48 Mr 2017

BRING THE SPA HOME K. S. BOX cartoon *Better Homes & Gardens* v95 no2 p18 F 2016

congrats, you just found time for a pedicure! M. MATTHEWS BROWN color *Parents* v92 no6 p84 Je 2017

En Plein Derrière img *New York* v50 no15 p44 Jl 24 2017

From Our Editor S. Donelson color *House Beautiful* v159 no4 p10 My 2017

HEALING WATERS M. M. GOLDSTEIN color *Martha Stewart Living* no271 p36 Ja/F 2017

How Clean Is Your Pet? A. Levi color *Health* v31 no7 p104 S 2017

HOW TO Troubleshoot Tub Time J. RAINEY MARQUEZ *Parents* v92 no11 p117 N 2017

Making Bath Time Better *Your Dog (10780343)* v22 no10 p11 O 2016

RADIATE BEAUTY from the Inside Out color *Better Nutrition* v79 no4 p41 Ap 2017

Baths—Equipment & supplies

Wash-Stall Organizer color *Horse & Rider* v56 no8 p34 Ag 2017

Baths—Equipment & supplies—Evaluation

Bath & Beyond C. ELLENBERG color *Vogue* v207 no11 p162 N 2017

Baths—Evaluation

SUPERB SOAKER color *Esquire* p27 Ag 2017

Baths—Psychological aspects

Cold Showers B. Dolnick *New York Times Magazine* p26 Jl 23 2017

Bathtubs

REVIVAL BATHS *Design Center Sourcebook* p41 2016

Why I Love LAVENDER BATH SALTS I. Glazer color *InStyle* v24 no7 p142 Jl 2017

Batino, Clarissa

Philippine Casinos Are Cleaning Up color graph *Bloomberg Businessweek* no4521 p19 My 8 2017

Batista, Dave, 1969-

A Brooklyn Bridge Too Far M. AGRESTA *Texas Monthly* v45 no3 p66 Mr 2017

THE PICTURES: CAN IT HAPPEN HERE? D. Steinberg bw *New Yorker* v93 no33 p37 O 23 2017

Batista, Ed

A Checklist for Someone About to Take on a Tougher Job *Harvard Business Review Digital Articles* p2 Ja 6 2015

How Great Coaches Ask, Listen, and Empathize *Harvard Business Review Digital Articles* p2 F 18 2015

How to Not Fight with Your Spouse When You Get Home from Work *Harvard Business Review Digital Articles* p2 Ap 12 2016

Tips for Coaching Someone Remotely *Harvard Business Review Digital Articles* p2 Mr 18 2015

To Stay Focused, Manage Your Emotions *Harvard Business Review Digital Articles* p2 F 2 2015

Batista, Facundo D.

A switch from canonical to noncanonical autophagy shapes B cell responses bibl graph *Science* v355 no6325 p641 F 10 2017

Batiste, Jonathan, 1987-

JON BATISTE: 'Reservoir of Positivity' [Cover story] A. Morrison color *Downbeat* v84 no4 p28 Ap 2017

Batman (Fictitious character)

NO. 3 Batman J. Jensen color *Entertainment Weekly* no1436/1437 p46 O 21 2016

Batman films

A TALE OF TWO BATMANS J. Hibberd color *Entertainment Weekly* no1454/1455 p18 F 24 2017

Batman v. Superman: Dawn of Justice (Film)

BATMAN V SUPERMAN: DAWN OF JUSTICE C. Chiarella color *Sound & Vision* v81 no9 p70 N 2016

Batmanglij, Rostam

Hot Secret Weapon Rostam Batmanglij P. DOYLE color *Rolling Stone* no1274 p37 N 17 2016

Baton Rouge (La.)

TSUNAMI SUSHI J. BENSON color *Louisiana Life* v37 no4 p22 Mr/Ap 2017

Baton Rouge (La.). Recreation & Park Commission

Member Spotlight: Carolyn McKnight S. Bartram *Parks & Recreation* v51 no10 p84 O 2016

Baton Rouge (La.)—Description & travel

BATON ROUGE T. DAY color *Louisiana Life* v37 no4 p54 Mr/Ap 2017

Baton Rouge (La.)—History

BATON ROUGE AT 200 E. Laborde *Louisiana Life* v37 no3 p4 Ja/F 2017

Batra, Ritesh

Our Souls at Night L. Greenblatt color *Entertainment Weekly* no1485 p39 O 6 2017

Batra, Sanjit S.

De novo assembly of the Aedes aegypti genome using Hi-C yields chromosome-length scaffolds chart color diag *Science* v356 no6333 p92 Ap 7 2017

Batrachotoxin

Asymmetric synthesis of batrachotoxin: Enantiomeric toxins show functional divergence against NaV M. M. Logan, Tatsuya Toma et al bibl diag graph *Science* v354 no6314 p865 N 18 2016

Bats

Acoustic mirrors as sensory traps for bats S. Greif, S. Zsebök et al diag *Science* v357 no6355 p1045 S 8 2017

Bats and human health J. H. KUHN *Issues in Science & Technology* v33 no4 p15 Summ 2017

BATS' EARS MAY SOLVE AN EVOLUTIONARY PUZZLE *Physics Today* v70 no3 p22 Mr 2017

Bats S. ELDER color *National Geographic Kids* no474 p22 O 2017

Brain Bogglers S. W. DRIMMMER color *National Geographic Kids* no470 p34 My 2017

Christmas Island bat is officially no more color *Science* v357 no6357 p1216 S 22 2017

How glass fronts deceive bats P. Stilz color diag *Science* v357 no6355 p977 S 8 2017

Retro Virus A. Braun color *Natural History* v125 no5 p6 My 2017

Bats as carriers of disease

As the bat flies D. T. S. Hayman bibl color *Science* v354 no6316 p1099 D 2 2016

Bats—Behavior

Bats in the Bronx K. Pierre-Louis color *Scientific American* v316 no1 p15 Ja 2017

Batsheva Dance Co. (Performer)

An American in Tel Aviv B. BARRY *Dance Magazine* v91 no1 p101 Ja 2017

Bats—Psychology

Cognition-mediated evolution of low-quality floral nectars V. Nachev, K. P. Stich et al bibl graph *Science* v355 no6320 p1 Ja 6 2017

Perception drives the evolution of observable traits H. Farris bibl color *Science* v355 no6320 p25 Ja 6 2017

Bats—Research

Vectorial representation of spatial goals in the hippocampus of bats A. Finkelstein, L. Las et al bibl graph *Science* v355 no6321 p1 Ja 13 2017

BATTAGLIA, EVELYN

CREATURE COMFORTS color *Martha Stewart Living* no271 p48 Ja/F 2017

DECODING DOG-SPEAK *Martha Stewart Living* no267 p68 S 2016

DOG DAYS OF WINTER *Martha Stewart Living* no270 p82 D 2016

GROUND RULES color *Martha Stewart Living* p64 Ap 2017

Homeward Bound color *Martha Stewart Living* p74 O 2017

SCRATCH AND SNIFFLE color *Martha Stewart Living* no275 p56 Je 2017

Battaglin Cycles Srl

OFFICINA BATTAGLIN POWER+ B. STRICKLAND color *Bicycling* v58 no4 p92 My 2017

Battan, Carrie

APPROACHING AUTHENTICITY cartoon color *New Yorker* v93 no18 p60 Je 26 2017

CYBERKIDS cartoon *New Yorker* v92 no44 p20 Ja 9 2017

FRESH cartoon *New Yorker* v93 no18 p18 Je 26 2017

GETTING TO YES cartoon *New Yorker* v93 no15 p72 My 29 2017

Madame Butterfly color *Vogue* v207 no10 p290 O 2017

NO SCOOP NECESSARY color *Bloomberg Businessweek* no4498 p90 N 7 2016

NOT A NORMAL WORK TRIP color *Bloomberg Businessweek* no4504 p60 D 19 2016

ON THE BACK OF A BREEZE cartoon *New Yorker* v92 no48 p70 F 6 2017

StairMaster to Heaven color *GQ: Gentlemen's Quarterly* v86 no11 p76 N 2016

WEIRD WAR cartoon *New Yorker* v92 no41 p70 D 12 2016

ZEN AND THE ART OF CLOSET MAINTENANCE color *Bloomberg Businessweek* no4524 p67 My 29 2017

Battan, Carrie—Interviews

GQ HQ bw color *GQ: Gentlemen's Quarterly* v86 no11 p30 N 2016

BATTERSBY, JEFFERY

Citrix ShareFile: Secure cloud-based file-sharing for the workplace color *Macworld - Digital Edition* v34 no9 p79 S 2017

The difference between backing up an iPhone to iCloud and iTunes cartoon color *Macworld - Digital Edition* v33 no11 p123 N 2016

Digit review: Online account service needs better controls color *Macworld - Digital Edition* p88 Je 13 2017

How to manage your network with iNet Network Scanner color *Macworld - Digital Edition* p108 F 2017

How to set up the Calendar Service in macOS Sierra Server color *Macworld - Digital Edition* p97 D 2016

How to use NetSpot to map out your Wi-Fi network color *Macworld - Digital Edition* p105 F 2017

How to use the advanced Calendar Service features in macOS Sierra Server color *Macworld - Digital Edition* p103 D 2016

MacOS High Sierra: The new Safari takes steps to reduce persistent user tracking, but is it enough? color *Macworld - Digital Edition* v34 no9 p82 S 2017

Timely: Time tracking Mac app hampered by required Internet connection color *Macworld - Digital Edition* v34 no10 p89 O 2017

Battersby, Martin

TEFAF M. Bartolucci color *Magazine Antiques* v184 no3 p38 My/ Je 2017

BATTERSON, JIM

PROGRAMMING FOR ALL color *Scientific American* v315 no6 p8 D 2016

Battery chargers

See also

Battery charging stations (Electric vehicles)

BATTERY CHARGERS: THE NEED FOR SPEED TO JUMP-START AN ENGINE DETERMINES WHICH CHARGER TO GET D. Mowitz *Successful Farming* v115 no12 p41 O 2017

Battery chargers—Evaluation

ANKER POWERCORE+ 26800 PD: QUICKLY RECHARGE YOUR USB-C MACBOOK OR MACBOOK PRO G. FLEISH-MAN color *Macworld - Digital Edition* v34 no10 p27 O 2017

BEZALEL OMNIA: STYLISH WIRELESS AUTOMOBILE CHARGER FOR IPHONE 6/7 J. R. BOOKWALTER color *Macworld - Digital Edition* v34 no11 p71 N 2017

CABLE MATTERS 72W 4-PORT USB CHARGER WITH USB-C POWER DELIVERY: HIGHWATTAGE USB-C CHARGER DELIVERS THE GOODS G. FLEISHMAN color *Macworld - Digital Edition* v34 no10 p29 O 2017

CHARGETECH PLUG PRO REVIEW: SUPER—SIZED POR-TABLE BATTERY CHARGER J. R. BOOKWALTER color *Macworld - Digital Edition* v34 no9 p51 S 2017

Electric Omnivore If the plug fits... F. Markus color *Motor Trend* v69 no10 p24 O 2017

FINSIX DART-C CHARGER: TINY, POWERFUL, AND WORTH THE EXPENSE G. MAH UNG chart color *Macworld - Digital Edition* v34 no6 p33 Je 2017

FLI CHARGE: VERSATILE WIRELESS CHARGING PAD WORKS WITH USB GADGETS, TOO J. R. BOOKWALTER color *Macworld - Digital Edition* p54 Je 13 2017

iOS Accessories J. Mathis color *Macworld - Digital Edition* v34 no4 p60 My 2017

KANEX GOPOWER WATCH AND ZENS POWERBANK FOR APPLE WATCH: CONVENIENT CHARGING SUSIE OCHS color *Macworld - Digital Edition* p55 F 2017

NONDA ZUS SMART CAR CHARGER J. R. BOOKWALTER color *Macworld - Digital Edition* p36 Mr 2017

RAVPOWER 26800MAH PORTABLE CHARGER: COMPACT, AFFORDABLE BATTERY DELIVERS USB-C LAPTOP CHARGING G. FLEISHMAN color *Macworld - Digital Edition* v34 no10 p25 O 2017

Tested: The truth behind the MacBook Pro's 'terrible' battery life G. MAH UNG color graph *PCWorld* p53 Mr 2017

WHAT'S NEW? *USA Today Magazine* v146 no2868 p74 S 2017

Battery charging stations (Electric vehicles)

Electric Vehicles Are Here. Now We Need to Figure Out How to Charge Them J. Worland color *Time* v190 no16/17 p34 O 23 2017

Battery charging stations (Electric vehicles)—Equipment & supplies

Electric Omnivore If the plug fits... F. Markus color *Motor Trend* v69 no10 p24 O 2017

Battery charging stations (Electric vehicles)—Evaluation

DRONE CHARGING STATION *Successful Farming* v114 no10 p30 O 2016

Getting Juiced by the Roadside C. SMITH *Weekly Standard* v22 no6 p14 O 17 2016

Battilana, Jessica

FOLLOW YOUR GUT chart color *Sunset* v238 no6 p30 Je 2017

Batting (Baseball)

Philosopher Up to Bat M. KINGWELL cartoon *Walrus* v14 no2 p59 Mr 2017

Batting (Baseball)—History

Leading Off color *Sports Illustrated* v127 no4 p6 Ag 7 2017

Nobody Home S. Apstein and T. Keith chart color *Sports Illustrated* v125 no12 p18 O 10 2016

Batting (Baseball)—Charts, diagrams, etc.

CONTACT HIGH T. Verducci color diag *Sports Illustrated* v127 no8 p44 S 18 2017

WAITING GAME chart color *Sports Illustrated* v126 no18 p39 Je 26 2017

Battini, Michele

Jew-Blaming *Commentary* v141 no9 p1 N 2016

Jew-Blaming *Commentary* v142 no4 p1 N 2016

Battison, Heather

Learn From the Credit-Score Elite L. GERSTNER chart *Kiplinger's Personal Finance* v71 no3 p43 Mr 2017

Battisti, Giuliana

Tesla Is Betting on Solar, Not Just Batteries *Harvard Business Review Digital Articles* p2 Jl 2 2015

BATTLE, CLEO A.

STORIES WE TELL OURSELVES color *Vanity Fair* v58 no11 p88 N 2016

Battle, Helen

Outstanding in the Fields bw *Canadian Wildlife* v23 no1 p9 Mr/ Ap 2017

Battle, Kathleen, 1948-

Dazzling *Opera News* v81 no5 p20 N 2016

Battle of the Network Stars (TV program)

GAME ON! The classic Battle of the Network Stars is back, and your TV favorites are ready to wage war--on each other! J. HALTERMAN *TV Guide* v65 no27 p24 Je 26 2017

Battle of the Sexes (Film)

BATTLE OF THE SEXES D. Coggan color *Entertainment Weekly* no1478 / 1479 p42 Ag 18-25 2017

Chauvinist Racket J. PODHORETZ color *Weekly Standard* v23 no5 p46 O 9 2017

Double Plays T. Keith color *Sports Illustrated* v127 no4 p22 Ag 7 2017

MIXED SINGLES A. Carter color *Esquire* p28 O 2017

NOW PLAYING color *Entertainment Weekly* no1485 p43 O 6 2017

OSCAR RACE TAKES SHAPE S. Vilkomerson color *Entertainment Weekly* no1484 p38 S 29 2017

Venus and Mars Duke It Out on the Tennis Court S. Zacharek color *Time* v190 no13 p64 O 2 2017

When King Was Queen S. E. ERICKSON bw color *Los Angeles Magazine* v62 no10 p94 O 2017

A WOMAN'S WORK A. LANE color *New Yorker* v93 no29 p104 S 25 2017

Battlefield monuments

A MONUMENTAL Decision: What to Do with Confederate Monuments? P. Gilbert *Parks & Recreation* v52 no10 p36 O 2017

Battlefields

The Best of Scribblers: Edward Gibbon and the importance of great writing to great history J. Epstein *Commentary* v140 no2 p48 S 2015

Battle of Aachen, Germany, 1944

WEREWOLVES OF AACHEN K. Bell bw color *Military History* v34 no2 p22 Jl 2017

Battle of Algiers, The (Film)

THE BATTLE OF ALGIERS AT FIFTY: END OF EMPIRE CINEMA AND THE FIRST BANUEUE FILM A. O'Leary *Film Quarterly* v70 no2 p17 Wint 2016

Battle of Bushy Run, Pa., 1763

Hallowed Ground Bushy Run Battlefield, Pennsylvania W. J. Shepherd color *Military History* v34 no2 p76 Jl 2017

Battle of Culloden, Scotland, 1746

Blades not bullets M. Pittock *History Today* v67 no1 p45 Ja 2017

Battle of Dunbar, Scotland, 1650

AFTER THE BATTLE D. WEISS bw color *Archaeology* v70 no3 p50 My/Je 2017

Battle of Franklin, Tenn., 1864

What We Learned From... The Battle of Franklin, 1864 J. Byrne *Military History* v33 no5 p18 Ja 2017

Battle of Gettysburg, Pa., 1863

Reflections on Leadership from Gettysburg P. Merrild *Harvard Business Review Digital Articles* p2 O 12 2015

Battle of Hamburger Hill, Vietnam, 1969

HAMBURGER HILL *AARP: The Magazine* v59 no3A p67 Ap/My 2016

Battle of Hastings, England, 1066

The Other Invasion: The Anglo-Norman invasion of Ireland in 1167 sowed the seeds for centuries of tension between England and the Irish C. Ellis *History Today* v67 no9 p12 S 2017

Battle of Hürtgen, 1944

THE FOREST FOR THE TREES M. D. Hull bw color *Military History* v34 no5 p30 Ja 2018

Slog Through the Hürtgen Forest M. Hull bw color map *Military History* v34 no5 p36 Ja 2018

Battle of Lexington, Mass., 1775

Revolutionary Roles D. FOX *National Parks* v91 no4 p10 Fall 2017

Battle of Leyte Gulf, Philippines, 1944

SURIGAO STRAIT color *AARP: The Magazine* v59 no3A p65 Ap/My 2016

Battle of Lutzen, Germany, 1632

LAST STAND OF THE BLUE BRIGADE D. WEISS color *Archaeology* v70 no5 p14 S/O 2017

Battle of Nagashino, Japan, 1575

What We Learned From... Nagashino, 1575 C. Lyons color *Military History* v34 no4 p18 N 2017

Battle of New Orleans, La., 1815

Cross Current C. KOLB bw *New Orleans Magazine* v51 no12 p48 O 2017

Battle of Poltava, Ukraine, 1709

THE MAP POLTAVA, 1709 K. Wiles *History Today* v67 no10 p4 O 2017

Battle of San Jacinto, Tex., 1836

THE BATTLE OF SAN JACINTO DIORAMA A. GUSTAFSON and F. CURATOR *Texas Monthly* v44 no11 p100 N 2016

Battle of Stalingrad, Volgograd, Russia, 1942-1943

THE SURVIVOR A. Holl *MHQ: Quarterly Journal of Military History* v29 no3 p14 Spr 2017

Battle of the Argonne, France, 1918

MYSTERY AT MONTFAUCON W. Walker *MHQ: Quarterly Journal of Military History* v29 no3 p28 Spr 2017

Battle of the Chosin Reservoir, Korea, 1950

CHOSIN RESERVOIR *AARP: The Magazine* v59 no3A p66 Ap/My 2016

Battle of Trafalgar, 1805

A Trafalgar Square Deal color *Forbes* v199 no4 p20 Ap 25 2017

Battle of Vimy Ridge, France, 1917

Monumental event B. BETHUNE bw color *Maclean's* v129 no51/52 p38 D 26 2016

ON THE MAP AT THE VIMY RIDGE CENTENNIAL color *Canadian Geographic* v137 no3 p76 My 2017

Battles

See also

Naval battles

THE FRENCH ARE COMING! [Cover story] D. T. Zabecki bw color map *Military History* v34 no4 p22 N 2017

HEARTS AND MINDS IN MINDANAO [Cover story] P. Maggioni bw color map *Military History* v34 no4 p48 N 2017

Lightbox color *Time* v188 no18 p16 O 31 2016

Battleships

THE TRAGEDY OF FORCE Z: The sinking by Japanese aircraft of HMS Prince of Wales and HMS Repulse in December 1941 and the subsequent loss of Singapore was a grievous blow to British morale. But have historians misunderstood what really happened? A. Boyd *History Today* v67 no9 p64 S 2017

Battlestar Galactica television programs

A REUNION OF GALACTICA PROPORTIONS J. Hibberd color diag *Entertainment Weekly* no1471 p14 Je 23 2017

Batts, Krys

Not Flowers but Love *Publishers Weekly* v264 no14 p60 Ap 3. 2017

Batuman, Elif

THE BAGGY MONSTER E. KINDLEY color *Nation* v304 no12 p31 Ap 10 2017

CONSTRUCTED WORLDS cartoon color *New Yorker* v92 no46 p56 Ja 23 2017

A Defiant Imperfection P. Christman color *Commonweal* v144 no12 p37 Jl 7 2017

EPICTETUS *New Yorker* v92 no42 p84 D 19 2016

The Fiction of Everyday Life E. ALTER color *Publishers Weekly* v264 no8 p52 F 20 2017

The Freedoms of Fiction A. Domestico bw *Commonweal* v144 no8 p26 My 5 2017

NO FOOL M. Fischer *Harper's Magazine* v334 no2002 p91 Mr 2017

On the Rebound bw *Vogue* v207 no11 p154 N 2017

The Possessed: Adventures with Russian Books and the People Who Read Them color *Publishers Weekly* v264 no17 p89 Ap 24 2017

The Reading Lesson P. SEHGAL *New York Times Book Review* p12 Ap 2 2017

Story Time V. STEIKER *Vogue* v207 no3 p392 Mr 2017

The Wisdom of the Yard C. Schine color *New York Review of Books* v64 no6 p33 Ap 6 2017

Batygin, Konstantin

COULD PLANET NINE TILT OUR SOLAR SYSTEM? J. Wenz color *Astronomy* v45 no2 p12 F 2017

Looking for Planet Nine K. HAYNES color *Discover* v38 no1 p19 Ja/F 2017

THE SEARCH FOR PLANET NINE S. W. DRIMMER *National Geographic Kids* no468 p18 Mr 2017

Baublebar Inc.

AMY JAIN J. Chen *Bloomberg Businessweek* no4521 p67 My 8 2017

BAUCELLS, ADRIÀ LÓPEZ

Bats and human health *Issues in Science & Technology* v33 no4 p16 Summ 2017

Baudisch, M.

Ultrafast electron diffraction imaging of bond breaking in di-ionized acetylene bibl graph *Science* v354 no6310 p308 O 21 2016

Bauer, Belinda

The Beautiful Dead R. Kinane color *Entertainment Weekly* no1449 p63 Ja 20 2017

Bauer, Bob

A Cruel Blow *Sail* v48 no11 p4 N 2017

BAUER, CARLENE

Higher Yearning *New York Times Book Review* p17 F 19 2017

Bauer, Carolyn

ARTISTIC AFFINITIES color *Magazine Antiques* v183 no6 p98 N/D 2016

Bauer, Claudia

California Dreaming: Benjamin Millepied is taking L.A. Dance Project to new horizons *Dance Magazine* v91 no6 p31 Je 2017

Collaborative Learning *Dance Magazine* v91 no1 p136 Ja 2017

Keep On Turning: New artistic director Marc Brew has big plans for AXIS *Dance Magazine* v91 no10 p16 O 2017

Sofiane Sylve: San Francisco Ballet's enigmatic ballerina opens

or *Dressage Today* v24 no1 p28 O 2017

DRESSAGE TWEET OF THE MONTH *Dressage Today* v23 no6 p12 F 2017

How STRETCHING Can BENEFIT Your Horse [Cover story] color *Dressage Today* p32 My 2017

How to Improve the Basics [Cover story] color *Dressage Today* v23 no6 p26 F 2017

In Search of Balance bw color *Dressage Today* v23 no12 p34 S 2017

INSIGHTS from Lilo Fore and Hans-Christian Matthiesen color graph *Dressage Today* v23 no8 p36 Ap 2017

PUSHING AWAY FROM THE BIT [Cover story] color *Dressage Today* v23 no4 p24 D 2016

The Secret to Free, Forward Collection color *Dressage Today* v23 no9 p24 Je 2017

The Swinging Back color *Dressage Today* v23 no7 p26 Mr 2017

Tips From a World Cup Champion color *Dressage Today* v23 no9 p40 Je 2017

To develop the ability to use your whip with accuracy and finesse... color *Dressage Today* v24 no2 p72 N 2017

Baumgaertner, Gabriel

The Case for ... KLUBOT AS MVP color *Sports Illustrated* v127 no10 p24 O 2 2017

Leading Men color *Sports Illustrated* v125 no14 p54 O 24-31 2016

Baumgaertner, Jill Peláez

Building Jerusalem: Elegies on Parish Churches *Christian Century* v134 no3 p35 F 2017

Baumgartner, Mark

Eavesdropping on Whales off New York City: BUOY DETECTS WHALES AND ALERTS SHIPS TO SLOW DOWN K. Madin *Oceanus* v52 no2 p14 Spr 2017

Baumgartner, Natalie

One Engagement Strategy Does Not Fit All *Harvard Business Review Digital Articles* p2 N 26 2014

Baumgartner, Thomas

Why Salespeople Need to Develop "Machine Intelligence" *Harvard Business Review Digital Articles* p2 Je 10 2016

Baumjohann, W.

Structure, force balance, and topology of Earth's magnetopause diag graph *Science* v356 no6341 p960 Je 1 2017

Bäumler, Andreas J.

Microbiota-activated PPAR-γ signaling inhibits dysbiotic Enterobacteriaceae expansion graph *Science* v357 no6351 p570 Ag 11 2017

Bäumler, Polly

TRENDING FRIENDS K. NEITZ color *Runner's World* v52 no1 p28 Ja/F 2017

Baumol, William J., 1922-2017

Is America Encouraging the Wrong Kind of Entrepreneurship? R. E. Litan and I. Hathaway *Harvard Business Review Digital Articles* p2 Je 13 2017

Bausch, Richard

Storm Front: Life can be threatening for the characters in Richard Bausch's stories D. SMITH *New York Times Book Review* p21 Ap 30 2017

Bausch, William J.

KEEP THE MISSALETTES! A. J. Distefano *Commonweal* v144 no5 p2 Mr 10 2017

MORE ON THE MASS D. W. Byers *Commonweal* v144 no5 p2 Mr 10 2017

What Not to Do at Mass bw *Commonweal* v143 no20 p2 D 16 2016

Bausilio, Giuseppe

GIUSEPPE BAUSILIO G. M. Garrett color *Dance Magazine* v91 no3 p22 Mr 2017

Bautista, Jose

IN THE RIGHT FIELD M. MURPHY color *Muscle & Performance* v9 no8 p36 Ag 2017

BAVER, KRISTIN

M-E Girard color *Publishers Weekly* v263 no52 p68 D 19 2016

Bavis, Peter

Detracked — And going strong chart color graph *Phi Delta Kappan* v98 no4 p37 D 2016/Ja 2017

Bavishi, Krutika

Characterization of a dynamic metabolon producing the defense

compound dhurrin in sorghum bibl graph *Science* v354 no6314 p890 N 18 2016

BAWANY, MOHAMMAD H.

The Unbreakable Relationship *Islamic Horizons* v45 no6 p48 N/D 2016

Bawer, Bruce

The Age of Anxiety *Weekly Standard* v22 no33 p42 My 8 2017

The Girl Who Loved Hollywood: The story of my mother *Commentary* v144 no2 p32 S 2017

Last Chance For Holland? *National Review* v69 no5 p20 Mr 20 2017

BAX, NICHOLAS J.

Assessing National Biodiversity Trends for Rocky and Coral Reefs through the Integration of Citizen Science and Scientific Monitoring Programs *BioScience* v67 no2 p134 F 2017

Bax, Nicolas A.

Vinculin forms a directionally asymmetric catch bond with F-actin chart color *Science* v357 no6352 p703 Ag 18 2017

Bax, Pauline

The Mauritania Exploit bw *Bloomberg Businessweek* no4508 p48 Ja 23 2017

Baxandall, Michael

Seeing Renaissance Art Anew G. Warwick *History Today* v67 no2 p61 F 2017

Baxendale, Shane

What Really Makes Customers Buy a Product *Harvard Business Review Digital Articles* p2 N 9 2015

Baxter, Charles

Chattering Spirits bw *New York Review of Books* v64 no7 p30 Ap 20 2017

THE GODS NEVER LEFT US il *Nation* v303 no22 p27 N 28 2016

Baxter, Randall

PARODY color *Weekly Standard* v22 no16 p40 D 26 2016

Baxter, Robbie Kellman

Subscription Business Models Are Great for Some Businesses and Terrible for Others *Harvard Business Review Digital Articles* p2 Jl 13 2016

Baxter, Scott

THE MAVERICK: "Doc "Doc; Luce" "The Maverick Doctor"... these are just some of the names people use when referring to Sam Luce. The names vary, but the regal'd is the same: Sam Luce is a legend down in the Blue K. VAUGHN *Arizona Highways* v96 no7 p34 Jl 2017

Baxter, Stephen

The Massacre of Mankind *Publishers Weekly* v264 no27 p57 Jl 3 2017

BAXTROM, GREG

r.s.v.p bw *Bon Appetit* v62 no4 p10 Ap 2017

Bay, Laura

The Pros and Cons of Federally Funded School Choice Programs *Congressional Digest* v96 no7 p12 S 2017

Bay, Michael, 1964-

Anthony Hopkins M. ZIMMERMAN *Men's Health* v32 no5 p148 Je 2017

TRANSFORMERS: THE LAST KNIGHT A. Breznican color *Entertainment Weekly* no1463/1464 p52 Ap/My 2017

WHAT'S NEXT FOR THE TRANSFORMERS? A. Breznican color *Entertainment Weekly* no1472 p43 Je 30 2017

Bay, Sarah

The Seeds of Life *Science* v356 no6342 p1009 Je 9 2017

BAYARD, LOUIS

Bookworms Anonymous *New York Times Book Review* p27 Ag 27 2017

Dangerous Journey *New York Times Book Review* p32 N 13 2016

Bay Area Laboratory Co-Operative

Victor CONTE T. Layden color *Sports Illustrated* v127 no1 p66 Jl 3 2017

Baydatch, Shaked

Global mRNA polarization regulates translation efficiency in the intestinal epithelium diag *Science* v357 no6357 p1299 S 22 2017

Bayer, Kayce

KIDS THESE DAYS A. RAO cartoon *Chicago* v66 no4 p40 Ap 2017

BAYER, LEW

RULES OF ENGAGEMENT *O, The Oprah Magazine* p100 Ap 2017

Bayerische Motoren Werke AG
10 Best Bikes 2017 color diag *Cycle World* v56 no10 p35 N 2017

1991 BMW 325i E. DYER color *Popular Mechanics* p60 Mr 2017

2016 BMW 740i E. Tingwall color *Car & Driver* v63 no1 p82 Jl 2017

2017 BMW HP4 RACER B. Conner color *Cycle World* v56 no8 p34 S 2017

2018 BMW K1600B P. Jones color *Cycle World* v56 no10 p12 N 2017

2018 BMW R nineT URBAN G/S S. MacDonald color *Cycle World* v56 no8 p10 S 2017

ACE OF AN 8 J. Meiners color *Car & Driver* v63 no2 p19 Ag 2017

The Apostate S. Oldham color *Car & Driver* v63 no2 p84 Ag 2017

THE BAVARIAN BEAST CIVILIZED F. Markus chart color *Motor Trend* v69 no7 p90 Jl 2017

Best FAST CAR for Around $50K K. SINTUMUANG color *Esquire* v166 no4 p74 N 2016

BMW 8 Series Concept K. Pleskot color *Motor Trend* v69 no9 p16 S 2017

BMW to Staff: Be Afraid, Be Very Afraid E. Behrmann graph *Bloomberg Businessweek* no4520 p25 My 1 2017

BMW X1 chart color *Motor Trend* v69 no1 p43 Ja 2017

BRUSH YOUR TEETH WITH GASOLINE J. Snyder color *Esquire* v167 no2 p28 Mr 2017

DRIVE A WEDGE J. Tate color *Car & Driver* v63 no5 p17 N 2017

Ian Robertson A. Priddle color *Motor Trend* v69 no5 p24 My 2017

MAKING IT S. MacDonald chart color *Cycle World* v55 no10 p38 N 2016

MICROMANAGEMENT E. Tingwall diag graph *Car & Driver* v63 no2 p28 Ag 2017

"M" IS FOR MOST P. LERNER color *Road & Track* v68 no8 p92 My 2017

M Means Something New. Again J. PearleyHuffman color *Car & Driver* v62 no11 p104 My 2017

NEW FIVE, SAME JIVE C. CHILTON color *Road & Track* v68 no7 p88 Mr/Ap 2017

A NEW HOPE B. Kong chart color *Motor Trend* v69 no3 p64 Mr 2017

What BMW's Corporate VC Offers That Regular Investors Can't G. Gimmy, D. Kanbach et al *Harvard Business Review Digital Articles* p2 Jl 27 2017

Bayerische Motoren Werke AG. Segment Motorräder
2017 BMW R nineT SCRAMBLER J. Gustafson color *Cycle World* v56 no1 p8 Ja/F 2017

2018 BMW G310R D. Canet color *Cycle World* v56 no2 p48 Mr 2017

Your Getaway Vehicle M. R. SALLEE bw cartoon color *Men's Health* v32 no5 p32 Je 2017

Bayerl, Katie
A Psalm for Lost Girls *Publishers Weekly* v264 no2 p70 Ja 9 2017

BAYERS, PETER L.
Spirituality and the Reclamation of Lakota Masculinity in Chris Eyre's Skins (2002) *American Indian Quarterly* v40 no3 p191 Summ 2016

Bayesian analysis
LEARNING CODE J. LOEWEN and B. MALETZKY color *Scientific American* v317 no4 p8 O 2017

Baykusheva, Denitsa
Time-resolved x-ray absorption spectroscopy with a water window high-harmonic source bibl graph *Science* v355 no6322 p264 Ja 20 2017

Bayles, Martha
Elizabethan Virtues *Claremont Review of Books* v17 no3 p85 Summ 2017

Horror Show *Claremont Review of Books* v16 no4 p87 Fall 2016

Le Carré's People *Claremont Review of Books* v17 no1 p95 Wint 2016/2017

A Long-Form Miracle *Claremont Review of Books* v17 no2 p93 Spr 2017

BAYLESS, KATE
your no-panic guide to fever *Parents* p58 2015

Bayless, Rick, 1953-

63 GREAT THINGS TO DO THIS MONTH J. FOUMBERG, J. HARDBERGER et al color *Chicago* v66 no7 p87 Jl 2017

Bayley-Schindelholz, Charlotte
An Ambassador of Dressage J. Pescatrice color *Dressage Today* v23 no5 p60 Ja 2017

BAYLISS, GRAEME
Deeds of Mercy cartoon *Walrus* v13 no9 p14 N 2016

Bayliss, Richard
Neurodevelopmental protein Musashi-1 interacts with the Zika genome and promotes viral replication diag *Science* v357 no6346 p83 Jl 7 2017

Baylor, Don, 1949-2017
TRIBUTES T. Keith, J. Fuchs et al color *Sports Illustrated* v127 no5 p22 Ag 14 2017

Baylor University
CALLED to Lead T. TALIAFERRO *Texas Monthly* v45 no9 p42 S 2017

Bayona, J. A.
A MONSTER CALLS N. Sperling color *Entertainment Weekly* no1438 p39 N 4 2016

Bayrle, Thomas
PART TO WHOLE K. Bell bw color *Art in America* v104 no10 p122 N 2016

Baywatch (Film)
Baywatch C. Nashawaty color *Entertainment Weekly* no1468/1469 p88 Je 2-9 2017

BAYWATCH L. Rice color *Entertainment Weekly* no1446/1447 p56 D 2016/Ja 2017

Baywatch Proves There's Nothing Wrong With a Little Skin, Sand and Surf S. Zacharek color *Time* v189 no21 p57 Je 5 2017

LINES IN THE SAND A. LANE cartoon *New Yorker* v93 no16 p110 Je 5 2017

STOP RIGHT THERE, MISTER E. Sullivan color *Esquire* p108 Je/Jl 2017

Summer Movie Preview: May S. Begley, E. Berman et al color *Time* v189 no20 p48 My 29 2017

Bazan, Jessie
Beyond the bubble color *U.S. Catholic* v82 no5 p45 My 2017

From roommates to riches: Christian tradition is clear about the way people should live together--and it doesn't include fine dining on the first floor color *U.S. Catholic* v82 no8 p18 Ag 2017

Life's work: Building the church takes everyone [Cover story] color *U.S. Catholic* v82 no8 p22 Ag 2017

Raise your voice: To be a lector is to live out the Catholic commitment to prayer, community, and storytelling color *U.S. Catholic* v82 no10 p45 O 2017

BAZAN, JUSTIN
ASK RW color *Runner's World* v52 no4 p35 My 2017

BAZAR, EMILY
How to Dispose of Drugs Safely color *Kiplinger's Personal Finance* v70 no12 p69 D 2016

Bazaruto Islands (Mozambique)
the Best Beaches for Black Women B. Atufunwa color *Essence* v48 no3 p94 Jl 2017

Bazelon, Emily
ANTONIN SCALIA *New York Times Magazine* p34 D 25 2016

Basic Instinct *New York Times Magazine* p13 O 23 2016

Democracy vs. Math *New York Times Magazine* p48 S 3 2017

DEPARTMENT OF JUSTIFICATION *New York Times Magazine* p36 Mr 5 2017

Family Planning color *New York Times Magazine* p17 O 9 2016

Ground Rules *New York Times Magazine* p9 Jl 16 2017

GUILT BY OMISSION color *New York Times Magazine* p40 Ag 6 2017

Pennsylvania *New York Times Magazine* p47 N 20 2016

STOP THE PRESSES *New York Times Magazine* p50 N 27 2016

Bazenet, Chantal
Lee Rubin: Our mentor and role model *Science* v355 no6327 p806 F 24 2017

Bazer, Gerald
Q: Who Is the Worst Leader of All Time? color *Atlantic* v319 no1 p100 Ja/F 2017

Bazer, Mark
CHICAGOANS OF THE YEAR [Cover story] color *Chicago* v65 no12 p74 D 2016

The Duke of Diversion *Chicago* v66 no10 p72 O 2017

WHO'S GOT NEXT? [Cover story] color *Chicago* v66 no6 p78 Je 2017

Bazerman, Max

How to Take the Bias Out of Interviews I. Bohnet *Harvard Business Review Digital Articles* p2 Ap 18 2016

Bazeyo, William

Applying Deliberative Democracy in Africa: Uganda's First Deliberative Polls *Daedalus* v146 no3 p140 Summ 2017

BAZILE, VINCENT

Pitcher Plants Shape Up color diag *Natural History* v125 no5 p12 My 2017

Bazille, Jean-Frédéric, 1841-1870—Exhibitions

Of an artist dying young J. Gardner color *Magazine Antiques* v184 no3 p96 My/Je 2017

SECOND IMPRESSIONS P. SCHJELDAHL cartoon *New Yorker* v93 no9 p74 Ap 17 2017

BAZIS, NICOLE

Through the Motions color *America* v215 p27 N 28 2016

Bazykin, Georgii A.

Negative selection in humans and fruit flies involves synergistic epistasis chart graph *Science* v356 no6337 p539 My 5 2017

B. -B., ALICE

François-Henri Pinault bw *Vanity Fair* v58 no12 p137 D 2016

BBQ Pitmasters (TV program)

PITMASTER TUFFY STONE: THE ZEN OF BARBECUE C. Kettlewell *Virginia Living* p28 2017 Smoke & Salt

BBVA Bancomer SA

Skidmore, Owings & Merrill H. Corcoran *Architectural Record* v205 no4 p112 Ap 2017

Bcaujon, Andrew

FREE BIRD: Anne Morrow Lindbergh's first plane could be hanging in a museum. Instead, it's still flying over Maryland *Washingtonian Magazine* v52 no12 p54 S 2017

Bdellovibrio bacteriovorus

Prescribing a Predator E. S. Eaton bw color diag graph *Science News* v191 no12 p22 Je 24 2017

Be Myself (Music)

How to choose a happy life, by Sheryl Crow M. Rollins color *Redbook* p103 Je 2017

Be Right Back (Film)

GOINGS ON ABOUT TOWN bw *New Yorker* v93 no9 p5 Ap 17 2017

Beach, Laura

A tastemaker and her rediscovered treasures bw cartoon color *Magazine Antiques* v184 no2 p42 Mr/Ap 2017

Beach, Lisa

Date-Night Do-Gooding color *Good Housekeeping* v265 no4 p65 O 2017

BEACH, NATALIE

10 TITLES TO PICK UP NOW color *O, The Oprah Magazine* p110 N 2017

GROWING PAINS cartoon color *O, The Oprah Magazine* p110 My 2017

JUST KIDS color *O, The Oprah Magazine* p90 S 2017

Lighten Up! color *O, The Oprah Magazine* p70 Ja 2017

WHAT A BOOK CAN DO [Cover story] color *O, The Oprah Magazine* p76 Jl 2017

BEACH, PATRICK

Murky WATERS *Texas Monthly* v44 no12 p55 D 2016

Beach, Ruth

Ta-da! The Bra bw color *Glamour* v115 no6 p24 Je 2017

The Test That Can Save a Newborn's Life bw color *Glamour* v115 no11 p26 N 2017

Beach house design & construction

PERFECT FIT K. BARNES color *Better Homes & Gardens* v95 no6 p35 Je 2017

Beach houses

BEAUTY & THE BEACH D. Keeps color *InStyle* p78 Home & Design 2016

HOMES by the sea J. DOWLE color *House Beautiful* p62 Ag 2017

Owning a slice of the seaside J. DOWLE color *House Beautiful* p61 Ag 2017

SEA CHANGE S. SMITH color *House Beautiful* p34 Ag 2017

WHY AREN'T YOU LAUGHING? D. SEDARIS bw cartoon *New Yorker* v93 no17 p30 Je 19 2017

Beach houses—Interior decoration

The Swell Life color *Martha Stewart Living* p96 My 2017

TOMMY'S GREAT ESCAPE H. Rubenstein color *InStyle* p70 Home & Design 2016

Beach Rats (Film)

Beach Rats M. Koresky color *Film Comment* v53 no4 p68 Jl/Ag 2017

Harris Dickinson Makes Waves in Beach Rats J. McGovern color *Entertainment Weekly* no1480 p40 S 1 2017

A Portrait of Male Beauty In Anguish S. Zacharek color *Time* v190 no9 p56 S 4 2017

Beach volleyball tournaments

THE END OF SAND D. OWEN cartoon color *New Yorker* v93 no15 p28 My 29 2017

Beach Boys, The (Performer)

Good Vibrations W. Werris *Publishers Weekly* v263 no41 p67 O 10 2016

The Salvation of Brian Wilson J. Fine bw color *Rolling Stone* no1295 p48 S 7 2017

Beaches

5 Reasons to Visit the First Free Black Republic O. RAYMOND and D. POINTDUJOUR color *Ebony* v72 no4 p68 F 2017

(A HAPPY) LIFE'S A BEACH A. K. LAIRD color *Women's Health* v14 no5 p8 Je 2017

The Beach Is for the Birds P. J. O'ROURKE cartoon *Reader's Digest* v190 no1132 p15 Jl/Ag 2017

BEACH, PLEASE help me calm down... STRENGTHEN MY LEGS... BRING ME CLOSER TO THE PEOPLE I LOVE. BUT BEACH, PLEASE DON'T burn my skin. OR WRECK MY ANKLES. OR CRUSH MY CONFIDENCE OKAY? [Cover story] color *Women's Health* v14 no5 p132 Je 2017

EDGE OF THE SEA P. STEFÁNSSON *Iceland Review* v55 no2 p74 Mr/Ap 2017

Endpaper *New York Times Magazine* p82 S 24 2017

Find an Empty Beach: There's no need to go far to find a deserted island--they're all along the Delmarva coast B. JENSEN *Washingtonian Magazine* v52 no11 p84 Ag 2017

FOR OUR GENERATION A. Tomlin color *Women's Health* v14 no5 p134 Je 2017

Get Away to Sea Island *New York* v50 no17 p146 Ag 21 2017

GET BEACHED A. RAO color *Chicago* v66 no7 p50 Jl 2017

Key Biscayne Parks and Recreation Protects Its Citizens from Severe Weather E. Carp *Parks & Recreation* v52 no5 p47 My 2017

Purging Plastic A. Skolnick *Sierra* v102 no3 p24 My/Je 2017

St. John Sojourn Z. Prochazka color *Sail* v48 no3 p66 Mr 2017

Walks of Life M. ALLEN bw color *Yankee* p12 Mr 2017

Beaches (Film)

Life's a BEACH D. HOLBROOK *TV Guide* v65 no4 p30 Ja 16 2017

Beaches—Australia

FAR OUT D. Prior color map *Conde Nast Traveler* v52 no2 p74 F 2017

Beaches—California

Beach Life A. HEROLD *Los Angeles Magazine* p86 Ag 2017

Mercy Rule E. KWAK-HEFFERAN color *Backpacker* p22 My 2017

Beaches—England

MEET THE FOLKESTONES J. MILLER *In These Times* v41 no2 p42 F 2017

Beaches—Environmental aspects

Selling a Beach Redesign Project S. Hudson *Parks & Recreation* v52 no4 p56 Ap 2017

Beaches—Environmental conditions

The Riddle of Rip Currents M. Moulton color *Oceanus* v51 no2 p44 Wint 2016

Beaches—Equipment & supplies

A Day at the Beach N. RICHARDSON color *Bon Appetit* v62 no7 p18 Jl 2017

Beaches—Evaluation

A Respite from the Crowds A. Graves color *Yankee* p86 Mr 2017

Beaches—Florida

Endless ADVENTURES *Atlanta* v57 no5 p69 S 2017

Beaches—France

More than Half the Fun color *Conde Nast Traveler* v52 no6 p16 Je/Jl 2017

Beaches—Maine

A Walk That Says Maine A. GRAVES color *Yankee* p88 Mr 2017

Beaches—Massachusetts

Almost Spring on Craigville Beach K. WHOULEY color *Yankee* p92 Mr 2017

Solitude by the Seashore J. K. DeFoe *Yankee* p89 Mr 2017

Beaches—Oregon

Shore up color *Backpacker* p16 My 2017

Beaches—United States

EASTERN VIRGINIA *Virginia Living* p58 2017 Best 20of Virginia

BEACHLER, HANNAH

Color Patterns color *Film Comment* v53 no1 p18 Ja/F 2017

THE SCENE MAKER color *Martha Stewart Living* p54 S 2017

Beachy, Philip A.

Stromal Gli2 activity coordinates a niche signaling program for mammary epithelial stem cells color *Science* v356 no6335 p284 Ap 21 2017

BEACHY-QUICK, DAN

The Made Thing Considers Itself *Nation* v305 no6 p31 S 11 2017

Beacom, John

Gary Steigman *Physics Today* v70 no8 p72 Ag 2017

Beacons

FORGOTTEN APPROACH OPTIONS: NDB/ADF diag *Flying* v144 no6 p22 Je 2017

Lost & Found [Cover story] B. ELLISON color *Power & Motoryacht* v34 no6 p46 Je 2017

Beadling, Laura L.

Tribal Television: Viewing Native People in Sitcoms *American Indian Quarterly* v41 no2 p193 Spr 2017

Beads—Evaluation

Global Warming L. Tudor *New Orleans Homes & Lifestyles* v20 no1 p32 Wint 2016

Beadwork—Exhibitions

DUANE LINKLATER E. Buhe color *Art in America* v105 no3 p128 Mr 2017

Beagle (Dog breed)

Guinness World Records J. KIFFEL-ALCHEH color *National Geographic Kids* no470 p8 My 2017

Beal, Bradley, 1993-

XBOX WIZARD: We challenged NBA star Bradley Beal to a game of basketball--on his couch J. KNAPP *Washingtonian Magazine* v53 no1 p19 O 2017

Beal, Daphne

INDIAN SUMMER color *Vogue* v207 no6 p130 Je 2017

BEALE, STEPHEN

The Essential Reagan bw *American Conservative* v16 no3 p6 My/Je 2017

Beale Road

SPRING VALLEY LOOP: Historic Route 66, the National Old Trails Road, the Beale Wagon Road ... some of the state's most iconic routes can be experienced along the Spring Valley Loop in Northern Arizona A. McGIVNEY *Arizona Highways* v96 no7 p52 Jl 2017

Beall, Mary Celeste

Renaissance Fare C. ELLENBERG color *Vogue* v207 no10 p222 O 2017

What loss taught me about life color *Redbook* p115 O 2017

BEALS, GREGORY

A VOICE IN THE NIGHT color *Foreign Policy* no226 p44 S/O 2017

Beals, Jennifer, 1963-

Taken I. Rudolph *TV Guide* v65 no2 p36 Ja 2 2017

Beals, Jennifer, 1963—Interviews

REunIons The L Word T. Stack color *Entertainment Weekly* no1471 p38 Je 23 2017

Beam, Alex

Axis of Envy P. BAUER bw *Weekly Standard* v22 no36 p33 My 29 2017

Pushkin Came to Shove E. BENNETT *New York Times Book Review* p29 D 11 2016

Beam, Judy

SADDLE CHAT bw color graph *Horse & Rider* v56 no7 p21 Jl 2017

Beam splitters

From lab to clinic C. Day *Physics Today* v70 no8 p8 Ag 2017

Beam Suntory Inc.

Raise a Glass color *American History* v52 no3 p31 Ag 2017

Beamon, Kelly L.

The Art Of Noise color *Architectural Record* v205 no8 p69 Ag 2017

Blurred Lines *Architectural Record* v205 no9 p65 S 2017

Entrance Exam *Architectural Record* v205 no10 p55 O 2017

Internal Affairs *Architectural Record* v205 no10 p61 O 2017

Knightsbridge Residence *Architectural Record* v205 no9 p148 S 2017

Light Work color *Architectural Record* v205 no8 p123 Ag 2017

Playing with Scale *Architectural Record* v205 no9 p153 S 2017

Bean, Aaron—Interviews

MEET AARON BEAN color *Sea Magazine* v109 no6 pPNW-8 Je 2017

Bean, Charlie

THE LEGO NINJAGO MOVIE D. Coggan color *Entertainment Weekly* no1474/1475 p48 Jl 21-28 2017

Bean, Matt

The Fathers of Our Wisdom bw color *Men's Health* v32 no5 p8 Je 2017

The Innovation Issue color *Men's Health* v32 no7 p4 S 2017

Let's Take This Outside color *Men's Health* v32 no6 p8 Ag 2017

Power to Transform bw *Men's Health* v32 no9 p6 N 2017

Thank You, Mom color *Men's Health* v32 no4 p4 My 2017

Why We Fight *Men's Health* v32 no8 p6 O 2017

Bean, Randy

How Machine Learning Is Helping Morgan Stanley Better Understand Client Needs *Harvard Business Review Digital Articles* p2 Ag 3 2017

How P&G and American Express Are Approaching AI *Harvard Business Review Digital Articles* p2 Mr 31 2017

Just Using Big Data Isn't Enough Anymore *Harvard Business Review Digital Articles* p2 F 9 2016

Your Data Should Be Faster, Not Just Bigger *Harvard Business Review Digital Articles* p2 F 4 2015

Bean, Sean, 1959-

My Most Excellent Death D. Coggan color *Entertainment Weekly* no1460/1461 p93 Ap 7-17 2017

Wasted A. D'ARMINIO *TV Guide* v65 no6 p43 Ja 30 2017

Beans

Go Stoveless A. JAMESON il *Backpacker* v45 no1 p34 Ja 2017

Q I'm craving comfort food. Recipes, please?! [Cover story] color *Good Housekeeping* v264 no2 p110 F 2017

BEANS, CAROLYN

The Microbiome of Green Design color *BioScience* v66 no10 p801 O 1 2016

Predicting Phenotypes in a Changing Climate *BioScience* v67 no7 p593 Jl 2017

Beans—Harvesting

THE GLORIES OF FENNEL *South Dakota Magazine* v33 no3 p32 S/O 2017

Bear, Julia

10 Myths About Negotiating Your First Salary *Harvard Business Review Digital Articles* p2 Jl 3 2017

Bear attack prevention

BEAR NECESSITIES C. AUSTIN color *Outdoor Life* v224 no7 p30 S 2017

Bear attacks

BIRD-DOGGING BEARS R. BRUGGEMAN and N. KREBS cartoon color *Outdoor Life* v224 no5 p12 Je/Jl 2017

I SURVIVED D. O'NEIL and A. DAWSON color *Men's Health* v32 no6 p128 Ag 2017

Bear attacks—News briefs

NEWSMAKERS: ANIMAL EDITION P. Treble color *Maclean's* v129 no48/49 p63 D 5 2016

Bear behavior

RIVER OF THE ICE GRIZZLIES M. ROSANO color *Canadian Geographic* v137 no5 p42 S/O 2017

Bear cubs

MOTHER AND MONSTER L. Moore color *Walrus* v14 no6 p48 Jl/Ag 2017

Bear hunting

See also

Black bear hunting

READ A BEAR'S MIND L. CASE color *Outdoor Life* v224 no8 pH11 O 2017

Bear populations

See also

Grizzly bear populations

LOST BEARS: WILL GRIZZLY BEARS RETURN TO THE NORTH CASCADES? K. SIBER *National Parks* v91 no3 p36 Summ 2017

Beard, Alison

Case Study: How Would You Save This Farm? *Harvard Business Review Digital Articles* p2 Ag 12 2016

Case Study: When You're Successful, Stretched Too Thin, and Indispensable *Harvard Business Review Digital Articles* p2 Ag 9 2017

Case Study: Which Customers Should This Restaurant Listen To? *Harvard Business Review Digital Articles* p2 Mr 29 2016

The Conference That's Trying to Reinvent How We Network *Harvard Business Review Digital Articles* p2 O 8 2015

CROWDED PLACES MAKE PEOPLE THINK MORE ABOUT THE FUTURE graph img *Harvard Business Review* v95 no4 p34 Jl/Ag 2017

GAME-CHANGING INVENTIONS: WHAT MAKES AN IDEA REVOLUTIONARY? color il *Harvard Business Review* v95 no5 p148 S/O 2017

HOW WORK STYLES INFORM LEADERSHIP [Cover story] color *Harvard Business Review* v95 no2 p58 Mr/Ap 2017

"IF YOU UNDERSTAND HOW THE BRAIN WORKS, YOU CAN REACH ANYONE" [Cover story] bw *Harvard Business Review* v95 no2 p60 Mr/Ap 2017

Leadership Lessons from 10 Wildly Successful People *Harvard Business Review Digital Articles* p2 D 29 2015

Life's Work: An Interview with Alice Waters color *Harvard Business Review* v95 no3 p176 My/Je 2017

Life's Work: An Interview with Brian Wilson bw *Harvard Business Review* v94 no12 p120 D 2016

Life's Work: An Interview with Marina Abramović color img *Harvard Business Review* v94 no11 p116 N 2016

Life's Work: An Interview with Mike Krzyzewski bw *Harvard Business Review* v95 no2 p164 Mr/Ap 2017

The Wheaties Box and the Why of Celebrity Endorsements *Harvard Business Review Digital Articles* p2 Ap 5 2016

YOUR SUCCESS IS SHAPED BY YOUR GENES *Harvard Business Review* v95 no1 p34 Ja/F 2017

Beard, David

auto no mo' us bw color diag graph *Car & Driver* v63 no5 p58 N 2017

Fleet Files color *Car & Driver* v63 no4 p90 O 2017

More Traction, Less Satisfaction color *Car & Driver* v62 no11 p112 My 2017

MOST PROMISING TECHNOLOGY cartoon color diag *Car & Driver* v62 no7 p28 Ja 2017

Pay Dirt color *Car & Driver* v63 no4 p102 O 2017

ROAD MASTER color *Car & Driver* v63 no1 p19 Jl 2017

Beard, Lanford

Will & Grace Reunion! color *Entertainment Weekly* no1434 p15 O 7 2016

BEARD, MARY

Lives in Ruins: Novels by Colm Toibin and David Vann reimagine two of the most savage Greek myths—the tales of Iphigenia and Medea *New York Times Book Review* p17 My 14 2017

Reading the Ruins of Rome color *New York Review of Books* v64 no12 p18 Jl 13 2017

Wrath in the Time of Choler: What the Greek myths teach us about anger in troubled times *New York Times Book Review* p18 S 10 2017

Beard, The (Poem)

THE BEARD A. Majmudar *New Yorker* v93 no19 p44 Jl 3 2017

Bearden, Romare, 1911-1988—Exhibitions

A Romare Bearden survey at the Taubman cartoon *Magazine Antiques* v184 no2 p32 Mr/Ap 2017

Beards

MAKE MINE NEAT J. Barger *Washingtonian Magazine* v52 no3 p119 D 2016

YOUR GUIDE TO WINNING MOVEMBER F. Katz cartoon *Esquire* p30 N 2017

Beards—Equipment & supplies

GQ's 2017: GROOMING AWARDS A. HURLY, C. WOLF et al bw color *GQ: Gentlemen's Quarterly* v97 no11 p56 N 2017

Beardsley, Felicia

Respect for the ancients color *Science* v354 no6317 p1242 D 9 2016

Shared history *Science* v356 no6338 p591 My 12 2017

Beardsley, Richard

Outsourcing and the Role of Strategic Alliances *Publishers Weekly* v263 no51 p6 D 12 2016

The Potential of Virtual Communities in the Publishing Ecosystem *Publishers Weekly* v264 no3 p12 Ja 16 2017

Beardsley, Rick

Challenges for Publishers in Uncertain Times *Publishers Weekly* v263 no40 p12 O 3 2016

Reflections on Metadata *Publishers Weekly* v263 no41 p8 O 10 2016

Bearings (Machinery)

See also

Ball bearings

Roller bearings

BEARING TIPS & TRICKS J. KOPYCINSKI color *Dirt Sports + Off-Road* v51 no5 p64 My 2017

LOADED FOR BEARING M. Davis bw color *Hot Rod* v70 no10 p88 O 2017

BEARMAN, JOSHUAH

THE PATIENT WHO FORGOT HE WAS A RAP LEGEND bw color *GQ: Gentlemen's Quarterly* v97 no10 p126 O 2017

Bears

A BAD DAY IN BEAR COUNTRY T. ORR cartoon color *Outdoor Life* v224 no8 p49 O 2017

Bear bum M. CAMPBELL color *Maclean's* no1 p16 F 17 2017

Bears G. TARLACH bw color *Discover* v38 no10 p74 D 2017

FUN FESTIVALS IN CABIN COUNTRY color *Cabin Living* p14 Je 2017

Grin & Bear It C. HEITGER-EWING color *Cabin Living* p16 O 2017

Laugh Out Loud color *National Geographic Kids* no465 p36 N 2016

Re: Conservation color *Canadian Wildlife* v23 no2 p11 My/Je 2017

Report Bear Dens *New York State Conservationist* v71 no4 p28 F 2017

STUMP YOUR PARENTS *National Geographic Kids* no466 p38 D 2016/Ja 2017

Bears Ears National Monument (Utah)

EYE ON 45 color *Science* v356 no6343 p1105 Je 16 2017

Native Americans press to keep Bears Ears land a national monument H. Gass *Christian Century* v134 no12 p17 Je 7 2017

New protected area in Utah includes land that's sacred for Native Americans H. Bruinius and H. Gass color *Christian Century* v134 no3 p13 F 2017

Trump Delays a Fight On Presidential Power E. E. Deprez and A. Natter color *Bloomberg Businessweek* no4520 p29 My 1 2017

Bears—Behavior

On the trail of the Nance County bear E. Schwartz cartoon *Nebraska Life* v20 no6 p16 N/D 2016

Bear's Heart, 1851-1882

The Drawing I Can't Stop Thinking About J. SALTZ img *New York* v50 no11 p112 My 29 2017

BEASLEY, JERRY

LESSONS LEARNED! color *Black Belt* v55 no6 p46 O/N 2017

Beasley, Kate

The Optimist E. EGAN *New York Times Book Review* p20 O 9 2016

Beasley, Matthew P.

Ocean mixing and ice-sheet control of seawater 234U/238U during the last deglaciation bibl graph *Science* v354 no6312 p626 N 4 2016

BEAS-LUNA, RODRIGO

Long-Term Studies Contribute Disproportionately to Ecology and Policy *BioScience* v67 no3 p271 Mr 2017

Beast Sports Nutrition (Company)

GET TO KNOW: BEAST SPORTS NUTRITION J. SCHILDHOUSE color *Muscle & Performance* v9 no6 p32 Je 2017

Beastie Boys

Mike D's Endless Summer J. WEINER bw *Rolling Stone* no1275 p20 D 1 2016

Beasts on the Street (Short story)

Beasts on the Street C. C. PETERS *Orion Magazine* v35 no3 p5
My/Je 2016

Beat of My Heart (Music)

Good Deals HADLEY color *Downbeat* v84 no5 p58 My 2017

Beat Shazam (TV program)

TV's Silly Season: A Guide D. D'addario color *Time* v189 no24
p48 Je 26 2017

Beath, Cynthia M.

Why Nordstrom's Digital Strategy Works (and Yours Probably
Doesn't) *Harvard Business Review Digital Articles* p2 Ja 14
2015

Beatification

See also

Blessed

Rutilio Grande: Is another saint on the way for El Salvador? il
America v216 no7 p17 Ap 3 2017

Beatles (Performer)

Beatles Open 'Sgt. Pepper' Vault R. SHEFFIELD bw color *Rolling Stone* no1286 p16 My 4 2017

IT WAS FIFTY YEARS AGO TODAY. . D. T. MORAN *Humanist*
v77 no3 p28 My/Je 2017

Love me Do, in Liverpool *British Heritage Travel* v37 no6 p59
N/D 2016

A New Trip Through Pepper-Land M. GILMORE color *Rolling
Stone* no1288 p49 Je 1 2017

THE REAL SGT. PEPPER color *MHQ: Quarterly Journal of
Military History* v30 no1 p15 Aut 2017

SGT. PEPPER'S LONELY HEARTS CLUB BAND TURNS 50
E. R. Brown color *Entertainment Weekly* no1467 p56 My 26
2017

That Magic Feeling J. ROSEN bw *National Review* v69 no17 p19
S 11 2017

Beatles: Eight Days a Week: The Touring Years, The (Film)

COME TOGETHER A. LANE cartoon *New Yorker* v92 no30 p78
S 26 2016

Beatrice (Neb.)

MEMORIES OF A MURDER R. AVIV bw cartoon *New Yorker*
v93 no17 p36 Je 19 2017

Beatriz at Dinner (Film)

Beatriz at Dinner Means Well but Flags Before the Last Course S.
Zacharek color *Time* v189 no23 p50 Je 19 2017

Beatriz at Dinner V. LUCCA color *Film Comment* v53 no3 p68
My/Je 2017

CRITICS' CHOICE chart *Film Comment* v53 no4 p12 Jl/Ag 2017

The lords of no mercy K. Reklis *Christian Century* v134 no17
p44 Ag 16 2017

A Masseuse in Newport Beach M. Rochlin color *AARP: The Magazine* v60 no4A p13 Je/Jl 2017

Beats Electronics LLC

BeatsX review: Just as magical as the AirPods, but more comfortable and convenient S. Ochs bw color *Macworld - Digital Edition* v34 no4 p72 My 2017

BEATTIE, ANN

A Dream of a Writer: Peter Taylor's stories reveal an artist im-
mersed in the quotidian who rose to the complexities of the heart
and psyche A. BEATTIE *American Scholar* v86 no4 p104 Aut
2017

FLOOD AIRLINES cartoon *New Yorker* v93 no12 p27 My 8 2017

Full Disclosure *American Scholar* v86 no2 p18 Spr 2017

Beattie, Sarah R.

Sterilizing immunity in the lung relies on targeting fungal apoptosis-like programmed cell death color diag *Science* v357 no6355
p1037 S 8 2017

Beatty, J. J.

Observation of a large-scale anisotropy in the arrival directions
of cosmic rays above 8×1018 eV *Science* v357 no6357 p1266
S 22 2017

BEATTY, J. KELLY

3122 Florence Flies By, Reveals Two Moons *Sky & Telescope*
v134 no6 p10 D 2017

Amateurs Find Asteroid's Moon color *Sky & Telescope* v134 no5
p8 N 2017

Charon & Company *Sky & Telescope* v132 no6 p36 D 2016

Epic Effort to Save the Night *Sky & Telescope* v134 no4 p67 O
2017

Europa Geysers Point to Subsurface Ocean *Sky & Telescope* v133

no2 p14 F 2017

Gallery *Sky & Telescope* v132 no6 p73 D 2016

Is New Horizons' Next Target a Binary Body? color *Sky & Telescope* v134 no5 p9 N 2017

More Evidence for Volcanoes on Venus *Sky & Telescope* v133 no2
p11 F 2017

Observers Track New Horizons' Next Target *Sky & Telescope*
v134 no4 p11 O 2017

Recent Briny Eruptions on Ceres? *Sky & Telescope* v134 no1 p10
Jl 2017

Beatty, John

How Small Businesses Can Increase Their Digital Capabilities
Harvard Business Review Digital Articles p1 Jl 25 2017

Beatty, Martin

GREAT MOMENTS IN VIDEO TUTORIALS J. LYNCH and L.
SOROKANICH color *Popular Mechanics* p94 O 2017

Beatty, Paul

Laughing to Keep from Crying D. Pinckney bw color *New York
Review of Books* v63 no20 p28 D 22 2016

Beatty, Tanaya

Night Shift's New Nurse A. D'Arminio *TV Guide* v65 no25 p8
Je 2017

Beatty, Warren, 1937-

Bonnie and Clyde at 50 M. AGRESTA *Texas Monthly* v45 no9
p50 S 2017

THE CHECKLIST *Texas Monthly* v44 no12 p72 D 2016

COME-BACK KID A. Wallace bw color *GQ: Gentlemen's Quarterly* v86 no12 p194 D 2016

Hollywood Can Wait S. KASHNER bw color *Vanity Fair* v58
no11 p186 N 2016

Rules Don't Apply L. Greenblatt color *Entertainment Weekly*
no1442 p42 D 2 2016 Rebellious Special Issue

Warren and Howard J. PODHORETZ *Weekly Standard* v22 no14
p39 D 12 2016

WarReN BEAtty An ORAL HISTORY C. Nashawaty, A. Breznican et al color *Entertainment Weekly* no1440 p30 N 18 2016

Where the #@$%! Have You Been, Warren Beatty? J. NEWMAN
color *AARP: The Magazine* v59 no6A p42 O/N 2016

Beatty, Warren, 1937—Interviews

Rich and Strange N. Rapold color *Film Comment* v52 no6 p10
N/D 2016

BEATY, KATELYN

Contemplative Activist color *Christianity Today* v60 no9 p48 N
2016

PRESSING AND PRESCIENT *Christianity Today* v60 no9 p9 N
2016

Beau Travail (Film)

FINDING MOONLIGHT J. McGovern color *Entertainment
Weekly* no1436/1437 p83 O 21 2016

Beaucamp, Stéphane

GROW, EAT, LOVE [Cover story] cartoon chart color *Yoga Journal* no291 p36 My 2017

Beauchamp, Katia, ca. 1982-

Katia Beauchamp J. Johnson color *Current Biography* v77 no11
p21 N 2016

BEAUCHAMP, SCOTT

Latest Language Abuse *American Conservative* v16 no3 p9 My/
Je 2017

Beaudette, Bronwen

THE BRITISH HERITAGE TRAVEL PUZZLER color *British
Heritage Travel* v38 no5 p78 S/O 2017

Beaudin, Laura

Your Data Isn't Helping Your Marketers If They Can't Access It
Harvard Business Review Digital Articles p2 N 5 2015

Beaudoin, Kimberlyn

The IDA School Horse: A Breed of its Own color *Dressage Today*
v23 no4 p36 D 2016

Three Cheers for the Coach of the Year color *Dressage Today* v23
no4 p66 D 2016

The Value of Equine Education color *Dressage Today* v23 no4
p42 D 2016

Beaudoin, Luc

Good Night, Toast K. DiNardo cartoon *O, The Oprah Magazine*
p103 My 2017

Beaudoin, P.

Reconciling solar and stellar magnetic cycles with nonlinear dynamo simulations diag *Science* v357 no6347 p185 Jl 14 2017

Beaufils, Julie

BRIGHT YOUNG ARTISTS *Interview* v46 no10 p106 D 2016/ Ja 2017

Julie BEAUFILS Z. STILLPASS *Interview* v46 no10 p108 D 2016/Ja 2017

Beaufort (S.C.)—Description & Travel

SOUTH'S BEST SMALL TOWN C. King color *Southern Living* v52 no4 p94 Ap 2017

Beaujolais (Wine)

Cru Cut B. Morton *Cincinnati Magazine* v50 no12 p104 S 2017

Beaujon, Andrew

19 THINGS YOU REALLY OUGHT TO 00 THIS MONTH *Washingtonian Magazine* v52 no3 p31 D 2016

CHANNEL 7, WHERE ARE YOU? *Washingtonian Magazine* v52 no6 p49 Mr 2017

THE COLOR OF RADIO *Washingtonian Magazine* v52 no9 p53 Je 2017

COMBAT REPORTING *Washingtonian Magazine* v52 no5 p45 F 2017

DC, WHERE POLITICAL ADS NEVER END *Washingtonian Magazine* v52 no5 p24 F 2017

INTRAMURAL POLITICS *Washingtonian Magazine* v52 no2 p53 N 2016

JIM VANCE: The newsman's life traced the history of our region-and we loved him for it. But in today's TV world, there can't be another like him *Washingtonian Magazine* v52 no12 p48 S 2017

MEET JOSHUA JOHNSON *Washingtonian Magazine* v52 no4 p22 Ja 2017

THE NEW JIM *Washingtonian Magazine* v52 no3 p45 D 2016

THE NEW WHITE HOUSE REPORTERS *Washingtonian Magazine* v52 no4 p49 Ja 2017

RON FOURNIER *Washingtonian Magazine* v52 no1 p43 O 2016

SLEEPER HIT color *Washingtonian Magazine* v52 no7 p13 Ap 2017

weekend getaways: just do it *Washingtonian Magazine* v52 no11 p82 Ag 2017

WHEN WHO MET SALLY? *Washingtonian Magazine* v52 no2 p21 N 2016

WHERE & WHEN color *Washingtonian Magazine* v52 no7 p31 Ap 2017

Beaulieu, Bradley P.

The Burning Light *Publishers Weekly* v263 no43 p61 O 24 2016

Beaulieu, Elizabeth

Local Strategies: Creating and Nurturing Collaborative Communities of Practice *Change* v49 no4 p20 Jl/Ag 2017

BEAULIEU, JAKE J.

Greenhouse Gas Emissions from Reservoir Water Surfaces: A New Global Synthesis *BioScience* v66 no11 p949 N 1 2016

Beaumont (Tex.)

KING ARTHUR'S PUB *Texas Monthly* v45 no1 p101 Ja 2017

Beaumont-Jones, Julia

The Brits Sure Do "Print" Well *USA Today Magazine* v146 no2868 p78 S 2017

Beauregard, G. T. (Gustave Toutant), 1818-1893

EASY CHAIR R. Solnit *Harper's Magazine* v334 no2000 p10 Ja 2017

Beauregard, Mario

Pseudoscience versus science *Physics Today* v69 no11 p10 N 2016

Beauties of the Night (Film)

Of Stars and Solitude: Two Mexican Documentaries P. J. Smith *Film Quarterly* v71 no1 p73 Fall 2017

Beauty & the Beast (Film : 2017)

Back to The Well R. DOUTHAT color *National Review* v69 no7 p46 Ap 17 2017

BE THEIR GUEST C. Collis color *Entertainment Weekly* no1439 p32 N 11 2016

BELLE OF THE BALL C. Collis color *Entertainment Weekly* no1439 p34 N 11 2016

BEAUTY AND THE BEAST B. A. DuHamel color *Sound & Vision* v82 no8 p71 O 2017

Beauty and the Beast Is Wonderfully Out of Step With the Times S. Zacharek color *Time* v189 no11 p57 Mr 27 2017

Becoming Gaston M. Snetiker color *Entertainment Weekly* no1457/1458 p78 Mr 17 2017

A BOX OFFICE BEAUTY D. Coggan color *Entertainment Week-*

ly no1459 p10 Mr 31 2017

The Game Plan: March bw chart color *Men's Health* v32 no2 p10 Mr 2017

Is Winter the New Summer? D. Coggan color *Entertainment Weekly* no1462 p18 Ap 21 2017

Money for Nothing J. PODHORETZ color *Weekly Standard* v22 no30 p39 Ap 10 2017

PRETTY AND GRITTY A. LANE cartoon *New Yorker* v93 no6 p78 Mr 27 2017

REBEL BELLE [Cover story] A. Breznican color *Entertainment Weekly* no1454/1455 p24 F 24 2017

Shall We Dance? C. Collis color *Entertainment Weekly* no1454/1455 p32 F 24 2017

TALE AS OLD AS TIME [Cover story] C. Collis color *Entertainment Weekly* no1439 p28 N 11 2016

Two Beauties and Some Beasts R. Alleva color *Commonweal* v144 no9 p26 My 19 2017

Beauty contests

HALIMA'S WORLD S. Kitchens color *Glamour* v115 no9 p200 S 2017

Beauty contests—United States

See also

Miss America Pageant

Beauty pageant contestants

2017 HBCU QUEENS B. WILLIAMS bw color *Ebony* v72/73 no12/1 p78 O/N 2017

PARODY color *Weekly Standard* v22 no36 p40 My 29 2017

Beauty shops

See also

Cosmetologists

Black Hair Now C. Martin color *Essence* v48 no6 p59 O 2017

Erecting Hammer & Nails Salons Nationwide C. M. Brown *Black Enterprise* v47 no2 p13 S 2016

Life IN THESE UNITED STATES color graph *Reader's Digest* v189 no1129 p32 Ap 2017

MEET Rock 'n' Roll Hair Stylists B. CALLOWAY and R. SHEL-LABARGER *Indianapolis Monthly* v40 no4 p24 D 2016

When Beauty Is Your 9-to-5 J. Militare and R. Nussbaum color *Glamour* v115 no10 p108 O 2017

Beauty shops—Evaluation

BARBERSHOP QUARTET *Atlanta* v57 no3 p40 Jl 2017

BAT CRAZY T. BRAND *Indianapolis Monthly* v40 no3 p42 N 2016

health & self img *New York* p92 Mr 6 2017

Beauty Queen of Leenane, The (Theatrical production)

ALLIES H. ALS cartoon *New Yorker* v92 no47 p74 Ja 30 2017

Beauvais, Brad

How to Pay for Health Care/The Case for Capitation: Interaction *Harvard Business Review* v94 no11 p20 N 2016

Beaux Arts architecture

These Waters Run Deep [Cover story] S. Blackwood color *Chicago* v66 no9 p94 S 2017

Beaver Valley Alloy Foundry Co.

How to Make a... EXTINCT STEEL K. DUPZYK color *Popular Mechanics* v193 no7 p78 S 2016

Beavers

Beavers as Ecopartners A. Bolen color *National Wildlife (World Edition)* v55 no5 p14 Ag/S 2017

Good Neighbors T. DEAN *American Scholar* v86 no1 p60 Wint 2017

BEAZLEY, KAREN F.

We Need a Biologically Sound North American Conservation Plan *BioScience* v67 no8 p685 Ag 2017

Because You Have To (Short story)

BECAUSE YOU HAVE TO C. Lacey *Harper's Magazine* v335 no2006 p18 Jl 2017

BECERRO, MIKEL A.

Assessing National Biodiversity Trends for Rocky and Coral Reefs through the Integration of Citizen Science and Scientific Monitoring Programs *BioScience* v67 no2 p134 F 2017

BÉCHARD, DENI ELLIS

On le Road cartoon *Walrus* v13 no10 p67 D 2016

BECHDEL, ALISON

The Fellowship cartoon *New Yorker* v92 no32 p82 O 10 2016

Becher, Sophie—Interviews

Meet the crew... K. Hahn *TV Guide* p17 D 5 2016

BECHERER, TIM
PRADAL SEREY bw color *Black Belt* v55 no5 p48 Ag/S 2017

Becht, Colin
Leading Men color *Sports Illustrated* v125 no14 p54 O 24-31 2016
WHO'S NO. 1? THESE PLAYERS COULD CHALLENGE JOSH ALLEN FOR THE TOP SPOT color *Sports Illustrated* v126 no14 p101 My 15-22 2017

Bechtel, Mark
BROWN POWER color *Sports Illustrated* v126 no11 p62 Ap 17-24 2017
A CITY ON FIRE color *Sports Illustrated* v126 no14 p86 My 15-22 2017
Farewell color *Sports Illustrated* v125 no21 p52 D 26 2016
PEAK CONCERN color *Sports Illustrated* v127 no9 p12 S 25 2017
The Standout color *Sports Illustrated* v125 no20 p102 D 19 2016

Bechtel, Stefan
However Improbable M. DIRDA bw *Weekly Standard* v22 no44 p34 Jl 31 2017

Beck, 1970-
Beck E. R. Brown color *Entertainment Weekly* no1486 p58 O 13 2017
Beck Goes Pop (Again) M. Miller color *Esquire* p24 N 2017
Beck's Colors Finds Joy In Its Time M. Ayers color *Time* v190 no16/17 p107 O 23 2017
Beck's Day-Glo Vision of Modern Pop W. HERMES color *Rolling Stone* no1298 p49 O 19 2017
Beck's Hard Road to Happy Songs A. GREENE bw *Rolling Stone* no1294 p19 Ag 24 2017
WHAT YOU SHOULD KNOW ABOUT BECK D. KAMP bw *Vanity Fair* v59 no11 p78 N 2017

Beck, Christina
Archaeologists restore floor from Second Temple period on Jerusalem mount *Christian Century* v133 no21 p17 O 12 2016

Beck, Glenn, 1964-
Glenn Beck's Regrets E. Hedegaard color *Rolling Stone* no1273 p44 N 3 2016
OBAMA'S AMERICA img *New York* v49 no20 p12 O 3 2016

Beck, Glenn, 1964- —Interviews
Charlie Rose talks to... Glenn Beck bw *Bloomberg Businessweek* no4497 p29 O 31 2016
Glenn Beck B. Luscombe color *Time* v189 no3 p64 Ja 16 2017
Glenn Beck Is Sorry About All That A. M. Cox color *New York Times Magazine* p70 N 27 2016

Beck, Glenn, 1964- —Political & social views
BAD GUYS N. Schmidle cartoon *New Yorker* v92 no37 p32 N 14 2016
Glenn Beck's Regrets P. BEINART color *Atlantic* v319 no1 p16 Ja/F 2017

Beck, Julia
Complying with Family-Friendly Leave Policies Is Not Enough *Harvard Business Review Digital Articles* p2 Ap 13 2016
How Some Companies Are Making Child Care Less Stressful for Their Employees *Harvard Business Review Digital Articles* p2 Ap 14 2017
What Nursing Parents Need to Know About Pumping During Work Travel *Harvard Business Review Digital Articles* p2 Je 14 2017

Beck, Kate—Interviews
Instyle Textiles J. DeBold *New Orleans Homes & Lifestyles* v20 no2 p30 Spr 2017

Beck, Kristin
For the Record color *Time* v190 no6 p6 Ag 7 2017

Beck, Laura—Interviews
When a Mid-Career Move Falls Flat: The Story of Stripedshirt D. McGinn *Harvard Business Review Digital Articles* p2 Je 1 2015

BECK, MARTHA
The Big Reveal cartoon *O, The Oprah Magazine* p40 My 2017
Degrees of Success color *O, The Oprah Magazine* p34 Je 2017
Down, Girl! color *O, The Oprah Magazine* p42 S 2017
Food of THE GODS color *O, The Oprah Magazine* p36 Jl 2017
Go Wild cartoon *O, The Oprah Magazine* p37 F 2017
Interior Decorating cartoon *O, The Oprah Magazine* p42 Mr 2017
Let There Be Light color *O, The Oprah Magazine* p51 D 2016
Make Yourself Clear color *O, The Oprah Magazine* p48 O 2017

Mission Critical color *O, The Oprah Magazine* p46 N 2017
Sleeping with the Enemy color *O, The Oprah Magazine* p40 Ag 2017
You Say You Want a Resolution... color *O, The Oprah Magazine* p34 Ja 2017
Zone DEFENSE cartoon *O, The Oprah Magazine* p42 Ap 2017

Beck, Megan
3 Ways to Get Your Own Digital Platform *Harvard Business Review Digital Articles* p2 Jl 22 2016
7 Questions to Ask Before Your Next Digital Transformation *Harvard Business Review Digital Articles* p2 Jl 14 2016
AI May Soon Replace Even the Most Elite Consultants *Harvard Business Review Digital Articles* p2 Jl 24 2017
GDP Is a Wildly Flawed Measure for the Digital Age *Harvard Business Review Digital Articles* p2 Jl 28 2016
How to Navigate a Digital Transformation *Harvard Business Review Digital Articles* p2 Je 22 2016
Investors Today Prefer Companies with Fewer Physical As sets *Harvard Business Review Digital Articles* p2 S 29 2016
The Rise of AI Makes Emotional Intelligence More Important *Harvard Business Review Digital Articles* p2 F 15 2017
To Go Digital, Leaders Have to Change Some Core Beliefs *Harvard Business Review Digital Articles* p2 Je 1 2016
What Airbnb, Uber, and Alibaba Have in Common *Harvard Business Review Digital Articles* p2 N 20 2014
What Apple, Lending Club, and AirBnB Know About Collaborating with Customers *Harvard Business Review Digital Articles* p2 Jl 3 2015
Why Are We Still Classifying Companies by Industry? *Harvard Business Review Digital Articles* p2 Ag 18 2016
Why Leaders Are Still So Hesitant to Invest in New Business Models *Harvard Business Review Digital Articles* p2 D 21 2016

Beck, Mordechai
What is a Jewish state? *Christian Century* v134 no13 p30 Je 21 2017

Beck, P.
Seasonal exposure of carbon dioxide ice on the nucleus of comet 67P/Churyumov-Gerasimenko bibl bw graph *Science* v354 no6319 p1563 D 23 2016

BECK, STEFAN
Camo Criminals bw *Weekly Standard* v23 no2 p42 S 18 2017
Hatred for Thee color *Weekly Standard* v22 no15 p30 D 19 2016

Beck, Steven
CLASSICAL MUSIC *New Yorker* v93 no25 p8 Ag 28 2017
IN CONVERSATION *In These Times* v41 no10 p4 O 2017

Beck, Ulrich, 1944-2015—Political & social views
Is the 'Common Good' Obsolete? [Cover story] A. Latham and J. R. Bowlin bw color *Commonweal* v143 no19 p12 D 2 2016

Becker, Alida
COUNTRY LIVING color *New York Times Book Review* p22 D 4 2016
Freezer Burn: The atmosphere at a polar research station heats up when a climate-change denier arrives *New York Times Book Review* p15 Ag 13 2017

Becker, Amelia—Interviews
Do You Even Code, Bro? T. CONFOY cartoon color *Esquire* v166 no5 p48 D 2016/Ja 2017

Becker, B.
Observation of coherent elastic neutrino-nucleus scattering diag *Science* v357 no6356 p1123 S 15 2017

Becker, Bob
Bob Becker L. Monk Carter color *New Orleans Magazine* v51 no5 p28 Mr 2017

Becker, Brett
BECKER STABLES and Kheanne G. DEARTH *Arabian Horse World* v57 no6 p1 Mr 2017

Becker, Denise
Three-dimensional Ca2+ imaging advances understanding of astrocyte biology diag *Science* v356 no6339 p715 My 19 2017

Becker, Holly
ALFRESCO PARTY PREP E. PECK color *House Beautiful* p135 Ag 2017

Becker, Justin S.
Mitotic transcription and waves of gene reactivation during mitotic exit color graph *Science* v357 no6359 p119 O 6 2017

Becker, K. H.

Observation of a large-scale anisotropy in the arrival directions of cosmic rays above 8 × 1018 eV *Science* v357 no6357 p1266 S 22 2017

Becker, Martha

HEALING HANDS L. F. Prater *Successful Farming* v115 no4 p63 Mr 2017

Becker, Nicole A.

Cyclin A2 is an RNA binding protein that controls Mre11 mRNA translation bibl graph *Science* v353 no6307 p1549 S 30 2016

BECKER, ROBERT

THE LIFE AQUATIC color *Architectural Digest* no6 p142 Je 1 2017

Becker, Thomas

The cryo-EM structure of a ribosome–Ski2-Ski3-Ski8 helicase complex bibl color graph *Science* v354 no6318 p1431 D 16 2016

Becker, Walter, 1950-2017

Steely Dan's Quiet Hero [Cover story] D. BROWNE bw color *Rolling Stone* no1297 p15 O 5 2017

Beckerman, Carly

BEYOND BALFOUR AND SYKES-PICOT: Steering clear of Orientalist fantasy and patriotic British myth, this innovative analysis brings clarity to the complexities of the Middle East in the early 20th century *History Today* v67 no9 p100 S 2017

Beckerman, Gal

Essay *New York Times Book Review* p14 My 28 2017

The 'Iron Wall' of Israel *New York Times Book Review* p28 D 11 2016

Beckerman, James

ASK THE EXPERTS color *Runner's World* v52 no1 p50 Ja/F 2017

Beckerman, Joel

Muting Unwanted Noise in an Open Office *Harvard Business Review Digital Articles* p2 D 17 2015

Beckerman, Stacie

She Was My Prosecutor T. HALLMAN *Reader's Digest* v188 no1124 p90 O 2016

Becket Fund for Religious Liberty

New Jersey case tests whether historic churches can get state grants B. Allen *Christian Century* v134 no17 p16 Ag 16 2017

BECKETT, LOUISA

Bright Future color *Power & Motoryacht* v33 no2 p58 F 2017

Day Tripper color *Power & Motoryacht* v33 no3 p50 Mr 2017

How It's Done chart color diag *Power & Motoryacht* v34 no10 p88 O 2017

Queen of the Fleet chart color *Power & Motoryacht* v34 no9 p90 S 2017

Star Quality color *Power & Motoryacht* v33 no4 p46 Ap 2017

Beckett, Paul

BACK-TO-BACK color *Spin to Win Rodeo* v21 no6 p14 Ag 2017

Beckham, David

Icons color *Time* v189 no16/17 p122 My 1-8 2017

Beckham, J. David

Zika virus produces noncoding RNAs using a multi-pseudoknot structure that confounds a cellular exonuclease bibl color graph *Science* v354 no6316 p1148 D 2 2016

Beckham, Odell, 1992-

The Ten Who'll Be Next D. GORDON, S. SCHUBE et al color *GQ: Gentlemen's Quarterly* v97 no11 p114 N 2017

Beckham, Victoria, 1975-

her style color *InStyle* v24 no4 p34 Ap 2017

"I feel my best in this dress" L. Garcia and F. Kane color *Glamour* v115 no4 p55 Ap 2017

Just Us girls [Cover story] E. Wilson color *InStyle* v24 no4 p180 Ap 2017

Pop Chart R. Bruner, C. Lang et al color *Time* v189 no15 p54 Ap 24 2017

Tuck IN color *Vogue* v206 no12 p150 D 2016

VICTORIA BECKHAM L. ARMSTRONG color *Vogue* v207 no3 p422 Mr 2017

BECKIUS, KIM KNOX

Fall Foliage Trains: All aboard for autumn thrills on New England's historic rails *Yankee* v81 no5 p76 S/O 2017

Green Hotels and Inns color *Yankee* p74 Mr 2017

Holiday Shopping Towns color *Yankee* v80 no6 p94 N/D 2016

Retro Summer-Fun Spots: Where a vintage vibe and timeless ap-

peal keep the generations coming back color *Yankee* p66 Jl 2017

Winter Ocean Weekends *Yankee* v81 no1 p74 Ja/F 2017

Beckmann, Max, 1884-1950

The Good Germany R. Platt cartoon *New Yorker* v92 no33 p16 O 17 2016

Beckmann, Max, 1884-1950—Exhibitions

ART *New Yorker* v92 no37 p25 N 14 2016

BECKMANN, MICHAEL

Harmonizing Biodiversity Conservation and Productivity in the Context of Increasing Demands on Landscapes graph *BioScience* v66 no10 p890 O 1 2016

Beckmann, Roland

The cryo-EM structure of a ribosome–Ski2-Ski3-Ski8 helicase complex bibl color graph *Science* v354 no6318 p1431 D 16 2016

Becktold, Wendy

A Desert Classic *Sierra* v102 no3 p68 My/Je 2017

Desert Guardian *Sierra* v101 no4 p67 Jl/Ag 2016

THE GREAT DISCONNECT *Sierra* v102 no1 p34 Ja/F 2017

Parent Power *Sierra* v102 no2 p59 Mr/Ap 2017

Phone Book Pencil Holder *Sierra* v101 no4 p13 Jl/Ag 2016

Real-World Wind Power *Sierra* v101 no5 p63 S/O 2016

Rewilding the Kids *Sierra* v101 no5 p10 S/O 2016

Student, Hiker, Sprogger *Sierra* v102 no5 p63 St/O 2017

Beckwith, Ryan Teague

How Can I Afford to Live to 100? color *Time* v189 no7/8 p96 F 27 2017

Long-Term Saving Strategies for the Self-Employed color *Time* v189 no3 p12 Ja 30 2017

What CEOs Think of Trump color *Time* v189 no6 p10 F 20 2017

Beckwith-Wiedemann syndrome—Genetic aspects

FATEFUL IMPRINTS J. Couzin-Frankel color diag *Science* v355 no6321 p122 Ja 13 2017

Becky G (Performer)

Becky G, Actor S. Lansky color *Time* v189 no12 p58 Ap 3 2017

Bed & breakfast accommodations

FLORIDA *New York Times Magazine* p74 Mr 26 2017

HIDDEN GOLD: A VERMONT INSIDERS GUIDE to finding UNDERTHERADAR, OVERTHETOP COLOR B. SCHELLER *Yankee* v81 no5 p96 S/O 2017

Bed & breakfast accommodations—Evaluation

School House Inn N. AUSTIN *Arizona Highways* v93 no4 p14 Ap 2017

Up the Creek B&B N. AUSTIN *Arizona Highways* v92 no7 p14 Jl 2016

Bed Bath & Beyond Inc.

Bed Bath & Beyond's Persistent Coupons and the Return of Thrifty Consumers R. Mohammed *Harvard Business Review Digital Articles* p2 O 6 2015

Pack a Wallop T. WILLEY color *Bon Appetit* v61 no12 p56 D 2016 /Jan2017

Bedard, Greg A.

CENTER STAGE color *Sports Illustrated* v125 no16 p38 N 14 2016

Players Of the Year color *Sports Illustrated* v125 no20 p92 D 19 2016

SCAR'S TO PROVE IT color *Sports Illustrated* v126 no4 p36 Ja 30 2017

SUPER BOWL LI: THE PICK color *Sports Illustrated* v126 no4 p39 Ja 30 2017

SUSPENDED DISBELIEF [Cover story] color *Sports Illustrated* v126 no5 p26 F 13 2017

BEDDIA, JOE

kitchen color *Bon Appetit* v62 no4 p31 Ap 2017

Bedding

See also

Blankets

Pillows

The More the Merrier Z. Gowen color *Southern Living* v52 no5 p50 My 2017

Bedding plants

How to Make a... RAISED FLOWER BED [Cover story] bw chart *Popular Mechanics* p70 S 2017

Bedding—Equipment & supplies

my style color *InStyle* v24 no8 p96 Ag 2017

Bedding—Evaluation

Sweet Talk on TV Ads *Consumer Reports* v82 no2 p25 F 2017

Beddit (Company)

Sleep Gadgets: What Works, What Doesn't K. A. FETTERS color *Men's Health* v32 no8 p76 O 2017

Bede, Pamela Nisevich

HOLIDAY TRIMMINGS [Cover story] cartoon color *Runner's World* v51 no11 p46 D 2016

Bedford, Sybille

Mexico in the Full Light of Day [Cover story] E. Krauze and H. Heifetz bw color *New York Review of Books* v64 no10 p48 Je 8 2017

Bedford (Westchester County, N.Y.)

LA VIE EN ROSE A. WITCHEL color *Vanity Fair* v59 no9 p168 S 2017

Bedke, Tanja

A pathogenic role for T cell–derived IL-22BP in inflammatory bowel disease bibl graph *Science* v354 no6310 p358 O 21 2016

Bednar, Michael

Boards Aren't the Right Way to Monitor Companies *Harvard Business Review Digital Articles* p2 My 10 2016

Bedord, Laurie

10 SUCCESSFUL FARMERS: JEFF BROWN *Successful Farming* v115 no8 p24 Je/Jl 2017

10 UP & COMERS: PEOPLE TO WATCH IN AGRICULTURE *Successful Farming* v115 no8 p32 Je/Jl 2017

AHEAD OF THE CURVE *Successful Farming* v115 no2 p54 F 2017

BETTING ON AG *Successful Farming* v115 no3 p30 Mid-F 2017

CONTEST WINNERS SELECTED *Successful Farming* v115 no1 p55 Ja 2017

Defend The Bottom Line *Successful Farming* v114 no12 p14 Mid-N 2016

Got data? Now what? *Successful Farming* v114 no12 p10 Mid-N 2016

IRRIGATION + INNOVATION = SAVING WATER IN KANSAS *Successful Farming* v115 no6 p47 Ap 2017

JOHN DEERE 4640 UNIVERSAL DISPLAY UNVEILED: PORTABLE DISPLAY FEATURES THE LATEST TECHNOLOGY IN A USER-FRIENDLY GEN 4 EXPERIENCE *Successful Farming* v115 no11 p24 S 2017

LONG WINTER LAYOFF *Successful Farming* v114 no13 p46 D 2016

MAKING TRACKS: SOFTWARE LETS YOU BETTER MANAGE NITROGEN'S FOOTPRINT IN YOUR SOIL AS WELL AS THE ENVIRONMENT *Successful Farming* v115 no6 p33 Ap 2017

MATCH MAKING *Successful Farming* v115 no2 p10 F 2017

NEW AND IMPROVED *Successful Farming* v115 no3 p24 Mid-F 2017

ONE MASSIVE MACHINE *Successful Farming* v115 no2 p32 F 2017

PICTURE THIS: THE QUESTIONS THAT IMAGERY CAN HELP ANSWER ARE SIMPLE YET IMPORTANT *Successful Farming* v115 no11 p50 S 2017

THE PLANTING SQUAD *Successful Farming* v115 no4 p41 Mr 2017

Precision: PAIN POINTS *Successful Farming* v115 no9 p43 Ag 2017

PUT YOUR POWER USE UNDER THE MICROSCOPE *Successful Farming* v114 no10 p50 O 2016

Q&A *Successful Farming* v114 no12 p30 Mid-N 2016

Q&A *Successful Farming* v114 no12 p56 Mid-N 2016

RECEIVER REBOOT *Successful Farming* v115 no1 p32 Ja 2017

SEEDING SUCCESS *Successful Farming* v114 no12 p42 Mid-N 2016

SHOOT STARTER WITH SEED *Successful Farming* v114 no10 p30 O 2016

SIDEDRESS AND SEED COVER CROPS *Successful Farming* v115 no1 p32 Ja 2017

SMARTPHONE SECURITY *Successful Farming* v114 no11 p18 N 2016

SPACE FARMING: HUMANS MUST MASS-PRODUCE FOOD ON THE RED PLANET IF THE JOURNEY IS TO BE SUSTAINABLE *Successful Farming* v115 no12 p32 O 2017

TAGGED *Successful Farming* v115 no2 p32 F 2017

THE VALUE PROPOSITION *Successful Farming* v114 no12 p6

Mid-N 2016

WHAT'S YOUR BIN'S IQ? GROWERS PROTECT STORED GRAIN BY BOOSTING THEIR BIN'S BRAIN POWER color *Successful Farming* v115 no7 p40 My 2017

WIRELESS WATCHDOG *Successful Farming* v115 no3 p25 Mid-F 2017

ZERO TO 140 *Successful Farming* v115 no1 p44 Ja 2017

BEDOSKY, LAUREN

Prep Your Legs for Winter color *Men's Health* v32 no9 p54 N 2017

SAVE THE DAY color *Runner's World* v52 no9 p28 O 2017

STRAIGHT UP [Cover story] color *Runner's World* v52 no3 p48 Ap 2017

Bedoya-Pinto, Amilcar

A molecular spin-photovoltaic device color diag *Science* v357 no6352 p677 Ag 18 2017

BEDRICK, JASON

Suing Choice Away *National Review* v68 no19 p35 O 24 2016

Bedroom (Music)

MABEL *Interview* v47 no5 p14 Je/Jl 2017

Bedroom furniture

See also

Beds

Dressing tables

DIMINUTIVE QUEEN ANNE CHERRY SCALLOPED TOP LOWBOY FROM THE CONNECTICUT RIVER VALLEY color *Magazine Antiques* v184 no3 p2 My/Je 2017

Bedrooms

See also

Guest rooms

Adding On D. MULFINGER diag *Cabin Living* p22 Je 2017

Ask Max *National Geographic Kids* no469 p35 Ap 2017

Bedroom Basics L. Elliott cartoon *Old House Journal* v44 no8 p52 D 2016

BEDROOM DOORBELL! J. SCHADEWALD bw chart color *Popular Mechanics* p102 S 2017

BEDROOM DOORBELL! J. SCHADEWALD chart color diag *Popular Mechanics* v193 no7 p102 S 2016

BEST BEDROOMS color *Log Home Living* p44 2017 SpecialIssue

CREATIVE CORNER L. MOWRY *Atlanta* v56 no7 p54 N 2016

LITTLE TRICKS FOR A LOVELY BEDROOM S. J. SHELTON color *Redbook* p130 F 2017

Bedrooms—Design & construction

BEST BEDROOM color *Timber Home Living* p22 2017 SpecialIssue

Sweet Dreams are Made of This C. Johnson color diag *Cabin Living* p72 Je 2017

Sweet Dreams are Made of This C. Johnson color *Timber Home Living* v27 no5 p58 O 2017

Bedrooms—Equipment & supplies

15 WAYS TO SLEEP BETTER TONIGHT C. FORTÉ and L. SACHS color *Good Housekeeping* v265 no4 p77 O 2017

Bedrooms—Interior decoration

#1: For a dapper New Yorker, Nick Olsen crafts a kaleidoscopic fantasia of freewheeling color, one-of a-kind auction finds, and yin-yang contrasts—plus a bedroom as handsomely tailored as a bespoke suit K. RENDA color *House Beautiful* v159 no2 p82 Mr 2017

House Beautiful GUIDE TO Family Style color *House Beautiful* v159 no7 p21 S 2017

Room for Two S. Evans color *Southern Living* v52 no3 p18 Mr 2017

THE SLOWER LANE S. ORR *Better Homes & Gardens* v95 no1 p2 Ja 2017

Bedrooms—Remodeling

A GLAM BEDROOM H. BROWN color *House Beautiful* v159 no2 p55 Mr 2017

Beds

DESIGN DILEMMA: My Home Has Tiny Closets. How Do I Store My Stuff? C. KENT and T. STRINGER color *Chicago* v66 no9 p89 S 2017

GOOD NIGHTS J. Francisco *Good Housekeeping* v265 no4 p14 O 2017

MAKING A PROPER BED M. B. EYERS color diag *Better Homes & Gardens* v95 no10 p38 O 2017

The Reader Page B. Shanley, J. Petkiewicz et al color *Popular Mechanics* p5 F 2017

SCREEN MAGIC E. N. GAGE color *Martha Stewart Living* p25 S 2017

Stack 'Em Up color *Log Home Living* v34 no6 p8 Ag 2017

Beds (Gardens)

How to Make a... RAISED FLOWER BED [Cover story] bw chart *Popular Mechanics* p70 S 2017

How to Make a... RAISED FLOWER BED [Cover story] bw chart *Popular Mechanics* v193 no7 p70 S 2016

Beds—Design & construction

Size matters L. DELAP color *Maclean's* v129 no44 p60 N 7 2016

Beds—Evaluation

A Little Bit Luxe F. L. Wright color *Log Home Living* v34 no5 p44 Jl 2017

Need a New Bed? Sleep on It J. Vrabel color *GQ: Gentlemen's Quarterly* v86 no11 p52 N 2016

REST EASY color *Martha Stewart Living* p35 Jl/Ag 2017

WEAVE IT IN C. Hong color *Martha Stewart Living* p94 Jl/Ag 2017

Bedtime

How to Spend the Last 10 Minutes of Your Day R. Friedman *Harvard Business Review Digital Articles* p2 N 10 2014

Bee, Olivia

Olivia Bee J. Johnson color *Current Biography* v78 no6 p10 Je 2017

WOMEN WHO DARE bw color *Harper's Bazaar* no3648 p246 N 2016

Bee, Samantha, 1969-

BEE NOT AFRAID D. CORN *Mother Jones* v42 no3 p62 My/Je 2017

FULL FRONTAL FRIENDS color *TV Guide* v65 no7 p47 F 13 2017

HACKER CRACK-UP E. D. Jennings, J. Alexander et al color *Wired* v25 no6 p10 Je 2017

The New Rules of Engaging with Women color *GQ: Gentlemen's Quarterly* v87 no1 p22 Ja 2017

No Joke color *GQ: Gentlemen's Quarterly* v87 no1 p20 Ja 2017

THE REAL GWYNETH color *Harper's Bazaar* no3648 p232 N 2016

SAMANTHA BEE R. Rahman color *Entertainment Weekly* no1444/1445 p18 D 16 2016

WELCOME TO THE ISSUE color *Harper's Bazaar* no3648 p42 N 2016

Bee, Samantha, 1969-—Interviews

FULL-FRONTAL ASSAULT V. HEFFERNAN cartoon color *Wired* v25 no4 p68 Ap 2017

MEET THE NEW (ISH) GUY color *Wired* v25 no4 p8 Ap 2017

Bee behavior

Antisocial bees share gene activity with people with autism color *Science* v357 no6350 p433 Ag 4 2017

A Helping Hand for Early Bees J. Marinelli color *National Wildlife (World Edition)* v55 no6 p16 O/N 2017

Bee colonies

visual statement PARISEAU color *Foreign Policy* no221 p26 N/D 2016

Bee culture

Bees Prefer Country Blossoms to City Blooms *USA Today Magazine* v145 no2865 p6 Je 2017

Busy Bees P. Marquis *New Orleans Homes & Lifestyles* v20 no1 p26 Wint 2016

BUZZ WORTHY color *Martha Stewart Living* p112 Ap 2017

Country Lore J. Poindexter, A. Sezak-Blatt et al *Mother Earth News* no280 p85 F/Mr 2017

When the hive mind is wrong C. MCINTYRE *Maclean's* v130 no9 p16 O 2017

Bee genetics

Antisocial bees share gene activity with people with autism color *Science* v357 no6350 p433 Ag 4 2017

Bee pollen

A Helping Hand for Early Bees J. Marinelli color *National Wildlife (World Edition)* v55 no6 p16 O/N 2017

Pollution confuses bees color *National Wildlife (World Edition)* v55 no3 p10 Ap/My 2017

You missed a spot, bee M. Temming color *Science News* v192 no5 p32 S 30 2017

Bee stings

the Sting R. K. JOHNSON cartoon *New Yorker* v93 no7 p40 Ap 3 2017

Beebe, Jeanette

Robo Pizzaiolo color *Scientific American* v316 no6 p22 Je 2017

Beebe, William

1930: Nonsuch Island *Lapham's Quarterly* v10 no2 p128 Spr 2017

Beebout, Connor J.

A SUMO-ubiquitin relay recruits proteasomes to chromosome axes to regulate meiotic recombination bibl graph *Science* v355 no6323 p403 Ja 27 2017

Beeby, Morgan

Nanoscale-length control of the flagellar driveshaft requires hitting the tethered outer membrane color diag graph *Science* v356 no6334 p197 Ap 14 2017

Beech, Hannah

Battling for Blood Jade color map *Time* v189 no10 p40 Mr 20 2017

Beijing Welcomes Trump color *Time* v188 no22-23 p31 N/D 2016

FALLEN IDOL bw cartoon *New Yorker* v93 no30 p22 O 2 2017

Hollywood East color *Time* v189 no4 p40 F 6 2017

TIME's Foreign Correspondents on How the World Sees the U.S. Election *Time* v188 no16/17 p34 O 24 2016

Why America Is Losing Asia color *Time* v188 no27-28 p66 D 26 2016

Beechcraft (Airplanes)

BEECHCRAFT: KING AIR 250 S. POPE chart color *Flying* v144 no10 p42 O 2017

KING AIR MODS R. MARK color *Flying* v144 no10 p52 O 2017

Beecher, Catharine Esther, 1800-1878

1841: Cincinnati C. Beecher *Lapham's Quarterly* v10 no1 p32 Wint 2017

BEECHIE, TIMOTHY J.

Envisioning, Quantifying, and Managing Thermal Regimes on River Networks *BioScience* v67 no6 p506 Je 2017

Beecroft, Alex

Foxglove Copse *Publishers Weekly* v264 no31 p69 Jl 31 2017

Sons of Devils: Arising #1 *Publishers Weekly* v264 no6 p51 F 6 2017

Beef

See also

Dried beef

Steak (Beef)

BY-PRODUCTS NO MORE G. Johnston *Successful Farming* v115 no1 p64 Ja 2017

CONFESSIONS OF A BEEF EATER A. KUMAR color *Nation* v305 no11 p32 O 30 2017

Eat these to stress less M. TAYLOR, D. Ramsey et al cartoon *Redbook* p92 F 2017

How to Make... JERKY F. MAROUKIAN and T. AIAZZI color *Popular Mechanics* p80 S 2017

I Love My Library I. GARTEN color *House Beautiful* v159 no3 p124 Ap 2017

Increased Consumer Sensitivity to Food Safety Raised Financial Costs of Ground Beef Recalls F. Kuchler and R. M. Morrison *Amber Waves: The Economics of Food, Farming, Natural Resources, & Rural America* p1 O 2016

Itty-Bitty Taco Cups color *Good Housekeeping* v264 no5 p111 My 2017

Know Your Ribs: A guide to the perfect rack *Virginia Living* p53 2017 Smoke & Salt

The LONG GAME R. Haskell color *Vogue* v207 no10 p292 O 2017

THE TRIUMPHANT RETURN OF RED MEAT M. Heid color *Men's Health* v32 no2 p88 Mr 2017

Beef cattle

BEYOND WAGYU A. Spiegel color *Washingtonian Magazine* v52 no7 p143 Ap 2017

Beef industry—Brazil

How to Quantify Sustainability's Impact on Your Bottom Line T. Whelan, B. Zappa et al *Harvard Business Review Digital Articles* p2 S 13 2017

Beef industry—United States

BEEF INDUSTRY PAST, PRESENT, AND FUTURE: NCBA PRESIDENT CRAIG UDEN HAS A FAMILY HISTORY OF INDUSTRY ACTIVISM AND HOPES TO UNITE PRODUC-

In Brazil, It's Now Beer—Without the Babes F. Moura and J. Brice color *Bloomberg Businessweek* no4508 p20 Ja 23 2017

Beers, Cyndi
HATCH OF THE MAYFLIES *South Dakota Magazine* v33 no2 p94 Jl/Ag 2017

Beers, Jody M.
Hydraulic control of tuna fins: A role for the lymphatic system in vertebrate locomotion color *Science* v357 no6348 p310 Jl 21 2017

Beers, Mike
TODAY'S TEAM-ROPING TALENT POOL RUNS DEEP K. Santos color *Spin to Win Rodeo* v21 no6 p36 Ag 2017

Beer—Sales & prices
GREATER NEW ORLEANS J. FROIS color map *Louisiana Life* v37 no4 p98 Mr/Ap 2017

Beer—Social aspects
A Better Brew M. WALTHER color *National Review* v69 no6 p23 Ap 3 2017

Beer—Taxation
Changes On Tap for Japan's Beer Tax G. Huang, G. Reidy et al color *Bloomberg Businessweek* no4513 p29 Mr 6 2017

Beer—United States
99 BOTTLES OF IPA ON THE WALL J. DETWILER and M. ALLYN chart color *Popular Mechanics* p71 Ap 2017
America Thirst chart color *GQ: Gentlemen's Quarterly* v97 no7 p58 Jl 2017

Bees
> *See also*
> Bee behavior
> Honeybees

A Bee or Not a Bee, That is the Question G. Lemmo *New York State Conservationist* v71 no6 p14 Je 2017
Bees once again making headlines color map *National Wildlife (World Edition)* v55 no5 p8 Ag/S 2017
BUZZKILL S. VOLK color graph map *Discover* v38 no2 p30 Mr 2017
Nerve agents in honey C. N. Connolly color diag *Science* v357 no6359 p38 O 6 2017
STUFF Nature SCREWED UP D. Botti cartoon *Old House Journal* v44 no8 p54 D 2016

Bees—Health
Bee Ecotoxicology and Data Veracity: Appreciating the GLP Process G. C. CUTLER and C. D. SCOTT-DUPREE *BioScience* v66 no12 p1066 D 1 2016

BEESON, MARK
Trump and the Asia-Pacific: Do the Ties Still Bind? *Current History* v116 no791 p235 S 2017

Beet juice
Taste the Rainbow J. DEMELO color *Bon Appetit* v62 no7 p17 Jl 2017

Beethoven, Ludwig van, 1770-1827
Fidelio *Opera News* v81 no9 p61 Mr 2017

Beetle behavior
Beetle manipulates microbes to benefit young color *Science* v357 no6354 p851 S 1 2017

Beetles
Just Joking bw color *National Geographic Kids* no474 p32 O 2017
SUMMER BUMMERS: PESTS, WEEDS, STRESSED PLANTS. EVERY YEAR, THEY SHOW UP OUT OF NOWHERE. SEND THEM PACKING WITH THESE EASY TIPS E. Liskey color *Successful Farming* v115 no7 p54 My 2017

Beets
> *See also*
> Sugar beet

ASK TUFTS EXPERTS A. H. Lichtenstein *Tufts University Health & Nutrition Letter* v35 no1 p8 Mr 2017
BEET THE COMPETITION D. N. JACKSON color *Muscle & Performance* v9 no9 p16 S 2017
GREAT GREENS MADE EASY C. Thompson color *Men's Health* v31 no10 p61 D 2016
THE HEART HELPER *Prevention* v69 no4 p15 Ap 2017
PASTRAMI TROUT J. Miles color *Field & Stream* v121 no9 p20 Ap 2017
What Is Nitric Oxide? V. TWEED color *Better Nutrition* v79 no7 p22 Jl 2017

Beets—Therapeutic use
just beet it! J. Challem color *Amazing Wellness* v9 no1 p56 Wint 2017

Beetz, Zazie
Zazie BEETZ D. Glover *Interview* v47 no5 p53 Je/Jl 2017

Beetz, Zazie—Interviews
ZAZIE BEETZ S. Pulia color *InStyle* v24 no1 p44 Ja 2017

Beevor, Antony
The Very Drugged Nazis bw *New York Review of Books* v64 no4 p14 Mr 9 2017

BEEZAT, ROBERT
READING (AND MORE) TOGETHER *Commonweal* v144 no8 p2 My 5 2017

BEFORE, JOHN
REVENGE OF THE FILM NERDS *Texas Monthly* v45 no7 p70 Jl 2017

Before I Fall (Film)
CRITICS' CHOICE N. Davis, R. Horton et al bw chart color *Film Comment* v53 no2 p12 Mr/Ap 2017

Before I Go (Short story)
Before I Go L. M. MOORE *Saturday Evening Post* v289 no2 p60 Mr/Ap 2017

Before the Dawn (Music)
What to Stream color *Entertainment Weekly* no1443 p59 D 9 2016

Before the Flood (Film)
Why the Climate Gets Top Billing color *National Geographic* v230 no5 p3 N 2016

Begay, Derrick
BUCKLE UP with Derrick Begay C. Toy color *Spin to Win Rodeo* v20 no11 p15 Ja 2017
FIVE FLAT C. Toy color *Spin to Win Rodeo* v21 no2 p33 Ap 2017
Why do I rope? color *Team Roping Journal* p160 S 2017

Bégay, Valérie
Fructose-driven glycolysis supports anoxia resistance in the naked mole-rat diag graph *Science* v356 no6335 p307 Ap 21 2017

Begeman, Christian
LIGHT IN THE DARKNESS, Salt of the Earth *South Dakota Magazine* v32 no6 p30 Mr/Ap 2017
SCUFFLE IN THE LOOP *South Dakota Magazine* v33 no3 p94 S/O 2017

Beggar on the Dublin Bridge, The (Short story)
THE BEGGAR ON DUBLIN BRIDGE R. Bradbury *Saturday Evening Post* v288 no6 p68 N/D 2016

Beggars
The Riches of the Church J. MARTIN *America* v216 no1 p12 Ja 2 2017

BEGGS, ALEX
starters color *Bon Appetit* v62 no6 p17 Je 2017
A Very Organized Thanksgiving color *Bon Appetit* no11 p19 N 2017

Beggs, Mack
Wrestle Mania T. Keith and R. Demak color *Sports Illustrated* v126 no7 p20 Mr 6 2017

Beghe, Jason
Chicago P.D.'s New Detective I. Rudolph *TV Guide* v65 no19 p10 My 1 2017

Beginning reading—Physiological aspects
We All Speed-Read R. Jacobson color *Scientific American* v315 no3 p23 S 2016

Beginning teachers—Services for
Show what you know D. Brown and D. E. Rhodes color *Phi Delta Kappan* v98 no8 p38 My 2017

Beglarian, Eve
Ansel Elgort E. Berman color *Time* v190 no4 p48 Jl 24 2017

Begley, Adam
His Lofty Ascent: Gaspard-Félix Tournachon, the great French photographer, had an antic personality and a gift for self-promotion L. SANTE *New York Times Book Review* p23 Jl 23 2017
A Wink and a Nod: The French artist Nadar at his most subversive and sly *American Scholar* v86 no3 p102 Summ 2017

Begley, Andrew J.
Searching for Captain Blye *Prologue* v49 no1 p58 Spr 2017

Begley, Louis
Departure Lounge W. H. PRITCHARD *Weekly Standard* v22 no5 p32 O 10 2016

Begley, Sarah

The 10 Best Nonfiction Books color *Time* v188 no25-26 p150 D 19 2016 Double Issue

The 10 Best Novels color *Time* v188 no25-26 p149 D 19 2016 Double Issue

2017 Fall Books Preview color *Time* v190 no12 p54 S 25 2017

The Advantage of Universal Pre-K color *Time* v190 no9 p24 S 4 2017

Advertising Is Dead; Long Live Advertising color *Time* v190 no1 p18 Jl 3 2017

All the President's Exes color *Time* v189 no19 p55 My 22 2017

America's Canine Protectors color *Time* v188 no19 p16 N 7 2016

America's Newest, Oldest Nomads color *Time* v190 no12 p22 S 25 2017

Anthony Gonzalez As an Explorer of the Afterlife color *Time* v190 no10/11 p110 S 18 2017

Armchair Traveler color map *Time* v189 no22 p52 Je 12 2017

Bartending Is Better Than Business School color *Time* v190 no2/3 p20 Jl 10-17 2017

The Birth of Britain's Global Palate color *Time* v190 no14 p22 O 9 2017

Body Language color *Time* v189 no4 p49 Ja 23 2017

The Campus Culture Wars color *Time* v190 no16/17 p48 O 23 2017

Celeste Ng, Novelist color *Time* v190 no12 p58 S 25 2017

Chimamanda Ngozi Adichie color *Time* v189 no9 p60 Mr 13 2017

A Collection of Tales That Bind color *Time* v188 no27-28 p112 D 26 2016

Crimes, Cover-Ups and Competition color *Time* v189 no6 p53 F 20 2017

Crimes of the Heart color *Time* v188 no20 p55 N 14 2016

Derek Walcott color *Time* v189 no12 p19 Ap 3 2017

Do-Gooders In Gangland color *Time* v190 no5 p62 Jl 31 2017

Double Homicide color *Time* v189 no24 p52 Je 26 2017

Elizabeth Strout color *Time* v189 no18 p60 My 15 2017

Emotion, the Great Manipulator color *Time* v190 no13 p22 O 2 2017

The Empathizer color *Time* v189 no5 p52 F 13 2017

The Essential Power of the Hive Mind color *Time* v189 no10 p20 Mr 20 2017

The Evolution of Sleep color *Time* v189 no9 p20 Mr 13 2017

The Fallacy of Finding Your One True Love color *Time* v189 no4 p22 Ja 23 2017

Fall's Heavy Hitters color *Time* v190 no12 p61 S 25 2017

The First 'Mission-Driven' Companies color *Time* v190 no6 p22 Ag 7 2017

A Found Novel of Harlem Works As a Time Capsule color *Time* v189 no5 p53 F 13 2017

Four Roads Diverge In a Wood color *Time* v189 no4 p54 F 6 2017

The Girls Off the Cliff color *Time* v189 no18 p56 My 15 2017

Grace and Gumption In Irish-Catholic Brooklyn color *Time* v190 no13 p67 O 2 2017

Heartthrobs and Hellscapes color *Time* v189 no4 p54 F 6 2017

A Heroine for Our Time color *Time* v190 no15 p58 O 16 2017

The Hidden (and Not-So-Hidden) Racism In Kids' Lit color *Time* v190 no6 p56 Ag 7 2017

The Hidden Stars of Champion Teams color *Time* v189 no18 p22 My 15 2017

The Hidden Truth In Every Ghost Story color *Time* v188 no18 p20 O 31 2016

History's Best Overlooked Inventions color *Time* v190 no10/11 p26 S 18 2017

House of Bards color *Time* v189 no7/8 p101 F 27 2017

How Beauty Drives Evolution color *Time* v189 no19 p18 My 22 2017

How Hidden Factors Drive What We Think color *Time* v190 no15 p18 O 16 2017

How Lawsuits Help Democracy color *Time* v189 no4 p18 F 6 2017

How Thelma & Louise Changed Hollywood color *Time* v190 no4 p18 Jl 24 2017

How to Work With Generation Z color *Time* v189 no11 p24 Mr 27 2017

How Video Games Can Save the World color *Time* v189 no3 p20 Ja 30 2017

Ina Garten color *Time* v190 no2/3 p100 Jl 10-17 2017

In Defense of 'Bad' Wine color *Time* v189 no12 p24 Ap 3 2017

The Inevitability of the iPhone color *Time* v189 no24 p18 Je 26 2017

In George Saunders' Debut Novel, Moving Tales from the Crypt color *Time* v189 no7/8 p99 F 27 2017

It's Not Over Yet color *Time* v190 no7 p53 Ag 21 2017

Jesmyn Ward, Heir to Faulkner, Probes the Specter of Race In the South color *Time* v190 no9 p58 S 4 2017

Julie Andrews color *Time* v189 no12 p54 Ap 3 2017

Lisa Lucas color *Time* v189 no3 p60 Ja 30 2017

Love In the Time of Refugees color *Time* v189 no10 p56 Mr 20 2017

Mark Kurlansky color *Time* v190 no1 p56 Jl 3 2017

The Moving Spirit color *Time* v190 no4 p54 Jl 24 2017

Murder, She Wrote color *Time* v188 no15 p61 O 17 2016

The New Conspicuous Consumption color *Time* v189 no20 p18 My 29 2017

A New Look at the Next Generation color *Time* v190 no8 p20 Ag 28 2017

Not Totally Deplorable color *Time* v188 no27-28 p110 D 26 2016

Paradise Lost: The Mysterious Case of the Missing Utopian Novels color *Time* v190 no14 p52 O 9 2017

The Perks of Being Weird In the Workplace color *Time* v189 no23 p20 Je 19 2017

The Pitfalls of Giving It All Away color *Time* v189 no15 p18 Ap 24 2017

The Politics of Art color *Time* v189 no3 p16 Ja 16 2017

Pop Music Is Smarter Than It Appears color *Time* v188 no14 p22 O 10 2016

Problem Colleagues and How to Deal color *Time* v189 no14 p22 Ap 17 2017

Read a Novel: It's Just What the Doctor Ordered color *Time* v188 no19 p58 N 7 2016

The Real Elena Ferrante Surfaces-In Books color *Time* v188 no20 p54 N 14 2016

Rebels With Causes color *Time* v189 no22 p53 Je 12 2017

Refugees Through the Looking Glass color *Time* v188 no27-28 p110 D 26 2016

The Risky Business of Angel Investing color *Time* v190 no5 p26 Jl 31 2017

Roy's Return to Form color *Time* v189 no22 p50 Je 12 2017

Roz Chast color *Time* v190 no15 p60 O 16 2017

Saints, Elsewhere color *Time* v189 no19 p55 My 22 2017

The Silver Linings of Big Sky color *Time* v189 no3 p57 Ja 30 2017

Smart Cities, Smarter Citizens color *Time* v189 no13 p18 Ap 10 2017

Something to Talk About ... color *Time* v189 no22 p54 Je 12 2017

Something Twisted This Way Comes color *Time* v190 no1 p54 Jl 3 2017

Summer Movie Preview: August color *Time* v189 no20 p58 My 29 2017

Summer Movie Preview: July color *Time* v189 no20 p56 My 29 2017

Summer Movie Preview: June color *Time* v189 no20 p50 My 29 2017

Summer Movie Preview: May color *Time* v189 no20 p48 My 29 2017

Teen Angst With a New Edge color *Time* v188 no22-23 p104 N/D 2016

This Land Is Our Land color *Time* v188 no18 p46 O 31 2016

Thrill Seekers color *Time* v189 no22 p51 Je 12 2017

Triviality Is the Mother of Invention color *Time* v188 no20 p18 N 14 2016

The Upside of the AI Revolution color *Time* v189 no7/8 p24 F 27 2017

What's In a Board Game? color *Time* v189 no22 p16 Je 12 2017

When Less Plot Is Actually More color *Time* v189 no3 p58 Ja 16 2017

Why Aliens Would (Probably) Come In Peace color *Time* v189 no18 p21 My 15 2017

Why Cats Rule the World color *Time* v188 no15 p14 O 17 2016

Why Table Manners Still Matter color *Time* v188 no16/17 p14 O 24 2016

Will Millennials Start Running for Office? color *Time* v189 no6 p20 F 20 2017

The Workaholic's Case for a Four-Hour Day color *Time* v188 no22-23 p18 N/D 2016

Begley, Sharon

High Anxiety S. MNOOKIN *New York Times Book Review* p20 Mr 12 2017

Begonias

Blue is high-energy color for begonias E. Conover bw color *Science News* v190 no12 p4 D 10 2016

Beguiled, The (Film : 2017)

ACROSS THE DIVIDE A. LANE color *New Yorker* v93 no18 p76 Je 26 2017

The Beguiled Explores the Dark Side of Female Desire S. Zacharek color *Time* v190 no1 p51 Jl 3 2017

The Beguiled L. Greenblatt color *Entertainment Weekly* no1472 p44 Je 30 2017

Blockbusting R. Alleva color *Commonweal* v144 no13 p21 Ag 11 2017

CRITICS' CHOICE chart *Film Comment* v53 no4 p12 Jl/Ag 2017

He Shot, She Shot: With The Beguiled, Sofia Coppola remakes a 1971 movie from a radically new perspective img *New York* v50 no12 p106 Je 12 2017

Love Is a Battlefield P. Travers color *Rolling Stone* no1290 p55 Je 29 2017

The Must List color *Entertainment Weekly* no1472 p1 Je 30 2017

Nicole Kidman C. Ianzito color *AARP: The Magazine* v60 no4A p68 Je/Jl 2017

SOFIA COPPOLA'S THE BEGUILED D. Coggan color *Entertainment Weekly* no1453 p46 F 17 2017

Summer's New Heroes P. Travers color *Rolling Stone* no1288 p52 Je 1 2017

Swept Away N. Heller color *Vogue* v207 no6 p87 Je 2017

Begun, Bret

GIVE ME A BREAK color *Bloomberg Businessweek* no4521 p62 My 8 2017

Begun, Rachel

Veggies du jour chart color *Yoga Journal* no289 p70 F 2017

Beha, Christopher

HEAD--SCRATCHER *Harper's Magazine* v334 no2004 p88 My 2017

NEW BOOKS *Harper's Magazine* v334 no2002 p83 Mr 2017

Quadruple Vision color *Esquire* v167 no1 p20 F 2017

BEHAL, AMBIKA

Asia's Rising Stars color *Forbes* v199 no5 p20 My 16 2017

BEHAR, MICHAEL

COMFY CARVING color *Bloomberg Businessweek* no4506 p59 Ja 9 2017

THE FORECAST IS CLOUDY *New York Times Magazine* p26 O 23 2016

BEHAR, RICHARD

ALL THE (POTENTIAL) PRESIDENT'S MEN bw color *Forbes* v198 no5 p77 O 25 2016

Béhar, Yves, 1967-

Yves Béhar E. HOLT color *Architectural Digest* v74 no10 p57 O 1 2017

Behari, Jo

MAKE + MEND color *House Beautiful* p142 Ag 2017

Beharie, Nicole, 1985-

Sleepy Hollow's New Team M. Roffman *TV Guide* v64 no48 p10 N 21 2016

Behavior

See also

    Animal behavior

    Bereavement

    Curiosity

    Drinking behavior

    Human behavior

    Normative theory (Communication)

    Organizational behavior

DOWN WITH EXTREMES! HEALTH, WELL-BEING, AND SUCCESS REST ON ONE PRINCIPLE: IN ALL THINGS MODERATION C. FLORA *Psychology Today* v50 no4 p80 Ag 2017

I Make All Things New M. R. Simone *America* v216 no8 p50 Ap 17 2017

POISON PEOPLE CAUTION [Cover story] K. SCHREIBER *Psychology Today* v50 no3 p50 My/Je 2017

Safety Pins For Slackers: Does the like button impede social change? D. FELDMAN *Psychology Today* v50 no4 p40 Ag 2017

SMOOTH CRIMINALS S. POLAN *Psychology Today* v50 no3 p19 My/Je 2017

Watch This Weight-Loss Saboteur *Health* v31 no6 p12 Jl 2017

Behavior disorders

See also

    Attention-deficit hyperactivity disorder

    Behavior disorders in adolescence

    Conduct disorders in children

Boys with the Same Behavior Problems as Girls Tend to Complete Less Schooling *Education Digest* v82 no8 p63 Ap 2017

Behavior disorders in adolescence

Managing stress for at-risk students E. J. Spiegel color il *Phi Delta Kappan* v98 no6 p42 Mr 2017

Behavior disorders in children

See also

    Anxiety in children

    Attention-deficit hyperactivity disorder

Getting Through *USA Today Magazine* v146 no2868 p36 S 2017

NOW THAT SOUNDS POSITIVE D. MILLER *USA Today Magazine* v146 no2868 p36 S 2017

Behavior disorders in children—Prevention

HOW TO Wipe Out Whining R. FELSENTHAL STEWART *Parents* v92 no11 p120 N 2017

Behavior disorders in children—Treatment

Road to Recovery *Psychology Today* v49 no5 p42 S/O 2016

Behavior modification

See also

    Behavior therapy

Do a Digital Detox J. Andriakos color *Health* v31 no5 p22 Je 2017

From Obese to Ironman A. Levi color *Health* v31 no5 p51 Je 2017

How to Give a Stellar Presentation R. Knight *Harvard Business Review Digital Articles* p2 N 25 2014

HOW TO WIN AT Wellness L. Goldman color *O, The Oprah Magazine* p83 F 2017

QUITTING TIME M. Burklund color *Better Nutrition* v79 no4 p50 Ap 2017

Situational Awareness B. ARRINGTON color *Power & Motoryacht* v34 no11 p54 N 2017

SLIM CHANCE *Indianapolis Monthly* v40 no3 p78 N 2016

Squeeze More Joy Out of Life J. Andriakos color *Health* v31 no3 p24 Ap 2017

Trick Yourself into Breaking a Bad Habit J. Grenny *Harvard Business Review Digital Articles* p2 Ja 18 2016

Why New Personal Productivity Efforts Don't Stick M. Thomas and S. Thomas *Harvard Business Review Digital Articles* p2 Ja 19 2016

Why You Need an Imaginary Scapegoat N. Eyal bw *Harvard Business Review Digital Articles* p2 F 6 2017

Behavior therapy

Improving Cognitive Function in Behavioral Health Treatment: Sovereign Health asks Veena Kumari, Ph.D., about Cognitive Remediation Therapy V. Kumari *Psychology Today* v50 no5 p12 S/O 2017

Nudged Out T. Newcombe *Governing* v30 no5 p62 F 2017

A Trance to Remember J. KHAWAJA *Los Angeles Magazine* p22 Ja 2017

Behavioral assessment

Examining Attention I. MCGILCHRIST cartoon *Tricycle: The Buddhist Review* v26 no3 p24 Spr 2017

Behavioral economics

The Behavioral Economics of Why Executives Underinvest in Cybersecurity A. Blau color *Harvard Business Review Digital Articles* p2 Je 7 2017

How Google Optimized Healthy Office Snacks Z. Chance, R. Dhar et al *Harvard Business Review Digital Articles* p2 Mr 3 2016

The Rise of Behavioral Economics and Its Influence on Organizations F. Gino *Harvard Business Review Digital Articles* p2 O 10 2017

WAIT, WHAT IS MONEY? S. METTES color *Christianity Today* v61 no1 p30 Ja/F 2017

Behavioral objectives (Education)

See also

    Cognitive objectives (Education)

Got grit? Maybe... B. Duckor color diag il *Phi Delta Kappan* v98

no7 p61 Ap 2017

Behavioral targeting (Internet advertising)

The Online Ad Scams Every Marketer Should Watch Out For B. Edelman *Harvard Business Review Digital Articles* p2 O 13 2015

Targeted Ads Don't Just Make You More Likely to Buy—They Can Change How You Think About Yourself R. W. Reczek, C. Summers et al *Harvard Business Review Digital Articles* p2 Ap 4 2016

Behaviorism (Psychology)

See also

Behavior modification

BEHAVIORISM K. NAHIGIAN *Humanist* v77 no2 p36 Mr/Ap 2017

Project Pigeon J. Ingram color *Canadian Wildlife* v23 no2 p14 My/Je 2017

Beheading in art

R. H. QUAYTMAN *Interview* v46 no8 p98 O 2016

Behemoth (Film)

BEHEMOTH color *Tricycle: The Buddhist Review* v27 no1 p7 Fall 2017

BEHEN, MADONNA

preemie primer *Parents* v92 no2 p100 F 2017

Behind the Door (Film)

TO WATCH *Film Comment* v53 no3 p75 My/Je 2017

Behjati, Sam

Retracing embryological fate bibl diag *Science* v354 no6316 p1109-B D 2 2016

Behlendorf, Brian

Betting on the Blockchain T. Simonite il *MIT Technology Review* v120 no1 p29 Ja/F 2017

Behm, Allyson

This Is Our Time color *Glamour* v115 no7 p14 Jl 2017

Behn, Jan

Statin Denialism? *Skeptical Inquirer* v41 no5 p63 S/O 2017

Behnia, Kamran

The fragility of distant Cooper pairs bibl diag *Science* v355 no6320 p26 Ja 6 2017

Behrens, Adam M.

Fabrication of fillable microparticles and other complex 3D microstructures color diag *Science* v357 no6356 p1138 S 15 2017

Behrens, Alfredo

Are Bad Managers Holding Back Your Best Talent? *Harvard Business Review Digital Articles* p2 Ap 23 2015

Behrens, M. Margarita

Single-cell methylomes identify neuronal subtypes and regulatory elements in mammalian cortex diag *Science* v357 no6351 p600 Ag 11 2017

Behrens, Michael

THE SKINNY ON BLACK COW FAT PIG S. W. KANSTEINER color *Nebraska Life* v21 no2 p28 Mr/Ap 2017

Behrmann, Elisabeth

BMW to Staff: Be Afraid, Be Very Afraid graph *Bloomberg Businessweek* no4520 p25 My 1 2017

Carmakers Could Hit That Wall, Too chart color graph *Bloomberg Businessweek* no4500 p20 N 21 2016

Sketching a High-Voltage Future color *Bloomberg Businessweek* no4494 p43 O 10 2016

Surviving a Classic Car Slump color *Bloomberg Businessweek* no4530 p64 Jl 17 2017

Why Mexico's Autoworkers Aren't Prospering color graph *Bloomberg Businessweek* no4521 p12 My 8 2017

Will Bosch Choke on VW's Exhaust? bw color *Bloomberg Businessweek* no4534 p12 Ag 14 2017

Behson, Scott

Complying with Family-Friendly Leave Policies Is Not Enough *Harvard Business Review Digital Articles* p2 Ap 13 2016

Flex Time Doesn't Need to Be an HR Policy *Harvard Business Review Digital Articles* p2 D 4 2014

Just Because You're Happy Doesn't Mean You're Not Burned Out *Harvard Business Review Digital Articles* p2 Jl 13 2015

Work-Life Balance Is Easier When Your Manager Knows How to Assess Performance *Harvard Business Review Digital Articles* p2 Ap 6 2016

Would Amazon's 30-Hour- Week Experiment Work in Your Company? *Harvard Business Review Digital Articles* p2 S 26 2016

Beidao, 1949-

City Gate, Open Up *Publishers Weekly* v264 no9 p86 F 27 2017

Beier, David

The Fight Against Zika Can't Wait for a Vaccine *Harvard Business Review Digital Articles* p2 Ag 18 2016

The World Is Completely Unprepared for a Global Pandemic *Harvard Business Review Digital Articles* p2 Mr 15 2017

BEIER, ELIZABETH

Leaving the Flatiron bw *Publishers Weekly* v264 no35 p132 Ag 28 2017

Beier, Kevin T.

Gating of social reward by oxytocin in the ventral tegmental area color graph *Science* v357 no6358 p1406 S 29 2017

Beige, Howard

Alakazam! C. Suddath color diag *Bloomberg Businessweek* no4495 p56 O 17 2016

Beijing (China)

Factory Finish A. A. SENO *Architectural Record* v205 no9 p110 S 2017

A Soft Touch S. STEPHENS *Architectural Record* v205 no4 p152 Ap 2017

Beil, Christian

Trispecific broadly neutralizing HIV antibodies mediate potent SHIV protection in macaques color graph *Science* v357 no6359 p85 O 6 2017

Beil, Kim

CANDY JERNIGAN color *Art in America* v105 no8 p127 S 2017

Beil, Laura

BAD AIR [Cover story] bw graph map *Science News* v192 no5 p18 S 30 2017

Celebrex's risk to heart debated color *Science News* v190 no12 p6 D 10 2016

CREATURE FROM THE GREEN LAGOON *Texas Monthly* v45 no9 p72 S 2017

DEFLATING CANCER [Cover story] color graph *Science News* v191 no4 p24 Mr 4 2017

'Exercise pill' boosts mice's endurance *Science News* v191 no11 p7 Je 10 2017

Heart problems tied to mom's diet cartoon *Science News* v190 no12 p14 D 10 2016

IS YOUR SUPPLEMENT TOXIC? color *Men's Health* v32 no3 p86 Ap 2017

Mind Your Meds color *Prevention* v69 no2 p74 F 2017

One and Done [Cover story] color graph *Science News* v192 no7 p18 O 28 2017

Poor sleep tied to heart rhythm issue *Science News* v190 no12 p7 D 10 2016

Roller coaster knocks out stones in kidney model color *Science News* v190 no10 p4 N 12 2016

THE STATIN UMBRELLA cartoon diag graph *Science News* v191 no9 p22 My 13 2017

Sugar industry shifted health focus *Science News* v190 no8 p7 O 15 2016

THE TRUE COLORS OF PROBIOTICS color *Women's Health* v14 no6 p140 Jl 2017

Zika virus went undetected for months map *Science News* v191 no12 p12 Je 24 2017

Beinart, Peter

Breaking Faith color *Atlantic* v319 no3 p15 Ap 2017

THE DEMOCRATS' IMMIGRATION MISTAKE color *Atlantic* v320 no1 p60 Jl/Ag 2017

Glenn Beck's Regrets color *Atlantic* v319 no1 p16 Ja/F 2017

Quiet Time *New Republic* v248 no4 p4 Ap 2017

The Rise of the Violent Left color *Atlantic* v320 no2 p13 S 2017

Schumer or Later color *New Republic* v248 no11 p5 N 2017

Being John Malkovich (Film)

50 Things Black Mirror Is Made Of J. SINGAL img *New York* v49 no21 p106 O 17 2016

Being Mary Jane (TV program)

Being Mary Jane T. Stack color *Entertainment Weekly* no1448 p37 Ja 13 2017

THE GIFT OF GAB [Cover story] C. Connors color *Women's Health* v14 no2 p115 Mr 2017

Beirendonck, Walter van

Matters of taste G. Adamson color *Magazine Antiques* v184 no1 p24 Ja/F 2017

Beirut (Lebanon)—Social conditions

A Shrinking Island K. GHATTAS color *Foreign Policy* no226 p67 S/O 2017

Beischel, Cynthia Kuhn

Lunch Ladies C. ROSE *Cincinnati Magazine* v50 no7 p156 Ap 2017

BEISER, VINCE

protection plan *Parents* v91 no10 p136 O 2016

A TREE GROWS IN CHINA color *Mother Jones* v42 no5 p38 S/O 2017

Beisson, Fred

An algal photoenzyme converts fatty acids to hydrocarbons color graph *Science* v357 no6354 p903 S 1 2017

BEITO, DAVID

Roosevelt's War Against the Press bw color *Reason* v49 no1 p54 My 2017

Bejan, Teresa M.

CIVILITY AND ITS LIMITS S. Yenor *Claremont Review of Books* v17 no3 p59 Summ 2017

Bejerano, Gill

Deriving genomic diagnoses without revealing patient genomes chart *Science* v357 no6352 p692 Ag 18 2017

Bekaert, D. V.

Xenon isotopes in 67P/Churyumov-Gerasimenko show that comets contributed to Earth's atmosphere diag *Science* v356 no6342 p1069 Je 9 2017

Bekker, Andrey

Titanium isotopic evidence for felsic crust and plate tectonics 3.5 billion years ago bw color graph *Science* v357 no6357 p1271 S 22 2017

Bekker, Linda-Gail

We still need to beat HIV color *Science* v357 no6349 p335 Jl 28 2017

Bekoff, Marc

Mutt Morality: DOGS KNOW HOW TO HAVE FUN, AND ENCODED IN THEIR ANTICS IS A DEEP UNDERSTANDING OF FAIR PLAY *Psychology Today* v50 no5 p77 S/O 2017

What's Good for the Goose D. MARTINDALE *In These Times* v41 no4 p50 Ap 2017

Bel, Jérôme, 1964-

Jérôme Bel M. Hagan color *Current Biography* v78 no5 p12 My 2017

Bel, Shai

Paneth cells secrete lysozyme via secretory autophagy during bacterial infection of the intestine color diag *Science* v357 no6355 p1047 S 8 2017

Belafonte, Harry

Artists color *Time* v189 no16/17 p40 My 1-8 2017

POWER TRIO G. BLACK bw *Ebony* v72 no3 p138 D 2016/Ja 2017

When Harry Met Late Night J. WALSH bw color *Nation* v304 no7 p20 Mr 6 2017

BELANGER, CHRISTIAN

WAR STORIES bw *Chicago* v66 no11 p26 N 2017

Belay devices

Climbr: Climbing Partner Reviews K. CORRIGAN*Climbing* no356 p32 S/O 2017

THE DEADLY VALLEY A. Flower and M. Oakley bw color *Climbing* no356 p44 S/O 2017

Protect Your Belay, Protect Your Belayer R. COPPOLILLO and M. CHAUVIN color *Climbing* no354 p42 Jl 2017

Belbin, Lee

Publish openly but responsibly color *Science* v357 no6347 p141 Jl 14 2017

Belcher, Cornell

TECH TRENDS CHANGING OUR WORLD color *Black Enterprise* v47 no2 p46 S 2016

Belcher, Tina

Page after page color *Equus* no482 p65 N 2017

Belcher, Wendy Laura

Of Saints and Kings *History Today* v66 no11 p52 N 2016

Belching

That's Outrageous! color *Reader's Digest* v189 no1130 p120 My 2017

Belcourt, Christi—Interviews

Christi Belcourt N. WALKER color *Canadian Geographic* v135 no6 p23 D 2015

BELCOVE, JULIE L.

ANSWERED PRAYERS color *Architectural Digest* v74 no9 p162 S 2017

PAINT THE TOWN color *Architectural Digest* v74 no2 p68 F 2017

Provocative Statements color *Architectural Digest* v74 no2 p22 F 2017

Belcram, Katia

The preprophase band of microtubules controls the robustness of division orientation in plants graph *Science* v356 no6334 p186 Ap 14 2017

Beldea, Catalin

Shadow Play E. MASTROIANNI color *Discover* v38 no1 p96 Ja/F 2017

Belden, Brace

Comments img *New York* v50 no8 p10 Ap 17 2017

The Dirtbag Left's Man in Syria R. Wiedeman img *New York* v50 no7 p40 Ap 3 2017

Belding, Shaun

KICK-ASS CUSTOMER SERVICE: INTERACTION color *Harvard Business Review* v95 no3 p16 My/Je 2017

Belfast (Northern Ireland)—Description & travel

BELFAST N. M. Wulfhart color *Runner's World* v52 no2 p64 Mr 2017

Belfer, Inna

miR-183 cluster scales mechanical pain sensitivity by regulating basal and neuropathic pain genes diag graph *Science* v356 no6343 p1168 Je 16 2017

Belfiore, Andrea

An accreting pulsar with extreme properties drives an ultraluminous x-ray source in NGC 5907 bibl chart graph *Science* v355 no6327 p817 F 24 2017

Belfiore, Michael

Bringing CAD To the Cloud *Bloomberg Businessweek* no4511 p30 F 13 2017

Education Robot Fight Club color *Bloomberg Businessweek* no4505 p35 D 26 2016

Gryphon Router bw color *Bloomberg Businessweek* no4499 p51 N 14 2016

Handheld 3D Mapper color *Bloomberg Businessweek* no4514 p37 Mr 13 2017

Innovation bw color *Bloomberg Businessweek* no4521 p35 My 8 2017

Innovation color *Bloomberg Businessweek* no4505 p37 D 26 2016

Innovation color *Bloomberg Businessweek* no4511 p33 F 13 2017

Innovation: Needle-Free Injections color *Bloomberg Businessweek* no4494 p37 O 10 2016

Innovation: Spray-On Touchpad color *Bloomberg Businessweek* no4532 p23 Jl 31 2017

Innovation Synthetic Cartilage bw color diag *Bloomberg Businessweek* no4518 p37 Ap 10 2017

Innovation: Tiny Blood Pump color *Bloomberg Businessweek* no4540 p29 O 2 2017

Innovation Yardbot color *Bloomberg Businessweek* no4504 p33 D 19 2016

Man vs. Machine: Architecture cartoon *Bloomberg Businessweek* no4539 p25 S 25 2017

Metal Devices, in Miniature bw *Scientific American* v316 no3 p16 Mr 2017

Needle Camera bw color *Bloomberg Businessweek* no4512 p35 F 20 2017

A New Leader in the Suborbital Space Race color *Bloomberg Businessweek* no4497 p35 O 31 2016

Pocket DSLR bw color *Bloomberg Businessweek* no4508 p31 Ja 23 2017

Supersensor color *Bloomberg Businessweek* no4538 p25 S 18 2017

Belfor Holdings Inc.

SHELDON YELLEN'S BIG SECRET D. ALEXANDER bw color map *Forbes* v199 no2 p80 F 28 2017

Belfort, Jordan

Way of the Wolf: Master the Art of Persuasion and Build Massive Wealth color *Publishers Weekly* v264 no32 p63 Ag 7 2017

Belfrey, Dianne

ADRIFT D. BELFREY cartoon color *New Yorker* v92 no36 p20

N 7 2016

Belgard (Company)

CURB APPEAL bw color *Good Housekeeping* v264 no5 p90 My 2017

Belichick, Bill, 1952-

Pats' Solutions C. CALDWELL color *Weekly Standard* v22 no21 p16 F 6 2017

A Real Winner G. NORMAN *Weekly Standard* v22 no6 p26 O 17 2016

Belief & doubt

See also

Credibility of the press

Superstition

Believe It J. LOGAN *USA Today Magazine* v145 no2864 p31 My 2017

The Courage of His Convictions B. Doyle color *U.S. Catholic* v82 no11 p23 N 2017

Great Leaders Know They're Not Perfect R. Carucci *Harvard Business Review Digital Articles* p2 D 4 2015

Kids' learning curve not so smooth B. BOWER *Science News* v190 no11 p6 N 26 2016

My Dirty Little Secret: I'm Happy A. Libers and S. G. Levy color *Glamour* v114 no12 p156 D 2016

My son's organ donation taught me death is not the last word E. Gregory il *America* v216 no13 p40 Je 12 2017

Network science on belief system dynamics under logic constraints N. E. Friedkin, A. V. Proskurnikov et al bibl diag graph *Science* v354 no6310 p321 O 21 2016

The Others W. Morris *New York Times Magazine* p15 N 20 2016

SELF, CENTERED E. GILBERT color *O, The Oprah Magazine* p39 S 2017

What Is Truth, Anyway? M. Shermer color *Scientific American* v316 no4 p78 Ap 2017

Why I know but don't believe C. T. Butts bibl diag *Science* v354 no6310 p286 O 21 2016

Why We Believe--Long After We Shouldn't C. TAVRIS and E. ARONSON *Skeptical Inquirer* v41 no2 p51 Mr/Ap 2017

Belisle, Rebecca A.

Perovskite-perovskite tandem photovoltaics with optimized band gaps bibl chart graph *Science* v354 no6314 p861 N 18 2016

Belk, Lisa—Awards

Patents and Awards *Science & Technology Review* p23 Ja/F 2017

Belkhadir, Youssef

The receptor kinase FER is a RALF-regulated scaffold controlling plant immune signaling graph *Science* v355 no6322 p287 Ja 20 2017

Root diffusion barrier control by a vasculature-derived peptide binding to the SGN3 receptor color *Science* v355 no6322 p280 Ja 20 2017

Belkin International Inc.

BELKIN LIGHTNING AUDIO + CHARGE ROCKSTAR ADAPTER L. YAMSHON color *Macworld - Digital Edition* v33 no11 p53 N 2016

Belko Experiment, The (Film)

The Belko Experiment D. Franich color *Entertainment Weekly* no1457/1458 p75 Mr 17 2017

NOW PLAYING color *Entertainment Weekly* no1462 p50 Ap 21 2017

Belkora, Jeff

Patients Make Better Medical Choices with Coaching *Harvard Business Review Digital Articles* p2 N 11 2016

Bell, Albert A.

Fortune's Fool: A Sixth Case from the Notebooks of Pliny the Younger *Publishers Weekly* v264 no7 p53 F 13 2017

Bell, Alexander Graham, 1847-1922

A Look at 2017, From 1917 A. G. Bell bw color *National Geographic* v231 no6 p20 Je 2017

Bell, Aran—Interviews

ARAN BELL *Dance Spirit* v21 no3 p37 Mr 2017

Bell, Baxter

practice safely color *Yoga Journal* p16 2017 SpecialIssue

Bell, Charles C.

Click chemistry enables preclinical evaluation of targeted epigenetic therapies diag *Science* v356 no6345 p1397 Je 30 2017

Bell, Christine

Grievance *Publishers Weekly* v264 no21 p74 My 22 2017

Bell, Christopher M.

Winston's Folly A. ROBERTS bw *Weekly Standard* v22 no41 p27 Jl 3 2017

BELL, DANIEL A.

Western Critics of China Need to Avoid a Colonial Mindset *NPQ: New Perspectives Quarterly* v33 no4 p23 O 2016

BELL, DAVID A.

HAITI'S JACOBIN color *Nation* v33 no21 p40 N 21 2016

Bell, Donald

Lineage-dependent spatial and functional organization of the mammalian enteric nervous system color graph *Science* v356 no6339 p722 My 19 2017

Bell, Duncan, 1976-

Reordering the World: Essays on Liberalism and Empire G. J. Ikenberry *Foreign Affairs* v95 no6 p172 N/D 2016

Bell, Edward

CASSINI AT SATURN color *Scientific American* v317 no4 p78 O 2017

Bell, Emily

The Facebook rescue that wasn't color graph *Columbia Journalism Review* v56 no1 p19 Spr 2017

Paying for Our Attention *New York Times Book Review* p13 N 13 2016

The tech/editorial culture clash cartoon *Columbia Journalism Review* p24 Fall/Wint 2016

Bell, Gabrielle

Mothers and Daughters G. BELLO color *Publishers Weekly* v264 no20 p29 My 15 2017

Bell, Greg

Good Cybersecurity Doesn't Try to Prevent Every Attack *Harvard Business Review Digital Articles* p2 O 25 2016

Bell, Jerri

It's My Country Too: Women's Military Stories from the American Revolution to Afghanistan *Publishers Weekly* v264 no18 p48 My 1 2017

Bell, Jillian

SLAY, GIRL, SLAY J. Black color *Esquire* p29 Je/Jl 2017

Bell, Johann D.

Biodiversity redistribution under climate change: Impacts on ecosystems and human well-being color *Science* v355 no6332 p1389 Mr 31 2017

Bell, Jordan

ALL-GLUE TEAM S. Davis color *Sports Illustrated* v126 no8 p61 Mr 20 2017

Bell, Joshua, 1967-

Armed & Musical C. Wren color *Commonweal* v144 no6 p22 Mr 24 2017

Bell, Julian

The Flash of the Blade color *New York Review of Books* v64 no11 p4 Je 22 2017

Looking for 'Life Itself' [Cover story] color *New York Review of Books* v64 no8 p42 My 11 2017

The Perennial Student color *New York Review of Books* v64 no12 p23 Jl 13 2017

Turner: High Ambition for Deep Truth color *New York Review of Books* v63 no18 p8 N 24 2016

Bell, Julie

People *Christian Century* v134 no14 p19 Jl 5 2017

Bell, Katherine

The CEO of Children's National Health System on Leadership, Innovation, and Delivering Specialized Care *Harvard Business Review Digital Articles* p1 Je 22 2017

The Management Ideas That Mattered Most in 2016 *Harvard Business Review Digital Articles* p2 D 22 2016

Bell, Kelly

The On-Demand Economy Is Growing, and Not Just for the Young and Wealthy *Harvard Business Review Digital Articles* p2 Ap 14 2016

THE RIVER RAN RED bw color map *Military History* v34 no5 p62 Ja 2018

WEREWOLVES OF AACHEN bw color *Military History* v34 no2 p22 Jl 2017

Bell, Kimberly

The Importance of Being Scandalous: A Tale of Two Sisters, Book 1 *Publishers Weekly* v264 no26 p162 Je 26 2017

Bell, Kirsty

PART TO WHOLE bw color *Art in America* v104 no10 p122 N 2016

Bell, Kristen, 1980-
family kitchen *Parents* v91 no11 p118 N 2016
THE GOOD PLACE BREAKS BAD D. Snierson color *Entertainment Weekly* no1472 p14 Je 30 2017
THE GOOD PLACE J. Russell *TV Guide* v65 no39 p47 S 18 2017
HEAVEN HELP US J. McDERMOT color *America* v215 no14 p37 N 7 2016
a note from Kristen *Parents* v91 no11 p8 N 2016
Points to Ponder *Reader's Digest* v188 no1126 p23 D 2016/Ja 2017
teaching little ones to give *Parents* v91 no11 p48 N 2016

Bell, Kristen, 1980----Interviews
Chill lessons from Kristen Bell [Cover story] J. PRESSLER color *Redbook* p104 O 2017
HOUSE OF LIES I. Rudolph *TV Guide* v64 no15 p50 Ap 4 2016

Bell, Lake, 1979-
Land O' Lake M. WAKIM *Los Angeles Magazine* v62 no9 p62 S 2017
A WEEK OF Awesome Outfits L. BELL color *Good Housekeeping* v265 no3 p36 S 2017

Bell, Le'Veon
BELL EPOCH A. Murphy color *Sports Illustrated* v126 no3 p30 Ja 23 2017

BELL, MADISON SMARTT
THE IMPENDING CRISIS *Nation* v305 no4 p36 Ag 14 2017

Bell, Mary H.
ask the experts color *Dressage Today* v23 no6 p64 F 2017

Bell, Matt
The Boys in the Band: Flashpoints of Cinema, History, and Queer Politics ed M. BETANCOURT *Film Quarterly* v71 no1 p118 Fall 2017
The Shape She's Shifting *New York Times Book Review* p11 O 2 2016

Bell, Matthew
MISSING THE POETRY J. M. Ellis *Claremont Review of Books* v16 no4 p73 Fall 2016

Bell, Otto
The Eagle Huntress J. Nolfi color *Entertainment Weekly* no1438 p47 N 4 2016

BELL, RYAN
HOW POVERTY KILLS wondeR and what we can do about it *Humanist* v77 no5 p16 S/O 2017

Bell, Scott C.
Emergence and spread of a human-transmissible multidrug-resistant nontuberculous mycobacterium bibl diag graph *Science* v354 no6313 p751 N 11 2016

Bell, Vanessa, 1879-1961
English Visionary D. GREEN color *Weekly Standard* v22 no32 p41 My 1 2017

Bell, W. Kamau
THE AGITATOR N. PARSI color *Chicago* v66 no5 p48 My 2017
Humor as It's Meant to Be Heard: In W. Kamau Bell's memoir, timing is everything N. Orr *New York Times Book Review* p20 My 21 2017
I NEED A (BLACK) HERO bw *Wired* v25 no6 p15 Je 2017

Bell Helicopter Textron Inc.
BELL FCX CONCEPT OFFERS A GLIMPSE OF THE FUTURE color *Flying* v144 no5 p14 My 2017

Bell Sports Inc.
BELL PRO STAR HELMET B. Adams color *Cycle World* v56 no3 p22 Ap 2017

Bella, Federico
Improving efficiency and stability of perovskite solar cells with photocurable fluoropolymers bibl chart graph *Science* v354 no6309 p203 O 14 2016

Bella, Peter
TALK TO US color graph *Chicago* v66 no11 p16 N 2017

Bella, Timothy
Purple Drank, Corpotate Bank color *Bloomberg Businessweek* no4514 p60 Mr 13 2017

Bella: An American Tall Tale (Theatrical production)
THE THEATRE *New Yorker* v93 no14 p10 My 22 2017
Westward Journey M. S. Eddy *Stage Directions* v29 no11 p36 N 2016

Bella Coola (North American people)
BETTER WITH BEAVERS R. Rich color *Earth Island Journal* v32 no1 p30 Spr 2017

Bella Donna (Music)
WHAT THE HEART SAYS A. PETRUSICH bw cartoon *New Yorker* v92 no39 p82 N 28 2016

BELLAFANTE, GINIA
Fighting the Power Broker *New York Times Book Review* p17 O 9 2016
The Way We Were: The creator of the blog 'Jeremiah's Vanishing New York' tracks hyper-gentrification and its discontents *New York Times Book Review* p15 O 1 2017

Bellamy, Francis, 1855-1931
The Pledge at 125 B. BROWN *New York Times Upfront* v149 no9 p20 F 20 2017

Bellamy, Jay
A Stalwart of Stalwarts *Prologue* v48 no3 p36 Fall 2016
The Zimmermann *Prologue* v48 no4 p18 Wint 2016

BELLAMY, SEAMUS
Bose Soundlink Revolve+: An all-around excellent indoor/outdoor Bluetooth speaker color *Macworld - Digital Edition* v34 no9 p93 S 2017
CANON PIXMA iP110: THIS INKJET PRINTER'S PORTABILITY COMES AT A PRICE color *Macworld - Digital Edition* v34 no4 p19 My 2017
DJI SPARK: A FANTASTIC, AFFORDABLE DRONE THAT DEMANDS EXPENSIVE EXTRAS color *Macworld - Digital Edition* v34 no11 p73 N 2017
GAEMS M155 PERFORMANCE MONITOR: PORTABLE DISPLAY SHOWS ITS PROMISE—AND FAULTS color graph *Macworld - Digital Edition* p19 Je 13 2017
LIFEPROOF NÜÜD FOR THE 9.7-INCH iPAD PRO color *Macworld - Digital Edition* p37 Mr 2017
TORMENT: TIDES OF NUMENERA: ONE OF THE BEST BOOKS YOU'LL EVER PLAY color *Macworld - Digital Edition* p26 Je 13 2017
URBAN ARMOR GEAR RUGGED CASE: AN EXCELLENT TOUGH CASE FOR YOUR DELICATE FLOWER OF A LAPTOP color *Macworld - Digital Edition* v34 no9 p33 S 2017
URBAN ARMOR GEAR RUGGED CASE color *Macworld - Digital Edition* v34 no8 p49 Ag 2017
ZAGG RUGGED BOOK KEYBOARD CASE FOR THE iPAD PRO color *Macworld - Digital Edition* v33 no11 p54 N 2016

Belle, Camilla
Dior and Me J. Davison and S. Iglehart bw color *Glamour* no8 p66 Ag 2017

Belle, John, 1932-2016
Obituary: John Belle, 1932-2016 F. A. BERNSTEIN *Architectural Record* v204 no10 p27 O 2016

Belle, Kimberly
The Marriage Lie *Publishers Weekly* v263 no41 p53 O 10 2016

Bellegarde, Perry—Interviews
THE INTERVIEW N. MACDONALD color *Maclean's* v130 no6 p24 Jl 2017

Bellesi, Michele
Ultrastructural evidence for synaptic scaling across the wake/sleep cycle bibl diag graph *Science* v355 no6324 p507 F 3 2017

Bellettini, Alisa Marie
ALISA BELLETTINI W. MORRIS *New York Times Magazine* p52 D 25 2016

Bellevue (Neb.)
Flock to Fontenelle D. FARNSWORTH-LIVINGSTON bw color *Nebraska Life* v21 no6 p72 N/D 2017
Winter fun heats up in Bellevue S. W. Kansteiner color *Nebraska Life* v21 no1 p66 Ja/F 2017

Bellevue Hospital
Take Me to Bellevue J. Neugeboren color *New York Review of Books* v64 no1 p19 Ja 19 2017

Bellezza, Silvia
Research: Why Americans Are So Impressed by Busyness *Harvard Business Review Digital Articles* p2 D 15 2016
Why We Are So Careless with the Things We Own *Harvard Business Review Digital Articles* p2 D 2 2016

Bellido, J. A.
Observation of a large-scale anisotropy in the arrival directions of cosmic rays above 8×10^{18} eV *Science* v357 no6357 p1266

S 22 2017

Bellingham Marine (Company)

WHAT'S NEW *Sea Magazine* v109 no8 pCA-12 Ag 2017

Bellingrath, Walter

ETC M. Cameran color *New Orleans Magazine* v51 no9 p135 Jl 2017

Bellini, Andrea

Relativistic deflection of background starlight measures the mass of a nearby white dwarf star chart color graph *Science* v356 no6342 p1046 Je 9 2017

Bellini, Vincenzo, 1801-1835

Norma-tivity N. M. GALLAGHER color *Weekly Standard* v23 no6 p39 O 16 2017

SHOWS OF FORCE A. ROSS cartoon *New Yorker* v93 no32 p94 O 16 2017

Bellis, Gil

Dispersals and genetic adaptation of Bantu-speaking populations in Africa and North America diag *Science* v356 no6337 p543 My 5 2017

Bellisario, Troian, 1986-

THE TELEVISION INDUSTRY ADVOCACY AWARDS, LOS ANGELES *TV Guide* v65 no41 p2 O 2 2017

Bellmann, Karin

ASSEMBLE color *Art in America* p133 O 2017

DANIEL RICHTER color *Art in America* v105 no5 p139 My 2017

NATHALIE DU PASQUIER color *Art in America* v104 no10 p163 N 2016

Secession *Art in America* v105 no1 p92 Ja 2017

Bellmar, Rob

4 Ways to Make Conference Calls Less Terrible *Harvard Business Review Digital Articles* p2 Ja 28 2015

BELLO, GRACE

Mothers and Daughters color *Publishers Weekly* v264 no20 p29 My 15 2017

Bello, Maria, 1967-—Interviews

NCIS A. D'Arminio *TV Guide* v65 no43 p32 O 16 2017

Bellon, Klaus

38 REASONS TO GO GA-GA FOR THE TOUR DE FRANCE color *Bicycling* v58 no7 p24 Ag 2017

Belloni, Matthew

THE MOST TRUSTED NAME IN NEWS bw color *Popular Mechanics* p52 O 2017

Bellos, Alex

Here's Why Seven Is Most Likely Your Favorite Number B. SPECKTOR color *Reader's Digest* v190 no1133 p134 S 2017

Bellos, David

Something Grander Than a Novel P. Brooks color *New York Review of Books* v64 no12 p44 Jl 13 2017

Songs From the Barricades T. GREY *New York Times Book Review* p13 Ap 2 2017

Bellows, George, 1882-1925

ART color *New Yorker* v93 no28 p6 S 18 2017

BELLOWS, LAYLA

CANCER SCANNERS *Atlanta* v56 no10 p22 F 2017

A LEAGUE OF YOUR OWN *Atlanta* v56 no11 p102 Mr 2017

Bellprat, Omar

Using climate models to estimate the quality of global observational data sets bibl graph *Science* v354 no6311 p452 O 28 2016

Bells

Ring a Bell? *Arizona Highways* v93 no4 p56 Ap 2017

Bells For The South Side (Music)

Bells For The South Side B. Bambarger color *Downbeat* v84 no10 p65 O 2017

Bells—History

THE MUSIC OF TIME NO 1: FOR WHOM THE BELLS TOLL: In Renaissance Florence, church and civic bells frequently rang out across the city's crowded soundscape. Their calls were far from impartial A. Lee *History Today* v67 no7 p86 Jl 2017

Bellstrom, Kristen

100 BEST COMPANIES TO WORK FOR 2017 [Cover story] color diag map *Fortune* v175 no4 p79 Mr 15 2017

THE 2017 Fortune Crystal Ball color diag *Fortune* v174 no7 p11 D 1 2016

APPLE REBOOTS IN CHINA color *Fortune* v176 no5 p106 O 1 2017

THE BLACK CEILING color *Fortune* v176 no5 p94 O 1 2017

BOXED IN color diag *Fortune* v176 no5 p86 O 1 2017

Fortune on the Global Stage color *Fortune* v176 no1 p18 Jl 1 2017

MOST POWERFUL WOMEN color *Fortune* v176 no5 p54 O 1 2017

MOST POWERFUL WOMEN INTERNATIONAL color *Fortune* v176 no5 p111 O 1 2017

THE QUEEN OF POP [Cover story] color diag *Fortune* v176 no5 p70 O 1 2017

TECH TAKEOVER IN TOYLAND color diag *Fortune* v176 no5 p76 O 1 2017

Bellucci, G.

Seasonal exposure of carbon dioxide ice on the nucleus of comet 67P/Churyumov-Gerasimenko bibl bw graph *Science* v354 no6319 p1563 D 23 2016

Bellucci, Monica, 1964-

Kimono A-Go-Go E. Wilson color *InStyle* v24 no10 p88 O 2017

Belmabkhout, Youssef

Hydrolytically stable fluorinated metal-organic frameworks for energy-efficient dehydration diag *Science* v356 no6339 p731 My 19 2017

Belniak, Alan

Expanding Your Social Footprint color *Black Enterprise* v47 no2 p16 S 2016

Belonging (Social psychology)

Creating Belonging color *Alternatives Journal (AJ) - Canada's Environmental Voice* v42 no3 p72 2016

Dare to Belong color *Alternatives Journal (AJ) - Canada's Environmental Voice* v42 no3 p18 2016

Diversity Efforts Fall Short Unless Employees Feel That They Belong P. Wadors *Harvard Business Review Digital Articles* p2 Ag 10 2016

For the Common Good cartoon diag graph *Alternatives Journal (AJ) - Canada's Environmental Voice* v42 no3 p20 2016

Our Emotional Attachment to Local Currencies C. de Anca *Harvard Business Review Digital Articles* p2 N 5 2014

State of Belonging T. Barton color diag *Alternatives Journal (AJ) - Canada's Environmental Voice* v42 no3 p42 2016

BELOTE, R. TRAVIS

Mapping Conservation Strategies under a Changing Climate *BioScience* v67 no6 p494 Je 2017

Belott, Brian—Exhibitions

Brian Belott B. POWERS color *ARTnews* v115 no3 p24 Fall 2016

Belotti, Amy

Glimpses of Home *American Scholar* v86 no4 p17 Aut 2017

BELOU, REBECCA

Grant-Writing Bootcamp: An Intervention to Enhance the Research Capacity of Academic Women in STEM *BioScience* v67 no7 p638 Jl 2017

Beloufa, Neil

OCCIDENTAL J. Romney color *Film Comment* v53 no2 p22 Mr/Ap 2017

Belov, V.

Observation of coherent elastic neutrino-nucleus scattering diag *Science* v357 no6356 p1123 S 15 2017

Belsky, Daniel—Interviews

YOUR SUCCESS IS SHAPED BY YOUR GENES A. Beard *Harvard Business Review* v95 no1 p34 Ja/F 2017

Belt buckles

What Should I Do With My Father's Nazi Keepsake? K. A. Appiah *New York Times Magazine* p28 Mr 26 2017

Belth, Alex

2017 MaVeRicks OF Style bw color *Esquire* p81 S 2017

DIFFICULT MEN color *Esquire* p38 O 2017

Ichiro SUZUKI bw *Esquire* p70 Ap 2017

John McENROE color *Esquire* p104 Ag 2017

THE MAVERICKS OF HOLLYWOOD 2017 bw color *Esquire* v167 no2 p89 Mr 2017

MYSTERY MAN color *Esquire* p20 Ag 2017

NEW YORK GIANT color *Esquire* p30 O 2017

NO FILTER bw color *Esquire* p26 N 2017

BELTON, KEITH B.

A Second Act for Risk-Based Chemicals Regulation *Issues in Science & Technology* v33 no1 p77 Fall 2016

Beltramone, Natalia

A disynaptic feedback network activated by experience promotes the integration of new granule cells bibl graph *Science* v354 no6311 p459 O 28 2016

Beltran, Himisha

SOX2 promotes lineage plasticity and antiandrogen resistance in TP53- and RB1-deficient prostate cancer bibl graph *Science* v355 no6320 p1 Ja 6 2017

Beltrao, Pedro

Evolution of protein phosphorylation across 18 fungal species bibl graph *Science* v354 no6309 p229 O 14 2016

Beltre, Adrian, 1979-

Leading Off color *Sports Illustrated* v127 no4 p6 Ag 7 2017

Belts & belting

Tack Room color *Practical Horseman* v45 no10 p69 O 2017

Belts & belting—Evaluation

Into the Wild color *Glamour* no8 p130 Ag 2017

Tack Room color *Practical Horseman* v45 no4 p68 Ap 2017

Belts (Clothing)

black POWER O. J. WILLIAMS color *Ebony* v72/73 no12/1 p44 O/N 2017

The Get-It Guide *Glamour* v115 no1 p98 Ja 2017

Get the Look O. J. WILLIAMS color *Ebony* v72 no11 p46 S 2017

In FORMATION *Interview* v46 no10 p64 D 2016/Ja 2017

Matchbox Car Belt! J. SCHADEWALD chart color diag *Popular Mechanics* p104 Mr 2017

Belts (Clothing)—Evaluation

Bathleisure: It's a Thing N. Silverstein and J. Harman color *Glamour* v115 no1 p16 Ja 2017

Buckle Up E. Wilson color *InStyle* v24 no2 p56 F 2017

THE GOODS *Atlanta* v57 no5 p37 S 2017

GREAT BUYS UNDER $100 color *O, The Oprah Magazine* p52 Ap 2017

PATROL BELT J. B. SNOW color *Outdoor Life* v224 no1 pR5 D 2016/Ja 2017

PLAY WITH YOUR clothes [Cover story] color *Redbook* p68 Ap 2017

Skins Game color *Esquire* v166 no5 p62 D 2016/Ja 2017

SO YOU'RE NOT INTO LEATHER? color *Esquire* p50 My 2017

Statement Belts R. WALDMAN, M. HOLGATE et al color *Vogue* v207 no9 p382 S 2017

THE TIP SHEET M. Hainey, N. Sullivan color *Esquire* p36 Ag 2017

WEIGHING In E. ELWICK color *Vogue* v207 no3 p500 Mr 2017

WHERE TO BUY color *Harper's Bazaar* no3652 p248 Ap 2017

Beltways—Washington (D.C.)

DIARY OF A BELTWAY HIKE *Washingtonian Magazine* v52 no12 p61 S 2017

A WALK AROUND THE BEAT BELTWAY: THE HIGHWAY RINGING WASHINGTON IS G4 MILES LONG. NO ONE EVER CONFUSED IT WITH A SCENIC NATURE TRAIL. BUT ON A SIX-DAY HIKE ALONG ITS PERIPHERY, A BDRN AND BRED WASHINGTONIAN FOUND MOMENTS OF SURPRISING BEAUTY,... J. HIMMELMAN *Washingtonian Magazine* v52 no12 p58 S 2017

Belyaev, Spartak Timofeevich

Spartak Timofeevich Belyaev A. Barabanov and V. Zelevinsky *Physics Today* v70 no6 p72 Je 2017

Bemas (Architecture)

GLOSSARY *History Today* v67 no8 p110 Ag 2017

Bement, Jerry

A Family Affair color *Log Home Living* v33 no9 p20 D 2016

BEMROSE, JOHN

WENJACK color *Maclean's* v129 no43 p60 O 31 2016

Ben l'Oncle Soul (Performer)

Under My Skin S. J. O'Connell color *Downbeat* v84 no3 p64 Mr 2017

Ben Nye Co. Inc.

Ben Nye Makeup Celebrates 50th Anniversary *Stage Directions* v30 no3 p59 Mr 2017

Benalcazar, Wladimir A.

Quantized electric multipole insulators bw color graph *Science* v357 no6346 p61 Jl 7 2017

Benally, Kalvin

Flight Club C. YU color *Runner's World* v52 no4 p48 My 2017

BENANAV, MICHAEL

THE TIGER WATCHERS *Sierra* v102 no4 p36 Jl/Ag 2017

Benaroch, Philippe

Mapping the human DC lineage through the integration of high-dimensional techniques diag *Science* v356 no6342 p1044 Je 9 2017

Benartzi, Shlomo

Retirement Planning Needs a Better UX *Harvard Business Review Digital Articles* p2 My 1 2015

Benavidez, Roy P., 1935-1998

War Heroes bw cartoon color *American Cowboy* p30 LEGENDS OF TEXAS Special Issue 2017

Benazzo, Andrea

Chimpanzee genomic diversity reveals ancient admixture with bonobos bibl diag graph map *Science* v354 no6311 p477 O 28 2016

Benbarak, Nadav

Every Company Needs a Growth Manager *Harvard Business Review Digital Articles* p2 F 19 2016

Bence, Evelyn

There are places I'll remember color *U.S. Catholic* v82 no7 p23 Jl 2017

Bench design & construction

Bench Mark H. MARTIN bw color *Architectural Digest* no6 p30 Je 1 2017

Bench press

All Gain, No Pain [Cover story] T. BUMGARDNER color *Men's Health* v32 no4 p50 My 2017

Bench Your Best J. Gilpatrick chart color *Men's Health* v32 no1 p52 Ja/F 2017

Call a Workout Audible cartoon chart color *Men's Health* v32 no8 p52 O 2017

THE (NEXT) 10 BEST CHEST EXERCISES M. BERG color *Muscle & Performance* v9 no8 p44 Ag 2017

Benches

Sitting Pretty *Indianapolis Monthly* v12 no40 p31 Ag 2017

Benches—Evaluation

Snow Business color *Log Home Living* v34 no1 p26 F 2017

Benchmarking (Management)

Learning New Things Means Getting Up From Your Desk B. Power *Harvard Business Review Digital Articles* p2 N 27 2014

Parks, Recreation and Resilience R. Richardson and J. Cox *Parks & Recreation* v51 no12 p26 D 2016

Smart Benchmarking Starts with Knowing Whom to Compare Yourself To R. Valdes-Perez *Harvard Business Review Digital Articles* p2 O 30 2015

The Stretch Goal Paradox S. B. SITKIN, C. C. MILLER et al color diag il img *Harvard Business Review* v95 no1 p92 Ja/F 2017

Bencic, Belinda

Belinda Bencic's Running Backhand L. ROLLEY bw chart color *Tennis* v53 no2 p64 Mr/Ap 2017

Bencie, Luke

Everyday Business Travelers Are Easy Targets for Espionage *Harvard Business Review Digital Articles* p2 N 10 2015

How an Airplane Laptop Ban Would Expose Company Data to Espionage *Harvard Business Review Digital Articles* p2 My 25 2017

Why You Really Need to Stop Using Public Wi-Fi *Harvard Business Review Digital Articles* p2 My 3 2017

Ben-David, Eyal

A genetic signature of the evolution of loss of flight in the Galapagos cormorant color diag *Science* v356 no6341 p921 Je 1 2017

A maternal-effect selfish genetic element in Caenorhabditis elegans diag *Science* v356 no6342 p1051 Je 9 2017

Ben-David, Roi

Wild emmer genome architecture and diversity elucidate wheat evolution and domestication color *Science* v357 no6346 p93 Jl 7 2017

Bender, Bryan

What Is Russia's Military Up To? *Hoover Digest: Research & Opinion on Public Policy* no4 p119 Fall 2016

Bender, Mark

The Eclipse Megamovie Project bw color *Sky & Telescope* v134 no2 p20 Ag 2017

WATCH A TOTAL SOLAR ECLIPSE: GONE IN A FLASH color *Wired* v25 no8 p30 Ag 2017

Bender, Matthias

Ruthenium-catalyzed insertion of adjacent diol carbon atoms into C-C bonds: Entry to type II polyketides diag *Science* v357 no6353 p779 Ag 25 2017

Bender, Mike
JUST HIT! color *Golf Magazine* v59 no2 p52 F 2017

Bender, Steve
AROUND THE GARDEN color map *Southern Living* v51 no11 p54 N 2016
AROUND THE GARDEN color *Southern Living* v52 no10 p50 O 2017
AROUND THE GARDEN color *Southern Living* v52 no3 p42 Mr 2017
AROUND THE GARDEN color *Southern Living* v52 no7 p36 Jl 2017
ask THE GRUMPY GARDENER color *Southern Living* v51 no12 p60 D 2016
Best Christmas Tree Ever color *Southern Living* v51 no12 p48 D 2016
The Best New Plants for 2017 color *Southern Living* v52 no1 p34 Ja 2017
THE GRUMPY GARDEN color *Southern Living* v52 no3 p38 Mr 2017
THE GRUMPY GARDENER color *Southern Living* v52 no10 p46 O 2017
THE GRUMPY GARDENER color *Southern Living* v52 no4 p48 Ap 2017
THE GRUMPY GARDENER color *Southern Living* v52 no7 p31 Jl 2017
THE GRUMPY GARDENER'S Guide to Hydrangeas color *Southern Living* v52 no5 p106 My 2017
Roll Out the Green Carpet color *Southern Living* v51 no11 p38 N 2016
Waterfalls of Mums color *Southern Living* v52 no10 p36 O 2017

Bendiksen, Jonas
MESSIAH COMPLEX color *National Geographic* v232 no2 p82 Ag 2017

Bendis, Debra
The Blood of Emmett Till *Christian Century* v134 no12 p36 Je 7 2017
Inviting controversy color *Christian Century* v134 no15 p10 Jl 19 2017

Bendix, Will
In the Wind bw color *Surfing Magazine* v53 no3 p50 Mr 2017
THE LAGOSIAN OASIS color *Surfer* v58 no5 p54 S 2017

Bendoris, Matt
Wicked Leaks *Publishers Weekly* v264 no30 p42 Jl 24 2017

Bendroth, Margaret
The Many Captivities of Esther Wheelwright *Christian Century* v134 no7 p40 Mr 29 2017

Benduhn, Francois
Global atmospheric particle formation from CERN CLOUD measurements bibl graph map *Science* v354 no6316 p1119 D 2 2016

Benecke, Norbert
Ancient genomic changes associated with domestication of the horse color diag *Science* v356 no6336 p442 Ap 28 2017

Benedict, C.
Sex matters: Report experimenter gender *Science* v356 no6341 p916 Je 1 2017

Benedict, Helen
Women and WAR W. SMITH color *Publishers Weekly* v264 no33 p42 Ag 14 2017

Benedict, Saint, Abbot of Monte Cassino
c. 540: Monte Cassino *Lapham's Quarterly* v10 no1 p85 Wint 2017

Benedictines
Life Among the Monks: As archivists at Augustana University sift through Blue Cloud Abbey's treasured photo collection, we learn more about how the Benedictines lived and worked J. ANDREWS *South Dakota Magazine* v33 no2 p56 Jl/Ag 2017

Benedict XVI, Pope, 1927-
JAMES CARROLL'S RATZINGER P. Baumann *Commonweal* v144 no1 p8 Ja 6 2017
Last Testament: In His Own Words J. M. Sweeney *Christian Century* v134 no5 p40 Mr 1 2017

Benedikt, Joseph von
THE ULTIMATE DEER AR color *Field & Stream* v122 no6 p28 N 2017

Benediktsson, Bjarni

TAKING COMMAND E. S. ARNARSÓTTIR *Iceland Review* v55 no2 p52 Mr/Ap 2017
Timeline of Events *Iceland Review* v55 no1 p74 Ja/F 2017

Beneficiaries
THE BENEFICIARY *Atlanta* v56 no7 p14 N 2016

BENEFIELD, NATHAN
Turning Pennsylvania color *Weekly Standard* v22 no13 p22 D 5 2016

Benefit corporations (Business structure)
Why Companies Are Becoming B Corporations S. Kim, M. J. Karlesky et al *Harvard Business Review Digital Articles* p2 Je 17 2016

Benefit Cosmetics LLC
Ace Your FOUNDATION K. FOSTER color *Seventeen* v76 no5 p40 S 2017

Benefit parties
2017 WASHINGURAL INAUGURAL BALL color *Washingtonian Magazine* v52 no7 p28 Ap 2017
THE NEW BRUNCH S. Lyon cartoon *New Yorker* v93 no6 p17 Mr 27 2017

Benefit performances
The Battle of Standing Rock A. GREENE color *Rolling Stone* no1275 p23 D 1 2016
MANCHESTER UNITED A. Bacle color *Entertainment Weekly* no1470 p11 Je 16 2017
A Prom for My Mom M. Sherman color *Money* v46 no5 p80 Je 2017

Benefunder Inc.
Ambitious web fundraising startup fails to meet big goals M. Harris *Science* v354 no6312 p534 N 4 2016

Benelli, Matteo
SOX2 promotes lineage plasticity and antiandrogen resistance in TP53- and RB1-deficient prostate cancer bibl graph *Science* v355 no6320 p1 Ja 6 2017

Benelli Armi SpA
OVER UNDER AND IN-BETWEEN A. McKEAN color *Outdoor Life* v224 no5 p90 Je/Jl 2017

Benenson, A. E.
MORE OF LESS color diag *Art in America* v105 no3 p100 Mr 2017

Beneteau Group (Company)
BENETEAU GRAN TURISMO 40 Z. PROCHAZKA *Sea Magazine* v109 no1 p38 Ja 2017
Beneteau Gran Turismo 46 J. Y. Wood color *Power & Motoryacht* v33 no2 p44 F 2017
Beneteau Sense 57 Z. Prochazka color *Sail* v48 no11 p26 N 2017
BENETEAU SWIFT TRAWLER 30 Z. PROCHAZKA *Sea Magazine* v108 no9 p32 S 2016

Bénéteau SA

Benetti, Jason—Interviews
THE SOX'S NEW VOICE W. MOSER color *Chicago* v66 no8 p26 Ag 2017

Benevolence
I'M ALL FOR BEING NICE P. Gulley *Saturday Evening Post* v288 no6 p19 N/D 2016

Benezra, Jorge
Lightbox color *Time* v190 no7 p14 Ag 21 2017

Benfeitas, Rui
A pathology atlas of the human cancer transcriptome diag *Science* v357 no6352 p660 Ag 18 2017

Benfey, Christopher
Building the American Dream color *New York Review of Books* v64 no6 p18 Ap 6 2017
Emily: The Quiet Earthquake cartoon color *New York Review of Books* v64 no1 p43 Ja 19 2017
The Long-Distance Reader bw *New York Review of Books* v63 no18 p21 N 24 2016
When British Eyes Were Smiling color *New York Times Book Review* p13 S 25 2016

Benford, Gregory, 1941-
The Berlin Project *Publishers Weekly* v264 no13 p80 Mr 27 2017

Bengal tiger
TIGER TOMBSTONE K. RANDALL *Washingtonian Magazine* v52 no9 p24 Je 2017

Benglis, Lynda, 1941-
LYNDA BENGLIS E. Buhe cartoon *Art in America* v104 no11

p118 D 2016

Bengsch, Bertram

Epigenetic stability of exhausted T cells limits durability of reinvigoration by PD-1 blockade bibl graph *Science* v354 no6316 p1160 D 2 2016

Bengtsson Gonzales, Carolina

miR-183 cluster scales mechanical pain sensitivity by regulating basal and neuropathic pain genes diag graph *Science* v356 no6343 p1168 Je 16 2017

Benhabib, Seyla

Learn From History *New Republic* v248 no3 p33 Mr 2017

THE RETURN OF FASCISM color *New Republic* v248 no11 p36 N 2017

Ben-Hamo, Rotem

The linker histone H1.0 generates epigenetic and functional intratumor heterogeneity bibl graph *Science* v353 no6307 paaf1644-1 S 30 2016

BENICH, ERIC

America's Original Frontier color *Backpacker* v45 no2 p28 Mr 2017

BÉNICHOU, LO

HOW TO PROTECT YOUR DIGITAL SELF color *Wired* v25 no6 p36 Je 2017

TROLLS ACROSS AMERICA map *Wired* v25 no9 p90 S 2017

Benilova, Iryna

De novo design of a biologically active amyloid bibl graph *Science* v354 no6313 paah4949-1 N 11 2016

Benincasa, Robyn

FLEX TIME A. Oglethorpe color *O, The Oprah Magazine* p78 S 2017

Bening, Annette, 1958-

Annette Bening Is Radiant In 20th Century Women S. Zacharek color *Time* v189 no3 p52 Ja 30 2017

BEST ACTRESS CONTENDER ANNETTE BENING N. Sperling color *Entertainment Weekly* no1446/1447 p104 D 2016/Ja 2017

Bening, Annette, 1958—Interviews

"Kiss all the people you want to kiss" K. Branch and E. Mahaney color *Glamour* v115 no2 p82 F 2017

NATURAL PROGRESSION M. HASKELL color *Film Comment* v53 no1 p38 Ja/F 2017

Beninga, Jochen

Trispecific broadly neutralizing HIV antibodies mediate potent SHIV protection in macaques color graph *Science* v357 no6359 p85 O 6 2017

Benini, Maurizio

Leoncavallo: Zazà R. Pines *Opera News* v81 no5 p55 N 2016

Benintendi, Andrew

Swing Shift J. Stowell *Cincinnati Magazine* v50 no12 p48 S 2017

Benion, Payton

THE LOOK BOOK img *New York* v50 no18 p57 S 4 2017

Benitez, Lydia

mTOR regulates metabolic adaptation of APCs in the lung and controls the outcome of allergic inflammation graph *Science* v357 no6355 p1014 S 8 2017

Benítez-López, A.

The impact of hunting on tropical mammal and bird populations graph map *Science* v356 no6334 p180 Ap 14 2017

Beniwal, Vrishti

India's Cash-Canceling Experiment color *Bloomberg Businessweek* no4501 p12 N 28 2016

Benjak, Andrej

Red squirrels in the British Isles are infected with leprosy bacilli bibl color diag map *Science* v354 no6313 p744 N 11 2016

Benjamin, Ali

Ali Benjamin R. Means color *Current Biography* v78 no5 p16 My 2017

Big Dreams *New York Times Book Review* p19 Ja 15 2017

Benjamin, Alice

INVEST IN YOURSELF IN 2017 color *Black Enterprise* v47 no5 p46 Ja/F 2017

Benjamin, Allie

ORANGUTAN WHISTLES *National Geographic Kids* no466 p13 D 2016/Ja 2017

Benjamin, Beth

Listen to Your Employees, Not Just Your Customers *Harvard*

Business Review Digital Articles p2 Ag 15 2016

A Study of 46,000 Shoppers Shows That Omnichannel Retailing Works color *Harvard Business Review Digital Articles* p2 Ja 3 2017

BENJAMIN, JENNIFER

gotta have it! *Parents* p134 2015

is he just acting his age? *Parents* v91 no10 p54 O 2016

Scale Stuck? color *Health* v31 no3 p47 Ap 2017

SEX TONIGHT color *Good Housekeeping* v264 no5 p107 My 2017

squirmy solutions *Parents* v92 no3 p110 Mr 2017

Benjamin, Kasey

10 BEST WALKS IN AMERICA cartoon *Prevention* p46 Mr 2017

Benjamin, Medea

ACTIVE DUTY: My Dedication to Liberty, Justice, and an End to Wars M. Benjamin *Humanist* v76 no6 p17 N/D 2016

MEDEA BENJAMIN AND THE POLITICS OF DISRUPTION R. Conniff color *Progressive* p58 D 2016/Ja 2017

Benjamin, Meredith

get into GEAR: Your four-year college-prep timeline *Dance Magazine* p28 2016/2017

get into GEAR: Your four-year college-prep timeline *Dance Magazine* v90 p28 2016/2017 Supplement College Guide

MUST-KNOW Commercial DANCE TERMS color *Dance Spirit* v20 no10 p60 D 2016

THE Theme Park LIFE color *Dance Spirit* v21 no2 p56 F 2017

BENJAMIN, MICHAEL

BIOHACKING FOR MARTIAL ARTISTS color *Black Belt* v55 no1 p39 D 2016/Ja 2017

Benjamin, S. C.

Entanglement distillation between solid-state quantum network nodes diag *Science* v356 no6341 p928 Je 1 2017

Benjamin Moore & Co. Inc.

BRIGHT YELLOW + CELADON color *Martha Stewart Living* p37 Ap 2017

FORM AND FUNCTION J. Sergent *Washingtonian Magazine* v52 no4 p185 Ja 2017

RESOURCES color *House Beautiful* v159 no4 p126 My 2017

Resources *House Beautiful* v159 no7 p122 S 2017

Rolling in the Deep K. RENDA color *House Beautiful* v159 no4 p32 My 2017

Benji B (Performer)

NIGHT LIFE *New Yorker* v93 no33 p10 O 23 2017

Benke, Ryan

Emission of volatile organic compounds from petunia flowers is facilitated by an ABC transporter diag *Science* v356 no6345 p1386 Je 30 2017

Benkhoff, J.

Seasonal exposure of carbon dioxide ice on the nucleus of comet 67P/Churyumov-Gerasimenko bibl bw graph *Science* v354 no6319 p1563 D 23 2016

Benko, Cathy—Interviews

The Solution to the Skills Gap Could Already Be Inside Your Company E. Harrell *Harvard Business Review Digital Articles* p2 S 27 2016

Benko, Jessica

HOT ZONES *New York Times Magazine* p54 Ap 23 2017

BenMark, Gadi

Messaging Apps Are Changing How Companies Talk with Customers *Harvard Business Review Digital Articles* p2 S 23 2016

Benmeleh, Yaacov

The Difficulties Of Cloning A CEO color graph *Bloomberg Businessweek* no4535 p50 Ag 28 2017

One Winner, One Loser After a Fortune's Split color *Bloomberg Businessweek* no4506 p33 Ja 9 2017

BENN, EVAN S.

Miami Heat color *Bon Appetit* v62 no10 p56 O 2017

Benna, M.

Mars' atmospheric history derived from upper-atmosphere measurements of 38 Ar/36Ar diag *Science* v355 no6332 p1408 Mr 31 2017

Bennani, Meriem—Exhibitions

"COMMERCIAL BREAK" W. S. Smith color *Art in America* v105 no5 p125 My 2017

Benneke, Björn

HAT-P-26b: A Neptune-mass exoplanet with a well-constrained

heavy element abundance chart diag graph *Science* v356 no6338 p628 My 12 2017

Bennell, Kale
MY DIY KITCHEN RENO: How I built my dream kitchen on a budget-no pricey professional designer needed *Washingtonian Magazine* v52 no11 p148 Ag 2017

Benner, Erica
Be like the Fox: Machiavelli in His World color *Publishers Weekly* v264 no10 p50 Mr 6 2017
CYNICAL, DETERMINED, INTELLIGENT AND WITTY: A rich and complex portrait of the author of The Prince manages to combine scholarly analysis with the imagination of the historical novelist S. Dunant *History Today* v67 no10 p98 O 2017
Princely Provocateur: An account of Niccolò Machiavelli traces the career of a tricky personality in a politically stormy era E. FAWCETT *New York Times Book Review* p12 Je 18 2017

BENNER, JERRY
COURT APPEAL *Missouri Life* v43 no6 p34 O/N 2016

Benner, Richard
Friends in Need M. CONNOLLY color *Film Comment* v53 no2 p18 Mr/Ap 2017

Benner Smidt, Margaret
From the Editor color *Weatherwise* v70 no4 p4 Jl/Ag 2017
From the Editor *Weatherwise* v69 no6 p4 N-D 2016

Bennet, Bindu
Systemic pan-AMPK activator MK-8722 improves glucose homeostasis but induces cardiac hypertrophy graph *Science* v357 no6350 p507 Ag 4 2017

Bennet, Chloe
MARVEL'S AGENTS OF S.H.I.E.L.D M. Roffman *TV Guide* v64 no15 p46 Ap 4 2016

BENNET, MOLLY
The Kids Are Not All Right *Audubon* v118 no6 p12 Wint 2016

Bennett (B.C.)—History
The Best Former Whorehouse in Canada N. O. Pearson color *Bloomberg Businessweek* no4497 p28 O 31 2016

Bennett, Alexis
Fit for Your Ride [Cover story] color *Horse & Rider* v56 no5 p60 My 2017

BENNETT, ANDY
Chill'n color *Cabin Living* p87 Ja/F 2017
Have a Seat color *Cabin Living* p74 Ja/F 2017

BENNETT, BETH
Use It ... and Lose It? *Climbing* no356 p39 S/O 2017

Bennett, Bob
Model a TRAILER HOME scene color *Model Railroader* v84 no9 p36 S 2017

Bennett, Brian R.
Is America great? graph *America* v216 no5 p6 Mr 6 2017

Bennett, Brit
The Mothers color *Publishers Weekly* v264 no5 p197 Ja 30 2017
The Mothers E. A. KAPLAN *Ms.* v26 no4 p40 Wint 2016
What the Church Ladies Know M. JACOB *New York Times Book Review* p10 N 6 2016

Bennett, Bruce R.
A Walrus Tribute color *Walrus* v14 no2 p56 Mr 2017

BENNETT, CHARLES L.
A COSMIC CONTROVERSY color *Scientific American* v317 no1 p5 Jl 2017

Bennett, Christopher
Bosnia's Paralyzed Peace R. Legvold *Foreign Affairs* v96 no2 p182 Mr/Ap 2017

Bennett, Claire-Louise
READINGS *Harper's Magazine* v333 no1998 p13 N 2016
The Recordings of Pauline Oliveros *New York Times Magazine* p20 F 12 2017

Bennett, Dawn
Do Do That Voodoo That You Do So Well color *Weekly Standard* v23 no1 p3 S 11 2017

Bennett, Deb
AMERICA'S MAJOR HORSE BREEDS EMERGE bw color *Equus* no473 p45 F 2017
BONES SPEAK VOLUMES bw color *Equus* no482 p43 N 2017
A DIFFERENT WORLD bw color *Equus* no475 p60 Ap 2017
HORSES OF THE CIVIL WAR bw color *Equus* no477 p55 Je 2017

THE REGISTERED MORGAN bw color *Equus* no471 p43 D 2016

BENNETT, DIANNE
THE ILLUSTRATED AVIARY color *Audubon* v119 no3 p52 Fall 2017

Bennett, Drake
Poor Little Rich Folks cartoon *Bloomberg Businessweek* no4539 p74 S 25 2017
Refugees, immigrants, expatriates. For some politicians, they're scapegoats. For Western Union, they're customers color *Bloomberg Businessweek* no4527 p74 Je 19 2017
REMEMBER NOKIA? color *Bloomberg Businessweek* no4529 p66 Jl 3 2017
The Wall bw *Bloomberg Businessweek* no4517 p31 Ap 3 2017

BENNETT, DREW E.
Addressing the Gender Gap in Distinguished Speakers at Professional Ecology Conferences *BioScience* v67 no5 p464 My 2017

BENNETT, ELENA M.
When, Where, and How Nature Matters for Ecosystem Services: Challenges for the Next Generation of Ecosystem Service Models *BioScience* v67 no9 p820 S 2017

BENNETT, ELIZABETH L.
Conserving the World's Megafauna and Biodiversity: The Fierce Urgency of Now *BioScience* v67 no3 p197 Mr 2017
Saving the World's Terrestrial Megafauna color *BioScience* v66 no10 p807 O 1 2016

BENNETT, ERIC
Pushkin Came to Shove *New York Times Book Review* p29 D 11 2016

Bennett, Haley, 1988-
HALEY BENNETT'S BEAUTY DIARY Guarnieri color *Harper's Bazaar* no3657 p192 O 2017
HALEY'S COMET I. Biedenharn color *Entertainment Weekly* no1435 p26 O 14 2016
Hot Actress Haley Bennett A. MORRIS color *Rolling Stone* no1274 p40 N 17 2016
STYLE CRUSH Haley Bennett S. Simon color *InStyle* v24 no9 p192 S 2017

Bennett, Jana
The Charlie Gard case reveals a persistent bias against disability *America* v217 no3 p10 Ag 7 2017

Bennett, Jay
The Iditarod Air Force color map *Popular Mechanics* p15 Mr 2017
POPULAR MECHANICS EVERYWHERE color *Popular Mechanics* p6 F 2017

Bennett, Jeffrey
A Global Warming Primer Answering Your Questions about the Science, the Consequences, and the Solutions J. Abraham *Physics Today* v70 no3 p60 Mr 2017

BENNETT, JESSICA
THE MOVEMENT IN MOTION: 4 ESSENTIAL CIVIL RIGHTS FILMS bw color *Ebony* v72/73 no12/1 p84 O/N 2017
SPOTLIGHT ON: STERLING K. BROWN color *Ebony* v72/73 no12/1 p82 O/N 2017

Bennett, Joan Wennstrom
H. Boyd Woodruff (1917–2017) bw *Science* v356 no6336 p381 Ap 28 2017

BENNETT, JOHN
Artifact exposure color *Canadian Geographic* v137 no1 p31 F 2017
Deep impact color *Canadian Geographic* v137 no2 p29 Mr/Ap 2017
Flora finders color *Canadian Geographic* v136 no6 p31 D 2016
Kestrel mystery color *Canadian Geographic* v137 no3 p31 My 2017
Knowledge keepers color *Canadian Geographic* v137 no5 p29 S/O 2017
Northern exposure color *Canadian Geographic* v135 no6 p33 D 2015
Umingmak in danger color *Canadian Geographic* v137 no4 p31 Jl/Ag 2017

Bennett, Jonathan A.
Plant-soil feedbacks and mycorrhizal type influence temperate forest population dynamics bibl graph map *Science* v355 no6321 p1 Ja 13 2017

Bennett, Jules

Caught Up in You *Publishers Weekly* v263 no44 p58 O 31 2016

BENNETT, KATE

Know Your Trumps *Washingtonian Magazine* v52 no4 p98 Ja 2017

RAISING AN EYEBROW *Washingtonian Magazine* v52 no3 p117 D 2016

Bennett, Kyle David

SPIRITUAL DISCIPLINES ARE NOT ABOUT YOU K. D. JOHNSON color *Christianity Today* v61 no7 p77 S 2017

Bennett, Nathan J.

Committing to socially responsible seafood color *Science* v356 no6341 p912 Je 1 2017

Bennett, Nigel C.

Fructose-driven glycolysis supports anoxia resistance in the naked mole-rat diag graph *Science* v356 no6335 p307 Ap 21 2017

BENNETT, ROGER

The Fifty Greatest Living Athletes bw color *GQ: Gentlemen's Quarterly* v97 no11 p96 N 2017

Bennett, Ryan

Dafnis Prieto's A World of Rhythmic Possibilities color *Downbeat* v84 no1 p106 Ja 2017

LP Peruvian Cajons color *Downbeat* v83 no11 p80 N 2016

Vic Firth Modern Jazz Collection color *Downbeat* v84 no6 p86 Je 2017

Bennett, Susan

My love triangle color *Equus* no480 p70 S 2017

Bennett, Tara

The Making of Outlander: The Series: The Official Guide to Seasons One & Two *British Heritage Travel* v37 no6 p78 N/D 2016

Bennett, Tony, 1926-—Interviews

TONY BENNETT E. SPITZNAGEL bw *Men's Health* v31 no10 p120 D 2016

TONY BENNETT He's Still Got That SWING! I. RUDOLPH *TV Guide* p32 D 19 2016

Tony Turns 90 D. Ross color *Entertainment Weekly* no1443 p21 D 9 2016

Bennett Demaio, Krista

HOW TO BE A HAIRCOLOR GENIUS color *O, The Oprah Magazine* p128 O 2017

Bennetts, Leslie

CAN WE TALK? M. DARGIS *New York Times Book Review* p16 D 4 2016

Last Girl Before Freeway T. Jordan color *Entertainment Weekly* no1440 p62 N 18 2016

Bennetts, Leslie—Interviews

A Hoot and a Horror color *Publishers Weekly* v263 no43 p66 O 24 2016

Benning, Sadie

SADIE BENNING T. Istomina *Art in America* v104 no9 p153 O 2016

Benning, Sarah K.

One Stitch at a Time M. OZAWA color *Martha Stewart Living* p34 My 2017

Bennington (Company)

Bennington Q27RSD Custom 10 *Boating World* v38 no1 p55 Ja 2017

Bennington, Chester, 1976-2017

BENNINGTON'S MOST SOUL-BARING SONGS E. R. Brown color *Entertainment Weekly* no1476 p62 Ag 4 2017

Chester Bennington E. Berman color *Time* v190 no6 p17 Ag 7 2017

Chester's Last Days K. GROW and S. Appleford color *Rolling Stone* no1294 p13 Ag 24 2017

BENNIS, PHYLLIS

Diplomacy Over War color *Nation* v304 no2 p18 Ja 16 2017

THIS MONTH: The U.S. Is Bombing at Least Six Countries. How Can the Anti-War Movement Step Up? *In These Times* v41 no10 p14 O 2017

Toward a New Foreign Policy [Cover story] bw *Nation* v304 no2 p12 Ja 16 2017

THE WAR IN SYRIA CANNOT BE WON. BUT IT CAN BE ENDED color *Nation* v303 no22 p12 N 28 2016

Bennison Fabrics (Company)

Resources *House Beautiful* v159 no7 p122 S 2017

Benno Bikes LLC

"I WANT TO DRIVE LESS." color *Bicycling* v58 no3 p32 Ap 2017

Benoist, Melissa, 1988-

Melissa Benoist J. Johnson color *Current Biography* v78 no6 p15 Je 2017

Supergirl N. Abrams, C. Holub et al *Entertainment Weekly* no1482/1483 p49 S 22 2017

Benoit, Andy

A GOOD DAY'S WORK color *Sports Illustrated* v126 no17 p58 Je 19 2017

INTO THE FIRE color *Sports Illustrated* v126 no13 p40 My 8 2017

MOVING RIGHT ALONG ... color *Sports Illustrated* v126 no5 p42 F 13 2017

PATFALLS color *Sports Illustrated* v127 no7 p43 S 4 2017

THE PATRIOTS PROBLEM [Cover story] color *Sports Illustrated* v127 no7 p32 S 4 2017

SAFETY First color *Sports Illustrated* v126 no12 p38 My 1 2017

SCOUTING Reports color *Sports Illustrated* v127 no7 p62 S 4 2017

TONY JEFFERSON'S Wild Ride color *Sports Illustrated* v126 no8 p68 Mr 20 2017

UPSIDE-DOWNSIDE color *Sports Illustrated* v126 no11 p40 Ap 17-24 2017

Benoit, Lindsey

AT MY HOUSE with Katie Lee color *Good Housekeeping* v264 no6 p30 Je 2017

I Love My Bar color *House Beautiful* p96 Jl 2017

a week of AWESOME OUTFITS color *Good Housekeeping* v265 no4 p34 O 2017

BenQ Corp.

Contrast and Color A. Griffin bw color graph *Sound & Vision* v82 no4 p62 My 2017

Bense, Kiley

AUGUSTA ROYALTY color *Golf Magazine* v58 no12 p34 D 2016

Ben Shalom, M.

High-temperature quantum oscillations caused by recurring Bloch states in graphene superlattices color *Science* v357 no6347 p181 Jl 14 2017

Benson, Ashley, 1989-

Look Who We Met! color *Seventeen* v76 no3 p8 My 2017

Benson, Eric

...AND NINE THEY NEED TO PROTECT *New York* v50 no7 p31 Ap 3 2017

flush with power *Texas Monthly* v45 no2 p84 F 2017

THE ICON OCLAST *Texas Monthly* v44 no11 p92 N 2016

INSIDE THE TEXAS QUARTERBACK FACTORY *Texas Monthly* v45 no9 p56 S 2017

THE NOT-SO-SECRET LIFE OF TERRENCE MALICK *Texas Monthly* v45 no4 p114 Ap 2017

UP AGAINST the Wall *Texas Monthly* v44 no11 p66 N 2016

BENSON, HARRY

50 Years in 15 Photos bw color *AARP: The Magazine* v30 no6A p58 O/N 2017

SHOOTING STARS L. SCHNEIDER bw *Vanity Fair* v59 no11 p69 N 2017

Benson, Jim

Transformation of bulk alloys to oxide nanowires color graph *Science* v355 no6322 p267 Ja 20 2017

Benson, Jyl

Brunches by the Bunches color *New Orleans Magazine* v51 no7 p60 My 2017

CULINARY HERITAGE color *Louisiana Life* v37 no6 p26 Jl/Ag 2017

FEASTING AND FROLICKING color *Louisiana Life* v37 no5 p50 My/Je 2017

FRESH PICKINGS color *Louisiana Life* v38 no1 p50 S/O 2017

HOME PLATE color *Louisiana Life* v37 no5 p52 My/Je 2017

LA GUNS color *Louisiana Life* v37 no6 p50 Jl/Ag 2017

MARKET FRESH color *Louisiana Life* v37 no3 p20 Ja/F 2017

Thy Daily Bread Pudding color *New Orleans Magazine* v51 no1 p64 N 2016

THE TIME IS RIGHT color *Louisiana Life* v37 no2 p22 N/D 2016

TSUNAMI SUSHI color *Louisiana Life* v37 no4 p22 Mr/Ap 2017

BENSON, SALLY M.
Advancing clean energy *Issues in Science & Technology* v33 no3 p5 Spr 2017

Benson, Tiffany
How I Solved My Horse's Problem cartoon *Horse & Rider* v56 no1 p72 Ja 2017

BENSON, TOM
Shipbuilding Docks as Experimental Systems for Realistic Assessments of Anthropogenic Stressors on Marine Organisms *BioScience* v67 no9 p853 S 2017

Benson, Tracy
Motivating Millennials Takes More than Flexible Work Policies *Harvard Business Review Digital Articles* p2 F 11 2016

Benson-Allott, Caetlin
LEARNING FROM HORROR *Film Quarterly* v70 no2 p58 Wint 2016
Telling Her Story *Film Quarterly* v70 no4 p88 Summ 2017

Benson-Gyles, Dick
The Boy in the Mask: The Hidden World of Lawrence of Arabia D. Saunders *Military History* v33 no5 p69 Ja 2017

Bensouda, Fatou, 1961—Interviews
The International Criminal Court on Trial color *Foreign Affairs* v96 no1 p48 Ja/F 2017

Bent, Stacey
Perovskite-perovskite tandem photovoltaics with optimized band gaps bibl chart graph *Science* v354 no6314 p861 N 18 2016

Benten, Brook
A Strong, Flexible Core for Back-Pain Relief color *Prevention* v68 no12 p18 D 2016

Benten, Daniel
A pathogenic role for T cell–derived IL-22BP in inflammatory bowel disease bibl graph *Science* v354 no6310 p358 O 21 2016

Benthic ecology
"The Importance of Benthic Habitats for Coastal Fisheries" (Kritzer et al. 2016): Soft Bottoms Are Biologically Productive, Not "Abiotic" L. B. CAHOON *BioScience* v67 no9 p781 S 2017

Bentley, Daniel
HOW TO BUY CLASSIC CARS color *Fortune* v175 no4 p53 Mr 15 2017
IN THE BELLY OF THE BRAZEN BULL color *Fortune* v176 no3 p37 S 1 2017
THIS BRAND DWARFS YOUR COMPANY *Fortune* v175 no8 p46 Je 15 2017
WORLD'S 50 GREATEST LEADERS [Cover story] color *Fortune* v175 no5 p46 Ap 1 2017

Bentley, Jeanine
U.S. Diets Still Out of Balance With Dietary Recommendations *Amber Waves: The Economics of Food, Farming, Natural Resources, & Rural America* p18 Jl 2017
U.S. Per Capita Availability of Red Meat, Poultry, and Fish Lowest Since 1983 *Amber Waves: The Economics of Food, Farming, Natural Resources, & Rural America* p18 F 2017

Bentley, Ross
ANALYZE THIS K. KINARD color *Road & Track* v69 no3 p102 O 2017

Bentley automobile
Aaron Robinson A. Robinson color *Car & Driver* v63 no2 p32 Ag 2017
The New Luxury Trucks E. DYER color *Popular Mechanics* v193 no7 p50 S 2016

Bentley automobile—Evaluation
Industrial, Heavy, and Magic K. A. Wilson color *Car & Driver* v62 no11 p114 My 2017
YACHT ROCK T. Quiroga chart color *Car & Driver* v62 no6 p64 D 2016

Bentley Motors Ltd.
Industrial, Heavy, and Magic K. A. Wilson color *Car & Driver* v62 no11 p114 My 2017

Bently, Peter
The Prince and the Porker *Publishers Weekly* v264 no1 p55 Ja 2 2017

Benton, Jan
Belonging J. S. Jordan color *U.S. Catholic* v82 no5 p28 My 2017

Benton, Janet—Interviews
Mothers from the Past V. S. FLYNN color *Publishers Weekly* v264 no13 p68 Mr 27 2017

Benton, Thomas Hart, 1889-1975
Old Kansas City color *Magazine Antiques* v183 no6 p6 N/D 2016

Benton, Thomas Hart, 1889-1975—Exhibitions
THE PERIL OF WAR bw color *Military History* v34 no4 p56 N 2017

Bentota River (Sri Lanka)
bentota, sri lanka F. A. BERNSTEIN color *Architectural Digest* no5 p84 My 2017

Bents (Structural engineering)
Timber Home Anatomy diag *Timber Home Living* p45 2017 Annual Buyers

BENVIE, BEN "ROOSTER"
Tell Your Story color diag *Backpacker* v45 no1 p38 Ja 2017

Benz, Bruce
Genomic estimation of complex traits reveals ancient maize adaptation to temperate North America diag *Science* v357 no6350 p512 Ag 4 2017

Benz, Felix
Single-molecule optomechanics in "picocavities" bibl graph *Science* v354 no6313 p726 N 11 2016

Benzakein, Erin
the no-stress, annuals-only CUTTING GARDEN color *Better Homes & Gardens* v95 no3 p78 Mr 2017

BEN-ZEÉV, AARON
MILD LOVE *Psychology Today* v50 no3 p76 My/Je 2017

Ben-Zvi, Batsheva
Wild emmer genome architecture and diversity elucidate wheat evolution and domestication color *Science* v357 no6346 p93 Jl 7 2017

Ben-Zvi, Gil
Wild emmer genome architecture and diversity elucidate wheat evolution and domestication color *Science* v357 no6346 p93 Jl 7 2017

BEOORD, LAURIE
FLIGHT PLAN *Successful Farming* v114 no12 p32 Mid-N 2016

Beowulf—Adaptations
Beowulf Is Back! J. PARKER color *Atlantic* v319 no3 p30 Ap 2017

Beowulf—Film adaptations
Beowulf Is Back! J. PARKER color *Atlantic* v319 no3 p30 Ap 2017

Beppler, Casey
Visualizing dynamic microvillar search and stabilization during ligand detection by T cells color *Science* v356 no6338 p598 My 12 2017

Bequia Island (Saint Vincent & the Grenadines)
Beautiful Bequia Z. Prochazka color *Sail* v48 no10 p93 O 2017

BERAM, NELL
Hey, Ho, Let's Go *New York Times Book Review* p29 Ag 27 2017

Beramendi, Rolando
Autentico: Cooking Italian, the Authentic Way *Publishers Weekly* v264 no40 p129 O 2 2017

Beran, Anja
The Dressage Seat color *Dressage Today* v24 no1 p46 O 2017

BERAN, MICHAEL KNOX
After The Fall *National Review* v69 no1 p19 Ja 23 2017
Castle Gothic *National Review* v69 no11 p30 Je 12 2017
Grand Alliance bw diag *National Review* v69 no5 p41 Mr 20 2017
Grande Dame bw color *National Review* v69 no21 p39 N 21 2016
Light in The Night color *National Review* v68 no19 p42 O 24 2016
The New Manichaeans *National Review* v69 no16 p39 Ag 28 2017

Beranek, Leo L., 1914-2016
Leo Leroy Beranek G. C. Maling Jr and E. J. W. Wood *Physics Today* v70 no10 p74 O 2017

BERARDI, GIGI
Carla Körbes *Dance Magazine* v91 no1 p44 Ja 2017
The Musicality Question *Dance Magazine* v91 no8 p30 Ag 2017
Seth Orza *Dance Magazine* v91 no8 p44 Ag 2017

Beras, Erika
INVENTORS color il *MIT Technology Review* v120 no5 p56 S/O 2017

Berat, C.
Observation of a large-scale anisotropy in the arrival directions of cosmic rays above 8×10^{18} eV *Science* v357 no6357 p1266 S 22 2017

BERCKEMEYER, JACK
Why Johnny Can't Sing, Dance, Saw, or Bake *Education Digest* v82 no4 p25 D 2016

Berdichevsky, Gene
Transformation of bulk alloys to oxide nanowires color graph *Science* v355 no6322 p267 Ja 20 2017

Berdingand, Jeff
GOAL ORIENTED J. A. MILLER *Cincinnati Magazine* v50 no7 p24 Ap 2017

Berdych, Tomáš, 1985-
Tomas Berdych *Tennis* v53 no1 p30 Ja/F 2017

Berea College
The Appalachian Work College A. B. LLOYD color *Weekly Standard* v22 no10 p26 N 14 2016

BEST BANG FOR THE BUCK SOUTHERN COLLEGES chart *Washington Monthly* v49 no9/10 p52 S/O 2017

LIBERAL ARTS COLLEGES chart *Washington Monthly* v49 no9/10 p96 S/O 2017

Bereavement
There are places I'll remember E. Bence color *U.S. Catholic* v82 no7 p23 Jl 2017

What matters most C. Gorrell color *Yoga Journal* no294 p12 S 2017

Bereavement & psychology
Returning to Work When You're Grieving [Cover story] S. Nawaz *Harvard Business Review Digital Articles* p2 Ap 28 2017

Bereavement—Psychological aspects
How to Handle Shared Grief at Work A. Ranieri *Harvard Business Review Digital Articles* p2 My 26 2015

Berenbaum, Sheri
Born this way? color *Science* v355 no6322 p254 Ja 20 2017

BERENBEIM, RONALD
ETHICAL LEADERSHIP—WINNING WITH INTEGRITY *Vital Speeches of the Day* v83 no1 p22 Ja 2017

BERENDSOHN, ROY
ASK ROY color diag *Popular Mechanics* p48 Mr 2017

ASK ROY color *Popular Mechanics* p36 F 2017

THE BARN JOB color *Popular Mechanics* p46 Ap 2017

CREATE A WORKSHOP ON WHEELS color *Popular Mechanics* p16 Je 2017

Earplugs color *Popular Mechanics* p35 S 2017

Earplugs color *Popular Mechanics* v193 no7 p35 S 2016

FURNITURE BUILDING bw color *Popular Mechanics* p31 F 2017

The New Yardwork Essentials color *Popular Mechanics* p14 Ap 2017

AN OPEN LETTER TO THE MAN WHO BOUGHT CRAFTSMAN color *Popular Mechanics* p81 Jl 2017

THE Right TOOL color *Popular Mechanics* p80 N 2017

THE SECRET GUIDE TO FINDING THE RIGHT HOUSE color *Popular Mechanics* p66 Je 2017

Shaving Razors: A Reckoning chart color *Popular Mechanics* p20 Mr 2017

THINGS YOU NEED TO KNOW ABOUT FUEL bw chart color *Popular Mechanics* p29 Mr 2017

TILLERS color *Popular Mechanics* p28 Ap 2017

Berenson, Tessa
After the Massacre [Cover story] color diag *Time* v190 no15 p22 O 16 2017

Hacking the Voter [Cover story] color *Time* v188 no14 p30 O 10 2016

How Neil Gorsuch Is Shaking Up the Supreme Court color *Time* v190 no15 p9 O 16 2017

J.D. Vance color *Time* v188 no20 p60 N 14 2016

Proposal Keeps Two Key Benefits for Moms *Time* v189 no10 p15 Mr 20 2017

The Return of 'Drill, Baby, Drill' color *Time* v188 no22-23 p33 N/D 2016

The Suite of Power [Cover story] color *Time* v189 no23 p22 Je 19 2017

Trump Goes to War [Cover story] color *Time* v188 no16/17 p20 O 24 2016

Trump's American Vision [Cover story] color *Time* v189 no3 p24 Ja 30 2017

Trump's Loyalty Test [Cover story] color *Time* v189 no20 p24 My 29 2017

Trump's Supreme Court Pick Puts Democrats In a Bind color diag *Time* v189 no5 p10 F 13 2017

Trump's Travel Ban Might Escape Judgment map *Time* v190 no14 p12 O 9 2017

The Truth Is Out There color *Time* v188 no15 p28 O 17 2016

Undocumented Immigrants May Get Less Time to Make Their Case map *Time* v190 no8 p12 Ag 28 2017

Will Bob Mueller Separate Fact from Fiction? [Cover story] color *Time* v190 no1 p24 Jl 3 2017

BERENZ, RYAN A.
13 MUST-SEE EVENTS *TV Guide* v65 no23 p44 My 29 2017

COMPLETE MADNESS *TV Guide* v65 no11 p50 Mr 6 2017

DERBY DAY *TV Guide* v65 no19 p46 My 1 2017

GREENS & GRIDIRON *TV Guide* v65 no39 p66 S 18 2017

HUSKIES GET STAR ROLES *TV Guide* v65 no8 p40 F 27 2017

THE MASTERS *TV Guide* v65 no14 p46 Ap 3 2017

MLB'S "SURREAL" SEASON OPENER *TV Guide* v65 no13 p48 Mr 20 2017

NASCAR SHOWDOWN *TV Guide* v65 no21 p46 My 15 2017

NBA JUMPSTART *TV Guide* v65 no43 p45 O 16 2017

NFL PREVIEW TOP 10 CONTENDERS *TV Guide* v65 no37 p55 S 4 2017

NFL WARM-UP *TV Guide* v65 no31 p43 Jl 24 2017

OCTOBER MAGIC *TV Guide* v65 no41 p43 O 2 2017

ON COURSE FOR DRAMA *TV Guide* v65 no25 p43 Je 2017

WIMBLEDON HOLDS SERVE *TV Guide* v65 no27 p41 Je 26 2017

Berets
Berets Berated color *Weekly Standard* v22 no24 p2 F 27 2017

Beretta shotguns
BERETTA 690 FIELD I J. B. SNOW chart color *Outdoor Life* v224 no7 p66 S 2017

BERFANGER, REBECCA
Hooray for Bollywood! *Indianapolis Monthly* v12 no40 p13 Ag 2017

Berfield, Susan
DELIVERING A $9 BILLION EMPIRE color *Bloomberg Businessweek* no4515 p42 Mr 20 2017

The Man Who Invented Wellness bw color *Bloomberg Businessweek* no4533 p62 Ag 7 2017

MEAT MARKETER [Cover story] color graph map *Bloomberg Businessweek* no4511 p42 F 13 2017

THE SUBTERRANEAN TRASH FIRE NEXT DOOR color *Bloomberg Businessweek* no4540 p52 O 2 2017

Supermall, Superstalled color *Bloomberg Businessweek* no4504 p44 D 19 2016

Welcome to America! Here's How Your Investment Is Doing color *Bloomberg Businessweek* no4493 p74 O 3 2016

BERG, A. SCOTT
History's FIRST DRAFT color *Vanity Fair* v59 no10 p158 O 2017

Berg, A. Scott—Interviews
A. Scott Berg *New York Times Book Review* p7 Jl 9 2017

Berg, Gretchen J.
STAR TREK'S NEW FRONTIER J. Hibberd color *Entertainment Weekly* no1472 p20 Je 30 2017

BERG, JENNY
ALEXIS NIDO-RUSSO cartoon color *Chicago* v66 no3 p56 Mr 2017

DONNA DAVIES color *Chicago* v65 no11 p46 N 2016

Everyone should try bw *Science* v355 no6322 p227 Ja 20 2017

GLORIA GROOM color *Chicago* v66 no6 p40 Je 2017

JENNIFFER WEIGEL color *Chicago* v66 no4 p46 Ap 2017

JOSHUA BLAKE CARTER color *Chicago* v66 no5 p54 My 2017

KATRINA MARKOFF color *Chicago* v66 no1 p50 Ja 2017

KENDALL REYNOLDS color *Chicago* v66 no7 p34 Jl 2017

KEVIN IEGA JEFF color *Chicago* v66 no2 p32 F 2017

LARRY YANDO color *Chicago* v65 no12 p56 D 2016

Looking inward at gender issues color *Science* v355 no6323 p329 Ja 27 2017

Berg, Jeremy
Awesome universal chirp color *Science* v354 no6319 p1507 D 23 2016

A family analysis color *Science* v355 no6320 p9 Ja 6 2017

Gene–environment interplay color *Science* v354 no6308 p15 O 7 2016

March for science color *Science* v356 no6333 p7 Ap 7 2017

Measuring and managing bias color *Science* v357 no6354 p849 S 1 2017

Preprint ecosystems color *Science* v357 no6358 p1331 S 29 2017

Reunifying America color *Science* v354 no6314 p807 N 18 2016

Science of preparedness color *Science* v357 no6356 p1073 S 15 2017

Science's rightful place color *Science* v354 no6318 p1355 D 16 2016

A short presidential reading list color *Science* v354 no6310 p265 O 21 2016

Shortsighted priorities color *Science* v356 no6341 p887 Je 1 2017

Berg, Joshua Lewis

BELIEF IN A SHARED FUTURE: AN INTERVIEW WITH Abdul El-Sayed, MUSLIM-AMERICAN CANDIDATE FOR GOVERNOR OF MICHIGAN *Humanist* v77 no4 p28 Jl/Ag 2017

The Case for Re-Enfranchisement *Humanist* v76 no6 p6 N/D 2016

BERG, MADDIE

America's Richest Celebrities color *Forbes* v198 no9 p18 D 30 2016

Streaming Stars color *Forbes* v198 no8 p28 D 20 2016

Berg, Madeline

Counter-Counter-Programming color *Forbes* v199 no4 p50 Ap 25 2017

If You Build It, They Will Come bw *Forbes* v199 no7 p102 Je 29 2017

LESSONS AND IDEAS BY THE 100 GREATEST LIVING BUSINESS MINDS bw color *Forbes* v200 no3 p115 S 28 2017

Old World, Young Promise color *Forbes* v199 no1 p20 Ja 24 2017

We Knew Them When color *Forbes* v199 no1 p22 Ja 24 2017

BERG, MICHAEL

Ascend & Deliver chart color *Muscle & Performance* v9 no10 p24 O 2017

Define & Conquer chart color *Muscle & Performance* v9 no10 p22 O 2017

"Fail" of the Century color *Muscle & Performance* v9 no9 p22 S 2017

Go The Distance chart color *Muscle & Performance* v9 no8 p20 Ag 2017

The HEX Effect chart color *Muscle & Performance* v9 no5 p34 My 2017

MASTER THE SLED cartoon *Muscle & Performance* v9 no4 p20 Ap 2017

the (next) 10 BEST BACK exercises color *Muscle & Performance* v9 no6 p36 Je 2017

THE (NEXT) 10 BEST CHEST EXERCISES color *Muscle & Performance* v9 no8 p44 Ag 2017

ONE MONTH TO A BIGGER 1RM bw *Muscle & Performance* v9 no6 p18 Je 2017

Perfectly BALANCED bw color *Muscle & Performance* v9 no11 p44 N 2017

POWER PLAY color *Muscle & Performance* v9 no1 p18 Ja 2017

[RE]BALANCING ACT chart color *Muscle & Performance* v9 no1 p20 Ja 2017

THE TOP 10 BEST FUNCTIONAL EXERCISES bw color *Muscle & Performance* v8 no12 p46 D 2016

TURN UP THE HEAT color *Muscle & Performance* v9 no6 p20 Je 2017

Berg, Peter

Blowed Up J. PODHORETZ color *Weekly Standard* v22 no7 p39 O 24 2016

DEEPWATER HORIZON D. Vaughn color *Sound & Vision* v82 no5 p65 Je 2017

Deepwater Horizon L. Greenblatt color *Entertainment Weekly* no1434 p40 O 7 2016

Patriots Day J. McGovern color *Entertainment Weekly* no1446/1447 p106 D 2016/Ja 2017

A SHARED REALITY bw *Vanity Fair* v59 no1 p156 Holiday 2017

Berg, Peter—Interviews

Pledging Allegiance D. Franich color *Entertainment Weekly* no1448 p17 Ja 13 2017

Berg, Rick

Stop Trump!: A Conservative's Perspective *Progressive* v81 no6 p23 Ag/S 2017

Bergamotto, Lori

HOW TO WEAR IT... anywhere! color *Good Housekeeping* v264 no3 p16 Mr 2017

HOW TO WEAR IT... anywhere! color *Good Housekeeping* v265 no5 p16 N 2017

HOW TO WEAR IT color *Good Housekeeping* v264 no2 p16 F 2017

HOW TO WEAR IT... color *Good Housekeeping* v265 no2 p14 Ag 2017

Mother's Day gift guide color *Good Housekeeping* v264 no5 p68I My 2017

Bergara Barrels Inc.

LONG-RANGE/TACTICAL RIFLES D. E. Petzal and R. Mann color *Field & Stream* v122 no5 p80 O 2017

Bergasse, Josh, 1973-

A Dancer's Choreographer J. Stahl *Dance Magazine* v91 no4 p10 Ap 2017

The Golden Ticket [Cover story] S. GOLD *Dance Magazine* v91 no4 p26 Ap 2017

Bergdoll, Barry

At Long Last, Labrouste: A newly restored masterwork reopens in Paris color map *Architectural Record* v205 no8 p52 Ag 2017

CLEAR VISION color *Architectural Digest* v73 no12 p106 D 2016

Look Up color *Architectural Digest* v74 no4 p178 Ap 2017

The Wright Stuff bw color diag *Architectural Digest* no6 p65 Je 1 2017

Bergdorf Goodman Inc.

LINDA'S CLOSET cartoon color *Harper's Bazaar* no3653 p148 My 2017

Bergé, Pierre, 1930-2017

Milestones *Time* v190 no12 p15 S 25 2017

Bergen, Erich

MADAM SECRETARY DECLASSIFIED M. LOGAN *TV Guide* v64 no15 p42 Ap 4 2016

Bergen, Mark

The AI Doctor Orders More Tests cartoon *Bloomberg Businessweek* no4526 p39 Je 12 2017

Apple's Alternative to Virtual Reality color *Bloomberg Businessweek* no4516 p29 Mr 27 2017

Downsizing Google's Dream color *Bloomberg Businessweek* no4519 p36 Ap 24 2017

FURY ROAD color *Bloomberg Businessweek* no4515 p54 Mr 20 2017

A Giant in Search, But a Wisp in the Cloud *Bloomberg Businessweek* no4498 p53 N 7 2016

Google Returns to Earth color *Bloomberg Businessweek* no4503 p44 D 12 2016

Google's Opioid Ad Addiction color *Bloomberg Businessweek* no4540 p21 O 2 2017

Kicking the Self-Driving Tires color *Bloomberg Businessweek* no4506 p26 Ja 9 2017

Man vs. Machine: Dermatology color *Bloomberg Businessweek* no4529 p23 Jl 3 2017

A Slow-Motion, Self-Driving Car Crash *Bloomberg Businessweek* no4537 p22 S 11 2017

A Spotlight on Harassment at Google *Bloomberg Businessweek* no4525 p33 Je 5 2017

Toto, I've a Feeling We're Still In Kansas (or Missouri) color *Bloomberg Businessweek* no4514 p33 Mr 13 2017

Waze Wants to Help You Hitch a Ride *Bloomberg Businessweek* no4523 p34 My 22 2017

Berger, Arthur

A Discourse on Discourse Studies color *Society* v53 no6 p597 D 2016

Berger, Bruce K.

Communicating in the Workplace *USA Today Magazine* v145 no2863 p13 Ap 2017

Berger, Carin

Good Night! Good Night! color *Publishers Weekly* v263 no44 p73 O 31 2016

Berger, Caroline M.

Gene duplication can impart fragility, not robustness, in the yeast protein interaction network bibl color graph *Science* v355 no6325 p630 F 10 2017

Berger, Cynthia

Silent Seashores? color *National Wildlife (World Edition)* v55 no5 p28 Ag/S 2017

Berger, Daniel

ATTACK MODE J. Leishman and D. Denunzio color *Golf Magazine* v59 no10 p42 O 2017

DIALING LONG DISTANCE D. M. Clarke color *Golf Magazine* v59 no3 p11 Mr 2017

Practice Like a Pro [Cover story] color *Golf Magazine* v59 no3 p65 Mr 2017

Berger, Frédéric

DNA replication–coupled histone modification maintains Polycomb gene silencing in plants diag *Science* v357 no6356 p1146 S 15 2017

Berger, James M.

Mechanisms for initiating cellular DNA replication graph *Science* v355 no6327 p811 F 24 2017

BERGER, JEANNINE

Mare Won't Use Her Paddock *Horse & Rider* v56 no4 p14 Ap 2017

Berger, Jody

ROLLING WITH IT color *Sunset* v239 no1 p19 Jl 2017

Berger, John, 1926-2017

John Berger of the Haute-Savoie J. White *Film Quarterly* v70 no4 p93 Summ 2017

Berger, Jonah

The Goldilocks Theory of Product Success *Harvard Business Review Digital Articles* p2 Jl 7 2016

The Language of Government M. Funkhouser *Governing* v30 no3 p59 D 2016

BERGER, JOSEPH

THE FORGER *New York Times Upfront* v149 no8 p16 Ja 30 2017

The Six-Day War, THEN & NOW: Fifty years after the 1967 war that redrew the Middle East map, here's what you need to know about the ongoing Israeli-Palestinian conflict *New York Times Upfront* v149 no12 p18 Ap 24 2017

When the City Stopped Sleeping: A history of the 20 years that made New York City *New York Times Book Review* p17 O 15 2017

Berger, Kavita M.

What life scientists should know about security threats bibl color diag *Science* v354 no6317 p1237 D 9 2016

Berger, Lauren

6 Things New Grads Should Know Before Joining a Startup *Harvard Business Review Digital Articles* p1 My 1 2017

Berger, Lee R., 1965-

Homo Naledi Likely Coexisted With Humans J. Kluger color *Time* v189 no19 p13 My 22 2017

Berger, Lee R., 1965—Interviews

THE HOMININ HUNTER L. BERGER color *National Geographic* v231 no5 pC10 My 2017

BERGER, LORI

EVA [Cover story] color *Redbook* p102 D 2016

I Love My Kitchen color *House Beautiful* v159 no1 p104 F 2017

Berger, Peter L., 1929-2017

People A. M. Banks *Christian Century* v134 no16 p16 Ag 2 2017

Berger, Richard A.

Less Pain, More Gain K. H. QUEEN color *Forbes* v200 no4 p(Sp)1 O 24 2017

Berger, Shelley L.

Epigenetic stability of exhausted T cells limits durability of reinvigoration by PD-1 blockade bibl graph *Science* v354 no6316 p1160 D 2 2016

Berger, Shoshana

Capitalism Needs Design Thinking *Harvard Business Review Digital Articles* p2 D 8 2014

Berger, Warren

Why Curious People Are Destined for the C-Suite *Harvard Business Review Digital Articles* p2 S 11 2015

Bergeron, David

BEYOND THE SURFACE J. Roedel color *Louisiana Life* v38 no1 p18 S/O 2017

Bergeron, Pierre

Relativistic deflection of background starlight measures the mass of a nearby white dwarf star chart color graph *Science* v356 no6342 p1046 Je 9 2017

Bergeron, Tom, 1955—Interviews

Dancing King J. RUSSELL *TV Guide* v64 no40 p40 O 3 2016

Bergeson, Bob

It's a One-derful Life R. Reilly and C. Barrett color *Golf Magazine* v59 no1 p28 Ja 2017

Berggruen, Nicolas

How Social Media Splits the Global Conversation *NPQ: New Perspectives Quarterly* v34 no1 p6 Ja 2017

New Institutions that Embrace Participation Without Populism *NPQ: New Perspectives Quarterly* v34 no1 p9 Ja 2017

Salvaging Globalization *NPQ: New Perspectives Quarterly* v34 no1 p67 Ja 2017

Bergh, Chip—Interviews

How Did I Get Here? CHIP BERGH bw color *Bloomberg Businessweek* no4507 p68 Ja 16 2017

Berghahn, Volker R.

The U.S.'s "Special Relationship" Is with Germany, Not Britain *Harvard Business Review Digital Articles* p2 Je 29 2016

Bergholz, Max

Violence as a Generative Force: Identity, Nationalism, and Memory in a Balkan Community R. Legvold *Foreign Affairs* v96 no3 p168 My/Je 2017

Bergl, Paul

THE DEADLY MEDICAL MISTAKE YOU CAN AVOID color *Men's Health* v32 no2 p75 Mr 2017

Berglin, Jacob

An interview with Olivia Gude about connecting school and community arts practice *Arts Education Policy Review* v118 no1 p60 2017

Bergman, Rachel

Using M&A to Increase Your Capacity for Growth *Harvard Business Review Digital Articles* p2 Jl 13 2016

Bergmann, Bastian

6 Ways to Recruit Superstar Talent to Your New Company *Harvard Business Review Digital Articles* p2 F 17 2016

A Data-Driven Approach to Group Creativity *Harvard Business Review Digital Articles* p2 Jl 12 2016

BERGMANN, BORIS

PIERRE-Ange CARLOTTI *Interview* v47 no3 p78 Ap 2017

Bergmann, Dominique C.

Mobile MUTE specifies subsidiary cells to build physiologically improved grass stomata bibl diag *Science* v355 no6330 p1215 Mr 17 2017

Bergmann, Uwe

Metalloprotein entatic control of ligand-metal bonds quantified by ultrafast x-ray spectroscopy diag *Science* v356 no6344 p1276 Je 23 2017

Bergmiller, Tobias

Biased partitioning of the multidrug efflux pump AcrAB-TolC underlies long-lived phenotypic heterogeneity diag *Science* v356 no6335 p311 Ap 21 2017

Bergner, Daniel

The Voice T. CHATTERTON WILLIAMS *New York Times Book Review* p12 O 9 2016

BERGNER, JEFF

Affairs of State color *Weekly Standard* v22 no20 p12 Ja 30 2017

The Liberal Ideological Complex color *Weekly Standard* v22 no16 p26 D 26 2016

What Good Is Military Force? *Weekly Standard* v22 no6 p16 O 17 2016

Bergner, Joel

Mural at Zaatari Syrian refugee camp, Jordan, 2013 L. Copan color *Christian Century* v134 no6 p47 Mr 15 2017

Bergonzi, Jerry—Interviews

Chords & Discords J. BOWMAN, R. SOMMER et al bw *Downbeat* v84 no1 p10 Ja 2017

THE MYSTIC C. Daly bw *Downbeat* v83 no11 p40 N 2016

Bergquist, Sharon Horesh

Ask anything bw color *Women's Health* v14 no2 p18 Mr 2017

BERGQVIST, PIA

THE ART OF AIR RACING color diag *Flying* v144 no9 p50 S 2017

FLIGHTSAFETY'S HONDAJET TRAINING bw color *Flying* v144 no5 p52 My 2017

GEAR ESSENTIALS FOR NEW PILOTS color *Flying* v144 no3 p62 Mr 2017

GENERAL AVIATION IN CHINA color map *Flying* v144 no10 p58 O 2017

IMMACULATE PROTECTION color *Flying* v144 no4 p60 Ap 2017

LEARNING TO FLY THE ICON A5 color *Flying* v144 no1 p38 Ja 2017

PILATUS PC-12 NG chart color *Flying* v144 no8 p42 Ag 2017

SPEED SECRETS color *Flying* v144 no8 p52 Ag 2017

TAMARACK'S ACTIVE WINGLETS color diag *Flying* v143 no12 p14 D 2016

Bergreen, Laurence

The Rake's Progress A. GOTTLIEB *New York Times Book Review* p14 Ja 8 2017

Bergson, Terilyn

When I Was a Horse-Crazy Kid, I... color *Horse & Rider* v56 no2 p72 F 2017

Bergstein, Brian

We Need More Alternatives to Facebook color diag *MIT Technology Review* v120 no3 p86 My/Je 2017

Bergström, Anders

A Neolithic expansion, but strong genetic structure, in the independent history of New Guinea diag *Science* v357 no6356 p1160 S 15 2017

Berigan, Bunny

The Tragic Trumpeter T. TEACHOUT *Commentary* v143 no6 p52 Je 2017

Berinato, Scott

AIR POLLUTION BRINGS DOWN THE STOCK MARKET *Harvard Business Review* v95 no2 p38 Mr/Ap 2017

Apple: Luxury Brand or Mass Marketer? *Harvard Business Review Digital Articles* p2 O 2 2014

Apple vs. the FBI Is Really, Really Complicated *Harvard Business Review Digital Articles* p2 F 19 2016

Cable Providers Win Even in an a La Carte World *Harvard Business Review Digital Articles* p2 O 22 2014

Flying COWs and Other Drone Apps *Harvard Business Review Digital Articles* p2 My 17 2017

HOW HABIT BEATS NOVELTY [Cover story] color diag *Harvard Business Review* v95 no1 p60 Ja/F 2017

INSIDE FACEBOOK'S AI WORKSHOP: At the social network behemoth, machine learning has become a platform for the platform *Harvard Business Review Digital Articles* p14 Jl 1 2017

The Personality Traits That Make Us Feel Like Frauds *Harvard Business Review Digital Articles* p2 O 22 2015

The Persuasiveness of a Chart Depends on the Reader, Not Just the Chart *Harvard Business Review Digital Articles* p2 My 27 2015

Sometimes, Less Innovation Is Better *Harvard Business Review* v95 no3 p38 My/Je 2017

There's No Such Thing as Anonymous Data *Harvard Business Review Digital Articles* p2 F 9 2015

Visualizing Sun Tzu's The Art of War *Harvard Business Review Digital Articles* p2 F 18 2015

WE LOOK LIKE OUR NAMES color img *Harvard Business Review* v95 no5 p32 S/O 2017

What Do We Know About Loneliness and Work? *Harvard Business Review Digital Articles* p2 S 28 2017

What HoloLens Has That Google Glass Didn't *Harvard Business Review Digital Articles* p2 Ja 29 2015

Why the Remain Campaign's Persuasion Strategy Backfired *Harvard Business Review Digital Articles* p2 Je 24 2016

Berinato, Scott—Interviews

Why It's So Hard for Us to Visualize Uncertainty N. Torres *Harvard Business Review Digital Articles* p2 N 11 2016

Bering, Henrik

Italian for Beginners color *Weekly Standard* v22 no23 p5 F 20 2017

Bering Land Bridge

STANDING STILL IN BERINGIA? N. SWAMINATHAN *Archaeology* v70 no3 p19 My/Je 2017

Bering Strait—History

BERING STRAIT, 1860S K. Wiles *History Today* v67 no8 p4 Ag 2017

BERINGER, ROBERT

we done reach color map *Sail* v48 no10 p58 O 2017

Berk, Brett

A Hypercar Made to Measure color *Bloomberg Businessweek* no4539 p70 S 25 2017

THE MERCEDES-BENZ G-WAGEN color *Car & Driver* v63 no2 p24 Ag 2017

THINK VERTICAL color *Road & Track* v69 no4 p68 N 2017

THE VOLVO WAGON bw color *Car & Driver* v62 no8 p20 F 2017

Berke, Allison

How Safe Are Blockchains? It Depends color *Harvard Business Review Digital Articles* p2 Mr 7 2017

Berkeley, Busby, 1895-1976

Whorled Series R. Brody bw *New Yorker* v92 no41 p12 D 12 2016

Berkeley, George, 1685-1753

Make Patriotism Great Again H. Bordwell color *Commonweal* v143 no20 p30 D 16 2016

BERKERY, PETER

The Importance of Scholarship *Publishers Weekly* v264 no38 p76 S 18 2017

BERKHOUT, JUST

Assessing National Biodiversity Trends for Rocky and Coral Reefs through the Integration of Citizen Science and Scientific Monitoring Programs *BioScience* v67 no2 p134 F 2017

Berklee College of Music

Cross-Disciplinary Heaven H. Rolfe *Dance Spirit* v21 no7 p104 S 2017

Berkley, Seth

Syria, slums, and health security color *Science* v356 no6336 p353 Ap 28 2017

Berkoff, Nancy

Cooking with Tempeh *Vegetarian Journal* v35 no1 p9 2016

Make Your Own Vegan Condiments *Vegetarian Journal* v36 no1 p6 2017

Portable Picnic Feasts *Vegetarian Journal* v36 no2 p6 2017

Quick and Easy Pear Dishes *Vegetarian Journal* v36 no1 p10 2017

Vegan Cooking Tips. Quick and Easy Hot Beverages *Vegetarian Journal* v35 no4 p32 2016

Vegan Cooking Tips. Quick and Easy Sandwich Ideas *Vegetarian Journal* v35 no2 p32 2016

Vegan Cooking Tips. Quick and Easy Taco Fillings *Vegetarian Journal* v35 no1 p34 2016

Vegan Cooking Tips. QUINOA DISHES *Vegetarian Journal* v36 no2 p32 2017

Berkooz, Gahl

CEOs Need to Ask the Right Questions About Their Digital Businesses *Harvard Business Review Digital Articles* p2 N 16 2016

Figuring Out How IT, Analytics, and Operations Should Work Together *Harvard Business Review Digital Articles* p2 Ag 3 2016

How Chief Data Officers Can Get Their Companies to Collect Clean Data *Harvard Business Review Digital Articles* p2 F 16 2017

Reducing Noise in Decision Making: Interaction color *Harvard Business Review* v94 no12 p18 D 2016

BERKOWITZ, BILL

Hate Crimes *In These Times* v41 no1 p23 Ja 2017

Berkowitz, Joe

The Best Vanilla Sex of Your Life color *Glamour* v115 no6 p102 Je 2017

Berkowitz, Peter

Before Push Comes to Shove: What the president needs to learn-fast *Hoover Digest: Research & Opinion on Public Policy* no2 p70 Spr 2017

Speak Up!: Colleges and universities honor free inquiry in theory, but not always in fact. How to keep higher education true to its values *Hoover Digest: Research & Opinion on Public Policy* no3 p125 Summ 2017

Berkshire, Dennis

Multipurpose Pools *Parks & Recreation* v52 no3 p56 Mr 2017

Berkshire, Jennifer

The Long Game of Betsy DeVos color *Progressive* v81 no2 p28 F 2017

Berkshire Corp.

Berkshire 25 Sport RFX9 *Boating World* v38 no1 p56 Ja 2017

Berkshire Hathaway Inc.

Buffett's Bet on Canadian Real Estate N. Buhayar and K. Dmitrieva bw *Bloomberg Businessweek* no4529 p27 Jl 3 2017

Buffett Likes Solar, But Not the Price Tag B. Eckhouse and N. Buhayar bw *Bloomberg Businessweek* no4534 p26 Ag 14 2017

Deal Snapshot: Oncor Electric Delivery Co R. Collins, J. Polson et al bw graph *Bloomberg Businessweek* no4530 p19 Jl 17 2017

The Fading Financial Magic Of Reinsurance S. BASAK and N. BUHAYAR cartoon *Bloomberg Businessweek* no4496 p52 O 24 2016

IN BRIEF K. Stock bw color graph *Bloomberg Businessweek* no4541 p8 O 9 2017

The Pensions Warren Buffett Runs N. Buhayar and K. Chiglinsky color *Bloomberg Businessweek* no4540 p32 O 2 2017

Stock X-Ray: Berkshire Hathaway T. Tepper color diag *Money* v46 no6 p42 Jl 2017

Warren Buffett's All-In Clean-Energy Bet S. Gandel and K. Fehrenbacher color diag map *Fortune* v174 no8 p158 D 15 2016

What It's Like to Be Owned by Berkshire Hathaway D. Larcker and B. Tayan *Harvard Business Review Digital Articles* p2 D 14 2015

'YOU CAN'T STOP THIS COUNTRY.' color *Fortune* v174 no8 p165 D 15 2016

Berkus, Nate, 1971-

I Love My Collections color *House Beautiful* v158 no10 p104 D 2016/Ja 2017

thanks, bro color diag *Better Homes & Gardens* v95 no10 p54 O 2017

Berla, Kathryn

Dream Me *Publishers Weekly* v264 no21 p94 My 22 2017

BERLAND, ADAM

Ecology for the Shrinking City *BioScience* v66 no11 p965 N 1 2016

Berlanti, Greg

ALL IN THE FAMILY [Cover story] J. Jensen and N. Abrams color *Entertainment Weekly* no1440 p20 N 18 2016

BERLATSKY, NOAH

The Limits of Expertise bw *Reason* v48 no11 p66 Ap 2017

Berlet, Chip

CLASSIC HUMANIST *Humanist* v77 no5 p10 S/O 2017

BERLEY, MARC

Fee-Free Submissions color *Publishers Weekly* v264 no14 p80 Ap 3. 2017

Berlin (Germany)—Description & travel

ROYAL FLUSH G. Pines color *Conde Nast Traveler* v52 no2 p96 F 2017

BERLIN, JEFF

BACK IN THE SADDLE color *Flying* v144 no6 p60 Je 2017

Berlin, Jeremy

COLORING OUTSIDE THE LINES cartoon *National Geographic* v231 no6 pC19 Je 2017

EYES IN THE SKY color *National Geographic* v231 no2 p132 F 2017

Flower Men color map *National Geographic* v231 no5 p112 My 2017

FOODS FOR THOUGHT diag *National Geographic* v232 no3 p20 S 2017

On All Floors color *National Geographic* v232 no4 p130 O 2017

SO THAT'S WHY THE LONG FACE color *National Geographic* v232 no4 p26 O 2017

Tiny Ruins color *National Geographic* v231 no4 p124 Ap 2017

WELL SUITED FOR SPACE WORK color *National Geographic* v232 no2 p18 Ag 2017

Berlin, Johann

Why You Should Tell Your Team to Take a Break and Go Outside *Harvard Business Review Digital Articles* p2 Je 26 2017

Berlin, Leslie

Q: What is the most significant fad of all time? color *Atlantic* v319 no3 p96 Ap 2017

Berlin Marathon

Racing to Run A Two-Hour Marathon R. Penty and R. Weiss color graph *Bloomberg Businessweek* no4538 p18 S 18 2017

Berlin Station (TV program)

Berlin Station J. Halterman *TV Guide* v65 no43 p36 O 16 2017

Berliner Philharmoniker

Orchestras and Nazis: When music could not transcend evil T. TEACHOUT *Commentary* v144 no1 p58 Jl/Ag 2017

To Do img *New York* v49 no22 p116 O 31 2016

Berlinerblau, Jacques

Teaching and the Bottom Line K. PHILLIPS-FEIN *New York Times Book Review* p21 Ag 27 2017

Teach or Die Trying J. MARKS *Commentary* v144 no1 p52 Jl/

Ag 2017

Berlinger, Max

FASHION FORWARD color *Bloomberg Businessweek* no4510 p60 F 6 2017

MODERN CLASSIC color *Bloomberg Businessweek* no4494 p67 O 10 2016

Berlingieri, Giuseppe

A Study of 16 Countries Shows That the Most Productive Firms (and Their Employees) Are Pulling Away from Everyone Else *Harvard Business Review Digital Articles* p2 Jl 13 2017

BERLINSKI, CLAIRE

The Dark Continent diag *National Review* v69 no5 p40 Mr 20 2017

A Megacity Old and New color *National Review* v68 no24 p38 D 31 2016

Berlinsky, Robin

The power of the arts: Evaluating a community artist-in-residence program through the lens of studio thinking bibl chart *Arts Education Policy Review* v118 no1 p19 2017

BERMAN, ARI

AMERICAN DEMOCRACY BESIEGED [Cover story] color *Nation* v305 no3 p18 Jl 31 2017

How Republicans Rigged the Election bw color *Nation* v303 no23/24 p12 D 5 2016

Judging Jeff Sessions *Nation* v304 no4 p5 F 6 2017

A Means and an End: Three longtime commentators lament the current state of American politics and look to its future *New York Times Book Review* p22 O 1 2017

RIGGED [Cover story] color map *Mother Jones* v42 no6 p24 N/D 2017

RIGHT TO VOTE? WRONG *Sierra* v101 no5 p34 S/O 2016

Texas's Jim Crow Voting Laws color *Nation* v303 no18 p14 O 31 2016

A Voting-Rights Victory *Nation* v304 no17 p4 Je 5 2017

Berman, Avis

"Miss Dimock is not orthodox at all": The life and career of Edith Dimock Glackens bw cartoon color *Magazine Antiques* v184 no5 p84 S/O 2017

BERMAN, BOB

Eclipse chasing color *Astronomy* v45 no8 p10 Ag 2017

Finding aliens color *Astronomy* v45 no9 p10 S 2017

Going for gold color *Astronomy* v45 no3 p10 Mr 2017

Just an arcsecond! *Astronomy* v44 no12 p10 D 2016

Lessons of Mir color *Astronomy* v45 no4 p10 Ap 2017

Love affair with a saros color *Astronomy* v45 no11 p10 N 2017

Moon motion color *Astronomy* v45 no7 p10 Jl 2017

A perfect circle color *Astronomy* v45 no5 p10 My 2017

Perfect totality color *Astronomy* v45 no6 p10 Je 2017

Say Betelgeuse color *Astronomy* v45 no10 p10 O 2017

Stellar rhythm color *Astronomy* v45 no2 p10 F 2017

Talking totality *Astronomy* v45 no1 p9 Ja 2017

Berman, Eliza

Anna Deavere Smith color *Time* v188 no19 p64 N 7 2016

Ansel Elgort color *Time* v190 no4 p48 Jl 24 2017

Art In the Age of Trump: The Whitney Biennial Takes a First Crack color *Time* v189 no13 p47 Ap 10 2017

Aubrey Plaza's Status Update color *Time* v190 no7 p47 Ag 21 2017

Barry Jenkins color *Time* v189 no5 p56 F 13 2017

The Best 25 Inventions of 2016 color *Time* v188 no22-23 p43 N/D 2016

The Best of Everything This Year-So Far color *Time* v189 no21 p61 Je 5 2017

Bette Midler color *Time* v188 no27-28 p117 D 26 2016

Calendar: Culture color *Time* v188 no27-28 p106 D 26 2016

Chester Bennington color *Time* v190 no6 p17 Ag 7 2017

Christopher Nolan's Great War color *Time* v190 no5 p53 Jl 31 2017

A Comeback King Fights His Way Back Into the Ring color *Time* v188 no22-23 p102 N/D 2016

The Definitive Guide to Random Oscar Facts color *Time* v189 no7/8 p112 F 27 2017

Disney Makes Its Maiden Voyage to the South Pacific color *Time* v188 no20 p52 N 14 2016

Disney's Renaissance Revival color *Time* v189 no11 p58 Mr 27 2017

Dustin Hoffman on Playing Fathers color *Time* v190 no16/17 p105 O 23 2017

Ewan McGregor color *Time* v189 no11 p59 Mr 27 2017

Gabrielle Union color *Time* v188 no18 p56 O 31 2016

Hamilton Nation color *Time* v188 no14 p50 O 10 2016

Helen Mirren color *Time* v188 no24 p64 D 12 2016

Hidden Figures Calculates the Sum of a Story Untold color *Time* v188 no22-23 p94 N/D 2016

John Cho color *Time* v190 no7 p51 Ag 21 2017

John Leguizamo, Actor color *Time* v189 no15 p50 Ap 24 2017

Jordan Peele Made Us Seriously Laugh. Now He's Going to Scare Us Silly color *Time* v189 no7/8 p108 F 27 2017

Lakeith Stanfield, Contemporary Chameleon color *Time* v190 no8 p47 Ag 28 2017

Lisa Kudrow color *Time* v189 no10 p51 Mr 20 2017

McConaughey Goes Carly Rae In Animated Sing color *Time* v188 no22-23 p109 N/D 2016

M. Night Shyamalan, Filmmaker color *Time* v189 no3 p54 Ja 30 2017

A New Kind of Star Power color *Time* v190 no2/3 p24 Jl 10-17 2017

On Broadway, It's Déjà Vu All Over-and Not Just for Groundhog Day color *Time* v189 no18 p51 My 15 2017

Putting the Fast In Fast Food color *Time* v189 no3 p53 Ja 30 2017

The Reboot Playbook Expands color *Time* v188 no27-28 p116 D 26 2016

The Romantic Comedian color *Time* v190 no1 p49 Jl 3 2017

Sam Elliott *Time* v189 no23 p51 Je 19 2017

Sam Richardson color *Time* v189 no6 p48 F 20 2017

Sigourney Weaver color *Time* v189 no3 p57 Ja 16 2017

Summer Movie Preview: August color *Time* v189 no20 p58 My 29 2017

Summer Movie Preview: July color *Time* v189 no20 p56 My 29 2017

Summer Movie Preview: June color *Time* v189 no20 p50 My 29 2017

Summer Movie Preview: May color *Time* v189 no20 p48 My 29 2017

Under the Giant Heads of Mascots Live Absurd Humans Just Like Us color *Time* v188 no16/17 p85 O 24 2016

Your Golden Globes Workout Plan color diag *Time* v189 no3 p55 Ja 16 2017

Berman, Emily

Ensuring scientific integrity in the Age of Trump bibl cartoon *Science* v355 no6326 p696 F 17 2017

Berman, Jonathan

3 Ways to Take Action in the Face of Uncertainty *Harvard Business Review Digital Articles* p2 D 8 2015

Africa's Unique Opportunity to Promote Inclusive Growth *Harvard Business Review Digital Articles* p2 Jl 9 2015

IBM's Emerging Market Strategy Has 3 Pillars *Harvard Business Review Digital Articles* p2 N 27 2014

Meet the Tech Companies Creating Opportunity in Africa *Harvard Business Review Digital Articles* p2 Ap 12 2016

New MBAs Should Start Their Careers in Frontier Markets *Harvard Business Review Digital Articles* p2 Ap 28 2015

Berman, Josh—Interviews

JOSH BERMAN J. HALTERMAN *TV Guide* v64 no40 p14 O 3 2016

Berman, Lazar

Bibi the Strategist: A close look at Benjamin Netanyahu's foreign policy reveals an underappreciated and misunderstood record of accomplishment *Commentary* v142 no2 p33 S 2016

Berman, Mandy

On Camp J. C. SULLIVAN *New York Times Book Review* p13 Je 4 2017

Berman, Marshall, 1940-2013

Freestyle Marxism M. HOLLERAN *New Republic* v248 no5 p69 My 2017

Berman, Miranda

Inside the Hot Mess Kitchen color *Glamour* v115 no9 p111 S 2017

Berman, Nina

The victims of fake news color *Columbia Journalism Review* v56 no2 p60 Fall 2017

BERMAN, PAUL

The Insurrectionist *New York Times Book Review* p30 D 11 2016

Berman, Pete

OUR 11TH ANNUAL APPRECIATION OF Angels AMONG US I. Aldrich and D. Smith color *Yankee* v80 no6 p130 N/D 2016

Berman, Rachel

CAROLYN ADAMS *Dance Magazine* v90 no12 p50 D 2016

Berman, Russell A.

Ten Ways to Rescue Mideast Policy: In the Middle East the previous administration established neither democracy nor security--and now Russia is on the scene *Hoover Digest: Research & Opinion on Public Policy* no2 p62 Spr 2017

Berman, Sara

ART color *New Yorker* v93 no10 p14 Ap 24 2017

Berman, Sheri

Populism Is Not Fascism bw *Foreign Affairs* v95 no6 p39 N/D 2016

Berman, Tzeporah

#CreateChange *Alternatives Journal (AJ) - Canada's Environmental Voice* v42 no3 p74 2016

Our Obama Moment *Alternatives Journal (AJ) - Canada's Environmental Voice* v42 no2 p75 2016

Bermuda Island (Bermuda Islands)

Find Bliss in Bermuda *New York* v50 no17 p149 Ag 21 2017

Bern, Jess

Technology and the Great Outdoors: How an LED sign is aiding the fight against aquatic invasive species *Parks & Recreation* v52 no5 p52 My 2017

Bernacki, Rachelle

Changing How Patients and Doctors Talk About Death *Harvard Business Review Digital Articles* p2 D 1 2016

Bernal, Antonio Arias

COMO UN SOLO HOMBRE C. Lindsey and A. Roberts *Hoover Digest: Research & Opinion on Public Policy* no1 p219 Wint 2017

Bernáldez, Andrés

DEATH SENTENCE *Lapham's Quarterly* v10 no3 p164 Summ 2017

Bernard, Carlos

24: Legacy M. Roffman *TV Guide* v65 no11 p41 Mr 6 2017

Bernard, David—Interviews

David Bernard A. McLellan color *New Orleans Magazine* v51 no8 p30 Je 2017

BERNARD, EMILY

Interstates *American Scholar* v86 no2 p43 Spr 2017

Bernard, Felix

Walking in a Winter Wonderland *Publishers Weekly* v263 no39 p92 S 26 2016

BERNARD, KATHERINE

Change AGENTS color *Vogue* v206 no11 p124 N 2016

Bernard, M. J.

Long-term pattern and magnitude of soil carbon feedback to the climate system in a warming world chart graph *Science* v357 no6359 p101 O 6 2017

Bernard, Riese

THE BIG QUESTION cartoon *Atlantic* v320 no4 p124 N 2017

I would like to try dating women bw *Glamour* v115 no6 p98 Je 2017

Bernard, Warren

A U-BOAT'S U-TURN [Cover story] bw color map *MHQ: Quarterly Journal of Military History* v29 no4 p40 Summ 2017

Bernard M. Baruch College

Not Without My Brothers [Cover story] J. C. Kang *New York Times Magazine* p30 Ag 13 2017

Bernardes, Gonçalo J. L.

Posttranslational mutagenesis: A chemical strategy for exploring protein side-chain diversity diag *Science* v354 no6312 p597 N 4 2016

Bernardi, Francesca

How boundaries shape chemical delivery in microfluidics bibl diag graph *Science* v354 no6317 p1252 D 9 2016

Bernardin, Joseph, 1928-1996

Signs of the Times [Cover story] B. J. Cupich color *Commonweal* v144 no10 p12 Je 2 2017

Bernardo, Brian

OLD FLAMES color *Field & Stream* v122 no1 p10 My 2017

Bernardo, Dolores

You Just Had a Difficult Conversation at Work. Here's What to Do

Next *Harvard Business Review Digital Articles* p2 My 29 2017

Bernardo, Melissa Rose

2 — FALSETTOS color *Entertainment Weekly* no1444/1445 p118 D 16 2016

4 — NOISES OFF *Entertainment Weekly* no1444/1445 p118 D 16 2016

6 — LONG DAY'S JOURNEY INTO NIGHT *Entertainment Weekly* no1444/1445 p118 D 16 2016

7 — DEAR EVAN HANSEN *Entertainment Weekly* no1444/1445 p118 D 16 2016

No. 1 THE HUMANS color *Entertainment Weekly* no1444/1445 p116 D 16 2016

Bernd, Candice

AMERICA'S TOXIC PRISONS color map *Earth Island Journal* v32 no2 p17 Summ 2017

BERNE, SUZANNE

The Roads Both Taken: A time-traveling novel follows two immigrant sisters on their very different paths *New York Times Book Review* p13 Jl 9 2017

True Grit *New York Times Book Review* p14 N 13 2016

Berne, Tim

NIGHT LIFE *New Yorker* v93 no28 p5 S 18 2017

Berne Convention for the Protection of Literary & Artistic Works

MAP OF THE ARAB LITERARY WORLD map *Publishers Weekly* v263 no43 p(Sp)20 O 24 2016

Bernevig, B. Andrei

Quantized electric multipole insulators bw color graph *Science* v357 no6346 p61 Jl 7 2017

BERNHARD, JIM

WHAT ON EARTH IS IT? chart *Phi Kappa Phi Forum* v97 no1 p32 Spr 2017

Bernhard, Toni

16 LIFE LESSONS *Psychology Today* v49 no5 p62 S/O 2016

BERNHARDT-RÖMERMANN, MARKUS

Combining Biodiversity Resurveys across Regions to Advance Global Change Research *BioScience* v67 no1 p73 Ja 2017

Bernholz, Malte

Why and How to Build an In-House Consulting Team *Harvard Business Review Digital Articles* p2 S 11 2015

Bernick, Karen

BERRY GOOD: PAUL AND SHELLY DETWILER WELCOME THE PUBLIC TO THEIR OHIO STRAWBERRY AND RASPBERRY FARM color *Successful Farming* v115 no7 p50 My 2017

Bernien, Hannes

Atom-by-atom assembly of defect-free one-dimensional cold atom arrays bibl diag graph *Science* v354 no6315 p1024 N 25 2016

Bernier, Debbie

CABIN art color *Cabin Living* p9 S 2017

Bernier, Maxime—Political & social views

THE POWER OF NO S. PROUDFOOT color *Maclean's* v130 no4 p30 My 2017

Berninghausen, Otto

The cryo-EM structure of a ribosome–Ski2-Ski3-Ski8 helicase complex bibl color graph *Science* v354 no6318 p1431 D 16 2016

Bernoff, Josh

Bad Writing Is Destroying Your Company's Productivity *Harvard Business Review Digital Articles* p2 S 6 2016

Corporate Writing Doesn't Have to Sound Like It's Written by Committee *Harvard Business Review Digital Articles* p2 S 15 2016

Why Your Organization Needs a Writing Center *Harvard Business Review Digital Articles* p2 F 21 2017

Your Writing Isn't as Good as You Think It Is *Harvard Business Review Digital Articles* p2 S 28 2016

Bernoulli effect (Fluid dynamics)

TUBULAR DUDE E. Tingwall bw color *Car & Driver* v63 no4 p24 O 2017

Bernsen, Corbin, 1954-

AMERICAN GODS M. Snetiker color *Entertainment Weekly* no1446/1447 p62 D 2016/Ja 2017

Bernstam, Michael S.

Inconvenient Math? On climate change, the uncertainties multiply--literally *Hoover Digest: Research & Opinion on Public Policy* no2 p133 Spr 2017

BERNSTEIN, ALEX

NIGHT MOVES *Cincinnati Magazine* v50 no8 p40 My 2017

Bernstein, Amy

Amazon's Brick-and-Mortar Store Shouldn't Come as a Surprise *Harvard Business Review Digital Articles* p2 O 10 2014

Bernstein, Andrew J.

THANKS FOR THE RIDE color *Bicycling* v58 no10 p15 N/D 2017

Bernstein, Aron M.

Virginia Ruth Brown *Physics Today* v69 no10 p67 O 2016

Bernstein, Bradley E.

Decoupling genetics, lineages, and microenvironment in IDH-mutant gliomas by single-cell RNA-seq diag *Science* v355 no6332 p1391 Mr 31 2017

Epigenetic plasticity and the hallmarks of cancer diag *Science* v357 no6348 p266 Jl 21 2017

BERNSTEIN, CARL

The Year in Reading [Cover story] *New York Times Book Review* p8 D 25 2016

Bernstein, David

INMATE NO. 40892-424 color *Chicago* v66 no10 p60 O 2017

THE RECKONING color *Chicago* v65 no12 p84 D 2016

Bernstein, Ethan

Case Study: Can an Airline Cut "Turn Times" Without Adding Staff? *Harvard Business Review Digital Articles* p2 Ja 27 2016

Flat Organizations Like Zappos Need Pockets of Privacy *Harvard Business Review Digital Articles* p2 N 28 2014

How Self-Managed Companies Help People Learn on the Job *Harvard Business Review Digital Articles* p2 Ag 3 2016

The Sales Director Who Turned Work into a Fantasy Sports Competition *Harvard Business Review Digital Articles* p2 Mr 27 2015

Why Is Micromanagement So Infectious? *Harvard Business Review Digital Articles* p2 Ag 17 2016

Why We Need to Outsmart Our Smart Devices *Harvard Business Review Digital Articles* p2 O 23 2014

BERNSTEIN, FRED A.

bentota, sri lanka color *Architectural Digest* no5 p84 My 2017

Border Wall Divides Profession *Architectural Record* v205 no4 p30 Ap 2017

Design as Salvation *Architectural Record* v205 no1 p43 Ja 2017

DIAMONDS ARE FOREVER color *Architectural Digest* v73 no11 p90 N 2016

Fertile Imaginations color *Architectural Digest* v74 no10 p60 O 1 2017

In Case of Emergency color *Architectural Digest* no6 p78 Je 1 2017

LESSON PLAN color *Architectural Digest* v73 no11 p84 N 2016

Linked In *Architectural Record* v204 no11 p84 N 2016

A Look at New York's Ambitious Infrastructure Plans color *Architectural Record* v205 no2 p20 F 2017

Mark Wigley and Beatriz Colomina *Architectural Record* v204 no10 p28 O 2016

MUSIC IN THE AIR color *Architectural Digest* v74 no2 p72 F 2017

Obituary: John Belle, 1932-2016 *Architectural Record* v204 no10 p27 O 2016

Oscar Winner color *Architectural Digest* no5 p158 My 2017

Pair of Aces bw color *Architectural Digest* v74 no3 p60 Mr 2017

Record's Innovation Conference Explores Craft color *Architectural Record* v204 no12 p17 D 2016

Stake in the Neighborhood: Two buildings open on a new campus in upper Manhattan, with a promise to enhance the community color map *Architectural Record* v205 no5 p80 My 2017

Studio Andrea Dragoni bw color *Architectural Record* v204 no12 p52 D 2016

A Surprising Critique of a Modernist Landmark *Architectural Record* v204 no11 p53 N 2016

Bernstein, Jane

HELLO MY NAME IS JANE *Saturday Evening Post* v289 no1 p18 Ja/F 2017

Bernstein, Jeremy

Great Scientists Against Terrible Odds bw *New York Review of Books* v63 no19 p52 D 8 2016

Spooky Physics Up Close: An Exchange bw *New York Review of Books* v63 no19 p62 D 8 2016

BERNSTEIN, JESSE

Masterpiece Theater *Commentary* v142 no3 p11 O 2016

Bernstein, Jonathan

Glen Campbell color *Entertainment Weekly* no1478 / 1479 p105 Ag 18-25 2017

Haim color *Entertainment Weekly* no1473 p57 Jl 7 2017

Bernstein, Joshua M.

home & help img *New York* p96 Mr 6 2017

Bernstein, Melissa—Interviews

MARK JOHNSON AND MELISSA BERNSTEIN J. HALTERMAN *TV Guide* p11 D 5 2016

Bernstein, Richard

Thailand: The Permanent Coup color *New York Review of Books* v64 no14 p69 S 28 2017

Bernstein, Shelley

VIEWER POSITIONING SYSTEM J. Enxuto and E. Love *Art in America* v104 no9 p122 O 2016

Bernstein, Sophie

Go Healthy STL S. Myrick *Parks & Recreation* v52 no2 p30 F 2017

BERNSTEIN-MACHLAY, LAURA

Tales From Motor City *American Scholar* v86 no1 p82 Wint 2017

Urban Wild: IN SLOWLY GENTRIFYING DETROIT, YOU MIGHT SEE A FOX, OR EVEN A COYOTE, BUT WHERE HAVE ALL THE STRAY DOGS GONE? *American Scholar* v86 no4 p76 Aut 2017

Bernthal, Jon

Marvel's The Punisher S. Li, A. Bacle et al color *Entertainment Weekly* no1482/1483 p106 S 22 2017

Berrahmouni, Nora

The extent of forest in dryland biomes [Cover story] chart map *Science* v356 no6338 p635 My 12 2017

Berrecloth, Darren

BIKE MAGAZINE PHOTO ANNUAL 2017 bw color *Bike Magazine* v24 no6 p72 Ag 2017

Berrett-Koehler Publishers (Company)

At 25, Berrett-Koehler Looks Forward A. Gross color *Publishers Weekly* v264 no18 p12 My 1 2017

Berridge, Scott

Young adults and trends in household formation *Monthly Labor Review* p1 S 2016

Berries

THE BIG CHEESE M. ALLAN *Iceland Review* v55 no4 p54 Jl/Ag 2017

BERRIGAN, FRIDA

Striking Back Against Empire bw color *In These Times* v40 no11 p33 N 2016

Berroa, Ignacio

Berroa's Jazz Crossroads J. Potter color *Downbeat* v84 no9 p22 S 2017

Berry, Amy

AN OPEN INVITATION A. Preiser color *Southern Living* v52 no6 p84 Je 2017

Berry, Barnett

Microcredentials color il *Phi Delta Kappan* v98 no3 p34 N 2016

Micro-Credentials: The Badges of Professional Growth *Education Digest* v82 no9 p21 My 2017

Solving the teacher shortage color *Phi Delta Kappan* v98 no8 p8 My 2017

Berry, Chuck, 1926-2017

Chuck Berry 1926-2017 M. GILMORE bw color *Rolling Stone* no1285 p22 Ap 20 2017

CHUCK BERRY K. O'Donnell color *Entertainment Weekly* no1459 p14 Mr 31 2017

Chuck Berry's Final Gift P. DOYLE color *Rolling Stone* no1284 p16 Ap 6 2017

Essential Chuck D. Browne, J. Dolan et al color *Rolling Stone* no1285 p36 Ap 20 2017

Founding Rocker A. CLINE bw *National Review* v69 no7 p24 Ap 17 2017

Riding With Chuck M. JACOBSON color *Rolling Stone* no1285 p35 Ap 20 2017

'The Granddaddy of Us All' K. RICHARDS bw *Rolling Stone* no1285 p34 Ap 20 2017

Berry, Eugene B.

LIFE: ***½ N. Irvin color *Art in America* v104 no10 p100 N 2016

Berry, Halle, 1966-

Halle Berry C. Ianzito color *AARP: The Magazine* v59 no5A p80 Ag/S 2016

Sound Bites color *Entertainment Weekly* no1476 p6 Ag 4 2017

Berry, Halle, 1966-—Interviews

Storm's Secret Mutant Love color *Entertainment Weekly* no1478 / 1479 p20 Ag 18-25 2017

Berry, Jason

AFTER PETE color *New Orleans Magazine* v51 no1 p56 N 2016

Barack Obama and the Limits of Optimism color *America* v216 no9 p25 Ap 24 2017

Best of Brass bw *New Orleans Magazine* v51 no5 p54 Mr 2017

Big Chiefs Coming color *New Orleans Magazine* v51 no4 p52 F 2017

BOOK AND BANJO color *New Orleans Magazine* v51 no3 p50 Ja 2017

Deb Cotton, Now and Forever: The Final Goodbye color *New Orleans Magazine* v51 no10 p64 Ag 2017

DYLAN IN STOCKHOLM bw *New Orleans Magazine* v51 no2 p56 D 2016

Lured to New Orleans color *New Orleans Magazine* v51 no6 p52 Ap 2017

Making Music Bounce color *New Orleans Magazine* v51 no12 p62 O 2017

A Melodic Zone color *New Orleans Magazine* v51 no9 p50 Jl 2017

A Record of Time color *New Orleans Magazine* v52 no1 p60 S 2017

Storyville in Time color *New Orleans Magazine* v51 no8 p52 Je 2017

Tom Sancton color *New Orleans Magazine* v51 no9 p28 Jl 2017

Tribute to Satchmo color *New Orleans Magazine* v51 no7 p54 My 2017

Berry, John—Interviews

ALMOST FAMOUS T. REHAGEN *Atlanta* v56 no10 p36 F 2017

Berry, Joseph A.

Mobile MUTE specifies subsidiary cells to build physiologically improved grass stomata bibl diag *Science* v355 no6330 p1215 Mr 17 2017

Berry, Kiel

What Happened When Linkin Park Asked Harvard for Help with Its Business Model *Harvard Business Review Digital Articles* p2 Je 23 2015

Berry, Leonard L.

Giving Seriously Ill Patients More Choices About Their Care *Harvard Business Review Digital Articles* p2 My 23 2017

How Service Companies Can Earn Customer Trust and Keep It *Harvard Business Review Digital Articles* p2 Ap 19 2017

Berry, Malinda Elizabeth

"A BOOK I'D LIKE MY ELECTED OFFICIALS TO READ" color *Christian Century* v133 no21 p28 O 12 2016

Berry, Mary

How the Cookie Crumbles D. Coggan color *Entertainment Weekly* no1434 p18 O 7 2016

'The Great British Baking Show' N. Englander *New York Times Magazine* p40 O 8 2017

Berry, Michael

Approaches to studying our history *Physics Today* v70 no3 p11 Mr 2017

BERRY, NANCY E.

Reclaiming the Past color diag *Timber Home Living* v27 no6 p26 D 2017

Berry, Paul

Communication Tips for Global Virtual Teams *Harvard Business Review Digital Articles* p2 O 30 2014

Berry, Scott

Distinct phases of Polycomb silencing to hold epigenetic memory of cold in Arabidopsis diag *Science* v357 no6356 p1142 S 15 2017

Berry, Wendell

The Bad Modern History of Farming bw *Progressive* v81 no5 p46 Je/Jl 2017

Berry growing

CSA CONFIDENTIAL: If you've splurged on a COMMUNITY

SUPPORTED AGRICULTURE membership, take these simple steps to protect your investment. Because thyme is money S. KROWIAK *Indianapolis Monthly* v12 no40 p65 Ag 2017

Sweet and WILD T. MARRONE color *Cabin Living* p55 Ag 2017

Bersabe, Ofelia

The Home Health Aide E. Craig *New York Times Magazine* p38 F 26 2017

Berselius, Fredrik

Aska D. Wenger color *New Yorker* v93 no2 p19 F 27 2017

Bershidsky, Leonid

Why We Need Cyberwar Rules of Engagement Now *Bloomberg Businessweek* no4531 p40 Jl 24 2017

Bersin, Josh

The 5 Elements of a Strong Leadership Pipeline *Harvard Business Review Digital Articles* p2 O 6 2016

Digital Leadership Is Not an Optional Part of Being a CEO *Harvard Business Review Digital Articles* p2 D 1 2016

Good Presentations Need to Make People Uncomfortable *Harvard Business Review Digital Articles* p2 S 9 2016

Using Design Thinking to Embed Learning in Our Jobs *Harvard Business Review Digital Articles* p2 Jl 25 2016

WHY FACEBOOK IS KEEPING PERFORMANCE REVIEWS: INTERACTION color *Harvard Business Review* v95 no1 p18 Ja/F 2017

Bertaina, M. E.

Observation of a large-scale anisotropy in the arrival directions of cosmic rays above 8 × 1018 eV *Science* v357 no6357 p1266 S 22 2017

Bertarelli, Ernesto

The World's Top 200 COLLECTORS bw cartoon chart color *ARTnews* v115 no3 p76 Fall 2016

Bertaux, J.-L.

Rosetta's comet 67P/Churyumov-Gerasimenko sheds its dusty mantle to reveal its icy nature bibl graph *Science* v354 no6319 p1566 D 23 2016

Surface changes on comet 67P/Churyumov-Gerasimenko suggest a more active past bw graph *Science* v355 no6332 p1392 Mr 31 2017

Bertelsmann SE & Co. KGaA

Europe K. Stock color *Bloomberg Businessweek* no4530 p9 Jl 17 2017

Spread Your Wings and Fly, Penguin S. Nicola, R. Penty et al color graph *Bloomberg Businessweek* no4509 p17 Ja 30 2017

Berthelier, J.-J.

Xenon isotopes in 67P/Churyumov-Gerasimenko show that comets contributed to Earth's atmosphere diag *Science* v356 no6342 p1069 Je 9 2017

Berthelsen, Christian

Data Mining to Find Tax Cheaters color *Bloomberg Businessweek* no4524 p41 My 29 2017

Berthiaume, Heidi

Fill Me In J. TRUPP *D: The Magazine of Dallas* v43 no10 p48 O 2016

Bertini, I.

Rosetta's comet 67P/Churyumov-Gerasimenko sheds its dusty mantle to reveal its icy nature bibl graph *Science* v354 no6319 p1566 D 23 2016

Surface changes on comet 67P/Churyumov-Gerasimenko suggest a more active past bw graph *Science* v355 no6332 p1392 Mr 31 2017

Bertini, Marco

Case Study: When You Have to Choose Between Core and New Customers: An extreme sports company considers a VIP tier il *Harvard Business Review* v95 no5 p143 S/O 2017

Case Study: When You Have to Choose Between Core and New Customers *Harvard Business Review Digital Articles* p2 Je 26 2017

Bertino, Bryan

The Monster C. Collis color *Entertainment Weekly* no1440 p45 N 18 2016

Bertoia, Harry, 1915-1978

Fine Art, Furniture, and Fun *Treasures* v6 no5 p6 Ap/My 2017

Bertoncini, Gene

NIGHT LIFE *New Yorker* v93 no28 p5 S 18 2017

BERTONI, STEVEN

LESSONS AND IDEAS BY THE 100 GREATEST LIVING BUSINESS MINDS bw color *Forbes* v200 no3 p115 S 28 2017

The Other Brother [Cover story] color *Forbes* v199 no4 p70 Ap 25 2017

The Son-in-Law Also Rises [Cover story] color *Forbes* v198 no8 p70 D 20 2016

THE WAY WE WORK [Cover story] color *Forbes* v200 no4 p64 O 24 2017

Bertotti, Candace

How to Talk Politics at Work Without Alienating People *Harvard Business Review Digital Articles* p2 S 14 2016

Bertou, X.

Observation of a large-scale anisotropy in the arrival directions of cosmic rays above 8 × 1018 eV *Science* v357 no6357 p1266 S 22 2017

Bertram Yacht Inc.

Bertram 35 D. J. Harding color *Power & Motoryacht* v32 no11 p64 N 2016

Bertram 60 S. Murray color *Power & Motoryacht* v34 no9 p52 S 2017

Bertram Yachts (Company)

Return of a Legend B. PIKE chart color *Power & Motoryacht* v34 no7 p42 Jl 2017

Bertrand, J. B.

Soft x-ray excitonics bw diag *Science* v357 no6356 p1134 S 15 2017

Bertrand, Jean-Louis

Severe Weather Threatens Businesses. It's Time to Measure and Disclose the Risks *Harvard Business Review Digital Articles* p2 S 14 2017

Bertrand, John

PRELUDE TO REVOLUTION *Military History* v33 no5 p61 Ja 2017

Bertsch, Dave

TURNED SCREWS GONE LOOSE color *Powder* v45 no6 p90 F 2017

BERTSCHE, RACHEL

BEST PRIVATE SCHOOLS [Cover story] chart color *Chicago* v66 no9 p104 S 2017

Bertschek, Irene

Does Engaging with Customers on Facebook Lead to Better Product Ideas? *Harvard Business Review Digital Articles* p2 O 12 2017

Bertulani, Carlos

Key Nuclear Reaction Experiments Discoveries and Consequences *Physics Today* v69 no11 p58 N 2016

Bertz, Josefine

Site-specific phosphorylation of tau inhibits amyloid-β toxicity in Alzheimer's mice bibl graph *Science* v354 no6314 p904 N 18 2016

Berube, David

Delayed Gratification color *Arts & Crafts Homes & the Revival* v12 no5 p18 Wint 2018

Berube, Joyce

Delayed Gratification color *Arts & Crafts Homes & the Revival* v12 no5 p18 Wint 2018

Berube, Kate

Hannah and Sugar color *Publishers Weekly* v263 no49 p22 D 7 2016

BERWALD, JULI

The Immortal Jellyfish color diag *Discover* v38 no10 p58 D 2017

BESCHTA, ROBERT L.

Conserving the World's Megafauna and Biodiversity: The Fierce Urgency of Now *BioScience* v67 no3 p197 Mr 2017

Saving the World's Terrestrial Megafauna color *BioScience* v66 no10 p807 O 1 2016

Beshear, Andy

Bluegrass Blood Feud A. Greenblatt *Governing* v30 no1 p9 O 2016

Beshears, John

Experiment with Organizational Change Before Going All In *Harvard Business Review Digital Articles* p2 O 13 2014

Identifying the Biases Behind Your Bad Decisions *Harvard Business Review Digital Articles* p2 O 31 2014

Besley, Adrian

Monty Python's Flying Circus: Hidden Treasures *Publishers Weekly* v264 no9 p92 F 27 2017

Besougloff, Neil

But how did he build that? *Model Railroader* v84 no2 p8 F 2017

Celebrate a hobby journey color *Model Railroader* v84 no1 p8 Ja 2017

Circles, figure numbers, and our buddy Lou *Model Railroader* v84 no6 p8 Je 2017

Enough theory; where do I put the wires? *Model Railroader* v84 no9 p8 S 2017

Guess who built another incredible layout? color *Model Railroader* v84 no5 p8 My 2017

Keeping your hobby hoard manageable [Cover story] color *Model Railroader* v84 no7 p8 Jl 2017

Layout names from a more playful era color *Model Railroader* v84 no8 p8 Ag 2017

Model railroading present, past, and future *Model Railroader* v84 no4 p8 Ap 2017

The next game changer? *Model Railroader* v83 no12 p8 D 2016

Realism? Use white paint *Model Railroader* v84 no3 p8 Mr 2017

TrainClap 2000 audio DCC controller color *Model Railroader* v84 no4 p98 Ap 2017

Besse, S.

Rosetta's comet 67P/Churyumov-Gerasimenko sheds its dusty mantle to reveal its icy nature bibl graph *Science* v354 no6319 p1566 D 23 2016

Surface changes on comet 67P/Churyumov-Gerasimenko suggest a more active past bw graph *Science* v355 no6332 p1392 Mr 31 2017

Besselink, Clara T.

An interactive three-dimensional digital atlas and quantitative database of human development bibl color graph *Science* v354 no6315 paag0053-1 N 25 2016

Bessen, James

Computers Don't Kill Jobs but Do Increase Inequality *Harvard Business Review Digital Articles* p2 Mr 24 2016

Free Community College Would Help Fix the Skills Gap *Harvard Business Review Digital Articles* p2 Ja 12 2015

How Technology Has Affected Wages for the Last 200 Years *Harvard Business Review Digital Articles* p2 Ap 29 2015

How Technology Has Affected Wages for the Last 200 Years J. Bessen *Harvard Business Review Digital Articles* p2 Ap 29 2015

Lobbyists Are Behind the Rise in Corporate Profits *Harvard Business Review Digital Articles* p2 My 26 2016

Stop Trying to Control How Ex-Employees Use Their Knowledge *Harvard Business Review Digital Articles* p2 O 9 2014

Bessette, Joan

When I Was a Horse-Crazy Kid, I... color *Horse & Rider* v56 no2 p72 F 2017

Bessette, Joseph M.

MORE JUSTICE, LESS CRIME *Claremont Review of Books* v17 no3 p15 Summ 2017

BESSINGER, JEANNETTE

Bake-Ahead Breakfast color *Better Nutrition* p62 My 2017

Cooking with Coconut Oil color *Amazing Wellness* v9 no2 p80 Spr 2017

Eat-The-Bowl Summer Salad [Cover story] color *Better Nutrition* v79 no6 p62 Je 2017

Fresh & Fast Chicken color *Better Nutrition* v79 no1 p66 Ja 2017

Ham-Yam Quiche Dijon color *Better Nutrition* v79 no4 p70 Ap 2017

Peanut Butter Power Snack Dip color *Better Nutrition* v79 no7 p56 Jl 2017

Post-Holiday Fast Food color *Better Nutrition* v79 no11 p78 N 2017

Quick & Healthy Homemade Sausage color *Better Nutrition* v79 no10 p78 O 2017

Soup's On color *Better Nutrition* v78 no11 p86 N 2016

Trout: The Perfect Catch color *Better Nutrition* v79 no9 p70 S 2017

Zoodle Ramen Bowl color *Better Nutrition* v79 no3 p70 Mr 2017

Besson, Luc, 1959-

GOING THE DISTANCE color map *Wired* v25 no7 p8 Jl 2017

LUC BESSON'S OUTER LIMITS A. ROGERS cartoon color *Wired* v25 no7 p64 Jl 2017

ORAL HISTORY THE FIFTH ELEMENT L. Greenblatt color *Entertainment Weekly* no1474/1475 p80 Jl 21-28 2017

Space Oddity A. Bhattacharji color *Bloomberg Businessweek* no4531 p70 Jl 24 2017

Valerian and the City of a Thousand Planets J. McGovern color *Entertainment Weekly* no1473 p44 Jl 7 2017

Valerian's Half-Crazed Space Race S. Zacharek color *Time* v190 no5 p59 Jl 31 2017

BESSOUDO, MARK

Energy efficiency color *Issues in Science & Technology* v33 no1 p12 Fall 2016

Best & Most Beautiful Things (Film)

Best and Most Beautiful Things K. P. Sullivan color *Entertainment Weekly* no1443 p48 D 9 2016

Best, Charles—Interviews

Funding Teachers' Dreams for Their Students S. MAUGHAN color *Publishers Weekly* v264 no34 p64 Ag 21 2017

Best, Eric

Beth Akers and Matthew M. Chingos, Game of Loans: The Rhetoric and Reality of Student Debt *Society* v54 no4 p372 Ag 2017

Best, Joel

Beth Akers and Matthew M. Chingos, Game of Loans: The Rhetoric and Reality of Student Debt *Society* v54 no4 p372 Ag 2017

BEST, MICHAEL

A Day's Work *Reader's Digest* v188 no1126 p64 D 2016/Ja 2017

Best, Rachel

Party Time! color *Vegetarian Times* v43 no2 p52 N/D 2016

Best books

ILA's Choices Reading Lists graph map *Literacy Today (2411-7862)* v34 no6 p12 My/Je 2017

VALUING THEIR VOICES P. J. Farris color *Literacy Today (2411-7862)* v34 no6 p14 My/Je 2017

WHAT'S YOUR SUMMER BOOK? A. BROWN color *Forbes* v199 no7 p34 Je 29 2017

Best Buy Co. Inc.

Leader Board color *Forbes* v198 no9 p20 D 30 2016

To Grandmother's House We Go M. Boyle color *Bloomberg Businessweek* no4541 p15 O 9 2017

Best Coast (Performer)

NIGHT LIFE *New Yorker* v93 no31 p5 O 9 2017

Best in the Desert (Company)

A NATION'S DATEBOOK *Dirt Sports + Off-Road* v51 no6 p72 Je 2017

Best practices

4 Things Successful Change Leaders Do Well D. A. Ready *Harvard Business Review Digital Articles* p2 Ja 28 2016

An Alternative to Health Care M&A D. Hayes *Harvard Business Review Digital Articles* p2 D 22 2014

A Checklist for Making Faster, Better Decisions E. Larson *Harvard Business Review Digital Articles* p2 Mr 7 2016

Getting the Most from an Online Customer Community C. Trevail *Harvard Business Review Digital Articles* p2 Je 3 2016

How to Fire Someone Without Destroying Them A. Cavanaugh *Harvard Business Review Digital Articles* p2 Ja 28 2016

Research: Why Best Practices Don't Translate Across Cultures P. Hinds *Harvard Business Review Digital Articles* p2 Je 27 2016

Smart Benchmarking Starts with Knowing Whom to Compare Yourself To R. Valdes-Perez *Harvard Business Review Digital Articles* p2 O 30 2015

Striving for Quality Mosques *Islamic Horizons* v46 no1 p18 Ja/F 2017

The Two Things Killing Your Ability to Focus W. Treseder *Harvard Business Review Digital Articles* p2 Ag 3 2016

Best sellers

AUDIO BESTSELLERS J. Maher chart color *Publishers Weekly* v263 no51 p14 D 12 2016

BESTSELLERS chart *Publishers Weekly* v264 no25 p17 Je 19 2017

BESTSELLERS chart *Publishers Weekly* v264 no29 p10 Jl 17 2017

BESTSELLERS chart *Publishers Weekly* v264 no5 p9 Ja 30 2017

BESTSELLERS C. JURIS chart *Publishers Weekly* v263 no50 p17 D 5 2016

Best Sellers *New York Times Book Review* p23 Ag 13 2017

Best Sellers *New York Times Book Review* p28 O 9 2016

Best Sellers *New York Times Book Review* p34 My 14 2017

CATEGORY BESTSELLERS chart *Publishers Weekly* v264 no25 p20 Je 19 2017

CATEGORY BESTSELLERS chart *Publishers Weekly* v264 no29 p13 Jl 17 2017

CHILDREN'S BESTSELLERS chart *Publishers Weekly* v263 no43 p16 O 24 2016

CHILDREN'S BESTSELLERS chart *Publishers Weekly* v264 no25 p19 Je 19 2017

CHILDREN'S BESTSELLERS chart *Publishers Weekly* v264 no29 p12 Jl 17 2017

CHILDREN'S BESTSELLERS chart *Publishers Weekly* v264 no36 p17 S 4 2017

CHILDREN'S BEST SELLERS *New York Times Book Review* p25 F 26 2017

CHILDREN'S BEST SELLERS *New York Times Book Review* p29 O 8 2017

CHILDREN'S BEST SELLERS *New York Times Book Review* p31 N 20 2016

CHILDREN'S BEST SELLERS *New York Times Book Review* p37 My 14 2017

CHILDREN'S BESTSELLERS *Publishers Weekly* v264 no5 p11 Ja 30 2017

COMBINED PRINT AND E-BOOK BEST SELLERS *New York Times Book Review* p19 Mr 5 2017

COMBINED PRINT AND E-BOOK BEST SELLERS *New York Times Book Review* p23 Ag 6 2017

COMBINED PRINT AND E-BOOK BEST SELLERS *New York Times Book Review* p23 F 26 2017

COMBINED PRINT AND E-BOOK BEST SELLERS *New York Times Book Review* p28 N 20 2016

Correction *Publishers Weekly* v264 no36 p13 S 4 2017

From MOOC to Bestseller A. Green color *Publishers Weekly* v264 no24 p6 Je 12 2017

FROM THE EDITOR P. Lay *History Today* v67 no2 p2 F 2017

Game Face C. JURIS chart color graph *Publishers Weekly* v264 no32 p10 Ag 7 2017

iBook Bestsellers chart color *Publishers Weekly* v264 no25 p21 Je 19 2017

iBook Bestsellers C. Juris chart color *Publishers Weekly* v264 no30 p15 Jl 24 2017

iBooks Bestsellers chart color *Publishers Weekly* v264 no1 p13 Ja 2 2017

iBooks Bestsellers chart color *Publishers Weekly* v264 no36 p18 S 4 2017

iBooks Bestsellers chart color *Publishers Weekly* v264 no5 p12 Ja 30 2017

Local Favorites Top in Italy, Spain, Sweden J. Maher chart color *Publishers Weekly* v264 no5 p13 Ja 30 2017

MISCELLANEOUS BEST SELLERS *New York Times Book Review* p24 Ja 22 2017

MISCELLANEOUS BEST SELLERS *New York Times Book Review* p28 O 30 2016

MISCELLANEOUS BEST SELLERS *New York Times Book Review* p32 N 20 2016

OCTOBER INTERNATIONAL BESTSELLERS chart *Publishers Weekly* v263 no48 p18 N 28 2016

PRINT / HARDCOVER BEST SELLERS *New York Times Book Review* p22 D 18 2016

PRINT / HARDCOVER BEST SELLERS *New York Times Book Review* p24 Ag 20 2017

PRINT/HARDCOVER BEST SELLERS *New York Times Book Review* p28 O 8 2017

PRINT / HARDCOVER BEST SELLERS *New York Times Book Review* p36 My 14 2017

Prize Winners On Top in France, Spain J. Maher chart *Publishers Weekly* v264 no1 p14 Ja 2 2017

Royal Family C. JURIS chart color graph *Publishers Weekly* v264 no8 p11 F 20 2017

SMASHWORDS SELF-PUBLISHED BESTSELLERS LIST, APRIL 2017 chart color *Publishers Weekly* v264 no25 p22 Je 19 2017

SMASHWORDS SELF-PUBLISHED BESTSELLERS LIST, JULY 2017 bw chart color *Publishers Weekly* v264 no36 p19 S 4 2017

SMASHWORDS SELF-PUBLISHED BESTSELLERS LIST, OCTOBER 2016 chart color *Publishers Weekly* v263 no52 p19 D 19 2016

Taking a Look at Apple's and Amazon's E-book Bestsellers C.

Reid chart *Publishers Weekly* v264 no29 p8 Jl 17 2017

'Trees' Takes Root in France, Germany J. Milliot and C. JURIS chart color *Publishers Weekly* v264 no39 p21 S 25 2017

Best sellers—Bibliographies

Best Sellers *New York Times Book Review* p23 Je 18 2017

CHILDREN'S BEST SELLERS *New York Times Book Review* p25 Je 18 2017

PRINT/HARDCOVER BEST SELLERS *New York Times Book Review* p24 Je 18 2017

Beste, Simon

Deliberative Citizens, (Non)Deliberative Politicians: A Rejoinder *Daedalus* v146 no3 p106 Summ 2017

Bestelink, Brad

WILD GAME OF THRONES K. HAHN *TV Guide* v64 no48 p24 N 21 2016

Bestor, Barbara

beach boys M. DIAMOND color *Architectural Digest* v74 no3 p108 Mr 2017

Best sellers—Charts, diagrams, etc.

AUDIO BESTSELLERS chart *Publishers Weekly* v263 no46 p19 N 14 2016

AUDIO BESTSELLERS C. JURIS chart *Publishers Weekly* v264 no28 p16 Jl 10 2017

AUDIO BESTSELLERS C. JURIS chart *Publishers Weekly* v264 no7 p15 F 13 2017

AUDIO BESTSELLERS J. Maher chart color *Publishers Weekly* v264 no33 p20 Ag 14 2017

BESTSELLERS chart color *Publishers Weekly* v264 no32 p11 Ag 7 2017

BESTSELLERS chart *Publishers Weekly* v264 no6 p13 F 6 2017

BESTSELLERS C. JURIS chart *Publishers Weekly* v264 no21 p15 My 22 2017

BESTSELLERS C. JURIS *Publishers Weekly* v263 no39 p17 S 26 2016

Best Sellers *New York Times Book Review* p23 Mr 19 2017

Best Sellers *New York Times Book Review* p24 N 6 2016

BESTSELLERS OCTOBER 17–23 2016 C. JURIS chart color *Publishers Weekly* v263 no44 p13 O 31 2016

Calendar Girl Strikes in France E. Nawotka chart map *Publishers Weekly* v264 no9 p17 F 27 2017

CATEGORY BESTSELLERS chart *Publishers Weekly* v263 no47 p17 N 21 2016

CATEGORY BESTSELLERS C. JURIS chart *Publishers Weekly* v264 no28 p17 Jl 10 2017

CATEGORY BESTSELLERS C. JURIS chart *Publishers Weekly* v264 no38 p20 S 18 2017

CATEGORY BESTSELLERS C. JURIS chart *Publishers Weekly* v264 no3 p18 Ja 16 2017

CHILDREN'S BESTSELLERS chart *Publishers Weekly* v263 no47 p16 N 21 2016

CHILDREN'S BESTSELLERS chart *Publishers Weekly* v263 no52 p16 D 19 2016

CHILDREN'S BESTSELLERS chart *Publishers Weekly* v264 no23 p13 Je 5 2017

CHILDREN'S BESTSELLERS chart *Publishers Weekly* v264 no33 p16 Ag 14 2017

CHILDREN'S BESTSELLERS chart *Publishers Weekly* v264 no6 p15 F 6 2017

CHILDREN'S BESTSELLERS chart *Publishers Weekly* v264 no8 p14 F 20 2017

CHILDREN'S BESTSELLERS C. JURIS chart *Publishers Weekly* v264 no21 p17 My 22 2017

CHILDREN'S BESTSELLERS C. JURIS chart *Publishers Weekly* v264 no38 p19 S 18 2017

CHILDREN'S BEST SELLERS *New York Times Book Review* p25 Je 25 2017

CHILDREN'S BEST SELLERS *New York Times Book Review* p25 Jl 2 2017

CHILDREN'S BEST SELLERS *New York Times Book Review* p25 Mr 19 2017

CHILDREN'S BEST SELLERS *New York Times Book Review* p27 N 27 2016

CHILDREN'S BESTSELLERS OCTOBER 17–23 2016 chart *Publishers Weekly* v263 no44 p16 O 31 2016

COMBINED PRINT AND E-BOOK BEST SELLERS *New York Times Book Review* p23 F 12 2017

COMBINED PRINT AND E-BOOK BEST SELLERS *New York Times Book Review* p23 Je 25 2017

COMBINED PRINT AND E-BOOK BEST SELLERS *New York Times Book Review* p24 N 27 2016

Escapist Favorites Top in Europe E. Nawotka chart color *Publishers Weekly* v264 no21 p19 My 22 2017

Ferrante Hits in Germany, Sweden J. Maher *Publishers Weekly* v263 no39 p22 S 26 2016

HARDCOVER BEST SELLERS *New York Times Book Review* p24 F 12 2017

iBook Bestsellers chart color *Publishers Weekly* v264 no32 p14 Ag 7 2017

iBook Bestsellers C. JURIS chart color *Publishers Weekly* v264 no21 p18 My 22 2017

iBooks Bestsellers chart color *Publishers Weekly* v263 no44 p17 O 31 2016

iBooks Bestsellers chart color *Publishers Weekly* v264 no6 p16 F 6 2017

iBooks Bestsellers C. JURIS chart color *Publishers Weekly* v264 no39 p20 S 25 2017

MISCELLANEOUS BEST SELLERS *New York Times Book Review* p28 N 27 2016

PRINT/HARDCOVER BEST SELLERS *New York Times Book Review* p24 Je 25 2017

PRINT/HARDCOVER BEST SELLERS *New York Times Book Review* p26 N 27 2016

SMASHWORDS SELF-PUBLISHED BESTSELLERS LIST, DECEMBER 2016 chart color *Publishers Weekly* v264 no6 p17 F 6 2017

SMASHWORDS SELF-PUBLISHED BESTSELLERS LIST, JUNE 2017 chart color *Publishers Weekly* v264 no32 p15 Ag 7 2017

SMASHWORDS SELF-PUBLISHED BESTSELLERS LIST, MAY 2017 C. JURIS chart color *Publishers Weekly* v264 no28 p19 Jl 10 2017

SMASHWORDS SELF-PUBLISHED BESTSELLERS LIST, NOVEMBER 2016 C. JURIS chart color *Publishers Weekly* v264 no3 p20 Ja 16 2017

SMASHWORDS SELF-PUBLISHED BESTSELLERS LIST, SEPTEMBER 2016 chart color *Publishers Weekly* v263 no46 p20 N 14 2016

Bestul, Scott

2016 BEST OF THE BEST bw color *Field & Stream* v121 no7 p96 D 2016/Ja 2017

THE BEST DAYS OF THE Rut [Cover story] color *Field & Stream* v122 no6 p37 N 2017

The Big Bully color *Field & Stream* v122 no3 pW1 Ag 2017

BLOOD SWEAT & DEER [Cover story] color *Field & Stream* v121 no7 p44 D 2016/Ja 2017

Chase the Rut color *Field & Stream* v122 no5 pW11 O 2017

DEKE ATTACK D. HURTEAU bw color *Field & Stream* v122 no5 p16 O 2017

The Easy Bird color *Field & Stream* v121 no9 pT1 Ap 2017

Fresh Takes color *Field & Stream* v122 no6 pW1 N 2017

Halloween Treat color *Field & Stream* v122 no5 pW1 O 2017

Hard Times color *Field & Stream* v122 no4 pW1 S 2017

Hone Sweet Hone color *Field & Stream* v122 no3 pB4 Ag 2017

Make a Mega Mock Scrape color *Field & Stream* v122 no5 pW7 O 2017

Read the Beans color *Field & Stream* v122 no4 pW5 S 2017

Seven BEST DAYS of The Rut color map *Field & Stream* v121 no6 p39 N 2016

Small Wonders color *Field & Stream* v122 no3 pW5 Ag 2017

Stop That Buck! color *Field & Stream* v122 no6 pW4 N 2017

YEAR OF THE GIANT color graph *Field & Stream* v122 no3 p30 Ag 2017

Beswick, Paul

Leading Digital Transformation Is Like Urban Planning *Harvard Business Review Digital Articles* p2 Ag 2 2017

Beta (Finance)

Markets/Personal Finance D. Burger color graph *Bloomberg Businessweek* no4498 p48 N 7 2016

Betancourt, Angela

BOOKS FOR EVERY CHILD: How the Greenbrier Bookcase Project ensures young readers have access to quality books at home *Literacy Today (2411-7862)* v35 no2 p36 S/O 2017

Betancourt, Ingrid

Leaders color *Time* v189 no16/17 p64 My 1-8 2017

BETANCOURT, MANUEL

The Boys in the Band: Flashpoints of Cinema, History, and Queer Politics ed *Film Quarterly* v71 no1 p118 Fall 2017

New Maricón Cinema: Outing Latin American Film *Film Quarterly* v70 no3 p95 Spr 2017

WHOSE LATIN AMERICAN CINEMA? *Film Quarterly* v70 no2 p9 Wint 2016

Betchart, Graham

Mind Over Mascot D. Leung and T. Keith color *Sports Illustrated* v125 no13 p23 O 17 2016

Beth, Jehnny

Melody-Makers img *New York* v50 no9 p90 My 1 2017

Bethea, Charles

BEHIND THE SCENES *Atlanta* v57 no1 p86 My 2017

CHANNEL SURFING WITH RODNEY HO *Atlanta* v57 no1 p90 My 2017

CHUCK TODD color *Runner's World* v52 no2 p96 Mr 2017

DOPE cartoon *New Yorker* v93 no27 p25 S 11 2017

Fast on a Different Track color *Runner's World* v52 no9 p56 O 2017

Jim Stacy, 2.0 3.0 4.0 *Atlanta* v56 no10 p53 F 2017

MONKEY DO cartoon *New Yorker* v92 no45 p23 Ja 16 2017

NEWS-ISH cartoon *New Yorker* v93 no5 p32 Mr 20 2017

ONE TEAM TO UNITE THEM ALL *Atlanta* v56 no11 p100 Mr 2017

PRO CANVASSER cartoon *New Yorker* v93 no10 p38 Ap 24 2017

REBOUND *Atlanta* v56 no7 p37 N 2016

Where There's SmoQue: Nigerian-born chef Seni Alabi-Isama is about to open a sous-vide barbecue restaurant called the SmoQue Pit in Statesboro. Yes, Statesboro *Atlanta* v57 no3 p50 Jl 2017

Bethell, Leslie

iViva Hobsbawm! P. Drinot *History Today* v67 no3 p63 Mr 2017

Bethesda (Md.)

TAPABAR A. Limpert *Washingtonian Magazine* v52 no2 p259 N 2016

BETHGE, GERRY

THE ABYSS color *Outdoor Life* v224 no3 pF1 Ap 2017

ALIVE AND FISHING color *Outdoor Life* v224 no3 p67 Ap 2017

THE ART OF THE EEL color *Outdoor Life* v224 no4 p66 My 2017

BASS OF A DIFFERENT STRIPE color *Outdoor Life* v224 no4 p64 My 2017

BOMBS AWAY BUCKS color *Outdoor Life* v223 no9 pH12 N 2016

BRING ON THE NIGHT color *Outdoor Life* v224 no5 p36 Je/Jl 2017

BROWN UNIVERSITY color *Outdoor Life* v224 no2 p28 F/Mr 2017

THE CHAMPS color *Outdoor Life* v224 no5 p34 Je/Jl 2017

CHOKE JOB chart color *Outdoor Life* v224 no2 p20 F/Mr 2017

CUTT AND RUN 2.0 color *Outdoor Life* v224 no3 pT1 Ap 2017

DIRTY BIRDS color *Outdoor Life* v223 no9 pH14 N 2016

THE DISH ON THE SPOONS color *Outdoor Life* v224 no3 p64 Ap 2017

THE DUCKS STOP HERE color *Outdoor Life* v224 no1 p70 D 2016/Ja 2017

FOR YOUR 'EYES ONLY color map *Outdoor Life* v224 no2 p30 F/Mr 2017

GET TO THE POINT cartoon *Outdoor Life* v224 no2 p32 F/Mr 2017

THE HEART OF A TURKEY DOG color *Outdoor Life* v224 no6 p52 Ag 2017

LIGHTS OUT FOR HOGS color *Outdoor Life* v224 no8 p24 O 2017

LOOK OUT BELOW color *Outdoor Life* v224 no5 p38 Je/Jl 2017

NEXT-LEVEL TURKEY CALLS color *Outdoor Life* v224 no3 p50 Ap 2017

PIMP YOUR SHRIMP diag *Outdoor Life* v224 no3 p66 Ap 2017

RETHINK YOUR TURKEY VEST color *Outdoor Life* v224 no3 pT5 Ap 2017

RUNNING OF THE BULLS color *Outdoor Life* v224 no3 p59 Ap 2017

THE SAILFISH COAST color map *Outdoor Life* v224 no2 p25 F/Mr 2017

SPEED KILLS color *Outdoor Life* v224 no4 p68 My 2017

SUMMER SURFACE BASS color *Outdoor Life* v224 no5 p31 Je/Jl 2017

TURKEY RECOVERY color *Outdoor Life* v224 no3 pT7 Ap 2017

THE UGLY FISH color *Outdoor Life* v224 no3 p62 Ap 2017

THE WEATHER RULES color *Outdoor Life* v224 no4 p67 My 2017

THE WEEKENDERS color map *Outdoor Life* v224 no4 p59 My 2017

WINDS OF CHANGE color map *Outdoor Life* v224 no5 p33 Je/Jl 2017

BETHUNE, BRIAN

The admiration of horror color *Maclean's* v129 no42 p50 O 24 2016

ALL THINGS MADE NEW color *Maclean's* v129 no41 p56 O 17 2016

AMERICAN WAR color *Maclean's* v130 no3 p68 Ap 2017

THE ARCHAEOLOGISTS bw color *Maclean's* v129 no44 p112 N 7 2016

Award Kremlinology color *Maclean's* v129 no44 p108 N 7 2016

The battles inside the battle bw *Maclean's* v130 no3 p54 Ap 2017

'Be true to the parrot' color *Maclean's* v129 no42 p46 O 24 2016

Blinking like moles bw *Maclean's* v130 no8 p60 S 2017

CanLit gets lit up color *Maclean's* v129 no48/49 p32 D 5 2016

CHARLEMAGNE color *Maclean's* v129 no47 p62 N 28 2016

CLIMATE CHANGE AND THE HEALTH OF NATIONS color *Maclean's* no1 p60 F 17 2017

CONFRONTING THE OCCUPATION color *Maclean's* p58 Je 2017

THE CURSE OF CASH color *Maclean's* v129 no40 p77 O 10 2016

THE DEATH AND RESURRECTION OF ELVIS PRESLEY color *Maclean's* v129 no45 p56 N 14 2016

Fighting their way home bw *Maclean's* v130 no7 p62 Ag 2017

FREUD bw *Maclean's* v129 no50 p60 D 19 2016

GAME OF TOMES [Cover story] color *Maclean's* v129 no51/52 p66 D 26 2016

The ghost orchard color *Maclean's* v130 no8 p58 S 2017

'I felt like quitting many times' color *Maclean's* v129 no44 p41 N 7 2016

Inside 'Scorpion block' color *Maclean's* v129 no46 p14 N 21 2016

THE INTERVIEW color *Maclean's* p20 Je 2017

THE INTERVIEW color *Maclean's* v130 no9 p22 O 2017

Monumental event bw color *Maclean's* v129 no51/52 p38 D 26 2016

'MY CURIOSITY FLARES UP WHEN I HEAR ABOUT...' color *Maclean's* v129 no45 p51 N 14 2016

'Never such a thing as arrival' color *Maclean's* v129 no43 p47 O 31 2016

The new Neanderthals color *Maclean's* v130 no4 p68 My 2017

Noah and the Liberal flood color *Maclean's* v129 no41 p24 O 17 2016

'No part of my life is immune' color *Maclean's* v129 no44 p40 N 7 2016

ON HUMAN NATURE color *Maclean's* v130 no2 p68 Mr 2017

THE ORANGE BALLOON DOG color *Maclean's* v130 no3 p68 Ap 2017

THE OTHER HELL color *Maclean's* v129 no43 p14 O 31 2016

A Protestant miracle color graph *Maclean's* v129 no47 p54 N 28 2016

RUSSIA: THE STORY OF WAR color *Maclean's* v130 no4 p70 My 2017

Second chances and Shakespeare color *Maclean's* v129 no41 p54 O 17 2016

SHAKESPEARE REIMAGINED color *Maclean's* p62 Je 2017

'THE SINGULAR GOAL OF MY ADULT LIFE' color *Maclean's* v129 no41 p40 O 17 2016

The wisdom of the blots bw cartoon *Maclean's* v130 no2 p66 Mr 2017

Betley, Matthew

Oath of Honor color *Publishers Weekly* v264 no3 p42 Ja 16 2017

Betrayal—Moral & ethical aspects

What Should We Have Told A Betrayed Wife? K. A. Appiah *New York Times Magazine* p22 Ja 22 2017

Betrothal

See also

Mate selection

The Case of the Ring and The Broken Engagement V. GLEMBOCKI color *Reader's Digest* v189 no1131 p19 Je 2017

Betrothal—Charts, diagrams, etc.

Reporting Dates T. Keith chart color *Sports Illustrated* v125 no20 p24 D 19 2016

Bettadapur, Akhila

Mobile MUTE specifies subsidiary cells to build physiologically improved grass stomata bibl diag *Science* v355 no6330 p1215 Mr 17 2017

Bettany, Paul, 1971-

HIDE AND SEEK: A new series takes you inside the life and capture of Unabomber Ted Kaczynski K. HAHN *TV Guide* v65 no31 p26 Jl 24 2017

Manhunt: Unabomber K. Hahn *TV Guide* v65 no35 p34 Ag 21 2017

Paul Bettany Is the Unabomber D. Snierson color *Entertainment Weekly* no1467 p13 My 26 2017

WHAT YOU SHOULD KNOW ABOUT PAUL BETTANY L. STRAUSS bw *Vanity Fair* v59 no9 p142 S 2017

Better Call Saul (TV program)

Better Call Saul J. Halterman *TV Guide* v65 no13 p31 Mr 20 2017

Better Call Saul J. Halterman *TV Guide* v65 no25 p32 Je 2017

Lord of the Fring img *New York* v50 no6 p76 Mr 20 2017

RETURN OF THE KINGPIN D. Snierson color *Entertainment Weekly* no1462 p54 Ap 21 2017

Better Neighbourhoods Inc.

Fix It Up B. LOI *Alternatives Journal (AJ) - Canada's Environmental Voice* v42 no2 p52 2016

Better Things (TV program)

All Happy Families, Alike D. D'addario color *Time* v190 no14 p48 O 9 2017

Ask Matt Jen and Doretta *TV Guide* v64 no48 p4 N 21 2016

Better Things N. Abrams, B. L. Heldman et al color *Entertainment Weekly* no1482/1483 p91 S 22 2017

Mikey MADISON *Interview* v47 no5 p70 Je/Jl 2017

Mom, Interrupted R. SYME il *New Republic* v248 no11 p58 N 2017

Better Angels of Our Nature: Why Violence Has Declined, The (Book)

Channel Your Inner Bill Gates With These Beach Reads C. Howorth, S. P. Jacobs et al color *Money* v46 no7 p19 Ag 2017

Why I Love Books-and Which Ones You'll Enjoy B. Gates, C. Howorth et al color *Time* v189 no21 p25 Je 5 2017

Betterments

back at the lake D. ZIRBEL color map *Cabin Living* p14 O 2017

Bettes, Hannah, 1996-

Ballet's Backbone A. RIVERS *Dance Magazine* v90 no12 p54 D 2016

BETTIGOLE, CHARLES

Society Is Ready for a New Kind of Science--Is Academia? *BioScience* v67 no7 p591 Jl 2017

Bettinelli, Marco

Nanophotonic rare-earth quantum memory with optically controlled retrieval diag graph *Science* v357 no6358 p1392 S 29 2017

Bettinger, Christopher J.

Polymeric peptide pigments with sequence-encoded properties color graph *Science* v356 no6342 p1064 Je 9 2017

BETTINSON, GARY

New Hong Kong Cinema: Transitions to Becoming Chinese in 21st-Century East Asia *Film Quarterly* v70 no2 p113 Wint 2016

Bettison, Stacy L.

AN EQUITARIAN MISSION color map *Equus* no471 p32 D 2016

Betts, Alexander

Alexander Betts A. Cohen color *Bloomberg Businessweek* no4532 p68 Jl 31 2017

the challengers bw *Foreign Policy* no221 p58 N/D 2016

BETTS, KATE

Crazy Years *New York Times Book Review* p11 O 16 2016

minding the manor color *Architectural Digest* v74 no3 p86 Mr 2017

Under the Breton Sun: Two novels set later-life awakenings in idyllic French towns *New York Times Book Review* p18 Ag 20 2017

BETTS, REGINALD DWAYNE

The Lord Might Have Given Him Wings *Progressive* v81 no4 p69 Ap/My 2017

Betty's Battalion (Company)

BETTY'S BATTALION *Texas Monthly* v45 no1 p100 Ja 2017

BETZ, ERIC

Auroras color diag *Discover* v38 no6 p30 Jl/Ag 2017

Battle for Access color *Discover* v38 no1 p34 Ja/F 2017

Beware the Blue-Collar Bots color *Discover* v38 no2 p12 Mr 2017

The CRISPR Antidote color *Discover* v38 no10 p10 D 2017

Digging Deep for New Bacteria color *Discover* v38 no1 p85 Ja/F 2017

Earth's Surprise Neighbor Hints at Exoplanet Abundance color diag *Discover* v38 no1 p10 Ja/F 2017

THE END OF THE PERIODIC TABLE? color *Discover* v38 no1 p32 Ja/F 2017

The Falcon Has Landed. Now SpaceX Is Eyeing Mars color *Discover* v38 no1 p27 Ja/F 2017

Inside the Historic Mission to Europa bw color *Discover* v38 no2 p58 Mr 2017

THE LAST SOVIET CITIZEN bw cartoon color *Discover* v27 no10 p40 D 2016

MELTDOWN [Cover story] color diag map *Discover* v38 no5 p36 Je 2017

Movin' On Up map *Discover* v38 no3 p13 Ap 2017

New Law Lets EPA Ban Toxic Chemicals color *Discover* v38 no1 p78 Ja/F 2017

The Next Horizon color *Discover* v38 no10 p44 D 2017

Nikola Tesla color *Discover* v38 no4 p43 My 2017

No. 1 FOUND: Einstein's Ripples in Space-Time bw color diag graph *Discover* v38 no1 p7 Ja/F 2017

The Pace — and Problems — of Climate Change Accelerate diag *Discover* v38 no1 p16 Ja/F 2017

PLANETS OF THE MILKY WAY diag *Discover* v38 no1 p40 Ja/F 2017

Protecting America's Last Dark Skies cartoon color map *Discover* v38 no4 p60 My 2017

The Tully Monster Mystery color *Discover* v38 no1 p56 Ja/F 2017

The Vanishing Eels bw color map *Discover* v38 no8 p22 O 2017

What Carbon Really Costs color *Discover* v38 no6 p10 Jl/Ag 2017

Betzig, Eric

Increased spatiotemporal resolution reveals highly dynamic dense tubular matrices in the peripheral ER bibl bw color graph *Science* v354 no6311 paaf3928-1 O 28 2016

Visualizing dynamic microvillar search and stabilization during ligand detection by T cells color *Science* v356 no6338 p598 My 12 2017

Beukeboom, Leo W.

Male sex in houseflies is determined by Mdmd, a paralog of the generic splice factor gene CWC22 bw color *Science* v356 no6338 p642 My 12 2017

Bevacqua, Brian

Bringing Whitewater Kayaking to Your Community *Parks & Recreation* v52 no4 p20 Ap 2017

BEVAN, ANDREW

cool customer color *Architectural Digest* v74 no9 p130 S 2017

Bever, Katherine M.

Mismatch repair deficiency predicts response of solid tumors to PD-1 blockade chart graph *Science* v357 no6349 p409 Jl 28 2017

Beverage industry

See also

Brewing industry

Soft drink industry

TAKING FLIGHT S. KROWIAK color *Indianapolis Monthly* v42 no2 p44 O 2017

Beverage industry—Equipment & supplies—Evaluation

ECO-FRIENDLY AND HEALTHY color *Iceland Review* v54 no5 p93 S-O 2016

Beverage industry—United States

An Energy Drink That Tastes of the Amazon J. Kaplan and A. Willis graph *Bloomberg Businessweek* no4503 p39 D 12 2016

Beverage refrigerators & coolers—Evaluation

BOTTLE SERVICE color *Architectural Digest* v73 no11 p130 N 2016

Beverages

See also

Alcoholic beverages

Carbonated beverages

Coffee

Drinking water

Fruit juices

Smoothies (Beverages)

Soft drinks

Tea

APRIL FOOLS L. MOYER and B. LIEBMAN *Nutrition Action Health Letter* v44 no3 p8 Ap 2017

BLEND ambition M. RABBITT color *Yoga Journal* no290 p77 Mr 2017

The Buzz Feed *Nutrition Action Health Letter* v44 no1 p9 Ja/F 2017

cheat, drink, & still shrink A. Rios color *Yoga Journal* no291 p29 My 2017

cheat, drink, & still shrink A. Rios color *Yoga Journal* no294 p11 S 2017

cheat, drink, & still shrink A. Rios color *Yoga Journal* p19 2017 Special Issue

Coffee Talk V. TWEED color *Better Nutrition* v78 no12 p54 D 2016

A Day at the Beach... L. Desantis color *Health* v31 no6 p34 Jl 2017

FOOD FOR THOUGHT *Nutrition Action Health Letter* v44 no5 p16 Je 2017

FOOD FOR THOUGHT *Nutrition Action Health Letter* v44 no6 p16 Jl/Ag 2017

Fresh Smoothie Bowls B. Lipton color *Health* v31 no6 p121 Jl 2017

Hello antioxidants. Goodbye free radicals *Psychology Today* v50 no3 p7 My/Je 2017

kick back & DRINK UP M. GLISAN color *Better Homes & Gardens* v95 no7 p124 Jl 2017

Not Your Average Joe J. Calderone, J. Lee et al chart color *Consumer Reports* v82 no10 p8 O 2017

One Minute to a Healthier You J. Migala color *Health* v31 no6 p63 Jl 2017

The other nut milks A. Gorin chart color *Yoga Journal* no290 p80 Mr 2017

Party Smart M. DiTrolio color *Men's Health* v31 no10 p68 D 2016

Power Up Your Smoothie color *Health* v31 no8 p9 O 2017

PROTEIN POWDERS FOR EVERYDAY PEOPLE [Cover story] L. Turner color *Better Nutrition* v79 no7 p46 Jl 2017

QUICK STUDIES *Nutrition Action Health Letter* v44 no5 p10 Je 2017

RAISE A GLASS C. K. Jackson color *Essence* v47 no10 p105 F 2017

Rigged! Supermarket shelves for sale *Nutrition Action Health Letter* v43 no9 p8 N 2016

Sneaky Forms of Sugar M. D. SMITH color *Better Nutrition* v79 no3 p60 Mr 2017

Sour Power *Atlanta* v56 no9 p56 Ja 2017

STRANGE BREW M. P. Lowry color *O, The Oprah Magazine* p32 My 2017

TAKE OM HOME T. Eichenseher color *Yoga Journal* no294 p96 S 2017

Taste the Rainbow J. DEMELO color *Bon Appetit* v62 no7 p17 Jl 2017

Vegan Cooking Tips. Quick and Easy Hot Beverages N. Berkoff *Vegetarian Journal* v35 no4 p32 2016

would you let your child eat 50 pounds of sugar? K. CICERO *Parents* v91 no6 p32 Je 2016

XTREME EATING 2017 L. MOYER and B. LIEBMAN *Nutrition Action Health Letter* v44 no6 p13 Jl/Ag 2017

Beverages—Economic aspects

NEWSBITES [Cover story] *Tufts University Health & Nutrition Letter* v34 no9 p1 N 2016

Beverages—Evaluation

CHEAT, DRINK & STILL SHRINK A. RIOS color *Runner's World* v52 no6 p45 Jl 2017

Purple Coffee, Rainbow Toast and the Politics of Unicorns N.

Hopper color *Time* v189 no18 p27 My 15 2017

Beverages—Labeling

Should Soda Have a Warning Label? *Scholastic Choices* v32 no7 p2 Ap 2017

BEVERLY, JONATHAN

BEST in SHOE [Cover story] bw color *Runner's World* v51 no10 p96 N 2016

Catching Fire color *Runner's World* v52 no7 p52 Ag 2017

THE LOVELY LONELINESS cartoon *Runner's World* v51 no11 p26 D 2016

THE RUN TO THE RACE cartoon *Runner's World* v52 no2 p24 Mr 2017

Today I Get to Run color *Runner's World* v52 no5 p52 Je 2017

When the Race Wins color *Runner's World* v52 no9 p60 O 2017

Beverly Hills (Calif.)—Description & travel

Beverly Hills Street Map, 1926 K. Wiles *History Today* v67 no1 p26 Ja 2017

Bevier, Charles

Celebrate Our Log Home Heritage in July color *Log Home Living* v34 no5 p14 Jl 2017

Bevin, Matt, 1967-

Bluegrass Blood Feud A. Greenblatt *Governing* v30 no1 p9 O 2016

The Evolution of Matt Bevin F. LUCAS color *Weekly Standard* v22 no32 p24 My 1 2017

Bevis, Matthew

IT WANTS TO GO TO BED WITH US: John Ashbery's well-spent youth color *Harper's Magazine* v335 no2005 p88 Je 2017

Bew, John

Mr. Attlee's Hour A. ROBERTS bw color *Weekly Standard* v22 no27 p34 Mr 20 2017

Realpolitik: A History G. J. Ikenberry *Foreign Affairs* v96 no3 p155 My/Je 2017

Beware the Slenderman (Film)

A Bogeyman Who Drove Kids to Attempt Murder M. Chan color *Time* v189 no4 p50 F 6 2017

Beware the Slenderman (TV program)

20. Watch Beware the Slenderman *New York* p87 F 9 2017

Bey, Adia

The extent of forest in dryland biomes [Cover story] chart map *Science* v356 no6338 p635 My 12 2017

BEY, LEE

WHY We LOVE CHICAGO bw cartoon color *Chicago* v66 no3 p75 Mr 2017

Beyer, Andrew D.

Nanophotonic rare-earth quantum memory with optically controlled retrieval diag graph *Science* v357 no6358 p1392 S 29 2017

Beyer, Axel

The Rydberg constant and proton size from atomic hydrogen bw chart color diag graph *Science* v357 no6359 p79 O 6 2017

Beyer, Christina

mom wins... ...and fails color *Working Mother* v40 no2 p8 Je/ Jl 2017

Beyer, Don

GUEST LIST *Washingtonian Magazine* v52 no2 p24 N 2016

Beyer, Marc

Mapping the human DC lineage through the integration of high-dimensional techniques diag *Science* v356 no6342 p1044 Je 9 2017

Beyer, Rick

THE BIG QUESTION cartoon *Atlantic* v318 no4 p112 N 2016

Beyer, Scott

Build, Baby, Build *Governing* v30 no6 p24 Mr 2017

Growing Smart: The right kind of transit is crucial for growing cities *Governing* v30 no12 p23 S 2017

Managing Chaos: How cities can handle the demands that density puts on services *Governing* v30 no8 p23 My 2017

The Right Mix: Portland's Eastside neighborhoods offer easy living and shopping *Governing* v30 no10 p23 Jl 2017

Unlikely Neighbors *Governing* v30 no2 p24 N 2016

When Local Control Backfires *Governing* v30 no4 p24 Ja 2017

Beyerdynamic GmbH & Co. KG

BEYERDYNAMIC AMIRON HOME HEADPHONES T. NICO-LAKIS color *Macworld - Digital Edition* p35 Mr 2017

Jewels for the Ear S. Guttenberg color *Sound & Vision* v82 no7

p20 S 2017

Take It Easy S. Guttenberg color *Sound & Vision* v82 no4 p24 My 2017

Beyerdynamic Inc.

The Sweet Spot S. Guttenberg and C. Crowley color *Sound & Vision* v82 no2 p20 F/Mr 2017

Beyers, Emma

So Long, Summer! color *Missouri Life* v44 no6 p18 S 2017

Beykpour, Kayvon, 1988-

Kayvon Beykpour J. Crelin color *Current Biography* v78 no2 p12 F 2017

BEYL, JEFF

Hemingway's Fishing Rod *Idaho Magazine* v16 no3 p24 D 2016

Beyoncé, 1981-

Beyoncé M. Harris-perry color *Time* v188 no25-26 p124 D 19 2016 Double Issue

MUSIC N. Feeney, K. O'Donnell et al color *Entertainment Weekly* no1444/1445 p88 D 16 2016

Pop Chart R. Bruner, C. Lang et al color *Time* v189 no5 p54 F 13 2017

Pop Chart R. Bruner, C. Lang et al color *Time* v190 no1 p55 Jl 3 2017

Predicting Pop's Big Night S. KNOPPER color *Rolling Stone* no1280 p18 F 9 2017

SOLANGE by BEYONCÉ *Interview* v47 no1 p40 F 2017

Sound Bites color *Entertainment Weekly* no1444/1445 p10 D 16 2016

What can Beyoncé and Pope Francis teach us about love? O. Segura color *America* v216 no11 p56 My 15 2017

WHO'S YOUR DREAM GRAD SPEAKER? color *Seventeen* v76 no3 p10 My 2017

Beyond Now (Music)

Donny McCaslin's Tenor Sax Solo on 'Faceplant' J. DURSO bw color *Downbeat* v84 no6 p84 Je 2017

Bezdek, Máté J.

Coordination-induced weakening of ammonia,water, and hydrazine X–H bonds in a molybdenum complex bibl diag *Science* v354 no6313 p730 N 11 2016

BEZERRA-NETO, JOSÉ F.

Greenhouse Gas Emissions from Reservoir Water Surfaces: A New Global Synthesis *BioScience* v66 no11 p949 N 1 2016

Bezginov, Alexandr

The role of dimer asymmetry and protomer dynamics in enzyme catalysis diag *Science* v355 no6322 p262 Ja 20 2017

BEZMOZGIS, DAVID

Homeland: Revisiting her roots in Latvia, a woman learns what happened to her family in World War II *New York Times Book Review* p8 S 17 2017

Bezos, Jeffrey, 1964-

2 JEFF BEZOS L. Rao color *Fortune* v174 no7 p74 D 1 2016

Data-Driven Management Can Also Be Compassionate M. Schrage *Harvard Business Review Digital Articles* p2 Ag 24 2015

THE NEW ESTABLISHMENT 2017 N. BILTON, W. ISAAC-SON et al bw color *Vanity Fair* v59 no11 p87 N 2017

NEW ESTABLISHMENT N. Bilton, W. D. Cohan et al bw cartoon color *Vanity Fair* v58 no11 p124 N 2016

THE PLANET'S RICHEST PERSON K. VINTON bw color graph *Forbes* v200 no2 p30 S 5 2017

ROCKETEER C. FISHMAN *Smithsonian* v47 no8 p36 D 2016

Titans B. Aldrin, A. Park et al color *Time* v189 no16/17 p94 My 1-8 2017

Bgd&c Corp.

(SUB)URBAN E. EICHINGER color *Chicago* v66 no9 p90 S 2017

Bgreen Apparel (Company)

FUNDIES GALORE! G. TOMAINE color *Rodale's Organic Life* v3 no1 p16 Ja 2017

Bhabha, Jacqueline

Half a Century of a Right to Health? *UN Chronicle* v53 no4 p1 2016

Half a Century of a Right to Health? *UN Chronicle* v54 no4 p13 2017

Bhabha, Leah

home & help img *New York* p96 Mr 6 2017

Bhagat, Sanjai

Board Directors Should Be Paid Only in Equity *Harvard Business Review Digital Articles* p2 My 3 2017

Bhakta, Raj
THE EDUCATION OF RAJ BHAKTA W. CURTIS color *Yankee* p126 Jl 2017

Bhalla, Ajay
60 Countries' Digital Competitiveness, Indexed *Harvard Business Review Digital Articles* p2 Jl 12 2017

Bhandari, S.
The magnetic field and turbulence of the cosmic web measured using a brilliant fast radio burst bibl chart graph *Science* v354 no6317 p1249 D 9 2016

Bharadwaj, Monisha
HEALING Spices [Cover story] color *Yoga Journal* no290 p83 Mr 2017

BHARADWAJ, SUNDAR
COMPETING ON SOCIAL PURPOSE: BRANDS THAT WIN BY TYING MISSION TO GROWTH chart diag il img *Harvard Business Review* v95 no5 p94 S/O 2017

Bharata natyam dancers
Bharatanatyam: A STORY FOR THE GODS color *Dance Spirit* v21 no8 p88 O 2017

Bharatiya Janata Party—Elections
India's Weakened Unions Face a Push for Reform E. TEITEL-BAUM *Current History* v116 no789 p142 Ap 2017

Bharrhan, Sushma
A "Trojan horse" bispecific-antibody strategy for broad protection against ebolaviruses bibl graph *Science* v354 no6310 p350 O 21 2016

Bhasin, Kim
KΣ$ color graph *Bloomberg Businessweek* no4495 p16 O 17 2016
Pants on Fyre color *Bloomberg Businessweek* no4524 p33 My 29 2017
WHERE DID YOU GET THAT LOVELY SUPPLY CHAIN? color *Bloomberg Businessweek* no4505 p62 D 26 2016

Bhasin, Rachna
CRACKING FASHION'S CODE color *Harper's Bazaar* no3654 p142 Je/Jl 2017

Bhaskar, M. K.
An integrated diamond nanophotonics platform for quantum-optical networks bibl graph *Science* v354 no6314 p847 N 18 2016

Bhat, Faizan
Ad Blocking's Unintended Consequences *Harvard Business Review Digital Articles* p2 Ag 12 2015

Bhat, N. D. R.
The magnetic field and turbulence of the cosmic web measured using a brilliant fast radio burst bibl chart graph *Science* v354 no6317 p1249 D 9 2016

BHATIA, JUHIE
A SUSTAINABLE SOLUTION *Ms.* v27 no1 p38 Spr 2017

Bhatia, Sangeeta N.
Potential role of intratumor bacteria in mediating tumor resistance to the chemotherapeutic drug gemcitabine diag *Science* v357 no6356 p1156 S 15 2017

Bhatia, Tanay
Manufacturing Companies Need to Sell Outcomes, Not Products *Harvard Business Review Digital Articles* p2 Je 2 2016

Bhatnagar, Jyotsna
Case Study: Should You Rehire Someone Who Left for a Competitor? bw color il *Harvard Business Review* v94 no12 p103 D 2016

Bhatt, Neelay
Five Steps to Unlock Your Agency's Marketing and Branding Potential *Parks & Recreation* v52 no9 p20 S 2017

Bhatt, Prashant M.
Hydrolytically stable fluorinated metal-organic frameworks for energy-efficient dehydration diag *Science* v356 no6339 p731 My 19 2017

Bhatt, Shubhang K.
A SUMO-ubiquitin relay recruits proteasomes to chromosome axes to regulate meiotic recombination bibl graph *Science* v355 no6323 p403 Ja 27 2017

BHATTACHARJEE, YUDHIJIT
PAD LAUNCH color *New York Times Magazine* p78 N 13 2016
WHY WE LIE cartoon color graph *National Geographic* v231 no6 p30 Je 2017

Bhattacharji, Alex
PIERCE BROSNAN RIDES AGAIN bw color *Esquire* p116 Ap 2017
Risky Business color *Bloomberg Businessweek* no4538 p62 S 18 2017
Space Oddity color *Bloomberg Businessweek* no4531 p70 Jl 24 2017

BHATTACHARYA, SANJIV
DAVID HOCKNEY color *Esquire* v167 no2 p134 Mr 2017
KIDS AREN'T US color *Esquire* p112 Ap 2017

Bhattacharyya, Onil
Expanding the Reach of Primary Care in Developing Countries color *Harvard Business Review Digital Articles* p2 Je 6 2017

Bhattacharyya, Roby P.
Nucleic acid detection with CRISPR-Cas13a/C2c2 color diag *Science* v356 no6336 p438 Ap 28 2017

Bhattacharyya, Sudipta
Structure of histone-based chromatin in Archaea diag *Science* v357 no6351 p609 Ag 11 2017

Bhattacherjee, Aditi
Femtosecond x-ray spectroscopy of an electrocyclic ring-opening reaction diag graph *Science* v356 no6333 p54 Ap 7 2017

Bhatti, Jabeen
Chancellor Angela Merkel of Germany calls for a ban of burqas as election nears *Christian Century* v134 no1 p15 Ja 4 2017

BHATTI, SAQIB
Solidarity *In These Times* v41 no1 p29 Ja 2017

Bhaumik, Siddhartha Kumar
IgG antibodies to dengue enhanced for FcγRIIIA binding determine disease severity bibl graph *Science* v355 no6323 p395 Ja 27 2017

Bhaw, Leena
Lineage-dependent spatial and functional organization of the mammalian enteric nervous system color graph *Science* v356 no6339 p722 My 19 2017

Bhawal, Benjamin N.
Palladium-catalyzed carbon-sulfur or carbon-phosphorus bond metathesis by reversible arylation diag *Science* v356 no6342 p1059 Je 9 2017

Bhikkhu, Thanissaro
THE BUDDHA'S BAGGAGE bw *Tricycle: The Buddhist Review* v26 no2 p78 Wint 2016
WHY SHAME GETS A BAD RAP (BUT SHOULDN'T) color *Tricycle: The Buddhist Review* v26 no4 p64 Summ 2017

Bhumibol Adulyadej, King of Thailand, 1927-2016
Bhumibol Adulyadej C. Campbell color *Time* v188 no18 p13 O 31 2016
Thailand's Royal Mess D. DEVOSS *Weekly Standard* v22 no8 p14 O 31 2016

Bhushan, Bharat
Bioinspired Hierarchical-Structured Surfaces for Green Science and Technology M. Srinivasarao *Physics Today* v70 no9 p60 S 2017

Bi, Pengpeng
Control of muscle formation by the fusogenic micropeptide myomixer diag *Science* v356 no6335 p323 Ap 21 2017

Bialik, Mayim, 1975-
BLOSSOM D. Franich color *Entertainment Weekly* no1486 p36 O 13 2017
Studio City J. HERBST *Los Angeles Magazine* p76 Mr 2017

Bialik, Mayim, 1975——Interviews
From TV to Lab, and Back N. D. TYSON color *National Geographic* v231 no6 p26 Je 2017
MAYIM BIALIK I. Biedenharn color *Entertainment Weekly* no1466 p61 My 19 2017

Bialosky, Jill
HOT TUB AFTER SKIING, DECEMBER, 2016 *New Yorker* v93 no7 p60 Ap 3 2017

Bian, Lin
Gender stereotypes about intellectual ability emerge early and influence children's interests bibl graph *Science* v355 no6323 p389 Ja 27 2017

Biancalana, Mary
UNDER PRESSURE A. SHAFFER cartoon color *Better Homes & Gardens* v95 no4 p158 Ap 2017

Bianchi, Emily C.

CEOs Who Began Their Careers During Booms Tend to Be Less Ethical *Harvard Business Review Digital Articles* p2 My 12 2017

Bianchi, Fabrizio

Reticulon 3–dependent ER-PM contact sites control EGFR non-clathrin endocytosis color diag graph *Science* v356 no6338 p617 My 12 2017

Bianchi, Federico

Global atmospheric particle formation from CERN CLOUD measurements bibl graph map *Science* v354 no6316 p1119 D 2 2016

Bianchi, Jane

How Top Docs Avoid Cancer color *Men's Health* v32 no7 p82 S 2017

Kiddie Car Service [Cover story] color *Working Mother* v40 no2 p22 Je/Jl 2017

Top Wealth Adviser Moms chart color *Working Mother* v40 no4 p85 O/N 2017

"What Are You?" *Scholastic Choices* v32 no7 p20 Ap 2017

Bianchi, Stefania

Gulf Rulers Try Fighting Deficits With Taxes cartoon *Bloomberg Businessweek* no4497 p18 O 31 2016

Bianchi bicycles—Evaluation

"I WANT A BIANCHI." M. Yozell and B. STRICKLAND color *Bicycling* v58 no3 p98 Ap 2017

Bianculli, David

CLONES, TWINS & DOPPELGÄNGERS: TV'S BEST DOUBLE FEATURES *TV Guide* v65 no27 p8 Je 26 2017

HOW THE FUGITIVE FINALE MADE TV BETTER *TV Guide* v65 no35 p8 Ag 21 2017

KEEPING UP WITH THE KARDASHIANS: TEN YEARS AND COUNTING... *TV Guide* v65 no39 p20 S 18 2017

THE PLATINUM AGE OF TELEVISION *TV Guide* v65 no25 p10 Je 2017

SALUTE THE OLD GUARD *TV Guide* v65 no31 p10 Jl 24 2017

WE CROSSED OVER INTO THE TWILIGHT ZONE. . .AND NEVER LOOKED BACK *TV Guide* v65 no41 p8 O 2 2017

WHAT'S NEXT FOR O'REILLY? *TV Guide* v65 no19 p16 My 1 2017

Bianzino, Nicola Morini

When AI Becomes the New Face of Your Brand *Harvard Business Review Digital Articles* p2 Je 27 2017

Biao Kan

Expert consensus on point-of-care testing *Science* v354 no6319 p15 D 23 2016

Recommendations on the management and use of POCT in medical institutions (nosocomial) *Science* v354 no6319 p13 D 23 2016

Bias, Kelvin C.

WHAT THE F? color *Sports Illustrated* v126 no11 p49 Ap 17-24 2017

Biba, Erin

High Robot graph *Scientific American* v316 no5 p21 My 2017

STD Results in Minutes color *Scientific American* v316 no3 p18 Mr 2017

BIBAS, STEPHANOS

Simplify The Law color *National Review* v69 no15 p20 Ag 14 2017

Biber, Eric

Merging paleobiology with conservation biology to guide the future of terrestrial ecosystems color *Science* v355 no6325 p594 F 10 2017

Biber-Freudenberger, Lisa

A global map of roadless areas and their conservation status bibl color graph map *Science* v354 no6318 p1423 D 16 2016

Bible

See also

Bible—Criticism, interpretation, etc.

Violence in the Bible

Bearing with the Patience of God D. RISHMAWY *Christianity Today* p28 Mr 2017

Benjamin Moser *New York Times Book Review* p27 F 19 2017

CAN YOU CONTROL YOURSELF? [Cover story] B. WRIGHT and D. CARREON color graph *Christianity Today* v61 no4 p34 My 2017

Famines, fasts, and feasts A. Camille il *U.S. Catholic* v82 no6 p47 Je 2017

Francis' Heavy Lift H. Alvaré color *America* v216 no7 p54 Ap 3 2017

From 'Enemy of the People' to Friend K. A. ELLIS *Christianity Today* v60 no9 p30 N 2016

Get to Work J. W. MARTENS il *America* v215 no14 p39 N 7 2016

Good News Bears A. WILSON *Christianity Today* v61 no1 p26 Ja/F 2017

Is the Bible infallible? A. Camille color *U.S. Catholic* v81 no11 p49 N 2016

I Will Call You Each By Name *America* v216 no10 p52 My 1 2017

THE LINGUISTIC ORIGINS OF THE QUESTION D. ESTES color *Christianity Today* v61 no7 p64 S 2017

LIVING BY The Word *Christian Century* v134 no13 p18 Je 21 2017

More than a Plain Reading M. LABBERTON cartoon *Christianity Today* v61 no1 p64 Ja/F 2017

Reflections on the lectionary A. West *Christian Century* v134 no22 p21 O 25 2017

Reflections on the lectionary J. H. Lee *Christian Century* v134 no13 p19 Je 21 2017

Show Us the Father M. S. J. Simone *America* v216 no10 p53 My 1 2017

Take Lord, Receive M. Simone *America* v217 no4 p56 Ag 21 2017

The word on women A. Camille il *U.S. Catholic* v82 no2 p47 F 2017

'You Are the One!' M. Simone *America* v217 no4 p54 Ag 21 2017

BIBLE, AARON H.

APPAREL color *Backpacker* p55 N 2017

Bikepacking color *Backpacker* p52 My 2017

Footwear color diag graph il *Backpacker* v45 no3 p43 Ap 2017

Your Buyer's Guide to the New 4K TVs cartoon color *Men's Health* v32 no8 p28 O 2017

Bible. Acts

LIVING BY The Word *Christian Century* v134 no9 p18 Ap 26 2017

Bible. English

GLEANINGS graph *Christianity Today* v60 no9 p20 N 2016

Bible. Epistles of John

LIVING BY The Word A. H. K. Apple *Christian Century* v134 no10 p25 My 10 2017

Bible. Ezekiel

I Will Raise You Up M. R. Simone *America* v216 no6 p52 Mr 20 2017

Bible. Genesis

LIVING BY The Word *Christian Century* v134 no14 p20 Jl 5 2017

Bible. Gospels

A DECADE OF CHANGE H. B. SMITH color *Christianity Today* v60 no8 p11 O 2016

EDITOR'S NOTE T. OLSEN color *Christianity Today* v61 no1 p7 Ja/F 2017

Gospel Feelings (gospelfeelings.com) L. Copan color *Christian Century* v134 no2 p47 Ja 18 2017

KEEPING THE FAITH in Seminary K. MILLER color *Christianity Today* v60 no8 p87 O 2016

Manga Mania A. Foxwell-Barajas color *Christianity Today* v60 no8 p24 O 2016

A new frontier L. Eppinger color *U.S. Catholic* v81 no12 p45 D 2016

Not My Will, But Yours M. R. Simone *America* v216 no7 p50 Ap 3 2017

Reflections on the lectionary D. Thomas *Christian Century* v134 no20 p21 S 27 2017

The Rewards of the Harvest *America* v217 no6 p58 S 18 2017

Tune Out the Noise M. Simone *America* v217 no3 p50 Ag 7 2017

Turning Over Our Will M. R. Simone *America* v216 no4 p55 F 20 2017

Where Is God at Work? M. Simone *America* v217 no6 p60 S 18 2017

Bible. Hebrews

Release Me M. LABASH color *Weekly Standard* v22 no25 p5 Mr 6 2017

Bible. Isaiah

LIVING BY The Word C. Chakoian *Christian Century* v134 no6 p21 Mr 15 2017

The Rewards of the Harvest *America* v217 no6 p58 S 18 2017

Bible. Jeremiah
  We are God's artwork S. Wells *Christian Century* v134 no3 p31
  F 2017
Bible. Joel
  LIVING BY The Word *Christian Century* v134 no4 p20 F 15 2017
Bible. John
  Becoming the Body of Christ M. R. Simone *America* v216 no13
  p58 Je 12 2017
  Go Out to All Nations M. S. J. Simone *America* v216 no11 p60
  My 15 2017
  I Will Call You Each By Name *America* v216 no10 p52 My 1 2017
  The Light of New Life M. R. Simone *America* v216 no5 p69 Mr
  6 2017
  LIVING BY The Word *Christian Century* v134 no5 p18 Mr 1
  2017
  Reflections on the lectionary *Christian Century* v134 no10 p23
  My 10 2017
  Submerged in the Spirit M. SIMONE *America* v216 no1 p43 Ja
  2 2017
Bible. Luke
  LIVING BY The Word *Christian Century* v134 no10 p22 My 10
  2017
  LIVING BY The Word S. D. Anderson *Christian Century* v133
  no22 p23 O 26 2016
  Reflections on the lectionary W. D. Francois III *Christian Century*
  v133 no21 p21 O 12 2016
Bible. Mark
  Retell me a story M. Clark color *U.S. Catholic* v82 no7 p10 Jl
  2017
Bible. Matthew
  6 Surprising Times You Are Quoting the Bible F. ADDIS *Reader's
  Digest* v188 no1126 p124 D 2016/Ja 2017
  A Life of Boldness M. R. Simone *America* v216 no13 p60 Je 12
  2017
  LIVING BY The Word *Christian Century* v133 no24 p22 N 23
  2016
  LIVING BY The Word *Christian Century* v134 no4 p20 F 15 2017
  On Earth as It Is in Heaven M. R. Simone *America* v216 no5 p66
  Mr 6 2017
  Reflections on the lectionary K. Hines-Shah *Christian Century*
  v133 no24 p23 N 23 2016
  Reflections on the lectionary W. J. Jennings *Christian Century*
  v134 no14 p21 Jl 5 2017
  To Show the Way M. R. SIMONE *America* v216 no1 p42 Ja 2
  2017
Bible. New Testament
  Suggestions or Commands? S. Zahl and D. Bentley Hart bw *Com-
  monweal* v143 no20 p9 D 16 2016
  Why Don't the Gospel Writers Tell the Same Story? New Testament scholar and apologist Michael Licona's new book argues
  that ancient literary devices are the answer—and that's a good
  thing for Christians C. LINDGREN color *Christianity Today*
  v61 no4 p42 My 2017
Bible. Old Testament
  6 Surprising Times You Are Quoting the Bible F. ADDIS *Reader's
  Digest* v188 no1126 p124 D 2016/Ja 2017
  Between Past & Future R. Ferrone color *Commonweal* v144 no7
  p7 Ap 14 2017
  THE GREAT EXPEDITION: A Danish-German survey sought to
  unearth the roots of the Hebrew Bible in Arabia. It became the
  first to comprehend a new Islamic ideology, which now threat-
  ens the West M. Ronan *History Today* v67 no6 p72 Je 2016
  Moses and DeMille W. SCHIMMERLING *Commentary* v143 no6
  p7 Je 2017
  The OLDER TESTAMENT: An Origin Story A. Gregory cartoon
  Esquire p136 O 2017
  The Presence M. S. J. Simone *America* v216 no11 p58 My 15
  2017
  Researchers identify author of tenth-century biblical text M.
  Buckley *Christian Century* v134 no17 p17 Ag 16 2017
Bible. Proverbs
  Proverbial Politics color *Weekly Standard* v22 no43 p3 Jl 24 2017
Bible. Psalms
  The Jesus Who Cannot Be M. R. Simone *America* v216 no6 p50
  Mr 20 2017
Bible. Revelation

  Over It P. GULLEY color *Indianapolis Monthly* p52 Ap 2017
Bible. Romans
  Reflections on the lectionary W. J. Jennings *Christian Century*
  v134 no14 p21 Jl 5 2017
Bible—Commentaries
  Let's Try This Again M. R. SIMONE *America* v215 p39 N 28
  2016
Bible—Criticism, interpretation, etc.
  Bodies in the vernacular B. Bantum color *Christian Century* v134
  no7 p26 Mr 29 2017
  Clothing Ourselves in Love M. Simone *America* v217 no7 p53
  O 2 2017
  I Will Raise You Up M. R. Simone *America* v216 no6 p52 Mr
  20 2017
  The Jesus Who Cannot Be M. R. Simone *America* v216 no6 p50
  Mr 20 2017
  Truth to Power *America* v217 no7 p52 O 2 2017
Bible—Exhibitions
  CROSS PURPOSES: The Museum of the Bible will bring religion
  near the Mall. Does it belong there? R. Brunner *Washingtonian
  Magazine* v53 no1 p15 O 2017
Bible—History of Biblical events—Art
  Gospel Feelings (gospelfeelings.com) L. Copan color *Christian
  Century* v134 no2 p47 Ja 18 2017
Bible—Manuscripts
  Seminary returns rare manuscript to Greek Orthodox C. Kennel-
  Shank color *Christian Century* v133 no26 p14 D 21 2016
Bible. Matthew—Criticism, interpretation, etc.
  Clothing Ourselves in Love M. Simone *America* v217 no7 p53
  O 2 2017
  Truth to Power *America* v217 no7 p52 O 2 2017
Bible—Meditations
  The Freedom of the Father's Children M. R. Simone *America*
  v216 no3 p52 F 6 2017
  Keep and Ponder M. R. SIMONE *America* v215 no19 p39 D 19
  2016
  LIVING BY The Word *Christian Century* v133 no26 p20 D 21
  2016
  LIVING BY The Word *Christian Century* v134 no2 p20 Ja 18
  2017
  Reflections on the lectionary M. Earley *Christian Century* v133
  no25 p21 D 7 2016
Bible—Numerical division
  Marvel and behold J. Bleem il *U.S. Catholic* v82 no8 p50 Ag 2017
Bible—Parables
      See also
      Jesus Christ—Parables
  Reflections on the lectionary A. West *Christian Century* v134
  no22 p21 O 25 2017
Bible—Prayers
  Prayer that echoes God L. F. Winner *Christian Century* v134 no18
  p26 Ag 30 2017
Bible—Publication & distribution—History
  Monks, memes, and medieval art S. Johnson color *U.S. Catholic*
  v82 no7 p32 Jl 2017
Bible—Reading
  Reflections on the lectionary D. B. Laytham *Christian Century*
  v134 no11 p21 My 24 2017
  Word Files B. SHIRLEY color *America* v215 no11 p22 O 17 2016
Bible—Societies, etc.
  Refugee work H. Simon, P. Blackwell et al *Christian Century*
  v134 no2 p6 Ja 18 2017
Bible—Study & teaching
  BEST SELLERS *Christian Century* v133 no21 p12 O 12 2016
  How to Prevent Bible Study Dropouts J. Wilkin *Christianity To-
  day* v61 no6 p28 Jl/Ag 2017
  Let Bible Studies Be Bible Studies J. WILKIN *Christianity Today*
  p26 Mr 2017
  MY COUNTRY, PRAYERS FOR THEE M. Reynolds color
  Christianity Today v61 no6 p21 Jl/Ag 2017
  Why Africa Needed Its Own Study Bible M. LEE map *Christian-
  ity Today* v60 no9 p22 N 2016
Bible—Theology
      See also
      Biblical teaching on the apocalypse
  INVESTING IN THE KINGDOM J. HAANEN color *Christianity*

"I'VE GOT $3,000. CAN I GET A BIKE WITH NICE WHEELS?" L. Tanner and B. STRICKLAND color *Bicycling* v58 no3 p56 Ap 2017

"I WANT A BIKE THAT GIVES ME EVERY SPEED ADVANTAGE." J. Lindsey and B. STRICKLAND color *Bicycling* v58 no3 p104 Ap 2017

"I WANT A BIKE THAT MAKES CLIMBING EASY." M. Phillips and B. STRICKLAND color *Bicycling* v58 no3 p34 Ap 2017

"I WANT A BIKE THAT WILL STAND OUT." C. McSherry and B. STRICKLAND color *Bicycling* v58 no3 p22 Ap 2017

"I WANT A BIKE WITH HERITAGE." M. Phillips and B. STRICKLAND color *Bicycling* v58 no3 p58 Ap 2017

"I WANT A GOOD ROAD BIKE, BUT I DON'T WANT TO SPEND MORE THAN $1,000." T. Rojek and B. STRICKLAND color *Bicycling* v58 no3 p50 Ap 2017

"I WANT TO DRINK MY COFFEE WHILE I RIDE TO WORK." E. Furia and B. STRICKLAND color *Bicycling* v58 no3 p40 Ap 2017

"I WANT TO GO BIKE CAMPING." R. Koch and B. STRICKLAND color *Bicycling* v58 no3 p24 Ap 2017

"I WANT TO GO FAST." G. Liu and B. STRICKLAND color *Bicycling* v58 no3 p68 Ap 2017

"I WANT TO RIDE TO WORK EVERY DAY." color *Bicycling* v58 no3 p90 Ap 2017

"I WANT TO TAKE MORE RISKS." L. Mazzante and B. STRICKLAND color *Bicycling* v58 no3 p70 Ap 2017

"I WANT TO TRY CYCLOCROSS." J. Hart and B. STRICKLAND color *Bicycling* v58 no3 p66 Ap 2017

"I WISH MY RIDES COULD GO ON FOREVER." C. Giddings and B. STRICKLAND color *Bicycling* v58 no3 p110 Ap 2017

JAEGHER TS-38 INTERCEPTOR S-STIFF J. Southerland color *Bicycling* v58 no10 p52 N/D 2017

JAMIS ICON ELITE M. YOZELL color *Bicycling* v58 no1 p68 Ja/F 2017

jamis R. Palmer color *Bike Magazine* v24 no2 p82 Mr 2017

LITESPEED GRAVEL J. Lindsey color *Bicycling* v58 no9 p86 O 2017

MARIN WOLF RIDGE PRO M. Phillips color *Bicycling* v58 no9 p80 O 2017

niner jet 9 T. Engel color *Bike Magazine* v24 no3 p104 My 2017

OFFICINA BATTAGLIN POWER+ B. STRICKLAND color *Bicycling* v58 no4 p92 My 2017

Off the Chain R. ANNIS *Indianapolis Monthly* p30 My 2017

ON THE MOUNTAIN G. Liu and B. STRICKLAND color *Bicycling* v58 no3 p84 Ap 2017

orbea occam R. Palmer color *Bike Magazine* v24 no3 p100 My 2017

ORBEA ORCA M11ILTD E. Huyett color *Bicycling* v58 no8 p70 S 2017

Santa Cruz: HIGHTOWER LT X01/CARBON CC W/ RESERVE 30 WHEEL UPGRADE J. Weber color *Bike Magazine* v24 no8 p66 N 2017

santa cruz tallboy c B. Minnigh color *Bike Magazine* v24 no3 p108 My 2017

"SHOULD I GET A DROP-BAR OR A FLAT-BAR ROAD BIKE?" E. Furia and B. STRICKLAND color *Bicycling* v58 no3 p108 Ap 2017

"SHOULD I GET AN ENDURO BIKE?" R. Koch and B. STRICKLAND color *Bicycling* v58 no3 p94 Ap 2017

"SHOULD I GET A PLUS BIKE OR A 29ER?" J. Lindsey and B. STRICKLAND color *Bicycling* v58 no3 p100 Ap 2017

"SHOULD I GET CARBON OR ALUMINUM?" color *Bicycling* v58 no3 p36 Ap 2017

SPECIALIZED WOMEN'S DIVERGE COMP L. Flickinger color *Bicycling* v58 no9 p66 O 2017

SPEEDVAGEN ROAD DISC M. Phillips color *Bicycling* v58 no4 p61 My 2017

Spot: MAYHEM 27.5+ 4-STAR BUILD T. Engel and A. Emanuel color *Bike Magazine* v24 no8 p74 N 2017

TERN CARGO NODE R. KOCH color *Bicycling* v58 no1 p70 Ja/F 2017

trek color *Bike Magazine* v24 no2 p80 Mr 2017

TREK ÉMONDA SLR 9 DISC, PROJECT ONE M. Yozell color *Bicycling* v58 no9 p74 O 2017

TREK SILQUE SLR 7 S. Yeager color *Bicycling* v58 no4 p64

My 2017

TRUST THE BIKE J. DETWILER color *Popular Mechanics* p92 Mr 2017

"WHAT'S A GOOD FIRST ROAD BIKE?" L. Flickinger and B. STRICKLAND color *Bicycling* v58 no3 p18 Ap 2017

Wheels Up L. BAILEY *Indianapolis Monthly* v40 no11 p25 Jl 2017

WOWZA! color *Bicycling* v58 no4 p76 My 2017

YETI SB5+ TURQ X01 EAGLE G. Liu color *Bicycling* v58 no4 p84 My 2017

Bicycles—Exhibitions

Your Fall To-Do List: Mark your calendars for these can't-miss artsy autumn events C. COX *Atlanta* v57 no6 p83 O 2017

Bicycles—History

VELOCI-RAPTURE A. Murphy color *Sports Illustrated* v127 no3 p98 Jl 24 2017

Bicycles—Maintenance & repair

The Accidental Bike Shop M. HURFORD color *Bicycling* v58 no4 p50 My 2017

Bicycles—Marketing

Wheels Up L. BAILEY *Indianapolis Monthly* v40 no11 p25 Jl 2017

Bicycles—Purchasing

TAYLOR ROJEK T. ROJEK color *Bicycling* v58 no3 p116 Ap 2017

WHAT BIKE SHOULD I BUY? B. STRICKLAND color *Bicycling* v58 no3 p16 Ap 2017

Bicycles—Social aspects

small decisions k. butcher color *Bike Magazine* v24 no3 p58 My 2017

Bicycles—Tires

WHY WHEELS MATTER R. Koch and B. STRICKLAND color *Bicycling* v58 no3 p57 Ap 2017

Bicycling (Periodical)

JOIN THE RIDE L. FLICKINGER color *Bicycling* v58 no6 p12 Jl 2017

Bidart, Frank

MOURNING WHAT WE THOUGHT WE WERE *New Yorker* v92 no46 p40 Ja 23 2017

Bidart, Frank, 1939-

GOLDEN BOY H. ALS cartoon *New Yorker* v93 no27 p76 S 11 2017

Half-Light: Collected Poems, 1965–2016 C. M. TEICHER color *Publishers Weekly* v264 no29 p194 Jl 17 2017

'Making Is the Mirror': A career retrospective shows how Frank Bidart shed the masks of his early poems to create a kind of self-mythology M. JACKSON *New York Times Book Review* p14 O 8 2017

The Tragic Sense of Frank Bidart H. Vendler color *New York Review of Books* v64 no16 p42 O 26 2017

Biddle, Stephen

Building Security Forces & Stabilizing Nations: The Problem of Agency *Daedalus* v146 no4 p126 Fall 2017

Biddlecombe, Wendy Joan

Amanda Giacomini color *Tricycle: The Buddhist Review* v27 no1 p26 Fall 2017

Denise Di Novi *Tricycle: The Buddhist Review* v26 no3 p22 Spr 2017

South Carolina Dharma Group color *Tricycle: The Buddhist Review* v27 no1 p24 Fall 2017

Biden, Jill, 1951-

THE UNSTOPPABLES N. Weldon color *Runner's World* v51 no10 p112 N 2016

BIDEN, JOE

OBAMA'S AMERICA img *New York* v49 no20 p12 O 3 2016

Biden, Joseph R., 1942-

TO DEFEND THE LIBERAL INTERNATIONAL ORDER J. BIDEN *Vital Speeches of the Day* v83 no3 p75 Mr 2017

When Politics Get Personal S. Detrow *America* v217 no7 p54 O 2 2017

Biden, Joseph R., 1942—Political & social views

I WISH TO HELL I'D JUST KEPT SAYING THE EXACT SAME THING J. Alter *New York Times Magazine* p40 Ja 22 2017

Biderman, Assaf

FROM PARKING LOT TO PARADISE color diag *Scientific*

N 11 2016

VAL EMMICH color *Entertainment Weekly* no1468/1469 p110 Je 2-9 2017

A WALK ON THE WILD SIDE color *Entertainment Weekly* no1438 p66 N 4 2016

What's Next for Hamilton's Breakout Stars? color *Entertainment Weekly* no1454/1455 p104 F 24 2017

WHAT THE H IS HYGGE? color *Entertainment Weekly* no1459 p62 Mr 31 2017

What to Watch color *Entertainment Weekly* no1457/1458 p88 Mr 17 2017

What to Watch color *Entertainment Weekly* no1465 p50 My 12 2017

THE WHOLE WIDE WORLD OF JOAN DIDION color map *Entertainment Weekly* no1457/1458 p104 Mr 17 2017

WHY ROCK MEMOIRS RULE color *Entertainment Weekly* no1438 p64 N 4 2016

WONDER color *Entertainment Weekly* no1478 / 1479 p65 Ag 18-25 2017

Your Sunshiny, Stupendous, Seriously Spectacular SUMMER BUCKET LIST color *Entertainment Weekly* no1470 p32 Je 16 2017

Biederman, Rob

Companies Need an Option Between Contractor and Employee *Harvard Business Review Digital Articles* p2 Ag 21 2015

The Dawning of the Age of Flex Labor *Harvard Business Review Digital Articles* p2 S 4 2015

Biegert & Funk (Company)

Look, No Hands! *Indianapolis Monthly* v40 no5 p23 Ja 2017

Biegert, J.

Ultrafast electron diffraction imaging of bond breaking in di-ionized acetylene bibl graph *Science* v354 no6310 p308 O 21 2016

Biehl, Brigitte

Four-to-the-Floor: The Techno Discourse and Aesthetic Work in Berlin color *Society* v53 no6 p608 D 2016

Biel, Jessica, 1982-

Darkness Under the Sun on USA's Gripping Drama the Sinner D. D'addario color *Time* v190 no6 p51 Ag 7 2017

FROM HEAVEN TO HELL A. D'ARMINIO *TV Guide* v65 no31 p16 Jl 24 2017

The Sinner J. Jensen color *Entertainment Weekly* no1476 p50 Ag 4 2017

THE SINNER T. Stack color *Entertainment Weekly* no1468/1469 p62 Je 2-9 2017

Biele, Teo

AN IMPROBABLE CONVERGENCE A. GULLEY color *Bicycling* v58 no1 p44 Ja/F 2017

Bielejec, E.

An integrated diamond nanophotonics platform for quantum-optical networks bibl graph *Science* v354 no6314 p847 N 18 2016

Bieler, A.

Xenon isotopes in 67P/Churyumov-Gerasimenko show that comets contributed to Earth's atmosphere diag *Science* v356 no6342 p1069 Je 9 2017

BIELER, RÜDIGER

Worm-snail Ships Out! bw color *Natural History* v125 no6 p10 Je 2017

Biello, David

Our Invasive Species R. SULLIVAN *New York Times Book Review* p31 D 11 2016

Time and the River *New York Times Book Review* p13 My 28 2017

Biemans, Ward

A fearless look at the tragedy of abortion C. C. Camosy color *America* v216 no5 p42 Mr 6 2017

BIEN-KAHN, JOSEPH

A.I. PEI cartoon *Wired* v25 no4 p30 Ap 2017

STRONG TO THE HOOP cartoon *Wired* v25 no3 p22 Mr 2017

THE ULTIMATE AIRPORT OF TOMORROW cartoon *Wired* v24 no12 p88 D 2016

WISH LIST 2016 color *Wired* v24 no12 p45 D 2016

Biennale di Venezia

U.S. Pavilion to Explore Citizenship at 2018 Venice Architecture Biennale M. SITZ *Architectural Record* v205 no10 p28 O 2017

Biennale internationale des antiquaires

Around and about at the Biennale des Antiquaires in Paris M. Bartolucci color *Magazine Antiques* v183 no6 p56 N/D 2016

Biennial & triennial exhibitions

See also

Shanghai Biennale

11th SHANGHAI BIENNALE Y. FUCA color *ARTnews* v116 no1 p122 Spr 2017

Art In the Age of Trump: The Whitney Biennial Takes a First Crack E. Berman color *Time* v189 no13 p47 Ap 10 2017

EDITORS' PICKS A. Greenberger, J. Chiaverina et al color *ARTnews* v115 no4 p26 Wint 2016/2017

KOCHI-MUZIRIS BIENNALE B. Augustine color *Art in America* v105 no3 p140 Mr 2017

Bier, Arielle

GÜLSÜN KARAMUSTAFA cartoon *Art in America* v104 no11 p130 D 2016

BIER, DAVID

WHY THE WALL, WON'T WORK bw color graph map *Reason* v49 no1 p20 My 2017

Bier, Susanne

The Night Manager J. Krebs chart color *Sound & Vision* v82 no1 p68 Ja 2017

Bierer, Barbara E.

What do revised U.S. rules mean for human research? color *Science* v357 no6352 p650 Ag 18 2017

Bierig, Aleksandr

The Perplexities of Keeping Fit *Architectural Record* v205 no4 p81 Ap 2017

Bierke, Russell

Perfect Day, New South Wales, Australia color *Surfer* v58 no3 p90 Je 2017

Perfect Day, New South Wales, Australia R. Bierke color *Surfer* v58 no3 p90 Je 2017

Bierman, Stephen

PUMP IT LIKE THE RUSSIANS color *Bloomberg Businessweek* no4496 p78 O 24 2016

Biermann, P. L.

Observation of a large-scale anisotropy in the arrival directions of cosmic rays above 8×1018 eV *Science* v357 no6357 p1266 S 22 2017

BIERSDORFER, J. D.

Caped Women *New York Times Book Review* p27 Je 4 2017

Serial Fiction on Tap *New York Times Book Review* p12 My 14 2017

STAR WARS *New York Times Book Review* p29 D 4 2016

Tech Decoder: The pioneering programmer Ellen Ullman discusses her career and the dangers the internet poses to privacy and civility *New York Times Book Review* p14 Ag 20 2017

Bies, Dawn

A chemical genetic roadmap to improved tomato flavor bibl graph *Science* v355 no6323 p391 Ja 27 2017

Biesheuvel, Thomas

500,000 Tons of Steel. 14 Jobs color *Bloomberg Businessweek* no4528 p16 Je 26 2017

Diamonds Aren't A Bank's Best Friend color *Bloomberg Businessweek* no4537 p26 S 11 2017

We're Going To Need More Lithium diag graph map *Bloomberg Businessweek* no4537 p60 S 11 2017

Bifidobacterium

Probiotics Are No Panacea F. Jabr color *Scientific American* v317 no1 p26 Jl 2017

Bifocal lenses

SHOP NOTES D. Owen bw color *Popular Mechanics* p104 Jl 2017

Biftu, Tesfaye

Systemic pan-AMPK activator MK-8722 improves glucose homeostasis but induces cardiac hypertrophy graph *Science* v357 no6350 p507 Ag 4 2017

Big 12 Conference

BIG TROUBLE IN THE BIG XII A. Staples color diag *Sports Illustrated* v127 no5 p54 Ag 14 2017

CONFERENCE BATTLE T. Taylor diag *Sports Illustrated* v126 no4 p66 Ja 30 2017

HOT | NOT T. Keith color *Sports Illustrated* v125 no15 p22 N 7 2016

Big Agnes Inc.

round up: Sleep Better W. M. ROCHFORT JR. color *Backpacker* p48 S 2017

Big Baby D.R.A.M. (Music)
WHO D.R.A.M J. Goodman color *Entertainment Weekly* no1439 p59 N 11 2016

Big bands
7 IDEAS FOR ORCHESTRATING BIG BAND BRASS M. Buselli color *Downbeat* v84 no4 p80 Ap 2017

Big bang theory
Microwave background teams mull a grand unification A. Cho color *Science* v357 no6358 p1339 S 29 2017

POP goes the universe A. Ijjas, P. J. Steinhardt et al color graph *Scientific American* v316 no2 p32 F 2017

Shock waves rocked baby universe E. CONOVER *Science News* v190 no9 p7 O 29 2016

WHAT CAME BEFORE THE BIG BANG? R. FELTMAN and M. R. FRANCIS color *Popular Science* v289 no5 p52 S/O 2017

Big Bend (Tex.)
High Sierras, Low Stress E. D. Klepper color map *American Cowboy* p78 LEGENDS OF TEXAS Special Issue 2017

Big Bend Ranch State Park (Tex.)
LOST IN BIG BEND C. FRYE color map *Reader's Digest* v190 no1132 p88 Jl/Ag 2017

Big Boat (Music)
The Jam Kings Come Down to Earth W. HERMES color *Rolling Stone* no1272 p49 O 20 2016

Big box stores
Big-Box Retailers Have Two Options If They Want to Survive D. L. Yohn *Harvard Business Review Digital Articles* p2 Je 22 2016

Big Brother (TV program)
Big Brother M. Logan *TV Guide* v65 no35 p32 Ag 21 2017

Confessions of a Reality TV FELON L. Rice color *Entertainment Weekly* no1463/1464 p80 Ap/My 2017

Big brown bat
Active Perception N. Wilson *Natural History* v125 no2 p6 F 2017

Big business
4 Tips for Launching Minimum Viable Products Inside Big Companies D. Madden *Harvard Business Review Digital Articles* p2 S 30 2015

Big Companies Don't Pay as Well as They Used To W. Frick *Harvard Business Review Digital Articles* p2 F 13 2017

Big Companies Should Collaborate with Startups E. Yoon and S. Hughes *Harvard Business Review Digital Articles* p2 F 25 2016

Great Businesses Scale Their Learning, Not Just Their Operations J. Hagel III and J. S. Brown color *Harvard Business Review Digital Articles* p2 Je 7 2017

The Neo-Brandeisian Attack on Big Business R. D. ATKINSON and M. LIND bw color *National Review* v69 no18 p18 O 2 2017

Stop Saying Big Companies Can't Innovate V. Govindarajan *Harvard Business Review Digital Articles* p2 Je 6 2016

WHO ARE YOU CALLING 'BORING'? D. Lyons color *Fortune* v175 no3 p52 Mr 1 2017

Big business—Social aspects
How Big Business Created the Politics of Anger M. R. Kramer *Harvard Business Review Digital Articles* p2 Mr 8 2016

Big business—United States
THE CONVERSATION B. Parks, J. Bade et al color *Atlantic* v319 no1 p10 Ja/F 2017

HOW AM I DOING? H. Clancy color *Fortune* v175 no3 p34 Mr 1 2017

IF YOU BET ON THE FORTUNE 500, YOU BEAT THE MARKET diag *Fortune* v175 no8 p36 Je 15 2017

REBEL TERRITORY C. Leaf color *Fortune* v175 no8 p24 Je 15 2017

Titans of Business Think Small V. Zarya color *Fortune* v175 no8 p44 Je 15 2017

Big churches
Seminary at the megachurch R. Lockhart and J. Byassee color *Christian Century* v134 no4 p24 F 15 2017

Big Cypress National Preserve (Fla.)
Bad Vibes in Big Cypress K. NIELSEN *Sierra* v101 no4 p50 Jl/Ag 2016

Secret Garden: Big Cypress National Preserve, Florida M. RADZICKI MCMANUS color *Backpacker* p16 N 2017

Big data
Beyond prediction: Using big data for policy problems S. Athey bibl color *Science* v355 no6324 p483 F 3 2017

Big-data approaches to protein structure prediction J. Söding bibl color diag graph *Science* v355 no6322 p248 Ja 20 2017

Big-Data Gurus See What the Cadres Don't *Bloomberg Businessweek* no4502 p24 D 5 2016

Big Data Is Only Half the Data Marketers Need M. B. Rasmussen and A. W. Hansen *Harvard Business Review Digital Articles* p2 N 16 2015

Big Data May Lead to Earlier Alzheimer's Diagnosis L. MARSA color graph *Discover* v38 no1 p23 Ja/F 2017

Big Data Opens Promising Career Paths for Biologists B. BAKER *BioScience* v67 no1 p100 Ja 2017

Brewing Big Data: The Tea-Bag Index L. E. OGDEN *BioScience* v67 no7 p680 Jl 2017

Connect Inventors with the Right Problems J. Walker and R. Litan *Harvard Business Review Digital Articles* p2 Ap 1 2015

How an Early Adopter of Electronic Health Records Uses Big Data A. R. Erskine, B. Karunakaran et al *Harvard Business Review Digital Articles* p2 D 15 2016

How Big Data Is Changing Disruptive Innovation M. Wessel *Harvard Business Review Digital Articles* p2 Ja 27 2016

How the Big Data Explosion Has Changed Decision Making M. Schrage *Harvard Business Review Digital Articles* p2 Ag 25 2016

An Important Data Lesson from an Inconsequential Football Scandal Kaiser Fung *Harvard Business Review Digital Articles* p2 Ja 30 2015

Inventory Management in the Age of Big Data M. A. Cohen *Harvard Business Review Digital Articles* p2 Je 24 2015

Just Using Big Data Isn't Enough Anymore R. Bean *Harvard Business Review Digital Articles* p2 F 9 2016

LAND HO! HERE ARE THE TOP 10 THINGS YOU NEED TO KNOW ABOUT FARMLAND B. Freese *Successful Farming* v115 no8 p56 Je/Jl 2017

Machines Learning Astronomy: The new era of artificial intelligence & Big Data is changing how we do astronomy M. Young *Sky & Telescope* v134 no6 p20 D 2017

Most Industries Are Nowhere Close to Realizing the Potential of Analytics N. Henke, J. Bughin et al *Harvard Business Review Digital Articles* p2 D 16 2016

The Promise and Challenge of Big Data for Pharma R. Copping and M. Li *Harvard Business Review Digital Articles* p2 N 29 2016

Run Field Experiments to Make Sense of Your Big Data S. Zoumpoulis, D. Simester et al *Harvard Business Review Digital Articles* p2 N 12 2015

THE SCIENTISTS' APPRENTICE [Cover story] T. Appenzeller color *Science* v357 no6346 p16 Jl 7 2017

Should Antitrust Regulators Stop Companies from Collecting So Much Data? J. Kennedy *Harvard Business Review Digital Articles* p2 Ap 17 2017

There's No Such Thing as Big Data in HR P. Cappelli color *Harvard Business Review Digital Articles* p1 Je 2 2017

Use Big Data to Create Value for Customers, Not Just Target Them N. Dawar *Harvard Business Review Digital Articles* p2 Ag 16 2014

Using an Algorithm to Figure Out What Luxury Customers Really Want A. Brant *Harvard Business Review Digital Articles* p2 Jl 18 2016

Using Big Data to Make Wiser Medical Decisions J. D. Halamka *Harvard Business Review Digital Articles* p2 D 14 2015

Weather Front K. Cutlip color *Weatherwise* v69 no6 p6 N-D 2016

What People Analytics Can't Capture D. Goleman *Harvard Business Review Digital Articles* p2 Jl 7 2015

What Popular Baby Names Teach Us About Data Analytics K. Fung *Harvard Business Review Digital Articles* p2 Ap 3 2015

WHAT YOUR THERAPIST DOESN'T KNOW T. ROUSMANIERE color *Atlantic* v319 no3 p50 Ap 2017

When Real-Time Intel Still Isn't Fast Enough J. O'Connor *Harvard Business Review Digital Articles* p2 O 30 2014

Why Health Care May Finally Be Ready for Big Data N. D. Shah and J. Pathak *Harvard Business Review Digital Articles* p2 D 3 2014

Big data—Management
The 4 Mistakes Most Managers Make with Analytics A. Lambrecht and C. Tucker *Harvard Business Review Digital Articles* p2 Jl 12 2016

How Chief Data Officers Can Get Their Companies to Collect Clean Data G. Berkooz *Harvard Business Review Digital Articles* p2 F 16 2017

You Don't Need Big Data—You Need the Right Data M. Wessel *Harvard Business Review Digital Articles* p2 N 3 2016

Big Fish Cider Co.—Awards

MADE IN VIRGINIA 2016 AWARDS E. PARKHURST, T. PILKINGTON et al *Virginia Living* v15 no1 p82 D 2016

Big Fish Theory (Music)

Vince Staples E. R. Brown color *Entertainment Weekly* no1472 p59 Je 30 2017

Big Five Chord (Performer)

Glimpses into a Grand Vision B. MILKOWSKI color *Downbeat* v83 no12 p69 D 2016

Big game animals

URSUS MAJOR C. NEWCOMB and A. McKEAN color *Outdoor Life* v224 no5 p89 Je/Jl 2017

Big game hunting

See also

   Bear hunting

   Deer hunting

   Elk hunting

   Moose hunting

DEER of the YEAR color *Outdoor Life* v224 no7 p49 S 2017

THE FIXER B. HEAVEY color *Field & Stream* v122 no6 p90 N 2017

LONG-RANGE SHOOTOUT R. Mann color *Field & Stream* v121 no6 p28 N 2016

Big game hunting—North America

BIG GAME, SMALL BUDGETS D. McDOUGAL color *Outdoor Life* v224 no8 pH1 O 2017

Big Little Lies (TV program)

BEACHES E. NUSSBAUM cartoon *New Yorker* v93 no3 p82 Mr 6 2017

Big Little Lies J. Jensen and R. Rahman color *Entertainment Weekly* no1453 p50 F 17 2017

Big Little Lies S. Vilkomerson color *Entertainment Weekly* no1448 p34 Ja 13 2017

THE DEADLIEST KLATCH B. HANDY bw *Vanity Fair* p170 Hollywood 2017 Supplement

THE GUIDE TO LIES L. Acken *TV Guide* v65 no7 p26 F 13 2017

The Must List color *Entertainment Weekly* no1454/1455 p1 F 24 2017

The Roush Review M. Roush color *TV Guide* v65 no7 p18 F 13 2017

Television Manages to Put a New Twist on the California State of Mind D. D'Addario color *Time* v189 no6 p47 F 20 2017

Total (and equal) depravity K. Reklis color *Christian Century* v134 no11 p44 My 24 2017

Big Phat Band (Performer)

BIG PHAT PRODUCTION VALUES G. Goodwin color *Downbeat* v84 no2 p88 F 2017

Big Sioux River (S.D. & Iowa)

WHERE THE BRIDGES ARE *South Dakota Magazine* v32 no6 p29 Mr/Ap 2017

Big Star Little Star (TV program)

ALSO COMING... A. D'Arminio and J. Russell *TV Guide* v65 no23 p27 My 29 2017

Big Sur (Calif.)

Over the Edge S. F. HAYWARD bw color *Weekly Standard* v22 no44 p27 Jl 31 2017

Big Sur (Calif.)—Description & travel

Back to Big Sur J. WOGAN color *Conde Nast Traveler* v52 no10 p32 N 2017

Big Ten Conference (U.S.)

A LEAGUE AHEAD M. Rosenberg color *Sports Illustrated* v125 no19 p32 D 12 2016

Bigard, Ashana

Monuments Fall, but Racism Stands Tall in New Orleans Schools color *Progressive* v81 no6 p43 Ag/S 2017

Big Bang Theory, The (TV program)

America's Most Watched 25 TOP SHOWS *TV Guide* v65 no31 p13 Jl 24 2017

Fall Sneak Peek: What to Expect J. HALTERMAN *TV Guide* v65 no23 p6 My 29 2017

HOT YOGA HOT BOD [Cover story] L. Majewski cartoon color

Women's Health v13 no10 p65 D 2016

The image of scientists in The Big Bang Theory M. A. Weitekamp *Physics Today* v70 no1 p40 Ja 2017

Bigda, Carolyn

FAST-GROWING ECONOMIES, FOR CHEAP *Fortune* v174 no8 p115 D 15 2016

How to Brace Yourself color diag *Money* v45 no11 p45 D 2016

TOP PICKS FROM TOP PROS color diag *Money* v46 no1 p58 Ja/F 2017

X-Ray: Walmart diag *Money* v45 no10 p43 N 2016

Big data—Charts, diagrams, etc.

HOW COMPANIES REALLY USE BIG DATA graph il img *Harvard Business Review* v95 no5 p26 S/O 2017

Bigelow, Kathryn, 1951-

10 THINGS WE'RE ALREADY OBSESSING OVER IN 2017 C. Hope color *Essence* v47 no9 p41 Ja 2017

Artists color *Time* v189 no16/17 p40 My 1-8 2017

Detroit L. Greenblatt color *Entertainment Weekly* no1476 p44 Ag 4 2017

The myth of white innocence K. Reklis color *Christian Century* v134 no19 p44 S 13 2017

Reliving '67 Algiers Motel Incident A. Tinubu color *Ebony* v72 no9 p20 Jl/Ag 2017

Bigert, Mats, 1965-

Sweden's Solar Egg Sauna J. Zorthian color *Time* v189 no20 p19 My 29 2017

Biggar, Jacquie

The Guardian *Publishers Weekly* v264 no17 p58a Ap 24 2017

Bigger Splash, A (Film)

9 — "MOVES LIKE FIENNES" L. Greenblatt *Entertainment Weekly* no1444/1445 p61 D 16 2016

Biggerstaff, Lee

Is Your Firm Underperforming? Your CEO Might Be Golfing Too Much *Harvard Business Review Digital Articles* p2 N 30 2016

Biggs, Duan

After Chile's fires, reforest private land color *Science* v356 no6334 p147 Ap 14 2017

BIGGS, JOANNA

BABY HAMLET il *Nation* v33 no21 p37 N 21 2016

Bighorn Mountains (Wyo. & Mont.)

EASY CHAIR: The Spaceship and the Moose W. Kirn *Harper's Magazine* p5 O 2017

Bighorn sheep

Bighorn Sheep color *Nebraska Life* v21 no4 p66 Jl/Ag 2017

Bighorn sheep hunting

The Bighorns Are Back K. MILLGATE *Idaho Magazine* v16 no5 p20 F 2017

Bight redfish

Fish on the Half Shell E. Laborde *New Orleans Magazine* v51 no9 p14 Jl 2017

Bigley, James

THE 33 YEAR SEARCH FOR MY BIRTH MOTHER J. BIGLEY II *Reader's Digest* v189 no1127 p77 F 2017

Big Sean, 1988-

BIG SEAN M. Vain *Entertainment Weekly* no1446/1447 p73 D 2016/Ja 2017

NIGHT LIFE *New Yorker* v93 no8 p8 Ap 10 2017

The "Underdog" Rises L. CROSS color *Ebony* v72 no8 p28 Je 2017

Big Sean, 1988-—Interviews

BIG SEAN M. Vain color *Entertainment Weekly* no1453 p58 F 17 2017

Big Sick, The (Film)

ACROSS THE DIVIDE A. LANE color *New Yorker* v93 no18 p76 Je 26 2017

The Best of Sundance C. Nashawaty color *Entertainment Weekly* no1451/1452 p90 F 3-10 2017

THE BIGGEST SUMMER BREAKOUTS (SO FAR) E. R. Brown, D. Coggan et al color diag *Entertainment Weekly* no1474/1475 p15 Jl 21-28 2017

The Big Sick C. Nashawaty color *Entertainment Weekly* no1472 p42 Je 30 2017

KUMAIL NANJIANI S. Vilkomerson color *Entertainment Weekly* no1463/1464 p54 Ap/My 2017

The Little Sick J. PODHORETZ color *Weekly Standard* v22 no44 p39 Jl 31 2017

Love and Its Complications R. DOUTHAT color *National Review* v69 no17 p42 S 11 2017

Biing-Hwan Lin
Shares of Food Commodities Purchased Away From Home Vary by Commodity *Amber Waves: The Economics of Food, Farming, Natural Resources, & Rural America* p26 Ap 2017

Bijan (Company)
Fresh Prince of Beverly Hills A. FELDMAN color *Forbes* v199 no4 p54 Ap 25 2017

Bijan, Nicolas
Fresh Prince of Beverly Hills A. FELDMAN color *Forbes* v199 no4 p54 Ap 25 2017

Bijian, Zheng
China's 'One Belt, One Road' Plan Marks The Next Phase Of Globalization *NPQ: New Perspectives Quarterly* v34 no3 p27 Jl 2017

Bijur, George
LEARNING TO WORK THE NIGHT SHIFT: With the war effort, suddenly many more factories were working around the clock to fulfill their defense contracts *Saturday Evening Post* v289 no4 p96 Jl/Ag 2017

Bikinis
BEST Summer Ever! [Cover story] color *Chicago* v66 no7 p48 Jl 2017

Bikinis—Evaluation
ONE & DONE color *Essence* v48 no2 p18 Je 2017
ROSY ROMANCE color *Harper's Bazaar* no3653 p110 My 2017
SUIT YOURSELF color *Women's Health* v14 no4 p52 My 2017
Well Suited A. R. Williams color *Southern Living* v52 no6 p45 Je 2017

Biko, Steve, 1946-1977
STEVE BIKO WITH THE BRUTAL TRUTH *Lapham's Quarterly* v10 no3 p171 Summ 2017

Bikoff, David
BEST OF ATLANTA *Atlanta* v56 no8 p106 D 2016

BIKOFF, MARY LOGAN
ATLANTA *Atlanta* v56 no10 p70 F 2017
BEST OF ATLANTA *Atlanta* v56 no8 p106 D 2016
Clay Time *Atlanta* v56 no12 p48 Ap 2017
Feel Good, Look Great *Atlanta* v56 no9 p106 Ja 2017
FLIGHT PATTERNS *Atlanta* v56 no9 p28 Ja 2017
Trendspotting *Atlanta* v56 no11 p44 Mr 2017
Wearable Sculpture *Atlanta* v56 no10 p43 F 2017
WESTSIDE STORY *Atlanta* v56 no7 p50 N 2016

Bikram yoga
The A-LIST K. Jenner color *Harper's Bazaar* no3653 p86 My 2017
THE CASE OF BIKRAM YOGA A. JAIN color *Tricycle: The Buddhist Review* v26 no3 p53 Spr 2017
DOWNWARD-FACING BULL J. Fuchs, T. Keith et al color *Sports Illustrated* v127 no7 p24 S 4 2017

Bila, Jedediah—Interviews
THE VIEW M. LOGAN *TV Guide* v64 no46 p40 N 7 2016

Bilal, Parker, 1960-
Dark Water *Publishers Weekly* v264 no19 p38 My 8 2017

BILAS, ZENON
Get Yer Slalom On *Boating World* v38 no6 p16 Je 2017
WATERSPORTS HOTSPOTS color *Boating World* v38 no7 p46 Jl 2017

Bilbao, Tatiana
house of the month P. VILADAS *Architectural Record* v205 no10 p31 O 2017

Bildner, Jim
Why Social Ventures Need Systems Thinking *Harvard Business Review Digital Articles* p2 Jl 25 2016

Bile ducts—Tumors
New Hope at Stage 4 M. Fetterman color *AARP: The Magazine* v30 no6A p27 O/N 2017

Biles, Simone, 1997-
Dancing With the Stars THE COUPLES TO WATCH E. ASLANIAN *TV Guide* v65 no14 p6 Ap 3 2017
MAKING THE COVER color *Ebony* v72 no3 p26 D 2016/Ja 2017
Simone BILES color *Vanity Fair* v59 no1 p129 Holiday 2017

Biles, Simone, 1997—Interviews
Simone BILES S. Dreisbach color *Glamour* v114 no12 p210 D

2016

Bilger, Burkhard
2013: Sierra Juárez *Lapham's Quarterly* v10 no2 p85 Spr 2017
FEATHERED GLORY bw cartoon color *New Yorker* v93 no29 p68 S 25 2017

BILHORN, CLEMENT
Jews, Christians, and the Law *Commentary* v144 no2 p6 S 2017

Bilibashi, Ardian
Changing climate shifts timing of European floods color graph *Science* v357 no6351 p588 Ag 11 2017

Bililies, Charles
SOUVLAKI SECRETS M. True color *Sunset* v238 no5 p85 My 2017

Bilingual education—California
California's Bilingual-Ed Mistake J. J. MILLER il *National Review* v69 no6 p19 Ap 3 2017

Bilingual students
The arts, educational policy, and emergent bilingual learners: Introductory remarks S. V. Chappell bibl *Arts Education Policy Review* v118 no4 p189 2017
BILINGUAL MATTERS C. España color *Literacy Today (2411-7862)* v34 no3 p26 N/D 2016

Bilingual teachers
The arts, educational policy, and emergent bilingual learners: Introductory remarks S. V. Chappell bibl *Arts Education Policy Review* v118 no4 p189 2017
Shifting discourses in teacher education: Performing the advocate bilingual teacher B. Caldas bibl *Arts Education Policy Review* v118 no4 p190 2017

Bilingualism
Hearing from you C. Day *Physics Today* v70 no4 p8 Ap 2017

Biliopancreatic diversion
OPERATION: DIABETES F. Rubino color *Scientific American* v317 no1 p60 Jl 2017

Bill, Frank
Bloody Good: The reigning king of "grit lit," Hoosier author Frank Bill returns with his third novel, The Savage C. FEHRMAN *Indianapolis Monthly* p29 N 2017

Bill, Hillary & Chelsea Clinton Foundation
To Innovate, Think Like a 19th-Century Barn Raiser J. Geraci and C. Chavez *Harvard Business Review Digital Articles* p2 Ag 4 2016

Bill Blass Inc.
Adopt the new kitten heel color *Redbook* p63 O 2017
Tote Couture color *O, The Oprah Magazine* p53 Mr 2017

Bill Charlap Trio (Performer)
BEST ALBUMS OF 2016 bw color *Downbeat* v84 no1 p51 Ja 2017

Bill Evans Trio (Performer)
Sonic Portrait of Evans in '68 P. Lutz bw *Downbeat* v84 no10 p13 O 2017

Billboards—Design & construction
Billboards That Don't Block the View J. Zorthian color *Time* v189 no10 p21 Mr 20 2017
Piccadilly Circus Goes Dark for the Summer *British Heritage Travel* v38 no2 p7 Mr/Ap 2017

Biller, Anna
THE BIG QUESTION cartoon *Atlantic* v319 no2 p100 Mr 2017
The Love Witch V. LUCCA color *Film Comment* v52 no6 p87 N/D 2016

Biller, David
Brazilian Police Strike, And Violence Spikes color *Bloomberg Businessweek* no4512 p14 F 20 2017
Brazilians Look for a Trump of Their Own cartoon *Bloomberg Businessweek* no4508 p15 Ja 23 2017
Brazil's Great Leap Backward diag *Bloomberg Businessweek* no4535 p30 Ag 28 2017
A Development Bank Stops Lending Abroad color *Bloomberg Businessweek* no4503 p13 D 12 2016
INTO THE URBAN JUNGLE color *Bloomberg Businessweek* no4534 p60 Ag 14 2017
Where Are All the Tourists? color diag *Bloomberg Businessweek* no4514 p15 Mr 13 2017

Billerbeck, Eva
Mouse models of acute and chronic hepacivirus infection *Science* v357 no6347 p204 Jl 14 2017

Billett, D.
An ecosystem-based deep-ocean strategy bibl color map *Science* v355 no6324 p452 F 3 2017

Billfish fishing
Backyard Billfish J. BROWNLEE color *Power & Motoryacht* v34 no10 p46 O 2017
EXPOSURE S. Murray color *Power & Motoryacht* v34 no7 p40 Jl 2017

Billiard parlors
Do *Los Angeles Magazine* p51 Ag 2017

Billimoria, Zahan
Z L. Hittmeier color *Skiing* p58 D 2016

Billing services—Software
Timing 2.0 review: Mac software for professionals to track billable time K. MCELHEARN color *Macworld - Digital Edition* p83 Je 13 2017

BILLINGE, MANDI
Connecting Kids with Nature color *Earth Island Journal* v32 no4 p15 Wint 2017

Billingham, Mark
Rush of Blood *Publishers Weekly* v263 no52 p98 D 19 2016

Billinghurst, Roy A.
Skepticism Should Be Nonpartisan *Skeptical Inquirer* v41 no3 p63 My/Je 2017

Billings, Lee
Apollo 8: The Thrilling Story of the First Mission to the Moon color *Scientific American* v316 no5 p74 My 2017
China's Moment graph *Scientific American* v317 no4 p72 O 2017
Hope Springs Eternal for Easy Access to Water on Europa color *Scientific American* v315 no6 p20 D 2016

Billionaires
BIG GUN'S BIG FAIL S. Witt img *New York* v49 no23 p42 N 14 2016
Government By Gazzillionaires N. Tabor and J. D. Walsh img *New York* p30 Ja 23 2017
Here's How the Backlash Against Tech Billionaires Will Play Out S. Wilkin *Harvard Business Review Digital Articles* p2 Je 24 2016
He's the Youngest Self-Made Billionaire R. Wile color *Money* v46 no5 p16 Je 2017
THE INTEREST GRAPH A. WILSON graph *Forbes* v199 no4 p30 Ap 25 2017
POORER PRESIDENT D. ALEXANDER and M. DRANGE color *Forbes* v200 no5 p62 N 14 2017
THE PRESIDENT'S MEN PART I: Frenemy of the State A. CIRALSKY color *Vanity Fair* v59 no11 p118 N 2017
SPRINGFIELD OR BUST C. FELSENTHAL color *Chicago* v66 no11 p24 N 2017
TEE FOR 'TUDE M. BURKE color *Forbes* v200 no5 p81 N 14 2017
THE TOP 20 chart color *Forbes* v198 no5 p128 O 25 2016
Who's the Richest Person Your Age? T. Tepper color *Money* v46 no7 p12 Ag 2017
THE WORLD'S BILLIONAIRES L. KROLL, K. A. DOLAN et al bw color diag graph map *Forbes* v199 no3 p84 Mr 28 2017

Billionaires—Charts, diagrams, etc.
The Class of 2016 L. KROLL and J. WANG cartoon chart *Forbes* v198 no5 p36 O 25 2016
Drop-Offs A. BROWN chart color graph *Forbes* v198 no5 p48 O 25 2016
Three Decades of Ten-Figure Fortunes K. BLANKFELD and M. TINDERA graph *Forbes* v199 no3 p30 Mr 28 2017
The Young and the Rich K. VINTON color graph *Forbes* v198 no5 p40 O 25 2016

Billionaires—China
THE EMPEROR'S NEW MUSEUM JIAYANG FAN cartoon *New Yorker* v92 no36 p28 N 7 2016

Billionaires—Economic conditions—21st century
Hello, Dollars! M. TINDERA color *Forbes* v199 no6 p18 Je 13 2017

Billionaires—Japan
She Became a Billionaire at Age 82 R. Wile color diag *Money* v46 no4 p14 My 2017

Billionaires—Political activity
Billionaire Ballot Boxes K. BLANKFELD and D. SIRTORI-CORTINA color *Forbes* v198 no5 p50 O 25 2016

Billionaires vs. Bombardiers M. T. KLARE diag *Nation* v304 no8 p3 Mr 13 2017
THE DEFINITIVE LOOK AT DONALD TRUMP'S WEALTH C. PETERSON-WITHORN and J. WANG color *Forbes* v198 no5 p80 O 25 2016

Billions (TV program)
Billions *TV Guide* v65 no19 p31 My 1 2017
Yes, They Can J. Harman color *Glamour* v115 no9 p39 S 2017

Billoir, P.
Observation of a large-scale anisotropy in the arrival directions of cosmic rays above 8×1018 eV *Science* v357 no6357 p1266 S 22 2017

Billon, Emmanuelle
An algal photoenzyme converts fatty acids to hydrocarbons color graph *Science* v357 no6354 p903 S 1 2017

Billoo, Zahra
Islamophobia K. ABIADE *In These Times* v41 no1 p24 Ja 2017

Bills, Joe
Beyond Camelot color *Yankee* p76 Mr 2017
Caring for Books You Value color *Yankee* v80 no6 p28 N/D 2016
FEEDING FRENZY: WHEN COMPETITIVE EATERS TACKLE LOBSTER ROLLS, YOU MIGHT WANT TO AVERT YOUR EYES. WE COULDN'T color *Yankee* p94 Jl 2017
How to Carry Your Wife: Giving new meaning to "spousal support" Elliot and Giana Storey share their secrets for winning a sports competition like no other *Yankee* v81 no5 p28 S/O 2017
How to Get Squirrels Out of Your Attic color *Yankee* p28 Mr 2017
How to Take the Plunge *Yankee* v81 no1 p26 Ja/F 2017
A New Chapter *Yankee* v81 no1 p76 Ja/F 2017
We Remember color *Yankee* v80 no6 p96 N/D 2016
Yankees guide to top events this season... color diag *Yankee* v80 no6 p100 N/D 2016

Bills of sale
Hire Extra Muscle to Reduce Monthly Bills J. Chatzky cartoon *AARP: The Magazine* v60 no1A p25 D 2016/Ja 2017

Billy Bee Honey Products Ltd.
Buzz Feud J. SMITH cartoon *Walrus* v13 no9 p19 N 2016

Billy Graham Evangelistic Association
SHOULD YOUR MINISTRY BE A 'CHURCH'? T. TOWNSEND color *Christianity Today* v60 no10 p19 D 2016

Billy Lynn's Long Halftime Walk (Film)
BEN FOUNTAIN'S LONG HOLLYWOOD TALK S. HARRIGAN *Texas Monthly* v44 no11 p116 N 2016
BILLY LYNN'S LONG HALFTIME WALK D. Vaughn color *Sound & Vision* v82 no6 p69 Jl/Ag 2017
Billy Lynn's Long Halftime Walk N. RAPOLD color *Film Comment* v52 no6 p84 N/D 2016
INTO THE COUNTRY J. BLACK color *Esquire* v166 no5 p122 D 2016/Ja 2017
NEWLY AVAILABLE MOVIES M. FELL *TV Guide* v65 no31 p40 Jl 24 2017
PORTRAITS OF AMERICA J. ANDERSON color *America* v215 no16 p29 N 21 2016

Billy on the Street (TV program)
Billy on How to Lighten Up C. LEE cartoon color *Men's Health* v32 no9 p26 N 2017
BILLY TAKES A STAND C. Agard color *Entertainment Weekly* no1470 p50 Je 16 2017
Man of the People C. Bagley color *InStyle* v24 no1 p88 Ja 2017

Billykirk Inc.
PUT YOUR GEAR IN HERE color *Men's Health* v32 no2 p(Sp)11 Mr 2017

Bilmes, Alex
Only If It SUITS YOU bw color *Esquire* p66 BigBlackBook
PLAY ANYTHING color *Esquire* p27 O 2017

Bilotta, Ruth
Everyday Kindnesses *Reader's Digest* v188 no1125 p97 N 2016

Biloxi, Kristen H.
On Rebels and Role Models color *Glamour* v115 no10 p34 O 2017

Bilson, Rachel, 1981-
Meet Nashville's Newbies S. Highfill color *Entertainment Weekly* no1468/1469 p91 Je 2-9 2017

Biltmore Estate (Asheville, N.C.)
GRAND TOUR K. BARNES *Better Homes & Gardens* v94 no12 pZ1 D 2016

Bilton, Diana

Emergence and spread of a human-transmissible multidrug-resistant nontuberculous mycobacterium bibl diag graph *Science* v354 no6313 p751 N 11 2016

Bilton, Nick

BRAVE NEW UNDERWORLD N. BILTON color *Vanity Fair* v59 no6 p68 My 2017

Denting the Universe *New York Times Book Review* p18 F 19 2017

THE NEW ESTABLISHMENT 2017 bw color *Vanity Fair* v59 no11 p87 N 2017

NEW ESTABLISHMENT bw cartoon color *Vanity Fair* v58 no11 p124 N 2016

THE RAND PACK cartoon *Vanity Fair* v58 no11 p120 N 2016

Selling the Silk Road Soap Opera B. DOHERTY color *Reason* v49 no4 p68 Ag/S 2017

THE SEVEN HABITS OF HIGHLY EFFECTIVE DRUG DEALERS M. Chafkin color *Bloomberg Businessweek* no4520 p74 My 1 2017

Tales From the Dark Web: The downfall of the Silk Road's creator is the startup hero's journey in a black mirror N. TIKU *New York Times Book Review* p13 Je 18 2017

That'S All Folks! color *Vanity Fair* p140 Hollywood 2017 Supplement

TRUMP, BETWEEN TAKES color *Vanity Fair* v59 no2 p52 F 2017

Bimpe, Israel

Promoting human rights through science color *Science* v357 no6359 p34 O 6 2017

Bin Liu

Photoactivation and inactivation of Arabidopsis cryptochrome 2 bibl graph *Science* v354 no6310 p343 O 21 2016

Bin Yang

Save the world's primates in peril bibl color *Science* v354 no6311 p425 O 28 2016

Bin Zhang

Quality management for precision medicine clinical applications: A consensus from the China Precision Medicine Clinical Research and Application Association bibl *Science* v354 no6319 p11 D 23 2016

Binary stars

Deep-sky objects in Cancer P. HARRINGTON color *Astronomy* v45 no5 p66 My 2017

Double star marathon redux G. CHAPLE color *Astronomy* v45 no3 p64 Mr 2017

Double your observing fun G. CHAPLE color *Astronomy* v44 no12 p65 D 2016

Paired Stars in Cygnus En Route to Merger? C. M. CARLISLE *Sky & Telescope* v133 no4 p11 Ap 2017

Binary stars—Charts, diagrams, etc.

Eyes of the Dragon M. Wedel bw chart color diag *Sky & Telescope* v134 no2 p22 Ag 2017

Bindeman, Ilya N.

Titanium isotopic evidence for felsic crust and plate tectonics 3.5 billion years ago bw color graph *Science* v357 no6357 p1271 S 22 2017

Binder, Amy

POLITICS ON CAMPUS: A Q&A WITH AMY BINDER color *Phi Kappa Phi Forum* v97 no2 p20 Summ 2017

Binder, Christof

Why Strong Customer Relationships Trump Powerful Brands *Harvard Business Review Digital Articles* p2 Ap 14 2015

Binder, John J.

SIN CITY H. NYHART bw *Chicago* v66 no6 p22 Je 2017

Binder, Leah

Don't Bother Complaining About High-Deductible Health Plans *Harvard Business Review Digital Articles* p2 N 13 2014

U.S. Health Care Reform Can't Wait for Quality Measures to Be Perfect *Harvard Business Review Digital Articles* p2 O 4 2017

BINDER, MELISSA

EVANGELISM Is Alive in Portland color *Christianity Today* p36 Ap 2017

Binder, Meredith

"Do I need to take a daily multi-vitamin and mineral in order to be healthy?" *Vegetarian Journal* v35 no1 p14 2016

Binding agents

See also

Adhesives

Glue

Highly elastic binders integrating polyrotaxanes for silicon microparticle anodes in lithium ion batteries S. Choi, Kwon et al diag *Science* v357 no6348 p279 Jl 21 2017

How to Glue Anything color *Popular Mechanics* p44 Mr 2017

Binding energy

Experimental measurement of binding energy, selectivity, and allostery using fluctuation theorems J. Camunas-Soler, A. Alemany et al bibl graph *Science* v355 no6323 p412 Ja 27 2017

Binding sites (Biochemistry)

See also

Cell receptors

Principles for designing proteins with cavities formed by curved β sheets E. Marcos, B. Basanta et al bibl color graph *Science* v355 no6321 p1 Ja 13 2017

BINDLER, RICHARD

The Arctic in the Twenty-First Century: Changing Biogeochemical Linkages across a Paraglacial Landscape of Greenland *BioScience* v67 no2 p118 F 2017

Bindocci, Erika

Three-dimensional Ca2+ imaging advances understanding of astrocyte biology diag *Science* v356 no6339 p715 My 19 2017

Binelli, Mark

THE FIRE LAST TIME bw *New Republic* v248 no5 p28 My 2017

The Happy Warrior [Cover story] bw color *Rolling Stone* no1289 p46 Je 15 2017

THE MICHIGAN EXPERIMENT *New York Times Magazine* p50 S 10 2017

TRUMP COUNTY, USA bw color *Rolling Stone* no1280 p26 F 9 2017

Binet, Laurent, 1972-

BITTERSWEET ESCAPE J. Black, A. Carter et al color *Esquire* p21 Ag 2017

The Death of the Theorist: Laurent Binet's detective novel reimagines the death and life of Roland Barthes N. DAMES *New York Times Book Review* p17 Ag 20 2017

Theory Conspiracy S. BIRKERTS bw color *New Republic* v248 no10 p51 O 2017

Word Games E. POWERS *National Review* v69 no18 p40 O 2 2017

Bing (Web resource)

4 REASONS WHY I SWITCHED FROM GOOGLE TO BING M. Hachman color *PCWorld* v35 no9 p83 S 2017

Bing, Dane Anine

THE DANISH GIRL E. FLORIO color *Conde Nast Traveler* v52 no4 p20 Ap 2017

Bing, Stanley

Immortal Life: A Soon to Be True Story *Publishers Weekly* v264 no41 p48 O 9 2017

Bing Chen

Quality management for precision medicine clinical applications: A consensus from the China Precision Medicine Clinical Research and Application Association bibl *Science* v354 no6319 p11 D 23 2016

BINGA, TIMOTHY

Information Bias in Library Catalogs *Skeptical Inquirer* v41 no3 p9 My/Je 2017

Notable Articles about the Creation of CSICOP and SKEPTICAL INQUIRER *Skeptical Inquirer* v41 no1 p19 Ja/F 2017

Bingaman, Joshua

SOLE OBSESSION color *Men's Health* v32 no2 p(Sp)16 Mr 2017

Bingcheng Hu

Synthesis and characterization of the pentazolate anion cyclo-N5⁻ in (N5)6(H3O)3(NH4)4Cl bibl diag graph *Science* v355 no6323 p374 Ja 27 2017

Binge watching (Television)

The real taboo in 13 Reasons Why A. KINGSTON color *Maclean's* p8 Je 2017

What's the Most Bingeworthy Show? S. Highfill, K. P. Sullivan et al color *Entertainment Weekly* no1443 p21 D 9 2016

Bingham, Clara

Revolution for What? H. WILHELM *Commentary* v142 no2 p60 S 2016

The Revolution Will Be Analyzed N. Kelley *Washington Monthly* p9 N/D 2016

Bingham, Joan

Deals R. DEAHL bw color *Publishers Weekly* v264 no40 p6 O 2 2017

Bingham, Sue

If Employees Don't Trust You, It's Up to You to Fix It bw *Harvard Business Review Digital Articles* p2 Ja 2 2017

Bingle, Richard J.

HALCYON DAYS, INDIAN SUMMERS *History Today* v67 no5 p98 My 2017

Binion, Justin—Interviews

MEET 'MR. WEALTH MANAGEMENT' JUSTIN BINION D. PRESSLEY color *Black Enterprise* v47 no8 p36 Jl/Ag 2017

Bin Laden, Osama, 1957-2011

The Final Obama Scandal [Cover story] S. F. HAYES and T. JOSCELYN color *Weekly Standard* v22 no21 p22 F 6 2017

Binns, Andy

Data Can Do for Change Management What It Did for Marketing *Harvard Business Review Digital Articles* p2 Jl 31 2017

Email and Calendar Data Are Helping Firms Understand How Employees Work *Harvard Business Review Digital Articles* p2 Ag 28 2017

Binocular vision

WAYPOINT N. KREBS color *Outdoor Life* v224 no5 p7 Je/Jl 2017

Binoculars

Best Bins for Your Buck *Audubon* v118 no6 p44 Wint 2016

The Easy Bird S. Bestul color *Field & Stream* v121 no9 pT1 Ap 2017

Eyes of the Dragon M. Wedel bw chart color diag *Sky & Telescope* v134 no2 p22 Ag 2017

THE LEADING EDGE OF SHOOTING, FISHING AND WILDLIFE MANAGEMENT color *Outdoor Life* v224 no2 p34 F/Mr 2017

Pickin' up good librations M. RATCLIFFE and A. LING bw *Astronomy* v45 no5 p37 My 2017

SECRETS OF A SCOUTMASTER N. KREBS color *Outdoor Life* v224 no7 pW6 S 2017

Sparkling star clusters P. HARRINGTON color *Astronomy* v45 no11 p68 N 2017

Binoculars—Evaluation

25 HOT ECLIPSE PRODUCTS P. Harrington color *Astronomy* v45 no6 p54 Je 2017

COASTAL CRUISING Gear P. Nielsen color *Sail* v48 no5 p26 My 2017

EYES IN THE SKIES P. Saha color *Audubon* v119 no3 p46 Fall 2017

GO-TO GLASS D. Hurteau and J. Zavislan color *Field & Stream* v121 no6 p75 N 2016

LOOKING GLASSES A. McKEAN chart color *Outdoor Life* v224 no5 p22 Je/Jl 2017

NEW PRODUCTS bw color *Astronomy* v45 no9 p69 S 2017

NEW PRODUCTS color *Astronomy* v45 no1 p68 Ja 2017

NEW PRODUCTS color *Astronomy* v45 no6 p68 Je 2017

Observe with both eyes open P. Harrington color *Astronomy* v45 no11 p58 N 2017

The Outdoorsman's Essentials S. RINELLA color *Men's Health* v32 no6 p32 Ag 2017

PEAK GLASS D. Hurteau, R. Mann et al color *Field & Stream* v122 no4 p69 S 2017

THE ULTIMATE KIDS' KIT A. Opar color *Audubon* v119 no3 p44 Fall 2017

Bins

A Community Affair D. Sanford *Parks & Recreation* v52 no5 p80 My 2017

Rubber Tub Captures Sawdust color *Popular Mechanics* p29 F 2017

Bins—Design & construction

Blank Canvas color *Martha Stewart Living* p22 My 2017

Bins—Evaluation

coat check color *Better Homes & Gardens* v95 no3 p44 Mr 2017

Binte Shadan, Nurhidaya

Mapping the human DC lineage through the integration of high-dimensional techniques diag *Science* v356 no6342 p1044 Je 9 2017

Binyam, Maya

Ghosting bw *New York Times Magazine* p24 Ag 6 2017

Biobanks

A Flood of Tears N. Caldwell color *Scientific American* v315 no3 p15 S 2016

BioBots Inc.—Finance

Body Parts on Demand K. DILL color *Forbes* v198 no7 p56 N 29 2016

Biochar

The Biochar Solution E. Strickland *Sierra* v102 no4 p25 Jl/Ag 2017

Biochemical markers

Cutting Calories Reduces Dangerous Inflammation [Cover story] *Tufts University Health & Nutrition Letter* v34 no10 p1 D 2016

Biochemistry

See also

Biogeochemistry

Body composition

Enzymology

Metabolism

Molecular biology

Rest and renew color *Yoga Journal* no291 p80 My 2017

Biochemists

Oliver Smithies (1925-2017) A. Sancar color *Science* v355 no6326 p695 F 17 2017

Biodegradation

See also

Human decomposition

A Columbia Lab Is Trying to Turn Corpses Into Glowing Installation Art Under the Manhattan Bridge B. WALLACE img *New York* v49 no25 p82 D 12 2016

Biodiesel fuels & the environment

A push for low-carbon fuels pays off in California R. F. Service color graph *Science* v357 no6347 p120 Jl 14 2017

Biodiesel fuels industry

BIODIESEL POWER: HOW IDAHO RESEARCH CHANGED THE WORLD J. CROCKETT *Idaho Magazine* v16 no8 p12 My 2017

Biodiesel fuels research

BIODIESEL POWER: HOW IDAHO RESEARCH CHANGED THE WORLD J. CROCKETT *Idaho Magazine* v16 no8 p12 My 2017

Biodiesel fuels—Government policy

A push for low-carbon fuels pays off in California R. F. Service color graph *Science* v357 no6347 p120 Jl 14 2017

Biodiversity

See also

Animal diversity

Aquatic biodiversity

Freshwater biodiversity

Marine biodiversity

Urban biodiversity

An Anthropocene map of genetic diversity A. Miraldo, Sen Li et al bibl graph map *Science* v353 no6307 p1532 S 30 2016

Birthday Bioblitzes D. Ireland color *Canadian Wildlife* v23 no2 p30 My/Je 2017

Border Walls and Biodiversity L. E. OGDEN *BioScience* v67 no6 p498 Je 2017

Combining Biodiversity Resurveys across Regions to Advance Global Change Research K. VERHEYEN, P. DE FRENNE et al *BioScience* v67 no1 p73 Ja 2017

Corrigendum: Assessing National Biodiversity Trends for Rocky and Coral Reefs through the Integration of Citizen Science and Scientific Monitoring Programs *BioScience* v67 no8 p774 Ag 2017

CROP DIVERSITY PAYDAY B. Spielgel *Successful Farming* v114 no11 p44 N 2016

EDITING EVOLUTION P. Koberstein diag *Earth Island Journal* v32 no1 p36 Spr 2017

Getting Back to the Basics: Museum Collections and Satellite Imagery Are Critical to Analyzing Species Diversity N. U. DE LA SANCHA, S. A. BOYLE et al *BioScience* v67 no5 p405 My 2017

The Nagoya Protocol: Big Steps, New Problems M. E. WATANABE *BioScience* v67 no4 p400 Ap 2017

Pitcher Plants Shape Up L. GAUME, V. BAZILE et al color diag *Natural History* v125 no5 p12 My 2017

Share & Share Alike J. Mark *Sierra* v102 no1 p4 Ja/F 2017

Biased inheritance protects older bacteria from harm T. C. Barrett, W. W. K. Mok et al diag *Science* v356 no6335 p247 Ap 21 2017

Biological evolution education

Helping Teachers Teach Evolution in the United States B. VAZQUEZ *Skeptical Inquirer* v41 no3 p49 My/Je 2017

Biological fitness

BEYOND CHICKEN M. KADEY cartoon color *Muscle & Performance* v9 no4 p54 Ap 2017

Biological invasions

Scientific and Normative Foundations for the Valuation of Alien-Species Impacts: Thirteen Core Principles F. ESSL, P. E. HULME et al *BioScience* v67 no2 p166 F 2017

Biological laboratories

Getting my feet wet E. S. Wright color *Science* v356 no6333 p106 Ap 7 2017

Biological manufacturing

Industrial biomanufacturing: The future of chemical production J. M. Clomburg, A. M. Crumbley et al bibl chart color diag graph *Science* v355 no6320 p1 Ja 6 2017

Biological membranes

In situ architecture, function, and evolution of a contractile injection system D. Böck, J. M. Medeiros et al color diag *Science* v357 no6352 p713 Ag 18 2017

The most perfect thing, explained C. N. Spottiswoode diag *Science* v356 no6344 p1234 Je 23 2017

Nanoscale-length control of the flagellar driveshaft requires hitting the tethered outer membrane E. J. Cohen, J. L. Ferreira et al color diag graph *Science* v356 no6334 p197 Ap 14 2017

Biological nomenclature

Carl Linnaeus color *Discover* v38 no4 p49 My 2017

Biological pigments

See also

Carotenoids

Color Me Dino M. Rosen bw color diag *Science News* v190 no11 p24 N 26 2016

Biological products

See also

Microbial products

BUGS IN A JUG G. GULLICKSON *Successful Farming* v114 no12 p48 Mid-N 2016

Biological research

Applying Science R. E. GROPP *BioScience* v67 no9 p779 S 2017

Biology and Light Sources R. BLAUSTEIN *BioScience* v67 no3 p201 Mr 2017

Critics challenge NIH finding that bigger labs aren't necessarily better J. Kaiser color *Science* v356 no6342 p997 Je 9 2017

NIH's massive health study is off to a slow start J. Kaiser color *Science* v357 no6355 p955 S 8 2017

Put Science Back in Congress color *Scientific American* v317 no4 p10 O 2017

Biological research—Government policy

Rethinking biosecurity J. REPPY diag *Issues in Science & Technology* v33 no2 p11 Wint 2017

Biological research—Moral & ethical aspects

Biosecurity Governance lor the Real World S. W. EVANS *Issues in Science & Technology* v33 no1 p84 Fall 2016

Biological rhythms

See also

Circadian rhythms

Jet lag

ON THE CLOCK L. B. Ray and J. Travis color *Science* v354 no6315 p986 N 25 2016

Biological systems

CRISPR-Cas: Adapting to change S. A. Jackson, R. E. McKenzie et al color *Science* v356 no6333 p40 Ap 7 2017

Biological warfare

Glaring gaps: America needs a biodefense upgrade D. M. Gerstein bibl *Bulletin of the Atomic Scientists* v73 no2 p86 Mr 2017

Biological weapons

Can everyone help verify the bioweapons convention? Perhaps, via open source monitoring G. Jeremias and M. Himmel bibl *Bulletin of the Atomic Scientists* v72 no6 p412 N 2016

Biologicals

See also

Vaccines

Are Drugs Samsung's Next Big Thing? N. Khan and S. Kim color graph *Bloomberg Businessweek* no4523 p23 My 22 2017

Biologists

See also

Ecologists

Neurobiologists

Women biologists

Big Data Opens Promising Career Paths for Biologists B. BAKER *BioScience* v67 no1 p100 Ja 2017

Extreme bird nests bring comforts, catastrophe S. Milius color *Science News* v190 no8 p4 O 15 2016

THE LION KING B. COSSAVELLA *Arizona Highways* v93 no1 p48 Ja 2017

Peter C. Nowell (1928–2016) M. I. Greene and J. S. Moore color *Science* v355 no6328 p913 Mr 3 2017

Rattlesnakes have lost venom genes L. HAMERS color *Science News* v190 no8 p9 O 15 2016

SOUTHERN JOURNAL R. Bragg color *Southern Living* v52 no7 p130 Jl 2017

Susan Lindquist (1949–2016) L. Whitesell and S. Santagata color *Science* v354 no6315 p974 N 25 2016

Yoshinori Ohsumi J. Crelin color *Current Biography* v78 no6 p78 Je 2017

Biology

See also

Biodiversity

Biophysics

Cells

Ecology

Evolution (Biology)

Extinction (Biology)

Fertilization (Biology)

Parthenogenesis

Pollinators

Reproduction

Space biology

Synthetic biology

Corrigendum: Biology and Light Sources *BioScience* v67 no8 p774 Ag 2017

Fossil data lacking for insects and fungi A. Hochkirch bibl color *Science* v355 no6329 p1032 Mr 10 2017

GLOSSARY *Equus* no471 p71 D 2016

Biology education

Dreamscapes of Maine: Kathleen Buchanan's handmade prints reveal a misty world of islands, seabirds, and coastal sheep A. GRAVES color *Yankee* p36 Jl 2017

Getting my feet wet E. S. Wright color *Science* v356 no6333 p106 Ap 7 2017

Teaching Biology in the Field: Importance, Challenges, and Solutions T. L. FLEISCHNER, R. E. ESPINOZA et al *BioScience* v67 no6 p558 Je 2017

Biology teachers

RUTH HUBBARD S. CORBETT *New York Times Magazine* p46 D 25 2016

Biology—Classification

See also

Species

Tension in Taxonomy K. Long cartoon *Scientific American* v315 no5 p13 N 2016

Biology—Study & teaching (Graduate)

The problem with 'alternative' M. Zaringhalam color *Science* v354 no6313 p798 N 11 2016

Bioluminescence

Strange creatures light up the polar 'twilight zone' color *Science* v354 no6313 p688 N 11 2016

Bioluminescence in insects

See also

Fireflies

Glowworms keep their fishing lines sticky with a surprising ingredient color *Science* v354 no6319 p1509 D 23 2016

Biomass

Formaldehyde stabilization facilitates lignin monomer production during biomass depolymerization Li Shuai, M. T. Amiri et al bibl diag graph *Science* v354 no6310 p329 O 21 2016

Biomass energy

BIOFUELS ARE DIRTIER THAN YOU THINK cartoon diag graph *Reason* v48 no8 p42 Ja 2017

Cellulosic biofuel contributions to a sustainable energy future: Choices and outcomes G. P. Robertson, S. K. Hamilton et al color *Science* v356 no6345 p1349 Je 30 2017

Biomechanics

See also

Plant mechanics

Stretch (Physiology)

Jogging With Junior: When you push your children, you need to push yourself too G. Reynolds *New York Times Magazine* p22 Ag 27 2017

Biomedical Research Laboratories (Company)

Cheat Your Way to Lean! A. RIOS *Runner's World* v52 no3 p41 Ap 2017

Biomedical Research Laboratories LLC

ADD FUEL TO THE FIRE WITH MORE OXYGEN M. HANSEN color *Bicycling* v58 no7 p19 Ag 2017

CHEAT, DRINK & STILL SHRINK A. RIOS color *Runner's World* v52 no6 p45 Jl 2017

SMARTEN UP TO SHRINK YOUR GUT C. Hansen color *Men's Health* v32 no6 p69 Ag 2017

Biomes

See also

Deserts

Rain forests

Taigas

Wetlands

The broad footprint of climate change from genes to biomes to people B. R. Scheffers, L. De Meester et al bibl chart color *Science* v354 no6313 paaf7671-1 N 11 2016

Biometric identification

From Man to Machine *New York Times Magazine* p12 O 16 2016

India's Answer to Safe Payments A. Chaudhary color *Bloomberg Businessweek* no4514 p44 Mr 13 2017

Passwords Are Terrible, but Will Biometrics Be Any Better? A. Rjeily and C. Jacco *Harvard Business Review Digital Articles* p1 My 11 2017

Technology beats corruption R. Hanna bibl color *Science* v355 no6322 p244 Ja 20 2017

What life scientists should know about security threats K. M. Berger bibl color diag *Science* v354 no6317 p1237 D 9 2016

Biometric identification laws

Biometrics Regulation: The State (by State) of Play *Bloomberg Businessweek* no4531 p42 Jl 24 2017

Saving Face K. Mehrotra color *Bloomberg Businessweek* no4531 p42 Jl 24 2017

Biometric identification—Equipment & supplies

Small to Big Vision-Box color diag graph *Bloomberg Businessweek* no4495 p40 O 17 2016

Biometry

m-Commerce Growth in Sales and Fraud *USA Today Magazine* v145 no2858 p6 N 2016

Biomimetic materials

Synthetic nacre by predesigned matrix-directed mineralization Li-Bo Mao, Huai-Ling Gao et al bibl bw diag graph *Science* v354 no6308 p107 O 7 2016

Biomimetic synthesis

Growing a synthetic mollusk shell F. Barthelat bibl color diag *Science* v354 no6308 p32 O 7 2016

Biomimicry

5 TRENDS TO RIDE IN 2017 V. Harnish color *Fortune* v175 no4 p32 Mr 15 2017

Biomineralization

Growing a synthetic mollusk shell F. Barthelat bibl color diag *Science* v354 no6308 p32 O 7 2016

Minerals Made by Microbes E. Estes color *Oceanus* v51 no2 p72 Wint 2016

Synthetic nacre by predesigned matrix-directed mineralization Li-Bo Mao, Huai-Ling Gao et al bibl bw diag graph *Science* v354 no6308 p107 O 7 2016

Biomolecules

See also

Biopolymers

Carbohydrates

Fossil biomolecules

Nucleic acids

Proteins

Nucleic acid detection with CRISPR-Cas13a/C2c2 J. S. Gootenberg, O. O. Abudayyeh et al color diag *Science* v356 no6336 p438 Ap 28 2017

Biophysics

See also

Biomechanics

Electrophysiology

Circular DNA throws biologists for a loop E. Pennisi color *Science* v356 no6342 p996 Je 9 2017

The Electric Touch J. KEATS color *Discover* v38 no9 p10 N 2017

Biopolymers

From sequence to color M. d'Ischia and P. B. Messersmith diag *Science* v356 no6342 p1011 Je 9 2017

Bioprinting—Equipment & supplies

Body Parts on Demand K. DILL color *Forbes* v198 no7 p56 N 29 2016

Biosecurity

10 UP & COMERS: NATHAN KATZER J. Scott *Successful Farming* v115 no8 p42 Je/Jl 2017

Biosecurity Governance for the Real World S. W. EVANS *Issues in Science & Technology* v33 no1 p84 Fall 2016

Boundaries for biosecurity N. EVANS *Issues in Science & Technology* v33 no4 p18 Summ 2017

EHV-1 VIABILITY HAS IMPLICATIONS FOR BIOSECURITY C. Barakat and M. McCluskey color *Equus* no478 p16 Jl 2017

Rethinking biosecurity J. REPPY diag *Issues in Science & Technology* v33 no2 p11 Wint 2017

Biosecurity—Law & legislation

Glaring gaps: America needs a biodefense upgrade D. M. Gerstein bibl *Bulletin of the Atomic Scientists* v73 no2 p86 Mr 2017

Biosensors—Evaluation

new products color *Science* v357 no6353 p822 Ag 25 2017

Biosphere

An Ecoregion-Based Approach to Protecting Half the Terrestrial Realm E. DINERSTEIN, D. OLSON et al *BioScience* v67 no6 p534 Je 2017

The laws of life C. S. Cockell *Physics Today* v70 no3 p42 Mr 2017

Our changing view of MARS A. R. Vasavada *Physics Today* v70 no3 p34 Mr 2017

Biosphere reserves

'Listen to what the land wants, listen to what the lake wants, listen to what the animals want' L. SARKADI color map *Canadian Geographic* v137 no1 p34 F 2017

Biotechnology

See also

Reproductive technology

Vaccines—Biotechnology

Managing cell and human identity J. Moreno, J. Gearhart et al cartoon *Science* v356 no6334 p139 Ap 14 2017

Rethinking biosecurity J. KUZMA diag *Issues in Science & Technology* v33 no2 p12 Wint 2017

Biotechnology industries

LIFE WITHOUT END E. KEEP *Smithsonian* v48 no3 p43 Je 2017

Biotechnology industries—United States

Flacking for GMOs: How the Biotech Industry Cultivates Positive Media P. D. Thacker color *Progressive* v81 no6 p34 Ag/S 2017

Biotechnology—Computer network resources

23ANDME.COM R. BAILEY *Reason* v48 no8 p60 Ja 2017

Biotechnology—Research—United States

Rethinking biosecurity M. J. PALMER bw *Issues in Science & Technology* v33 no2 p13 Wint 2017

Biotechnology—Safety measures

Rethinking biosecurity M. J. PALMER bw *Issues in Science & Technology* v33 no2 p13 Wint 2017

Bioterrorism

TIME TO WORRY ABOUT ANTHRAX AGAIN P. S. Keim, D. H. Walker et al color diag *Scientific American* v316 no4 p70 Ap 2017

Bioterrorism—Prevention

Rapid Recovery of Critical Infrastructure L. L. Helms color *Science & Technology Review* p20 O/N 2016

Biotherapy

Medications for rheumatoid arthritis *Harvard Health Letter* v42 no6 p3 Ap 2017

Biotic communities

PATRICK MCCARTHY cartoon color *Snowboarder* v29 no5 p32 Ja 2017

BIRD, WINIFRED

THE TREE GUARDIANS OF KYOTO color *Tricycle: The Buddhist Review* v27 no1 p66 Fall 2017

Bird banding

SWAN SONG H. Macdonald *New York Times Magazine* p24 Ja 8 2017

Bird behavior

Dividends of Diversity N. Wilson color *Natural History* v125 no6 p8 Je 2017

Jail Birds M. WEBER *Orion Magazine* v35 no6 p11 N/D 2016

MOST BIRDS LIVE THREE-DIMENSIONAL LIVES K. Kaufman color *Audubon* v119 no3 p46 Fall 2017

Bird breeding

ESTERO LLANO GRANDE *Texas Monthly* v45 no4 p107 Ap 2017

Follow the Birds L. Greenow *New York State Conservationist* v71 no3 p32 D 2016

The Secret Lives of Birds R. KWOK *Audubon* v119 no2 p18 Summ 2017

Bird care

Ask the Biologist *New York State Conservationist* v71 no4 p31 F 2017

Bird conservation

Bird's-Eye View H. FURFARO *Audubon* v119 no1 p12 Spr 2017

A Call for Hope D. YARNOLD *Audubon* v118 no6 p8 Wint 2016

CAMP MACAW M. Harbison *Audubon* v119 no1 p26 Spr 2017

Dovekies Have a New Diet and Workout Plan B. DRAXLER *Audubon* v119 no2 p16 Summ 2017

Oases in a Dry Land D. OWEN *Audubon* v119 no2 p22 Summ 2017

Talon Show L. VACCARIELLO *Cincinnati Magazine* v50 no3 p160 D 2016

A Voice You Can Trust M. JANNOT *Audubon* v119 no2 p7 Summ 2017

Bird control

Fowl play on campus R. COUNTER color *Maclean's* p11 Je 2017

Bird declines

Safeguarding Summer's Bounty L. MOORE *National Wildlife (World Edition)* v55 no5 p4 Ag/S 2017

Silent Seashores? C. Berger color *National Wildlife (World Edition)* v55 no5 p28 Ag/S 2017

'We know that insect species are being lost across the planet ... but no one is really looking.' L. ANTHONY color *Canadian Geographic* v135 no6 p50 D 2015

Bird droppings

REAL OR FAKE? E. KRIEGER *National Geographic Kids* no469 p18 Ap 2017

Bird eggs

Flight may have steered egg evolution L. HAMERS color *Science News* v192 no1 p9 Ag 5 2017

Bird evolution

Birds rebounded quickly after dinosaur mass extinction color *Science* v357 no6347 p114 Jl 14 2017

Taking Wing [Cover story] S. Brusatte color *Scientific American* v316 no1 p48 Ja 2017

Bird extinctions

Going... Going...? P. Tolmé color *National Wildlife (World Edition)* v55 no2 p22 F/Mr 2017

The Lucky Ones S. Milius cartoon diag *Science News* v191 no2 p26 F 4 2017

Safety Net M. JANNOT color *Audubon* v119 no3 p18 Fall 2017

Wake-Up Call M. JANNOT color *Audubon* v119 no3 p5 Fall 2017

Bird feeders

Bird Feeding: No Feeders Required M. Mayntz color *National Wildlife (World Edition)* v55 no1 p12 D/Ja 2016

Bird flight

First Flight color *Earth Island Journal* v32 no4 p5 Wint 2017

Flight may have steered egg evolution L. HAMERS color *Science News* v192 no1 p9 Ag 5 2017

Bird genetics

'Supergenes' drive evolution E. Pennisi color *Science* v357 no6356 p1083 S 15 2017

Bird habitats

5 Tropical Birding Hot Spots *Audubon* v118 no6 p46 Wint 2016

Black-capped chickadee A. Kylie color *Canadian Geographic* v135 no6 p71 D 2015

Choose Your Adventure A. Opar *Audubon* v119 no2 p54 Summ 2017

Bird migration

See also

Duck migration

Goose migration

BLIND FAITH T. T. WILLIAMS *Audubon* v119 no2 p40 Summ 2017

CHASING THE GHOSTS OF APRIL R. MARR color *Missouri Life* v44 no2 p62 Ap 2017

Conserving Transborder Migratory Bats, Preserving Nature's Benefits to Humans: The Lesson from North America's Bird Conservation Treaties L. LÓPEZ-HOFFMAN, C. C. CHESTER et al *BioScience* v67 no4 p321 Ap 2017

Follow the Birds L. Greenow *New York State Conservationist* v71 no3 p32 D 2016

Malheur Refuge on the Rebound P. Tolmé color *National Wildlife (World Edition)* v55 no1 p14 D/Ja 2016

Mapping Melodies B. TSUI *Audubon* v119 no1 p14 Spr 2017

Microtracker maps a rare bird's migration color *Science* v355 no6329 p998 Mr 10 2017

New insights on birds in flight color *National Wildlife (World Edition)* v55 no3 p8 Ap/My 2017

ON THE MOVE: ANIMAL MIGRATION IN THE 21ST CENTURY A. FUDICKAR color *Phi Kappa Phi Forum* v96 no4 p26 Wint 2016

Bird mitochondrial DNA

'Supergenes' drive evolution E. Pennisi color *Science* v357 no6356 p1083 S 15 2017

Bird mortality

When Windows Kill D. Bird color *Canadian Wildlife* v23 no2 p40 My/Je 2017

Bird nests

4 Tips for Teachers *Audubon* v119 no3 p44 Fall 2017

back porch visitors S. UMLAND color *Cabin Living* p52 Ag 2017

Bane—or Blessing? J. Heimbuch color *National Wildlife (World Edition)* v55 no6 p36 O/N 2017

Elusive blue-throated macaw nests discovered color *Science* v355 no6332 p1356 Mr 31 2017

Home Sweet Dome K. Long color *Scientific American* v316 no5 p16 My 2017

Search for the blue goose J. Pearce bw color *Canadian Geographic* v137 no5 p22 S/O 2017

Bird populations

The pet trade's role in defaunation M. W. Tingley, J. B. C. Harris et al color *Science* v356 no6341 p916 Je 1 2017

Bird refuges

Forest "Islands" Offer Refuge to Birds *USA Today Magazine* v145 no2865 p7 Je 2017

weekend getaways: woods *Washingtonian Magazine* v52 no11 p87 Ag 2017

Bird reproduction

In The Wild color *Nebraska Life* v21 no1 p58 Ja/F 2017

Bird trapping

THE JUMP-SHOOTER'S PLAYBOOK A. ROBINSON color *Outdoor Life* v224 no8 pW8 O 2017

Bird vocalizations

The Crow's Song B. HEINRICH color *Natural History* v125 no11 p10 N 2017

Game On N. Lund color *Audubon* v119 no3 p45 Fall 2017

Bird watchers

3 Ways to Get Stoked *Audubon* v119 no3 p45 Fall 2017

4 Tips for Lofty Birding *Audubon* v119 no3 p47 Fall 2017

Jail Birds M. WEBER *Orion Magazine* v35 no6 p11 N/D 2016

Nest Quest R. Shivni color *Audubon* v119 no3 p46 Fall 2017

Take It Up a Notch M. Bartels color *Audubon* v119 no3 p47 Fall 2017

Those flighty millennials C. MCINTYRE color *Maclean's* v130 no8 p14 S 2017

Bird watching

3 Ways to Get Stoked *Audubon* v119 no3 p45 Fall 2017

4 Tips for Lofty Birding *Audubon* v119 no3 p47 Fall 2017

4 Tips for Teachers *Audubon* v119 no3 p44 Fall 2017

5 Fantastic Festivals *Audubon* v119 no1 p46 Spr 2017

The Afterlife List D. KOEPPEL *Audubon* v119 no1 p34 Spr 2017

BIRD CRAZY B. Andrews color *Prevention* v69 no6 p64 Je 2017

BIRDING T. Winston *Audubon* v119 no1 p44 Spr 2017

BLIND FAITH T. T. WILLIAMS *Audubon* v119 no2 p40 Summ 2017

CALL OF THE WILD M. OZAWA color *Martha Stewart Living* p40 Mr 2017

CONTIGUOUS U.S. & CANADA *Sierra* v102 no1 p57 Ja/F 2017

A Day in the Life of a Teen Birder N. Koszycki color *Audubon* v119 no3 p45 Fall 2017

Feed a Child's Urge to Bird L. McCarthy color *Audubon* v119 no3 p44 Fall 2017

For the Birds K. POPE color *Backpacker* p18 N 2017

Game On N. Lund color *Audubon* v119 no3 p45 Fall 2017

Head For the Treetops color *Audubon* v119 no3 p47 Fall 2017

The Lovebirds G. MUNROE color *Walrus* v14 no7 p62 S 2017

MONITORING NESTING BIRDS *New York State Conservationist* v71 no5 p10 Ap 2017

MOST BIRDS LIVE THREE-DIMENSIONAL LIVES K. Kaufman color *Audubon* v119 no3 p46 Fall 2017

Nine Brilliant Birds to Bring to Your Yard This Spring *Audubon* v119 no1 p44 Spr 2017

Take It Up a Notch M. Bartels color *Audubon* v119 no3 p47 Fall 2017

Bird watching—Equipment & supplies

THE ULTIMATE KIDS' KIT A. Opar color *Audubon* v119 no3 p44 Fall 2017

Birdcages—Evaluation

WOWZA! color *Bicycling* v58 no6 p66 Jl 2017

Birdhouses

The Gratitude Meter Z. Donaldson color *O, The Oprah Magazine* p22 Ap 2017

BirdLife International

Bird's-Eye View H. FURFARO *Audubon* v119 no1 p12 Spr 2017

Birds

See also

Birds of prey

Migratory birds

Penguins

Photography of birds

Poultry

Birdbrain Is a Misnomer: New Studies Show Birds' Remarkable Cognitive Skills J. Kluger color *Time* v190 no7 p24 Ag 21 2017

Built-in Peril M. N. MITRA color *Earth Island Journal* v32 no1 p27 Spr 2017

Chili Out! R. Melvin color *Health* v31 no1 p113 Ja 2017

The Crow and the Cup J. RAO color *Natural History* v125 no4 p44 Ap 2017

EDITING EVOLUTION P. Koberstein diag *Earth Island Journal* v32 no1 p36 Spr 2017

Fresh & Fast Chicken J. BOWDEN and J. BESSINGER color *Better Nutrition* v79 no1 p66 Ja 2017

Grail Bird K. Kaufman *Audubon* v118 no6 p46 Wint 2016

The Greatness of the Grackle N. NICHOLS *D: The Magazine of Dallas* v43 no10 p45 O 2016

Guinness World Records K. JAZYNKA color *National Geographic Kids* no473 p5 S 2017

Master Carver M. BARTELS color *Audubon* v119 no3 p15 Fall 2017

Noah and Penguin *Orion Magazine* v35 no3 p1 My/Je 2016

Sparrows, swallows, and us M. Florer-Bixler *Christian Century* v134 no17 p12 Ag 16 2017

TOUCAN GETS NEW BEAK! R. Davidson *National Geographic Kids* no466 p12 D 2016/Ja 2017

veggie bits: Chicken-less Legs S. Gendler *Vegetarian Journal* v35 no4 p29 2016

Winks on the Wing A. Braun *Natural History* v124 no10 p6 N 2016

Bird's-eye views in art

AMERICAN PLACES *American Scholar* v86 no3 p128 Summ 2017

Birds in art

See also

Falcons in art

THE BIRDMAN OF SALEM E. O'NEILL color *Missouri Life* v44 no2 p26 Ap 2017

A Peaceable Kingdom J. Skelly color *Orion Magazine* v35 no6 p32 N/D 2016

Birds of a Passage (Film)

Ship of Fools N. Rapold bw color *Film Comment* v53 no5 p8 S/O 2017

Birds of prey

Golden Eagle color *Audubon* v119 no3 p46 Fall 2017

Raptors on the Mountain G. NORMAN *Weekly Standard* v22 no5 p16 O 10 2016

Birdsall, John

AVOCADO TOAST color *Bon Appetit* no8 p92 Ag 2017

Birdsall, William C.

A Brush of the Butterfly's Wing color *Commonweal* v143 no19 p39 D 2 2016

Birds—Arctic regions

Dovekies Have a New Diet and Workout Plan B. DRAXLER *Audubon* v119 no2 p16 Summ 2017

Birds—Behavior

Ask the Biologist *New York State Conservationist* v71 no4 p31 F 2017

Birds—Behavior—Research

Coping with Chronic Clamor M. Wexler color *National Wildlife (World Edition)* v55 no2 p40 F/Mr 2017

New insights on birds in flight color *National Wildlife (World Edition)* v55 no3 p8 Ap/My 2017

Birds—Canada

COMMENT A. Abbott, Spence et al color *Canadian Geographic* v137 no1 p72 F 2017

Birds—Charts, diagrams, etc.

The Lucky Ones S. Milius cartoon diag *Science News* v191 no2 p26 F 4 2017

Birdseed

PLANTING A NEW HOBBY, OUTLOOK ON LIFE D. HEITMAN *Phi Kappa Phi Forum* v96 no4 p36 Wint 2016

Birds—Exhibitions

THE IMAGE-MAKER P. STEFÁNSSON *Iceland Review* v55 no4 p68 Jl/Ag 2017

Birds—Feeding & feeds

Bird Feeding: No Feeders Required M. Mayntz color *National Wildlife (World Edition)* v55 no1 p12 D/Ja 2016

FEED the BIRDS *Better Homes & Gardens* v94 no11 p70 N 2016

Please, Feed the Birds color *Canadian Wildlife* v22 no5 p40 N/D 2016

Birds—Genetics

Lost in Translation M. L. Callaghan *Audubon* v119 no1 p15 Spr 2017

Birds—Iceland

ISLAND OF OPPORTUNITY E. S. ARNARSDÓTTIR color *Iceland Review* v54 no5 p52 S-O 2016

Birds—New York (State)

BLUEBIRD COUNTRY J. Taylor *New York State Conservationist* v71 no5 p6 Ap 2017

Birds—North America

Quick Hits map *Scientific American* v315 no6 p22 D 2016

Birdsong, Pete

Build a WIRING HARNESS color diag *Model Railroader* v84 no2 p54 F 2017

Birdsongs

Encoding vocal culture O. Tchernichovski and D. Lipkind bibl color *Science* v354 no6317 p1234 D 9 2016

Songs on the Wing E. A. WCELA *America* v216 no1 p29 Ja 2 2017

Birds—Research

Seeing Double *Earth Island Journal* v32 no1 p12 Spr 2017

Birds—Tropics

1930: Nonsuch Island *Lapham's Quarterly* v10 no2 p128 Spr 2017

5 Tropical Birding Hot Spots *Audubon* v118 no6 p46 Wint 2016

Birenbaum, Jeffrey

Suppressing relaxation in superconducting qubits by quasiparticle pumping bibl graph *Science* v354 no6319 p1573 D 23 2016

Birgeneau, Robert

Not just Salk color *Science* v357 no6356 p1105 S 15 2017

Birgersson, Göran

A key malaria metabolite modulates vector blood seeking, feeding, and susceptibility to infection bibl chart diag *Science* v355 no6329 p1076 Mr 10 2017

Birgmeier, Johannes A.
Deriving genomic diagnoses without revealing patient genomes chart *Science* v357 no6352 p692 Ag 18 2017

Birhanzel, Rich
Navigating Health Care's Transition to Private Exchanges *Harvard Business Review Digital Articles* p2 N 7 2014

Birk, Ben
"HOLY SHIT." color *Snowboarder* v29 no5 p14 Ja 2017

Birk, Harjus S.
CRISPRi-based genome-scale identification of functional long noncoding RNA loci in human cells bibl graph *Science* v355 no6320 p1 Ja 6 2017

BIRKERTS, SVEN
Theory Conspiracy bw color *New Republic* v248 no10 p51 O 2017

Birkinshaw, Julian
The 3 Preconditions for an Entrepreneurial Society *Harvard Business Review Digital Articles* p2 Ag 17 2016
Manage Your Team's Attention *Harvard Business Review Digital Articles* p2 Ja 29 2015
To Grow a Digital Business, Learn from the Startup Community *Harvard Business Review Digital Articles* p2 Je 11 2015

Birkmeyer, John D.
Why Health Care Mergers Can Be Good for Patients *Harvard Business Review Digital Articles* p2 S 30 2015

Birks, H. B. John
The fourth dimension of vegetation bibl color graph *Science* v354 no6311 p412 O 28 2016

Birks, Hilary H.
The fourth dimension of vegetation bibl color graph *Science* v354 no6311 p412 O 28 2016

Birmingham
HOOK-PROOF YOUR SWING color diag *Golf Magazine* v59 no2 p54 F 2017

Birmingham (Ala.)—Politics & government
The Political Revolution's Southern Front K. WEBB-HEHN *In These Times* v41 no10 p6 O 2017

Birnbach, Lisa
Lisa Birnbach color *Vanity Fair* p169 Hollywood 2017 Supplement

BIRNBAUM, CARA
balance is BS *Parents* v91 no9 p126 S 2016
the ultimate guide to a blissful family vacation *Parents* v91 no6 p42 Je 2016

Birney, Bernadette
take the leap! color *Yoga Journal* p62 2017 Special Issue

Birney, Gus
Gus BIRNEY C. KELSEY *Interview* v46 no10 p28 D 2016/Ja 2017

Birney, Perri
Pure Vision: The Magdalene Revelation *Publishers Weekly* v263 no52 p90b D 19 2016

Birney, Reed
No. 1 THE HUMANS M. Snetiker and M. R. Bernardo color *Entertainment Weekly* no1444/1445 p116 D 16 2016

Birns, Jonah
THE ART OF COOL S. GEARHART color *Bicycling* v58 no4 p18 My 2017

Birse, Kenzie
Vaginal bacteria modify HIV tenofovir microbicide efficacy in African women chart graph *Science* v356 no6341 p938 Je 1 2017

Birsel, Ayse
To Come Up with a Good Idea, Start by Imagining the Worst Idea Possible *Harvard Business Review Digital Articles* p2 2017

Birshan, Michael
What Makes a Great Chief Strategy Officer *Harvard Business Review Digital Articles* p2 My 14 2015

Birth certificates
Happy Birthday to Me! L. Myers color *Missouri Life* v44 no6 p64 S 2017

Birth control
See also
Abortion
31 Days of Giving C. de Len chart color *Glamour* v114 no12 p192 D 2016
Access Denied A. Cunningham cartoon color diag graph *Science News* v192 no3 p20 S 2 2017

Can I Keep A Baby My Boyfriend Doesn't Want? K. Anthony Appiah cartoon *New York Times Magazine* p22 Ag 6 2017
keeping score *Ms.* v26 no4 p6 Wint 2016
#THXBIRTHCONTROL C. K. Jackson color *Essence* v47 no7 p104 N 2016
'To Perish in These Sordid, Abnormal Experiences' [Cover story] K. D. WILLIAMSON color *National Review* v69 no11 p24 Je 12 2017
WHAT'S BEHIND THE NEW ATTACK ON BIRTH CONTROL? R. BOSTON *Humanist* v77 no4 p36 Jl/Ag 2017

Birth control—Government policy
See also
Abortion—Government policy

Birth control—History—20th century
America's first birth control clinic R. Cavendish *History Today* v66 no10 p9 O 2016

Birth control—India
Contraception mans up A. KINGSTON color *Maclean's* v130 no4 p8 My 2017

Birth control—Psychological aspects
This Just In J. Zorthian *Time* v188 no16/17 p15 O 24 2016

Birth injuries
WELCOME TO MY WORLD: Living with a disability, I'm the one my peers call when their bodies start to fail. How sympathetic, or surprised, should I be? L. MILK *Washingtonian Magazine* v52 no12 p176 S 2017

Birth order
How One Law Measurably Lifted the Status of Women in India P. Kalsi *Harvard Business Review Digital Articles* p2 Mr 16 2017

Birth rate
Implications of the Baby Bust: Lower birth rates in America will have a wide range of policy consequences M. Maciag *Governing* v30 no10 p56 Jl 2017
This Just In J. Zorthian *Time* v190 no4 p19 Jl 24 2017

Birth weight
WHITE-TAILED DEER FAWN color *Canadian Wildlife* v23 no2 p6 My/Je 2017

Birthday cakes
CAKES FOR any OCCASION [Cover story] B. PORTER KATZ, S. BOCAR et al color *Martha Stewart Living* p70 My 2017

Birthday parties
Birthday Bash! cartoon *National Geographic Kids* no472 p30 Ag 2017
THE BITE THAT CHANGED MY LIFE cartoon *Chicago* v66 no2 p78 F 2017
An Interstellar Party color *Martha Stewart Living* p15 Mr 2017
TRAUMARAMA cartoon color *Seventeen* v76 no12 p108 D 2016/Ja 2017
When Norah Met Mr. Dan T. WOOD color *Reader's Digest* v189 no1129 p94 Ap 2017

Birthdays
Benicio Del Toro C. Ianzito color *AARP: The Magazine* v60 no2A p82 F/Mr 2017
Canada's indigenous peoples are crashing its 150th birthday D. Dettloff color *America* v217 no4 p15 Ag 21 2017
Cindy Crawford C. Ianzito color *AARP: The Magazine* v59 no2A p84 F/Mr 2016
COMIC STRIP E. STEED cartoon *New Yorker* v93 no14 p65 My 22 2017
When Norah Met Mr. Dan T. WOOD color *Reader's Digest* v189 no1129 p94 Ap 2017

Birthing centers
SPECIAL DELIVERY K. DINAN *Cincinnati Magazine* v50 no4 p74 Ja 2017

Birthmarks
See also
Mongolian spot
My Mongolian Spot: AN EPHEMERAL BIRTHMARK IS A RARE GIFT, CONNECTING ME TO GENERATIONS SPANNING THE CENTURIES J. H. CHOI *American Scholar* v86 no3 p62 Summ 2017

Birthmothers
'Who's My Tummy Mommy?' S. SILVERMAN color *Reader's Digest* v190 no1135 p102 N 2017

Birth of a Nation, The (Film : 2016)
An American Spartacus R. Alleva bw *Commonweal* v143 no18

p28 N 11 2016

The Birth of a Nation L. Greenblatt color *Entertainment Weekly* no1435 p44 O 14 2016

The Birth of a Star N. Sperling color *Entertainment Weekly* no1435 p14 O 14 2016

BLACK WOMEN IN HOLLYWOOD R. R. Robertson and K. G. Marable color *Essence* v47 no11 p87 Mr 2017

Bold and Fraught, the Birth of a Nation Merits Your Attention S. Zacharek color *Time* v188 no15 p51 O 17 2016

GHOST STORY V. CUNNINGHAM cartoon *New Yorker* v92 no32 p102 O 10 2016

LET FREEDOM RING M. M. Lewis color *Essence* v47 no7 p50 N 2016

Nat Turner's Confessions D. EDELSTEIN img *New York* v49 no20 p127 O 3 2016

NEWLY AVAILABLE MOVIES M. FELL *TV Guide* v65 no25 p40 Je 2017

Racial Fury Unleashed P. Travers color *Rolling Stone* no1272 p52 O 20 2016

Today's Nat Turner R. DOUTHAT bw *National Review* v68 no20 p46 N 7 2016

The visions of Nat Turner K. Reklis *Christian Century* v133 no24 p43 N 23 2016

Birthplaces

One mother's brave choice T. GLAVIN color *Maclean's* v129 no40 p28 O 10 2016

Points of Origin M. Fabry map *Time* v189 no16/17 p12 My 1-8 2017

Birthplaces—Research

In Search of King Arthur's Roots G. TARLACH color *Discover* v38 no1 p86 Ja/F 2017

Birthright citizenship (U.S.)

Should Birthright Citizenship Be Abolished? S. D. VITTER and M. WASLIN *New York Times Upfront* v149 no3 p22 O 10 2016

Births to unmarried women

The "marriage premium" and the economic impact it can have on children J. C. Roach *Monthly Labor Review* p1 My 2017

Birzer, Bradley J.

Bradley J. Birzer, Russell Kirk: American Conservative J. Litke *Society* v54 no3 p299 Je 2017

Viva Margaret Atwood! il *American Conservative* v15 no6 p38 N/D 2016

Bisbee (Ariz.)

School House Inn N. AUSTIN *Arizona Highways* v93 no4 p14 Ap 2017

Biscayne automobile

Along for the Ride R. Bragg color *Southern Living* v52 no6 p146 Je 2017

Mothers 1959 SEDAN DELIVERY B. Gillogly color *Hot Rod* v70 no11 p56 N 2017

Biscotti

Boo-scotti color *Good Housekeeping* v265 no4 p131 O 2017

SWEETER BY THE DOZEN S. DIGREGORIO *Martha Stewart Living* no270 p136 D 2016

Biscuits

Buttermilk Biscuit G. LOFTS color *Martha Stewart Living* p79 Ap 2017

CHERRY COBBLER WITH WHITE CHOCOLATE-ALMOND BISCUITS *Successful Farming* v115 no5 p63 Mid-Mr 2017

CROWD CONTROL M. GLISAN color *Better Homes & Gardens* v95 no11 p72 N 2017

Does it taste good? D. GOLDMAN chart color *Popular Mechanics* p23 My 2017

Finger-Lickin' Biscuit Loaf color *Good Housekeeping* v264 no2 p107 F 2017

HIP TO BE SQUARE M. HENNESSY color *Chicago* v66 no1 p56 Ja 2017

It's All in the Hands: So much of the pleasure of baking is tied to touch D. Greenspan *New York Times Magazine* p28 Ap 30 2017

Rabbit Biscuits & Gravy *Indianapolis Monthly* v40 no5 p40 Ja 2017

RECIPES A. Larson *Idaho Magazine* v16 no8 p56 My 2017

RISING STARS: The humble biscuit goes big-time S. KROWI-AK color *Indianapolis Monthly* v41 no2 p41 S 2017

SINGULAR Sensation M. Kiesel cartoon color *O, The Oprah Magazine* p169 My 2017

Three-Bite Turkey "Dinner" color *Good Housekeeping* v263 no5 p173 N 2016

YOUR PANTRY chart color *Good Housekeeping* v263 no5 p191 N 2016

Bisexual activists

THE MOTHER OF PRIDE: THE FIRST PRIDE WAS ORGANIZED BY A BISEXUAL WOMAN E. CRUZ and D. GUERRERO bw *Advocate* no1091 p120 Je/Jl 2017

Bisexual actors

GINGER SNAPS: The Walking Dead's bi star on being the change he wants to see in Hollywood D. ARTAVIA *Advocate* no1093 p28 O/N 2017

Bisexual actresses—United States

QUESTIONS FOR MEGAN MULLALLY D. ANDERSON-MINSHALL color *Advocate* no1090 p58 Ap 2017

Bisexual men

5 THINGS I LEARNED FROM DATING A BI GUY: Lasting lessons learned from a relationship with a bisexual man. BY-ALEXENDERCHEVES *Advocate* no1093 p57 O/N 2017

Bisexuality

SEXUAL RELATIVITY AND GENDER REVOLUTION N. CATALANO *Humanist* v77 no4 p42 Jl/Ag 2017

Bisexuals

MAINTAINING BISEXUAL SEXUAL HEALTH AND WELLNESS D. GUERRERO and J. ANDERSON-MINSHALL bw *Advocate* no1090 p46 Ap 2017

NUMBER CRUNCH: BISEXUALITY chart *Advocate* no1088 p32 D 2016/Ja 2017

Bishop, André, 1948-

André BISHOP J. O'BRIEN color *Vanity Fair* v58 no12 p130 D 2016

Bishop, Anna

2017 Egyptian Event D. Hearst *Arabian Horse World* v57 no11 p26 Ag 2017

Bishop, Brent—Interviews

Summit Talk T. Keith color *Sports Illustrated* v126 no4 p23 Ja 30 2017

Bishop, Deborah

Birdman color *American Craft* v77 no2 p22 Ap/My 2017

Culture Shocks bw color *American Craft* v76 no6 p74 D 2016-Ja 2017

Julian Watts color *American Craft* v76 no6 p12 D 2016-Ja 2017

Kicks Meister color *American Craft* v77 no2 p26 Ap/My 2017

Plot Lines color diag *American Craft* v77 no3 p34 Je/Jl 2017

BISHOP, DONALD M.

DON'T KNOW MUCH ABOUT HISTORY *Vital Speeches of the Day* v83 no7 p208 Jl 2017

Bishop, Elizabeth, 1911-1979

'This Suffering Business' B. D. McClay bw *Commonweal* v144 no8 p23 My 5 2017

Bishop, Greg

... And Now What? color *Sports Illustrated* v125 no20 p64 D 19 2016

BIGGER, STRONGER, FASTER, BROKENER color diag *Sports Illustrated* v127 no6 p38 Ag 28 2017

The Case for ... Boxing's Big Summer color *Sports Illustrated* v126 no17 p30 Je 19 2017

DIVIDE AND CONQUER color *Sports Illustrated* v126 no2 p40 Ja 16 2017

DON'T HOLD BACK color *Sports Illustrated* v126 no10 p60 Ap 10 2017

Finding Myself color *Sports Illustrated* v126 no16 p80 Je 5 2017

FOOTBALL IN AMERICA [Cover story] color *Sports Illustrated* v125 no17 p40 N 21 2016 Double Issue

GET-RIGHT DAY color *Sports Illustrated* v125 no19 p68 D 12 2016

MISS UNDERSTOOD color *Sports Illustrated* v127 no7 p128 S 4 2017

PACK IT UP, PACK IT IN color *Sports Illustrated* v126 no3 p33 Ja 23 2017

SHADOWBOXING color *Sports Illustrated* v127 no6 p52 Ag 28 2017

SUSPENDED DISBELIEF [Cover story] color *Sports Illustrated* v126 no5 p26 F 13 2017

THIS IS 40 color *Sports Illustrated* v127 no3 p76 Jl 24 2017

Vince YOUNG color *Sports Illustrated* v127 no1 p40 Jl 3 2017

WAIT FOR IT ... color *Sports Illustrated* v126 no13 p36 My 8 2017

THE X-MAN FACTOR color *Sports Illustrated* v127 no7 p46 S 4 2017

Bishop, Jesse

GARAGE chart color diag *Motor Trend* v69 no11 p106 N 2017

GARAGE chart color diag *Motor Trend* v69 no8 p96 Ag 2017

Bishop, Joseph

Sticky schools color graph *Phi Delta Kappan* v98 no8 p19 My 2017

Bishop, Lori

Committing to socially responsible seafood color *Science* v356 no6341 p912 Je 1 2017

BISHOP, MICHAEL F.

Inside the Circus color *National Review* v68 no19 p49 O 24 2016

BISHOP, PAMELA

Synthesis Centers as Critical Research Infrastructure *BioScience* v67 no8 p750 Ag 2017

Bishop, Richard C.

Contingent valuation: Flawed logic? color *Science* v357 no6349 p363 Jl 28 2017

Putting a value on injuries to natural assets: The BP oil spill chart *Science* v356 no6335 p253 Ap 21 2017

Bishop, Stephanie

Way Down Under S. COLL *New York Times Book Review* p20 O 2 2016

Bishops

Armagh Archbishop Martin contemplates changing times in Ireland R. Tarrant color *America* v216 no4 p15 F 20 2017

George Carey quits role as Anglicans confront sexual abuse scandal C. Pepinster *Christian Century* v134 no16 p15 Ag 2 2017

IN SOUTHERN MEXICO, TRACKING THE LEGACY OF BISHOP SAMUEL RUIZ Hootsen color *America* v217 no4 p18 Ag 21 2017

Sketchbook: Graphic Review H. Bliss *New York Times Book Review* p31 S 24 2017

Bishops—England—History

The Perils of PIETY K. Harvey *History Today* v67 no1 p11 Ja 2017

Bishops—United States

AUXILIARY ANNOUNCEMENT T. QUIGLEY *Commonweal* v144 no12 p2 Jl 7 2017

Bishops—United States—Societies, etc.

Signs of the Times [Cover story] B. J. Cupich color *Commonweal* v144 no10 p12 Je 2 2017

BISKIND, PETER

A Case of Do or Die: Examining the cultural and political context of 'Casablanca' and 'High Noon' *New York Times Book Review* p9 Mr 5 2017

BISLEY, ALEXANDER

ANTHONY BOURDAIN ON SMUG LIBERALS AND EATING DOGS color *Reason* v48 no10 p67 Mr 2017

Bismuth

At low temps, bismuth superconducts E. CONOVER color *Science News* v190 no13 p14 D 24 2016

The fragility of distant Cooper pairs K. Behnia bibl diag *Science* v355 no6320 p26 Ja 6 2017

Bisnette, Nancy

AGING GRACEFULLY on the Homestead *Mother Earth News* no280 p34 F/Mr 2017

Bison

American Bison K. Vaughn *Arizona Highways* v93 no4 p13 Ap 2017

Bison welcomed home on Wind River Reservation color map *National Wildlife (World Edition)* v55 no2 p44 F/Mr 2017

Closing the Loop G. R. Schiavino color *Team Roping Journal* p94 S 2017

Extraordinary Encounter *South Dakota Magazine* v33 no3 p55 S/O 2017

Bispecific antibodies

A "Trojan horse" bispecific-antibody strategy for broad protection against ebolaviruses A. Z. Wec, E. K. Nyakatura et al bibl graph *Science* v354 no6310 p350 O 21 2016

Hitting Ebola, to the power of two A. F. Labrijn and P. W. H. I. Parren bibl diag *Science* v354 no6310 p284 O 21 2016

Biss, Levon

A Bug's Life color *Entertainment Weekly* no1485 p62 O 6 2017

Bissell, Tom

WHO'S LAUGHING NOW? The tragicomedy of Donald Trump on Saturday Night Live *Harper's Magazine* p61 O 2017

Bissell-Siders, Aidan

Blasphemy Laws Attack Free Expression—Can Freethought Hit Back? *Humanist* v76 no6 p9 N/D 2016

Bissett, Marshall

To See; To Hear *Stage Directions* v30 no10 p14 O 2017

BISSEY, JUDY

GIFTS that UPLIFT! cartoon *O, The Oprah Magazine* p148 D 2016

Bissiere, S.

A microtubule-organizing center directing intracellular transport in the early mouse embryo diag *Science* v357 no6354 p925 S 1 2017

Bisson-Filho, Alexandre W.

Treadmilling by FtsZ filaments drives peptidoglycan synthesis and bacterial cell division bibl graph *Science* v355 no6326 p739 F 17 2017

BISSONNETTE, GILLES

Should 'Ballot Box Selfies' Be Banned? *New York Times Upfront* v149 no4 p22 O 31 2016

Bistline, Maria

HUNGRY SOULS *Harper's Magazine* v333 no1999 p18 D 2016

Bistrova, Julia

Many CEOs Aren't Breakthrough Innovators (and That's OK) *Harvard Business Review Digital Articles* p2 S 4 2015

Biswas, Surojit

Phytochromes function as thermosensors in Arabidopsis bibl graph *Science* v354 no6314 p886 N 18 2016

Biswell, Dennis

Craft Your Own COONSKIN CAP: Turn a raccoon hide into a warm and hardy hat *Mother Earth News* no284 p24 O/N 2017

How to Make Your Own MOCCASINS *Mother Earth News* no280 p26 F/Mr 2017

Bit-mapped graphics

At a Glance *Sea Magazine* v108 no8 p42 Ag 2016

Bitariho, Robert

Positive biodiversity-productivity relationship predominant in global forests bibl chart graph map *Science* v354 no6309 paaf8957-1 O 14 2016

Bitcoin

THE 21ST-CENTURY BANK ROBBERY J. Wieczner color *Fortune* v176 no3 p52 S 1 2017

BITCOIN MINING R. Chun color *Atlantic* v320 no2 p26 S 2017

BITCOIN'S BLUE CHIP L. SHIN color graph *Forbes* v198 no8 p88 D 20 2016

BREAKING THE BITCOIN BANK J. J. Roberts color *Fortune* v176 no5 p26 O 1 2017

CASHLESS I. Parker bw *New Yorker* v93 no28 p18 S 18 2017

COUNTING COINS J. J. Roberts *Fortune* v175 no5 p15 Ap 1 2017

The Impact of the Blockchain Goes Beyond Financial Services D. Tapscott and A. Tapscott *Harvard Business Review Digital Articles* p2 My 10 2016

Meltdown Comics' Bitcoin Experience J. Boog chart color *Publishers Weekly* v264 no32 p5 Ag 7 2017

THE SECRET, DANGEROUS WORLD OF VENEZUELAN BITCOIN MINING J. EPSTEIN *Reason* v48 no8 p27 Ja 2017

SPAWN OF BITCOIN: BLOCKCHAIN-FUELED STARTUPS C. METZ color graph *Wired* v25 no7 p18 Jl 2017

Bitcoin—Economic aspects

BITCOIN IS BACK R. Hackett diag *Fortune* v175 no2 p11 F 1 2017

Bitcoin—Government policy

Movers K. Stock color graph *Bloomberg Businessweek* no4521 p11 My 8 2017

Biteau, J.

Observation of a large-scale anisotropy in the arrival directions of cosmic rays above 8×10^{18} eV *Science* v357 no6357 p1266 S 22 2017

Bitenc, Josefa

EVENTS color *Magazine Antiques* v184 no3 p130 My/Je 2017

Bites & stings

How to Treat Canine Snakebites S. Cox *Mother Earth News*

no282 p89 Je/Jl 2017

Second opinion *Mayo Clinic Health Letter* v34 no12 p8 D 2016

Bits (Bridles)

Bits for Head Horses: Tips from Professional Headers color *Team Roping Journal* p72 O 2017

Bits for Heel Horses: Tips from Professional Heelers color *Team Roping Journal* p76 S 2017

Bits That Go Ouch! [Cover story] R. Gollehon and A. Harrison color *Horse & Rider* v56 no1 p44 Ja 2017

Cowboy Up: How a Curb Bit Works L. FELDMAN color *American Cowboy* v23 no5 p64 F/Mr 2017

Get Snaffle-Bit Smart A. DUNNING and J. PAULSON color *Horse & Rider* v56 no8 p48 Ag 2017

Simplify the Turn S. PARKINSON and J. PAULSON color *Horse & Rider* v56 no8 p42 Ag 2017

Uncover the Mystery of "On the Bit" D. Hannon and A. Morris color diag *Dressage Today* v23 no11 p24 Ag 2017

BitSight Technologies Inc.—Officials & employees

The Septuagenarian Whiz Kid A. FELDMAN color *Forbes* v198 no9 p44 D 30 2016

Bittencourt, Ela

L'Important c'est d'aimer color *Film Comment* v53 no4 p71 Jl/Ag 2017

BITTERMAN, PATRICK

Incorporating Sociocultural Phenomena into Ecosystem-Service Valuation: The Importance of Critical Pluralism *BioScience* v67 no3 p233 Mr 2017

BITTERMANN, JEREMY

High Note color diag *Architectural Record* v204 no12 p96 D 2016

Bitterroot Range (Idaho & Mont.)

From Darkness to Light M. BRINKMAN *Idaho Magazine* v16 no2 p24 N 2016

Spring Campaign T. WAITE *Idaho Magazine* v16 no2 p28 N 2016

Bitter Stems, The (Film)

No Peace of Mind R. Brody color *New Yorker* v93 no28 p12 S 18 2017

Bittersweet (Plant)

Bittersweet in the Preserve W. K. Stoos *South Dakota Magazine* v33 no3 p93 S/O 2017

Bitter Tears of Petra von Kant, The (Theatrical production)

Cinema Scope H. Als cartoon *New Yorker* v93 no2 p16 F 27 2017

Bittle, Jake

Meridian Center for Health *Architectural Record* v205 no4 p188 Ap 2017

Bittman, Mark

Char a Different Course color *GQ: Gentlemen's Quarterly* v97 no7 p64 Jl 2017

EVERY DAY I'M BRUSSELIN' color *Runner's World* v52 no1 p54 Ja/F 2017

Bittner, Katie C.

Behavioral time scale synaptic plasticity underlies CA1 place fields diag *Science* v357 no6355 p1033 S 8 2017

Bittner, Stefani

Harvest: Unexpected Projects Using 47 Extraordinary Garden Plants *Publishers Weekly* v263 no45 p56 N 7 2016

Bitto, Emily

Neglectful Bohemians S. GILBERT *New York Times Book Review* p18 Ja 8 2017

The Strays *Publishers Weekly* v263 no40 p96 O 3 2016

Bitumen

Acceptable R. Gibson *Alternatives Journal (AJ) - Canada's Environmental Voice* v42 no3 p80 2016

Bitumen—Export & import trade

SOMETHING NEW FOR SUTTON HOO J. URBANUS bw color *Archaeology* v70 no2 p14 Mr/Ap 2017

Bivalve culture

SINGING PINK SCALLOPS color *Sea Magazine* v109 no6 pPNW-5 Je 2017

Biver, N.

Seasonal exposure of carbon dioxide ice on the nucleus of comet 67P/Churyumov-Gerasimenko bibl bw graph *Science* v354 no6319 p1563 D 23 2016

Bix, Cynthia Overbeck

Q: What is the most significant fad of all time? color *Atlantic* v319 no3 p96 Ap 2017

Bjarke Ingels Group ApS

Let's Do the Twist S. STEPHENS *Architectural Record* v205 no10 p84 O 2017

Bjerga, Alan

BOOM That You Hear Is Ukraine's Agriculture color *Bloomberg Businessweek* no4495 p12 O 17 2016

Designed in Davos, Tested in Zimbabwe color *Bloomberg Businessweek* no4507 p37 Ja 16 2017

How to Help Africa Feed Itself *Bloomberg Businessweek* no4520 p20 My 1 2017

Should Farmers Fear Him? color graph *Bloomberg Businessweek* no4512 p13 F 20 2017

Trump's Real Jobs Crisis chart *Bloomberg Businessweek* no4528 p32 Je 26 2017

Why Florida Farmers Want to Kill Nafta color graph *Bloomberg Businessweek* no4535 p35 Ag 28 2017

Bjerk, Paul

Julius Nyerere N. van de Walle *Foreign Affairs* v96 no6 p172 N/D 2017

Björk, 1965-

The Playlist color *Rolling Stone* no1298 p10 O 19 2017

Björk, 1965—Exhibitions

BIG TIME VIRTUAL REALITY E. Hancox *Iceland Review* v55 no1 p6 Ja/F 2017

Bjork, B. J.

Direct frequency comb measurement of OD + CO→DOCO kinetics bibl graph *Science* v354 no6311 p444 O 28 2016

Björk, Lars

A subcellular map of the human proteome color *Science* v356 no6340 p820 My 26 2017

Bjorken, James D.

Sidney David Drell *Physics Today* v70 no9 p69 S 2017

Bjorkman, Pamela

Not just Salk color *Science* v357 no6356 p1105 S 15 2017

BJÖRNSDÓTTIR, INGIBJÖRG RÓSA

CLOTHING A GENERATION *Iceland Review* v54 no6 p12 N/D 2016

ON A QUEST *Iceland Review* v54 no6 p76 N/D 2016

Bjornsson, Hafthor Julius

BIG BOY J. DEAN *Men's Health* v32 no4 p111 My 2017

Bjørnevik, Kjetil

β2-Adrenoreceptor is a regulator of the a-synuclein gene driving risk of Parkinson's disease cartoon chart graph *Science* v357 no6354 p891 S 1 2017

Black, Ashley Nicole

FULL FRONTAL WITH SAMANTHA BEE J. RUSSELL *TV Guide* v64 no40 p63 O 3 2016

Black, Benjamin A.

Global drainage patterns and the origins of topographic relief on Earth, Mars, and Titan diag graph *Science* v356 no6339 p727 My 19 2017

Black, Bernard

Protecting unauthorized immigrant mothers improves their children's mental health diag *Science* v357 no6355 p1041 S 8 2017

Black, Dustin Lance, 1974-

EYES ON THE RISE M. Snetiker color *Entertainment Weekly* no1454/1455 p87 F 24 2017

When We Rise M. ROUSH *TV Guide* v65 no8 p16 F 27 2017

Black, Dustin Lance, 1974—Interviews

RISING TIDES LIFT ALL BOATS D. ANDERSON-MINSHALL color *Advocate* no1090 p22 Ap 2017

BLACK, GEOFFREY

COUTURE SHOCK bw *Ebony* v72 no6 p98 Ap/My 2017

GLORY ON THE GREEN color *Ebony* v72 no4 p106 F 2017

THE HIGH PRIESTESS OF SOUL bw *Ebony* v72 no5 p98 Mr 2017

POWER TRIO bw *Ebony* v72 no3 p138 D 2016/Ja 2017

VIRTUOSO VOCALIST color *Ebony* v72 no8 p98 Je 2017

Black, George Nixon

The House That Changed Everything J. GOODRICH and B. MORGAN bw color *Yankee* p30 Mr 2017

BLACK, JANE

HOME AGAIN color *Better Homes & Gardens* v95 no11 p106 N 2017

Joy's BIG EASY LUNCH color *Better Homes & Gardens* v95 no9 p126 S 2017

Black, Jeff

Possibly color *Bloomberg Businessweek* no4507 p14 Ja 16 2017

Black, Jeremy

A Brief History of Entrepreneurship *History Today* v67 no2 p59 F 2017

Thundersticks: Firearms and the Violent Transformation of Native America *History Today* v67 no1 p58 Ja 2017

Black, Jonathan

To The Editor color *American Craft* v76 no6 p10 D 2016-Ja 2017

Black, Julia

2017 MaVeRicks OF Style bw color *Esquire* p81 S 2017

AMERICAN BEAUTIES bw *Esquire* p30 Ap 2017

BITTERSWEET ESCAPE color *Esquire* p21 Ag 2017

CHIN UP! bw *Esquire* p65 Ap 2017

DAMIAN MARLEY color *Esquire* p37 My 2017

HACKING CHIVALRY color *Esquire* p26 Ag 2017

INTO THE COUNTRY color *Esquire* v166 no5 p122 D 2016/Ja 2017

James PATTERSON color *Esquire* p76 S 2017

KELLER INSTINCT color *Esquire* v167 no2 p54 Mr 2017

THE MAVERICKS OF HOLLYWOOD 2017 bw color *Esquire* v167 no2 p89 Mr 2017

Mike WiLL Made-It color *Esquire* p46 Ag 2017

MIX MASTER color *Esquire* v167 no1 p88 F 2017

OUT OF HER SHELL color *Esquire* p36 Ap 2017

SLAY, GIRL, SLAY color *Esquire* p29 Je/Jl 2017

SMELLS LIKE TRUMP SPIRIT color *Esquire* p45 Ap 2017

Black, Lee

Greener Pastures *Arabian Horse World* v57 no2 p137 N 2016

Black, Libby

LIBBY BLACK M. Sussman *Art in America* v104 no9 p161 O 2016

Black, Mhairi, 1994-

A Fiery Scotswoman: The youngest MP in 350 years, Mhairi Black is making a name for herself as a leader on the left B. HEING *Ms.* v27 no2 p16 Summ 2017

BLACK, MICHAEL IAN

My Bad Genes *Reader's Digest* v189 no1127 p106 F 2017

BLACK, ROBIN

Below Base Camp *New York Times Book Review* p22 My 7 2017

Black, Sara

CAN GEO CHALLENGE FINALISTS EXPLORE THE EAST COAST color *Canadian Geographic* v137 no5 p77 S/O 2017

Black, Saul

Love Murder *Publishers Weekly* v264 no19 p37 My 8 2017

Black, Shane, 1961-

THE NICE GUYS C. Gunnestad color *Sound & Vision* v82 no1 p71 Ja 2017

Black, Sophie Cabot

CHORUS AND ANTI-CHORUS *New Yorker* v93 no12 p50 My 8 2017

BLACK, STEVEN

Out of Place *Natural History* v125 no2 p48 F 2017

Black, Thomas

CHINA'S ROBOT REVOLUTION color graph *Bloomberg Businessweek* no4520 p32 My 1 2017

Houston and the Politics of Immigration color *Bloomberg Businessweek* no4537 p31 S 11 2017

NASA says it's got the secret to quiet supersonic planes. Now comes the hard part color *Bloomberg Businessweek* no4532 p19 Jl 31 2017

Private Jets Aren't So Private Anymore *Bloomberg Businessweek* no4498 p33 N 7 2016

Trump's Uncertainty Principle color *Bloomberg Businessweek* no4509 p6 Ja 30 2017

Black actresses

See also

African American actresses

10 THINGS WE'RE ALREADY OBSESSING OVER IN 2017 C. Hope color *Essence* v47 no9 p41 Ja 2017

Black America Again (Music)

THE COMMON CAUSE M. Vain color *Entertainment Weekly* no1439 p56 N 11 2016

Common E. R. Brown color *Entertainment Weekly* no1439 p57 N 11 2016

Marrying Genres C. TART color *Downbeat* v84 no3 p62 Mr 2017

Black art—Exhibitions

Lynne Cooke R. Simonini color *Art in America* v105 no1 p25 Ja 2017

Black bean

15-Minute All-Organic Meal Under $15 [Cover story] color *Prevention* v69 no6 p12 Je 2017

Horror D'Oeuvres color *Martha Stewart Living* p36 O 2017

MELT WITH ME [Cover story] M. Kadey cartoon color *Runner's World* v51 no11 p48 D 2016

Black bear

The Confrontation C. Ritchie color *New York Times Magazine* p38 N 27 2016

PEDALS THE BEAR J. MOOALLEM *New York Times Magazine* p22 D 25 2016

WILD THINGS: FIVE ANIMALS YOU COULD SPOT IN SHENANDOAH NATIONAL PARK *Washingtonian Magazine* v53 no1 p106 O 2017

Black bear hunting

THE BEAR AT LAST LIGHT C. KEARNS color *Field & Stream* v122 no4 p48 S 2017

THE SHORE BOAR D. DRAPER bw color *Field & Stream* v122 no1 p15 My 2017

URSUS MAJOR C. NEWCOMB and A. McKEAN color *Outdoor Life* v224 no5 p89 Je/Jl 2017

Black-capped chickadee

in a snap color *Canadian Geographic* v137 no5 p14 S/O 2017

Please Feed the Birds color *Canadian Wildlife* v22 no5 p40 N/D 2016

Black-capped chickadee—Behavior

Black-capped chickadee A. Kylie color *Canadian Geographic* v135 no6 p71 D 2015

Black children—Crimes against

PROTECT AND DEFEND S. Gibney *Lapham's Quarterly* v10 no3 p44 Summ 2017

Black Diamond Equipment Ltd.

Packs N. BOUCHARD bw color diag graph il *Backpacker* v45 no3 p29 Ap 2017

Black directors

THE BUSINESS OF BLACK COMIC BOOKS S. LYNN bw cartoon color *Black Enterprise* v47 no8 p56 Jl/Ag 2017

POWER IN THE BOARDROOM bw color *Black Enterprise* v47 no8 p67 Jl/Ag 2017

Black Dog Salvage (Company)

Shopping *Virginia Living* p127 2017 Best 20of Virginia

Black duck

Operation Black Duck M. D. Johnson color *Field & Stream* v122 no5 p80 O 2017

Black Elk Energy LLC

Black Elk Down L. STEFFY *Texas Monthly* v45 no4 p82 Ap 2017

Black feminists

Transformation of Consciousness: The National Women's Studies Association and the Combahee River Collective's "Black Feminist Statement" turn 40 J. HOBSON and K. JOLNA *Ms.* v27 no3 p48 Fall 2017

Black Forest Decor LLC

DECOR & FURNISHINGS color *Timber Home Living* p60 2017 SpecialIssue

Black Friday (Retail trade)

STORES' BLEAK BLACK FRIDAY P. Wahba *Fortune* v174 no6 p11 N 1 2016

Why Spending Dipped on Black Friday K. Close color *Time* v188 no24 p18 D 12 2016

Black gay men

BECOMING MY OWN WARRIOR: HE WASN'T EVEN OUT TO HIS PARENTS YET, BUT JOSHUA THOMAS HAD TO TELL THEM HE WAS HIV-POSITIVE. HE SURVIVED AND TELLS OTHERS HOW YOU CAN, TOO D. GUERRERO *Advocate* no1093 p33 O/N 2017

Stuck in the Middle with You: A black gay activist ponders midLife C. STEPHENS *Advocate* no1093 p51 O/N 2017

Black gay men—Health

REAL HIV PREVENTION REQUIRES MORE THAN UNDERWEAR ADS: IF WE WANT BLACK GAY MEN TO USE PREP, WE HAVE TO CHANGE THE WAY WE'RE BRANDING IT C. STEPHENS *Advocate* no1093 p33 O/N 2017

Black high school students

THE A.P. CALCULUS A. TUGEND *New York Times Magazine*

p66 S 10 2017

Black Hills (S.D. & Wyo.)

The Legendary Black Hills A. Radke color *American Cowboy* v23 no4 p28 D 2016/Ja 2017

Black Hills (S.D. & Wyo.)—Description & travel

LITTLE DEVILS TOWER TRAIL *South Dakota Magazine* v32 no6 p93 Mr/Ap 2017

Plan It: Black Hills Adventure *American Cowboy* v23 no4 p39 D 2016/Ja 2017

Black Hills Energy (Company)

POWER HUNGRY N. SAVKA *Sierra* v102 no5 p44 St/O 2017

Black Hills Wild Horse Sanctuary (S.D.)

Spirit of the Black Hills A. PAVIA color *Trail Rider* v29 no1 p44 Ja/F 2017

Black holes (Astronomy)

See also

Stellar black holes

Anatomy of a Black Hole C. M. Carlisle *Sky & Telescope* v133 no2 p16 F 2017

Black Holes and Revelations S. NADIS color *Discover* v38 no9 p70 N 2017

BLACK HOLES from the Beginning of Time J. García-Bellido and S. Clesse color graph *Scientific American* v317 no1 p38 Jl 2017

CAN TONS OF XENON FINALLY FIND DARK MATTER? J. Wenz color *Astronomy* v45 no7 p12 Jl 2017

Chandra snaps a deep-field X-ray image color *Astronomy* v45 no5 p19 My 2017

Cosmic lens sees black hole's burps L. GROSSMAN color graph *Science News* v192 no4 p16 S 16 2017

Debate heats up over black holes as dark matter A. Cho color *Science* v355 no6325 p560 F 10 2017

FROM OUR READERS C. Simpson, T. Wright et al *Sky & Telescope* v133 no6 p6 Je 2017

Gravitational waves offer new view of dynamic cosmos E. Conover color *Science News* v190 no13 p16 D 24 2016

HOW DOES A BLACK HOLE FORM? color diag *Astronomy* v45 no7 p15 Jl 2017

How to Swallow a Sun S. B. Cenko and N. Gehrels color *Scientific American* v316 no4 p38 Ap 2017

LIGO Detects Third Black Hole Merger C. M. CARLISLE *Sky & Telescope* v134 no3 p10 S 2017

Milky Way's black hole may hurl galactic spitballs our way C. Crockett color *Science News* v191 no2 p11 F 4 2017

More gravitational waves detected E. CONOVER color *Science News* v191 no12 p6 Je 24 2017

No. 1 FOUND: Einstein's Ripples in Space-Time E. BETZ bw color diag graph *Discover* v38 no1 p7 Ja/F 2017

Of Black Holes and Galaxies C. M. Carlisle *Sky & Telescope* v133 no2 p18 F 2017

POPULAR MECHANICS color *Popular Mechanics* p14 Jl 2017

Portrait of a giant D. J. Eicher color *Astronomy* v45 no11 p8 N 2017

Potential "Failed Supernova" Discovered M. YOUNG *Sky & Telescope* v134 no3 p10 S 2017

Second black hole spotted in famous galaxy color *Astronomy* v45 no9 p13 S 2017

Skipping through the Virgo Cluster S. J. O'Meara color *Astronomy* v45 no4 p58 Ap 2017

Space ripples may untangle black hole tango A. Cho color *Science* v356 no6341 p895 Je 1 2017

Superfluid behaves like black holes E. CONOVER *Science News* v191 no7 p11 Ap 15 2017

Superluminous event caused by spinning black hole swallowing star color *Astronomy* v45 no4 p16 Ap 2017

Supersonic gas streams enhance the formation of massive black holes in the early universe S. Hirano, T. Hosokawa et al diag graph *Science* v357 no6358 p1375 S 29 2017

Trio tracks source of gravity waves E. CONOVER color *Science News* v192 no7 p8 O 28 2017

What Would Happen? C. BOYER *National Geographic Kids* no467 p8 F 2017

Year's biggest stories D. J. EICHER *Astronomy* v45 no1 p6 Ja 2017

Black Is...Black Ain't (Film)

Black Is... Black Ain't G. SHAMBU color *Film Comment* v53 no1

p62 Ja/F 2017

Black-ish (TV program)

black-ish I. Ratledge color *TV Guide* v65 no7 p36 F 13 2017

black-ish I. Ratledge *TV Guide* v65 no19 p28 My 1 2017

black-ish N. Abrams, A. Bacle et al *Entertainment Weekly* no1482/1483 p63 S 22 2017

The Must List color *Entertainment Weekly* no1485 p8 O 6 2017

Black Lightning (TV program)

BLACK LIGHTNING N. Abrams color *Entertainment Weekly* no1474/1475 p73 Jl 21-28 2017

Black Lives Matter movement

Black Lives Matter Because All Lives Matter [Cover story] J. E. JONES *Islamic Horizons* v46 no1 p20 Ja/F 2017

Black Lives Matter in Canada, Too D. DETTLOFF *America* v215 no14 p11 N 7 2016

Catholic Universities And #BlackLivesMatter R. K. VISCHER color *America* v215 no12 p22 O 24 2016

THE FUTURE OF BLM [Cover story] D. McCLAIN color *Nation* v305 no8 p12 O 9 2017

JIMMY CARTER: PURSUING AN ARC OF RECONCILIATION R. CLARK bw *Christianity Today* v60 no8 p66 O 2016

NATIONAL TREASURE [Cover story] P. Lutz color *Downbeat* v83 no11 p30 N 2016

On the Matter of Black Lives Matter L. NICHOLS *Commentary* v143 no2 p8 F 2017

Protests Get Results color *Weekly Standard* v22 no36 p2 My 29 2017

STILL CLIMBING J. WILLIAMS *Cincinnati Magazine* v50 no2 p22 N 2016

The Truth About Black Lives Matter: The movement paints a false and disturbing portrait of America in order to justify its even more disturbing aims J. Muravchik *Commentary* v142 no5 p20 D 2016

WHY BLACK LIVES MATTER STILL MATTERS [Cover story] P. E. JOSEPH bw *New Republic* v248 no5 p16 My 2017

WHY THE GUN-CONTROL MOVEMENT FAILS G. YOUNGE color *Nation* v303 no19 p12 N 7 2016

Black Love (TV program)

The Truth About 'Black Love' S. E. Jamison color *Ebony* v72 no9 p66 Jl/Ag 2017

Black men

LAST TABOO W. Morris *New York Times Magazine* p48 O 30 2016

Black Men Run Inc.

HEALTHY BROTHERHOOD M. WORTHINGTON color *Runner's World* v52 no1 p22 Ja/F 2017

Black Mirror (TV program)

Back to Black: Inside the Making of Mirror J. Hibberd color *Entertainment Weekly* no1436/1437 p91 O 21 2016

Black Mirror *TV Guide* v64 no40 p39 O 3 2016

Sci-fi Evolves Into Disturbing Reality In Black Mirror and Westworld E. Dockterman color *Time* v188 no16/17 p90 O 24 2016

A 'Twilight Zone' for the iPhone Era R. SHEFFIELD color *Rolling Stone* no1274 p19 N 17 2016

WORST-CASE SCENARIO G. HARVEY cartoon *New Yorker* v92 no39 p46 N 28 2016

Black Mountains (Wales & England)

Biking the Legends of Wales S. Gutierrez and S. Levine *British Heritage Travel* v38 no1 p10 Ja/F 2017

Black musicians—Awards

EXAMINING THE GRAMMYS' RACE ISSUE E. R. Brown, K. O'Donnell et al color *Entertainment Weekly* no1454/1455 p13 F 24 2017

Black Muslims (Nation of Islam)

Masjid Muhammad: The Nation's Mosque S. SWETZOFF *Islamic Horizons* v46 no1 p26 Ja/F 2017

Black nationalism—United States

The Black Power Renaissance S. MUWAKKIL *In These Times* v41 no8 p12 Ag 2017

Black Panther (Fictitious character)

Comic book truth A. Hearlson color *Christian Century* v134 no2 p43 Ja 18 2017

NO. 9 BLACK PANTHER A. Breznican color *Entertainment Weekly* no1436/1437 p51 O 21 2016

Black Panther (Film)

BLACK PANTHER A. Breznican color *Entertainment Weekly*

p20 Jl 24 2017

ENTERTAINMENT WEEKLY PRESENTS COMIC-CON 2017 color *Entertainment Weekly* no1474/1475 p27 Jl 21-28 2017

THE KINGDOM & THE POWER [Cover story] A. Breznican color *Entertainment Weekly* no1474/1475 p30 Jl 21-28 2017

PANTHER PACK A. Breznican color *Entertainment Weekly* no1474/1475 p34 Jl 21-28 2017

Black Panther Party—History

Bobby Seale L. Rothman color *Time* v188 no15 p64 O 17 2016

Black pepper (Plant)

Shamelessly French F. Lam color *New York Times Magazine* p26 D 4 2016

Black pine bark beetle

TINY INSECT—BIG IMPACT S. Walsh *New York State Conservationist* v71 no3 p14 D 2016

Black politicians

The blackest man on council A. DOMISE color *Maclean's* v129 no44 p20 N 7 2016

Black power

50, 100 & 150 YEARS AGO color *Scientific American* v316 no4 p82 Ap 2017

Black power—United States

The Black Power Renaissance S. MUWAKKIL *In These Times* v41 no8 p12 Ag 2017

Black radicalism

THE UNTOLD BLACK HISTORY OF THE SECOND WAVE M. CAPORALE *In These Times* v41 no7 p39 Jl 2017

Black Sails (TV program)

Black Sails I. Rudolph *TV Guide* v65 no4 p40 Ja 16 2017

Black Sails' New Adversary *TV Guide* v65 no2 p13 Ja 2 2017

Black scientists

See also

African American scientists

Doing science while black E. J. Smith color *Science* v353 no6307 p1586 S 30 2016

Black students

With Just One Black Teacher, Black Students Are More Likely to Graduate *Education Digest* v83 no2 p52 O 2017

Black students—Education

The candidates are out there A. DOMISE *Maclean's* p10 Je 2017

Black students—Social conditions

Monuments Fall, but Racism Stands Tall in New Orleans Schools A. Bigard color *Progressive* v81 no6 p43 Ag/S 2017

Black teachers

The Case for a Teacher Like Me cartoon *Education Digest* v82 no9 p4 My 2017

With Just One Black Teacher, Black Students Are More Likely to Graduate *Education Digest* v83 no2 p52 O 2017

Black women

See also

African American women

BACK TO SCHOOL V. K. De Luca color *Essence* v48 no5 p10 S 2017

CHANGING THE FACE OF THERAPY J. Thompson color *O, The Oprah Magazine* p84 S 2017

Here We Go! O. Winfrey color *O, The Oprah Magazine* p23 S 2017

A MATTER OF LIFE & DEATH M. Winter color *Essence* v48 no6 p106 O 2017

TALK TV'S BREAKOUT STARS color *Essence* v48 no5 p62 S 2017

THEN AND NOW Drama Queens C. Murray and B. Danielle color *Essence* v48 no5 p64 S 2017

WE LOVE HEARING FROM YOU! color diag *Essence* v47 no7 p10 N 2016

WE LOVE HEARING FROM YOU! color diag *Essence* v48 no5 p24 S 2017

Black women authors

THE PATH TO PEACE C. V. CLARKE color *Black Enterprise* v47 no5 p36 Ja/F 2017

Black women executives

EXECUTIVE MEMO color *Black Enterprise* v47 no5 p8 Ja/F 2017

Black women musicians

ESSENCE'S GLAM GRAMMY WARM-UP R. Kinane color *Entertainment Weekly* no1454/1455 p14 F 24 2017

Black women—Mental health

THERAPY SAVED ME G. Roberts-grey color *Essence* v47 no7 p107 N 2016

Black women—Psychology

BATTLING THE BURDEN OF SUCCESS T. E. Holmes color *Essence* v47 no7 p92 N 2016

Black women—Sexual behavior

SISTERS ARE DOING IT FOR THEMSELVES: BLACK QUEER WOMEN TAKE SEXUAL HEALTH INTO THIER OWN HANDS R. NEIRENE color *Advocate* no1091 p112 Je/Jl 2017

Blackall, Sophie

Because the Night *New York Times Book Review* p14 Ap 9 2017

Blackbaud Inc.

RISING STARS S. Agus and J. Vanian color *Fortune* v176 no4 p89 S 15 2017

Blackberries

muffins remixed *Martha Stewart Living* no267 p88 S 2016

r.s.v.p P. JACOBSEN, P. O'CAIN et al color *Bon Appetit* no8 p14 Ag 2017

BLACKBIRD, MIKE

Trial by Fire color *Idaho Magazine* v16 no1 p14 O 2016

Black Box, The (Short story)

THE BLACK BOX M. OLDER cartoon *Wired* v25 no1 p76 Ja 2017

Blackburn, Danny

The Real-Deal DIYer [Cover story] C. Raymond Herbert color *Horse & Rider* v55 no11 p60 N 2016

Blackburn, Doug

BOUNTY HUNTERS J. Miller *Harper's Magazine* v334 no2000 p68 Ja 2017

Blackburn, Howard

Taking it all with you P. Nielsen *Sail* v48 no8 p4 Ag 2017

Triumph of Will [Cover story] P. Nielsen color *Sail* v48 no8 p10 Ag 2017

Blackburn, Jennifer

Ask anything bw color *Women's Health* v14 no4 p18 My 2017

Blackburn, Mark

HIT A DRAW... RIGHT NOW! color diag *Golf Magazine* v58 no12 p80 D 2016

HOOK-PROOF YOUR SWING color diag *Golf Magazine* v59 no2 p54 F 2017

THE LOW DOWN ON LEFT HAND LOW color *Golf Magazine* v59 no11 p72 N 2017

Blackburn, Tom

An Ordinary Sunday [Cover story] color *Commonweal* v144 no15 p11 S 22 2017

Blackcoat's Daughter, The (Film)

KIERNAN SHIPKA A. Salazar color *InStyle* v24 no5 p57 My 2017

Blackfire (Company)

Flash Forward S. MURRAY color *Power & Motoryacht* v34 no8 p36 Ag 2017

Blackford, Carol

CONNECTING WITH NATURE *South Dakota Magazine* v33 no2 p69 Jl/Ag 2017

Blackhawk Modifications Inc.

KING AIR MODS R. MARK color *Flying* v144 no10 p52 O 2017

Blackhurst, Rod

Amanda Knox K. P. Sullivan color *Entertainment Weekly* no1434 p42 O 7 2016

Blackhurst, Rod—Interviews

The Most Infamously Accused Female Villain L. Brody and E. Mahaney color *Glamour* v114 no11 p143 N 2016

Blacklist, The (TV program)

The Blacklist I. Rudolp *TV Guide* p37 Ap 17 2017

The Blacklist N. Abrams, B. L. Heldman et al color *Entertainment Weekly* no1482/1483 p74 S 22 2017

The Blacklist's Big Reveal N. Abrams color *Entertainment Weekly* no1467 p14 My 26 2017

My Obsessions... *TV Guide* v65 no41 p9 O 2 2017

SPY GAME J. Russell color *TV Guide* v65 no7 p28 F 13 2017

Blackman, Andrew

Preparing to Pop a Bubble, Just in Case color *Bloomberg Businessweek* no4535 p29 Ag 28 2017

BLACKMAN, JOSH

Fair-Weather Originalists color *National Review* v69 no3 p20 F 20 2017

Blackmar, Trisha

Flying Start *Sports Illustrated* v126 no1 p52 Ja 9 2017

BLACKMER, EMILY

Invasive Species, Indigenous Stewards, and Vulnerability Discourse chart diag map *American Indian Quarterly* v41 no3 p201 Summ 2017

Blackmer, Stephen

THE PRIEST IN THE TREES F. Bahnson *Harper's Magazine* v333 no1999 p45 D 2016

Black Mesa (Okla., New Mexico & Colo.)

The First American Revolution E. A. POWELL color *Archaeology* v70 no2 p42 Mr/Ap 2017

Blackmon, Julie

Off Center M. Ryan bw color *Popular Photography* v81 no1 p82 Ja/F 2017

Time Out color *Art in America* v104 no10 p64 N 2016

BLACKMORE, ANDREW

International Wildlife Law: Understanding and Enhancing Its Role in Conservation *BioScience* v67 no9 p784 S 2017

Blackmore, Willy

Seed Catalogs *New York Times Magazine* p20 F 5 2017

Black Power Mixtape 1967-1975, The (Film)

THE MOVEMENT IN MOTION: 4 ESSENTIAL CIVIL RIGHTS FILMS J. BENNETT bw color *Ebony* v72/73 no12/1 p84 O/N 2017

BlackRock Inc.

19 LARRY FINK J. Wieczner color *Fortune* v174 no7 p89 D 1 2016

BlackRock Inc.—Finance

BlackRock Fights A Price War, Selectively C. Stein graph *Bloomberg Businessweek* no4520 p39 My 1 2017

Blacks

See also

African Americans

Black students

Black teachers

Black women

All of ME color *InStyle* v24 no8 p156 Ag 2017

DREAD RECKONING J. WARD color *O, The Oprah Magazine* p140 My 2017

Girl Who Codes J. BLAEC *O, The Oprah Magazine* p145 My 2017

Hair Apparent J. WEAVER *Walrus* v14 no7 p66 S 2017

Powered Up K. Kyles color *Ebony* v72 no3 p20 D 2016/Ja 2017

Spotlight on Brittani "Brittsense" Sensabaugh L. CROSS color *Ebony* v72 no3 p43 D 2016/Ja 2017

The Vegetarian Journal's 2016 Essay Contest Winner *Vegetarian Journal* v35 no4 p11 2016

Blackshaw, Robert

Sexism in Silicon Valley color *Atlantic* v319 no5 p10 Je 2017

Blackshaw, Seth

A nuclease that mediates cell death induced by DNA damage and poly(ADP-ribose) polymerase-1 bw graph *Science* v354 no6308 paad6872-1 O 7 2016

Blacks—Health

HOW I'M THRIVING WITH HIV G. Roberts-Grey color *Essence* v47 no8 p144 D 2016

Blacksmithing

Fleur de Lis Forge L. S. FORD *Texas Monthly* v45 no5 p27 My 2017

Q & A WITH ROB FLURRY *Texas Monthly* v45 no5 p28 My 2017

Blacks—New York (State)—New York

Black Gotham J. L. HESTER bw color map *Atlantic* v320 no1 p30 Jl/Ag 2017

Blacks—Social conditions

See also

African Americans—Social conditions

Basic Instinct E. Bazelon *New York Times Magazine* p13 O 23 2016

Blacks—South Africa

FROM THE ARCHIVES bw color *Reason* v48 no8 p62 Ja 2017

Blackstar (Music)

ALBUMS OF THE YEAR bw color *Rolling Stone* no1276 p13 D 15 2016

The Ten Best Pop Albums of the Year C. Jenkins img *New York* v49 no25 p118 D 12 2016

Blackstock, Traci

Congratulations on Your New Job! B. HOROVITZ color *AARP: The Magazine* v59 no2A p33 F/Mr 2016

Blackstone, Craig

Increased spatiotemporal resolution reveals highly dynamic dense tubular matrices in the peripheral ER bibl bw color graph *Science* v354 no6311 paaf3928-1 O 28 2016

Blackstone, Robin P.

Measuring and Communicating Health Care Value with Charts *Harvard Business Review Digital Articles* p2 O 26 2015

BLACKSTONE, TIFFANY

Confidence Lessons [Cover story] color *Redbook* p70 Je 2017

Blacks—United States

STEP OUT OF YOUR COMFORT ZONE D. BACKSTROM color *Ebony* v72/73 no12/1 p65 O/N 2017

Blacks—United States—Crimes against

A Presumption of Guilt B. Stevenson color *New York Review of Books* v64 no12 p8 Jl 13 2017

Blacks—United States—Social conditions—21st century

Do You See Me? J. Legend color *Time* v188 no16/17 p60 O 24 2016

Blackwell, John

TEMPTING THE TOIYABE K. GENSHEIMER bw color *Bike Magazine* v23 no9 p70 D 2016

Blackwell, Philip

Refugee work *Christian Century* v134 no2 p6 Ja 18 2017

Blackwood, Algernon, 1869-1951

Algernon Blackwood: The Master of the Supernatural M. Dirda bw *New York Review of Books* v63 no20 p92 D 22 2016

Blackwood, Gary

Bucket's List: A Charley Field Victorian Mystery *Publishers Weekly* v264 no40 p118 O 2 2017

Blackwood, Scott

These Waters Run Deep [Cover story] color *Chicago* v66 no9 p94 S 2017

BLAD, EVIE

Atlanta Schools Start Over with Police *Education Digest* v82 no8 p38 Ap 2017

Bladder stones

STUD FARM DIARIES: A Very Curious Case, Plus Answers to Common Foaling Questions C. Reich *Arabian Horse World* v57 no9 p161 Je 2017

Blade Runner (Film : 1982)

Blade Runner J. HOGAN *TV Guide* v65 no41 p39 O 2 2017

RIDLEY SCOTT A LIFE IN PICTURES S. Vilkomerson color *Entertainment Weekly* no1465 p34 My 12 2017

Blade Runner 2049 (Film)

2049 Is a Love Letter to Blade Runner S. Zacharek *Time* v190 no15 p55 O 16 2017

BLADE NEW WORLD S. Vilkomerson color *Entertainment Weekly* no1486 p32 O 13 2017

Blade Runner 2049 L. Greenblatt color *Entertainment Weekly* no1486 p42 O 13 2017

The Bullseye M. Snetiker color *Entertainment Weekly* no1486 p64 O 13 2017

How to Replicate a Hit P. Travers color *Rolling Stone* no1298 p53 O 19 2017

Pop Chart E. Dockterman color *Time* v190 no6 p58 Ag 7 2017

REAL OR REPLICANT? S. Vilkomerson color *Entertainment Weekly* no1446/1447 p45 D 2016/Ja 2017

REBORN TO RUN [Cover story] S. Vilkomerson color *Entertainment Weekly* no1446/1447 p40 D 2016/Ja 2017

THE REPLICANT B. RAFTERY bw cartoon chart color *Wired* v25 no10 p76 O 2017

REPLICANT REDUX A. LANE color *New Yorker* v93 no32 p96 O 16 2017

Replicants' Return J. PODHORETZ color *Weekly Standard* v23 no6 p46 O 16 2017

Replicating The Replicants M. WAKIM color *Los Angeles Magazine* v62 no10 p140 O 2017

RYAN GOSLING IN Blade Runner 2049 S. Vilkomerson color *Entertainment Weekly* no1478 / 1479 p52 Ag 18-25 2017

Blades (Hydraulic machinery)

ADVENTURE TECHNOLOGY color *Canoe & Kayak Magazine* v45 no1 p66 Wint 2017

Blades (Hydraulic machinery)—Evaluation
STOCK & TRADE color *Equus* no481 p76 O 2017

BLADES, LINCOLN
DETACHING MONEY FROM MANHOOD color *Ebony* v72 no5 p69 Mr 2017
SEXUAL HEALING color *Ebony* v72 no4 p77 F 2017
STRANGERS IN A STRANGE LAND color *Ebony* v72 no6 p69 Ap/My 2017

Blades, Nicole
I Tried a Runcation color *Health* v31 no6 p57 Jl 2017
The Real Reason I Work Out color *Health* v31 no2 p120 Mr 2017

BLAEC, JAGGER
Girl Who Codes *O, The Oprah Magazine* p145 My 2017

Blaedel, Sara
The Lost Woman *Publishers Weekly* v263 no50 p49 D 5 2016

Blaess, S. G.
Observation of a large-scale anisotropy in the arrival directions of cosmic rays above 8×10^{18} eV *Science* v357 no6357 p1266 S 22 2017

Blagojevich, Rod R., 1956-
INMATE NO. 40892-424 D. BERNSTEIN color *Chicago* v66 no10 p60 O 2017
TALK TO US P. Bella, B. Antcliff et al color graph *Chicago* v66 no11 p16 N 2017

Blagorodnova, N.
iPTF16geu: A multiply imaged, gravitationally lensed type Ia supernova color diag graph *Science* v356 no6335 p291 Ap 21 2017

Blahous, Charles
Debt? What Debt? *Hoover Digest: Research & Opinion on Public Policy* no4 p18 Fall 2016
Work Long and Prosper *Hoover Digest: Research & Opinion on Public Policy* no1 p57 Wint 2017

Blaine, David, 1973-
TOP PICKS F. Esker bw color *New Orleans Magazine* v51 no9 p26 Jl 2017

Blair, Bill
A POLICE CHIEF LEGALIZES MARIJUANA S. PROUDFOOT color *Maclean's* v129 no40 p24 O 10 2016

Blair, David M.
Formation of the Orientale lunar multiring basin bibl graph *Science* v354 no6311 p441 O 28 2016

Blair, David N.
Are We Any Safer? color *Atlantic* v318 no4 p14 N 2016

Blair, Elaine
BEHIND THE FIG LEAF *Harper's Magazine* p94 Ap 2017
Fathers & Daughters color *New York Review of Books* v64 no12 p4 Jl 13 2017
A FEMALE ANTIHERO cartoon color *New Yorker* v92 no38 p42 N 21 2016
Ferrante's World [Cover story] *New York Times Book Review* p1 N 6 2016
Robert B. Silvers (1929–2017) [Cover story] bw color *New York Review of Books* v64 no8 p31 My 11 2017

BLAIR, JASON
CHART WISE map *Flying* v144 no11 p25 N 2017
CONSIDER THE OPERATING ENVIRONMENT AROUND AN ILS APPROACH color *Flying* v144 no10 p27 O 2017
EVEN AN ILS APPROACH DEMANDS ATTENTION bw *Flying* v144 no7 p25 Jl 2017
A NEW GPS PROCEDURE DEMANDS SOME STUDY map *Flying* v144 no9 p23 S 2017
THE UPS AND DOWNS OF VISUAL APPROACHES map *Flying* v144 no8 p23 Ag 2017

Blair, Macon
I Don't Feel at Home Aims for the Heart S. Zacharek color *Time* v189 no7/8 p110 F 27 2017
I don't feel at home in this world anymore C. Collis color *Entertainment Weekly* no1454/1455 p83 F 24 2017

BLAIR, PEGGY
La nueva Cuba [Cover story] color *Canadian Geographic* v135 no6 p42 D 2015

Blair, Tony, 1953-
How Bad Was Tony Blair? B. Barder, G. Wheatcroft et al bw *New York Review of Books* v64 no1 p64 Ja 19 2017

Blair Witch Project, The (Film)
THE BLAIR WITCH PROJECT R. Kinane color *Entertainment Weekly* no1460/1461 p75 Ap 7-17 2017

BLAIS, MADELEINE
Kay's Kind of Summer color *Vanity Fair* v59 no7 p110 Summ 2017

Blais, Richard
So Good: Recipes from My Kitchen to Yours color *Publishers Weekly* v264 no12 p63 Mr 20 2017

Blais-Billie, Braudie
HOME TOWN HERO color *Glamour* v115 no9 p174 S 2017

Blake, Alma Pringle
Still worried *U.S. Catholic* v82 no10 p5 O 2017

Blake, Ashley Herring
How to Make a Wish *Publishers Weekly* v264 no12 p74 Mr 20 2017

BLAKE, BRIAN
The Opioid Crisis color graph *Weekly Standard* v22 no9 p19 N 7 2016

Blake, Chris
Will Beijing Also Have A Friend at State? bw *Bloomberg Businessweek* no4504 p26 D 19 2016

Blake, D. F.
Redox stratification of an ancient lake in Gale crater, Mars color *Science* v356 no6341 p922 Je 1 2017

Blake, David Haven
Addicted to Fame: From the Greeks to Lady Gaga *Humanities* v38 no4 p1 Fall 2017

Blake, Eubie, d. 1983
EUBIE BLAKE: 'NOTHING STAYS THE SAME' T. Panken bw *Downbeat* v84 no8 p37 Ag 2017

Blake, H. Emerson
Preamble color *Orion Magazine* v35 no6 p1 N/D 2016
Preamble *Orion Magazine* v35 no4/5 p1 Jl-O 2016

Blake, James, 1979-
James Blake's Next Challenge B. KALLET *Tennis* v52 no6 p22 N/D 2016
US Open Special bw color *Tennis* v53 no5 p30 S/O 2017

Blake, James, 1979——Interviews
THE TENNIS CONVERSATION: GEAR A. FRIEDMAN bw color *Tennis* v53 no2 p22 Mr/Ap 2017
THE TENNIS CONVERSATION: Wimbledon A. FRIEDMAN *Tennis* v53 no4 p38 Jl/Ag 2017

Blake, Jenny
How to Decide Which Tasks to Delegate *Harvard Business Review Digital Articles* p2 Jl 26 2017

BLAKE, MELISSA
"MY DAD MADE ME FEEL BEAUTIFUL, teaching me to see the beauty beyond my disability." color *Good Housekeeping* v264 no6 p63 Je 2017

Blake, Michael
Genomic estimation of complex traits reveals ancient maize adaptation to temperate North America diag *Science* v357 no6350 p512 Ag 4 2017

BLAKE, RICHARD A.
A MERCURIAL CHARACTER *America* v215 no18 p38 D 5 2016

Blake, Thomas
Step Into Tom's Shoes M. WAKIM *Los Angeles Magazine* p54 My 2017

BLAKE, WILLIAM
THOUGHTS ON Property *Forbes* v199 no5 p124 My 16 2017

Blake, William, 1757-1827
Confront & Forgive N. Enright color *Commonweal* v144 no15 p46 S 22 2017

Blake Island State Park (Wash.)
ANYTIME GETAWAY S. SHIBATA *Sea Magazine* v109 no2 pPNW-1 F 2017

Blakelock, Ralph Albert, 1847-1919
The Last Red Canoe color *Magazine Antiques* v183 no6 p19 N/D 2016

Blakely, Sarah
HOW TO GET TO $1 MILLION [Cover story] color *Money* v46 no8 p44 S 2017

BLAKEMORE, ERIN

Raging Belle *Smithsonian* v48 no1 p16 Ap 2017

Blakemore, Richard

The Civil Wars' Troubled Waters *History Today* v67 no2 p29 F 2017

BLAKENEY, JUSTINA

THE FREE SPIRIT color *Martha Stewart Living* p56 Jl/Ag 2017

BLAKER, ELIZABETH

Discovering the Perilous Life of Monarchs *Natural History* v125 no1 p12 D 2016/Ja 2017

Blakeslee, Nate

American Wolf G. Bowser color *Science* v357 no6355 p966 S 8 2017

Running With the Pack: Running With the Pack V. Klinkenborg *American Scholar* v86 no4 p120 Aut 2017

Streets of Laredo *New York Times Book Review* p9 O 16 2016

Blalock, Catherine

College Promise: Pathway to the 21 Century *Change* v48 no6 p6 N/D 2016

Blanc, Paul David

Toxic textiles E. Monosson bibl bw color *Science* v354 no6315 p977 N 25 2016

BLANCHARD, BRENDAN

Augmented Climbing Games color *Climbing* no351 p20 F/Mr 2017

Climbing Missionaries color *Climbing* no350 p18 D 2016/Ja 2017

Levitation 29 color *Climbing* no351 p38 F/Mr 2017

Swiss Precision Instrument color *Climbing* no353 p40 My/Je 2017

A Theoretical Climbing Rope *Climbing* no349 p10 N 2016

TRAIN SMART color *Climbing* no351 p54 F/Mr 2017

Blanchard, Jenny

bold INTENTIONS R. COLE color *Old House Journal* v45 no2 p22 Ap 2017

BLANCHARD, JULIA L.

Assessing National Biodiversity Trends for Rocky and Coral Reefs through the Integration of Citizen Science and Scientific Monitoring Programs *BioScience* v67 no2 p134 F 2017

Biodiversity redistribution under climate change: Impacts on ecosystems and human well-being color *Science* v355 no6332 p1389 Mr 31 2017

Blanchard, Rowan, 2001-

Dressing the Part color *InStyle* v24 no3 p182 Mr 2017

Blanchard, Scott

Finding common ground over barbecue color *Columbia Journalism Review* v56 no1 p42 Spr 2017

Blanchard, Terence

Mutually Beneficial Exchange B. REED color *Downbeat* v84 no9 p8 S 2017

Blanchard, Terence—Interviews

Blanchard Helps Fans Process Anger B. Reed color *Downbeat* v84 no10 p20 O 2017

Blanchenay, Patrick

A Study of 16 Countries Shows That the Most Productive Firms (and Their Employees) Are Pulling Away from Everyone Else *Harvard Business Review Digital Articles* p2 Jl 13 2017

Blanchett, Cate, 1969-

Artists color *Time* v189 no16/17 p40 My 1-8 2017

50 BEST DRESSED LIST J. Ferrise, E. Wilson et al color *InStyle* v24 no11 p186 N 2017

Cate Blanchett HER BEST EVER E. Wilson color *InStyle* v24 no11 p78 N 2017

My Obsessions... *TV Guide* v65 no11 p10 Mr 6 2017

Blanchett, Cate, 1969-—Interviews

I AM THAT GIRL Cate Blanchett A. Synnott color *InStyle* v23 no13 p282 D 2016

BLANCKE, STEFAAN

Creationism in Europe *Skeptical Inquirer* v41 no1 p48 Ja/F 2017

Blanco, A.

Observation of a large-scale anisotropy in the arrival directions of cosmic rays above 8×10^{18} eV *Science* v357 no6357 p1266 S 22 2017

Seasonal exposure of carbon dioxide ice on the nucleus of comet 67P/Churyumov-Gerasimenko bibl bw graph *Science* v354 no6319 p1563 D 23 2016

Blanco, Cesar

THE LOYAL OPPOSITION *Texas Monthly* v45 no2 p92 F 2017

BLANCO, JUAN CARLOS

An Unparalleled Opportunity for an Important Ecological Study *BioScience* v67 no10 p875 O 2017

Blanco, Mario

Xist recruits the X chromosome to the nuclear lamina to enable chromosome-wide silencing bibl graph *Science* v354 no6311 p468 O 28 2016

Blanco, Tia

Surf's Up L. McGLASHAN bw color *Muscle & Performance* v9 no7 p34 Jl 2017

Blanco-Aparicio, Carmen

Tissue damage and senescence provide critical signals for cellular reprogramming in vivo bibl chart graph *Science* v354 no6315 paaf4445-1 N 25 2016

Blancon, J.-C.

Extremely efficient internal exciton dissociation through edge states in layered 2D perovskites bibl graph *Science* v355 no6331 p1288 Mr 24 2017

Blangy, Stéphanie

An algal photoenzyme converts fatty acids to hydrocarbons color graph *Science* v357 no6354 p903 S 1 2017

Blank, Christopher

New Building, New Direction *Dance Magazine* v91 no8 p16 Ag 2017

Blank, Steve

Why You Can't Just Tell a Company "Be More Like a Startup" *Harvard Business Review Digital Articles* p2 Je 19 2017

Blankenship, Anne M.

Christianity, Social Justice, and the Japanese American Incarceration during World War II P. Harvey color *Christian Century* v134 no10 p41 My 10 2017

Blankenship, Robert E.

How Cyanobacteria went green color *Science* v355 no6332 p1372 Mr 31 2017

Blankets

See also

Horse blankets

CLIPPING & BLANKETING Insights from Top Grooms K. Brittle color *Dressage Today* v24 no1 p56 O 2017

GET IT ALL OUT T. WALRATH color *Outdoor Life* v224 no7 pH12 S 2017

Snuggly Vestments cartoon *Weekly Standard* v22 no25 p3 Mr 6 2017

Under Pressure L. Krieger color *O, The Oprah Magazine* p100 N 2017

Blankets—Evaluation

1968 ORANGE L. HEDRICK color *Better Homes & Gardens* v95 no3 p156 Mr 2017

Beard, Bath & Beyond S. DAILY *Indianapolis Monthly* v40 no5 p25 Ja 2017

CHERRY + SKY BLUE color *Martha Stewart Living* no275 p27 Je 2017

COLD WEATHER FRIENDS color *Equus* no481 p24 O 2017

Let's get Cozy N. DAYTON *Better Homes & Gardens* v95 no1 p88 Ja 2017

MATERIAL WORLD E. ELWICK-BATES color *Vogue* v207 no4 p254 Ap 2017

ROLL CALL color *Martha Stewart Living* p36 Jl/Ag 2017

A TO Z GUIDE TO YOUR BEST NIGHT'S SLEEP D. DICKINSON *Better Homes & Gardens* v95 no1 p41 Ja 2017

Blankfein, Lloyd, 1954-

IS GOLDMAN SACHS STILL NO. 1 ON WALL STREET? W. D. Cohan chart color diag *Fortune* v175 no8 p184 Je 15 2017

New Lloyd D. Campbell color *Bloomberg Businessweek* no4530 p26 Jl 17 2017

BLANKFELD, KEREN

The $4.5 Billion Cabinet color *Forbes* v199 no1 p26 Ja 24 2017

America's Richest Celebrities color *Forbes* v198 no9 p18 D 30 2016

Billionaire Ballot Boxes color *Forbes* v198 no5 p50 O 25 2016

Three Decades of Ten-Figure Fortunes graph *Forbes* v199 no3 p30 Mr 28 2017

THE WORLD'S BILLIONAIRES bw color diag graph map *Forbes* v199 no3 p84 Mr 28 2017

Blankfort, Jeff

Defending the State *Commentary* v140 no2 p11 S 2015

BLANTON, CAROLYN

I Survived! [Cover story] *Reader's Digest* v189 no1128 p62 Mr 2017

BLANTON, THOMAS H.
KNOW THE RISKS OF CRYPTOCURRENCIES color *Kiplinger's Personal Finance* v71 no12 p10 D 2017
LIVE LARGE ON A SUBSCRIPTION PLAN color *Kiplinger's Personal Finance* v71 no7 p15 Jl 2017

Blanz, Judith
Dopamine oxidation mediates mitochondrial and lysosomal dysfunction in Parkinson's disease graph *Science* v357 no6357 p1255 S 22 2017

Blas, Javier
Fat Wallets Come To the Shale Patch *Bloomberg Businessweek* no4516 p34 Mr 27 2017
Help Wanted in Saudi Arabia: Savvy Investors color graph *Bloomberg Businessweek* no4513 p41 Mr 6 2017
Peak Oil Could Be Here Sooner Than You Think bw *Bloomberg Businessweek* no4530 p32 Jl 17 2017
Russia's Deadly Mideast Game *Bloomberg Businessweek* no4505 p16 D 26 2016
A SAUDI ABOUT-FACE graph *Bloomberg Businessweek* no4496 p82 O 24 2016
The Tables Have Turned cartoon graph *Bloomberg Businessweek* no4493 p47 O 3 2016
Why the Oil Glut Isn't Gone Yet graph *Bloomberg Businessweek* no4514 p39 Mr 13 2017

BLASBERG, DEREK
ELLA'S A-POPPIN' color *Vanity Fair* v59 no5 p142 Ap 2017
A FEMININE MYSTIQUE color *Vanity Fair* v59 no2 p88 F 2017
GOOD GOLLY, MISS MARLEY! color *Vanity Fair* v59 no11 p132 N 2017
HAVEN IN A HASHTAG color *Vanity Fair* v58 no11 p174 N 2016
horse country color *Architectural Digest* no5 p102 My 2017
MAYE IN AUTUMN color *Vanity Fair* v59 no4 p172 Mr 2017
MODERN ENGLISH color *Architectural Digest* no11 p152 N 1 2017
NICK KROLL color *Vanity Fair* v58 no12 p92 D 2016
PARIS IN APRIL color *Vanity Fair* v59 no6 p90 My 2017
The Rebel Belle bw color *Vanity Fair* v59 no4 p152 Mr 2017
sea for days color *Architectural Digest* no6 p98 Je 1 2017
SPEAKING OF FIRST DAUGHTERS... color *Vanity Fair* v59 no10 p190 O 2017
TRUE BLUES color *Vanity Fair* v59 no10 p125 O 2017
WHOLLY MOSELEY color *Vanity Fair* v58 no12 p160 D 2016
zen spirit color *Architectural Digest* v74 no2 p86 F 2017

Blaschke, Janet Winter
Shelf Awareness cartoon *O, The Oprah Magazine* p63 Ap 2017

Blasco, Maria A.
Tissue damage and senescence provide critical signals for cellular reprogramming in vivo bibl chart graph *Science* v354 no6315 paaf4445-1 N 25 2016

Blaser, Tom—Interviews
Managers Shouldn't Fear Algorithm-Based Decision Making E. Harrell *Harvard Business Review Digital Articles* p2 S 7 2016

Blashaw, Matt
Crash & Learn D. Peak color *Log Home Living* v34 no5 p18 Jl 2017

Blasim, Hassan
Sci-Fi Iraq M. L. QUALEY *In These Times* v40 no12 p36 D 2016

Blaskey, Sarah
How local is the local news at Gannett? diag *Columbia Journalism Review* v56 no1 p69 Spr 2017

Blaskiewicz, Robert
Burzynski Sanctioned by Texas Medical Board *Skeptical Inquirer* v41 no4 p7 Jl/Ag 2017
Burzynski Update: Texas Hearings End, Judges Sifting Evidence *Skeptical Inquirer* v40 no6 p5 N/D 2016

Blasphemy
Indonesian Christian leader jailed under blasphemy law C. Kennel-Shank *Christian Century* v134 no12 p16 Je 7 2017

Blasphemy laws
Where Artists Fall Afoul of Blasphemy Laws T. John color *Time* v189 no19 p13 My 22 2017

Blasphemy—Law & legislation
Blasphemy Laws Attack Free Expression—Can Freethought Hit

Back? A. Bissell-Siders *Humanist* v76 no6 p9 N/D 2016

Blass, Gregory
Fructose-driven glycolysis supports anoxia resistance in the naked mole-rat diag graph *Science* v356 no6335 p307 Ap 21 2017

Blasucci, Tony
UNSOLICITED BETA color *Climbing* no352 p8 Ap 2017

Blatchford, Garnet
A greater good color *Equus* no480 p27 S 2017

Blatner, Dawn Jackson
The Snacking Diaries color *Women's Health* v14 no2 p106 Mr 2017

BLATT, BEN
Have Bestsellers become Dumber? color diag graph *Reader's Digest* v190 no1133 p118 S 2017

Blättermann, A.
Observing the ultrafast buildup of a Fano resonance in the time domain bibl graph *Science* v354 no6313 p738 N 11 2016

Blatt-Gross, Carolina
Creating community from the inside out: A concentric perspective on collective artmaking bibl *Arts Education Policy Review* v118 no1 p51 2017

Blatty, William Peter, 1928-2017
Evil to Good to God J. Haldane bw *Commonweal* v144 no5 p13 Mr 10 2017

Blatz, Emily
Control of species-dependent cortico-motoneuronal connections underlying manual dexterity diag graph *Science* v357 no6349 p400 Jl 28 2017

Blau, Alex
The Behavioral Economics of Why Executives Underinvest in Cybersecurity color *Harvard Business Review Digital Articles* p2 Je 7 2017

BLAU, MAX
DEATH ROW RUSH *Atlanta* v56 no12 p28 Ap 2017
UPPER WESTSIDE *Atlanta* v56 no12 p52 Ap 2017

BLAU, PETER
Trump Theory *Commentary* v142 no1 p7 Jl/Ag 2016

Blau, Steven K.
Proton structure seen in a new light *Physics Today* v70 no5 p14 My 2017

BLAUNER, PETER
Coming Home bw *Publishers Weekly* v264 no13 p79 Mr 27 2017

BLAUSTEIN, RICHARD
Biology and Light Sources *BioScience* v67 no3 p201 Mr 2017
Phytoremediation of Lead: What Works, What Doesn't *BioScience* v67 no9 p868 S 2017

Blavity Inc.
Black News Matters C. Brooks Jr. color *Wired* v25 no3 p64 Mr 2017

BLAYLOCK, JIM
our happy place color map *Cabin Living* p15 S 2017

BLAYLOCK, KAREN
our happy place color map *Cabin Living* p15 S 2017

Blazar, Bruce R.
Rescue of exhausted CD8 T cells by PD-1-targeted therapies is CD28-dependent bw diag graph *Science* v355 no6332 p1423 Mr 31 2017

Blazek, J.
Observation of a large-scale anisotropy in the arrival directions of cosmic rays above 8×1018 eV *Science* v357 no6357 p1266 S 22 2017

Blazers (Jackets)
THE ABROAD-ROBE N. SULLIVAN bw color *Esquire* p46 My 2017
The STYLE color *Harper's Bazaar* no3656 p277 S 2017
Who Are You Wearing? M. Wildgen color *O, The Oprah Magazine* p119 Mr 2017

Blazers (Jackets)—Evaluation
The Evening Suit S. P. Nadella color *Glamour* v114 no12 p94 D 2016
First, Get a Bomber color *Glamour* v114 no7 p46 Jl 2016
JANELLE LANGFORD J. Wilson color *Essence* v48 no2 p26 Je 2017
Miuccia Prada E. Wilson color *InStyle* v24 no9 p190 S 2017
My Clothes Don't Fit My New Job B. Boyé color *Men's Health* v31 no10 p76 D 2016

Our Fall Favorites F. Kane and E. Velluto color *Glamour* no8 p62 Ag 2017

Outfits for Days color *Glamour* v114 no12 p102 D 2016

Outfits for Days color *Glamour* v115 no11 p60 N 2017

the start color *InStyle* v24 no11 p51 N 2017

Stella McCartney E. Wilson color *InStyle* v24 no9 p188 S 2017

Track Pants Everywhere! color *Glamour* v114 no7 p50 Jl 2016

a "tuxedo" blazer color *Good Housekeeping* v263 no6 p28 D 2016

VELVET CRUSH color *Ebony* v72 no3 p64 D 2016/Ja 2017

Bleaching of skin—Equipment & supplies

Cute for CLASS M. ABERMAN color *Seventeen* v76 no5 p48 S 2017

Bleaching powder

PALE Fire K. Molvar color *Vogue* v206 no12 p198 D 2016

Blecha, Ben

Benkelman hero PLUGGED INTO HIS DESTINY K. LONG color *Nebraska Life* v20 no6 p45 N/D 2016

DUNDY COUNTY Road Trip A. J. BARTELS color *Nebraska Life* v20 no6 p40 N/D 2016

Blecka, M. I.

Seasonal exposure of carbon dioxide ice on the nucleus of comet 67P/Churyumov-Gerasimenko bibl bw graph *Science* v354 no6319 p1563 D 23 2016

Bledel, Alexis, 1981-

The 3-Minute Interview J. Radloff and J. Harman color *Glamour* v114 no12 p82 D 2016

Gilmore Girls: A Year in the Life S. Highfill, A. Writing et al color *Entertainment Weekly* no1439 p18 N 11 2016

The Handmaid and the Despot J. Stites *In These Times* v41 no5 p38 My 2017

Bledsoe, Alex

Gather Her Round: Tufa, Book 5 *Publishers Weekly* v264 no5 p184 Ja 30 2017

Bleed for This (Film)

A Comeback King Fights His Way Back Into the Ring E. Berman color *Time* v188 no22-23 p102 N/D 2016

THE DEVIL GETS HIS DUE B. Baskin color *Sports Illustrated* v125 no18 p42 D 5 2016

Bleeding Edge, The (Film)

THE BLEEDING EDGE E. BOEHM color *Reason* v49 no1 p68 My 2017

Bleem, Jerry

Contemporary crucifixion il *U.S. Catholic* v82 no4 p50 Ap 2017

A difficult choice color *U.S. Catholic* v82 no3 p50 Mr 2017

A gesture for continual peace color *U.S. Catholic* v82 no2 p50 F 2017

Hungry for more color *U.S. Catholic* v82 no6 p50 Je 2017

Looking ahead color *U.S. Catholic* v82 no10 p50 O 2017

Marvel and behold il *U.S. Catholic* v82 no8 p50 Ag 2017

Of the world color *U.S. Catholic* v82 no3 p26 Mr 2017

One man's trash color *U.S. Catholic* v82 no7 p50 Jl 2017

Redefining family color *U.S. Catholic* v81 no12 p50 D 2016

Sow kindness color *U.S. Catholic* v82 no9 p50 S 2017

Stitches of change color *U.S. Catholic* v81 no11 p50 N 2016

A storm is coming color *U.S. Catholic* v82 no1 p50 Ja 2017

We are one color *U.S. Catholic* v82 no5 p50 My 2017

What lies ahead color *U.S. Catholic* v82 no11 p50 N 2017

BLEIBERG, LARRY

WEEKEND GETAWAYS cartoon *Better Homes & Gardens* v95 no7 p170 Jl 2017

winter wonderlands *Better Homes & Gardens* v94 no11 p166 N 2016

Bleichert, Franziska

Mechanisms for initiating cellular DNA replication graph *Science* v355 no6327 p811 F 24 2017

BLEIFUSS, JOEL

40 Years bw *In These Times* v40 no11 p9 N 2016

A Budget for the Rest of Us *In These Times* v41 no7 p5 Jl 2017

The Children's Crusade *In These Times* v41 no10 p48 O 2017

Ellison's 3,143-County Strategy *In These Times* v41 no1 p5 Ja 2017

Fixing Electoral Mechanics *In These Times* v41 no2 p5 F 2017

GOP Death Panels *In These Times* v41 no8 p5 Ag 2017

Lighting a Fire on the Prairie *In These Times* v41 no7 p30 Jl 2017

Resistance *In These Times* v40 no12 p5 D 2016

Robert Reich's Plan To Save the Democrats *In These Times* v41 no1 p30 Ja 2017

Single Payer Here We Come *In These Times* v41 no5 p5 My 2017

Tweetstorms and Circuses *In These Times* v41 no4 p5 Ap 2017

Bleikasten, André, 1933-2009

The Big Thing on His Mind T. Powers bw *New York Review of Books* v64 no7 p41 Ap 20 2017

Blended learning

Takeaways from the 2016 Blended and Personalized Learning Conference J. F. FISHER and J. WHITE *Education Digest* v82 no6 p42 F 2017

Blenders (Cooking)

The 8 Best Kitchen Essentials color *Men's Health* v32 no8 p81 O 2017

YOUR MAIN SUMMER TEST KITCHEN SQUEEZE color *Better Homes & Gardens* v95 no5 p118 My 2017

Blenders (Cooking)—Evaluation

Blenders color *Good Housekeeping* v265 no1 p60 Jl 2017

For the Get Up and Go-Getter color *Consumer Reports* v81 no12 p46 D 2016

the (mostly) clean eater color *House Beautiful* v159 no8 p74 O 2017

STIR CRAZY color *Runner's World* v52 no7 p24 Ag 2017

Vitamix A3500 Blender color *Bloomberg Businessweek* no4541 p67 O 9 2017

Blenniidae

What big fangs you have, little blenny S. Milius color *Science News* v191 no10 p4 My 27 2017

Blepharoplasty

Brow Growth Serums L. Desantis color *Health* v31 no2 p41 Mr 2017

Eyelid surgery *Mayo Clinic Health Letter* v35 no3 p7 Mr 2017

Blériot, Louis, 1872-1936

STRANGE WINGS P. Garrison bw color *Flying* v144 no5 p80 My 2017

Blessed

BLESS IS MORE E. Dwyer *Saturday Evening Post* v289 no4 p28 Jl/Ag 2017

Blessing & cursing

THE INDEPENDENT CUSS V. HOFER *South Dakota Magazine* v33 no2 p96 Jl/Ag 2017

Bletery, Quentin

Mega-earthquakes rupture flat megathrusts bibl graph *Science* v354 no6315 p1027 N 25 2016

Bleu (Music)

FORGING HIS OWN PATH D. Ouellette color *Downbeat* v84 no6 p56 Je 2017

Bleve, C.

Observation of a large-scale anisotropy in the arrival directions of cosmic rays above 8×1018 eV *Science* v357 no6357 p1266 S 22 2017

Bleyer, Bill

The Hard Way cartoon color *Sail* v47 no12 p12 D 2016

Bleyer, Jennifer

day tripping *Psychology Today* v49 no6 p96 N/D 2016

A DOORWAY TO CHANGE *Psychology Today* v50 no3 p60 My/Je 2017

Mastering Your Mental Game... TANIA SACHDEV *Psychology Today* v50 no2 p96 Mr/Ap 2017

My Funny Valentine: ONE QUESTION FOR KUMAIL NANJIANI AND EMILY V. GORDON *Psychology Today* v50 no4 p96 Ag 2017

Tend and Defend *Psychology Today* v50 no2 p38 Mr/Ap 2017

Vision Quest... Isaac Lidsky *Psychology Today* v50 no3 p96 My/Je 2017

Blickstead, Rick

LIVING WELL WITH DIABETES IS POSSIBLE *Maclean's* v129 no48/49 p39 D 5 2016

Blickstein, Andrew

Shutting Down Your Business Gracefully *Harvard Business Review Digital Articles* p2 Mr 20 2017

Blige, Mary J., 1971-

THE NEW FACE OF R&B S. Scott color *Essence* v48 no6 p68 O 2017

WHAT'S THE 411? color *Ebony* v72 no11 p42 S 2017

Blige, Mary J., 1971---Interviews

MARY J. BLIGE IN Mudbound K. P. Sullivan color *Entertain-*

ment Weekly no1478 / 1479 p61 Ag 18-25 2017

Blind

Save Your Eyesight G. DEGROOT REDFORD color *AARP: The Magazine* v60 no2A p26 F/Mr 2017

Blind athletes

Steven Holcomb (1980-2017) J. Fuchs and T. Keith color *Sports Illustrated* v126 no15 p20 My 29 2017

Blind children

Noah Is Blind N. CARVER and J. PRESS *Scholastic Choices* v32 no3 p16 N/D 2016

Blind students

What a blind student taught me to see C. Caswell bw chart color diag *Phi Delta Kappan* v98 no3 p68 N 2016

Blinder, Alan

Emmett Till Revisited img *New York Times Upfront* v149 no11 p16 Ap 3 2017

Blindness

TOXICITY AS A STEALTH TEACHER *Psychology Today* v50 no3 p4 My/Je 2017

Blindness—Prevention

CANADA'S ELITE VISION-IMPAIRED ATHLETES ARE RAISING AWARENESS FOR UNIVERSAL EYE HEALTH D. F. McCourt bw *Maclean's* v129 no42 p33 O 24 2016

VISION LOSS DUE TO DIABETES ON THE RISE M. Sponagle cartoon *Maclean's* v129 no48/49 p43 D 5 2016

Blind—Orientation & mobility

The Blind Community Has High Hopes for Self-Driving Cars E. Woyke il *MIT Technology Review* v120 no1 p20 Ja/F 2017

Blindspot (TV program)

Blindspot N. Abrams, S. Highfill et al color *Entertainment Weekly* no1482/1483 p95 S 22 2017

Season Finale Shockers! I. Rudolph, M. Logan et al *TV Guide* v65 no25 p4 Je 2017

Blink (Music)

THE ULTIMATE FALL SINGLES SWAP color *Entertainment Weekly* no1440 p56 N 18 2016

BLINN, DAN

A THANKSGIVING PRAYER *Humanist* v76 no6 p43 N/D 2016

Bliss, Harry

Sketchbook: Graphic Review *New York Times Book Review* p31 S 24 2017

Blister rust

Blisters, Beetles and British Columbia: Global ReLeaf in Canada D. Irvin *American Forests* v123 no1 p6 Wint/Spr 2017

BLITT, BARRY

Hillary 2016 CAMPAIGN MEMORABILIA cartoon *New Yorker* v92 no33 p55 O 17 2016

A LITTLE CONTEXT, PLEASE! cartoon *New Yorker* v92 no36 p44 N 7 2016

Blitz, Jeffrey

Table 19 C. Nashawaty color *Entertainment Weekly* no1456 p56 Mr 10 2017

BLITZ, MARK

Stand on Tradition color *Weekly Standard* v22 no27 p38 Mr 20 2017

Blitz, Matt

6 CONFEDERATE MEMORIALS THAT ARE STILL HERE *Washingtonian Magazine* v52 no2 p22 N 2016

6 WEIRD WINTER SITES AROUND WASHINGTON *Washingtonian Magazine* v52 no4 p18 Ja 2017

WASHINGTON GHOST STORIES *Washingtonian Magazine* v52 no1 p24 O 2016

Blitzer, Jonathan

AMERICAN STUDIES cartoon *New Yorker* v93 no14 p40 My 22 2017

CALLED AWAY cartoon *New Yorker* v92 no46 p30 Ja 23 2017

PRO BONO cartoon *New Yorker* v93 no27 p24 S 11 2017

Something's Brewing color *Esquire* v166 no4 p42 N 2016

TIME TRAVEL cartoon *New Yorker* v92 no42 p46 D 19 2016

Blizzards

In Case of Blizzard, Do Nothing D. DUDLEY *Reader's Digest* v189 no1127 p16 F 2017

Bloat (Physiology)

Soothe Your Stomach T. Low Dog color *Prevention* v69 no11 p24 N 2017

Bloch, Ernst, 1885-1977

THE DEVIL YOU KNOW E. Bloch *Lapham's Quarterly* v10 no3 p55 Summ 2017

Bloch, Immanuel

Quantum simulations with ultracold atoms in optical lattices cartoon color diag *Science* v357 no6355 p995 S 8 2017

Revealing hidden antiferromagnetic correlations in doped Hubbard chains via string correlators bw diag graph *Science* v357 no6350 p484 Ag 4 2017

Bloch, Serge

The Big Adventure of a Little Line *Publishers Weekly* v263 no49 p11 D 7 2016

Bloch, Yoni

ALTERNATE ENDINGS R. KHATCHADOURIAN cartoon *New Yorker* v92 no47 p46 Ja 30 2017

Bloch equations (Physics)

Large, valley-exclusive Bloch-Siegert shift in monolayer WS2 E. J. Sie, C. Hung Lui et al bibl diag *Science* v355 no6329 p1066 Mr 10 2017

Bloch Inc.

STRAP - Happy H. Rolfe color *Dance Spirit* v21 no8 p86 O 2017

Block, Adam

POINT-SIZED UNIVERSE? color *Astronomy* v45 no2 p34 F 2017

READER GALLERY color *Astronomy* v44 no12 p70 D 2016

Block, Barbara A.

Hydraulic control of tuna fins: A role for the lymphatic system in vertebrate locomotion color *Science* v357 no6348 p310 Jl 21 2017

Block, Frederic

Race to Judgment *Publishers Weekly* v264 no34 p92 Ag 21 2017

Block, Lawrence

In Sunlight or in Shadow: Stories Inspired by the Paintings of Edward Hopper *Publishers Weekly* v263 no43 p53 O 24 2016

Keller's Fedora *Publishers Weekly* v264 no9 p79 F 27 2017

Block, Lawrence—Interviews

Art Noir L. PICKER color *Publishers Weekly* v263 no44 p50 O 31 2016

Block, Martin Moses

Martin Moses Block F. L. Halzen *Physics Today* v69 no10 p66 O 2016

BLOCK, SANDRA

Best Places to Retire [Cover story] color *Kiplinger's Personal Finance* v71 no8 p56 Ag 2017

BROKERS CHANGE THEIR GAME PLAN cartoon *Kiplinger's Personal Finance* v71 no4 p9 Ap 2017

Cut Your Tax Bill Now color *Kiplinger's Personal Finance* v70 no12 p36 D 2016

De-Stress Your Life cartoon *Kiplinger's Personal Finance* v71 no2 p64 F 2017

EMPLOYERS EXPAND PAID FAMILY LEAVE color *Kiplinger's Personal Finance* v70 no12 p15 D 2016

EXPATS FIND A HOME FOR THEIR MONEY color *Kiplinger's Personal Finance* v71 no3 p14 Mr 2017

GAME PLAN cartoon *Kiplinger's Personal Finance* v71 no7 p40 Jl 2017

GAME PLAN color *Kiplinger's Personal Finance* v71 no6 p39 Je 2017

GET INCOME FOR LIFE [Cover story] chart color *Kiplinger's Personal Finance* v71 no10 p26 O 2017

HOW A BORDER TAX WOULD AFFECT YOU color *Kiplinger's Personal Finance* v71 no5 p11 My 2017

HOW TO HIDE YOUR ONLINE FOOTPRINT cartoon *Kiplinger's Personal Finance* v71 no7 p13 Jl 2017

How to Save If You Don't Have a 401(k) chart color *Kiplinger's Personal Finance* v71 no1 p24 Ja 2017

Last-Minute Tax Savers cartoon *Kiplinger's Personal Finance* v71 no4 p46 Ap 2017

LIVING WITH CANCER color *Kiplinger's Personal Finance* v71 no6 p58 Je 2017

MAKE THE MOST OF YOUR DONOR DOLLARS color *Kiplinger's Personal Finance* v71 no12 p9 D 2017

Money Help for Aging Parents color *Kiplinger's Personal Finance* v71 no11 p34 N 2017

Q: I'd like to invest in a rental property. Can I use my IRA to buy real estate? color *Kiplinger's Personal Finance* v70 no12 p43 D 2016

Q: My property tax bill has skyrocketed. How can I reduce it? color *Kiplinger's Personal Finance* v71 no5 p37 My 2017

Roll Your Money Into an IRA? color *Kiplinger's Personal Finance* v71 no5 p38 My 2017

STATE TAXES SPIRAL UPWARD cartoon *Kiplinger's Personal Finance* v71 no1 p13 Ja 2017

STRESS-BUSTING VACATIONS color *Kiplinger's Personal Finance* v71 no7 p62 Jl 2017

Trim Your Tax Bill color *Kiplinger's Personal Finance* v71 no12 p38 D 2017

WHAT'S KEEPING YOU UP AT NIGHT? S. Block cartoon *Kiplinger's Personal Finance* v71 no3 p64 Mr 2017

YOUR NEXT PAY RAISE WILL LOOK FAMILIAR *Kiplinger's Personal Finance* v71 no11 p9 N 2017

Block copolymers

Molecular stitches for enhanced recycling of packaging C. Creton bibl diag *Science* v355 no6327 p797 F 24 2017

Block grants

Block Grant Jitters A. Greenblatt *Governing* v30 no7 p10 Ap 2017

Block Island (R.I. : Island)

Exploring a 'Last Great Place' P. Voskamp *Yankee* p93 Mr 2017

Blockchains

Amber Baldet M. Leising color *Bloomberg Businessweek* no4536 p72 S 4 2017

Blockchain Can Grow More Than Just Money M. Leising color diag *Bloomberg Businessweek* no4516 p33 Mr 27 2017

Blockchain Could Help Artists Profit More from Their Creative Works D. Tapscott and A. Tapscott *Harvard Business Review Digital Articles* p2 Mr 22 2017

Blockchain Could Help Musicians Make Money Again I. Heap color *Harvard Business Review Digital Articles* p2 Je 5 2017

Blockchain Could Help Us Reclaim Control of Our Personal Data M. Mainelli *Harvard Business Review Digital Articles* p2 O 5 2017

BLOCKCHAIN IN REAL LIFE J. J. Roberts *Fortune* v176 no3 p49 S 1 2017

BLOCKCHAIN MANIA! [Cover story] R. Hackett color *Fortune* v176 no3 p44 S 1 2017

The Blockchain Will Do to the Financial System What the Internet Did to Media Joichi Ito, N. Narula et al color *Harvard Business Review Digital Articles* p2 Mr 8 2017

Blockchain Will Help Us Prove Our Identities in a Digital World M. Mainelli *Harvard Business Review Digital Articles* p2 Mr 16 2017

Blockchain Will Transform Customer Loyalty Programs D. Kowalewski, J. McLaughlin et al *Harvard Business Review Digital Articles* p2 Mr 14 2017

A Brief History of Blockchain V. Gupta bw *Harvard Business Review Digital Articles* p2 F 28 2017

BUILDING BLOCKS: BLOCKCHAIN TECHNOLOGY COULD REMAKE GOVERNMENT SERVICES FROM THE GROUND UP L. Farmer *Governing* v30 no12 p44 S 2017

Cloud Armor That's Not Quite So Fluffy D. Lawrence *Bloomberg Businessweek* no4504 p32 D 19 2016

CRYSTAL CLEAR PROVENANCE J. J. Roberts color *Fortune* v176 no4 p44 S 15 2017

DIGITAL DOINGS IN DELAWARE J. J. Roberts *Fortune* v176 no3 p50 S 1 2017

E Pluribus Unum And The Blockchain L. BRODY color *Forbes* v200 no1 p78 Jl 27 2017

Global Supply Chains Are About to Get Better, Thanks to Blockchain M. J. Casey and P. Wong *Harvard Business Review Digital Articles* p2 Mr 13 2017

How Blockchain Could Help Emerging Markets Leap Ahead V. Gupta and R. Knight *Harvard Business Review Digital Articles* p2 My 17 2017

How Blockchain Is Changing Finance A. Tapscott and D. Tapscott color *Harvard Business Review Digital Articles* p2 Mr 1 2017

How Safe Are Blockchains? It Depends A. Berke color *Harvard Business Review Digital Articles* p2 Mr 7 2017

How Utilities Are Using Blockchain to Modernize the Grid J. Basden and M. Cottrell *Harvard Business Review Digital Articles* p2 Mr 23 2017

ICO Is the New IPO D. Lawrence *Bloomberg Businessweek* no4527 p35 Je 19 2017

NEW KIDS ON THE BLOCKCHAIN C. Leaf color *Fortune*

v176 no3 p9 S 1 2017

The Potential for Blockchain to Transform Electronic Health Records J. D. Halamka, A. Lippman et al bw *Harvard Business Review Digital Articles* p2 Mr 3 2017

The Promise of Blockchain Is a World Without Middlemen V. Gupta color *Harvard Business Review Digital Articles* p2 Mr 6 2017

SPAWN OF BITCOIN: BLOCKCHAIN-FUELED STARTUPS C. METZ color graph *Wired* v25 no7 p18 Jl 2017

THE TRUTH ABOUT BLOCKCHAIN M. IANSITI and K. R. LAKHANI bw color diag img *Harvard Business Review* v95 no1 p118 Ja/F 2017

Using Blockchain to Keep Public Data Public B. Forde *Harvard Business Review Digital Articles* p2 Mr 31 2017

What Blockchain Means for the Sharing Economy P. De Filippi *Harvard Business Review Digital Articles* p2 Mr 15 2017

Will OpenBazaar Succeed Where Silk Road Failed? S. W. Malone color *Reason* v48 no7 p46 D 2016

Blockchains—Economic aspects

THE BLOCKCHAIN REVOLUTION: INTERACTION M. IANSITI, K. R. LAKHANI et al color *Harvard Business Review* v95 no2 p20 Mr/Ap 2017

Blockchains—Social aspects

Blockchain May Help Walmart Stop Bad Food O. Kharif cartoon *Bloomberg Businessweek* no4501 p20 N 28 2016

Blocker, John

John Blocker's Road Brand B. Welch color *American Cowboy* v23 no6 p72 Ap/My 2017

Blocks (Toys)

AYAH BDEIR S. BUSHWICK color *Popular Science* v288 no6 p26 N/D 2016

The Lego House J. Zorthian color *Time* v190 no9 p25 S 4 2017

Blocks (Toys)—Evaluation

A Lego-Like Tape J. Zorthian color *Time* v189 no12 p25 Ap 3 2017

Blockstack Labs (Company)

One Startup's Vision to Reinvent the Web for Better Privacy T. Simonite il *MIT Technology Review* v120 no2 p20 Mr/Ap 2017

Blodgett, Sequoia

5 Black-Owned Startups to Watch [Cover story] cartoon color *Black Enterprise* v47 no3 p29 O 2016

THE 5 HOTTEST BLACK-OWNED BEAUTY TECH START-UPS color *Black Enterprise* v47 no8 p28 Jl/Ag 2017

KEEPING IT LOCAL color *Black Enterprise* v47 no8 p13 Jl/Ag 2017

Blodgett, Susan

THE BRITISH HERITAGE TRAVEL PUZZLER color *British Heritage Travel* v38 no5 p78 S/O 2017

Bloggers

THE COUNTRY CUISINIÉRE M. Thorisson *Martha Stewart Living* no269 p58 N 2016

Deb Cotton, Now and Forever: The Final Goodbye J. Berry color *New Orleans Magazine* v51 no10 p64 Ag 2017

In Her Shoes color *Southern Living* v52 no11 p55 N 2017

Niyah Jackson A. BRANDT *Cincinnati Magazine* v50 no7 p32 Ap 2017

Spice Girl S. KROWIAK *Indianapolis Monthly* p43 F 2017

The World According to Huda F. Valdesolo color *Glamour* v115 no11 p82 N 2017

Bloggers—Interviews

Twisted Sisters P. GABBARA color *Ebony* v72 no8 p43 Je 2017

Blogs

See also

Microblogs

The Aging Process E. C. PEYTON color *New Orleans Magazine* v52 no1 p54 S 2017

BUZZWORTHY *Indianapolis Monthly* v40 no3 p14 N 2016

Have LinkedIn and Medium Killed the Old-Fashioned Blog? A. Samuel *Harvard Business Review Digital Articles* p2 Je 30 2015

NO FILTER E. LOECHNER *Indianapolis Monthly* v40 no5 p54 Ja 2017

THE PROBLEM WITH COMMENTERS cartoon *New Orleans Magazine* v51 no3 p18 Ja 2017

SHARE WHAT YOU KNOW J. SCOTT *Successful Farming* v114 no13 p20 D 2016

STILL SLAYED J. AMAY color *Ebony* v72/73 no12/1 p42 O/N

2017
VERY NECESSARY BROTHAS Z. HILL color *Ebony* v72/73 no12/1 p25 O/N 2017
War Cry E. C. Peyton color *New Orleans Magazine* v51 no9 p44 Jl 2017
Your Best Cyberself G. D. MELTON cartoon *O, The Oprah Magazine* p35 Ap 2017

Blogs—Social aspects
Instamom B. BOSKER cartoon *Atlantic* v319 no2 p16 Mr 2017

Blois, Jessica
Merging paleobiology with conservation biology to guide the future of terrestrial ecosystems color *Science* v355 no6325 p594 F 10 2017

Blom, Jinny
BLOM COUNTY V. LOWRY color *Architectural Digest* v74 no3 p126 Mr 2017

Blonde (Music)
The 10 Best Albums J. Cox color *Time* v188 no25-26 p152 D 19 2016 Double Issue

BLONDEEL, HABEN
Combining Biodiversity Resurveys across Regions to Advance Global Change Research *BioScience* v67 no1 p73 Ja 2017

Blonder, Benjamin
Without inclusion, diversity initiatives may not be enough color *Science* v357 no6356 p1101 S 15 2017

Blondes
GOING Blondie L. REGENSDORF color *Vogue* v206 no12 p200 D 2016
NOT SO DUMB BLONDE color *Women's Health* v14 no4 p30 My 2017
POLITICAL PEROXIDE: Blonde privilege A. LAROCCA img *New York* v50 no16 p44 Ag 7 2017

Blondiau, Eloise
The British Michael Moore investigates the Church of Scientology color *America* v216 no6 p46 Mr 20 2017
CHARACTER STUDIES color *America* v215 no13 p31 O 31 2016
Faith, Feminism and 'The Handmaid's Tale' [Cover story] color *America* v216 no11 p46 My 15 2017
A Human Hero color *America* v216 no1 p21 Ja 2 2017

Blondiaux, Nicolas
Reversion of antibiotic resistance in Mycobacterium tuberculosis by spiroisoxazoline SMARt-420 bibl diag *Science* v355 no6330 p1206 Mr 17 2017

Blonigen, Bruce A.
Mergers May Be Profitable, but Are They Good for the Economy? *Harvard Business Review Digital Articles* p2 N 15 2016

BLOOD, HAL
AT HOME IN THE TIMBER color *Outdoor Life* v224 no1 p42 D 2016/Ja 2017

Blood analysis
A New Way to Define Value in Drug Pricing P. B. Bach *Harvard Business Review Digital Articles* p2 O 6 2015

Blood-brain barrier
Resveratrol Boosts Blood-Brain Barrier *USA Today Magazine* v145 no2861 p14 F 2017

Blood cancer—Treatment
Could a Special Diet Replace Chemotherapy? K. Weintraub color *Scientific American* v316 no1 p14 Ja 2017

Blood cell physiology
DEFICIENCY NATION B12 K. Dold color *Women's Health* v14 no7 p82 S 2017

Blood circulation—Equipment & supplies
Innovation: Tiny Blood Pump M. Belfiore color *Bloomberg Businessweek* no4540 p29 O 2 2017

Blood coagulation
travel smartly J. ASHTON *Parents* v91 no12 p118 D 2016

Blood coagulation factors
Innovations Improving Lives in Canada's Hemophilia Community D. F. McCourt *Maclean's* v130 no9 p33 O 2017

Blood collection
Blood money A. KINGSTON color *Maclean's* no1 p18 F 17 2017

Blood disease treatment
BLOOD HEALTH & ORGAN TRANSPLANTS D. Wong-Rieger *Maclean's* v130 no9 p31 O 2017
STEM CELLS TO THE RESCUE! C. Hasilo *Maclean's* v130 no9

Blood Father (Film)
Blood Father M. FELL *TV Guide* v65 no11 p48 Mr 6 2017
The Gibson Quandary J. PODHORETZ *Weekly Standard* v22 no4 p38 O 3 2016
Troubled Genius R. DOUTHAT color *National Review* v68 no19 p51 O 24 2016

Blood groups
See also
RH factor
Everything You Know about Being Rh-Negative Is Wrong D. E. K. TARR *Skeptical Inquirer* v41 no3 p53 My/Je 2017

Blood plasma
Blood money A. KINGSTON color *Maclean's* no1 p18 F 17 2017
WHEN THE LAB RAT IS A SNAKE D. Engber color *New York Times Magazine* p65 My 21 2017

Blood pressure
Health Notebook color *Prevention* v69 no11 p10 N 2017
Should I be eating less salt? A. Weil color graph *Prevention* v68 no12 p26 D 2016
To Control Blood Pressure chart color *AARP: The Magazine* v59 no3A p34 Ap/My 2016

Blood pressure measurement—Equipment & supplies
iOS Accessories J. Mathis color *Macworld - Digital Edition* p66 F 2017

Blood pressure measurement—Evaluation
The (Blood) Pressure's ON C. DOW *Nutrition Action Health Letter* v43 no10 p7 D 2016

Blood pressure—Regulation
just beet it! J. Challem color *Amazing Wellness* v9 no1 p56 Wint 2017

Blood proteins
See also
Blood coagulation factors
Immunoglobulins
Broadly neutralizing antibodies to prevent HIV-1 M. S. Cohen and L. Corey diag *Science* v357 no6359 p46 O 6 2017

Blood sugar
50 SMART WAYS TO Feel Great Now! color *AARP: The Magazine* v59 no3A p31 Ap/My 2016
6 Strategies for Better Blood Sugar After Meals *Tufts University Health & Nutrition Letter* v35 no3 p7 My 2017
β-cell–mimetic designer cells provide closed-loop glycemic control Mingqi Xie, Haifeng Ye et al bibl graph *Science* v354 no6317 p1296 D 9 2016
Cinnamon and Blood Sugar *Tufts University Health & Nutrition Letter* v35 no8 p3 O 2017
A Dumpling Through the Digestive Tract A. MACMILLAN img *New York* v49 no25 p108 D 12 2016
FEEL YOUR BEST C. Guthrie color *Yoga Journal* p12 2017 Special Issue
For Lower Blood Sugar chart color *AARP: The Magazine* v59 no3A p38 Ap/My 2016
Found! A Simple Way to Slim Down C. Mchugh color *Health* v31 no1 p4 Ja 2017
Healthy Buzz color *Better Nutrition* v78 no11 p20 N 2016
Is Fruit Keeping You from Losing Weight? J. BOWDEN color *Better Nutrition* v79 no10 p64 O 2017
New Insights: Glycemic Index: The glycemic index may help predict the blood sugar effects of a food, but it doesn't tell the whole story, especially when combining foods *Tufts University Health & Nutrition Letter* v35 no7 p3 S 2017
Roughing It M. KADEY color *Muscle & Performance* v9 no9 p56 S 2017
Why You Can't Rely on the Glycemic Index for Healthy Eating *Tufts University Health & Nutrition Letter* v34 no10 p6 D 2016

Blood sugar monitoring
The Most Significant Advance in Diabetes Care Since Insulin B. Keyes-Bevan color *Maclean's* v129 no48/49 p46 D 5 2016

Blood sugar—Analysis
Take steps to prevent or reverse stress-related health problems *Harvard Health Letter* v42 no5 p1 Mr 2017

Blood transfusion
Call to halt heart trial raises vexing questions J. Couzin-Frankel color *Science* v357 no6351 p538 Ag 11 2017

Blood-vessels

Organotypic vasculature: From descriptive heterogeneity to functional pathophysiology H. G. Augustin and G. Young Koh color *Science* v357 no6353 p771 Ag 25 2017

Bloodbuy (Company)

The Harvard Contest That's Trying to Improve Health Care Delivery R. G. Hamermesh, R. Huckman et al *Harvard Business Review Digital Articles* p2 O 2 2015

Blood—Equipment & supplies

new products color *Science* v356 no6334 p209 Ap 14 2017

Bloodgood, Moon

Moon Bloodgood Joins Code Black J. Halterman *TV Guide* v65 no37 p14 S 4 2017

Bloodline (TV program)

Bloodline K. Hahn *TV Guide* v65 no25 p21 Je 2017

Bloodstains

Adulting 101 L. SAXTON color *Seventeen* v76 no12 p100 D 2016/Ja 2017

Bloodsucking animals

real vampires of planet earth [Cover story] S. Milius color graph *Science News* v192 no7 p22 O 28 2017

Bloodworth, Sandra

The Subterranean Scene M. Guerber color il *American Craft* v77 no3 p80 Je/Jl 2017

Bloody Marys (Cocktails)

Proud Mary L. Cericola and K. Rankin color *Southern Living* v52 no4 p138 Ap 2017

Bloom, Allison

COMING CLEAN K. P. Badal color *Sunset* v239 no1 p43 Jl 2017

Bloom, Amy

Jane's Addictions: A BBC presenter tells Austen's admirers what they want to know about how and where she lived *New York Times Book Review* p9 Jl 16 2017

Bloom, B. J.

A Fermi-degenerate three-dimensional optical lattice clock color diag graph *Science* v357 no6359 p90 O 6 2017

Bloom, Cameron

Penguin Bloom T. Brorby *Orion Magazine* v35 no3 p60 My/Je 2016

Thank God for That Crazy Little Bird *Audubon* v119 no1 p20 Spr 2017

Bloom, Claudia

A Happy Medium color *Martha Stewart Living* p66 Ap 2017

Bloom, Harold, 1930-

Falstaff: Give Me Life bw *Publishers Weekly* v264 no9 p89 F 27 2017

FALSTAFF: Give Me Life J. Winterson bw *New York Times Book Review* p1 Ap 23 2017

The Year in Reading [Cover story] *New York Times Book Review* p8 D 25 2016

BLOOM, J. ARTHUR

William Lind's Way of War bw *American Conservative* v15 no6 p6 N/D 2016

Bloom, Jane Ira

JANE IRA BLOOM: CHASING A MERCURIAL SOUND J. Hale bw *Downbeat* v84 no8 p46 Ag 2017

Jane Ira Bloom's Soprano Saxophone Solo on 'Big Bill' J. DURSO bw color *Downbeat* v84 no2 p96 F 2017

Bloom, Jessi

9 PERMACULTURE PRACTICES: Apply permaculture to your land to nurture its natural features *Mother Earth News* no282 p22 Je/Jl 2017

Bloom, Linda

Methodist agency leaves NYC as other institutions face rising property costs color *Christian Century* v133 no23 p17 N 9 2016

UMC court rules against consecrating gay bishops color *Christian Century* v134 no11 p13 My 24 2017

Bloom, Nicholas

WHY DO WE UNDERVALUE COMPETENT MANAGEMENT? NEITHER GREAT LEADERSHIP NOR BRILLIANT STRATEGY MATTERS WITHOUT OPERATIONAL EXCELLENCE graph il img *Harvard Business Review* v95 no5 p120 S/O 2017

A Working from Home Experiment Shows High Performers Like It Better *Harvard Business Review Digital Articles* p2 Ja 23 2015

Bloom, Paul

The Danger of Empathy S. BARON-COHEN *New York Times Book Review* p12 Ja 1 2017

Feeling No Pain N. Lagerfeld img *American Scholar* v86 no1 p124 Wint 2017

Feeling Your Pain M. M. ROSEN color *Weekly Standard* v22 no28 p38 Mr 27 2017

I Don't Feel Your Pain S. Pope color *Commonweal* v144 no11 p33 Je 16 2017

Bloom, Rachel, 1987-

CHEERS & JEERS D. HOLBROOK *TV Guide* v65 no27 p76 Je 26 2017

The CHIC I Seek color *InStyle* v24 no8 p83 Ag 2017

Crazy Ex-Girlfriend J. Jensen color *Entertainment Weekly* no1436/1437 p92 O 21 2016

Crazy Ex-Girlfriend S. Highfill, N. Abrams et al color *Entertainment Weekly* no1482/1483 p98 S 22 2017

Why TV Musicals Matter *TV Guide* v64 no48 p16 N 21 2016

Bloom, Rachel, 1987—Interviews

Wild West Covina M. WAKIM *Los Angeles Magazine* v61 no11 p76 N 2016

Bloom, Tricia Laughlin

SHARED AUTHORITY bw *Art in America* p76 O 2017

Bloomberg, Michael R.

Government and the Rise of Automation *Bloomberg Businessweek* no4528 p10 Je 26 2017

U.S. Where Washington Fails to Drive Progress, Cities Will Act color *Time* v188 no27-28 p28 D 26 2016

Bloomfield, Doni

Fighting Hearing Loss cartoon chart *Bloomberg Businessweek* no4497 p37 O 31 2016

How do you maximize the profits of a drug that treats a very rare disease? [Cover story] color *Bloomberg Businessweek* no4524 p42 My 29 2017

Pharma's Worst Nightmare cartoon *Bloomberg Businessweek* no4508 p18 Ja 23 2017

BLOOMINGDALE, HAYLEY

With GUSTO color *Vogue* v206 no12 p170 D 2016

Blooms & Linen (Company)

Little Bit Country L. BAILEY *Indianapolis Monthly* p27 F 2017

Bloomsbury Publishing PLC

Deals R. DEAHL color *Publishers Weekly* v264 no13 p10 Mr 27 2017

BLOOR, CAROLINE

ON THE ROAD color *House Beautiful* p162 Ag 2017

Blöschl, Günter

Changing climate shifts timing of European floods color graph *Science* v357 no6351 p588 Ag 11 2017

Blossom (TV program)

BLOSSOM D. Franich color *Entertainment Weekly* no1486 p36 O 13 2017

Blossom, Christopher

Master of the Seascape T. WILKINSON *Saturday Evening Post* v289 no2 p34 Mr/Ap 2017

Blotting paper

OFFICE UPGRADE: Work from home in style B. L. GRANT color *Chicago* v66 no9 p80 S 2017

BLOUNT, ROY, JR.

Life *Reader's Digest* v188 no1126 p36 D 2016/Ja 2017

Blount, Sally

Overcome Resistance to Change with Two Conversations *Harvard Business Review Digital Articles* p2 My 16 2017

Blouses

7 KEY PIECES J. HILLMAN color *Harper's Bazaar* no3656 p187 S 2017

CARE LESS, LOOK BETTER N. Sullivan bw cartoon color *Esquire* v167 no2 p66 Mr 2017

GRAPHIC CONTENT bw color *Harper's Bazaar* no3656 p262 S 2017

real style color *InStyle* v24 no2 p18 F 2017

Blouses—Evaluation

5 reasons to wear more prints color *Redbook* p68 Mr 2017

The Get-It Guide *Glamour* v114 no12 p243 D 2016

INSTANT STYLE color *InStyle* v24 no1 p46 Ja 2017

Katherine WATERSTON: EMERGING, AS SHE HAS, FROM PRESTIGIOUS DIRECTOR-DRIVEN FILMS AND. BEFORE THAT, A WHOLE LOT OF HUSTLE AND TOIL. THE

FIERCELY TALENTED ACTRESS IS BRINGING A LITTLE SCRAPPINESS BACK TO THE BLOCKBUSTER N. LYONNE *Interview* v47 no3 p80 My 2017

off the chain A. Syrett color *InStyle* v24 no1 p82 Ja 2017

Onward March bw color *Vogue* v207 no4 p220 Ap 2017

O'S FALL FASHION Look Book color *O, The Oprah Magazine* p55 S 2017

Outfits for Days R. Wang color *Glamour* v115 no9 p74 S 2017

Own The Night color *Glamour* v114 no12 p224 D 2016

Pop Art S. FRISCIA *Dance Magazine* v90 no12 p86 D 2016

Pretty Little Things color *Glamour* v114 no12 p232 D 2016

shoes you can't lose color *InStyle* v24 no3 p336 Mr 2017

the start color *InStyle* v24 no6 p25 Je 2017

STRATEGIST img *New York* v50 no13 p53 Je 26 2017

Summer Scores color *InStyle* v24 no6 p71 Je 2017

SUMMER STOCK color *Equus* no477 p26 Je 2017

Super Style E. Wilson color *InStyle* v24 no3 p310 Mr 2017

Twice? Nice! F. Kane, S. P. Nadella et al color *Glamour* v115 no3 p74 Mr 2017

A WEEK OF Awesome Outfits S. Walter color *Good Housekeeping* v264 no4 p38 Ap 2017

THE WELL-SPENT $ DOLLAR color *Harper's Bazaar* no3650 p92 F 2017

We Made Plus-Size Jeans! L. Chan color *Glamour* no8 p54 Ag 2017

WE'VE GOT YOUR BACK M. Horjus color *Backpacker* p43 Je 2017

WHERE FASHION GETS PERSONAL color *Harper's Bazaar* no3649 p181 D 2016/Ja 2017

Wide-Leg Wonders S. P. Nadella and A. Hou color *Glamour* no8 p46 Ag 2017

THE WOMAN Emma Stone E. Wilson color *InStyle* v24 no5 p92 My 2017

Blow, Jonathan

8 — THE WITNESS D. Franich *Entertainment Weekly* no1444/1445 p122 D 16 2016

Blowflies

Cooperative Undertaking B. HEINRICH color *Natural History* v125 no6 p14 Je 2017

Blown glass—Evaluation

Brad Pearce Glass L. S. FORD *Texas Monthly* v44 no11 p35 N 2016

BLOXHAM, ELEANOR

MISSION: RETHINK HIGHER ED color *Phi Kappa Phi Forum* v97 no2 p14 Summ 2017

UPWARD MOBILITY STALLS color *Phi Kappa Phi Forum* v96 no4 p16 Wint 2016

Bloxham, J.

Jupiter's interior and deep atmosphere: The initial pole-to-pole passes with the Juno spacecraft [Cover story] color graph *Science* v356 no6340 p821 My 26 2017

Blu-ray discs

THE ADVENTURES OF K'SCAPE R. SABIN *Sound & Vision* v81 no10 p8 D 2016

MQA Explained A. GRIFFIN color *Sound & Vision* v82 no8 p24 O 2017

Blu-ray technology

See also
Blu-ray discs

ULTRA HD SETTLES IN R. SABIN *Sound & Vision* v82 no1 p8 Ja 2017

Blue

color of the month: NAVY color *Good Housekeeping* v265 no4 p64a O 2017

Why So Blue? K. Owen color *Southern Living* v52 no5 p46 My 2017

BLUE, ALEXIS

TAKING A SHOT IN "TERROR" *USA Today Magazine* v145 no2860 p66 Ja 2017

Blue, Bella

ETC M. Cameran color *New Orleans Magazine* v51 no7 p151 My 2017

Blue, Debbie

WRITERS' FEAST color *Christian Century* v134 no10 p30 My 10 2017

Blue Bloods (TV program)

Blue Bloods I. Rudolph *TV Guide* v65 no19 p26 My 1 2017

Blue Bloods N. Abrams, S. Highfill et al color *Entertainment Weekly* no1482/1483 p99 S 22 2017

Blue Bloods *TV Guide* v65 no6 p37 Ja 30 2017

Blue Bottle (Company)

New York's Finest... Coffee L. HARTMAN color *Publishers Weekly* v264 no20 p(Sp)90 My 15 2017

Blue chip stocks

Blue Chips Gain Advantage chart diag *Money* v46 no9 p88 O 2017

SURVIVORS' GILT A. GARA bw chart *Forbes* v200 no3 p48 S 28 2017

Blue Chips 7000 (Music)

WHAT TO STREAM color *Entertainment Weekly* no1480 p49 S 1 2017

Blue collar workers

See also
Industrial workers

Blue-Collar HS Training Leaves Women Behind *USA Today Magazine* v145 no2859 p14 D 2016

Blue collar workers—Employment

CODE IS KING C. THOMPSON cartoon *Wired* v24 no12 p40 D 2016

Blue jay

In The Wild color *Nebraska Life* v21 no1 p58 Ja/F 2017

Blue light—Physiological effect

Blue Light Blues F. Jabr cartoon *Scientific American* v315 no5 p24 N 2016

Blue Marble Microinsurance (Company)

Designed in Davos, Tested in Zimbabwe A. Bjerga color *Bloomberg Businessweek* no4507 p37 Ja 16 2017

Blue Microphones (Company)

Out of the Blue S. Guttenberg and C. Crowley color *Sound & Vision* v82 no5 p22 Je 2017

Blue Origin LLC

A New Leader in the Suborbital Space Race M. Belfiore color *Bloomberg Businessweek* no4497 p35 O 31 2016

ROCKETEER C. FISHMAN *Smithsonian* v47 no8 p36 D 2016

Blue Ridge Mountains

An Hour Away, a World Apart D. Peak color diag *Log Home Living* v34 no3 p68 Ap 2017

the play list color *Backpacker* p8 O 2017

Blue Ridge Parkway (N.C. & Va.)

the play list color diag il *Backpacker* v45 no2 p14 Mr 2017

Blue Velvet (Film)

LAURA DERN D. Franich color *Entertainment Weekly* no1459 p34 Mr 31 2017

Blue zones (Medical geography)

The dying of the blue zones C. ROCA color *Maclean's* v129 no48/49 p30 D 5 2016

Blueberries

12 Smart Food Choices J. SCHILDHOUSE cartoon color *Muscle & Performance* v9 no5 p55 My 2017

PURPLE POWER color *Vegetarian Today* no2 p20 Ap 2017

Ripe for Easy Picking P. S. York color *Southern Living* v52 no6 p29 Je 2017

Sweet and WILD T. MARRONE color *Cabin Living* p55 Ag 2017

TANGLED UP IN BLUE[BERRIES] Y. LEE color *Runner's World* v52 no7 p18 Ag 2017

Bluebirds in art

THE ILLUSTRATED AVIARY D. BENNETT color *Audubon* v119 no3 p52 Fall 2017

Bluefin tuna

East not least for Pacific bluefin tuna D. J. Madigan, A. Boustany et al color diag *Science* v357 no6349 p356 Jl 28 2017

Bluegill

THE EVERYTHING GUIDE TO: Catching Your Lunch A. VADUKUL img *New York* v50 no13 p58 Je 26 2017

Bluegill fishing

RUNNING OF THE BULLS S. RYAN and G. BETHGE color *Outdoor Life* v224 no3 p59 Ap 2017

SLAB WORK M. Modoski color *Field & Stream* v122 no3 p24 Ag 2017

WAYNE'S WORLD J. JOHNSTON color *Outdoor Life* v224 no8 p69 O 2017

Bluegrass festivals

The Small Festival with a Big Heart Z. Glasgow color *Missouri*

Life v44 no6 p24 S 2017

Bluegrass music

THE BLUEGRASS BLUES M. JANSSEN *Washingtonian Magazine* v52 no1 p21 O 2016

Bluemner, Oscar, 1867-1938

A House in the Night color *Magazine Antiques* v184 no3 p8 My/ Je 2017

Blueprint Specials (Theatrical production)

BLUEPRINT Specials: SOLDIER MUSICALS *Stage Directions* v30 no6 p24 Je 2017

G.I. Jive M. Schulman cartoon *New Yorker* v92 no44 p9 Ja 9 2017

Blueprints

Elements of a Blueprint for ACA Replacement O. Spurgeon, III *Parks & Recreation* v52 no3 p22 Mr 2017

Blueprints for St. Louis (Short story)

Blueprints for St. Louis B. Marcus cartoon *New Yorker* v93 no30 p56 O 2 2017

BlueRail Trains (Company)

BlueRail Trains App upgrade D. Kawala *Model Railroader* v84 no9 p63 S 2017

Blues & Lonesome (Music)

Back to the Blues [Cover story] B. HIATT bw color *Rolling Stone* no1275 p40 D 1 2016

Blues Farm (Music)

Christian McBride D. OUELLETTE color *Downbeat* v84 no1 p114 Ja 2017

Blues I Felt (Music)

DAVID L. HARRIS P. Lutz color *Downbeat* v84 no7 p27 Jl 2017

Blues music—Reviews

Essential Allman D. Fricke *Rolling Stone* no1290 p49 Je 29 2017

Blues music—2011-2020—Reviews

The Late Shows HADLEY color *Downbeat* v84 no10 p64 O 2017

Bluestein, Paul

Laid Low: Inside the Crisis That Overwhelmed Europe and the IMF A. Moravcsik *Foreign Affairs* v96 no2 p177 Mr/Ap 2017

Bluetooth technology

Bluetooth Headphones: You're Killing Me K. C. POHLMANN color *Sound & Vision* v81 no10 p30 D 2016

Bose Soundlink Revolve+: An all-around excellent indoor/outdoor Bluetooth speaker S. BELLAMY color *Macworld - Digital Edition* v34 no9 p93 S 2017

HOW TO BLUETOOTH AN OLD CAR E. DYER color *Popular Mechanics* p44 Jl 2017

INVOXIA NVX 200: TURN YOUR iPHONE INTO A DESK PHONE J. R. BOOKWALTER color *Macworld - Digital Edition* v34 no9 p48 S 2017

Now Hear This K. PITSKER cartoon *Kiplinger's Personal Finance* v71 no10 p70 O 2017

Party Animal B. Ankosko and C. Crowley color *Sound & Vision* v82 no1 p18 Ja 2017

Streamin' in the Shower M. ANTONOFF cartoon color *Sound & Vision* v81 no10 p28 D 2016

Bluetooth technology—Equipment & supplies

Astell&Kern AK XB10 Bluetooth DAC and amp: Wireless, hires audio for any headphones T. NICOLAKIS color *Macworld - Digital Edition* v34 no11 p129 N 2017

smart SPEAKERS D. DICKINSON color *Better Homes & Gardens* v95 no6 p65 Je 2017

SOUND OFF N. SANTOS color *Ebony* v72 no11 p90 S 2017

Bluetooth technology—Equipment & supplies—Evaluation

CHIPOLO PLUS: A BLUETOOTH TRACKER LOUD ENOUGH TO FIND MOST ANYTHING J. R. BOOKWALTER color *Macworld - Digital Edition* p57 Mr 2017

Bluetooth technology—Evaluation

The WIRELESS RUNNER J. Dengate color *Runner's World* v52 no4 p1 My 2017

Blum, Andrew

This forecast brought to you by math color diag *Popular Science* v289 no4 p66 Jl/Ag 2017

Blum, Ben

Camo Criminals S. BECK bw *Weekly Standard* v23 no2 p42 S 18 2017

BLUM, DAN

What Do Writers Have a Right to Write? *Publishers Weekly* v263 no50 p76 D 5 2016

Blum, Edward J.

Critics of a savage empire *Christian Century* v133 no24 p36 N 23 2016

Taking white America to church color *Christian Century* v134 no9 p32 Ap 26 2017

BLUM, HOWARD

THE KREMLIN CONNECTION color *Vanity Fair* v59 no5 p85 Ap 2017

Blum, Jason

CHEAP THRILLS: FOR THE PRODUCER JASON BLUM, 'GET OUT' IS JUST THE LATEST HORROR BLOCKBUSTER IN AN EIGHT-YEAR RUN OF LEAN, INVENTIVE AND SCARILY PROFITABLE HITS R. Bradley *New York Times Magazine* p44 My 14 2017

Blum, Scott

SCOTT BLUM T. Monterosso color *Snowboarder* v29 no5 p34 Ja 2017

Blum, Travis R.

Enantioselective photochemistry through Lewis acid–catalyzed triplet energy transfer bibl chart diag graph *Science* v354 no6318 p1391 D 16 2016

Bluman, Daniel

LEG BEFORE REIN color *Practical Horseman* v45 no1 p50 Ja 2017

BLUMBERG, PERRI ORMONT

12 Superfoods You Should Be Eating [Cover story] color *Prevention* v69 no4 p60 Ap 2017

Good Food eat to Beat inflammation color *Prevention* v69 no9 p20 O 2017

Good Food: Protect Your vision color *Prevention* v69 no8 p34 Ag 2017

Healthy Choices That Really Aren't color *Prevention* v69 no5 p30 My 2017

What to Eat When You're Tired [Cover story] color *Prevention* v69 no6 p28 Je 2017

Blumberg, Peter

This Lawsuit Is Brought To You by Our Sponsors *Bloomberg Businessweek* no4502 p34 D 5 2016

Blumberg, Richard S.

The road to Crohn's disease diag *Science* v357 no6355 p976 S 8 2017

Blumberg, Rishon

Whose Job Is It to Manage Freelancers? *Harvard Business Review Digital Articles* p2 Mr 14 2016

Blume, Fred H., b. 1875

THE LAW ACCORDING TO JUSTINIAN A. Cameron *History Today* v67 no8 p91 Ag 2017

BLUME, LESLEY M. M.

Boy on Film bw color *Vogue* v207 no9 p458 S 2017

GILLIAN JACOBS bw *Vanity Fair* v59 no4 p124 Mr 2017

STEPHEN STARR bw *Vanity Fair* v59 no2 p48 F 2017

Blumenauer, Earl

Honorable Earl Blumenauer *Congressional Digest* v95 no9 p29 N 2016

Blumenthal, Daniel M.

Do Doctors Get Worse as They Get Older? *Harvard Business Review Digital Articles* p2 My 23 2017

Blumenthal, David

The Critical Skills for Leading Major Change in America's Health System *Harvard Business Review Digital Articles* p2 O 3 2017

Speeding Up the Digitization of American Health Care *Harvard Business Review Digital Articles* p2 F 22 2016

Where Both the ACA and AHCA Fall Short, and What the Health Insurance Market Really Needs *Harvard Business Review Digital Articles* p2 Mr 21 2017

White Americans' Mortality Rates Are Rising. Something Similar Happened in Russia from 1965 to 2005 *Harvard Business Review Digital Articles* p2 Je 26 2017

Blumenthal, Sidney, 1948-

Debate Prep: How the Lincoln-Douglas rivalry defined a nation F. M. BORDEWICH *New York Times Book Review* p21 Ag 20 2017

Wrestling with His Angel: The Political Life of Abraham Lincoln, Vol. II, 1849-1856 *Publishers Weekly* v264 no13 p96 Mr 27 2017

Blumhagen, Myron

AN EYE FOR NEW CROPS R. Nickel *Successful Farming* v114

no13 p37 D 2016

Blumner, Robyn

The Enlightenment Wrapped Up in an Organizational Package *Skeptical Inquirer* v41 no2 p9 Mr/Ap 2017

Blumstein, Daniel T.

Skiing for science cartoon *Science* v356 no6334 p214 Ap 14 2017

Blumstein, Jodi

How to move from High Lunge to Dhanurasana color *Yoga Journal* no294 p55 S 2017

Q: For stress relief, what is your go-to practice or pose? color *Yoga Journal* no294 p14 S 2017

Blundell, Emma

Hail to the MARES P. Schofler color *Dressage Today* v23 no11 p28 Ag 2017

Blundell, Tom L.

DNA-PKcs structure suggests an allosteric mechanism modulating DNA double-strand break repair bibl graph *Science* v355 no6324 p520 F 3 2017

Blunden, Hayley

The Sales Director Who Turned Work into a Fantasy Sports Competition *Harvard Business Review Digital Articles* p2 Mr 27 2015

Blunder, Monika

5 beauty tricks I just learned V. Kirby color *Redbook* p64 F 2017

Blundon, Jay A.

Restoring auditory cortex plasticity in adult mice by restricting thalamic adenosine signaling graph *Science* v356 no6345 p1352 Je 30 2017

Blundy, Jonathan D.

Vertically extensive and unstable magmatic systems: A unified view of igneous processes color *Science* v355 no6331 p1280 Mr 24 2017

Blunk, Jonathan

James Wright: A Life in Poetry *Publishers Weekly* v264 no27 p63 Jl 3 2017

Blunt, Emily, 1983-

The Art of Being Blunt [Cover story] A. Synnott color *InStyle* v23 no12 p238 N 2016

The Cover color *InStyle* v23 no12 p26 N 2016

Emily Blunt's Girl on a Train In Vain S. Zacharek color *Time* v188 no15 p53 O 17 2016

A GOOD YEAR FOR BAD WOMEN D. Coggan color *Entertainment Weekly* no1444/1445 p54 D 16 2016

The List color *InStyle* v23 no12 p28 N 2016

PARTY LINES img *New York* v49 no21 p118 O 17 2016

Blunt, James, 1977- Interviews

James Blunt D. Snierson color *Entertainment Weekly* no1459 p60 Mr 31 2017

Bluth, Don

The Wonderful World of Bluth M. AGRESTA *Texas Monthly* v45 no8 p40 Ag 2017

Blyskal, Jeff

GROUP GIVING: THE MORE THE MERRIER *Consumer Reports* v81 no12 p65 D 2016

Save Money il *Consumer Reports* v82 no3 p30 Mr 2017

What You Don't Know About Home Insurance chart il *Consumer Reports* v82 no8 p36 Ag 2017

Blyth, Mark

Fixing the Euro Zone and Reducing Inequality, Without Fleecing the Rich *Harvard Business Review Digital Articles* p2 Ja 9 2015

BLYTH, MYRNA

An Alluring Compromise color *AARP: The Magazine* v60 no2A p42 F/Mr 2017

Blythe, A.

Burned *Publishers Weekly* v263 no51 p129 D 12 2016

Blythe, Will

Denis Johnson: A Lot Like Prayer *New York Times Book Review* p14 Jl 30 2017

Your Angst Is Served: Marriage, career, life—disappointment comes from everywhere in these Joshua Ferris stories *New York Times Book Review* p29 My 14 2017

BMC Group Holding AG

BMC TEAMMACHINE SLR01 [Cover story] M. Phillips color *Bicycling* v58 no10 p70 N/D 2017

BMW 3 series automobiles

What Do We Mean by "Wagon"? J. Sabatini bw color *Car &*

Driver v63 no4 p72 O 2017

BMW 5 series automobiles—Evaluation

CLIMB EVERY MOUNTAIN T. Quiroga chart color *Car & Driver* v62 no11 p54 My 2017

A NEW HOPE B. Kong chart color *Motor Trend* v69 no3 p64 Mr 2017

BMW 6 series automobiles

The Apostate S. Oldham color *Car & Driver* v63 no2 p84 Ag 2017

BMW 6 series automobiles—Evaluation

B6 VS M6 J. Cammisa chart color *Motor Trend* v69 no4 p80 Ap 2017

BMW 7 series automobiles—Evaluation

DESIGNATED RIDES C. J. WASHINGTON color *Ebony* v72 no11 p91 S 2017

M Means Something New. Again J. PearleyHuffman color *Car & Driver* v62 no11 p104 My 2017

BMW automobiles

See also

BMW 3 series automobiles

BMW Z4 automobile

Easy Rider B. LUTZ, T. ANDERSON et al color *Road & Track* v68 no8 p108 My 2017

THE ONE S. SMITH color *Road & Track* v68 no10 p30 Jl 2017

SIX YEARS LATER, WE DRIVE THE MULLIGAN BMW 5-SERIES THROUGH COASTAL PORTUGAL ONCE AGAIN E. TINGWALL color *Car & Driver* v62 no8 p44 F 2017

BMW automobiles—Equipment & supplies

TACO BELL FANTASIES J. P. Huffman color *Car & Driver* v62 no7 p30 Ja 2017

BMW automobiles—Evaluation

1991 BMW 325i E. DYER color *Popular Mechanics* p60 Mr 2017

2016 BMW 740i E. Tingwall color *Car & Driver* v63 no1 p82 Jl 2017

$80K+ CARS A. Wendler color *Car & Driver* v62 no7 p22 Ja 2017

ACE OF AN 8 J. Meiners color *Car & Driver* v63 no2 p19 Ag 2017

THE BAVARIAN BEAST CIVILIZED F. Markus chart color *Motor Trend* v69 no7 p90 Jl 2017

BMW 8 Series Concept K. Pleskot color *Motor Trend* v69 no9 p16 S 2017

BMW X1 chart color *Motor Trend* v69 no1 p43 Ja 2017

CROSSBREEDING D. ZENLEA color *Road & Track* v69 no1 p88 Ag 2017

DRIVE A WEDGE J. Tate color *Car & Driver* v63 no5 p17 N 2017

FIRST LOOK: BMW Concept Z4 S. Evans color *Motor Trend* v69 no11 p16 N 2017

GARAGE M. Rechtin, K. Pleskot et al chart color diag *Motor Trend* v69 no8 p96 Ag 2017

"M" IS FOR MOST P. LERNER color *Road & Track* v68 no8 p92 My 2017

New Car Ratings chart diag *Consumer Reports* v82 no4 p40 Ap 2017

NEW FIVE, SAME JIVE C. CHILTON color *Road & Track* v68 no7 p88 Mr/Ap 2017

Road Test chart color *Consumer Reports* v82 no2 p54 F 2017

SECOND CHANCES E. JOHNSON color *Car & Driver* v62 no7 p52 Ja 2017

Silky Sophisticate *Consumer Reports* v82 no7 p63 Jl 2017

BMW M automobiles

THE 10 BEST CARS FOR 2017 color *Car & Driver* v62 no7 p114 Ja 2017

BMW M automobiles—Evaluation

B6 VS M6 J. Cammisa chart color *Motor Trend* v69 no4 p80 Ap 2017

Best FAST CAR for Around $50K K. SINTUMUANG color *Esquire* v166 no4 p74 N 2016

Redemption Songs A. Robinson color graph *Car & Driver* v62 no7 p110 Ja 2017

ROAD TESTED E. DYER color *Popular Mechanics* p36 Ap 2017

BMW motorcycle

Service R. NIERLICH color *Cycle World* v55 no10 p56 N 2016

WHY I LOVE IT E. GAUKEL color *Treasures* v5 no5 p64 Ap/My 2016

Your Getaway Vehicle M. R. SALLEE bw cartoon color *Men's*

Health v32 no5 p32 Je 2017

BMW motorcycle—Evaluation

2017 BMW R nineT SCRAMBLER J. Gustafson color *Cycle World* v56 no1 p8 Ja/F 2017

2018 BMW G310R D. Canet color *Cycle World* v56 no2 p48 Mr 2017

BMW X3 sport utility vehicle

CROSSING OVER S. SMITH color diag *Road & Track* v68 no10 p54 Jl 2017

BMX Bandits (Film)

Hello! L. Brown color *InStyle* v24 no7 p16 Jl 2017

BNSF Railway

9 THINGS I CAN'T LOOK AWAY FROM P. FRIEDERICI *Orion Magazine* v36 no1 p6 Ja/F 2017

Bo-hae Yu

COURT of APPEALS WITH REBEL GOOD *Tennis* v52 no6 p6 N/D 2016

Bo Hu

The DNA-sensing AIM2 inflammasome controls radiation-induced cell death and tissue injury bibl color graph *Science* v354 no6313 p765 N 11 2016

Bo Wen

Electron optics with p-n junctions in ballistic graphene bibl graph *Science* v353 no6307 p1522 S 30 2016

Bo Xu

Rb1 and Trp53 cooperate to suppress prostate cancer lineage plasticity, metastasis, and antiandrogen resistance bibl graph *Science* v355 no6320 p1 Ja 6 2017

Bo Zhang

A chemical genetic roadmap to improved tomato flavor bibl graph *Science* v355 no6323 p391 Ja 27 2017

Generation of influenza A viruses as live but replication-incompetent virus vaccines bibl graph *Science* v354 no6316 p1170 D 2 2016

Boachon, Benoît

Emission of volatile organic compounds from petunia flowers is facilitated by an ABC transporter diag *Science* v356 no6345 p1386 Je 30 2017

Boada, Jason

Expand innovation finance via crowdfunding bibl color graph map *Science* v354 no6319 p1526 D 23 2016

Boahen, Kwabena

Selective modulation of cortical state during spatial attention bibl graph *Science* v354 no6316 p1140 D 2 2016

Boal, Mark—Interviews

The view from Hollywood V. M. Gezari color *Columbia Journalism Review* p42 Fall/Wint 2016

Boal, Peter

SHINE ON: George Balanchine's Jewels celeb rates its 50th anniversary this year. But what is it that makes this plotless full-length so timeless? *Danee Magazine* v91 no7 p35 Jl 2017

Stuck in the Middle K. SCHWAB *Dance Magazine* v91 no1 p126 Ja 2017

Bo'an Li

Expert consensus on point-of-care testing *Science* v354 no6319 p15 D 23 2016

Recommendations on the management and use of POCT in medical institutions (nosocomial) *Science* v354 no6319 p13 D 23 2016

Board books—Sales & prices

Board Book Sales Soar chart *Publishers Weekly* v264 no17 p5 Ap 24 2017

Board Books Have Big Week chart *Publishers Weekly* v264 no30 p5 Jl 24 2017

Sales Bounce for Board Books chart *Publishers Weekly* v264 no16 p5 Ap 17 2017

Board gamers

Game changers A. Chuang bibl color *Science* v355 no6325 p587 F 10 2017

Board games

See also

Chess

Monopoly (Game)

Board-Game Theory J. MORIARITY cartoon *Walrus* v13 no9 p23 N 2016

LAST CHANCE: A classic board game gets a climate-change

makeover J. BROWNING and S. BROWNING color *Orion Magazine* v36 no1 p32 Ja/F 2017

Monopoly's Feminist History J. Lance bw color *Glamour* v115 no5 p20 My 2017

Pop-Tarts for Dinner J. KAY *Walrus* v14 no4 p66 My 2017

Sorry Not Sorry M. Rubino *Indianapolis Monthly* v12 no40 p10 Ag 2017

What's In a Board Game? S. Begley color *Time* v189 no22 p16 Je 12 2017

Board games—Evaluation

SECRET HITLER J. WALKER color *Reason* v49 no4 p76 Ag/S 2017

Board games—Reviews

Game changers A. Chuang bibl color *Science* v355 no6325 p587 F 10 2017

Board of Governors of the Federal Reserve System (U.S.)

'Chairman Cohn' Has a Nice Ring to It J. Smialek, M. Abelson et al color graph *Bloomberg Businessweek* no4533 p32 Ag 7 2017

DON'T LET THE FED BE ANOTHER OBAMACARE color *Forbes* v199 no4 p13 Ap 25 2017

The Fed Keeps Its Eye on Swings in the Stock Market M. Boesler color *Bloomberg Businessweek* no4518 p15 Ap 10 2017

The Fed Primes the Stock Pump T. Tepper chart *Money* v45 no10 p96 N 2016

GET READY FOR A BOND MELTDOWN D. DREMAN *Forbes* v198 no8 p66 D 20 2016

A Preview of the Fed Under Trump J. J. SIEGEL color *Kiplinger's Personal Finance* v71 no2 p59 F 2017

The Push and Pull Of Politics P. Coy cartoon *Bloomberg Businessweek* no4493 p22 O 3 2016

Resources *Bridges (Federal Reserve Bank of St. Louis)* p6 Spr 2017

Rutgers Over Princeton In Epic Nerd Fight L. Nguyen color *Bloomberg Businessweek* no4510 p34 F 6 2017

Trump And Yellen: Besties? P. Coy, S. Matthews et al color *Bloomberg Businessweek* no4502 p12 D 5 2016

UNLOCKING THE VAULT FOR SHAREHOLDERS diag *Fortune* v174 no8 p112 D 15 2016

U.S. ECONOMY NEARS GOALS OF MAXIMUM EMPLOYMENT AND PRICE STABILITY *Vital Speeches of the Day* v82 no10 p307 O 2016

Board of Governors of the Federal Reserve System (U.S.). Consumer Financial Protection Bureau

Consumer Bureau at Risk *Congressional Digest* v96 no2 p11 F 1 2017

The Fall of Warren's CFPB? S. Woolley and E. Dexheimer bw *Bloomberg Businessweek* no4500 p36 N 21 2016

How long can a progressive federal agency, the Consumer Financial Protection Bureau, stand firm against the deregulatory pressures of the Trump administration? G. Rivlin *New York Times Magazine* p18 Ap 23 2017

How to Make Lawsuits Work for Consumers *Bloomberg Businessweek* no4532 p10 Jl 31 2017

Lending Giant Gets Sued K. Mulhere color *Money* v46 no2 p21 Mr 2017

Protecting Consumers' Right to Arbitration T. J. DONOHUE *Weekly Standard* v22 no46 p29 Ag 14 2017

Board of Governors of the Federal Reserve System (U.S.)—Officials & employees

The Fed Is Driving Blind P. Coy color graph *Bloomberg Businessweek* no4527 p43 Je 19 2017

THE FED NEEDS A NEW HEAD—AND POLICY *Forbes* v198 no8 p15 D 20 2016

A Safe Choice to Regulate Banks P. Coy color *Bloomberg Businessweek* no4519 p35 Ap 24 2017

Boarding school students

Q&A: Beyond Boarding School color *Maclean's* v130 no9 p66 O 2017

Boarding schools—United States—History—19th century

Acting Out Assimilation J. R. GRAM *American Indian Quarterly* v40 no3 p251 Summ 2016

BOARDMAN, CRAIG

Future of space color *Issues in Science & Technology* v33 no1 p15 Fall 2016

Boards of directors

Boards Aren't as Global as Their Businesses G. L. Davis *Harvard*

v108 no8 p46 Ag 2016

Dealers Choice D. J. HARDING color *Power & Motoryacht* v34 no11 p132 N 2017

Delusions of Grandeur M. PETERS color *Power & Motoryacht* v32 no11 p44 N 2016

Private Party D. Harding and S. MURRAY color *Power & Motoryacht* v33 no2 p32 F 2017

TAKE THE BEACH M. WERLING *Sea Magazine* v109 no4 p6 Ap 2017

TENDER CHOICES T. HALE color *Sail* v48 no4 p50 Ap 2017

Boat ramps

Learn to Launch C. CASWELL *Boating World* v38 no6 p14 Je 2017

RULE THE RAMP D. T. CLARKE *Boating World* v38 no5 p54 My 2017

Boat restoration

Living History J. Y. Wood color *Power & Motoryacht* v34 no6 p16 Je 2017

The More Things Change... D. J. Harding color *Power & Motoryacht* v34 no6 p12 Je 2017

Boat sales & prices

currents *Boating World* v38 no6 p10 Je 2017

SHOWCASE: FEATURED BROKERAGE BOATS color *Sea Magazine* v109 no8 p69 Ag 2017

SUMMER SHOWTIME: THE PREMIER BOATING SHOW FOR THE SAN DIEGO AREA IS BACK ON FATHER'S DAY WEEKEND S. SHIBATA color *Sea Magazine* v109 no6 pCA-1 Je 2017

Sweat the Details: It's a great time to sell a boat. Here's how to get it ready G. MANSFIELD color *Sea Magazine* v109 no8 p52 Ag 2017

Boat trailers

Create a User-Friendly Trailer C. CASWELL *Boating World* v38 no2 p14 F 2017

Learn to Launch C. CASWELL *Boating World* v38 no6 p14 Je 2017

Trailers Get Personal G. MANSFIELD *Boating World* v38 no4 p12 Ap 2017

Boat trailers—Maintenance & repair

12 Trailer Tire Maintenance Tips C. CASWELL *Boating World* v38 no5 p14 My 2017

Procrastination Doesn't Pay C. Caswell *Boating World* v37 no9 p12 N/D 2016

Year-Round Trailer Maintenance C. CASWELL *Boating World* v38 no1 p18 Ja 2017

Boat Trouble (Short story)

Boat Trouble S. SWAN color *Walrus* v14 no6 p50 Jl/Ag 2017

Boatbuilders

Don Aronow: The Legend in My Corner M. PETERS color *Power & Motoryacht* v33 no2 p36 F 2017

The Future Faces of Boatbuilding D. HARDING JR. color *Power & Motoryacht* v33 no1 p32 Ja 2017

Walking the Walk M. PETERS color *Power & Motoryacht* v34 no10 p42 O 2017

Boatbuilding

Aussie Adventure D. Harding Jr. *Power & Motoryacht* v34 no9 p18 S 2017

Creating Comfort M. SMITH color *Power & Motoryacht* v34 no9 p105 S 2017

Cutting Class color *Power & Motoryacht* v34 no8 p18 Ag 2017

DON'T MISS LIST SEPTEMBER 2016 *Sea Magazine* v108 no9 pCA-7 S 2016

HOT ROD's Sea Monster T. Taylor bw color *Hot Rod* v69 no12 p52 D 2016

Seeing into the Future [Cover story] J. MOSER color *Power & Motoryacht* v34 no6 p22 Je 2017

A Solid Half-Century P. Nielsen *Sail* v48 no10 p6 O 2017

Time for a Change M. SMITH color *Power & Motoryacht* v33 no4 p99 Ap 2017

What a Concept *Sea Magazine* v109 no4 p14 Ap 2017

Boaters (Persons)

See also

Sailors

7 REASONS FOR BOATING'S EXPANDING APPEAL: OWNING AND OPERATING A VESSEL HAS BECOME EASIER AND MORE ACCESSIBLE FOR A WIDER VARIETY OF

PEOPLE Z. PROCHAZKA *Sea Magazine* v109 no9 p48 S 2017

Acing the Tests *Boating World* v38 no1 p40 Ja 2017

ANCHORS, OBEY M. WERLING *Sea Magazine* v109 no9 p6 S 2017

At a Glance *Sea Magazine* v109 no9 p58 S 2017

BET YOU DON'T KNOW SPORTFISHING BOATS T. SERIO *Sea Magazine* v109 no9 p54 S 2017

Budget Cuts Bad for Boaters A. JONES *Boating World* v38 no5 p4 My 2017

CAPTIVATED BY CRUISING H. Steinberger *Sea Magazine* v108 no9 p20 S 2016

CRUISING INTO TRANQUILITY D. Hislop *Sea Magazine* v109 no4 p20 Ap 2017

DON'T MISS LIST: SEPTEMBER 2017 *Sea Magazine* v109 no9 pCA-6 S 2017

DON'T MISS LIST SEPTEMBER 2017 *Sea Magazine* v109 no9 pPNW-15 S 2017

A Draining Experience G. MICHAL *Boating World* v38 no1 p36 Ja 2017

Drill Instructor B. ARRINGTON color *Power & Motoryacht* v34 no9 p34 S 2017

HOT TIME IN MEXICO P. RAINS *Sea Magazine* v108 no9 p18 S 2016

Keyboard Warriors M. PETERS color *Power & Motoryacht* v34 no9 p28 S 2017

LONG NIGHT IN FOSSIL BAY E. LEE *Sea Magazine* v109 no9 p22 S 2017

MEET DEBBIE DUNNE color *Sea Magazine* v109 no8 pCA-8 Ag 2017

METAL BOAT Q & A B. M. KENYON *Sea Magazine* v108 no9 p54 S 2016

MUSEUMS FOR EVERYONE IN BRITISH COLUMBIA *Sea Magazine* v108 no9 pPNW-1 S 2016

MY TOWN J. Sugarman color *Washingtonian Magazine* v52 no7 p159 Ap 2017

NAME GAME *Sea Magazine* v109 no9 p11 S 2017

NAME THE BOAT S. SHIBATA *Sea Magazine* v109 no9 p12 S 2017

NEW & IMPROVED MARINA PUERTO ESCONDIDO: THE MARINA NEAR LORETO BENEFITS FROM AN OWNERSHIP GROUP THAT LOVES TO GO BOATING P. RAINS *Sea Magazine* v109 no9 p18 S 2017

THE NEW KAYAKTIVISM C. MIHELL color *Canoe & Kayak Magazine* v45 no1 p34 Wint 2017

NEW KID IN THE WATER: THE SOUTHERN CALIFORNIA BOAT SHOW WILL FILL CABRILLO WAY MARINA WITH 200 BOATS IN LATE SEPTEMBER *Sea Magazine* v109 no9 pCA-1 S 2017

ONBOARD HERB GARDENS: NO ONE HAS TO GIVE UP THE TASTE OF FRESH HERBS WHILE CRUISING D. HISLOP *Sea Magazine* v109 no9 pPNW-13 S 2017

READY, SET, GO D. HISLOP *Sea Magazine* v108 no10 pPNW-8 O 2016

RUN IT HARD D. HISLOP *Sea Magazine* v108 no10 p34 O 2016

SAFE & SECURE BY SUNSET P. RAINS *Sea Magazine* v109 no4 p18 Ap 2017

SEPTEMBER QUESTIONS *Sea Magazine* v109 no9 p61 S 2017

Silver Lining D. J. Harding color *Power & Motoryacht* v34 no11 p38 N 2017

Situational Awareness B. ARRINGTON color *Power & Motoryacht* v34 no11 p54 N 2017

TAKING HEAT *Sea Magazine* v109 no9 p30 S 2017

TGIF: FRIDAY HARBOR IS HOME TO ART, WHALES AND LOCAL FLAVOR D. HISLOP *Sea Magazine* v109 no9 pPNW-1 S 2017

Boaters (Persons)—Interviews

MEET HALEY STICKLER *Sea Magazine* v108 no10 pCA-9 O 2016

Boaters (Persons)—Services for

MEXICO MADE EASIER C. P. RAINS *Sea Magazine* v109 no1 p18 Ja 2017

Boaters (Persons)—Societies, etc.

UP FOR A CHALLENGE? WHETHER IT'S THE GETTING THERE OR THE RELAXING ATMOSPHERE, YOU'LL FIND SOMETHING TO ENJOY AND REMEMBER ABOUT SILVA BAY *Sea Magazine* v108 no9 pPNW-12 S 2016

Boathouses

THE HOUSE AT ALLEN COVE M. ALLEN *Yankee* v81 no5 p40 S/O 2017

SHOWCASE: FEATURED BROKERAGE BOATS. color *Sea Magazine* v109 no8 p69 Ag 2017

Boating accidents

BROKEN WINDOWS K. TENNEFOSS *Sea Magazine* v109 no1 p24 Ja 2017

cabin capers P. SULLIVAN cartoon *Cabin Living* p88 Ap 2017

Darkness, Speed, and Bad Decisions B. ELLISON color *Power & Motoryacht* v32 no12 p24 D 2016

ESCAPE FROM STATEN ISLAND K. Pears color *Sail* v48 no1 p42 Ja 2017

Head toward the Island B. Wagner map *Sail* v48 no9 p26 S 2017

LUCKY AND GOOD J. MACDONALD and S. MACDONALD *Sea Magazine* v109 no4 p12 Ap 2017

Boating equipment

See also

Electronics on boats

Be Safer at Sea: Know what to inspect, what equipment to have and which procedures to practice Z. Prochazka color *Sea Magazine* v109 no7 p40 Jl 2017

Be Your Own Boat Doctor M. SMITH color *Power & Motoryacht* v34 no7 p71 Jl 2017

Breeze On! S. Fortescue chart color *Sail* v48 no11 p50 N 2017

Cloak and Dagger B. PIKE bw *Power & Motoryacht* v34 no7 p136 Jl 2017

Coam Over J. JOHNSON *Boating World* v38 no6 p24 Je 2017

DOCKBOX: GEAR, TOOLS AND TOYS *Sea Magazine* v109 no9 p34 S 2017

Gear P. NIELSEN color *Sail* v48 no11 p30 N 2017

Gear P. Nielsen color *Sail* v48 no6 p30 Je 2017

Ice Boxes & Refrigeration D. Everitt color *Sail* v48 no7 p47 Jl 2017

KEEP PONTOON TUBES SHIPSHAPE: They keep the family afloat, so make sure the pontoon's logs are ready for action B. M. KENYON color *Boating World* v38 no7 p52 Jl 2017

Let's Go Racing A. JONES color *Boating World* v38 no7 p24 Jl 2017

MOUNTING OPTIONS F. LANIER *Sea Magazine* v109 no9 p28 S 2017

Queen of the Fleet L. BECKETT chart color *Power & Motoryacht* v34 no9 p90 S 2017

TUBE CARE S. SHIBATA color *Boating World* v38 no7 p54 Jl 2017

Boating equipment—Maintenance & repair

Think First G. MICHAL *Boating World* v38 no6 p22 Je 2017

Boating industry

See also

Canoe industry

Yacht industry

Attitude Adjustment D. Harding *Power & Motoryacht* v33 no2 p26 F 2017

MAKE THE SWITCH F. LANIER *Sea Magazine* v109 no4 p28 Ap 2017

Minorca 42 Islander J. Y. Wood color *Power & Motoryacht* v34 no9 p50 S 2017

NEWPORT BOAT SHOW XLIV *Sea Magazine* v109 no4 p8 Ap 2017

Private Party D. Harding and S. MURRAY color *Power & Motoryacht* v33 no2 p32 F 2017

TAKE THE BEACH M. WERLING *Sea Magazine* v109 no4 p6 Ap 2017

XO 270 Cabin OB B. Pike color *Power & Motoryacht* v34 no9 p47 S 2017

Boating industry—Congresses

On The Road Again A. Jones *Boating World* v37 no9 p4 N/D 2016

Boating industry—Equipment & supplies

Let the Sun Shine In A. JONES color *Boating World* v38 no7 p38 Jl 2017

A new Gunboat Takes Shape color *Sail* v48 no3 p22 Mr 2017

STUFF YOU WANT color *Boating World* v38 no7 p32 Jl 2017

Boating industry—Law & legislation

THINKING CAP M. WERLING *Sea Magazine* v108 no10 p6 O 2016

Boating injuries

Fine-tune Your Endgame J. BROWNLEE color *Power & Motoryacht* v34 no7 p24 Jl 2017

Boating instruction

WATERFRONT D. J. HARDING color *Power & Motoryacht* v32 no11 p40 N 2016

Boating laws

OFF THE CHARTERS: AUTHORITIES ARE CRACKING DOWN ON UNAUTHORIZED PASSENGER-FOR-HIRE ACTIVITIES IN SOUTHERN CALIFORNIA color *Sea Magazine* v109 no7 pCA-6 Jl 2017

Boating techniques

HOW TO HOP DOWN BAJA IN NOVEMBER P. RAINS *Sea Magazine* v108 no10 p18 O 2016

RUN IT HARD D. HISLOP *Sea Magazine* v108 no10 p34 O 2016

BOATNER, KAY

CHEW ON THIS SWEDISH MEATBALLS *National Geographic Kids* no466 p9 D 2016/Ja 2017

Guinness Guinness Records color *National Geographic Kids* no474 p5 O 2017

History's Greatest Hits cartoon *National Geographic Kids* no473 p10 S 2017

History's Greatest Hits color *National Geographic Kids* no465 p7 N 2016

History's Greatest Hits *National Geographic Kids* no469 p11 Ap 2017

Boats & boating

See also

Boating industry

Canoes & canoeing

Catamarans

Electric boats

Houseboats

Inflatable boats

Motorboats

Pontoon boating

Rafting (Sports)

Sailboats

Skiffs

Steamboats

Yachting

100 years OF BOATS [Cover story] A. Cort color *Sail* v48 no8 p30 Ag 2017

The 12s are Better than Ever! color *Sail* v48 no6 p18 Je 2017

2017 A Look Ahead D. Harding Jr., B. Pike et al color map *Power & Motoryacht* v32 no12 p38 D 2016

25 TRENDS ARE MAKING BOATING BETTER Z. PROCHAZKA *Sea Magazine* v109 no4 p50 Ap 2017

7 REASONS FOR BOATING'S EXPANDING APPEAL: OWNING AND OPERATING A VESSEL HAS BECOME EASIER AND MORE ACCESSIBLE FOR A WIDER VARIETY OF PEOPLE Z. PROCHAZKA *Sea Magazine* v109 no9 p48 S 2017

8 Safety Hacks T. KEER *Boating World* v38 no1 p20 Ja 2017

Acing the Tests *Boating World* v38 no1 p40 Ja 2017

ADVANCEMENT FOR ALL C. CASWELL color *Sea Magazine* v109 no7 p46 Jl 2017

All Hands on Deck color *Sail* v48 no6 p8 Je 2017

Anchor Locker Arrangement D. Everitt cartoon *Sail* v48 no6 p56 Je 2017

ANCHORS, OBEY M. WERLING *Sea Magazine* v109 no9 p6 S 2017

Are You Ready? G. MICHAL *Boating World* v38 no4 p18 Ap 2017

ART AND CULTURE PIT STOPS IN PUGET SOUND: LEARN THE RICH HISTORY OF THE SAN JUAN ISLANDS AT ONE OF THESE MUSEUMS ON PUGET SOUND D. HISLOP *Sea Magazine* v109 no9 pPNW-8 S 2017

ASK A BROKER *Sea Magazine* v108 no12 p57 D 2016

ASK SAIL D. CASEY, B. HANCOCK et al color *Sail* v48 no2 p70 F 2017

ask the experts *Boating World* v38 no3 p24 Mr 2017

AT LEISURE *Sea Magazine* v109 no4 p1 Ap 2017

Aussie Adventure D. Harding Jr. *Power & Motoryacht* v34 no9 p18 S 2017

BAIT & SWITCH color *Sea Magazine* v109 no6 p30 Je 2017

BAY AREA BOAT STOP: REDWOOD CITY IS A LUXURIOUS AND WELCOMING RETREAT IN THE HEART OF

SILICON VALLEY color map *Sea Magazine* v109 no6 pCA-6 Je 2017

Bedding Hardware B. Pike color *Power & Motoryacht* v34 no10 p120 O 2017

Be Safer at Sea: Know what to inspect, what equipment to have and which procedures to practice Z. Prochazka color *Sea Magazine* v109 no7 p40 Jl 2017

Best Boating Week A. JONES *Boating World* v38 no4 p4 Ap 2017

BOAT BUILDERS BUILD BETTER BOATS Z. PROCHAZKA *Sea Magazine* v109 no2 p50 F 2017

BOAT-CRAZY DAKOTANS K. Hunhoff *South Dakota Magazine* v33 no2 p6 Jl/Ag 2017

BOATING MONOGAMY *Sea Magazine* v109 no7 p25 Jl 2017

Cabin Condensation D. Everitt cartoon *Sail* v48 no11 p58 N 2017

A Canoeist's Eureka Moment bw color *Yankee* p24 Jl 2017

Catalina 425 P. Nielsen cartoon color *Sail* v48 no1 p26 Ja 2017

Charged Up N. Calder color *Sail* v47 no12 p46 D 2016

CLOSE TO HOME N. WARREN color *Canoe & Kayak Magazine* v45 no1 p36 Wint 2017

COMMON SENSE AND THE GOLDEN RULE GO A LONG WAY D. HISLOP *Sea Magazine* v109 no1 p46 Ja 2017

A COMMUNITY EFFORT D. HISLOP *Sea Magazine* v109 no1 pPNW-14 Ja 2017

Creating Comfort M. SMITH color *Power & Motoryacht* v34 no9 p105 S 2017

CROSSOVER CAT S. SHIBATA *Boating World* v38 no3 p8 Mr 2017

CRUISING TIPS T. Cunliffe color *Sail* v48 no10 p62 O 2017

Diesel Issues N. Calder color *Sail* v48 no3 p54 Mr 2017

The Difference Matters G. MICHAL *Boating World* v38 no2 p30 F 2017

DINGHIES DONE RIGHT G. MANSFIELD *Sea Magazine* v109 no1 p50 Ja 2017

DO AS I SAY, NOT AS I DO B. CALVERT *Sea Magazine* v109 no1 p23 Ja 2017

DOCKBOX: GEAR, TOOLS AND TOYS *Sea Magazine* v109 no9 p34 S 2017

Do Como Right K. LAGRAVE color *Conde Nast Traveler* v52 no2 p14 F 2017

DON'T GET HOLIDAZED M. WERLING *Sea Magazine* v108 no12 p5 D 2016

DON'T MISS LIST AUGUST 2016 *Sea Magazine* v108 no8 pPNW-14 Ag 2016

DON'T MISS LIST JULY 2017 *Sea Magazine* v109 no7 pPNW-18 Jl 2017

DON'T MISS LIST: JUNE 2017 *Sea Magazine* v109 no6 pPNW-14 Je 2017

DON'T MISS LIST: SEPTEMBER 2017 *Sea Magazine* v109 no9 pCA-6 S 2017

DON'T MISS LIST SEPTEMBER 2017 *Sea Magazine* v109 no9 pPNW-15 S 2017

DOWN MEXICO WAY D. McLennan color *Sail* v48 no10 p64 O 2017

A Draining Experience G. MICHAL *Boating World* v38 no1 p36 Ja 2017

EVENTS *Sea Magazine* v109 no7 pCA-10 Jl 2017

Exploring Parts Unknown J. Y. Wood color *Power & Motoryacht* v33 no4 p24 Ap 2017

EXPOSURE D. j. Harding color *Power & Motoryacht* v32 no11 p70 N 2016

EXPOSURE S. Murray color *Power & Motoryacht* v33 no4 p48 Ap 2017

EXPOSURE S. Murray color *Power & Motoryacht* v34 no8 p38 Ag 2017

Fact or Superstition? J. BROWNLEE color *Power & Motoryacht* v34 no9 p32 S 2017

Fine-tune Your Endgame J. BROWNLEE color *Power & Motoryacht* v34 no7 p24 Jl 2017

Following the Dream P. Nielsen *Sail* v48 no2 p4 F 2017

Forever Oil G. MICHAL *Boating World* v38 no3 p47 Mr 2017

FORMIDABLE FEATURES M. WERLING *Sea Magazine* v109 no7 p4 Jl 2017

Frankenboat S. SHIBATA and A. Jones *Boating World* v38 no4 p6 Ap 2017

A FRESH LOOK M. WERLING *Sea Magazine* v108 no10 p6 O 2016

Fuel's Paradise P. Gutowski color diag *Sail* v48 no2 p64 F 2017

GAME ON! H. STEINBERGER *Boating World* v38 no2 p54 F 2017

GATEWAY TO THE ISLANDS: CHANNEL ISLANDS HARBOR IS FAMILY AND FOODIE FRIENDLY, AND ITS LOCATION IS IDEAL FOR A TRIP TO THE OFFSHORE PARK AND SANCTUARY S. SHIBATA color map *Sea Magazine* v109 no7 pCA-1 Jl 2017

Go Big, or Go Small P. FREDERIKSEN color *Power & Motoryacht* v32 no12 p22 D 2016

The Hard Way B. Bleyer cartoon color *Sail* v47 no12 p12 D 2016

Havana, Cuba S. Murray color *Power & Motoryacht* v33 no2 p60 F 2017

HEALING WATERS D. SHIVELY color *Canoe & Kayak Magazine* v45 no1 p46 Wint 2017

HELP CREATE THE NEXT GENERATION OF BOATERS M. WERLING *Sea Magazine* v108 no8 p5 Ag 2016

HOT TIME IN MEXICO P. RAINS *Sea Magazine* v108 no9 p18 S 2016

How Do You Know When It's Time to Give Up? B. Wagner color *Sail* v48 no2 p13 F 2017

How to Choose a Cruising Crew J. Fredrick bw color *Sail* v48 no6 p10 Je 2017

I'm the Son of a Sailor K. Danielewicz color *Sail* v48 no2 p10 F 2017

Installing Deck Lighting C. REYNOLDS *Boating World* v38 no4 p20 Ap 2017

THE INTERPRETATION OF DREAMS B. PIKE bw *Power & Motoryacht* v34 no6 p144 Je 2017

IN THE SHOP, ON THE WATER color *Popular Mechanics* p57 S 2017

Intro to Electronic Charts F. LANIER *Sea Magazine* v108 no8 p40 Ag 2016

Land Rover BAR in the Driver's Seat? color *Sail* v48 no2 p24 F 2017

Light Refreshment P. Nielsen color *Sail* v48 no3 p56 Mr 2017

LOGBOOK D. Harding Jr. *Power & Motoryacht* v33 no3 p26 Mr 2017

The Long Run B. PIKE color *Power & Motoryacht* v33 no1 p84 Ja 2017

THE LONG WAY HOME J. HARTJOY color map *Sail* v48 no2 p52 F 2017

Look! Kangaroos? B. PIKE cartoon *Power & Motoryacht* v34 no8 p160 Ag 2017

Make it Final with Vinyl W. SHEPPARD *Boating World* v38 no1 p28 Ja 2017

Making Do D. Casey color *Sail* v48 no8 p11 Ag 2017

Making Sound Choices P. FREDERIKSEN color *Power & Motoryacht* v34 no7 p22 Jl 2017

A Mark in Time M. PETERS color *Power & Motoryacht* v34 no7 p20 Jl 2017

Martha's Summer chart color *Martha Stewart Living* p4 Jl/Ag 2017

MAY'S QUESTION: Is a marine survey absolutely necessary, and how can my broker help with it? *Sea Magazine* v109 no5 p61 My 2017

MEET EAMON O'BYRNE *Sea Magazine* v108 no8 pCA-4 Ag 2016

MIDSEASON PREVENTIVE MAINTENANCE: PERFORM SOME QUICK AND SIMPLE CHECKS FOR A CAREFREE BALANCE OF THE BOATING SEASON D. HISLOP bw color *Sea Magazine* v109 no8 p28 Ag 2017

Monohulls Forever! color *Sail* v48 no2 p8 F 2017

MOUNTING OPTIONS F. LANIER *Sea Magazine* v109 no9 p28 S 2017

Move Over, Gilligan! B. PIKE bw *Power & Motoryacht* v33 no4 p184 Ap 2017

NAME GAME *Sea Magazine* v109 no9 p11 S 2017

name the boat *Boating World* v38 no3 p64 Mr 2017

NAMETHEBOAT *Sea Magazine* v109 no2 p96 F 2017

NAME THE BOAT *Sea Magazine* v109 no4 p12 Ap 2017

NAME THE BOAT S. SHIBATA *Sea Magazine* v109 no9 p12 S 2017

New Adventures, Same Kid From the Boatyard D. Harding Jr. *Power & Motoryacht* v33 no1 p24 Ja 2017

NEW & IMPROVED MARINA PUERTO ESCONDIDO: THE

MARINA NEAR LORETO BENEFITS FROM AN OWNER-SHIP GROUP THAT LOVES TO GO BOATING P. RAINS *Sea Magazine* v109 no9 p18 S 2017

NEW KID IN THE WATER: THE SOUTHERN CALIFORNIA BOAT SHOW WILL FILL CABRILLO WAY MARINA WITH 200 BOATS IN LATE SEPTEMBER *Sea Magazine* v109 no9 pCA-1 S 2017

New Wave A. JONES *Boating World* v38 no2 p44 F 2017

OFFSHORE AND MORE S. SHIBATA *Boating World* v38 no2 p8 F 2017

ONBOARD HERB GARDENS: NO ONE HAS TO GIVE UP THE TASTE OF FRESH HERBS WHILE CRUISING D. HISLOP *Sea Magazine* v109 no9 pPNW-13 S 2017

The Other French Boats D. Kent cartoon color *Sail* v48 no1 p24 Ja 2017

Oy of the Hurricane G. MICHAL *Boating World* v38 no4 p46 Ap 2017

PICTURESQUE PORT OF EDMONDS: EDMONDS HAS NOT LOST SIGHT OF WHAT MAKES IT UNIQUE D. HISLOP color map *Sea Magazine* v109 no6 pPNW-10 Je 2017

Pretty & Practical J. WOOLDRIDGE color *Power & Motoryacht* v34 no9 p78 S 2017

Pro-style Racing for the Masses color *Sail* v48 no2 p26 F 2017

PURSUIT OF PASSION D. HARDING JR. bw chart color *Power & Motoryacht* v34 no8 p52 Ag 2017

Q + A *Boating World* v38 no1 p30 Ja 2017

Q+A *Boating World* v38 no2 p23 F 2017

Q+A G. Michal, Z. Prochazka et al *Boating World* v38 no5 p26 My 2017

Rebuild a Rotten Transom J. JOHNSON *Boating World* v38 no3 p22 Mr 2017

THE ROARING FORTIES J. HARTJOY color map *Sail* v48 no1 p36 Ja 2017

The SAILING SCENE C. Hughson, J. Edenfield et al color *Sail* v48 no10 p8 O 2017

Self-Inflicted Wounds C. J. Doane color *Sail* v48 no2 p96 F 2017

SET IT STRAIGHT: MAKE SURE THE MAGNETIC COM-PASS IS READY WHEN NEEDED D. HISLOP color *Sea Magazine* v109 no7 p22 Jl 2017

THE SHORE BOAR D. DRAPER bw color *Field & Stream* v122 no1 p15 My 2017

SHOWCASE FEATURED BROKERAGE BOATS *Sea Magazine* v109 no9 p61 S 2017

Smart Provisioning Z. Prochazka color *Sail* v48 no4 p75 Ap 2017

So Close, Yet... P. FREDERIKSEN color *Power & Motoryacht* v32 no11 p48 N 2016

A Solid Half-Century P. Nielsen *Sail* v48 no10 p6 O 2017

Sorry, Mr Roboto! B. PIKE cartoon *Power & Motoryacht* v33 no3 p208 Mr 2017

A Speck In the Sea J. ALDRIDGE and A. SOSINSKI bw color *Power & Motoryacht* v34 no7 p48 Jl 2017

STAY SHARP! Z. Prochazka *Sea Magazine* v109 no1 p56 Ja 2017

STEER CLEAR OF SCAMS *Sea Magazine* v109 no1 p61 Ja 2017

SUMMER SHOWTIME: THE PREMIER BOATING SHOW FOR THE SAN DIEGO AREA IS BACK ON FATHER'S DAY WEEKEND S. SHIBATA color *Sea Magazine* v109 no6 pCA-1 Je 2017

Take It Easy B. PIKE cartoon *Power & Motoryacht* v34 no9 p184 S 2017

TAKING HEAT *Sea Magazine* v109 no9 p30 S 2017

TGIF: FRIDAY HARBOR IS HOME TO ART, WHALES AND LOCAL FLAVOR D. HISLOP *Sea Magazine* v109 no9 pPNW-1 S 2017

That Was Then *National Parks* v91 no1 p60 Wint 2017

THIS TOO SHALL PASS . . N. GOLDBERG *Sea Magazine* v108 no10 p20 O 2016

Triple Threat A. JONES *Boating World* v38 no3 p36 Mr 2017

A VISIT FROM OLD SALT NICK *Sea Magazine* v108 no12 p96 D 2016

Water Dog M. PETERS color *Power & Motoryacht* v33 no4 p28 Ap 2017

WATERFRONT D. J. HARDING color *Power & Motoryacht* v32 no11 p40 N 2016

Weather Cloths D. Everitt cartoon *Sail* v48 no2 p68 F 2017

we done reach R. BERINGER color map *Sail* v48 no10 p58 O 2017

WENONAH color *Canoe & Kayak Magazine* v45 no1 p110 Wint 2017

WEST COAST FOCUS S. SHIBATA *Sea Magazine* v108 no10 p10 O 2016

What's in a Name? B. PIKE bw *Power & Motoryacht* v32 no11 p256 N 2016

WHAT'S NEW *Sea Magazine* v109 no7 pCA-12 Jl 2017

WHAT'S OLD IS NEW M. YOUNGBLOOD *Sea Magazine* v108 no10 p22 O 2016

When and Why to Use a Charter Broker Z. Prochazka color *Sail* v48 no2 p73 F 2017

When stuff happens... K. Westman cartoon *Sail* v48 no4 p30 Ap 2017

WILDERNESS SYSTEMS color *Canoe & Kayak Magazine* v45 no1 p108 Wint 2017

A World Apart S. MURRAY bw color *Power & Motoryacht* v33 no4 p56 Ap 2017

YARD CARE T. Hale color *Sail* v48 no10 p72 O 2017

Boats & boating in art

Seal color *Magazine Antiques* v183 no6 pC1 N/D 2016

Boats & boating—Chartering

Checkout Tips Z. Prochazka color *Sail* v48 no1 p64 Ja 2017

Five Essential Questions for Your Chart Briefing Z. Prochazka color *Sail* v47 no12 p55 D 2016

Boats & boating—Chartering—Evaluation

SCANDINAVIAN STYLE S. SHIBATA and M. Werling *Boating World* v38 no1 p6 Ja 2017

Boats & boating—Competitions

DON'T MISS LIST BOAT SHOWS :EVENTS *Sea Magazine* v109 no1 pCA-7 Ja 2017

DON'T MISS LIST FEBRUARY 2017 BOAT SHOWS *Sea Magazine* v109 no2 pPNW-10 F 2017

Boats & boating—Congresses

THE BOAT SHOW'S HERE *Sea Magazine* v109 no1 pPNW-1 Ja 2017

Bound by Boating D. Harding *Power & Motoryacht* v33 no4 p18 Ap 2017

Class Is in Session color *Power & Motoryacht* v34 no9 p24 S 2017

Boats & boating—Design & construction

    See also

        Houseboats—Design & construction

Adventures in Boat Buying S. Gateley color *Sail* v48 no5 p10 My 2017

Big, Bold and Classy P. Nielsen color *Sail* v48 no2 p28 F 2017

Bound by Boating D. Harding *Power & Motoryacht* v33 no4 p18 Ap 2017

Extreme Boating A. JONES *Boating World* v38 no1 p4 Ja 2017

Find YOUR Center T. Serio *Boating World* v37 no9 p54 N/D 2016

NAME THE BOAT S. SHIBATA *Sea Magazine* v108 no9 p12 S 2016

SCANDINAVIAN STYLE S. SHIBATA and M. Werling *Boating World* v38 no1 p6 Ja 2017

What Were They Thinking? B. PIKE color *Power & Motoryacht* v33 no4 p102 Ap 2017

Boats & boating—Economic aspects

Find YOUR Center T. Serio *Boating World* v37 no9 p54 N/D 2016

Boats & boating—Electric equipment

Extreme Boating A. JONES *Boating World* v38 no1 p4 Ja 2017

Boats & boating—Electronic equipment

In 2017, I Resolve to... M. SMITH color *Power & Motoryacht* v33 no1 p96 Ja 2017

Informational overload? P. Nielsen color *Sail* v48 no5 p4 My 2017

Put the Hammer Down J. Y. WOOD color *Power & Motoryacht* v33 no1 p40 Ja 2017

What's Next? J. Y. WOOD color *Power & Motoryacht* v33 no2 p48 F 2017

Boats & boating—Electronic equipment—Evaluation

NEW ELECTRONICS J. Y. WOOD color *Power & Motoryacht* v33 no1 p44 Ja 2017

Boats & boating—Electronic equipment—Maintenance & repair

Helm Hacks J. Y. WOOD color *Power & Motoryacht* v32 no11 p50 N 2016

Boats & boating—Equipment & supplies

    See also

Boats & boating—Electronic equipment

Attitude Adjustment T. Serio *Boating World* v37 no9 p50 N/D 2016

BELT & SUSPENDERS Z. Prochazka *Sea Magazine* v108 no10 p60 O 2016

CLEAN FUEL, HAPPY BOAT F. LANIER *Sea Magazine* v108 no9 p48 S 2016

Features, Features *Boating World* v38 no4 p50 Ap 2017

gear *Boating World* v38 no4 p28 Ap 2017

gear STUFF YOU WANT *Boating World* v38 no3 p28 Mr 2017

GIFT GUIDE *Sea Magazine* v108 no12 p40 D 2016

Helm Hacks J. Y. WOOD color *Power & Motoryacht* v32 no11 p50 N 2016

METAL BOAT Q & A B. M. KENYON *Sea Magazine* v108 no9 p54 S 2016

Mouthy MFD Z. PROCHAZKA *Boating World* v38 no4 p48 Ap 2017

Non-traditional Anchoring *Boating World* v38 no4 p57 Ap 2017

POWER PROGRESSION G. MICHAL *Boating World* v38 no2 p48 F 2017

Stay Put F. LANIER *Boating World* v38 no4 p54 Ap 2017

Boats & boating—Equipment & supplies—Evaluation

Gear P. Nielsen color *Sail* v48 no1 p22 Ja 2017

Gift Guide *Boating World* v37 no9 p43 N/D 2016

NEW ELECTRONICS J. Y. WOOD bw color *Power & Motoryacht* v33 no4 p36 Ap 2017

NEW ELECTRONICS J. Y. WOOD color *Power & Motoryacht* v33 no1 p44 Ja 2017

PLAY TIME *Sea Magazine* v108 no12 p41 D 2016

Smooth Operator D. HARDING JR. color *Power & Motoryacht* v33 no1 p95 Ja 2017

Boats & boating—Evaluation

Absolute 50 Fly color *Power & Motoryacht* v32 no12 p32 D 2016

Aquila 36 D. J. Harding color *Power & Motoryacht* v34 no7 p34 Jl 2017

Axopar 37 Sport Cabin D. J. Harding color *Power & Motoryacht* v33 no4 p42 Ap 2017

Bennington Q27RSD Custom 10 *Boating World* v38 no1 p55 Ja 2017

Berkshire 25 Sport RFX9 *Boating World* v38 no1 p56 Ja 2017

BEST BOATS 2017 N. Calder, A. Cort et al color *Sail* v47 no12 p24 D 2016

BEST BOATS 2018 [Cover story] color *Sail* v48 no9 p30 S 2017

Big, Bold and Classy P. Nielsen color *Sail* v48 no2 p28 F 2017

Big on Innovation S. SHIBATA *Sea Magazine* v108 no10 p10 O 2016

Boat of all Trades color *Power & Motoryacht* v34 no6 p18 Je 2017

Boston Whaler 330 Outrage D. Harding Jr. color *Power & Motoryacht* v33 no3 p52 Mr 2017

Breaking the Mold P. Nielsen color *Sail* v48 no7 p20 Jl 2017

Charger 210 Elite *Boating World* v38 no1 p65 Ja 2017

Coach 250RL *Boating World* v38 no1 p57 Ja 2017

Cranchi E56F J. Y. Wood color *Power & Motoryacht* v34 no8 p32 Ag 2017

Crest III 250 SLC *Boating World* v38 no1 p58 Ja 2017

Crown Jewel A. JONES *Boating World* v38 no5 p32 My 2017

Cypress Cay Cabana 220 *Boating World* v38 no1 p59 Ja 2017

Dehler 34 Z. Prochazka cartoon color *Sail* v48 no1 p28 Ja 2017

A Different Breed of Cat R. THIEL chart color *Power & Motoryacht* v33 no4 p78 Ap 2017

Dragonfly 28 Performance A. Cort color *Sail* v48 no4 p28 Ap 2017

Duffield 58 S. Murray color *Power & Motoryacht* v34 no8 p28 Ag 2017

Elan E4 A. Cort cartoon color *Sail* v48 no2 p30 F 2017

ENDURING LEGACY D. HARDING chart color *Power & Motoryacht* v33 no1 p72 Ja 2017

European Newcomers P. Nielsen color *Sail* v48 no6 p24 Je 2017

FAMILY FISHER S. SHIBATA *Boating World* v38 no5 p8 My 2017

Fareast 23R C. J. Doane color *Sail* v48 no5 p22 My 2017

Formula 310 Bowrider *Boating World* v38 no1 p42 Ja 2017

FULL THROTTLE TO FT. LAUDERDALE [Cover story] color *Power & Motoryacht* v34 no11 p104 N 2016

Glastron GS 259 *Boating World* v38 no1 p46 Ja 2017

Going Dutch S. SHIBATA *Sea Magazine* v108 no10 p11 O 2016

The Good Life In the Fast Lane: You don't have to give up go-fast performance to embrace the pontoon lifestyle A. JONES *Boating World* v38 no5 p42 My 2017

Greenline 65 OceanClass J. Y. Wood color *Power & Motoryacht* v34 no8 p34 Ag 2017

Gulfstream 52 D. HARDING JR. color *Power & Motoryacht* v32 no12 p34 D 2016

Hallberg-Rassy 40 Mk II Z. Prochazka color *Sail* v48 no8 p24 Ag 2017

Harris Cruiser 220 *Boating World* v38 no1 p60 Ja 2017

HH55 C. Caswell color *Sail* v48 no11 p24 N 2017

HH66 P. Nielsen cartoon color *Sail* v48 no2 p32 F 2017

Hitting the Spot A. JONES *Boating World* v38 no6 p42 Je 2017

Hurricane 187 IO *Boating World* v38 no1 p48 Ja 2017

Hybrid Happiness A. JONES *Boating World* v38 no4 p30 Ap 2017

J/112e A. Cort cartoon color diag *Sail* v48 no4 p26 Ap 2017

Jeanneau Leader 10.5 D. Harding Jr. color *Power & Motoryacht* v34 no8 p30 Ag 2017

JEANNEAU LEADER 30 M. WERLING *Sea Magazine* v109 no2 p38 F 2017

KOKOPELLI PACKRAFT color *Canoe & Kayak Magazine* v45 no1 p87 Wint 2017

Lexus Sport Yacht 42 S. Murray color *Power & Motoryacht* v33 no4 p44 Ap 2017

Locked and Loaded A. JONES *Boating World* v38 no6 p38 Je 2017

Lowe Infinity 250 RFL *Boating World* v38 no1 p61 Ja 2017

Make It a Double A. JONES *Boating World* v38 no4 p38 Ap 2017

Malibu Did What? Malibu's new 21 VLX is the boat many people wanted to own but didn't think they could afford A. JONES *Boating World* v38 no6 p34 Je 2017

Malibu M235 *Boating World* v38 no1 p70 Ja 2017

Maritimo X60 S. Murray color *Power & Motoryacht* v34 no11 p82 N 2017

MasterCraft X26 *Boating World* v38 no1 p71 Ja 2017

MEDITERRANEAN PASSAGE A. HARPER chart color *Power & Motoryacht* v33 no4 p68 Ap 2017

Minorca 42 Islander J. Y. Wood color *Power & Motoryacht* v34 no9 p50 S 2017

Moody DS54 Z. Prochazka cartoon color *Sail* v48 no2 p34 F 2017

A new Gunboat Takes Shape color *Sail* v48 no3 p22 Mr 2017

New-look VOR Boats B. Hancock color *Sail* v48 no8 p20 Ag 2017

Nordic Tug 44 B. Pike color *Power & Motoryacht* v32 no11 p66 N 2016

Out from the Crowd A. HARPER chart color *Power & Motoryacht* v34 no9 p58 S 2017

Platinum Upgrade: The Catalina series gets elevated styling and remains multitalented A. JONES color *Boating World* v38 no7 p42 Jl 2017

The Power of Proportion J. Y. WOOD chart color *Power & Motoryacht* v33 no4 p92 Ap 2017

Premier 220 SunSation *Boating World* v38 no1 p62 Ja 2017

Princecraft Sport 164 *Boating World* v38 no1 p68 Ja 2017

Princecraft Ventura 220 WS *Boating World* v38 no1 p50 Ja 2017

Princess 40M D. Harding color *Power & Motoryacht* v33 no4 p40 Ap 2017

Propless Surfing A. JONES *Boating World* v38 no6 p46 Je 2017

Pursuit S 328 J. Y. Wood color *Power & Motoryacht* v34 no7 p30 Jl 2017

Queen of the Fleet L. BECKETT chart color *Power & Motoryacht* v34 no9 p90 S 2017

Qwest For the Best A. JONES color *Boating World* v38 no7 p34 Jl 2017

Qwest LS 818 XRE Cruise *Boating World* v38 no1 p63 Ja 2017

Ranger Rover A. JONES *Boating World* v38 no4 p42 Ap 2017

Ranger RT 198P *Boating World* v38 no1 p69 Ja 2017

Return of the Beast: Light weight converges with extreme power and channels a bit of checkered (flag) history A. JONES *Boating World* v38 no5 p38 My 2017

Rinker QX 29 Bow Rider *Boating World* v38 no1 p44 Ja 2017

Riva 76 Bahamas J. Y. Wood color *Power & Motoryacht* v32 no12 p30 D 2016

The 'Roboat' J. Zorthian color *Time* v188 no15 p15 O 17 2016

Sage 15 A. Cort color *Sail* v48 no3 p27 Mr 2017

Seascape 18 C. J. Doane color *Sail* v48 no5 p23 My 2017

Seas the Day [Cover story] D. HARDING color *Power & Motoryacht* v33 no4 p50 Ap 2017

A SECOND LOOK Z. PROCHAZKA *Boating World* v38 no5 p48 My 2017

Sirena 64 J. Y. Wood color *Power & Motoryacht* v33 no4 p38 Ap 2017

Skiff's Notes: A skiff provides an inexpensive alternative to the big boat and delivers a different sort of boating experience A. JONES *Boating World* v38 no8 p48 S/O 2017

Smart and Stylish A. HARPER chart color *Power & Motoryacht* v33 no4 p62 Ap 2017

Splendor 239 SunStar *Boating World* v38 no1 p52 Ja 2017

Starcraft Star Step 221 E I/O *Boating World* v38 no1 p53 Ja 2017

THE STAR OF THE SHOW [Cover story] J. Y. Wood, B. Pike et al color *Power & Motoryacht* v32 no11 p76 N 2016

Stingray 186cc Deck Boat *Boating World* v38 no1 p54 Ja 2017

Sweetwater 2286 SB *Boating World* v38 no1 p64 Ja 2017

TOP 10 TENDERS C. CASWELL color *Power & Motoryacht* v33 no4 p84 Ap 2017

Transformer A. Jones *Boating World* v37 no9 p34 N/D 2016

TRIXX Aren't Just For Kids: The Spark TRIXX makes everyone a PWC trick artist hero in a matter of minutes A. JONES *Boating World* v38 no5 p36 My 2017

Wake Up A. JONES *Boating World* v38 no4 p34 Ap 2017

Xcat A. Cort color *Sail* v48 no11 p22 N 2017

XO 270 Cabin OB B. Pike color *Power & Motoryacht* v34 no9 p47 S 2017

Xquisite X5 C. J. Doane color *Sail* v48 no3 p24 Mr 2017

Yacht Royalty J. WOOLDRIDGE color *Power & Motoryacht* v33 no4 p74 Ap 2017

You Can Go Home Again P. A. JANSSEN chart color *Power & Motoryacht* v33 no1 p54 Ja 2017

YOU GOT A LOTTA VERVE S. SHIBATA *Sea Magazine* v109 no2 p6 F 2017

Boats & boating—Exhibitions

CHANGE OF VENUE, CHANGE OF NAME M. Werling *Sea Magazine* v108 no9 p6 S 2016

DON'T-MISS LIST: APRIL 2017 *Sea Magazine* v109 no4 p15 Ap 2017

DON'T MISS LIST: AUGUST 2017 *Sea Magazine* v109 no8 pCA-11 Ag 2017

DON'T MISS LIST: JUNE 2017 color *Sea Magazine* v109 no6 pCA-10 Je 2017

DON'T MISS LIST MAY 2017 *Sea Magazine* v109 no5 pCA-15 My 2017

NEWPORT BOAT SHOW XLIV *Sea Magazine* v109 no4 p8 Ap 2017

The Other French Boats D. Kent cartoon color *Sail* v48 no1 p24 Ja 2017

WATERFRONT D. HARDING JR. color *Power & Motoryacht* v32 no12 p18 D 2016

Welcome to Paradise P. JORDAN color *Power & Motoryacht* v32 no11 p92 N 2016

Boats & boating—Inspection

GET READY FOR THE SEASON color *Sail* v48 no4 p56 Ap 2017

HIGH-TECH BOAT TESTING B. PIKE chart color diag *Power & Motoryacht* v33 no2 p104 F 2017

Boats & boating—Maintenance & repair

See also

Boatyards

BOATING MAINTENANCE color *Cabin Living* p70 Ap 2017

Checkout Tips Z. Prochazka color *Sail* v48 no1 p64 Ja 2017

EXPOSURE color *Power & Motoryacht* v32 no12 p36 D 2016

A Little Tape'll Do Ya! B. PIKE color *Power & Motoryacht* v33 no4 p104 Ap 2017

Q + A *Boating World* v38 no4 p22 Ap 2017

Q+A F. Lanier, G. Michal et al *Boating World* v37 no9 p24 N/D 2016

Refit Tips C. Lawson color *Sail* v48 no1 p46 Ja 2017

Save Money: Burn Less Fuel M. SMITH color *Power & Motoryacht* v33 no1 p98 Ja 2017

Surgery Gone Bad A. Dike color *Sail* v48 no1 p52 Ja 2017

Temperature Check R. THIEL color *Power & Motoryacht* v32 no11 p46 N 2016

Time for a Change M. SMITH color *Power & Motoryacht* v33 no4 p99 Ap 2017

A Timely Save B. PIKE color *Power & Motoryacht* v32 no11 p156 N 2016

What Were They Thinking? B. PIKE color *Power & Motoryacht* v33 no4 p102 Ap 2017

Boats & boating—Maintenance & repair—Equipment & supplies

Batteries and Boom G. Michal *Boating World* v37 no9 p28 N/D 2016

Boats & boating—News briefs

DON'T MISS LIST JANUARY 2017: BOAT SHOWS *Sea Magazine* v109 no1 pPNW-19 Ja 2017

Boats & boating—Painting

Ghost Busters B. PIKE color *Power & Motoryacht* v32 no11 p141 N 2016

Letter Perfect B. PIKE color *Power & Motoryacht* v32 no12 p68 D 2016

Boats & boating—Safety measures

11 COMMONSENSE TIPS FOR SAFE BOATING F. LANIER *Sea Magazine* v108 no12 p36 D 2016

ACTING A LITTLE DINGHY P. BACICH and M. BACICH *Sea Magazine* v109 no1 p26 Ja 2017

Protect Your Rig From Theft: Every year, about 5,000 boats are stolen. Here's how to keep it from happening A. JONES *Boating World* v38 no8 p14 S/O 2017

UNINTENDED ENTANGLEMENTS K. PAINTER *Sea Magazine* v109 no1 p25 Ja 2017

Boats & boating—Sales & prices

SHOWCASE FEATURED BROKERAGE BOATS *Sea Magazine* v109 no2 p57 F 2017

Boats & boating—Societies, etc.

DON'T MISS LIST SEPTEMBER 2016 *Sea Magazine* v108 no9 pPNW-15 S 2016

EXPOSURE color *Power & Motoryacht* v32 no12 p36 D 2016

Keyboard Warriors M. PETERS color *Power & Motoryacht* v34 no9 p28 S 2017

Boatwright, Abigail

Ace Your Pivot color *Horse & Rider* v56 no9 p86 S 2017

Get It Right, Keep It Right [Cover story] color *Horse & Rider* v56 no6 p48 Je 2017

No More Saddle Sore color *Horse & Rider* v56 no8 p86 Ag 2017

Show-Time COUNTDOWN color *Horse & Rider* v55 no11 p56 N 2016

Boatyards

Crunch Time B. PIKE *Power & Motoryacht* v33 no3 p118 Mr 2017

DISCOVER PORT SAN LUIS *Sea Magazine* v108 no9 pCA-1 S 2016

In 2017, I Resolve to... M. SMITH color *Power & Motoryacht* v33 no1 p96 Ja 2017

Boazman, Derrick

SAVING MORRIS BROWN T. WHEATLEY *Atlanta* v56 no12 p92 Ap 2017

Bobbi Brown Professional Cosmetics Inc.

Slick Days L. REGENSDORF color *Vogue* v207 no7 p54 Jl 2017

Bobbitt, Philip

A Way Forward on the North Korea Crisis color *Time* v190 no13 p35 O 2 2017

Bobby pins

Welcome Back, Bobby Pins M. R. Sulcov color *Glamour* v115 no4 p46 Ap 2017

Bobby pins—Evaluation

CHIC WAVES color *Harper's Bazaar* no3649 p254 D 2016/Ja 2017

your GLAMSTROLOGY guide K. FOSTER color *Seventeen* p120 Ja 1 2017

Bobcat

Bobcats N. Austin *Arizona Highways* v93 no8 p13 Ag 2017

THE CAT GAME BACK B. Freed *Washingtonian Magazine* v52 no6 p13 Mr 2017

HERE, KITTY C. KETTLEWELL *Virginia Living* v15 no2 p15 F 2017

Tough Love color *National Wildlife (World Edition)* v55 no5 p50 Ag/S 2017

WILD THINGS: FIVE ANIMALS YOU COULD SPOT IN SHENANDOAH NATIONAL PARK *Washingtonian Magazine*

v53 no1 p106 O 2017

BOBENRIETH, MARIA

PLAY IT FORWARD *UN Chronicle* v53 no2 p17 2016

Bober, Joanna

SERENE QUEEN [Cover story] color *InStyle* p4 Home & Design 2016

Winner, Winner, Turkey Dinner color *InStyle* v23 no12 p283 N 2016

Boblitt, Kacie

Learn How to Learn New Rep color *Dance Magazine* v91 no3 p32 Mr 2017

BOBO, MARIELLE

ART & CRAFT bw *Ebony* v72 no3 p62 D 2016/Ja 2017

Beauty Unwrapped color *Ebony* v72 no5 p43 Mr 2017

Better With Time color *Ebony* v72 no4 p57 F 2017

The Blueprint color *Ebony* v72 no5 p50 Mr 2017

Bright Ideas color *Ebony* v72 no5 p35 Mr 2017

CHARM SCHOOL color *Ebony* v72 no4 p45 F 2017

COUTURE CURATOR color *Ebony* v72 no4 p56 F 2017

Date Ready! color *Ebony* v72 no4 p58 F 2017

Great Innovators color *Ebony* v72 no5 p44 Mr 2017

HOLIDAY GIFT GUIDE color *Ebony* v72 no3 p51 D 2016/Ja 2017

IN THE BUFF color *Ebony* v72 no4 p50 F 2017

THE LOOK OF LOVE color *Ebony* v72 no4 p55 F 2017

MAN-I-CURE! color *Ebony* v72 no3 p70 D 2016/Ja 2017

ONE-CLICK WONDERS color *Ebony* v72 no5 p42 Mr 2017

PARTY ON color *Ebony* v72 no3 p56 D 2016/Ja 2017

SEEING GREEN color *Ebony* v72 no5 p40 Mr 2017

Bobolink

The Bobolink Dilemma E. CLARK color *Yankee* p14 My/Je 2017

BOBROW, JONATHAN

HOW TO MAKE ANYTHING [Cover story] color diag *Popular Mechanics* p56 S 2017

Bob's Burgers (TV program)

Bob's Burgers A. Bacle, D. Coggan et al *Entertainment Weekly* no1482/1483 p34 S 22 2017

Bob's Burgers M. Logan *TV Guide* v64 no48 p36 N 21 2016

Bobseine, Liza

On Patrol color *New York State Conservationist* v71 no2 p17 O 2016

On Patrol *New York State Conservationist* v71 no3 p25 D 2016

On Patrol *New York State Conservationist* v71 no4 p27 F 2017

On Patrol *New York State Conservationist* v71 no6 p25 Je 2017

On Patrol: Real stories from Conservation Officers and Forest Rangers in the field *New York State Conservationist* v72 no1 p33 Ag 2017

Bob-Waksberg, Raphael

American Horse Story M. Z. SEITZ img *New York* v49 no15 p87 Jl 25 2016

Boca Systems Inc.

Box Office Supplies *Stage Directions* v30 no7 p19 Jl 1 2017

BOCAR, SHIRA

CAKES FOR any OCCASION [Cover story] color *Martha Stewart Living* p70 My 2017

INTO THE SPOTLIGHT color *Martha Stewart Living* p62 My 2017

LIFE'S A PICNIC color *Martha Stewart Living* no275 p78 Je 2017

NEW WAY TO EAT color *Martha Stewart Living* p92 Ap 2017

TAPPED POTENTIAL color *Martha Stewart Living* p82 My 2017

Use Your Voodles color *Martha Stewart Living* p74 S 2017

Boccara, C. N.

Superficial layers of the medial entorhinal cortex replay independently of the hippocampus bibl graph *Science* v355 no6321 p1 Ja 13 2017

Boccio, Frank Jude

BE THE SKY color *Yoga Journal* p110 2017 Special Issue

BOCH, CHARLES

The Resilience of Marine Ecosystems to Climatic Disturbances *BioScience* v67 no3 p208 Mr 2017

Boch, Ronny

Response to Comments on "Reconciliation of the Devils Hole climate record with orbital forcing" bibl chart graph *Science* v354 no6310 p296-e O 21 2016

Bochanski, John

Brown Dwarfs Mimic Stellar Siblings *Sky & Telescope* v134 no4 p10 O 2017

STILL IN THE FAMILY color *Astronomy* v45 no1 p34 Ja 2017

Bochmann, Manfred

High-performance light-emitting diodes based on carbene-metal-amides chart graph *Science* v356 no6334 p159 Ap 14 2017

Bochove, Danielle

A Gold Rush in Mexico's Deadly South color *Bloomberg Businessweek* no4497 p20 O 31 2016

Bochy, Bruce, 1955-

Bruce Bochy J. Crelin color *Current Biography* v77 no10 p10 O 2016

BOCK, ALAN W.

FROM THE ARCHIVES bw cartoon *Reason* v48 no11 p70 Ap 2017

Böck, Désirée

In situ architecture, function, and evolution of a contractile injection system color diag *Science* v357 no6352 p713 Ag 18 2017

Bock, Halley

GETTING TO KNOW YOU *Saturday Evening Post* v289 no2 p67 Mr/Ap 2017

BOCK, JOSEPH G.

HOW TO SEE INVISIBLE PEOPLE color map *Phi Kappa Phi Forum* v96 no4 p18 Wint 2016

Bock, Mary

The Role of the Citizen Journalist *USA Today Magazine* v145 no2859 p2 D 2016

Bock, Robert

What the Companies on the Right Side of the Digital Business Divide Have in Common color *Harvard Business Review Digital Articles* p2 Ja 31 2017

Bockelee-Morvan, D.

Seasonal exposure of carbon dioxide ice on the nucleus of comet 67P/Churyumov-Gerasimenko bibl bw graph *Science* v354 no6319 p1563 D 23 2016

Bockmaster, Shaun

How to be a Video Star color *Sail* v48 no9 p10 S 2017

Bodanis, David

Einstein's Greatest Mistake: A Biography A. D. Stone *Physics Today* v70 no5 p58 My 2017

Boddy, Jessica

Catching ancient maize domestication in the act color *Science* v354 no6315 p953 N 25 2016

Energy pulses reveal possible new state of memory *Science* v354 no6316 p1089 D 2 2016

Bode, Jeffrey W.

A radical approach to posttranslational mutagenesis bibl diag *Science* v354 no6312 p553 N 4 2016

BODE, KIM

THE WORLD'S BILLIONAIRES bw color diag graph map *Forbes* v199 no3 p84 Mr 28 2017

Bode, Matthias

Robust spin-polarized midgap states at step edges of topological crystalline insulators bibl graph *Science* v354 no6317 p1269 D 9 2016

Bodega Bay (Calif. : Bay)—Description & travel

WAY UP THE COAST S. SHIBATA *Sea Magazine* v109 no2 pCA-1 F 2017

Bodewes, Rogier

Role for migratory wild birds in the global spread of avian influenza H5N8 bibl graph map *Science* v354 no6309 p213 O 14 2016

Bodewits, D.

Surface changes on comet 67P/Churyumov-Gerasimenko suggest a more active past bw graph *Science* v355 no6332 p1392 Mr 31 2017

Bodgas, Meredith

Blessings in Disguise color *Working Mother* v40 no4 p6 O/N 2017

Candid Camerota [Cover story] color *Working Mother* v40 no4 p20 O/N 2017

Less Guilt, More Sweet Success color *Working Mother* v40 no2 p7 Je/Jl 2017

A New Chapter S. Barry *Working Mother* p5 F/Mr 2017

BODGE, TRAE

42 new ALL-STAR PRODUCTS of the year [Cover story] color *Redbook* p27 Jl/Ag 2017

Bodhimaya Ltd.

Clean ESCAPES L. GÖKSENIN color *Vogue* v206 no12 p184 D 2016

Bodies of water

See also

Lakes

Keeping Illinois waters clean color *National Wildlife (World Edition)* v55 no2 p46 F/Mr 2017

The Quiz T. BALAZO *Maclean's* v130 no9 p80 O 2017

Bodies of water—Government policy

WET AND WILD: New York's waterfront, once home to pirates and robber barons, fell into dangerous decline. But with a new wave of money and creativity the city is rediscovering its maritime spirit T. PERROTTET *Smithsonian* v48 no2 p26 My 2017

Bodin, Örjan

Collaborative environmental governance: Achieving collective action in social-ecological systems color *Science* v357 no6352 p659 Ag 18 2017

Bodkin, Sam

Keeping It Classic: GROUPMUSE TAKES MOZART, STRAVINSKY, AND HANDEL OUT OF THE CONCERT HALL AND PUTS THEM IN THE MIDDLE OF YOUR LIVING ROOM M. WAKIM *Los Angeles Magazine* v62 no9 p64 S 2017

Bodnar, Janet

Active or Index Funds? *Kiplinger's Personal Finance* v71 no3 p6 Mr 2017

All in the Fund Family color *Kiplinger's Personal Finance* v70 no12 p21 D 2016

All-Stars of the Kip 25 color *Kiplinger's Personal Finance* v71 no5 p22 My 2017

Blazing a Trail in Finance cartoon *Kiplinger's Personal Finance* v71 no1 p18 Ja 2017

Build Your Own Company cartoon *Kiplinger's Personal Finance* v71 no3 p37 Mr 2017

Charitable Giving May Be in Your Genes color *Kiplinger's Personal Finance* v71 no7 p24 Jl 2017

Getting Women to Talk About Money color *Kiplinger's Personal Finance* v71 no10 p24 O 2017

Great Places to Retire *Kiplinger's Personal Finance* v71 no8 p6 Ag 2017

How to Buy Bonds Now *Kiplinger's Personal Finance* v71 no6 p8 Je 2017

How to Get Good Advice *Kiplinger's Personal Finance* v71 no5 p6 My 2017

Is a Bear on the Prowl? *Kiplinger's Personal Finance* v71 no1 p8 Ja 2017

Our 70th Anniversary *Kiplinger's Personal Finance* v71 no4 p4 Ap 2017

Our Personal Best List *Kiplinger's Personal Finance* v70 no12 p8 D 2016

Our Top 300 Colleges *Kiplinger's Personal Finance* v71 no2 p8 F 2017

What Single Women Need to Know color *Kiplinger's Personal Finance* v71 no11 p25 N 2017

Bodo, Peter

A Big Return color *Tennis* v53 no2 p4 Mr/Ap 2017

A Grand Slump *Tennis* v53 no3 p6 My/Je 2017

The Name Game color *Tennis* v53 no5 p6 S/O 2017

Serving Notice *Tennis* v53 no4 p8 Jl/Ag 2017

Body cavities

Boning up on belly size E. DeMarco cartoon *Science News* v190 no12 p32 D 10 2016

Body composition

Ask Men's Health color *Men's Health* v31 no10 p14 D 2016

COMPOSITION Class G. GRAVES and C. ELLENBERG color *Vogue* v207 no3 p382 Mr 2017

The food swap that changed my body K. Canning color *Health* v31 no9 p51 N 2017

What your mom's body says about you H. Levine color *Health* v31 no9 p59 N 2017

Body doubles

Lights, Camera, Ride! L. FELDMAN color *American Cowboy* v23 no5 p69 F/Mr 2017

Body hair

See also

Pubic hair

In Defense of Body Hair K. Erickson color *Glamour* v115 no6

p60 Je 2017

Body image

See also

Body image in adolescence

Body image in women

The 5-Minute Smoky Eye color *Health* v31 no1 p32 Ja 2017

AT HOME IN EVERY POSE [Cover story] color *Yoga Journal* no292 p72 Je 2017

Black Lives Matter C. Meyerson color *Glamour* v114 no12 p218 D 2016

Celebrate Your Post-Baby Body color *Health* v30 no10 p23 D 2016

Dads Are So Hot Right Now S. James *Parents* v91 no12 p11 D 2016

THE EVOLUTION OF THE "IDEAL" BODY *Scholastic Choices* v32 no3 p4 N/D 2016

EYES OFF THE PRIZE C. PARK *Psychology Today* v49 no5 p18 S/O 2016

glam it up! T. PEREZ *Parents* p82 2015

How not to be a wallflower color *Health* v31 no9 p13 N 2017

ISKRA LAWRENCE "BODY POSITIVE IS A CHOICE" J. Naftulin color *Health* v31 no7 p26 S 2017

I Want Her Polished Pony! L. Desantis color *Health* v31 no7 p50 S 2017

Jessamyn Stanley Y. MOROZ ALPERT color *Yoga Journal* no287 p78 N 2016

LAWS OF ATTRACTION: Who we desire is driven by powerful evolutionary forces, but while most of us are drawn to looks first (whether or not we admit it), human attraction is far more complex than it appears at first sight [Cover story] W. PARIS *Psychology Today* v50 no4 p52 Ag 2017

Let's Talk About... BODY IMAGE A. STANLEY cartoon color *Seventeen* v75 no11 p76 N 2016

Passion's Frontier P. Thungkasemvathana *Psychology Today* v50 no1 p12 Ja/F 2017

PERFECTLY ME A. STANLEY bw cartoon color *Seventeen* v75 no11 p80 N 2016

Stop the Fat Talk J. Andriakos color *Health* v31 no2 p24 Mr 2017

Tokens of Our Affection M. KAUFMAN, E. SPINNER et al cartoon *O, The Oprah Magazine* p17 F 2017

Tracee Ellis Ross: "I DIDN'T WAKE UP LIKE THIS" [Cover story] A. Spencer color *Health* v31 no3 p82 Ap 2017

UNITED BY YOGA [Cover story] bw color *Yoga Journal* no292 p40 Je 2017

What Love Really Looks Like M. Huston *Psychology Today* v50 no1 p9 Ja/F 2017

Your Most-Googled Summer Body Issues... M. Choi color *Glamour* v114 no7 p71 Jl 2017

You + your Body M. Jesser color diag graph *Seventeen* v76 no5 p86 S 2017

Zendaya A. Morris color *Glamour* v114 no12 p216 D 2016

Body image in adolescence

Stronger together H. Khouri color *Yoga Journal* no295 p19 O 2017

Body image in women

everyone has an opinion about a woman's BODY color *Women's Health* v14 no7 p140 S 2017

PORTRAIT OF A Naked Woman K. Dold chart color graph *Women's Health* v14 no7 p130 S 2017

Body language

See also

Facial expression

Gesture

AD SENSES: THE NEW BODY LANGUAGE A. POWELL cartoon *Wired* v25 no8 p22 Ag 2017

Leashed To the Here and Now: DO DOGS KNOW THAT WE KNOW THAT THEY'RE THINKING OF US? J. Bradshaw *Psychology Today* v50 no5 p90 S/O 2017

Nonverbal Cues Get Employees to Open Up—or Shut Down J. R. Detert and E. R. Burris *Harvard Business Review Digital Articles* p2 D 11 2015

YOU LOOKIN' AT ME? S. POLAN *Psychology Today* v49 no5 p21 S/O 2016

Body Language (Music)

15 Fresh Songs for Fall color *Entertainment Weekly* no1434 p54 O 7 2016

Body mass index
> *See also*
> Body weight

HOW HEALTHY ARE YOU? J. THOMPSON color *Martha Stewart Living* p48 Mr 2017

Body movement

STRETCH AWAY A SLICE T. Cooke and D. DeNunzio color *Golf Magazine* v59 no7 p50 Jl 2017

Tailor-Made SQUATS E. CALDERONE color *Muscle & Performance* v9 no4 p40 Ap 2017

Body movement—Research

Simple Moves Can Lead to a Less Stressed-Out You M. Oaklander color *Time* v189 no4 p56 F 6 2017

Body odor

This Woman Was So Mortified… C. Shortsleeve color *Women's Health* v14 no2 p90 Mr 2017

Body oils (Cosmetics)

NOT YOUR DAD'S AFTER-SHAVE A. Mangum color *Bloomberg Businessweek* no4523 p62 My 22 2017

Body oils (Cosmetics)—Evaluation

Best. Bath. Ever! K. FOSTER cartoon color *Seventeen* v76 no12 p47 D 2016/Ja 2017

the buzz color *InStyle* v24 no5 p160 My 2017

The HELLO, WORLD O List color *O, The Oprah Magazine* p37 Ja 2017

How to Stress Less color *InStyle* v24 no4 p160 Ap 2017

The O List color *O, The Oprah Magazine* p55 F 2017

Body painting

MYSTERIOUS SKIN J. ANDERSON-MINSHALL *Advocate* no1088 p32 D 2016/Ja 2017

Body piercing

body-art q+a's T. RICE *Parents* v92 no5 p115 My 2017

Body scanners (Apparel design)

Hands-on: ShapeScale 3D color *PCWorld* v35 no6 p162 Je 2017

Body size
> *See also*
> Body weight

Brides Above Size 14, Read This! K. Miller color *Glamour* v115 no5 p60 My 2017

Head decor linked to bigger dinos H. Thompson graph *Science News* v191 no2 p32 F 4 2017

Killer drillers got bigger over time S. MILIUS color graph *Science News* v192 no1 p16 Ag 5 2017

Why midsize animals have the most zip H. Thompson graph *Science News* v192 no2 p32 Ag 19 2017

Body weight
> *See also*
> Obesity

The 20-Minute Turkey Buster L. MCGLASHAN color *Muscle & Performance* v9 no11 p24 N 2017

6 Things Every Woman Should Know About Her Heart H. Levine color *Health* v31 no1 p83 Ja 2017

KHLOÉ [Cover story] A. Prato color *Health* v31 no1 p86 Ja 2017

Lose Weight Your Way [Cover story] E. SPENCE color *Prevention* v69 no9 p32 O 2017

Our Doc Will See You Now R. Rajapaksa color *Health* v31 no5 p63 Je 2017

Scale Stuck? J. Benjamin color *Health* v31 no3 p47 Ap 2017

THE SECRETS OF HEALTHY PEOPLE L. HANEY *Martha Stewart Living* no267 p58 S 2016

Social Media Changed My Body A. Levi color *Health* v31 no7 p66 S 2017

STRONGER & FASTER A. SHAFFER and S. BRICKELL cartoon color *Better Homes & Gardens* v95 no2 p132 F 2016

The truth about competition *Redbook* p152 O 2017

Body weight—Physiological aspects

BARE MINIMUM [Cover story] M. Gainsburg color *Women's Health* v14 no7 p73 S 2017

Body weight—Regulation

Age-proof your knees *Harvard Health Letter* v42 no7 p1 My 2017

The "Body Kindness" Workout R. Scritchfield color *Amazing Wellness* v9 no1 p78 Wint 2017

Is your salad dressing hurting your healthy diet? Bottled dressings are often rich sources of saturated fat, calories, sodium, and added sugar chart *Harvard Health Letter* v42 no7 p5 My 2017

Mastering Portion Control *Tufts University Health & Nutrition*

Letter v34 no11 p4 Ja 2017

The Simple Trick to Eating Less Dessert color *Health* v31 no4 p14 My 2017

Your Best Diet N. Quistgard color *Yoga Journal* p105 2017 Special Issue

Bodybuilders

20 ESSENTIAL FIT-FLUENCERS B. COURT bw color *Men's Health* v32 no9 p108 N 2017

BODIES AND SOULS color *Los Angeles Magazine* v62 no10 p176 O 2017

Flexing His Muscle: Can Ah-nold create buzz around one of Indiana's most neglected issues come November 22? M. RUBINO *Indianapolis Monthly* p20 N 2017

A POSITION OF STRENGTH *Interview* v47 no2 p132 Mr 2017

Bodybuilders—Interviews

Jojo's Got the Mojo J. SCHILDHOUSE color *Muscle & Performance* v9 no9 p32 S 2017

THE NEW MR. OLYMPIA? J. KINDELA chart color *Muscle & Performance* v9 no5 p30 My 2017

Bodybuilders—Nutrition

Gain Strength, Power and More color *Muscle & Performance* v9 no7 p64 Jl 2017

Bodybuilders—Substance use

HOT | NOT T. Keith and S. Kwak color *Sports Illustrated* v127 no5 p24 Ag 14 2017

Bodybuilding

Are You Ready for MetaShred Extreme? B. J. Gaddour bw color *Men's Health* v32 no1 p132 Ja/F 2017

BODIES AND SOULS color *Los Angeles Magazine* v62 no10 p176 O 2017

The Core Principles M. Barroso color *Men's Health* v32 no2 p50 Mr 2017

Define & Conquer M. BERG chart color *Muscle & Performance* v9 no10 p22 O 2017

GET A LEG UP ON THE TEE B. O'neal and D. Denunzio color *Golf Magazine* v59 no2 p56 F 2017

JUST 3 MOVES FIRM UP, FAST! bw color *Good Housekeeping* v263 no5 p156 N 2016

Load of Doggcrapp J. GRINNELL chart color *Muscle & Performance* v9 no11 p30 N 2017

Lou Ferrigno M. ZIMMERMAN color *Men's Health* v32 no4 p128 My 2017

Milk Your Inflammation! J. WUEBBEN and D. JACKSON color *Muscle & Performance* v9 no11 p32 N 2017

MUSCLE IN THE AGE OF INSTAGRAM D. KUNITZ color *Men's Health* v32 no9 p90 N 2017

Bodyguards

Armed Guards *Lapham's Quarterly* v10 no3 p104 Summ 2017

Bodysuits

the start color *InStyle* v24 no8 p43 Ag 2017

Bodysuits—Evaluation

Intimate Affairs color *O, The Oprah Magazine* p62 Mr 2017

Boe, Alicia

Community Caves: Short and Steep *South Dakota Magazine* v33 no2 p93 Jl/Ag 2017

Boebinger, Greg

Lev Petrovich Gor'kov *Physics Today* v70 no5 p68 My 2017

Boeckle, Markus

A raven's memories are for the future color *Science* v357 no6347 p126 Jl 14 2017

BOEGEL, ELLEN K.

Blowing the Whistle *America* v215 no13 p20 O 31 2016

Sanctuary cities draw Trump administration threat color *America* v216 no4 p16 F 20 2017

Still Tinkering With Death *America* v215 no16 p18 N 21 2016

WHAT CAN WE EXPECT FROM THE SUPREME COURT'S NEW TERM? color *America* v215 no12 p13 O 24 2016

BOEGER, WALTER

Transformational Principles for NEON Sampling of Mammalian Parasites and Pathogens: A Response to Springer and Colleagues *BioScience* v66 no11 p917 N 1 2016

BOEHLERT, BART

Out of the Woods color *Architectural Digest* v74 no10 p44 O 1 2017

Boehlert, Paul

BUILD A LAYOUT IN A WEEKEND color *Model Railroader*

v84 no9 p26 S 2017
LAYOUT IN A WEEKEND UPDATE [Cover story] color diag *Model Railroader* v84 no10 p40 O 2017
A SHELF TRACK PLAN for a switching line map *Model Railroader* v84 no2 p64 F 2017

Boehm, Barbara Drake
An Armorial Age J. Livingstone cartoon color *Art in America* v104 no11 p41 D 2016
Recapturing Jerusalem at the Met P. Brown color *New York Review of Books* v63 no19 p10 D 8 2016
SACRED CITY R. NAMDAR color *New York Times Book Review* p67 D 4 2016

BOEHM, ERIC
AIRBNB: PUBLIC ENEMY NO. 1? cartoon *Reason* v49 no1 p6 My 2017
A Baby Dies in Virginia cartoon *Reason* v48 no11 p46 Ap 2017
THE BLEEDING EDGE color *Reason* v49 no1 p68 My 2017
CHARLOTTESVILLE AND THE PERILS OF COLLECTIVISM color *Reason* v49 no6 p7 N 2017
DALLAS IS ABOUT TO GO BROKE color *Reason* v48 no10 p17 Mr 2017
AN EXPENSIVE EXPERIMENT WITH SINGLE-PAYER HEALTH CARE color *Reason* v49 no5 p15 O 2017
GETTING VETERANS BACK TO WORK color *Reason* v49 no6 p38 N 2017
High-Speed Waste *Reason* v48 no7 p8 D 2016
OUT OF PRISON. OUT OF WORK *Reason* v49 no3 p12 Jl 2017

BOEHM, JIM
A Day's Work *Reader's Digest* v188 no1126 p64 D 2016/Ja 2017

Boehme, Karl W.
Reovirus infection triggers inflammatory responses to dietary antigens and development of celiac disease color diag *Science* v356 no6333 p44 Ap 7 2017

Boehmer, Tegan
Creating Safe Routes to Parks *Parks & Recreation* v52 no9 p46 S 2017

Boehnke, Kevin F.
Selling out science? cartoon *Science* v354 no6314 p934 N 18 2016
When personal becomes professional color *Science* v357 no6352 p726 Ag 18 2017

Boeing 757 (Jet transport)
ABSENCE MAKES THE HEART GROW FONDER S. Weigel bw color *Flying* v144 no6 p38 Je 2017

Boeing 777 (Jet transport)
FLYING WITH A HERO L. Abend color *Flying* v144 no6 p74 Je 2017

Boeing 777 (Jet transport)—Sales & prices
Big Jets Get Squeezed C. Jasper, J. Johnsson et al color *Bloomberg Businessweek* no4539 p16 S 25 2017

Boeing airplanes—Sales & prices
Big Jets Get Squeezed C. Jasper, J. Johnsson et al color *Bloomberg Businessweek* no4539 p16 S 25 2017

Boeing Co.
For the Man on a Mission J. Nosek cartoon color *Men's Health* v32 no4 p36 My 2017
Hardware AH-64D Apachen Longbow J. Guttman *Military History* v33 no6 p16 Mr 2017
Movers K. Stock color *Bloomberg Businessweek* no4509 p11 Ja 30 2017

Boeing Co.—Finance
Will Boeing Become Collateral Damage? J. Johnsson color graph *Bloomberg Businessweek* no4500 p23 N 21 2016

Boeke, Jef D.
3D organization of synthetic and scrambled chromosomes diag *Science* v355 no6329 p1050 Mr 10 2017
Bug mapping and fitness testing of chemically synthesized chromosome X diag *Science* v355 no6329 p1048 Mr 10 2017
Deep functional analysis of synII, a 770-kilobase synthetic yeast chromosome diag *Science* v355 no6329 p1047 Mr 10 2017
Design of a synthetic yeast genome bibl chart color graph *Science* v355 no6329 p1040 Mr 10 2017
Engineering the ribosomal DNA in a megabase synthetic chromosome diag *Science* v355 no6329 p1049 Mr 10 2017
"Perfect" designer chromosome V and behavior of a ring derivative diag *Science* v355 no6329 p1046 Mr 10 2017
Synthesis, debugging, and effects of synthetic chromosome consolidation: synVI and beyond color *Science* v355 no6329 p1045 Mr 10 2017

Boelte, Kyle
Ultralight Baggage *Sierra* v102 no1 p19 Ja/F 2017

Boerboom, Marvin
Cheers & Jeers color *Field & Stream* v122 no2 p14 Je/Jl 2017

Boerio-Goates, Juliana
Patriotism in the pews color *U.S. Catholic* v82 no11 p5 N 2017

Boerner, Heather
Stanford's Big Health Care Idea color *Washington Monthly* v49 no3-5 p48 Mr-My 2017

Boernke, Phyllis
dust of creation *South Dakota Magazine* v32 no6 p90 Mr/Ap 2017

Boers, Carly
CAKES, PASTRIES, PIES, COOKIES, HOT FUDGE, GALATO, BROWNIES & MORE! chart color *Chicago* v65 no11 p70 N 2016
EAT THEIR WORDS color *Chicago* v65 no12 p62 D 2016
HAUTE MADE EASY color *Chicago* v65 no11 p55 N 2016
KID STUFF color *Chicago* v66 no7 p38 Jl 2017
Level Up Your Grilling Game color *Chicago* v66 no7 p54 Jl 2017
MOVE OVER, HARD CIDER color *Chicago* v66 no5 p70 My 2017
THE NEW FITNESS FOOD TREND chart color *Chicago* v66 no1 p58 Ja 2017
SHARPEN YOUR KNIVES [Cover story] color *Chicago* v66 no11 p60 N 2017
Thirsty? color diag *Chicago* v66 no2 p57 F 2017

Boersema, Paul J.
Cell-wide analysis of protein thermal unfolding reveals determinants of thermostability color *Science* v355 no6327 p812 F 24 2017

Boesch, Christophe
Chimpanzee genomic diversity reveals ancient admixture with bonobos bibl diag graph map *Science* v354 no6311 p477 O 28 2016

Boeser, Brock
WHO IS THE NEXT BREAKOUT STAR? J. Fuchs color *Sports Illustrated* v127 no11 p43 O 9 2017

Boesing, Andrea Larissa
Higher predation risk for insect prey at low latitudes and elevations graph *Science* v356 no6339 p742 My 19 2017

Boesler, Matthew
The Fed Keeps Its Eye on Swings in the Stock Market color *Bloomberg Businessweek* no4518 p15 Ap 10 2017
Neel Kashkari color *Bloomberg Businessweek* no4527 p92 Je 19 2017

Boesmans, Werend
Lineage-dependent spatial and functional organization of the mammalian enteric nervous system color graph *Science* v356 no6339 p722 My 19 2017

Boeth, Jenny
We Say Goodbye to One of Our Own H. Goldblatt, D. Snierson et al color *Entertainment Weekly* no1480 p3 S 1 2017

BOETTIGER, CARL
Skills and Knowledge for Data-Intensive Environmental Research *BioScience* v67 no6 p546 Je 2017

BOFFERDING, R. LOUIS
Magnate School color *Architectural Digest* v74 no4 p69 Ap 2017

Bogachev, Evgeniy Mikhailovich
CHASING THE PHANTOM G. M. GRAFF map *Wired* v25 no4 p52 Ap 2017

BOGAERT, ELIZABETH
Life IN THESE UNITED STATES *Reader's Digest* v189 no1128 p38 Mr 2017

Bogart, Anne
Power Games R. Platt cartoon *New Yorker* v93 no22 p8 Jl 31 2017

Bogart, Humphrey, 1899-1957
BOGIE'S DARK SIDE *Saturday Evening Post* v289 no3 p93 My/Je 2017

Bogdan, Sarah
APPLIANCE ANALYST color *Good Housekeeping* v264 no6 p6 Je 2017
SPRING CLEANING LAUNDRY SPECIAL color *Good Housekeeping* v264 no5 p81 My 2017

Bogdanoff, Alec

Through the Looking-Glass of the Ocean Surface color *Oceanus* v51 no2 p106 Wint 2016

Bogdanor, Vernon

How Bad Was Tony Blair? bw *New York Review of Books* v64 no1 p64 Ja 19 2017

Bogdanović, Ozren

Germ line–inherited H3K27me3 restricts enhancer function during maternal-to-zygotic transition diag *Science* v357 no6347 p212 Jl 14 2017

Bogdanovich, Peter, 1939-

THE LAST PICTURE SHOW C. Nashawaty color *Entertainment Weekly* no1460/1461 p14 Ap 7-17 2017

Boger, Richard

FATHER OF THE NAVY D. Harris bw color *Military History* v34 no5 p22 Ja 2018

Boggild, Lars

Investors Watch Tesla *Alternatives Journal (AJ) - Canada's Environmental Voice* v42 no3 p11 2016

Boggs, Belle

The Art of Waiting K. Schwehn color *Orion Magazine* v35 no6 p61 N/D 2016

Bogle, Jack

THE OUTSIDER [Cover story] color *Money* v46 no4 p38 My 2017

Bogle, Jennifer

COURT of APPEALS color *Tennis* v53 no5 p10 S/O 2017

Bogle, John C., 1929-

Fear of Finance? J. Otter color *AARP: The Magazine* v60 no5A p44 Ag/S 2017

Bognanni, Peter

Things I'm Seeing Without You *Publishers Weekly* v264 no33 p80 Ag 14 2017

Bogo, Jennifer

The Owl and the Photographer *Audubon* v118 no6 p48 Wint 2016

BOGOMOLNI, ANDREA

Google Haul Out: Earth Observation Imagery and Digital Aerial Surveys in Coastal Wildlife Management and Abundance Estimation *BioScience* v67 no8 p760 Ag 2017

BOGOST, IAN

A POCKET GUIDE TO THE ROBOT REVOLUTION color *Atlantic* v318 no4 p84 N 2016

Bogotá (Colombia)

Secret Garden A. FIXSEN *Architectural Record* v205 no7 p120 Jl 2017

Bogotá (Colombia)—Description & travel

Bogotá, Colombia L. DIXON color *Foreign Policy* no224 p82 My/Je 2017

Rediscovering Bogotá L. WARD *Virginia Living* v15 no3 p62 Ap 2017

Bogs

Bogs H. Wismayer *New York Times Magazine* p24 N 20 2016

Bogue, Sarah

YOU GAIN, YOU WIN color *Women's Health* v14 no7 p114 S 2017

Bohacz, Ray

DIFFERENCE IN PARTS *Successful Farming* v115 no2 p30 F 2017

DUALS ON DIESELS *Successful Farming* v115 no5 p24 Mid-Mr 2017

EFI FUEL PUMP PRIME STRATEGY: EVERYTHING GAS IS NOW RUNING ON EFI SYSTEMS *Successful Farming* v115 no9 p32 Ag 2017

GM'S HEI MODULE DWELL: THIS PRIMER WILL HELP YOU ADJUST THE DWELL ON ALL ENGINE TYPES *Successful Farming* v115 no6 p26 Ap 2017

HARMONIC BALANCER REPAIR SLEEVE: MAKE IT A POINT TO CHECK THE BALANCER FOR WEAR *Successful Farming* v115 no12 p40 O 2017

IT'S A RECYCLING CENTER: UNDERSTANDING EXHAUST GAS RECIRCULATION *Successful Farming* v115 no9 p33 Ag 2017

KEY SUMMER MAINTENANCE CHORES *Successful Farming* v115 no8 p52 Je/Jl 2017

OIL VISCOSITY DEBATE *Successful Farming* v115 no3 p29 Mid-F 2017

ORGANIZING PARTS *Successful Farming* v114 no11 p28 N 2016

SWAPPING OUT BRAKE FLUID: HERE ARE SEVERAL METHODS FOR BLEEDING AIR OUT OF A SYSTEM *Successful Farming* v115 no7 p20 My 2017

THROTTLED ENGINE? *Successful Farming* v115 no4 p32 Mr 2017

UNDERSTANDING WORKING FLUIDS: EVERYTHING GAS IS NOW RUNNING ON EFI SYSTEMS *Successful Farming* v115 no11 p26 S 2017

Bohannon, John

Artificial intelligence ups its game color *Science* v354 no6319 p1518 D 23 2016

THE CYBERSCIENTIST color diag *Science* v357 no6346 p18 Jl 7 2017

THE PULSE OF THE PEOPLE color graph *Science* v355 no6324 p470 F 3 2017

Raising the drawbridge graph *Science* v355 no6328 p896 Mr 3 2017

RESTLESS MINDS color graph *Science* v356 no6339 p690 My 19 2017

U.S. charges journal publisher with misleading authors *Science* v354 no6308 p23 O 7 2016

Boha.ova, M.

Observation of a large-scale anisotropy in the arrival directions of cosmic rays above 8×1018 eV *Science* v357 no6357 p1266 S 22 2017

BOHBOT, AMIR

How Israel Took a Toy and Made It a High-Tech Weapon [Cover story] *Commentary* v143 no1 p19 Ja 2017

Bohem, Les

Shut Eye J. Halterman *TV Guide* v64 no40 p32 O 3 2016

Bohemian glass

A Fresh Breath for Czech Glass C. Matlack color *Bloomberg Businessweek* no4535 p42 Ag 28 2017

Bohen, Colleen

FOLLOW Like a Boss *Dance Spirit* v21 no7 p100 S 2017

Bohjalian, Chris

The Sleepwalker *Publishers Weekly* v263 no46 p32 N 14 2016

Bohlin Cywinski Jackson (Company)

Wine Country Farmhouse S. Kim *Architectural Record* v205 no9 p142 S 2017

Böhmer, A. E.

Discovery of orbital-selective Cooper pairing in FeSe diag *Science* v357 no6346 p75 Jl 7 2017

Böhmermann, Jan

the chroniclers bw color *Foreign Policy* no221 p79 N/D 2016

Bohn, John L.

Cold molecules: Progress in quantum engineering of chemistry and quantum matter bw color *Science* v357 no6355 p1002 S 8 2017

Bohnenstiehl, DelWayne R.

Seismic constraints on caldera dynamics from the 2015 Axial Seamount eruption bibl color graph *Science* v354 no6318 p1395 D 16 2016

Bohnet, Iris

How to Take the Bias Out of Interviews *Harvard Business Review Digital Articles* p2 Ap 18 2016

Bohnet, Iris—Interviews

Women leaders still need to be trailblazers C. NEWBERY *People Management* p40 F 2017

BÖHNING-GAESE, KATRIN

When, Where, and How Nature Matters for Ecosystem Services: Challenges for the Next Generation of Ecosystem Service Models *BioScience* v67 no9 p820 S 2017

Bohns, Vanessa K.

The best way to get a little help color *Redbook* p103 My 2017

Bohus, Allie

Behind the Chutes color *American Cowboy* v24 no1 p69 Je/Jl 2017

Boilers

HOMESTEAD HACKS *Mother Earth News* no279 p66 D/Ja 2017

Pellet Boilers for Off-Grid Living *Mother Earth News* no280 p9 F/Mr 2017

Boire, Ronald D., 1962-

The Big Stories of 2016 J. Milliot color *Publishers Weekly* v263

no52 p6 D 19 2016

Boise (Idaho)

BEST VALUE TOWNS 2017 [Cover story] C. Ryan color *Sunset* v238 no2 p48 F 2017

Boise National Forest (Idaho)

Tangled Lines P. D. McQUADE *Idaho Magazine* v16 no2 p6 N 2016

Boise State University—Sports

BLOWING UP THE BCS L. Schnell color *Sports Illustrated* v125 no19 p52 D 12 2016

Week 3 color *Sports Illustrated* v127 no5 p61 Ag 14 2017

Boismoreau, F.

The sacral autonomic outflow is sympathetic bibl color diag *Science* v354 no6314 p893 N 18 2016

BOITANI, LUIGI

International Wildlife Law: Understanding and Enhancing Its Role in Conservation *BioScience* v67 no9 p784 S 2017

An Unparalleled Opportunity for an Important Ecological Study *BioScience* v67 no10 p875 O 2017

Boivie, Steven

Boards Aren't the Right Way to Monitor Companies *Harvard Business Review Digital Articles* p2 My 10 2016

How Companies Use Strategically Timed Announcements to Confuse the Market *Harvard Business Review Digital Articles* p2 Ap 26 2016

Research: Board Directors Are More Likely to Leave When a Firm Is Getting Criticized *Harvard Business Review Digital Articles* p2 Ag 9 2017

Serving on Boards Helps Executives Get Promoted *Harvard Business Review Digital Articles* p2 My 20 2016

When Star CEOs and Star Analysts Disagree, the Market Trusts the Analysts *Harvard Business Review Digital Articles* p2 Ap 18 2016

Boivin, Diane B.

Wake up smiling color *Redbook* p71 Mr 2017

Boivin, Karen

SURPRISE *Christian Century* v134 no12 p22 Je 7 2017

BoJack Horseman (TV program)

The 10 Best Episodes D. D'Addario color *Time* v188 no25-26 p140 D 19 2016 Double Issue

American Horse Story M. Z. SEITZ img *New York* v49 no15 p87 Jl 25 2016

STREAMING A. D'ARMINIO *TV Guide* v65 no37 p50 S 4 2017

Bojang, Kalifa A.

Resistance to malaria through structural variation of red blood cell invasion receptors diag *Science* v356 no6343 p1139 Je 16 2017

Bojowald, Martin

Now The Physics of Time *Physics Today* v70 no2 p57 F 2017

Bok choy

new ways with CHARD M. XERAKIA *Better Homes & Gardens* v94 no12 p92 D 2016

Bokaer, Jonah

DANCE *New Yorker* v92 no37 p23 N 14 2016

Making His Own Rules C. ESCOYNE *Dance Magazine* v90 no11 p37 N 2016

Bokeh (Film)

Bokeh C. Nashawaty color *Entertainment Weekly* no1459 p48 Mr 31 2017

Boknam Lee

Positive biodiversity-productivity relationship predominant in global forests bibl chart graph map *Science* v354 no6309 paaf8957-1 O 14 2016

Boko Haram (Organization)

Boko Haram's Other Victims A. Baker color *Time* v190 no2/3 p40 Jl 10-17 2017

THE BOYS FROM BAGA: THE FOUR OF THEM, CHILDREN FROM A FISHING VILLAGE IN NORTHEASTERN NIGERIA, WERE AMONG THOUSANDS ABDUCTED BY BOKO HARAM AND TRAINED AS CHILD SOLDIERS. THEY LEARNED TO SURVIVE, BUT ONLY BY FORGETTING WHO THEY WERE S. A. Topol *New York Times Magazine* p42 Je 25 2017

CENTURY marks cartoon graph *Christian Century* v134 no5 p8 Mr 1 2017

GOOD NEWS color *Maclean's* v129 no43 p8 O 31 2016

NIGERIA'S INVISIBLE CRISIS [Cover story] L. Roberts color

map *Science* v356 no6333 p18 Ap 7 2017

Bokor, Jeffrey

MoS2 transistors with 1-nanometer gate lengths bibl color graph *Science* v354 no6308 p99 O 7 2016

Boksenbaum-Granier, Alexandre

The Duck That Clipped Fillon's Wings color *Bloomberg Businessweek* no4518 p17 Ap 10 2017

Where YouTube Meets The Boob Tube graph *Bloomberg Businessweek* no4512 p44 F 20 2017

Bol, Bol

WHOLE NEW BOL GAME L. Winn color *Sports Illustrated* v127 no2 p50 Jl 17 2017

Bol, Manute

WHOLE NEW BOL GAME L. Winn color *Sports Illustrated* v127 no2 p50 Jl 17 2017

Boland, Conor S.

Sensitive electromechanical sensors using viscoelastic graphene-polymer nanocomposites bibl graph *Science* v354 no6317 p1257 D 9 2016

Boland, John J.

Nanocrystalline copper films are never flat diag graph *Science* v357 no6349 p397 Jl 28 2017

BOLAND, WHITNEY

FROM PORTUGAL WITH LOVE bw color *Climbing* no353 p66 My/Je 2017

Bolande, Jennifer

Billboards That Don't Block the View J. Zorthian color *Time* v189 no10 p21 Mr 20 2017

Bolcom, William

Dinner Is Served J. ROBINSON *Opera News* v81 no9 p20 Mr 2017

Bold & the Beautiful, The (TV program)

BEST OF DAYTIME 2016 M. LOGAN *TV Guide* p44 D 19 2016

THE BOLD AND THE BEAUTIFUL M. LOGAN *TV Guide* p48 D 5 2016

THE BOLD AND THE BEAUTIFUL M. LOGAN *TV Guide* v65 no13 p44 Mr 20 2017

DAYTIME M. LOGAN *TV Guide* v65 no23 p42 My 29 2017

DAYTIME M. LOGAN *TV Guide* v65 no35 p42 Ag 21 2017

Bold Type, The (TV program)

THE 20-WORD REVIEW S. Highfill color *Entertainment Weekly* no1473 p50 Jl 7 2017

The Bold Type's IRL Inspo S. Highfill color *Entertainment Weekly* no1478 / 1479 p89 Ag 18-25 2017

Bolduc, Remi

Dispatches from the Great White North K. MCDOWALL color *Downbeat* v84 no7 p53 Jl 2017

BOLE, WILLIAM

DISABLED AND BETRAYED color *America* v215 no10 p30 O 10 2016

Bolen, Anne

Beavers as Ecopartners color *National Wildlife (World Edition)* v55 no5 p14 Ag/S 2017

Nature's Jewels color *National Wildlife (World Edition)* v55 no4 p22 Je/Jl 2017

Unexpected Bounties color *National Wildlife (World Edition)* v55 no2 p18 F/Mr 2017

Boler-Davis, Alicia

How GM Uses Social Media to Improve Cars and Customer Service *Harvard Business Review Digital Articles* p2 F 12 2016

Boles, John B.

Prodigy of Freedom G. S. WOOD color *Weekly Standard* v22 no38 p30 Je 12 2017

Bolin, Bryce

Identification of a primordial asteroid family constrains the original planetesimal population diag graph *Science* v357 no6355 p1026 S 8 2017

Boling, Dave

The Lost History of Stars *Publishers Weekly* v264 no17 p63 Ap 24 2017

Bolino, Mark C.

7 Ways People Quit Their Jobs *Harvard Business Review Digital Articles* p2 S 15 2016

How to Motivate Employees to Go Beyond Their Jobs *Harvard Business Review Digital Articles* p2 S 15 2017

Will Refusing an International Assignment Derail Your Career?

Harvard Business Review Digital Articles p2 Ap 18 2017

Bolivia

NATIONAL GALLERY BOLIVIA R. Griffiths *History Today* v67 no8 p76 Ag 2017

Boll, Martin

Revealing hidden antiferromagnetic correlations in doped Hubbard chains via string correlators bw diag graph *Science* v357 no6350 p484 Ag 4 2017

Bollen, Christopher

The ACCRA ART Scene *Interview* v46 no10 p44 D 2016/Ja 2017

CHRISTOPHER BOLLEN *Interview* v47 no5 p18 Je/Jl 2017

The Destroyers *Publishers Weekly* v264 no16 p37 Ap 17 2017

Édouard LOUIS: THE YOUNG FRENCH WRITER BRINGS HIS RUTHLESSLY BEAUTIFUL NOVEL ABOUT IDENTITY AND CLASS TO AMERICA *Interview* v47 no3 p20 My 2017

JAMES IVORY *Interview* v47 no3 p94 My 2017

A Passion *Interview* v46 no10 p54 D 2016/Ja 2017

The Society PAGE *Interview* v47 no1 p38 F 2017

Wish You Were Here: Money, murder and a missing heir combine on a Greek island in this literary thriller T. ZIOLKOWSKI *New York Times Book Review* p8 Ag 20 2017

Bollenbach, Tobias

Decoding of position in the developing neural tube from antiparallel morphogen gradients diag *Science* v356 no6345 p1379 Je 30 2017

Boller, Caroline

COUCH TO 50K E. Strout color *Runner's World* v52 no3 p34 Ap 2017

BOLLIER, DAVID

THE NEXT BIG THING WILL BE A LOT OF... SMALL THINGS bw color *Nation* v305 no5 p16 Ag 28 2017

BOLLING, RUBEN

TOM the DANCING BUG *In These Times* v41 no3 p34 Mr 2017

Bollinger, Lee C.

Can the First Amendment save us? *Columbia Journalism Review* v56 no2 p10 Fall 2017

Is free speech under threat IN THE UNITED STATES? WE RECEIVED TWENTY-SEVEN RESPONSES. WE PUBLISH THEM HERE, IN ALPHABETICAL ORDER *Commentary* v144 no1 p13 Jl/Ag 2017

Bolman, Chris

Can Your Mobile Customers Afford to Watch Your Ads? *Harvard Business Review Digital Articles* p2 D 8 2015

Bolo ties

The Style Guy M. Anthony Green color *GQ: Gentlemen's Quarterly* v97 no10 p70 O 2017

Bologna sausages

Tony Baloney J. SPALDING *Indianapolis Monthly* p43 My 2017

Bolognafiere (Company)

BolognaFiere Confirms 2018 N.Y.C. Rights Show J. Milliot *Publishers Weekly* v264 no15 p13 Ap 10 2017

Bolonik, Kera

Finding Herself at 36 color *Prevention* v69 no1 p38 Ja 2017

Mourning Becomes Her color *Prevention* v68 no11 p34 N 2016

Moving Toward Joy color *Prevention* v69 no2 p36 F 2017

Voted Most Inappropriate: Samantha Irby took up her confessional writing to "impress a dude"--and wound up marrying a woman. She also picked up a lot of famous fans img *New York* v50 no11 p120 My 29 2017

Bolozdynya, A.

Observation of coherent elastic neutrino-nucleus scattering diag *Science* v357 no6356 p1123 S 15 2017

Bolster, Mary

Poses to last a lifetime [Cover story] color *Yoga Journal* p14 2017 Special Issue

Bolt, Clay

Getting Youth to Focus on Nature color *National Wildlife (World Edition)* v55 no4 p14 Je/Jl 2017

Bolt, Laura

See the Light color graph *Bloomberg Businessweek* no4509 p60 Ja 30 2017

Bolt, Robert

A More for All Seasons J. Paul *History Today* v66 no12 p6 D 2016

Bolt, Usain, 1986-

FAST FASTER, FASTEST D. Friedman color *GQ: Gentlemen's*

Quarterly v86 no12 p212 D 2016

THE INTERSECTION bw color *Runner's World* v52 no1 p26 Ja/F 2017

Leading Off color *Sports Illustrated* v127 no5 p10 Ag 14 2017

Reign Over T. Layden, T. Keith et al color *Sports Illustrated* v127 no5 p22 Ag 14 2017

Usain Bolt S. Gregory color *Time* v190 no7 p13 Ag 21 2017

Bolton, Alexander D.

Will Federal Employees Work for a President They Disagree With? color graph *Harvard Business Review Digital Articles* p2 F 10 2017

BOLTON, BRIAN

Fundamentalism ON TRIAL *Humanist* v77 no2 p18 Mr/Ap 2017

Bolton, Michael, 1953——Interviews

Michael Bolton's Funny Valentine R. Rahman color *Entertainment Weekly* no1453 p52 F 17 2017

Bolton, Robyn

Whole Foods' Misguided Play for Millennials *Harvard Business Review Digital Articles* p2 My 14 2015

Why Online Retailers Are Starting to Care About Your Feelings *Harvard Business Review Digital Articles* p2 Ja 12 2015

Bolton, S. J.

Jupiter's interior and deep atmosphere: The initial pole-to-pole passes with the Juno spacecraft [Cover story] color graph *Science* v356 no6340 p821 My 26 2017

Jupiter's magnetosphere and aurorae observed by the Juno spacecraft during its first polar orbits diag graph *Science* v356 no6340 p826 My 26 2017

Bolton, Scott J.

Cassini finds molecular hydrogen in the Enceladus plume: Evidence for hydrothermal processes chart graph *Science* v356 no6334 p155 Ap 14 2017

Bolton, Sharon

Dead Woman Walking *Publishers Weekly* v264 no29 p197 Jl 17 2017

Bolts & nuts

How to reeve a new halyard D. Everitt cartoon color *Sail* v48 no1 p56 Ja 2017

THE NUTS AND BOLTS D. HISLOP *Sea Magazine* v109 no2 p30 F 2017

Bolyai, János

1823: Timisoara *Lapham's Quarterly* v10 no2 p40 Spr 2017

Bomb squads

Safety and Freedom and Magazines R. D'AGOSTINO *Popular Mechanics* p4 Ap 2017

BOMBACI, SARA P.

Addressing the Gender Gap in Distinguished Speakers at Professional Ecology Conferences *BioScience* v67 no5 p464 My 2017

Bombardier Inc.

Bombardier's Painful Double Whammy F. Tomesco and A. Mayeda *Bloomberg Businessweek* no4540 p23 O 2 2017

Bombardier Recreational Products Inc.

Appetite for Destruction J. Jacquot color *Car & Driver* v62 no10 p90 Ap 2017

Bombardment

See also

Aerial bombing

Bombay Stock Exchange Ltd.

Checkup: India graph *Bloomberg Businessweek* no4532 p35 Jl 31 2017

Bombeck, Erma

Laugh Lines *Reader's Digest* v188 no1126 p91 D 2016/Ja 2017

Bombers (Terrorists)—Psychology

Unmasking the Mad Bomber M. CANNELL *Smithsonian* v48 no1 p25 Ap 2017

Bombings

Critics with Bombs J. BOTTUM color *Weekly Standard* v22 no20 p21 Ja 30 2017

TERROR AROUND THE GLOBE color *Maclean's* v129 no48/49 p52 D 5 2016

UPDATE: Syria's Civil War P. Smith *New York Times Upfront* v149 no5 p16 N 21 2016

Bombproof building

See also

Nuclear bomb shelters

Hardware R621 Gruppenstand J. Guttman color *Military History*

v34 no5 p20 Ja 2018

Bombs

See also

Guided missiles

The Legacy of Fake Bomb Detectors in Iraq B. RADFORD *Skeptical Inquirer* v41 no1 p7 Ja/F 2017

The Warrior Rides Again G. R. Schiavino color *American Cowboy* v24 no1 p58 Je/Jl 2017

Bombycilla garrulus

do you know your waxwings? color *Cabin Living* p10 Mr 2017

Bomer, Matthew, 1977-

Amazon Tries to Complete F. Scott Fitzgerald's Unfinished Novel D. D'addario color *Time* v190 no5 p60 Jl 31 2017

The Last Tycoon M. ROUSH *TV Guide* v65 no31 p15 Jl 24 2017

Bommakanti, Gayathri

mTOR regulates metabolic adaptation of APCs in the lung and controls the outcome of allergic inflammation graph *Science* v357 no6355 p1014 S 8 2017

Bommarco, Riccardo

Ten policies for pollinators bibl color *Science* v354 no6315 p975 N 25 2016

Bommarito, Michael J. II

Harnessing legal complexity diag graph *Science* v355 no6332 p1377 Mr 31 2017

Bon Iver (Performer)

Bon Iver E. R. Brown color *Entertainment Weekly* no1434 p57 O 7 2016

Winter Preview M. Trammell cartoon *New Yorker* v92 no37 p12 N 14 2016

Bon Jovi (Performer)

WHOA, LIVIN ON $10.4 MILLION color *Bloomberg Businessweek* no4519 p66 Ap 24 2017

Bon-Ton Stores Inc.

FRESH ON THE SCENE C. LAUTERBACH *Atlanta* v57 no1 p66 My 2017

Bonacci, Ognjen

Changing climate shifts timing of European floods color graph *Science* v357 no6351 p588 Ag 11 2017

Bonaccorsi, Lucilla

Bella Sicilia H. BOWLES color *Vogue* v207 no9 p408 S 2017

Bonafide (Music)

Empowerment HADLEY color *Downbeat* v84 no2 p76 F 2017

Bonal, L.

Seasonal exposure of carbon dioxide ice on the nucleus of comet 67P/Churyumov-Gerasimenko bibl bw graph *Science* v354 no6319 p1563 D 23 2016

Bonaldi, Tiziana

Reticulon 3–dependent ER-PM contact sites control EGFR non-clathrin endocytosis color diag graph *Science* v356 no6338 p617 My 12 2017

Bonanos, Christopher

Arbus, Unearthed: Eight rarely seen New York moments img *New York* v50 no9 p84 My 1 2017

Can Bob Dole Make America Great Again? img *New York* v49 no19 p12 S 19 2016

The Circus Comes to America img *New York* p8 Ja 23 2017

Excuse Me, Sir, How Much Do You Make? img *New York* v50 no10 p14 My 15 2017

The Last Time New York Felt Blue img *New York* v49 no24 p26 N 28 2016

Letter Head color *Conde Nast Traveler* v52 no3 p102 Mr 2017

Loft Life: The Early Years img *New York* v50 no8 p12 Ap 17 2017

Long Island City's Slow Sizzle img *New York* v50 no18 p12 S 4 2017

The Loudest Voice in 'New York' img *New York* v49 no15 p10 Jl 25 2017

On the House color *Conde Nast Traveler* v52 no7 p98 Ag 2017

Sixteen Trumps img *New York* v49 no22 p12 O 31 2016

Slosh, Slosh, Zzzzz: The hot (if you turned on the heater) mattress craze of 1970 img *New York* v50 no9 p10 My 1 2017

This Isn't Fun Anymore: When Molly Haskell offered to take porn seriously, the movies didn't perform on command img *New York* v50 no12 p14 Je 12 2017

Tomorrow: David Wallace-Wells img *New York* v50 no18 p15 S 4 2017

Two Views of Homelessness img *New York* v50 no6 p8 Mr 20 2017

The Universally Acknowledged Dump That Is La Guardia Airport Is Finally Getting an Upgrade img *New York* v49 no25 p72 D 12 2016

When Bobby Met Billie Jean img *New York* v50 no17 p28 Ag 21 2017

When Trump Tower Was Luxurious img *New York* p10 F 20 2017

The Year New York Almost Lost the Right to Choose img *New York* p10 F 9 2017

Bonanza (Private planes)

BEST USED SIX SEATERS S. POPE chart color *Flying* v144 no6 p42 Je 2017

MORE THAN HE COULD HANDLE P. Garrison *Flying* v144 no4 p40 Ap 2017

Bonaparte, Anne

Sexism in Silicon Valley color *Atlantic* v319 no5 p10 Je 2017

Bonaventura, Jordi

Chemogenetics revealed: DREADD occupancy and activation via converted clozapine graph *Science* v357 no6350 p503 Ag 4 2017

BONAVOGLIA, ANGELA

WHAT WOULD IT MEAN FOR 24 MILLION AMERICANS TO LOSE HEALTH INSURANCE? color *Nation* v304 no12 p20 Ap 10 2017

Bonchek, Mark

The Best Digital Strategists Don't Think in Terms of Either/Or *Harvard Business Review Digital Articles* p2 Je 16 2015

Build Your Brand as a Relationship *Harvard Business Review Digital Articles* p2 My 9 2016

A Cheat Sheet for Marketers on the Future of Digital Platforms *Harvard Business Review Digital Articles* p2 My 5 2015

Design How Your Team Thinks *Harvard Business Review Digital Articles* p2 Je 24 2016

Focus on Keeping Up with Your Customers, Not Your Competitors *Harvard Business Review Digital Articles* p2 Ap 28 2016

A Good Digital Strategy Creates a Gravitational Pull color *Harvard Business Review Digital Articles* p2 Ja 25 2017

How Leaders Can Let Go Without Losing Control *Harvard Business Review Digital Articles* p2 Je 2 2016

How to Build a Strategic Narrative *Harvard Business Review Digital Articles* p2 Mr 25 2016

How to Create an Exponential Mindset *Harvard Business Review Digital Articles* p2 Jl 27 2016

How to Discover Your Company's DNA *Harvard Business Review Digital Articles* p2 D 12 2016

How to Stop Worrying About Becoming Obsolete at Work *Harvard Business Review Digital Articles* p2 Ja 11 2016

Making Sense of Owned Media *Harvard Business Review Digital Articles* p2 O 10 2014

There Are 4 Futures for CMOs (Some Better Than Others) *Harvard Business Review Digital Articles* p2 S 8 2017

To Change Your Strategy, First Change How You Think *Harvard Business Review Digital Articles* p2 My 17 2017

What Creativity in Marketing Looks Like Today *Harvard Business Review Digital Articles* p2 Mr 22 2017

What If You Could Learn Design from Apple? *Harvard Business Review Digital Articles* p2 S 14 2016

What Kind of Thinker Are You? *Harvard Business Review Digital Articles* p2 N 23 2015

Why Apple Music Missed a Beat *Harvard Business Review Digital Articles* p2 S 25 2015

Why Customer Gratitude Trumps Loyalty *Harvard Business Review Digital Articles* p2 O 19 2015

Why the Problem with Learning Is Unlearning *Harvard Business Review Digital Articles* p2 N 3 2016

You Don't Need to Be a Silicon Valley Startup to Have a Network-Based Strategy *Harvard Business Review Digital Articles* p2 Jl 14 2017

Boncher, Mark

BUYING A USED SNOWMOBILE color *Cabin Living* p10 D 2016

MOVING DIRT & GRAVEL color *Cabin Living* p68 S 2017

Bonci, Antonello

Chemogenetics revealed: DREADD occupancy and activation via converted clozapine graph *Science* v357 no6350 p503 Ag 4 2017

Boncioli, D.

Observation of a large-scale anisotropy in the arrival directions of cosmic rays above 8 × 1018 eV *Science* v357 no6357 p1266 S 22 2017

Bond, Alan

Cognition-mediated evolution of low-quality floral nectars bibl graph *Science* v355 no6320 p1 Ja 6 2017

BOND, COURTNEY

Black Tiger Shrimp *Texas Monthly* v45 no5 p34 My 2017

Chicken and Dumplings *Texas Monthly* v45 no1 p32 Ja 2017

Garne Guisada *Texas Monthly* v45 no2 p36 F 2017

KNIVES OUT *Texas Monthly* v44 no12 p90 D 2016

Pan de Campo *Texas Monthly* v44 no11 p42 N 2016

Peach Ice Cream *Texas Monthly* v45 no6 p28 Je 2017

Sopaipillas *Texas Monthly* v45 no3 p42 Mr 2017

Tamales *Texas Monthly* v44 no12 p44 D 2016

Bond, Gemma

Gemma BOND color *Dance Spirit* v21 no2 p28 F 2017

Bond, Gemma—Interviews

Gemma Bond M. HARSS *Dance Magazine* v91 no8 p18 Ag 2017

BOND, GWENDA

The Refrigerator Monologues color *Publishers Weekly* v264 no16 p50 Ap 17 2017

Bond, Howard E.

Relativistic deflection of background starlight measures the mass of a nearby white dwarf star chart color graph *Science* v356 no6342 p1046 Je 9 2017

BOND, J. RICHARD

A COSMIC CONTROVERSY color *Scientific American* v317 no1 p5 Jl 2017

Bond, Jennifer

Pulses Production Expanding as Consumers Cultivate a Taste for U.S. Lentils and Chickpeas *Amber Waves: The Economics of Food, Farming, Natural Resources, & Rural America* p35 F 2017

Bond, Jeremy Gibson

Stage Presence: A Collaboration That Resulted in a New Approach to Design Communication *Stage Directions* v30 no10 p32 O 2017

Bond, Jon

FOREIGN FOODS J. A. MCELIECE *Dance Magazine* v91 no4 p50 Ap 2017

BOND, JOSH

THE KILLER NEXT DOOR color *Reader's Digest* v189 no1130 p122 My 2017

BOND, JUSTIN VIVIAN

APPARATUS *Interview* v46 no9 p30 N 2016

Bond formation mechanism

Transition metal-catalyzed alkyl-alkyl bond formation: Another dimension in cross-coupling chemistry J. Choi and G. C. Fu diag *Science* v356 no6334 p152 Ap 14 2017

Bond funds

WORRIED ABOUT THE STOCK MARKET? D. FONDA cartoon *Kiplinger's Personal Finance* v71 no6 p13 Je 2017

Bond market

Why Trump Is Making Bond Markets Nervous S. Barton, Y. Li et al *Bloomberg Businessweek* no4500 p39 N 21 2016

Bond market—Corrupt practices

China's Bond Market Has a Forgery Problem *Bloomberg Businessweek* no4509 p36 Ja 30 2017

Bondar, Ana-Nicoleta

A three-dimensional movie of structural changes in bacteriorhodopsin bibl diag graph *Science* v354 no6319 p1552 D 23 2016

Bondar, Roberta, 1945-

DOWN TO EARTH S. DOYLE color *Canadian Geographic* v137 no4 p58 Jl/Ag 2017

Bondette, Neal E.

DRIVEN TO DISTRACTION *New York Times Upfront* v149 no10 p10 Mr 13 2017

Bond funds—Charts, diagrams, etc.

Infrastructure Wins Fans D. FONDA chart *Kiplinger's Personal Finance* v71 no1 p60 Ja 2017

Trump Bump Suffers Slump T. Tepper chart *Money* v46 no5 p76 Je 2017

Bonds (Finance)

Earn Up to 10% D. FONDA cartoon *Kiplinger's Personal Finance*

v71 no6 p42 Je 2017

Finding Bargains Across the Pond N. S. HUANG chart *Kiplinger's Personal Finance* v71 no8 p54 Ag 2017

The Future of Cities Depends on Innovative Financing J. D. Macomber *Harvard Business Review Digital Articles* p2 Ja 11 2016

How to Buy Bonds Now J. BODNAR *Kiplinger's Personal Finance* v71 no6 p8 Je 2017

Replot Your Income Plan C. Fried color diag *Money* v45 no10 p39 N 2016

When a Tree Falls, Who Pays? K. LANKFORD *Kiplinger's Personal Finance* v71 no8 p38 Ag 2017

When Everything Is Working, Sit Tight J. R. KOSNETT color *Kiplinger's Personal Finance* v71 no7 p53 Jl 2017

When to Step Back From Stocks J. Waggoner diag *Money* v46 no9 p51 O 2017

Why Interest Rates Matter D. FONDA cartoon graph *Kiplinger's Personal Finance* v71 no2 p57 F 2017

Bonds (Finance)—Evaluation

Three Ways to Join in Europe's Recovery R. ERMEY chart *Kiplinger's Personal Finance* v71 no8 p55 Ag 2017

Bonds (Finance)—Prices

Shift Your Bond Gears C. Fried color diag *Money* v46 no2 p47 Mr 2017

TAX-SMART BOND SWAPPING M. COHEN *Forbes* v198 no8 p67 D 20 2016

You'll Still Make Money in Bonds J. R. KOSNETT *Kiplinger's Personal Finance* v71 no1 p49 Ja 2017

Bonds (Finance)—Rate of return

Best Ways to Invest in Bonds Now J. K. GLASSMAN chart *Kiplinger's Personal Finance* v71 no3 p18 Mr 2017

What Happened to the New Normal for Bonds? B. Chappatta and J. Gittelsohn bw *Bloomberg Businessweek* no4504 p36 D 19 2016

Bonds (Finance)—Taxation

TAX-SMART BOND SWAPPING M. COHEN *Forbes* v198 no8 p67 D 20 2016

Bonds (Finance)—United States

What Happened to the New Normal for Bonds? B. Chappatta and J. Gittelsohn bw *Bloomberg Businessweek* no4504 p36 D 19 2016

You'll Still Make Money in Bonds J. R. KOSNETT *Kiplinger's Personal Finance* v71 no1 p49 Ja 2017

Bonds, Barry, 1964-—Substance use

Leap Year T. Keith color diag *Sports Illustrated* v126 no2 p16 Ja 16 2017

Bonds (Finance)—Charts, diagrams, etc.

We Add a Real Estate Fund D. FONDA chart *Kiplinger's Personal Finance* v71 no3 p62 Mr 2017

Bonds (Finance)—Prices—Charts, diagrams, etc.

THE FUND REPORT D. I. Salisbury diag *Money* v46 no1 p108 Ja/F 2017

Bonds (Finance)—Rate of return—Charts, diagrams, etc.

Markets Reactions D. Burger and L. Kawa graph *Bloomberg Businessweek* no4536 p31 S 4 2017

Bondy, Dianne

Dianne Bondy J. Calderone bw *Rodale's Organic Life* v3 no1 p82 Ja 2017

Bone, Kenneth

Sound Bites color *Entertainment Weekly* no1436/1437 p12 O 21 2016

Bone abnormalities

BONES SPEAK VOLUMES D. Bennett bw color *Equus* no482 p43 N 2017

Bone density

advice for dancers L. HAMILTON *Dance Magazine* v91 no4 p24 Ap 2017

Bone growth

BONE SMART T. G. HOPE cartoon *Better Homes & Gardens* v95 no5 p164 My 2017

Bone morphogenetic proteins

Decoding of position in the developing neural tube from antiparallel morphogen gradients M. Zagorski, Y. Tabata et al diag *Science* v356 no6345 p1379 Je 30 2017

Bone physiology

Bones tell other organs a thing or two C. MARTIN chart color *Science News* v191 no13 p12 Jl 8 2017

Bone remodeling
Lovely BONES C. Krucoff color *Yoga Journal* p60 2017 Special Issue

Bonebrake, Timothy C.
Biodiversity redistribution under climate change: Impacts on ecosystems and human well-being color *Science* v355 no6332 p1389 Mr 31 2017
Higher predation risk for insect prey at low latitudes and elevations graph *Science* v356 no6339 p742 My 19 2017

Bonebreaker (Short story)
BONEBREAKER N. Zink color *Harper's Magazine* v335 no2005 p77 Je 2017

Boneh, Dan
Deriving genomic diagnoses without revealing patient genomes chart *Science* v357 no6352 p692 Ag 18 2017

Bonello, Bertrand
BLANK GENERATION H. HAMPTON bw color *Film Comment* v53 no3 p52 My/Je 2017
FRAME TO FRAME V. LUCCA *Film Comment* v53 no3 p54 My/Je 2017

Bonello, Bertrand—Interviews
Next Steps V. Lucca color *Film Comment* v53 no1 p10 Ja/F 2017

Bones
See also
Cartilage
Femur
BONE SMART T. G. HOPE cartoon *Better Homes & Gardens* v95 no5 p164 My 2017
Had to Share! color *Better Nutrition* p20 My 2017
IF THEY CAN'T SAY SOMETHING NICE... J. GALLOWAY color *Runner's World* v52 no7 p29 Ag 2017
Meet the Denisovans B. ALEX color map *Discover* v27 no10 p64 D 2016

Bones (TV program)
THE BEST OF BOOTH'S WORLD K. Connolly color *Entertainment Weekly* no1457/1458 p87 Mr 17 2017
BONES BIDS ADIEU M. ROFFMAN *TV Guide* v65 no13 p16 Mr 20 2017
Bones' Big Send-Off M. Roffman *TV Guide* v65 no8 p10 F 27 2017
BONES M. Roffman *TV Guide* v64 no15 p54 Ap 4 2016
Bones M. Roffman *TV Guide* v65 no2 p26 Ja 2 2017
Booth Searches for Brennan on Bones M. Roffman *TV Guide* p12 D 19 2016

Bones—Diseases—Prevention
EXERCISE AND BONE HEALTH color *Harvard Health Letter* v42 no2 p5 D 2016

Bonessi, Dominique
After coup attempt, Turkey cracks down on Protestants color *Christian Century* v134 no1 p14 Ja 4 2017
The Waiting Room color *Commonweal* v144 no5 p39 Mr 10 2017

Bonet, Clarissa
Head Space color *Popular Photography* v81 no2 p12 Mr/Ap 2017

BONEVELLE, ANDREA
RISK MANAGEMENT *Psychology Today* v50 no4 p6 Ag 2017

Bonfires
Bonfire Basics E. Millard color *Log Home Living* v33 no9 p38 D 2016
OUR TOP PICKS F. ESKER color *New Orleans Magazine* v51 no2 p28 D 2016

Bonfond, B.
Jupiter's magnetosphere and aurorae observed by the Juno spacecraft during its first polar orbits diag graph *Science* v356 no6340 p826 My 26 2017

Bongers, F.
Persistent effects of pre-Columbian plant domestication on Amazonian forest composition bibl chart graph map *Science* v355 no6328 p925 Mr 3 2017

Bongers, Frans
Forest conservation: Humans' handprints bibl color *Science* v355 no6324 p466 F 3 2017

BongWoo Kim
A nuclease that mediates cell death induced by DNA damage and poly(ADP-ribose) polymerase-1 bw graph *Science* v354 no6308 paad6872-1 O 7 2016

Bonham, William

CAPTIVE HEARTS W. Bonham color *AARP: The Magazine* v59 no3A p70 Ap/My 2016

Bonhoeffer, Sebastian
Reducing antimicrobial use in food animals color graph *Science* v357 no6358 p1350 S 29 2017

BONHOMME, VINCENT
Pitcher Plants Shape Up color diag *Natural History* v125 no5 p12 My 2017

Boni, Maciej F.
Role for migratory wild birds in the global spread of avian influenza H5N8 bibl graph map *Science* v354 no6309 p213 O 14 2016

Bonifacio, Adrian
THE CONVERSATION color *Atlantic* v320 no2 p8 S 2017

Bonifazi, C.
Observation of a large-scale anisotropy in the arrival directions of cosmic rays above 8×10^{18} eV *Science* v357 no6357 p1266 S 22 2017

Bonilla, Peter
FIT TO PRINT bw color *Wired* v25 no5 p14 My 2017

Bonin, Jeremy
Small-House Design Strategies color diag *Timber Home Living* v27 no3 p56 Je 2017

Bonior, Andrea
FRIENDSHIP {decoded} color *Seventeen* v76 no4 p86 Jl/Ag 2017

Bonis, Peter
An Online Medical Database Is Reducing Diagnostic Errors *Harvard Business Review Digital Articles* p2 O 27 2015

BONK, CHYRLE
AHSAHKA: WHERE RIVERS MEET AND LINES ARE CAST *Idaho Magazine* v16 no8 p32 My 2017
Packing the Tot *Idaho Magazine* v16 no5 p23 F 2017

Bonkowski, Michael S.
A conserved NAD+ binding pocket that regulates protein-protein interactions during aging bibl graph *Science* v355 no6331 p1312 Mr 24 2017

BONN, ALETTA
National Ecosystem Assessments in Europe: A Review chart *BioScience* v66 no10 p813 O 1 2016
When, Where, and How Nature Matters for Ecosystem Services: Challenges for the Next Generation of Ecosystem Service Models *BioScience* v67 no9 p820 S 2017

Bonnell, Kimberly
10-Year-Old-Girl Powers We Should All Reclaim color *Glamour* v115 no5 p195 My 2017
12 Sex Things We Still Don't Understand color *Glamour* v115 no7 p109 Jl 2017
13 Accomplishments That Are Bigger Than They Seem color *Glamour* v115 no6 p147 Je 2017
13 Resolutions Other People Really Need to Make This Year color *Glamour* v115 no1 p99 Ja 2017
13 Things That Should Be A Thing color *Glamour* v114 no11 p183 N 2016
14 Totally Legit Expectations in Love color *Glamour* v115 no2 p127 F 2017
32 Weirdly Random Thoughts We've Had During Yoga color *Glamour* v115 no9 p215 S 2017
My First Year bw color *Glamour* v115 no1 p48 Ja 2017

Bonner, Jordan Sebastian
10 TITLES TO PICK UP NOW color *O, The Oprah Magazine* p99 O 2017

Bonner, Laurie
1977: A LOOK BACK bw color *Equus* no482 p39 N 2017
Beyond basic care color *Equus* no476 p62 My 2017
Botulism color *Equus* no481 p31 O 2017
Colic bw color *Equus* no470 p26 N 2016
EPM color *Equus* no478 p29 Jl 2017
Heaves flare-up color *Equus* no472 p18 Ja 2017
LAMINITIS PREVENTION BASICS bw color *Equus* no475 p52 Ap 2017
Large laceration color *Equus* no473 p20 F 2017
Parasite control color *Equus* no476 p37 My 2017
Rhinopneumonitis color diag *Equus* no480 p35 S 2017
Scratches color *Equus* no474 p18 Mr 2017
Test your knowledge of POISONOUS PLANTS [Cover story] color *Equus* no477 p34 Je 2017

West Nile encephalitis bw color *Equus* no475 p36 Ap 2017

Bonnet, Didier

The Best Digital Business Models Put Evolution Before Revolution *Harvard Business Review Digital Articles* p2 Ja 20 2015

Bonneville motorcycle—Evaluation

2017 TRIUMPH BONNEVILLE BOBBER S. MacDonald color *Cycle World* v56 no2 p58 Mr 2017

Bonneville Salt Flats (Utah)

HONORING BURT MUNRO, CELEBRATING SPEED K. Cameron bw color *Cycle World* v56 no10 p52 N 2017

Bonnie & Clyde (Film)

Bonnie and Clyde at 50 M. AGRESTA *Texas Monthly* v45 no9 p50 S 2017

BONNIER, JORDAN S.

10 TITLES TO PICK UP NOW color *O, The Oprah Magazine* p110 N 2017

Bonnier Corp.

REWARDING EXCELLENCE S. Pope *Flying* v144 no2 p10 F 2017

Bono, 1960-

What Makes a Woman of the Year in 2016? C. Leive color *Glamour* v114 no12 p48 D 2016

Bono, 1960-—Awards

Movers K. Stock bw color graph *Bloomberg Businessweek* no4498 p19 N 7 2016

Bono, 1960-—Interviews

Bono C. Amanpour color *Glamour* v114 no12 p212 D 2016

Bono, Joyce E.

The Powerful Effect of Noticing Good Things at Work *Harvard Business Review Digital Articles* p2 S 4 2015

Bonobo—Reproduction

Chimps, bonobos interbred long ago T. Hesman Saey color *Science News* v190 no11 p19 N 26 2016

Bonora, Massimo

Reticulon 3–dependent ER-PM contact sites control EGFR nonclathrin endocytosis color diag graph *Science* v356 no6338 p617 My 12 2017

Bonsai

Green Room J. K. DE VALLE color *Architectural Digest* no6 p39 Je 1 2017

Grow Your Own Miniature Fruit Trees M. L. Shaw *Mother Earth News* no282 p89 Je/Jl 2017

Bonus Army, 1932

THE BATTLE OF ANACOSTIA FLATS B. Hogan *MHQ: Quarterly Journal of Military History* v29 no2 p66 Wint 2017

Bonuses (Employee fringe benefits)

Career Coach J. Barberio color *Working Mother* v40 no4 p8 O/N 2017

Do Conservative Managers Give Smaller Bonuses to Women? F. Briscoe and A. Joshi *Harvard Business Review Digital Articles* p2 D 2 2016

Sales Bonuses Are Supposed to Motivate, So Don't Waste Them on Easy Targets A. A. Zoltners, P. K. Sinha et al *Harvard Business Review Digital Articles* p2 S 14 2017

Should a CEO's Bonus Be Based on Financial Performance Alone? G. Kenny *Harvard Business Review Digital Articles* p2 My 25 2017

Time for a reward rethink P. Cheese *People Management* p5 O 2016

What's the Right Kind of Bonus to Motivate Your Sales Force? D. J. Chung and D. Narayandas *Harvard Business Review Digital Articles* p2 S 12 2017

Bonvicini, Monica

MONICA BONVICINI R. Wetzler color *Art in America* v105 no5 p126 My 2017

BOODMAN, ERIC

Blow-Up Bomb Shelter bw color *Discover* v27 no10 p16 D 2016

BOOEY, BABA

Always Watching color *Popular Mechanics* p38 Mr 2017

Boog, Jason

Bookstagrammers Gain Influence in a Diffuse Marketplace bw chart color *Publishers Weekly* v264 no38 p6 S 18 2017

Chronicle Books at 50 color *Publishers Weekly* v264 no24 p7 Je 12 2017

How Kepler's Books Prepared For the Retail Bloodbath color *Publishers Weekly* v264 no28 p8 Jl 10 2017

Independent Bookstore Day 2017: A Perfect Storm for Sales color map *Publishers Weekly* v264 no17 p6 Ap 24 2017

Is Poetry "the New Adult Coloring Book"? color *Publishers Weekly* v264 no35 p12 Ag 28 2017

Meltdown Comics' Bitcoin Experience chart color *Publishers Weekly* v264 no32 p5 Ag 7 2017

Moppet Books Moves Forward With KinderGuides Line color *Publishers Weekly* v264 no33 p8 Ag 14 2017

The Steady Rise of 'Not Giving a F*ck' bw color *Publishers Weekly* v264 no31 p6 Jl 31 2017

"The Library Saved My Life" color *Publishers Weekly* v264 no22 p29 My 29 2017

THROUGH THE LOOKING GLASS bw color *Publishers Weekly* v264 no41 p24 O 9 2017

Book auctions

Deals R. DEAHL bw color *Publishers Weekly* v264 no41 p6 O 9 2017

Book clubs (Bookselling)

KIDS' SUBSCRIPTION SERVICES TAKE OFF C. KIRCH color *Publishers Weekly* v264 no11 p26 Mr 13 2017

Book clubs (Discussion groups)

A Shared Passion for Reading D. A. WOOD color *Missouri Life* v44 no6 p10 S 2017

Who Will Win the Newbery Medal? S. MAUGHAN color *Publishers Weekly* v263 no52 p56 D 19 2016

Book collecting

CELEBRATING THE STORY OF CANADA E. NAWOTKA color *Publishers Weekly* v264 no41 p3 O 9 2017

Book cover art

Cover Redesign color *Publishers Weekly* v264 no13 p44 Mr 27 2017

Book cover design

See also

Book cover art

11 Tips for Successfully Working With a Cover Designer J. FRIEDLANDER *Publishers Weekly* v264 no9 p47 F 27 2017

Cover Redesign color *Publishers Weekly* v264 no17 p40 Ap 24 2017

Book covers

The Best Book Covers of 2016 M. DORFMAN *New York Times Book Review* p18 D 11 2016

Book design

Design Options for Self-Publishers J. FRIEDLANDER *Publishers Weekly* v263 no43 p42 O 24 2016

Book editors

A Different Feel at BookExpo 2017 J. Milliot color *Publishers Weekly* v264 no23 p4 Je 5 2017

"Pinch Me, I'm Dreaming" bw color *Publishers Weekly* v263 no49 p6 D 7 2016

Robert B. Silvers (1929-2017) D. Mendelsohn bw *New York Review of Books* v64 no7 p8 Ap 20 2017

Book equipment

How to Make a... BOOK SAFE color *Popular Mechanics* p81 S 2017

Book illustration—Awards

SHARJAH CHILDREN'S BOOK ILLUSTRATION PRIZES 2016 cartoon *Publishers Weekly* v263 no43 p(Sp)10 O 24 2016

Book industry

See also

Booksellers & bookselling

Publishers & publishing

Stationery

BOOKSELLING IN THE TWIN CITIES C. KIRCH color *Publishers Weekly* v264 no3 p10 Ja 16 2017

Celebrating the Holidays With Favorite Friends K. Raugust color *Publishers Weekly* v263 no50 p21 D 5 2016

Deals D. LEFFERTS color *Publishers Weekly* v263 no50 p14 D 5 2016

Georgetown Group Celebrates 50 Years E. NAWOTKA *Publishers Weekly* v263 no39 p22 S 26 2016

HERE IT IS: OUR BIG FALL BOOKS PREVIEW J. SEGURA *Publishers Weekly* v264 no26 p20 Je 26 2017

Indie Spirits E. NAWOTKA *Publishers Weekly* v263 no39 p16 S 26 2016

An International Press Looks to 2017 J. Maher color *Publishers Weekly* v263 no50 p15 D 5 2016

News Briefs *Publishers Weekly* v264 no4 p4 Ja 23 2017

The Next Steps in Digitization L. Dawson *Publishers Weekly* v264 no4 p20 Ja 23 2017

Taiwan's Indie Booksellers and Publishers Join Forces to Tackle Challenges T. Tan color *Publishers Weekly* v264 no8 p6 F 20 2017

Book industry exhibitions

Andrew Wylie Makes First FIL Appearance L. Ahuile and E. Nawotka color *Publishers Weekly* v263 no50 p25 D 5 2016

A Big Week for Children's Books J. Rosen, D. Roback et al color *Publishers Weekly* v264 no16 p4 Ap 17 2017

BolognaFiere Confirms 2018 N.Y.C. Rights Show J. Milliot *Publishers Weekly* v264 no15 p13 Ap 10 2017

A Bonanza of Book Events for Toddlers to Teens L. Hartman bw color *Publishers Weekly* v263 no44 p(Sp)29 O 31 2016

By the Community, for the Community L. Hartman bw *Publishers Weekly* v263 no44 p(Sp)6 O 31 2016

Consolidation in Book Plus And the Evolution of Coloring K. Raugust color *Publishers Weekly* v264 no9 p7 F 27 2017

DATING IN SHARJAH M. MOUSHABECK *Publishers Weekly* v263 no43 p(Sp)16 O 24 2016

Despite Embargo, U.S., Cuba Publishers Invoke Solidarity, Cultural Exchange C. Reid color *Publishers Weekly* v264 no8 p5 F 20 2017

A Different Feel at BookExpo 2017 J. Milliot color *Publishers Weekly* v264 no23 p4 Je 5 2017

Diversity on Display L. Ahuile color *Publishers Weekly* v263 no50 p24 D 5 2016

An Energetic Season of Regional Shows Wraps Up J. Rosen color *Publishers Weekly* v263 no45 p10 N 7 2016

A Gallery of Hot Titles from China T. TAN color *Publishers Weekly* v264 no12 p32 Mr 20 2017

The Goddard Riverside Book Fair, 30 Years In J. Maher *Publishers Weekly* v263 no42 p10 O 17 2016

Highlights of the Fair bw color *Publishers Weekly* v263 no44 p(Sp)3 O 31 2016

Librarians, Check This Out A. R. ALBANESE color *Publishers Weekly* v264 no20 p(Sp)28 My 15 2017

THE PLAY'S THE THIHG T. MALONE *Atlanta* v56 no7 p38 N 2016

PRINTS & EDITIONS color *Art in America* v105 no1 p42 Ja 2017

PROFESSIONAL PROGRAM PROFILE D. WALLACE *Publishers Weekly* v263 no43 p(Sp)17 O 24 2016

Publishers Keep Calm And Carry On A. Albanese, N. Denn et al color *Publishers Weekly* v264 no12 p5 Mr 20 2017

Reed Sets a New Direction for BEA J. Milliot color *Publishers Weekly* v263 no44 p5 O 31 2016

SELECT BOOK CONFERENCES, FESTIVALS, AND FAIRS IN 2017 J. MAHER *Publishers Weekly* v264 no1 p23 Ja 2 2017

Thirty Years of Telling Great Stories L. AHUILE *Publishers Weekly* v263 no46 p4 N 14 2016

Wednesday's Focus L. HARTMAN *Publishers Weekly* v264 no20 p(Sp)16 My 15 2017

Weekend Closeup November 19–20 L. Hartman cartoon *Publishers Weekly* v263 no44 p(Sp)4 O 31 2016

What's Cookin'? L. Hartman bw color *Publishers Weekly* v263 no44 p(Sp)14 O 31 2016

Book industry exhibitions—New York (State)—New York

A New Look For New York J. MILLIOT color *Publishers Weekly* v264 no20 p(Sp)6 My 15 2017

Book Industry Study Group Inc.

O'Leary Takes the Reins at BISG J. Milliot *Publishers Weekly* v263 no39 p5 S 26 2016

Book industry—Awards

The Rising Stars of the Industry L. Hartman bw color *Publishers Weekly* v264 no36 p(Sp)3 S 4 2017

Book industry—Canada

Canadian Kids Publishers Extend Reach into U.S., TV E. NAWOTKA *Publishers Weekly* v263 no39 p14 S 26 2016

Book industry—Congresses

See also

Publishers & publishing—Congresses

BookCon 2017: More of the Same, but Better L. HARTMAN color *Publishers Weekly* v264 no20 p(Sp)32 My 15 2017

An Energetic Season of Regional Shows Wraps Up J. Rosen color

Publishers Weekly v263 no45 p10 N 7 2016

PW Holds Education, Training Program for South Korean Publishers E. Nawotka color *Publishers Weekly* v264 no40 p12 O 2 2017

Book industry—Exhibitions—Germany

The Big Deal at the Frankfurt Book Fair: Free Speech A. Albanese and E. Nawotka color *Publishers Weekly* v263 no43 p4 O 24 2016

FRANKFURT BRIEFCASE 2016 R. DEAHL and J. MAHER *Publishers Weekly* v263 no39 p34 S 26 2016

WORLDVIEWS A. R. ALBANESE *Publishers Weekly* v263 no39 p32 S 26 2016

Book industry—Exhibitions—Great Britain

See You in London A. R. ALBANESE *Publishers Weekly* v264 no9 p20 F 27 2017

Book industry—Finance

Ready to Launch J. FRIEDMAN color *Publishers Weekly* v264 no4 p42 Ja 23 2017

Book industry—News briefs

Deals D. LEFFERTS color *Publishers Weekly* v263 no48 p12 N 28 2016

Deals D. LEFFERTS color *Publishers Weekly* v264 no4 p7 Ja 23 2017

Deals R. DEAHL bw color *Publishers Weekly* v264 no16 p12 Ap 17 2017

Deals R. DEAHL color *Publishers Weekly* v264 no32 p7 Ag 7 2017

News Briefs *Publishers Weekly* v264 no16 p6 Ap 17 2017

News Briefs *Publishers Weekly* v264 no31 p8 Jl 31 2017

Book industry—United States

Bookstores Engage in Diverse Forms of Protest E. Nawotka and C. Kirch color *Publishers Weekly* v264 no11 p6 Mr 13 2017

Estimates Show a 6.6% Decline in Industry J. Milliot chart *Publishers Weekly* v264 no25 p5 Je 19 2017

Release of 'What Happened' Can't Stop Sales Slide chart *Publishers Weekly* v264 no39 p5 S 25 2017

Book reviewing

Those Amazon Numbers P. RIVA color *Publishers Weekly* v263 no44 p80 O 31 2016

Book sales & prices

See also

Textbooks—Sales & prices

Adler-Olsen Ruled March E. Nawotka color *Publishers Weekly* v264 no17 p18 Ap 24 2017

Bargain Books in the Digital Age J. Rosen color *Publishers Weekly* v264 no39 p4 S 25 2017

BESTSELLERS chart *Publishers Weekly* v264 no33 p14 Ag 14 2017

BESTSELLERS C. JURIS chart *Publishers Weekly* v264 no24 p13 Je 12 2017

The Bestsellers of 2017 (So Far) J. Maher *Publishers Weekly* v264 no28 p5 Jl 10 2017

A Big Week for Adult Fiction chart *Publishers Weekly* v264 no21 p5 My 22 2017

Bookselling As a Second Career C. Kirch color *Publishers Weekly* v264 no34 p11 Ag 21 2017

Books Suffer from Potter Curse, Sales Tumble 17% chart *Publishers Weekly* v264 no33 p6 Ag 14 2017

Bookstagrammers Gain Influence in a Diffuse Marketplace J. Boog bw chart color *Publishers Weekly* v264 no38 p6 S 18 2017

CATEGORY BESTSELLERS C. JURIS chart *Publishers Weekly* v264 no24 p17 Je 12 2017

Estimates Show a 6.6% Decline in Industry J. Milliot chart *Publishers Weekly* v264 no25 p5 Je 19 2017

Everybody Falls Sometimes B. ECKSTEIN color *Publishers Weekly* v264 no40 p144 O 2 2017

FALL 2017 AUDIO ANNOUNCEMENTS S. MAUGHAN color *Publishers Weekly* v264 no27 p21 Jl 3 2017

Fast, Cheap, and Good J. FRIEDMAN *Publishers Weekly* v264 no21 p50 My 22 2017

Favorites Drive 7% Gain in Units chart *Publishers Weekly* v264 no27 p5 Jl 3 2017

Flat Sales Identified as Top Industry Problem J. Milliot graph *Publishers Weekly* v264 no40 p5 O 2 2017

How Kepler's Books Prepared For the Retail Bloodbath J. Boog color *Publishers Weekly* v264 no28 p8 Jl 10 2017 iBook Bestsellers C. JURIS chart color *Publishers Weekly* v264 no24 p18 Je 12 2017

In a Quiet Week, Hardcover Gains Offset Declines in Audio, Mass Market Paperback chart *Publishers Weekly* v264 no22 p7 My 29 2017

Juvenile Categories Had Double-Digit Gains in the Week chart *Publishers Weekly* v264 no31 p5 Jl 31 2017

Juvenile Nonfiction Stays Hot chart *Publishers Weekly* v264 no32 p5 Ag 7 2017

Print, Audio Keep Publishers Moving Ahead J. Milliot chart *Publishers Weekly* v264 no36 p4 S 4 2017

Print Sales Get an Easter Bump chart *Publishers Weekly* v264 no15 p9 Ap 10 2017

Print Units Through September Up 2% J. Milliot chart *Publishers Weekly* v264 no41 p4 O 9 2017

Release of 'What Happened' Can't Stop Sales Slide chart *Publishers Weekly* v264 no39 p5 S 25 2017

The Rise in Print Continues J. Milliot chart *Publishers Weekly* v264 no28 p4 Jl 10 2017

Sales Stay Flat for a Second Consecutive Week chart *Publishers Weekly* v264 no35 p12 Ag 28 2017

Solid Gains in the Juvenile Categories Help Drive Units Up chart *Publishers Weekly* v264 no24 p6 Je 12 2017

Spring Fever C. JURIS chart color graph *Publishers Weekly* v264 no15 p17 Ap 10 2017

Thrillers Hot In May E. Nawotka chart *Publishers Weekly* v264 no26 p17 Je 26 2017

Trade a Bright Spot In a Down Year for Book Sales J. Milliot chart *Publishers Weekly* v264 no32 p4 Ag 7 2017

Unit Sales Rise 4% chart *Publishers Weekly* v264 no40 p6 O 2 2017

Unit Sales Rose 3% at the End of April chart *Publishers Weekly* v264 no19 p5 My 8 2017

Unit Sales Slide 3% from 2016 chart *Publishers Weekly* v264 no38 p6 S 18 2017

With Late Easter, Juvenile Sales Tumble chart *Publishers Weekly* v264 no14 p5 Ap 3. 2017

Yep, There Are Books C. JOHNSON color *Publishers Weekly* v264 no32 p76 Ag 7 2017

Bookends (Music)

Essential Paul Simon D. Fricke bw color *Rolling Stone* no1275 p62 D 1 2016

Booker, Benjamin

Benjamin Booker's L.A. Punk Chic P. DOYLE bw color *Rolling Stone* no1287 p16 My 18 2017

Booker, Charles

Urban Oasis: Stylish New Orleans outdoor living spaces large, small and everything between V. Hart *New Orleans Homes & Lifestyles* v20 no3 p56 Summ 2017

Booker, Cory, 1969-

Cory Booker's Challenge K. B. VLAHOS *American Conservative* v16 no3 p28 My/Je 2017

Icons color *Time* v189 no16/17 p122 My 1-8 2017

Who, Me? Nah... *Weekly Standard* v22 no19 p3 Ja 23 2017

Booker, Kristin

HIDING IN PLAIN SIGHT color *Women's Health* v14 no8 p46 O 2017

Booker, Tricia

Catch Me Is Uncatchable *In Stride* v12 no2 p18 Mr 2017

Cuba: Conquers the $268,550 USHJA International Hunter Derby Championship *In Stride* v12 no5 p12 S 2017

EDUCATING THE NEXT GENERATION color *Practical Horseman* v45 no8 p40 Ag 2017

Gracie Marlowe Is Golden at the USHJA Emerging Athletes Program National Training Session *In Stride* v12 no1 p16 Ja 2017

John French Wins Wire-To-Wire in the WCHR Professional Finals *In Stride* v11 no6 p22 N 2016

Kavar Kerr's Legacy of Service *In Stride* v12 no3 p45 My 2017

Mary Babick Arrives for the 'Formative Years' *In Stride* v11 no6 p32 N 2016

McLain Ward's Flawless World Cup Finish Was No Fluke *In Stride* v12 no3 p16 My 2017

Millions of Reasons to Celebrate the USHJA International Hunter Derby Program: After less than a decade, the program pays out more than $10 million--and the numbers are only increasing *In Stride* v12 no4 p20 Jl 2017

Nancy Crary Jones: An Amateur with a Professional Mindset *In Stride* v12 no4 p39 Jl 2017

Playbook Draft & Victory in the $218,04 Platinum Performance/ USJHA Green Hunter Incentive Championship *In Stride* v12 no5 p20 S 2017

St. Jacques and Iwasaki Claim Hunterdon Cup Titles *In Stride* v12 no5 p42 S 2017

Book industry—Charts, diagrams, etc.

THE WEEKLY SCORECARD chart *Publishers Weekly* v263 no52 p7 D 19 2016

THE WEEKLY SCORECARD chart *Publishers Weekly* v264 no8 p6 F 20 2017

THE WEEKLY SCORECARD Tracking Unit Print Sales (in thousands) chart *Publishers Weekly* v263 no44 p6 O 31 2016

Book industry—Societies, etc.

PW Holds Education, Training Program for South Korean Publishers E. Nawotka color *Publishers Weekly* v264 no40 p12 O 2 2017

Book industry—United States—Charts, diagrams, etc.

THE WEEKLY SCORECARD chart *Publishers Weekly* v263 no51 p2 D 12 2016

Book of Henry, The (Film)

THE BOOK OF HENRY R. Kinane color *Entertainment Weekly* no1463/1464 p57 Ap/My 2017

Dancing Acting Taking Over the World [Cover story] A. STANLEY bw color *Seventeen* v76 no4 p60 Jl/Ag 2017

Book of Love, The (Film)

The Book of Love C. Nashawaty color *Entertainment Weekly* no1449 p45 Ja 20 2017

Book of Simon, The (Short story)

THE BOOK OF SIMON S. RICH cartoon *New Yorker* v92 no30 p31 S 26 2016

Bookouture (Company)

Britain's Hottest Digital Publisher J. Maher *Publishers Weekly* v263 no39 p8 S 26 2016

Books

    See also
    Books & reading
    Children's books
    Cookbooks
    Electronic books
    Guidebooks
    Manuscripts
    Notebooks
    Picture books

5 Books for Raising Respectful Children *Parents* v91 no10 p20 O 2016

THE APPROVAL MATRIX img *New York* v50 no8 p164 Ap 17 2017

AYESHA CURRY "I Believe You Can Have It All" A. Prato color *Health* v30 no9 p24 N 2016

believe E. ZAMMETT RUDDY *Parents* v91 no12 p82 D 2016

Boxes for Everyone! K. Cicero color *Parents* v92 no9 p148 S 2017

CREATIVITY UNLEASHED S. COCHRAN color *Architectural Digest* v73 no12 p144 D 2016

downtime finds *Parents* v91 no11 p46 N 2016

Easiest Picnic Ever color *Health* v31 no5 p13 Je 2017

Editors' Choice: Staff Picks From the Book Review *New York Times Book Review* p22 S 3 2017

funny finds E. ELVERU color *Parents* v92 no6 p79 Je 2017

GEAR ESSENTIALS H. Dowdle color *Yoga Journal* p18 2017 Special Issue

Green Gazette *Mother Earth News* no280 p10 F/Mr 2017

Happiness on Your Bookshelf color *Health* v31 no8 p14 O 2017

Headed for the Graveyard of Books J. ATLAS *New York Times Book Review* p21 F 12 2017

HEALTHY LIVING MADE EASY color *Health* v31 no1 p12 Ja 2017

Here We Go! O. Winfrey color *O, The Oprah Magazine* p20 N 2017

How SHE-roes Raise Girls M. LaScala color *Parents* v92 no5 p17 My 2017

How to Make a... BOOK SAFE color *Popular Mechanics* p81 S 2017

the inside story K. CICERO *Parents* v91 no12 p60 D 2016

It's Cheesy N. Brechka color *Better Nutrition* v79 no11 p76 N 2017

kids * health news *Parents* v92 no2 p28 F 2017

Letting Go R. BROOKHISER *National Review* v69 no11 p43 Je 12 2017

Listen Up! color *Health* v31 no6 p14 Jl 2017

media to go E. ELVERU color *Parents* v92 no8 p85 Ag 2017

nighty night, everyone! L. SMITH BRODY color graph *Parents* v92 no8 p44 Ag 2017

A NOTE FROM OUR PUBLISHER S. Katz *Mother Jones* v42 no3 p44 My/Je 2017

Organic and Non-GMO, Simplified! M. D. SMITH color *Better Nutrition* v79 no10 p72 O 2017

parent-pleasing media picks color *Parents* v92 no4 p76 Ap 2017

popular authors' favorite children's books J. PACTON color *Parents* v92 no5 p48 My 2017

Portable & Affordable Vegan color *Better Nutrition* v79 no6 p60 Je 2017

Remainders of the Day J. STEIN cartoon *New York Times Book Review* p29 S 25 2016

Reviews Roundup *Publishers Weekly* v263 no43 p50 O 24 2016

Sales at Mass Merchandisers Continue to Bounce Back *Publishers Weekly* v264 no18 p5 My 1 2017

Savannah and Her Stories L. Vaccariello color *Parents* v92 no11 p8 N 2017

shelf help L. FENTON color *Parents* v92 no8 p121 Ag 2017

Sketchbook A. Nilsen *New York Times Book Review* p27 Je 25 2017

spread the word! K. CICERO *Parents* p29 2015

SPRING 2017 ADULT ANNOUNCEMENTS L. ERMELINO color *Publishers Weekly* v263 no51 p18 D 12 2016

Stories for the Memory Books *Southern Living* v51 no12 p130 D 2016

Stuff we love color *Yoga Journal* no292 p24 Je 2017

This Year's Winning Reads K. CICERO color *Parents* v92 no11 p64 N 2017

Vegan Family Meals N. BRECHKA color *Better Nutrition* v79 no10 p76 O 2017

Veganize Your Meal N. BRECHKA color *Better Nutrition* v79 no9 p60 S 2017

WHAT'S YOUR FAVORITE YOGA READ? [Cover story] color *Yoga Journal* no292 p20 Je 2017

Where He Stands *Arizona Highways* v93 no9 p56 S 2017

THE WORST BOOKS OF THE YEAR color *Entertainment Weekly* no1444/1445 p108 D 16 2016

YA Stories You Should Snatch Up K. Kemp color *Parents* v92 no7 p16 Jl 2017

Your starter toolkit color *Yoga Journal* p118 2016 Special Issue

Books & reading

See also

Best sellers

BOOKS FOR EVERY CHILD: How the Greenbrier Bookcase Project ensures young readers have access to quality books at home A. Betancourt *Literacy Today (2411-7862)* v35 no2 p36 S/O 2017

DAVIDE GRASSO IS THE CEO OF CONVERSE D. GRASSO *Harvard Business Review* v95 no3 p160 My/Je 2017

Harry Potter, holy writ S. Paulsell *Christian Century* v133 no22 p35 O 26 2016

Here We Go! Oprah color *O, The Oprah Magazine* p21 Ag 2017

How to Read a Book a Week P. Bregman *Harvard Business Review Digital Articles* p2 F 8 2016

ILA's Choices Reading Lists graph map *Literacy Today (2411-7862)* v34 no6 p12 My/Je 2017

Keeping Faith M. LANE *American Scholar* v86 no2 p74 Spr 2017

KNOW IT ALL K. SCHULZ cartoon color *New Yorker* v93 no32 p76 O 16 2017

Match Book N. Lamy *New York Times Book Review* p53 Je 4 2017

Match Book N. Lamy *New York Times Book Review* p9 O 8 2017

Parneshia Jones C. Kirch color *Publishers Weekly* v264 no19 p6 My 8 2017

PRINT / HARDCOVER BEST SELLERS *New York Times Book Review* p24 Ag 20 2017

PRINT/HARDCOVER BEST SELLERS *New York Times Book Review* p26 N 27 2016

READ, WHITE AND BLUE: Which books do Americans take on vacation? Our analysis uncovered some surprises A. Clemens *Smithsonian* v48 no4 p14 Jl/Ag 2017

So Many Books H. STERNBERG *Publishers Weekly* v264 no7 p80 F 13 2017

Those Amazon Numbers P. RIVA color *Publishers Weekly* v263 no44 p80 O 31 2016

THREE COMPONENTS TO READING SUCCESS: Guide readers from striving to thriving through reading volume A. Ward color *Literacy Today (2411-7862)* v34 no6 p10 My/Je 2017

VALUING THEIR CHOICES: Fuel students' love for literature with their own reading picks C. Maloney map *Literacy Today (2411-7862)* v34 no6 p12 My/Je 2017

VALUING THEIR VOICES P. J. Farris color *Literacy Today (2411-7862)* v34 no6 p14 My/Je 2017

Why Businesspeople Should Join Book Clubs J. Coleman *Harvard Business Review Digital Articles* p2 F 23 2016

Books & reading—Great Britain

FROM THE EDITOR P. Lay *History Today* v67 no2 p2 F 2017

Books & reading—Humor

Laugh Lines color *Reader's Digest* v190 no1133 p117 S 2017

Books & reading—Social aspects

A CLASSIC DEBATE E. Chiariello color *Literacy Today (2411-7862)* v34 no6 p26 My/Je 2017

Books & reading—United States

Research: How Investors' Reading Habits Influence Stock Prices A. Fedyk *Harvard Business Review Digital Articles* p2 S 2 2016

Book sales & prices—Charts, diagrams, etc.

BESTSELLERS C. JURIS chart *Publishers Weekly* v264 no19 p12 My 8 2017

CATEGORY BESTSELLERS C. JURIS chart *Publishers Weekly* v264 no19 p16 My 8 2017

CHILDREN'S BESTSELLERS C. JURIS chart *Publishers Weekly* v264 no19 p14 My 8 2017

Books—Charts, diagrams, etc.

BESTSELLERS chart *Publishers Weekly* v264 no2 p14 Ja 9 2017

BESTSELLERS C. JURIS chart *Publishers Weekly* v264 no21 p15 My 22 2017

BESTSELLERS C. JURIS chart *Publishers Weekly* v264 no38 p17 S 18 2017

BestSellers *New York Times Book Review* p22 Ap 2 2017

Best Sellers *New York Times Book Review* p23 Mr 26 2017

Board Books Have Big Week chart *Publishers Weekly* v264 no30 p5 Jl 24 2017

CATEGORY BESTSELLERS C. JURIS chart *Publishers Weekly* v264 no34 p21 Ag 21 2017

COMBINED PRINT AND E-BOOK BEST SELLERS *New York Times Book Review* p19 Jl 9 2017

HARDCOVER BEST SELLERS *New York Times Book Review* p24 F 12 2017

iBook Bestsellers C. JURIS chart color *Publishers Weekly* v264 no34 p22 Ag 21 2017

iBooks Bestsellers C. JURIS chart color *Publishers Weekly* v264 no38 p21 S 18 2017

iBooks Bestsellers C. JURIS chart color *Publishers Weekly* v264 no7 p17 F 13 2017

Prize Winners On Top in France, Spain J. Maher chart *Publishers Weekly* v264 no1 p14 Ja 2 2017

THE WEEKLY SCORECARD chart *Publishers Weekly* v264 no1 p4 Ja 2 2017

Books—China—History

A Gallery of Hot Titles from China T. TAN color *Publishers Weekly* v264 no12 p32 Mr 20 2017

Books—Computer network resources

Goodreads Marks 10 Years of Supporting Books, Reading C. Reid color *Publishers Weekly* v264 no39 p12 S 25 2017

Books—Congresses

That Was the Week That Was color *Publishers Weekly* v264 no24 p26 Je 12 2017

Booksellers & bookselling

See also

Book auctions

Book sales & prices

Bookstores

Serial publication of books

B&N Still Searching For "Magic Bullet" to Stop Sales Slide J. Milliot chart *Publishers Weekly* v264 no10 p4 Mr 6 2017

Bookselling As a Second Career C. Kirch color *Publishers Weekly* v264 no34 p11 Ag 21 2017

Deals D. LEFFERTS color *Publishers Weekly* v264 no1 p6 Ja 2 2017

HERE IT IS: OUR BIG FALL BOOKS PREVIEW J. SEGURA *Publishers Weekly* v264 no26 p20 Je 26 2017

In Memoriam: Dave Dutton B. VICKREY color *Publishers Weekly* v264 no5 p208 Ja 30 2017

Juvenile Nonfiction Stays Hot chart *Publishers Weekly* v264 no32 p5 Ag 7 2017

Kinokuniya Seeing Steady Growth In the U.S E. Nawotka color *Publishers Weekly* v264 no35 p15 Ag 28 2017

Making Book: How Booksellers Are Becoming Publishers J. Rosen chart color *Publishers Weekly* v263 no47 p6 N 21 2016

Print Units Through September Up 2% J. Milliot chart *Publishers Weekly* v264 no41 p4 O 9 2017

Publishers Plan for Future Without Family Christian J. Milliot and E. Koonse *Publishers Weekly* v264 no9 p5 F 27 2017

Rowling, O'Reilly, Hawkins All Soared in 2016 J. Maher *Publishers Weekly* v264 no4 p6 Ja 23 2017

Summer in the Bookstore C. Kirch color *Publishers Weekly* v264 no27 p5 Jl 3 2017

What's Ahead for Bookselling in 2017 J. Rosen color *Publishers Weekly* v264 no1 p3 Ja 2 2017

Booksellers & bookselling—Congresses

Chilling Out in Minneapolis J. ROSEN color *Publishers Weekly* v264 no3 p3 Ja 16 2017

REGIONAL SHOW HIGHLIGHTS bw color *Publishers Weekly* v264 no36 p36 S 4 2017

To Sell or Not to Sell: Censorship Or Free Speech for Bookstores? C. Reid color *Publishers Weekly* v264 no26 p9 Je 26 2017

Booksellers & bookselling—Economic aspects

The Answer is... Scholastic J. Milliot *Publishers Weekly* v264 no9 p4 F 27 2017

Booksellers & bookselling—Exhibitions

Independent Bookstore Day 2017: A Perfect Storm for Sales E. Nawotka, J. Boog et al color map *Publishers Weekly* v264 no17 p6 Ap 24 2017

Booksellers & bookselling—History—21st century

BESTSELLERS chart *Publishers Weekly* v264 no4 p11 Ja 23 2017

Europeans Cheer Move Toward Flexible VAT for E-books E. Nawotka color *Publishers Weekly* v264 no4 p8 Ja 23 2017

Booksellers & bookselling—Marketing

Amazon Buy-Button Change Raises Alarms, Questions J. Milliot *Publishers Weekly* v264 no20 p4 My 15 2017

Booksellers & bookselling—News briefs

Deals R. DEAHL bw color *Publishers Weekly* v264 no41 p6 O 9 2017

News Briefs *Publishers Weekly* v264 no41 p5 O 9 2017

News Briefs *Publishers Weekly* v264 no4 p4 Ja 23 2017

Booksellers & bookselling—United States

Bookstores of Every Kind A. GROSS color *Publishers Weekly* v263 no47 p50 N 21 2016

Indie Booksellers See Early Holiday Boost J. Rosen, C. Kirch et al color *Publishers Weekly* v263 no50 p4 D 5 2016

Juvenile Nonfiction Stays Hot, Up 10% in Week chart *Publishers Weekly* v264 no25 p6 Je 19 2017

Trade a Bright Spot In a Down Year for Book Sales J. Milliot chart *Publishers Weekly* v264 no32 p4 Ag 7 2017

Booksellers & bookselling—United States—Congresses

Bookselling in a Time of Political Upheaval J. Rosen color *Publishers Weekly* v264 no6 p5 F 6 2017

Booksellers & bookselling—Charts, diagrams, etc.

2017's SFF Bestsellers So Far chart color *Publishers Weekly* v264 no41 p38 O 9 2017

AUDIO BESTSELLERS J. Maher and C. JURIS chart color *Publishers Weekly* v264 no41 p16 O 9 2017

BESTSELLERS C. JURIS chart *Publishers Weekly* v264 no41 p12 O 9 2017

CATEGORY BESTSELLERS C. JURIS chart *Publishers Weekly* v264 no41 p15 O 9 2017

CHILDREN'S BESTSELLERS C. JURIS chart *Publishers Weekly* v264 no41 p14 O 9 2017

iBooks Bestsellers C. JURIS chart color *Publishers Weekly* v264 no41 p17 O 9 2017

SMASHWORDS SELF-PUBLISHED BESTSELLERS LIST, AUGUST 2017 C. JURIS bw chart color *Publishers Weekly* v264 no41 p18 O 9 2017

THE WEEKLY SCORECARD chart *Publishers Weekly* v263 no47 p6 N 21 2016

THE WEEKLY SCORECARD chart *Publishers Weekly* v264 no10 p5 Mr 6 2017

Booksellers & bookselling—Colportage, subscription trade, etc.

KIDS' SUBSCRIPTION SERVICES TAKE OFF C. KIRCH color *Publishers Weekly* v264 no11 p26 Mr 13 2017

Booksellers & bookselling—Societies, etc.

FALL REGIONALS NAVIGATE TURBULENT TIMES J. ROSEN color *Publishers Weekly* v264 no36 p28 S 4 2017

REGIONAL SHOW HIGHLIGHTS bw color *Publishers Weekly* v264 no36 p36 S 4 2017

Books—History—Exhibitions

Asylums and after A. Robinson bibl bw *Science* v354 no6309 p188 O 14 2016

Books—Marketing

ALWAYS IN SEASON D. DILWORTH color *Publishers Weekly* v264 no16 p24 Ap 17 2017

Cultivating Superfans M. COKER *Publishers Weekly* v264 no31 p40 Jl 31 2017

Despite Some Editors' Weariness, Psychological Suspense Is Still Hot R. Deahl *Publishers Weekly* v263 no41 p5 O 10 2016

First Go Narrow, Then Go Wide J. FRIEDMAN *Publishers Weekly* v264 no39 p64 S 25 2017

Juvenile Categories Had Double-Digit Gains in the Week chart *Publishers Weekly* v264 no31 p5 Jl 31 2017

An Overview of the Children's Book Market in China T. TAN color *Publishers Weekly* v264 no12 p3 Mr 20 2017

Print Sales Slowed in Third Quarter J. Milliot chart *Publishers Weekly* v263 no42 p4 O 17 2016

Social Fabric C. LASOTA color *Publishers Weekly* v264 no31 p18 Jl 31 2017

Social Media Marketing Takes Center Stage T. TAN color *Publishers Weekly* v264 no12 p30 Mr 20 2017

THE WEEKLY SCORECARD chart *Publishers Weekly* v264 no5 p3 Ja 30 2017

Books—News briefs

Deals R. DEAHL color *Publishers Weekly* v264 no27 p9 Jl 3 2017

Deals R. DEAHL color *Publishers Weekly* v264 no31 p8 Jl 31 2017

Guardians of the Galley color *Publishers Weekly* v264 no20 p(Sp)38 My 15 2017

News Briefs *Publishers Weekly* v264 no30 p4 Jl 24 2017

Books & reading—Charts, diagrams, etc.

MISCELLANEOUS BEST SELLERS *New York Times Book Review* p28 N 27 2016

Books—Sales & prices

Adult Nonfiction Stayed Hot in 2016 J. Milliot chart *Publishers Weekly* v264 no3 p4 Ja 16 2017

BESTSELLERS chart *Publishers Weekly* v263 no43 p14 O 24 2016

Books on Politics, Trump Rise After Election J. Maher chart *Publishers Weekly* v263 no47 p5 N 21 2016

Bookstore Sales Rose Again in 2016 J. Milliot chart color *Publishers Weekly* v264 no8 p10 F 20 2017

HOW TO GET RID OF ANYTHING M. SHIH and C. SULLIVAN cartoon color *Martha Stewart Living* p118 Ap 2017

iBooks Bestsellers bw chart color *Publishers Weekly* v263 no45 p18 N 7 2016

Print Sales Slowed in Third Quarter J. Milliot chart *Publishers Weekly* v263 no42 p4 O 17 2016

Regnery Publishing: More Than Just Politics J. Milliot color *Publishers Weekly* v264 no12 p10 Mr 20 2017

Books—Sales & prices—History—21st century

Trump Bump C. JURIS bw color *Publishers Weekly* v264 no6 p37 F 6 2017

Books—Sales & prices—Charts, diagrams, etc.

BESTSELLERS chart *Publishers Weekly* v264 no6 p13 F 6 2017

BESTSELLERS C. JURIS chart *Publishers Weekly* v263 no42 p14 O 17 2016

CATEGORY BESTSELLERS C. JURIS chart *Publishers Weekly* v263 no42 p17 O 17 2016

iBooks Bestsellers C. JURIS chart color *Publishers Weekly* v263

no42 p20 O 17 2016

Springsteen Plays Well Abroad C. JURIS chart map *Publishers Weekly* v263 no42 p18 O 17 2016

THE WEEKLY SCORECARD chart *Publishers Weekly* v263 no47 p6 N 21 2016

THE WEEKLY SCORECARD chart *Publishers Weekly* v264 no9 p5 F 27 2017

Books—Social aspects

CELEBRATING THE STORY OF CANADA E. NAWOTKA color *Publishers Weekly* v264 no41 p3 O 9 2017

Forever Frankfurt D. H. SMYK color *Publishers Weekly* v264 no41 p72 O 9 2017

Books—Societies, etc.

READING THAT UNITES US: Discovering the science of literature through our favorite books N. Smetannikova color *Literacy Today (2411-7862)* v34 no6 p46 My/Je 2017

Bookstores

THE ACCIDENTAL BOOKSHOP D. KAMP color *Vanity Fair* v58 no12 p112 D 2016

Amazon Books Spreads Out J. Milliot *Publishers Weekly* v264 no13 p4 Mr 27 2017

Amazon Books Will Be the Nation's Fifth-Largest Bookstore Chain J. Milliot chart color *Publishers Weekly* v264 no23 p6 Je 5 2017

Bargain Books in the Digital Age J. Rosen color *Publishers Weekly* v264 no39 p4 S 25 2017

A Book Lover's Cultural Department Store E. NAWOTKA *Publishers Weekly* v263 no39 p10 S 26 2016

BOOK NOOK KOOKS *Reader's Digest* v189 no1130 p69 My 2017

BOOKSELLING IN THE TWIN CITIES C. KIRCH color *Publishers Weekly* v264 no3 p10 Ja 16 2017

Bookstore Sales Rose Again in 2016 J. Milliot chart color *Publishers Weekly* v264 no8 p10 F 20 2017

Bookstores of Every Kind A. GROSS color *Publishers Weekly* v263 no47 p50 N 21 2016

Caring for Books You Value J. BILLS and S. SHEFFIELD color *Yankee* v80 no6 p28 N/D 2016

CHILDREN'S BOOKS FOR FALL color *Publishers Weekly* v264 no29 p21 Jl 17 2017

Favorites Drive 7% Gain in Units chart *Publishers Weekly* v264 no27 p5 Jl 3 2017

Juvenile & Children Reading Experience Wonderland: A New Business Model color *Publishers Weekly* v264 no12 p4 Mr 20 2017

Lessons from Some of the Country's Oldest Children's Bookstores J. ROSEN color *Publishers Weekly* v264 no29 p22 Jl 17 2017

News Briefs *Publishers Weekly* v264 no3 p7 Ja 16 2017

Niche Stores Find Their Way J. Rosen *Publishers Weekly* v263 no40 p10 O 3 2016

Pop-Up Bookstores Proliferate E. Nawotka color *Publishers Weekly* v264 no21 p11 My 22 2017

Real books, fake store A. Frykholm *Christian Century* v133 no21 p10 O 12 2016

Summer in the Bookstore C. Kirch color *Publishers Weekly* v264 no27 p5 Jl 3 2017

Bookstores—Awards

Wild Rumpus: PW's Bookstore of the Year C. KIRCH color *Publishers Weekly* v264 no20 p(Sp)8 My 15 2017

Bookstores—California

Bricks and Amour-tar color *Publishers Weekly* v264 no23 p20 Je 5 2017

Dialogue *Los Angeles Magazine* p10 F 2017

Meltdown Comics' Bitcoin Experience J. Boog chart color *Publishers Weekly* v264 no32 p5 Ag 7 2017

Bookstores—Design & construction

interiors C. A. PEARSON *Architectural Record* v205 no1 p31 Ja 2017

Bookstores—Evaluation

Little Shop of Hoarders F. WHEEN bw color *Vanity Fair* v59 no2 p100 F 2017

A NEW CHAPTER C. COX *Atlanta* v56 no7 p48 N 2016

SHOPPING & STYLE *Atlanta* v56 no8 p130 D 2016

Shopping *Virginia Living* p47 2017 Best 20of Virginia

Soapbox B. Eckstein color *Publishers Weekly* v264 no17 p96 Ap 24 2017

Bookstores—Georgia

A NEW CHAPTER C. COX *Atlanta* v56 no7 p48 N 2016

Bookstores—History

Archive Dive: The Last Time the Cubs Won the World Series... bw *Publishers Weekly* v263 no45 p3 N 7 2016

Bookstores—Massachusetts

For a Few Months, A Spanish-Language Bookstore in Boston A. Green color *Publishers Weekly* v264 no10 p18 Mr 6 2017

Bookstores—New York (State)—New York

We Three Kings County Booksellers color *Publishers Weekly* v264 no33 p84 Ag 14 2017

Bookstores—Social aspects

Bookstores Engage in Diverse Forms of Protest E. Nawotka and C. Kirch color *Publishers Weekly* v264 no11 p6 Mr 13 2017

Positive Proximity D. WILLIAMS color *Publishers Weekly* v264 no34 p116 Ag 21 2017

Bookstores—Tennessee

Soapbox B. Eckstein color *Publishers Weekly* v264 no17 p96 Ap 24 2017

Bookstores—Virginia

Shopping *Virginia Living* p151 2017 Best 20of Virginia

BookWalker (Company)

BookWalker Offers Digital Manga And Light Novels in English B. Alverson *Publishers Weekly* v263 no46 p12 N 14 2016

BOOKWALTER, J. R.

ADOBE AUDITION CC (2015.2): AUDIO EDITING BECOMES MORE USER-FRIENDLY color *Macworld - Digital Edition* p37 D 2016

BEZALEL OMNIA: STYLISH WIRELESS AUTOMOBILE CHARGER FOR IPHONE 6/7 color *Macworld - Digital Edition* v34 no11 p71 N 2017

BUSYCAL 3: THE BETTER MAC CALENDAR EXPERIENCE, NOW ON iOS color *Macworld - Digital Edition* v33 no11 p33 N 2016

CHARGETECH PLUG PRO REVIEW: SUPER—SIZED PORTABLE BATTERY CHARGER color *Macworld - Digital Edition* v34 no9 p51 S 2017

CHIPOLO PLUS: A BLUETOOTH TRACKER LOUD ENOUGH TO FIND MOST ANYTHING color *Macworld - Digital Edition* p57 Mr 2017

DISKASHUR PRO2: CROSS-PLATFORM, MAXIMUM SECURITY PORTABLE HARD DRIVE color *Macworld - Digital Edition* v34 no8 p44 Ag 2017

DISK DRILL 3: MAC UTILITY NOW RECOVERS DATA FROM iOS DEVICES, TOO cartoon color *Macworld - Digital Edition* p26 D 2016

EPSON DS-320 REVIEW: PORTABLE PRODUCTIVITY SCANNER, SANS WIRELESS color *Macworld - Digital Edition* v34 no6 p42 Je 2017

EPSON FASTFOTO FF-640: QUICK, CONVENIENT PHOTO SCANS DON'T COME CHEAP color *Macworld - Digital Edition* p31 Mr 2017

FINAL DRAFT 10: NEW WAYS TO PLOT YOUR NEXT OSCAR-WORTHY SCREENPLAY color *Macworld - Digital Edition* p31 F 2017

FLI CHARGE: VERSATILE WIRELESS CHARGING PAD WORKS WITH USB GADGETS, TOO color *Macworld - Digital Edition* p54 Je 13 2017

GRIDS 4.0 FOR INSTAGRAM: POST PHOTOS FROM MAC, BUT SHARING IS LIMITED color *Macworld - Digital Edition* p36 F 2017

iMazing 2.2: Use your Mac to manage your iPhone and iPad color *Macworld - Digital Edition* p93 Je 13 2017

INVOXIA NVX 200: TURN YOUR iPHONE INTO A DESK PHONE color *Macworld - Digital Edition* v34 no9 p48 S 2017

iSCRAPBOOK 7: COLOR TOOLS KEEP MAC DESIGN SOFTWARE ATOP SCRAP HEAP color *Macworld - Digital Edition* v34 no4 p37 My 2017

K'ABLEKEY REVIEW: VERSATILE IPHONE FLASH DRIVE DOUBLES AS LIGHTNING CHARGE CABLE color *Macworld - Digital Edition* p51 Je 13 2017

LIFECRAFT: RETOOLED MAC JOURNAL APP EMBRACES CLOUD SYNC, IOS SUPPORT color *Macworld - Digital Edition* v34 no9 p29 S 2017

MARBOTIC SMART LETTERS AND SMART NUMBERS: TOYS + TABLETS = EDUCATIONAL FUN color *Macworld -*

Digital Edition p53 Mr 2017

NONDA ZUS SMART CAR CHARGER color *Macworld - Digital Edition* p36 Mr 2017

O6 PORTABLE SMART BLUETOOTH REMOTE color *Macworld - Digital Edition* v34 no10 p36 O 2017

Paragon NTFS for Mac 15: Slick, native performance for accessing NTFS Windows drives color *Macworld - Digital Edition* v34 no10 p83 O 2017

PERI DUO: BULKY iPHONE BATTERY CASE WITH SPEAKERS DOESN'T QUITE GO TO 11 color *Macworld - Digital Edition* v34 no6 p65 Je 2017

PICTURE KEEPER CONNECT: SIMPLE PHOTO BACKUP FOR THE ENTIRE FAMILY color *Macworld - Digital Edition* v33 no11 p92 N 2016

PIXIE SMART TAGS color *Macworld - Digital Edition* v34 no4 p43 My 2017

READIRIS PRO 16: OCR SOFTWARE MORE FOCUSED ON SPEED THAN ACCURACY color *Macworld - Digital Edition* v34 no6 p29 Je 2017

REELGOOD: ONE APP, SO MANY STREAMING OR THEATRICAL MOVIES TO DISCOVER color *Macworld - Digital Edition* p69 D 2016

REOLINK KEEN: BATTERY-POWERED CAMERA OFFERS WIRELESS SECURITY FOR CHEAP color *Macworld - Digital Edition* p23 Je 13 2017

SECRETS FOR MAC AND SECRETS TOUCH: A SIMPLE, NO-FRILLS PASSWORD MANAGER color *Macworld - Digital Edition* p21 Mr 2017

TRACKR BRAVO: IT'S LIKE FIND MY iPHONE FOR EVERYTHING ELSE YOU OWN color *Macworld - Digital Edition* p65 D 2016

Boom, Benny

ALL EYEZ ON ME C. Holub color *Entertainment Weekly* no1463/1464 p50 Ap/My 2017

DEAR TUPAC W. L. Wilson color *Essence* v48 no2 p58 Je 2017

Boom Technology Inc.

BOOM UNVEILS SUPERSONIC PROTOTYPE color *Flying* v144 no2 p18 F 2017

Boom Technology Inc.—Officials & employees

SUPERSONIC TRAVEL IS BOOMING C. Dillow color *Fortune* v174 no8 p34 D 15 2016

Boomer, Eric

EXPANDING THE REALM C. Mihell color *Canoe & Kayak Magazine* v45 no1 p28 Wint 2017

Boon, Adrianus C. M.

The microbial metabolite desaminotyrosine protects from influenza through type I interferon graph *Science* v357 no6350 p498 Ag 4 2017

Boone, Amelia

Conquer Any Obstacle J. COVERT cartoon color *Men's Health* v32 no4 p23 My 2017

The Queen of Pain L. McGLASHAN color *Muscle & Performance* v9 no9 p36 S 2017

Boone, Charles

Exploring genetic suppression interactions on a global scale diag *Science* v354 no6312 p599 N 4 2016

Boone, Claire E.

Exploring genetic suppression interactions on a global scale diag *Science* v354 no6312 p599 N 4 2016

Boone, Debby

THE DARK SIDE OF "YOU LIGHT UP MY LIFE" D. Coggan color *Entertainment Weekly* no1451/1452 p78 F 3-10 2017

Boone, Graham

Does employer bias affect worker performance? *Monthly Labor Review* p1 Mr 2017

How banning boxes encourages discrimination *Monthly Labor Review* p1 Ja 2017

Boone, Megan, 1983-

My Obsessions... *TV Guide* v65 no41 p9 O 2 2017

Boone Isaacs, Cheryl, 1950——Interviews

The Academy Will See Us Now E. Strauss and J. Harman color *Glamour* v115 no3 p50 Mr 2017

Boonyabancha, Somsook

Cities for People and by People *UN Chronicle* v53 no3 p1 2016

BOOT, MAX

CLEANING UP OBAMA'S SYRIA MESS *Commentary* v142

no4 p20 N 2016

He Has Returned *Commentary* v142 no1 p48 Jl/Ag 2016

The Original Supersoldiers *New York Times Book Review* p16 N 6 2016

The Pipes of Peace: A history of the international pact that promised to bring an end to war *New York Times Book Review* p25 S 24 2017

Saving Syria *Commentary* v143 no1 p8 Ja 2017

Teams of Warriors color *National Review* v69 no8 p35 My 2017

Boot design & construction

Fall Re-Boot color *Seventeen* v76 no5 p34 S 2017

Booth, Carmen J.

A pathogenic role for T cell–derived IL-22BP in inflammatory bowel disease bibl graph *Science* v354 no6310 p358 O 21 2016

Booth, Danielle DiMartino

CASSANDRA OF THE CRASH B. DOHERTY color *Reason* v49 no3 p71 Jl 2017

Booth, David

Australian plan would roll back marine protections color *Science* v357 no6349 p338 Jl 28 2017

BOOTH, GEORGE

SKETCHBOOK cartoon *New Yorker* v92 no41 p59 D 12 2016

Booth, Mary Louise, 1831-1889

EDITOR'S LETTER G. Bailey color *Harper's Bazaar* no3649 p118 D 2016/Ja 2017

BOOTH, MICHAEL

Science and History Get Personal *Skeptical Inquirer* v41 no3 p32 My/Je 2017

Booth, Stephanie

heads up! color *Parents* v92 no8 p34 Ag 2017

WE ARE DIFFERENT WE ARE FRIENDS color *Parents* v92 no11 p30 N 2017

Booth, Susan

Susan Booth *Atlanta* v57 no2 p92 Je 2017

Booth-Binczik, Susan

The Challenge of Suburban Deer Management *New York State Conservationist* v72 no2 p19 O 2017

Boothe, Jas

Be a hero to homeless veterans J. PRESS color *Redbook* p114 D 2016

Boothe, Powers, 1948-2017

Milestones *Time* v189 no20 p11 My 29 2017

POWERS BOOTHE A. Breznican color *Entertainment Weekly* no1467 p17 My 26 2017

Things Left Unsaid: POWERS BOOTHE ALWAYS HELD SOMETHING BACK. MAYBE THAT'S WHY HE NEVER BECAME A STAR. AND MAYBE THAT'S WHY HE WAS SO FASCINATING TO WATCH T. CARSON *Texas Monthly* v45 no7 p56 Jl 2017

TRIBUTES I. Rudolph *TV Guide* v65 no23 p11 My 29 2017

Bootlaces

The Anatomy of the Shoe color *Esquire* p134 BigBlackBook

Bootlegging

BOOTLEGGER'S MAP OF THE UNITED STATES, 1926 K. Wiles *History Today* v67 no6 p4 Je 2016

Boots

BIG RED BOOTS color *InStyle* v24 no9 p414 S 2017

BREATHE color *Prevention* v69 no2 p42 F 2017

COLOR THERAPY color *Harper's Bazaar* no3656 p448 S 2017

Contact High A. WHITTLE color *Conde Nast Traveler* v51 no10 p182 N 2016

COZY UP *Indianapolis Monthly* v40 no4 p161 D 2016

EDITOR'S LETTER Glenda color *Harper's Bazaar* no3654 p54 Je/Jl 2017

The Legs Have It color *Vogue* v207 no7 p116 Jl 2017

SPARKLE & SHINE, TWINKLE TOES! C. WALTER color *Ebony* v72 no11 p41 S 2017

The STYLE FILE bw color *Harper's Bazaar* no3656 p335a S 2017

TAILOR-MADE color *Harper's Bazaar* no3656 p255 S 2017

TRUE WEST N. Silva-Jelly bw color *Harper's Bazaar* no3656 p430 S 2017

Who Are You Wearing? M. Wildgen color *O, The Oprah Magazine* p119 Mr 2017

WINE COUNTRY color *Harper's Bazaar* no3656 p316 S 2017

THE WORLD ACCORDING TO Gayle G. King bw color *O, The*

Oprah Magazine p36 S 2017

Boots, Christopher

Rock Star H. MARTIN color *Architectural Digest* v74 no9 p36 S 2017

BOOTS, MIKE

Using Social Network Measures in Wildlife Disease Ecology, Epidemiology, and Management *BioScience* v67 no3 p245 Mr 2017

Boots—Evaluation

ALL IS NOT LOST - A MODERN WALLFLOWER FINDS HER WAY THROUGH A 70s LANDSCAPE OF FLORAL-WALLPAPER PRINTS AND SEPIA-TONED WARDROBE STAPLES. SHE INTERPRETS THE ERAS LOUNGE MOOD WITH A CASUAL NEW LANGUAGE THAT IS ALL HER OWN *Interview* v47 no3 p60 My 2017

ANGELA BRANTLEY H. MITCHELL color *Chicago* v66 no11 p44 N 2017

BEST IN SHOE E. ELWICK-BATES color *Vogue* v207 no1 p106 Ja 2017

THE BEST OF WHAT'S NEW color *Harper's Bazaar* no3655 p107 Ag 2017

THE BIG CHILL bw *Harper's Bazaar* no3648 p260 N 2016

BLOCK PARTY color *Harper's Bazaar* no3653 p128 My 2017

BOOT CAMP A. GARDNER *Indianapolis Monthly* p34 N 2017

Boot Forecast color *InStyle* v23 no12 p148 N 2016

BOOTING UP color *Equus* no473 p22 F 2017

Boots Are on the Rise *Los Angeles Magazine* p34 F 2017

BOOT UP N. Sullivan color *Esquire* p60 S 2017

Bringing Booties Back! color *Glamour* v114 no11 p64 N 2016

BUCKLE UP color *Esquire* p48 N 2017

CADET CHIC color *Harper's Bazaar* no3648 p156 N 2016

DEEP PURPLE J. MOAZAMI color *Chicago* v66 no10 p42 O 2017

Denim Always [Cover story] color *Glamour* no8 p152 Ag 2017

digital directory color *InStyle* v24 no9 p74 S 2017

DOPE STUFF ON MY DESK J. Wilson color *Essence* v48 no6 p32 O 2017

Dressed to Chill N. SULLIVAN bw color *Esquire* v166 no5 p64 D 2016/Ja 2017

EASILY SUEDE color *Esquire* p38 Ag 2017

emporium bw color *Dressage Today* v23 no5 p62 Ja 2017

emporium color *Dressage Today* v23 no8 p64 Ap 2017

Equip the Kids L. H. Oh *Sierra* v101 no4 p20 Jl/Ag 2016

EVERY SHOE TELLS A STORY color *Esquire* p112 My 2017

Finding Her Feet L. YAEGER color *Vogue* v207 no10 p202 O 2017

Forecast A. ROUSH *Texas Monthly* v45 no3 p190 Mr 2017

GET DOWN color *Vogue* v207 no9 p698 S 2017

THE GIRL Zendaya E. Wilson color *InStyle* v24 no6 p53 Je 2017

Holiday Gift Guide *Missouri Life* v43 no7 p22 D 2016/Ja 2017

I Can't Believe It's RUBBER! color *Women's Health* v14 no3 p50 Ap 2017

The In/Out LIST color *Harper's Bazaar* no3657 p122 O 2017

Insta-Outfit color *InStyle* v24 no11 p115 N 2017

IT'S PERSONAL *Interview* v47 no5 p94 Je/Jl 2017

KICK IT! color *InStyle* v24 no10 p143 O 2017

KINKY BOOTS color *Harper's Bazaar* no3654 p60 Je/Jl 2017

KORKERS HATCHBACK BOOTS color *Field & Stream* v121 no8 p96 F/Mr 2017

Last Look V. SMITH color *Vogue* v207 no9 p753 S 2017

LIGHT ON YOUR FEET S. L. White, Peterson et al color *Field & Stream* v121 no9 p74 Ap 2017

Manolo Blahnik boots, $1,065 V. SMITH color *Vogue* v207 no11 p240 N 2017

Mix and Remix F. Kane color *Glamour* v115 no4 p60 Ap 2017

NEW PRODUCTS color *Spin to Win Rodeo* v21 no1 p30 Mr 2017

on demand color *InStyle* v24 no4 p49 Ap 2017

PACKING FOR THE ADIRONDACKS BRING ON THE KNITS AND HOT TODDYS L. DECARLO color *Conde Nast Traveler* v52 no10 p46 N 2017

Power Puff color *Glamour* v115 no11 p52 N 2017

PRETTY IN PINK color *Harper's Bazaar* no3648 p158 N 2016

Put Your Sole Into It *Los Angeles Magazine* p32 Ja 2017

SOLE OBSESSION J. Bingaman color *Men's Health* v32 no2 p(Sp)16 Mr 2017

SO YOU'RE NOT INTO LEATHER? color *Esquire* p50 My 2017

STOCK & TRADE color *Equus* no478 p76 Jl 2017

Tack Room color *Practical Horseman* v45 no5 p78 My 2017

Tapped Off B. Welch color *American Cowboy* v24 no1 p42 Je/Jl 2017

TREK STAR VOYAGERS J. BROWN color *Popular Science* p11 Ja/F 2017

a week of awesome outfits color *Good Housekeeping* v264 no2 p30 F 2017

When Two Labels Love Each Other Very Much... color *GQ: Gentlemen's Quarterly* v97 no10 p64 O 2017

WHERE FASHION GETS PERSONAL G. MAHARY color *Harper's Bazaar* no3648 p139 N 2016

Wish List! color *Glamour* v114 no7 p62 Jl 2016

Boozer, Lyndon

DAN ABOUT TOWN color *Washingtonian Magazine* v52 no7 p26 Ap 2017

Bopp, Daniel

Male sex in houseflies is determined by Mdmd, a paralog of the generic splice factor gene CWC22 bw color *Science* v356 no6338 p642 My 12 2017

Boquillod, Yann

Air pollution, in real time color *Science* v354 no6315 p949 N 25 2016

Borando, Silvia

Near, Far *Publishers Weekly* v263 no49 p23 D 7 2016

Borch, Jonas

Characterization of a dynamic metabolon producing the defense compound dhurrin in sorghum bibl graph *Science* v354 no6314 p890 N 18 2016

Bordas, Camille

Most Die Young cartoon color *New Yorker* v92 no43 p56 Ja 2 2017

Bordeaux (Aquitaine, France)—Description & travel

Bordeaux's Fresh Fantasy E. McCoy bw color *Bloomberg Businessweek* no4538 p55 S 18 2017

Stomping Ground C. TATTOLI color *Conde Nast Traveler* v52 no5 p22 My 2017

Borden, Clifford

Letter of the Month color *Powder* v45 no6 p96 F 2017

Borden, Jane

The Case of the Christmas Stockings color *Southern Living* v51 no12 p136 D 2016

Classic Country color *Southern Living* v52 no11 p36 N 2017

The Tomato Man color *Southern Living* v52 no7 p24 Jl 2017

Borden, John H.

A retirement 'hobby' color *Science* v355 no6324 p542 F 3 2017

Borden, Lizzie, 1860-1927

LIZZIE BORDEN'S POP CULTURE PANOPLY I. Biedenharn color *Entertainment Weekly* no1477 p61 Ag 11 2017

Borden, Sam

Star-Spangled PROTEST [Cover story] *New York Times Upfront* v149 no3 p8 O 10 2016

Border, Terry

Merry Christmas, Peanut! *Publishers Weekly* v264 no36 p93 S 4 2017

Border barriers

The Border Wall: Immigration, Security, and U.S.-Mexico Relations *Congressional Digest* v96 no8 p2 O 2017

Don't Mess With Texas R. MONROE color *New Republic* v248 no5 p10 My 2017

Let's talk about RACE color *O, The Oprah Magazine* p134 My 2017

North of the Border, South of the Wall L. Etter and K. Luce color *Bloomberg Businessweek* no4518 p62 Ap 10 2017

On Today's Refugee Road M. Ruthven and N. Thorpe color map *New York Review of Books* v63 no18 p27 N 24 2016

Over the Edge L. Lalami *New York Times Magazine* p13 Ap 30 2017

Taxing Mexico. Or Not P. Coy diag *Bloomberg Businessweek* no4510 p12 F 6 2017

Trump's Wall L. Chavez *Commentary* v142 no2 p9 S 2016

The Wall Needs the Consent of Many L. Etter and J. Sink map *Bloomberg Businessweek* no4510 p13 F 6 2017

Wall to Wall A. FIXSEN color *Architectural Record* v205 no5 p33 My 2017

WHAT WALL? C. BALLÍ *Texas Monthly* v45 no5 p101 My 2017

Border barriers—Design & construction

Bad Math Props Up Border Wall K. Kakaes diag graph il *MIT*

Technology Review v119 no6 p18 N/D 2016

Barriers to a Border Wall color diag map *Time* v189 no18 p16 My 15 2017

Border Wall Divides Profession F. A. BERNSTEIN *Architectural Record* v205 no4 p30 Ap 2017

Executive Order on Border Security: Directing the Establishment of a Physical Wall and Other Deterrents *Congressional Digest* v96 no8 p5 O 2017

For the Record color *Time* v189 no4 p5 F 6 2017

Mexican Border Wall *Congressional Digest* v96 no2 p10 F 1 2017

The Wall D. Bennett bw *Bloomberg Businessweek* no4517 p31 Ap 3 2017

Border barriers—Economic aspects

A Wall Won't Secure the U.S.-Mexico Border, but Economic Policy Could D. McAdams *Harvard Business Review Digital Articles* p2 F 14 2017

Border crossing

Borderlands R. MISRACH color *National Geographic* v232 no3 p128 S 2017

THE NEW UNDERGROUND RAILROAD [Cover story] J. Markusoff color *Maclean's* v130 no2 p20 Mr 2017

Refugees risk lives to flee the U.S. for Canada D. Dettloff color *America* v217 no5 p17 S 4 2017

Border Patrol Agent (Poem)

Border Patrol Agent E. C. CORRAL *New Republic* v247 no11 p59 N 2016

Border patrol agents

Activists Work to Stop Militarization of the Border J. WEST color *Progressive* p12 D 2016/Ja 2017

Border Patrol *Congressional Digest* v96 no7 p31 S 2017

CROSSING THE LINE IN EL CENIZO L. REIGSTAD *Texas Monthly* v45 no9 p76 S 2017

Border patrols

CROSSING THE LINE IN EL CENIZO L. REIGSTAD *Texas Monthly* v45 no9 p76 S 2017

Border security

See also
Border barriers

BOARDER SECURITY P. BRIDGES color *Snowboarder* v29 no2 p26 O 2016

Border security—United States

Border Wall Divides Profession F. A. BERNSTEIN *Architectural Record* v205 no4 p30 Ap 2017

Keep Out! How the U.S. Is Militarizing Mexico's Southern Border J. Abbott color *Progressive* v81 no7 p40 O/N 2017

Legislative Background on Border Security: Legislative Background on Border Security *Congressional Digest* v96 no8 p7 O 2017

The Pros and Cons of a Mexico Border Wall *Congressional Digest* v96 no8 p8 O 2017

Same Old, Same Old color *Weekly Standard* v23 no3 p10 S 25 2017

U.S. Border Enforcement: Federal Laws and Requirements *Congressional Digest* v96 no8 p3 O 2017

Border security—United States—Environmental aspects

Weaponized Wilderness J. Mark *Sierra* v102 no5 p4 St/O 2017

Border stations

HOW ISRAEL PRIVATIZED ITS OCCUPATION OF PALESTINE A. LOEWENSTEIN and M. KENNARD color il *Nation* v303 no20 p20 N 14 2016

Border security—Mexican-American Border Region

North of the Border, South of the Wall L. Etter and K. Luce color *Bloomberg Businessweek* no4518 p62 Ap 10 2017

Bordetella diseases—Prevention

Dear Doctor *Your Dog (10780343)* v22 no10 p15 O 2016

BORDEWICH, FERGUS M.

Debate Prep: How the Lincoln-Douglas rivalry defined a nation *New York Times Book Review* p21 Ag 20 2017

Bordoloi, Rongmon

Our black hole's last known feast color *Astronomy* v45 no7 p13 Jl 2017

Bordwell, David

Beyond the Kael S. BUNCH *Commentary* v142 no2 p69 S 2016

Bordwell, Harold

Make Patriotism Great Again color *Commonweal* v143 no20 p30 D 16 2016

Boréal Sarl

The Bones of the Beast C. J. Doane color *Sail* v48 no4 p96 Ap 2017

Boreanaz, David

THE BEST OF BOOTH'S WORLD K. Connolly color *Entertainment Weekly* no1457/1458 p87 Mr 17 2017

My 20 Years on Television D. BOREANAZ and M. Roffman *TV Guide* v65 no41 p12 O 2 2017

SEAL Team N. Abrams, B. L. Heldman et al color *Entertainment Weekly* no1482/1483 p76 S 22 2017

Boreanaz, David—Interviews

DAVID BOREANAZ M. Roffman *TV Guide* v65 no37 p32 S 4 2017

DAVID BOREANAZ ON BUFFY, BONES, AND BEYOND C. M. Smith color *Entertainment Weekly* no1457/1458 p86 Mr 17 2017

Borecki, Ingrid B.

Distribution and clinical impact of functional variants in 50,726 whole-exome sequences from the DiscovEHR study chart graph *Science* v354 no6319 paaf6814-1 D 23 2016

Genetic identification of familial hypercholesterolemia within a single U.S. health care system chart graph *Science* v354 no6319 paaf7000-1 D 23 2016

Boredom

BORED AT WORK? YOU'RE NOT ALONE color *Fortune* v175 no4 p18 Mr 15 2017

Confessions of a Short Attention Span Man: Boredom is the enemy, and fear of boredom the spur J. Epstein *Commentary* v144 no3 p41 O 2017

Make Time for Boredom J. STEWART cartoon *Atlantic* v319 no5 p23 Je 2017

BOREL, BROOKE

ENGINEERING A BETTER MOUSETRAP *Audubon* v119 no2 p48 Summ 2017

Message Control color graph *Scientific American* v317 no4 p68 O 2017

Borenstein, Joram

11 Things the Health Care Sector Must Do to Improve Cybersecurity *Harvard Business Review Digital Articles* p2 Je 1 2017

BORENSTEIN, PHYLLIS

Righting Words color *O, The Oprah Magazine* p17 Jl 2017

Borescopes

INSPECTION CAMERAS: MECHANIC'S BORESCOPE HAS ENDLESS USES D. Mowitz *Successful Farming* v115 no6 p30 Ap 2017

Borg, Marcus J., 1942-2015

Borg's Jesus S. King *Christian Century* v134 no17 p6 Ag 16 2017

Out of unbelief T. G. Long color *Christian Century* v134 no15 p30 Jl 19 2017

Borga, Marco

Changing climate shifts timing of European floods color graph *Science* v357 no6351 p588 Ag 11 2017

Borge, Erik

HOW TO OWN A SKI AREA J. Brown color *Powder* v45 no4 p46 D 2016

Borger, Julian

PURSUIT OF JUSTICE D. WALSH *America* v215 no11 p34 O 17 2016

Borges, Jorge Luis, 1899-1986

1935: Ramos Mejía *Lapham's Quarterly* v10 no2 p151 Spr 2017

Portrait of the Author as a Historian A. Lee *History Today* v66 no10 p54 O 2016

Borgford-Parnell, N.

A climate policy pathway for near- and long-term benefits color *Science* v356 no6337 p493 My 5 2017

Borghese, Cecilia M.

Interacting amino acid replacements allow poison frogs to evolve epibatidine resistance chart diag graph *Science* v357 no6357 p1261 S 22 2017

Borg-Karlson, Anna-Karin

A key malaria metabolite modulates vector blood seeking, feeding, and susceptibility to infection bibl chart diag *Science* v355 no6329 p1076 Mr 10 2017

Borglum, Marilyn

Where Dressage Meets the Canvas K. M. Brittle color *Dressage Today* v23 no4 p60 D 2016

Borg/McEnroe (Film)

Double Plays T. Keith color *Sports Illustrated* v127 no4 p22 Ag 7 2017

Borgognone, Alessandro

BRASH LANDING: The "most hated restaurateur in America" comes to DC J. Sidman *Washingtonian Magazine* v53 no1 p153 O 2017

Boring machinery

Tunnel Vision *Los Angeles Magazine* p32 Mr 2017

Borini, Joe

Athens as Analogy color *Atlantic* v319 no5 p12 Je 2017

Boris Godunov (Theatrical production)

Mussorgsky: Boris Godunov D. J. Baker *Opera News* v81 no7 p46 Ja 2017

Borisov, Boĭko, 1959-

On Putting Our Leaders in a Cage bw *Black Belt* v55 no5 p16 Ag/S 2017

Boritt, Beowulf

"Look What We Did!" *Stage Directions* v30 no10 p19 O 2017

Borjas, George J.

The Facts on Immigration M. KRIKORIAN color *National Review* v68 no20 p39 N 7 2016

Harvard's George J. Borjas R. VERBRUGGEN graph *American Conservative* v16 no1 p37 Ja/F 2017

THE HIDDEN COSTS OF IMMIGRATION C. Caldwell *Claremont Review of Books* v16 no4 p47 Fall 2016

Two Immigrants Debate Immigration color *Reason* v48 no7 p28 D 2016

Winners and Losers P. J. HANSEN bw *Weekly Standard* v22 no36 p32 My 29 2017

Borm, Lars E.

The promise of spatial transcriptomics for neuroscience in the era of molecular cell typing color diag *Science* v357 no6359 p64 O 6 2017

Bormans, Guy

De novo design of a biologically active amyloid bibl graph *Science* v354 no6313 paah4949-1 N 11 2016

Bormel, Laney

Article So Long Love Songs *Commentary* v140 no2 p5 S 2015

Born, Scott—Interviews

LEAF SPRINGS 101 J. HEADLEE color *Dirt Sports + Off-Road* v51 no9 p34 S 2017

Born in an Urban Ruin (Music)

Born In An Urban Ruin J. D. Considine bw *Downbeat* v84 no2 p81 F 2017

Born on the Fourth of July (Film)

THE ALL-TIME GREATEST TOM CRUISE PERFORMANCES C. Nashawaty color *Entertainment Weekly* no1485 p39 O 6 2017

Born to Run (Music : Springsteen)

Runaway American Dream R. Ford color *New York Times Book Review* p1 S 25 2016

A Troubadour in the Age of Trump *Commentary* v141 no10 p1 D 2016

A Troubadour in the Age of Trump *Commentary* v142 no5 p1 D 2016

Working Man's Bard R. D. LURIE bw *National Review* v68 no24 p40 D 31 2016

Bornean orangutan

FOR DEAR LIFE K. MOORE color *Natural History* v125 no5 p2 My 2017

Börner, G. Valentin

Control of meiotic pairing and recombination by chromosomally tethered 26S proteasome bibl graph *Science* v355 no6323 p408 Ja 27 2017

Bornholdt, Zachary A.

A "Trojan horse" bispecific-antibody strategy for broad protection against ebolaviruses bibl graph *Science* v354 no6310 p350 O 21 2016

Borns, Garrett

BØRNS M. MULLEN *Interview* v46 no8 p40 O 2016

STREET FIGHTING MAN L. LOWE color *Esquire* p112 Big-BlackBook

Borodai, N.

Observation of a large-scale anisotropy in the arrival directions of cosmic rays above 8×10^{18} eV *Science* v357 no6357 p1266

S 22 2017

Boronat, Mercedes

"Ab initio" synthesis of zeolites for preestablished catalytic reactions bibl chart diag *Science* v355 no6329 p1051 Mr 10 2017

Boronic acids

Decarboxylative borylation C. Li, J. Wang et al color *Science* v356 no6342 p1045 Je 9 2017

Boros, Tracy

One horse's journey color *Equus* no476 p85 My 2017

BOROSAGE, ROBERT L.

Beyond Resistance *Nation* v304 no7 p4 Mr 6 2017

FROM THE REARVIEW MIRROR color *Nation* v304 no15 p35 My 8 2017

How We Can Fight Trump *Nation* v303 no23/24 p22 D 5 2016

The Lawless Suites *Nation* v303 no16 p4 O 17 2016

A Taxing Debate color *Nation* v305 no5 p3 Ag 28 2017

Trump Budget, GOP Values color *Nation* v304 no12 p3 Ap 10 2017

Was Barack Obama a Transformational President? color *Nation* v304 no1 p40 Ja 2 2017 The Obama Years

What Bannon Wrought *Nation* v305 no6 p6 S 11 2017

Borowitz, Anthony

Double Homicide S. Begley color *Time* v189 no24 p52 Je 26 2017

Borowski, Craig

What a Great Digital Customer Experience Actually Looks Like *Harvard Business Review Digital Articles* p2 N 9 2015

Borowski, Tadeusz

LAST ORDERS *Lapham's Quarterly* v10 no3 p58 Summ 2017

Borregaard, J.

An integrated diamond nanophotonics platform for quantum-optical networks bibl graph *Science* v354 no6314 p847 N 18 2016

Borregaard, Michael K.

An Anthropocene map of genetic diversity bibl graph map *Science* v353 no6307 p1532 S 30 2016

Island biogeography: Taking the long view of nature's laboratories map *Science* v357 no6354 p885 S 1 2017

Borrelia burgdorferi

Homegrown Medical Mystery M. LALIBERTE color map *Reader's Digest* v190 no1132 p42 Jl/Ag 2017

Borrell, Brendan

The Curse of the Bahia Emerald cartoon *Wired* v25 no3 p84 Mr 2017

Flight School color *National Geographic* v232 no1 p98 Jl 2017

Walk This Way chart color diag graph *Consumer Reports* v82 no8 p8 Ag 2017

Borromeo String Quartet (Performer)

CLASSICAL MUSIC *New Yorker* v93 no33 p27 O 23 2017

BORS, MATT

COMICS *In These Times* v41 no10 p46 O 2017

Borshchevskiy, Valentin

Mechanism of transmembrane signaling by sensor histidine kinases color *Science* v356 no6342 p1043 Je 9 2017

Borthne, Johanne

Tipping the Scales A. FIXSEN *Architectural Record* v204 no10 p33 O 2016

Bortz, Daniel

Crafting a Big Business color *Money* v45 no10 p33 N 2016

Drive Home a Better Deal color diag *Money* v45 no11 p23 D 2016

Tweet Your Way to Better Service chart *Money* v46 no2 p32 Mr 2017

Borylation

Decarboxylative borylation C. Li, J. Wang et al color *Science* v356 no6342 p1045 Je 9 2017

Photoinduced decarboxylative borylation of carboxylic acids A. Fawcett, J. Pradeilles et al diag *Science* v357 no6348 p283 Jl 21 2017

BORZYKOWSKI, BRYAN

The best of both worlds color *Maclean's* v130 no2 p50 Mr 2017

Borzynski, Lisa

ask the experts color *Dressage Today* v23 no4 p67 D 2016

Bos

See also

Cattle

That's Outrageous! *Reader's Digest* v188 no1124 p121 O 2016

BOS, KIRSTEN I.

Tracking Ancient Plagues bw color *Natural History* v125 no9 p18

S 2017

Bosa, Joey, 1994-
BIG BEAR, PAPA BEAR AND SMALLER BEAR M. Rosenberg color *Sports Illustrated* v127 no9 p26 S 25 2017

Bosa, John
BIG BEAR, PAPA BEAR AND SMALLER BEAR M. Rosenberg color *Sports Illustrated* v127 no9 p26 S 25 2017

Bosack, Maria
Creating a Special Space for Their Buddies *Parks & Recreation* v51 no11 p36 N 2016

Bosche, Anne
"This Cat Is Meant to Be Here" [Cover story] A. LEWIS *Reader's Digest* v188 no1126 p79 D 2016/Ja 2017

Boschen, Jessica
Homegrown Nebraskans hit early baseball home run color *Nebraska Life* v21 no2 p17 Mr/Ap 2017
Nebraskans' bridge past and present with photography color *Nebraska Life* v21 no1 p14 Ja/F 2017
Superstitious Huskers win with skill and a little luck color *Nebraska Life* v21 no5 p16 S/O 2017

Bosdosh, Steve
Why Do My Putts Jump Off Line? *Golf Magazine* v59 no4 p65 Ap 2017

Bose, Maitrayee
Rapid cooling and cold storage in a silicic magma reservoir recorded in individual crystals color diag graph *Science* v356 no6343 p1154 Je 16 2017

Bose, Mihir
A Hatred for Hindus *History Today* v66 no12 p3 D 2016
The troubled history of the 'jewel in the Crown' *History Today* v67 no1 p59 Ja 2017

BOSE, SUDIP
The Old Master *American Scholar* v86 no1 p103 Wint 2017

Bose audio equipment—Evaluation
AIRPODS REVIEW: They sound great, but Siri holds them back S. Ochs color *Macworld - Digital Edition* p72 F 2017

Bose Corp.
THE BEST BET img *New York* p53 Ja 9 2017
TUNE OUT TRAVEL STRESS color *Men's Health* v31 no10 p(Sp)22 D 2016

Bose-Einstein condensation
Bloch oscillations in the absence of a lattice F. Meinert, M. Knap et al graph *Science* v356 no6341 p945 Je 1 2017
Classical precursor to turbulence observed in a superfluid M. Wilson *Physics Today* v70 no1 p19 Ja 2017
Cold atoms twisting spin and momentum M. Aidelsburger bibl diag *Science* v354 no6308 p35 O 7 2016
The new era of POLARITON CONDENSATES D. W. Snoke and J. Keeling *Physics Today* v70 no10 p54 O 2017
Supersolids made from exotic matter E. CONOVER *Science News* v190 no12 p8 D 10 2016
TRAPPED IN ORBIT A. Cho color diag graph *Science* v357 no6355 p986 S 8 2017

Bose-Einstein gas
Two- and three-body contacts in the unitary Bose gas R. J. Fletcher, R. Lopes et al bibl diag graph *Science* v355 no6323 p377 Ja 27 2017

Boselli, Pietro
THE PERFECT FIT B. HANSEN-BUNDY color *GQ: Gentlemen's Quarterly* v87 no1 p68 Ja 2017

Boseman, Chadwick, 1982-
CHADWICK BOSEMAN UPS HIS GAME [Cover story] B. SCHMIDT and C. Saunders color *Ebony* v72/73 no12/1 p70 O/N 2017
HIS MARSHALL PLAN K. SMITH color *Vanity Fair* v59 no11 p122 N 2017
MAKING THE COVER color *Ebony* v72/73 no12/1 p14 O/N 2017

Boser, Ulrich
Talking to Yourself (Out Loud) Can Help You Learn *Harvard Business Review Digital Articles* p2 My 5 2017

Boshara, Ray
Does College Level the Playing Field? *Bridges (Federal Reserve Bank of St. Louis)* p7 Spr 2017

Bosideng International Holdings Ltd.
China's Elusive Goal: A Global Apparel Brand R. Chang and L.

Rupp color *Bloomberg Businessweek* no4532 p12 Jl 31 2017

BOSILKOVSKI, IGOR
TRUMP UNFILTERED bw color graph *Forbes* v200 no5 p50 N 14 2017
THE WORLD'S MOST INNOVATIVE COMPANIES chart color *Forbes* v200 no2 p72 S 5 2017

Bosinger, Steven
mTOR regulates metabolic adaptation of APCs in the lung and controls the outcome of allergic inflammation graph *Science* v357 no6355 p1014 S 8 2017

Bosker, Bianca
Haute Concrete color *Atlantic* v319 no3 p28 Ap 2017
In Defense of 'Bad' Wine S. Begley color *Time* v189 no12 p24 Ap 3 2017
Instamom cartoon *Atlantic* v319 no2 p16 Mr 2017
The Mayo Mogul color *Atlantic* v320 no4 p76 N 2017
TRISTAN HARRIS BELIEVES SILICON VALLEY IS ADDICTING US TO OUR PHONES. HE'S DETERMINED TO MAKE IT STOP color *Atlantic* v318 no4 p56 N 2016

Bosley, Catherine
Pins and Needles in The Heart of the Alps color *Bloomberg Businessweek* no4531 p31 Jl 24 2017

Boslough, Mark
Is the MOON HOUSE an AMERICAN STONEHENGE? color map *Astronomy* v45 no7 p50 Jl 2017
Michael Mann and the Climate Wars *Skeptical Inquirer* v40 no6 p17 N/D 2016

BOSNIC, TYRA
HIT THE ROAD, BILL *In These Times* v41 no6 p11 Je 2017
STARVING THE BLACK SNAKE *In These Times* v41 no5 p11 My 2017

Bosons
See also
Axions
Bose-Einstein condensation
Higgs bosons
Plasmons that won't stick D. Faccio diag *Science* v356 no6345 p1336 Je 30 2017
Universal space-time scaling symmetry in the dynamics of bosons across a quantum phase transition L. W. Clark, Lei Feng et al bibl graph *Science* v354 no6312 p606 N 4 2016

Boss, J. M.
Quantum sensing with arbitrary frequency resolution diag graph *Science* v356 no6340 p837 My 26 2017

Boss, Suzie
PDK Connection *Phi Delta Kappan* v98 no8 p79 My 2017

Boss, The (Film)
The Boss M. FELL *TV Guide* v65 no4 p47 Ja 16 2017

Bossa nova music
A Foot In Two Worlds A. Morrison color *Downbeat* v83 no11 p27 N 2016

Boss Baby, The (Film)
CHILD IN CHARGE D. Walters color *Bloomberg Businessweek* no4517 p71 Ap 3 2017

Boston (Mass.)—Description & travel
BOSTON, MASSACHUSETTS color *Runner's World* v52 no3 p8 Ap 2017
CHRISTMAS in Boston A. Traverso, G. SCHIAVONE et al color *Yankee* v80 no6 p108 N/D 2016
Tall Tales on the High Seas L. ADDISON color *AARP: The Magazine* v59 no2A p42 F/Mr 2016

Boston (Mass.)—Economic conditions
Turning Capital Against Capitalism C. MERRIAM *In These Times* v41 no6 p10 Je 2017

BOSTON, ROB
CHURCH, STATE, AND TAXPAYER SUPPORT: Is America Moving Toward a European Model? *Humanist* v77 no5 p36 S/O 2017
THE GREAT "PERSECUTION OF CHRISTIANS" MYTH *Humanist* v77 no3 p34 My/Je 2017
LAND OF CONFUSION: THE RELIGIOUS RIGHT, TRUMP, AND 'POST-TRUTH' AMERICA *Humanist* v77 no2 p32 Mr/Ap 2017
NO MOORE: ALABAMA IS FINALLY RID OF THE WORST JUDGE IN AMERICA *Humanist* v76 no6 p38 N/D 2016
WANT TO SURVIVE THE NEXT FOUR YEARS? FIRST STEP:

OPEN YOUR MOUTH *Humanist* v77 no1 p30 Ja/F 2017
WHAT'S BEHIND THE NEW ATTACK ON BIRTH CON-
TROL? *Humanist* v77 no4 p36 Jl/Ag 2017

Boston Ballet
DANCE THAT ADAPTS TO DISABILITIES J. ANDERSON
and I. RASTEGARI *USA Today Magazine* v145 no2864 p60
My 2017
My Final Season S. WROTH *Dance Magazine* v91 no4 p56 Ap
2017

Boston Celtics (Basketball team)
2 CELTICS color *Sports Illustrated* v127 no12 p58 O 16 2017
2 Celtics R. Nadkarni, B. Golliver et al *Sports Illustrated* v125
no14 p74 O 24-31 2016
How an NBA Team Thinks About Data, Talent, and Pricing D.
Rousmaniere *Harvard Business Review Digital Articles* p2 Mr
23 2015

Boston Conservatory—Students
Cross-Disciplinary Heaven H. Rolfe *Dance Spirit* v21 no7 p104
S 2017

Boston Marathon
BOSTON, MASSACHUSETTS color *Runner's World* v52 no3
p8 Ap 2017
Going the Distance B. Marston and T. Keith color *Sports Illustrated* v126 no11 p26 Ap 17-24 2017
PREPARING TO LAUNCH D. WILLEY color *Runner's World*
v52 no3 p10 Ap 2017

Boston Pizza International Inc.
Pizza to go. And go. And go C. MCINTYRE color *Maclean's* v130
no9 p70 O 2017

Boston Public Library
Boston Public Library D. S. Glenn *Architectural Record* v205 no4
p180 Ap 2017

Boston Red Sox (Baseball team)
1 RED SOX color *Sports Illustrated* v126 no9 p76 Mr 27 2017
7 AFTER BIG PAPI, THE LITTLE THINGS T. Verducci color
Sports Illustrated v126 no9 p49 Mr 27 2017
Out of Left Field M. Malamut color *Rodale's Organic Life* v3 no1
p84 Ja 2017
The Week color *National Review* v69 no18 p4 O 2 2017

Boston Red Sox (Baseball team)—History—21st century
CONTACT HIGH T. Verducci color diag *Sports Illustrated* v127
no8 p44 S 18 2017
Leading Off color *Sports Illustrated* v127 no3 p4 Jl 24 2017
THE PAPI PAPERS D. Ortiz and M. Holley color *Sports Illus-
trated* v126 no14 p68 My 15-22 2017
WHAT IF? ... THE PLAYERS' UNION HADN'T REJECTED A-
ROD'S 2003 TRADE TO THE RED SOX? C. P. Pierce and J.
Feldman color *Sports Illustrated* v126 no11 p55 Ap 17-24 2017

Boston Scientific Corp.
A SURGICAL ALTERNATIVE TO PRESCRIPTION BLOOD
THINNERS V. Prevish *Cincinnati Magazine* v50 no12 p84 S
2017

Boston Symphony Orchestra
Contemporary Boston R. Platt cartoon *New Yorker* v93 no3 p15
Mr 6 2017

Boston University
ART SCHOOLS *Art in America* v105 no1 p94 Ja 2017
SUMMER STUDY DIRECTORY *Stage Directions* v30 no1 p23
Ja 2017

Boston Whaler Inc.
Boston Whaler 330 Outrage D. Harding Jr. color *Power & Motoryacht* v33 no3 p52 Mr 2017
DON'T BE ALL WET D. THOMPSON *Sea Magazine* v108 no10
p42 O 2016

Boston Tea Party, 1773
Revolutionary Road color *AARP: The Magazine* v59 no5A p60
Ag/S 2016

BOSTWICK, WILLIAM
THE IMPOSSIBLE LIST bw cartoon color *Esquire* v167 no1 p70
F 2017
Learning to Love the Hog color *Esquire* v166 no4 p44 N 2016

Bosurgi, Lidia
Macrophage function in tissue repair and remodeling requires
IL-4 or IL-13 with apoptotic cells diag *Science* v356 no6342
p1072 Je 9 2017

Boswell, Andrew

Strengthening the Precautionary Principle in the Post-Paris Climate Regime bibl *Environment* v59 no5 p26 S/O 2017

BOSWELL, FRANCES
EASTER FEAST color *Martha Stewart Living* p100 Ap 2017

Bosworth, Jeremy
ROCKET MAN B. Haugen color *American Craft* v76 no6 p50
D 2016-Ja 2017

Bosworth, Kate, 1983-
InSTYLE November 2016 color *InStyle* v23 no12 p237 N 2016
RED HOT N. Vargas-cooper color *InStyle* v23 no12 p244 N 2016

Bosworth, Patricia
20-Something P. GREEN *New York Times Book Review* p14 F 5
2017
His Skunk Hours: A psychological biography of Robert Lowell
explores the overlap of poetry and pathology *New York Times
Book Review* p13 Mr 5 2017

Bosworth, R. J. B.
Fascists in Love J. BACHRACH color *Weekly Standard* v22 no31
p39 Ap 17 2017

Bosworth, Richard
The pain behind the pleasure *History Today* v67 no2 p47 F 2017

Botanical gardens
COLOR crescendo J. A. BAGGET color *Better Homes & Gardens*
v95 no10 p95 O 2017
The Role of Botanical Gardens in the Conservation of Cactaceae
K. R. HULTINE, L. C. MAJURE et al *BioScience* v66 no12
p1057 D 1 2016

Botanical gardens—Evaluation
Secret Gardens Z. MATTHEW color *Los Angeles Magazine* v62
no10 p88 O 2017
Your CHECKLIST E. Jardina and C. Salwitz color *Sunset* v237
no6 p50 D 2016

Botanical gardens—United States
Broader Role for Botanical Gardens D. Cubie color *National
Wildlife (World Edition)* v55 no3 p12 Ap/My 2017

Botanical research
THE SECRET LIFE OF PLANTS D. Stone and Takao Fujiwara
color *National Geographic* v231 no5 p26 My 2017

Botanical specimens
Collection in limbo *Science* v356 no6333 p9 Ap 7 2017

Botanists
BOTANY E. S. SOTO color *Better Homes & Gardens* v95 no5
p10 My 2017
Engineered crops could have it made in the shade E. Stokstad
color *Science* v354 no6314 p816 N 18 2016
Seeds of the Future J. Mark *Sierra* v102 no2 p45 Mr/Ap 2017

Botany
See also
Aquatic plants
Ferns
Fruit
Plant hybridization
Trees
Weeds
Nature's Industry C. TUDOR ERLER *Virginia Living* v15 no3
p79 Ap 2017

Botany—Tropics
Eating ecosystems J. S. Brashares and K. M. Gaynor color *Science*
v356 no6334 p136 Ap 14 2017

Botchan, Michael R.
Mechanisms for initiating cellular DNA replication graph *Science*
v355 no6327 p811 F 24 2017
Not just Salk color *Science* v357 no6356 p1105 S 15 2017

Botelho, Elena L.
The Dangers of Hiring a Nice CEO *Harvard Business Review
Digital Articles* p2 Je 7 2016

BOTELHO, ELENA LYTKINA
What Sets Successful CEOs Apart [Cover story] color *Harvard
Business Review* v95 no3 p70 My/Je 2017

Botha, Johan, 1965-2016
JOHAN BOTHA. RUSTENBERG, SOUTH AFRICA, AUGUST
19,1965—VIENNA, AUSTRIA, SEPTEMBER 8, 2016 H.
Stewart *Opera News* v81 no5 p60 N 2016

Bothwell, Javier
Specializing in Unique *Stage Directions* v30 no3 p68 Mr 2017

Botnets (Computer networks)

BOTNETS of Things B. SCHNEIER chart color map *MIT Technology Review* v120 no2 p88 Mr/Ap 2017

Twitter Votes diag graph *MIT Technology Review* v120 no3 p9 My/Je 2017

Botsman, Rachel

The Changing Rules of Trust in the Digital Age *Harvard Business Review Digital Articles* p2 O 20 2015

Botstein, David

Systems-level analysis of mechanisms regulating yeast metabolic flux bibl diag graph *Science* v354 no6311 paaf2786-1 O 28 2016

Botstein, Leon

Hand in Glove R. Platt cartoon *New Yorker* v92 no47 p13 Ja 30 2017

Botstein, Sarah

An interview about interviewing with Lynn Novick and Sarah Botstein of The Vietnam War M. Hindley *Humanities* v38 no4 p1 Fall 2017

Botswana—Description & travel

BEAUTY AND THE BEASTS S. Roberts bw color *Conde Nast Traveler* v51 no10 p158 N 2016

DELTA FORCE C. TATTOLI color *Conde Nast Traveler* v51 no10 p165 N 2016

ZAMBIA + BOTSWANA P. GUZMAN color *Conde Nast Traveler* v52 no4 p44 Ap 2017

Bott, Kristina

Research: Moral Appeals Can Help Reduce Tax Evasion *Harvard Business Review Digital Articles* p2 Jl 20 2017

Böttcher, René

Evolution of protein phosphorylation across 18 fungal species bibl graph *Science* v354 no6309 p229 O 14 2016

Bottega Veneta SA

Fold 'Em E. Wilson color *InStyle* v24 no1 p33 Ja 2017

VIENNA BOTH THE CLASSIC AND MODERN SIDES R. MISNER color *Conde Nast Traveler* v52 no8 p32 S 2017

Botti, A. M.

Observation of a large-scale anisotropy in the arrival directions of cosmic rays above 8×1018 eV *Science* v357 no6357 p1266 S 22 2017

Botti, Deb

STUFF Nature SCREWED UP cartoon *Old House Journal* v44 no8 p54 D 2016

Botticelli, Sandro, 1444 or 5-1510

Adoration of the Magi H. J. Hornik and M. C. Parsons *Christian Century* v133 no25 p47 D 7 2016

Botticelli, Sandro, 1444 or 5-1510—Exhibitions

SEARCH FOR THE DIVINE B. Glose *Virginia Living* v15 no2 p19 F 2017

Bottle feeding

Breast and Bottle for the Win! H. Pevzner color *Parents* v92 no9 p40 S 2017

Formula for Feeding *Parents* v91 no11 p34 N 2016

Bottled water

See also

Enriched bottled water

Bottled Water M. J. WEEDMAN img *New York* p56 F 9 2017

THE EVERYTHING GUIDE TO: Bottled Water M. J. WEEDMAN img *New York* p56 Ja 9 2017

Flint: a day by the bottle R. Feltman color *Popular Science* v289 no2 p11 Mr/Ap 2017

High-tech Hydration [Cover story] S. KLEIN color *Prevention* v69 no7 p28 Jl 2017

Bottled water industry & the environment

The Nestlé Bottled Water Cycle C. Winter cartoon color *Bloomberg Businessweek* no4539 p56 S 25 2017

Bottled water—Evaluation

That Fizzy Feeling J. BAINBRIDGE *Atlanta* v57 no6 p54 O 2017

The Water Taste Test img *New York* p58 Ja 9 2017

Bottled water—Sales & prices

ALMOST FAMOUS: Waterfront the Blue Ridge hasn't won any contests--yet R. NELSON *Virginia Living* v15 no6 p112 O 2017

Bottles

See also

Carbonated beverage bottles

Liquor bottles

Wine bottles

GEAR A. Opar *Audubon* v118 no6 p47 Wint 2016

Bottles—Evaluation

Adam's Home STYLE SHEET color *O, The Oprah Magazine* p59 Ap 2017

Cleaning House color *Bon Appetit* v62 no4 p27 Ap 2017

SMALL BATCH, HIGH YIELD D. MICHEL color *Men's Health* v32 no2 p(Sp)14 Mr 2017

BOTTOM, STEPHANA

soup up dinner *Parents* v91 no12 p50 D 2016

Bottomley, Paul

Leicester City FC and the Benefits of an Underdog Brand *Harvard Business Review Digital Articles* p2 Ag 12 2016

BOTTOMS, GLEN D.

An Infrastructure Fix il *American Conservative* v16 no1 p15 Ja/F 2017

Bottoms, Keisha Lance

OFF TO THE RACES S. HENRY *Atlanta* v56 no10 p32 F 2017

BOTTUM, JOSEPH

Artificial Intelligence color *Weekly Standard* v22 no16 p5 D 26 2016

Core Dogma color *Weekly Standard* v22 no34 p16 My 15 2017

Critics with Bombs color *Weekly Standard* v22 no20 p21 Ja 30 2017

A Crying Shame color *Weekly Standard* v22 no21 p5 F 6 2017

An Extraordinary Career color *Weekly Standard* v22 no25 p15 Mr 6 2017

I Don't Want a Bargain cartoon *Weekly Standard* v22 no38 p5 Je 12 2017

The Joy of Destruction color *Weekly Standard* v23 no3 p21 S 25 2017

Mnemonic Possession color *Weekly Standard* v22 no26 p5 Mr 13 2017

Time Bandits color *Weekly Standard* v22 no30 p5 Ap 10 2017

Bottura, Massimo, 1962-

Massimo Bottura M. Rich color *Current Biography* v78 no4 p12 Ap 2017

Botulinum toxin—Research

The Drug That's Treating Everything [Cover story] A. Sifferlin color diag *Time* v189 no3 p38 Ja 16 2017

Botulinum toxin—Therapeutic use

The Drug That's Treating Everything [Cover story] A. Sifferlin color diag *Time* v189 no3 p38 Ja 16 2017

Boublil, Alain

Why Are We in Miss Saigon? img *New York* v50 no7 p83 Ap 3 2017

Bouchard, Fred

MEHMET ALI SANLIKOL color *Downbeat* v84 no1 p22 Ja 2017

Monk Dreams, Hallucinations And Nightmares bw *Downbeat* v84 no5 p57 My 2017

Bouchard, Jay

The Chicago Cubs and the mystery of faith color *U.S. Catholic* v82 no4 p19 Ap 2017

Peripheral vision color *U.S. Catholic* v82 no5 p12 My 2017

Bouchard, Loren

Bob's Burgers M. Logan *TV Guide* v64 no48 p36 N 21 2016

BOUCHARD, NANCY

EQUIPMENT color *Backpacker* p73 N 2017

Little Big Packs color diag *Backpacker* p49 My 2017

Making a Splash color *Backpacker* p43 O 2017

Packs bw color diag graph il *Backpacker* v45 no3 p29 Ap 2017

BOUCHER, BRUCE

Between Fable and Fact: A biography of a pioneering natural scientist *New York Times Book Review* p9 S 10 2017

LIKE AN EGYPTIAN *New York Times Book Review* p23 D 4 2016

Boucher, Chris

SLIM'S CHANCE [Cover story] L. Winn color *Sports Illustrated* v125 no15 p40 N 7 2016

Boucher, Jean-Philippe

Row bots *Physics Today* v70 no6 p82 Je 2017

Boucher, Nathalie

Intercellular communication and conjugation are mediated by ESX secretion systems in mycobacteria bibl diag graph *Science* v354 no6310 p347 O 21 2016

Boucheron, Patrick

A Buffet of French History R. Darnton color *New York Review of Books* v64 no8 p40 My 11 2017

Bouchery, Tiffany
Specific repair by discerning macrophages diag *Science* v356 no6342 p1014 Je 9 2017

Bouchet, Amanda
Breath of Fire color *Publishers Weekly* v263 no48 p54 N 28 2016

BOUCHET, FRANCOIS
A COSMIC CONTROVERSY color *Scientific American* v317 no1 p5 Jl 2017

Bouchez, David
The preprophase band of microtubules controls the robustness of division orientation in plants graph *Science* v356 no6334 p186 Ap 14 2017

BOUDET, ANA MARIA MUNOZ
WOMEN'S WORK color graph *Scientific American* v317 no3 p72 S 2017

Boudett, Kathryn Parker
Using data wisely at the system level chart color *Phi Delta Kappan* v99 no1 p25 S 2017

Boudreau, Curt
FROM OUR READERS color *Sky & Telescope* v134 no2 p6 Ag 2017

Boudreau, John
The Big Disconnect in Your Talent Strategy and How to Fix It *Harvard Business Review Digital Articles* p2 D 23 2016
The Case for Lending Out Your Star Performers *Harvard Business Review Digital Articles* p2 Ja 19 2015
HR Must Make People Analytics More User-Friendly *Harvard Business Review Digital Articles* p2 Je 16 2017
The Right Kind of Conflict Leads to Better Products *Harvard Business Review Digital Articles* p2 D 23 2016
Tongal, eLance, and Topcoder Will Change How You Compete *Harvard Business Review Digital Articles* p2 N 7 2014
Uber Is Finally Realizing HR Isn't Just for Recruiting color *Harvard Business Review Digital Articles* p2 Mr 7 2017
We Need to Move Beyond the Employee vs. Contractor Debate *Harvard Business Review Digital Articles* p2 Jl 8 2015
When Investors Want to Know How You Treat People *Harvard Business Review Digital Articles* p2 F 10 2015
Why More Executives Should Consider Becoming a CHRO *Harvard Business Review Digital Articles* p2 My 3 2017
Work in the Future Will Fall into These 4 Categories *Harvard Business Review Digital Articles* p2 Mr 17 2016

Boudreaux's Fine Jewelers (Company)
Finest of the FINE M. Cameran color *New Orleans Magazine* v51 no1 p72 N 2016

BOUDRY, MAARTEN
THE FALLACY FORK: Why It's time to Get Rid of Fallacy Theory *Skeptical Inquirer* v41 no5 p46 S/O 2017

Boudway, Ira
Americas color map *Bloomberg Businessweek* no4532 p7 Jl 31 2017
Asia color *Bloomberg Businessweek* no4532 p6 Jl 31 2017
BALLERS color *Bloomberg Businessweek* no4535 p44 Ag 28 2017
Europe color *Bloomberg Businessweek* no4532 p6 Jl 31 2017
GET IN THE HOLE! cartoon color *Bloomberg Businessweek* no4497 p63 O 31 2016
GOT ANY IDEAS? [Cover story] color graph *Bloomberg Businessweek* no4517 p48 Ap 3 2017
How MusclePharm Went From Swole to Twig bw color *Bloomberg Businessweek* no4497 p56 O 31 2016
It's the End of the World as We Know It color *Bloomberg Businessweek* no4510 p58 F 6 2017
JUST DO IT REDO IT TRY NOT TO UNDO IT DON'T LOSE TO ADIDAS color *Bloomberg Businessweek* no4523 p42 My 22 2017
Liberal Nonprofits Ride The Anti-Trump Wave color *Bloomberg Businessweek* no4500 p30 N 21 2016
THE LIFE OF BEEF JOHNSTON color *Bloomberg Businessweek* no4523 p59 My 22 2017
Mary Kay Henry color *Bloomberg Businessweek* no4496 p24 O 24 2016
Q&A color *Bloomberg Businessweek* no4496 p72 O 24 2016
This New Test Could Crush The NFL color *Bloomberg Businessweek* no4510 p48 F 6 2017
What's Your One Shining Moment? cartoon *Bloomberg Business-*

week no4514 p73 Mr 13 2017
When League Pass Takes You Courtside color *Bloomberg Businessweek* no4498 p42 N 7 2016

Boudway, Matthew
Children of God? bw color *Commonweal* v143 no18 p18 N 11 2016

Boué, Géori
GÉORI BOUÉ *Opera News* v81 no10 p66 Ap 2017

Bouée, Charles-Edouard
Digital Transformation Doesn't Have to Leave Employees Behind *Harvard Business Review Digital Articles* p2 S 30 2015

Boufaied, Othman
Europe Can Find Better Ways to Get Refugees into Workforces *Harvard Business Review Digital Articles* p2 O 5 2015

Bouffard, Suzanne M.
The Advantage of Universal Pre-K S. Begley color *Time* v190 no9 p24 S 4 2017

Bougouma, Edith C.
Resistance to malaria through structural variation of red blood cell invasion receptors diag *Science* v356 no6343 p1139 Je 16 2017

Bouie, Jamelle
Jamelle Bouie M. Hagan color *Current Biography* v77 no10 p14 O 2016

Boulatov, Roman
Experimentally realized mechanochemistry distinct from force-accelerated scission of loaded bonds diag graph *Science* v357 no6348 p299 Jl 21 2017

Bould, Fred
The Point- and-Shoot Reborn color *Bloomberg Businessweek* no4518 p71 Ap 10 2017

Boulder Philharmonic Orchestra (Performer)
RITE OF SPRING A. ROSS cartoon *New Yorker* v93 no9 p76 Ap 17 2017

Boulders
THE DESCENT A. BURR color *Climbing* no354 p80 Jl 2017
Highball Tactics N. WILLIAMS color *Climbing* no350 p50 D 2016/Ja 2017
It's Not a Free Solo, It's a Highball, DAD! ". CORRIGAN color *Climbing* no354 p35 Jl 2017
A New Joc's C. WEBBER color *Climbing* no353 p22 My/Je 2017

Boulger Canyon (Utah)
Something Very Clear color *Arizona Highways* v93 no5 p5 My 2017

Bouligny, Edgar
World War I CENTENNIAL B. ALTOBELLO bw *New Orleans Magazine* v51 no12 p92 O 2017

Boullay, P.
Hydrogen positions in single nanocrystals revealed by electron diffraction bibl color *Science* v355 no6321 p1 Ja 13 2017

Bouloc, Philippe
Guanine glycation repair by DJ-1/Park7 and its bacterial homologs chart color diag graph *Science* v357 no6347 p208 Jl 14 2017

Boulogne-Billancourt (France)
Machine in the Garden S. STEPHENS *Architectural Record* v205 no6 p92 Je 2017

BOULOUQUE, CLÉMENCE
MOSES, THE MAN *New York Times Book Review* p56 D 4 2016

Boulware, Chase
X-ray sterilization with accelerators is viable in US *Physics Today* v70 no1 p11 Ja 2017

Boumgarden, Peter
Good Christian Sex: Why Chastity Isn't the Only Option—And Other Things the Bible Says about Sex color *Christian Century* v133 no21 p48 O 12 2016
How a Cartoon Caption Contest Can Make You a Better Writer *Harvard Business Review Digital Articles* p2 Jl 21 2015

Bound, John
Crossing borders along an endless frontier color *Science* v356 no6339 p694 My 19 2017

Boundaries
Border Walls and Biodiversity L. E. OGDEN *BioScience* v67 no6 p498 Je 2017
COLLATERAL DAMAGE *Sierra* v102 no5 p34 St/O 2017
DO YOU LIVE IN A BORDER ZONE? C. J. CIARAMELLA color map *Reason* v49 no1 p36 My 2017

The Great Struggle of Our Era P. J. BUCHANAN *American Conservative* v16 no2 p11 Mr/Ap 2017

IS TRUMP ENDING THE AMERICAN ERA? E. A. COHEN color map *Atlantic* v320 no3 p68 O 2017

THE ULTIMATE CANADIAN GEOGRAPHY QUIZ CITIES EDITION N. WALKER color map *Canadian Geographic* v137 no3 p41 My 2017

Boundaries (Film)

BOUNDARIES (PAYS) J. Teodoro color *Film Comment* v53 no2 p22 Mr/Ap 2017

Boundaries—Economic aspects

Unlikely Neighbors S. Beyer *Governing* v30 no2 p24 N 2016

Boundaries—Government policy

WHAT WALL? C. BALLÍ *Texas Monthly* v45 no5 p101 My 2017

Boundary disputes

China's Deep Logic M. Maochun Yu *Hoover Digest: Research & Opinion on Public Policy* no4 p128 Fall 2016

Course Correction E. Ratner color *Foreign Affairs* v96 no4 p64 Jl/Ag 2017

A SEA'S FADING BOUNTY R. BALE color map *National Geographic* v231 no3 p74 Mr 2017

Shadow on the South China Sea B. Hayton *History Today* v66 no10 p3 O 2016

Bouquet, Alexis

Cassini finds molecular hydrogen in the Enceladus plume: Evidence for hydrothermal processes chart graph *Science* v356 no6334 p155 Ap 14 2017

Bouquets

Make a bouquet last and last color *Redbook* p131 My 2017

Bourbon Street Parade (Music)

Best of Brass J. Berry bw *New Orleans Magazine* v51 no5 p54 Mr 2017

Bourbon whiskey

American Spirits J. deBary color *Bloomberg Businessweek* no4528 p73 Je 26 2017

Bourbon. In Ohio F. MAROUKIAN color *Popular Mechanics* p16 S 2017

Bourbon. In Ohio F. MAROUKIAN color *Popular Mechanics* v193 no7 p16 S 2016

Raise a Glass color *American History* v52 no3 p31 Ag 2017

Bourbon whiskey—Evaluation

THE RICHEST POURS color *Forbes* v198 no9 p49 D 30 2016

Bourc'his, Déborah

The DNA methyltransferase DNMT3C protects male germ cells from transposon activity bibl diag graph *Science* v354 no6314 p909 N 18 2016

Bourdain, Anthony, 1956-

ANTHONY BOURDAIN A. BOURDAIN color *Esquire* v166 no4 p141 N 2016

JOURNEYMAN P. R. KEEFE cartoon color *New Yorker* v92 no49 p52 F 13 2017

MAN of the WORLD O. Strand color *Vogue* v206 no11 p236 N 2016

Bourdain, Anthony, 1956—Interviews

ANTHONY BOURDAIN ON SMUG LIBERALS AND EATING DOGS A. BISLEY color *Reason* v48 no10 p67 Mr 2017

THE INTERVIEW A. LEE color *Maclean's* v129 no45 p14 N 14 2016

Bourdette-Donon, Fanny

Secrets of the Foundation Free F. Valdesolo color *Glamour* v115 no6 p66 Je 2017

Bourdin, Guy

Flipping the Switch color *InStyle* v24 no3 p178 Mr 2017

Bourelly, Bibi

BIBI BOURELLY L. N. Williams color map *Essence* v47 no8 p80 D 2016

Bourenkov, Gleb

Mechanism of transmembrane signaling by sensor histidine kinases color *Science* v356 no6342 p1043 Je 9 2017

Bourg, Norman A.

Plant diversity increases with the strength of negative density dependence at the global scale diag *Science* v356 no6345 p1389 Je 30 2017

BOURGEOIS, JEAN-PAUL

UP IN SMOKE color *Field & Stream* v122 no2 p66 Je/Jl 2017

Bourgeois, Louise, 1911-2010—Exhibitions

ART color *New Yorker* v93 no33 p12 O 23 2017

Bourgeois, Trudy

People Suffer at Work When They Can't Discuss the Racial Bias They Face Outside of It *Harvard Business Review Digital Articles* p2 Jl 10 2017

Bourguignon, François

RISING TIDES AND MEGA-YACHTS D. Lal *Claremont Review of Books* v16 no4 p55 Fall 2016

Bourguignon, Marc

UNSOLICITED BETA color *Climbing* no351 p18 F/Mr 2017

Bouriaud, Olivier

Positive biodiversity-productivity relationship predominant in global forests bibl chart graph map *Science* v354 no6309 paaf8957-1 O 14 2016

Bourjaily, Phil

2016 BEST OF THE BEST bw color *Field & Stream* v121 no7 p96 D 2016/Ja 2017

A 20 FOR TOM cartoon color *Field & Stream* v121 no9 p28 Ap 2017

THE BIG 1-5-0 color *Field & Stream* v121 no6 p64 N 2016

A BRACE IN THE SUN color *Field & Stream* v121 no8 p16 F/Mr 2017

CHEAP SHOTS color *Field & Stream* v121 no7 p30 D 2016/Ja 2017

DOUBLE VISION color *Field & Stream* v121 no8 p34 F/Mr 2017

DREAM GUNS cartoon color *Field & Stream* v122 no1 p28 My 2017

FIELD TEST color *Field & Stream* v122 no2 p99 Je/Jl 2017

FIRE DRILLS bw color *Field & Stream* v121 no8 p64 F/Mr 2017

FIT AND SHIM color *Field & Stream* v122 no3 p28 Ag 2017

FIVE REASONS YOU MISSED THAT DOVE color *Field & Stream* v122 no4 p34 S 2017

The Jump Shot color *Field & Stream* v122 no4 pF10 S 2017

Make a Splash color *Field & Stream* v122 no4 pF5 S 2017

OVERNIGHT FLIGHT color *Field & Stream* v122 no5 p30 O 2017

SHOTGUN SHOOTOUT 2017 [Cover story] color *Field & Stream* v122 no6 p72 N 2017

SOUTHERN SWING color *Field & Stream* v122 no2 p32 Je/Jl 2017

THE TAGGED-OUT DEER HUNTER'S GUIDE TO FALL [Cover story] color *Field & Stream* v122 no6 p59 N 2017

Bourke, Stephen

Emergence and spread of a human-transmissible multidrug-resistant nontuberculous mycobacterium bibl diag graph *Science* v354 no6313 p751 N 11 2016

Bourke-White, Margaret, 1904-1971

FOR YOUR CONSID-HER-ATION bw color *O, The Oprah Magazine* p22 Ja 2017

Pioneers bw color *Forbes* v199 no6 p108 Je 13 2017

Bourlange, Sylvain

Release of mineral-bound water prior to subduction tied to shallow seismogenic slip off Sumatra graph *Science* v356 no6340 p841 My 26 2017

Bournazos, Stylianos

IgG antibodies to dengue enhanced for FcγRIIIA binding determine disease severity bibl graph *Science* v355 no6323 p395 Ja 27 2017

Bourne, David G.

Seagrass ecosystems reduce exposure to bacterial pathogens of humans, fishes, and invertebrates bibl graph *Science* v355 no6326 p731 F 17 2017

Bourne, Sarah L.

A SUMO-ubiquitin relay recruits proteasomes to chromosome axes to regulate meiotic recombination bibl graph *Science* v355 no6323 p403 Ja 27 2017

Bourque, Charles W.

Neurons that drive and quench thirst color diag *Science* v357 no6356 p1092 S 15 2017

Bourzac, Katherine

Carbon color il *MIT Technology Review* v120 no4 p62 Jl/Ag 2017

INSIDE THE FAR-OUT GLASS LAB bw color *MIT Technology Review* v120 no2 p100 Mr/Ap 2017

To Feed the World, Improve Photosynthesis color *MIT Technology Review* v120 no5 p80 S/O 2017

Boushey, Heather, 1970-

How Should Governments Address Inequality? M. S. Kearney color *Foreign Affairs* v96 no6 p133 N/D 2017

Boussata, Souad

ELABELA deficiency promotes preeclampsia and cardiovascular malformations in mice color diag graph *Science* v357 no6352 p707 Ag 18 2017

Boustany, Andre

East not least for Pacific bluefin tuna color diag *Science* v357 no6349 p356 Jl 28 2017

Boutella, Sofia, 1982-

Arms Up! E. Wilson color *InStyle* v24 no11 p74 N 2017

Sofia Boutella J. Crelin color *Current Biography* v78 no9 p3 S 2017

SOFIA BOUTELLA K. SMITH color *Vanity Fair* v59 no7 p41 Summ 2017

Bouter, Lex

Addressing scientific integrity scientifically *Science* v357 no6357 p1248 S 22 2017

Boutique hotels

BRINGING HERITAGE TO LIFE color *Walrus* v14 no7 p28 S 2017

THE ORIGINAL HOSPITALITY DISRUPTER L. Gallagher color *Fortune* v175 no8 p87 Je 15 2017

Boutique hotels—Evaluation

north adams, massachusetts T. McKEOUGH bw color *Architectural Digest* no5 p82 My 2017

An ODE to HOTELS in Marrakech R. MISNER bw color *Conde Nast Traveler* v52 no1 p78 Ja 2017

They're SORT OF OUT OF THE WAY BUT WORTH THE TRIP color *Conde Nast Traveler* v52 no1 p80 Ja 2017

Bouton, Katie

Recruiting for Cultural Fit *Harvard Business Review Digital Articles* p2 Jl 17 2015

Bouton, Shannon

Technology Is Changing Transportation, and Cities Should Adapt *Harvard Business Review Digital Articles* p2 S 13 2017

Boutros-Ghali, Boutros, 1922-2016

In memoriam bw color *Maclean's* v129 no48/49 p82 D 5 2016

Boutry, Marc

Emission of volatile organic compounds from petunia flowers is facilitated by an ABC transporter diag *Science* v356 no6345 p1386 Je 30 2017

Bouvier, Brendan

Posthole color *Powder* v45 no4 p146 D 2016

Bouvier, Ives

Paint, by Numbers cartoon *Forbes* v199 no4 p24 Ap 25 2017

Bouwstra, Ruth

Role for migratory wild birds in the global spread of avian influenza H5N8 bibl graph map *Science* v354 no6309 p213 O 14 2016

Bouzereau, Laurent

The Long Way Home S. MEARS bw color *Film Comment* v53 no3 p74 My/Je 2017

When the Film Greats Went to War S. Zacharek color *Time* v189 no13 p50 Ap 10 2017

Bouziat, Romain

Reovirus infection triggers inflammatory responses to dietary antigens and development of celiac disease color diag *Science* v356 no6333 p44 Ap 7 2017

Bova, Dan

Can TV Make You Slim? color *Health* v31 no7 p55 S 2017

Bova, Tiffani

Reinvent Your Sales Process While Still Hitting Your Numbers *Harvard Business Review Digital Articles* p2 F 18 2015

What Salespeople Need to Know About the New B2B Landscape *Harvard Business Review Digital Articles* p2 Ag 5 2015

Bove, Vincenzo

Why Mass Migration Is Good for Long-Term Economic Growth *Harvard Business Review Digital Articles* p2 Ap 18 2017

Bovee, Roger

#trailchat color il map *Backpacker* p6 Je 2017

Bovine respiratory syncytial virus diseases

MORE PREVENTION, LESS TREATMENT G. Johnston *Successful Farming* v115 no5 p52 Mid-Mr 2017

Bovine spongiform encephalopathy

New blood tests make strides in detecting prion disease K. Servick color *Science* v354 no6319 p1512 D 23 2016

Bovine viral diarrhea

ERADICATE? CATTLE INDUSTRY CONTEMPLATES THE POTENTIAL TO ELIMINATE BVD AS A SIGNIFICANT DISEASE G. Johnston *Successful Farming* v115 no6 p58 Ap 2017

Bovy, Phoebe Maltz

The Privilege Enforcers T. H. WARREN color *Christianity Today* p72 Ap 2017

Bow & arrow

Archers Make Ready K. Massicot color *New Orleans Magazine* v51 no8 p150 Je 2017

THE BOW BUBBLE W. Brantley color *Field & Stream* v121 no8 p36 F/Mr 2017

DOG DAYS color *Field & Stream* v122 no2 p83 Je/Jl 2017

NO PAIN, NO GAME D. Hurteau color diag *Field & Stream* v122 no3 p57 Ag 2017

OLD FLAMES G. Kendall, J. Kacena et al color *Field & Stream* v122 no1 p10 My 2017

Bow & arrow—Evaluation

BOW SHOOTOUT 2017 W. Brantley and D. Hurteau bw color *Field & Stream* v122 no3 p69 Ag 2017

BOW TEST 2017 T. HANSEN and A. McKEAN chart color *Outdoor Life* v224 no6 p17 Ag 2017

Bow Truss Coffee Roasters (Company)

THE BOW TRUSS BEEF E. KANG color *Chicago* v66 no5 p28 My 2017

Bowannie, Mary K.

Choctaw Code Talkers *American Indian Quarterly* v40 no4 p385 Fall 2016

Bowden, Brett

Civilization: 'It Means Just What I Choose It to Mean' *Society* v54 no2 p126 Ap 2017

BOWDEN, CHARLES

THE SANTA CATALINAS: TUCSON'S NEARBY WILDERNESS *Arizona Highways* v93 no6 p46 Je 2017

Bowden, Jonny

AUTOIMMUNE DISEASE: NATURAL SOLUTIONS color *Amazing Wellness* p30 Fall 2017

Bake-Ahead Breakfast color *Better Nutrition* p62 My 2017

CRAZY ABOUT COLLAGEN color *Better Nutrition* v78 no12 p40 D 2016

CREATE A capsule cabinet J. Rice chart color *Amazing Wellness* v9 no2 p54 Spr 2017

DEFEATING ALZHEIMER'S color *Better Nutrition* v79 no11 p54 N 2017

Eat-The-Bowl Summer Salad [Cover story] color *Better Nutrition* v79 no6 p62 Je 2017

Fresh & Fast Chicken color *Better Nutrition* v79 no1 p66 Ja 2017

Ham-Yam Quiche Dijon color *Better Nutrition* v79 no4 p70 Ap 2017

Hope for Fibromyalgia color *Amazing Wellness* v9 no1 p36 Wint 2017

Is Fruit Keeping You from Losing Weight? color *Better Nutrition* v79 no10 p64 O 2017

NATURAL TREATMENT FOR PAIN color *Amazing Wellness* v9 no2 p34 Spr 2017

ON THE A-LIST color *Amazing Wellness* v9 no3 p22 EarlySumm 2017

Peanut Butter Power Snack Dip color *Better Nutrition* v79 no7 p56 Jl 2017

Post-Holiday Fast Food color *Better Nutrition* v79 no11 p78 N 2017

Quick & Healthy Homemade Sausage color *Better Nutrition* v79 no10 p78 O 2017

THE REAL DEAL ON FIBER color *Amazing Wellness* v8 no6 p42 Early Winter2016

THE THYROID MISTAKE color *Amazing Wellness* v9 no3 p34 EarlySumm 2017 SECRETS TO ZEN [Cover story] color *Amazing Wellness* v9 no6 p36 EarlyWint 2017

SMARTER FATS color *Amazing Wellness* v8 no2 p36 Spr 2016

Soup's On color *Better Nutrition* v78 no11 p86 N 2016

SUMMER "TEA-TOX" color *Amazing Wellness* v9 no4 p47 Summ 2017

Trout: The Perfect Catch color *Better Nutrition* v79 no9 p70 S 2017

WEIGHT-LOSS SUCCESS STORY color *Amazing Wellness* v8

no2 p60 Spr 2016

Zoodle Ramen Bowl color *Better Nutrition* v79 no3 p70 Mr 2017

Bowden, Mark, 1951-

444 DAYS IN HELL R. Soodalter *Military History* v33 no6 p18 Mr 2017

Tet Turnaround J. D. Morelock color *Military History* v34 no4 p70 N 2017

THE WORST PROBLEM ON EARTH color diag *Atlantic* v320 no1 p66 Jl/Ag 2017

Bowdoin, Jarred

WAYPOINT N. KREBS color *Outdoor Life* v224 no4 p5 My 2017

Bowe, Christopher

Fixing Pharma's Incentives Problem in the Wake of the U.S. Opioid Crisis *Harvard Business Review Digital Articles* p2 Je 13 2016

Identifying the Skills That Can Help You Change Careers *Harvard Business Review Digital Articles* p2 Ag 6 2015

Bowe, Julie

Big & Little Questions (According to Wren Jo Byrd) *Publishers Weekly* v264 no3 p59 Ja 16 2017

Bowe, Whitney

Age-proof your hands M. OLIVA color *Redbook* p36 Mr 2017

Arches de Triumph A. Finney color *Women's Health* v14 no1 p49 Ja/F 2017

Bowen, Cynthia

The Economic Benefit of Downtown Parks *Parks & Recreation* v52 no9 p54 S 2017

BOWEN, DANA

it's going to be a / ROAST *Martha Stewart Living* no268 p106 O 2016

Bowen, Daniel H.

The art of partnerships color graph il *Phi Delta Kappan* v98 no7 p8 Ap 2017

Bowen, Julie, 1970-

Julie Bowen C. M. Smith color *Entertainment Weekly* no1454/1455 p20 F 24 2017

Bowen, Kelly

Between the Devil and the Duke: A Season for Scandal Romance *Publishers Weekly* v263 no51 p131 D 12 2016

Bowen, Kevin, 1947-

The Stubborn Optimist N. DAMES color *Atlantic* v319 no3 p38 Ap 2017

Bowen, Rhys

In Farleigh Field: A Novel of World War II *Publishers Weekly* v263 no47 p88 N 21 2016

On Her Majesty's Frightfully Secret Service *Publishers Weekly* v264 no26 p158 Je 26 2017

Bowen Jewelry (Company)

SPECIAL WEDDINGS ADVERTISING SECTION *Virginia Living* v15 no2 p90 F 2017

Bower, Ben J.

Posttranslational mutagenesis: A chemical strategy for exploring protein side-chain diversity diag *Science* v354 no6312 p597 N 4 2016

BOWER, BRUCE

Abuse hinders children's social learning *Science News* v191 no5 p10 Mr 18 2017

African farmers' kids ace willpower test *Science News* v192 no1 p13 Ag 5 2017

Americas' first settlers debated color *Science News* v191 no10 p7 My 27 2017

Ancient peoples reshaped Amazon *Science News* v191 no6 p13 Ap 1 2017

Apes recognize others' false beliefs *Science News* v190 no10 p8 N 12 2016

Australia's interior colonized quickly color *Science News* v190 no11 p18 N 26 2016

Big Viking families nurtured murder *Science News* v190 no10 p16 N 12 2016

Burials give peek at Philistines' lives *Science News* v190 no13 p8 D 24 2016

Chipped teeth hint at Homo naledi diet color graph *Science News* v192 no4 p12 S 16 2017

Clay army made from custom pastes color *Science News* v192 no4 p19 S 16 2017

Clovis spearpoints absorbed shock color *Science News* v191 no9

p8 My 13 2017

Duty Bound Killings bw chart color map *Science News* v192 no2 p22 Ag 19 2017

Foragers first settled Tibetan Plateau color *Science News* v191 no2 p8 F 4 2017

Fossil offers clues to ape evolution color *Science News* v192 no3 p13 S 2 2017

Fossils push back origin of humans color *Science News* v191 no13 p6 Jl 8 2017

Genetics alone won't explain how humans left Africa color *Science News* v190 no13 p25 D 24 2016

Herders helped shape Silk Road color *Science News* v191 no7 p9 Ap 15 2017

Hominid roots may go back to Europe color *Science News* v191 no12 p9 Je 24 2017

Homo naledi's age surprises scientists color *Science News* v191 no11 p6 Je 10 2017

Humanlike helpers teach social skills color *Science News* v192 no6 p19 O 14 2017

Human sleep patterns show flexibility graph *Science News* v191 no3 p13 F 18 2017

THE HYBRID FACTOR color map *Science News* v190 no8 p22 O 15 2016

Iron Age trade secrets revealed color *Science News* v191 no4 p17 Mr 4 2017

Kids' learning curve not so smooth *Science News* v190 no11 p6 N 26 2016

Lasting mental health may be unusual chart graph *Science News* v191 no4 p7 Mr 4 2017

Low-status chimps are trendsetters *Science News* v191 no6 p8 Ap 1 2017

Lucy had taller kin, footprints suggest color *Science News* v191 no1 p8 Ja 21 2017

Maya codex real, analysis claims cartoon *Science News* v190 no9 p16 O 29 2016

MEETING NOTES color *Science News* v190 no13 p9 D 24 2016

Monkey flakes resemble hominid tools color *Science News* v190 no11 p16 N 26 2016

Monkey lives revealed color *Science News* v191 no5 p30 Mr 18 2017

Neandertal tar-making reconstructed color *Science News* v192 no5 p13 S 30 2017

Networking was key to human success color *Science News* v192 no7 p7 O 28 2017

New views snag science Nobels bw *Science News* v192 no7 p6 O 28 2017

NUDGE BACKLASH color diag graph *Science News* v191 no5 p18 Mr 18 2017

Oldest alphabet identified as Hebrew color *Science News* v190 no13 p8 D 24 2016

Oldest indigo-dyed fabric found color *Science News* v190 no8 p8 O 15 2016

Rise of civilization came at a big cost, book claims color *Science News* v192 no6 p28 O 14 2017

Romans, Huns sometimes got along color *Science News* v191 no8 p18 Ap 29 2017

Seeing CHACO in a NEW LIGHT color map *Science News* v191 no10 p16 My 27 2017

Skeleton ignites Viking warrior debate bw *Science News* v192 no6 p6 O 14 2017

Stone Age injuries lack modern analog color *Science News* v191 no10 p13 My 27 2017

Stone Age people treated cavities color *Science News* v191 no9 p15 My 13 2017

Bower, Deborah S.

Amphibians on the brink color map *Science* v357 no6350 p454 Ag 4 2017

Bower, Joseph L.

Another Year Has Passed, but the List of Massive Global Problems Has Stayed the Same *Harvard Business Review Digital Articles* p2 D 14 2015

The Error at the Heart of Corporate Leadership chart img *Harvard Business Review* v95 no3 p50 My/Je 2017

THE ERROR AT THE HEART OF CORPORATE LEADERSHIP: INTERACTION color *Harvard Business Review* v95 no4 p16 Jl/Ag 2017

THE ERROR AT THE HEART OF CORPORATE LEADER-SHIP: INTERACTION J. L. BOWER and L. S. PAINE color *Harvard Business Review* v95 no4 p16 Jl/Ag 2017

More Insiders Are Becoming CEOs, and That's a Good Thing *Harvard Business Review Digital Articles* p2 Mr 18 2016

Bower, Joseph—Interviews

Google's Alphabet Move Is Reorganizing 101 S. Cliffe *Harvard Business Review Digital Articles* p2 Ag 13 2015

Bower, Sara

Adopt a Critter chart color *Good Housekeeping* v264 no4 p140 Ap 2017

Ellen's Gone to the Dogs color *Good Housekeeping* v265 no1 p122 Jl 2017

THE FRIDGE color *Good Housekeeping* v265 no3 p104 S 2017

happiness is a warm puppy color *Good Housekeeping* v264 no3 p156 Mr 2017

"How Shelter Dogs Rescued Me" color *Good Housekeeping* v263 no6 p166 D 2016

Kitty Myths — Busted! color *Good Housekeeping* v265 no2 p136 Ag 2017

Spooktacular Decorating color *Good Housekeeping* v265 no4 p47 O 2017

Teach Safe Snuggling color *Good Housekeeping* v264 no5 p142 My 2017

Bowerbirds

Birds, Bees, and Beauty B. HEINRICH color *Natural History* v125 no4 p14 Ap 2017

Bowering, George

THE DAD DIALOGUES B. JOSEF GRUBISIC color *Maclean's* v129 no42 p60 O 24 2016

Bowers, Courtney

AFTER THE SHOW *Dance Spirit* v21 no4 p42 Ap 2017

Behind the Scenes of "Crazy Ex-Girlfriend" *Dance Spirit* v21 no1 p23 Ja 2017

BEST ALL AROUND *Dance Spirit* v20 no10 p24 D 2016

Candy Land color *Dance Spirit* v21 no4 p15 Ap 2017

Can't Stop the Beat *Dance Spirit* v20 no10 p19 D 2016

CIRQUE Queen *Dance Spirit* v21 no7 p52 S 2017

Dear Diary *Dance Spirit* v21 no3 p15 Mr 2017

THE DIRT *Dance Spirit* v21 no1 p24 Ja 2017

THE DIRT with Nicole Ciapponi *Dance Spirit* v20 no10 p20 D 2016

Extra! color *Dance Spirit* v21 no2 p17 F 2017

a fresh start *Dance Spirit* v20 no10 p2 D 2016

Greta HODGKINSON color *Dance Spirit* v21 no1 p28 Ja 2017

letter to my teenage self color *Dance Spirit* v21 no2 p24 F 2017

Melanie MOORE *Dance Spirit* v21 no7 p46 S 2017

Sarah WROTH color *Dance Spirit* v21 no4 p20 Ap 2017

TAKING THE Radio City STAGE color *Dance Spirit* v20 no10 p30 D 2016

Travis Wall: Puts His Stamp on Ballet *Dance Spirit* v21 no7 p41 S 2017

Val CHMERKOVSKIY *Dance Spirit* v21 no3 p22 Mr 2017

Vernard J. GILMOR bw *Dance Spirit* v20 no10 p24 D 2016

WHAT DO COLLEGE DANCE PROGRAMS really LOOK for? *Dance Spirit* v21 no7 p76 S 2017

BOWERS, KATHERINE

Powerful Partnerships chart color graph *Working Mother* v40 no2 p28 Je/Jl 2017

Bowersock, G. W.

The Bible and the Perils of 'Evolution' cartoon *New York Review of Books* v63 no16 p35 O 27 2016

Lost on the Road to Damascus color *New York Review of Books* v64 no7 p60 Ap 20 2017

ON RELIGION AND HISTORICAL NARRATIVE: A leading scholar's new history of Islam has a gaping hole at its centre T. Holland *History Today* v67 no10 p94 O 2017

Bowes, John

D'Addario Select Jazz Tenor Saxophone Mouthpiece color *Downbeat* v84 no5 p86 My 2017

Rampone & Cazzani 'Two Voices' color *Downbeat* v84 no5 p84 My 2017

Bowfin

Bow Hunting J. Cermele color *Field & Stream* v122 no1 pF4 My 2017

THE UGLY FISH M. VINCENT and G. BETHGE color *Outdoor Life* v224 no3 p62 Ap 2017

Bowhunters

Halloween Treat S. Bestul color *Field & Stream* v122 no5 pW1 O 2017

Bowhunters—Accidents

ONE FELL SWOOP D. W. Grable cartoon *Outdoor Life* v223 no9 p16 N 2016

Bowhunters—Interviews

SUPER WOMAN N. Krebs color *Outdoor Life* v223 no9 p13 N 2016

Bowhunting

Cheers & Jeers J. Nichols, M. Matuszak et al *Field & Stream* v122 no5 p12 O 2017

ELK THE KANE WAY T. CHRISTIE color *Outdoor Life* v224 no6 p37 Ag 2017

THE PROCRASTINATOR'S PLAYBOOK T. Hansen color *Outdoor Life* v224 no6 p55 Ag 2017

RECORD-BUSTING BULLS color *Outdoor Life* v224 no7 p12 S 2017

TRANSITION SEASON T. HANSEN color *Outdoor Life* v224 no8 pB1 O 2017

WORLD RECORD S. FELIX color *Outdoor Life* v224 no7 p34 S 2017

Bowhunting equipment

MAKING THE CASE FOR PROTECTION T. HANSEN color *Outdoor Life* v224 no8 pB4 O 2017

Bowhunting—Physiological aspects

NO PAIN, NO GAME D. Hurteau color diag *Field & Stream* v122 no3 p57 Ag 2017

Bowie, David, 1947-2016

THE BEST OF BOWIE'S NEW BOX SET E. R. Brown color *Entertainment Weekly* no1485 p59 O 6 2017

Bowie's Touring Alumni Say Goodbye A. GREENE color *Rolling Stone* no1280 p14 F 9 2017

DAVID BOWIE J. C. Mitchell and L. Greenblatt color *Entertainment Weekly* no1446/1447 p88 D 2016/Ja 2017

David Bowie's Parting Gift A. GREENE color *Rolling Stone* no1273 p16 N 3 2016

The Playlist color *Rolling Stone* no1274 p10 N 17 2016

Sound and Vision J. SLATE bw color *Esquire* v166 no4 p27 N 2016

BOWIE, MATTHEW J.

Opportunities for Improved Transparency in the Timber Trade through Scientific Verification *BioScience* v66 no11 p990 N 1 2016

BOWIE LARSON, PARKER

A Grand Gesture color *Architectural Digest* v73 no12 p128 D 2016

Bowl games (College football)

A Basket of Deplora-Bowls G. NORMAN color *Weekly Standard* v22 no18 p21 Ja 16 2017

Bowl games (College football)—History

School Book T. Keith color *Sports Illustrated* v125 no14 p22 O 24-31 2016

Bowl games (College football)—History—21st century

BEST OF THE BOWLS C. Johnson color *Sports Illustrated* v126 no2 p31 Ja 16 2017

Bowler, Gerry

Cleaning Up Christmas cartoon *Walrus* v13 no10 p71 D 2016

The Ghosts of Wars on Christmas Past T. S. KIDD color *Christianity Today* v60 no10 p70 D 2016

Bowler, Grant

Still Star-Crossed M. Logan *TV Guide* v65 no23 p20 My 29 2017

Bowler, Ian C. J. W.

Emergence and spread of a human-transmissible multidrug-resistant nontuberculous mycobacterium bibl diag graph *Science* v354 no6313 p751 N 11 2016

Bowles, F. P.

Long-term pattern and magnitude of soil carbon feedback to the climate system in a warming world chart graph *Science* v357 no6359 p101 O 6 2017

Bowles, Hamish

Bella Sicilia color *Vogue* v207 no9 p408 S 2017

CIRCUS MAXIMUS color *Vogue* v207 no9 p718 S 2017

Fashion HOUSE bw color *Vogue* v207 no4 p212 Ap 2017

GIVENCHY'S Giacomettis color *Vogue* v207 no3 p350 Mr 2017

The Merchants of Venice color *Vogue* v207 no11 p130 N 2017

My New Career color *Vogue* v207 no11 p142 N 2017

Not Your Mother's Dior bw color *Vogue* v206 no12 p256 D 2016

On with the SHOWS color *Vogue* v206 no11 p136 N 2016

SARAH BURTON color *Vogue* v207 no3 p430 Mr 2017

SPLASH of the TITANS bw color *Vogue* v207 no3 p372 Mr 2017

WILD at HEART color *Vogue* v207 no1 p88 Ja 2017

Bowles, Hamish—Exhibitions

Certain WOMEN A. Wintour color *Vogue* v207 no4 p84 Ap 2017

Bowles, Hannah Riley

Research: When Men Have Lower Status at Work, They're Less Likely to Negotiate *Harvard Business Review Digital Articles* p2 S 8 2017

Bowles, Jane Auer, 1917-1973

On the Edge of Something N. AZIMI bw *New York Times Book Review* p13 Ap 23 2017

Bowles, Tom Parker

HOT SPOT color *Conde Nast Traveler* v52 no9 p88 O 2017

Bowlin, John R.

Endure or Resist? M. Farneth cartoon *Commonweal* v144 no3 p32 F 10 2017

Is the 'Common Good' Obsolete? [Cover story] bw color *Commonweal* v143 no19 p12 D 2 2016

Bowling

BOWLED OVER R. O'CONNOR cartoon *Chicago* v66 no4 p34 Ap 2017

DRINKING GAMES D. Garner bw color *Esquire* v166 no4 p82 N 2016

Take a Small Knee J. LILEKS *National Review* v69 no19 p51 O 16 2017

THIS IS HOW YOU ROLL J. Nosek cartoon *Men's Health* v32 no3 p32 Ap 2017

Bowling, Michael

DeepStack: Expert-level artificial intelligence in heads-up no-limit poker [Cover story] chart diag *Science* v356 no6337 p508 My 5 2017

Bowling alleys—Evaluation

THE COMET PUB & LANES C. VAN DUSEN *Atlanta* v56 no7 p60 N 2016

Bowling games

See also

Bowling

THIS IS HOW YOU ROLL J. Nosek cartoon *Men's Health* v32 no3 p32 Ap 2017

Bowls (Tableware)

1939 PET GEAR L. HEDRICK color *Better Homes & Gardens* v95 no8 p184 Ag 2017

Adam's Home STYLE SHEET Adam color *O, The Oprah Magazine* p52 Jl 2017

GREAT HEIGHTS L. HEDRICK *Better Homes & Gardens* v94 no12 p141 D 2016

HOMESPUN RUSTIC color *House Beautiful* v159 no8 p120 O 2017

MODERN BRIDE color *Harper's Bazaar* no3654 p88 Je/Jl 2017

Bowls (Tableware)—Evaluation

Clay Time M. L. BIKOFF *Atlanta* v56 no12 p48 Ap 2017

Dune K. RENDA color *House Beautiful* v159 no4 p25 My 2017

A LADIES' BRUNCH H. BROWN color *House Beautiful* v159 no2 p58 Mr 2017

OBSESSED WITH CATS E. S. SOTO color *Better Homes & Gardens* v95 no2 p10 F 2016

Bowman, Akemi Dawn

Starfish *Publishers Weekly* v264 no29 p221 Jl 17 2017

BOWMAN, ALISA

THE TROUBLE WITH TIME-OUTS color *Parents* v92 no4 p60 Ap 2017

Bowman, Conor

Horace Winter Says Goodbye color *Publishers Weekly* v264 no16 p39 Ap 17 2017

BOWMAN, JAMES

Fantasia on a Theme color *Weekly Standard* v23 no2 p45 S 18 2017

BOWMAN, JEFF S.

Microbial Community Dynamics in Two Polar Extremes: The Lakes of the McMurdo Dry Valleys and the West Antarctic Peninsula Marine Ecosystem chart color graph *BioScience* v66

no10 p829 O 1 2016

BOWMAN, JOHN

Chords & Discords bw *Downbeat* v84 no1 p10 Ja 2017

Bowman, Karen

HUSTLE BUSTLE M. SEYMOUR color *New York Times Book Review* p40 D 4 2016

Bowman, Maria

Conservation Compliance in the Crop Insurance Era *Amber Waves: The Economics of Food, Farming, Natural Resources, & Rural America* p29 Jl 2017

An Economic Perspective on Soil Health *Amber Waves: The Economics of Food, Farming, Natural Resources, & Rural America* p18 S 2016

Voluntary Labeling of Chicken "Raised Without Antibiotics" Has Posed Challenges for Firms and Consumers *Amber Waves: The Economics of Food, Farming, Natural Resources, & Rural America* p35 S 2016

BOWMAN, MICHAEL

International Wildlife Law: Understanding and Enhancing Its Role in Conservation *BioScience* v67 no9 p784 S 2017

Bowman, Nina

4 Ways to Improve Your Strategic Thinking Skills *Harvard Business Review Digital Articles* p2 D 27 2016

Bowman, Zach

THE NORTH RIM color *Cycle World* v56 no10 p24 N 2017

THE UNNECESSARY EXPRESS [Cover story] color *Cycle World* v56 no5 p32 Je 2017

Bowser, Gillian

American Wolf color *Science* v357 no6355 p966 S 8 2017

Bowser, Muriel, 1972-

MOST POWERFUL WOMEN: More than 100 of the area's most influential women in government, business, law, education, media, nonprofits, and the arts L. MILK *Washingtonian Magazine* v53 no1 p50 O 2017

Trump-Watching from City Hall: His policy choices will challenge places from Manhattan to Mobile, Ala P. A. Harkness *Governing* v30 no8 p16 My 2017

BOWSHER, MIKE

#Climbing Training color *Climbing* no352 p9 Ap 2017

Box, C. J.

Paradise Valley *Publishers Weekly* v264 no20 p36 My 15 2017

BOX, KATE SANDOVAL

BRING THE SPA HOME cartoon *Better Homes & Gardens* v95 no2 p18 F 2016

cool aids color *Parents* v92 no8 p88 Ag 2017

navigate the beauty aisle [Cover story] color *Parents* v92 no7 p72 Jl 2017

play with your ponytail color *Parents* v92 no8 p90 Ag 2017

the secret to GLOWY SKIN color *Better Homes & Gardens* v95 no3 p16 Mr 2017

Box, Mathew S.

Phytochromes function as thermosensors in Arabidopsis bibl graph *Science* v354 no6314 p886 N 18 2016

Box office revenue (Motion pictures)

Harry Potter: By the Numbers D. Coggan color *Entertainment Weekly* no1435 p10 O 14 2016

Hollywood East H. Beech color *Time* v189 no4 p40 F 6 2017

Hollywood's Search for a Blockbuster Algorithm T. J. Huddleston color *Fortune* v175 no6 p12 My 1 2017

HOLLYWOOD WRAPS ONE OF ITS WORST SUMMERS EVER T. J. Huddleston color *Fortune* v176 no4 p27 S 15 2017

Is Winter the New Summer? D. Coggan color *Entertainment Weekly* no1462 p18 Ap 21 2017

SUMMER'S WINNERS AND LOSERS J. Nolfi color *Entertainment Weekly* no1477 p18 Ag 11 2017

TO INFINITY WAR AND BEYOND! C. Collis color *Entertainment Weekly* no1466 p12 My 19 2017

Box office revenue (Theatrical productions)

Box Office Supplies *Stage Directions* v30 no7 p19 Jl 1 2017

BOXBERGER, TEDDY

HOW TO MAKE ANYTHING [Cover story] color diag *Popular Mechanics* p56 S 2017

BOXER, SARAH

Growing Up Arab cartoon color *New York Review of Books* v63 no16 p8 O 27 2016

Move Over, Michelangelo color *Atlantic* v318 no5 p44 D 2016

Yayoi Kusama's Existential Circus color *Atlantic* v320 no1 p94 Jl/Ag 2017

Boxer shorts—Evaluation

72 SOUTHERN-MADE GIFTS UNDER $100 SL color *Southern Living* v51 no12 p91 D 2016

Boxers (Sports)

THE BALLAD OF ED "BAD BOY" BROWN B. SMITH bw color *Chicago* v66 no4 p106 Ap 2017

Boxing vs. Boxe Francaise: A History Lesson M. Hatmaker cartoon *Black Belt* v55 no5 p20 Ag/S 2017

Boxers (Sports)—Attitudes

MUHAMMAD ALI L. Gast and J. Labrecque color *Entertainment Weekly* no1446/1447 p90 D 2016/Ja 2017

Boxers (Sports)—United States

JAKE LAMOTTA (1922-2017) J. Fuchs and S. Kwak color *Sports Illustrated* v127 no10 p22 O 2 2017

MUHAMMAD ALI G. HOWARD *New York Times Magazine* p54 D 25 2016

Boxes

See also
  Jewelry boxes
  Mailboxes
  Toolboxes
  Trunks (Luggage)

BOX SET F. VIGNA color *Martha Stewart Living* p120 Mr 2017

Kitchen Cabinets for Period Houses M. E. POLSON bw cartoon color diag *Old House Journal* v45 no2 p40 Ap 2017

Let It Go B. O'Dair *Prevention* v69 no4 p3 Ap 2017

Boxes—Evaluation

BEST OF THE WEST C. Dash color *Sunset* v237 no6 p11 D 2016

Boxing

BOXING SHADOWS A. HUTCHINS bw *Maclean's* v130 no9 p72 O 2017

The Good Fight color *O, The Oprah Magazine* p90 Jl 2017

Boxing equipment—Evaluation

ESSENTIAL GEAR color *Black Belt* v55 no5 p72 Ag/S 2017

Boxing gloves—Evaluation

ESSENTIAL GEAR color *Black Belt* v55 no5 p72 Ag/S 2017

Boxing matches—History

Fighting Words T. Keith color *Sports Illustrated* v127 no6 p22 Ag 28 2017

Boxing techniques

Battling Nelson and the Scissor Punch M. Hatmaker bw *Black Belt* v55 no3 p18 Ap/My 2017

Boxing—Competitions

The Case for ... Boxing's Big Summer G. Bishop and T. Keith color *Sports Illustrated* v126 no17 p30 Je 19 2017

Boxing matches—Charts, diagrams, etc.

PICK A FIGHT T. Keith chart color *Sports Illustrated* v127 no8 p18 S 18 2017

Box office revenue (Motion pictures)—Charts, diagrams, etc.

THREE STRIKES OUT D. Coggan color diag *Entertainment Weekly* no1439 p13 N 11 2016

Boxster automobile

2017 PORSCHE 718 BOXSTER S E. Tingwall color graph *Car & Driver* v63 no2 p78 Ag 2017

Boxster automobile—Evaluation

BEST PORSCHE of the Year B. WASEF bw color *Esquire* v166 no4 p75 N 2016

Boxwood

The Shapely Boxwood K. Owen color *Southern Living* v52 no9 p24 S 2017

Boy & the World (Film)

BOY & THE WORLD T. J. Norton color *Sound & Vision* v81 no10 p69 D 2016

Boy Band (TV program)

Boy Band I. Ratledge *TV Guide* v65 no25 p38 Je 2017

Emma Bunton N. Feeney color *Entertainment Weekly* no1472 p50 Je 30 2017

THE RACE TO FIND THE NEXT ONE DIRECTION N. Feeney color *Entertainment Weekly* no1478 / 1479 p22 Ag 18-25 2017

Boy Scouts of America

A New Scouting Experience S. A. CATOVIC *Islamic Horizons* v45 no6 p38 N/D 2016

outer edge g. averill bw color *Bike Magazine* v23 no9 p32 D 2016

Scouts' Honor M. Hemingway color *Weekly Standard* v22 no36

p8 My 29 2017

Boyagoda, Randy

Worth the Wait color *Commonweal* v114 no14 p35 S 8 2017

Boyajian, Tabetha

FAST AND CURIOUS D. Clery color map *Science* v356 no6337 p476 My 5 2017

The Most Mysterious Star in the Galaxy *Sky & Telescope* v133 no6 p16 Je 2017

Party of One C. S. POWELL color graph *Discover* v27 no10 p60 D 2016

Boyar, Jeff

WINDOW WASHING BUCKHEAD 6 MILES NORTH OF DOWNTOWN J. GREEN *Atlanta* v56 no7 p236 N 2016

Boyatzis, Richard E.

Emotional Intelligence Has 12 Elements. Which Do You Need to Work On? color graph *Harvard Business Review Digital Articles* p2 F 6 2017

How to Handle Rebellion on Your Team *Harvard Business Review Digital Articles* p2 Jl 9 2015

BOYCE, LEE

Aerobic vs. Anaerobic Exercise color *Muscle & Performance* v9 no11 p22 N 2017

All About the Deadlift color *Muscle & Performance* v9 no8 p22 Ag 2017

BE ECCENTRIC color *Muscle & Performance* v8 no12 p20 D 2016

BULK SEASON chart color *Muscle & Performance* v8 no12 p38 D 2016

Core Moves You've Never Tried color *Muscle & Performance* v9 no7 p41 Jl 2017

HEIGHT TRAINING HACKS color *Muscle & Performance* v9 no1 p24 Ja 2017

Put Your Best Foot Forward color *Muscle & Performance* v9 no8 p18 Ag 2017

THE ULTIMATE SPLIT-STANCE TRAINING GUIDE color *Muscle & Performance* v9 no6 p44 Je 2017

Unassailable Ankles color *Muscle & Performance* v9 no8 p53 Ag 2017

WARM UP LIKE A PRO color *Muscle & Performance* v8 no12 p26 D 2016

Boyce, Sandy

People H. Meyer *Christian Century* v134 no17 p19 Ag 16 2017

Boycott Divestment & Sanctions (Movement)

BDS Beat Down D. DANON *USA Today Magazine* v145 no2860 p53 Ja 2017

Boycotts

About a Boycott *Commentary* v143 no3 p4 Mr 2017

The Culture Business: Mark Harris img *New York* p14 Ja 23 2017

India's War Over Water—and Soft Drinks P. R. Sanjai and A. Chaudhary map *Bloomberg Businessweek* no4515 p15 Mr 20 2017

LET THEM EAT MEAT R. Serkin *History Today* v67 no8 p50 Ag 2017

PARODY color *Weekly Standard* v22 no31 p44 Ap 17 2017

Recouping their losses N. MACDONALD *Maclean's* v130 no4 p15 My 2017

SHOP TILL THEY DROP J. Surowiecki cartoon *New Yorker* v92 no44 p23 Ja 9 2017

Boyd, Andy

THE TRAGEDY OF FORCE Z: The sinking by Japanese aircraft of HMS Prince of Wales and HMS Repulse in December 1941 and the subsequent loss of Singapore was a grievous blow to British morale. But have historians misunderstood what really happened? *History Today* v67 no9 p64 S 2017

Boyd, Carolyn

The White Shaman Mural *Texas Monthly* v45 no2 p34 F 2017

BOYD, CARRIE

crank up the heat *Better Homes & Gardens* v94 no11 p102 N 2016

for the love of CHOCOLATE color *Better Homes & Gardens* v95 no4 p94 Ap 2017

IT'S SHOW TIME color *Better Homes & Gardens* v95 no8 p70 Ag 2017

Lighten up color *Better Homes & Gardens* v95 no6 p134 Je 2017

POP ART color *Better Homes & Gardens* v95 no7 p108 Jl 2017

BOYD, D. ERIC

THE POWER PARTNERSHIP: CMO & CIO *Harvard Business*

Review v95 no4 p55 Jl/Ag 2017

Boyd, David R.

The Rights of Nature: A Legal Revolution That Could Save the World color *Publishers Weekly* v264 no31 p78 Jl 31 2017

BOYD, ELENA

r.s.v.p bw *Bon Appetit* v62 no4 p10 Ap 2017

Boyd, Herb

In Praise of a City: Herb Boyd's 'Black Detroit' celebrates the freedom fighters on history's margins T. J. SUGRUE *New York Times Book Review* p10 S 10 2017

Boyd, Ian L.

Toward pesticidovigilance chart color *Science* v357 no6357 p1232 S 22 2017

BOYD, JOHN W. JR.

BUILDING A SMALL-SCALE FARMING REVOLUTION *Nation* v305 no11 p17 O 30 2017

Boyd, Liza Towell

6 EXERCISES TO NAIL YOUR HUNTER DERBY: Part 2: Master rollbacks, the hand gallop and finish with flair [Cover story] color *Practical Horseman* v45 no7 p34 Jl 2017

Boyd, Michael

Rapid development of a DNA vaccine for Zika virus bibl graph *Science* v354 no6309 p237 O 14 2016

Boyd, R. W.

Breaking Lorentz reciprocity to overcome the time-bandwidth limit in physics and engineering bw diag graph *Science* v356 no6344 p1260 Je 23 2017

BOYD, WILLIAM

Pity the Prince: Sally Bedell Smith's biography offers a sympathetic view of the English heir *New York Times Book Review* p18 My 14 2017

Boyden, Joseph

'I believe that Chanie Wenjak chose me' bw color *Maclean's* v129 no44 p16 N 7 2016

WENJACK J. BEMROSE color *Maclean's* v129 no43 p60 O 31 2016

Who gets to be Indigenous? bw color *Maclean's* v130 no8 p36 S 2017

Boydstun, Amber E.

The Trump Conundrum color graph *Columbia Journalism Review* v56 no2 p42 Fall 2017

Boyé, Brian

ACTIVE STYLE AWARDS bw color *Men's Health* v32 no7 p(Sp)17 S 2017

THE EXCHANGE bw cartoon color graph *Men's Health* v32 no5 p16 Je 2017

Find Your Strong Suit cartoon color *Men's Health* v32 no4 p57 My 2017

LOOK BETTER INSTANTLY cartoon color *Men's Health* v32 no2 p(Sp)12 Mr 2017

Look Your Best color *Men's Health* v32 no5 p99 Je 2017

MOTOR CITY MADE bw color *Men's Health* v32 no2 p(Sp)20 Mr 2017

My Clothes Don't Fit My New Job color *Men's Health* v31 no10 p76 D 2016

SPIC AND SPAN color *Men's Health* v32 no5 p108 Je 2017

SPORTY SOLES color *Men's Health* v32 no7 p(Sp)8 S 2017

Time Honored color *Men's Health* v32 no5 p64 Je 2017

Boyega, John, 1992-

American Horror Story P. Travers color *Rolling Stone* no1294 p56 Ag 24 2017

Next Generation Leaders E. Dockterman, N. Kumar et al color *Time* v190 no16/17 p74 O 23 2017

Boyen, Hans-Gerd

Perovskite-perovskite tandem photovoltaics with optimized band gaps bibl chart graph *Science* v354 no6314 p861 N 18 2016

BOYER, CRISPIN

5 SMART Toys *National Geographic Kids* no466 p18 D 2016/Ja 2017

ACCIDENTS Happen color *National Geographic Kids* no465 p20 N 2016

PRANKSTERS IN CHIEF *National Geographic Kids* no467 p26 F 2017

The Secret Language Of Dolphins color *National Geographic Kids* no471 p14 Je/Jl 2017

What Would Happen? cartoon color *National Geographic Kids*

no473 p6 S 2017

What Would Happen? cartoon *National Geographic Kids* no470 p7 My 2017

What Would Happen? *National Geographic Kids* no467 p8 F 2017

What Would Happen? *National Geographic Kids* no468 p7 Mr 2017

Boyer, Martine

SIMMER ALL DAY, PARTY ALL NIGHT color *Southern Living* v52 no2 p110 F 2017

Boyer, Peter

OLD MONEY C. R. JOYNT *Washingtonian Magazine* v52 no4 p26 Ja 2017

BOYER, PETER J.

Now More Than Ever [Cover story] color *Weekly Standard* v23 no5 p21 O 9 2017

White House Divided color *Weekly Standard* v22 no47 p9 Ag 21 2017

A White House on a War Footing color *Weekly Standard* v22 no38 p9 Je 12 2017

Boyer, Stéphane

Nature's treasure hunt *Science* v356 no6336 p387 Ap 28 2017

Boyer-Kelly, Michelle Nicole

Survivance, Sovereignty, and Story: Teaching American Indian Rhetorics *American Indian Quarterly* v41 no2 p190 Spr 2017

Boyett, Steven R.

Fata Morgana *Publishers Weekly* v264 no11 p62 Mr 13 2017

Boykin, Le'alani S.

Grassroots Park Stewardship: A Force of Change *Parks & Recreation* v51 no10 p36 O 2016

BOYKO, C. P.

In the Palace of Cats color *Walrus* v14 no6 p54 Jl/Ag 2017

Boylan, Catherine

THE MAN IN CARRIAGE NO.2013: Leo Steveni was a British officer based in St Petersburg at the time of the Russian Revolution. He became an active eyewitness to the chaos of the Civil War that followed *History Today* v67 no10 p68 O 2017

BOYLAN, JENNIFER FINNEY

The Best Draft of the Self *New York Times Book Review* p19 Je 18 2017

Boylan, Jennifer Finney, 1958-

Transitioning in Life And Literature L. MATHEWS color *Publishers Weekly* v264 no13 p37 Mr 27 2017

Boyle, Danny, 1956-

Middle Age in Revolt P. Travers color *Rolling Stone* no1284 p54 Ap 6 2017

T2 Trainspotting C. Nashawaty color *Entertainment Weekly* no1457/1458 p72 Mr 17 2017

Boyle, Deirdre

EXILE, WITHIN AND WITHOUT: NEWWORK IN TWO MODES FROM RITHY PANH *Film Quarterly* v71 no1 p10 Fall 2017

Boyle, Edward

Nitrogen pollution knows no bounds color *Science* v356 no6339 p700 My 19 2017

Boyle, Evan A.

Detection of human adaptation during the past 2000 years bibl graph *Science* v354 no6313 p760 N 11 2016

Boyle, Greg

I thought I could 'save' gang members. I was wrong bw *America* v216 no11 p41 My 15 2017

Knead to heal G. Boyle S.J. bw *U.S. Catholic* v82 no6 p18 Je 2017

Boyle, Helen

The Death of a Hero E. J. Dionne Jr. color *Commonweal* v144 no5 p8 Mr 10 2017

Boyle, Kevin J.

Contingent valuation: Flawed logic? color *Science* v357 no6349 p363 Jl 28 2017

Deciphering dueling analyses of clean water regulations color *Science* v357 no6359 p49 O 6 2017

Putting a value on injuries to natural assets: The BP oil spill chart *Science* v356 no6335 p253 Ap 21 2017

Boyle, Leo V.

Are We Any Safer? color *Atlantic* v318 no4 p14 N 2016

Boyle, Mariah

Committing to socially responsible seafood color *Science* v356 no6341 p912 Je 1 2017

Boyle, Matt

BREITBART'S (OTHER) MAN IN THE WHITE HOUSE L. MULLINS *Washingtonian Magazine* v52 no9 p70 Je 2017

Boyle, Matthew

AMAZON WON'T KNOW WHAT HIT 'EM! [Cover story] color graph *Bloomberg Businessweek* no4521 p42 My 8 2017

Target Slips Up color graph *Bloomberg Businessweek* no4528 p13 Je 26 2017

To Grandmother's House We Go color *Bloomberg Businessweek* no4541 p15 O 9 2017

Wal-Mart Cracks the Whip on Suppliers *Bloomberg Businessweek* no4531 p14 Jl 24 2017

Who's Who in Trump Town E. PLOTT *Washingtonian Magazine* v52 no4 p100 Ja 2017

BOYLE, MICHAEL J.

The Tragedy of Obama's Foreign Policy *Current History* v116 no786 p10 Ja 2017

Boyle, Robert H., 1928-2017

Robert H. Boyle (1928-2017) J. Fuchs and T. Keith color *Sports Illustrated* v126 no16 p32 Je 5 2017

BOYLE, SARAH A.

Getting Back to the Basics: Museum Collections and Satellite Imagery Are Critical to Analyzing Species Diversity *BioScience* v67 no5 p405 My 2017

Boyle, Susie

Around the Campfire color *Trail Rider* v29 no1 p6 Ja/F 2017

Boyle, T. Coraghessan, 1948-

ARE WE NOT MEN? T. C. Boyle cartoon *New Yorker* v92 no36 p56 N 7 2016

Sex Under the Dome J. MILES *New York Times Book Review* p11 N 13 2016

Boylen, Danny

LOCKED AND LOADED J. Sidman *Washingtonian Magazine* v52 no4 p180 Ja 2017

Boyles, Denis

A TO Z R. Brookhiser *Claremont Review of Books* v17 no1 p87 Wint 2016/2017

Boyls, Marshall

To the Editor *Commentary* v142 no2 p1 S 2016

Boynton, Andy

When a Prototype Isn't Enough, Use Theatrical Tricks to Sell Your Idea *Harvard Business Review Digital Articles* p2 Je 16 2017

Boynton, Lucy, 1994-

LUCY BOYNTON K. SMITH color *Vanity Fair* v59 no11 p59 N 2017

Boys

SUGAR RAUTBORD B. Zehme cartoon *Chicago* v66 no4 p132 Ap 2017

Boys, Alaina

Discussion *Smithsonian* v48 no1 p10 Ap 2017

Boyz N the Hood (Film)

BOYZ N THE HOOD S. Li color *Entertainment Weekly* no1460/1461 p76 Ap 7-17 2017

DETACHING MONEY FROM MANHOOD L. BLADES and S. T. BROWN color *Ebony* v72 no5 p69 Mr 2017

Bozadzhieva, Martina

Why Multinationals Are Doubling Down on Russia *Harvard Business Review Digital Articles* p2 Ap 4 2016

Bozell, Brent

Speeches and Herb S. F. HAYES color *Weekly Standard* v22 no7 p5 O 24 2016

Bozella, Dewey, 1959-

Fighter's Heart K. B. ZOOK *New York Times Book Review* p24 D 11 2016

Bozikovic, Alex

KPMB Architects *Architectural Record* v205 no4 p108 Ap 2017

Bozo, Frédéric

A History of the Iraq Crisis: France, the United States, and Iraq, 1991–2003 A. Moravcsik *Foreign Affairs* v96 no3 p162 My/Je 2017

Bozorgmehr, Cyrus

HOW THE WU-TANG CLAN MET PHARMA BRO L. Entis color *Fortune* v176 no3 p18 S 1 2017

Bozzato, Fabio

Positive biodiversity-productivity relationship predominant in global forests bibl chart graph map *Science* v354 no6309

paaf8957-1 O 14 2016

BP Deepwater Horizon Explosion & Oil Spill, 2010

Contingent valuation: Flawed logic? J. Baron, R. C. Bishop et al color *Science* v357 no6349 p363 Jl 28 2017

BPI Sports (Company)

ABCs of BCAAs color *Muscle & Performance* v9 no8 p34 Ag 2017

Intense Supps color *Muscle & Performance* v9 no10 p62 O 2017

The Keto Kraze color *Muscle & Performance* v9 no7 p32 Jl 2017

Brabec, Ricky

2017 SONORA RALLY J. RETTIE color *Dirt Sports + Off-Road* v51 no8 p18 Ag 2017

Brace, Charles Loring, 1826-1890

Reading Charles Darwin Utterly Changed How Charles Loring Brace Thought about Social Reform R. Fuller *Humanities* v38 no1 p1 Wint 2017

Bracelets

Fully STACKED R. WALDMAN color *Vogue* v206 no11 p120 N 2016

THE GOLD STANDARD color *Harper's Bazaar* no3656 p458 S 2017

Heiress and GRACES E. ELWICK-BATES color *Vogue* v206 no11 p114 N 2016

Hermès bracelet cartoon *Vogue* v206 no11 p264 N 2016

LINKED IN color *Conde Nast Traveler* v52 no8 p26 S 2017

PRECIOUS MOMENTS color *Harper's Bazaar* no3656 p270 S 2017

WHERE TO BUY color *Harper's Bazaar* no3655 p166 Ag 2017

Bracelets—Design & construction

COPPER BRACELETS N. MOREAU color *Popular Mechanics* p97 Mr 2017

Bracelets—Evaluation

BLANK SLATE color *Harper's Bazaar* no3652 p142 Ap 2017

#BUYBLACK T. A. Christian, C. Market et al color *Essence* v47 no8 p19 D 2016

Check LIST color *Harper's Bazaar* no3648 p114 N 2016

FABULOUS at Every Age color *Harper's Bazaar* no3655 p85 Ag 2017

Gifts for riders color *Equus* no470 p28 N 2016

GREEN PARTY color *Harper's Bazaar* no3657 p177 O 2017

heartfelt L. Tudor color *New Orleans Magazine* v51 no4 p72 F 2017

HOLIDAY GIFT GUIDE A. Wisch color *Sail* v47 no12 p22 D 2016

INTO THE WILD color *Harper's Bazaar* no3652 p121 Ap 2017

IT'S ALL IN THE WRIST color *Conde Nast Traveler* v52 no3 p26 Mr 2017

LEATHER HEADS *Cincinnati Magazine* v50 no7 p30 Ap 2017

MATCH POINT color *O, The Oprah Magazine* p41 Ja 2017

Modern Love A. Tarttelin bw color *Glamour* v115 no7 p94 Jl 2017

MODERN ROMANCE J. MOAZAMI color *Chicago* v66 no2 p34 F 2017

Mother's Day gift guide L. BERGAMOTTO color *Good Housekeeping* v264 no5 p681 My 2017

PEARL JAM color *Harper's Bazaar* no3655 p75 Ag 2017

The Sign S. Miller color *InStyle* v23 no12 p31 N 2016

SILVER STREAK color *Harper's Bazaar* no3655 p74 Ag 2017

SPRING REVIVAL bw *Harper's Bazaar* no3650 p147 F 2017

STYLE YOUR GUY A. Dorsey color *Essence* v48 no2 p28 Je 2017

TAKE THE PLUNGE color *Harper's Bazaar* no3649 p213 D 2016/Ja 2017

Wait LIST color *Harper's Bazaar* no3652 p94 Ap 2017

WARM FRONT color *Harper's Bazaar* no3648 p155 N 2016

THE WELL-SPENT $ DOLLAR color *Harper's Bazaar* no3654 p76 Je/Jl 2017

Wish LIST N. Fritton color *Harper's Bazaar* no3648 p110 N 2016

Brach, Brad

5 FIREMEN IN THE HOLE S. Apstein color *Sports Illustrated* v126 no9 p47 Mr 27 2017

Brachial plexus surgery

A Spare Hand D. Robitzski color *Scientific American* v316 no5 p17 My 2017

Brachtel, Elena

Origins of lymphatic and distant metastases in human colorectal cancer diag graph *Science* v357 no6346 p55 Jl 7 2017

Brack, J.

Observation of a large-scale anisotropy in the arrival directions of cosmic rays above 8×1018 eV *Science* v357 no6357 p1266 S 22 2017

Brack, Reginald K., 1937-2016

Milestones *Time* v188 no16/17 p9 O 24 2016

BRACKEN, AMBER

Alex Janvier color *Canadian Geographic* v137 no4 p19 Jl/Ag 2017

Bracken, Conor

DAMAGED VILLANELLE *New Yorker* v93 no10 p62 Ap 24 2017

Brackets

ASK OLD HOUSE JOURNAL M. E. Polson color *Old House Journal* v45 no3 p60 My 2017

GEARBOX color *Dirt Sports + Off-Road* v51 no12 p70 D 2017

ONE-HOUR WONDERS M. EMERY color *Dirt Sports + Off-Road* v51 no3 p44 Mr 2017

ROOMS FOR IMPROVEMENT S. MORROW *Martha Stewart Living* no267 p100 S 2016

Shelf Brackets Rehab B. D. Coleman color *Old House Journal* v45 no2 p56 Ap 2017

Brackett, Marc

Teaching Teenagers to Develop Their Emotional Intelligence *Harvard Business Review Digital Articles* p2 My 19 2015

Brackett, Marc—Interviews

On the science and teaching of emotional intelligence R. Heller color *Phi Delta Kappan* v98 no6 p20 Mr 2017

Brackley, Chris

CITY WIDE B. BANKS map *Canadian Geographic* v137 no3 p62 My 2017

Brackley, Dean

Beyond the bubble J. Bazan color *U.S. Catholic* v82 no5 p45 My 2017

Brad Cunningham Band (Performer)

MISSOURI TO TEXAS BY WAY OF OKLAHOMA M. W. SCHWARTZ *Missouri Life* v43 no6 p22 O/N 2016

BRADBURN, DOUGLAS

Curious George color *Weekly Standard* v22 no41 p24 Jl 3 2017

BRADBURY, ALEXANDRA

IN THE AGE OF TRUMP, CAN LABOR UNITE? [Cover story] *In These Times* v41 no5 p18 My 2017

BRADBURY, DOMINIC

peak performance color *Architectural Digest* no11 p114 N 1 2017

Bradbury, Ray, 1920-2012

THE BEGGAR ON DUBLIN BRIDGE R. Bradbury *Saturday Evening Post* v288 no6 p68 N/D 2016

BRADFIELD, SCOTT

Hard Places *New York Times Book Review* p18 Ja 29 2017

Bradford, Mark—Exhibitions

National Treasure S. COCHRAN color *Architectural Digest* no5 p62 My 2017

Bradford, Mark—Interviews

Mark BRADFORD: THE AMERICAN ARTIST HEADS TO VENICE WITH THE HOPE OF TURNING ACTIVISM INTO AN ART FORM B. Jenkins *Interview* v47 no5 p106 Je/Jl 2017

Bradford, Peter A.

Wasting time: Subsidies, operating reactors, and melting ice *Bulletin of the Atomic Scientists* v73 no1 p13 Ja 2017

Bradley, Alice

Can You Zap Away the Blues? color *Health* v31 no5 p69 Je 2017

Bradley, Allan

Priming HIV-1 broadly neutralizing antibody precursors in human Ig loci transgenic mice bibl graph *Science* v353 no6307 p1557 S 30 2016

BRADLEY, ANTHONY B.

You Are the Manure of the Earth bw color *Christianity Today* v60 no8 p72 O 2016

BRADLEY, BILL

THE POWDER AND THE GLORY color *Vanity Fair* v58 no11 p184 N 2016

Bradley, Bob—Interviews

American Abroad G. Wahl color *Sports Illustrated* v125 no17 p96 N 21 2016 Double Issue

Bradley, Charles

'Changes' C. AARON *New York Times Magazine* p61 Mr 12 2017

Bradley, Charles, 1948-2017

Milestones color *Time* v190 no14 p12 O 9 2017

Bradley, Gerard V.

ONE NATION, UNDER GOD? *Claremont Review of Books* v17 no1 p46 Wint 2016/2017

Bradley, Heather L.

Switch Off: The Clergy Guide to Preserving Energy and Passion for Ministry C. Lindner *Christian Century* v134 no6 p41 Mr 15 2017

Bradley, Jackie

Leading Off color *Sports Illustrated* v127 no3 p4 Jl 24 2017

Bradley, Jon

THE CONVERSATION color *Atlantic* v319 no1 p10 Ja/F 2017

Bradley, Keegan

Modern Love J. Passov and C. Barrett color *Golf Magazine* v58 no11 p36 N 2016

BRADLEY, KIMBERLY BRUBAKER

Profiles in Courage *New York Times Book Review* p32 N 13 2016

BRADLEY, LLOYD

Jazzie B *Interview* v47 no1 p74 F 2017

Bradley, Mark Philip

The World Reimagined: Americans and Human Rights in the Twentieth Century G. J. Ikenberry *Foreign Affairs* v96 no6 p151 N/D 2017

BRADLEY, RICHARD

The Front Page *New York Times Book Review* p8 N 13 2016

BRADLEY, ROBERT D.

Transformational Principles for NEON Sampling of Mammalian Parasites and Pathogens: A Response to Springer and Colleagues *BioScience* v66 no11 p917 N 1 2016

Bradley, Ryan

'BAROK MAIN' color *New York Times Magazine* p36 Mr 12 2017

CHEAP THRILLS: FOR THE PRODUCER JASON BLUM, 'GET OUT' IS JUST THE LATEST HORROR BLOCKBUSTER IN AN EIGHT-YEAR RUN OF LEAN, INVENTIVE AND SCARILY PROFITABLE HITS *New York Times Magazine* p44 My 14 2017

Infrastructure, the Trump Way color *Fortune* v75 no1 p13 Ja 1 2017

Not Breathing *New York Times Magazine* p16 Ja 1 2017

TALK TO ME: PEAK TV HAS BROUGHT A FLOOD OF GLOBAL ACTING TALENT TO HOLLYWOOD. IT'S THE JOB OF DIALECT COACHES LIKE SAMARA BAY TO HELP THEM ALL SOUND RIGHT *New York Times Magazine* p32 Jl 23 2017

Bradley, Sara

Celebrity, Politics and Francis Drake *History Today* v67 no3 p3 Mr 2017

BRADLEY, SEAN MICHAEL

SCARY THINGS color *Cabin Living* p80 O 2017

Bradley, Simon

Fifty English Steeples *History Today* v67 no2 p64 F 2017

Bradner, Liesl

BIRD MAN OF AMERICA color *American History* v52 no4 p68 O 2017

Interview Paul Golz A German View of D-Day bw *Military History* v34 no5 p14 Ja 2018

Brad's Status (Film)

ALSO PLAYING D. Heching color *Entertainment Weekly* no1478 / 1479 p44 Ag 18-25 2017

ENVY T. Friend cartoon *New Yorker* v93 no28 p20 S 18 2017

Measuring Up J. PODHORETZ color *Weekly Standard* v23 no4 p39 O 2 2017

Bradshaw, Chris

CHRIS BRADSHAW T. Monterosso color *Snowboarder* v29 no2 p39 O 2016

Bradshaw, John, 1950-

In Favor of Feline Felicity S. Mirsky color *Scientific American* v315 no3 p90 S 2016

Leashed To the Here and Now: DO DOGS KNOW THAT WE KNOW THAT THEY'RE THINKING OF US? *Psychology Today* v50 no5 p90 S/O 2017

Bradshaw, Justin

ENDURO ESCAPE color *Cycle World* v55 no10 p52 N 2016

Bradway, Robert A.

Business backs the basics color *Science* v354 no6309 p151 O 14 2016

Brady, A. F.
Inside the Asylum color *Publishers Weekly* v264 no30 p42 Jl 24 2017

BRADY, BURL
READERS' THOUGHTS ON PAST ISSUES color *Motor Trend* v69 no2 p26 F 2017

Brady, David
NEW WAYS OF SEEING: A painter and a critic discuss the visual past in a beguiling and provocative way, but do they engage the reader? *History Today* v67 no6 p96 Je 2016
No, Prime Minister *Hoover Digest: Research & Opinion on Public Policy* no1 p19 Wint 2017
Westminster, D.C.? No, the United States does not need a prime minister *Commentary* v142 no2 p51 S 2016

Brady, David—Interviews
A Foretaste of 2018: Hoover fellow David Brady, surveying the political landscape, sees "knife-edge electoral instability" L. Simmons *Hoover Digest: Research & Opinion on Public Policy* no3 p28 Summ 2017

Brady, Ethan
Pool Pals chart color *Sports Illustrated* v127 no3 p24 Jl 24 2017

Brady, James S., 1940-2014
The White House briefing room gets its 15 minutes J. Friedman color *Columbia Journalism Review* v56 no2 p84 Fall 2017

Brady, Justin
Don't Be a Hypocrite About Failure *Harvard Business Review Digital Articles* p2 Ag 4 2016

Brady, Kristyn
All the World's a Stage color *Dance Spirit* v21 no4 p40 Ap 2017
I Got Fired: Rebuild your career after you've been shown the door *Dance Magazine* v91 no7 p56 Jl 2017
Make 'Em Laugh *Dance Magazine* v90 no11 p34 N 2016
no average day *Dance Magazine* p18 2016/2017
no average day: The busy lives of dancers at Juilliard, Indiana University and Harvard *Dance Magazine* v90 p18 2016/2017 Supplement College Guide
One-on-Wonderful: What makes a good competition coach and how do you find one? *Dance Magazine* v91 no10 p42 O 2017
Resolutions Nutritionists Wish You'd Make *Dance Magazine* v91 no1 p116 Ja 2017
a taste of COLLEGE: College fairs can help you narrow down your options *Dance Magazine* v90 p6 2016/2017 Supplement College Guide
a taste of COLLEGE *Dance Magazine* p6 2016/2017
Tourist Traps: Tricks for eating healthy on tour *Dance Magazine* v91 no10 p38 O 2017

Brady, Meredith
The Mayo Clinic Model for Running a Value-Improvement Program *Harvard Business Review Digital Articles* p2 O 22 2015

Brady, Michael A.
BET ON FRIENDSHIP *Psychology Today* v50 no4 p10 Ag 2017
SCREEN GRAB *Psychology Today* v50 no3 p20 My/Je 2017
Two-dimensional sp2 carbon–conjugated covalent organic frameworks diag graph *Science* v357 no6352 p673 Ag 18 2017

BRADY, PAUL
Chicago Culture Fix color *Conde Nast Traveler* v52 no8 p18 S 2017
CHOOSE YOUR Cruise bw color *Conde Nast Traveler* v52 no1 p72 Ja 2017
Face Time color *Conde Nast Traveler* v52 no4 p102 Ap 2017
Going Back to Cali Wine Country color *Conde Nast Traveler* v52 no3 p50 Mr 2017
MADE IN MÉRIDA color *Conde Nast Traveler* v52 no5 p118 My 2017
ON A DREAM VACATION YOU WOULD bw color *Conde Nast Traveler* v52 no7 p48 Ag 2017
Second Coming color *Conde Nast Traveler* v52 no5 p56 My 2017
Take a River Cruise color *Conde Nast Traveler* v51 no11 p23 D 2016
TRAVEL SPECIALISTS 2016 color *Conde Nast Traveler* v51 no11 p78 D 2016
Water to Wine bw color diag *Conde Nast Traveler* v52 no7 p72 Ag 2017
WE'RE TURNING 30 bw chart color *Conde Nast Traveler* v52

no8 p55 S 2017

Brady, Sharon M.
How to Negotiate for Vacation Time *Harvard Business Review Digital Articles* p2 Je 19 2015

Brady, Tim
Out of the Shadow T. TROY *Weekly Standard* v22 no41 p35 Jl 3 2017

Brady, Tom, 1977-
ALL ABOUT CONNECTIONS [Cover story] T. Layden color *Sports Illustrated* v126 no3 p22 Ja 23 2017
For the Record color *Time* v189 no6 p8 F 20 2017
THE GREAT SUPER BOWL JERSEY CAPER R. Klemko and J. Vrentas color *Sports Illustrated* v126 no11 p98 Ap 17-24 2017
THE NEW ABNORMAL *Claremont Review of Books* v17 no2 p8 Spr 2017
PERSONALLY BRANDED T. Keith color *Sports Illustrated* v127 no9 p15 S 25 2017
THIS IS 40 G. Bishop color *Sports Illustrated* v127 no3 p76 Jl 24 2017
Tom Brady S. Gregory color *Time* v189 no6 p13 F 20 2017
Tom Brady's Payback Play S. Gregory color *Time* v189 no4 p55 F 6 2017

Brady, Tom, 1977—Awards
FIVE WILL GET YOU ZEN P. King color *Sports Illustrated* v126 no7 p74 Mr 6 2017
Happily Ever After ... color *Sports Illustrated* v126 no5 p112 F 13 2017

Brady, Wayne
THE ART OF THE DEAL D. HOLBROOK *TV Guide* v64 no46 p20 N 7 2016

Brady Bunch, The (TV program)
FLORENCE HENDERSON L. Rice color *Entertainment Weekly* no1443 p26 D 9 2016

Bradypus
THE NATURAL EXPLANATION K. MOORE color *Natural History* v125 no7 p4 Jl/Ag 2017

Braeden, Eric—Interviews
Eric Braeden's RESTLESS LIFE M. LOGAN *TV Guide* v65 no6 p26 Ja 30 2017

Braff, Meg
AN INVITING POOL PAVILION color *House Beautiful* v159 no4 p60 My 2017
THE TRANSFORMATIVE POWER OF BLUE & WHITE color *Redbook* p116 Mr 2017

Braff, Zach, 1975-
7. See The Films of Martin Brest D. EDELSTEIN *New York* v50 no7 p88 Ap 3 2017

Braga, Sônia, 1951-
Super Mom color *AARP: The Magazine* v59 no5A p9 Ag/S 2016

Braga Junqueira, André
Forest conservation: Humans' handprints bibl color *Science* v355 no6324 p466 F 3 2017

Braganza, Ramona
The Wherever Workout color *AARP: The Magazine* v59 no4A p62 Je/Jl 2016

Bragg, Amy
Pack & Play D. DeNunzio color *Golf Magazine* v59 no5 p60 My 2017

Bragg, Billy
Roots, Radicals and Rockers: How Skiffle Changed the World *Publishers Weekly* v264 no16 p57 Ap 17 2017

BRAGG, MEREDITH
THE SLANTS color *Reason* v48 no11 p36 Ap 2017

Bragg, Rick
Along for the Ride color *Southern Living* v52 no6 p146 Je 2017
The Best of Who We Are color *Southern Living* v52 no10 p136 O 2017
Can I Get an Amen? color *Southern Living* v51 no11 p172 N 2016
The Canned Stuff color *Southern Living* v52 no11 p140 N 2017
The Chariots of My People color *Southern Living* v52 no1 p132 Ja 2017
Fishing for the Moon color *Southern Living* v52 no3 p140 Mr 2017
Let's Eat Pig's Feet color *Southern Living* v52 no4 p150 Ap 2017
Mama Loves Me Anyway color *Southern Living* v52 no5 p154 My 2017

Old Men Behaving Badly color *Southern Living* v52 no2 p146 F 2017

The Roses of Fairhope color *Reader's Digest* v189 no1130 p22 My 2017

Seeing The Lights *Reader's Digest* v188 no1126 p108 D 2016/ Ja 2017

Socks, Underwear, and a Camaro color *Southern Living* v51 no12 p234 D 2016

SOUTHERN JOURNAL color *Southern Living* v52 no7 p130 Jl 2017

The Superfan color *Southern Living* v52 no9 p150 S 2017

When Your Best Fish Story Is About Catching ... A Goat color *Reader's Digest* v190 no1135 p17 N 2017

Bragg, Rick—Interviews

Rick Bragg L. Monk Carter color *New Orleans Magazine* v51 no6 p28 Ap 2017

Braham, Lewis

Bearing the Financial Burden of Alzheimer's *Bloomberg Businessweek* no4493 p54 O 3 2016

How to Prepare for Your Star's Exit *Bloomberg Businessweek* no4517 p46 Ap 3 2017

Planning for a Low-Tax, High-Deficit World *Bloomberg Businessweek* no4516 p42 Mr 27 2017

Sizing Up Trump's Tax Proposal color graph *Bloomberg Businessweek* no4520 p42 My 1 2017

Brahler-Smith, Annie

Bridle Party K. RENDA color *House Beautiful* v159 no5 p78 Je 2017

CORRECTION *House Beautiful* p94 Jl 2017

Brahm, Gabriel

Killing the Messenger: Mark Lilla's 'End of Identity Liberalism' and its Critics *Society* v54 no4 p326 Ag 2017

Brahmachari, Saurav

Pathological α-synuclein transmission initiated by binding lymphocyte-activation gene 3 bibl graph *Science* v353 no6307 paah3374-1 S 30 2016

Brahmaputra River

How China Could Weaponize Water T. John color *Time* v190 no13 p14 O 2 2017

Brahms: Lieder & Liebeslieder Waltzes (Music)

Brahms: Lieder and Liebeslieder Waltzes J. Rosenblum *Opera News* v81 no5 p58 N 2016

Braids (Hairdressing)

Braided Beauty bw *Ebony* v72 no4 p52 F 2017

double-duty dos K. Foster color *Seventeen* p194 Ja 1 2017

The Hair Braider J. Hughes *New York Times Magazine* p40 F 26 2017

HAIRSTORY M. Leuchter color *Popular Photography* v81 no1 p106 Ja/F 2017

How to Win at Holiday Hair M. Choi color *Glamour* v114 no12 p138 D 2016

Your Hair Lookbook J. Mulrow color *Glamour* v115 no9 p92 S 2017

Your Ponytail Lookbook J. Mulrow and Ying Chu color *Glamour* v115 no3 p106 Mr 2017

Brailsford, Dave, 1964-—Interviews

How 1% Performance Improvements Led to Olympic Gold E. Harrell *Harvard Business Review Digital Articles* p2 O 30 2015

Brain

See also
Cerebrospinal fluid
Mind & body

AARP Is Good for Your Brain Health E. J. Schneidewind *AARP: The Magazine* v59 no5A p75 Ag/S 2016

AGE PROOF YOUR BRAIN [Cover story] J. VanTine cartoon chart *Prevention* v69 no5 p60 My 2017

Aging? What's That? T. FERRISS bw cartoon color *Men's Health* v32 no5 p34 Je 2017

Brains, environments, and policy responses to addiction K. Humphreys, R. C. Malenka et al color *Science* v356 no6344 p1237 Je 23 2017

BUSY BODY C. THOMPSON cartoon *Wired* v25 no6 p30 Je 2017

Can't Get That Song Out of Your Head? color *Prevention* v69 no2 p12 F 2017

Crime Doesn't Pay color *Prevention* v69 no9 p12 O 2017

Disrupting Dopamine Dogma M. LOCKLEAR diag *Discover* v38 no1 p39 Ja/F 2017

editor's note. THE 100-YEAR PLAN K. Perina *Psychology Today* v50 no4 p3 Ag 2017

Emotions Are Cognitive, not Innate *USA Today Magazine* v146 no2867 p10 Ag 2017

Finding Your Mind B. DiDomenico color *Prevention* v69 no9 p3 O 2017

Good Night, Toast K. DiNardo cartoon *O, The Oprah Magazine* p103 My 2017

Headaches and spinal fluid leaks *Mayo Clinic Health Letter* v35 no9 p7 S 2017

Hearts and MINDS M. OZ color *O, The Oprah Magazine* p78 Je 2017

Hearts & Minds B. Gifford cartoon color *Men's Health* v32 no3 p112 Ap 2017

How ApoE4 endangers brains E. Underwood color *Science* v357 no6357 p1224 S 22 2017

How Dog Brains Work: DOGS USE THE SAME NEURAL PATHWAYS WE DO TO GET WHERE THEY CANT GO H. Estroff Marano *Psychology Today* v50 no5 p78 S/O 2017

How Signals: Get Skewed An imbalance of omega-3 and omega-6 fatty acids may be a stealth cause of depression and other disorders K. GOLDYNIA *Psychology Today* v50 no4 p29 Ag 2017

How to nurture a high-performing brain J. Brockis *People Management* p50 F 2017

I WAS CRAZY NOW I'M NOT cartoon color *Men's Health* v32 no3 p118 Ap 2017

Mind Games *Prevention* v69 no5 p3 My 2017

Our Brains Love New Stuff, and It's Killing the Planet Duhaime *Harvard Business Review Digital Articles* p2 Mr 17 2017

PRIME YOUR MIND D. DeNunzio color *Golf Magazine* v59 no8 p52 Ag 2017

Protein mobs selectively kill brain cells T. H. SAEY *Science News* v190 no12 p14 D 10 2016

Stay Sharp color *Prevention* v69 no8 p96 Ag 2017

TALES & TRIVIA: WHEREIN WE CONSIDER THE LOBSTER, A CREATURE AS FASCINATING AS IT IS DELICIOUS S. SHOCKERS color *Yankee* p96 Jl 2017

This Is You on Sugar A. Levi color *Health* v31 no3 p68 Ap 2017

Training BY Reward J. L. Jones bw color *Equus* no481 p46 O 2017

Two areas for familiar face recognition in the primate brain S. M. Landi and W. A. Freiwald color graph *Science* v357 no6351 p591 Ag 11 2017

The Ways Your Brain Manages Overload, and How to Improve Them S. Pillay color *Harvard Business Review Digital Articles* p2 Je 7 2017

WHEN HEALING IS A NO-BRAINER S. VEISSIEÈE *Psychology Today* v50 no4 p62 Ag 2017

Word Play [Cover story] color *Prevention* v69 no5 p96 My 2017

World of Medicine S. RIDEOUT *Reader's Digest* v188 no1125 p81 N 2016

Young human plasma renews old mice L. SANDERS color *Science News* v191 no9 p7 My 13 2017

YOUR BRAIN C. FLORA color *Redbook* p80 Mr 2017

your brain: time machine C. Maldarelli color *Popular Science* v289 no5 p6 S/O 2017

Brain aging

On the Brain's Path B. Lang *Discover* v38 no8 p6 O 2017

This Old Brain [Cover story] J. WHEELWRIGHT bw color *Discover* v38 no8 p26 O 2017

Brain-computer interfaces

Better Typing Through Mind Control J. Wise color *Bloomberg Businessweek* no4537 p74 S 11 2017

Help, hope, and hype: Ethical dimensions of neuroprosthetics J. Clausen, E. Fetz et al color *Science* v356 no6345 p1338 Je 30 2017

Brain concussion

4 Ways to Help Prevent Concussions R. Fierberg *Parents* p54 2015

Boost Your Burn color *Health* v31 no5 p6 Je 2017

THE CONCUSSION COUNT T. FOSTER *Texas Monthly* v45 no9 p60 S 2017

SHOCK WAVES J. HOUSMAN color *Surfer* v57 no12 p42 Ja/F 2017

(Music)

THE BRAIN BOX M. Mettler bw color *Sound & Vision* v82 no6 p72 Jl/Ag 2017

Brain—Concussion—Risk factors

THE TRUTH ABOUT WOMEN AND CONCUSSIONS H. Levine color *Health* v30 no9 p132 N 2016

Brain—Magnetic resonance imaging

What Happens to Your Brain When You Negotiate About Money K. Sehgal *Harvard Business Review Digital Articles* p2 O 26 2015

Brainstorm Golf Inc.

GET SMART M. Chwasky and R. Sauerhaft color *Golf Magazine* v59 no7 p85 Jl 2017

Brainstorming

10 UP & COMERS: AUBREY FLETCHER L. Prater *Successful Farming* v115 no8 p50 Je/Jl 2017

Leading a Brainstorming Session with a Cross-Cultural Team D. Livermore *Harvard Business Review Digital Articles* p2 My 27 2016

The Problem-Solving Process That Prevents Groupthink A. Markman *Harvard Business Review Digital Articles* p2 N 25 2015

Research: For Better Brainstorming, Tell an Embarrassing Story L. Thompson *Harvard Business Review Digital Articles* p2 O 2 2017

Why Brainstorming Works Better Online T. Chamorro-Premuzic *Harvard Business Review Digital Articles* p2 Ap 2 2015

Why Group Brainstorming Is a Waste of Time T. Chamorro-Premuzic *Harvard Business Review Digital Articles* p2 Mr 25 2015

Your Team Is Brainstorming All Wrong A. Markman *Harvard Business Review Digital Articles* p2 My 18 2017

Brain—Wounds & injuries

HEADSTRONG M. PRINCE *Road & Track* v68 no8 p98 My 2017

Worries, confusion after cancer trial deaths J. Couzin-Frankel color *Science* v354 no6317 p1211 D 9 2016

Brain—Wounds & injuries—Prevention

Target for Preventing Long-Term Effects *USA Today Magazine* v145 no2861 p13 F 2017

Brain—Wounds & injuries—Risk factors

Play Hard and Still Stay Safe C. Mehugh color *Health* v30 no9 p8 N 2016

Brain—Wounds & injuries—Treatment

Drug Couriers for Brain Injuries T. BURRELL color *Discover* v38 no1 p33 Ja/F 2017

Braitman, Stephen

FILIAL POETRY *Harper's Magazine* v334 no2002 p16 Mr 2017

Brake, Alan G.

A Kentucky Classic *Architectural Record* v205 no7 p86 Jl 2017

ROBERTO BURLE MARX color *Art in America* v104 no10 p149 N 2016

Brake design & construction

PIT STOP M. Davis color diag *Hot Rod* v70 no10 p96 O 2017

Brake fluids

SWAPPING OUT BRAKE FLUID: HERE ARE SEVERAL METHODS FOR BLEEDING AIR OUT OF A SYSTEM R. Bohacz *Successful Farming* v115 no7 p20 My 2017

Brakes

See also

Automobile brakes

Disc brakes

Motor vehicles—Brakes

"I WANT TO DRINK MY COFFEE WHILE I RIDE TO WORK." E. Furia and B. STRICKLAND color *Bicycling* v58 no3 p40 Ap 2017

SLOW LEARNERS K. KINARD cartoon *Road & Track* v68 no7 p96 Mr/Ap 2017

WHY WHEELS MATTER R. Koch and B. STRICKLAND color *Bicycling* v58 no3 p57 Ap 2017

Brakes—Evaluation

PARTS & STUFF color *Hot Rod* v70 no11 p124 N 2017

STEADY PULL: SHIMANO'S SLX BRAKES ARE SO GOOD, IT'S ALMOST BORING J. Weber color *Bike Magazine* v24 no7 p120 S 2017

Brakhage, Stan

Metaphors on Vision M. J. Rowin bw *Film Comment* v53 no5 p78 S/O 2017

Brako, Lois

What do revised U.S. rules mean for human research? color *Science* v357 no6352 p650 Ag 18 2017

Bralower, Timothy

The formation of peak rings in large impact craters bibl color graph *Science* v354 no6314 p878 N 18 2016

BRAM, CHRISTOPHER

The Story of O *New York Times Book Review* p13 Mr 12 2017

Brammer, Greg

TINTYPE TRICK? *Popular Photography* v81 no2 p27 Mr/Ap 2017

BRAMMER, SHELBY

STORIES WE TELL OURSELVES color *Vanity Fair* v58 no11 p88 N 2016

Bramsiepe, Jonathan

RETINOBLASTOMA RELATED1 mediates germline entry in Arabidopsis color diag *Science* v356 no6336 p396 Ap 28 2017

Branagh, Kenneth, 1960-

Back on the Train T. Appelo color *AARP: The Magazine* v30 no6A p14 O/N 2017

How to GET AWAY WITH MURDER ON THE ORIENT EXPRESS [Cover story] C. Collis color *Entertainment Weekly* no1465 p22 My 12 2017

MURDER ON THE ORIENT EXPRESS C. Collis color *Entertainment Weekly* no1478 / 1479 p69 Ag 18-25 2017

Branca (Poem)

BRANCA R. Pinsky *New Yorker* v93 no4 p64 Mr 13 2017

Branca, John

GHOST LAWYER D. Leonard color *Bloomberg Businessweek* no4510 p42 F 6 2017

BRANCACCIO, DAVID

IS YOUR JOB ROBOT-PROOF? color *Popular Mechanics* p78 Jl 2017

My Wrench cartoon *Popular Mechanics* p54 D 2016/Ja 2017

Branch, Billy—Interviews

THE STATE OF BLUES M. POLLOCK color *Chicago* v66 no6 p33 Je 2017

BRANCH, GLENN

Creating Scientific Controversies: Uncertainty and Bias in Science and Society *Skeptical Inquirer* v41 no3 p60 My/Je 2017

Skepticism Should Be Nonpartisan *Skeptical Inquirer* v41 no3 p63 My/Je 2017

Understanding Gallup's Latest Poll on Evolution *Skeptical Inquirer* v41 no5 p5 S/O 2017

Branch, Kate

The 3-Minute Interview color *Glamour* v115 no1 p18 Ja 2017

Alexa's New Gig color *Glamour* v115 no7 p21 Jl 2017

Boy-Band Heaven color *Glamour* v114 no7 p38 Jl 2016

Braless Nation [Cover story] bw color *Glamour* v114 no11 p48 N 2016

Gloss Castle color *Vogue* v207 no10 p219 O 2017

Groomed! bw color *Glamour* v115 no2 p116 F 2017

"Kiss all the people you want to kiss" color *Glamour* v115 no2 p82 F 2017

Now meet 39 more beauty game changers—each defining themselves [Cover story] bw color *Glamour* v115 no4 p166 Ap 2017

The Power of an Outsider color *Glamour* v115 no1 p62 Ja 2017

"True badassery has no gender" color diag *Glamour* v115 no1 p60 Ja 2017

The Ultimate Beauty How-tos... color *Glamour* v115 no4 p204 Ap 2017

"You've got to break your back!" color *Glamour* v115 no4 p153 Ap 2017

BRANCH, MICHAEL

Finding Home: What happens when a desert baby visits the meadows of Yosemite? *National Parks* v91 no3 p18 Summ 2017

Raising Wild S. Prentiss color *Orion Magazine* v36 no2 p58 Mr/Ap 2017

Utopia Drive color *Orion Magazine* v36 no1 p59 Ja/F 2017

Branch, Michelle, 1983-

3 REINVENTIONS WE CAN'T WAIT TO HEAR M. Vain and J. Goodman color *Entertainment Weekly* no1446/1447 p76 D 2016/Ja 2017

Michelle Branch's Second Act J. HUDAK color *Rolling Stone* no1283 p14 Mr 23 2017

Branch, William

THE FUTURE IS FEMALE... INSPIRED color *Women's Health* v14 no4 p38 My 2017

Branched chain amino acids
See also
Leucine
ABCs of BCAAs color *Muscle & Performance* v9 no8 p34 Ag 2017
Depleting dietary valine permits nonmyeloablative mouse hematopoietic stem cell transplantation Yuki Taya, Yasunori Ota et al bibl graph *Science* v354 no6316 p1152 D 2 2016
GET ENERGIZED D. N. JACKSON color *Muscle & Performance* v9 no10 p18 O 2017

Branches (Business enterprises)
Innovative Partnership Brings Hope to Small Towns C. Williams *Bridges (Federal Reserve Bank of St. Louis)* p8 Summ 2016
The Publisher with All of Speculative Fiction in Its Orbit J. Maher color *Publishers Weekly* v264 no38 p12 S 18 2017

Branco, Luis M.
Structural basis for antibody-mediated neutralization of Lassa virus [Cover story] color diag *Science* v356 no6341 p923 Je 1 2017

Brancus, I.
Observation of a large-scale anisotropy in the arrival directions of cosmic rays above 8×1018 eV *Science* v357 no6357 p1266 S 22 2017

Brand, Amy
How MIT and the Internet Archive Made Free E-books A. Green *Publishers Weekly* v264 no39 p10 S 25 2017

Brand, Donald
Philip Hamburger, Is Administrative Law Unlawful? *Society* v53 no6 p668 D 2016

BRAND, TRISHA
54th and Monon *Indianapolis Monthly* p30 F 2017
BAT CRAZY *Indianapolis Monthly* v40 no3 p42 N 2016
best of Indy *Indianapolis Monthly* v40 no4 p73 D 2016
BIG DEAL *Indianapolis Monthly* v40 no7 p32 Mr 2017
FRESH HEIR color *Indianapolis Monthly* p34 Ap 2017
HOT PROPERTY *Indianapolis Monthly* v40 no4 p42 D 2016
JUST ADD WATER *Indianapolis Monthly* v40 no5 p26 Ja 2017
PILLAR OF WISDOM *Indianapolis Monthly* v40 no5 p22 Ja 2017
SHOW HOME *Indianapolis Monthly* v40 no3 p44 N 2016
SPINNING WOOLLEN *Indianapolis Monthly* p33 F 2017

Brand awareness
6 Ways to Tell Stories with Data Throughout the Customer Lifecycle A. Samuel *Harvard Business Review Digital Articles* p2 O 2 2015

Brand choice
See also
Brand loyalty
A Simple Way to Measure How Much Customers Love Your Brand T. Halloran *Harvard Business Review Digital Articles* p2 F 3 2015

Brand communities
Should You Compete with Amazon or Sell on Amazon? H. Schmid *Harvard Business Review Digital Articles* p2 My 23 2016

Brand differentiation
Your Company Culture Shouldn't Just Be Great— It Should Be Distinctive D. L. Yohn *Harvard Business Review Digital Articles* p2 S 14 2015

Brand equity
Why Is the NFL's Brand More Valuable than Ever? W. Anson *Harvard Business Review Digital Articles* p2 N 26 2015

Brand identification
THE MOST IMPORTANT QUARTER-INCH IN BUSINESS LOGO R. Walker color *Fortune* v175 no8 p210 Je 15 2017

Brand integration
See also
Branded entertainment
Who Provides Tech Support for the Internet of Things? P. Weichselbaum *Harvard Business Review Digital Articles* p2 D 31 2014

Brand loyalty
A Simple Way to Measure How Much Customers Love Your Brand T. Halloran *Harvard Business Review Digital Articles* p2 F 3 2015

Brand name product advertising
DC, WHERE POLITICAL ADS NEVER END A. BEAUJON and C. CUNNINGHAM *Washingtonian Magazine* v52 no5 p24 F 2017
Off-Color Ads by Beauty Brands K. Samuelson color *Time* v190 no16/17 p16 O 23 2017

Brand name product sales & prices
THIS BRAND DWARFS YOUR COMPANY D. Bentley *Fortune* v175 no8 p46 Je 15 2017

Brand name products
13 Things Savvy Shoppers Look for in Online Reviews C. HILTON ANDERSEN *Reader's Digest* v188 no1126 p120 D 2016/Ja 2017
Apple: Luxury Brand or Mass Marketer? W. Frick and S. Berinato *Harvard Business Review Digital Articles* p2 O 2 2014
Brand Report Card J. S. Bartlett chart *Consumer Reports* v82 no4 p36 Ap 2017
The Brands That Make Customers Feel Respected C. Trevail, M. Austin et al *Harvard Business Review Digital Articles* p2 N 1 2016
HOW TO GET RID OF ANYTHING M. SHIH and C. SULLIVAN cartoon color *Martha Stewart Living* p118 Ap 2017
Know When to Kill Your Brand D. L. Yohn *Harvard Business Review Digital Articles* p2 Jl 17 2015
My Favorite Brand B. Welch color *American Cowboy* v24 no1 p72 Je/Jl 2017
This + That A. LAROCCA img *New York* v49 no23 p49 N 14 2016
When AI Becomes the New Face of Your Brand H. J. Wilson, P. Daugherty et al *Harvard Business Review Digital Articles* p2 Je 27 2017
Why Do We Get So Emotional About Brands? A. O'Connell *Harvard Business Review Digital Articles* p2 Ap 21 2015

Brand name products—Management
Seizing Our Brand's Destiny L. D'VORKIN *Forbes* v198 no7 p16 N 29 2016

Brand name products—Ratings & rankings
Why Simple Brands Win M. Molloy *Harvard Business Review Digital Articles* p2 N 9 2015

Brand name products—Social aspects
CUSTOMER LOYALTY IS OVERRATED [Cover story] A. G. LAFLEY and R. L. MARTIN color *Harvard Business Review* v95 no1 p45 Ja/F 2017

Brandão, Hugo B.
Bacillus subtilis SMC complexes juxtapose chromosome arms as they travel from origin to terminus bibl graph *Science* v355 no6324 p524 F 3 2017

Brandeau, Greg
The Capabilities Your Organization Needs to Sustain Innovation *Harvard Business Review Digital Articles* p2 Ja 14 2015
The Inescapable Paradox of Managing Creativity *Harvard Business Review Digital Articles* p2 D 12 2014

Branded entertainment
A Standalone Podcast Network, Just Maybe L. Shaw cartoon *Bloomberg Businessweek* no4499 p50 N 14 2016

Brandeker, A.
iPTF16geu: A multiply imaged, gravitationally lensed type Ia supernova color diag graph *Science* v356 no6335 p291 Ap 21 2017

Brandenberg, Nathalie
Decoding of position in the developing neural tube from antiparallel morphogen gradients diag *Science* v356 no6345 p1379 Je 30 2017

Brand equity—Charts, diagrams, etc.
The Most Valuable Sports Brands M. K. OZANIAN chart color *Forbes* v198 no8 p34 D 20 2016

Brandimarte, Walter
Brazilian Police Strike, And Violence Spikes color *Bloomberg Businessweek* no4512 p14 F 20 2017

Branding (Marketing)
See also
Rebranding (Marketing)
The Best Salespeople Do What the Best Brands Do D. L. Yohn *Harvard Business Review Digital Articles* p2 Ag 15 2016
The Brand Benefits of Places Like the Guinness Storehouse C. Lachel *Harvard Business Review Digital Articles* p2 O 20 2015
The Branding Logic Behind Google's Creation of Alphabet K. L.

Keller *Harvard Business Review Digital Articles* p2 Ag 14 2015

BREAKTHROUGH BRANDS 2017 L. Gallagher, A. Nusca et al color diag *Fortune* v75 no1 p64 Ja 1 2017

Build Your Brand as a Relationship M. Bonchek and C. France *Harvard Business Review Digital Articles* p2 My 9 2016

Don't Overlook the Small Brands You Already Own E. Yoon *Harvard Business Review Digital Articles* p2 D 30 2016

Get Buy-in for Your Global Strategy with Local Partners K. Knight *Harvard Business Review Digital Articles* p2 O 21 2014

HOBBLED HOTEL? B. Freed *Washingtonian Magazine* v52 no1 p17 O 2016

HOW AIRBNB FOUND A MISSION—AND A BRAND [Cover story] L. Gallagher color *Fortune* v75 no1 p56 Ja 1 2017

How Tesla, Under Armour, and Sonos Do Branding R. B. Hansen *Harvard Business Review Digital Articles* p2 O 8 2015

How to Change Your Name and Keep Your Professional Identity D. Clark *Harvard Business Review Digital Articles* p2 O 9 2014

How to Rebrand Yourself as Creative When You're Not Perceived That Way D. Clark *Harvard Business Review Digital Articles* p2 My 25 2017

Know When to Kill Your Brand D. L. Yohn *Harvard Business Review Digital Articles* p2 Jl 17 2015

The More Experience You Have, the Worse You Are at Bootstrapping J. M. Olejarz *Harvard Business Review Digital Articles* p2 Jl 22 2015

Physical Graffiti N. SULLIVAN cartoon color *Esquire* v167 no1 p31 F 2017

A Simple Graph Explains the Complex Logic of the Big Beer Merger N. Dawar and C. K. Bagga *Harvard Business Review Digital Articles* p2 O 20 2015

What an OTT Future Means for Brands J. Balis *Harvard Business Review Digital Articles* p2 My 13 2015

What Apple, Lending Club, and AirBnB Know About Collaborating with Customers B. Libert, Y. (. Wind et al *Harvard Business Review Digital Articles* p2 Jl 3 2015

What It Takes to Build a Startup into a Brand M. J. Silverstein *Harvard Business Review Digital Articles* p2 Mr 9 2016

WHAT'S IN A NAME? J. Surowiecki cartoon *New Yorker* v92 no37 p35 N 14 2016

Why Do We Get So Emotional About Brands? A. O'Connell *Harvard Business Review Digital Articles* p2 Ap 21 2015

Why Simple Brands Win M. Molloy *Harvard Business Review Digital Articles* p2 N 9 2015

Why We Welcome the Seven-Year Itch L. D'VORKIN *Forbes* v200 no4 p8 O 24 2017

Your Content Marketing Strategy Doesn't Have to Be Complicated N. Westergaard *Harvard Business Review Digital Articles* p2 My 26 2016

Branding (Marketing)—China

China's Elusive Goal: A Global Apparel Brand R. Chang and L. Rupp color *Bloomberg Businessweek* no4532 p12 Jl 31 2017

Brandis, Alexander

Potential role of intratumor bacteria in mediating tumor resistance to the chemotherapeutic drug gemcitabine diag *Science* v357 no6356 p1156 S 15 2017

Brandl, Susanne

Positive biodiversity-productivity relationship predominant in global forests bibl chart graph map *Science* v354 no6309 paaf8957-1 O 14 2016

Brandolini d'Adda, Marcantonio

Glass House H. MARTIN color *Architectural Digest* v74 no9 p58 S 2017

Brands, H. W.

Even Headstrong Generals Must Answer to Someone M. Duffy color *Time* v188 no18 p48 O 31 2016

The General vs. the President: MacArthur and Truman at the Brink of Nuclear War L. D. Freedman *Foreign Affairs* v96 no2 p172 Mr/Ap 2017

Brands, H. W.—Interviews

H. W. Brands *New York Times Book Review* p8 O 9 2016

Brands, Hal

THE DIFFERENCE REAGAN MADE H. R. Nau *Claremont Review of Books* v17 no1 p66 Wint 2016/2017

Not Too Cold, Not Too Hot color *Weekly Standard* v23 no2 p10 S 18 2017

Restoring Solvency color *Weekly Standard* v22 no25 p23 Mr 6

2017

Saving Realism from the So-Called Realists: A foreign-policy approach based in security and pragmatism is now characterized by retrenchment and radicalism *Commentary* v144 no2 p15 S 2017

Should America Retrench? *Foreign Affairs* v95 no6 p164 N/D 2016

Trump and Terrorism color *Foreign Affairs* v96 no2 p28 Mr/Ap 2017

Brandshaft, Richard

Unfamiliar Terms *Skeptical Inquirer* v41 no3 p64 My/Je 2017

BRANDSTETTER, MICHELLE

CHIP SHOT *Cincinnati Magazine* v50 no7 p154 Ap 2017

DOG DAZE *Cincinnati Magazine* v50 no10 p52 Jl 2017

THE FLOATING WORLD *Cincinnati Magazine* v50 no5 p24 F 2017

LONG SERVE *Cincinnati Magazine* v50 no11 p24 Ag 2017

NIGHT MOVES *Cincinnati Magazine* v50 no8 p40 My 2017

RUN AROUND *Cincinnati Magazine* v50 no8 p20 My 2017

BRANDT, ALYSSA

Alma Bartos *Cincinnati Magazine* v50 no4 p40 Ja 2017

Asheville, North Carolina *Cincinnati Magazine* p60 Je 2017

BE OUR GUEST *Cincinnati Magazine* v50 no6 p44 Mr 2017

BLUES STREAK *Cincinnati Magazine* v50 no10 p26 Jl 2017

Cannes Do!: French burgers that rival the fries *Cincinnati Magazine* v50 no10 p120 Jl 2017

CAN WE TALK? *Cincinnati Magazine* v50 no4 p72 Ja 2017

Catalytic Converters: Emily Wolff and Paul Weckman aim to stabilize Covington's MainStrasse one property at time *Cincinnati Magazine* v50 no11 p80 Ag 2017

DOG DAZE *Cincinnati Magazine* v50 no10 p52 Jl 2017

ENDLESS LOVE *Cincinnati Magazine* v50 no2 p56 N 2016

FEAST YOUR EYES *Cincinnati Magazine* v50 no6 p65 Mr 2017

FIELD GOALS *Cincinnati Magazine* p26 Je 2017

GO TEAM! *Cincinnati Magazine* v50 no4 p76 Ja 2017

HIT PARADE *Cincinnati Magazine* v50 no5 p26 F 2017

Jill Franco color *Cincinnati Magazine* v51 no1 p32 O 2017

Kevin Jones *Cincinnati Magazine* v50 no2 p32 N 2016

Kitchen Ritual *Cincinnati Magazine* v50 no5 p162 F 2017

Lauren Doolittle *Cincinnati Magazine* p34 Je 2017

METALHEAD *Cincinnati Magazine* v50 no4 p42 Ja 2017

Nicole Gunderman *Cincinnati Magazine* v50 no3 p44 D 2016

Niyah Jackson *Cincinnati Magazine* v50 no7 p32 Ap 2017

ONE SIZE FITS ALL *Cincinnati Magazine* v50 no12 p36 S 2017

Pam Kravetz *Cincinnati Magazine* v50 no10 p38 Jl 2017

Pho Keeps *Cincinnati Magazine* p111 Je 2017

POWER OF THE PRESS *Cincinnati Magazine* v50 no5 p38 F 2017

RIDE ALONG *Cincinnati Magazine* v50 no7 p25 Ap 2017

Shell Game *Cincinnati Magazine* v50 no5 p158 F 2017

THEY PERSISTED bw *Cincinnati Magazine* v51 no1 p20 O 2017

WALTZ THIS WAY *Cincinnati Magazine* v50 no3 p36 D 2016

Brandt, Amy

Coached by Gelsey *Dance Magazine* v91 no1 p134 Ja 2017

PART-TIME POST-GRAD *Dance Magazine* p27 2016/2017

PART-TIME POST-GRAD *Dance Magazine* v90 p27 2016/2017 Supplement College Guide

PETER WEIL *Dance Spirit* v21 no3 p38 Mr 2017

Brandt, Anthony

GAME-CHANGING INVENTIONS: WHAT MAKES AN IDEA REVOLUTIONARY? A. BEARD color il *Harvard Business Review* v95 no5 p148 S/O 2017

Losing the West bw color map *American History* v52 no3 p32 Ag 2017

SKY ABOVE, MUD BELOW bw color *Military History* v34 no1 p32 My 2017

Brandt, Grace

Art Meets Organization R. Minetor *Stage Directions* v30 no3 p28 Mr 2017

BRANDT, JAMES

CHEAP ADVENTURES cartoon color *Outdoor Life* v224 no4 p30 My 2017

THE GREATEST RIG EVER MADE color *Outdoor Life* v224 no1 p97 D 2016/Ja 2017

LOAD THE BOAT color diag *Outdoor Life* v224 no4 p48 My 2017

PITCH PERFECT color *Outdoor Life* v224 no6 pH1 Ag 2017

SPACE-AGE LURES THAT LOOK, SOUND, ACT—AND EVEN SMELL—LIKE LIVE BAIT color *Outdoor Life* v224 no2 p44 F/Mr 2017

THE TIE THAT BINDS color *Outdoor Life* v224 no8 p66 O 2017

BRANDT, JODI

Invasive Species, Indigenous Stewards, and Vulnerability Discourse chart diag map *American Indian Quarterly* v41 no3 p201 Summ 2017

A looming tragedy of the sand commons color *Science* v357 no6355 p970 S 8 2017

Brandy—Evaluation

BEYOND HENNESSY J. Clarke color *Bloomberg Businessweek* no4503 p68 D 12 2016

Brangwynne, Clifford P.

Liquid phase condensation in cell physiology and disease *Science* v357 no6357 p1253 S 22 2017

Braniss, Ilan

Antibiotic tolerance facilitates the evolution of resistance bibl bw chart diag graph *Science* v355 no6327 p826 F 24 2017

Branka, Nancy

Graduating the Future color *Forbes* v198 no6 p51 N 8 2016

Brann, Eva

Next Question I. LINDQUIST color *Weekly Standard* v22 no9 p38 N 7 2016

Brannigan, Mikey

MIKEY BRANNIGAN J. HANC color *Runner's World* v52 no1 p88 Ja/F 2017

Brannock, Larry

SHOP NOTES cartoon chart color *Popular Mechanics* v193 no7 p36 S 2016

Brannon, Holmes

THE CONVERSATION color *Atlantic* v319 no1 p10 Ja/F 2017

Brannon, Ike

Harry Caray Is My Wingman color *Weekly Standard* v22 no7 p14 O 24 2016

Housing's Drag on the Economy *Weekly Standard* v22 no22 p24 F 13 2017

Ode to a Couch color *Weekly Standard* v22 no47 p5 Ag 21 2017

Revenge of the Nerds color *Weekly Standard* v22 no23 p26 F 20 2017

Time to Fix Fannie and Freddie color *Weekly Standard* v22 no30 p18 Ap 10 2017

The Ture-Kennedy Blueprint *National Review* v69 no9 p37 My 15 2017

Branom, Mike

Maxx Echt: Huntington Botanical Department Systems Manager *Weatherwise* v70 no5 p40 S/O 2017

On the Job color map *Weatherwise* v70 no4 p32 Jl/Ag 2017

Weather Front map *Weatherwise* v70 no4 p6 Jl/Ag 2017

Weather Front *Weatherwise* v70 no1 p6 Ja/F 2017

Weather Front *Weatherwise* v70 no2 p6 Mr/Ap 2017

weather front *Weatherwise* v70 no5 p6 S/O 2017

Bransen, Ted

Cultivating Choreographers L. Winship *Dance Magazine* v91 no4 p14 Ap 2017

Branson, Richard, 1950-

Life IN THESE UNITED STATES color *Reader's Digest* v190 no1135 p32 N 2017

Looking for Answers to the World's Biggest Challenges In the Eternal City color *Time* v188 no24 p31 D 12 2016

Branstad, Terry E., 1946——Interviews

TERRY BRANSTAND A. McConnell *Successful Farming* v115 no8 p8 Je/Jl 2017

BRANSTETTER, HEATHER

You Don't Have to Obey the Laws: But You Do Have to Follow the Rules *Idaho Magazine* v16 no10 p19 Jl 2017

Brant, Ana

The Best Luxury Services Are Customized, Not Standardized *Harvard Business Review Digital Articles* p2 Mr 2 2016

Everyone Says They Listen to Their Customers— Here's How to Really Do It *Harvard Business Review Digital Articles* p2 O 28 2015

How Our Hotel Used Data to Make Our Laundry Service Glamorous color *Harvard Business Review Digital Articles* p2 Mr 1 2017

Using an Algorithm to Figure Out What Luxury Customers Really Want *Harvard Business Review Digital Articles* p2 Jl 18 2016

Brant, John

Running for Her Life [Cover story] bw color *Runner's World* v52 no6 p82 Jl 2017

BRANTLEY, STEVEN T.

Crossing Scales: The Complexity of Barrier-Island Processes for Predicting Future Change *BioScience* v67 no1 p39 Ja 2017

BRANTLEY, WILL

10-RINGERS [Cover story] color *Field & Stream* v122 no6 p77 N 2017

ADVENTURES IN SQUIRREL COUNTRY cartoon *Field & Stream* v122 no5 p59 O 2017

ANGRY BIRDS bw cartoon color *Field & Stream* v121 no9 p47 Ap 2017

AUTUMN IN AUGUST color *Field & Stream* v122 no3 p14 Ag 2017

THE BIG GAMERS cartoon color *Field & Stream* v121 no7 p82 D 2016/Ja 2017

THE BOW BUBBLE color *Field & Stream* v121 no8 p36 F/Mr 2017

BO WHOOP COMES HOME color *Field & Stream* v121 no6 p52 N 2016

BOW SHOOTOUT 2017 bw color *Field & Stream* v122 no3 p69 Ag 2017

BREAK OUT! cartoon color *Field & Stream* v121 no9 p35 Ap 2017

CARRY ON color *Field & Stream* v122 no1 p52 My 2017

DREAM LAND color *Field & Stream* v122 no2 p92 Je/Jl 2017

THE FAMILY GUIDE TO NOODLING color *Field & Stream* v122 no2 p76 Je/Jl 2017

FIELD TEST color *Field & Stream* v122 no2 p99 Je/Jl 2017

FOUR OF A KIND cartoon *Field & Stream* v121 no9 p30 Ap 2017

HOLIDAY GIFT GUIDE 2016 color *Field & Stream* v121 no7 p92 D 2016/Ja 2017

NO REGRETS color *Field & Stream* v122 no4 p30 S 2017

Reed Section color *Field & Stream* v121 no9 pT8 Ap 2017

THE SQUIRREL RUT color *Field & Stream* v121 no7 p24 D 2016/Ja 2017

STUDY ABROAD color *Field & Stream* v122 no6 p30 N 2017

THE TAGGED-OUT DEER HUNTER'S GUIDE TO FALL [Cover story] color *Field & Stream* v122 no6 p59 N 2017

THE WATERFOWL FRONTIER color diag *Field & Stream* v121 no7 p76 D 2016/Ja 2017

Young Blood color *Field & Stream* v122 no4 p54 S 2017

YOUR Wildest DREAMS color *Field & Stream* v122 no5 p38 O 2017

Branton, Paul

Visual Artist Paul Branton L. CROSS color *Ebony* v72 no6 p20 Ap/My 2017

BRARA, NOOR

chandigarh, india color *Architectural Digest* no5 p78 My 2017

Earthly Pleasures color *Vogue* v207 no11 p166 N 2017

Brashares, Justin

Eating ecosystems color *Science* v356 no6334 p136 Ap 14 2017

Merging paleobiology with conservation biology to guide the future of terrestrial ecosystems color *Science* v355 no6325 p594 F 10 2017

Brass

ASK ROY R. BERENDSOHN cartoon *Popular Mechanics* p47 D 2016/Ja 2017

Brass instruments

See also

Bugle

Blessing BFH-1541 Flugelhorn B. Zimmerman color *Downbeat* v84 no8 p90 Ag 2017

B&S MBX3 Heritage X-Line Trumpet B. Zimmerman color *Downbeat* v84 no10 p194 O 2017

BRASSAW, BRIAN

Isles of Debris color *Natural History* v125 no11 p18 N 2017

Brassell, Danny

AFFILIATES AT WORK *Literacy Today (2411-7862)* v35 no1 p38 Jl/Ag 2017

Brassieres

See also

Sports bras

Braless Nation [Cover story] K. Branch bw color *Glamour* v114 no11 p48 N 2016

Rachael Heger Do-gooder M. RUBINO *Indianapolis Monthly* v40 no4 p60 D 2016

Brassieres—Evaluation

7 genius underwear updates color *Redbook* p74 S 2017

Adam's TOP FIT TIPS color *O, The Oprah Magazine* p56 Ap 2017

Delicate Subject: Bust a move to Carmel's new lingerie boutique S. BAHR *Indianapolis Monthly* p36 N 2017

Intimate Affairs color *O, The Oprah Magazine* p62 Mr 2017

PRETTY INTIMATE color *Essence* v47 no10 p21 F 2017

SHOW of SUPPORT K. BASTONE color *Runner's World* v52 no7 p78 Ag 2017

Brassieres—History

Ta-da! The Bra R. Beach bw color *Glamour* v115 no6 p24 Je 2017

Brassinga, Angela

A FOOLPROOF FEAST color *Sunset* v237 no5 p81 N 2016

PARTY ON THE GO color *Sunset* v239 no4 p83 O 2017

Toast of the TOWN [Cover story] color *Sunset* v237 no5 p70 N 2016

WEEKNIGHT COOKING color *Sunset* v237 no6 p96 D 2016

WEEKNIGHT COOKING color *Sunset* v239 no3 p96 S 2017

Brasswork—Evaluation

Top Brass M. Khemsurov color *Bloomberg Businessweek* no4509 p58 Ja 30 2017

Brastianos, Priscilla K.

Decoupling genetics, lineages, and microenvironment in IDH-mutant gliomas by single-cell RNA-seq diag *Science* v355 no6332 p1391 Mr 31 2017

Brastoff, Sascha, 1918-1993

CERAMICS TRIAD JOHNSON *Treasures* v6 no4 p28 F/Mr 2017

Bratcher, Drew

HELENA, FALLING: And the human impulse, from the youngest age,to keep going *Washingtonian Magazine* v52 no11 p176 Ag 2017

Bratton, Mark

Faith and Science at a Crossroad *Sky & Telescope* v134 no3 p6 S 2017

BRATTSTROM, BAYARD

Anesthesia and Euthanasia of Amphibians and Reptiles Used in Scientific Research: Should Hypothermia and Freezing Be Prohibited? *BioScience* v67 no1 p53 Ja 2017

BRÄU, WALTER

EXERCISING RESTRAINT color *Scientific American* v316 no6 p5 Je 2017

Braudy, Leo

Haunted: On Ghosts,Witches, Vampires, Zombies, and Other Monsters of the Natural and Supernatural C. RICKEY *Film Quarterly* v71 no1 p111 Fall 2017

Where the Wild Things Come From G. MAGUIRE *New York Times Book Review* p13 O 30 2016

Brauer, Dave

FROM OUR READERS *Archaeology* v70 no4 p8 Je-Ag 2017

Brauer, M.

A climate policy pathway for near- and long-term benefits color *Science* v356 no6337 p493 My 5 2017

Braun, Allen

Publication ban upends NIH lab, collaborators J. Couzin-Frankel color *Science* v355 no6327 p783 F 24 2017

Braun, Ashley

Benign Selection *Natural History* v125 no1 p7 D 2016/Ja 2017

Clearing Memory color *Natural History* v125 no4 p8 Ap 2017

A Crimp on Crops graph *Scientific American* v316 no4 p21 Ap 2017

Dry Plants? Add Vinegar color *Natural History* v125 no10 p8 O 2017

Fleshing Out Dinosaurs color *Natural History* v125 no6 p6 Je 2017

Fungal Feedback color *Natural History* v125 no3 p8 Mr 2017

Getting Out of One's Own Way color *Natural History* v125 no7 p6 Jl/Ag 2017

Monumental Feats *Natural History* v125 no2 p7 F 2017

Retro Virus color *Natural History* v125 no5 p6 My 2017

Winks on the Wing *Natural History* v124 no10 p6 N 2016

Braun, Dieter

Wild Animals of the South *Publishers Weekly* v264 no12 p72 Mr 20 2017

Braun, Eddie

Rocket Redux D. KEISER *Idaho Magazine* v16 no2 p40 N 2016

Braun, H. J.

Improving global integration of crop research color *Science* v357 no6349 p359 Jl 28 2017

Braun, Josh

THE BIG QUESTION cartoon *Atlantic* v320 no3 p100 O 2017

Braun, Martin Z.

Raising Private Money For Public Projects *Bloomberg Businessweek* no4513 p46 Mr 6 2017

Braun, Michael

Don't Treat Innovation as a Cure-All *Harvard Business Review Digital Articles* p2 D 8 2014

Braun, Sebastian Felix

Transforming Ethnohistories: Narrative, Meaning, and Community G. A. Rogers *American Indian Quarterly* v40 no3 p285 Summ 2016

Braun, Wendy

BRAIN-ZAP WEIGHT LOSS PROGRAM *Saturday Evening Post* v289 no5 p69 S/O 2017

Braun, William R.

ALL NATURAL *Opera News* v81 no7 p22 Ja 2017

Berg: Wozzeck *Opera News* v81 no10 p54 Ap 2017

Debussy/Orledge: Poe Operas *Opera News* v81 no6 p52 D 2016

Hitting the Mark *Opera News* v81 no7 p32 Ja 2017

L'Amour de Loin *Opera News* v81 no9 p32 Mr 2017

Philippe Jaroussky: Sacred Cantatas *Opera News* v81 no9 p55 Mr 2017

Shchedrin: The Left-Hander *Opera News* v81 no6 p50 D 2016

Braund, Anna

Dreamy Hues K. Owen color *Southern Living* v52 no2 p24 F 2017

YOU CAN GO HOME AGAIN V. Rains color *Southern Living* v52 no9 p92 S 2017

Braunger, Katharina

The cryo-EM structure of a ribosome–Ski2-Ski3-Ski8 helicase complex bibl color graph *Science* v354 no6318 p1431 D 16 2016

Braunohler, Robert

Capitol Crossing M. M. KASHINO color *Washingtonian Magazine* v52 no7 p103 Ap 2017

Braus, Gerhard H.

Sterilizing immunity in the lung relies on targeting fungal apoptosis-like programmed cell death color diag *Science* v357 no6355 p1037 S 8 2017

Braut-Hegghammer, Malfrid

Unclear Physics: Why Iraq and Libya Failed to Build Nuclear Weapons L. D. Freedman *Foreign Affairs* v96 no2 p173 Mr/Ap 2017

Brautlecht, Nicholas

Global Trade Is Slowing color *Bloomberg Businessweek* no4500 p16 N 21 2016

Bravard, Jean-Louis

All Boards Need a Technology Expert *Harvard Business Review Digital Articles* p2 S 23 2015

Brave, The (TV program)

The Brave N. Abrams, C. Holub et al color *Entertainment Weekly* no1482/1483 p55 S 22 2017

Network TV's Calorie-Free Take on American Patriotism D. D'addario color *Time* v190 no13 p63 O 2 2017

Primetime Combat T. Appelo color *AARP: The Magazine* v30 no6A p15 O/N 2017

Braverman, Beth

Pull Down the Best Rate chart color *Money* v46 no3 p21 Ap 2017

Shop Online With Confidence graph il *Consumer Reports* v82 no12 p20 D 2017

Braverman, Blair

The Great White Hope *Smithsonian* v47 no10 p11 Mr 2017

Bravo, Ellen

YOU: THE INSTANT EXPERT ACTIVISM color *Women's Health* v14 no3 p161 Ap 2017

Bravo, Janicza, 1981-

Janicza Bravo J. Johnson color *Current Biography* v78 no8 p8 Ag 2017

Braxton-Smith, Ananda
Merrow color *Publishers Weekly* v263 no49 p99 D 7 2016
Bray, Duane
IDEO's Employee Engagement Formula *Harvard Business Review Digital Articles* p2 D 18 2015
Bray, Paden
MAKING IT HAPPEN color *Spin to Win Rodeo* v21 no2 p16 Ap 2017
BRAY, SHELLY
Beyond Words color *O, The Oprah Magazine* p17 Ap 2017
Brázda, P.
Hydrogen positions in single nanocrystals revealed by electron diffraction bibl color *Science* v355 no6321 p1 Ja 13 2017
BRAZIER, BRENDAN
To Fast or To Feed? color *Muscle & Performance* v9 no9 p64 S 2017
BRAZIER, DAVID
THE GIFT OF FEAR bw *Tricycle: The Buddhist Review* v27 no1 p52 Fall 2017
Understand, Realize, Give Up, Develop color *Tricycle: The Buddhist Review* v27 no1 p44 Fall 2017
Brazile, Trevor
DEPUTIZED color *Spin to Win Rodeo* v21 no5 p12 Jl 2017
Sports Figures bw cartoon color *American Cowboy* p36 LEGENDS OF TEXAS Special Issue 2017
Team Roping Spices Up World All-Around Race K. Santos *Spin to Win Rodeo* v21 no6 p28 Ag 2017
Brazil—Economic conditions—1985-
BRAZIL'S SPORTS, SCANDAL, AND MARKET RALLY E. Fry diag *Fortune* v174 no8 p21 D 15 2016
Brazil—Emigration & immigration
INTO THE URBAN JUNGLE D. Biller color *Bloomberg Businessweek* no4534 p60 Ag 14 2017
Brazilian Development Bank (Company)
A Development Bank Stops Lending Abroad D. Biller, J. Brice et al color *Bloomberg Businessweek* no4503 p13 D 12 2016
Brazilian pepper tree—Therapeutic use
A WEED THAT BUSTS BACTERIA A. R. Williams color *National Geographic* v232 no3 p18 S 2017
Brazil—Politics & government—1822-
Brazil's Never-Ending Corruption Crisis B. Winter color *Foreign Affairs* v96 no3 p87 My/Je 2017
Brazil—Politics & government—2003-
Brazilians Look for a Trump of Their Own B. Douglas and D. Biller cartoon *Bloomberg Businessweek* no4508 p15 Ja 23 2017
Brazil's Crisis Reflects Demise of Representative Democracy Across the West F. H. CARDOSO *NPQ: New Perspectives Quarterly* v33 no4 p35 O 2016
A coalition to impeach C. Carvalhaes and R. Barreto *Christian Century* v133 no23 p11 N 9 2016
Who will watch the Amazon? E. Stokstad *Science* v356 no6338 p569 My 12 2017
Brazos Bend State Park (Tex.)
Pay Your Respects A. SAIKIN color map *Backpacker* p28 My 2017
BRCA genes
Hidden Agenda N. Casey color *Vogue* v207 no10 p224 O 2017
I'M FLAT AND I'M PROUD C. Guthrie bw color *O, The Oprah Magazine* p90 O 2017
Brea, Jennifer
See Through Me E. HYNES color *Film Comment* v53 no2 p14 Mr/Ap 2017
Bread
See also
Bread crumbs
Corn bread
Dough
Toast (Bread)
Baguette Basics color *Vegetarian Today* no1 p38 F 2017
BRAND-NAME RATING *Nutrition Action Health Letter* v44 no2 p15 Mr 2017
BREAD IS NOT THE ENEMY J. Stout color *Bicycling* v58 no8 p36 S 2017
BREAD WINNERS L. MOYER and B. LIEBMAN *Nutrition Action Health Letter* v44 no2 p13 Mr 2017
Capital Grilled Cheese F. Largeman-Roth color *Parents* v92 no9

p46 S 2017
D-NAME RATING *Nutrition Action Health Letter* v44 no2 p14 Mr 2017
GIVE THANKS UNDER THE STARS [Cover story] A. LONGOBUCCO color *Good Housekeeping* v263 no5 p76 N 2016
Lyman Lemon Zucchini Bread A. Larson *Idaho Magazine* v16 no12 p57 S 2017
Missouriana M. W. SCHWARTZ *Missouri Life* v43 no7 p98 D 2016/Ja 2017
MMM...MORNING color *Good Housekeeping* v264 no5 p129 My 2017
Modern Vegan Comfort Food D. Daneils-Zeller *Vegetarian Journal* v35 no1 p18 2016
Raise the Crostini Bar color *Vegetarian Today* no2 p34 Ap 2017
Sneaky Forms of Sugar M. D. SMITH color *Better Nutrition* v79 no3 p60 Mr 2017
The Taste of Regret: How you should—and should not—cook with garlic S. Nosrat *New York Times Magazine* p26 O 1 2017
Trim your table with new holiday recipes color *Nebraska Life* v21 no6 p36 N/D 2017
Unexpected Encounters M. ALLEN *Yankee* v81 no5 p12 S/O 2017
Vegan Cooking Tips. Quick and Easy Sandwich Ideas N. Berkoff *Vegetarian Journal* v35 no2 p32 2016
White Castle Removes L-Cysteine from Veggie Slider Bun; Prompted by Vegans J. Yacoubou *Vegetarian Journal* v35 no4 p36 2016
Bread crumbs
ШЕLCOMɘ TO CUTLET COUЯTЯɣ E. WARTZMAN color *Bon Appetit* p124 S 2017
Bread puddings
Thy Daily Bread Pudding J. BENSON color *New Orleans Magazine* v51 no1 p64 N 2016
Bread—Evaluation
Bread WINNERS T. MALONE *Atlanta* v56 no7 p85 N 2016
Breadwinner Cycles (Company)
breadwinner color *Bike Magazine* v24 no2 p77 Mr 2017
WHAT BIKE SHOULD I BUY? B. STRICKLAND color *Bicycling* v58 no3 p16 Ap 2017
Break-even analysis
A Refresher on Breakeven Quantity A. Gallo *Harvard Business Review Digital Articles* p2 Je 22 2015
Breaker, The (Music)
Country That Melds Tried-and-True With Utterly New M. Johnston color *Time* v189 no7/8 p107 F 27 2017
LITTLE BIG TOWN K. O'Donnell color *Entertainment Weekly* no1446/1447 p77 D 2016/Ja 2017
The Must List color *Entertainment Weekly* no1454/1455 p1 F 24 2017
What to Stream color *Entertainment Weekly* no1454/1455 p96 F 24 2017
BREAKEY, SHARLENE
Stronger, Shinier, Silkier! color *Parents* v92 no11 p75 N 2017
Breakfast cereals
Extreme Makeover: Breakfast Edition [Cover story] L. Sampedro color *Women's Health* v14 no1 p111 Ja/F 2017
Breakfast Club, The (Film : 1985)
A Gym Teacher Visited The Breakfast Club D. Coggan color *Entertainment Weekly* no1460/1461 p40 Ap 7-17 2017
Breakfasts
25 BREAKFASTS OVER EASY K. CICERO color *Parents* v92 no11 p46 N 2017
5 minute breakfasts K. SULLIVAN MORFORD *Parents* v91 no9 p150 S 2016
Bake-Ahead Breakfast J. BOWDEN and J. BESSINGER color *Better Nutrition* p62 My 2017
BLOCK PARTY A. BROWNLEE *Cincinnati Magazine* v50 no2 p62 N 2016
BOOST your breakfast M. RABBITT color *Yoga Journal* no288 p73 D 2016
Boost Your Burn color *Health* v31 no5 p6 Je 2017
BREAKFASTS OF CHAMPIONS A. GORIN color *Runner's World* v52 no8 p26 S 2017
Congee: The Original Grain Bowl R. Patronite and R. Raisfeld img *New York* v50 no6 p68 Mr 20 2017
Dialogue *Los Angeles Magazine* p10 F 2017
Easter together J. HOWARD color *Parents* v92 no4 p108 Ap 2017

Get Down, Melt Pounds color *Health* v31 no1 p6 Ja 2017

GRAB A BISCUIT G. SNYDER *Los Angeles Magazine* p116 Ap 2017

GREAT STARTS *Washingtonian Magazine* v52 no1 p100 O 2016

Happy Apple Discs F. LARGEMAN-ROTH color *Parents* v92 no11 p70 N 2017

Laughter THE BEST MEDICINE color *Reader's Digest* v189 no1129 p92 Ap 2017

Le Bristol Paris A. WHITTLE color *Conde Nast Traveler* v51 no11 p62 D 2016

Make Over Your Breakfast *Parents* v91 no9 p154 S 2016

The Mercer Sevilla color *Conde Nast Traveler* v52 no6 p49 Je/Jl 2017

MORNING *Atlanta* v56 no12 p73 Ap 2017

MORNING GLORIES Y. KIM *Martha Stewart Living* no270 p91 D 2016

The NEW L.A. BREAKFAST *Los Angeles Magazine* p106 Ap 2017

Nutrition Then and Now: The science of nutrition is ever-evolving, resulting in small changes and larger shifts in dietary advice over time *Tufts University Health & Nutrition Letter* v35 no7 p4 S 2017

The PURSUIT of Life S. UMLAND color *Cabin Living* p88 Je 2017

Rock Your Morning B. Lipton color *Health* v30 no9 p148 N 2016

A Sunny Start to the Day C. MOROCCO color *Bon Appetit* no11 p52 N 2017

Time for Breakfast! C. THORP color *Seventeen* v76 no5 p68 S 2017

What's for Breakfast? color *Health* v31 no5 p115 Je 2017

WHY YOU SHOULD GO BIG AT BREAKFAST color *Health* v31 no9 p16 N 2017

XTREME EATING 2017 L. MOYER and B. LIEBMAN *Nutrition Action Health Letter* v44 no6 p13 Jl/Ag 2017

Your Three-Course Fix color *Tennis* v53 no5 p18 S/O 2017

Breakfasts—Physiological aspects

FAFQ K. Patel and J. WUEBBEN *Muscle & Performance* v9 no5 p14 My 2017

Breakfasts—Social aspects

MAKE A POWER PLAY D. HOCHMAN *Los Angeles Magazine* p114 Ap 2017

Breaking Away (Film)

Reel Talk M. Rubino *Indianapolis Monthly* v41 no2 p14 S 2017

Breaking the Waves (Film)

Breaking the Waves D. Shengold *Opera News* v81 no6 p42 D 2016

From Screen to Stage R. VAVREK *Opera News* v81 no6 p20 D 2016

Breakout Labs (Company)

BRINGING 'HARD SCIENCE' TO THE MASSES E. Griffith color *Fortune* v176 no4 p35 S 15 2017

Breakspear, Andrew

Fatty acids in arbuscular mycorrhizal fungi are synthesized by the host plant diag graph *Science* v356 no6343 p1175 Je 16 2017

Breakwell, James

My husband's been totally focused on our baby color *Glamour* v115 no1 p52 Ja 2017

BREAL, JORDAN

El Paso *Texas Monthly* v45 no5 p30 My 2017

Galveston: NEITHER SHIFTING SANDS NOR FLUCTUATING FORTUNES CAN ERODE THIS ISLAND TOWN'S INDOMITABLE SPIRIT *Texas Monthly* v45 no7 p28 Jl 2017

Near Southside *Texas Monthly* v45 no1 p28 Ja 2017

OBJECTS OF OUR AFFECTION *Texas Monthly* v44 no11 p99 N 2016

OFF the BEATEN PATH color *GQ: Gentlemen's Quarterly* v97 no9 p154 S 2017

Route 66 *Texas Monthly* v45 no3 p38 Mr 2017

SIGHTS UNSEEN *Texas Monthly* v45 no3 p100 Mr 2017

Breast

Battle of the Brains E. SPITZNAGEL color *Men's Health* v31 no10 p110 D 2016

Sports Support L. McGLASHAN color *Muscle & Performance* v9 no7 p26 Jl 2017

Breast cancer

Awareness Is Good. Attention Is Better M. Loftus *Christianity To-*

day v60 no8 p31 O 2016

Four Weeks to the Finish Line K. LOREN chart color *Muscle & Performance* v9 no9 p30 S 2017

THE INVASION EQUATION S. MUKHERJEE cartoon color *New Yorker* v93 no27 p40 S 11 2017

I Treated Breast Cancer for Years As a Doctor. Then I Was Diagnosed P. Munster color *Time* v190 no15 p46 O 16 2017

A Little Bit Braver Now D. DEE THOMAS, D. SCARBOROUGH et al color *O, The Oprah Magazine* p18 D 2016

Rethinking Drinking color *Prevention* v68 no11 p10 N 2016

Breast cancer diagnosis

Breast Cancer Warrior K. ZALAN *Ms.* v26 no4 p17 Wint 2016

An Individual Approach to Breast Cancer A. Park color *Time* v190 no15 p40 O 16 2017

A STRANGER in My House color *Vogue* v207 no6 p42 Je 2017

Breast cancer patients

A BEAUTIFUL LIFE color *Women's Health* v14 no8 p52 O 2017

Bouncing Back After Breast Cancer K. Johnson and A. GUMBS color *Black Enterprise* v47 no3 p69 O 2016

A MATTER OF LIFE AND BREAST K. Corrigan *O, The Oprah Magazine* p84 O 2017

MEET A WARRIOR V. Jonas color *Essence* v48 no6 p118 O 2017

NEWS FROM THE World of Medicine S. RIDEOUT color *Reader's Digest* v189 no1129 p56 Ap 2017

October, Whoa color *Glamour* v114 no12 p64 D 2016

A Prom for My Mom M. Sherman color *Money* v46 no5 p80 Je 2017

"THE LAST THING I EXPECTED when I was expecting was breast cancer." K. MALMO color *Good Housekeeping* v265 no4 p95 O 2017

"We never expected cancer to be part of our marriage" M. Mertens bw color *Glamour* v115 no10 p130 O 2017

Breast cancer prevention

Every Woman Needs These Breast Cancer Lessons L. Floyd bw color *Glamour* v115 no10 p117 O 2017

New imaging center by women, for women *Successful Farming* v115 no1 p41 Ja 2017

Pink Power S. Leach color *Glamour* v115 no10 p36 O 2017

Reduce Cancer Risk E. A. Kane color *Amazing Wellness* v9 no1 p28 Wint 2017

TESTING, TESTING T. G. HOPE color *Better Homes & Gardens* v95 no8 p177 Ag 2017

Wanda's Latest Treat color *AARP: The Magazine* v59 no6A p9 O/N 2016

Breast cancer risk factors

KNOW YOUR RISKS K. ASP color *Better Homes & Gardens* v95 no10 p180 O 2017

Breast cancer surgery

See also

Lumpectomy

HOW MY BODY CHANGED... AND HOW IT CHANGED ME color *Women's Health* v14 no7 p117 S 2017

"THE LAST THING I EXPECTED when I was expecting was breast cancer." K. MALMO color *Good Housekeeping* v265 no4 p95 O 2017

Breast cancer treatment

6 Surprising Things That May Improve Breast-Cancer Treatment A. Sifferlin color *Time* v190 no15 p45 O 16 2017

THE CUT-OFF POINT S. Sea Gold color *O, The Oprah Magazine* p86 O 2017

LEARNING CURVE C. Guthrie cartoon *O, The Oprah Magazine* p129 Mr 2017

Perfect Match *Virginia Living* v15 no1 p111 D 2016

Precision medicine for Chinese women with familial breast cancer: Opportunities and challenges Xinyi Chen, Cong Fan et al bibl *Science* v354 no6319 p43 D 23 2016

"We never expected cancer to be part of our marriage" M. Mertens bw color *Glamour* v115 no10 p130 O 2017

Why More Women Are Getting a Double Mastectomy A. Sifferlin diag *Time* v190 no15 p41 O 16 2017

Breast cancer—Etiology

New Frontiers In Breast Cancer A. Park color diag *Time* v188 no15 p34 O 17 2016

Breast cancer—Gene therapy

PI3K pathway regulates ER-dependent transcription in breast cancer through the epigenetic regulator KMT2D E. Toska, H.

U. Osmanbeyoglu et al bibl graph *Science* v355 no6331 p1324 Mr 24 2017

Breast cancer—Patients—Research

Avoid Chemo with This Gene Test color *Prevention* v68 no12 p13 D 2016

Breast cancer—Research

Breast cancer research in the era of precision medicine Yi-Zhou Jiang and Zhi-Ming Shao bibl color *Science* v354 no6319 p30 D 23 2016

New Frontiers In Breast Cancer A. Park color diag *Time* v188 no15 p34 O 17 2016

Breast diseases—Diagnosis

Our Doc Will See You Now R. Rajapaksa color *Health* v31 no2 p86 Mr 2017

Breast exams

See also

Mammograms

Why do mammograms squeeze my breasts between two x-ray plates when x-rays of other body parts don't? color *Prevention* v69 no9 p8 O 2017

Breast implants

breast reconstruction, on my own time C. Maldarelli color *Popular Science* v289 no6 p78 N/D 2017

THE CROWNING TOUCH K. Hobson bw color diag *O, The Oprah Magazine* p95 O 2017

Breast milk

Bikers Who Deliver Breast Milk S. James color *Parents* v92 no5 p14 My 2017

breast practices J. MIGALA *Parents* v92 no7 p122 Jl 2017

bursting with goodness A. PALANJIAN color *Parents* v92 no8 p96 Ag 2017

crushing it L. SMITH BRODY *Parents* v91 no10 p98 O 2016

Breast pumps

preemie primer M. BEHEN *Parents* v92 no2 p100 F 2017

Breast surgery

See also

Mammaplasty

THE BENEFITS D. L. Colgan *Washingtonian Magazine* v52 no1 p117 O 2016

Breast tumor treatment

Women and heart disease [Cover story] *Mayo Clinic Health Letter* v35 no7 p1 Jl 2017

Breast tumors—Diagnosis

Breast Cancer Breaking News H. Levine color *Health* v31 no8 p74 O 2017

Breast tumors—Prevention

Breast Cancer Breaking News H. Levine color *Health* v31 no8 p74 O 2017

Top screenings to avoid cancer *Harvard Health Letter* v42 no2 p6 D 2016

Breast tumors—Risk factors

DON'T WORRY—IVF DOES NOT CAUSE CANCER *Health* v30 no9 p16 N 2016

Sleep & Your Health N. Brechka color *Better Nutrition* v79 no10 p6 O 2017

Breastfeeding (Humans)

Breast and Bottle for the Win! H. Pevzner color *Parents* v92 no9 p40 S 2017

breast practices J. MIGALA *Parents* v92 no7 p122 Jl 2017

HOW TO Wean When Your Toddler Resists A. KLEIN *Parents* v92 no11 p119 N 2017

IT'S COME TO THIS *Parents* v91 no9 p15 S 2016

Pumping on the Job *Glamour* v115 no5 p134 My 2017

Think About Pacifiers L. Anastasia *Parents* v92 no9 p163 S 2017

This Just In J. Zorthian *Time* v189 no13 p19 Ap 10 2017

The Unbreakable Relationship M. H. BAWANY, A. MILHAN et al *Islamic Horizons* v45 no6 p48 N/D 2016

Breastfeeding (Humans)—Humor

Life IN THESE UNITED STATES *Reader's Digest* v188 no1125 p50 N 2016

Breastfeeding (Humans)—Law & legislation

Proposal Keeps Two Key Benefits for Moms T. Berenson and M. Farber *Time* v189 no10 p15 Mr 20 2017

Breath holding

FREE FALLING PURSUITS P. Scott color *Bloomberg Businessweek* no4527 p83 Je 19 2017

Breathe (Film)

Love Takes Bravery Too S. Zacharek color *Time* v190 no16/17 p103 O 23 2017

Breathing exercises

The best medicine S. Sexton color *Yoga Journal* p108 2017 Special Issue

CHELSEA JACKSON ROBERTS color *Yoga Journal* no292 p12 Je 2017

Get Her in the Zen Zone S. SEA GOLD color *Parents* v92 no4 p30 Ap 2017

Goodnight, SLEEP ISSUES T. Eichenseher color *Yoga Journal* p102 2017 Special Issue

IN THIS SECTION color *Yoga Journal* p92 2017 Special Issue

Just breathe J. Levine color *Yoga Journal* p42 2017 Special Issue

POST-PRACTICE PAUSE H. Dowdle color *Yoga Journal* p112 2017 Special Issue

simple everyday practice K. HOLCOMBE color *Yoga Journal* p12 2017 Special Issue

The Stress Problems No One Talks About G. Saltz color *Health* v31 no3 p72 Ap 2017

You're in a funk S. Kempton color *Yoga Journal* p39 2016 Special Issue

ZEN FOR MEN [Cover story] M. EASTER cartoon color *Men's Health* v32 no1 p118 Ja/F 2017

Breathing exercises—Psychological aspects

Just breathe J. Levine color *Yoga Journal* p42 2017 Special Issue

Breaux Bridge (La.)

Adventures in Acadiana H. Hayes color map *Southern Living* v52 no5 p77 My 2017

Brechbuhler Architects PLLC

BIG SKY BEAUTY color *Timber Home Living* v27 no2 p80 Ap 2017

BRECHER, FRANK W.

A Peaceless Process *Commentary* v142 no2 p12 S 2016

Brecher, Piers

UNKNOWN: LOST LEADER bw *MHQ: Quarterly Journal of Military History* v30 no1 p87 Aut 2017

Brecher, Ron

Bright-Sky Imaging color *Sky & Telescope* v134 no5 p68 N 2017

CLUSTERS IN CONTRAST *Sky & Telescope* v133 no6 p74 Je 2017

READER GALLERY color *Astronomy* v45 no1 p72 Ja 2017

Restoring Detail with Deconvolution *Sky & Telescope* v134 no1 p68 Jl 2017

Brechka, Nicole

Don't Stress About It *Better Nutrition* v79 no9 p6 S 2017

Fun Gift Ideas *Better Nutrition* v78 no12 p6 D 2016

A Healthier & Happier 2017 *Better Nutrition* v79 no1 p6 Ja 2017

It's Cheesy color *Better Nutrition* v79 no11 p76 N 2017

Simply Superior *Better Nutrition* v78 no11 p6 N 2016

Sleep & Your Health color *Better Nutrition* v79 no10 p6 O 2017

Special Beauty Issue color *Better Nutrition* v79 no4 p6 Ap 2017

Stiff Competition *Better Nutrition* v79 no11 p6 N 2017

Stroke Awareness *Better Nutrition* p6 My 2017

Transform Yourself color *Better Nutrition* v79 no7 p62 Jl 2017

Vegan Family Meals color *Better Nutrition* v79 no10 p76 O 2017

Veganize Your Meal color *Better Nutrition* v79 no9 p60 S 2017

What Are You Missing? color *Better Nutrition* v79 no3 p6 Mr 2017

Brecht, M.

Neural correlates of ticklishness in the rat somatosensory cortex bibl graph *Science* v354 no6313 p757 N 11 2016

Breckels, Lisa M.

A subcellular map of the human proteome color *Science* v356 no6340 p820 My 26 2017

Breckenridge, Donald

And Then *Publishers Weekly* v264 no13 p71 Mr 27 2017

Bredenoord, Annelien L.

Human tissues in a dish: The research and ethical implications of organoid technology diag *Science* v355 no6322 p260 Ja 20 2017

Bredhoff, Stacey

JFK 100 Milestones & Mementos *Prologue* v49 no1 p48 Spr 2017

Breech delivery

baby's position A. PALANJIAN *Parents* v92 no7 p118 Jl 2017

Breed, Andrew C.

Role for migratory wild birds in the global spread of avian influenza H5N8 bibl graph map *Science* v354 no6309 p213 O 14 2016

Breeder reactors

50, 100 & 150 YEARS AGO color *Scientific American* v316 no5 p79 My 2017

Closing Japan's Monju fast breeder reactor: The possible implications M. Takubo bibl *Bulletin of the Atomic Scientists* v73 no3 p182 My 2017

Breeding

Season of Birth Can Affect Foal Size S. Dulai Wenholz color *Practical Horseman* v45 no11 p68 N 2017

Seeing Double *Earth Island Journal* v32 no1 p12 Spr 2017

wildlife quiz color *Cabin Living* p10 O 2017

Breen, Erin

2017 Southern Beauties C. Mckenzie and M. M. Brown color *Southern Living* v52 no10 p53 O 2017

Breen, Hannah Paramore—Interviews

HANNAH PARAMORE BREEN J. Chen color *Bloomberg Businessweek* no4525 p63 Je 5 2017

BREEN, JON L.

The Big Trial *Weekly Standard* v22 no41 p33 Jl 3 2017

Felonious Monk color *Weekly Standard* v22 no13 p42 D 5 2016

BREEN, KERRI

That's Dr. Clinton, to MSVU color *Maclean's* v129 no44 p48 N 7 2016

BREEN, MATTHEW

2016 YEAR IN REVIEW *Advocate* no1088 p32 D 2016/Ja 2017

OUR OWN ODYSSEY bw color *Advocate* no1089 p48 F/Mr 2017

Breen, T. H.

The Inventor of the Presidency G. S. Wood color *New York Review of Books* v64 no9 p34 My 25 2017

Breer, Albert

OUT OF OPTIONS color *Sports Illustrated* v127 no7 p112 S 4 2017

Brees, Drew, 1979-

CSI: MIAMI M. Rosenberg and J. Feldman color *Sports Illustrated* v126 no11 p52 Ap 17-24 2017

Breeze, Joe

VELOCI-RAPTURE A. Murphy color *Sports Illustrated* v127 no3 p98 Jl 24 2017

Bregman, Alexander—Interviews

Q&A WITH ALEXANDER BREGMAN color *Publishers Weekly* v263 no43 p(Sp)23 O 24 2016

Bregman, Peter

3 Timeless Rules for Making Tough Decisions *Harvard Business Review Digital Articles* p2 N 2 2015

3 Ways to Stop Yourself from Being Passive-Aggressive *Harvard Business Review Digital Articles* p2 Je 13 2016

5 Steps to Investing Your Energy More Wisely *Harvard Business Review Digital Articles* p2 Mr 8 2016

Are You Trying to Solve the Wrong Problem? *Harvard Business Review Digital Articles* p2 D 7 2015

Employees Can't Be Summed Up by a Personality Test *Harvard Business Review Digital Articles* p2 Ag 19 2015

Execution Is a People Problem, Not a Strategy Problem bw diag *Harvard Business Review Digital Articles* p2 Ja 4 2017

Get More Done During Your Commute *Harvard Business Review Digital Articles* p2 Ja 27 2015

A Healthier Approach to Business Travel *Harvard Business Review Digital Articles* p2 N 17 2015

The High Cost of Conformity, and How to Avoid It *Harvard Business Review Digital Articles* p2 O 21 2015

How Gratitude Can Help Your Career *Harvard Business Review Digital Articles* p2 O 1 2015

How Leaders Should React When Someone Disappoints *Harvard Business Review Digital Articles* p2 F 20 2015

How to Ask for Feedback That Will Actually Help You *Harvard Business Review Digital Articles* p2 D 5 2014

How to Read a Book a Week *Harvard Business Review Digital Articles* p2 F 8 2016

If You Want People to Listen, Stop Talking *Harvard Business Review Digital Articles* p2 My 25 2015

It's Your Job to Tell the Hard Truths *Harvard Business Review Digital Articles* p2 O 17 2014

The Magic of 30-Minute Meetings *Harvard Business Review Digital Articles* p2 F 22 2016

Managing the Critical Voices Inside Your Head *Harvard Business Review Digital Articles* p2 Ap 6 2015

Outsmart Your Next Angry Outburst *Harvard Business Review Digital Articles* p2 My 6 2016

Quash Your Bad Habits by Knowing What Triggers Them *Harvard Business Review Digital Articles* p2 O 8 2015

A Simple Formula for Changing Our Behavior *Harvard Business Review Digital Articles* p2 O 14 2015

The Small Personal Risks That Actually Change Behavior *Harvard Business Review Digital Articles* p2 N 17 2014

Stop Worrying About How Much You Matter *Harvard Business Review Digital Articles* p2 Je 25 2015

You Need to Practice Being Your Future Self *Harvard Business Review Digital Articles* p2 Mr 28 2016

Bregman, Rutger

MOVE OVER REALPOLITIK, IT'S TIME FOR UTOPIA *In These Times* v41 no3 p40 Mr 2017

Breguet SA

BREGUET 18K ROSE GOLD color *Magazine Antiques* v183 no6 p57 N/D 2016

Brehm, Alexander

Blocking promiscuous activation at cryptic promoters directs cell type–specific gene expression diag *Science* v356 no6339 p717 My 19 2017

Breijo, Stephanie

TAKE A DRIVE: RICHMOND color *Washingtonian Magazine* v52 no7 p123 Ap 2017

Breitbart News Network LLC

Breitbart Advertisers Take Political Fire, Too C. Giammona and G. Smith color *Bloomberg Businessweek* no4502 p31 D 5 2016

COMBAT REPORTING A. Beaujon *Washingtonian Magazine* v52 no5 p45 F 2017

THE RABBLE-ROUSER *Texas Monthly* v45 no2 p90 F 2017

Breitbart News Network LLC—Officials & employees

THE MEGAPHONE W. S. HYLTON *New York Times Magazine* p30 Ag 20 2017

BREITBERG, FRED

An Engineer's Approach to Modern Big Band Recording color *Downbeat* v84 no2 p92 F 2017

Breitenlechner, Martin

Global atmospheric particle formation from CERN CLOUD measurements bibl graph map *Science* v354 no6316 p1119 D 2 2016

Breitling SA

BREITLING AEROSPACE EVO CIRRUS AIRCRAFT WATCH color *Flying* v144 no2 p15 F 2017

BREITLING'S LATEST color *Flying* v144 no6 p13 Je 2017

FLOATS LIKE A BUTTERFLY N. Sullivan color *Esquire* p41 O 2017

LET'S MEET IN NEW YORK color *Flying* v144 no11 p82 N 2017

Breker, Joe

10 SUCCESSFUL FARMERS: JOE BREKER G. Johnson *Successful Farming* v115 no8 p14 Je/Jl 2017

Brekke, Gregg

Hundreds of clergy gather in North Dakota to back people blocking pipeline color *Christian Century* v133 no25 p13 D 7 2016

Brekke, Torkel

Faithonomics: Religion and the Free Market R. N. Cooper *Foreign Affairs* v96 no2 p170 Mr/Ap 2017

Brekken, Isaac

Nevada voted twice for President Obama, but Republicans have spent millions trying to win its U.S. Senate seat—and perhaps the state color *Bloomberg Businessweek* no4498 p39 N 7 2016

Brem, Tommi

Projecting the Reflected Soul: San Francisco Opera's Mirror Solution for Don Giovanni M. S. Eddy *Stage Directions* v30 no9 p16 S 2017

BREMERICH, VANESSA

Freshwater Megafauna: Flagships for Freshwater Biodiversity under Threat *BioScience* v67 no10 p919 O 2017

Bremmer, Ian

2017 Might Not Be Europe's 'Year of the Populist' After All *Time* v189 no9 p12 Mr 13 2017

Argentina's Mauricio Macri on the Challenge of Change color *Time* v188 no18 p12 O 31 2016

Britain's Theresa May Is All-In on Brexit With Lousy Cards *Time* v189 no4 p12 F 6 2017

Can Tunisia Remain a Beacon of Democracy for the Arab World? color *Time* v190 no5 p21 Jl 31 2017

Chile's President on Her Country's Fitful Progress and Future Challenges color *Time* v189 no22 p10 Je 12 2017

The Countries That Fear Trump Most color map *Time* v189 no3 p44 Ja 30 2017

Dealt a Weak Hand, Rex Tillerson Is Still In the Game at State color *Time* v190 no7 p12 Ag 21 2017

Egypt's al-Sisi Finds a Kindred Spirit In President Trump *Time* v189 no14 p14 Ap 17 2017

The Era of American Global Leadership Is Over. Here's What Comes Next color *Time* v188 no27-28 p21 D 26 2016

Five World Leaders Who Are Less Popular Than President Trump color *Time* v189 no21 p12 Je 5 2017

The Harsh Reality of Brexit Sets In *Time* v188 no16/17 p8 O 24 2016

How Singapore Sees Asia-and America *Time* v188 no19 p10 N 7 2016

Indefatigable Merkel Complicates Europe's Need to Reform color *Time* v189 no20 p10 My 29 2017

India's Youth and Liberty Are Looking Less Like Advantages Over China color *Time* v190 no10/11 p17 S 18 2017

Kiev and the Kremlin Face Narrowing Options In Ukraine *Time* v189 no12 p16 Ap 3 2017

Liberal Democracy Is Eroding Right In Europe's Backyard *Time* v190 no6 p16 Ag 7 2017

Lightbox color *Time* v190 no4 p14 Jl 24 2017

Merkel May Be Struggling, but Don't Count Her Out *Time* v189 no6 p12 F 20 2017

Middle East Rifts Are Widening Amid a Global Power Vacuum *Time* v189 no24 p10 Je 26 2017

Peru Is a Bright Spot on the Global Stage color *Time* v188 no24 p19 D 12 2016

The Qatar Rift Is the Middle East's 'Trump Effect' In Action color *Time* v189 no23 p14 Je 19 2017

The Real Cost of 'Forced Transparency' *Time* v189 no11 p14 Mr 27 2017

The Real Story in U.S.-Russia Relations Can Be Seen In the Skies Above Syria *Time* v190 no1 p12 Jl 3 2017

The Saga of Kenya's Disputed Election Is a Good-News Story *Time* v190 no12 p14 S 25 2017

Sorry, Brits: Abe and Trump Have the Real 'Special Relationship' *Time* v189 no7/8 p18 F 27 2017

South Korea's Familial Presidential Family Scandal *Time* v188 no20 p10 N 14 2016

The Startling Rise of the Brash Young Man Who Would Be King of Saudi Arabia color *Time* v190 no2/3 p10 Jl 10-17 2017

The Top Global Risks for 2017, a Year of Geopolitical Recession color *Time* v189 no3 p8 Ja 16 2017

To Reinvent Itself, Saudi Arabia Must Empower Its Women *Time* v189 no10 p10 Mr 20 2017

Trump's Desire for a Better Deal With Iran Could Isolate the U.S *Time* v190 no15 p12 O 16 2017

Trump's Foreign Policy Is Unilateral-and Worrying color *Time* v188 no21 p22 N 21 2016

Trump's Hard Line on Mexico Gives Left-Wing Populist an Opening *Time* v189 no5 p12 F 13 2017

Trump's New World Order Puts Nation Over Globe color *Time* v189 no4 p24 Ja 23 2017

Trump Will Thaw Chilly U.S.-Russia Relationship *Time* v188 no22-23 p12 N/D 2016

Turkey's Erdogan Threatens a Breakup With the E.U *Time* v189 no13 p10 Ap 10 2017

Turkey-U.S. Relations are Going from Bad to Much, Much Worse *Time* v190 no16/17 p16 O 23 2017

The U.S. Can Win a Trade War With China. That Doesn't Mean It Should Try color *Time* v190 no8 p19 Ag 28 2017

The U.S. Has a Weak Hand In Syria-and Russia Knows It *Time* v188 no14 p10 O 10 2016

Venezuela Nears a Tipping Point, and a Violent Endgame color *Time* v189 no18 p14 My 15 2017

Viktor Orban Is Turning Hungary Into Europe's Black Sheep color *Time* v189 no15 p12 Ap 24 2017

The Wave to Come color *Time* v189 no19 p38 My 22 2017

Why Referendums Have Been Backfiring *Time* v188 no15 p8 O

17 2016

Will Nigeria's Ailing President Name a Successor? *Time* v190 no9 p14 S 4 2017

Yes, Merkel Won Again. But the Fires of European Populism Are Still Raging color *Time* v190 no14 p16 O 9 2017

Bremmer, Ian—Interviews

What's at Stake in an Economy with Low Oil Prices J. Kehoe *Harvard Business Review Digital Articles* p2 F 15 2016

Why Europe Tops 2015's List of Global Risks J. Kehoe *Harvard Business Review Digital Articles* p2 Ja 9 2015

Bren, Kara L.

Locked and loaded for apoptosis diag *Science* v356 no6344 p1236 Je 23 2017

Brende, Eric

DISPUTED MATERIAL *Commonweal* v144 no13 p2 Ag 11 2017

No One Expects the Inquisition [Cover story] color *Commonweal* v144 no10 p17 Je 2 2017

Brendel, Alfred

The Growing Charm of Dada bw cartoon color *New York Review of Books* v63 no16 p22 O 27 2016

Brendel, David

Asking Open-Ended Questions Helps New Managers Build Trust *Harvard Business Review Digital Articles* p2 S 17 2015

How Mindfulness Improves Executive Coaching *Harvard Business Review Digital Articles* p2 Ja 29 2016

Manage Stress by Knowing What You Value *Harvard Business Review Digital Articles* p2 S 8 2015

There Are Risks to Mindfulness at Work *Harvard Business Review Digital Articles* p2 F 11 2015

To Succeed as a First-Time Leader, Relax *Harvard Business Review Digital Articles* p1 S 30 2016

Brenden, Kevin

UNSOLICITED BETA *Climbing* no355 p14 Ag 2017

Brennaman, Marty, 1942-

LOUD & CLEAR C. FEHRMAN bw color *Cincinnati Magazine* v51 no1 p74 O 2017

BRENNAN, ANN MARIE

Exploring God's Call color *America* v215 no18 p27 D 5 2016

Brennan, Cait

POP ROCKS: Meet rock's next big thing: middle-aged, but still nerdy, trans girl Cait Brennan J. ANDERSON-MINSHALL *Advocate* no1093 p24 O/N 2017

BRENNAN, CALEB

THE BERNIECRATS PAINTING TRUMP COUNTRY BLUE *In These Times* v41 no7 p11 Jl 2017

THE GHOST OF CAPITALISM PAST *In These Times* v41 no8 p39 Ag 2017

Brennan, Jack—Interviews

JACK BRENNAN J. WILLIAMS *Cincinnati Magazine* v50 no5 p80 F 2017

Brennan, Jason

BLAMING THE PEOPLE MÜLLER color *Nation* v305 no8 p31 O 9 2017

NONE OF THE ABOVE C. CRAIN cartoon *New Yorker* v92 no36 p67 N 7 2016

Brennan, Kevin

Occasional Soulmates *Publishers Weekly* v264 no21 p68 My 22 2017

Brennan, Marc A.

Community network for deaf scientists color *Science* v356 no6336 p386 Ap 28 2017

Brennan, Marie

Within the Sanctuary of Wings: A Memoir by Lady Trent *Publishers Weekly* v264 no9 p81 F 27 2017

Brennan, Michael

To Persuade People, Trade PowerPoint for Papier-Mâché *Harvard Business Review Digital Articles* p2 N 29 2016

Brennan, Thomas J.

The Emotional Fallout from War F. O'reilly color *Publishers Weekly* v264 no30 p34 Jl 24 2017

Shooting Ghosts: A U.S. Marine, a Combat Photographer, and Their Journey Back from War *Publishers Weekly* v264 no40 p134 O 2 2017

A Veteran's Odyssey G. GURLEY *Publishers Weekly* v264 no23 p42 Je 5 2017

Brennan, Tom

RIDE YOUR HUNTER ROUND LIKE A PRO color *Practical Horseman* v45 no3 p36 Mr 2017

RIDE YOUR HUNTER ROUND LIKE A PRO [Cover story] color *Practical Horseman* v45 no2 p28 F 2017

We Deserve Fair Play *In Stride* v12 no2 p25 Mr 2017

BRENNAN, WILLIAM

Bulletproofing bw color *Atlantic* v319 no1 p26 Ja/F 2017

Brenneman, Amy

The Leftovers *TV Guide* v65 no21 p34 My 15 2017

Brennen, Linda

What My Horse Wears on His Feet cartoon *Horse & Rider* v56 no5 p80 My 2017

BRENNER, AL

YEA BOXY BRONCOS, NAY BEATNIK BOLSHEVIKS bw color *Forbes* v200 no2 p31 S 5 2017

BRENNER, DOUGLAS

BACK TO THE LAND color *House Beautiful* v159 no8 p96 O 2017

Call of the Wild color *House Beautiful* p76 Jl 2017

FAMILY STYLE bw color *Architectural Digest* v74 no4 p168 Ap 2017

GARDEN STATE OF MIND color *House Beautiful* v159 no4 p80 My 2017

A New Americana color *House Beautiful* v159 no9 p94 N 2017

Brenner, Jamie

The Forever Summer *Publishers Weekly* v264 no9 p73 F 27 2017

Brenner, Joel

Pain POINTERS H. Rolfe color *Dance Spirit* v21 no8 p48 O 2017

BRENNER, MARIE

DEAL with the DEVIL bw color *Vanity Fair* v59 no8 p84 Ag 2017

OSLO CONFIDENTIAL color *Vanity Fair* v59 no5 p133 Ap 2017

BRENNER, YONI

SURPRISE OUTCOMES TO THE MUELLER PROBE cartoon *New Yorker* v93 no20 p33 Jl 10 2017

Brentwood Home LLC

... And 15 Other Casper Types *New York* v50 no9 p70 My 1 2017

Bresch, Heather, 1969-

LAST CALL / 2016 cartoon *Vanity Fair* v59 no1 p134 Holiday 2017

Breshears, Danielle

Bourbon, Brews, BBQ & Blues color *Missouri Life* v44 no4 p44 Je 2017

DELI DELIGHTS color *Missouri Life* v44 no3 p72 My 2017

EAT MO NUTS! *Missouri Life* v43 no7 p70 D 2016/Ja 2017

from groceries to gossip bw color *Missouri Life* v44 no6 p52 S 2017

Noble Parentage color *Missouri Life* v44 no2 p98 Ap 2017

Breslauer, George W.

Images of the Future diag *Daedalus* v146 no2 p142 Spr 2017

Breslaw, Anna

FIRST COMES LOVE... color *Women's Health* v14 no6 p114 Jl 2017

GET UP Stand Up [Cover story] bw color *Women's Health* v13 no10 p103 D 2016

Hotter Sex in Just Minutes! *Men's Health* v32 no6 p97 Ag 2017

In Defense of Emotional Cheating color *Glamour* v115 no3 p140 Mr 2017

"My face told me to stop partying" *Glamour* v115 no6 p76 Je 2017

We Retired Before 35 color *Glamour* v115 no10 p136 O 2017

WORK-LIFE BALANCE IS A SHAM cartoon diag *Women's Health* v14 no3 p146 Ap 2017

BRESLER, ROBERT J.

Game On!!! *USA Today Magazine* v145 no2862 p10 Mr 2017

If Given the Chance, the Dems Will Make the U.S. into a "Flabby Europe" *USA Today Magazine* v146 no2868 p10 S 2017

The Long March to Bedlam *USA Today Magazine* v146 no2866 p13 Jl 2017

The Polarization Trap *USA Today Magazine* v145 no2864 p13 My 2017

TRUMP'S OPPORTUNITY AND AGENDA *USA Today Magazine* v145 no2860 p12 Ja 2017

The Way We Were/Are *USA Today Magazine* v145 no2858 p13 N 2016

Breslin, Abigail, 1996-

BABY'S BACK: The cast of ABC's reimagined Dirty Dancing

gives the classic '80s film a musical lift A. D'ARMINIO *TV Guide* v65 no21 p26 My 15 2017

Dirty Dancing's Dynamic Duo A. D'Arminio *TV Guide* v65 no14 p9 Ap 3 2017

JUNE @ GH color *Good Housekeeping* v264 no6 p10 Je 2017

Breslin, Jimmy, 1928-2017

Jimmy Breslin G. Troy color *Time* v189 no12 p18 Ap 3 2017

Bresman, Henrik

What Millennials Want from Work, Charted Across the World *Harvard Business Review Digital Articles* p2 F 23 2015

Bresson, Robert, 1901-1999

L'Argent R. Brody *New Yorker* v92 no33 p13 O 17 2016

PREACHING WHAT YOU PRACTICE D. SULLIVAN bw color *Film Comment* v52 no6 p78 N/D 2016

Bresteau, Enzo

Tubular clathrin/AP-2 lattices pinch collagen fibers to support 3D cell migration color *Science* v356 no6343 p1138 Je 16 2017

Breton, Thierry

Some Companies Are Banning Email and Getting More Done D. Burkus *Harvard Business Review Digital Articles* p2 Je 8 2016

Bretscher, Hope

Promoting human rights through science color *Science* v357 no6359 p34 O 6 2017

Brett, Jeanne

How to Handle a Disagreement on Your Team *Harvard Business Review Digital Articles* p2 Jl 10 2017

What Chinese Companies Want from International Deals *Harvard Business Review Digital Articles* p2 F 12 2015

Brettel, Klaus

An algal photoenzyme converts fatty acids to hydrocarbons color graph *Science* v357 no6354 p903 S 1 2017

Brettel, Malte

Research: How a New CEO Can Make a Firm More Entrepreneurial *Harvard Business Review Digital Articles* p2 N 17 2016

Brettell, Logan

Anything You Can Do ... J. Fuchs and T. Keith color *Sports Illustrated* v126 no2 p23 Ja 16 2017

Brettell, Steve

Shelf Life D. L. NG color *Field & Stream* v121 no6 p10 N 2016

Brettschneider, Brian

Hot Alaska: As the Climate Warms, Alaska Experiences Record High Temperatures color graph map *Weatherwise* v69 no6 p12 N-D 2016

Bretz, T.

Observation of a large-scale anisotropy in the arrival directions of cosmic rays above 8×10^{18} eV *Science* v357 no6357 p1266 S 22 2017

Breuillac, Antoine

High-performance vitrimers from commodity thermoplastics through dioxaborolane metathesis color diag *Science* v356 no6333 p62 Ap 7 2017

Brevard, Aleshia

GOODBYE, BOMBSHELL: Aleshia Brevard was one of the first trans actresses on the silver screen D. ARTAVIA *Advocate* no1093 p13 O/N 2017

Breville Group Ltd.

THE BLENDER color *Men's Health* v32 no8 p84 O 2017

Breviro Caviar (Company)

GOVERNMENT DREAMS AND CAVIAR WISHES M. CAMPBELL color *Maclean's* v129 no43 p18 O 31 2016

Brew, Mark

Keep On Turning: New artistic director Marc Brew has big plans for AXIS C. Bauer *Dance Magazine* v91 no10 p16 O 2017

BrewDog PLC

INVASION OF THE PUNKS B. Warner color *Fortune* v174 no8 p176 D 15 2016

Brewer, Brad

THE SWING OF A KING color *Golf Magazine* v58 no12 p67 D 2016

Brewer, Carolyn Glenn

Breaking Jazz's Glass Ceiling T. PERKINS color *Downbeat* v84 no7 p65 Jl 2017

BREWER, JACK

USING SPORT TO END HUNGER AND ACHIEVE FOOD SECURITY *UN Chronicle* v53 no2 p39 2016

Brewer, John

Ben Franklin: Caught Between Worlds color *New York Review of Books* v63 no17 p42 N 10 2016

BREWER, MARK

Blue Laws? Blame the Puritans color *Yankee* v80 no6 p24 N/D 2016

Brewer, William

For Better, for Verse color *Publishers Weekly* v264 no14 p42 Ap 3. 2017

I Know Your Kind *Publishers Weekly* v264 no26 p151 Je 26 2017

Breweries

See also

Microbreweries

Before Prohibition, Breweries Made Advertising an Art E. Machulak *Humanities* v37 no4 p1 Fall 2016

FROM DIRT TO GLASS E. J. Wallace *Virginia Living* v15 no2 p21 F 2017

HOPPY TRAILS M. P. SPENCER bw color *Louisiana Life* v37 no5 p32 My/Je 2017

JULIA STREET / WITH POYDRAS THE PARROT J. STREET bw *New Orleans Magazine* v51 no3 p20 Ja 2017

Palace Diner: With the greatest tuna melt in lunch counter history, a 15-seat dining car becomes an anchor for a Maine mill town's revival A. TRAVERSO color *Yankee* p50 Jl 2017

YOUR BEDTIME IS 9 PM *Indianapolis Monthly* p67 F 2017

Breweries—Competitions

BEST NEW Breweries R. Annis, A. Lynch et al *Indianapolis Monthly* v40 no11 p57 Jl 2017

Breweries—Evaluation

Belgian Bites M. MCLAUGHLIN color *Indianapolis Monthly* v41 no2 p39 S 2017

Better With Age M. Rubino *Indianapolis Monthly* v40 no11 p10 Jl 2017

News From the Kitchens R. Peyton color *New Orleans Magazine* v51 no9 p82 Jl 2017

SOUTH'S BEST BREWERY K. Purvis color *Southern Living* v52 no4 p72 Ap 2017

Breweries—Management

BEST NEW Breweries R. Annis, A. Lynch et al *Indianapolis Monthly* v40 no11 p57 Jl 2017

Better With Age M. Rubino *Indianapolis Monthly* v40 no11 p10 Jl 2017

Breweries—Remodeling for other use

Farewell, Lebanon's First Brewery D. KENNER color *Foreign Policy* no225 p21 Jl/Ag 2017

Brewing

See also

Beer brewing

BREWING BEER The Basic: Bottle your own beer by using four ingredients and following four steps C. Colby *Mother Earth News* no284 p35 O/N 2017

Real Ginger Beer F. MAROUKIAN color *Popular Mechanics* p22 Jl 2017

Verde Brewing Co K. MONTGOMERY *Arizona Highways* v93 no2 p12 F 2017

Brewing industry

Raising the Bar color *O, The Oprah Magazine* p28 S 2017

Brewing industry laws

The Bavarian beer purity law is adopted *History Today* v67 no4 p9 Ap 2017

Brewing industry—United States

Tipping Point J. VOREL *Atlanta* v56 no8 p70 D 2016

BREWITT, KIMBERLY

Long-Term Studies Contribute Disproportionately to Ecology and Policy *BioScience* v67 no3 p271 Mr 2017

Brewpubs

This Month in Beer N. RICHARDSON, A. DELANY et al color *Bon Appetit* no8 p24 Ag 2017

Brewster, Jack

Beyond Repeal and Replace color diag map *Time* v190 no2/3 p30 Jl 10-17 2017

Jeff Flake color *Time* v190 no7 p56 Ag 21 2017

The Secret History of Election 2016 [Cover story] color map *Time* v190 no5 p32 Jl 31 2017

Brewster, Janice

2017 Renovation SHOWCASE color *Cabin Living* p47 Je 2017

all-inclusive space SAVERS color *Cabin Living* p54 Mr 2017

Better Together color *Cabin Living* p44 Ja/F 2017

BUILDING small color *Cabin Living* p42 Mr 2017

chance OF SHOWERS color *Cabin Living* p51 S 2017

CLOSETS color *Cabin Living* p40 Ja/F 2017

Creating a Getaway to Share color diag *Log Home Living* v34 no3 p38 Ap 2017

DESIGNING a dream color diag *Cabin Living* p66 D 2016

EXPERT ADVICE FROM LOG PROVIDERS FOR FINISHING YOUR CABIN BUILD color *Cabin Living* p43 S 2017

Home with a View color diag *Log Home Living* v34 no5 p52 Jl 2017

Just Add Water color *Timber Home Living* v27 no5 p26 O 2017

Lakeside Living color diag *Log Home Living* v34 no9 p36 D 2017

make a SPLASH color *Cabin Living* p52 Ap 2017

Midwestern Masterpiece [Cover story] color diag *Log Home Living* p76 2018 Annual Buyers Guide

THE NATURE OF ALL Things [Cover story] color *Cabin Living* p44 Ag 2017

Past and Present color diag *Log Home Living* v34 no7 p42 S 2017

PERFECTLY Seasoned color *Cabin Living* p44 Je 2017

polishing a gem [Cover story] color diag *Cabin Living* p26 O 2017

Ranch with a View color diag *Log Home Living* v34 no4 p40 My 2017

ReTRO-A-Go-Go color *Cabin Living* p38 D 2016

RISE AND SHINE color *Cabin Living* p46 O 2017

Rolling on the River bw color diag *Log Home Living* v34 no6 p40 Ag 2017

A SHORE THING color *Cabin Living* p38 Ap 2017

two's better than one [Cover story] color diag *Cabin Living* p28 Ag 2017

Brexit Referendum, 2016

As Brexit Negotiations Start, Companies Need Contingency Plans P. Ghemawat *Harvard Business Review Digital Articles* p2 Je 16 2017

THE BATTLE FOR BRITAIN E. CAESAR color *Esquire* p124 O 2017

Brexit Could Deepen Europe's Digital Recession B. Chakravorti *Harvard Business Review Digital Articles* p2 Jl 5 2016

The Brexit Door *Hoover Digest: Research & Opinion on Public Policy* no4 p33 Fall 2016

Brexit's Irish Question F. O'toole color *New York Review of Books* v64 no14 p43 S 28 2017

The Brexit Voter and the Trump Voter J. MILLER *In These Times* v40 no12 p42 D 2016

BRITAIN'S MIDSUMMER FEVER DREAM J. Harris color *Nation* v305 no4 p16 Ag 14 2017

Britain's Theresa May Is All-In on Brexit With Lousy Cards I. Bremmer *Time* v189 no4 p12 F 6 2017

A BUDDHIST BREXIT S. BATCHELOR color *Tricycle: The Buddhist Review* v26 no3 p68 Spr 2017

Dover and Out [Cover story] J. Freedland color *New York Review of Books* v64 no8 p22 My 11 2017

Election 2017: the key issues: Which battlegrounds will shape Britain's trip to the polls this June? *People Management* p15 My 2017

Figuring Out Which Companies and Industries Will Be Most Damaged by Brexit P. Ghemawat *Harvard Business Review Digital Articles* p2 Mr 29 2017

Five Paths for the EU D. GREEN color *Weekly Standard* v22 no28 p14 Mr 27 2017

In 2016, Lies, the Whole Lies and Nothing but the Lies J. Stein color *Time* v188 no25-26 p158 D 19 2016 Double Issue

Jeremy Corbyn's Judgment Day J. MILLER *In These Times* v41 no6 p41 Je 2017

A Lesson for America G. Younge il *Nation* v303 no20 p10 N 14 2016

May Day G. Wood color *Vogue* v207 no4 p204 Ap 2017

May Poll C. CALDWELL color *Weekly Standard* v22 no32 p16 My 1 2017

OUR VISION FOR BRITAIN AFTER THE BREXIT *Vital Speeches of the Day* v82 no12 p378 D 2016

Preparing for Brexit Just Got Harder T. Ross color *Bloomberg Businessweek* no4507 p15 Ja 16 2017

The Prime Minister Goes All In D. GREEN color *Weekly Standard* v22 no20 p14 Ja 30 2017

Publishers Keep Calm And Carry On A. Albanese, N. Denn et al

Weekly no1478 / 1479 p30 Ag 18-25 2017
STEPHEN KING & SON color *Entertainment Weekly* no1484 p60 S 29 2017
SUPER FUNNY color *Entertainment Weekly* no1436/1437 p52 O 21 2016
Tom Holland color *Entertainment Weekly* no1444/1445 p59 D 16 2016
TRANSFORMERS: THE LAST KNIGHT color *Entertainment Weekly* no1463/1464 p52 Ap/My 2017
WarReN BEAtty An ORAL HISTORY color *Entertainment Weekly* no1440 p30 N 18 2016
What Really Happened After This Kiss in E.T.? color *Entertainment Weekly* no1460/1461 p46 Ap 7-17 2017
WHAT'S NEXT FOR THE TRANSFORMERS? color *Entertainment Weekly* no1472 p43 Je 30 2017
Who Is The Last Jedi? color *Entertainment Weekly* no1451/1452 p13 F 3-10 2017
Your Sunshiny, Stupendous, Seriously Spectacular SUMMER BUCKET LIST color *Entertainment Weekly* no1470 p32 Je 16 2017

Breznitz, Dan
What the U.S. Should Be Doing to Protect Intellectual Property *Harvard Business Review Digital Articles* p2 Ja 27 2016
Why Silicon Valley Shouldn't Be the Model for Innovation *Harvard Business Review Digital Articles* p2 N 18 2014

Briant, Pierre
AN IDEA OF ALEXANDER P. Cartledge *History Today* v67 no8 p94 Ag 2017

Brianton, Kevin
Hollywood Divided: The 1950 Screen Directors Guild Meeting and the Impact of the Blacklist J. HEMPHILL *Film Quarterly* v71 no1 p117 Fall 2017

Bribery
The best way to get a little help color *Redbook* p103 My 2017
A Development Bank Stops Lending Abroad D. Biller, J. Brice et al color *Bloomberg Businessweek* no4503 p13 D 12 2016
UPSIDE DOWN, ON THE CEILING J. FIELDEN color *Esquire* v167 no2 p36 Mr 2017

Bribery—Latin America
BRAZIL'S CARWASH SCANDAL T. Padgett color *Bloomberg Businessweek* no4524 p8 My 29 2017
Will Bad Beef Taint Brazil's Meat Master? G. Freitas Jr., J. Brice et al cartoon chart *Bloomberg Businessweek* no4516 p20 Mr 27 2017

Bribicseas, Richard G.
Men, and Mortality *Natural History* v124 no10 p28 N 2016

Brice, Jessica
Brazil Has a School Problem diag *Bloomberg Businessweek* no4513 p24 Mr 6 2017
A Development Bank Stops Lending Abroad color *Bloomberg Businessweek* no4503 p13 D 12 2016
A Gold Rush in Mexico's Deadly South color *Bloomberg Businessweek* no4497 p20 O 31 2016
In Brazil, It's Now Beer—Without the Babes color *Bloomberg Businessweek* no4508 p20 Ja 23 2017
Will Bad Beef Taint Brazil's Meat Master? cartoon chart *Bloomberg Businessweek* no4516 p20 Mr 27 2017

BRICKELL, SUSAN
coming up ROSES color *Better Homes & Gardens* v95 no2 p16 F 2016
it's a colorful life cartoon color *Better Homes & Gardens* v95 no4 p10 Ap 2017
STRONGER & FASTER cartoon color *Better Homes & Gardens* v95 no2 p132 F 2016

Bricker Labs (Company)
Autumn Crush color *Amazing Wellness* p96 Fall 2017

BRICKLIN, JONATHAN
Walking Backward Toward the Future cartoon *Tricycle: The Buddhist Review* v26 no3 p26 Spr 2017

BRICKMAN, LAUREN
These Are Your Sexual Rights color *Glamour* v114 no7 p94 Jl 2016

Bricks
10 Misunderstood Materials color *Old House Journal* v45 no3 p44 My 2017
Brick by Brick M. Cockram bw color *Architectural Record* v205

no2 p100 F 2017
Postwar Challenges M. E. POLSON color *Old House Journal* v45 no3 p40 My 2017

BRICS countries—Congresses
USHERING IN THE NEXT GOLDEN DECADE Zhou Xiaoyan and P. Tobey *Bloomberg Businessweek* no4536 p4 S 4 2017

BRICS countries—Foreign economic relations
USHERING IN THE NEXT GOLDEN DECADE Zhou Xiaoyan and P. Tobey *Bloomberg Businessweek* no4536 p4 S 4 2017

Bridal shops—Evaluation
Go Get Your Gown! color *Glamour* v115 no5 p62 My 2017
WESTSIDE STORY M. L. BIKOFF *Atlanta* v56 no7 p50 N 2016

Bridenstine, Jim, 1975-
Oklahoma politician picked to lead NASA back to the moon P. Voosen color *Science* v357 no6355 p957 S 8 2017

Brideshead Revisited (Film)
Brideshead Reunited M. LINDSAY-HOGG color *Vanity Fair* v58 no12 p148 D 2016

Brideshead Revisited (TV program)
CLASH OF THE TITANS W. T. GULLETTE, F. K. PLOUS et al cartoon *Vanity Fair* p84 Hollywood 2017 Supplement

Bridesmaids (Film)
Paul Rudd Was a Nightmare in Bridesmaids N. Sperling color *Entertainment Weekly* no1460/1461 p94 Ap 7-17 2017

Brideson, Cynthia
Dancin' in the Rain J. BASINGER *New York Times Book Review* p46 Je 4 2017

Bridge, Candice—Interviews
TO CATCH A PREDATOR J. Thompson color *Essence* v47 no10 p66 F 2017

Bridge, Rebecca
we asked you answered color *Cabin Living* p8 D 2016

Bridge, Tom C. L.
The broad footprint of climate change from genes to biomes to people bibl chart color *Science* v354 no6313 paaf7671-1 N 11 2016

Bridge demolition
TO THE BRIDGE D. Smith cartoon *New Yorker* v93 no24 p16 Ag 21 2017

Bridge Alternative Middle School (Lowell, Mass.)
Managing stress for at-risk students E. J. Spiegel color il *Phi Delta Kappan* v98 no6 p42 Mr 2017

Bridgeman, A.
Observation of a large-scale anisotropy in the arrival directions of cosmic rays above 8×1018 eV *Science* v357 no6357 p1266 S 22 2017

Bridger Bowl (Bozeman, Mont.)
Old School E. STIFLER WOLFE bw color *Powder* v46 no2 p48 O 2017

Bridges
ELK RIVER K. WRIGHT color *Idaho Magazine* v16 no1 p32 O 2016

Bridges, Craig A.
Neutron scattering in the proximate quantum spin liquid a-RuCl3 bw diag *Science* v356 no6342 p1055 Je 9 2017

Bridges, Fidelia, 1834 or 5-1923 or 4
WOMEN AND WATER COLOR K. A. Foster cartoon color *Magazine Antiques* v184 no2 p84 Mr/Ap 2017

Bridges, Mark—Interviews
A Fine Cut C. LAVERTY bw cartoon *Film Comment* v53 no5 p16 S/O 2017

Bridges, Pat
ANGLE GRINDERS bw color *Snowboarder* v29 no2 p142 O 2016
BOARDER SECURITY color *Snowboarder* v29 no2 p26 O 2016
FOURTHCOMING bw color *Snowboarder* v29 no4 p68 D 2016
GEAR TO TIE DYE FOR color *Snowboarder* v29 no3 p128 N 2016
POWDER 80'S color *Snowboarder* v29 no2 p138 O 2016
SHORTIES — LESS IS MORE cartoon color *Snowboarder* v29 no4 p132 D 2016
SNOW BALLERS color *Snowboarder* v29 no4 p128 D 2016
SQUAD GOALS cartoon color *Snowboarder* v29 no5 p118 Ja 2017
SUPER FRIENDS color *Snowboarder* v29 no5 p24 Ja 2017
SUPER PARK 20 bw cartoon color *Snowboarder* v29 no5 p42

Ja 2017

TOP OF THE FALL LINE color *Snowboarder* v29 no3 p132 N 2016

ZERO DEGREES OF SEPERATION cartoon color *Snowboarder* v29 no4 p26 D 2016

Bridges, Ruby, 1954-

A child leads P. W. Marty *Christian Century* v134 no7 p3 Mr 29 2017

Bridges—California—Design & construction

Sixth Street Viaduct D. S. Glenn *Architectural Record* v205 no4 p207 Ap 2017

Bridges—Design & construction

DC HAS ITS BEST SHOT AT BRIDGING THE EAST/WEST-OF-THE-RIVER DIVIDE S. COURTNEY *Washingtonian Magazine* v52 no7 p106 Ap 2017

No Cars Allowed A. Marshall *Governing* v30 no3 p22 D 2016

A preacher builds bridges B. K. Modahl color *Christian Century* v134 no3 p24 F 2017

Bridges—Indiana

BRIDGE TO THE PAST E. Taylor color *Indianapolis Monthly* v41 no2 p70 S 2017

Bridges—Maintenance & repair

Boulevard Dreams A. Ehrenhalt *Governing* v30 no3 p14 D 2016

BRIDGING THE JAMES B. HUNHOFF *South Dakota Magazine* v32 no6 p20 Mr/Ap 2017

Bridges—New York (State)—New York

TO THE BRIDGE D. Smith cartoon *New Yorker* v93 no24 p16 Ag 21 2017

Bridgespan Group (Company)

An Open Office Experiment That Actually Worked P. Rosenberg and K. Campbell *Harvard Business Review Digital Articles* p2 O 3 2014

Bridges—South Dakota

WHERE THE BRIDGES ARE *South Dakota Magazine* v32 no6 p29 Mr/Ap 2017

Bridget Jones's Baby (Film)

COME TOGETHER A. LANE cartoon *New Yorker* v92 no30 p78 S 26 2016

Bridgewater Associates LP

Radical Transparency Can Reduce Bias—but Only If It's Done Right F. Gino *Harvard Business Review Digital Articles* p2 O 10 2017

Bridgham, Jamie T.

Predicting the basis of convergent evolution bibl color *Science* v354 no6310 p289 O 21 2016

Bridles

See also

Bits (Bridles)

Tack Room color *Practical Horseman* v45 no7 p69 Jl 2017

Bridles—Evaluation

emporium color *Dressage Today* p64 My 2017

Brie, Alison, 1982-

Budget Wrestling Lights Up the Screen In Glow D. D'addario color *Time* v190 no2/3 p93 Jl 10-17 2017

GLOW *TV Guide* v65 no27 p34 Je 26 2017

Briechle, F. L.

Observation of a large-scale anisotropy in the arrival directions of cosmic rays above 8 × 1018 eV *Science* v357 no6357 p1266 S 22 2017

Bried, Erin

31 DAY HAPPY * LIFE MAKEOVER color *Good Housekeeping* v264 no1 p81 Ja 1 2017

What Children Can Teach Us About Acceptance *Parents* v91 no10 p16 O 2016

Why it's COOL to be KIND [Cover story] color *Good Housekeeping* v265 no3 p85 S 2017

Briefcases

60 FOR 60: THE INSPIRATION BOARD bw color *GQ: Gentlemen's Quarterly* v97 no10 p182 O 2017

A FANTASTIC BEAST... ...And where to FIND it J. Roth color *Esquire* p40 O 2017

Briefcases—Evaluation

THE HARD STUFF J. Roth color *Esquire* p47 Ap 2017

Briegel, Hans J.

Versatile cluster entangled light bibl diag *Science* v354 no6311 p416 O 28 2016

Brienen, R.

Persistent effects of pre-Columbian plant domestication on Amazonian forest composition bibl chart graph map *Science* v355 no6328 p925 Mr 3 2017

Brier, Bob

LOOKING FOR NEEDLES IN OBELISKS R. Janssen *History Today* v67 no8 p96 Ag 2017

Briere, Emily—Interviews

WHY I 'M SENDING A TIME CAPSULE TO MARS color *National Geographic* v230 no6 pc13 D 2016

Brigande, John V.

Community network for deaf scientists color *Science* v356 no6336 p386 Ap 28 2017

Briggs & Stratton Commercial Power (Company)

Generators [Cover story] color *Popular Mechanics* v193 no7 p32 S 2016

Briggs, Brian

Because the Night S. Blackall *New York Times Book Review* p14 Ap 9 2017

Briggs, Cherri

TRAVEL SPECIALISTS 2016 P. BRADY and M. WYNNE color *Conde Nast Traveler* v51 no11 p78 D 2016

Briggs, David

Pay gap for women clergy is decreasing color *Christian Century* v134 no18 p12 Ag 30 2017

The rise and fall (and rise?) of Christian nationalism color *Christian Century* v133 no26 p16 D 21 2016

Studies reveal how faith counts in placing spiritual before material goods *Christian Century* v134 no1 p17 Ja 4 2017

Studies show help, hurt that can come from how clergy talk about end-of-life care *Christian Century* v134 no15 p16 Jl 19 2017

Briggs, David W.

The Age of Misinformation *Skeptical Inquirer* v41 no5 p63 S/O 2017

Caring for Aging Loved Ones color *Consumer Reports* v82 no12 p6 D 2017

Briggs, Gordon

THE CASE FOR Robot Disobedience [Cover story] color *Scientific American* v316 no1 p44 Ja 2017

Briggs, John A. G.

The structure and flexibility of conical HIV-1 capsids determined within intact virions bibl color *Science* v354 no6318 p1434 D 16 2016

Briggs, Kenneth A.

Kenneth A. Briggs J. Riess color *Publishers Weekly* v263 no45 p20 N 7 2016

Briggs, Patricia

Silence Fallen: Mercy Thompson, Book 10 *Publishers Weekly* v264 no5 p183 Ja 30 2017

Briggs, Stephen

Making climate science more relevant bibl color *Science* v354 no6311 p421 O 28 2016

Brigham, Lawson W.

The Arctic Waterway to Russia's Economic Future color map *Wilson Quarterly* p1 Summ 2017

Brigham, Tonya

Can a Franchise Make You Rich? J. Thompson color *Essence* v47 no12 p83 Ap 2017

Bright (Film)

BRIGHT D. Franich color *Entertainment Weekly* no1478 / 1479 p78 Ag 18-25 2017

Bright, Deborah

How to Deliver Criticism So Employees Pay Attention color *Harvard Business Review Digital Articles* p2 Ja 17 2017

Bright, Susan

HUMANIST PROFILE *Humanist* v77 no4 p2 Jl/Ag 2017

Bright Star (Theatrical production)

3 — BRIGHT STAR M. Snetiker *Entertainment Weekly* no1444/1445 p118 D 16 2016

Brighter in the Dark (Music)

OUT OF THE MOUTHS OF BABES JAM color *Advocate* no1091 p34 Je/Jl 2017

Brightfield, Amy

the health nut *Better Homes & Gardens* v94 no11 p158 N 2016

the health nut cartoon *Better Homes & Gardens* v95 no4 p150 Ap 2017 the health nut color *Better Homes & Gardens* v95 no10 p184 O 2017

the health nut color *Better Homes & Gardens* v95 no8 p178 Ag 2017

Brigsby Bear (Film)

BRAIN TRUST T. Friend cartoon *New Yorker* v93 no22 p19 Jl 31 2017

Brigsby Bear C. Nashawaty color *Entertainment Weekly* no1476 p46 Ag 4 2017

Dude Nostalgia Done Right S. Zacharek color *Time* v190 no6 p54 Ag 7 2017

Briles, Art, 1955-

The System Is the Star P. Thamel chart color *Sports Illustrated* v125 no14 p50 O 24-31 2016

Briles, Art, 1955—Trials, litigation, etc.

HOT | NOT T. Keith color *Sports Illustrated* v125 no20 p24 D 19 2016

Brill, Alan—Interviews

DON'T LET HACKERS KIDNAP YOUR DATA N. S. HUANG color *Kiplinger's Personal Finance* v71 no8 p12 Ag 2017

Brill, Callista

Tugboat Bill and the River Rescue *Publishers Weekly* v263 no46 p55 N 14 2016

Brill, Janet

shake it off color *Better Homes & Gardens* v95 no7 p168 Jl 2017

Brill, Michael H.

Colour How We See It and How We Use It *Physics Today* v70 no4 p56 Ap 2017

Brill, Steven

DONALD TRUMP, PALANTIR, AND THE CRAZY BATTLE TO CLEAN UP A MULTIBILLION-DOLLAR MILITARY PROCUREMENT SWAMP color diag *Fortune* v175 no5 p78 Ap 1 2017

Brillhart, Jessica—Interviews

Q+A: Jessica Brillhart J. Pontin color *MIT Technology Review* v120 no2 p28 Mr/Ap 2017

Brilliant, Jennifer

STRIKE a Pose *Dance Spirit* v21 no7 p56 S 2017

BRILLS, STEVE

Soup's On color *Backpacker* v45 no2 p36 Mr 2017

Brilot, Axel F.

Assembly of a nucleus-like structure during viral replication in bacteria bibl color graph *Science* v355 no6321 p1 Ja 13 2017

Brimm, Linda

What the Best Cross Cultural Managers Have in Common *Harvard Business Review Digital Articles* p2 Je 29 2016

Brin, Sergey, 1973-

Google's Other Founder Wants to Fly, Too A. Vance color *Bloomberg Businessweek* no4521 p32 My 8 2017

Brincks, Jocelyn

oops *Parents* v92 no7 p132 Jl 2017

Brinda, Mark

Your Data Isn't Helping Your Marketers If They Can't Access It *Harvard Business Review Digital Articles* p2 N 5 2015

Briner, Rob

Branch event to tackle changing world of work: Midlands conference is one of a raft of CIPD activities taking place around the UK and Ireland *People Management* p58 S 2017

Briney, Bryan

Priming HIV-1 broadly neutralizing antibody precursors in human Ig loci transgenic mice bibl graph *Science* v353 no6307 p1557 S 30 2016

Bring your own device policies

Tracking the Trends in Bringing Our Own Devices to Work J. McConnell *Harvard Business Review Digital Articles* p2 My 4 2016

BRINKERHOFF, TAKISHA

Poor but Happy: The Wisdom of the Elders *Idaho Magazine* v16 no9 p42 Je 2017

Brinkley, Christie, 1954-

So What Do You Do, CHRISTIE BRINKLEY? color *InStyle* v24 no7 p84 Jl 2017

Brinkley, Douglas

After the hurricane, Larry McMurtry's Houston trilogy lives on *New York Times Book Review* p22 O 8 2017

The Campaign Issue You Won't Hear About color *AARP: The Magazine* v59 no6A p30 O/N 2016

This Is the Most Enlightening Election In More Than a Century and Here's Why J. Stein color *Time* v188 no18 p55 O 31 2016

Thoreau and the Legacy of Wilderness *New York Times Book Review* p12 Jl 9 2017

BRINKMAN, MELINDA

From Darkness to Light *Idaho Magazine* v16 no2 p24 N 2016

Brinkman, Paul D.

Beyond the museum's mandate color *Science* v357 no6352 p652 Ag 18 2017

Brinkmanship

The Perils of Brinkmanship *America* v217 no7 p8 O 2 2017

Brinkworth, Jessica F.

Social status alters immune regulation and response to infection in macaques bibl graph *Science* v354 no6315 p1041 N 25 2016

Briois, C.

Xenon isotopes in 67P/Churyumov-Gerasimenko show that comets contributed to Earth's atmosphere diag *Science* v356 no6342 p1069 Je 9 2017

Briquets

TOP 5: ... Healthy Ways to Cook Thanksgiving Turkey L. McGLASHAN color *Muscle & Performance* v9 no11 p66 N 2017

Briquets—Evaluation

open-air Deliciousness E. HARE color *Cabin Living* p56 S 2017

Brisbane (Qld.)

DIARY OF A SEASON S. Johnson *Tennis* v53 no1 p36 Ja/F 2017

BRISBY, DALE

At Home With... color *American Cowboy* v23 no6 p16 Ap/My 2017

Briscoe, Dolph

Great Texas Ranches color *American Cowboy* p71 LEGENDS OF TEXAS Special Issue 2017

Briscoe, Forrest

Do Conservative Managers Give Smaller Bonuses to Women? *Harvard Business Review Digital Articles* p2 D 2 2016

Briscoe, James

Decoding of position in the developing neural tube from antiparallel morphogen gradients diag *Science* v356 no6345 p1379 Je 30 2017

Brisse, Dan—Interviews

DAN BRISSE T. Monterosso color *Snowboarder* v29 no2 p38 O 2016

BRISTER, EVELYN

Genome Fidelity and the American Chestnut *Issues in Science & Technology* v33 no4 p41 Summ 2017

Bristol, Michael

MY LATEST DIY PROJECT, COMPLETED bw color *Old House Journal* v45 no4 p32 Je 2017

Bristol, Peter

Peter Bristol B. LIBBY color *Architectural Digest* v74 no10 p112 O 1 2017

Bristol Bay (Alaska)

SEARCHING FOR SILVER J. R. Sullivan color *Field & Stream* v122 no2 p26 Je/Jl 2017

Bristow, Matthew

Colombians Yank The Welcome Mat color *Bloomberg Businessweek* no4537 p30 S 11 2017

A Failed Peace Process Could Mean More Pain bw color *Bloomberg Businessweek* no4494 p17 O 10 2016

Bristow, Paul

BASS OF A DIFFERENT STRIPE S. RYAN and G. BETHGE color *Outdoor Life* v224 no4 p64 My 2017

British

THE FRENCH ARE COMING! [Cover story] D. T. Zabecki bw color map *Military History* v34 no4 p22 N 2017

How to be British J. Sens color *Golf Magazine* v59 no7 p73 Jl 2017

British Airways PLC

WOLE SOYINKA AIRS A GRIEVANCE *Lapham's Quarterly* v10 no3 p140 Summ 2017

British architecture

Our Exotic Architecture: An Imperial Legacy S. Reeves *British Heritage Travel* v38 no4 p32 Jl/Ag 2017

British art—Exhibitions

ANGLO-FILE S. Gutierrez *British Heritage Travel* v38 no4 p12 Jl/Ag 2017

British atlases—History—17th century

'The Road from London to Dover', 1675 K. Wiles *History Today* v67 no2 p18 F 2017

British Broadcasting Corp.

"Our staff are now proud to work here": How a complex restructure, HR shake-up and cultural revamp prepared the broadcaster for its digital future *People Management* p20 Je 2017

British colonial architecture

Artful Living M. SLENSKE color *Architectural Digest* v74 no7 p88 Jl 2017

British Columbia

Spared by the blaze M. HEMMADI color *Maclean's* v130 no8 p18 S 2017

British Columbia—Commerce

JUST CALL IT SILICON COAST C. Dillow color *Fortune* v176 no2 p30 Ag 1 2017

British Columbia—Description & travel

BEACHCOMBING IN GIBSONS D. HISLOP *Sea Magazine* v108 no8 pPNW-10 Ag 2016

UP IN THE AIR C. Pfeuffer color *Sunset* v238 no1 p28 Ja 2017

Where the Wild Things Are P. Rauber *Sierra* v101 no5 p18 S/O 2016

British Columbia—Environmental conditions

missed connections d. tolnai color *Bike Magazine* v24 no7 p40 S 2017

British Columbia—Politics & government—21st century

Big money, big problems N. MACDONALD color *Maclean's* v130 no2 p32 Mr 2017

British cooking

For the Love of Welsh Rarebit C. TAN color *Foreign Policy* no225 p84 Jl/Ag 2017

British Gas PLC

Employers 'must prepare to add commission to holiday pay' after landmark ruling M. CALNAN *People Management* p8 N 2016

British history

HEARTS OF OAK S. Lawrence *British Heritage Travel* v38 no3 p54 My/Je 2017

It Happened Here: The Great Plains, 1867 G. R. Schiavino bw *American Cowboy* v24 no1 p41 Je/Jl 2017

British kings & rulers

See also

British monarchy

The Quiz T. BALAZO color *Maclean's* v130 no8 p64 S 2017

READY TO RULE L. Roach *History Today* v67 no5 p24 My 2017

British monarchy

A Letter from a Person of Quality *Lapham's Quarterly* v10 no3 p211 Summ 2017

British Open (Golf tournament)

Jordan Spieth S. Gregory color *Time* v190 no6 p17 Ag 7 2017

MAN on a MISSION [Cover story] C. Barrett color *Golf Magazine* v59 no8 p62 Ag 2017

British painting—Exhibitions

All along the watchtowers at Yale color *Magazine Antiques* v184 no2 p30 Mr/Ap 2017

British Virgin Islands—Description & travel

CLOSE to the Madding Crowd [Cover story] A. CORT color *Sail* v48 no10 p36 O 2017

Operation Vacation! J. Raycroft color *Power & Motoryacht* v34 no10 p94 O 2017

British withdrawal from the European Union, 2016-

BREXIT COULD GET MESSY *Fortune* v175 no7 p11 Je 1 2017

Brexit Could Hurt the Most Here A. Tartar, J. Scott Diamond et al graph map *Bloomberg Businessweek* no4527 p20 Je 19 2017

Business is braced for Brexit *People Management* p6 Jl 2017

Continental Divide I. Vesper color *Scientific American* v317 no4 p70 O 2017

Delusions of Power G. Younge *Nation* v304 no16 p10 My 22 2017

The Fog Lifts M. Campbell and S. Morris color *Bloomberg Businessweek* no4525 p48 Je 5 2017

Hysterical History Tour color *Weekly Standard* v22 no35 p2 My 22 2017

I'LL DEFEND FRANCE. I'LL DEFEND EUROPE E. FRÉDÉRIC *Vital Speeches of the Day* v83 no7 p201 Jl 2017

London Strives to Remain a Place the World Will Call Home D. Stewart color *Time* v189 no23 p18 Je 19 2017

May Should Go Easy On Brexit Promises color *Bloomberg Business-*

nessweek no4521 p8 My 8 2017

A More Imperfect Union: Britain's separation from the EU: not merely a new political and legal arrangement but a deep and permanent schism N. Ferguson *Hoover Digest: Research & Opinion on Public Policy* no3 p88 Summ 2017

Most employment rights 'indispensable', say businesses: Survey finds majority want to avoid post-Brexit 'bonfire' *People Management* p13 Je 2017

No Way Out T. Ross bw *Bloomberg Businessweek* no4539 p41 S 25 2017

A Pregnant Pause: Brexit is now certain, but the terms are not. Britain still has time to work with the EU, head off political strife, and minimize economic pain T. G. Ash *Hoover Digest: Research & Opinion on Public Policy* no3 p93 Summ 2017

So Much for That Brexit Mandate G. Smith color *Fortune* v176 no1 p11 Jl 1 2017

Those Who Leave and Those Who Stay J. MILLER *In These Times* v41 no7 p41 Jl 2017

What does HARD BREXIT mean? Skilled and unskilled labour may be treated very differently when the UK leaves the single market - and that means many businesses are already concerned about talent G. GYTON *People Management* p8 Mr 2017

What the World Needs Now M. DiChristina *Scientific American* v317 no4 p5 O 2017

WHY CAN'T BRITS DO ALL THE JOBS? [Cover story] J. FARAGHER *People Management* p26 Je 2017

Britnell, Mark

Transforming Health Care Takes Continuity and Consistency *Harvard Business Review Digital Articles* p2 D 28 2015

Britney Ever After (Film)

Britney Ever After A. D'arminio color *TV Guide* v65 no7 p38 F 13 2017

BRITO, JOSÉ C.

An Ecoregion-Based Approach to Protecting Half the Terrestrial Realm *BioScience* v67 no6 p534 Je 2017

Britschgi, Christian

Chip Implants Make It Impossible to Forget Your Keys bw *Reason* v48 no7 p64 D 2016

Britt, Paige

Peace, Love and Understanding R. J. PALACIO *New York Times Book Review* p24 Ag 27 2017

Brittle, Karen

CLIPPING & BLANKETING Insights from Top Grooms color *Dressage Today* v24 no1 p56 O 2017

Coaching Youth Toward USDF MEDALS [Cover story] color *Dressage Today* v24 no2 p30 N 2017

EQUUS Film Festival bw color *Dressage Today* v23 no7 p54 Mr 2017

Holistic Care FOR THE DRESSAGE HORSE color *Dressage Today* v23 no6 p40 F 2017

Keep Your COOL at SUMMER SHOWS chart color *Dressage Today* v23 no10 p58 Jl 2017

Managing Your Horse's Joints with Injections color *Dressage Today* v23 no5 p56 Ja 2017

TACK CHANGES color *Dressage Today* p48 My 2017

Vaccinating Your Dressage Horse color *Dressage Today* v23 no7 p58 Mr 2017

Welcome OLD MAN WINTER color *Dressage Today* v23 no12 p56 S 2017

Where Dressage Meets the Canvas color *Dressage Today* v23 no4 p60 D 2016

Britton, Connie, 1967-

America's top TV critic Matt Roush answers your burning questions M. Roush *TV Guide* v65 no13 p4 Mr 20 2017

FRIDAY NIGHT LIGHTS S. Highfill color *Entertainment Weekly* no1434 p48 O 7 2016

Nashville M. ROUSH *TV Guide* v65 no2 p19 Ja 2 2017

true beauties inside & out L. MAJEWSKI color *Good Housekeeping* v264 no5 p44 My 2017

BRITTON, ZOY

ONE OF THE LUCKY ONES bw *Ebony* v72/73 no12/1 p20 O/N 2017

Britz, David

FROM OUR READERS color *Sky & Telescope* v134 no2 p6 Ag 2017

Brizé, Stéphane, 1966-

HARD TIMES K. M. JONES color *Film Comment* v53 no3 p36 My/Je 2017

Brizo, Roy—Interviews

Take 5 With ROY BRIZIO T. Taylor color *Hot Rod* v70 no6 p14 Je 2017

Brizuela, Natalia

A SENSE OF PLACE: PAZ ENCINA'S RADICAL POETICS *Film Quarterly* v70 no4 p49 Summ 2017

Brjansdottir, Birna

THE CASE OF BIRNA Z. ROBERT *Iceland Review* v55 no2 p42 Mr/Ap 2017

Bro, Susan

keeping score *Ms.* v27 no3 p6 Fall 2017

Broad, Kenny

TRUE DISCOVERY color *National Geographic* v232 no1 p26 Jl 2017

Broad City (TV program)

Abbi Jacobson Didn't Expect Hillary to Come On Her Show D. Itzkoff *New York Times Magazine* p54 O 23 2016

Broad City N. Abrams, B. L. Heldman et al color *Entertainment Weekly* no1482/1483 p79 S 22 2017

BROAD CITY R. Rahman color *Entertainment Weekly* no1468/1469 p50 Je 2-9 2017

Broadband communication systems

Governing the Smart, Connected City S. Crawford *Harvard Business Review Digital Articles* p2 O 31 2014

How streaming TV services are coping with ISP data caps J. NEWMAN color *Macworld - Digital Edition* v34 no8 p120 Ag 2017

Internet for All K. Vick color *Time* v189 no13 p34 Ap 10 2017

Will Not-Quite-Fiber Make the Grade? E. Pfanner and M. Scaturro diag *Bloomberg Businessweek* no4495 p27 O 17 2016

Broadband communication systems—United States

FCC Proposed Privacy Rules: Choice, Transparency, and Security of Personal Broadband Data *Congressional Digest* v96 no5 p4 My 2017

Broadbelt, Kathryn

Housing Heals and Saves color *Alternatives Journal (A.J) - Canada's Environmental Voice* v42 no2 p34 2016

Broadbent, Ed

LIFETIME ACHIEVEMENT AWARD J. GEDDES color *Maclean's* v129 no47 p24 N 28 2016

Broadcast journalism

Consuming Negative News Can Make You Less Effective at Work S. Achor and M. Gielan *Harvard Business Review Digital Articles* p2 S 14 2015

The Man. The Myth. The Moustache K. MANGU-WARD bw color *Reason* v48 no10 p36 Mr 2017

Broadcasters

See also

Sportscasters

Television personalities

DAVID ATTENBOROUGH T. Obreht cartoon *New Yorker* v92 no42 p104 D 19 2016

Broadcasters—Government policy

More Panic from Politico and the Post *Weekly Standard* v22 no16 p2 D 26 2016

Broadcasting industry—Awards

Out & About *TV Guide* v64 no40 p6 O 3 2016

Broadcasting industry—Canada

What Is the CBC Good For? [Cover story] T. JOKINEN bw color *Walrus* v14 no7 p20 S 2017

Broadchurch (TV program)

Broadchurch I. Rudolph *TV Guide* v65 no27 p29 Je 26 2017

Broadchurch: The detective drama goes out on an emotional high M. ROUSH *TV Guide* v65 no27 p12 Je 26 2017

Broadcom Corp.

Designing nutritional games and brains for space color *Science News* v190 no11 p27 N 26 2016

Broadfoot, Marla

BUILDING A BETTER HARVEST color *Scientific American* v317 no2 p66 Ag 2017

BROADHEAD, ROBERT S.

Chords & Discords bw color *Downbeat* v84 no10 p10 O 2017

Broadheads (Arrowheads)

Hone Sweet Hone S. Bestul color *Field & Stream* v122 no3 pB4

Ag 2017

Broadie, Mark

All Mixed Up color *Golf Magazine* v59 no9 p36 S 2017

The Big Breakthrough color *Golf Magazine* v59 no1 p35 Ja 2017

Brutish Empire color *Golf Magazine* v59 no3 p36 Mr 2017

DJ's Secret Sauce color *Golf Magazine* v59 no6 p28 Je 2017

Dustin' the Competition chart color *Golf Magazine* v59 no1 p72 Ja 2017

Go the Distance color *Golf Magazine* v58 no11 p32 N 2016

Let the Gains Begin color *Golf Magazine* v59 no2 p36 F 2017

Major Pain chart color *Golf Magazine* v59 no8 p70 Ag 2017

One for the Money color *Golf Magazine* v59 no4 p38 Ap 2017

Season's Readings chart color *Golf Magazine* v59 no11 p32 N 2017

The Short Story chart color *Golf Magazine* v59 no10 p31 O 2017

What in the World? color *Golf Magazine* v59 no5 p38 My 2017

Your Lucky Number: 13 color *Golf Magazine* v59 no7 p34 Jl 2017

Broadway Dance Center (Company)

SCHOOL DIRECTORY *Dance Spirit* v20 no10 p70 D 2016

Broadway Ltd. Imports LLC

Broadway Limited Imports HO scale P70 D. Kawala color *Model Railroader* v84 no11 p66 N 2017

RAILWAY POST OFFICE J. Holt, K. Olsen et al color *Model Railroader* v83 no12 p18 D 2016

Broadway theatrical productions

BROADWAY'S GAME CHANGERS M. Snetiker color *Entertainment Weekly* no1434 p63 O 7 2016

BUILDING A Fitness Empire K. McGuire color *Dance Spirit* v21 no2 p58 F 2017

Waitresses and Witches: Broadway's new formula for success T. TEACHOUT *Commentary* v142 no4 p49 N 2016

WELCOME G. M. Holt *Cincinnati Magazine* v50 no8 p2 My 2017

A WORD FROM OUR SPONSORS T. Elsbrock and M. Clement *Cincinnati Magazine* v50 no8 p4 My 2017

Broadway theatrical productions—Economic aspects

Hello, Dollars! M. TINDERA color *Forbes* v199 no6 p18 Je 13 2017

Broadway theatrical productions—Reviews

Spring Awakening S. GOLD *Dance Magazine* v91 no4 p20 Ap 2017

Broadway Wig Co.

Costumes, Makeup & Wigs *Stage Directions* v30 no7 p20 Jl 1 2017

Broadway (New York, N.Y.)

Two Cuisines, Two Menus, Too Much A. PLATT *New York* v50 no7 p64 Ap 3 2017

Wet Hot American Sandwich R. RAISFELD and R. PATRONITE *New York* p52 Ja 23 2017

Broan-NuTone LLC

Bug Off color *Log Home Living* v34 no6 p20 Ag 2017

Broccoli

but how much does food drink? M. Koziol cartoon *Popular Science* v289 no2 p16 Mr/Ap 2017

Eat your greens! B. Lipton color *Health* v31 no9 p107 N 2017

One-Pan Wonders color *Health* v31 no2 p129 Mr 2017

TOP PICKS J. BALL, S. DUGGER et al *Indianapolis Monthly* v12 no40 p62 Ag 2017

Brochere, Lizzie

Falling Water J. Jensen color *Entertainment Weekly* no1435 p48 O 14 2016

Brochures

UPCOMING ISSUES *Arabian Horse World* v57 no3 p293 D 2016

Brocious, Tiffany Erdos

GOT IT! color *Literacy Today (2411-7862)* v34 no3 p34 N/D 2016

Brock, Allison

5 Tips to Improve MENTAL FOCUS color *Dressage Today* v24 no1 p36 O 2017

BROCK, BO

The Most Handsome Man in the World color *Reader's Digest* v190 no1133 p22 S 2017

Brock, Chris

Chris BROCK M. B. DOUGHERTY *Interview* v47 no2 p66 Mr 2017

BROCK, DANIEL J.

Assessing National Biodiversity Trends for Rocky and Coral

Reefs through the Integration of Citizen Science and Scientific Monitoring Programs *BioScience* v67 no2 p134 F 2017

Brock, David, 1962-—Political & social views

Liberals Plot Revenge M. Scherer color *Time* v189 no3 p38 Ja 30 2017

BROCK, LEXI

"What Are You?" *Scholastic Choices* v32 no7 p20 Ap 2017

Brock, Sean

THE CHEF LOSES IT B. Martin bw color *GQ: Gentlemen's Quarterly* v86 no12 p208 D 2016

BROCK, WENDELL

ACTING OUT *Atlanta* v56 no12 p38 Ap 2017

Chick-fil-Aloha! *Atlanta* v56 no7 p89 N 2016

Rye Revival *Atlanta* v56 no11 p55 Mr 2017

Brockann, Suzanne

Some Kind of Hero: A Troubleshooters Novel *Publishers Weekly* v264 no14 p58 Ap 3. 2017

Brockbank, Wayne

Your Company Culture Can't Be Disconnected from Your Customers *Harvard Business Review Digital Articles* p2 Mr 18 2016

Brock-Broido, Lucie

THE AMERICAN SECURITY AGAINST FOREIGN ENEMIES ACT *New Yorker* v92 no30 p54 S 26 2016

Brockdorff, Neil

PCGF3/5–PRC1 initiates Polycomb recruitment in X chromosome inactivation color *Science* v356 no6342 p1081 Je 9 2017

Brockelman, Warren Y.

Plant diversity increases with the strength of negative density dependence at the global scale diag *Science* v356 no6345 p1389 Je 30 2017

Brockenbrough, Martha

Love, Santa *Publishers Weekly* v264 no36 p100 S 4 2017

BROCKETT, ZANDIE

LOOK OVER HERE bw color *Conde Nast Traveler* v52 no3 p88 Mr 2017

Brockis, Jenny

How to nurture a high-performing brain *People Management* p50 F 2017

Brockman, Hank

Of troughs and trophies G. Albert color *Magazine Antiques* v184 no3 p110 My/Je 2017

Brockman, John

Know This: Today's Most Interesting and Important Scientific Ideas, Discoveries, and Developments *Publishers Weekly* v263 no52 p115 D 19 2016

Brockman, Terra

Much ado about mulching *Christian Century* v134 no17 p32 Ag 16 2017

Planting garlic color *Christian Century* v133 no26 p11 D 21 2016

Brockmann, Leonie

A pathogenic role for T cell–derived IL-22BP in inflammatory bowel disease bibl graph *Science* v354 no6310 p358 O 21 2016

Brockmire (TV program)

Broadcast Muse T. Keith color *Sports Illustrated* v126 no12 p17 My 1 2017

Brockschmidt, Bill—Interviews

STARTING FRESH M. K. QUINLAN color *House Beautiful* v159 no4 p108 My 2017

Brockway, Anna—Interviews

What I Wear to Work: ANNA BROCKWAY J. Chen color *Bloomberg Businessweek* no4499 p87 N 14 2016

BROCKWELL, JOSHUA

Investing Basics: When Is It Halal? *Islamic Horizons* v46 no1 p46 Ja/F 2017

Brockwell, Tim

Cassini finds molecular hydrogen in the Enceladus plume: Evidence for hydrothermal processes chart graph *Science* v356 no6334 p155 Ap 14 2017

BRODAK, MOLLY

Home After Dark *New York Times Book Review* p18 Ap 2 2017

BRODD, YEFIM

Life IN THESE UNITED STATES *Reader's Digest* v189 no1128 p38 Mr 2017

Life *Reader's Digest* v188 no1126 p36 D 2016/Ja 2017

Brodesser-Akner, Taffy

ALL THE PETTY HORSESHIT bw color *GQ: Gentlemen's*

Quarterly v86 no11 p124 N 2016

APOSTATES ANONYMOUS *New York Times Magazine* p36 Ap 2 2017

LOSING IT bw color *New York Times Magazine* p34 Ag 6 2017

Mr. Popular *New York Times Magazine* p34 Ja 15 2017

OUTSIDERS THE EXILE *New York Times Magazine* p41 O 30 2016

The Realest Face in "Fake News" color *GQ: Gentlemen's Quarterly* v97 no5 p56 My 2017

THE SECOND COMING OF ROBERT PATTINSON [Cover story] bw color *GQ: Gentlemen's Quarterly* v97 no9 p142 S 2017

Springtime for SALLY color *AARP: The Magazine* v59 no3A p48 Ap/My 2016

TOM FORD'S WILD KINGDOM color *GQ: Gentlemen's Quarterly* v86 no12 p178 D 2016

WE ♥ T. H [Cover story] color *GQ: Gentlemen's Quarterly* v97 no3 p108 Mr 2017

what will the kids think? bw *Bon Appetit* v62 no10 p48 O 2017

BRODIN, ERIC

FROM THE ARCHIVES cartoon *Reason* v49 no2 p70 Je 2017

Brodin, Priscille

Reversion of antibiotic resistance in Mycobacterium tuberculosis by spiroisoxazoline SMARt-420 bibl diag *Science* v355 no6330 p1206 Mr 17 2017

Brodowy, Richard J.

Thoughts on previous issues color *American Cowboy* v23 no4 p26 D 2016/Ja 2017

Brodrick, William

Felonious Monk J. L. BREEN color *Weekly Standard* v22 no13 p42 D 5 2016

A friar turned detective M. J. Sweeney color *America* v217 no4 p50 Ag 21 2017

Brodsky, Andrew

The Dos and Don'ts of Work Email, from Emojis to Typos *Harvard Business Review Digital Articles* p2 Ap 23 2015

Brodsky, Joseph, 1940-1996

Brodsky and His Muses: A new collection shows where the great émigré poet Joseph Brodsky found friendship, love, and inspiration C. L. Haven *Hoover Digest: Research & Opinion on Public Policy* no3 p188 Summ 2017

Brody, Adam, 1980-

StartUp A. Bacle, K. Connolly et al *Entertainment Weekly* no1482/1483 p109 S 22 2017

BRODY, BARBARA

GREAT GRAINS *Better Homes & Gardens* v94 no12 p152 D 2016

HEART-HEALTH WAKE-UPCALL bw cartoon color *Better Homes & Gardens* v95 no2 p125 F 2016

Brody, Ben

THE BEST YARD SALE color *Bloomberg Businessweek* no4501 p22 N 28 2016

Chillary Clinton color *Bloomberg Businessweek* no4493 p35 O 3 2016

How to Lobby But Not Be a Lobbyist *Bloomberg Businessweek* no4511 p25 F 13 2017

Selling Trump's D.C. Hotel Wouldn't Be Easy *Bloomberg Businessweek* no4505 p40 D 26 2016

Until Donald Trump, U.S. presidents and vice presidents went to extremes to avoid conflicts of interest... real or apparent bw color *Bloomberg Businessweek* no4503 p22 D 12 2016

BRODY, BOB

The Oldest Kid on The Job color *Reader's Digest* v190 no1134 p22 O 2017

Brody, Caitlin

Daria: 20 Years Later color *Entertainment Weekly* no1460/1461 p68 Ap 7-17 2017

THE Fan Girl color *Glamour* v115 no10 p172 O 2017

A GAY Old Timeline color diag *Entertainment Weekly* no1471 p32 Je 23 2017

Harriet the Spy: Behind the Blue Paint Scene color *Entertainment Weekly* no1440 p44 N 18 2016

INSIDE THE HANDMAID'S STUDIO color *Entertainment Weekly* no1467 p50 My 26 2017

My TV Motto: You Go High; I'll Go Low color *Glamour* v115 no10 p40 O 2017

RISKY BUSINESS color *Entertainment Weekly* no1449 p38 Ja

20 2017

The Sex and the City Opening Credits color *Entertainment Weekly* no1460/1461 p72 Ap 7-17 2017

TV chart color *Entertainment Weekly* no1444/1445 p66 D 16 2016

Your Sunshiny, Stupendous, Seriously Spectacular SUMMER BUCKET LIST color *Entertainment Weekly* no1470 p32 Je 16 2017

YVONNE ORJI color *Entertainment Weekly* no1441 p49 N 25 2016

Brody, Jessica

In Some Other Life *Publishers Weekly* v264 no24 p66 Je 12 2017

BRODY, LAUREN SMITH

crushing it *Parents* v91 no10 p98 O 2016

nighty night, everyone! color graph *Parents* v92 no8 p44 Ag 2017

You've Got a Job. And a Baby... ...And You're Gonna Be Fine color *Glamour* v115 no5 p126 My 2017

BRODY, LEONARD

Artificial Intelligence Goes Microbial bw chart color *Forbes* v199 no5 p82 My 16 2017

Coming Soon To A Device Near You color *Forbes* v200 no2 p64 S 5 2017

E Pluribus Unum And The Blockchain color *Forbes* v200 no1 p78 Jl 27 2017

Fresh-Squeezed Insurance color *Forbes* v198 no7 p92 N 29 2016

Virtual Plan, Real Surgery color *Forbes* v198 no9 p82 D 30 2016

Brody, Liz

Chayce Doesn't Want to Be One of Them color *Glamour* v115 no10 p149 O 2017

"I'm Doing This for Hadiya" color *Glamour* v114 no7 p102 Jl 2016

The Most Infamously Accused Female Villain color *Glamour* v114 no11 p143 N 2016

(The Big)Salary Reveal [Cover story] bw color *Glamour* v115 no3 p146 Mr 2017

"We keep choosing each other" bw color *Glamour* v115 no3 p159 Mr 2017

Who Are You Sexually? color *Glamour* v115 no7 p68 Jl 2017

"You've got to break your back!" color *Glamour* v115 no4 p153 Ap 2017

Brody, Richard

Building Blocks color *New Yorker* v93 no17 p6 Je 19 2017

Caught in the Act cartoon *New Yorker* v93 no23 p10 Ag 7 2017

Fall Preview color *New Yorker* v93 no25 p16 Ag 28 2017

Family Business color *New Yorker* v93 no24 p6 Ag 21 2017

First Person Singular bw *New Yorker* v92 no36 p9 N 7 2016

L'Argent *New Yorker* v92 no33 p13 O 17 2016

Leading Ladies bw *New Yorker* v93 no9 p11 Ap 17 2017

The Memory Card color *New Yorker* v92 no42 p30 D 19 2016

Mother's Day color *New Yorker* v93 no16 p26 Je 5 2017

Mother Tongue color *New Yorker* v92 no45 p14 Ja 16 2017

No Peace of Mind color *New Yorker* v93 no28 p12 S 18 2017

On the Wild Side color *New Yorker* v93 no19 p12 Jl 3 2017

Past Tense color *New Yorker* v93 no10 p22 Ap 24 2017

Revolutions per Minute color *New Yorker* v93 no33 p16 O 23 2017

Sanctuary City bw *New Yorker* v92 no49 p12 F 13 2017

Site Lines color *New Yorker* v92 no39 p17 N 28 2016

Spring Preview cartoon *New Yorker* v93 no4 p6 Mr 13 2017

Summer Preview cartoon *New Yorker* v93 no14 p20 My 22 2017

Two from the Heart color *New Yorker* v93 no30 p8 O 2 2017

Whorled Series bw *New Yorker* v92 no41 p12 D 12 2016

Winter Preview cartoon *New Yorker* v92 no37 p18 N 14 2016

BRODY, WILLIAM R.

WE MAY KNOW WHAT WE KNOW WITHOUT UNDERSTANDING PRECISELY HOW WE KNOW IT *Vital Speeches of the Day* v83 no8 p237 Ag 2017

Broene, Scott

QUIRK APPEAL M. LAWLER color *Chicago* v66 no2 p16 F 2017

Broering, Bill

ALL AROUND THE FARM® *Successful Farming* v115 no6 p77 Ap 2017

Broida, Rick

The Best Tech Gifts for $50 or Less color *Money* v45 no11 p18 D 2016

Trick Out Your Phone color *Money* v46 no1 p23 Ja/F 2017

Wireless for Less color *Money* v45 no10 p23 N 2016

Broken symmetry (Physics)

Physicists make 'time crystal' in lab E. CONOVER *Science News* v190 no10 p12 N 12 2016

Brokers

See also

Stockbrokers

BUYING OR SELLING SOLO D. THOMPSON *Sea Magazine* v108 no8 p46 Ag 2016

JULY'S QUESTION: It sounds so simple: Find a yacht broker who can help you find the right yacht. But how do you know you're working with a good broker? *Sea Magazine* v109 no7 p53 Jl 2017

SEPTEMBER'S QUESTION: What can a broker do to help me get a loan for the yacht I want to purchase? *Sea Magazine* v108 no9 p61 S 2016

Brokers—Corrupt practices

Traders' New Favorite Way to Swap Secrets L. J. Keller color *Bloomberg Businessweek* no4518 p41 Ap 10 2017

Brokers—Legal status, laws, etc.

NOVEMBER'S QUESTION *Sea Magazine* v108 no10 p49 O 2016

Brolin, Josh, 1968-

THE RIDE OF HIS LIFE M. POTTER bw color *Esquire* p100 S 2017

Bromo, Mount (Indonesia)

INDONESIA color *National Geographic* v232 no5 p8 N 2017

Bromodomain-containing protein 1

Click chemistry enables preclinical evaluation of targeted epigenetic therapies Chan, A. Hienzsch et al diag *Science* v356 no6345 p1397 Je 30 2017

Bromotrifluoromethane

The Halon Tragedy B. PIKE bw *Power & Motoryacht* v34 no11 p264 N 2017

Bromund, K. R.

Structure, force balance, and topology of Earth's magnetopause diag graph *Science* v356 no6341 p960 Je 1 2017

BROMUND, TED

Churchill in Washington color *Weekly Standard* v22 no10 p12 N 14 2016

One Tory's Story color *Weekly Standard* v22 no40 p27 Je 26 2017

Bromwich, David

In Praise of Ambiguity bw *New York Review of Books* v64 no16 p50 O 26 2017

Bromwich, Jonah Engel

How Trump Could Change America *New York Times Upfront* v149 no7 p8 Ja 9 2017

Bronc riding

Feel the Footfalls L. LaPlante color *Horse & Rider* v56 no3 p23 Mr 2017

Bronchitis

Your True Stories IN 100 WORDS color *Reader's Digest* v190 no1135 p25 N 2017

Bronco truck

COOL MOVE [Cover story] B. W. SMITH color *Dirt Sports + Off-Road* v51 no12 p62 D 2017

FSB REBIRTH PART 2: E40D OVERHAUL B. SMITH color *Dirt Sports + Off-Road* v51 no5 p52 My 2017

GIVE THE PEOPLE WHAT THEY WANT M. Emery color *Dirt Sports + Off-Road* v51 no5 p6 My 2017

IN THE COMFORT ZONE B. W. SMITH color *Dirt Sports + Off-Road* v51 no9 p46 S 2017

TIME HAS COME M. Emery color *Dirt Sports + Off-Road* v51 no2 p4 F 2017

WORLD DOMINATION M. EMERY color *Dirt Sports + Off-Road* v51 no10 p20 O 2017

Bronfman, Hannah, 1988-

IN TREATMENT WITH Hannah Bronfman D. Mazzone color *InStyle* v24 no4 p146 Ap 2017

Brongersma, Mark L.

Applying plasmonics to a sustainable future color *Science* v356 no6341 p908 Je 1 2017

Optically resonant dielectric nanostructures bibl graph *Science* v354 no6314 paag2472-1 N 18 2016

Bronner, Ethan

The Arranger color *Bloomberg Businessweek* no4503 p60 D 12

2016
A TV Bonanza From the Homeland of Homeland *Bloomberg Businessweek* no4526 p20 Je 12 2017

Bronski, Peter
How to Better Manage Your Company's Utility Bills *Harvard Business Review Digital Articles* p2 N 24 2015
Lost Skills of tracking bw *American Cowboy* p52 LEGENDS OF TEXAS Special Issue 2017

Bronson, A. A.—Exhibitions
GENERAL IDEA B. Droitcour color *Art in America* v105 no4 p120 Ap 2017

Bronstein, Michael—Interviews
WE ARE THE LAW: We took employment lawyers from top firms and asked them about what really matters to HR - from Brexit and the Taylor review to staying out of court *People Management* p34 S 2017

Bronsther, Jacob
Stay the Hand of Justice? Evaluating Claims that War Crimes Trials Do More Harm than Good *Daedalus* v146 no1 p83 Wint 2017

Bronx Tale, A (Theatrical production)
Robert De Niro's Bronx Cheer J. Mcgovern color *Entertainment Weekly* no1438 p70 N 4 2016

Bronze
THE GOLDEN AGE OF BRONZE JOHNSON *Treasures* v6 no6 p24 Je/Jl 2017

Bronze age
PONDERING THE PAST E. MASTROIANNI color *Discover* v38 no3 p9 Ap 2017

Bronze age—England
THINKING BACK, LOOKING AHEAD cartoon *Archaeology* v70 no1 p6 Ja/F 2017

Bronze age—Greece
Town Beneath the Waves D. WEISS color *Archaeology* v70 no2 p30 Mr/Ap 2017

Bronze sculpture—20th century
Accordeoniste color *Magazine Antiques* v183 no6 p8 N/D 2016
Der Judische Maler color *Magazine Antiques* v183 no6 p9 N/D 2016

Bronzers (Cosmetics)
42 new ALL-STAR PRODUCTS of the year [Cover story] G. WAY, T. HALL et al color *Redbook* p27 Jl/Ag 2017

Brooches
Mountain Men E. FLORIO color *Conde Nast Traveler* v51 no11 p130 D 2016
PRECIOUS MOMENTS color *Harper's Bazaar* no3656 p270 S 2017

Brooches—Evaluation
A CUT ABOVE bw color *Harper's Bazaar* no3652 p149 Ap 2017
IT'S SPECIAL OUTFIT SEASON! color *Redbook* p70 D 2016
SO BAZAAR bw *Harper's Bazaar* no3649 p342 D 2016/Ja 2017

Brood X (Music)
What to Stream color *Entertainment Weekly* no1459 p59 Mr 31 2017

Brook, Barry W.
Biodiversity losses and conservation responses in the Anthropocene color diag graph map *Science* v356 no6335 p270 Ap 21 2017

Brook, Daniel
HERE A CITY SHALL BE WROUGHT: What's forgotten in China's time-lapse urbanism color *Harper's Magazine* v335 no2005 p49 Je 2017

BROOK, ELIZABETH
Understanding Academic Language and Its Connection to School Success *Education Digest* v82 no6 p58 F 2017

Brook, Larry
shalom y'all *Successful Farming* v115 no1 p3 Ja 2017

Brooker, Charlie
Black Mirror *TV Guide* v64 no40 p39 O 3 2016
WORST-CASE SCENARIO G. HARVEY cartoon *New Yorker* v92 no39 p46 N 28 2016

Brooker, Charlie—Interviews
MAN IN THE MIRROR M. Mechanic color *Mother Jones* v41 no6 p57 N/D 2016
THE Punch List A. PEELE bw *GQ: Gentlemen's Quarterly* v86 no11 p69 N 2016

Brooker, Gary—Interviews
Gary Brooker and Procol Harum Fuse Sonic Shades of Both Past and Present With Novum M. METTLER and C. Crowley color *Sound & Vision* v82 no6 p24 Jl/Ag 2017

BROOKER, KATRINA
Airbnb Hits the Road color *Vanity Fair* v59 no1 p158 Holiday 2017

Brookhiser, Richard
THE ANDREW BROTHERS bw color *American History* v52 no3 p18 Ag 2017
Apple-Picking Time color il *National Review* v68 no20 p47 N 7 2016
Bird's-Eye View il *National Review* v69 no1 p43 Ja 23 2017
Center of The World bw *National Review* v69 no7 p47 Ap 17 2017
Children of The Night *National Review* v69 no15 p46 Ag 14 2017
A City of Shopkeepers il *National Review* v69 no5 p47 Mr 20 2017
Down These Lonely Streets bw *National Review* v69 no17 p43 S 11 2017
Eagle's View Of a Nation il *National Review* v68 no23 p43 D 19 2016
FIRST FAMILIES bw color *American History* v52 no4 p20 O 2017
The Gimlet-Eyed bw color *National Review* v68 no20 p24 N 7 2016
Letting Go *National Review* v69 no11 p43 Je 12 2017
Notes from Underground il *National Review* v69 no3 p55 F 20 2017
OF SCALES AND THUMBS *American History* v52 no1 p18 Ap 2017
ORGAN RECITAL *American History* v51 no6 p18 F 2017
SPY VS. SPY VS. SPY bw color *American History* v52 no2 p22 Je 2017
The Staff Of Life *National Review* v69 no9 p43 My 15 2017
A TO Z *Claremont Review of Books* v17 no1 p87 Wint 2016/2017
True Inventions color *National Review* v69 no2 p44 F 6 2017
Urban Symphony il *National Review* v69 no19 p59 O 16 2017

Brooking, Emerson T.
WAR GOES VIRAL HOW SOCIAL MEDIA IS BEING WEAPONIZED color *Atlantic* v318 no4 p70 N 2016

Brooklyn Academy of Music
GOINGS ON ABOUT TOWN color *New Yorker* v92 no35 p12 O 31 2016

Brooklyn Museum
The Animal Mummy Business J. KEATS color *Discover* v38 no10 p64 D 2017
THE BRIEF color *Art in America* v104 no10 p21 N 2016
GOINGS ON ABOUT TOWN color *New Yorker* v93 no30 p4 O 2 2017
THE UNTOLD BLACK HISTORY OF THE SECOND WAVE M. CAPORALE *In These Times* v41 no7 p39 Jl 2017

Brooklyn Nets (Basketball team)
14 NETS color *Sports Illustrated* v127 no12 p73 O 16 2017

Brooklyn Nets (Basketball team)—Finance
15 Nets R. Nadkarni, B. Golliver et al color *Sports Illustrated* v125 no14 p92 O 24-31 2016

Brooklyn Navy Yard (New York, N.Y.)
One Building, 41 Moon Shots A. TSOULIS-REAY img *New York* v49 no21 p64 O 17 2016

Brooklyn (New York, N.Y.)
BARTENDERS' CHOICE J. Sidman *Washingtonian Magazine* v52 no2 p260 N 2016
The Finch C. Kormann color *New Yorker* v93 no8 p15 Ap 10 2017
Mettä J. Fan color *New Yorker* v93 no27 p18 S 11 2017
Take Root B. Cooper color *New Yorker* v92 no37 p29 N 14 2016

Brooklyn (New York, N.Y.)—Social conditions
Hillary Clinton Thought Brooklyn Could Be the Capital of America N. MALONE img *New York* v49 no25 p86 D 12 2016

Brooklyn Nine-Nine (TV program)
BROOKLYN NINE-NINE D. Holbrook *TV Guide* p30 D 5 2016
DIVE INTO Brooklyn Nine-Nine D. Snierson, N. Abrams et al color *Entertainment Weekly* no1482/1483 p67 S 22 2017
Nathan Fillion Heads to Brooklyn D. Holbrook *TV Guide* v65 no11 p14 Mr 6 2017
WHaT'S WORTH WaTCHING *TV Guide* v64 no15 p47 Ap 4 2016

Brooks, Adrian
Memorial Community Development Corporation: Putting Faith to
Work R. Jackson *Bridges (Federal Reserve Bank of St. Louis)*
p11 Wint 2016/2017
Brooks, Alison Wood
Explaining Gender Differences at the Top *Harvard Business Re-
view Digital Articles* p2 S 23 2015
Research: Cracking a Joke at Work Can Make You Seem More
Competent color *Harvard Business Review Digital Articles* p2
Ja 11 2017
Research: Performing a Ritual Before a Stressful Task Improves
Performance color *Harvard Business Review Digital Articles* p2
Ja 10 2017
Brooks, Amanda
how sweet it is color *Architectural Digest* v74 no9 p166 S 2017
Yes, You Can Do Low-Key St. Barts color *Conde Nast Traveler*
v52 no1 p60 Ja 2017
Brooks, Arthur
'This Economy Kills' A. Annett color *Commonweal* v144 no11
p21 Je 16 2017
Brooks, Arthur C.
CONFESSIONS OF A CAPITALIST CONVERT [Cover story]
color *America* v216 no4 p18 F 20 2017
The Dignity Deficit bw *Foreign Affairs* v96 no2 p106 Mr/Ap 2017
Brooks, Burt Vernon
Photographer of a Lost Valley M. Allen *Yankee* v81 no1 p140 Ja/F
2017
Brooks, Carl, Jr.
Black News Matters color *Wired* v25 no3 p64 Mr 2017
Brooks, Carleton
SHARPEN YOUR COURSE-RIDING SKILLS color diag *Prac-
tical Horseman* v45 no8 p30 Ag 2017
Brooks, Cassandra M.
Science-based management in decline in the Southern Ocean bibl
map *Science* v354 no6309 p185 O 14 2016
Brooks, Dan
Pedialyte color *New York Times Magazine* p22 Ja 29 2017
BROOKS, DANIEL R.
Transformational Principles for NEON Sampling of Mamma-
lian Parasites and Pathogens: A Response to Springer and Col-
leagues *BioScience* v66 no11 p917 N 1 2016
Brooks, David
EDITOR'S NOTE J. BARDI *Humanist* v77 no2 p3 Mr/Ap 2017
Life together as an empire collapses color *Christian Century* v134
no8 p1 Ap 12 2017
No Surrender bw *Atlantic* v318 no4 p44 N 2016
Brooks, David Benjamin, 1961——Interviews
Chasing beauty, finding grace M. Fitzgerald color *Christian Cen-
tury* v134 no3 p27 F 2017
Brooks, Geraldine
Everything Happens to King David C. Kirch bw *Publishers Week-
ly* v263 no44 p(Sp)16 O 31 2016
The King's Man A. W. SCHACHTER color *National Review* v68
no21 p44 N 21 2016
Sleep and Dreams *New York Times Book Review* p7 F 5 2017
Brooks, Gwendolyn, 1917-2000
AN HOMAGE TO BRONZEVILLE'S BARD color *Chicago* v66
no10 p78 O 2017
Brooks, James L.
GRANT TINKER color *Entertainment Weekly* no1446/1447 p89
D 2016/Ja 2017
Brooks, Jonathan
Ears to Mouth J. Gorant and T. Keith color *Sports Illustrated* v126
no15 p24 My 29 2017
Brooks, Karen R.
CNN *New York Times Magazine* p10 Ap 23 2017
Brooks, Kate
Woman Warrior M. Wappler and E. Mahaney color *Glamour* v115
no6 p106 Je 2017
Brooks, Lonnie, 1933-2017
Milestones color *Time* v189 no14 p15 Ap 17 2017
Brooks, Max
George Romero color *Time* v190 no5 p17 Jl 31 2017
Brooks, Max——Interviews
MAX BROOKS I. Biedenharn color *Entertainment Weekly*
no1457/1458 p106 Mr 17 2017

Brooks, Mel, 1926-
HIGH ANXIETY'S OBSCENE PHONE CALL D. Franich color
Entertainment Weekly no1460/1461 p28 Ap 7-17 2017
Mel BROOKS *Interview* v47 no5 p24 Je/Jl 2017
Brooks, Mel, 1926-——Interviews
Mel Brooks A. PEELE *GQ: Gentlemen's Quarterly* v97 no6 p130
Je 2017
Brooks, Oliver——Interviews
THE LOOK BOOK A. SWERDLOFF img *New York* p41 Ja 23
2017
Brooks, Peter
Flaubert: The Tragic Historian bw color *New York Review of
Books* v64 no4 p24 Mr 9 2017
Something Grander Than a Novel color *New York Review of Books*
v64 no12 p44 Jl 13 2017
Brooks, Rahiem
A Butler Christmas *Publishers Weekly* v264 no40 p123 O 2 2017
BROOKS, RAY
THE MAMMOTH MINE *Idaho Magazine* v16 no5 p12 F 2017
Brooks, Rosa
How David Became Goliath *New York Times Book Review* p21
F 5 2017
How Everything Became War and the Military Became Every-
thing: Tales From the Pentagon L. D. Freedman *Foreign Affairs*
v96 no1 p160 Ja/F 2017
Warriors and Citizens *Hoover Digest: Research & Opinion on
Public Policy* no4 p73 Fall 2016
Brooks, Sam
Micro-Credentials: The Badges of Professional Growth B. BER-
RY *Education Digest* v82 no9 p21 My 2017
Brooks, Sarah
THE CONVERSATION color *Atlantic* v320 no2 p8 S 2017
BROOKS, TAMI
Brave Hearts color *O, The Oprah Magazine* p14 Mr 2017
Brooks, Terry, 1944-——Interviews
THE BLACK ELFSTONE I. Biedenharn color *Entertainment
Weekly* no1446/1447 p82 D 2016/Ja 2017
BROOKS, TIFFANY
How Can I Add Excitement to a Boxy, Bland Room? cartoon color
Chicago v66 no4 p72 Ap 2017
Spring Forward color *Ebony* v72 no5 p53 Mr 2017
Brooks, Traci
SHARPEN YOUR COURSE-RIDING SKILLS color diag *Prac-
tical Horseman* v45 no8 p30 Ag 2017
Brooks, Walt
SO YOU WANT TO BE A WINEMAKER? S. Schneider color
Sunset v238 no1 p92 Ja 2017
Brooks + Scarpa (Company)
THE SIX J. Zara *Architectural Record* v205 no4 p194 Ap 2017
Brooks-Dalton, Lily
Women Who Ride *New York Times Magazine* p25 Ja 15 2017
Brookshire, Bethany
An eye-opening role for a cancer drug color *Science News* v191
no11 p4 Je 10 2017
Science News for Students color *Science News* v192 no4 p33 S
16 2017
Brookshire, Judy Wiles
Caring for Aging Loved Ones color *Consumer Reports* v82 no12
p6 D 2017
Broom, Sarah M.
What's Up With the Orgasm Double Standard? color *Glamour*
v115 no7 p70 Jl 2017
BROOME, BETH
Feast for the Senses *Architectural Record* v204 no11 p116 N 2016
Record Hosts 19th Innovation Conference, in San Francisco *Ar-
chitectural Record* v205 no7 p34 Jl 2017
Richardson Revival *Architectural Record* v205 no9 p78 S 2017
Southern Revival *Architectural Record* v205 no7 p80 Jl 2017
White Hot color diag *Architectural Record* v204 no12 p90 D 2016
Brooms & brushes——Evaluation
Southern Comfort color *Log Home Living* v34 no2 p38 Mr 2017
Brophy, Ben
BABACOMARI: 50 Years Later B. Cossavella *Arizona Highways*
v93 no4 p43 Ap 2017
BROPHY, CATHERINE
GUIDE TO Restfulness color *House Beautiful* v159 no2 p61 Mr

2017

BROPHY, FRANK CULLEN
SAN IGNACIO DEL BABACOMARI *Arizona Highways* v93 no4 p36 Ap 2017

Brorby, Taylor
Industrial Scars color *Orion Magazine* v35 no6 p62 N/D 2016
Nature and Politics color *Orion Magazine* v36 no1 p62 Ja/F 2017
Penguin Bloom *Orion Magazine* v35 no3 p60 My/Je 2016
Rooftop *Orion Magazine* v35 no4/5 p111 Jl-O 2016
Through Darkness to Light color *Orion Magazine* v36 no2 p62 Mr/Ap 2017
Waiting for High Tide *Orion Magazine* v35 no3 p57 My/Je 2016
Wilderness to Wasteland *Orion Magazine* v35 no3 p58 My/Je 2016

Brosch, Roland
Leprosy in red squirrels bibl color diag *Science* v354 no6313 p702 N 11 2016

Brosgol, Vera
ABOUT OUR COVER ARTIST VERA BROSGOL color *Publishers Weekly* v263 no49 p3 D 7 2016
She Persisted *New York Times Book Review* p17 Mr 12 2017
Vera Brosgol J. Crelin *Current Biography* v78 no8 p13 Ag 2017

Brosi, Berry
Ten policies for pollinators bibl color *Science* v354 no6315 p975 N 25 2016

Brosnahan, Rachel—Interviews
RACHEL BROSNAHAN S. Pulia color *InStyle* v23 no13 p128 D 2016

Brosnan, Pierce, 1953-
Oilmen and Indians In a Saga of American West D. D'Addario color *Time* v189 no14 p52 Ap 17 2017
PIERCE BROSNAN RIDES AGAIN A. Bhattacharji bw color *Esquire* p116 Ap 2017
Pierce BROSNAN S. HAYEK *Interview* v47 no3 p34 My 2017

Brosnan, Pierce, 1953-—Interviews
PIERCE BROSNAN GOES WEST I. RUDOLPH *TV Guide* v65 no14 p20 Ap 3 2017
Pierce Brosnan J. Wolf *Saturday Evening Post* v289 no3 p25 My/Je 2017

Bross, Tim
Plaintiffs' Lawyers ? St. Louis *Bloomberg Businessweek* no4493 p31 O 3 2016

Brossard, Dominique
Mapping the Landscape of Public Attitudes on Synthetic Biology *BioScience* v67 no3 p290 Mr 2017
U.S. attitudes on human genome editing color graph *Science* v357 no6351 p553 Ag 11 2017

Brossat, Alain
Shouting From the Steppes G. Miller *History Today* v67 no3 p61 Mr 2017

Brothels
BRINGING LIGHT TO THE TRAFFICKING FIGHT [Cover story] K. SHELLNUTT color graph *Christianity Today* v61 no5 p26 Je 2017
A business doing pleasure M. CAMPBELL *Maclean's* v130 no7 p12 Ag 2017

Brotherhood of the Snake (Music)
Metal Guitarist Skolnick Gets Jazzy on Trio Project B. Milkowski color *Downbeat* v84 no1 p15 Ja 2017

Brotherliness
A Deadly Campus Tradition K. Reilly color *Time* v190 no16/17 p56 O 23 2017

Brothers
The Brothers Kim D. P. HALPIN color *Weekly Standard* v22 no27 p22 Mr 20 2017
The Courage of His Convictions B. Doyle color *U.S. Catholic* v82 no11 p23 N 2017

Brothers & sisters
See also
Brothers
Twins
A CHILD VOID? H. ESTROFF MARANO *Psychology Today* v50 no4 p21 Ag 2017
Getting slim with my sister A. Levi color *Health* v31 no8 p46 O 2017
Handle a Sibling's Playdate J. W. Dubin *Parents* v92 no9 p169

S 2017
let the bonding begin! S. JOHNSON color *Parents* v92 no5 p52 My 2017
love times two L. IANNOTTI *Parents* v91 no9 p134 S 2016
My best Halloween costume ever was ... map *Reader's Digest* v190 no1134 p26 O 2017
raise happy siblings R. SAGIV RIEBLING *Parents* v91 no6 p56 Je 2016
Sketchbook J. Tamaki *New York Times Book Review* p27 Ag 20 2017
Teddy's Wisdom Made Me Weep H. Levine color *Parents* v92 no5 p10 My 2017

Brothers & sisters—Social aspects
The ORIGINAL KARDASHIANS N. Gabler *Los Angeles Magazine* p112 D 2016

Brothers & sisters—Substance use
I watched his addiction take hold H. Gellar *Scholastic Choices* v32 no3 p9 N/D 2016

BROTHERS, SOREN
Translating Regime Shifts in Shallow Lakes into Changes in Ecosystem Functions and Services *BioScience* v67 no10 p928 O 2017

Brothers of the Night (Film)
Making Ends Meet M. Koresky color *Film Comment* v53 no3 p8 My/Je 2017

Brotons, L.
Using fire to promote biodiversity bibl color *Science* v355 no6331 p1264 Mr 24 2017

Brotton, Jerry
ISLAMIC OVERTURES A. F. LANG JR. color *America* v215 no16 p36 N 21 2016
QUEEN'S ISLAM J. GOODWIN *New York Times Book Review* p50 D 4 2016

Broudy, Berne
CLIMBING TO A BETTER FUTURE color *Climbing* no351 p64 F/Mr 2017
FLORIDA'S NATURAL WONDERS *Sierra* v102 no3 p28 My/Je 2017
GO AHEAD, OVERTHINK IT color *Bicycling* v58 no8 p32 S 2017
A Shoe Sole That Won't Slip on Ice color *Popular Science* v288 no6 p58 N/D 2016
These skis fold in half! color diag *Popular Science* v289 no6 p30 N/D 2017

Brough Superior motorcycle—Evaluation
ALL-NEW BROUGH SUPERIOR SS 100 P. d'Orléans bw color *Cycle World* v56 no1 p44 Ja/F 2017

Brough Superior Motorcycles SAS
ALL-NEW BROUGH SUPERIOR SS 100 P. d'Orléans bw color *Cycle World* v56 no1 p44 Ja/F 2017

BROUGHTON, JANE
TRIPS THAT TRANSPORT AND TRANSFORM color *Martha Stewart Living* p102 Mr 2017

Brouillette, Monique
Organelle Overhaul *Scientific American* v315 no6 p18 D 2016
To Treat Primates More Humanely: Transparency color *Scientific American* v316 no2 p14 F 2017

Brouns, Stan J. J.
CRISPR-Cas: Adapting to change color *Science* v356 no6333 p40 Ap 7 2017

Broussard, Lyle
LOUISIANA PROUD M. SIMONEAUX color *Louisiana Life* v37 no2 p20 N/D 2016

BROVERMAN, NEAL
SAY HER NAME: As one murder case is closed, another begins, marking 16 trans women killed before August *Advocate* no1093 p8 O/N 2017

Browaeys, Antoine
An atom-by-atom assembler of defect-free arbitrary two-dimensional atomic arrays bibl bw diag graph *Science* v354 no6315 p1021 N 25 2016

Browder, Joshua
PIONEERS R. E. Mullin, S. Parkin et al color il *MIT Technology Review* v120 no5 p50 S/O 2017

Browe, Brigitte M.
Fructose-driven glycolysis supports anoxia resistance in the naked

mole-rat diag graph *Science* v356 no6335 p307 Ap 21 2017

Brower, Elena

Fall fuel color *Yoga Journal* no296 p22 N 2017

Brower, Holly Henderson

Business Professors Need to Spend Time in Companies *Harvard Business Review Digital Articles* p2 N 27 2015

Want Your Employees to Trust You? Show You Trust Them *Harvard Business Review Digital Articles* p2 Jl 5 2017

Brower, Kate Andersen

The House As a Home color *Time* v189 no4 p37 Ja 23 2017

Brown

THAT '70s COLOR M. Prince color *Esquire* p32 O 2017

Brown, A.

Observation of coherent elastic neutrino-nucleus scattering diag *Science* v357 no6356 p1123 S 15 2017

Brown, Aaquil

Meet the Black Beatles B. SPANOS color *Rolling Stone* no1278/1279 p15 Ja 12 2017

Brown, Abram

The $150 BILLION MOMENT color *Forbes* v200 no5 p21 N 14 2017

THE DONALD OF THE DESERT color *Forbes* v199 no3 p62 Mr 28 2017

Drop-Offs chart color graph *Forbes* v198 no5 p48 O 25 2016

The Expense of Exclusive Living color graph *Forbes* v198 no5 p46 O 25 2016

February 1, 1935: America's Secret Strength color *Forbes* v198 no7 p34 N 29 2016

FORBES @ 100 bw color *Forbes* v198 no8 p32 D 20 2016

FORBES @ 100 bw *Forbes* v199 no6 p30 Je 13 2017

FORBES @ 100 color *Forbes* v199 no3 p38 Mr 28 2017

Founder's Remorse color *Forbes* v198 no9 p40 D 30 2016

July 1, 1958: Rocket Men bw color *Forbes* v199 no1 p30 Ja 24 2017

July 1, 1968: HOUSTON, WE'VE GOT YOUR BACK bw color *Forbes* v200 no2 p32 S 5 2017

JULY 15, 1931: DRIVING FORCE bw color *Forbes* v200 no1 p30 Jl 27 2017

JUNE 12, 1989: CYBER-SOVIETS bw color *Forbes* v199 no7 p36 Je 29 2017

LESSONS AND IDEAS BY THE 100 GREATEST LIVING BUSINESS MINDS bw color *Forbes* v200 no3 p115 S 28 2017

LIFE AS A PARTY color *Forbes* v200 no3 p80 S 28 2017

March 1, 1948: A Fortunate Time bw color *Forbes* v199 no5 p36 My 16 2017

March 15, 1967: Tuned In to the Future bw color *Forbes* v198 no9 p26 D 30 2016

May 1, 1971: Financing Fantasyland bw color *Forbes* v199 no4 p28 Ap 25 2017

NINE ZEROS: OCTOBER 9, 2006 color *Forbes* v200 no5 p36 N 14 2017

Pablo's Pots color *Forbes* v198 no6 p32 N 8 2016

THE POSTWAR DREAM: NOV. 15, 1947 bw color *Forbes* v200 no4 p30 O 24 2017

RICHEST BY STATE bw map *Forbes* v199 no4 p22 Ap 25 2017

Sept. 13, 1982: The First Forbes 400 bw color *Forbes* v198 no5 p54 O 25 2016

THE SHELL GAME color *Forbes* v200 no3 p84 S 28 2017

THE STRONGMAN'S MIDDLEMAN color *Forbes* v199 no3 p60 Mr 28 2017

Time Machines And War Machines color *Forbes* v199 no6 p20 Je 13 2017

THE TRUMP CLONE [Cover story] bw color *Forbes* v199 no3 p50 Mr 28 2017

WHAT'S YOUR SUMMER BOOK? color *Forbes* v199 no7 p34 Je 29 2017

WHERE SHOULD YOU RETIRE? color *Forbes* v200 no1 p20 Jl 27 2017

THE WORLD'S BILLIONAIRES bw color diag graph map *Forbes* v199 no3 p84 Mr 28 2017

Brown, Alan

The structure of the yeast mitochondrial ribosome bibl color *Science* v355 no6324 p528 F 3 2017

Translational termination without a stop codon bibl color *Science* v354 no6318 p1437 D 16 2016

Brown, Alton, 1962-

The Best Tech. EveryDay color *Popular Science* v288 no6 p8 N/D 2016

Brown, Ann

People and posts *People Management* p55 D 2016/Ja 2017

Brown, Anna J.

From thought to action color *America* v216 no5 p43 Mr 6 2017

Brown, Antonio, 1988——Interviews

Playing Catch-up T. Keith color *Sports Illustrated* v127 no3 p14 Jl 24 2017

Brown, Anya

Creating our own community color *Science* v355 no6332 p1446 Mr 31 2017

Brown, Archie

How Did the Huge War Really End? bw color *New York Review of Books* v64 no5 p55 Mr 23 2017

Reagan's Most Convincing Role *History Today* v67 no2 p63 F 2017

Brown, Ari

advice every new mom needs [Cover story] color *Parents* v92 no7 p32 Jl 2017

bizarre behavior *Parents* v92 no1 p72 Ja 2017

BROWN, BEVERLEY

Return TO GLORY color *House Beautiful* p48 Ag 2017

Brown, Billy

SPOTLIGHT ON: BILLY BROWN A. TINUBU color *Ebony* v72 no11 p76 S 2017

Brown, Binta Niambi

A new kind of music J. M. Griffith color *U.S. Catholic* v82 no3 p45 Mr 2017

Brown, Bob

Out of the Woods color *Log Home Living* v34 no5 p20 Jl 2017

Brown, Bobbi, 1957-

COUNTER INTELLIGENCE M. MILRAD GOLDSTEIN color *Martha Stewart Living* p38 My 2017

Feed Your FACE color *Vogue* v206 no12 p188 D 2016

Brown, Bobby

To think, three thousand years from now people will still be asking, "Who?" *Texas Monthly* v45 no1 p88 Ja 2017

Brown, Brandon

THE MUSIC OF CHANCE color *Art in America* v105 no1 p54 Ja 2017

BROWN, BRYAN

THE ART OF PROTEST: When it comes to swaying public opinion, a provocative image can be a powerful tool [Cover story] *New York Times Upfront* v149 no13 p18 My 15 2017

The Debate Ober COLUMBUS *New York Times Upfront* p18 S 18 2017

HAITI IN CRISIS *New York Times Upfront* v149 no6 p8 D 12 2016

The Pledge at 125 *New York Times Upfront* v149 no9 p20 F 20 2017

THE PRESIDENT VS. THE PRESS *New York Times Upfront* v149 no10 p18 Mr 13 2017

PROTEST NATION: From the Boston Tea Party to the modern-day Tea Party and the Women's March, America has been shaped by protest movements *New York Times Upfront* v149 no13 p16 My 15 2017

The Right to LOVE *New York Times Upfront* v149 no7 p18 Ja 9 2017

Brown, Carolyn M.

The Board Game That Is Bringing Conversation Back color *Black Enterprise* v47 no4 p10 N/D 2016

Competing for Up to $1Million for Your Startup [Cover story] color *Black Enterprise* v47 no4 p40 N/D 2016

Daring To Be Different color *Black Enterprise* v47 no3 p19 O 2016

Designing Women color *Black Enterprise* v47 no5 p40 Ja/F 2017

Erecting Hammer & Nails Salons Nationwide *Black Enterprise* v47 no2 p13 S 2016

Get Your Feet Wet in Business Ownership color *Black Enterprise* v47 no3 p13 O 2016

How Millenials Manage Their Money color *Black Enterprise* v47 no3 p23 O 2016

Make Stock Investing Affordable color *Black Enterprise* v47 no4 p16 N/D 2016

MAKING A BEELINE TO SELF-EMPLOYMENT color *Black*

Enterprise v47 no5 p13 Ja/F 2017

THREE MOST IMPORTANT MONEY LESSONS color *Black Enterprise* v47 no2 p18 S 2016

brown, casey

A GUIDE TO VEGAN CHEESE *Vegetarian Journal* v36 no2 p12 2017

It's all in the hips color *Bike Magazine* v23 no9 p98 D 2016

Vegetarian Action. Vesanto Melina, Passionate Vegan Dietitian and Author *Vegetarian Journal* v36 no2 p35 2017

Veggie Meals in (or near!) National Parks *Vegetarian Journal* v36 no1 p25 2017

Where Are They Now? Catching Up with the Past VRG Interns and Scholarships Winners *Vegetarian Journal* v36 no3 p9 2017

Brown, Celia

Knowing When to Fire Someone *Harvard Business Review Digital Articles* p2 Ja 7 2015

Brown, Charlie

3 Questions to Ask Before Adopting a Platform Business Model *Harvard Business Review Digital Articles* p2 Ap 5 2016

Too Many Executives Are Missing the Most Important Part of CRM *Harvard Business Review Digital Articles* p2 Ag 24 2016

Brown, Charlie (Fictitious character)

TIDINGS OF GREAT JOY J. McDERMOTT *America* v215 no19 p29 D 19 2016

Brown, Chip

Making a Man cartoon color *National Geographic* v231 no1 p74 Ja 2017

Brown, Christina

Visible and Indivisible: The Birth of a Resistance Movement K. Aronoff color *Progressive* v81 no6 p15 Ag/S 2017

Brown, Christopher

Tropic of Kansas *Publishers Weekly* v264 no21 p76 My 22 2017

Brown, Clair

Buddhist Economics: An Enlightened Approach to the Dismal Science *Publishers Weekly* v263 no51 p141 D 12 2016

A More Mindful Economy *American Scholar* v86 no2 p14 Spr 2017

BROWN, CLAIRE

National Ecosystem Assessments in Europe: A Review chart *Bio-Science* v66 no10 p813 O 1 2016

Brown, Coral

TAP YOUR CORE POWER SOURCE color *Yoga Journal* p42 2017 Special Issue

Brown, Cyndi

CONFORMATION CLINIC color *Horse & Rider* v56 no5 p39 My 2017

Brown, Dale

ARABIAN HORSE WORLD'S TRAINERS ALMANAC G. DEARTH *Arabian Horse World* v57 no1 p49 O 2016

Brown, Dan

Show what you know color *Phi Delta Kappan* v98 no8 p38 My 2017

Brown, Dan, 1964-

DAN BROWN I. Biedenharn color *Entertainment Weekly* no1486 p62 O 13 2017

Brown, Danielle

Danielle Brown C. Seidman color *Dance Magazine* v91 no3 p44 Mr 2017

How Did I Get Here? DANIELLE BROWN bw color *Bloomberg Businessweek* no4514 p76 Mr 13 2017

Brown, David

Caught Between Reform and a Hard Place J. Buntin *Governing* v30 no2 p40 N 2016

NINJA GIRAFFES *National Geographic Kids* no468 p24 Mr 2017

Opioids and Paternalism: TO HELP END THE CRISIS, BOTH DOCTORS AND PATIENTS NEED TO FIND A NEW WAY TO THINK ABOUT PAIN [Cover story] *American Scholar* v86 no4 p22 Aut 2017

PCGF3/5–PRC1 initiates Polycomb recruitment in X chromosome inactivation color *Science* v356 no6342 p1081 Je 9 2017

SCALY SUPERHEROES color map *National Geographic Kids* no470 p22 My 2017

BROWN, DAVID A.

PANFISH AND PALM REELS color *Outdoor Life* v224 no1 p100 D 2016/Ja 2017

PIMP YOUR SHRIMP diag *Outdoor Life* v224 no3 p66 Ap 2017

SUMMER SURFACE BASS color *Outdoor Life* v224 no5 p31 Je/Jl 2017

Brown, David S., 1966-

IN EQUILIBRIO D. SCHLOZMAN color *Nation* v305 no7 p35 S 25 2017

Moderates: The Vital Center of American Politics, from the Founding to Today *Publishers Weekly* v263 no43 p70 O 24 2016

Shimmering Visions S. TANENHAUS bw color *New Republic* v248 no6 p66 Je 2017

Tender Is the Fall J. Banville bw *New York Review of Books* v64 no17 p40 N 9 2017

Trails of the Jazz Age W. H. PRITCHARD bw color *Weekly Standard* v22 no40 p30 Je 26 2017

Brown, David—Interviews

David Brown B. Luscombe color *Time* v189 no23 p56 Je 19 2017

BROWN, DIALLO TELLI

Here's the Pitch: Analytics for Managing School Buildings *Education Digest* v82 no6 p20 F 2017

Brown, Don, 1949-

Older Than Dirt: A Wild But True History of Earth *Publishers Weekly* v264 no29 p222 Jl 17 2017

Brown, Douglas

Leadership Takes Self-Control. Here's What We Know About It color *Harvard Business Review Digital Articles* p2 Je 5 2017

Brown, Ed

THE BALLAD OF ED "BAD BOY" BROWN B. SMITH bw color *Chicago* v66 no4 p106 Ap 2017

Brown, Eddie—Interviews

Daring To Be Different K. Meeks and C. M. BROWN color *Black Enterprise* v47 no3 p19 O 2016

Brown, Elaine Meryl

CONFESSIONS OF DIVORCED MEN color *Essence* v48 no6 p115 O 2017

Brown, Elizabeth Nolan

AMERICAN SEX POLICE color *Reason* v48 no11 p16 Ap 2017

The Case for Gender Anarchy color *Reason* v49 no4 p74 Ag/S 2017

Why Buy Sex? *Reason* v48 no7 p10 D 2016

Brown, Emily

Let's celebrate AMAZING MOMS J. PRESS bw color *Redbook* p110 My 2017

BROWN, EMMA

ANDY'S Candy *Interview* v47 no3 p37 Ap 2017

Brown, Eric Renner

10 ARTISTS WHO WILL RULE 2017 color *Entertainment Weekly* no1450 p56 Ja 27 2017

1950-2017 Tom Petty color *Entertainment Weekly* no1486 p18 O 13 2017

3 ROUNDS WITH HANSON color *Entertainment Weekly* no1467 p40 My 26 2017

Arcade Fire color *Entertainment Weekly* no1476 p59 Ag 4 2017

The Beautiful, Bizarre Mind of Father John Misty color *Entertainment Weekly* no1462 p62 Ap 21 2017

Beck color *Entertainment Weekly* no1486 p58 O 13 2017

BENNINGTON'S MOST SOUL-BARING SONGS color *Entertainment Weekly* no1476 p62 Ag 4 2017

THE BEST ALBUMS OF 2017 (SO FAR) color *Entertainment Weekly* no1468/1469 p98 Je 2-9 2017

THE BEST OF BOWIE'S NEW BOX SET color *Entertainment Weekly* no1485 p59 O 6 2017

The Best Stocking Stuffers (And A Few Lumps Of Coal) color *Entertainment Weekly* no1442 p56 D 2 2016 Rebellious Special Issue

THE BIGGEST SUMMER BREAKOUTS (SO FAR) color diag *Entertainment Weekly* no1474/1475 p15 Jl 21-28 2017

BILLIE JOE ARMSTRONG color *Entertainment Weekly* no1435 p54 O 14 2016

Bon Iver color *Entertainment Weekly* no1434 p57 O 7 2016

Chester Bennington color *Entertainment Weekly* no1476 p62 Ag 4 2017

Common color *Entertainment Weekly* no1439 p57 N 11 2016

Danger Mouse's 30th Century Vision color *Entertainment Weekly* no1438 p60 N 4 2016

DAVID BOWIE'S GOLDEN YEAR color *Entertainment Weekly* no1434 p56 O 7 2016

AN ECLECTIC SONIC SQUAD color *Entertainment Weekly* no1438 p60 N 4 2016

EXAMINING THE GRAMMYS' RACE ISSUE color *Entertainment Weekly* no1454/1455 p13 F 24 2017

THE FLAMING LIPS' WAYNE COYNE color *Entertainment Weekly* no1449 p58 Ja 20 2017

THE FOUR-HOUR GRATEFUL DEAD FILM... REVIEWED BY A DEADHEAD color *Entertainment Weekly* no1468/1469 p89 Je 2-9 2017

THE GOLDEN AGE OF HAIM color *Entertainment Weekly* no1467 p32 My 26 2017

Grizzly Bear's Vital New Tunes color *Entertainment Weekly* no1477 p57 Ag 11 2017

Kesha color *Entertainment Weekly* no1478 / 1479 p103 Ag 18-25 2017

Migos: The Viral MCs Are Here to Stay color *Entertainment Weekly* no1451/1452 p107 F 3-10 2017

MUSIC color *Entertainment Weekly* no1444/1445 p88 D 16 2016

Music Royalty's Next Generation color *Entertainment Weekly* no1457/1458 p96 Mr 17 2017

PRINCE color *Entertainment Weekly* no1446/1447 p87 D 2016/ Ja 2017

QUEENS OF THE STONE AGE'S JOSHUA HOMME color *Entertainment Weekly* no1480 p48 S 1 2017

RUN THE JEWELS color *Entertainment Weekly* no1446/1447 p72 D 2016/Ja 2017

SGT. PEPPER'S LONELY HEARTS CLUB BAND TURNS 50 color *Entertainment Weekly* no1467 p56 My 26 2017

SHARON JONES color *Entertainment Weekly* no1446/1447 p96 D 2016/Ja 2017

SOUNDTRACK SOUND-OFF: VOL. 2'S BEST TRACKS color *Entertainment Weekly* no1465 p41 My 12 2017

ST. VINCENT color *Entertainment Weekly* no1462 p63 Ap 21 2017

THE TRANSFORMATION OF KATY PERRY color *Entertainment Weekly* no1467 p28 My 26 2017

THE ULTIMATE 2016 ALBUM SWAP color *Entertainment Weekly* no1446/1447 p116 D 2016/Ja 2017

"Video Killed the Radio Star" color *Entertainment Weekly* no1460/1461 p45 Ap 7-17 2017

Vince Staples color *Entertainment Weekly* no1472 p59 Je 30 2017

We Like Big Hits and We Cannot Lie color *Entertainment Weekly* no1480 p51 S 1 2017

What's Next for Kanye West? color *Entertainment Weekly* no1443 p17 D 9 2016

What to Watch color *Entertainment Weekly* no1453 p54 F 17 2017

What to Watch color *Entertainment Weekly* no1473 p52 Jl 7 2017

Your Sunshiny, Stupendous, Seriously Spectacular SUMMER BUCKET LIST color *Entertainment Weekly* no1470 p32 Je 16 2017

Brown, Erica L.
Dark at the Crossing: A Novel/Exit West: A Novel color *Christian Century* v134 no10 p39 My 10 2017

Homegoing: A Novel *Christian Century* v133 no23 p41 N 9 2016

Mischling: A Novel color *Christian Century* v133 no21 p37 O 12 2016

Brown, Flavian D.
The epigenetic landscape of T cell exhaustion bibl graph *Science* v354 no6316 p1165 D 2 2016

Brown, Fred
KICKING IT OLD-SCHOOL K. FOX color *Runner's World* v51 no10 p24 N 2016

Brown, Garrett—Interviews
AMAZING GRACE J. BAILEY bw color *Film Comment* v52 no6 p24 N/D 2016

Brown, Guy C.
Deciphering microglial diversity in Alzheimer's disease color *Science* v356 no6343 p1123 Je 16 2017

BROWN, HARRIET
Every Bite You Take [Cover story] color *Prevention* v68 no12 p30 D 2016

BROWN, HILLARY
the best of THE BEST 120 color *House Beautiful* v158 no9 p57 N 2016

THE BIG MIX-UP [Cover story] color *House Beautiful* v159 no8 p57 O 2017

Book Report: A+ color *House Beautiful* v159 no8 p42 O 2017

A COZIER DINING color *House Beautiful* v159 no8 p62 O 2017

A DARLING SITTING ROOM color *House Beautiful* v159 no1 p38 F 2017

AN ENCHANTED GARDEN color *House Beautiful* p34 Jl 2017

Faux Arts color *House Beautiful* v159 no1 p30 F 2017

A GLAM BEDROOM color *House Beautiful* v159 no2 p55 Mr 2017

A HOLIDAY SOIREE color *House Beautiful* v158 no10 p36 D 2016/Ja 2017

JUST ADD WATER color *House Beautiful* v159 no1 p47 F 2017

A LADIES' BRUNCH color *House Beautiful* v159 no2 p58 Mr 2017

LET THE GOOD TIMES ROLL color *House Beautiful* v159 no8 p112 O 2017

Roped In color *House Beautiful* v159 no3 p38 Ap 2017

A SERENE DRAWING ROOM color *House Beautiful* v159 no7 p65 S 2017

SERVING UP SIMPLICITY color *House Beautiful* v159 no7 p58 S 2017

shopping secrets OF THE PROS color *House Beautiful* v159 no3 p46 Ap 2017

UNDER A CANOPY OF FLOWERS... color *House Beautiful* p154 Ag 2017

Velvet for All Seasons color *House Beautiful* v159 no3 p36 Ap 2017

WORK IN PROGRESS color *House Beautiful* v159 no1 p42 F 2017

Brown, Ian H.
Role for migratory wild birds in the global spread of avian influenza H5N8 bibl graph map *Science* v354 no6309 p213 O 14 2016

BROWN, INDYA
THE VERY RED CARPET: And other trends that most caught our eye on the runways img *New York* v50 no16 p58 Ag 7 2017

Brown, Janelle
Watch Me Disappear *Publishers Weekly* v264 no21 p66 My 22 2017

BROWN, JANET
School of Quant color *Forbes* v200 no2 p54 S 5 2017

Brown, Jason W., 1983-
Sweet Pickings A. JUNG *Reader's Digest* v188 no1125 p14 N 2016

Brown, Jeff
10 SUCCESSFUL FARMERS: JEFF BROWN L. Bedord *Successful Farming* v115 no8 p24 Je/Jl 2017

Brown, Jennifer
Deconstructing behavioral neuropharmacology with cellular specificity color *Science* v356 no6333 p42 Ap 7 2017

Show your money some love S. M. FERNÁNDEZ color *Redbook* p97 Je 2017

Brown, Jera
On Living *Christian Century* v134 no4 p52 F 15 2017

Brown, Jerry, 1938-
Becau$e That'$ Democracy, Baby color *Weekly Standard* v22 no33 p2 My 8 2017

CALIFORNIA IS NOT TURNING BACK. NOT NOW, NOT EVER J. BROWN *Vital Speeches of the Day* v83 no3 p79 Mr 2017

Jerry BROWN D. EGGERS color *Vanity Fair* v59 no8 p76 Ag 2017

The New Nullifiers D. F. Kettl *Governing* v30 no7 p16 Ap 2017

The Philosopher King K. Steinmetz color *Time* v190 no10/11 p58 S 18 2017

This Land Is Their Land D. DEVOSS color *Weekly Standard* v22 no22 p20 F 13 2017

Brown, Jerry, 1938—Interviews
Jerry Brown's California Dream T. Dickinson bw color *Rolling Stone* no1298 p32 O 19 2017

BROWN, JESSICA
Good Food: Meat Without Meds color *Prevention* v69 no11 p28 N 2017

Brown, Jessica Wambach
Valor He Built, He Fought bw color *Military History* v34 no2 p16 Jl 2017

Brown, Jim, 1936—Awards
The Activist Minds W. Lowery color *Sports Illustrated* v125 no20

p52 D 19 2016

Brown, Joe

AMERICAN RENAISSANCE color *Popular Science* v289 no5 p66 S/O 2017

BACK TO THE FUTURE color *Popular Science* v289 no6 p4 N/D 2017

LIFE IS THIRSTY *Popular Science* v289 no2 p6 Mr/Ap 2017

LIFE MADE IN CHINA color *Popular Science* p36 Ja/F 2017

MIRACLE IN ICE color *Popular Science* v289 no2 p28 Mr/Ap 2017

THE ORIGIN OF ICE-IES color *Popular Science* v289 no2 p29 Mr/Ap 2017

Shock and awe [Cover story] color diag *Popular Science* v289 no6 p38 N/D 2017

A SINGLE MOMENT OF LIGHT *Popular Science* p8 Ja/F 2017

STORM'S COMING color *Popular Science* v289 no4 p6 Jl/Ag 2017

TIME DIFFERENCES *Popular Science* v289 no5 p5 S/O 2017

TREK STAR VOYAGERS color *Popular Science* p11 Ja/F 2017

WHERE WE'RE GOING, WE WON'T NEED ROADS color *Popular Science* v289 no6 p42 N/D 2017

Brown, John

STOP US IF YOU'VE HEARD THIS ... M. Piellucci color *Sports Illustrated* v127 no8 p60 S 18 2017

Brown, John M.

Weather Queries color graph *Weatherwise* v70 no4 p35 Jl/Ag 2017

Brown, John Seely

Great Businesses Scale Their Learning, Not Just Their Operations color *Harvard Business Review Digital Articles* p2 Je 7 2017

Help Employees Create Knowledge—Not Just Share It *Harvard Business Review Digital Articles* p2 2017

Brown, John, 1800-1859

From Revolution to Rhythm & Blues S. Richardson bw color *American History* v52 no3 p6 Ag 2017

Brown, Jolene

CAN THEIR PROBLEM BE SOLVED? *Successful Farming* v115 no4 p68 Mr 2017

PROBLEM: GROWN SONS ARE ACTING LIKE 2-YEAR-OLDS IN ADULT BODIES *Successful Farming* v115 no1 p70 Ja 2017

THE PROBLEM: WHAT FINANCIAL MATTERS DOES A CITY GIRL NEED TO CONSIDER BEFORE MARRYING HER FARMER? *Successful Farming* v115 no11 p64 S 2017

Brown, Joseph A.

Daniel Berrigan prays the rosary at a supermarket: in July *America* v216 no10 p45 My 1 2017

Brown, Joy

HEAVY P. Williams cartoon *New Yorker* v93 no16 p42 Je 5 2017

Brown, Judy J.

Reovirus infection triggers inflammatory responses to dietary antigens and development of celiac disease color diag *Science* v356 no6333 p44 Ap 7 2017

Brown, Julia A.

Enhancement of Zika virus pathogenesis by preexisting antiflavivirus immunity graph *Science* v356 no6334 p175 Ap 14 2017

Brown, Julie

A DESERT ISLAND bw color *Powder* v45 no5 p28 Ja 2017

HOW TO OWN A SKI AREA color *Powder* v45 no4 p46 D 2016

I Can See Clearly Now color *Powder* v45 no4 p40 D 2016

LATITUES color *Powder* v45 no4 p60 D 2016

SERENDIPITY IN ALASKA color *Powder* v45 no6 p46 F 2017

The Skis of the Year color *Powder* p82 S 2017

SKI TOWN TINDER cartoon *Powder* v45 no3 p60 N 2016

WONDERLAND bw color *Powder* v45 no3 p82 N 2016

Brown, Kahlana Barfield

Bella Hadid color *InStyle* v24 no6 p102 Je 2017

Drew Barrymore color *InStyle* v24 no11 p145 N 2017

Emilia Clarke color *InStyle* v24 no9 p349 S 2017

Emma Watson color *InStyle* v24 no5 p152 My 2017

Joan Smalls color *InStyle* v24 no3 p290 Mr 2017

Lily Aldridge color *InStyle* v24 no10 p187 O 2017

Penélope Cruz color *InStyle* v24 no8 p111 Ag 2017

Sir John color *InStyle* v24 no6 p86 Je 2017

Taraji P. Henson color *InStyle* v24 no7 p91 Jl 2017

Taylor Hill color *InStyle* v24 no4 p148 Ap 2017

Brown, Kane

On Tour With... KANE BROWN J. Abidor color *Seventeen* v75 no11 p20 N 2016

Brown, Kara

Mother. Daughter. Repeat color *Glamour* v115 no5 p189 My 2017

Brown, Karamo

WRITING OUR OWN STORIES: Reality star Karamo Brown says it's time for LGBT people to "take the pen out of Hollywood's hands." J. ANDERSON-MINSHALL *Advocate* no1093 p30 O/N 2017

Brown, Karen A.

The Decline of the Rural American Hospital and How to Reverse It *Harvard Business Review Digital Articles* p2 Ja 30 2015

Brown, Karen P.

Emergence and spread of a human-transmissible multidrug-resistant nontuberculous mycobacterium bibl diag graph *Science* v354 no6313 p751 N 11 2016

Brown, Karma

Karma Brown color *Publishers Weekly* v264 no9 p11 F 27 2017

Brown, Kevin

Hope in the Humanless Economy color *Christianity Today* v61 no6 p30 Jl/Ag 2017

BROWN, LANE

Ryan Adams img *New York* p20 Mr 6 2017

Brown, Laura

CP WHEN CHRISTY MET PIERPAOLO color *InStyle* v24 no3 p330 Mr 2017

DESERT ROSE color *InStyle* v24 no8 p144 Ag 2017

digital directory color *InStyle* v24 no7 p14 Jl 2017

Hello! color *InStyle* v24 no10 p28 O 2017

Hello! color *InStyle* v24 no2 p12 F 2017

Hello! color *InStyle* v24 no4 p24 Ap 2017

Hello! color *InStyle* v24 no7 p16 Jl 2017

KARLIE KLOSS SUPER MODEL [Cover story] color *InStyle* v24 no6 p118 Je 2017

LADY IN RED color *InStyle* v24 no3 p320 Mr 2017

The Most Trusted Name in News color *InStyle* v24 no9 p386 S 2017

SAM MCKNIGHT color *InStyle* v24 no1 p72 Ja 2017

Selena On Fire [Cover story] color *InStyle* v24 no9 p366 S 2017

SJP [Cover story] color *InStyle* v24 no1 p76 Ja 2017

A Star is Reborn [Cover story] color *InStyle* v24 no7 p104 Jl 2017

Welcome color *InStyle* v23 no12 p20 N 2016

BROWN, LEE E.

The Multitrophic Effects of Climate Change and Glacier Retreat in Mountain Rivers *BioScience* v67 no10 p897 O 2017

BROWN, LEVI

THE BURNING QUESTION cartoon color *Men's Health* v32 no5 p142 Je 2017

Brown, Lindy

TAKING FLIGHT S. KROWIAK color *Indianapolis Monthly* v42 no2 p44 O 2017

Brown, Lisa

Girls, Interrupted: An abandoned orphanage fascinates a lonely daughter in this eerie illustrated novel with echoes of "Jane Eyre" *New York Times Book Review* p17 O 8 2017

HOW to READ PROUST in the ORIGINAL *New York Times Book Review* p23 Mr 5 2017

Brown, Luke

Brown and Nogueira Split $11K at Windy Ryon K. Gustave color *Spin to Win Rodeo* v21 no6 p20 Ag 2017

FREEZE FRAME C. Toy color *Spin to Win Rodeo* v20 no10 p52 D 2016

Luke Brown & Jake Long Master the BFI Mountain [Cover story] K. Santos color *Spin to Win Rodeo* v21 no6 p56 Ag 2017

LUKE BROWN'S "ROCKSTAR" A. Wilson color *Spin to Win Rodeo* v20 no12 p52 F 2017

Brown, Lyn Mikel

Powered by Girl: A Field Guide for Supporting Youth Activists *Ms.* v26 no4 p42 Wint 2016

BROWN, MARK

They Did the Right Thing cartoon *Reader's Digest* v190 no1134 p88 O 2017

The travel paradox color graph *Maclean's* v130 no10 p72 N 2017

BROWN, MARLEY

BEHIND THE CURTAIN *Archaeology* v70 no2 p17 Mr/Ap 2017

BRONZE AGE BLING color *Archaeology* v70 no3 p14 My/Je

2017

COMMON GROUND color *Archaeology* v70 no3 p18 My/Je 2017

THE GRAND ARMY DIET color *Archaeology* v70 no4 p22 Je-Ag 2017

HOUSE RULES color *Archaeology* v70 no4 p14 Je-Ag 2017

KNIGHT WATCH [Cover story] color *Archaeology* v70 no4 p21 Je-Ag 2017

TO DIE LIKE AN EGYPTIAN color *Archaeology* v70 no5 p44 S/O 2017

Brown, Mary Ann

Power of Goal Setting C. Toy color *Spin to Win Rodeo* v21 no4 p22 Je 2017

BROWN, MATT

Home of the Brave cartoon *Reader's Digest* v190 no1132 p99 Jl/Ag 2017

Brown, McLeod

The effect of natural disasters on local economies *Monthly Labor Review* p1 Jl 2017

Brown, Meaghen

Lift Off cartoon *Vogue* v206 no11 p170 N 2016

Brown, Melissa Matthews

2017 Southern Beauties color *Southern Living* v52 no10 p53 O 2017

beauty wishes from moms color *Parents* v92 no5 p70 My 2017

Coats of Many Colors color *Southern Living* v52 no9 p48 S 2017

congrats, you just found time for a pedicure! color *Parents* v92 no6 p84 Je 2017

harness your hair envy color *Parents* v92 no4 p88 Ap 2017

A Playground Hug Means Everything color *Parents* v92 no7 p18 Jl 2017

Brown, Michael

Amazon Echo Dot: This is the Echo most people should buy color *PCWorld* v35 no1 p101 Ja 2017

The Art of Seeing Things Invisible R. Armstrong *History Today* v67 no4 p56 Ap 2017

Eero Home WiFi System 2 review: Beacons make this system even easier to install color diag graph *Macworld - Digital Edition* v34 no8 p98 Ag 2017

Google Wifi: Mesh networking made easy color graph *PCWorld* v35 no1 p59 Ja 2017

How I Started a BACKYARD FARM: This suburbanite transformed a patch of grass into food and established a lucrative farm *Mother Earth News* no283 p12 Ag/S 2017

How to set up a wireless router color *PCWorld* v35 no8 p144 Ag 2017

Linksys announces the all-new mid-range EA9300 Wi-Fi router color *Macworld - Digital Edition* p86 Je 13 2017

Linksys Velop Wi-Fi router: One of the best mesh network systems to date color diag graph *PCWorld* v35 no2 p93 F 2017

Logitech ZeroTouch: This Android smartphone holder puts Amazon's Alexa in your car color map *PCWorld* v35 no5 p132 My 2017

Meridian Audio Explorer2 USB DAC review: An inexpensive path to high-resolution audio color *Macworld - Digital Edition* p97 Je 13 2017

Roost Smart Water Leak and Freeze Detector: One feature short of perfection color *PCWorld* v35 no4 p98 Ap 2017

Sony's Bravia OLED: the first flat-screen TV with sound that doesn't suck color *PCWorld* v35 no2 p21 F 2017

TERK TRINITY XTEND: THIS TV ANTENNA TRIES TO PULL DOUBLE-DUTY AS A WI-FI RANGE EXTENDER color *Macworld - Digital Edition* v34 no11 p25 N 2017

Tivoli Audio Model One Digital review: Big sound from a small footprint color *Macworld - Digital Edition* v34 no8 p124 Ag 2017

WATCHAIR SMART ANTENNA color *Macworld - Digital Edition* p40 F 2017

Wi-Fi Alliance introduces a certification program for new smart home construction color diag *PCWorld* v35 no7 p44 Jl 2017

Brown, Mike

"A VERY LIMITED PLAYER" C. Fehrman *Cincinnati Magazine* v50 no12 p66 S 2017

THE SEARCH FOR PLANET NINE S. W. DRIMMER *National Geographic Kids* no468 p18 Mr 2017

Brown, Millard D.

How the U.S. Army Personalized Its Mental Health Care *Harvard Business Review Digital Articles* p2 D 7 2016

Brown, Millie Bobby, 2004-

Just Kids J. CHANEY img *New York* v50 no17 p92 Ag 21 2017

MILLIE BOBBY BROWN M. ZIEGLER *Interview* v46 no9 p56 N 2016

THINGS ARE LOOKING UP... SIDE DOWN [Cover story] T. Stack and S. Li color *Entertainment Weekly* no1485 p16 O 6 2017

Upside Down All Over Again Z. BARON color *GQ: Gentlemen's Quarterly* v97 no11 p68 N 2017

Brown, Molly McCully

The Virginia State Colony for Epileptics and Feebleminded: Poems A. K. Silver color *Christian Century* v134 no10 p55 My 10 2017

Brown, Myles

Rb1 and Trp53 cooperate to suppress prostate cancer lineage plasticity, metastasis, and antiandrogen resistance bibl graph *Science* v355 no6320 p1 Ja 6 2017

Brown, Neal

Neal Brown Restaurateur *Indianapolis Monthly* v40 no11 p46 Jl 2017

ROASTED ASPARAGUS *Indianapolis Monthly* v12 no40 p76 Ag 2017

BROWN, NICHOLAS J. L.

Public Debate, Scientific Skepticism, and Science Denial *Skeptical Inquirer* v41 no1 p40 Ja/F 2017

Brown, Noleen

Publish openly but responsibly color *Science* v357 no6347 p141 Jl 14 2017

Brown, Patrick T.

Catholic campuses should look outward to the larger church *America* v217 no4 p10 Ag 21 2017

Reporting on global warming: A study in headlines *Physics Today* v69 no10 p10 O 2016

Brown, Paula R.

Elimination of the male reproductive tract in the female embryo is promoted by COUP-TFII in mice color graph *Science* v357 no6352 p717 Ag 18 2017

Brown, Peter

At the Center of a Roiling World [Cover story] color *New York Review of Books* v64 no8 p48 My 11 2017

The Cats Come Back *New York Times Book Review* p31 N 13 2016

Dialogue With God color *New York Review of Books* v64 no16 p45 O 26 2017

Recapturing Jerusalem at the Met color *New York Review of Books* v63 no19 p10 D 8 2016

Brown, Peter T.

Spin-imbalance in a 2D Fermi-Hubbard system diag graph *Science* v357 no6358 p1385 S 29 2017

Brown, Peter, 1979-

The Wild Robot *Publishers Weekly* v263 no49 p69 D 7 2016

Brown, Richard

The Door of No Return color *Commonweal* v144 no9 p39 My 19 2017

Panel 42W, Row 39 color *Commonweal* v114 no14 p38 S 8 2017

Brown, Robert

Research, practice, and policy connections: The ArtPlay case study bibl chart diag *Arts Education Policy Review* v118 no1 p37 2017

Brown, Roger, 1942-1997

A storm is coming J. Bleem color *U.S. Catholic* v82 no1 p50 Ja 2017

Brown, Ryan Lenora

56 MILES OF FREEDOM color *Runner's World* v52 no9 p84 O 2017

Brown, S.

Jupiter's interior and deep atmosphere: The initial pole-to-pole passes with the Juno spacecraft [Cover story] color graph *Science* v356 no6340 p821 My 26 2017

BROWN, SARA

THE Accessible CABIN color *Cabin Living* p64 Ja/F 2017

American Beauty color *Timber Home Living* v27 no5 p10 O 2017

editor's note *Timber Home Living* p8 2017 SpecialIssue

Enjoy the Ride color *Timber Home Living* p6 2017 Annual Buyers

Eye on Design *Timber Home Living* v27 no2 p6 Ap 2017

I'M FLAT AND I'M PROUD C. Guthrie bw color *O, The Oprah Magazine* p90 O 2017

Say Hello to Summer! *Timber Home Living* v27 no4 p8 Ag 2017

The Space Issue *Timber Home Living* v27 no3 p10 Je 2017

Brown, Scott

Navigating Health Care's Transition to Private Exchanges *Harvard Business Review Digital Articles* p2 N 7 2014

Brown, Scott—Interviews

Four Questions for Scott Brown *Texas Monthly* v45 no2 p6 F 2017

Brown, Selina

Ladies With Lassos: Four women known as the Cowgirls of Color have found a niche within the rodeo community L. PEOPLES img *New York* v50 no13 p46 Je 26 2017

Brown, Shannon

Honor Roles J. VRABEL *Indianapolis Monthly* p17 F 2017

Brown, Sherrod, 1952-

BACK IN THE SPOTLIGHT *Successful Farming* v114 no13 p16 D 2016

Brown, Stacy—Interviews

Sharing a Taste of the South P. MERTZ ESSWEIN color *Kiplinger's Personal Finance* v71 no5 p16 My 2017

Brown, Sterling K.

FAMILY ALBUM I. RATLEDGE *TV Guide* v64 no46 p24 N 7 2016

SPOTLIGHT ON: STERLING K. BROWN J. BENNETT color *Ebony* v72/73 no12/1 p82 O/N 2017

Sterling K. Brown A. Wilkinson color *Entertainment Weekly* no1444/1445 p30 D 16 2016

Sterling K. Brown J. ZAMBRANO color *O, The Oprah Magazine* p30 S 2017

TOASTING THIS IS US color *Entertainment Weekly* no1486 p49 O 13 2017

Brown, Sterling K.—Interviews

STERLING K. BROWN D. Zepeda color *Runner's World* v52 no8 p96 S 2017

Brown, Taylor

MYSTIC RIVER A. ENJETI *Atlanta* v56 no11 p38 Mr 2017

BROWN, TERI

Trek and Toast color *Backpacker* p19 My 2017

BROWN, THERESA CARDINAL

DRUG SMUGGLERS HAVE ALREADY BEATEN TRUMP'S WALL color *Reason* v49 no1 p32 My 2017

Brown, Thomas M.

Relativistic deflection of background starlight measures the mass of a nearby white dwarf star chart color graph *Science* v356 no6342 p1046 Je 9 2017

Brown, Tia

50-State Sisterhood color *Glamour* v115 no9 p30 S 2017

I Love You—Now Go Home color *Glamour* v115 no11 p105 N 2017

BROWN, TIA S.

7 Habits That Will Save Your Long-Distance Relationship color *Ebony* v72 no6 p68 Ap/My 2017

Bae Watch color *Ebony* v72 no4 p82 F 2017

Cleaning House bw color *Ebony* v72 no5 p68 Mr 2017

CROWNED jewels color *Ebony* v72 no6 p90 Ap/My 2017

DETACHING MONEY FROM MANHOOD color *Ebony* v72 no5 p69 Mr 2017

Failure to Launch color *Ebony* v72 no8 p66 Je 2017

Genius at Work color *Ebony* v72 no4 p80 F 2017

GIFTS THAT GIVE color *Ebony* v72 no3 p92 D 2016/Ja 2017

Holiday Happiness: Will You Fake It or Make It? color *Ebony* v72 no3 p98 D 2016/Ja 2017

How to Be Divorceproof cartoon *Ebony* v72 no4 p74 F 2017

Killer Crossover color *Ebony* v72 no6 p74 Ap/My 2017

Killing the Competition color *Ebony* v72 no5 p66 Mr 2017

'ME TIME' FOR MOMS cartoon *Ebony* v72 no6 p66 Ap/My 2017

Mixing Dollars and Sense color *Ebony* v72 no5 p74 Mr 2017

Moving to the Middle color *Ebony* v72 no6 p70 Ap/My 2017

#RelationshipGoals color *Ebony* v72 no4 p78 F 2017

SEXUAL HEALING color *Ebony* v72 no4 p77 F 2017

STRANGERS IN A STRANGE LAND color *Ebony* v72 no6 p69 Ap/My 2017

Sugar Mama color *Ebony* v72 no6 p75 Ap/My 2017

Tightening Your Bond With Boo color *Ebony* v72 no4 p76 F 2017

Total Boz Moves color *Ebony* v72 no5 p72 Mr 2017

WOMEN'S WORK color *Ebony* v72 no5 p84 Mr 2017

WOMEN UP color *Ebony* v72 no5 p70 Mr 2017

Brown, Tim

Capitalism Needs Design Thinking *Harvard Business Review Digital Articles* p2 D 8 2014

Capitalism Needs Design Thinking T. Brown, R. L. Martin et al *Harvard Business Review Digital Articles* p2 D 8 2014

Leaders Can Turn Creativity into a Competitive Advantage *Harvard Business Review Digital Articles* p2 N 2 2016

When Everyone Is Doing Design Thinking, Is It Still a Competitive Advantage? *Harvard Business Review Digital Articles* p2 Ag 27 2015

BROWN, TINA

Recalling the People's Princess bw color *Maclean's* v130 no7 p55 Ag 2017

S.I. Newhouse color *Time* v190 no15 p13 O 16 2017

BROWN, TOM JR.

Aluminum Foil color *Backpacker* p40 O 2017

Raingear color *Backpacker* p46 My 2017

saved by: Lip Balm color *Backpacker* p42 S 2017

Snowshoes color *Backpacker* v45 no2 p42 Mr 2017

Brown, Trisha, 1936-2017

Moments in Time *Dance Magazine* v91 no7 p67 Jl 2017

When Worlds Collide J. Acocella bw *New Yorker* v92 no48 p11 F 6 2017

Brown, Vernon

TOP 7 *South Dakota Magazine* v32 no6 p17 Mr/Ap 2017

Brown, Victoria

Drama as a valuable learning medium in early childhood bibl *Arts Education Policy Review* v118 no3 p164 2017

Brown, Virginia Ruth

Virginia Ruth Brown A. M. Bernstein, R. P. Redwine et al *Physics Today* v69 no10 p67 O 2016

Brown, William

Can't Hurry Love N. WILSON color *Natural History* v125 no4 p48 Ap 2017

BROWN, YVETTE NICOLE

Gale Anne HURD *Interview* v47 no3 p26 My 2017

Why I Still Love The Walking Dead *TV Guide* v65 no11 p18 Mr 6 2017

Brown dwarf stars

Brown Dwarfs Mimic Stellar Siblings J. BOCHANSKI *Sky & Telescope* v134 no4 p10 O 2017

Zones, spots, and planetary-scale waves beating in brown dwarf atmospheres D. Apai, T. Karalidi et al color graph *Science* v357 no6352 p683 Ag 18 2017

Brown dwarf stars—Research

BROWN DWARFS FORMING PLANETS K. Haynes color *Astronomy* v45 no1 p10 Ja 2017

Brown Girls (TV program)

BROWN GIRL AUTEUR B. GOLDEN color *Chicago* v66 no2 p25 F 2017

Brown sugar

THE ART OF THE ROAST M. True color *Sunset* v237 no6 p70 D 2016

Brown trout fishing

BROWN UNIVERSITY D. KARCZYNSKI and G. BETHGE color *Outdoor Life* v224 no2 p28 F/Mr 2017

BRUISER BROWNS S. RYAN color *Outdoor Life* v224 no7 p55 S 2017

Brown widow spider

Urban Biodiversity J. KEATS color *Discover* v38 no10 p12 D 2017

Brownback, Sam, 1956-

If They Only Had a Brain S. MOORE color *Weekly Standard* v22 no36 p16 My 29 2017

Browne, Alix

RUNWAY L. NEILSON *Interview* v46 no8 p38 O 2016

Browne, Daniel

Summer learning that sticks color *Phi Delta Kappan* v98 no4 p15 D 2016/Ja 2017

Browne, David

THE 50 GREATEST CONCERTS OF THE LAST 50 YEARS bw color *Rolling Stone* no1286 p30 My 4 2017

Bob Weir bw *Rolling Stone* no1273 p58 N 3 2016

p38 D 2016

Backyard Billfish color *Power & Motoryacht* v34 no10 p46 O 2017

The Beauty of Baja color *Power & Motoryacht* v33 no2 p38 F 2017

The Bite Is On! color *Power & Motoryacht* v33 no3 p38 Mr 2017

Boater Beware color *Power & Motoryacht* v34 no11 p58 N 2017

A Conch's Life color *Power & Motoryacht* v34 no7 p64 Jl 2017

Fact or Superstition? color *Power & Motoryacht* v34 no9 p32 S 2017

Fine-tune Your Endgame color *Power & Motoryacht* v34 no7 p24 Jl 2017

Fishing for Kids color *Power & Motoryacht* v33 no4 p30 Ap 2017

A Fishing Life color *Power & Motoryacht* v34 no8 p20 Ag 2017

Reinventing a Classic chart color *Power & Motoryacht* v34 no7 p60 Jl 2017

Rigged for Tuna color *Power & Motoryacht* v34 no6 p24 Je 2017

Brownlee, Shannon

The Health Care Debate We're Not Having color *Washington Monthly* v49 no9/10 p122 S/O 2017

Introduction: A Cure for High Health Care Costs color *Washington Monthly* v49 no3-5 p38 Mr-My 2017

Brownmiller, Susan, 1935-

THREAT OF FORCE S. Brownmiller *Lapham's Quarterly* v10 no3 p182 Summ 2017

Brown-Philpot, Stacy—Awards

And the Award Goes to... S. Lynn color *Black Enterprise* v47 no2 p22 S 2016

Brown-Philpot, Stacy—Political & social views

PERSON OF INTEREST K. Kokalitcheva color *Fortune* v174 no8 p40 D 15 2016

Brownrigg, Sylvia

Old Flames Die Hard: A sequel by Sylvia Brownrigg reunites former lovers two decades later S. GILBERT *New York Times Book Review* p19 S 3 2017

Brown-Saracino, Brooke

How to Work with Colleagues Who Are Less Creative than You *Harvard Business Review Digital Articles* p2 S 16 2015

BROWNSTEIN, CARRIE

The Year in Reading [Cover story] *New York Times Book Review* p8 D 25 2016

Brownstein, Carrie, 1974-—Interviews

Portlandia's "Put a Bird on It!" D. Snierson color *Entertainment Weekly* no1454/1455 p89 F 24 2017

Brownstein, Joan R.

Art therapy cartoon *Magazine Antiques* v184 no1 p54 Ja/F 2017

Brownstein, John

How a Startup Accelerator at Boston Children's Hospital Helps Launch Companies color *Harvard Business Review Digital Articles* p2 Je 5 2017

Browsers (Computer programs)

    See also

    Google Chrome (Computer software)

    Mozilla Firefox (Computer software)

    Safari (Computer software)

10 ALTERNATIVE BROWSERS I. PAUL color *PCWorld* v35 no9 p91 S 2017

10 Best Edge (SO FAR) Extensions I. PAUL *PCWorld* v35 no8 p127 Ag 2017

Another 40 million people bolt from Microsoft's browsers as mass exodus continues G. KEIZER color graph *PCWorld* p58 D 2016

Get more Edge extensions by installing beta versions I. PAUL color *PCWorld* v35 no11 p141 N 2016

MR. KNOW-IT-ALL J. MOOALLEM cartoon *Wired* v25 no7 p28 Jl 2017

Browsers (Computer programs)—Evaluation

Anonymous browsing with Tor reduces exposure but still has risks G. FLEISHMAN cartoon color *Macworld - Digital Edition* p99 Mr 2017

Become an expert at Safari for iOS with these 8 tips and tricks B. PATTERSON color *Macworld - Digital Edition* v34 no8 p51 Ag 2017

Best web browsers of 2017: Chrome, Edge, Firefox, and Opera go head-to-head I. PAUL color graph *PCWorld* v35 no9 p43 S 2017

Meet Opera Neon, Opera's radical vision for the future of web browsers M. HACHMAN color *PCWorld* v35 no2 p17 F 2017

BROYARD, BLISS

the fun one color *Parents* v92 no8 p102 Ag 2017

Brubaker, Matt

Embracing the Hack Attack *Parks & Recreation* v52 no5 p70 My 2017

The Mistakes PE Firms Make When They Pick CEOs for Portfolio Companies *Harvard Business Review Digital Articles* p2 S 6 2016

Brubaker, Rogers

Rogers Brubaker, Trans: Gender and Race in an Age of Unsettled Identities J. Davis *Society* v54 no1 p78 F 2017

Thinking with trans L. Curry diag *Christian Century* v134 no2 p34 Ja 18 2017

TRANS S. DHANVANTARI color *Maclean's* v129 no50 p61 D 19 2016

Brubaker, Sarah Morice

Theology through prayer [Cover story] color *Christian Century* v133 no24 p24 N 23 2016

Brubert, Jacob—Interviews

Three Qs *Science* v354 no6312 p531 N 4 2016

Bruce, Al—Interviews

MEET CAPT. AL BRUCE *Sea Magazine* v108 no12 pPNW-12 D 2016

Bruce, Dannie

Thoughts on previous issues color *American Cowboy* v23 no5 p24 F/Mr 2017

Bruce, Stephanie

MARATHON MOM S. L. Butler color *Runner's World* v52 no2 p34 Mr 2017

BRUCK, CONNIE

A HOLLYWOOD STORY cartoon *New Yorker* v93 no11 p34 My 1 2017

Bruckbauer, Andreas

A switch from canonical to noncanonical autophagy shapes B cell responses bibl graph *Science* v355 no6325 p641 F 10 2017

BRUCKNER, JULIA MICHIE

More Than Skin Deep color *Discover* v38 no10 p20 D 2017

Bruckner, Pascal

Material World: A French essayist and intellectual looks at financial considerations philosophically F. SALMON *New York Times Book Review* p15 My 14 2017

Bruder, Jessica

America's Newest, Oldest Nomads S. Begley color *Time* v190 no12 p22 S 25 2017

SNOWDEN'S BOX *Harper's Magazine* v334 no2004 p25 My 2017

Bruder, Jessica—Interviews

Q&A: JESSICA BRUDER A. Taylor *Nation* v305 no9 p5 O 16 2017

Brueggemann, Walter

Longing for Home: Forced Displacement and Postures of Hospitality *Christian Century* v134 no1 p38 Ja 4 2017

Saul and David's destructive powers *Christian Century* v134 no16 p30 Ag 2 2017

A Unique Time of God: Karl Barth's WWI Sermons *Christian Century* v134 no13 p37 Je 21 2017

Uses and Abuses of Moses: Literary Representations since the Enlightenment color *Christian Century* v133 no21 p54 O 12 2016

WRITERS' FEAST color *Christian Century* v134 no10 p30 My 10 2017

Bruelheide, Helge

Positive biodiversity-productivity relationship predominant in global forests bibl chart graph map *Science* v354 no6309 paaf8957-1 O 14 2016

Bruenig, Elizabeth

Augustine gets a makeover color *America* v217 no4 p44 Ag 21 2017

EVER ANCIENT, EVER NEW color *America* v217 no3 p18 Ag 7 2017

LUTHER'S REVOLUTION *Nation* v305 no3 p31 Jl 31 2017

A MORAL BULWARK bw *Nation* v304 no3 p33 Ja 30 2017

Brugge, Joan

Not just Salk color *Science* v357 no6356 p1105 S 15 2017

BRUGGEMAN, RICK

BIRD-DOGGING BEARS cartoon color *Outdoor Life* v224 no5 p12 Je/Jl 2017

Brugière, Sabine
An algal photoenzyme converts fatty acids to hydrocarbons color graph *Science* v357 no6354 p903 S 1 2017

Bruinius, Harry
New protected area in Utah includes land that's sacred for Native Americans color *Christian Century* v134 no3 p13 F 2017
Refugee plan divides religious leaders color *Christian Century* v134 no5 p12 Mr 1 2017

BRUINTJES, RICK
Shipbuilding Docks as Experimental Systems for Realistic Assessments of Anthropogenic Stressors on Marine Organisms *BioScience* v67 no9 p853 S 2017

Bruises
POP QUIZ? C. Barakat and M. Freckleton color *Equus* no474 p14 Mr 2017

Brûlé, Tyler, 1968-
Nowhere Mag K. CHAYKA *New Republic* v248 no7 p64 Jl 2017

Brulliard, Nicolas
THE BURRO QUANDARY *National Parks* v91 no1 p28 Wint 2017
Desert Gator: The life and times of Clem of Grand Canyon-Parashant *National Parks* v91 no3 p58 Summ 2017
Esther of the Rockies *National Parks* v91 no4 p58 Fall 2017
Mercury Rising? *National Parks* v91 no2 p24 Spr 2017
Soaking It All In: The woods are lovely, dark and deep—perfect for forest bathers searching for a little peace of mind *National Parks* v91 no3 p12 Summ 2017
Unearthing a Lost City *National Parks* v91 no2 p66 Spr 2017
Vulture Vandals *National Parks* v91 no4 p24 Fall 2017
Wild West Josie *National Parks* v91 no1 p58 Wint 2017

Brumback, Claire
Hot on the TRAILS: A ROAD-FREE GUIDE TO EXPLORING CENTRAL INDIANA *Indianapolis Monthly* v40 no10 p59 Je 2017

BRUMBAUGH, DANIEL R.
Long-Term Studies Contribute Disproportionately to Ecology and Policy *BioScience* v67 no3 p271 Mr 2017

Brun, A. S.
Reconciling solar and stellar magnetic cycles with nonlinear dynamo simulations diag *Science* v357 no6347 p185 Jl 14 2017

BRUN, JULIEN
Skills and Knowledge for Data-Intensive Environmental Research *BioScience* v67 no6 p546 Je 2017

Brun, Yves V.
Treadmilling by FtsZ filaments drives peptidoglycan synthesis and bacterial cell division bibl graph *Science* v355 no6326 p739 F 17 2017

Brunches
Golden Age P. SHARPE *Texas Monthly* v44 no11 p44 N 2016
Happy Grandmother's Day S. Evans color *Southern Living* v52 no5 p12 My 2017
MOST EXPENNSIVE BRUNCH *Washingtonian Magazine* v52 no1 p92 O 2016

BRUNDAGE, ELIZABETH
The Devil's Detail *New York Times Book Review* p12 Mr 26 2017

Brundage, Vernon, Jr.
Unemployment holds steady for much of 2016 but edges down in the fourth quarter bibl chart color graph *Monthly Labor Review* p1 Mr 2017

Brune, Mary
Explore, Enjoy--and Parent *Sierra* v102 no5 p6 St/O 2017

Brune, Michael
Explore, Enjoy--and Parent *Sierra* v102 no5 p6 St/O 2017
Get Out There *Sierra* v101 no4 p4 Jl/Ag 2016
History Lessons and Future Dreams *Sierra* v102 no3 p6 My/Je 2017
Time to March *Sierra* v102 no2 p7 Mr/Ap 2017
To Change Everything, It Takes Everyone: The Sierra Club is part of a larger ecosystem of progressive change-makers *Sierra* v102 no4 p6 Jl/Ag 2017
Turning Walls Into Bridges *Sierra* v102 no1 p6 Ja/F 2017
We the People *Sierra* v101 no5 p4 S/O 2016
Yes We Did *Sierra* v101 no6 p4 N/D 2016

Brunel, Valentin
'This Girl' L. KIESLING *New York Times Magazine* p34 Mr 12 2017

Brunelli, Jennifer
Fix It Faster with Food K. Morell bw cartoon *Men's Health* v32 no3 p62 Ap 2017

Brunello Cucinelli SpA
My Stuff bw color *Vanity Fair* v58 no11 p80 N 2016
Why Does This Sweater Cost $4,925? E. Wilson color *InStyle* v24 no10 p71 O 2017

Bruner, Raisa
The 2017 Album Watch List color *Time* v188 no27-28 p106 D 26 2016
The Agony and the Ecstasy of Perfume Genius color *Time* v189 no19 p52 My 22 2017
The Best of Everything This Year-So Far color *Time* v189 no21 p61 Je 5 2017
Demi Lovato color *Time* v190 no14 p54 O 9 2017
Esperanza Spalding As a Real-Time Innovator color *Time* v190 no10/11 p106 S 18 2017
How Khalid Makes Music color *Time* v189 no14 p51 Ap 17 2017
Jeff Garlin color *Time* v189 no19 p50 My 22 2017
La La Land, a Truly Modern Hollywood Musical, Strikes All the Best Chords color *Time* v188 no24 p61 D 12 2016
A New Kind of Star Power color *Time* v190 no2/3 p24 Jl 10-17 2017
New Music Containing Multitudes color *Time* v189 no14 p50 Ap 17 2017
The New Science of the Truly Unstoppable, Impossible-to-Resist Summer Jam color *Time* v190 no9 p53 S 4 2017
Next Generation Leaders color *Time* v190 no16/17 p74 O 23 2017
Pop Chart color *Time* v188 no19 p62 N 7 2016
Pop Chart color *Time* v189 no12 p62 Ap 3 2017
Pop Chart color *Time* v189 no18 p58 My 15 2017
Pop Chart color *Time* v190 no5 p63 Jl 31 2017
Songs That Won the Summer color *Time* v190 no9 p54 S 4 2017
Summer Movie Preview: August color *Time* v189 no20 p58 My 29 2017
Summer Movie Preview: July color *Time* v189 no20 p56 My 29 2017
Summer Movie Preview: June color *Time* v189 no20 p50 My 29 2017
Summer Movie Preview: May color *Time* v189 no20 p48 My 29 2017

Brunet, J.-F.
The sacral autonomic outflow is sympathetic bibl color diag *Science* v354 no6314 p893 N 18 2016

BRUNET, JÖRG
Combining Biodiversity Resurveys across Regions to Advance Global Change Research *BioScience* v67 no1 p73 Ja 2017

Bruni, Carla, 1967-
CARLA UNCENSORED M. Heyman bw *Harper's Bazaar* no3656 p325 S 2017

Bruning, Jennifer
FOODS FOR THOUGHT J. Berlin diag *National Geographic* v232 no3 p20 S 2017

Brunker, Cal
When Art Imitates Park Life: "The Nut Job 2: Nutty by Nature" animates land conservation V. Paynich *Parks & Recreation* v52 no8 p42 Ag 2017

Brunner, Claudia
Male sex in houseflies is determined by Mdmd, a paralog of the generic splice factor gene CWC22 bw color *Science* v356 no6338 p642 My 12 2017

Brunner, Rob
CROSS PURPOSES: The Museum of the Bible will bring religion near the Mall. Does it belong there? *Washingtonian Magazine* v53 no1 p15 O 2017

Brunner, Tracy
You Never Forget Your First Time diag il *Backpacker* v45 no2 p64 Mr 2017

Brunner-Winkle Aircraft Corp.
FREE BIRD: Anne Morrow Lindbergh's first plane could be hanging in a museum. Instead, it's still flying over Maryland A. Beaujon *Washingtonian Magazine* v52 no12 p54 S 2017

Brunnström, Hans
A pathology atlas of the human cancer transcriptome diag *Science* v357 no6352 p660 Ag 18 2017

Bruno, A.

Demonstration of an ac Josephson junction laser bibl diag *Science* v355 no6328 p939 Mr 3 2017

Bruno, Debra

A COMMUNITY, UNLEASHED: The NoMa dog park opens this fall. It got built thanks to 400 neighbors who sneaked onto a vacant, muddy lot *Washingtonian Magazine* v53 no1 p213 O 2017

NOT-FOREVER FAMILIES color *Washingtonian Magazine* v52 no7 p161 Ap 2017

A SHARP APPROACH *Washingtonian Magazine* v52 no3 p181 D 2016

Bruno, James

Advice for Trump on Post-Fidel Cuba *Washington Monthly* p1 Ja/F 2017

BRUNO, R. STEPHANIE

THE UPTOWN EXPERIENCE [Cover story] color *New Orleans Magazine* v51 no6 p58 Ap 2017

BRUNS, RICHARD

DRUG ADVERTISING color *Scientific American* v315 no3 p5 S 2016

Brunskill, Andrew

A multifunctional catalyst that stereoselectively assembles prodrugs diag *Science* v356 no6336 p426 Ap 28 2017

Brunskill, Emma

Playtime's Over *MIT Technology Review* v120 no2 p10 Mr/Ap 2017

Brunt, Douglas

By the Book *New York Times Book Review* p7 N 13 2016

Brusatte, Stephen

A Mesozoic aviary bibl color diag *Science* v355 no6327 p792 F 24 2017

Taking Wing [Cover story] color *Scientific American* v316 no1 p48 Ja 2017

T. rex Evolution: Smarts First, Size Second G. TARLACH color diag map *Discover* v38 no1 p42 Ja/F 2017

Bruse, Shannon

Distribution and clinical impact of functional variants in 50,726 whole-exome sequences from the DiscovEHR study chart graph *Science* v354 no6319 paaf6814-1 D 23 2016

Brush, Silla

Are Banking Rules About To Go the Other Way? color *Bloomberg Businessweek* no4520 p37 My 1 2017

BRUSKOTTER, JEREMY T.

Conserving the World's Megafauna and Biodiversity: The Fierce Urgency of Now *BioScience* v67 no3 p197 Mr 2017

Modernization, Risk, and Conservation of the World's Largest Carnivores *BioScience* v67 no7 p646 Jl 2017

Saving the World's Terrestrial Megafauna color *BioScience* v66 no10 p807 O 1 2016

Brustein, Joshua

The Bot That Bluffed Me color *Bloomberg Businessweek* no4511 p29 F 13 2017

Captain Ahab Doesn't Live Here Anymore color *Bloomberg Businessweek* no4540 p26 O 2 2017

China's Twitter Returns From the Dead color graph *Bloomberg Businessweek* no4526 p28 Je 12 2017

D.C. Is Building an Uber-Fighting Test Lab color *Bloomberg Businessweek* no4524 p34 My 29 2017

Juno Got Sold, and Its Drivers Got Stiffed *Bloomberg Businessweek* no4521 p33 My 8 2017

Keep Austin ... Tough To Get Around? *Bloomberg Businessweek* no4515 p31 Mr 20 2017

Making VR Matter cartoon color *Bloomberg Businessweek* no4496 p32 O 24 2016

A New Sports Authority *Bloomberg Businessweek* no4532 p20 Jl 31 2017

No Use for Old School Ties color *Bloomberg Businessweek* no4526 p32 Je 12 2017

THE PECULIAR PARABLE OF THE LYFT LOT cartoon *Bloomberg Businessweek* no4534 p58 Ag 14 2017

Reinventions: Scrip color *Bloomberg Businessweek* no4494 p46 O 10 2016

A Reputation for Badoo Behavior color *Bloomberg Businessweek* no4526 p30 Je 12 2017

Time for Some Traffic Problems on Netflix? *Bloomberg Businessweek* no4500 p34 N 21 2016

Brustein, William I.

MEMBER NEWS *Phi Kappa Phi Forum* v97 no1 p7 Spr 2017

A ROAD MAP TO THE GLOBAL UNIVERSITY map *Phi Kappa Phi Forum* v97 no2 p16 Summ 2017

Brutalism (Architecture)

A Concrete Vision J. McDERMOTT *America* v216 no1 p11 Ja 2 2017

Last days of the Smithsons' Robin Hood Gardens H. PEARMAN *Architectural Record* v205 no9 p32 S 2017

Brutt, Ryan

Automotive Archaeology A Junkyard That No Longer Is color *Hot Rod* v70 no3 p14 Mr 2017

Automotive Archaeology: Junkyard Jewels color *Hot Rod* v70 no8 p22 Ag 2017

Automotive Archaeology: Mopars in the Trees color *Hot Rod* v70 no11 p16 N 2017

Automotive Archaeology: The Bee in the Garage color *Hot Rod* v70 no12 p14 D 2017

Automotive Archaeology This Olds 442 Is Waiting to be Saved color *Hot Rod* v70 no1 p26 Ja 2017

Automotive Archaeology Train Station in the Junkyard?! color *Hot Rod* v69 no12 p16 D 2016

Barn Full of Mopars! color *Hot Rod* v70 no2 p16 F 2017

Birds in the Barn—and a Charger! color *Hot Rod* v70 no7 p20 Jl 2017

Buried Treasure in Backyard color *Hot Rod* v70 no9 p22 S 2017

Macho Wagon Heading to New Home color *Hot Rod* v70 no6 p24 Je 2017

Mopar Sacrifice color *Hot Rod* v70 no5 p14 My 2017

Shortened 1957 Bel-Air Convertible color *Hot Rod* v70 no4 p18 Ap 2017

Bruxism—Treatment

Protect Your Teeth [Cover story] A. Weil color *Prevention* v69 no5 p24 My 2017

Bry, Dave

THE FIFTH QUARTER color *Esquire* p24 Je/Jl 2017

Talking About the Weather *New York Times Magazine* p18 My 14 2017

Bry, Kent—Interviews

MAGIC CARPET RIDE K. Krichko color *Powder* v45 no4 p52 D 2016

Bryan, Ashley—Exhibitions

PAINTER AND POET *Atlanta* v56 no12 p34 Ap 2017

BRYAN, BILL

THE ROAD TO RIDE bw color *Missouri Life* v44 no5 p48 Ag 2017

Bryan, Gregory

THE STORYTELLER'S STORY: Celebrated illustrator Paul Goble is the subject of a new biography *South Dakota Magazine* v33 no2 p71 Jl/Ag 2017

Bryan, Meredith

SELF-HEALTH cartoon *O, The Oprah Magazine* p97 My 2017

Bryan, Wesley—Interviews

Bank On Him P. Madden and C. Barrett color *Golf Magazine* v59 no3 p25 Mr 2017

Bryant, Aidy, 1987-

Red-Carpet Revolution L. Chan, F. Kane et al color *Glamour* v115 no3 p82 Mr 2017

Bryant, Cathy Lynn

Sarah Anne's Faithful Friends *Publishers Weekly* v264 no7 p58 F 13 2017

Bryant, Daryn

What My Horse Wears on His Feet cartoon *Horse & Rider* v56 no5 p80 My 2017

Bryant, Don

Deliberate Moves A. Cohen color *Downbeat* v84 no9 p27 S 2017

Bryant, Doug Jr.

TECH TRENDS CHANGING OUR WORLD color *Black Enterprise* v47 no2 p46 S 2016

Bryant, Edwin F.

Bhakti Yoga: Tales and Teachings from the Bhagavata Purana color *Publishers Weekly* v264 no19 p55 My 8 2017

Bryant, Elizabeth

HOW WORK STYLES INFORM LEADERSHIP [Cover story] A. BEARD color *Harvard Business Review* v95 no2 p58 Mr/Ap 2017

Bryant, Greg

Treasures of the Tarantula color graph *Sky & Telescope* v134 no5 p24 N 2017

Bryant, Jeff
A Southern California District Resists Bad Education Policy color *Progressive* v81 no6 p40 Ag/S 2017

Bryant, Jefferson
BATTERY CHARGERS: THE NEED FOR SPEED TO JUMP-START AN ENGINE DETERMINES WHICH CHARGER TO GET D. Mowitz *Successful Farming* v115 no12 p41 O 2017
Beyond the Iron Curtain color *Hot Rod* v70 no10 p74 O 2017
GEAR UP color *Hot Rod* v70 no7 p76 Jl 2017
SLIPPED DISC color *Hot Rod* v70 no8 p84 Ag 2017
Step by Step: Solid Foundations color *Hot Rod* v70 no12 p84 D 2017

Bryant, Jennifer O.
Dressage Movers and Shakers Gather in St. Louis color *Practical Horseman* v45 no3 p64 Mr 2017

Bryant, Jerry L.
Never Dull in Deadwood *South Dakota Magazine* v32 no6 p46 Mr/Ap 2017

Bryant, Josephine M.
Emergence and spread of a human-transmissible multidrug-resistant nontuberculous mycobacterium bibl diag graph *Science* v354 no6313 p751 N 11 2016

Bryant, Joyce
Who's That Lady? bw color *O, The Oprah Magazine* p127 Mr 2017

Bryant, Kobe, 1978–
Seven for The Road B. Golliver, A. Lawrence et al color *Sports Illustrated* v125 no20 p122 D 19 2016

Bryant, Kris
9 BORN TO WIN [Cover story] T. Verducci color diag *Sports Illustrated* v126 no9 p52 Mr 27 2017

Bryant, Martavis
MARTAVIS BRYANT WILL … J. Feldman color *Sports Illustrated* v127 no4 p44 Ag 7 2017

Bryant, Phil, 1954–
IN THE HOLLOW C. Offutt *Harper's Magazine* v333 no1998 p53 N 2016
SNAP JUDGMENT D. d'Amora graph *Mother Jones* v41 no6 p14 N/D 2016

Bryk, Anthony S.
The right network for the right problem color diag *Phi Delta Kappan* v98 no3 p8 N 2016

Brynildsen, Mark P.
Biased inheritance protects older bacteria from harm diag *Science* v356 no6335 p247 Ap 21 2017

Brynjolfsson, Erik
ARTIFICIAL INTELLIGENCE, FOR REAL: YOU'VE BEEN TOLD IT WILL TRANSFORM EVERYTHING. YOU'VE BEEN TOLD YOU NEED TO INVEST IN IT. BUT YOU HAVEN'T BEEN TOLD HOW. START HERE *Harvard Business Review Digital Articles* p1 Jl 1 2017
THE BUSINESS OF ARTIFICIAL INTELLIGENCE: WHAT IT CAN—AND CANNOT—DO FOR YOUR ORGANIZATION *Harvard Business Review Digital Articles* p3 Jl 1 2017
The Rise of Data-Driven Decision Making Is Real but Uneven *Harvard Business Review Digital Articles* p2 F 3 2016
THREE SUMMARIES: HUMAN, EXTRACTIVE, AND ABSTRACTIVE *Harvard Business Review Digital Articles* p26 Jl 1 2017
What's Driving the Machine Learning Explosion? *Harvard Business Review Digital Articles* p2 Jl 18 2017
WHAT'S DRIVING THE MACHINE LEARNING EXPLOSION? Three factors make this AI's moment *Harvard Business Review Digital Articles* p12 Jl 1 2017

Bryson, Alex
Profit Sharing Boosts Employee Productivity and Satisfaction *Harvard Business Review Digital Articles* p2 D 13 2017

Bryson, Joanna J.
Semantics derived automatically from language corpora contain human-like biases chart graph *Science* v356 no6334 p183 Ap 14 2017

Brzezinski, Mika, 1967–
Donald Trump Is Not Invited to the Wedding: Joe, Mika and their star-crossed relationship with the president O. Nuzzi img *New York* v50 no15 p16 Jl 24 2017

Brzezinski, Zbigniew, 1928-2017
How To Address Strategic Insecurity In A Turbulent Age *NPQ: New Perspectives Quarterly* v34 no2 p29 My 2017
Milestones color *Time* v189 no22 p10 Je 12 2017
Zbigniew Brzezinski P. Elliott color *Time* v189 no22 p10 Je 12 2017

BT Group PLC
Will Not-Quite-Fiber Make the Grade? E. Pfanner and M. Scaturro diag *Bloomberg Businessweek* no4495 p27 O 17 2016

Bu, Jeffrey
Potential role of intratumor bacteria in mediating tumor resistance to the chemotherapeutic drug gemcitabine diag *Science* v357 no6356 p1156 S 15 2017

Bu, Zack
BY THE NUMBERS *Washingtonian Magazine* v52 no3 p78 D 2016
Destination: The Airports *Washingtonian Magazine* v52 no2 p80 N 2016

Buatta, Mario
Hall of Fame color *Architectural Digest* v74 no1 p92 Ja 2017

Bubar, Lorraine
Slices of the World J. Lovelace il *American Craft* v77 no3 p38 Je/Jl 2017

Bubbles
See also
Soap bubbles
Soap bubbles show their dark side E. Conover color *Science News* v191 no1 p32 Ja 21 2017

Bubbly Black Girl Sheds Her Chameleon Skin, The (Theatrical production)
THE THEATRE color *New Yorker* v93 no22 p10 Jl 31 2017

Bubela, T.
Fostering reproducibility in industry-academia research color *Science* v357 no6353 p759 Ag 25 2017

Buber, Martin, 1878-1965
A LADDER IS TO CLIMB L. G. STONE *Humanist* v77 no3 p40 My/Je 2017
To Love Another T. MARKATOS *Weekly Standard* v22 no46 p36 Ag 14 2017

Bublé, Michael, 1975——Interviews
Bubbles comes back to life E. IANNACCI color *Maclean's* v129 no41 p50 O 17 2016

Buc-ee's Ltd.
Game of Porcelain Thrones P. CARBONARA and W. BALDWIN color *Forbes* v200 no2 p37 S 5 2017

Bucay, Yemile
America's growing news deserts map *Columbia Journalism Review* v56 no1 p34 Spr 2017

BUCCA, MIKE
10! cartoon color *Field & Stream* v122 no1 p30 My 2017

Buccini, Beth
HOME FOR THE HOLIDAYS L. McCarthy color *Harper's Bazaar* no3649 p245 D 2016/Ja 2017

Buchan, Eugenie
A Few Planes for China: The Birth of The Flying Tigers M. W. McCarty *Military History* v34 no5 p74 Ja 2018

BUCHANAN, EUGENE
PADDLING color *Backpacker* v45 no3 p110 Ap 2017

Buchanan, Gale A.
MAKING THE CASE FOR US AGRICULTURAL RESEARCH D. I. GUSTAFSON *BioScience* v67 no3 p311 Mr 2017

Buchanan, James M., 1919-2013
The Architect of the Radical Right S. TANENHAUS color *Atlantic* v320 no1 p40 Jl/Ag 2017

Buchanan, Joe
Wit and Wisdom from Our Early Breeders: Garth and Joe Buchanan M. J. PARKINSON *Arabian Horse World* v57 no9 p134 Je 2017

Buchanan, Kyle
Is There Really Such a Thing As "Oscar Bait"? img *New York* v49 no22 p97 O 31 2016
Is There Really Such a Thing As "Oscar Bait"? M. HARRIS and K. BUCHANAN img *New York* v49 no22 p97 O 31 2016
NICOLE KIDMAN'S BAD WOMEN img *New York* v49 no24 p130 N 28 2016

Runaway Starlets img *New York* p71 F 20 2017

Buchanan, Patrick J. (Patrick Joseph), 1938-
All the Right Moves [Cover story] J. Klein *New York Times Book Review* p1 My 14 2017
Buchanan on Nixon: Triumph and Tragedy J. R. COYNE JR. *American Conservative* v16 no3 p48 My/Je 2017
CALL IT, FRIENDO J. FIELDEN color *Esquire* p18 My 2017
CHARGE OF THE RIGHT BRIGADE S. TANENHAUS bw color *Esquire* p80 My 2017
Father of Trumpism M. SCULLY color *National Review* v69 no11 p35 Je 12 2017
Gatekeepers and Barbarians S. HEBBAR *Commentary* v142 no2 p10 S 2016
Grandmasters of Fake News *American Conservative* v16 no1 p26 Ja/F 2017
The Great Struggle of Our Era *American Conservative* v16 no2 p11 Mr/Ap 2017
The Impeach-Trump Conspiracy *American Conservative* v16 no4 p12 Jl/Ag 2017
No-Win War in Syria *American Conservative* v15 no6 p11 N/D 2016
A Populist-Nationalist Right? No Thanks! W. Kristol color *Weekly Standard* v22 no9 p7 N 7 2016
Stop the War Party Now *American Conservative* v16 no3 p11 My/Je 2017
Trump's Dangerous Kill Box *American Conservative* v16 no5 p12 S/O 2017
Why I Read The American Conservative R. C. Young color *American Conservative* v16 no1 p2 Ja/F 2017

Buchanan, Rowan Hisayo
Harmless Like You *Publishers Weekly* v263 no48 p40 N 28 2016
Reaction *New York Times Book Review* p36 Je 4 2017

Buchanan, Tracy
No Turning Back *Publishers Weekly* v264 no15 p55 Ap 10 2017

Buchanan, Travis L.
Illuminating amination bibl diag *Science* v355 no6326 p690 F 17 2017

BUCHAS, LAWRENCE
Chords & Discords color *Downbeat* v84 no9 p10 S 2017

Buchbinder, Mara
Embodied inequality D. Goldberg color *Science* v354 no6315 p978 N 25 2016

Büchel, C.
Interactions between brain and spinal cord mediate value effects in nocebo hyperalgesia color *Science* v357 no6359 p105 O 6 2017

Bucher, Kathleen
Country Lore *Mother Earth News* no281 p84 Ap/My 2017

Buchholz, P.
Observation of a large-scale anisotropy in the arrival directions of cosmic rays above 8×1018 eV *Science* v357 no6357 p1266 S 22 2017

BUCK, BILL
Paths Forged by Man and Beast color *Earth Island Journal* v32 no4 p54 Wint 2017

Buck, Joan Juliet
A FAST LIFE bw color *Harper's Bazaar* no3651 p288 Mr 2017
Flipping the Switch color *InStyle* v24 no3 p178 Mr 2017
Her Beau Monde T. L. FORCE *New York Times Book Review* p17 Ap 2 2017
A KEY TO ANJELICA color *Vanity Fair* v59 no10 p180 O 2017

Buck, Joe
Book of Joe T. Keith color *Sports Illustrated* v125 no16 p20 N 14 2016

Buck, Joe—Interviews
Bucking the Trend R. Asselta and J. Marksbury color *Golf Magazine* v59 no11 p21 N 2017
Joe Buck Knows Why You Hate Him A. M. Cox *New York Times Magazine* p50 F 5 2017

Buck, Nina
Behemoth 'Coffee Burger' Rides Again in Sioux County color *Nebraska Life* v21 no1 p15 Ja/F 2017
DO-IT-YOURSELF Treasures color *Nebraska Life* v21 no5 p69 S/O 2017
Nebraskans of a feather let new crane book fly cartoon color *Nebraska Life* v21 no2 p77 Mr/Ap 2017
PALEON TOLOGY in Action color *Nebraska Life* v21 no4 p96

Jl/Ag 2017
STATEWIDE color *Nebraska Life* v21 no2 p63 Mr/Ap 2017
STATEWIDE EVENTS color *Nebraska Life* v21 no4 p85 Jl/Ag 2017
STATEWIDE EVENTS color *Nebraska Life* v21 no6 p70 N/D 2017
Traveling exhibit remembers fallen Nebraskan heroes color *Nebraska Life* v21 no4 p84 Jl/Ag 2017
Washing COLOR into Nebraska skies cartoon color *Nebraska Life* v21 no2 p76 Mr/Ap 2017
Winter WARMER-UPPERS color *Nebraska Life* v21 no6 p64 N/D 2017
Woodwork builds on pioneering vision color *Nebraska Life* v21 no5 p92 S/O 2017

Buck, S.
Fostering reproducibility in industry-academia research color *Science* v357 no6353 p759 Ag 25 2017

Buckhead (Atlanta, Ga.)
BUCKHEAD, REFASHIONED K. ABNEY *Atlanta* v56 no11 p44 Mr 2017

Buckholtz, Alison
How to Work Remotely Without Losing Motivation *Harvard Business Review Digital Articles* p2 S 22 2016

Buckhurst, Bill
PARTNERS H. ALS color *New Yorker* v93 no4 p82 Mr 13 2017

BUCKINGHAM, JOHN
Brand Boys color *Forbes* v199 no2 p58 F 28 2017
Warning Signs color *Forbes* v200 no4 p46 O 24 2017

Buckingham, Lindsey, 1949-
Fleetwood Mac's New Spinoff J. WEINER bw color *Rolling Stone* no1290 p19 Je 29 2017

Buckingham, Lindsey, 1949——Interviews
Fleetwood Mac's Dynamic Duo K. O'donnell color *Entertainment Weekly* no1472 p58 Je 30 2017

Buckingham, Marcus
Most HR Data Is Bad Data *Harvard Business Review Digital Articles* p2 F 9 2015
Team Leaders Need Better Data, Faster *Harvard Business Review Digital Articles* p2 Mr 4 2015

Buckland, Kevin
Remodeling a Sedan Plant for the SUV Era bw *Bloomberg Businessweek* no4529 p18 Jl 3 2017

Buckler, Edward S.
Genomic estimation of complex traits reveals ancient maize adaptation to temperate North America diag *Science* v357 no6350 p512 Ag 4 2017

Buckles
See also
Belt buckles
Matchbox Car Belt! J. SCHADEWALD chart color diag *Popular Mechanics* p104 Mr 2017

Buckles—Evaluation
Day Help color *American Cowboy* v23 no5 p46 F/Mr 2017

Buckley, Chris
The Cultural Revolution *New York Times Upfront* v149 no5 p18 N 21 2016

BUCKLEY, CHRISTOPHER
LAUGHING MATTERS *Forbes* v200 no3 p90 S 28 2017
Life on His Mississippi *New York Times Book Review* p14 N 20 2016
Travels of a Lifetime *New York Times Book Review* p1 Jl 30 2017
The Year in Reading [Cover story] *New York Times Book Review* p8 D 25 2016

Buckley, Craig D.
Vinculin forms a directionally asymmetric catch bond with F-actin chart color *Science* v357 no6352 p703 Ag 18 2017

BUCKLEY, F. H.
Great Chain of Contempt *American Conservative* v15 no6 p27 N/D 2016

Buckley, Frank
HOW TO RESTORE THE U.S.'s ECONOMIC MOBILITY *USA Today Magazine* v145 no2860 p18 Ja 2017
'THE AMERICAN DREAM MOVED TO CANADA' J. GEDDES color *Maclean's* v129 no47 p28 N 28 2016

Buckley, Gail Lumet
The first and last Christian? color *America* v216 no9 p54 Ap 24

dhist Review v26 no2 p50 Wint 2016

Buddhist sanghas

ONLY CONNECT S. Wilhelm color *Tricycle: The Buddhist Review* v26 no4 p84 Summ 2017

The Web of Shared Support J. Shaheen color *Tricycle: The Buddhist Review* v27 no1 p10 Fall 2017

Buddhist scholars

BHUTAN on the Brink color *Tricycle: The Buddhist Review* v26 no3 p42 Spr 2017

Buddhist sculpture

Amanda Giacomini W. J. Biddlecombe color *Tricycle: The Buddhist Review* v27 no1 p26 Fall 2017

THE CASE OF THE DISEMBODIED MONK M. SCARLES color *Tricycle: The Buddhist Review* v26 no2 p18 Wint 2016

Buddhist temples

THE TREE GUARDIANS OF KYOTO W. BIRD color *Tricycle: The Buddhist Review* v27 no1 p66 Fall 2017

Buddhists

10,000 Dharma Doors J. Shaheen *Tricycle: The Buddhist Review* v26 no2 p12 Wint 2016

Brighton, Rocked color *Weekly Standard* v23 no5 p2 O 9 2017

Buddhist Bad Boys M. Scarles color *Tricycle: The Buddhist Review* v26 no4 p17 Summ 2017

DHARMA DIRECTORY color *Tricycle: The Buddhist Review* v26 no4 p114 Summ 2017

Buddhists—Attitudes

ONLY CONNECT S. Wilhelm color *Tricycle: The Buddhist Review* v26 no4 p84 Summ 2017

Budgen, Andy

Mix of Boats for Round-Barbados Race color *Sail* v48 no4 p22 Ap 2017

Budget

See also

Budget cuts

Budget-Friendly Airport Tips for the CONSCIOUS VEGAN TRAVELER S. GENDLER *Vegetarian Journal* v35 no1 p6 2016

Can This State Be Saved? A. B. LLOYD color *Weekly Standard* v23 no6 p27 O 16 2017

Did We Say That? K. Barrett and R. Greene *Governing* v30 no4 p58 Ja 2017

How Republicans Might Bring About Single-Payer Health Care: The long-term consequences of the failure of 2017 T. Troy *Commentary* v144 no3 p31 O 2017

The Price We've Paid chart graph *Chicago* v66 no7 p69 Jl 2017

Woman on Fire [Cover story] T. C. Fishman color *Chicago* v66 no7 p64 Jl 2017

Budget, The (Newspaper)

THE BUDGET S. Hepworth bw *Columbia Journalism Review* v56 no1 p85 Spr 2017

Budget cuts

ARTLESS T. Genoways cartoon chart *Mother Jones* v42 no5 p60 S/O 2017

Athwart J. LILEKS *National Review* v69 no6 p39 Ap 3 2017

BioScience®: A Forum for Integrating the Life Sciences R. E. GROPP *BioScience* v67 no5 p403 My 2017

Budget Cuts Bad for Boaters A. JONES *Boating World* v38 no5 p4 My 2017

EYE ON 45 color *Science* v355 no6331 p1245 Mr 24 2017

Lawmakers balk at most Trump cuts D. Malakoff and J. Mervis color *Science* v357 no6346 p11 Jl 7 2017

Library Advocacy Efforts Gaining Steam S. MAUGHAN color *Publishers Weekly* v264 no25 p64 Je 19 2017

Modern Medicis A. CLINE *Weekly Standard* v22 no34 p18 My 15 2017

Ready or Not? Not T. Donnelly *Hoover Digest: Research & Opinion on Public Policy* no4 p83 Fall 2016

A Social Security Proposal We Can All Live With R. C. Pozen *Harvard Business Review Digital Articles* p2 Je 17 2017

"The Challenge of a Lifetime" A. RICHARD ALBANESE color *Publishers Weekly* v264 no25 p29 Je 19 2017

Trump Budget, GOP Values R. L. BOROSAGE color *Nation* v304 no12 p3 Ap 10 2017

U.N. biodiversity group confronts cash crunch E. Stokstad color *Science* v355 no6332 p1358 Mr 31 2017

Budget cuts—Universities & colleges

STARVING THE SCHOOLS L. Farmer *Governing* v30 no9 p44 Je 2017

Budget deficits

Deficit in Dallas A. Greenblatt *Governing* v30 no7 p11 Ap 2017

Budget deficits—Government policy

Gulf Rulers Try Fighting Deficits With Taxes Z. Fattah and S. Bianchi cartoon *Bloomberg Businessweek* no4497 p18 O 31 2016

Budget deficits—United States

A Fiscal Collision Course K. D. WILLIAMSON *National Review* v68 no21 p17 N 21 2016

Budget in business

See also

Zero-base budgeting

The Right Way to Prepare Your Budget *Harvard Business Review Digital Articles* p2 Jl 20 2015

Zero-Based Budgeting Is Not a Wonder Diet for Companies D. Mahler *Harvard Business Review Digital Articles* p2 Je 30 2016

Budget management

Budgeting Tools for Every Style L. GERSTNER cartoon *Kiplinger's Personal Finance* v71 no1 p34 Ja 2017

Budget—Great Britain

Spring budget was a damp squib *People Management* p6 Ap 2017

Budget—India

The Costs of India's Annual Budget Guessing Game V. Nayar *Harvard Business Review Digital Articles* p2 Ap 6 2016

Budget—United States

A BIG FAT FREAK-OUT OVER DONALD TRUMP'S 'SKINNY' BUDGET K. MANGU-WARD color *Reason* v49 no2 p4 Je 2017

Budget proposal would slash science L. Hamers, M. Rosen et al *Science News* v191 no7 p15 Ap 15 2017

Cutting Off Your Base To Spite Your Foes S. J. DOUGLAS *In These Times* v41 no5 p16 My 2017

A Debt to Posterity J. Cost cartoon *Weekly Standard* v22 no29 p17 Ap 3 2017

Fiscal Fakery bw *National Review* v69 no5 p14 Mr 20 2017

Speak Up B. TULIPANE *Parks & Recreation* v52 no4 p8 Ap 2017

Tweetstorms and Circuses J. BLEIFUSS *In These Times* v41 no4 p5 Ap 2017

Budget—United States—States

Burying Bad News A. Greenblatt *Governing* v30 no4 p11 Ja 2017

FINANCIAL STRESS L. Farmer *Governing* v30 no4 p31 Ja 2017

Budiansky, Stephen

Spy vs. Spy *Commentary* v141 no10 p1 D 2016

Spy vs. Spy H. KLEHR *Commentary* v142 no5 p38 D 2016

BUDREAU, DELPHINE J.

Life IN THESE UNITED STATES *Reader's Digest* v189 no1128 p38 Mr 2017

Budson, Andrew E.

Seven Steps to Managing Your Memory: What's Normal, What's Not, and What to Do About It color *Publishers Weekly* v264 no18 p54 My 1 2017

Buecher, Dave

BLACK AND BLUE MOON color *Astronomy* v44 no12 p44 D 2016

Buecking, Alex

The Best Boots of 2018 color *Powder* p95 S 2017

The Skis of the Year color *Powder* p82 S 2017

Buelens, Lukas C.

Super-dry reforming of methane intensifies CO2 utilization via Le Chatelier's principle bibl diag graph *Science* v354 no6311 p449 O 28 2016

Buell, Courtney E.

Ratchet-like polypeptide translocation mechanism of the AAA+ disaggregase Hsp104 diag *Science* v357 no6348 p273 Jl 21 2017

Buell, Ryan W.

Case Study: Can an Airline Cut "Turn Times" Without Adding Staff? *Harvard Business Review Digital Articles* p2 Ja 27 2016

How Self-Service Kiosks Are Changing Customer Behavior G. Gavett *Harvard Business Review Digital Articles* p2 Mr 11 2015

A Transformation Is Underway at U.S. Veterans Affairs. We Got an Inside Look *Harvard Business Review Digital Articles* p2 D 22 2016

Buell, Samuel

Capital Offenses: Business Crime and Punishment in America's

Corporate Age R. N. Cooper *Foreign Affairs* v96 no1 p158 Ja/F 2017

Buell Motorcycle Co.

The Very Long-Term Buell P. Egan bw color *Cycle World* v55 no10 p48 N 2016

Bueno, A.

Observation of a large-scale anisotropy in the arrival directions of cosmic rays above 8 × 1018 eV *Science* v357 no6357 p1266 S 22 2017

Buenos Aires (Argentina : Province)

open house M. R. MERCADO *Opera News* v81 no6 p29 D 2016

Buenos Aires (Argentina)—Description & travel

DOING BUSINESS IN: BUENOS AIRES A. Erace color *Fortune* v175 no6 p27 My 1 2017

Buenos Aires National Wildlife Refuge (Ariz.)

PRONGHORN DRIVE N. AUSTIN *Arizona Highways* v93 no3 p52 Mr 2017

Buenzli, E.

Zones, spots, and planetary-scale waves beating in brown dwarf atmospheres color graph *Science* v357 no6352 p683 Ag 18 2017

Buergin, Rainer

An Establishment Firebrand in Germany color *Bloomberg Businessweek* no4514 p28 Mr 13 2017

How Facebook Could Stop bw color *Bloomberg Businessweek* no4524 p56 My 29 2017

This Just Got Awkward color graph *Bloomberg Businessweek* no4532 p36 Jl 31 2017

Buescher, Craig

A LIFE IN FARMING: THE NEXT CHAPTER D. KURNS *Successful Farming* v115 no3 p4 Mid-F 2017

Buesing, Debbie

Life's work: Building the church takes everyone [Cover story] color *U.S. Catholic* v82 no8 p22 Ag 2017

Buettel, Jessie C.

Biodiversity losses and conservation responses in the Anthropocene color diag graph map *Science* v356 no6335 p270 Ap 21 2017

BUETTNER, DAN

The Blue Zones of Happiness: Lessons from the World's Happiest People color *Publishers Weekly* v264 no32 p67 Ag 7 2017

THE WORLD'S HAPPIEST PLACES [Cover story] color diag graph *National Geographic* v232 no5 p30 N 2017

Bufete, Tercius

Bring on the Joy chart il *Consumer Reports* v82 no3 p31 Mr 2017

Home Sweet Home Office color graph il *Consumer Reports* v82 no9 p8 S 2017

Picture Perfect chart color diag graph *Consumer Reports* v82 no12 p14 D 2017

Save Money il *Consumer Reports* v82 no3 p30 Mr 2017

Save Time and Add Convenience il *Consumer Reports* v82 no3 p24 Mr 2017

Buffalo (N.Y.)—Economic conditions

POSTCARDS FROM THE PAST M. NOER color *Forbes* v200 no3 p76 S 28 2017

Buffalo Bill's Wild West Co.

William 'Buffalo Bill' Cody dies *History Today* v67 no1 p9 Ja 2017

Buffalo Bills (Football team)

3 Buffalo Bills color *Sports Illustrated* v127 no7 p67 S 4 2017

BUFFALOED J. Dickey and J. Feldman color *Sports Illustrated* v126 no11 p60 Ap 17-24 2017

Buffalo River (N.Y.)

RIVER REBORN K. Davidson, D. Skaros et al *New York State Conservationist* v71 no4 p10 F 2017

Buffalo Bill, 1846-1917

Lost Skills L. FELDMAN bw *American Cowboy* v24 no1 p66 Je/Jl 2017

ON THE TRAIL OF THE INDIANS color *MHQ: Quarterly Journal of Military History* v29 no4 p20 Summ 2017

William 'Buffalo Bill' Cody dies *History Today* v67 no1 p9 Ja 2017

Buffalomeat, Kobe

HOT | NOT T. Keith color *Sports Illustrated* v126 no5 p18 F 13 2017

Buffat, Jeanne

82% D. Denunzio color *Golf Magazine* v58 no11 p54 N 2016

Buffet, Bernard

A BECKONING ANGST B. Adams color *Art in America* v105 no5 p102 My 2017

BUFFETT, JIMMY

THE KEYS TO MARGARITAVILLE color *Vanity Fair* v59 no11 p151 N 2017

Buffett, Jimmy, 1946-—Interviews

Jimmy Buffett A. MCLELLAN color *New Orleans Magazine* v51 no12 p32 O 2017

Buffett, Warren, 1930-

7 Cool Things I Learned Editing This Issue R. Love *AARP: The Magazine* v59 no4A p2 Je/Jl 2016

CONVERSATION A. WILSON color graph *Forbes* v199 no7 p38 Je 29 2017

The Master Chides His Students N. Buhayar color *Bloomberg Businessweek* no4512 p37 F 20 2017

Stock X-Ray: Berkshire Hathaway T. Tepper color diag *Money* v46 no6 p42 Jl 2017

Warren Buffett's Risky Final Bet J. Baron and R. Lachenauer *Harvard Business Review Digital Articles* p2 Ap 21 2016

What You Can Learn When Winners Lose T. Tepper color diag *Money* v46 no5 p33 Je 2017

The Wisdom of Warren D. CAPLINGER color *AARP: The Magazine* v59 no4A p32 Je/Jl 2016

Buffett, Warren, 1930-—Finance

The Best in Business 2016 color diag *Fortune* v174 no8 p18 D 15 2016

Buffett, Warren, 1930-—Interviews

'YOU CAN'T STOP THIS COUNTRY.' color *Fortune* v174 no8 p165 D 15 2016

Buffy the Vampire Slayer (Fictitious character)

NO. 11 Buffy J. Hibberd color *Entertainment Weekly* no1436/1437 p52 O 21 2016

Buffy the Vampire Slayer (TV program)

Bring "Your Ugly Stuff" M. K. Schilling img *New York* v50 no13 p74 Je 26 2017

DAVID BOREANAZ ON BUFFY, BONES, AND BEYOND C. M. Smith color *Entertainment Weekly* no1457/1458 p86 Mr 17 2017

The / EDITOR'S NOTE H. Goldblatt color *Entertainment Weekly* no1460/1461 p8 Ap 7-17 2017

My 20 Years on Television D. BOREANAZ and M. Roffman *TV Guide* v65 no41 p12 O 2 2017

THE REDEMPTION OF SPIKE T. Stack color *Entertainment Weekly* no1460/1461 p60 Ap 7-17 2017

UNDEAD AGAIN [Cover story] T. Stack color *Entertainment Weekly* no1460/1461 p50 Ap 7-17 2017

Bufo marinus

TOADZILLA! B. Wright *National Geographic Kids* no469 p13 Ap 2017

Buford, Kay Stone

VERACITY KSB *Arabian Horse World* v56 no12 p62 S 2016

Bugaboos (B.C.)

CANADA'S GRANDEST TRAVERSE A. Findlay color map *Skiing* p88 D 2016

Bugatti automobile

THE BENCHMARK A. MacKenzie chart color *Motor Trend* v69 no7 p94 Jl 2017

The Bugatti Buyer H. Elliott color *Bloomberg Businessweek* no4531 p67 Jl 24 2017

URGE OVERKILL C. CHILTON color *Road & Track* v69 no1 p54 Ag 2017

Bugatti automobile—Evaluation

On a Highway in Hell J. Zoellter color *Car & Driver* v62 no6 p48 D 2016

Bugatti Automobiles SAS

THE BENCHMARK A. MacKenzie chart color *Motor Trend* v69 no7 p94 Jl 2017

On a Highway in Hell J. Zoellter color *Car & Driver* v62 no6 p48 D 2016

URGE OVERKILL C. CHILTON color *Road & Track* v69 no1 p54 Ag 2017

Bugbane

Black COHOSH D. Kalmansohn color *Vegetarian Times* v43 no2 p30 N/D 2016

Bugbee, Bruce

Come Along for the Ride D. PEAK *Log Home Living* v34 no9 p6 D 2017

Man vs. Machine: Architecture M. Belfiore cartoon *Bloomberg Businessweek* no4539 p25 S 25 2017

Navajo Nation Council Chamber N. AUSTIN *Arizona Highways* v93 no6 p6 Je 2017

Plan on It diag *Log Home Living* p52 2018 Annual Buyers Guide

Building design & construction—History—20th century

EMPIRE BUILDING, MARIETTA & BROAD 1900 T. Wheatley *Atlanta* v57 no5 p160 S 2017

Building information modeling

3D CAD — Not Your Father's Blue Prints color *Log Home Living* v33 no9 p67 D 2016

Building inspection—Government policy

Winning the Permit Game A. Greenblatt *Governing* v30 no1 p12 O 2016

Building inspectors

The CR Guide to Smarter Remodeling P. Hope chart color il *Consumer Reports* v82 no7 p44 Jl 2017

Building layout

A SHELF TRACK PLAN for a switching line P. Boehlert map *Model Railroader* v84 no2 p64 F 2017

Building maintenance

See also

Floor maintenance & repair

Historic building maintenance & repair

Museum maintenance & repair

Wall maintenance & repair

Those Old Houses: 8K Construction is out to save Cincinnati's historic fabric, one home at a time L. MURTHA *Cincinnati Magazine* v50 no11 p78 Ag 2017

Building materials

See also

Bricks

Cement

Composite building materials

Flooring

Shingles (Building materials)

Tiles

Timber

Wood

Wood veneers & veneering

CLAPBOARD, DUTCH LAP & OTHER NOVELTIES diag *Old House Journal* v45 no5 p21 Ag 2017

Concrete Block color *Old House Journal* v45 no3 p46 My 2017

GREAT UNKNOWNS cartoon *Popular Mechanics* p33 D 2016/Ja 2017

HEAVY METAL *Architectural Record* v205 no1 p57 Ja 2017

Wrap It Up: These weather-tight products will seal the deal for a variety of project categories and programs R. C. Orrell color *Architectural Record* v205 no5 p71 My 2017

Building permits—Lawsuits & claims

Mosque wins $3.25 million in legal settlement from New Jersey township L. Markoe *Christian Century* v134 no14 p16 Jl 5 2017

Building repair

See also

Adaptive reuse of buildings

Church building remodeling

Farmhouse remodeling

Historic building maintenance & repair

Historic building remodeling

Hotel remodeling

Hotels—Repair & reconstruction

Office building remodeling

Vacation home remodeling

THE FIX P. Carlsen cartoon *Old House Journal* v45 no7 p52 O 2017

A Fresh Spin A. FIXSEN *Architectural Record* v205 no6 p42 Je 2017

Long Road for NYC Public Projects H. CORCORAN color *Architectural Record* v205 no5 p26 My 2017

New in New Orleans Real Estate K. FINN color *New Orleans Magazine* v52 no1 p34 S 2017

Renovations Done Right P. MERTZ ESSWEIN color *Kiplinger's Personal Finance* v71 no11 p64 N 2017

Urban Symphony R. BROOKHISER il *National Review* v69 no19 p59 O 16 2017

Well Schooled L. CUTRONE color *New Orleans Magazine* v51 no12 p64 O 2017

Building—Accidents

A CHRISTMAS RIFLE J. ARTERBURN cartoon *Outdoor Life* v224 no1 p114 D 2016/Ja 2017

Building—China

Hong Kong and Shenzhen Band Together to Lure Startups N. Khan and E. Curran color *Bloomberg Businessweek* no4527 p44 Je 19 2017

Building—Estimates

Money Saving Design Tips: A Builder's Point of View D. Mitchell color *Log Home Living* v33 no9 p26 D 2016

Building—Planning

Coping with Steep Slopes J. COOPER color *Cabin Living* p64 Ap 2017

Buildings

See also

Church buildings

Dwellings

Historic buildings

Monasteries

Museum buildings

Observatories

Pavilions

School buildings

Down These Lonely Streets R. BROOKHISER bw *National Review* v69 no17 p43 S 11 2017

Wherebraska? color *Nebraska Life* v20 no6 p17 N/D 2016

WITH POYDRAS THE PARROT J. STREET color *New Orleans Magazine* v51 no1 p24 N 2016

Buildings & structures for model railroads

See also

Model railroad stations

CASTING PLASTER WALLS for a scratchbuilt structure [Cover story] R. Howard color diag *Model Railroader* v84 no10 p24 O 2017

Make a hill from foam peanuts C. Grivno color *Model Railroader* v84 no10 p22 O 2017

Trackside Photos color *Model Railroader* v84 no10 p64 O 2017

Buildings—Additions

DIAMONDS ARE FOREVER F. A. BERNSTEIN color *Architectural Digest* v73 no11 p90 N 2016

News B. Manley *Military History* v33 no6 p8 Mr 2017

Buildings—Cleaning

See also

Industrial housekeeping

Company's Coming! [Cover story] color *Good Housekeeping* v263 no5 p57 N 2016

Buildings—Design & construction

See also

Art centers—Design & construction

Bus terminals—Design & construction

Community centers—Design & construction

Courthouses—Design & construction

Cultural centers—Design & construction

Dwellings—Design & construction

Exhibition buildings—Design & construction

Floors—Design & construction

Hotels—Design & construction

Library buildings—Design & construction

Memorials—Design & construction

Monuments—Design & construction

Office buildings—Design & construction

Offices—Design & construction

Pavilions—Design & construction

Public buildings—Design & construction

Public spaces—Design & construction

Railroad stations—Design & construction

Roofs—Design & construction

School buildings—Design & construction

Subways—Design & construction

Theaters—Design & construction

Towers—Design & construction

Are You and Your Builder Speaking the Same Language? D. Mitchell color *Log Home Living* v34 no2 p22 Mr 2017

Our Snow-Salt Sheds Look Like Museums J. DAVIDSON img *New York* v49 no25 p76 D 12 2016

Buildings—Energy conservation

Energy efficiency M. BESSOUDO color *Issues in Science & Technology* v33 no1 p12 Fall 2016

Old Buildings Are U.S. Cities' Biggest Sustainability Challenge I. Campbell and K. Calhoun *Harvard Business Review Digital Articles* p2 Ja 21 2016

Buildings—England—Design & construction

Saving the Skyline D. STEWART *America* v215 no12 p11 O 24 2016

Buildings—Environmental engineering

See also

Plumbing

Buildings—Evaluation

BEST OF DESIGN J. P. Klingman color *New Orleans Magazine* v51 no5 p74 Mr 2017

The Mapparium K. LIEBENSON-MORSE *Yankee* v81 no1 p28 Ja/F 2017

Buildings—Maintenance

See also

Airports—Maintenance & repair

Buildings—Mechanical equipment—Installation

Roughin' It S. Murphy color *Log Home Living* v34 no2 p20 Mr 2017

Buildings—New York (State)

Cost of 666 Fifth Avenue D. Kocieniewski and C. Melby color diag graph *Bloomberg Businessweek* no4537 p39 S 11 2017

Buildings—Pennsylvania

Ode to the Corner Store B. Martin color *American Craft* v77 no3 p30 Je/Jl 2017

Buildings—Repair & reconstruction

See also

Adaptive reuse of buildings

Airport remodeling

Art museums—Remodeling

Carriage houses—Remodeling

Railroad stations—Remodeling

Restaurants—Remodeling

School buildings—Remodeling

Vacation homes—Remodeling

BRING VINTAGE WINDOWS BACK TO LIFE S. HERTZ *Yankee* v81 no1 p40 Ja/F 2017

HANG ON TO THE "GOOD STUFF" *Yankee* v81 no1 p37 Ja/F 2017

Modern Reboot J. GONCHAR bw color *Architectural Record* v205 no2 p52 F 2017

PEACEFUL GRANDEUR B. WARREN color *New Orleans Magazine* v51 no3 p52 Ja 2017

QUIRK APPEAL M. LAWLER color *Chicago* v66 no2 p16 F 2017

U.K. Antarctic stations poised for upgrades color *Science* v355 no6321 p113 Ja 13 2017

Buildings—Repair & reconstruction—Evaluation

BUILD & REMODEL color *Arts & Crafts Homes & the Revival* v12 no1 p58 2017 Resouce Guide

Buildings—Retrofitting

Old Buildings Are U.S. Cities' Biggest Sustainability Challenge I. Campbell and K. Calhoun *Harvard Business Review Digital Articles* p2 Ja 21 2016

Built-in furniture

Better Built-Ins C. MARTIN color *Timber Home Living* v27 no5 p21 O 2017

Built to Last (Music)

Lockn' Roll J. HOLT *Weekly Standard* v22 no6 p37 O 17 2016

Built to Spill (Performer)

Spilling Over M. Trammell cartoon *New Yorker* v92 no32 p25 O 10 2016

Buirski, Nancy

By Sidney Lumet C. Nashawaty color *Entertainment Weekly* no1438 p49 N 4 2016

Buitink, S.

Observation of a large-scale anisotropy in the arrival directions of cosmic rays above 8×1018 eV *Science* v357 no6357 p1266 S 22 2017

BUITRAGO, ALEJANDRA

No Peace in the Peace Corps: Women volunteers face sexual assault and victim-blaming *Ms.* v27 no3 p16 Fall 2017

Bukatman, Scott

Hellboy's World: Comics and Monsters on the Margins P. YOUNG *Film Quarterly* v70 no3 p99 Spr 2017

BUKER, SARRAH

Islamic Schools Face the Future: Independent schools are usually not required to adhere to education policy regulations if they receive no state or federal government funds *Islamic Horizons* v46 no3 p38 My/Je 2017

Bukh, Jens

Mouse models of acute and chronic hepacivirus infection *Science* v357 no6347 p204 Jl 14 2017

Bukowski, Robert

Genomic estimation of complex traits reveals ancient maize adaptation to temperate North America diag *Science* v357 no6350 p512 Ag 4 2017

Bukvich, Daniel

What My Music Teacher Taught Me About Money C. Kornelis color *Money* v46 no6 p80 Jl 2017

Bulbs (Plants)

AROUND THE GARDEN S. Bender color *Southern Living* v52 no10 p50 O 2017

Branching Out K. Hammonds color *Southern Living* v52 no2 p17 F 2017

Büldt, Georg

Mechanism of transmembrane signaling by sensor histidine kinases color *Science* v356 no6342 p1043 Je 9 2017

Bulgari, Nicola

Mountain Men E. FLORIO color *Conde Nast Traveler* v51 no11 p130 D 2016

Bulgari SpA

Bulgari/Nicholas Kirkwood Bags E. ELWICK-BATES, M. HOLGATE et al color *Vogue* v207 no9 p368 S 2017

the pick color *InStyle* v24 no10 p176 O 2017

SNAKES AND THE CITY bw color *Harper's Bazaar* no3657 p251 O 2017

Wait LIST color *Harper's Bazaar* no3652 p94 Ap 2017

Bulimia

"How Shelter Dogs Rescued Me" S. Bower color *Good Housekeeping* v263 no6 p166 D 2016

Is Your Period Making YOU SICK? S. Colino cartoon *O, The Oprah Magazine* p101 My 2017

Bull (TV program)

Bull N. Abrams, A. Bacle et al color *Entertainment Weekly* no1482/1483 p66 S 22 2017

THE NEW TV SHOWS YOU CAN'T GET ENOUGH OF J. Hibberd color *Entertainment Weekly* no1436/1437 p20 O 21 2017

Bull markets

Is a Bear on the Prowl? J. Bodnar *Kiplinger's Personal Finance* v71 no1 p8 Ja 2017

When Will the Bull Market End? A. K. SMITH color *Kiplinger's Personal Finance* v71 no10 p59 O 2017

Bull racing

Chicken Among Bulls T. MECIA color *Weekly Standard* v22 no45 p33 Ag 7 2017

San Fermin en Nueva Orleans color *New Orleans Magazine* v51 no9 p27 Jl 2017

Bull riders

BUCKLE UP with Derrick Begay C. Toy color *Spin to Win Rodeo* v20 no11 p15 Ja 2017

DOWNWARD-FACING BULL J. Fuchs, T. Keith et al color *Sports Illustrated* v127 no7 p24 S 4 2017

Leading Off color *Sports Illustrated* v126 no4 p6 Ja 30 2017

Bull shark

Stayin' Alive A. JONES *Boating World* v38 no3 p18 Mr 2017

Bullard, E. John

Ceramics dynamic: The only thing more remarkable than John Bullard's studio pottery collection is how quickly he became a connoisseur of the field C. Waddington color *Magazine Antiques* v184 no4 p108 Jl/Ag 2017

BULLARD, JOANNA E.

The Arctic in the Twenty-First Century: Changing Biogeochemical Linkages across a Paraglacial Landscape of Greenland *Bioscience* v67 no2 p118 F 2017

Bullard, John

BLUEGRASS TO BACH C. Kettlewell *Virginia Living* v15 no2 p11 F 2017

Bullard, Martyn Lawrence

debut: Popular Demand M. RUS color *Architectural Digest* no11 p44 N 1 2017

minding the manor K. BETTS color *Architectural Digest* v74 no3 p86 Mr 2017

sand castle M. RUS color *Architectural Digest* v74 no4 p158 Ap 2017

Bulldog

BUTLER BLUE III, AKA TRIP M. WELCH *Indianapolis Monthly* p24 N 2017

DAWG DAYS J. Gorant, T. Keith et al color *Sports Illustrated* v127 no5 p28 Ag 14 2017

Handsome Is ... B. Marks, T. Keith et al color *Sports Illustrated* v127 no5 p28 Ag 14 2017

Bulldozers

BULLDOZERS VS. CHAINSAWS Z. S. George color *Powder* v45 no3 p50 N 2016

Buller, Jeffrey L.

Is Collegiality a Weapon or a Shield? *Change* v49 no1 p54 Ja/F 2017

Bulletin of the Atomic Scientists (Periodical)

Addendum *Bulletin of the Atomic Scientists* v73 no2 p143 Mr 2017

Minutes to Midnight *Lapham's Quarterly* v10 no3 p117 Summ 2017

Bullets

THE INSANE TURBONIQUE TALE OF MAGIC BULLET MADNESS T. Taylor bw color diag *Hot Rod* v70 no4 p52 Ap 2017

JOURNEY TO GUNLAND M. Wenner Moyer color graph *Scientific American* v317 no4 p54 O 2017

LONG-RANGE SHOOTOUT R. Mann color *Field & Stream* v121 no6 p28 N 2016

Bullets—Evaluation

.38 SPECIALS J. B. SNOW color *Outdoor Life* v224 no8 pP8 O 2017

FRESH MAG D. E. Petzal color *Field & Stream* v121 no9 p26 Ap 2017

GRAND OPENING J. B. SNOW color *Outdoor Life* v224 no1 p95 D 2016/Ja 2017

THREE NEW, AND ACCURATE, .243-CALIBER BULLETS THAT WILL DUKE IT OUT IN COMPETITION THIS YEAR J. B. SNOW color *Outdoor Life* v224 no2 p41 F/Mr 2017

Bullfrog

Bet You Didn't Know V. C. CLARK color *National Geographic Kids* no471 p11 Je/Jl 2017

Blame Canada J. RAPP LEARN map *Canadian Geographic* v135 no6 p34 D 2015

Photos from the Field *Mother Earth News* no281 p128 Ap/My 2017

THE SPORT OF KINGS M. R. Shea cartoon *Field & Stream* v122 no1 p22 My 2017

Bulliet, Richard W.

Revolution, evolution or reinvention? H. Giffard *History Today* v66 no10 p58 O 2016

Bulling, Ian

RIDE ALONG A. BRANDT *Cincinnati Magazine* v50 no7 p25 Ap 2017

BULLINGTON, JOSEPH

AN EXHIBIT TO END ALL EXHIBITS *In These Times* v41 no5 p39 My 2017

The Folk Singer vs. the Millionaire *In These Times* v41 no6 p8 Je 2017

Bullock, Emma S.

Large gem diamonds from metallic liquid in Earth's deep mantle bibl color *Science* v354 no6318 p1403 D 16 2016

Bullock, J. M.

Country-specific effects of neonicotinoid pesticides on honey bees and wild bees diag map *Science* v356 no6345 p1393 Je 30 2017

Bullock, Sandra, 1964-

Ocean's 8: Everything We Know So Far D. Coggan color *Entertainment Weekly* no1442 p10 D 2 2016 Rebellious Special Issue

Bullock, Seth

ONLY ON OUR WEBSITE *South Dakota Magazine* v33 no3 p19

S/O 2017

Bull riders—Societies, etc.

WRANGLER NFR AFTER PARTIES color *Horse & Rider* v56 no11 p84 N 2017

Bulls

Incredible Animal Friends K. GALLAGHER color *National Geographic Kids* no471 p9 Je/Jl 2017

Lightbox color *Time* v190 no5 p22 Jl 31 2017

Bullying

Besting The Bullies T. PATKIN *USA Today Magazine* v145 no2860 p36 Ja 2017

Let's talk about bullies M. Rollins *Redbook* p12 O 2017

MY KIND of PEOPLE color *Good Housekeeping* v265 no2 p8 Ag 2017

Navigating a world of bullies M. Jacob color *Redbook* p108 O 2017

A Pledge to Bullies P. GULLEY *Indianapolis Monthly* v40 no5 p42 Ja 2017

Bullying in the workplace

No one will challenge this bully S. Sales *People Management* p53 S 2017

Bullying in the workplace—Prevention

How to Deal with a Mean Colleague A. Gallo *Harvard Business Review Digital Articles* p2 O 16 2014

How to Respond to an Offensive Comment at Work A. Gallo color *Harvard Business Review Digital Articles* p2 F 8 2017

Bullying in universities & colleges

Bullied out of research R. Poole color *Science* v354 no6311 p514 O 28 2016

Bullying prevention

See also

Prevention of school bullying

How any one of us can stop bullying J. PRESS color *Redbook* p109 F 2017

Bulstrode, Samantha

Samantha BULSTRODE N. Loeffler-Gladstone *Dance Spirit* v21 no4 p71 Ap 2017

Bum Steer Awards

EDITOR'S LETTER T. TALIAFERRO *Texas Monthly* v45 no2 p14 F 2017

Bumblebees

Endangered: The Rusty Patched Bumblebee R. J. Dolesh *Parks & Recreation* v52 no3 p30 Mr 2017

Protection for Bees *Earth Island Journal* v32 no1 p10 Spr 2017

Bumblebees—Behavior

Bumble bees prove their smarts color *Science* v354 no6309 p154 O 14 2016

Bumblebees show cognitive flexibility by improving on an observed complex behavior O. J. Loukola, C. J. Perry et al bibl diag *Science* v355 no6327 p833 F 24 2017

Unexpected rewards induce dopamine-dependent positive emotion–like state changes in bumblebees C. J. Perry, L. Baciadonna et al bibl graph *Science* v353 no6307 p1529 S 30 2016

Bumblebees—Psychology

Bee happy M. T. Mendl and E. S. Paul bibl color diag *Science* v353 no6307 p1499 S 30 2016

Bumblebees exhibit signs of emotions E. UNDERWOOD *Science News* v190 no9 p12 O 29 2016

BUMGARDNER, TODD

All Gain, No Pain [Cover story] color *Men's Health* v32 no4 p50 My 2017

A New Take on Classic Lifts L. SCHULER cartoon *Men's Health* v32 no4 p48 My 2017

Bumiller, Elisabeth

The Big Lie the New York Missed J. NAURECKAS *In These Times* v41 no3 p19 Mr 2017

Bump, Philip

SEEN & HEARD *Humanist* v77 no3 p7 My/Je 2017

Bumper stickers

John Phillips J. Phillips color *Car & Driver* v63 no1 p30 Jl 2017

Bumppo, Natty (Fictitious character)

NO. 49 Hawkeye D. Coggan color *Entertainment Weekly* no1436/1437 p78 O 21 2016

Bumstead, Chris—Interviews

THE NEW MR. OLYMPIA? J. KINDELA chart color *Muscle & Performance* v9 no5 p30 My 2017

Bunbury, Kylie
 BEAT STREET color *Essence* v47 no7 p84 N 2016
BUNCE, TOM
 Shipbuilding Docks as Experimental Systems for Realistic Assessments of Anthropogenic Stressors on Marine Organisms *BioScience* v67 no9 p853 S 2017
Bunce, Valerie
 The Prospects for a Color Revolution in Russia *Daedalus* v146 no2 p19 Spr 2017
Bunch, Lonnie G.
 Double Exposure: Fighting for Freedom *Publishers Weekly* v264 no17 p85 Ap 24 2017
BUNCH, SONNY
 Beyond the Kael *Commentary* v142 no2 p69 S 2016
Bundles (Music)
 Allan Holdsworth's Guitar Solo on 'Land Of The Bag Snake' J. DURSO bw *Downbeat* v84 no3 p112 Mr 2017
Bundles, A'Lelia
 Looking Ahead *Prologue* v49 no2 p70 Summ 2017
 NATIONAL ARCHIVES FOUNDATION *Prologue* v48 no4 p64 Wint 2016
 Thank You Greetings To Our Special Partners *Prologue* v48 no3 p70 Fall 2016
Bundling (Marketing)
 Cable Providers Win Even in an a La Carte World S. Berinato *Harvard Business Review Digital Articles* p2 O 22 2014
 A Different Kind of Bundle L. Dawson *Publishers Weekly* v264 no12 p24 Mr 20 2017
Bunduc, Paul
 Enhancement of Zika virus pathogenesis by preexisting antiflavivirus immunity graph *Science* v356 no6334 p175 Ap 14 2017
Bungalow design & construction
 Monrovia/Greater Los Angeles, California J. C. Massey and S. Maxwell bw color *Old House Journal* v45 no6 p34 S 2017
Bungalows
 DATA IN THE HOUSE: WHERE TO MOVE NOW S. KADISH color graph *Wired* v25 no8 p18 Ag 2017
 Forever home K. WILSON color *House Beautiful* p54 Ag 2017
 a perfect marriage D. PIZZA color *Arts & Crafts Homes & the Revival* v12 no3 p40 Summ 2017
 Tenleytown/Washington, D.C J. C. Massey and S. Maxwell bw color *Old House Journal* v45 no3 p34 My 2017
Bungalows—Conservation & restoration
 Tug of the familiar P. Poore bw cartoon *Old House Journal* v45 no1 p8 F 2017
Bungalows—Design & construction
 Gentle Stewards for a 1908 house D. PIZZI color *Arts & Crafts Homes & the Revival* v12 no2 p40 Spr 2017
Bungalows—Interior decoration
 ELEMENTAL VISION W. James color *Old House Journal* v45 no3 p32 My 2017
Bungalows—Remodeling
 Remuddling color *Old House Journal* v44 no8 p96 D 2016
Bungalows—Sales & prices
 Compound Interest C. NICHOLS color *Los Angeles Magazine* v62 no10 p128 O 2017
Bunge, Marcia J.
 Honoring children *Christian Century* v134 no5 p36 Mr 1 2017
Bunge, Mario, 1919-
 The Scientist and the Philosopher J. E. ALCOCK *Skeptical Inquirer* v41 no2 p58 Mr/Ap 2017
Bungee jumping
 Cashing In on The Fear Factor J. Clenfield and P. Alpeyev color *Bloomberg Businessweek* no4495 p35 O 17 2016
Bunion
 advice for dancers L. HAMILTON *Dance Magazine* v91 no7 p24 Jl 2017
Bunion surgery
 For Feet's sake [Cover story] A. Weil color *Prevention* v69 no7 p22 Jl 2017
Bunker, Jack
 True Grit color *Publishers Weekly* v264 no26 p173 Je 26 2017
Bunker, Steve
 Why We Ride: Great bikes and the people who love them W. Sheppard bw color *Virginia Living* v15 no5 p90 Ag 2017
Bunkers (Fortification)—Social aspects

 A Resort for the Apocalypse B. ROWEN bw cartoon color diag map *Atlantic* v319 no2 p30 Mr 2017
Bunkers (Golf)
 Turn In, Plug Out D. Pelz and C. Barrett color *Golf Magazine* v59 no8 p33 Ag 2017
Bunn, Andrew
 Traverse of the Clods L. HAAS color *Climbing* no353 p36 My/Je 2017
Bunn, Davis
 Davis Bunn color *Publishers Weekly* v264 no2 p35 Ja 9 2017
Bunn, Matthew
 Doomed to Cooperate How American and Russian Scientists Joined Forces to Avert Some of the Greatest Post-Cold War Nuclear Dangers *Physics Today* v69 no11 p56 N 2016
Bunn, Michael
 Mitigating coastal landslide damage color *Science* v357 no6355 p981 S 8 2017
Bunnell, David Hugh
 Good Friday on the Rez *Publishers Weekly* v263 no48 p57 N 28 2016
Bunnett, Jane
 Bunnett Continues Cuban Journey Y. Kato color *Downbeat* v83 no11 p13 N 2016
Buns (Bread)
 Cinnamon twirl L. DELAP color *Maclean's* v129 no44 p72 N 7 2016
 Morning Glories J. DEMELO color diag *Bon Appetit* v61 no11 p30 N 2016
 One Bao to Rule All *Los Angeles Magazine* v61 no11 p68 N 2016
 The Second Coming of the Schnecken J. Kramer *Bon Appetit* v61 no12 p82 D 2016 /Jan2017
Buntin, John
 Bailing OUT: Everyone agrees that America's bail system is broken. So why is it so hard to get anything done? *Governing* v31 no1 p30 O 2017
 Caught Between Reform and a Hard Place *Governing* v30 no2 p40 N 2016
 THE COP NEXT DOOR: Can police rebuild trust by moving into the neighborhood? *Governing* v30 no10 p24 Jl 2017
 The Mayors Goodman *Governing* v30 no4 p46 Ja 2017
 THE MISSING MIDDLE: We talk endlessly about affordable housing, but we don't produce much. Could that change? *Governing* v30 no8 p24 My 2017
 PUBLIC OFFICIALS OF THE YEAR *Governing* v30 no3 p26 D 2016
Buntin, Julie
 Burning Brief and Bright: Past and present overlap in a portrait of an electric friendship cut short D. SHAPIRO color *New York Times Book Review* p16 Ap 23 2017
 Home Away from Home color *Publishers Weekly* v264 no34 p78 Ag 21 2017
 OIL Boom color *Vogue* v207 no6 p78 Je 2017
 PW'S TOP AUTHORS PICK THEIR FAVORITE BOOKS OF 2016 bw color *Publishers Weekly* v263 no50 p38 D 5 2016
Bunting, Daniel E.
 A large fraction of HLA class I ligands are proteasome-generated spliced peptides bibl graph *Science* v354 no6310 p354 O 21 2016
Bunton, Emma—Interviews
 Emma Bunton N. Feeney color *Entertainment Weekly* no1472 p50 Je 30 2017
Buntz, Sam
 The Power of Negative Tweeting color *Washington Monthly* v49 no3-5 p61 Mr-My 2017
Buntz, Samuel
 What Drives Social Justice? *Washington Monthly* p13 N/D 2016
 What Would Donald Do? color *Washington Monthly* v49 no9/10 p131 S/O 2017
Bunyan, Maureen
 CHANNEL 7, WHERE ARE YOU? A. Beaujon *Washingtonian Magazine* v52 no6 p49 Mr 2017
Bunyavejchewin, Sarayudh
 Plant diversity increases with the strength of negative density dependence at the global scale diag *Science* v356 no6345 p1389 Je 30 2017
Bünz, S.

Massive blow-out craters formed by hydrate-controlled methane expulsion from the Arctic seafloor graph map *Science* v356 no6341 p948 Je 1 2017

Bunzel, Michelle

Systemic pan-AMPK activator MK-8722 improves glucose homeostasis but induces cardiac hypertrophy graph *Science* v357 no6350 p507 Ag 4 2017

Buolamwini, Joy A.

Joy Buolamwini A. Cohen color *Bloomberg Businessweek* no4529 p80 Jl 3 2017

Buonanno, Linda

JUST LIKE MEDICINE T. G. HOPE *Prevention* v69 no5 p54 My 2017

Buonassisi, Tonio

Terawatt-scale photovoltaics: Trajectories and challenges chart graph *Science* v356 no6334 p141 Ap 14 2017

Buoniconti, Nick

Man in the MIDDLE S. L. Price color *Sports Illustrated* v126 no14 p102 My 15-22 2017

Buonomano, Dean

Your Brain Is a Time Machine: The Neuroscience and Physics of Time *Publishers Weekly* v264 no8 p78 F 20 2017

Buoro, Mathieu

Precipitation drives global variation in natural selection bibl chart diag map *Science* v355 no6328 p959 Mr 3 2017

Buote, Vanessa

Most Employees Feel Authentic at Work, but It Can Take a While *Harvard Business Review Digital Articles* p2 My 11 2016

Buprenorphine—Therapeutic use

Inspired Health *Psychology Today* v49 no5 p16 S/O 2016

A New Paradigm for Opioid Addiction: More Drugs A. Park color *Time* v188 no16/17 p48 O 24 2016

Burak, Asi

How Video Games Can Save the World S. Begley color *Time* v189 no3 p20 Ja 30 2017

Buran, Brad N.

Community network for deaf scientists color *Science* v356 no6336 p386 Ap 28 2017

Buratto, Eleonora

Lyric Tradition S. HASTINGS *Opera News* v81 no7 p16 Ja 2017

Burbach, Roger

Home—So Different, So Appealing R. Feinberg *Foreign Affairs* v96 no6 p163 N/D 2017

Burbage, Marianne

A switch from canonical to noncanonical autophagy shapes B cell responses bibl graph *Science* v355 no6325 p641 F 10 2017

Burbano, Hernán A.

Genomic estimation of complex traits reveals ancient maize adaptation to temperate North America diag *Science* v357 no6350 p512 Ag 4 2017

Neandertal and Denisovan DNA from Pleistocene sediments bw color *Science* v356 no6338 p605 My 12 2017

Burbidge, David

Complex multifault rupture during the 2016 Mw 7.8 Kaikōura earthquake, New Zealand color map *Science* v356 no6334 p154 Ap 14 2017

Burbulla, Lena F.

Dopamine oxidation mediates mitochondrial and lysosomal dysfunction in Parkinson's disease graph *Science* v357 no6357 p1255 S 22 2017

Burch, Cary

How Thomson Reuters Is Creating a Culture of Innovation *Harvard Business Review Digital Articles* p2 O 2 2014

BURCH, DRUIN

Morbid Curiosity color *Natural History* v125 no9 p3 S 2017

Burch, J. L.

Structure, force balance, and topology of Earth's magnetopause diag graph *Science* v356 no6341 p960 Je 1 2017

Burch, Neil

DeepStack: Expert-level artificial intelligence in heads-up no-limit poker [Cover story] chart diag *Science* v356 no6337 p508 My 5 2017

Burch, Tory, 1966-

PERFECT FIT color *Architectural Digest* v74 no10 pCover O 1 2017

TORY'S GLORY H. Rubenstein color *InStyle* p46 Home & De-

sign 2016

Burcham, Christopher L.

Kilogram-scale prexasertib monolactate monohydrate synthesis under continuous-flow CGMP conditions chart diag *Science* v356 no6343 p1144 Je 16 2017

Burcham, John—Interviews

Q&A: John Burcham *Arizona Highways* v92 no11 p9 N 2016

Burchfield, Charles Ephraim, 1893-1967

Sunflowers at Late Dusk cartoon *Magazine Antiques* v184 no1 p23 Ja/F 2017

Burchfield, Charles Ephraim, 1893-1967—Exhibitions

Current and coming N. Anderson, S. Dalati et al bw color *Magazine Antiques* v184 no5 p26 S/O 2017

Burchfield, Donna Faye

WHAT DO COLLEGE DANCE PROGRAMS really LOOK for? C. Bowers *Dance Spirit* v21 no7 p76 S 2017

Burchman, Seymour

How Incentives for Long-Term Management Backfire *Harvard Business Review Digital Articles* p2 My 6 2016

It's Time to Tie Executive Compensation to Sustainability *Harvard Business Review Digital Articles* p2 2017

Why Companies Should Measure "Share of Growth," Not Just Market Share color *Harvard Business Review Digital Articles* p1 Je 2 2017

Burd, Stephen

BORROWER'S REMORSE color *Washington Monthly* v49 no9/10 p76 S/O 2017

Burda, Chris

WIRE-ARM CHANDELIERS color *Old House Journal* v44 no8 p84 D 2016

Burdette, Kacy

SAVING SCIENCE color *Fortune* v175 no5 p18 Ap 1 2017

Burdick, Alan

Body's perception of time still a puzzle L. Sanders bw *Science News* v191 no3 p28 F 18 2017

The Human Clock T. EHRENFELD *Weekly Standard* v22 no41 p34 Jl 3 2017

It's Not Really on Your Side C. ROVELLI *New York Times Book Review* p10 F 12 2017

PRESENT TENSE cartoon *New Yorker* v92 no42 p68 D 19 2016

Why Time Flies: A Mostly Scientific Investigation L. A. MARSCHALL color *Natural History* v125 no3 p47 Mr 2017

Burdick, Joe

Do-It-Yourself OFF-GRID SOLAR: Explore the components and considerations for creating your own off-grid photovoltaic system *Mother Earth News* no282 p16 Je/Jl 2017

Burdine, Kenneth

Historical Analysis of MPP-Dairy Suggests Limited Impact on Average Margins but Considerable Potential for Risk Reduction *Amber Waves: The Economics of Food, Farming, Natural Resources, & Rural America* p7 F 2017

Bureaucracy

See also

Bureaucratization

Bureaucracy Is Keeping Health Care from Getting Better K. T. Segel *Harvard Business Review Digital Articles* p2 O 13 2017

Bureaucracy Must Die G. Hamel *Harvard Business Review Digital Articles* p2 N 4 2014

Excess Management Is Costing the U.S. $3 Trillion Per Year G. Hamel and M. Zanini *Harvard Business Review Digital Articles* p2 S 5 2016

The Greatest Barriers to Growth, According to Executives C. Zook *Harvard Business Review Digital Articles* p2 My 17 2016

What We Learned About Bureaucracy from 7,000 HBR Readers G. Hamel and M. Zanini *Harvard Business Review Digital Articles* p2 Ag 10 2017

Bureaucracy—Management

How to Stop People Who Bog Things Down with Bureaucracy J. Allen *Harvard Business Review Digital Articles* p2 Jl 12 2016

Bureaucracy—United States

Deep State of Affairs S. GRONSKI *Commentary* v143 no4 p4 Ap 2017

Bureaucratization

What We Learned About Bureaucracy from 7,000 HBR Readers G. Hamel and M. Zanini *Harvard Business Review Digital Articles* p2 Ag 10 2017

Burek, M. J.

An integrated diamond nanophotonics platform for quantum-optical networks bibl graph *Science* v354 no6314 p847 N 18 2016

BURES, FRANK

THE FUTURE STARTS IN A MUDDY FIELD color *Bicycling* v58 no4 p52 My 2017

In the Deep Dark: Stargazing color *Backpacker* p18 My 2017

Buress, Hannibal

WHY We LOVE CHICAGO bw cartoon color *Chicago* v66 no3 p75 Mr 2017

Buress, Hannibal—Interviews

HANNIBAL LECTURE A. FLANGO *Cincinnati Magazine* v50 no2 p18 N 2016

Burfield, Brian

Magic, medicine and the Viking way of war *History Today* v67 no4 p19 Ap 2017

Burfoot, Amby

CAROLYN MATHER color *Runner's World* v52 no2 p25 Mr 2017

STREAKER KING S. Douglas bw color *Runner's World* v51 no10 p46 N 2016

Use It Or Lose It bw color *Runner's World* v52 no5 p84 Je 2017

Burga, Alejandro

A genetic signature of the evolution of loss of flight in the Galapagos cormorant color diag *Science* v356 no6341 p921 Je 1 2017

A maternal-effect selfish genetic element in Caenorhabditis elegans diag *Science* v356 no6342 p1051 Je 9 2017

Burgasser, A. J.

Zones, spots, and planetary-scale waves beating in brown dwarf atmospheres color graph *Science* v357 no6352 p683 Ag 18 2017

Burgaud, Gaetan

Life Dwells Deep Within Earth's Crust G. Schanker *Oceanus* v52 no1 p48 Summ 2016

Burgdörfer, J.

Observing the ultrafast buildup of a Fano resonance in the time domain bibl graph *Science* v354 no6313 p738 N 11 2016

BURGE, KATHLEEN

My Swimming Instructor bw color *Reader's Digest* v189 no1129 p18 Ap 2017

Burgelman, Robert A.

Remembering Andy Grove, the Teacher *Harvard Business Review Digital Articles* p2 Mr 23 2016

Burgener, Adam D.

Vaginal bacteria modify HIV tenofovir microbicide efficacy in African women chart graph *Science* v356 no6341 p938 Je 1 2017

Burgener, Simon

A synthetic pathway for the fixation of carbon dioxide in vitro bibl graph *Science* v354 no6314 p900 N 18 2016

Burger, Amy

CURTAIN CALL color *Missouri Life* v44 no2 p46 Ap 2017

HAND JIVE *Missouri Life* v43 no7 p25 D 2016/Ja 2017

Nice Cream St. Louis color *Missouri Life* v44 no3 p16 My 2017

SON'S RISE color *Missouri Life* v44 no2 p24 Ap 2017

Under Cover Bands Go as Greats St. Louis color *Missouri Life* v44 no5 p24 Ag 2017

Burger, Christoph

The 3 Stages of a Country Embracing Renewable Energy *Harvard Business Review Digital Articles* p2 Ap 17 2017

Burger, Dani

I Can Haz Make You Money? color *Bloomberg Businessweek* no4525 p37 Je 5 2017

Lies, Damn Lies, and Financial Statistics cartoon *Bloomberg Businessweek* no4518 p8 Ap 10 2017

Markets/Personal Finance color graph *Bloomberg Businessweek* no4498 p48 N 7 2016

Markets Reactions graph *Bloomberg Businessweek* no4536 p31 S 4 2017

Stock Investors Nervously Do the Math color *Bloomberg Businessweek* no4520 p41 My 1 2017

Burger, William C.

EVOLUTION AND COMPLEXITY IN BIOTA AND HUMAN CULTURES N. H. CARTER *BioScience* v67 no1 p92 Ja 2017

Burger Boat Co.

Yacht Royalty J. WOOLDRIDGE color *Power & Motoryacht* v33 no4 p74 Ap 2017

Burgess, Matthew

An Infrastructure Plan From Down Under diag *Bloomberg Businessweek* no4534 p37 Ag 14 2017

Burgess, Matthew G.

U.S. seafood import restriction presents opportunity and risk bibl color map *Science* v354 no6318 p1372 D 16 2016

BURGESS, NEIL D.

An Ecoregion-Based Approach to Protecting Half the Terrestrial Realm *BioScience* v67 no6 p534 Je 2017

BURGESS, REBECCA

French Adoption color *Weekly Standard* v22 no44 p19 Jl 31 2017

Giving Madison His Due color *Weekly Standard* v22 no30 p14 Ap 10 2017

Burgess, Tituss, 1979-

Tituss Burgess J. Crelin color *Current Biography* v78 no3 p3 Mr 2017

Burgess, Tituss, 1979-—Interviews

HAPPY HOUR! B. Keith color *Entertainment Weekly* no1465 p28 My 12 2017

Burgess, Tony

Railway Post Office color *Model Railroader* v84 no8 p16 Ag 2017

BURGESS, TREENA I.

Pathogens on the Move: A 100-Year Global Experiment with Planted Eucalypts *BioScience* v67 no1 p14 Ja 2017

Burgess, Wade

A Bad Reputation Costs a Company at Least 10% More Per Hire *Harvard Business Review Digital Articles* p2 Mr 29 2016

Burgess, Wayne

Wayne Burgess A. Priddle color *Motor Trend* v69 no10 p26 O 2017

Burgess Shale (B.C.)

Online Exhibitions color *Natural History* v125 no10 p5 O 2017

SHALE GAME L. ANTHONY color map *Canadian Geographic* v137 no1 p50 F 2017

BURGHARDT, GORDON M.

Anesthesia and Euthanasia of Amphibians and Reptiles Used in Scientific Research: Should Hypothermia and Freezing Be Prohibited? *BioScience* v67 no1 p53 Ja 2017

Burgie, E. Sethe

Phytochrome B integrates light and temperature signals in Arabidopsis bibl graph *Science* v354 no6314 p897 N 18 2016

Burglary

Frank Rich: Just Wait Watergate did't become Watergate overnight, either img *New York* v50 no13 p22 Je 26 2017

Burglary lawsuits

The Handshake M. Wolfe color *New Republic* v248 no8/9 p36 Ag/S 2017

Burglary—Law & legislation

A second charge of falling to put his dirty plate in the dishwasher is pending R. Martinez II *Texas Monthly* v45 no1 p87 Ja 2017

BURGMAN, MARK A.

Metaresearch for Evaluating Reproducibility in Ecology and Evolution *BioScience* v67 no3 p282 Mr 2017

Bürgmann, Roland

Seasonal water storage, stress modulation, and California seismicity diag graph *Science* v356 no6343 p1161 Je 16 2017

Burgmeier, Steve

Built to Last C. Wood color diag *Log Home Living* v34 no1 p28 F 2017

Burgo, Joseph

Grim: Dark Fairy Tales for the Psychologically Minded *Publishers Weekly* v264 no13 p64e Mr 27 2017

Burgundy (Wine)

Why You Should Become a Wine Snob R. HARGREAVE, J. SALCITO et al color *GQ: Gentlemen's Quarterly* v97 no10 p80 O 2017

BURHAN, JENNY

BALLER FROM THE HOLLER: JEAN DOWELL WAS A GROUND-BREAKING ATHLETE and collegiate basketball coach. Now, with an unlikely second act (and a guitar), she is bringing it all back home *Cincinnati Magazine* v50 no11 p82 Ag 2017

Burial

See also

Cemeteries

Crypts

Mass burials

Above Old Bones M. Phillips color *Commonweal* v114 no14 p22 S 8 2017

Burials give peek at Philistines' lives B. BOWER *Science News* v190 no13 p8 D 24 2016

My Snow Angel L. Wright color *Good Housekeeping* v264 no2 p63 F 2017

WHO LIES IN THE CUSTER GRAVES? J. ANDREWS *South Dakota Magazine* v32 no4 p40 N/D 2016

Burial at sea

Turned to Stone M. Greshko color *National Geographic* v231 no6 p92 Je 2017

Burial clothing

NO LONGER LOST C. Valentino color *Archaeology* v70 no5 p4 S/O 2017

TO DIE LIKE AN EGYPTIAN M. BROWN color *Archaeology* v70 no5 p44 S/O 2017

Burial—Religious aspects

Don't Scatter the Ashes—or Wear Them R. Ferrone color *Commonweal* v143 no20 p6 D 16 2016

Burial—Social aspects

MEMENTO MORI J. A. LOBELL color *Archaeology* v70 no2 p38 Mr/Ap 2017

Burj Khalifa (Dubai, United Arab Emirates)

'Oh, DUBAI. I do not understand you' H. O'Neill color map *Canadian Geographic* v137 p30 2017 Travel

Burk, Floyd

BILL WALLACE [Cover story] color *Black Belt* v55 no2 p40 F/Mr 2017

HOW A SENIOR SALVAGED HIS MARTIAL ARTS CAREER — TWICE! color *Black Belt* v55 no3 p14 Ap/My 2017

KARATE WINS ITS OLYMPIC BID color *Black Belt* v55 no1 p44 D 2016/Ja 2017

BURK, MARTHA

Trump's Starvation Budget *Ms.* v27 no2 p35 Summ 2017

BURKE, BRITTANY

17 HAPPY, HEALTHY CHOICES for 2017 [Cover story] color *Redbook* p13 F 2017

Burke, Chris

Look Sharp L. VACCARIELLO *Cincinnati Magazine* v50 no4 p160 Ja 2017

Burke, Donald S.

Forecasting the opioid epidemic color *Science* v354 no6312 p529 N 4 2016

Burke, Edmund, 1729-1797

The Republican Challenge W. Kristol *Weekly Standard* v22 no23 p6 F 20 2017

BURKE, INGRID C.

Society Is Ready for a New Kind of Science--Is Academia? *BioScience* v67 no7 p591 Jl 2017

Burke, Karen

OBSESSED WITH HUNTER-GATHERERS M. B. EYERS color *Better Homes & Gardens* v95 no9 p16 S 2017

BURKE, KATHLEEN

HOW TO SNEAK UP ON AN EMPIRE *Smithsonian* v48 no4 p114 Jl/Ag 2017

Burke, Larry

A Fight for What's Right color *Power & Motoryacht* v32 no12 p12 D 2016

A Man You Could Count On color *Power & Motoryacht* v32 no11 p34 N 2016

Burke, Martin D., 1976-

A moonshot for chemistry R. F. Service color *Science* v356 no6335 p231 Ap 21 2017

Restored iron transport by a small molecule promotes absorption and hemoglobinization in animals color graph *Science* v356 no6338 p608 My 12 2017

Burke, Maya

STUFF WATER INFILTRATION SCREWED UP cartoon *Old House Journal* v45 no2 p54 Ap 2017

Burke, Miles

STUFF WATER INFILTRATION SCREWED UP cartoon *Old House Journal* v45 no2 p54 Ap 2017

BURKE, MONTE

THE AMERICAN DREAM IS ALIVE AND WELL...ON THE FORBES 400 color graph map *Forbes* v198 no5 p58 O 25 2016

The Flip Turn color *Forbes* v199 no1 p100 Ja 24 2017

TEE FOR 'TUDE color *Forbes* v200 no5 p81 N 14 2017

Burke, Peter, 1937-

CULTURAL AND INTELLECTUAL ENRICHMENT EN-MASSE: One of our foremost cultural historians examines the impact of immigration on the transfer of knowledge D. Snowman *History Today* v67 no10 p91 O 2017

Secret History and Historical Consciousness D. Snowman *History Today* v67 no2 p57 F 2017

Burke, Raymond L., 1948-

No One Expects the Inquisition [Cover story] E. Brende color *Commonweal* v144 no10 p17 Je 2 2017

Of Popes & Trumpists cartoon *Commonweal* v144 no5 p5 Mr 10 2017

Burke, Robert

HORSE POWER bw color *Esquire* p104 2017 BigBlackBook

Burke, Siobhan

Adrenaline Rush *Dance Magazine* v91 no4 p35 Ap 2017

Leslie Andrea Williams *Dance Magazine* v91 no7 p22 Jl 2017

LYNN GARAFOLA *Dance Magazine* v90 no12 p52 D 2016

Burke, Thomas

The dishonest HONEST Act color *Science* v356 no6342 p989 Je 9 2017

BURKE, TYRONE

Savouring SINALOA color map *Canadian Geographic* v135 no6 p34 D 2015

Burke-Spolaor, S.

The magnetic field and turbulence of the cosmic web measured using a brilliant fast radio burst bibl chart graph *Science* v354 no6317 p1249 D 9 2016

Burkett, Kira

THE EXPEDITIONS color map *Canadian Geographic* v137 no4 p49 Jl/Ag 2017

BURKETT, NANCY

A Little Bit Braver Now color *O, The Oprah Magazine* p18 D 2016

Burkett, Virginia—Interviews

WE'RE SINKING P. O'Donnell *Washingtonian Magazine* v52 no6 p37 Mr 2017

Burkhart, Brett W.

Structure of histone-based chromatin in Archaea diag *Science* v357 no6351 p609 Ag 11 2017

Burkhart, Ian

Bypassing Paralysis Altogether J. KEATS color *Discover* v38 no1 p81 Ja/F 2017

Burkhart, Timothy

CONVERGENCE E. Fishman color *Chicago* v65 no11 p92 N 2016

Burkinis—Government policy

What the Burqini Ban Reveals N. GARDELS *NPQ: New Perspectives Quarterly* v33 no4 p28 O 2016

Burkins, Glenn H.

Where have all the black digital publishers gone? color *Columbia Journalism Review* v56 no1 p23 Spr 2017

Burkle, Frederick M.

The right planning now will save countless lives after a nuclear attack bibl *Bulletin of the Atomic Scientists* v73 no4 p220 Jl 2017

Burklund, Michele

His & Hers color *Amazing Wellness* v9 no1 p32 Wint 2017

QUITTING TIME color *Better Nutrition* v79 no4 p50 Ap 2017

A Sip of Summer color *Better Nutrition* v79 no7 p28 Jl 2017

Burkman, Deborah

A home practice for Better balance color *Yoga Journal* p57 2017 Special Issue

A home practice to get grounded and stable color *Yoga Journal* p93 2017 SpecialIssue

Burko, Diane

Elegy Series color *Issues in Science & Technology* v33 no1 p96 Fall 2016

Burks, Edward C.

Chiral Majorana fermion modes in a quantum anomalous Hall insulator–superconductor structure diag *Science* v357 no6348 p294 Jl 21 2017

Burkus, David

3 Ways Leaders Accidentally Undermine Their Teams' Creativity *Harvard Business Review Digital Articles* p2 Jl 7 2015

Everyone Likes Flex Time, but We Punish Women Who Use It

Harvard Business Review Digital Articles p2 F 20 2017

For Leaders, Looking Healthy Matters More than Looking Smart *Harvard Business Review Digital Articles* p2 Ja 2 2015

Former Colleagues Are More Valuable than You Think *Harvard Business Review Digital Articles* p2 Ja 13 2016

Get Buy-In for Your Crazy Idea *Harvard Business Review Digital Articles* p2 Je 3 2015

How Adobe Structures Feedback Conversations *Harvard Business Review Digital Articles* p2 Jl 20 2017

How to Make Unlimited Vacation Time Work at Your Company *Harvard Business Review Digital Articles* p2 Je 15 2015

How to Tell if Your Company Has a Creative Culture *Harvard Business Review Digital Articles* p2 D 2 2014

If You Want to Be the Boss, Say "We" Not "I" *Harvard Business Review Digital Articles* p2 Mr 6 2015

Inside Adobe's Innovation Kit *Harvard Business Review Digital Articles* p2 F 23 2015

Let Your Frontline Workers Be Creative *Harvard Business Review Digital Articles* p2 D 4 2015

No, That Meeting Could Not Have Been an Email *Harvard Business Review Digital Articles* p2 Ap 21 2015

Research: Keeping Work and Life Separate Is More Trouble than It's Worth *Harvard Business Review Digital Articles* p2 Ag 9 2016

Research Shows That Organizations Benefit When Employees Take Sabbaticals *Harvard Business Review Digital Articles* p2 Ag 10 2017

Some Companies Are Banning Email and Getting More Done *Harvard Business Review Digital Articles* p2 Je 8 2016

Why Keeping Salaries a Secret May Hurt Your Company *Harvard Business Review Digital Articles* p2 Mr 10 2016

Why Managers Are More Likely to Be Depressed *Harvard Business Review Digital Articles* p2 S 23 2015

Work Friends Make Us More Productive (Except When They Stress Us Out) *Harvard Business Review Digital Articles* p2 My 26 2017

BURLEIGH, NINA

Terrorism's Child *New York Times Book Review* p20 N 27 2016

Burle Marx, Roberto, 1909-1994

ROBERTO BURLE MARX A. G. Brake color *Art in America* v104 no10 p149 N 2016

Burlesque (Theater)

WITH A GROUP *Indianapolis Monthly* p60 F 2017

Burley, Ingrid—Interviews

RAPPER'S DELIGHT B. B. Royall color *Essence* v47 no7 p18 N 2016

Burlingame, Michael

Q: What was the most important letter in history? color *Atlantic* v320 no2 p104 S 2017

BURLINGHAM, BO

STARTING OVER color *Forbes* v199 no5 p92 My 16 2017

What Price Growth? color *Forbes* v198 no6 p56 N 8 2016

Burlington College (Burlington, Vt.)

The Little College That Couldn't A. B. LLOYD color *Weekly Standard* v22 no45 p17 Ag 7 2017

Burma-Shave signs

ROUTE 66: SELIGMAN TO KINGMAN N. AUSTIN *Arizona Highways* v93 no2 p52 F 2017

Burma—Description & travel

Spires in the Sky Myanmar lifts the curtain on the Golden Land of Burma T. PEARSALL *Virginia Living* v15 no6 p52 O 2017

Burma—Foreign relations—1948-

We Hope That All Stakeholders Can Work Together to Find a Solution in Myanmar *Vital Speeches of the Day* v83 no10 p287 O 2017

BURMAN, JENNY

NIGHT MOVES *Cincinnati Magazine* v50 no8 p40 My 2017

Burman, Peter

Rating the English Proficiency of Countries and Industries Around the World *Harvard Business Review Digital Articles* p2 N 21 2016

Burn, Daily

JUST 3 MOVES TO More Energy color *Good Housekeeping* v264 no2 p99 F 2017

Burn care teams

HEALING THE WHOLE CHILD A. BROWNLEE *Cincinnati*

Magazine v50 no4 p70 Ja 2017

Burnell, Susan

Florida color *Forbes* v198 no9 p27 D 30 2016

Promoting a Culture of Health and Well-Being in the Workplace color *Forbes* v200 no3 p46 S 28 2017

Burners (Technology)—Evaluation

New Flame color *Indianapolis Monthly* p25 Ap 2017

Burnett, Carol, 1933-—Interviews

Carol Burnett *Saturday Evening Post* v289 no1 p29 Ja/F 2017

Burnett, David

Caring for Aging Loved Ones color *Consumer Reports* v82 no12 p6 D 2017

BURNETT, DEREK

GREED, GUILE & LIES *Reader's Digest* v188 no1124 p100 O 2016

Burnett, Frances Hodgson, 1849-1924

1911: Yorkshire F. H. Burnett *Lapham's Quarterly* v10 no2 p135 Spr 2017

BURNETT, KRISTIN

Jordan's Principle *American Indian Quarterly* v41 no2 p101 Spr 2017

BURNETT, MATIA

Changing the World, One Reader at a Time color *Publishers Weekly* v264 no35 p60 Ag 28 2017

The Subtle Art of Finding A Niche color *Publishers Weekly* v264 no31 p34 Jl 31 2017

Burnett, Walter

MR. NICER GUY E. McCLELLAND color *Chicago* v66 no9 p33 S 2017

BURNETT-KIRK, PAUL

Chords & Discords bw color *Downbeat* v84 no2 p10 F 2017

Burney, Matthew J.

The linker histone H1.0 generates epigenetic and functional intratumor heterogeneity bibl graph *Science* v353 no6307 paaf1644-1 S 30 2016

Burnham, Jennifer

Brownsburg: Pit stops worth making in the west side's other racing town color diag *Indianapolis Monthly* v41 no2 p36 S 2017

Fulton Street *Indianapolis Monthly* v40 no7 p30 Mr 2017

Hot on the TRAILS: A ROAD-FREE GUIDE TO EXPLORING CENTRAL INDIANA *Indianapolis Monthly* v40 no10 p59 Je 2017

Speedway *Indianapolis Monthly* v40 no5 p28 Ja 2017

BURNLEY, RIC

THE POWER 'YAK REVIEW chart color *Outdoor Life* v224 no4 p14 My 2017

Burnout (Psychology)

advice for dancers L. HAMILTON *Dance Magazine* v91 no6 p24 Je 2017

Avoid Burnout by Asking This Question N. Pasricha *Harvard Business Review Digital Articles* p2 Je 21 2016

Burnout at Work Isn't Just About Exhaustion. It's Also About Loneliness E. Seppala and M. King *Harvard Business Review Digital Articles* p2 Je 29 2017

The Burnout Quiz M. DiTrolio and J. Covert color *Men's Health* v32 no1 p31 Ja/F 2017

FEEL THE BURNOUT K. Schaefer cartoon *Bloomberg Businessweek* no4516 p68 Mr 27 2017

If You Live in an Area with High Income Inequality, You're More Likely to Burn Out at Work Lixin Jiang and T. Probst *Harvard Business Review Digital Articles* p2 My 17 2017

Just Because You're Happy Doesn't Mean You're Not Burned Out S. Behson *Harvard Business Review Digital Articles* p2 Jl 13 2015

One Way to Prevent Clinician Burnout D. E. Mylod *Harvard Business Review Digital Articles* p2 O 12 2017

PHYSICIAN BURNOUT: The number of overworked, emotionally exhausted doctors has reached epidemic proportions. Stressed-out doctors have less time with patients and are more prone to making medical errors. Fixing the problem is a matter of national... N. STEDMAN *Saturday Evening Post* v289 no4 p46 Jl/Ag 2017

Prevent Your Star Performers from Losing Passion for Their Work M. E. Kibler *Harvard Business Review Digital Articles* p2 Ja 14 2015

Staying Motivated After a Major Achievement R. Friedman *Har-*

vard Business Review Digital Articles p2 F 3 2015

Steps to Take When You're Starting to Feel Burned Out M. Valcour *Harvard Business Review Digital Articles* p2 Je 20 2016

Surviving scientist burnout L. D. Site *Physics Today* v70 no9 p10 S 2017

Burnout (Psychology)—Prevention

Don't Get Surprised by Burnout S. D'Souza *Harvard Business Review Digital Articles* p2 Je 17 2016

How One California Medical Group Is Decreasing Physician Burnout S. Arabadjis and E. E. Sullivan color *Harvard Business Review Digital Articles* p2 Je 7 2017

How to Overcome Burnout and Stay Motivated R. Knight *Harvard Business Review Digital Articles* p2 Ap 2 2015

Prevent Burnout by Making Compassion a Habit A. McKee and K. Wiens *Harvard Business Review Digital Articles* p1 My 11 2017

Why Some People Get Burned Out and Others Don't K. Wiens and A. McKee *Harvard Business Review Digital Articles* p2 N 23 2016

Burnout (Psychology)—Research

Mismatched needs and wants cause burnout *People Management* p61 O 2016

Burnout (Psychology)—Risk factors

Beating Burnout M. Valcour il img *Harvard Business Review* v94 no11 p98 N 2016

Burnout (Psychology)—Treatment

Beating Burnout M. Valcour il img *Harvard Business Review* v94 no11 p98 N 2016

Burns & scalds

CATRIN'S LONG WAY BACK R. KINER *Reader's Digest* v189 no1128 p112 Mr 2017

Second opinion *Mayo Clinic Health Letter* v35 no6 p8 Je 2017

Burns, Chelsea Traber

How to Talk So Your Stylist Will Listen color *Health* v31 no8 p108 O 2017

Melt-Proof Your Makeup color *Health* v31 no5 p96 Je 2017

Talk to the hand(s) color *Health* v31 no9 p33 N 2017

Your Happiest Summer Hair color *Health* v31 no6 p112 Jl 2017

Your Travel Beauty Problems, Solved color *Health* v31 no6 p27 Jl 2017

Burns, Christine

Hidden but not lost *History Today* v67 no5 p8 My 2017

Burns, Christopher

Examining Farm Sector and Farm Household Income *Amber Waves: The Economics of Food, Farming, Natural Resources, & Rural America* p23 Ag 2017

Farm Households Experience High Levels of Income Volatility *Amber Waves: The Economics of Food, Farming, Natural Resources, & Rural America* p43 F 2017

The Number of Midsize Farms Declined From 1992 to 2012, But Their Household Finances Remain Strong color graph *Amber Waves: The Economics of Food, Farming, Natural Resources, & Rural America* p19 D 2016

Burns, Curtis

NO FILTER A. B. WALTERS *Cincinnati Magazine* p24 Je 2017

Burns, Jennifer

Objectively Speaking, Rand Is History: The recent presidential race made it obvious: conservatives have shrugged off Ayn Rand *Hoover Digest: Research & Opinion on Public Policy* no3 p170 Summ 2017

Burns, Kathryn

Funny Girl M. SCHROCK *Dance Magazine* v91 no4 p58 Ap 2017

Burns, Kathryn—Interviews

Behind the Scenes of "Crazy Ex-Girlfriend" C. Bowers *Dance Spirit* v21 no1 p23 Ja 2017

Burns, Ken, 1953-

GOOD EVENING, VIETNAM D. KAMP bw *Vanity Fair* v59 no8 p58 Ag 2017

How Americans Lost Faith in the Presidency bw *Atlantic* v320 no3 p24 O 2017

Ken Burns revisits the division and bloodshed wrought by 'a barbaric war' R. A. Schroth bw *America* v217 no7 p50 O 2 2017

MR. AMERICA I. PARKER cartoon *New Yorker* v93 no26 p50 S 4 2017

NEW EYES on VIETNAM A. Grant color *Esquire* p69 S 2017

THE VIETNAM WAR: How the film story of the most divisive

event in America since the Civil War came to life in a small New Hampshire town M. ALLEN *Yankee* v81 no5 p136 S/O 2017

The Vietnam War: Ken Burns's moving history of the grueling war that divided America M. ROUSH *TV Guide* v65 no39 p26 S 18 2017

Burns, Ken, 1953-—Interviews

Documentarian Ken Burns on How Vietnam Explains the Current Political Moment N. Gillespie color *Reason* v49 no5 p79 O 2017

INTO THE VOID P. KLAY bw cartoon color *Mother Jones* v42 no5 p56 S/O 2017

Ken Burns on "The Roosevelts" and American Leadership D. McGinn *Harvard Business Review Digital Articles* p2 S 18 2017

KEN BURNS: VIETNAM J. WOLF *Saturday Evening Post* v289 no5 p32 S/O 2017

Burns, Kida

Contemporary ALL OVER color *Dance Spirit* v20 no10 p14 D 2016

KIDA K. Holmes color *Dance Spirit* v20 no10 p36 D 2016

#TeamHipHop *Dance Spirit* v20 no10 p22 D 2016

Burns, Mark

Virtually Yours color *Sports Illustrated* v125 no17 p30 N 21 2016 Double Issue

Burns, Noah Z.

Mechanochemical unzipping of insulating polyladderene to semiconducting polyacetylene [Cover story] diag *Science* v357 no6350 p475 Ag 4 2017

Burns, Nora

GOINGS ON ABOUT TOWN bw *New Yorker* v93 no19 p4 Jl 3 2017

Burns, Rebecca

-A - NEW DEAL FOR WALL STREET: Trump's plan to sell off our infrastructure, and the Democrats who paved the way *In These Times* v41 no8 p14 Ag 2017

THE SECOND BURNING OF ATLANTA *Atlanta* v56 no10 p84 F 2017

Socialism, Coming to a State Fair Near You *In These Times* v41 no10 p7 O 2017

Burns, Robert, 1759-1796

Robert Burns of the Ages F. Inglis color *British Heritage Travel* v38 no5 p33 S/O 2017

Burns, Shari

from you, the reader D. Hubbard, C. Willoughby et al color graph *Horse & Rider* v56 no8 p22 Ag 2017

Burns, Theresa

KNIGHTS OF COLUMBUS *America* v216 no9 p37 Ap 24 2017

Burns, Ursula

The Summer Job I'll Never Forget color *Time* v190 no2/3 p55 Jl 10-17 2017

Burns Stainless LLC

IMPERFECT PIPES P. LERNER color *Road & Track* v69 no3 p98 O 2017

Burnsed, Brian

Clinton PORTIS color *Sports Illustrated* v127 no1 p98 Jl 3 2017

BURNS ROSS, JULIE

Indigenous Intergenerational Teachings bw chart il map *American Indian Quarterly* v40 no3 p216 Summ 2016

Burow, Liz

7 Factors of Great Office Design *Harvard Business Review Digital Articles* p2 My 20 2016

BURPEE, BENJAMIN T.

The Arctic in the Twenty-First Century: Changing Biogeochemical Linkages across a Paraglacial Landscape of Greenland *BioScience* v67 no2 p118 F 2017

Burqas (Islamic clothing)

Chancellor Angela Merkel of Germany calls for a ban of burqas as election nears D. Iaconangelo and J. Bhatti *Christian Century* v134 no1 p15 Ja 4 2017

Europe in Transition *American Conservative* v16 no2 p58 Mr/Ap 2017

TWO WOMEN IN BURKAS E. LABORDE cartoon *New Orleans Magazine* v51 no1 p184 N 2016

BÚRQUEZ, ALBERTO

The Role of Botanical Gardens in the Conservation of Cactaceae *BioScience* v66 no12 p1057 D 1 2016

Burr, Andrew

THE DESCENT color *Climbing* no350 p80 D 2016/Ja 2017
THE DESCENT color *Climbing* no353 p80 My/Je 2017
THE DESCENT color *Climbing* no354 p80 Jl 2017
THE DESCENT color *Climbing* no356 p80 S/O 2017
Eye Candy Z. GATES color *Climbing* no354 p28 Jl 2017
FLASH bw color *Climbing* no349 p12 N 2016
Where the Waves Meet the Rock color *Climbing* no354 p46 Jl 2017

Burr, Chuck
LEAKY PIPE CAN COST YOU $32 PER ACRE: A THIRD OF PUMPED WATER CAN LEAK OUT OF WORN GATES AND GASKETS D. Mowitz *Successful Farming* v115 no12 p58 O 2017

Burr, Devon
Defining the topography of a planetary body map *Science* v356 no6339 p708 My 19 2017

BURR, RICHARD
Sorry to Disappoint You, Mr. President color *Weekly Standard* v22 no31 p26 Ap 17 2017

Burr, Tom—Interviews
Tom BURR C. MAUM *Interview* v46 no10 p143 D 2016/Ja 2017

Burr, Ty
THE BIG QUESTION cartoon *Atlantic* v319 no2 p100 Mr 2017
Virtually There bw *MIT Technology Review* v120 no2 p96 Mr/Ap 2017

Burrell, Kenny
Unlimited 1 J. McDonough color *Downbeat* v84 no2 p69 F 2017

BURRELL, PAUL
REMEMBERING DIANA color *AARP: The Magazine* v60 no5A p50 Ag/S 2017

BURRELL, TEAL
Are Facial Expressions Universal? color *Discover* v38 no5 p18 Je 2017
Drug Couriers for Brain Injuries color *Discover* v38 no1 p33 Ja/F 2017
Not Your Kid's ADHD cartoon *Discover* v38 no1 p65 Ja/F 2017
Redefining the Brain's Divisions color *Discover* v38 no1 p55 Ja/F 2017

Burrell, Ty, 1967-
Casting Call: The Jetsons M. L. Lenker color *Entertainment Weekly* no1480 p43 S 1 2017

BURRESS, RICK
Understanding Aperture *Arizona Highways* v93 no6 p9 Je 2017

Burrington, Ingrid
The Internet Is Under This Manhole M. READ img *New York* v49 no25 p75 D 12 2016

Burris, Ethan R.
Don't Let Your Brain's Defense Mechanisms Thwart Effective Feedback *Harvard Business Review Digital Articles* p2 Ag 18 2016
Employee Suggestion Schemes Don't Have to Be Exercises in Futility *Harvard Business Review Digital Articles* p2 Ja 26 2016
Nonverbal Cues Get Employees to Open Up—or Shut Down *Harvard Business Review Digital Articles* p2 D 11 2015
Research: Insecure Managers Don't Want Your Suggestions *Harvard Business Review Digital Articles* p2 N 24 2014
When It's Tough to Speak Up, Get Help from Your Coworkers *Harvard Business Review Digital Articles* p2 Mr 4 2016

Burritos (Cooking)
The Sweetness of Fall S. Evans color *Southern Living* v52 no9 p12 S 2017
WANT SPROUTS WITH THAT? [Cover story] G. Hamadey color *Women's Health* v14 no5 p96 Je 2017

Burro Creek (Mohave County, Ariz.)
Misty Morning *Arizona Highways* v93 no2 p5 F 2017

BURROUGH, BRYAN
FIELD OF NIGHTMARES color *Vanity Fair* v58 no11 p164 N 2016
INVADING APPLE color *Vanity Fair* v59 no1 p144 Holiday 2017
It Seemed Like a Good Idea color *Vanity Fair* v59 no8 p70 Ag 2017
The Old Terrorists H. KLEHR *Commentary* v140 no2 p61 S 2015

Burroughs, Augusten
day tripping *Psychology Today* v49 no5 p96 S/O 2016
LUST LESSONS cartoon *Men's Health* v32 no3 p25 Ap 2017

BURROUGHS, GAYLYNN
NOT GOING BACK *Ms.* v26 no4 p20 Wint 2016
The War on Women's Health: Trumpcare leaves 23 million more people uninsured and slashes $834 billion from Medicaid, rewarding the wealthy while penalizing low-income women *Ms.* v27 no2 p36 Summ 2017

Burroughs, Jordan
HOT | NOT T. Keith and S. Kwak color *Sports Illustrated* v127 no7 p22 S 4 2017

Burroughs, Nannie Helen, 1879-1961
Last Look D. Kidd *Governing* v30 no7 p64 Ap 2017

Burrowing animals
Wasps are experts at crypt escape S. Milius color *Science News* v191 no6 p4 Ap 1 2017

Burrowing owl
CRiTTER CHAT A. SHAW color *National Geographic Kids* no470 p31 My 2017

Burrows, Julia
WOMAN in government *Governing* v30 no5 p48 F 2017

Burrows, Ken
The Sanctity of Human Life Act: Politicians Playing God *Humanist* v77 no5 p9 S/O 2017

Burrows, Peter
Elon Musk's House of Giga-cards graph il *MIT Technology Review* v119 no6 p58 N/D 2016
Eyeing a Dropbox IPO il *MIT Technology Review* v120 no2 p24 Mr/Ap 2017
PIONEERS color il *MIT Technology Review* v120 no5 p50 S/O 2017

Burruss, Kandi
Still Shining On [Cover story] C. Penn color *Essence* v48 no6 p94 O 2017

BURSA, FRANCIS
Estimation of Relative Potency from Bioassay Data that Include Values below the Limit of Quantitation *BioScience* v66 no11 p983 N 1 2016

Bursztyn, Leonardo
The Ambition-Marriage Trade-Off Too Many Single Women Face *Harvard Business Review Digital Articles* p2 My 8 2017

Burt & Co.
Val's Guide to GORGEOUS V. Monroe color *O, The Oprah Magazine* p50 Ja 2017

BURT, EMILY
189,245 graduates. 19,732 vacancies *People Management* p44 F 2017
It'll cost you... *People Management* p27 S 2017
THE PM GUIDE TO Video learning: Video is one of the most effective ways to deliver learning. So where do L&D professionals go for resources? We asked readers for their tips *People Management* p46 Jl 2017
"We deliberately don't call it 'engagement'": Why HR put employees in the driving seat in its quest to reinvigorate the company's culture *People Management* p20 Mr 2017

Burt, Gabor George
Keeping Customers Continuously Infatuated *Harvard Business Review Digital Articles* p2 Ag 9 2016
What We Can Learn from One of the World's Most-Mocked Cars *Harvard Business Review Digital Articles* p2 Ap 22 2016

Burt, Jake
Greetings from Witness Protection! *Publishers Weekly* v264 no31 p88 Jl 31 2017

Burt, Randy
Chicago Style C. KUZMA color *Runner's World* v52 no9 p50 O 2017

Burt, S. P.
Selective oxidative dehydrogenation of propane to propene using boron nitride catalysts bibl diag graph *Science* v354 no6319 p1570 D 23 2016

BURT, SHEILA
RUN, PILGRIM, RUN color map *Tricycle: The Buddhist Review* v26 no2 p50 Wint 2016

BURT, STEPH
SINGING IN THE DARK color *Nation* v305 no6 p35 S 11 2017
SPACE TRAVELS color *Nation* v304 no18 p12 Je 19 2017

Burt, Stephen
After Callimachus S. Burt *American Scholar* v86 no2 p59 Spr 2017

Anubis S. Burt *American Scholar* v86 no2 p62 Spr 2017
'A Place for the Genuine'; A new volume does justice to one of the 20th century's most singular poets *New York Times Book Review* p12 Ag 13 2017
LAMB'S EAR *New Yorker* v93 no14 p72 My 22 2017
Shorter Means Sweeter L. HAMMER *American Scholar* v86 no2 p58 Spr 2017

Burtch, Patrick
Speed Read R. ANNIS color *Indianapolis Monthly* p15 Ap 2017

BURT COTE, JACQUELINE
babyish behavior *Parents* v92 no8 p132 Ag 2017

Burton, Bonnie
'Star Wars' at 40 bw color *AARP: The Magazine* v60 no3A p10 Ap/My 2017

Burton, Brent
Brent's Beauties J. Oltion *Sky & Telescope* v133 no5 p72 My 2017

Burton, Dennis R.
Developing an HIV vaccine bibl diag *Science* v355 no6330 p1129 Mr 17 2017
Priming HIV-1 broadly neutralizing antibody precursors in human Ig loci transgenic mice bibl graph *Science* v353 no6307 p1557 S 30 2016
Trispecific broadly neutralizing HIV antibodies mediate potent SHIV protection in macaques color graph *Science* v357 no6359 p85 O 6 2017

Burton, Gary—Interviews
Vibes Legend Burton Bids Fond Farewell A. Druout color *Downbeat* v84 no6 p13 Je 2017

Burton, James
Saving the saola from extinction color *Science* v357 no6357 p1248 S 22 2017

Burton, Katherine
THE COMEBACK KID color *Bloomberg Businessweek* no4509 p62 Ja 30 2017
Hot Tickets and Wall Street Marks *Bloomberg Businessweek* no4540 p33 O 2 2017
Mystery Deal *Bloomberg Businessweek* no4510 p33 F 6 2017
THE SINS OF THE FATHER color *Bloomberg Businessweek* no4524 p70 My 29 2017
Stock Investors Nervously Do the Math color *Bloomberg Businessweek* no4520 p41 My 1 2017

Burton, Robert
HARM DONE *Lapham's Quarterly* v10 no3 p85 Summ 2017

Burton, Rodrick—Interviews
Climate Steward J. Spring *Sierra* v101 no6 p63 N/D 2016

Burton, Sarah
SARAH BURTON H. Bowles color *Vogue* v207 no3 p430 Mr 2017

Burton, Susan
Becoming Ms. Burton: From Prison to Recovery to Leading the Fight for Incarcerated Women color *Publishers Weekly* v264 no11 p71 Mr 13 2017
Life on the Outside J. ROSEN color *Publishers Weekly* v264 no18 p31 My 1 2017
Susan Burton J. HERBST *Los Angeles Magazine* v62 no9 p92 S 2017

Burton, Suzanne L.
Serve and return: Communication foundations for early childhood music policy stakeholders bibl *Arts Education Policy Review* v118 no3 p140 2017

Burton, Thomas
Opera Omaha *Opera News* v81 no7 p60 Ja 2017

Burton, Tim, 1958-
Burton Loses the Plot In Peregrine S. Zacharek color *Time* v188 no14 p56 O 10 2016
Grossed Out J. PODHORETZ *Weekly Standard* v22 no6 p39 O 17 2016
Miss Peregrine's Home for Peculiar Children B. Diones *New Yorker* v92 no35 p24 O 31 2016
TIM BURTON'S SCORE CARD color *Entertainment Weekly* no1434 p42 O 7 2016

BURTON, VALERIE
A Woman's Place Is in the Marathon color *Reader's Digest* v189 no1129 p20 Ap 2017

Burton, Valorie
REVIVE YOUR Soul color *Essence* v47 no9 p72 Ja 2017

Burton, Walter John, 1836-1880
THE LOOKING GLASS A. BROWNLEE *Cincinnati Magazine* v50 no4 p26 Ja 2017

Burton Snowboards (Company)
2017 HOLIDAY GIFT GUIDE T. Monterosso bw *Snowboarder* v29 no4 p108 D 2016

Burtynsky, Ed
The admiration of horror B. BETHUNE color *Maclean's* v129 no42 p50 O 24 2016
THE LONG VIEW R. KHATCHADOURIAN cartoon color *New Yorker* v92 no42 p80 D 19 2016

BURUM, LINDA
HALO-HALO REMIX *Los Angeles Magazine* v61 no11 p133 N 2016

Buruma, Ian
DANCE WITH THE DRAGON cartoon color *New Yorker* v93 no17 p61 Je 19 2017
Exit Wounds *New York Times Magazine* p38 D 4 2016
The 'Indescribable Fragrance' of Youths [Cover story] color *New York Review of Books* v64 no8 p29 My 11 2017
Japan: Beautiful, Savage, Mute color *New York Review of Books* v64 no2 p27 F 9 2017
LE CARRÉ'S OTHER COLD WAR color *Nation* v303 no17 p27 O 24 2016
Oscar Wilde's 'Living Death' bw *New York Review of Books* v63 no18 p66 N 24 2016
Robert B. Silvers (1929–2017) [Cover story] bw color *New York Review of Books* v64 no8 p31 My 11 2017
The Weird Success of Guy Burgess bw *New York Review of Books* v63 no20 p77 D 22 2016

Burwell, Sylvia M. (Sylvia Mathews), 1965-
QUAD GOALS: A political insider takes on a new challenge: running American University P. O'Donnell *Washingtonian Magazine* v53 no1 p41 O 2017

Burwick, Dave
DAVE BURWICK bw color *Bloomberg Businessweek* no4517 p76 Ap 3 2017

Bury, Edward M.
TALK TO US bw *Chicago* v66 no3 p23 Mr 2017

Bury, Erin—Interviews
3 TIPS FOR FUTURE ENTREPRENEURS color *Maclean's* v130 no3 p64 Ap 2017

Buryakov, Evgeny
The Spy Who Added Me on LinkedIn G. M. Graff color *Bloomberg Businessweek* no4500 p54 N 21 2016

Burz, Michael F.
Rechargeable nickel–3D zinc batteries: An energy-dense, safer alternative to lithium-ion bw chart diag *Science* v356 no6336 p415 Ap 28 2017

Burzynski, S. R., 1943-
Burzynski Sanctioned by Texas Medical Board R. Blaskiewicz *Skeptical Inquirer* v41 no4 p7 Jl/Ag 2017

Burzynski, Stanislaw—Trials, litigation, etc.
Burzynski Update: Texas Hearings End, Judges Sifting Evidence R. BLASKIEWICZ *Skeptical Inquirer* v40 no6 p5 N/D 2016

Bus terminals—Design & construction
Newport Transit Station *Architectural Record* v205 no4 p206 Ap 2017

Bus transportation
A Lot on the Line C. RITCHIE *Indianapolis Monthly* v40 no3 p68 N 2016
REROUTED: Big-city bus systems are finding ways to dig out from decades of stagnation D. C. Vock *Governing* v30 no12 p38 S 2017
WHERE THE BUS IS THE NEW TRAIN D. Heed *Washingtonian Magazine* v52 no1 p55 O 2016

Bus travel
LEAF PEOPLE: A WEEK ON A GUIDED FOLIAGE TOUR SHOWS OFF NOT ONLY NEW ENGLAND BUT A BIT OF HUMAN NATURE, TOO I. ALDRICH *Yankee* v81 no5 p110 S/O 2017
MY BUS: A LOVE LETTER: What Metrobus's most popular route can tell us about our city D. Reed *Washingtonian Magazine* v52 no12 p51 S 2017
WHERE THE BUS IS THE NEW TRAIN D. Heed *Washingtonian Magazine* v52 no1 p55 O 2016

Busby, George B. J.
Resistance to malaria through structural variation of red blood cell invasion receptors diag *Science* v356 no6343 p1139 Je 16 2017

Buscemi, M.
Observation of a large-scale anisotropy in the arrival directions of cosmic rays above 8 × 1018 eV *Science* v357 no6357 p1266 S 22 2017

Busch, Kurt, 1978-
Leading Off A. Lawrence color *Sports Illustrated* v126 no7 p6 Mr 6 2017

Busch, Marc L.
Executives Need to Know How Trade Deals Shape Their Markets *Harvard Business Review Digital Articles* p2 O 13 2016

Busch, Philipp
A pathogenic role for T cell–derived IL-22BP in inflammatory bowel disease bibl graph *Science* v354 no6310 p358 O 21 2016

Buschauer, Robert
Assembly of a nucleus-like structure during viral replication in bacteria bibl color graph *Science* v355 no6321 p1 Ja 13 2017

Buselli, Mark
7 IDEAS FOR ORCHESTRATING BIG BAND BRASS color *Downbeat* v84 no4 p80 Ap 2017

Bush (Performer)
GAVIN ROSSDALE R. Rahman color *Entertainment Weekly* no1457/1458 p97 Mr 17 2017

Bush, Barbara
Dear Sasha and Malia ... color *Time* v189 no4 p43 Ja 23 2017

Bush, Barbara Pierce
SPEAKING OF FIRST DAUGHTERS... D. BLASBERG color *Vanity Fair* v59 no10 p190 O 2017

Bush, George W. (George Walker), 1946-
The CIA, Post-Obama R. M. GERECHT color *Weekly Standard* v22 no15 p24 D 19 2016
Crispy Duck *New Republic* v247 no12 p4 D 2016
Empathetic Eye J. GARDNER color *Weekly Standard* v22 no41 p31 Jl 3 2017
AN EVEN GREATER NATION FOR GENERATIONS TO COME G. W. BUSH *Vital Speeches of the Day* v82 no11 p349 N 2016
FROM THE ARCHIVES N. GILLESPIE, A. C. KORS et al bw cartoon *Reason* v48 no11 p70 Ap 2017
LIVE FROM DC *Washingtonian Magazine* v53 no1 p70 O 2017
Nicolle Wallace Thinks White House Staffers Need to Have a Limit A. M. Cox color *New York Times Magazine* p54 Ag 6 2017
One Brainchild Left Behind P. E. Peterson *Hoover Digest: Research & Opinion on Public Policy* no4 p138 Fall 2016
Portraits of Courage W. W. Horne color *AARP: The Magazine* v60 no3A p56 Ap/My 2017
The Rehabilitation of Dubya G. Younge bw color *Nation* v304 no10 p10 Mr 27 2017
Searching for George W. Bush in his portraits of soldiers he sent to war J. Malesic color *America* v216 no7 p48 Ap 3 2017
Sounds of Silence A. Sullivan *New Republic* v248 no3 p4 Mr 2017
War Paint: The unexpected power of George W. Bush's book of paintings J. ALTER color *New York Times Book Review* p17 Ap 23 2017

Bush, George W. (George Walker), 1946-—Interviews
The Art of Warriors M. Duffy color *Time* v189 no9 p49 Mr 13 2017

Bush, George, 1924-
How Climate Change Became a Political Issue J. Worland *Time* v190 no6 p25 Ag 7 2017

Bush, Harold K.
For a Little While: New and Selected Stories *Christian Century* v134 no1 p41 Ja 4 2017

Bush, John-Morgan
BEST BETS L. Schwartzberg and B. Doherty img *New York* v49 no19 p61 S 19 2016

Bush, Jonathan
Bringing the Power of Platforms to Health Care *Harvard Business Review Digital Articles* p2 N 10 2016
Making Appointments Fast and Easy Must Be Health Care's Top Priority *Harvard Business Review Digital Articles* p2 Je 4 2015

Bush, Kevin A.
Perovskite-perovskite tandem photovoltaics with optimized band gaps bibl chart graph *Science* v354 no6314 p861 N 18 2016

Bush, Lauren, 1984-
THE DO-GOOD DESIGNER L. B. LAUREN color *Martha Stewart Living* p42 Mr 2017

Bush, Michael C.
100 BEST COMPANIES TO WORK FOR 2017 [Cover story] color diag map *Fortune* v175 no4 p79 Mr 15 2017
HOW TO GET ON THIS LIST color *Fortune* v175 no4 p89 Mr 15 2017

BUSH, SETH D.
Origins of Science Faculty with Education Specialties: Hiring Motivations and Prior Connections Explain Institutional Differences in the SFES Phenomenon *BioScience* v67 no5 p452 My 2017

Bush, Sophia, 1982-
Chicago P.D N. Abrams, B. L. Heldman et al *Entertainment Weekly* no1482/1483 p79 S 22 2017
My Obsessions... *TV Guide* v65 no11 p10 Mr 6 2017
Your Hair This Summer K. Erickson color *Glamour* v115 no6 p55 Je 2017

Bush family
Politicians bw cartoon color *American Cowboy* p26 LEGENDS OF TEXAS Special Issue 2017

Bush pilots
The Iditarod Air Force J. BENNETT color map *Popular Mechanics* p15 Mr 2017

Bush v. Gore (Supreme Court case)
GETTING IT RIGHT A. J. BAER *Washingtonian Magazine* v52 no4 p216 Ja 2017

Bushido
PASCAL FAULIOT cartoon *Tricycle: The Buddhist Review* v26 no3 p19 Spr 2017

Bushmarinov, Ivan S.
Density functional theory is straying from the path toward the exact functional bibl chart graph *Science* v355 no6320 p1 Ja 6 2017

Bushnell, Ed
DEDICATED K. BEEKMAN color *Skiing* p18 D 2016

Bushnell, James
Reforming the U.S. coal leasing program color graph *Science* v354 no6316 p1096 D 2 2016

Bushnell Corp.
FIXED FOCUS A. McKEAN color *Outdoor Life* v224 no9 p34 N 2017

Bushong, Eric A.
Ultrastructural evidence for synaptic scaling across the wake/sleep cycle bibl diag graph *Science* v355 no6324 p507 F 3 2017

Bushwick (Film)
A Brooklyn Bridge Too Far M. AGRESTA *Texas Monthly* v45 no3 p66 Mr 2017
THE PICTURES: CAN IT HAPPEN HERE? D. Steinberg bw *New Yorker* v93 no33 p37 O 23 2017

Bushwick, Sophie
AERO-SPACE color *Popular Science* v288 no6 p52 N/D 2016
AYAH BDEIR color *Popular Science* v288 no6 p26 N/D 2016
How Long Is a Year? bw color graph *Popular Science* v289 no5 p50 S/O 2017
How to Eat As Much As Possible (ACCORDING TO SCIENCE) color *Reader's Digest* v190 no1135 p128 N 2017
it's coming from inside the house color *Popular Science* v289 no6 p88 N/D 2017
Make a Sextant from Junk color *Popular Science* p84 Ja/F 2017
Smartest. Cooker. Ever [Cover story] color diag *Popular Science* v289 no6 p60 N/D 2017
Snap the Night Sky on a Phone cartoon *Popular Science* p78 Ja/F 2017
a stroke erased my sense of past or future cartoon *Popular Science* v289 no5 p75 S/O 2017
that time i bombed antarctica cartoon *Popular Science* v289 no2 p75 Mr/Ap 2017
THIS IS YOUR UNIVERSE color *Popular Science* p20 Ja/F 2017

Bushwick Starr, The (Performer)
GOINGS ON ABOUT TOWN color *New Yorker* v93 no15 p4 My 29 2017

BUSICO, MICHALENE
Changes In the 'Bu color *Los Angeles Magazine* v62 no10 p18 O 2017

A Consultant's Guide to Difficult Client Feedback R. Ashkenas *Harvard Business Review Digital Articles* p2 Ag 21 2015

Corporate Writing Doesn't Have to Sound Like It's Written by Committee J. Bernoff *Harvard Business Review Digital Articles* p2 S 15 2016

For Better Presentations, Start with a Villain G. Stone *Harvard Business Review Digital Articles* p2 N 12 2015

Good Communication Requires Experimenting with Your Language M. Luca and O. Hauser *Harvard Business Review Digital Articles* p2 F 4 2016

How Experts Can Help a General Audience Understand Their Ideas N. Duarte *Harvard Business Review Digital Articles* p2 S 12 2016

How to Calm Your Nerves Before a Big Presentation Amy Jen Su *Harvard Business Review Digital Articles* p2 O 27 2016

How to Get Employees Excited to Do Their Work K. Decker and B. Decker *Harvard Business Review Digital Articles* p2 My 18 2015

How to Get Your Colleagues' Attention A. Gallo *Harvard Business Review Digital Articles* p2 My 14 2015

How to Handle 3 Types of Difficult Conversations K. Dillon *Harvard Business Review Digital Articles* p2 D 29 2014

How to Improve Your Business Writing C. O'Hara *Harvard Business Review Digital Articles* p2 N 20 2014

How to Write Email with Military Precision K. Sehgal *Harvard Business Review Digital Articles* p2 N 22 2016

If You Want People to Listen, Stop Talking P. Bregman *Harvard Business Review Digital Articles* p2 My 25 2015

Learning the Language of Indirectness A. Molinsky and M. Hahn *Harvard Business Review Digital Articles* p2 My 6 2015

No, That Meeting Could Not Have Been an Email D. Burkus *Harvard Business Review Digital Articles* p2 Ap 21 2015

"Poor Communication" Is Often a Symptom of a Different Problem A. Markman *Harvard Business Review Digital Articles* p2 F 22 2017

"Rally the Troops" and Other Business Metaphors You Can Do Without M. Chussil *Harvard Business Review Digital Articles* p2 N 24 2016

Stop Trying to Sound Smart When You're Writing L. Davey *Harvard Business Review Digital Articles* p2 O 5 2016

Tailor Your Presentation to Fit the Culture E. Meyer *Harvard Business Review Digital Articles* p2 O 29 2014

They launched an internal social network. What happened next will blow your mind... *People Management* p40 My 2017

What Email, IM, and the Phone Are Each Good For K. Decker and B. Decker *Harvard Business Review Digital Articles* p2 Jl 30 2015

What Makes a Boss Too Formal? E. Meyer *Harvard Business Review Digital Articles* p2 Ja 6 2015

Why Your Organization Needs a Writing Center J. Bernoff *Harvard Business Review Digital Articles* p2 F 21 2017

You Can Have Constructive Conflict Over Email J. Grenny *Harvard Business Review Digital Articles* p2 Mr 24 2015

Your Company Needs a Communications Plan for Data Breaches H. Rollo and P. Tran *Harvard Business Review Digital Articles* p2 O 7 2016

Your Customers Still Want to Talk to a Human Being G. Johnson *Harvard Business Review Digital Articles* p2 Jl 26 2017

Your Late-Night Emails Are Hurting Your Team M. Thomas *Harvard Business Review Digital Articles* p2 Mr 16 2015

Business conditions
 See also
  Industrywide conditions
Business conditions—Louisiana—New Orleans
What Makes New Orleans a Startup City to Rival the "Big Three" T. Williamson *Harvard Business Review Digital Articles* p2 Mr 8 2016

Business conditions—Singapore
How Singapore Became an Entrepreneurial Hub S. Anthony *Harvard Business Review Digital Articles* p2 F 25 2015
Business consultants
A Consultant's Guide to Firing a Client D. Clark *Harvard Business Review Digital Articles* p2 Ja 26 2015
Business continuity planning
When to Tell Your Employees to Stay Home K. Firestone *Harvard Business Review Digital Articles* p2 F 27 2015

Business conversion
How to (Gradually) Become a Different Company H. Vantrappen and D. Deneffe *Harvard Business Review Digital Articles* p2 O 15 2014
Business cycles
 See also
  Economic forecasting
  Economic recovery
  Stagnation (Economics)
10 SUCCESSFUL FARMERS: JOHN SCHWARTZ B. Freese *Successful Farming* v115 no8 p23 Je/Jl 2017
Employed workers leaving the labor force: an analysis of recent trends H. Frazis bibl *Monthly Labor Review* p1 My 2017
The impact of business cycles on job mobility D. Wile *Monthly Labor Review* p1 Je 2017
Why No One Will Implement the Best Solution to Economic Stagnation U. Haque *Harvard Business Review Digital Articles* p2 N 26 2015
You Can't Understand China's Slowdown Without Understanding Supply Chains D. Simchi-Levi *Harvard Business Review Digital Articles* p2 S 4 2015
Business development
 See also
  Partnership (Business)
The 3 Preconditions for an Entrepreneurial Society J. Birkinshaw *Harvard Business Review Digital Articles* p2 Ag 17 2016
7 SECRETS OF A SIDE HUSTLER K. Johnson color *Black Enterprise* v47 no7 p14 My/Je 2017
BE 100s MILESTONES D. T. Dingle bw color *Black Enterprise* v47 no7 p76 My/Je 2017
A CONVERSATION with Jon and Krista Henningsgard S. Andersen *Arabian Horse World* v57 no6 p70 Mr 2017
GHESQUIÈRE'S VIEW E. Wilson color *InStyle* v23 no13 p238 D 2016
Business ecosystems
The Rise of Social Graphs for Businesses S. P. Choudary *Harvard Business Review Digital Articles* p2 F 2 2015
What I Learned from Trying to Innovate at the New York Times J. Geraci *Harvard Business Review Digital Articles* p2 Ap 7 2016
Business education
 See also
  Master of business administration degree
Business Professors Need to Spend Time in Companies H. H. Brower and M. D. Steward *Harvard Business Review Digital Articles* p2 N 27 2015
Making Business School Research More Relevant J. Eckhardt and J. C. Wetherbe *Harvard Business Review Digital Articles* p2 D 24 2014
Why I Challenged My Kids to Start Companies Before College R. Sheen *Harvard Business Review Digital Articles* p2 Ja 22 2016
You Can Learn and Get Work Done at the Same Time L. Davey *Harvard Business Review Digital Articles* p2 Ja 11 2016
Business education—Canada
Business Education Gets Personal G. Bauer color *Maclean's* v129 no43 p40 O 31 2016
Business enterprises
 See also
  Architectural firms
  Big business
  Bookstores
  Branches (Business enterprises)
  Contractors
  Employment agencies
  Executive search firms
  Family-owned business enterprises
  Foreign business enterprises
  For-profit universities & colleges
  International business enterprises
  Music industry
  New business enterprises
  Partnership (Business)
  Real estate business
  Restaurants
  Small business
  Travel agents
The 4 Types of Small Businesses, and Why Each One Matters K.

N. Torres *Harvard Business Review Digital Articles* p2 Ag 6 2015

Business enterprises—Finance—Management

How to Better Manage Your Company's Utility Bills J. Mandel, M. Dyson et al *Harvard Business Review Digital Articles* p2 N 24 2015

Business enterprises—Finance—News briefs

Movers K. Stock bw color *Bloomberg Businessweek* no4493 p19 O 3 2016

Business enterprises—Great Britain

Tackling the gender pay gap P. Cheese *People Management* p5 Ap 2017

Business enterprises—Japan

NEW OPPORTUNITY UNDER THE ABE ADMINISTRATION M. Foster and D. W. Russell color *Forbes* v199 no1 p(Sp)1 Ja 24 2017

Business enterprises—Latin America

SOUTH OF THE WALL D. Alexander, D. Sirtori-Cortina et al bw *Forbes* v199 no3 p74 Mr 28 2017

Business enterprises—Marketing

To Get More Out of Social Media, Think Like an Anthropologist S. Fournier, J. Quelch et al *Harvard Business Review Digital Articles* p2 Ag 17 2016

Business enterprises—News briefs

IN BRIEF color graph *Bloomberg Businessweek* no4533 p6 Ag 7 2017

Movers K. Stock color *Bloomberg Businessweek* no4517 p13 Ap 3 2017

Movers K. Stock color *Bloomberg Businessweek* no4519 p15 Ap 24 2017

Business enterprises—Purchasing

From the Editor *MIT Technology Review* v119 no6 p2 N/D 2016

Is AT&T Buying a Big Dog to Get a Fancy Tail? O. Kharif *Bloomberg Businessweek* no4498 p30 N 7 2016

Why Buying a Company Can Be Better than Starting One R. S. Ruback and R. Yudkoff *Harvard Business Review Digital Articles* p2 Ap 5 2016

Business enterprises—Ratings & rankings

100 BEST COMPANIES TO WORK FOR 2017 [Cover story] M. C. Bush, S. Lewis-kulin et al color diag map *Fortune* v175 no4 p79 Mr 15 2017

HOW TO GET ON THIS LIST M. C. Bush and S. Lewis-kulin color *Fortune* v175 no4 p89 Mr 15 2017

A New Way to Rate Retailers on Providing Good Jobs Z. Ton *Harvard Business Review Digital Articles* p2 S 3 2015

THE WORLD'S MOST ADMIRED COMPANIES S. Decarlo color *Fortune* v175 no3 p113 Mr 1 2017

Business enterprises—Ratings & rankings—History

LEGENDS LIST C. Zillman color *Fortune* v175 no4 p92 Mr 15 2017

Business enterprises—Software

How Companies Are Benefiting from "Lite" Artificial Intelligence S. Earley *Harvard Business Review Digital Articles* p2 Jl 19 2016

Business enterprises—Technological innovations

7 Questions to Ask Before Your Next Digital Transformation B. Libert, M. Beck et al *Harvard Business Review Digital Articles* p2 Jl 14 2016

The Best Digital Strategists Don't Think in Terms of Either/Or M. Bonchek and C. France *Harvard Business Review Digital Articles* p2 Je 16 2015

Great Innovators Create the Future, Manage the Present, and Selectively Forget the Past V. Govindarajan *Harvard Business Review Digital Articles* p2 Mr 31 2016

High-Tech Tools Won't Automatically Improve Your Operations S. Thomke *Harvard Business Review Digital Articles* p2 Je 10 2015

Business enterprises—United States

See also

African American business enterprises

3 Ways Companies Are Building a Business Around AI Q. Hardy *Harvard Business Review Digital Articles* p2 2017

63 DELTA J. J. Roberts color *Fortune* v175 no4 p106 Mr 15 2017

93 AT&T A. Pressman color *Fortune* v175 no4 p124 Mr 15 2017

AMERICA: A GROWTH INDUSTRY L. Entis color diag *Fortune* v175 no8 p149 Je 15 2017

AMERICA'S TOP 50 COMPANIES 1917-2017 M. NOER and J. KAUFLIN chart graph *Forbes* v200 no3 p38 S 28 2017

Establishment, firm, or enterprise: does the unit of analysis matter? bibl chart color graph *Monthly Labor Review* p1 N 2016

Even for Companies, the U.S. Is Split Between Haves and Have-Nots S. Wilkin *Harvard Business Review Digital Articles* p2 Ag 27 2015

HOW THE COMPANIES STACK UP chart *Fortune* v175 no8 pF29 Je 15 2017

LARGEST U.S. CORPORATIONS [Cover story] chart color *Fortune* v175 no8 pF1 Je 15 2017

The Omissions That Make So Many Sexual Harassment Policies Ineffective D. S. Dougherty *Harvard Business Review Digital Articles* p2 My 31 2017

The Potential and Pitfalls of Doing Business in Cuba P. G. Alonso and A. Lee *Harvard Business Review Digital Articles* p2 Mr 16 2016

Protecting the Right to Take a Risk T. J. DONOHUE *Weekly Standard* v22 no42 p15 Jl 17 2017

TURNOVER chart *Fortune* v175 no8 pF27 Je 15 2017

What Should U.S. Companies Do If Congress Ever Passes a Tax Holiday? A. Rappaport *Harvard Business Review Digital Articles* p1 Je 21 2017

Business enterprises—United States—Finance

IT PAYS TO BE A DIGITAL LEADER graph img *Harvard Business Review* v95 no3 p34 My/Je 2017

Business enterprises—Valuation

See also

Debt-to-equity ratio

Economic value added (Corporations)

Investors Fawning over Uber Should Recall AOL's Stumbles R. G. McGrath *Harvard Business Review Digital Articles* p2 Ja 9 2015

A Refresher on Debt-to-Equity Ratio A. Gallo *Harvard Business Review Digital Articles* p2 Jl 13 2015

The Top 20 Start-Up Accelerators in the U.S Y. Hochberg, S. Cohen et al *Harvard Business Review Digital Articles* p2 Mr 31 2015

What Airbnb, Uber, and Alibaba Have in Common B. Libert, Y. (. Wind et al *Harvard Business Review Digital Articles* p2 N 20 2014

Business ethics

See also

Nepotism

Social responsibility of business

5 Questions to Ask Before You Call Out Someone Powerful M. Reitz and J. Higgins *Harvard Business Review Digital Articles* p2 Ap 7 2017

Being an Ethical Business in a Corrupt Environment S. R. Velamuri, W. S. Harvey et al *Harvard Business Review Digital Articles* p2 Mr 23 2017

CEOs Who Began Their Careers During Booms Tend to Be Less Ethical E. C. Bianchi and A. Mohliver *Harvard Business Review Digital Articles* p2 My 12 2017

Corporate Ethics Can't Be Reduced to Compliance P. Rea, A. Kolp et al *Harvard Business Review Digital Articles* p2 Ap 29 2016

Cultural Stereotypes May Make You a Less Ethical Negotiator Yu Yang and D. De Cremer *Harvard Business Review Digital Articles* p2 Ja 8 2014

Does Stating What Your Company Stands for Affect Your Bottom Line? W. Frick *Harvard Business Review Digital Articles* p2 Ag 3 2015

The Ethicist K. A. Appiah *New York Times Magazine* p26 N 6 2016

The Ethics Conversation We're Not Having About Data K. Fung *Harvard Business Review Digital Articles* p2 N 12 2015

How to Survive a Company Scandal You Had Nothing to Do With B. Groysberg, E. Lin et al *Harvard Business Review Digital Articles* p2 Ag 31 2016

Keep a List of Unethical Things You'll Never Do M. Chussil *Harvard Business Review Digital Articles* p2 My 30 2016

The Latest Victim of Uber's Bold Disruption May Be Itself R. Hackett color *Time* v189 no10 p22 Mr 20 2017

THE MORAL IMPERATIVE FOR LEADERS A. Murray color *Fortune* v174 no7 p6 D 1 2016

The Most Important Leadership Competencies, According to Leaders Around the World S. Giles *Harvard Business Review Digital Articles* p2 Mr 15 2016

Powerful People React More Unethically to Incentives J. M. Olejarz *Harvard Business Review Digital Articles* p2 Mr 9 2016

Should ethics determine who you do business with? K. KIPLINGER *Kiplinger's Personal Finance* v71 no12 p12 D 2017

We Studied 38 Incidents of CEO Bad Behavior and Measured Their Consequences D. Larcker and B. Tayan *Harvard Business Review Digital Articles* p2 Je 9 2016

What You Can Do to Improve Ethics at Your Company C. McLaverty and A. McKee *Harvard Business Review Digital Articles* p2 D 29 2016

Why Companies Are Blind to Child Labor D. Zane, J. Irwin et al *Harvard Business Review Digital Articles* p2 Ja 28 2016

Why We're Seeing So Many Corporate Scandals A. S. Mukherjee *Harvard Business Review Digital Articles* p2 D 28 2016

Business etiquette

Collection Rejection color *Money* v45 no11 p16 D 2016

How to choose the perfect leaving present: Row over Tate chief's boat gift shines a light on tricky area of office etiquette *People Management* p15 Je 2017

How to Respond When Someone Takes Credit for Your Work A. Gallo *Harvard Business Review Digital Articles* p2 Ap 29 2015

Pay Attention and Be Nice *USA Today Magazine* v145 no2859 p13 D 2016

Texting Is Turning Into Serious Business M. C. White color *Money* v46 no2 p20 Mr 2017

What Makes a Boss Too Formal? E. Meyer *Harvard Business Review Digital Articles* p2 Ja 6 2015

Business failures

6 Reasons Platforms Fail M. W. Van Alstyne, G. G. Parker et al *Harvard Business Review Digital Articles* p2 Mr 31 2016

G IS FOR GRAVEYARD R. Hackett color *Fortune* v175 no4 p40 Mr 15 2017

How Dell, HP, and Apple Rediscovered Their Founders' Vision C. Zook *Harvard Business Review Digital Articles* p2 Jl 15 2016

Last call at Le Mas J. RICHLER color *Maclean's* v129 no40 p75 O 10 2016

Let's Cancel B. LUTZ *Road & Track* v69 no3 p108 O 2017

PASSION AND BUSINESS M. HOYER *Cycle World* v56 no3 p5 Ap 2017

Rituals: The Last Pastrami J. D. Stein and J. Rothman img *New York* p18 Ja 9 2017

Shutting Down Your Business Gracefully A. Blickstein and J. Mullins *Harvard Business Review Digital Articles* p2 Mr 20 2017

What the Death of Topsy Tells Us About Today's Social Web A. Samuel *Harvard Business Review Digital Articles* p2 D 23 2015

Young People Need to Know Entrepreneurship Is Hard S. Osborne *Harvard Business Review Digital Articles* p2 Ap 6 2015

Business failures—Canada

Why Target's Canadian Expansion Failed D. Dahlhoff *Harvard Business Review Digital Articles* p2 Ja 20 2015

Business failures—Case studies

A Case Study of Crowdsourcing Gone Wrong S. K. Fixson and T. J. Marion *Harvard Business Review Digital Articles* p2 D 15 2016

Business failures—Prevention

Getting an Intricate Operation Back in Sync E. Mady *Harvard Business Review Digital Articles* p2 My 20 2016

Is Your Company Experiencing Good Times? Time for a Plan B W. Johnson *Harvard Business Review Digital Articles* p2 N 18 2016

Business failures—Research

THE SCARY TRUTH ABOUT CORPORATE SURVIVAL il *Harvard Business Review* v94 no12 p24 D 2016

Business finance

See also

Financing of new business enterprises

The Data: Where Long-Termism Pays Off D. BARTON, J. MANYIKA et al graph img *Harvard Business Review* v95 no3 p67 My/Je 2017

Direct listing (n.) *Bloomberg Businessweek* no4523 p39 My 22 2017

Finance Can Be a Noble Profession (Yes, Really) M. A. Desai

Harvard Business Review Digital Articles p2 Jl 17 2017

STARTING OVER B. BURLINGHAM color *Forbes* v199 no5 p92 My 16 2017

Business forecasting

See also

Sales forecasting

Stock price forecasting

5 TRENDS TO RIDE IN 2017 V. Harnish color *Fortune* v175 no4 p32 Mr 15 2017

The Forecasting Sweet Spot Between Micro and Macro E. Yoon, J. Bartlow et al *Harvard Business Review Digital Articles* p2 Ag 26 2016

How Our Company Learned to Make Better Predictions About Everything D. Hernandez *Harvard Business Review Digital Articles* p2 My 15 2017

Predict the Future of Your Business M. Wessel *Harvard Business Review Digital Articles* p2 Ap 13 2015

SALESFORCE SETS ITS SIGHTS ON $20 BILLION H. Clancy color *Fortune* v174 no8 p38 D 15 2016

Want Growth? Focus on Sales J. K. GLASSMAN color *Kiplinger's Personal Finance* v70 no12 p18 D 2016

Business improvement districts

The Rise of Urban Innovation Districts B. J. Katz and J. Wagner *Harvard Business Review Digital Articles* p2 N 12 2014

Business incubators

Europe's Startup Factory Sputters J. Kahn, S. Nicola et al color *Bloomberg Businessweek* no4495 p31 O 17 2016

How Brigham & Women's Funds Health Care Innovation K. Laskowski and J. Dudley *Harvard Business Review Digital Articles* p2 O 15 2015

'Hustlers Are Entrepreneurs Denied Opportunity' M. Ewing color *Bloomberg Businessweek* no4502 p82 D 5 2016

Business incubators—Design & construction

ArtHouse: A Social Kitchen *Architectural Record* v205 no4 p185 Ap 2017

Business information services

A Dedicated Team of Problem Solvers Can Help Big Companies Act Like Lean Startups G. Satell *Harvard Business Review Digital Articles* p2 Ag 24 2016

Business intelligence

Companies Collect Competitive Intelligence, but Don't Use It B. Gilad *Harvard Business Review Digital Articles* p2 Jl 31 2015

"Competitive Intelligence" Shouldn't Just Be About Your Competitors B. Gilad *Harvard Business Review Digital Articles* p2 My 18 2015

Industrial Espionage Is More Effective Than R&D C. Nickisch il img *Harvard Business Review* v94 no11 p30 N 2016

Only Half of Companies Actually Use the Competitive Intelligence They Collect B. Gilad and L. M. Fuld *Harvard Business Review Digital Articles* p2 Ja 26 2016

The Right Way to Use Competitive Intelligence B. Gilad and M. Hoppe *Harvard Business Review Digital Articles* p2 Je 16 2016

Why the Best Salespeople Get So Lucky J. Le Bon *Harvard Business Review Digital Articles* p2 Ap 13 2015

Business intelligence—Economic aspects

Stealing industrial secrets pays off—at first C. Matacic bw graph *Science* v357 no6350 p434 Ag 4 2017

Business journalism

100 YEARS OF HITS AND FLOPS M. SCHIFRIN color *Forbes* v200 no3 p54 S 28 2017

Business losses

THE GLOBAL MACROECONOMIC SITUATION *Economic Indicators* p119 S 2016

Investments You Can Do Without J. K. GLASSMAN color *Kiplinger's Personal Finance* v71 no7 p18 Jl 2017

NEW-TECH'S PROFIT BLACK HOLE D. Lyons color *Fortune* v174 no8 p82 D 15 2016

Business meetings

5 Ways Meetings Get Off Track, and How to Prevent Each One R. Schwarz *Harvard Business Review Digital Articles* p2 My 3 2016

6 Reasons to Get Better at Leading Meetings P. Axtell *Harvard Business Review Digital Articles* p2 D 8 2016

7 Ways to Stop a Meeting from Dragging On J. Grenny *Harvard Business Review Digital Articles* p2 Ap 25 2016

8 Ground Rules for Great Meetings R. Schwarz *Harvard Business*

Wedellsborg and P. Miller *Harvard Business Review Digital Articles* p2 N 25 2014

THE GOOD BUSINESS ISSUE *Bloomberg Businessweek* no4505 p53 D 26 2016

A Good Digital Strategy Creates a Gravitational Pull M. Bonchek color *Harvard Business Review Digital Articles* p2 Ja 25 2017

Google may slam the brakes on its self-driving car to partner with auto makers P. SAYER color *PCWorld* v35 no1 p33 Ja 2017

How Companies Escape the Traps of the Past V. Govindarajan and H. Faber *Harvard Business Review Digital Articles* p2 Ap 26 2016

How Entrepreneurs Can Keep Their Passion from Fading V. Collewaert and F. Anseel *Harvard Business Review Digital Articles* p2 Je 16 2016

How to Discover Your Company's DNA M. Bonchek *Harvard Business Review Digital Articles* p2 D 12 2016

How to Set More-Realistic Growth Targets R. G. McGrath and A. van Putten *Harvard Business Review Digital Articles* p2 Jl 12 2017

HOW TO TURN SECOND PLACE INTO A WIN M. Heimer *Fortune* v176 no2 p72 Ag 1 2017

Hybrid Business Models Look Ugly, but They Work N. Furr *Harvard Business Review Digital Articles* p2 Mr 30 2016

Lessons from Companies That Put Purpose Ahead of Short-Term Profits A. White *Harvard Business Review Digital Articles* p2 Je 9 2016

A List of Goals Is Not a Strategy G. Kenny *Harvard Business Review Digital Articles* p2 N 19 2014

Navigating the Dozens of Different Strategy Options M. Reeves, K. Haanaes et al *Harvard Business Review Digital Articles* p2 Je 24 2015

Only 8% of Leaders Are Good at Both Strategy and Execution P. Leinwand, C. Mainardi et al *Harvard Business Review Digital Articles* p2 D 30 2015

Research: Writing a Business Plan Makes Your Startup More Likely to Succeed F. J. Greene and C. Hopp *Harvard Business Review Digital Articles* p2 Jl 14 2017

The Right Kind of Conflict Leads to Better Products D. S. Thompson, G. Butkus et al *Harvard Business Review Digital Articles* p2 D 23 2016

Sometimes the Best Ideas Come from Outside Your Industry M. Poetz, N. Franke et al *Harvard Business Review Digital Articles* p2 N 21 2014

Stop Distinguishing Between Execution and Strategy R. L. Martin *Harvard Business Review Digital Articles* p2 Mr 13 2015

Stop Making Excuses for Your Flawed Data T. C. Redman *Harvard Business Review Digital Articles* p2 F 12 2015

Strategic Plans Are Less Important than Strategic Planning G. Kenny *Harvard Business Review Digital Articles* p2 Je 21 2016

The Strategic Value of APIs B. Iyer and M. Subramaniam *Harvard Business Review Digital Articles* p2 Ja 7 2015

Strategy as Jazz vs. Symphony A. K. Tjan *Harvard Business Review Digital Articles* p2 Mr 3 2017

There's No Excuse for Avoiding Strategy F. V. Cespedes *Harvard Business Review Digital Articles* p2 O 28 2014

To Come Up with a Good Idea, Start by Imagining the Worst Idea Possible A. Birsel *Harvard Business Review Digital Articles* p2 2017

To Jumpstart Growth, Flip the Company's Priorities R. ". Wang *Harvard Business Review Digital Articles* p2 My 11 2015

Video Marketing: Now with a Bigger Bang for Park and Rec Agencies J. Dysart *Parks & Recreation* v51 no11 p18 N 2016

Wall Street Rewards CEOs Who Talk About Their Strategies R. Whittington, B. Yakis-Douglas et al *Harvard Business Review Digital Articles* p2 D 28 2015

What's Your Data Strategy? L. DALLEMULE and T. H. DAVENPORT color diag img *Harvard Business Review* v95 no3 p112 My/Je 2017

What the Best Change Leaders Know, and Why They're So Hard to Copy B. Taylor *Harvard Business Review Digital Articles* p2 D 21 2016

What to Do When Your Future Strategy Clashes with Your Present M. W. Johnson *Harvard Business Review Digital Articles* p2 Ap 29 2015

What to Know About Doing Business in Iran M. Spivack *Harvard Business Review Digital Articles* p2 My 5 2016

When It Comes to Digital Innovation, Less Action, More Thought S. Anthony *Harvard Business Review Digital Articles* p2 Ja 21 2015

Why Leaders Are Still So Hesitant to Invest in New Business Models B. Libert, M. Beck et al *Harvard Business Review Digital Articles* p2 D 21 2016

Why Talking About Strategy "Execution" Is Still Dangerous R. L. Martin *Harvard Business Review Digital Articles* p2 S 15 2015

You Don't Need to Adopt Holacracy to Get Some of Its Benefits G. Satell *Harvard Business Review Digital Articles* p2 Ag 28 2015

You Don't Need to Be a Silicon Valley Startup to Have a Network-Based Strategy M. Bonchek and B. Libert *Harvard Business Review Digital Articles* p2 Jl 14 2017

Business planning—France

Peugeot on the Go J. MULLER and J. DOBOSZ color *Forbes* v200 no2 p48 S 5 2017

Business planning—Great Britain

Our agenda is crystal clear P. Cheese *People Management* p5 Ag 2017

Business planning—Management

A Refresher on Discovery-Driven Planning A. Gallo *Harvard Business Review Digital Articles* p2 F 13 2017

Your Whole Company Needs to Be Distinctive, Not Just Your Product P. Leinwand and C. Mainardi *Harvard Business Review Digital Articles* p2 My 19 2016

Business planning—United States

Elon Musk's House of Giga-cards P. Burrows graph il *MIT Technology Review* v119 no6 p58 N/D 2016

The World Just Got More Uncertain and Your Strategy Needs to Adjust M. Reeves *Harvard Business Review Digital Articles* p2 N 11 2016

Business presentations

6 Ways to Disagree with Senior Management P. Claman *Harvard Business Review Digital Articles* p2 Je 14 2016

6 Ways to Look More Confident During a Presentation [Cover story] K. Wezowski *Harvard Business Review Digital Articles* p2 Ap 6 2017

6 Ways to Reduce the Stress of Presenting J. Grenny *Harvard Business Review Digital Articles* p2 Ag 31 2015

The Best Presentations Are Tailored to the Audience *Harvard Business Review Digital Articles* p2 Ap 17 2015

Conquer Your Nerves Before Your Presentation N. Duarte *Harvard Business Review Digital Articles* p2 Ap 28 2015

Create a Conversation, Not a Presentation J. Coleman *Harvard Business Review Digital Articles* p2 Jl 29 2015

Fighting the clicker wars T. Koester *Model Railroader* v84 no9 p78 S 2017

Finding the Right Metaphor for Your Presentation N. Duarte *Harvard Business Review Digital Articles* p2 N 17 2014

For Better Presentations, Start with a Villain G. Stone *Harvard Business Review Digital Articles* p2 N 12 2015

Getting an Audience to Remember Your Presentation A. Markman *Harvard Business Review Digital Articles* p2 S 21 2015

Get Your Message Across to a Skeptical Audience S. Martin *Harvard Business Review Digital Articles* p2 My 28 2015

How Experts Can Help a General Audience Understand Their Ideas N. Duarte *Harvard Business Review Digital Articles* p2 S 12 2016

How to Calm Your Nerves Before a Big Presentation Amy Jen Su *Harvard Business Review Digital Articles* p2 O 27 2016

How to Give a Data-Heavy Presentation A. Samuel *Harvard Business Review Digital Articles* p2 O 16 2015

A Refresher on Storytelling 101 J. D. Schramm *Harvard Business Review Digital Articles* p2 O 8 2014

Tailor Your Presentation to Fit the Culture E. Meyer *Harvard Business Review Digital Articles* p2 O 29 2014

To Persuade People, Trade PowerPoint for Papier-Mâché M. Brennan *Harvard Business Review Digital Articles* p2 N 29 2016

Your Presentation Needs a Punch Line A. Ferrara *Harvard Business Review Digital Articles* p2 My 21 2015

Business presentations—Planning

How to Give a Stellar Presentation R. Knight *Harvard Business Review Digital Articles* p2 N 25 2014

Business process management

Business Processes Are Learning to Hack Themselves H. J. Wilson, A. Alter et al *Harvard Business Review Digital Articles* p2 Je 27 2016

Companies Are Reimagining Business Processes with Algorithms H. J. Wilson, A. Alter et al *Harvard Business Review Digital Articles* p2 F 8 2016

What Knowledge Workers Stand to Gain from Automation M. C. Lacity and L. Willcocks *Harvard Business Review Digital Articles* p2 Je 19 2015

Business process outsourcing

How the Philippines Became Tech Startups' New Source for Talent O. Segovia *Harvard Business Review Digital Articles* p2 Ag 5 2015

Business referrals

Love Your Ex-Employees and They'll Love You Back M. Schrage *Harvard Business Review Digital Articles* p2 N 18 2015

Business relocation

Letting Go R. BROOKHISER *National Review* v69 no11 p43 Je 12 2017

A Sea Change at America's Test Kitchen A. Green *Publishers Weekly* v264 no27 p10 Jl 3 2017

Toronto's Beguiling Comics Store Relocates E. Nawotka color *Publishers Weekly* v264 no20 p9 My 15 2017

Wayne's New World: Wayne McGregor isn't keeping his state-of-the-art space to himself L. Cappelle *Dance Magazine* v91 no7 p14 Jl 2017

Business relocation—Government policy

Paris and Frankfurt Vie For Brexit's Spoils F. B. Valentini, S. Arons et al *Bloomberg Businessweek* no4530 p30 Jl 17 2017

Business report writing

The One Unbreakable Rule in Business Writing T. Max *Harvard Business Review Digital Articles* p2 S 13 2016

Business revenue

GOOD STUFF M. J. V *Atlanta* v56 no7 p32 N 2016

Indie Booksellers See Early Holiday Boost J. Rosen, C. Kirch et al color *Publishers Weekly* v263 no50 p4 D 5 2016

Price Pointe J. CARMAN *Dance Magazine* v91 no6 p37 Je 2017

THIS BRAND DWARFS YOUR COMPANY D. Bentley *Fortune* v175 no8 p46 Je 15 2017

TOTAL OUTPUT, INCOME, AND SPENDING *Economic Indicators* p1 Mr 2017

We've Forgotten What "Greatness" Really Means D. Seidman *Harvard Business Review Digital Articles* p2 Mr 4 2016

When Should Multinationals Move Back into Venezuela? P. González Alonso and A. Valerio *Harvard Business Review Digital Articles* p2 S 1 2017

Business school graduates

New MBAs Should Start Their Careers in Frontier Markets J. Berman *Harvard Business Review Digital Articles* p2 Ap 28 2017

You Should Consider Buying a Small Business. But When? R. S. Ruback and R. Yudkoff *Harvard Business Review Digital Articles* p2 F 15 2017

Business schools—Alumni & alumnae

Top 30 U.S. Schools chart *Bloomberg Businessweek* no4500 p42 N 21 2016

Business schools—Faculty

How Women Are Faring at Business Schools Worldwide A. Wittenberg-Cox and L. Symons *Harvard Business Review Digital Articles* p2 Ap 27 2015

Business schools—United States

B-Schools Aren't Bothering to Produce HR Experts P. Cappelli *Harvard Business Review Digital Articles* p2 Jl 27 2015

Gifts The Rising Price of B-School Glory J. Lorin color *Bloomberg Businessweek* no4522 p51 My 15 2017

MBA Programs Tout Entrepreneurship L. Lambert diag *Bloomberg Businessweek* no4522 p50 My 15 2017

U.S. B-Schools Grapple With the 'Trump Effect' N. Leiber color *Bloomberg Businessweek* no4522 p49 My 15 2017

Business skills

HBR's Best on Saying No to More Work A. Gallo color *Harvard Business Review Digital Articles* p2 Ja 30 2017

Business software

See also

Customer relations—Management

Artificial Intelligence Is Almost Ready for Business B. Power *Harvard Business Review Digital Articles* p2 Mr 19 2015

The Reason So Many Analytics Efforts Fall Short C. McShea, D.

Oakley et al *Harvard Business Review Digital Articles* p2 Ag 29 2016

The Technology Trends That Matter to Sales Teams A. A. Zoltners, P. K. Sinha et al *Harvard Business Review Digital Articles* p2 My 7 2015

Too Many Executives Are Missing the Most Important Part of CRM C. Brown *Harvard Business Review Digital Articles* p2 Ag 24 2016

You Don't Have to Be a Software Company to Think Like One V. Gurbaxani *Harvard Business Review Digital Articles* p2 Ap 20 2016

Business students

4 CAREER GEMS FROM BLACK BUSINESS MASTER-MINDS C. RHINEHART and N. K. Webb color *Black Enterprise* v47 no7 p25 My/Je 2017

Business tax

See also

Payroll tax

Business teachers

Business Professors Need to Spend Time in Companies H. H. Brower and M. D. Steward *Harvard Business Review Digital Articles* p2 N 27 2015

Business-to-business electronic markets

How B2B Marketers Can Get Started with Social Media L. Minsky and K. A. Quesenberry *Harvard Business Review Digital Articles* p2 D 24 2015

Stop Treating B2B Customers Like Digital Novices A. Di Fiore and S. Schneider *Harvard Business Review Digital Articles* p2 My 10 2016

Business-to-business transactions

4 Ways for B2B Businesses to Keep Their Customers B. Maguire and J. Hiscock *Harvard Business Review Digital Articles* p2 D 6 2016

B2B Salespeople Can Survive If They Reimagine Their Roles J. A. Narus *Harvard Business Review Digital Articles* p2 Ap 17 2015

How B2B Sales Can Benefit from Social Selling L. Minsky and K. A. Quesenberry *Harvard Business Review Digital Articles* p2 N 8 2016

Social Media Works for B2B Sales, Too M. Kovac *Harvard Business Review Digital Articles* p2 Ja 4 2016

Business-to-business transactions—Research

THE NEW SALES IMPERATIVE N. TOMAN, B. ADAMSON et al color diag il img *Harvard Business Review* v95 no2 p118 Mr/Ap 2017

Business travel

Bringing Luxury to Business Travel C. Williams color *Black Enterprise* v47 no3 p70 O 2016

Dealing with Loneliness While Traveling for Work A. Gallo *Harvard Business Review Digital Articles* p2 N 19 2015

DOING BUSINESS IN: BUENOS AIRES A. Erace color *Fortune* v175 no6 p27 My 1 2017

The Health Risks of Business Travel T. Chamorro-Premuzic *Harvard Business Review Digital Articles* p2 N 3 2015

The Hidden Benefits of Short-Term Business Travel A. Molinsky and M. Hahn *Harvard Business Review Digital Articles* p2 Je 13 2016

How Smart Business Travelers Get More from Hotels E. Mady *Harvard Business Review Digital Articles* p2 Ja 7 2016

How the Sharing Economy Can Improve Your Next Business Trip A. Samuel *Harvard Business Review Digital Articles* p2 N 2 2015

How to Avoid Frustrating Business Travel Mishaps S. G. Carmichael *Harvard Business Review Digital Articles* p2 N 6 2015

Intel bw color *Conde Nast Traveler* v52 no6 p99 Je/Jl 2017

PASSING LANE: UBERS ARE BUMPING TAXIS OFF TRAVELERS' EXPENSE REPORTS color *Fortune* v176 no3 p16 S 1 2017

Purpose Matters for Business Travel, Too *Harvard Business Review Digital Articles* p2 N 11 2015

Secrets to Better Business Travel J. Thompson color *Essence* v48 no6 p83 O 2017

A Step-by-Step Guide to Packing for a Complicated Work Trip S. G. Carmichael *Harvard Business Review Digital Articles* p2 N 18 2015

Business travel—Equipment & supplies

Cures for the business travel blues J. Chen and K. Morell color *Bloomberg Businessweek* no4522 p89 My 15 2017

Business travelers

How Smart Business Travelers Get More from Hotels E. Mady *Harvard Business Review Digital Articles* p2 Ja 7 2016

Traveling for Work? You're a Prime Target for Hackers P. Everton *Harvard Business Review Digital Articles* p2 S 29 2016

What to Do with All the Business Cards from Your Last Conference A. Samuel *Harvard Business Review Digital Articles* p2 N 13 2015

Business travel—Health aspects

A Healthier Approach to Business Travel P. Bregman *Harvard Business Review Digital Articles* p2 N 17 2015

Jet Lag Doesn't Have to Ruin Your Business Trip C. M. Barnes *Harvard Business Review Digital Articles* p2 N 4 2015

Business writing

Bad Writing Is Destroying Your Company's Productivity J. Bernoff *Harvard Business Review Digital Articles* p2 S 6 2016

Corporate Writing Doesn't Have to Sound Like It's Written by Committee J. Bernoff *Harvard Business Review Digital Articles* p2 S 15 2016

How to Improve Your Business Writing C. O'Hara *Harvard Business Review Digital Articles* p2 N 20 2014

How to Make Sure Your Emails Give the Right Impression S. Harmon color *Harvard Business Review Digital Articles* p2 F 6 2017

Improve Your Writing to Improve Your Credibility B. Wallraff *Harvard Business Review Digital Articles* p2 S 13 2016

The One Unbreakable Rule in Business Writing T. Max *Harvard Business Review Digital Articles* p2 S 13 2016

A Quick Guide to Avoiding Common Writing Errors M. Fogarty *Harvard Business Review Digital Articles* p2 Jl 22 2015

Stop Trying to Sound Smart When You're Writing L. Davey *Harvard Business Review Digital Articles* p2 O 5 2016

What Your Professional Bio Needs to Get Noticed M. Fineman *Harvard Business Review Digital Articles* p2 Mr 2 2015

Why I Write in PowerPoint N. Duarte *Harvard Business Review Digital Articles* p2 Jl 27 2015

You Can Talk About Innovation Without Resorting to Cliches K. Gordon *Harvard Business Review Digital Articles* p2 F 4 2016

Business—Awards

Leading Businesses Make a Difference T. J. DONOHUE *Weekly Standard* v22 no12 p21 N 28 2016

Business—California

take OM HOME T. Eichenseher color *Yoga Journal* no289 p108 F 2017

Business—Charts, diagrams, etc.

Movers K. Stock cartoon color *Bloomberg Businessweek* no4510 p11 F 6 2017

Business—China

New Opportunities In Our New Century L. D'VORKIN color *Forbes* v199 no1 p12 Ja 24 2017

Business—Congresses

The Conference That's Trying to Reinvent How We Network A. Beard *Harvard Business Review Digital Articles* p2 O 8 2015

When Someone Gloms On to You at a Conference D. Clark *Harvard Business Review Digital Articles* p2 O 5 2015

Business cycles—United States—Charts, diagrams, etc.

PRICES *Economic Indicators* p22 D 2016

Business enterprises—Charts, diagrams, etc.

AMERICA: A GROWTH INDUSTRY L. Entis color diag *Fortune* v175 no8 p149 Je 15 2017

HOW THE COMPANIES STACK UP chart *Fortune* v175 no8 pF29 Je 15 2017

NOTES *Fortune* v175 no8 pF28 Je 15 2017

RANKED WITHIN INDUSTRIES chart diag *Fortune* v175 no8 pF33 Je 15 2017

RANKED WITHIN STATES chart map *Fortune* v175 no8 pF41 Je 15 2017

Business enterprises—Ratings & rankings—Charts, diagrams, etc.

THE COMPANIES OF THE YEAR C. Austin color diag *Fortune* v174 no8 p62 D 15 2016

Business enterprises—Societies, etc.

Party Hopping D. MANN *Texas Monthly* v45 no5 p18 My 2017

Business enterprises—Valuation—Charts, diagrams, etc.

The Most Valuable NFL Teams K. BADENHAUSEN, M. OZANIAN et al color graph *Forbes* v198 no5 p32 O 25 2016

Business—Environmental aspects

See also

Pollution

9 Sustainable Business Stories That Shaped 2016 A. Winston *Harvard Business Review Digital Articles* p2 D 20 2016

Business—Great Britain

Figuring Out Which Companies and Industries Will Be Most Damaged by Brexit P. Ghemawat *Harvard Business Review Digital Articles* p2 Mr 29 2017

Business—History

DIGITAL DEATH STAR R. KARLGAARD color *Forbes* v198 no6 p44 N 8 2016

Here's How the Backlash Against Tech Billionaires Will Play Out S. Wilkin *Harvard Business Review Digital Articles* p2 Je 24 2016

Business—History—20th century

Nov. 15, 1971: High Tech, High Anxiety bw color *Forbes* v198 no6 p38 N 8 2016

Business literature—Charts, diagrams, etc.

Turbocharge Your Business in 2017 M. SOLOMON color diag *Forbes* v198 no8 p24 D 20 2016

Businessmen

High Score G. CHUNG color *Forbes* v198 no6 p30 N 8 2016

A HOLLYWOOD STORY C. BRUCK cartoon *New Yorker* v93 no11 p34 My 1 2017

A HOT RODDING Hero: THE LEGACY OF VIC EDELBROCK JR T. Taylor bw color *Hot Rod* v70 no11 p66 N 2017

How Manufacturers Can Get Faster, More Flexible, and Cheaper R. Narsalay, A. Sen et al bw *Harvard Business Review Digital Articles* p2 F 27 2017

How Startup "Joiners" Are (and Aren't) Like Founders W. Frick *Harvard Business Review Digital Articles* p2 Jl 20 2015

THE LIFE EXPANDERS N. Barzilai chart color *Men's Health* v32 no7 p116 S 2017

The Potem kin Prince R. COHEN color *Vanity Fair* v59 no11 p124 N 2017

Top CI Trends from CEDIA 2016 J. SCIACCA color *Sound & Vision* v82 no1 p19 Ja 2017

TOUGH TIMES LEAD TO TOUGH KENNELS *South Dakota Magazine* v32 no6 p14 Mr/Ap 2017

VULTURE CAPITALISTS DEVOUR THE NEWS J. REYNOLDS color map *Nation* v305 no9 p12 O 16 2017

Wit and Wisdom From Our Early Breeders: THE ED TWEED FAMILY M. J. PARKINSON *Arabian Horse World* v57 no11 p94 Ag 2017

Businessmen—Attitudes

Good Leaders Aren't Afraid to Be Nice J. Panepinto *Harvard Business Review Digital Articles* p2 Ap 8 2015

Understanding Trust, In China and the West D. De Cremer *Harvard Business Review Digital Articles* p2 F 11 2015

Businessmen—Finance

The Toll Collector [Cover story] A. GARA color map *Forbes* v199 no5 p68 My 16 2017

Businessmen—Interviews

How Did I Get Here? CHIP BERGH bw color *Bloomberg Businessweek* no4507 p68 Ja 16 2017

Businessmen—Japan

Bowled Over C. SORVINO color *Forbes* v199 no5 p26 My 16 2017

Businessmen—United States

As Time Goes By W. Kristol bw *Weekly Standard* v22 no43 p7 Jl 24 2017

Business—News briefs

Americas C. Suddath and I. Boudway color map *Bloomberg Businessweek* no4532 p7 Jl 31 2017

Asia C. Suddath and I. Boudway color *Bloomberg Businessweek* no4532 p6 Jl 31 2017

Asia K. Stock color graph *Bloomberg Businessweek* no4529 p9 Jl 3 2017

Europe K. Stock color *Bloomberg Businessweek* no4529 p8 Jl 3 2017

Europe K. Stock color *Bloomberg Businessweek* no4530 p9 Jl 17 2017

IN BRIEF K. Stock bw color *Bloomberg Businessweek* no4537

p10 S 11 2017

IN BRIEF K. Stock color graph *Bloomberg Businessweek* no4527 p14 Je 19 2017

INDIA'S SICKENING AND IMMORAL MOVE S. FORBES *Forbes* v199 no1 p15 Ja 24 2017

Movers K. Stock color *Bloomberg Businessweek* no4500 p15 N 21 2016

Movers K. Stock color *Bloomberg Businessweek* no4509 p11 Ja 30 2017

Movers K. Stock color graph *Bloomberg Businessweek* no4524 p13 My 29 2017

SCORECARD G. CHUNG color *Forbes* v198 no6 p30 N 8 2016

Businesspeople

    See also

       Businessmen

       Businesswomen

       Capitalists & financiers

       Corporate founders

       Real estate agents

       Self-employed

       Young businesspeople

25 People Who Bust the Myths M. B. CORTEZ, C. IANZITO et al color *AARP: The Magazine* v59 no4A p42 Je/Jl 2016

40 and Under (and Underperforming) J. Tarmy bw *Bloomberg Businessweek* no4502 p88 D 5 2016

4 Reasons to Kill the Office Holiday Party—and One Reason to Save It J. Kirby *Harvard Business Review Digital Articles* p2 D 17 2014

6 Signs You're Living in an Entrepreneurial Society E. Ojomo *Harvard Business Review Digital Articles* p2 O 4 2016

Anne Mahlum's Battles C. RUBIN *Washingtonian Magazine* v52 no3 p54 D 2016

Bad Hair Daze W. DURST cartoon *Progressive* v81 no5 p66 Je/Jl 2017

The Best Entrepreneurs Are Missionaries, Not Mercenaries B. Taylor *Harvard Business Review Digital Articles* p2 Ap 11 2016

Break Bad Habits with a Simple Checklist S. Nawaz chart color *Harvard Business Review Digital Articles* p2 F 10 2017

BUSINESSPERSON OF THE YEAR *Fortune* v174 no7 p65 D 1 2016

The C-Suite Needs a Chief Entrepreneur A. Osterwalder *Harvard Business Review Digital Articles* p2 Je 25 2015

DECEASED, DECLINED OR LEFT BEHIND M. TINDERA color *Forbes* v200 no5 p28 N 14 2017

Desert Days C. Lalli Music and A. Carroll color *Bon Appetit* v62 no7 p84 Jl 2017

Do as I Say, Not What I'm Accused Of M. Campbell bw *Bloomberg Businessweek* no4494 p34 O 10 2016

Doorman Design P. Marquis *New Orleans Homes & Lifestyles* v20 no1 p93 Wint 2016

THE EDUCATION OF RAJ BHAKTA W. CURTIS color *Yankee* p126 Jl 2017

Entrepreneurs Take On Manufacturing M. Muro *Harvard Business Review Digital Articles* p2 F 22 2016

FINANCIAL AIDE E. WEINER *Smithsonian* v47 no8 p44 D 2016

FRIDAY NIGHT AT THE COLONNADE J. BAINBRIDGE *Atlanta* v57 no6 p94 O 2017

GLOBAL GAME CHANGERS bw *Forbes* v199 no6 p38 Je 13 2017

A Global Survey Explains Why Your Employees Don't Innovate D. Sturt and J. Rogers *Harvard Business Review Digital Articles* p2 F 24 2016

How Freelancers Can Make Sure They Get Paid on Time R. Knight *Harvard Business Review Digital Articles* p2 2017

How Israeli Startups Can Scale J. Bussgang and O. Stern *Harvard Business Review Digital Articles* p2 S 10 2015

How to Make Feedback Feel Normal J. Grenny *Harvard Business Review Digital Articles* p2 Ag 19 2016

Learning How to Collaborate When You're Self-Employed D. Clark *Harvard Business Review Digital Articles* p2 D 28 2016

Male and Female Entrepreneurs Get Asked Different Questions by VCs—and It Affects How Much Funding They Get D. Kanze, L. Huang et al *Harvard Business Review Digital Articles* p2 Je 27 2017

Managing 3 Types of Bad Bosses V. Nayar *Harvard Business Review Digital Articles* p2 D 1 2014

Meet "The Wine Maker" André Hueston Mack D. Pressley and K. MEEKS chart color *Black Enterprise* v47 no4 p33 N/D 2016

The Myth of the Tech Whiz Who Quits College to Start a Company M. Goodwin *Harvard Business Review Digital Articles* p2 Ja 9 2015

Negotiating with Clients You Can't Afford to Lose R. K. Holden *Harvard Business Review Digital Articles* p2 Je 10 2016

A New Way for Entrepreneurs to Think About IT B. Iyer and T. H. Davenport *Harvard Business Review Digital Articles* p2 Je 28 2016

A Note to Our Readers *Current Biography* v78 no9 p2 S 2017

Recognizing the Role of Emotional Labor in the On-Demand Economy L. Stark *Harvard Business Review Digital Articles* p2 Ag 26 2016

REVENGE OF THE FILM NERDS D. SOLOMON, C. KELLY et al *Texas Monthly* v45 no7 p70 Jl 2017

The Sharing Economy's New Middlemen Moatti *Harvard Business Review Digital Articles* p2 Mr 5 2015

To Get Over Something, Write About It M. F. R. Kets de Vries *Harvard Business Review Digital Articles* p2 N 26 2014

TRADING VS. TRUMP S. Marikar cartoon *New Yorker* v92 no33 p24 O 17 2016

Two Digital Myths That Trip Up the C-Suite D. K. Rigby *Harvard Business Review Digital Articles* p2 F 24 2016

The Two Traits Every Entrepreneur Needs J. Dougherty *Harvard Business Review Digital Articles* p2 Mr 21 2016

We Recorded VCs' Conversations and Analyzed How Differently They Talk About Female Entrepreneurs M. Malmstrom, J. Johansson et al *Harvard Business Review Digital Articles* p2 My 17 2017

WOMEN'S WORK S. T. BROWN color *Ebony* v72 no5 p84 Mr 2017

The Worry-Free Life J. KITA color *AARP: The Magazine* v59 no2A p28 F/Mr 2016

You Don't Have to Go to a Conference to Enjoy It S. Kaplan *Harvard Business Review Digital Articles* p2 O 6 2015

Businesspeople—Attitudes

The Case Against Competing W. Kiechel *Harvard Business Review Digital Articles* p2 Ap 30 2015

HIRING AN ENTREPRENEURIAL LEADER T. BUTLER color il *Harvard Business Review* v95 no2 p84 Mr/Ap 2017

How Hard Do Company Founders Really Work? K. Firestone *Harvard Business Review Digital Articles* p2 D 17 2014

People Favor Naturals Over Strivers—Even Though They Say Otherwise S. B. Kaufman and Chia-Jung Tsay *Harvard Business Review Digital Articles* p2 My 19 2016

Powerful People Underperform When They Work Together A. Hildreth and C. Anderson *Harvard Business Review Digital Articles* p2 F 24 2016

The Snow People S. LOCKLEAR *Idaho Magazine* v17 no1 p27 Ja 2017

Businesspeople—Congresses

ABOVE & BEYOND cartoon *New Yorker* v93 no3 p18 Mr 6 2017

Brain Gain K. Finn color *New Orleans Magazine* v51 no6 p30 Ap 2017

CALLING ALL ENTREPRENEURS S. HILL color *Black Enterprise* v47 no8 p42 Jl/Ag 2017

FORGING A NEW SOCIAL COMPACT C. Leaf color *Fortune* v174 no7 p8 D 1 2016

THE MORAL IMPERATIVE FOR LEADERS A. Murray color *Fortune* v174 no7 p6 D 1 2016

Businesspeople—Education

MBA Programs Tout Entrepreneurship L. Lambert diag *Bloomberg Businessweek* no4522 p50 My 15 2017

Businesspeople—Europe, Western

Old World, Young Promise M. BERG, A. CALA et al color *Forbes* v199 no1 p20 Ja 24 2017

Businesspeople—Finance

How Venture Capitalists Really Assess a Pitch bw *Harvard Business Review* v95 no3 p26 My/Je 2017

Businesspeople—Mental health

How Founders Can Recognize and Combat Depression J. Valencia *Harvard Business Review Digital Articles* p2 F 17 2017

Businesspeople—New York (State)—New York

N.Y.C.'S MOST ELIGIBLE PIGEONS W. McPHAIL color *New*

Yorker v93 no24 p49 Ag 21 2017

Businesspeople—Psychology

FACING THE DARKNESS L. Entis color *Fortune* v174 no8 p64 D 15 2016

HIRING AN ENTREPRENEURIAL LEADER T. BUTLER color il *Harvard Business Review* v95 no2 p84 Mr/Ap 2017

Businesspeople—Religious life

What Would Jesus Disrupt? Entrepreneurs from Crossroads Church try to scale their startups without selling their souls M. Farzier color *Bloomberg Businessweek* no4518 p56 Ap 10 2017

Businesspeople—Travel

The Health Risks of Business Travel T. Chamorro-Premuzic *Harvard Business Review Digital Articles* p2 N 3 2015

How to Use Your Travel Time Productively D. Clark *Harvard Business Review Digital Articles* p2 N 5 2015

Businesspeople—United States

The Climate Movement Needs More Corporate Lobbyists S. Whitehouse *Harvard Business Review Digital Articles* p2 F 25 2016

Does the Mensch Have Staying Power? M. Townsend color graph *Bloomberg Businessweek* no4503 p37 D 12 2016

FOREVER YOUNG bw *Forbes* v200 no3 p70 S 28 2017

How the Navy SEALs Train for Leadership Excellence M. Schrage *Harvard Business Review Digital Articles* p2 My 28 2015

Teri Arvesu N. RHEE color *Chicago* v66 no6 p81 Je 2017

'THE HARDER I FALL, THE HIGHER THE BOUNCE' D. Eng color *Fortune* v175 no8 p72 Je 15 2017

Businesspeople—United States—Political activity

Do Business Leaders Make Good Presidents? J. Meacham color *Time* v189 no3 p36 Ja 30 2017

Businesspeople—United States—Legal status, laws, etc.

Bulls On Parole E. Huet cartoon *Bloomberg Businessweek* no4496 p33 O 24 2016

Business—Periodicals

New Opportunities In Our New Century L. D'VORKIN color *Forbes* v199 no1 p12 Ja 24 2017

Business—Periodicals—History

FORBES @ 100 A. BROWN bw color *Forbes* v198 no8 p32 D 20 2016

Business—Periodicals—Management

Our Innovative Game Plan L. D'VORKIN *Forbes* v198 no8 p12 D 20 2016

Business planning—Charts, diagrams, etc.

ASK A FLOWCHART R. CAPPS diag *Wired* v25 no6 p96 Je 2017

Business—Research

Making Business School Research More Relevant J. Eckhardt and J. C. Wetherbe *Harvard Business Review Digital Articles* p2 D 24 2014

Why the Future of Social Science Is with Private Companies M. Schrage *Harvard Business Review Digital Articles* p2 S 1 2015

Business schools—Ratings & rankings—Charts, diagrams, etc.

Top 30 U.S. Schools chart *Bloomberg Businessweek* no4500 p42 N 21 2016

Business—United States

HOPE FOR THE DAY AFTER A. Murray color *Fortune* v174 no6 p6 N 1 2016

TAKE A FAMILY 'FIELD' TRIP: MAKE AG A PART OF YOUR VACATION PLANS - NO MATTER WHERE YOU'RE HEADED L. F. Prater color *Successful Farming* v115 no7 p57 My 2017

Businesswomen

See also

Women capitalists & financiers

Alpha Male vs. Alpha Female T. RICHTER *USA Today Magazine* v145 no2862 p66 Mr 2017

BLACK WOMEN'S MENTOR IN YOUR POCKET T. A. Sykes color *Essence* v47 no12 p100 Ap 2017

THE BLOGGER AND THE TROLLS E. TEMPLE-WOOD color *Scientific American* v317 no3 p70 S 2017

A BOARDROOM OF ONE'S OWN D. GILMORE color *Vanity Fair* v59 no7 p55 Summ 2017

The Different Reasons Men and Women Leave Their Successful Startups R. Justo color *Harvard Business Review Digital Articles* p2 F 8 2017

Finder Not Keeper D. DANIEL color *American Craft* v77 no2 p14 Ap/My 2017

FORTUNE'S MPW VIPs C. Leaf color *Fortune* v176 no5 p10 O 1 2017

How I Found My Purpose C. de León color *Glamour* v114 no11 p138 N 2016

Instyle Textiles J. DeBold *New Orleans Homes & Lifestyles* v20 no2 p30 Spr 2017

LA WOMAN *Los Angeles Magazine* v62 no9 p90 S 2017

MOST POWERFUL WOMEN INTERNATIONAL C. Austin, L. Entis et al color *Fortune* v176 no5 p111 O 1 2017

The People's Princess C. FLANAGAN and T. O'Brien img *New York* v50 no10 p46 My 15 2017

SIGHTS ON SUCCESS bw color *Martha Stewart Living* no271 p13 Ja/F 2017

Sock it to 'Em! C. V. Clarke color *Black Enterprise* v47 no2 p30 S 2016

Traveling the World Made Me a Better Entrepreneur G. Morris *Harvard Business Review Digital Articles* p2 My 26 2015

Virginia C. PETERSON-WITHORN color *Forbes* v199 no2 p26 F 28 2017

WELL BEINGS N. SPORTELLI color *Forbes* v200 no1 p18 Jl 27 2017

WHEN LINKEDIN ISN'T ENOUGH J. Osterheldt color *Essence* v48 no6 p86 O 2017

WOMEN UP G. JEFFERS and S. T. BROWN color *Ebony* v72 no5 p70 Mr 2017

Businesswomen—Attitudes

A Friend's Support Can Make Women Better Entrepreneurs E. Field, S. Jayachandran et al *Harvard Business Review Digital Articles* p2 Je 19 2015

Businesswomen—Awards

2017 Southern Beauties C. Mckenzie and M. M. Brown color *Southern Living* v52 no10 p53 O 2017

A Few Good Deeds S. Evans color *Southern Living* v52 no10 p12 O 2017

Businesswomen—Congresses

EXECUTIVE MEMO color *Black Enterprise* v47 no5 p8 Ja/F 2017

She's Gotta Have Grit E. JANE FOX bw color *Vanity Fair* v59 no9 p174 S 2017

Businesswomen—History

Ceiling Crasher C. SORVINO color *Forbes* v199 no2 p24 F 28 2017

Businesswomen—Interviews

JODY GERSON bw color *Bloomberg Businessweek* no4506 p68 Ja 9 2017

MOSAIC OF CULTURES M. STREET color *Ebony* v72 no8 p42 Je 2017

THE POWER OF THE PIVOT J. Thompson color *Essence* v47 no7 p74 N 2016

Startup Queen Z. HUGHES color *Ebony* v72 no8 p72 Je 2017

Businesswomen's clothing

Nothing to Wear To Work R. Greenfield color *Bloomberg Businessweek* no4535 p68 Ag 28 2017

Businesswomen—Social conditions

NO MEN ALLOWED A. Igneri color *Bloomberg Businessweek* no4506 p66 Ja 9 2017

What's the Password? Tech startups in Indianapolis are booming, but where are all the women founders? A. Denton *Indianapolis Monthly* v40 no10 p53 Je 2017

Businesswomen—United States

Family Flock E. Conant bw color *National Geographic* v230 no5 p140 N 2016

I, TINA P. H. Bass color *Essence* v47 no8 p104 D 2016

MIXING IT UP K. FINN color *Louisiana Life* v37 no3 p8 Ja/F 2017

The Queen of Trump Swag J. McCormick color *Bloomberg Businessweek* no4528 p36 Je 26 2017

top female achievers A. McLellan color *New Orleans Magazine* v51 no8 p70 Je 2017

THE WEED WARRIORS E. GARBER-PAUL color *Rolling Stone* no1295 p45 S 7 2017

When a Mid-Career Move Falls Flat: The Story of Stripedshirt D. McGinn *Harvard Business Review Digital Articles* p2 Je 1 2015

Words to Live By G. PALMIERI *Indianapolis Monthly* p28 F

2017

Busk, Peter Linde

PETER LINDE BUSK E. Sutphin *Art in America* v104 no9 p152 O 2016

Buslaev, Pavel

Mechanism of transmembrane signaling by sensor histidine kinases color *Science* v356 no6342 p1043 Je 9 2017

BUSSEY, CARL

ALL IN A Day's Work cartoon *Reader's Digest* v190 no1132 p54 Jl/Ag 2017

Bussgang, Jeff

Every Company Needs a Growth Manager *Harvard Business Review Digital Articles* p2 F 19 2016

How Israeli Startups Can Scale *Harvard Business Review Digital Articles* p2 S 10 2015

BUSSINGER, BUZZ

Serena's Love Match bw color *Vanity Fair* v59 no8 p62 Ag 2017

Busso, Philippe

Red squirrels in the British Isles are infected with leprosy bacilli bibl color diag map *Science* v354 no6313 p744 N 11 2016

BUSSOLA, MATTEO

does love end? color *Parents* v92 no6 p106 Je 2017

Sleepless Nights and Kisses for Breakfast: Reflections on Fatherhood *Publishers Weekly* v264 no15 p66 Ap 10 2017

Bussotti, Filippo

Positive biodiversity-productivity relationship predominant in global forests bibl chart graph map *Science* v354 no6309 paaf8957-1 O 14 2016

Bustamante, Carlos D.

Dispersals and genetic adaptation of Bantu-speaking populations in Africa and North America diag *Science* v356 no6337 p543 My 5 2017

Bustamante, Mercedes M. C.

Undervaluing and Overexploiting the Brazilian Cerrado at Our Peril bibl *Environment* v58 no6 p4 N/D 2016

Bustillo, Richard

MARTIAL ARTS COMMUNITY BIDS FAREWELL TO RICHARD BUSTILLO bw color *Black Belt* v55 no4 p10 Je/Jl 2017

RICHARD BUSTILLO (1942-2017) M. JACOBS bw color *Black Belt* v55 no5 p42 Ag/S 2017

Butadiene

Controlling guest conformation for efficient purification of butadiene Liao, Huang et al bw diag *Science* v356 no6343 p1193 Je 16 2017

Butane

THINGS YOU NEED TO KNOW ABOUT FUEL R. BERENDSOHN and E. Dyer bw chart color *Popular Mechanics* p29 Mr 2017

Butchart, Stuart H. M.

The broad footprint of climate change from genes to biomes to people bibl chart color *Science* v354 no6313 paaf7671-1 N 11 2016

Butcher, kristin

ask me no questions... color *Bike Magazine* v23 no9 p50 D 2016

aspirations of mediocrity color *Bike Magazine* v24 no7 p48 S 2017

FORWARD MOMENTUM color *Bike Magazine* v24 no1 p116 Ja/F 2017

Land of OZ bw cartoon color *Bike Magazine* v24 no1 p74 Ja/F 2017

lose the moment color *Bike Magazine* v24 no6 p56 Ag 2017

low tide color *Bike Magazine* v24 no2 p44 Mr 2017

lying in wait: THE LOST ART OF PATIENCE color *Bike Magazine* v24 no8 p38 N 2017

master of (dis)repair color *Bike Magazine* v24 no1 p60 Ja/F 2017

small decisions color *Bike Magazine* v24 no3 p58 My 2017

solo mission bw *Bike Magazine* v24 no4 p50 Je 2017

sweet relief bw *Bike Magazine* v24 no5 p46 Jl 2017

trail wizards color *Bike Magazine* v24 no1 p56 Ja/F 2017

BUTCHER, STERRY

The Earth Below *Texas Monthly* v45 no1 p64 Ja 2017

Let Fly the Loop *Texas Monthly* v44 no11 p70 N 2016

The Purest Type *Texas Monthly* v45 no7 p60 Jl 2017

Snake! *Texas Monthly* v45 no3 p90 Mr 2017

THIS AMERICAN LIFE *Texas Monthly* v45 no5 p94 My 2017

Butcher Block Co.

Hardworking ISLANDS D. Howland color *Cabin Living* p7 Mr

2017

Butchers

The Butcher's Wife color *New York Times Magazine* p26 F 12 2017

CALL OF THE WILD: No need for camo. Catch these beasts at your local butcher shop J. BALL *Indianapolis Monthly* v12 no40 p75 Ag 2017

THE MEAT ROOM M. Pendley color *Field & Stream* v122 no6 p32 N 2017

WILDTHINGS J. ROEDEL bw color *Louisiana Life* v37 no4 p16 Mr/Ap 2017

Butchers—Evaluation

The Raw and the Cooked img *New York* p58 F 20 2017

Butigan, Ken

The gospel of nonviolence color *U.S. Catholic* v82 no2 p20 F 2017

Butkus, Gary

The Right Kind of Conflict Leads to Better Products *Harvard Business Review Digital Articles* p2 D 23 2016

Butler, Andrew

Single-cell RNA-seq reveals new types of human blood dendritic cells, monocytes, and progenitors color *Science* v356 no6335 p283 Ap 21 2017

Butler, Brandon

Field Guides color *Missouri Life* v44 no3 p46 My 2017

Loss of the Wild color *National Wildlife (World Edition)* v54 no6 p36 O/N 2016

on a wing and a prayer color *Missouri Life* v44 no6 p38 S 2017

BUTLER, CAROL A.

Gynandromorphism [Cover story] color *Natural History* v125 no5 p20 My 2017

BUTLER, CHARLIE

STRENGTH SERVICE cartoon color *Men's Health* v32 no4 p116 My 2017

Butler, Jeff

How to Make Electronic Health Records an Asset Instead of a Burden *Harvard Business Review Digital Articles* p2 D 8 2015

Butler, Jennifer

Vaginal bacteria modify HIV tenofovir microbicide efficacy in African women chart graph *Science* v356 no6341 p938 Je 1 2017

Butler, Jimmy

JIMMY BUTLER [Cover story] L. Jenkins color *Sports Illustrated* v127 no12 p34 O 16 2017

BUTLER, JOSHUA RYAN

Evangelism, Without the Weird Aftertaste bw color *Christianity Today* v60 no9 p72 N 2016

Butler, Juliet

A twin tale to keep you up at night J. M. Craig color *Science* v357 no6352 p653 Ag 18 2017

Butler, Kathryn L.

A Critical Care Surgeon Meets the Great Physician color *Christianity Today* p80 Mr 2017

BUTLER, KIERA

INCONCEIVABLE color *Mother Jones* v42 no5 p34 S/O 2017

What to Extopect cartoon diag graph *Mother Jones* v42 no1 p38 Ja/F 2017

Butler, Logan R.

ZATT (ZNF451)–mediated resolution of topoisomerase 2 DNA-protein cross-links diag *Science* v357 no6358 p1412 S 29 2017

Butler, Lucas P.

The social origins of persistence color *Science* v357 no6357 p1236 S 22 2017

Butler, Marcia

The Skin Above My Knee color *Publishers Weekly* v263 no51 p138 D 12 2016

Butler, Mike

New electronic lure may catch too many fish; one state bans it color *Field & Stream* v121 no9 p29 Ap 2017

New electronic lure may catch too many fish; one state bans it color *Field & Stream* v122 no2 p35 Je/Jl 2017

Butler, Nickolas

The Hearts of Men L. Greenblatt color *Entertainment Weekly* no1459 p65 Mr 31 2017

Lord of the Flaws D. STRAUSS *New York Times Book Review* p9 Mr 12 2017

Butler, Nickolas—Interviews

A Muscle That Makes Us Feel M. HARVKEY color *Publishers Weekly* v263 no48 p41 N 28 2016

Butler, Octavia E., 1947-2006

Kindred N. Serrao color *Entertainment Weekly* no1450 p63 Ja 27 2017

BUTLER, PAUL

When Black America Was Pro-Police bw *Atlantic* v319 no5 p37 Je 2017

Butler, Robert Olen

The Long Shadow M. UPCHURCH color *New York Times Book Review* p21 S 25 2016

Butler, Sarah

Checkout charity [Cover story] color *U.S. Catholic* v82 no7 p12 Jl 2017

Don't forget the kids *U.S. Catholic* v82 no11 p4 N 2017

Solidarity in action *U.S. Catholic* v82 no5 p4 My 2017

BUTLER, SARAH LORGE

MARATHON MOM color *Runner's World* v52 no2 p34 Mr 2017

RW 2016 COVER SEARCH [Cover story] color *Runner's World* v51 no11 p62 D 2016

Butler, Shannon

FIT TO PRINT bw color *Wired* v25 no5 p14 My 2017

BUTLER, SIMONE

The Question *O, The Oprah Magazine* p12 Mr 2017

Butler, Stuart

All of Africa Will Be Bright *Sierra* v101 no5 p24 S/O 2016

Once We Were Lions *Sierra* v101 no5 p16 S/O 2016

BUTLER, TIMOTHY

HIRING AN ENTREPRENEURIAL LEADER color il *Harvard Business Review* v95 no2 p84 Mr/Ap 2017

BUTLER, TRAY

TERMINAL ILLNESS *Atlanta* v56 no12 p36 Ap 2017

Butler, Win

ARCADE FIRE'S WIN BUTLER L. Greenblatt color *Entertainment Weekly* no1476 p58 Ag 4 2017

Butler Maps (Company)

SCOUTING PARTY color *Popular Science* p12 Ja/F 2017

Butman, Oleg

OLEG BUTMAN T. Panken color *Downbeat* v83 no12 p24 D 2016

Butor, Michel, 1926-2016

MICHEL BUTOR L. DAVIS *New York Times Magazine* p58 D 25 2016

Butt, Hans-Jürgen

Biological fabrication of cellulose fibers with tailored properties color *Science* v357 no6356 p1118 S 15 2017

Butter

ghee WIZ M. RABBITT color *Yoga Journal* no287 p63 N 2016

gold standard S. VanGilder color *Yoga Journal* p114 2017 Special Issue

Mixing Bowl color *O, The Oprah Magazine* p110 Ja 2017

super sticks color *Good Housekeeping* v265 no2 p140 Ag 2017

Buttercups

Flash of Gold: In the Flower Season J. W. DAVIS *Idaho Magazine* v16 no7 p24 Ap 2017

Butter—Evaluation

BEST FOODS FOR RUNNERS [Cover story] M. KADEY, A. Rumsey et al cartoon color *Runner's World* v52 no3 p54 Ap 2017

BETTER BUTTER J. DRILLING *Cincinnati Magazine* v50 no6 p144 Mr 2017

Bust Out of Your Nut Rut color *Men's Health* v31 no10 p64 D 2016

EDITORS' CHOICE FOOD AWARDS 2016 A. Traverso and K. Liebenson-Morse color *Yankee* v80 no6 p73 N/D 2016

The RUNNER'S HIGH [Cover story] C. DANILOFF color diag *Runner's World* v52 no3 p68 Ap 2017

Butterfield, Asa

Boys Are from Mars, Girls Are from Earth S. Zacharek color *Time* v189 no5 p50 F 13 2017

Butterfield, Stewart, 1973-

The Summer Job I'll Never Forget color *Time* v190 no2/3 p55 Jl 10-17 2017

Butterfield, Stewart, 1973—Interviews

Loneliness and the Digital Workplace L. Amico *Harvard Business Review Digital Articles* p2 S 29 2017

SLACK'S QUEST TO MAKE WORK EASIER M. Lev-ram color *Fortune* v176 no1 p21 Jl 1 2017

Butterflies

BLUE BY DESIGN E. MASTROIANNI color *Discover* v38 no4 p15 My 2017

The Butterfly, in Fact: Stuff You Probably Didn't Know L. TANNER *Idaho Magazine* v16 no10 p46 Jl 2017

Discovering the Perilous Life of Monarchs E. BLAKER *Natural History* v125 no1 p12 D 2016/Ja 2017

VISIONS color *National Geographic* v232 no3 p10 S 2017

WILDLIFE color *Canadian Geographic* v137 no3 p22 My 2017

Butterflies in art

ART THERAPY C. Zuckerman cartoon color *National Geographic* v231 no4 p154 Ap 2017

Butterflies—Migration

Peril at Journey's End J. Marinelli color *National Wildlife (World Edition)* v55 no1 p34 D/Ja 2016

Butterfly behavior

See also

Butterfly migration

Butterfly migration

on a wing and a prayer B. BUTLER and L. Heck color *Missouri Life* v44 no6 p38 S 2017

Butternut squash

Playing Squash L. TYRELL color *Martha Stewart Living* p90 O 2017

Vastly Variable Veggies *Mother Earth News* no280 p10 F/Mr 2017

Butters, Jamie

Come for the Treadmill Desk, Stay for the ... color *Bloomberg Businessweek* no4522 p40 My 15 2017

The Everyman Ride For the Upper Half bw *Bloomberg Businessweek* no4533 p14 Ag 7 2017

Ford Has Some Catching Up to Do color diag *Bloomberg Businessweek* no4524 p20 My 29 2017

It's happening again color graph *Bloomberg Businessweek* no4531 p23 Jl 24 2017

The Real Cause of the U.S. Car Slide: SUVs diag *Bloomberg Businessweek* no4518 p24 Ap 10 2017

Rental Cars to The Rescue cartoon graph *Bloomberg Businessweek* no4526 p18 Je 12 2017

Butterworth, Moses

A Lot of What Is Known about Pirates Is Not True, and a Lot of What Is True Is Not Known M. G. Hanna *Humanities* v38 no1 p1 Wint 2017

Buttigieg, Pete—Interviews

DO MAYORS DO IT BETTER? E. KILGORE img *New York* v50 no18 p30 S 4 2017

Pete Buttigieg A. WREN color *Indianapolis Monthly* p48 Ap 2017

Büttner, Karina A.

A disynaptic feedback network activated by experience promotes the integration of new granule cells bibl graph *Science* v354 no6311 p459 O 28 2016

Buttocks

5 Moves to Reinvent Your Rear T. Anderson color *Health* v30 no10 p42 D 2016

Hip & glute pain color *Yoga Journal* p67 2017 SpecialIssue

LEA MICHELE'S BETTER-BUTT SECRET color *Health* v31 no2 p15 Mr 2017

Your greatest asset K. SIBER color *Yoga Journal* p80 2017 SpecialIssue

Buttocks exercises

See also

Squat (Weight lifting)

5 WAYS ...TO BUILD ON THE CLASSIC SQUAT J. CONNOR cartoon *Muscle & Performance* v9 no1 p66 Ja 2017

FRONT SQUAT color *Muscle & Performance* v9 no1 p17 Ja 2017

HEIGHT TRAINING HACKS L. BOYCE color *Muscle & Performance* v9 no1 p24 Ja 2017

TRX, REDEFINED L. MCGLASHAN chart color *Muscle & Performance* v9 no1 p22 Ja 2017

Work That Body L. Leicht color *Glamour* v114 no7 p138 Jl 2016

Buttocks—Muscles

3 GYM-FRIENDLY EXERCISE TECHNIQUES FOR GREAT GLUTES L. McGLASHAN color *Muscle & Performance* v9

no5 p28 My 2017
Fire Up Your Hustle Muscles bw color *Men's Health* v31 no10 p127 D 2016
The Strength Secret Most Men Ignore K. Dold bw color *Men's Health* v31 no10 p56 D 2016

BUTTON, GRAHAM
THE WORLD'S BILLIONAIRES bw color diag graph map *Forbes* v199 no3 p84 Mr 28 2017

Buttons
PIN IT TO WIN IT color *Bloomberg Businessweek* no4508 p58 Ja 23 2017

Buttons—Evaluation
Handles With Flair color *Martha Stewart Living* p28 Jl/Ag 2017

Butts, Carter T.
Why I know but don't believe bibl diag *Science* v354 no6310 p286 O 21 2016

Butts, Gary
How to build an operating switch stand [Cover story] diag *Model Railroader* v84 no7 p52 Jl 2017

Butts, Gerald
FRIENDS OF GERRY N. TAYLOR-VAISEY bw *Maclean's* v130 no10 p28 N 2017

BUTTS, LISA
Austen at the Theater color *Publishers Weekly* v264 no22 p53 My 29 2017

Butts, Marcus
We're All Capable of Being an Abusive Boss [Cover story] *Harvard Business Review Digital Articles* p2 O 14 2016

Butyric acid
From Food to Mood: The bugs in your gut have hidden ways of helping you master your emotions H. ESTROFF MARANO *Psychology Today* v50 no5 p31 S/O 2017

BUWALDA, ANN
UNDER DISCUSSION *Christianity Today* p17 Ap 2017

Buxton, Rachel T.
Noise pollution is pervasive in U.S. protected areas graph map *Science* v356 no6337 p531 My 5 2017

Buxton, Ryan
Niecy Nash Nails It color *Entertainment Weekly* no1470 p14 Je 16 2017

BUXTON, VALERIE L.
Reproductive Decisions in Anurans: A Review of How Predation and Competition Affects the Deposition of Eggs And Tadpoles *BioScience* v67 no1 p26 Ja 2017

Buy national policy
BUYING BRITISH S. Dyer *History Today* v67 no8 p56 Ag 2017

Buy national policy—United States
'BUY AMERICAN' IS UN-AMERICAN N. Gillespie *Reason* v49 no5 p18 O 2017
John Phillips J. Phillips color *Car & Driver* v63 no1 p30 Jl 2017

BUZEK, SCARLETT
Life *Reader's Digest* v188 no1126 p36 D 2016/Ja 2017

Buzzell, Colby
THE BATTLE OF NEW YORK color *Popular Mechanics* p80 My 2017

Buzzelli, Elizabeth Kane
She Stopped for Death: A Little Library Mystery *Publishers Weekly* v263 no46 p35 N 14 2016

BuzzFeed Inc.
29 Reasons Why BuzzFeed Is Getting Into the TV Game G. Smith and F. Gillette color *Bloomberg Businessweek* no4526 p60 Je 12 2017

By Sidney Lumet (Film)
By Sidney Lumet C. Nashawaty color *Entertainment Weekly* no1438 p49 N 4 2016
The Must List color *Entertainment Weekly* no1438 p5 N 4 2016

By the Way (Poem)
BY THE WAY J. Harjo *New Yorker* v92 no40 p52 D 5 2016

Byam Shaw School of Art (London, England)
Helen Marten M. Rich color *Current Biography* v78 no4 p52 Ap 2017

Byassee, Jason
Evangelically liberal color *Christian Century* v133 no23 p26 N 9 2016
Evangelizing the parish color *Christian Century* v134 no15 p26 Jl 19 2017

Seminary at the megachurch color *Christian Century* v134 no4 p24 F 15 2017
Why Niebuhr mattered *Christian Century* v134 no7 p44 Mr 29 2017

Byatt, Michael
A Prized Commodity color *Arabian Horse World* v57 no7 p112 Ap 2017

Byatt, Michael—Interviews
A Conversation with Michael Byatt C. R. REICH *Arabian Horse World* v57 no3 p265 D 2016

Bye, Erik
Is Your Property Lake-Friendly? color *Cabin Living* p54 S 2017

Byeonghyun Jeon
A three-dimensional movie of structural changes in bacteriorhodopsin bibl diag graph *Science* v354 no6319 p1552 D 23 2016

Byer, Nicole
Ask anything [Cover story] cartoon color *Women's Health* v13 no10 p22 D 2016

Byer, Robert L.
A fully programmable 100-spin coherent Ising machine with all-to-all connections bibl diag graph *Science* v354 no6312 p614 N 4 2016

Byerly, Grace
A meal for many color *U.S. Catholic* v82 no6 p5 Je 2017

Byers, Brook
SAND HILL ROAD: AN ORAL HISTORY color *Wired* v25 no9 p24 S 2017

Byers, Dohrman W.
MORE ON THE MASS *Commonweal* v144 no5 p2 Mr 10 2017

Byers, Michael—Interviews
Michael Byers A. POPE color *Canadian Geographic* v137 no2 p17 Mr/Ap 2017

BYFORD, MARK
Onboarding Isn't Enough color diag graph il img *Harvard Business Review* v95 no3 p78 My/Je 2017

Byington, Dyannah
COLD FISH *Harper's Magazine* v333 no1999 p75 D 2016

Bykofsky, Melissa
CELEB CHAT *Parents* p20 2015

Bykov, Dmitry
The Russian We Need C. YOUNG bw *Weekly Standard* v22 no46 p35 Ag 14 2017

Bykova, Julia
Harvesting electrical energy from carbon nanotube yarn twist diag graph *Science* v357 no6353 p773 Ag 25 2017

Bylander, Jonas
Suppressing relaxation in superconducting qubits by quasiparticle pumping bibl graph *Science* v354 no6319 p1573 D 23 2016

Byle, Ann
What It Means To Live Christian color *Publishers Weekly* v263 no43 p20 O 24 2016

Bylin, Victoria
The Two of Us *Publishers Weekly* v264 no26 p164 Je 26 2017

Bylinskii, A.
Magnetic resonance spectroscopy of an atomically thin material using a single-spin qubit bibl color diag graph *Science* v355 no6324 p503 F 3 2017

Byman, Daniel
How to Hunt a Lone Wolf cartoon *Foreign Affairs* v96 no2 p96 Mr/Ap 2017

Byndloss, Austin J.
Microbiota-activated PPAR-γ signaling inhibits dysbiotic Enterobacteriaceae expansion graph *Science* v357 no6351 p570 Ag 11 2017

Byndloss, Mariana X.
Microbiota-activated PPAR-γ signaling inhibits dysbiotic Enterobacteriaceae expansion graph *Science* v357 no6351 p570 Ag 11 2017

Bynum, Helen
Tuberculosis today color *Science* v357 no6354 p879 S 1 2017

Bynum, Sarah Shun-Lien
Likes S. Shun-lien Bynum cartoon color *New Yorker* v93 no31 p58 O 9 2017

Byock, Ira
The Ultimate Gift color *Prevention* v69 no8 p28 Ag 2017

Byrareddy, Siddappa N.

Sustained virologic control in SIV+ macaques after antiretroviral and α4β7 antibody therapy bibl graph *Science* v354 no6309 p197 O 14 2016

Byrd, Dennis, 1966-2016

Dennis Byrd 1966-2016 P. King and T. Keith color *Sports Illustrated* v125 no14 p22 O 24-31 2016

Milestones *Time* v188 no18 p13 O 31 2016

Byrd, Donald

Truthiness color *Dance Magazine* v91 no3 p12 Mr 2017

Byrd, Jason

Animal CSI [Cover story] color *Scientific American* v316 no1 p56 Ja 2017

Byrd, Mark

Using Longitudinal Data on Career Outcomes to Promote Improvements and Diversity in Graduate Education *Change* v48 no6 p42 N/D 2016

BYRD, MAX

Original Sin *New York Times Book Review* p18 Je 25 2017

Byrd, P. Ann

Microcredentials color il *Phi Delta Kappan* v98 no3 p34 N 2016

Byrd, Tommy Lee

DROP THE HAMMER color *Hot Rod* v70 no12 p32 D 2017

LS All the Things! color *Hot Rod* v70 no2 p68 F 2017

Byrd, Troy

One Man's Junk T. Lee Byrd color *Hot Rod* v70 no4 p26 Ap 2017

Byredo (Company)

Coming Up Roses color *Good Housekeeping* v265 no5 p15 N 2017

Byrne, David

Eliminating the Human il *MIT Technology Review* v120 no5 p8 S/O 2017

Byrne, David—Interviews

A Thought Experiment color *National Geographic* v231 no6 p14 Je 2017

Byrne, Dominic P.

Local protein kinase A action proceeds through intact holoenzymes color diag graph *Science* v356 no6344 p1288 Je 23 2017

Byrne, Gabriel, 1950-

6 — LONG DAY'S JOURNEY INTO NIGHT M. R. Bernardo *Entertainment Weekly* no1444/1445 p118 D 16 2016

Byrne, James

What We Learned From... The Battle of Franklin, 1864 *Military History* v33 no5 p18 Ja 2017

What We Learned From... The Fall of Singapore, 1942 *Military History* v33 no6 p14 Mr 2017

What We Learned From... The Haitian Revolution color *Military History* v34 no5 p18 Ja 2018

Byrne, Julie

NIGHT LIFE *New Yorker* v92 no47 p5 Ja 30 2017

Byrne, Katharine M.

'Happy Little Wives and Mothers' *America* v216 no11 p42 My 15 2017

Byrne, Kerrigan

The Duke color *Publishers Weekly* v263 no52 p105 D 19 2016

Byrne, Kyle R.

Structure of histone-based chromatin in Archaea diag *Science* v357 no6351 p609 Ag 11 2017

BYRNE, MARK

EVERY DAY I'M SIDE-HUSTLIN' cartoon color *GQ: Gentlemen's Quarterly* v97 no4 p60 Ap 2017

home & help img *New York* p96 Mr 6 2017

THE IMPOSSIBLE LIST bw cartoon color *Esquire* v167 no1 p70 F 2017

Magnum Force color *Esquire* p58 BigBlackBook

The Secret to Drinking More Is... Drinking Less color *GQ: Gentlemen's Quarterly* v97 no6 p42 Je 2017

Too Cool to Fail: Why Trump Can't Kill D.C.'s Mojo color *GQ: Gentlemen's Quarterly* v97 no4 p52 Ap 2017

Byrne, Paula

Austen at the Theater L. BUTTS color *Publishers Weekly* v264 no22 p53 My 29 2017

Byrne, Peter—Awards

AAAS Kavli Science Journalism Award winners named E. Lane color *Science* v355 no6323 p362 Ja 27 2017

Byrne, Rose, 1979-

DESERT ROSE L. Brown color *InStyle* v24 no8 p144 Ag 2017

Half Ponies color *InStyle* v23 no12 p182 N 2016

Byrne, Sean—Interviews

Hell Houses L. KERN color *Film Comment* v53 no3 p22 My/Je 2017

Byrne, Sue

Weird Foods Worth Trying color *Consumer Reports* v82 no7 p14 Jl 2017

Byrnes, Nanette

The Business Issue color *MIT Technology Review* v120 no4 p2 Jl/Ag 2017

ENTREPRENEURS color il *MIT Technology Review* v120 no5 p48 S/O 2017

Goldman Sachs Embraces Automation, Leaving Many Behind il *MIT Technology Review* v120 no3 p22 My/Je 2017

HUMANITARIANS color il *MIT Technology Review* v120 no5 p62 S/O 2017

Learning to Prosper in a Factory Town color map *MIT Technology Review* v119 no6 p64 N/D 2016

TREATING ADDICTION WITH AN APP color *MIT Technology Review* v120 no3 p34 My/Je 2017

BYROM, ANDREA E.

New Zealand Shouldn't Ignore Feral Cats *BioScience* v67 no8 p686 Ag 2017

Bystander effect (Psychology)

WOULD YOU STAND UP TO HATE? K. TRANELL *Scholastic Choices* v32 no6 p6 Mr 2017

Byzantine Empire—History—527-1081

Death of the Byzantine Emperor Theophilus *History Today* v67 no1 p8 Ja 2017

C

C3 Inc.

SIEBEL'S SECOND ACT A. KONRAD color *Forbes* v200 no1 p90 Jl 27 2017

Caballero, Papo

A sequence for Healing and strength color *Yoga Journal* no296 p69 N 2017

Caballero-Mora, K. S.

Observation of a large-scale anisotropy in the arrival directions of cosmic rays above 8×1018 eV *Science* v357 no6357 p1266 S 22 2017

Cabane, Olivia Fox

UNLOCKING YOUR BIG IDEAS color *Fortune* v175 no4 p142 Mr 15 2017

Cabaret (Theatrical production)

ATLANTA NOIR *Atlanta* v57 no4 p24 Ag 2017

Cabbage

Ancient Superfoods You Should Eat Now N. Frehsee color *Health* v30 no10 p94 D 2016

better S. LIAO color *Better Homes & Gardens* v95 no3 p134 Mr 2017

Come Meet the Grand Dames of the Brassica Family! Z. Allen *Vegetarian Journal* v36 no1 p14 2017

GOOD FOR WHAT AILS YOU? L. MOYER *Nutrition Action Health Letter* v44 no2 p8 Mr 2017

Cabela's Inc.

Nature's Bounty S. SCHAEFER color *Forbes* v199 no2 p34 F 28 2017

Cabeleira, Pedro

DAMNED SUMMER J. Cronk color *Film Comment* v53 no5 p22 S/O 2017

Cabello, Camila, 1997-

BEHIND THE SCENES WITH Camila Cabello color *Seventeen* v76 no2 p12 Mr 2017

Camila Cabello B. Muteba color *Current Biography* v78 no9 p7 S 2017

FIFTH HARMONY HIT A SOUR NOTE J. Goodman color *Entertainment Weekly* no1446/1447 p28 D 2016/Ja 2017

From Cuba, With Dreams E. Hayasaki bw *Glamour* v115 no5 p176 My 2017

JUST camila M. TOPRAN color *Seventeen* v76 no2 p102 Mr 2017

Cabello, Gabriela

Latino Outdoors J. ELLISON color *Climbing* no353 p20 My/Je 2017

Cabernet Sauvignon (Wine)
CALIFORNIA'S BEST-KEPT SECRETS S. Schneider color *Sunset* v238 no3 p86 Mr 2017
WINE 1, 2, 3 F. COHEN color *Better Homes & Gardens* v95 no11 p139 N 2017

Cabeza-Cabrerizo, Mar
Macrophage function in tissue repair and remodeling requires IL-4 or IL-13 with apoptotic cells diag *Science* v356 no6342 p1072 Je 9 2017

Cabido, Marcel
Forest conservation: Remember Gran Chaco bibl color *Science* v355 no6324 p465 F 3 2017

Cabin in the Sky (Film)
AL HIRSCHFELD A. Curry color *Film Comment* v53 no2 p80 Mr/Ap 2017

Cabinet hardware
CAN YOU HANDLE IT? Statement-making cabinet hardware F. Stephanie *Washingtonian Magazine* v53 no1 p160 O 2017
HARDWARE & METALWORK *Design Center Sourcebook* p101 2016

Cabinet officers
See also
    Education ministers
    Prime ministers

Cabinet officers—Canada
A POLICE CHIEF LEGALIZES MARIJUANA S. PROUDFOOT color *Maclean's* v129 no40 p24 O 10 2016

Cabinet officers—Selection & appointment—United States
How Trump Is Restocking the Washington Swamp Z. J. Miller color *Time* v188 no27-28 p14 D 26 2016
IF SILICON VALLEY WENT TO WASHINGTON R. Hackett color *Fortune* v175 no2 p26 F 1 2017
Power Players T. Keith color *Sports Illustrated* v125 no20 p22 D 19 2016
The Schoolyard Rebel H. S. Edwards color *Time* v188 no27-28 p64 D 26 2016
Team Trump [Cover story] color *Commonweal* v144 no1 p5 Ja 6 2017
Trump's Gilded Team A. Abrams color diag *Time* v189 no3 p37 Ja 30 2017
Trump: The Gang M. Tomasky cartoon color *New York Review of Books* v64 no1 p4 Ja 19 2017

Cabinet officers—Selection & appointment—United States—News briefs
Movers K. Stock bw color *Bloomberg Businessweek* no4504 p11 D 19 2016

Cabinet officers—United States
The Muck Starts Here D. DAYEN *Nation* v303 no23/24 p4 D 5 2016
TRANSITIONS A. Davidson cartoon *New Yorker* v92 no40 p21 D 5 2016

Cabinet system
The Awfulest of the Awful J. HIGHTOWER color *Progressive* v81 no6 p70 Ag/S 2017
Presidents and Parliaments M. MOORE and R. H. SHULMAN *Commentary* v142 no4 p13 N 2016

Cabinets (Furniture)
THE affordable LOG CABIN M. R. JOHNSON color diag *Cabin Living* p28 Ap 2017
all-inclusive space SAVERS J. BREWSTER color *Cabin Living* p54 Mr 2017
Block Party [Cover story] color *Martha Stewart Living* p30 S 2017
Declutter that cabinet! J. Jones color *Redbook* p26 N 2017
FIND MORE ROOM IN EVERY ROOM A. LONGOBUCCO color diag *Good Housekeeping* v264 no3 p60 Mr 2017
From Our Editor S. Donelson color *House Beautiful* v159 no2 p4 Mr 2017
i did it! J. GARLOCK color *Better Homes & Gardens* v95 no4 p50 Ap 2017
Kitchen Cabinets for Period Houses M. E. POLSON bw cartoon color diag *Old House Journal* v45 no2 p40 Ap 2017
SAVING MONEY ON YOUR PROJECT color *Cabin Living* p11 Je 2017
STUFF USE & TIME SCREWED UP T. Petty cartoon *Old House Journal* v45 no3 p54 My 2017
Your DREAM KITCHEN is right here N. Voulgaris color *Red-*

book p134 My 2017

Cabinets (Furniture)—Design & construction
A TALE OF TWO BAR CARTS H. Kelly and H. Garrison Phillips *Washingtonian Magazine* v52 no3 p170 D 2016

Cabinets (Furniture)—Evaluation
Age of Opulence color *Architectural Digest* v74 no4 p46 Ap 2017
ESCAPE FROM L.A K. P. Badal color *Sunset* v239 no3 p72 S 2017
Good times, beautifully organized J. Jones color *Redbook* p18 Je 2017
LILAC, TAUPE & WHITE color *Martha Stewart Living* p38 Jl/Ag 2017

Cabinets (Furniture)—Exhibitions
"THE ARTIST'S MUSEUM" C. Barliant color *Art in America* v105 no3 p133 Mr 2017

Cabinetwork
See also
    Kitchen cabinets
    Wood veneers & veneering
Draw Close A. HEROLD *Los Angeles Magazine* p52 Mr 2017
Los Angeles 03/17 *Los Angeles Magazine* p6 Mr 2017

CABLE, AMANDA
Katie RUSHWORTH color *House Beautiful* p178 Ag 2017

Cable, Dan
The Powerful Way Onboarding Can Encourage Authenticity *Harvard Business Review Digital Articles* p2 N 26 2015
The Pros and Cons of Competition Among Employees *Harvard Business Review Digital Articles* p2 Mr 20 2017
Stop Paying Executives for Performance *Harvard Business Review Digital Articles* p2 F 23 2016

Cable cars (Streetcars)
Lessons From a Streetcar E. Laborde bw *New Orleans Magazine* v51 no6 p160 Ap 2017
TROLLEY TROUBLE J. GREEN *Atlanta* v56 no7 p28 N 2016

Cable modems—Performance
Maximizing Your Network Performance J. SCIACCA color *Sound & Vision* v82 no3 p21 Ap 2017

Cable News Network
Another War, Another Blitzerkrieg S. J. DOUGLAS *In These Times* v41 no6 p13 Je 2017
A BILLIONAIRE FOR THE BEARS W. H. Funk *Sierra* v102 no1 p44 Ja/F 2017
Candid Camerota [Cover story] M. BODGAS color *Working Mother* v40 no4 p20 O/N 2017
CNN K. R. Brooks and A. Heyman *New York Times Magazine* p10 Ap 23 2017
The Halcyon Days of Ted Turner bw color *Weekly Standard* v22 no9 p2 N 7 2016
PARODY color *Weekly Standard* v22 no11 p44 N 21 2016
Upside-Down Days E. Alterman il *Nation* v304 no9 p6 Mr 20 2017

Cable television
Cutting the Cord G. DELL'ABATE color *Popular Mechanics* p16 Ap 2017

Cable television industry
BAD RATINGS S. Kolhatkar color *New Yorker* v93 no23 p23 Ag 7 2017
Cable Providers Win Even in an a La Carte World S. Berinato *Harvard Business Review Digital Articles* p2 O 22 2014

Cable television—Computer network resources
How to watch the news without cable TV: 2017 edition J. NEWMAN color *PCWorld* v35 no5 p197 My 2017

Cable television—Economic aspects
Cord cutting is a bigger bargain than ever J. NEWMAN cartoon color *PCWorld* p123 O 2016

Cable television—Government policy
Time for Some Traffic Problems on Netflix? J. Brustein *Bloomberg Businessweek* no4500 p34 N 21 2016

Cable television—United States
This Just In... M. Fleischmann color *Sound & Vision* v82 no4 p17 My 2017

Cables
Working with DCC cables color diag *Model Railroader* v84 no3 p62 Mr 2017

Cabot, Andreu
Oxidation at the atomic scale diag *Science* v356 no6335 p245 Ap

21 2017

Cabral, Angelique
Life in Pieces N. Abrams, B. L. Heldman et al *Entertainment Weekly* no1482/1483 p88 S 22 2017

Cabrera, Beth
Women Need Mindfulness Even More than Men Do *Harvard Business Review Digital Articles* p2 Je 21 2016

Cabrera, Santiago
Salvation I. Rudolph *TV Guide* v65 no23 p23 My 29 2017

Cabrera-Palmer, B.
Observation of coherent elastic neutrino-nucleus scattering diag *Science* v357 no6356 p1123 S 15 2017

Cacao
BLEND ambition M. RABBITT color *Yoga Journal* no290 p77 Mr 2017
haute COCOA M. RABBITT color *Yoga Journal* no289 p67 F 2017
reviews. SUPERFOODS FOR LIFE, CACAO R. Mangels *Vegetarian Journal* v35 no1 p31 2016
STACKING THE DECK? [Cover story] *Nutrition Action Health Letter* v44 no2 p3 Mr 2017
Stuff we love color *Yoga Journal* no292 p24 Je 2017
veggie bits. Vegan Ben & Jerry's Hana Takemoto *Vegetarian Journal* v35 no4 p28 2016

Cacao beans—Sales & prices
Ghana Pays the Price Of Cheap Cocoa E. Dontoh color *Bloomberg Businessweek* no4539 p28 S 25 2017

Cacao—Therapeutic use
SUPERFOOD SWEETS D. Wise color *Health* v31 no9 p98 N 2017

Cacchione, Robert E.
50 Years of IHSA L. A. Pomeroy bw *Practical Horseman* v45 no4 p72 Ap 2017

Caccianiga, L.
Observation of a large-scale anisotropy in the arrival directions of cosmic rays above 8 × 1018 eV *Science* v357 no6357 p1266 S 22 2017

Caceres, Eva F.
Genomic exploration of the diversity, ecology, and evolution of the archaeal domain of life color *Science* v357 no6351 p563 Ag 11 2017

Caceres, Hernan
After Chile's fires, reforest private land color *Science* v356 no6334 p147 Ap 14 2017

Cacioppo, John T.
The Social Muscle *Harvard Business Review Digital Articles* p2 O 2 2017

Cacioppo, Stephanie
The Social Muscle *Harvard Business Review Digital Articles* p2 O 2 2017

Cactus
GREEN GIANTS I. Cobb color *Sunset* v237 no6 p32 D 2016
The Role of Botanical Gardens in the Conservation of Cactaceae K. R. HULTINE, L. C. MAJURE et al *BioScience* v66 no12 p1057 D 1 2016

Cactus Saddlery (Company)
Stirrup Style color *American Cowboy* v23 no6 p42 Ap/My 2017

Cadagin, Joe
Agnes Obel: Citizen of Glass *Opera News* v81 no6 p54 D 2016
Anne Sofie von Otter: So Many Things *Opera News* v81 no9 p54 Mr 2017
Eotvos: Paradise Reloaded (Lilith) *Opera News* v81 no7 p47 Ja 2017
Pluhar: Orfeo Chamán *Opera News* v81 no10 p53 Ap 2017

Cadaval, Eduardo
Cadaval & Solà-Morales I. VOLNER color *Architectural Digest* v74 no10 p114 O 1 2017

Cadavid, Doris
Oxidation at the atomic scale diag *Science* v356 no6335 p245 Ap 21 2017

CADDELL, RICHARD
International Wildlife Law: Understanding and Enhancing Its Role in Conservation *BioScience* v67 no9 p784 S 2017

Caddies
Out of The Loop S. Zak and T. Keith color *Sports Illustrated* v127 no1 p16 Jl 3 2017

Caddisflies
ONE LASTING CAST T. E. Nickens color *Field & Stream* v121 no9 p22 Ap 2017

Cadiau, Amandine
Hydrolytically stable fluorinated metal-organic frameworks for energy-efficient dehydration diag *Science* v356 no6339 p731 My 19 2017

Cadillac (Company)
Cadillac CT6 chart color *Motor Trend* v69 no1 p137 Ja 2017
Cadillac XT5 chart color *Motor Trend* v69 no1 p44 Ja 2017
THE ESCALADE DILEMMA A. MacKenzie color *Motor Trend* v69 no11 p120 N 2017
TO MILL OR NOT TO MILL M. HOYER *Cycle World* v56 no1 p5 Ja/F 2017

Cadillac automobile
Comparing Customs From 1956 T. Taylor bw *Hot Rod* v70 no5 p88 My 2017

Cadillac automobile—Evaluation
$80K+ CARS A. Wendler color *Car & Driver* v62 no7 p22 Ja 2017
Cadillac CT6 chart color *Motor Trend* v69 no1 p137 Ja 2017
Cadillac XT5 chart color *Motor Trend* v69 no1 p44 Ja 2017
Proceed With Caution color *Consumer Reports* v82 no4 p20 Ap 2017
Road Report color *Consumer Reports* v81 no12 p74 D 2016

Cadillac automobile—Marketing
Where Cadillac Is Still Prized D. Welch and Y. Zhang color graph *Bloomberg Businessweek* no4510 p16 F 6 2017

Cadillac CTS automobile—Evaluation
The End of an Era D. V. Werp color *Car & Driver* v62 no7 p92 Ja 2017
SIZE MATTERS C. Seabaugh chart color *Motor Trend* v69 no2 p72 F 2017

Cadman, Emily
Active Funds Still Rule Down Under. For Now color *Bloomberg Businessweek* no4526 p33 Je 12 2017
An Infrastructure Plan From Down Under diag *Bloomberg Businessweek* no4534 p37 Ag 14 2017

Cadnum, Michael
COYOTE *Commonweal* v144 no7 p26 Ap 14 2017
EGRET *Commonweal* v144 no7 p26 Ap 14 2017
ELEPHANT AT THE MALL GRAND OPENING *Commonweal* v144 no16 p16 O 6 2017
THE GIRAFFE *Commonweal* v144 no12 p25 Jl 7 2017
MOSQUITO *Commonweal* v144 no12 p25 Jl 7 2017

Cadoch, Lilly
Busy Mom's Cheat Sheet: Raising Happy Healthy Kids *Publishers Weekly* v264 no9 p66g F 27 2017

Cadotsch, Lucia
Center of the Storm B. Bambarger bw *Downbeat* v84 no10 p32 O 2017

Cady, J. V.
Strong coupling of a single electron in silicon to a microwave photon bibl graph *Science* v355 no6321 p1 Ja 13 2017

Caelus Energy LLC—Finance
Biting the Hand That Feeds You C. HELMAN color map *Forbes* v198 no7 p48 N 29 2016

Caenorhabditis elegans
A global brain state underlies C. elegans sleep behavior A. L. A. Nichols, T. Eichler et al diag *Science* v356 no6344 p1247 Je 23 2017
A maternal-effect selfish genetic element in Caenorhabditis elegans E. Ben-David, A. Burga et al diag *Science* v356 no6342 p1051 Je 9 2017
Transgenerational transmission of environmental information in C. elegans A. Klosin, E. Casas et al diag *Science* v356 no6335 p320 Ap 21 2017

Caenorhabditis elegans genetics
Selfish DNA fooled scientists for years S. MILIUS bw *Science News* v191 no12 p10 Je 24 2017

Caenorhabditis elegans—Behavior
Lunch Breaks L. E. Ogden bw *Natural History* v125 no11 p8 N 2017

CAESAR, E. D.
1:59:59 color *Wired* v25 no7 p84 Jl 2017
THE BATTLE FOR BRITAIN color *Esquire* p124 O 2017

TWILIGHT cartoon color *New Yorker* v92 no30 p48 S 26 2016

Caesar, Julius, 100 B.C.-44 B.C.

COWS TO DOLLARS: RANSOMS IN HISTORY *History Today* v67 no5 p22 My 2017

The Quiz *History Today* v67 no4 p71 Ap 2017

Caesar, Shirley

'Hold My Mule' G. HOWARD bw *New York Times Magazine* p46 Mr 12 2017

Caesar salads

CAESAR SALAD *Martha Stewart Living* no268 p81 O 2016

Cafardi, Nicholas

A housing policy built on sand *America* v217 no7 p48 O 2 2017

A journey of healing color *America* v217 no5 p49 S 4 2017

Cafe Society (Film)

CAFÉ SOCIETY J. Krebs color *Sound & Vision* v82 no5 p67 Je 2017

Cafeteria (New York, N.Y.)

New York's Finest... Coffee L. HARTMAN color *Publishers Weekly* v264 no20 p(Sp)90 My 15 2017

Cafeterias

KEY *Indianapolis Monthly* v40 no11 p112 Jl 2017

Cafeterias—Evaluation

BELOVED BACKWARDNESS E. S. ARNARSDÓTTIR *Iceland Review* v55 no1 p38 Ja/F 2017

Magnolia Room Cafeteria C. LAUTERBACH *Atlanta* v57 no3 p58 Jl 2017

Caffeine

The Buzz Feed *Nutrition Action Health Letter* v44 no1 p9 Ja/F 2017

Caffeine 101 O. Manno color *Dance Spirit* v21 no2 p30 F 2017

Energy Patches color *Prevention* v68 no11 p16 N 2016

Get Hydrated ... With Coffee? K. LOREN chart color *Muscle & Performance* v9 no11 p36 N 2017

Our Doc Will See You Now R. Rajapaksa color *Health* v31 no3 p65 Ap 2017

A Red-Hot Supplement J. WUEBBEN color *Muscle & Performance* v9 no7 p13 Jl 2017

Caffeine—Physiological effect

How Caffeine Works J. COVERT cartoon color *Men's Health* v32 no4 p72 My 2017

PUT FAT AT A LOSS D. N. JACKS color *Muscle & Performance* v9 no5 p12 My 2017

Silent Signs Your Body Craves a Diet Tweak M. LALIBERTE *Reader's Digest* v188 no1126 p46 D 2016/Ja 2017

Supplement Support For Your New Year's Resolutions D. N. JACKSON color *Muscle & Performance* v9 no1 p58 Ja 2017

Caffeine—Therapeutic use

Caffeine D. SCHARDT *Nutrition Action Health Letter* v44 no1 p7 Ja/F 2017

COFFEE NAP *Health* v31 no9 p20 N 2017

Caftans—Evaluation

O'S SPRING FASHION LOOK BOOK color *O, The Oprah Magazine* p57 Mr 2017

Çağaptay, Soner

The New Sultan: Erdogan and the Crisis of Modern Turkey J. Waterbury *Foreign Affairs* v96 no6 p168 N/D 2017

Cage, Luke (Fictitious character)

NO. 29 LUKE CAGE D. Coggan color *Entertainment Weekly* no1436/1437 p68 O 21 2016

Cagle, Jess

FIGHT CLUB [Cover story] color *Entertainment Weekly* no1450 p22 Ja 27 2017

Sarah Jessica Parker Isn't a Carrie D. Coggan color *Entertainment Weekly* no1436/1437 p20 O 21 2016

Caglieris, Giovanni Maria

Who Discovered the Ring Nebula? [Cover story] *Sky & Telescope* v133 no6 p32 Je 2017

Cahal, Sherman

FINDING BEAUTY IN DECAY S. Dalati color *Magazine Antiques* v183 no6 p122 N/D 2016

Cahan, Richard

THE LIFE OF A CITY E. FISHMAN bw *Chicago* v66 no1 p39 Ja 2017

THE WAR AT HOME J. HARDBERGER bw *Chicago* v65 no11 p40 N 2016

Cahill, Daniel P.

Decoupling genetics, lineages, and microenvironment in IDH-mutant gliomas by single-cell RNA-seq diag *Science* v355 no6332 p1391 Mr 31 2017

Cahill, Elizabeth Kirkland

The Garden of Learning color *America* v216 no9 p62 Ap 24 2017

Girl Uncorrupted color *Commonweal* v144 no3 p25 F 10 2017

An Ordinary Sunday [Cover story] color *Commonweal* v144 no15 p11 S 22 2017

PORTRAIT OF A MARTYR *America* v216 no1 p37 Ja 2 2017

Cahill, Jill

St. Ursula Academy *Cincinnati Magazine* v51 no1 p113 O 2017

Cahokia Mounds State Historic Park (Ill.)

Breaking Cahokia's Glass Ceiling E. A. POWELL bw color *Archaeology* v69 no6 p16 N/D 2016

Hard Times at Mid-Continent S. Richardson color *American History* v52 no2 p10 Je 2017

CAHOON, LAWRENCE B.

"The Importance of Benthic Habitats for Coastal Fisheries" (Kritzer et al. 2016): Soft Bottoms Are Biologically Productive, Not "Abiotic" *BioScience* v67 no9 p781 S 2017

CAHOON, SEAN M. P.

The Arctic in the Twenty-First Century: Changing Biogeochemical Linkages across a Paraglacial Landscape of Greenland *BioScience* v67 no2 p118 F 2017

Cai, En

Visualizing dynamic microvillar search and stabilization during ligand detection by T cells color *Science* v356 no6338 p598 My 12 2017

Cai, J.

Eye patches: Protein assembly of index-gradient squid lenses bw color graph *Science* v357 no6351 p564 Ag 11 2017

Cai, Shang

Stromal Gli2 activity coordinates a niche signaling program for mammary epithelial stem cells color *Science* v356 no6335 p284 Ap 21 2017

Cai, Tianxi

Origins of lymphatic and distant metastases in human colorectal cancer diag graph *Science* v357 no6346 p55 Jl 7 2017

Cai, Weizhao

Quantum and isotope effects in lithium metal color diag graph *Science* v356 no6344 p1254 Je 23 2017

Cai, Wen-Qi

Satellite-based entanglement distribution over 1200 kilometers diag graph *Science* v356 no6343 p1140 Je 16 2017

Cai, Yizhi

3D organization of synthetic and scrambled chromosomes diag *Science* v355 no6329 p1050 Mr 10 2017

Bug mapping and fitness testing of chemically synthesized chromosome X diag *Science* v355 no6329 p1048 Mr 10 2017

Deep functional analysis of synII, a 770-kilobase synthetic yeast chromosome diag *Science* v355 no6329 p1047 Mr 10 2017

Design of a synthetic yeast genome bibl chart color graph *Science* v355 no6329 p1040 Mr 10 2017

Engineering the ribosomal DNA in a megabase synthetic chromosome diag *Science* v355 no6329 p1049 Mr 10 2017

"Perfect" designer chromosome V and behavior of a ring derivative diag *Science* v355 no6329 p1046 Mr 10 2017

Synthesis, debugging, and effects of synthetic chromosome consolidation: synVI and beyond color *Science* v355 no6329 p1045 Mr 10 2017

Cailan, Alvin

FIESTA TIME I. Edwards color *Sunset* v238 no3 p4 Mr 2017

Meet Me in Vegas N. RICHARDSON and L. BALLA color *Bon Appetit* v62 no4 p24 Ap 2017

Caillat, J.

Attosecond dynamics through a Fano resonance: Monitoring the birth of a photoelectron bibl graph *Science* v354 no6313 p734 N 11 2016

Caillat, Marjolaine

Poor fisheries struggle with U.S. import rule bibl color *Science* v355 no6329 p1031 Mr 10 2017

Caillet, Alexander

4 Steps to Dispel a Bad Mood *Harvard Business Review Digital Articles* p2 Ap 6 2015

How Your State of Mind Affects Your Performance *Harvard Business Review Digital Articles* p2 D 8 2014

Caillier, Stacey
Getting better together color il *Phi Delta Kappan* v98 no3 p16 N 2016

Caimi, Greg
Hackathons Aren't Just for Coders *Harvard Business Review Digital Articles* p2 Ap 1 2016

Cain, Chuck
Caring for Aging Loved Ones color *Consumer Reports* v82 no12 p6 D 2017

Cain, Curtis
PDK Connection color *Phi Delta Kappan* v99 no1 p46 S 2017

Cain, Dana
Mile-High Modern E. GAUKEL color *Treasures* v5 no5 p14 Ap/My 2016

CAIN, HAMILTON
AND THEN THERE WERE NONE color *O, The Oprah Magazine* p90 Ap 2017
Moonlight Sonata cartoon color *O, The Oprah Magazine* p103 Mr 2017
TENDER IS THE PAST color *O, The Oprah Magazine* p82 Je 2017
WHAT A BOOK CAN DO [Cover story] color *O, The Oprah Magazine* p76 Jl 2017

Cain, Susan—Interviews
How Introverts Can Make the Most of Conferences D. Rousmaniere *Harvard Business Review Digital Articles* p2 O 9 2015
How to Talk in Meetings When You Hate Talking in Meetings D. Rousmaniere *Harvard Business Review Digital Articles* p2 Ap 21 2016

Caine, Brett
Your Mobile Strategy Can't Just Be About Phones *Harvard Business Review Digital Articles* p2 Jl 27 2017

Caine, Stephen
How Customers Perceive a Price Is as Important as the Price Itself color *Harvard Business Review Digital Articles* p2 Ja 3 2017

Caine-Barrett, Myokei
The Great Divide color *Tricycle: The Buddhist Review* v26 no4 p80 Summ 2017

Cainion, Eritha Akilè
Meet Eritha Akilè Cainion, Millennial of Change S. E. Jamison color *Ebony* v72 no9 p25 Jl/Ag 2017

Cairn terrier
Living a Good Life *Mother Earth News* no283 p5 Ag/S 2017

Cairney, Julie
Atoms on the move—finding the hydrogen bibl diag *Science* v355 no6330 p1128 Mr 17 2017

Cairns, Kay
Letter from... IRELAND *Advocate* no1088 p28 D 2016/Ja 2017

Cairns, Marian Cooper
HAUTE CHOCOLATE color *Southern Living* v52 no1 p110 Ja 2017
JUST CHILL color *Southern Living* v52 no6 p106 Je 2017
A LAID-BACK Easter Lunch color *Southern Living* v52 no4 p100 Ap 2017
TRUE GRITS color *Southern Living* v52 no10 p78 O 2017

CAIRNS, ROSE
Climate engineering *Issues in Science & Technology* v33 no4 p9 Summ 2017

Cairns, Scott
From Nothing: Poems *Christian Century* v134 no5 p39 Mr 1 2017

Cajón (Musical instrument)—Evaluation
LP Peruvian Cajons R. Bennett color *Downbeat* v83 no11 p80 N 2016

Cajun musicians
HEARTFELT VOCALS A. WICKS color *Louisiana Life* v37 no3 p112 Ja/F 2017

Cajuns—Social life & customs
PLANTATION COUNTRY J. FROIS color *Louisiana Life* v37 no3 p99 Ja/F 2017

Cake
See also
    Bars (Desserts)
    Brownies (Cooking)
    Coffee cakes
    Cookies
    Doughnuts

All Men Must Dine R. Kinane color *Entertainment Weekly* no1480 p44 S 1 2017
Apple Custard Cake: Re-creating a recipe from memory ... when the memory isnt yours A. TRAVERSO *Yankee* v81 no5 p68 S/O 2017
bake the season D. Greenspan and M. GLISAN color *Better Homes & Gardens* v95 no10 p122 O 2017
Cake Fit for a Queen R. Kinane color diag *Entertainment Weekly* no1474/1475 p24 Jl 21-28 2017
Catch Your FANCY C. Stone color *O, The Oprah Magazine* p110 Jl 2017
Cinnamon Crumb Cake R. Kinane color *Entertainment Weekly* no1465 p18 My 12 2017
CUT TO THE CAKES E. N. Hall, P. Lolley et al color *Southern Living* v51 no12 p156 D 2016
EASY AS PIE *Martha Stewart Living* no269 p96 N 2016
Edd Kimber's Nanna's Gingerbread S. Gutierrez *British Heritage Travel* v38 no2 p77 Mr/Ap 2017
Fruity Teatime Sweets S. Gutierrez *British Heritage Travel* v38 no4 p74 Jl/Ag 2017
HEART-HEALTHY CHOCOLATE CAKE L. F. Prater *Successful Farming* v115 no2 p65 F 2017
Hit the Sweet Spot L. Cericola color *Southern Living* v52 no2 p140 F 2017
Home Sweet Home color *House Beautiful* v159 no8 p29 O 2017
IT'S PARTY TIME! WHERE'S THE CAKE? J. TRINH *Los Angeles Magazine* v61 no11 p128 N 2016
LET THEM EAT CAKE J. O'Connor and S. Castle color *Southern Living* v52 no3 p106 Mr 2017
Let Them Eat Cake S. LODGE color *Weekly Standard* v22 no39 p34 Je 19 2017
Masking Like a Baby Cake M. Gunch color *New Orleans Magazine* v51 no4 p44 F 2017
a new (old) TRADITION A. Saltsman *Better Homes & Gardens* v94 no12 p88 D 2016
On the Road: A cake you can take with you anywhere D. Greenspan *New York Times Magazine* p24 O 8 2017
Pound Cake Perfection L. Cericola color *Southern Living* v52 no5 p146 My 2017
RECIPES A. Larson *Idaho Magazine* v16 no7 p56 Ap 2017
S'mores Icebox Cake color *Good Housekeeping* v265 no3 p113 S 2017
Soak It Up B. ESPARZA *Los Angeles Magazine* v61 no11 p129 N 2016
Spice Things Up *Martha Stewart Living* no268 p92 O 2016
SUNNY DELIGHTS [Cover story] H. Hayes color *Southern Living* v52 no2 p88 F 2017
Tastes like Fall [Cover story] color *Good Housekeeping* v265 no4 p109 O 2017
Toffee Date Cake img *New York* p64 F 9 2017
Wake to Cake E. HARE color *Cabin Living* p66 Mr 2017
What Can I Bring? E. Heiskell color *Southern Living* v52 no10 p124 O 2017
THE WORKBOOK color *Martha Stewart Living* p104 My 2017

Cake decorating competitions
8TH ANNUAL SWEET VICTORY *Cincinnati Magazine* v50 no6 p49 Mr 2017

Cake stands
AN ENCHANTED GARDEN H. BROWN color *House Beautiful* p34 Jl 2017

Cake stands—Evaluation
Editors' Picks color *Prevention* v68 no11 p5 N 2016

Cake—Evaluation
SWEET ELEGANCE bw color *Harper's Bazaar* no3654 p84 Je/Jl 2017
Toffee Date Cake img *New York* p64 Ja 9 2017

CALA, ANDRÉS
Old World, Young Promise color *Forbes* v199 no1 p20 Ja 24 2017

Cala, Ismael—Interviews
Ismael Cala: CNN Host Turned Life Strategist L. Ahuile color *Publishers Weekly* v264 no18 p18 My 1 2017

Calabrese, Alex
Defense with Dignity D. C. Vock *Governing* v30 no6 p50 Mr 2017

Calabresi, Guido, 1932-
Listen, Economists! C. R. Sunstein color *New York Review of Books* v63 no17 p53 N 10 2016

Calabresi, Massimo
  The Art of the Hostage Deal color *Time* v190 no6 p30 Ag 7 2017
  Can Trump Clean Up His Messy World of Conflicts? color *Time* v188 no24 p13 D 12 2016
  Christopher Wray color *Time* v189 no23 p15 Je 19 2017
  The Comey Misfire color *Time* v189 no19 p20 My 22 2017
  Country First [Cover story] color *Time* v190 no7 p26 Ag 21 2017
  Donald Trump's Loyalty Pledge for the FBI Challenges the Nation color *Time* v189 no23 p11 Je 19 2017
  Family First [Cover story] color *Time* v189 no22 p24 Je 12 2017
  Hacking Democracy Inside Russia's Social Media War on America color *Time* v189 no20 p30 My 29 2017
  Hacking the Voter [Cover story] color *Time* v188 no14 p30 O 10 2016
  Hot Spots and Double-Talk color *Time* v188 no22-23 p29 N/D 2016
  How Castro Will Be Trump's First Foreign Policy Test color *Time* v188 no24 p46 D 12 2016
  How Donald Trump Jr.'s Emails Have Cranked Up the Heat on His Family [Cover story] color *Time* v190 no4 p22 Jl 24 2017
  Inside Donald Trump's War Against the State [Cover story] color *Time* v189 no10 p26 Mr 20 2017
  The Lost Colony color *Time* v190 no15 p32 O 16 2017
  Russia, a Dossier of Rumors and a President-Elect color diag *Time* v189 no4 p9 Ja 23 2017
  Russia's Election Meddling Hampers Trump Transition *Time* v188 no27-28 p16 D 26 2016
  The Secret History of Election 2016 [Cover story] color map *Time* v190 no5 p32 Jl 31 2017
  The Troublemaker color *Time* v189 no3 p22 Ja 16 2017
  The Trouble With Russia color map *Time* v189 no7/8 p44 F 27 2017
  Trump and His Allies Stumble As Russia Probe Moves Closer to the White House color *Time* v189 no21 p9 Je 5 2017
  Trump's Immigration Order Is Legal-for Now color diag *Time* v189 no5 p7 F 13 2017
  Unmasking and Leaks: Trump's Russia Retort color *Time* v189 no14 p15 Ap 17 2017
  U.S.-Russia Tensions Reach Dangerous New Level color *Time* v188 no16/17 p5 O 24 2016
  The White Helmets of Syria [Cover story] color *Time* v188 no15 p20 O 17 2016
  Why James Comey Couldn't Keep the FBI Above Politics color *Time* v188 no20 p7 N 14 2016
  Will Bob Mueller Separate Fact from Fiction? [Cover story] color *Time* v190 no1 p24 Jl 3 2017

Calacanis, Jason
  The Risky Business of Angel Investing S. Begley color *Time* v190 no5 p26 Jl 31 2017

Calagione, Sam
  Drink the Beer, Skip the Gut P. KITA color *Men's Health* v32 no5 p67 Je 2017
  The Founder of Dogfish Head on Flouting a 500- Year-Old Beer Law *Harvard Business Review Digital Articles* p2 My 5 2016

Calah (Extinct city)
  REVIVING A RUINED CITY A. R. Williams bw color *National Geographic* v232 no1 p28 Jl 2017

Calamida, Annalisa
  Relativistic deflection of background starlight measures the mass of a nearby white dwarf star chart color graph *Science* v356 no6342 p1046 Je 9 2017

Calcagni, Alessia
  Transcriptional activation of RagD GTPase controls mTORC1 and promotes cancer growth diag *Science* v356 no6343 p1188 Je 16 2017

Calcite
  Specks in the Spectrometer S. Rosengard color *Oceanus* v51 no2 p86 Wint 2016

Calcium
  ASK TUFTS EXPERTS A. H. Lichtenstein *Tufts University Health & Nutrition Letter* v34 no12 p8 F 2017
  Behavioral time scale synaptic plasticity underlies CA1 place fields K. C. Bittner, A. D. Milstein et al diag *Science* v357 no6355 p1033 S 8 2017
  Find Your Dream Mask L. Desantis color *Health* v31 no2 p38 Mr 2017

  Take 5 L. McGLASHAN color *Muscle & Performance* v9 no10 p32 O 2017

Calcium channels
  See also
    Ryanodine receptors
  Structural basis for the gating mechanism of the type 2 ryanodine receptor RyR2 Wei Peng, Huaizong Shen et al bibl color graph *Science* v354 no6310 paah5324-1 O 21 2016

Calcium in human nutrition
  Calcium Myths and Facts [Cover story] V. Tweed chart color *Better Nutrition* v79 no11 p26 N 2017
  Say Cheese: Pitfalls on the path to a better cheddar L. MOYER and B. LIEBMAN *Nutrition Action Health Letter* v44 no7 p14 S 2017

Calcium—Therapeutic use
  Bone Smarts... Bess Dawson-Hughes [Cover story] B. Liebman *Nutrition Action Health Letter* v44 no6 p3 Jl/Ag 2017

Calculators
  Ada Lovelace color *Discover* v38 no4 p46 My 2017

Calculus
  What to do about Enteroliths H. S. Thomas color *Equus* no481 p36 O 2017

Caldarone, Barbara J.
  β2-Adrenoreceptor is a regulator of the a-synuclein gene driving risk of Parkinson's disease cartoon chart graph *Science* v357 no6354 p891 S 1 2017

Caldas, Blanca
  Shifting discourses in teacher education: Performing the advocate bilingual teacher bibl *Arts Education Policy Review* v118 no4 p190 2017

Calder, Alexander Milne, 1846-1923
  Family Circus A. S. C. Rower and L. Anne Miller bw *Art in America* v104 no10 p79 N 2016
  Summer Preview A. K. Scott cartoon *New Yorker* v93 no14 p14 My 22 2017

Calder, Barnabas
  Raw Concrete The Beauty of Brutalism A. Higgott *History Today* v67 no1 p60 Ja 2017

Calder, Ned
  How Industrial Systems Are Turning into Digital Services *Harvard Business Review Digital Articles* p2 Je 23 2015

Calder, Nigel
  BEST BOATS 2017 color *Sail* v47 no12 p24 D 2016
  Charged Up color *Sail* v47 no12 p46 D 2016
  Diesel Issues color *Sail* v48 no3 p54 Mr 2017

Calderas
  Fields of Fire R. JUSKALIAN color map *Discover* v38 no9 p32 N 2017

Calderone, Athena
  getting ready with ATHENA CALDERONE *Better Homes & Gardens* v94 no12 p26 D 2016

CALDERONE, ERIN
  DYNAMIC RELIEF color *Muscle & Performance* v9 no6 p24 Je 2017
  Spinal T(ap) color *Muscle & Performance* v9 no10 p28 O 2017
  Tailor-Made SQUATS color *Muscle & Performance* v9 no4 p40 Ap 2017

Calderone, Julia
  Dianne Bondy bw *Rodale's Organic Life* v3 no1 p82 Ja 2017
  Eat Smarter, Eat Healthier [Cover story] color *Consumer Reports* v82 no11 p18 N 2017
  Get Healthier il *Consumer Reports* v82 no3 p25 Mr 2017
  Is Whole-Milk Yogurt a Whole Lot Better? chart color *Consumer Reports* v82 no8 p18 Ag 2017
  No More Suffering in Silence? color graph il *Consumer Reports* v82 no3 p15 Mr 2017
  Not Your Average Joe chart color *Consumer Reports* v82 no10 p8 O 2017
  Weird Foods Worth Trying color *Consumer Reports* v82 no7 p14 Jl 2017

Calderone, Michael
  In Trump's America, Protest Is Criminalized While Reporters Are Literally Assaulted J. Jackson *Extra!* v30 no6 p1 Jl/Ag 2017

Calderwood, Randi
  Last Call J. SHIPLEY *Yankee* v81 no1 p124 Ja/F 2017

Caldesi, Giancarlo

Salad DAYS [Cover story] color *Yoga Journal* no292 p28 Je 2017

Caldesi, Katie

Salad DAYS [Cover story] color *Yoga Journal* no292 p28 Je 2017

Caldieri, Giusi

Reticulon 3–dependent ER-PM contact sites control EGFR non-clathrin endocytosis color diag graph *Science* v356 no6338 p617 My 12 2017

CalDigit Inc.

CALDIGIT USB-C DOCK: A FULLFEATURED USB-C DOCK WITH BOTH DISPLAYPORT AND HDMI PORTS G. FLEISHMAN color *Macworld - Digital Edition* p25 Mr 2017

Caldwell, Allen

Making a statement about parameter ranges *Physics Today* v70 no8 p12 Ag 2017

Caldwell, Alva R.

CHARACTER *Christian Century* v134 no17 p22 Ag 16 2017

CALDWELL, CHRISTOPHER

Barack to the Future color *Weekly Standard* v22 no18 p27 Ja 16 2017

Bumped Off cartoon *Weekly Standard* v22 no27 p9 Mr 20 2017

Catalanguish color *Weekly Standard* v23 no6 p17 O 16 2017

The Dutch Give Up on Trumpism color *Weekly Standard* v22 no28 p24 Mr 27 2017

Fillon Falling *Weekly Standard* v22 no22 p14 F 13 2017

First Taste of Japan color *Weekly Standard* v22 no36 p5 My 29 2017

France Picks a Novice color *Weekly Standard* v22 no35 p23 My 22 2017

The Germans Turn Right color *Weekly Standard* v23 no5 p30 O 9 2017

THE HIDDEN COSTS OF IMMIGRATION *Claremont Review of Books* v16 no4 p47 Fall 2016

HOW TO -NOT WHAT TO- THINK ABOUT PUTIN *USA Today Magazine* v146 no2866 p35 Jl 2017

In My Solitude *Weekly Standard* v22 no8 p5 O 31 2016

An Insider's Outsider color *Weekly Standard* v22 no33 p8 My 8 2017

Japan Returns color *Weekly Standard* v22 no37 p17 Je 5 2017

Les Déplorables *Weekly Standard* v22 no5 p23 O 10 2016

Make America **eat Again cartoon *Weekly Standard* v22 no19 p5 Ja 23 2017

May Poll color *Weekly Standard* v22 no32 p16 My 1 2017

Merkel Makes an Enemy color *Weekly Standard* v22 no38 p12 Je 12 2017

Once Bitten, Twice Shy color *Weekly Standard* v22 no11 p18 N 21 2016

Party at the End of the World color *Weekly Standard* v22 no10 p23 N 14 2016

Pats' Solutions color *Weekly Standard* v22 no21 p16 F 6 2017

Quelle Histoire! *New York Times Book Review* p16 N 27 2016

SANCTIMONY CITIES *Claremont Review of Books* v17 no1 p25 Wint 2016/2017

SENDING JOBS OVERSEAS *Claremont Review of Books* v17 no2 p20 Spr 2017

Start to Finnish bw color *Weekly Standard* v22 no47 p44 Ag 21 2017

Caldwell, Elizabeth

Liquefied gas electrolytes for electrochemical energy storage devices graph *Science* v356 no6345 p1351 Je 30 2017

Caldwell, Laura

Anatomy of Innocence: Testimonies of the Wrongfully Convicted *Publishers Weekly* v264 no3 p51 Ja 16 2017

CALDWELL, LUCY

Conservatism In the Desert color *National Review* v69 no17 p15 S 11 2017

Caldwell, Noah

A Flood of Tears color *Scientific American* v315 no3 p15 S 2016

CALDWELL, PATRICK

Who Moved My Teachers? cartoon *Mother Jones* v42 no2 p36 Mr/Ap 2017

Caldwell, Tommy

NEW DAWN J. LUCAS color *Climbing* no351 p72 F/Mr 2017

THE PUSH color *Climbing* no353 p52 My/Je 2017

Caldwell-Tautges, Dean

Moving First-Time Buyers Off the Fence: Solving the Millennial Homebuyer Puzzle with Proven Online Solutions and Partner-

ships *Bridges (Federal Reserve Bank of St. Louis)* p6 Summ 2016

Cale, John, 1942-

IN RETROSPECT A. PETRUSICH cartoon color *New Yorker* v92 no47 p64 Ja 30 2017

Caleb, M.

The magnetic field and turbulence of the cosmic web measured using a brilliant fast radio burst bibl chart graph *Science* v354 no6317 p1249 D 9 2016

Calendar

See also

Jewish calendar

REEL BEAUTY L. IMMEDIATO *Los Angeles Magazine* p36 Ap 2017

Calendar reform

THE MAN WHO WOULD KILL YOUR HOLIDAYS M. Hongoltz-Hetling color *Popular Science* v289 no5 p22 S/O 2017

Calendars (Publications)

See also

Advent calendars

Organize the whole family! J. Jones color *Redbook* p32 D 2016

Calendar—Software

How to set up the Calendar Service in macOS Sierra Server J. BATTERSBY color *Macworld - Digital Edition* p97 D 2016

How to use the advanced Calendar Service features in macOS Sierra Server J. BATTERSBY color *Macworld - Digital Edition* p103 D 2016

Calendrical Reform (Poem)

CALENDRICAL REFORM J. C. PETTY *Humanist* v77 no2 p31 Mr/Ap 2017

Calendula (Genus)

Your CHECKLIST M. Irvine and E. Jardina color *Sunset* v239 no1 p58 Jl 2017

Calf roping

(At home with) C. Shaffer color *Team Roping Journal* p50 S 2017

Cowboy Up: Backhand Slip Catch color *American Cowboy* v23 no6 p65 Ap/My 2017

FIVE FLAT with Zane Bruce C. Toy color *Spin to Win Rodeo* v21 no6 p31 Ag 2017

FREEZE FRAME WITH CHRIS GLOVER C. Toy color *Spin to Win Rodeo* v21 no5 p38 Jl 2017

FREEZE FRAME WITH WHITNEY DESALVO K. Gustave color *Spin to Win Rodeo* v21 no6 p42 Ag 2017

HORSEPOWER IS NEVER TO BE TAKEN FOR GRANTED K. Santos color *Spin to Win Rodeo* v21 no6 p44 Ag 2017

MIDNIGHT: THE HORSE WHO COULDN'T BE RIDDEN L. Feldman bw *Spin to Win Rodeo* v21 no5 p96 Jl 2017

PRIME PRACTICE PAYS PREMIUMS K. Santos color *Spin to Win Rodeo* v20 no9 p34 N 2016

SHARING THE WEALTH color *Spin to Win Rodeo* v21 no6 p68 Ag 2017

SILVER STANDARD C. Toy color *Spin to Win Rodeo* v21 no6 p70 Ag 2017

TALK IT OVER, MAKE A PLAN AND EXECUTE K. Santos color *Spin to Win Rodeo* v21 no5 p30 Jl 2017

TODAY'S TEAM-ROPING TALENT POOL RUNS DEEP K. Santos color *Spin to Win Rodeo* v21 no6 p36 Ag 2017

Why do I rope? D. Begay color *Team Roping Journal* p160 S 2017

YOUNG GUNS with Kyle Lockett C. Toy color *Spin to Win Rodeo* v21 no6 p24 Ag 2017

Calf roping—Competitions

Brown and Nogueira Split $11K at Windy Ryon K. Gustave color *Spin to Win Rodeo* v21 no6 p20 Ag 2017

Operations cont. USTRC & WSTR *Spin to Win Rodeo* v21 no6 p10 Ag 2017

Tyler Merrill: Weatherford, Texas A. Gentry color *Spin to Win Rodeo* v21 no6 p26 Ag 2017

USTRC CHANGES OWNERSHIP color *Spin to Win Rodeo* v21 no6 p8 Ag 2017

The WestStar Open color *Spin to Win Rodeo* v20 no9 p20 N 2016

Calfas, Jennifer

5 Cheap Things Restaurants Love to Overcharge You For color *Money* v46 no6 p15 Jl 2017

9 Secrets to Scoring First-Class Upgrades on the Cheap color *Money* v46 no9 p30 O 2017

Grab This $10 Parks Bargain ... Quick! color *Money* v46 no7 p26

Ag 2017

How Many Avocado Toasts It Takes to Buy a Home color *Money* v46 no7 p14 Ag 2017

These Are Airbnb's Most Wished-For Rentals color *Money* v46 no9 p18 O 2017

Calgary Stampede

One of a Kind color *American Cowboy* v23 no5 p72 F/Mr 2017

Calhoun, Ada

THE EMOTIONAL WAKE color *Women's Health* v14 no7 p122 S 2017

Married, Bored, and Confused N. S. RILEY bw *Weekly Standard* v23 no3 p37 S 25 2017

Searching for a Soul Mate Is Futile. The Ideal Partner Is the One You Create color *Time* v189 no20 p22 My 29 2017

CALHOUN, CRAIG

Campus Choices *New York Times Book Review* p22 Ag 27 2017

Calhoun, Koben

A New Way to Think About Office Lighting *Harvard Business Review Digital Articles* p2 Je 27 2017

Old Buildings Are U.S. Cities' Biggest Sustainability Challenge *Harvard Business Review Digital Articles* p2 Ja 21 2016

Calhoun, Laurie

Death from above: The perils of lethal drone strikes bibl *Bulletin of the Atomic Scientists* v73 no2 p138 Mr 2017

Calico Labs (Company)

Google's Long Strange Life Span Trip A. Regalado color *MIT Technology Review* v120 no1 p52 Ja/F 2017

Twitter Votes graph *MIT Technology Review* v120 no2 p9 Mr/Ap 2017

California

California vs. Trump Over Car Emissions bw *Bloomberg Businessweek* no4517 p10 Ap 3 2017

the Disney park that's right for your family [Cover story] K. CICERO chart color *Parents* v92 no3 p34 Mr 2017

Glow, Baby, Glow D. ROTHBART color *Los Angeles Magazine* v62 no7 p45 Jl 2017

Going Nuts color *Los Angeles Magazine* v62 no7 p16 Jl 2017

Mesa Verde Restaurant J. Lewis color *Vegetarian Times* v43 no2 p20 N/D 2016

California, Gulf of (Mexico)

Requiem for the Vaquita E. Vance color map *Scientific American* v317 no2 p36 Ag 2017

California, Southern—Description & travel

Winter-Riding Opportunities R. EVERSOLE color *Trail Rider* v29 no1 p22 Ja/F 2017

California, Southern—Politics & government

The Fight of His Life M. FLEMING color *Weekly Standard* v22 no7 p15 O 24 2016

California condor

First Flight color *Earth Island Journal* v32 no4 p5 Wint 2017

California. Dept. of Transportation

The High Sign J. HERBST *Los Angeles Magazine* v61 no11 p32 N 2016

Swim-up Bar *Los Angeles Magazine* p22 Ap 2017

California Institute of Technology

John D. Roberts (1918–2016) G. M. Whitesides color *Science* v354 no6318 p1382 D 16 2016

NEWSMAKERS *Science* v357 no6351 p533 Ag 11 2017

SCIENCE JOURNALISM D. CORDELL, T. J. MARTIN et al color *Scientific American* v316 no2 p5 F 2017

California Institute of the Arts

2017 HIGHER ED GUIDE *Dance Spirit* v21 no7 p106 S 2017

SUMMER STUDY DIRECTORY *Stage Directions* v30 no1 p23 Ja 2017

California. Legislature. Senate

BLUE REPUBLIC M. TINOCO *Mother Jones* v42 no4 p38 Jl/Ag 2017

California. Legislature. Senate—Elections

California's Woeful Republicans M. FLEMING *Weekly Standard* v22 no4 p18 O 3 2016

California Pizza Kitchen Inc.—Finance

SAVED BY BARBECUE CHICKEN PIZZA D. Eng color *Fortune* v174 no8 p58 D 15 2016

California state history

California Dreaming: A contemporary visual journey color *Orion Magazine* v36 no1 p46 Ja/F 2017

Decalifornication S. Richardson bw *American History* v52 no4 p6 O 2017

California State Prison at San Quentin

Prison University Project P. Wasley *Humanities* v37 no4 p1 Fall 2016

California State University

California State University—Long Beach *Dance Magazine* v90 p114 2016/2017 Supplement College Guide

CSULB Students Meet High Standards J. Hale color *Downbeat* v84 no8 p94 Ag 2017

California Typewriter (Film)

The Soul of an Old Machine S. Zacharek color *Time* v190 no9 p56 S 4 2017

California—Commerce

Abuzz In the Drone Age P. LERNER *Los Angeles Magazine* p76 Ja 2017

California—Description & travel

Best Places to Retire [Cover story] S. BLOCK, P. MERTZ ESSWEIN et al color *Kiplinger's Personal Finance* v71 no8 p56 Ag 2017

CALIFORNIA S. Doyle color map *Canadian Geographic* v135 no6 p32 D 2015

Cambria M. JAFFE *Los Angeles Magazine* p90 Ap 2017

CITY OF PALM DESERT *Los Angeles Magazine* p84 F 2017

HIDDEN GEMS P. RAINS *Sea Magazine* v108 no8 p14 Ag 2016

HOW TO PLAN A BETTER BASH: WHILE THE CONDITIONS FOR THE BAJA BASH ARE INEVITABLE, FACING THEM DOESN'T HAVE TO BE *Sea Magazine* v109 no5 p14 My 2017

Sea World K. BASTONE map *Backpacker* p20 Ag 2017

STRANDED... AND LOVING IT R. Levin color *Sunset* v238 no3 p13 Mr 2017

This country is incredible [Cover story] K. VALENTINI color *Redbook* p105 Mr 2017

Tour de California C. GRAHAM color *Backpacker* p12 My 2017

THE Trip M. Rapkin and M. Salcido color *Sunset* v238 no1 p48 Ja 2017

WAY UP THE COAST S. SHIBATA *Sea Magazine* v109 no2 pCA-1 F 2017

WHERE THE WILD THINGS ARE Z. Schaeffer color *Sunset* v238 no4 p32 Ap 2017

A WORLD AWAY IN ALAMEDA *Sea Magazine* v108 no8 pCA-1 Ag 2016

California—Economic conditions

100 FASTEST-GROWING COMPANIES S. Decarlo, D. G. Elam et al chart color diag map *Fortune* v176 no4 p157 S 15 2017

California—History

Get Your Kicks *Los Angeles Magazine* p28 Mr 2017

California Maritime Academy (Vallejo, Calif.)

BEST BANG FOR THE BUCK WESTERN COLLEGES chart *Washington Monthly* v49 no9/10 p56 S/O 2017

California—Politics & government

The California Republic Comes Roaring Back K. Steinmetz color diag map *Time* v189 no5 p34 F 13 2017

California—Politics & government—21st century

A Brief History of Secession [Cover story] R. STRINER *American Scholar* v86 no2 p20 Spr 2017

CIVIL WAR II? CALIFORNIA'S FEVERED FANTASIES S. FORBES *Forbes* v199 no2 p17 F 28 2017

Doing something on climate *Christian Century* v134 no4 p7 F 15 2017

Look to Cities and States G. Newsom *New Republic* v248 no3 p33 Mr 2017

California—Politics & government—1951-

California's Dream J. Nash and E. E. Deprez color *Bloomberg Businessweek* no4500 p26 N 21 2016

California—Social aspects

West Coast Modern color *Treasures* v5 no5 p24 Ap/My 2016

California—Social conditions

CIVIL WAR II? CALIFORNIA'S FEVERED FANTASIES S. FORBES *Forbes* v199 no2 p17 F 28 2017

Californication (TV program)

THE RISE OF THE FAKE FAMOUS JACKASS NOVELIST J. LARSON img *New York* v50 no6 p80 Mr 20 2017

Calipers

In the Bag L. SCHLEY color *Discover* v38 no2 p14 Mr 2017

Calisi, Christopher

Stop Noise from Ruining Your Open Office *Harvard Business Review Digital Articles* p2 Mr 16 2015

Caliskan, Aylin

Semantics derived automatically from language corpora contain human-like biases chart graph *Science* v356 no6334 p183 Ap 14 2017

Call, Andrew

Research: Firms Give More Stock Options When They're Committing Fraud color *Harvard Business Review Digital Articles* p2 Ja 26 2017

Call, Josep

Great apes anticipate that other individuals will act according to false beliefs bibl chart diag graph *Science* v354 no6308 p110 O 7 2016

Call center agents—Psychology

Abuse at work linked to shopping binges *People Management* p57 S 2017

Call centers—Officials & employees

CALLED AWAY J. BLITZER cartoon *New Yorker* v92 no46 p30 Ja 23 2017

Call Me by Your Name (Film)

CALL ME BY YOUR NAME J. Nolfi color *Entertainment Weekly* no1478 / 1479 p63 Ag 18-25 2017

Making a Name M. GUIDUCCI color *Vogue* v207 no11 p168 N 2017

A Summer Place bw color *Film Comment* v53 no5 p6 S/O 2017

Call Me Francis (TV program)

A political life of Pope Francis, from Argentina to the Vatican J. Anderson color *America* v216 no8 p48 Ap 17 2017

STREAM THESE OTHER FOREIGN-LANGUAGE SHOWS ON NETFLIX NOW C. Agard color *Entertainment Weekly* no1449 p51 Ja 20 2017

Call the Midwife (TV program)

And Don't Miss... J. Russell *TV Guide* v65 no13 p37 Mr 20 2017

Callaghan, Adrian H.

Turbulence in breaking waves *Physics Today* v69 no10 p86 O 2016

CALLAGHAN, CAROLYN

'Neonics' and Other Pesticides color *Canadian Wildlife* v23 no2 p44 My/Je 2017

Callaghan, Meaghan Lee

Lost in Translation *Audubon* v119 no1 p15 Spr 2017

Recycle Plastic at Home cartoon color *Popular Science* p89 Ja/F 2017

Callahan, Dan

Cinema by Design: Art Nouveau, Modernism, and Film History color *Film Comment* v53 no3 p78 My/Je 2017

Callahan, Daniel

End Games color *Commonweal* v144 no4 p26 F 24 2017

Callahan, David

A Bigger Seat at the Table: Are the new megadonors distorting American society? M. COTTLE *New York Times Book Review* p19 Ap 30 2017

The Givers: Money, Power, and Philanthropy in a New Gilded Age *Publishers Weekly* v264 no6 p58 F 6 2017

Our Philanthropic Overlords C. LEHMANN *In These Times* v41 no5 p37 My 2017

The Pitfalls of Giving It All Away S. Begley color *Time* v189 no15 p18 Ap 24 2017

Callahan, Michael

GETTING THE GLAMOURPUSSES BACK bw color *Bloomberg Businessweek* no4521 p64 My 8 2017

The McGinnis Look cartoon color *Vanity Fair* v59 no5 p134 Ap 2017

THE QUEEN OF CHRISTMAS color *Bloomberg Businessweek* no4499 p79 N 14 2016

Callahan, Sidney

How to build a better preacher *America* v217 no3 p46 Ag 7 2017

A NUANCED THINKER color *America* v215 no14 p34 N 7 2016

Callahan, Tom

Palmer's Method G. NORMAN bw *Weekly Standard* v22 no41 p30 Jl 3 2017

CALLANAN, MARK

Experiment *Walrus* v13 no9 p34 N 2016

Callaway (Company)

MAX GAME IMPROVEMENT IRONS M. Chwasky, M. Dee et al color *Golf Magazine* v59 no4 p117 Ap 2017

CALLAWAY, EWEN

Freedom in Exile [Cover story] color graph map *Natural History* v125 no3 p18 Mr 2017

Callaway Golf Co.

GOOD WOOD M. Chwasky and R. Sauerhaft color *Golf Magazine* v59 no8 p86 Ag 2017

LONG SHOTS M. Chwasky and R. Sauerhaft color *Golf Magazine* v59 no1 p84 Ja 2017

Patrick Reed C. Barrett color *Golf Magazine* v59 no1 p25 Ja 2017

Calle, Nastenka

Pipelines imperil Canada's ecosystem *Science* v355 no6321 p140 Ja 13 2017

Calle, Sophie

GOINGS ON ABOUT TOWN color *New Yorker* v93 no11 p4 My 1 2017

Calleja, Jonas

A general catalytic β-C–H carbonylation of aliphatic amines to β-lactams bibl diag *Science* v354 no6314 p851 N 18 2016

Callery, Sean—Interviews

Meet the crew... E. Aslanian *TV Guide* v65 no43 p8 O 16 2017

CALLIAN, MIKE

FIND YOUR CALLING color *Field & Stream* v122 no5 p50 O 2017

Callier, Viviane

Aspirin vs. Cancer color *Scientific American* v316 no5 p24 My 2017

Fossils shake up fish family tree color *Science News* v192 no5 p5 S 30 2017

Callies, Sarah Wayne—Interviews

Prison Break M. Roffman *TV Guide* v65 no14 p35 Ap 3 2017

CALLIMACHI, RUKMINI

OBAMA'S AMERICA img *New York* v49 no20 p12 O 3 2016

Obama's JV Jibe Still Stings E. PEPPERS *USA Today Magazine* v145 no2864 p47 My 2017

Rukmini Callimachi D. Kiper color *Current Biography* v78 no2 p17 F 2017

Calliope

Tool Sweet E. STYRON color *Missouri Life* v44 no2 p40 Ap 2017

Callo, Joseph

Heligoland: Britain, Germany and the Struggle for the North Sea *Military History* v34 no2 p73 Jl 2017

CALLO, JOSEPH F.

Victory (?) at Sea bw *Weekly Standard* v22 no40 p37 Je 26 2017

CALLOS, TOM

A MARTIAL ARTIST'S GUIDE TO HIP HEALTH color *Black Belt* v55 no1 p32 D 2016/Ja 2017

A MARTIAL ARTIST'S GUIDE TO HIP HEALTH [Cover story] bw color *Black Belt* v55 no2 p54 F/Mr 2017

Callow, Simon

The Lion in Autumn D. A. HOFFMAN bw *Weekly Standard* v22 no12 p34 N 28 2016

Sherlock Out Loud: Stephen Fry narrates Arthur Conan Doyle's tales of a certain obsessive detective *New York Times Book Review* p16 My 21 2017

CALLOWAY, BRITYN

MEET Rock 'n' Roll Hair Stylists *Indianapolis Monthly* v40 no4 p24 D 2016

Calloway, Kirk

These Supersavers Spend a Little J. KOSNETT color *Kiplinger's Personal Finance* v71 no11 p72 N 2017

Calmness

Open your mind to calm color *Redbook* p95 N 2017

Your Mindful Day [Cover story] C. Gregoire color *Prevention* v69 no9 p80 O 2017

Calmonte, U.

Xenon isotopes in 67P/Churyumov-Gerasimenko show that comets contributed to Earth's atmosphere diag *Science* v356 no6342 p1069 Je 9 2017

CALNAN, MARIANNE

DO NOT READ THIS ARTICLE: Delivering learning exactly when it's needed isn't just common sense - it's a revolution for the L&D department *People Management* p46 Ap 2017

Employers 'must prepare to add commission to holiday pay' after landmark ruling *People Management* p8 N 2016

Get ready for #HRmegamonth: From gender pay reporting to the minimum wage, People Management rounds up key legal and practical changes coming to the UK in April *People Management* p8 Ap 2017

It'll cost you... *People Management* p27 S 2017

We're serious about putting patients at the heart of learning *People Management* p22 F 2017

We wanted to prove learning can be fun *People Management* p25 O 2016

Who I am *People Management* p51 F 2017

Who I am *People Management* p53 O 2016

Calonzo, Andreo
Philippine Casinos Are Cleaning Up color graph *Bloomberg Businessweek* no4521 p19 My 8 2017

Calore, Michael
FETISH SAFE HOUSE bw *Wired* v25 no6 p33 Je 2017

OK, HOUSE. GET SMART chart color *Wired* v25 no6 p39 Je 2017

SHAPIN' SAFARI color *Wired* v25 no7 p46 Jl 2017

TOP THREE: SOUND WAVES color *Wired* v25 no8 p40 Ag 2017

WISH LIST 2016 color *Wired* v24 no12 p45 D 2016

Caloric content of foods
Bodyweight Fat Blast K. LOREN chart color *Muscle & Performance* v9 no7 p20 Jl 2017

Caloric expenditure
Jogging With Junior: When you push your children, you need to push yourself too G. Reynolds *New York Times Magazine* p22 Ag 27 2017

Calorie
better S. LIAO color *Better Homes & Gardens* v95 no2 p123 F 2016

EXERCISING RESTRAINT A. AZEVEDO, W. BRÄU et al color *Scientific American* v316 no6 p5 Je 2017

THE MESSY TRUTH ABOUT WEIGHT LOSS S. B. Roberts and S. Krupa Das color graph *Scientific American* v316 no6 p36 Je 2017

Nutrion SCHOOL [Cover story] color *Redbook* p81 Ap 2017

The truth about CALORIES color *Redbook* p88 Ap 2017

Calrissian, Lando (Fictitious character)
STAR WARS: MEET THE NEW LANDO D. Franich color *Entertainment Weekly* no1438 p20 N 4 2016

CALSTER, HANS VAN
Combining Biodiversity Resurveys across Regions to Advance Global Change Research *BioScience* v67 no1 p73 Ja 2017

CALVERT, BRIAN
DO AS I SAY, NOT AS I DO *Sea Magazine* v109 no1 p23 Ja 2017

Calvert, Cynthia Thomas
What Young vs. UPS Means for Pregnant Workers and Their Bosses *Harvard Business Review Digital Articles* p2 Mr 26 2015

Calvert, Kay—Awards
MEMBER SPOTLIGHT color *Literacy Today (2411-7862)* v34 no3 p40 N/D 2016

Calves—Vaccination
MORE PREVENTION, LESS TREATMENT G. Johnston *Successful Farming* v115 no5 p52 Mid-Mr 2017

Calvet, Nuria
Spiral density waves in a young protoplanetary disk bibl graph *Science* v353 no6307 p1519 S 30 2016

Calvillo, Michael
Employment expansion continues but at a slower pace bibl *Monthly Labor Review* p1 Ap 2017

One hundred years of Current Employment Statistics: busting CES myths bibl chart color graph *Monthly Labor Review* p1 O 2016

Calvin, Jean
DUNE BUGGIES RACING ACROSS AMERICA J. OBER bw *Dirt Sports + Off-Road* v51 no6 p74 Je 2017

Calvin, Jean, 1509-1564
Dethroning the idols M. Sanchez *Christian Century* v134 no18 p30 Ag 30 2017

Calvin, Linda
The California Leafy Greens Industry Provides an Example of an Established Food Safety System *Amber Waves: The Economics of Food, Farming, Natural Resources, & Rural America* p43 Je 2017

Calvin Klein Inc.
Calvin Klein 205W39NYC earrings, $1,190 V. SMITH color *Vogue* v207 no10 p310 O 2017

STYLE CRUSH Laura Harrier J. Ferrise color *InStyle* v24 no10 p110 O 2017

Calvinists
Dethroning the idols M. Sanchez *Christian Century* v134 no18 p30 Ag 30 2017

MARILYNNE ROBINSON'S THREAT ASSESSMENT *Lapham's Quarterly* v10 no3 p75 Summ 2017

Calvino, Italo, 1923-1985
THE ADVENTURE OF A SKIER I. CALVINO color *New Yorker* v93 no19 p58 Jl 3 2017

Calvo, Trisha
Don't Get Burned! chart color *Consumer Reports* v82 no7 p8 Jl 2017

Eat Smarter, Eat Healthier [Cover story] color *Consumer Reports* v82 no11 p18 N 2017

Step Away From the Sticky Bun! chart color *Consumer Reports* v82 no3 p36 Mr 2017

Weird Foods Worth Trying color *Consumer Reports* v82 no7 p14 Jl 2017

Calvocoressi, Gabrielle
The Poetic Is Political C. M. TEICHER bw color *Publishers Weekly* v264 no14 p38 Ap 3. 2017

Calvo-Enrique, Laura
Multipotent peripheral glial cells generate neuroendocrine cells of the adrenal medulla color *Science* v357 no6346 p46 Jl 7 2017

Calzone
CAST-IRON SKILLET CALZONE L. F. Prater *Successful Farming* v115 no3 p59 Mid-F 2017

Cam, 1984-
Cam B. Muteba color *Current Biography* v78 no6 p20 Je 2017

CAM, DENIZ
DOCTORATE, DEGREE OR DROPOUT? diag graph *Forbes* v200 no5 p24 N 14 2017

THE WORLD'S BILLIONAIRES bw color diag graph map *Forbes* v199 no3 p84 Mr 28 2017

Camacho, R. M.
An integrated diamond nanophotonics platform for quantum-optical networks bibl graph *Science* v354 no6314 p847 N 18 2016

CÁMARA, GABRIELA
r.s.v.p bw *Bon Appetit* v62 no4 p10 Ap 2017

Camargo, J. L.
Persistent effects of pre-Columbian plant domestication on Amazonian forest composition bibl chart graph map *Science* v355 no6328 p925 Mr 3 2017

Camaro automobile
2016 CHEVROLET CAMARO SS J. Jacquot color graph *Car & Driver* v63 no2 p72 Ag 2017

2017 COPO CAMARO: DIRECT INJECTION GOES DRAG RACING M. Davis bw chart color *Hot Rod* v70 no10 p64 O 2017

The 50 Quickest Cars of Drag Week 2016 —and Then Some B. Gillogly chart color *Hot Rod* v70 no2 p18 F 2017

Big Red Redemption P. Thomas color *Hot Rod* v70 no12 p18 D 2017

CHEVROLET GT4.R CAMARO J. Machaqueiro color *Hot Rod* v70 no11 p78 N 2017

Dream Test E. J. Smith color *Hot Rod* v70 no10 p54 O 2017

Drive to the Super Bowl T. Keith color *Sports Illustrated* v127 no4 p17 Ag 7 2017

FINISH LINE D. Freiburger color *Hot Rod* v70 no6 p122 Je 2017

THE FOREVER WAR [Cover story] J. Lieberman chart color diag graph *Motor Trend* v69 no8 p48 Ag 2017

THE GOOD, BAD, AND UGLY OF GLOBE-TREKKING DRAG WEEK COMPETITORS T. Taylor color *Hot Rod* v70 no2 p32 F 2017

Greg Zoetmulder's Supercharged Small-Block Jeep Runs 8s With Ease J. Reiss color *Hot Rod* v70 no1 p50 Ja 2017

The HOT ROD Archives D. Wallace color *Hot Rod* v70 no4 p14 Ap 2017

INFERNO [Cover story] B. Gillogly color *Hot Rod* v70 no8 p24 Ag 2017

LS All the Things! T. L. Byrd color *Hot Rod* v70 no2 p68 F 2017

Why Are There 1970 1/2 Camaros? T. Taylor color *Hot Rod* v70

no10 p84 O 2017

Your Say... D. PASQUALE, R. LODATO et al color *Motor Trend* v69 no1 p32 Ja 2017

Z/409: The '69 Camaro Chevrolet Should Have Built B. Gillogly color *Hot Rod* v70 no10 p24 O 2017

ZR71 B. Gillogly color *Hot Rod* v70 no5 p26 My 2017

Camaro automobile—Evaluation

Ballistic Leaf Blower [Cover story] J. Jacquot color diag *Car & Driver* v62 no6 p42 D 2016

BRUTE SQUAD GOALS J. Lieberman chart color *Motor Trend* v69 no4 p62 Ap 2017

CHEMISTRY LESSON K. KINARD color *Road & Track* v68 no6 p80 F 2017

DRIVE AWAY WITH A BEAUTY color *Men's Health* v31 no10 p(Sp)28 D 2016

GARAGE chart color diag *Motor Trend* v69 no2 p90 F 2017

GARAGE color *Motor Trend* v69 no5 p88 My 2017

The Ringbrothers' G-Code Camaro BLUEPRINTED B. Gillogly color *Hot Rod* v70 no6 p50 Je 2017

THROWBACK P. LERNER color diag graph *Road & Track* v68 no8 p68 My 2017

TRIPLE THREAT B. Gillogly color *Hot Rod* v70 no5 p64 My 2017

TWO FOR THE PRICE OF ONE D. Pund color graph *Car & Driver* v62 no7 p106 Ja 2017

Camassa, Roberto

How boundaries shape chemical delivery in microfluidics bibl diag graph *Science* v354 no6317 p1252 D 9 2016

CAMBANIS, THANASSIS

Youth Was Not Enough *New York Times Book Review* p12 F 12 2017

Camblin, Victoria

Buildings Seeking Art bw color *Art in America* v104 no11 p48 D 2016

Cambodia—Description & travel

RELATED LINKS T. OLSEN *Christianity Today* v61 no5 p9 Je 2017

Cambodia—History

NATIONAL GALLERY CAMBODIA R. Griffiths *History Today* v67 no5 p78 My 2017

Cambodia—Politics & government—1979-

The Minesweeper Sok Chenda A. SEIFF color *Foreign Policy* no221 p24 N/D 2016

Cambodia—Religion

UNLOCKING CAMBODIAN CHRISTIANITY K. SHELL-NUTT color *Christianity Today* v61 no5 p34 Je 2017

Cambridge (England)—History

COMMON GROUND M. BROWN color *Archaeology* v70 no3 p18 My/Je 2017

Cambridge, Catherine, Duchess of, 1982-

BUSTING THE RECYCLING MYTH P. TREBLE color *Maclean's* v129 no40 p53 O 10 2016

DRESSING THE DUCHESS OF CAMBRIDGE M. CAMPBELL color *Maclean's* v129 no40 p54 O 10 2016

A New Leaf color *Vogue* v207 no11 p124 N 2017

Cambridge Analytica (Company)

AI'S KILLER APP? DUH ... MARKETING D. Lyons color *Fortune* v175 no5 p40 Ap 1 2017

Cambridge Analytica's Low-Tech Fisticuffs S. Baker, D. Kocieniewski et al color *Bloomberg Businessweek* no4516 p23 Mr 27 2017

Camcorders—Equipment & supplies

6 ACCESSORIES that make the iPhone an even BETTER VIDEO CAMERA [Cover story] T. Larson and D. Masaoka color *Macworld - Digital Edition* v34 no6 p83 Je 2017

Camcorders—Evaluation

NEW PRODUCTS color *Astronomy* v45 no1 p68 Ja 2017

Camden, Elizabeth

To the Farthest Shores *Publishers Weekly* v264 no2 p48 Ja 9 2017

Camel racing

High-Tech Camel Races *New York Times Upfront* v149 no9 p2 F 20 2017

CamelBak Products LLC

CAMELBAK K.U.D.U. PROTECTOR 10 R. Koch color *Bicycling* v58 no9 p70 O 2017

Camellias

See also

Tea

AROUND THE GARDEN S. Bender color map *Southern Living* v51 no11 p54 N 2016

SHOVELING BLOSSOMS G. KLEINER color *Orion Magazine* v36 no1 p64 Ja/F 2017

Camels

Tale from the Land of Oz A. Mitchell color *Canadian Wildlife* v23 no4 p14 S/O 2017

Cameo performances in motion pictures

Two for the Road D. Franich color *Entertainment Weekly* no1466 p13 My 19 2017

Camera bags—Evaluation

SMALL WONDERS color *Essence* v47 no7 p16 N 2016

THE WELL-SPENT $ DOLLAR color *Harper's Bazaar* no3651 p248 Mr 2017

Camera equipment—Evaluation

Get the Shot L. ALBANESE and J. SCHNEIDER color *Backpacker* p61 Je 2017

Camera phones

Do You Still Need a 'Real' Camera? M. Leuchter color *Popular Photography* v81 no2 p60 Mr/Ap 2017

Camera tripods

Make a tripod holder for your smart phone L. Sassi color diag *Model Railroader* v84 no5 p56 My 2017

photo school: Get Serial G. FULLERTON color *Backpacker* p36 S 2017

Camera tripods—Evaluation

NEW PRODUCTS color *Astronomy* v45 no8 p85 Ag 2017

Cameran, Mirella

DINING GUIDE color *New Orleans Magazine* v51 no2 p92 D 2016

DINING GUIDE color *New Orleans Magazine* v51 no5 p96 Mr 2017

ETC color *New Orleans Magazine* v51 no10 p215 Ag 2017

ETC color *New Orleans Magazine* v51 no12 p167 O 2017

ETC color *New Orleans Magazine* v51 no4 p143 F 2017

ETC color *New Orleans Magazine* v51 no9 p135 Jl 2017

Fall into Festival Fashion color *New Orleans Magazine* v52 no1 p44 S 2017

Finest of the FINE color *New Orleans Magazine* v51 no1 p72 N 2016

Golden Opportunity: Pair gold and green for an enviable interior *New Orleans Homes & Lifestyles* v20 no4 p100 Aut 2017

In the Spirit color *New Orleans Magazine* v51 no12 p46 O 2017

Cameraperson (Film)

HUMAN PRESENCE S. KLAWANS *Nation* v303 no17 p36 O 24 2016

Cameras

360° CAMERAS color *Popular Mechanics* p80 D 2016/Ja 2017

DIGITIZED MENAGERIE R. H. Shea color *National Geographic* v231 no5 p8 My 2017

FROM OUR READERS G. Gladfelter, A. Cugnini et al *Sky & Telescope* v134 no1 p6 Jl 2017

GARMIN VIRB ULTRA 30 D. Canet color *Cycle World* v56 no7 p22 Ag 2017

Get Your Kicks... D. KNOWLES *USA Today Magazine* v146 no2866 p74 Jl 2017

Hardware Update Is Available K. SINTUMUANG color *Esquire* p74 BigBlackBook

How to choose the right camera for the eclipse M. E. Bakich color *Astronomy* v45 no4 p50 Ap 2017

How to Shoot Great Video T. Sullivan chart color *Consumer Reports* v82 no5 p18 My 2017

INSPECTION CAMERAS: MECHANIC'S BORESCOPE HAS ENDLESS USES D. Mowitz *Successful Farming* v115 no6 p30 Ap 2017

Make Your Camera a Tool D. Owen cartoon *Popular Mechanics* p102 Je 2017

New Wave S. BAHR color *Indianapolis Monthly* v42 no2 p31 O 2017

Trigger Trash D. GEORGE *Idaho Magazine* v16 no6 p6 Mr 2017

Cameras—Design & construction

THE 360-Degree Selfie E. WOYKE color *MIT Technology Review* v120 no2 p36 Mr/Ap 2017

Cameras—Equipment & supplies—Evaluation

OUR PICKS color *Popular Photography* v81 no1 p14 Ja/F 2017

Cameras—Evaluation

A 360-DEGREE VIEW color *Flying* v144 no8 p13 Ag 2017

The ASI 1600MC Cooled Camera J. Horne *Sky & Telescope* v133 no4 p58 Ap 2017

The Camera That Makes Movies for You D. DUBNO cartoon color *Popular Mechanics* p20 Ap 2017

DOCK BOX *Sea Magazine* v109 no1 p28 Ja 2017

FETISH MATINEE IDOL T. MOYNIHAN color *Wired* v25 no5 p43 My 2017

Gadgets for the Edge of the World A. George color *Popular Mechanics* p46 Mr 2017

GEARHEAD A. DAVIES color *Wired* v25 no3 p34 Mr 2017

Gear of the Year color *Popular Photography* v80 no11 p56 D 2016

Gear P. Nielsen color *Sail* v48 no8 p28 Ag 2017

Get the Shot L. ALBANESE and J. SCHNEIDER color *Backpacker* p61 Je 2017

GoPro cartoon color *Snowboarder* v29 no4 p113 D 2016

HAPPY MEDIUM P. Ryan color *Popular Photography* v80 no11 p14 D 2016

HOLIDAY ON ICE color *Forbes* v198 no7 p65 N 29 2016

LUCIDCAM: STEREOSCOPIC 3D VR CREATION COMES TO THE MASSES J. DOVE color *Macworld - Digital Edition* v34 no10 p102 O 2017

MallinCarrVs SkyRaider DS2.3 Plus: This device promises to be three cameras in one convenient package R. Mollise *Sky & Telescope* v134 no4 p58 O 2017

Needle Camera M. Belfiore bw color *Bloomberg Businessweek* no4512 p35 F 20 2017

NEW PRODUCTS color *Astronomy* v45 no3 p67 Mr 2017

New Product Showcase *Sky & Telescope* v132 no6 p64 D 2016

NEW PRODUCT SHOWCASE *Sky & Telescope* v134 no1 p66 Jl 2017

The No-Frills, Full-Fun Snapshot Is Back A. Fitzpatrick and K. Bachor color *Time* v190 no4 p52 Jl 24 2017

ONE OF A KIND P. Ryan color diag *Popular Photography* v80 no11 p72 D 2016

PLUG 'N' PLAY D. Canet color *Cycle World* v56 no1 p17 Ja/F 2017

Power Play: Amplify your next adventure with these cutting-edge outdoor gadgets R. HORJUS color *Backpacker* p45 S 2017

SKY EYE A. Ryder color *Popular Photography* v81 no1 p18 Ja/F 2017

SOLUTIONS chart color *Horse & Rider* v56 no1 p20 Ja 2017

Star Quality L. BECKETT color *Power & Motoryacht* v33 no4 p46 Ap 2017

A STAR'S TURN M. Leuchter color *Popular Photography* v81 no1 p64 Ja/F 2017

TIME EXPOSURE bw color *Popular Photography* v80 no11 p82 D 2016

TOP THREE: TRICK SHOTS B. ROSE color *Wired* v25 no7 p44 Jl 2017

WHY WAIT? color *Popular Photography* v80 no11 p16 D 2016

YEAR'S END color *Popular Photography* v80 no11 p10 D 2016

Cameras—History

The Golden Age of the Instant Camera... Just Got Started F. Woodward bw color *GQ: Gentlemen's Quarterly* v97 no3 p70 Mr 2017

Cameras—Software

WHAT'S NEW AT THE APP STORE color *Macworld - Digital Edition* v34 no8 p79 Ag 2017

Cameron, Averil

THE LAW ACCORDING TO JUSTINIAN *History Today* v67 no8 p91 Ag 2017

Mount Sinai *History Today* v66 no10 p64 O 2016

Cameron, Claire

The new Neanderthals B. BETHUNE color *Maclean's* v130 no4 p68 My 2017

Cameron, Dove, 1996-

Disney's Next Teen Queen M. Snetiker color *Entertainment Weekly* no1474/1475 p106 Jl 21-28 2017

Cameron, Eleanor, 1912-1997

A Boy Becomes a Writer J. FINDER *Publishers Weekly* v264 no21 p96 My 22 2017

Cameron, Erin K.

Higher predation risk for insect prey at low latitudes and eleva-

tions graph *Science* v356 no6339 p742 My 19 2017

Cameron, James

Bill Paxton color *Time* v189 no9 p14 Mr 13 2017

Cameron, James, 1954-—Interviews

TERMINATOR 2: JUDGMENT DAY 3D C. Collis color *Entertainment Weekly* no1480 p34 S 1 2017

Cameron, Kevin

BIG color *Cycle World* v56 no5 p68 Je 2017

CHOOSING MATERIALS color *Cycle World* v56 no8 p20 S 2017

DADDY, WHAT'S A CARBURETOR? color *Cycle World* v56 no10 p22 N 2017

DYNAMIC CHANGES ATHARLEY-DAVIDSON: ADIOS, DYNA! color *Cycle World* v56 no9 p30 O 2017

GREAT EXPECTATIONS *Cycle World* v56 no9 p28 O 2017

HONORING BURT MUNRO, CELEBRATING SPEED bw color *Cycle World* v56 no10 p52 N 2017

HOW DID WE GET HERE? diag *Cycle World* v56 no7 p52 Ag 2017

INDIAN THROWS DOWN THE GLOVE color *Cycle World* v55 no11 p26 D 2016

NOT SO FAST *Cycle World* v56 no3 p28 Ap 2017

ON BEING A FAN color *Cycle World* v56 no1 p58 Ja/F 2017

RUBBER REVOLUTION *Cycle World* v55 no11 p24 D 2016

Service color *Cycle World* v56 no10 p66 N 2017

SERVICE color *Cycle World* v56 no7 p54 Ag 2017

SIMPLE AND STRAIGHT-FORWARD *Cycle World* v56 no2 p26 Mr 2017

SUZUKI'S NEW SWORLD [Cover story] color *Cycle World* v55 no10 p30 N 2016

THEN AND NOW *Cycle World* v55 no10 p24 N 2016

THE TIRE REVOLUTION SPREADS *Cycle World* v56 no7 p28 Ag 2017

TOAST *Cycle World* v56 no1 p22 Ja/F 2017

TWO-STROKES LIVE ON *Cycle World* v56 no4 p34 My 2017

THE VERSATILE MOTORCYCLE *Cycle World* v56 no6 p27 Jl 2017

WHAT IS THE FOUR-STROKE CYCLE? color *Cycle World* v56 no5 p30 Je 2017

WHERE IS WORLD SUPERBIKE GOING? color *Cycle World* v56 no9 p50 O 2017

WILL KTM'S CLEAN TWO-STROKE MAKE IT TO THE STREET? color *Cycle World* v56 no8 p14 S 2017

Cameron, Kim

Happy Workplaces Can Also Be Candid Workplaces *Harvard Business Review Digital Articles* p2 My 31 2016

Proof That Positive Work Cultures Are More Productive *Harvard Business Review Digital Articles* p2 D 1 2015

Cameron, Marc

Field of Fire *Publishers Weekly* v263 no48 p50 N 28 2016

Cameron, Peter John

A Re-Appreciation: The Imitation of Christ color *America* v216 no3 p36 F 6 2017

CAMERON, SILVER DONALD

Treasured ISLANDS color map *Canadian Geographic* v135 no6 p44 D 2015

Cameron-Bure, Candace, 1976-

Fuller House A. Bacle, K. Connolly et al *Entertainment Weekly* no1482/1483 p106 S 22 2017

Cameroon

A TALE OF Two Christmases I. Mbue cartoon color *Good Housekeeping* v263 no6 p81 D 2016

Camerota, Alisyn

Candid Camerota [Cover story] M. BODGAS color *Working Mother* v40 no4 p20 O/N 2017

Camhi, Leslie

Avant Guards color *Vogue* v207 no10 p190 O 2017

Being Bardot bw *Vogue* v206 no11 p100 N 2016

Borderlands color *Vogue* v207 no9 p620 S 2017

Face TIME color *Vogue* v206 no12 p202 D 2016

MODESTY BLAZES! color *Vogue* v207 no7 p90 Jl 2017

Staying Power color *Vogue* v207 no11 p212 N 2017

Camille, Alice

Beginner's mind color *U.S. Catholic* v82 no1 p47 Ja 2017

Be the peace il *U.S. Catholic* v81 no12 p47 D 2016

Brave new world color *U.S. Catholic* v82 no4 p47 Ap 2017

Composition notes: The New Testament letters give us a window into the early church color *U.S. Catholic* v82 no10 p47 O 2017

Faith in the balance color *U.S. Catholic* v82 no7 p47 Jl 2017

Famines, fasts, and feasts il *U.S. Catholic* v82 no6 p47 Je 2017

Forge ahead! color *U.S. Catholic* v82 no5 p47 My 2017

Hold your lamp high color *U.S. Catholic* v82 no11 p47 N 2017

Is the Bible infallible? color *U.S. Catholic* v81 no11 p49 N 2016

Jesus is the question: Knowing the 'Catholic answer' does little good if we're not asking the right questions color *U.S. Catholic* v82 no9 p47 S 2017

Strong and unwavering color *U.S. Catholic* v82 no3 p47 Mr 2017

Was Jesus a refugee? color *U.S. Catholic* v82 no8 p49 Ag 2017

Were women at the Last Supper? color *U.S. Catholic* v82 no4 p49 Ap 2017

What's new? The Eucharist may not immediately transform the faithful into better Christians, but stick around for a lifetime and see what happens il *U.S. Catholic* v82 no8 p47 Ag 2017

When the sky falls color *U.S. Catholic* v81 no11 p47 N 2016

Where and who you are color *U.S. Catholic* v82 no1 p12 Ja 2017

Why was Mary a virgin? *U.S. Catholic* v81 no12 p49 D 2016

The word on women il *U.S. Catholic* v82 no2 p47 F 2017

Caminero, Alberto

How infection can incite sensitivity to food diag *Science* v356 no6333 p29 Ap 7 2017

Camino, Micaela

Forest conservation: Remember Gran Chaco bibl color *Science* v355 no6324 p465 F 3 2017

Camino de Santiago de Compostela

The Hardest Blessing R. Collins color *Commonweal* v144 no10 p39 Je 2 2017

Caminos, Ximena

The X Factor D. KAZANJIAN color *Vogue* v206 no12 p126 D 2016

Cammack, Angela

College Promise: Pathway to the 21 Century *Change* v48 no6 p6 N/D 2016

Cammisa, Jason

2018 Volkswagen Atlas color *Motor Trend* v69 no8 p26 Ag 2017

B6 VS M6 chart color *Motor Trend* v69 no4 p80 Ap 2017

The finalist round color *Motor Trend* v69 no1 p64 Ja 2017

FIVE-SEAT FURY color *Motor Trend* v69 no6 p54 Je 2017

the leftovers... [Cover story] chart color *Motor Trend* v69 no4 p36 Ap 2017

SHOOTING BRAKE chart color *Motor Trend* v69 no7 p98 Jl 2017

SUPERCAR SLAYER SEEKS WORTHY OPPONENT chart color *Motor Trend* v68 no12 p52 D 2016

Camosy, Charles

A fearless look at the tragedy of abortion color *America* v216 no5 p42 Mr 6 2017

Sex and the Catholic college campus *America* v217 no6 p55 S 18 2017

Camouflage (Biology)

AN EYE FOR CAMOUFLAGE E. MASTROIANNI color *Discover* v38 no5 p9 Je 2017

Find the Hidden Animals color *National Geographic Kids* no475 p31 N 2017

Camouflage (Military science)

NEW HIDES color *Outdoor Life* v224 no6 p42 Ag 2017

Camouflage (Sporting goods)

KRYLON CAMO T. FREEL and A. McKEAN bw color *Outdoor Life* v224 no5 p94 Je/Jl 2017

Camouflage (Textiles)

backstory color *New Republic* v247 no11 p64 N 2016

A NEW LOOK: Langford farmer develops lighter camouflage pattern *South Dakota Magazine* v33 no3 p14 S/O 2017

TECH THROWBACK N. KREBS bw color *Outdoor Life* v224 no2 p12 F/Mr 2017

Camp, Kate

As you are: logan killen interiors renews northshore house lo reflect couples personalities and lifestyle L. CUTRONE *New Orleans Homes & Lifestyles* v20 no3 p46 Summ 2017

Camp, W. Hunter II

POWER [Cover story] color *Christian Century* v134 no1 p22 Ja 4 2017

Camp stoves

Get int Gear: Everything You Need for Your Next Camping Trip color *GQ: Gentlemen's Quarterly* v97 no5 p122 My 2017

The Great Escape B. HANSEN-BUNDY color *GQ: Gentlemen's Quarterly* v97 no5 p114 My 2017

Camp stoves—Evaluation

BIOLITE CAMPSTOVE K. Dupzyk color *Popular Mechanics* p18 Ap 2017

GEAR FOR THE LONG HAUL G. MILLIKEN color *Popular Science* p18 Ja/F 2017

Campagna, Dean R.

UBE2O remodels the proteome during terminal erythroid differentiation diag *Science* v357 no6350 p471 Ag 4 2017

Campagna, Soren

WALTZ THIS WAY A. BRANDT *Cincinnati Magazine* v50 no3 p36 D 2016

Campaign debates

MILLENNIALISM J. Cobb cartoon *New Yorker* v92 no32 p33 O 10 2016

TALKING HEADS A. Marantz cartoon *New Yorker* v92 no32 p36 O 10 2016

Campaign debates—United States

How to talk (down) to the town-hall voter S. FESCHUK color *Maclean's* v129 no41 p61 O 17 2016

Trump Exposed J. WALSH il *Nation* v303 no16 p3 O 17 2016

Campaign funds

Governing in the Dark A. Greenblatt *Governing* v30 no9 p10 Je 2017

'NATIONAL LAMPOON''S PRESIDENTIAL VACATION G. CARTER *Vanity Fair* v59 no10 p80 O 2017

A party with a cover charge J. MARKUSOFF color diag *Maclean's* p13 Je 2017

Swamp Creature A. KROLL cartoon *Mother Jones* v42 no1 p16 Ja/F 2017

TRUMP'S MONEY MAN J. MAYER cartoon color *New Yorker* v93 no6 p34 Mr 27 2017

Campaign funds—Canada

Big money, big problems N. MACDONALD color *Maclean's* v130 no2 p32 Mr 2017

Campaign funds—United States

How to Win Congress With a Polar Bear Outfit, Cheez-Its, and a Bunch of iPads Z. Mider color *Bloomberg Businessweek* no4495 p20 O 17 2016

Sheldon Adelson's Not-So-Winning Year C. Palmeri, B. Allison et al bw *Bloomberg Businessweek* no4530 p40 Jl 17 2017

Campaign management

BOOMING S. Marikar cartoon *New Yorker* v92 no37 p33 N 14 2016

Campaign management—Officials & employees

How to make a candidate M. PATRIQUIN and C. GILLIS color *Maclean's* no1 p26 F 17 2017

Campaign management—United States

TAMING TRUMP R. LIZZA cartoon *New Yorker* v92 no33 p30 O 17 2016

Campaign promises

Promises, Promises *Bloomberg Businessweek* no4499 p30 N 14 2016

Campaign Speech (Music)

The Bullseye M. Snetiker color *Entertainment Weekly* no1438 p72 N 4 2016

CAMPANO, GABRIELLE

The Visual Food Encyclopedia *America* v215 no11 p30 O 17 2016

Campano, Gerald

THE REAL SUMMER EXPERIENCE: Going beyond the vacation essay to foster deeper school-community relationships *Literacy Today (2411-7862)* v35 no1 p8 Jl/Ag 2017

Campanula rotundifolia

WHERE THE WILD ORCHID GROWS A. McGIVNEY *Arizona Highways* v93 no8 p38 Ag 2017

CAMPBELL, ADAM

PICK A MOVE! ANY MOVE! [Cover story] bw *Women's Health* v13 no10 p140 D 2016

CAMPBELL, ALEX

4 Linux projects for newbies and intermediate users cartoon color *PCWorld* v35 no2 p184 F 2017

4 ways to block political posts on Facebook color *PCWorld* v35 no2 p189 F 2017

Confederation smackdown! *Maclean's* v130 no3 p17 Ap 2017

Dealer beware color *Maclean's* v130 no4 p46 My 2017

Down on the border color *Maclean's* v130 no7 p24 Ag 2017

DRESSING THE DUCHESS OF CAMBRIDGE color *Maclean's* v129 no40 p54 O 10 2016

Eureka in the Arctic color *Maclean's* v130 no3 p18 Ap 2017

Framed by fortune bw color *Maclean's* v129 no50 p16 D 19 2016

FRIENDS IN HIGH PLACES color *Maclean's* p32 Je 2017

GOVERNMENT DREAMS AND CAVIAR WISHES color *Maclean's* v129 no43 p18 O 31 2016

THE GREAT-GRAND-DAUGHTERS OF CONFEDERATION [Cover story] bw color *Maclean's* v130 no6 p46 Jl 2017

Hating on Canadian art *Maclean's* v130 no4 p12 My 2017

INSPIRATION, REWARDED color *Maclean's* v130 no10 p74 N 2017

Little monks of Little Sands color *Maclean's* v130 no7 p16 Ag 2017

Lost and broken [Cover story] color *Maclean's* v130 no9 p24 O 2017

The luckiest man in Canada color *Maclean's* v130 no2 p14 Mr 2017

Men in tights color *Maclean's* v129 no43 p63 O 31 2016

A moment of painful truth color *Maclean's* v130 no2 p18 Mr 2017

Ottawa's slimiest problem color *Maclean's* v130 no9 p18 O 2017

Retelling a tragedy bw *Maclean's* v129 no51/52 p33 D 26 2016

Town for sale: needs work *Maclean's* v130 no2 p13 Mr 2017

A Western weekend chart color *Maclean's* v130 no2 p60 Mr 2017

Whose kids are these? *Maclean's* p15 Je 2017

Campbell, Michele

It's Always the Husband *Publishers Weekly* v264 no10 p40 Mr 6 2017

CAMPBELL, MORGAN

African-Americans and the Diamond color *Ebony* v72 no6 p88 Ap/My 2017

UNEVEN PLAYING FIELD color *Ebony* v72 no5 p92 Mr 2017

Campbell, N. J.

Found Audio bw *Publishers Weekly* v264 no15 p46 Ap 10 2017

Campbell, Naomi, 1970-

Forever Young J. Amay color *Ebony* v72 no9 p92 Jl/Ag 2017

Icons color *Time* v189 no16/17 p122 My 1-8 2017

In the Navy E. Wilson color *InStyle* v23 no12 p66 N 2016

Skirts vs. Skins E. Wilson color *InStyle* v23 no12 p64 N 2016

Campbell, Norie—Interviews

Commitment to Diversity Puts Women in the Lead color *Maclean's* v130 no3 p57 Ap 2017

Campbell, Peter J.

Mutational signatures associated with tobacco smoking in human cancer bibl graph *Science* v354 no6312 p618 N 4 2016

Campbell, Phil

Drawn Away B. D. SMITH *Indianapolis Monthly* p49 F 2017

CAMPBELL, ROBERT

The Power of Persuasion color *Architectural Record* v205 no8 p90 Ag 2017

Scenes from a Lost World *American Scholar* v86 no2 p102 Spr 2017

Campbell, S. L.

A Fermi-degenerate three-dimensional optical lattice clock color diag graph *Science* v357 no6359 p90 O 6 2017

Campbell, Scott D.

Striking the right chord bibl bw color *Science* v354 no6311 p423 O 28 2016

Campbell, Shannon

CAMPBELLS CRUSH IT AT KOH M. EMERY and E. MILLER color *Dirt Sports + Off-Road* v51 no7 p12 Jl 2017

FROM NAPKIN NOTES TO WORLD PHENOMENA C. COLLARD color *Dirt Sports + Off-Road* v51 no7 p20 Jl 2017

Campbell, Thomas P. (Thomas Patrick), 1962-

The MET'S POWER FAILURE W. D. COHAN color *Vanity Fair* v59 no5 p122 Ap 2017

WHAT BROKE THE MET? B. KACHKA img *New York* v50 no8 p44 Ap 17 2017

Campbell, Thomas—Interviews

THOMAS CAMPBELL 47, FILMMAKER/PHOTOGRAPHER/ARTIST M. Shaw color *Surfer* v57 no13 p34 Mr 2017

Campbell, Veronica

ART ADVOCATES color *Christianity Today* v60 no8 p21 O 2016

Campbell Soup Co.

Firsts & Lasts O. B. Waxman color diag *Time* v188 no25-26 p23 D 19 2016 Double Issue

The Key to Campbell Soup's Turnaround? Civility C. Porath and D. R. Conant *Harvard Business Review Digital Articles* p2 O 5 2017

Campbell-Staton, Shane C.

Winter storms drive rapid phenotypic, regulatory, and genomic shifts in the green anole lizard graph *Science* v357 no6350 p495 Ag 4 2017

Campbell Winters, Kandy

THE BEST PLAYHOUSE *Idaho Magazine* v17 no1 p49 Ja 2017

Campeau, Louis-Charles

A multifunctional catalyst that stereoselectively assembles prodrugs diag *Science* v356 no6336 p426 Ap 28 2017

Campers (Persons)

THE DESCENT D. SMITH color *Climbing* no349 p80 N 2016

Campf, Shelley

The Trainer Certification Program Moves From Tortoise to Hare *In Stride* v12 no3 p8 My 2017

Campfire (Poem)

TWO POEMS A. Amsterdam *Harper's Magazine* no2007 p67 Ag 2017

Campfires

Indoor S'mores color *Good Housekeeping* v264 no2 p139 F 2017

Campillo, Robin

Through the Darkness color *Film Comment* v53 no4 p6 Jl/Ag 2017

Camping

See also

Backpacking

Better With Two J. Fiedler color *Parents* v92 no7 p13 Jl 2017

BORN TO BE WILD D. OKO *Texas Monthly* v45 no4 p102 Ap 2017

Branding Time Bob color *American Cowboy* v23 no6 p8 Ap/My 2017

CABIN LOOP K. VAUGHN *Arizona Highways* v92 no7 p32 Jl 2016

CAMP Grandma ...AND GRANDPAA. TOO P. MEAD color *Cabin Living* p120 Ja/F 2017

Campspo! A. KOZOLCHYK color *Women's Health* v14 no4 p130 My 2017

Champ Out in Church *British Heritage Travel* v38 no3 p9 My/Je 2017

Change of Pace Q. HARPER color *Backpacker* p24 My 2017

Connecting People & Nature L. DiBetta *New York State Conservationist* v72 no1 p15 Ag 2017

Cool off color *Backpacker* p18 Ag 2017

DAZE OF THE RUT B. Heavey cartoon *Field & Stream* v121 no6 p90 N 2016

The Dragon's Lair V. LILLO color map *Backpacker* p16 Ag 2017

Get Out There M. BRUNE *Sierra* v101 no4 p4 Jl/Ag 2016

Goat Lake Loop, Gifford-Pinchot National Forest, Washington [Cover story] T. VANDERMOLEN diag *Backpacker* p96 Ag 2017

Go Camping, Sleep Better V. TWEED color *Better Nutrition* v79 no6 p10 Je 2017

Gone Glamping R. S. Frazier color *Health* v31 no5 p54 Je 2017

HAPPY CAMPERS J. Haddad *Virginia Living* v15 no1 p23 D 2016

HOW TO GET AWAY color *Popular Mechanics* p65 Mr 2017

In Praise of Smallness: Fishing the Little Creeks L. TANNER *Idaho Magazine* v16 no8 p6 My 2017

IRREGULAR JOE J. ARTERBURN cartoon *Outdoor Life* v224 no4 p78 My 2017

"I WANT TO GO BIKE CAMPING." R. Koch and B. STRICKLAND color *Bicycling* v58 no3 p24 Ap 2017

Laundering My History: For a Cleaner America S. CARR *Idaho Magazine* v16 no11 p54 Ag 2017

Mountains to Sea R. WICHELNS color map *Backpacker* v45 no1 p17 Ja 2017

A New Scouting Experience S. A. CATOVIC *Islamic Horizons* v45 no6 p38 N/D 2016

On Two Wheels N. YORK *Idaho Magazine* v16 no6 p24 Mr 2017

Pioneer Days K. PETERSON diag *Backpacker* p22 Je 2017

A PLACE IN THE SUN M. SIMMS color *O, The Oprah Magazine* p130 S 2017

RIVER TALES D. A. WOOD color *Missouri Life* v44 no4 p10 Je 2017

ROLLING WITH IT J. Berger color *Sunset* v239 no1 p19 Jl 2017

UNDER THE STARS AND UNDER THE RADAR J. D. TUCCILLE color *Reason* v49 no3 p14 Jl 2017

THE WILDERNESS WAY T. E. Nickens cartoon *Field & Stream* v122 no1 p26 My 2017

WILD THINGS I. Edwards color *Sunset* v238 no5 p8 My 2017

WORK YOUR BODY CLOCK: A USER'S MANUAL H. Levine color *Health* v31 no7 p109 S 2017

Camping instruction

Keep Your Cool in the Cold il *Backpacker* v45 no2 p43 Mr 2017

Left Behind O. DWYER *Backpacker* p20 N 2017

the play list color il map *Backpacker* p6 N 2017

Camping trailers

INTO THE BLUE I. Edwards color *Sunset* v239 no1 p8 Jl 2017

Camping trailers—Evaluation

TOW TAPPERS J. Chamberlain color *Sunset* v239 no1 p32 Jl 2017

Camping with dogs

Canine Campers N. B. McGough and P. S. York color *Southern Living* v52 no7 p35 Jl 2017

Camping—Arizona

Goodnight Moonscape *Arizona Highways* v93 no8 p5 Ag 2017

Camping—California

FROM BACKYARD TO BACKCOUNTRY [Cover story] E. Kwak-hefferan, C. Ferreira et al color *Sunset* v238 no5 p60 My 2017

Camping—Equipment & supplies

See also

Tents

Camp Season on a Budget *Parks & Recreation* v52 no4 p52 Ap 2017

FROM BACKYARD TO BACKCOUNTRY [Cover story] E. Kwak-hefferan, C. Ferreira et al color *Sunset* v238 no5 p60 My 2017

PACK-AND-GO CHECKLISTS B. DAVIS color *Trail Rider* v29 no3 p62 Ap 2017

Portable Hydropower O. Kharif cartoon color *Bloomberg Businessweek* no4493 p45 O 3 2016

Camping—Equipment & supplies—Evaluation

GEAR FOR THE LONG HAUL G. MILLIKEN color *Popular Science* p18 Ja/F 2017

Camping—Research

This Just In J. Zorthian *Time* v189 no6 p21 F 20 2017

Camping—United States

BASE CAMP *Sierra* v102 no1 p69 Ja/F 2017

Campion, Jane, 1954——Interviews

Diving into the Wreck N. Davis color *Film Comment* v53 no5 p10 S/O 2017

Campisi, Judith

Senescent intimal foam cells are deleterious at all stages of atherosclerosis bibl *Science* v354 no6311 p472 O 28 2016

Camplin, Jamie

From signs in clay tablets to digital data *History Today* v66 no10 p59 O 2016

LEXICON TOTIUS ANGLICITATIS *History Today* v67 no5 p96 My 2017

Campolo, Bart

BEYOND UNBELIEF M. OPPENHEIMER *New York Times Magazine* p42 Ja 1 2017

Campolo, Tony

Why I left, Why I Stayed: Conversations on Christianity Between an Evangelical Father and His Humanist Son D. CHIVERS *Humanist* v77 no5 p44 S/O 2017

Campolongo, Susan

Multiple jobholding in states in 2015 bibl chart color map *Monthly Labor Review* p1 F 2017

Campos, António

Christine L. Greenblatt color *Entertainment Weekly* no1436/1437 p85 O 21 2016

Campos, Francisco

Teaching personal initiative beats traditional training in boosting small business in West Africa chart graph *Science* v357 no6357 p1287 S 22 2017

Campos, Luis

Crops on demand bw *Science* v354 no6313 p713 N 11 2016

Our synthetic moment color *Science* v355 no6330 p1136 Mr 17 2017

CAMPOSARCEIZ, AHIMSA

Conserving the World's Megafauna and Biodiversity: The Fierce Urgency of Now *BioScience* v67 no3 p197 Mr 2017

Saving the World's Terrestrial Megafauna color *BioScience* v66 no10 p807 O 1 2016

Camps

See also

Refugee camps

Tourist camps, hostels, etc.

70 YEARS OF MAGIC AT DEC SUMMER CAMPS C. McLaughlin *New York State Conservationist* v72 no2 p12 O 2017

CAMP RZR WEST M. EMERY color *Dirt Sports + Off-Road* v51 no5 p10 My 2017

DITCH THE JITTERS! J. YOUNG *Indianapolis Monthly* v40 no7 p86 Mr 2017

DIVE IN THE DEEP END L. ROBERTS *Indianapolis Monthly* v40 no7 p88 Mr 2017

Off-Grid in Northern Ontario F. SIGURDSSON color *Cabin Living* p22 S 2017

Open Book J. WILLIAMS *New York Times Book Review* p4 O 2 2016

A PLACE TO GET AWAY W. CURTIS and W. L. Duncan color *Yankee* p92 My/Je 2017

Setting the Table for a Successful Summer at South Burlington Recreation and Parks H. Baker and B. Leonard *Parks & Recreation* v51 no12 p28 D 2016

So You Want to Be a (Social Media) Star D. DEVOSS color *Weekly Standard* v22 no46 p26 Ag 14 2017

Summer Camp on Capitol Hill: Play On to Protect Programming at Parks M. Acquino *Parks & Recreation* v52 no8 p60 Ag 2017

That's Outrageous! color *Reader's Digest* v189 no1131 p84 Je 2017

UPCOMING IN 2017 *Washingtonian Magazine* v52 no2 p218 N 2016

Camps for children

CAMPS color *New Orleans Magazine* v51 no5 p122 Mr 2017

Camps for girls

CAMPS color *New Orleans Magazine* v51 no5 p122 Mr 2017

Camps—Food service

TRAILBLAZERS E. Johnson color *Sunset* v238 no5 p74 My 2017

WILD THINGS I. Edwards color *Sunset* v238 no5 p8 My 2017

Camp sites, facilities, etc.

See also

Tourist camps, hostels, etc.

Before CAMP DAVID R. SKLAREW *Washingtonian Magazine* v53 no1 p101 O 2017

The Big Pictures: THE WHITE MOUNTAINS *Arizona Highways* v96 no7 p18 Jl 2017

Pitch the Perfect Camp color *Backpacker* p33 My 2017

The Shady Dell K. VAUGHN *Arizona Highways* v93 no9 p16 S 2017

UNDER THE STARS AND UNDER THE RADAR J. D. TUCCILLE color *Reason* v49 no3 p14 Jl 2017

THE WILD CONGAREE G. M. PETERS *National Parks* v91 no4 p44 Fall 2017

Camp sites, facilities, etc.—Michigan

Oh! The Stories They Tell M. R. JOHNSON *Cabin Living* p5 S 2017

Camry automobile

It's Alive! R. Ceppos color *Car & Driver* v63 no4 p104 O 2017

Camry automobile—Evaluation

BOLDLY GOING F. Markus chart color *Motor Trend* v69 no9 p80 S 2017

Camunas-Soler, Joan

Experimental measurement of binding energy, selectivity, and allostery using fluctuation theorems bibl graph *Science* v355 no6323 p412 Ja 27 2017

Can-Am (Company)

MOSSY OAK DEFENDER B. SMITH color *Dirt Sports + Off-Road* v51 no5 p24 My 2017

X-FACTOR TURBO RS B. SMITH color *Dirt Sports + Off-Road*

v51 no2 p48 F 2017

Can I Get a Witness? The Gospel of James Baldwin (Theatrical production)
Stoking the Fire H. Als cartoon *New Yorker* v92 no40 p13 D 5 2016

Can You Forgive Her? (Theatrical production)
THE THEATRE *New Yorker* v93 no14 p10 My 22 2017

Canaanites
DNA reveals Canaanites' fate M. TEMMING color *Science News* v192 no3 p8 S 2 2017
Great Is Your Faith! M. Simone *America* v217 no3 p52 Ag 7 2017

Canada
Grandfather D. COLES *Walrus* v13 no10 p61 D 2016
The Quiz T. BALAZO *Maclean's* v130 no2 p72 Mr 2017
Vacation! [Cover story] color *Reader's Digest* v189 no1131 p66 Je 2017
WHERE'S THIS? color *Canadian Geographic* v135 no6 p77 D 2015

Canada, Nathan
Pressure-Testing Equine Leg Wraps S. Wenholz color *Practical Horseman* v45 no1 p69 Ja 2017

Canada. Forest Service
Wildfire watch J. PEARCE and H. WILSON map *Canadian Geographic* v137 no5 p30 S/O 2017

Canada goose
Don't Call Him Goofy D. AGUIRRE *Idaho Magazine* v16 no2 p43 N 2016

Canada Mortgage & Housing Corp.
WHAT IT TOOK TO TAME CMHC K. CARMICHAEL color *Maclean's* v130 no4 p53 My 2017

Canada. National Capital Commission
A NEW HOME FOR THE RCGS: 50 SUSSEX N. Walker color *Canadian Geographic* v136 no6 p74 D 2016

Canada. National Energy Board
HOW TO KILL A PIPELINE C. GILLIS color *Maclean's* v129 no51/52 p20 D 26 2016
Why BC Is Standing Up to Kinder Morgan D. Cayley-Daoust *Alternatives Journal (AJ) - Canada's Environmental Voice* v42 no2 p10 2016

Canada Science & Technology Museum
CLIMATE CHANGE AND THE ECONOMY N. Walker diag *Canadian Geographic* v137 no2 p69 Mr/Ap 2017

Canada—Anniversaries, etc.
Second to none *Maclean's* v130 no6 p6 Jl 2017

Canada—Armed Forces
Being trans in the military Z. MCKNIGHT color *Maclean's* v130 no9 p17 O 2017

Canada—Armed Forces—History
The battles inside the battle B. BETHUNE bw *Maclean's* v130 no3 p54 Ap 2017

Canada—Description & travel
BEAUTY STOLE THE ROYAL SHOW P. TREBLE color *Maclean's* v129 no41 p46 O 17 2016
BRINGING HERITAGE TO LIFE color *Walrus* v14 no7 p28 S 2017
Road to Everywhere N. RICHLER cartoon map *Walrus* v14 no6 p19 Jl/Ag 2017
SIERRA CLUB OUTINGS *Sierra* v101 no6 p52 N/D 2016

Canada—Economic conditions—21st century
Canada's rocky path ahead E. SOLOMON *Maclean's* no1 p10 F 17 2017

Canada—Economic policy
This one's on the house J. GEDDES color *Maclean's* v129 no45 p22 N 14 2016
THE UNEVEN JOURNEY TO THE NEW NORMAL E. SOLOMON color *Maclean's* v129 no45 p23 N 14 2016
WAITING FOR THE PAYOFF FROM BIGGER DEFICITS C. SORENSEN color *Maclean's* v129 no42 p16 O 24 2016

Canada—Economic conditions—1991-
Rough seas ahead for trade C. SORENSEN color *Maclean's* v129 no45 p40 N 14 2016
THE UNEVEN JOURNEY TO THE NEW NORMAL E. SOLOMON color *Maclean's* v129 no45 p23 N 14 2016

Canada—Emigration & immigration
GOOD NEWS color *Maclean's* v129 no41 p8 O 17 2016
THE PROBLEM WITH REFUGEES T. GLAVIN color *Maclean's* v130 no3 p34 Ap 2017

Canada—Emigration & immigration—Government policy
Canada's Brain Gain Strategy C. Matthews color *Fortune* v174 no6 p12 N 1 2016
The Merit System C. MALCOLM color *Weekly Standard* v23 no1 p11 S 11 2017
The true test of Canadianness T. GLAVIN chart color *Maclean's* v130 no6 p20 Jl 2017

Canada—Foreign economic relations
WHAT CHINA WANTS J. CASTALDO color *Maclean's* v130 no9 p67 O 2017

Canada—Foreign economic relations—United States
THE DAWN OF THE STRONGMAN ERA IS HERE E. SOLOMON color *Maclean's* v129 no48/49 p12 D 5 2016
Trade Fears Grip America's Northern Neighbor C. Goujard *Wilson Quarterly* p4 Spr 2017
What happens when the walls go up C. SORENSEN color *Maclean's* v129 no47 p34 N 28 2016

Canada—Foreign relations
China is no friend of ours T. GLAVIN *Maclean's* v130 no4 p10 My 2017
Rough Road Ahead? *Change* v82 no3 p26 Mr 2017

Canada—Foreign relations—United States
THE TRUE NORTH P. Lay *History Today* v67 no8 p3 Ag 2017

Canada—Geography
WHAT'S THIS? color *Canadian Geographic* v135 no6 p76 D 2015

Canada—History
Confederation smackdown! M. CAMPBELL *Maclean's* v130 no3 p17 Ap 2017
WHAT'S THIS? color *Canadian Geographic* v135 no6 p76 D 2015

Canada—Maps
The Great Canadian Song Map: Road Trip Edition H. WILSON color map *Canadian Geographic* v137 no4 p32 Jl/Ag 2017

Canada—Military relations
Quagmire A. R. KHAN color *Maclean's* v129 no45 p30 N 14 2016

Canada—News briefs
BAD NEWS color *Maclean's* v129 no50 p9 D 19 2016
GOOD NEWS color *Maclean's* v129 no50 p8 D 19 2016
WILDLIFE color *Canadian Geographic* v137 no2 p20 Mr/Ap 2017

Canada—Politics & government
Back to Basics A. COYNE color *Walrus* v14 no4 p32 My 2017
Dealer beware M. CAMPBELL color *Maclean's* v130 no4 p46 My 2017
The Quiz T. BALAZO color *Maclean's* v129 no50 p64 D 19 2016
The Wingman J. KAY *Walrus* v14 no3 p66 Ap 2017

Canada—Politics & government—21st century
Canada Punts on Electoral Reform *America* v216 no5 p8 Mr 6 2017
Canada's rocky path ahead E. SOLOMON *Maclean's* no1 p10 F 17 2017
JUSTIN TRUDEAU IS JUST NOT THAT INTO YOU A. KINGSTON color *Maclean's* v129 no51/52 p12 D 26 2016
JUSTIN TRUDEAU'S LONG GAME P. WELLS color *Maclean's* v130 no7 p36 Ag 2017
The last lines of defence J. GEDDES color *Maclean's* v130 no3 p22 Ap 2017
The Liberal lowlights J. GEDDES color *Maclean's* p29 Je 2017
More than just America's foil *Maclean's* v130 no2 p4 Mr 2017
OUTSIDE THE OTTAWA BUBBLE S. GILMORE color *Maclean's* p28 Je 2017
WHY FEAR AND DIVISION REMAIN UNDEFEATED A. DOMISE color *Maclean's* v129 no41 p11 O 17 2016

Canada—Politics & government—1867-
King among PMs S. AZZI and N. HILLMER bw chart color *Maclean's* v129 no41 p19 O 17 2016

Canada—Politics & government—1980-
CHILLY TIMES AHEAD FOR THE LIBERALS E. SOLOMON color *Maclean's* v129 no40 p12 O 10 2016
Some days, it just isn't #2016 S. PROUDFOOT color *Maclean's* v129 no45 p24 N 14 2016

Canada—Relations—United States
Wooing America N. TAYLOR-VAISEY color graph *Maclean's* v130 no8 p20 S 2017

Canada—Social conditions—21st century
MISPLACED PRIDE S. GILMORE color *Maclean's* v130 no6 p22 Jl 2017

Canada—Social life & customs
What it means to belong A. Chunilall color *Walrus* v14 no9 p12 N 2017

Canadeo, Anne
Knit to Kill color *Publishers Weekly* v264 no39 p85 S 25 2017

Canadian-American Border Region
A border runs through it A. ABEL color *Maclean's* v130 no7 p15 Ag 2017
Down on the border J. MARKUSOFF, N. MACDONALD et al color *Maclean's* v130 no7 p24 Ag 2017

Canadian-American Challenge Cup
2017 CAN-AM RACING TEAM AND X-TEAM CONTINGENCY PROGRAM color *Dirt Sports + Off-Road* v51 no8 p8 Ag 2017

Canadian arts
'I believe that Chanie Wenjak chose me' J. BOYDEN bw color *Maclean's* v129 no44 p16 N 7 2016

Canadian Broadcasting Corp.
What Is the CBC Good For? [Cover story] T. JOKINEN bw color *Walrus* v14 no7 p20 S 2017

Canadian coins
big picture color *Canadian Geographic* v137 no2 p10 Mr/Ap 2017
big picture color *Canadian Geographic* v137 no4 p12 Jl/Ag 2017

Canadian cooking
Kill What You Eat J. RICHLER color *Walrus* v14 no4 p15 My 2017

Canadian films—Exhibitions
Ten Facts about National Canadian Film Day 150 bw color *Walrus* v14 no3 p1 Ap 2017

Canadian history
The Quiz T. BALAZO color *Maclean's* v130 no6 p88 Jl 2017
Second to none *Maclean's* v130 no6 p6 Jl 2017
THE TRUE NORTH P. Lay *History Today* v67 no8 p3 Ag 2017

Canadian literature—History & criticism
Blinking like moles B. BETHUNE bw *Maclean's* v130 no8 p60 S 2017

Canadian national characteristics
The Back Page color *Maclean's* v130 no6 p90 Jl 2017
Dreams of Canada [Cover story] A. Abel color *Maclean's* v130 no6 p28 Jl 2017
The true test of Canadianness T. GLAVIN chart color *Maclean's* v130 no6 p20 Jl 2017

Canadian National Exhibition
Pop Chart R. Bruner, C. Lang et al color *Time* v190 no9 p60 S 4 2017

Canadian painting—Exhibitions
Dusting off some faces S. PROUDFOOT color *Maclean's* p16 Je 2017

Canadian provinces
COUNTRIES CLOSEST IN SIZE TO EACH PROVINCE J. KIRBY map *Maclean's* v130 no2 p15 Mr 2017

Canadian Rockies (B.C. & Alta.)
Cold Comfort M. HORJUS color *Backpacker* v45 no2 p24 Mr 2017

Canadian students—Foreign countries
BRIDGING THE EAST-WEST GAP [Cover story] J. DEHAAS color *Maclean's* v129 no44 p44 N 7 2016

Canadian Timberframes Ltd.—Awards
BEST ENTRY DOOR color *Timber Home Living* p27 2017 SpecialIssue

Canadian Wildlife Federation
Canada's 150th Nature Celebration color *Canadian Wildlife* v23 no1 p42 Mr/Ap 2017

Canadian women authors
THE PROPHET OF DYSTOPIA R. MEAD cartoon color *New Yorker* v93 no9 p38 Ap 17 2017

Canadian women poets
Rupi Kaur: Bestselling Poet C. Kirch *Publishers Weekly* v263 no52 p28 D 19 2016

Canadian history, 1867-
MACLEAN'S ON CANADA bw color *Maclean's* v130 no6 p85 Jl 2017

Canadians
Sketchbook J. Tamaki *New York Times Book Review* p27 Ag 20 2017
Trailblazers bw color *Maclean's* v130 no6 p64 Jl 2017

Canadians—Attitudes
150 YEARS THE CANADA PROJECT [Cover story] color *Maclean's* v130 no6 p8 Jl 2017
Denial of a nation M. WILLIAMS chart color *Maclean's* v130 no6 p18 Jl 2017
Dreams of Canada [Cover story] A. Abel color *Maclean's* v130 no6 p28 Jl 2017
National anthems S. FESCHUK chart color *Maclean's* v130 no6 p14 Jl 2017
A SUGAR CUBE BESIDE A GALLON OF COFFEE F. PELLETIER chart color *Maclean's* v130 no6 p17 Jl 2017
What a delicious mess J. RICHLER chart color *Maclean's* v130 no6 p16 Jl 2017
Who we are P. WELLS chart color *Maclean's* v130 no6 p10 Jl 2017

Canadians—Employment
Old Growth, New Shoots A. MANDEL-CAMPBELL cartoon *Walrus* v13 no10 p44 D 2016

Canadians—Finance
Maxed Out [Cover story] R. Robin color *Walrus* v14 no5 p28 Je 2017

Canadians—Travel
State Secrets map *Canadian Geographic* v135 no6 p21 D 2015

Canados Yachts (Company)
Canados 808 Maximus J. Y. Wood color *Power & Motoryacht* v34 no11 p82 N 2017
NEW FROM THE ETERNAL CITY: AN ITALIAN BUILDER RECALLS GLORIES PAST FOR ITS LATEST MODEL NAME, AND GLORIES PRESENT FOR ITS DESIGN AND BUILD S. SHIBATA color *Sea Magazine* v109 no7 p6 Jl 2017

CANAL, EMILY
Shark Tank's Toothless Deals color graph *Forbes* v198 no7 p24 N 29 2016

Canal maintenance
Revisiting New York's Historic Canals on the Sailing Schooner Lois McClure E. Tichonuk *New York State Conservationist* v71 no6 p18 Je 2017

Canali SpA
THIS COAT'S A CINCH FOR FALL J. Roth color *Esquire* p55 S 2017

Canals—England
LIFE ON LONDON'S WATERWAYS S. Gutierrez *British Heritage Travel* v37 no6 p36 N/D 2016

Canals—Idaho
What Happens Next? After the Near Drowning S. CARR *Idaho Magazine* v16 no5 p54 F 2017

Canary Islands
Postcard From the Moon J. MILLER *In These Times* v41 no3 p42 Mr 2017

Cancer
See also
   Breast cancer
   Melanoma
2017 CANCER REPORT J. H. REDMOND *Cincinnati Magazine* p78 Je 2017
ALL ABOUT EVE L. Rodriguez color *Los Angeles Magazine* v62 no10 p156 O 2017

Cancer cells
Origins of lymphatic and distant metastases in human colorectal cancer K. Naxerova, J. G. Reiter et al diag graph *Science* v357 no6346 p55 Jl 7 2017
Reprogramming to resist K. Kelly and S. P. Balk bibl diag *Science* v355 no6320 p29 Ja 6 2017
Some cells survive attempted suicide T. HESMAN SAEY color *Science News* v191 no1 p10 Ja 21 2017

Cancer diagnosis
Cancer Moonshot Misses the Mark R. BAILEY color *Reason* v48 no9 p6 F 2017
CANCER'S INVISIBLE INJURY S. HELD color *Indianapolis Monthly* v42 no2 p88 O 2017
EAT, MEMORY D. Wong Louie *Harper's Magazine* no2007 p39 Ag 2017

It's O.K. to Be a Coward About Cancer J. Friedman color *Time* v190 no6 p21 Ag 7 2017

WHAT CANCER TAUGHT ME B. Zehme color *Chicago* v66 no1 p70 Ja 2017

Cancer gene therapy

Drugging RAS: Know the enemy B. Papke and C. J. Der bibl diag *Science* v355 no6330 p1158 Mr 17 2017

FDA OKs cancer gene therapy *Science* v357 no6355 p952 S 8 2017

Cancer genetics

Cancer Gene Tests Provide Few Answers J. Wapner color *Scientific American* v315 no3 p24 S 2016

How tobacco smoke changes the (epi)genome G. P. Pfeifer bibl color diag *Science* v354 no6312 p549 N 4 2016

Rb1 and Trp53 cooperate to suppress prostate cancer lineage plasticity, metastasis, and antiandrogen resistance Sheng Yu Ku, S. Rosario et al bibl graph *Science* v355 no6320 p1 Ja 6 2017

SOX2 promotes lineage plasticity and antiandrogen resistance in TP53- and RB1-deficient prostate cancer Ping Mu, Z. Zhang et al bibl graph *Science* v355 no6320 p1 Ja 6 2017

Cancer hospitals

Breast Cancer Warrior K. ZALAN *Ms.* v26 no4 p17 Wint 2016

Cancer hospitals—Design & construction

Building Confidence M. LAMSTER *Architectural Record* v205 no7 p114 Jl 2017

Green House Effect C. FOGES *Architectural Record* v205 no7 p109 Jl 2017

Cancer immunotherapy

Cancer immunotherapy comes of age A. Dance color *Science* v355 no6330 p1220 Mr 17 2017

CANCER KILLERS A. D. J. Posey, C. H. June et al color *Scientific American* v316 no3 p38 Mr 2017

Can immunotherapy treat neurodegeneration? M. Schwartz color *Science* v357 no6348 p254 Jl 21 2017

A new cancer ecosystem S. J. Horning color *Science* v355 no6330 p1103 Mr 17 2017

Skin Deep *Virginia Living* v15 no1 p97 D 2016

What you need to know about... Immuno therapy [Cover story] A. PATUREL color *Prevention* v68 no11 p68 N 2016

Cancer in children

At Peace in the Sun J. Tomlinson color *Money* v45 no11 p92 D 2016

Children with cancer get more access to experimental drugs C. Schmidt color *Science* v357 no6351 p540 Ag 11 2017

Game Changers K. DOLD color *Women's Health* v14 no8 p122 O 2017

INCONCEIVABLE? PERHAPS. IMPOSSIBLE? NEVER! A. KELLER LAIRD color *Women's Health* v14 no8 p8 O 2017

Cancer in children—Treatment

The War Without And the War Within C. Hogan *New York Times Magazine* p36 Ag 13 2017

Cancer in women—Prevention

Every Woman Needs These Breast Cancer Lessons L. Floyd bw color *Glamour* v115 no10 p117 O 2017

Cancer patient attitudes

RITA WILSON ON LIFE AFTER BREAST CANCER color *Harper's Bazaar* no3657 p196 O 2017

Cancer patient psychology

Grief Is a Genesis. Not a Finale S. SABBAGE *Psychology Today* v50 no3 p44 My/Je 2017

A MATTER OF LIFE AND BREAST K. Corrigan *O, The Oprah Magazine* p84 O 2017

Cancer patients

Cancer's Newest Miracle Cure A. Park color *Time* v190 no7 p32 Ag 21 2017

Down Off The Cross D. JARVIS *Reader's Digest* v188 no1124 p18 O 2016

FATHER FIGURE: Franciscan Health's cancer center has a secret weapon: a medical director who knows what it's like to be the parent of a leukemia patient A. GARCEAU *Indianapolis Monthly* p76 N 2017

Forward Motion D. HOWARD color *Prevention* v69 no7 p76 Jl 2017

"I'LL NEVER FORGET WHERE I WAS the moment I learned I had melanoma." N. O'DONNELL color *Good Housekeeping* v264 no6 p89 Je 2017

Knowledge that Empowers K. RIDDERBUSCH *Atlanta* v56 no7 p218 N 2016

Learning How to Live B. SHEIFFER color *Powder* v46 no2 p94 O 2017

MY LAST PATIENT D. SCHEINER color *Chicago* v66 no1 p80 Ja 2017

My Mr. Chemotherapy Contest L. Mullins *Washingtonian Magazine* v52 no3 p60 D 2016

A New Approach to Safely Sharing Cancer Patients' Data K. Giusti and R. G. Hamermesh *Harvard Business Review Digital Articles* p1 Je 21 2017

A pathology atlas of the human cancer transcriptome M. Uhlen, C. Zhang et al diag *Science* v357 no6352 p660 Ag 18 2017

T.J. Day T. Keith color *Sports Illustrated* v126 no13 p18 My 8 2017

A Whole Lot to Celebrate color *Cincinnati Magazine* v51 no1 p84 O 2017

Cancer patients—Attitudes

SHARON JONES B. Kopple and E. R. Brown color *Entertainment Weekly* no1446/1447 p96 D 2016/Ja 2017

Cancer patients—Education

The Power of Virtual Chemo S. SEA GOLD color *Parents* v92 no5 p26 My 2017

Cancer patients—Medical care

LIVE STRONGISH A. Murphy and J. Feldman color *Sports Illustrated* v126 no11 p54 Ap 17-24 2017

Cancer patients—Psychology

The Forgotten Side of Cancer Care A. Park color *Time* v188 no19 p20 N 7 2016

Cancer patients—Social conditions

MISSION POSSIBLE J. YOUNG color *Indianapolis Monthly* v41 no2 p33 S 2017

Cancer prevention

Cancer Moonshot *Congressional Digest* v96 no2 p6 F 1 2017

Cancer Moonshot Misses the Mark R. BAILEY color *Reason* v48 no9 p6 F 2017

Five Foods to Fend Off Cancer M. YOUNG color *Men's Health* v32 no9 p64 N 2017

How Top Docs Avoid Cancer J. BIANCHI color *Men's Health* v32 no7 p82 S 2017

What doctors tell their friends about cancer S. WOOD and J. Detwiler color *Redbook* p77 N 2017

Cancer relapse—Risk factors

Health risks after cancer *Mayo Clinic Health Letter* v358 no8 p4 Ag 2017

Cancer-related mortality

Dying while Alive C. TAYLOR color *Tricycle: The Buddhist Review* v27 no1 p86 Fall 2017

Cancer research

FROM THE EDITOR *Popular Mechanics* p4 Je 2017

THE INFORMATION CURE T. CHIARELLA cartoon color *Chicago* v66 no1 p74 Ja 2017

IT'LL TAKE AN ARMY TO KILL THE EMPEROR [Cover story] J. DETWILER color *Popular Mechanics* p74 Je 2017

Mighty Mouse J. Adler *Smithsonian* v47 no8 p54 D 2016

Mixed results from cancer replications unsettle field J. Kaiser graph *Science* v355 no6322 p234 Ja 20 2017

A pathology atlas of the human cancer transcriptome M. Uhlen, C. Zhang et al diag *Science* v357 no6352 p660 Ag 18 2017

Zebrafish larvae could help to personalize cancer treatments M. Leslie color *Science* v357 no6353 p745 Ag 25 2017

Cancer treatment

See also

　　Cancer gene therapy

　　Cancer immunotherapy

　　Chemotherapy (Cancer)

Burzynski Update: Texas Hearings End, Judges Sifting Evidence R. BLASKIEWICZ *Skeptical Inquirer* v40 no6 p5 N/D 2016

Cancer Breakthroughs Can Happen Anywhere - Including Your Community *Texas Monthly* v44 no11 p74 N 2016

The cancer epigenome: Concepts, challenges, and therapeutic opportunities M. A. Dawson bibl diag *Science* v355 no6330 p1147 Mr 17 2017

Cancer Moonshot *Congressional Digest* v96 no2 p6 F 1 2017

CANCER'S INVISIBLE INJURY S. HELD color *Indianapolis Monthly* v42 no2 p88 O 2017

Candy (Music)

Ron Rambach's Music Matters Closes Shop K. Micallef color *Downbeat* v84 no4 p17 Ap 2017

Candy Crush (TV program)

Candy Crush M. Roffman *TV Guide* v65 no23 p26 My 29 2017

Candy dispensers

Candy Dispenser! J. SCHADEWALD chart color *Popular Mechanics* p108 D 2016/Ja 2017

Candy—History

Kiss of Summer: The first families of salt water taffy stir up another season of making history by the bite A. Owens *Smithsonian* v48 no4 p9 Jl/Ag 2017

Candy—Sales & prices

Wanda's Latest Treat color *AARP: The Magazine* v59 no6A p9 O/N 2016

Canel, Tomoko Takeda

Gorgeous Skin All Winter color *Health* v31 no1 p27 Ja 2017

MAKE YOUR EYES POP color *Health* v31 no2 p116 Mr 2017

What's Hot in Natural Beauty color *Health* v31 no3 p27 Ap 2017

CANELO, TARA

The Oxidative Cost of Reproduction: Theoretical Questions and Alternative Mechanisms *BioScience* v67 no3 p258 Mr 2017

Canepa, Thomas

To The Editor color *American Craft* v77 no3 p10 Je/Jl 2017

Cañeque, Tatiana

Click chemistry enables preclinical evaluation of targeted epigenetic therapies diag *Science* v356 no6345 p1397 Je 30 2017

CANES, MICHAEL

A Messy World *Commentary* v143 no1 p6 Ja 2017

Canet, Don

2016 SUZUKI GSX-S1000 chart color *Cycle World* v56 no1 p52 Ja/F 2017

2017 DUCATI 1299 SUPER-LEGGERA color *Cycle World* v56 no7 p48 Ag 2017

2017 DUCATI DIAVEL DIESEL color *Cycle World* v56 no7 p18 Ag 2017

2017 HONDA CBR1000RR/SP color *Cycle World* v56 no3 p10 Ap 2017

2017 HONDA REBEL 300 AND 500 color *Cycle World* v56 no5 p20 Je 2017

2017 INDIAN CHIEFTAIN LIMITED/ELITE color *Cycle World* v56 no4 p20 My 2017

2017 INDIAN ROADMASTER CLASSIC color *Cycle World* v56 no3 p16 Ap 2017

2017 KAWASAKI Z900 color *Cycle World* v56 no4 p22 My 2017

2017 TRIUMPH STREET TRIPLE RS color *Cycle World* v56 no4 p10 My 2017

2017 YAMAHA YZF-R6 color *Cycle World* v56 no5 p14 Je 2017

2018 BMW G310R color *Cycle World* v56 no2 p48 Mr 2017

2018 SUZUKI GSX-S750 color *Cycle World* v56 no10 p16 N 2017

ANSWERING THE R QUESTION chart color diag *Cycle World* v56 no10 p44 N 2017

BATTLE LA BREEZE color *Cycle World* v56 no3 p20 Ap 2017

CHARACTER ADJUSTMENT color *Cycle World* v56 no2 p18 Mr 2017

FASTRAX BACKROADS LUGGAGE color *Cycle World* v56 no2 p20 Mr 2017

GARMIN VIRB ULTRA 30 color *Cycle World* v56 no7 p22 Ag 2017

GENUINE ACCESSORIES color *Cycle World* v56 no5 p22 Je 2017

HIGH ADVENTURE color *Cycle World* v55 no10 p16 N 2016

PEAK PERFORMANCE color *Cycle World* v56 no10 p18 N 2017

PERPENDICULAR TWINS chart color *Cycle World* v56 no2 p42 Mr 2017

PLUG 'N' PLAY color *Cycle World* v56 no1 p17 Ja/F 2017

RIDERS 'ON THE STORM color *Cycle World* v55 no11 p12 D 2016

RIDING GLOVES color *Cycle World* v56 no4 p26 My 2017

RIDING WITH THE KING cartoon chart color *Cycle World* v56 no8 p22 S 2017

ROADSIDE ASSISTANCE color *Cycle World* v56 no6 p20 Jl 2017

SUPER MIDDLEWEIGHT MATCHUP chart color *Cycle World* v56 no6 p50 Jl 2017

TRACKDAY DELIGHTS color *Cycle World* v56 no7 p20 Ag 2017

YOSHIMURA SIGNATURE SERIES ALPHA SLIP-ON color *Cycle World* v56 no1 p19 Ja/F 2017

Canfield, P. C.

Discovery of orbital-selective Cooper pairing in FeSe diag *Science* v357 no6346 p75 Jl 7 2017

Canfora, F.

Observation of a large-scale anisotropy in the arrival directions of cosmic rays above 8 × 1018 eV *Science* v357 no6357 p1266 S 22 2017

Cang Hui

Invasion Dynamics: From Invasion Biology to Invasion Science H. MOONEY *BioScience* v67 no9 p860 S 2017

Cangialosi, Angelo

DNA sequence–directed shape change of photopatterned hydrogels via high-degree swelling color diag *Science* v357 no6356 p1126 S 15 2017

Cani, Patrice D.

Gut cell metabolism shapes the microbiome color *Science* v357 no6351 p548 Ag 11 2017

Canidae

See also

Canis

Foxes

DISASTER DOGS M. D. G. Kaplan *Washingtonian Magazine* v52 no6 p185 Mr 2017

Canis

See also

Dogs

Wolves

The wolf of Juan de Fuca R. COUNTER color *Maclean's* v130 no3 p13 Ap 2017

Canis Major (Constellation)

Between the Dogs F. Schaaf *Sky & Telescope* v133 no2 p45 F 2017

Canis minor (Constellation)

Between the Dogs F. Schaaf *Sky & Telescope* v133 no2 p45 F 2017

Čanjevac, Ivan

Changing climate shifts timing of European floods color graph *Science* v357 no6351 p588 Ag 11 2017

Cannabinoids

CBD OIL L. Turner color *Amazing Wellness* p22 Fall 2017

Cannabis

See also

Cannabinoids

CBD Oil: Anxiety Aid & Much More [Cover story] L. Turner color *Better Nutrition* v79 no11 p34 N 2017

Hemp Harvest in Virginia S. Richardson *American History* v52 no1 p8 Ap 2017

Marijuana L. SCHLEY color diag *Discover* v38 no6 p56 Jl/Ag 2017

A TIMELINE OF MARIJUANA IN THE NEW YORK TIMES J. SULLUM bw color *Reason* v49 no4 p52 Ag/S 2017

Cannabis—Law & legislation

Dealer beware M. CAMPBELL color *Maclean's* v130 no4 p46 My 2017

Cannabis—Physiological aspects

A new neglected crop: cannabis E. Pennisi color *Science* v356 no6335 p232 Ap 21 2017

Cannabis—Physiological effect

A new neglected crop: cannabis E. Pennisi color *Science* v356 no6335 p232 Ap 21 2017

Cannabis—Therapeutic use

POT AND PAIN G. Miller color map *Science* v354 no6312 p566 N 4 2016

TINY TREATS A. Bartz color *Women's Health* v14 no8 p84 O 2017

Cannadine, David, 1950-

In Search of Mrs. T G. HIMMELFARB bw *Weekly Standard* v22 no25 p34 Mr 6 2017

Cannatella, David C.

Interacting amino acid replacements allow poison frogs to evolve epibatidine resistance chart diag graph *Science* v357 no6357 p1261 S 22 2017

CANNATO, VINCENT J.
Fuzzy History color *Weekly Standard* v22 no42 p33 Jl 17 2017
Mother Brooklyn *Commentary* v143 no4 p44 Ap 2017

Cannavale, Bobby, 1970-
REAL WORK I. Parker cartoon *New Yorker* v93 no18 p19 Je 26 2017

Cannavino, Jessica
Control of muscle formation by the fusogenic micropeptide myomixer diag *Science* v356 no6335 p323 Ap 21 2017

Canned beans—Evaluation
THE SOUTHERN LIVING FOOD AWARDS H. Hayes color *Southern Living* v52 no6 p109 Je 2017

Canned foods—Evaluation
SUPERMARKET HEROES color *Women's Health* v14 no9 p106 N 2017

Canned tomatoes—Evaluation
THE SOUTHERN LIVING FOOD AWARDS H. Hayes color *Southern Living* v52 no6 p109 Je 2017

Canned tuna
Scientists share 50 food facts to help you live longer (and lose weight too) [Cover story] M. CROUCH *Reader's Digest* v189 no1127 p63 F 2017

CANNELL, MICHAEL
Unmasking the Mad Bomber *Smithsonian* v48 no1 p25 Ap 2017

Cannella, Megan E.
Spaces between Us: Queer Settler Colonialism and Indigenous Decolonization *American Indian Quarterly* v41 no1 p96 Wint 2017

Canner, Niko
How Self-Managed Companies Help People Learn on the Job *Harvard Business Review Digital Articles* p2 Ag 3 2016
Why Is Micromanagement So Infectious? *Harvard Business Review Digital Articles* p2 Ag 17 2016

Cannes Film Festival
EDITOR'S LETTER N. Rapold color *Film Comment* v53 no4 p4 Jl/Ag 2017
A Fraught Cannes, Inside Screening Rooms and Out S. Zacharek color *Time* v189 no22 p55 Je 12 2017
FREE RANGE A. Taubin color *Film Comment* v53 no4 p28 Jl/Ag 2017
In the Beginning N. Rapold bw color *Film Comment* v53 no3 p10 My/Je 2017
Ooh La La! N. Sperling color *Entertainment Weekly* no1468/1469 p22 Je 2-9 2017
The Speed of Light in a Vacuum Λ. Taubin bw color *Film Comment* v53 no4 p54 Jl/Ag 2017
VIRTUOUS REALITY color *Vanity Fair* v59 no8 p47 Ag 2017

Cannibalism
The Case for Cannibalism B. SCHUTT cartoon *Discover* v38 no3 p56 Ap 2017
FOOD FOR THOUGHT R. Nelson color *Virginia Living* v15 no5 p96 Ag 2017

Canning, Kristin
Do you need a second opinion? color *Health* v31 no9 p68 N 2017
Escape the Gym color *Health* v31 no5 p39 Je 2017
The Everything Guide to Seafood color *Health* v31 no5 p111 Je 2017
The food swap that changed my body color *Health* v31 no9 p51 N 2017
They shared their health secrets with the world color *Health* v31 no8 p81 O 2017
Think Yourself Thin? color *Health* v31 no6 p51 Jl 2017
This Is Your Body on Exercise color *Health* v31 no7 p72 S 2017
Three Ways to Walk Off the Weight color *Health* v31 no4 p53 My 2017
Wake Up and Work Out! color *Health* v31 no6 p24 Jl 2017
Worried about the weight room? color *Health* v31 no8 p55 O 2017

Canning, Patrick
The Relationship Between Energy Prices and Food-Related Energy Use in the United States *Amber Waves: The Economics of Food, Farming, Natural Resources, & Rural America* p17 Je 2017

Canning, Wayne
BED REST color *Sail* v48 no9 p58 S 2017
Play it Safe color *Sail* v48 no7 p50 Jl 2017

Cannizzaro, Becky

GO-TO GIRL chart color *Team Roping Journal* p56 O 2017

Cannizzaro, Jessie—Interviews
Interview with a ... K. Green color *Career Outlook* p1 O 2016

Cannon, Jean McElwee
A Bomb to Remember *Hoover Digest: Research & Opinion on Public Policy* no1 p184 Wint 2017
Hoover and the Great Outdoors *Hoover Digest: Research & Opinion on Public Policy* no2 p187 Spr 2017
Weapon on the Wall: As World War I raged, posters encouraged, enticed, and even shamed young Americans into joining the great conflict *Hoover Digest: Research & Opinion on Public Policy* no2 p199 Spr 2017

Cannon, Kay—Interviews
"You've got to break your back!" A. Eler, L. Brody et al color *Glamour* v115 no4 p153 Ap 2017

Cannon, Nick, 1980-
The Bullseye M. Snetiker color *Entertainment Weekly* no1454/1455 p108 F 24 2017

Cannon, Peter
Mysteries & Thrillers bw color *Publishers Weekly* v264 no26 p90 Je 26 2017
Mysteries & Thrillers color *Publishers Weekly* v263 no51 p80 D 12 2016
The Night Ocean bw *Publishers Weekly* v263 no51 p120 D 12 2016

Cannon, Sarah
How Uber and the Sharing Economy Can Win Over Regulators *Harvard Business Review Digital Articles* p2 O 13 2014

Cannon, Walter B. (Walter Bradford), 1871-1945
SCARED TO DEATH W. Cannon *Lapham's Quarterly* v10 no3 p176 Summ 2017

Cannon-Brookes, Mike
The Wizards From Oz N. KIRSCH color *Forbes* v199 no6 p36 Je 13 2017

Cannondale Bicycle Corp.
BOOYAH, E-BIKES! color *Bicycling* v58 no8 p(Sp)2 S 2017
Cannondale R. Cleek color *Bike Magazine* v24 no7 p108 S 2017
CANNONDALE SCALPEL SE 2 M. Yozell color *Bicycling* v58 no8 p62 S 2017
QUICK NEO M. Yozell color *Bicycling* v58 no8 p(Sp)4 S 2017

Cano, A.
Persistent effects of pre-Columbian plant domestication on Amazonian forest composition bibl chart graph map *Science* v355 no6328 p925 Mr 3 2017

Cano, Lucía
Extraterrestrial Encounter: Spanish firm SelgasCano pays respect to nature by jolting it with the surreal A. COHN color *Architectural Record* v205 no8 p64 Ag 2017

Canoa: A Shameful Memory (Film)
Day of the Dead M. Nelson color *Film Comment* v53 no2 p11 Mr/Ap 2017

Canoe camping
AHSAHKA: WHERE RIVERS MEET AND LINES ARE CAST C. BONK *Idaho Magazine* v16 no8 p32 My 2017

Canoe design & construction
A BRIEF HISTORY OF THE CANOE: From postwar 'canoedling' to unplugging from our smartphones, the elegantly simple and efficient conveyance takes us back to simpler days M. NEUZIL *Saturday Evening Post* v289 no4 p82 Jl/Ag 2017

Canoe industry
Connected by Canoe color *Walrus* v14 no9 p39 N 2017

Canoeists
Rediscovering Canada by Canoe S. Loney color *Walrus* v14 no9 p42 N 2017

Canoes & canoeing
    See also
      Kayaking
2016 PHOTO ANNUAL color *Canoe & Kayak Magazine* v45 no1 p14 Wint 2017
The Back Story G. WOOD color *Missouri Life* v44 no5 p98 Ag 2017
Beacon of Strength: In troubled waters, it helps to remember the courage of a remarkable family friend E. CLARK *Yankee* v81 no5 p14 S/O 2017
A Canoeist's Eureka Moment bw color *Yankee* p24 Jl 2017
DOUBLE JEOPARDY M. SHANKLIN and N. KREBS cartoon

color *Outdoor Life* v224 no3 p12 Ap 2017

FAR FROM THE MADDING CROWD C. TOMLIN cartoon color *Missouri Life* v44 no4 p30 Je 2017

The Great North L. WARNER color *Backpacker* p13 O 2017

Learning To Take A Stand N. DEUEL *Los Angeles Magazine* p88 Mr 2017

LODGE *Sierra* v102 no1 p78 Ja/F 2017

Our New Home on the Water S. Loney color *Walrus* v14 no9 p44 N 2017

Paddling Forward C. Fisher Tully color *Walrus* v14 no9 p41 N 2017

POND HOPPING E. Stegemann *New York State Conservationist* v72 no1 p6 Ag 2017

Q&A C. Fisher Tully color *Walrus* v14 no9 p40 N 2017

Rediscovering Canada by Canoe S. Loney color *Walrus* v14 no9 p42 N 2017

ROCKING THE BOAT J. Roth color *Esquire* p50 2017 BigBlackBook

Silence Like a Symphony: Canoeing Silver Creek M. RIPPLE *Idaho Magazine* v16 no11 p10 Ag 2017

Why the Boundary Waters Matter M. Ingram color *Progressive* v81 no5 p31 Je/Jl 2017

WORLD ROUNDUP J. URBANUS color map *Archaeology* v70 no5 p24 S/O 2017

Canoes & canoeing—Accidents

On Patrol L. Bobseine and S. Scherry *New York State Conservationist* v71 no6 p25 Je 2017

Canoes & canoeing—Evaluation

CLIPPER CANOES color *Canoe & Kayak Magazine* v45 no1 p71 Wint 2017

NOVA CRAFT CANOE color *Canoe & Kayak Magazine* v45 no1 p94 Wint 2017

PADDLING E. BUCHANAN color *Backpacker* v45 no3 p110 Ap 2017

PLACID BOATWORKS color *Canoe & Kayak Magazine* v45 no1 p100 Wint 2017

SEA EAGLE BOATS color *Canoe & Kayak Magazine* v45 no1 p104 Wint 2017

WENONAH color *Canoe & Kayak Magazine* v45 no1 p110 Wint 2017

Canoes & canoeing—History

A BRIEF HISTORY OF THE CANOE: From postwar 'canoodling' to unplugging from our smartphones, the elegantly simple and efficient conveyance takes us back to simpler days M. NEUZIL *Saturday Evening Post* v289 no4 p82 Jl/Ag 2017

Canola oil

Breaking up exercise ... Canola oil ... Probiotics ... Roasting vegetables A. H. Lichtenstein *Tufts University Health & Nutrition Letter* v34 no11 p8 Ja 2017

JUST ASK color *Vegetarian Today* no2 p6 Ap 2017

STEAK AU POIVRE color *AARP: The Magazine* v59 no5A p67 Ag/S 2016

Canon camera

Choosing Equipment for Eclipse Photography K. Sklute and D. Henry color *Astronomy* v45 no7 p7 Jl 2017

Canon Inc.

CANON PIXMA iP110: THIS INKJET PRINTER'S PORTABILITY COMES AT A PRICE S. BELLAMY color *Macworld - Digital Edition* v34 no4 p19 My 2017

Choosing Equipment for Eclipse Photography K. Sklute and D. Henry color *Astronomy* v45 no7 p7 Jl 2017

A Sharper Focus on Constant Transformation M. Foster and D. W. Russell color *Forbes* v199 no1 p(Sp)6 Ja 24 2017

Canonization

People C. Kennel-Shank color *Christian Century* v133 no21 p19 O 12 2016

Canora, Marco

Chicken Fight! color *Men's Health* v32 no8 p88 O 2017

EXPENSIVE TASTE M. LAISKONIS color *Women's Health* v14 no8 p30 O 2017

Canova, Antonio, 1757-1822—Exhibitions

A curious George at the Frick color *Magazine Antiques* v184 no4 p40 Jl/Ag 2017

Cantacuzino, Marina—Interviews

What is forgiveness? A. Frykholm color *Christian Century* v134 no7 p10 Mr 29 2017

Cantalapiedra, J. L.

Decoupled ecomorphological evolution and diversification in Neogene-Quaternary horses bibl graph *Science* v355 no6325 p627 F 10 2017

Cantarini, Martha Crawford

Mixed signals bw color *Equus* no475 p88 Ap 2017

Cantering (Horsemanship)

Canter with Confidence J. GOODNIGHT and H. MELOCCO color *Trail Rider* v29 no4 p44 My 2017

The Clinic S. von Dietze color *Dressage Today* v23 no10 p24 Jl 2017

MAINTAIN FITNESS THROUGH CANTERING C. Barakat and M. McCluskey color *Equus* no477 p16 Je 2017

The Priceless School Horse J. Mellace *Dressage Today* v23 no4 p8 D 2016

THE RIGHT CANTER FOR EVERY SITUATION [Cover story] E. Gingras bw chart color *Practical Horseman* v45 no10 p28 O 2017

Cantilevers

Force spectroscopy unveils hidden protein-folding states J. Miller *Physics Today* v70 no5 p16 My 2017

Canto, Adan

ADAN CANTO C. Agard color *Entertainment Weekly* no1440 p49 N 18 2016

CANTOR, AMY

BUZZER BEATERS [Cover story] color *Runner's World* v52 no5 p32 Je 2017

Cantor, Ellen

IS TRAGEDY A CHOICE? B. SCHWABSKY bw *Nation* v304 no2 p32 Ja 16 2017

Pornography of Power D. E. Howe *Art in America* v104 no9 p29 O 2016

Cantor, Eric, 1963-

CATCHING UP WITH ERIC CANTOR: Neither his own ouster nor Trump's election convinced the former Virginia pol that the establishment needs to change E. Plott *Washingtonian Magazine* v52 no11 p47 Ag 2017

CANTOR, HALLIE

Mating bw color *GQ: Gentlemen's Quarterly* v86 no11 p58 N 2016

THE WRITER'S PROCESS cartoon *New Yorker* v93 no15 p27 My 29 2017

Cantor Fitzgerald & Co.

Tears of the Times color *Weekly Standard* v22 no34 p2 My 15 2017

Can't Stop, Won't Stop (Film)

Diddy Doesn't Like To Get Hot W. Staley *New York Times Magazine* p58 Jl 9 2017

Cantú, Francisco

TUCSON, ARIZONA *Harper's Magazine* p28 O 2017

Cantu, Michael

NEW CARS 2018-2019 [Cover story] chart color *Motor Trend* v69 no9 p34 S 2017

NEW SUVS & TRUCKS 2018-2019 [Cover story] color *Motor Trend* v69 no10 p32 O 2017

SUVOCABULARY bw *Motor Trend* v69 no10 p65 O 2017

Toyota FT-4X Concept color *Motor Trend* v69 no7 p22 Jl 2017

TRUCK TIRE TECH color *Motor Trend* v69 no10 p80 O 2017

Cantwell, Kevin

OLD MIAMI *Commonweal* v144 no17 p12 O 20 2017

Cantwell, Patrick R.

Segregation-induced ordered superstructures at general grain boundaries in a nickel-bismuth alloy color *Science* v357 no6359 p97 O 6 2017

Canyon Bicycles GmbH

CANYON ENDURAGE CF SIX 9.0 M. PHILLIPS color *Bicycling* v58 no1 p74 Ja/F 2017

CANYON SPECTRAL CF 9.0 EX L. Tanner color *Bicycling* v58 no7 p78 Ag 2017

CANYON ULTIMATE WMN CF SLX DISC 9.0 TEAM CSR G. Liu color *Bicycling* v58 no9 p90 O 2017

Canyon de Chelly National Monument (Ariz.)

National Parks Guide *Arizona Highways* v92 no8 p52 Ag 2016

Canyon Lake (Ariz.)

CHEVELON CANYON LAKE: The Mogollon Rim gets busy this time of year, especially at Woods Canyon Lake. However, not far from there, along a scenic road lined with giant ponderosas, is an isolated lake that's every bit as beautiful N. AUSTIN *Arizona Highways* v93 no8 p52 Ag 2017

Canyoneering

out alive: flooded color *Backpacker* p43 Ag 2017

Reality Check J. ELLISON color *Climbing* no350 p15 D 2016/ Ja 2017

UNSOLICITED BETA J. Wong and D. Josey color *Climbing* no350 p16 D 2016/Ja 2017

Canyonlands National Park (Utah)

REFLECTIONS FROM THE CENTER OF THE UNIVERSE M. Ingram color *Progressive* p40 D 2016/Ja 2017

Canyons

POSTCARDS FROM THE CANYON K. Vaughn *Arizona Highways* v93 no10 p28 O 2017

Weatherscapes: The Grand Canyon of the Colorado River – Earth's Dynamic Past Opened by the Sky E. Darack *Weatherwise* v70 no2 p8 Mr/Ap 2017

Canyons—Arizona

See also

Chelly, Canyon de (Ariz.)

Chevelon Canyon (Ariz.)

Grand Canyon (Ariz.)

Goodnight Moonscape *Arizona Highways* v93 no8 p5 Ag 2017

HE KNOWS WHAT HE'S TALKING ABOUT M. JAFFE *Arizona Highways* v93 no10 p46 O 2017

INSIDE OUT K. VAUGHN *Arizona Highways* v93 no10 p32 O 2017

PHOTOGENIC CANYON DE CHELLY *Arizona Highways* v93 no10 p33 O 2017

Canyons—Idaho

See also

Hells Canyon (Idaho & Or.)

TRAILING THE HERD P. WILSON *Idaho Magazine* v16 no2 p48 N 2016

Cao, Athena

$1,388 Average spending for the holidays color *Money* v45 no11 p13 D 2016

BEST IN TRAVEL 2017 color *Money* v46 no3 p58 Ap 2017

Get Smart About Mobile Payments color *Money* v46 no2 p34 Mr 2017

The MONEY Do List color *Money* v46 no1 p19 Ja/F 2017

Cao, Cong

Challenges of S&T system reform in China bibl color *Science* v355 no6329 p1019 Mr 10 2017

Cao, Jessica

Exploring genetic suppression interactions on a global scale diag *Science* v354 no6312 p599 N 4 2016

Cao, Jing

IBM's Big Jobs Dodge color *Bloomberg Businessweek* no4509 p30 Ja 30 2017

LEAVE my ETSY ALONE bw color *Bloomberg Businessweek* no4523 p48 My 22 2017

Cao, Junyue

Comprehensive single-cell transcriptional profiling of a multicellular organism diag *Science* v357 no6352 p661 Ag 18 2017

Cao, Kaixiang

PAF1 regulation of promoter-proximal pause release via enhancer activation color *Science* v357 no6357 p1294 S 22 2017

Cao, Peng

Structure and assembly mechanism of plant C2S2M2-type PSII-LHCII supercomplex color *Science* v357 no6353 p815 Ag 25 2017

Cao, Qing

Carbon nanotube transistors scaled to a 40-nanometer footprint color graph *Science* v356 no6345 p1369 Je 30 2017

Cao, Wenxuan, 1954-

Bronze and Sunflower *Publishers Weekly* v263 no52 p124 D 19 2016

Join Together: Two lonely kids form a lifesaving friendship in a tale from one of China's most popular authors L. SEE *New York Times Book Review* p21 My 14 2017

Cao, Xueqin, ca. 1717-1763

Dream of the Red Chamber R. M. Rinaldi *Opera News* v81 no6 p40 D 2016

Cao, Y.

High-temperature quantum oscillations caused by recurring Bloch states in graphene superlattices color *Science* v357 no6347 p181 Jl 14 2017

iPTF16geu: A multiply imaged, gravitationally lensed type Ia supernova color diag graph *Science* v356 no6335 p291 Ap 21 2017

Cao, Y. Grace

Macrophage function in tissue repair and remodeling requires IL-4 or IL-13 with apoptotic cells diag *Science* v356 no6342 p1072 Je 9 2017

Cao, Yuan

Satellite-based entanglement distribution over 1200 kilometers diag graph *Science* v356 no6343 p1140 Je 16 2017

Cap Beauty (Company)

DIY MATCHA color *Women's Health* v14 no9 p144 N 2017

Going Hollywood L. REGENSDORF and C. ELLENBERG color *Vogue* v207 no9 p444 S 2017

Capaccioni, F.

Localized aliphatic organic material on the surface of Ceres bibl graph *Science* v355 no6326 p719 F 17 2017

Seasonal exposure of carbon dioxide ice on the nucleus of comet 67P/Churyumov-Gerasimenko bibl bw graph *Science* v354 no6319 p1563 D 23 2016

Capacitors

The next game changer? N. Besougloff *Model Railroader* v83 no12 p8 D 2016

Capaldi, Peter, 1958-

DOCTOR WHO C. Collis color *Entertainment Weekly* p26 Jl 24 2017

Doctor Who Christmas Special A. D'Arminio *TV Guide* p38 D 19 2016

DOCTOR WHO CHRISTMAS SPECIAL C. Collis color *Entertainment Weekly* no1474/1475 p72 Jl 21-28 2017

Caparon, Michael G.

Lactobacillus reuteri induces gut intraepithelial CD4+CD8αα+ T cells diag graph *Science* v357 no6353 p806 Ag 25 2017

Capasso, Federico

Leonid Keldysh *Physics Today* v70 no6 p75 Je 2017

Capasso, Michael

GOINGS ON ABOUT TOWN color *New Yorker* v93 no16 p9 Je 5 2017

Capay, Adam

1,560 DAYS [Cover story] M. Patriquin and N. Macdonald color *Maclean's* v129 no45 p16 N 14 2016

52 months of torture and zero answers S. GILMORE color *Maclean's* v129 no45 p20 N 14 2016

Capcom Co. Ltd.

Thai Temple Soundtrack Tangle M. SCARLES color *Tricycle: The Buddhist Review* v27 no1 p17 Fall 2017

Cape Cod (Mass.)—Description & travel

HOME IS WHERE THE BOAT IS A. Cort and P. Nielsen color map *Sail* v48 no3 p38 Mr 2017

Cape Cod Doormats (Company)

MEET AND GREET E. MOODY color *Martha Stewart Living* p28 My 2017

Cape Cod houses

CAPE CATASTROPHE bw color *Old House Journal* v45 no1 p88 F 2017

Great Old Capes color *Old House Journal* v45 no1 p36 F 2017

PLANNING FOR adding on M. E. POLSON color diag *Old House Journal* v45 no7 p62 O 2017

Cape Fear River (N.C.)

MAKING A SPLASH R. Annis, S. Bahr et al color *Indianapolis Monthly* v41 no2 p76 S 2017

Cape Hatteras National Seashore (N.C.)

That Was Then *National Parks* v91 no3 p60 Summ 2017

Cape Horn (Calif : Cliff)

Because It's There [Cover story] S. MURRAY color *Power & Motoryacht* v34 no6 p54 Je 2017

Cape Town (South Africa)—Description & travel

Great Escapes C. Stern color *InStyle* v24 no8 p163 Ag 2017

Čapek, Karel, 1890-1938

c. 2000 BC: Sodom K. Čapek *Lapham's Quarterly* v10 no1 p174 Wint 2017

CAPELLI, CHRIS

POSTHOLE color *Powder* v46 no2 p94 O 2017

CAPITAIN, JENNY

FOOD FOR THOUGHT color *O, The Oprah Magazine* p14 Ag 2017

Capital

See also
> Profit
> Saving & investment
> Venture capital
> Working capital

Capital cities

The Quiz T. BALAZO color *Maclean's* p64 Je 2017

Capital Cities/ABC Inc.—Finance

One for Mickey's Mantel A. GARA color *Forbes* v199 no6 p24 Je 13 2017

Capital costs

A Refresher on Cost of Capital A. Gallo *Harvard Business Review Digital Articles* p2 Ap 30 2015

Capital gains tax

Start Your Retirement With a Tax Break! K. A. Renzulli color *Money* v46 no8 p30 S 2017

Capital investments

See also
> Free cash flow
> Investment tax credit
> Net present value
> Rate of return

Joint Ventures Reduce the Risk of Major Capital Investments H. Vantrappen and D. Deneffe *Harvard Business Review Digital Articles* p2 Ap 6 2016

Capital market

See also
> Bond market
> Stock exchanges

Capital market—Africa

Bogus Audited Statements Are Holding Africa Back N. Ekekwe *Harvard Business Review Digital Articles* p2 Ag 22 2016

Capital market—United States

Capital Markets: Fueling Our Economic Growth T. J. Donohue *Weekly Standard* v22 no5 p22 O 10 2016

Capital movements—China

Beijing Moves to Curb Overseas Investments D. Roberts *Bloomberg Businessweek* no4504 p17 D 19 2016

Capital punishment

See also
> Capital punishment sentencing

LIFE ON THE LINE C. G. Reid *Harper's Magazine* v334 no2002 p58 Mr 2017

People B. Allen color *Christian Century* v134 no11 p18 My 24 2017

Capital punishment sentencing

DEATH PENALTY'S DECLINE CONTINUES K. Clarke color graph *America* v216 no3 p12 F 6 2017

Capital punishment—Arkansas

OUT OF TIME J. Cobb cartoon *New Yorker* v93 no12 p15 My 8 2017

Capital punishment—Georgia

DEATH ROW RUSH M. BLAU *Atlanta* v56 no12 p28 Ap 2017

Capital punishment—Law & legislation

Still Tinkering With Death E. K. BOEGEL *America* v215 no16 p18 N 21 2016

Capital punishment—Religious aspects

Death Penalty on the Ropes? M. O'LOUGHLIN *America* v215 no11 p8 O 17 2016

Capital punishment—United States

DEATH PENALTY'S DECLINE CONTINUES K. Clarke color graph *America* v216 no3 p12 F 6 2017

A MATTER OF LIFE M. Cuddehe *Harper's Magazine* v334 no2002 p59 Mr 2017

Should the Death Penalty Be Abolished? D. RUST-TIERNEY and J. MARQUIS *New York Times Upfront* v149 no9 p22 F 20 2017

Still Tinkering With Death E. K. BOEGEL *America* v215 no16 p18 N 21 2016

Capital punishment—United States—Social aspects

The Case for Mercy: Some of the Unlikeliest People Oppose the Death Penalty E. Gunn color *Progressive* v81 no7 p26 O/N 2017

Capital—Accounting

A Better Scorecard for Your Company's Sustainability Efforts M. Thomas and M. W. McElroy *Harvard Business Review Digital Articles* p2 D 10 2015

Capitalism

See also
> Corporate capitalism
> Crony capitalism
> Entrepreneurship
> Monopoly capitalism
> Technocracy

Another Year Has Passed, but the List of Massive Global Problems Has Stayed the Same J. L. Bower *Harvard Business Review Digital Articles* p2 D 14 2015

CAPITALISM, BY GEORGE! M. KINSLEY color *Vanity Fair* v59 no10 p142 O 2017

CONFESSIONS OF A CAPITALIST CONVERT [Cover story] A. C. Brooks color *America* v216 no4 p18 F 20 2017

Conservatives in Denial C. G. RYN *American Conservative* v15 no6 p32 N/D 2016

The Emperor Has No Clothes G. TETT cartoon *Foreign Policy* no222 p70 Ja/F 2017

EXIT LEFT J. Gamble, P. Mason et al bw color *Nation* v304 no16 p16 My 22 2017

The Promise of a Truly Entrepreneurial Society R. Straub *Harvard Business Review Digital Articles* p2 Mr 25 2016

Rescuing Capitalism from Itself H. Mintzberg *Harvard Business Review Digital Articles* p2 D 3 2015

To fight climate change, we need to improve capitalism, not get rid of it P. Kellner *America* v216 no11 p10 My 15 2017

Why Monopolistic Pension Funds Undermine Capitalism R. L. Martin *Harvard Business Review Digital Articles* p2 O 6 2014

Capitalism—Exhibitions

THE GHOST OF CAPITALISM PAST C. BRENNAN *In These Times* v41 no8 p39 Ag 2017

Capitalism—India

Of Sun Gods and Solar Energy K. SINGH color *Issues in Science & Technology* v33 no2 p48 Wint 2017

Capitalism—Research

You Can't Avoid Failure Unless You Do Nothing R. Garvin color *MIT Technology Review* v120 no1 p8 Ja/F 2017

Capitalism—United States

The Crumbs of Capitalism D. MAYER-FOULKES *Commentary* v142 no2 p11 S 2016

ETHICS--THE ESSENCE OF SUCCESSFUL CAPITALISM S. FORBES *Vital Speeches of the Day* v83 no4 p128 Ap 2017

THE GHOST OF CAPITALISM PAST C. BRENNAN *In These Times* v41 no8 p39 Ag 2017

Shark Tank J. Lowe *New York Times Magazine* p24 O 1 2017

Trump Theory P. MARTIN *Commentary* v142 no1 p9 Jl/Ag 2016

You Can't Avoid Failure Unless You Do Nothing R. Garvin color *MIT Technology Review* v120 no1 p8 Ja/F 2017

Capitalism—United States—History

IMMIGRANTS KEEP CAPITALISM FRESH R. KARLGAARD *Forbes* v198 no5 p56 O 25 2016

Capitalist & financier surveys

SURPRISE, SURPRISE WOMEN ARE OUTPERFORMING MEN A. Gumbs graph *Black Enterprise* v47 no7 p18 My/Je 2017

Capitalists & financiers

See also
> Stockholders
> Women capitalists & financiers

Cover *Fortune* v174 no8 pC1 D 15 2016

The Data Says Climate Change Could Cost Investors Trillions A. Winston *Harvard Business Review Digital Articles* p2 Ap 14 2016

Everyone's Jumping on the Yield Bandwagon M. Hobson color *Black Enterprise* v47 no2 p20 S 2016

From the Ashes of Liberal Democracy S. ŽIŽEK *In These Times* v41 no3 p17 Mr 2017

Funders groan under growing review burden J. de Vrieze color *Science* v357 no6349 p343 Jl 28 2017

GAMM ON: The Humanist Interview with Philanthropist Gordon Gamm J. BARDI *Humanist* v77 no5 p20 S/O 2017

How CEOs Can Best Manage Their Boards M. Useem *Harvard Business Review Digital Articles* p2 D 9 2014

How CFOs Can Take the Long-Term View in a Short-Term Economy J. Sinfield and A. Trotter *Harvard Business Review Digital Articles* p2 Mr 15 2016

Investors Watch Tesla L. Boggild *Alternatives Journal (AJ) - Canada's Environmental Voice* v42 no3 p11 2016

Memphis & Beyond: Assessing the Market for CRA Investment N. Logan-Robinson, I. Nunley et al *Bridges (Federal Reserve Bank of St. Louis)* p1 Spr 2017

NO TIME TO WAIT C. Leaf color *Fortune* v174 no8 p11 D 15 2016

OFFSHORE BLUES K. FINN color *New Orleans Magazine* v51 no2 p32 D 2016

Private Equity Can Make Firms More Innovative N. Torres *Harvard Business Review Digital Articles* p2 Je 29 2015

Profit From Being a Patient Investor J. K. GLASSMAN chart *Kiplinger's Personal Finance* v71 no8 p17 Ag 2017

RISKY BUSINESS S. THORNTON color *ARTnews* v115 no3 p102 Fall 2016

This Man Will Purify Your Portfolio W. BALDWIN chart color *Forbes* v199 no4 p62 Ap 25 2017

UBER AND OUT S. Kolhatkar cartoon *New Yorker* v93 no20 p27 Jl 10 2017

What Kind of Investor Are You? A. K. SMITH *Kiplinger's Personal Finance* v71 no6 p25 Je 2017

What VCs Can Teach Executives About What Drives Returns M. Wessel *Harvard Business Review Digital Articles* p2 Je 25 2015

Wheeler-Dealer cartoon *Forbes* v199 no4 p20 Ap 25 2017

Women in Asia Are More Financially Savvy than Women in the U.S. S. A. Hewlett and A. T. Moffitt *Harvard Business Review Digital Articles* p2 Ag 25 2015

Capitalists & financiers—Attitudes

"I PASSED ON TESLA" Regrets of the VCs P. Marinova *Fortune* v174 no8 p36 D 15 2016

The Master Chides His Students N. Buhayar color *Bloomberg Businessweek* no4512 p37 F 20 2017

Capitalists & financiers—China

Hedge City Blues P. ROBERTS color graph *Mother Jones* v42 no3 p40 My/Je 2017

Capitalists & financiers—Economic conditions—21st century

INFLATION PLAY W. BALDWIN chart color graph *Forbes* v198 no9 p88 D 30 2016

The Unreformed Stock Picker A. GARA color *Forbes* v200 no1 p56 Jl 27 2017

Capitalists & financiers—History—21st century

Stay Cool and Stay Invested [Cover story] M. Heimer color diag *Fortune* v174 no8 p84 D 15 2016

Capitalists & financiers—Political activity

4 Types of Activist Investors and How to Spot Them D. Romito *Harvard Business Review Digital Articles* p2 O 7 2015

Capitalists & financiers—United States

See also

African American capitalists & financiers

Best Places to Get Investment Advice N. S. HUANG cartoon *Kiplinger's Personal Finance* v71 no1 p52 Ja 2017

Cracking the Bro Code S. McBride, L. Chapman et al cartoon *Bloomberg Businessweek* no4533 p18 Ag 7 2017

GONE BABY GONE R. MONROE color *New Republic* v248 no10 p34 O 2017

My Portfolio's Uninvited Guests K. KRISTOF *Kiplinger's Personal Finance* v71 no1 p56 Ja 2017

A Stodgy Fund Still Delights Investors N. S. HUANG chart *Kiplinger's Personal Finance* v71 no11 p61 N 2017

Where to Invest in 2017 A. K. SMITH cartoon graph *Kiplinger's Personal Finance* v71 no1 p42 Ja 2017

WORLDLY WEALTH R. HENAGER il *Phi Kappa Phi Forum* v97 no1 p17 Spr 2017

Capitalists & financiers—United States—Attitudes

Stock Investors Nervously Do the Math K. Burton, K. Porzecanski et al color *Bloomberg Businessweek* no4520 p41 My 1 2017

Capitalization rate

Big-Cap Growth Stocks Are Back N. S. HUANG chart *Kiplinger's Personal Finance* v71 no6 p55 Je 2017

Capitation fees (Medical care)

How to Pay for Health Care/The Case for Capitation: Interaction B. Beauvais, C. Habig et al *Harvard Business Review* v94 no11 p20 N 2016

Capitol Records Inc.

COMIC S. Marikar cartoon *New Yorker* v93 no27 p27 S 11 2017

Capitol Hill (Washington, D.C.)

THE WHOLE HILL J. SIDMAN, M. D. G. KAPLAN et al *Washingtonian Magazine* v52 no9 p162 Je 2017

Caplan, Liz

Go From Sucking to 60 K. SCHAEFER and L. SCHWARTZBERG img *New York* v49 no23 p68 N 14 2016

Lizzy Caplan M. WAKIM *Los Angeles Magazine* v61 no11 p80 N 2016

CAPLAN, NATHAN S.

TRIAL JUDGMENT *Scientific American* v317 no2 p5 Ag 2017

Caplan-Auerbach, Jacqueline

Seismic constraints on caldera dynamics from the 2015 Axial Seamount eruption bibl color graph *Science* v354 no6318 p1395 D 16 2016

Caplin, Joan

Creating Smart Tools color *Money* v45 no11 p20 D 2016

Empowering Woman color *Money* v46 no1 p24 Ja/F 2017

Nurturing Success color *Money* v46 no2 p26 Mr 2017

A Passion for Teaching color *Money* v45 no10 p26 N 2016

CAPLINGER, DAN

The Wisdom of Warren color *AARP: The Magazine* v59 no4A p32 Je/Jl 2016

Caponigro, Dara

My New Career H. BOWLES color *Vogue* v207 no11 p142 N 2017

CAPORALE, MICCO

THE UNTOLD BLACK HISTORY OF THE SECOND WAVE *In These Times* v41 no7 p39 Jl 2017

Capota, Emanuela

Anticancer sulfonamides target splicing by inducing RBM39 degradation via recruitment to DCAF15 color diag *Science* v356 no6336 p397 Ap 28 2017

CAPPA, JOHN

BIG-IRON BOONDOCKING [Cover story] color *Dirt Sports + Off-Road* v51 no12 p34 D 2017

Capparella, Joseph

And the Beat Goes On color *Car & Driver* v63 no2 p96 Ag 2017

A Boost for the Soul color *Car & Driver* v62 no8 p82 F 2017

A Crude Awakening color *Car & Driver* v63 no2 p88 Ag 2017

Sui Generis cartoon color *Car & Driver* v62 no7 p88 Ja 2017

Cappelen, Alexander W.

Is It OK to Get Paid More for Being Lucky? color graph *Harvard Business Review Digital Articles* p2 Mr 9 2017

Research: Moral Appeals Can Help Reduce Tax Evasion *Harvard Business Review Digital Articles* p2 Jl 20 2017

Cappelle, Laura

Against All Odds color *Dance Magazine* v91 no3 p52 Mr 2017

A Bold Leap *Dance Magazine* v90 no12 p77 D 2016

Julian MacKay *Dance Magazine* v91 no9 p26 S 2017

Upheaval at Staatsballett Berlin *Dance Magazine* v91 no1 p40 Ja 2017

Wayne's New World: Wayne McGregor isn't keeping his state-of-the-art space to himself *Dance Magazine* v91 no7 p14 Jl 2017

Cappelletti, Valentina

Cell-wide analysis of protein thermal unfolding reveals determinants of thermostability color *Science* v355 no6327 p812 F 24 2017

Cappelli, Peter

B-Schools Aren't Bothering to Produce HR Experts *Harvard Business Review Digital Articles* p2 Jl 27 2015

The Common Myths About Performance Reviews, Debunked *Harvard Business Review Digital Articles* p2 Jl 26 2016

Engaging Your Older Workers *Harvard Business Review Digital Articles* p2 N 5 2014

Google Adds Benefits, Walmart Cuts Them; Oddly, the Logic Is the Same *Harvard Business Review Digital Articles* p2 N 7 2014

There's No Such Thing as Big Data in HR color *Harvard Business Review Digital Articles* p1 Je 2 2017

What It Really Takes to Attract Top Talent *Harvard Business Review Digital Articles* p2 N 24 2015

Why the U.S. Decided That Managers Deserve Overtime Too *Harvard Business Review Digital Articles* p2 My 26 2016

CAPPS, KRISTON

Hanged, Burned, Shot, Drowned, Beaten color *Atlantic* v320 no4

p30 N 2017

CAPPS, ROBERT

ASK A FLOWCHART diag *Wired* v24 no12 p144 D 2016

ASK A FLOWCHART diag *Wired* v25 no4 p96 Ap 2017

ASK A FLOWCHART diag *Wired* v25 no7 p96 Jl 2017

ASK A FLOWCHART HOW STRONG IS MY GENETIC TOLERANCE TO PAIN? diag *Wired* v25 no5 p120 My 2017

Knoll color *Wired* v24 no12 p124 D 2016

WHAT TECHNOLOGY SHOULD I USE TO ENSURE MY LEGACY LIVES ON? diag *Wired* v25 no8 p96 Ag 2017

Capps, Ron—Interviews

RON CAPPS T. Taylor color *Hot Rod* v70 no5 p16 My 2017

CAPRETTA, JAMES C.

Cut the Payroll Tax *National Review* v69 no19 p22 O 16 2017

Capria, M. T.

Localized aliphatic organic material on the surface of Ceres bibl graph *Science* v355 no6326 p719 F 17 2017

Seasonal exposure of carbon dioxide ice on the nucleus of comet 67P/Churyumov-Gerasimenko bibl bw graph *Science* v354 no6319 p1563 D 23 2016

Capricornus (Constellation)

Exploring Capricornus P. HARRINGTON bw color *Astronomy* v45 no10 p68 O 2017

Caprimulgidae

See also

Eurostopodus

A Diabolical Pair B. HEINRICH color *Natural History* v125 no7 p14 Jl/Ag 2017

CAPRIO, DENNIS

Break From Tradition chart color *Power & Motoryacht* v34 no11 p118 N 2017

Caps & closures—Equipment & supplies

new products: sample prep-handling color *Science* v356 no6343 p1197 Je 16 2017

Caps & closures—Evaluation

Labels We Love J. ORTVED bw color *GQ: Gentlemen's Quarterly* v86 no12 p106 D 2016

TEST KITCHEN TALK C. L. Music color *Bon Appetit* no1 p102 F 2017

Two Words: No, Plastic R. Spinks *Sierra* v101 no5 p12 S/O 2016

Caps (Headgear)

See also

Baseball caps

HAPPY TRAILS J. Dengate color *Runner's World* v52 no9 p78 O 2017

Caps (Headgear)—Evaluation

CAPS LOCK *Cincinnati Magazine* v50 no8 p28 My 2017

POWDER 80'S P. Bridges color *Snowboarder* v29 no2 p138 O 2016

Capsaicin

5 Fat-Loss Hacks S. STIEFEL color *Muscle & Performance* v9 no7 p24 Jl 2017

HEAT A. C. Shilton color *Men's Health* v32 no4 p112 My 2017

Capshaw, Jessica—Interviews

Grey's Anatomy M. Logan *TV Guide* v65 no4 p35 Ja 16 2017

Capsids (Viruses)

The structure and flexibility of conical HIV-1 capsids determined within intact virions S. Mattei, B. Glass et al bibl color *Science* v354 no6318 p1434 D 16 2016

Captain America (Fictitious character)

NO. 7 Captain America A. Breznican color *Entertainment Weekly* no1436/1437 p50 O 21 2016

Captain America: Civil War (Film)

CAPTAIN AMERICA: CIVIL WAR C. Chiarella color *Sound & Vision* v82 no1 p71 Ja 2017

No. 10 CAPTAIN AMERICA: CIVIL WAR C. Nashawaty color diag *Entertainment Weekly* no1444/1445 p56 D 16 2016

Captain Fantastic (Film)

Captain Fantastic A. D'ARMINIO *TV Guide* v65 no8 p36 F 27 2017

Captain Planet & the Planeteers (TV program)

Green from the Get-Go: At 24, Atlanta's new sustainability director has already spent a lifetime in the field E. Daigneau *Governing* v31 no1 p20 O 2017

Captain Underpants (Film)

CAPTAIN UNDERPANTS D. Coggan color *Entertainment Week-*

ly no1446/1447 p51 D 2016/Ja 2017

CAPTAIN UNDERPANTS: THE FIRST EPIC MOVIE D. Coggan color *Entertainment Weekly* no1463/1464 p53 Ap/My 2017

Captivity

Boko Haram's Other Victims A. Baker color *Time* v190 no2/3 p40 Jl 10-17 2017

Capturing Everest (Film)

Peak Season color *Sports Illustrated* v126 no13 p12 My 8 2017

Summit Talk T. Keith color *Sports Illustrated* v126 no4 p23 Ja 30 2017

CAPUA, ENZO

Chords & Discords bw color *Downbeat* v84 no6 p10 Je 2017

Capuano, Katie

mom wins... ...and fails color *Working Mother* v40 no2 p8 Je/Jl 2017

Capuchin monkeys

Monkey flakes resemble hominid tools B. BOWER color *Science News* v190 no11 p16 N 26 2016

Capuchin monkeys—Behavior

Whose Tools Are These? K. Wong color *Scientific American* v316 no1 p10 Ja 2017

CAPUTI, GARY

BATTLE TESTED chart color diag *Power & Motoryacht* v33 no2 p76 F 2017

Caputo, Nina

FROM THE EDITOR P. Lay *History Today* v66 no11 p2 N 2016

Caputo, Philip

Rat On Me, Father S. AKAM *New York Times Book Review* p11 Je 25 2017

Car & Driver (Periodical)

Editor's Letter E. Alterman *Car & Driver* v63 no2 p12 Ag 2017

Car Seat Headrest (Performer)

STAGE RIGHT *Cincinnati Magazine* v50 no12 p26 S 2017

Car sharing

Baby, You Can Rent My Car N. Leiber *Bloomberg Businessweek* no4494 p36 O 10 2016

Car 54, Where Are You? (TV program)

The 'Car 54' Model W. Kristol bw *Weekly Standard* v22 no27 p10 Mr 20 2017

Cara, Alessia, 1996-

Alessia Cara B. Muteba color *Current Biography* v77 no11 p26 N 2016

Cara, Alessia, 1996-—Interviews

Alessia Cara B. HIATT color *Rolling Stone* no1283 p18 Mr 23 2017

Carabello, Laura

Employers Are Destined for Health Quality and Cost Savings: Health City Cayman Islands color *Forbes* v199 no7 p(Sp2)1 Je 29 2017

Carabiners

The Carabiner A. DENNIS color graph *Climbing* no350 p28 D 2016/Ja 2017

Caracas (Venezuela)—Social conditions

Leading a Double Life In Caracas A. Rosati color *Bloomberg Businessweek* no4531 p30 Jl 24 2017

Caramel

FOOD GIFTS M. GLISAN color *Better Homes & Gardens* v95 no11 p14 N 2017

Caramete, L.

Observation of a large-scale anisotropy in the arrival directions of cosmic rays above 8×10^{18} eV *Science* v357 no6357 p1266 S 22 2017

Carande, Carl

How to Integrate Data and Analytics into Every Part of Your Organization *Harvard Business Review Digital Articles* p2 Je 23 2017

Carandini, Andrea

On books J. Gardner color *Magazine Antiques* v184 no5 p42 S/O 2017

Reading the Ruins of Rome M. Beard color *New York Review of Books* v64 no12 p18 Jl 13 2017

Caraoke Showdown (TV program)

CARAOKE SHOWDOWN L. ACKEN *TV Guide* v65 no4 p45 Ja 16 2017

Caras, Jim

Burns Fat, Improves Sleep... and Beautifies Hair, Skin & Nails!

The limits of carbon reduction roadmaps J. Urpelainen *Science* v356 no6342 p1019 Je 9 2017

PILING UP CO[subscript 2] SAVINGS B. O'Keefe diag *Fortune* v175 no7 p88 Je 1 2017

Rightsizing carbon dioxide removal C. B. Field and K. J. Mach chart color *Science* v356 no6339 p706 My 19 2017

Toolset Promotes Carbon-Capture Solution M. Garrison color *Science & Technology Review* p14 Ja/F 2017

The trouble with negative emissions K. Anderson and G. Peters bibl graph *Science* v354 no6309 p182 O 14 2016

Carbon dioxide—Absorption & adsorption

Gene offers clues to grasses' success L. HAMERS color *Science News* v191 no7 p12 Ap 15 2017

Hidden Battles Reefs T. DeCarlo color *Oceanus* v51 no2 p32 Wint 2016

Up to Speed: Two Months, One Page P. Rauber *Sierra* v101 no4 p26 Jl/Ag 2016

Carbon dioxide—Environmental aspects

For the Record color diag *Time* v189 no11 p8 Mr 27 2017

Point of No Return color *Earth Island Journal* v32 no4 p4 Wint 2017

Carbon fibers

The Miracle Material E. DYER color *Popular Mechanics* p51 Mr 2017

THE ONE S. SMITH color *Road & Track* v68 no10 p30 Jl 2017

shaping the now m. ferrentino bw *Bike Magazine* v24 no5 p44 Jl 2017

Carbon-hydrogen bonds (Chemistry)

Low-temperature activation of methane on the IrO2(110) surface Z. Liang, T. Li et al bw diag graph *Science* v356 no6335 p299 Ap 21 2017

Carbon in soils

Long-term pattern and magnitude of soil carbon feedback to the climate system in a warming world J. M. Melillo, S. D. Frey et al chart graph *Science* v357 no6359 p101 O 6 2017

RESEARCH color *Science* v355 no6332 p1386 Mr 31 2017

The whole-soil carbon flux in response to warming [Cover story] C. E. Hicks Pries, C. Castanha et al chart graph *Science* v355 no6332 p1420 Mr 31 2017

Carbon Inc.

Carbon K. Bourzac color il *MIT Technology Review* v120 no4 p62 Jl/Ag 2017

Carbon nanotubes

The carbon nanotube integrated circuit goes three-dimensional: Chip makers have a mantra: smaller, cheaper, and faster. They may now need a new adjective--taller M. Wilson *Physics Today* v70 no9 p14 S 2017

Carbon nanotube transistors scaled to a 40-nanometer footprint Q. Cao, J. Tersoff et al color graph *Science* v356 no6345 p1369 Je 30 2017

Enhanced water permeability and tunable ion selectivity in sub-nanometer carbon nanotube porins R. H. Tunuguntla, R. Y. Henley et al chart color *Science* v357 no6353 p792 Ag 25 2017

Harvesting electrical energy from carbon nanotube yarn twist S. Hyeong Kim, C. S. Haines et al diag graph *Science* v357 no6353 p773 Ag 25 2017

Scaling carbon nanotube complementary transistors to 5-nm gate lengths C. Qiu, Z. Zhang et al bibl chart graph *Science* v355 no6322 p271 Ja 20 2017

Carbon offsetting

Credit Check K. WEISUL cartoon color *Rodale's Organic Life* v2 no7 p18 D 2016/Ja 2017

Carbon pricing

See also

Carbon taxes

GOOD NEWS color *Maclean's* v129 no41 p8 O 17 2016

Carbon sequestration

The Biochar Solution E. Strickland *Sierra* v102 no4 p25 Jl/Ag 2017

Carbon sequestration beyond tree longevity L. C. R. Silva bibl *Science* v355 no6330 p1141 Mr 17 2017

Christoph Gebald and Jan Wurzbacher B. Parkin cartoon *Bloomberg Businessweek* no4537 p76 S 11 2017

Cost of carbon capture drops, but does anyone want it? R. F. Service color graph *Science* v354 no6318 p1362 D 16 2016

A matter of tree longevity C. Körner bibl color *Science* v355

no6321 p130 Ja 13 2017

The promise of negative emissions K. Anderson and G. Peters bibl *Science* v354 no6313 p714 N 11 2016

Rightsizing carbon dioxide removal C. B. Field and K. J. Mach chart color *Science* v356 no6339 p706 My 19 2017

Carbon sequestration in the ocean

'Mucus houses' catch sea carbon fast S. MILIUS color *Science News* v191 no11 p13 Je 10 2017

Carbon sequestration—Methodology

Toolset Promotes Carbon-Capture Solution M. Garrison color *Science & Technology Review* p14 Ja/F 2017

Carbon taxes

A Different Carbon Tax: The Sustainable Green Tariff P. Lorenzi *Society* v54 no4 p342 Ag 2017

The Shifting Politics of Taxing Carbon C. Flavelle *Bloomberg Businessweek* no4519 p52 Ap 24 2017

Carbon taxes—Canada

CAN CANADA STILL HAVE A CARBON TAX? J. MARKU-SOFF color *Maclean's* v129 no47 p36 N 28 2016

THE TORIES ARE STUCK IN THE PAST ON CARBON E. SOLOMON *Maclean's* v129 no42 p10 O 24 2016

CARBONARA, PETER

Game of Porcelain Thrones color *Forbes* v200 no2 p37 S 5 2017

GAMING THE SYSTEM color *Forbes* v199 no4 p98 Ap 25 2017

Carbonated beverage bottles

ATLANTA IN 50 OBJECTS T. MALONE *Atlanta* v56 no8 p50 D 2016

Carbonated beverages

See also

Root beer

Eating to Beat Belly Fat [Cover story] *Tufts University Health & Nutrition Letter* v34 no11 p1 Ja 2017

How to Make a... ROOT BEER B. KAUFMAN color *Popular Mechanics* p76 S 2017

How to Make a... ROOT BEER B. KAUFMAN color *Popular Mechanics* v193 no7 p76 S 2016

Jeff Sluman J. Marksbury and C. Barrett color *Golf Magazine* v59 no8 p39 Ag 2017

NEW New Year's Resolutions color *Prevention* v69 no1 p13 Ja 2017

Nutrients in carrot peels ... Lemon-lime soda ... Rinsing canned beans R. A. Fielding *Tufts University Health & Nutrition Letter* v35 no8 p8 O 2017

Carbone, Jason

YOU DA AQUAMAN! color *Golf Magazine* v59 no2 p48 F 2017

Carbon—Export & import trade

Emission Permission L. Laursen color *Scientific American* v317 no2 p17 Ag 2017

Carbon fiber-reinforced plastics

CHOOSING MATERIALS K. CAMERON color *Cycle World* v56 no8 p20 S 2017

Carbon—Therapeutic use

On the value of carbon-ion therapy M. Story, A. Pompos et al *Physics Today* v69 no11 p14 N 2016

Carboxylic acid derivatives

Photoinduced decarboxylative borylation of carboxylic acids A. Fawcett, J. Pradeilles et al diag *Science* v357 no6348 p283 Jl 21 2017

Carbray, Julie

What Your SELFIE Says ABOUT YOU A. STANLEY color *Seventeen* v76 no12 p68 D 2016/Ja 2017

Carburetors

Boost-Ready M. Gearhart color *Hot Rod* v70 no5 p20 My 2017

Service R. NIERLICH color *Cycle World* v56 no6 p62 Jl 2017

THROTTLED ENGINE? R. Bohacz *Successful Farming* v115 no4 p32 Mr 2017

The Thumpr-Cammed 383 Small-Block in Don Kwiatkowski's 1971 Nova Hesitates and Stumbles Off Idle. We're Gonna Fix It M. Davis chart color *Hot Rod* v70 no6 p104 Je 2017

CARBYN, LUDWIG

An Unparalleled Opportunity for an Important Ecological Study *BioScience* v67 no10 p875 O 2017

Carcassés, Bobby

Artists Collaborate, Celebrate at Jazz Day Events in Havana J. Murph color *Downbeat* v84 no7 p14 Jl 2017

Carcinogens

Cardiovascular fitness

GO LONG K. LOREN chart color *Muscle & Performance* v9 no5 p20 My 2017

THE NEW CARDIO L. McGLASHAN cartoon *Muscle & Performance* v8 no12 p30 D 2016

Cardiovascular system

See also

Blood-vessels

is yoga enough? color *Yoga Journal* p28 2017 Special Issue

Cardiovascular system physiology

Get into Fighting Shape Like Ruby Rose color *Health* v31 no1 p16 Ja 2017

A home practice to Boost heart health S. Nardini color *Yoga Journal* p33 2017 Special Issue

CARDONE, GARY

'Tis the Season for ID Theft *USA Today Magazine* v145 no2860 p37 Ja 2017

CARDOSO, FERNANDO HENRIQUE

Brazil's Crisis Reflects Demise of Representative Democracy Across the West *NPQ: New Perspectives Quarterly* v33 no4 p35 O 2016

Cardoso, Hugo

The growth pattern of Neandertals, reconstructed from a juvenile skeleton from El Sidrón (Spain) color graph *Science* v357 no6357 p1282 S 22 2017

CARDOZA, RILEY

FRIENDSHIP {decoded} color *Seventeen* v76 no4 p86 Jl/Ag 2017

Cardoza, Russell

Broc Cresta K. Santos color *Spin to Win Rodeo* v21 no5 p60 Jl 2017

Cards (TV program)

Cards Returns With a Thud D. D'Addario color *Time* v189 no21 p63 Je 5 2017

Care of Alzheimer's patients

The Forgotten Y. Stines color *Ebony* v72 no9 p60 Jl/Ag 2017

Care of people

See also

Child care

The Guys Next Door D. Stattmann, P. Kita et al *Women's Health* v14 no2 p20 Mr 2017

Careem (Company)

Dial-a-Caravan P. OLSON color *Forbes* v199 no7 p41 Je 29 2017

Career changes

4 Things That Sink New Executives, and How to Overcome Them R. Carucci *Harvard Business Review Digital Articles* p2 F 9 2016

5 Signs It's Time for a New Job T. Chamorro-Premuzic *Harvard Business Review Digital Articles* p2 Ap 7 2015

Are You Sure You Want to Be a Manager? J. Grenny *Harvard Business Review Digital Articles* p2 S 22 2015

Change Your Career Without Having to Start All Over Again D. Clark *Harvard Business Review Digital Articles* p2 My 24 2016

Don't Talk Yourself Out of Trying a Second Career L. Smith *Harvard Business Review Digital Articles* p2 Ap 27 2016

Extraordinary and poor P. Yuan color *Science* v356 no6345 p1406 Je 30 2017

Find the Career Coach Who's Right for You D. Clark *Harvard Business Review Digital Articles* p2 Mr 31 2015

GET A BETTER JOB NOW K. Bahler and M. C. White color diag *Money* v46 no2 p76 Mr 2017

GIRL CODE R. SAUJANI color *Scientific American* v317 no3 p66 S 2017

HOW TO BE A NON-TEXAN *Texas Monthly* v45 no4 p6 Ap 2017

How to Become a Coach or Consultant After You Retire D. Clark *Harvard Business Review Digital Articles* p2 My 12 2017

How to Use Your LinkedIn Profile to Power a Career Transition J. Heifetz *Harvard Business Review Digital Articles* p2 My 28 2015

It's Mama's Turn! How to Start Your Second Career K. PALMER color *AARP: The Magazine* v59 no4A p26 Je/Jl 2016

Leaving a Stable Job to Create Your Dream Career M. Valcour *Harvard Business Review Digital Articles* p2 Ja 26 2016

Navigating the Emotional Side of a Career Transition R. Ashkenas *Harvard Business Review Digital Articles* p2 Ap 5 2016

New year, new career: 5 tips for changing occupations E. Torpey *Career Outlook* p4 F 2017

Not Taking Risks Is the Riskiest Career Move of All A. Kreamer *Harvard Business Review Digital Articles* p2 Ap 16 2015

A retirement 'hobby' J. H. Borden color *Science* v355 no6324 p542 F 3 2017

A Tourist's Guide to Changing Careers J. Acuff *Harvard Business Review Digital Articles* p2 Ap 13 2015

When You're Leaving Your Job Because of Your Kids [Cover story] D. W. Dowling *Harvard Business Review Digital Articles* p2 Ap 11 2017

Career changes—United States

Doctors Without Patients A. Mostue *Bloomberg Businessweek* no4537 p34 S 11 2017

Career development

See also

Teacher development

The 3 Ways People React to Career Disasters P. Mirvis, M. Marks et al *Harvard Business Review Digital Articles* p2 Je 18 2015

4 Tools to Help You Identify the Skills You Need to Grow D. Rousmaniere *Harvard Business Review Digital Articles* p2 Ag 8 2016

6 Things Every Mentor Should Do V. Chopra and S. Saint *Harvard Business Review Digital Articles* p2 Mr 29 2017

The Ambition-Marriage Trade-Off Too Many Single Women Face L. Bursztyn, T. Fujiwara et al *Harvard Business Review Digital Articles* p2 My 8 2017

Backtalk S. van der Veen and E. M. Furtak color *Phi Delta Kappan* v98 no8 p80 My 2017

The Best Advice I Never Got N. Gibbs color *InStyle* v24 no9 p210 S 2017

Career Question: Should You Take More Risks? W. Naugle color *Glamour* v115 no10 p134 O 2017

the case for ballet in college K. RICHTER *Dance Magazine* p14 2016/2017

The Case for Lending Out Your Star Performers R. Jesuthasan, D. Creelman et al *Harvard Business Review Digital Articles* p2 Ja 19 2015

Change Your Career Without Having to Start All Over Again D. Clark *Harvard Business Review Digital Articles* p2 My 24 2016

Companies Drain Women's Ambition After Only 2 Years O. Gadiesh and J. Coffman *Harvard Business Review Digital Articles* p2 My 18 2015

COULD YOUR PERSONALITY DERAIL YOUR CAREER? DON'T TAKE THESE TRAITS TO THE EXTREME T. CHAMORRO-PREMUZIC chart il img *Harvard Business Review* v95 no5 p138 S/O 2017

Divorce Doesn't Have to Derail Your Career A. Bassuk and J. Glickman *Harvard Business Review Digital Articles* p2 Ap 15 2015

DON CHERRY: ORGANIC FLOW P. Lutz bw *Downbeat* v84 no8 p32 Ag 2017

DO NOT READ THIS ARTICLE: Delivering learning exactly when it's needed isn't just common sense - it's a revolution for the L&D department M. CALNAN *People Management* p46 Ap 2017

Don't Set Too Many Goals for Yourself D. Clark *Harvard Business Review Digital Articles* p2 D 16 2016

The Energizing Impact of Micro-Credentials in Kettle Moraine P. Deklotz *Education Digest* v82 no9 p24 My 2017

Episcopal Divinity School to join Union Seminary, Brown Douglas named dean C. Kennel-Shank *Christian Century* v134 no13 p15 Je 21 2017

Establish Expertise Inside Your Company D. Clark *Harvard Business Review Digital Articles* p2 Ag 19 2015

EUBIE BLAKE: 'NOTHING STAYS THE SAME' T. Panken bw *Downbeat* v84 no8 p37 Ag 2017

Everyone's Network Should Provide Two Things L. Davey *Harvard Business Review Digital Articles* p1 S 30 2016

An Experiment in India Shows How Much Companies Have to Gain by Investing in Their Employees A. Adhvaryu, L. Garg et al *Harvard Business Review Digital Articles* p1 Jl 25 2017

Extraordinary and poor P. Yuan color *Science* v356 no6345 p1406 Je 30 2017

Finding Your Lane B. Welch bw *Horse & Rider* v56 no7 p17 Jl 2017

The Fine Line Between a Collaborative Employee and One Who Doesn't Get Enough Done R. Shambaugh *Harvard Business Review Digital Articles* p2 Je 30 2016

Free Yourself from What You "Should" Be Doing A. Molinsky color *Harvard Business Review Digital Articles* p2 Ja 18 2017

GET A BETTER JOB NOW K. Bahler and M. C. White color diag *Money* v46 no2 p76 Mr 2017

Getting Your Career Back on Track After a Catastrophic Error M. Peabody and L. Stybel *Harvard Business Review Digital Articles* p2 My 12 2016

Get Your Passion Project Moving Without Quitting Your Day Job R. Knight *Harvard Business Review Digital Articles* p2 F 19 2015

HERBIE NICHOLS: RIGHTFUL HONOR J. Hale bw *Downbeat* v84 no8 p36 Ag 2017

HERE'S WHY BRITISH VOGUE'S NEW EDITOR-IN-CHIEF MATTERS M. HARRIS color *Ebony* v72 no11 p30 S 2017

HOLDING COURT B. HENLEY color *Tennis* v53 no5 p38 S/O 2017

How Stay-at-Home Parents Can Transition Back to Work D. Clark *Harvard Business Review Digital Articles* p2 Ap 24 2017

How to Ask for the Job Title You Deserve R. Knight *Harvard Business Review Digital Articles* p2 Jl 17 2017

How to Build a Meaningful Career A. Gallo *Harvard Business Review Digital Articles* p2 F 4 2015

How to Decide What Skill to Work On Next E. Andersen *Harvard Business Review Digital Articles* p2 Ja 25 2016

How to Help Someone Discover Work That Excites Them A. Jen Su *Harvard Business Review Digital Articles* p2 S 13 2017

How to Know If Joining a Startup Is Right for You R. Knight *Harvard Business Review Digital Articles* p2 My 16 2016

How to Launch a Successful Portfolio Career M. Greenspan *Harvard Business Review Digital Articles* p2 My 4 2017

Identifying the Skills That Can Help You Change Careers C. Bowe *Harvard Business Review Digital Articles* p2 Ag 6 2015

I'LL TELL YOU SOMETHING NADEEM KARBHARI N. KARBHARI *People Management* p18 F 2017

Increase the Odds of Achieving Your Goals by Setting Them with Your Spouse J. Coleman and J. Coleman *Harvard Business Review Digital Articles* p2 F 3 2015

JANE IRA BLOOM: CHASING A MERCURIAL SOUND J. Hale bw *Downbeat* v84 no8 p46 Ag 2017

The Kind of Homework That Helps Coaching Stick M. Valcour *Harvard Business Review Digital Articles* p2 Mr 3 2015

KRIS DAVIS: 'Open To Surprise' B. Bambarger color *Downbeat* v84 no8 p51 Ag 2017

THE LAST LONG ROAD R. ZUMMALLEN color *Road & Track* v69 no2 p64 S 2017

LIVING THE Dream color *Dance Spirit* v21 no2 p12 F 2017

Local Strategies: Creating and Nurturing Collaborative Communities of Practice D. Bauer, E. Beaulieu et al *Change* v49 no4 p20 Jl/Ag 2017

Lonely at the Top K. SCHWAB *Dance Magazine* v90 no11 p50 N 2016

MARIJUANA MOMS [Cover story] C. MOSCATELLO color *Working Mother* v40 no3 p20 Ag/S 2017

MARY HALVORSON: 'MORE THAN I WOULD'VE HOPED FOR' D. Ouellette color *Downbeat* v84 no8 p42 Ag 2017

Maximize Your Learning in Short-Term Assignments J. Coleman *Harvard Business Review Digital Articles* p2 Jl 15 2016

Micro-Credentials: The Badges of Professional Growth B. BERRY *Education Digest* v82 no9 p21 My 2017

Nevertheless, She Persisted M. Halpin color *Glamour* v115 no5 p162 My 2017

The next step *People Management* p54 F 2017

The next step *People Management* p55 D 2016/Ja 2017

Not Taking Risks Is the Riskiest Career Move of All A. Kreamer *Harvard Business Review Digital Articles* p2 Ap 16 2013

NOT THE PRESIDENT'S MEN: Top lawyers are passing up a career-making opportunity. Why? M. M. Kashina *Washingtonian Magazine* v52 no11 p16 Ag 2017

Once Upon a Time in America M. HOLGATE bw color *Vogue* v207 no9 p706 S 2017

One Engagement Strategy Does Not Fit All N. Baumgartner *Harvard Business Review Digital Articles* p2 N 26 2014

ONLY CONNECT M. Daum bw *Vogue* v207 no9 p680 S 2017

On Tour With... KANE BROWN J. Abidor color *Seventeen* v75 no11 p20 N 2016

O's GO-FOR-IT GUIDE to Getting Unstuck cartoon chart *O, The Oprah Magazine* p114 F 2017

PASSION PLAYER J. Powers color *Vogue* v207 no9 p676 S 2017

Plan Your Professional Development for the Year D. Clark *Harvard Business Review Digital Articles* p2 Ja 7 2016

Quantifying the evolution of individual scientific impact R. Sinatra, Dashun Wang et al graph *Science* v354 no6312 p596 N 4 2016

Reading List: Midcareer Crisis Series *Harvard Business Review Digital Articles* p2 My 4 2015

Rebel In the House W. HOPPS, D. TREISMAN et al *Los Angeles Magazine* v62 no6 p60 Je 2017

Research: The More Essential Your Job Is to Your Company, the Happier You'll Be Lixin Jiang, T. Tripp et al *Harvard Business Review Digital Articles* p2 My 10 2017

SINGER OF SECRETS N. PAUMGARTEN cartoon color *New Yorker* v93 no25 p60 Ag 28 2017

The "So You Think You Can Dance" Effect S. FRISCIA *Dance Magazine* v91 no6 p34 Je 2017

Teachable Moments: Structures don't store memories or build character--people do *Indianapolis Monthly* p168 N 2017

TECH OF ALL TRADES S. Tedesco color *Good Housekeeping* v265 no2 p6 Ag 2017

Think Strategically About Your Career Development D. Clark *Harvard Business Review Digital Articles* p2 D 6 2016

To Boost Your Career, Get to Know Your Boss's Boss R. Knight *Harvard Business Review Digital Articles* p2 S 2 2016

To Get Promoted, Get Feedback from Your Critics S. Nawaz *Harvard Business Review Digital Articles* p2 N 10 2016

Turning Your Complex Career Path into a Coherent Story A. Ranieri *Harvard Business Review Digital Articles* p2 Ag 14 2015

TWINNING AS BOSSES IS A LIFESTYLE B. VIERA color *Ebony* v72/73 no12/1 p26 O/N 2017

Using Harsh Feedback to Fuel Your Career W. Treseder color *Harvard Business Review Digital Articles* p2 O 12 2016

WADADA Leo Smith: RISING UP IN PURITY [Cover story] T. Panken color *Downbeat* v84 no8 p22 Ag 2017

What does a 'professional' do? P. Cheese *People Management* p5 Mr 2017

What Do I Do Now? A Midlife Career Change May Be Just the Challenge You Need K. V. Ogtrop color *Time* v190 no8 p59 Ag 28 2017

What Having a "Growth Mindset" Actually Means C. Dweck *Harvard Business Review Digital Articles* p2 Ja 13 2016

WHAT'S NEXT? J. FARAGHER *People Management* p36 Mr 2017

What to Do If You Feel Stuck in the Wrong Career D. Rousmaniere *Harvard Business Review Digital Articles* p2 Ap 6 2015

What to Do When People Don't Support Your Next Career Move D. Clark *Harvard Business Review Digital Articles* p2 Ag 26 2016

What to Do When Your Heart Isn't in Your Work Anymore A. Molinsky *Harvard Business Review Digital Articles* p2 Jl 10 2017

What to Do When Your Personal Growth Stalls W. Johnson *Harvard Business Review Digital Articles* p2 S 28 2015

WHAT YOU WANT TO BE (AND HOW TO GET THERE) img *Scholastic Choices* p7 O 2017 Supplement

When Authenticity Does More Harm than Good M. Schrage *Harvard Business Review Digital Articles* p2 O 26 2015

When You Realize You'll Never Get Your Dream Job S. Friedman *Harvard Business Review Digital Articles* p2 Ap 1 2015

Who I am Catherine Shutt *People Management* p51 Ap 2017

Why Certain Managers Thrive in Tough New Jobs While Others Get Fed Up Yuntao Dong, Myeong-Gu Seo et al *Harvard Business Review Digital Articles* p2 Ap 22 2015

Why IBM Gives Top Employees a Month to Do Service Abroad R. Chong and M. Fleming *Harvard Business Review Digital Articles* p2 N 5 2014

Why "Network More" Is Bad Advice for Women S. G. Carmichael *Harvard Business Review Digital Articles* p2 F 26 2015

Why That Risky Career Move Could Be a Safer Bet than You Think K. Firestone *Harvard Business Review Digital Articles* p2 Mr 11 2016

WITHOUT A NET J. Gay color *Vogue* v207 no9 p630 S 2017

You Can't Move Up If You're Stuck in Your Boss's Shadow R. Knight *Harvard Business Review Digital Articles* p2 My 8 2015

You Don't Need a Promotion to Grow at Work J. Stark and K. S. Milway *Harvard Business Review Digital Articles* p2 Je 24 2015

You Need to Practice Being Your Future Self P. Bregman *Harvard Business Review Digital Articles* p2 Mr 28 2016

Your Career Needs Many Mentors, Not Just One D. Clark color *Harvard Business Review Digital Articles* p2 Ja 19 2017

Career development—Congresses

Why learning has never mattered more *People Management* p10 Je 2017

Career development—United States

Melanie MOORE C. Bowers *Dance Spirit* v21 no7 p46 S 2017

Career education

See also

Professional education

Washington View M. Ferguson *Phi Delta Kappan* v99 no1 p42 S 2017

Career education—United States

Where Career Plans Start Early C. Gewertz *Education Digest* v83 no1 p54 S 2017

Careers & Enterprise Co.

Volunteers boost careers support: Members share their HR expertise with local schools to help young people prepare for work *People Management* p56 Mr 2017

Careful What You Wish For (Film)

NEW AVAILABLE MOVIES M. FELL *TV Guide* v64 no40 p60 O 3 2016

Caregiver education

Watch, Play, Learn cartoon *AARP: The Magazine* v60 no2A p78 F/Mr 2017

Caregivers

See also

Women caregivers

CAREGIVER'S PREP GUIDE L. GOLDMAN color *Better Homes & Gardens* v95 no11 p146 N 2017

Getting Help at Home P. Wang color *Consumer Reports* v82 no12 p40 D 2017

A HELPING HAND: What to do when it's time to find care for your parents Rin-rin Yu *Washingtonian Magazine* v52 no8 p156 My 2017

THE RIGHT WAY TO PAY A CAREGIVER T. Stanger *Consumer Reports* v82 no12 p51 D 2017

What Has the Biggest Impact on Hospital Readmission Rates C. Senot and A. Chandrasekaran *Harvard Business Review Digital Articles* p2 S 23 2015

Caregivers—United States

Help AARP Help Family Caregivers E. J. Schneidewind *AARP: The Magazine* v59 no6A p76 O/N 2016

Society Needs to Care for All Our Caregivers M. Gates color *Time* v188 no16/17 p43 O 24 2016

Videos Showcase Diverse Caregiving color *AARP: The Magazine* v59 no5A p74 Ag/S 2016

Carell, Steve, 1962-

MEET THE NEW MINION M. Snetiker color *Entertainment Weekly* no1467 p13 My 26 2017

Carell, Steve, 1962-—Interviews

Steve Carell M. ZIMMERMAN *Men's Health* v32 no8 p128 O 2017

Carens, Joseph H.

Calling the Shots W. Voegeli *Claremont Review of Books* v17 no3 p11 Summ 2017

Carew, Keggie, 1957-

Dadland *Publishers Weekly* v263 no44 p61 O 31 2016

Carex

FINDING A GRASSY PATCH color *Martha Stewart Living* p33 My 2017

Carey, David

MAN OF THE (VERY RICH) PEOPLE [Cover story] color *Bloomberg Businessweek* no4509 p38 Ja 30 2017

Shopping the Retail Apocalypse color *Bloomberg Businessweek* no4523 p37 My 22 2017

Why Suppliers Will Still Play With Toys 'R' Us color *Bloomberg Businessweek* no4539 p17 S 25 2017

Carey, David J.

Distribution and clinical impact of functional variants in 50,726 whole-exome sequences from the DiscovEHR study chart graph *Science* v354 no6319 paaf6814-1 D 23 2016

Genetic identification of familial hypercholesterolemia within a single U.S. health care system chart graph *Science* v354 no6319 paaf7000-1 D 23 2016

Carey, Dennis

How Companies Are Using Simulations, Competitions, and Analytics to Hire *Harvard Business Review Digital Articles* p2 Ap 22 2016

Your Board Should Think Like Activists *Harvard Business Review Digital Articles* p2 F 9 2015

Carey, George, 1935-

George Carey quits role as Anglicans confront sexual abuse scandal C. Pepinster *Christian Century* v134 no16 p15 Ag 2 2017

Carey, Glen

Help Wanted in Saudi Arabia: Savvy Investors color graph *Bloomberg Businessweek* no4513 p41 Mr 6 2017

The War in Yemen Tests Saudi Arabia's Clout color *Bloomberg Businessweek* no4508 p12 Ja 23 2017

Carey, Greg

The Beatitudes/Jesus and the Prodigal Son: The God of Radical Mercy *Christian Century* v133 no24 p37 N 23 2016

Carey, Jacqueline

The Shortlist *New York Times Book Review* p26 Ag 20 2017

Carey, Jim, 1974-

PARTY LINES T. Ferber and K. Van Syckle img *New York* v50 no12 p112 Je 12 2017

Carey, John

The Cat Conundrum color *National Wildlife (World Edition)* v55 no6 p30 O/N 2017

CAREY, JONATHAN

The Kiwi Connection *Audubon* v118 no6 p16 Wint 2016

Carey, Kevin

INTRODUCTION: A DIFFERENT KIND OF COLLEGE RANKING chart *Washington Monthly* v49 no9/10 p21 S/O 2017

Introduction: A Different Kind of College Ranking *Washington Monthly* p1 S/O 2016

Carey, Leo

Liszt: The Reluctant Superstar bw *New York Review of Books* v63 no17 p31 N 10 2016

Carey, M. R.

The Boy on the Bridge *Publishers Weekly* v264 no13 p84 Mr 27 2017

Carey, Mariah, 1970-

Mariah Carey Sounds Off J. Hibberd color *Entertainment Weekly* no1448 p10 Ja 13 2017

New Year's Eve Roundup I. Ratledge *TV Guide* p41 D 19 2016

CAREY, SARAH

BROWNIE POINTS *Martha Stewart Living* no269 p86 N 2016

CAKES FOR any OCCASION [Cover story] color *Martha Stewart Living* p70 My 2017

FISH FRY color *Martha Stewart Living* p86 Jl/Ag 2017

FRESH IN A FLASH color *Martha Stewart Living* p72 S 2017

JUST ADD GREENS color *Martha Stewart Living* p84 Ap 2017

LOVE AT FIRST BITE color *Martha Stewart Living* p76 S 2017

THE TIME IS RIPE (TO BAKE WITH FRUIT) color *Martha Stewart Living* no275 p98 Je 2017

CAREY, STEPHANIE

"Said to Be" color *Natural History* v125 no9 p48 S 2017

Cargill Inc.

Leadership Development Should Focus on Experiments R. Ashkenas and R. Hausmann *Harvard Business Review Digital Articles* p2 Ap 12 2016

Cargo ships

STORM TROOPERS T. KORTEN color map *Reader's Digest* v190 no1135 p116 N 2017

TITANS of the Great Lakes I. COUTTS color map *Canadian Geographic* v137 no4 p34 Jl/Ag 2017

WEST COAST FOCUS S. SHIBATA *Sea Magazine* v108 no12 p12 D 2016

Cargo ships—Passenger traffic

UP AND OVER D. Stone diag *National Geographic* v231 no3 p22 Mr 2017

Caribbean Area—Description & travel

An Alluring Compromise M. BLYTH color *AARP: The Magazine* v60 no2A p42 F/Mr 2017

SOUTH for the SUMMER Z. Prochazka color map *Sail* v48 no3 p32 Mr 2017

Caribbean Area—Foreign economic relations

The Red Tide Sweeping the Caribbean E. Fieser color *Bloomberg Businessweek* no4526 p14 Je 12 2017

Caribbean cooking

Jamaica Style J. Forman color *New Orleans Magazine* v51 no9 p80 Jl 2017

Caribbean music

Integrating Afro Caribbean Rhythms into Straightahead Jazz L. PERDOMO bw *Downbeat* v84 no10 p190 O 2017

Caribe, Roman

Confidential Source Ninety-Six color *Publishers Weekly* v264 no27 p68 Jl 3 2017

Caribou

See also

Woodland caribou

Build habitats, not fences, for caribou G. Proulx and R. A. Powell bibl *Science* v353 no6307 p1506 S 30 2016

consider the caribou K. Pierre-Louis chart color *Popular Science* v289 no5 p10 S/O 2017

THE DISTANCE J. ARTERBURN cartoon *Outdoor Life* v224 no8 p78 O 2017

exposure color *Canadian Geographic* v137 no2 p12 Mr/Ap 2017

PORCUPINE CARIBOU color *Canadian Wildlife* v23 no1 p10 Mr/Ap 2017

RACK ATTACK K. EVANS cartoon color *Outdoor Life* v224 no6 p14 Ag 2017

Wolves, Lies & Logging E. C. ALBERTS color *Alternatives Journal (AJ) - Canada's Environmental Voice* v42 no2 p66 2016

Caribou populations

Out of Time? L. Warren color *National Wildlife (World Edition)* v55 no6 p40 O/N 2017

Caricatures & cartoons

See also

Comic books, strips, etc.

Political cartoons

Good on Paper S. L. Johnson cartoon *O, The Oprah Magazine* p128 Mr 2017

Laugh Out Loud *National Geographic Kids* no468 p32 Mr 2017

"Over There" Becomes "Over Here" *USA Today Magazine* v146 no2866 p38 Jl 2017

'Pinky and the Brain' J. Weiner *New York Times Magazine* p22 N 6 2016

TRANSFORMATIONS A. SHRESTHA cartoon *Wired* v25 no1 p3 Ja 2017

UnLeaShed *National Geographic Kids* no467 p32 F 2017

Caricatures & cartoons—Competitions

EVIL EYE *MHQ: Quarterly Journal of Military History* v29 no3 p96 Spr 2017

Carilli, Chris L.

[C II] 158-μm emission from the host galaxies of damped Lyman-alpha systems bibl color graph *Science* v355 no6331 p1285 Mr 24 2017

Molecular gas in the halo fuels the growth of a massive cluster galaxy at high redshift bibl graph *Science* v354 no6316 p1128 D 2 2016

CARILLO, MARY

US Open Special bw color *Tennis* v53 no5 p30 S/O 2017

Carillo, Mary—Interviews

THE TENNIS CONVERSATION: GEAR A. FRIEDMAN bw color *Tennis* v53 no2 p22 Mr/Ap 2017

Caring

Care and FEEDING E. GILBERT color *O, The Oprah Magazine* p29 Je 2017

The Compassionate Care You Need M. L. Tellado *Consumer Reports* v82 no10 p4 O 2017

get through your child's hospital stay V. SOLE-SMITH color *Parents* v92 no4 p34 Ap 2017

raise a kid who cares B. STEPHENS *Parents* p66 2015

Caring for Plants (Short story)

CARING FOR PLANTS Hye-young Pyun cartoon color *New Yorker* v93 no20 p64 Jl 10 2017

CARINI, WAYNE

YEA BOXY BRONCOS, NAY BEATNIK BOLSHEVIKS bw color *Forbes* v200 no2 p31 S 5 2017

Caris, Shell E.

THE RUN N. HONACHEFSKY color *Outdoor Life* v224 no8 p65 O 2017

CARL, JEREMY

First Principles diag *National Review* v69 no4 p36 Mr 6 2017

The Red Wall color *National Review* v68 no22 p26 D 5 2016

Carlberg, Frank

Monk Dreams, Hallucinations And Nightmares F. Bouchard bw *Downbeat* v84 no5 p57 My 2017

Carlen, Joe

A Brief History of Entrepreneurship J. Black *History Today* v67 no2 p59 F 2017

Carleo, Giuseppe

Solving the quantum many-body problem with artificial neural networks bibl diag *Science* v355 no6325 p602 F 10 2017

Carleton, Gregory

RUSSIA: THE STORY OF WAR B. BETHUNE color *Maclean's* v130 no4 p70 My 2017

War Stories S. PINKHAM color *New Republic* v248 no10 p62 O 2017

CARLEY, BRENNAN

Hunt Down the Next Camo color *GQ: Gentlemen's Quarterly* v97 no10 p68 O 2017

Lighten Your Workload color *GQ: Gentlemen's Quarterly* v97 no7 p84 Jl 2017

Carlin, George, 1937-2008

Funny Never Gets Old R. Love color *AARP: The Magazine* v60 no4A p2 Je/Jl 2017

JURY RIGGING ENGINES - AND LANGUAGE *Sea Magazine* v108 no9 p31 S 2016

Carlin, Peter Ames

Another Side of Paul Simon A. GREENE bw *Rolling Stone* no1272 p16 O 20 2016

Carlisle, Brian A.

The Evolution of in loco parentis Plus *Change* v49 no1 p48 Ja/F 2017

Carlisle, Camille M.

7 Earth-Size Planets Orbit Dim Star *Sky & Telescope* v133 no6 p12 Je 2017

Anatomy of a Black Hole *Sky & Telescope* v133 no2 p16 F 2017

ASTRONOMERS HAVE COMBINED *Sky & Telescope* v133 no4 p12 Ap 2017

Atmosphere Lost to Space *Sky & Telescope* v134 no1 p11 Jl 2017

Coming in from the Void? *Sky & Telescope* v133 no1 p12 Ja 2017

Enceladus's Hydrothermal Heating, Europa's Leaks color *Sky & Telescope* v134 no2 p10 Ag 2017

EXOPLANETS t World Found Around Proxima Centauri *Sky & Telescope* v132 no6 p10 D 2016

The First Black Holes *Sky & Telescope* v133 no1 p24 Ja 2017

History Of MARKS MISSIONS *Sky & Telescope* v134 no5 p16 N 2017

LIGO Detects Third Black Hole Merger *Sky & Telescope* v134 no3 p10 S 2017

Milky Way May Be Made with Swapped Gas color *Sky & Telescope* v134 no5 p10 N 2017

Of Black Holes and Galaxies *Sky & Telescope* v133 no2 p18 F 2017

Paired Stars in Cygnus En Route to Merger? *Sky & Telescope* v133 no4 p11 Ap 2017

Proxima Centauri b Likely a Desert World *Sky & Telescope* v133 no5 p10 My 2017

Solar Waves Reveal Core's Spin color *Sky & Telescope* v134 no5 p10 N 2017

Subsurface Ocean on Dione? *Sky & Telescope* v133 no2 p14 F 2017

TRAPPIST-1 Star Is Old *Sky & Telescope* v134 no6 p10 D 2017

Two Routes to the Truth *Sky & Telescope* v133 no6 p84 Je 2017

Void "Repels" Milky Way's Galaxy Group *Sky & Telescope* v133 no5 p8 My 2017

Carlisle, Kate

Deals D. LEFFERTS color *Publishers Weekly* v263 no52 p10 D 19 2016

Once upon a Spine: A Bibliophile Mystery *Publishers Weekly* v264 no17 p71 Ap 24 2017

CARLO, TOMÁS A.

Using Plant-Animal Interactions to Inform Tree Selection in Tree-Based Agroecosystems for Enhanced Biodiversity *BioScience* v66 no12 p1046 D 1 2016

Carlo Ratti Associati (Company)

Tour de Seine *Boating World* v38 no3 p12 Mr 2017

CARLON, MICK

Chords & Discords bw *Downbeat* v83 no12 p10 D 2016

Carlos, Marjon

Force of Nature color *Essence* v48 no3 p43 Jl 2017

IN FULL BLOOM color *Vogue* v207 no6 p114 Je 2017

Carlos, the Jackal, 1949-

The Week color il *National Review* v69 no7 p6 Ap 17 2017

Carlos Cuevas, Juan

Quantized thermal transport in single-atom junctions bibl diag graph *Science* v355 no6330 p1192 Mr 17 2017

CARLOTTI, PAIGE

Raise a Fitter Family cartoon color *Men's Health* v32 no5 p92 Je 2017

Carlsen, Frands

Chimpanzee genomic diversity reveals ancient admixture with bonobos bibl diag graph map *Science* v354 no6311 p477 O 28 2016

Carlsen, Magnus

Checkmate A. Fenwick and T. Keith color *Sports Illustrated* v125 no19 p26 D 12 2016

Carlsen, Peter

THE FIX cartoon *Old House Journal* v45 no7 p52 O 2017

Carlsen, Spike

DETAIL YOUR DIGS cartoon *Men's Health* v32 no3 p28 Ap 2017

IT'S A SMALL World M. R. JOHNSON *Cabin Living* p5 Je 2017

Carlsen, Andrea

Growing Organic Demand Provides High-Value Opportunities for Many Types of Producers *Amber Waves: The Economics of Food, Farming, Natural Resources, & Rural America* p51 F 2017

CARLSON, ANNE A.

Mapping Conservation Strategies under a Changing Climate *BioScience* v67 no6 p494 Je 2017

Carlson, Arne

School of Hard Knocks C. E. Finn Jr. and B. L. Wright *Hoover Digest: Research & Opinion on Public Policy* no4 p142 Fall 2016

Carlson, Benjamin

LICENSE-PLATE MARRIAGES color *Atlantic* v320 no3 p22 O 2017

CARLSON, CLAYTON

I AM PLURAL cartoon *Christianity Today* v60 no9 p60 N 2016

Carlson, David J.

Imagining Sovereignty: Self-Determination in American Indian Law and Literature A. Nemmers *American Indian Quarterly* v41 no2 p195 Spr 2017

Carlson, Erin

Affairs to Remember: An entertainment journalist argues that Nora Ephron took a Hollywood genre and made it her own L. SCHWARZBAUM *New York Times Book Review* p13 S 3 2017

Carlson, Gretchen, 1966-

All the Presidents' Men *Time* v189 no3 p45 Ja 30 2017

Gretchen Carlson's Next Fight [Cover story] B. Luscombe color *Time* v188 no18 p26 O 31 2016

GROWING INTO Feminism G. Carlson color *InStyle* v24 no11 p208 N 2017

how do you COME BACK from PERSONAL DISASTER? color *Good Housekeeping* v264 no2 p72 F 2017

WHO IS GRETCHEN CARLSON? [Cover story] color *Good Housekeeping* v264 no2 p66 F 2017

Why I Decided to Make My Future About Fighting Back G. Carlson *Time* v190 no16/17 p33 O 23 2017

Carlson, Gretchen, 1966-—Interviews

February @ GH color *Good Housekeeping* v264 no2 p10 F 2017

CARLSON, JEFF

Best USB-C memory card readers color graph *Macworld - Digital Edition* v34 no9 p71 S 2017

How to unlock your iPhone on Verizon, AT&T, Sprint, T-Mobile, and Virgin Mobile color *Macworld - Digital Edition* v34 no8 p61 Ag 2017

The iPad Pro: Now a true photographer's tool color *Macworld - Digital Edition* v34 no8 p57 Ag 2017

SD memory cards: The features and specifications to look for color *Macworld - Digital Edition* v34 no9 p76 S 2017

VERBATIM USB-C POCKET CARD READER: A GREAT COMBINATION OF PRICE AND PERFORMANCE color *Macworld - Digital Edition* v34 no11 p32 N 2017

Carlson, Julie

Remodelista: The Organized Home; Simple, Stylish Storage Ideas for All Over the House *Publishers Weekly* v264 no38 p66 S 18 2017

Carlson, Melissa

Holistic Care FOR THE DRESSAGE HORSE K. Brittle color *Dressage Today* v23 no6 p40 F 2017

Carlson, Peter

Becoming Barnum *American History* v51 no6 p26 F 2017

DENNIS, CHARLIE... CHARLIE, DENNIS *American History* v52 no1 p14 Ap 2017

IMPERIAL WALKER bw color *American History* v52 no3 p16 Ag 2017

SONNY NIGHTS, NORMAN DAYS *American History* v51 no6 p14 F 2017

T FOR TEXAS, G FOR A GOOD TIME bw color *American History* v52 no4 p18 O 2017

W. LEE "PAPPY" O'DANIEL bw color *American History* v52 no2 p18 Je 2017

Carlson, R.

Seasonal exposure of carbon dioxide ice on the nucleus of comet 67P/Churyumov-Gerasimenko bibl bw graph *Science* v354 no6319 p1563 D 23 2016

Carlson, Richard W.

Building Archean cratons from Hadean mafic crust bibl graph *Science* v355 no6330 p1199 Mr 17 2017

CARLSON, RON

LONG LIVE THE LANDLINE *Saturday Evening Post* v289 no2 p30 Mr/Ap 2017

Carlson, Stephanie M.

Precipitation drives global variation in natural selection bibl chart diag map *Science* v355 no6328 p959 Mr 3 2017

Carlson, Susan

Get to Know: Carlson Laboratories J. SCHILDHOUSE color *Muscle & Performance* v9 no11 p42 N 2017

Carlson, Tucker

ON THE CONTRARY K. SANNEH cartoon color *New Yorker* v93 no8 p50 Ap 10 2017

TUCKER CARLSON IS SORRY FOR BEING MEAN S. RODRICK color graph *GQ: Gentlemen's Quarterly* v97 no10 p84 O 2017

Carlson Laboratories (Company)

CARLSON MAXIMUM OMEGA 2000 color *Muscle & Performance* v9 no6 p62 Je 2017

Get to Know: Carlson Laboratories J. SCHILDHOUSE color *Muscle & Performance* v9 no11 p42 N 2017

Carlson's Choke Tubes LLC

CHOKE JOB G. BETHGE and T. HANSEN chart color *Outdoor Life* v224 no2 p20 F/Mr 2017

Carlson-Wee, Olaf

THE EMPEROR'S NEW COINS [Cover story] L. SHIN chart color diag *Forbes* v200 no1 p62 Jl 27 2017

Carlsson, M.

On the generation of solar spicules and Alfvénic waves diag *Science* v356 no6344 p1269 Je 23 2017

Carlsson-Szlezak, Philipp

A CEO's Guide to Navigating Brexit *Harvard Business Review Digital Articles* p2 Je 29 2016

Companies Shouldn't Wait to Prepare for the Post-Brexit World *Harvard Business Review Digital Articles* p2 N 3 2016

Carlstrom, Gregg

Hebron, Palestine color *Foreign Policy* no221 p102 N/D 2016

How Long Will Israel Survive?: The Threat from Within *Publishers Weekly* v264 no35 p114 Ag 28 2017

Carlton, Deborah A.

Tsunami-driven rafting: Transoceanic species dispersal and implications for marine biogeography color graph *Science* v357 no6358 p1402 S 29 2017

Carlton, James T.

Tsunami-driven rafting: Transoceanic species dispersal and implications for marine biogeography color graph *Science* v357 no6358 p1402 S 29 2017

Carmack, Eddy C.

Greater role for Atlantic inflows on sea-ice loss in the Eurasian Basin of the Arctic Ocean chart diag graph *Science* v356 no6335 p285 Ap 21 2017

Carman, Joseph

The Arc of Artistry *Dance Magazine* v91 no1 p91 Ja 2017

The MOST INFLUENTIAL PEOPLE IN DANCE TODAY: THE MOVERS, SHAKERS AND CHANGEMAKERS HAVING THE BIGGEST IMPACT ON DANCE RIGHT NOW *Dance Magazine* v91 no7 p27 Jl 2017

Price Pointe *Dance Magazine* v91 no6 p37 Je 2017

Carmel (Calif.)

FIVE PLACES YOU HAVE TO RIDE BEFORE THEY CHANGE FOREVER E. SPENCE color *Bicycling* v58 no7 p36 Ag 2017

Carmel (Ind.)

SPA *Indianapolis Monthly* v40 no7 p84 Mr 2017

WHERE TO SHOP? color *Indianapolis Monthly* v41 no2 p90 S 2017

Carmel Valley (Calif.)

Ride California's Wine Country A. PAVIA color *Trail Rider* v29 no3 p42 Ap 2017

Carmeliet, Peter

De novo design of a biologically active amyloid bibl graph *Science* v354 no6313 paah4949-1 N 11 2016

Carmichael, Jerrod, 1987-

Super-Bright (and Pretty Dark) Future cartoon color *GQ: Gentlemen's Quarterly* v97 no5 p51 My 2017

Why I Push the Social Envelope: Actor-writer Jerrod Carmichael takes on tough subjects--like gun control, euthanasia and using the N-word--all while getting major laughs M. Roffman *TV Guide* v65 no27 p10 Je 26 2017

Carmichael, Jerrod, 1987-—Interviews

Jerrod Carmichael: 8 I. Ratledge *TV Guide* v65 no11 p38 Mr 6 2017

Super-Bright (and Pretty Dark) Future J. Carmichael cartoon color *GQ: Gentlemen's Quarterly* v97 no5 p51 My 2017

CARMICHAEL, KEVIN

New world disorder color *Maclean's* v129 no48/49 p60 D 5 2016

WHAT IT TOOK TO TAME CMHC color *Maclean's* v130 no4 p53 My 2017

Carmichael, Sarah Green

Advice from a Serial Life Reinventor *Harvard Business Review Digital Articles* p2 Ap 2 2015

Everything You Need to Know About Becoming a Better Listener *Harvard Business Review Digital Articles* p2 F 6 2015

Feeling Like a Winner Changes What You Think Is Fair *Harvard Business Review Digital Articles* p2 D 15 2014

Female CEOs Find Stock-Based Pay Harder to Get, Easier to Lose *Harvard Business Review Digital Articles* p2 Ag 28 2015

Hiring C-Suite Executives by Algorithm *Harvard Business Review Digital Articles* p2 Ap 6 2015

The House That Actually Makes the Internet of Things Easy *Harvard Business Review Digital Articles* p2 N 12 2014

How America's Wealthiest Black Families Invest Money *Harvard Business Review Digital Articles* p2 F 10 2015

How to Avoid Frustrating Business Travel Mishaps *Harvard Business Review Digital Articles* p2 N 6 2015

How to Coach, According to 5 Great Sports Coaches *Harvard Business Review Digital Articles* p2 F 25 2015

It Might Be Time to Spill Your Corporate Secrets *Harvard Business Review Digital Articles* p2 Ap 13 2015

Lots of Companies Still Have No Senior Executives Who Are Women color graph *Harvard Business Review Digital Articles* p2 Mr 8 2017

Millennials Are Actually Workaholics, According to Research *Harvard Business Review Digital Articles* p2 Ag 17 2016

Putting the Right Information on Twitter in a Crisis *Harvard Business Review Digital Articles* p2 N 20 2015

The Reason Smart People Sometimes Struggle with "Aha" Moments *Harvard Business Review Digital Articles* p2 Ag 26 2015

Research: For a Corporate Apology to Work, the CEO Should Look Sad *Harvard Business Review Digital Articles* p2 Ag 24

2015

The Research Is Clear: Long Hours Backfire for People and for Companies *Harvard Business Review Digital Articles* p2 Ag 19 2015

The Ripple Effects of Parents Not Using Their Vacation Time *Harvard Business Review Digital Articles* p2 O 12 2015

A Step-by-Step Guide to Packing for a Complicated Work Trip *Harvard Business Review Digital Articles* p2 N 18 2015

Study: Employers Are Less Likely to Hire a Woman Who Wears a Headscarf *Harvard Business Review Digital Articles* p2 My 26 2017

Training Police Departments to Be Less Biased *Harvard Business Review Digital Articles* p2 Mr 6 2015

What MIT Is Learning About Online Courses and Working from Home *Harvard Business Review Digital Articles* p2 Mr 30 2015

Why ESPN Won't Pull an HBO *Harvard Business Review Digital Articles* p2 O 21 2014

Why "Network More" Is Bad Advice for Women *Harvard Business Review Digital Articles* p2 F 26 2015

Working Long Hours Makes Us Drink More *Harvard Business Review Digital Articles* p2 Ap 10 2015

Yes, Your Uber Driver Is Judging You *Harvard Business Review Digital Articles* p2 F 20 2015

Carmichael Show, The (TV program)

ALSO COMING... A. D'Arminio *TV Guide* v65 no23 p35 My 29 2017

Jerrod Carmichael: 8 I. Ratledge *TV Guide* v65 no11 p38 Mr 6 2017

Why I Push the Social Envelope: Actor-writer Jerrod Carmichael takes on tough subjects--like gun control, euthanasia and using the N-word--all while getting major laughs M. Roffman *TV Guide* v65 no27 p10 Je 26 2017

Carmichel, Jim

GOING LIGHT J. B. SNOW color *Outdoor Life* v224 no2 p83 F/Mr 2017

Carnarvon, Fiona, 1965-

THE BRITISH HERITAGE TRAVEL INTERVIEW Lady Carnarvon of Highclere S. GUTIERREZ *British Heritage Travel* v38 no4 p42 Jl/Ag 2017

Carnegie, Cloudy

Single-molecule optomechanics in "picocavities" bibl graph *Science* v354 no6313 p726 N 11 2016

Carnegie Medal

The Carnegie Medals Turn Six A. RICHARD ALBANESE color *Publishers Weekly* v264 no25 p38 Je 19 2017

Carnegie Hall (New York, N.Y.)

CLASSICAL MUSIC *New Yorker* v93 no11 p5 My 1 2017

GOINGS ON ABOUT TOWN color *New Yorker* v92 no41 p7 D 12 2016

Winter Preview R. Platt cartoon *New Yorker* v92 no37 p14 N 14 2016

Carnes, Aaron

Packing It Out *Sierra* v102 no2 p25 Mr/Ap 2017

CARNES, MATTHEW E.

The Challenges of Formalizing Labor in Latin America *Current History* v116 no787 p43 F 2017

Carney, Dana

Power Poses: Plus or Bust? A. PATUREL color *Discover* v38 no2 p18 Mr 2017

Carney, George

Gatekeepers and Barbarians *Commentary* v142 no2 p1 S 2016

Carney, J. J.

The problem of violence in the modern world *America* v216 no12 p51 My 29 2017

Carney, John, 1972-

No. 9 SING STREET L. Greenblatt color *Entertainment Weekly* no1444/1445 p56 D 16 2016

SING STREET D. Vaughn color *Sound & Vision* v81 no10 p71 D 2016

Carney, Laura

"My dad had a bucket list of 60 things. He'd only checked off 5 when his life was cut short." bw color *Good Housekeeping* v264 no4 p81 Ap 2017

Carney, Margaret

To The Editor color *American Craft* v76 no6 p10 D 2016-Ja 2017

Carney, Mark, 1965-

GOOD NEWS color *Maclean's* v129 no45 p8 N 14 2016

Carney, Sean J. Patrick

Andrew Ross color *Art in America* p27 O 2017

BRIAN BELOTT color *Art in America* v105 no8 p123 S 2017

David Leggett color *Art in America* v105 no6 p37 Je/Jl 2017

Carnitine

AMAZING NEWS V. Tweed color *Amazing Wellness* v9 no4 p12 Summ 2017

carnitine V. Tweed color *Amazing Wellness* v9 no4 p12 Summ 2017

Energy Essential V. TWEED chart color *Better Nutrition* p22 My 2017

Carnival

February Events F. Esker color *New Orleans Magazine* v51 no4 p26 F 2017

Krewesin' for a Brewsin' C. Rose color *New Orleans Magazine* v51 no4 p42 F 2017

Lundi Gras E. Laborde *New Orleans Magazine* v51 no4 p14 F 2017

ON THE RUN M. Romer color *Louisiana Life* v37 no3 p38 Ja/F 2017

THE QUIZ OF KINGS E. LABORDE color *Louisiana Life* v37 no3 p110 Ja/F 2017

Carnival—Brazil—Rio de Janeiro

Lightbox color *Time* v189 no9 p16 Mr 13 2017

Carnival—Louisiana—New Orleans

HIT PARADE A. BRANDT *Cincinnati Magazine* v50 no5 p26 F 2017

JANUARY/FEBRUARY K. MASSICOT color *Louisiana Life* v37 no3 p108 Ja/F 2017

Laissez Les Bon Temps Roulez! J. DeBold color *New Orleans Magazine* v51 no4 p142 F 2017

Masking Like a Baby Cake M. Gunch color *New Orleans Magazine* v51 no4 p44 F 2017

Picturing Mardi Gras C. Kolb bw *New Orleans Magazine* v51 no4 p38 F 2017

Carnival—Louisiana—New Orleans—History

Custer at Mardi Gras E. Laborde bw *New Orleans Magazine* v51 no4 p144 F 2017

Carnivals

Mardi Gras bw *New Orleans Magazine* v51 no4 p20 F 2017

That's a Wrap E. Crawford Peyton color *New Orleans Magazine* v51 no6 p46 Ap 2017

Caro, Anthony, 1924-2013—Exhibitions

ANTHONY CARO D. Ebony color *Art in America* v105 no4 p111 Ap 2017

CARO, EDGAR

Brasa Bound color *New Orleans Magazine* v51 no12 p110 O 2017

Caro, Mark

The Lonely Crusade of Jim DeRogatis color *Chicago* v66 no11 p90 N 2017

Caro, Tim

The biology of color color *Science* v357 no6350 p470 Ag 4 2017

The Consequences of Internal Migration in Sub-Saharan Africa: A Case Study *BioScience* v67 no7 p664 Jl 2017

Carolina Panthers (Football team)

3 Carolina Panthers color *Sports Illustrated* v127 no7 p98 S 4 2017

NFC + SOUTH color *Sports Illustrated* v126 no5 p50 F 13 2017

Caroline, or Change (Theatrical production)

WHERE & WHEN *Washingtonian Magazine* v52 no4 p31 Ja 2017

Caroll, Robert

Philosopher and CSI Fellow Robert Carroll, Creator of Skeptics Dictionary, Dies at Seventy-One S. GERBIC *Skeptical Inquirer* v41 no1 p11 Ja/F 2017

Carollo, Nancie

Get to know... your QL muscles color *Yoga Journal* p54 2017 SpecialIssue

Carols

Rock these reboots around the tree S. FESCHUK color *Maclean's* v129 no45 p61 N 14 2016

Caron, Leslie, 1931-

ONCE IN LOVE WITH GIGI L. JACOBS cartoon *Vanity Fair* v59 no4 p212 Mr 2017

Carotenoids

CAN YOU HEAR ME NOW? How to prevent—or deal with—hearing loss [Cover story] *Nutrition Action Health Letter* v43 no10 p3 D 2016

Potent Pigments E. A. KANE color *Better Nutrition* v79 no10 p30 O 2017

RELIEVE EYE STRAIN J. Martin color *Amazing Wellness* v9 no3 p28 EarlySumm 2017

Carousel (Theatrical production)

Musicals! (Now for Men!) R. McCAMMON and J. WILLIS bw color *GQ: Gentlemen's Quarterly* v97 no9 p116 S 2017

Carp

SO SUBTLE A CATCH S. Parkin *Harper's Magazine* v333 no1999 p67 D 2016

CARP, ALEX

WHITENESS UNDER THE MICROSCOPE img *New York* v50 no6 p21 Mr 20 2017

Carp, Elizabeth

Key Biscayne Parks and Recreation Protects Its Citizens from Severe Weather *Parks & Recreation* v52 no5 p47 My 2017

Carp fishing

RED STATE VENTURE CAPITAL P. ROBISON color *Bloomberg Businessweek* no4508 p42 Ja 23 2017

Carpal tunnel syndrome

THAT TWIST OF YOUR WRIST J. L. Stein color *Cycle World* v56 no2 p22 Mr 2017

Carpal tunnel syndrome treatment

Yog-ahhh N. PAIN color *Yoga Journal* p6 2017 SpecialIssue

Carpal tunnel syndrome—Alternative treatment

THE NEW BUZZ S. Cristobal color *Harper's Bazaar* no3648 p266 N 2016

Carpal tunnel syndrome—Prevention

Best ways to cope with hand pain *Harvard Health Letter* v42 no9 p4 Jl 2017

Carpenter, Anne M.

Beauty's Vineyard: A Theological Aesthetic of Anguish and Anticipation *Christian Century* v133 no22 p39 O 26 2016

Carpenter, Annie

Seat of Power color *Yoga Journal* p24 2017 Special Issue

Carpenter, Bruce

A signal system to FIT ANY RAILROAD color diag *Model Railroader* v84 no4 p66 Ap 2017

CARPENTER, BRYAN

THE LONG ROAD BACK *USA Today Magazine* v145 no2864 p42 My 2017

Carpenter, Emily

20. Read The Weight of Lies *New York* v50 no13 p88 Je 26 2017

Carpenter, John M.

Spiral density waves in a young protoplanetary disk bibl graph *Science* v353 no6307 p1519 S 30 2016

Carpenter, John, 1948-

Next Steps V. Lucca color *Film Comment* v53 no1 p10 Ja/F 2017

CARPENTER, LAUREN

best of Indy *Indianapolis Monthly* v40 no4 p73 D 2016

Carpenter, Sabrina, 1999-

BEHIND THE SCENES WITH Sabrina Carpenter color *Seventeen* p28 Ja 1 2017

girl meets prom J. ABIDOR color *Seventeen* p150 Ja 1 2017

CARPENTER, SHELBY

Stepping Out of YouTube's Shadow color *Forbes* v198 no6 p52 N 8 2016

CARPENTER, SHELLEY

Jesus and Magdalene *Humanist* v77 no4 p46 Jl/Ag 2017

Carpenter, Stephen

Social norms as solutions bibl color *Science* v354 no6308 p42 O 7 2016

CARPENTER, SUSAN

The Road Ahead: BIKE LANES, CROSSWALKS, RAMPED-UP POLICE ENFORCEMENT— THERE'S LOTS OF CHANGE AFOOT AS LOS ANGELES MOVES TO REDUCE TRAFFIC-RELATED DEATHS *Los Angeles Magazine* v62 no9 p76 S 2017

CARPENTER, TED GALEN

Geopolitical Shell Game: Washington and the fraudulent freedom fighters *American Conservative* v16 no5 p31 S/O 2017

No More Anti-War Liberals? *USA Today Magazine* v145 no2862 p15 Mr 2017

Carpenter, Tom

7 WAYS TO TAKE TOUGH ELK color *Outdoor Life* v223 no9 pH1 N 2016

COYOTE NATION color *Outdoor Life* v224 no1 p74 D 2016/ Ja 2017

GET YOUR GOBBLER color *Outdoor Life* v224 no4 p43 My 2017

HUNT THE PUDDLE DIVER color *Outdoor Life* v224 no8 pW6 O 2017

INCOMING GREENHEADS color *Outdoor Life* v224 no8 pW1 O 2017

RETHINK YOUR TURKEY VEST color *Outdoor Life* v224 no3 pT5 Ap 2017

SECRETS OF THE SHED MASTERS color *Outdoor Life* v224 no2 p80 F/Mr 2017

SO, YOU WANT A RABBIT DOG? color *Outdoor Life* v224 no7 pH11 S 2017

TAIL TALES color *Outdoor Life* v224 no7 pH14 S 2017

THE TEAL ZONE color *Outdoor Life* v224 no7 pW5 S 2017

TWEAK THE DEKES color *Outdoor Life* v224 no7 pW9 S 2017

Carpenter, Zoë

BLACK BIRTHS MATTER color il *Nation* v304 no7 p12 Mr 6 2017

THE FUTURE OF FOOD [Cover story] color *Nation* v305 no11 p14 O 30 2017

The Journeys of Ursula K. Le Guin bw color *Nation* v303 no17 p22 O 24 2016

Senator Jeff Merkley, Working-Class Hero color *Nation* v304 no17 p22 Je 5 2017

CARPENTER-NOLTING, DEB

Oshkosh: Heart of Garden County color *Nebraska Life* v21 no5 p52 S/O 2017

Carpenters

Carpenter Logic D. MULFINGER color *Cabin Living* p20 D 2016

Character Building: Carpenter and designer Matthew Holdren creates custom wood pieces with reclaimed materials J. DeBold *New Orleans Homes & Lifestyles* v20 no3 p30 Summ 2017

Nailed It M. OZAWA *Martha Stewart Living* no268 p44 O 2016

Carpentry tools

ADD A STORAGE BUILDING J. Cooper color *Cabin Living* p65 O 2017

From Attic to the Basement L. Elliott color *Old House Journal* v45 no7 p46 O 2017

Carpets

ADDITIONAL LISTINGS *Arts & Crafts Homes & the Revival* v12 no1 p21 2017 Resouce Guide

curtains to carpets *Design Center Sourcebook* p68 2017

design ideas FROM THE PAST FOR TODAY'S STYLE P. POORE *Design Center Sourcebook* p10 2017

TAPESTRY PORTIÈRES B. Sullivan color *Arts & Crafts Homes & the Revival* v12 no2 p72 Spr 2017

Carpets—Evaluation

Golden Opportunity: Pair gold and green for an enviable interior M. Cameron *New Orleans Homes & Lifestyles* v20 no4 p100 Aut 2017

History Lesson M. OWENS color *Architectural Digest* no5 p48 My 2017

LATEST LOOKS UPDATE H. GILBERT color *House Beautiful* p96 Ag 2017

True Colorist K. O'SHEA-EVANS color *House Beautiful* v159 no7 p55 S 2017

Carpinus

Martha's Month chart color *Martha Stewart Living* p6 S 2017

CARR, CALEB

Brains Take the Stand *New York Times Book Review* p19 Mr 12 2017

Carr, Deborah

A meal for many color *U.S. Catholic* v82 no6 p5 Je 2017

Carr, Derek

HOT | NOT T. Keith color *Sports Illustrated* v127 no1 p18 Jl 3 2017

Carr, Derek—Interviews

JUST MY TYPE D. Patrick and T. Keith color *Sports Illustrated* v125 no14 p28 O 24-31 2016

Carr, Frances

CENTURY marks cartoon *Christian Century* v134 no3 p8 F 2017

Carr, Jim

U.S. AND CANADA: SHARING A CONTINENT BY CHANCE; BUT FRIENDS AND ECONOMIC PARTNERS BY CHOICE *Vital Speeches of the Day* v83 no5 p147 My 2017

USING ENERGY EFFICIENTLY IN THE FIGHT AGAINST CLIMATE CHANGE color *Maclean's* v129 no50 p38 D 19 2016

CARR, JOHN

Georgetown Steps Up color *America* v215 no10 p14 O 10 2016

In the Time of Trump *America* v215 no18 p12 D 5 2016

Value-Free Politics color *America* v215 no14 p12 N 7 2016

CARR, JULIE PALAKOVICH

AIBS Photo Contest Brings Biology into Focus *BioScience* v67 no4 p323 Ap 2017

Evolution Education and State Politics *BioScience* v67 no8 p687 Ag 2017

President Obama's Scientific Legacy *BioScience* v66 no12 p1011 D 1 2016

CARR, MARK H.

Long-Term Studies Contribute Disproportionately to Ecology and Policy *BioScience* v67 no3 p271 Mr 2017

Carr, Nicholas

Amazon's Next Big Move: Take Over the Mall il *MIT Technology Review* v120 no1 p96 Ja/F 2017

CARR, STEVE

Dinner with Arnold: And Burying the Sail-Cats *Idaho Magazine* v16 no7 p54 Ap 2017

Going Full Circle: In the Adult Diaper Aisle *Idaho Magazine* v16 no10 p54 Jl 2017

Gratitude *Idaho Magazine* v16 no3 p54 D 2016

I Have a Dream, Too *Idaho Magazine* v16 no1 p54 O 2016

Laundering My History: For a Cleaner America *Idaho Magazine* v16 no11 p54 Ag 2017

Purple Pose *Idaho Magazine* v16 no6 p54 Mr 2017

The Rapture or a Rupture? *Idaho Magazine* v17 no1 p54 Ja 2017

The Reluctant Reunioner: Amid Friends and Strangers *Idaho Magazine* v16 no12 p54 S 2017

Suckers and Cemeteries *Idaho Magazine* v16 no2 p54 N 2016

What Happens Next? After the Near Drowning *Idaho Magazine* v16 no5 p54 F 2017

Who's the Wise One? Ask the Marshmallow Bunny *Idaho Magazine* v16 no9 p54 Je 2017

CARR, STEVEN

OBAMA'S AMERICA img *New York* v49 no20 p12 O 3 2016

Carr, Teresa

Should Drugs Do Double Duty? il *Consumer Reports* v82 no2 p12 F 2017

Too Many Meds? [Cover story] color *Consumer Reports* v82 no9 p24 S 2017

Carradine, Keith

Madam Secretary M. Logan *TV Guide* v65 no19 p27 My 1 2017

Carranza, Mario E.

Managing nuclear risk in South Asia bibl *Bulletin of the Atomic Scientists* v73 no1 p64 Ja 2017

Carrasco, Jesús

A Life in Flight: In this debut novel a young boy flees his tormentors into an unforgiving landscape N. SERBER *New York Times Book Review* p17 S 3 2017

Carré, B.

Attosecond dynamics through a Fano resonance: Monitoring the birth of a photoelectron bibl graph *Science* v354 no6313 p734 N 11 2016

CARRÉ, MICHEL

Roméo et Juliette *Opera News* v81 no7 p56 Ja 2017

CARREIRO, JESSICA

A Tiny Village By Little Tokyo *Los Angeles Magazine* v61 no11 p24 N 2016

CARREON, DAVID

CAN YOU CONTROL YOURSELF? [Cover story] color graph *Christianity Today* v61 no4 p34 My 2017

Carrera (Company)

CLUTCH MOVE color *Esquire* p42 Je/Jl 2017

Carrera, Lianna

A Tale of Two Sisters color *Glamour* v115 no2 p69 F 2017

Carrère, Emmanuel, 1957-

Church history as memoir P. Christman color *Christian Century*

v134 no22 p38 O 25 2017

Lost on the Road to Damascus G. W. Bowersock color *New York Review of Books* v64 no7 p60 Ap 20 2017

NEW BOOKS C. Beha *Harper's Magazine* v334 no2002 p83 Mr 2017

PAUL IS DEAD J. WOOD color *New Yorker* v93 no20 p82 Jl 10 2017

Telling the Truth W. Mason *New York Times Magazine* p50 Mr 5 2017

Carrero, C. A.

Selective oxidative dehydrogenation of propane to propene using boron nitride catalysts bibl diag graph *Science* v354 no6319 p1570 D 23 2016

Carretero, Juan—Interviews

Rolling the Dice K. RENDA color *House Beautiful* v159 no9 p84 N 2017

Carrey, Jim

Jerry Lewis color *Time* v190 no9 p17 S 4 2017

Carriage House Door Co.

ADDITIONAL LISTINGS *Arts & Crafts Homes & the Revival* v12 no1 p62 2017 Resouce Guide

Carriage houses—Interior decoration

Halloween All Year W. GOODMAN and A. Schlechter img *New York* v49 no15 p69 Jl 25 2016

Carriage houses—Remodeling

Halloween All Year W. GOODMAN and A. Schlechter img *New York* v49 no15 p69 Jl 25 2016

Carriages & carts

See also

Handcarts

Horse-drawn buggies

Bar Carts We Love *Treasures* v6 no4 p10 F/Mr 2017

IDEA OF THE MONTH P. Barbour *Successful Farming* v115 no2 p80 F 2017

Carrier Corp.

Bribe Bully Beg Borrow Steal D. R. HENDERSON color *Reason* v48 no10 p18 Mr 2017

Chiling Effect color *National Review* v68 no24 p14 D 31 2016

Superman Politics K. D. WILLIAMSON il *National Review* v68 no24 p16 D 31 2016

THE WORKERS TRUMP FORGOT S. JAFFE color *Nation* v304 no15 p18 My 8 2017

Carrier proteins

See also

Synucleins

Protein helps push petunia's scent out A. YEAGER color *Science News* v192 no1 p15 Ag 5 2017

Carriero, Giovanni

Three-dimensional Ca2+ imaging advances understanding of astrocyte biology diag *Science* v356 no6339 p715 My 19 2017

CARRIGAN, HENRY

A History of Southern Food color *Publishers Weekly* v264 no17 p78 Ap 24 2017

Carrigan, Richard A.

Edwin Leo Goldwasser *Physics Today* v70 no9 p70 S 2017

CARRILLO, SOPHIA

Provoking Thoughts color *O, The Oprah Magazine* p18 N 2017

Carrington, Ann

AD visits: Change Agent S. RIEGLER color *Architectural Digest* no11 p46 N 1 2017

Carrington, Leonora, 1917-2011

International Literature: Writers have found freedom and restriction working in other languages. For Leonora Carrington, alternatives to English offered her access to secret selves P. Sehgal *New York Times Book Review* p59 Je 4 2017

New Sentences S. Anderson *New York Times Magazine* p13 Jl 30 2017

CARRIVICK, JONATHAN L.

The Arctic in the Twenty-First Century: Changing Biogeochemical Linkages across a Paraglacial Landscape of Greenland *BioScience* v67 no2 p118 F 2017

The Multitrophic Effects of Climate Change and Glacier Retreat in Mountain Rivers *BioScience* v67 no10 p897 O 2017

CARRIZO, SAVRINA F.

Freshwater Megafauna: Flagships for Freshwater Biodiversity under Threat *BioScience* v67 no10 p919 O 2017

Carroll, Alison

Desert Days color *Bon Appetit* v62 no7 p84 Jl 2017

Carroll, Andrew

Hail to the Chieftain M. Yockelson *Weekly Standard* v22 no29 p36 Ap 3 2017

CARROLL, CARLOS

Mapping Conservation Strategies under a Changing Climate *Bio-Science* v67 no6 p494 Je 2017

Carroll, Christopher

The Knight Errant of Music Criticism bw *New York Review of Books* v64 no7 p38 Ap 20 2017

Carroll, James, 1943-

JAMES CARROLL'S RATZINGER P. Baumann *Commonweal* v144 no1 p8 Ja 6 2017

Why We Can't Stop Talking About Pope Francis *Harvard Business Review Digital Articles* p2 N 10 2014

Carroll, Jay

Desert Days C. Lalli Music and A. Carroll color *Bon Appetit* v62 no7 p84 Jl 2017

Carroll, Joe

How Exxon Is Learning To Let Go color *Bloomberg Businessweek* no4519 p49 Ap 24 2017

Tillerson's Got a Private State Department *Bloomberg Businessweek* no4505 p30 D 26 2016

Will Beijing Also Have A Friend at State? bw *Bloomberg Businessweek* no4504 p26 D 19 2016

CARROLL, JOHN J.

SUPERVOID *Scientific American* v315 no6 p9 D 2016

Carroll, Jonathan, 1949-

The Crow's Dinner color *Publishers Weekly* v264 no23 p43 Je 5 2017

Carroll, Leah

Home After Dark M. BRODAK *New York Times Book Review* p18 Ap 2 2017

Carroll, Michael

Cassini's Grand Finale: 20 years in the making bw color diag *Astronomy* v45 no9 p28 S 2017

The hunt for Earth's BIGGER COUSINS [Cover story] color diag *Astronomy* v45 no4 p22 Ap 2017

Your guide to the oceans of our solar system color *Astronomy* v45 no11 p24 N 2017

Carroll, P. Brandon

Mirror asymmetry in life and in space *Physics Today* v69 no11 p86 N 2016

Carroll, Rebecca

Is Bigotry a Parking Ticket or a Capital Offense? *New York* v49 no23 p27 N 14 2016

OBAMA'S AMERICA img *New York* v49 no20 p12 O 3 2016

OUR FATHERS IN THEIR OWN WORDS color *Essence* v48 no2 p94 Je 2017

Carroll, Rocky

NCIS A. D'Arminio *TV Guide* v65 no43 p32 O 16 2017

CARROLL, SEAN

A COSMIC CONTROVERSY color *Scientific American* v317 no1 p5 Jl 2017

Carroll, Sean B.

Rattlesnakes have lost venom genes L. HAMERS color *Science News* v190 no8 p9 O 15 2016

The Serengeti Rules: The Quest to Discover How Life Works and Why It Matters J. A. DEWOODY *BioScience* v66 no12 p1079 D 1 2016

Carroll, Sean M.

The Big Picture B. Keating *Physics Today* v69 no12 p55 D 2016

Carroll, Shana

Overcome Resistance to Change with Two Conversations *Harvard Business Review Digital Articles* p2 My 16 2017

Carroll, Shay

LIVIN' IT UP IN THE CITY A. WILSON color *Spin to Win Rodeo* v20 no10 p86 D 2016

Carrón, Julián

The Christian Encounter T. S. HIBBS *National Review* v69 no18 p41 O 2 2017

Carrot growing

Taming the Wild Carrot M. STONE *BioScience* v66 no10 p912 O 1 2016

Carrots

CARROTS S. PUCKETT *Atlanta* v56 no12 p62 Ap 2017

A MATTER OF TASTE D. DICKINSON chart color *Better Homes & Gardens* v95 no5 p98 My 2017

Nutrients in carrot peels ... Lemon-lime soda ... Rinsing canned beans R. A. Fielding *Tufts University Health & Nutrition Letter* v35 no8 p8 O 2017

Carrots—Varieties

Taming the Wild Carrot M. STONE *BioScience* v66 no10 p912 O 1 2016

Carrozza, Ann-Margaret

Family + money = happiness?! L. FREEDMAN color *Redbook* p105 N 2017

Carrozzo, F. G.

Localized aliphatic organic material on the surface of Ceres bibl graph *Science* v355 no6326 p719 F 17 2017

Carruthers, Charlene

Charlene Carruthers D. HOLLIDAY color *Chicago* v66 no6 p93 Je 2017

Carruthers, Dana

ALL AROUND THE FARM® color *Successful Farming* v115 no7 p67 My 2017

CARRUTHERS, JOHN

HOMEGROWN HOPS color *Chicago* v66 no8 p54 Ag 2017

Carruthers, Susan L.

Debunking America's 'Good' Occupation A. J. BACEVICH *American Conservative* v16 no1 p46 Ja/F 2017

Cars 3 (Film)

CARS 3 ADDS TO ITS FLEET M. Snetiker color *Entertainment Weekly* no1448 p13 Ja 13 2017

Cars 3 Makes Career Anxiety (Almost) Fun S. Zacharek color *Time* v189 no24 p50 Je 26 2017

CARS 3 M. Snetiker color *Entertainment Weekly* no1463/1464 p50 Ap/My 2017

THE POSTHUMOUS RETURN OF PAUL NEWMAN M. Snetiker color *Entertainment Weekly* no1471 p49 Je 23 2017

CARSE, ASHLEY

The infrastructure challenge *Issues in Science & Technology* v33 no3 p5 Spr 2017

Carsen, Robert

Der Rosenkavalier G. Hall *Opera News* v81 no9 p44 Mr 2017

ROBERT CARSEN F. P. Driscoll *Opera News* v81 no10 p26 Ap 2017

Time Capsule R. Platt cartoon *New Yorker* v93 no9 p13 Ap 17 2017

Carsenty, U.

Seasonal exposure of carbon dioxide ice on the nucleus of comet 67P/Churyumov-Gerasimenko bibl bw graph *Science* v354 no6319 p1563 D 23 2016

Carslaw, Kenneth S.

Global atmospheric particle formation from CERN CLOUD measurements bibl graph map *Science* v354 no6316 p1119 D 2 2016

Carson, Anne, 1950-

Back the Way You Went cartoon *New Yorker* v92 no35 p80 O 31 2016

CLIVE SONG A. Carson *New Yorker* v93 no23 p54 Ag 7 2017

Carson, Ben, 1951-

Home Is Where the Market Is: What we should do--and stop doing--in the quest for "affordable housing" R. A. Epstein *Hoover Digest: Research & Opinion on Public Policy* no3 p137 Summ 2017

Is Anybody Home at HUD? A. MacGillis img *New York* v50 no17 p40 Ag 21 2017

Shelter and the Storm F. Shafroth *Governing* v30 no6 p62 Mr 2017

Carson, Clare

Orkney Twilight *Publishers Weekly* v264 no17 p69 Ap 24 2017

Carson, Clayborne

Q: What was the most important letter in history? color *Atlantic* v320 no2 p104 S 2017

Carson, Jackie

KITCHEN-TESTED TIPS color *Vegetarian Today* no2 p4 Ap 2017

Carson, Jennifer

The Sun spotters color *Science* v357 no6347 p137 Jl 14 2017

Carson, Johnny, 1925-2005

GETTING TO KNOW JOHNNY CARSON *Saturday Evening Post* v288 no6 p105 N/D 2016

Carson, Richard T.

Contingent valuation: Flawed logic? color *Science* v357 no6349 p363 Jl 28 2017

Putting a value on injuries to natural assets: The BP oil spill chart *Science* v356 no6335 p253 Ap 21 2017

Carson, Ted

USEF Pegasus Award Banquet C. Reich *Arabian Horse World* v57 no5 p235 F 2017

THE USEF RULING ON SHANKING C. REICH *Arabian Horse World* v56 no12 p71 S 2016

CARSON, TOM

Things Left Unsaid: POWERS BOOTHE ALWAYS HELD SOMETHING BACK. MAYBE THAT'S WHY HE NEVER BECAME A STAR. AND MAYBE THAT'S WHY HE WAS SO FASCINATING TO WATCH *Texas Monthly* v45 no7 p56 Jl 2017

Carstarphen, Meria

Meria Carstarphen *Atlanta* v57 no2 p93 Je 2017

CARSWELL, CALLY

Critics pan wolf plan color map *Science* v357 no6358 p1341 S 29 2017

PEOPLE AND THE PLANET *Sierra* v101 no5 p25 S/O 2016

The Place Where Happiness Dwelled *Sierra* v102 no5 p24 St/O 2017

Cartacci, M.

Seasonal exposure of carbon dioxide ice on the nucleus of comet 67P/Churyumov-Gerasimenko bibl bw graph *Science* v354 no6319 p1563 D 23 2016

Cartagena (Colombia)—Description & travel

In Colombia, You'll Get Beach and Then Some L. MORRIS color *Conde Nast Traveler* v52 no1 p51 Ja 2017

Cartagena, Maria

Business Perks S. KROWIAK *Indianapolis Monthly* v40 no4 p52 D 2016

Cartagena, Rosa

AFTER "CHOCOLATE CITY" *Washingtonian Magazine* v52 no8 p21 My 2017

BLADE BONNER *Washingtonian Magazine* v52 no3 p16 D 2016

DOUBLE AGENTS, DEAD DROPS, AND SEXPIONAGE *Washingtonian Magazine* v52 no6 p20 Mr 2017

FOTOWEEKDC *Washingtonian Magazine* v52 no2 p35 N 2016

GIVING BACK *Washingtonian Magazine* v52 no3 p106 D 2016

HOW TO BE A BLEACHER-STOMPING, BEER-TOSSING D.C. UNITED FAN *Washingtonian Magazine* v52 no6 p70 Mr 2017

WHERE & WHEN: 17 THINGS YOU REALLY OUGHT TO DO THIS MONTH *Washingtonian Magazine* v53 no1 p31 O 2017

WHERE & WHEN: 18 THINGS YOU REALLY OUGHT TO DO THIS MONTH *Washingtonian Magazine* v52 no11 p31 Ag 2017

WHERE & WHEN color *Washingtonian Magazine* v52 no7 p31 Ap 2017

Cartels

the DRUG RUNNERS R. GOLDBERG *Texas Monthly* v45 no8 p74 Ag 2017

THE MAKING OF A MASSACRE G. Thompson color *National Geographic* v232 no1 p120 Jl 2017

Cartels—Government policy

Justice Served With a Dash of Chili K. Salna color *Bloomberg Businessweek* no4524 p18 My 29 2017

Carter, Abby

ALLOW YOUR HORSE TO 'HEAR' YOU color diag *Practical Horseman* v45 no10 p42 O 2017

CREATING HARMONY AND EXPRESSION color *Practical Horseman* v45 no2 p36 F 2017

EXERCISES AND ADVICE FROM ROBERT DOVER color diag *Practical Horseman* v45 no9 p38 S 2017

Carter, Ash

BITTERSWEET ESCAPE color *Esquire* p21 Ag 2017

DEEP DIVES color *Esquire* p50 S 2017

DIFFICULT MEN color *Esquire* p38 O 2017

ERROL MORRIS: THREE SELF-IMPROVEMENT BOOKS THAT CHANGED MY LIFE *Esquire* p29 Je/Jl 2017

ET TU, MURRAY? cartoon *Esquire* v167 no2 p58 Mr 2017

FIGHT THE POWER color *Esquire* p32 N 2017

THE MAVERICKS OF HOLLYWOOD 2017 bw color *Esquire*

v167 no2 p89 Mr 2017

MIXED SINGLES color *Esquire* p28 O 2017

PROJECT RED LIGHT bw color *Esquire* p37 S 2017

Ray DALIO color *Esquire* p62 O 2017

The Rebalance and Asia-Pacific Security color *Foreign Affairs* v95 no6 p65 N/D 2016

The Selfie Samurai bw *Vanity Fair* v59 no10 p182 O 2017

What I Learned from Transforming the U.S. Military's Approach to Talent *Harvard Business Review Digital Articles* p2 My 23 2017

Yanis VAROUFAKIS color *Esquire* p58 N 2017

Carter, Ashton B., 1954-

Guns and Robots: We've paid too much attention to weapons of the future and too little to our forces today T. Donnelly *Hoover Digest: Research & Opinion on Public Policy* no3 p59 Summ 2017

Carter, Blue Ivy, 2012-

GREAT EXPECTATIONS C. Agard color *Entertainment Weekly* no1463/1464 p18 Ap/My 2017

CARTER, BRIAN

Halo Effect *Architectural Record* v205 no10 p70 O 2017

CARTER, CAMERON

Gator Growth and Reproduction color graph map *Natural History* v125 no7 p10 Jl/Ag 2017

CARTER, CHARLES W., JR.

An Alternative to the RNA World *Natural History* v125 no1 p28 D 2016/Ja 2017

Carter, Chris

I Am Death: A Robert Hunter Thriller color *Publishers Weekly* v264 no11 p59 Mr 13 2017

Carter, Clint

Cooler Gear, Hotter Deals color *Men's Health* v32 no2 p24 Mr 2017

MH WORLD color *Men's Health* v32 no9 p4 N 2017

THE NEW TURN-ONS color *Men's Health* v32 no7 p114 S 2017

Take Up the Slack color graph *Men's Health* v32 no9 p84 N 2017

Carter, Darryl

DARRYL CARTER ON MIXING MODERN WITH TRADITIONAL K. O'SHEA-EVANS color *House Beautiful* v159 no2 p56 Mr 2017

CARTER, ELLIOT

RED STARE *Washingtonian Magazine* v52 no3 p22 D 2016

Carter, Erika

Lucky You *Publishers Weekly* v264 no5 p171 Ja 30 2017

CARTER, GRAYDON

ALL THE PRESIDENT'S MEN 2.0 *Vanity Fair* v59 no8 p34 Ag 2017

THE DECIDERS AND THE DAMNED *Vanity Fair* v58 no12 p62 D 2016

A FARCE TO BE RECKONED WITH color *Vanity Fair* v59 no7 p32 Summ 2017

FROM 9/11 to 11/9 *Vanity Fair* v59 no1 p42 Holiday 2017

THE GANG That COULDN'T SHOOT STRAIGHT *Vanity Fair* v59 no4 p90 Mr 2017

HIGH RISK, LOW ENERGY *Vanity Fair* v59 no9 p92 S 2017

A JOKE CERTAINLY, but NO LAUGHING MATTER *Vanity Fair* v59 no5 p40 Ap 2017

A LIFE IN FOCUS bw *Vanity Fair* v59 no6 p100 My 2017

'NATIONAL LAMPOON"S PRESIDENTIAL VACATION *Vanity Fair* v59 no10 p80 O 2017

A PILLAR of IGNORANCE and CERTITUDE *Vanity Fair* p72 Hollywood 2017 Supplement

THE RECKONING *Vanity Fair* v59 no11 p46 N 2017

TRUMP FAMILY VALUES *Vanity Fair* v59 no6 p40 My 2017

THE UGLY AMERICAN *Vanity Fair* v58 no11 p48 N 2016

WELCOME TO TRUMPISTAN *Vanity Fair* v59 no2 p20 F 2017

Carter, Heath W.

THE DEEPER ROOTS of the Christian Right color *Christianity Today* v61 no6 p60 Jl/Ag 2017

Ghetto: The Invention of a Place, the History of an Idea color *Christian Century* v133 no21 p42 O 12 2016

Wilson's troubling faith *Christian Century* v134 no14 p36 Jl 5 2017

CARTER, HOLLY

THE Beauty OF Giving color *O, The Oprah Magazine* p76 N 2017

Softer Skin, REVEALED color *O, The Oprah Magazine* p120 N 2017

Carter, Jacqueline

How to Practice Mindfulness Throughout Your Work Day *Harvard Business Review Digital Articles* p2 Mr 4 2016

Spending 10 Minutes a Day on Mindfulness Subtly Changes the Way You React to Everything color *Harvard Business Review Digital Articles* p2 Ja 18 2017

Carter, James—Interviews

Following WISE MEN J. EPHLAND color *Downbeat* v83 no12 p54 D 2016

Carter, Jimmy, 1924-

1977: A LOOK BACK L. Bonner bw color *Equus* no482 p39 N 2017

The Great Carter Mystery A. Schlesinger Jr. *New Republic* v248 no6 p4 Je 2017

OBAMA FINALLY FINDS HIS CLEMENCY PEN J. SULLUM graph *Reason* v48 no11 p44 Ap 2017

Renée ZELLWEGER cartoon *Vanity Fair* p196 Hollywood 2017 Supplement

Carter, Jimmy, 1924-—Interviews

JIMMY CARTER: PURSUING AN ARC OF RECONCILIATION R. CLARK bw *Christianity Today* v60 no8 p66 O 2016

Carter, John E.

Photographer was eyewitness to Nebraska's birth E. Schwartz bw *Nebraska Life* v20 no6 p60 N/D 2016

Carter, Joshua Blake

JOSHUA BLAKE CARTER J. BERG color *Chicago* v66 no5 p54 My 2017

Carter, Kate

Memory Maker A. PATUREL color *Good Housekeeping* v264 no1 p69 Ja 1 2017

Carter, Kelley

#BUYBLACK color *Essence* v47 no8 p19 D 2016

CARTER, KIERA

THE NEW TURN-ONS color *Men's Health* v32 no7 p114 S 2017

Carter, Kyle

DITCH YOUR DITCH TROUBLES color diag *Practical Horseman* v45 no11 p32 N 2017

Carter, Lauren

Global analysis of protein folding using massively parallel design, synthesis, and testing color diag *Science* v357 no6347 p168 Jl 14 2017

Carter, Lucie Monk

Adonis Expose color *New Orleans Magazine* v51 no4 p28 F 2017

Bob Becker color *New Orleans Magazine* v51 no5 p28 Mr 2017

Rick Bragg color *New Orleans Magazine* v51 no6 p28 Ap 2017

Carter, Lynda

50 Reasons to Love Being 50+ color *AARP: The Magazine* v59 no6A p63 O/N 2016

Carter, Michelle

The Girl from Plainville J. Barron bw color *Esquire* p100 O 2017

CARTER, NEIL H.

EVOLUTION AND COMPLEXITY IN BIOTA AND HUMAN CULTURES *BioScience* v67 no1 p92 Ja 2017

Modernization, Risk, and Conservation of the World's Largest Carnivores *BioScience* v67 no7 p646 Jl 2017

Carter, Nick, 1980-—Interviews

BACKSTREET'S BACK, ALL RIGHT! N. Feeney color *Entertainment Weekly* no1454/1455 p58 F 24 2017

Carter, Raven

EIGHT PEOPLE TO WHIP YOU INTO SHAPE C. Cunningham *Washingtonian Magazine* v52 no4 p108 Ja 2017

CARTER, REBECCA

THE NEXT JCVD? color *Black Belt* v55 no1 p52 D 2016/Ja 2017

Carter, Regina

Saluting ELLA D. Ouellette color *Downbeat* v84 no10 p46 O 2017

Carter, Ryan

ADD WATER TO DIRT AND YOU GET MUD. ADD BEER, WEED, AND 15,000 PEOPLE TO MUD AND YOU GET MICHIGAN MUD JAM M. DUFF color *Car & Driver* v63 no5 p106 N 2017

Carter, Shaun

Popular money-saving strategies prove elusive for low-income households *Monthly Labor Review* p1 S 2016

Carter, Shawn
Our Bail-Bond System Is Predatory and Destroys Families color *Time* v190 no2/3 p28 Jl 10-17 2017

Carter, Taliya
GENERATION EXCELLENT E. Craig bw *Wired* v24 no11 p58 N 2016

Carter, Victoria
Race & Dating: It's Complicated color *Glamour* v115 no6 p91 Je 2017

Carter, Vince, 1977-
sports funnies K. MILLER color *National Geographic Kids* no465 p9 N 2016

CARTER-BEY, ALVIN
Chords & Discords color *Downbeat* v83 no11 p10 N 2016

Cartica Management LLC
The Trump Discount S. SCHAEFER color *Forbes* v199 no1 p60 Ja 24 2017

Cartier, Kimberly
STRANGE NEWS FROM Another Star color diag graph *Scientific American* v316 no5 p36 My 2017

Cartier International AG
100 YEARS OLD AND STILL A KNOCKOUT M. Hainey bw color *Esquire* p56 S 2017
Bling RING *Interview* v47 no5 p30 Je/Jl 2017
CARTIER BRINGS IT HOME color *Harper's Bazaar* no3649 p332 D 2016/Ja 2017
THE CARTIER TANK AT 100 M. SOLOMON bw color *Forbes* v200 no4 p20 O 24 2017
FOREVER LINKED color *Harper's Bazaar* no3648 p112 N 2016
LINKED IN color *Conde Nast Traveler* v52 no8 p26 S 2017
Secret Ginza color *Conde Nast Traveler* v52 no1 p52 Ja 2017

Cartilage
LIVING BETTER WITH ARTHRITIS J. HOGAN REDMOND *Cincinnati Magazine* v50 no7 p90 Ap 2017

Cartilage cells
FACTORS FOR GROWTH A. GONZALEZ color *Muscle & Performance* v9 no9 p50 S 2017

Cartledge, Paul
An Alexander for the social media age? *History Today* v66 no10 p60 O 2016
AN IDEA OF ALEXANDER *History Today* v67 no8 p94 Ag 2017

Cartlidge, Edwin
Eastern Europe's laser centers will debut without a star color *Science* v355 no6327 p785 F 24 2017
European XFEL to shine as brightest, fastest x-ray source chart color *Science* v354 no6308 p22 O 7 2016
Giant radio telescope faces downsizing color *Science* v356 no6334 p124 Ap 14 2017

Cartographers
Lunar Hall of Fame: Beginning in 1645, obsessed observers drew maps of the Moon's face in ever-greater detail C. Wood *Sky & Telescope* v134 no6 p52 D 2017
The Map K. Wiles *History Today* v67 no3 p26 Mr 2017

Cartography
See also
Geological mapping
You Had To Be There C. TATTOLI color *Conde Nast Traveler* v52 no5 p132 My 2017

Cartography—Equipment & supplies
Handheld 3D Mapper M. Belfiore color *Bloomberg Businessweek* no4514 p37 Mr 13 2017

Cartography—History
Ask Smithsonian K. Nodjimbadem *Smithsonian* v47 no7 p104 N 2016

Carton, Andrew M.
People Remember What You Say When You Paint a Picture *Harvard Business Review Digital Articles* p2 Je 12 2015

Cartonia, Ray
OLD FLAMES color *Field & Stream* v122 no1 p10 My 2017

Cartoon captions
How a Cartoon Caption Contest Can Make You a Better Writer P. Boumgarden *Harvard Business Review Digital Articles* p2 Jl 21 2015

Cartoon characters
Put a Great Spin on the Gift-Giving Season *USA Today Magazine* v145 no2858 p78 N 2016

Cartoonists
A\J at 45 cartoon *Alternatives Journal (AJ) - Canada's Environmental Voice* v42 no2 p12 2016
CARTOON COUNTY, U.S.A C. MURPHY bw cartoon color *Vanity Fair* v59 no9 p158 S 2017
Drawing from Life P. Nielsen cartoon *Sail* v48 no4 p6 Ap 2017
Gene Luen Yang Thinks Superheroes Are For Everyone D. Itzkoff *New York Times Magazine* p66 N 20 2016
Views From Abroad *New York Times Upfront* p1 Mr 13 2017 Supplement World Week

Cartoonists—United States
JACK T. CHICK D. BARRY *New York Times Magazine* p20 D 25 2016

Cartridges (Ammunition)
6.5 CREEDMOOR J. B. SNOW color *Outdoor Life* v224 no5 p57 Je/Jl 2017
Q & A D. E. Petzal cartoon *Field & Stream* v121 no8 p24 F/Mr 2017
Q&A D. E. Petzal color *Field & Stream* v122 no2 p23 Je/Jl 2017

Cartridges (Ammunition)—Design & construction
HOW OL'S WILDCAT CAME TO DOMINATE LONG-RANGE PRECISION-RIFLE SHOOTING J. B. SNOW color graph *Outdoor Life* v224 no2 p36 F/Mr 2017

Cartridges (Ammunition)—Evaluation
22 NOSLER J. B. SNOW chart color *Outdoor Life* v224 no4 p28 My 2017
BALLISTIC BELLY FLOPS B. M. TOWSLEY color *Outdoor Life* v224 no1 p87 D 2016/Ja 2017
THE ENDURING .45/70 J. B. SNOW color *Outdoor Life* v224 no7 p62 S 2017

Cartwright, Gary, 1934-2017
The Writer's Life J. SPONG *Texas Monthly* v45 no4 p18 Ap 2017

Cartwright, Kelly B.
EXECUTIVE-LEVEL THINKING: Teaching 21st-century skills for effective reading comprehension color *Literacy Today (2411-7862)* v34 no6 p38 My/Je 2017

Cartwright, Ryan
Kevin Can Wait J. Halterman *TV Guide* v65 no19 p30 My 1 2017

Carty, Kevin
The Constitutional Case for Equality color *Washington Monthly* v49 no9/10 p133 S/O 2017
Power to the People *Washington Monthly* p13 Ja/F 2017

Carucci, Elinor
UNCONDITIONAL M. SAGER color *Men's Health* v32 no5 p112 Je 2017

Carucci, Ron
A 10-Year Study Reveals What Great Executives Know and Do *Harvard Business Review Digital Articles* p2 Ja 19 2016
3 Ways Leaders Undermine Cohesion by Trying to Create It *Harvard Business Review Digital Articles* p2 D 23 2015
4 Things That Sink New Executives, and How to Overcome Them *Harvard Business Review Digital Articles* p2 F 9 2016
4 Ways Leaders Fritter Their Power Away *Harvard Business Review Digital Articles* p2 O 29 2015
The Better You Know Yourself, the More Resilient You'll Be *Harvard Business Review Digital Articles* p2 S 4 2017
Big Companies Don't Have to Be Soulless Places to Work *Harvard Business Review Digital Articles* p2 Mr 23 2016
Great Leaders Know They're Not Perfect *Harvard Business Review Digital Articles* p2 D 4 2015
How Corporate Values Get Hijacked and Misused *Harvard Business Review Digital Articles* p2 My 29 2017
How to Make Raising Difficult Issues Everyone's Job *Harvard Business Review Digital Articles* p2 My 19 2017
How to Nourish Your Team's Creativity *Harvard Business Review Digital Articles* p2 My 9 2017
How to Tell Your Boss to Stop Doing Your Job color *Harvard Business Review Digital Articles* p2 Mr 27 2017
Leading Effectively When You Inherit a Mess *Harvard Business Review Digital Articles* p2 Ag 7 2017
Midsize Companies Shouldn't Confuse Growth with Scaling *Harvard Business Review Digital Articles* p2 Jl 25 2016
Most Reorgs Aren't Ambitious Enough color *Harvard Business Review Digital Articles* p2 F 10 2017
Stress Leads to Bad Decisions. Here's How to Avoid Them *Harvard Business Review Digital Articles* p2 Ag 29 2017

Why Self-Improvement Should Be a Group Activity *Harvard Business Review Digital Articles* p2 F 22 2017

Caruso, Catherine

Grandma's Robot Helper color *Scientific American* v317 no1 p24 Jl 2017

Make Earth Great Again graph *Scientific American* v316 no3 p20 Mr 2017

Caruso, Christina M.

Precipitation drives global variation in natural selection bibl chart diag map *Science* v355 no6328 p959 Mr 3 2017

CARUSO, FRANK

The Main Harmonic Movement Principles Used in Jazz Composition bw color *Downbeat* v84 no3 p108 Mr 2017

Caruso, Jim—Interviews

Free Speech, No Shit N. GILLESPIE color *Reason* v49 no3 p50 Jl 2017

Caruso, R.

Observation of a large-scale anisotropy in the arrival directions of cosmic rays above 8×10^{18} eV *Science* v357 no6357 p1266 S 22 2017

Carusone, Angelo

WASHINGTON CONFIDENTIAL: Why a Tinseltown insider publication is suddenly a player in DC E. Plott *Washingtonian Magazine* v52 no11 p52 Ag 2017

Carvalhaes, Cláudio

A coalition to impeach *Christian Century* v133 no23 p11 N 9 2016

Carvalho, F. A.

Persistent effects of pre-Columbian plant domestication on Amazonian forest composition bibl chart graph map *Science* v355 no6328 p925 Mr 3 2017

Carvalho, Mónica R.

Eocene lantern fruits from Gondwanan Patagonia and the early origins of Solanaceae bibl color diag *Science* v355 no6320 p1 Ja 6 2017

Carver, Martin Oswald Hugh, 1941-

PICTS, PINS, STONES AND BONES: A vivid account of groundbreaking archaeological excavations at a Scottish site of crucial importance to the North Sea world R. Hodges *History Today* v67 no9 p92 S 2017

CARVER, NOAH

Noah Is Blind *Scholastic Choices* v32 no3 p16 N/D 2016

Carver, Robert

From Levantine glory to dystopian wreck *History Today* v66 no10 p65 O 2016

HACKER CRACK-UP color *Wired* v25 no6 p10 Je 2017

SAVAGE NOBLES AND NOBLE SAVAGES *History Today* v67 no8 p101 Ag 2017

What the British Did *History Today* v67 no3 p57 Mr 2017

Carver Yachts (Company)

CARVER 52 COMMAND BRIDGE T. SERIO *Sea Magazine* v109 no1 p34 Ja 2017

Carver Wees, Beth

A gem of a discovery color *Magazine Antiques* v183 no6 p48 N/D 2016

Carving (Decorative arts)

See also

Wood carving

Chester's Pencil Lady S. W. Kansteiner color *Nebraska Life* v21 no1 p62 Ja/F 2017

I JUST STARTED READING THE T. A. Johnson, M. McQuaid et al *Arizona Highways* v92 no11 p4 N 2016

RIPE FOR DECORATING E. N. GAGE color *Martha Stewart Living* p104 S 2017

Carving (Decorative arts)—Exhibitions

CABIN art color *Cabin Living* p11 Mr 2017

Pocket-size punch B. L. Scherer color *Magazine Antiques* v184 no2 p52 Mr/Ap 2017

Caryl, Christian

The Kurds Are Nearly There C. Caryl color map *New York Review of Books* v63 no19 p42 D 8 2016

Casa Grande Ruins National Monument (Ariz.)

NATIONAL PARKS TIMELINE E. LIERLE *Arizona Highways* v92 no8 p10 Ag 2016

Casablanca (Morocco)

VICTOR LASZLO'S BLOG I. FRAZIER bw *New Yorker* v93 no28 p27 S 18 2017

CASADA, JIM

The GOBFATHER color *Outdoor Life* v224 no2 p52 F/Mr 2017

Casal, Jorge J.

Phytochrome B integrates light and temperature signals in Arabidopsis bibl graph *Science* v354 no6314 p897 N 18 2016

Casaleggio, Davide

Participate. Don't Delegate *NPQ: New Perspectives Quarterly* v34 no2 p14 My 2017

Casals, Cristina

Local amplifiers of IL-4Rα-mediated macrophage activation promote repair in lung and liver diag *Science* v356 no6342 p1076 Je 9 2017

Casals, Ferran

Chimpanzee genomic diversity reveals ancient admixture with bonobos bibl diag graph map *Science* v354 no6311 p477 O 28 2016

Casals, Pablo, 1876-1973

Knock, Knock, Knocking ... color *Weekly Standard* v22 no9 p4 N 7 2016

Casanova, Fèlix

A molecular spin-photovoltaic device color diag *Science* v357 no6352 p677 Ag 18 2017

Casarett, David

The Missing Guests of the Magic Grove Hotel: An Ethical Chiang Mai Detective Agency Novel *Publishers Weekly* v264 no41 p43 O 9 2017

Casas, Eduard

Transgenerational transmission of environmental information in C. elegans diag *Science* v356 no6335 p320 Ap 21 2017

Casasanto, Daniel

Sleight of hand color *Science* v357 no6357 p1246 S 22 2017

Casas-Zamora, Kevin

Beyond the Scandals: The Changing Context of Corruption in Latin America R. Feinberg *Foreign Affairs* v96 no3 p166 My/Je 2017

CASAUS, JORDI CARDONER

The Barça Foundation *UN Chronicle* v53 no2 p44 2016

Casavant, David

DAVID CASAVANT J. Roth color *Esquire* p54 Ap 2017

Cascade connections

THE UNFOLDING AND CONTROL OF NETWORK CASCADES A. E. Motter and Yang Yang *Physics Today* v70 no1 p32 Ja 2017

Cascades (Fluid dynamics)

THE UNFOLDING AND CONTROL OF NETWORK CASCADES A. E. Motter and Yang Yang *Physics Today* v70 no1 p32 Ja 2017

Caschetta, M. B.

Pretend I'm Your Friend I. Biedenharn color *Entertainment Weekly* no1441 p62 N 25 2016

Case, Anne, 1958-

Anne Case M. Rich color *Current Biography* v78 no3 p8 Mr 2017

Case, Emily

Chapman's RV campers host riverside trick-or-treat adventure color *Nebraska Life* v21 no5 p81 S/O 2017

Final salute in Alliance: Nebraska Veterans Cemetery *Nebraska Life* v20 no6 p17 N/D 2016

Front porch music sessions take center stage in Hastings color *Nebraska Life* v21 no5 p76 S/O 2017

Hastings traditions inspire ageless symphonic voices color *Nebraska Life* v20 no6 p64 N/D 2016

Nebraska music scene growing color *Nebraska Life* v21 no4 p74 Jl/Ag 2017

CASE, HOLLY

Shape-Shifting Illiberalism in East-Central Europe *Current History* v116 no788 p112 Mr 2017

Case, Ingrid

Enjoy a Senior Term Abroad color *Money* v46 no2 p43 Mr 2017

Grab a Spot in the Sharing Economy diag *Money* v46 no2 p44 Mr 2017

CASE, JENNIFER

Baby Center *Orion Magazine* v35 no4/5 p38 Jl-O 2016

Case, John

Treat Employees Like Business Owners *Harvard Business Review Digital Articles* p2 D 8 2015

Case, Joshua

People D. Paulsen color *Christian Century* v133 no26 p19 D 21 2016

CASE, LARRY

READ A BEAR'S MIND color *Outdoor Life* v224 no8 pH11 O 2017

Case, Leland D. (Leland Davidson), 1900-1986

OUR CASE FOR HISTORY: Historian Leland Case's spirit can be felt in certain South Dakota places P. Higbee *South Dakota Magazine* v33 no3 p42 S/O 2017

CASE, NEKO

The Year in Reading [Cover story] *New York Times Book Review* p8 D 25 2016

Case, Stephanie

STEPHANIE CASE A. C. SHILTON color *Runner's World* v52 no1 p85 Ja/F 2017

Case, Steve

Looking for Answers to the World's Biggest Challenges In the Eternal City color *Time* v188 no24 p31 D 12 2016

Case Farms LLC

CUT TO THE BONE M. GRABELL cartoon *New Yorker* v93 no12 p46 My 8 2017

Case study (Research)

Case Study: When You're Successful, Stretched Too Thin, and Indispensable A. Beard *Harvard Business Review Digital Articles* p2 Ag 9 2017

Case Western Reserve University

Case Western Reserve University *Dance Magazine* v90 p114 2016/2017 Supplement College Guide

Case for Christ, The (Film)

The case for (and problem with) Christian movies P. S. J. Lickteig color *America* v216 no10 p50 My 1 2017

Casella, Jean

America's Invisible Inferno M. Garbus color *New York Review of Books* v63 no19 p24 D 8 2016

Hell Is a Very Small Place K. Vandenberg *Orion Magazine* v35 no3 p56 My/Je 2016

Casella, Piergiorgio

An accreting pulsar with extreme properties drives an ultraluminous x-ray source in NGC 5907 bibl chart graph *Science* v355 no6327 p817 F 24 2017

Casemate Publishers & Distributors LLC

TARGETING HISTORY color *Publishers Weekly* v264 no30 p32 Jl 24 2017

Casertano, Stefano

Relativistic deflection of background starlight measures the mass of a nearby white dwarf star chart color graph *Science* v356 no6342 p1046 Je 9 2017

Casetify (Company)

CASETIFY iPHONE 7 CASES AND COVERS S. J. PUREWAL color *Macworld - Digital Edition* v34 no4 p42 My 2017

CASEY, BERNIE

MEN BEHAVING BADLY color *Vanity Fair* v59 no11 p54 N 2017

Casey, Brian

How the Insurance Industry Can Push Us to Prepare for Climate Change *Harvard Business Review Digital Articles* p2 Ag 28 2017

Casey, Caroline

Open Book J. WILLIAMS *New York Times Book Review* p6 S 10 2017

CASEY, CONSTANCE

Animal House: Isobel Charman recounts the London Zoo's 19th-century origins *New York Times Book Review* p8 Jl 9 2017

Casey, Don

ASK SAIL color *Sail* v47 no12 p50 D 2016

ASK SAIL *Sail* v48 no5 p50 My 2017

Core Principles color *Sail* v48 no6 p50 Je 2017

Making Do color *Sail* v48 no8 p11 Ag 2017

Casey, Ginny

Half E. Sutphin color *Art in America* v105 no1 p81 Ja 2017

CASEY, MAUD

Twenty Thousand Leagues Under the Sea *American Scholar* v86 no4 p94 Aut 2017

Casey, Michael J.

Global Supply Chains Are About to Get Better, Thanks to Blockchain *Harvard Business Review Digital Articles* p2 Mr 13 2017

Casey, Nell

Hidden Agenda color *Vogue* v207 no10 p224 O 2017

Casey, Nicholas

One Family's Tragic Tale: Their story became a symbol of the nation's collapse *New York Times Upfront* v149 no13 p15 My 15 2017

CASEY, RYAN P.

The Bandleader: Sarah Reich is bringing tap to new audiences with innovative collaborations and daring creativity *Dance Magazine* v91 no9 p58 S 2017

Get Booked *Dance Magazine* v91 no1 p105 Ja 2017

Cash, Johnny, 1932-2003

Forever Words: The Unknown Poems J. Johnson *Christian Century* v134 no6 p42 Mr 15 2017

Cash crops

GET READY TO MAKE MORE SALES: HERE ARE THE KEY WEEKS YOU'LL WANT TO WATCH IN 2017 A. Kluis graph *Successful Farming* v115 no7 p14 My 2017

Cash flow

Cheap Shares, Plenty of Cash R. ERMEY chart color *Kiplinger's Personal Finance* v71 no11 p58 N 2017

Cash flow statements

Lend Online and Earn Up to 11% E. LEARY cartoon *Kiplinger's Personal Finance* v71 no1 p58 Ja 2017

A Stodgy Fund Still Delights Investors N. S. HUANG chart *Kiplinger's Personal Finance* v71 no11 p61 N 2017

Cash flow—Taxation

Will the BAT Be the Tax That Changes Everything? H. S. Edwards color diag *Time* v189 no11 p28 Mr 27 2017

Cash position of corporations

APPLE IS SITTING ON A HUGE PILE OF CASH diag *Fortune* v176 no3 p15 S 1 2017

Cash transactions

Why the Doctor Takes Only Cash H. S. Edwards color diag *Time* v189 no4 p34 F 6 2017

Cashel Co.

Battle the Bugs color *Horse & Rider* v56 no7 p34 Jl 2017

PRACTICAL PRODUCTS L. Back color *Trail Rider* v29 no2 p57 Mr 2017

Cashew

The other nut milks A. Gorin chart color *Yoga Journal* no290 p80 Mr 2017

Cash flow—Charts, diagrams, etc.

CASH HOARDERS B. O'Keefe diag *Fortune* v174 no7 p108 D 1 2016

Cashman, Brian, 1967-

1 THE NEW TESTAMENT B. Reiter, S. Apstein et al color *Sports Illustrated* v126 no9 p40 Mr 27 2017

Cashman, Jim

Kilogram-scale prexasertib monolactate monohydrate synthesis under continuous-flow CGMP conditions chart diag *Science* v356 no6343 p1144 Je 16 2017

Cashman, Katharine V.

Vertically extensive and unstable magmatic systems: A unified view of igneous processes color *Science* v355 no6331 p1280 Mr 24 2017

Cashman, Sherry

ALL ABOUT THAT BASE! color *Practical Horseman* v44 no12 p32 D 2016

Casino finance

Phil Falcone's Last Resort M. CAMPBELL color *Bloomberg Businessweek* no4527 p66 Je 19 2017

Casinos

LOSING It ALL J. ROSENGREN color *Atlantic* v318 no5 p66 D 2016

Narragansett, Rhode Island: In this town, a mile-long beach is the local playground A. GRAVES color map *Yankee* p56 Jl 2017

Casinos—Asia

Philippine Casinos Are Cleaning Up D. Wei, B. Einhorn et al color graph *Bloomberg Businessweek* no4521 p19 My 8 2017

Casinos—Economic aspects

Should Casinos Court Senior Citizens? color *Kiplinger's Personal Finance* v71 no1 p16 Ja 2017

Casinos—Evaluation

THE COSMOPOLITAN OF LAS VEGAS *Los Angeles Magazine* p78 Mr 2017

PUT YOUR CARDS ON THE DINING TABLE B. VAN ZANDT bw color *Louisiana Life* v38 no1 p36 S/O 2017

Casinos—Florida
The Alligator Wrestler and the Casino Boss L. GENSLER bw color *Forbes* v198 no6 p104 N 8 2016

Casinos—Nevada—Las Vegas
What Happens in Vegas Doesn't Stay There D. Wei and C. Palmeri color *Bloomberg Businessweek* no4497 p24 O 31 2016

Casinos—Texas
Low Stakes on the High Seas D. COURTNEY *Texas Monthly* v45 no1 p151 Ja 2017

Casinos—United States
PLACE YOUR BETS: WHAT TO KNOW ABOUT THE FOUR AREA CASINOS *Washingtonian Magazine* v52 no11 p112 Ag 2017

Casio America Inc.
FACES OF INNOVATION D. MICHEL color *Men's Health* v32 no7 p(Sp)14 S 2017

Casiraghi, Luca
From Russia, With Debt color *Bloomberg Businessweek* no4517 p42 Ap 3 2017
A Sun-Dappled Tuscan Banking Mess color *Bloomberg Businessweek* no4511 p36 F 13 2017

Casitas, Lake (Calif.)
OJAI VALLEY, CALIFORNIA C. Ress *Harper's Magazine* p38 O 2017

Caskey, Judson
Research: Workplace Injuries Are More Common When Companies Face Earnings Pressure *Harvard Business Review Digital Articles* p2 My 18 2017

Casner, Steve
Make your home truly safe [Cover story] color *Redbook* p65 Je 2017

Casnocha, Ben
Marissa Mayer Was Right to Ask Executives to Commit to Staying at Yahoo *Harvard Business Review Digital Articles* p2 N 11 2015
Reid Hoffman's Two Rules for Strategy Decisions *Harvard Business Review Digital Articles* p2 Mr 5 2015

Casola, Francesco
Control and local measurement of the spin chemical potential in a magnetic insulator bw diag *Science* v357 no6347 p195 Jl 14 2017

Casonhua, Lauren
Fabricating the World's Thinnest Plastic Wrap color *Science & Technology Review* p16 Ja/F 2017

Caspe, David
HAPPY ENDINGS D. Snierson, A. Writing et al color *Entertainment Weekly* no1439 p20 N 11 2016

Casper (Company)
DREAM WEAVER E. Griffith, A. Vandermey et al color *Fortune* v176 no3 p74 S 1 2017

Casper, Jayson
Five-Star Pilgrimage *Christianity Today* v61 no6 p18 Jl/Ag 2017
LET MY PEOPLE BUILD color *Christianity Today* v60 no9 p17 N 2016
They Will Know We Are Christians by Our Drinks *Christianity Today* p20 Ap 2017
WHO AWAITS THE MESSIAH MOST? MUSLIMS cartoon *Christianity Today* v61 no1 p17 Ja/F 2017

Casper Sleep Inc.
SOFT LANDINGS IN MATTRESSES L. Entis color *Fortune* v75 no1 p26 Ja 1 2017

CASPERMEYER, JOE
IT'S NOT A WASH *USA Today Magazine* v145 no2862 p54 Mr 2017

Caspers, Barbara
The biology of color color *Science* v357 no6350 p470 Ag 4 2017

Caspian Sea
VACATION IN IRAN N. Tavakolian color map *New Yorker* v93 no10 p74 Ap 24 2017

Caspit, Ben
The Netanyahu Years *Publishers Weekly* v264 no18 p50 My 1 2017

Cass, Danielle
Bringing the Customer's Voice into Medicine *Harvard Business Review Digital Articles* p2 N 24 2014

CASS, OREN
Trump the Climate-Slayer *National Review* v68 no23 p16 D 19 2016
What Counts as Climate Consensus? *National Review* v69 no11 p2 Je 12 2017
Who's The Denier Now? color *National Review* v69 no8 p23 My 2017

Cassavetes, John, 1929-1989
The Kid Slays in the Picture S. ENELOW color *Film Comment* v53 no5 p20 S/O 2017

Cassegrainian telescopes
Build Your Own On-Axis Guider J. Oltion *Sky & Telescope* v133 no1 p72 Ja 2017

Cassegrainian telescopes—Evaluation
Hot Products 2017 *Sky & Telescope* v133 no1 p32 Ja 2017

CASSELMAN, BARRY
Will Minnesota Finally Go Red? color *Weekly Standard* v22 no46 p24 Ag 14 2017

Cassels, Laura
Scaling pain threshold with microRNAs diag *Science* v356 no6343 p1124 Je 16 2017

Casserole cooking
MORNING GLORIES Y. KIM *Martha Stewart Living* no270 p91 D 2016
the new CASSEROLE M. GLISAN color *Better Homes & Gardens* v95 no8 p110 Ag 2017
NOT-COOL CASSEROLE E. Passarella color *Southern Living* v52 no5 p97 My 2017
OYSTER CASSEROLE L. Cericola, K. Hammonds et al color *Southern Living* v51 no12 p188 D 2016
SLOW, STEADY... READY! *Martha Stewart Living* no268 p84 O 2016

Cassidy, Bill
Remaking Public Schools D. Ruth Wilson color *New Orleans Magazine* v51 no6 p32 Ap 2017
To Pass Health Care, The Senate Needs Him S. T. Dennis color *Bloomberg Businessweek* no4524 p28 My 29 2017

Cassidy, Butch, b. 1866
Wild West Josie N. BRULLIARD *National Parks* v91 no1 p58 Wint 2017

Cassidy, Clayton Kenneth
Clayton Kenneth Cassidy A. A. DAVIS color *Maclean's* v130 no7 p66 Ag 2017

Cassidy, Donna M.
"My native continent" cartoon *Magazine Antiques* v184 no2 p100 Mr/Ap 2017

CASSIDY, EMMA
Standing Rock Says No to the Dakota Access Pipeline color *Progressive* v81 no10 p10 N 2016

Cassidy, M. C.
Demonstration of an ac Josephson junction laser bibl diag *Science* v355 no6328 p939 Mr 3 2017

Cassidy, Michelle
Making Marriage: Husbands, Wives, and the American State in Dakota and Ojibwe Country *American Indian Quarterly* v40 no3 p288 Summ 2016

Cassidy, Shaun, 1958-
SHAUN CASSIDY M. Logan color *TV Guide* v65 no7 p11 F 13 2017

Cassigneul, Jean Pierre, 1935-
Modèle dans l'Atelier color *Architectural Digest* v73 no11 p134 N 2016

Cassin, Barbara
Barbara Cassin, ed; Emily Apter, Jacques Lezra, and Michael Wood, English trans. eds; translated by Christian Hubert, Jeffrey Mehlman, Steven Rendall, Nathaniel Stein, and Michael Syrotinsky. Dictionary of Untranslatables: A Philosophical Lexicon L. Rosenwald *Society* v53 no6 p662 D 2016

Cassini (Spacecraft)
Age of Saturn's rings debated C. CROCKETT bw *Science News* v190 no10 p10 N 12 2016
CASSINI AT SATURN C. Porco and E. Bell color *Scientific American* v317 no4 p78 O 2017
Cassini embarks on twilight mission at Saturn P. Voosen color *Science* v356 no6334 p120 Ap 14 2017

Cassini Finds Empty Space on First Finale Pass D. Dickinson color *Sky & Telescope* v134 no2 p12 Ag 2017

The Cassini-Huygens space probe [Cover story] A. ABEL color *Maclean's* v129 no51/52 p74 D 26 2016

Cassini's Closing Act E. MASTROIANNI color *Discover* v38 no7 p14 S 2017

CASSINI'S Curtain Call L. Lisa Grossman bw color *Science News* v192 no3 p16 S 2 2017

Cassini's Grand Finale: 20 years in the making M. Carroll bw color diag *Astronomy* v45 no9 p28 S 2017

Cassini spacecraft gets a proper send-off C. Crockett color *Science News* v192 no3 p26 S 2 2017

Cassini weaves through Saturn's rings color *Astronomy* v45 no8 p18 Ag 2017

Detecting molecular hydrogen on Enceladus J. S. Seewald color *Science* v356 no6334 p132 Ap 14 2017

A fiery finish to Cassini's long run at Saturn P. Voosen color *Science* v357 no6357 p1219 S 22 2017

THE FINAL DAYS OF CASSINI K. N. Smith bw color diag *Astronomy* v45 no1 p26 Ja 2017

A legacy of discovery P. Voosen color *Science* v357 no6357 p1220 S 22 2017

Mission Extraordinaire *Sky & Telescope* v134 no3 p4 S 2017

Patience is one virtue scientists must embrace *Science News* v192 no3 p2 S 2 2017

Subsurface Ocean on Dione? C. M. CARLISLE *Sky & Telescope* v133 no2 p14 F 2017

Worlds of Wonder L. Dones *Sky & Telescope* v134 no3 p16 S 2017

Cassino, Dan

Earning Less Than Their Wives Makes U.S. Men More Partisan *Harvard Business Review Digital Articles* p2 Ap 14 2017

Even the Thought of Earning Less than Their Wives Changes How Men Behave *Harvard Business Review Digital Articles* p2 Ap 19 2016

How Fox News Created the War on Christmas *Harvard Business Review Digital Articles* p2 D 9 2016

How Polls Overestimate Support for Third-Party Candidates *Harvard Business Review Digital Articles* p2 N 4 2016

How Today's Political Polling Works *Harvard Business Review Digital Articles* p2 Ag 1 2016

Trump's Low Approval Numbers Matter — Here's Why color graph *Harvard Business Review Digital Articles* p2 F 3 2017

When Male Unemployment Rates Rise, So Do Sexual Harassment Claims *Harvard Business Review Digital Articles* p2 2017

Why More American Men Feel Discriminated Against *Harvard Business Review Digital Articles* p2 S 29 2016

Why Pollsters Were Completely and Utterly Wrong *Harvard Business Review Digital Articles* p2 N 9 2016

The 'Wisdom of the Crowd' Has a Pretty Bad Track Record at Predicting Jobs Reports *Harvard Business Review Digital Articles* p2 Jl 8 2016

Cassiopeia (Constellation)

Four for the Road M. Wedel *Sky & Telescope* v134 no4 p42 O 2017

Cassouto, Dror

agenda *Successful Farming* v115 no1 p5 Ja 2017

Cast, Jodi

Dairy family raises COWS AND QUADRUPLETS S. OLSON and B. OLSON color *Nebraska Life* v21 no2 p44 Mr/Ap 2017

Cast Aways (Short story)

CAST AWAYS *Harper's Magazine* v335 no2006 p15 Jl 2017

Cast-iron

Lucky Iron Fish to Add Iron to Food [Cover story] color *Prevention* p13 Mr 2017

Cast-iron cookware

CAST-IRON LOVE L. F. Prater *Successful Farming* v115 no3 p58 Mid-F 2017

Cookware 101 color *Prevention* v69 no6 p15 Je 2017

From Our Editor S. Donelson color *House Beautiful* v159 no8 p8 O 2017

Iron Will L. Claverie *New Orleans Homes & Lifestyles* v20 no1 p28 Wint 2016

THAT SWEET CHAR A. RAPOPORT color *Bon Appetit* no11 p128 N 2017

Cast-iron pipe

it's coming from inside the house S. Bushwick color *Popular Science* v289 no6 p88 N/D 2017

Cast steel

WHY WIRES? M. Lindemann color *Cycle World* v56 no10 p32 N 2017

CASTALDO, JOE

BANKING ON THE BUBBLE color *Maclean's* p44 Je 2017

Intrigue at Sloan's Curve color *Maclean's* v130 no8 p45 S 2017

Realtors gone wild color *Maclean's* p14 Je 2017

THROUGH THE ROOF [Cover story] color *Maclean's* v130 no4 p48 My 2017

TOUGH LOVE REQUIRED color *Maclean's* v130 no10 p46 N 2017

WHAT CHINA WANTS color *Maclean's* v130 no9 p67 O 2017

Castañares, Tina

Urgent Care *Harper's Magazine* v334 no2000 p3 Ja 2017

Castanha, C.

The whole-soil carbon flux in response to warming [Cover story] chart graph *Science* v355 no6332 p1420 Mr 31 2017

CASTAÑON, KELSEY

beauty NEWSFEED color *Seventeen* v75 no11 p54 N 2016

How School MESSES WITH YOUR SKIN color *Seventeen* v75 no11 p52 N 2016

Oh Zit! cartoon color *Seventeen* v76 no12 p84 D 2016/Ja 2017

Score Your HAIR GOALS cartoon color *Seventeen* v75 no11 p39 N 2016

TIME TO SHINE color *Seventeen* v75 no11 p86 N 2016

Castanon, Rosa

Single-cell methylomes identify neuronal subtypes and regulatory elements in mammalian cortex diag *Science* v357 no6351 p600 Ag 11 2017

A transcription factor hierarchy defines an environmental stress response network diag *Science* v354 no6312 p598 N 4 2016

Casteel, Jordan

Jordan CASTEEL K. HERRIMAN *Interview* v47 no6 p22 Ag 2017

CASTEEL, KATHY

THE HEAT IS ON color *Missouri Life* v44 no5 p80 Ag 2017

TICKED OFF color *Missouri Life* v44 no4 p64 Je 2017

Work It Out(side) color *Missouri Life* v44 no6 p76 S 2017

Casteel, Seth

Leaping Cats! color *Good Housekeeping* v263 no5 p204 N 2016

Castel, Pau

PI3K pathway regulates ER-dependent transcription in breast cancer through the epigenetic regulator KMT2D bibl graph *Science* v355 no6331 p1324 Mr 24 2017

CASTELIER, SEBASTIAN

Balancing Act: Morocco's circus school takes women to new heights--though many in the country may not approve *Ms.* v27 no3 p18 Fall 2017

Castellano, Brian M.

Lysosomal cholesterol activates mTORC1 via an SLC38A9–Niemann-Pick C1 signaling complex bibl diag graph *Science* v355 no6331 p1306 Mr 24 2017

CASTELLANO, RICH

Smile, and the Sun Will Come Shining Through *USA Today Magazine* v145 no2862 p62 Mr 2017

Castellano, Sergi

Chimpanzee genomic diversity reveals ancient admixture with bonobos bibl diag graph map *Science* v354 no6311 p477 O 28 2016

Castellano Pulido, Javier

CUAC Arquitectura M. Sitz bw color *Architectural Record* v204 no12 p56 D 2016

Castellanos, H.

Persistent effects of pre-Columbian plant domestication on Amazonian forest composition bibl chart graph map *Science* v355 no6328 p925 Mr 3 2017

Castellanos-Galindo, Gustavo A.

Panama's impotent mangrove laws bibl *Science* v355 no6328 p918 Mr 3 2017

Castellarin, Attilio

Changing climate shifts timing of European floods color graph *Science* v357 no6351 p588 Ag 11 2017

Castellina, A.

Observation of a large-scale anisotropy in the arrival directions of cosmic rays above 8 × 1018 eV *Science* v357 no6357 p1266

S 22 2017

Castelluccio, Lorenzo
palace coup M. OWENS color *Architectural Digest* no5 p122 My 2017

Casten, Thomas R.
CSI Fellows in the News *Skeptical Inquirer* v41 no5 p8 S/O 2017

Castile, Philando
RELEASE NOTES cartoon color *Wired* v24 no12 p12 D 2016

Castilho, C. V.
Persistent effects of pre-Columbian plant domestication on Amazonian forest composition bibl chart graph map *Science* v355 no6328 p925 Mr 3 2017

Castilho, Leda R.
Rapid development of a DNA vaccine for Zika virus bibl graph *Science* v354 no6309 p237 O 14 2016

Castillo, Johanna
Deals D. LEFFERTS color *Publishers Weekly* v263 no51 p5 D 12 2016

Deals R. DEAHL color *Publishers Weekly* v264 no21 p10 My 22 2017

CASTILLO, LINDA
Exploring a Hidden World *Publishers Weekly* v264 no21 p75 My 22 2017

Castillo, Stephanie
WORLD'S 50 GREATEST LEADERS [Cover story] color *Fortune* v175 no5 p46 Ap 1 2017

Castillo Blanco LLC
Floating in Space J. DeBold color *New Orleans Magazine* v51 no5 p150 Mr 2017

Castillo-Rogez, J.
Extensive water ice within Ceres' aqueously altered regolith: Evidence from nuclear spectroscopy bibl graph *Science* v355 no6320 p1 Ja 6 2017

Casting (Fishing)
FLY-FISHING J. GLUCK cartoon color *Popular Mechanics* p29 Je 2017

hooked color *Women's Health* v14 no8 p150 O 2017
ONE LASTING CAST T. E. Nickens color *Field & Stream* v121 no9 p22 Ap 2017

Casting directors
Marisa Ross B. GOLDEN color *Chicago* v66 no6 p86 Je 2017

Casting directors—Interviews
Leah Daniels-Butler, Casting Director, Empire M. Logan color *TV Guide* v64 no42 p13 O 10 2016

Casting JonBenet (Film)
Casting JonBenét C. Nashawaty color *Entertainment Weekly* no1463/1464 p88 Ap/My 2017
OFF THE RECORD: REENACTMENT AND INTIMACY IN CASTING JONBENET M. Francis and L. Hussein *Film Quarterly* v71 no1 p32 Fall 2017

Castle, James
Seeing Beauty in the Mundane S. S. PATEL bw cartoon color *Archaeology* v70 no1 p46 Ja/F 2017

Castle, Sheri
Asparagus color *Better Homes & Gardens* v95 no4 p132 Ap 2017
CHEERS to MOM color *Southern Living* v52 no5 p90 My 2017
GENEROUS GRAVY color *Southern Living* v52 no5 p104 My 2017
LET'S HAVE SUPPER color *Southern Living* v52 no10 p96 O 2017
LET THEM EAT CAKE color *Southern Living* v52 no3 p106 Mr 2017
SLOW vs FAST *Better Homes & Gardens* v95 no10 p100 Ja 2017
TRUE GRITS color *Southern Living* v52 no10 p78 O 2017

Castle Connolly Medical Ltd.
WHO DECIDES? *New York* v50 no11 p56 My 29 2017

Castle Geyser (Wyo.)
WORKS IN PROGRESS *American Scholar* v86 no1 p12 Wint 2017

Castle on the Hill (Music)
The Must List color *Entertainment Weekly* no1449 p3 Ja 20 2017

Castleman, Amanda
The Most Silent Night *Sierra* v101 no6 p14 N/D 2016

CASTLEMAN, BEN
Learn to Ad: Madison Avenue Strategies to Strengthen School Communication *Education Digest* v82 no6 p34 F 2017

CastleOak Securities LP
STRONG AS OAK D. T. Dingle color *Black Enterprise* v47 no7 p72 My/Je 2017

Castles
Castle Gothic M. KNOX BERAN *National Review* v69 no11 p30 Je 12 2017

Castles—England
KING COAL'S CASTLES S. Ellis *British Heritage Travel* v38 no2 p68 Mr/Ap 2017

Castles—Europe
The Castle Matchmaker J. Tarmy bw color *Bloomberg Businessweek* no4536 p67 S 4 2017

Castles—France
Bordeaux's Fresh Fantasy E. McCoy bw color *Bloomberg Businessweek* no4538 p55 S 18 2017

Castles—France—Conservation & restoration
FRENCH EVOLUTION N. ARIKHA color *Architectural Digest* no11 p126 N 1 2017

Castles—History
Expanding the Story [Cover story] S. TOTH STUB bw color *Archaeology* v69 no6 p26 N/D 2016
Korea's Half Moon Palace KIM color *Archaeology* v69 no6 p44 N/D 2016

Castles—Ireland—Conservation & restoration
Kingdom by the Sea D. KAMP color *Vanity Fair* v59 no10 p198 O 2017

Castles—Israel
Expanding the Story [Cover story] S. TOTH STUB bw color *Archaeology* v69 no6 p26 N/D 2016

Caston, Marcus
FAREWELL FACIAL L. COHEN color *Skiing* p104 D 2016
SADDLE UP D. Pogge bw color *Skiing* p48 Wint 2017

Castor, Helen
ON THE SPOT HELEN CASTOR *History Today* v67 no5 p112 My 2017

Castor, Helen—Interviews
ON THE SPOT HELEN CASTOR H. Castor *History Today* v67 no5 p112 My 2017

CASTRO, ALI
Freelance Nation *Dance Magazine* v91 no9 p34 S 2017

Castro, Fidel, 1926-2016
Advice for Trump on Post-Fidel Cuba J. Bruno *Washington Monthly* p1 Ja/F 2017
After Fidel P. KORNBLUH bw color *Nation* v303 no25/26 p4 D 19 2016
Cozying Up to the Dictator F. BARNES bw *Weekly Standard* v22 no14 p11 D 12 2016
The Cuban Litmus Test A. J. Stavridis *Time* v188 no24 p49 D 12 2016
Faithless Fidel T. Quigley color *Commonweal* v144 no4 p10 F 24 2017
Fidel Castro 1926-2016 [Cover story] T. Padgett color *Time* v188 no24 p40 D 12 2016
Fidel Castro: Death of a Tyrant bw *National Review* v68 no23 p14 D 19 2016
From Cuba to the Ka'ba: Yes, Cuba has a past, present, and future of Islam W. DÍAZ *Islamic Horizons* v46 no3 p52 My/Je 2017
History Will Not Absolve Him E. ABRAMS bw color *Weekly Standard* v22 no14 p19 D 12 2016
How Castro Will Be Trump's First Foreign Policy Test K. Vick, D. Mascareñas et al color *Time* v188 no24 p46 D 12 2016
How to Keep U.S.-Cuba Relations on Track bw *Bloomberg Businessweek* no4502 p14 D 5 2016
A New Day for Cuba? R. ZISSOU *New York Times Upfront* v149 no7 p12 Ja 9 2017
PARODY *Weekly Standard* v22 no14 p40 D 12 2016
Purpose Pitch S. L. Price and T. Keith color *Sports Illustrated* v125 no18 p17 D 5 2016
The Refit That Sparked Revolution P. SWANSON bw color *Power & Motoryacht* v34 no8 p74 Ag 2017
Style Over Substance: Why Fidel Castro's Revolutionary Chic Was a Fraud J. Klein color *Time* v188 no24 p38 D 12 2016
That's a Lot of Broken Eggs J. LILEKS *National Review* v68 no23 p33 D 19 2016

Castro, Raúl, 1930-
Human Rights in Cuba *Congressional Digest* v95 no10 p9 D 2016

Castro, Rene

The extent of forest in dryland biomes [Cover story] chart map *Science* v356 no6338 p635 My 12 2017

Castro, Vern

THE CASTRO BROTHERS B. Welch bw *Spin to Win Rodeo* v21 no2 p96 Ap 2017

Castrogiovanni, Nick

How Dixie Got Its 45 E. LABORDE color *New Orleans Magazine* v52 no1 p168 S 2017

Castrol Ltd.

Sump, dude? The 90-second oil change F. Markus color *Motor Trend* v69 no4 p30 Ap 2017

Casualties in the Iraq War, 2003-2011

STORIES OF SERVICE AND SACRIFICE S. Goldberg color *National Geographic* v232 no5 p2 N 2017

Caswell, Caroline

What a blind student taught me to see bw chart color diag *Phi Delta Kappan* v98 no3 p68 N 2016

CASWELL, CHRIS

12 Trailer Tire Maintenance Tips *Boating World* v38 no5 p14 My 2017

ADVANCEMENT FOR ALL color *Sea Magazine* v109 no7 p46 Jl 2017

BEST OF BOTH WORLDS chart color *Power & Motoryacht* v34 no7 p54 Jl 2017

Create a User-Friendly Trailer *Boating World* v38 no2 p14 F 2017

HH55 color *Sail* v48 no11 p24 N 2017

Keep 'Em Rollin' *Boating World* v38 no3 p14 Mr 2017

Learn to Launch *Boating World* v38 no6 p14 Je 2017

THE OTHER AMERICA chart color *Power & Motoryacht* v34 no11 p92 N 2017

Procrastination Doesn't Pay *Boating World* v37 no9 p12 N/D 2016

Room and a View chart color diag *Power & Motoryacht* v33 no2 p70 F 2017

TOP 10 TENDERS color *Power & Motoryacht* v33 no4 p84 Ap 2017

Year-Round Trailer Maintenance *Boating World* v38 no1 p18 Ja 2017

Caswell Stoddard, Mary

The biology of color color *Science* v357 no6350 p470 Ag 4 2017

Cat behavior

The Cat Conundrum J. Carey color *National Wildlife (World Edition)* v55 no6 p30 O/N 2017

DO YOU REALLY KNOW YOUR CAT? N. Strochlic color *National Geographic* v232 no4 p12 O 2017

Cat owners

See also

Women cat owners

Domestic Abuse and Protecting Pets C. Lindner *Catnip* v24 no10 p7 O 2016

Cat training

DO YOU REALLY KNOW YOUR CAT? N. Strochlic color *National Geographic* v232 no4 p12 O 2017

Catacombs

Lasers reveal long-hidden catacomb frescoes that have biblical themes J. McKenna color *Christian Century* v134 no15 p16 Jl 19 2017

Çatal Mound (Turkey)

FIGURE OF DISTINCTION J. A. LOBELL color *Archaeology* v70 no1 p22 Ja/F 2017

Catalano, Cosmo

38 REASONS TO GO GA-GA FOR THE TOUR DE FRANCE color *Bicycling* v58 no7 p24 Ag 2017

CATALANO, NICK

SEXUAL RELATIVITY AND GENDER REVOLUTION *Humanist* v77 no4 p42 Jl/Ag 2017

Cataldi, G.

Observation of a large-scale anisotropy in the arrival directions of cosmic rays above 8 × 1018 eV *Science* v357 no6357 p1266 S 22 2017

Catalina Yachts Inc.

Catalina 425 P. Nielsen cartoon color *Sail* v48 no1 p26 Ja 2017

Catalinac, Amy

Electoral Reform and National Security in Japan: From Pork to Foreign Policy *Foreign Affairs* v96 no2 p187 Mr/Ap 2017

Catalini, Christian

KNOW THE RISKS OF CRYPTOCURRENCIES T. H. BLANTON color *Kiplinger's Personal Finance* v71 no12 p10 D 2017

When early adopters don't adopt graph *Science* v357 no6347 p135 Jl 14 2017

Catalogs

See also

Lists

CINDY LINDGREN M. E. Polson color *Arts & Crafts Homes & the Revival* v11 no5 p46 Wint 2017

Graveyard of cold slabs mapped in Earth's mantle P. Voosen color map *Science* v354 no6315 p954 N 25 2016

Kepler Team Releases Final Catalog S. HALL *Sky & Telescope* v134 no4 p10 O 2017

VRG Catalog *Vegetarian Journal* v35 no4 p33 2016

Catalogs—Evaluation

Dream Homes JOHNSON color *Treasures* v5 no5 p44 Ap/My 2016

Catalogs—Marketing

Dream Homes JOHNSON color *Treasures* v5 no5 p44 Ap/My 2016

Catalonia (Spain)—Economic conditions

Anatomy of a Bad Marriage P. Coy, C. Penty et al color *Bloomberg Businessweek* no4541 p10 O 9 2017

Catalonia (Spain)—History—Autonomy & independence movements

The Pressure Rises In Catalonia E. Duarte color *Bloomberg Businessweek* no4539 p36 S 25 2017

Catalonia (Spain)—Politics & government

A Secessionist Abroad B. Soloway color *Foreign Policy* no224 p30 My/Je 2017

Catalonia (Spain)—Politics & government—21st century

The Pressure Rises In Catalonia E. Duarte color *Bloomberg Businessweek* no4539 p36 S 25 2017

Catalysis

See also

Catalysts

Photosensitized, energy transfer-mediated organometallic catalysis through electronically excited nickel(II) E. R. Welin, D. M. Arias-Rotondo et al bibl diag graph *Science* v355 no6323 p380 Ja 27 2017

Catalysts

See also

Enzymes

Iron catalysts

Zeolite catalysts

Biaxially strained PtPb/Pt core/shell nanoplate boosts oxygen reduction catalysis Lingzheng Bu, Nan Zhang et al bibl color graph *Science* v354 no6318 p1410 D 16 2016

Built for SPEED L. Hamers bw color diag graph *Science News* v191 no4 p20 Mr 4 2017

A multifunctional catalyst that stereoselectively assembles prodrugs D. A. DiRocco, Y. Ji et al diag *Science* v356 no6336 p426 Ap 28 2017

Catamaran Co.

Sunreef Power Day Cat: Sunreef 's latest is a 60-knot, 41-foot catamaran with a penchant for dayboating S. SHIBATA *Sea Magazine* v109 no9 p10 S 2017

Catamaran design & construction

BETTER WITH AGE C. SISSON bw color *Power & Motoryacht* v34 no10 p106 O 2017

CAT BE NIMBLE, CAT BE QUICK D. J. HARDING chart color *Power & Motoryacht* v34 no10 p100 O 2017

Catamarans

Green Machine C. Sisson color *Power & Motoryacht* v34 no10 p38 O 2017

Herdin' Cats color *Sail* v48 no7 p8 Jl 2017

JUST ANOTHER DAY ON INDIGO E. SANFORD cartoon color *Sail* v48 no11 p48 N 2017

Land Rover BAR in the Driver's Seat? color *Sail* v48 no2 p24 F 2017

SAILING AN ACC CATAMARAN A. Campbell color map *Sail* v48 no5 p31 My 2017

SHOWCASE FEATURED BROKERAGE BOATS *Sea Magazine* v109 no9 p61 S 2017

WESTCOASTFOCUS *Sea Magazine* v109 no1 p12 Ja 2017

Catamarans—Design & construction

WONDERFUL FLYING MACHINES C. Museler color *Sail* v48 no5 p32 My 2017

Catamarans—Evaluation

HH55 C. Caswell color *Sail* v48 no11 p24 N 2017

Xcat A. Cort color *Sail* v48 no11 p22 N 2017

Catanese, Nicole

HOW DO I GET A GREAT NIGHT'S SLEEP color *Harper's Bazaar* no3651 p332 Mr 2017

HOW TO SHRINK YOUR WAIST color *Harper's Bazaar* no3648 p222 N 2016

LOSE 5 POUNDS FAST color *Harper's Bazaar* no3649 p270 D 2016/Ja 2017

Cataract—Risk factors

MULTI-TASKING [Cover story] D. SCHARDT *Nutrition Action Health Letter* v43 no9 p3 N 2016

Catastrophe (TV program)

What's Love Got To Do With It? E. GOULD color *New Republic* v247 no11 p50 N 2016

Catastrophe Management Solutions Inc.

The Case of the Disqualifying Dreads V. GLEMBOCKI *Reader's Digest* v189 no1128 p25 Mr 2017

Catch, The (TV program)

The Catch M. Logan *TV Guide* v65 no11 p36 Mr 6 2017

A KNIGHT'S Tale N. Abrams color *Entertainment Weekly* no1454/1455 p64 F 24 2017

A Lighter Touch L. Rice color *Entertainment Weekly* no1456 p30 Mr 10 2017

Catchen, Julian

Winter storms drive rapid phenotypic, regulatory, and genomic shifts in the green anole lizard graph *Science* v357 no6350 p495 Ag 4 2017

Catchers (Baseball)

Gary Sánchez M. Hagan color *Current Biography* v78 no5 p77 My 2017

Catching Salinger (Film)

Being Salinger K. ANG cartoon color *Esquire* v167 no1 p21 F 2017

CATCHINGS, VELMA

SEEING THE LIGHT color *O, The Oprah Magazine* p18 Ag 2017

Catelani, Gianluigi

Suppressing relaxation in superconducting qubits by quasiparticle pumping bibl graph *Science* v354 no6319 p1573 D 23 2016

Catering services

See also

Breakfasts

Luncheons

All the Fixin's color *American Cowboy* p68 LEGENDS OF TEXAS Special Issue 2017

DINING GUIDE M. Cameran color *New Orleans Magazine* v51 no4 p92 F 2017

JOCKS AND TOQUES A. SPIEGEL color *Washingtonian Magazine* v52 no7 p18 Ap 2017

Caterpillar Inc.

How Does Tax Avoidance Play in Peoria? B. Gruley, D. Voreacos et al color *Bloomberg Businessweek* no4525 p42 Je 5 2017

People and posts: Who's making HR headlines? *People Management* p56 Je 2017

Caterpillars

Higher predation risk for insect prey at low latitudes and elevations S. Huang, B. Koane et al graph *Science* v356 no6339 p742 My 19 2017

Reading Tree Leaves B. HEINRICH *Natural History* v125 no1 p10 D 2016/Ja 2017

RESEARCH color *Science* v356 no6339 p712 My 19 2017

Cates, Hannah M.

Early life stress confers lifelong stress susceptibility in mice via ventral tegmental area OTX2 diag *Science* v356 no6343 p1185 Je 16 2017

Cates, Jobi

Working Together to Address the Wealth Gap *Bridges (Federal Reserve Bank of St. Louis)* p5 Wint 2016/2017

Cates, Kaitlynn

Stronger Than EVER C. SHMERLER *Tennis* v52 no6 p48 N/D 2016

CATES, MERYL

Life *Reader's Digest* v188 no1124 p40 O 2016

Catfight (Film)

Catfight *New Yorker* v93 no4 p6 Mr 13 2017

Catfishes

Seeing the Light R. KOBELL *National Parks* v91 no1 p24 Wint 2017

Catfishing (Sport)

CAT HACKS K. SUTTON color *Outdoor Life* v224 no6 p35 Ag 2017

CAT NIP J. Cermele cartoon color *Field & Stream* v121 no7 p32 D 2016/Ja 2017

Cathay Pacific Airways Ltd.

Everything Is Fine at Cathay Pacific K. Park and D. Lyu cartoon graph *Bloomberg Businessweek* no4516 p17 Mr 27 2017

Cathedral Rocks (Calif.)

over drive d. o'neil bw color *Bike Magazine* v24 no7 p66 S 2017

Cathedrals

Lightbox color *Time* v188 no27-28 p18 D 26 2016

Cathedrals—Italy

Florence's gift to the people, believers and nonbelievers alike E. W. Schmidt color *America* v217 no4 p52 Ag 21 2017

Cathedrals—Maintenance & repair

AFTER SHOCK B. FREED *Washingtonian Magazine* v52 no1 p28 O 2016

Cather, Willa, 1873-1947

THOUGHTS ON Property *Forbes* v199 no5 p124 My 16 2017

A Winter's Journey M. Sandor *Opera News* v81 no5 p32 N 2016

Catheterization

Advances in emergency stroke care *Mayo Clinic Health Letter* v35 no9 p4 S 2017

Catholic bishops

Solidarity in action S. Butler *U.S. Catholic* v82 no5 p4 My 2017

Catholic bishops—Attitudes

San Diego's Bishop McElroy encourages Catholics to be hopefilled 'disruptors' J. McDermott color *America* v216 no6 p16 Mr 20 2017

Catholic Charities USA

AFTER HARVEY'S RAGE ACROSS TEXAS, CATHOLIC CHARITIES RAMPS UP ITS RESPONSE K. Clarke color *America* v217 no6 p12 S 18 2017

Real life R. McCarty *U.S. Catholic* v82 no4 p4 Ap 2017

Catholic Christian sociology

American Carnage *Commonweal* v144 no3 p5 F 10 2017

Free-Market Folly C. Wilber color *Commonweal* v144 no9 p15 My 19 2017

The gospel of nonviolence K. Butigan color *U.S. Catholic* v82 no2 p20 F 2017

Catholic Church

Age is just a number R. McCarty *U.S. Catholic* v82 no10 p4 O 2017

and the survey says *U.S. Catholic* v82 no6 p35 Je 2017

Answering Our Daughters H. ALVARÉ *America* v215 no15 p14 N 14 2016

BOHEMIAN CATASTROPHY D. Hollway color map *Military History* v34 no5 p40 Ja 2018

Can every sin be forgiven? B. Haile *U.S. Catholic* v82 no9 p49 S 2017

CATHOLICS AT A CROSSROADS I. Johnson color map *America* v217 no7 p18 O 2 2017

Church leaders urge Senate fix on G.O.P. Obamacare repeal K. Clarke color *America* v216 no12 p17 My 29 2017

The church must build 'spiritual ramps' for abuse survivors L. Karen Kivi *America* v216 no12 p10 My 29 2017

Collars on the Corner offers prayers on the streets of Milwaukee D. Paulsen *Christian Century* v134 no17 p18 Ag 16 2017

CONFESSIONS OF A CAPITALIST CONVERT [Cover story] A. C. Brooks color *America* v216 no4 p18 F 20 2017

Consecrated in Mexico M. Taboada color map *National Geographic* v230 no5 p130 N 2016

Critical Mass R. ROSS *Texas Monthly* v45 no6 p70 Je 2017

A Crossroads in Oakland K. OAKES color *America* v215 no16 p14 N 21 2016

Evangelizing the parish J. Byassee color *Christian Century* v134 no15 p26 Jl 19 2017

EVER ANCIENT, EVER NEW E. Bruenig color *America* v217 no3 p18 Ag 7 2017

Find Your Tribe N. SCHNEIDER *America* v215 p14 N 28 2016

For crying out loud R. M. McKenny color *U.S. Catholic* v82 no4 p36 Ap 2017

Get your money in order C. Zech color graph *U.S. Catholic* v82 no1 p30 Ja 2017

Jesus is the question: Knowing the 'Catholic answer' does little good if we're not asking the right questions A. Camille color *U.S. Catholic* v82 no9 p47 S 2017

Just War? G. W. Schlabach bw *Commonweal* v144 no11 p11 Je 16 2017

LAND O' LAKES 50 YEARS ON J. I. Jenkins bw color *America* v217 no2 p28 Jl 24 2017

THE LARGEST PARISH IN AMERICA [Cover story] L. Libresco color *America* v216 no10 p18 My 1 2017

A Millennial walks into a church: Young qualified Catholics don't need to earn their stripes before taking on church leadership roles N. Perone color *U.S. Catholic* v82 no10 p27 O 2017

New Leader of Jesuits Worldwide Is Latin American 'Historic Choice' G. O'CONNELL color *America* v215 no13 p9 O 31 2016

One church? R. Mack, J. Keough et al *U.S. Catholic* v82 no7 p5 Jl 2017

A quiet grief J. S. Collazo color *U.S. Catholic* v81 no11 p30 N 2016

Ready or not color *U.S. Catholic* v82 no5 p5 My 2017

The redemption of ex-prisoners is a duty of the church J. McGreevey *America* v217 no7 p10 O 2 2017

SEEKING SIGNS OF A CATHOLIC REVIVAL IN FRANCE Gobry color *America* v216 no8 p26 Ap 17 2017

UNDER THE GAZE OF DOROTHY K. Hennessy bw *America* v216 no12 p36 My 29 2017

Urban presence [Cover story] P. H. Nettleton color *U.S. Catholic* v82 no1 p25 Ja 2017

U.S. CHURCH WRESTLES WITH CHANGING ATTITUDES, PASTORAL PRACTICE TOWARD L.G.B.T. CATHOLICS M. J. O'Loughlin chart color *America* v216 no12 p12 My 29 2017

WELCOMED HOME S. Evans il *America* v216 no8 p32 Ap 17 2017

Where do hosts come from? V. M. Tufano *U.S. Catholic* v82 no6 p49 Je 2017

you follow? LOLs and hashtags from Twitter *U.S. Catholic* v82 no9 p8 S 2017

you may be right J. Czarkowski, J. Krane-Calvert et al chart *U.S. Catholic* v82 no9 p5 S 2017

Your presence is needed S. Johnson *U.S. Catholic* v82 no7 p4 Jl 2017

Catholic Church & philosophy

Churched Philosophy J. J. CONLEY *America* v215 no11 p26 O 17 2016

Catholic church buildings

NEIGHBOR TO ALL K. Oakes color *America* v216 no7 p18 Ap 3 2017

Catholic church buildings—Design & construction

A Concrete Vision J. McDERMOTT *America* v216 no1 p11 Ja 2 2017

Catholic Church doctrines

A good death J. M. Griffith color *U.S. Catholic* v82 no1 p38 Ja 2017

One church? R. Mack, J. Keough et al *U.S. Catholic* v82 no7 p5 Jl 2017

A prescription for human dignity M. Clark color *U.S. Catholic* v82 no1 p8 Ja 2017

Seek Out and Save J. W. MARTENS il *America* v215 no12 p39 O 24 2016

Catholic Church. Collegium Cardinalium

Cardinal Virtues R. Ferrone color *Commonweal* v144 no11 p8 Je 16 2017

Catholic Church. United States Conference of Catholic Bishops

CHURCH LEADERS SCRUTINIZE BUDGET AND HEALTH CARE PRIORITIES K. Clarke color graph *America* v216 no13 p12 Je 12 2017

Still Welcoming the Stranger J. G. Young color *Commonweal* v144 no5 p9 Mr 10 2017

Catholic Church—Africa

The Catholic surge in Africa P. Jenkins *Christian Century* v134 no6 p45 Mr 15 2017

Swazi Catholics march against human trafficking and gender-

based violence R. Pollitt color *America* v217 no7 p17 O 2 2017

Catholic Church—Bishops—Congresses

Bishops Await President Trump M. O'LOUGHLIN *America* v215 no18 p9 D 5 2016

Catholic Church—Congresses

A New Form of Collaboration *America* v217 no2 p8 Jl 24 2017

Catholic Church—France

After the Macron-Le Pen race, how will 'new Catholics' reshape French politics? Gobry color *America* v216 no13 p16 Je 12 2017

Catholic Church—Political activity

The Enemy Within [Cover story] M. J. Hollerich color *Commonweal* v143 no19 p10 D 2 2016

Politics As Usual *Commonweal* v143 no18 p5 N 11 2016

Catholic Church—Relations—Islam

What Catholics owe their Muslim brothers and sisters J. Denari Duffner *America* v216 no3 p10 F 6 2017

Catholic Church—Relations—Judaism

Standing With Our Jewish Brothers and Sisters *America* v216 no6 p8 Mr 20 2017

Catholic Church—Relations—Protestant churches

The Ecumenical Pope G. O'CONNELL *America* v215 p24 N 28 2016

Catholic Church—United States

CATHOLIC BETWEEN THE COASTS W. Massey color *America* v216 no5 p24 Mr 6 2017

Church Advocates on the Alert As Transition Begins in Washington *America* v215 p10 N 28 2016

From Chapels to Condos M. M. ROBARE bw *American Conservative* v16 no1 p6 Ja/F 2017

A Hispanic Moment? *America* v215 no11 p5 O 17 2016

How would you rate your experience of parish-based religious education? chart diag graph *America* v216 no3 p6 F 6 2017

INSIDE THE CHANGING U.S. CATHOLIC CHURCH L. Libresco color diag *America* v216 no5 p12 Mr 6 2017

The Religious Right & Wrong *Commonweal* v144 no13 p5 Ag 11 2017

Catholic clergy

See also

Cardinals

New Wine, New Wineskins M. Coleridge *America* v216 no3 p54 F 6 2017

Catholic converts

Find Your Tribe N. SCHNEIDER *America* v215 p14 N 28 2016

Catholic education

A drive to thrive: energy and innovation in the Catholic schools of Los Angeles J. McDermott color *America* v217 no7 p16 O 2 2017

Give us this day our daily lesson *Maclean's* p4 Je 2017

Jesus is the question: Knowing the 'Catholic answer' does little good if we're not asking the right questions A. Camille color *U.S. Catholic* v82 no9 p47 S 2017

OF MANY THINGS M. MALONE *America* v215 no12 p2 O 24 2016

Catholic fiction

Present in Every Page R. E. Lauder *Commonweal* v144 no16 p39 O 6 2017

Catholic health facilities

See also

Catholic hospitals

GOING TO THE MARGINS K. Clarke color *America* v216 no13 p32 Je 12 2017

Catholic historians

A Luther Renaissance in Catholic Thought W. W. MacDonald *America* v217 no3 p33 Ag 7 2017

Catholic hospitals

ACLU V CATHOLIC HEALTH CARE [Cover story] S. Slade color il *America* v216 no3 p18 Je 12 2017

Catholic institutions

Congo's churches face rising violence C. Kennel-Shank *Christian Century* v134 no13 p12 Je 21 2017

A Dry Time for Catholics M. W. Higgins color *Commonweal* v144 no15 p8 S 22 2017

Catholic institutions—Buildings

Miracle Tableau: Knock, Ireland, 1879 J. NICKELL *Skeptical Inquirer* v41 no2 p26 Mr/Ap 2017

Catholic LGBT people

U.S. CHURCH WRESTLES WITH CHANGING ATTITUDES, PASTORAL PRACTICE TOWARD L.G.B.T. CATHOLICS M. J. O'Loughlin chart color *America* v216 no12 p12 My 29 2017

Catholic literature

The Catholic Imagination bw *Commonweal* v144 no11 p6 Je 16 2017

Catholic liturgy

Evening's light M. Centore color *U.S. Catholic* v82 no7 p45 Jl 2017

They Only Look like Zombies F. Nonomen color *Commonweal* v144 no17 p8 O 20 2017

Catholic missions

The Catholic Vision J. P. Hochschild color *Commonweal* v144 no9 p8 My 19 2017

Catholic nuns

Consecrated in Mexico M. Taboada color map *National Geographic* v230 no5 p130 N 2016

Catholic philosophers

An Extraordinary Career J. BOTTUM color *Weekly Standard* v22 no25 p15 Mr 6 2017

Friend of Freedom C. DEMUTH SR. color *Weekly Standard* v22 no25 p17 Mr 6 2017

Catholic preaching

Francis the Preacher G. O'CONNELL *America* v215 no18 p24 D 5 2016

Catholic priests

LAWYERS LEAD, PASTORAL WORKERS LAG ON PAY SCALE IN CATHOLIC CHURCH M. O'Loughlin il *America* v217 no5 p12 S 4 2017

Why do priests wear green in Ordinary Time? V. M. Tufano color *U.S. Catholic* v82 no1 p49 Ja 2017

Catholic priests—Crimes against

Three Priests Killed Over Two Days color *America* v215 no10 p10 O 10 2016

Catholic priests—History—16th century

SECRET SPACES J. A. LOBELL bw color *Archaeology* v70 no2 p12 Mr/Ap 2017

Catholic Relief Services

Catholic Relief Services responds to misery in Mosul K. Clarke color *America* v217 no3 p17 Ag 7 2017

Four ways to strengthen humanitarian aid C. Y. Woo *America* v216 no5 p10 Mr 6 2017

Catholic religious education

How would you rate your experience of parish-based religious education? chart diag graph *America* v216 no3 p6 F 6 2017

READER COMMENTS J. McGlynn, M. Conk et al *America* v216 no3 p7 F 6 2017

Catholic schools

Building on Diversity T. G. MATHEWSON *America* v215 no13 p12 O 31 2016

Filling Empty Seats A. J. ZAVAGNIN color *America* v215 no13 p25 O 31 2016

Schools ... with superpowers M. S. Winters color diag *U.S. Catholic* v82 no3 p12 Mr 2017

Catholic schools—Economic aspects

Catholic campuses should look outward to the larger church P. T. Brown *America* v217 no4 p10 Ag 21 2017

Catholic schools—United States

A drive to thrive: energy and innovation in the Catholic schools of Los Angeles J. McDermott color *America* v217 no7 p16 O 2 2017

OPEN HOUSE GUIDE color *Cincinnati Magazine* v51 no1 p001 O 2017

Catholic spiritual life

Raise your voice: To be a lector is to live out the Catholic commitment to prayer, community, and storytelling J. Bazan color *U.S. Catholic* v82 no10 p45 O 2017

Catholic theological seminaries

KEEPING THE FAITH in Seminary K. MILLER color *Christianity Today* v60 no8 p87 O 2016

Catholic universities & colleges

and the survey says *U.S. Catholic* v82 no8 p19 Ag 2017

The Catholic Vision J. P. Hochschild color *Commonweal* v144 no9 p8 My 19 2017

LAND O' LAKES 50 YEARS ON J. I. Jenkins bw color *America* v217 no2 p28 Jl 24 2017

Mission before Identity D. O'Brien color *Commonweal* v144 no6 p8 Mr 24 2017

READING (AND MORE) TOGETHER R. BEEZAT *Commonweal* v144 no8 p2 My 5 2017

Catholic universities & colleges—Faculty

Hiring for Mission J. Garvey and M. W. Roche color *Commonweal* v144 no3 p10 F 10 2017

Catholic universities & colleges—United States

Catholic Universities And #BlackLivesMatter R. K. VISCHER color *America* v215 no12 p22 O 24 2016

Should Catholics be feeling March Madness? P. Kelly color *America* v216 no6 p36 Mr 20 2017

Catholic Worker Movement

WELCOMED HOME S. Evans il *America* v216 no8 p32 Ap 17 2017

Catholic bishops—Appointment, call, & election

Beijing and Holy See near accord? G. O'Connell color *America* v216 no5 p17 Mr 6 2017

Catholic hospitals—Trials, litigation, etc.

GLEANINGS graph *Christianity Today* v61 no5 p16 Je 2017

Catholic League, 1609-1648

BOHEMIAN CATASTROPHY D. Hollway color map *Military History* v34 no5 p40 Ja 2018

Catholics

See also

Catholic priests

Age is just a number R. McCarty *U.S. Catholic* v82 no10 p4 O 2017

Beginner's mind A. Camille color *U.S. Catholic* v82 no1 p47 Ja 2017

Can Catholics celebrate the Reformation? J. Kohlhaas color *U.S. Catholic* v82 no2 p49 F 2017

Catholics Must Combat Racism and Bigotry at Every Turn *America* v217 no5 p8 S 4 2017

Confessions of an Interloper R. R. Cooper bw color *Commonweal* v114 no14 p15 S 8 2017

Hate.Net J. MARTIN *America* v215 no13 p14 O 31 2016

In a Cape Cod fishing town, Catholic culture is a blessing M. J. O'Loughlin color *America* v217 no2 p17 Jl 24 2017

I THOUGHT GOOD CATHOLICS DIDN'T NEED THERAPY. THEN I WENT S. Fisher color *America* v217 no2 p36 Jl 24 2017

KOCH-FUELED DYSTOPIA M. L. O'NEILL *Commonweal* v114 no14 p2 S 8 2017

Live on the margins B. Massingale color *U.S. Catholic* v82 no9 p10 S 2017

A Millennial walks into a church: Young qualified Catholics don't need to earn their stripes before taking on church leadership roles N. Perone color *U.S. Catholic* v82 no10 p27 O 2017

A not so cookie-cutter Christmas R. McCarty color *U.S. Catholic* v81 no12 p33 D 2016

Pro-Life's Reformation Ripples K. SHELLNUTT *Christianity Today* v61 no1 p21 Ja/F 2017

Protecting the Confessional Seal *America* v217 no6 p8 S 18 2017

Real & Unimaginable J. Ryan color *Commonweal* v144 no8 p46 My 5 2017

A Shrine That Endures P. JASKUNAS color *America* v215 no16 p25 N 21 2016

A sorta CATHOLIC'S very CATHOLIC WEDDING [Cover story] T. Wigfield bw *America* v216 no10 p34 My 1 2017

Speak up T. B. Neal, V. Y. Piccorossi et al color *U.S. Catholic* v82 no4 p5 Ap 2017

Start with a cup of coffee M. J. Rose color *U.S. Catholic* v81 no11 p25 N 2016

Survey: U.S. Protestants and Catholics have more in common than not E. M. Miller *Christian Century* v134 no20 p16 S 27 2017

Unchosen Hardships L. Kosa color *Commonweal* v144 no6 p47 Mr 24 2017

UNDER THE GAZE OF DOROTHY K. Hennessy bw *America* v216 no12 p36 My 29 2017

WHEN A JEW & A CATHOLIC MARRY M. Oppenheimer color *America* v217 no5 p18 S 4 2017

WHEN THE K.K.K. CAME TO CHARLOTTESVILLE HOW SHOULD CATHOLICS RESPOND TO THE SIN OF RACISM? [Cover story] N. M. Flores color *America* v217 no5 p34

S 4 2017

Where and who you are N. Flores, J. Essmann et al color *U.S. Catholic* v82 no1 p12 Ja 2017

Catholics vs. Convicts (Film)

CATHOLICS VS. CONVICTS K. ROSEN *TV Guide* p52 D 5 2016

Catholics—Canada

A Dry Time for Catholics M. W. Higgins color *Commonweal* v144 no15 p8 S 22 2017

Northern Warning J. T. KEANE *America* v215 no16 p12 N 21 2016

Catholics—United States

See also

African American Catholics

and the survey says... *U.S. Catholic* v81 no11 p27 N 2016

What does Catholic health care reform look like? graph *America* v216 no8 p6 Ap 17 2017

you follow? LOLs and hashtags from Twitter *U.S. Catholic* v82 no1 p10 Ja 2017

Catholics—United States—Political activity

THIRD PARTY REVOLUTION R. McCULLOUGH color *America* v215 no12 p24 O 24 2016

Catino, Erme

LATITUDES bw color *Powder* v45 no5 p46 Ja 2017

SALT OF THE EARTH bw color *Skiing* p30 D 2016

Catledge, Oraien

CABBAGE TOWN 1996 T. WHEATLEY *Atlanta* v57 no2 p160 Je 2017

Catlow, C. Richard A.

Identification of single-site gold catalysis in acetylene hydrochlorination bw diag graph *Science* v355 no6332 p1399 Mr 31 2017

Catone, Lara

A home practice to awaken your sexual vitality [Cover story] color *Yoga Journal* no289 p51 F 2017

CATOVIC, SAFFET A.

A New Scouting Experience *Islamic Horizons* v45 no6 p38 N/D 2016

The World United to Save the Earth: The global movement of serious investment in renewable energy continues, despite President Trump's campaign pledge to focus on the domestic coal and oil industries *Islamic Horizons* v46 no3 p42 My/Je 2017

Cats

See also

Feral cats

Kittens

Animal House color *Parents* v92 no9 p64 S 2017

Ask Martha Martha color *Martha Stewart Living* p56 Mr 2017

CATS GONE WILD P. S. TAYLOR color *Maclean's* v130 no3 p50 Ap 2017

Friends, Foes, and Felines J. HERBST color *Los Angeles Magazine* v62 no10 p98 O 2017

GOINGS ON ABOUT TOWN color *New Yorker* v93 no30 p4 O 2 2017

The Gratitude Meter Z. Donaldson color *O, The Oprah Magazine* p26 N 2017

Here, Kitty, Kitty color *Weekly Standard* v22 no35 p3 My 22 2017

Homebodies K. MORI *American Scholar* v86 no1 p70 Wint 2017

HOW TO SAVE A CAT M. GUNCH color *New Orleans Magazine* v51 no3 p42 Ja 2017

I Can Haz Make You Money? D. Burger color *Bloomberg Businessweek* no4525 p37 Je 5 2017

KITTEN ON BOARD S. Schwartz *National Geographic Kids* no469 p13 Ap 2017

Kitty Myths — Busted! S. Bower color *Good Housekeeping* v265 no2 p136 Ag 2017

My Shot *National Geographic Kids* no466 p39 D 2016/Ja 2017

Naughty Pets color *National Geographic Kids* no474 p7 O 2017

Settling In B. HEWITT and P. HEWITT color *Yankee* v80 no6 p16 N/D 2016

Should I Stop Bringing Up My Cat? J. JOHN *Reader's Digest* v189 no1127 p14 F 2017

"This Cat Is Meant to Be Here" [Cover story] A. LEWIS *Reader's Digest* v188 no1126 p79 D 2016/Ja 2017

Unleashed color *National Geographic Kids* no465 p38 N 2016

Cats (Theatrical production)

Becoming a Cats Cat R. MILZOFF img *New York* v49 no15 p82

Jl 25 2016

The Best of 2016 G. PEREZ, M. SCHROCK et al *Dance Magazine* v90 no12 p84 D 2016

What's a Jellicle Cat? L. KAY *Dance Magazine* v90 no12 p70 D 2016

Cats in motion pictures

GOINGS ON ABOUT TOWN color *New Yorker* v92 no35 p12 O 31 2016

Cats—Behavior

Adopting the Right Cat for You J. Singer *Catnip* v24 no10 p10 O 2016

CAT GOES TO HIGH SCHOOL S. Jose and K. Jazynka color map *National Geographic Kids* no465 p13 N 2016

Cats—Diseases

How to Combat Car Sickness *Catnip* v24 no10 p3 O 2016

Primary Hyperparathyroidism A. Plotnick *Catnip* v24 no10 p12 O 2016

Cats—Health

Concerns about Cat Care *Catnip* v24 no10 p16 O 2016

No Time Like the Present E. Vecsi *Catnip* v24 no10 p2 O 2016

Prolapse of the rectum; feline plasma cell pododermatitis; finding the culprit in multicat home *Catnip* v24 no10 p14 O 2016

Catskill Mountains (N.Y.)—Economic conditions

HER REVOLUTION Zephyr Teachout S. JAFFE bw color *Nation* v303 no20 p12 N 14 2016

Cats—Research

A LITTLE CAT GOES A LONG WAY M. JAFFE *Arizona Highways* v93 no9 p48 S 2017

Cats—Social aspects

The Cat Conundrum J. Carey color *National Wildlife (World Edition)* v55 no6 p30 O/N 2017

Cattan, Nacha

In Mexico, Pricier Gas Lures the Gangs color *Bloomberg Businessweek* no4507 p16 Ja 16 2017

Let's Make Mexico Great Again color *Bloomberg Businessweek* no4510 p15 F 6 2017

No Wall to Stop Migrant Cash From Going South color *Bloomberg Businessweek* no4502 p23 D 5 2016

Photostat: Mexico City Earthquake bw color *Bloomberg Businessweek* no4539 p38 S 25 2017

Why Mexico's Autoworkers Aren't Prospering color graph *Bloomberg Businessweek* no4521 p12 My 8 2017

Cattani, Kate

Marley Jordan's 'Village' Expands to Florida and Beyond *In Stride* v12 no3 p41 My 2017

Cattelan, Maurizio, 1960-

Watch the Throne img *New York* v49 no23 p80 N 14 2016

Catterson, Brian

2015 YAMAHA YZF-R1 color *Cycle World* v56 no5 p56 Je 2017

2016 TRIUMPH TIGER 800 XCx chart color *Cycle World* v56 no1 p53 Ja/F 2017

2016 TRIUMPH TIGER 800 XCx chart color *Cycle World* v56 no3 p54 Ap 2017

2017 YAMAHA FZ-09 color *Cycle World* v56 no4 p18 My 2017

HIGHWAY TO HELL chart color *Cycle World* v56 no1 p36 Ja/F 2017

Cattivelli, Luigi

Wild emmer genome architecture and diversity elucidate wheat evolution and domestication color *Science* v357 no6346 p93 Jl 7 2017

Cattle

See also

Bulls

COW SAVVY: QUIET HANDLING AND STRATEGIC PRESSURE HELP CATTLE CHOOSE THE RIGHT DIRECTION R. Nickel *Successful Farming* v115 no6 p55 Ap 2017

DON'T HAVE A COW: It seemed like a bright idea to raise cattle, but the average cow is a disaster waiting to happen P. Gulley *Saturday Evening Post* v289 no5 p16 S/O 2017

The Long Rope C. Hutchison color *American Cowboy* v23 no4 p42 D 2016/Ja 2017

Wagonhound Land and Livestock B. Welch color *American Cowboy* v23 no4 p96 D 2016/Ja 2017

Cattle breeds

BEYOND WAGYU A. Spiegel color *Washingtonian Magazine* v52 no7 p143 Ap 2017

Cattle drives
Git Along *Arizona Highways* v93 no2 p56 F 2017
Lost Skills of the cattle drive L. Miller bw *American Cowboy* p66 LEGENDS OF TEXAS Special Issue 2017

Cattle drives—History—19th century
John Blocker's Road Brand B. Welch color *American Cowboy* v23 no6 p72 Ap/My 2017
The Old CHISHOLM TRAIL [Cover story] B. Welch color map *American Cowboy* v23 no6 p54 Ap/My 2017

Cattle handling
HANDLES ARE SPEEDING UP WITH THE TIMES K. Santos color *Spin to Win Rodeo* v20 no12 p38 F 2017
IDEA OF THE MONTH: CATTLE HANDLING CAN BE A ONE-PERSON JOB P. Barbour color *Successful Farming* v115 no7 p68 My 2017

Cattle herding
BEEF IS BOUNCING BACK A. McConnell *Successful Farming* v114 no10 p31 O 2016
Handy Hints color *American Cowboy* v24 no1 p50 Je/Jl 2017

Cattle industry
Cattle Queen L. Feldman bw color *American Cowboy* v24 no1 p18 Je/Jl 2017

Cattle industry—Management
LOOKING UNDER THE HOOD G. Johnston *Successful Farming* v115 no3 p50 Mid-F 2017
OLD and RIGHT W. F. LLOYD *American Conservative* v16 no1 p25 Ja/F 2017

Cattle trails—Kansas
See also
Chisholm Trail
Trail Broke B. Welch bw color *American Cowboy* v23 no6 p62 Ap/My 2017

Cattle—Cloning
Why, That Son of a Steak! L. STEFFY *Texas Monthly* v45 no1 p56 Ja 2017

Cattle—Growth
OLD and RIGHT W. F. LLOYD *American Conservative* v16 no1 p25 Ja/F 2017

Cattle—Marking
Branding Time Bob color *American Cowboy* v23 no6 p8 Ap/My 2017

Cattle—Pregnancy—Nutritional aspects
BEFORE THEY'RE BORN G. Johnston *Successful Farming* v115 no3 p54 Mid-F 2017

Catton, Bruce, 1899-1978
THE CIVIL WARRIOR J. Vacha bw *MHQ: Quarterly Journal of Military History* v30 no1 p74 Aut 2017

Catton, Eleanor, 1985-
Eleanor Catton J. Pritchard *Current Biography* v77 no10 p18 O 2016

CATTON, PIA
Up from Macaroni bw *Weekly Standard* v22 no20 p33 Ja 30 2017

Cauberghe, Verolien
Companies Fare Worse When the Press Exposes Their Problems Before They Do *Harvard Business Review Digital Articles* p2 Ag 22 2016

CAUDILL, S. AMANDA
Using Plant-Animal Interactions to Inform Tree Selection in Tree-Based Agroecosystems for Enhanced Biodiversity *BioScience* v66 no12 p1046 D 1 2016

Caudron, Fabrice
Aggregation of the Whi3 protein, not loss of heterochromatin, causes sterility in old yeast cells bibl diag *Science* v355 no6330 p1184 Mr 17 2017

Caught (Film)
CAUGHT L. Kern color *Film Comment* v53 no3 p24 My/Je 2017

CAULEY, H. M.
BIG NEWS ON CAMPUS *Atlanta* v56 no11 p128 Mr 2017
GETTING IN *Atlanta* v56 no7 p112 N 2016
HANGING ONTO HOPE *Atlanta* v56 no11 p124 Mr 2017
THE RIGHT SCHOOL *Atlanta* v56 no7 p110 N 2016

Cauliflower
Cauliflower Is the New It Vegetable M. Gajanan color *Time* v190 no5 p28 Jl 31 2017
Come Meet the Grand Dames of the Brassica Family! Z. Allen *Vegetarian Journal* v36 no1 p14 2017

EAT, DRINK, AND BE WARY C. Zuckerman color *National Geographic* v232 no3 p14 S 2017
FOOD FOR THOUGHT *Nutrition Action Health Letter* v44 no3 p16 Ap 2017
YOU WON'T FIND THIS IN LAOS. AND THAT'S THE POINT J. SYHABOUT color *Bon Appetit* v62 no2 p72 Mr 2017

Cauliflower—Therapeutic use
Good To Go-To K. Massicot color *New Orleans Magazine* v51 no7 p36 My 2017

Caulkin, Simon
Staying Human in the Robot Age *Harvard Business Review Digital Articles* p2 O 6 2015

Caulkins, Jon
Nip It in the Bud *Washington Monthly* p10 Ja/F 2017

Causa, Tim
FEEDING AND READING A. WHITING *Washingtonian Magazine* v52 no3 p17 D 2016

Causes of death
See also
Drowning
Suicide
ACCIDENTAL KILLERS A. GREGORY cartoon color *New Yorker* v93 no28 p28 S 18 2017

Causey, Amy
Junior Arabian Mares color *Horse & Rider* v56 no7 p57 Jl 2017

Causey, James Michael
FOTOWEEKDC *Washingtonian Magazine* v52 no2 p35 N 2016
WHERE & WHEN color *Washingtonian Magazine* v52 no7 p31 Ap 2017
WHERE & WHEN *Washingtonian Magazine* v52 no5 p31 F 2017

Cautivo, Kelly M.
An adipo-biliary-uridine axis that regulates energy homeostasis diag *Science* v355 no6330 p1173 Mr 17 2017

Cava, R. J.
Observation of a nematic quantum Hall liquid on the surface of bismuth bibl graph *Science* v354 no6310 p316 O 21 2016

Cavalieri, A. J.
Improving global integration of crop research color *Science* v357 no6349 p359 Jl 28 2017

Cavalieri, Jimmy
THANKS FOR THE RIDE color *Bicycling* v58 no10 p15 N/D 2017
Totally Worth It! color *Bicycling* v58 no4 p22 My 2017

Cavalleria Rusticana (Theatrical production)
Cavalleria Rusticana/Sancta Susanna S. J. Mudge *Opera News* v81 no9 p47 Mr 2017

Cavalletti
Cavalletti Training for Every Horse and Discipline I. Klimke color diag *Practical Horseman* v45 no5 p58 My 2017

Cavalli, Enrico
Nanophotonic rare-earth quantum memory with optically controlled retrieval diag graph *Science* v357 no6358 p1392 S 29 2017

Cavalli, Francesco
Eliogabalo S. J. Mudge *Opera News* v81 no6 p48 D 2016

Cavan, Jennifer
AMERICAN PLACES *American Scholar* v86 no1 p128 Wint 2017

Cavanaugh, Anese
How to Fire Someone Without Destroying Them *Harvard Business Review Digital Articles* p2 Ja 28 2016

Cavanaugh, Ray
Joyce and His Jesuits color *America* v216 no9 p18 Ap 24 2017

Cave, Nick, 1957-
THE GOOD SEED C. HEATH bw color *GQ: Gentlemen's Quarterly* v97 no5 p124 My 2017

Cave, Nick, 1959—Interviews
DREAM DUO E. FISHMAN bw *Chicago* v66 no9 p49 S 2017

Cave divers
EXPLORER-IN-RESIDENCE SCHOOL VISITS S. Doyle color *Canadian Geographic* v136 no6 p77 D 2016

Cave paintings
Return of the Aurochs J. KEATS color *Discover* v38 no2 p24 Mr 2017

Cavender family
Legends in the Making B. Welch color *American Cowboy* p72

LEGENDS OF TEXAS Special Issue 2017

Cavender's Out of State Stores Ltd.

Legends in the Making B. Welch color *American Cowboy* p72 LEGENDS OF TEXAS Special Issue 2017

Cavendish, Margaret

1666: Blazing World *Lapham's Quarterly* v10 no2 p117 Spr 2017

Cavendish, Richard

America's first birth control clinic *History Today* v66 no10 p9 O 2016

King John dies in Newark *History Today* v66 no10 p8 O 2016

Cavert, William M.

Through the Fog and Filthy Air G. Tindall *History Today* v67 no2 p65 F 2017

Caves

See also

Ice caves

ENTER THE UNDERWORLD *Iceland Review* v54 no6 p106 N/D 2016

THE FIRST AUSTRALIANS [Cover story] K. RAVILIOUS color *Archaeology* v70 no4 p49 Je-Ag 2017

NO PLACE LIKE HOME C. Valentino color *Archaeology* v70 no4 p4 Je-Ag 2017

Caves—Mexico

Mine crystals harbor bizarre microbes A. YEAGER color *Science News* v191 no5 p15 Mr 18 2017

Caves—South Dakota

Community Caves: Short and Steep A. Boe *South Dakota Magazine* v33 no2 p93 Jl/Ag 2017

ONLY ON OUR WEBSITE *South Dakota Magazine* v32 no4 p19 N/D 2016

Caves—Uzbekistan

Into the Deep M. Synnott color map *National Geographic* v231 no3 p104 Mr 2017

Caviar

The Chinese Caviar Connection K. Krader color *Bloomberg Businessweek* no4539 p73 S 25 2017

Empowerment P. Chakrabarty, S. Negi et al color *Science* v356 no6335 p242 Ap 21 2017

Caviar—Sales & prices

GOVERNMENT DREAMS AND CAVIAR WISHES M. CAMPBELL color *Maclean's* v129 no43 p18 O 31 2016

Caviness, Ylonda Gault

KEEPING YOUR NEW YEAR'S RESOLUTIONS color *Essence* v47 no9 p45 Ja 2017

Cawthorne, Ellie

Red Dawn *Hoover Digest: Research & Opinion on Public Policy* no2 p108 Spr 2017

Cayago AG

WESTCOASTFOCUS *Sea Magazine* v109 no5 p12 My 2017

Cayenne automobile

The Complete Package H. Elliott chart color *Bloomberg Businessweek* no4538 p60 S 18 2017

Cayley-Daoust, Daniel

Why BC Is Standing Up to Kinder Morgan *Alternatives Journal (AJ) - Canada's Environmental Voice* v42 no2 p10 2016

Cayman Islands—Description & travel

Caymankind of Vacation *New York* v50 no17 p150 Ag 21 2017

Cayne, Alison

EASY AS PIE ACTUALLY, EASIER color *Redbook* p154 My 2017

Cayne, Candis—Interviews

TRANS BEAUTY SECRETS DAM color *Advocate* no1091 p76 Je/Jl 2017

Caza, Brianna

When Work Satisfaction Comes from Having 4 Jobs *Harvard Business Review Digital Articles* p2 My 4 2015

Cazals, Felipe

Day of the Dead M. Nelson color *Film Comment* v53 no2 p11 Mr/Ap 2017

CAZARES, GLORIA

Righting Words color *O, The Oprah Magazine* p17 Jl 2017

Cazon, L.

Observation of a large-scale anisotropy in the arrival directions of cosmic rays above 8×1018 eV *Science* v357 no6357 p1266 S 22 2017

CBRE Inc.

Gensler J. M. McKnight *Architectural Record* v205 no4 p118 Ap 2017

CBS Corp.

THE CHANGE AGENT R. R. Robertson color *Essence* v47 no8 p88 D 2016

CBS Interactive Inc.

Bingeing on CBS Assets M. ANTONOFF color *Sound & Vision* v82 no6 p25 Jl/Ag 2017

CBS This Morning (TV program)

My Days in Morning TV G. KING and I. Rudolph *TV Guide* v65 no2 p16 Ja 2 2017

CD1 antigen

Researchers Finally ID Poison Ivy Suspect M. BARNA color *Discover* v38 no1 p88 Ja/F 2017

CD28 antigen

Rescue of exhausted CD8 T cells by PD-1–targeted therapies is CD28-dependent A. O. Kamphorst, A. Wieland et al bw diag graph *Science* v355 no6332 p1423 Mr 31 2017

T cell costimulatory receptor CD28 is a primary target for PD-1–mediated inhibition E. Hui, J. Cheung et al color diag graph *Science* v355 no6332 p1428 Mr 31 2017

CD46 antigen

Lactobacillus reuteri induces gut intraepithelial CD4+CD8αα+ T cells L. Cervantes-Barragan, J. N. Chai et al diag graph *Science* v357 no6353 p806 Ag 25 2017

Ceaser, James W.

Eleven Nine [Cover story] color *Weekly Standard* v22 no11 p11 N 21 2016

A Lack of Ideas Has Consequences *Weekly Standard* v23 no3 p14 S 25 2017

POWER TO THE PEOPLE *Claremont Review of Books* v17 no3 p38 Summ 2017

Shaken and Stirred *Hoover Digest: Research & Opinion on Public Policy* no1 p9 Wint 2017

Ceaser, James—Interviews

The Demagogues Move In E. Green *Hoover Digest: Research & Opinion on Public Policy* no4 p56 Fall 2016

CEAUŞU, SILVIA

Harmonizing Biodiversity Conservation and Productivity in the Context of Increasing Demands on Landscapes graph *BioScience* v66 no10 p890 O 1 2016

Ceballos, Gerardo

Merging paleobiology with conservation biology to guide the future of terrestrial ecosystems color *Science* v355 no6325 p594 F 10 2017

Cebon, Peter

The 3 Company Crises Boards Should Watch For color *Harvard Business Review Digital Articles* p2 Ja 16 2017

CEC Entertainment Inc.

CHUCK'S NEW CHEDDAR M. Pilon color *Bloomberg Businessweek* no4494 p74 O 10 2016

Cecchi, Guillermo A.

Predicting human olfactory perception from chemical features of odor molecules bibl diag graph *Science* v355 no6327 p820 F 24 2017

Cecchi-Dimeglio, Paola

How Gender Bias Corrupts Performance Reviews, and What to Do About It *Harvard Business Review Digital Articles* p2 Ap 12 2017

Cech, Richo

MEDICINAL HERBS for Difficult Growing Conditions *Mother Earth News* no281 p20 Ap/My 2017

Cech, Tom

Not just Salk color *Science* v357 no6356 p1105 S 15 2017

Cecil, David, 1902-1986

c. 1800: England D. Cecil *Lapham's Quarterly* v10 no1 p89 Wint 2017

CECIL, ELIZABETH

HOLIDAY KITCHEN color *Yankee* v80 no6 p58 N/D 2016

Cedar

RUSTIC CEDAR PICKET SIGN D. Kuczynski color *Cabin Living* p62 Ag 2017

That Was Then *National Parks* v91 no2 p68 Spr 2017

Cedar, Jonathan

How One Startup Developed a Sales Model That Works in Emerging Markets *Harvard Business Review Digital Articles* p2 S 7

2016

Cederberg, Aki

Journeys in the Kali Yuga: A Pilgrimage from Esoteric India to Pagan Europe *Publishers Weekly* v264 no41 p61 O 9 2017

Cederman, Lars-Erik

Predicting armed conflict: Time to adjust our expectations? bibl color map *Science* v355 no6324 p474 F 3 2017

Cederquist, Caroline

NOT THE SPIRIT color *Women's Health* v14 no2 p36 Mr 2017

Cederström, Carl

Like It or Not, "Smart Drugs" Are Coming to the Office *Harvard Business Review Digital Articles* p2 My 19 2016

The Research We've Ignored About Happiness at Work *Harvard Business Review Digital Articles* p2 Jl 21 2015

What Companies Should Ask Before Embracing Wearables *Harvard Business Review Digital Articles* p2 My 20 2015

Cegelski, Lynette

Mechanochemical unzipping of insulating polyladderene to semi-conducting polyacetylene [Cover story] diag *Science* v357 no6350 p475 Ag 4 2017

Ceiling decoration

HIGH STYLE: Want to make your new house stand out? Don't forget about the ceilings A. Cochran *Washingtonian Magazine* v52 no8 p184 My 2017

WALLS & CEILINGS *Design Center Sourcebook* p47 2016

Ceiling fans

SHOP NOTES cartoon color *Popular Mechanics* p100 My 2017

Ceiling fans—Evaluation

Summer Style color *Timber Home Living* v27 no4 p14 Ag 2017

Ceiling tiles

A Ceiling That Wirelessly Charges Devices J. Zorthian color *Time* v189 no3 p21 Ja 30 2017

WHEN TIN CEILINGS WERE HIGH-TECH V. Postrel *Reason* v49 no5 p16 O 2017

Ceilings

Architectural Ceilings P. Poore color *Old House Journal* v45 no3 p64 My 2017

Framed by Tin Ceiling B. D. Coleman bw color *Old House Journal* v44 no8 p56 D 2016

Ceilings—Decoration

WALLS & CEILINGS color *Old House Journal* v44 p47 2016 Design Center source Book

Ceilings—Design & construction

Revolutionizing Ceiling and Wall Surfaces with Parametrics and Digital Fabrication C. A. Novak color *Architectural Record* v204 no12 p194 D 2016

Ceilings—Equipment & supplies

Over Our Heads J. Taraska color *Architectural Record* v205 no2 p46 F 2017

Ceilings—Evaluation

Finishes & Surfacing color *Architectural Record* v204 no12 p116 D 2016

Celant, Germano

EDGAR ARCENEAUX K. Swenson color *Art in America* v105 no1 p86 Ja 2017

Celarier, Michelle

HIDDEN TREASURES OR MONEY PITS? color diag *Fortune* v175 no5 p33 Ap 1 2017

Celebrities

See also

Celebrity chefs
Celebrity couples
Internet celebrities
Radio personalities
Television personalities

17 Eat-Clean Secrets from Top Chefs J. Andriakos color *Health* v31 no3 p42 Ap 2017

3 Celeb Nutrition Trends to Try (and 3 to Skip!) C. Sass color *Health* v30 no9 p73 N 2016

THE ANDY COHEN INDEX I. Biedenharn color *Entertainment Weekly* no1441 p58 N 25 2016

At Jimmy Fallon's House M. LaScala color *Parents* v92 no11 p11 N 2017

AYESHA CURRY "I Believe You Can Have It All" A. Prato color *Health* v30 no9 p24 N 2016

Best Face Forward A. Serrano and D. Mazzone color *InStyle* v24

no11 p125 N 2017

Can TV Make You Slim? D. Bova color *Health* v31 no7 p55 S 2017

Can We Get Real About Having It All? B. Hauser color *Health* v31 no6 p91 Jl 2017

CARRIE'S FLAT-BELLY SECRET color *Health* v31 no5 p13 Je 2017

CELEB CHAT M. Bykofsky *Parents* p20 2015

A Celeb Glow at Home color *Health* v31 no2 p36 Mr 2017

CELEBRITIES ... img *New York* v50 no9 p40 My 1 2017

Celebrity science J. GREENBERG color *Issues in Science & Technology* v33 no1 p19 Fall 2016

Celebs Bare All color *Health* v31 no1 p18 Ja 2017

Celebs Dabble in Weird Food J. Kell color *Fortune* v176 no1 p14 Jl 1 2017

CHRISTIE BRINKLEY "Feeling Good Is Looking Good" J. Andriakos color *Health* v31 no5 p19 Je 2017

Crowning Glory color *Health* v30 no9 p20 N 2016

Dads Across Decades bw color *Parents* v92 no6 p24 Je 2017

Domhnall Gleeson Proves (Once More) He Can Do Almost Anything K. Samuelson color *Time* v190 no16/17 p104 O 23 2017

Everything Is 25 This Summer C. Rosa and J. Harman color *Glamour* no8 p38 Ag 2017

From the Mouths of (Celebs') Babes J. Hartshorn color *Parents* v92 no8 p20 Ag 2017

harness your hair envy M. MATTHEWS BROWN color *Parents* v92 no4 p88 Ap 2017

Heartthrob Celeb Dads, and What We Fantasize They're Good At J. Hartshorn color *Parents* v92 no6 p16 Je 2017

THE HOT SEAT M. HUSTON *Psychology Today* v49 no5 p9 S/O 2016

HOW TO WEAR PINK EYE SHADOW IRL color *Health* v31 no7 p24 S 2017

"I'M REALLY LUCKY" [Cover story] A. Spencer color *Health* v31 no6 p100 Jl 2017

Jennifer Aniston on Dry Eye: "I Was Addicted to Eye Drops" L. Lombardi color *Health* v30 no9 p80 N 2016

Jillian Gets You Strong [Cover story] A. Spencer color *Health* v30 no9 p116 N 2016

KHLOE [Cover story] A. Prato color *Health* v31 no1 p86 Ja 2017

LAST CALL / 2016 cartoon *Vanity Fair* v59 no1 p134 Holiday 2017

LOVE BEYOND GENDER A. Abbott *Psychology Today* v49 no5 p72 S/O 2016

Nina Dobrev's Total-Body Toner color *Health* v30 no9 p16 N 2016

padma heat up [Cover story] A. Prato color *Health* v31 no8 p96 O 2017

PADMA LAKSHMI What I love color *Health* v31 no8 p18 O 2017

PARTY LINES J. Vineyard img *New York* v50 no6 p88 Mr 20 2017

PARTY LINES S. W. Hunt, J. Yuan et al img *New York* v50 no10 p104 My 15 2017

Pop Goes German Philosophy S. JEFFRIES color *Foreign Policy* no225 p70 Jl/Ag 2017

THE POWER (AND PERIL) OF PRIDE E. SILBER *Psychology Today* v49 no5 p10 S/O 2016

QUOTE MARKS P. Lockwood cartoon *New Yorker* v92 no39 p42 N 28 2016

RACHEL BRATHEN "Life Takes You Where You're Supposed to Go" J. Andriakos color *Health* v31 no3 p22 Ap 2017

Random Notes color *Rolling Stone* no1281/1282 p26 F 23 2017

The right (and wrong) ways to get a hot Hollywood bod J. Andriakos color *Health* v31 no8 p43 O 2017

SAY HELLO TO THE NEW GIRL T. M. Ferguson *Ebony* v72 no11 p12 S 2017

Sculpt your body like a celeb T. Anderson color *Health* v31 no9 p48 N 2017

The Society PAGE *Interview* v47 no2 p62 Mr 2017

So You Want to Be a (Social Media) Star D. DEVOSS color *Weekly Standard* v22 no46 p26 Ag 14 2017

star scents T. PEREZ *Parents* p80 2015

Steal Selena's Leg-Sculpting Secret color *Health* v31 no7 p22 S 2017

TEAM CURRY [Cover story] A. SHIPNUCK *Parents* v91 no6

p88 Je 2016

They shared their health secrets with the world K. Canning color *Health* v31 no8 p81 O 2017

Tracee Ellis Ross: "I DIDN'T WAKE UP LIKE THIS" [Cover story] A. Spencer color *Health* v31 no3 p82 Ap 2017

WHEN HEALING IS A NO-BRAINER S. VEISSIEÈE *Psychology Today* v50 no4 p62 Ag 2017

Who to Follow on Snapchat Now J. Smith color *Health* v31 no2 p66 Mr 2017

Why we practice C. Gorrell *Yoga Journal* no290 p12 Mr 2017

Celebrities' correspondence

The Girl Who Loved Hollywood: The story of my mother B. Bawer *Commentary* v144 no2 p32 S 2017

Celebrities—Charts, diagrams, etc.

Pop Chart R. Bruner, C. Lang et al color *Time* v189 no18 p58 My 15 2017

Celebrities—Clothing

Best-Dressed LIST L. McCarthy color *Harper's Bazaar* no3649 p140 D 2016/Ja 2017

Buckle Up E. Wilson color *InStyle* v24 no2 p56 F 2017

Hailey Gates S. Pulia color *InStyle* v24 no2 p68 F 2017

MET GALA MADNESS R. Kinane color *Entertainment Weekly* no1465 p12 My 12 2017

Mix & Match E. Wilson color *InStyle* v24 no2 p58 F 2017

Celebrities—Death

Are Some Years More Important Than Others? L. Rothman *Time* v189 no3 p19 Ja 16 2017

In the Future, Everyone Will Be Dead for 15 Minutes C. Rosen color *Commentary* v143 no2 p1 F 2017

In the Future, Everyone Will Be Dead for 15 Minutes C. ROSEN *Commentary* v143 no2 p4 F 2017

Celebrities—History

Celebrity Squabbles for the Ages C. Lang color *Time* v189 no9 p53 Mr 13 2017

Celebrities—Homes & haunts

Beverly Hills Street Map, 1926 K. Wiles *History Today* v67 no1 p26 Ja 2017

Celebrities—News briefs

Feuds M. Gajanan color *Time* v188 no25-26 p34 D 19 2016 Double Issue

Celebrities—Political activity

CELEBRITIES AREN'T REQUIRED TO BE ACTIVISTS B. VIERA color *Ebony* v72 no11 p26 S 2017

Household Names A. Greenblatt *Governing* v30 no5 p19 F 2017

Celebrities—Travel

Flying in Style E. Wilson color *InStyle* v23 no13 p65 D 2016

Celebrities—United States

America's Richest Celebrities Z. O. GREENBURG, N. ROBEHMED et al color *Forbes* v198 no9 p18 D 30 2016

Fairgroup color *Vanity Fair* v59 no2 p43 F 2017

A fresh take C. Gorrell color *Yoga Journal* no289 p12 F 2017

Household Names A. Greenblatt *Governing* v30 no5 p19 F 2017

Idol Minds P. GULLEY *Indianapolis Monthly* v40 no7 p48 Mr 2017

L.A. Bohème K. SMITH color *Vanity Fair* v59 no9 p198 S 2017

N.Y.C.'S MOST ELIGIBLE PIGEONS W. McPHAIL color *New Yorker* v93 no24 p49 Ag 21 2017

PARTY LINES T. Rami and K. Van Syckle img *New York* v50 no16 p110 Ag 7 2017

Celebrities—United States—Political activity

Hollywood Takes a Knee J. Hibberd and C. Sosenko color *Entertainment Weekly* no1485 p14 O 6 2017

Celebrities—United States—Charts, diagrams, etc.

The Full-Court Parent Trap T. Keith chart color *Sports Illustrated* v126 no8 p24 Mr 20 2017

Celebrity athletes

The AFTER-PARTY L. J. Wertheim color *Sports Illustrated* v127 no1 p48 Jl 3 2017

The World's Unlikeliest Star Athletes T. John color *Time* v189 no9 p12 Mr 13 2017

Celebrity chefs

15 MINUTES *Cincinnati Magazine* v50 no12 p39 S 2017

Emeril Lagasse J. Forman color *New Orleans Magazine* v51 no2 p68 D 2016

THE INTERVIEW A. LEE color *Maclean's* v129 no45 p14 N 14 2016

Celebrity couples

IN UTERO POWER LIST D. Coggan color *Entertainment Weekly* no1454/1455 p21 F 24 2017

Verify My Love J. Ganz color *Entertainment Weekly* no1477 p16 Ag 11 2017

WHEN REALITY ATTACKS D. Coggan color *Entertainment Weekly* no1434 p14 O 7 2016

Celebrity Family Feud (TV program)

ALSO COMING... A. D'Arminio and J. Russell *TV Guide* v65 no23 p27 My 29 2017

America's Most Watched 25 TOP SHOWS *TV Guide* v65 no31 p13 Jl 24 2017

Celebrity impersonators

One NaTiON UNDER PencE L. LARSON color *GQ: Gentlemen's Quarterly* v97 no6 p112 Je 2017

Celebrity interviews

FINANCIAL ADVICE FROM THE STARS J. YUAN color *Bloomberg Businessweek* no4519 p86 Ap 24 2017

Celebrity Apprentice, The (TV program)

The Quiz T. BALAZO color *Maclean's* no1 p64 F 17 2017

Celecoxib

Celebrex's risk to heart debated L. BEIL color *Science News* v190 no12 p6 D 10 2016

Celecoxib—Therapeutic use

Before You Take It S. KLEIN color *Prevention* v69 no2 p22 F 2017

CELESTE, ERIC

Who Would Vote Against This? *D: The Magazine of Dallas* v43 no10 p82 O 2016

Celestial mechanics

See also

Galactic dynamics

A Cornucopia of Celestial Curiosities: The year's end prompts reminiscences of stellar things past F. SCHAAF *Sky & Telescope* v134 no6 p45 D 2017

OBSERVING December 2017 M. WEDEL *Sky & Telescope* v134 no6 p41 D 2017

Celestial sphere

The Return of Uranus and Neptune *Sky & Telescope* v134 no4 p50 O 2017

Celestin, Louis Kevin

KAY-TRANADA D. Valdez color *Surfing Magazine* v53 no1 p30 Ja 2017

Celestin, Ray

Dead Man's Blues *Publtshers Weekly* v264 no39 p84 S 25 2017

Celestron LLC

Celestron's CGX Mount D. d. Cicco color *Sky & Telescope* v134 no5 p62 N 2017

NEW PRODUCTS color *Astronomy* v45 no6 p68 Je 2017

Smart Astronomy: The NexStar Evolution 9,25 R. Mollise *Sky & Telescope* v133 no5 p60 My 2017

TELESCOPE K. Dupzyk color diag *Popular Mechanics* p18 F 2017

Celiac disease

How infection can incite sensitivity to food E. F. Verdu and A. Caminero diag *Science* v356 no6333 p29 Ap 7 2017

One bread? J. P. Kelly color *U.S. Catholic* v82 no6 p28 Je 2017

Celiac disease diagnosis

FAFQ (FREQUENTLY ASKED FOOD QUESTIONS) K. Patel and J. WUEBBEN color *Muscle & Performance* v9 no9 p18 S 2017

Céline, Louis-Ferdinand, 1894-1961

1847: Vienna Celine *Lapham's Quarterly* v10 no2 p65 Spr 2017

Celine SA

CARINE ON THE COLLECTIONS. A NEW PERSPECTIVE C. ROITFELD color *Harper's Bazaar* no3651 p349 Mr 2017

SMALL WONDER color *Harper's Bazaar* no3656 p311 S 2017

Celiz, A. D.

Tough adhesives for diverse wet surfaces diag *Science* v357 no6349 p378 Jl 28 2017

Cell compartmentation

Assembly principles and structure of a 6.5-MDa bacterial microcompartment shell M. Sutter, B. Greber et al color diag *Science* v356 no6344 p1293 Je 23 2017

Cell culture

Are labmade human eggs coming soon? G. Vogel color *Science*

v354 no6310 p272 O 21 2016

Cells gobble up strands of silicon M. ROSEN *Science News* v191 no1 p9 Ja 21 2017

Cell culture—Equipment & supplies

bioengineering color *Science* v355 no6330 p1223 Mr 17 2017

new products: cell culture color *Science* v356 no6333 p99 Ap 7 2017

Cell culture—Equipment & supplies—Evaluation

new products: cell/tissue culture color *Science* v355 no6329 p1085 Mr 10 2017

Cell cycle

Mitotic transcription and waves of gene reactivation during mitotic exit K. C. Palozola, G. Donahue et al color graph *Science* v357 no6359 p119 O 6 2017

RNA interference is essential for cellular quiescence B. Roche, B. Arcangioli et al bibl diag graph *Science* v354 no6313 paah5651-1 N 11 2016

Cell death

See also

Apoptosis

The MIFstep in parthanatos E. Jonas bibl diag *Science* v354 no6308 p36 O 7 2016

Some cells survive attempted suicide T. HESMAN SAEY color *Science News* v191 no1 p10 Ja 21 2017

Cell determination

Notch-Jagged complex structure implicates a catch bond in tuning ligand sensitivity V. C. Luca, B. Choul Kim et al bibl diag graph *Science* v355 no6331 p1320 Mr 24 2017

Cell differentiation

Amoeba gives clues to animal origins L. HAMERS *Science News* v190 no10 p7 N 12 2016

Cell division in plants

The preprophase band of microtubules controls the robustness of division orientation in plants E. Schaefer, K. Belcram et al graph *Science* v356 no6334 p186 Ap 14 2017

Cell imaging

RESEARCH color *Science* v357 no6354 p882 S 1 2017

Cell imaging—Equipment & supplies

new products color *Science* v357 no6359 p123 O 6 2017

Cell interaction (Biology)

Costimulation, a surprising connection for immunotherapy D. L. Clouthier and P. S. Ohashi color diag *Science* v355 no6332 p1373 Mr 31 2017

Intercellular communication and conjugation are mediated by ESX secretion systems in mycobacteria T. A. Gray, R. R. Clark et al bibl diag graph *Science* v354 no6310 p347 O 21 2016

Intracellular signaling in CRISPR-Cas defense G. Amitai and R. Sorek color *Science* v357 no6351 p550 Ag 11 2017

Is the cell's garbage disposal sending messages? M. Leslie color *Science* v355 no6332 p1361 Mr 31 2017

Optical control of cell signaling by single-chain photoswitchable kinases X. X. Zhou, L. Z. Fan et al bibl diag *Science* v355 no6327 p836 F 24 2017

Cell membranes

See also

Membrane proteins

Biological tissue can behave like a liquid crystal M. Wilson *Physics Today* v70 no6 p19 Je 2017

Membrane proteins scrambling through a folding landscape D. J. Müller and H. E. Gaub bibl diag *Science* v355 no6328 p907 Mr 3 2017

Cell metabolism

Gut cell metabolism shapes the microbiome P. D. Cani color *Science* v357 no6351 p548 Ag 11 2017

Inflammation and metabolism in tissue repair and regeneration S. A. Eming, T. A. Wynn et al diag *Science* v356 no6342 p1026 Je 9 2017

Cell migration

Tubular clathrin/AP-2 lattices pinch collagen fibers to support 3D cell migration N. Elkhatib, E. Bresteau et al color *Science* v356 no6343 p1138 Je 16 2017

Cell morphology

Adding depth to cell culture K. Powell color *Science* v356 no6333 p96 Ap 7 2017

Cell nuclei

The genome—seeing it clearly now D. R. Larson and T. Misteli

diag *Science* v357 no6349 p354 Jl 28 2017

Cell organelles

See also

Endoplasmic reticulum

Lysosomes

Assembly principles and structure of a 6.5-MDa bacterial microcompartment shell M. Sutter, B. Greber et al color diag *Science* v356 no6344 p1293 Je 23 2017

Organelle inheritance—what players have skin in the game? U. Gruneberg and F. Barr bibl color *Science* v355 no6324 p459 F 3 2017

Reticulon 3–dependent ER-PM contact sites control EGFR non-clathrin endocytosis G. Caldieri, E. Barbieri et al color diag graph *Science* v356 no6338 p617 My 12 2017

Cell organelles—Research

Organelle Overhaul M. Brouillette *Scientific American* v315 no6 p18 D 2016

Cell phone advertising

Can Your Mobile Customers Afford to Watch Your Ads? J. Gross and C. Bolman *Harvard Business Review Digital Articles* p2 D 8 2015

In Mobile Advertising, Timing Is Everything S. Gupta *Harvard Business Review Digital Articles* p2 N 4 2015

Where YouTube Meets The Boob Tube S. Nicola, A. Boksenbaum-Granier et al graph *Bloomberg Businessweek* no4512 p44 F 20 2017

Cell phone batteries

Galaxy S8 battery life tips: How to control battery drain F. ION color *PCWorld* v35 no10 p116 O 2017

Cell phone equipment

GEARHEAD AWAY GAME D. PIERCE bw color *Wired* v25 no6 p34 Je 2017

Cell phone photographs

PHOTO ops D. DICKINSON color *Better Homes & Gardens* v95 no8 p74 Ag 2017

Cell phone security measures

6 easy ways to keep your Android phone secure B. PATTERSON color *PCWorld* v35 no6 p39 Je 2017

Cell phone systems—Evaluation

The Best Cell Phone Plan for You M. Leonhardt and K. Mulhere color diag *Money* v46 no6 p64 Jl 2017

Cell phone users

CELLPHONE ACCESS HAS SKYROCKETED. THE WORLD IS BETTER FOR IT M. Tupy graph *Reason* v49 no5 p44 O 2017

Cell phone videos

THE MOBILE DATA SQUEEZE IS COMING A. Pressman diag *Fortune* v174 no8 p16 D 15 2016

Cell phones

See also

Smartphones

Airplane Mode T. Johnston color *Practical Horseman* v45 no11 p16 N 2017

Aziz Ansari Is From a Red State, Too: Even though he is the latest comic ambassador for New York neuroses J. Yuan img *New York* v50 no9 p79 My 1 2017

Conserve Your Cell Data (and Your Money) M. CUTOLO color *Reader's Digest* v189 no1130 p46 My 2017

Just Hearing Your Phone Buzz Hurts Your Productivity N. Torres *Harvard Business Review Digital Articles* p2 Jl 10 2015

LANDLINES BETTER THAN CELL PHONES FOR 911 *USA Today Magazine* v146 no2868 p7 S 2017

LAST PAGE P. STEFÁNSSON *Iceland Review* v55 no2 p128 Mr/ Ap 2017

THE LIFE CYCLE OF A CELL PHONE *New York State Conservationist* v71 no4 p6 F 2017

A Side Table That Can Charge Your Phone A. GEORGE color *Popular Mechanics* p110 Ap 2017

STAY WELL ON THE WAY L. Goldman color *Good Housekeeping* v264 no5 p101 My 2017

Trick Out Your Phone R. Broida color *Money* v46 no1 p23 Ja/F 2017

Unplug a little, gain a lot color *Redbook* p101 D 2016

What's on Jillian Michaels's Phone? J. Hartshorn *Parents* v91 no11 p22 N 2016

Your Mobile Strategy Can't Just Be About Phones B. Caine *Har-*

vard Business Review Digital Articles p2 Jl 27 2017

Cell phones & automobiles

HOW TO Arrive alive color *Good Housekeeping* v264 no4 p83 Ap 2017

Cell phones & teenagers

Terms and conditions: Parents can make smartphone use for kids safer by writing their own fine print A. Scobey color *U.S. Catholic* v82 no9 p43 S 2017

Cell phones—China

The Cheap Phone Is Dead In China B. Einhorn cartoon color *Bloomberg Businessweek* no4496 p36 O 24 2016

Cell phones—Equipment & supplies—Evaluation

FLIR One Smartphone Thermal-Imaging Attachment J. Y. WOOD color *Power & Motoryacht* v33 no3 p46 Mr 2017

Cell phones—History

Microsoft halts Minecraft updates for Windows 10 phones M. HACHMAN cartoon color *PCWorld* v35 no2 p14 F 2017

We Could Have Had Cellphones Four Decades Earlier T. W. HAZLETT color *Reason* v49 no3 p60 Jl 2017

Cell phones—Physiological aspects

The Perils of Smartphones R. BACHER *AARP: The Magazine* v59 no5A p19 Ag/S 2016

Cell phones—Social aspects

Codebreakers M. Gunch cartoon *New Orleans Magazine* v51 no9 p42 Jl 2017

Cell physiology

See also

Blood cell physiology

Liquid phase condensation in cell physiology and disease Y. Shin and C. P. Brangwynne *Science* v357 no6357 p1253 S 22 2017

Single-cell epigenomics: Recording the past and predicting the future G. Kelsey, O. Stegle et al diag *Science* v357 no6359 p69 O 6 2017

Cell receptors

See also

Antigen receptors

Protein receptors

CAR T-cell–based therapeutic modality in solid tumors: How to achieve precision Yang Liu, Hanren Dai et al bibl color *Science* v354 no6319 p27 D 23 2016

Cella, Marina

Lactobacillus reuteri induces gut intraepithelial CD4+CD8αα+ T cells diag graph *Science* v357 no6353 p806 Ag 25 2017

CELLI, DAN

Chords & Discords bw color *Downbeat* v84 no10 p10 O 2017

Cellists

Akua Dixon: PLAYING WITH POWER D. Ouellette color *Downbeat* v84 no4 p44 Ap 2017

Cells

See also

Cartilage cells

Fertilization (Biology)

Neurons

Ovum

Stem cells

ChromEMT: Visualizing 3D chromatin structure and compaction in interphase and mitotic cells H. D. Ou, S. Phan et al color *Science* v357 no6349 p370 Jl 28 2017

Comprehensive single-cell transcriptional profiling of a multicellular organism J. Cao, J. S. Packer et al diag *Science* v357 no6352 p661 Ag 18 2017

In situ architecture, function, and evolution of a contractile injection system D. Böck, J. M. Medeiros et al color diag *Science* v357 no6352 p713 Ag 18 2017

Paneth cells secrete lysozyme via secretory autophagy during bacterial infection of the intestine S. Bel, M. Pendse et al color diag *Science* v357 no6355 p1047 S 8 2017

The promise of spatial transcriptomics for neuroscience in the era of molecular cell typing E. Lein, L. E. Borm et al color diag *Science* v357 no6359 p64 O 6 2017

RESEARCH color *Science* v357 no6352 p656 Ag 18 2017

Synthetic cell may reveal what is necessary for life R. Ehrenberg color *Science News* v190 no13 p26 D 24 2016

Writ large: Genomic dissection of the effect of cellular environment on immune response N. Yosef and A. Regev bibl diag *Science* v354 no6308 p64 O 7 2016

Cells—Analysis

Variations on a cell T. H. Saey color *Science News* v191 no8 p40 Ap 29 2017

Cells—Imaging

Biggest organelle gets image update L. HAMERS color *Science News* v190 no11 p10 N 26 2016

Variations on a cell T. H. Saey color *Science News* v191 no8 p40 Ap 29 2017

Cells—Imaging—Equipment & supplies

LIFE SCIENCE TECHNOLOGIES color *Science* v355 no6322 p313 Ja 20 2017

Cellular aging

Killing old cells to stay young M. Leslie color *Science* v354 no6319 p1519 D 23 2016

Senescent intimal foam cells are deleterious at all stages of atherosclerosis B. G. Childs, D. J. Baker et al bibl *Science* v354 no6311 p472 O 28 2016

Tissue damage and senescence provide critical signals for cellular reprogramming in vivo L. Mosteiro, C. Pantoja et al bibl chart graph *Science* v354 no6315 paaf4445-1 N 25 2016

Cellular growth—Abstracts

Coupling organelle inheritance with mitosis to balance growth and differentiation A. Asare, J. Levorse et al diag *Science* v355 no6324 p493 F 3 2017

Cellular mappings (Mathematics)

A subcellular map of the human proteome P. J. Thul, L. Åkesson et al color *Science* v356 no6340 p820 My 26 2017

Cellular mechanics

Ancestral alliances: Plant mutualistic symbioses with fungi and bacteria F. M. Martin, S. Uroz et al color *Science* v356 no6340 p819 My 26 2017

Cellular signal transduction

See also

Plant cellular signal transduction

Mechanism of transmembrane signaling by sensor histidine kinases I. Gushchin, I. Melnikov et al color *Science* v356 no6342 p1043 Je 9 2017

Multisite phosphorylation by MAPK A. J. Whitmarsh and R. J. Davis bibl diag *Science* v354 no6309 p179 O 14 2016

Cellulitis

Cellulitis in Your Dressage Partner K. L. Marcella color *Dressage Today* v23 no10 p20 Jl 2017

Cellulitis—Diagnosis

Cellulitis *Mayo Clinic Health Letter* v35 no1 p7 Ja 2017

Cellulitis—Prevention

Stop the Fat Talk J. Andriakos color *Health* v31 no2 p24 Mr 2017

Cellulitis—Risk factors

Cellulitis *Mayo Clinic Health Letter* v35 no1 p7 Ja 2017

Cellulose

SCOTCH MAGIC TAPE C. LEU color *Wired* v24 no12 p36 D 2016

Celmins, Vija, 1938—Exhibitions

NEW LIVES P. SCHJELDAHL cartoon *New Yorker* v93 no2 p72 F 27 2017

Celtic antiquities

A PRINCELY UPDATE J. URBANUS color *Archaeology* v70 no5 p16 S/O 2017

Cement

Using multiple techniques to build a CEMENT PLANT E. White color *Model Railroader* v84 no6 p34 Je 2017

Cement plants

River Ruins *South Dakota Magazine* v32 no6 p48 Mr/Ap 2017

Cemeteries

See also

National cemeteries

Above Old Bones M. Phillips color *Commonweal* v114 no14 p22 S 8 2017

Burials give peek at Philistines' lives B. BOWER *Science News* v190 no13 p8 D 24 2016

WHO LIES IN THE CUSTER GRAVES? J. ANDREWS *South Dakota Magazine* v32 no4 p40 N/D 2016

Cemeteries—England

Real & Unimaginable J. Ryan color *Commonweal* v144 no8 p46 My 5 2017

Cemeteries—Georgia

UPPER WESTSIDE M. BLAU *Atlanta* v56 no12 p52 Ap 2017

Cemeteries—Missouri
St. Louis Parks and Green Spaces P. M. Jacoby-Garrett *Parks & Recreation* v51 no10 p66 O 2016

Cemeteries—Nebraska
Final salute in Alliance: Nebraska Veterans Cemetery E. Case *Nebraska Life* v20 no6 p17 N/D 2016

Cemeteries—New York (State)
See also
Green-Wood Cemetery (New York, N.Y.)
"Said to Be" S. CAREY color *Natural History* v125 no9 p48 S 2017

Cemetery of Splendor (Film)
Cemetery of Splendor D. Lim *Film Comment* v53 no1 p46 Ja/F 2017

Cemex SAB de CV
TRUMP'S STOCK SCORECARD color *Fortune* v175 no3 p18 Mr 1 2017

Cem Tasan, Cemal
Bone-like crack resistance in hierarchical metastable nanolaminate steels bibl color diag *Science* v355 no6329 p1055 Mr 10 2017

Cena, John, 1977-—Interviews
TRUE GRIT: WWE phenom John Cena transforms average Joes into G.I. Joes on Season 2 of Fox's reality competition American Grit I. RATLEDGE *TV Guide* v65 no27 p22 Je 26 2017

Cena, John—Interviews
AMERICAN GRIT G. E. Miller *TV Guide* v64 no15 p52 Ap 4 2016

Cenac, Wyatt
People of Earth A. D'Arminio *TV Guide* v65 no31 p31 Jl 24 2017

CENDES, YVETTE
Figuring Out FRBs color *Discover* v38 no1 p71 Ja/F 2017
GAME OVER cartoon *Discover* v38 no2 p46 Mr 2017
Supernova Shocker! color *Discover* v38 no1 p84 Ja/F 2017

Cendrowski, Scott
10 JACK MA color *Fortune* v174 no7 p85 D 1 2016
16 WANG JIANLIN color *Fortune* v174 no7 p88 D 1 2016
THE 2017 Fortune Crystal Ball color diag *Fortune* v174 no7 p11 D 1 2016
8 CHENG WEI color *Fortune* v174 no7 p85 D 1 2016
CHINA'S NEW CRAFT-BEER BULLY color diag *Fortune* v175 no4 p152 Mr 15 2017
China Spreads the Wealth Around color map *Fortune* v174 no8 p138 D 15 2016
IS THE WORLD BIG ENOUGH FOR HUAWEI? color diag *Fortune* v175 no2 p66 F 1 2017
THE PGA TOUR TAKES ON CHinA color *Fortune* v174 no6 p116 N 1 2016
POSTAL SAVINGS BANK OF CHINA GOES BIG diag *Fortune* v174 no8 p24 D 15 2016
TESLA MAKES A U-TURN IN CHINA chart color diag *Fortune* v175 no8 p128 Je 15 2017
WORLD'S 50 GREATEST LEADERS [Cover story] color *Fortune* v175 no5 p46 Ap 1 2017
THE WORLD'S NEW ANTAGONIZER-IN-CHIEF *Fortune* v75 no1 p22 Ja 1 2017

Cenko, S. Bradley
Cornelis A. Gehrels *Physics Today* v70 no10 p75 O 2017
How to Swallow a Sun color *Scientific American* v316 no4 p38 Ap 2017

Cenovus Energy Inc.
Cheap Stocks for a Pricey Market T. PETRUNO color *Kiplinger's Personal Finance* v71 no8 p50 Ag 2017

Censorship
See also
Freedom of the press
To Sell or Not to Sell: Censorship Or Free Speech for Bookstores? C. Reid color *Publishers Weekly* v264 no26 p9 Je 26 2017
Winnie the Pooh and Homer Too K. Samuelson color *Time* v190 no5 p16 Jl 31 2017

Censorship—Egypt
Freedom of The Press is Not a Given R. ASPDEN *Publishers Weekly* v264 no9 p104 F 27 2017

Censorship—United States
FROM THE ARCHIVES bw color *Reason* v49 no5 p78 O 2017
The Right to Speech Vs. the Right to Censor B. Walsh color *Time*

v189 no9 p19 Mr 13 2017

Census—Canada
The space between us J. KIRBY map *Maclean's* v130 no3 p19 Ap 2017

Census—Methodology
Adding questions on certifications and licenses to the Current Population Survey bibl chart color *Monthly Labor Review* p1 N 2016

Centaur objects
3122 Florence Flies By, Reveals Two Moons J. K. BEATTY and B. KING *Sky & Telescope* v134 no6 p10 D 2017

Centaurus (Constellation)
EXPLORE CENTAURUS' DEEP-SKY TREASURES M. E. Bakich color *Astronomy* v45 no6 p44 Je 2017

Centenarians
Faces of a Century M. Pollock color *Chicago* v66 no5 p110 My 2017
How Can I Afford to Live to 100? R. T. Beckwith color *Time* v189 no7/8 p96 F 27 2017

Centennial Olympic Park (Atlanta, Ga.)
Saving Atlanta's Centennial Olympic Park from Concert Damage R. W. Cohen *Parks & Recreation* v51 no12 p48 D 2016

Centennials
Common Ground J. Mark *Sierra* v101 no4 p6 Jl/Ag 2016
FORBES @ 100 A. BROWN bw color *Forbes* v198 no8 p32 D 20 2016
FORBES @ 100 A. BROWN bw *Forbes* v199 no6 p30 Je 13 2017
That man Robert Mitchum: remembering an enigmatic American original C. Sandford bw *America* v217 no5 p38 S 4 2017

Centeno, Josef
Bringing It All Back Home color *Bon Appetit* p56 S 2017

Center (Politics)
Germany Stays in the Center M. Champion *Bloomberg Businessweek* no4538 p12 S 18 2017
Trump the Triangulator? R. SALAM color *National Review* v68 no22 p33 D 5 2016

Center, Erika
THE PATH TO EXEMPLARY color *Literacy Today (2411-7862)* v34 no4 p34 Ja/F 2017

Center for American Progress
Liberal Think Tank Freaks Out *Weekly Standard* v22 no8 p3 O 31 2016

Center for the Arts at Yerba Buena Gardens
THE MASTER PLANS cartoon color *Vanity Fair* v58 no11 p68 N 2016

Center of mass
A Bit Tipsy H. Leifert map *Natural History* v125 no3 p7 Mr 2017

Center for Immigration Studies (Washington, D.C.)
Trump's Fuzzy Border Math L. RESTON color *New Republic* v248 no4 p6 Ap 2017

Centerpieces
Budding Artist G. Haynes color *Southern Living* v52 no5 p22 My 2017
a grateful spread J. Tung *Martha Stewart Living* no269 p114 N 2016
MAKE + MEND J. Behari color *House Beautiful* p142 Ag 2017

Centers for Disease Control & Prevention (U.S.)
GENERATION: America's opioid epidemic is leaving an entire generation of children behind J. B. Wogan *Governing* v30 no10 p32 Jl 2017
Living with Autism: Early intervention is critical to helping children diagnosed with autism reach their full potential I. MURTUZA *Islamic Horizons* v46 no3 p44 My/Je 2017
MOTHER SUCKER! L. Haney color *Women's Health* v14 no5 p72 Je 2017
Sexual assault— it's on us *Christian Century* v133 no24 p7 N 23 2016
The Silent Battle: Surviving Sexual Trauma D. POINTDUJOUR color *Ebony* v72 no4 p72 F 2017

Centers for Disease Control & Prevention (U.S.)—Officials & employees
Is the U.S. Ready for Future Disease Threats? D. Fine Maron color *Scientific American* v316 no4 p24 Ap 2017

Centers for Medicare & Medicaid Services (U.S.)
Andy Slavitt Wants to Unite America on Health Care A. M. Cox *New York Times Magazine* p50 Ag 13 2017

How Safe Does a Hospital Need to Be? M. Quinn *Governing* v30 no6 p18 Mr 2017

Centers for Medicare & Medicaid Services (U.S.)—Officials & employees

A Passion for Teaching J. Caplin color *Money* v45 no10 p26 N 2016

CENTONI, DANIELLE

POP ART color *Better Homes & Gardens* v95 no7 p108 Jl 2017

CENTORCELLI, KRISTIN

Jessica Cluess color *Publishers Weekly* v263 no52 p69 D 19 2016

Centore, Michael

Evening's light color *U.S. Catholic* v82 no7 p45 Jl 2017

Central African Republic—Economic conditions

The Burning Heart of Africa P. Gwin color map *National Geographic* v231 no5 p56 My 2017

Central Asia

SAND TRICKS N. Strochlic color *National Geographic* v232 no5 p144 N 2017

Central Bank of Iceland (Company)

News Roundup V. HAFSTAÐ *Iceland Review* v55 no3 p8 My/ Je 2017

Central banking industry

It's Wrong to Bully Central Banks cartoon *Bloomberg Businessweek* no4501 p8 N 28 2016

Central banking industry—News briefs

Resources *Bridges (Federal Reserve Bank of St. Louis)* p12 Wint 2016/2017

Central business districts

THE FORGOTTEN HISTORY OF U STREET B. THOMAS *Washingtonian Magazine* v52 no5 p60 F 2017

TOWN CENTERS EVERYWHERE! D. Reed *Washingtonian Magazine* v52 no2 p57 N 2016

Central business districts—Design & construction

Time-Travel Therapy A. KOLSON HURLEY bw color *Atlantic* v319 no1 p28 Ja/F 2017

Central Connecticut State University—Sports

The New Marshall Plan J. Fuchs and T. Keith color diag *Sports Illustrated* v125 no15 p20 N 7 2016

Central economic planning

Agricultural Recovery in Russia and the Rise of Its South N. Rada, W. Liefert et al *Amber Waves: The Economics of Food, Farming, Natural Resources, & Rural America* p10 Ap 2017

Central Intelligence (Film)

CENTRAL INTELLIGENCE D. Vaughn color *Sound & Vision* v82 no2 p70 F/Mr 2017

Central Intelligence M. FELL *TV Guide* v65 no6 p47 Ja 30 2017

DWAYNE JOHNSON ROCKS D. Coggan color *Entertainment Weekly* no1441 p11 N 25 2016

Kevin Hart L. Greenblatt color *Entertainment Weekly* no1444/1445 p22 D 16 2016

Streaming S. Li color *Entertainment Weekly* no1451/1452 p94 F 3-10 2017

Central nervous system

See also

Brain

THE POWER OF NEGATIVITY L. McGLASHAN color *Muscle & Performance* v9 no4 p16 Ap 2017

Central nervous system stimulants—Therapeutic use

a game changer for ADHD V. SOLE-SMITH color *Parents* v92 no5 p30 My 2017

Central processing units (Computers)

AMD Ryzen Threadripper: Everything we know so far about this monster CPU [Cover story] G. MAH UNG color *PCWorld* v35 no6 p9 Je 2017

AMD's Ryzen 3 lineup brings competitive quad-core CPUs to the masses B. CHACOS color *PCWorld* v35 no8 p14 Ag 2017

AMD Threadripper prices undercut Intel's Core i9 by as much as $1,000 M. HACHMAN chart color *PCWorld* v35 no8 p9 Ag 2017

Facepalm: Intel's upcoming Coffee Lake CPUs won't work with today's motherboards G. M. UNG color *PCWorld* v35 no9 p11 S 2017

Ryzen CPUs explained: Everything you need to know about AMD's disruptive multicore chips B. CHACOS color *PCWorld* v35 no5 p13 My 2017

Ryzen Threadripper: AMD's monster stomps on other CPUs G.

M. UNG chart color graph *PCWorld* v35 no9 p27 S 2017

Central High School (Little Rock, Ark.)

The Little Rock Nine: Sixty years ago this month, President Eisenhower sent federal troops into Arkansas to enforce the desegregation of Little Rock's Central High School S. ROBERTS and C. Staffers *New York Times Upfront* v150 no1 p18 S 4 2017

Central Mexico Earthquake, 2017

Another deadly quake rocks Mexico color *Science* v357 no6358 p1332 S 29 2017

Photostat: Mexico City Earthquake E. Martin and N. Cattan bw color *Bloomberg Businessweek* no4539 p38 S 25 2017

Central Park Five, The (Film)

quick takes bw color *U.S. Catholic* v82 no5 p39 My 2017

Centre Georges Pompidou

THE BRIEF bw color *Art in America* v105 no1 p19 Ja 2017

Centrowitz, Matt, 1989-

MATTHEW CENTROWITZ E. STROUT color *Runner's World* v52 no1 p82 Ja/F 2017

Century Cycle (Theatrical production)

GOINGS ON ABOUT TOWN color *New Yorker* v92 no43 p6 Ja 2 2017

Century LLC

ESSENTIAL GEAR color *Black Belt* v55 no2 p60 F/Mr 2017

Return of the Kicking Jeans R. W. Young color *Black Belt* v55 no4 p76 Je/Jl 2017

Ceo, Mari-An

Meet the crew... I. Rudolph *TV Guide* v64 no48 p12 N 21 2016

Cephalopoda

Cephalopod smarts tied to RNA edits T. H. SAEY color *Science News* v191 no8 p6 Ap 29 2017

Drawing on the Past M. Jones *Natural History* v124 no10 p16 N 2016

Cephalosomatic anastomosis

WARNING, STRANGE DAYS AHEAD [Cover story] A. HUTCHINS color *Maclean's* v129 no51/52 p65 D 26 2016

Cepheids—Research

No new stellar births in the galaxy's center color *Astronomy* v44 no12 p12 D 2016

Ceppos, Rich

It's Alive! color *Car & Driver* v63 no4 p104 O 2017

Ceramic bowls—Evaluation

It's Spring - Say Yes to Yellow! color *Treasures* v5 no5 p6 Ap/ My 2016

Ceramic sculpture

ANIMAL ATTRACTION F. VIGNA color *Martha Stewart Living* p116 My 2017

DISPOSABLE GODS D. WEISS color *Archaeology* v70 no5 p16 S/O 2017

Ceramic sculpture—Exhibitions

KEN PRICE G. Coxhead color *Art in America* v105 no3 p138 Mr 2017

Ceramic tiles

ADDITIONAL LISTINGS *Arts & Crafts Homes & the Revival* v12 no1 p40 2017 Resouce Guide

wall & floor tiles *Design Center Sourcebook* p36 2017

Ceramics

See also

Ceramic tiles

Glass

ABOVE & BEYOND cartoon *New Yorker* v93 no14 p22 My 22 2017

BH&G throwback 1956 HANDMADE CERAMICS K. K. CONDON color *Better Homes & Gardens* v95 no9 p172 S 2017

fired up color *Architectural Digest* v74 no1 p208 Ja 2017

Guten Co L. S. FORD *Texas Monthly* v45 no8 p17 Ag 2017

Ceramics—Exhibitions

CALENDAR OF SHOWS *Magazine Antiques* v184 no1 p212 Ja/F 2017

EMILY MULLIN J. Kreimer color *Art in America* v105 no3 p124 Mr 2017

Ceramics—Study & teaching

Eleven Things You're Likely to Do Poorly (But Love Anyway) L. SCHWARTZBERG img *New York* v49 no23 p66 N 14 2016

Ceramides

GET FLAWLESS SKIN color *Harper's Bazaar* no3653 p295 My 2017

Cerase, Andrea

PCGF3/5–PRC1 initiates Polycomb recruitment in X chromosome inactivation color *Science* v356 no6342 p1081 Je 9 2017

Xist recruits the X chromosome to the nuclear lamina to enable chromosome-wide silencing bibl graph *Science* v354 no6311 p468 O 28 2016

Ceratocystis diseases

Alien fungus blights Hawaii's native trees I. Vesper color *Science* v354 no6310 p273 O 21 2016

Tree-Killing Fungus Continues to Spread on Hawaii's Biggest Island M. STONE *BioScience* v67 no8 p776 Ag 2017

Cerchio, Salvatore

A New Whale Species Is Discovered in the Wild E. Koenig *Oceanus* v52 no1 p10 Summ 2016

Cerda Jara, Cledi Alicia

Loss of a mammalian circular RNA locus causes miRNA deregulation and affects brain function color *Science* v357 no6357 p1254 S 22 2017

Cerebellum—Development

Modular brain construction P. J. H color *Science* v354 no6308 p78 O 7 2016

Cerebral atrophy

More Mediterranean Diet Magic color *Prevention* v69 no4 p10 Ap 2017

Cerebral cortex

See also

Hippocampus (Brain)

Conversion of object identity to object-general semantic value in the primate temporal cortex K. Tamura, M. Takeda et al color graph *Science* v357 no6352 p687 Ag 18 2017

Redefining the Brain's Divisions T. BURRELL color *Discover* v38 no1 p55 Ja/F 2017

Cerebral cortex—Physiology

Microstructural proliferation in human cortex is coupled with the development of face processing J. Gomez, M. A. Barnett et al bibl graph *Science* v355 no6320 p1 Ja 6 2017

Cerebral hemispheres

Your Pun-Divided Attention R. Jacobson color *Scientific American* v315 no6 p17 D 2016

Cerebral palsied

"ALL I WANNA DO IS STAND UP and DANCE! " J. SMALL color *Good Housekeeping* v265 no4 p69 O 2017

Atlanta v57 no2 p100 Je 2017

JUSTIN GALLEGOS color *Runner's World* v52 no1 p86 Ja/F 2017

Cerebral palsy treatment

"ALL I WANNA DO IS STAND UP and DANCE! " J. SMALL color *Good Housekeeping* v265 no4 p69 O 2017

Cerebrospinal fluid

Headaches and spinal fluid leaks *Mayo Clinic Health Letter* v35 no9 p7 S 2017

Zika hides out in hard-to-reach spots L. HAMERS color *Science News* v191 no10 p10 My 27 2017

CEREN, OMRI

Let's Make a Bad Deal *Commentary* v142 no3 p48 O 2016

Middle East Misjudgment *Commentary* v142 no5 p41 D 2016

Ceres (Dwarf planet)

CERES HAS AN ABUNDANCE OF ICE J. Wenz color *Astronomy* v45 no4 p12 Ap 2017

Dawn spacecraft maps Ceres water C. CROCKETT color *Science News* v191 no1 p8 Ja 21 2017

Dwarf planet Ceres and the ingredients of life M. Küppers bibl color *Science* v355 no6326 p692 F 17 2017

Extensive water ice within Ceres' aqueously altered regolith: Evidence from nuclear spectroscopy T. H. Prettyman, N. Yamashita et al bibl graph *Science* v355 no6320 p1 Ja 6 2017

Organic compounds detected on Ceres color *Science* v355 no6326 p706 F 17 2017

Organic compounds found on Ceres E. S. EATON color *Science News* v191 no5 p8 Mr 18 2017

Recent Briny Eruptions on Ceres? J. K. BEATTY *Sky & Telescope* v134 no1 p10 Jl 2017

Separated at Birth N. T. REDD chart color diag *Discover* v38 no10 p38 D 2017

Ceres (Dwarf planet)—Exploration

Dawn of Discovery at Ceres M. D. Rayman *Sky & Telescope* v132

no6 p16 D 2016

Cerf, David C.

A selective insecticidal protein from Pseudomonas for controlling corn rootworms bibl chart graph *Science* v354 no6312 p634 N 4 2016

Cerf, Moran—Interviews

BOX-OFFICE MIND READERS C. ZULKEY color *Chicago* v66 no6 p24 Je 2017

Cericola, Lisa

THE 5-INGREDIENT Farmers' Market Cookbook color *Southern Living* v52 no7 p61 Jl 2017

BEST OF WHAT'S LEFT color *Southern Living* v51 no11 p156 N 2016

A CAROLINA CHRISTMAS color *Southern Living* v51 no12 p170 D 2016

COOKING SCHOOL color *Southern Living* v52 no11 p132 N 2017

Eat Your Greens color *Southern Living* v52 no4 p119 Ap 2017

A FESTIVE FEAST color *Southern Living* v51 no12 p142 D 2016

Full of Flavor color *Southern Living* v52 no6 p123 Je 2017

A Great Pot of Gumbo color *Southern Living* v52 no3 p126 Mr 2017

Hit the Sweet Spot color *Southern Living* v52 no2 p140 F 2017

Light Pasta with a Kick color *Southern Living* v52 no1 p124 Ja 2017

A Month of Simple Suppers color *Southern Living* v52 no2 p117 F 2017

THE NEW SOUTHERN SIDEBOARD color *Southern Living* v52 no11 p80 N 2017

OYSTER CASSEROLE color *Southern Living* v51 no12 p188 D 2016

Pound Cake Perfection color *Southern Living* v52 no5 p146 My 2017

Proud Mary color *Southern Living* v52 no4 p138 Ap 2017

The Scoop on Cobbler color *Southern Living* v52 no9 p142 S 2017

THE SOUTHERN LIVING CAST-IRON COOKBOOK color *Southern Living* v52 no9 p106 S 2017

THE SOUTHERN LIVING COMFORT FOOD COOKBOOK [Cover story] color *Southern Living* v52 no1 p74 Ja 2017

THE SOUTHERN LIVING COOKIE COOKBOOK color *Southern Living* v51 no12 p190 D 2016

SPECTACULAR SIDES color *Southern Living* v51 no11 p100 N 2016

Spring Chicken! color *Southern Living* v52 no3 p119 Mr 2017

Super Dips color *Southern Living* v52 no2 p136 F 2017

A TALE OF TWO TURKEYS color *Southern Living* v51 no11 p96 N 2016

TORTILLAS TONIGHT color *Southern Living* v52 no1 p115 Ja 2017

Weeknight Wonders color *Southern Living* v52 no9 p123 S 2017

Cerio, Gregory

EDITOR'S LETTER color *Magazine Antiques* v183 no6 p16 N/D 2016

EDITOR'S LETTER color *Magazine Antiques* v184 no3 p16 My/Je 2017

EDITOR'S LETTER *Magazine Antiques* v184 no1 p20 Ja/F 2017

EDITOR'S LETTER *Magazine Antiques* v184 no5 p14 S/O 2017

Glass act bw color *Magazine Antiques* v183 no6 p76 N/D 2016

Old guard avant-garde color *Magazine Antiques* v184 no3 p124 My/Je 2017

Ceriotti, Aldo

Wild emmer genome architecture and diversity elucidate wheat evolution and domestication color *Science* v357 no6346 p93 Jl 7 2017

Cerise, Frederick P.

Health Care Innovation Doesn't Have to Be Driven by Profit *Harvard Business Review Digital Articles* p2 D 4 2015

Cermak, Jenny

Put the "and" Back in "Sales and Marketing" *Harvard Business Review Digital Articles* p2 O 30 2014

Cermele, Joe

Bow Hunting color *Field & Stream* v122 no1 pF4 My 2017

BREAK OUT! cartoon color *Field & Stream* v121 no9 p35 Ap 2017

BURNING RUBBER cartoon color *Field & Stream* v121 no8 p72 F/Mr 2017

CAT NIP cartoon color *Field & Stream* v121 no7 p32 D 2016/Ja 2017

Current Trends color *Field & Stream* v122 no1 pF7 My 2017

FEEDING THE COWS color *Field & Stream* v122 no6 p22 N 2017

FRESH BAITS color *Field & Stream* v122 no1 p68 My 2017

HELL ON REELS 2017 color *Field & Stream* v121 no9 p67 Ap 2017

HOLIDAY GIFT GUIDE 2016 color *Field & Stream* v121 no7 p92 D 2016/Ja 2017

HOT RODS 2017 cartoon color *Field & Stream* v122 no1 p59 My 2017

Mining for Bronze color *Field & Stream* v121 no9 pF7 Ap 2017

PITCH-BLACK BRONZEBACKS color *Field & Stream* v122 no4 p36 S 2017

RELISH THE WEENIE color *Field & Stream* v122 no3 p22 Ag 2017

THE SLAB HARVEST cartoon color *Field & Stream* v121 no6 p59 N 2016

SPEED BUGS color *Field & Stream* v121 no7 p26 D 2016/Ja 2017

SUMMER CRUSH color *Field & Stream* v122 no2 p18 Je/Jl 2017

SURFACE SEDUCER DOUBLE BARREL POPPER BODIES color *Field & Stream* v121 no8 p90 F/Mr 2017

THE TAGGED-OUT DEER HUNTER'S GUIDE TO FALL [Cover story] color *Field & Stream* v122 no6 p59 N 2017

TREASURE CHEST color *Field & Stream* v122 no1 p24 My 2017

UNDER-DOGFISH color *Field & Stream* v121 no8 p20 F/Mr 2017

WEATHER STRIPPING cartoon color *Field & Stream* v121 no9 p16 Ap 2017

WELCOME TO THE JUNGLE bw color *Field & Stream* v122 no2 p51 Je/Jl 2017

Cernan, Eugene, 1934-2017

Eugene Cernan J. Kluger color *Time* v189 no3 p11 Ja 30 2017

Cernovich, Mike

Spin Cycle J. Silverman *New York Times Magazine* p11 S 3 2017

TROLLS FOR TRUMP A. MARANTZ cartoon *New Yorker* v92 no35 p42 O 31 2016

Wow If True M. Hemingway color *Weekly Standard* v22 no33 p17 My 8 2017

CERNY-CHIPMAN, ELIZABETH B.

Long-Term Studies Contribute Disproportionately to Ecology and Policy *BioScience* v67 no3 p271 Mr 2017

Cerón, C.

Persistent effects of pre-Columbian plant domestication on Amazonian forest composition bibl chart graph map *Science* v355 no6328 p925 Mr 3 2017

Cerqueira, João

Jesus and Magdalene S. CARPENTER *Humanist* v77 no4 p46 Jl/Ag 2017

Cerrado ecology

The Cerrado: One of Many Cinderellas of Global Hotspots T. O'Riordan *Environment* v58 no6 p2 N/D 2016

Cerrados—Brazil

The Cerrado: One of Many Cinderellas of Global Hotspots T. O'Riordan *Environment* v58 no6 p2 N/D 2016

Civil Society and Environmental Change in Brazil's Cerrado D. Sawyer and M. Lahsen bibl *Environment* v58 no6 p16 N/D 2016

Undervaluing and Overexploiting the Brazilian Cerrado at Our Peril M. Lahsen, M. M. C. Bustamante et al bibl *Environment* v58 no6 p4 N/D 2016

Cerroni, P.

Seasonal exposure of carbon dioxide ice on the nucleus of comet 67P/Churyumov-Gerasimenko bibl bw graph *Science* v354 no6319 p1563 D 23 2016

Certain Women (Film)

Certain Women Burns Slow but True S. Zacharek color *Time* v188 no16/17 p88 O 24 2016

Certain Women color *New Yorker* v92 no35 p22 O 31 2016

Just Enough D. CHEW-BOSE color *Film Comment* v52 no6 p16 N/D 2016

PASSING TIME WITH CERTAIN WOMEN A. Hastie *Film Quarterly* v70 no3 p74 Spr 2017

Total Eclipse img *New York* v49 no21 p114 O 17 2016

Certification

See also

Air pilot certification

CPRP Certification: The Key to Career Advancement S. Ghose *Parks & Recreation* v52 no1 p44 Ja 2017

Have You Thought About Certification as an Alternative Educational Experience? M. Sullivan *Parks & Recreation* v52 no2 p42 F 2017

The Next Wave K. Logan and J. Gonchar *Architectural Record* v205 no9 p131 S 2017

PROTEIN POWDERS: Certifications & Label Lingo V. Tweed chart color *Amazing Wellness* v9 no1 p14 Wint 2017

The Trainer Certification Program Moves From Tortoise to Hare S. Campf *In Stride* v12 no3 p8 My 2017

Trainers Will Have 2 Tracks & 4 Levels for Certification L. Taylor *In Stride* v12 no3 p24 My 2017

Will I need a license or certification for my job? E. Torpey color graph *Career Outlook* p2 S 2016

Cervantes, M.

Observation of coherent elastic neutrino-nucleus scattering diag *Science* v357 no6356 p1123 S 15 2017

Cervantes-Barragan, Luisa

Lactobacillus reuteri induces gut intraepithelial CD4+CD8αα+ T cells diag graph *Science* v357 no6353 p806 Ag 25 2017

Cervantes Saavedra, Miguel de, 1547-1616

In Exile With 'Don Quixote' *New York Times Book Review* p33 O 9 2016

Cervelli, Peter

Volcanic tremor and plume height hysteresis from Pavlof Volcano, Alaska bibl graph *Science* v355 no6320 p1 Ja 6 2017

Cervélo Cycles Inc.

CERVÉLO R5 M. Phillips color *Bicycling* v58 no7 p88 Ag 2017

"I'M GOING THROUGH A MIDLIFE CRISIS AND WANT SOMETHING BETTER THAN A CORVETTE." R. Koch and B. STRICKLAND color *Bicycling* v58 no3 p96 Ap 2017

Cervenka, Igor

Kynurenines: Tryptophan's metabolites in exercise, inflammation, and mental health color *Science* v357 no6349 p369 Jl 28 2017

Cerveny, Catherine

The Rule of Luck *Publishers Weekly* v264 no38 p58 S 18 2017

Cerveny, Randy

Rainbow Detectives: When Art Gets Meteorology Wrong *Weatherwise* v70 no2 p24 Mr/Ap 2017

Cervical cancer—Diagnosis

THE OTHER BIG C C. Anton *Women's Health* v14 no4 p86 My 2017

Cervical cancer—Prevention

Critics assail paper claiming harm from cancer vaccine D. Normile color graph *Science* v354 no6319 p1514 D 23 2016

Cervical cancer—Risk factors

About Those HPV Rumors... B. Lieberman color *Glamour* v115 no7 p57 Jl 2017

Cervical cancer—Treatment

THE PAIN YOU CAN'T SEE E. Kaplan color *Sports Illustrated* v126 no4 p40 Ja 30 2017

Cervical vertebrae abnormalities

A greater good G. Blatchford and H. Arington color *Equus* no480 p27 S 2017

Cervix uteri tumors—Diagnosis

"I'M REALLY LUCKY" [Cover story] A. Spencer color *Health* v31 no6 p100 Jl 2017

Cervix uteri—Diseases—Prevention

CERVICAL DYSPLASIA & CERVICAL CANCER: NATURAL THERAPIES FOR TREATMENT & PREVENTION M. Schauch color *Better Nutrition* p41 My 2017

Cervix uteri—Physiology

THE OTHER BIG C C. Anton *Women's Health* v14 no4 p86 My 2017

Cervone, Tony

SOUVLAKI SECRETS M. True color *Sunset* v238 no5 p85 My 2017

Cesal, Eric—Interviews

Eric Cesal M. SITZ *Architectural Record* v205 no1 p23 Ja 2017

Cesarean section

baby's position A. PALANJIAN *Parents* v92 no7 p118 Jl 2017

A Mother's Journey A. NADELLA color *Good Housekeeping*

v265 no5 p62 N 2017

CESARI, JOCELYNE

The Nationalist Origins of Political Islam *Current History* v116 no786 p31 Ja 2017

Cescatti, Alessandro

Satellites reveal contrasting responses of regional climate to the widespread greening of Earth diag *Science* v356 no6343 p1180 Je 16 2017

Cesium iodide

NEUTRINO DETECTION GOES SMALL *Physics Today* v70 no10 p29 O 2017

Cespedes, Frank V.

4 Ways to Build a Productive Sales Culture *Harvard Business Review Digital Articles* p2 Je 16 2015

Any Value Proposition Hinges on the Answer to One Question *Harvard Business Review Digital Articles* p2 Ja 13 2015

The Best Ways to Hire Salespeople *Harvard Business Review Digital Articles* p2 N 2 2015

Don't Turn Your Sales Team Loose Without a Strategy *Harvard Business Review Digital Articles* p2 D 15 2015

Find the Right Metrics for Your Sales Team *Harvard Business Review Digital Articles* p2 2017

Get More from Your Event Spending *Harvard Business Review Digital Articles* p2 Mr 31 2015

How Merck Is Trying to Keep Disrupters at Bay *Harvard Business Review Digital Articles* p2 Je 8 2015

Is Social Media Actually Helping Your Company's Bottom Line? *Harvard Business Review Digital Articles* p2 Mr 3 2015

It Doesn't Matter If Competitors Know Your Strategy *Harvard Business Review Digital Articles* p2 N 25 2014

More Universities Need to Teach Sales *Harvard Business Review Digital Articles* p2 Ap 26 2016

Reinvent Your Sales Process While Still Hitting Your Numbers *Harvard Business Review Digital Articles* p2 F 18 2015

Selling to Customers Who Do Their Homework Online *Harvard Business Review Digital Articles* p2 Mr 16 2016

Stop Using Battle Metaphors in Your Company Strategy *Harvard Business Review Digital Articles* p2 D 19 2014

There's No Excuse for Avoiding Strategy *Harvard Business Review Digital Articles* p2 O 28 2014

To Increase Sales, Get Customers to Commit a Little at a Time *Harvard Business Review Digital Articles* p2 Jl 20 2016

What Salespeople Need to Know About the New B2B Landscape *Harvard Business Review Digital Articles* p2 Ag 5 2015

Your Sales Training Is Probably Lackluster. Here's How to Fix It *Harvard Business Review Digital Articles* p2 Je 12 2017

CESSNA, JANICE

Global Rush to Harness Drones Yields Ups and Downs *BioScience* v67 no10 p944 O 2017

The Indomitable Dung Beetle Plays Key Role in Parasite Regulation *BioScience* v67 no6 p583 Je 2017

Cessna, Jerry

Changes in Herd Composition a Key to Indian Dairy Production *Amber Waves: The Economics of Food, Farming, Natural Resources, & Rural America* p5 Je 2017

Historical Analysis of MPP-Dairy Suggests Limited Impact on Average Margins but Considerable Potential for Risk Reduction *Amber Waves: The Economics of Food, Farming, Natural Resources, & Rural America* p7 F 2017

Managing Agricultural Risk Under Different Scenarios: Selected 2014 Farm Act Programs *Amber Waves: The Economics of Food, Farming, Natural Resources, & Rural America* p22 F 2017

Cessna 150 (Private plane)

IN THE REGION OF REVERSED COMMANDS P. Garrison *Flying* v144 no9 p34 S 2017

Cessna 172 (Private plane)

BENCHMARK: SAFE PASSAGE J. KEATS color *Wired* v25 no10 p52 O 2017

Cessna 182 (Private plane)

THE PRIVILEGE OF BEING A PILOT M. Lunken color *Flying* v144 no7 p64 Jl 2017

Cessna aircraft

See also

Cessna 150 (Private plane)

Cessna 172 (Private plane)

AVIATION SIGHTS D. Karl color *Flying* v144 no6 p70 Je 2017

CESSNA 206 [Cover story] R. MARK chart color *Flying* v144 no9 p42 S 2017

LOST SOUL OR GUARDIAN ANGEL? T. TEXTOR color *Flying* v144 no4 p30 Ap 2017

THERE, I SAID IT D. Karl bw color *Flying* v144 no3 p78 Mr 2017

WE FLY: CESSNA CITATION CJ3+ D. KARL chart color *Flying* v144 no11 p40 N 2017

Cessna Aircraft Co.

WE FLY: CESSNA CITATION CJ3+ D. KARL chart color *Flying* v144 no11 p40 N 2017

Cessna aircraft—Accidents

THE UNSEEN P. Garrison *Flying* v144 no11 p34 N 2017

Cetina, Marko

Ultrafast many-body interferometry of impurities coupled to a Fermi sea bibl diag graph *Science* v354 no6308 p96 O 7 2016

Cetinbas, Naniye Malli

The DNA-sensing AIM2 inflammasome controls radiation-induced cell death and tissue injury bibl color graph *Science* v354 no6313 p765 N 11 2016

Cettina, Teri

Best Bets: Online Banks cartoon color *Working Mother* p56 F/Mr 2017

help with hygiene *Parents* v92 no8 p138 Ag 2017

Cevallos, Stephanie A.

Microbiota-activated PPAR-γ signaling inhibits dysbiotic Enterobacteriaceae expansion graph *Science* v357 no6351 p570 Ag 11 2017

Ceverino, D.

Molecular gas in the halo fuels the growth of a massive cluster galaxy at high redshift bibl graph *Science* v354 no6316 p1128 D 2 2016

Ceviche

OCEAn TO TABLE C. Leschin-Hoar color *Sunset* v238 no2 p68 F 2017

CG Technologies (Company)

A Wall Street Legend Flops in Sports Betting B. Louis and C. Palmeri *Bloomberg Businessweek* no4515 p35 Mr 20 2017

Cha, Victor

North Korea: How to Stop Kim Jong Un color *Time* v189 no12 p40 Ap 3 2017

Powerplay: The Origins of the American Alliance System in Asia A. J. Nathan *Foreign Affairs* v95 no6 p190 N/D 2016

Cha, Wonsuk

Bragg coherent diffractive imaging of single-grain defect dynamics in polycrystalline films color graph *Science* v356 no6339 p739 My 19 2017

Chabal, Patrick

Guinea-Bissau: Micro-State to "Narco-State" N. van de Walle *Foreign Affairs* v96 no2 p190 Mr/Ap 2017

Chabin, Michele

American Jews campaign to change Israeli minds about Judaism's diversity *Christian Century* v134 no17 p15 Ag 16 2017

Archaeologists discover ancient Jewish artifacts, part of Jerusalem walls color *Christian Century* v133 no24 p16 N 23 2016

Archaeologists find more signs of Babylonian destruction of Jerusalem color *Christian Century* v134 no18 p15 Ag 30 2017

Christian and Jewish groups form partnerships to care for Holocaust survivors color *Christian Century* v134 no6 p15 Mr 15 2017

Clashes over security at Jerusalem Temple Mount *Christian Century* v134 no17 p14 Ag 16 2017

Hobby Lobby purchase shows ethical problems in the antiquities trade color *Christian Century* v134 no19 p15 S 13 2017

Nonprofit offers Talmud in English online for free *Christian Century* v134 no8 p1 Ap 12 2017

People color *Christian Century* v134 no19 p17 S 13 2017

Chabon, Michael, 1963-

A lover of fiction sets out to find the truth J. G. Phelan *America* v216 no3 p46 F 6 2017

The Amazing Adventures of Wernher von Braun C. LORENTZEN img *New York* v49 no24 p142 N 28 2016

CONFRONTING THE OCCUPATION B. BETHUNE color *Maclean's* p58 Je 2017

Down the Memory Hole *Commentary* v143 no3 p61 Mr 2017

Immoral Equivalence D. J. GREENBAUM *Commentary* v144 no1 p50 Jl/Ag 2017

MOONGLOW E. DONALDSON color *Maclean's* v129 no47 p60 N 28 2016

Nick LAIRD M. Chabon *Interview* v47 no5 p16 Je/Jl 2017

Story After Story [Cover story] A. O. Scott *New York Times Book Review* p1 N 20 2016

The Triumph of Foxy Grandpa F. Prose color *New York Review of Books* v63 no20 p56 D 22 2016

Chabon, Michael, 1963—Interviews

Family Lore B. Kachka img *New York* v49 no23 p78 N 14 2016

Chabris, Christopher

Decision Making *New York Times Book Review* p30 S 24 2017

Chacko, Leslie

Can You Put a Dollar Amount on Your Company's Cyber Risk? *Harvard Business Review Digital Articles* p2 O 5 2016

Chaco Canyon (N.M.)

Seeing CHACO in a NEW LIGHT B. Bower color map *Science News* v191 no10 p16 My 27 2017

Chacon-Cruz, Arturo

Macbeth S. Williams *Opera News* v81 no6 p40 D 2016

CHACOS, BRAD

7 technologies killed in Apple's new MacBook Pro color *Macworld - Digital Edition* p19 D 2016

7 WAYS TO SAVE MONEY WHEN YOU BUILD A PC color *PCWorld* p131 Mr 2017

AMD, Nvidia coin-mining cards appear as gaming GPU shortage intensifies color *PCWorld* v35 no8 p21 Ag 2017

AMD Radeon RX 550: A thrilling budget graphics card with a perplexing price chart color graph *PCWorld* v35 no6 p74 Je 2017

AMD Radeon RX Vega: Vega 56, Vega 64, and liquid-cooled Vega 64 tested chart color graph *PCWorld* v35 no10 p23 O 2017

AMD's FreeSync 2 tech debuts in a wild 49-inch Samsung HDR monitor color *PCWorld* v35 no7 p25 Jl 2017

AMD's Ryzen 3 lineup brings competitive quad-core CPUs to the masses color *PCWorld* v35 no8 p14 Ag 2017

AMD's Ryzen processors will launch before March 3, GDC slip-up reveals color *PCWorld* v35 no2 p9 F 2017

Equifax hack: How to know if you're affected color *PCWorld* v35 no10 p7 O 2017

Every custom GeForce GTX 1080 Ti graphics card revealed so far color *PCWorld* v35 no4 p14 Ap 2017

Everything Microsoft revealed: Surface Studio, Windows 10 Creators Update, and more color *PCWorld* p8 D 2016

EVGA GTX 1060 3GB: A compelling $200 graphics card with a questionable future color graph *PCWorld* p81 O 2016

EVGA GTX 1080 Ti SC2: A ferocious graphics card with a radical cooler chart color graph *PCWorld* v35 no6 p55 Je 2017

EVGA's sensor-laden iCX technology revolutionizes graphics card cooling color graph *PCWorld* p102 Mr 2017

GeForce GTX 970 settlement website opens, Nvidia will pay graphics card owners $30 color *PCWorld* p32 O 2016

Google Chrome will start blocking noisy autoplay videos in January color *PCWorld* v35 no10 p14 O 2017

Go PC! 5 killer MacBook Pro alternatives for disappointed Apple fans [Cover story] color *PCWorld* p41 D 2016

Meet the Corsair One, Corsair's 'category-defying' gaming PC debut color *PCWorld* p27 Mr 2017

Microsoft Build's biggest reveals: building the future color *PCWorld* v35 no6 p14 Je 2017

Nvidia GeForce GTX 1080 Ti: The monster graphics card 4K gamers have been waiting for chart color graph *PCWorld* v35 no4 p110 Ap 2017

Nvidia's beastly Titan Xp steals the performance crown from the GTX 1080 Ti color *PCWorld* v35 no5 p31 My 2017

Nvidia's GeForce GTX 1050 and GTX 1050 Ti can give prebuilt PCs a big boost bw chart color *PCWorld* v35 no11 p13 N 2016

Nvidia supercharges GeForce DirectX 12 performance with new Game Ready driver color *PCWorld* v35 no4 p24 Ap 2017

Ryzen 51600X: Building a versatile work-and-play PC with AMD's 6-core CPU champion color graph *PCWorld* v35 no5 p175 My 2017

Ryzen CPUs explained: Everything you need to know about AMD's disruptive multicore chips color *PCWorld* v35 no5 p13 My 2017

Sapphire Radeon RX 570 Pulse and RX 580 Pulse: Solid gaming

on a tight budget chart color graph *PCWorld* v35 no7 p128 Jl 2017

VIRTUAL REALITY, ONE YEAR OUT: What went right, what didn't color *PCWorld* p141 Mr 2017

WHY YOU SHOULD TRY LINUX TODAY: 6 compelling reasons color *PCWorld* p157 D 2016

Windows 10 Creators Update FAQ: Everything you need to know [Cover story] color *PCWorld* v35 no5 p9 My 2017

The Windows 10 CREATORS UPDATE'S BEST NEW FEATURES: Dynamic Lock, Game Mode, privacy tweaks color *PCWorld* v35 no2 p151 F 2017

Windows 10's Game Mode makes unplayable games playable—sometimes color graph *PCWorld* v35 no5 p86 My 2017

Xbox Project Scorpio specs revealed: Microsoft's next console is a Radeon-infused monster chart color *PCWorld* v35 no5 p46 My 2017

CHADBURN, MELISSA

Uncanny Powers: Feminist fiction by one of the Philippines' greatest (male) writers *New York Times Book Review* p8 S 3 2017

Chade-Meng Tan

Just 6 Seconds of Mindfulness Can Make You More Effective *Harvard Business Review Digital Articles* p2 D 30 2015

Chadwick, Bruce

Birth of the Blue: Bumbling constables led to the rise of New York's police force W. JAMIESON *New York Times Book Review* p16 Jl 2 2017

Fuzzy History V. J. CANNATO color *Weekly Standard* v22 no42 p33 Jl 17 2017

CHADWICK, JEF

THANKS FOR THE RIDE color *Bicycling* v58 no10 p15 N/D 2017

Chadwick, Justin, 1968-

Love in a Bubble J. Weisenthal cartoon *Bloomberg Businessweek* no4536 p70 S 4 2017

Chadwick, Melanie

Is your skin freaking out? color *Health* v31 no8 p25 O 2017

the secret to lush lashes color *Better Homes & Gardens* v95 no11 p26 N 2017

your get-real SUN-CARE GUIDE cartoon color *Better Homes & Gardens* v95 no6 p18 Je 2017

Chadwick, William W., Jr.

Inflation-predictable behavior and co-eruption deformation at Axial Seamount bibl graph map *Science* v354 no6318 p1399 D 16 2016

Chae, Doyoun (Grace)

Why a Messy Workspace Undermines Your Persistence *Harvard Business Review Digital Articles* p2 Ja 22 2015

Chaetognatha

Ancient sea worm had a head full of spines L. Hamers bw color *Science News* v192 no3 p4 S 2 2017

CHAEY, CHRISTINA

Steam Power color *Bon Appetit* v62 no4 p46 Ap 2017

Chaffetz, Jason

PARODY J. Chaffetz color *Weekly Standard* v22 no27 p44 Mr 20 2017

Resist and Persist J. NICHOLS color *Nation* v304 no7 p3 Mr 6 2017

CHAFFIN, BRIAN C.

Ecology for the Shrinking City *BioScience* v66 no11 p965 N 1 2016

Chafkin, Max

All the News That's Fit to Click color *Bloomberg Businessweek* no4498 p81 N 7 2016

America's relationship with Mark Zuckerberg is It's complicated color graph *Bloomberg Businessweek* no4539 p50 S 25 2017

THE BILLION-DOLLAR WAR Over an $18 Part color graph *Bloomberg Businessweek* no4541 p52 O 9 2017

Can a lonely man in a tiny bedroom deliver a real October surprise? color *Bloomberg Businessweek* no4495 p62 O 17 2016

Changing Lanes color *Bloomberg Businessweek* no4528 p60 Je 26 2017

Dropbox's Drew Houston color *Bloomberg Businessweek* no4526 p40 Je 12 2017

FURY ROAD color *Bloomberg Businessweek* no4515 p54 Mr 20 2017

Get Your Own Broadband cartoon map *Bloomberg Businessweek*

no4496 p38 O 24 2016

Google Returns to Earth color *Bloomberg Businessweek* no4503 p44 D 12 2016

GOT ANY IDEAS? [Cover story] color graph *Bloomberg Businessweek* no4517 p48 Ap 3 2017

In Case of Low Revenue cartoon *Bloomberg Businessweek* no4497 p50 O 31 2016

Innovation color *Bloomberg Businessweek* no4522 p41 My 15 2017

Insta-fluencer color *Bloomberg Businessweek* no4502 p66 D 5 2016

IS WIKIPEDIA WOKE? color *Bloomberg Businessweek* no4505 p70 D 26 2016

LEAVE my ETSY ALONE bw color *Bloomberg Businessweek* no4523 p48 My 22 2017

Lifestyles of the Rich and Not-Quite Internet Famous color *Bloomberg Businessweek* no4524 p63 My 29 2017

THE SEVEN HABITS OF HIGHLY EFFECTIVE DRUG DEALERS color *Bloomberg Businessweek* no4520 p74 My 1 2017

The Slow-Motion Bust cartoon graph *Bloomberg Businessweek* no4496 p30 O 24 2016

This Kushner Likes Obamacare bw *Bloomberg Businessweek* no4527 p22 Je 19 2017

TUNNEL VISION color *Bloomberg Businessweek* no4512 p52 F 20 2017

Chagall, Marc, 1887-1985

Contemporary crucifixion J. Bleem il *U.S. Catholic* v82 no4 p50 Ap 2017

Chagall, Marc, 1887-1985—Exhibitions

A symphony of Chagall in Montreal cartoon *Magazine Antiques* v184 no1 p38 Ja/F 2017

Chahed, Youssef

Can Tunisia Remain a Beacon of Democracy for the Arab World? I. Bremmer color *Time* v190 no5 p21 Jl 31 2017

Chahine, Teresa

The business of doing good O. Bagasra color *Science* v354 no6310 p294 O 21 2016

CHAHINIAN, HAIG

Walking the Walk *O, The Oprah Magazine* p136 My 2017

Chai, Jiani N.

Lactobacillus reuteri induces gut intraepithelial CD4+CD8αα+ T cells diag graph *Science* v357 no6353 p806 Ag 25 2017

CHAI, JULIE

garden IN A VASE color *Better Homes & Gardens* v95 no5 p80 My 2017

A Garden of Her Own *Martha Stewart Living* no268 p52 O 2016

Chaigne, Antoine

Acoustics of Musical Instruments B. Greenhut *Physics Today* v70 no4 p58 Ap 2017

Chaikeeratisak, Vorrapon

Assembly of a nucleus-like structure during viral replication in bacteria bibl color graph *Science* v355 no6321 p1 Ja 13 2017

Chaikin, Carly

Carly Chaikin P. KITA cartoon color *Men's Health* v32 no9 p38 N 2017

CHAIKIN, MARC

Build the Wall! Por Favor color *Forbes* v199 no6 p66 Je 13 2017

Chain, The (Music)

SOUNDTRACK SOUND-OFF: VOL. 2'S BEST TRACKS E. R. Brown color *Entertainment Weekly* no1465 p41 My 12 2017

Chain of being (Philosophy)

Great Chain of Contempt F. H. BUCKLEY *American Conservative* v15 no6 p27 N/D 2016

Chain restaurants

13 AND COUNTING N. E. WILLIAMS color *Black Enterprise* v47 no8 p16 Jl/Ag 2017

FOR WHICH WICH, SUCCESS IS IN THE BAG D. Eng color *Fortune* v175 no6 p17 My 1 2017

How a Fast Casual Chain Shows Employees Their Work Matters J. Olinto *Harvard Business Review Digital Articles* p2 N 19 2015

Chain restaurants management

Pizza to go. And go. And go C. MCINTYRE color *Maclean's* v130 no9 p70 O 2017

Chain saws

AGAINST THE GRAIN W. Cornwall bw color map *Science* v357 no6359 p24 O 6 2017

BULLDOZERS VS. CHAINSAWS Z. S. George color *Powder* v45 no3 p50 N 2016

Chain saws—Evaluation

CORDLESS ELECTRIC CHAINSAWS R. ROMANSKI color *Popular Mechanics* p94 N 2017

Chain stores

Amazon Books Will Be the Nation's Fifth-Largest Bookstore Chain J. Milliot chart color *Publishers Weekly* v264 no23 p6 Je 5 2017

Shopping Spree L. Murtha *Cincinnati Magazine* v50 no5 p66 F 2017

SOMETHING WITCHY THIS WAY COMES S. MIKULAN *Los Angeles Magazine* p128 D 2016

CHAINANI, SOMAN

Saints and Sinners *New York Times Book Review* p19 O 9 2016

Chains

How to reeve a new halyard D. Everitt cartoon color *Sail* v48 no1 p56 Ja 2017

The Key to Your Next Fashion Move color *GQ: Gentlemen's Quarterly* v97 no5 p32 My 2017

Chainsmokers, The (Performer)

The Chainsmokers J. Goodman color *Entertainment Weekly* no1444/1445 p29 D 16 2016

DUDES OF THE DANCE J. Weiner color *Rolling Stone* no1272 p38 O 20 2016

Chair design & construction

Power Bloc H. MARTIN color *Architectural Digest* no6 p46 Je 1 2017

Securing Loose Stretchers R. Tschoepe diag *Old House Journal* v45 no6 p60 S 2017

Chairish (Company)

What I Wear to Work: ANNA BROCKWAY J. Chen color *Bloomberg Businessweek* no4499 p87 N 14 2016

Chairman of the board

Meet the New Chair *Parks & Recreation* v51 no10 p10 O 2016

Chairman Spaceman (Short story)

CHAIRMAN SPACEMAN T. PIERCE cartoon color *New Yorker* v92 no45 p68 Ja 16 2017

Chairs

See also

Armchairs

Folding chairs

Rocking chairs

A Day at the Beach N. RICHARDSON color *Bon Appetit* v62 no7 p18 Jl 2017

Fun For the Kids *Treasures* v6 no3 p6 D 2016/Ja 2017

furniture & decorative accessories *Design Center Sourcebook* p56 2017

GOINGS ON ABOUT TOWN color *New Yorker* v93 no22 p6 Jl 31 2017

Hot Seat H. MARTIN bw color *Architectural Digest* v74 no2 p12 F 2017

More Room More Seats More Money R. Minetor *Stage Directions* v29 no12 p14 D 2016

scandinavian STORYBOOK B. D. Coleman color *Old House Journal* v45 no3 p14 My 2017

Shell Shock H. MARTIN color *Architectural Digest* v74 no9 p30 S 2017

Chairs in art

William and Mary Carved crest leather back side chair with pierced front stretcher color *Magazine Antiques* v183 no6 p13 N/D 2016

Chairs—Design & construction

Movable Chairs S. Myrick *Parks & Recreation* v51 no11 p64 N 2016

PORCH PREP B. THORKELSON color *Better Homes & Gardens* v95 no5 p54 My 2017

Take Make a Seat J. Oltion *Sky & Telescope* v132 no6 p70 D 2016

Chairs—Design & construction—Evaluation

ReTRO-A-Go-Go J. BREWSTER color *Cabin Living* p38 D 2016

Chairs—Evaluation

Adam's Home STYLE SHEET Adam color *O, The Oprah Magazine* p44 Ja 2017

Back to Mid-century M. E. Polson color *Old House Journal* v45 no3 p76 My 2017

BH&G throwback 1961 MIDCENTURY MODERN L. HED-

RICK color *Better Homes & Gardens* v95 no10 p186 O 2017

Big Ideas for Tight Spots C. SWANSON color *House Beautiful* v159 no5 p59 Je 2017

Blurred Lines K. L. Beamon *Architectural Record* v205 no9 p65 S 2017

DELFT BLUE M. B. EYERS color *Better Homes & Gardens* v95 no8 p26 Ag 2017

EDITORS' CHOICE AWARDS color map *Backpacker* v45 no3 p13 Ap 2017

Have a Seat A. BENNETT color *Cabin Living* p74 Ja/F 2017

The House Always Wins K. O'SHEA-EVANS color *House Beautiful* v159 no8 p35 O 2017

I LOVE IT E. GAUKEL *Treasures* v6 no3 p48 D 2016/Ja 2017

My Dog Reviews the Furniture He Has Eaten A. SIMMONS *Reader's Digest* v188 no1124 p15 O 2016

OBSESSED WITH RUSHES, REEDS & GRASSES E. S. SOTO color *Better Homes & Gardens* v95 no3 p10 Mr 2017

ONYX AND ECRU L. BIRCH color *House Beautiful* p17 Ag 2017

PERSONAL EFFECTS S. Morrow color *Martha Stewart Living* no271 p96 Ja/F 2017

A ROOM OF HER OWN Y. Huh color *House Beautiful* v159 no5 p54 Je 2017

THE SHAKER CHAIR color *Old House Journal* v45 no2 p78 Ap 2017

SHOULDER ON color *Esquire* v167 no2 p68 Mr 2017

Thoroughly Modern Charlotte color *House Beautiful* v159 no1 p35 F 2017

TROPICAL PUNCH color *Better Homes & Gardens* v95 no2 p24 F 2016

Welcome Effects A. Kwun *Architectural Record* v205 no4 p93 Ap 2017

Werk It P. BOWIE LARSON color *Architectural Digest* v74 no10 p42 O 1 2017

Chairs—History

Up Rising H. MARTIN color *Architectural Digest* v74 no10 p30 O 1 2017

Chairs—Maintenance & repair

Securing Loose Stretchers R. Tschoepe diag *Old House Journal* v45 no6 p60 S 2017

Chaisson, Patrick J.

PASSING THE TORCH: Volunteers Keep Outdoor Traditions Alive *New York State Conservationist* v72 no2 p26 O 2017

Chait, Jonathan

Citizens, United img *New York* v49 no23 p12 N 14 2016

Cleveland: Four Days in Donald Trump's America img *New York* v49 no15 p13 Jl 25 2016

Dead Center T. SHENK color il *New Republic* v248 no1/2 p61 Ja/F 2017

Fact Finders *New Republic* v248 no5 p4 My 2017

FROM THE REARVIEW MIRROR R. L. BOROSAGE color *Nation* v304 no15 p35 My 8 2017

THE GOP'S AGE OF AUTHORITARIANISM HAS ONLY JUST BEGUN AND IT WILL NOT END WITH A CLINTON PRESIDENCY img *New York* v49 no22 p52 O 31 2016

The Kleptocracy Preps for Pennsylvania Avenue img *New York* v49 no24 p29 N 28 2016

Mythical President B. DOMENECH color *National Review* v69 no3 p43 F 20 2017

The National Interest: Jonathan Chait img *New York* v50 no8 p15 Ap 17 2017

OBAMA'S AMERICA img *New York* v49 no20 p12 O 3 2016

Obama's Considerable, if Shaky, Legacy M. Cooper *Washington Monthly* p11 Ja/F 2017

A Pat on My Own Back *Weekly Standard* v22 no8 p2 O 31 2016

The White Nationalist House The GOP once drew the line at Nazis img *New York* v50 no17 p31 Ag 21 2017

Yes He Did P. BAKER *New York Times Book Review* p9 Ja 22 2017

Chaix, L.

Femtosecond electron-phonon lock-in by photoemission and x-ray free-electron laser chart diag *Science* v357 no6346 p71 Jl 7 2017

Chaker, Zayna

Hypothalamic regulation of regionally distinct adult neural stem cells and neurogenesis diag *Science* v356 no6345 p1383 Je 30 2017

Chaker-Margot, Malik

Architecture of the yeast small subunit processome bibl color *Science* v355 no6321 p1 Ja 13 2017

Chakoian, Christine

LIVING BY The Word *Christian Century* v134 no6 p21 Mr 15 2017

Chakrabarti, Tamoghna

Quantum dot–induced phase stabilization of α-CsPbI3 perovskite for high-efficiency photovoltaics bibl chart graph *Science* v354 no6308 p92 O 7 2016

Chakrabarti, Vishaan—Interviews

Vishaan Chakrabarti S. STEPHENS *Architectural Record* v204 no11 p30 N 2016

Chakrabarty, Prosanta

Empowerment color *Science* v356 no6335 p242 Ap 21 2017

Chakraborty, Raja

Clonal hematopoiesis associated with TET2 deficiency accelerates atherosclerosis development in mice bibl diag *Science* v355 no6327 p842 F 24 2017

Chakras

MEET YOUR CHAKRAS Zya color *Essence* v48 no5 p116 S 2017

Chakravarty, Probir

The linker histone H1.0 generates epigenetic and functional intra-tumor heterogeneity bibl graph *Science* v353 no6307 paaf1644-1 S 30 2016

Chakravorti, Bhaskar

60 Countries' Digital Competitiveness, Indexed *Harvard Business Review Digital Articles* p2 Jl 12 2017

The Battle Over iPhones in India *Harvard Business Review Digital Articles* p2 Ap 19 2016

Brexit Could Deepen Europe's Digital Recession *Harvard Business Review Digital Articles* p2 Jl 5 2016

China's New Development Bank Is a Wake-Up Call for Washington *Harvard Business Review Digital Articles* p2 Ap 20 2015

The Countries That Would Profit Most from a Cashless World *Harvard Business Review Digital Articles* p2 My 31 2016

Early Lessons from India's Demonetization Experiment *Harvard Business Review Digital Articles* p2 Mr 14 2017

Europe's Other Crisis: A Digital Recession *Harvard Business Review Digital Articles* p2 O 27 2015

How Benchmarking Can Help Countries Become More Digital *Harvard Business Review Digital Articles* p2 Mr 8 2016

How Companies Can Champion Sustainable Development *Harvard Business Review Digital Articles* p2 Mr 14 2017

Lessons from Facebook's Fumble in India *Harvard Business Review Digital Articles* p2 F 16 2016

The Missing Political Debate Over the Digital Economy *Harvard Business Review Digital Articles* p2 O 6 2016

The "Smart Society" of the Future Doesn't Look Like Science Fiction *Harvard Business Review Digital Articles* p2 O 5 2017

Unilever's Big Strategic Bet on the Dollar Shave Club *Harvard Business Review Digital Articles* p2 Jl 28 2016

What Businesses Need to Know About Sustainable Development Goals *Harvard Business Review Digital Articles* p2 N 20 2015

What the CEO of the "New" Google Needs to Do Next *Harvard Business Review Digital Articles* p2 S 1 2015

Where the Digital Economy Is Moving the Fastest *Harvard Business Review Digital Articles* p2 F 19 2015

Would a Hard Brexit Cripple the EU's Digital Economy? *Harvard Business Review Digital Articles* p2 Jl 18 2017

CHAKRAVORTY, SWAGATO

Cinema without Reflection: Jacques Derrida's Echopoiesis and Narcissism Adrift *Film Quarterly* v70 no3 p98 Spr 2017

Chalamet, Timothee

Making a Name M. GUIDUCCI color *Vogue* v207 no11 p168 N 2017

Timothée CHALAMET M. Mcconaughey *Interview* v47 no5 p42 Je/Jl 2017

Chalets

TNT E. TNT color *Vogue* v207 no4 p162 Ap 2017

Chalfont (Pa.)—History

Friendsgiving A. Fenwick and T. Keith color *Sports Illustrated* v125 no18 p24 D 5 2016

Chalices

See also
Grail

Take and drink D. Philippart color *U.S. Catholic* v82 no6 p33 Je 2017

Chalker, Justin M.

Posttranslational mutagenesis: A chemical strategy for exploring protein side-chain diversity diag *Science* v354 no6312 p597 N 4 2016

Challem, Jack

HEAD OFF MIGRAINES color *Amazing Wellness* v8 no6 p32 Early Winter2016

just beet it! color *Amazing Wellness* v9 no1 p56 Wint 2017

KEEP YOUR MIND SHARP color *Amazing Wellness* v8 no2 p32 Spr 2016

Challenge, The (Film)

The Challenge V. LUCCA color *Film Comment* v53 no5 p71 S/O 2017

Challenger (Spacecraft)—Accidents

Fire in the Sky C. Klosterman color *AARP: The Magazine* v59 no1A p26 D 2015/Ja 2016

Challenger, John A.

Have I Got a Job for You *USA Today Magazine* v145 no2864 p25 My 2017

Start Me Up ... or not *USA Today Magazine* v145 no2863 p12 Ap 2017

Challenger automobile

2018 Dodge Challenger SRT Demon C. Walton color *Motor Trend* v69 no10 p18 O 2017

9.65 AT 140 [Cover story] D. R. Glad color *Hot Rod* v70 no7 p22 Jl 2017

The Drivetrain in Kevin Maher's 1971 Dodge Challenger Has a Serious and Constant Vibration. We're Gonna Fix It M. Davis chart color diag *Hot Rod* v70 no4 p88 Ap 2017

One Tool to Rule Them All K. C. Colwell color *Car & Driver* v63 no4 p96 O 2017

RETURN OF THE T/A B. Iger color *Hot Rod* v70 no8 p48 Ag 2017

the year in review *Car & Driver* v62 no7 p17 Ja 2017

Challenge XXX: Dirty Thirty, The (TV program)

The Challenge Hall of Fame B. L. Heldman color *Entertainment Weekly* no1474/1475 p107 Jl 21-28 2017

Challman, Becca

Terror's Afterlife: Do suicide bombers think their victims are headed to paradise as well? *Humanist* v77 no4 p6 Jl/Ag 2017

Challoner, Jack

The Cell S. Hurtley color *Science* v354 no6317 p1229 D 9 2016

Cham, James

The Competitive Landscape for Machine Intelligence *Harvard Business Review Digital Articles* p2 N 2 2016

Chamber music

ABOVE & BEYOND cartoon *New Yorker* v93 no17 p16 Je 19 2017

Chamber of Commerce of the United States of America

Fighting Government's Fourth Branch T. J. DONOHUE *Weekly Standard* v22 no15 p9 D 19 2016

A Growth Agenda to Unite All Americans T. J. DONOHUE *Weekly Standard* v22 no18 p9 Ja 16 2017

IP: The Roots of Innovation T. J. Donohue *Weekly Standard* v22 no23 p11 F 20 2017

It's Time to Build T. J. DONOHUE *Weekly Standard* v22 no35 p29 My 22 2017

Meet Small Business Owners Who Depend on Trade T. J. DONOHUE *Weekly Standard* v22 no39 p31 Je 19 2017

Opportunity by the Truckload T. J. DONOHUE *Weekly Standard* v22 no16 p8 D 26 2016

Progress on Limiting Health Insurance Costs Still Possible T. J. DONOHUE *Weekly Standard* v23 no2 p27 S 18 2017

Speaking Up for Free Speech T. J. DONOHUE *Weekly Standard* v22 no43 p8 Jl 24 2017

Trade and Growth Protect Against Global Turmoil T. J. DONOHUE *Weekly Standard* v22 no21 p19 F 6 2017

Welcome to the Neighborhood, President Trump T. J. DONOHUE *Weekly Standard* v22 no20 p8 Ja 30 2017

When Disaster Strikes, Businesses Rise to Help T. J. Donohue *Weekly Standard* v22 no8 p19 O 31 2016

When Disaster Strikes, Businesses Step Up T. J. DONOHUE *Weekly Standard* v23 no3 p9 S 25 2017

Chamber of Commerce of the United States of America—Congresses

Innovation That's Out of This World T. J. Donohue *Weekly Standard* v22 no26 p25 Mr 13 2017

Chamberlain, Andrew

What Matters More to Your Workforce than Money color *Harvard Business Review Digital Articles* p2 Ja 17 2017

Chamberlain, Jess

Beauty color *Sunset* v237 no5 p60 N 2016

BEST OF THE WEST color *Sunset* v238 no1 p11 Ja 2017

BEST OF THE WEST color *Sunset* v238 no4 p17 Ap 2017

BEST OF THE WEST color *Sunset* v238 no6 p9 Je 2017

TINY HOME BIG DREAMS color *Sunset* v238 no1 p70 Ja 2017

TOW TAPPERS color *Sunset* v239 no1 p32 Jl 2017

TREASURE ISLAND color *Sunset* v238 no3 p29 Mr 2017

Chamberlain, Sarah

THE TALK STOPS HERE: For a year, this GOP strategist listened to voters' problems. Now she's ready to act E. Plott *Washingtonian Magazine* v52 no8 p22 My 2017

Chambers, Ernest William, 1937-

I AM WHAT I AM AND OTHER TRUTHS E. Chambers *Humanist* v76 no6 p25 N/D 2016

Chambers, James—Finance

The Class of 2016 L. KROLL and J. WANG cartoon chart *Forbes* v198 no5 p36 O 25 2016

CHAMBERS, LORI

Jordan's Principle *American Indian Quarterly* v41 no2 p101 Spr 2017

Chambers, Sam

Marlboro color *Bloomberg Businessweek* no4514 p46 Mr 13 2017

CHAMBERS, THOMAS

TRUMP TAKES UP THE MANTLE OF OLD HICKORY *USA Today Magazine* v145 no2864 p14 My 2017

Chambers, Veronica

Finding more happiness in the holidays color *Redbook* p116 D 2016

The Meaning of Michelle: 15 Writers on the Iconic First Lady and How Her Journey Inspires Our Own *Publishers Weekly* v263 no44 p62 O 31 2016

Michelle, Our Belle P. H. Bass color *Essence* v47 no10 p60 F 2017

Things Fall Apart *New York Times Book Review* p17 N 20 2016

Chambers, Veronica—Interviews

The Meaning of Michelle E. Egan, B. Little et al bw color *Glamour* v114 no12 p198 D 2016

Chamblee, Brandel, 1962-

ON THE ROAD WITH... BRANDEL CHAMBLEE J. Passov color *Golf Magazine* v59 no3 p110 Mr 2017

CHAMBLISS, LAUREN

Society Is Ready for a New Kind of Science--Is Academia? *BioScience* v67 no7 p591 Jl 2017

Chambon, Pierre

Regeneration of fat cells from myofibroblasts during wound healing bibl color graph *Science* v355 no6326 p748 F 17 2017

Chameleon (Music)

Herbie Hancock's Synthesizer Solo on 'Chameleon' J. DURSO color *Downbeat* v84 no9 p96 S 2017

Chameleons

OFF LINE color *Bike Magazine* v24 no4 p114 Je 2017

Chamessian, Alexander

Pain regulation by non-neuronal cells and inflammation bibl diag *Science* v354 no6312 p572 N 4 2016

Chamois

master of (dis)repair k. butcher color *Bike Magazine* v24 no1 p60 Ja/F 2017

Chamorro-Premuzic, Tomas

3 Emerging Alternatives to Traditional Hiring Methods *Harvard Business Review Digital Articles* p2 Je 26 2015

5 Signs It's Time for a New Job *Harvard Business Review Digital Articles* p2 Ap 7 2015

Are CEOs Overhyped and Overpaid? *Harvard Business Review Digital Articles* p2 N 1 2016

The Best Managers Are Boring Managers *Harvard Business Review Digital Articles* p2 S 28 2015

Can AI Ever Be as Curious as Humans? color *Harvard Business Review Digital Articles* p2 Ap 5 2017

A CEO's Personality Can Undermine Succession Planning *Harvard Business Review Digital Articles* p2 S 15 2016

COULD YOUR PERSONALITY DERAIL YOUR CAREER? DON'T TAKE THESE TRAITS TO THE EXTREME chart il img *Harvard Business Review* v95 no5 p138 S/O 2017

The Dark Side of Creativity *Harvard Business Review Digital Articles* p2 N 24 2015

The Dark Side of High Employee Engagement *Harvard Business Review Digital Articles* p2 Ag 16 2016

Does Diversity Actually Increase Creativity? *Harvard Business Review Digital Articles* p2 Je 28 2017

The Downsides of Being Very Emotionally Intelligent color *Harvard Business Review Digital Articles* p2 Ja 12 2017

Great Teams Are About Personalities, Not Just Skills color *Harvard Business Review Digital Articles* p2 Ja 25 2017

The Health Risks of Business Travel *Harvard Business Review Digital Articles* p2 N 3 2015

How and Why We Lie at Work *Harvard Business Review Digital Articles* p2 Ja 2 2015

How to Deal with a Boss Who Stresses You Out *Harvard Business Review Digital Articles* p2 Jl 19 2017

How to Make Work More Meaningful for Your Team *Harvard Business Review Digital Articles* p2 Ag 9 2017

How to Manage a Team of B Players *Harvard Business Review Digital Articles* p2 Jl 13 2015

How to Tell Leaders They're Not as Great as They Think They Are *Harvard Business Review Digital Articles* p2 Mr 29 2017

How to Work with People Who Aren't Good at Working with People *Harvard Business Review Digital Articles* p2 My 26 2015

If You Want to Motivate Employees, Stop Trusting Your Instincts color *Harvard Business Review Digital Articles* p2 F 8 2017

Is How You Deliver Feedback Doing More Harm than Good? *Harvard Business Review Digital Articles* p2 Ag 10 2015

It's the Company's Job to Help Employees Learn *Harvard Business Review Digital Articles* p2 Jl 18 2016

Marissa Mayer's Departure from Yahoo and the Challenge of Drawing Lessons from an N of 1 *Harvard Business Review Digital Articles* p2 Je 15 2017

Maybe Your Team Doesn't Need to Be More Creative *Harvard Business Review Digital Articles* p2 N 27 2015

More Data Won't Turn Employees into High- Performing Machines *Harvard Business Review Digital Articles* p2 O 30 2014

Personality Tests Can Help Balance a Team *Harvard Business Review Digital Articles* p2 Mr 19 2015

The Personality Traits of Good Negotiators *Harvard Business Review Digital Articles* p2 Ag 7 2017

Persuasion Depends Mostly on the Audience *Harvard Business Review Digital Articles* p2 Je 2 2015

The Pros and Cons of Robot Managers *Harvard Business Review Digital Articles* p2 D 12 2016

The Psychological Underpinnings of This Strange Political Summer *Harvard Business Review Digital Articles* p2 Jl 14 2016

Should Your Voice Determine Whether You Get Hired? *Harvard Business Review Digital Articles* p2 Ap 20 2015

Strengths-Based Coaching Can Actually Weaken You *Harvard Business Review Digital Articles* p2 Ja 4 2016

The Talent Delusion *People Management* p52 Mr 2017

To Motivate Employees, Help Them Do Their Jobs Better *Harvard Business Review Digital Articles* p2 N 12 2014

The Underlying Psychology of Office Politics *Harvard Business Review Digital Articles* p2 D 25 2014

What Leadership Looks Like in Different Cultures *Harvard Business Review Digital Articles* p2 My 6 2016

What Science Says About Identifying High-Potential Employees *Harvard Business Review Digital Articles* p2 O 3 2017

When Leaders Are Hired for Talent but Fired for Not Fitting In *Harvard Business Review Digital Articles* p2 Je 14 2017

Why Bad Guys Win at Work *Harvard Business Review Digital Articles* p2 N 2 2015

Why Brainstorming Works Better Online *Harvard Business Review Digital Articles* p2 Ap 2 2015

Why Group Brainstorming Is a Waste of Time *Harvard Business Review Digital Articles* p2 Mr 25 2015

Why We Keep Hiring Narcissistic CEOs *Harvard Business Review Digital Articles* p2 N 29 2016

Why We're So Hypocritical About Online Privacy *Harvard Business*

ness Review Digital Articles* p1 My 1 2017

You Can Teach Someone to Be More Creative *Harvard Business Review Digital Articles* p2 F 23 2015

Chamovitz, Daniel A.

Wild emmer genome architecture and diversity elucidate wheat evolution and domestication color *Science* v357 no6346 p93 Jl 7 2017

Champagne (Wine)

BETTER BUBBLES J. Hoy color *Rodale's Organic Life* v2 no7 p41 D 2016/Ja 2017

Bubbling Up: Afton's Thibaut-Janisson Winery brings sparkling wine to the forefront W. SHEPPARD *Virginia Living* v15 no6 p45 O 2017

A GOLDEN RAY Cynthia and K. Hansen color *Cabin Living* p16 Ja/F 2017

HAPPY TO HOST R. DOLGIN color *Martha Stewart Living* no275 p28 Je 2017

Large and in Charge M. A. ROSS color *Bon Appetit* v61 no12 p58 D 2016 /Jan2017

LETTER FROM THE EDITOR J. STOWE *Cincinnati Magazine* v50 no3 p24 D 2016

Notes from Underground M. Krigbaum color *Conde Nast Traveler* v51 no11 p118 D 2016

Champagne, Michael

THE ROAD TO MERCY S. Livingston color *America* v217 no5 p26 S 4 2017

Champagne Louis Roederer SA

Bubble Bath B. MORTON *Cincinnati Magazine* v50 no3 p136 D 2016

Champion, David

Brexit and the Triumph of Insularity *Harvard Business Review Digital Articles* p2 Je 24 2016

A CONVERSATION WITH INTUIT CHAIRMAN AND CO-FOUNDER SCOTT COOK [Cover story] color *Harvard Business Review* v95 no1 p62 Ja/F 2017

A CONVERSATION WITH JØRGEN VIG KNUDSTORP, CO-CHAIRMAN OF THE LEGO BRAND GROUP [Cover story] color *Harvard Business Review* v95 no1 p58 Ja/F 2017

The Leadership Behaviors That Make or Break a Global Team *Harvard Business Review Digital Articles* p2 Je 22 2015

Champion, Marc

Après le Champagne, More Campaign color graph *Bloomberg Businessweek* no4522 p34 My 15 2017

Blame Automation, Not Immigration color *Bloomberg Businessweek* no4513 p30 Mr 6 2017

Erdogan's Empire State of Mind color *Bloomberg Businessweek* no4511 p14 F 13 2017

Germany Stays in the Center *Bloomberg Businessweek* no4538 p12 S 18 2017

Give This Man A Party color *Bloomberg Businessweek* no4520 p27 My 1 2017

In Poland, the Stench Of Swamp Clearing color map *Bloomberg Businessweek* no4505 p17 D 26 2016

Iran Has a 1 Percent Too, and It's Pro-West cartoon *Bloomberg Businessweek* no4495 p14 O 17 2016

Iran's Islamic Evolution color *Bloomberg Businessweek* no4524 p14 My 29 2017

Russia's Deadly Mideast Game *Bloomberg Businessweek* no4505 p16 D 26 2016

Championships

See also

World championships

2017 SCHEDULE chart *Dirt Sports + Off-Road* v51 no5 p72 My 2017

Duel of the Duals T. Taylor color *Hot Rod* v70 no4 p10 Ap 2017

Holding All the Cards B. Hall color *AARP: The Magazine* v60 no5A p64 Ag/S 2017

Omaha: A World Cup Legacy N. Jaffer *In Stride* v12 no3 p20 My 2017

TALK color graph *Horse & Rider* v56 no6 p24 Je 2017

Wrangler TRC color *Spin to Win Rodeo* v20 no10 p28 D 2016

WRCA World Championship Ranch Rodeo color *Horse & Rider* v56 no11 p28 N 2017

Zippos ATM N. Chirico color *Horse & Rider* v56 no6 p23 Je 2017

Championships—History

Double Trouble M. Rosenberg color *Sports Illustrated* v126 no3

p60 Ja 23 2017

Dreams Redeemed W. Leitch and T. Keith color *Sports Illustrated* v127 no1 p24 Jl 3 2017

Misery Index T. Keith color *Sports Illustrated* v125 no16 p18 N 14 2016

Run It Back W. Leitch and T. Keith color *Sports Illustrated* v126 no11 p17 Ap 17-24 2017

Championships—History—21st century

The Last Leap J. Fuchs and T. Keith color *Sports Illustrated* v126 no18 p20 Je 26 2017

Streakless In Seattle G. Wahl and T. Keith color *Sports Illustrated* v125 no20 p22 D 19 2016

Championships—Psychological aspects

Entitled Behavior W. Leitch and T. Keith color *Sports Illustrated* v125 no20 p20 D 19 2016

Champlain, Samuel de, d. 1635

Confluence of history A. Pope color map *Canadian Geographic* v137 no4 p26 Jl/Ag 2017

Champlain Valley

First Harvest: Moving a homestead also means planting in new soil color *Yankee* p14 Jl 2017

Vermont Charm E. GAUKEL *Treasures* v6 no3 p10 D 2016/Ja 2017

Chamuya, Nurdin

Positive biodiversity-productivity relationship predominant in global forests bibl chart graph map *Science* v354 no6309 paaf8957-1 O 14 2016

Chan, Adam

The Strongest Branch of Liberty *Washington Monthly* p10 N/D 2016

Chan, Addison

Cuba On the Rocks color *Sail* v48 no10 p34 O 2017

CHAN, ANDREW

BETWEEN the LINES color *Film Comment* v52 no6 p72 N/D 2016

THE GREAT DIVIDE bw *Film Comment* v53 no1 p54 Ja/F 2017

The Ornithologist color *Film Comment* v53 no3 p66 My/Je 2017

Chan, Carmen

PI3K pathway regulates ER-dependent transcription in breast cancer through the epigenetic regulator KMT2D bibl graph *Science* v355 no6331 p1324 Mr 24 2017

Chan, Charles K. F.

Fibroblasts become fat to reduce scarring bibl diag *Science* v355 no6326 p693 F 17 2017

Chan, Claudia

This Is How We Rise: Reach Your Highest Potential, Empower Women, Lead Change in the World *Publishers Weekly* v264 no35 p120 Ag 28 2017

Chan, Edwin

How to Fight Quantum Cybercrooks *Bloomberg Businessweek* no4531 p43 Jl 24 2017

Chan, Elsa T.

If There's Only One Woman in Your Candidate Pool, There's Statistically No Chance She'll Be Hired *Harvard Business Review Digital Articles* p2 Ap 26 2016

Chan, Gemma, 1982-

When the Most Human Human Isn't Actually Human D. D'Addario color *Time* v189 no7/8 p104 F 27 2017

Chan, Jackie, 1954-

STILL KICKING A. PAPPADEMAS bw color *GQ: Gentlemen's Quarterly* v97 no10 p104 O 2017

Chan, Jerry K. Y.

Mapping the human DC lineage through the integration of high-dimensional techniques diag *Science* v356 no6342 p1044 Je 9 2017

CHAN, KAI M. A.

ECONOMIZING NATURE AS A POLITICAL STRATEGY: IS IT WORKING? *BioScience* v67 no8 p770 Ag 2017

Chan, Lauren

Coats for All Sizes color *Glamour* v114 no12 p104 D 2016

Four Truths About Dressing Your Shape color *Glamour* v114 no11 p90 N 2016

Hey, Stores: Where's My Size? cartoon color *Glamour* v115 no4 p76 Ap 2017

"It's OK to be whatever size you are" color *Glamour* v114 no12 p116 D 2016

Jamie Does Juicy color *Glamour* v115 no9 p76 S 2017

Queen of Everything [Cover story] bw color *Glamour* v115 no7 p78 Jl 2017

Red-Carpet Revolution color *Glamour* v115 no3 p82 Mr 2017

This Model Belongs on the Runway color *Glamour* v115 no9 p70 S 2017

Three Writers. Three Sizes. Three Perfect Pairs of Jeans color *Glamour* v115 no2 p38 F 2017

WE ARE HERE color map *Glamour* v115 no9 p206 S 2017

We Made Plus-Size Jeans! color *Glamour* no8 p54 Ag 2017

What to Know NOW color *Glamour* v114 no11 p72 N 2016

What to Know Now color *Glamour* v115 no6 p52 Je 2017

Chan, Margaret

The Slow-Motion Disaster *Nutrition Action Health Letter* v44 no3 p7 Ap 2017

Unhealthy Agency E. Epstein color *Weekly Standard* v22 no38 p8 Je 12 2017

Chan, Melissa

America's New Clown Panic color *Time* v188 no15 p9 O 17 2016

A Bogeyman Who Drove Kids to Attempt Murder color *Time* v189 no4 p50 F 6 2017

The Fire Season color map *Time* v190 no16/17 p40 O 23 2017

The Kindness of Strangers color *Time* v190 no12 p42 S 25 2017

A New Kind of Star Power color *Time* v190 no2/3 p24 Jl 10-17 2017

Next Generation Leaders color *Time* v190 no16/17 p74 O 23 2017

Chan, Sylvia W.

Higher and Higher We Go A. Wintour *Vogue* v207 no1 p24 Ja 2017

Chan, Yih-Chih

Click chemistry enables preclinical evaluation of targeted epigenetic therapies diag *Science* v356 no6345 p1397 Je 30 2017

Chanama, Sumalee

Dengue diversity across spatial and temporal scales: Local structure and the effect of host population size bibl graph *Science* v355 no6331 p1302 Mr 24 2017

Chance

THE STORIES WE FALL FOR R. Lowenstein color *Fortune* v175 no4 p28 Mr 15 2017

Chance (TV program)

Chance A. D'Arminio *TV Guide* v64 no40 p28 O 3 2016

Laurie's New Healing Sleuth Takes a Dubious Chance D. D'Addario color *Time* v188 no18 p45 O 31 2016

Chance, Karen

Ride the Storm color *Publishers Weekly* v264 no24 p45 Je 12 2017

Chance, Maia

Gin and Panic *Publishers Weekly* v264 no28 p63 Jl 10 2017

Chance, Zoe

How Google Optimized Healthy Office Snacks *Harvard Business Review Digital Articles* p2 Mr 3 2016

Chancellor, Bryn

Sycamore color *Publishers Weekly* v264 no12 p3 Mr 20 2017

Chance the Rapper, 1993-

THE ARTIST WAY C. Murray color *Essence* v48 no2 p57 Je 2017

B-BOY ON THE BALLOT! PLEASE. MAYBE? [Cover story] A. SAMUELS GIBBS color *Ebony* v72 no8 p74 Je 2017

MAKING THE COVER T. PAYNE color *Ebony* v72 no8 p20 Je 2017

Musically Inclined K. Kyles color *Ebony* v72 no8 p16 Je 2017

PUT THE BASEBALL CAP BACK IN YOUR ROTATION color *Esquire* p52 O 2017

Random Notes color *Rolling Stone* no1295 p26 S 7 2017

Chance the Rapper, 1993-—Interviews

Hot Tracks L. ROBINSON bw *Vanity Fair* p102 Hollywood 2017 Supplement

Chandeliers

BACKYARD RETREAT L. MOWRY *Atlanta* v57 no4 p32 Ag 2017

editor's note S. BROWN *Timber Home Living* p8 2017 SpecialIssue

lighting *Design Center Sourcebook* p44 2017

Sweat Equity S. Murphy color *Log Home Living* v34 no3 p20 Ap 2017

Chandeliers—Design & construction

WIRE-ARM CHANDELIERS color *Old House Journal* v44 no8 p84 D 2016

Chandeliers—Evaluation

Golden Opportunity: Pair gold and green for an enviable interior M. Cameron *New Orleans Homes & Lifestyles* v20 no4 p100 Aut 2017

Home Stretch color *House Beautiful* v159 no5 p48 Je 2017

Rustic Lighting M. R. JOHNSON color *Cabin Living* p38 Ja/F 2017

CHANDLEE, PATTY

THE SECRET LIFE OF ANIMALS cartoon *Reader's Digest* v190 no1134 p38 O 2017

Chandler, Bob

What I'd Do Differently Bob Chandler, 75 J. PEARLEY HUFFMAN color *Car & Driver* v63 no1 p112 Jl 2017

Chandler, Claire J.

Spiral density waves in a young protoplanetary disk bibl graph *Science* v353 no6307 p1519 S 30 2016

Chandler, Clay

CHANGE THE WORLD !!!! color diag map *Fortune* v176 no4 p74 S 15 2017

INDIA'S MARATHON MAN color diag *Fortune* v176 no2 p94 Ag 1 2017

CHANDLER, CURTIS

Improving Student Note-Taking Skills *Education Digest* v82 no7 p54 Mr 2017

Chandler, Jennifer

Help, hope, and hype: Ethical dimensions of neuroprosthetics color *Science* v356 no6345 p1338 Je 30 2017

Chandler, Kim

Firebrand Moore wins GOP primary runoff color *Christian Century* v134 no22 p15 O 25 2017

Chandler, Kyle, 1965-

ACCORDING TO: Kyle Chandler J. DUBOFF color *Vanity Fair* v58 no12 p90 D 2016

In a Tragedy, Casey Affleck Finds Triumph S. Lansky color *Time* v188 no22-23 p98 N/D 2016

Chandler, Rachel

Change AGENTS K. BERNARD color *Vogue* v206 no11 p124 N 2016

Chandler, Raymond, 1888-1959

1949: Los Angeles R. Chandler *Lapham's Quarterly* v10 no2 p139 Spr 2017

Chandon, Pierre

Customers Aren't Very Good at Judging Product Sizing *Harvard Business Review Digital Articles* p2 N 11 2015

The Customers Who Are Happy to Pay More for Less *Harvard Business Review Digital Articles* p2 O 29 2015

The Reasons We Buy (and Eat) Too Much Food *Harvard Business Review Digital Articles* p2 D 20 2016

Research: Customers Notice When Products Shrink More Than When They Get Bigger color *Harvard Business Review Digital Articles* p2 Mr 7 2017

Chandra, A.

How economics can shape precision medicines bibl color *Science* v355 no6330 p1131 Mr 17 2017

Chandra, Amitabh

It's Easier to Measure the Cost of Health Care than Its Value *Harvard Business Review Digital Articles* p2 N 18 2014

Research: Perhaps Market Forces Do Work in Health Care After All *Harvard Business Review Digital Articles* p2 D 5 2016

A Simple Way to Measure Health Care Outcomes *Harvard Business Review Digital Articles* p2 D 8 2016

Understanding Health Care's Short-Termism Problem *Harvard Business Review Digital Articles* p2 S 28 2015

Chandra, Shobhana

Trump Says, 'Dig.' Wall Street Asks, 'Why?' *Bloomberg Businessweek* no4500 p19 N 21 2016

Chandran, Kartik

A "Trojan horse" bispecific-antibody strategy for broad protection against ebolaviruses bibl graph *Science* v354 no6310 p350 O 21 2016

Structural basis for antibody-mediated neutralization of Lassa virus [Cover story] color diag *Science* v356 no6341 p923 Je 1 2017

Chandrasegaran, Srinivasan

Design of a synthetic yeast genome bibl chart color graph *Science* v355 no6329 p1040 Mr 10 2017

Chandrasekaran, Aravind

What Has the Biggest Impact on Hospital Readmission Rates *Harvard Business Review Digital Articles* p2 S 23 2015

Chandrasekaran, Natarajan, 1963-

INDIA'S MARATHON MAN C. Chandler color diag *Fortune* v176 no2 p94 Ag 1 2017

Chandra X-ray Observatory (U.S.)

Chandra snaps a deep-field X-ray image color *Astronomy* v45 no5 p19 My 2017

Chanel, Coco, 1883-1971

Chanel's Costume Drama S. KASHNER bw color *Vanity Fair* p158 Hollywood 2017 Supplement

Chanel Inc.

Coco Served HOT *Interview* v47 no6 p33 Ag 2017

Chanel SA

Blooming BRILLIANT! cartoon *O, The Oprah Magazine* p75 Mr 2017

GET GORGEOUS SKIN Guarnieri color *Harper's Bazaar* no3649 p262 D 2016/Ja 2017

The In/Out LIST color *Harper's Bazaar* no3649 p134 D 2016/Ja 2017

My Cuba Diary color *Glamour* v114 no11 p84 N 2016

Not Your Basic Bag, Man N. Silverstein color *Glamour* v115 no4 p48 Ap 2017

Chaney, Jen

Just Kids img *New York* v50 no17 p92 Ag 21 2017

Rise of the Neo Rom-Com img *New York* p70 F 20 2017

CHANEY, KATHY

FLAWLESS BEAUTY bw color *Ebony* v72 no6 p42 Ap/My 2017

Logan Browning's Black Face in a White Place color *Ebony* v72 no6 p28 Ap/My 2017

STARCATION: WASHINGTON, D.C color *Ebony* v72 no8 p56 Je 2017

Chaney, Roy

Seven Times Dead *Publishers Weekly* v263 no40 p102 O 3 2016

Chang, Calvin

A nuclease that mediates cell death induced by DNA damage and poly(ADP-ribose) polymerase-1 bw graph *Science* v354 no6308 paad6872-1 O 7 2016

Chang, Christopher J.

Redox-based reagents for chemoselective methionine bioconjugation bibl diag graph *Science* v355 no6325 p597 F 10 2017

CHANG, CLIO

The Anti-Protest Backlash *New Republic* v248 no4 p8 Ap 2017

Not So Fast, Blue Cities il *New Republic* v248 no6 p12 Je 2017

Repeal and Replace il *New Republic* v248 no11 p12 N 2017

Chang, David

The Cheap Man's Guide to a Better Kitchen cartoon *GQ: Gentlemen's Quarterly* v97 no4 p54 Ap 2017

Chang, E. F.

Intonational speech prosody encoding in the human auditory cortex diag *Science* v357 no6353 p797 Ag 25 2017

Chang, Gordon G.

Bibles and Ginseng *New York Times Book Review* p19 Ap 9 2017

Chang, Howard Y.

CRISPRi-based genome-scale identification of functional long noncoding RNA loci in human cells bibl graph *Science* v355 no6320 p1 Ja 6 2017

Chang, Jade

No Place Is Home K. NGUYEN *New York Times Book Review* p19 O 16 2016

South of West Egg *New York Times Book Review* p17 Ap 9 2017

The Wangs vs. the World L. Greenblatt color *Entertainment Weekly* no1436/1437 p102 O 21 2016

Chang, Kabrina Krebel

What Companies Can Do When Work and Religion Conflict *Harvard Business Review Digital Articles* p2 Mr 15 2016

Chang, Li-Wan

Plant diversity increases with the strength of negative density dependence at the global scale diag *Science* v356 no6345 p1389 Je 30 2017

Chang, Mu-Chieh

Locked synchronous rotor motion in a molecular motor diag *Science* v356 no6341 p964 Je 1 2017

Chang, Rachel

China's Elusive Goal: A Global Apparel Brand color *Bloomberg*

Businessweek no4532 p12 Jl 31 2017

China's Foodmakers Try New Growth Recipes color diag *Bloomberg Businessweek* no4524 p22 My 29 2017

CHINA'S ROBOT REVOLUTION color graph *Bloomberg Businessweek* no4520 p32 My 1 2017

Chang, Siwei

The complex effects of ocean acidification on the prominent N2-fixing cyanobacterium Trichodesmium graph *Science* v356 no6337 p527 My 5 2017

CHANG, STEPHANIE

THE ULTIMATE GUIDE TO TECH @50+ color *AARP: The Magazine* v59 no1A p34 D 2015/Ja 2016

Chang, Tom Y.

Air Pollution Is Making Office Workers Less Productive *Harvard Business Review Digital Articles* p2 S 29 2016

Research: When a Retail Store Closes, Crime Increases Around It *Harvard Business Review Digital Articles* p2 Je 29 2017

Chang, Wenrui

Structure and assembly mechanism of plant C2S2M2-type PSII-LHCII supercomplex color *Science* v357 no6353 p815 Ag 25 2017

Chang, Xiang

Satellite-based entanglement distribution over 1200 kilometers diag graph *Science* v356 no6343 p1140 Je 16 2017

Chang, Ya-Wen

Transition from turbulent to coherent flows in confined three-dimensional active fluids color *Science* v355 no6331 p1284 Mr 24 2017

Chang, Yong-Gang

Structural basis of the day-night transition in a bacterial circadian clock bibl diag *Science* v355 no6330 p1174 Mr 17 2017

Chang-Seon Song

Role for migratory wild birds in the global spread of avian influenza H5N8 bibl graph map *Science* v354 no6309 p213 O 14 2016

Chang Wen Ke

Role for migratory wild birds in the global spread of avian influenza H5N8 bibl graph map *Science* v354 no6309 p213 O 14 2016

Changala, P. B.

Direct frequency comb measurement of OD + CO→DOCO kinetics bibl graph *Science* v354 no6311 p444 O 28 2016

Changalucha, John

Seasonal cycling in the gut microbiome of the Hadza hunter-gatherers of Tanzania diag *Science* v357 no6353 p802 Ag 25 2017

Change

See also

    Career changes

    Educational change

    Innovations in business

    Organizational change

    Political change

    Social change

    Technological innovations

CHEWING IT OVER R. Mead cartoon *New Yorker* v93 no10 p37 Ap 24 2017

Consortial Leadership Toward Large-Scale Change A. Kezar *Change* v48 no6 p50 N/D 2016

editor's note. WHAT DOES IT MEAN TO BE ON THE RIGHT SIDE OF THE FUTURE? K. Perina *Psychology Today* v49 no6 p3 N/D 2016

Embracing Change Means Disrupting Your Day K. Sweetman and S. Cragun *Harvard Business Review Digital Articles* p2 Jl 22 2016

Even Life-Saving Innovations Don't Sell Themselves T. Hussein and M. Plummer *Harvard Business Review Digital Articles* p2 F 16 2017

Change agents

6 Signs You're Living in an Entrepreneurial Society E. Ojomo *Harvard Business Review Digital Articles* p2 O 4 2016

Africa's Maker Movement Offers Opportunity for Growth N. Ekekwe *Harvard Business Review Digital Articles* p2 My 29 2015

the innovators bw *Foreign Policy* no221 p62 N/D 2016

INNOVATORS UNDER 35 *MIT Technology Review* v120 no5 p40 S/O 2017

Old World, Young Promise M. BERG, A. CALA et al color *Forbes* v199 no1 p20 Ja 24 2017

Tackling Big Global Challenges with Low-Cost Innovation N.

Radjou *Harvard Business Review Digital Articles* p2 F 17 2016

This Year's 35 Innovators Under the Age of 35 *MIT Technology Review* v120 no5 p2 S/O 2017

Why Innovators Should Study the Rise and Fall of the Venetian Empire P. Formica color *Harvard Business Review Digital Articles* p2 Ja 17 2017

Change management

5 Ways to Help Employees Keep Up with Digital Transformation D. Henretta and A. Chopra-McGowan *Harvard Business Review Digital Articles* p2 S 27 2017

Change Efforts Can Fail Unless They're Coordinated R. Newton *Harvard Business Review Digital Articles* p2 Ja 22 2016

Change Management Meets Social Media S. Clayton *Harvard Business Review Digital Articles* p2 N 10 2015

Changing Company Culture Requires a Movement, Not a Mandate B. Walker and S. A. Soule *Harvard Business Review Digital Articles* p2 Je 20 2017

Data Can Do for Change Management What It Did for Marketing M. L. Tushman, A. Kahn et al *Harvard Business Review Digital Articles* p2 Jl 31 2017

The Elusive Easy-Peasy D. T. PUTERBAUGH *USA Today Magazine* v146 no2868 p80 S 2017

Experiment with Organizational Change Before Going All In J. Beshears and F. Gino *Harvard Business Review Digital Articles* p2 O 13 2014

Getting Employees Excited About a New Direction D. A. Ready *Harvard Business Review Digital Articles* p2 N 20 2015

How IDEO Designers Persuade Companies to Accept Change A. Powell *Harvard Business Review Digital Articles* p2 My 17 2016

HR Can't Change Company Culture by Itself R. Newton *Harvard Business Review Digital Articles* p2 N 2 2016

The Key to Change Is Middle Management B. Tabrizi *Harvard Business Review Digital Articles* p2 O 27 2014

Leading Effectively When You Inherit a Mess R. Carucci *Harvard Business Review Digital Articles* p2 Ag 7 2017

Rethinking the Corporate Love Affair with Change Z. First *Harvard Business Review Digital Articles* p2 Mr 20 2017

A Way to Assess and Prioritize Your Change Efforts P. Keenan, S. Mingardon et al *Harvard Business Review Digital Articles* p2 Jl 9 2015

We Still Don't Know the Difference Between Change and Transformation R. Ashkenas *Harvard Business Review Digital Articles* p2 Ja 15 2015

What FDR Knew About Managing Fear in Times of Change V. Govindarajan and H. Faber *Harvard Business Review Digital Articles* p2 My 4 2016

What Spinning Off a GE Business Taught Me About Managing Ultra-Fast Change M. Keane *Harvard Business Review Digital Articles* p2 Jl 24 2017

Change management—Case studies

Case Study: How Much Should a New CEO Shake Things Up? P. M. Healy *Harvard Business Review Digital Articles* p2 O 26 2016

Changes (Music)

'Changes' C. AARON *New York Times Magazine* p61 Mr 12 2017

Change—Social aspects

Wicket Cool J. Feldman and T. Keith color *Sports Illustrated* v127 no3 p12 Jl 24 2017

Changhyun Ko

Anomalously low electronic thermal conductivity in metallic vanadium dioxide bibl graph *Science* v355 no6323 p371 Ja 27 2017

Changqing Lin

Expert consensus on point-of-care testing *Science* v354 no6319 p15 D 23 2016

Recommendations on the management and use of POCT in medical institutions (nosocomial) *Science* v354 no6319 p13 D 23 2016

Changyong Song

A three-dimensional movie of structural changes in bacteriorhodopsin bibl diag graph *Science* v354 no6319 p1552 D 23 2016

Channel Islands (Company)

Summer Gear Guide color *Surfer* v58 no3 p84 Je 2017

Channel Islands National Park (Calif.)

National Moments *Natural History* v125 no2 p5 F 2017

Chantecaille Beaute Inc.
The Pick color *InStyle* v23 no13 p184 D 2016
Chanterelle
Do You Know the Mushroom Man? R. O'CONNOR color *Chicago* v66 no4 p100 Ap 2017
Chantim, Andra
AT MY HOUSE with Katie Lee color *Good Housekeeping* v264 no6 p30 Je 2017
A LITTLE BIT COUNTRY color *Good Housekeeping* v265 no2 p46 Ag 2017
TURN AN UNUSED GARAGE INTO A Guest Retreat color diag *Good Housekeeping* v265 no1 p44 Jl 2017
Chao, Elaine L., 1953-
GUEST LIST color *Washingtonian Magazine* v52 no7 p20 Ap 2017
Will There Be An Internal Revolt Against Trump? T. Troy color *Commentary* v143 no2 p1 F 2017
Chaoming Song
Quantifying the evolution of individual scientific impact graph *Science* v354 no6312 p596 N 4 2016
Chaon, Dan
THE DARK SIDE M. HARVKEY color *Publishers Weekly* v264 no3 p30 Ja 16 2017
The Devil's Detail E. BRUNDAGE *New York Times Book Review* p12 Mr 26 2017
Ill Will I. Biedenharn color *Entertainment Weekly* no1456 p70 Mr 10 2017
Lie, Memory D. Preziosi color *Commonweal* v144 no12 p35 Jl 7 2017
Chaparral automobile
1966 CHAPARRAL 2E D. Kimble bw color *Hot Rod* v70 no1 p60 Ja 2017
Chaparral Boats Inc.
Ski, Fish, Cruise, Save: The flagship of Chaparral's H2O line has something never seen before: outboard power A. JONES *Boating World* v38 no8 p32 S/O 2017
Chapel design & construction
Halo Effect B. CARTER *Architectural Record* v205 no10 p70 O 2017
The Rothko Chapel J. Shine *New York Times Magazine* p26 Ag 27 2017
Chapels
Chapel of the Holy Dove N. AUSTIN *Arizona Highways* v93 no9 p6 S 2017
THE DUSTY TRAIL: The Fort Meade National Backcountry Byway might be our most historic gravel road J. Andrews *South Dakota Magazine* v33 no3 p74 S/O 2017
Prophet Elias' Chapel N. AUSTIN color *Arizona Highways* v93 no5 p6 My 2017
Chapels—Design & construction
Sanctuary for the Stars S. AMELAR color diag *Architectural Record* v205 no2 p90 F 2017
Chapels—History
THE SAINTS OF PITTSBURGH: A TINY NEIGHBORHOOD CHURCH IS HOME TO THE GREATEST COLLECTION OF RELICS OUTSIDE OF THE VATICAN R. WILKINSON *Smithsonian* v48 no4 p98 Jl/Ag 2017
Chapin, Adele
KICK IT WITH YOUR COLLEAGUES color *Bloomberg Businessweek* no4525 p55 Je 5 2017
Chapin, F. Stuart III
Social norms as solutions bibl color *Science* v354 no6308 p42 O 7 2016
Chapin, Sasha
Marching Orders *New York Times Magazine* p11 S 10 2017
Your Move color *Walrus* v14 no9 p75 N 2017
Chaplains
See also
Military chaplains
Out-of-control ministry C. L. Howard *Christian Century* v134 no12 p10 Je 7 2017
With More Than a Prayer N. ZAKI *Islamic Horizons* v46 no1 p38 Ja/F 2017
Chaple, Glenn
ASK ASTRO color diag *Astronomy* v45 no3 p34 Mr 2017
Celebrate with Charles color *Astronomy* v45 no2 p20 F 2017

Double star marathon redux color *Astronomy* v45 no3 p64 Mr 2017
Double your observing fun color *Astronomy* v44 no12 p65 D 2016
The final four bw color *Astronomy* v45 no9 p64 S 2017
Grab Explore Scientific's 80mm APO, and go! color *Astronomy* v45 no4 p64 Ap 2017
Hitching a ride bw *Astronomy* v45 no7 p66 Jl 2017
January's top 10 targets color *Astronomy* v45 no1 p66 Ja 2017
Keep your eyes on the eclipse color *Astronomy* v45 no8 p84 Ag 2017
Priceless royalty color *Astronomy* v45 no11 p14 N 2017
Shadow transit double header color *Astronomy* v45 no5 p18 My 2017
A smartphone lunar atlas color *Astronomy* v45 no6 p62 Je 2017
Track an asteroid pair color *Astronomy* v45 no10 p18 O 2017
Trekking the terminator color *Astronomy* v45 no4 p68 Ap 2017
Chaplin, Charlie, 1889-1977
REJECTED! C. Barrett color *MHQ: Quarterly Journal of Military History* v29 no4 p17 Summ 2017
Chaplin, George
The biology of color color *Science* v357 no6350 p470 Ag 4 2017
Chaplin, Heather
Turn On, Burn Out: A memoir recalls a tumultuous journey of self-discovery J. Attenberg *New York Times Book Review* p21 Ag 13 2017
Chaplin, Oona—Interviews
Taboo's Biggest Taboo R. Rahman color *Entertainment Weekly* no1450 p53 Ja 27 2017
CHAPLIN-KRAMER, REBECCA
Society Is Ready for a New Kind of Science--Is Academia? *BioScience* v67 no7 p591 Jl 2017
When, Where, and How Nature Matters for Ecosystem Services: Challenges for the Next Generation of Ecosystem Service Models *BioScience* v67 no9 p820 S 2017
Chapman & Cutler LLP
Best Law Firms for Women 2017 *Working Mother* v40 no3 p30 Ag/S 2017
Chapman, Anne
Evidence in the Precautionary Assessment of Novel Substances bibl *Environment* v59 no5 p16 S/O 2017
Chapman, C. D.
Sex matters: Report experimenter gender *Science* v356 no6341 p916 Je 1 2017
Chapman, David
Contingent valuation: Flawed logic? color *Science* v357 no6349 p363 Jl 28 2017
Putting a value on injuries to natural assets: The BP oil spill chart *Science* v356 no6335 p253 Ap 21 2017
Chapman, Georgina
MEMORIES are MADE of THIS bw color *Vogue* v207 no3 p276 Mr 2017
CHAPMAN, GRAY
EAST ATLANTA VILLAGE *Atlanta* v56 no10 p50 F 2017
Gabi Lee *Atlanta* v57 no6 p48 O 2017
In the Spirit: Step right up to Costumes Etc, Atlanta's 17,000-square-foot dress-up box *Atlanta* v57 no6 p43 O 2017
Shani James *Atlanta* v57 no3 p42 Jl 2017
Yes, Atlanta Has "Bodegas" *Atlanta* v57 no2 p49 Je 2017
Chapman, Jason W.
From Agricultural Benefits to Aviation Safety: Realizing the Potential of Continent-Wide Radar Networks *BioScience* v67 no10 p912 O 2017
Mass seasonal bioflows of high-flying insect migrants bibl graph *Science* v354 no6319 p1584 D 23 2016
Chapman, Jeff
Whoa-o-oh, Listen to the Music E. Wood color *Missouri Life* v44 no4 p14 Je 2017
CHAPMAN, JEFFREY
Think It, Speak It, Live It *USA Today Magazine* v145 no2860 p69 Ja 2017
CHAPMAN, JIM
AIR STRIKE color *Outdoor Life* v224 no1 p29 D 2016/Ja 2017
Chapman, John W.
Tsunami-driven rafting: Transoceanic species dispersal and implications for marine biogeography color graph *Science* v357 no6358 p1402 S 29 2017

Chapman, Lizette

Cracking the Bro Code cartoon *Bloomberg Businessweek* no4533 p18 Ag 7 2017

Hacking the Need For a Full-Time Job cartoon *Bloomberg Businessweek* no4518 p33 Ap 10 2017

A Heightened State Of Security graph *Bloomberg Businessweek* no4514 p45 Mr 13 2017

Security Software, Insecurity Culture color *Bloomberg Businessweek* no4519 p38 Ap 24 2017

Stalking the Next Zuckerberg color *Bloomberg Businessweek* no4502 p39 D 5 2016

Chapman, Rex

Our National Pain color *Sports Illustrated* v126 no17 p72 Je 19 2017

CHAPMAN, RUTH

My Stuff color *Vanity Fair* v59 no2 p32 F 2017

Chapman, Stephen J.

Emergence and spread of a human-transmissible multidrug-resistant nontuberculous mycobacterium bibl diag graph *Science* v354 no6313 p751 N 11 2016

Chapman, Steven Curtis, 1962—Interviews

Don't Miss Steven Curtis Chapman's Point S. TURNER bw *Christianity Today* p60 Mr 2017

Chapman, Terri

last look: TERRI CHAPMAN *American Forests* v123 no2 p48 Summ 2017

Chapman University

A CAREER & LEARNING RESOURCE GUIDE *Dance Magazine* v91 no10 p68 O 2017

Survey Shows Americans Fear Ghosts, the Government, and Each Other C. POPPY *Skeptical Inquirer* v41 no1 p16 Ja/F 2017

Chapotin, S.

Improving global integration of crop research color *Science* v357 no6349 p359 Jl 28 2017

Chappaquiddick (Film)

A Bridge Too Far bw cartoon *Weekly Standard* v23 no3 p2 S 25 2017

Chappatta, Brian

What Happened to the New Normal for Bonds? bw *Bloomberg Businessweek* no4504 p36 D 19 2016

CHAPPEL, MARY MARGARET

Pesto Perfection color *Better Nutrition* v79 no4 p60 Ap 2017

Chappell, Ben G. N.

A general catalytic β-C–H carbonylation of aliphatic amines to β-lactams bibl diag *Science* v354 no6314 p851 N 18 2016

Chappell, Duane E.

Horse Owner's Spring Notebook color *Trail Rider* v29 no4 p38 My 2017

Chappell, Kevin

PAINT A PERFECT SWING [Cover story] color *Golf Magazine* v59 no5 p71 My 2017

Chappell, Mary Margaret

COOK THE BOOKS color *Vegetarian Times* v43 no2 p58 N/D 2016

DIY Delicious [Cover story] color *Vegetarian Times* v43 no2 p45 N/D 2016

It's the Great Pumpkin color *Vegetarian Times* v43 no2 p66 N/D 2016

Chappell, Sharon Verner

The arts, educational policy, and emergent bilingual learners: Introductory remarks bibl *Arts Education Policy Review* v118 no4 p189 2017

CHAPPELLE, DAVE

Kendrick LAMAR *Interview* v47 no6 p34 Ag 2017

Points to Ponder color *Reader's Digest* v190 no1134 p35 O 2017

Chappelle, Dave, 1973-

Sound Bites color *Entertainment Weekly* no1463/1464 p8 Ap/My 2017

THE WORLD ACCORDING TO Gayle Gayle color *O, The Oprah Magazine* p28 Jl 2017

Chapple, Clint

Formaldehyde stabilization facilitates lignin monomer production during biomass depolymerization bibl diag graph *Science* v354 no6310 p329 O 21 2016

Chapple, Iain

Flossing — What Is It Good For? B. ALEX bw color *Discover*

v27 no10 p12 D 2016

Chapple, Justin

Mad Genius Tips: Over 90 Expert Hacks and 100 Delicious Recipes color *Publishers Weekly* v263 no42 p63 O 17 2016

Chappo, Beth

Style Blogger *Indianapolis Monthly* v40 no4 p94 D 2016

Chapron, Guillaume

Conserving the World's Megafauna and Biodiversity: The Fierce Urgency of Now *BioScience* v67 no3 p197 Mr 2017

Europe's biodiversity avoids fatal setback color *Science* v355 no6321 p140 Ja 13 2017

International Wildlife Law: Understanding and Enhancing Its Role in Conservation *BioScience* v67 no9 p784 S 2017

Modernization, Risk, and Conservation of the World's Largest Carnivores *BioScience* v67 no7 p646 Jl 2017

Saving the World's Terrestrial Megafauna color *BioScience* v66 no10 p807 O 1 2016

Character

The Mindset That Leads People to Be Dangerously Overconfident H. G. Halvorson *Harvard Business Review Digital Articles* p2 Ap 19 2016

a modest proposal [Cover story] D. SKOLNIK color *Parents* v92 no3 p52 Mr 2017

Character actors & actresses

Interview with a ... Character actor D. Angeles *Career Outlook* p1 F 2017

The Robert Pattinson Career-Makeover Playbook K. LINCOLN img *New York* v50 no8 p128 Ap 17 2017

Character tests

CHARACTER RECOGNITION: Private preschools are judging the "character" of applicants as well as their aptitude-even when children are as young as three G. Cook *Washingtonian Magazine* v53 no1 p129 O 2017

Characters & characteristics

See also

Antiheroes

An undivided life P. W. Marty *Christian Century* v134 no16 p3 Ag 2 2017

Characters & characteristics in literature

Ask the Editor B. K. SARGENT *Publishers Weekly* v264 no9 p51 F 27 2017

Characters & characteristics in motion pictures

THE BEST, BADDEST ACTION HERO NAMES K. P. Sullivan color *Entertainment Weekly* no1449 p44 Ja 20 2017

CARS 3 ADDS TO ITS FLEET M. Snetiker color *Entertainment Weekly* no1448 p13 Ja 13 2017

Ever ANDERSON SOKO *Interview* v46 no10 p48 D 2016/Ja 2017

Gabrielle Union E. Berman color *Time* v188 no18 p56 O 31 2016

GIRL POWER LIST I. Biedenharn color *Entertainment Weekly* no1435 p41 O 14 2016

How Jack Reacher Got His Name I. Biedenharn color *Entertainment Weekly* no1466 p62 My 19 2017

My Most Excellent Death D. Coggan color *Entertainment Weekly* no1460/1461 p93 Ap 7-17 2017

NOW AND JEN A. Sedaris color *Harper's Bazaar* no3657 p205 O 2017

PANTHER PACK A. Breznican color *Entertainment Weekly* no1474/1475 p34 Jl 21-28 2017

ROGUE ONE A. Breznican color *Entertainment Weekly* no1460/1461 p93 Ap 7-17 2017

Sound Bites 2017 Preview color *Entertainment Weekly* no1446/1447 p16 D 2016/Ja 2017

Sound Bites color *Entertainment Weekly* no1457/1458 p12 Mr 17 2017

Sound Bites color *Entertainment Weekly* no1468/1469 p12 Je 2-9 2017

SOUND BITES color *Entertainment Weekly* p10 Jl 24 2017

SPIDEY SQUAD S. Vilkomerson color *Entertainment Weekly* no1473 p21 Jl 7 2017

STAR WARS' FEMINIST FORCE A. Breznican color *Entertainment Weekly* no1462 p12 Ap 21 2017

Storm's Secret Mutant Love color *Entertainment Weekly* no1478 / 1479 p20 Ag 18-25 2017

TOM HIDDLESTON B. CUMBERBATCH *Interview* v46 no8 p62 O 2016

Characters & characteristics on television
See also
LGBT people on television
Are Arrogant Men Still Funny? J. M. Goldstein color *Glamour* v115 no5 p152 My 2017
A Bloody Good Time at Code Black J. HALTERMAN *TV Guide* v64 no46 p9 N 7 2016
A CLASH OF QUEENS J. Hibberd color *Entertainment Weekly* no1474/1475 p62 Jl 21-28 2017
Daria: 20 Years Later C. Brody color *Entertainment Weekly* no1460/1461 p68 Ap 7-17 2017
Fake Lives, Real Paydays C. Agard color *Entertainment Weekly* no1485 p48 O 6 2017
Getting Med-ucated M. Snetiker color *Entertainment Weekly* no1462 p53 Ap 21 2017
How Jack Reacher Got His Name I. Biedenharn color *Entertainment Weekly* no1466 p62 My 19 2017
How the 'Game' Changed Everything R. Sheffield bw color *Rolling Stone* no1291/1292 p50 Jl 13 2017
Nashville's Life After Death S. Highfill color *Entertainment Weekly* no1456 p16 Mr 10 2017
OUTLANDER'S NEW LADS L. Rice color *Entertainment Weekly* no1434 p23 O 7 2016
THE PLAYERS color *Entertainment Weekly* no1434 p48 O 7 2016
THE REDEMPTION OF SPIKE T. Stack color *Entertainment Weekly* no1460/1461 p60 Ap 7-17 2017
Sound Bites 2017 Preview color *Entertainment Weekly* no1446/1447 p16 D 2016/Ja 2017
Sound Bites color *Entertainment Weekly* no1442 p7 D 2 2016 Rebellions Special Issue
Sound Bites color *Entertainment Weekly* no1453 p8 F 17 2017
Sound Bites color *Entertainment Weekly* no1463/1464 p8 Ap/My 2017
Sound Bites color *Entertainment Weekly* no1477 p5 Ag 11 2017
TV J. Jensen, R. Rahman et al chart color *Entertainment Weekly* no1444/1445 p66 D 16 2016
When Fonzie Lost His Cool: He was the epitome of '50s chill on TV's family-friendly "Happy Days." And then he went over the top J. MacGregor *Smithsonian* v48 no5 p20 S 2017
WHICH FICTIONAL CHARACTER'S WARDROBE DO YOU COVET THE MOST? C. M. Smith color *Entertainment Weekly* no1449 p18 Ja 20 2017

Characters & characteristics in motion pictures—Charts, diagrams, etc.
SIZE KINGS D. Coggan color diag *Entertainment Weekly* no1456 p54 Mr 10 2017

Characters & characteristics on television—Charts, diagrams, etc.
Showbiz's Multiple-Personality Meter R. Rahman color *Entertainment Weekly* no1472 p49 Je 30 2017

Character—Social aspects
In the Year of Character, Issues Still Matter N. Gibbs color diag *Time* v188 no16/17 p30 O 24 2016

Charan, Ram
Boards Can't Wait for CEOs to Prioritize Digital Change *Harvard Business Review Digital Articles* p2 S 6 2017
How to Transform a Traditional Giant into a Digital One *Harvard Business Review Digital Articles* p2 F 26 2016
The Secrets of Great CEO Selection color *Harvard Business Review* v94 no12 p52 D 2016
Your Board Should Think Like Activists *Harvard Business Review Digital Articles* p2 F 9 2015

Charan, Ram—Interviews
How Boards Can Set a New CEO Up for Success E. Harrell *Harvard Business Review Digital Articles* p2 N 28 2016
Leaders should spend as much time on people as they do on money *People Management* p11 Jl 2017

Charas, Solange
Why Men Have More Help Getting to the C-Suite *Harvard Business Review Digital Articles* p2 N 16 2015

Charbonneau, P.
Reconciling solar and stellar magnetic cycles with nonlinear dynamo simulations diag *Science* v357 no6347 p185 Jl 14 2017

Charcoal
See also

Biochar
Gut Check C. DOW *Nutrition Action Health Letter* v44 no4 p9 My 2017

Charcoal grills—Evaluation
Fire Power: SOUTHERN CALIFORNIA GRILL MAKERS TURN UP THE HEAT ON ALFRESCO COOKING A. HEROLD color *Los Angeles Magazine* v62 no7 p30 Jl 2017

Charcoal—Evaluation
Holiday Gift Guide *Missouri Life* v43 no7 p22 D 2016/Ja 2017

Charcoal—Therapeutic use
Charcoal: A Go-To Remedy V. TWEED color *Better Nutrition* v78 no11 p24 N 2016

Charcuterie
IT HAPPENED AT THE FAIR *Mother Earth News* no283 p56 Ag/S 2017
THE LOVE color *Women's Health* v14 no6 p29 Jl 2017

Chardonnay (Wine)
WINE 1, 2, 3 F. COHEN color *Better Homes & Gardens* v95 no11 p139 N 2017

Chardonnay (Wine)—Evaluation
OUR 2017 GOLD & SILVER MEDAL WINNERS color *Sunset* v239 no4 p100 O 2017

Chareau, Pierre, 1883-1950
Glass act G. Cerio bw color *Magazine Antiques* v183 no6 p76 N/D 2016

Chareau, Pierre, 1883-1950—Exhibitions
exhibition J. MINUTILLO color *Architectural Record* v204 no12 p31 D 2016

CHAREN, MONA
Books for Children: A Symposium *National Review* v69 no19 p48 O 16 2017

Charette, Allison M.
Beyond the Rice Fields *Publishers Weekly* v264 no36 p62 S 4 2017

Charge carriers (Nuclear physics)
Semiconductor metamaterial fools the Hall effect J. Miller *Physics Today* v70 no2 p21 F 2017

Charge transfer
See also
Proton transfer reactions
Spectroscopic snapshots of the proton-transfer mechanism in water C. T. Wolke, J. A. Fournier et al bibl diag graph *Science* v354 no6316 p1131 D 2 2016

Charge transfer in biology
The [4Fe4S] cluster of human DNA primase functions as a redox switch using DNA charge transport E. O'Brien, M. E. Holt et al color *Science* v355 no6327 p813 F 24 2017

Chargebacks
Collaboration Can Help Merchants and Issuers *USA Today Magazine* v145 no2859 p8 D 2016

Chargebacks911 (Company)
Purchases, Chargebacks Are on the Rise *USA Today Magazine* v145 no2859 p7 D 2016

Chargebacks—Software
Disputing Credit Card Charges Gets Easy J. Surane color *Bloomberg Businessweek* no4529 p28 Jl 3 2017

Charger, Jasilea Rose
Power Move C. de Len color *Glamour* v114 no12 p63 D 2016

Charger, Jasilyn
THE SEVENTH GENERATION S. Elbein *New York Times Magazine* p24 F 5 2017

Charger Boats (Company)
Charger 210 Elite *Boating World* v38 no1 p65 Ja 2017

ChargeTech (Company)
CHARGETECH PLUG PRO REVIEW: SUPER—SIZED PORTABLE BATTERY CHARGER J. R. BOOKWALTER color *Macworld - Digital Edition* v34 no9 p51 S 2017

Charifou, Romina
Sensitive electromechanical sensors using viscoelastic graphene-polymer nanocomposites bibl graph *Science* v354 no6317 p1257 D 9 2016

Charisma (Personality trait)
Fidel Castro 1926-2016 [Cover story] T. Padgett color *Time* v188 no24 p40 D 12 2016
The little prince P. TREBLE color *Maclean's* v129 no40 p52 O 10 2016

When Charismatic Leadership Goes Too Far D. Ciampa *Harvard Business Review Digital Articles* p2 N 21 2016

Charismatic authority

Too Much Charisma Can Make Leaders Look Less Effective J. Vergauwe, B. Wille et al *Harvard Business Review Digital Articles* p2 S 26 2017

Charitable giving

Checkout charity [Cover story] S. Butler color *U.S. Catholic* v82 no7 p12 Jl 2017

Collection Rejection color *Money* v45 no11 p16 D 2016

Come Together. M. DUPLASS *USA Today Magazine* v145 no2864 p21 My 2017

Donor-Advised Funds: The Fastest-Growing Vehicle For Charitable Giving J. MULLICH color *Forbes* v200 no5 p88 N 14 2017

FAMILY L. Foust Prater *Successful Farming* v114 no13 p75 D 2016

Feeding Our App-etite D. CHEN *Reader's Digest* v188 no1125 p8 N 2016

FEED THE KIND-O-METER diag *Good Housekeeping* v263 no5 p92 N 2016

FOODSTUFFS *Atlanta* v56 no12 p58 Ap 2017

FOOLPROOF FOUNDATIONS A. Ebeling color *Forbes* v198 no9 p96 D 30 2016

GIFT OF GRUB color *Women's Health* v14 no3 p31 Ap 2017

Give Well, Give Wisely F. TORABI cartoon color graph *O, The Oprah Magazine* p56 D 2016

How a New Generation of Business Leaders Views Philanthropy P. Goldman *Harvard Business Review Digital Articles* p2 F 29 2016

JOHN MUIR SOCIETY *Sierra* v101 no4 p56 Jl/Ag 2016

MAKING GOOD: HUMANIST PHILANTHROPY & THE DUTY TO GIVE M. TRAFAS *Humanist* v77 no5 p12 S/O 2017

Strengthening a Force for Good *American Forests* v123 no3 p10 Fall 2017

The Summer of Change C. GRISE *Scholastic Choices* v32 no8 p20 My 2017

SUMMIT CIRCLE *Sierra* v101 no4 p55 Jl/Ag 2016

UNCHARTED WATERS A. RAPOPORT color *Bon Appetit* v61 no11 p12 N 2016

Wayne State Faces Bright Future J. Hale color *Downbeat* v84 no9 p102 S 2017

Charitable giving—Moral & ethical aspects

Is It O.K. to Give Cigarettes To a Homeless Person? K. A. Appiah *New York Times Magazine* p18 O 8 2017

Charitable giving—Charts, diagrams, etc.

America's Top Philanthropists K. SAVCHUK color graph *Forbes* v198 no5 p44 O 25 2016

THE GREATEST GIVERS J. WANG color graph *Forbes* v200 no5 p30 N 14 2017

Charitable uses, trusts, & foundations (Law)

See also
Family foundations

Funding the Right Projects: Lessons from the Elton John AIDS Foundation D. Furnish *Harvard Business Review Digital Articles* p2 D 1 2015

Get more cash for what you care about N. Lapin color *Redbook* p33 Ap 2017

Lessons from Boston's Experiment with The One Fund M. Weiss *Harvard Business Review Digital Articles* p2 Ja 22 2016

NEWS FROM THE DRESSAGE FOUNDATION bw color *Dressage Today* v24 no2 p12 N 2017

Planning to Live to 100? Volunteer! E. J. Schneidewind *AARP: The Magazine* v60 no4A p65 Je/Jl 2017

Charitable uses, trusts, & foundations (Law)—Taxation— United States

FOOLPROOF FOUNDATIONS A. Ebeling color *Forbes* v198 no9 p96 D 30 2016

Charitable uses, trusts, & foundations (Law)—United States

A GOP Plan to Tax Gifts For Wealthy Schools J. Lorin *Bloomberg Businessweek* no4506 p23 Ja 9 2017

Looking Ahead A. Bundles *Prologue* v49 no2 p70 Summ 2017

Why Major Philanthropists Are Giving More Money to Just One Cause W. Foster and A. Powell color *Harvard Business Review Digital Articles* p2 Ja 19 2017

Charities

See also

Asylums (Institutions)
Charitable uses, trusts, & foundations (Law)
Food relief
Sisterhoods
Social workers

ALLISON WILLIAMS' HOPE ON THE HORIZON M. L. Lenker color *Entertainment Weekly* no1474/1475 p18 Jl 21-28 2017

BIG BET PHILANTHROPY K. A. DOLAN color graph map *Forbes* v198 no8 p100 D 20 2016

CHRISTINA APPLEGATE FIGHTS FOR WOMEN'S HEALTH CARE M. L. Lenker color *Entertainment Weekly* no1486 p45 O 13 2017

Cocoa for a Cause A. Paturel color *Good Housekeeping* v264 no2 p59 F 2017

Driven to Succeed *Tennis* v52 no6 p42 N/D 2016

FAMILY L. Foust Prater *Successful Farming* v114 no13 p75 D 2016

GET STARTED T. A. Christian *Essence* v47 no8 p117 D 2016

Getting It Done K. H. McINTOSH *Idaho Magazine* v17 no1 p50 Ja 2017

How Large NGOs Are Using Data to Transform Themselves K. Campbell, S. Virani et al *Harvard Business Review Digital Articles* p2 My 18 2016

Italian for Beginners H. Bering color *Weekly Standard* v22 no23 p5 F 20 2017

MAKE THE MOST OF YOUR DONOR DOLLARS S. BLOCK color *Kiplinger's Personal Finance* v71 no12 p9 D 2017

Out of the Margins E. Parker *History Today* v66 no11 p25 N 2016

Solving Complex Social Problems Through Collaboration C. Conaway *Harvard Business Review Digital Articles* p2 Je 17 2015

Sweet Pickings A. JUNG *Reader's Digest* v188 no1125 p14 N 2016

THIS NEW HOUSE color *O, The Oprah Magazine* p114 N 2017

Why Mark Zuckerberg and Priscilla Chan Should Use Their Money for Fundraising D. Pallotta *Harvard Business Review Digital Articles* p2 D 3 2015

Charities—California

BBVA COMPASS & LINC HOUSING CHARITY EVENT *TV Guide* v64 no42 p4 O 10 2016

Charities—Charts, diagrams, etc.

TRUMP'S SECRET SANTAS C. Melby and M. Abelson color *Bloomberg Businessweek* no4505 p84 D 26 2016

Charities—Great Britain

"Cybersecurity is now an essential part of our values": How a growing charity secured its data by changing behaviours C. NEWBERRY *People Management* p23 Mr 2017

We used to withhold information from staff - now we tell them the truth: Why transparent communication means the charitys HR director can cross the car park without facing angry employees *People Management* p20 My 2017

Charities—Investments

See also

Donor-advised funds

Q: My alma mater is offering a charitable gift annuity. Is that a good way to generate income? E. AMBROSE color *Kiplinger's Personal Finance* v71 no11 p46 N 2017

Charities—Marketing

The Economics of Charity Telemarketing D. Pallotta *Harvard Business Review Digital Articles* p2 Ap 15 2015

Charities—Social aspects

Take this $500 and do good in the world L. S. Truax and A. Campbell color *Christian Century* v134 no8 p1 Ap 12 2017

Charities—United States

America's Largest Charities W. P. BARRETT color *Forbes* v198 no9 p24 D 30 2016

Arts, Culture & Entertainment *Virginia Living* p116 2017 Best 20of Virginia

BEHIND THE SCENES E. PARKHURST *Virginia Living* v15 no2 p7 F 2017

Don't Stop Now! Give, Give! K. Pollitt color diag *Nation* v304 no2 p10 Ja 16 2017

Give Your Best K. A. Renzulli color diag *Money* v45 no11 p82 D 2016

A TRULY HEARTFELT GIFT A. Giorgianni color *Consumer Reports* v81 no12 p50 D 2016

Charity

See also
Kindness

Arts, Culture & Entertainment *Virginia Living* p140 2017 Best 20of Virginia

crafts for a cause! *Parents* v91 no11 p52 N 2016

A Flexible Way to Give to Charity K. LANKFORD color *Kiplinger's Personal Finance* v70 no12 p44 D 2016

Good buys E. Marglin color *Yoga Journal* no295 p22 O 2017

How to Help Hurricane Victims Rebuild K. LANKFORD color *Kiplinger's Personal Finance* v71 no11 p18 N 2017

kids * health news *Parents* v91 no9 p27 S 2016

a modest proposal [Cover story] D. SKOLNIK color *Parents* v92 no3 p52 Mr 2017

playing with purpose J. HARTSHORN color *Parents* v92 no5 p60 My 2017

presents with purpose H. M. BAUER *Parents* v91 no12 p89 D 2016

raise a kid who cares B. STEPHENS *Parents* p66 2015

Show Me The Money E. KELSEY *Psychology Today* v49 no6 p35 N/D 2016

sweet charity color *Parents* v92 no5 p19 My 2017

teaching little ones to give K. BELL *Parents* v91 no11 p48 N 2016

A truly happy way to spend your money N. Lapin color *Redbook* p36 D 2016

A TRULY HEARTFELT GIFT A. Giorgianni color *Consumer Reports* v81 no12 p50 D 2016

Your presence is needed S. Johnson *U.S. Catholic* v82 no7 p4 Jl 2017

Charity Navigator Inc.

Overhead Overhaul K. Shellnutt color *Christianity Today* v60 no8 p25 O 2016

Charity organization

Cause & Effect C. Shanahan color *InStyle* v23 no12 p58 N 2016

Charity—Moral & ethical aspects

Giving from the Heart *Christianity Today* v61 no6 p15 Jl/Ag 2017

Charity—Religious aspects

Giving from the Heart *Christianity Today* v61 no6 p15 Jl/Ag 2017

Charity—Social aspects

Ride for a Cause J. Sullivan color *Trail Rider* v29 no2 p28 Mr 2017

Charlamagne Tha God (Performer), 1980-

BOOK IT: FAVORITE READS FROM CHARLAMAGNE THA GOD S. E. JAMISON color *Ebony* v72/73 no12/1 p85 O/N 2017

Charlamagne Tha God Loves Telling Middle America About Black Privilege J. Hughes color *New York Times Magazine* p82 My 21 2017

CHARLES, MARISSA

Jurnee toward justice color *Ebony* v72 no5 p76 Mr 2017

No Longer 'Hidden Figures' color *Ebony* v72 no3 p30 D 2016/ Ja 2017

Charles, Prince of Wales, 1948-

THE Lonely Heir S. B. SMITH bw color *Vanity Fair* v59 no5 p144 Ap 2017

MOST LIKELY TO SUCCEED Z. HELLER cartoon *New Yorker* v93 no8 p66 Ap 10 2017

Recalling the People's Princess T. BROWN bw color *Maclean's* v130 no7 p55 Ag 2017

Charles, Prince of Wales, 1948-—Political & social views

Apocalypse Now color *Weekly Standard* v22 no37 p3 Je 5 2017

Charles, Ray, 1930-2004

Genius at Work J. Johnson color *Downbeat* v83 no12 p91 D 2016

Charles, Tina, 1988-

Tina Charles M. Hagan color *Current Biography* v78 no5 p18 My 2017

Charles H. Stewart (Company)

Backdrops by Charles H. Stewart ...a timeless tradition since 1893 *Stage Directions* v30 no3 p7 Mr 2017

Charles Rose Architects Inc.

By Design color *Working Mother* p8 F/Mr 2017

Charles Schwab & Co. Inc.

Schwab's Cut-Rate ETFs Are Catching On C. Stein color graph *Bloomberg Businessweek* no4494 p39 O 10 2016

Charles-Donatien, Eric

FEATHERED GLORY B. BILGER bw cartoon color *New Yorker* v93 no29 p68 S 25 2017

Charleston (S.C.)

CHARLESTON, SOUTH CAROLINA color *Washington Monthly* v49 no3-5 p26 Mr-My 2017

City Bountiful K. ABBONDANZA *Sierra* v102 no2 p60 Mr/Ap 2017

Charleston (S.C.)—Description & travel

FIELD NOTES color *Martha Stewart Living* p112 My 2017

SOUTH'S BEST CITY J. Mischner color *Southern Living* v52 no4 p74 Ap 2017

Charleston (W. Va.)

The Other Charleston C. Balestier color *Southern Living* v52 no10 p67 O 2017

Charleston Harbor (S.C.)

Plenty of Breeze at Charleston color *Sail* v48 no7 p17 Jl 2017

Charleston Church Shooting, Charleston, S.C., 2015

DOPE C. Bethea cartoon *New Yorker* v93 no27 p25 S 11 2017

For the Record color *Time* v189 no4 p8 Ja 23 2017

In black Charleston, a struggle to find both justice and mercy P. Jonsson color *Christian Century* v134 no4 p13 F 15 2017

THE MAKING AND UNMAKING OF DYLANN ROOF R. KAADZI GHANSAH bw color *GQ: Gentlemen's Quarterly* v97 no9 p186 S 2017

Charlie & the Chocolate Factory (Theatrical production)

IT'S A WONKA WORLD D. KAMP color *Vanity Fair* p187 Hollywood 2017 Supplement

Our Ridiculously Early Tony Preview M. Snetiker color *Entertainment Weekly* no1462 p14 Ap 21 2017

THE SOUND OF IMAGINATION: Andrew Keister's Sound Design for Charlie and the Chocolate Factory B. Reesman *Stage Directions* v30 no6 p12 Je 2017

Spring Preview M. Schulman cartoon *New Yorker* v93 no4 p15 Mr 13 2017

Charlie Brown Christmas, A (TV program)

TIDINGS OF GREAT JOY J. McDERMOTT *America* v215 no19 p29 D 19 2016

Charlier, Philippe

When Science Sheds Light on History: Forensic Science and Anthropology *Publishers Weekly* v264 no35 p122 Ag 28 2017

Charli XCX, 1992-

Charli XCX Gets Down With the Robots C. R. WEINGARTEN color *Rolling Stone* no1284 p52 Ap 6 2017

CHARLI XCX N. Feeney *Entertainment Weekly* no1446/1447 p75 D 2016/Ja 2017

NIGHT LIFE *New Yorker* v93 no9 p10 Ap 17 2017

Charlotte Hornets (Basketball team)

5 Hornets R. Mahoney, B. Golliver et al color *Sports Illustrated* v125 no14 p78 O 24-31 2016

6 HORNETS color *Sports Illustrated* v127 no12 p62 O 16 2017

Charlottesville (Va.)—Description & travel

SOUTH'S BEST SMALL TOWN C. King color *Southern Living* v52 no4 p94 Ap 2017

Charly Bliss (Performer)

STAGE RIGHT *Cincinnati Magazine* v50 no12 p26 S 2017

Charm (Theatrical production)

THE THEATRE *New Yorker* v93 no26 p7 S 4 2017

Charman, Isobel

Animal House: Isobel Charman recounts the London Zoo's 19th-century origins C. CASEY *New York Times Book Review* p8 Jl 9 2017

Shocking stories tell tale of zoo's founding M. Rosen cartoon color *Science News* v191 no6 p28 Ap 1 2017

Charmed (TV program)

OUR CHARMED REBOOT WISH LIST N. Abrams color *Entertainment Weekly* no1449 p22 Ja 20 2017

Charmed Circle (Music)

A Trail of Cedars C. WOLFF bw *Downbeat* v84 no9 p70 S 2017

CHARMOZ, ALEX

Backcountry First Aid *Climbing* no350 p47 D 2016/Ja 2017

Charms

PUMP It UP *Interview* v47 no1 p36 F 2017

Charner-Laird, Megin

What real high performance looks like chart diag *Phi Delta Kappan* v98 no7 p38 Ap 2017

Charney, Amanda

AMANDA CHARNEY C. FENNESSY color *Runner's World* v52 no1 p89 Ja/F 2017

Charney, Dov, 1969-
The Resurrection of Dov Charney *Los Angeles Magazine* p12 Mr 2017

Charney, Dov, 1969—Trials, litigation, etc.
Second Act: Dov Charney M. Townsend color *Bloomberg Businessweek* no4531 p17 Jl 24 2017

CHARNEY, NICHOLAS
25 BIG IDEAS THAT BEGAN HERE *Psychology Today* v50 no4 p44 Ag 2017

Charney, Tamar
The gift of friendship color *Equus* no477 p88 Je 2017

Charnock, Garry
the stewards bw color *Foreign Policy* no221 p86 N/D 2016

Charo (Performer)
CHARO CHA-CHAS ONTO DWTS L. Rice color *Entertainment Weekly* no1456 p18 Mr 10 2017

Charo, R. Alta
Evolving policy with science color *Science* v355 no6328 p889 Mr 3 2017

Charoen Pokphand Group (Company)
A Case of Chicken vs. Machine P. Ho and J. Gale cartoon color *Bloomberg Businessweek* no4507 p18 Ja 16 2017

Charoensawan, Varodom
Phytochromes function as thermosensors in Arabidopsis bibl graph *Science* v354 no6314 p886 N 18 2016

Charon (Satellite)
Charon & Company J. K. BEATTY *Sky & Telescope* v132 no6 p36 D 2016

Charrerias
Pride and Joy E. PARKHURST *Virginia Living* v15 no2 p36 F 2017

Charter schools
Does school choice create better choices? color *Christian Century* v134 no8 p1 Ap 12 2017
Highlighted & Underlined graph il *Phi Delta Kappan* v99 no2 p6 O 2017
The Long Game of Betsy DeVos J. Berkshire color *Progressive* v81 no2 p28 F 2017
THE MICHIGAN EXPERIMENT M. BINELLI *New York Times Magazine* p50 S 10 2017

Charter schools—Administration
The War over Education and Civil Rights J. V. Heilig *Progressive* v81 no10 p13 N 2016

Charter schools—California
Teachers Union Head Casts School Choice as Racism S. Shackford color *Reason* v49 no5 p14 O 2017

Charter schools—Illinois
The Other Chicago Teachers Union M. UETRICHT *In These Times* v41 no5 p10 My 2017

Charter schools—United States
5 Issues That Deserve More Love-or Hate N. Hopper *Time* v188 no16/17 p36 O 24 2016
Burnout factories M. Fusco color il *Phi Delta Kappan* v98 no8 p26 My 2017
Charter schools don't serve black children well J. Richardson color *Phi Delta Kappan* v98 no5 p41 F 2017
Improve governance for charters C. E. Finn, B. V. Manno et al *Phi Delta Kappan* v98 no6 p63 Mr 2017
A Quiet Revolution A. SMARICK color *Weekly Standard* v22 no7 p20 O 24 2016
Reclaim Charter Schools M. J. PETRILLI color *National Review* v69 no19 p44 O 16 2017
School of Hard Knocks C. E. Finn Jr. and B. L. Wright *Hoover Digest: Research & Opinion on Public Policy* no4 p142 Fall 2016

Chartered Institute of Personnel & Development
Branch activities step up a gear: Webinars and walks among the new initiatives CIPD branches are embracing to support members *People Management* p60 Je 2017
EXTRA EXTRA *People Management* p65 N 2016
Get collaborative with new HR platform *People Management* p58 My 2017
New platform for evidence-based HR: CIPD invites practitioners and experts to contribute their ideas and views to online community forum *People Management* p58 Jl 2017
Our agenda is crystal clear P. Cheese *People Management* p5 Ag 2017

Pulling the levers of change P. Cheese *People Management* p5 Je 2017

Chartered Institute of Personnel & Development—Awards
Are you 2017's HR champion? Enter now to be in with a chance to win a CIPD People Management Award *People Management* p11 Mr 2017

Chartered Institute of Personnel & Development—Congresses
Branch event to tackle changing world of work: Midlands conference is one of a raft of CIPD activities taking place around the UK and Ireland *People Management* p58 S 2017
Committee helps shape CIPD framework: Members of the Membership and Professional Development Committee share their views *People Management* p56 Ap 2017
IF YOU THOUGHT YOU KNEW L&D... THINK AGAIN: Discover new ideas and trends at this year's CIPD Learning and Development Show *People Management* p42 My 2017
Members help shape CIPD framework: HR professionals were encouraged to share their views and experiences at a Manchester event *People Management* p54 Ag 2017
Social media boosts event's success *People Management* p58 D 2016/Ja 2017

Charteris, John A.
Humor in Uniform *Reader's Digest* v188 no1126 p134 D 2016/Ja 2017

Charters
Your Project Needs a Charter. Here's What That Means *Harvard Business Review Digital Articles* p2 N 3 2016

Chartway Federal Credit Union (Company)
ABOUT TOWN *Virginia Living* v15 no1 p37 D 2016

Charvat, Alex
The Keys to a Log Home Renovation color *Log Home Living* v34 no7 p64 S 2017

Charyk, Chris
The Pros and Cons of Pros-and-Cons Lists color *Harvard Business Review Digital Articles* p2 Ja 6 2017

Charyn, Jerome
Jerzy *Publishers Weekly* v264 no4 p52 Ja 23 2017
LIFE AS FICTION R. FRANKLIN bw *New Yorker* v93 no6 p73 Mr 27 2017
Prometheus Unbound: Emily Dickinson comes confidently alive *American Scholar* v86 no3 p104 Summ 2017
Stranger as Fiction B. MARKOVITS *New York Times Book Review* p9 Ap 2 2017

CHASE, CHLOE
Win GAME DAY color *Seventeen* v75 no11 p65 N 2016

Chase, Debra Martin
STAYING POWER S. Fales-hill color *Essence* v47 no12 p104 Ap 2017

Chase, Jennifer
grow a GARDEN RUG K. BARNES color *Better Homes & Gardens* v95 no3 p84 Mr 2017

Chase, Jill
Building a Good Picket Fence color *Old House Journal* v45 no5 p48 Ag 2017

Chase, Kathy
Taking Nebraska Life Doorstep to Doorstep C. Amundson *Nebraska Life* v20 no6 p9 N/D 2016

Chase, Loretta
A Duke in Shining Armor *Publishers Weekly* v264 no38 p59 S 18 2017

Chase, Robin
We Need to Expand the Definition of Disruptive Innovation *Harvard Business Review Digital Articles* p2 Ja 7 2016
Who Benefits from the Peer-to-Peer Economy? *Harvard Business Review Digital Articles* p2 Jl 28 2015

Chase, Samantha
A Sky Full of Stars *Publishers Weekly* v264 no15 p58 Ap 10 2017

Chase scenes in motion pictures
BABY, YOU CAN FLY MY CAR D. Franich color *Entertainment Weekly* no1462 p11 Ap 21 2017

Chase-Lubitz, Jesse
Language Haven color *Foreign Policy* no226 p10 S/O 2017
They Can't Go Home Again color *Foreign Policy* no226 p16 S/O 2017

Chasing Coral (Film)
An unseen environmental disaster N. M. Flores *America* v217 no6

p57 S 18 2017

Chasing Honey (Short story)

Chasing Honey S. B. SAUM *Orion Magazine* v35 no3 p10 My/
Je 2016

Chasing Paper LLC

BEST OF THE WEST J. Sexton color *Sunset* v238 no2 p7 F 2017

Chasing Trane: The John Coltrane Documentary (Film)

Chasing Trane: The John Coltrane Documentary *New Yorker* v93
no13 p16 My 15 2017

Chaskalson, Michael

How to Bring Mindfulness to Your Company's Leadership *Harvard Business Review Digital Articles* p2 D 1 2016

Mindfulness Works but Only If You Work at It *Harvard Business
Review Digital Articles* p2 N 4 2016

Chason, Eric

Epitaxial lift-off of electrodeposited single-crystal gold foils for
flexible electronics bibl bw diag *Science* v355 no6330 p1203
Mr 17 2017

CHAST, ROZ

THE KNIFE cartoon *New Yorker* v93 no30 p30 O 2 2017

One Cartoonist's Rather Particular Guide to Manhattan cartoon
Conde Nast Traveler v52 no9 p110 O 2017

THE SEVEN AGES OF ME AND TV cartoon *New Yorker* v93
no26 p31 S 4 2017

Chast, Roz—Interviews

Roz Chast *New York Times Book Review* p8 O 8 2017

Chastain, Jessica, 1977-

Crewel Summer E. Wilson color *InStyle* v24 no8 p72 Ag 2017

Emma WATSON: THE FUTURE IS TERRIFYING. THE FUTURE IS UNCERTAIN. THE FUTURE IS ... HERE. AND
IF EMMA WATSON HAS ANYTHING TO SAY ABOUT IT,
THE FUTURE IS GOING TO BE MAGICAL *Interview* v47
no3 p46 My 2017

Jessica Chastain vs. the Machine L. Schallon color *Glamour* v115
no11 p74 N 2017

REALITY BITES D. Walters color *Bloomberg Businessweek*
no4501 p62 N 28 2016

Chastain, Jessica, 1977-—Interviews

"True badassery has no gender" K. Branch and E. Mahaney color
diag *Glamour* v115 no1 p60 Ja 2017

Chasteen, Stephanie

Teaching and Learning STEM: A Practical Guide *Physics Today*
v70 no5 p57 My 2017

Chastity

THE LUST LOCKDOWN L. L. Joiner color *Essence* v47 no11
p107 Mr 2017

Chatbots

Artificial People E. Huet cartoon color *Bloomberg Businessweek*
no4496 p40 O 24 2016

These are the experts deciding the future of HR... ...shouldn't you
know who they are? [Cover story] G. GYTON and R. JEFFSRY
People Management p24 Ag 2017

Château de Versailles (Versailles, France)

Mom and Me: 4 Destinations to Explore with Your Mother O.
RAYMOND and D. POINTDUJOUR color *Ebony* v72 no6 p58
Ap/My 2017

Chatel, Peter

Fox and His Friends color *New Yorker* v93 no26 p10 S 4 2017

Chatman, Kelly

Potential role of intratumor bacteria in mediating tumor resistance
to the chemotherapeutic drug gemcitabine diag *Science* v357
no6356 p1156 S 15 2017

Chatsworth (England)

CHATSWORTH: THE PALACE OF THE PEAKS *British Heritage Travel* v38 no2 p60 Mr/Ap 2017

Chattahoochee River

ATLANTA'S BLUE-RIBBON TROUT STREAM C. Scalley *Atlanta* v57 no4 p50 Ag 2017

THE FUTURE OF THE CHATTAHOOCHEE: Long overlooked,
the river s segment along Atlanta's west side has endless opportunity T. WHEATLEY *Atlanta* v57 no4 p57 Ag 2017

OUR RIVER K. EDELSTEIN *Atlanta* v57 no4 p58 Ag 2017

RIVER: SIGNS OF CIVILIZATIONS PAST T. WHEATLEY *Atlanta* v57 no4 p55 Ag 2017

WATER: CAST A LURE, GRAB A TUBE, AND PADDLE AN
OAR J. GREEN *Atlanta* v57 no4 p51 Ag 2017

Chattahoochee River—Environmental conditions

A RIVER RUNS THROUGH IT S. FENNESSY *Atlanta* v57 no4
p12 Ag 2017

Chattanooga (Tenn.)

Southern Super Nova E. Elliott color *Climbing* no350 p22 D 2016/
Ja 2017

Chattanooga (Tenn.)—Description & travel

CHATTANOOGA, TENNESSEE R. J. Smith *Cincinnati Magazine* v50 no12 p38 S 2017

Chatterjee, Anjan

TALENTED & GIFTED S. LEBLANC color *Martha Stewart Living* no275 p46 Je 2017

Chatterjee, Arnab K.

Decarboxylative borylation color *Science* v356 no6342 p1045 Je
9 2017

Chatterji, Aaron

Starbucks' "Race Together" Campaign and the Upside of CEO
Activism *Harvard Business Review Digital Articles* p2 Mr 24
2015

Chaturvedi, Ravi Shankar

60 Countries' Digital Competitiveness, Indexed *Harvard Business
Review Digital Articles* p2 Jl 12 2017

The Countries That Would Profit Most from a Cashless World
Harvard Business Review Digital Articles p2 My 31 2016

Europe's Other Crisis: A Digital Recession *Harvard Business Review Digital Articles* p2 O 27 2015

How Benchmarking Can Help Countries Become More Digital
Harvard Business Review Digital Articles p2 Mr 8 2016

The "Smart Society" of the Future Doesn't Look Like Science
Fiction *Harvard Business Review Digital Articles* p2 O 5 2017

Where the Digital Economy Is Moving the Fastest *Harvard Business Review Digital Articles* p2 F 19 2015

Chatzky, Jean

Going Cold Turkey color *AARP: The Magazine* v59 no5A p30
Ag/S 2016

Hire Extra Muscle to Reduce Monthly Bills cartoon *AARP: The
Magazine* v60 no1A p25 D 2016/Ja 2017

Read This Before You Cosign *AARP: The Magazine* v59 no6A
p27 O/N 2016

Spend on Values to Feel Good color *AARP: The Magazine* v60
no4A p24 Je/Jl 2017

Teach the Children Well: Money lessons for the grandkids cartoon
color *AARP: The Magazine* v60 no5A p27 Ag/S 2017

Tidy Up Your Files color *AARP: The Magazine* v59 no3A p26
Ap/My 2016

Time to Weed Out Your Wallet? *AARP: The Magazine* v59 no4A
p28 Je/Jl 2016

Chaudhary, Archana

How India Tripped Itself Up graph *Bloomberg Businessweek*
no4538 p30 S 18 2017

India's Answer to Safe Payments color *Bloomberg Businessweek*
no4514 p44 Mr 13 2017

India's Cash-Canceling Experiment color *Bloomberg Businessweek* no4501 p12 N 28 2016

India's War Over Water—and Soft Drinks map *Bloomberg Businessweek* no4515 p15 Mr 20 2017

Chaudhry, Lakshmi

Can the digital revolution save Indian journalism? cartoon color
Columbia Journalism Review p80 Fall/Wint 2016

Chauhan, Anaahita

FOLLOWING MY dreams: How a love for reading led me to become an author--at just 8 years old color *Literacy Today (2411-
7862)* v34 no6 p52 My/Je 2017

Chauliodontidae

Halloween Under The Sea B. F. SUMMERS color *National Geographic Kids* no474 p26 O 2017

Chaussee, Jennifer

WISH LIST 2016 color *Wired* v24 no12 p45 D 2016

Chauvet, Adrien

Time-resolved x-ray absorption spectroscopy with a water window high-harmonic source bibl graph *Science* v355 no6322
p264 Ja 20 2017

Chauvet Professional (Company)

Profile of a Profile C. Rutherford *Stage Directions* v30 no3 p76
Mr 2017

Chauvin, Jean-Philippe R.

Synthesis of resveratrol tetramers via a stereoconvergent radical equilibrium bibl diag graph *Science* v354 no6317 p1260 D 9 2016

CHAUVIN, MARC

Fast, Safe, and Easy Anchoring color *Climbing* no355 p50 Ag 2017

The LSD Lower color *Climbing* no353 p50 My/Je 2017

Protect Your Belay, Protect Your Belayer color *Climbing* no354 p42 Jl 2017

Chavali, Pavithra L.

Neurodevelopmental protein Musashi-1 interacts with the Zika genome and promotes viral replication diag *Science* v357 no6346 p83 Jl 7 2017

Chavan, Archana

Structural basis of the day-night transition in a bacterial circadian clock bibl diag *Science* v355 no6330 p1174 Mr 17 2017

Chavez, A. G.

Observation of a large-scale anisotropy in the arrival directions of cosmic rays above 8×10^{18} eV *Science* v357 no6357 p1266 S 22 2017

Chavez, Amy

RUN, PILGRIM, RUN S. BURT color map *Tricycle: The Buddhist Review* v26 no2 p50 Wint 2016

Chavez, Chris

Great Barrier Reach color *Sports Illustrated* v126 no8 p22 Mr 20 2017

Running Man Challenge color *Sports Illustrated* v126 no5 p20 F 13 2017

Chavez, Christopher

To Innovate, Think Like a 19th-Century Barn Raiser *Harvard Business Review Digital Articles* p2 Ag 4 2016

Chavez, Gregorio Rosa

AUXILIARY ANNOUNCEMENT T. QUIGLEY *Commonweal* v144 no12 p2 Jl 7 2017

New cardinal wants to revive legacy of Óscar Romero in El Salvador M. Vida color *America* v217 no5 p15 S 4 2017

Chávez, Hugo

AMID THE RUINS OF A REVOLUTION, THE CHURCH ENDURES [Cover story] J. D. Hirst color il *America* v216 no11 p26 My 15 2017

Chavez, Jose

Interview with a ... Park interpreter E. Torpey *Career Outlook* p1 Jl 2017

CHAVEZ, LINDA

The Happiest in the World *Commentary* v143 no1 p41 Ja 2017

Trump's Massive Miscalculation color *Foreign Policy* no226 p64 S/O 2017

Trump's Wall *Commentary* v142 no2 p9 S 2016

Chavez, Shannon

Hotter Sex in Just Minutes! A. BRESLAW *Men's Health* v32 no6 p97 Ag 2017

Chávez Frías, Hugo, 1954-2013

Venezuela's Manmade Disaster M. M. MCCARTHY *Current History* v116 no787 p61 F 2017

Chavez Qureshi, Shannon

Ask anything bw color *Women's Health* v14 no2 p18 Mr 2017

Chavira, Ricardo

BACK IN THE WHITE HOUSE M. LOGAN *TV Guide* v65 no4 p26 Ja 16 2017

Chavkin, Rachel

Turning a Theater Inside Out: Problem No. 1: Move your musical from a cabaret into a Broadway theater. Problem No. 2: Make that theater feel like a cabaret J. McHenry img *New York* v50 no11 p114 My 29 2017

Chawla, Ajay

Immunity around the clock bibl diag graph *Science* v354 no6315 p999 N 25 2016

Chaya, Masazumi

Learn How to Learn New Rep color *Dance Magazine* v91 no3 p32 Mr 2017

Chayes, Antonia

What Comes Next *Daedalus* v146 no1 p125 Wint 2017

Chayka, Doug

A Man in Need R. J. Smith *Cincinnati Magazine* v50 no3 p92 D 2016

CHAYKA, KYLE

High and Mighty color *New Republic* v248 no5 p66 My 2017

Nowhere Mag *New Republic* v248 no7 p64 Jl 2017

CHAYKOWSKI, KATHLEEN

Avenging MySpace color *Forbes* v199 no7 p46 Je 29 2017

Bricks and Clicks color *Forbes* v200 no4 p40 O 24 2017

Build, Race, Fight... and Chat color *Forbes* v200 no1 p46 Jl 27 2017

Class App color *Forbes* v199 no6 p50 Je 13 2017

Hoarder Control color *Forbes* v200 no2 p42 S 5 2017

LESSONS AND IDEAS BY THE 100 GREATEST LIVING BUSINESS MINDS bw color *Forbes* v200 no3 p115 S 28 2017

THE WORLD'S BILLIONAIRES bw color diag graph map *Forbes* v199 no3 p84 Mr 28 2017

Chazelle, Damien, 1985-

BEST PICTURE CONTENDER LA LA LAND N. Sperling color *Entertainment Weekly* no1442 p44 D 2 2016 Rebellious Special Issue

CAN ANYTHING STOP LA LA LAND? N. Sperling color *Entertainment Weekly* no1449 p12 Ja 20 2017

Damien Chazelle D. Kiper color *Current Biography* v78 no6 p25 Je 2017

DANCING WITH THE STARS A. LANE cartoon *New Yorker* v92 no41 p88 D 12 2016

The Entertainer S. MARCHE cartoon color *Esquire* v166 no5 p45 D 2016/Ja 2017

FINDING LA LA LAND J. McGovern color *Entertainment Weekly* no1443 p44 D 9 2016

La La Land C. Chiarella color *Sound & Vision* v82 no7 p66 S 2017

LA LA LAND IS A MUSICAL LOVE LETTER TO THE CITY M. WAKIM *Los Angeles Magazine* p124 D 2016

LA LA LAND J. Mcgovern color *Entertainment Weekly* no1438 p36 N 4 2016

Let's Face the Music and Dance G. O'Brien color *New York Review of Books* v64 no6 p16 Ap 6 2017

The Missing Piece M. KORESKY color *Film Comment* v53 no1 p50 Ja/F 2017

No. 1 LA LA LAND C. Nashawaty and L. Greenblatt color *Entertainment Weekly* no1444/1445 p48 D 16 2016

ORNAMENTS TO THE SEASON S. KLAWANS color *Nation* v304 no2 p35 Ja 16 2017

A Star Is Born J. PODHORETZ color *Weekly Standard* v22 no16 p39 D 26 2016

UNDER THE INFLUENCE D. MARCHESE img *New York* v49 no24 p120 N 28 2016

Chazin, Walter J.

The [4Fe4S] cluster of human DNA primase functions as a redox switch using DNA charge transport color *Science* v355 no6327 p813 F 24 2017

Che, Michael

WHERE & WHEN *Washingtonian Magazine* v52 no9 p35 Je 2017

Che, Michael—Interviews

"When life gets bad, make it funny" [Cover story] W. Paskin color *Glamour* v115 no3 p190 Mr 2017

Che, Xiaoyu

Chiral Majorana fermion modes in a quantum anomalous Hall insulator–superconductor structure diag *Science* v357 no6348 p294 Jl 21 2017

Chebankova, Elena

Ideas, Ideology & Intellectuals in Search of Russia's Political Future *Daedalus* v146 no2 p76 Spr 2017

Chechnia (Russia)—Politics & government

RUSSIAN ROULETTE: Alarming reports indicate that Chechnya is detaining hundreds of gay men and some aren't making it out alive color *Advocate* no1091 p16 Je/Jl 2017

CHECK, JOHN

The Master's Voice color *Weekly Standard* v22 no41 p36 Jl 3 2017

Checking accounts

Online Bill Paying Isn't Foolproof L. GERSTNER chart *Kiplinger's Personal Finance* v71 no7 p45 Jl 2017

Checks—Computer network resources

Mobile Deposit: Give It a Shot L. GERSTNER chart *Kiplinger's Personal Finance* v71 no1 p41 Ja 2017

Checks—Management

The Road to Freedom: How One Woman Became Debt-Free S. E. Jamison color *Ebony* v72 no9 p71 Jl/Ag 2017

Checks—Security measures
Mobile Deposit: Give It a Shot L. GERSTNER chart *Kiplinger's Personal Finance* v71 no1 p41 Ja 2017

Cheddar cheese
English Cheddar Cheese D. Huntley *British Heritage Travel* v38 no1 p77 Ja/F 2017

Chediak, Mark
The Coming War On Gas color graph *Bloomberg Businessweek* no4519 p51 Ap 24 2017

CHEDLER, CARRIES
THE WORLD'S LOUDES INNER MONOLOGUE color *Chicago* v66 no5 p94 My 2017

CHEE, ALEXANDER
'A Woman's Face — Reprise (Sonnet 20)' *New York Times Magazine* p47 Mr 12 2017
Novelist, Interrupted bw color *New Republic* v247 no12 p56 D 2016
WAKEFIELD POOLE *Interview* v47 no3 p28 My 2017

Chee, Traci
Traci Chee S. GROCHOWSKI color *Publishers Weekly* v263 no52 p70 D 19 2016

Cheek
Super Natural A. FINNEY color *Women's Health* v14 no8 p138 O 2017

CHEEK, LAWRENCE W.
BORN SURVIVOR *Arizona Highways* v93 no3 p44 Mr 2017

Cheerleading
The New York Liberty's Dancers, the Timeless Torches, Are All 40-Plus A. TSOULIS-REAY img *New York* v49 no25 p54 D 12 2016
WHY I LOVE R. Zellweger color *InStyle* v24 no11 p220 N 2017

Cheese
Capital Grilled Cheese F. Largeman-Roth color *Parents* v92 no9 p46 S 2017
Cheesy dips for the win! color *Redbook* p150 O 2017
Expiration Dates You Should Never Ignore T. GAGNON color *Reader's Digest* v189 no1129 p42 Ap 2017
A Fine Meze color *Vegetarian Today* no1 p34 F 2017
THE FRIDGE S. Bower color *Good Housekeeping* v265 no3 p104 S 2017
Get the Party Started A. BARAGHANI color *Bon Appetit* v61 no12 p60 D 2016 /Jan2017
Gnocchi Two Ways color *Vegetarian Today* no2 p38 Ap 2017
A GUIDE TO VEGAN CHEESE C. Brown and S. Keenan *Vegetarian Journal* v36 no2 p12 2017
It's Cheesy N. Brechka color *Better Nutrition* v79 no11 p76 N 2017
Let's do brunch B. Risher color *Yoga Journal* no290 p78 Mr 2017
March 2017 color *O, The Oprah Magazine* p107 Mr 2017
RECIPES *Bon Appetit* v61 no12 p99 D 2016 /Jan2017
Say Cheese: Pitfalls on the path to a better cheddar L. MOYER and B. LIEBMAN *Nutrition Action Health Letter* v44 no7 p14 S 2017
What's your craving? Start snacking here B. Lipton color *Health* v31 no8 p127 O 2017

Cheese, Peter
CIPD helps boost civil service HR *People Management* p65 N 2016
Money's too tight to mention *People Management* p5 F 2017
Our agenda is crystal clear *People Management* p5 Ag 2017
Pulling the levers of change *People Management* p5 Je 2017
Putting People before profit *People Management* p5 D 2016/Ja 2017
Tackling the gender pay gap *People Management* p5 Ap 2017
Time for a reward rethink *People Management* p5 O 2016
Time for purposeful leadership *People Management* p5 Jl 2017
What does a 'professional' do? *People Management* p5 Mr 2017
What is the point of pay? *People Management* p5 S 2017
Who can we Trust? *People Management* p5 N 2016

Cheese shops
THE CHEESEMAKERS *South Dakota Magazine* v33 no3 p22 S/O 2017

Cheese spreads—Evaluation
Enjoy Nebraska Spreadables color *Nebraska Life* v21 no1 p55 Ja/F 2017

Cheese substitutes

MAC AND CHEESE E. McNamara color *Women's Health* v14 no5 p36 Je 2017

Cheeseburgers
That Sublime Slice of American Cheese J. SCHERER *Los Angeles Magazine* p46 Ja 2017

Cheeseburgers—Evaluation
THE LOOP K. B. GROSS, C. GAFFNEY et al bw color *Runner's World* v51 no11 p18 D 2016

Cheesecake
ALL GROWN UP *Martha Stewart Living* no267 p84 S 2016
A BRIGHT IDEA M. Sinclair color *O, The Oprah Magazine* p122 Ag 2017
CHRISTMAS CREATIONS D. CURRY color *New Orleans Magazine* v51 no2 p88 D 2016
Fluff and Fold L. TYRELL color *Martha Stewart Living* p80 Jl/Ag 2017
for the love of CHOCOLATE C. BOYD color *Better Homes & Gardens* v95 no4 p94 Ap 2017
HEALTHY HOLIDAY DESSERTS K. HYMORE color *Prevention* v68 no12 p40 D 2016
Here's the dessert that bakes itself! C. Hall color *Redbook* p23 Mr 2017
MMM...MORNING color *Good Housekeeping* v263 no5 p188 N 2016
Red, White & Berry Bars D. Wise color *Southern Living* v52 no7 p124 Jl 2017
YOUR PANTRY color *Good Housekeeping* v264 no5 p131 My 2017

Cheesecloth
THE WRINGER N. RICHARDSON color *Bon Appetit* no8 p102 Ag 2017

Cheese—Evaluation
BEST FOODS FOR RUNNERS [Cover story] M. KADEY, A. Rumsey et al cartoon color *Runner's World* v52 no3 p54 Ap 2017
Bone Char Pearl Cheese: It's made in Maine, aged in Brooklyn, and coated in animal-bone charcoal from Blue Hill at Stone Barns *New York* v50 no11 p106 My 29 2017
The RUNNER'S HIGH [Cover story] C. DANILOFF color diag *Runner's World* v52 no3 p68 Ap 2017
WHIZ KID A. STANEK color *Bon Appetit* no1 p101 F 2017

Cheese—Fat content
Silent Signs Your Body Craves a Diet Tweak M. LALIBERTE *Reader's Digest* v188 no1126 p46 D 2016/Ja 2017

Cheese—History
English Cheddar Cheese D. Huntley *British Heritage Travel* v38 no1 p77 Ja/F 2017

Cheetah
Art Zone *National Geographic Kids* no466 p36 D 2016/Ja 2017
DISPLACED C. Cox *Orion Magazine* v35 no3 p18 My/Je 2016
TURBO-CHEETAH A. E. HURT cartoon color map *National Geographic Kids* no470 p16 My 2017

Cheetah behavior
TURBO-CHEETAH A. E. HURT cartoon color map *National Geographic Kids* no470 p16 My 2017

Cheever, Meg
From Steel to Green: Revitalizing Pittsburgh Through Its Park System: The Pittsburgh Parks Conservancy shares lessons learned as it celebrates 20 years S. Roller *Parks & Recreation* v52 no8 p18 Ag 2017

Cheez Whiz (Company)
WHIZ KID A. STANEK color *Bon Appetit* no1 p101 F 2017

Chef'd (Company)
New Meal Services That Deliver color *Men's Health* v32 no7 p66 S 2017

Chekhov, Anton Pavlovich, 1860-1904
TEMPS PERDU I. Parker cartoon *New Yorker* v92 no33 p28 O 17 2016

Chelan Fresh (Company)
GROCERY SHOPPING MADE EASY J. London color *Good Housekeeping* v263 no5 p152 N 2016

CHELETTE, BEATE
The Shadow Knows *USA Today Magazine* v145 no2858 p19 N 2016

CHELLEL, KIT
THE HIJACKING OF THE BRILLANTE VIRTUOSO color map

Bloomberg Businessweek no4532 p48 Jl 31 2017

LIBYA VS GOLDMAN cartoon *Bloomberg Businessweek* no4493 p66 O 3 2016

Chelly, Canyon de (Ariz.)

The Big Pictures: CANYON DE CHELLY *Arizona Highways* v93 no10 p16 O 2017

Canyon de Chelly National Monument K. FROST *Arizona Highways* v92 no7 p7 Jl 2016

Chelsea (TV program)

Chelsea's Back for More J. HALTERMAN *TV Guide* v65 no14 p10 Ap 3 2017

What, Me Worry? color *InStyle* v24 no6 p156 Je 2017

Chelsea Flower Show

AROUND THE GARDEN S. Bender color *Southern Living* v52 no3 p42 Mr 2017

Chelsom, Peter

BIRTH OF A MARTIAN K. M. MCFARLAND cartoon *Wired* v24 no12 p34 D 2016

Chelydra serpentina

In the Company of DINOSAURS W. S. Hoffman *New York State Conservationist* v71 no5 p28 Ap 2017

Chelys (Genus)

awesome 8 S. W. FLYNN color *National Geographic Kids* no470 p6 My 2017

Chemainus (Vancouver Island, B.C.)

MURAL TOWN D. HISLOP *Sea Magazine* v108 no10 pPNW-1 O 2016

Chemale, Farid Jr.

Release of mineral-bound water prior to subduction tied to shallow seismogenic slip off Sumatra graph *Science* v356 no6340 p841 My 26 2017

Chemerinsky, Erwin

Closing the Courthouse Door: How Your Constitutional Rights Became Unenforceable *Publishers Weekly* v263 no43 p68 O 24 2016

Chemical biology

A chemical biology route to site-specific authentic protein modifications A. Yang, S. Ha et al bibl diag graph *Science* v354 no6312 p623 N 4 2016

Chemical bonds

Directed evolution of cytochrome c for carbon–silicon bond formation: Bringing silicon to life S. B. J. Kan, R. D. Lewis et al bibl diag graph *Science* v354 no6315 p1048 N 25 2016

Chemical elements

See also

Siderophile elements

Feng Shui Beauty S. STRAUSFOGEL color *Better Nutrition* v79 no1 p54 Ja 2017

Chemical industry laws

Evidence in the Precautionary Assessment of Novel Substances A. Chapman bibl *Environment* v59 no5 p16 S/O 2017

Chemical kinetics

Direct frequency comb measurement of OD + CO→DOCO kinetics B. J. Bjork, T. Q. Bui et al bibl graph *Science* v354 no6311 p444 O 28 2016

Chemical laboratory equipment

Natural Eye Creams S. STRAUSFOGEL color *Better Nutrition* v79 no10 p34 O 2017

Chemical modification of proteins

Posttranslational mutagenesis: A chemical strategy for exploring protein side-chain diversity T. H. Wright, B. J. Bower et al diag *Science* v354 no6312 p597 N 4 2016

Proteins by design R. F. Service color *Science* v354 no6319 p1520 D 23 2016

A radical approach to posttranslational mutagenesis R. Hofmann and J. W. Bode bibl diag *Science* v354 no6312 p553 N 4 2016

Chemical mutagenesis

Posttranslational mutagenesis: A chemical strategy for exploring protein side-chain diversity T. H. Wright, B. J. Bower et al diag *Science* v354 no6312 p597 N 4 2016

Chemical peel

What Happens Between Before and After: A rarely seen side of plastic surgery L. Wells img *New York* v50 no11 p46 My 29 2017

Chemical peel—Equipment & supplies

Mask appeal E. Marglin color *Yoga Journal* no289 p20 F 2017

Chemical products manufacturing

Industrial biomanufacturing: The future of chemical production J. M. Clomburg, A. M. Crumbley et al bibl chart color diag graph *Science* v355 no6320 p1 Ja 6 2017

Chemical purification—Equipment & supplies

new products: protein analysis color *Science* v356 no6341 p973 Je 1 2017

Chemical reactions

See also

Borylation

Coupling reactions (Chemistry)

Polymerization

AYAH BDEIR S. BUSHWICK color *Popular Science* v288 no6 p26 N/D 2016

Detonation Science Blasts into a New Frontier H. Auten *Science & Technology Review* p12 Jl/Ag 2017

How boundaries shape chemical delivery in microfluidics M. Aminian, F. Bernardi et al bibl diag graph *Science* v354 no6317 p1252 D 9 2016

Single-particle mapping of nonequilibrium nanocrystal transformations Xingchen Ye, M. R. Jones et al bibl bw graph *Science* v354 no6314 p874 N 18 2016

Time-resolved x-ray absorption spectroscopy with a water window high-harmonic source Y. Pertot, C. Schmidt et al bibl graph *Science* v355 no6322 p264 Ja 20 2017

Chemical terrorism—Prevention

Rapid Recovery of Critical Infrastructure L. L. Helms color *Science & Technology Review* p20 O/N 2016

Chemical testing

Chemical safety must extend to ecosystems J. R. Rohr, C. J. Salice et al *Science* v356 no6341 p917 Je 1 2017

Chemical tests & reagents

Synthesis of mixed hypermetallic oxide BaOCa+ from laser-cooled reagents in an atom-ion hybrid trap P. Puri, M. Mills et al diag graph *Science* v357 no6358 p1370 S 29 2017

Chemical warfare

See also

Poisonous gases—War use

CHEMICAL WEAPONS CONUNDRUM J. M. ORIENT *USA Today Magazine* v146 no2866 p34 Jl 2017

Chemical weapons testing

AGENT DEFEAT Efforts Strike Gold R. Hansen *Science & Technology Review* p12 Mr 2017

Chemical weapons—Social aspects

CHEMICAL WEAPONS CONUNDRUM J. M. ORIENT *USA Today Magazine* v146 no2866 p34 Jl 2017

Military impulse *Christian Century* v134 no10 p7 My 10 2017

Chemicals safety measures

Policy reforms to update chemical safety testing A. E. Nel and T. F. Malloy bibl color *Science* v355 no6329 p1016 Mr 10 2017

Protect Yourself A. JONES *Boating World* v38 no5 p24 My 2017

Chemicals—Law & legislation—United States

New toxic chemical regulations J. A. ROBERTS *Issues in Science & Technology* v33 no2 p9 Wint 2017

Chemicals—Safety measures—Law & legislation

Not'Til the Fat Lady Sings TSCA's Next Act D. GOLDSTON *Issues in Science & Technology* v33 no1 p73 Fall 2016

A Second Act for Risk-Based Chemicals Regulation K. B. BELTON and J. E. S. W. CONRAD JR. *Issues in Science & Technology* v33 no1 p77 Fall 2016

Chemistry

See also

Chemical reactions

Color

Condensation

Forensic chemistry

Pharmacy

Stereochemistry

Why We Still Don't Have Better Batteries R. Martin il *MIT Technology Review* v119 no6 p22 N/D 2016

Chemists

See also

Pharmacists

Neural networks learn the art of chemical synthesis R. F. Service *Science* v357 no6346 p27 Jl 7 2017

Chemists—Biography

MEG HE color *Bloomberg Businessweek* no4518 p79 Ap 10 2017

Peak Performance bw color *Esquire* v166 no5 p56 D 2016/Ja 2017

Pull Yourself Together, Man! color *Esquire* v166 no4 p65 N 2016

STEVEN TRISTAN YOUNG color *Bloomberg Businessweek* no4511 p67 F 13 2017

The Superhero Sweater color *Esquire* v166 no5 p55 D 2016/Ja 2017

What I Wear to Work: ANNA BROCKWAY color *Bloomberg Businessweek* no4499 p87 N 14 2016

What I Wear to Work color *Bloomberg Businessweek* no4504 p67 D 19 2016

What I Wear to Work color *Bloomberg Businessweek* no4523 p67 My 22 2017

What I Wear to Work: JOAN INSEL color *Bloomberg Businessweek* no4516 p71 Mr 27 2017

What I Wear to Work: MAURICIO URIBE color *Bloomberg Businessweek* no4507 p67 Ja 16 2017

What I Wear to Work: NOA SANTOS color *Bloomberg Businessweek* no4520 p75 My 1 2017

What I Wear to Work: REIHAN SALAM color *Bloomberg Businessweek* no4495 p75 O 17 2016

What I Wear to Work: SHOSHANA FISHER color *Bloomberg Businessweek* no4514 p75 Mr 13 2017

What I Wear to Work: TALI EDUT color *Bloomberg Businessweek* no4515 p67 Mr 20 2017

XINJIANG, CHINA color *Conde Nast Traveler* v52 no1 p32 Ja 2017

Chen, Jennifer

Aloha Adventure color *Popular Photography* v80 no11 p48 D 2016

Anti-Bullying Buddies color *Good Housekeeping* v265 no2 p67 Ag 2017

GIFTS that UPLIFT! cartoon *O, The Oprah Magazine* p148 D 2016

The Grass Menagerie color *Popular Photography* v81 no2 p42 Mr/Ap 2017

Promoting human rights through science color *Science* v357 no6359 p34 O 6 2017

Chen, Jingguang G.

Active sites for CO2 hydrogenation to methanol on Cu/ZnO catalysts bibl graph *Science* v355 no6331 p1296 Mr 24 2017

TECHNICAL COMMENT ABSTRACTS *Science* v357 no6354 p881 S 1 2017

Chen, Jinmiao

Mapping the human DC lineage through the integration of high-dimensional techniques diag *Science* v356 no6342 p1044 Je 9 2017

Chen, Joanne

First Aid for Eye Ouches *Parents* v92 no8 p33 Ag 2017

Teeth: an owner's manual color *Redbook* p77 Jl/Ag 2017

Chen, Joel

The Accidental Collector E. YOUNG *Los Angeles Magazine* p52 D 2016

Chen, Judy

China's Bridge and Tunnel Addiction color *Bloomberg Businessweek* no4513 p47 Mr 6 2017

Chen, Julie, 1970——Interviews

THE TALK M. LOGAN *TV Guide* v65 no27 p40 Je 26 2017

Chen, Ken

"Perfect" designer chromosome V and behavior of a ring derivative diag *Science* v355 no6329 p1046 Mr 10 2017

Chen, Lanhee J.

The Drug Marketplace at Work: Competition already lowers the price of drugs--and it works better than price fixing ever could *Hoover Digest: Research & Opinion on Public Policy* no3 p51 Summ 2017

Chen, Lixin

DNA damage is a pervasive cause of sequencing errors, directly confounding variant identification bibl graph *Science* v355 no6326 p752 F 17 2017

Chen, Lulu Yilun

Airbnb Inches Its Way Into China color *Bloomberg Businessweek* no4503 p30 D 12 2016

OUT-UBERING Uber How CHENG WEI, founder of China's DIDI, drove the Americans OFF THE ROAD in CHINA color *Bloomberg Businessweek* no4494 p60 O 10 2016

Patience You Must Have, My Young Investors color *Bloomberg Businessweek* no4503 p27 D 12 2016

TENCENT GOES GLOBAL MAYBE color diag *Bloomberg Businessweek* no4529 p50 Jl 3 2017

Chen, Man, 1980-

Chen Man J. Crelin *Current Biography* v78 no9 p53 S 2017

Chen, Michael Z.

Thirst-associated preoptic neurons encode an aversive motivational drive diag *Science* v357 no6356 p1149 S 15 2017

CHEN, MICHELLE

Bad Credit *Nation* v305 no9 p6 O 16 2017

Chen, Nathan, 1999-

FIGURE SKATING K. ROSEN *TV Guide* v65 no4 p48 Ja 16 2017

Chen, Peng

Robust epitaxial growth of two-dimensional heterostructures, multiheterostructures, and superlattices color *Science* v357 no6353 p788 Ag 25 2017

Chen, Pingfan

All-oxide–based synthetic antiferromagnets exhibiting layer-resolved magnetization reversal diag *Science* v357 no6347 p191 Jl 14 2017

Chen, Qingfeng

Mapping the human DC lineage through the integration of high-dimensional techniques diag *Science* v356 no6342 p1044 Je 9 2017

Chen, Qingzhi

Epitaxial lift-off of electrodeposited single-crystal gold foils for flexible electronics bibl bw diag *Science* v355 no6330 p1203 Mr 17 2017

Chen, Qiuhong

Two-dimensional sp2 carbon–conjugated covalent organic frameworks diag graph *Science* v357 no6352 p673 Ag 18 2017

Chen, S. R. Wayne

Structural basis for the gating mechanism of the type 2 ryanodine receptor RyR2 bibl color graph *Science* v354 no6310 paah5324-1 O 21 2016

Chen, Sarah

A FRAGILE BORDER color *Bloomberg Businessweek* no4539 p33 S 25 2017

Chen, Sean

Deficiency of microRNA miR-34a expands cell fate potential in pluripotent stem cells diag *Science* v355 no6325 p596 F 10 2017

Chen, Shihong

Deep functional analysis of synII, a 770-kilobase synthetic yeast chromosome diag *Science* v355 no6329 p1047 Mr 10 2017

CHEN, SHU-CHING JEAN

THE WORLD'S BILLIONAIRES bw color diag graph map *Forbes* v199 no3 p84 Mr 28 2017

Chen, Si

"Perfect" designer chromosome V and behavior of a ring derivative diag *Science* v355 no6329 p1046 Mr 10 2017

Chen, Steven

GET MORE OUT OF YOUR DRUGSTORE C. Ratcliff color *Men's Health* v32 no1 p85 Ja/F 2017

Chen, Tai

Deep functional analysis of synII, a 770-kilobase synthetic yeast chromosome diag *Science* v355 no6329 p1047 Mr 10 2017

Chen, Tiffany Q.

A catalytic fluoride-rebound mechanism for C(sp3)-CF3 bond formation diag *Science* v356 no6344 p1272 Je 23 2017

Chen, Weisheng V.

Multicluster Pcdh diversity is required for mouse olfactory neural circuit assembly diag *Science* v356 no6336 p411 Ap 28 2017

Pcdhαc2 is required for axonal tiling and assembly of serotonergic circuitries in mice diag *Science* v356 no6336 p406 Ap 28 2017

Chen, Wenhuang

Release of mineral-bound water prior to subduction tied to shallow seismogenic slip off Sumatra graph *Science* v356 no6340 p841 My 26 2017

Chen, X.

High-temperature quantum oscillations caused by recurring Bloch states in graphene superlattices color *Science* v357 no6347 p181 Jl 14 2017

Chen, Xiao-Ming

Controlling guest conformation for efficient purification of butadiene bw diag *Science* v356 no6343 p1193 Je 16 2017

Chen, Xiaoya

Plants transfer lipids to sustain colonization by mutualistic mycorrhizal and parasitic fungi diag graph *Science* v356 no6343 p1172 Je 16 2017

Chen, Xuejun

Trispecific broadly neutralizing HIV antibodies mediate potent SHIV protection in macaques color graph *Science* v357 no6359 p85 O 6 2017

Chen, Y.

A human-driven decline in global burned area chart graph map *Science* v356 no6345 p1356 Je 30 2017

Chen, Y. -S.

Direct observation of individual hydrogen atoms at trapping sites in a ferritic steel bibl diag *Science* v355 no6330 p1196 Mr 17 2017

Chen, Yan

Bug mapping and fitness testing of chemically synthesized chromosome X diag *Science* v355 no6329 p1048 Mr 10 2017

Chen, Yang

History of winning remodels thalamo-PFC circuit to reinforce social dominance color *Science* v357 no6347 p162 Jl 14 2017

Chen, Yi-Chi

21st-century rise in anthropogenic nitrogen deposition on a remote coral reef diag graph *Science* v356 no6339 p749 My 19 2017

Chen, Yu-Ao

Satellite-based entanglement distribution over 1200 kilometers diag graph *Science* v356 no6343 p1140 Je 16 2017

Chen, Zhenqing

Glia relay differentiation cues to coordinate neuronal development in Drosophila color *Science* v357 no6354 p886 S 1 2017

Chen, Zhijie

Chiral Majorana fermion modes in a quantum anomalous Hall insulator–superconductor structure diag *Science* v357 no6348 p294 Jl 21 2017

Chen, Zhixing

Mechanochemical unzipping of insulating polyladderene to semiconducting polyacetylene [Cover story] diag *Science* v357 no6350 p475 Ag 4 2017

Chen, Zhou-Feng

Molecular and neural basis of contagious itch behavior in mice bibl diag *Science* v355 no6329 p1072 Mr 10 2017

Chen, Zibo

A cargo-sorting DNA robot color *Science* v357 no6356 p1112 S 15 2017

Chen Chen

Self-Portrait as So Much Potential Chen Chen *New York Times Magazine* p17 Mr 5 2017

Self-Portrait as So Much Potential *New York Times Magazine* p17 Mr 5 2017

Chen Qi

Pathological α-synuclein transmission initiated by binding lymphocyte-activation gene 3 bibl graph *Science* v353 no6307 paah3374-1 S 30 2016

Chen Wang

Quality management for precision medicine clinical applications: A consensus from the China Precision Medicine Clinical Research and Application Association bibl *Science* v354 no6319 p11 D 23 2016

Chen Zhao

The DNA-sensing AIM2 inflammasome controls radiation-induced cell death and tissue injury bibl color graph *Science* v354 no6313 p765 N 11 2016

Chen Zhenghao

Who's Benefiting from MOOCs, and Why *Harvard Business Review Digital Articles* p2 S 22 2015

Chenault, Paige

How I Found My Purpose C. de León color *Glamour* v114 no11 p138 N 2016

CHENEY, KAREN

home renovation without the hassle *Parents* v91 no6 p118 Je 2016

Cheney, Liz, 1966-

Return to the Dark Side T. MURPHY bw *Mother Jones* v42 no1 p22 Ja/F 2017

Cheney, Richard B., 1941-

Cheney Was Right E. EDELMAN and R. JOSEPH color *Weekly Standard* v23 no5 p27 O 9 2017

Cheng, Carl

CARL CHENG W. Vogel *Art in America* v104 no9 p159 O 2016

Cheng, Christine

High-resolution interrogation of functional elements in the noncoding genome bibl graph *Science* v353 no6307 p1545 S 30 2016

Cheng, Erchao

Engineering the ribosomal DNA in a megabase synthetic chromosome diag *Science* v355 no6329 p1049 Mr 10 2017

Cheng, G. J.

High dislocation density–induced large ductility in deformed and partitioned steels bw color diag *Science* v357 no6355 p1029 S 8 2017

Cheng, Hui-Ming

Charge delivery goes the distance color *Science* v356 no6338 p582 My 12 2017

Cheng, Ian

Portal_Ranch.txt color *Art in America* v105 no4 p42 Ap 2017

Cheng, Ian—Exhibitions

Never-Ending Story A. K. Scott cartoon *New Yorker* v93 no13 p10 My 15 2017

Cheng, J. Yo-Jud

7 Charts Show How Political Affiliation Shapes U.S. Boards *Harvard Business Review Digital Articles* p2 Ag 23 2016

The Political Issues Board Directors Care Most About *Harvard Business Review Digital Articles* p2 F 16 2016

Cheng, Jack

See You in the Cosmos, Carl Sagan color *Publishers Weekly* v263 no50 p73 D 5 2016

Somewhere Out There: In this middle-grade novel, a boy's quest to connect with alien life turns into a family affair N. STANDIFORD *New York Times Book Review* p19 My 14 2017

Cheng, Jing-Sheng

"Perfect" designer chromosome V and behavior of a ring derivative diag *Science* v355 no6329 p1046 Mr 10 2017

CHENG, MARK

STILL KICKING! (and Punching and Grappling) [Cover story] bw color *Black Belt* v55 no1 p26 D 2016/Ja 2017

Cheng, Susan J.

How I'm standing up for science color *Science* v355 no6327 p878 F 24 2017

Cheng, Tammy M.

Opposing effects of Elk-1 multisite phosphorylation shape its response to ERK activation bibl graph *Science* v354 no6309 p233 O 14 2016

Cheng, Xiaodong

A placental growth factor is silenced in mouse embryos by the zinc finger protein ZFP568 color graph *Science* v356 no6339 p757 My 19 2017

Cheng Chin

Universal space-time scaling symmetry in the dynamics of bosons across a quantum phase transition bibl graph *Science* v354 no6312 p606 N 4 2016

Cheng Li

Chinese Politics in the Xi Jinping Era: Reassessing Collective Leadership A. J. Nathan and V. SHIH *Foreign Affairs* v96 no1 p177 Ja/F 2017

Cheng-Ming Chuong

The "tao" of integuments bibl color diag *Science* v354 no6319 p1533 D 23 2016

Cheng Wei

8 CHENG WEI S. Cendrowski color *Fortune* v174 no7 p85 D 1 2016

Chengcheng Jin

The DNA-sensing AIM2 inflammasome controls radiation-induced cell death and tissue injury bibl color graph *Science* v354 no6313 p765 N 11 2016

Chengfeng Wang

Opportunities and challenges for precision medicine in pancreatic cancer prevention and treatment bibl *Science* v354 no6319 p42 D 23 2016

Chengguo Sun

Synthesis and characterization of the pentazolate anion cyclo-N5⁻ in (N5)6(H3O)3(NH4)4Cl bibl diag graph *Science* v355 no6323 p374 Ja 27 2017

CHENG-TOZUN, DORCAS

CAUGHT BETWEEN TWO WORLDS cartoon *Christianity Today* p42 Mr 2017

Cheng Yu-tung
Hail and Farewell color *Forbes* v199 no3 p36 Mr 28 2017

Chenhui Peng
Command of active matter by topological defects and patterns bibl graph *Science* v354 no6314 p882 N 18 2016

Chenjie Zeng
Emergence of hierarchical structural complexities in nanoparticles and their assembly bibl color *Science* v354 no6319 p1580 D 23 2016

Chenming Hu
MoS2 transistors with 1-nanometer gate lengths bibl color graph *Science* v354 no6308 p99 O 7 2016

Chenot, Elise
The formation of peak rings in large impact craters bibl color graph *Science* v354 no6314 p878 N 18 2016

Chenoweth, Kristin, 1968-
GODS GONE WILD M. Snetiker color *Entertainment Weekly* no1462 p26 Ap 21 2017

Chentao Lin
Photoactivation and inactivation of Arabidopsis cryptochrome 2 bibl graph *Science* v354 no6310 p343 O 21 2016

CHENXI LU
Optimal Tree Canopy Cover during Ecological Restoration: A Case Study of Possible Ecological Thresholds in Changting, China *BioScience* v67 no3 p221 Mr 2017

Chenxin Zhu
Highly stretchable polymer semiconductor films through the nanoconfinement effect bibl graph *Science* v355 no6320 p1 Ja 6 2017

Cheong, Suah
How Panamanians and Trees Are Saving Each Other *American Forests* v123 no2 p6 Summ 2017

Cheoy Lee Shipyards Ltd.
NEW TRADITIONS P. FREDERIKSEN chart color *Power & Motoryacht* v34 no9 p72 S 2017

Cher, 1946-
For the Record color *Time* v190 no15 p6 O 16 2017

Cherepanov, Peter
A supramolecular assembly mediates lentiviral DNA integration bibl color *Science* v355 no6320 p1 Ja 6 2017

Chergui, Majed
Ahmed Hassan Zewail *Physics Today* v69 no12 p69 D 2016

Cherkassy Pocket, Battle of the, Ukraine, 1944
THE KORSUN NOOSE R. M. Citino *MHQ: Quarterly Journal of Military History* v29 no2 p26 Wint 2017

CHERNILA, ALANA
Every Recipe Has a Story color *Parents* v92 no11 p99 N 2017

Chernobyl Nuclear Accident, Chornobyl, Ukraine, 1986
Quick Hits map *Scientific American* v316 no2 p16 F 2017

Chernobyl Nuclear Accident, Chornobyl, Ukraine, 1986—Health aspects
Chernobyl nuclear-meltdown consequences A. DeVolpi *Physics Today* v69 no11 p13 N 2016

Chernomordik, Boris D.
Quantum dot–induced phase stabilization of α-CsPbI3 perovskite for high-efficiency photovoltaics bibl chart graph *Science* v354 no6308 p92 O 7 2016

Chernow, Ron
The Rest Is History L. Rothman color *Time* v190 no15 p48 O 16 2017
Ron Chernow A. MacLean *Humanities* v37 no4 p1 Fall 2016
The Unlikely Grant B. Clinton *New York Times Book Review* p1 O 15 2017

Cherny, Andrei
Low Fees, Low Minimum, Big Return R. ERMEY chart *Kiplinger's Personal Finance* v71 no6 p57 Je 2017

Cherokee automobile
5 THINGS TO KNOW ABOUT THE 2017 JEEP GRAND CHEROKEE SUMMIT C. Seabaugh color *Motor Trend* v69 no2 p57 F 2017

Cherokee Inc.
OVER LANDER'S DREAM C. Seabaugh chart color *Motor Trend* v69 no2 p54 F 2017

Cherry

At Home with Moose J. KEEBLE color *Natural History* v125 no7 p48 Jl/Ag 2017
Fruits of Summer: The season's bounty in flavor-packed parcels M. W. Spencer *New Orleans Homes & Lifestyles* v20 no3 p112 Summ 2017
Japan color *National Geographic* v231 no4 p8 Ap 2017

Cherry, Don, 1936-1995
DON CHERRY: ORGANIC FLOW P. Lutz bw *Downbeat* v84 no8 p32 Ag 2017

Cherry-Sakura (Music)
Cherry–Sakura J. Corbett color *Downbeat* v84 no5 p49 My 2017
The Hot Box J. McDonough, P. de Barros et al chart *Downbeat* v84 no5 p51 My 2017

Cherry—History
The Surprising History of Cherry Blossoms O. B. Waxman *Time* v189 no12 p25 Ap 3 2017

Chertoff, Michael
8 Ways Governments Can Improve Their Cybersecurity [Cover story] *Harvard Business Review Digital Articles* p2 Ap 25 2017

CHERUVELIL, KENDRA S.
Conceptions of Good Science in Our Data-Rich World chart *BioScience* v66 no10 p1 O 1 2016

Chervin, Christopher N.
Rechargeable nickel–3D zinc batteries: An energy-dense, safer alternative to lithium-ion bw chart diag *Science* v356 no6336 p415 Ap 28 2017

Chesapeake Bay (Md. & Va.)—Description & travel
THE EASTERN SHORE J. Sugarman color *Washingtonian Magazine* v52 no7 p149 Ap 2017
HOME IS WHERE THE BOAT IS A. Cort and P. Nielsen color map *Sail* v48 no3 p38 Mr 2017

Chesapeake Bay (Md. & Va.)—Environmental conditions
Submersed Aquatic Vegetation in Chesapeake Bay: Sentinel Species in a Changing World R. J. ORTH, W. C. DENNISON et al *BioScience* v67 no8 p698 Ag 2017

Chesapeake Bay Catering Co.
SPECIAL WEDDINGS ADVERTISING SECTION *Virginia Living* v15 no2 p90 F 2017

Chesapeake Shores (TV program)
Chesapeake Shores K. Freeze *TV Guide* v65 no31 p34 Jl 24 2017

Cheshire, James
Where the Animals Go: Tracking Wildlife with Technology in 50 Maps and Graphics A. Gawrylewski color map *Scientific American* v317 no3 p88 S 2017

Chesman, Andrea
MAKE JAMS WITH LESS SUGAR: These recipes and tips offer a variety of options for preserving low-sugar jams without commercial pectin *Mother Earth News* no283 p16 Ag/S 2017
WINTER SOUPS FROM THE CELLAR *Mother Earth News* no280 p50 F/Mr 2017

Chesney, Kenny, 1968-
Kenny Chesney N. Feeney color *Entertainment Weekly* no1438 p59 N 4 2016

Chesney, Kenny, 1968—Interviews
THE TAO OF KENNY CHESNEY M. Vain color *Entertainment Weekly* no1438 p58 N 4 2016

Chess
Meeting the God of Chess W. So color *Christianity Today* v61 no7 p88 S 2017

Chess, Andrew
Intersection of diverse neuronal genomes and neuropsychiatric disease: The Brain Somatic Mosaicism Network color *Science* v356 no6336 p395 Ap 28 2017

Chess players
Game of Kings J. Tarmy color *Bloomberg Businessweek* no4539 p67 S 25 2017
Garry KASPAROV J. Dickey color *Sports Illustrated* v127 no1 p78 Jl 3 2017
Meeting the God of Chess W. So color *Christianity Today* v61 no7 p88 S 2017
Your Move S. CHAPIN color *Walrus* v14 no9 p75 N 2017

Chess tournaments
ALL AROUND Missouri color *Missouri Life* v44 no3 p83 My 2017
CALENDAR OF EVENTS *Idaho Magazine* v16 no3 p58 D 2016

Chessboards

Power Tools: Pioneers C. Alter color *Time* v189 no16/17 p36 My 1-8 2017

Chess—Competitions

WHY ROBOTS WON'T FARM R. Holtzmann *South Dakota Magazine* v33 no2 p44 Jl/Ag 2017

Chest exercises

THE (NEXT) 10 BEST CHEST EXERCISES M. BERG color *Muscle & Performance* v9 no8 p44 Ag 2017

Chest pain

How to Survive Your First Heart Attack *AARP: The Magazine* v59 no2A p18 F/Mr 2016

CHESTER, CHARLES C.

Conserving Transborder Migratory Bats, Preserving Nature's Benefits to Humans: The Lesson from North America's Bird Conservation Treaties *BioScience* v67 no4 p321 Ap 2017

CHESTER, SAM

Assessing Bibi *Commentary* v142 no4 p14 N 2016

Chesterton, G. K. (Gilbert Keith), 1874-1936

1910: London G. K. Chesterton *Lapham's Quarterly* v10 no1 p26 Wint 2017

Chesterton's Throne M. W. Jones bw *Commonweal* v144 no13 p39 Ag 11 2017

THOUGHTS ON Property *Forbes* v199 no5 p124 My 16 2017

Chestnut, Morris

The Cut: Lose Up to 10 Pounds in 10 Days and Sculpt Your Best Body *Publishers Weekly* v264 no6 p64 F 6 2017

Chestnut, Morris—Interviews

MAKING THE CUT L. McGLASHAN chart color *Muscle & Performance* v9 no4 p34 Ap 2017

Chests (Furniture)

THE ALMY FAMILY CHIPPENDALE CHEST ON CHEST color *Magazine Antiques* v184 no3 p1 My/Je 2017

THE ODDS AND ENDS OF ZEN L. Haney color *Women's Health* v14 no4 p121 My 2017

Queen Anne figured maple high chest with stylized lobster tail scrolled apron color *Magazine Antiques* v184 no3 p13 My/Je 2017

SPEED-CLEANING *Good Housekeeping* v264 no3 p54 Mr 2017

Tame that junk drawer for good [Cover story] J. Jones color *Redbook* p32 My 2017

Chests (Furniture)—Evaluation

Nordic White color *House Beautiful* v158 no10 p16 D 2016/Ja 2017

Chétrite, Evelyne

Perfect Match N. Silverstein bw color *Glamour* v115 no5 p54 My 2017

Chétrite, Evelyne—Interviews

SISTER ACT color *Harper's Bazaar* no3649 p186 D 2016/Ja 2017

Chettouh, Z.

The sacral autonomic outflow is sympathetic bibl color diag *Science* v354 no6314 p893 N 18 2016

Chetty, Raj

The fading American dream: Trends in absolute income mobility since 1940 bw graph *Science* v356 no6336 p398 Ap 28 2017

Improving Opportunities for Economic Mobility *Bridges (Federal Reserve Bank of St. Louis)* p1 Fall 2016

Cheu, Ryan

Vaginal bacteria modify HIV tenofovir microbicide efficacy in African women chart graph *Science* v356 no6341 p938 Je 1 2017

Cheung, Jeanne

T cell costimulatory receptor CD28 is a primary target for PD-1–mediated inhibition color diag graph *Science* v355 no6332 p1428 Mr 31 2017

Cheung, Man Kit

Research night owls color *Science* v354 no6315 p964 N 25 2016

Cheung, Ruby

New Hong Kong Cinema: Transitions to Becoming Chinese in 21st-Century East Asia G. BETTINSON *Film Quarterly* v70 no2 p113 Wint 2016

Cheung, William W. L.

Large benefits to marine fisheries of meeting the 1.5°C global warming target bibl graph *Science* v354 no6319 p1591 D 23 2016

Chevalier, Aaron

Global analysis of protein folding using massively parallel design,

synthesis, and testing color diag *Science* v357 no6347 p168 Jl 14 2017

Chevee, Maxime

Multicluster Pcdh diversity is required for mouse olfactory neural circuit assembly diag *Science* v356 no6336 p411 Ap 28 2017

Chevelle automobile

The 350 Crate Engine in Carl Arentz's 1964 Chevelle Has Severe Driveability Issues. We're Gonna Fix It M. Davis chart color *Hot Rod* v70 no9 p94 S 2017

Larry Musto Ask... Which Edelbrock Head Yields 9.5:1 Compression on a Stock 1971 402? M. Davis color *Hot Rod* v70 no1 p104 Ja 2017

TWO YEARS, TWO TURBOS: THE AUSSIE CHEVELLE RETURNS! P. Thomas color *Hot Rod* v70 no2 p38 F 2017

Chevelle automobile—Evaluation

Big-Block Beauty T. Taylor color *Hot Rod* v70 no6 p32 Je 2017

Chevelon Canyon (Ariz.)

CHEVELON CANYON LAKE: The Mogoiion Rim gets busy this time of year, especially at Woods Canyon Lake. However, not far from there, along a scenic road lined with giant ponderosas, is an isolated lake that's every bit as beautiful N. AUSTIN *Arizona Highways* v93 no8 p52 Ag 2017

Cheviron, Zachary A.

Winter storms drive rapid phenotypic, regulatory, and genomic shifts in the green anole lizard graph *Science* v357 no6350 p495 Ag 4 2017

Chevlen, Dorie

The Age of Consequences *Science* v356 no6337 p481 My 5 2017

Chevrolet (Company)

2016 CHEVROLET CAMARO SS J. Jacquot color graph *Car & Driver* v63 no2 p72 Ag 2017

2017 COPO CAMARO: DIRECT INJECTION GOES DRAG RACING M. Davis bw chart color *Hot Rod* v70 no10 p64 O 2017

2018 Chevrolet Equinox F. Markus color *Motor Trend* v69 no1 p20 Ja 2017

ATOMIC PROSPECTOR A. Robinson chart color diag *Car & Driver* v63 no2 p42 Ag 2017

Ballistic Leaf Blower [Cover story] J. Jacquot color diag *Car & Driver* v62 no6 p42 D 2016

BIG BET F. Markus chart color *Motor Trend* v69 no8 p56 Ag 2017

Big-Block Beauty T. Taylor color *Hot Rod* v70 no6 p32 Je 2017

BRUTE SQUAD GOALS J. Lieberman chart color *Motor Trend* v69 no4 p62 Ap 2017

Chevrolet Cruze chart color *Motor Trend* v69 no1 p121 Ja 2017

Chevrolet FNR-X concept E. Tahaney color *Motor Trend* v69 no8 p18 Ag 2017

Chevrolet Volt chart color *Motor Trend* v69 no1 p122 Ja 2017

A Crude Awakening J. Capparella color *Car & Driver* v63 no2 p88 Ag 2017

DRIVE AWAY WITH A BEAUTY color *Men's Health* v31 no10 p(Sp)28 D 2016

Evolutionary Success D. Sherman color *Car & Driver* v63 no1 p100 Jl 2017

FIRST DRIVE "1963" Superformance Corvette Grand Sport C. Walton color *Motor Trend* v68 no12 p46 D 2016

Functional but Not Much Zip color *Consumer Reports* v82 no8 p59 Ag 2017

GARAGE color *Motor Trend* v69 no5 p88 My 2017

POWER HITTER B. MCALEER color *Road & Track* v68 no7 p84 Mr/Ap 2017

RUNNING WITH THE DEVIL M. EMERY color *Dirt Sports + Off-Road* v51 no3 p18 Mr 2017

Slow Roll M. WAKIM *Los Angeles Magazine* p96 My 2017

Sub-Suburban J. Sabatini color *Car & Driver* v63 no5 p116 N 2017

THROWBACK P. LERNER color diag graph *Road & Track* v68 no8 p68 My 2017

TIME MACHINE R. PINTO color *Road & Track* v69 no2 p82 S 2017

TRIPLE THREAT B. Gillogly color *Hot Rod* v70 no5 p64 My 2017

Z/409: The '69 Camaro Chevrolet Should Have Built B. Gillogly color *Hot Rod* v70 no10 p24 O 2017

Chevrolet automobile

See also

Biscayne automobile
Camaro automobile
Corvette automobile
Impala automobile
AMERICAN GLADIATOR J. BARUTH color *Road & Track* v69 no4 p88 N 2017
Batanides Asks... Why Is White Smoke Coming Out My Exhaust Pipes? M. Davis color *Hot Rod* v70 no6 p112 Je 2017
Blue Steel cartoon *Road & Track* v69 no4 p24 N 2017
High Voltage [Cover story] C. Seabaugh chart color graph *Motor Trend* v69 no2 p30 F 2017
The HOT ROD Archives D. Wallace color *Hot Rod* v70 no7 p14 Jl 2017
JEFF OPPENHEIM WINS SPIRIT OF DRAG WEEK P. Thomas color *Hot Rod* v70 no2 p48 F 2017
NOT YOUR FATHER'S SHOEBOX P. Thomas color *Hot Rod* v70 no5 p46 My 2017
A RACER'S SENDOFF E. Perkins color *Hot Rod* v70 no2 p46 F 2017
Scott A. Sawyer From Pacifica, California, Asks... M. Davis color *Hot Rod* v70 no2 p96 F 2017
Shortened 1957 Bel-Air Convertible R. Brutt color *Hot Rod* v70 no4 p18 Ap 2017
STREET MACHINE ELIMINATOR'S ELITE EIGHT B. Gillogly color *Hot Rod* v70 no3 p80 Mr 2017
Thom On Design Oddity Allure T. Taylor *Hot Rod* v70 no6 p98 Je 2017

Chevrolet automobile—Awards
CHEVY CHANGES THE GAME. AGAIN A. MacKenzie chart color *Motor Trend* v69 no1 p150 Ja 2017

Chevrolet automobile—Equipment & supplies
Mike Davis Asks... What Distributor Gear, Break-In Procedure, and Lifter-Adjustment Method Works on a Small-Block Chevy Hydraulic-Roller Cam? M. Davis color *Hot Rod* v70 no12 p104 D 2017

Chevrolet automobile—Evaluation
THE 2017 AUTOMOTIVE EXCELLENCE AWARDS chart color *Popular Mechanics* p46 My 2017
2017 Chevrolet Colorado ZR2 E. DYER color *Popular Mechanics* p36 N 2017
2018 Chevrolet Camaro ZL1 1LE A. Nishimoto color *Motor Trend* v69 no6 p20 Je 2017
American SPEED, Served TWO WAYS color *Esquire* v166 no4 p77 N 2016
ATOMIC PROSPECTOR A. Robinson chart color diag *Car & Driver* v63 no2 p42 Ag 2017
CHARGE! M. Duff color graph *Car & Driver* v62 no7 p78 Ja 2017
Chevrolet FNR-X concept E. Tahaney color *Motor Trend* v69 no8 p18 Ag 2017
CHEVROLET GT4.R CAMARO J. Machaqueiro color *Hot Rod* v70 no11 p78 N 2017
CHEVY CHANGES THE GAME. AGAIN A. MacKenzie chart color *Motor Trend* v69 no1 p150 Ja 2017
A Crude Awakening J. Capparella color *Car & Driver* v63 no2 p88 Ag 2017
Functional but Not Much Zip color *Consumer Reports* v82 no8 p59 Ag 2017
GARAGE C. Walton, J. Bishop et al chart color diag *Motor Trend* v69 no9 p104 S 2017
Memory LANE E. Perkins color *Hot Rod* v70 no11 p60 N 2017
Mothers 1959 SEDAN DELIVERY B. Gillogly color *Hot Rod* v70 no11 p56 N 2017
New Life for the Gas Engine C. ATIYEH color *Popular Science* v288 no6 p42 N/D 2016
POWER HITTER B. MCALEER color *Road & Track* v68 no7 p84 Mr/Ap 2017
REVIEWS E. DYER color *Popular Mechanics* v193 no7 p54 S 2016
Sub-Suburban J. Sabatini color *Car & Driver* v63 no5 p116 N 2017
THUNDERSTRUCK D. ZENLEA color *Road & Track* v68 no9 p84 Je 2017
TIME MACHINE R. PINTO color *Road & Track* v69 no2 p82 S 2017
TWO FOR THE PRICE OF ONE D. Pund color graph *Car & Driver* v62 no7 p106 Ja 2017

Chevrolet Cruze automobile
NEW PERSPECTIVE ON THE ROAD R. HOWELL color *Car & Driver* v62 no6 p15 D 2016

Chevrolet Cruze automobile—Evaluation
Chevrolet Cruze chart color *Motor Trend* v69 no1 p121 Ja 2017

Chevrolet Equinox automobile
BIG BET F. Markus chart color *Motor Trend* v69 no8 p56 Ag 2017
Evolutionary Success D. Sherman color *Car & Driver* v63 no1 p100 Jl 2017

Chevrolet Equinox sport utility vehicle—Evaluation
2018 Chevrolet Equinox F. Markus color *Motor Trend* v69 no1 p20 Ja 2017

Chevrolet Traverse automobile
FUTURE CARS [Cover story] bw color *Motor Trend* v69 no7 p36 Jl 2017

Chevrolet trucks
PUFF DADDY M. EMERY color *Dirt Sports + Off-Road* v51 no1 p56 Ja 2017

Chew, Jonathan
CHANGE THE WORLD !!!! color diag map *Fortune* v176 no4 p74 S 15 2017
WORLD'S 50 GREATEST LEADERS [Cover story] color *Fortune* v175 no5 p46 Ap 1 2017

Chew-Bose, Durga
Durga CHEW--BOSE: THE CANADIAN WRITER'S FIRST BOOK OF ESSAYS SYNTHESIZES PUBLIC AND PRIVATE THOUGHTS INTO AN ANTHEM OF A DIFFICULT AGE A. STERN *Interview* v47 no3 p32 Ap 2017
Just Enough color *Film Comment* v52 no6 p16 N/D 2016

Chewing gum
Gum K. O. Knausgaard *New York Times Magazine* p18 Ag 13 2017
How to... DESTROY ANYTHING color *Popular Mechanics* p83 S 2017
Not an Act *Lapham's Quarterly* v10 no3 p216 Summ 2017

Chewing gum & health
BURST THE HEALTH BUBBLE! G. Hamadey color *Women's Health* v14 no8 p102 O 2017

Chewy Inc.
Pet Food That Comes With an Oil Painting O. Zaleski color *Bloomberg Businessweek* no4501 p30 N 28 2016
Pet Smarter S. ADAMS color *Forbes* v199 no1 p42 Ja 24 2017

Cheyenne (Wyo.)
MORNING CALM color *Team Roping Journal* p20 S 2017

Chezar, Ariella
SWEET ON CARNATIONS A. PANOS color *Better Homes & Gardens* v95 no2 p96 F 2016

Chhangawala, Sagar
Aerobic glycolysis promotes T helper 1 cell differentiation through an epigenetic mechanism bibl graph *Science* v354 no6311 p481 O 28 2016

Chi-Chao Chen
SOX2 promotes lineage plasticity and antiandrogen resistance in TP53- and RB1-deficient prostate cancer bibl graph *Science* v355 no6320 p1 Ja 6 2017

Chi-Raq (Film)
THE SHADOW BEHIND THE REAL: SPIKE LEE DOES CHI-CAGO J. D. Petermon *Film Quarterly* v70 no2 p30 Wint 2016

Chi Xiong
Kerson Huang *Physics Today* v70 no9 p71 S 2017

Chia
Cooking with Chia Seeds [Cover story] R. Robertson color *Amazing Wellness* v9 no6 p90 EarlyWint 2017

Chia, Sandro, 1946-
SANDRO CHIA D. Ebony color *Art in America* v105 no5 p127 My 2017

Chia-Jung Tsay
People Favor Naturals Over Strivers—Even Though They Say Otherwise *Harvard Business Review Digital Articles* p2 My 19 2016

Chiang, Dawn
Dawn Chiang Named to Tony Nominating Committee *Stage Directions* v30 no10 p4 O 2017

Chiang, Jyh-Min
Plant diversity increases with the strength of negative density de-

pendence at the global scale diag *Science* v356 no6345 p1389 Je 30 2017

Chiang, Ted
c. 2500: United States *Lapham's Quarterly* v10 no2 p133 Spr 2017

Chiapas Earthquake, Mexico, 2017
Lightbox I. Grillo color *Time* v190 no13 p18 O 2 2017

Chiappe, Luis M.
The Significance and Magnificence of Jehol Biota *Natural History* v124 no10 p20 N 2016

CHIAPPETTA, MARCO
If we show you how to back up your PC for free, will you finally do it? color *PCWorld* p155 Mr 2017

Chiarella, Chris
THE ACCOUNTANT color *Sound & Vision* v82 no5 p66 Je 2017
ALLIED color *Sound & Vision* v82 no6 p69 Jl/Ag 2017
Arrival chart color *Sound & Vision* v82 no5 p64 Je 2017
BATMAN V SUPERMAN: DAWN OF JUSTICE color *Sound & Vision* v81 no9 p70 N 2016
CAPTAIN AMERICA: CIVIL WAR color *Sound & Vision* v82 no1 p71 Ja 2017
FINDING DORY color *Sound & Vision* v82 no3 p70 Ap 2017
Getting Back on Track color *Sound & Vision* v82 no4 p66 My 2017
HENRY: PORTRAIT OF A SERIAL KILLER color *Sound & Vision* v82 no4 p69 My 2017
HIDDEN FIGURES color *Sound & Vision* v82 no7 p69 S 2017
HIGH NOON bw *Sound & Vision* v82 no5 p70 Je 2017
THE HILLS HAVE EYES color *Sound & Vision* v82 no2 p70 F/Mr 2017
THE JUNGLE BOOK color *Sound & Vision* v81 no10 p71 D 2016
La La Land color *Sound & Vision* v82 no7 p66 S 2017
THE LEGO BATMAN MOVIE color *Sound & Vision* v82 no8 p68 O 2017
Logan color *Sound & Vision* v82 no8 p66 O 2017
The Mermaid chart color *Sound & Vision* v81 no10 p68 D 2016
MOANA color *Sound & Vision* v82 no6 p70 Jl/Ag 2017
THE QUIET MAN color *Sound & Vision* v82 no3 p67 Ap 2017
X-MEN: APOCALYPSE color *Sound & Vision* v82 no2 p71 F/Mr 2017

Chiarella, Tom
Bold, Beautiful, Brutal color *Chicago* v66 no11 p82 N 2017
Found in Chicago color *Chicago* v66 no10 p86 O 2017
A House by the Lake bw color *Popular Mechanics* p88 D 2016/Ja 2017
HOW TO MAKE ICE CREAM bw color diag *Popular Mechanics* p80 S 2017
THE INFORMATION CURE cartoon color *Chicago* v66 no1 p74 Ja 2017
THE KEEPERS OF THE GAME color *Popular Mechanics* p48 Je 2017
"LANDLORD" color *Popular Mechanics* p78 Mr 2017
THE POPULAR MECHANICS GUIDE TO SELF-SUFFICIENCY [Cover story] color *Popular Mechanics* p55 F 2017
THE ULTIMATE BACKYARD MOVIE SETUP color diag *Popular Mechanics* p97 Jl 2017
THE WELL-MONITORED HOME color *Popular Mechanics* p78 My 2017
What I Learned AT MY Summer Job cartoon *Popular Mechanics* p64 Je 2017
WHY I HATE SUMMER color *Chicago* v66 no7 p63 Jl 2017
WHY We LOVE CHICAGO bw cartoon color *Chicago* v66 no3 p75 Mr 2017

Chiariello, Emily
A CLASSIC DEBATE color *Literacy Today (2411-7862)* v34 no6 p26 My/Je 2017

CHIASSON, DAN
THE ASCETIC bw *New Yorker* v93 no28 p67 S 18 2017
CROSS TALK color *New Yorker* v92 no38 p84 N 21 2016
FIRST LIGHT color *New Yorker* v93 no13 p88 My 15 2017
FROM "THE NAMES OF 1,001 STRANGERS" *New Yorker* v93 no11 p38 My 1 2017
THE FUGITIVE cartoon *New Yorker* v93 no7 p98 Ap 3 2017
HELL OF A DRUG cartoon *New Yorker* v92 no33 p100 O 17 2016
THE MANIA AND THE MUSE cartoon *New Yorker* v93 no5 p94 Mr 20 2017
MERRY WAR cartoon *New Yorker* v93 no26 p88 S 4 2017

OUT OF PRINT color *New Yorker* v92 no40 p77 D 5 2016
PAPER TRAIL cartoon color *New Yorker* v93 no23 p77 Ag 7 2017
SPOKEN FOR cartoon *New Yorker* v93 no30 p72 O 2 2017
TOUCHING SOULS color *New Yorker* v93 no31 p66 O 9 2017
Vanities & Regrets bw *New York Review of Books* v64 no10 p34 Je 8 2017

CHIASSON, EDWARD
TRACKING MYTHS color *Scientific American* v316 no4 p6 Ap 2017

Chiaverina, John
EDITORS' PICKS color *ARTnews* v115 no4 p26 Wint 2016/2017

Chiba, Kunitoshi
Mutations in the promoter of the telomerase gene TERT contribute to tumorigenesis by a two-step mechanism diag *Science* v357 no6358 p1416 S 29 2017

Chibnall, Chris
Broadchurch: The detective drama goes out on an emotional high M. ROUSH *TV Guide* v65 no27 p12 Je 26 2017

Chibok (African people)
GLEANINGS *Christianity Today* v60 no10 p22 D 2016

Chicago (Ill.)
2017 DINING GUIDE WHERE TO EAT P. POLLACK bw color *Chicago* v65 no12 p(Sp)1 D 2016
Chicago Architecture Biennial Preview A. FIXSEN *Architectural Record* v205 no4 p32 Ap 2017
Chicago Architecture Biennial to Kick Off Round 2 D. COHEN *Architectural Record* v205 no9 p29 S 2017
EAST MEETS MIDWEST C. SCHEDLER color *Chicago* v66 no1 p55 Ja 2017
EAT IT ON A STICK C. SCHEDLER color *Chicago* v66 no7 p58 Jl 2017
THE NEW FITNESS FOOD TREND C. BOERS chart color *Chicago* v66 no1 p58 Ja 2017
THE New POWER LUNCH S. Tishgart color *Bloomberg Businessweek* no4493 p89 O 3 2016
Out & About color *Martha Stewart Living* p8 My 2017
PLUNGE INTO COOL POOLS J. HARDBERGER color *Chicago* v66 no7 p62 Jl 2017
'Specimens' goes behind the scenes H. Wolinsky color *Science News* v191 no7 p28 Ap 15 2017
SPLIT DECISION J. RUBY color *Chicago* v66 no7 p46 Jl 2017
UPPER CRUST color *Chicago* v66 no1 p62 Ja 2017
UPSTAIRS, DOWNSTAIRS J. RUBY color *Chicago* v65 no12 p68 D 2016
WHY I HATE SUMMER T. CHIARELLA color *Chicago* v66 no7 p63 Jl 2017
WINGS OF DESIRE J. RUBY color *Chicago* v66 no1 p64 Ja 2017

Chicago (Ill.)—Description & travel
BEST of CHICAGO color *Chicago* v66 no8 p63 Ag 2017
BIKE AND BOOZE L. ARNETT color *Chicago* v66 no7 p56 Jl 2017
Chicago Culture Fix P. BRADY color *Conde Nast Traveler* v52 no8 p18 S 2017
THE CITY OF BROAD SHOULDERS A. Erace color *Fortune* v175 no4 p60 Mr 15 2017
GET BEACHED A. RAO color *Chicago* v66 no7 p50 Jl 2017
GET ON THE WATER J. DUGDALE color *Chicago* v66 no7 p60 Jl 2017
LAKE VIEW J. REESE color map *Chicago* v66 no8 p30 Ag 2017
NORTH CENTER J. REESE color map *Chicago* v66 no11 p29 N 2017
Top 5 Dog-Friendly Cities map *Good Housekeeping* v265 no3 p144 S 2017
WHY We LOVE CHICAGO T. CHIARELLA, T. J. Miller et al bw cartoon color *Chicago* v66 no3 p75 Mr 2017

Chicago (Ill.)—Environmental conditions
The Urban Wild A. Geni color *Chicago* v66 no8 p90 Ag 2017

Chicago (Ill.)—Social conditions
63 GREAT THINGS TO DO THIS MONTH J. FOUMBERG, J. HARDBERGER et al color *Chicago* v66 no8 p105 Ag 2017
CONFESSIONS OF A BI-SIDER B. SAVAGE color *Chicago* v66 no8 p86 Ag 2017
Murder No. 605 A. HUTCHINS color graph *Maclean's* v129 no45 p34 N 14 2016
PENNY'S NEW FAVE color *Chicago* v66 no8 p58 Ag 2017

SUSHI FOR ADULTS J. RUBY color *Chicago* v66 no8 p60 Ag 2017

WATER WORKS J. FOUMBERG cartoon *Chicago* v66 no8 p40 Ag 2017

Chicago (Ill.)—Social life & customs

Chicago Culture Fix P. BRADY color *Conde Nast Traveler* v52 no8 p18 S 2017

MASTER OF FIRE J. R. FULLER color *Chicago* v66 no8 p51 Ag 2017

SECOND TO NONE [Cover story] J. KRAMER bw color *Bon Appetit* p134 S 2017

Chicago (Performer)

Lee Loughnane and Chicago Assert Their 4.0 Authority on Blu-ray M. METTLER and C. Crowley bw color *Sound & Vision* v81 no9 p22 N 2016

Chicago (Theatrical production)

THE REAL WOMEN OF "MURDERESS ROW" AND THE WOMAN WHO TOLD THEIR STORY R. Price *Cincinnati Magazine* v50 no8 p16 My 2017

Chicago Bears (Football team)

3 Chicago Bears color *Sports Illustrated* v127 no7 p94 S 4 2017

Chicago Bulls (Basketball team)

11 Bulls A. Sharp, B. Golliver et al color *Sports Illustrated* v125 no14 p86 O 24-31 2016

15 BULLS color *Sports Illustrated* v127 no12 p74 O 16 2017

THE CALL OF THE NORTH R. O'CONNOR color *Chicago* v66 no7 p13 Jl 2017

WORDS WITH... Dwyane Wade R. Nadkarni color *Sports Illustrated* v125 no14 p120 O 24-31 2016

Chicago Cubs (Baseball team)

1 CUBS color *Sports Illustrated* v126 no9 p102 Mr 27 2017

The Chicago Cubs and Their Unlikely Ace Could Make History S. Gregory color *Time* v188 no18 p50 O 31 2016

Chi Society M. Rosenberg color *Sports Illustrated* v126 no9 p116 Mr 27 2017

The Cubs N. AUSTIN *Arizona Highways* v93 no3 p8 Mr 2017

Harry Caray Is My Wingman I. BRANNON color *Weekly Standard* v22 no7 p14 O 24 2016

HOT | NOT T. Keith color *Sports Illustrated* v125 no14 p24 O 24-31 2016

HOT | NOT T. Keith color *Sports Illustrated* v127 no4 p22 Ag 7 2017

Joy in Mudville [Cover story] J. EPSTEIN bw color *Weekly Standard* v22 no10 p17 N 14 2016

Leading Off color *Sports Illustrated* v125 no16 p8 N 14 2016

MLB PLAYOFFS K. ROSEN *TV Guide* v64 no40 p66 O 3 2016

Money for Something S. Apstein and T. Keith color *Sports Illustrated* v126 no9 p24 Mr 27 2017

THE WHITE SOX PUZZLE R. WATT color graph *Chicago* v66 no4 p21 Ap 2017

Chicago Cubs (Baseball team)—History

C of Joy T. Verducci color *Sports Illustrated* v125 no17 p32 N 21 2016 Double Issue

Ghostbusters [Cover story] T. Verducci, B. Reiter et al color *Sports Illustrated* v125 no12 p24 O 10 2016

How to Be a Winner M. Rosenberg color *Sports Illustrated* v125 no17 p120 N 21 2016 Double Issue

The Rainmaker T. Verducci color *Sports Illustrated* v125 no20 p110 D 19 2016

Suffer Club color *Sports Illustrated* v125 no16 p60 N 14 2016

VIEWERS TUNE IN FOR CUBS' EPIC WIN, TUNE OUT THE REST T. J. Huddleston color *Fortune* v174 no8 p22 D 15 2016

WORLD SERIES It Happened [Cover story] T. Verducci color *Sports Illustrated* v125 no16 p24 N 14 2016

WORLD SERIES Timeless T. Verducci color *Sports Illustrated* v125 no15 p30 N 7 2016

Chicago Cubs (Baseball team)—History—21st century

THE CUBS WAY T. Verducci color *Sports Illustrated* v126 no8 p78 Mr 20 2017

Hibernating Cubs T. Keith chart color *Sports Illustrated* v127 no3 p14 Jl 24 2017

WHAT THE F? K. C. Bias and J. Feldman color *Sports Illustrated* v126 no11 p49 Ap 17-24 2017

Chicago Fire (TV program)

ALL GEARED UP I. RUDOLPH *TV Guide* p36 D 5 2016

Chicago Fire I. Rudolph *TV Guide* v65 no43 p34 O 16 2017

Chicago Fire's Severide in Custody! I. Rudolph *TV Guide* p13 D 19 2016

The Heat Is On I. RUDOLPH *TV Guide* p20 Ap 17 2017

THE VOICE R. O'CONNOR cartoon *Chicago* v66 no5 p40 My 2017

Chicago Justice (TV program)

ALSO COMING . . J. Russell *TV Guide* v65 no2 p40 Ja 2 2017

JUSTICE LEAGUE I. RUDOLPH *TV Guide* v65 no8 p24 F 27 2017

Chicago Med (TV program)

ELSEWHERE IN CHICAGO... *TV Guide* p24 Ap 17 2017

Chicago Milwaukee St. Paul & Pacific Railroad Co.

Z SCALE IN A CLOSET V. Sargent color *Model Railroader* v84 no11 p50 N 2017

Chicago P.D. (TV program)

CHICAGO P.D I. Rudolph *TV Guide* v65 no39 p44 S 18 2017

Chicago P.D.'s New Detective I. Rudolph *TV Guide* v65 no19 p10 My 1 2017

ELSEWHERE IN CHICAGO... *TV Guide* p24 Ap 17 2017

Chicago Public Schools

BEST PRIVATE SCHOOLS [Cover story] R. BERTSCHE chart color *Chicago* v66 no9 p104 S 2017

Chicago River (Ill.)

SEEDS OF CHANGE J. PFEIFER cartoon map *Chicago* v66 no5 p34 My 2017

These Waters Run Deep [Cover story] S. Blackwood color *Chicago* v66 no9 p94 S 2017

Chicago Shakespeare Theater

THE BARD'S YARD B. GOLDEN color *Chicago* v66 no9 p52 S 2017

Chicago Stock Exchange

A China Moonshot for Chicago's Exchange A. Massa, D. Lawrence et al *Bloomberg Businessweek* no4514 p40 Mr 13 2017

Chicago Symphony Orchestra

67 GREAT THINGS TO DO THIS MONTH J. FOUMBERG, J. HARDERGER et al color *Chicago* v66 no3 p129 Mr 2017

THE IMPROBABLE ENCORE E. FISHMAN bw color *Chicago* v66 no2 p72 F 2017

Chicago Teachers Union

KAREN LEWIS B. Zehme *Chicago* v66 no9 p160 S 2017

Chicago White Sox (Baseball team)

5 WHITE SOX color *Sports Illustrated* v126 no9 p87 Mr 27 2017

BASEBALL BLOOD C. Jones *New York Times Magazine* p38 S 17 2017

The Case for ... The White Sox J. Fuchs and T. Keith color *Sports Illustrated* v126 no12 p21 My 1 2017

WHAT IF? ... BABE RUTH HAD BEEN DEALT TO THE WHITE SOX—GASP!—INSTEAD OF TO THE YANKEES? D. Greene and J. Feldman color *Sports Illustrated* v126 no11 p57 Ap 17-24 2017

THE WHITE SOX PUZZLE R. WATT color graph *Chicago* v66 no4 p21 Ap 2017

Chicago (Ill.)—Buildings, structures, etc.

Parkside of Oldtown, Phase Mb A. Fixsen *Architectural Record* v205 no4 p197 Ap 2017

Chicago Public Library (Chicago, Ill.)

Musically Inclined K. Kyles color *Ebony* v72 no8 p16 Je 2017

Chicago Race Riot, Chicago, Ill., 1919

Faces of a Century M. Pollock color *Chicago* v66 no5 p110 My 2017

Chiccine, Lisa

TALKING HEADS color *O, The Oprah Magazine* p128 Ap 2017

Chick, Kristen

Freed Iraqi Christians tell of life under the IS color *Christian Century* v134 no1 p12 Ja 4 2017

People color *Christian Century* v134 no22 p20 O 25 2017

Chick-fil-A Inc.

CLUCK OFF JAM bw *Advocate* no1091 p26 Je/Jl 2017

Chickadees

Forest "Islands" Offer Refuge to Birds *USA Today Magazine* v145 no2865 p7 Je 2017

Chicken industry

A VAST WING CON-SPIRACY? C. Leonard color *Bloomberg Businessweek* no4512 p62 F 20 2017

Chicken Salad Chick (Company)

Sharing a Taste of the South P. MERTZ ESSWEIN color *Kip-*

IS GE DUE FOR A COMEBACK? color *Fortune* v176 no1 p11 Jl 1 2017

KEEPING IT LOCAL S. Blodgett and S. Lynn color *Black Enterprise* v47 no8 p13 Jl/Ag 2017

Looking for Answers to the World's Biggest Challenges In the Eternal City R. Foroohar, C. D. Wuerl et al color *Time* v188 no24 p31 D 12 2016

MARK HOPLAMAZIAN bw color *Bloomberg Businessweek* no4524 p72 My 29 2017

The Mistakes PE Firms Make When They Pick CEOs for Portfolio Companies M. Brubaker and M. Durrant *Harvard Business Review Digital Articles* p2 S 6 2016

The Most Innovative Companies Have Long- Term Leadership M. Wessel *Harvard Business Review Digital Articles* p2 D 30 2014

Most Likely to succeed bw color *Bloomberg Businessweek* no4526 p67 Je 12 2017

MR. NICE GUY: INSTAGRAM'S KEVIN SYSTROM WANTS TO CLEAN UP THE &#%$@! INTERNET N. THOMPSON bw cartoon color *Wired* v25 no9 p80 S 2017

Please Don't Hire a Chief Artificial Intelligence Officer K. J. Hammond *Harvard Business Review Digital Articles* p2 Mr 29 2017

Research: Companies See a Stock Bump After Executives Visit the White House G. Gavett *Harvard Business Review Digital Articles* p2 Jl 5 2017

Research: Executives Who Flatter Their CEOs Are More Likely to Criticize Them to the Press G. Keeves, J. Westphal et al bw *Harvard Business Review Digital Articles* p2 Ap 5 2017

Research: How a New CEO Can Make a Firm More Entrepreneurial B. Grühn, S. Strese et al *Harvard Business Review Digital Articles* p2 N 17 2016

Resisting the Lure of Short-Termism [Cover story] D. McGinn *Harvard Business Review* v94 no11 p42 N 2016

THE ROLE OF GLOBAL COMPANIES IN BRIDGING WEALTH DISPARITY *Vital Speeches of the Day* v82 no10 p315 O 2016

SAP's CEO on Being the American Head of a German Multinational B. McDermott bw graph img *Harvard Business Review* v94 no11 p35 N 2016

Should a CEO's Bonus Be Based on Financial Performance Alone? G. Kenny *Harvard Business Review Digital Articles* p2 My 25 2017

Should CEOs Respond When Employees Complain About Them Online? S. Clayton color *Harvard Business Review Digital Articles* p2 Ap 3 2017

Should Older CEOs Be Forced to Retire? W. Frick *Harvard Business Review Digital Articles* p2 F 15 2016

Starbucks' "Race Together" Campaign and the Upside of CEO Activism A. Chatterji and M. Toffel *Harvard Business Review Digital Articles* p2 Mr 24 2015

THINK VERTICAL B. BERK color *Road & Track* v69 no4 p68 N 2017

Tips for Working Under a Type-A Boss M. Raffoni *Harvard Business Review Digital Articles* p2 N 21 2014

To Lead a Digital Transformation, CEOs Must Prioritize Baculard color *Harvard Business Review Digital Articles* p2 Ja 2 2017

We Studied 38 Incidents of CEO Bad Behavior and Measured Their Consequences D. Larcker and B. Tayan *Harvard Business Review Digital Articles* p2 Je 9 2016

What 11 CEOs Have Learned About Championing Diversity S. K. Johnson *Harvard Business Review Digital Articles* p2 2017

What CEO Activism Looks Like in the Trump Era L. Gaines-Ross *Harvard Business Review Digital Articles* p2 O 2 2017

What CEOs Are Afraid Of R. Jones *Harvard Business Review Digital Articles* p2 F 24 2015

What CEOs Have Learned About Social Media L. Gaines-Ross *Harvard Business Review Digital Articles* p2 My 18 2015

What CEOs Should Know About Speaking Up on Political Issues L. Gaines-Ross *Harvard Business Review Digital Articles* p2 F 17 2017

What Executives Value in Their CEOs L. Gaines-Ross *Harvard Business Review Digital Articles* p2 Mr 5 2015

What Frugal Innovators Do N. Radjou and J. Prabhu *Harvard Business Review Digital Articles* p2 D 10 2014

What Happens When an Interim CEO Takes Over? W. Frick *Harvard Business Review Digital Articles* p2 Je 12 2015

What I'd Do Differently Fake Elon Musk, not 45 J. P. HUFFMAN

cartoon *Car & Driver* v62 no7 p120 Ja 2017

What I Didn't Know About Becoming a CEO K. Firestone *Harvard Business Review Digital Articles* p2 N 9 2015

What the CEO of the "New" Google Needs to Do Next B. Chakravorti *Harvard Business Review Digital Articles* p2 S 1 2015

What U.S. CEOs Can Learn from GM's India Failure V. Govindarajan and G. Bagla *Harvard Business Review Digital Articles* p2 Je 15 2017

When Star CEOs and Star Analysts Disagree, the Market Trusts the Analysts S. Boivie, S. D. Graffin et al *Harvard Business Review Digital Articles* p2 Ap 18 2016

Where the Women Were M. Maerz and I. Kaplan bw color *Glamour* no8 p142 Ag 2017

Why CEOs Can't Stay Silent in the Wake of Events Like Charlottesville N. Kteily and F. Gino *Harvard Business Review Digital Articles* p2 2017

Why CEOs Should Commit to Many Small Battles Instead of a Single Big One J. Allen *Harvard Business Review Digital Articles* p2 D 14 2014

Why Top Management Should Listen to Activist Investors P. Leinwand and A. Gilcreast *Harvard Business Review Digital Articles* p2 N 30 2016

Chief executive officers—Attitudes

4 Ways CEOs Can Conquer Short-Termism K. Isaacs, D. Langstaff et al *Harvard Business Review Digital Articles* p2 F 24 2017

Are Most CEOs Too Old to Innovate? W. Frick *Harvard Business Review Digital Articles* p2 N 20 2014

THE BALLAD OF KELCY WARREN J. H. Richardson cartoon *Mother Jones* v42 no2 p12 Mr/Ap 2017

BURSTING THE CEO BUBBLE H. GREGERSEN color *Harvard Business Review* v95 no2 p76 Mr/Ap 2017

CEOs with Lots of Stock Options Are More Likely to Break Laws D. Minor *Harvard Business Review Digital Articles* p2 My 26 2016

The Dangers of Hiring a Nice CEO E. L. Botelho, D. Wang et al *Harvard Business Review Digital Articles* p2 Je 7 2016

The Family Dynamics We Grew Up with Shape How We Work R. Jones *Harvard Business Review Digital Articles* p2 Jl 19 2016

How Did I Get Here? A. Cohen bw color *Bloomberg Businessweek* no4526 p72 Je 12 2017

INDIA'S MARATHON MAN C. Chandler color diag *Fortune* v176 no2 p94 Ag 1 2017

Research: When CEOs Don't Win Awards, They Make More Acquisitions Wei Shi, Yan Anthea Zhang et al *Harvard Business Review Digital Articles* p2 Mr 27 2017

A Survey of How 1,000 CEOs Spend Their Day Reveals What Makes Leaders Successful O. Bandiera, S. Hansen et al *Harvard Business Review Digital Articles* p2 O 12 2017

Your Company's Networks Might Matter More than Its Strategy G. Satell *Harvard Business Review Digital Articles* p2 Je 10 2015

Chief executive officers—Canada

YOUR PAL HARRY C. MCINTYRE color *Maclean's* v130 no2 p46 Mr 2017

Chief executive officers—Congresses

Fairground color *Vanity Fair* v59 no1 p102 Holiday 2017

Chief executive officers—Employment

UNEASY LIES THE HEAD J. Surowiecki cartoon *New Yorker* v92 no36 p19 N 7 2016

Chief executive officers—Evaluation

COMP TARGETS THAT WORK: HOW TO KEEP EXECUTIVES FROM GAMING THE SYSTEM R. GOPALAN, J. HORN et al color graph img *Harvard Business Review* v95 no5 p102 S/O 2017

MBAS ARE MORE SELF-SERVING THAN OTHER CEOS N. Torres color *Harvard Business Review* v94 no12 p32 D 2016

Chief executive officers—Finance

CEOs Earn Less at More-Prestigious Firms F. Focke, E. Maug et al color *Harvard Business Review Digital Articles* p2 F 2 2017

Chief executive officers—Interviews

BURSTING THE CEO BUBBLE H. GREGERSEN color *Harvard Business Review* v95 no2 p76 Mr/Ap 2017

The Business of Getting Dirty color *Fortune* v176 no5 p19 O 1 2017

Finding the Green in Your Junk P. M. ESSWEIN color *Kiplinger's*

Personal Finance v71 no4 p14 Ap 2017

Free Speech, No Shit N. GILLESPIE color *Reason* v49 no3 p50 Jl 2017

Håkan Samuelsson A. Priddle *Motor Trend* v69 no7 p30 Jl 2017

Her Headphones Lull You to Sleep P. M. ESSWEIN color *Kiplinger's Personal Finance* v71 no3 p17 Mr 2017

MARK POESCHL: FFA CEO TALKS ABOUT THE ORGANIZATION'S UPS AND DOWNS, AND THE NEXT GENERATION OF AG LEADERS J. Davey *Successful Farming* v115 no12 p10 O 2017

Muslin, Paint and Light M. S. Eddy *Stage Directions* v30 no4 p18 Ap 2017

Ridding the World of Bad Sound bw color *Sound & Vision* v82 no3 p16 Ap 2017

THE TALK STOPS HERE: For a year, this GOP strategist listened to voters' problems. Now she's ready to act E. Plott *Washingtonian Magazine* v52 no8 p22 My 2017

"WE NEED PEOPLE TO LEAN INTO THE FUTURE" A. IGNATIUS color img *Harvard Business Review* v95 no2 p94 Mr/Ap 2017

What CEOs Really Worry About [Cover story] A. Ignatius bw color img *Harvard Business Review* v94 no11 p52 N 2016

Chief executive officers—Psychology

THE ANXIETY EFFECT *Harvard Business Review* v95 no1 p32 Ja/F 2017

How Anxiety Affects CEO Decision Making M. Mannor, A. Wowak et al *Harvard Business Review Digital Articles* p2 Jl 19 2016

THE INSULATED LEADER A. IGNATIUS bw img *Harvard Business Review* v95 no2 p12 Mr/Ap 2017

What Sets Successful CEOs Apart [Cover story] E. L. BOTELHO, K. R. POWELL et al color *Harvard Business Review* v95 no3 p70 My/Je 2017

Chief executive officers—Recreation

Is Your Firm Underperforming? Your CEO Might Be Golfing Too Much L. Biggerstaff, D. C. Cicero et al *Harvard Business Review Digital Articles* p2 N 30 2016

Chief executive officers—Selection & appointment

The Bull Case for Uber's New Chief Executive A. Lashinsky color *Fortune* v176 no4 p26 S 15 2017

EXECUTIVE SUMMARIES *Harvard Business Review* v94 no12 p116 D 2016

How Boards Can Set a New CEO Up for Success E. Harrell *Harvard Business Review Digital Articles* p2 N 28 2016

How to Bring in a New CEO for Your Startup S. Dutia *Harvard Business Review Digital Articles* p2 F 29 2016

More Insiders Are Becoming CEOs, and That's a Good Thing J. L. Bower *Harvard Business Review Digital Articles* p2 Mr 18 2016

The Secrets of Great CEO Selection R. CHARAN color *Harvard Business Review* v94 no12 p52 D 2016

Succession Planning: What the Research Says E. HARRELL color img *Harvard Business Review* v94 no12 p70 D 2016

WHEN HIRING EXECS, CONTEXT MATTERS MOST bw *Harvard Business Review* v95 no5 p20 S/O 2017

Why CEOs Don't Get Fired as Often as They Used To Karlsson *Harvard Business Review Digital Articles* p2 Je 15 2015

Chief executive officers—Social aspects

When Charismatic Leadership Goes Too Far D. Ciampa *Harvard Business Review Digital Articles* p2 N 21 2014

Chief executive officers—United States

How Did I Get Here? BLAKE IRVING bw color *Bloomberg Businessweek* no4497 p72 O 31 2016

Remembering Andy Grove, the Teacher R. A. Burgelman *Harvard Business Review Digital Articles* p2 Mr 23 2016

STORM CHASERS A. Nusca color *Fortune* v175 no8 p62 Je 15 2017

Chief executive officers—United States—Attitudes

CEO SOOTHSAYERS A. Murray diag *Fortune* v175 no8 p340 Je 15 2017

Chief financial officers

C-SUITE GIGS: A WEB OF MAD SKILLS S. KADISH diag *Wired* v25 no9 p18 S 2017

How CFOs Can Take the Long-Term View in a Short-Term Economy J. Sinfield and A. Trotter *Harvard Business Review Digital Articles* p2 Mr 15 2016

How the CFO and General Counsel Can Partner More Effectively

B. W. Heineman Jr. *Harvard Business Review Digital Articles* p2 Jl 25 2016

Who's Better at Strategy: CFOs or CSOs? A. Agrawal, E. Gibbs et al *Harvard Business Review Digital Articles* p2 Ja 11 2016

Chief information officers

How Three Top CIOs Turn IT Into "Empowerment Organizations" J. MULLICH color *Forbes* v200 no1 p92 Jl 27 2017

Letting the Little Guy In T. Newcombe *Governing* v30 no6 p60 Mr 2017

THE POWER PARTNERSHIP: CMO & CIO K. A. WHITLER, D. E. BOYD et al *Harvard Business Review* v95 no4 p55 Jl/Ag 2017

Why CIOs Make Great Board Directors C. Stephenson and N. Olson *Harvard Business Review Digital Articles* p2 Mr 15 2017

Chief legal officers

How the CFO and General Counsel Can Partner More Effectively B. W. Heineman Jr. *Harvard Business Review Digital Articles* p2 Jl 25 2016

Chief marketing officers

6-STEP RECIPE FOR SUCCESS C. V. CLARKE color *Black Enterprise* v47 no8 p38 Jl/Ag 2017

The Best CMOs Combine 4 Leadership Styles J. Sorofman *Harvard Business Review Digital Articles* p2 My 12 2015

Big Data Is Only Half the Data Marketers Need M. B. Rasmussen and A. W. Hansen *Harvard Business Review Digital Articles* p2 N 16 2015

EXECUTIVE SUMMARIES K. A. WHITLER and N. MORGAN bw color *Harvard Business Review* v95 no4 p146 Jl/Ag 2017

How CMOs and CROs Can Be Allies B. Ellis, B. Gregg et al *Harvard Business Review Digital Articles* p2 Mr 26 2015

THE POWER PARTNERSHIP: CMO & CIO K. A. WHITLER, D. E. BOYD et al *Harvard Business Review* v95 no4 p55 Jl/Ag 2017

Put the "and" Back in "Sales and Marketing" J. Cermak, M. Hancock et al *Harvard Business Review Digital Articles* p2 O 30 2014

REDUCING CMO TURNOVER: A Recruiter's Prescription G. WELCH color *Harvard Business Review* v95 no4 p59 Jl/Ag 2017

A Step-by-Step Plan to Improve CMO-COO Collaboration D. C. Edelman, D. Stone et al *Harvard Business Review Digital Articles* p2 Ja 28 2015

Technology Questions Every CMO Must Ask A. Joshi *Harvard Business Review Digital Articles* p2 O 2 2014

There Are 4 Futures for CMOs (Some Better Than Others) M. Bonchek and G. Cornfield *Harvard Business Review Digital Articles* p2 S 8 2017

WHY CMOs NEVER LAST AND WHAT TO DO ABOUT IT K. A. WHITLER and N. MORGAN chart color graph img *Harvard Business Review* v95 no4 p46 Jl/Ag 2017

Chief marketing officers—Education

JOY HOWARD bw color *Bloomberg Businessweek* no4512 p84 F 20 2017

Chief marketing officers—Interviews

REFLECTIONS OF A SIX-TIME CMO: A CONVERSATION WITH JOE TRIPODI D. MCGINN color *Harvard Business Review* v95 no4 p56 Jl/Ag 2017

Chief operating officers

Operating Room K. Barrett and R. Greene *Governing* v30 no6 p58 Mr 2017

A Step-by-Step Plan to Improve CMO-COO Collaboration D. C. Edelman, D. Stone et al *Harvard Business Review Digital Articles* p2 Ja 28 2015

Chief operating officers—Interviews

Q & A: Long-term Care S. Goldberg *Cincinnati Magazine* v50 no10 p74 Jl 2017

Chief risk officers

How CMOs and CROs Can Be Allies B. Ellis, B. Gregg et al *Harvard Business Review Digital Articles* p2 Mr 26 2015

Research: Hiring Chief Risk Officers Led Banks to Take on Even More Risk K. Pernell, J. Jung et al *Harvard Business Review Digital Articles* p2 Jl 13 2017

Chief strategy officers

What Makes a Great Chief Strategy Officer M. Birshan, E. Gibbs et al *Harvard Business Review Digital Articles* p2 My 14 2015

Who's Better at Strategy: CFOs or CSOs? A. Agrawal, E. Gibbs et al *Harvard Business Review Digital Articles* p2 Ja 11 2016

Chief sustainability officers

Leading in a World of Resource Constraints and Extreme Weather A. Winston *Harvard Business Review Digital Articles* p2 Je 16 2015

Chief technical officers

GADGET GIRL R. Rothman color *Good Housekeeping* v265 no5 p12 N 2017

How Did I Get Here? THUAN PHAM bw color *Bloomberg Businessweek* no4499 p88 N 14 2016

Chief executive officers—Salaries, wages, etc.

DECODING CEO PAY: *THE TRUTH IS BURIED IN THE FINE PRINT—AND THAT'S A PROBLEM R. C. POZEN and S. P. KOTHARI color graph img *Harvard Business Review* v95 no4 p78 Jl/Ag 2017

GOLDEN PARACHUTE, MEET GLASS CLIFF G. Colvin color *Fortune* v175 no5 p14 Ap 1 2017

Stop Making CEO Pay a Political Issue A. Edmans *Harvard Business Review Digital Articles* p2 Jl 18 2016

We Know Female CEOs Get Paid More, But We Don't Know Why M. Ormiston and J. R. Bailey *Harvard Business Review Digital Articles* p2 Mr 13 2017

Why Is CEO Pay Rising? Maybe There Aren't Enough Good CEOs N. Donatiello, D. Larcker et al *Harvard Business Review Digital Articles* p2 O 5 2017

Chief information officers—Salaries, wages, etc.

HOW MUCH IS SECURITY WORTH? J. J. Roberts *Fortune* v175 no2 p14 F 1 2017

Chief marketing officers—Charts, diagrams, etc.

The Evolution of the CMO C. FLEIT color *Harvard Business Review* v95 no4 p60 Jl/Ag 2017

Chien, Huan-Chieh

A placental growth factor is silenced in mouse embryos by the zinc finger protein ZFP568 color graph *Science* v356 no6339 p757 My 19 2017

Chien, Windy

Learning the Ropes M. OZAWA color *Martha Stewart Living* p42 S 2017

Chien Lu

Highly stretchable polymer semiconductor films through the nanoconfinement effect bibl graph *Science* v355 no6320 p1 Ja 6 2017

Chieng, Ronny

PARTY LINES img *New York* v49 no22 p114 O 31 2016

Chieregato, A.

Selective oxidative dehydrogenation of propane to propene using boron nitride catalysts bibl diag graph *Science* v354 no6319 p1570 D 23 2016

Chiglinsky, Katherine

Blowing Down That Fiduciary Rule color *Bloomberg Businessweek* no4511 p35 F 13 2017

The Pension Hole color graph *Bloomberg Businessweek* no4533 p27 Ag 7 2017

The Pensions Warren Buffett Runs color *Bloomberg Businessweek* no4540 p32 O 2 2017

Chigurupati, Anuraag

How the U.S. Can Reduce Waste in Health Care Spending by $1 Trillion *Harvard Business Review Digital Articles* p2 O 13 2015

Chih-Yen Chen

Ultrafine jagged platinum nanowires enable ultrahigh mass activity for the oxygen reduction reaction bibl chart graph *Science* v354 no6318 p1414 D 16 2016

Chiha, Patric

Making Ends Meet M. Koresky color *Film Comment* v53 no3 p8 My/Je 2017

Chihuahuan Desert

JENNA LYONS K. MOLVAR bw color *Conde Nast Traveler* v52 no3 p30 Mr 2017

Chihuly, Dale, 1941-—Exhibitions

Shows to See color *American Craft* v77 no3 p18 Je/Jl 2017

Chikkaraddy, Rohit

Single-molecule optomechanics in "picocavities" bibl graph *Science* v354 no6313 p726 N 11 2016

Chilczuk, Lucas

The Gallim Dream color *Dance Spirit* v21 no2 p34 F 2017

QUICK CHANGE color *Dance Spirit* v21 no2 p48 F 2017

Child, Lee

PRINT / HARDCOVER BEST SELLERS *New York Times Book Review* p78 D 4 2016

THINK TWICE J. LANCHESTER cartoon *New Yorker* v92 no37 p85 N 14 2016

Child abuse

See also

Child pornography

The Cry of Abel's Blood J. A. Miller cartoon *Commonweal* v144 no7 p16 Ap 14 2017

HOW FAKE NEWS TURNED A SMALL TOWN UPSIDE DOWN: AT THE HEIGHT OF THE 2016 ELECTION, EXAGGERATED REPORTS OF A JUVENILE SEX CRIME BROUGHT A MEDIA MAELSTROM TO TWIN FALLS—ONE THE IDAHO CITY STILL HASN'T RECOVERED FROM C. DICKERSON *New York Times Magazine* p46 O 1 2017

THE SEPARATION L. MACFARQUHAR cartoon *New Yorker* v93 no23 p36 Ag 7 2017

WE ALL SCREAM FOR THE ICE CREAM MAN'S HEAD L. SKENAZY cartoon *Reason* v49 no2 p6 Je 2017

Child abuse—Psychological aspects

Abuse hinders children's social learning B. BOWER *Science News* v191 no5 p10 Mr 18 2017

UP FROM CHAOS M. HUSTAD *Psychology Today* v50 no2 p72 Mr/Ap 2017

Child actors

Anthony Gonzalez As an Explorer of the Afterlife S. Begley color *Time* v190 no10/11 p110 S 18 2017

JACOB TREMBLAY 2.0? S. Li color *Entertainment Weekly* no1442 p10 D 2 2016 Rebellious Special Issue

Meet the New Faces of Avatar 2 J. Hibberd color *Entertainment Weekly* no1485 p40 O 6 2017

The Rebel Belle D. BLASBERG bw color *Vanity Fair* v59 no4 p152 Mr 2017

Child athletes

EARLY DAZE C. Johnson *Sports Illustrated* v127 no6 p49 Ag 28 2017

Child car seats

Ask Our Experts il *Consumer Reports* v82 no3 p21 Mr 2017

Child car seats—Evaluation

The Safest Car Seat for Your Child M. Naranjo chart color *Consumer Reports* v82 no1 p56 Ja 2017

Child care

See also

Child rearing

100 BEST COMPANIES: HIGHLIGHTS graph map *Working Mother* v40 no4 p28 O/N 2017

Annunciation R. Miska color *U.S. Catholic* v81 no12 p11 D 2016

balance is BS C. BIRNBAUM *Parents* v91 no9 p126 S 2016

Does Having Grandchildren Persuade Women to Retire Early? K. Firestone *Harvard Business Review Digital Articles* p2 My 19 2015

Family Matters L. Lavelle color *Working Mother* v40 no4 p96 O/N 2017

I thought the babysitter would quit after my kid ... *Parents* v91 no10 p148 O 2016

Kids Incorporated K. REYNOLDS LEWIS color *Working Mother* v40 no4 p80 O/N 2017

LET'S GET REAL *Parents* v92 no11 p14 N 2017

Remote Chance S. BARRY color *Working Mother* v40 no4 p83 O/N 2017

A System from the North A. OHLIN cartoon *Walrus* v13 no10 p62 D 2016

When Your Kid Is Sick and You're Tired A. MENCEL color *Parents* v92 no8 p28 Ag 2017

win your flextime fight K. ASHFORD color *Parents* v92 no7 p90 Jl 2017

YES LIST S. Marikar cartoon *New Yorker* v93 no28 p19 S 18 2017

Child care costs

How Some Companies Are Making Child Care Less Stressful for Their Employees J. Beck *Harvard Business Review Digital Articles* p2 Ap 14 2017

The Terrible, Horrible, No Good, Very Bad Child-Care Problem E. Dias color *Time* v188 no16/17 p38 O 24 2016

Child care services—United States
Family Planning E. Bazelon color *New York Times Magazine* p17 O 9 2016

Child care—Economic aspects
THE JUGGLE IS REAL D. Cunha cartoon *Parents* v92 no9 p112 S 2017

Child dancers
Lior MELNIKOV N. Loeffler-Gladstone *Dance Spirit* v20 no10 p71 D 2016
Samantha BULSTRODE N. Loeffler-Gladstone *Dance Spirit* v21 no4 p71 Ap 2017
TALK TO US color *Dance Spirit* v21 no2 p14 F 2017

Child development
> *See also*
> Child psychology

ages+stages color *Parents* v92 no4 p123 Ap 2017
ages+stages color *Parents* v92 no7 p117 Jl 2017
all the feels M. CROUCH *Parents* v92 no8 p136 Ag 2017
babyish behavior J. BURT COTE *Parents* v92 no8 p132 Ag 2017
baring it all J. NESBIT *Parents* v91 no10 p138 O 2016
bless the mess K. M. REILLY *Parents* v92 no5 p118 My 2017
a case for coding B. THORKELSON *Parents* v92 no7 p130 Jl 2017
Child growth sensitivity to rainfall variability color *Science* v355 no6325 p593 F 10 2017
CHINA'S CHILDHOOD EXPERIMENT D. Normile color diag *Science* v357 no6357 p1226 S 22 2017
cutting the cord *Parents* p45 2015
DIRT IS GOOD FOR YOU J. Jetsohn *Saturday Evening Post* v289 no2 p26 Mr/Ap 2017
good sports H. A. ROTBART *Parents* v92 no3 p114 Mr 2017
HOW TO Avoid Losing Things T. REECE *Parents* v92 no11 p120 N 2017
HOW TO Talk About Periods M. COHEN *Parents* v92 no11 p122 N 2017
how to teach time R. HARTMAN *Parents* v92 no8 p133 Ag 2017
HOW TO Troubleshoot Tub Time J. RAINEY MARQUEZ *Parents* v92 no11 p117 N 2017
HOW TO Wean When Your Toddler Resists A. KLEIN *Parents* v92 no11 p119 N 2017
imitation game T. REECE *Parents* v92 no3 p108 Mr 2017
innocent mistakes J. TEEMAN *Parents* v92 no5 p121 My 2017
Introduce Team Sports L. Anastasia *Parents* v92 no9 p168 S 2017
nighty night, everyone! L. SMITH BRODY color graph *Parents* v92 no8 p44 Ag 2017
pet perks A. MENCEL color *Parents* v92 no8 p25 Ag 2017
Safe Browsing, by Age *Parents* v91 no12 p44 D 2016
the skinny on thin kids J. MONINGER *Parents* v91 no9 p46 S 2016
social influence T. REECE *Parents* v92 no5 p119 My 2017
tiny teenagers I. COHEN *Parents* v91 no12 p124 D 2016
vocabulary lessons J. VASQUEZ *Parents* v92 no7 p126 Jl 2017
What I Learned at My Parent's Job M. LaScala color *Parents* v92 no4 p13 Ap 2017
When Everything Is "Mine!" M. DAHL color *Parents* v92 no11 p38 N 2017
WHY WE LIE Y. BHATTACHARJEE cartoon color graph *National Geographic* v231 no6 p30 Je 2017

Child development deviations
coming attractions J. DETZ *Parents* v91 no9 p52 S 2016

Child health services
In Session: School Clinics: More and more, they're seen as an important part of the social safety net M. Quinn *Governing* v30 no9 p18 Je 2017
Pediatric Predicament C. Schmidt color *Scientific American* v317 no3 p24 S 2017

Child labor
Business Can Help End Child Labor V. Govindarajan *Harvard Business Review Digital Articles* p2 Ap 9 2015
Is It OK to Buy Cheap Clothes? *Scholastic Choices* v32 no8 p2 My 2017
Why Companies Are Blind to Child Labor D. Zane, J. Irwin et al *Harvard Business Review Digital Articles* p2 Ja 28 2016

Child labor—Law & legislation
History of child labor in the United States--part 1: little children working M. Schuman bibl bw color *Monthly Labor Review* p1

Ja 2017

Child labor—United States
History of child labor in the United States--part 1: little children working M. Schuman bibl bw color *Monthly Labor Review* p1 Ja 2017
History of child labor in the United States--part 2: the reform movement M. Schuman bibl bw color *Monthly Labor Review* p1 Ja 2017

Child marriage
It's Time to Change the Story About Child Marriage color *Maclean's* v130 no3 p61 Ap 2017
Too Young to Say 'I Do'? Underage teens can still get married in most states. But some lawmakers and advocacy groups are trying to change that P. SMITH and L. W. Foderaro *New York Times Upfront* v149 no12 p6 Ap 24 2017

Child mental health
Growing Up In Public B. Luscombe color *Time* v189 no20 p42 My 29 2017

Child molesters
Should I Tell Someone That His Father-in-Law Is a Child Molester? K. A. Appiah *New York Times Magazine* p22 Jl 9 2017

Child mortality
Unpaid Bills J. McGowan color *Commonweal* v144 no15 p6 S 22 2017

Child nutrition
CHAPTER 4 INEQUALITY IN EARLY CHILDHOOD AND EFFECTIVE PUBLIC POLICY INTERVENTIONS *Economic Indicators* p153 O 2016
Double Down on Your Veggie Efforts S. SEA GOLD color *Parents* v92 no5 p22 My 2017
simplify your lunch strategy K. CICERO *Parents* v91 no9 p92 S 2016

Child pornography
Project Spade R. KOLKER bw *Walrus* v14 no7 p44 S 2017
SAFE SEX, DANGEROUS STATE K. MANGU-WARD color *Reason* v48 no11 p4 Ap 2017

Child pornography—United States—Law & legislation
SEX AND KIDS J. SULLUM color *Reason* v48 no11 p26 Ap 2017

Child psychologists
Diane Caprioia *Atlanta* v57 no2 p98 Je 2017

Child psychology
> *See also*
> Anxiety in children
> Childhood friendships
> Color vision in children
> Curiosity in children
> Grandparent & child
> Self-control in children

birthday-party blues M. COHEN *Parents* v92 no4 p134 Ap 2017
Giggles *Parents* v92 no11 p124 N 2017
MAKING AI MORE HUMAN A. Gopnik color *Scientific American* v316 no6 p60 Je 2017
Responding to Defiance in the Moment *Education Digest* v82 no7 p46 Mr 2017
Science vs. Silliness for Parents: Debunking the Myths of Child Psychology S. HUPP, A. STARY et al *Skeptical Inquirer* v41 no1 p44 Ja/F 2017
When Big Brother Parents J. Darrow img *New York* v50 no18 p34 S 4 2017
When Everything Is "Mine!" M. DAHL color *Parents* v92 no11 p38 N 2017
WHEN SEX AND GENDER COLLIDE K. R. OLSON color *Scientific American* v317 no3 p44 S 2017

Child rearing
> *See also*
> Discipline of children
> Parenting
> Toilet training

5 Books for Raising Respectful Children *Parents* v91 no10 p20 O 2016
75 ways to be a grown-up E. ZAMMETT RUDDY, J. DUNN et al *Parents* v91 no11 p95 N 2016
are asian kids really better at math? M. THIAGARAJAN *Parents* v91 no9 p58 S 2016
avoid the homework trap E. ZAMMETT RUDDY *Parents* v91

no9 p96 S 2016

behind the scenes *Parents* v91 no12 p8 D 2016

believe E. ZAMMETT RUDDY *Parents* v91 no12 p82 D 2016

bus behavior R. DELANEY *Parents* v91 no9 p170 S 2016

class wars J. MANN *Parents* v92 no1 p78 Ja 2017

cultivate caring J. TORRES SIDERS *Parents* v91 no12 p122 D 2016

eating out B. HILL *Parents* v92 no2 p102 F 2017

fair ground H. GOWEN WALSH *Parents* v91 no11 p146 N 2016

fickle friendships E. KENNEDY-MOORE *Parents* v92 no1 p76 Ja 2017

first teacher C. WIRA DINEEN *Parents* v91 no9 p168 S 2016

future focus D. Points *Parents* v92 no1 p4 Ja 2017

Good Grief G. D. MELTON cartoon *O, The Oprah Magazine* p36 Mr 2017

good sports H. A. ROTBART *Parents* v92 no3 p114 Mr 2017

guess my power move L. Vaccariello *Parents* v92 no3 p6 Mr 2017

'Happy Little Wives and Mothers' K. M. Byrne *America* v216 no11 p42 My 15 2017

hard truths J. DETZ *Parents* v92 no2 p106 F 2017

how to raise an optimist V. GLEMBOCKI color *Parents* v92 no4 p50 Ap 2017

if you ask Kristen *Parents* v91 no11 p82 N 2016

imitation game T. REECE *Parents* v92 no3 p108 Mr 2017

IT'S COME TO THIS *Parents* v92 no2 p13 F 2017

the kind of mom i am L. Vaccariello *Parents* v92 no2 p10 F 2017

Know Your Options *Parents* v91 no12 p48 D 2016

manage your kid's digital life M. CROUCH *Parents* v91 no12 p42 D 2016

me to we J. Francisco *Good Housekeeping* v264 no3 p8 Mr 2017

a note from Kristen K. Bell *Parents* v91 no11 p8 N 2016

playing favorites K. KEMP *Parents* v91 no12 p128 D 2016

powerful emotions L. GARISTO PFAFF *Parents* v91 no11 p144 N 2016

PROBLEM: GROWN SONS ARE ACTING LIKE 2-YEAR-OLDS IN ADULT BODIES J. Brown *Successful Farming* v115 no1 p70 Ja 2017

quiet child L. NARGI *Parents* v92 no2 p104 F 2017

quiz: are you raising an emotional eater? [Cover story] chart color *Parents* v92 no3 p42 Mr 2017

raise a science lover M. CROUCH *Parents* v92 no2 p56 F 2017

Safe Browsing, by Age *Parents* v91 no12 p44 D 2016

Safeguard Your Smartphone *Parents* v91 no12 p46 D 2016

school support L. GARISTO PFAFF *Parents* v91 no11 p148 N 2016

A Single Mom Plans Her Next Act K. LANKFORD color *Kiplinger's Personal Finance* v71 no8 p72 Ag 2017

the skinny on thin kids J. MONINGER *Parents* v91 no9 p46 S 2016

the sleep fix H. GOWEN WALSH *Parents* v91 no11 p58 N 2016

squirmy solutions J. T. BENJAMIN *Parents* v92 no3 p110 Mr 2017

teach your child to be a FORCE FOR GOOD S. Dolgoff color *Good Housekeeping* v264 no4 p138 Ap 2017

tech confessions D. Points *Parents* v91 no12 p6 D 2016

tiny teenagers I. COHEN *Parents* v91 no12 p124 D 2016

TRIUMPH AND TURMOIL C. HIATT *USA Today Magazine* v145 no2864 p74 My 2017

watch this way *Parents* v91 no11 p29 N 2016

When Getting the Gear Isn't a Given S. MAHONEY color *Parents* v92 no11 p92 N 2017

when kids interrupt E. ZAMMETT RUDDY *Parents* v92 no2 p42 F 2017

Child rearing ethics

Is There a Case to be Made Against Baby Making? color *Foreign Policy* no224 p26 My/Je 2017

Child restraint systems in automobiles—Evaluation

The Safest Car Seat for Your Child M. Naranjo chart color *Consumer Reports* v82 no1 p56 Ja 2017

Child sexual abuse

See also

Child sexual abuse by clergy

Reflections on the Scandal at Choate L. SMITH color *Weekly Standard* v22 no35 p17 My 22 2017

talking to strangers J. WIENER *Parents* v92 no7 p128 Jl 2017

Child sexual abuse by clergy

An elite school's dark past M. FRISCOLANTI bw color *Maclean's* v130 no10 p32 N 2017

the silence of the lambs K. JOYCE color *New Republic* v248 no7 p38 Jl 2017

Child sexual abuse lawsuits

Criminal Background Checks for Youth Sport Coaches J. C. Kozlowski *Parks & Recreation* v52 no6 p20 Je 2017

Child sexual abuse—Lawsuits & claims

SEE NO EVIL HEAR NO EVIL SPEAK NO EVIL E. LEWIS bw color *Esquire* v166 no5 p114 D 2016/Ja 2017

Child sexual abuse—United States

The Great Day-Care Sexual-Abuse Panic P. TERZIAN bw *Weekly Standard* v22 no42 p12 Jl 17 2017

SEX AND KIDS J. SULLUM color *Reason* v48 no11 p26 Ap 2017

Child surfers

BEST 14 AND UNDER color *Surfing Magazine* v53 no1 p56 Ja 2017

BEST FEMALE color *Surfing Magazine* v53 no1 p54 Ja 2017

BEST OVERALL bw color *Surfing Magazine* v53 no1 p60 Ja 2017

BEST TUBE RIDER color *Surfing Magazine* v53 no1 p44 Ja 2017

BIGGEST LADYKILLER color *Surfing Magazine* v53 no1 p58 Ja 2017

Ethan Ewing color *Surfing Magazine* v53 no1 p22 Ja 2017

GROM GAMES 2016 T. Paul color *Surfing Magazine* v53 no1 p76 Ja 2017

MOST FEARLESS color *Surfing Magazine* v53 no1 p50 Ja 2017

MOST POWERFUL color *Surfing Magazine* v53 no1 p46 Ja 2017

MOST PROGRESSIVE color *Surfing Magazine* v53 no1 p48 Ja 2017

MOST UNDERRATED color *Surfing Magazine* v53 no1 p52 Ja 2017

Sebastian Williams color *Surfing Magazine* v53 no1 p32 Ja 2017

TARO WATANABE M. Ciaramella color *Surfing Magazine* v53 no1 p34 Ja 2017

TEEN AGE *Surfing Magazine* v53 no1 p42 Ja 2017

YOUTH-FUL EXUBERANCE Z. Morton color *Surfing Magazine* v53 no1 p12 Ja 2017

Child victims

A System from the North A. OHLIN cartoon *Walrus* v13 no10 p62 D 2016

Child volunteers

FEED THE KIND-O-METER diag *Good Housekeeping* v263 no5 p92 N 2016

Child welfare

Home Alone P. HARRIMAN and H. ASHBACH *USA Today Magazine* v145 no2864 p29 My 2017

Child welfare—Arizona

Put the Kids First N. S. RILEY color *Weekly Standard* v22 no41 p18 Jl 3 2017

Child writing

EARLY WRITING EXPERIENCES: What every teacher and parent should know about why young children need to write D. Wells Rowe *Literacy Today (2411-7862)* v35 no2 p30 S/O 2017

Childbirth

See also

Delivery (Obstetrics)

Implications of the Baby Bust: Lower birth rates in America will have a wide range of policy consequences M. Maciag *Governing* v30 no10 p56 Jl 2017

IT'S COME TO THIS *Parents* v91 no9 p15 S 2016

A MATTER OF LIFE & DEATH M. Winter color *Essence* v48 no6 p106 O 2017

Social Science and the Public Interest *Society* v53 no6 p571 D 2016

Childbirth—Charts, diagrams, etc.

The Baby Spike M. Fischetti and Z. Armstrong diag *Scientific American* v317 no1 p76 Jl 2017

Childbirth—Psychological aspects

a labor to love A. PATUREL *Parents* v91 no9 p119 S 2016

Childbirth—Statistics

Birth rate craters as housing costs rise *America* v216 no3 p8 F 6 2017

KIDS AREN'T US S. BHATTACHARYA color *Esquire* p112 Ap 2017

Solid Gains in the Juvenile Categories Help Drive Units Up chart *Publishers Weekly* v264 no24 p6 Je 12 2017

Xinjiang Juvenile Publishing House color *Publishers Weekly* v264 no12 p24 Mr 20 2017

Zhejiang Juvenile & Children's Publishing House color *Publishers Weekly* v264 no12 p26 Mr 20 2017

Children's books—Congresses

AUTHORS AND ILLUSTRATORS TO MEET AT CI 5 bw color *Publishers Weekly* v264 no11 p30 Mr 13 2017

CHILDREN'S INSTITUTE HEADS TO PORTLAND J. ROSEN cartoon *Publishers Weekly* v264 no11 p21 Mr 13 2017

Covering The World of Children's Publishing C. Reid and J. Maher color *Publishers Weekly* v263 no51 p1 D 12 2016

Children's books—Economic aspects

Canadian Kids Publishers Extend Reach into U.S., TV E. NAWOTKA *Publishers Weekly* v263 no39 p14 S 26 2016

Children's books—Exhibitions

A Big Week for Children's Books J. Rosen, D. Roback et al color *Publishers Weekly* v264 no16 p4 Ap 17 2017

Children's books—Sales & prices

CHILDREN'S BESTSELLERS chart *Publishers Weekly* v264 no4 p13 Ja 23 2017

Penguin Random House Rules The Children's Book Market J. Milliot chart *Publishers Weekly* v263 no45 p4 N 7 2016

Children's clothing

See also

Children's clothing design

Margherita Missoni J. K. DE VALLE color *Architectural Digest* v74 no2 p26 F 2017

Shirts Without Snark *Parents* v91 no12 p18 D 2016

Children's clothing design

CLOTHING A GENERATION I. R. BJÖRNSDÓTTIR *Iceland Review* v54 no6 p12 N/D 2016

Children's clothing stores

Little Darlings: A Fishers-based shop for children's clothing rental offers storybook styles at fairytale prices L. BAILEY *Indianapolis Monthly* v40 no11 p27 Jl 2017

Children's clothing stores—Evaluation

Shopping *Virginia Living* p103 2017 Best 20of Virginia

Children's conduct of life

advice every new mom needs [Cover story] D. SPARROW, W. Fleisig et al color *Parents* v92 no7 p32 Jl 2017

ages+stages color *Parents* v92 no7 p117 Jl 2017

babyish behavior J. BURT COTE *Parents* v92 no8 p132 Ag 2017

back talk boot camp V. GLEMBOCKI *Parents* p72 2015

Brush Up on Mealtime Manners H. G. Walsh *Parents* v92 no9 p170 S 2017

easily embarrassed T. REECE *Parents* v92 no6 p138 Je 2017

help with hygiene T. CETTINA *Parents* v92 no8 p138 Ag 2017

HOW TO Avoid Losing Things T. REECE *Parents* v92 no11 p120 N 2017

HOW TO Wipe Out Whining R. FELSENTHAL STEWART *Parents* v92 no11 p120 N 2017

I Am a Toddler, Ask Me Anything R. D'apice color *Parents* v92 no9 p62 S 2017

Just Ignore It C. Pearlman color *Parents* v92 no9 p58 S 2017

oops J. Garcia, S. R. Wright et al *Parents* v92 no7 p132 Jl 2017

pants on fire E. ZAMMETT RUDDY color graph *Parents* v92 no8 p56 Ag 2017

perspective, please! K. CICERO *Parents* v91 no6 p146 Je 2016

quirky quotes from kids *Parents* p42 2015

vocabulary lessons J. VASQUEZ *Parents* v92 no7 p126 Jl 2017

the weirdest thing my child has slept with is... *Parents* v91 no6 p148 Je 2016

Children's dental care

Does Your Seven-Year-Old Really Need Braces? [Cover story] *USA Today Magazine* v146 no2869 p8 O 2017

A Mouthful of Answers J. Miller color *Parents* v92 no9 p30 S 2017

Children's drawings

Art Zone color *National Geographic Kids* no472 p35 Ag 2017

Children's films

Streaming Jr S. Li color *Entertainment Weekly* no1449 p46 Ja 20 2017

Yankees favorite events this season chart *Yankee* v81 no1 p78 Ja/F 2017

Children's furniture—Evaluation

WHOA, BABY H. Kelly *Washingtonian Magazine* v52 no5 p148 F 2017

Children's health

See also

Obesity in children

Pediatric Predicament C. Schmidt color *Scientific American* v317 no3 p24 S 2017

scrap the nap [Cover story] R. R. PEACHMAN *Parents* v92 no7 p124 Jl 2017

SCREEN TIME RULES L. GOLDMAN *Better Homes & Gardens* v95 no6 p165 Je 2017

sweets worth saluting [Cover story] J. HOWARD color *Parents* v92 no7 p60 Jl 2017

Children's hospitals

The CEO of Children's National Health System on Leadership, Innovation, and Delivering Specialized Care K. Bell *Harvard Business Review Digital Articles* p1 Je 22 2017

Children's hospitals—Design & construction

Seattle Children's Hospital, South Clinic C. Gavin *Architectural Record* v205 no4 p189 Ap 2017

Children's literature

See also

Children's nonfiction

Children's poetry

A Bonanza of Book Events for Toddlers to Teens L. Hartman bw color *Publishers Weekly* v263 no44 p(Sp)29 O 31 2016

CHILDREN'S BESTSELLERS chart *Publishers Weekly* v264 no20 p15 My 15 2017

CHILDREN'S BEST SELLERS *New York Times Book Review* p25 Jl 2 2017

CHILDREN'S BEST SELLERS *New York Times Book Review* p33 My 21 2017

SEPARATING FACT FROM FICTION J. ROSEN color *Publishers Weekly* v264 no5 p16 Ja 30 2017

Children's literature—Authorship

FAIL FUNNIER R. GALCHEN cartoon *New Yorker* v92 no48 p28 F 6 2017

"Pinch Me, I'm Dreaming" bw color *Publishers Weekly* v263 no49 p6 D 7 2016

Children's literature—China

Hunan Juvenile & Children's Publishing House color *Publishers Weekly* v264 no12 p18 Mr 20 2017

Children's literature—Congresses

Covering The World of Children's Publishing C. Reid and J. Maher color *Publishers Weekly* v263 no51 p1 D 12 2016

PUTTING BOOKS TO WORK: Create lessons based on children's and YA books, side by side with the authors themselves, at ILA 2017 M. Cotillo and E. O'Leary color *Literacy Today (2411-7862)* v34 no6 p30 My/Je 2017

Children's literature—Marketing

News Briefs *Publishers Weekly* v264 no30 p4 Jl 24 2017

Children's Museum of Manhattan

225 MINUTES WITH... Asahd Khaled: Touring the Children's Museum of Manhattan with the busiest baby in hip-hop A. P. DAVIS img *New York* v50 no18 p18 S 4 2017

Children's museums

Big rig rolls statewide to celebrate Nebraska's big birthday A. J. BARTELS cartoon color *Nebraska Life* v21 no4 p82 Jl/Ag 2017

Children's nonfiction

SEPARATING FACT FROM FICTION J. ROSEN color *Publishers Weekly* v264 no5 p16 Ja 30 2017

Children's paraphernalia

See also

Children's books

Children's clothing

Infants' supplies

Toys

Bringing Up Bébé E. A. ACHARA color *Vogue* v206 no11 p164 N 2016

WHAT'S NEW? *USA Today Magazine* v145 no2860 p74 Ja 2017

Children's parties

dive into summer A. MAZE color *Better Homes & Gardens* v95 no7 p49 Jl 2017

Children's periodicals

Nature's Ambassador Hits the Big 5-0 L. Moore color *National*

Wildlife (World Edition) v55 no1 p18 D/Ja 2016

Children's playhouses
See also
Tree houses
BRICK HOUSE: DENMARK'S LEGO LANDMARK C. HAR-RINGTON diag *Wired* v25 no9 p22 S 2017

Children's poetry
See also
Lullabies
Tongue twisters
BEYOND NATIONAL borders O. Aina color *Literacy Today (2411-7862)* v34 no5 p52 Mr/Ap 2017

Children's rooms
See also
Nurseries (Children's rooms)
From Our Editor S. Donelson color *House Beautiful* v159 no1 p4 F 2017

Children's rooms—Interior decoration
room to grow K. BARNES *Better Homes & Gardens* v94 no12 pN1 D 2016

Children's stories
With Late Easter, Juvenile Sales Tumble chart *Publishers Weekly* v264 no14 p5 Ap 3. 2017

Children's television programs
Afternoons and Popeye Cartoons M. W. SCHWARTZ *Missouri Life* v43 no7 p38 D 2016/Ja 2017
Streaming Jr S. Li color *Entertainment Weekly* no1436/1437 p88 O 21 2016

Children's television programs—History
Street Cred B. Luscombe color *Time* v189 no14 p44 Ap 17 2017

Children's television programs—United States
HERE'S THE DIRT S. STALL *Indianapolis Monthly* p18 F 2017
A New PBS, Just for Kids J. Halterman *TV Guide* v65 no4 p9 Ja 16 2017

Children's Book Fair (Bologna, Italy)
21st Century Publishing Group color *Publishers Weekly* v264 no12 p8 Mr 20 2017
Bologna 2017 Preview E. NAWOTKA color *Publishers Weekly* v264 no12 p26 Mr 20 2017
Trend Watching color *Publishers Weekly* v264 no12 p28 Mr 20 2017

Children's book sales & prices—Charts, diagrams, etc.
CHILDREN'S BESTSELLERS chart *Publishers Weekly* v264 no26 p15 Je 26 2017

Children's books—Charts, diagrams, etc.
CHILDREN'S BESTSELLERS chart *Publishers Weekly* v263 no43 p16 O 24 2016
CHILDREN'S BESTSELLERS chart *Publishers Weekly* v264 no32 p13 Ag 7 2017
CHILDREN'S BESTSELLERS chart *Publishers Weekly* v264 no8 p14 F 20 2017
CHILDREN'S BESTSELLERS C. JURIS chart *Publishers Weekly* v263 no42 p16 O 17 2016
CHILDREN'S BESTSELLERS C. JURIS chart *Publishers Weekly* v263 no50 p19 D 5 2016
CHILDREN'S BESTSELLERS C. JURIS chart *Publishers Weekly* v264 no10 p16 Mr 6 2017
CHILDREN'S BESTSELLERS C. JURIS chart *Publishers Weekly* v264 no21 p17 My 22 2017
CHILDREN'S BESTSELLERS C. Juris chart *Publishers Weekly* v264 no30 p14 Jl 24 2017
CHILDREN'S BESTSELLERS C. JURIS chart *Publishers Weekly* v264 no34 p20 Ag 21 2017
CHILDREN'S BESTSELLERS C. JURIS chart *Publishers Weekly* v264 no38 p19 S 18 2017
CHILDREN'S BESTSELLERS C. JURIS chart *Publishers Weekly* v264 no41 p14 O 9 2017
CHILDREN'S BEST SELLERS *New York Times Book Review* p25 Ag 20 2017
CHILDREN'S BEST SELLERS *New York Times Book Review* p25 Ag 6 2017
CHILDREN'S BEST SELLERS *New York Times Book Review* p25 Mr 19 2017
CHILDREN'S BEST SELLERS *New York Times Book Review* p27 N 27 2016
CHILDREN'S BEST SELLERS *New York Times Book Review*

p27 O 2 2016
CHILDREN'S BESTSELLERS OCTOBER 17–23 2016 chart *Publishers Weekly* v263 no44 p16 O 31 2016
CHILDREN'S BOOKS FOR FALL color *Publishers Weekly* v264 no29 p21 Jl 17 2017

Children's books—Sales & prices—Charts, diagrams, etc.
CHILDREN'S BESTSELLERS chart *Publishers Weekly* v264 no6 p15 F 6 2017
The Year in Children's Bestsellers J. MILLIOT chart color *Publishers Weekly* v264 no6 p34 F 6 2017

Children's literature—Charts, diagrams, etc.
CHILDREN'S BEST SELLERS *New York Times Book Review* p25 Je 25 2017

Children—Social aspects
ON THE SPOT CAROLINE DODDS PENNOCK: We ask leading historians 20 questions on why their research matters, one book everyone should read and their views on the Tudors ... C. D. Pennock *History Today* v67 no7 p112 Jl 2017

Children's stories—Charts, diagrams, etc.
CHILDREN'S BESTSELLERS C. JURIS chart *Publishers Weekly* v264 no7 p14 F 13 2017
CHILDREN'S BESTSELLERS SEPT. 26–OCT. 2, 2016 *Publishers Weekly* v263 no41 p17 O 10 2016

Children's television programs—Plots, themes, etc.
What They Really Couldn't Do on You Can't Do That on Television A. Wilkinson color *Entertainment Weekly* no1460/1461 p41 Ap 7–17 2017

Children—United States
BIG REACH color *Spin to Win Rodeo* v20 no12 p16 F 2017
A Plea to America's Adults A. POWELL and C. POWELL color *Reader's Digest* v190 no1132 p20 Jl/Ag 2017

Children—United States—Health
Suffer the Children *In These Times* v41 no6 p32 Je 2017

Childress, Jessica
Beyond the Letter of the Law C. Kettlewell color *Virginia Living* v15 no5 p60 Ag 2017

Childress, Kyle
The hard blue glow *Christian Century* v134 no13 p10 Je 21 2017
The ministry of showing up *Christian Century* v133 no23 p10 N 9 2016

Childs, Bennett G.
Senescent intimal foam cells are deleterious at all stages of atherosclerosis bibl *Science* v354 no6311 p472 O 28 2016

CHILDS, CRAIG
THE SOUND OF FALLEN TREES *Arizona Highways* v92 no8 p4 Ag 2016

CHILDS, JESSIE
ON THE SPOT: We ask 20 questions of leading historians on why their research matters, one book everyone should read and their views on the Tudors ... *History Today* v67 no9 p112 S 2017

Chile
Chile's glacial lakes pose newly recognized flood threat J. Palmer color *Science* v355 no6329 p1004 Mr 10 2017

Chile—Description & travel
7 Days of LOCURA L. Hittmeier color *Skiing* p58 Wint 2017

Chilemba, Ellen
60 Years of Campus Changemakers J. Militare color *Glamour* v115 no5 p138 My 2017

Chile—Politics & government
When Allende TOLD US HAPPINESS IS A HUMAN RIGHT L. SEPÚLVEDA bw *Nation* v305 no6 p16 S 11 2017

Chili con carne
Cook Like a Texanist D. COURTNEY *Texas Monthly* v44 no12 p272 D 2016
THE FULL LEADED JACKET AT LEADBELLY A. Staples color *Sports Illustrated* v127 no5 p74 Ag 14 2017

Chillers (Refrigeration)
new products color *Science* v356 no6345 p1402 Je 30 2017

Chilly Scenes of Winter (Film)
STRONGER TOGETHER S. ENELOW bw color *Film Comment* v53 no5 p50 S/O 2017

Chilton, Andrew
The Goblin's Puzzle: Being the Adventures of a Boy with No Name and Two Girls Called Alice color *Publishers Weekly* v263 no49 p78 D 7 2016

CHILTON, CHRIS

GREEN HELLION color *Road & Track* v68 no7 p80 Mr/Ap 2017

NEW FIVE, SAME JIVE color *Road & Track* v68 no7 p88 Mr/Ap 2017

SHOW STEALER color *Road & Track* v68 no8 p86 My 2017

STINGS SO GOOD color *Road & Track* v69 no3 p94 O 2017

SUPERHERO color *Road & Track* v68 no10 p46 Jl 2017

URGE OVERKILL color *Road & Track* v69 no1 p54 Ag 2017

Chimeric antigen receptors

Supply of promising T cell therapy is strained J. Couzin-Frankel color *Science* v356 no6343 p1112 Je 16 2017

Chimerism

Human-animal chimeras created T. H. SAEY color *Science News* v191 no3 p6 F 18 2017

Chimney linings

Do you need a chimney liner? R. Tschoepe color *Old House Journal* v45 no7 p42 O 2017

Chimneys

ASK OLD HOUSE JOURNAL P. Poore color *Old House Journal* v45 no2 p60 Ap 2017

Romantic Revivals color *Old House Journal* v45 no3 p36 My 2017

Chimneys—Design & construction

Do you need a chimney liner? R. Tschoepe color *Old House Journal* v45 no7 p42 O 2017

Chimowitz, Eldred

Statistical Physics: A Prelude and Fugue for Engineers *Physics Today* v70 no10 p62 O 2017

Chimpanzee behavior

DOCTOR WHO? M. Velasquez-Manoff color *New York Times Magazine* p68 My 21 2017

Under the Microscope color *Earth Island Journal* v32 no3 p12 Aut 2017

Chimpanzees

Becoming Jane [Cover story] T. GERBER bw color map *National Geographic* v232 no4 p30 O 2017

Chimpanzee genomic diversity reveals ancient admixture with bonobos J. Novembre, M. Gut et al bibl diag graph map *Science* v354 no6311 p477 O 28 2016

Chimpanzees as laboratory animals

CHIMPS IN WAITING D. Grimm color *Science* v356 no6343 p1114 Je 16 2017

Chimpanzees—Behavior

Low-status chimps are trendsetters B. BOWER *Science News* v191 no6 p8 Ap 1 2017

Chimpanzees—Diseases

Elderly chimps may get Alzheimer's disease R. Cross color *Science* v357 no6350 p440 Ag 4 2017

Chimpanzees—Reproduction

Chimps, bonobos interbred long ago T. Hesman Saey color *Science News* v190 no11 p19 N 26 2016

Chimpanzees—Research

Save the world's primates in peril Bin Yang, J. R. Anderson et al bibl color *Science* v354 no6311 p425 O 28 2016

The Trees of Gombe J. GOODALL and D. Rothkopf *Foreign Policy* no224 p84 My/Je 2017

Chin, Jimmy

Frozen Assets J. ROTH color *Esquire* p72 BigBlackBook

Chin, Lynda

How Physicians Can Keep Up with the Knowledge Explosion in Medicine *Harvard Business Review Digital Articles* p2 D 19 2016

Chin, Mel—Exhibitions

"PERPETUAL REVOLUTION: THE IMAGE AND SOCIAL CHANGE" E. Heartney color *Art in America* v105 no4 p114 Ap 2017

China

Anhui Children's Publishing House color *Publishers Weekly* v264 no12 p10 Mr 20 2017

How China's Government Helps—and Hinders—Innovation A. Gupta and Haiyan Wang *Harvard Business Review Digital Articles* p2 N 16 2016

An Overview of the Children's Book Market in China T. TAN color *Publishers Weekly* v264 no12 p3 Mr 20 2017

China Euro Vehicle Technology AB

Mats Fägerhag A. MacKenzie color *Motor Trend* v69 no2 p24 F 2017

China National Petroleum Corp.

Linked In L. Yu *Bloomberg Businessweek* no4538 pC1 S 18 2017

China. National Space Administration

China selects a lunar target color *Science* v356 no6343 p1104 Je 16 2017

China Ocean Shipping (Group) Co.

Shipping News J. PSAROPOULOS color map *Weekly Standard* v22 no45 p24 Ag 7 2017

China Railway Construction Corp. Ltd.

Mega-Eye on the Sky Renjiang Xie *Sky & Telescope* v133 no2 p26 F 2017

China—Antiquities

THE BUDDHA OF THE LAKE S. S. PATEL color *Archaeology* v70 no3 p23 My/Je 2017

China—Commerce—United States

Did Trade with China Make U.S. Manufacturing Less Innovative? W. Frick *Harvard Business Review Digital Articles* p2 D 8 2016

Where Trump Does (and Doesn't) Have Leverage with China T. Hout *Harvard Business Review Digital Articles* p2 D 16 2016

China—Description & travel

CHINA *New York Times Magazine* p40 S 24 2017

FINE CHINA K. GLOWCZEWSKA bw color map *Harper's Bazaar* no3655 p95 Ag 2017

XINJIANG, CHINA J. CHEN color *Conde Nast Traveler* v52 no1 p32 Ja 2017

China—Economic conditions

Asia & Oceania img *New York Times Upfront* v149 no6 p28 D 12 2016

What China's 13th Five-Year Plan Means for Business M. Reeves and D. He *Harvard Business Review Digital Articles* p2 D 7 2015

China—Economic policy

China and the World E. A. Feigenbaum color *Foreign Affairs* v96 no1 p33 Ja/F 2017

China—Economic conditions—1949-

Milton Friedman's Misadventures in China J. B. GEWIRTZ *American Scholar* v86 no1 p30 Wint 2017

China—Economic conditions—2000-

China's Growth: A Brief History L. Yueh *Harvard Business Review Digital Articles* p2 D 9 2015

China's Slowdown: The First Stage of the Bullwhip Effect Y. Sheffi *Harvard Business Review Digital Articles* p2 S 9 2015

China Still Isn't Ready to Be a True Global Leader W. C. Kirby and F. W. McFarlan *Harvard Business Review Digital Articles* p2 Ja 5 2015

"Economic Openness Serves Everyone Better" L. Keqiang bw *Bloomberg Businessweek* no4509 p8 Ja 30 2017

China—Economic policy—1949-

The Cruise That Changed China J. Baird Gewirtz bw *Foreign Affairs* v95 no6 p101 N/D 2016

China—Economic policy—2000-

China's Big Play for Small Chips R. Hackett color *Fortune* v175 no3 p16 Mr 1 2017

"Economic Openness Serves Everyone Better" L. Keqiang bw *Bloomberg Businessweek* no4509 p8 Ja 30 2017

It's Hard to Label China A Currency Manipulator E. Curran, S. Mohsin et al *Bloomberg Businessweek* no4500 p17 N 21 2016

The Once and Future Financial Crisis M. Schuman color *Bloomberg Businessweek* no4529 p10 Jl 3 2017

China—Foreign economic relations

China Spreads the Wealth Around S. Cendrowski color map *Fortune* v174 no8 p138 D 15 2016

Salesman Xi M. STINSON *National Review* v69 no12 p18 Je 26 2017

WHAT CHINA WANTS J. CASTALDO color *Maclean's* v130 no9 p67 O 2017

China—Foreign economic relations—United States

THE ASIA PIVOT: PROBLEMS, PROBLEMS, PROBLEMS D. BANDOW *USA Today Magazine* v145 no2862 p32 Mr 2017

CHINA'S GREAT LEAP BACKWARD [Cover story] J. Fallows color *Atlantic* v318 no5 p58 D 2016

Here's How Donald Trump Can Win a Trade War With China C. Matthews color diag *Fortune* v75 no1 p22 Ja 1 2017

"HOLLYWOOD" A. Sakoui and J. Yang color *Bloomberg Businessweek* no4511 p18 F 13 2017

Hollywood Hunts for Its Next Pot of Gold A. Sakoui and J. Y. de

Morel bw *Bloomberg Businessweek* no4540 p24 O 2 2017

How to Win a Trade War With China M. Schuman bw *Bloomberg Businessweek* no4512 p6 F 20 2017

Professor Propaganda K. D. WILLIAMSON color *National Review* v69 no6 p28 Ap 3 2017

Trump's Trade War With … Boeing? chart color *Bloomberg Businessweek* no4502 p36 D 5 2016

Will Beijing Also Have A Friend at State? T. Shi, D. Tweed et al bw *Bloomberg Businessweek* no4504 p26 D 19 2016

China—Foreign relations—21st century

As Distrust Mounts, US and China Battle Over New Rules of Global Order W. JISI *NPQ: New Perspectives Quarterly* v33 no4 p44 O 2016

Western Critics of China Need to Avoid a Colonial Mindset D. A. BELL *NPQ: New Perspectives Quarterly* v33 no4 p23 O 2016

China—Foreign relations—India

Border Trouble: China and India Face Off D. TWEED bw map *Bloomberg Businessweek* no4534 p32 Ag 14 2017

China—Foreign relations—Korea

Beijing Is Mad About Thaad B. Einhorn, Sohee Kim et al color *Bloomberg Businessweek* no4514 p16 Mr 13 2017

China—Foreign relations—Soviet Union

50, 100 & 150 YEARS AGO bw color *Scientific American* v315 no5 p79 N 2016

China—Foreign relations—United States

All Quiet(ed) on the Eastern Front A. WALDRON *Weekly Standard* v22 no5 p14 O 10 2016

Asia's Other Revisionist Power J. Lind color *Foreign Affairs* v96 no2 p74 Mr/Ap 2017

Beijing Welcomes Trump H. Beech color *Time* v188 no22-23 p31 N/D 2016

Dealing With North Korea Is a Team Sport, and the U.S. Needs China on Its Side A. J. Stavridis color *Time* v189 no6 p24 F 20 2017

THE MONTH IN REVIEW *Current History* v116 no789 p160 Ap 2017

The Thucydides Trap G. ALLISON color *Foreign Policy* no224 p80 My/Je 2017

Trade Reciprocity With China [Cover story] D. SCISSORS color *National Review* v69 no2 p25 F 6 2017

With North Korea, No Alternative to Patience *Bloomberg Businessweek* no4530 p12 Jl 17 2017

China—Foreign relations—United States—History—21st century

China Makes Nice With Ivanka and Jared *Bloomberg Businessweek* no4511 p27 F 13 2017

Course Correction E. Ratner color *Foreign Affairs* v96 no4 p64 Jl/Ag 2017

Trump and China S. Shirk color *Foreign Affairs* v96 no2 p20 Mr/Ap 2017

Why China Fears a 'Color Revolution' Incited by the West N. GARDELS *NPQ: New Perspectives Quarterly* v33 no4 p8 O 2016

Will Boeing Become Collateral Damage? J. Johnsson color graph *Bloomberg Businessweek* no4500 p23 N 21 2016

THE WORLD'S NEW ANTAGONIZER-IN-CHIEF S. Cendrowski *Fortune* v75 no1 p22 Ja 1 2017

China—Foreign relations—1976-

China's Deep Logic M. Maochun Yu *Hoover Digest: Research & Opinion on Public Policy* no4 p128 Fall 2016

China—Government policy

The Real Reason Uber Is Giving Up in China W. C. Kirby *Harvard Business Review Digital Articles* p2 Ag 2 2016

China—History—Charts, diagrams, etc.

The Cultural Revolution V. MAJEROL, J. Yardley et al *New York Times Upfront* v149 no5 p18 N 21 2016

China—History—Cultural Revolution, 1966-1976

A Beijing Model? R. Terrill color *Weekly Standard* v22 no23 p18 F 20 2017

The Cultural Revolution V. MAJEROL, J. Yardley et al *New York Times Upfront* v149 no5 p18 N 21 2016

When the Chinese Were Unspeakable I. Johnson color map *New York Review of Books* v64 no1 p22 Ja 19 2017

China—History—Xi Xia dynasty, 1038-1227

BRINGING LEGENDS TO LIFE K. McLaughlin color *Science* v354 no6316 p1094 D 2 2016

China—Officials & employees

Working Together to Usher In the Second "Golden Decade" of BRICS Cooperation *Vital Speeches of the Day* v83 no10 p277 O 2017

China—Politics & government

China Gambles on Modernizing Through Urbanization M. RITHMIRE and K. LOONEY *Current History* v116 no791 p203 S 2017

Technocracy Chinese style ZHIHUI ZHANG *Issues in Science & Technology* v33 no3 p18 Spr 2017

China—Politics & government—21st century

See also

China—Politics & government—2002-

Western Critics of China Need to Avoid a Colonial Mindset D. A. BELL *NPQ: New Perspectives Quarterly* v33 no4 p23 O 2016

China—Politics & government—History

China's Corruption Crackdown: War Without End? A. WEDEMAN *Current History* v116 no791 p210 S 2017

China—Politics & government—2002-

Chinese technocracy R. OLSON *Issues in Science & Technology* v33 no2 p15 Wint 2017

China—Religion

CATHOLICS AT A CROSSROADS I. Johnson color map *America* v217 no7 p18 O 2 2017

China—Social conditions

THE MONTH IN REVIEW *Current History* v116 no786 p40 Ja 2017

NUMBER CRUNCH: QUEER CHINA bw color *Advocate* no1089 p28 F/Mr 2017

China—Social conditions—2000-

THE EMPEROR'S NEW MUSEUM JIAYANG FAN cartoon *New Yorker* v92 no36 p28 N 7 2016

Chinchar, Gerald

Home Remedy A. Gorman color *Washington Monthly* v49 no3-5 p43 Mr-My 2017

Chinellato, J. A.

Observation of a large-scale anisotropy in the arrival directions of cosmic rays above 8×10^{18} eV *Science* v357 no6357 p1266 S 22 2017

CHINEN, NATE

Free Jazzmeia *Texas Monthly* v45 no6 p88 Je 2017

Chinese art—Exhibitions

AROUND BEIJING Y. FUCA color *ARTnews* v115 no4 p131 Wint 2016/2017

Spring Preview A. K. Scott cartoon *New Yorker* v93 no4 p18 Mr 13 2017

Chinese arts—Exhibitions

ART'S SAKE: BRIGHT AND SHINY J. Fan bw *New Yorker* v93 no33 p38 O 23 2017

Chinese authors

Sexual Life in Modern China I. Johnson color *New York Review of Books* v64 no16 p63 O 26 2017

Chinese authors—Biography

Peng Xuejun color *Publishers Weekly* v264 no12 p33 Mr 20 2017

Chinese calligraphy

Asia Society D. Ebony color *Art in America* v105 no1 p77 Ja 2017

Chinese Communist Party—Congresses

The riddle of Xi D. Roberts color *Bloomberg Businessweek* no4496 p17 O 24 2016

Chinese cooking

See also

Sichuan cooking

Guilin Mi Fen Noodles M. J. WEEDMAN img *New York* v50 no16 p95 Ag 7 2017

THE JOY OF NOT COOKING L. Goldman color *Women's Health* v14 no2 p102 Mr 2017

Not All Ragùs Are Italian S. Sifton *New York Times Magazine* p28 N 6 2016

OLD CHiNESE IS THE NEIII CHiNESə [Cover story] J. KRAMER and A. MASON color *Bon Appetit* p114 S 2017

What My Chinese Mother Made F. Lam *New York Times Magazine* p22 F 5 2017

Chinese corporations

What Chinese Companies Want from International Deals Li Ma, J. Brett et al *Harvard Business Review Digital Articles* p2 F 12 2015

Chinese diaspora

Opportunities and Anxieties for the Chinese Diaspora in Southeast Asia HONG LIU *Current History* v115 no784 p312 N 2016

Chinese investments

THE TALKING CAT AND THE PEROXIDE CORPORATION A. SATARIANO, D. Ramli et al color *Bloomberg Businessweek* no4523 p54 My 22 2017

Chinese investments—Africa

The World's Next Great Manufacturing Center I. Y. SUN color *Harvard Business Review* v95 no3 p122 My/Je 2017

Chinese investments—Government policy

Beijing Moves to Curb Overseas Investments D. Roberts *Bloomberg Businessweek* no4504 p17 D 19 2016

Chinese investments—United States

CHINA BUYS INTO THE U.S B. O'keefe diag *Fortune* v175 no4 p196 Mr 15 2017

So you want to move to the U.S P. Robison, K. Weise et al color diag graph *Bloomberg Businessweek* no4538 p48 S 18 2017

Chinese language

TO SPEAK IS TO BLUNDER YIYUN LI cartoon *New Yorker* v92 no43 p30 Ja 2 2017

Chinese martial arts

AFGHANISTAN'S FEMALE KUNG FU FIGHTERS M. SCARLES color *Tricycle: The Buddhist Review* v27 no1 p16 Fall 2017

Chinese New Year

ABOVE & BEYOND cartoon *New Yorker* v92 no47 p14 Ja 30 2017

Chinese poetry

The Ancient Art of Imbibing L. TONINO color *Tricycle: The Buddhist Review* v27 no1 p30 Fall 2017

Chinese porcelain

Steven Chait H. MARTIN color *Architectural Digest* v74 no10 p34 O 1 2017

Chinese restaurants—Evaluation

DINING GUIDE *Cincinnati Magazine* v50 no4 p153 Ja 2017

Little Tong Noodle Shop Jiayang Fan color *New Yorker* v93 no31 p15 O 9 2017

NORTHERN TASTE C. SCHEDLER color *Chicago* v66 no10 p54 O 2017

Progressive Chinese A. PLATT, R. Patronite et al img *New York* v49 no15 p66 Jl 25 2016

Q BY PETER CHANG: The famed Chinese chef puts down roots in Bethesda A. Limpert *Washingtonian Magazine* v53 no1 p143 O 2017

Tim Ho Wan Jiayang Fan color *New Yorker* v93 no9 p16 Ap 17 2017

Chinese students in foreign countries

THE NEW KIDS B. LARMER *New York Times Magazine* p40 F 5 2017

Chinese art—Qin & Han dynasties, 221 B.C.-220 A.D.—Exhibitions

ART color *New Yorker* v93 no9 p8 Ap 17 2017

Chinese—Attitudes

Uncle Sam in Midlife Crisis? Da Wei *Wilson Quarterly* p6 Spr 2017

Chinese—Foreign countries

See also

Chinese diaspora

Opportunities and Anxieties for the Chinese Diaspora in Southeast Asia HONG LIU *Current History* v115 no784 p312 N 2016

Chinese history, 1949-

Assignment: China A. J. Nathan *Foreign Affairs* v96 no6 p170 N/D 2017

Chinese—Travel

Tourists: China's New Political Weapon C. Dillow color *Fortune* v175 no8 p42 Je 15 2017

Chingo Bling (Performer)

LEMME HEAR YOU Say, "Ha!" A. LANGER *Texas Monthly* v45 no6 p66 Je 2017

Chinn, Calvin

Reflections on the lectionary *Christian Century* v133 no23 p21 N 9 2016

Chinn, Cindy

Chester's Pencil Lady S. W. Kansteiner color *Nebraska Life* v21 no1 p62 Ja/F 2017

Chinook salmon

big picture color *Canadian Geographic* v135 no6 p16 D 2015

Chinook salmon fishing

From the Wild: You don't need much more than butter to pan-roast Alaskan king salmon. But a little jalapeño is nice S. Sifton *New York Times Magazine* p26 Jl 9 2017

Chinstrap penguin

PENGUIN CITY S. ELDER *National Geographic Kids* no467 p14 F 2017

Chion, Michel

Words on Screen P. RANGAN *Film Quarterly* v71 no1 p119 Fall 2017

Chipaumire, Nora

DANCE *New Yorker* v93 no28 p8 S 18 2017

Chipchase, Jan

Postcards From The Edge J. Pavlus color *Bloomberg Businessweek* no4494 p44 O 10 2016

Chiperi, Cristina

My Dilemma Is You. Un nuevo amor. O dos.../My Dilemma Is You: A New Love... or Two *Publishers Weekly* v263 no46 p17 N 14 2016

Chipman, Kim

Buy Today. Take a Close Look Tomorrow color *Bloomberg Businessweek* no4518 p39 Ap 10 2017

Canadian Finance Gets Less Boring. That's Bad graph *Bloomberg Businessweek* no4521 p41 My 8 2017

Chipmunks

Aerial Picnic color *National Wildlife (World Edition)* v55 no2 p50 F/Mr 2017

Goldilocks, the Chipmunk C. HEITGER-EWING color *Cabin Living* p20 Je 2017

Chippendale furniture

COUNTRY CHIPPENDALE CANDLESTAND WITH CABINET color *Magazine Antiques* v183 no6 p25 N/D 2016

THE SIGNED DANIEL SPENCER (1741-1801) CHIPPENDALE DESK AND BOOKCASE color *Magazine Antiques* v183 no6 p1 N/D 2016

Chips (Film)

CHIPS L. Rice color *Entertainment Weekly* no1446/1447 p49 D 2016/Ja 2017

MICHAEL PEÑA D. Franich color *Entertainment Weekly* no1459 p46 Mr 31 2017

Chiquet, Maureen

Beyond the Label: Women, Leadership, and Success on Our Own Terms *Publishers Weekly* v264 no8 p76 F 20 2017

CHIRA, SUSAN

The Comforts of Jane *New York Times Book Review* p25 D 25 2016

Chirac, Jacques, 1932-

Jacques Chirac in New Orleans E. Laborde cartoon *New Orleans Magazine* v51 no8 p152 Je 2017

Chirality

Mirror asymmetry in life and in space B. A. McGuire and P. B. Carroll *Physics Today* v69 no11 p86 N 2016

Mirror-Image Molecule Far, Far Away N. SCHARPING cartoon color *Discover* v38 no1 p68 Ja/F 2017

Mirror Molecules in Space N. Collins color *Scientific American* v315 no3 p14 S 2016

Quantum optical circulator controlled by a single chirally coupled atom M. Scheucher, A. Hilico et al bibl graph *Science* v354 no6319 p1577 D 23 2016

Chirbes, Rafael, 1949-2015

A Masterpiece from the Muck N. Rush bw color *New York Review of Books* v63 no16 p18 O 27 2016

Chirgadze, Dimitri Y.

DNA-PKcs structure suggests an allosteric mechanism modulating DNA double-strand break repair bibl graph *Science* v355 no6324 p520 F 3 2017

Chiriboga, Luis

Mouse models of acute and chronic hepacivirus infection *Science* v357 no6347 p204 Jl 14 2017

Chiricahua Mountains (Ariz.)

The Big Pictures: THE CHIRICAHUA MOUNTAINS *Arizona Highways* v93 no9 p18 S 2017

THE CHIRICAHUA IS A STUDY IN ROCKS AND HISTORY N. N. DODGE *Arizona Highways* v93 no9 p36 S 2017

SHE HAS AMAZING FOCUS *Arizona Highways* v93 no9 p44

S 2017

SMALL WONDERS K. VAUGHN *Arizona Highways* v93 no9 p30 S 2017

Chirico, Giovanni B.

Changing climate shifts timing of European floods color graph *Science* v357 no6351 p588 Ag 11 2017

Chirico, Nichole

Captive Style color *Horse & Rider* v55 no11 p17 N 2016

Chics Smart Lena color *Horse & Rider* v56 no1 p17 Ja 2017

The Company You Keep color *Horse & Rider* v56 no4 p19 Ap 2017

Fallon Taylor's Best Advice for Any Rider color *Horse & Rider* v56 no11 p118 N 2017

Get Through the Line color *Horse & Rider* v56 no7 p86 Jl 2017

Gotta Lota Good color *Horse & Rider* v56 no2 p15 F 2017

The Immortal color *Horse & Rider* v55 no12 p15 D 2016

Just Joe color *Horse & Rider* v56 no3 p15 Mr 2017

Let's Talk TAPE color *Horse & Rider* v56 no1 p58 Ja 2017

The 'Man of Trail' SHARES HIS TIPS color *Horse & Rider* v55 no12 p52 D 2016

Ride Off the Rail color *Horse & Rider* v56 no8 p92 Ag 2017

Seniors That Still Have It color *Horse & Rider* v56 no2 p60 F 2017

Solve Blanket Problems color *Horse & Rider* v56 no10 p63 O 2017

Wranglered color *Horse & Rider* v56 no5 p19 My 2017

Zippos ATM color *Horse & Rider* v56 no6 p23 Je 2017

Chirik, Paul J.

Coordination-induced weakening of ammonia,water, and hydrazine X–H bonds in a molybdenum complex bibl diag *Science* v354 no6313 p730 N 11 2016

Chirp modulation

NEXT-GEN FISH FINDERS: ENHANCED CHIRP AND BEYOND J. RAGUSO graph *Outdoor Life* v224 no2 p46 F/Mr 2017

Chisholm, Dave

Blending Skill Sets C. Tart color *Downbeat* v84 no9 p16 S 2017

Instrumental *Publishers Weekly* v264 no16 p54 Ap 17 2017

CHISHOLM, PAUL

HIKE MORE, DRIVE LESS color *Backpacker* p56 My 2017

TREKKING POLES/SOCKS color *Backpacker* v45 no3 p126 Ap 2017

Chisholm, Sallie W., 1947-

MAKING WAVES E. Pennisi bw color *Science* v355 no6329 p1006 Mr 10 2017

Chisholm Trail

It Happened Here: The Great Plains, 1867 G. R. Schiavino bw *American Cowboy* v24 no1 p41 Je/Jl 2017

Making his Mark E. Putfark bw *American Cowboy* v23 no6 p19 Ap/My 2017

The Old CHISHOLM TRAIL [Cover story] B. Welch color map *American Cowboy* v23 no6 p54 Ap/My 2017

Chism, Robin

A Bridge Back to Life K. RIDDERBUSCH *Atlanta* v56 no7 p214 N 2016

Chittka, Lars

Bumblebees show cognitive flexibility by improving on an observed complex behavior bibl diag *Science* v355 no6327 p833 F 24 2017

Unexpected rewards induce dopamine-dependent positive emotion–like state changes in bumblebees bibl graph *Science* v353 no6307 p1529 S 30 2016

Chittum, Randy

How Your Company Can Better Retain Employees Who Are Veterans *Harvard Business Review Digital Articles* p2 Jl 11 2017

Chiu, David

A Tip From a Stroke Expert color *Prevention* v69 no5 p8 My 2017

Chiu, Lucinda

Branch-specific plasticity of a bifunctional dopamine circuit encodes protein hunger graph *Science* v356 no6337 p534 My 5 2017

CHIU, MYRNA

SUPER FLY: YOU'RE GONNA LARVA IT cartoon *Wired* v25 no8 p32 Ag 2017

Chiuri, Maria Grazia, 1960-

DIOR'S NEW GUARD J. Picardie color *Harper's Bazaar* no3651 p410 Mr 2017

Maria Grazia Chiuri E. Wilson color *InStyle* v24 no11 p90 N 2017

MARIA GRAZIA CHIURI S. MOWER cartoon color *Vogue* v207 no3 p415 Mr 2017

MEETING OF THE (FLORAL) MINDS bw color *Harper's Bazaar* no3653 p136 My 2017

The NEWS color *Harper's Bazaar* no3649 p221 D 2016/Ja 2017

Not Your Mother's Dior H. Bowles bw color *Vogue* v206 no12 p256 D 2016

Chive growing

The Versatile Herb K. Hammonds color *Southern Living* v52 no4 p31 Ap 2017

Chivers, C. J.

THE FIGHTER C. J. CHIVERS *New York Times Magazine* p28 Ja 1 2017

How to Make a... BAIT BARREL bw *Popular Mechanics* p77 S 2017

How to Make a... BAIT BARREL cartoon *Popular Mechanics* v193 no7 p77 S 2016

Chivers, David

The Book That Changed America: How Darwin's Theory of Evolution Ignited a Nation *Humanist* v77 no3 p46 My/Je 2017

The Boundaries Around Your Industry Are About to Change *Harvard Business Review Digital Articles* p2 N 3 2014

Why I left, Why I Stayed: Conversations on Christianity Between an Evangelical Father and His Humanist Son *Humanist* v77 no5 p44 S/O 2017

Chivvis, Christopher S.

Hybrid war: Russian contemporary political warfare bibl *Bulletin of the Atomic Scientists* v73 no5 p316 2017

Chiwan Choi

From 'The Yellow House' *New York Times Magazine* p19 Ja 22 2017

Chloé SAS

La Femme Natacha M. HOLGATE color *Vogue* v207 no7 p94 Jl 2017

Chloe x Halle (Performer)

SXSW'S GREATEST HITS color *Entertainment Weekly* no1459 p16 Mr 31 2017

Chlorella as food

Go Green V. Tweed color *Amazing Wellness* v9 no1 p24 Wint 2017

Chlorhexidine

KEEP YOUR HANDS CLEAN C. Barakat and M. McCluskey color *Equus* no480 p18 S 2017

Chlorofluorocarbons—Environmental aspects

Antarctic ozone hole officially on the mend A. Witze color *Science News* v190 no13 p28 D 24 2016

Chlorofluorocarbons—International cooperation

Climate-friendly coolants needed T. SUMNER *Science News* v190 no11 p13 N 26 2016

Chlorogenic acid

This Just In J. Zorthian *Time* v190 no2/3 p23 Jl 10-17 2017

Chlorophyll

CHLOROPHYLL J. WUEBBEN color *Muscle & Performance* v9 no9 p17 S 2017

DON'T FORGET SULFUR K. Birchmier *Successful Farming* v115 no1 p49 Ja 2017

THE SECRET LIFE OF PLANTS D. Stone and Takao Fujiwara color *National Geographic* v231 no5 p26 My 2017

Chlorophyll—Therapeutic use

green foods supplements V. Tweed color *Amazing Wellness* v8 no2 p12 Spr 2016

Chloroplasts

Blue is high-energy color for begonias E. Conover bw color *Science News* v190 no12 p4 D 10 2016

Holliday junction resolvases mediate chloroplast nucleoid segregation Y. Kobayashi, O. Misumi et al diag *Science* v356 no6338 p631 My 12 2017

Chlorpyrifos—Government policy

Better Living Through Chemistry? A. Lappé *Earth Island Journal* v32 no2 p12 Summ 2017

Chlumsky, Anna, 1980-—Interviews

Halt and Catch Fire J. Russell *TV Guide* v65 no35 p37 Ag 21 2017

Chmerkovskiy, Valentin, 1986-

Val CHMERKOVSKIY C. Bowers *Dance Spirit* v21 no3 p22 Mr 2017

Chng, Serene C.

ELABELA deficiency promotes preeclampsia and cardiovascular malformations in mice color diag graph *Science* v357 no6352 p707 Ag 18 2017

Cho, Adrian

AI's early proving ground: the hunt for new particles color *Science* v357 no6346 p20 Jl 7 2017

Can dark matter vanquish controversial rival theory? color *Science* v355 no6323 p337 Ja 27 2017

The cosmos aquiver color *Science* v354 no6319 p1516 D 23 2016

Cresting a gravitational wave color *Science* v355 no6332 p1380 Mr 31 2017

Debate heats up over black holes as dark matter color *Science* v355 no6325 p560 F 10 2017

In familiar decays, a whiff of new physics color diag *Science* v356 no6335 p229 Ap 21 2017

In search for unseen matter, physicists turn to dark sector color diag *Science* v355 no6331 p1251 Mr 24 2017

Microwave background teams mull a grand unification color *Science* v357 no6358 p1339 S 29 2017

Odd computer zips through knotty tasks color *Science* v354 no6310 p269 O 21 2016

Plot to redefine the kilogram nears climax color *Science* v356 no6339 p670 My 19 2017

Space ripples may untangle black hole tango color *Science* v356 no6341 p895 Je 1 2017

TRAPPED IN ORBIT color diag graph *Science* v357 no6355 p986 S 8 2017

Trio surfs gravitational waves to Nobel glory color *Science* v357 no6359 p17 O 6 2017

Trio wins Nobel for effects of topology on exotic matter color *Science* v354 no6308 p21 O 7 2016

THE UNBEARABLE LIGHTNESS OF NEUTRINOS color diag map *Science* v356 no6345 p1322 Je 30 2017

Will Nobel Prize overlook LIGO's master builder? color *Science* v353 no6307 p1478 S 30 2016

Cho, John

The Exorcist S. Li, N. Abrams et al color *Entertainment Weekly* no1482/1483 p92 S 22 2017

Cho, John—Interviews

John Cho E. Berman color *Time* v190 no7 p51 Ag 21 2017

Cho, Kyeongjae

Harvesting electrical energy from carbon nanotube yarn twist diag graph *Science* v357 no6353 p773 Ag 25 2017

Cho, Mark

HOW I GOT MY STYLE: MARK CHO J. Roth color *Esquire* p32 Ag 2017

Cho, Min Y.

CRISPRi-based genome-scale identification of functional long noncoding RNA loci in human cells bibl graph *Science* v355 no6320 p1 Ja 6 2017

Cho, Seong-Yong

Double-heterojunction nanorod light-responsive LEDs for display applications bibl color graph *Science* v355 no6325 p616 F 10 2017

Cho, Youn Kyoung

Double-heterojunction nanorod light-responsive LEDs for display applications bibl color graph *Science* v355 no6325 p616 F 10 2017

Choate, Mabel, 1870-1958

Lessons from NAUMKEAG R. COLE color *Arts & Crafts Homes & the Revival* v12 no3 p58 Summ 2017

Out & About *Martha Stewart Living* no267 p10 S 2016

CHOATE, MICHELLE

A Day's Work *Reader's Digest* v188 no1126 p64 D 2016/Ja 2017

Choate Rosemary Hall (Wallingford, Conn.)

Reflections on the Scandal at Choate L. SMITH color *Weekly Standard* v22 no35 p17 My 22 2017

Choates, Harry

JOLE BLON'S ANNIVERSARY E. Laborde *Louisiana Life* v38 no1 p6 S/O 2017

Chobani LLC

Chobani Welcomes an Old Enemy to Its Dairy Case C. Giammona color *Bloomberg Businessweek* no4529 p16 Jl 3 2017

Chocano, Carina

Attention Deficit *New York Times Magazine* p11 O 1 2017

False Front color *New York Times Magazine* p13 My 21 2017

Freckles, Lace, and Curls img *New York* v50 no6 p49 Mr 20 2017

Lying Low color *New York Times Magazine* p13 Ja 29 2017

No Prob *New York Times Magazine* p13 Jl 23 2017

When Life Imitates Artifacts img *New York* p75 F 9 2017

Chocolate

Bet you didn't know S. THOMPSON and J. SCHAFER color *National Geographic Kids* no465 p10 N 2016

coffee mug mixers color *Good Housekeeping* v263 no6 p30 D 2016

Eat these to stress less M. TAYLOR, D. Ramsey et al cartoon *Redbook* p92 F 2017

EXPENSIVE TASTE M. LAISKONIS color *Women's Health* v14 no8 p30 O 2017

FOOD GIFTS M. GLISAN color *Better Homes & Gardens* v95 no11 p14 N 2017

HEALTH Q & A cartoon color *Good Housekeeping* v264 no2 p91 F 2017

High on CottonHi L. RABINOVITCH *Los Angeles Magazine* v61 no11 p132 N 2016

THE KITCHEN COOKBOOK *Better Homes & Gardens* v94 no12 p118 D 2016

LET THEM EAT CAKE J. O'Connor and S. Castle color *Southern Living* v52 no3 p106 Mr 2017

SWEETS FOR YOUR SWEETIE G. LOFTS and S. DiGREGORIO color *Martha Stewart Living* no271 p90 Ja/F 2017

What'S New, Cookie? D. GREENSPAN *Better Homes & Gardens* v94 no12 p112 D 2016

Chocolate candy

See also

Truffles (Confectionery)

Holiday Peppermint Bark *Saturday Evening Post* v288 no6 p27 N/D 2016

Melts in Your Mouth N. SCHMIDT cartoon *Walrus* p22 Ja\F 2017

RAISING THE BAR E. STUART *Virginia Living* v15 no3 p23 Ap 2017

Chocolate chip cookies

LOVE AT FIRST BITE S. CAREY color *Martha Stewart Living* p76 S 2017

Chocolate chip cookies—Evaluation

Cookie Town L. BALLA *Los Angeles Magazine* v61 no11 p130 N 2016

Chocolate desserts

CHOCOLATE PARTY! E. Johnson color *Sunset* v238 no2 p77 F 2017

Chocolate drinks

See also

Hot chocolate (Beverage)

HAUTE CHOCOLATE M. C. Cairns color *Southern Living* v52 no1 p110 Ja 2017

Chocolate drinks—Evaluation

Get Cultured Chelsea Leu *Sierra* v101 no5 p8 S/O 2016

Chocolate milk

For the Record color *Time* v190 no1 p6 Jl 3 2017

Perk Up Your Iced Coffee K. O'SHEA-EVANS and LULU color *House Beautiful* v159 no5 p64 Je 2017

Chocolate processing

The Melting Point D. HOCHMAN *Los Angeles Magazine* p118 D 2016

Chocolate stores

By the Numbers The Sweetest Countries J. BEER and M. HARRIS *National Geographic Kids* no466 p6 D 2016/Ja 2017

C'est Bon Bon *Atlanta* v57 no1 p60 My 2017

Chocolate stores—Evaluation

Acalli Chocolate J. Forman color *New Orleans Magazine* v51 no2 p71 D 2016

Chocolate—Evaluation

Beard, Bath & Beyond S. DAILY *Indianapolis Monthly* v40 no5 p25 Ja 2017

For Your Favorite Foodie color *Consumer Reports* v81 no12 p34 D 2016

Mixing Bowl color *O, The Oprah Magazine* p137 S 2017

Chocolate—Physiological effect

I ♥ CHOCOLATE color *Prevention* v69 no2 p11 F 2017

Chocolate—Sales & prices

The Melting Point D. HOCHMAN *Los Angeles Magazine* p118

D 2016

Chocolate—Therapeutic use

What to Eat When You're Tired [Cover story] P. O. BLUMBERG color *Prevention* v69 no6 p28 Je 2017

Choctaw Code Talkers (Film)

Choctaw Code Talkers M. K. Bowannie *American Indian Quarterly* v40 no4 p385 Fall 2016

Chodosh, Sara

BOIL BARONS color *Popular Science* v289 no5 p28 S/O 2017

the case of the cat-scented faucet cartoon *Popular Science* v289 no2 p82 Mr/Ap 2017

CINDY LEE VAN DOVER cartoon *Popular Science* p48 Ja/F 2017

going for boeing color *Popular Science* v289 no6 p80 N/D 2017

HOLES IN THE MAP map *Popular Science* p22 Ja/F 2017

I WISH SOMEONE WOULD INVENT... cartoon *Popular Science* p98 Ja/F 2017

I WISH SOMEONE WOULD INVENT... cartoon *Popular Science* v289 no2 p98 Mr/Ap 2017

KING OF THRONES color *Popular Science* v289 no2 p33 Mr/Ap 2017

THE LAST UMBRELLA YOU'LL EVER NEED color *Popular Science* v289 no4 p34 Jl/Ag 2017

The Modern Explorer's Survival Kit color *Popular Science* p80 Ja/F 2017

one crazy month in Montana color *Popular Science* v289 no4 p18 Jl/Ag 2017

Rocket to the Red Planet color diag *Popular Science* v289 no6 p54 N/D 2017

say "cheese" for border security color *Popular Science* v289 no6 p78 N/D 2017

THIS IS CLEAN COAL color *Popular Science* v289 no2 p24 Mr/Ap 2017

the water (re)cycle diag *Popular Science* v289 no2 p14 Mr/Ap 2017

where does the day go? color *Popular Science* v289 no5 p12 S/O 2017

Choe, Florence

A SOLDIER'S LAST BEDTIME Story K. MILLER *Reader's Digest* v189 no1128 p80 Mr 2017

Choe, Misook

Trispecific broadly neutralizing HIV antibodies mediate potent SHIV protection in macaques color graph *Science* v357 no6359 p85 O 6 2017

Choi, Amy

Happy Mix J. HERBST color *Los Angeles Magazine* v62 no7 p41 Jl 2017

Choi, Changsoon

Harvesting electrical energy from carbon nanotube yarn twist diag graph *Science* v357 no6353 p773 Ag 25 2017

CHOI, JENNIFER HOPE

My Mongolian Spot: AN EPHEMERAL BIRTHMARK IS A RARE GIFT, CONNECTING ME TO GENERATIONS SPANNING THE CENTURIES *American Scholar* v86 no3 p62 Summ 2017

Choi, Junwon

Transition metal-catalyzed alkyl-alkyl bond formation: Another dimension in cross-coupling chemistry diag *Science* v356 no6334 p152 Ap 14 2017

Choi, Maureen

How to Win at Holiday Hair color *Glamour* v114 no12 p138 D 2016

MAUREEN CHOI J. Hale color *Downbeat* v84 no9 p25 S 2017

Your Most-Googled Summer Body Issues... color *Glamour* v114 no7 p71 Jl 2016

Choi, Peter

CALVIN INSTITUTE OF CHRISTIAN WORSHIP color *America* v216 no8 p11 Ap 17 2017

Choi, S.

Magnetic resonance spectroscopy of an atomically thin material using a single-spin qubit bibl color diag graph *Science* v355 no6324 p503 F 3 2017

Choi, Soon-sil

South Korea's Familial Presidential Family Scandal I. Bremmer *Time* v188 no20 p10 N 14 2016

Choi, Sunghun

Highly elastic binders integrating polyrotaxanes for silicon microparticle anodes in lithium ion batteries diag *Science* v357 no6348 p279 Jl 21 2017

Choi, Thomas Y.

Hidden Suppliers Can Make or Break Your Operations *Harvard Business Review Digital Articles* p2 My 29 2015

The Rise of FinTech in Supply Chains *Harvard Business Review Digital Articles* p2 Je 22 2016

Choice (Psychology)

See also

    Commitment (Psychology)

    Decision making

    Nudge theory

3 Timeless Rules for Making Tough Decisions P. Bregman *Harvard Business Review Digital Articles* p2 N 2 2015

Decisions Are More Effective When More People Are Involved from the Start J. Whitehurst *Harvard Business Review Digital Articles* p2 Mr 15 2016

To Make Better Choices, Look at All Your Options Together S. Basu and K. Savani *Harvard Business Review Digital Articles* p2 Je 28 2017

What to Do When You've Made a Bad Decision D. Clark *Harvard Business Review Digital Articles* p2 Ag 11 2016

Choirs (Musical groups)

Choir S. Manguso *New York Times Magazine* p22 O 23 2016

CHOJNACKY, CINDY COFFER

The Long Way Home: Returns *Backpacker* p13 S 2017

Chokephaibulkit, Kulkanya

IgG antibodies to dengue enhanced for FcγRIIIA binding determine disease severity bibl graph *Science* v355 no6323 p395 Ja 27 2017

Chokshi, Roshani

The Star-Touched Queen color *Publishers Weekly* v263 no49 p111 D 7 2016

Choldenko, Gennifer

Dad and the Dinosaur color *Publishers Weekly* v263 no51 p146 D 12 2016

Cholecalciferol

Potent Cancer Fighters K. Gazella *Amazing Wellness* v9 no1 p30 Wint 2017

Cholera

Battling for Yemen's survival C. Martin color *Science News* v192 no2 p4 Ag 19 2017

Cholera crisis grows in Middle Eastern war zone color *Science* v356 no6340 p787 My 26 2017

For the Record color *Time* v190 no8 p7 Ag 28 2017

PRODUCING MIRACLES IS ALL IN A DAY'S WORK FOR NAVY MEDIC *Saturday Evening Post* v289 no5 p34 S/O 2017

Cholera vaccination

Cholera vaccine faces major test in Yemen K. Kupferschmidt color *Science* v356 no6345 p1316 Je 30 2017

Cholesterol

FAFQ K. Patel and J. WUEBBEN color *Muscle & Performance* v9 no4 p12 Ap 2017

Genetic identification of familial hypercholesterolemia within a single U.S. health care system N. S. Abul-Husn, K. Manickam et al chart graph *Science* v354 no6319 paaf7000-1 D 23 2016

GOOD EGGS *Amazing Wellness* v8 no2 p8 Spr 2016

THE STATIN UMBRELLA L. Beil cartoon diag graph *Science News* v191 no9 p22 My 13 2017

Where the worst type of fat is hiding in supermarket foods chart *Harvard Health Letter* v42 no3 p5 Ja 2017

Which DIY Health Tests Are Worth It? S. S. Gold color *Health* v31 no2 p77 Mr 2017

Cholesterol testing

PLAYING DOCTOR T. GERBER HOPE color *Prevention* v69 no8 p48 Ag 2017

Cholesterol—Physiological effect

Lysosomal cholesterol activates mTORC1 via an SLC38A9–Niemann-Pick C1 signaling complex B. M. Castellano, A. M. Thelen et al bibl diag graph *Science* v355 no6331 p1306 Mr 24 2017

Choline

The Case for Choline H. ESTROFF MARANO *Psychology Today* v50 no1 p31 Ja/F 2017

CHOLLET, DEREK

What Would America Do? color *Foreign Policy* no225 p82 Jl/Ag

2017

Chollet, Matthieu

Metalloprotein entatic control of ligand-metal bonds quantified by ultrafast x-ray spectroscopy diag *Science* v356 no6344 p1276 Je 23 2017

Choma, Russ

HERE COMES THE BRIBE chart color *Mother Jones* v42 no4 p8 Jl/Ag 2017

REMOTE CONTROLLED color graph *Mother Jones* v42 no6 p48 N/D 2017

Chomsky, Noam, 1928-

IN THESE TIMES ALUMNI bw *In These Times* v40 no11 p16 N 2016

LANGUAGE IN A NEW KEY P. Ibbotson and M. Tomasello cartoon *Scientific American* v315 no5 p70 N 2016

Chondronasiou, Dafni

Tissue damage and senescence provide critical signals for cellular reprogramming in vivo bibl chart graph *Science* v354 no6315 paaf4445-1 N 25 2016

Chong, Jun

From the Archives color *Black Belt* v55 no6 p82 O/N 2017

CHONG, KEVIN

Tough Act to Follow cartoon *Walrus* v14 no6 p64 Jl/Ag 2017

Chong, Pooi Koon

ON CHINESE AQUACULTURE FARMS, THE FISH ARE PUMPED WITH ANTIBIOTICS, AS ARE THE PIGS, WHOSE WASTE FEEDS THE FISH. SO LET'S TALK ABOUT THAT SEAFOOD PLATTER [Cover story] color graph *Bloomberg Businessweek* no4504 p38 D 19 2016

Chong, Rachael

Why IBM Gives Top Employees a Month to Do Service Abroad *Harvard Business Review Digital Articles* p2 N 5 2014

Chong Ding

Oral precision medicine: Identification of microbes from saliva by mass spectrometry bibl *Science* v354 no6319 p60 D 23 2016

Chong Liu

Direct and continuous strain control of catalysts with tunable battery electrode materials bibl graph *Science* v354 no6315 p1031 N 25 2016

Photosynthesis reinvented L. Hamers color diag *Science News* v192 no6 p20 O 14 2017

Chong-Yu Ruan

Molecular imaging at 1-femtosecond resolution bibl diag *Science* v354 no6310 p283 O 21 2016

Chong Zhang

Synthesis and characterization of the pentazolate anion cyclo-N5⁻ in (N5)6(H3O)3(NH4)4Cl bibl diag graph *Science* v355 no6323 p374 Ja 27 2017

Chontorotzea, Tatiana

Multipotent peripheral glial cells generate neuroendocrine cells of the adrenal medulla color *Science* v357 no6346 p46 Jl 7 2017

Choo, Jimmy

JIMMY CHOO'S OWN ADVENTURE M. SOLOMON color *Forbes* v200 no2 p28 S 5 2017

Cho Oh-Hyun

Waves C. OH-HYUN color *Tricycle: The Buddhist Review* v26 no2 p116 Wint 2016

Choppers (Motorcycles)

DEATH OF THE NEO-CUSTOM M. HOYER *Cycle World* v56 no2 p6 Mr 2017

Chopra, Aneesh

Speeding Up the Digitization of American Health Care *Harvard Business Review Digital Articles* p2 F 22 2016

Chopra, Deepak

Discover your true potential *Yoga Journal* no291 p4 My 2017

THE REVOLUTION STARTS HERE color *Fortune* v174 no7 p26 D 1 2016

Chopra, Kabeer

HOT SEATS M. HARRIS *New York Times Magazine* p64 N 13 2016

Chopra, Priyanka, 1982-

Feel the BURN E. Wilson color *InStyle* v23 no12 p69 N 2016

PARTY LINES img *New York* v49 no22 p114 O 31 2016

Pop Chart R. Bruner, C. Lang et al color *Time* v189 no23 p54 Je 19 2017

Priyanka Chopra B. COURT color *Men's Health* v32 no1 p34 Ja/F

2017

Quotable Quotes *Reader's Digest* v188 no1125 p148 N 2016

War of the Greens color *Glamour* v114 no12 p244 D 2016

Why I Love P. Chopra color *InStyle* v24 no1 p104 Ja 2017

Chopra, Priyanka, 1982-—Interviews

"Don't Be Afraid of Who You Are" M. Jacob color *Glamour* v115 no6 p116 Je 2017

Priyanka Chopra S. Zuckerman color *InStyle* v24 no2 p112 F 2017

Chopra, Vineet

6 Things Every Mentor Should Do *Harvard Business Review Digital Articles* p2 Mr 29 2017

Chopra-McGowan, Anand

5 Ways to Help Employees Keep Up with Digital Transformation *Harvard Business Review Digital Articles* p2 S 27 2017

Choral music—Performance—Reviews

Baltic Baton R. Platt cartoon *New Yorker* v92 no30 p14 S 26 2016

Choral singing

Off-Key but In Sync A. Gurwitch cartoon *Prevention* v69 no1 p34 Ja 2017

Chordata—Physiology

WHEN SEX IS SO RIGHT (OR LEFT) P. Edmonds color *National Geographic* v231 no4 p29 Ap 2017

Chordoma—Treatment

THE WAY BACK T. Balf and S. SHEFFIELD color *Yankee* v80 no6 p124 N/D 2016

Choreographers

See also

Women choreographers

35 Years Ago This Month *Dance Magazine* v90 no11 p67 N 2016

Adrenaline Rush S. BURKE *Dance Magazine* v91 no4 p35 Ap 2017

Behind the Scenes of "Crazy Ex-Girlfriend" C. Bowers *Dance Spirit* v21 no1 p23 Ja 2017

Both Sides of the Curtain G. HENDERSON *Dance Magazine* v91 no8 p50 Ag 2017

California Dreaming: Benjamin Millepied is taking L.A. Dance Project to new horizons C. BAUER *Dance Magazine* v91 no6 p31 Je 2017

Cinematic Sword Fighters and the Mistakes They Make D. Lowry color *Black Belt* v55 no5 p26 Ag/S 2017

C'mon, Get Happy M. McNamara bw color *Dance Spirit* v20 no10 p44 D 2016

dance finder *Dance Magazine* v90 no11 p60 N 2016

A Dancer's Choreographer J. Stahl *Dance Magazine* v91 no4 p10 Ap 2017

Defying Tradition J. BAYOD ESPOZ *Dance Magazine* v90 no11 p58 N 2016

Gemma BOND color *Dance Spirit* v21 no2 p28 F 2017

The Golden Ticket [Cover story] S. GOLD *Dance Magazine* v91 no4 p26 Ap 2017

JACK OF ALL TRADES, OR MASTER OF ONE? G. Larsen color *Dance Spirit* v21 no2 p40 F 2017

Jérôme Bel M. Hagan color *Current Biography* v78 no5 p12 My 2017

LAR LUBOVITCH M. Schrock *Dance Magazine* v90 no12 p48 D 2016

My Obsessions. . *TV Guide* v65 no31 p7 Jl 24 2017

Network to Success L. WINGENROTH *Dance Magazine* v91 no4 p54 Ap 2017

A New Home for Choreograpers: NCCAkron launches its first official residency this month S. Sucato *Dance Magazine* v91 no7 p16 Jl 2017

On the Circuit K. SCHWAB *Dance Magazine* v90 no11 p54 N 2016

Prima, Puppies, Premieres J. Stahl *Dance Magazine* v91 no9 p10 S 2017

The Tax-Season Dance J. Peters color *Dance Magazine* v91 no3 p50 Mr 2017

TRICIA MIRANDA'S TOP 10 WAYS TO OWN YOUR CAREER N. Loeffler-Gladstone color *Dance Spirit* v21 no2 p46 F 2017

Choreographers—Attitudes

Not Just a YouTube Star A. Feller color *Dance Magazine* v91 no3 p26 Mr 2017

Choreographers—Interviews

Diana Vishneva W. PERRON *Dance Magazine* v90 no11 p18 N

2016

Choreographers—Training of

What It Takes to Create a Choreographer J. G. SADAN *Dance Magazine* v90 no12 p65 D 2016

Choreographers—United States

Andrew WINGHART N. Zisa bw color *Dance Spirit* v21 no4 p24 Ap 2017

Choreography

See also

Choreographers

RITUAL WORK T. J. Rosenthal bw color *Art in America* v105 no3 p82 Mr 2017

WHERE ARE YOU GOING? A. Rudolph color *O, The Oprah Magazine* p116 O 2017

Choreography—Social aspects

TAKE A STAND J. Stahl *Dance Magazine* v90 no12 p22 D 2016

Choreography—Study & teaching

Smith College, FCDD *Dance Magazine* v90 p121 2016/2017 Supplement College Guide

The University of Arizona *Dance Magazine* v90 p113 2016/2017 Supplement College Guide

Virginia Commonwealth University *Dance Magazine* v90 p107 2016/2017 Supplement College Guide

Choreography—Study & teaching (Higher)

Columbia College Chicago *Dance Magazine* v90 p55 2016/2017 Supplement College Guide

Ohio University *Dance Magazine* v90 p89 2016/2017 Supplement College Guide

The University of North Carolina—Greensboro *Dance Magazine* v90 p87 2016/2017 Supplement College Guide

Chores

FOLDING LAUNDRY S. ORR *Better Homes & Gardens* v95 no11 p10 N 2017

A WOMAN'S WORK M. Ruiz color *Women's Health* v14 no8 p113 O 2017

Chorkendorff, Ib

Combining theory and experiment in electrocatalysis: Insights into materials design bibl color graph *Science* v355 no6321 p1 Ja 13 2017

TECHNICAL COMMENT ABSTRACTS *Science* v357 no6354 p881 S 1 2017

Toward sustainable fuel cells bibl graph *Science* v354 no6318 p1378 D 16 2016

Chorneau, Tom

Making the Case for More Civics in the Classroom *Education Digest* v83 no3 p10 N 2017

Chorus & Orchestra of the Deutsche Oper Berlin (Performer)

Meyerbeer: Dinorah D. J. Baker *Opera News* v81 no5 p58 N 2016

Chorus & Anti-Chorus (Poem)

CHORUS AND ANTI-CHORUS S. C. Black *New Yorker* v93 no12 p50 My 8 2017

Chorus Line, A (Music)

Livin' the DREAM J. D. Hench color *Dance Spirit* v21 no8 p72 O 2017

Chotiner, Isaac

Revisiting the Raj *New York Times Book Review* p13 S 10 2017

"We Have to Hold the Line" *Hoover Digest: Research & Opinion on Public Policy* no4 p155 Fall 2016

Chou, Eileen Y.

The Link Between Income Inequality and Physical Pain *Harvard Business Review Digital Articles* p2 Mr 21 2016

Chou, Tracy

VISIONARIES J. Surowiecki, M. Orcutt et al color il *MIT Technology Review* v120 no5 p42 S/O 2017

Choudary, Sangeet Paul

6 Reasons Platforms Fail *Harvard Business Review Digital Articles* p2 Mr 31 2016

The Rise of Social Graphs for Businesses *Harvard Business Review Digital Articles* p2 F 2 2015

Choudhary, Alok

Customers Who Like Santa Also Like...Nicotine Gum? *Harvard Business Review Digital Articles* p2 O 22 2015

Choudhury, Ambereen

HOW TO MAKE A €367 MILLION LOSS DISAPPEAR *Bloomberg Businessweek* no4508 p36 Ja 23 2017

Choudhury, Bikram, 1946-

THE CASE OF BIKRAM YOGA A. JAIN color *Tricycle: The Buddhist Review* v26 no3 p53 Spr 2017

Choudhury, Kushanava

The Epic City: The World on the Streets of Calcutta *Publishers Weekly* v264 no39 p95 S 25 2017

Choul Kim, Byoung

Notch-Jagged complex structure implicates a catch bond in tuning ligand sensitivity bibl diag graph *Science* v355 no6331 p1320 Mr 24 2017

Chou Yu-Cheng

CHOU YU-CHENG W. Vogel color *Art in America* v104 no11 p133 D 2016

Chow, Alex

Hong Kong Jails Its First Prisoners of Conscience F. Solomon color *Time* v190 no9 p13 S 4 2017

Chow, Amy

Xist recruits the X chromosome to the nuclear lamina to enable chromosome-wide silencing bibl graph *Science* v354 no6311 p468 O 28 2016

Chow, Stephen, 1962-

The Mermaid C. Chiarella chart color *Sound & Vision* v81 no10 p68 D 2016

Chowdhury, Abhijit

The impact of training informal health care providers in India: A randomized controlled trial chart diag *Science* v354 no6308 paaf7384-1 O 7 2016

CHOWELL, GERARDO

Death March of 1918 bw color *Natural History* v125 no9 p11 S 2017

Chown, Steven L.

Tsunami debris spells trouble map *Science* v357 no6358 p1356 S 29 2017

Chrepa, Eleni

THE MAYOR IS IN color *Bloomberg Businessweek* no4534 p66 Ag 14 2017

CHRISINGER, DAVID

A Lifesaving Golf Date with His Dad color *Reader's Digest* v190 no1134 p48 O 2017

Chrisler, Lindsay

I would like to try dating women bw *Glamour* v115 no6 p98 Je 2017

My husband's been totally focused on our baby color *Glamour* v115 no1 p52 Ja 2017

Chrisman, Jacobe

Game On! D. Sax color *Bloomberg Businessweek* no4509 p55 Ja 30 2017

Chrissopoulos, Christos

The Parthenon Bomber *Publishers Weekly* v264 no15 p49 Ap 10 2017

Christ & Gantenbein Architekten AG

Linked In F. A. BERNSTEIN *Architectural Record* v204 no11 p84 N 2016

Christ, Carol

Confronting the Crisis in Higher Ed *Issues in Science & Technology* v33 no3 p89 Spr 2017

Christ, Emanuel

Pair of Aces F. A. BERNSTEIN bw color *Architectural Digest* v74 no3 p60 Mr 2017

CHRISTAKIS, ERIKA

The War on Public Schools color *Atlantic* v320 no3 p15 O 2017

Christe, Karl O.

Polynitrogen chemistry enters the ring bibl diag *Science* v355 no6323 p351 Ja 27 2017

Christenberry, William, 1936-2016

Returning to the same landscape gives photographers the chance to catch time itself at work T. Cole *New York Times Magazine* p14 F 5 2017

CHRISTENSEN, ALISON

r.s.v.p cartoon *Bon Appetit* no1 p10 F 2017

Christensen, Clay—Interviews

Clay Christensen on Peter Drucker J. Kirby *Harvard Business Review Digital Articles* p2 N 10 2014

CHRISTENSEN, CLAYTON M.

AFRICA'S NEW GENERATION OF INNOVATORS color il img *Harvard Business Review* v95 no1 p128 Ja/F 2017

Know the Job Your Product Was Hired for (with Help from Cus-

Christian leadership—Catholic Church

A New Form of Collaboration *America* v217 no2 p8 Jl 24 2017

Christian life

Addicted to piety B. Haile color *U.S. Catholic* v82 no5 p10 My 2017

Faith away from home: Early faith formation prepares young adults for college--years before the admission letters arrive A. Scobey color *U.S. Catholic* v82 no9 p23 S 2017

Faith Matters S. Wells *Christian Century* v133 no24 p44 N 23 2016

THE GRACE OF CHURCH DISCIPLINE M. GALLI color *Christianity Today* v60 no10 p27 D 2016

SOCIAL STUDIES G. Hardy color *America* v216 no5 p30 Mr 6 2017

Who Is My Neighbor? C. GONZÁLEZ-ANDRIEU color *America* v215 no13 p21 O 31 2016

Christian Life Community

Exploring God's Call A. M. BRENNAN color *America* v215 no18 p27 D 5 2016

Christian life—Catholic authors

Anxious Hearts [Cover story] G. POPCAK color *America* v216 no1 p19 Ja 2 2017

Digital Growth [Cover story] C. J. COYNE color *America* v215 no11 p19 O 17 2016

Christian life—Pentecostal authors

The fasts we choose T. Larsen *Christian Century* v134 no5 p10 Mr 1 2017

Christian literature—Bibliographies

BEST SELLERS *Christian Century* v133 no21 p12 O 12 2016

Christian missionaries

Early Algonquian Tomes Displayed S. Richardson color *American History* v52 no2 p8 Je 2017

Christian pilgrims & pilgrimages

The Hardest Blessing R. Collins color *Commonweal* v144 no10 p39 Je 2 2017

A Shrine That Endures P. JASKUNAS color *America* v215 no16 p25 N 21 2016

Christian pilgrims & pilgrimages—Jerusalem

Egyptian Copts finally fulfilling dream of Jerusalem pilgrimage J. Wirtschafter and M. Nader color *Christian Century* v134 no9 p15 Ap 26 2017

Christian saints

Upstart from Assisi: St. Francis is probably our most popular saint. But do we know who he really is? [Cover story] K. Manning color *U.S. Catholic* v82 no10 p12 O 2017

Christian sects

See also

Catholic Church

Mennonites

Protestant churches

Protestantism

Critical Mass R. ROSS *Texas Monthly* v45 no6 p70 Je 2017

Division is not necessarily Scandal J. P. MCNUTT color *Christianity Today* v61 no1 p42 Ja/F 2017

Christian sects—United States

See also

Episcopal Church

Karen refugees revitalize two mainline churches, inspire film All Saints A. Sowder and H. Hahn color *Christian Century* v134 no20 p15 S 27 2017

Christian transgender people

HOW DO YOU HOLD TOGETHER YOUR TRANS IDENTITY AND YOUR LIFE OF FAITH? M. Himschoot, C. Robinson et al color *Christian Century* v134 no2 p22 Ja 18 2017

Christian union

Can the Churches Be Reunited? [Cover story] G. Hunsinger color *Commonweal* v144 no17 p14 O 20 2017

Christian universities & colleges

WHAT CHRISTIAN COLLEGE PROFESSORS WANT YOU TO KNOW J. JONES bw chart color *Christianity Today* v60 no9 p75 N 2016

Christian Zionism

Christian Zionism G. R. McDermott color *Christian Century* v134 no20 p6 S 27 2017

Peter Pettit replies *Christian Century* v134 no20 p6 S 27 2017

Christiani, Pamela Edwards

Get Your Vita-Fix color *Essence* v47 no7 p36 N 2016

Christianity

See also

Catholic Church

Christianity & history

Church

Confession (Christianity)

Doctrinal theology

Euthanasia—Religious aspects—Christianity

Gay rights—Religious aspects—Christianity

God (Christianity)

Pornography—Religious aspects—Christianity

Spirituality—Christianity

Theology

A basic income K. Clarke color *U.S. Catholic* v82 no4 p42 Ap 2017

CENTURY marks bw *Christian Century* v134 no15 p8 Jl 19 2017

CENTURY marks *Christian Century* v134 no22 p8 O 25 2017

The Chicago Cubs and the mystery of faith J. Bouchard color *U.S. Catholic* v82 no4 p19 Ap 2017

Christianity's Russian Temptation S. Ahmari color *America* v216 no7 p26 Ap 3 2017

The Church Is Not a Single-Parent Family J. WILKIN *Christianity Today* v60 no10 p30 D 2016

DO YOU KNOW THIS SONG? T. OLSEN *Christianity Today* p7 Ap 2017

A Former Shoplifter Takes Stock E. Chen color *Christianity Today* v61 no4 p80 My 2017

From roommates to riches: Christian tradition is clear about the way people should live together--and it doesn't include fine dining on the first floor J. Bazan color *U.S. Catholic* v82 no8 p18 Ag 2017

From Scotland to Sicily [Cover story] W. Storrar color *Commonweal* v144 no17 p9 O 20 2017

...from the farthest lands of the English C. O'Brien *History Today* v66 no11 p44 N 2016

Grace stet OR Grace ALONE? B. R. BARRON and R. E. OLSON bw *Christianity Today* p42 Ap 2017

Inclusive or exclusive? *Christian Century* v134 no15 p7 Jl 19 2017

THE INVENTION OF ST. PATRICK'S DAY M. Cronin *Saturday Evening Post* v289 no2 p78 Mr/Ap 2017

Leap of Faith S. DAILY *Indianapolis Monthly* p52 My 2017

LIVING BY The Word *Christian Century* v134 no15 p20 Jl 19 2017

LOVING ALL TYPES OF SOJOURNERS M. GALLI color *Christianity Today* v61 no5 p19 Je 2017

MARILYNNE ROBINSON'S THREAT ASSESSMENT *Lapham's Quarterly* v10 no3 p75 Summ 2017

MESSIAH COMPLEX J. Bendiksen color *National Geographic* v232 no2 p82 Ag 2017

People H. Meyer *Christian Century* v134 no17 p19 Ag 16 2017

Scorning America R. R. Reilly *Claremont Review of Books* v17 no3 p44 Summ 2017

Speak of the devil P. Jenkins *Christian Century* v134 no20 p44 S 27 2017

Speak up T. B. Neal, V. Y. Piccorossi et al color *U.S. Catholic* v82 no4 p5 Ap 2017

'Still She Is a Wonderful Girl' J. McGowan color *Commonweal* v144 no12 p6 Jl 7 2017

UNLOCKING CAMBODIAN CHRISTIANITY K. SHELLNUTT color *Christianity Today* v61 no5 p34 Je 2017

What It Means To Live Christian A. Byle color *Publishers Weekly* v263 no43 p20 O 24 2016

WHO COMES TO STEAL KILL AND DESTROY? C. KEENER *Christianity Today* p48 Ap 2017

WHY CHRISTIANITY TODAY REVISITED T. OLSEN color *Christianity Today* v60 no8 p46 O 2016

Christianity & antisemitism

READER COMMENTS W. Bagley, R. Killoren et al *America* v216 no7 p7 Ap 3 2017

Christianity & art

We are God's artwork S. Wells *Christian Century* v134 no3 p31 F 2017

Christianity & culture

Religion vs. Culture R. ASLAN and B. Allen-Ebrahimian color

Foreign Policy no225 p112 Jl/Ag 2017

Christianity & gender
L.G.B.T. Catholics Should Be 'Accompanied,' Pope Francis Urges *America* v215 no11 p8 O 17 2016
Permeable savior J. Morris *Christian Century* v134 no2 p12 Ja 18 2017

Christianity & history
A God by any other name P. J. Kreeft *Christian Century* v134 no19 p24 S 13 2017

Christianity & law
Jews, Christians, and the Law C. BILHORN *Commentary* v144 no2 p6 S 2017

Christianity & literature
The Catholic Imagination bw *Commonweal* v144 no11 p6 Je 16 2017

Christianity & other religions—Islam
See also
Catholic Church—Relations—Islam
Christians, Muslims stump together in Jordan T. Luck color *Christian Century* v133 no22 p14 O 26 2016
When Muslims talk to Jews D. Heim color *Christian Century* v134 no4 p41 F 15 2017

Christianity—China
Beijing and Holy See near accord? G. O'Connell color *America* v216 no5 p17 Mr 6 2017
Pearl River Delta Christians P. Jenkins *Christian Century* v134 no16 p36 Ag 2 2017

Christianity—Congresses
Global church leaders hold historic meeting *Christian Century* v134 no14 p15 Jl 5 2017

Christianity—Customs & practices
New rituals for new realities C. H. Merritt *Christian Century* v133 no21 p61 O 12 2016

Christianity—Europe
To Save the EU, Citizens Need to Wake Up and Refuse to Be Lied to A. GÖRLACH *NPQ: New Perspectives Quarterly* v33 no4 p39 O 2016

Christianity—India
PRESSING AND PRESCIENT K. BEATY *Christianity Today* v60 no9 p9 N 2016

Christianity—Japan
Finding Jesus in Japan J. R. Shelton color *Christianity Today* v60 no10 p79 D 2016

Christianity—Korea (South)
Evangelical Christian Discourse in South Korea on the LGBT: the Politics of Cross-Border Learning J. Yi, G. Jung et al *Society* v54 no1 p29 F 2017

Christianity—News briefs
1 IN 5 *Christianity Today* v61 no1 p20 Ja/F 2017
CENTURY marks bw graph *Christian Century* v133 no24 p8 N 23 2016
GLEANINGS *Christianity Today* p18 Ap 2017
GLEANINGS *Christianity Today* v60 no10 p22 D 2016
GLEANINGS *Christianity Today* v61 no6 p16 Jl/Ag 2017
NEWS color *Christianity Today* v60 no8 p23 O 2016

Christianity—Nigeria
RADICAL ISLAM IS NOT THE NIGERIAN CHURCH'S GREATEST THREAT S. B. AGANG color *Christianity Today* v61 no4 p54 My 2017

Christianity—Philosophy
LIVING BY THE WORD *Christian Century* v134 no18 p18 Ag 30 2017
Reflections on the lectionary C. Dorsey *Christian Century* v134 no18 p19 Ag 30 2017

Christianity—Social aspects
DIFFERENTLY MORAL T. OLSEN cartoon *Christianity Today* p23 Ap 2017
The Most Astonishing Easter Miracle [Cover story] M. Galli bw *Christianity Today* p28 Ap 2017
Pronoun tensions P. W. Marty *Christian Century* v134 no14 p3 Jl 5 2017
Revelation Versus Revolution K. A. ELLIS *Christianity Today* p26 Ap 2017
A Tale of Two Churches A. WILSON *Christianity Today* p25 Ap 2017
They Will Know We Are Christians by Our Drinks J. CASPER

Christianity Today p20 Ap 2017

Christianity—Societies, etc.
UNDER DISCUSSION J. KING, T. JOHNSON et al *Christianity Today* p17 Ap 2017

Christianity—United States
CENTURY marks cartoon graph *Christian Century* v133 no23 p8 N 9 2016
Christianity Without an Adjective K. A. ELLIS *Christianity Today* v61 no1 p28 Ja/F 2017
Saviour-in-Chief M. COREN color *Walrus* v14 no3 p16 Ap 2017
UNDER DISCUSSION J. KING, T. JOHNSON et al *Christianity Today* p17 Ap 2017

Christians
See also
Catholics
Missionaries
After coup attempt, Turkey cracks down on Protestants D. Bonessi color *Christian Century* v134 no1 p14 Ja 4 2017
A basic income K. Clarke color *U.S. Catholic* v82 no4 p42 Ap 2017
Bearing Burdens After Obamacare K. SHELLNUTT *Christianity Today* v61 no4 p18 My 2017
Becoming a Christian Almost Got Me Killed V. Prodan bw *Christianity Today* v60 no8 p111 O 2016
The Chicago Cubs and the mystery of faith J. Bouchard color *U.S. Catholic* v82 no4 p19 Ap 2017
Christianity Without an Adjective K. A. ELLIS *Christianity Today* v61 no1 p28 Ja/F 2017
THE CHURCH'S INTEGRITY IN THE TRUMP YEARS M. GALLI cartoon *Christianity Today* v61 no1 p23 Ja/F 2017
Confessions of an Interloper R. R. Cooper bw color *Commonweal* v114 no14 p15 S 8 2017
Contentious Christians J. Kinlaw color *Commonweal* v144 no16 p14 O 6 2017
Division is not necessarily Scandal J. P. MCNUTT color *Christianity Today* v61 no1 p42 Ja/F 2017
Get to Work J. W. MARTENS il *America* v215 no14 p39 N 7 2016
God Is a Homemaker A. J. SWOBODA bw color *Christianity Today* v61 no4 p62 My 2017
Love and the Law M. Y. SOLOVEICHIK *Commentary* v143 no6 p13 Je 2017
Michigan's Iraqi Christians fear deportation T. Bach color *Christian Century* v134 no15 p12 Jl 19 2017
The other Eastern churches P. Jenkins *Christian Century* v134 no14 p44 Jl 5 2017
Out of service H. G. Gary color *U.S. Catholic* v82 no4 p26 Ap 2017
Payday Predators E. J. WEISENBURGER *America* v215 no15 p24 N 14 2016
A REAL OPTION M. GALLI *Christianity Today* p9 Mr 2017
The sound of silence B. Massingale color *U.S. Catholic* v82 no3 p10 Mr 2017
Sparrows, swallows, and us M. Florer-Bixler *Christian Century* v134 no17 p12 Ag 16 2017
THE SPIRITUAL ACT OF SUBSCRIPTION M. GALLI color *Christianity Today* v60 no8 p29 O 2016
That Loving Feeling graph *Christianity Today* v61 no4 p15 My 2017
What's new? The Eucharist may not immediately transform the faithful into better Christians, but stick around for a lifetime and see what happens A. Camille il *U.S. Catholic* v82 no8 p47 Ag 2017
The word on women A. Camille il *U.S. Catholic* v82 no2 p47 F 2017

Christians, Jeffrey A.
Quantum dot–induced phase stabilization of α-CsPbI3 perovskite for high-efficiency photovoltaics bibl chart graph *Science* v354 no6308 p92 O 7 2016

Christians—Attitudes
SAINTS NOT SUPERHEROES [Cover story] R. Ellsberg color *America* v216 no6 p28 Mr 20 2017

Christians—Crimes against
Lightbox J. Malsin color *Time* v189 no15 p14 Ap 24 2017

Christians—Egypt
LET MY PEOPLE BUILD J. CASPER color *Christianity Today* v60 no9 p17 N 2016

Christmas lights—Exhibitions
EVENTS *Sea Magazine* v108 no12 pPNW-14 D 2016

Christmas Memories (Music)
Yuletide Joy HADLEY color *Downbeat* v83 no12 p84 D 2016

Christmas of Many Colors: Circle of Love (TV program)
DOLLY'S TRUE COLORS I. RUDOLPH *TV Guide* v64 no48 p28 N 21 2016

Christmas parties
Editor's Letter M. Hansche color *Rodale's Organic Life* v2 no7 p9 D 2016/Ja 2017

Christmas shopping
See also
Black Friday (Retail trade)

Christmas stockings
The Case of the Christmas Stockings J. Borden color *Southern Living* v51 no12 p136 D 2016

Christmas tree ornaments
MERRY AND MOD L. HOWARD *Better Homes & Gardens* v94 no12 p56 D 2016
O TANNENBAUM S. Davidson color *Southern Living* v51 no12 p58 D 2016
UP YOUR TREE GAME B. THORKELSON *Better Homes & Gardens* v94 no12 p48 D 2016

Christmas trees
See also
Artificial Christmas trees
Best Christmas Tree Ever S. Bender color *Southern Living* v51 no12 p48 D 2016
DECK THE HALLS T. A. Christian color *Essence* v47 no8 p138 D 2016
Ethical Evergreens Z. SCHAEFFER and T. ROSS color *Rodale's Organic Life* v2 no7 p94 D 2016/Ja 2017
GOING OUT ON A LIMB J. L. Ney color *Rodale's Organic Life* v2 no7 p96 D 2016/Ja 2017
GOINGS ON ABOUT TOWN color *New Yorker* v92 no42 p17 D 19 2016
GRAND TOUR K. BARNES *Better Homes & Gardens* v94 no12 pZ1 D 2016
The Perfect Tree J. A. ABEL *Idaho Magazine* v16 no3 p20 D 2016

Christmas trees—Design & construction
Artificial Intelligence J. BOTTUM color *Weekly Standard* v22 no16 p5 D 26 2016

Christmas Carol, A (Theatrical production)
Making Christmas Magic R. Minetor *Stage Directions* v29 no10 p8 O 2016

Christmas—Humor
Rock these reboots around the tree S. FESCHUK color *Maclean's* v129 no45 p61 N 14 2016
SETTING THE RECORD STRAIGHT B. FRANZEN cartoon *New Yorker* v92 no41 p35 D 12 2016

Christmas—Social aspects
CHRISTMAS OF '89 E. LABORDE bw *New Orleans Magazine* v51 no2 p152 D 2016
SETTING THE RECORD STRAIGHT B. FRANZEN cartoon *New Yorker* v92 no41 p35 D 12 2016

Christmas Story, A (Film)
Santa Gets His Claws S. KASHNER bw cartoon color *Vanity Fair* v59 no1 p168 Holiday 2017

Christmas Story: The Musical, A (Theatrical production)
IRREVERENT NOSTALGIA: ENDURING AFFECTION FOR A CULT HOLIDAY CLASSIC *Cincinnati Magazine* v50 no8 p10 My 2017

Christmas—United States
Feeling Grateful M. R. JOHNSON *Cabin Living* p5 D 2016
A TALE OF Two Christmases I. Mbue cartoon color *Good Housekeeping* v263 no6 p81 D 2016

Christodoulides, Demetrios N.
Spatiotemporal mode-locking in multimode fiber lasers color *Science* v357 no6359 p94 O 6 2017

Christodoulou, Neophytos
Assembly of embryonic and extraembryonic stem cells to mimic embryogenesis in vitro diag *Science* v356 no6334 p153 Ap 14 2017

Christoffels, Vincent M.
An interactive three-dimensional digital atlas and quantitative database of human development bibl color graph *Science* v354 no6315 paag0053-1 N 25 2016

CHRISTOPHER, THOMAS
THE NATURAL ORDER OF THINGS color *Martha Stewart Living* p108 Jl/Ag 2017

Christopher, William, 1932-2016
1932-2016 William Christopher L. Rice color *Entertainment Weekly* no1448 p53 Ja 13 2017

Christopher Farr (Company)
Skate color *Architectural Digest* v73 no11 p102c N 2016

Christopher Kimball's Milk Street (Company)
Kimball Returns to Cookbook Publishing J. Rosen color *Publishers Weekly* v264 no5 p3 Ja 30 2017

Christopher Speakers (Company)
Christopher Speakers CSP1 Reference Monitors J. Velasco color *Downbeat* v84 no2 p98 F 2017

Christopher Beard, K.
Chew on this color *Science* v356 no6339 p710 My 19 2017

Christopher Garcia, K.
Notch-Jagged complex structure implicates a catch bond in tuning ligand sensitivity bibl diag graph *Science* v355 no6331 p1320 Mr 24 2017

Christophi, George P.
The microbial metabolite desaminotyrosine protects from influenza through type I interferon graph *Science* v357 no6350 p498 Ag 4 2017

CHRISTY, BRYAN
DEADLY TRADE bw color graph map *National Geographic* v230 no4 p56 O 2016

Christy, Mark
A Fresh Slice of Orange County A. ABEL color *Forbes* v198 no8 p106 D 20 2016

CHRITARO, GUSTAVO
Chords & Discords bw color *Downbeat* v84 no6 p10 Je 2017

CHROBAK, ULA
Yosemite Rockfall color *Climbing* no357 p24 N 2017

Chroma (Theatrical production)
Trans-Atlantic Treat *Dance Magazine* v90 no11 p12 N 2016

Chromag Bikes (Company)
chromag T. Engel color *Bike Magazine* v24 no2 p78 Mr 2017

Chromatin
See also
Histones
Building chromosomes without bricks [Cover story] Y. Kakui and F. Uhlmann diag *Science* v356 no6344 p1233 Je 23 2017
Crystal structure of the overlapping dinucleosome composed of hexasome and octasome D. Kato, A. Osakabe et al graph *Science* v356 no6334 p205 Ap 14 2017
Distortion of histone octamer core promotes nucleosome mobilization by a chromatin remodeler K. K. Sinha, J. D. Gross et al diag *Science* v355 no6322 p263 Ja 20 2017
Mitotic chromosome assembly despite nucleosome depletion in Xenopus egg extracts K. Shintomi, F. Inoue et al diag *Science* v356 no6344 p1284 Je 23 2017
Propagation of Polycomb-repressed chromatin requires sequence-specific recruitment to DNA F. Laprell, K. Finkl et al diag *Science* v356 no6333 p85 Ap 7 2017
Structure of histone-based chromatin in Archaea F. Mattiroli, S. Bhattacharyya et al diag *Science* v357 no6351 p609 Ag 11 2017

Chromatin assembly factors
Unlocking the nucleosome A. Flaus and T. Owen-Hughes bibl diag *Science* v355 no6322 p245 Ja 20 2017

Chromatin—Molecular structure
Chromatin untangled: New methods map genomic structure J. M. Perkel color *Science* v354 no6308 p118 O 7 2016
Mutation of a nucleosome compaction region disrupts Polycomb-mediated axial patterning M. Sheng Lau, M. G. Schwartz et al bibl chart diag *Science* v355 no6329 p1081 Mr 10 2017
Unlocking the nucleosome A. Flaus and T. Owen-Hughes bibl diag *Science* v355 no6322 p245 Ja 20 2017

Chromatographic analysis equipment
new products color *Science* v356 no6337 p547 My 5 2017

Chrome (Music)
Chrome/Vertical P. Margasak color *Downbeat* v84 no10 p61 O 2017

Chromebook (Computer)
Hands-on: Running Android apps on a Chromebook could be the

best of both worlds M. RIOFRIO color *PCWorld* p112 Mr 2017

The timing is perfect for a new Chromebook Pixel M. SIMON color *PCWorld* v35 no10 p16 O 2017

USING CROSSOVER ANDROID TO RUN WINDOWS APPS ON A CHROME-BOOK J. NEWMAN color *PCWorld* p148 D 2016

Why Google plans to stop supporting your Chromebook after five years J. NEWMAN color *PCWorld* p43 O 2016

Chromium

A Healthier Way to Celebrate V. TWEED color *Better Nutrition* v78 no11 p12 N 2016

MICROMINERALS FOR MAXIMUM PERFORMANCE D. N. JACKSON color *Muscle & Performance* v9 no4 p58 Ap 2017

Chromosome duplication

Gene duplication can impart fragility, not robustness, in the yeast protein interaction network G. Diss, I. Gagnon-Arsenault et al bibl color graph *Science* v355 no6325 p630 F 10 2017

Chromosome numbers

Fertile offspring from sterile sex chromosome trisomic mice T. Hirota, H. Ohta et al chart diag *Science* v357 no6354 p932 S 1 2017

Chromosome segregation

Actin divides to conquer H. Maiato and C. Ferrás color diag *Science* v357 no6353 p756 Ag 25 2017

When degradation spurs segregation M. Zetka bibl diag *Science* v355 no6323 p349 Ja 27 2017

Chromosome structure

Chromosomal chaos silences immune surveillance M. Zanetti bibl chart color *Science* v355 no6322 p249 Ja 20 2017

Chromosome stitch-up? D. J. Sherratt bibl color *Science* v355 no6324 p460 F 3 2017

Chromosomes

   See also

      Alleles

      Chromatin

Building chromosomes without bricks [Cover story] Y. Kakui and F. Uhlmann diag *Science* v356 no6344 p1233 Je 23 2017

Mitotic chromosome assembly despite nucleosome depletion in Xenopus egg extracts K. Shintomi, F. Inoue et al diag *Science* v356 no6344 p1284 Je 23 2017

Tracking Telomeres: Short telomeres are bad. Can you lengthen yours? D. SCHARDT *Nutrition Action Health Letter* v44 no4 p7 My 2017

Chromosomes—Research

"Perfect" designer chromosome V and behavior of a ring derivative Xie, Li et al diag *Science* v355 no6329 p1046 Mr 10 2017

Chroneos, Zissis C.

Local amplifiers of IL-4Rα-mediated macrophage activation promote repair in lung and liver diag *Science* v356 no6342 p1076 Je 9 2017

Chronic disease risk factors

LOW-CAL SWEETENERS: Do low-calorie sweeteners like aspartame and sucralose cause cancer? Make you gain weight? Give you diabetes? Here's what the best evidence shows C. DOW *Nutrition Action Health Letter* v44 no7 p7 S 2017

NEWS BITES [Cover story] *Tufts University Health & Nutrition Letter* v35 no8 p1 O 2017

Chronic disease treatment

BEAT THE HEAT C. W. KIRSHNER color *Prevention* v69 no6 p58 Je 2017

Chronic diseases

   See also

      Chronic pain

MY LAST PATIENT D. SCHEINER color *Chicago* v66 no1 p80 Ja 2017

WHAT IS A MICROHOSPITAL? St. Vincent and Franciscan introduce a new type of treatment center A. GARCEAU *Indianapolis Monthly* p83 N 2017

Chronic diseases & psychology

A chronic issue A. Scobey color *U.S. Catholic* v82 no7 p29 Jl 2017

Chronic diseases—Prevention

Belly fat *Mayo Clinic Health Letter* v34 no12 p7 D 2016

New Evidence for the Benefits of Whole Grains *Tufts University Health & Nutrition Letter* v34 no9 p4 N 2016

Whole grains *Mayo Clinic Health Letter* v35 no1 p6 Ja 2017

Chronic diseases—Psychological aspects

Let joy in [Cover story] R. Miller *Yoga Journal* no289 p22 F 2017

Chronic diseases—Risk factors

Belly fat *Mayo Clinic Health Letter* v34 no12 p7 D 2016

Cutting Calories Reduces Dangerous Inflammation [Cover story] *Tufts University Health & Nutrition Letter* v34 no10 p1 D 2016

Chronic fatigue syndrome

FIGHTING Fatigue N. Loeffler-Gladstone *Dance Spirit* v20 no10 p34 D 2016

Chronic fatigue syndrome diagnosis

LOST AND FOUND J. REHMEYER color *O, The Oprah Magazine* p102 Je 2017

Chronic fatigue syndrome—Research

For chronic fatigue syndrome, a 'shifting tide' at NIH M. Wadman color *Science* v354 no6313 p691 N 11 2016

Chronic kidney failure—Prevention

NEWSBITES [Cover story] *Tufts University Health & Nutrition Letter* v34 no9 p1 N 2016

Chronic pain

HEALING With Light A. PATUREL and A. Jung color *Prevention* v69 no11 p72 N 2017

The Secret Behind Chronic Pain [Cover story] S. Colino cartoon *Prevention* v69 no4 p68 Ap 2017

A sequence for Healing and strength P. Caballero color *Yoga Journal* no296 p69 N 2017

Chronic pain treatment

Acupuncture *Mayo Clinic Health Letter* v35 no7 p4 Jl 2017

Chronic pain update *Mayo Clinic Health Letter* v34 no11 p7 N 2016

The downside of taking pills to treat chronic pain *Harvard Health Letter* v42 no5 p6 Mr 2017

Relief is here! C. Gorrell *Yoga Journal* p3 2017 SpecialIssue

TINY TREATS A. Bartz color *Women's Health* v14 no8 p84 O 2017

THE TRANSITION OF CANNABIS TO MAINSTREAM PAIN MEDICATION D. F. MCCOURT *Maclean's* v130 no3 p48 Ap 2017

Chronic traumatic encephalopathy

American Gladiators *America* v217 no5 p8 S 4 2017

THE CTE Diaries R. Forgrave color *GQ: Gentlemen's Quarterly* v87 no1 p88 Ja 2017

Chronic traumatic encephalopathy—Diagnosis

This New Test Could Crush The NFL I. Boudway color *Bloomberg Businessweek* no4510 p48 F 6 2017

TURNING HEADS J. Vrentas and S. Kwak color *Sports Illustrated* v127 no10 p14 O 2 2017

Chronic traumatic encephalopathy—Patients

Head Games C. P. Pierce color *Sports Illustrated* v127 no4 p68 Ag 7 2017

Chronic wasting disease

Loss of the Wild B. Butler color *National Wildlife (World Edition)* v54 no6 p36 O/N 2016

Norway seeks to stamp out prion disease E. Stokstad color map *Science* v356 no6333 p12 Ap 7 2017

Chronic wasting disease—Risk factors

THE UNKNOWNS T. HANSEN color *Outdoor Life* v224 no2 p67 F/Mr 2017

Chronic wounds & injuries—Treatment

ARTIFICIAL SKIN FROM THE SEA L. Parshley color diag *Bloomberg Businessweek* no4529 p58 Jl 3 2017

Chronicle Books LLC

Chronicle Books at 50 J. Boog color *Publishers Weekly* v264 no24 p7 Je 12 2017

Chronobiology disorders

   See also

      Jet lag

Chronograph

GOOD AS GOLD color *Forbes* v199 no7 p65 Je 29 2017

Chronograph—Evaluation

LAPS OF LUXURY color *Conde Nast Traveler* v52 no4 p22 Ap 2017

Chronometers

GLOSSARY *Lapham's Quarterly* v10 no2 p220 Spr 2017

Chronos Inc.

iSCRAPBOOK 7: COLOR TOOLS KEEP MAC DESIGN SOFTWARE ATOP SCRAP HEAP J. R. BOOKWALTER color *Macworld - Digital Edition* v34 no4 p37 My 2017

LIFECRAFT: RETOOLED MAC JOURNAL APP EMBRACES CLOUD SYNC, IOS SUPPORT J. R. BOOKWALTER color *Macworld - Digital Edition* v34 no9 p29 S 2017

Chr. Stenseth, Nils

Merging paleobiology with conservation biology to guide the future of terrestrial ecosystems color *Science* v355 no6325 p594 F 10 2017

Chrusciel, Ewa

Of Annunciations *Publishers Weekly* v264 no38 p52 S 18 2017

Chrysanthemums

New genes give mums the blues E. DEMARCO color *Science News* v192 no2 p12 Ag 19 2017

Waterfalls of Mums S. Bender color *Southern Living* v52 no10 p36 O 2017

Chrysanthemums—Varieties

rare BEAUTIES M. OZAWA *Martha Stewart Living* no269 p120 N 2016

Chrysler automobile

See also

Chrysler Sebring automobile

Plymouth automobile

Where's My Barn Find? E. Perkins color *Hot Rod* v70 no6 p8 Je 2017

Chrysler automobile—Evaluation

2017 Chrysler Pacifica Hybrid A. Priddle color *Motor Trend* v69 no3 p29 Mr 2017

A Frugal Family-Friendly Ride color *Consumer Reports* v82 no10 p63 O 2017

Chrysler Pacifica automobile

2017 Chrysler Pacifica Hybrid E. DYER color *Popular Mechanics* p37 Je 2017

Fleet Files D. VanderWerp, J. Sabatini et al color diag *Car & Driver* v63 no1 p88 Jl 2017

Learning to LOVE the MINIVAN 2017 CHRYSLER PACIFICA color *Esquire* v166 no4 p81 N 2016

Chrysler Pacifica automobile—Evaluation

Chrysler Pacifica chart color *Motor Trend* v69 no1 p138 Ja 2017

Chrysler Sebring automobile

RUNWAY MODEL C. Csere diag *Car & Driver* v62 no10 p20 Ap 2017

Chu, Jeff

Family fears color *Christian Century* v134 no3 p37 F 2017

Chu, Jon M. (Jon Murray), 1979-

NOW YOU SEE ME 2 D. Vaughn color *Sound & Vision* v82 no5 p66 Je 2017

Chu, Lenora

Study Skills A. PAUL *New York Times Book Review* p22 Ag 27 2017

Chu, Steven, 1948- —Interviews

Taking stock: Steven Chu, former secretary of the Energy Department, on fracking, renewables, nuclear weapons, and his work, post-Nobel Prize D. Drollette color *Bulletin of the Atomic Scientists* v72 no6 p351 N 2016

Chu, William T.

Moo-Young Han *Physics Today* v69 no11 p70 N 2016

Chu, Ying

Fashion Does Fragrance color *Glamour* v114 no11 p106 N 2016

Fiery Ombré Lips color *Glamour* v115 no1 p39 Ja 2017

Mermaid Eyes color *Glamour* v115 no1 p36 Ja 2017

The New Matte color *Glamour* v115 no1 p38 Ja 2017

Read My Lips color *Glamour* v114 no11 p166 N 2016

Supermodel Makeup School color *Glamour* v114 no12 p119 D 2016

This Is What a Beauty Icon Looks Like color *Glamour* v115 no10 p87 O 2017

This woman is about to cut her hair off [Cover story] color *Glamour* no8 p136 Ag 2017

Waves Like This [Cover story] bw color *Glamour* v114 no11 p97 N 2016

Your New Beauty Meal Plan color *Glamour* v114 no11 p108 N 2016

Chua, Sook Wern

Site-specific phosphorylation of tau inhibits amyloid-β toxicity in Alzheimer's mice bibl graph *Science* v354 no6314 p904 N 18 2016

Chuang, Angela

Game changers bibl color *Science* v355 no6325 p587 F 10 2017

Chuang, Edward

Ratchet-like polypeptide translocation mechanism of the AAA+ disaggregase Hsp104 diag *Science* v357 no6348 p273 Jl 21 2017

Chuang, Y.-D.

Femtosecond electron-phonon lock-in by photoemission and x-ray free-electron laser chart diag *Science* v357 no6346 p71 Jl 7 2017

Chuangye Yan

Structure of a yeast step II catalytically activated spliceosome bibl diag *Science* v355 no6321 p1 Ja 13 2017

Chuanling Zhang

Generation of influenza A viruses as live but replication-incompetent virus vaccines bibl graph *Science* v354 no6316 p1170 D 2 2016

Chuanming Yu

Synthesis and characterization of the pentazolate anion cyclo-N5⁻ in (N5)6(H3O)3(NH4)4Cl bibl diag graph *Science* v355 no6323 p374 Ja 27 2017

Chubbuck, Christine

Rebecca Hall S. Lansky color *Time* v188 no16/17 p89 O 24 2016

Chuchill, Winston

Statesmanship and Geopolitics J. Muller *Society* v54 no2 p188 Ap 2017

Chuck (Film)

ALSO PLAYING: MAY J. Nolfi color *Entertainment Weekly* no1463/1464 p40 Ap/My 2017

OUT-GUTTING T. Friend cartoon *New Yorker* v93 no14 p30 My 22 2017

WE ARE FAMILY A. LANE cartoon *New Yorker* v93 no13 p94 My 15 2017

Chuck (Music)

Chuck Berry's Final Gift P. DOYLE color *Rolling Stone* no1284 p16 Ap 6 2017

What to Stream color *Entertainment Weekly* no1470 p58 Je 16 2017

Chuck, Martin

CLEAN CONTACT! color *Golf Magazine* v59 no4 p49 Ap 2017

HIT LIKE A KID color *Golf Magazine* v59 no10 p38 O 2017

Is My Setup Hurting My Swing? *Golf Magazine* v59 no6 p42 Je 2017

NIX YOUR CHILI-DIP color *Golf Magazine* v59 no9 p64 S 2017

Chudoba, J.

Observation of a large-scale anisotropy in the arrival directions of cosmic rays above 8 × 1018 eV *Science* v357 no6357 p1266 S 22 2017

CHUDOMELOVÁ, MARKÉTA

Combining Biodiversity Resurveys across Regions to Advance Global Change Research *BioScience* v67 no1 p73 Ja 2017

Chufa

THE MYTH OF SUPERFOOD C. Weinberg color *Men's Health* v32 no2 p53 Mr 2017

Chui, Michael

25% of CEOs' Time Is Spent on Tasks Machines Could Do color *Harvard Business Review Digital Articles* p2 F 3 2017

The Countries Most (and Least) Likely to be Affected by Automation *Harvard Business Review Digital Articles* p2 Ap 12 2017

Most Industries Are Nowhere Close to Realizing the Potential of Analytics *Harvard Business Review Digital Articles* p2 D 16 2016

A Survey of 3,000 Executives Reveals How Businesses Succeed with AI *Harvard Business Review Digital Articles* p2 Ag 28 2017

Chuma, Izumi

Evolution of the wheat blast fungus through functional losses in a host specificity determinant diag map *Science* v357 no6346 p80 Jl 7 2017

Chumack, John

READER GALLERY bw color *Astronomy* v45 no11 p72 N 2017

CHUN, RENE

BITCOIN MINING color *Atlantic* v320 no2 p26 S 2017

DEATH BY TECH HAS GONE VIRAL color *Los Angeles Magazine* v62 no7 p76 Jl 2017

HEAD-TO-HEAD: FINE TUNERS color *Wired* v25 no8 p44 Ag 2017

MY SPACE: SYNTH CITY color *Wired* v25 no8 p46 Ag 2017

SCENE STEALERS color *Wired* v25 no3 p78 Mr 2017

Chun, Rosa

Samsung, Shame, and Corporate Atonement *Harvard Business Review Digital Articles* p2 My 17 2017

What Aristotle Can Teach Firms About CSR *Harvard Business Review Digital Articles* p2 S 12 2016

Chun-Hao Huang

SOX2 promotes lineage plasticity and antiandrogen resistance in TP53- and RB1-deficient prostate cancer bibl graph *Science* v355 no6320 p1 Ja 6 2017

Chun-Kan Chen

Xist recruits the X chromosome to the nuclear lamina to enable chromosome-wide silencing bibl graph *Science* v354 no6311 p468 O 28 2016

Chung, Alexa, 1983-

Alexa's New Gig K. Branch color *Glamour* v115 no7 p21 Jl 2017

BEST DRESS E. Wilson color *InStyle* v24 no6 p41 Je 2017

Chung, Doug J.

Study: More Frequent Sales Quotas Help Volume but Hurt Profits *Harvard Business Review Digital Articles* p2 2017

What's the Right Kind of Bonus to Motivate Your Sales Force? *Harvard Business Review Digital Articles* p2 S 12 2016

Chung, Frances

why i dance *Dance Magazine* v91 no8 p88 Ag 2017

Chung, Grace

THE AMERICAN DREAM IS ALIVE AND WELL...ON THE FORBES 400 color graph map *Forbes* v198 no5 p58 O 25 2016

High Score color *Forbes* v198 no6 p30 N 8 2016

SCORECARD color *Forbes* v198 no6 p30 N 8 2016

Chung, Hoon T.

Direct atomic-level insight into the active sites of a high-performance PGM-free ORR catalyst diag graph *Science* v357 no6350 p479 Ag 4 2017

Chung, Hyeseung

Liquefied gas electrolytes for electrochemical energy storage devices graph *Science* v356 no6345 p1351 Je 30 2017

Chung, Raymond T.

The epigenetic landscape of T cell exhaustion bibl graph *Science* v354 no6316 p1165 D 2 2016

Chung Yip, Chan

Mapping the human DC lineage through the integration of high-dimensional techniques diag *Science* v356 no6342 p1044 Je 9 2017

Chunhua Zhang

Expert consensus on inborn errors of metabolism screening bibl chart diag *Science* v354 no6319 p62 D 23 2016

Chunilall, Andrew

Is Canadian Philanthropy Ready for the Future? color *Walrus* v14 no5 p36 Je 2017

What it means to belong color *Walrus* v14 no9 p12 N 2017

Church

    See also

    Christian union

    Church membership

    Church polity

    Church work

Aid groups seek funds as Sudan crisis worsens F. Nzwili color *Christian Century* v134 no20 p14 S 27 2017

FROM RUSSIA WITH LOVE C. TATTOLI color *Conde Nast Traveler* v52 no2 p26 F 2017

The gospel of nonviolence K. Butigan color *U.S. Catholic* v82 no2 p20 F 2017

A hard knot to untie: It's difficult to ensure parishioners from different cultures all feel welcome F. B. Barman color *U.S. Catholic* v82 no8 p31 Ag 2017

Leap of Faith S. DAILY *Indianapolis Monthly* p52 My 2017

Let Bible Studies Be Bible Studies J. WILKIN *Christianity Today* p26 Mr 2017

THE MAINLINE'S SAVING GRACE? Even in secular Canada's declining denominations, conservative theology correlates with church growth K. SHELLNUTT color *Christianity Today* v61 no4 p13 My 2017

Orphaned by War M. Doe color *Christianity Today* v60 no9 p95 N 2016

OUTPACING PERSECUTION [Cover story] J. WEBER color *Christianity Today* v60 no9 p38 N 2016

Policing the Communion Line F. Nonomen color *Commonweal* v144 no8 p8 My 5 2017

RADICAL ISLAM IS NOT THE NIGERIAN CHURCH'S GREATEST THREAT S. B. AGANG color *Christianity Today* v61 no4 p54 My 2017

A REAL OPTION M. GALLI *Christianity Today* p9 Mr 2017

room with a pew c. reid color *Bike Magazine* v24 no7 p36 S 2017

'Unjust Discrimination' *America* v215 no14 p5 N 7 2016

A WISDOM ECCLESIOLOGY: The cosmic church on earth A. P. Pauw *Christian Century* v134 no16 p20 Ag 2 2017

THE YEAR OF LIVING HOPELESSLY R. CLARK cartoon *Christianity Today* v60 no9 p25 N 2016

Church & Dwight Co. Inc.

CONDOMS color *Women's Health* v14 no6 p42 Jl 2017

Church & politics—Catholic Church

As Trump Era Begins, Church Leaders Defend Health Care, Immigration, Worker Rights M. O'Loughlin color *America* v216 no3 p16 F 6 2017

Faithless Fidel T. Quigley color *Commonweal* v144 no4 p10 F 24 2017

Re-enchanting the World P. GILGER color *America* v215 no10 p16 O 10 2016

Church & social problems—Canada

In rural Canada, churches find a new connection in welcoming Syrian refugees B. Ross Jr. color *Christian Century* v134 no10 p16 My 10 2017

Church & state

IN JEFFERSON'S SHADOW N. M. Flores color *America* v216 no12 p28 My 29 2017

Not in Our Name J. GALLAGHER color *America* v215 p16 N 28 2016

Church & state—England

CHURCH, STATE, AND TAXPAYER SUPPORT: Is America Moving Toward a European Model? R. BOSTON *Humanist* v77 no5 p36 S/O 2017

Church & state—Poland

Christ, King, and Corporate Savior M. Strzelecki, D. Bartyzel et al bw *Bloomberg Businessweek* no4531 p33 Jl 24 2017

Church & state—United States

CHURCH, STATE, AND TAXPAYER SUPPORT: Is America Moving Toward a European Model? R. BOSTON *Humanist* v77 no5 p36 S/O 2017

Church, Audrey

Reflections on a "Busy and Wonderful Year" S. MAUGHAN *Publishers Weekly* v264 no25 p75 Je 19 2017

Church, Curtis

FOR THE Love of SHIPLAP D. Howland color *Cabin Living* p9 Ap 2017

Church, Eric—Interviews

Eric Church P. DOYLE bw *Rolling Stone* no1272 p58 O 20 2016

Church, George M.

Inactivation of porcine endogenous retrovirus in pigs using CRISPR-Cas9 diag *Science* v357 no6357 p1303 S 22 2017

Church, Henry, 1836-1908

Folk fun in Williamsburg color *Magazine Antiques* v184 no4 p28 Jl/Ag 2017

Church, John

Three Centuries, One Scope *Sky & Telescope* v132 no6 p84 D 2016

Church, Jonathan D.

Examining price transmission across labor compensation costs, consumer prices, and finished-goods prices bibl *Monthly Labor Review* p1 Ap 2017

Church, Matthew

Connecting the Collective color *Canadian Wildlife* v23 no4 p42 S/O 2017

Church, Steven

Can Puerto Rico Corral Its Tax Dodgers? color graph *Bloomberg Businessweek* no4524 p17 My 29 2017

Church architecture—Conservation & restoration

Fund supports historic congregations C. Kennel-Shank color *Christian Century* v134 no4 p12 F 15 2017

Church attendance

Love becomes fruitful S. Wells *Christian Century* v134 no19 p35 S 13 2017

Understanding Gallup's Latest Poll on Evolution G. BRANCH *Skeptical Inquirer* v41 no5 p5 S/O 2017

you follow? LOLs and hashtags from Twitter *U.S. Catholic* v82 no1 p10 Ja 2017

Church bells—History

THE MUSIC OF TIME NO 1: FOR WHOM THE BELLS TOLL: In Renaissance Florence, church and civic bells frequently rang out across the city's crowded soundscape. Their calls were far from impartial A. Lee *History Today* v67 no7 p86 Jl 2017

Church building design & construction

The Fire Within; Sky Steps L. Copan color *Christian Century* v134 no22 p47 O 25 2017

Church building remodeling

ANSWERED PRAYERS J. L. BELCOVE color *Architectural Digest* v74 no9 p162 S 2017

Church buildings

See also

Chapels

ARE CHURCHES GOOD NEIGHBORS? In otherwise hopping neighborhoods, a building that's empty six days a week can be a drain. Now a surprising solution is emerging D. Reed *Washingtonian Magazine* v52 no8 p53 My 2017

Belonging J. S. Jordan color *U.S. Catholic* v82 no5 p28 My 2017

Can a parish ever have clutter? J. Ferrari *U.S. Catholic* v82 no3 p35 Mr 2017

Churches see benefits in sponsoring art shows G. J. MacDonald *Christian Century* v134 no13 p16 Je 21 2017

Church, State & Playgrounds R. W. Garnett color *Commonweal* v114 no14 p12 S 8 2017

The Last Prairie S. C. Cooper color *American Cowboy* v24 no1 p28 Je/Jl 2017

LIGHT IN THE DARKNESS, Salt of the Earth C. BEGEMAN *South Dakota Magazine* v32 no6 p30 Mr/Ap 2017

Lutheran church wins Supreme Court case to get public funding L. Markoe *Christian Century* v134 no15 p13 Jl 19 2017

Sanctuary B. Doyle color *U.S. Catholic* v82 no8 p29 Ag 2017

Who is us? color *U.S. Catholic* v82 no5 p18 My 2017

Church buildings—Design & construction

THE BRITISH HERITAGE TRAVEL PUZZLER *British Heritage Travel* v38 no2 p78 Mr/Ap 2017

LET MY PEOPLE BUILD J. CASPER color *Christianity Today* v60 no9 p17 N 2016

snapshot A. Klimoski *Architectural Record* v205 no1 p160 Ja 2017

Church buildings—Economic aspects

Church of England sees its cathedrals at risk C. Pepinster color *Christian Century* v134 no10 p19 My 10 2017

Church buildings—England

And The Winning Photo Is... T. Zamboni *British Heritage Travel* v38 no1 p80 Ja/F 2017

Church buildings—Fires & fire prevention

Fire and Faith: The coverage of a disaster in Chile revealed religious divisions among the world's press S. J. Martland *History Today* v67 no7 p14 Jl 2017

Church buildings—History—11th century

THE CHURCH THAT TRANSFORMED NORWAY Z. ZORICH color *Archaeology* v70 no2 p22 Mr/Ap 2017

Church buildings—Jordan

CENTURY marks graph *Christian Century* v134 no10 p8 My 10 2017

Church buildings—New York (State)—New York

Not Yet a Saint J. MARTIN color *America* v215 no12 p27 O 24 2016

Church buildings—Remodeling for other use

After 500 years, a new synagogue opens in Sicily J. McKenna color *Christian Century* v134 no4 p15 F 15 2017

Second Coming M. PEPCHINSKI color diag *Architectural Record* v205 no2 p70 F 2017

SEEKING SANCTUARY M. M. Kashino *Washingtonian Magazine* v52 no2 p274 N 2016

Church closures—History—21st century

From Chapels to Condos M. M. ROBARE bw *American Conservative* v16 no1 p6 Ja/F 2017

Church controversies

DISPUTED MATERIAL B. A. RAGEN and E. BRENDE *Commonweal* v144 no13 p2 Ag 11 2017

Church discipline

THE GRACE OF CHURCH DISCIPLINE M. GALLI color *Christianity Today* v60 no10 p27 D 2016

Church finance

The Science of Giving I. BAGBY *Islamic Horizons* v46 no2 p44 Mr/Ap 2017

Church fund raising

Recycling Religiously? T. Eastland color *Weekly Standard* v22 no10 p7 N 14 2016

Church growth

What to know before you plant C. H. Merritt *Christian Century* v133 no25 p45 D 7 2016

Church history

See also

Christian sects

Protestantism

SEEING IS BELIEVING J. M. KATZ *Smithsonian* v48 no4 p77 Jl/Ag 2017

Church management

Six & Six F. Nonomen color *Commonweal* v144 no10 p6 Je 2 2017

Church membership

See also

Church attendance

A Bell for the Queen: In a High-Desert Haven M. N. O'MALLEY *Idaho Magazine* v16 no10 p24 Jl 2017

A hard knot to untie: It's difficult to ensure parishioners from different cultures all feel welcome F. B. Barman color *U.S. Catholic* v82 no8 p31 Ag 2017

It takes a parish R. McCarty color *U.S. Catholic* v82 no5 p23 My 2017

An Ordinary Sunday [Cover story] T. Baker, J. Schwenkler et al color *Commonweal* v144 no15 p11 S 22 2017

Policing the Communion Line F. Nonomen color *Commonweal* v144 no8 p8 My 5 2017

Second Coming [Cover story] J. BARDE color *Walrus* v14 no9 p22 N 2017

Church music

See also

Choirs (Musical groups)

Music and the Aesthetic in Worship and Collective Singing: England since 1840 D. Martin *Society* v53 no6 p647 D 2016

THANKS, ROBOTS A. Olsen *Christianity Today* v61 no6 p7 Jl/Ag 2017

Church music—Reviews

THE HAMILTON MIXTAPE M. J. Rose color *U.S. Catholic* v82 no3 p40 Mr 2017

Church of England—Clergy—Biography

FROM THE EDITOR *History Today* v66 no10 p2 O 2016

Church of England—History

Church of England sees its cathedrals at risk C. Pepinster color *Christian Century* v134 no10 p19 My 10 2017

Church of God

THE LOOK BOOK img *New York* v50 no18 p57 S 4 2017

Church of Misery (Performer)

'Make Them Die Slowly (John George Haigh)' J. DARNIELLE color *New York Times Magazine* p34 Mr 12 2017

Church of the Flying Spaghetti Monster (Social movement)

THE CHURCH OF THE FLYING SPAGHETTI MONSTER K. Gilsinan cartoon *Atlantic* v318 no4 p23 N 2016

Church polity

See also

Church membership

Clergy

Parishes

The ministry of convening D. R. Nelson *Christian Century* v134 no20 p12 S 27 2017

Church records & registers

Glory Bound L. VACCARIELLO *Cincinnati Magazine* v50 no6 p160 Mr 2017

Church schools

See also

Catholic schools

TAKING A CHARTERED PATH cartoon *New Orleans Magazine* v51 no2 p22 D 2016

Church schools—Canada

Give us this day our daily lesson *Maclean's* p4 Je 2017

Church vestments

Why do priests wear green in Ordinary Time? V. M. Tufano color *U.S. Catholic* v82 no1 p49 Ja 2017

Church work

See also

Pastoral care

Pastoral theology

Senior LIVING R. Bird color *Cincinnati Magazine* v51 no1 p141 O 2017

Church work with immigrants

Sanctuary churches, cities may face consequences from federal authorities K. Winston and A. Hoover color *Christian Century* v134 no9 p13 Ap 26 2017

Church work with transgender people

Ministry with trans people E. Palmer color *Christian Century* v134 no2 p28 Ja 18 2017

UNITED, BODY & SOUL A. COLBERT *Commonweal* v144 no11 p4 Je 16 2017

Church work—News briefs

People color *Christian Century* v134 no10 p21 My 10 2017

Church year

See also

Advent

Christmas

Feast of the Holy Innocents

Shrove Tuesday

LIVING BY The Word *Christian Century* v133 no23 p20 N 9 2016

Reflections on the lectionary C. Chinn *Christian Century* v133 no23 p21 N 9 2016

Church history—Primitive & early church, ca. 30-600—Economic aspects

Suggestions or Commands? S. Zahl and D. Bentley Hart bw *Commonweal* v143 no20 p9 D 16 2016

Churchill (Film)

ALSO PLAYING: JUNE J. Nolfi color *Entertainment Weekly* no1463/1464 p53 Ap/My 2017

Churchill, Chester Lindsay

The Mapparium K. LIEBENSON-MORSE *Yankee* v81 no1 p28 Ja/F 2017

Churchill, Winston, Sir, 1874-1965

Churchill Challenged *Commentary* v143 no4 p12 Ap 2017

Churchill in Washington T. BROMUND color *Weekly Standard* v22 no10 p12 N 14 2016

CHURCHILL'S IMPROBABLE ARMY J. A. Raymond *MHQ: Quarterly Journal of Military History* v29 no3 p78 Spr 2017

Grandmasters of Fake News P. J. BUCHANAN *American Conservative* v16 no1 p26 Ja/F 2017

Question Time W. Kristol cartoon *Weekly Standard* v22 no38 p6 Je 12 2017

Churchman, Leidy—Exhibitions

ART color *New Yorker* v93 no16 p14 Je 5 2017

Church of Jesus Christ Christian, Aryan Nations

Idaho town stares down so-called Aryan church D. Struck *Christian Century* v134 no22 p19 O 25 2017

Church of Jesus Christ of Latter-day Saints

Scouts' Honor M. Hemingway color *Weekly Standard* v22 no36 p8 My 29 2017

Church—Social aspects

Sunday Crybaby V. Schultz *America* v216 no4 p58 F 20 2017

Church—United States

Sanctuary B. Doyle color *U.S. Catholic* v82 no8 p29 Ag 2017

Churchwell, Kevin

How a Startup Accelerator at Boston Children's Hospital Helps Launch Companies color *Harvard Business Review Digital Articles* p2 Je 5 2017

Churton, Tobias

Deconstructing Gurdjieff: Biography of a Spiritual Magician *Publishers Weekly* v264 no15 p68 Ap 10 2017

Churyumov-Gerasimenko comet

Comet's oxygen may be homegrown A. YEAGER color *Science News* v191 no11 p9 Je 10 2017

More than a day in the life of a comet N. D. Russo bibl bw diag *Science* v354 no6319 p1536 D 23 2016

RESEARCH color *Science* v355 no6332 p1386 Mr 31 2017

Rosetta's comet 67P/Churyumov-Gerasimenko sheds its dusty mantle to reveal its icy nature S. Fornasier, S. Mottola et al bibl graph *Science* v354 no6319 p1566 D 23 2016

Rosetta's Grand Finale D. DICKINSON *Sky & Telescope* v133 no1 p12 Ja 2017

Surface changes on comet 67P/Churyumov-Gerasimenko suggest a more active past M. Ramy El-Maarry, O. Groussin et al bw graph *Science* v355 no6332 p1392 Mr 31 2017

Xenon isotopes in 67P/Churyumov-Gerasimenko show that comets contributed to Earth's atmosphere B. Marty, K. Altwegg et al diag *Science* v356 no6342 p1069 Je 9 2017

Churyumov-Gerasimenko comet—Research

Rosetta ends 2-year comet mission with final descent D. Clery bw *Science* v353 no6307 p1482 S 30 2016

Chussil, Mark

Don't Let Your Mistakes Go to Waste *Harvard Business Review Digital Articles* p2 Mr 1 2016

Don't Spend Your Life Making Up Your Mind *Harvard Business Review Digital Articles* p2 My 15 2017

Keep a List of Unethical Things You'll Never Do *Harvard Business Review Digital Articles* p2 My 30 2016

No One Can Think Outside the Box *Harvard Business Review Digital Articles* p2 Je 5 2015

Question What You "Know" About Strategy *Harvard Business Review Digital Articles* p2 Jl 30 2015

"Rally the Troops" and Other Business Metaphors You Can Do Without *Harvard Business Review Digital Articles* p2 N 24 2016

Slow Deciders Make Better Strategists *Harvard Business Review Digital Articles* p2 Jl 8 2016

A Tournament Pits Strategists Against Each Other to See What Works *Harvard Business Review Digital Articles* p2 Je 8 2015

Two Words to Help You Gut Check Your Career *Harvard Business Review Digital Articles* p2 N 5 2015

Why Being Unpredictable Is a Bad Strategy color *Harvard Business Review Digital Articles* p2 Ja 5 2017

Chutes

ASK SAIL D. CASEY, G. WEST et al color *Sail* v48 no1 p58 Ja 2017

Chutney

LIFE AT LULU'S: A Seasonal "Sneeky" K. O'SHEA-EVANS color *House Beautiful* v159 no9 p62 N 2017

Chuyong, George B.

Plant diversity increases with the strength of negative density dependence at the global scale diag *Science* v356 no6345 p1389 Je 30 2017

Chwasky, Michael

And the Techy Goes To... color *Golf Magazine* v58 no11 p66 N 2016

BETTER PLAYER DRIVERS color diag *Golf Magazine* v59 no3 p82 Mr 2017

BETTER PLAYER FAIRWAY WOODS color *Golf Magazine* v59 no5 p86 My 2017

BETTER PLAYER HYBRIDS color *Golf Magazine* v59 no5 p94 My 2017

BETTER PLAYER IRONS color *Golf Magazine* v59 no4 p112 Ap 2017

BLADE PUTTERS color *Golf Magazine* v59 no6 p84 Je 2017

DISTANCE BLADES color *Golf Magazine* v59 no11 p82 N 2017

The DJ Universe color *Golf Magazine* v59 no1 p68 Ja 2017

G400 Drivers and Irons color *Golf Magazine* v59 no9 p84 S 2017

GAME IMPROVEMENT DRIVERS color diag *Golf Magazine* v59 no3 p74 Mr 2017

GAME IMPROVEMENT FAIRWAY WOODS color *Golf Magazine* v59 no5 p82 My 2017

GAME IMPROVEMENT HYBRIDS color *Golf Magazine* v59 no5 p90 My 2017

GAME IMPROVEMENT IRONS color *Golf Magazine* v59 no4 p104 Ap 2017

GET SMART color *Golf Magazine* v59 no7 p85 Jl 2017

GO BIG OR GO HOME color *Golf Magazine* v58 no11 p80 N 2016

GOOD WOOD color *Golf Magazine* v59 no8 p86 Ag 2017

HIGH-END HAMMERS color *Golf Magazine* v59 no7 p80 Jl 2017

IT'S HY TIME color *Golf Magazine* v58 no11 p56 N 2016

6 New Attractions for Summer *Parents* v91 no6 p16 Je 2016

beach towns with benefits color *Parents* v92 no8 p74 Ag 2017

BEAT-THE-BUS SCHOOL LUNCHES color *Parents* v92 no9 p78 S 2017

Boxes for Everyone! color *Parents* v92 no9 p148 S 2017

the Disney park that's right for your family [Cover story] chart color *Parents* v92 no3 p34 Mr 2017

double the number of foods your kid likes! *Parents* v91 no11 p64 N 2016

fickle friendships *Parents* v91 no10 p144 O 2016

food free-for-all color *Parents* v92 no4 p42 Ap 2017

Go Away Together! color *Parents* v92 no9 p152 S 2017

Health Care HERO color *Prevention* v69 no6 p34 Je 2017

the inside story *Parents* v91 no12 p60 D 2016

Last-Minute Spring Break Trips *Parents* v92 no2 p16 F 2017

make over your fridge *Parents* v91 no10 p110 O 2016

Nurses We Love color *Prevention* v69 no5 p42 My 2017

perspective, please! *Parents* v91 no6 p146 Je 2016

Santa's Watching *Parents* v91 no12 p14 D 2016

save on bucket-list trips *Parents* v91 no9 p64 S 2016

simplify your lunch strategy *Parents* v91 no9 p92 S 2016

spread the word! *Parents* p29 2015

This Year's Winning Reads color *Parents* v92 no11 p64 N 2017

warm up to winter fruit *Parents* v92 no1 p26 Ja 2017

What's Your Plan? color graph *Prevention* v68 no12 p86 D 2016

would you let your child eat 50 pounds of sugar? *Parents* v91 no6 p32 Je 2016

Cicerone, Ralph, 1943-2016

Ralph J. Cicerone (1943–2016) J. P. Holdren and M. K. McNutt color *Science* v354 no6316 p1107 D 2 2016

Ralph J. Cicerone M. Prather and R. Stolarski *Physics Today* v70 no2 p67 F 2017

Cici Zhang

99 fried weather balloons cartoon *Popular Science* v289 no4 p87 Jl/Ag 2017

cloud encounters of the third kind color *Popular Science* v289 no4 p92 Jl/Ag 2017

I WISH SOMEONE WOULD INVENT... cartoon *Popular Science* v289 no4 p102 Jl/Ag 2017

Cicli Pinarello SpA

"SHOULD I GET A ROAD BIKE WITH SUSPENSION?" M. Yozell and B. STRICKLAND color *Bicycling* v58 no3 p86 Ap 2017

Cider (Alcoholic beverage)

MOVE OVER, HARD CIDER C. BOERS color *Chicago* v66 no5 p70 My 2017

prep school N. RICHARDSON, A. DELANY et al bw color *Bon Appetit* v62 no10 p105 O 2017

Cider (Alcoholic beverage)—Evaluation

Drink L. LARSON color *GQ: Gentlemen's Quarterly* v86 no11 p50 N 2016

Cider vinegar

Quick-pickle anything C. Hall color *Redbook* p22 S 2017

Cider vinegar—Therapeutic use

QUICK FIXES J. Rice color *Amazing Wellness* v8 no2 p40 Spr 2016

Cid-Perea, Laura

A CAKE TO REMEMBER J. R. FULLER color *Chicago* v66 no4 p56 Ap 2017

Cie. de Saint-Gobain

Industry-Academic Partnerships Can Solve Bigger Problems A. Tanikella *Harvard Business Review Digital Articles* p2 My 2 2016

CiES Inc.

DIGITAL FUEL SENDERS color *Flying* v144 no1 p13 Ja 2017

Ciezadlo, Annia

fulCan Stories About Food Upend Familiar Narratives of War? K. SURANA bw *Foreign Policy* no225 p16 Jl/Ag 2017

Cigar Factory New Orleans (Company)

LIGHT 'EM UP! C. KOLB color *New Orleans Magazine* v51 no1 p42 N 2016

Cigarette cases

A gift from the czar, and a puzzle solved T. Adams color *Magazine Antiques* v184 no4 p46 Jl/Ag 2017

Cigarette industry

LIGHT 'EM UP! C. KOLB color *New Orleans Magazine* v51 no1

p42 N 2016

Cigarette smokers

Do Less Harm E. LEHRER *Weekly Standard* v22 no5 p18 O 10 2016

Is It O.K. to Have Another Man Satisfy Me Sexually, Since My Husband Can't? K. A. Appiah *New York Times Magazine* p26 O 9 2016

Cigarette tax laws

These Cigarettes Are Smokin' D. Voreacos and A. Martin color graph *Bloomberg Businessweek* no4532 p14 Jl 31 2017

Cigarettes

Cigarette Fiend color *Weekly Standard* v22 no21 p2 F 6 2017

CIGELSKE, TIMOTHY

RUN AWAY! [Cover story] color *Runner's World* v52 no7 p54 Ag 2017

Ciguatera poisoning

Trouble in Tropics K. Pitz color *Oceanus* v51 no2 p60 Wint 2016

Cilia & ciliary motion

Cost of Fast Food N. Wilson color *Natural History* v125 no3 p6 Mr 2017

Ciliata

When stop makes sense B. Zinshteyn and R. Green bibl diag *Science* v354 no6316 p1106 D 2 2016

Cilic, Marin

Marin Cilic *Tennis* v53 no1 p22 Ja/F 2017

Why There Is Crying In Baseball, and Tennis, and Golf, and Soccer ... S. Gregory color *Time* v190 no5 p25 Jl 31 2017

Cilliers, Jacobus

The dual components of mental health—Response bibl color *Science* v354 no6314 p840 N 18 2016

CILLIERS, SAREL S.

Planning for the Future of Urban Biodiversity: A Global Review of City-Scale Initiatives *BioScience* v67 no4 p332 Ap 2017

CILLS, HAZEL

'Side to Side' color *New York Times Magazine* p52 Mr 12 2017

Cimbro, Raffaello

Sustained virologic control in SIV+ macaques after antiretroviral and α4β7 antibody therapy bibl graph *Science* v354 no6309 p197 O 14 2016

CIMICS, JOHN THOMAS

Your True Stories IN 100 WORDS *Reader's Digest* v189 no1128 p36 Mr 2017

Cimino, Michael, 1939-2016

On the Wild Side R. Brody color *New Yorker* v93 no19 p12 Jl 3 2017

Cimino-Isaacs, Cathleen

Trans-Pacific Partnership: An Assessment R. N. Cooper *Foreign Affairs* v95 no6 p174 N/D 2016

Cimitile, Matthew

Working Lands as Wild Lands color *National Wildlife (World Edition)* v55 no5 p40 Ag/S 2017

Cimpian, Andrei

THE BRILLIANCE TRAP color graph *Scientific American* v317 no3 p60 S 2017

Gender stereotypes about intellectual ability emerge early and influence children's interests bibl graph *Science* v355 no6323 p389 Ja 27 2017

Cincinnati (Ohio)

BIG WOOF C. ROSE *Cincinnati Magazine* v50 no5 p19 F 2017

CHAIN GANG A. AHUJA *Cincinnati Magazine* v50 no5 p156 F 2017

Cold Comfort L. VACCARIELLO *Cincinnati Magazine* v50 no5 p176 F 2017

DINING GUIDE *Cincinnati Magazine* v50 no5 p164 F 2017

Down Under A. BROWNLEE color *Cincinnati Magazine* v51 no1 p176 O 2017

EYES WIDE SHUT J. Williams *Cincinnati Magazine* v50 no12 p65 S 2017

THE GEOGRAPHY OF MEMORY A. B. WALTERS *Cincinnati Magazine* v50 no5 p72 F 2017

Help Keep Cincinnati Safe S. HARRISON *Cincinnati Magazine* v50 no5 p118 F 2017

HISTORICALLY BLACK *Cincinnati Magazine* v50 no5 p166 F 2017

THE ILLUMINATI L. MURTHA *Cincinnati Magazine* v50 no5 p36 F 2017

IN THE ASHES L. Vaccariello *Cincinnati Magazine* v50 no5 p70 F 2017

LETTER FROM THE EDITOR J. FOX cartoon *Cincinnati Magazine* v51 no1 p14 O 2017

LETTER FROM THE EDITOR J. STOWE *Cincinnati Magazine* v50 no5 p14 F 2017

On behalf of the Greater Cincinnati Automobile Dealers Association, it is my pleasure to welcome you to the Cincinnati Auto Expo 2017! T. R. Fiehrer *Cincinnati Magazine* v50 no5 p116 F 2017

PENTHOUSE VIEWS: A TIP-TOP CONDO IN THE HEART OF DOWNTOWN L. MURTHA *Cincinnati Magazine* v50 no11 p36 Ag 2017

Pull a Pint J. K. WOLFE *Cincinnati Magazine* v50 no5 p159 F 2017

RUN AROUND H. BRANDSTETTER *Cincinnati Magazine* v50 no8 p20 My 2017

Shell Game A. BRANDT *Cincinnati Magazine* v50 no5 p158 F 2017

Sparkle and Dance K. LAUR *Cincinnati Magazine* v50 no7 p38 Ap 2017

VINTAGE STOCK J. DRILLING *Cincinnati Magazine* v50 no5 p160 F 2017

Cincinnati (Ohio)—Politics & government

The Polls Are Open A. Spear color *Bloomberg Businessweek* no4498 p34 N 7 2016

Cincinnati Ballet (Performer)

One for the Ladies: Cincinnati Ballet shows even more love for women choreographers this season C. Thompson *Dance Magazine* v91 no9 p18 S 2017

Travis Wall: Puts His Stamp on Ballet C. Bowers *Dance Spirit* v21 no7 p41 S 2017

Cincinnati Bengals (Football team)

3 Cincinnati Bengals color *Sports Illustrated* v127 no7 p72 S 4 2017

AFC + NORTH color *Sports Illustrated* v126 no5 p45 F 13 2017

Hard Knocks Revisited M. Graham *Cincinnati Magazine* v50 no12 p44 S 2017

Cincinnati Children's Hospital Medical Center

Hello. The Dog Will See You Now J. WILLIAMS *Cincinnati Magazine* v50 no4 p78 Ja 2017

Cincinnati Reds (Baseball team)

13 THE REDS' BIG MACHINE J. Dickey color *Sports Illustrated* v126 no9 p66 Mr 27 2017

5 REDS color *Sports Illustrated* v126 no9 p107 Mr 27 2017

Cincinnati Symphony Orchestra

FABLES OF THE RECONSTRUCTION R. J. SMITH *Cincinnati Magazine* v50 no11 p86 Ag 2017

Cincinnati/Northern Kentucky International Airport

AIR CARE: How CVG shed its costly reputation A. FLANGO *Cincinnati Magazine* v50 no11 p21 Ag 2017

Cincinnati riots, Ohio, 2001

LETTER FROM THE EDITOR J. STOWE *Cincinnati Magazine* v50 no7 p14 Ap 2017

Cinderella Christmas, A (TV program)

COZY UP! IT'S YOUR HOLIDAY TV-MOVIE CHEAT SHEET D. Snierson color *Entertainment Weekly* no1443 p51 D 9 2016

Cinel, Jessica—Interviews

THE LOOK BOOK A. SWERDLOFF img *New York* v50 no6 p57 Mr 20 2017

Cinema Paradiso (Film)

CINEMA PARADISO B. A. DuHamel color *Sound & Vision* v82 no5 p68 Je 2017

Cinematographers

Fated J. Stifter bw cartoon color *Powder* v45 no5 p52 Ja 2017

Cinematography awards

CYRUS SUTTON J. HOUSMAN color *Surfer* v58 no3 p36 Je 2017

Cingl, Lubomír

Behavior management color *Science* v356 no6335 p244 Ap 21 2017

Cinnamon (Spice)

Bake-Ahead Breakfast J. BOWDEN and J. BESSINGER color *Better Nutrition* p62 My 2017

Cinnamon Crumb Cake R. Kinane color *Entertainment Weekly* no1465 p18 My 12 2017

EAT TO BEAT THE HOLIDAY SPREAD color *Men's Health* v31 no10 p67 D 2016

HEALING Spices [Cover story] J. Jibrin and M. Bharadwaj color *Yoga Journal* no290 p83 Mr 2017

La Morada N. Niarchos color *New Yorker* v93 no30 p15 O 2 2017

Spice of Life: Take 2 cups of ginger tea and call me in the morning D. SCHARDT *Nutrition Action Health Letter* v44 no5 p6 Je 2017

SWEET TO THE CORE S. COLLINS color *Martha Stewart Living* p96 O 2017

Cinnamon (Spice)—Research

GENIUS SPICE color *Prevention* v68 no11 p8 N 2016

Cinque Terre (Italy)

Room 8 Albergo Barbara L. LAUCHT color *Conde Nast Traveler* v52 no8 p122 S 2017

Cinsaut (Wine)

Summer... Reds?! J. SMELT *Atlanta* v57 no4 p40 Ag 2017

Cinta Romay, M.

Genomic estimation of complex traits reveals ancient maize adaptation to temperate North America diag *Science* v357 no6350 p512 Ag 4 2017

Cintra, B. B. L.

Persistent effects of pre-Columbian plant domestication on Amazonian forest composition bibl chart graph map *Science* v355 no6328 p925 Mr 3 2017

Cioffi, Alexander G.

Restored iron transport by a small molecule promotes absorption and hemoglobinization in animals color graph *Science* v356 no6338 p608 My 12 2017

CIOLFE, TERRA

Cross-Canada spell check map *Maclean's* v130 no7 p17 Ag 2017

How safe is your province? map *Maclean's* v130 no8 p17 S 2017

They come from away map *Maclean's* v130 no10 p17 N 2017

CIOLFI, ANGELA

Busting the School-to-Prison Pipeline *Education Digest* v82 no5 p42 Ja 2017

Ciombor, Kristen K.

Mismatch repair deficiency predicts response of solid tumors to PD-1 blockade chart graph *Science* v357 no6349 p409 Jl 28 2017

Ciphers

Apple vs. the FBI Is Really, Really Complicated S. Berinato *Harvard Business Review Digital Articles* p2 F 19 2016

Girl Who Codes J. BLAEC *O, The Oprah Magazine* p145 My 2017

UNRAVELING A SECRET B. ALEX bw color map *Discover* v38 no8 p40 O 2017

CIPRI, NINO

Picking Up the Pieces color *Publishers Weekly* v264 no1 p34 Ja 2 2017

CIPRIANI, JASON

TERK TRINITY XTEND: THIS TV ANTENNA TRIES TO PULL DOUBLE-DUTY AS A WI-FI RANGE EXTENDER color *Macworld - Digital Edition* v34 no11 p25 N 2017

Cipriano, Robert E.

Is Collegiality a Weapon or a Shield? *Change* v49 no1 p54 Ja/F 2017

CIRALSKY, ADAM

THE PRESIDENT'S MEN PART I: Frenemy of the State color *Vanity Fair* v59 no11 p118 N 2017

Circadian rhythms

Circadian clocks: Not your grandfather's clock F. W. Turek bibl diag *Science* v354 no6315 p992 N 25 2016

Circadian physiology of metabolism S. Panda bibl diag *Science* v354 no6315 p1008 N 25 2016

Circadian time signatures of fitness and disease J. Bass and M. A. Lazar bibl diag map *Science* v354 no6315 p994 N 25 2016

EIGHT WAYS NATURE CAN HEAL YOU F. Williams cartoon *Rodale's Organic Life* v3 no1 p83 Ja 2017

The Ideal Work Schedule, as Determined by Circadian Rhythms C. M. Barnes *Harvard Business Review Digital Articles* p2 Ja 28 2015

Immunity around the clock K. Man, A. Loudon et al bibl diag graph *Science* v354 no6315 p999 N 25 2016

Keeping time *Mayo Clinic Health Letter* v34 no12 p6 D 2016

Mechanisms linking circadian clocks, sleep, and neurodegeneration E. S. Musiek and D. M. Holtzman bibl diag *Science* v354 no6315 p1004 N 25 2016

ON THE CLOCK L. B. Ray and J. Travis color *Science* v354 no6315 p986 N 25 2016

START OF DARKNESS T. G. HOPE color *Better Homes & Gardens* v95 no11 p154 N 2017

Circadian rhythms in animals—Research

Structural basis of the day-night transition in a bacterial circadian clock R. Tseng, N. F. Goularte et al bibl diag *Science* v355 no6330 p1174 Mr 17 2017

Circadian rhythms in cyanobacteria

Structural basis of the day-night transition in a bacterial circadian clock R. Tseng, N. F. Goularte et al bibl diag *Science* v355 no6330 p1174 Mr 17 2017

Structures of the cyanobacterial circadian oscillator frozen in a fully assembled state J. Snijder, J. M. Schuller et al bibl diag *Science* v355 no6330 p1181 Mr 17 2017

Circadian rhythms—Genetic aspects

Structures of the cyanobacterial circadian oscillator frozen in a fully assembled state J. Snijder, J. M. Schuller et al bibl diag *Science* v355 no6330 p1181 Mr 17 2017

Circle, The (Film)

Dahmer, Docs, and Godfathers J. McGovern color *Entertainment Weekly* no1462 p48 Ap 21 2017

Circular DNA

Circular DNA throws biologists for a loop E. Pennisi color *Science* v356 no6342 p996 Je 9 2017

Circular RNA

Circular RNAs hint at new realm of genetics K. Servick color *Science* v355 no6332 p1363 Mr 31 2017

Circulators (Electrical engineering)

See also

Optical circulators

Optical circulators reach the quantum level W. J. Munro and Kae Nemoto bibl diag *Science* v354 no6319 p1532 D 23 2016

Circus

Circus at Sunset C. ALLEN color *Weekly Standard* v22 no35 p36 My 22 2017

EXTREME ANNAPOLIS: A spurned action-sports starwoos his hometown A. WHITING *Washingtonian Magazine* v52 no12 p20 S 2017

Ringling Bros. Strikes Its Tent color *Time* v189 no3 p11 Ja 30 2017

Circus cyaneus

SNOWBIRDS C. Hoh *New York State Conservationist* v71 no3 p2 D 2016

Circus performers

See also

Aerialists

Clowns

Faith in the balance A. Camille color *U.S. Catholic* v82 no7 p47 Jl 2017

Circus—History

CIRCUS DAYS R. Smith bw *American History* v52 no3 p56 Ag 2017

Circus Maximus T. Keith color *Sports Illustrated* v126 no15 p19 My 29 2017

STEP RIGHT UP! SEE THE REINVENTION OF THE GREAT AMERICAN CIRCUS H. MILLEA *Smithsonian* v48 no4 p38 Jl/Ag 2017

Circus—Law & legislation

The Last Act D. Von Drehle color *Time* v189 no18 p44 My 15 2017

Circus—Study & teaching

Balancing Act: Morocco's circus school takes women to new heights--though many in the country may not approve S. CASTELIER and P. MASSY *Ms.* v27 no3 p18 Fall 2017

Circus—United States

The Circus is Not in Town S. Richardson color *American History* v52 no2 p7 Je 2017

Sky Driver color *Reader's Digest* v189 no1130 p20 My 2017

Cirelli, Chiara

Ultrastructural evidence for synaptic scaling across the wake/sleep cycle bibl diag graph *Science* v355 no6324 p507 F 3 2017

Cirelli, Marco

Particle Physics in the LHC Era *Physics Today* v70 no6 p62 Je

2017

Cirque du Soleil

IF I RAN THE CIRCUS M. Lev-ram color *Fortune* v175 no3 p132 Mr 1 2017

TORUK: The First Flight F. Esker color *New Orleans Magazine* v51 no4 p27 F 2017

Cirrus Aircraft Corp.

CIRRUS SF50 VISION JET ENTERS MARKET color *Flying* v144 no3 p16 Mr 2017

CIRRUS SR22 G6 S. POPE bw chart color *Flying* v144 no3 p52 Mr 2017

FLIGHT'S NEXT ACE R. KARLGAARD color *Forbes* v200 no1 p22 Jl 27 2017

WE FLY: CIRRUS VISION [Cover story] S. POPE chart color *Flying* v144 no7 p44 Jl 2017

Cirrus clouds

A cirrus cloud climate dial? U. Lohmann and B. Gasparini map *Science* v357 no6348 p248 Jl 21 2017

Cirrus Design Corp.

The Cheap(er) Private Jet A. Fitzpatrick color *Time* v189 no23 p21 Je 19 2017

Cirrus Products (Company)

MIRACLE IN ICE J. Brown color *Popular Science* v289 no2 p28 Mr/Ap 2017

Cis-regulatory elements (Genetics)

Decoding the evolution of species K. L. Cooper color *Science* v356 no6341 p904 Je 1 2017

Cisco fisheries

Cisco Time K. MILLGATE *Idaho Magazine* v17 no1 p18 Ja 2017

Wild Goose Chase J. DAVIS *Idaho Magazine* v17 no1 p21 Ja 2017

Cisco Systems Inc.

How We Think About Innovation at Cisco S. Monterde *Harvard Business Review Digital Articles* p2 Je 8 2016

Managing Multiparty Innovation N. Furr, K. O'Keeffe et al color img *Harvard Business Review* v94 no11 p76 N 2016

Cisgender people

The Gender Issue color *National Geographic* v231 no1 p12 Ja 2017

A PORTRAIT OF GENDER TODAY cartoon *National Geographic* v231 no1 p14 Ja 2017

REDEFINING GENDER *National Geographic* v231 no1 p14 Ja 2017

STRAIGHT CIS FOLKS STILL DON'T GET US: Data reveals cisgender attitudes towards trans people haven't changed that much Z. ZAMF color *Advocate* no1091 p21 Je/Jl 2017

CISSIK, JOHN

FULL FRONTAL chart color *Muscle & Performance* v9 no5 p18 My 2017

Ja, Ja — Muskeln Machen! bw chart *Muscle & Performance* v9 no7 p18 Jl 2017

RIDE THE WAVE color *Muscle & Performance* v9 no6 p22 Je 2017

Cissoko, Adji

why i dance A. Cissoko *Dance Magazine* v91 no4 p72 Ap 2017

Cistaceae

Gulf of St Lawrence Beach Pinweed M. WALWYN color *Canadian Wildlife* v23 no4 p37 S/O 2017

Citadel LLC

Maybe a Good Manager Can't Run Everything M. Leising and A. Massa *Bloomberg Businessweek* no4510 p32 F 6 2017

Cities & towns

See also

Communities

Neighborhoods

Plazas

Public spaces

Urbanization

Villages

30 Cool Things About Cities S. McCOLLUM color *National Geographic Kids* no472 p28 Ag 2017

Are the Super-Rich Really Ruining the World's Great Cities? R. Florida *Harvard Business Review Digital Articles* p2 Je 9 2017

The Autonomobile and the City M. SORKIN *Architectural Record* v205 no4 p64 Ap 2017

CITIES color *Conde Nast Traveler* v52 no10 p76 N 2017

Delaware's Odd, Beautiful, Contentious, Private Utopia J. WALKER bw color *Reason* v49 no6 p62 N 2017

Designing the City of Tomorrow Today M. DiChristina color *Scientific American* v317 no1 p4 Jl 2017

THE EASTERN SHORE J. Sugarman color *Washingtonian Magazine* v52 no7 p149 Ap 2017

First, a Note About Napoli... D. COGGINS color *Esquire* p158 BigBlackBook

GHOST TOWNE J. GREEN *Atlanta* v56 no11 p24 Mr 2017

Great Places to Retire J. Bodnar *Kiplinger's Personal Finance* v71 no8 p6 Ag 2017

HIDDEN SPRINGS J. KARAMALES *Idaho Magazine* v17 no1 p32 Ja 2017

HISTORIC GROUNDS *Iceland Review* v54 no6 p104 N/D 2016

HÓLMAVÍK'S HUTS P. STEFÁNSSON *Iceland Review* v54 no6 p7 N/D 2016

THE INNOCENT WHO TRAVELED ABROAD *Missouri Life* v43 no7 p10 D 2016/Ja 2017

In Your Words P. Guzmán color *Conde Nast Traveler* v52 no10 p20 N 2017

LETTER FROM THE EDITOR J. STOWE *Cincinnati Magazine* v50 no5 p14 F 2017

The Limits of Café Urbanism A. Ehrenhalt *Governing* v30 no6 p14 Mr 2017

Midsize Cities Are Entrepreneurship's Real Test D. Isenberg and V. Onyemah color *Harvard Business Review Digital Articles* p2 Ja 24 2017

NAME-DROPPERS S. STALL *Indianapolis Monthly* v40 no3 p22 N 2016

The New Laboratories W. Fulton *Governing* v30 no7 p23 Ap 2017

NIGHT MOVES A. BERNSTEIN, M. BRANDSTETTER et al *Cincinnati Magazine* v50 no8 p40 My 2017

Not-So-New Urbanism: City revival has ceased to be a radical idea W. Fulton *Governing* v31 no1 p25 O 2017

THE OASIS OF PALMYRA P. Veyne *Lapham's Quarterly* v10 no1 p214 Wint 2017

Positive Proximity D. WILLIAMS color *Publishers Weekly* v264 no34 p116 Ag 21 2017

SUGAR CITY: SWEET TOWN, IDAHO J. D. EDLEFSEN *Idaho Magazine* v16 no11 p32 Ag 2017

TAPPING THE TRASH M. E. Webber color diag *Scientific American* v317 no1 p48 Jl 2017

WELCOME TO SNORRASTOFA *Iceland Review* v54 no6 p105 N/D 2016

Cities & towns—California

Why California Is Such a Talent Magnet O. Lobel *Harvard Business Review Digital Articles* p2 Ja 19 2016

The Wonder Years M. MELTON *Los Angeles Magazine* p24 D 2016

A WORLD AWAY IN ALAMEDA *Sea Magazine* v108 no8 pCA-1 Ag 2016

Cities & towns—Canada

BEACHCOMBING IN GIBSONS D. HISLOP *Sea Magazine* v108 no8 pPNW-10 Ag 2016

Town for sale: needs work M. CAMPBELL *Maclean's* v130 no2 p13 Mr 2017

Cities & towns—Canada—Maps

Waterloo Region map *Alternatives Journal (AJ) - Canada's Environmental Voice* v42 no3 p16 2016

Cities & towns—China—Environmental conditions

Adapting Chinese cities to climate change Qinhua Fang bibl *Science* v354 no6311 p425 O 28 2016

Cities & towns—Colombia

Colombians Yank The Welcome Mat M. Bristow color *Bloomberg Businessweek* no4537 p30 S 11 2017

Cities & towns—Colorado

How did a scientific Siberia turn into AstroBoulder? J. P. Bassi *Physics Today* v70 no2 p36 F 2017

Cities & towns—Developing countries

How to Manage The Sprawl P. Coy map *Bloomberg Businessweek* no4534 p8 Ag 14 2017

Cities & towns—Economic conditions

The 4 Types of Cities and How to Prepare Them for the Future J. D. Macomber *Harvard Business Review Digital Articles* p2 Ja 18 2016

Unlikely Neighbors S. Beyer *Governing* v30 no2 p24 N 2016

Cities & towns—History

Border, beach, buried wonders, Old Baldy & Bells C. AMUNDSON and A. J. BARTELS color *Nebraska Life* v21 no6 p56 N/D 2017

LETTER FROM THE EDITOR MARCH 2017 J. STOWE *Cincinnati Magazine* v50 no6 p18 Mr 2017

Cities & towns—Indiana—Marketing

CHANGE the CITY L. BAILEY, D. S. COMISKEY et al *Indianapolis Monthly* p55 Ap 2017

Cities & towns—Management

Not-So-New Urbanism: City revival has ceased to be a radical idea W. Fulton *Governing* v31 no1 p25 O 2017

Cities & towns—Population distribution

Build, Baby, Build S. Beyer *Governing* v30 no6 p24 Mr 2017

Cities & towns—Security measures

Driverless Cars: What Could Possibly Go Wrong? R. Hutchinson *Harvard Business Review Digital Articles* p2 Ja 15 2016

Cities & towns—South Africa

backstory color *New Republic* v248 no3 p72 Mr 2017

Cities & towns—Texas

On the Defensive A. Greenblatt *Governing* v31 no1 p9 O 2017

Cities & towns—United States

Back in Black: Cities that once faced bankruptcy have made remarkable recoveries F. Shafroth *Governing* v30 no10 p62 Jl 2017

THE BEST PLACES TO LIVE IN AMERICA [Cover story] K. A. Renzulli, I. S. Mangla et al chart color map *Money* v46 no9 p54 O 2017

City Fixers: Some city managers live in constant quest of new places with new problems to fix L. Farmer *Governing* v30 no8 p40 My 2017

Dear Readers *Reader's Digest* v190 no1132 p4 Jl/Ag 2017

The great divide K. Clarke color *U.S. Catholic* v82 no9 p42 S 2017

Nicest Place IN America 2017 color *Reader's Digest* v189 no1130 p12 My 2017

PRICEY PAYOUTS M. Maciag *Governing* v30 no2 p32 N 2016

SORRY, URBANITES: PEOPLE STILL LOVE SUNBELT SUBURBS diag map *Fortune* v175 no8 p36 Je 15 2017

TECH CRUNCH BUILD CITIES THAT WON'T TRASH THE WORKING CLASS R. FLORIDA color *Wired* v25 no5 p17 My 2017

Think Globally, Resist Locally B. BARBER color *Nation* v304 no4 p17 F 6 2017

The Urban Future We Can't See A. M. Renn *Governing* v30 no2 p22 N 2016

THE WELLTHIEST CITIES IN AMERICA K. DOLD and J. MOYE bw color *Women's Health* v14 no6 p120 Jl 2017

WHERE SHOULD YOU RETIRE? W. P. BARRETT and A. BROWN color *Forbes* v200 no1 p20 Jl 27 2017

Cities & towns—United States—Economic conditions

The Unaffordable Urban Paradise R. Florida color il *MIT Technology Review* v120 no4 p88 Jl/Ag 2017

Cities & towns—United States—Growth

Are Cities Growing or Not? W. Fulton *Governing* v30 no1 p24 O 2016

Cities & towns—United States—History

NOT REALLY LOOKING TO GROW J. D. EDLEFSEN *Idaho Magazine* v16 no2 p33 N 2016

Cities Between Us (Music)

Memorable Melodies A. Morrison color *Downbeat* v84 no6 p30 Je 2017

Cities & towns—United States—Charts, diagrams, etc.

NO, REALLY, DON'T CALL IT "SILICON BEACH" diag *Fortune* v175 no4 p13 Mr 15 2017

Citigroup Inc.

BANKING L. Shen *Fortune* v175 no7 p64 Je 1 2017

Why Citi Got Rid of Assigned Desks E. Galinsky and E. Tahmincioglu *Harvard Business Review Digital Articles* p2 N 12 2014

Citino, Robert M.

D-DAY THROUGH A GERMAN LENS color *MHQ: Quarterly Journal of Military History* v29 no4 p68 Summ 2017

THE KORSUN NOOSE *MHQ: Quarterly Journal of Military History* v29 no2 p26 Wint 2017

Citizen journalism

Fake News B. LUEDERS chart *Progressive* v81 no4 p14 Ap/My

2017

THE NEW CITIZEN JOURNALISTS cartoon color *Popular Mechanics* p38 O 2017

Citizen journalists

The Role of the Citizen Journalist *USA Today Magazine* v145 no2859 p2 D 2016

Citizen of Glass (Music)

Agnes Obel: Citizen of Glass J. Cadagin *Opera News* v81 no6 p54 D 2016

Citizen participation in crime prevention

I Accidentally Killed a Child. May I Contact The Family? K. A. Appiah *New York Times Magazine* p26 My 21 2017

Citizen participation in police administration

Undocumented on Patrol K. SURANA color *Foreign Policy* no226 p11 S/O 2017

Citizen science

See also

Biohacking

Citizen scientists join the hunt for Planet 9 A. Yeager color *Science News* v191 no11 p28 Je 10 2017

See Change, Change Sea A. Wisch color *Sail* v48 no3 p10 Mr 2017

Citizens

Deliberative Citizens, (Non)Deliberative Politicians: A Rejoinder A. Bächtiger and S. Beste *Daedalus* v146 no3 p106 Summ 2017

News Splash: Elated by the word that World War II had ended, Indy citizens took to the streets to cheer, party, wave flags—and even skivvies-dip on Monument Circle C. ZEIGLER bw *Indianapolis Monthly* v41 no2 p22 S 2017

Try This! cartoon *O, The Oprah Magazine* p152 My 2017

Citizens United v. Federal Election Commission (Supreme Court case)

Our Legitimacy Crisis R. FEINGOLD *Nation* v304 no11 p4 Ap 3 2017

Citizens Budget Commission (New York, N.Y.)

Long Road for NYC Public Projects H. CORCORAN color *Architectural Record* v205 no5 p26 My 2017

Citizens for Responsibility & Ethics in Washington (Organization)—Trials, litigation, etc.

A Trump Lawsuit Gets a Boost From Restaurants B. Van Voris color *Bloomberg Businessweek* no4519 p34 Ap 24 2017

Citizenship

See also

Undocumented immigrants

The America I believe in H. A. Lashuel cartoon *Science* v355 no6326 p706 F 17 2017

Could You Pass the U.S. CITIZENSHIP TEST? *New York Times Upfront* v149 no11 p10 Ap 3 2017

How to Launder A Russian Y. Onaran and V. Silver graph *Bloomberg Businessweek* no4522 p17 My 15 2017

SHOWCASE SHOTS color *Nebraska Life* v21 no4 p106 Jl/Ag 2017

Citizenship Act (Canada)

EMERGENCY CANADIAN RESIDENCE APPLICATION B. MCCALL cartoon *New Yorker* v92 no39 p45 N 28 2016

Citizenship—Canada

HOUSE OF SPIES [Cover story] M. Friscolanti color *Maclean's* v130 no8 p30 S 2017

Citizenship—Japan

THE BOY WITHOUT A COUNTRY J. Weisberg *Harper's Magazine* p73 Ap 2017

Citizenship—Switzerland

A SPORT AND A PASSPORT *Harper's Magazine* p15 O 2017

Citizenship—United States

FLIGHT 1040 M. Mechanic color *Mother Jones* v42 no3 p46 My/Je 2017

How American Are You, Really? The Citizenship Test for Citizens S. SHERRILL color graph *GQ: Gentlemen's Quarterly* v97 no6 p62 Je 2017

Realizing the Dream of Citizenship *Saturday Evening Post* v289 no2 p104 Mr/Ap 2017

Should Birthright Citizenship Be Abolished? S. D. VITTER and M. WASLIN *New York Times Upfront* v149 no3 p22 O 10 2016

Citizens—Social conditions

ACCORDING TO THE LATEST POLL... P. SMITH and G. C. TYLER *New York Times Upfront* v149 no3 p16 O 10 2016

Citric acid

Sour Patch Citrus L. MENNIES color *Bon Appetit* no11 p22 N 2017

Citrin, James M.

What Parents Should Tell Their Kids About Finding a Career *Harvard Business Review Digital Articles* p2 My 15 2015

Citron

A lot of holiday recipes call for candied citron. What exactly is it? *Martha Stewart Living* no270 p86 D 2016

Citron, Jason

Build, Race, Fight... and Chat K. CHAYKOWSKI color *Forbes* v200 no1 p46 Jl 27 2017

Citron, Stephanie

Coeur d'Alene Resort, Idaho *Saturday Evening Post* v289 no3 p27 My/Je 2017

Citrulline

CITRULLINE MALATE: FUEL FOR FEMALES color *Muscle & Performance* v9 no1 p14 Ja 2017

Citrulline in the body

BOOST YOUR BENCH WITH CITRULLINE J. WUEBBEN color *Muscle & Performance* v9 no9 p15 S 2017

Citrus

See also

Citrus fruits

Lemon

Key Lime Cookies color *Vegetarian Today* no1 p46 F 2017

Start Your Day Strong L. Murray color *Health* v31 no2 p69 Mr 2017

Citrus fruit industry

SAFETY HARBOR, FLORIDA color *Runner's World* v52 no9 p8 O 2017

Citrus fruit industry—Florida

Apocalypse Now N. Abebe *New York Times Magazine* p11 O 8 2017

Citrus fruits

See also

Grapefruit

OUR GH DO DIET PROMISE TO YOU J. LONDON color *Good Housekeeping* v264 no3 p99 Mr 2017

Citrus—Charts, diagrams, etc.

FOR CITRUS, IT'S ALL RELATIVE D. Stone color *National Geographic* v231 no2 p20 F 2017

City 40 (Film)

City 40 C. Gramling *Science* v356 no6337 p482 My 5 2017

City Builders (Film)

BREAKING THE ICE N. DUNNE bw *Film Comment* v53 no1 p72 Ja/F 2017

City College of San Francisco

Making College Free Again S. E. SMITH *In These Times* v41 no4 p8 Ap 2017

City council members

Money Talks—in My Case Softly J. Epstein cartoon *Weekly Standard* v22 no29 p5 Ap 3 2017

City council members—Elections

Ensuring Representation A. Greenblatt *Governing* v30 no7 p17 Ap 2017

City council members—United States

AYANNA PRESSLEY L. N. Williams color map *Essence* v47 no7 p62 N 2016

In Chicago, There's Pork on the Menu *Governing* v30 no10 p10 Jl 2017

City council personnel

Carlos Ramirez-Rosa E. KANG color *Chicago* v66 no6 p95 Je 2017

City councils—Elections

Ensuring Representation A. Greenblatt *Governing* v30 no7 p17 Ap 2017

City dwellers

METROPOLIS M. Roemers color *National Geographic* v231 no3 p120 Mr 2017

Split Personalities W. Fulton *Governing* v30 no3 p24 D 2016

City dwellers—Health

Doses of Neighborhood Nature: The Benefits for Mental Health of Living with Nature D. T. C. COX, D. F. SHANAHAN et al *BioScience* v67 no2 p147 F 2017

The state of Health map *Prevention* v69 no9 p9 O 2017

color *Time* v190 no1 p17 Jl 3 2017

Civil rights—United States

THE CIVIL RIGHTS ERA *New York Times Upfront* v149 no7 p20 Ja 9 2017

FROM 9/11 to 11/9 G. CARTER *Vanity Fair* v59 no1 p42 Holiday 2017

Judging Jeff Sessions A. BERMAN *Nation* v304 no4 p5 F 6 2017

Civil rights—United States—Cases

CIVIL RIGHTS WRONGED C. N. BAKER *Ms.* v27 no3 p20 Fall 2017

Civil service

HR should stand for humane rigour R. JEFFERY *People Management* p42 N 2016

Save Our Bureaucrats! A. FERGUSON *Commentary* v144 no1 p9 Jl/Ag 2017

Civil service positions

Slow Confirmations Are Thwarting Progress T. J. DONOHUE *Weekly Standard* v23 no6 p9 O 16 2017

Civil service retirement

THE MOST HATED MAN IN PENSIONLAND L. Farmer *Governing* v30 no7 p38 Ap 2017

Civil service—Attitudes

Why Government Workers Are Harder to Motivate R. Lavigna *Harvard Business Review Digital Articles* p2 N 28 2014

Civil service—Awards

The Heroine of the FDA N. KRIPLEN bw *Discover* v38 no2 p68 Mr 2017

Civil service—Great Britain

CIPD helps boost civil service HR P. Cheese *People Management* p65 N 2016

Civil service—United States

See also

United States armed forces—Civilian employees

The Treason of the Bureaucrats: The internal governmental revolt against Trump may backfire on 'the resistance' D. DiSalvo *Commentary* v143 no4 p23 Ap 2017

Weak! G. Edelman cartoon color *Washington Monthly* v49 no6-8 p24 Je-Ag 2017

Civil society

CHINA'S GREAT LEAP BACKWARD [Cover story] J. Fallows color *Atlantic* v318 no5 p58 D 2016

Containing Trump P. Leach *Atlantic* v319 no5 p10 Je 2017

Foundering Fathers J. COST color *Weekly Standard* v22 no39 p21 Je 19 2017

Medical crises M. SAGOFF color *Issues in Science & Technology* v33 no1 p8 Fall 2016

What arguments motivate citizens to demand nuclear disarmament? A. I. Harrington, E. Gheorghe et al bibl *Bulletin of the Atomic Scientists* v73 no4 p255 Jl 2017

Civil society—United States

Civil Society and a Public Argument M. Malone *America* v217 no7 p3 O 2 2017

Civil war

See also

Insurgency

Civil Wars as Challenges to the Modern International System H. Spruyt *Daedalus* v146 no4 p112 Fall 2017

Civil Wars & the Post–Cold War International Order B. D. Jones and S. J. Stedman *Daedalus* v146 no4 p33 Fall 2017

Civil Wars & the Structure of World Power B. R. Posen *Daedalus* v146 no4 p167 Fall 2017

Civil Wars & Transnational Threats: Mapping the Terrain, Assessing the Links S. Patrick *Daedalus* v146 no4 p45 Fall 2017

Civil War & the Current International System J. D. Fearon chart graph *Daedalus* v146 no4 p18 Fall 2017

Civil War & the Global Threat of Pandemics P. H. Wise and M. Barry *Daedalus* v146 no4 p71 Fall 2017

France at the Epicenter S. McCONNELL diag *American Conservative* v16 no3 p12 My/Je 2017

Introduction K. Eikenberry and S. D. Krasner *Daedalus* v146 no4 p6 Fall 2017

It's Time to Plan for Civil War In Venezuela A. J. Stavridis color *Time* v190 no10/11 p35 S 18 2017

THE NUMBER THAT NO MAN COULD NUMBER A. Heilbut *Harper's Magazine* v334 no2001 p60 F 2017

Stars in His Eyes *Commentary* v142 no1 p1 Jl/Ag 2016

Stop the War Party Now P. J. BUCHANAN *American Conservative* v16 no3 p11 My/Je 2017

Venezuela's Agony G. HETLAND *Nation* v305 no5 p4 Ag 28 2017

With Peace, Colombia Is Poised for Greater Prosperity R. H. K. Vietor *Harvard Business Review Digital Articles* p2 Jl 7 2016

Civil war—Colombia

The Colombian Paradox: Peace Processes, Elite Divisions & Popular Plebiscites A. M. Matanock and M. García-Sánchez graph *Daedalus* v146 no4 p152 Fall 2017

Civil war—History

ASK MHQ J. GUTTMAN *MHQ: Quarterly Journal of Military History* v29 no2 p11 Wint 2017

Civilian evacuation

Storm Surge C. Acevedo color *Vogue* v207 no11 p84 N 2017

Civilians in war

INSIDE MOSUL A. R. KHAN color *Maclean's* v129 no50 p14 D 19 2016

Civilization

See also

Education

Enlightenment

Learning & scholarship

Manners & customs

Migrations of nations

Religions

Social sciences

ALTERNATIVE ARCHAEOLOGY G. HANCOCK and M. SHERMER *Scientific American* v317 no4 p9 O 2017

Are We Civilized Yet? S. Montgomery *Society* v54 no2 p133 Ap 2017

'Civilization' and the Self-Critical Tradition D. Gordon *Society* v54 no2 p106 Ap 2017

Civilization: 'It Means Just What I Choose It to Mean' B. Bowden *Society* v54 no2 p126 Ap 2017

Early Civilization Uncovered in Southeast *USA Today Magazine* v145 no2865 p11 Je 2017

HOW CIVILIZATION STARTED J. LANCHESTER cartoon *New Yorker* v93 no28 p22 S 18 2017

Civil rights—Charts, diagrams, etc.

THE CIVIL RIGHTS ERA *New York Times Upfront* v149 no7 p20 Ja 9 2017

Civil service—Salaries, etc.—Government policy

IN DEFENSE OF EXPERTISE A. Whiting *Washingtonian Magazine* v52 no5 p15 F 2017

Civil War: Chicago, A (Film)

WAR STORIES C. BELANGER bw *Chicago* v66 no11 p26 N 2017

C. K., Louis, 1967-

THE 50 FUNNIEST PEOPLE RIGHT NOW! R. SHEFFIELD color *Rolling Stone* no1287 p35 My 18 2017

Fathers & Daughters E. Blair color *New York Review of Books* v64 no12 p4 Jl 13 2017

Points to Ponder color *Reader's Digest* v190 no1133 p25 S 2017

WHERE & WHEN *Washingtonian Magazine* v52 no4 p31 Ja 2017

CKE Restaurants Inc.

MEAT MARKETER [Cover story] S. BERFIELD, C. GIAMMONA et al color graph map *Bloomberg Businessweek* no4511 p42 F 13 2017

Claassen, Manfred

Cell-wide analysis of protein thermal unfolding reveals determinants of thermostability color *Science* v355 no6327 p812 F 24 2017

CLAASSEN, PAIGE

Breakfast (and Dinner) of Champions color *Climbing* no353 p29 My/Je 2017

Claassen, Roger

Conservation Compliance in the Crop Insurance Era *Amber Waves: The Economics of Food, Farming, Natural Resources, & Rural America* p29 Jl 2017

Clack, Odin—Interviews

Odin Leather Goods L. S. FORD *Texas Monthly* v45 no2 p32 F 2017

Claes, Filip

De novo design of a biologically active amyloid bibl graph *Sci-*

ence v354 no6313 paah4949-1 N 11 2016

Claessen, R.

Bismuthene on a SiC substrate: A candidate for a high-temperature quantum spin Hall material diag graph *Science* v357 no6348 p287 Jl 21 2017

Claeys, An-Sofie

Companies Fare Worse When the Press Exposes Their Problems Before They Do *Harvard Business Review Digital Articles* p2 Ag 22 2016

Claeys, Philippe

The formation of peak rings in large impact craters bibl color graph *Science* v354 no6314 p878 N 18 2016

Claflin, Sam, 1986——Interviews

THE THINKING MAN SAM CLAFLIN M. Khidekel color *Women's Health* v14 no5 p106 Je 2017

Claims

BRICKBATS C. OLIVER color *Reason* v49 no3 p72 Jl 2017

Questioning Claims That Are Too Good to Be True K. Firestone *Harvard Business Review Digital Articles* p2 S 7 2016

Clair, Judy

Coping with the Effects of Emotionally Difficult Work *Harvard Business Review Digital Articles* p2 Ag 16 2016

The Right and Wrong Ways to Help Pregnant Workers *Harvard Business Review Digital Articles* p2 S 27 2016

Clam populations

School of tides R. Stuart color *Canadian Geographic* v137 no5 p24 S/O 2017

Claman, Priscilla

6 Ways to Disagree with Senior Management *Harvard Business Review Digital Articles* p2 Je 14 2016

How to Get Out from Under Your Boss's Shadow *Harvard Business Review Digital Articles* p2 D 2 2014

How to Get the Most Out of Reference Checks *Harvard Business Review Digital Articles* p2 Mr 10 2016

How to Interview and Assess a Serial Job Hopper *Harvard Business Review Digital Articles* p2 Ja 27 2016

How to Spark Creativity When You're in a Rut *Harvard Business Review Digital Articles* p2 Ap 19 2017

Stop Doing Low-Value Work *Harvard Business Review Digital Articles* p2 Je 1 2016

Clambakes

Seaside Suppers P. S. York and K. Rankin color *Southern Living* v52 no7 p101 Jl 2017

Clamps (Engineering)

Hose Clamp Smarts B. PIKE color *Power & Motoryacht* v34 no6 p79 Je 2017

HOSE HEALTH: USING THE CORRECT CLAMP IS VITAL FOR HOSES' LONG-TERM VIABILITY D. HISLOP color *Sea Magazine* v109 no6 p28 Je 2017

Clams

prep school C. SAFFITZ, A. MASON et al bw color *Bon Appetit* v62 no4 p112 Ap 2017

Clancy, Heather

HOW AM I DOING? color *Fortune* v175 no3 p34 Mr 1 2017

A NEW MIND-SET color *Fortune* v75 no1 p30 Ja 1 2017

SALESFORCE SETS ITS SIGHTS ON $20 BILLION color *Fortune* v174 no8 p38 D 15 2016

TECH TAKES THE FIELD color *Fortune* v175 no3 p32 Mr 1 2017

Clancy, Matthew

U.S. Agricultural R&D in an Era of Falling Public Funding *Amber Waves: The Economics of Food, Farming, Natural Resources, & Rural America* p1 N 2016

Clancy, Nicole

How Sore Is TOO SORE? color *O, The Oprah Magazine* p72 Jl 2017

Clandinin, Thomas R.

Glia put visual map in sync color *Science* v357 no6354 p867 S 1 2017

Clanet, Christophe

Row bots *Physics Today* v70 no6 p82 Je 2017

Clans

The ORIGINAL KARDASHIANS N. Gabler *Los Angeles Magazine* p112 D 2016

Clanton, Alan

ARABIAN HORSE WORLD'S TRAINERS ALMANAC G.

DEARTH *Arabian Horse World* v57 no1 p49 O 2016

Clanton, Ben

Boo Who? *Publishers Weekly* v264 no22 p65 My 29 2017

Clanton, Zach

THE SOLOIST [Cover story] D. Page bw *Powder* v45 no6 p78 F 2017

Clapham, Christopher

The Horn of Africa: State Formation and Decay N. van de Walle *Foreign Affairs* v96 no6 p173 N/D 2017

Clapper, James R. (James Robert), 1941-

U.S. INTELLIGENCE AS A PILLAR OF STABILITY DURING TRANSITION J. R. CLAPPER *Vital Speeches of the Day* v82 no11 p340 N 2016

WATCHING THE WATCHER G. M. Graff bw *Wired* v24 no12 p132 D 2016

WHY BLACK LIVES MATTER TO U.S. INTELLIGENCE *Vital Speeches of the Day* v83 no2 p55 F 2017

Clappier, Eric

BOXED VODKA JUST WANTS TO BE LOVED J. Miller cartoon *Bloomberg Businessweek* no4507 p64 Ja 16 2017

Claps, Pierluigi

Changing climate shifts timing of European floods color graph *Science* v357 no6351 p588 Ag 11 2017

Clapton, Eric, 1945-

Random Notes color *Rolling Stone* no1285 p20 Ap 20 2017

Clara Labs (Company)

Your Next Assistant: A Cyborg C. O'CONNOR color *Forbes* v199 no4 p48 Ap 25 2017

Claravall, Eric B.

THINKING LIKE A HISTORIAN: Developing disciplinary literacy in history among middle school struggling readers *Literacy Today (2411-7862)* v35 no1 p32 Jl/Ag 2017

Clardy, Jon

Unequivocal determination of complex molecular structures using anisotropic NMR measurements color *Science* v356 no6333 p43 Ap 7 2017

Clare (Ireland)

SMALL HOUSE, BIG LIFE D. McGLYNN color *O, The Oprah Magazine* p26 Jl 2017

Clare, Cassandra——Interviews

Q&A WITH CASSANDRA CLARE bw *Publishers Weekly* v263 no43 p(Sp)12 O 24 2016

Clare, Kerry

Little Truths color *Walrus* v14 no5 p56 Je 2017

Clare, Olivia

Tales of the Unhinged: The characters in these insightful stories are often unstable, possibly even deranged A. ERVIN *New York Times Book Review* p18 Jl 30 2017

Claremont Trio (Performer)

ABOVE & BEYOND cartoon *New Yorker* v93 no29 p32 S 25 2017

Claridge, Timothy D. W.

Posttranslational mutagenesis: A chemical strategy for exploring protein side-chain diversity diag *Science* v354 no6312 p597 N 4 2016

Clarifai Inc.

Battling Giants A. TILLEY chart color *Forbes* v200 no1 p50 Jl 27 2017

Clarinetists

David Krakauer's Clarinet Solos on 'Tribe Number Thirteen' J. DURSO bw *Downbeat* v83 no12 p104 D 2016

Clarins SA

The BUY Beauty color *Harper's Bazaar* no3656 p180 S 2017

MUST-BUYS M. Santos color *Working Mother* v40 no2 p20 Je/Jl 2017

CLARK, ASHLEY

O SAY CAN YOU SEE bw *Film Comment* v53 no1 p57 Ja/F 2017

THIS IS US color *Film Comment* v53 no5 p32 S/O 2017

CLARK, BRIAN E.

Yes, You Can Ski and Ride in October bw *Conde Nast Traveler* v51 no10 p172 N 2016

Clark, Bryan W.

The genomic landscape of rapid repeated evolutionary adaptation to toxic pollution in wild fish bibl graph *Science* v354 no6317 p1305 D 9 2016

Clark, Cathy

The Exile: The Stunning Inside Story of Osama bin Laden and Al Qaeda in Flight L. D. Freedman *Foreign Affairs* v96 no6 p155 N/D 2017

Clark, Charles Dismas

Father Hood W. E. Mueller bw *Commonweal* v144 no2 p31 Ja 27 2017

Clark, Cheryl

ORANGE CRUSH J. N. LOMAX *Texas Monthly* v44 no11 p112 N 2016

Clark, Christopher

Flight School B. Borrell color *National Geographic* v232 no1 p98 Jl 2017

Clark, Claire D.

Breaking Addicts in Order to Fix Them M. Szalavitz color *Reason* v49 no5 p72 O 2017

Clark, Colleen Patrice

EMBRACING THE UNKNOWN [Cover story] color *Literacy Today (2411-7862)* v34 no5 p28 Mr/Ap 2017

LITERACY IS THE KEY *Literacy Today (2411-7862)* v35 no1 p3 Jl/Ag 2017

A MOST DESERVING RECOGNITION *Literacy Today (2411-7862)* v35 no2 p2 S/O 2017

PROMOTING EMPATHY *Literacy Today (2411-7862)* v34 no3 p2 N/D 2016

WHAT'S HOT 2017 *Literacy Today (2411-7862)* v34 no4 p3 Ja/F 2017

WRITING YOURSELF INTO EXISTENCE color *Literacy Today (2411-7862)* v34 no5 p20 Mr/Ap 2017

Clark, Cristen

SNAPS OF REALITY J. Scott *Successful Farming* v115 no4 p20 Mr 2017

Clark, D. S.

An artificial metalloenzyme with the kinetics of native enzymes bibl diag graph *Science* v354 no6308 p102 O 7 2016

Clark, Don

INTO THE WOOD A. FLANGO *Cincinnati Magazine* v50 no8 p34 My 2017

Clark, Dorie

3 Productivity Tips You Can Start Using Today *Harvard Business Review Digital Articles* p2 Mr 2 2016

3 Rules for Experts Who Want More Influence *Harvard Business Review Digital Articles* p2 My 22 2015

3 Small Things Every Person Can Do to Reduce Stress in Their Office *Harvard Business Review Digital Articles* p2 Mr 31 2017

3 Ways to Make Time for the Little Tasks You Never Make Time For *Harvard Business Review Digital Articles* p2 F 14 2017

4 Ways to Overcome a Bad First Impression *Harvard Business Review Digital Articles* p2 My 13 2016

5 Ways to Make Conference Networking Easier *Harvard Business Review Digital Articles* p2 O 13 2015

Actually, You Should Check Email First Thing in the Morning *Harvard Business Review Digital Articles* p2 Mr 7 2016

Change Your Career Without Having to Start All Over Again *Harvard Business Review Digital Articles* p2 My 24 2016

A Consultant's Guide to Firing a Client *Harvard Business Review Digital Articles* p2 Ja 26 2015

Create a "Mastermind Group" to Help Your Career *Harvard Business Review Digital Articles* p2 Ag 13 2015

Don't Set Too Many Goals for Yourself *Harvard Business Review Digital Articles* p2 D 16 2016

Establish Expertise Inside Your Company *Harvard Business Review Digital Articles* p2 Ag 19 2015

Fending Off a Colleague Who Keeps Wasting Your Time *Harvard Business Review Digital Articles* p2 Mr 28 2016

Find the Career Coach Who's Right for You *Harvard Business Review Digital Articles* p2 Mr 31 2015

Get People to Listen to You When You're Not Seen as an Expert *Harvard Business Review Digital Articles* p2 My 13 2015

Harper Lee and Dr. Seuss Won't Save Publishing *Harvard Business Review Digital Articles* p2 Jl 24 2015

Help Your Employees Be Themselves at Work *Harvard Business Review Digital Articles* p2 N 3 2014

How Stay-at-Home Parents Can Transition Back to Work *Harvard Business Review Digital Articles* p2 Ap 24 2017

How Successful People Network with Each Other *Harvard Business Review Digital Articles* p2 Ja 21 2016

How to Become a Coach or Consultant After You Retire *Harvard Business Review Digital Articles* p2 My 12 2017

How to Change Your Name and Keep Your Professional Identity *Harvard Business Review Digital Articles* p2 D 9 2014

How to Decide Which Conferences Are Worth Your Time color *Harvard Business Review Digital Articles* p2 Ja 10 2017

How to Promote Yourself Without Looking Like a Jerk *Harvard Business Review Digital Articles* p2 D 22 2014

How to Protect Your Time Without Alienating Your Network *Harvard Business Review Digital Articles* p2 F 6 2015

How to Rebrand Yourself as Creative When You're Not Perceived That Way *Harvard Business Review Digital Articles* p2 My 25 2017

How to Say No to Things You Want to Do *Harvard Business Review Digital Articles* p2 Ja 4 2016

How to Stay Motivated When Everyone Else Is on Vacation *Harvard Business Review Digital Articles* p2 Ag 8 2016

How to Take a Productive Yet Refreshing Vacation [Cover story] *Harvard Business Review Digital Articles* p2 Je 4 2015

How to Tell If Someone Wants to Stop Talking to You *Harvard Business Review Digital Articles* p2 O 19 2015

How to Use Your Travel Time Productively *Harvard Business Review Digital Articles* p2 N 5 2015

Learning How to Collaborate When You're Self-Employed *Harvard Business Review Digital Articles* p2 D 28 2016

Managing Your Professional Identity During a Gender Change *Harvard Business Review Digital Articles* p2 F 3 2015

Networking When You Hate Talking to Strangers *Harvard Business Review Digital Articles* p2 My 5 2015

Planning Your Post-Retirement Career *Harvard Business Review Digital Articles* p2 Ap 28 2016

Plan Your Professional Development for the Year *Harvard Business Review Digital Articles* p2 Ja 7 2016

The Right (and Wrong) Way to Network *Harvard Business Review Digital Articles* p2 Mr 10 2015

Scheduling Meetings Effectively When You're Self-Employed color *Harvard Business Review Digital Articles* p2 Mr 8 2017

Stop Believing That You Have to Be Perfect *Harvard Business Review Digital Articles* p2 O 8 2014

Stop Wasting Your Time on Work Calls *Harvard Business Review Digital Articles* p2 Mr 31 2016

Thinking About a "Work from Anywhere" Arrangement? Ask These Questions First *Harvard Business Review Digital Articles* p2 S 26 2017

Think Strategically About Your Career Development *Harvard Business Review Digital Articles* p2 D 6 2016

What to Do When People Don't Support Your Next Career Move *Harvard Business Review Digital Articles* p2 Ag 26 2016

What to Do When You Don't Feel Comfortable Being Yourself at Work *Harvard Business Review Digital Articles* p2 Ja 29 2016

What to Do When Your Colleague Comes Out as Transgender *Harvard Business Review Digital Articles* p2 F 5 2015

What to Do When You've Made a Bad Decision *Harvard Business Review Digital Articles* p2 Ag 11 2016

What You Need to Stand Out in a Noisy World color *Harvard Business Review Digital Articles* p2 Ja 6 2017

When It's OK to Ignore Feedback *Harvard Business Review Digital Articles* p2 Ag 4 2015

When Someone Gloms On to You at a Conference *Harvard Business Review Digital Articles* p2 O 5 2015

When You Agree to a Networking Meeting But Don't Know What You're Going to Talk About *Harvard Business Review Digital Articles* p2 Mr 21 2017

Why Tim Cook's Coming Out Matters for Apple, and Business *Harvard Business Review Digital Articles* p2 O 30 2014

Your Career Needs Many Mentors, Not Just One color *Harvard Business Review Digital Articles* p2 Ja 19 2017

Clark, Doug Bock

Fast Forward color graph *Wired* v25 no10 p58 O 2017

The UNTOLD STORY of the ACCIDENTAL ASSASSINS of NORTH KOREA color *GQ: Gentlemen's Quarterly* v97 no10 p168 O 2017

CLARK, EDIE

Beacon of Strength: In troubled waters, it helps to remember the courage of a remarkable family friend *Yankee* v81 no5 p14 S/O 2017

The Bobolink Dilemma color *Yankee* p14 My/Je 2017

Hard Drive *Yankee* v81 no1 p14 Ja/F 2017

Plane-Spotting at Edgar's color *Yankee* p14 Mr 2017

Clark, Elyse V.

Walk This Way: FIVE OF SHENANDOAH NATIONAL PARK'S BEST DAY HIKES *Washingtonian Magazine* v53 no1 p96 O 2017

CLARK, ERICA

cupcakes in costume *Parents* v91 no10 p82 O 2016

make thanksgiving in four hours *Parents* v91 no11 p112 N 2016

PLANT POWER! color *Parents* v92 no7 p106 Jl 2017

Clark, Gary, Jr., 1984-

Gary Clark Jr.'s Juke-Joint Couture P. DOYLE color *Rolling Stone* no1278/1279 p16 Ja 12 2017

MAVERICKS OF STYLE D. ROOKWOOD color *Esquire* v166 no5 p98 D 2016/Ja 2017

CLARK, GEORGE DAVID

Adoration of the Christ Child color *America* v215 no19 p30 D 19 2016

CLARK, GRAEME F.

Assessing National Biodiversity Trends for Rocky and Coral Reefs through the Integration of Citizen Science and Scientific Monitoring Programs *BioScience* v67 no2 p134 F 2017

CLARK, J. BLAKE

Ecological Forecasting and the Science of Hypoxia in Chesapeake Bay *BioScience* v67 no7 p614 Jl 2017

Clark, J. P.

Generational Warfare M. T. OWENS color *National Review* v69 no8 p40 My 2017

CLARK, JANE BENNETT

After a Few Do-Overs, Success color *Kiplinger's Personal Finance* v71 no2 p72 F 2017

Avoid Social Security Screwups *Kiplinger's Personal Finance* v71 no1 p32 Ja 2017

Merging Their Money and Their Goals color *Kiplinger's Personal Finance* v71 no5 p72 My 2017

MONEY MADE SIMPLE [Cover story] color *Kiplinger's Personal Finance* v71 no5 p24 My 2017

Moving to Be Near the Grandkids *Kiplinger's Personal Finance* v71 no5 p46 My 2017

RETIRE WHEN YOU WANT color *Kiplinger's Personal Finance* v71 no3 p22 Mr 2017

Clark, Jason

Twin Peaks Cheat Sheet: Showtime's revival has (finally!) ended--here's a guide to the essential episodes *TV Guide* v65 no39 p18 S 18 2017

Clark, Jayne

TORONTO ... FOR WASHINGTONIANS *Washingtonian Magazine* v52 no2 p241 N 2016

Clark, Jennifer—Interviews

Expert OPINION: FIVE WEDDING VETERANS GIVE US THEIR TIPS AND TRICKS FOR GETTING THE MOST OUT OF VENDORS L. Roberts *Indianapolis Monthly* v12 no40 p18 Ag 2017

Clark, Jeremiah

Short Rib Mole *Indianapolis Monthly* v40 no4 p58 D 2016

Clark, Jerry

Mania and Marjorie Diehl-Armstrong: Inside the Mind of a Female Serial Killer *Publishers Weekly* v264 no28 p78 Jl 10 2017

Clark, Jonathan Russell

Danger Position: An ambitious collegiate wrestler has one last shot at the title he seeks *New York Times Book Review* p18 Jl 23 2017

The Shortlist *New York Times Book Review* p26 F 12 2017

Clark, Kate

Complex multifault rupture during the 2016 Mw 7.8 Kaikōura earthquake, New Zealand color map *Science* v356 no6334 p154 Ap 14 2017

CLARK, KAYLA

r.s.v.p color *Bon Appetit* no8 p14 Ag 2017

Clark, Kelly

Amusement Mountain color *Snowboarder* v29 no4 p77 D 2016

Clark, Kevin—Interviews

KEVIN CLARK P. O'Donnell *Washingtonian Magazine* v52 no9 p45 Je 2017

Clark, Kim

THE 2017 WASHINGTON WISH LIST color diag *Money* v46 no1 p96 Ja/F 2017

3 FAMILY CONVERSATIONS diag *Money* v46 no1 p118 Ja/F 2017

5 Things to Know About the New FAFSA *Money* v45 no10 p37 N 2016

THE BEST COLLEGES FOR YOUR MONEY 2017 chart color *Money* v46 no7 p52 Ag 2017

BEST CREDIT CARDS color *Money* v46 no9 p72 O 2017

Best State Schools for Out-of-Staters chart *Money* v45 no11 p31 D 2016

FIVE STEPS TO WIN MORE AID color *Money* v46 no3 p52 Ap 2017

Mom, Dad: Your House Isn't Safe color *Money* v46 no5 p22 Je 2017

THE MONEY CHAMPIONS [Cover story] color *Money* v45 no11 p52 D 2016

Rip-Off Alert color *Money* v46 no5 p23 Je 2017

What Children Should Chip In diag *Money* v46 no2 p35 Mr 2017

CLARK, KURTIS

THE OTHER SIDE OF DEATH VALLEY color *Dirt Sports + Off-Road* v51 no6 p36 Je 2017

Clark, Lane

FLY-IN FORT M. Coté bw color *Skiing* p24 Wint 2017

GLASS J. FOERSTERLING color *Powder* v46 no2 p18 O 2017

Clark, Leith

NEW ROMANTICS color *Harper's Bazaar* no3654 p154 Je/Jl 2017

Clark, Linda

Just Joe N. Chirico color *Horse & Rider* v56 no3 p15 Mr 2017

Clark, Logan W.

Universal space-time scaling symmetry in the dynamics of bosons across a quantum phase transition bibl graph *Science* v354 no6312 p606 N 4 2016

Clark, Luke

The Morning After R. Jeremy color *Field & Stream* v122 no4 pF12 S 2017

Clark, Matt

Along for the Ride G. Ellis color *Surfer* v57 no13 p14 Mr 2017

MATT CLARK A. Goggans bw color *Surfer* v57 no13 p62 Mr 2017

Clark, Meghan

A Good Friday people color *U.S. Catholic* v82 no4 p10 Ap 2017

A leap of fidelity *U.S. Catholic* v82 no10 p10 O 2017

A prescription for human dignity color *U.S. Catholic* v82 no1 p8 Ja 2017

Retell me a story color *U.S. Catholic* v82 no7 p10 Jl 2017

Clark, Melissa

DINNER IS SERVED N. DANFORD color *Publishers Weekly* v264 no10 p34 Mr 6 2017

Clark, Meredith

Owning Your Vote cartoon *Glamour* v114 no11 p36 N 2016

Clark, Missy—Interviews

Missy Clark: "Riding is a Master Class in Life" T. Conahan color *Practical Horseman* v44 no12 p18 D 2016

CLARK, NEIL

The Greatest of Ghost Stories bw *American Conservative* v15 no6 p55 N/D 2016

Clark, Noelene

THE GREATEST DISNEY SONGS OF ALL TIME color *Entertainment Weekly* no1454/1455 p36 F 24 2017

ORPHAN BLACK A TO Z color *Entertainment Weekly* no1470 p24 Je 16 2017

Clark, Patrick

THE CORPORATE BEDROOM color *Bloomberg Businessweek* no4503 p74 D 12 2016

Unsweetened bw color *Bloomberg Businessweek* no4516 p27 Mr 27 2017

Clark, Peter U.

Regional and global sea-surface temperatures during the last interglaciation color graph *Science* v355 no6322 p276 Ja 20 2017

CLARK, RICHARD

JIMMY CARTER: PURSUING AN ARC OF RECONCILIATION bw *Christianity Today* v60 no8 p66 O 2016

OUR FIRST COMMUNITY cartoon *Christianity Today* p23 Mr 2017

OUR SUSTAINING FORCE *Christianity Today* v60 no10 p9 D 2016

We Need More Odd Couples color *Christianity Today* v60 no8 p83 O 2016

THE YEAR OF LIVING HOPELESSLY cartoon *Christianity Today* v60 no9 p25 N 2016

Clark, Ryan R.

Intercellular communication and conjugation are mediated by ESX secretion systems in mycobacteria bibl diag graph *Science* v354 no6310 p347 O 21 2016

Clark, Sean

MARRIED TO MY BUSINESS PARTNER N. Jordan color *Essence* v47 no12 p113 Ap 2017

Clark, Shelby

Critical consciousness A key to student achievement bw il *Phi Delta Kappan* v98 no5 p18 F 2017

Clark, Stephen

Alpine Sublime color *Climbing* no355 p15 Ag 2017

Clark, Suzanne J.

Mass seasonal bioflows of high-flying insect migrants bibl graph *Science* v354 no6319 p1584 D 23 2016

Clark, Tiana

NASHVILLE *New Yorker* v93 no31 p42 O 9 2017

CLARK, TIM

December 1941 bw *Yankee* v80 no6 p20 N/D 2016

Clark, Timothy D.

Biodiversity redistribution under climate change: Impacts on ecosystems and human well-being color *Science* v355 no6332 p1389 Mr 31 2017

Clark, Todd

3 Things Are Holding Back Your Analytics, and Technology Isn't One of Them *Harvard Business Review Digital Articles* p2 Je 8 2017

3 Things Are Holding Back Your Analytics, and Technology Isn't One of Them *Harvard Business Review Digital Articles* p2 Je 9 2017

To Survive, Health Care Data Providers Need to Stop Selling Data *Harvard Business Review Digital Articles* p2 Je 14 2017

CLARK, VALERIE C.

Bet You Didn't Know color *National Geographic Kids* no471 p11 Je/Jl 2017

Clark, Wendel

Dear Auston ... color *Sports Illustrated* v125 no12 p60 O 10 2016

Clark County (Wash.)

DOUBLE THE FUN *South Dakota Magazine* v33 no3 p92 S/O 2017

Clarke, Antony

Global atmospheric particle formation from CERN CLOUD measurements bibl graph map *Science* v354 no6316 p1119 D 2 2016

Clarke, Arthur C.

A Personality of Its Own color *MIT Technology Review* v120 no5 p20 S/O 2017

Clarke, Ava

The Eye of the Beholder color *Essence* v47 no9 p23 Ja 2017

CLARKE, CAITLIN

Opportunities for Improved Transparency in the Timber Trade through Scientific Verification *BioScience* v66 no11 p990 N 1 2016

CLARKE, CAROLINE V.

6-STEP RECIPE FOR SUCCESS color *Black Enterprise* v47 no8 p38 Jl/Ag 2017

Journaling: A Timeless Tool for Growth color *Black Enterprise* v47 no2 p31 S 2016

Lean, Green, Business Machine color *Black Enterprise* v47 no4 p31 N/D 2016

THE PATH TO PEACE color *Black Enterprise* v47 no5 p36 Ja/F 2017

Sock it to 'Em! color *Black Enterprise* v47 no2 p30 S 2016

Turning Networking On Its Head color *Black Enterprise* v47 no3 p40 O 2016

Clarke, Daniel J.

Disasters Should Be Dull S. HAEFFELE-BALCH and D. M. ROTHSCHILD color *Reason* v48 no9 p66 F 2017

Clarke, David

How David Clarke Became the American Right's Sheriff E. Gunn color *Progressive* p32 D 2016/Ja 2017

Milestones color *Time* v190 no10/11 p16 S 18 2017

Clarke, David M.

THE BIG EASY, STILL DOING IT color *Golf Magazine* v59 no8 p9 Ag 2017

DANNY GETS HIS DUE color *Golf Magazine* v59 no4 p13 Ap 2017

DIALING LONG DISTANCE color *Golf Magazine* v59 no3 p11 Mr 2017

DUSTIN'S YEAR TO REMEMBER color *Golf Magazine* v59 no1 p12 Ja 2017

MAKE YOUR GAME PRESSURE-PROOF color *Golf Magazine* v58 no11 p10 N 2016

MASTERFUL SERGIO color *Golf Magazine* v59 no6 p15 Je 2017

PICTURE PERFECT color *Golf Magazine* v59 no5 p11 My 2017

THIS YOUNG GUN HAS FIREPOWER color *Golf Magazine* v59 no7 p11 Jl 2017

WHEN WE WERE KINGS color *Golf Magazine* v58 no12 p11 D 2016

YOUNG GUN, OLD SOUL color *Golf Magazine* v59 no2 p10 F 2017

Clarke, Dean Travis

22 AVOIDABLE ON-THE-WATER MISTAKE *Boating World* v38 no3 p54 Mr 2017

After the Catch... : The trip back to the dock after a day of fishing should be used wisely, for cleaning up color *Boating World* v38 no7 p20 Jl 2017

Choose the Right Light- Tackle Rod: Know a little lingo and how a rod will be used before purchasing one *Boating World* v38 no8 p18 S/O 2017

How to Tuck Your Tackle In *Boating World* v37 no9 p18 N/D 2016

RULE THE RAMP *Boating World* v38 no5 p54 My 2017

Clarke, Emilia, 1987-

Game of Thrones K. Hahn *TV Guide* v65 no23 p28 My 29 2017

The Queen of Dragons Tells All A. MORRIS color *Rolling Stone* no1291/1292 p46 Jl 13 2017

Yes, Queen! color *Glamour* v114 no7 p28 Jl 2016

Clarke, Emilia, 1987--Interviews

Emilia Clarke K. B. Brown color *InStyle* v24 no9 p349 S 2017

CLARKE, GEORGE ELLIOTT

A story in STONE bw color *Canadian Geographic* v137 no4 p42 Jl/Ag 2017

Clarke, Geraldine M.

Resistance to malaria through structural variation of red blood cell invasion receptors diag *Science* v356 no6343 p1139 Je 16 2017

Clarke, Jennifer Kotler

How any one of us can stop bullying J. PRESS color *Redbook* p109 F 2017

Clarke, Jessica A.

Should Employers Fire Employees Who Attend White Supremacist Rallies? *Harvard Business Review Digital Articles* p2 S 19 2017

Clarke, Jim

BEYOND HENNESSY color *Bloomberg Businessweek* no4503 p68 D 12 2016

KICK IT WITH YOUR COLLEAGUES color *Bloomberg Businessweek* no4525 p55 Je 5 2017

TURBO DOGS C. Csere color *Car & Driver* v63 no4 p30 O 2017

Uncharted Terroir color *Bloomberg Businessweek* no4517 p72 Ap 3 2017

Clarke, John

Suppressing relaxation in superconducting qubits by quasiparticle pumping bibl graph *Science* v354 no6319 p1573 D 23 2016

Clarke, Kevin

AFTER HARVEY'S RAGE ACROSS TEXAS, CATHOLIC CHARITIES RAMPS UP ITS RESPONSE color *America* v217 no6 p12 S 18 2017

As elections approach, a fragile peace holds in Liberia color *America* v216 no8 p15 Ap 17 2017

As Mass Extinction Threatens, Are Catholics Listening to 'Laudato Si"? color *America* v215 no15 p9 N 14 2016

A basic income color *U.S. Catholic* v82 no4 p42 Ap 2017

Catholic hospitals' C.E.O. ready to fix health care after G.O.P. 'skinny repeal' fails color *America* v217 no4 p17 Ag 21 2017

Catholic Relief Services responds to misery in Mosul color *America* v217 no3 p17 Ag 7 2017

Check the budget *U.S. Catholic* v82 no7 p42 Jl 2017

Church Agencies Prepare Emergency Response in Haiti color *America* v215 no12 p8 O 24 2016

CHURCH LEADERS SCRUTINIZE BUDGET AND HEALTH CARE PRIORITIES color graph *America* v216 no13 p12 Je 12 2017

Church leaders urge Senate fix on G.O.P. Obamacare repeal color *America* v216 no12 p17 My 29 2017

The church's peacekeepers color *U.S. Catholic* v82 no2 p42 F 2017

THE CLASH OF POPULATIONS? color graph *America* v216 no10 p12 My 1 2017

DEATH PENALTY'S DECLINE CONTINUES color graph *America* v216 no3 p12 F 6 2017

The decline of unions is part of a bad 50 years for American workers *America* v217 no5 p10 S 4 2017

Don't fence us in color *U.S. Catholic* v82 no5 p42 My 2017

Fight for Mosul Drags On While Displaced Numbers Grow *America* v216 no1 p8 Ja 2 2017

Flood warning color *U.S. Catholic* v82 no11 p42 N 2017

For whose benefit? color *U.S. Catholic* v82 no1 p42 Ja 2017

Georgetown seeks forgiveness for sale of 272 enslaved people color *America* v216 no11 p16 My 15 2017

GOING TO THE MARGINS color *America* v216 no13 p32 Je 12 2017

The great divide color *U.S. Catholic* v82 no9 p42 S 2017

Green works of mercy color *U.S. Catholic* v81 no11 p42 N 2016

How long, O Lord? color *U.S. Catholic* v81 no12 p42 D 2016

Job insecurity color *U.S. Catholic* v82 no8 p42 Ag 2017

Locally grown color *U.S. Catholic* v82 no3 p42 Mr 2017

The manhunt for a martyr's killers *America* v216 no4 p49 F 20 2017

MASTER OF WARS color map *America* v216 no7 p12 Ap 3 2017

Pope Francis calls for action as famine declared in South Sudan color *America* v216 no6 p15 Mr 20 2017

PREVENTIVE STRIKES ON NORTH KOREA FAIL JUST WAR CRITERIA color *America* v217 no3 p12 Ag 7 2017

Record Homelessness Hits a High Rent City *America* v215 no19 p12 D 19 2016

Recovery Will Take Long-term Effort color *America* v215 no13 p10 O 31 2016

Travel ban confusion continues even after Supreme Court weighs in color *America* v217 no2 p16 Jl 24 2017

UNDOCUMENTED IN AMERICA chart color graph *America* v216 no4 p12 F 20 2017

U.S.–Russian Tensions Thwart Cooperation color *America* v215 no12 p9 O 24 2016

Watch what you eat color *U.S. Catholic* v82 no6 p42 Je 2017

The world is watching *U.S. Catholic* v82 no10 p42 O 2017

Clarke, Michael F.

Stromal Gli2 activity coordinates a niche signaling program for mammary epithelial stem cells color *Science* v356 no6335 p284 Ap 21 2017

Clarke, Michael John, 1981-

sports funnies K. MILLER color *National Geographic Kids* no465 p9 N 2016

Clarke, Molly

Take your yoga to go color *Yoga Journal* no293 p24 Ag 2017

Clarke, Peter

The Locomotive of War: Money, Empire, Power, and Guilt K. M. KOSTYAL bw *MHQ: Quarterly Journal of Military History* v29 no4 p92 Summ 2017

The Locomotive of War: Money, Empire, Power and Guilt W. Wilkins *Military History* v34 no5 p73 Ja 2018

CLARKE, TRAVIS

Work the Water Column *Boating World* v38 no4 p16 Ap 2017

Clarkson, Adrienne

The Back Page color *Maclean's* v130 no6 p90 Jl 2017

State of Belonging T. Barton color diag *Alternatives Journal (AJ) - Canada's Environmental Voice* v42 no3 p42 2016

Clarkson, Chris

The first Australians arrived early A. Gibbons color map *Science* v357 no6348 p238 Jl 21 2017

Clarkson, Kelly, 1982-

Kelly Clarkson I. Biedenharn color *Entertainment Weekly* no1435 p58 O 14 2016

THE WORLD ACCORDING TO Gayle color *O, The Oprah Magazine* p32 F 2017

Clarkson, Kelly, 1982——Interviews

STRONGER than EVER C. KOPACZEWSKI color *Good Housekeeping* v263 no6 p85 D 2016

CLARKSON, TOM

A SNACK BEFORE THE BANQUET *Commonweal* v144 no11 p2 Je 16 2017

Clarren, Rebecca

LEFT BEHIND color *Nation* v305 no4 p12 Ag 14 2017

Clasen, Raili

Farm, Fresher K. Renda color *House Beautiful* p41 Jl 2017

Clash of the Grandmas (TV program)

CAMERON MATHISON M. LOGAN *TV Guide* v64 no46 p42 N 7 2016

Class (TV program)

BREAKING BIG CLASS C. Collis color *Entertainment Weekly* no1446/1447 p64 D 2016/Ja 2017

Class A. D'Arminio *TV Guide* v65 no14 p38 Ap 3 2017

Class actions (Civil procedure)—United States

SMOKE'EM OUT [Cover story] E. E. Deprez and P. M. Barrett bw color *Bloomberg Businessweek* no4541 p40 O 9 2017

Class relations in literature

Books on Politics, Trump Rise After Election J. Maher chart *Publishers Weekly* v263 no47 p5 N 21 2016

Class reunions

See also

High school reunions

Class size

The Effectiveness of Class Size Reduction W. J. MATHIS *Education Digest* v82 no5 p60 Ja 2017

Class 73 (Electro-diesel locomotives)

IT'S A DISCOUNT MARKET ON CLASS 7 COMBINES: EXPECT FURTHER DISCOUNTS ON LATE-MODEL HARVESTERS THIS SUMMER AS WE WORK THROUGH A GLUT OF MACHINES D. Mowitz *Successful Farming* v115 no9 p26 Ag 2017

ClassDojo (Company)

Class App K. CHAYKOWSKI and J. DOBOSZ color *Forbes* v199 no6 p50 Je 13 2017

Classic Cakes Ltd.

DECADENT DESSERTS *Indianapolis Monthly* v40 no5 p16 Ja 2017

Classic Equine (Company)

SOLUTIONS A. White chart color *Horse & Rider* v56 no6 p28 Je 2017

Classical conditioning

Pavlovian conditioning–induced hallucinations result from overweighting of perceptual priors A. R. Powers, C. Mathys et al diag *Science* v357 no6351 p596 Ag 11 2017

Classical literature

The Modern Hamzanama: A epic project in memory of a departed son *Islamic Horizons* v46 no4 p40 Jl/Ag 2017

Classical mythology

See also

Sphinxes (Mythology)

The Return of the Fairies M. POLIDORO *Skeptical Inquirer* v41 no3 p21 My/Je 2017

Classic Savoy Bebop Sessions: 1945-1949 (Music)

Boppin' Savoy Sessions T. PANKEN bw *Downbeat* v84 no3 p64 Mr 2017

Classification of galaxies

Observing on the edge R. Pommier color *Astronomy* v45 no3 p50 Mr 2017

The Road Less Traveled T. Forte color *Sky & Telescope* v134 no5 p34 N 2017

Classification of minerals

Animal, Vegetable, or Mineral? P. J. HEANEY *Natural History* v125 no2 p32 F 2017

Classification of plants

See also

Plant species

bloom time color *Better Homes & Gardens* v95 no3 p106 Mr 2017

Canopies of many colors L. Hamers color map *Science News* v191 no5 p32 Mr 18 2017

Classification of stars

See also
Stellar populations
The Name Game: Have a go at this celestial sport. You might just win gold S. Mazlin *Sky & Telescope* v134 no4 p84 O 2017
Virgo's Flames F. Schaaf *Sky & Telescope* v133 no5 p45 My 2017

Classified advertising
A Garage Sale on Your Phone A. GEORGE cartoon chart color *Popular Mechanics* p24 My 2017

Classroom activities
Is This the Perfect Power Snack? *Scholastic Choices* pT8 S 2017 Supplement
Your Future: Dear Younger Me *Scholastic Choices* pT9 S 2017 Supplement
Your Relationships: They Changed Their School *Scholastic Choices* pT4 S 2017 Supplement

Classroom environment
TEACHER TALK AS AN INSTRUCTIONAL TOOL: Tips for making use of the "third turn" E. Ford-Connors and D. A. Robertson *Literacy Today (2411-7862)* v35 no1 p34 Jl/Ag 2017

Classroom management—Software
Class App K. CHAYKOWSKI and J. DOBOSZ color *Forbes* v199 no6 p50 Je 13 2017

Classrooms
How Kids Learn in Nature R. Szczytko and K. Stevenson *Parks & Recreation* v52 no5 p36 My 2017
THE LOOK BOOK A. SWERDLOFF img *New York* v50 no13 p55 Je 26 2017
YOUR OWN BACK YARD J. L. Hester cartoon *New Yorker* v93 no30 p19 O 2 2017

Classrooms—Equipment & supplies—Evaluation
Get Schooled J. Taraska *Architectural Record* v204 no11 p61 N 2016

Classrooms—Research
Teacher self-captured video M. G. Sherin and E. B. Dyer color il *Phi Delta Kappan* v98 no7 p49 Ap 2017

Clathrate compounds
Clathrate colloidal crystals H. Lin, S. Lee et al bibl color *Science* v355 no6328 p931 Mr 3 2017

Claude Debussy (Music)
Debussy/Orledge: Poe Operas W. R. Braun *Opera News* v81 no6 p52 D 2016

Claudel, Matthew
If Work Is Digital, Why Do We Still Go to the Office? *Harvard Business Review Digital Articles* p2 Ap 13 2016

Claure, Marcelo
Looking for Answers to the World's Biggest Challenges In the Eternal City color *Time* v188 no24 p31 D 12 2016

Clausen, Jens
Help, hope, and hype: Ethical dimensions of neuroprosthetics color *Science* v356 no6345 p1338 Je 30 2017

Clauses (Law)
See also
Arbitration clauses (Contracts)

Clauset, Aaron
Data-driven predictions in the science of science bibl color diag *Science* v355 no6324 p477 F 3 2017

Clausing, Kimberly
The Real (and Imagined) Problems with the U.S. Corporate Tax Code *Harvard Business Review Digital Articles* p2 D 6 2016

Claustrophobia
Don't Take This Quiz Before Bed A. CLAYBOURNE color diag *National Geographic Kids* no474 p20 O 2017

Claverie, Laura
At Play: Antique toys add history and whimsy to any room *New Orleans Homes & Lifestyles* v20 no3 p28 Summ 2017
Freeze Frame: Antique and vintage frames make a comeback *New Orleans Homes & Lifestyles* v20 no4 p28 Aut 2017
Iron Will *New Orleans Homes & Lifestyles* v20 no1 p28 Wint 2016
Renewed Beauty *New Orleans Homes & Lifestyles* v20 no2 p28 Spr 2017

CLAVIJO, MARCELA
WHAT GREEN TARA CAN TEACH US ABOUT FEAR: A CALMING EXERCISE bw *Tricycle: The Buddhist Review* v27 no1 p60 Fall 2017

Clavin, Paul
Combustion Waves and Fronts in Flows: Flames, Shocks, Detonations, Ablation Fronts and Explosion of Stars T. Poinsot *Physics Today* v70 no8 p62 Ag 2017

Clavin, Tom
Dodge City: Wyatt Earp, Bat Masterson, and the Wickedest Town in the American West *Publishers Weekly* v264 no5 p192 Ja 30 2017

Clawbacks (Finance)
Executive Clawbacks J. Zorthian *Time* v189 no15 p19 Ap 24 2017

Claws
SIZE MATTERS: For fiddler crabs, it's all about the claw C. Kettlewell color *Virginia Living* v15 no5 p21 Ag 2017

Claws (TV program)
Claws J. Halterman *TV Guide* v65 no23 p32 My 29 2017
Niecy Nash Nails It R. Buxton color *Entertainment Weekly* no1470 p14 Je 16 2017
On TNT's New Soap, Utopia Among the Manicurists D. D'addario color *Time* v189 no24 p49 Je 26 2017

Claxton, Louis M.
Ocean mixing and ice-sheet control of seawater 234U/238U during the last deglaciation bibl graph *Science* v354 no6312 p626 N 4 2016

Clay, Andrew Dice—Interviews
DICE G. E. Miller *TV Guide* v64 no15 p49 Ap 4 2016

Clay, Cassius Marcellus, 1810-1903
FISTS OF CLAY S. RICHARDSON *American History* v52 no1 p24 Ap 2017

Clay, Dawn Marie
USDA's FoodAPS: Providing Insights Into U.S. Food Demand and Food Assistance Programs *Amber Waves: The Economics of Food, Farming, Natural Resources, & Rural America* p42 Ag 2017

Clay, Henry, 1777-1852
Remember Henry Clay W. Kristol bw *Weekly Standard* v22 no25 p7 Mr 6 2017

Clay, Keith
Plant diversity increases with the strength of negative density dependence at the global scale diag *Science* v356 no6345 p1389 Je 30 2017

Clay, R. W.
Observation of a large-scale anisotropy in the arrival directions of cosmic rays above 8×1018 eV *Science* v357 no6357 p1266 S 22 2017

Clay figurines
DOLL STORY KIM bw *Archaeology* v70 no5 p12 S/O 2017

CLAYBOURNE, ANNA
Don't Take This Quiz Before Bed color diag *National Geographic Kids* no474 p20 O 2017

Claycomb, Ann
The Mermaid's Daughter *Publishers Weekly* v264 no5 p172 Ja 30 2017

Clayton, Andrew
Emergence and spread of a human-transmissible multidrug-resistant nontuberculous mycobacterium bibl diag graph *Science* v354 no6313 p751 N 11 2016

Clayton, Garrett
THE BEAT GOES ON J. HALTERMAN *TV Guide* p34 D 5 2016

Clayton, Jace
COSMOPOLITAN POP A. A. ABRAHAMIAN color *Nation* v33 no21 p20 N 21 2016

Clayton, Jay
Movers K. Stock color graph *Bloomberg Businessweek* no4506 p11 Ja 9 2017

CLAYTON, JEFFREY J.
BAIL OUT *USA Today Magazine* v145 no2858 p22 N 2016

CLAYTON, JOHN J.
The Friedman Pharmacy *Commentary* v142 no4 p33 N 2016

Clayton, Nicola S.
A raven's memories are for the future color *Science* v357 no6347 p126 Jl 14 2017

Clayton, Robert W.
Localized seismic deformation in the upper mantle revealed by dense seismic arrays bibl graph *Science* v354 no6308 p88 O 7 2016

Clayton, Russell
How to Do Walking Meetings Right *Harvard Business Review*

Digital Articles p2 Ag 5 2015

Clayton, Sarah

Change Management Meets Social Media *Harvard Business Review Digital Articles* p2 N 10 2015

Should CEOs Respond When Employees Complain About Them Online? color *Harvard Business Review Digital Articles* p2 Ap 3 2017

Clayton, Victoria

Hungry for sleep color *Yoga Journal* no294 p41 S 2017

HYDRATE your plate color *Yoga Journal* no293 p43 Ag 2017

CLAYTON-GEORGE, BETH

best of Indy *Indianapolis Monthly* v40 no4 p73 D 2016

Clean & Clear (Company)

cheap THRILLS E. STOVALL color *Seventeen* v76 no5 p62 S 2017

Clean, Cleaner, Cleanest (Short story)

CLEAN, CLEANER, CLEANEST S. ALEXIE bw *New Yorker* v93 no16 p48 Je 5 2017

Clean coal technologies

'Clean Coal' Is Far From Clean cartoon *Bloomberg Businessweek* no4495 p8 O 17 2016

Clean energy

    See also

    Nuclear energy

    Solar energy

    Wind power

Australia eyes clean energy goal color *Science* v356 no6343 p1105 Je 16 2017

Clean Energy Mind Games: If policy makers want to accelerate the transition to a low-carbon economy, they should heed the lessons of the decision sciences and take another look at nuclear energy D. ROPEIK *Issues in Science & Technology* v33 no4 p59 Summ 2017

Climate Steward J. Spring *Sierra* v101 no6 p63 N/D 2016

Combining theory and experiment in electrocatalysis: Insights into materials design Zhi Wei Seh, J. Kibsgaard et al bibl color graph *Science* v355 no6321 p1 Ja 13 2017

Divestment Alone Won't Beat Climate Change G. Serafeim and M. Fulton *Harvard Business Review Digital Articles* p2 N 4 2014

GO WEST TO SEE THE FUTURE OF GREEN BUILDINGS K. Tam Wu color *Maclean's* v129 no50 p39 D 19 2016

HIGH-SEAS POWER P. RAUBER *Sierra* v102 no1 p46 Ja/F 2017

Our Renewable Future: Laying the Path for One Hundred Percent Clean Energy C. A. S. HALL *BioScience* v66 no12 p1080 D 1 2016

Pittsburgh's Transformation Is a Model for Clean Energy Innovation G. Unruh color *Harvard Business Review Digital Articles* p2 Je 6 2017

President Obama's science legacy is big on climate change and clean energy D. Kramer *Physics Today* v69 no12 p26 D 2016

Renewables Power Up color *Earth Island Journal* v32 no4 p7 Wint 2017

Turning Walls Into Bridges M. BRUNE *Sierra* v102 no1 p6 Ja/F 2017

Unlocking Clean Energy V. SIVARAM bw color *Issues in Science & Technology* v33 no2 p31 Wint 2017

Clean energy industries

6 Ways the North American Clean Economy Agreement Will Affect Business A. Winston *Harvard Business Review Digital Articles* p2 Jl 6 2016

Advancing clean energy F. N. LAIRD, D. M. KAMMEN et al *Issues in Science & Technology* v33 no3 p5 Spr 2017

Clean energy industries—Finance

A Cloud Hangs Over a Clean-Energy Fund A. Natter color graph *Bloomberg Businessweek* no4513 p33 Mr 6 2017

Clean energy—Economic aspects

THE BEST ENERGY REVOLUTION MONEY CAN BUY J. Ball color diag map *Fortune* v175 no4 p172 Mr 15 2017

The irreversible momentum of clean energy B. Obama color *Science* v355 no6321 p126 Ja 13 2017

Clean energy—Government policy

Setting the PACE E. Daigneau *Governing* v30 no7 p20 Ap 2017

Clean energy—International cooperation

Global clean energy in 2017 D. King color *Science* v355 no6321

p111 Ja 13 2017

Clean Water Act of 1977 (U.S.)

CHANGE OF COURSE *Successful Farming* v115 no1 p12 Ja 2017

Cleaning

    See also

    Graffiti removal

    House cleaning

38 Easy Ways to CLEAN HOUSE C. Forte and S. Walter color *Good Housekeeping* v265 no3 p60A S 2017

9 Tidy Resolutions J. PHILLIP color *Good Housekeeping* v264 no1 p46 Ja 1 2017

ASK CAROLYN [Cover story] C. FORTÉ bw color *Good Housekeeping* v264 no2 p57 F 2017

fall CLEANING B. THORKELSON color *Better Homes & Gardens* v95 no10 p50 O 2017

How to Freshen Up a Guest Room, Fast! color *Good Housekeeping* v263 no5 p60 N 2016

Cleaning compounds

    See also

    Soap

ALL LATHERED UP color *Health* v31 no4 p10 My 2017

Hey Mr. Green! What's a good ecofriendly tile cleaner? B. Schildgen *Sierra* v102 no1 p14 Ja/F 2017

MAKE YOUR HOME HEALTHIER K. Rockwood color *Health* v31 no4 p59 My 2017

Super Naturals M. M. GOLDSTEIN color *Martha Stewart Living* p60 Ap 2017

Cleaning compounds—Evaluation

erica explores MICELLAR WATER E. Metzger color *Better Homes & Gardens* v95 no9 p24 S 2017

grime fighter [Cover story] color *Good Housekeeping* v265 no5 p61 N 2017

Strong Yet Gentle M. SMITH color *Power & Motoryacht* v34 no11 p148 N 2017

Cleaning equipment

CLEANING TRICKS FOR PEOPLE WHO HATE TO CLEAN color *Redbook* p127 N 2017

Maintain your layers R. WICHELNS diag il *Backpacker* p46 O 2017

Cleaning personnel

THE WORK YOU DO, THE PERSON YOU ARE T. MORRISON cartoon *New Yorker* v93 no16 p66 Je 5 2017

Cleaning—Equipment & supplies

    See also

    Cleaning compounds

The Logophile A. Hollandbeck *Saturday Evening Post* v289 no2 p24 Mr/Ap 2017

Cleaning—Equipment & supplies—Evaluation

MAN-I-CURE! M. BOBO color *Ebony* v72 no3 p70 D 2016/Ja 2017

PRESSURE WASHERS R. ROMANSKI color *Popular Mechanics* p28 My 2017

Cleanup of marine debris

Sea trash traps face doubts E. Stokstad *Science* v356 no6339 p671 My 19 2017

Cleanup of radioactive waste sites—Equipment & supplies

It's a Dirty Job, But Something's Gotta Do It A. Satariano color *Bloomberg Businessweek* no4512 p31 F 20 2017

ClearHealth Costs (Company)

It's Absurd That Health Care Costs Are So Confusing J. Pinder *Harvard Business Review Digital Articles* p2 N 26 2014

Clearing of land

The Consequences of Internal Migration in Sub-Saharan Africa: A Case Study J. SALERNO, J. MWALYOYO et al *BioScience* v67 no7 p664 Jl 2017

UP IN SMOKE Z. LOFTUS-FARREN *Earth Island Journal* v32 no4 p44 Wint 2017

Clearinghouses (Banking)

The Ways Americans Pay for Things Are Woefully Out of Date J. Lampe *Harvard Business Review Digital Articles* p2 O 14 2015

ClearWater Inc.

FLOOR PLAN gallery color diag *Log Home Living* v34 no7 p44 S 2017

Cleary, Brian

Systematic mapping of functional enhancer–promoter connections with CRISPR interference bibl graph *Science* v354 no6313 p769 N 11 2016

Cleary, Daniel
It takes a village, actually S. DEZIEL color *Maclean's* p52 Je 2017

Cleary Gottlieb Steen & Hamilton LLP
We're accessing a whole new pool of talent *People Management* p18 N 2016

Cleaveland, Sarah
Driving improvements in emerging disease surveillance through locally relevant capacity strengthening color diag *Science* v357 no6347 p146 Jl 14 2017

Cleaver, Joanne
What to Do When a "Devil's Advocate" Tries to Derail Your Project *Harvard Business Review Digital Articles* p2 Ja 18 2016

Cleavers (Knives)—Evaluation
LEAVE IT TO CLEAVER color *Bon Appetit* v61 no12 p168 D 2016 /Jan2017

Clee, Nicholas
SHARJAH PUBLISHING CITY color *Publishers Weekly* v263 no43 p(Sp)4 O 24 2016

cleek, ryan
AGNOSTIC AGGRESSION color *Bike Magazine* v24 no1 p106 Ja/F 2017
BEATDOWN *Bike Magazine* v24 no3 p120 My 2017
Cannondale color *Bike Magazine* v24 no7 p108 S 2017
EVEN FLOW bw color *Bike Magazine* v24 no1 p94 Ja/F 2017
full service color *Bike Magazine* v24 no6 p126 Ag 2017
GET IN GEAR bw color *Bike Magazine* v24 no1 p122 Ja/F 2017
Niner RIP 9 color *Bike Magazine* v24 no6 p114 Ag 2017
old dog's tricks bw color *Bike Magazine* v24 no4 p42 Je 2017

Cleerline Technology Group LLC
The Future of Fiber C. Crowley color *Sound & Vision* v82 no1 p16 Ja 2017

Cleeves, Ann
The Crow Trap: A Vera Stanhope Mystery *Publishers Weekly* v263 no48 p46 N 28 2016

Cleft palate—Genetic aspects
LIP-READING C. Zuckerman color *National Geographic* v232 no3 p22 S 2017

CLEGG, RIVER
HONEST MUSEUM AUDIO TOUR cartoon *New Yorker* v92 no40 p32 D 5 2016
MILLION-DOLLAR SUBWAY FIXES cartoon *New Yorker* v93 no24 p29 Ag 21 2017

Clegg, Sonya M.
Precipitation drives global variation in natural selection bibl chart diag map *Science* v355 no6328 p959 Mr 3 2017

CLEHANE, DIANE
VICTORIA STARS JENNA COLEMAN AND RUFUS SEWELL *British Heritage Travel* v38 no1 p32 Ja/F 2017

Cleinge, Henri
interiors A. KLIMOSKI color *Architectural Record* v204 no12 p29 D 2016

Clem, Bachman Brown
#4: In a New York apartment, Bachman Brown Clem performs an about-face: The moldings and trim—not walls—are in gleaming blue, framing a neutral backdrop filled with antiques and treasures T. McKEOUGH color *House Beautiful* v159 no2 p108 Mr 2017

Clemence, Sara
The Esquire Travel Dossier 2017 color *Esquire* v166 no5 p42 D 2016/Ja 2017
FRESH DIRECT color *Conde Nast Traveler* v52 no9 p32 O 2017
THE SWEET SPOT TRIP cartoon color *Esquire* v167 no2 p39 Mr 2017

Clemency
After Life M. Rhodan color diag *Time* v188 no19 p38 N 7 2016
I PARDONED A CONVICT WHO KILLED AGAIN M. S. Singel color *America* v217 no3 p34 Ag 7 2017

Clemens, Austin
READ, WHITE AND BLUE: Which books do Americans take on vacation? Our analysis uncovered some surprises *Smithsonian* v48 no4 p14 Jl/Ag 2017

Clemens, Raymond
Secret Knowledge—or a Hoax? E. Duffy cartoon *New York Review of Books* v64 no7 p44 Ap 20 2017

Clemens, Roger, 1962-—Substance use
Leap Year T. Keith color diag *Sports Illustrated* v126 no2 p16 Ja 16 2017

Clemens, Telfar
Show of Strength R. WALDMAN cartoon color *Vogue* v207 no11 p226 N 2017

Clement, C. R.
Persistent effects of pre-Columbian plant domestication on Amazonian forest composition bibl chart graph map *Science* v355 no6328 p925 Mr 3 2017

Clement, Charles R.
Forest conservation: Humans' handprints bibl color *Science* v355 no6324 p466 F 3 2017

Clement, Jemaine, 1974-
LEGION C. Collis color *Entertainment Weekly* no1474/1475 p69 Jl 21-28 2017

Clement, Mark
A WORD FROM OUR SPONSORS *Cincinnati Magazine* v50 no8 p4 My 2017

Clemente, Deirdre
DRESSING DOWN *Saturday Evening Post* v289 no3 p80 My/Je 2017

Clementine
MEDITATE ON THE MANDARIN color *Prevention* v68 no12 p8 D 2016

Clementine, Benjamin
TRUE BLUES D. BLASBERG color *Vanity Fair* v59 no10 p125 O 2017

Clements, -Alan
The Best Remedy color *Tricycle: The Buddhist Review* v26 no2 p42 Wint 2016

Clements, Andrew, 1949-
Bookworms Anonymous L. BAYARD *New York Times Book Review* p27 Ag 27 2017

Clements, Mike
How to Make a... TELESCOPE J. NOBEL cartoon color *Popular Mechanics* v193 no7 p72 S 2016
How to Make a... TELESCOPE J. NOBEL color *Popular Mechanics* p72 S 2017

Clements, Ron
MOANA C. Chiarella color *Sound & Vision* v82 no6 p70 Jl/Ag 2017
MOANA M. Snetiker color *Entertainment Weekly* no1438 p44 N 4 2016

Clements, Ron—Interviews
MAKING WAVES WITH MOANA M. Snetiker color *Entertainment Weekly* no1442 p12 D 2 2016 Rebellious Special Issue

Clemmons, Zinzi
MOURNING GLORY N. DENNIS-BENN color *O, The Oprah Magazine* p84 Ag 2017

Clemons, Kiersey, 1993-
Clemons' Time color *InStyle* v24 no9 p221 S 2017
KIERSEY CLEMONS K. SMITH color *Vanity Fair* v59 no8 p41 Ag 2017
KIERSEY'S GUIDE TO Feeling Good color *InStyle* v24 no9 p232 S 2017

Clemson University—Sports
7 Clemson color *Sports Illustrated* v127 no5 p95 Ag 14 2017
CASE FOR ... CLEMSON B. Hamilton color *Sports Illustrated* v125 no19 p40 D 12 2016
LEARNING TO FLY [Cover story] B. Hamilton color *Sports Illustrated* v126 no2 p24 Ja 16 2017
Lightbox color *Time* v189 no4 p18 Ja 23 2017
LINE OF FIRE B. Hamilton color *Sports Illustrated* v126 no1 p36 Ja 9 2017
Week 7 color *Sports Illustrated* v127 no5 p70 Ag 14 2017

Clenfield, Jason
THE AGE OF BIG VET color *Bloomberg Businessweek* no4506 p48 Ja 9 2017
The Asian Jobs Ladder Is Broken *Bloomberg Businessweek* no4528 p58 Je 26 2017
Cashing In on the Fear Factor color *Bloomberg Businessweek* no4495 p35 O 17 2016
Changes On Tap for Japan's Beer Tax color *Bloomberg Businessweek* no4513 p29 Mr 6 2017
The Curse Of Zombie Inc color *Bloomberg Businessweek* no4519

p16 Ap 24 2017

How to Lose $6 Billion color graph *Bloomberg Businessweek* no4512 p19 F 20 2017

Japan's Furniture King Caters to the Plebes color *Bloomberg Businessweek* no4526 p19 Je 12 2017

Japan's Priests Turn to Property Development color *Bloomberg Businessweek* no4521 p38 My 8 2017

Why Japan's Idemitsu Isn't Feeling Blue color *Bloomberg Businessweek* no4520 p34 My 1 2017

Clerestories (Architecture)

NEW CENTURY FOR A WRIGHT ROOF S. Jordan color *Old House Journal* v45 no3 p31 My 2017

Clergy

See also
Bishops
Cardinals
Child sexual abuse by clergy
Confidential communications—Clergy
Missionaries
Monks
Nuns
Priests
Spouses of clergy
Women clergy

BEYOND UNBELIEF M. OPPENHEIMER *New York Times Magazine* p42 Ja 1 2017

CALVARY CHAPEL GOES GLOBAL K. SHELLNUTT cartoon *Christianity Today* p15 Mr 2017

How do I respond when ICE comes for my flock? R. P. Roden color *America* v216 no10 p38 My 1 2017

Lonelier Than Thou K. STILLER color *Walrus* v14 no8 p66 O 2017

The ministry of convening D. R. Nelson *Christian Century* v134 no20 p12 S 27 2017

'M' Is for Mysterious Marks B. RADFORD *Skeptical Inquirer* v40 no6 p30 N/D 2017

The pastors I worry about M. C. Barnes *Christian Century* v134 no1 p35 Ja 4 2017

Clergy conferences

Post-traumatic ministry [Cover story] L. Kraus, D. Holyan et al color *Christian Century* v134 no7 p22 Mr 29 2017

Clergy—Appointment, call, & election

Discerning Desire A. HEYER color *America* v216 no1 p30 Ja 2 2017

Clergy—Attitudes

How Small Churches Make Disciples chart *Christianity Today* v61 no7 p17 S 2017

Clergy—Crimes against

Muslim clerics disappearing near Kenya-Somalia border F. Nzwili *Christian Century* v134 no1 p13 Ja 4 2017

Clergy—Employment

Pay gap for women clergy is decreasing D. Briggs color *Christian Century* v134 no18 p12 Ag 30 2017

Clergy—Interviews

REV. R. TONY RICARD F. DAWSON color *New Orleans Magazine* v51 no2 p30 D 2016

We Need More Odd Couples R. Clark color *Christianity Today* v60 no8 p83 O 2016

Clergy—Office

PUTTING PASTORS TO PASTURE S. OGUNTOLA cartoon *Christianity Today* p15 Ap 2017

Clergy—Political activity

Hundreds of clergy gather in North Dakota to back people blocking pipeline G. Brekke color *Christian Century* v133 no25 p13 D 7 2016

Clergy—Psychology

Blurring the lines L. G. Irwin color *Christian Century* v134 no3 p20 F 2017

Clergy—Public relations

Pastor resists extremism in Nigeria C. Kennel-Shank *Christian Century* v134 no14 p14 Jl 5 2017

Clergy—Relocation

Six & Six F. Nonomen color *Commonweal* v144 no10 p6 Je 2 2017

Clergy—Salaries, etc.

HOW TO GOVERN YOUR CHURCH EFFECTIVELY color

graph *Christianity Today* v60 no8 p22 O 2016

Clergy—Services for

Pastor resists extremism in Nigeria C. Kennel-Shank *Christian Century* v134 no14 p14 Jl 5 2017

Clergy—United States

I've Got Mail J. V. LAST color *Weekly Standard* v22 no22 p5 F 13 2017

Life in a fishbowl: Survey reveals stresses and joys of pastors' spouses A. M. Banks color *Christian Century* v134 no22 p18 O 25 2017

Survey reveals public's skepticism about pastors E. M. Miller *Christian Century* v134 no5 p13 Mr 1 2017

Clerkenwell (London, England)

Peel Back the Centuries in Smithfield and Clerkenwell *British Heritage Travel* v38 no4 p26 Jl/Ag 2017

Clerks

Attention, office workers! color *Health* v31 no9 p10 N 2017

'For £750,000 Per Dear, I'll Call Anyone Sir' S. AKAM color *Bloomberg Businessweek* no4524 p48 My 29 2017

Clerks—United States

Anna Valencia E. KANG color *Chicago* v66 no6 p89 Je 2017

Clery, Daniel

As Hawaii deliberates, giant telescope considers new home color *Science* v354 no6309 p156 O 14 2016

Astrophysics missions vie for NASA money color *Science* v357 no6352 p634 Ag 18 2017

European gravitational wave detector falters color *Science* v355 no6326 p673 F 17 2017

The exoplanet next door color *Science* v354 no6319 p1518 D 23 2016

FAST AND CURIOUS color map *Science* v356 no6337 p476 My 5 2017

Global telescope gears up to image black holes color map *Science* v355 no6328 p893 Mr 3 2017

Hubble uses galactic lens to study universe's first stars color *Science* v354 no6316 p1087 D 2 2016

Hurricane damage threatens Arecibo's future color *Science* v357 no6358 p1336 S 29 2017

Mars lander crash adds to 2020 rover worries color *Science* v354 no6311 p397 O 28 2016

NSF says: Out with the old telescopes, in with the new chart color *Science* v354 no6313 p693 N 11 2016

Private fusion machines aim to beat massive global effort chart color *Science* v356 no6336 p360 Ap 28 2017

Rosetta ends 2-year comet mission with final descent bw *Science* v353 no6307 p1482 S 30 2016

Survey finds galaxy clumps stirred up by dark energy color *Science* v357 no6351 p537 Ag 11 2017

Treaty tested by space miners color *Science* v357 no6359 p19 O 6 2017

U.S. observers seek a more perfect union chart color *Science* v355 no6324 p442 F 3 2017

XPrize finalists mull payloads to the moon color diag *Science* v354 no6319 p1510 D 23 2016

Your self-driving car could kill radio astronomy color *Science* v355 no6322 p232 Ja 20 2017

Clesse, Sébastien

BLACK HOLES from the Beginning of Time color graph *Scientific American* v317 no1 p38 Jl 2017

Cleveland (Miss.)

REUNION E. RIOS color *Mother Jones* v42 no6 p6 N/D 2017

Cleveland (Ohio)—History—20th century

A CITY ON FIRE M. Bechtel color *Sports Illustrated* v126 no14 p86 My 15-22 2017

Cleveland (Ohio)—Politics & government

Ian Leahy, Director of Urban Forests Programs *American Forests* v123 no1 p8 Wint/Spr 2017

Cleveland, David A.

Prioritizing good diets bibl color *Science* v354 no6318 p1385 D 16 2016

Cleveland Browns (Football team)

4 Cleveland Browns color *Sports Illustrated* v127 no7 p73 S 4 2017

Dawg Pounded J. Dickey and T. Keith color *Sports Illustrated* v125 no17 p22 N 21 2016 Double Issue

Cleveland Browns (Football team)—History—20th century

BROWN POWER M. Bechtel and J. Feldman color *Sports Illustrated* v126 no11 p62 Ap 17-24 2017

Cleveland Cavaliers (Basketball team)

1 Cavaliers A. Sharp, B. Golliver et al color *Sports Illustrated* v125 no14 p72 O 24-31 2016

FO' BETTER OR FO' WORSE? [Cover story] L. Jenkins color *Sports Illustrated* v126 no16 p34 Je 5 2017

HOT | NOT T. Keith and R. Demak color *Sports Illustrated* v126 no7 p23 Mr 6 2017

Leading Off color *Sports Illustrated* v125 no20 p10 D 19 2016

Leading Off color *Sports Illustrated* v126 no12 p6 My 1 2017

The Stopper L. Jenkins color *Sports Illustrated* v125 no14 p64 O 24-31 2016

This Old House E. Laase and T. Keith color *Sports Illustrated* v127 no6 p16 Ag 28 2017

Cleveland Cavaliers (Basketball team)—History—21st century

1 CAVALIERS color *Sports Illustrated* v127 no12 p56 O 16 2017

Cleveland Clinic Foundation

14 DELOS "TOBY" COSGROVE C. Leaf color *Fortune* v174 no7 p88 D 1 2016

Building Confidence M. LAMSTER *Architectural Record* v205 no7 p114 Jl 2017

Why Cleveland Clinic Shares Its Outcomes Data with the World M. W. Kattan *Harvard Business Review Digital Articles* p2 S 22 2015

Cleveland Indians (Baseball team)

1 INDIANS color *Sports Illustrated* v126 no9 p82 Mr 27 2017

4 A QUEST CALLED TRIBE J. Dickey color *Sports Illustrated* v126 no9 p46 Mr 27 2017

For the Record color *Time* v190 no13 p10 O 2 2017

PEAK CONCERN M. Bechtel and T. Keith color *Sports Illustrated* v127 no9 p12 S 25 2017

SEVENTH SONS T. Verducci color *Sports Illustrated* v127 no10 p40 O 2 2017

Streak Show M. Rosenberg color *Sports Illustrated* v127 no9 p56 S 25 2017

Cleveland Indians (Baseball team)—History

Pieces of a Dream B. Reiter color *Sports Illustrated* v125 no16 p33 N 14 2016

Cleveland Park (Washington, D C.)—Economic conditions

WHAT'S EATING CLEVELAND PARK? Explaining an upscale neighborhood's restaurant die-off J. SIDMAN *Washingtonian Magazine* v52 no11 p20 Ag 2017

CLEVENGER, BRENDA

The Question *O, The Oprah Magazine* p12 Mr 2017

Clevenger, Tony

IN SEARCH OF THE WOLVERINE F. LOS color map *Canadian Geographic* v136 no6 p46 D 2016

Clevers, Hans

Human tissues in a dish: The research and ethical implications of organoid technology diag *Science* v355 no6322 p260 Ja 20 2017

Lineage-dependent spatial and functional organization of the mammalian enteric nervous system color graph *Science* v356 no6339 p722 My 19 2017

THE ORGANOID ARCHITECT G. Sinha color *Science* v357 no6353 p746 Ag 25 2017

Origins of lymphatic and distant metastases in human colorectal cancer diag graph *Science* v357 no6346 p55 Jl 7 2017

Cliburn, Van, 1934-2013

Van Cliburn, To Russia With Love T. TEACHOUT *Commentary* v142 no3 p50 O 2016

Clichés

It Was a Dark and Stormy Night ... color *Weekly Standard* v22 no40 p2 Je 26 2017

SLEUTHING FOR CLICHÉS bw color *Reader's Digest* v190 no1133 p124 S 2017

Click, Melissa

Campus Chaos K. C. Johnson *Commentary* v142 no1 p15 Jl/Ag 2016

Click chemistry

Click chemistry enables preclinical evaluation of targeted epigenetic therapies Chan, A. Hienzsch et al diag *Science* v356 no6345 p1397 Je 30 2017

RESEARCH color *Science* v356 no6345 p1346 Je 30 2017

ClickSeed LLC

Building His Audience J. Hyatt color *Money* v45 no11 p27 D 2016

Client relations

See also

Investment advisor-client relationships

A Consultant's Guide to Firing a Client D. Clark *Harvard Business Review Digital Articles* p2 Ja 26 2015

How to Handle Losing a Major Client K. Firestone *Harvard Business Review Digital Articles* p2 Ja 27 2015

Run B2B Sales on Data, Not Hunches R. Markey *Harvard Business Review Digital Articles* p2 S 12 2016

Why Our Trust in Banks Hasn't Been Restored D. De Cremer *Harvard Business Review Digital Articles* p2 Mr 3 2015

Client satisfaction

MR. KNOW-IT-ALL J. MOOALLEM cartoon *Wired* v25 no6 p22 Je 2017

Clients

IN DEFENSE OF LAWYERS: The widely held belief that lawyers are untrustworthy and unprincipled is dead wrong L. Tesser *Saturday Evening Post* v289 no5 p12 S/O 2017

Cliff, Nigel

Keyboard Diplomacy J. BARRON bw *New York Times Book Review* p23 S 25 2016

Cliff diving—Competitions

LEGAL FOR A DAY J. LUCAS color *Climbing* no350 p64 D 2016/Ja 2017

Cliffe, Sarah

The Board View: Directors Must Balance All Interests color *Harvard Business Review* v95 no3 p64 My/Je 2017

The CEO View: Defending a Good Company from Bad Investors color *Harvard Business Review* v95 no3 p61 My/Je 2017

Google's Alphabet Move Is Reorganizing 101 *Harvard Business Review Digital Articles* p2 Ag 13 2015

"Leadership Qualities" vs. Competence: Which Matters More? *Harvard Business Review Digital Articles* p2 N 5 2015

A Partial Defense of Our Obsession with Short-Term Earnings *Harvard Business Review Digital Articles* p2 My 7 2015

Reflecting on David Garvin's Imprint on Management *Harvard Business Review Digital Articles* p2 My 18 2017

What Climate Change Means for Business Before and After Paris *Harvard Business Review Digital Articles* p2 D 15 2015

Clifford, Nicholas

Open & Shut color *Commonweal* v144 no5 p32 Mr 10 2017

CLIFFORD, STEPHANIE

A SHOT TO THE HEART cartoon *New Yorker* v92 no34 p26 O 24 2016

Clifford, Steven

BREAKING THE CEO PAY CYCLE R. Lowenstein diag *Fortune* v175 no6 p58 My 1 2017

Cliffs

"Cliff Camping": The Latest Bucket-List Tick J. FLASHMAN color *Climbing* no355 p16 Ag 2017

RIMCOUNTRY E. H. Peplow Jr. *Arizona Highways* v92 no7 p16 Jl 2016

Where the Waves Meet the Rock A. BURR color *Climbing* no354 p46 Jl 2017

Clift, Eleanor—Interviews

SUFFRAGE SHIFT N. TAPPAN bw color *American History* v52 no3 p14 Ag 2017

Clifton, Scott

THE BOLD AND THE BEAUTIFUL M. LOGAN *TV Guide* v65 no13 p44 Mr 20 2017

Climate change

See also

Effect of climate on biodiversity

Effect of climate on wildlife resources

Radiative forcing

515" L. Anthony color *Powder* p66 S 2017

Adrift Upon the Open Sea *Earth Island Journal* v32 no3 p5 Aut 2017

Apocalypse Hound J. LILEKS *National Review* v69 no16 p37 Ag 28 2017

As Oceans Rise, Insurers Flee B. Kowitt, P. Wahba et al color *Fortune* v176 no2 p18 Ag 1 2017

THE AUTHOR RESPONDS img *New York* v50 no15 p7 Jl 24 2017

BUILDING A SMALL-SCALE FARMING REVOLUTION J. W. J. BOYD *Nation* v305 no11 p17 O 30 2017

Burning Down the House P. J. Williams diag il *Nation* v305 no1 p12 Jl 3 2017

Can America's Blue States Tackle Climate Change on Their Own? J. Eyer and M. E. Kahn color *Harvard Business Review Digital Articles* p2 Je 6 2017

Changing climate shifts timing of European floods G. Blöschl, J. Hall et al color graph *Science* v357 no6351 p588 Ag 11 2017

China can lead on climate change C. Wang and F. Wang color *Science* v357 no6353 p764 Ag 25 2017

CLIMATE CHANGE: IN FOCUS color *National Geographic* v231 no5 p2 My 2017

Climate Change Is Changing the Face of Outdoor Recreation R. J. Dolesh *Parks & Recreation* v52 no10 p30 O 2017

Climate Change, Parks and Health R. J. Dolesh *Parks & Recreation* v52 no6 p30 Je 2017

Climate Change Poses a Threat to Our Oceans I. Lövin *UN Chronicle* v54 no1/2 p1 2017

Climate change scenarios and risks M. J. Gerver *Physics Today* v70 no9 p11 S 2017

Climate engineering J. APT *Issues in Science & Technology* v33 no4 p5 Summ 2017

Climate Justice Marchers Bring the Heat J. COMER color *Progressive* v81 no5 p12 Je/Jl 2017

A climate policy pathway for near- and long-term benefits D. Shindell, N. Borgford-Parnell et al color *Science* v356 no6337 p493 My 5 2017

Climate Trauma color *Earth Island Journal* v32 no2 p4 Summ 2017

Consensual Tools C. De Robertis color *Weekly Standard* v22 no32 p2 My 1 2017

THE DELUGE J. Mooallem *New York Times Magazine* p36 Ap 23 2017

Discord: Can states and cities really uphold the Paris climate accord on their own? N. Delgadillo color *Governing* v30 no11 p20 Ag 2017

Does Silicon Valley Still Care About Climate Change? W. Frick *Harvard Business Review Digital Articles* p2 My 30 2017

Evolution, climate change, and extreme events P. R. Grant color *Science* v357 no6350 p451 Ag 4 2017

exit, pursued by bear K. Pierre-Louis cartoon *Popular Science* v289 no4 p83 Jl/Ag 2017

Exposed M. B. Griggs color *Popular Science* v289 no4 p70 Jl/Ag 2017

From abalone to advocacy A. R. Frederick color *Science* v357 no6349 p422 Jl 28 2017

THE FUTURE OF FOOD [Cover story] Z. Carpenter color *Nation* v305 no11 p14 O 30 2017

Getting Back to the Basics: Museum Collections and Satellite Imagery Are Critical to Analyzing Species Diversity N. U. DE LA SANCHA, S. A. BOYLE et al *BioScience* v67 no5 p405 My 2017

Global climatic drivers of leaf size [Cover story] I. J. Wright, N. Dong et al graph *Science* v357 no6354 p917 S 1 2017

Greenbelt Earns Its Cooperative Stripes A. N. IFATEYO *In These Times* v41 no8 p8 Ag 2017

Hot and bothered about climate color *Science* v356 no6337 p468 My 5 2017

HOT ZONES J. Benko *New York Times Magazine* p54 Ap 23 2017

If You Think Fighting Climate Change Will Be Expensive, Calculate the Cost of Letting It Happen D. Disparte *Harvard Business Review Digital Articles* p2 Je 12 2017

Inclusion Is the Solution G. MULLINS-COHEN *Parks & Recreation* v52 no10 p10 O 2017

'It's been raining! In the High Arctic!' C. WILKINS color map *Canadian Geographic* v137 no4 p62 Jl/Ag 2017

Jerry BROWN D. EGGERS color *Vanity Fair* v59 no8 p76 Ag 2017

The Life and Death of Pando C. KETCHAM color graph map *Discover* v38 no10 p24 D 2017

Life in the Balance C. Solomon chart color map *National Geographic* v231 no6 p52 Je 2017

Life on the Edge G. Raygorodetsky bw color graph map *National Geographic* v232 no4 p108 O 2017

Lifetime experience #19 A. White color *Canadian Geographic* v137 no4 p11 Jl/Ag 2017

The limits of carbon reduction roadmaps J. Urpelainen *Science*

v356 no6342 p1019 Je 9 2017

LOST AT SEA D. L. Dixson color *Scientific American* v316 no6 p42 Je 2017

Measuring the changing pulse of rivers L. J. Slater and R. L. Wilby color *Science* v357 no6351 p552 Ag 11 2017

The Multitrophic Effects of Climate Change and Glacier Retreat in Mountain Rivers S. C. FELL, J. L. CARRIVICK et al *BioScience* v67 no10 p897 O 2017

No Time for Rubbernecking K. FINNERAN *Issues in Science & Technology* v33 no4 p19 Summ 2017

Out of Paris color *National Review* v69 no12 p12 Je 26 2017

PARODY color *Weekly Standard* v22 no39 p44 Je 19 2017

Protecting Small Island Developing States from Pollution and the Effects of Climate Change A. Sareer *UN Chronicle* v54 no1/2 p1 2017

Protecting the Coral Sea-the Cradle to the Great Barrier Reef A. Pedder *UN Chronicle* v54 no1/2 p1 2017

Research News color *Canadian Wildlife* v23 no4 p11 S/O 2017

The Road to Hakha K. PIERRE-LOUIS *Sierra* v102 no5 p64 St/O 2017

The Roots of Science Denial K. Hayhoe and J. Schwartz color *Scientific American* v317 no4 p66 O 2017

Russia heightens defenses against climate change A. Davydova color *Science* v357 no6357 p1221 S 22 2017

Satellites reveal contrasting responses of regional climate to the widespread greening of Earth G. Forzieri, R. Alkama et al diag *Science* v356 no6343 p1180 Je 16 2017

Science in litigation, the third branch of U.S. climate policy S. McCormick, S. J. Simmens et al graph *Science* v357 no6355 p979 S 8 2017

The Science Police: On highly charged issues, such as climate change and endangered species, peer review literature and public discourse are aggressively patrolled by self-appointed sheriffs in the scientific community K. KLOOR *Issues in Science & Technology* v33 no4 p78 Summ 2017

Seeing Silver Linings *Mother Earth News* no282 p5 Je/Jl 2017

Skiing for science D. T. Blumstein cartoon *Science* v356 no6334 p214 Ap 14 2017

States of Denial M. SHAER color map *New Republic* v248 no11 p16 N 2017

Sulfur injections for a cooler planet U. Niemeier and S. Tilmes color graph *Science* v357 no6348 p246 Jl 21 2017

Surprisingly Ordinary Allergy Triggers A. NUÑEZ and L. GELMAN color *Reader's Digest* v189 no1129 p54 Ap 2017

Think Healthy Across the Board G. Mullins-Cohen *Parks & Recreation* v52 no6 p10 Je 2017

This Is What Climate Change Sounds Like K. Stock color *Bloomberg Businessweek* no4535 p20 Ag 28 2017

To fight climate change, we need to improve capitalism, not get rid of it P. Kellner *America* v216 no11 p10 My 15 2017

Toward a Responsible Solar Geoengineering Research Program D. W. KEITH *Issues in Science & Technology* v33 no3 p71 Spr 2017

AN UNCERTAIN FUTURE K. Siber *National Parks* v91 no4 p36 Fall 2017

AN UNLIKELY OPTIMIST color *National Geographic* v232 no1 p10 Jl 2017

Unmask temporal trade-offs in climate policy debates I. B. Ocko, S. P. Hamburg et al color *Science* v356 no6337 p492 My 5 2017

Vietnam's Urgent Task: Adapting to Climate Change P. MCELWEE *Current History* v116 no791 p223 S 2017

Weather Front M. Branom map *Weatherwise* v70 no4 p6 Jl/Ag 2017

weather front M. Branom *Weatherwise* v70 no5 p6 S/O 2017

What Counts as Climate Consensus? D. Sylvan, P. Howard et al *National Review* v69 no11 p2 Je 12 2017

WHAT SEA RISE? C. Solomon color *National Geographic* v231 no5 p158 My 2017

What's the Deal? S. Mirsky color *Scientific American* v317 no2 p82 Ag 2017

Why carbon capture is not enough J. LOVERING and A. TREMBATH *Issues in Science & Technology* v33 no4 p12 Summ 2017

Why the Revolution Will Not (but Must) Be Televised J. Naureckas *Extra!* v30 no7 p1 S 2017

Without Apology E. Alterman *Nation* v305 no9 p10 O 16 2017

Yeah, THE WEATHER Has Been WEIRD K. Hayhoe color *For-*

eign Policy no224 p40 My/Je 2017

Climate change & economics

Estimating economic damage from climate change in the United States S. Hsiang, R. Kopp et al color graph *Science* v356 no6345 p1362 Je 30 2017

What's the damage from climate change? W. A. Pizer *Science* v356 no6345 p1330 Je 30 2017

Climate change & health

Climate Change: We Are What We Eat *USA Today Magazine* v145 no2865 p4 Je 2017

THIS COULD HAPPEN IN YOUR HOMETOWN J. Schwartz, T. Middleton et al bw color *Women's Health* v14 no7 p88 S 2017

Climate change & politics

Cooling-Off Period J. Pasztor *MIT Technology Review* v120 no3 p10 My/Je 2017

Dam Politics: The drought is over, but don't expect Sacramento to take any meaningful action to avert the next water crisis. That well is still bone dry V. D. Hanson *Hoover Digest: Research & Opinion on Public Policy* no3 p83 Summ 2017

Discord: Can states and cities really uphold the Paris climate accord on their own? N. Delgadillo color *Governing* v30 no11 p20 Ag 2017

How Climate Change Became a Political Issue J. Worland *Time* v190 no6 p25 Ag 7 2017

Lean In to Climate Change G. MCCARTHY color *Foreign Policy* no224 p76 My/Je 2017

THE Timely DISAPPEARANCE of CLIMATE CHANGE DENIAL IN CHINA G. Dembicki color *Foreign Policy* no224 p58 My/Je 2017

WORTH NOTING K. A. GAJEWSKI *Humanist* v77 no5 p48 S/O 2017

Climate change insurance

How the Insurance Industry Can Push Us to Prepare for Climate Change M. E. Kahn, B. Casey et al *Harvard Business Review Digital Articles* p2 Ag 28 2017

Climate change mitigation

Climate Change Adaptation and Traditional Cultures in Northern Russia S. CRATE *Current History* v116 no792 p277 O 2017

Climate change research cut as Canada focuses on mitigation: Barring a reversal, government-academia research networks will lapse and facilities in the high Arctic will shut down T. Feder *Physics Today* v70 no9 p28 S 2017

A Climate Hawk Among the Deniers Z. Mider color *Bloomberg Businessweek* no4498 p70 N 7 2016

DIRTY POWER PLAN D. SLATER *Sierra* v101 no5 p36 S/O 2016

Enemy of Humanity M. HERTSGAARD *Nation* v305 no1 p10 Jl 3 2017

GO WEST TO SEE THE FUTURE OF GREEN BUILDINGS K. Tam Wu color *Maclean's* v129 no50 p39 D 19 2016

The incredible shrinking nuclear offset to climate change S. Squassoni bibl *Bulletin of the Atomic Scientists* v73 no1 p17 Ja 2017

Invite annoys French scientists *Science* v356 no6343 p1104 Je 16 2017

Making SDGs Work for Climate Change Hotspots S. Szabo, R. J. Nicholls et al bibl *Environment* v58 no6 p24 N/D 2016

Up to Speed: Two Months, One Page P. Rauber *Sierra* v101 no4 p26 Jl/Ag 2016

USING ENERGY EFFICIENTLY IN THE FIGHT AGAINST CLIMATE CHANGE J. Carr color *Maclean's* v129 no50 p38 D 19 2016

Climate change mitigation—Government policy

WORTH NOTING K. A. GAJEWSKI *Humanist* v77 no5 p48 S/O 2017

Climate change mitigation—International cooperation

Is the Oil and Gas Industry Serious About Climate Action? M. S. Bach bibl chart color graph *Environment* v59 no2 p4 Mr/Ap 2017

Making Paris Work S. Herz bibl color map *Environment* v59 no2 p29 Mr/Ap 2017

Putting the Paris Agreement to the Test T. O'Riordan and A. McGowan *Environment* v59 no2 p2 Mr/Ap 2017

Climate change prevention

See also

Prevention of global warming

Inconvenient Math? On climate change, the uncertainties multiply--literally M. S. Bernstam *Hoover Digest: Research & Opinion on Public Policy* no2 p133 Spr 2017

Climate change research

The Arctic Environment in the Age of Man R. A. Virginia color *Wilson Quarterly* p1 Summ 2017

Cooling-Off Period J. Pasztor *MIT Technology Review* v120 no3 p10 My/Je 2017

SO, WHAT DO YOU BELIEVE? N. DRAKE *USA Today Magazine* v146 no2868 p72 S 2017

Climate Change Science Program (U.S.)

SO, WHAT DO YOU BELIEVE? N. DRAKE *USA Today Magazine* v146 no2868 p72 S 2017

Climate change skepticism

AAAS Leshner Fellows help confront climate impacts M. Jarvis color *Science* v353 no6307 p1508 S 30 2016

Climate Denialism Kills M. HERTSGAARD *Nation* v305 no7 p3 S 25 2017

GOSPEL OF THE CLIMATE DENIERS A. Kroll cartoon color *Rolling Stone* no1274 p24 N 17 2016

Stay Out of Scientists' E-mails K. Cowtan and Z. Hausfather *Scientific American* v316 no4 p12 Ap 2017

Climate change—Management

MANAGING CLIMATE CHANGE: LESSONS FROM THE U.S. NAVY F. L. REINHARDT and M. W. TOFFEL chart color il img *Harvard Business Review* v95 no4 p102 Jl/Ag 2017

Climatic changes

See also

Biodiversity—Climatic factors

The 10 Most Important Sustainable Business Stories from 2014 A. Winston *Harvard Business Review Digital Articles* p2 D 19 2014

Alaska's Big Problem With Warmer Winters C. Flavelle color *Bloomberg Businessweek* no4514 p26 Mr 13 2017

The Apostate A. COOPER *Sierra* v101 no6 p34 N/D 2016

Artifact exposure J. BENNETT color *Canadian Geographic* v137 no1 p31 F 2017

The broad footprint of climate change from genes to biomes to people B. R. Scheffers, L. De Meester et al bibl chart color *Science* v354 no6313 paaf7671-1 N 11 2016

Business Is Taking Action on LGBT Rights. Will Climate Change Be Next? A. Winston *Harvard Business Review Digital Articles* p2 My 9 2016

The case for American nuclear leadership D. B. Poneman *Bulletin of the Atomic Scientists* v73 no1 p44 Ja 2017

Civil Society and Environmental Change in Brazil's Cerrado D. Sawyer and M. Lahsen bibl *Environment* v58 no6 p16 N/D 2016

Climate Change cartoon color graph map *National Geographic* v231 no4 p30 Ap 2017

Climate change: The 2015 Paris Agreement thresholds and Mediterranean basin ecosystems J. Guiot and W. Cramer bibl *Science* v354 no6311 p465 O 28 2016

The Climate Movement Needs More Corporate Lobbyists S. Whitehouse *Harvard Business Review Digital Articles* p2 F 25 2016

Climate Wars Heat Up R. A. Epstein *Hoover Digest: Research & Opinion on Public Policy* no4 p150 Fall 2016

Coal and Climate Change in Kentucky T. Cole color *Progressive* v81 no2 p16 F 2017

A Conservative Takes on Climate Change S. F. Hayward color *Weekly Standard* v22 no29 p22 Ap 3 2017

Corporations Will Never Solve Climate Change N. Oreskes and A. Schendler *Harvard Business Review Digital Articles* p2 D 4 2015

Corrigendum *Bulletin of the Atomic Scientists* v73 no2 p144 Mr 2017

Could His Hip-Hop Save the Earth? C. GRISE and J. Shotz *Scholastic Choices* v32 no6 p22 Mr 2017

The Data Says Climate Change Could Cost Investors Trillions A. Winston *Harvard Business Review Digital Articles* p2 Ap 14 2016

The Day Warming Began D. FOX bw cartoon color *Discover* v27 no10 p54 D 2016

Defending the Earth from Donald Trump D. Helvarg cartoon *Progressive* v81 no2 p21 F 2017

DRY AS DEATH P. Edmonds color *National Geographic* v231

Trump's Irreversible Threat il *Nation* v303 no23/24 p3 D 5 2016

Why Republicans Are Embracing Climate Change J. Worland color *Time* v189 no11 p23 Mr 27 2017

Climatic changes—Prevention

3 Ways to Incorporate Sustainability into Everyday Work M. W. Lamach *Harvard Business Review Digital Articles* p2 O 1 2015

Doing something on climate *Christian Century* v134 no4 p7 F 15 2017

Editor's Letter M. Hansche color *Rodale's Organic Life* v3 no1 p10 Ja 2017

Climatic changes—Prevention—Congresses

Dealing with details in Marrakesh P. Espinosa color *Science* v354 no6311 p393 O 28 2016

Climatic changes—Prevention—Economic aspects

Movers K. Stock bw cartoon color *Bloomberg Businessweek* no4516 p11 Mr 27 2017

Climatic changes—Prevention—International cooperation

6 Ways the North American Clean Economy Agreement Will Affect Business A. Winston *Harvard Business Review Digital Articles* p2 Jl 6 2016

Dealing with details in Marrakesh P. Espinosa color *Science* v354 no6311 p393 O 28 2016

Making climate science more relevant C. F. Kennel, S. Briggs et al bibl color *Science* v354 no6311 p421 O 28 2016

Climatic changes—Research

Biodiversity redistribution under climate change: Impacts on ecosystems and human well-being G. T. Pecl, M. B. Araújo et al color *Science* v355 no6332 p1389 Mr 31 2017

Climate adaptation funding: Getting the money to those who need it M. Mostafa, M. F. Rahman et al bibl *Bulletin of the Atomic Scientists* v72 no6 p396 N 2016

Climate Knows no Ideology *Parks & Recreation* v52 no3 p12 Mr 2017

Coral - Current Connections A. Alpert color *Oceanus* v51 no2 p48 Wint 2016

Climatic changes—Social aspects

THE GHOSTS OF KANGEQ H. HARMSEN color *Archaeology* v70 no3 p55 My/Je 2017

OFF-TARGET M. KLARE and P. A. DUR *Foreign Affairs* v95 no6 p196 N/D 2016

Trusting the Climate: Catastrophe Vs. Stability N. Stehr and A. Machin graph *Society* v53 no6 p573 D 2016

Who's The Denier Now? O. CASS color *National Review* v69 no8 p23 My 2017

Climatologists—Interviews

WILL WE MISS OUR LAST CHANCE? J. Goodell bw color *Rolling Stone* no1278/1279 p28 Ja 12 2017

Climatology

See also

Atmospheric pressure

Climate change

Global warming

Seasons

China's Moment L. Billings graph *Scientific American* v317 no4 p72 O 2017

Climate-data rescue efforts gear up T. Feder *Physics Today* v70 no3 p31 Mr 2017

Requiring Companies to Disclose Climate Risks Helps Everyone M. E. Kahn *Harvard Business Review Digital Articles* p2 F 16 2017

Science in litigation, the third branch of U.S. climate policy S. McCormick, S. J. Simmens et al graph *Science* v357 no6355 p979 S 8 2017

Time to codify scientific integrity P. D. Tonko *Science* v356 no6344 p1241 Je 23 2017

Time to March M. BRUNE *Sierra* v102 no2 p7 Mr/Ap 2017

The Weather and Climate of Nebraska: The Heartland of Extremes K. Dewey and H. M. Mogil bw chart color diag graph map *Weatherwise* v70 no4 p12 Jl/Ag 2017

Climatology—Government policy

Identifying the policy space for climate loss and damage R. Mechler and T. Schinko bibl color diag *Science* v354 no6310 p290 O 21 2016

Climbing gyms

Scary (and true) tales from a crag near you Brandon and Spencer *Climbing* no353 p21 My/Je 2017

Climbing gyms—Evaluation

Welcome to Sendhaus™: America's Hippest New Climbing Gym K. CORRIGAN color *Climbing* no355 p38 Ag 2017

Climbing knots

THE DESCENT A. BURR color *Climbing* no353 p80 My/Je 2017

The LSD Lower R. COPPOLILLO and M. CHAUVIN color *Climbing* no353 p50 My/Je 2017

Climeworks AG

Christoph Gebald and Jan Wurzbacher B. Parkin cartoon *Bloomberg Businessweek* no4537 p76 S 11 2017

Giant machine to suck CO2 from the air color *Science* v356 no6342 p990 Je 9 2017

Clinciu, Daniel L.

Human health color *Science* v356 no6338 p590 My 12 2017

CLINE, ANDREW

Founding Rocker bw *National Review* v69 no7 p24 Ap 17 2017

Modern Medicis *Weekly Standard* v22 no34 p18 My 15 2017

Cline, Emma

David SALLE *Interview* v46 no9 p110 N 2016

Emma Cline M. Rich color *Current Biography* v78 no8 p17 Ag 2017

No. 7 THE GIRLS L. Greenblatt color *Entertainment Weekly* no1444/1445 p106 D 16 2016

NORTH EAST REGIONAL cartoon *New Yorker* v93 no8 p58 Ap 10 2017

Cline, Eric H., 1960-

Digging Into the Future *American Scholar* v86 no3 p12 Summ 2017

Three Stones Make a Wall: The Story of Archaeology V. H. Pennanen *Christian Century* v134 no14 p40 Jl 5 2017

Clines, Peter

Paradox Bound color *Publishers Weekly* v264 no33 p55 Ag 14 2017

Clinger, John

More on 'WhySkepticism?' *Skeptical Inquirer* v41 no4 p63 Jl/Ag 2017

Clinical drug trials

6 ways to stay on your medication plan *Harvard Health Letter* v42 no5 p7 Mr 2017

Avoiding winter heart attacks *Harvard Health Letter* v41 no12 p3 O 2016

HUMAN-FREE HUMAN TRIALS S. PALUS color *Popular Science* v288 no6 p32 N/D 2016

Should you take a drug holiday? *Harvard Health Letter* v42 no1 p1 N 2016

Clinical psychologists—Interviews

The Trauma of Saving Animals R. Nuwer color *Scientific American* v316 no2 p20 F 2017

Clinical trials

Cancer Breakthroughs Can Happen Anywhere - Including Your Community *Texas Monthly* v44 no11 p74 N 2016

Failed spinal cord trial offers cautionary tale K. Servick color *Science* v355 no6326 p679 F 17 2017

Mending a Broken Heart D. Fine Maron color *Scientific American* v317 no2 p19 Ag 2017

A RARE SUCCESS AGAINST ALZHEIMER'S [Cover story] M. Kivipelto and K. Håkansson color graph *Scientific American* v316 no4 p32 Ap 2017

Clinical trials—Government policy

NIH redefines clinical trials, attracting critics J. Kaiser color *Science* v357 no6348 p236 Jl 21 2017

Clinical trials—Management

Improving vaccine trials in infectious disease emergencies M. Lipsitch and N. Eyal graph *Science* v357 no6347 p153 Jl 14 2017

Clinics

See also

Family planning services

Is Your Doc Getting It Wrong? K. Mickle bw color *Glamour* v115 no9 p116 S 2017

MBODY—MODERN BODY CONTOURING & LASER CENTER *Washingtonian Magazine* v53 no1 p112 O 2017

A Shot In the Arm M. Quinn *Governing* v30 no3 p18 D 2016

Clinics—Evaluation

SPECIALTY MEDICINE color *New Orleans Magazine* v51 no5 p131 Mr 2017

O 24 2016

Hillary Milhous Clinton J. PODHORETZ *Commentary* v142 no2 p1 S 2016

Hillary Opens the Overton Window P. Glastris *Washington Monthly* p2 N/D 2016

HILLARYS FOR PRESIDENT! J. HITT il *New Republic* v247 no11 p18 N 2016

Hillary's Second Amendment Nonsense C. C. W. COOKE color *National Review* v68 no21 p20 N 21 2016

Hillary Takes Your Questions [Cover story] bw color *Glamour* v114 no11 p172 N 2016

A Hill Too Steeped in Lies T. ROSENWASSER *USA Today Magazine* v145 no2862 p25 Mr 2017

How Do Young Women Feel About Hillary Clinton? [Cover story] H. Kelly *Glamour* v114 no11 p174 N 2016

How Hillary Became 'Hillary' R. Draper *New York Times Magazine* p46 O 16 2016

How She Lost P. Elliott, S. Frizell et al color *Time* v188 no21 p58 N 21 2016

HOW TRUMP DID IT J. SALAMON *Texas Monthly* v45 no1 p52 Ja 2017

I Came Here for an Argument G. NORMAN color *Weekly Standard* v22 no16 p16 D 26 2016

In Chicago, Librarians Get Their Mojo Back A. Albanese color *Publishers Weekly* v264 no27 p4 Jl 3 2017

It's Election Time Are You Ready? C. Leive color *Glamour* v114 no11 p30 N 2016

It Still Takes a Village R. A. Fox color *Commonweal* v143 no17 p14 O 21 2016

James Comey's Dereliction [Cover story] A. C. McCARTHY color *National Review* v68 no19 p21 O 24 2016

KEEPING IT 100 S. MEHTA color *Vanity Fair* v58 no11 p42 N 2016

Lessons from an Election G. NORMAN map *Weekly Standard* v22 no13 p15 D 5 2016

Liberal Think Tank Freaks Out *Weekly Standard* v22 no8 p3 O 31 2016

The Long View R. LONG *National Review* v68 no21 p38 N 21 2016

Maine M. Paterniti *New York Times Magazine* p36 N 20 2016

MATCHUP color *Vanity Fair* v58 no11 p58 N 2016

Men Behaving Badly K. Pollitt color *Nation* v33 no21 p10 N 21 2016

Minnesota C. Homans *New York Times Magazine* p46 N 20 2016

Ms. letter E. Smeal and K. Spillar *Ms.* v26 no3 p2 Fall 2016

No Coattails for Hillary? K. A. HASSETT *National Review* v68 no20 p8 N 7 2016

Noisy Desperation H. WILHELM *National Review* v69 no9 p44 My 15 2017

None of the Above C. GRAIZBORD *Commentary* v142 no5 p6 D 2016

THE NOT–SO–CRAZY CASE AGAINST CLINTON S. GILMORE color *Maclean's* v129 no44 p36 N 7 2016

November Surprise color *Esquire* v166 no4 p46 N 2016

OCTOBER SURPRISES A. Davidson cartoon *New Yorker* v92 no36 p15 N 7 2016

The Old Electoral College Try J. COST color *Weekly Standard* v22 no12 p18 N 28 2016

PARODIES BY THE NUMBERS *Washingtonian Magazine* v53 no1 p76 O 2017

PARODY *Weekly Standard* v22 no48 p44 S 4 2017

Pledging Allegiance E. Felten color *Weekly Standard* v22 no33 p16 My 8 2017

The Redistribution Fallacy: The federal government knows how to support a welfare state. It does not know how to transfer money from the rich to the poor J. Piereson *Commentary* v140 no2 p27 S 2015

SANCTIMONY CITIES C. Caldwell *Claremont Review of Books* v17 no1 p25 Wint 2016/2017

Science in the Elections color *Scientific American* v315 no5 p22 N 2016

Secret History C. Homans *New York Times Magazine* p17 O 2 2016

Shattered R. Traister img *New York* v49 no23 p28 N 14 2016

The Shelter of Mother's Little Helper color *Weekly Standard* v23 no3 p2 S 25 2017

She Runs WE WIN R. SCHREIBER *Ms.* v27 no1 p28 Spr 2017

The Soap Opera Comes to an End N. EMERY color *Weekly Standard* v22 no20 p23 Ja 30 2017

STATES VS. TRUMP J. Cobb cartoon *New Yorker* v92 no39 p31 N 28 2016

STILL HERE D. REMNICK cartoon color *New Yorker* v93 no29 p58 S 25 2017

Tearing Up N. EMERY color *Weekly Standard* v22 no12 p11 N 28 2016

That's Dr. Clinton, to MSVU K. BREEN color *Maclean's* v129 no44 p48 N 7 2016

THAT'S WHAT HE SAID M. Talbot cartoon *New Yorker* v92 no34 p19 O 24 2016

Their Town M. Dowd *New York Times Magazine* p30 N 6 2016

THERE'S NO OTHER DONALD TRUMP. THIS IS IT *Vital Speeches of the Day* v82 no10 p299 O 2016

THERE'S ONLY ONE PRESIDENT CLINTON A. ABEL color *Maclean's* v129 no45 p36 N 14 2016

They Weren't with Her *Commentary* v141 no10 p1 D 2016

They Weren't with Her C. ROSEN *Commentary* v142 no5 p4 D 2016

THIS LOSS HURTS, BUT PLEASE NEVER STOP BELIEVING THAT FIGHTING FOR WHAT'S RIGHT IS WORTH IT H. CLINTON *Vital Speeches of the Day* v83 no1 p4 Ja 2017

The Thread J. Browder *New York Times Magazine* p12 N 20 2016

To the Bitchhouse *Commentary* v141 no9 p1 N 2016

To the Bitchhouse *Commentary* v142 no4 p1 N 2016

Tragical Herstory Tour color *Weekly Standard* v23 no1 p2 S 11 2017

TRUMP IS STILL STANDING BUT DOES IT MATTER? S. GILMORE color *Maclean's* v129 no42 p43 O 24 2016

Trump Theory S. KLEIN *Commentary* v142 no1 p8 Jl/Ag 2016

Trump Wins [Cover story] R. ZISSOU and P. SMITH *New York Times Upfront* v149 no5 p6 N 21 2016

Two Clintons Too Many *American Conservative* v15 no6 p58 N/D 2016

THE UNCONNECTED G. PACKER cartoon color *New Yorker* v92 no35 p48 O 31 2016

Value-Free Politics J. CARR color *America* v215 no14 p12 N 7 2016

Virginia Slim: The Race Tightens F. BARNES *Weekly Standard* v22 no4 p9 O 3 2016

WE ARE THE INDISPENSABLE NATION *Vital Speeches of the Day* v82 no10 p291 O 2016

What Hillary Clinton's Insiders Know That Voters Don't–Yet S. Frizell and P. Elliott color *Time* v188 no18 p14 O 31 2016

WHAT'S WRONG WITH THE DEMOCRATS? F. FOER color *Atlantic* v320 no1 p48 Jl/Ag 2017

When a Cough Is Not Just a Cough M. CONTINETTI *Commentary* v142 no3 p56 O 2016

Where Do We Go From Here? B. D. SWEANY *Texas Monthly* v44 no12 p26 D 2016

Which Candidate Will Better Exploit the Irrational Fear of Terrorism? A. Johnson *Extra!* v29 no9 p3 N 2016

WHO THEY REALLY ARE *Reader's Digest* v188 no1125 p102 N 2016

Why Hillary Failed N. EMERY bw color *Weekly Standard* v23 no4 p30 O 2 2017

Why I'm For Hillary Clinton [Cover story] V. KIM *New York Times Upfront* v149 no4 p12 O 31 2016

Why Stephen Bannon Doesn't Scare Washington Anymore A. Altman and P. Elliott color *Time* v190 no12 p11 S 25 2017

Will They Roll the Dice with Him? E. EPSTEIN color *Weekly Standard* v22 no9 p15 N 7 2016

WILL WE BE LEFT BEHIND, OR WILL WE CONTINUE TO LEAD THE WAY? *Vital Speeches of the Day* v83 no6 p176 Je 2017

THE WOMAN WHO MIGHT HAVE BEEN PRESIDENT S. J. DOUGLAS *In These Times* v40 no12 p44 D 2016

The year of the 'nasty woman' A. KINGSTON color *Maclean's* v129 no48/49 p73 D 5 2016

YOU DIDN'T CREATE THESE CIRCUMSTANCES BUT YOU HAVE THE POWER TO CHANGE THEM H. R. CLINTON *Vital Speeches of the Day* v83 no7 p202 Jl 2017

Clinton, Hillary Rodham, 1947——Health

CLINTON'S SICK DAYS A. Davidson cartoon *New Yorker* v92

no30 p21 S 26 2016

Clinton, Hillary Rodham, 1947—-Political & social views

The Debate Stage Reveals Character, Preparation and the Candidate Who Is Still a Child J. Klein color *Time* v188 no14 p28 O 10 2016

Don't Blame the Message P. TERZIAN color *Weekly Standard* v22 no16 p14 D 26 2016

For the Record color *Time* v188 no14 p6 O 10 2016

Hillary Clinton's Acceptance Speech *Congressional Digest* v95 no8 p4 O 2016

TALE OF THE TAPE: CLINTON VS. TRUMP T. Newmyer color *Fortune* v174 no6 p79 N 1 2016

A Tale of Two Tax Plans E. Barone color diag *Time* v188 no16/17 p37 O 24 2016

The Ultimate Insider Who Could Still Change the Game In the Oval Office J. Klein color *Time* v188 no19 p24 N 7 2016

The Unionista L. SAND il *National Review* v68 no19 p33 O 24 2016

Why the Russian Hacks of Hillary Clinton's Campaign Should Reassure Us All J. Klein color *Time* v188 no16/17 p18 O 24 2016

CLINTON, KATE

The American Bardo *Progressive* v81 no6 p67 Ag/S 2017

Chris Hayes's Book for the Times *Progressive* v81 no5 p67 Je/Jl 2017

The Eagle Has Landed color *Progressive* v81 no4 p67 Ap/My 2017

Eleanor to Hillary: Just Do It cartoon *Progressive* v81 no10 p43 N 2016

In the Darkroom/Backlash: The Undeclared War Against American Women/Stiffed: The Betrayal of the American Man... color *Progressive* p61 D 2016/Ja 2017

I Renounce Hair Trump *Progressive* v81 no2 p44 F 2017

A Life in the Family color *Progressive* v81 no7 p67 O/N 2017

CLIQUET, A. N.

International Wildlife Law: Understanding and Enhancing Its Role in Conservation *BioScience* v67 no9 p784 S 2017

Clive Song (Poem)

CLIVE SONG A. Carson *New Yorker* v93 no23 p54 Ag 7 2017

Cloaking devices

What Would Happen? C. BOYER cartoon color *National Geographic Kids* no473 p6 S 2017

Cloaks—Evaluation

DOPE STUFF ON MY DESK J. Wilson color *Essence* v48 no5 p34 S 2017

Clock & watch makers

BOSTON F. MAROUKIAN bw color *Popular Mechanics* p26 Je 2017

TIME OUT G. SHTEYNGART cartoon *New Yorker* v93 no5 p36 Mr 20 2017

Clock & watch making

The Second Time Around R. NAAS color *Forbes* v199 no6 p106 Je 13 2017

Time Crunch color *Esquire* v166 no5 p58 D 2016/Ja 2017

Clock & watch sales & prices

Case Study: Competing Against Bling S. NASON, J. SALVACRUZ et al il *Harvard Business Review* v95 no3 p155 My/Je 2017

The Imperial Rolex M. SOLOMON color *Forbes* v199 no5 p34 My 16 2017

Time Machines And War Machines A. BROWN color *Forbes* v199 no6 p20 Je 13 2017

Clock & watch stores

WANNA BUY A WATCH? S. Watson color *Esquire* p46 Je/Jl 2017

Clocks & watches

See also

Wrist watches

ABOUT FACE color *Harper's Bazaar* no3648 p164 N 2016

BREGUET 18K ROSE GOLD color *Magazine Antiques* v183 no6 p57 N/D 2016

THE CARTIER TANK AT 100 M. SOLOMON bw color *Forbes* v200 no4 p20 O 24 2017

The New Vows of Wedding Style J. MOORE and B. HANSEN-BUNDY color *GQ: Gentlemen's Quarterly* v97 no6 p23 Je 2017

The Tick List J. Sens and J. Passov color *Golf Magazine* v59 no3

p108 Mr 2017

Time Bandits J. BOTTUM color *Weekly Standard* v22 no30 p5 Ap 10 2017

a timely Idea *Saturday Evening Post* v289 no5 p26 S/O 2017

Clocks & watches—Congresses

ZADOK JEWELERS SWISS WATCH AFFAIR *Texas Monthly* v45 no3 p81 Mr 2017

Clocks & watches—Equipment & supplies

The Anatomy of the Watch color *Esquire* p135 BigBlackBook

Clocks & watches—Evaluation

ALTITUDE ADJUSTMENT S. Watson color *Esquire* p29 Ag 2017

BEST BETS img *New York* v50 no10 p68 My 15 2017

BUILT TO LAST color *Esquire* v166 no4 p128 N 2016

Can a gadget make you skinny? A. Sweeney color *Redbook* p26 Ap 2017

hitting the BIG TIME N. SULLIVAN bw color *Esquire* p38 2017 BigBlackBook

Hold, PLEASE *Interview* v47 no6 p32 Ag 2017

HOLIDAY OUTFITS color *InStyle* v23 no13 p143 D 2016

Look, No Hands! *Indianapolis Monthly* v40 no5 p23 Ja 2017

Market: SUPER 70S color *Vanity Fair* v59 no9 p118 S 2017

MOTHERLY LOVE color *Martha Stewart Living* p48 My 2017

MUSEUM GIFT GUIDE *Los Angeles Magazine* p89 D 2016

ONES TO WATCH color *Harper's Bazaar* no3652 p141 Ap 2017

ORANGE CRUSH *Cincinnati Magazine* v50 no12 p34 S 2017

Time Crunch color *Esquire* v166 no5 p58 D 2016/Ja 2017

TIMELESS bw color *Vanity Fair* v58 no11 p78 N 2016

TRISTAN 'MACK' WILDS T. Payne and L. CROSS color *Ebony* v72 no4 p34 F 2017

THE UPGRADE color *Conde Nast Traveler* v51 no10 p44 N 2016

Weight Watches color *InStyle* v24 no4 p122 Ap 2017

Clocks & watches—Exhibitions

Once Upon A Time bw color *Architectural Digest* v74 no7 p24 Jl 2017

Clockwork (Music)

VICTOR GOULD J. Murph color *Downbeat* v83 no12 p20 D 2016

Clockwork Orange, A (Theatrical production)

THE THEATRE *New Yorker* v93 no29 p14 S 25 2017

Clogs—Evaluation

BEST IN SHOE E. ELWICK-BATES color *Vogue* v207 no1 p106 Ja 2017

CLOKE, SUSAN

The Naked Man at the Door: City ordinances seek to protect hotel workers from sexual harassment and assault *Ms.* v27 no3 p11 Fall 2017

Clomburg, James M.

Industrial biomanufacturing: The future of chemical production bibl chart color diag graph *Science* v355 no6320 p1 Ja 6 2017

Clonazepam

Diagnosis L. Sanders *New York Times Magazine* p20 Je 11 2017

Cloning

Horse DNA Trading A. Popescu color *Bloomberg Businessweek* no4534 p20 Ag 14 2017

Retracing embryological fate S. Behjati bibl diag *Science* v354 no6316 p1109-B D 2 2016

Clonts, Chris

GARAGE chart color diag *Motor Trend* v69 no10 p102 O 2017

GARAGE chart color diag *Motor Trend* v69 no8 p96 Ag 2017

SOLVING A PROBLEMATIC LINEUP chart color *Motor Trend* v69 no3 p74 Mr 2017

VOLKSWAGEN GOES UPMARKET chart color *Motor Trend* v69 no9 p96 S 2017

Clooney, Amal, 1978-

DON'T LET ISIS GET AWAY WITH GENOCIDE *Vital Speeches of the Day* v83 no5 p160 My 2017

Milestones *Time* v189 no23 p15 Je 19 2017

Clooney, George, 1961-

Quotable Quotes color *Reader's Digest* v190 no1133 p140 S 2017

SUBURBICON C. Collis color *Entertainment Weekly* no1478 / 1479 p51 Ag 18-25 2017

CLOOS, KASSONDRA

Pack Ice Cream il *Backpacker* p30 Je 2017

Clorox Co.

Must-Buys M. Santos color *Working Mother* v40 no4 p16 O/N

2017

Clos, Joan

Habitat III Is the Citizens' Conference of the United Nations *UN Chronicle* v53 no3 p9 2016

Close, Chuck, 1940-

People Watching S. COCHRAN color *Architectural Digest* v74 no3 p146 Mr 2017

Underground Art J. Gardner color *Weekly Standard* v22 no24 p39 F 27 2017

Close, Frank

Goodnight, Sun W. HERBERT color *Weekly Standard* v22 no36 p30 My 29 2017

Close, Glenn, 1947-

92 MINUTES WITH ... Glenn Close C. SWANSON img *New York* p16 F 20 2017

Dancing with the Stars S. Gold color *Dance Magazine* v91 no3 p20 Mr 2017

Glenn Close on the Meaning of Alex D. Coggan color *Entertainment Weekly* no1484 p44 S 29 2017

MAD ABOUT THE BOY H. ALS cartoon *New Yorker* v93 no2 p76 F 27 2017

READY FOR HER CLOSE-UP AGAIN C. Collis color *Entertainment Weekly* no1451/1452 p34 F 3-10 2017

Close, Kerry

ASK THE EXPERT diag *Money* v45 no10 p31 N 2016

Get Your House in Shape This Winter color *Money* v46 no1 p32 Ja/F 2017

HOME PRICES RETURN TO PRE-CRASH LEVELS color *Money* v46 no1 p21 Ja/F 2017

STORE CARDS POSE CREDIT HAZARDS color *Money* v45 no11 p14 D 2016

WHY BUYING A FIXER-UPPER MIGHT NOT BE WORTH IT color *Money* v45 no10 p21 N 2016

Why Spending Dipped on Black Friday color *Time* v188 no24 p18 D 12 2016

YOUR 20 BEST MONEY MOVES FOR 2017 color diag *Money* v45 no11 p60 D 2016

CLOSE, SARAH L.

Long-Term Studies Contribute Disproportionately to Ecology and Policy *BioScience* v67 no3 p271 Mr 2017

Closed loop systems

A Body Computer to Manage Insulin L. PANDELL color *AARP: The Magazine* v30 no6A p32 O/N 2017

Closeness (Film)

Blood Ties N. Rapold color *Film Comment* v53 no4 p8 Jl/Ag 2017

Closet doors

From Our Editor S. Donelson color *House Beautiful* v159 no2 p4 Mr 2017

Closing the River No Name (Short story)

CROSSING THE RIVER NO NAME W. MACKIN bw *New Yorker* v93 no16 p55 Je 5 2017

Closing the sale

7 Reasons Salespeople Don't Close the Deal S. W. Martin *Harvard Business Review Digital Articles* p2 Ag 2 2017

Closser, Kristina D.

Femtosecond x-ray spectroscopy of an electrocyclic ring-opening reaction diag graph *Science* v356 no6333 p54 Ap 7 2017

Clostridia

Neonatal acquisition of Clostridia species protects against colonization by bacterial pathogens Kim, K. Sakamoto et al diag *Science* v356 no6335 p315 Ap 21 2017

Clostridium botulinum

Botulism L. Bonner color *Equus* no481 p31 O 2017

Clostridium difficile

Nourishing Your Microbiota *Tufts University Health & Nutrition Letter* v35 no3 p4 My 2017

TRUST YOUR GUT [Cover story] R. EBERSOLE cartoon *Prevention* v69 no9 p60 O 2017

Clostridium disease treatment

Edible CRISPR Could Precisely Target Dangerous Germs E. Mullin color *MIT Technology Review* v120 no4 p23 Jl/Ag 2017

Clostridium diseases—Risk factors

C. difficile *Mayo Clinic Health Letter* v35 no5 p6 My 2017

Clothes closets

The $55,000 Closet S. HOLLAND MURPHY *D: The Magazine of Dallas* v43 no10 p66 O 2016

DESIGN DILEMMA: My Home Has Tiny Closets. How Do I Store My Stuff? C. KENT and T. STRINGER color *Chicago* v66 no9 p89 S 2017

Hey, Jenna! F. Kane, S. P. Nadella et al color *Glamour* v115 no3 p92 Mr 2017

I Love My Dressing Room J. ADLER color *House Beautiful* v159 no2 p128 Mr 2017

Clothes closets—Design & construction

CLOSETS J. BREWSTER color *Cabin Living* p40 Ja/F 2017

Clothes closets—Evaluation

Alexa's New Gig K. Branch color *Glamour* v115 no7 p21 Jl 2017

Clothes dryers

Energy-Saving $avings S. FRANKE color *Good Housekeeping* v264 no4 p87 Ap 2017

Clothes dryers—Evaluation

Dynamic Duos K. Janeway chart color graph *Consumer Reports* v82 no8 p12 Ag 2017

Clothing & dress

See also

Belts (Clothing)

Burial clothing

Business attire

Coats

Costume

Custom-made clothing

Dresses

Fashion accessories

Footwear

Fur garments

Gloves

Headgear

Islamic clothing & dress

Jackets

Leggings

Men's clothing

Pants

Pet clothing & dress

Petite clothing

Ponchos

Scarves

Shoulder straps

Sleepwear

Sport clothes

Sweaters

Underwear

Uniforms

Vintage clothing

Women's clothing

5 ways to be fearless in color color *Redbook* p55a S 2017

8 COOL COATS THAT'LL KEEP YOU WARM O. J. WILLIAMS color *Ebony* v72/73 no12/1 p40 O/N 2017

Adam's STYLE SHEET color *O, The Oprah Magazine* p66 N 2017

AGE BEFORE BEAUTY G. Sheehy color *Harper's Bazaar* no3652 p155 Ap 2017

AMERICAN DREAMING: Take a sophisticated approach to patriotic fashion E. STUART *Virginia Living* v15 no4 p37 Je 2017

...And this is what our judges say bw color *Redbook* p67 S 2017

ask REDBOOK color *Redbook* p20 Ap 2017

BACK to BLACK *Interview* v47 no1 p33 F 2017

Best Dress E. Wilson color *InStyle* v23 no12 p61 N 2016

THE BIG TEN J. FIELDEN color *Esquire* p32 BigBlackBook

Black & White, Amirite? color *Glamour* v115 no5 p196 My 2017

Boxes for Everyone! K. Cicero color *Parents* v92 no9 p148 S 2017

The Business of Casual color *InStyle* v24 no4 p100 Ap 2017

Celeb Labels You'll Love R. S. Frazier color *Health* v30 no10 p48 D 2016

CHIC STREET L. TUDOR color *New Orleans Magazine* v51 no12 p84 O 2017

COME FOR THE SHOES, STAY FOR THE CLOTHES color *Esquire* p50 O 2017

Cozy & Cruelty-Free A. Piper color *Vegetarian Times* v43 no2 p15 N/D 2016

COZY UP TO THIS R. DOLGIN *Martha Stewart Living* no268 p48 O 2016

The CROWN *Interview* v47 no6 p45 Ag 2017

DEBATE *Scholastic Choices* v32 no8 p4 My 2017

DENIM'S Besties color *Seventeen* v76 no5 p28 S 2017

Doesn't Look Fake color *Women's Health* v14 no1 p70 Ja/F 2017

DOES YOUR Style MATCH YOUR Soul? color *O, The Oprah Magazine* p116 Mr 2017

Downright Cool K. Shapiro color *Health* v30 no9 p37 N 2016

Earthly Delights *Los Angeles Magazine* p37 Mr 2017

Electric Brights S. FRISCIA *Dance Magazine* v91 no8 p38 Ag 2017

Fitness Fashion *Parents* v91 no9 p124 S 2016

Fix That Beauty Oops H. Dawsey color *Health* v30 no10 p29 D 2016

Folk TALES color *Vogue* v206 no11 p258 N 2016

GAME-CHANGING GIFTS L. Desantis, R. S. Frazier et al color *Health* v30 no10 p116 D 2016

The Grand Essentials *D: The Magazine of Dallas* v43 no10 p64 O 2016

GREAT BEFORE, GREATER AFTER! A. K. LAIRD *Women's Health* v14 no1 p12 Ja/F 2017

GREAT BUYS: UNDER $100 color *O, The Oprah Magazine* p64 N 2017

have a better morning G. O'CONNOR *Parents* v91 no9 p86 S 2016

Hello! L. Brown color *InStyle* v24 no2 p12 F 2017

Hey, Jenna! F. Kane, S. P. Nadella et al color *Glamour* v115 no3 p92 Mr 2017

Hey, Jenna! J. Lyons color *Glamour* v115 no2 p42 F 2017

if you ask me... S. JAMES bw color *Parents* v92 no8 p106 Ag 2017

I Love My Dressing Room J. ADLER color *House Beautiful* v159 no2 p128 Mr 2017

THE IN CROWD color *Seventeen* v76 no5 p92 S 2017

The Innovation Issue M. Bean color *Men's Health* v32 no7 p4 S 2017

The INTERNATIONAL BEST-DRESSED List color *Vanity Fair* v59 no10 p97 O 2017

In This Issue *Vogue* v206 no11 p262 N 2016

Is It OK to Buy Cheap Clothes? *Scholastic Choices* v32 no8 p2 My 2017

Italian Styling, Japanese Engineering color *Esquire* v167 no1 p42 F 2017

Jamie Does Juicy L. Chan color *Glamour* v115 no9 p76 S 2017

Learn to Layer R. S. Frazier color *Health* v31 no2 p54 Mr 2017

Left Behind J. SALTZ img *New York* v49 no23 p76 N 14 2016

Look Good Half Naked D. MICHEL color *Men's Health* v32 no6 p80 Ag 2017

The Magic of Michelle color *Glamour* v115 no1 p100 Ja 2017

Maintain your layers R. WICHELNS diag il *Backpacker* p46 O 2017

MAJOR LEAGUE STYLE *Atlanta* v56 no11 p104 Mr 2017

Mating M. A. GREEN, L. LARSON et al bw color *GQ: Gentlemen's Quarterly* v86 no11 p58 N 2016

Mom Wins & Fails color *Working Mother* v40 no4 p7 O/N 2017

THE MOST FLATTERING SWIMSUITS of 2017 R. S. Frazier and K. Shapiro color *Health* v31 no4 p34 My 2017

My Collection color *Horse & Rider* v56 no8 p104 Ag 2017

My Stuff JENNIFER FISHER color *Vanity Fair* v59 no8 p42 Ag 2017

my style color *InStyle* v24 no11 p108 N 2017

Natalie Portman HER BEST EVER E. Wilson color *InStyle* v24 no6 p50 Je 2017

New Shape, New Style [Cover story] G. Monahan color *Women's Health* v14 no1 p65 Ja/F 2017

Nostalgia for Now img *New York* v50 no7 p49 Ap 3 2017

THE OFFICE *Interview* v46 no9 p98 N 2016

Our Favorite Designer Collections (as Worn by Our Favorite Human Collections) J. MOORE bw color *GQ: Gentlemen's Quarterly* v97 no11 p33 N 2017

OUT SIDE THE BOX: THESE NINE TRENDSETTERS ARE STEPPING UP WASHINGTON STYLE WITH UNEXPECTED PAIRINGS, BOLD PRINTS, AND PERFECT TAILORING A. MOELLER *Washingtonian Magazine* v52 no12 p78 S 2017

Parallel LINES F. Noyes bw color *Esquire* p136 S 2017

Period Pieces *Parents* v91 no9 p16 S 2016

Pipe Up E. Wilson color *InStyle* v23 no12 p62 N 2016

QUIET STORM *Interview* v47 no6 p78 Ag 2017

The Real Reason I Work Out N. Blades, J. Dunn et al color *Health* v31 no2 p120 Mr 2017

RETHINK YOUR ... Shearling Coat color *InStyle* v23 no13 p148 D 2016

Running Skirts Rock! color *Health* v31 no4 p12 My 2017

The Secrets of Southern Comfort S. NYGAARD color *Men's Health* v32 no6 p73 Ag 2017

Shabby Chic J. EPSTEIN color *Weekly Standard* v23 no1 p5 S 11 2017

Sit in style E. Marglin color *Yoga Journal* no291 p24 My 2017

SOCK IT TO ME L. BAILEY *Indianapolis Monthly* v40 no3 p34 N 2016

Sole Survivor: How I found myself at the special store for special people with broken-down feet requiring special footwear D. Paul *Indianapolis Monthly* v12 no40 p192 Ag 2017

solutions color *Parents* v92 no6 p110 Je 2017

Space COWBOY *Interview* v46 no9 p50 N 2016

Start Your Day Strong L. Murray color *Health* v31 no2 p69 Mr 2017

Street APPEAL *Interview* v46 no9 p52 N 2016

STYLE AHOY! color *Seventeen* v75 no11 p27 N 2016

The Style Guy M. A. Green color *GQ: Gentlemen's Quarterly* v86 no11 p44 N 2016

Suit Up for Less J. Smith color *Health* v31 no1 p53 Ja 2017

SUPER Furry ANIMALS *Interview* v46 no9 p46 N 2016

SURPRISE ME *Vogue* v207 no11 p171 N 2017

SWEATER SONGS color *Vogue* v206 no11 p204 N 2016

Take Summer into Winter color *Esquire* v166 no5 p68 D 2016/Ja 2017

think inside the box *Parents* v91 no10 p68 O 2016

transition WITH STYLE color *Yoga Journal* no294 p18 S 2017

Trendspotting M. L. BIKOFF *Atlanta* v56 no11 p44 Mr 2017

WELCOME TO THE ISSUE color *Harper's Bazaar* no3656 p80 S 2017

What, This Old Thing? [Cover story] S. HOTCHKISS color *Esquire* p98 BigBlackBook

WORK *Interview* v47 no1 p91 F 2017

Your New Summer Uniform: The Doily Dress A. Edwards Walker color *Glamour* v114 no7 p35 Jl 2016

Clothing & dress—Alteration

Stitches in Time C. Kolb color *New Orleans Magazine* v51 no8 p40 Je 2017

Clothing & dress—Care

Winter Clothing-Care Guide *Good Housekeeping* v264 no3 p57 Mr 2017

Clothing & dress—Care—Equipment & supplies

Case closed L. BIRCH color *House Beautiful* p76 Ag 2017

Clothing & dress—Environmental aspects

Amour Vert *American Forests* v122 no3 p10 Fall 2016

Clothing & dress—Equipment & supplies

SHOCKER! color *Women's Health* v14 no2 p28 Mr 2017

Clothing & dress—Evaluation

5 reasons to wear more prints color *Redbook* p68 Mr 2017

Adam's STYLE SHEET Adam color *O, The Oprah Magazine* p43 Ja 2017

Back To Basics color *Glamour* v114 no11 p148 N 2016

BARE ESSENTIALS color *Indianapolis Monthly* p26 Ap 2017

BASE TURN ATTIRE color *Flying* v144 no8 p14 Ag 2017

Boring Gloves Get the Finger color *GQ: Gentlemen's Quarterly* v86 no11 p40 N 2016

Burn RUBBER *Interview* v47 no6 p28 Ag 2017

BUTTFESSIONS color *Women's Health* v14 no2 p62 Mr 2017

Changing the Game color *Glamour* v115 no2 p110 F 2017

CHECK THIS OUT S. Kennedy color *Bloomberg Businessweek* no4504 p64 D 19 2016

City Chic S. FRISCIA *Dance Magazine* v91 no6 p40 Je 2017

Coats? Check color *Glamour* v115 no11 p51 N 2017

DESERT FLOWERS color *Vogue* v207 no3 p492 Mr 2017

EVERY-SIZE STYLE color *Good Housekeeping* v264 no3 p18 Mr 2017

the FAB five J. ROTH color *Esquire* p64 2017 BigBlackBook

Fashion FORMULA OVERSIZE SWEATER + SLIP SKIRT color *InStyle* v23 no12 p130 N 2016

FASHION UNDER $100 color *Redbook* p55 Mr 2017

FIND YOUR PERFECT Skirt Suit & Faux-Fur Collar color *In-*

Private clubs
Riding clubs
Travel clubs
Women's societies & clubs
BACK TO Barbados H. Silva color diag *Conde Nast Traveler* v52 no1 p82 Ja 2017
Fasching Fosters Creativity J. Ephland color *Downbeat* v84 no2 p60 F 2017
fun img *New York* p78 Mr 6 2017
It Takes TWO M. SWANN bw color *Conde Nast Traveler* v52 no10 p114 N 2017
LET'S HAVE SUPPER S. Castle color *Southern Living* v52 no10 p96 O 2017
Nothing in Moderation B. Court color *Men's Health* v32 no7 p10 S 2017
Retreating Inside the Bubble *Commentary* v143 no4 p22 Ap 2017
That's Outrageous! *Reader's Digest* v189 no1128 p87 Mr 2017
THEY OWNED THE NIGHT M. THOMAS bw color *Chicago* v66 no11 p96 N 2017

Clubs—Evaluation
Blue Whale Nurtures Creativity K. Silsbee color *Downbeat* v84 no2 p51 F 2017
Rock 'n' Roll 'n' Romance at (le) Poisson Rouge K. Gottschalk color *Downbeat* v84 no2 p46 F 2017
WEST color *Downbeat* v84 no2 p58 F 2017

Clubs—Management
EAST color *Downbeat* v84 no2 p47 F 2017

Clubs—Social aspects
195 Clubs Where Music Thrives [Cover story] color *Downbeat* v84 no2 p45 F 2017

Cluess, Jessica
Jessica Cluess K. CENTORCELLI color *Publishers Weekly* v263 no52 p69 D 19 2016

Cluff, Priscilla
Wonderful Women of World *Arabian Horse World* v57 no9 p164 Je 2017

Clumsiness
TRAUMARAMA color *Seventeen* v76 no3 p108 My 2017

Cluster theory (Nuclear physics)
Versatile cluster entangled light H. J. Briegel bibl diag *Science* v354 no6311 p416 O 28 2016

Clutch bags—Evaluation
Christmas Clutches color *Good Housekeeping* v263 no6 p40 D 2016
CULTURE CLUB color *Harper's Bazaar* no3648 p134 N 2016
The Dress REPORT color *Harper's Bazaar* no3648 p175 N 2016
Dress Your Western Best color *Horse & Rider* v56 no11 p36 N 2017
Get Personal L. IMMEDIATO *Los Angeles Magazine* p29 F 2017
GET THE LOOK color *Seventeen* p66 Ja 1 2017
HOW TO WEAR IT... anywhere! K. SALADINO and L. BERGAMOTTO color *Good Housekeeping* v264 no5 p20 My 2017
THE LADY Laura Linney E. Wilson color *InStyle* v24 no4 p92 Ap 2017
on demand color *InStyle* v24 no9 p135 S 2017
PANTSUIT NATION color *Harper's Bazaar* no3654 p75 Je/Jl 2017
ROCK SOLID color *Vogue* v207 no4 p228 Ap 2017
SEW CUTE L. BAILEY *Indianapolis Monthly* p28 My 2017
Shop Guide color *O, The Oprah Magazine* p173 My 2017
So CLUTCH color *Seventeen* p54 Ja 1 2017
STRATEGIST img *New York* v50 no16 p87 Ag 7 2017
STYLE color *Horse & Rider* v55 no12 p20 D 2016
To Give And To Get color *Conde Nast Traveler* v51 no11 p29 D 2016
WILD THINGS S. Zlotnick *Washingtonian Magazine* v52 no1 p107 O 2016
THE WOMAN Naomie Harris E. Wilson color *InStyle* v24 no6 p54 Je 2017

Clutches (Machinery)
SLIPPED DISC J. Bryant color *Hot Rod* v70 no8 p84 Ag 2017

Clutter, Adriane—Interviews
Member Spotlight: Adriane Clutter V. Paynich *Parks & Recreation* v52 no4 p54 Ap 2017

Clutter Inc.
Hoarder Control K. CHAYKOWSKI, S. SHARF et al color

Forbes v200 no2 p42 S 5 2017

Clutterbuck, David
DAVID CLUTTERBUCK: HR must 'upcycle' outdated approaches to survive the future *People Management* p19 Je 2017

CLUTTERBUCK-COOK, HANNA
Fall from Grace bw *Publishers Weekly* v264 no31 p75 Jl 31 2017

CLYNES, TOM
A PIPELINE RUNS THROUGH IT *Audubon* v118 no6 p18 Wint 2016

Co-Operative Group Ltd.
"We don't talk a corporate language - neither should our colleagues": The Co-op is back from the brink of disaster, and its staff are re-energised thanks to a huge series of immersive road-shows *People Management* p22 Je 2017

Coach-athlete relationships
Is the Tough Trainer Worth It? J. Susser *Dressage Today* v23 no10 p18 Jl 2017

Coach Inc.
COACH'S DINO-MITE YEAR S. Cristobal color *Harper's Bazaar* no3649 p322 D 2016/Ja 2017
COACH THINKS OUTSIDE THE BAG P. Wahba color diag *Fortune* v175 no7 p80 Je 1 2017
COAST to Coach E. ELWICK-BATES color *Vogue* v207 no4 p134 Ap 2017
The High-Fashion Varsity Jacket J. MOORE color *GQ: Gentlemen's Quarterly* v97 no3 p59 Mr 2017

Coachella Valley Music & Arts Festival
The Chainsmokers J. Goodman color *Entertainment Weekly* no1444/1445 p29 D 16 2016
COACHELLA IS HELLA QUEER THIS YEAR D. GUERRERO color *Advocate* no1090 p51 Ap 2017
DESERT COOL J. Scatena chart color *Sunset* v238 no5 p26 My 2017
THE IMMACULATE LINEUP J. SEABROOK cartoon *New Yorker* v93 no9 p30 Ap 17 2017
KENDRICK & GAGA HEAT UP THE DESERT G. Hall color *Entertainment Weekly* no1463/1464 p106 Ap/My 2017

Coaches (Athletics)
See also
Golf coaches
Soccer coaches
Tennis coaches
GOOD LUCK, COACH *USA Today Magazine* v145 no2864 p74 My 2017
'I Love Watching You Play' S. ECKELBERRY *Parks & Recreation* v52 no5 p8 My 2017
THE OLD COLLEGE TRY C. FEHRMAN *Cincinnati Magazine* v50 no2 p17 N 2016
Understanding What You're Part Of A. Ashley color *Climbing* no353 p24 My/Je 2017

Coaches (Athletics)—Employment—Charts, diagrams, etc.
Rebounders T. Keith color diag *Sports Illustrated* v126 no1 p14 Ja 9 2017

Coaching (Athletics)
See also
Time outs (Sports)
How to Coach, According to 5 Great Sports Coaches S. G. Carmichael *Harvard Business Review Digital Articles* p2 F 25 2015
A PORTRAIT IN SPEED A. LUBBEN color *Climbing* no356 p72 S/O 2017

Coaching of employees
Mentor People Who Aren't Like You R. Farnell *Harvard Business Review Digital Articles* p2 Ap 17 2017
When Coaching Finds That an Executive Isn't in the Right Role B. Dattner and E. Wood *Harvard Business Review Digital Articles* p2 Jl 31 2017

COACHMAN WARD, ERIKA
Q: What adventure would you love to share with your best friend? color *O, The Oprah Magazine* p12 Ja 2017

Coacoochee, Seminole chief, b. ca. 1810
Spheres of Influence E. GRAHAM *American Scholar* v86 no2 p15 Spr 2017

Coakley, Jacob
AUTHENTIC for the festival *Stage Directions* v29 no10 p22 O 2016
Buyer's Guide *Stage Directions* v30 no1 p12 Ja 2017

Conversing with Colleges *Stage Directions* v29 no11 p29 N 2016

Exit, Pursued by a Bear *Stage Directions* v30 no2 p2 F 2017

Expanding to Improve *Stage Directions* v29 no10 p30 O 2016

Golden Age of Gear *Stage Directions* v29 no12 p2 D 2016

Illuminations Debuts Online *Stage Directions* v29 no10 p2 O 2016

LED ERS-Style Fixtures *Stage Directions* v30 no2 p8 F 2017

Paying My Dues *Stage Directions* v30 no1 p2 Ja 2017

See Clearly *Stage Directions* v29 no12 p20 D 2016

Show Offs *Stage Directions* v29 no12 p6 D 2016

The Show's the Thing *Stage Directions* v29 no11 p2 N 2016

The skills of scenic artists can take a design to the next level *Stage Directions* v30 no2 p16 F 2017

Coakley, Sarah, 1951-

Theology through prayer [Cover story] S. M. Brubaker color *Christian Century* v133 no24 p24 N 23 2016

Coal

Renewables Power Up color *Earth Island Journal* v32 no4 p7 Wint 2017

Coal & the environment

Cleaning up coal—cost-effectively R. F. Service color *Science* v356 no6340 p798 My 26 2017

Coal ash—Environmental aspects

State of Denial T. Korteti *Sierra* v101 no5 p22 S/O 2016

Coal Barons (Poem)

Coal Barons G. STERN *Progressive* v81 no2 p43 F 2017

Coal gasification

Negative Energy K. Wong *Sierra* v101 no6 p26 N/D 2016

Coal industry

The Future of Yesterday's Fuel B. H. Potts color *Weekly Standard* v22 no29 p14 Ap 3 2017

UNDERMINED E. GRISWOLD cartoon color *New Yorker* v93 no19 p48 Jl 3 2017

Coal industry—United States

'Clean Coal' Is Far From Clean cartoon *Bloomberg Businessweek* no4495 p8 O 17 2016

Footing the Bill D. Slater *Sierra* v101 no6 p22 N/D 2016

Reforming the U.S. coal leasing program K. Gillingham, J. Bushnell et al color graph *Science* v354 no6316 p1096 D 2 2016

Coal industry—Wyoming

THE GREAT DISCONNECT T. Wilkinson and W. Becktold *Sierra* v102 no1 p34 Ja/F 2017

Coal miners—Employment

Sorry, Coal: Solar Is Where the Jobs Are E. Fry color *Fortune* v175 no3 p12 Mr 1 2017

Coal miners—United States—Training of

What If All U.S. Coal Workers Were Retrained to Work in Solar? J. M. Pearce *Harvard Business Review Digital Articles* p2 Ag 8 2016

Coal mines & mining—Economic aspects

Saving Coal Country P. M. Barrett color graph *Bloomberg Businessweek* no4507 p46 Ja 16 2017

Coal mines & mining—Law & legislation

Stream Protection *Congressional Digest* v96 no3 p30 Mr 2017

Coal mines & mining—United States

Demise of stream rule won't revitalize coal industry W. Cornwall color *Science* v355 no6326 p674 F 17 2017

Coal mines & mining—West Virginia

Coal's Last Kick J. Worland color diag *Time* v189 no14 p38 Ap 17 2017

Saving Coal Country P. M. Barrett color graph *Bloomberg Businessweek* no4507 p46 Ja 16 2017

Coal sales & prices

In Coal Country, Signing Bonuses Are the Buzz T. Loh color graph *Bloomberg Businessweek* no4521 p28 My 8 2017

Coal transportation

Coal port terminal may reach its last stop color *National Wildlife (World Edition)* v55 no4 p48 Je/Jl 2017

Coalbed methane

Methane production from coal by a single methanogen Daisuke Mayumi, Hanako Mochimaru et al bibl graph *Science* v354 no6309 p222 O 14 2016

Coal—Canada

Up to Speed: Two Months, One Page P. Rauber *Sierra* v102 no2 p22 Mr/Ap 2017

Coalescence (Chemistry)

Quantitative 3D evolution of colloidal nanoparticle oxidation in

solution Y. Sun, X. Zuo et al diag graph *Science* v356 no6335 p303 Ap 21 2017

Coalitions

Inaugural Parade Regulations Constitutional Challenge J. C. Kozlowski *Parks & Recreation* v52 no1 p20 Ja 2017

Coal—Microbiology

A microbial route from coal to gas C. U. Welte bibl color *Science* v354 no6309 p184 O 14 2016

Coal miners—Salaries, wages, etc.

Scenes from the Front Lines F. F. PIVEN bw color *In These Times* v40 no11 p29 N 2016

Coan, Linda

KITCHEN-TESTED TIPS color *Vegetarian Today* no1 p4 F 2017

Coast defenses

Beat Back the Sea J. Worland color *Time* v189 no13 p41 Ap 10 2017

Coast live oak

Coast live oak *American Forests* v122 no3 p11 Fall 2016

Coast Mountains (B.C. & Alaska)

Coast Mountains of British Columbia—Wilderness of Sky and Ice E. Darack *Weatherwise* v70 no5 p8 S/O 2017

Coast redwood

Return of Giants Z. S. GEORGE color *Orion Magazine* v36 no1 p7 Ja/F 2017

Coastal plants

The Whole Earth Is Medicine W. JOHNSON color *Tricycle: The Buddhist Review* v27 no1 p29 Fall 2017

Coastal surveillance

"A MASS RESCUE OPERATION" *Smithsonian* v48 no4 p68 Jl/Ag 2017

BOARDING PASS G. MANSFIELD *Sea Magazine* v109 no4 p46 Ap 2017

Coastal zone management

THE FIRST LINE OF DEFENSE J. NOBEL color *Audubon* v119 no3 p30 Fall 2017

COASTER, EDWIN JOHN

The COASTER CORRESPONDENCE bw *Vanity Fair* v59 no10 p87 O 2017

Coastline changes

How high will the seas rise? M. Oppenheimer and R. B. Alley bibl color graph *Science* v354 no6318 p1375 D 16 2016

Coaston, Jane

High Horses *New York Times Magazine* p9 Ag 13 2017

Coasts

See also

Coastal zone management

Cajun Son: A Louisiana native has spent his career working to save the state's coastline and the communities he loves S. Netter *Sierra* v102 no4 p24 Jl/Ag 2017

City of Sand S. THOMAS bw *Orion Magazine* v35 no6 p9 N/D 2016

Coasts—California

Sea World K. BASTONE map *Backpacker* p20 Ag 2017

Coasts—Iceland

EDGE OF THE SEA P. STEFÁNSSON *Iceland Review* v55 no2 p74 Mr/Ap 2017

Coasts—Maine

The Natural J. CRAIG color *Power & Motoryacht* v33 no1 p66 Ja 2017

Coasts—United States

ON THE TRAIL OF ANCIENT MARINERS [Cover story] L. Wade color map *Science* v357 no6351 p542 Ag 11 2017

SHORT-BILLED DOWITCHERS color *Canadian Wildlife* v23 no4 p6 S/O 2017

Coat hangers

NO MORE CHIPPING HANG-UPS D. Rader and D. DeNunzio color *Golf Magazine* v58 no12 p81 D 2016

Coated vesicles

Tubular clathrin/AP-2 lattices pinch collagen fibers to support 3D cell migration N. Elkhatib, E. Bresteau et al color *Science* v356 no6343 p1138 Je 16 2017

Coates, Alaina

She Got Game N. Santos color *Ebony* v72 no9 p31 Jl/Ag 2017

Coates, Geoffrey W.

Combining polyethylene and polypropylene: Enhanced performance with PE/iPP multiblock polymers bibl chart graph *Sci-*

ence v355 no6327 p814 F 24 2017

COATES, KAREN

THE HEIGHTS WE GO TO color *Archaeology* v70 no5 p38 S/O 2017

A SINGULAR LANDSCAPE color *Archaeology* v70 no1 p55 Ja/F 2017

COATES, MICHELLE B.

Shaping Up at the Butte *Idaho Magazine* v16 no6 p48 Mr 2017

Coates, Ta-Nehisi, 1975-

Comic book truth A. Hearlson color *Christian Century* v134 no2 p43 Ja 18 2017

THE FIRST WHITE PRESIDENT bw *Atlantic* v320 no3 p74 O 2017

My President Was Black [Cover story] bw color *Atlantic* v319 no1 p46 Ja/F 2017

Coates, Ta-Nehisi, 1975---Interviews

Ta-Nehisi Coates Is Retooling America's Myth Factory E. Dockterman color *Time* v189 no5 p47 F 13 2017

Coates, Timothy

Using Supply Chains to Grow Your Businesss *Harvard Business Review Digital Articles* p2 N 20 2015

Coatracks

Coat Rack from a Porch Post B. D. Coleman color *Old House Journal* v45 no6 p58 S 2017

Coats

See also

Trenchcoats

8 COOL COATS THAT'LL KEEP YOU WARM O. J. WILLIAMS color *Ebony* v72/73 no12/1 p40 O/N 2017

BAZAAR THINGS S. Doonan color *Harper's Bazaar* no3656 p462 S 2017

Business Non-Casual A. Edwards color *AARP: The Magazine* v60 no2A p68 F/Mr 2017

A CLASSIC COAT GOES ROGUE color *Esquire* p48 O 2017

Cool in the Cold color *Seventeen* v76 no5 p35 S 2017

FABULOUS at Every Age color *Harper's Bazaar* no3656 p361 S 2017

Get the LOOK O. J. WILLIAMS color *Ebony* v72/73 no12/1 p41 O/N 2017

GO LONG color *Esquire* p76 BigBlackBook

In the Navy E. Wilson color *InStyle* v23 no12 p66 N 2016

Model Beauty K. Diamond color *InStyle* v24 no3 p342 Mr 2017

Nostalgia for Now img *New York* v50 no7 p49 Ap 3 2017

Peak Performance J. CHEN bw color *Esquire* v166 no5 p56 D 2016/Ja 2017

RETHINK YOUR ... Shearling Coat color *InStyle* v23 no13 p148 D 2016

RYAN GOSLING HAS ANOTHER KILLER LOOK cartoon color *Esquire* p64 S 2017

WILD & WOOLLY color *Harper's Bazaar* no3656 p260 S 2017

Coats, Frank

CHARACTER *Christian Century* v134 no17 p22 Ag 16 2017

Coats---Evaluation

...And Even More Coats color *Glamour* v115 no11 p58 N 2017

Back To Basics color *Glamour* v114 no11 p148 N 2016

The Buy color *Harper's Bazaar* no3657 p100 O 2017

CHECK YOUR COAT C. SKIPPER color *GQ: Gentlemen's Quarterly* v97 no9 p172 S 2017

Coats? Check color *Glamour* v115 no11 p51 N 2017

Coats for All Sizes L. CHAN color *Glamour* v114 no12 p104 D 2016

Coats of Many Colors M. M. Brown color *Southern Living* v52 no9 p48 S 2017

Cold comforts color *Equus* no482 p20 N 2017

Cold Relief E. Wilson color *InStyle* v24 no3 p144 Mr 2017

COZY UP color *Essence* v48 no6 p30 O 2017

DILONE J. Ferrise color *InStyle* v24 no9 p143 S 2017

FABULOUS at Every Age color *Harper's Bazaar* no3657 p185 O 2017

FRESH COATS bw color *Vogue* v207 no10 p296 O 2017

Her Style color *InStyle* v23 no13 p38 D 2016

HOW TO WEAR IT... anywhere! color *Good Housekeeping* v265 no4 p18 O 2017

HOW TO WEAR IT K. SALADINO and L. BERGAMOTTO color *Good Housekeeping* v264 no2 p16 F 2017

INTO THE WILD color *Harper's Bazaar* no3652 p121 Ap 2017

Love your coat! color *Redbook* p57 N 2017

Mansur Gavriel Coats R. WALDMAN, M. HOLGATE et al color *Vogue* v207 no9 p386 S 2017

Onward March bw color *Vogue* v207 no4 p220 Ap 2017

Packing LIST G. Bailey color *Harper's Bazaar* no3653 p90 My 2017

Puffer Coats L. Indvik color *InStyle* v23 no13 p205 D 2016

Pump Up the volume! color *Essence* v48 no6 p100 O 2017

SEE NOW, BUY NOW C. HORYN img *New York* v49 no19 p55 S 19 2016

Self-less Portrait C. L'HEUREUX img *New York* v49 no22 p65 O 31 2016

She Wears The Pants color *Glamour* v114 no7 p128 Jl 2016

SHOWSTOPPERS color *Essence* v48 no5 p90 S 2017

STAND TO ATTENTION color *Harper's Bazaar* no3648 p138 N 2016

The STYLE color *Harper's Bazaar* no3655 p77 Ag 2017

SUIT YOURSELF A. R. Williams color *Southern Living* v51 no11 p57 N 2016

These Jackets Are the Bomb S. Kennedy color *Bloomberg Businessweek* no4498 p88 N 7 2016

THINK pink color *Harper's Bazaar* no3649 p298 D 2016/Ja 2017

THIS COAT'S A CINCH FOR FALL J. Roth color *Esquire* p55 S 2017

TRAIL & CAMPING GEAR L. Berger O'connor color *Trail Rider* v29 no2 p54 Mr 2017

TRISTAN 'MACK' WILDS T. Payne and L. CROSS color *Ebony* v72 no4 p34 F 2017

Weekend in West Virginia J. B. Hager color *Southern Living* v52 no2 p74 F 2017

WHERE TO BUY color *Essence* v47 no10 p112 F 2017

WHO'S THAT GIRL? E. CIUFO bw color *Harper's Bazaar* no3648 p124 N 2016

Your Utility Layer S. Nygaard color *Men's Health* v32 no2 p(Sp)28 Mr 2017

Cobain, Kurt, 1967-1994

Kurt Cobain, Remembered N. Feeney and M. Vain color *Entertainment Weekly* no1454/1455 p97 F 24 2017

Cobalt Boats LLC

New Wave A. JONES *Boating World* v38 no2 p44 F 2017

Cobalt isotopes

NUCLEAR POWER S. MacGregor *Maclean's* v129 no50 p53 D 19 2016

Cobaría (South American people)

People N. Rojas color *Christian Century* v134 no1 p18 Ja 4 2017

Cobb, Adam

Inequality Isn't Just Due to Market Forces — It's Caused by Decisions the Boss Makes, Too *Harvard Business Review Digital Articles* p2 Mr 30 2017

Cobb, Bill

BILL COBB color *Bloomberg Businessweek* no4518 p80 Ap 10 2017

Cobb, Daniel M.

Clyde Warrior: Tradition, Community, and Red Power *American Indian Quarterly* v41 no1 p93 Wint 2017

Say We Are Nations: Documents of Politics and Protest in Indigenous America since 1887 R. S. W. Soldier *American Indian Quarterly* v41 no3 p294 Summ 2017

Cobb, Isaac

GREEN GIANTS color *Sunset* v237 no6 p32 D 2016

COBB, JAY

Goldwater Revisited *Commentary* v144 no3 p53 O 2017

Cobb, Jelani

AFTER BANNON cartoon *New Yorker* v93 no26 p19 S 4 2017

BIRTHDAY WISHES bw cartoon *New Yorker* v92 no45 p21 Ja 16 2017

MILLENNIALISM cartoon *New Yorker* v92 no32 p33 O 10 2016

OUT OF TIME cartoon *New Yorker* v93 no12 p15 My 8 2017

PRODIGY OF HATE cartoon *New Yorker* v92 no48 p20 F 6 2017

REVERSAL OF JUSTICE cartoon *New Yorker* v93 no10 p35 Ap 24 2017

A STATE AWAY cartoon *New Yorker* v93 no4 p27 Mr 13 2017

STATES VS. TRUMP cartoon *New Yorker* v92 no39 p31 N 28 2016

TAKING IT TO THE STREETS cartoon *New Yorker* v92 no44 p19 Ja 9 2017

Cobb, Matthew

The Brave New World of Gene Editing color *New York Review of Books* v64 no12 p31 Jl 13 2017

How biologists pioneered preprints—with paper and postage J. Kaiser bw *Science* v357 no6358 p1348 S 29 2017

Cobb, Paul

A better research-practice partnership color *Phi Delta Kappan* v98 no3 p23 N 2016

COBB, PAUL M.

ON THE SPOT *History Today* v67 no6 p112 Je 2016

Cobb County (Ga.)

The Charm of Cobb *Atlanta* v57 no2 p117 Je 2017

Cobblers (Cooking)

RECIPES A. Larson *Idaho Magazine* v16 no11 p56 Ag 2017

The Scoop on Cobbler L. Cericola and P. Lolley color *Southern Living* v52 no9 p142 S 2017

Cobbs, Elizabeth

Staying Power *Hoover Digest: Research & Opinion on Public Policy* no1 p80 Wint 2017

WAR BY TELEPHONE N. Tappan bw color *American History* v52 no3 p68 Ag 2017

Winning Women: Woodrow Wilson at first found himself scandalized by protesting women, but soon he championed their cause. How President Trump and feminists might likewise make common cause *Hoover Digest: Research & Opinion on Public Policy* no2 p58 Spr 2017

COBI GmbH

BUILD A BETTER BIKE *Saturday Evening Post* v289 no2 p21 Mr/Ap 2017

Cobia Boats (Company)

COBIA 277 Z. PROCHAZKA *Sea Magazine* v108 no10 p34 O 2016

Coble, Colleen

Because You're Mine *Publishers Weekly* v263 no45 p42 N 7 2016

COBLENTZ, KYLE E.

Long-Term Studies Contribute Disproportionately to Ecology and Policy *BioScience* v67 no3 p271 Mr 2017

Cobos, A.

Observation of a large-scale anisotropy in the arrival directions of cosmic rays above 8 × 1018 eV *Science* v357 no6357 p1266 S 22 2017

Cobra (Company)

GREAT LENGTHS A. Johnson and R. Sauerhaft color *Golf Magazine* v59 no1 p86 Ja 2017

SMART MISSILES M. Chwasky, A. Johnson et al color *Golf Magazine* v59 no1 p82 Ja 2017

Cobra Golf Inc.

LIGHT & LONG M. Chwasky color *Golf Magazine* v59 no11 p86 N 2017

Coburn, Derek

Don't Waste Your Time on Networking Events *Harvard Business Review Digital Articles* p2 S 26 2016

Cobweb weavers

Laughter cartoon *Reader's Digest* v190 no1134 p96 O 2017

Coca-Cola Co.

The Intelligent Way to Market *Foreign Affairs* v95 no6 p(Sp)18 N/D 2016

Kent Is Leaving, but Coke's Problems Remain J. Reingold color *Fortune* v75 no1 p16 Ja 1 2017

OFF THE MAT S. Marikar cartoon *New Yorker* v93 no14 p31 My 22 2017

Coca-Cola Co.—Officials & employees

Interview Coke's James Quincey J. Kaplan color *Bloomberg Businessweek* no4522 p28 My 15 2017

Cocaine

DAVID HOCKNEY S. BHATTACHARYA color *Esquire* v167 no2 p134 Mr 2017

Cocaine abuse

ZAPPING COCAINE ADDICTION M. Wadman color *Science* v357 no6355 p960 S 8 2017

Cocaine—Physiological aspects

ALMOST THERE P. Garrison *Flying* v144 no7 p36 Jl 2017

WWI'S WONDER DRUG Ł. Kamiński *MHQ: Quarterly Journal of Military History* v29 no2 p44 Wint 2017

Cochineal insect

BUGS ARE IN OUR FOOD—AND THAT'S OK D. Stone color *National Geographic* v231 no2 p22 F 2017

Cochlear implants

Cochlear implants and electronic hearing M. Svirsky *Physics Today* v70 no8 p52 Ag 2017

Cochlear Implants - Life Beyond Hearing Aids J. Herzog *Saturday Evening Post* v289 no5 p101 S/O 2017

Cochran, Ann

CROSSING OVER: Yes, I have cancer, but no treatment's needed--yet. And then? *Washingtonian Magazine* v52 no8 p224 My 2017

DOWNSIZING MY DAD *Washingtonian Magazine* v52 no2 p279 N 2016

Find Some Peace: A spiritual retreat can let you not only achieve some calm but also contemplate the important things in life *Washingtonian Magazine* v52 no11 p96 Ag 2017

HIGH STYLE: Want to make your new house stand out? Don't forget about the ceilings *Washingtonian Magazine* v52 no8 p184 My 2017

HOME SWEET HOMESTEAD *Washingtonian Magazine* v52 no3 p16 D 2016

NASHVILLE... FOR WASHINGTONIANS *Washingtonian Magazine* v52 no1 p111 O 2016

REMEMBER WHEN? *Washingtonian Magazine* v52 no6 p167 Mr 2017

Cochran, Brice

Build a Backyard Retreat color *Timber Home Living* v27 no2 p8 Ap 2017

tip Take Cover color *Timber Home Living* v27 no3 p18 Je 2017

Cochran, David Carroll

An Ordinary Sunday [Cover story] color *Commonweal* v144 no15 p11 S 22 2017

Cochran, Kelly E.

Vitamin B3 modulates mitochondrial vulnerability and prevents glaucoma in aged mice bibl graph *Science* v355 no6326 p756 F 17 2017

COCHRAN, SAM

Alley-Oop color *Architectural Digest* v74 no9 p184 S 2017

Bright Eyes color *Architectural Digest* v74 no3 p44 Mr 2017

CREATIVITY UNLEASHED color *Architectural Digest* v73 no12 p144 D 2016

CURVES AHEAD color *Architectural Digest* v74 no2 p106 F 2017

DISCO FEVER bw color *Architectural Digest* v73 no11 p82 N 2016

Girl Just Wants to Have Fun color *Architectural Digest* v74 no9 p94 S 2017

Good Medicine color *Architectural Digest* no6 p154 Je 1 2017

Green Acres color *Architectural Digest* v74 no9 p90 S 2017

A group effort—led by AD100 designer Dan Fink—transforms the dancers' lounge for American Ballet Theatre into a triumphant tour de force bw color *Architectural Digest* v74 no7 p76 Jl 2017

High Heat color *Architectural Digest* v74 no3 p51 Mr 2017

ISLAND TIME bw color *Architectural Digest* v73 no11 p94 N 2016

LEGACY BUILDING color *Architectural Digest* v74 no1 p232 Ja 2017

LOOK AGAIN color *Architectural Digest* v73 no12 p64 D 2016

Molto Bene color *Architectural Digest* v74 no7 p96 Jl 2017

National Treasure color *Architectural Digest* no5 p62 My 2017

People Watching color *Architectural Digest* v74 no3 p146 Mr 2017

PYRAMID POWER color *Architectural Digest* v73 no11 p208 N 2016

Rock Steady color *Architectural Digest* v74 no8 p110 Ag 2017

TWIST AND SHOUT color *Architectural Digest* no11 p138 N 1 2017

UNITED FRONT color *Architectural Digest* no5 p138 My 2017

Voutsa color *Architectural Digest* v74 no10 p102 O 1 2017

Wish Fulfillment color *Architectural Digest* v74 no1 p84 Ja 2017

Cochran, Tom

How I Led Change in the U.S. State Department Bureaucracy color *Harvard Business Review Digital Articles* p2 Ja 4 2017

Cochrane, Joe

TRUMP'S TRAVEL BAN *New York Times Upfront* v149 no10 p6 Mr 13 2017

Cochrane, John H.

Make America Exceptional Again: The rule of law, the centerpiece of American exceptionalism, is under assault. How to halt the predations of the regulatory state *Hoover Digest: Research & Opinion on Public Policy* no2 p32 Spr 2017

Only a Clean Sweep Will Do *Hoover Digest: Research & Opinion on Public Policy* no4 p9 Fall 2016

Cochrane, John H.—Interviews

"A Thousand Things Going Wrong" C. Yip *Hoover Digest: Research & Opinion on Public Policy* no1 p44 Wint 2017

"Growth Is the Problem": Lower tax rates, broaden the base. Such simple changes are all that we need, says Hoover fellow John H. Cochrane P. Robinson *Hoover Digest: Research & Opinion on Public Policy* no3 p143 Summ 2017

Cockburn, Andrew

CRIME AND PUNISHMENT Will the 9/11 case finally go to trial? *Harper's Magazine* p41 O 2017

IT'S MY PARTY: The Democrats struggle to rise from the ashes *Harper's Magazine* v335 no2006 p33 Jl 2017

THE NEW RED SCARE *Harper's Magazine* v333 no1999 p25 D 2016

TEXAS IS THE FUTURE *Harper's Magazine* v334 no2002 p26 Mr 2017

Turning Blue *Harper's Magazine* v334 no2004 p2 My 2017

Cockburn, Patrick

Why bombs won't stop terrorism Z. SCHWARTZ color *Maclean's* v129 no42 p60 O 24 2016

COCKBURN, TERRY

REAL SLOW [Cover story] bw color *Runner's World* v52 no6 p24 Jl 2017

Cockell, Charles

The formation of peak rings in large impact craters bibl color graph *Science* v354 no6314 p878 N 18 2016

The laws of life *Physics Today* v70 no3 p42 Mr 2017

Cockerham, Kimberly

THE EXCHANGE cartoon color graph *Men's Health* v32 no8 p16 O 2017

Cockfighter (Film)

Cockfighter color *New Yorker* v93 no29 p24 S 25 2017

Cockram, Michael

The Big Idea *Architectural Record* v205 no1 p70 Ja 2017

Brick by Brick bw color *Architectural Record* v205 no2 p100 F 2017

Home Grown *Architectural Record* v205 no6 p120 Je 2017

On the Waterfront *Architectural Record* v205 no10 p123 O 2017

COCKRELL, CHRISTOPHER

FUMIO DEMURA [Cover story] bw color *Black Belt* v55 no2 p34 F/Mr 2017

Cockroaches

Lessons From a Streetcar E. Laborde bw *New Orleans Magazine* v51 no6 p160 Ap 2017

Melodies in the Mind B. Lutz color *New Orleans Magazine* v51 no6 p34 Ap 2017

Cockroaches—Environmental aspects

Roach Buster B. Lutz color *New Orleans Magazine* v51 no5 p34 Mr 2017

Cockrum, Betty

Pieces de Résistance: Outgoing Planned Parenthood CEO Betty Cockrum packs up a collection of quirky office tchotchkes K. Kendall *Indianapolis Monthly* v40 no10 p18 Je 2017

Cocktail Kingdom (Company)

LIQUID ASSETS A. Shaffer color *Wired* v24 no12 p78 D 2016

Cocktail parties

DAVID YURMAN'S PURE FORM COLLECTION LAUNCH *Washingtonian Magazine* v52 no2 p238 N 2016

HAND to MOUTH J. Steingarten cartoon *Vogue* v207 no3 p474 Mr 2017

Cocktails

See also

Non-alcoholic cocktails

2016 WASHINGTONIAN STYLE SETTERS *Washingtonian Magazine* v52 no3 p116 D 2016

ALL-STAR PITCHERS L. TYRELL color *Martha Stewart Living* p58 My 2017

BAR EXAM [Cover story] T. McNally color *New Orleans Magazine* v51 no3 p56 Ja 2017

A BIG BATCH OF CHEER F. MAROUKIAN color *Popular Mechanics* p34 N 2017

CHICAGO'S COZIEST BARS M. HENNESSY color *Chicago* v66 no10 p47 O 2017

COCK TAIL OF THE MONTH D. ALAN *Texas Monthly* v45 no1 p36 Ja 2017

Coming Around Again T. Mcnally color *New Orleans Magazine* v51 no9 p86 Jl 2017

Cover *Southern Living* v52 no6 pC1 Je 2017

Day-Drinking Essentials color *Glamour* v115 no5 p24 My 2017

EAT THIS NOW CARDAMOM COCKTAILS *Better Homes & Gardens* v94 no12 p81 D 2016

family matters P. P. FISCHER color *Better Homes & Gardens* v95 no5 p46 My 2017

Fancy a Nightcap? S. Tishgart color *Bloomberg Businessweek* no4501 p58 N 28 2016

Fancy Cocktails? A Breeze! K. O'Shea-Evans and C. SWANSON color *House Beautiful* v159 no4 p65 My 2017

FEAST WITH BENEFITS [Cover story] L. Gnat and J. Albert color *O, The Oprah Magazine* p128 N 2017

Good Blood R. Schaap *New York Times Magazine* p32 O 30 2016

GOVERNMENT ALMOST KILLED THE COCKTAIL P. Suderman color *Reason* v49 no5 p54 O 2017

GREAT UNKNOWNS cartoon *Popular Mechanics* p26 My 2017

HIT ME WITH YOUR BEST SHOTS M. Reyes color *Bloomberg Businessweek* no4506 p63 Ja 9 2017

Hold the Liquor R. Schaap *New York Times Magazine* p22 Ja 1 2017

HOLIDAYS ON ICE A. Vorrasi color *InStyle* v23 no13 p276 D 2016

I Love My Bar L. BENOIT color *House Beautiful* p96 Jl 2017

IN THE FIELD I. Edwards color *Sunset* v239 no4 p10 O 2017

Is It Cocktailing Season Yet? color *Glamour* v115 no5 p23 My 2017

IT'S COCKTAIL O'CLOCK! E. N. GAGE *Martha Stewart Living* no270 p128 D 2016

Kick back with a cocktail color *Redbook* p107 Je 2017

LOVAGE color *Better Homes & Gardens* v95 no5 p120 My 2017

Martini, Please, No BS J. GORDINIER color *Esquire* v166 no5 p46 D 2016/Ja 2017

May Showers Bring... T. McNally color *New Orleans Magazine* v51 no7 p88 My 2017

THE NEW APERITIF S. Schneider color *Sunset* v238 no2 p90 F 2017

The No-Frills NEGRONI A. Rapoport and J. Harman color *Glamour* v115 no1 p96 Ja 2017

On the Bubble T. BAIOCCHI color *Bon Appetit* v61 no12 p53 D 2016 /Jan2017

PAINT IT BLACK C. Jones color *Bloomberg Businessweek* no4497 p67 O 31 2016

PINK IS THE NEW BLACK: We could sip Etto's sprightly vermouth cocktail all afternoon long *Washingtonian Magazine* v52 no8 p134 My 2017

PRAISE (JUST) JACK—WILL & GRACE IS BACK! R. Kinane color *Entertainment Weekly* no1484 p50 S 29 2017

Punch Up Your Summer N. RICHARDSON color *Bon Appetit* no8 p42 Ag 2017

REDBEARD COCKTAIL J. Sidman *Washingtonian Magazine* v52 no4 p184 Ja 2017

Sandra Lee Favorites *TV Guide* v65 no6 p14 Ja 30 2017

SCHEDULE OF EVENTS *Cincinnati Magazine* p90 Je 2017

SHOT IN A BEER T. Willey color *Bon Appetit* v62 no6 p86 Je 2017

Spring Goes Fancy T. McNally color *New Orleans Magazine* v51 no6 p90 Ap 2017

starters J. BAINBRIDGE, E. WARTZMAN et al color *Bon Appetit* p25 S 2017

starters N. RICHARDSON, J. BAINBRIDGE et al bw color diag *Bon Appetit* v62 no2 p19 Mr 2017

Suprfood cocktails T. Darlington and A. Darlington color *Rodale's Organic Life* v3 no1 p85 Ja 2017

THE TIPSY TEXAN'S COCKTAIL OF THE MONTH D. ALAN *Texas Monthly* v45 no3 p48 Mr 2017

A TOAST TO GREATNESS N. H. REEDER and D. POINTDUJOUR color *Ebony* v72 no5 p58 Mr 2017

YOU'RE INVITED TO DINNER WITH FRIENDS M. Crowell

color *Sunset* v239 no4 p54 O 2017

Cocktails—Equipment & supplies

Catch Him If You Can S. Grobart color *Bloomberg Businessweek* no4504 p62 D 19 2016

Cocktails—Evaluation

FIGHTING SPIRITS D. Wondrich, N. Gordon-Loebl et al *Nation* v305 no11 p41 O 30 2017

Ready to Rum-ble E. G. Dunn color *Bloomberg Businessweek* no4523 p64 My 22 2017

Coco (Film)

COCO M. Snetiker color *Entertainment Weekly* no1446/1447 p46 D 2016/Ja 2017

COCO M. Snetiker color *Entertainment Weekly* no1478 / 1479 p58 Ag 18-25 2017

Coco, Giovanni

Shadows on the Lake *Publishers Weekly* v263 no52 p100 D 19 2016

Coconino National Forest (Ariz.)

CAMPBELL MESA LOOP R. STIEVE *Arizona Highways* v92 no7 p54 Jl 2016

PUMPHOUSE WASH R. STIEVE *Arizona Highways* v93 no10 p54 O 2017

Coconut

CHEAT YOUR WAY TO LEAN A. RIOS color *Yoga Journal* no290 p7 Mr 2017

Coconut Water with a Conscience V. TWEED color *Better Nutrition* v79 no1 p12 Ja 2017

NUTRITION HOTLINE R. MANGELS *Vegetarian Journal* v35 no4 p2 2016

Smashing the Coconut Oil Myth color *Health* v31 no2 p11 Mr 2017

Thai-Style Curry color *Vegetarian Today* no2 p12 Ap 2017

Coconut crab—Behavior

Don't shake hands with this crab S. Milius color *Science News* v191 no4 p4 Mr 4 2017

Coconut oil

7 SURPRISING USES FOR COCONUT OIL color *Prevention* v69 no4 p12 Ap 2017

MAKE HEALTHY COME TO YOU *Los Angeles Magazine* p113 Ap 2017

NATURAL GLOW color *Better Homes & Gardens* v95 no7 p20 Jl 2017

prep school C. SAFFITZ, A. MASON et al bw color *Bon Appetit* v62 no4 p112 Ap 2017

Coconut Oil (Music)

Lizzo's Feel-Good Revolution N. Feeney color *Entertainment Weekly* no1435 p56 O 14 2016

Coconut oil—Evaluation

In the SUNSET KITCHEN E. Johnson and S. Spencer color *Sunset* v238 no5 p94 My 2017

Ready for the Summer? color *Amazing Wellness* v9 no3 p88 EarlySumm 2017

Coconut oil—Therapeutic use

STRETCH MARK SMOOTHERS L. Turner color *Amazing Wellness* v8 no2 p76 Spr 2016

Coconut products—Evaluation

FILIPINO BOUNTY C. SCHEDLER color *Chicago* v65 no12 p59 D 2016

Coconut—History

KNOW YOUR COCONUTS B. McCALL color *New Yorker* v93 no10 p60 Ap 24 2017

Cocote (Film)

COCOTE N. Rapold color *Film Comment* v53 no5 p22 S/O 2017

Cocozza, Paula

Fox and Friend E. McKENZIE *New York Times Book Review* p13 Je 25 2017

Code 42 Software Inc.

How to move from CrashPlan for Home to another backup solution G. FLEISHMAN color *Macworld - Digital Edition* v34 no10 p12 O 2017

Code Black (TV program)

A Bloody Good Time at Code Black J. HALTERMAN *TV Guide* v64 no46 p9 N 7 2016

Moon Bloodgood Joins Code Black J. Halterman *TV Guide* v65 no37 p14 S 4 2017

Code Noir (Music)

Code Noir J. Mcdonough color *Downbeat* v84 no4 p49 Ap 2017

The Hot Box chart *Downbeat* v84 no4 p51 Ap 2017

Coded language (Linguistics)

How Political Language Got So Coded K. Steinmetz *Time* v188 no16/17 p65 O 24 2016

Codeine

Purple Drank, Corpotate Bank T. Bella color *Bloomberg Businessweek* no4514 p60 Mr 13 2017

Codes of ethics

GAME FACES color *Outdoor Life* v224 no8 p9 O 2017

Codevilla, Angelo M.

THE RISE OF POLITICAL CORRECTNESS *Claremont Review of Books* v16 no4 p37 Fall 2016

THE TIPPING POINT *Claremont Review of Books* v17 no2 p68 Spr 2017

WAR WITHOUT END *Claremont Review of Books* v17 no3 p23 Summ 2017

Coding House (Woodside, Calif.)

Code School's Out S. McBride color *Bloomberg Businessweek* no4504 p29 D 19 2016

CODINHA, ALESSANDRA

CAROLINA HERRERA color *Vogue* v207 no3 p409 Mr 2017

Cody, L.

AGING GRACEFULLY on the Homestead *Mother Earth News* no280 p34 F/Mr 2017

Coe, Alexis

Presidential Biographies *New York Times Magazine* p18 F 19 2017

Coe, Andrew

Steady Diet of Depression *American History* v52 no1 p56 Ap 2017

Coe, Jonathan, 1961-

Neoliberalism, Cranked Up to 11 C. LEHMANN *In These Times* v41 no2 p39 F 2017

Coe, Steve

Observe winter planetary nebulae color *Astronomy* v45 no2 p50 F 2017

Coelho, Janet Tappin

Brazil's iconic statue Christ the Redeemer is in need of restoration color *Christian Century* v134 no3 p14 F 2017

Coelho, João

All-printed thin-film transistors from networks of liquid-exfoliated nanosheets diag *Science* v356 no6333 p69 Ap 7 2017

COELHO, PAULA NUNES

Copepods Against Aedes Mosquitoes: A Very Risky Strategy *BioScience* v67 no6 p489 Je 2017

Coelho, Rogério

Boat of Dreams *Publishers Weekly* v263 no45 p60 N 7 2016

Coen, Cheré

ALABAMA COASTING color *Louisiana Life* v37 no6 p48 Jl/ Ag 2017

MOST OF THE COAST [Cover story] color *New Orleans Magazine* v51 no5 p60 Mr 2017

WELL TRAVELED cartoon *Louisiana Life* v37 no2 p80 N/D 2016

Coenzyme A

Fixing carbon, unnaturally Fuyu Gong and Yin Li bibl diag *Science* v354 no6314 p830 N 18 2016

A synthetic pathway for the fixation of carbon dioxide in vitro T. Schwander, L. S. von Borzyskowski et al bibl graph *Science* v354 no6314 p900 N 18 2016

Coenzymes

See also

Biotin

Coenzyme A

The biosynthetic pathway of coenzyme F430 in methanogenic and methanotrophic archaea Kaiyuan Zheng, P. D. Ngo et al bibl diag graph *Science* v354 no6310 p339 O 21 2016

Coetzee, J. M., 1940-

The Apathy of J. M. Coetzee C. LORENTZEN img *New York* p73 F 20 2017

The Gospel Dance P. BAUER *Weekly Standard* v22 no31 p38 Ap 17 2017

A Great Writer We Should Know bw cartoon *New York Review of Books* v64 no1 p59 Ja 19 2017

Losing His Way C. Nelson bw *Commonweal* v144 no12 p33 Jl 7 2017

Play of Passions J. MILES *New York Times Book Review* p13 F 26 2017

Shadows & Ghosts C. Tóibín bw color *New York Review of Books* v64 no8 p37 My 11 2017

Coeur d'Alene (Idaho)

COEUR D'ALENE, ID L. Ladoceour color *Sunset* v238 no4 p34 Ap 2017

RUN AWAY! [Cover story] E. STROUT, M. PRELLE et al color *Runner's World* v52 no7 p54 Ag 2017

Coffee

10 Foods to Tame Your Pain L. TURNER color *Better Nutrition* v79 no10 p68 O 2017

Break That Bad Habit—for Good J. Migala color *Health* v31 no1 p63 Ja 2017

Caffeine 101 O. Manno color *Dance Spirit* v21 no2 p30 F 2017

calm & bright H. DOWDLE color *Yoga Journal* no288 p58 D 2016

COFFEE PERKS A. MACMILLAN color *Runner's World* v52 no5 p29 Je 2017

Coffee Talk V. TWEED color *Better Nutrition* v78 no12 p54 D 2016

cool beans color *Parents* v92 no8 p112 Ag 2017

Drink Coffee, Live Longer? Growing evidence suggests enjoying a daily cup (or more) of this popular beverage may help decrease risk of an early death *Tufts University Health & Nutrition Letter* v35 no8 p6 O 2017

For the Record color *Time* v190 no4 p6 Jl 24 2017

Fun Party Snacks B. Lipton color *Health* v31 no2 p132 Mr 2017

HOT SIP: NITRO COFFEE color *Health* v31 no8 p10 O 2017

kick back & DRINK UP M. GLISAN color *Better Homes & Gardens* v95 no7 p124 Jl 2017

MANDY MOORE "I'm never going to deprive myself" J. Naftulin color *Health* v31 no9 p25 N 2017

Not Your Average Joe J. Calderone, J. Lee et al chart color *Consumer Reports* v82 no10 p8 O 2017

Power Tools: Icons C. Alter color *Time* v189 no16/17 p150 My 1-8 2017

Sip Before You Sweat color *Health* v31 no2 p12 Mr 2017

SMALL TOWN COFFEE P. Higbee *South Dakota Magazine* v33 no2 p64 Jl/Ag 2017

A Stodgy Barroom Syrup Gets a Jolt F. MAROUKIAN color *Popular Mechanics* p14 Je 2017

This Just In J. Zorthian *Time* v190 no10/11 p29 S 18 2017

Coffee beans

ARE YOU Worthy OF THIS MAN'S Coffee? C. SCHEDLER cartoon color *Chicago* v66 no5 p104 My 2017

Coffee cakes

Coffeeless Coffeecakes: No caffeine required color *Nebraska Life* v21 no5 p46 S/O 2017

MAKING WAVES L. TYRELL color *Martha Stewart Living* p86 O 2017

the SWEET spot [Cover story] K. Hammonds color *Southern Living* v52 no7 p86 Jl 2017

Coffee filters

Craft a New Coffee Rig S. Vaglica and P. Kita color *Men's Health* v32 no2 p34 Mr 2017

Coffee mills

THE BEST BET img *New York* v49 no23 p55 N 14 2016

Power Tools: Artists C. Alter color *Time* v189 no16/17 p62 My 1-8 2017

Coffee services (Tableware)

1951 COFFEE K. K. CONDON color *Better Homes & Gardens* v95 no5 p178 My 2017

Tiffany Applied Japanese Influence Coffee Set color *Magazine Antiques* v183 no6 p24 N/D 2016

Coffee shops

Tout Sweet *Los Angeles Magazine* p10 Ja 2017

Coffee shops—Evaluation

Breakfast Town M. RIGBY color *Bon Appetit* v62 no2 p46 Mr 2017

A coffee shop for Christ color *U.S. Catholic* v82 no6 p8 Je 2017

Fulton Street J. BURNHAM *Indianapolis Monthly* v40 no7 p30 Mr 2017

NEWPORT M. SULLIVAN *Cincinnati Magazine* v50 no7 p33 Ap 2017

NITRO COFFEE *Washingtonian Magazine* v52 no1 p90 O 2016

Play Station J. DRILLING *Cincinnati Magazine* v50 no4 p146 Ja 2017

Roast of the Town color *Los Angeles Magazine* v62 no7 p73 Jl 2017

Coffee shops—Government policy

DOUBLE SHOT J. SIDMAN *Washingtonian Magazine* v52 no1 p20 O 2016

Coffee stains

GET ANYTHING OUT C. FORTÉ chart color *Good Housekeeping* v263 no6 p90 D 2016

Coffee tables

Get Off The Loop E. GLUSAC color *Conde Nast Traveler* v52 no2 p36 F 2017

THE WAR TRUNK J. DETWILER color *Popular Mechanics* p97 S 2017

Coffee tables—Evaluation

HIGH or LOW? color *Good Housekeeping* v264 no5 p60 My 2017

Italian Modern Table color *Treasures* v5 no5 p11 Ap/My 2016

Coffee—Equipment & supplies

See also

Coffee filters

Coffee mills

Craft a New Coffee Rig S. Vaglica and P. Kita color *Men's Health* v32 no2 p34 Mr 2017

For the Coffee Connoisseur color *Consumer Reports* v81 no12 p58 D 2016

Coffee—Equipment & supplies—Evaluation

GOOD MORNING, NEAL! N. POLLACK color *Popular Mechanics* p72 My 2017

Morning Glory M. Khemsurov color *Bloomberg Businessweek* no4494 p72 O 10 2016

Coffee—Evaluation

ONE FRESH CUP color *Good Housekeeping* v264 no3 p160 Mr 2017

Coffeehouses

Board-Game Theory J. MORIARITY cartoon *Walrus* v13 no9 p23 N 2016

Business Perks S. KROWIAK *Indianapolis Monthly* v40 no4 p52 D 2016

CALIFORNIA'S SONORA A. Deabler color map *Sunset* v239 no1 p28 Jl 2017

Here, Kitty, Kitty color *Weekly Standard* v22 no35 p3 My 22 2017

Rainbow Salad img *New York* v49 no23 p60 N 14 2016

The U.S. of yum color *O, The Oprah Magazine* p92 Jl 2017

Coffeehouses—Evaluation

Broth With Froth img *New York* v49 no23 p63 N 14 2016

Dialogue *Los Angeles Magazine* p8 My 2017

Englewood: This up-and-coming stretch of East Washington Street is sprouting some quirky gems JUSSI KENT-DOOLAN *Indianapolis Monthly* v40 no11 p30 Jl 2017

Fish Milanese img *New York* v50 no9 p75 My 1 2017

Paradise Point Café: Known as "Old Town's sweet retreat," Paradise Point Café has built a loyal following with its baked goods, including a signature carrot cake and salted caramel apple pie that's made with house-made caramel. Mmmm ... K. MONTGOMERY *Arizona Highways* v96 no7 p12 Jl 2017

UPPER CRUST color *Chicago* v66 no1 p62 Ja 2017

Coffee—Physiological effect

Coffee: The Latest Antidote to Aging? A. Park color *Time* v189 no3 p22 Ja 30 2017

Coffeepots—Evaluation

THE EASY PATH TO AWESOME COFFEE color *Redbook* p128 S 2017

For the Coffee Connoisseur color *Consumer Reports* v81 no12 p58 D 2016

Morning Glory M. Khemsurov color *Bloomberg Businessweek* no4494 p72 O 10 2016

STRANGE BREW G. Megroz color *Bloomberg Businessweek* no4514 p74 Mr 13 2017

Coffee—Social aspects

This Just In J. Zorthian *Time* v188 no19 p17 N 7 2016

Coffey, Frank

The Free Spirit A. Barronian color *Powder* v45 no3 p42 N 2016

Coffey, Terrance

Valley of the Kings: The 18th Dynasty *Publishers Weekly* v263

no50 p47 D 5 2016

Coffey, Terry

Cash In on Your Good Health K. LANKFORD color *Kiplinger's Personal Finance* v70 no12 p62 D 2016

Coffey, Wayne

At Any Cost color *Sports Illustrated* v125 no12 p44 O 10 2016

Coffin, Pierre

Despicable Me 3 L. Greenblatt color *Entertainment Weekly* no1473 p42 Jl 7 2017

Minions, Delightfully Relegated to Their Proper Place S. Zacharek color *Time* v190 no2/3 p90 Jl 10-17 2017

Coffin, Sarah D.

MELTING POT MODERN cartoon color *Magazine Antiques* v184 no2 p110 Mr/Ap 2017

Coffman, Julie

Companies Drain Women's Ambition After Only 2 Years *Harvard Business Review Digital Articles* p2 My 18 2015

Cogan, Christina—Interviews

MEET BETSY DAVIS AND CHRISTINA COGAN S. SHIBATA *Sea Magazine* v108 no10 pPNW-1 O 2016

Cogan, D.

Deterministic generation of a cluster state of entangled photons bibl diag graph *Science* v354 no6311 p434 O 28 2016

Cogan, John F.

America the Fixer-Upper *Hoover Digest: Research & Opinion on Public Policy* no4 p14 Fall 2016

Cogan, Marin

First She Marched, Then She Ran: Alexis Frank, a 26-year-old political novice, never considered vying for Congress--until she saw Hillary Clinton lose img *New York* v50 no11 p42 My 29 2017

OBAMA'S AMERICA img *New York* v49 no20 p12 O 3 2016

Cogar, Matt

THE JOY OF AX A. ZALESKI cartoon color *Men's Health* v32 no8 p100 O 2017

COGDILL, OLINE H.

A Dark Fairy Tale color *Publishers Weekly* v264 no15 p52 Ap 10 2017

Coggan, Devan

1917-2016 Zsa Zsa Gabor color *Entertainment Weekly* no1446/1447 p26 D 2016/Ja 2017

THE 25 MOST PATRIOTIC MOVIES OF ALL TIME color *Entertainment Weekly* no1472 p30 Je 30 2017

39 Perfect Pop Culture Presents color *Entertainment Weekly* no1442 p31 D 2 2016 Rebellious Special Issue

6 — "YOU'RE WELCOME" *Entertainment Weekly* no1444/1445 p60 D 16 2016

ADAM SCOTT AND CRAIG ROBINSON color *Entertainment Weekly* no1482/1483 p42 S 22 2017

After the Verdict color *Entertainment Weekly* no1482/1483 p62 S 22 2017

Ali Wentworth Talks the Talk color *Entertainment Weekly* no1440 p16 N 18 2016

Almost Christmas color *Entertainment Weekly* no1440 p43 N 18 2016

ALSO PLAYING color *Entertainment Weekly* no1438 p44 N 4 2016

ANNABELLE: CREATION color *Entertainment Weekly* no1474/1475 p48 Jl 21-28 2017

BATTLE OF THE SEXES color *Entertainment Weekly* no1478 / 1479 p42 Ag 18-25 2017

THE BEGUILED color *Entertainment Weekly* no1463/1464 p56 Ap/My 2017

BEST ACTOR color diag *Entertainment Weekly* no1451/1452 p54 F 3-10 2017

BEST ACTRESS color diag *Entertainment Weekly* no1451/1452 p44 F 3-10 2017

BEST SUPPORTING ACTOR color diag *Entertainment Weekly* no1451/1452 p50 F 3-10 2017

BEST SUPPORTING ACTRESS color diag *Entertainment Weekly* no1451/1452 p62 F 3-10 2017

THE BIGGEST SUMMER BREAKOUTS (SO FAR) color diag *Entertainment Weekly* no1474/1475 p15 Jl 21-28 2017

black-ish *Entertainment Weekly* no1482/1483 p63 S 22 2017

Bob's Burgers *Entertainment Weekly* no1482/1483 p34 S 22 2017

BONE DEEP color *Entertainment Weekly* no1476 p30 Ag 4 2017

A BOX OFFICE BEAUTY color *Entertainment Weekly* no1459 p10 Mr 31 2017

Breaking Big BRANDON MICHEAL HALL color *Entertainment Weekly* no1482/1483 p65 S 22 2017

Bull color *Entertainment Weekly* no1482/1483 p66 S 22 2017

THE BUNNY SUIT color *Entertainment Weekly* no1460/1461 p99 Ap 7-17 2017

CAPTAIN UNDERPANTS color *Entertainment Weekly* no1446/1447 p51 D 2016/Ja 2017

CAPTAIN UNDERPANTS: THE FIRST EPIC MOVIE color *Entertainment Weekly* no1463/1464 p53 Ap/My 2017

CASABLANCA REVISITED color *Entertainment Weekly* no1441 p38 N 25 2016

Curb Your Enthusiasm color *Entertainment Weekly* no1482/1483 p40 S 22 2017

THE DARK SIDE OF "YOU LIGHT UP MY LIFE" color *Entertainment Weekly* no1451/1452 p78 F 3-10 2017

DC's Legends of Tomorrow color *Entertainment Weekly* no1482/1483 p66 S 22 2017

The Deuce color *Entertainment Weekly* no1482/1483 p29 S 22 2017

Disney Brings Good Things to Life color *Entertainment Weekly* no1459 p11 Mr 31 2017

DIVE INTO Brooklyn Nine-Nine color *Entertainment Weekly* no1482/1483 p67 S 22 2017

DWAYNE JOHNSON ROCKS color *Entertainment Weekly* no1441 p11 N 25 2016

Eddie Redmayne Works His Magic color *Entertainment Weekly* no1441 p13 N 25 2016

EMMA'S Must-Reads color *Entertainment Weekly* no1454/1455 p30 F 24 2017

Family Guy *Entertainment Weekly* no1482/1483 p34 S 22 2017

The Flash color *Entertainment Weekly* no1482/1483 p66 S 22 2017

Fresh Off the Boat color *Entertainment Weekly* no1482/1483 p63 S 22 2017

FUTURE FRANCO FILMS color *Entertainment Weekly* no1454/1455 p82 F 24 2017

GENE WILDER color *Entertainment Weekly* no1446/1447 p90 D 2016/Ja 2017

The Girlfriend Experience color *Entertainment Weekly* no1482/1483 p38 S 22 2017

Glenn Close on the Meaning of Alex color *Entertainment Weekly* no1484 p44 S 29 2017

Good Behavior *Entertainment Weekly* no1482/1483 p39 S 22 2017

A GOOD YEAR FOR BAD WOMEN color *Entertainment Weekly* no1444/1445 p54 D 16 2016

THE GREATEST DISNEY SONGS OF ALL TIME color *Entertainment Weekly* no1454/1455 p36 F 24 2017

A Gym Teacher Visited The Breakfast Club color *Entertainment Weekly* no1460/1461 p40 Ap 7-17 2017

Hail to the Ulti mate Chief color diag *Entertainment Weekly* no1438 p32 N 4 2016

HALEY LU RICHARDSON color *Entertainment Weekly* no1478 / 1479 p86 Ag 18-25 2017

Harry Potter: By the Numbers color *Entertainment Weekly* no1435 p10 O 14 2016

Hit the Road *Entertainment Weekly* no1482/1483 p60 S 22 2017

How the Cookie Crumbles color *Entertainment Weekly* no1434 p18 O 7 2016

IN UTERO POWER LIST color *Entertainment Weekly* no1454/1455 p21 F 24 2017

Is Winter the New Summer? color *Entertainment Weekly* no1462 p18 Ap 21 2017

JASON RITTER OF Kevin (Probably) Saves the World color *Entertainment Weekly* no1482/1483 p61 S 22 2017

JUMANJI: WELCOME TO THE JUNGLE color *Entertainment Weekly* no1478 / 1479 p73 Ag 18-25 2017

KATE WALSH STANDS WITH WOMEN color *Entertainment Weekly* no1457/1458 p16 Mr 17 2017

Law & Order True Crime: The Menendez Murders color *Entertainment Weekly* no1482/1483 p62 S 22 2017

THE LEGO NINJAGO MOVIE color *Entertainment Weekly* no1478 / 1479 p47 Ag 18-25 2017

Lethal Weapon color *Entertainment Weekly* no1482/1483 p60 S

22 2017

The Little Hours color *Entertainment Weekly* no1473 p48 Jl 7 2017

Madam Secretary color *Entertainment Weekly* no1482/1483 p39 S 22 2017

Major Crimes *Entertainment Weekly* no1482/1483 p66 S 22 2017

Mascots color *Entertainment Weekly* no1435 p44 O 14 2016

MATT DAMON'S WATER FIGHT color *Entertainment Weekly* no1467 p14 My 26 2017

The Mick *Entertainment Weekly* no1482/1483 p67 S 22 2017

The Middle color *Entertainment Weekly* no1482/1483 p60 S 22 2017

Miss Peregrine's Home for Peculiar Children color *Entertainment Weekly* no1434 p43 O 7 2016

A Monster Calls color *Entertainment Weekly* no1448 p49 Ja 13 2017

The Most Insane Items in the Goop Gift Guide* color *Entertainment Weekly* no1442 p12 D 2 2016 Rebellious Special Issue

MULAN RIDES BACK INTO BATTLE—FOR REAL color *Entertainment Weekly* no1435 p10 O 14 2016

My Most Excellent Death color *Entertainment Weekly* no1460/1461 p93 Ap 7-17 2017

NCIS *Entertainment Weekly* no1482/1483 p60 S 22 2017

NCIS: Los Angeles *Entertainment Weekly* no1482/1483 p38 S 22 2017

NCIS: New Orleans *Entertainment Weekly* no1482/1483 p67 S 22 2017

The New Boy Next Door color *Entertainment Weekly* no1450 p44 Ja 27 2017

The New Crush color *Entertainment Weekly* no1440 p18 N 18 2016

NO. 29 LUKE CAGE color *Entertainment Weekly* no1436/1437 p68 O 21 2016

NO. 35 Falcon color *Entertainment Weekly* no1436/1437 p70 O 21 2016

NO. 49 Hawkeye color *Entertainment Weekly* no1436/1437 p78 O 21 2016

Ocean's 8: Everything We Know So Far color *Entertainment Weekly* no1442 p10 D 2 2016 Rebellious Special Issue

Outlander color *Entertainment Weekly* no1482/1483 p26 S 22 2017

PICTURE color diag *Entertainment Weekly* no1451/1452 p70 F 3-10 2017

Poldark *Entertainment Weekly* no1482/1483 p38 S 22 2017

ROUGH NIGHT color *Entertainment Weekly* no1463/1464 p54 Ap/My 2017

Sarah Jessica Parker Isn't a Carrie color *Entertainment Weekly* no1436/1437 p20 O 21 2016

Score: A Film Music Documentary color *Entertainment Weekly* no1471 p53 Je 23 2017

Seacrest IN! color *Entertainment Weekly* no1465 p17 My 12 2017

The Secret History of Twin Peaks color *Entertainment Weekly* no1436/1437 p106 O 21 2016

SEPARATION ANXIETY color *Entertainment Weekly* no1478 / 1479 p14 Ag 18-25 2017

Shameless color *Entertainment Weekly* no1482/1483 p30 S 22 2017

SHOCK of MOONLIGHT color *Entertainment Weekly* no1456 p42 Mr 10 2017

The Simpsons color *Entertainment Weekly* no1482/1483 p34 S 22 2017

Sing color *Entertainment Weekly* no1446/1447 p103 D 2016/Ja 2017

SIZE KINGS color diag *Entertainment Weekly* no1456 p54 Mr 10 2017

SMILF *Entertainment Weekly* no1482/1483 p43 S 22 2017

SOFIA COPPOLA'S THE BEGUILED color *Entertainment Weekly* no1453 p46 F 17 2017

Streaming color *Entertainment Weekly* no1472 p46 Je 30 2017

Ten Days in the Valley color *Entertainment Weekly* no1482/1483 p43 S 22 2017

This Is Us color *Entertainment Weekly* no1482/1483 p56 S 22 2017

THREE STRIKES OUT color diag *Entertainment Weekly* no1439 p13 N 11 2016

The Walking Dead color *Entertainment Weekly* no1482/1483 p38

S 22 2017

WAS THAT THE MOST POLITICAL SUPER BOWL EVER? color *Entertainment Weekly* no1453 p17 F 17 2017

WHAT NOW? *Entertainment Weekly* no1478 / 1479 p16 Ag 18-25 2017

What Really Happened After This Kiss in E.T.? color *Entertainment Weekly* no1460/1461 p46 Ap 7-17 2017

WHEN REALITY ATTACKS color *Entertainment Weekly* no1434 p14 O 7 2016

WHEN ZOMBIE SHARKS ATTACK color *Entertainment Weekly* no1468/1469 p84 Je 2-9 2017

White Famous color *Entertainment Weekly* no1482/1483 p36 S 22 2017

Wisdom of the Crowd color *Entertainment Weekly* no1482/1483 p34 S 22 2017

The Woman Changing the Face of Hollywood color *Entertainment Weekly* no1476 p46 Ag 4 2017

THE WORST FILMS OF THE YEAR color *Entertainment Weekly* no1444/1445 p62 D 16 2016

Your LGBTQ Pop Preview color *Entertainment Weekly* no1471 p44 Je 23 2017

Your Sunshiny, Stupendous, Seriously Spectacular SUMMER BUCKET LIST color *Entertainment Weekly* no1470 p32 Je 16 2017

Coggins, David

Ciao Napoli! bw color *Esquire* p142 BigBlackBook

Common Threads color map *Conde Nast Traveler* v52 no3 p64 Mr 2017

First, a Note About Napoli... color *Esquire* p158 BigBlackBook

Coggiola, John C.

Syracuse Music Students Keep Options Wide Open P. Lutz color *Downbeat* v84 no4 p94 Ap 2017

Cogman, Genevieve

The Burning Page *Publishers Weekly* v263 no46 p36 N 14 2016

Cognetta, Armand B. III

Activity-based protein profiling reveals off-target proteins of the FAAH inhibitor BIA 10-2474 chart color graph *Science* v356 no6342 p1084 Je 9 2017

Cognition

See also

Cognitive bias

Consciousness

Perception

BEWARE OF HAPPY MEMORIES C. Taylor color diag *Fortune* v175 no3 p40 Mr 1 2017

Deconstructing the sensation of pain: The influence of cognitive processes on pain perception K. Wiech bibl diag graph *Science* v354 no6312 p584 N 4 2016

Discover your true potential D. Chopra *Yoga Journal* no291 p4 My 2017

The long game [Cover story] R. Miller *Yoga Journal* no291 p26 My 2017

THE MAD GENIUS MYSTERY K. Perina *Psychology Today* v50 no4 p70 Ag 2017

Meet your next teacher [Cover story] *Yoga Journal* no291 p75 My 2017

ON THE RUN S. POLAN *Psychology Today* v50 no4 p16 Ag 2017

Quiet your mind color *Yoga Journal* p100 2016 Special Issue

Reactivation of latent working memories with transcranial magnetic stimulation N. S. Rose, J. J. LaRocque et al bibl graph *Science* v354 no6316 p1136 D 2 2016

Regular Exercise Is Part of Your Job R. Friedman *Harvard Business Review Digital Articles* p2 O 3 2014

Selective modulation of cortical state during spatial attention T. A. Engel, N. A. Steinmetz et al bibl graph *Science* v354 no6316 p1140 D 2 2016

Stroke Awareness N. Brechka *Better Nutrition* p6 My 2017

Sunny Side Up bw color *Better Nutrition* v79 no7 p20 Jl 2017

Webs of Perception J. Ingram color *Canadian Wildlife* v23 no4 p12 S/O 2017

Your Brain on Food L. TURNER color *Better Nutrition* v79 no3 p64 Mr 2017

Cognition disorder patients

Is Sex With A Brain-Damaged Man Assault? K. A. Appiah *New York Times Magazine* p22 S 10 2017

Cognition disorders
See also
    Delirium
    Dementia
    Memory disorders
Second opinion *Mayo Clinic Health Letter* v35 no9 p8 S 2017

Cognition disorders—Prevention
Better habits, better brain health *Harvard Health Letter* v42 no11 p4 S 2017

Cognition disorders—Risk factors
Health risks after cancer *Mayo Clinic Health Letter* v358 no8 p4 Ag 2017
How depression affects your thinking skills *Harvard Health Letter* v42 no7 p3 My 2017
Sweet Drinks: Bad for Your Brain? *Tufts University Health & Nutrition Letter* v35 no5 p6 Jl 2017

Cognition in animals
The Brainy Big Cats J. G. Goldman color *Scientific American* v315 no6 p18 D 2016
Cognition, behavior, and the globus pallidus *Science* v354 no6312 p594 N 4 2016

Cognitive ability
See also
    Cognitive training
Birdbrain Is a Misnomer: New Studies Show Birds' Remarkable Cognitive Skills J. Kluger color *Time* v190 no7 p24 Ag 21 2017
DO LESS, EARN MORE T. Ferriss color *Men's Health* v32 no7 p90 S 2017
Exercise your gray matter color *Good Housekeeping* v265 no2 p98 Ag 2017
KEEP YOUR MIND SHARP J. Challem color *Amazing Wellness* v8 no2 p32 Spr 2016
Selective modulation of cortical state during spatial attention T. A. Engel, N. A. Steinmetz et al bibl graph *Science* v354 no6316 p1140 D 2 2016
UPWARDLY MOBILE E. Williamson *Virginia Living* v15 no3 p24 Ap 2017

Cognitive ability—Research
BRAIN-BOOSTING SUPPLEMENT COMBO J. WUEBBEN color *Muscle & Performance* v8 no12 p14 D 2016
PIONEERS, DRIVERS, INTEGRATORS, & GUARDIANS [Cover story] S. M. J. VICKBERG and K. CHRISTFORT bw graph il img *Harvard Business Review* v95 no2 p50 Mr/Ap 2017

Cognitive bias
Canis Sapiens E. GRAHAM *American Scholar* v86 no3 p15 Summ 2017
FAIR-MINDED MACHINES M. Temming color graph map *Science News* v192 no4 p26 S 16 2017
How a Video Game Helped People Make Better Decisions C. K. Morewedge *Harvard Business Review Digital Articles* p2 O 13 2015
The Pros and Cons of Pros-and-Cons Lists C. Charyk color *Harvard Business Review Digital Articles* p2 Ja 6 2017

Cognitive development
Sensory overload hurts young brains L. SANDERS *Science News* v190 no12 p12 D 10 2016

Cognitive dissonance
BOMBARDIER SAFETY STANDDOWN R. MARK bw color *Flying* v144 no3 p70 Mr 2017
How Power Affects Your Productivity A. McKee *Harvard Business Review Digital Articles* p2 F 9 2015

Cognitive learning
See also
    Problem solving
Improving Student Note-Taking Skills C. CHANDLER *Education Digest* v82 no7 p54 Mr 2017

Cognitive objectives (Education)
Got grit? Maybe... B. Duckor color diag il *Phi Delta Kappan* v98 no7 p61 Ap 2017

Cognitive science
See also
    Cognitive styles
Cognitive science in the field: A preschool intervention durably enhances intuitive but not formal mathematics M. R. Dillon, H. Kannan et al chart color diag graph *Science* v357 no6346 p47 Jl 7 2017

Cognitive styles
Talking to Yourself (Out Loud) Can Help You Learn U. Boser *Harvard Business Review Digital Articles* p2 My 5 2017

Cognitive testing
HEAD TRAUMA HITS HOME B. Adams color *Cycle World* v56 no3 p18 Ap 2017

Cognitive therapy
Happy News for SAD People cartoon *Prevention* v69 no2 p8 F 2017
Improving Cognitive Function in Behavioral Health Treatment: Sovereign Health asks Veena Kumari, Ph.D., about Cognitive Remediation Therapy V. Kumari *Psychology Today* v50 no5 p12 S/O 2017
Unfamiliar Terms R. Brandshaft *Skeptical Inquirer* v41 no3 p64 My/Je 2017
YOUR LIFE *USA Today Magazine* v145 no2862 p6 Mr 2017

Cognitive training
Stay Sharp this Semester M. AIRHART *USA Today Magazine* v146 no2868 p45 S 2017
TRIAL JUDGMENT J. CHRISTIAN JENSENIUS and N. S. CAPLAN *Scientific American* v317 no2 p5 Ag 2017

Cognizant Technology Solutions Corp.
You Can't Delegate Talent Management to the HR Department R. Ashkenas *Harvard Business Review Digital Articles* p2 S 23 2016

Cohan, Lauren
LAUREN COHAN D. Ross color *Entertainment Weekly* no1438 p25 N 4 2016

Cohan, William D.
Can Wall Street Save Trump From Himself? color *Atlantic* v319 no3 p22 Ap 2017
HOW TO TEACH YOURSELF TO LOVE THE BANKS color *Fortune* v175 no4 p16 Mr 15 2017
IS GOLDMAN SACHS STILL NO. 1 ON WALL STREET? chart color diag *Fortune* v175 no8 p184 Je 15 2017
JAMES AND THE GIANT BREACH color *Vanity Fair* p114 Hollywood 2017 Supplement
The MET'S POWER FAILURE color *Vanity Fair* v59 no5 p122 Ap 2017
THE NEW ESTABLISHMENT 2017 bw color *Vanity Fair* v59 no11 p87 N 2017
NEW ESTABLISHMENT bw cartoon color *Vanity Fair* v58 no11 p124 N 2016
Paying Themselves Forward *New York Times Book Review* p16 Ap 9 2017
Send in the Clones color *Vanity Fair* v59 no2 p76 F 2017
STEPHEN MILLER'S WHITE RAGE bw color *Vanity Fair* v59 no7 p102 Summ 2017
A Very Goldman White House color *Vanity Fair* v59 no8 p90 Ag 2017

Cohane, Ondine
The Innkeeper's Diaries color *Conde Nast Traveler* v52 no3 p60 Mr 2017
Rome bw chart color map *Conde Nast Traveler* v52 no3 p52 Mr 2017

Cohen, Aaron
Deliberate Moves color *Downbeat* v84 no9 p27 S 2017
Stax Celebrateds 60 Years color *Downbeat* v84 no9 p18 S 2017

Cohen, Adam
Piece of Mind: At Ellis Island, a jigsaw challenge could seal an immigrant's fate *Smithsonian* v48 no2 p46 My 2017

Cohen, Alex
Players on a World Stage *Architectural Record* v205 no9 p61 S 2017
The Right Strategies color *Architectural Record* v204 no12 p33 D 2016

Cohen, Alina
ANDREA JOYCE HEIMER cartoon *Art in America* v105 no4 p116 Ap 2017
BELLA FOSTER color *Art in America* v105 no5 p130 My 2017
CRG color *Art in America* v105 no6 p137 Je/Jl 2017
MIRA DANCY color *Art in America* v105 no8 p121 S 2017

Cohen, Anat
Anat Cohen A. Morrison color *Downbeat* v84 no7 p38 Jl 2017

Cohen, Andrew Jay
THE HOUSE N. Sperling color *Entertainment Weekly*

no1463/1464 p49 Ap/My 2017

My Love Affair With Reality TV *TV Guide* v65 no21 p14 My 15 2017

Psychological Harm and Free Speech on Campus *Society* v54 no4 p320 Ag 2017

Cohen, Andy

Anderson Cooper S. STALL *Indianapolis Monthly* v40 no7 p25 Mr 2017

LOVE CONNECTION T. Stack color *Entertainment Weekly* no1468/1469 p49 Je 2-9 2017

Mr. Popular T. BRODESSER-AKNER *New York Times Magazine* p34 Ja 15 2017

WATCH WHAT HAPPENS LIVE L. ACKEN *TV Guide* v64 no46 p41 N 7 2016

Cohen, Anne L.

21st-century rise in anthropogenic nitrogen deposition on a remote coral reef diag graph *Science* v356 no6339 p749 My 19 2017

Cohen, Arianne

Alexander Betts color *Bloomberg Businessweek* no4532 p68 Jl 31 2017

BETTER DIETING THROUGH CHEMISTRY color *Bloomberg Businessweek* no4516 p70 Mr 27 2017

How Did I Get Here? bw color *Bloomberg Businessweek* no4526 p72 Je 12 2017

Joy Buolamwini color *Bloomberg Businessweek* no4529 p80 Jl 3 2017

KICK IT WITH YOUR COLLEAGUES color *Bloomberg Businessweek* no4525 p55 Je 5 2017

What I Wear to Work: DAVID ROSENBLATT color *Bloomberg Businessweek* no4497 p71 O 31 2016

Cohen, Armond

Nuclear power: Deployment speed—Response bibl *Science* v354 no6316 p1113 D 2 2016

COHEN, ASON

Rollerblading the Little Miami *Cincinnati Magazine* p62 Je 2017

Cohen, Ayelet-Hashahar Shapira

The linker histone H1.0 generates epigenetic and functional intra-tumor heterogeneity bibl graph *Science* v353 no6307 paaf1644-1 S 30 2016

COHEN, BEN

Jew-Blaming *Commentary* v142 no4 p43 N 2016

Cohen, Carol Fishman

Don't Lose Track of High Performers Who Take a Hiatus *Harvard Business Review Digital Articles* p2 Ja 5 2016

For Professionals Returning to Work, There's Power in the Cohort *Harvard Business Review Digital Articles* p2 Mr 30 2015

If You Offer Mid-Career Internships, Flaunt It *Harvard Business Review Digital Articles* p2 Jl 4 2016

Why Some People Intentionally Take a Pay Cut When Resuming Their Careers *Harvard Business Review Digital Articles* p2 Ja 28 2016

Cohen, Charles

REEL ESTATE color *Forbes* v199 no7 p19 Je 29 2017

COHEN, DANIELLE

Architectural Record Traveling Fellowships Awarded to Lea Oxenhandler and Benjamin Halpern color *Architectural Record* v205 no8 p20 Ag 2017

Chicago Architecture Biennial to Kick Off Round 2 *Architectural Record* v205 no9 p29 S 2017

Cohen, David

DAN ABOUT TOWN *Washingtonian Magazine* v52 no1 p30 O 2016

Cohen, Deborah

2006: Providence, RI *Lapham's Quarterly* v10 no1 p121 Wint 2017

Before Straight and Gay cartoon color *Atlantic* v319 no2 p40 Mr 2017

More Is More color *New York Review of Books* v64 no9 p42 My 25 2017

Cohen, Eli J.

Nanoscale-length control of the flagellar driveshaft requires hitting the tethered outer membrane color diag graph *Science* v356 no6334 p197 Ap 14 2017

Cohen, Eliot A.

Farewell, Obama M. T. OWENS *Weekly Standard* v22 no18 p36 Ja 16 2017

IS TRUMP ENDING THE AMERICAN ERA? color map *Atlantic* v320 no3 p68 O 2017

Restoring U.S. Strength A. HERMAN color *National Review* v69 no6 p42 Ap 3 2017

WAR WITHOUT END A. M. Codevilla *Claremont Review of Books* v17 no3 p23 Summ 2017

Cohen, Emmet

EMMET COHEN Student of History T. Panken color *Downbeat* v84 no2 p22 F 2017

COHEN, FRANCINE

WINE 1, 2, 3 color *Better Homes & Gardens* v95 no11 p139 N 2017

Cohen, Geoffrey L.

Closing global achievement gaps in MOOCs graph *Science* v355 no6322 p251 Ja 20 2017

COHEN, ILISA

sign up for fun *Parents* v92 no6 p134 Je 2017

tiny teenagers *Parents* v91 no12 p124 D 2016

Cohen, Jared

Cyberwars: We Must Prepare Ourselves for the Wars of the Future *Time* v188 no27-28 p25 D 26 2016

COHEN, JASON

Cinnaticin kid: justin doellman *Cincinnati Magazine* v50 no6 p86 Mr 2017

SLICE OF LIFE *Cincinnati Magazine* v50 no2 p24 N 2016

THERE AND BACK AGAIN *Texas Monthly* v45 no2 p94 F 2017

Cohen, Jason A.

BEST DENTISTS *Washingtonian Magazine* v52 no2 p244 N 2016

Cohen, Joel E.

More tornadoes in the most extreme U.S. tornado outbreaks bibl chart graph *Science* v354 no6318 p1419 D 16 2016

Cohen, Jon

AIDS epidemic nears control in three African countries color *Science* v354 no6317 p1213 D 9 2016

THE BIRTH OF CRISPR INC chart color diag *Science* v355 no6326 p680 F 17 2017

Controversial HIV vaccine strategy gets a second chance color *Science* v354 no6312 p535 N 4 2016

CRISPR patent ruling leaves license holders scrambling color *Science* v355 no6327 p786 F 24 2017

Dengue may bring out the worst in Zika color *Science* v355 no6332 p1362 Mr 31 2017

Easier cure for resistant TB color *Science* v355 no6326 p677 F 17 2017

EPIDEMIC INSURANCE color graph *Science* v356 no6334 p125 Ap 14 2017

A half-billion-dollar bid to head off emerging diseases color *Science* v355 no6322 p237 Ja 20 2017

MICE MADE EASY color *Science* v354 no6312 p539 N 4 2016

New Ebola outbreak rings alarm bells early color map *Science* v356 no6340 p788 My 26 2017

Pinpointing HIV spread in Africa poses risks color *Science* v356 no6338 p568 My 12 2017

A reporter does CRISPR color *Science* v354 no6312 p541 N 4 2016

Surprising treatment 'cures' monkey HIV infection color *Science* v354 no6309 p157 O 14 2016

SURVIVING THE CURE color diag *Science* v357 no6347 p122 Jl 14 2017

Where has all the Zika gone? color graph *Science* v357 no6352 p631 Ag 18 2017

Why is the flu vaccine so mediocre? color graph *Science* v357 no6357 p1222 S 22 2017

Zika rewrites maternal immunization ethics color *Science* v357 no6348 p241 Jl 21 2017

Cohen, Jordan

Put Yourself in Your Colleague's Shoes *Harvard Business Review Digital Articles* p2 O 6 2014

Use Subtle Cues to Encourage Better Meetings *Harvard Business Review Digital Articles* p2 S 12 2016

Cohen, Josh—Interviews

Finding the Green in Your Junk P. M. ESSWEIN color *Kiplinger's Personal Finance* v71 no4 p14 Ap 2017

COHEN, JOSHUA

A Balkans of the Mind *New York Times Book Review* p7 Ja 1 2017

THE CONFESSIONS cartoon *Wired* v25 no9 p70 S 2017

Evicted: The Israeli immigrants in Joshua Cohen's novel spend their days displacing delinquent tenants Z. Lazar *New York Times Book Review* p11 Ag 13 2017

The Moving Spirit S. Begley color *Time* v190 no4 p54 Jl 24 2017

West Meets East: A prize-winning French novelist presents a Viennese musicologist lost in dreams of a Levantine past *New York Times Book Review* p17 Jl 2 2017

COHEN, JUSTIN M.

Malaria Dollars and Sense bw color *Natural History* v125 no9 p28 S 2017

Cohen, Lauren H.

Patent Trolling Isn't Dead—It's Just Moving to Delaware *Harvard Business Review Digital Articles* p2 Je 28 2017

COHEN, LEAH HAGER

Bitter and Delicious: Tales that disclose the uncanny within the commonplace *New York Times Book Review* p12 Je 11 2017

COHEN, LEE

FAREWELL FACIAL color *Skiing* p104 D 2016

Cohen, Leonard, 1934-2016

By Your Side M. BARTON-FUMO color *Film Comment* v53 no1 p22 Ja/F 2017

Goodnight, grocer of despair M. BARCLAY color *Maclean's* v129 no47 p52 N 28 2016

How the Light Gets In C. Raab bw *Commonweal* v144 no8 p15 My 5 2017

HOW THE LIGHT GETS IN D. REMNICK bw cartoon *New Yorker* v92 no33 p46 O 17 2016

IN MEMORIAM M. SCARLES bw color *Tricycle: The Buddhist Review* v26 no3 p16 Spr 2017

Leonard Cohen 1934-2016 M. Vain, C. Collis et al color *Entertainment Weekly* no1441 p12 N 25 2016

Leonard Cohen J. Collins color *Time* v188 no22-23 p13 N/D 2016

Leonard Cohen's Golden Hour A. GREENE color *Rolling Stone* no1274 p15 N 17 2016

Leonard Cohen's Late-Night Serenade W. HERMES color *Rolling Stone* no1273 p49 N 3 2016

Leonard Cohen's Life of Poetry and Song D. COWAN bw *American Conservative* v16 no1 p54 Ja/F 2017

SO LONG, LEONARD color *Maclean's* v129 no47 p50 N 28 2016

'You Want It Darker' J. MAHLER bw *New York Times Magazine* p20 Mr 12 2017

Cohen, Lucas

Preventing mussel adhesion using lubricant-infused materials color diag graph *Science* v357 no6352 p668 Ag 18 2017

COHEN, MARILYN

TAX-SMART BOND SWAPPING *Forbes* v198 no8 p67 D 20 2016

Trash Tech color *Forbes* v199 no1 p46 Ja 24 2017

Cohen, Marisa

Alzheimer's and the 15-Year Window color *Prevention* v69 no8 p80 Ag 2017

birthday-party blues *Parents* v92 no4 p134 Ap 2017

HEART HEALTH color *Good Housekeeping* v264 no2 p101 F 2017

HOW TO Talk About Periods *Parents* v92 no11 p122 N 2017

"I THOUGHT I HAD ALZHEIMER'S" color *Prevention* v69 no11 p54 N 2017

let's talk about your mood color *Parents* v92 no6 p94 Je 2017

signs it's almost time *Parents* v92 no4 p124 Ap 2017

Cohen, Michael

INTERSTATE 5 KILLER color *Sports Illustrated* v125 no17 p108 N 21 2016 Double Issue

Cohen, Michael A.

A YEAR OF EXTREMES J. P. DOLAN *America* v215 no15 p32 N 14 2016

Cohen, Mike

Kenya Braces for Another Chaotic Election color *Bloomberg Businessweek* no4533 p28 Ag 7 2017

The Race to Lead South Africa Is On color *Bloomberg Businessweek* no4524 p15 My 29 2017

South Africa Tries to End a Leadership Crisis color *Bloomberg Businessweek* no4499 p40 N 14 2016

Cohen, Morris A.

Inventory Management in the Age of Big Data *Harvard Business Review Digital Articles* p2 Je 24 2015

COHEN, MUHAMMAD

THE WORLD'S BILLIONAIRES bw color diag graph map *Forbes* v199 no3 p84 Mr 28 2017

Cohen, Myron S.

Broadly neutralizing antibodies to prevent HIV-1 diag *Science* v357 no6359 p46 O 6 2017

Cohen, Nancy J.

Facials Can Be Fatal: A Bad Hair Day Mystery *Publishers Weekly* v263 no52 p102 D 19 2016

COHEN, NANCY L.

L.A. Women LEAD THE WAY *Ms.* v27 no1 p32 Spr 2017

COHEN, RACHEL M.

Bad Education color *New Republic* v248 no1/2 p11 Ja/F 2017

The New Fight for Labor Rights color *New Republic* v248 no10 p6 O 2017

Cohen, Rena Wish

Saving Atlanta's Centennial Olympic Park from Concert Damage *Parks & Recreation* v51 no12 p48 D 2016

COHEN, RICH

THE BESTEST GENERATION bw color *Vanity Fair* v59 no9 p152 S 2017

BEYOND OBSESSION color *Sports Illustrated* v127 no8 p50 S 18 2017

CALL TO STARDOM color *Vanity Fair* v59 no2 p62 F 2017

The Potemkin Prince color *Vanity Fair* v59 no11 p124 N 2017

STICKY BUSINESS color *Vanity Fair* v59 no1 p162 Holiday 2017

The Sun & the Moon & the Rolling Stones color *AARP: The Magazine* v59 no4A p52 Je/Jl 2016

Cohen, Richard

WHEN WHO MET SALLY? A. BEAUJON *Washingtonian Magazine* v52 no2 p21 N 2016

Cohen, Robin

A Mixed-Up World F. J. KOROM *Current History* v115 no784 p325 N 2016

Cohen, Roger Wolfe

Roger Wolfe Cohen P. Eisenberger, M. P. Fricke et al *Physics Today* v70 no8 p70 Ag 2017

Cohen, Ryan

Pet Smarter S. ADAMS color *Forbes* v199 no1 p42 Ja 24 2017

Cohen, Sam

FAREWELL FACIAL L. COHEN color *Skiing* p80 Wint 2017

Cohen, Sharonne

AL McLEAN Emphasis on Aesthetics color *Downbeat* v84 no2 p21 F 2017

Cohen, Sidney R.

Biological fabrication of cellulose fibers with tailored properties color *Science* v357 no6356 p1118 S 15 2017

More details on Israel's water story *Physics Today* v70 no6 p11 Je 2017

COHEN, STEPHEN F.

Against Kremlin-Baiting *Nation* v304 no8 p4 Mr 13 2017

Cohen, Stephen S.

YOU DIDN'T BUILD THAT R. Vedder *Claremont Review of Books* v17 no1 p79 Wint 2016/2017

Cohen, Steven, 1956——Finance

STEVE COHEN HAS NOTHING TO PROVE (BUT HE'S GOING TO PROVE IT ANYWAY) J. Wieczner color diag *Fortune* v174 no6 p94 N 1 2016

TOTAL RETURN S. KOLHATKAR cartoon *New Yorker* v92 no45 p34 Ja 16 2017

Cohen, Susan

The Top 20 Start-Up Accelerators in the U.S *Harvard Business Review Digital Articles* p2 Mr 31 2015

Cohen, Susan E.

Structural basis of the day-night transition in a bacterial circadian clock bibl diag *Science* v355 no6330 p1174 Mr 17 2017

Cohen-Sandler, Roni

FRIENDSHIP {decoded} color *Seventeen* v76 no4 p86 Jl/Ag 2017

Coherent scattering

From chaos to order in active fluids A. Morozov bibl color *Science* v355 no6331 p1262 Mr 24 2017

Cohn, David

Cloud Nine *Architectural Record* v205 no9 p92 S 2017

Extraterrestrial Encounter: Spanish firm SelgasCano pays respect to nature by jolting it with the surreal color *Architectural Record* v205 no8 p64 Ag 2017

MAGÉN ARCHITECTS bw color *Architectural Record* v204 no12 p46 D 2016

Norman Foster Foundation Hosts Inaugural Forum, Dedicates Building *Architectural Record* v205 no7 p29 Jl 2017

Spain: Looking Back 25 Years color *Architectural Record* v205 no8 p43 Ag 2017

Cohn, Fred

The Art of Conversation *Opera News* v81 no10 p62 Ap 2017

BACKSTORY: Joyce DiDonato *Opera News* v81 no6 p64 D 2016

BACKSTORY: Susan Graham *Opera News* v81 no5 p64 N 2016

Hawaii Opera Theatre *Opera News* v81 no6 p14 D 2016

Higher Power: Soprano Leah Crocetto views singing as a gift she is called to share *Opera News* v81 no12 p7 Je 2017

Soul SISTER *Opera News* v81 no5 p26 N 2016

Wagner: Die Walküre *Opera News* v81 no9 p51 Mr 2017

Cohn, Gabe

New York Spends $1.2 Billion a Year on Homelessness And yet the problem is only getting worse img *New York* v50 no6 p32 Mr 20 2017

OBAMA'S AMERICA img *New York* v49 no20 p12 O 3 2016

Cohn, Gary D., 1960-

The Adult in the Room M. Warren color *Weekly Standard* v22 no26 p12 Mr 13 2017

FROM WALL STREET TO PENNSYLVANIA AVENUE color *Fortune* v175 no2 p16 F 1 2017

The Swamp: Jessica Pressler: Gary Cohn's Gamble: Watching a risky career move unfold in real time img *New York* v50 no12 p24 Je 12 2017

'Chairman Cohn' Has a Nice Ring to It J. Smialek, M. Abelson et al color graph *Bloomberg Businessweek* no4533 p32 Ag 7 2017

SIX TRUMP ADVISERS WITH TIES TO THE WORLD'S BIGGEST PRIVATIZERS *In These Times* v41 no8 p19 Ag 2017

Cohn, Mary

The Pride of Shelburne Falls: This village in the Berkshire foothills has lots to be proud of—the famous Bridge of Flowers, for instance. But we recently discovered something else very special there color *Yankee* p40 Jl 2017

Cohn, Roy M., 1927-1986

DEAL with the DEVIL M. BRENNER bw color *Vanity Fair* v59 no8 p84 Ag 2017

My Name Is ROY COHN, and I MADE THIS man bw color *Esquire* p56 My 2017

Coin design

MINT CONDITION C. FEHRMAN *Cincinnati Magazine* v50 no4 p28 Ja 2017

Coin hoards

HOARDS OF THE VIKINGS D. WEISS color *Archaeology* v70 no1 p48 Ja/F 2017

KA-CHING! D. WEISS color *Archaeology* v70 no4 p9 Je-Ag 2017

Coinbase Inc.

THE 21ST-CENTURY BANK ROBBERY J. Wieczner color *Fortune* v176 no3 p52 S 1 2017

BITCOIN'S BLUE CHIP L. SHIN color graph *Forbes* v198 no8 p88 D 20 2016

Coincidence

SEPARATED AT BIRTH D. A. Rose *Harper's Magazine* v333 no1999 p33 D 2016

Coiné, Ted

The 7 Attributes of CEOs Who Get Social Media *Harvard Business Review Digital Articles* p2 D 3 2014

Coins

See also

Coin hoards

Gold coins

Silver coins

Brilliant Uses for Pennies B. SPECKTOR *Reader's Digest* v188 no1125 p68 N 2016

COKAL, SUSANN

Stormy Transports: Heavy weather catapults a woman into a stranger's body *New York Times Book Review* p11 Jl 2 2017

Coker, Joanna K. C.

Assembly of a nucleus-like structure during viral replication in bacteria bibl color graph *Science* v355 no6321 p1 Ja 13 2017

Coker, Keller

Coker Fosters Customized Learning at New School J. Hale color *Downbeat* v84 no7 p86 Jl 2017

COKER, MARK

Cultivating Superfans *Publishers Weekly* v264 no31 p40 Jl 31 2017

How to Market Self-Published E-books to Libraries *Publishers Weekly* v264 no13 p45 Mr 27 2017

Colabufo, Sandy

MOUNTAIN RAILROADING, NEW YORK STYLE color il *Model Railroader* v83 no12 p56 D 2016

COLACELLO, BOB

CAPTURING CALVIN KLEIN color *Vanity Fair* v59 no9 p218 S 2017

LIVING BY DESIGN bw color *Vanity Fair* v59 no4 p202 Mr 2017

THE LURE OF LACMA color *Vanity Fair* v58 no12 p138 D 2016

Made in Montauk color *Vanity Fair* v59 no8 p96 Ag 2017

Studio Fever bw color *Vanity Fair* v59 no9 p134 S 2017

SUZY HAD THE SCOOP! bw color *Vanity Fair* v59 no2 p106 F 2017

Colalillo, R.

Observation of a large-scale anisotropy in the arrival directions of cosmic rays above 8×10^{18} eV *Science* v357 no6357 p1266 S 22 2017

Colangeli, L.

Seasonal exposure of carbon dioxide ice on the nucleus of comet 67P/Churyumov-Gerasimenko bibl bw graph *Science* v354 no6319 p1563 D 23 2016

Colarusso, Laura

Making Nice With the Loan Sharks color *Washington Monthly* v49 no3-5 p63 Mr-My 2017

Colatch, John Patrick

SURPRISE *Christian Century* v134 no12 p22 Je 7 2017

COLBERT, AMY

UNITED, BODY & SOUL *Commonweal* v144 no11 p4 Je 16 2017

Colbert, David

IS A $2,000 FACIAL WORTH IT? E. Listfield color *Harper's Bazaar* no3655 p160 Ag 2017

Colbert, Stephen, 1964-

AUTHORITY ALWAYS WINS E. NUSSBAUM cartoon *New Yorker* v93 no9 p64 Ap 17 2017

Humor in Uniform *Reader's Digest* v189 no1128 p134 Mr 2017

Kennedy Center Honors M. Roffman *TV Guide* p39 D 19 2016

Showbiz's Multiple-Personality Meter R. Rahman color *Entertainment Weekly* no1472 p49 Je 30 2017

Sound Bites color *Entertainment Weekly* no1434 p6 O 7 2016

Titans color *Time* v189 no16/17 p94 My 1-8 2017

Colbert, Tyraia

Step Up to a Breakthrough color *Women's Health* v14 no9 p88 N 2017

Colbourne, John K.

The genomic landscape of rapid repeated evolutionary adaptation to toxic pollution in wild fish bibl graph *Science* v354 no6317 p1305 D 9 2016

Colby, Charles

The On-Demand Economy Is Growing, and Not Just for the Young and Wealthy *Harvard Business Review Digital Articles* p2 Ap 14 2016

Colby, Chris

BREWING BEER The Basic: Bottle your own beer by using four ingredients and following four steps *Mother Earth News* no284 p35 O/N 2017

Colby, Gordon

MTI ADVENTUREWEAR: ALL IN THE FAMILY J. MOAG color *Canoe & Kayak Magazine* v45 no1 p92 Wint 2017

Colby, Laura

Kaplan Sells Its College But Keeps Its Profits *Bloomberg Businessweek* no4521 p23 My 8 2017

L'Oréal's Problem With Men cartoon graph *Bloomberg Businessweek* no4537 p19 S 11 2017

Tired of Halal Chicken? Try the Eyeshadow color *Bloomberg Businessweek* no4505 p24 D 26 2016

Colby, Ruth

Making Hospital Partnerships Work *Harvard Business Review Digital Articles* p2 D 10 2015

Colby, Susan

What It Will Take to Make the Tech Industry More Diverse *Harvard Business Review Digital Articles* p2 Mr 15 2016

Cold (Disease)

Our Doc Will See You Now R. Rajapaksa color *Health* v31 no1 p80 Ja 2017

Started School and Sick Already color *Parents* v92 no9 p26 S 2017

Cold (Disease)—Prevention

10 Steps to Protect Yourself Against Colds and Flu *Tufts University Health & Nutrition Letter* v34 no8 p4 O 2016

Can vitamin C prevent a cold? *Harvard Health Letter* v42 no4 p7 F 2017

the cold (and flu) truth T. G. HOPE *Better Homes & Gardens* v94 no11 p150 N 2016

COLD BUSTERS [Cover story] M. Kadey color *Vegetarian Times* v43 no2 p26 N/D 2016

COLD RELIEF... IN A K-CUP! color *Health* v30 no10 p18 D 2016

HOW TO OUTSMART COLD+FLU SEASON [Cover story] J. MIGALA cartoon chart color *Good Housekeeping* v263 no5 p163 N 2016

immunity now! S. SEA GOLD *Parents* v91 no11 p38 N 2016

Keeping Winter Bugs at Bay V. TWEED color *Better Nutrition* v78 no12 p60 D 2016

STAGES OF COLDS & FLU J. Rice color *Amazing Wellness* v8 no6 p52 Early Winter2016

Cold (Disease)—Prevention—Research

Stay warm to beat a cold A. Iwasaki color *Redbook* p85 F 2017

Cold (Disease)—Treatment

5 Top Homeopathic Cold Remedies A. Constantinides color *Amazing Wellness* v9 no1 p72 Wint 2017

Cold (Temperature)

Chill Out to Burn Fat color *Health* v30 no10 p11 D 2016

COLD BUSTERS [Cover story] M. Kadey color *Vegetarian Times* v43 no2 p26 N/D 2016

Winterproof Your Pup L. Murray color *Health* v31 no1 p70 Ja 2017

Cold baths

Cold Showers B. Dolnick *New York Times Magazine* p26 Jl 23 2017

Cold Brew Labs Inc.

Movers K. Stock color *Bloomberg Businessweek* no4526 p13 Je 12 2017

What We Learned from Improving Diversity Rates at Pinterest C. Morgan *Harvard Business Review Digital Articles* p2 Jl 11 2017

Cold Comfort (Poem)

438 BC: Pherae Euripides *Lapham's Quarterly* v10 no1 p126 Wint 2017

Cold Fish (Short story)

COLD FISH D. Byington *Harper's Magazine* v333 no1999 p75 D 2016

Cold gases

The biggest spiderweb in the universe color *Astronomy* v45 no4 p14 Ap 2017

Galaxy formation through cosmic recycling N. Hatch color *Science* v354 no6316 p1102 D 2 2016

Cold prevention

4 Skills to Teach Him Before Cold Season A. Mencel color *Parents* v92 no11 p19 N 2017

DRUG-FREE COLD & FLU RELIEF [Cover story] J. Cosgrove color *Amazing Wellness* v9 no6 p62 EarlyWint 2017

fall immunity guide V. TWEED color *Better Nutrition* v79 no10 p42 O 2017

Cold Spring Harbor Laboratory

THE PREPRINT DILEMMA J. Kaiser chart color graph *Science* v357 no6358 p1344 S 29 2017

Cold therapy

THE BIG CHILL *Saturday Evening Post* v288 no6 p75 N/D 2016

Heat or Ice? C. W. Dineen color *Health* v30 no10 p65 D 2016

Cold therapy—Evaluation

Beauty S. GRINNELL cartoon color *Vanity Fair* p94 Hollywood 2017 Supplement

Cold therapy—Research

Cold Comfort D. F. Maron color *Scientific American* v316 no1 p22 Ja 2017

Cold treatments

The best cold & flu fighting secrets of all time E. Crain, K. Holland et al color *Health* v31 no9 p71 N 2017

Rhinopneumonitis L. Bonner color diag *Equus* no480 p35 S 2017

Cold weather clothing

The Art and Science of LAYERING E. Larsen color diag *Backpacker* p71 My 2017

THE BEST BET img *New York* p39 Ja 23 2017

COZY UP color *Essence* v48 no6 p30 O 2017

GET KOSELIG! L. F. Prater *Successful Farming* v115 no2 p64 F 2017

LIFTING THE DARKNESS T. ROSS color *Rodale's Organic Life* v2 no7 p80 D 2016/Ja 2017

The Popular Mechanics WINTER OUTFITTER color *Popular Mechanics* p50 N 2017

Winter Clothing-Care Guide *Good Housekeeping* v264 no3 p57 Mr 2017

Cold weather clothing—Evaluation

THE GEAR A. Shoalts *Canadian Geographic* v136 no6 p35 D 2016

LOOK CUTE ON YOUR COMMUTE S. Zlotnick *Washingtonian Magazine* v52 no5 p113 F 2017

SQUALL PARKA color *Good Housekeeping* v264 no1 p136 Ja 1 2017

What to Know NOW N. Silverstein, S. P. Nadella et al color *Glamour* v114 no11 p72 N 2016

Winter Is Coming [Cover story] J. K. de Valle and J. S. Van Lith color *Glamour* v114 no11 p53 N 2016

Cold weather conditions

Bacchus Takes an Ice Bath in Bordeaux G. Collins, R. Ruitenberg et al color *Bloomberg Businessweek* no4522 p24 My 15 2017

COLD-WEATHER PET-GROOMING GUIDE J. Szabo color *Amazing Wellness* v9 no6 p88 EarlyWint 2017

Staying Warm *Yankee* v81 no1 p24 Ja/F 2017

Coldplay (Performer)

The Playlist bw color *Rolling Stone* no1291/1292 p8 Jl 13 2017

Coldren, Faith

Transient compartmentalization of RNA replicators prevents extinction due to parasites bibl chart graph *Science* v354 no6317 p1293 D 9 2016

Cold War, 1945-1989

Cold-War Dangers color *Nation* v303 no19 p3 N 7 2016

FROM THE EDITOR P. Lay *History Today* v67 no4 p2 Ap 2017

'Tear Down This Big, Beautiful Wall' J. LILEKS *National Review* v68 no20 p37 N 7 2016

War can be fought with many things, sometimes even sandwiches M. Duff color *Car & Driver* v62 no11 p70 My 2017

Cold War, 1945-1991

Civil Wars & the Post–Cold War International Order B. D. Jones and S. J. Stedman *Daedalus* v146 no4 p33 Fall 2017

The Cold War's Modern Resistance M. LANDAS bw color *Discover* v38 no8 p74 O 2017

Stanislav Petrov S. Shuster color *Time* v190 no13 p17 O 2 2017

COLE, ALAN

The Case for Tax Reform color *National Review* v69 no8 p30 My 2017

COLE, ALISON

Living Out Loud: On good food, great reads, and strong women color *O, The Oprah Magazine* p20 S 2017

Cole, Brad

Niner RIP 9 color *Bike Magazine* v24 no6 p114 Ag 2017

COLE, BRANDON

SPACE ODDITY *Scientific American* v315 no3 p5 S 2016

Cole, Bruce

UNABASHED ELITISM *Claremont Review of Books* v16 no4 p78 Fall 2016

Cole, Daniel—Interviews

Baseball Bat to the Head P. G. ALLEN color *Publishers Weekly* v264 no6 p46 F 6 2017

Cole, David

Can the ACLU Stop Trump? G. Edelman color *Washington Monthly* v49 no3-5 p16 Mr-My 2017

The Court Moves Right *Nation* v305 no2 p4 Jl 17 2017

The Courts Fight Trump *Nation* v304 no16 p4 My 22 2017

The First Amendment vs. Trump color *Nation* v304 no4 p20 F 6 2017

How Voting Rights Are Being Rigged color *New York Review of Books* v63 no16 p26 O 27 2016

Making Trump Pay *Nation* v304 no17 p3 Je 5 2017

Obama's Civil-Rights Legacy—and Ours color *Nation* v304 no1 p34 Ja 2 2017 The Obama Years

Robert B. Silvers (1929–2017) [Cover story] bw color *New York Review of Books* v64 no8 p31 My 11 2017

Trump Is Violating the Constitution color *New York Review of Books* v64 no3 p4 F 23 2017

Trump's Constitutional Crisis [Cover story] color *New York Review of Books* v64 no10 p51 Je 8 2017

Trump's Travel Bans—Look Beyond the Text [Cover story] color *New York Review of Books* v64 no8 p4 My 11 2017

The Truth About Our Prison Crisis bw color *New York Review of Books* v64 no11 p29 Je 22 2017

What James Comey Did color *New York Review of Books* v63 no19 p4 D 8 2016

Why Free Speech Is Not Enough color *New York Review of Books* v64 no5 p34 Mr 23 2017

Why We Must Still Defend Free Speech color *New York Review of Books* v64 no14 p61 S 28 2017

Cole, David—Interviews

DAVID COLE M. M. Kashino *Washingtonian Magazine* v52 no5 p39 F 2017

'I've Never Seen Citizen Engagement of This Type' R. Conniff color *Progressive* v81 no5 p59 Je/Jl 2017

Cole, Desmond

Black Lives Matter in Canada, Too D. DETTLOFF *America* v215 no14 p11 N 7 2016

Cole, G. D.

Direct frequency comb measurement of OD + CO→DOCO kinetics bibl graph *Science* v354 no6311 p444 O 28 2016

Cole, Harold

A "Big Intellectual Risk" J. Wolf *Hoover Digest: Research & Opinion on Public Policy* no4 p195 Fall 2016

Cole, Jennifer V.

THE SOUTH'S BEST Biscuits color *Southern Living* v52 no1 p63 Ja 2017

Cole, Jim

Rapid cooling and cold storage in a silicic magma reservoir recorded in individual crystals color diag graph *Science* v356 no6343 p1154 Je 16 2017

COLE, JUAN

How to Beat ISIS *Nation* v304 no7 p5 Mr 6 2017

Cole, Kevin P.

Kilogram-scale prexasertib monolactate monohydrate synthesis under continuous-flow CGMP conditions chart diag *Science* v356 no6343 p1144 Je 16 2017

Cole, Lauren Lyons

Save Money il *Consumer Reports* v82 no3 p30 Mr 2017

Cole, Natalie, 1950-2015

2016: A LOOK BACK AT THE YEAR IN BLACK CULTURE D. Henderson color *Essence* v47 no8 p100 D 2016

NATALIE COLE R. HOERBURGER *New York Times Magazine* p28 D 25 2016

Cole, Paula

Cole Offers Exquisite Take on Standards B. Doerschuk color *Downbeat* v84 no10 p23 O 2017

COLE, REBECCA

Transformational Principles for NEON Sampling of Mammalian Parasites and Pathogens: A Response to Springer and Colleagues *BioScience* v66 no11 p917 N 1 2016

COLE, REGINA

1830 HOUSE IN ROSLYN color *Old House Journal* v45 no4 p22 Je 2017

bold INTENTIONS color *Old House Journal* v45 no2 p22 Ap 2017

GEORGIAN BY CANDLELIGHT color *Old House Journal* v45 no6 p24 S 2017

Lessons from NAUMKEAG color *Arts & Crafts Homes & the Revival* v12 no3 p58 Summ 2017

One Wright Pilgrimage color *Arts & Crafts Homes & the Revival* v12 no3 p20 Summ 2017

QUIET UPGRADES: A MODERN BUNGALOW MAKE color

Arts & Crafts Homes & the Revival v12 no5 p50 Wint 2018

A TASTE OF THE PAST color *Old House Journal* v45 no6 p30 S 2017

wright ON THE RIVER color *Arts & Crafts Homes & the Revival* v12 no2 p50 Spr 2017

Cole, Renée S.

From Dissemination to Propagation: A New Paradigm for Education Developers *Change* v49 no4 p35 Jl/Ag 2017

Cole, Richard—Interviews

WORLD OF WAR J. STOWELL *Cincinnati Magazine* v50 no7 p20 Ap 2017

Cole, Roger

plumb Perfect color *Yoga Journal* p34 2017 Special Issue

Cole, Sarah

Video Links Professors to Far-Flung Student Teachers B. IASEVOLI *Education Digest* v82 no9 p14 My 2017

Cole, Stewart T.

Red squirrels in the British Isles are infected with leprosy bacilli bibl color diag map *Science* v354 no6313 p744 N 11 2016

Cole, Tanner

Coal and Climate Change in Kentucky color *Progressive* v81 no2 p16 F 2017

Cole, Teju

A Burning Collection N. Rush color *New York Review of Books* v64 no6 p23 Ap 6 2017

Candid Camera R. PINSKY *New York Times Book Review* p15 Je 4 2017

A grandmother's death prompts a search for her in family snapshots. Photographs are our reservoirs of memory, our talismans of mourning *New York Times Magazine* p12 Jl 16 2017

Returning to the same landscape gives photographers the chance to catch time itself at work *New York Times Magazine* p14 F 5 2017

Taryn Simon's photographs — canny, unsentimental and meticulously made — attend to the details of how power works color *New York Times Magazine* p18 D 4 2016

Through blur, shadow and drift, the photographer Santu Mofokeng shows that black South Africans were more than their suffering *New York Times Magazine* p12 Ag 13 2017

With color photography of a dreamlike lushness, Marie Cosindas pioneered a magic all her own *New York Times Magazine* p16 S 10 2017

COLE, TERRY WOLFISCH

Home of the Brave cartoon *Reader's Digest* v190 no1132 p99 Jl/Ag 2017

Coleman, A.

Observation of a large-scale anisotropy in the arrival directions of cosmic rays above 8 × 1018 eV *Science* v357 no6357 p1266 S 22 2017

Coleman, Aaron

Too Far North T. Hayes *New York Times Magazine* p17 Jl 9 2017

Coleman, Angel—Interviews

the SPIN TWINS J. Thompson color *Essence* v47 no10 p76 F 2017

Coleman, Arica L.

Trail Sisters: Freedwomen in Indian Territory, 1850-1890 *American Indian Quarterly* v40 no3 p274 Summ 2016

Coleman, Brent

The Chair Maker *Cincinnati Magazine* v50 no5 p84 F 2017

ENCYCLOPEDIA CINCINNATI bw cartoon color *Cincinnati Magazine* v51 no1 p42 O 2017

END OF THE ROAD *Cincinnati Magazine* v50 no5 p66 F 2017

HIVE MIND *Cincinnati Magazine* p20 Je 2017

Coleman, Brian D.

All About Cabinet Hinges color *Old House Journal* v45 no1 p52 F 2017

Artist Shawn Krueger color *Arts & Crafts Homes & the Revival* v12 no5 p48 Wint 2018

THE Arts & Crafts ROOM color *Arts & Crafts Homes & the Revival* v12 no1 p10 2017 Resouce Guide

California ease color diag *Arts & Crafts Homes & the Revival* v12 no2 p58 Spr 2017

Chicken-wire Glass bw color *Old House Journal* v45 no1 p56 F 2017

Coat Rack from a Porch Post color *Old House Journal* v45 no6 p58 S 2017

A Colorful Welcome color *Old House Journal* v45 no7 p54 O 2017

The Conference Skinny bw color *Arts & Crafts Homes & the Revival* v12 no5 p20 Wint 2018

A Cottage All Grown Up color *Old House Journal* v44 no8 p16 D 2016

D. Porthault M. OWENS color *Architectural Digest* v74 no9 p46 S 2017

English Sensibility color *Old House Journal* v45 no6 p74 S 2017

Fire Screen to Window Grille color *Old House Journal* v45 no4 p56 Je 2017

Framed by Tin Ceiling bw color *Old House Journal* v44 no8 p56 D 2016

A Frank Lloyd Wright Rescue color *Arts & Crafts Homes & the Revival* v12 no4 p52 Fall 2017

Hanging Curtains & Drapery: 1900–1939 color *Arts & Crafts Homes & the Revival* v12 no4 p22 Fall 2017

Hanging Drapery bw color *Old House Journal* v45 no6 p52 S 2017

A House Rescued Simplicity Restored color *Old House Journal* v45 no5 p14 Ag 2017

Lost & Found ... a restoration tale color *Old House Journal* v45 no7 p14 O 2017

MOSAIC PATTERNS for Serviceable Floors color *Arts & Crafts Homes & the Revival* v12 no2 p29 Spr 2017

Powder Rooms & Half Baths color diag *Old House Journal* v45 no6 p64 S 2017

the profound delight in PERSONAL EXPRESSION [Cover story] color *Arts & Crafts Homes & the Revival* v12 no4 p40 Fall 2017

Reclaimed Wood Tables color *Old House Journal* v45 no3 p56 My 2017

scandinavian STORYBOOK color *Old House Journal* v45 no3 p14 My 2017

Shelf Brackets Rehab color *Old House Journal* v45 no2 p56 Ap 2017

SIMPLE LIVING in Santa Barbara chart color *Arts & Crafts Homes & the Revival* v11 no5 p38 Wint 2017

vernacular to a fare-thee-well color *Arts & Crafts Homes & the Revival* v11 no5 p56 Wint 2017

Window Boxes color *Old House Journal* v45 no5 p60 Ag 2017

Window Shades from Vintage Maps color *Old House Journal* v45 no5 p56 Ag 2017

Coleman, Christina

HOW BLACK WOMEN ATHLETES AT THE OLYMPICS HELPED RESTORE MY PATRIOTISM color *Essence* v47 no8 p102 D 2016

LEADERS of the NEW SCHOOL color *Essence* v47 no11 p100 Mr 2017

Coleman, Courtney—Interviews

STARTING FRESH M. K. QUINLAN color *House Beautiful* v159 no4 p108 My 2017

Coleman, David

modern getaway color *Cabin Living* p65 Ag 2017

Coleman, Dren—Interviews

the SPIN TWINS J. Thompson color *Essence* v47 no10 p76 F 2017

Coleman, Jackie

Don't Take Work Stress Home with You *Harvard Business Review Digital Articles* p2 Jl 28 2016

Increase the Odds of Achieving Your Goals by Setting Them with Your Spouse *Harvard Business Review Digital Articles* p2 F 3 2015

Coleman, Jackson

Untapped Revenue color *Weekly Standard* v22 no29 p16 Ap 3 2017

Coleman, Jenna, 1986-

Queen V P. Sykes color *Vogue* v207 no1 p74 Ja 2017

STYLE CRUSH Jenna Coleman S. Simon color *InStyle* v24 no6 p56 Je 2017

Victoria J. Russell *TV Guide* v65 no2 p34 Ja 2 2017

Victoria: The teenage queen's early reign gets the Masterpiece treatment M. ROUSH *TV Guide* v65 no2 p18 Ja 2 2017

Coleman, Jenna, 1986—Interviews

VICTORIA STARS JENNA COLEMAN AND RUFUS SEWELL D. CLEHANE *British Heritage Travel* v38 no1 p32 Ja/F 2017

YOUR NEXT ROYAL OBSESSION C. Collis color *Entertain-ment Weekly* no1449 p53 Ja 20 2017

Coleman, John

6 Ways to Make the Most of Your Internship *Harvard Business Review Digital Articles* p2 Jl 11 2016

The Best Strategic Leaders Balance Agility and Consistency bw color *Harvard Business Review Digital Articles* p2 Ja 4 2017

Create a Conversation, Not a Presentation *Harvard Business Review Digital Articles* p2 Jl 29 2015

Don't Take Work Stress Home with You *Harvard Business Review Digital Articles* p2 Jl 28 2016

Increase the Odds of Achieving Your Goals by Setting Them with Your Spouse *Harvard Business Review Digital Articles* p2 F 3 2015

Lifelong Learning Is Good for Your Health, Your Wallet, and Your Social Life color *Harvard Business Review Digital Articles* p2 F 7 2017

Make Learning a Lifelong Habit bw *Harvard Business Review Digital Articles* p2 Ja 24 2017

Maximize Your Learning in Short-Term Assignments *Harvard Business Review Digital Articles* p2 Jl 15 2016

Use Storytelling to Explain Your Company's Purpose *Harvard Business Review Digital Articles* p2 N 24 2015

Why Businesspeople Should Join Book Clubs *Harvard Business Review Digital Articles* p2 F 23 2016

Coleman, John A.

A theology that weeps color *America* v216 no6 p44 Mr 20 2017

Coleman, Jonathan N.

All-printed thin-film transistors from networks of liquid-exfoliated nanosheets diag *Science* v356 no6333 p69 Ap 7 2017

Sensitive electromechanical sensors using viscoelastic graphene-polymer nanocomposites bibl graph *Science* v354 no6317 p1257 D 9 2016

Coleman, M. Ruth

Why GE, Boeing, Lowe's, and Walmart Are Directly Buying Health Care for Employees *Harvard Business Review Digital Articles* p2 Je 9 2017

Coleman, Mary Sue, 1943-

SAVING PUBLIC HIGHER EDUCATION *Vital Speeches of the Day* v82 no12 p362 D 2016

Coleman, Oliver D.

Posttranslational mutagenesis: A chemical strategy for exploring protein side-chain diversity diag *Science* v354 no6312 p597 N 4 2016

Coleman, Ornette, 1930-2015

Lavish Box Set Salutes Ornette P. Freeman bw *Downbeat* v84 no4 p13 Ap 2017

Coleman, Peter T.

What to Do If Your Boss Asks You to Break the Rules *Harvard Business Review Digital Articles* p2 Ja 7 2016

Coleman, Piers

Introduction to Many-Body Physics M. Randeria *Physics Today* v70 no5 p59 My 2017

Coleman, Reed Farrel—Interviews

Private Investigator and Redeemer L. PICKER color *Publishers Weekly* v263 no51 p126 D 12 2016

Coleman, Rory T.

Causal role for inheritance of H3K27me3 in maintaining the OFF state of a Drosophila HOX gene diag *Science* v356 no6333 p41 Ap 7 2017

COLEMAN, SUSAN

Q: What was the greatest summer read of your life? color *O, The Oprah Magazine* p16 Jl 2017

Coleman, Tevin

DIVIDE AND CONQUER G. Bishop color *Sports Illustrated* v126 no2 p40 Ja 16 2017

Coleman-Jensen, Alisha

Food Insecurity Among Children Declined to Pre-Recession Levels in 2015 *Amber Waves: The Economics of Food, Farming, Natural Resources, & Rural America* p41 N 2016

USDA's National School Lunch Program Reduces Food Insecurity *Amber Waves: The Economics of Food, Farming, Natural Resources, & Rural America* p38 Ag 2017

What Is Very Low Food Security and Who Experiences It color *Amber Waves: The Economics of Food, Farming, Natural Resources, & Rural America* p38 D 2016

Coleman-Lochner, Lauren

Shopping the Retail Apocalypse color *Bloomberg Businessweek* no4523 p37 My 22 2017

Where Dead Celebrities Go to Live cartoon color *Bloomberg Businessweek* no4530 p16 Jl 17 2017

Colen, Dan, 1979-
Good Medicine S. COCHRAN color *Architectural Digest* no6 p154 Je 1 2017

Coleridge, Mark
Archbishop Coleridge: Resist 'False Clarity' M. O'LOUGHLIN *America* v216 no1 p9 Ja 2 2017
New Wine, New Wineskins *America* v216 no3 p54 F 6 2017

Coleridge, Samuel Taylor, 1772-1834
1802: Somerset *Lapham's Quarterly* v10 no2 p37 Spr 2017

COLES, DON
Grandfather *Walrus* v13 no10 p61 D 2016

Coles, Edward James
Grandfather D. COLES *Walrus* v13 no10 p61 D 2016

Coles, Gregory
Single, Gay, Christian: A Personal Journey of Faith and Sexual Identity *Publishers Weekly* v264 no24 p61 Je 12 2017

Coles, Joanna, 1962-
Comments img *New York* v50 no6 p6 Mr 20 2017

Coles, Ken
FROM OUR READERS *Sky & Telescope* v133 no5 p6 My 2017

Coles, Robert
A child leads P. W. Marty *Christian Century* v134 no7 p3 Mr 29 2017

Coles, Sloane
Here's How [Cover story] color *Practical Horseman* v45 no7 p62 Jl 2017

Coleus
The Best New Plants for 2017 S. Bender color *Southern Living* v52 no1 p34 Ja 2017

Coley, Claudia
ask the experts color *Dressage Today* p66 My 2017

Cölfen, Helmut
Synthetic nacre by predesigned matrix-directed mineralization bibl bw diag graph *Science* v354 no6308 p107 O 7 2016

Colfer, Chris, 1990-
Chris Colfer N. Serrao color *Entertainment Weekly* no1457/1458 p102 Mr 17 2017

Colfer, Eoin, 1965-
Strange New Worlds D. Stern color *Publishers Weekly* v263 no44 p(Sp)17 O 31 2016

Colgan, Diane L.
THE BENEFITS *Washingtonian Magazine* v52 no1 p117 O 2016

Colgan, Jeff
Moving Way Left W. Voegeli *Claremont Review of Books* v17 no3 p9 Summ 2017

Colgan, Jeff D.
The Liberal Order Is Rigged *Foreign Affairs* v96 no3 p36 My/Je 2017

Colic
Be ready for colic color *Horse & Rider* v56 no9 p32 S 2017

Colic in horses
GOOD NEWS ABOUT LIFE AFTER COLIC SURGERY C. Barakat and M. McCluskey color *Equus* no476 p18 My 2017

Colic in horses—Prevention
DOWNTIME FEEDING C. Barakat and M. Freckleton color *Equus* no475 p30 Ap 2017
WATCH WINTER WATER INTAKE C. Barakat and M. Freckleton *Equus* no473 p18 F 2017

Colic in horses—Treatment
Colic L. Bonner bw color *Equus* no470 p26 N 2016

Colicchio, Tom, 1962-
Top Chef I. Ratledge *TV Guide* v64 no48 p41 N 21 2016

Colic—Treatment
THE BEST WAY TO TREAT SAND COLIC C. Barakat and M. McCluskey color *Equus* no474 p11 Mr 2017

Colier, Nancy
Happily out of reach M. Rollins *Redbook* p12 D 2016
Unplug a little, gain a lot color *Redbook* p101 D 2016

COLIN, CHRIS
ADVENTURES IN DRONE HORTICULTURE color *Popular Mechanics* p7 My 2017
CLOSE ENCOUNTERS color *Sunset* v238 no3 p20 Mr 2017

LOVE IN A WAR ZONE bw color *Men's Health* v32 no6 p124 Ag 2017
TOUGH CALL color *O, The Oprah Magazine* p30 F 2017

Colin, Fred
Mozart: Le Nozze di Figaro *Opera News* v81 no6 p51 D 2016

Colino, Stacey
Is Your Period Making YOU SICK? cartoon *O, The Oprah Magazine* p101 My 2017
paging mother nature *Parents* v91 no9 p36 S 2016
The Secret Behind Chronic Pain [Cover story] cartoon *Prevention* v69 no4 p68 Ap 2017
What your DOCTOR needs to know color *Good Housekeeping* v264 no6 p97 Je 2017

Colin Prentice, I.
Global climatic drivers of leaf size [Cover story] graph *Science* v357 no6354 p917 S 1 2017

Colitt, Raymond
Brazil's Great Leap Backward diag *Bloomberg Businessweek* no4535 p30 Ag 28 2017
Latin America Drains Its Political Swamp bw *Bloomberg Businessweek* no4531 p38 Jl 24 2017

Coll, Steve
Finding new ways to follow the story *Columbia Journalism Review* p21 Fall/Wint 2016
INFO WARS cartoon *New Yorker* v92 no48 p15 F 6 2017
MADMEN THEORIES cartoon *New Yorker* v93 no30 p17 O 2 2017
THE POLITICS OF ANGER cartoon *New Yorker* v93 no18 p17 Je 26 2017
TRUMP'S INTERVENTION cartoon *New Yorker* v93 no9 p19 Ap 17 2017

COLL, SUSAN
Mystery at the Museum: A smart debut about a disappearance in the art world *New York Times Book Review* p18 Ag 20 2017
ROCK STAR MOM *Washingtonian Magazine* v52 no8 p84 My 2017
Size Matters *New York Times Book Review* p11 Mr 12 2017
Way Down Under *New York Times Book Review* p20 O 2 2016

Collaborative consumption
What Customers Want from the Collaborative Economy A. Samuel *Harvard Business Review Digital Articles* p2 O 8 2015

Collaborative learning
Tele-Mentoring Is Creating Global Communities of Practice in Health Care D. Barash *Harvard Business Review Digital Articles* p2 N 22 2017

Collage—Exhibitions
WERNER BÜTTNER A. Considine color *Art in America* v105 no3 p132 Mr 2017

Collagen
10 Trending Supplements FOR 2017 V. TWEED color *Better Nutrition* v79 no1 p16 Ja 2017
Get a Collagen Boost M. D. SMITH color *Better Nutrition* v79 no9 p62 S 2017
JUST BEAUTIFUL! color *Amazing Wellness* v8 no6 p100 Early Winter2016
Medical-Grade Collagen: 102 Million Doses, 35 Years, 4,700 Health Professionals J. Caras chart color *Amazing Wellness* v9 no6 p10 EarlyWint 2017
Medical-Grade Collagen: 102 Million Doses, 35 Years, 4,700 Health Professionals J. Caras chart color diag *Better Nutrition* p18 My 2017
Orthopedic Exam N. Wilson *Natural History* v125 no1 p6 D 2016/Ja 2017
PUMP IT UP! M. D. Smith color *Amazing Wellness* v9 no6 p32 EarlyWint 2017

Collagen—Physiology
Burns Fat, Improves Sleep... and Beautifies Hair, Skin & Nails! J. Caras color diag *Better Nutrition* v79 no3 p20 Mr 2017

Collagen—Therapeutic use
Burns Fat, Improves Sleep... and Beautifies Hair, Skin & Nails! J. Caras color diag *Better Nutrition* v79 no3 p20 Mr 2017
Medical-Grade Collagen: 102 Million Dose, 35 Years, 4,700 Health Professionals J. Caras chart color diag *Better Nutrition* v79 no4 p20 Ap 2017

Collar, J. I.
Observation of coherent elastic neutrino-nucleus scattering diag

Science v357 no6356 p1123 S 15 2017

COLLARD, CHRIS

FROM NAPKIN NOTES TO WORLD PHENOMENA color *Dirt Sports + Off-Road* v51 no7 p20 Jl 2017

VIVA LA BAJA! [Cover story] color *Dirt Sports + Off-Road* v51 no10 p10 O 2017

Collard, Rebecca

Malala Yousafzai color *Time* v190 no4 p56 Jl 24 2017

New Travel Ban Helps U.S.-Iraq Relations but Still Stings Elsewhere color *Time* v189 no10 p7 Mr 20 2017

Collards

EAT YOUR WAY TO PROSPERITY C. K. Jackson and N. Jordan color *Essence* v47 no9 p83 Ja 2017

Collars

COLLAR THEM BAD color *Esquire* v167 no1 p78 F 2017

TECH RX S. STANKORB *Cincinnati Magazine* v50 no4 p69 Ja 2017

Collateral Beauty (Film)

ALSO PLAYING D. Coggan color *Entertainment Weekly* no1438 p44 N 4 2016

Helen Mirren in LIGHT & SHADOW R. LOVE color *AARP: The Magazine* v60 no1A p26 D 2016/Ja 2017

HOLDING HIS OWN T. A. Christian color *Essence* v47 no8 p67 D 2016

NEWLY AVAILABLE MOVIES M. FELL *TV Guide* v65 no31 p40 Jl 24 2017

Collateral circulation

heart therapy [Cover story] G. Rubanyi color *Scientific American* v316 no1 p38 Ja 2017

Collatz, G. J.

A human-driven decline in global burned area chart graph map *Science* v356 no6345 p1356 Je 30 2017

Collazo, Julie Schwietert

A quiet grief color *U.S. Catholic* v81 no11 p30 N 2016

Collectibles

See also
Antiques

The Gratitude Meter Z. Donaldson color *O, The Oprah Magazine* p26 O 2017

Inside Lou Reed's Archives D. FRICKE color *Rolling Stone* no1283 p13 Mr 23 2017

U.S. 127 Yard Sale A. B. WALTERS *Cincinnati Magazine* p58 Je 2017

Collecting of accounts

See also
Collection agencies

Collection & preservation of zoological specimens

Joanna Suitors Taxidermist: A Putnam County artisan cutting it in a male-dominated industry L. Wright *Indianapolis Monthly* v40 no10 p48 Je 2017

Collection, The (TV program)

The Collection A. D'arminio color *TV Guide* v65 no7 p45 F 13 2017

MARK YOUR CALENDAR! *TV Guide* v65 no37 p46 S 4 2017

Collection agencies

Board of Confusion A. Greenblatt *Governing* v30 no10 p9 Jl 2017

Should colleges use collection agencies for overdue student bills? K. KIPLINGER *Kiplinger's Personal Finance* v71 no11 p12 N 2017

Collection management (Museums)

See also
Museum curatorship

Autocorrect R. WETZLER color *ARTnews* v115 no3 p38 Fall 2016

Collections

See also
Private art collections

My Collection S. Metcalf color *Horse & Rider* v56 no9 p104 S 2017

Obsessions K. McMAHON and M. DURÓN bw color *ARTnews* v115 no3 p54 Fall 2016

Collective action

See also
Crowdsourcing

Collaborative environmental governance: Achieving collective action in social-ecological systems Ö. Bodin color *Science* v357

no6352 p659 Ag 18 2017

Collective bargaining

The New Fight for Labor Rights R. M. COHEN color *New Republic* v248 no10 p6 O 2017

Collective behavior

See also
Demonstrations (Collective behavior)
Mobilization (Social action)

THE ART OF PROTEST: When it comes to swaying public opinion, a provocative image can be a powerful tool [Cover story] B. BROWN *New York Times Upfront* v149 no13 p18 My 15 2017

Collective labor agreements in sports

American Voices Meghan Klingenberg G. Wahl and T. Keith color *Sports Illustrated* v126 no11 p24 Ap 17-24 2017

More Perfect Unions L. J. Wertheim and T. Keith color *Sports Illustrated* v125 no19 p19 D 12 2016

Collective memory

Ventral CA1 neurons store social memory Teruhiro Okuyama, Takashi Kitamura et al bibl graph *Science* v353 no6307 p1536 S 30 2016

Collective memory & music

In the Groove D. HARSANYI color *National Review* v69 no7 p48 Ap 17 2017

Collective memory—Research

Social memory goes viral K. Saxena and R. G. M. Morris bibl diag *Science* v353 no6307 p1496 S 30 2016

Collectivism (Political science)

See also
Communism
Fascism
Socialism

CHARLOTTESVILLE AND THE PERILS OF COLLECTIVISM E. BOEHM color *Reason* v49 no6 p7 N 2017

Collectors & collecting

See also
Antiques
Automobile collecting
Book collecting
Fashion collecting

FD Gallery H. MARTIN color *Architectural Digest* v74 no9 p34 S 2017

Major League Memorabilia J. Paskin color *Bloomberg Businessweek* no4524 p68 My 29 2017

Obsessions K. McMAHON and M. DURÓN bw color *ARTnews* v115 no3 p54 Fall 2016

Steven Chait H. MARTIN color *Architectural Digest* v74 no10 p34 O 1 2017

TECH VS. TYRANNY color *Reason* v49 no2 p9 Je 2017

Colleen B.

r.s.v.p bw *Bon Appetit* v62 no4 p10 Ap 2017

College & school drama

Conversing with Colleges J. Coakley *Stage Directions* v29 no11 p29 N 2016

College administrators—United States

MEMBER NEWS color *Phi Kappa Phi Forum* v97 no2 p3 Summ 2017

College admission officers

Should colleges give preference to applicants from wealthy families? color *Kiplinger's Personal Finance* v71 no6 p16 Je 2017

College applicants—Services for

Small Nudges Can Improve How Students Apply to College L. Page *Harvard Business Review Digital Articles* p2 N 29 2016

College applications

Aligned Transitions T. J. PACE and J. J. GARCIA *Education Digest* v82 no5 p12 Ja 2017

MONEY MATTERS: Ways you can pay for school N. LOEFFLER-GLADSTONE *Dance Magazine* v90 p20 2016/2017 Supplement College Guide

POST-ACCEPTANCE LETTER Hurdles N. Loeffler-Gladstone *Dance Spirit* v21 no4 p56 Ap 2017

College applications—United States

Small Nudges Can Improve How Students Apply to College L. Page *Harvard Business Review Digital Articles* p2 N 29 2016

College athlete recruitment

COLLEGES RECRUIT A NEW KIND OF ATHLETE: VIDEO GAMERS C. Morris color *Fortune* v176 no5 p23 O 1 2017

College athlete recruitment—Methodology

THE STREAM TEAMS P. Thamel color *Sports Illustrated* v126 no4 p62 Ja 30 2017

College athletes

See also

College basketball players

Snow Monkey N. Zevnik color *Better Nutrition* v79 no7 p16 Jl 2017

College athletes—United States

FACES IN THE CROWD T. Keith color *Sports Illustrated* v125 no20 p26 D 19 2016

FACES IN THE CROWD T. Keith color *Sports Illustrated* v126 no4 p22 Ja 30 2017

FACES IN THE CROWD T. Keith color *Sports Illustrated* v127 no1 p26 Jl 3 2017

FACES IN THE CROWD T. Keith color *Sports Illustrated* v127 no3 p23 Jl 24 2017

College athletes—United States—Finance

ALLOWANCE TO PLAY S. Kwak color map *Sports Illustrated* v127 no10 p18 O 2 2017

College athletes—United States—Wounds & injuries

When Pain Surpasses Gain J. Lisanti and T. Keith color *Sports Illustrated* v126 no4 p20 Ja 30 2017

College baseball

On the Team: College Baseball As a Rite of Passage D. WINKEL-MAIER *Idaho Magazine* v16 no9 p45 Je 2017

College basketball

On Sports J. C. Kang *New York Times Magazine* p18 N 20 2016

College basketball coaches

LEGAL BRIEF M. McCann *Sports Illustrated* v127 no11 p24 O 9 2017

College basketball players

HERE WE GO, 'ZO B. Hamilton color *Sports Illustrated* v125 no13 p42 O 17 2016

Leading Off color *Sports Illustrated* v127 no1 p6 Jl 3 2017

SLIM'S CHANCE [Cover story] L. Winn color *Sports Illustrated* v125 no15 p40 N 7 2016

College basketball players—Awards

Flying Start T. Blackmar *Sports Illustrated* v126 no1 p52 Ja 9 2017

College basketball players—History—21st century

ALL-GLUE TEAM S. Davis color *Sports Illustrated* v126 no8 p61 Mr 20 2017

Back to the Basket J. Fuchs and T. Keith color *Sports Illustrated* v126 no14 p28 My 15-22 2017

SCOUTING REPORTS color *Sports Illustrated* v125 no15 p54 N 7 2016

College basketball teams

Last Losers L. Flynn and T. Keith chart color *Sports Illustrated* v125 no21 p22 D 26 2016

Life Lessons of the Anti-Coach L. PLATT bw color *GQ: Gentlemen's Quarterly* v97 no3 p100 Mr 2017

College basketball teams—History—21st century

10 ARIZONA WILDCATS P. Thamel chart color *Sports Illustrated* v125 no15 p69 N 7 2016

11 PURDUE BOILERMAKERS J. Fuchs chart color *Sports Illustrated* v125 no15 p70 N 7 2016

12 XAVIER MUSKETEERS D. Greene chart color *Sports Illustrated* v125 no15 p71 N 7 2016

13 LOUISVILLE CARDINALS S. Davis chart color *Sports Illustrated* v125 no15 p72 N 7 2016

14 INDIANA HOOSIERS S. Davis chart color *Sports Illustrated* v125 no15 p73 N 7 2016

15 SYRACUSE ORANGE P. Thamel chart color *Sports Illustrated* v125 no15 p74 N 7 2016

16 UCLA BRUINS B. Hamilton chart color *Sports Illustrated* v125 no15 p75 N 7 2016

1 DUKE BLUE DEVILS B. Hamilton chart color *Sports Illustrated* v125 no15 p60 N 7 2016

2017-18 TOP 10 S. Davis color *Sports Illustrated* v126 no10 p40 Ap 10 2017

2 KANSAS JAYHAWKS D. Gardner chart color *Sports Illustrated* v125 no15 p61 N 7 2016

3 KENTUCKY WILDCATS S. Davis chart color *Sports Illustrated* v125 no15 p62 N 7 2016

4 OREGON DUCKS L. Winn chart color *Sports Illustrated* v125 no15 p63 N 7 2016

5 VILLANOVA WILDCATS D. Greene chart color *Sports Illustrated* v125 no15 p64 N 7 2016

6 NORTH CAROLINA TAR HEELS B. Hamilton chart color *Sports Illustrated* v125 no15 p65 N 7 2016

7 VIRGINIA CAVALIERS D. Greene chart color *Sports Illustrated* v125 no15 p66 N 7 2016

8 WISCONSIN BADGERS L. Winn chart color *Sports Illustrated* v125 no15 p67 N 7 2016

9 GONZAGA BULLDOGS L. Schnell chart color *Sports Illustrated* v125 no15 p68 N 7 2016

INSIDE THE RANKINGS L. Winn and D. Hanner color *Sports Illustrated* v125 no15 p56 N 7 2016

SCOUTING REPORTS color *Sports Illustrated* v125 no15 p54 N 7 2016

College basketball—History—21st century

'Tis the Season M. Rosenberg color *Sports Illustrated* v125 no19 p80 D 12 2016

College buildings—Design & construction

COLLEGES & UNIVERSITIES *Architectural Record* v204 no11 p95 N 2016

Design for Social Animals C. McGuigan *Architectural Record* v204 no11 p21 N 2016

Feast for the Senses B. BROOME *Architectural Record* v204 no11 p116 N 2016

Full House J. GAUER *Architectural Record* v204 no11 p104 N 2016

Minding the Gap S. WILLIAMS GOLDHAGEN *Architectural Record* v204 no11 p122 N 2016

Paired Off J. MINUTILLO *Architectural Record* v204 no11 p110 N 2016

Serene Machine S. STEPHENS *Architectural Record* v204 no11 p96 N 2016

College campuses

The Campus Culture Wars K. Steinmetz, C. Alter et al color *Time* v190 no16/17 p48 O 23 2017

Choosing Your Fight: Political Correctness and Free Speech on Campus M. Dunbar *Humanist* v77 no4 p9 Jl/Ag 2017

Congress and Campus D. FRENCH color *National Review* v69 no19 p38 O 16 2017

The Injustice of the 'Rape-Culture' Theory: For those in the grips of hysteria, proof is the enemy C. Young *Commentary* v144 no3 p26 O 2017

Let there be peace M. Murphy-Gill *U.S. Catholic* v82 no2 p4 F 2017

The Professor's Dilemma J. RICE and J. Marks *Commentary* v144 no3 p6 O 2017

College campuses—Safety measures

In guns we trust? F. A. Fitzgerald color *U.S. Catholic* v82 no2 p24 F 2017

College chaplains

Campus ministry: Multifaith chaplains move onto the quad A. Weaver color *U.S. Catholic* v82 no9 p12 S 2017

Muslim cleric to lead national association of chaplains in higher ed C. Kennel-Shank *Christian Century* v134 no8 p1 Ap 12 2017

The ties that bind E. Sanna *U.S. Catholic* v82 no9 p4 S 2017

College clubs

Harvard Finds a Scapegoat N. S. RILEY color *Weekly Standard* v22 no44 p16 Jl 31 2017

Harvard's Club Brawl J. SEDGWICK color *Vanity Fair* v59 no9 p224 S 2017

College costs

FIVE STEPS TO WIN MORE AID K. Clark color *Money* v46 no3 p52 Ap 2017

What Children Should Chip In K. Clark diag *Money* v46 no2 p35 Mr 2017

College costs—Canada

The travel paradox M. BROWN color graph *Maclean's* v130 no10 p72 N 2017

College costs—United States

On Money G. Rivlin color *New York Times Magazine* p18 My 21 2017

College curriculum

See also

Interdisciplinary approach in education

Eugene Lana College The New School for Liberal Arts *Dance*

Magazine v90 p59 2016/2017 Supplement College Guide

FCDD Amherst College *Dance Magazine* v90 p60 2016/2017 Supplement College Guide

FCDD Hampshire College *Dance Magazine* v90 p61 2016/2017 Supplement College Guide

FCDD Mount Holyoke College *Dance Magazine* v90 p62 2016/2017 Supplement College Guide

FCDD University of Massachusetts Amherst *Dance Magazine* v90 p61 2016/2017 Supplement College Guide

Five College Dance Department (FCDD) *Dance Magazine* v90 p60 2016/2017 Supplement College Guide

Golden Age of Classicism: Notre Dame's architecture school is rebuilding the traditional city L. MCCRARY il *American Conservative* v16 no4 p48 Jl/Ag 2017

Origins of Science Faculty with Education Specialties: Hiring Motivations and Prior Connections Explain Institutional Differences in the SFES Phenomenon S. D. BUSH, M. T. STEVENS et al *BioScience* v67 no5 p452 My 2017

College dropouts

Changing the Praxis of Retention in Higher Education: A Plan to TEACH All Learners A. M. Eitzen, M. A. Kinney et al *Change* v48 no6 p58 N/D 2016

College football

Cheer and Trebling S. Rushin color *Sports Illustrated* v127 no5 p116 Ag 14 2017

College Football's Fumble: Empty Stands E. Novy-Williams color *Bloomberg Businessweek* no4506 p17 Ja 9 2017

SPORTS K. ROSEN *TV Guide* v64 no48 p48 N 21 2016

W STARTS WITH D J. Niesen color *Sports Illustrated* v125 no13 p36 O 17 2016

College football coaches

Life Coach J. A. MILLER *Cincinnati Magazine* v50 no4 p56 Ja 2017

College football coaches—Awards

Coach Ed Orgeron F. ESKER color *Louisiana Life* v37 no3 p66 Ja/F 2017

College football coaches—Employment

WHAT IF THE PIRATE NEVER LEFT THE ISLAND? A. Staples color *Sports Illustrated* v127 no9 p36 S 25 2017

College football players

Leading Men G. Baumgaertner and C. Becht color *Sports Illustrated* v125 no14 p54 O 24-31 2016

NEW YORK JET P. Thamel color *Sports Illustrated* v125 no21 p38 D 26 2016

College football players—Education

Three and Out P. Thamel and T. Keith color *Sports Illustrated* v125 no16 p16 N 14 2016

College football players—History—21st century

WHO'S NO. 1? THESE PLAYERS COULD CHALLENGE JOSH ALLEN FOR THE TOP SPOT C. Becht color *Sports Illustrated* v126 no14 p101 My 15-22 2017

College football—Competitions

SPORTS K. ROSEN *TV Guide* p48 D 19 2016

College football—History—19th century

FOUNDERS' DAY A. BARRA *American History* v52 no1 p22 Ap 2017

College football—History—21st century

10 Auburn color *Sports Illustrated* v127 no5 p98 Ag 14 2017

11 Michigan color *Sports Illustrated* v127 no5 p99 Ag 14 2017

12 Wisconsin color *Sports Illustrated* v127 no5 p100 Ag 14 2017

13 LSU color *Sports Illustrated* v127 no5 p101 Ag 14 2017

14 Louisville color *Sports Illustrated* v127 no5 p102 Ag 14 2017

15 Stanford color *Sports Illustrated* v127 no5 p104 Ag 14 2017

16 Georgia color *Sports Illustrated* v127 no5 p105 Ag 14 2017

17 South Florida color *Sports Illustrated* v127 no5 p106 Ag 14 2017

18 Florida color *Sports Illustrated* v127 no5 p107 Ag 14 2017

19 Kansas State color *Sports Illustrated* v127 no5 p108 Ag 14 2017

1 Alabama [Cover story] color *Sports Illustrated* v127 no5 p88 Ag 14 2017

2017 COLLEGE FOOTBALL PREVIEW color *Sports Illustrated* v127 no5 p49 Ag 14 2017

2017 SI'S (WAY TOO EARLY) TOP 10 A. Staples color *Sports Illustrated* v126 no2 p33 Ja 16 2017

20 Miami color *Sports Illustrated* v127 no5 p109 Ag 14 2017

21 West Virginia color *Sports Illustrated* v127 no5 p110 Ag 14 2017

22 Washington State color *Sports Illustrated* v127 no5 p111 Ag 14 2017

23 Texas color *Sports Illustrated* v127 no5 p112 Ag 14 2017

24 Virginia Tech color *Sports Illustrated* v127 no5 p113 Ag 14 2017

25 Texas A&M color *Sports Illustrated* v127 no5 p114 Ag 14 2017

2 Florida State color *Sports Illustrated* v127 no5 p90 Ag 14 2017

3 Ohio State color *Sports Illustrated* v127 no5 p91 Ag 14 2017

4 Oklahoma State color *Sports Illustrated* v127 no5 p92 Ag 14 2017

5 USC color *Sports Illustrated* v127 no5 p93 Ag 14 2017

6 Oklahoma color *Sports Illustrated* v127 no5 p94 Ag 14 2017

7 Clemson color *Sports Illustrated* v127 no5 p95 Ag 14 2017

8 Penn State color *Sports Illustrated* v127 no5 p96 Ag 14 2017

9 Washington color *Sports Illustrated* v127 no5 p97 Ag 14 2017

COLLEGE FOOTBALL SCOUTING REPORTS color *Sports Illustrated* v127 no5 p87 Ag 14 2017

Prep Rally color *Sports Illustrated* v127 no5 p16 Ag 14 2017

Surprise, Surprise A. Staples color *Sports Illustrated* v125 no14 p53 O 24-31 2016

College football—Safety measures

NEW TAKES ON TACKLING A. Staples color *Sports Illustrated* v127 no5 p64 Ag 14 2017

College fraternity members

A Deadly Campus Tradition K. Reilly color *Time* v190 no16/17 p56 O 23 2017

College freshmen

Siri: Alta, Utah J. C. DAVIES color *Powder* p9 S 2017

THROWN TO THE WOLVES A. Staples color *Sports Illustrated* v127 no8 p56 S 18 2017

College freshmen—Attitudes

"WHAT I WISH I'D KNOWN" A. Smith *Dance Spirit* v21 no7 p72 S 2017

College freshmen—Social aspects

"WHAT I WISH I'D KNOWN" A. Smith *Dance Spirit* v21 no7 p72 S 2017

College graduate recruitment

Firms Are Wasting Millions Recruiting on Only a Few Campuses L. Rivera *Harvard Business Review Digital Articles* p2 O 23 2015

College graduates

The Average Mid-Forties Male College Graduate Earns 55% More Than His Female Counterpart E. Barth, C. Goldin et al *Harvard Business Review Digital Articles* p2 Je 12 2017

College graduates—Employment

College All Stars: Galaxy of Success J. Southerst color *Maclean's* v129 no46 p44 N 21 2016

We've got too many graduates *People Management* p6 N 2016

College majors

See also

Double majors (Education)

DOES YOUR CHOICE MEASURE UP? Check out the numbers surrounding popular degree choices and careers J. H. REDMOND *Cincinnati Magazine* v50 no11 pCG8 Ag 2017

College of New Jersey

Addicted to Fame: From the Greeks to Lady Gaga D. H. Blake *Humanities* v38 no4 p1 Fall 2017

College preparation programs

get into GEAR: Your four-year college-prep timeline M. BENJAMIN *Dance Magazine* v90 p28 2016/2017 Supplement College Guide

Washington View M. Ferguson *Phi Delta Kappan* v99 no1 p42 S 2017

College presidents

CHALLENGES OF AN AGING GLOBAL POPULATION *Vital Speeches of the Day* v82 no12 p374 D 2016

Exiting Academe A. Greenblatt *Governing* v30 no3 p12 D 2016

Faculty Expressions of (No) Confidence in Institutional Leadership A. C. Frantz and J. N. Lawson *Change* v49 no1 p62 Ja/F 2017

Patrick Awuah E. Turner *Current Biography* v78 no6 p8 Je 2017

College presidents—Interviews

BRINGING BACK BAYLOR T. C. REAM color *Christianity Today* v61 no7 p54 S 2017

College sophomores
BEWARE THE RED ZONE S. KARDIAN *USA Today Magazine* v146 no2868 p42 S 2017

College sorority members
KΣ$ K. Bhasin color graph *Bloomberg Businessweek* no4495 p16 O 17 2016

College sports
See also
National Collegiate Athletic Association
On Sports J. C. Kang *New York Times Magazine* p18 N 20 2016
SPEARFISH: HIPPIE HAVEN? P. Higbee *South Dakota Magazine* v32 no4 p54 N/D 2016

College sports spectators
Best Colleges for Sports Lovers K. Mulhere chart *Money* v46 no3 p24 Ap 2017
Class Rank D. Greene and T. Keith color *Sports Illustrated* v126 no8 p17 Mr 20 2017

College sports—United States
A LEAGUE AHEAD M. Rosenberg color *Sports Illustrated* v125 no19 p32 D 12 2016

College sports—United States—History
Dreams Redeemed W. Leitch and T. Keith color *Sports Illustrated* v127 no1 p24 Jl 3 2017

College stores
College Stores—and the Businesses That Serve Them—in a Time of Change J. Rosen color *Publishers Weekly* v263 no48 p5 N 28 2016

College stores—Social aspects
National Association of College Stores Gears Up to Fight for Indies J. Rosen color *Publishers Weekly* v264 no11 p4 Mr 13 2017

College student development programs
College Promise: Pathway to the 21 Century M. J. Kanter, A. Armstrong et al *Change* v48 no6 p6 N/D 2016

College student mobility
OUTWARD BOUND J. CROWN cartoon graph *Chicago* v66 no2 p13 F 2017

College student travel
The travel paradox M. BROWN color graph *Maclean's* v130 no10 p72 N 2017

College students
See also
College freshmen
College sophomores
Undergraduates
5 Ways to Make the Most of College E. Y. REITZ *Christianity Today* p68 Mr 2017
back to school (again): Professional dancer Ida Saki on why she chose to return to college A. RIVERS *Dance Magazine* v90 p24 2016/2017 Supplement College Guide
CARNAL KNOWLEDGE A. Orr color *Louisiana Life* v38 no1 p16 S/O 2017
COLLEGE ELECTORAL S. Desai color *Washington Monthly* v49 no9/10 p58 S/O 2017
COLUMBIA'S IDENTITY CRISIS T. C. Fishman bw color graph *Chicago* v66 no1 p110 Ja 2017
From College to Career: The Struggle Is Real E. Y. Reitz color *Christianity Today* p63 Mr 2017
Help Create a Veggie World *Vegetarian Journal* v36 no3 p32 2017
MEET THE NU-NERDS T. TULATHIMUTTE color *Wired* v25 no5 p100 My 2017
There's No One Right Age to Be Awesome C. Leive color *Glamour* v115 no5 p16 My 2017
WAITING FOR THE GREAT LEAP FORWARD J. DeBrosse *Cincinnati Magazine* v50 no8 p60 My 2017
The Young Rocketeers J. PAPPALARDO color *Popular Mechanics* p26 N 2017

College students—Attitudes
Online Student Orientation: Guerrilla Style D. Swett *Change* v48 no5 p26 S/O 2016
STUDENT ISSUE A. HUTCHINS chart color graph *Maclean's* v130 no2 p57 Mr 2017
Why Are they Silent? H. Yu *Society* v53 no6 p625 D 2016

College students—Canada
The depth of despair A. HUTCHINS chart color *Maclean's* v130 no2 p59 Mr 2017
I'm moving to Canada J. LEWINGTON color *Maclean's* v130

no10 p64 N 2017
STUDENT DOWNLOADERS BEWARE M. ROBINSON color *Maclean's* v129 no44 p56 N 7 2016
STUDENT ISSUE A. HUTCHINS chart color graph *Maclean's* v130 no2 p57 Mr 2017
They come from away T. CIOLFE map *Maclean's* v130 no10 p17 N 2017
A Western weekend M. CAMPBELL chart color *Maclean's* v130 no2 p60 Mr 2017

College students—Competitions
Rutgers Over Princeton In Epic Nerd Fight L. Nguyen color *Bloomberg Businessweek* no4510 p34 F 6 2017

College students—Employment
The Appalachian Work College A. B. LLOYD color *Weekly Standard* v22 no10 p26 N 14 2016
Providing Students with Pathways to High-Value Careers R. Craig *Change* v48 no5 p58 S/O 2016

College students—Fiction
Economy Clash color *Money* v46 no1 p22 Ja/F 2017

College students—Finance
Every Student a Bond Seller J. HARTLEY color *National Review* v68 no19 p37 O 24 2016

College students—Health
Scrounging for sustenance J. LORINC color graph *Maclean's* v129 no44 p64 N 7 2016

College students—Mental health
The depth of despair A. HUTCHINS chart color *Maclean's* v130 no2 p59 Mr 2017
Introducing a Psychotherapy for the Collective: A Paradigm Shift for College Mental Health G. D. Glass *Change* v48 no6 p16 N/D 2016

College students—Political activity—United States
Congress and Campus D. FRENCH color *National Review* v69 no19 p38 O 16 2017

College students—Rating of
Narcissistic Students Get Better Grades from Narcissistic Professors N. Torres *Harvard Business Review Digital Articles* p2 Mr 4 2016

College students—Social aspects
The Birth of College Party Culture L. Wade *Time* v189 no3 p21 Ja 30 2017

College students—United States
Best Cards for College Students L. GERSTNER chart *Kiplinger's Personal Finance* v71 no10 p46 O 2017
Cowering on Campus color *Weekly Standard* v22 no11 p3 N 21 2016
How a College Kid Made His Honda Civic Self-Driving for $700 T. Simonite il *MIT Technology Review* v120 no3 p13 My/Je 2017
You Aren't From Around Here, Are You? color *Weekly Standard* v22 no27 p2 Mr 20 2017

College students—United States—Political activity
POLITICS ON CAMPUS: A Q&A WITH AMY BINDER color *Phi Kappa Phi Forum* v97 no2 p20 Summ 2017
TAKING IT TO THE STREETS M. TODD color *Phi Kappa Phi Forum* v97 no2 p2 Summ 2017

College students—United States—Sexual behavior
Talking Back A. Fenwick and T. Keith color *Sports Illustrated* v125 no16 p22 N 14 2016

College students—United States—Social conditions—20th century
Joe College Is Dead: In an essay directed at bewildered '60s-era parents, a noted historian attempts to explain the roots of student unrest A. SCHLESINGER JR. *Saturday Evening Post* v289 no4 p44 Jl/Ag 2017

College students—United States—Substance use
MARIJUANA ON CAMPUS: By the '60s, this former street drug had become the sacrament of the youth generation. Here, a recent college graduate describes the phenomenon and the attraction R. GOLDSTEIN *Saturday Evening Post* v289 no4 p42 Jl/Ag 2017

College teachers
Adam Grant M. Rich color *Current Biography* v78 no9 p27 S 2017
Arthur J. Freeman S. Bader, B. Harmon et al *Physics Today* v69 no11 p69 N 2016

BREAK THROUGH AWARDS 2017 [Cover story] L. Sorokan-ich, K. Dupzyk et al bw color *Popular Mechanics* p56 N 2017

Campus Chaos K. C. Johnson *Commentary* v142 no1 p15 Jl/Ag 2016

Fighting through the darkness C. G. Hoogstraten color *Science* v357 no6350 p522 Ag 4 2017

Inspired Lives R. Bird *Cincinnati Magazine* v50 no10 p71 Jl 2017

John David Jackson C. Quigg *Physics Today* v69 no10 p68 O 2016

Local news on public airways D. Emanuel and K. Sullivan graph *Columbia Journalism Review* v56 no1 p101 Spr 2017

LUTHER'S MONEY REFORMATION M. FOUST cartoon *Christianity Today* p30 Mr 2017

My Professor, My Mentor, My Rock E. RAPP BLACKK *Reader's Digest* v189 no1129 p44 Ap 2017

My second acts A. Mathur color *Science* v357 no6358 p1430 S 29 2017

On the Job: Tim Garrett K. Cutlip *Weatherwise* v70 no1 p40 Ja/F 2017

OUT OF Africa M. SWARTZ *Texas Monthly* v44 no12 p74 D 2016

Pacifism in action color *U.S. Catholic* v82 no2 p28 F 2017

Sara Goldrick-Rab J. Crelin color *Current Biography* v78 no1 p13 Ja 2017

The Seer of AI: Physicist MAX TEGMARK has borne witness to the rise of artificial intelligence and insists that we start thinking about what it means for humanity--before machines decide for us G. DREVITCH *Psychology Today* v50 no5 p27 S/O 2017

Stage Presence: A Collaboration That Resulted in a New Approach to Design Communication J. Hopgood and J. Gibson Bond *Stage Directions* v30 no10 p32 O 2017

Study: Employers Are Less Likely to Hire a Woman Who Wears a Headscarf S. G. Carmichael *Harvard Business Review Digital Articles* p2 My 26 2017

Taking on the PC Crowd: A Canadian professor gains fame and followers B. ANDERSON *American Conservative* v16 no4 p41 Jl/Ag 2017

College teachers—Awards

CLASS ACTS bw *Maclean's* v130 no2 p62 Mr 2017

College teachers—Canada

CLASS ACTS bw *Maclean's* v130 no2 p62 Mr 2017

College teachers—Evaluation

Making the Grade color diag *Weekly Standard* v22 no35 p3 My 22 2017

College teachers—Health

The walking man walks A. A. DAVIS color *Maclean's* v129 no44 p62 N 7 2016

College teachers—Interviews

Coming of age color *U.S. Catholic* v82 no9 p21 S 2017

How Self-Service Kiosks Are Changing Customer Behavior G. Gavett *Harvard Business Review Digital Articles* p2 Mr 11 2015

I am, through you: God is in the ties that bind all of creation together, says this African priest S. C. Ilo color *U.S. Catholic* v82 no9 p18 S 2017

KNOW THE RISKS OF CRYPTOCURRENCIES T. H. BLANTON color *Kiplinger's Personal Finance* v71 no12 p10 D 2017

College teachers—Selection & appointment

Hiring for Mission J. Garvey and M. W. Roche color *Commonweal* v144 no3 p10 F 10 2017

College teachers—United States

IN MEMORIAM *Phi Kappa Phi Forum* v97 no1 p33 Spr 2017

KEVIN CLARK P. O'Donnell *Washingtonian Magazine* v52 no9 p45 Je 2017

On the science and teaching of emotional intelligence R. Heller color *Phi Delta Kappan* v98 no6 p20 Mr 2017

College tennis

Stronger Than EVER C. SHMERLER *Tennis* v52 no6 p48 N/D 2016

College athlete recruitment—Charts, diagrams, etc.

CONFERENCE BATTLE T. Taylor diag *Sports Illustrated* v126 no4 p66 Ja 30 2017

College athletes—Salaries, wages, etc.

Should College Athletes Be Paid? J. NOCERA and B. WILLIAMS *New York Times Upfront* v149 no10 p22 Mr 13 2017

College basketball teams—Charts, diagrams, etc.

THE BRACKETS D. Greene and L. Winn *Sports Illustrated* v126 no8 p40 Mr 20 2017

College basketball—Tournaments—Charts, diagrams, etc.

Bracket of Brackets T. Keith color diag *Sports Illustrated* v125 no16 p18 N 14 2016

College Hoops Tip-Off Marathon (TV program)

COLLEGE HOOPS TIP-OFF MARATHON K. ROSEN *TV Guide* v64 no46 p46 N 7 2016

College of the Ozarks (Point Lookout, Mo.)

TOP 150 BACCALAUREATE COLLEGES chart *Washington Monthly* v49 no9/10 p114 S/O 2017

Collembola

Easter Island's Last Endemics Flirt With Extinction [Cover story] N. SCHARPING color *Discover* v38 no4 p24 My 2017

Colletier, Jacques-Philippe

The cytotoxic Staphylococcus aureus PSMα3 reveals a cross-α amyloid-like fibril bibl color diag graph *Science* v355 no6327 p831 F 24 2017

Collet-Serra, Jaume

THE SHALLOWS D. Vaughn color *Sound & Vision* v82 no2 p69 F/Mr 2017

Collett, Elizabeth

Destination: Europe cartoon *Foreign Affairs* v96 no2 p150 Mr/Ap 2017

Collett, Morgan

What, This Old Thing? [Cover story] S. HOTCHKISS color *Esquire* p98 BigBlackBook

Collette, Bruce B.

East not least for Pacific bluefin tuna color diag *Science* v357 no6349 p356 Jl 28 2017

Colletti, Ned

The Big Chair: The Smooth Hops and Bad Bounces from the Inside World of the Acclaimed Los Angeles Dodgers General Manager *Publishers Weekly* v264 no33 p63 Ag 14 2017

Collewaert, Veroniek

How Entrepreneurs Can Keep Their Passion from Fading *Harvard Business Review Digital Articles* p2 Je 16 2016

Colley, Linda

What Gets Called 'Civil War'? color *New York Review of Books* v64 no10 p42 Je 8 2017

Collica, L.

Observation of a large-scale anisotropy in the arrival directions of cosmic rays above 8×1018 eV *Science* v357 no6357 p1266 S 22 2017

Collier, Benjamin

Small and Young Businesses Are Especially Vulnerable to Extreme Weather *Harvard Business Review Digital Articles* p2 N 23 2016

Collier, Bill

Did you receive support from your faith community while you were experiencing depression and/or anxiety? graph *America* v216 no12 p6 My 29 2017

Collier, Winn

Dear potential pastor *Christian Century* v134 no20 p28 S 27 2017

Colligan, Philip

Look to Government—Yes, Government—for New Social Innovations *Harvard Business Review Digital Articles* p2 N 20 2014

Collin, Michaela—Interviews

NO BONES ABOUT IT D. ANDERSON-MINSHALL color *Advocate* no1090 p32 Ap 2017

Collingham, Lizzie

The Birth of Britain's Global Palate S. Begley color *Time* v190 no14 p22 O 9 2017

Collings, Clayton K.

PAF1 regulation of promoter-proximal pause release via enhancer activation color *Science* v357 no6357 p1294 S 22 2017

Collings, Kelsey

Q: What is the most interesting family in history? color *Atlantic* v318 no5 p96 D 2016

Collings, Randy

Prove It K. Birchmier *Successful Farming* v114 no12 p18 Mid-N 2016

COLLINI, STEFAN

POLITICS BY CANDLELIGHT color *Nation* v305 no1 p35 Jl 3 2017

COLLINS, AMY FINE

ALL ABOUT YVES color *Vanity Fair* v59 no10 p189 O 2017

BEAUTY QUEENS color *Vanity Fair* v59 no4 p200 Mr 2017

BONBON VOYAGE color *Vanity Fair* v59 no6 p88 My 2017

Renée FLEMING color *Vanity Fair* v59 no5 p114 Ap 2017

Collins, Bentley

WATERFRONT D. HARDING JR. color *Power & Motoryacht* v32 no12 p18 D 2016

Collins, Beth

DOWNTOWN PORTLAND color map *Sunset* v237 no6 p34 D 2016

COLLINS, BILLY

'DUCK BLIND' B. Collins bw *New York Times Book Review* p14 Ag 6 2017

EVENING WIND *Atlantic* v318 no4 p96 N 2016

The Year in Reading [Cover story] *New York Times Book Review* p8 D 25 2016

Collins, Cameron

TREASURE TROVE Z. GLASGOW color *Missouri Life* v44 no5 p21 Ag 2017

Collins, Charis

Beyond the forever home color *Equus* no470 p11 N 2016

COLLINS, CRAIG M.

FROM THE ARCHIVES color *Reason* v49 no4 p78 Ag/S 2017

Collins, Darron

Hard data and human empathy color *Science* v357 no6359 p142 O 6 2017

Collins, Eric

SPECIALISTS *New York* v50 no11 p60 My 29 2017

Collins, Francis S., 1950-

NIH's ineffective funding policies W. P. Wahls *Science* v356 no6343 p1132 Je 16 2017

Collins, Francis S., 1950——Political & social views

The Pros and of the 21st Century *Congressional Digest* v96 no2 p12 F 1 2017

Collins, Gareth S.

The formation of peak rings in large impact craters bibl color graph *Science* v354 no6314 p878 N 18 2016

Formation of the Orientale lunar multiring basin bibl graph *Science* v354 no6311 p441 O 28 2016

Collins, Guy

Bacchus Takes an Ice Bath in Bordeaux color *Bloomberg Businessweek* no4522 p24 My 15 2017

Collins, Harry

Are We All Scientific Experts Now? C. Mitcham color *Issues in Science & Technology* v33 no1 p89 Fall 2016

Collins, Harry——Interviews

Cresting a gravitational wave A. Cho color *Science* v355 no6332 p1380 Mr 31 2017

Collins, Ian

chemtrails b. minnigh bw *Bike Magazine* v24 no5 p42 Jl 2017

THE LIBRARY IS NOT DEAD *Saturday Evening Post* v289 no1 p10 Ja/F 2017

Collins, James J.

Nucleic acid detection with CRISPR-Cas13a/C2c2 color diag *Science* v356 no6336 p438 Ap 28 2017

Collins, James P.

Precaution and governance of emerging technologies bibl color *Science* v354 no6313 p710 N 11 2016

Collins, Judy

FLAMES J. Seabrook cartoon *New Yorker* v93 no29 p38 S 25 2017

Leonard Cohen color *Time* v188 no22-23 p13 N/D 2016

Sanity and Grace B. Hasselbring color *AARP: The Magazine* v59 no1A p54 D 2015/Ja 2016

Collins, Kathleen

THE BEST BOOKS OF 2016 P. H. Bass color *Essence* v47 no8 p72 D 2016

The Love We Don't Know V. Gornick color *New York Review of Books* v64 no6 p28 Ap 6 2017

One Day It Shall Please Us to REMEMBER THIS D. AKINTOYE color *O, The Oprah Magazine* p69 Ja 2017

Out of the Shadow M. JERKINS *New York Times Book Review* p24 D 11 2016

Collins, Latigo

Reaching the Next Level B. Welch color *American Cowboy* v24 no1 p20 Je/Jl 2017

Collins, Lauren

A BAD WIND cartoon *New Yorker* v92 no39 p33 N 28 2016

CAN THE CENTER HOLD? bw cartoon *New Yorker* v93 no12 p20 My 8 2017

THE CHILDREN'S ODYSSEY bw cartoon *New Yorker* v93 no2 p52 F 27 2017

GIFT WORDS cartoon *New Yorker* v93 no9 p21 Ap 17 2017

IDENTITY CRISIS color diag *New Yorker* v93 no23 p24 Ag 7 2017

IN SEARCH OF AMERICA cartoon *New Yorker* v93 no32 p22 O 16 2017

SECRETS IN THE SAUCE cartoon *New Yorker* v93 no10 p66 Ap 24 2017

SHELTERING cartoon *New Yorker* v92 no36 p18 N 7 2016

SIDELINE cartoon *New Yorker* v93 no17 p22 Je 19 2017

UNLUCKY JIM cartoon *New Yorker* v93 no4 p28 Mr 13 2017

WHAT WOULD BILLY DO? cartoon *New Yorker* v93 no8 p20 Ap 10 2017

Collins, Lily, 1989-

BONE DEEP D. Coggan color *Entertainment Weekly* no1476 p30 Ag 4 2017

Halter Dresses E. Wilson color *InStyle* v24 no5 p74 My 2017

Lily Collins J. Johnson color *Current Biography* v78 no8 p22 Ag 2017

MISS lily M. Wappler and L. Collins color *InStyle* v24 no3 p189 Mr 2017

My LIST L. Christensen color *Harper's Bazaar* no3655 p66 Ag 2017

Collins, Mariah

Why Big Health Systems Are Investing in Community Health *Harvard Business Review Digital Articles* p2 D 6 2016

Collins, Marie

Heeding Marie Collins's Voice *America* v216 no7 p8 Ap 3 2017

Collins, Marva, 1936-2015

Education For Us, By Us B. Packnett color *Essence* v47 no12 p132 Ap 2017

Collins, Michael S.

A MATTER OF DEGREES: America's long struggle with affirmative action *Harper's Magazine* p69 S 2017

Collins, Nathan

Mirror Molecules in Space color *Scientific American* v315 no3 p14 S 2016

Collins, Petra

A FEMININE MYSTIQUE D. BLASBERG color *Vanity Fair* v59 no2 p88 F 2017

Girls, Uninterrupted color *Vogue* v207 no10 p204 O 2017

Collins, Phil, 1951-

Drumbeats M. BAI *New York Times Book Review* p18 N 20 2016

Collins, Phil, 1951——Interviews

Phil Collins A. GREENE bw *Rolling Stone* no1275 p70 D 1 2016

Collins, Phil, 1970-

The Fred & Karl Show K. SMITH *National Review* v69 no16 p48 Ag 28 2017

Collins, Rebecca

The Hardest Blessing color *Commonweal* v144 no10 p39 Je 2 2017

Collins, Ryan

Deal Snapshot: Oncor Electric Delivery Co bw graph *Bloomberg Businessweek* no4530 p19 Jl 17 2017

Collins, Sara

Where Both the ACA and AHCA Fall Short, and What the Health Insurance Market Really Needs *Harvard Business Review Digital Articles* p2 Mr 21 2017

collins, sarah

FISH FRY color *Martha Stewart Living* p86 Jl/Ag 2017

RAISING YOUR HOME'S IQ color *Martha Stewart Living* p80 S 2017

SWEET TO THE CORE color *Martha Stewart Living* p96 O 2017

TAPPED POTENTIAL color *Martha Stewart Living* p82 My 2017

COLLINS, SCOTT L.

The Coming Era of Open Data *BioScience* v67 no3 p191 Mr 2017

Editorial *BioScience* v67 no1 p3 Ja 2017

A Forum for Integrating the Life Sciences *BioScience* v67 no10 p871 O 2017

Science Communication *BioScience* v67 no6 p487 Je 2017

Skills and Knowledge for Data-Intensive Environmental Research *BioScience* v67 no6 p546 Je 2017

COLLINS, SONYA

NO LIMITS *Atlanta* v56 no9 p110 Ja 2017

Collins, Steven H.
Human-in-the-loop optimization of exoskeleton assistance during walking diag *Science* v356 no6344 p1280 Je 23 2017

Collins, Suzanne, 1962-
Mapping "The Hunger Games": Using location quotients to find the Districts of Panem E. Cross *Career Outlook* p3 F 2017

Collins, Taylor
How I Did It color *Men's Health* v32 no3 p36 Ap 2017

COLLINS, TIMOTHY
Worm-snail Ships Out! bw color *Natural History* v125 no6 p10 Je 2017

Collinson, Angel—Interviews
THICKER THAN WATER K. Beekman bw *Skiing* p72 D 2016

Collinson, John—Interviews
THICKER THAN WATER K. Beekman bw *Skiing* p72 D 2016

Collinson, Lucy
A switch from canonical to noncanonical autophagy shapes B cell responses bibl graph *Science* v355 no6325 p641 F 10 2017

Collinsworth, Eden
Behaving Badly: The New Morality in Politics, Sex, and Business *Publishers Weekly* v264 no6 p56 F 6 2017

Collis, Clark
THE 25 MOST PATRIOTIC MOVIES OF ALL TIME color *Entertainment Weekly* no1472 p30 Je 30 2017

2 — BLACK PHILLIP SPEAKS *Entertainment Weekly* no1444/1445 p58 D 16 2016

ADAM SCOTT AND CRAIG ROBINSON color *Entertainment Weekly* no1482/1483 p42 S 22 2017

Afterlife color *Entertainment Weekly* no1473 p62 Jl 7 2017

All Our Wrong Todays color *Entertainment Weekly* no1453 p63 F 17 2017

ARI GRAYNOR IS NO JOKE... color *Entertainment Weekly* no1470 p48 Je 16 2017

Baby on Board color *Entertainment Weekly* no1471 p50 Je 23 2017

BELLE OF THE BALL color *Entertainment Weekly* no1439 p34 N 11 2016

BE THEIR GUEST color *Entertainment Weekly* no1439 p32 N 11 2016

Bob's Burgers *Entertainment Weekly* no1482/1483 p34 S 22 2017

Born to Run color *Entertainment Weekly* no1434 p58 O 7 2016

BREAKING BIG CLASS color *Entertainment Weekly* no1446/1447 p64 D 2016/Ja 2017

BROUGHT UP BAD color *Entertainment Weekly* no1441 p35 N 25 2016

Calling the Night Nurse color *Entertainment Weekly* no1436/1437 p37 O 21 2016

Curb Your Enthusiasm color *Entertainment Weekly* no1482/1483 p40 S 22 2017

DAN STEVENS TRANSFORMS LIKE THE DICKENS color *Entertainment Weekly* no1459 p12 Mr 31 2017

The Deuce color *Entertainment Weekly* no1482/1483 p29 S 22 2017

A DOCTOR WHO CHARACTER COMES OUT OF THE TARDIS color *Entertainment Weekly* no1462 p12 Ap 21 2017

DOCTOR WHO CHRISTMAS SPECIAL color *Entertainment Weekly* no1474/1475 p72 Jl 21-28 2017

DOCTOR WHO color *Entertainment Weekly* p26 Jl 24 2017

The Doctor Will See You Now [Cover story] color *Entertainment Weekly* no1436/1437 p34 O 21 2016

Family Guy *Entertainment Weekly* no1482/1483 p34 S 22 2017

Gamora the Merrier color *Entertainment Weekly* no1465 p20 My 12 2017

GHOUL TALK color *Entertainment Weekly* no1436/1437 p104 O 21 2016

The Girlfriend Experience color *Entertainment Weekly* no1482/1483 p38 S 22 2017

GLENN FREY color *Entertainment Weekly* no1446/1447 p91 D 2016/Ja 2017

Good Behavior *Entertainment Weekly* no1482/1483 p39 S 22 2017

GREAT MOMENTS IN RICKROLLING *Entertainment Weekly* no1435 p38 O 14 2016

GROWN-UP GRINT color *Entertainment Weekly* no1457/1458 p60 Mr 17 2017

GUARDIANS OF THE GALAXY VOL. 2 [Cover story] color *Entertainment Weekly* no1463/1464 p24 Ap/My 2017

HAPPY! color *Entertainment Weekly* no1474/1475 p70 Jl 21-28 2017

How to GET AWAY WITH MURDER ON THE ORIENT EXPRESS [Cover story] color *Entertainment Weekly* no1465 p22 My 12 2017

I don't feel at home in this world anymore color *Entertainment Weekly* no1454/1455 p83 F 24 2017

I'M DYING UP HERE color *Entertainment Weekly* no1446/1447 p63 D 2016/Ja 2017

I'M DYING UP HERE color *Entertainment Weekly* no1468/1469 p42 Je 2-9 2017

In the Rick of Time color *Entertainment Weekly* no1435 p36 O 14 2016

Is This Thing On? color *Entertainment Weekly* no1436/1437 p15 O 21 2016

IT COMES AT NIGHT color *Entertainment Weekly* no1463/1464 p58 Ap/My 2017

JAMES FRANCO IN The Disaster Artist color *Entertainment Weekly* no1478 / 1479 p74 Ag 18-25 2017

Jason Mantzoukas Bets On The House color *Entertainment Weekly* no1473 p48 Jl 7 2017

JIGSAW color *Entertainment Weekly* p19 Jl 24 2017

J Lee color *Entertainment Weekly* no1485 p45 O 6 2017

JOHN WICK: CHAPTER 2 color *Entertainment Weekly* no1446/1447 p51 D 2016/Ja 2017

KISS AND MAKEUP color *Entertainment Weekly* no1459 p66 Mr 31 2017

LEGION color *Entertainment Weekly* no1474/1475 p69 Jl 21-28 2017

Leonard Cohen 1934-2016 color *Entertainment Weekly* no1441 p12 N 25 2016

Madam Secretary color *Entertainment Weekly* no1482/1483 p39 S 22 2017

MEET THE DOCTOR'S NEW COMPANION! PEARL MACKIE color *Entertainment Weekly* no1446/1447 p64 D 2016/Ja 2017

Mick Rock color *Entertainment Weekly* no1460/1461 p27 Ap 7-17 2017

The Monster color *Entertainment Weekly* no1440 p45 N 18 2016

THE MONSTER MAN color *Entertainment Weekly* no1453 p62 F 17 2017

MURDER ON THE ORIENT EXPRESS color *Entertainment Weekly* no1478 / 1479 p69 Ag 18-25 2017

NAUGHTY BY NATURE color *Entertainment Weekly* no1441 p32 N 25 2016

NCIS: Los Angeles *Entertainment Weekly* no1482/1483 p38 S 22 2017

NO. 26 Doctor Strange color *Entertainment Weekly* no1436/1437 p64 O 21 2016

NO. 33 Human Torch color *Entertainment Weekly* no1436/1437 p69 O 21 2016

NO. 37 ANT-MAN color *Entertainment Weekly* no1436/1437 p72 O 21 2016

One Scary Mother color *Entertainment Weekly* no1459 p50 Mr 31 2017

Outlander color *Entertainment Weekly* no1482/1483 p26 S 22 2017

Poldark *Entertainment Weekly* no1482/1483 p38 S 22 2017

PREACHER color *Entertainment Weekly* no1474/1475 p74 Jl 21-28 2017

READY FOR HER CLOSE-UP AGAIN color *Entertainment Weekly* no1451/1452 p34 F 3-10 2017

The Rolling Stones, Recharged color *Entertainment Weekly* no1440 p58 N 18 2016

SEPARATION ANXIETY color *Entertainment Weekly* no1478 / 1479 p14 Ag 18-25 2017

SERIAL MOM color *Entertainment Weekly* no1465 p42 My 12 2017

Shall We Dance? color *Entertainment Weekly* no1454/1455 p32 F 24 2017

Shameless color *Entertainment Weekly* no1482/1483 p30 S 22 2017

The Simpsons color *Entertainment Weekly* no1482/1483 p34 S 22 2017

SMILF *Entertainment Weekly* no1482/1483 p43 S 22 2017

STAR SEARCH color *Entertainment Weekly* no1463/1464 p28 Ap/My 2017

Strange-r Danger: Mads Mikkelsen Evils Up color *Entertainment Weekly* no1439 p41 N 11 2016

SUBURBICON color *Entertainment Weekly* no1478 / 1479 p51 Ag 18-25 2017

TALE AS OLD AS TIME [Cover story] color *Entertainment Weekly* no1439 p28 N 11 2016

Ten Days in the Valley color *Entertainment Weekly* no1482/1483 p43 S 22 2017

TENNESSEE TITANS color *Entertainment Weekly* no1454/1455 p70 F 24 2017

TERMINATOR 2: JUDGMENT DAY 3D color *Entertainment Weekly* no1480 p34 S 1 2017

This New Animal Planet Show Will Make You Weep color *Entertainment Weekly* no1478 / 1479 p90 Ag 18-25 2017

To CATCH the ZODIAC Killer color *Entertainment Weekly* no1468/1469 p72 Je 2-9 2017

TO INFINITY WAR AND BEYOND! color *Entertainment Weekly* no1466 p12 My 19 2017

Trespass Against Us color *Entertainment Weekly* no1450 p46 Ja 27 2017

A True Texas Gentleman color *Entertainment Weekly* no1456 p12 Mr 10 2017

Under the Shadow color *Entertainment Weekly* no1435 p42 O 14 2016

The Walking Dead color *Entertainment Weekly* no1482/1483 p38 S 22 2017

WarReN BEAtty An ORAL HISTORY color *Entertainment Weekly* no1440 p30 N 18 2016

We Say Goodbye to One of Our Own color *Entertainment Weekly* no1480 p3 S 1 2017

What to Watch color *Entertainment Weekly* no1450 p54 Ja 27 2017

What to Watch color *Entertainment Weekly* no1466 p53 My 19 2017

What to Watch color *Entertainment Weekly* no1477 p50 Ag 11 2017

White Famous color *Entertainment Weekly* no1482/1483 p36 S 22 2017

Wisdom of the Crowd color *Entertainment Weekly* no1482/1483 p34 S 22 2017

YOUR NEXT ROYAL OBSESSION color *Entertainment Weekly* no1449 p53 Ja 20 2017

Your Sunshiny, Stupendous, Seriously Spectacular SUMMER BUCKET LIST color *Entertainment Weekly* no1470 p32 Je 16 2017

Your Ultimate Halloween Watch Guide color *Entertainment Weekly* no1436/1437 p86 O 21 2016

Collision damage to automobiles

When You Crash a Rental Car K. LANKFORD *Kiplinger's Personal Finance* v71 no7 p43 Jl 2017

Collisions (Astrophysics)

Synestia \sin-ES-ti-ə\ n A. Yeager color *Science News* v192 no1 p5 Ag 5 2017

Collisions (Nuclear physics)

ULTRAPERIPHERAL NUCLEAR COLLISIONS S. Klein and J. Nystrand *Physics Today* v70 no10 p40 O 2017

Collison, John

He's the Youngest Self-Made Billionaire R. Wile color *Money* v46 no5 p16 Je 2017

Paymasters K. VINTON color *Forbes* v198 no9 p20 D 30 2016

Collison, Patrick

CELTIC TIGERS A. Vance color *Bloomberg Businessweek* no4533 p38 Ag 7 2017

Paymasters K. VINTON color *Forbes* v198 no9 p20 D 30 2016

Colloca, Luana

Nocebo effects can make you feel pain color *Science* v357 no6359 p44 O 6 2017

COLLOFF, ED

ON THE RECORD *Scientific American* v317 no2 p6 Ag 2017

COLLOFF, PAMELA

CENTRAL INTELLIGENCE *Texas Monthly* v45 no2 p106 F 2017

INSIDE OUT *Texas Monthly* v45 no5 p96 My 2017

Colloid thrusters

The More Things Change... D. J. Harding color *Power & Motoryacht* v34 no6 p12 Je 2017

Colloquial language

See also

Conversation

Colloquium: J.T. Henry & Lady Simcoe on Early Ontario Petrocolonialism (Poem)

COLLOQUIUM: J.T. HENRY AND LADY SIMCOE ON EARLY ONTARIO PETROCOLONIALISM D. HUEBERT *Walrus* p73 Ja\F 2017

Collum, Danny Duncan

America's original sin color *U.S. Catholic* v82 no5 p38 My 2017

Common faith: Documentary film Sacred explores ritual and prayer as primary human experiences color *U.S. Catholic* v82 no8 p38 Ag 2017

A corner turned bw *U.S. Catholic* v82 no2 p38 F 2017

Flies on the wall color *U.S. Catholic* v81 no11 p38 N 2016

Still waiting color *U.S. Catholic* v82 no11 p38 N 2017

Collum, Marla

Troops for Fitness Engages Military Veterans in Community Health and Wellness Programming *Parks & Recreation* v51 no11 p34 N 2016

Collusion

Big-Bank Hegemony: They have seized control of their own regulators C. WHALEN *American Conservative* v16 no5 p25 S/O 2017

His Own Worst Enemy A. C. McCARTHY *National Review* v69 no12 p15 Je 26 2017

Collver, Jordan

an introduction to JERRY ANDRUS *Skeptical Inquirer* v41 no1 p65 Ja/F 2017

Colman, Allison

Celebrating Three Years of Healthy Out-of-School Time *Parks & Recreation* v52 no3 p32 Mr 2017

Community and Home Gardening Develop Lifelong Healthy Habits *Parks & Recreation* v52 no8 p34 Ag 2017

COLMAN, DAVID

SECRET HISTORY color *Architectural Digest* v73 no12 p120 D 2016

Colmer, Roy, 1935-

ROY COLMER E. Buhe color *Art in America* v105 no5 p124 My 2017

Colombia

COLOMBIA RISING A. GULLEY color *Bicycling* v58 no7 p54 Ag 2017

The Testing Life color *Backpacker* v45 no3 p136 Ap 2017

Colombia—Description & travel

SOMEWHERE NEW R. MISNER color *Conde Nast Traveler* v52 no5 p34 My 2017

Colombia—Economic conditions—21st century

A Failed Peace Process Could Mean More Pain M. Bristow bw color *Bloomberg Businessweek* no4494 p17 O 10 2016

Colombia—Foreign relations—1974-

There Has Been Too Much Hatred and Vengeance *Vital Speeches of the Day* v83 no10 p286 O 2017

Colombia—History

The Colombian Paradox: Peace Processes, Elite Divisions & Popular Plebiscites A. M. Matanock and M. García-Sánchez graph *Daedalus* v146 no4 p152 Fall 2017

Colombia—Politics & government—21st century

Getting to Peace in Colombia J. NORDLINGER color *National Review* v68 no23 p30 D 19 2016

How the West is winning S. GILMORE color *Maclean's* v129 no41 p32 O 17 2016

Colombia—Politics & government—History

The Distant Promise of a Negotiated Justice L. Vinjamuri *Daedalus* v146 no1 p100 Wint 2017

Colombia—Politics & government—1974-

What's Next After the Peace Deal In Colombia T. John color *Time* v188 no14 p9 O 10 2016

Colombia—Social conditions—21st century

When the Résumé Reads: 'GUERRILLA (1964-2016)' J. Otis color *Bloomberg Businessweek* no4528 p54 Je 26 2017

Colomina, Beatriz—Interviews

Mark Wigley and Beatriz Colomina F. A. BERNSTEIN *Architec-*

tural Record v204 no10 p28 O 2016

COLÓN, JOHN MICHAEL
Revenge of the Trolls *In These Times* v41 no8 p34 Ag 2017

COLON, TERRY
BRICKBATS color *Reason* v49 no6 p80 N 2017

Colon cancer
See also
Hereditary nonpolyposis colorectal cancer
Cancer bypasses the lymph nodes S. D. Markowitz diag *Science* v357 no6346 p35 Jl 7 2017
THE HEALTH REPORT cartoon *Men's Health* v32 no9 p72 N 2017
Should I Speak Up About a Green-Card Marriage? K. A. Appiah *New York Times Magazine* p24 Ja 29 2017

Colon cancer treatment
Potential role of intratumor bacteria in mediating tumor resistance to the chemotherapeutic drug gemcitabine L. T. Geller, M. Barzily-Rokni et al diag *Science* v357 no6356 p1156 S 15 2017

Colon cancer—Diagnosis
Save Your Butt J. Stewart cartoon *Men's Health* v32 no1 p88 Ja/F 2017
Taking On Colon Cancer J. W. Milsom *AARP: The Magazine* v59 no5A p22 Ag/S 2016

Colon cancer—Charts, diagrams, etc.
Taking On Colon Cancer J. W. Milsom *AARP: The Magazine* v59 no5A p22 Ag/S 2016

Colonel Lew Schlicter, Mercenary (Short story)
Colonel Lew Schlicter, Mercenary J. EPSTEIN *Commentary* v142 no3 p35 O 2016

Colonial architecture
A House Rescued Simplicity Restored B. D. Coleman color *Old House Journal* v45 no5 p14 Ag 2017
Hudson Valley Rebirth P. POORE color *Old House Journal* v45 no5 p22 Ag 2017
Remuddling color *Old House Journal* v45 no6 p88 S 2017

Colonial birds
WILD ABANDON B. KEVIN *Audubon* v118 no6 p38 Wint 2016

Colonial Pipeline Co.
A PIPELINE RUNS THROUGH IT [Cover story] C. Leonard color graph map *Bloomberg Businessweek* no4501 p36 N 28 2016

Colonial revival (Architecture)
Royal Barry Wills COLONIAL REVIVAL P. POORE color *Old House Journal* v45 no1 p14 F 2017

Colonies (Biology)
See also
Bacterial colonies
Coupling and sharing when life is hard V. Gordon color *Science* v356 no6338 p583 My 12 2017

Colonists
Byzantine Tale J. Hall *History Today* v67 no3 p66 Mr 2017
VOYAGES OF OLD A. R. Williams color *National Geographic* v232 no1 p20 Jl 2017

Colonization
See also
Space colonies
The land is the classroom M. ROSANO color *Canadian Geographic* v137 no2 p58 Mr/Ap 2017
Rethinking 'Structural Violence' K. Hirschfeld *Society* v54 no2 p156 Ap 2017

Colonization—Environmental aspects
A global map of roadless areas and their conservation status P. L. Ibisch, M. T. Hoffmann et al bibl color graph map *Science* v354 no6318 p1423 D 16 2016

Colonna, Marco
Lactobacillus reuteri induces gut intraepithelial CD4+CD8αα+ T cells diag graph *Science* v357 no6353 p806 Ag 25 2017

Colony (TV program)
Colony I. Rudolph *TV Guide* v65 no2 p27 Ja 2 2017
Colony Is Back in Action I. Rudolph *TV Guide* p12 D 5 2016

Colony collapse disorder of honeybees
When the hive mind is wrong C. MCINTYRE *Maclean's* v130 no9 p16 O 2017

Color
See also
Cosmetics—Color
1665: Cambridge I. Newton *Lapham's Quarterly* v10 no2 p88 Spr 2017

2017'S HOTTEST COLOR COMBOS color *Good Housekeeping* v264 no6 p48A Je 2017
20 Things You Didn't Know About ... Color S. MORROW color *Discover* v38 no9 p74 N 2017
Get Lush Lips L. Desantis color *Health* v30 no9 p31 N 2016
Hello, Color! L. Corona color *Parents* v92 no9 p129 S 2017
HOW TO WEAR PINK EYE SHADOW IRL color *Health* v31 no7 p24 S 2017
red alert *Parents* v92 no2 p65 F 2017

Color in clothing
Beach, Please! J. JONES CONDON color *House Beautiful* p28 Jl 2017

Color in interior decoration
HARVEST HUES M. B. EYERS color *Better Homes & Gardens* v95 no11 p34 N 2017
My favorite girl P. Poore color *Old House Journal* v45 no2 p8 Ap 2017

Color in marketing
THE POWER OF PINK J. Miller color *Bloomberg Businessweek* no4501 p55 N 28 2016

Color of birds
Birds, Bees, and Beauty B. HEINRICH color *Natural History* v125 no4 p14 Ap 2017

Color of fruit
Weird but true! J. SWAIN and A. E. HURT color map *National Geographic Kids* no470 p4 My 2017

Color photography—20th century
Pitch Perfect K. Olbermann and T. Keith color *Sports Illustrated* v125 no12 p18 O 10 2016

Color Theory (Music)
High Brass Fantasy B. ZIMMERMAN color *Downbeat* v84 no5 p54 My 2017

Color vision in children
Baby's Rainbow J. C. Hu color *Scientific American* v317 no3 p16 S 2017

Colorado
POLITICAL CLIMBERS R. Manning *Harper's Magazine* no2007 p45 Ag 2017
SHOULD YOU TELL THE COPS YOU HAVE A GUN? J. Sullum color graph *Reason* v49 no5 p7 O 2017

Colorado. Civil Rights Commission
Is a cake speech? *Christian Century* v134 no16 p7 Ag 2 2017

Colorado. Dept. of Transportation
Road Rage D. C. Vock *Governing* v30 no7 p44 Ag 2017

Colorado Plateau
STATES OF DECAY: A journey through America's nuclear heartland B. Mauk *Harper's Magazine* p48 O 2017

Colorado Rockies (Baseball team)
3 ROCKIES color *Sports Illustrated* v126 no9 p111 Mr 27 2017
HIGHLY DEVELOPED A. Chen color *Sports Illustrated* v127 no2 p36 Jl 17 2017

Colorado State University
Hall of Fame City Plays Host to Football Exhibit *USA Today Magazine* v146 no2867 p16 Ag 2017

Colorado. Supreme Court
CAN'T AFFORD A LAWYER? NO FREE SPEECH FOR YOU N. SIBILLA and J. KERR *Reason* v48 no8 p44 Ja 2017

Colorado Trail (Colo.)
Mountain Magic D. LEWON color *Backpacker* v45 no2 p70 Mr 2017
SILVERTON, COLORADO color *Runner's World* v51 no11 p14 D 2016
STAY AWHILE J. Montalvo color *Backpacker* v45 no1 p85 Ja 2017

Colorado truck
2017 Chevrolet Colorado ZR2 E. DYER color *Popular Mechanics* p36 N 2017
2017 CHEVY COLORADO ZR2 [Cover story] A. MANSOUR color *Dirt Sports + Off-Road* v51 no10 p42 O 2017
Clowns to the Left of Me, Jokers to the Right D. Pund chart color *Car & Driver* v63 no1 p104 Jl 2017
GARAGE chart color diag *Motor Trend* v69 no7 p106 Jl 2017
SHOCK DOCTRINE B. SOROKANICH color *Road & Track* v69 no1 p84 Ag 2017

Colorado truck—Evaluation

Four Powerful Pickups A. DEL-COLLE cartoon color *Men's Health* v32 no4 p30 My 2017

GARAGE cartoon chart color *Motor Trend* v68 no12 p106 D 2016

Colorado—Description & travel

SANDBOX IN THE SKY M. D. G. KAPLAN and M. HEIM *National Parks* v91 no2 p40 Spr 2017

See in color color *Backpacker* p8 Je 2017

Coloring Book (Music)

Hot Tracks L. ROBINSON bw *Vanity Fair* p102 Hollywood 2017 Supplement

Coloring books

Fill Me In J. TRUPP *D: The Magazine of Dallas* v43 no10 p48 O 2016

The Line King T. JOKINEN cartoon *Walrus* v14 no6 p12 Jl/Ag 2017

Coloring books for adults

BOOKS TO UNPLUG WITH A. GROSS color *Publishers Weekly* v264 no7 p28 F 13 2017

Coloring books—Evaluation

Tack Room color *Practical Horseman* v45 no2 p70 F 2017

Coloring matter in food

Brand new HUE M. WOLLAN *New York Times Magazine* p51 O 9 2016

Food Coloring S. KLEIN bw color *Prevention* v68 no12 p96 D 2016

Healthy Hues N. Zevnik color *Better Nutrition* v79 no11 p20 N 2017

True Colors J. DEMELO and J. EVERIST color *Bon Appetit* v61 no12 p92 D 2016 /Jan2017

true colors K. SULLIVAN MORFORD *Parents* v92 no2 p48 F 2017

What a Year! M. F. Jacobson *Nutrition Action Health Letter* v43 no10 p2 D 2016

Coloring matter—Evaluation

Take a Chance color *House Beautiful* v158 no10 p18 D 2016/Ja 2017

Color Purple, The (Film)

STAYING POWER S. Fales-hill color *Essence* v47 no12 p104 Ap 2017

Color Purple: The Musical, The (Theatrical production)

ONE NIGHT ONLY C. Murray color *Essence* v47 no8 p70 D 2016

Colors

    See also

    Blue

    Brown

    Palette (Color range)

    Pink

    Purple

    Structural colors

    Yellow

COLOR SCHEME E. Flake cartoon *New Yorker* v92 no39 p15 N 28 2016

Less Is More K. RENDA color *House Beautiful* v159 no4 p28 My 2017

Mix and Match color *House Beautiful* v159 no1 p21 F 2017

PAINT: Hue New? color *House Beautiful* v159 no9 p24 N 2017

Set the Stage K. RENDA and B. REYNAERT color *House Beautiful* v159 no7 p33 S 2017

Colors (Music)

Beck E. R. Brown color *Entertainment Weekly* no1486 p58 O 13 2017

Beck's Day-Glo Vision of Modern Pop W. HERMES color *Rolling Stone* no1298 p49 O 19 2017

Beck's Hard Road to Happy Songs A. GREENE bw *Rolling Stone* no1294 p19 Ag 24 2017

Colors—Evaluation

All About Ease color *House Beautiful* v159 no8 p30 O 2017

H2-Whoa! color *House Beautiful* v159 no5 p34 Je 2017

Colors—Physiological effect

A Short History of Muralism cartoon *Alternatives Journal (A.J)* - *Canada's Environmental Voice* v42 no3 p70 2016

Colossal (Film)

Big Monsters, Bigger Feelings S. Zacharek color *Time* v189 no14 p53 Ap 17 2017

Monster Mash J. PODHORETZ color *Weekly Standard* v22 no32

p43 My 1 2017

NOW PLAYING color *Entertainment Weekly* no1462 p50 Ap 21 2017

NOW PLAYING color *Entertainment Weekly* no1463/1464 p90 Ap/My 2017

Party Girl, Godzilla Girl P. Travers color *Rolling Stone* no1285 p55 Ap 20 2017

Two Beauties and Some Beasts R. Alleva color *Commonweal* v144 no9 p26 My 19 2017

Colostrum

CHEAT YOUR WAY TO LEAN A. RIOS color *Yoga Journal* no290 p7 Mr 2017

Milk Your Muscles color *Muscle & Performance* v9 no1 p13 Ja 2017

Colour in Anything, The (Music)

WAIT FOR THE DROP: THE YEAR THE SURPRISE ALBUM TOOK OVER MUSIC V. Staples color *GQ: Gentlemen's Quarterly* v86 no12 p147 D 2016

Colposcopy

JUST ANOTHER DAY AT THE OFFICE S. Dominus color *Glamour* v115 no9 p194 S 2017

Colquitt, Alan

The Right Kind of Conflict Leads to Better Products *Harvard Business Review Digital Articles* p2 D 23 2016

Colson, Tobias A.

Release of mineral-bound water prior to subduction tied to shallow seismogenic slip off Sumatra graph *Science* v356 no6340 p841 My 26 2017

Colt revolver

THE GUN THAT WON THE WEST N. Solheim bw cartoon color *American Cowboy* p46 LEGENDS OF TEXAS Special Issue 2017

COLTART, CORDELIA E. M.

From Contamination to Containment [Cover story] color *Natural History* v125 no9 p40 S 2017

Colter, Mike, 1976-

Build Muscle at Any Age—Like This Guy A. MCCARRON color *Men's Health* v32 no7 p52 S 2017

The First Black Lives Matter Superhero R. SHEFFIELD color *Rolling Stone* no1272 p29 O 20 2016

Marvel's Luke Cage M. Logan *TV Guide* v64 no40 p31 O 3 2016

Marvel's The Defenders M. ROUSH *TV Guide* v65 no35 p13 Ag 21 2017

Mike Colter C. Mari color *Current Biography* v78 no6 p30 Je 2017

Colter, Mike, 1976-—Interviews

THE THINKING MAN: MIKE COLTER M. Khidekel color *Women's Health* v14 no8 p118 O 2017

Colton, Aaron

MY INDIAN TAMING A THOROUGHBRED SCOUT IS TOUGH BUT FTR750 GRATIFYING EXPERIENCE color *Cycle World* v56 no9 p44 O 2017

Colton, Timothy J.

Introduction *Daedalus* v146 no2 p5 Spr 2017

Paradoxes of Putinism chart graph *Daedalus* v146 no2 p8 Spr 2017

Russia: What Everyone Needs to Know R. Legvold *Foreign Affairs* v96 no2 p182 Mr/Ap 2017

Coltrane, Ellar, 1994-—Interviews

Ellar COLTRANE T. E. SHULTS *Interview* v47 no1 p102 F 2017

Coltrane, John, 1926-1967

HISTORICAL ALBUM OF THE YEAR bw color *Downbeat* v83 no12 p40 D 2016

HOW TO USE PATTERNS TO ENHANGE YOUR CREATIVITY(AND NOT JUST PLAY LICKS) [Cover story] T. Nash bw color *Downbeat* v84 no5 p72 My 2017

PRAISE SONGS HUA HSU bw *New Yorker* v93 no10 p98 Ap 24 2017

Still Chasin' the Trane cartoon *Weekly Standard* v22 no43 p34 Jl 24 2017

Coltrane-Turiyasangitananda, A. (Alice)

PRAISE SONGS HUA HSU bw *New Yorker* v93 no10 p98 Ap 24 2017

Spiritual Awakenings K. GOTTSCHALK color *Downbeat* v84 no7 p61 Jl 2017

Coluccia, M. R.

Observation of a large-scale anisotropy in the arrival directions of cosmic rays above 8×1018 eV *Science* v357 no6357 p1266 S 22 2017

Columbia (S.C.)

Through Glasses, Darkly B. SWAIM cartoon *Weekly Standard* v22 no48 p5 S 4 2017

Columbia River

LOCKJAW LESSONS T. E. Nickens color *Field & Stream* v122 no4 p32 S 2017

Columbia River Highway (Or.)

Go color *Road & Track* v68 no9 p6 Je 2017

Columbia River Knife & Tool Inc.

FOLDING KNIVES color *Popular Mechanics* p30 My 2017

Columbia Sportswear Co.

MEMBRAINIAC S. Horaczek color *Popular Science* v289 no4 p38 Jl/Ag 2017

Columbia University

THE CAMERA MAN C. Iozzio color *Popular Photography* v81 no1 p76 Ja/F 2017

Christopher Kimball M. Rich color *Current Biography* v78 no6 p59 Je 2017

My Mentor: Grand Street editor Ben Sonnenberg was a great enthusiast S. MINOT *American Scholar* v86 no3 p16 Summ 2017

Columbia University—Buildings

Stake in the Neighborhood: Two buildings open on a new campus in upper Manhattan, with a promise to enhance the community F. A. BERNSTEIN color map *Architectural Record* v205 no5 p80 My 2017

Columbia College (New York, N.Y.)

COLUMBIA'S IDENTITY CRISIS T. C. Fishman bw color graph *Chicago* v66 no1 p110 Ja 2017

Columbia Years 1968-1969, The (Music)

REISSUES OF THE YEAR D. FRICKE bw *Rolling Stone* no1276 p20 D 15 2016

Studio Cuts: Tales of the Tape J. EPHLAND bw *Downbeat* v83 no11 p61 N 2016

Columbus (Film)

Building Blocks R. Brody color *New Yorker* v93 no17 p6 Je 19 2017

Columbus Begins a New Conversation About Modernism D. A. CIAMPAGLIA *Architectural Record* v205 no9 p36 S 2017

Columbus *New Yorker* v93 no23 p10 Ag 7 2017

HALEY LU RICHARDSON D. Coggan color *Entertainment Weekly* no1478 / 1479 p86 Ag 18-25 2017

Reel Talk M. Rubino *Indianapolis Monthly* v41 no2 p14 S 2017

SCENE STEALERS S. BAHR bw color *Indianapolis Monthly* v41 no2 p78 S 2017

Columbus (Ohio)—Description & travel

columbus, indiana T. McKEOUGH color *Architectural Digest* no5 p90 My 2017

Columbus, Christopher, 1451-1506

The Debate Ober COLUMBUS B. BROWN *New York Times Upfront* p18 S 18 2017

Examining Columbus's Complicated Leadership Legacy P. J. Murphy *Harvard Business Review Digital Articles* p2 O 13 2014

Columbus Blue Jackets (Hockey team)—History

Talking a BLUE STREAK A. Prewitt color *Sports Illustrated* v126 no2 p50 Ja 16 2017

Columbus Avenue (New York, N.Y.)

The Friedman Pharmacy *Commentary* v141 no9 p1 N 2016

The Friedman Pharmacy *Commentary* v142 no4 p1 N 2016

Columns

SECRETS OF THE GOLDEN GATE BRIDGE K. JAZYNKA *National Geographic Kids* no467 p20 F 2017

COLVIN, BETH

CITY OF THORNS *Phi Kappa Phi Forum* v96 no4 p30 Wint 2016

IRON MAN color *Phi Kappa Phi Forum* v96 no4 p3 Wint 2016

LOOKING BACK AT PHI KAPPA PHI'S FELLOWS color *Phi Kappa Phi Forum* v97 no2 p24 Summ 2017

MAKING WAVES color *Phi Kappa Phi Forum* v97 no1 p6 Spr 2017

Colvin, Geoff

THE 2017 Fortune Crystal Ball color diag *Fortune* v174 no7 p11 D 1 2016

6 BRAD SMITH color *Fortune* v174 no7 p84 D 1 2016

Automation Won't Replace People as Your Competitive Advantage T. H. Davenport and J. Kirby *Harvard Business Review Digital Articles* p2 Ag 10 2015

BUY. SQUEEZE. REPEAT [Cover story] chart color *Fortune* v175 no2 p74 F 1 2017

CAN WELLS FARGO GET WELL? chart color diag *Fortune* v175 no8 p138 Je 15 2017

CHANGE THE WORLD !!!! color diag map *Fortune* v176 no4 p74 S 15 2017

CHINA'S $43 BILLION BID FOR FOOD SECURITY color diag *Fortune* v175 no6 p78 My 1 2017

GOLDEN PARACHUTE, MEET GLASS CLIFF color *Fortune* v175 no5 p14 Ap 1 2017

MILLENNIALS ARE NOT MONOLITHIC color *Fortune* v174 no6 p48 N 1 2016

WORLD'S 50 GREATEST LEADERS [Cover story] color *Fortune* v175 no5 p46 Ap 1 2017

Colwell, Chip

Culture clash J. Younker color *Science* v356 no6335 p255 Ap 21 2017

COLWELL, K. C.

DATA CENTRAL cartoon diag graph *Car & Driver* v62 no7 p20 Ja 2017

LIGHTNING LAP [Cover story] color graph map *Car & Driver* v63 no4 p45 O 2017

One Tool to Rule Them All color *Car & Driver* v63 no4 p96 O 2017

RACING KEEPS GETTING FASTER, DESPITE ALL EFFORTS graph *Car & Driver* v63 no2 p26 Ag 2017

SPOOL SAMPLE color *Car & Driver* v63 no5 p20 N 2017

Three-Row Hero color *Car & Driver* v63 no1 p94 Jl 2017

Thunder(s)truck color *Car & Driver* v63 no4 p106 O 2017

TRANS-PLANT diag *Car & Driver* v62 no11 p26 My 2017

Colwell, Rita

Not just Salk color *Science* v357 no6356 p1105 S 15 2017

Colwell, Robert K.

Biodiversity redistribution under climate change: Impacts on ecosystems and human well-being color *Science* v355 no6332 p1389 Mr 31 2017

Coma Cluster

A LARGE GALAXY MADE ALMOST ENTIRELY OF DARK MATTER *Physics Today* v69 no11 p24 N 2016

Combat

See also

Battles

Martial Arts the Old-Fashioned Way M. Jacobs bw color *Black Belt* v55 no5 p24 Ag/S 2017

On a Question of the Day S. Marlow, J. Cordova et al color *Black Belt* v55 no6 p16 O/N 2017

The Pankration Flow J. ARVANITIS bw color *Black Belt* v55 no3 p54 Ap/My 2017

The Real Story in U.S.-Russia Relations Can Be Seen In the Skies Above Syria I. Bremmer *Time* v190 no1 p12 Jl 3 2017

WORLD OF WAR J. STOWELL *Cincinnati Magazine* v50 no7 p20 Ap 2017

Combat in art

Martial Arts Archeology and the Way of the Autodidact M. Hatmaker color *Black Belt* v55 no2 p18 F/Mr 2017

Combe, J.-Ph.

Seasonal exposure of carbon dioxide ice on the nucleus of comet 67P/Churyumov-Gerasimenko bibl bw graph *Science* v354 no6319 p1563 D 23 2016

Combes, M.

Seasonal exposure of carbon dioxide ice on the nucleus of comet 67P/Churyumov-Gerasimenko bibl bw graph *Science* v354 no6319 p1563 D 23 2016

Combi, M.

Xenon isotopes in 67P/Churyumov-Gerasimenko show that comets contributed to Earth's atmosphere diag *Science* v356 no6342 p1069 Je 9 2017

Combination drug therapy

Giant cell arteritis: New treatment for inflammation *Mayo Clinic Health Letter* v35 no11 p6 N 2017

Combinatorial optimization

A fully programmable 100-spin coherent Ising machine with all-to-all connections P. L. McMahon, A. Marandi et al bibl diag graph *Science* v354 no6312 p614 N 4 2016

Combs—Design & construction

NIT-PICKING IN ANCIENT CHILE A. R. Williams color *National Geographic* v231 no3 p20 Mr 2017

Combs—Evaluation

HAIR IT IS GROOMING J. WUEBBEN color *Muscle & Performance* v9 no8 p12 Ag 2017

LITTLE LUXURIES color *Martha Stewart Living* p54 Mr 2017

SPARKLE & SHINE color *Essence* v47 no8 p64 D 2016

THE WIND IN YOUR HAIR [Cover story] A. Finney bw color *Women's Health* v14 no6 p45 Jl 2017

Combs—History

NIT-PICKING IN ANCIENT CHILE A. R. Williams color *National Geographic* v231 no3 p20 Mr 2017

Combustion

VIRTUAL COMBUSTION P. JONES *Cycle World* v55 no11 p20 D 2016

Comcast Corp.

Comcast's 1TB data cap starts rolling out across the U.S I. PAUL color diag *PCWorld* v35 no11 p39 N 2016

Come, Labor On (Short story)

Come, Labor On T. JENKS *American Scholar* v86 no1 p92 Wint 2017

Come Before Winter (Film)

Fighting the Nazis With Fake News M. SHAER *Smithsonian* v48 no1 p22 Ap 2017

Come From Away (Theatrical production)

A 9/11 Musical With Heart and Nostalgia R. Zoglin color *Time* v189 no11 p62 Mr 27 2017

Canadian Nice: The Musical J. GREEN *New York* v50 no6 p86 Mr 20 2017

FORD'S THEATRE HONORS VETERANS WITH A SPECIAL SHOWING OF COME FROM AWAY *Washingtonian Magazine* v52 no2 p225 N 2016

THE THEATRE *New Yorker* v93 no2 p17 F 27 2017

Comeback City (Short story)

COMEBACK CITY N. Mackey *Harper's Magazine* v334 no2001 p20 F 2017

Comebacks (Success)

See also

Corporate turnarounds

Back to the Basket J. Fuchs and T. Keith color *Sports Illustrated* v126 no14 p28 My 15-22 2017

O.K. • CALL IT A • COME BACK A. Murphy color *Sports Illustrated* v125 no14 p32 O 24-31 2016

Comedian, The (Film)

You Laughin' at Me? J. McGovern color *Entertainment Weekly* no1436/1437 p20 O 21 2016

Comedians

See also

Women comedians

1926-2017 Jerry Lewis C. Nashawaty color *Entertainment Weekly* no1480 p16 S 1 2017

THE 50 FUNNIEST PEOPLE RIGHT NOW! R. SHEFFIELD color *Rolling Stone* no1287 p35 My 18 2017

AGING GRACEFULLY WITH HOWIE MANDEL B. Keyes-Bevan color *Maclean's* v129 no40 p58 O 10 2016

BEFORE THERE WAS NERD PROM T. Troy color *Washingtonian Magazine* v52 no7 p16 Ap 2017

Chris Rock C. WEAVER color *GQ: Gentlemen's Quarterly* v97 no6 p148 Je 2017

COMEDY CALENDAR J. HARDBERGER cartoon *Chicago* v66 no1 p46 Ja 2017

Comments img *New York* v50 no10 p12 My 15 2017

David Letterman B. MARTIN color *GQ: Gentlemen's Quarterly* v97 no6 p130 Je 2017

Deadpan Walking G. MUNROE cartoon *Walrus* v13 no9 p63 N 2016

THE DEVIL'S ADVOCATE S. RODRICK bw color *Esquire* p58 Ag 2017

DICE G. E. Miller *TV Guide* v64 no15 p49 Ap 4 2016

Dick Gregory T. Smiley color *Time* v190 no9 p17 S 4 2017

Dinner With Don—and AARP R. Love color *AARP: The Magazine* v30 no6A p4 O/N 2017

Don Rickles 1926-2017 M. Roush *TV Guide* p12 Ap 17 2017

'EGYPT'S JON STEWART' IN EXILE J. MONTICELLO color

Reason v49 no6 p44 N 2017

The Elephant in the Comedy Club K. SURANA color *Foreign Policy* no225 p23 Jl/Ag 2017

THE GUIDE / 10.17 M. WAKIM color *Los Angeles Magazine* v62 no10 p92 O 2017

HANNIBAL LECTURE A. FLANGO *Cincinnati Magazine* v50 no2 p18 N 2016

HECKLERS FOR HIRE A. Marantz cartoon *New Yorker* v93 no4 p29 Mr 13 2017

her style color *InStyle* v24 no5 p32 My 2017

Hot Comedian Brandon Wardell B. HIATT color *Rolling Stone* no1274 p43 N 17 2016

How to be Funny T. MALONE *Atlanta* v57 no6 p81 O 2017

"I BECAME A COMIC AT 41" T. Trespicio color *Women's Health* v13 no10 p107 D 2016

I GOT YOU, BABE D. MAGARY, B. HANSEN-BUNDY et al bw color *GQ: Gentlemen's Quarterly* v97 no6 p96 Je 2017

Issey Ogata M. Hagan color *Current Biography* v78 no8 p64 Ag 2017

Jerry Lewis J. Carrey color *Time* v190 no9 p17 S 4 2017

KUMAIL NANJIANI J. MILLER color *Vanity Fair* v59 no7 p60 Summ 2017

louie Anderson A. Wallace color *GQ: Gentlemen's Quarterly* v97 no6 p132 Je 2017

MODERN ROMANTIC J. PRESSLER *Smithsonian* v47 no8 p42 D 2016

ONE WAYANS WAY T. M. FERGUSON color *Ebony* v72 no11 p58 S 2017

Rob Delaney J. Crelin color *Current Biography* v77 no10 p21 O 2016

Stars We Loved and Lost A. D'Arminio *TV Guide* p28 D 19 2016

This Man Is the Future of Funny Kumail Nanjiani can see what's coming in comedy—including everything that's in this issue A. PEELE color *GQ: Gentlemen's Quarterly* v97 no6 p44 Je 2017

Tracy Morgan Z. BARON color *GQ: Gentlemen's Quarterly* v97 no6 p127 Je 2017

Words of Past Images W. D. GEHRING *USA Today Magazine* v146 no2868 p49 S 2017

Comedians in Cars Getting Coffee (TV program)

STREAMING A. D'ARMINIO *TV Guide* v65 no2 p42 Ja 2 2017

Comedians—Interviews

Fred Armisen A. GREENE color *Rolling Stone* no1272 p28 O 20 2016

Hasan Minhaj Thinks Comedy Is for Weirdos S. Dominus *New York Times Magazine* p66 Je 25 2017

Ricky GERVAIS color *Vanity Fair* v59 no9 p247 S 2017

Comedians—Political activity

FOLLOW THE FUNNY: SPEAKING JOKES TO POWER E. RAMPELL color *Progressive* v81 no6 p48 Ag/S 2017

Comedians—United States

Abbi Jacobson D. Kiper color *Current Biography* v77 no10 p68 O 2016

Billy Eichner Has a Few Questions img *New York* p66 Ja 23 2017

Don Rickles P. Oswalt color *Time* v189 no15 p13 Ap 24 2017

Garry Shandling M. Roush *TV Guide* v64 no15 p13 Ap 4 2016

JEFF GARLIN [Cover story] B. Zehme color *Chicago* v66 no6 p132 Je 2017

Larry David As the Social Critic Still In the Right D. D'addario color *Time* v190 no10/11 p104 S 18 2017

Sex, Drugs, Comedy J. WEINER color *Rolling Stone* no1297 p17 O 5 2017

T. J. MILLER color *Esquire* v166 no5 p156 D 2016/Ja 2017

WHERE & WHEN *Washingtonian Magazine* v52 no9 p35 Je 2017

Comedians—United States—Biography

Melissa Villaseñor M. Rich bw *Current Biography* v78 no2 p79 F 2017

Comedy

See also

Stand-up comedy

ARE YOU LAUGHIN' AT ME? O. ELLICKSON cartoon color *Wired* v25 no4 p64 Ap 2017

Brooklyn Nine-Nine D. Holbrook *TV Guide* v65 no19 p38 My 1 2017

CARRY A BIG SHTICK J. Lovett cartoon *Wired* v25 no4 p72 Ap 2017

COMEDY CALENDAR J. HARDBERGER cartoon *Chicago* v66 no1 p46 Ja 2017

GO J. FOUMBERG, J. HARDBERGER et al color *Chicago* v66 no4 p113 Ap 2017

How to be Funny T. MALONE *Atlanta* v57 no6 p81 O 2017

Jack Benny's Comic Program T. TEACHOUT *Commentary* v144 no3 p56 O 2017

Judd Apatow P. DOYLE bw *Rolling Stone* no1288 p58 Je 1 2017

Q+A *Cincinnati Magazine* v50 no2 p26 N 2016

THE QUEEN OF CLEAN CLAPS BACK L. MURROW cartoon color *Wired* v25 no4 p73 Ap 2017

Sasheer Zamata S. Pulia color *InStyle* v24 no7 p54 Jl 2017

VAUDEVILLE TONITE! JOHNSON *Treasures* v6 no4 p38 F/ Mr 2017

Comedy festivals

54 GREAT THINGS TO DO THIS MONTH J. FOUMBERG, J. HARDBERGER et al color *Chicago* v66 no1 p117 Ja 2017

62 GREAT THINGS TO DO THIS MONTH J. FOUMBERG, J. HARDBERGER et al color *Chicago* v66 no6 p97 Je 2017

ABOVE & BEYOND diag *New Yorker* v93 no24 p12 Ag 21 2017

The Little Comedy Fest That Could J. HERBST *Los Angeles Magazine* p57 Ja 2017

Comedy films

See also

Romantic comedy films

Central Intelligence M. FELL *TV Guide* v65 no6 p47 Ja 30 2017

MH WORLD color *Men's Health* v32 no6 p6 Ag 2017

NO JOKE V. LUCCA color *Film Comment* v53 no2 p52 Mr/Ap 2017

War Machine A. D'ARMINIO *TV Guide* v65 no21 p41 My 15 2017

Comedy sketches

GOINGS ON ABOUT TOWN bw *New Yorker* v93 no19 p4 Jl 3 2017

Comedy—Reviews

BLING RING E. NUSSBAUM cartoon *New Yorker* v93 no19 p70 Jl 3 2017

Comencini, Francesca

THE WOMEN A. Levy cartoon *New Yorker* v92 no39 p34 N 28 2016

Comer, Colin

1965 ALFA ROMEO GIULIA SPRINT SPECIALE color *Road & Track* v68 no8 p95 My 2017

1970-1973 DATSUN 240Z color *Road & Track* v69 no2 p92 S 2017

Comer, Jodie

Jodie COMER K. AFTAB *Interview* v47 no2 p64 Mr 2017

The White Princess B. Oates *TV Guide* v65 no13 p36 Mr 20 2017

COMER, JONATHAN

Climate Justice Marchers Bring the Heat color *Progressive* v81 no5 p12 Je/Jl 2017

Comesport SA

Commencal J. Weber color *Bike Magazine* v24 no4 p98 Je 2017

Cometary nuclei

Seasonal exposure of carbon dioxide ice on the nucleus of comet 67P/Churyumov-Gerasimenko G. Filacchione, A. Raponi et al bibl bw graph *Science* v354 no6319 p1563 D 23 2016

Cometary orbits

The Poleward Trek of Comet ASASSN1 A. MacRobert color *Sky & Telescope* v134 no5 p48 N 2017

Comets

See also

Churyumov-Gerasimenko comet

c. 60: Rome *Lapham's Quarterly* v10 no2 p27 Spr 2017

Comet viewing the whole night through M. RATCLIFFE and A. LING color *Astronomy* v45 no5 p42 My 2017

GALLERY *Sky & Telescope* v133 no5 p74 My 2017

Impostors in the asteroid belt N. T. Redd bw color diag *Astronomy* v45 no4 p28 Ap 2017

Napoleon's Comets R. Jakiel *Sky & Telescope* v133 no5 p52 My 2017

Some topics call for science reporting from many angles E. Quill *Science News* v191 no11 p2 Je 10 2017

Comets spectra

The Poleward Trek of Comet ASASSN1 A. MacRobert color *Sky & Telescope* v134 no5 p48 N 2017

Comets—Environmental aspects

Surface changes on comet 67P/Churyumov-Gerasimenko suggest a more active past M. Ramy El-Maarry, O. Groussin et al bw graph *Science* v355 no6332 p1392 Mr 31 2017

Comets—Formation

More than a day in the life of a comet N. D. Russo bibl bw diag *Science* v354 no6319 p1536 D 23 2016

Comey, James B., 1960-

The 10 best days in journalism P. Vernon color *Columbia Journalism Review* v56 no2 p50 Fall 2017

THE APPROVAL MATRIX img *New York* v50 no12 p128 Je 12 2017

THE APPROVAL MATRIX: Our deliberately oversimplified guide to who falls where on our taste hierarchies img *New York* v50 no10 p118 My 15 2017

THE BIG BUST T. WEINER bw color *Esquire* v167 no1 p102 F 2017

Blocking the Detectives L. RESTON color *New Republic* v248 no7 p6 Jl 2017

Comey Discredits Himself color *Nation* v33 no21 p3 N 21 2016

The Comey Misfire D. V. Drehle, A. Altman et al color *Time* v189 no19 p20 My 22 2017

COMEY'S LAW B. McLEAN color *Vanity Fair* v59 no4 p166 Mr 2017

Comey's People M. CONTINETTI *Commentary* v144 no1 p64 Jl/Ag 2017

Comey, Trump, and the GOP S. F. Hayes color *Weekly Standard* v22 no35 p6 My 22 2017

Comey v. Trump S. F. Hayes color *Weekly Standard* v22 no39 p7 Je 19 2017

The Fall Guy T. Schoenberg and C. Strohm bw *Bloomberg Businessweek* no4523 p24 My 22 2017

Fever Dreams: The 'witch hunt' once made scapegoats out of the defenseless. How did it become a complaint of the powerful? A. Quinn *New York Times Magazine* p13 Je 11 2017

Fired. But Not Finished S. T. Dennis, M. Talev et al bw *Bloomberg Businessweek* no4522 p30 My 15 2017

The Firing That Misfired M. WARREN color *Weekly Standard* v22 no35 p10 My 22 2017

HAPPY HUNGER GAMES J. FIELDEN color *Esquire* v167 no1 p10 F 2017

Investigations and Prosecutions T. EASTLAND color *Weekly Standard* v22 no35 p13 My 22 2017

Is Trump Inc. the President's Greatest Vulnerability? A group of enterprising lawyers thinks it might be, whether all roads lead to Russia or not A. Rice, K. Gold et al img *New York* v50 no12 p40 Je 12 2017

James Comey's Dereliction [Cover story] A. C. McCARTHY color *National Review* v68 no19 p21 O 24 2016

Let the Investigation Begin [Cover story] color *Weekly Standard* v22 no36 p6 My 29 2017

Making Trump Pay D. COLE *Nation* v304 no17 p3 Je 5 2017

THE MAN IN THE ROOM A. Davidson cartoon *New Yorker* v93 no17 p19 Je 19 2017

PARODY color *Weekly Standard* v22 no12 p40 N 28 2016

PLAYING THE TRUMP CARD C. Hollub color *Entertainment Weekly* no1470 p12 Je 16 2017

The Russia Mess color *National Review* v69 no11 p12 Je 12 2017

Sentencing Reversal Angers Both Sides M. Rhodan color *Time* v189 no20 p11 My 29 2017

Trump Gets Himself in Hot Water—Again F. BARNES color *Weekly Standard* v22 no35 p12 My 22 2017

What James Comey Did D. Cole color *New York Review of Books* v63 no19 p4 D 8 2016

What We Saw Is What We've Got R. Ponnuru bw *Bloomberg Businessweek* no4523 p10 My 22 2017

Why James Comey Couldn't Keep the FBI Above Politics S. Frizell and M. Calabresi color *Time* v188 no20 p7 N 14 2016

Yes, She Is Guilty color *National Review* v68 no21 p13 N 21 2016

Comey, James B., 1960-—Trials, litigation, etc.

A Memo-rable Hearing M. WARREN color *Weekly Standard* v22 no39 p10 Je 19 2017

Comfort food

COMFORT EATS & TREATS FROM SOME OF OUR FAVORITE CELEBS S. E. JAMISON color *Ebony* v72/73 no12/1 p62 O/N 2017

Ed Sheeran J. ZAMBRANO color *O, The Oprah Magazine* p25 Jl 2017

Granny Ambition: 22nd Street Diner gives comfort food a good, old-fashioned schooling J. SPALDING *Indianapolis Monthly* p50 N 2017

LET THEM EAT CAKE S. FENNESSY *Atlanta* v56 no9 p16 Ja 2017

Steve Coogan If you were a critic, what would get four stars? D. WALTERS color *Bon Appetit* p154 S 2017

Comfort food—Psychological aspects

EATING YOUR FEELINGS A. GLOCK *Atlanta* v56 no9 p68 Ja 2017

Comic book conventions

ABOVE & BEYOND cartoon *New Yorker* v92 no32 p30 O 10 2016

ABOVE & BEYOND cartoon *New Yorker* v93 no31 p14 O 9 2017

DC Entertainment at New York Comic Con color *Publishers Weekly* v264 no38 p28 S 18 2017

New York Comic Con 2017 Adds Library Programming R. SHIVENER color *Publishers Weekly* v264 no38 p25 S 18 2017

SAN DIEGO COMIC-CON 2017: Comics in Libraries and Schools C. REID color *Publishers Weekly* v264 no28 p54 Jl 10 2017

Selling Graphic Novels to a Diverse Audience C. Reid color *Publishers Weekly* v264 no31 p4 Jl 31 2017

Comic book stores

Graphic Novels Rise, Periodicals Struggle in 2016 S. O'LEARY color *Publishers Weekly* v264 no7 p36 F 13 2017

Toronto's Beguiling Comics Store Relocates E. Nawotka color *Publishers Weekly* v264 no20 p9 My 15 2017

Comic book writers

CAUGHT BETWEEN TWO WORLDS D. CHENG-TOZUN cartoon *Christianity Today* p42 Mr 2017

Comic book writers—Interviews

Ta-Nehisi Coates Is Retooling America's Myth Factory E. Dockterman color *Time* v189 no5 p47 F 13 2017

Comic strip characters in motion pictures

STAR SEARCH C. Collis color *Entertainment Weekly* no1463/1464 p28 Ap/My 2017

Comic books, strips, etc.

See also

Graphic novels

BEST COMIC BOOKS N. Serrao, C. Agard et al color *Entertainment Weekly* no1444/1445 p110 D 16 2016

BRUCE LEE ENTER THE COMIC BOOK - AND THEN ENTER THE TV! [Cover story] R. W. YOUNG bw color *Black Belt* v55 no4 p32 Je/Jl 2017

THE BUSINESS OF BLACK COMIC BOOKS S. LYNN bw cartoon color *Black Enterprise* v47 no8 p56 Jl/Ag 2017

COLORING OUTSIDE THE LINES J. Berlin cartoon *National Geographic* v231 no6 pC19 Je 2017

THE FUNNY PAPERS E. Dwyer *Saturday Evening Post* v288 no6 p36 N/D 2016

Good on Paper S. L. Johnson cartoon *O, The Oprah Magazine* p128 Mr 2017

A Real Treasure color *Indianapolis Monthly* v42 no2 p72 O 2017

UnLeaShed *National Geographic Kids* no467 p32 F 2017

Visual Literacy S. SHAFER *Publishers Weekly* v264 no24 p68 Je 12 2017

Comic books, strips, etc.—Canada

NOT SO FAST, CANADA! B. McCALL cartoon *New Yorker* v93 no22 p27 Jl 31 2017

Comic books, strips, etc.—Coloring

OUTSIDE THE LINES: An Adult Coloring Experience bw *GQ: Gentlemen's Quarterly* v86 no12 p234 D 2016

Comic books, strips, etc.—Sales & prices

See also

Manga (Art)—Sales & prices

NINE REASONS MANGA PUBLISHERS CAN SMILE IN 2017 D. AOKI color *Publishers Weekly* v264 no25 p80 Je 19 2017

Comic books, strips, etc.—Themes, motives

THE ULTIMATE SUPERHERO FACE-LIFT C. Holub color *Entertainment Weekly* no1456 p68 Mr 10 2017

Coming of age

Girls, Uninterrupted color *Vogue* v207 no10 p204 O 2017

Coming out (Sexual orientation)

THE ESCAPE ARTIST S. Vilkomerson color *Entertainment Weekly* no1457/1458 p44 Mr 17 2017

INSIDE ELLEN'S COMING-OUT D. Snierson color *Entertainment Weekly* no1465 p49 My 12 2017

RECENT OUTINGS B. HALEY and S. HERNANDEZ color *Advocate* no1090 p15 Ap 2017

COMINGS, SID

Chords & Discords bw color *Downbeat* v84 no2 p10 F 2017

COMISKEY, DANIEL S.

CHANGE the CITY *Indianapolis Monthly* p55 Ap 2017

Leading Lady *Indianapolis Monthly* v40 no4 p66 D 2016

Q+A *Indianapolis Monthly* p73 Ap 2017

The Wrecked, Rebuilt Life OF ALDO ANDRETTI *Indianapolis Monthly* p72 My 2017

Comiskey, J. A.

Persistent effects of pre-Columbian plant domestication on Amazonian forest composition bibl chart graph map *Science* v355 no6328 p925 Mr 3 2017

Comita, Liza S.

How latitude affects biotic interactions color *Science* v356 no6345 p1328 Je 30 2017

Comizzoli, Pierre

Saving the saola from extinction color *Science* v357 no6357 p1248 S 22 2017

Comma (Punctuation)

For Want of a Comma J. Servaas *Saturday Evening Post* v289 no3 p23 My/Je 2017

Command & Control (Film)

NOW PLAYING color *Entertainment Weekly* no1434 p45 O 7 2016

Command & control systems

A hybrid DCC system D. Kawala *Model Railroader* v84 no4 p47 Ap 2017

Command of troops

Guadalcanal Revisited: The official Japanese postmortem of World War II shows how rivalries, miscommunication, and poor leadership plagued the imperial military machine Yuma Totani *Hoover Digest: Research & Opinion on Public Policy* no3 p110 Summ 2017

TRUMP'S TROOPS D. Neiwert, S. Posner et al *Mother Jones* v41 no6 p31 N/D 2016

Commando troops

Fighting for the Enemy: European powers sought to colonise the world. They could not do so without the support of indigenous peoples R. Johnson *History Today* v67 no10 p8 O 2017

Commemorative Air Force

COMMEMORATIVE AIR FORCE DIXIE WING PEACHTREE CITY 36 MILES SOUTHWEST OF ATLANTA J. GREEN *Atlanta* v56 no12 p144 Ap 2017

Commencement ceremonies

Milestones *Time* v190 no2/3 p11 Jl 10-17 2017

Showing-Up Ribbon cartoon color *Weekly Standard* v22 no41 p3 Jl 3 2017

Commerce

See also

Auctions

Barter

Competition (Economics)

Electronic commerce

Fairs

International trade

Purchasing

Retail industry

Sales

Why Localizing Marketing Doesn't Always Work N. Dawar *Harvard Business Review Digital Articles* p2 S 1 2016

Commercial aeronautics

See also

Air taxis

Airline industry

Commercial aeronautics laws

Transport planes

EARLY BIRD BEATS THE CROWD: Providing the best service possible *Iceland Review* v55 no4 p60 Jl/Ag 2017

Economic productivity in the air transportation industry: multifactor and labor productivity trends, 1990-2014 M. Russell bibl chart color diag graph *Monthly Labor Review* p1 Mr 2017

TOAST TO TREO T. MCNALLY color *New Orleans Magazine* v51 no3 p118 Ja 2017

Commercial aeronautics chartering

Cessna Flights For the Masses P. Robison *Bloomberg Businessweek* no4524 p35 My 29 2017

Private Jets Aren't So Private Anymore T. Black *Bloomberg Businessweek* no4498 p33 N 7 2016

Commercial aeronautics laws

DO MILLENNIALS WANT TO LEARN TO FLY? *Flying* v144 no11 p10 N 2017

What to Do if You Get Bumped M. Leonhardt color *Money* v46 no6 p19 Jl 2017

Commercial aeronautics laws—United States

Commercial Space Flight *Congressional Digest* v96 no7 p30 S 2017

Commercial aeronautics—Law & legislation—United States

GA AND THE NTSB'S MOST WANTED LIST S. Pope *Flying* v144 no3 p10 Mr 2017

Commercial aeronautics—Vocational guidance

AVIATION CAREERS S. Pope color *Flying* v144 no9 p58 S 2017

WHOA, BUDDY! S. Pope *Flying* v144 no9 p8 S 2017

Commercial Aircraft Corp. of China Ltd.

China—With Western Help—Finds Its Wings B. Einhorn and D. Lyu diag *Bloomberg Businessweek* no4522 p25 My 15 2017

Commercial art

Sweet Memories J. Nilsson *Saturday Evening Post* v289 no5 p99 S/O 2017

Commercial art galleries

Angela King Gallery's 10th Anniversary color *New Orleans Magazine* v51 no5 p27 Mr 2017

EVERYBODY LOVES THE SUNSHINE C. G. WAGLEY cartoon color diag *ARTnews* v115 no3 p106 Fall 2016

Found and Formed: Glass artist Mitchell Gaudet finds the extraordinary in the ordinary J. DeBold *New Orleans Homes & Lifestyles* v20 no4 p30 Aut 2017

GALLERIES MUSEUMS AND ARTISTS *Art in America* v105 no7 p61 Ag 2017

GALLERY IN THE GARDEN M. M. Kashino *Washingtonian Magazine* v52 no3 p164 D 2016

HEART FOR ART V. HAFSTAÐ *Iceland Review* v55 no4 p18 Jl/Ag 2017

POOL PARTY A. KONERMANN *Cincinnati Magazine* v50 no4 p21 Ja 2017

Time travel through the Haymarket M. Masich color *Nebraska Life* v21 no2 p60 Mr/Ap 2017

Commercial art galleries—Evaluation

Cape Calm M. Guerber color il *American Craft* v77 no2 p66 Ap/My 2017

IN THE OEUVR S. Sargent *Virginia Living* v15 no3 p17 Ap 2017

THE NATIONAL GALLERY OF ICELAND *Iceland Review* v55 no4 p23 Jl/Ag 2017

SHOPS and STOPS *Texas Monthly* v45 no3 p108 Mr 2017

Commercial art galleries—New York (State)—New York

On the Ball A. K. Scott color *New Yorker* v93 no8 p12 Ap 10 2017

Commercial art galleries—Officials & employees

"FLYING ALONE FOR WORK IS LIKE A VACATION. FLYING WITH MY SON IS DEFINITELY WORK." A. WHITTLE color *Conde Nast Traveler* v52 no6 p30 Je/Jl 2017

Commercial art galleries—United States

Mom & Popped N. FREEMAN bw color *ARTnews* v115 no4 p116 Wint 2016/2017

Commercial art gallery owners

Outsider Art's Inner Santum D. HARVEY *Los Angeles Magazine* p30 Mr 2017

What Is Art Really Worth? M. GLUCK *Los Angeles Magazine* p36 D 2016

Commercial buildings

See also

Bars (Drinking establishments)

Funeral homes

Nightclubs

Retail stores

Store decoration

Terminals (Transportation)

Trump Overseas J. Sanburn color *Time* v189 no23 p28 Je 19 2017

Commercial buildings—California

The Wrecking Crew C. NICHOLS *Los Angeles Magazine* v62 no6 p18 Je 2017

Commercial buildings—Maintenance & repair

You Are Now Entering the Money Pit A. KONERMANN *Cincinnati Magazine* v50 no11 p77 Ag 2017

Commercial catalogs

Why the Print Catalog Is Back in Style D. L. Yohn *Harvard Business Review Digital Articles* p2 F 25 2015

Commercial credit fraud

Brokerage Account Fraud Protection K. LANKFORD *Kiplinger's Personal Finance* v71 no1 p40 Ja 2017

Commercial crimes

See also

Corporate corruption

Fraud

Monopolies

False Front C. Chocano color *New York Times Magazine* p13 My 21 2017

Commercial crimes—United States—Government policy

Fines Alone Won't Deter Corporate Crime bw *Bloomberg Businessweek* no4500 p12 N 21 2016

Commercial dog breeders—Moral & ethical aspects

The Dog Factory P. Solotaroff color *Rolling Stone* no1278/1279 p42 Ja 12 2017

Commercial law

See also

Arbitration & award

Auctions

Bankruptcy

Bills of sale

Contracts

Licenses

Liquidation

Payment

Sales

Suretyship & guaranty

Trade regulation

Corporations Need a Better Approach to Public Policy B. W. Heineman Jr. *Harvard Business Review Digital Articles* p2 Ap 1 2016

Commercial law—Japan

Japan's Big Bet B. Einhorn, G. Huang et al color *Bloomberg Businessweek* no4505 p20 D 26 2016

Commercial leases

How Businesses Can Support a Circular Economy Terence Tse, M. Esposito et al *Harvard Business Review Digital Articles* p2 F 1 2016

Commercial policy

See also

Protectionism

AG IN THE BALANCE *Successful Farming* v115 no3 p10 Mid-F 2017

Russia, Japan, and China Fill the Trade Gap B. Einhorn and I. Arkhipov *Bloomberg Businessweek* no4502 p22 D 5 2016

Commercial policy—United States

The Human Side of Trade: In a dynamic economy, short-term pain is real. But over the longer term? Free trade leads to better, richer lives R. Roberts *Hoover Digest: Research & Opinion on Public Policy* no2 p13 Spr 2017

Commercial product evaluation

15 Things You Need to Know About Sun Protection J. Edgar color *Health* v31 no5 p25 Je 2017

The A-LIST G. Hadid color *Harper's Bazaar* no3654 p58 Je/Jl 2017

Back in Style: White Kicks color *Health* v31 no5 p9 Je 2017

BB & CC Cream Benefits S. STRAUSFOGEL color *Better Nutrition* v79 no9 p28 S 2017

Beauty Loot We Love color *Health* v31 no5 p34 Je 2017

THE BEST BET img *New York* v50 no9 p59 My 1 2017

Beyond The Blender L. TURNER color *Better Nutrition* v79 no6 p26 Je 2017

BOHEMIAN RHAPSODY color *Harper's Bazaar* no3654 p92 Je/Jl 2017

cheat, drink, & still shrink A. Rios color *Yoga Journal* no294 p11 S 2017

Does It Really Work? L. Desantis color *Health* v31 no5 p31 Je 2017

Get the Wet Look color *Health* v31 no5 p16 Je 2017

GIFT GUIDE 2017 [Cover story] color *Amazing Wellness* v9 no6 p70 EarlyWint 2017

Gone Glamping R. S. Frazier color *Health* v31 no5 p54 Je 2017

Melt-Proof Your Makeup C. T. Burns color *Health* v31 no5 p96 Je 2017

navigate the beauty aisle [Cover story] K. S. BOX color *Parents* v92 no7 p72 Jl 2017

new products color *Science* v357 no6358 p1425 S 29 2017

Not Your Grandma's Gate color *Parents* v92 no11 p112 N 2017

open-air Deliciousness E. HARE color *Cabin Living* p56 S 2017

Products *Parks & Recreation* v52 no6 p50 Je 2017

Product Spotlights color *Better Nutrition* v79 no6 p63 Je 2017

Proven Car Care color *Good Housekeeping* v265 no4 p85 O 2017

Sensory Toys Are Having a Moment color *Parents* v92 no11 p24 N 2017

Snacks for Your Summer Travels M. DIANE SMITH color *Better Nutrition* v79 no6 p58 Je 2017

SO BAZAAR color *Harper's Bazaar* no3654 p166 Je/Jl 2017

Stop Wrestling with Your Razor S. STRAUSFOGEL color *Better Nutrition* v79 no6 p52 Je 2017

Summer Sizzlers color *Better Nutrition* v79 no6 p20 Je 2017

SWEET ELEGANCE bw color *Harper's Bazaar* no3654 p84 Je/Jl 2017

Time Honored B. BOYÉ color *Men's Health* v32 no5 p64 Je 2017

TOY JOY J. HARTSHORN color *Parents* v92 no11 p56 N 2017

veggie bits *Vegetarian Journal* v36 no3 p30 2017

virtual vacation T. PEREZ *Parents* v91 no6 p78 Je 2016

Wake Up Happy—with Tech! color *Health* v31 no7 p90 S 2017

WELCOME TO MIAMI color *Harper's Bazaar* no3654 p102 Je/Jl 2017

WHAT'S NEW? *USA Today Magazine* v145 no2864 p76 My 2017

Your Anti-Aging Lip Kit color *Health* v31 no5 p10 Je 2017

Commercial products
> *See also*
>> Animal products
>> Brand name products
>> Electric apparatus & appliances
>> Green products
>> Manufactures
>> Natural products
>> New product development
>> Synthetic products

FINDING THE PLATFORM IN YOUR PRODUCT: FOUR STRATEGIES THAT CAN REVEAL HIDDEN VALUE A. HAGIU and E. J. ALTMAN il *Harvard Business Review* v95 no4 p94 Jl/Ag 2017

LG's robot lineup for the lazy future color *PCWorld* v35 no2 p204 F 2017

Max Out Points for Holiday Shopping L. GERSTNER chart *Kiplinger's Personal Finance* v70 no12 p45 D 2016

PUT TOGETHER YOUR SEASONAL PLAN: WATCH WHAT TO DO EACH MONTH THIS SPRING AND SUMMER A. Kluis *Successful Farming* v115 no6 p18 Ap 2017

STYLE *New Orleans Homes & Lifestyles* v20 no2 p16 Spr 2017

Why Platform Disruption Is So Much Bigger than Product Disruption J. P. Vazquez Sampere *Harvard Business Review Digital Articles* p2 Ap 8 2016

Commercial products—China—Sales & prices

China's High – End Retail Emporium color *Bloomberg Businessweek* no4498 p29 N 7 2016

Commercial products—Evaluation

cheat, drink, & still shrink A. Rios color *Yoga Journal* no291 p29 My 2017

Cozy & Cruelty-Free A. Piper color *Vegetarian Times* v43 no2 p15 N/D 2016

FANTASTIC FINDS *Psychology Today* v49 no6 p94 N/D 2016

FOOD FOR THOUGHT *Nutrition Action Health Letter* v44 no3 p16 Ap 2017

food free-for-all K. CICERO color *Parents* v92 no4 p42 Ap 2017

For the Social Animal color *Consumer Reports* v81 no12 p38 D 2016

GIFTS WE Love color *Rodale's Organic Life* v2 no7 p20 D 2016/Ja 2017

Gorgeous Skin All Winter T. T. Canel color *Health* v31 no1 p27 Ja 2017

Had to Share! color *Better Nutrition* p20 My 2017

Her Style color *InStyle* v23 no13 p38 D 2016

In With the New color *Better Nutrition* v79 no1 p20 Ja 2017

I promise you a pain-free life or your money back T. Lemerond color *Better Nutrition* v78 no11 p76 N 2016

I ♥ SUPPLEMENTS color *Better Nutrition* v78 no11 p49 N 2016

Living in the Present D. POINTDUJOUR color *Ebony* v72 no3 p72 D 2016/Ja 2017

MATCHA'S SKIN-SAVING MAGIC color *Health* v31 no1 p16 Ja 2017

My Stuff R. CHAPMAN color *Vanity Fair* v59 no2 p32 F 2017

Our Favorite Sports Bras Now R. S. Frazier color *Health* v31 no3 p54 Ap 2017

PIZZA PARTY *Nutrition Action Health Letter* v44 no3 p14 Ap 2017

Power Ingredient: Gold! L. Desantis color *Health* v31 no1 p34 Ja 2017

Product Spotlights color *Better Nutrition* v79 no1 p67 Ja 2017

Product Spotlights color *Better Nutrition* v79 no4 p71 Ap 2017

RISE & SHINE bw color *Vogue* v207 no1 p45 Ja 2017

Sit in style E. Marglin color *Yoga Journal* no291 p24 My 2017

SLIM DOWN IN 2017 L. TURNER color *Better Nutrition* v79 no1 p36 Ja 2017

slow cooker vs. pressure cooker F. DURAND *Parents* v92 no2 p88 F 2017

STUFF WE LOVE color *Yoga Journal* no291 p22 My 2017

Style for Miles C. KUZMA cartoon color *Runner's World* v52 no4 p46 My 2017

Suit Up for Less J. Smith color *Health* v31 no1 p53 Ja 2017

Toxin-Free Hair Care S. STRAUSFOGEL color *Better Nutrition* v78 no11 p38 N 2016

UP YOUR BEAUTY GAME L. Desantis color *Health* v31 no1 p102 Ja 2017

The Very Best in Drugstore Lip Picks L. Desantis color *Health* v31 no3 p30 Ap 2017

VRG Catalog *Vegetarian Journal* v35 no4 p33 2016

Warming Trends color *Better Nutrition* v79 no4 p22 Ap 2017

What's Hot in Natural Beauty T. T. Canel color *Health* v31 no3 p27 Ap 2017

WHAT'S NEW? *USA Today Magazine* v145 no2862 p78 Mr 2017

White Castle Removes L-Cysteine from Veggie Slider Bun; Prompted by Vegans J. Yacoubou *Vegetarian Journal* v35 no4 p36 2016

Commercial products—Marketing
> *See also*
>> Brand integration

Customers Aren't Very Good at Judging Product Sizing P. Chandon *Harvard Business Review Digital Articles* p2 N 11 2015

Commercial products—Reviews
> *See also*
>> Consumers' reviews

This Winter, Be Ready for Anything color *Consumer Reports* v81 no12 p9 D 2016

Commercial products—Sales & prices

SHARK TANK'S WACKIEST MONEYMAKERS L. Rice color *Entertainment Weekly* no1439 p51 N 11 2016

Commercial products—Testing

Yes, A/B Testing Is Still Necessary K. Fung *Harvard Business Review Digital Articles* p2 D 10 2014

Commercial real estate
> *See also*
>> Shopping malls

KEEPING IT REAL: Thanks to our historic housing stock, Cincinnati's rehabbed real estate market is the anti-anytown, usa A. BROWNLEE *Cincinnati Magazine* v50 no11 p74 Ag 2017

Commercial space ventures

THEY CAME FOR OUTER SPACE A. Vance color graph map *Bloomberg Businessweek* no4529 p40 Jl 3 2017

Commercial treaties
> *See also*
>> North American Free Trade Agreement (NAFTA)

Asia K. Stock color *Bloomberg Businessweek* no4535 p8 Ag 28 2017

Don't Cry for the TPP C. Prestowitz color *Harvard Business Review Digital Articles* p2 Ja 26 2017

Executives Need to Know How Trade Deals Shape Their Markets M. L. Busch *Harvard Business Review Digital Articles* p2 O 13 2016

How Labor Standards Can Be Good for Growth E. Verhoogen *Harvard Business Review Digital Articles* p2 Ap 27 2016

Let's Grow: Ideas to Get Our Economy Moving T. J. DONOHUE *Weekly Standard* v22 no19 p23 Ja 23 2017

What Trade Deals Are Good For G. Grossman *Harvard Business Review Digital Articles* p2 My 24 2016

Why Wallonia wobbled S. HAYDEN color *Maclean's* v129 no45 p43 N 14 2016

Commercialization

Perovskite solar cells gear up to go commercial R. F. Service color *Science* v354 no6317 p1214 D 9 2016

STILL BAKING R. SABIN color *Sound & Vision* v82 no8 p8 O 2017

Commercial products—Charts, diagrams, etc.

ROAD TEST SUMMARY chart *Road & Track* v69 no2 p98 S 2017

Commingled funds (Mutual funds)

Low-Fee 401(k) Choices Are Hiding in Plain Sight E. O'Brien color diag *Money* v46 no6 p25 Jl 2017

Commitment (Psychology)

    See also

        Organizational commitment

7 ideas to ignite your passion for practice H. Dowdle color *Yoga Journal* p14 2017 Special Issue

Magic Words J. BIRCH *Psychology Today* v49 no5 p40 S/O 2016

MILD LOVE A. BEN-ZEÉV *Psychology Today* v50 no3 p76 My/Je 2017

take the leap! B. Birney color *Yoga Journal* p62 2017 Special Issue

Commitment (Psychology)—Religious aspects

Advice for Conflict A. Olendzki *Tricycle: The Buddhist Review* v26 no4 p29 Summ 2017

Committees

A Community Affair D. Sanford *Parks & Recreation* v52 no5 p80 My 2017

Commodities brokerage

The Rise and Fall of a Trading Giant in Asia A. Hoffman color graph map *Bloomberg Businessweek* no4525 p39 Je 5 2017

Commodity exchanges

    See also

        Gold markets

Gold Is for Cranks? Not So Fast W. BALDWIN chart color *Forbes* v199 no7 p128 Je 29 2017

Commodity exchanges—China

How to Trade a Donkey color *Bloomberg Businessweek* no4517 p38 Ap 3 2017

Commodity exchanges—Economic aspects

How to Trade a Donkey color *Bloomberg Businessweek* no4517 p38 Ap 3 2017

Common Core State Standards (Education)

Backtalk L. S. Goldstein diag *Phi Delta Kappan* v98 no6 p80 Mr 2017

THE COMMON CORE CONUNDRUM H. ARABADJIS *USA Today Magazine* v145 no2864 p54 My 2017

Common decency

The Church Isn't Called to Be 'Decent' D. RISHMAWY *Christianity Today* v61 no4 p30 My 2017

Common descent (Evolution)

Science's Confusion Concerning the Origin of Life M. AVERICK *USA Today Magazine* v145 no2862 p46 Mr 2017

Common fallacies

10 WEIGHT-LOSS MYTHS BUSTED V. Tweed color *Amazing Wellness* v8 no2 p54 Spr 2016

5 Myths of Great Workplaces R. Friedman *Harvard Business Review Digital Articles* p2 Mr 5 2015

6 FOOD MYTHS YOU CAN FORGET J. SCHILDHOUSE color *Muscle & Performance* v9 no5 p26 My 2017

Fake News and Fake Science in the Age of Misinformation K. FRAZIER *Skeptical Inquirer* v41 no3 p4 My/Je 2017

If You Gild It... K. D. HODES color *Women's Health* v14 no9 p45 N 2017

INSIDE THE ECHO CHAMBER W. Quattrociocchi color *Scientific American* v316 no4 p60 Ap 2017

Mass Misinformation Author David Helfand Warns of 'Google-Fed Zombies' *Skeptical Inquirer* v41 no2 p13 Mr/Ap 2017

NEWS BLUES A. Marantz cartoon *New Yorker* v92 no42 p44 D 19 2016

SURVIVING THE MIS INFORMATION AGE D. J. HELFAND *Skeptical Inquirer* v41 no3 p34 My/Je 2017

Common good

For whose benefit? K. Clarke color *U.S. Catholic* v82 no1 p42 Ja 2017

What is the common good? B. Haile *U.S. Catholic* v82 no11 p49 N 2017

Common good—Religious aspects

Is the 'Common Good' Obsolete? [Cover story] A. Latham and J. R. Bowlin bw color *Commonweal* v143 no19 p12 D 2 2016

Common murre

Seabirds negotiate parenting duties E. S. EATON color *Science News* v191 no13 p16 Jl 8 2017

Common sense

Wit's End D. Paul *Indianapolis Monthly* p172 My 2017

Common (Musician), 1972-

Common E. R. Brown color *Entertainment Weekly* no1439 p57 N 11 2016

Pioneers [Cover story] color *Time* v189 no16/17 p14 My 1-8 2017

Common (Musician), 1972—Interviews

THE COMMON CAUSE M. Vain color *Entertainment Weekly* no1439 p56 N 11 2016

Commons

    See also

        Parks

Commons, grounds, and DCC L. Puckett color diag *Model Railroader* v84 no9 p56 S 2017

How Companies Can Help Rebuild America's Common Resources K. Mills and C. Rudnicki *Harvard Business Review Digital Articles* p2 S 21 2015

Commune (Company)

BACK TO CALI M. RUS color *Architectural Digest* v74 no10 p140 O 1 2017

Hitmakers bw color *Architectural Digest* v74 no1 p140 Ja 2017

Commune, The (Film)

NOW PLAYING color *Entertainment Weekly* no1468/1469 p86 Je 2-9 2017

Communicable disease diagnosis

Diagnosis L. Sanders color *New York Times Magazine* p30 My 21 2017

Communicable disease epidemiology

    See also

        Influenza epidemiology

Driving improvements in emerging disease surveillance through locally relevant capacity strengthening J. E. B. Halliday, K. Hampson et al color diag *Science* v357 no6347 p146 Jl 14 2017

OUTBREAK [Cover story] C. Ash color *Science* v357 no6347 p144 Jl 14 2017

When an emerging disease becomes endemic G. F. Medley and A. Vassall color *Science* v357 no6347 p156 Jl 14 2017

Communicable diseases

    See also

        Bacterial diseases

        Mycoses

        Polio

        Tick-borne diseases

Contagions Make a Comeback [Cover story] S. Shah color *Science News* v190 no13 p32 D 24 2016

IT'S ALIIIIVE! color *Women's Health* v14 no1 p33 Ja/F 2017

Morbid Curiosity D. BURCH color *Natural History* v125 no9 p3 S 2017

TRAVELERS NEED TO EXERCISE CAUTION *USA Today Magazine* v146 no2869 p12 O 2017

What's Your STI-Q? K. MICKLE color *Seventeen* v76 no4 p52 Jl/Ag 2017

Communicable diseases—International cooperation

Opportunities and challenges in modeling emerging infectious diseases C. J. E. Metcalf and J. Lessler diag graph *Science* v357 no6347 p149 Jl 14 2017

Communicable diseases—Prevention

See also

Vaccination

CANADA LEADS GLOBAL HEALTH INITIATIVE G. Davidson color *Maclean's* v129 no50 p51 D 19 2016

SAVE YOUR VACATION D. Keating color *Maclean's* v129 no50 p54 D 19 2016

Communicable diseases—Social aspects

When an emerging disease becomes endemic G. F. Medley and A. Vassall color *Science* v357 no6347 p156 Jl 14 2017

Communication

See also

Business communication

Communication barriers

Communication in management

Communication in organizations

Communication in science

Interpersonal communication

Language & languages

Mass media

Political communication

Popular culture

Publications

Social media

Teacher-student communication

Writing

Written communication

10 discipline mistakes L. GARISTO PFAFF chart color *Parents* v92 no6 p48 Je 2017

75 ways to be a grown-up E. ZAMMETT RUDDY, J. DUNN et al *Parents* v91 no11 p95 N 2016

Be Rude at Your Own Risk K. Rockwood color *Parents* v92 no6 p28 Je 2017

CHAKRA ALIGNMENT M. RABBITT color *Yoga Journal* no288 p64 D 2016

COMMUNICATION IS KEY TO ALL SUCCESSFUL PARTNERSHIPS K. Santos color *Spin to Win Rodeo* v21 no5 p40 Jl 2017

Conversing with Canines: THINK CAT IN THE HAT FOR TALKING TO DOGS S. COREN *Psychology Today* v50 no5 p73 S/O 2017

cultivate caring J. TORRES SIDERS *Parents* v91 no12 p122 D 2016

Do you need a second opinion? K. Canning color *Health* v31 no9 p68 N 2017

EMOJIS FOR BEAUTY LOVERS color *Health* v31 no2 p12 Mr 2017

EYE TO EYE: A BOND BETWEEN MINDS MAY SHOW ITSELF IN OUR PUPILS K. GOLDYNIA *Psychology Today* v50 no4 p20 Ag 2017

Find Your Peace of Mind G. Saltz color *Health* v30 no10 p77 D 2016

Gabrielle Union J. STEWART and P. Kita color *Men's Health* v32 no2 p28 Mr 2017

How Leaderless Groups End Up with Leaders S. Pillay *Harvard Business Review Digital Articles* p2 F 19 2016

How not to be a wallflower color *Health* v31 no9 p13 N 2017

How to Talk So Your Stylist Will Listen C. T. Burns color *Health* v31 no8 p108 O 2017

How to Talk to a Loved One Who Is Suffering S. Sandberg and A. Grant color *Time* v189 no15 p43 Ap 24 2017

if you ask me… S. JAMES color *Parents* v92 no4 p100 Ap 2017

Just Ignore It C. Pearlman color *Parents* v92 no9 p58 S 2017

Listen Up C. HEADLEE *American Scholar* v86 no4 p16 Aut 2017

LIVING BY The Word *Christian Century* v134 no1 p20 Ja 4 2017

Mastering the Entering Game C. Toy color *Spin to Win Rodeo* v21 no3 p22 My 2017

Publishing's Bright Future (Really!) C. MAUM *Publishers Weekly* v264 no22 p72 My 29 2017

Standing up to fear A. Khaledi-Nasab color *Science* v356 no6336 p458 Ap 28 2017

stop fighting about money! M. LILES *Parents* v91 no9 p156 S 2016

Talking of Taste: Umami? Kokumi? The search for new tastes goes way beyond gastronomy K. GOLDYNIA *Psychology Today* v50 no5 p36 S/O 2017

That's Outrageous! color *Reader's Digest* v190 no1133 p129 S 2017

Tune In S. Oliynyk *Practical Horseman* v45 no11 p8 N 2017

Communication barriers

IT'S THE LITTLE THINGS: MANY OF THE DIFFERENCES BETWEEN CRUISING IN THE U.S AND CRUISING IN MEXICO ARE SUBTLE P. RAINS color *Sea Magazine* v109 no8 p14 Ag 2017

Let's talk about language barriers A. Deczkowska color *Science* v356 no6341 p978 Je 1 2017

Reinventing Sundays S. TURRENTINE bw color *Climbing* no354 p64 Jl 2017

Communication in industrial relations

How to Get Your Employees to Speak Up R. Knight *Harvard Business Review Digital Articles* p2 O 10 2014

Outsmart Your Next Angry Outburst P. Bregman *Harvard Business Review Digital Articles* p2 My 6 2016

Communication in management

The Assumptions That Make Giving Tough Feedback Even Tougher J. Zenger and J. Folkman *Harvard Business Review Digital Articles* p2 Ap 30 2015

Building Trust Between Your Employees and Freelancers J. Younger and M. Kearns *Harvard Business Review Digital Articles* p2 Mr 15 2017

Communicating a Corporate Vision to Your Team K. Decker and B. Decker *Harvard Business Review Digital Articles* p2 Jl 10 2015

Create a Culture Where Difficult Conversations Aren't So Hard J. Whitehurst *Harvard Business Review Digital Articles* p2 Ag 14 2015

Figure Out Your Manager's Communication Style *Harvard Business Review Digital Articles* p2 Jl 2 2015

Great CEOs See the Importance of Being Understood M. Schrage *Harvard Business Review Digital Articles* p2 D 16 2016

How to Give Feedback to People Who Cry, Yell, or Get Defensive Amy Jen Su *Harvard Business Review Digital Articles* p2 S 21 2016

How to Help an Employee Who Rubs People the Wrong Way R. Knight *Harvard Business Review Digital Articles* p2 S 21 2017

How to Tell Your Boss You Have Too Much Work R. Knight color *Harvard Business Review Digital Articles* p2 Ja 13 2017

If You Want to Be the Boss, Say "We" Not "I" D. Burkus *Harvard Business Review Digital Articles* p2 Mr 6 2015

It's Harder to Empathize with People If You've Been in Their Shoes R. Ruttan, McDonnell et al *Harvard Business Review Digital Articles* p2 O 20 2015

Just Because You're in Charge Doesn't Mean You Should Run Every Meeting P. Axtell *Harvard Business Review Digital Articles* p2 D 23 2016

Motivating Millennials Takes More than Flexible Work Policies T. Benson *Harvard Business Review Digital Articles* p2 F 11 2016

Nonverbal Cues Get Employees to Open Up—or Shut Down J. R. Detert and E. R. Burris *Harvard Business Review Digital Articles* p2 D 11 2015

The Top Complaints from Employees About Their Leaders L. Solomon *Harvard Business Review Digital Articles* p2 Je 24 2015

What's Worse than a Difficult Conversation? Avoiding One D. Rowland *Harvard Business Review Digital Articles* p2 Ap 8 2016

What to Do When You Get a New Boss Every Few Months R. Knight *Harvard Business Review Digital Articles* p2 Jl 1 2016

When to Skip a Difficult Conversation D. G. Riegel *Harvard Business Review Digital Articles* p2 Mr 1 2016

Your Team Can't Read Your Mind A. Ranieri *Harvard Business Review Digital Articles* p2 Jl 23 2015

Communication in marketing—Social aspects

Praising Customers for Ethical Purchases Can Backfire M. Kouchaki and A. Jami *Harvard Business Review Digital Articles* p2 O 6 2016

Communication in organizations

Actually, You Should Check Email First Thing in the Morning D. Clark *Harvard Business Review Digital Articles* p2 Mr 7 2016

How can I tell staff about pay rate cuts? PM's Fixer Samantha Sales tackles readers big issues *People Management* p53 Ap 2017

How the Best CEOs Get the Important Work Done J. Allen *Harvard Business Review Digital Articles* p2 S 27 2016

How to Communicate Clearly During Organizational Change E. Johnson *Harvard Business Review Digital Articles* p2 Je 13 2017

How to cultivate effective engagement N. Purse *People Management* p50 Ap 2017

"Poor Communication" Is Often a Symptom of a Different Problem A. Markman *Harvard Business Review Digital Articles* p2 F 22 2017

The Right Way to Bring a Problem to Your Boss A. Gallo *Harvard Business Review Digital Articles* p2 D 5 2014

The Top Complaints from Employees About Their Leaders L. Solomon *Harvard Business Review Digital Articles* p2 Je 24 2015

Two-Thirds of Managers Are Uncomfortable Communicating with Employees L. Solomon *Harvard Business Review Digital Articles* p2 Mr 9 2016

Your New Idea Is Worthless Unless You Know How to Sell It L. Davey *Harvard Business Review Digital Articles* p2 N 26 2015

Communication in personnel management

Do You Know How Each Person on Your Team Likes to Work? S. Nawaz *Harvard Business Review Digital Articles* p2 My 30 2017

How to Make Your One-on-Ones with Employees More Productive R. Knight *Harvard Business Review Digital Articles* p2 Ag 8 2016

How to Really Listen to Your Employees S. Stibitz *Harvard Business Review Digital Articles* p2 Ja 30 2015

If You Want to Get Promoted, Say So S. Nawaz color *Harvard Business Review Digital Articles* p2 Ja 5 2017

What to Say and Do When Your Employee Has Another Job Offer A. Gallo *Harvard Business Review Digital Articles* p2 My 31 2016

Communication in science

See also

Science journalism

Friendship L. Kingsley, R. Fiorenza et al *Science* v354 no6308 p46 O 7 2016

Promote scientific integrity via journal peer review data C. J. Lee and D. Moher color *Science* v357 no6348 p256 Jl 21 2017

Communication policy

See also

Information policy

Network neutrality

Learn to Ad: Madison Avenue Strategies to Strengthen School Communication B. CASTLEMAN and J. SKILLMAN *Education Digest* v82 no6 p34 F 2017

Communication styles

Figure Out Your Manager's Communication Style *Harvard Business Review Digital Articles* p2 Jl 2 2015

Communication—Methodology

THE POWER OF REVISION S. Coppola color *Literacy Today (2411-7862)* v34 no5 p40 Mr/Ap 2017

Communicative competence

How Doctors (or Anyone) Can Craft a More Persuasive Message S. Martin *Harvard Business Review Digital Articles* p2 Ja 29 2015

The Soft Skills of Great Digital Organizations A. Samuel *Harvard Business Review Digital Articles* p2 F 5 2016

Communion sermons

LIVING BY The Word *Christian Century* v134 no19 p18 S 13 2017

Communism

Caisson Communism color *Weekly Standard* v23 no6 p4 O 16 2017

A Flawed Portrait M. C. Ricklefs, *History Today* v67 no7 p6 Jl 2017

Communism—Cuba

WHIPLASH AND BACKLASH IN THE REPUBLIC OF CUBA S. Slade color *Reason* v49 no5 p28 O 2017

Communism—Europe

Stars in His Eyes *Commentary* v142 no1 p1 Jl/Ag 2016

Communism—Russia

Images of the Future G. W. Breslauer diag *Daedalus* v146 no2 p142 Spr 2017

Communist Party of the United States of America

Does the Left Bear Any Blame for Trump? J. THINDWA and K. GEIER *In These Times* v41 no2 p12 F 2017

Fixing Electoral Mechanics J. BLEIFUSS *In These Times* v41 no2 p5 F 2017

Communist revisionism

Asia's Other Revisionist Power J. Lind color *Foreign Affairs* v96 no2 p74 Mr/Ap 2017

Communists

Are We Heading Toward a New COLD WAR? C. STOFFERS and M. Wines *New York Times Upfront* v149 no3 p18 O 10 2016

Communitarianism

Understanding the Victors M. EIGEN, F. HEGGE et al *American Scholar* v86 no2 p3 Spr 2017

Communitech Corp.

Health Care Meets High Tech L. Snell color *Alternatives Journal (AJ) - Canada's Environmental Voice* v42 no3 p32 2016

Communities

See also

Community life

Gay community

LGBT communities

Neighborhoods

Become a Parks and Recreation Trendsetter: Use a hospitality mindset and choose your offerings wisely to do so S. Howell *Parks & Recreation* v52 no9 p108 S 2017

Border, beach, buried wonders, Old Baldy & Bells C. AMUNDSON and A. J. BARTELS color *Nebraska Life* v21 no6 p56 N/D 2017

Bread for the world B. Massingale color *U.S. Catholic* v82 no6 p10 Je 2017

Do Good, Feel Great cartoon *Good Housekeeping* v263 no5 p91 N 2016

Faith Matters S. Wells *Christian Century* v134 no15 p2 Jl 19 2017

First Go Narrow, Then Go Wide J. FRIEDMAN *Publishers Weekly* v264 no39 p64 S 25 2017

Five Steps to Unlock Your Agency's Marketing and Branding Potential N. Bhatt *Parks & Recreation* v52 no9 p20 S 2017

HIGHER GROUND Z. SLOBIG *Orion Magazine* v35 no4/5 p20 Jl-O 2016

How to Leverage Geocaching to Promote Park and Recreation Events A. Frank *Parks & Recreation* v52 no10 p52 O 2017

LETTER FROM THE EDITOR MARCH 2017 J. STOWE *Cincinnati Magazine* v50 no6 p18 Mr 2017

Localism Means Security W. S. LIND *American Conservative* v15 no6 p10 N/D 2016

LOSING HOME Z. Loftus-Farren color *Earth Island Journal* v32 no1 p19 Spr 2017

The Man in the Mirror D. C. Paris *Change* v48 no6 p4 N/D 2016

Member Spotlight: Maria Nardi C. Jones *Parks & Recreation* v52 no9 p97 S 2017

Mother Brooklyn *Commentary* v143 no4 p19 Ap 2017

THE Nicest Places IN America [Cover story] J. GREENFIELD color map *Reader's Digest* v190 no1135 p59 N 2017

Radical hospitality E. Sanna *U.S. Catholic* v82 no6 p4 Je 2017

Communities—Social aspects

A HOME OF LAST RESORT S. SMITH *Texas Monthly* v45 no5 p81 My 2017

The War over Education and Civil Rights J. V. Heilig *Progressive* v81 no10 p13 N 2016

Community & college

Campus Cowardice *Weekly Standard* v23 no4 p3 O 2 2017

New Hope for College Towns M. Funkhouser *Governing* v30 no7 p59 Ap 2017

Community arts projects

Creating community from the inside out: A concentric perspective on collective artmaking C. Blatt-Gross bibl *Arts Education Policy Review* v118 no1 p51 2017

High Line Art M. Jensen *Orion Magazine* v35 no4/5 p72 Jl-O 2016

Community banks—Congresses

Calendar *Bridges (Federal Reserve Bank of St. Louis)* p2 Summ 2016

Community-based social services

THE STORIES WE TELL C. Paxton cartoon *Louisiana Life* v37 no2 p50 N/D 2016

Community centers

See also

Recreation centers

Economy W. Frick *Harvard Business Review Digital Articles* p1 Jl 25 2017

A Moment of Reckoning for a Soaring Solar Industry J. Worland color *Time* v190 no12 p30 S 25 2017

Obsess Over Your Customers, Not Your Rivals Nelson *Harvard Business Review Digital Articles* p1 My 11 2017

The Real Reason Superstar Firms Are Pulling Ahead W. Frick *Harvard Business Review Digital Articles* p2 O 5 2017

Should Farmers Fear Him? A. Bjerga and L. Thomasson color graph *Bloomberg Businessweek* no4512 p13 F 20 2017

There Are Still Only Two Ways to Compete R. L. Martin *Harvard Business Review Digital Articles* p2 Ap 21 2015

Thirst for Fuel Drives Competition *Foreign Affairs* v95 no6 p(Sp)8 N/D 2016

Trial and Error Is No Way to Make Strategy T. Zenger *Harvard Business Review Digital Articles* p2 Ap 24 2015

What Driverless Cars Mean for Today's Automakers M. Wessel *Harvard Business Review Digital Articles* p2 Ag 27 2015

What Is Strategy, Again? A. Ovans *Harvard Business Review Digital Articles* p2 My 12 2015

Why Being Unpredictable Is a Bad Strategy M. Chussil color *Harvard Business Review Digital Articles* p2 Ja 5 2017

WHY RECALLS OFTEN HURT RIVALS *Harvard Business Review* v94 no11 p26 N 2016

Competition (Economics)—Case studies

The Boundaries Around Your Industry Are About to Change D. Chivers *Harvard Business Review Digital Articles* p2 N 3 2014

Competition (Economics)—Germany

The Real Reason the German Labor Market Is Booming A. Spitz-Oener *Harvard Business Review Digital Articles* p2 Mr 13 2017

Competition (Economics)—United States

Competition Is on the Decline, and That's Fueling Inequality W. Frick *Harvard Business Review Digital Articles* p2 Mr 24 2017

HEALTH CARE NEEDS REAL COMPETITION: INTERAC-TION C. Mendelson, R. D. King et al img *Harvard Business Review* v95 no2 p19 Mr/Ap 2017

Competition (Psychology)

Chill Out & Get Healthy Nicole *Better Nutrition* v79 no6 p6 Jc 2017

if you ask me .. S. JAMES *Parents* v91 no10 p96 O 2016

IN IT FOR THE LONG HAUL K. Santos color *Spin to Win Rodeo* v21 no1 p38 Mr 2017

The QUEEN BEE in the CORNER OFFICE O. Khazan color *Atlantic* v320 no2 p50 S 2017

Why We Fight M. Bean *Men's Health* v32 no8 p6 O 2017

Competition (Psychology) in children

raise a good sport E. ZAMMETT RUDDY color graph *Parents* v92 no5 p36 My 2017

Competition horses

See also

Dressage horses

Race horses

Pint-sized Dynamos: Tyler Hardin and "Zipy" C. Reich *Arabian Horse World* v57 no4 p110 Ja 2017

Sheikh Zayed bin sultan Al Nahyan Jewel Crown S. Andersen *Arabian Horse World* v57 no4 p156 Ja 2017

SHOWRING STARS *Arabian Horse World* v57 no3 p66 D 2016

STALLION Directory *Arabian Horse World* v57 no4 p190 Ja 2017

Competition horses—Health

ACUPUNCTURE A HOLISTIC TOOL FOR OPTIMUM HEALTH M. DEPAOLO *Arabian Horse World* v57 no4 p182 Ja 2017

Competition horses—Wounds & injuries

Pam's Blog color *Dressage Today* v23 no11 p12 Ag 2017

Competition in the banking industry

One Big Reason There's So Little Competition Among U.S. Banks M. Schmalz *Harvard Business Review Digital Articles* p2 Je 13 2016

Competition in the grocery industry

Jeff Bezos Goes Grocery Shopping S. Soper and O. Zaleski color *Bloomberg Businessweek* no4517 p21 Ap 3 2017

Competition in the high technology industries

MANAGING OUR HUB ECONOMY: STRATEGY, ETHICS, AND NETWORK COMPETITION IN THE AGE OF DIGI-TAL SUPERPOWERS M. IANSITI and K. R. LAKHANI color

diag graph img *Harvard Business Review* v95 no5 p84 S/O 2017

Competition in the information technology industry

How About a Bit More Room For Competition? P. Dwyer, D. McLaughlin et al *Bloomberg Businessweek* no4531 p8 Jl 24 2017

Competition in the manufacturing industries

COMPUTATIONAL Innovation Boosts MANUFACTURING A. Parker color *Science & Technology Review* p4 Ja/F 2017

Competition in the mass media industry

Apple TV gets cozy with Amazon Prime, so where does that leave Netflix? J. NEWMAN color *PCWorld* v35 no7 p50 Jl 2017

Competition horses—Charts, diagrams, etc.

2016 SPORT HORSE NATIONALS LEADING SIRES D. Tatelman *Arabian Horse World* v57 no4 p108 Ja 2017

Competitive advantage

3 Steps to Break Out in a Tired Industry F. Vermeulen *Harvard Business Review Digital Articles* p2 My 1 2015

Are You Using APIs to Gain Competitive Advantage? B. Iyer and M. Subramaniam *Harvard Business Review Digital Articles* p2 Ap 13 2015

The Basic Principles of Strategy Haven't Changed in 30 Years A. Campbell *Harvard Business Review Digital Articles* p2 Ap 23 2015

The Best Leaders Are Constant Learners K. Mikkelsen and H. Jarche *Harvard Business Review Digital Articles* p2 O 16 2015

CUSTOMER LOYALTY IS OVERRATED: INTERACTION M. Ionescu, J. Knowles et al color *Harvard Business Review* v95 no3 p18 My/Je 2017

Does Your Company Know What to Do with All Its Data? T. C. Redman *Harvard Business Review Digital Articles* p2 Je 15 2017

How Academics and Researchers Can Get More Out of Social Media L. Duque *Harvard Business Review Digital Articles* p2 Je 8 2016

How Can Companies Compete with Amazon? Netflix Has the Answer W. Frick *Harvard Business Review Digital Articles* p2 Je 19 2017

Immigration Is at the Heart of U.S. Competitiveness M. Ali *Harvard Business Review Digital Articles* p2 My 15 2017

Midsize Companies Shouldn't Confuse Growth with Scaling R. Carucci *Harvard Business Review Digital Articles* p2 Jl 25 2016

Most Reorgs Aren't Ambitious Enough R. Carucci color *Harvard Business Review Digital Articles* p2 F 10 2017

Neurodiversity as a Competitive Advantage R. D. AUSTIN and G. P. PISANO color *Harvard Business Review* v95 no3 p96 My/Je 2017

Profit Is Less About Good Management than You Think J. A. Marco-Izquierdo *Harvard Business Review Digital Articles* p2 S 28 2015

The Sharing Economy Isn't About Sharing at All G. M. Eckhardt and F. Bardhi *Harvard Business Review Digital Articles* p2 Ja 28 2015

Stop Comparing Management to Sports F. Vermeulen *Harvard Business Review Digital Articles* p2 Je 2 2016

There's No Excuse for Avoiding Strategy F. V. Cespedes *Harvard Business Review Digital Articles* p2 O 28 2014

To Reduce Complexity in Your Company, Start with Pen and Paper R. McGrath *Harvard Business Review Digital Articles* p2 Ag 22 2016

Trial and Error Is No Way to Make Strategy T. Zenger *Harvard Business Review Digital Articles* p2 Ap 24 2015

When Opportunity Resides Along the Edges A. Lewis and D. McKone *Harvard Business Review Digital Articles* p2 F 1 2016

Your Data Should Be Faster, Not Just Bigger R. Bean *Harvard Business Review Digital Articles* p2 F 4 2015

Your Whole Company Needs to Be Distinctive, Not Just Your Product P. Leinwand and C. Mainardi *Harvard Business Review Digital Articles* p2 My 19 2016

Competitive eating

EVERYWHERE color *Popular Mechanics* v193 no7 p10 S 2016

Extreme Weirdness A. SHAW color *National Geographic Kids* no473 p7 S 2017

FEEDING FRENZY: WHEN COMPETITIVE EATERS TACK-LE LOBSTER ROLLS, YOU MIGHT WANT TO AVERT YOUR EYES. WE COULDN'T J. BILLS color *Yankee* p94 Jl 2017

Complaints & complaining
MR. KNOW-IT-ALL J. MOOALLEM cartoon *Wired* v25 no6 p22 Je 2017

Complaints against police
ARRESTED DEVELOPMENT N. Baptiste *Mother Jones* v42 no4 p10 Jl/Ag 2017
The Bullet, the Cop, the Boy J. D. WALSH img *New York* v50 no12 p46 Je 12 2017

Complete Deaths, The (Theatrical production)
GO J. FOUMBERG, J. HARDBERGER et al color *Chicago* v65 no12 p119 D 2016

Complete Syllables Music, The (Music)
Language Games M. LONGLEY color *Downbeat* v84 no6 p66 Je 2017

Complex compounds
See also
Clathrate compounds
Coordination compounds
Bacillus subtilis SMC complexes juxtapose chromosome arms as they travel from origin to terminus X. Wang, H. B. Brandão et al bibl graph *Science* v355 no6324 p524 F 3 2017

Complexity (Philosophy)
The Complexity of Simplicity M. Funkhouser *Governing* v30 no6 p59 Mr 2017
Harnessing legal complexity J. B. Ruhl, D. Martin Katz et al diag graph *Science* v355 no6332 p1377 Mr 31 2017

Compliance
Compliance Alone Won't Make Your Company Safe D. De Cremer and B. Lemmich *Harvard Business Review Digital Articles* p2 My 18 2015
The Once and Future Order M. J. Mazarr color *Foreign Affairs* v96 no1 p25 Ja/F 2017
POLICING THE COLONY [Cover story] C. HAYES color *Nation* v304 no13 p12 Ap 17 2017

Compliance—Standards
KNOW YOUR NAV LIGHTS F. LANIER *Sea Magazine* v108 no8 p26 Ag 2016

Complications of alcoholism
Muscle health: Strong for life *Mayo Clinic Health Letter* v35 p1 2017 SepcialReport

Compliments
THOUGHTS FROM Our Readers K. Douglas, T. A. Edison et al bw *Forbes* v200 no3 p180 S 28 2017
THE ULTIMATE COMPLIMENT *Women's Health* v14 no9 p8 N 2017

Composers
See also
Film composers
Singer-songwriters
An American Outsider J. NORDLINGER *National Review* v69 no9 p40 My 15 2017
"Borning Cry" songwriter dies at age 79 *Christian Century* v134 no8 p1 Ap 12 2017
By Your Side M. BARTON-FUMO color *Film Comment* v53 no1 p22 Ja/F 2017
His Dark Materials A. WASSERMAN *Opera News* v81 no7 p14 Ja 2017
Justin Hurwitz D. Kiper color *Current Biography* v78 no8 p54 Ag 2017
LIN-MANUEL MIRANDA color *GQ: Gentlemen's Quarterly* v97 no9 p121 S 2017
MANY BRANCHES MAKE THE TREE R. Mercer color *Iceland Review* v54 no5 p38 S-O 2016
MY SPACE: SYNTH CITY R. CHUN color *Wired* v25 no8 p46 Ag 2017
String Theory: Classical music needs new superfans. Nadia Sirota is doing her best to create them J. Davidson img *New York* v50 no15 p60 Jl 24 2017
VICTOR PROVOST J. Murph color *Downbeat* v84 no3 p23 Mr 2017

Composers—Biography
Daniel Pemberton M. Hagan color *Current Biography* v78 no2 p62 F 2017

Composers—United States
Howlin' at the Moondog M. BARCLAY bw *Maclean's* v129 no48/49 p36 D 5 2016

The Recordings of Pauline Oliveros Bennett *New York Times Magazine* p20 F 12 2017

Composite building materials
See also
Terrazzo
Terrazzo color *Old House Journal* v45 no3 p46 My 2017

Composite materials
Installing Clapboards R. Tschoepe diag *Old House Journal* v45 no4 p58 Je 2017

Composition (Musical composition)
See also
Popular music—Writing & publishing
Applying 12-Tone Rows to Bass, Guitar J. DURSO color diag *Downbeat* v84 no7 p76 Jl 2017
CREATIVITY IN COMMON T. Perkins color *Downbeat* v84 no6 p122 Je 2017
CULTURAL DIPLOMACY J. Rosenblum and k. T. Garcia *Opera News* v81 no7 p28 Ja 2017
The Exposed Melodic Use OF BASS TROMBONE IN A BIG BAND B. Wallarab color *Downbeat* v84 no4 p82 Ap 2017
Gary Brooker and Procol Harum Fuse Sonic Shades of Both Past and Present With Novum M. METTLER and C. Crowley color *Sound & Vision* v82 no6 p24 Jl/Ag 2017
A Sense of the In-Between color *Idaho Magazine* v16 no1 p51 O 2016
The Sons Also Rise A. LANGER *Texas Monthly* v45 no2 p70 F 2017
Wolfgang Muthspiel's 5/4 Guitar Solo on 'Boogaloo' J. DURSO bw diag *Downbeat* v84 no7 p78 Jl 2017

Composition (Photography)
Art Watch: Three artists moving the Atlanta art scene forward F. FEASTER *Atlanta* v57 no6 p76 O 2017

Composters (Containers)
2017 Renovation SHOWCASE J. BREWSTER color *Cabin Living* p47 Je 2017

Composting
Breaking It Down E. Daigneau *Governing* v30 no2 p20 N 2016
COMPOSTING MANURE The Scoop on Poop J. Salatin *Mother Earth News* no280 p72 F/Mr 2017
Hey Mr. Green! Should receipts be recycled? B. Schildgen *Sierra* v102 no2 p12 Mr/Ap 2017
MORTALITY COMPOSTING J. Henke *Successful Farming* v115 no2 p32 F 2017
TRENCH COMPOSTING J. Henke *Successful Farming* v114 no13 p40 D 2016

Compotes (Stewed fruit)
Juicy Little Gems V. Willis color *Southern Living* v52 no5 p138 My 2017

Comprehension
See also
Learning
Listening
A love that heals A. Scobey color *U.S. Catholic* v82 no5 p36 My 2017

Compressed air
COLD-AIR CARBS J. Smith color graph *Hot Rod* v70 no11 p86 N 2017

Compression loads
How Much Cranking Compression Is Safe on Pump Gas? M. Davis color *Hot Rod* v70 no5 p90 My 2017

Compression stockings
Tight Club color *Health* v30 no9 p20 N 2016

Compressor industry
STATIONARY COMPRESSORS: IT'S ALL ABOUT CFM WHEN IT COMES TO GAUGING COMPRESSOR QUALITIES D. Mowitz *Successful Farming* v115 no9 p38 Ag 2017

Compressors
See also
Air compressors
Compressor industry
STATIONARY COMPRESSORS: IT'S ALL ABOUT CFM WHEN IT COMES TO GAUGING COMPRESSOR QUALITIES D. Mowitz *Successful Farming* v115 no9 p38 Ag 2017

Compromise (Law)
See also
Consent decrees

Compromise (Law)—United States

Uncommon Cooperation A. Greenblatt *Governing* v30 no12 p9 S 2017

Compromise (Law)—United States—History—21st century

VERIZON'S STRIKE SETTLEMENT A. Pressman color *Fortune* v174 no8 p20 D 15 2016

Compton, K. C.

BACKBONE FARM Growing Kids, Food, and Skills *Mother Earth News* no280 p12 F/Mr 2017

FARMING the Neighborhood *Mother Earth News* no279 p24 D/Ja 2017

SELF-RELIANCE Is a Family Affair *Mother Earth News* no281 p12 Ap/My 2017

SLOW FLOWERS and a Solar Home *Mother Earth News* no279 p16 D/Ja 2017

Compton, Robert N.

Laser Experiments for Chemistry and Physics J. Stalnaker *Physics Today* v70 no1 p60 Ja 2017

Compton, Tania

WILD at HEART H. Bowles color *Vogue* v207 no1 p88 Ja 2017

Compton-Phillips, Amy L.

The Antidote to Fragmented Health Care *Harvard Business Review Digital Articles* p2 D 15 2014

Compugen Inc.

GOING GREEN4GOOD IS ABOUT MORE THAN THE ENVIRONMENT C. Metler *Maclean's* v129 no50 p42 D 19 2016

Compulsive behavior

See also

Compulsive eating

Sex addiction

Video game addiction

"HERE'S WHAT IT REALLY FEELS LIKE to have OCD ...welcome to my brain" C. SCHEELER color *Good Housekeeping* v265 no1 p96 Jl 2017

Compulsive eating

Follow the "Bright Line" S. P. THOMPSON *USA Today Magazine* v146 no2868 p62 S 2017

How to Escape Zombie Eating K. Dinardo color *Health* v30 no9 p47 N 2016

Rapid binge-like eating and body weight gain driven by zona incerta GABA neuron activation X. Zhang and A. N. van den Pol graph *Science* v356 no6340 p853 My 26 2017

Compulsive gambling

THE CONVERSATION T. L. Cox, R. Moss et al color *Atlantic* v319 no3 p12 Ap 2017

Compulsive hoarding

The Hoarding Problem D. Freiburger color *Hot Rod* v69 no12 p113 D 2016

Compulsive skin picking

Addicted to PICKING cartoon *O, The Oprah Magazine* p102 My 2017

Computation laboratories

Code.org: A Resource for Computer Science in Your District J. A. Baskin *Education Digest* v83 no2 p31 O 2017

Computational learning theory

WHY AI CAN'T WRITE THIS ARTICLE (YET) W. Frick *Harvard Business Review Digital Articles* p24 Jl 1 2017

Computed tomography

The inside story on 20,000 vertebrates R. Cross color *Science* v357 no6353 p742 Ag 25 2017

New Horse Headset Records EEGs S. Dulai Wenholz color *Practical Horseman* v45 no8 p68 Ag 2017

Computer access control

See also

Passwords (Computers)

4 easy ways to keep your iCloud password safe B. PATTERSON color *Macworld - Digital Edition* v34 no6 p99 Je 2017

Computer adventure games

DISNEY MEETS FINAL FANTASY (AND TEDIUM) IN KINGDOM HEARTS UNION X[CROSS] A. HAYWARD color *Macworld - Digital Edition* v34 no10 p55 O 2017

TACOMA: THE MAKERS OF GONE HOME UNSPOOL A MESMERIZING SCIENCE FICTION STORY N. ALDERMAN color *Macworld - Digital Edition* v34 no10 p31 O 2017

Computer-aided design

3D CAD — Not Your Father's Blue Prints color *Log Home Living*

v33 no9 p67 D 2016

Computer-Aided Creativity D. Pogue color *Scientific American* v317 no1 p28 Jl 2017

The poetry and purpose of operations J. Dziedzic color *Model Railroader* v84 no1 p76 Ja 2017

Computer-aided design software

Bringing CAD To the Cloud M. Belfiore *Bloomberg Businessweek* no4511 p30 F 13 2017

Cover Up P. Gutowski color diag *Sail* v48 no10 p80 O 2017

Computer-aided design—Software—Evaluation

Drafting Made 'Easier than Pencil and Paper' *Stage Directions* v30 no5 p7 My 2017

Simply Powerful C. Rutherford *Stage Directions* v29 no10 p33 O 2016

Computer algorithms

See also

Computer programming

Algorithm of the Enlightenment E. FINN *Issues in Science & Technology* v33 no3 p21 Spr 2017

Companies Are Reimagining Business Processes with Algorithms H. J. Wilson, A. Alter et al *Harvard Business Review Digital Articles* p2 F 8 2016

PEOPLE LIKE THE ILLUSION OF CONTROL *Harvard Business Review* v95 no1 p26 Ja/F 2017

Reducing Noise in Decision Making: Interaction G. Berkooz, T. Mullie et al color *Harvard Business Review* v94 no12 p18 D 2016

Your Algorithms Are Not Safe from Hackers K. Radinsky *Harvard Business Review Digital Articles* p2 Ja 5 2016

Computer art

THE CLEANING CREW V. LUCCA color *Film Comment* v52 no6 p60 N/D 2016

Computer art—Exhibitions

Life in Picoseconds *Issues in Science & Technology* v33 no3 p6 Spr 2017

Never-Ending Story A. K. Scott cartoon *New Yorker* v93 no13 p10 My 15 2017

Computer assisted instruction

See also

Web-based instruction

May-June color *Yoga Journal* no292 p6 Je 2017

Computer crime prevention

See also

Internet fraud—Prevention

Limit Cyberattacks with a System-Wide Safe Mode C. Herbolzheimer *Harvard Business Review Digital Articles* p2 My 17 2017

To Guard Against Cybercrime, Follow the Money M. Gardiner *Harvard Business Review Digital Articles* p2 My 26 2017

Computer crimes

See also

Computer viruses

Cyberterrorism

Identity theft

Internet fraud

Can You Put a Dollar Amount on Your Company's Cyber Risk? L. Chacko, E. Sekeris et al *Harvard Business Review Digital Articles* p2 O 5 2016

Cyberwars: We Must Prepare Ourselves for the Wars of the Future E. Schmidt and J. Cohen *Time* v188 no27-28 p25 D 26 2016

KEYS TO THE KINGDOM C. Leaf color *Fortune* v176 no1 p4 Jl 1 2017

Computer crimes— International cooperation

The Flaws in Obama's Cybersecurity Initiative D. M. Upton *Harvard Business Review Digital Articles* p2 Ja 20 2015

Computer crimes—Prevention

Preparing for a Black Swan Cyberattack C. Herbolzheimer *Harvard Business Review Digital Articles* p2 S 14 2016

Computer drawing—Software

Hands-on: Paint 3D Preview remixes Paint for the HoloLens generation M. HACHMAN color *PCWorld* p32 D 2016

Computer engineering

Knowledge Is Infrastructure R. Dijkgraaf color *Scientific American* v316 no6 p8 Je 2017

A new Microsoft foldable device patent offers more grist for the Surface phone rumor mill M. HACHMAN cartoon *PCWorld*

v35 no2 p11 F 2017

one for all D. Pierce color diag *Wired* v25 no8 p86 Ag 2017

Xbox One X PC Build: Can you do it for $500? A. YEE chart color *PCWorld* v35 no8 p112 Ag 2017

Computer engineers

Sweetening The Deal A. Webb color *Bloomberg Businessweek* no4517 p33 Ap 3 2017

Computer file organization software

THE 10 MUST-HAVE UTILITIES FOR MACOS SIERRA G. Fleishman cartoon color *Macworld - Digital Edition* p82 F 2017

Paragon NTFS for Mac 15: Slick, native performance for accessing NTFS Windows drives J. R. BOOKWALTER color *Macworld - Digital Edition* v34 no10 p83 O 2017

Computer file sharing

Mac 911 G. FLEISHMAN color *Macworld - Digital Edition* v34 no6 p127 Je 2017

Computer fonts

Mac 911 G. FLEISHMAN and M. CONNELL color *Macworld - Digital Edition* p131 F 2017

Computer fonts—Software—Evaluation

FONTAGENT 7 AND FONTAGENT SYNC: ALL-NEW INTERFACE AND FONT SYNCING ACROSS USERS AND MACS J. J. NELSON color *Macworld - Digital Edition* p31 D 2016

Computer games

See also

Computer adventure games

Mobile games

StarCraft games

9 REASONS WHY PC GAMING IS A BETTER VALUE THAN CONSOLES H. DINGMAN bw color *PCWorld* p131 O 2016

Forza Horizon 3 (PC): Get ready to make your graphics card sweat H. DINGMAN color *PCWorld* v35 no11 p114 N 2016

Hackintosh: Build a DIY Mac for gaming R. GRIFFITHS color graph *Macworld - Digital Edition* v34 no8 p11 Ag 2017

Here's proof that Ryzen can benefit from optimized game code G. MAH UNG color graph *PCWorld* v35 no5 p120 My 2017

How a Video Game Helped People Make Better Decisions C. K. Morewedge *Harvard Business Review Digital Articles* p2 O 13 2015

Lost Highway J. Reichert color *Film Comment* v53 no4 p20 Jl/ Ag 2017

A New Level: When Gen Con lands on planet Indianapolis August 17 and turns 50, the annual gathering of gamers will look quite different than it did during the beta phase L. JOSS *Indianapolis Monthly* v12 no40 p16 Ag 2017

Total War Saga series focused on smaller 'powder-keg' moments in history H. DINGMAN color *PCWorld* v35 no8 p37 Ag 2017

Windows 10 Creators Update: Microsoft adds fun to its flagship OS M. HACHMAN color *PCWorld* v35 no5 p67 My 2017

Computer games software

See also

Mobile games

War game software

The best PC game recording software: 5 freeware capture tools compared I. PAUL color graph *PCWorld* v35 no10 p83 O 2017

Computer games—Evaluation

The best PC games of 2017 (so far) H. DINGMAN color *PCWorld* v35 no8 p25 Ag 2017

Titanfall 2: Prepare for more mech-dropping, wall-running action H. DINGMAN color *PCWorld* p133 D 2016

Tyranny: Obsidian's RPG ponders the nature of evil H. DINGMAN color *PCWorld* v35 no1 p137 Ja 2017

Windows 10's Game Mode makes unplayable games playable— sometimes B. CHACOS color graph *PCWorld* v35 no5 p86 My 2017

Computer-generated imagery

Risky Business J. Nolfi color *Entertainment Weekly* no1480 p15 S 1 2017

Computer graphics

See also

Computer-generated imagery

Sapphire Radeon RX 570 Pulse and RX 580 Pulse: Solid gaming on a tight budget B. CHACOS chart color graph *PCWorld* v35 no7 p128 Jl 2017

Computer graphics equipment

See also

Graphics processing units (Computers)

AMD Radeon RX 550: A thrilling budget graphics card with a perplexing price B. CHACOS chart color graph *PCWorld* v35 no6 p74 Je 2017

EVGA GTX 1080 Ti SC2: A ferocious graphics card with a radical cooler B. CHACOS chart color graph *PCWorld* v35 no6 p55 Je 2017

Nvidia's beastly Titan Xp steals the performance crown from the GTX 1080 Ti B. CHACOS color *PCWorld* v35 no5 p31 My 2017

Computer graphics equipment—Evaluation

AMD Radeon RX Vega: Vega 56, Vega 64, and liquid-cooled Vega 64 tested B. CHACOS chart color graph *PCWorld* v35 no10 p23 O 2017

Sapphire Radeon RX 570 Pulse and RX 580 Pulse: Solid gaming on a tight budget B. CHACOS chart color graph *PCWorld* v35 no7 p128 Jl 2017

Computer graphics—Equipment & supplies

Every custom GeForce GTX 1080 Ti graphics card revealed so far B. CHACOS color *PCWorld* v35 no4 p14 Ap 2017

Nvidia GeForce GTX 1080 Ti: The monster graphics card 4K gamers have been waiting for B. CHACOS chart color graph *PCWorld* v35 no4 p110 Ap 2017

Nvidia supercharges GeForce DirectX 12 performance with new Game Ready driver B. CHACOS color *PCWorld* v35 no4 p24 Ap 2017

Computer graphics—Evaluation

Xbox Project Scorpio specs revealed: Microsoft's next console is a Radeon-infused monster B. CHACOS chart color *PCWorld* v35 no5 p46 My 2017

Computer hackers

Build a Better Password D. Shadel cartoon *AARP: The Magazine* v60 no3A p24 Ap/My 2017

HACKER CRACK-UP E. D. Jennings, J. Alexander et al color *Wired* v25 no6 p10 Je 2017

The Hackers M. Vella color diag *Time* v188 no25-26 p102 D 19 2016 Double Issue

Identity Theft A. Hess *New York Times Magazine* p11 Ap 2 2017

MEET THE NU-NERDS T. TULATHIMUTTE color *Wired* v25 no5 p100 My 2017

SNAPPED SHOTS color *Wired* v25 no5 p10 My 2017

THINK LIKE A HACKER S. ORNES bw color graph *Discover* v38 no8 p48 O 2017

What It's Really Like to... img *New York* v50 no10 p54 My 15 2017

Why Companies Shouldn't Try to Hack Their Hackers C. E. Thomas *Harvard Business Review Digital Articles* p2 My 24 2017

Computer hackers—Employment

Not All Russian Hackers Are Bad V. Walt color *Fortune* v175 no2 p12 F 1 2017

Computer hackers—Humor

Hacking Myself Is the Most Surprisingly Humiliating Decision I've Ever Made J. Stein color *Time* v189 no12 p63 Ap 3 2017

Computer industry security measures

Why Do IoT Companies Keep Building Devices with Huge Security Flaws? [Cover story] A. Tannenbaum *Harvard Business Review Digital Articles* p2 Ap 27 2017

Computer industry—Mergers

THE GAMBLERS BEHIND TECH'S BIGGEST DEAL EVER M. Lev-ram color *Fortune* v75 no1 p82 Ja 1 2017

Computer literacy

4 Linux projects for newbies and intermediate users A. CAMPBELL cartoon color *PCWorld* v35 no2 p184 F 2017

4 Windows Command Prompt tricks everyone should know J. NOREM color *PCWorld* v35 no2 p200 F 2017

a case for coding B. THORKELSON *Parents* v92 no7 p130 Jl 2017

CLOSING THE FAMILIAL DIVIDE T. Lewis Ellison color *Literacy Today (2411-7862)* v34 no3 p16 N/D 2016

DIGITAL Responsibility color *Literacy Today (2411-7862)* v34 no3 p42 N/D 2016

How to incorporate keyboard shortcuts into your workflow I. PAUL color *PCWorld* v35 no2 p180 F 2017

PROMOTING EMPATHY C. Patrice Clark *Literacy Today (2411-*

7862) v34 no3 p2 N/D 2016

Computer literacy—Congresses

The literacy scene color *Literacy Today (2411-7862)* v34 no5 p5 Mr/Ap 2017

Computer maintenance & repair

How to install Windows 10 on a USB drive with Microsoft's Media Creation Tool I. PAUL color *PCWorld* v35 no7 p190 Jl 2017

Computer managed instruction

Reaching Full Digitization in the Classroom S. Wilson *Education Digest* v83 no3 p61 N 2017

Computer monitors

More high-end GPUs are now compatible with Dell's 8K monitor A. SHAH color *PCWorld* v35 no5 p43 My 2017

A USB device is all it takes to steal credentials from locked PCs L. CONSTANTIN color *PCWorld* p52 O 2016

Computer monitors—Evaluation

AMD's FreeSync 2 tech debuts in a wild 49-inch Samsung HDR monitor B. CHACOS color *PCWorld* v35 no7 p25 Jl 2017

COMPUTER MONITORS A. GEORGE color *Popular Mechanics* p30 Ap 2017

Dell's wild 8K monitor goes on sale with a just-as-stunning price tag I. PAUL color *PCWorld* v35 no5 p41 My 2017

TECH THE HALLS S. Grobart color *Bloomberg Businessweek* no4500 p78 N 21 2016

Why AMD FreeSync is beating Nvidia G-Sync on monitor selection and price J. NEWMAN color *PCWorld* v35 no11 p118 N 2016

Computer network protocols—Security measures

The Swedish Kings of Cyberwar H. Eakin color map *New York Review of Books* v64 no1 p56 Ja 19 2017

Computer network resources—Evaluation

POPULAR MECHANICS EVERYWHERE J. Bennett color *Popular Mechanics* p6 F 2017

Computer network security

Neighborhood Watch D. Lawrence cartoon *Bloomberg Businessweek* no4514 p42 Mr 13 2017

Computer network software

How to use NetSpot to map out your Wi-Fi network J. BATTERSBY color *Macworld - Digital Edition* p105 F 2017

Computer networking equipment

Tools of the Trade: Lighting Networking *Stage Directions* v30 no6 p6 Je 2017

Computer networks—Management—Software

How to manage your network with iNet Network Scanner J. BATTERSBY color *Macworld - Digital Edition* p108 F 2017

Computer operating system design & construction

ANDROID 8 OREO M. SIMON color *PCWorld* v35 no10 p95 O 2017

Computer operating system maintenance & repair

Confirmed: Windows 10 may cut off devices with older CPUs M. HACHMAN color *PCWorld* v35 no9 p20 S 2017

Computer password security

Best password managers of 2017: Reviews of the top products M. ANSALDO color *PCWorld* v35 no10 p79 O 2017

Computer peripherals—Evaluation

HEAD-TO-HEAD D. PIERCE color *Wired* v25 no3 p36 Mr 2017

THE WILD, WEIRD, AND POWERFUL PC HARDWARE of CES 2017 J. PHILLIPS color *PCWorld* v35 no2 p127 F 2017

Computer printers—Evaluation

You Can Find Just Your Type! chart color *Consumer Reports* v82 no3 p9 Mr 2017

Computer programmers

See also

Women computer programmers

Hacking the Need For a Full-Time Job L. Chapman cartoon *Bloomberg Businessweek* no4518 p33 Ap 10 2017

Computer programmers—Employment

Betting on the Blockchain T. Simonite il *MIT Technology Review* v120 no1 p29 Ja/F 2017

Computer programmers—Political activity

Startup Types Build Ready-Made Activism V. Vara *Bloomberg Businessweek* no4511 p32 F 13 2017

Computer programming

See also

Hackathons

Amrita took action when she discovered a local school was low on

laptops *Scholastic Choices* p24 O 2017

CODE IS KING C. THOMPSON cartoon *Wired* v24 no12 p40 D 2016

GENDER BINARY E. Ullman *Harper's Magazine* v335 no2006 p11 Jl 2017

Hackathons Aren't Just for Coders E. Spaulding and G. Caimi *Harvard Business Review Digital Articles* p2 Ap 1 2016

How to stop autoplay videos in Safari 11 R. LOYOLA color *Macworld - Digital Edition* v34 no11 p7 N 2017

Leading a Digital Transformation? Learn to Code S. Anthony *Harvard Business Review Digital Articles* p2 S 2 2015

A National Security Code Is Reborn for Industry A. Heller *Science & Technology Review* p20 Je 2017

UNDER THE HOOD: MAKE CODE MORE TINKER-FRIENDLY C. THOMPSON cartoon *Wired* v25 no7 p34 Jl 2017

Computer routing equipment

Linksys announces the all-new mid-range EA9300 Wi-Fi router M. BROWN color *Macworld - Digital Edition* p86 Je 13 2017

Computer science

See also

Computer engineering

Quantum computing

Women in computer science

Computer science education

Code.org: A Resource for Computer Science in Your District J. A. Baskin *Education Digest* v83 no2 p31 O 2017

Computer science—Study & teaching

PROGRAMMING FOR ALL J. BATTERSON, D. L. STREINER et al color *Scientific American* v315 no6 p8 D 2016

Computer scientists

The Disease Detectives C. GRABER color *New Republic* v248 no1/2 p10 Ja/F 2017

Computer scientists—Interviews

History Unwrapped M. BARNA color *Discover* v38 no5 p12 Je 2017

Computer security

See also

Data encryption (Computer science)

Internet security

Passwords (Computers)

Any website can crash your Windows 7 or 8 PC with these four characters I. PAUL color *PCWorld* v35 no7 p42 Jl 2017

How I deleted Google from my life S. AXON color diag *PCWorld* v35 no7 p179 Jl 2017

HOW TO PROTECT YOUR DIGITAL SELF L. BÉNICHOU color *Wired* v25 no6 p36 Je 2017

KEYS TO THE KINGDOM C. Leaf color *Fortune* v176 no1 p4 Jl 1 2017

A USB device is all it takes to steal credentials from locked PCs L. CONSTANTIN color *PCWorld* p52 O 2016

Yahoo's billion account breach: 5 things you should do to stay safe L. CONSTANTIN color *PCWorld* v35 no1 p41 Ja 2017

Computer security software

See also

Antivirus software

Little Flocker reincarnates as Xfence, a free beta from F-Secure G. FLEISHMAN color *Macworld - Digital Edition* v34 no6 p107 Je 2017

Computer security—Congresses

Calendar: Discovery L. Eadicicco color *Time* v188 no27-28 p84 D 26 2016

Computer security—Management

See Your Company Through the Eyes of a Hacker N. C. Fick *Harvard Business Review Digital Articles* p2 Mr 24 2015

Computer simulation

See also

Virtual reality

Supernovae, supercomputers, and galactic evolution P. F. Hopkins *Physics Today* v70 no4 p70 Ap 2017

TALKING TO THE DEAD M. A. Ahmad *Saturday Evening Post* v289 no2 p10 Mr/Ap 2017

THE UNSEEN P. Garrison *Flying* v144 no11 p34 N 2017

Computer software

See also

Application software

Artificial intelligence

Chatbots
Computer file organization software
Computer games
Computer software development
Electronic spreadsheets
Electronic wallets
Freeware (Computer software)
Malware (Computer software)
Microsoft software
Operating systems (Computers)
Search engines
Time management software

3 Cosmic Chirps & Counting V. Kalogera *Sky & Telescope* v134 no3 p24 S 2017

ART SERVICES *Art in America* v105 no1 p102 Ja 2017

Computer defeats master at ancient Chinese game T. Sumner color *Science News* v190 no13 p28 D 24 2016

The Computer Will See You Now D. Fine Maron color *Scientific American* v317 no2 p24 Ag 2017

The End of the Language Barrier D. GERSHGORN and L. KRA-TOCHWILL color *Popular Science* v288 no6 p84 N/D 2016

Get more Edge extensions by installing beta versions I. PAUL color *PCWorld* v35 no11 p141 N 2016

How Babelsoft Media Preview reveals less-common file types in Explorer J. JACOBI color *PCWorld* v35 no4 p152 Ap 2017

How to update your PC's BIOS T. RYAN color *PCWorld* v35 no4 p144 Ap 2017

How to use Night Light in the Windows 10 Creators Update I. PAUL color diag *PCWorld* v35 no7 p185 Jl 2017

ICELAND'S WISE SOLUTION *Iceland Review* v54 no6 p120 N/D 2016

Let Data Ask Questions, Not Just Answer Them M. Schrage *Harvard Business Review Digital Articles* p2 O 8 2014

Lurking in the Shadows T. Newcombe *Governing* v30 no7 p60 Ap 2017

MAKING TRACKS: SOFTWARE LETS YOU BETTER MAN-AGE NITROGEN'S FOOTPRINT IN YOUR SOIL AS WELL AS THE ENVIRONMENT L. Bedord *Successful Farming* v115 no6 p33 Ap 2017

SEO Beyond Google C. SIM *Publishers Weekly* v264 no28 p92 Jl 10 2017

the sorcerer's code m. hutson *Psychology Today* v49 no6 p78 N/D 2016

Computer software development
See also
Mobile app development

Building a Software Start- Up Inside GE B. Power *Harvard Business Review Digital Articles* p2 Ja 29 2015

Can Jigsaw's Designers Make the Internet Safer? D. Lawrence cartoon *Bloomberg Businessweek* no4539 p49 S 25 2017

Is Sex With A Brain-Damaged Man Assault? K. A. Appiah *New York Times Magazine* p22 S 10 2017

Make Enterprise Software People Actually Love J. Kolko *Harvard Business Review Digital Articles* p2 F 12 2015

The Secret History of Agile Innovation D. K. Rigby, J. Sutherland et al *Harvard Business Review Digital Articles* p2 Ap 20 2016

A STARTUP ON THE INSIDE I. Lapowsky color *Wired* v24 no11 p42 N 2016

WHAT'S NEW AT THE APP STORE J. MATHIS color *Macworld - Digital Edition* v34 no11 p79 N 2017

Computer software development—Government policy
Microsoft Isn't Feeling Any Russian Thaw I. Khrennikov, S. Kravchenko et al *Bloomberg Businessweek* no4500 p35 N 21 2016

Computer software evaluation
See also
Wireless communication system software—Evaluation

10 ALTERNATIVE BROWSERS I. PAUL color *PCWorld* v35 no9 p91 S 2017

12 Free Utilities THAT CAN GIVE YOU MORE CONTROL OVER YOUR PC [Cover story] M. VANHELDER color diag graph *PCWorld* v35 no7 p167 Jl 2017

Furuno TZTouch2 Software Update 4.01 J. Y. WOOD color *Power & Motoryacht* v33 no3 p46 Mr 2017

How to use Microsoft's Paint 3D app color *PCWorld* p174 Mr 2017

Innovation M. Cortez bw color *Bloomberg Businessweek* no4502 p43 D 5 2016

A MIGHTY WIND J. Pearley Huffman and J. Gall color *Car & Driver* v62 no6 p24 D 2016

NEW PRODUCTS *Physics Today* v69 no12 p64 D 2016

Product Hits of AES 2016 G. Petersen *Stage Directions* v29 no12 p11 D 2016

Timing 2.0 review: Mac software for professionals to track bill-able time K. MCELHEARN color *Macworld - Digital Edition* p83 Je 13 2017

Computer software industry
The Changing Economics of App Development P. A. Salz *Harvard Business Review Digital Articles* p2 N 4 2015

How Investors React When Companies Announce They're Mov-ing to a SaaS Business Model J. Nurkka, J. Waltl et al color *Harvard Business Review Digital Articles* p2 Ja 12 2017

To Predict the Trajectory of the Internet of Things, Look to the Software Industry B. Iyer *Harvard Business Review Digital Articles* p2 F 25 2016

Will AI Companies Make Any Money? T. H. Davenport *Harvard Business Review Digital Articles* p2 Jl 12 2016

THE WORLD'S MOST ADMIRED COMPANIES S. Decarlo color *Fortune* v175 no3 p113 Mr 1 2017

Computer software industry—Officials & employees
"Authenticity makes us stand out from our competitors": Why the software company had to revamp its employer brand to secure top talent *People Management* p25 Ap 2017

Computer software installation
How to have the Windows XP-style Quick Launch bar in Win-dows 10 I. PAUL color *PCWorld* p161 O 2016

How to reinstall Windows 10 without any bloatware J. NOREM color *PCWorld* v35 no1 p211 Ja 2017

Computer software termination
Adobe Flash will die by 2020, Adobe and browser makers say M. HACHMAN color *PCWorld* v35 no9 p23 S 2017

Google Drive dumps Windows XP and Vista, now what? I. PAUL color *PCWorld* v35 no1 p209 Ja 2017

Computer software training
Will Make AI Smarter For Cash M. Hutson *Bloomberg Business-week* no4537 p23 S 11 2017

Computer software—Correctness
How to repair Windows' master boot record and fix your bricked PC I. PAUL color *PCWorld* p146 O 2016

Computer software—Exhibitions
ABOVE & BEYOND cartoon *New Yorker* v92 no46 p14 Ja 23 2017

Computer software—Human factors
Make Enterprise Software People Actually Love J. Kolko *Harvard Business Review Digital Articles* p2 F 12 2015

Computer software—Upgrading
The new Apple TV update is no friend to cord cutters J. NEW-MAN color *PCWorld* v35 no1 p35 Ja 2017

Samsung to brick Galaxy Note7s through software M. SIMON color *PCWorld* v35 no1 p27 Ja 2017

Computer storage capacity
Intel Optane Memory has a mission: Make hard drives faster than SSDs G. MAH UNG color graph *PCWorld* v35 no5 p33 My 2017

Computer storage devices
See also
Hard disks (Computer science)

Quantum storage device fits on a chip M. TEMMING color *Science News* v192 no5 p8 S 30 2017

When to defrag a hard drive, TRIM an SSD and perform other storage tasks, or not J. NOREM color *PCWorld* v35 no6 p157 Je 2017

Computer storage devices—Evaluation
Optane Memory: Why you may want Intel's futuristic cache in your PC GORDON MAH UNG color diag graph *PCWorld* v35 no7 p101 Jl 2017

Samsung 960 Pro NVMe SSD: Ludicrously fast PC storage J. L. JACOBI color graph *PCWorld* v35 no2 p104 F 2017

WD My Passport SSD: Worthy competition for Samsung's T3 J. L. JACOBI color graph *PCWorld* v35 no9 p66 S 2017

Computer storage devices—Performance
Samsung 960 Pro NVMe SSD: Ludicrously fast PC storage J. L.

JACOBI color graph *PCWorld* v35 no2 p104 F 2017

Computer surveys

How to Click Your Way to Cash M. C. White color *Money* v46 no5 p24 Je 2017

Computer system failures

See also

Computer systems security vulnerabilities

How to stop Windows 10 from rebooting after updates J. NOREM color *PCWorld* p163 Mr 2017

Computer systems

See also

Computer input-output equipment

Computer software

Computers

Information storage & retrieval systems

Virtual machine systems

Laying the Groundwork for EXTREME-SCALE COMPUTING R. Hansen *Science & Technology Review* p5 S 2016

Computer systems security vulnerabilities

Hacker shows how easy it is to take over a city's public Wi-Fi network L. CONSTANTIN color *PCWorld* v35 no1 p51 Ja 2017

Why a Global Cyber Crisis Stalled-This Time R. Hackett color map *Time* v189 no20 p7 My 29 2017

Computer systems—Evaluation

WAHOO ELEMNT G. LIU color *Bicycling* v58 no1 p61 Ja/F 2017

Computer users

See also

Computer hackers

Internet users

How to easily switch between open windows of the same program I. PAUL color *PCWorld* v35 no5 p203 My 2017

Computer virus prevention

See also

Antivirus software

How to avoid the WannaCrypt virus if you run Windows on a Mac G. FLEISHMAN *Macworld - Digital Edition* p81 Je 13 2017

Computer viruses

7 Ways to Block Computer Viruses D. SHADEL color *AARP: The Magazine* v60 no5A p26 Ag/S 2017

Computer viruses—Economic aspects

BUG BARONESS AND LUTA SECURITY CEO KATIE MOUSSOURIS EXPLAINS THE ECONOMY OF EXPLOITS R. Hackett color *Fortune* v176 no1 p65 Jl 1 2017

Computer worms

How to avoid the WannaCrypt virus if you run Windows on a Mac G. FLEISHMAN *Macworld - Digital Edition* p81 Je 13 2017

Computer hackers—Charts, diagrams, etc.

ASK A FLOWCHART R. CAPPS diag *Wired* v25 no4 p96 Ap 2017

Computer hackers—Societies, etc.

Seriously, Beware the 'Shadow Brokers' D. Lawrence color *Bloomberg Businessweek* no4521 p34 My 8 2017

Computer input-output equipment

See also

Keyboards (Electronics)

Mac 911 G. FLEISHMAN color *Macworld - Digital Edition* v33 no11 p157 N 2016

Computer input-output equipment—Evaluation

Intel SSD 545s: The next great budget SSD has arrived J. L. JACOBI color graph *PCWorld* v35 no8 p82 Ag 2017

LOFREE KEYBOARD: THE FEELING OF A TYPEWRITER ON YOUR MAC OR iOS DEVICE R. LOYOLA color *Macworld - Digital Edition* v34 no4 p23 My 2017

Computer input-output equipment—Maintenance & repair

External drive died? Your data may still be easy to recover J. L. JACOBI color *PCWorld* v35 no7 p196 Jl 2017

Computerized instruments

This forecast brought to you by math A. Blum color diag *Popular Science* v289 no4 p66 Jl/Ag 2017

Computers

See also

Computers & children

Computers & literacy

Personal computers

Supercomputers

WILL A ROBOT TAKE YOUR JOB? E. SHERMAN and R. ZISSOU *New York Times Upfront* v149 no3 p10 O 10 2016

Computers & children

Inside the New Standards for Kids and Screen Time M. Heid color *Time* v188 no19 p15 N 7 2016

Computers & children—Psychological aspects

Growing Up with Alexa R. Metz color graph il *MIT Technology Review* v120 no5 p70 S/O 2017

Computers & college students

1-to-1 Computing Under Microscope in Maine Schools B. HEROLD and J. KAZI *Education Digest* v82 no5 p48 Ja 2017

Computers & literacy

TECHNOLOGY-SUPPORTED LEARNING R. Karchmer-Klein color *Literacy Today (2411-7862)* v34 no3 p8 N/D 2016

Computers & privacy

See also

Internet & privacy

Broadband Privacy: Protecting Personal Information in the Digital Age *Congressional Digest* v96 no5 p2 My 2017

Windows 10 privacy settings: What's new in the Creators Update I. PAUL color *PCWorld* v35 no6 p150 Je 2017

Computers in business

See also

Bring your own device policies

Mobile apps in business

How Companies Are Using Machine Learning to Get Faster and More Efficient H. J. Wilson, S. Sachdev et al *Harvard Business Review Digital Articles* p2 My 3 2016

Tracking the Trends in Bringing Our Own Devices to Work J. McConnell *Harvard Business Review Digital Articles* p2 My 4 2016

Computers in investment analysis

Faceless Returns N. VARDI color *Forbes* v199 no7 p148 Je 29 2017

Computers in medicine

See also

Artificial intelligence in medicine

Medical informatics

To Get Consumers to Trust AI, Show Them Its Benefits E. Enkel *Harvard Business Review Digital Articles* p2 Ap 17 2017

Computers in the health care industry

See also

Electronic health records

Bringing the Power of Platforms to Health Care J. Bush and J. Fox *Harvard Business Review Digital Articles* p2 N 10 2016

Hospitals Are Finally Starting to Put Real-Time Data to Use J. S. Toussaint and M. Mannon *Harvard Business Review Digital Articles* p2 N 12 2014

Computers—Economic aspects

Computers Don't Kill Jobs but Do Increase Inequality J. Bessen *Harvard Business Review Digital Articles* p2 Mr 24 2016

Computers—Equipment & supplies

See also

Personal computers—Equipment & supplies

USB (Computer bus)

How to update your PC's BIOS T. RYAN color *PCWorld* v35 no4 p144 Ap 2017

Computers—Equipment & supplies—Evaluation

AMD's Ryzen processors will launch before March 3, GDC slip-up reveals B. CHACOS color *PCWorld* v35 no2 p9 F 2017

Computers—Evaluation

Brix Gaming UHD (GBBNi7HG4-950): A lot of performance in a little PC A. YEE color graph *PCWorld* v35 no1 p123 Ja 2017

Computers—History—20th century

DIGGING UP DIGITAL MUSIC S. S. PATEL bw color *Archaeology* v70 no2 p9 Mr/Ap 2017

Comstock, Beth

Innovation Springs from the Unexpected Meeting of Minds *Harvard Business Review Digital Articles* p2 Mr 9 2016

Comunita di Sant'Egidio

CENTURY marks bw *Christian Century* v134 no15 p8 Jl 19 2017

Conahan, Tricia

6 EXERCISES TO NAIL YOUR HUNTER DERBY color diag *Practical Horseman* v45 no6 p44 Je 2017

6 EXERCISES TO NAIL YOUR HUNTER DERBY: Part 2: Master rollbacks, the hand gallop and finish with flair [Cover story]

color *Practical Horseman* v45 no7 p34 Jl 2017

Andre Dignelli: "Life is a Competition" color *Practical Horseman* v45 no8 p22 Ag 2017

Carol Kozlowski: 'Don't Ever Close Your Mind' color *Practical Horseman* v45 no5 p24 My 2017

HUNTING FOR PERFECTION [Cover story] color diag *Practical Horseman* v45 no11 p22 N 2017

John French: 'Try to Always Find the Good' color *Practical Horseman* v45 no2 p22 F 2017

Kai Handt: 'Never Blame the Horse' color *Practical Horseman* v45 no10 p22 O 2017

Max Corcoran: 'Not Just the Groom' color *Practical Horseman* v45 no1 p24 Ja 2017

Missy Clark: "Riding is a Master Class in Life" color *Practical Horseman* v44 no12 p18 D 2016

Conant, Douglas R.

CEOs Can't Give Feedback Only to Their Direct Reports *Harvard Business Review Digital Articles* p2 Ag 24 2015

The Connection Between Employee Trust and Financial Performance *Harvard Business Review Digital Articles* p2 Jl 18 2016

The Key to Campbell Soup's Turnaround? Civility *Harvard Business Review Digital Articles* p2 O 5 2017

Conant, Eve

CROWNING GLORY bw *National Geographic* v230 no6 p132 D 2016

DARKNESS FALLS color map *National Geographic* v232 no2 p24 Ag 2017

Family Flock bw color *National Geographic* v230 no5 p140 N 2016

I Am Nine Years Old color *National Geographic* v231 no1 p30 Ja 2017

REWIRING THE SENSE OF TOUCH color *National Geographic* v232 no3 p19 S 2017

A Sobering Race bw *National Geographic* v230 no4 p148 O 2016

Conant, Jeff

CRISIS AMONG The Palms color *Earth Island Journal* v32 no2 p33 Summ 2017

Conard, Edward

Dispelling the Myths J. S. GORDON *Commentary* v143 no2 p42 F 2017

In the Long Run M. M. ROSEN *Weekly Standard* v22 no11 p36 N 21 2016

A New Trade Consensus *National Review* v68 no22 p35 D 5 2016

Conarello, Stacey

Systemic pan-AMPK activator MK-8722 improves glucose homeostasis but induces cardiac hypertrophy graph *Science* v357 no6350 p507 Ag 4 2017

Conaway, Ann

I Wish My Horse's Mentor Could Be... color *Horse & Rider* v56 no6 p88 Je 2017

Conaway, Cameron

Solving Complex Social Problems Through Collaboration *Harvard Business Review Digital Articles* p2 Je 17 2015

Conaway, Michael

MIKE CONAWAY'S OTHER JOB *Successful Farming* v115 no7 p10 My 2017

WHAT ARE THE ODDS? *Successful Farming* v115 no5 p10 Mid-Mr 2017

Concave lenses

Stargaze Like Galileo M. KOZIOL color *Popular Science* p77 Ja/F 2017

Concealed weapons in schools

ARGYLE, TEXAS S. Johnson *Harper's Magazine* p29 O 2017

Under the Law J. Underwood il *Phi Delta Kappan* v98 no6 p74 Mr 2017

Concealed weapons in universities & colleges

Inside the Fight Over Guns on Campus B. WOFFORD color *Rolling Stone* no1284 p28 Ap 6 2017

Conceicao, R.

Observation of a large-scale anisotropy in the arrival directions of cosmic rays above 8×10^{18} eV *Science* v357 no6357 p1266 S 22 2017

Concentration camp inmates

The Search for Meaning A. OLENDZKI cartoon *Tricycle: The Buddhist Review* v26 no3 p28 Spr 2017

Concentration camps

FROM RUSSIA, WITH LIES *Harper's Magazine* v334 no2002 p14 Mr 2017

Slaves Are Catching Our Shrimp S. Ruden color *Commonweal* v144 no13 p8 Ag 11 2017

UNWANTED C. Omori *Saturday Evening Post* v289 no3 p30 My/Je 2017

Conception

See also

Human in vitro fertilization

Pregnancy

Conception—Law & legislation

The Sanctity of Human Life Act: Politicians Playing God K. Burrows *Humanist* v77 no5 p9 S/O 2017

Conceptual art

THERE AND BACK AGAIN J. COHEN *Texas Monthly* v45 no2 p94 F 2017

Tom BURR C. MAUM *Interview* v46 no10 p143 D 2016/Ja 2017

Concert agents

THE IMMACULATE LINEUP J. SEABROOK cartoon *New Yorker* v93 no9 p30 Ap 17 2017

Concert hall design & construction

noted graph *Architectural Record* v205 no8 p22 Ag 2017

Concert halls

Show Business A. Brownlee *Cincinnati Magazine* v50 no5 p62 F 2017

TEMPLES OF SOUND A. ROSS cartoon *New Yorker* v93 no14 p90 My 22 2017

Concert halls—Design & construction

For a Song S. AMELAR *Architectural Record* v205 no1 p58 Ja 2017

Show Boat S. STEPHENS color diag *Architectural Record* v204 no12 p76 D 2016

Concert halls—Evaluation

INTERNATIONAL color *Downbeat* v84 no2 p61 F 2017

Concert of the Century: A Tribute to Charlie Parker (Music)

Magic on the Bandstand K. Silsbee bw *Downbeat* v84 no4 p65 Ap 2017

Concert tours

Bowie's Touring Alumni Say Goodbye A. GREENE color *Rolling Stone* no1280 p14 F 9 2017

CALENDAR color *Advocate* no1090 p58 Ap 2017

ED SHEERAN M. Vain color *Entertainment Weekly* no1473 p54 Jl 7 2017

McCartney Shares His Touring Secrets K. GROW color *Rolling Stone* no1291/1292 p26 Jl 13 2017

Metallica's Monster Summer K. GROW color *Rolling Stone* no1290 p13 Je 29 2017

The Nineties Rise Again R. SHEFFIELD color *Rolling Stone* no1293 p23 Ag 10 2017

ON THE ROAD WITH TIM AND FAITH M. Vain color *Entertainment Weekly* no1471 p63 Je 23 2017

Petty's 'Last Big One'? A. GREENE color *Rolling Stone* no1278/1279 p13 Ja 12 2017

The Road Heats Up P. Doyle, D. Fricke et al bw color *Rolling Stone* no1288 p11 Je 1 2017

Summer Forecast S. KNOPPER color *Rolling Stone* no1291/1292 p28 Jl 13 2017

The Summer of Bad Blood A. GREENE bw color *Rolling Stone* no1295 p22 S 7 2017

Vibes Legend Burton Bids Fond Farewell A. Druout color *Downbeat* v84 no6 p13 Je 2017

WHAT'S NEXT FOR LADY GAGA M. Vain color *Entertainment Weekly* no1453 p17 F 17 2017

Your Sunshiny, Stupendous, Seriously Spectacular SUMMER BUCKET LIST I. Biedenharn, A. Breznican et al color *Entertainment Weekly* no1470 p32 Je 16 2017

Concertos (Cello)

L.A. Rhapsody A. Ross cartoon *New Yorker* v93 no5 p18 Mr 20 2017

Concerts

See also

Concert tours

ABOVE & BEYOND cartoon *New Yorker* v93 no29 p32 S 25 2017

After Dark on The Strip color *American Cowboy* v23 no4 p82 D 2016/Ja 2017

ALL AROUND Missouri color *Missouri Life* v44 no2 p103 Ap 2017

Artists Collaborate, Celebrate at Jazz Day Events in Havana J. Murph color *Downbeat* v84 no7 p14 Jl 2017

The Best of 2016 *Opera News* v81 no7 p52 Ja 2017

CALENDAR *New Orleans Magazine* v51 no1 p28 N 2016

CLASSICAL MUSIC *New Yorker* v92 no33 p18 O 17 2016

CLASSICAL MUSIC *New Yorker* v93 no15 p9 My 29 2017

CLASSICAL MUSIC *New Yorker* v93 no27 p13 S 11 2017

CLASSICAL MUSIC *New Yorker* v93 no6 p8 Mr 27 2017

Dateline *Opera News* v81 no12 p14 Je 2017

EAST RIVER EVENTS *South Dakota Magazine* v32 no6 p82 Mr/Ap 2017

GOINGS ON ABOUT TOWN color *New Yorker* v92 no32 p13 O 10 2016

GROOVE M. GRIFFITH color *New Orleans Magazine* v51 no8 p58 Je 2017

THE GUIDE / 07.17 M. WAKIM color *Los Angeles Magazine* v62 no7 p46 Jl 2017

THE GUIDE / 12.16 M. WAKIM *Los Angeles Magazine* p82 D 2016

Hot Weather, Cool Concerts: Escape the heat with great live music M. Griffith color *New Orleans Magazine* v51 no10 p60 Ag 2017

I Hear Music: Songs of Frank Loesser img *New York* v49 no24 p156 N 28 2016

Lyrical Isles S. LODGE color *Weekly Standard* v22 no46 p32 Ag 14 2017

Madonna: Rebel Heart Tour *TV Guide* p43 D 5 2016

Making Music Bounce J. BERRY color *New Orleans Magazine* v51 no12 p62 O 2017

Meanwhile, 3 Doors Down... R. Kinane color *Entertainment Weekly* no1451/1452 p19 F 3-10 2017

MUSICAL MARATHON G. MEYER cartoon *Chicago* v66 no3 p54 Mr 2017

MUSIC MADE THE PEOPLE COME TOGETHER R. Kinane, A. Writing et al color *Entertainment Weekly* no1439 p22 N 11 2016

Music's Best Month M. Griffith color *New Orleans Magazine* v51 no6 p48 Ap 2017

NIGHT LIFE cartoon *New Yorker* v93 no7 p25 Ap 3 2017

NIGHT LIFE color *New Yorker* v93 no29 p18 S 25 2017

NIGHT LIFE *New Yorker* v92 no34 p12 O 24 2016

NIGHT LIFE *New Yorker* v93 no15 p8 My 29 2017

NOVEMBER'S COOLEST EVENTS *Indianapolis Monthly* v40 no3 p28 N 2016

POP RULES M. GRIFFITH color *New Orleans Magazine* v51 no1 p52 N 2016

Reaching Youngsters B. REED color *Downbeat* v84 no7 p8 Jl 2017

Rock & Roll Can Never Die *USA Today Magazine* v145 no2858 p56 N 2016

SEPTEMBER 2017 *Idaho Magazine* v16 no12 p58 S 2017

SEPTEMBER'S COOLEST EVENTS color *Indianapolis Monthly* v41 no2 p24 S 2017

Speaking of Springfield Music... M. W. Schwartz color *Missouri Life* v44 no3 p22 My 2017

Stars Salute Ella at Lincoln Center R. Musto color *Downbeat* v84 no7 p13 Jl 2017

STATEWIDE EVENTS N. BUCK color *Nebraska Life* v21 no6 p70 N/D 2017

'Step, Step, Step' J. NORDLINGER *National Review* v69 no5 p26 Mr 20 2017

Summer Holiday: OPERA NEWS's spotlights the best of the U.S. Festival scene M. Mazzaro *Opera News* v81 no12 p27 Je 2017

Summer Preview M. Trammell cartoon *New Yorker* v93 no14 p18 My 22 2017

TAKE IT FROM THE TOP J. R. MARQUEZ *Atlanta* v56 no8 p52 D 2016

Toby Keith's Happy Hour S. KORNHABER cartoon *Atlantic* v320 no4 p20 N 2017

Viewpoint: As Thousands Cheer *Opera News* v81 no12 p69 Je 2017

We Were the Band R. ROBERTSON bw color *Vanity Fair* v58 no11 p176 N 2016

Concerts—Economic aspects

WHOA, LIVIN ON $10.4 MILLION color *Bloomberg Business-*week no4519 p66 Ap 24 2017

Concerts—Finance

Music Festivals Have A Volume Problem L. Shaw, J. E. Ellis et al color diag *Bloomberg Businessweek* no4512 p21 F 20 2017

Concerts—Reviews

AULD ACQUAINTANCES M. GRIFFITH color *New Orleans Magazine* v51 no3 p46 Ja 2017

CLASSICAL MUSIC *New Yorker* v92 no39 p24 N 28 2016

GOINGS ON ABOUT TOWN color *New Yorker* v92 no39 p9 N 28 2016

GOINGS ON ABOUT TOWN color *New Yorker* v93 no33 p9 O 23 2017

NIGHT LIFE *New Yorker* v92 no30 p7 S 26 2016

NIGHT LIFE *New Yorker* v93 no9 p10 Ap 17 2017

The Seer B. Shapiro color *New Yorker* v93 no18 p11 Je 26 2017

Under Cover Bands Go as Greats St. Louis A. Burger color *Missouri Life* v44 no5 p24 Ag 2017

VINCENT GARDNER T. Panken color *Downbeat* v84 no5 p25 My 2017

Concerts—Security measures

Can Anyone Keep Fans Safe? M. Vain color *Entertainment Weekly* no1486 p22 O 13 2017

Concert Security's New Frontier S. KNOPPER color *Rolling Stone* no1293 p16 Ag 10 2017

HOW SAFE ARE CONCERTS? K. O'Donnell, S. Helling et al color *Entertainment Weekly* no1468/1469 p16 Je 2-9 2017

Music's Scary New Reality S. KNOPPER, S. Hewitt et al color *Rolling Stone* no1289 p13 Je 15 2017

Concessions (Amusements, etc.)

THE GREASE-STAINED SUGAR-DUSTED INSANELY TEXAN TRUE BUT IMPROBABLE INSIDE STORY ABOUT THE INVENTION OF FRIED JELL~O A. LAUSSADE *D: The Magazine of Dallas* v43 no10 p138 O 2016

Concha, Joe

COMBAT REPORTING A. Beaujon *Washingtonian Magazine* v52 no5 p45 F 2017

Concierge Auctions LLC

New House on the Block S. SHARF color *Forbes* v199 no1 p40 Ja 24 2017

Concierge medical care

" I was only 9 WHEN MY MOM GOT SICK" T. KARRAS color *Good Housekeeping* v264 no4 p107 Ap 2017

Concord

We're Thinking About Organizational Culture All Wrong J. Traphagan color *Harvard Business Review Digital Articles* p2 Ja 6 2017

Concord—Social aspects

Shared Rituals Are the Tie That Binds S. Schrobsdorff color *Time* v189 no3 p59 Ja 30 2017

Concrete

Designing with Concrete in the 21st Century P. J. Arsenault color *Architectural Record* v204 no12 p174 D 2016

How to Make a... CONCRETE FRAME B. LOSLEBEN chart color *Popular Mechanics* p82 S 2017

Concrete & Gold (Music)

Foo Fighters' All-Star Return K. GROW color *Rolling Stone* no1293 p11 Ag 10 2017

Concrete blocks

Concrete Block color *Old House Journal* v45 no3 p46 My 2017

How to Make a... ROCKET STOVE color *Popular Mechanics* v193 no7 p74 S 2016

Concrete construction

How to Make a... CONCRETE FRAME B. LOSLEBEN chart color *Popular Mechanics* v193 no7 p82 S 2016

Concrete construction design

How to Make a... CONCRETE FRAME B. LOSLEBEN chart color *Popular Mechanics* v193 no7 p82 S 2016

Concrete slabs

"Camp Off the Grid" F. SIGURDSSON color *Cabin Living* p24 Ja/F 2017

Concrete walls

How to Make a... WALL color *Popular Mechanics* p80 S 2017

Concrete—Mixing

BEST OF THE WEST J. Scatena, C. Lamers et al color *Sunset* v238 no1 p11 Ja 2017

SHOP NOTES cartoon color *Popular Mechanics* p112 Ap 2017

CONDA, CESAR

A Friendship on the Rocks color *Weekly Standard* v22 no10 p14 N 14 2016

SPANISH-LANGUAGE TV IS EN FUEGO T. J. Huddleston color *Fortune* v75 no1 p34 Ja 1 2017

Condé Nast Press (Company)

S.I. Newhouse T. Brown color *Time* v190 no15 p13 O 16 2017

Conde Nast Traveler (Periodical)

Age of Experience color *Conde Nast Traveler* v52 no8 p16 S 2017

Condensation

See also

Bose-Einstein condensation

A Well That Sucks Water from Air J. Zorthian color *Time* v188 no19 p17 N 7 2016

Condie, Cami

SIDE-BY-SIDE LEARNING: A summer program focused on science disciplinary literacy *Literacy Today (2411-7862)* v35 no1 p30 Jl/Ag 2017

Condiments

See also

Salsas (Cooking)

Spices

Always Use a Condiment J. LEDOUX *Atlanta* v56 no7 p84 N 2016

Make Your Own Vegan Condiments N. Berkoff *Vegetarian Journal* v36 no1 p6 2017

On the SIDE A. NEASON color *House Beautiful* p169 Ag 2017

Pesto Perfection M. M. CHAPPEL color *Better Nutrition* v79 no4 p60 Ap 2017

VEGAN BURGER Condiments *Vegetarian Journal* v35 no2 p12 2016

Vegan Cooking Tips. Quick and Easy Sandwich Ideas N. Berkoff *Vegetarian Journal* v35 no2 p32 2016

Condit, Richard

Plant diversity increases with the strength of negative density dependence at the global scale diag *Science* v356 no6345 p1389 Je 30 2017

Conditional cash transfer programs

Technology beats corruption R. Hanna bibl color *Science* v355 no6322 p244 Ja 20 2017

Condliffe, Jamie

INVENTORS color il *MIT Technology Review* v120 no5 p56 S/O 2017

Laser Vision color *MIT Technology Review* v120 no5 p88 S/O 2017

PIONEERS color il *MIT Technology Review* v120 no5 p50 S/O 2017

The Robotic Grocery Store of the Future Is Here color *MIT Technology Review* v120 no2 p22 Mr/Ap 2017

Condominium design & construction

Let's Do the Twist S. STEPHENS *Architectural Record* v205 no10 p84 O 2017

OSCAR MUNOZ'S NEW DIGS M. LAWLER color *Chicago* v66 no8 p28 Ag 2017

Condominium hotels—Design & construction

DOMAIN IN THE SKYLINE K. FINN color *New Orleans Magazine* v51 no1 p32 N 2016

Condominiums

CLEAN SLATE [Cover story] H. MITCHELL color *Chicago* v66 no9 p73 S 2017

Industrial Lite: Designer Shauna Leftwich softens industrial edges of warehouse district condo L. Cutrone *New Orleans Homes & Lifestyles* v20 no4 p65 Aut 2017

OFF THE MARKET! color *Washingtonian Magazine* v52 no7 p169 Ap 2017

Condominiums—Canada

Fresh Start J. MINUTILLO color diag *Architectural Record* v205 no2 p86 F 2017

Condominiums—Design & construction

LESS SPACE. MORE GLAM J. Sergent *Washingtonian Magazine* v52 no6 p158 Mr 2017

The Region's Newest Sales Tool: Virtual reality cartoon *Washingtonian Magazine* v52 no7 p92 Ap 2017

Condominiums—Design & construction—Evaluation

THE RETURN OF LUXE LIVING J. CROWN color *Chicago* v65 no12 p27 D 2016

Condominiums—Evaluation

PENTHOUSE VIEWS: A TIP-TOP CONDO IN THE HEART OF DOWNTOWN L. MURTHA *Cincinnati Magazine* v50 no11 p36 Ag 2017

Condominiums—New York (State)—New York

Haute Concrete B. BOSKER color *Atlantic* v319 no3 p28 Ap 2017

Condominiums—Sales & prices

THE POTOMAC PROBLEM M. M. Kashino *Washingtonian Magazine* v52 no1 p183 O 2016

Condominiums—Washington (D.C.)

SEEKING SANCTUARY M. M. Kashino *Washingtonian Magazine* v52 no2 p274 N 2016

Condoms

Let's talk about birth control color *Health* v31 no9 p20 N 2017

This Just In J. Zorthian *Time* v190 no8 p21 Ag 28 2017

Condon, Bill, 1955-

Money for Nothing J. PODHORETZ color *Weekly Standard* v22 no30 p39 Ap 10 2017

Condon, Christopher

Janet Yellen Can't Help Retirees color *Bloomberg Businessweek* no4540 p50 O 2 2017

CONDON, JENNIFER JONES

15 Reasons to Become a Morning Person color *House Beautiful* v159 no7 p48 S 2017

Finishing Touch color *House Beautiful* v159 no4 p38 My 2017

Get in Line color *House Beautiful* v159 no4 p40 My 2017

Homecoming Season color *House Beautiful* v159 no7 p41 S 2017

Made to Measure color *House Beautiful* v159 no7 p51 S 2017

The New Blooms color *House Beautiful* v159 no4 p35 My 2017

Rise & Dine color *House Beautiful* v159 no7 p46 S 2017

CONDON, JOSH

Hauling Class color *Esquire* p62 BigBlackBook

CONDON, KATY KIICK

1951 COFFEE color *Better Homes & Gardens* v95 no5 p178 My 2017

1968 CRAFTING SPACE color *Better Homes & Gardens* v95 no7 p172 Jl 2017

BHG throw back 1953 UPDATED HEIRLOOMS *Better Homes & Gardens* v94 no11 p168 N 2016

BH&G throwback 1956 HANDMADE CERAMICS color *Better Homes & Gardens* v95 no9 p172 S 2017

BH&G throwback 1957 CLOSETS color *Better Homes & Gardens* v95 no2 p136 F 2016

GAME ON color *Better Homes & Gardens* v95 no7 p134 Jl 2017

go to your ROOM color *Better Homes & Gardens* v95 no8 p34 Ag 2017

LIVING LAID-BACK & DOWN UNDER color *Better Homes & Gardens* v95 no8 p142 Ag 2017

painting a BLUE STREAK color *Better Homes & Gardens* v95 no4 p38 Ap 2017

queen of COLORING color *Better Homes & Gardens* v95 no11 p20 N 2017

SIMPLY RED *Better Homes & Gardens* v94 no12 p102 D 2016

the thrill of the [ART] HUNT color *Better Homes & Gardens* v95 no10 p86 O 2017

Condon, Liam—Interviews

THE SUCCESSFUL INTERVIEW K. Birchmier *Successful Farming* v115 no11 p10 S 2017

Conduct disorders in children

The Problem with Measuring Effects of Delinquent Peers in Education—and How to Get Around It T. AHN and J. TROGDON *Education Digest* v82 no9 p18 My 2017

Conduct of life

See also

Altruism

Brotherliness

Caring

Charity

Courage

Etiquette

Exploitation of humans

Forgiveness

Friendship

Habit

Humanity

Justice

Kindness

Modesty

Patience

Pride & vanity

Respect

Sharing

Simplicity

Spirituality

Success

Sympathy

GIVE YOURSELF a Hand E. GILBERT cartoon *O, The Oprah Magazine* p45 D 2016

Here We Go! Oprah color *O, The Oprah Magazine* p21 Ag 2017

HOPE M. WERNER *Humanist* v76 no6 p42 N/D 2016

KINDER, GENTLER cartoon *O, The Oprah Magazine* p96 Ap 2017

LET'S DO THIS E. Graves color *Martha Stewart Living* p6 My 2017

Life K. SMITH, S. MUELLER et al cartoon *Reader's Digest* v190 no1132 p30 Jl/Ag 2017

Life With ISIS & After ISIS E. Trieb color *Glamour* no8 p117 Ag 2017

PRIVATE SELVES, PUBLIC LIES W. McPhail cartoon *Esquire* p40 S 2017

Still, the world is good J. Denari Duffner il *U.S. Catholic* v81 no11 p45 N 2016

To Form Successful Habits, Know What Motivates You G. Rubin *Harvard Business Review Digital Articles* p2 Mr 17 2015

Two Words to Help You Gut Check Your Career M. Chussil *Harvard Business Review Digital Articles* p2 N 5 2015

WELCOME HOME SIGN B. HEAVEY color *Field & Stream* v122 no4 p90 S 2017

What Ever Happened to the Romantic Gesture? L. LARSON color *GQ: Gentlemen's Quarterly* v97 no10 p78 O 2017

Zone DEFENSE M. BECK cartoon *O, The Oprah Magazine* p42 Ap 2017

Conductor interviews

MAGIC BATON K. DOANE *Cincinnati Magazine* v50 no10 p24 Jl 2017

Conductors (Musicians)

See also

Band directors

2020 VISION [Cover story] D. J. BAKER *Opera News* v81 no9 p22 Mr 2017

Leading Women M. YOUNG *Opera News* v81 no5 p22 N 2016

Metropolitan Opera M. MAZZARO *Opera News* v81 no9 p64 Mr 2017

The Old Master S. BOSE *American Scholar* v86 no1 p103 Wint 2017

Redefining the Gold Standard: As he winds down his New York Philharmonic tenure with Das Rheingold, Alan Gilbert looks forward to new beginnings H. Stewart *Opera News* v81 no12 p51 Je 2017

Cone, Allen

Cheers & Jeers cartoon color *Field & Stream* v121 no9 p14 Ap 2017

Cone, Michèle C.

Art into Fiction color *Art in America* v105 no8 p55 S 2017

Conepatus leuconotus

NEW FLY REPELLENT IN THE WORKS C. Barakat and M. McCluskey color *Equus* no471 p10 D 2016

CONERY, ROB

I WAS A MIDDLE-AGED LIFTIE color *Powder* p28 S 2017

Coney Island (New York, N.Y.)

NEIGHBORHOOD WATCHED J. GONNERMAN bw cartoon *New Yorker* v93 no18 p30 Je 26 2017

SUBWAY SUBSTITUTES L. GUTIÉRREZ cartoon *New Yorker* v93 no23 p53 Ag 7 2017

Confalonieri, Stefano

Reticulon 3–dependent ER-PM contact sites control EGFR non-clathrin endocytosis color diag graph *Science* v356 no6338 p617 My 12 2017

Confectionery

See also

Cake

Candy

Chewing gum

Desserts

Ice cream, ices, etc.

Icings (Confectionery)

Marshmallow (Confectionery)

All Tied Up C. SAFFITZ color *Bon Appetit* v61 no12 p85 D 2016 /Jan2017

Cake Fit for a Queen R. Kinane color diag *Entertainment Weekly* no1474/1475 p24 Jl 21-28 2017

ICE CREAM MAKERS M. XERAKIA color *Better Homes & Gardens* v95 no7 p154 Jl 2017

Pet-Safe Halloween Treats G. McClure color *Good Housekeeping* v265 no4 p134 O 2017

PEZ DISPENSERS color *Indianapolis Monthly* v42 no2 p70 O 2017

Sandra Lee Favorites color *TV Guide* v64 no42 p14 O 10 2016

Step Away From the Sticky Bun! T. Calvo chart color *Consumer Reports* v82 no3 p36 Mr 2017

Sweet Tooth Strategies C. Bauer color *Dance Magazine* v91 no3 p42 Mr 2017

Top This Ice Cream K. O'SHEA-EVANS and C. SWANSON color *House Beautiful* v159 no7 p74 S 2017

Confectionery competitions

See also

Cake decorating competitions

8TH ANNUAL SWEET VICTORY *Cincinnati Magazine* v50 no6 p49 Mr 2017

Confectionery stores—Evaluation

Candy Land J. ZYMAN *Atlanta* v56 no8 p69 D 2016

GREATER NEW ORLEANS J. FROIS color map *Louisiana Life* v37 no4 p98 Mr/Ap 2017

Raising Canes L. VACCARIELLO *Cincinnati Magazine* v50 no2 p136 N 2016

Confectionery—Evaluation

Mixing Bowl color *O, The Oprah Magazine* p138 O 2017

Confederate cemeteries

A MONUMENTAL Decision: What to Do with Confederate Monuments? P. Gilbert *Parks & Recreation* v52 no10 p36 O 2017

Confederate States of America—History

6 CONFEDERATE MEMORIALS THAT ARE STILL HERE M. Blitz *Washingtonian Magazine* v52 no2 p22 N 2016

Confederation of states

Content-Based Park Permit Decisions Unconstitutional J. C. Kozlowski *Parks & Recreation* v52 no10 p18 O 2017

A HALF A DOZEN BATTLES J. Goldberg bw *Atlantic* v320 no4 p10 N 2017

Confer, Brian—Interviews

Headshots Are Their Gig P. M. ESSWEIN color *Kiplinger's Personal Finance* v71 no6 p24 Je 2017

Conference rooms—Design & construction

THE MASTER PLANS cartoon color *Vanity Fair* v58 no11 p68 N 2016

Conferences & conventions

See also

Education—Congresses

Meetings

ABOVE & BEYOND diag *New Yorker* v93 no16 p31 Je 5 2017

Bahrain host of the 2017 WAHO CONFERENCE [Cover story] D. Hearst *Arabian Horse World* v56 no12 p1 S 2016

EVENTS *Literacy Today (2411-7862)* v34 no6 p48 My/Je 2017

How to Decide Which Conferences Are Worth Your Time D. Clark color *Harvard Business Review Digital Articles* p2 Ja 10 2017

Navigating Challenges and Seizing Opportunities S. NAGEEB and M. D. A. NIEMI *Islamic Horizons* v45 no6 p16 N/D 2016

On Wall Street, A Bipolar Diagnosis J. Pressler *New York* v49 no23 p26 N 14 2016

The Prose of Cons S. CORBETT color *Publishers Weekly* v264 no19 p25 My 8 2017

Small Stories, Big Picture A. R. Albanese color *Publishers Weekly* v263 no47 p19 N 21 2016

When It's Worth Having a Meeting Before Your Meeting A. Molinsky color *Harvard Business Review Digital Articles* p2 O 28 2016

Conferences & conventions—Nevada

The Show's the Thing J. Coakley *Stage Directions* v29 no11 p N 2016

Conferences & conventions—Ontario

Meanwhile, Up North K. J. TORRANCE color *Weekly Standard* v22 no36 p22 My 29 2017

Conferences & conventions—Security measures

STAYING SAFE AT SAN DIEGO COMIC-CON 2017 H. MACDONALD color *Publishers Weekly* v264 no28 p48 Jl 10 2017

Conferences & conventions—Social aspects

5 Ways to Make Conference Networking Easier D. Clark *Harvard Business Review Digital Articles* p2 O 13 2015

Confession (Christianity)

5 JUICY CONFESSIONS with... Keanu Reeves C. Keller color *Women's Health* v14 no2 p126 Mr 2017

CONFESSING color *Women's Health* v14 no2 p160 Mr 2017

READER COMMENTS L. Weber, K. Gallagher et al *America* v216 no6 p7 Mr 20 2017

THE ROAD TO MERCY S. Livingston color *America* v217 no5 p26 S 4 2017

YOUR BODY ON... A CONFESSION J. Migala color *Women's Health* v14 no2 p88 Mr 2017

Confession (Christianity)—Frequency of confession

Hate confession? J. Martin *America* v216 no5 p70 Mr 6 2017

Confession stories

FULL DISCLOSURE *Women's Health* v14 no2 p27 Mr 2017

Get More WH color *Women's Health* v14 no2 p14 Mr 2017

Confessionals (Architecture)

Protecting the Confessional Seal *America* v217 no6 p8 S 18 2017

Confessions, The (Short story)

THE CONFESSIONS J. COHEN cartoon *Wired* v25 no9 p70 S 2017

Confessions of a Free-Range Parent (Short story)

CONFESSIONS OF A FREE-RANGE PARENT C. KENLEY *Indianapolis Monthly* v40 no4 p100 D 2016

Confessore, Nicholas

ACCESS 2 PREZ WHILE U WAIT: THE BUCKS START HERE *New York Times Magazine* p32 S 3 2017

SEA OF MONEY *New York Times Magazine* p30 D 4 2016

Confidence

See also

Self-confidence

"Be your whole self" A. D. Barnett color *Glamour* v115 no9 p130 S 2017

Cleaning House S. T. BROWN bw color *Ebony* v72 no5 p68 Mr 2017

DON'T PANIC! G. Graves cartoon *O, The Oprah Magazine* p87 Mr 2017

Embrace Awkwardness G. DREVITCH *Psychology Today* v50 no3 p48 My/Je 2017

Happily out of reach M. Rollins *Redbook* p12 D 2016

THE HARDEST WORD [Cover story] C. FLORA *Psychology Today* v50 no5 p52 S/O 2017

Just Say Thanks A. Gurwitch cartoon *Prevention* p28 Mr 2017

Little steps to total body confidence A. Sweeney color *Redbook* p28 My 2017

Rest, reflect, and refresh color *Yoga Journal* p64 2016 Special Issue

Setbacks & Comebacks J. Paulson *Horse & Rider* v55 no11 p6 N 2016

Slow Deciders Make Better Strategists M. Chussil *Harvard Business Review Digital Articles* p2 Jl 8 2016

Sprints Are the Secret to Getting More Done J. Zeratsky *Harvard Business Review Digital Articles* p2 Mr 15 2016

Confidential communications

THE BREACH cartoon *Wired* v24 no11 p114 N 2016

Open Secrets A. Hess *New York Times Magazine* p11 My 14 2017

Your problems *People Management* p59 N 2016

Confidential communications—Clergy

See also

Seal of confession

Confidential records

Is Your Company Using Employee Data Ethically? Kon Leong *Harvard Business Review Digital Articles* p2 Mr 13 2017

Confidential records—Law & legislation

Yes, 'It's a Scandal' M. Hemingway color *Weekly Standard* v22 no9 p8 N 7 2016

Confirmation (Film)

Justice M. LOGAN *TV Guide* v64 no15 p40 Ap 4 2016

Confirmation (TV program)

Confirmation M. ROUSH *TV Guide* v64 no15 p20 Ap 4 2016

Confirmation bias (Psychology)

Root Out Bias from Your Decision-Making Process T. C. Redman color *Harvard Business Review Digital Articles* p2 Mr 10 2017

Conflict management

See also

Peacebuilding

A 3-Step Process to Break a Cycle of Frustration, Stress, and Fighting at Work A. McKee *Harvard Business Review Digital Articles* p2 Jl 12 2017

The 4 Types of Ineffective Apologies A. Molinsky *Harvard Business Review Digital Articles* p2 N 15 2016

6 Ways to Disagree with Senior Management P. Claman *Harvard Business Review Digital Articles* p2 Je 14 2016

Antagonistic Mediators Can Make Resolving Disputes Easier F. Gino *Harvard Business Review Digital Articles* p2 Ag 19 2016

Avoid Political Tension at Thanksgiving color *Time* v188 no22-23 p20 N/D 2016

Defusing an Emotionally Charged Conversation with a Colleague R. Friedman *Harvard Business Review Digital Articles* p2 Ja 12 2016

Don't Let Frustration Make You Say the Wrong Thing T. Healey and J. Roberts *Harvard Business Review Digital Articles* p2 D 24 2015

Even Experienced Executives Avoid Conflict R. Ashkenas *Harvard Business Review Digital Articles* p2 Mr 8 2016

How People with Different Conflict Styles Can Work Together A. Gallo *Harvard Business Review Digital Articles* p2 Jl 24 2017

How Self-Managed Teams Can Resolve Conflict A. Maimon *Harvard Business Review Digital Articles* p2 Ap 17 2017

How to Deal with the Irrational Parts of a Negotiation J. Grenny *Harvard Business Review Digital Articles* p2 Je 6 2016

How to De-Escalate an Argument with a Coworker L. Davey *Harvard Business Review Digital Articles* p2 Je 27 2017

How to Disagree with Someone More Powerful than You A. Gallo *Harvard Business Review Digital Articles* p2 Mr 17 2016

HOW TO FIGHT FAIR K. TRANELL and C. RIDSDALE *Scholastic Choices* v32 no4 p12 Ja 2017

How to Handle a Disagreement on Your Team J. Brett and S. B. Goldberg *Harvard Business Review Digital Articles* p2 Jl 10 2017

How to Have Difficult Conversations When You Don't Like Conflict J. Garfinkle *Harvard Business Review Digital Articles* p2 My 24 2017

How to Make Sure You're Heard in a Difficult Conversation A. Gallo *Harvard Business Review Digital Articles* p2 N 9 2015

How to Navigate a Turf War at Work A. Gallo *Harvard Business Review Digital Articles* p2 S 27 2017

How to Say No to Taking on More Work R. Knight *Harvard Business Review Digital Articles* p2 D 29 2015

How to Tell a Coworker They're Annoying You C. Webb *Harvard Business Review Digital Articles* p2 Mr 10 2016

Learning to Appreciate Disagreement at Work W. Johnson *Harvard Business Review Digital Articles* p2 Jl 6 2016

My Competitiveness Was Hurting My Sales Team. Here's How I Realized It R. Harris *Harvard Business Review Digital Articles* p2 S 29 2017

Put Yourself in Your Colleague's Shoes J. Cohen *Harvard Business Review Digital Articles* p2 O 6 2014

Resolve a Fight with a Remote Colleague A. Gallo *Harvard Business Review Digital Articles* p2 N 30 2015

There's more than one way to solve a dispute: Resolving workplace differences is a fine art - and many businesses have been getting it dramatically wrong J. SIMMS *People Management* p32 Ag 2017

What to Do If a Conversation Is Turning Loud and Aggressive J. Grenny *Harvard Business Review Digital Articles* p2 Mr 17 2016

What to Do If a Feud Threatens Your Family Business J. Baron and R. Lachenauer *Harvard Business Review Digital Articles* p2 Ap 15 2015

What to Do If Your Boss Asks You to Break the Rules P. T. Coleman and R. Ferguson *Harvard Business Review Digital Articles* p2 Ja 7 2016

What to Do When a Colleague Can't Stick to a Decision A. Jen

Su *Harvard Business Review Digital Articles* p2 Mr 25 2016

When an Argument Gets Too Heated, Here's What to Say L. Davey *Harvard Business Review Digital Articles* p2 Mr 3 2016

Why Is It So Hard for Us to Admit Our Mistakes? K. Firestone *Harvard Business Review Digital Articles* p2 Mr 28 2016

Conflict management—History

FROM THE EDITOR P. Lay *History Today* v67 no4 p2 Ap 2017

Conflict management—Methodology

If Your Team Agrees on Everything, Working Together Is Pointless L. Davey color *Harvard Business Review Digital Articles* p2 Ja 31 2017

Conflict of interests

Building Security Forces & Stabilizing Nations: The Problem of Agency S. Biddle *Daedalus* v146 no4 p126 Fall 2017

Conflict Resolution M. F. Jacobson *Nutrition Action Health Letter* v44 no2 p2 Mr 2017

IN TRUMP THEY TRUST D. ALEXANDER color map *Forbes* v199 no3 p42 Mr 28 2017

No Prob C. Chocano *New York Times Magazine* p13 Jl 23 2017

STACKING THE DECK? [Cover story] *Nutrition Action Health Letter* v44 no2 p3 Mr 2017

WATER K. ATHERTON *Popular Science* v289 no2 p64 Mr/Ap 2017

Conflict of interests—Canada

Industrialist vs. Indigenous R. RUSSELL color *Walrus* v14 no3 p24 Ap 2017

Conflict of interests—United States

THE BEST YARD SALE C. Melby, S. Baker et al color *Bloomberg Businessweek* no4501 p22 N 28 2016

Carl 'I can' Z. Mider and J. A. Dlouhy bw color graph *Bloomberg Businessweek* no4515 p23 Mr 20 2017

Until Donald Trump, U.S. presidents and vice presidents went to extremes to avoid conflicts of interest... real or apparent C. Melby, B. Allison et al bw color *Bloomberg Businessweek* no4503 p22 D 12 2016

Conflict of interests—United States—Law & legislation

The Quiet Official Who's Trump Enemy No. 1 B. Allison color *Bloomberg Businessweek* no4508 p24 Ja 23 2017

Conflict resources (Natural resources)

80% of Companies Don't Know If Their Products Contain Conflict Minerals Y. H. Kim and G. F. Davis color *Harvard Business Review Digital Articles* p2 Ja 4 2017

Conformational analysis

Controlling guest conformation for efficient purification of butadiene Liao, Huang et al bw diag *Science* v356 no6343 p1193 Je 16 2017

Conformity

See also

Dissenters

Persuasion (Psychology)

The High Cost of Conformity, and How to Avoid It P. Bregman *Harvard Business Review Digital Articles* p2 O 21 2015

Why Superstars Struggle to Bond with Their Teams A. O'Connell *Harvard Business Review Digital Articles* p2 O 27 2014

Conforti, Lana

Producer prices, 2016: goods inflation returns and price increases for services move higher bibl chart color graph *Monthly Labor Review* p1 Mr 2017

Confoy, Tyler

Do You Even Code, Bro? cartoon color *Esquire* v166 no5 p48 D 2016/Ja 2017

Learning to Love the Hog color *Esquire* v166 no4 p44 N 2016

THE MAVERICKS OF HOLLYWOOD 2017 bw color *Esquire* v167 no2 p89 Mr 2017

MY FIRST RIDE: T-PAIN cartoon color *Esquire* v167 no2 p62 Mr 2017

SCOTT TUROW: 3 BOOKS THAT CHANGED MY LIFE color *Esquire* p36 My 2017

The Valentine's Day Wine Survival Guide bw *Esquire* v167 no1 p17 F 2017

Confucianism

REGIME CHANGE He-Yin Zhen *Lapham's Quarterly* v10 no3 p47 Summ 2017

Confucius, 551 B.C.-479 B.C.

Education & Success bw color *Forbes* v200 no5 p172 N 14 2017

Of Meat and Men A. Chen color *Scientific American* v316 no5

p22 My 2017

Cong, Zhiyuan

Melting glaciers: Hidden hazards color *Science* v356 no6337 p495 My 5 2017

Cong Fan

Precision medicine for Chinese women with familial breast cancer: Opportunities and challenges bibl *Science* v354 no6319 p43 D 23 2016

Congaree National Park (S.C.)

THE WILD CONGAREE G. M. PETERS *National Parks* v91 no4 p44 Fall 2017

CongBao Kang

Crystal structure of unlinked NS2B-NS3 protease from Zika virus bibl color graph *Science* v354 no6319 p1597 D 23 2016

Congdon, Joy

Organize, Plan and Structure Your Ride color *Dressage Today* p30 My 2017

Congee

Congee: The Original Grain Bowl R. Patronite and R. Raisfeld img *New York* v50 no6 p68 Mr 20 2017

Congenital disorders

See also

Genetic disorders

Rapid development of a DNA vaccine for Zika virus K. A. Dowd, Sung-Youl Ko et al bibl graph *Science* v354 no6309 p237 O 14 2016

Congenital disorders—Case studies

The Test of a Lifetime A. Park color *Time* v190 no13 p52 O 2 2017

Congleton, Christina

Mindfulness Can Literally Change Your Brain *Harvard Business Review Digital Articles* p2 Ja 8 2015

Conglomerate corporations

3D Printing Will Revive Conglomerates R. D'Aveni *Harvard Business Review Digital Articles* p2 My 19 2015

Gentle Giants *Sierra* v102 no2 p10 Mr/Ap 2017

Conglomerate corporations—China

YOU'VE NEVER HEARD OF *HNA GROUP. HERE'S WHY YOU WILL V. Walt color diag *Fortune* v176 no2 p86 Ag 1 2017

Congregate housing

Caring for Aging Loved Ones R. L. Dilenschneider, T. Allen et al color *Consumer Reports* v82 no12 p6 D 2017

The Compassionate Care You Need M. L. Tellado *Consumer Reports* v82 no10 p4 O 2017

Death of a caregiver I. S. Villegas *Christian Century* v134 no3 p10 F 2017

DOWNSIZING MY DAD A. Cochran *Washingtonian Magazine* v52 no2 p279 N 2016

REMEMBER WHEN? A. Cochran *Washingtonian Magazine* v52 no6 p167 Mr 2017

Who Will Care for You? [Cover story] P. Wang, E. Stark et al chart color map *Consumer Reports* v82 no10 p28 O 2017

Congregate housing—Evaluation

LIVING WELL F. Esker color *Louisiana Life* v37 no2 p76 N/D 2016

Congregational churches

The hard blue glow K. Childress *Christian Century* v134 no13 p10 Je 21 2017

Red state, purple church B. D. McLaren *Christian Century* v134 no13 p26 Je 21 2017

Congregational singing (Sacred music)

Singing Isn't Just for Sunday S. GUTHRIE bw color *Christianity Today* v61 no7 p80 S 2017

Congregationalism

Disciple for Dakota: Joseph Ward came to Yankton to spread Congregationalism, but he also built schools and helped create a state J. ANDREWS *South Dakota Magazine* v33 no2 p32 Jl/Ag 2017

Congressional Gold Medal

OSS VETERANS RECEIVE CONGRESSIONAL GOLD MEDAL B. Manley bw *Military History* v34 no1 p10 My 2017

Congressional Review Act, 1996 (U.S.)

The Congressional Review Act: Congress Putting Our Forests in Jeopardy R. Turner *American Forests* v123 no2 p10 Summ 2017

Little-Known Law Makes a Big Difference T. J. DONOHUE *Weekly Standard* v22 no36 p9 My 29 2017

CONICK, HAL
THE NEW SODA TAX color *Chicago* v66 no7 p18 Jl 2017
Coniferous forests
Northern Exposure color *House Beautiful* v158 no10 p17 D 2016/ Ja 2017
PRESCOTT LAKES LOOP K. MONTGOMERY *Arizona Highways* v93 no4 p52 Ap 2017
Conifers
Conifer Cruising T. WILLIAM *American Forests* v122 no3 p24 Fall 2016
Conings, Bert
Perovskite-perovskite tandem photovoltaics with optimized band gaps bibl chart graph *Science* v354 no6314 p861 N 18 2016
Conjoint analysis (Marketing)
The Trade-Off Every AI Company Will Face A. Agrawal, J. Gans et al *Harvard Business Review Digital Articles* p2 Mr 28 2017
Conjugation (Biology)
The ATG conjugation systems are important for degradation of the inner autophagosomal membrane Kotaro Tsuboyama, Ikuko Koyama-Honda et al bibl graph *Science* v354 no6315 p1036 N 25 2016
Conjunctions (Astronomy)
November 2017: Venus meets Jupiter M. RATCLIFFE and A. LING color *Astronomy* v45 no11 p36 N 2017
A Pretty Pair: Venus and Mars dance at dawn. Saturn sets early in the evening F. Schaaf *Sky & Telescope* v134 no4 p46 O 2017
What's in the sky tonight? *Sky & Telescope* v133 no1 p84 Ja 2017
Conjunctivitis—Treatment
Common causes of eye redness [Cover story] *Mayo Clinic Health Letter* v35 no5 p1 My 2017
Conjuring, The (Film)
Dispelling Demons: Detective Work at The Conjuring House J. NICKELL *Skeptical Inquirer* v40 no6 p20 N/D 2016
Conk, Michael
READER COMMENTS *America* v216 no3 p7 F 6 2017
Conklin, Bruce R.
CRISPRi-based genome-scale identification of functional long noncoding RNA loci in human cells bibl graph *Science* v355 no6320 p1 Ja 6 2017
CONKLIN, LISA MARIE
I Survived! [Cover story] *Reader's Digest* v189 no1128 p62 Mr 2017
Conley, Chip
I Joined Airbnb at 52, and Here's What I Learned About Age, Wisdom, and the Tech Industry *Harvard Business Review Digital Articles* p2 Ap 18 2017
Conley, Jim
Johan Heilbron, French Sociology *Society* v54 no1 p86 F 2017
Conley, John
Readers Respond color *Publishers Weekly* v263 no51 pC4 D 12 2016
CONLEY, JOHN J.
Churched Philosophy *America* v215 no11 p26 O 17 2016
Game Show Philosophy *America* v216 no10 p54 My 1 2017
RESURRECTING THE IDEA OF A CHRISTIAN SOCIETY color *America* v215 no12 p36 O 24 2016
Teachers Who Teach *America* v215 no19 p28 D 19 2016
Undercover Grief *America* v215 no15 p29 N 14 2016
Conley, Mark A.
Male and Female Entrepreneurs Get Asked Different Questions by VCs—and It Affects How Much Funding They Get *Harvard Business Review Digital Articles* p2 Je 27 2017
Conley, Valerie Martin
Whither the Faculty? *Change* v49 no4 p43 Jl/Ag 2017
Conlin, Jonathan
Invisible Handler S. Miller bw color *Weekly Standard* v22 no23 p30 F 20 2017
CONLON, Edward
NYPD BLACK bw color *Esquire* p104 Ap 2017
Conn, David
Soccer's Culture of Corruption [Cover story] S. Kuper color *New York Review of Books* v64 no14 p55 S 28 2017
Connally, Bruce A.
CONSULTANTS bw *Equus* no474 p67 Mr 2017
CONSULTANTS color *Equus* no472 p67 Ja 2017
Coping with brittle hooves color *Equus* no478 p73 Jl 2017

ORTHOPEDICS: A late-in-life change in gaits? color *Equus* no480 p74 S 2017
Connect-the-dots puzzles
Connect the Dots N. HORVATH cartoon color *Prevention* p96 Mr 2017
Connecticut—Description & travel
CONNECTICUT *Yankee* p163 My/Je 2017
Green Acres S. COCHRAN color *Architectural Digest* v74 no9 p90 S 2017
Holiday Shopping Towns K. K. BECKIUS color *Yankee* v80 no6 p94 N/D 2016
Connecticut—Economic conditions
Can This State Be Saved? A. B. LLOYD color *Weekly Standard* v23 no6 p27 O 16 2017
RICHER AND POORER: How could the nation's wealthiest state become a fiscal basket case? A. Greenblatt *Governing* v30 no12 p30 S 2017
Connective tissue growth factor
Building bridges to regenerate axons P. R. Williams and Zhigang He bibl color diag *Science* v354 no6312 p544 N 4 2016
Injury-induced ctgfa directs glial bridging and spinal cord regeneration in zebrafish M. H. Mokalled, C. Patra et al bibl graph *Science* v354 no6312 p630 N 4 2016
Connective tissues
Adipocytes L. SCHLEY color *Discover* v38 no9 p20 N 2017
BE ECCENTRIC L. BOYCE and L. McGLASHAN color *Muscle & Performance* v8 no12 p20 D 2016
Connell, Evan S., 1924-2013
1912: Antarctica *Lapham's Quarterly* v10 no2 p59 Spr 2017
CONNELL, KATHERINE
Tocqueville And the Art Of Living diag *National Review* v69 no5 p43 Mr 20 2017
Connell, Kevin
"Failing" in the Classroom K. M. Mitchell *Stage Directions* v29 no10 p34 O 2016
CONNELL, MICHAEL
Mac 911 color *Macworld - Digital Edition* p131 F 2017
CONNELLY, BEN
ONENESS WITH EVERY STITCH color *Tricycle: The Buddhist Review* v26 no2 p74 Wint 2016
CONNELLY, BOB
50 YEARS AFTER THE HOMOSEXUALS bw *Advocate* no1089 p12 F/Mr 2017
CONNELLY, JOHN
Humanity's Conscience? color *Commonweal* v144 no4 p16 F 24 2017
JOHN CONNELLY REPLIES: *Commonweal* v144 no7 p2 Ap 14 2017
LESSONS LEARNED? J. CORNWELL *Commonweal* v144 no7 p2 Ap 14 2017
Conner, Blake
2017 BMW HP4 RACER color *Cycle World* v56 no8 p34 S 2017
2017 YAMAHA SCR950 color *Cycle World* v55 no10 p14 N 2016
COMMUNITY M. HOYER *Cycle World* v55 no10 p6 N 2016
Conner, Bruce, 1933-2008
A MOVIE color *Art in America* v104 no10 p20 N 2016
Conner, Cindy
Ask Our Experts *Mother Earth News* no281 p91 Ap/My 2017
Conner, Scott
Scott Conner F. P. DRISCOLL *Opera News* v81 no9 p10 Mr 2017
Connerney, J. E. P.
Jupiter's interior and deep atmosphere: The initial pole-to-pole passes with the Juno spacecraft [Cover story] color graph *Science* v356 no6340 p821 My 26 2017
Jupiter's magnetosphere and aurorae observed by the Juno spacecraft during its first polar orbits diag graph *Science* v356 no6340 p826 My 26 2017
Connerty, Michael
Manufacturing Companies Need to Sell Outcomes, Not Products *Harvard Business Review Digital Articles* p2 Je 2 2016
CONNERY, ANA
TRAVEL SMART color *Better Homes & Gardens* v95 no8 p182 Ag 2017
Connery, Gary, 1970-
DROP TEST P. Garrison color *Flying* v143 no12 p80 D 2016
Connery, Jason

Pairs for The Course T. Keith chart color *Sports Illustrated* v126 no11 p21 Ap 17-24 2017

THE TEES THAT BIND S. Gutierrez *British Heritage Travel* v38 no2 p34 Mr/Ap 2017

Connery, Jason—Interviews

Jason Connery J. Marksbury and C. Barrett color *Golf Magazine* v59 no4 p44 Ap 2017

Connick, Harry, 1967-

Happy Holidays, Harry! color *AARP: The Magazine* v60 no1A p7 D 2016/Ja 2017

Conniff, Richard

LOVED TO DEATH color graph *Scientific American* v317 no4 p40 O 2017

The New Age of Discovery color *Smithsonian* v47 no10 p21 Mr 2017

Weirdest Wonders on Wings bw color diag *National Geographic* v232 no5 p60 N 2017

CONNIFF, RUTH

After the Shock *Progressive* p5 D 2016/Ja 2017

Bigger and Better *Progressive* v81 no4 p5 Ap/My 2017

Building the Resistance *Progressive* v81 no3 p5 Mr 2017

Climate Warriors bw *Progressive* v81 no5 p6 Je/Jl 2017

Contempt for Democracy bw *Progressive* v81 no6 p6 Ag/S 2017

THE COURTESY OF THE OPPRESSED color *Progressive* v81 no7 p15 O/N 2017

Don't Worry, Be Happy cartoon *Progressive* v81 no4 p6 Ap/My 2017

Evicted: Poverty and Profit in the American City/Behind the Beautiful Forevers color *Progressive* p60 D 2016/Ja 2017

Impeachment Time *Progressive* v81 no6 p5 Ag/S 2017

It Can Happen Here cartoon *Progressive* v81 no2 p6 F 2017

'I've Never Seen Citizen Engagement of This Type' color *Progressive* v81 no5 p59 Je/Jl 2017

Life on Earth *Progressive* v81 no5 p5 Je/Jl 2017

MEDEA BENJAMIN AND THE POLITICS OF DISRUPTION color *Progressive* p58 D 2016/Ja 2017

A New American Rebellion *Progressive* v81 no10 p5 N 2016

Over the Wall *Progressive* v81 no7 p5 O/N 2017

Populist Revolt cartoon *Progressive* p6 D 2016/Ja 2017

Shattered Illusions in Lancaster, Ohio color *Progressive* v81 no5 p63 Je/Jl 2017

Solidarity and Struggle *Progressive* v81 no2 p5 F 2017

The Will to Resist cartoon *Progressive* v81 no3 p6 Mr 2017

Connolly, Christopher N.

Nerve agents in honey color diag *Science* v357 no6359 p38 O 6 2017

CONNOLLY, DANIEL

Getting It Right bw *Publishers Weekly* v264 no1 p60 Ja 2 2017

Connolly, Jerome

NEW LIFE MEMBERS *Sierra* v101 no4 p60 Jl/Ag 2016

Connolly, Katherine

The 3 Things CEOs Worry About the Most *Harvard Business Review Digital Articles* p2 Mr 16 2015

Connolly, Kelly

AFTER GLOW color *Entertainment Weekly* no1473 p24 Jl 7 2017

THE BEST OF BOOTH'S WORLD color *Entertainment Weekly* no1457/1458 p87 Mr 17 2017

CHECKING IN ON THE X-FILES color *Entertainment Weekly* no1485 p44 O 6 2017

Fuller House *Entertainment Weekly* no1482/1483 p106 S 22 2017

Future Man *Entertainment Weekly* no1482/1483 p106 S 22 2017

Marvel's The Punisher color *Entertainment Weekly* no1482/1483 p106 S 22 2017

Mindhunter color *Entertainment Weekly* no1482/1483 p107 S 22 2017

The Mindy Project *Entertainment Weekly* no1482/1483 p107 S 22 2017

PAIGE OF ALL TRADES color *Entertainment Weekly* no1476 p19 Ag 4 2017

Riviera color *Entertainment Weekly* no1482/1483 p106 S 22 2017

Ryan Hansen Solves Crimes on Television* *Entertainment Weekly* no1482/1483 p109 S 22 2017

SARAH SILVERMAN I Love You, America color *Entertainment Weekly* no1482/1483 p108 S 22 2017

Star Trek Discovery color *Entertainment Weekly* no1482/1483 p104 S 22 2017

StartUp *Entertainment Weekly* no1482/1483 p109 S 22 2017

Stranger Things 2 color *Entertainment Weekly* no1482/1483 p100 S 22 2017

Tin Star *Entertainment Weekly* no1482/1483 p109 S 22 2017

Transparent color *Entertainment Weekly* no1482/1483 p109 S 22 2017

What to Watch color *Entertainment Weekly* no1485 p52 O 6 2017

CONNOLLY, KEVIN

Don't Think *Walrus* v14 no3 p43 Ap 2017

Connolly, Matt

Friends in Need color *Film Comment* v53 no2 p18 Mr/Ap 2017

Labor of Love *Washington Monthly* p1 S/O 2016

Parting Glances color *Film Comment* v53 no1 p64 Ja/F 2017

Connolly, Myles

HOW THE WORLD WILL END P. ALMONTE *America* v215 p32 N 28 2016

Connolly, Sean M., 1965-

CONAGRA'S NEXT ACT J. CROWN color *Chicago* v65 no12 p32 D 2016

Connor, Erin

You're getting sleepy... color *National Wildlife (World Edition)* v55 no6 p50 O/N 2017

Connor, Frances

Aging increases cell-to-cell transcriptional variability upon immune stimulation color diag graph *Science* v355 no6332 p1433 Mr 31 2017

CONNOR, JENESSA

5 WAYS ...TO BUILD ON THE CLASSIC SQUAT cartoon *Muscle & Performance* v9 no1 p66 Ja 2017

5 WAYS ... TO DO A KETTLEBELL SWING color *Muscle & Performance* v9 no5 p66 My 2017

5 WAYS ...TO SURVIVE THE HOLIDAYS cartoon *Muscle & Performance* v8 no12 p66 D 2016

5 WAYS... TO USE THE RINGS color *Muscle & Performance* v9 no4 p66 Ap 2017

BALLS TO THE WALL color *Muscle & Performance* v9 no4 p24 Ap 2017

Connor, Joseph

Big Lie [Cover story] bw *American History* v52 no2 p30 Je 2017

Off Key *American History* v51 no6 p42 F 2017

Connor, Phillip

Muslim refugees to U.S. have decreased in 2017 M. Buckley *Christian Century* v134 no17 p17 Ag 16 2017

CONNOR, SARAH

SMART PEOPLE DO THE Dumbest THINGS! [Cover story] *Reader's Digest* v190 no1134 p62 O 2017

CONNOR, STEVE

The CELL Atlas bw color *MIT Technology Review* v120 no2 p58 Mr/Ap 2017

Connor, Steven

Quantifying culture C. J. Phillips color *Science* v354 no6308 p45 O 7 2016

Connors, Claire

AT LAST, SHE SPEAKS! color *Women's Health* v14 no5 p142 Je 2017

DON'T BELIEVE HER SPORTS BRA [Cover story] color *Women's Health* v14 no4 p61 My 2017

THE GIFT OF GAB [Cover story] color *Women's Health* v14 no2 p115 Mr 2017

Connors, Mark

Trispecific broadly neutralizing HIV antibodies mediate potent SHIV protection in macaques color graph *Science* v357 no6359 p85 O 6 2017

Connors, Mike, 1925-2017

Also In MEMORIAM C. Nashawaty, J. Jensen et al color *Entertainment Weekly* no1453 p39 F 17 2017

Connors, Philip

Crude Awakening *New York Times Book Review* p11 My 28 2017

A World of Wounds color *Commonweal* v143 no20 p22 D 16 2016

Conover, Cheryl A.

Senescent intimal foam cells are deleterious at all stages of atherosclerosis bibl *Science* v354 no6311 p472 O 28 2016

CONOVER, EMILY

Aloof light particles nudged to interact color *Science News* v192 no4 p7 S 16 2017

Antimatter hydrogen passes test diag *Science News* v191 no1 p1

Ja 21 2017

Artificial intelligence bests poker pros color *Science News* v191 no6 p12 Ap 1 2017

Astronomer hustles to find E.T color *Science News* v192 no1 p26 Ag 5 2017

At low temps, bismuth superconducts color *Science News* v190 no13 p14 D 24 2016

Black hole census results in big tally *Science News* v192 no4 p7 S 16 2017

Blue is high-energy color for begonias bw color *Science News* v190 no12 p4 D 10 2016

Charting the dark side of the universe color map *Science News* v192 no3 p32 S 2 2017

Collider data hint at new particle color *Science News* v191 no9 p16 My 13 2017

Compound defies helium's inertness color *Science News* v191 no5 p8 Mr 18 2017

Constant Connections chart color diag *Science News* v190 no10 p24 N 12 2016

CuriosityStream is for science-hungry viewers color *Science News* v191 no12 p27 Je 24 2017

Dark matter searches come up empty color *Science News* v190 no10 p14 N 12 2016

Drama of Einstein's life unfolds in new series color *Science News* v191 no8 p34 Ap 29 2017

Einstein principle passes quantum test *Science News* v191 no10 p8 My 27 2017

Entangled atoms break record *Science News* v191 no8 p8 Ap 29 2017

Fast-freezing hot water spurs debate *Science News* v191 no2 p14 F 4 2017

Faux particle commits physics faux pas *Science News* v191 no13 p14 Jl 8 2017

Gravitational waves offer new view of dynamic cosmos color *Science News* v190 no13 p16 D 24 2016

How lizards are like computer programs color *Science News* v191 no9 p32 My 13 2017

Long-standing gold mystery solved *Science News* v191 no3 p11 F 18 2017

Maxwell's demon's memory tested *Science News* v192 no2 p14 Ag 19 2017

Molecules face the biggest chill color *Science News* v192 no4 p18 S 16 2017

More gravitational waves detected color *Science News* v191 no12 p6 Je 24 2017

Movie celebrates NASA 'computers' bw color *Science News* v191 no1 p28 Ja 21 2017

Muon surplus may reveal new physics *Science News* v190 no11 p15 N 26 2016

Neutrinos caught bouncing off nuclei color *Science News* v192 no3 p7 S 2 2017

Neutron longevity remains elusive *Science News* v191 no4 p13 Mr 4 2017

New claim staked for metallic hydrogen color *Science News* v191 no3 p14 F 18 2017

New data fuel further debate on universe's expansion rate *Science News* v191 no4 p18 Mr 4 2017

New steps toward quantum internet *Science News* v190 no8 p13 O 15 2016

New views snag science Nobels bw *Science News* v192 no7 p6 O 28 2017

Nobels honor the small and exotic cartoon color *Science News* v190 no9 p6 O 29 2016

Philosopher dives into physics of nothingness color *Science News* v190 no11 p28 N 26 2016

Physicists discover 'bubble nucleus' color *Science News* v190 no11 p11 N 26 2016

Physicists make 'time crystal' in lab *Science News* v190 no10 p12 N 12 2016

Potential signs of quantum collapse *Science News* v192 no5 p10 S 30 2017

The Proton Puzzle chart color diag *Science News* v191 no8 p22 Ap 29 2017

Quantum Computers GET REAL chart color diag *Science News* v191 no13 p28 Jl 8 2017

Quantum effect passes space test *Science News* v191 no1 p12 Ja 21 2017

Quantum satellite sets distance record color *Science News* v192 no1 p14 Ag 5 2017

Quantum video chat links Asia, Europe *Science News* v192 no7 p14 O 28 2017

Rarest nucleus reluctant to decay *Science News* v190 no9 p11 O 29 2016

Shock waves rocked baby universe *Science News* v190 no9 p7 O 29 2016

Signs of Majorana fermion detected color *Science News* v192 no2 p8 Ag 19 2017

Singularities may reveal themselves *Science News* v191 no11 p12 Je 10 2017

Soap bubbles show their dark side color *Science News* v191 no1 p32 Ja 21 2017

Superfluid behaves like black holes *Science News* v191 no7 p11 Ap 15 2017

Supersolids made from exotic matter *Science News* v190 no12 p8 D 10 2016

Swirls possible in infant cosmos *Science News* v190 no12 p9 D 10 2016

Traveler in a vacuum might heat up *Science News* v192 no6 p12 O 14 2017

Trio tracks source of gravity waves color *Science News* v192 no7 p8 O 28 2017

Triplet of high-energy neutrinos detected from unknown source *Science News* v191 no6 p16 Ap 1 2017

Visionary wrangles light color *Science News* v192 no6 p23 O 14 2017

Waiting for a Supernova color diag *Science News* v191 no3 p24 F 18 2017

X-ray 'bump' hints at dark matter color *Science News* v191 no4 p8 Mr 4 2017

CONOVER, SARAH

WHEN MY SON BECAME A MONK color *Tricycle: The Buddhist Review* v27 no1 p72 Fall 2017

Conquerors

MASTER OF THE CONQUEST J. D. Lyons *Military History* v33 no6 p30 Mr 2017

Conrad, Edward

The Downside of Romneyism J. WILLICK color *National Review* v68 no20 p42 N 7 2016

CONRAD, JAM E S W., JR.

A Second Act for Risk-Based Chemicals Regulation *Issues in Science & Technology* v33 no1 p77 Fall 2016

Conrad, Kendall—Interviews

ACCESSORIES AND JEWELRY DESIGNER KENDALL CONRAD A. WHITTLE color *Conde Nast Traveler* v52 no7 p28 Ag 2017

Conrad, Lauren

Comfort JOY color *Good Housekeeping* v263 no6 p114 D 2016

Conrad, Lauren—Interviews

Lauren Conrad color *Maclean's* v130 no3 p56 Ap 2017

Conrad, Steve

PASSION FOR FARM AND COUNTRY: VIETNAM WAR VETERAN STEVE CONRAD HAS A DEEP LOVE FOR HIS EIGHTH-GENERATION FARM AND THE COUNTRY HE FOUGHT FOR J. Scott *Successful Farming* v115 no12 p60 O 2017

STEVE CONRAD N. PARSI bw color *Chicago* v66 no2 p30 F 2017

Conroy, Charles P.

READER COMMENTS *America* v216 no6 p7 Mr 20 2017

CONROY, NICOLAS

Lichen Adventure color *Canadian Wildlife* v23 no1 p7 Mr/Ap 2017

Conroy, Pat, 1945-2016

PAT CONROY B. Streisand and T. Jordan color *Entertainment Weekly* no1446/1447 p86 D 2016/Ja 2017

Conscience—Religious aspects—Christianity

Called to Conscience J. F. KEENAN color *America* v216 no1 p14 Ja 2 2017

Shaping a conscience P. W. Marty *Christian Century* v134 no18 p3 Ag 30 2017

Conscientiousness

6 Traits That Predict Ethical Behavior at Work D. De Cremer *Har-*

vard Business Review Digital Articles p2 N 22 2016

Consciousness

See also

Belief & doubt

Personality

Self-consciousness (Awareness)

Embodying the sutra N. Rizopoulos color *Yoga Journal* no296 p51 N 2017

Emergent consciousness decoded J. LaSala *Physics Today* v69 no12 p52 D 2016

THE GIFT OF FEAR D. BRAZIER bw *Tricycle: The Buddhist Review* v27 no1 p52 Fall 2017

IN THE DEAD ZONE I. Verzemnieks color *New York Times Magazine* p82 D 11 2016

No Cause for Alarm P. GULLEY *Indianapolis Monthly* p48 My 2017

STROKE AWARENESS color *New Orleans Magazine* v51 no6 p140 Ap 2017

We're Not Fine, and We Do CARE G. DOYLE MELTON color *O, The Oprah Magazine* p31 Jl 2017

Consecration

The host for most color *U.S. Catholic* v82 no8 p5 Ag 2017

Conselice, Christopher J.

Our trillion-galaxy universe [Cover story] color *Astronomy* v45 no6 p18 Je 2017

Consensus (Social sciences)

See also

Legitimacy of governments

Political stability

Social contract

The Most Innovative Companies Don't Worry About Consensus M. Wessel *Harvard Business Review Digital Articles* p2 O 3 2014

What is the common good? B. Haile *U.S. Catholic* v82 no11 p49 N 2017

Consent decrees

Cops May Get Freer Hand Under Trump M. Rhodan color *Time* v189 no14 p10 Ap 17 2017

Let the Police Police H. M. DONALD *National Review* v69 no9 p28 My 15 2017

Conservation & restoration

See also

Automobile restoration

Conservation of natural resources

Preservation of gardens

Ships—Conservation & restoration

Profiles in Courage J. Mark, H. Jensen et al *Sierra* v102 no4 p4 Jl/Ag 2017

Conservation biology

Conservation Biology: A New Hope? L. E. OGDEN *BioScience* v66 no12 p1088 D 1 2016

Conservation easements

EASEMENTS EXPLAINED J. C. Massey color *Old House Journal* v45 no1 p30 F 2017

Conservation of energy

Large-amplitude transfer motion of hydrated excess protons mapped by ultrafast 2D IR spectroscopy F. Dahms, B. P. Fingerhut et al graph *Science* v357 no6350 p491 Ag 4 2017

Conservation of natural resources

See also

Energy conservation

National parks & reserves

Nature conservation

Recycling (Waste, etc.)

Waste minimization

Water conservation

Wildlife conservation

Burrito on My Plate J. Yacoubou *Vegetarian Journal* v36 no2 p15 2017

The Caribbean's Crown Jewels color *National Geographic* v230 no5 p96 N 2016

Healthy Foods B. Liebman and J. Hurley *Nutrition Action Health Letter* v44 p1 Je 2017 Supplement

Living by the lessons of the planet J. Foley color *Science* v356 no6335 p251 Ap 21 2017

SAVE THE PLANET AT HOME T. A. Christian color *Essence*

v47 no12 p126 Ap 2017

take OM HOME T. Eichenseher color *Yoga Journal* no291 p86 My 2017

Uniting Americans for Wildlife C. O'MARA color *National Wildlife (World Edition)* v55 no1 p6 D/Ja 2016

VEGETARIAN DIETS AND WATER D. Wasserman and C. Stabler *Vegetarian Journal* v36 no2 p4 2017

Conservation of natural resources study & teaching

70 YEARS OF MAGIC AT DEC SUMMER CAMPS C. McLaughlin *New York State Conservationist* v72 no2 p12 O 2017

Conservation of natural resources—Congresses

A Seat at the Conservation Table color *Earth Island Journal* v32 no4 p10 Wint 2017

Conservation organizations

OVERNIGHT FLIGHT P. Bourjaily color *Field & Stream* v122 no5 p30 O 2017

Conservationists

On Patrol L. Bobseine and S. Scherry *New York State Conservationist* v71 no5 p20 Ap 2017

Conservationists—Awards

C.C. Lockwood F. ESKER color *Louisiana Life* v37 no3 p62 Ja/F 2017

Conservationists—United States

THE AUDACITY OF LIZ PUTNAM M. ALLEN and M. FLEMING bw color *Yankee* p86 My/Je 2017

Conservatism

As the Anglo-American right adopts the slogans of the left, it sounds the death knell of the neoliberal economic order it built. But what comes next? P. Mishra *New York Times Magazine* p14 Je 25 2017

Defining Jewish Conservatism G. EPSTEIN and J. STERN *Commentary* v144 no1 p4 Jl/Ag 2017

Gatekeepers and Barbarians G. Carney *Commentary* v142 no2 p1 S 2016

THE HISTORY TEST J. LEPORE cartoon *New Yorker* v93 no6 p66 Mr 27 2017

How to Be a Conservative in the Age of Trump: There can be no conservatism without ideas N. C. Rothman *Commentary* v143 no6 p24 Je 2017

How to Make Conservatism Great Again P. Longman color *Washington Monthly* p3 N/D 2016

The New Old Right M. Funkhouser *Governing* v30 no6 p4 Mr 2017

Those '60s Flashbacks C. MILORD, T. STRAKA et al *Commentary* v142 no4 p10 N 2016

What's the Story? J. EPSTEIN *Weekly Standard* v23 no3 p27 S 25 2017

Conservatism—History

Peter's Choice R. PERLSTEIN cartoon *Mother Jones* v42 no1 p9 Ja/F 2017

Conservatism—Periodicals

To the Editor M. Boyls *Commentary* v142 no2 p1 S 2016

Conservatism—United States

Fragmentation Of the Soul R. MOORE color *National Review* v68 no22 p45 D 5 2016

Principled Populism M. LEE *National Review* v68 no22 p32 D 5 2016

Trump and Conservatism M. INGALL and N. C. Rothman *Commentary* v144 no2 p5 S 2017

Conservative Judaism

Conservative Judaism and Its Discontents A. COOPER and S. GLICK *Commentary* v143 no6 p4 Je 2017

Saving Conservative Judaism: The case for ballasting the tent rather than widening it until it collapses R. Rosenthal Kwall *Commentary* v143 no4 p31 Ap 2017

Conservative Party (Great Britain)

One Tory's Story T. R. BROMUND color *Weekly Standard* v22 no40 p27 Je 26 2017

Conservative Party of Canada (2003-)

AW SHUCKS. ME? LEADER? J. GEDDES color *Maclean's* v130 no7 p32 Ag 2017

Back to Basics A. COYNE color *Walrus* v14 no4 p32 My 2017

CANADA'S OWN TWO TINY TRUMPS S. FESCHUK color *Maclean's* v130 no2 p73 Mr 2017

CONFESSIONS OF A SELF-LOATHING TORY S. GILMO

color *Maclean's* v130 no4 p32 My 2017

HARDEST WORKING S. PROUDFOOT color *Maclean's* v129 no47 p20 N 28 2016

It's not so bad. Really [Cover story] P. WELLS color *Maclean's* p24 Je 2017

Jasper Pride's Tory supporter J. MARKUSOFF color *Maclean's* v130 no8 p15 S 2017

MOST COLLEGIAL S. NEMIS color *Maclean's* v129 no47 p23 N 28 2016

Mr. Wonderful Goes to Ottawa? J. J. McCULLOUGH color *National Review* v69 no3 p25 F 20 2017

OUTSIDE THE OTTAWA BUBBLE S. GILMORE color *Maclean's* p28 Je 2017

THE TORIES ARE STUCK IN THE PAST ON CARBON E. SOLOMON *Maclean's* v129 no42 p10 O 24 2016

The Tories need to go gay S. GILMORE color *Maclean's* v130 no7 p10 Ag 2017

Conservatives

A Billionaire Resistance Targets President Trump from the Right P. Elliott color *Time* v189 no5 p31 F 13 2017

Britain Stumbles Toward Exit Talks With a Reinvigorated Europe D. Stewart color *Time* v189 no24 p7 Je 26 2017

CARTOONS *In These Times* v41 no5 p32 My 2017

A Crying Shame J. BOTTUM color *Weekly Standard* v22 no21 p5 F 6 2017

Here We Go! O. Winfrey color *O, The Oprah Magazine* p17 Mr 2017

Infrastructure Dangers Ahead Y. LEVIN map *Weekly Standard* v22 no18 p18 Ja 16 2017

In the Debate Over Campus Free Speech, Who Are the Real Special Snowflakes? E. S. J. Glaude color *Time* v190 no14 p25 O 9 2017

The last lines of defence J. GEDDES color *Maclean's* v130 no3 p22 Ap 2017

Moscow Cozies Up to the Right A. Altman, E. Dias et al color *Time* v189 no10 p32 Mr 20 2017

REACTIONARIES MUST BE TAKEN SERIOUSLY: A tricky exercise in our political climate—but a necessary one A. SULLIVAN img *New York* v50 no9 p28 My 1 2017

Reclaim Charter Schools M. J. PETRILLI color *National Review* v69 no19 p44 O 16 2017

THE SEEKER J. ROTHMAN cartoon color *New Yorker* v93 no11 p46 My 1 2017

The Strangest of Bedfellows J. V. LAST color *Weekly Standard* v22 no9 p12 N 7 2016

Visions of Entitlement T. Sowell *Hoover Digest: Research & Opinion on Public Policy* no4 p192 Fall 2016

Why I Read The American Conservative R. C. Young color *American Conservative* v15 no6 p2 N/D 2016

Conservatives—Attitudes

The Case For Trump [Cover story] V. D. HANSON il *National Review* v68 no19 p24 O 24 2016

Make Earth Great Again C. Caruso graph *Scientific American* v316 no3 p20 Mr 2017

Praying for an Imperfect President C. C. PECKNOLD color *America* v215 no18 p17 D 5 2016

The Religious Right's Demise I. TUTTLE color *National Review* v68 no20 p20 N 7 2016

Conservatives—Political activity

The Cronyist Threat Y. LEVIN *National Review* v68 no20 p32 N 7 2016

SECRET ADMIRERS K. SANNEH cartoon *New Yorker* v92 no44 p24 Ja 9 2017

Conservatories—Design & construction

CONSERVATORIES color *Old House Journal* v45 no6 p78 S 2017

Conservators (Conservation & restoration)

OLDIES AND GOODIES C. R. JOYNT *Washingtonian Magazine* v52 no3 p26 D 2016

Considine, Austin

JAMES COLEMAN color *Art in America* v105 no4 p110 Ap 2017

LÁSZLÓ MOHOLY-NAGY color *Art in America* v104 no10 p147 N 2016

MARK LECKEY color *Art in America* v105 no5 p123 My 2017

MARTIN CREED *Art in America* v104 no9 p153 O 2016

VERNER BÜTTNER color *Art in America* v105 no3 p132 Mr

2017

Considine, J.D.

Born In An Urban Ruin bw *Downbeat* v84 no2 p81 F 2017

Considine, Kevin P.

Does hell exist? color *U.S. Catholic* v82 no3 p49 Mr 2017

Move with God color *U.S. Catholic* v82 no2 p36 F 2017

What is sin? *U.S. Catholic* v82 no7 p49 Jl 2017

Consolati, G.

Observation of a large-scale anisotropy in the arrival directions of cosmic rays above 8×1018 eV *Science* v357 no6357 p1266 S 22 2017

Console, Cyrus

A MAN OF LIMITED *Harper's Magazine* v333 no1999 p22 D 2016

THE MOODS OF ANIMALS *Harper's Magazine* v334 no2001 p11 F 2017

Consoles (Furniture)

Wrensilva Loft Record Console B. Ankosko color *Sound & Vision* v82 no6 p74 Jl/Ag 2017

Consoles (Furniture)—Evaluation

PALE PINK + CAFÉ AU LAIT color *Martha Stewart Living* no271 p29 Ja/F 2017

sofa table update A. PALANJIAN *Better Homes & Gardens* v95 no1 pN6 Ja 2017

Consolidation & merger of corporations

See also

Railroad mergers

3 Ways M&A Is Different When You're Acquiring a Digital Company A. Leroi *Harvard Business Review Digital Articles* p2 Jl 1l 2017

A 5-Step Process for Reorganizing After a Merger S. Heidari-Robinson, S. Heywood et al *Harvard Business Review Digital Articles* p2 D 21 2016

The Amazon-Whole Foods Deal Means Every Other Retailer's Three-Year Plan Is Obsolete D. K. Rigby *Harvard Business Review Digital Articles* p1 Je 21 2017

BIG FOOD bw *Nation* v305 no11 p39 O 30 2017

Big Merger Review graph *Bloomberg Businessweek* no4496 p46 O 24 2016

Bombardier's Painful Double Whammy F. Tomesco and A. Mayeda *Bloomberg Businessweek* no4540 p23 O 2 2017

The CEO View: Defending a Good Company from Bad Investors S. CLIFFE color *Harvard Business Review* v95 no3 p61 My/Je 2017

A China Moonshot for Chicago's Exchange A. Massa, D. Lawrence et al *Bloomberg Businessweek* no4514 p40 Mr 13 2017

The Deal That Made an Industry Shudder B. Kowitt color diag *Fortune* v176 no1 p7 Jl 1 2017

Drink Local, Buy Global J. Kell color map *Fortune* v176 no1 p13 Jl 1 2017

How Disney Found Its Way Back to Creative Success V. Govindarajan *Harvard Business Review Digital Articles* p2 Je 3 2016

Is Intel's Buying Binge a Good Thing? K. KRISTOF *Kiplinger's Personal Finance* v71 no6 p54 Je 2017

Movers K. Stock color *Bloomberg Businessweek* no4525 p11 Je 5 2017

The New Barbarian at The Cate M. Campbell, J. Browning et al color graph *Bloomberg Businessweek* no4497 p39 O 31 2016

NO MORE MR. NICE GUY S. Kolhatkar cartoon *New Yorker* v93 no16 p44 Je 5 2017

The Pfizer-Allergan Deal Shouldn't Be Just About Tax Inversion B. Gomes-Casseres *Harvard Business Review Digital Articles* p2 N 24 2015

PRESTIGIOUS FIRMS MAKE RISKIER ACQUISITIONS *Harvard Business Review* v95 no4 p26 Jl/Ag 2017

The Problem of Bolt-On Acquisitions in a Digital World J. Kolko *Harvard Business Review Digital Articles* p2 Jl 5 2016

Research: Innovation Suffers When Drug Companies Merge J. Haucap and J. Stiebale *Harvard Business Review Digital Articles* p2 Ag 3 2016

Research: When CEOs Don't Win Awards, They Make More Acquisitions Wei Shi, Yan Anthea Zhang et al *Harvard Business Review Digital Articles* p2 Mr 27 2017

So Many M&A Deals Fail Because Companies Overlook This Simple Strategy A. Lewis and D. McKone *Harvard Business Review Digital Articles* p2 My 10 2016

Trade Publishers Focused on Strategic Deals In 2016 J. Milliot chart *Publishers Weekly* v264 no1 p7 Ja 2 2017

Using M&A to Increase Your Capacity for Growth M. Reeves, J. Harnoss et al *Harvard Business Review Digital Articles* p2 Jl 13 2016

What Does Whole Foods Get from Amazon? Alexa, for Starters B. Gomes-Casseres *Harvard Business Review Digital Articles* p2 Je 19 2017

What the Nonprofit Sector Needs to Reach Its Full Potential D. Pallotta *Harvard Business Review Digital Articles* p2 My 13 2016

Why Sprint and Radio Shack Are Shacking Up D. Dahlhoff *Harvard Business Review Digital Articles* p2 F 10 2015

Why Strong Customer Relationships Trump Powerful Brands C. Binder and D. M. Hanssens *Harvard Business Review Digital Articles* p2 Ap 14 2015

Consolidation & merger of corporations—China

The Conglomerate That Troubles China M. Campbell, Dong Lyu et al *Bloomberg Businessweek* no4533 p12 Ag 7 2017

Consolidation & merger of corporations—Economic aspects

Mergers May Be Profitable, but Are They Good for the Economy? B. A. Blonigen and J. R. Pierce *Harvard Business Review Digital Articles* p2 N 15 2016

STOCKS THAT ARE BETTER-OFF SINGLE L. Shen color *Fortune* v175 no4 p48 Mr 15 2017

Consolidation & merger of corporations—Research

SURVIVING M&A M. L. MARKS, P. MIRVIS et al color il *Harvard Business Review* v95 no2 p145 Mr/Ap 2017

Consolidation & merger of corporations—Social aspects

A Successful M&A Considers the Human Element R. Ashkenas *Harvard Business Review Digital Articles* p2 N 18 2014

Consolidation & merger of corporations—United States

SURVIVING M&A M. L. MARKS, P. MIRVIS et al color il *Harvard Business Review* v95 no2 p145 Mr/Ap 2017

What We Can Learn from Merger Deals That Never Happened B. Gomes-Casseres *Harvard Business Review Digital Articles* p2 Je 21 2016

Consolidation & merger of corporations—United States—Government policy

China Is Missing the Chips Rush I. King *Bloomberg Businessweek* no4529 p22 Jl 3 2017

Consortia

Consortial Leadership Toward Large-Scale Change A. Kezar *Change* v48 no6 p50 N/D 2016

Conspiracies—History—16th century

MURDER AT THE VATICAN: An unsolved Renaissance mystery casts light on the dark world of extortion, revenge and power politics at the heart of the Catholic Church C. Fletcher *History Today* v67 no10 p56 O 2017

Conspiracy

BRICKBATS C. Oliver bw color *Reason* v49 no5 p80 O 2017

CATCHING A CONSPIRACY R. DAVIS and C. PAVITT color *Scientific American* v317 no2 p5 Ag 2017

CLIMB ABOARD, YE WHO SEEK THE TRUTH! B. DICKEY color *Popular Mechanics* p84 S 2017

JFK CONSPIRACY COVERUP? *Saturday Evening Post* v289 no1 p100 Ja/F 2017

THE REAL AND THE FAKE: DC has always had conspiracy theories. Now they have actual addresses B. Freed *Washingtonian Magazine* v52 no12 p15 S 2017

snapshot P. KARMAN *In These Times* v41 no3 p7 Mr 2017

Conspiracy theories

THE '67 GREATEST, CRAZIEST, AND MOST PERSISTENT POP-CULTURE CONSPIRACY THEORIES OF ALL TIME A. K. RAYMOND img *New York* v49 no23 p72 N 14 2016

All the President's Phantoms J. WALKER color *New Republic* v248 no3 p14 Mr 2017

CLIMB ABOARD, YE WHO SEEK THE TRUTH! B. DICKEY color *Popular Mechanics* v193 no7 p84 S 2016

CONSPIRACY THEORIST IN CHIEF T. MURPHY cartoon *Mother Jones* v41 no6 p5 N/D 2016

FIRST AS TRAGEDY D. Remnick cartoon *New Yorker* v93 no5 p29 Mr 20 2017

THE NEW PARANOIA C. DICKEY color *New Republic* v248 no7 p22 Jl 2017

Constable, John, 1776-1837—Exhibitions

All along the watchtowers at Yale color *Magazine Antiques* v184 no2 p30 Mr/Ap 2017

Constand, Andrea

Cosby's Accusers On the Mistrial: "We wanted to stand witness." N. Malone img *New York* v50 no13 p10 Je 26 2017

Constant, Randy

10 SUCCESSFUL FARMERS: RANDY CONSTANT J. Henke *Successful Farming* v115 no8 p28 Je/Jl 2017

Constantakes, Peter

BREAKING BARRIERS *New York State Conservationist* v71 no3 p6 D 2016

Celebrating ADIRONDACK PARK'S 125th ANNIVERSARY *New York State Conservationist* v71 no6 p2 Je 2017

NEW LIFE FOR DEAD BATTERIES *New York State Conservationist* v71 no3 p26 D 2016

RESTORING LEAN-TOS, VOLUNTEERS WORK TO SAVE THESE HISTORIC STRUCTURES *New York State Conservationist* v72 no1 p34 Ag 2017

CONSTANTIN, LUCIAN

Hacker shows how easy it is to take over a city's public Wi-Fi network color *PCWorld* v35 no1 p51 Ja 2017

LastPass password manager fixes serious password leak vulnerabilities color *PCWorld* v35 no5 p59 My 2017

New macOS ransomware spotted color *Macworld - Digital Edition* p8 Ap 2017

Recent WordPress vulnerability used to deface 1.5 million pages color *PCWorld* p47 Mr 2017

A USB device is all it takes to steal credentials from locked PCs color *PCWorld* p52 O 2016

Yahoo's billion account breach: 5 things you should do to stay safe color *PCWorld* v35 no1 p41 Ja 2017

Constantine, David

His Past Discretions S. D'ERASMO *New York Times Book Review* p12 N 13 2016

Constantine, Dow

PUBLIC OFFICIALS OF THE YEAR A. Greenblatt, M. Maciag et al *Governing* v30 no3 p26 D 2016

Constantinides, Avghi

5 Top Homeopathic Cold Remedies color *Amazing Wellness* v9 no1 p72 Wint 2017

EASE ECZEMA color *Amazing Wellness* v8 no6 p38 Early Winter2016

Homeopathic Mood Boosters color *Better Nutrition* v78 no12 p34 D 2016

Post-Traumatic Stress color *Better Nutrition* v79 no3 p32 Mr 2017

TO VACCINATE OR NOT? color *Amazing Wellness* p36 Fall 2017

Constellations

See also

Andromeda (Constellation)

Capricornus (Constellation)

Cassiopeia (Constellation)

Leo (Constellation)

Pisces (Constellation)

Pleiades

Ursa Minor

The Crow and the Cup J. RAO color *Natural History* v125 no4 p44 Ap 2017

The Dark Wolf of Summer R. P. Wilds *Sky & Telescope* v133 no6 p64 Je 2017

Doodles in the Sky S. French *Sky & Telescope* v133 no6 p54 Je 2017

A Galaxy in the Giraffe M. Wedel *Sky & Telescope* v132 no6 p42 D 2016

Gemini City Sights K. Hewitt-White *Sky & Telescope* v133 no2 p58 F 2017

Great Ursa Major galaxies P. HARRINGTON color *Astronomy* v45 no6 p64 Je 2017

The Inconstant Star: The joys of observing variable stars are predictably wonderful S. French *Sky & Telescope* v134 no4 p54 O 2017

THE IRISH CONSTELLATION C. TRILLIN color *New Yorker* v93 no11 p27 My 1 2017

The Kneeler J. RAO color *Natural History* v125 no6 p45 Je 2017

LHS 1140b: A Super-Earth in the Habitable Zone D. Dickinson color *Sky & Telescope* v134 no2 p12 Ag 2017

Harvard Business Review Digital Articles p2 Jl 12 2017

How Customers Get Hooked on Products N. Eyal *Harvard Business Review Digital Articles* p2 N 12 2014

Keeping Customers Continuously Infatuated G. G. Burt *Harvard Business Review Digital Articles* p2 Ag 9 2016

Know the Job Your Product Was Hired for (with Help from Customer Selfies) C. M. Christensen and B. Moesta *Harvard Business Review Digital Articles* p2 Je 6 2016

OLD HABITS DIE HARD, BUT THEY DO DIE [Cover story] R. G. MCGRATH color *Harvard Business Review* v95 no1 p54 Ja/F 2017

The Power of Designing Products for Customers You Don't Have Yet K. Dillon *Harvard Business Review Digital Articles* p2 Ag 31 2016

Research: Consumers Prefer Products Created by Mistake T. Reich, D. Kupor et al *Harvard Business Review Digital Articles* p2 S 20 2017

Research: Customers Notice When Products Shrink More Than When They Get Bigger P. Chandon color *Harvard Business Review Digital Articles* p2 Mr 7 2017

Research: Missing Product Information Doesn't Bother Consumers as Much as It Should S. Sah and D. Read *Harvard Business Review Digital Articles* p2 S 28 2017

Store Brands Aren't Just about Price E. Yoon *Harvard Business Review Digital Articles* p2 Ap 15 2015

A Study of 46,000 Shoppers Shows That Omnichannel Retailing Works E. Sopadjieva, U. M. Dholakia et al color *Harvard Business Review Digital Articles* p2 Ja 3 2017

THINGS TO CONSIDER WHEN BUYING SOMETHING NEW... *New York State Conservationist* v71 no4 p4 F 2017

Wait in Line? I Can't Even J. STEIN *Los Angeles Magazine* p60 D 2016

What Really Makes Customers Buy a Product H. N. Wilson, E. K. Macdonald et al *Harvard Business Review Digital Articles* p2 N 9 2015

When a Simple Rule of Thumb Beats a Fancy Algorithm J. Fox *Harvard Business Review Digital Articles* p2 O 2 2014

When Customers Will (Willingly) Pay More for Less G. Morse *Harvard Business Review Digital Articles* p2 F 24 2015

Why We Are So Careless with the Things We Own S. Bellezza and F. Gino *Harvard Business Review Digital Articles* p2 D 2 2016

Your In-Store Customers Want More Privacy C. Esmark *Harvard Business Review Digital Articles* p2 D 28 2016

Consumer behavior—Moral & ethical aspects

Ethical Consumerism Isn't Dead, It Just Needs Better Marketing J. Irwin *Harvard Business Review Digital Articles* p2 Ja 12 2015

Consumer behavior—United States

Recessions Push People to Buy Cheap Things, Which Just Makes Everything Worse S. Rebelo *Harvard Business Review Digital Articles* p2 My 12 2017

Consumer complaints

How Much Does Customer Social Media Angst Really Matter? M. Aarons-Mele *Harvard Business Review Digital Articles* p2 Ap 3 2015

ONLINE MERCHANTS THAT DON'T DELIVER B. PEDERSEN color *Kiplinger's Personal Finance* v71 no11 p11 N 2017

Tweet Your Way to Better Service D. Bortz chart *Money* v46 no2 p32 Mr 2017

Consumer confidence

Movers K. Stock color graph *Bloomberg Businessweek* no4513 p19 Mr 6 2017

Consumer credit

See also

Credit cards

All Low- and Moderate-Income Areas Are Not Created Equal [Cover story] M. Eggleston *Bridges (Federal Reserve Bank of St. Louis)* p1 Summ 2016

Online Purchases Decrease After Fraud *USA Today Magazine* v145 no2859 p6 D 2016

Research: The Best Strategy for Paying Off Credit Card Debt R. Trudel *Harvard Business Review Digital Articles* p2 D 27 2016

Consumer credit—Research

Learn From the Credit-Score Elite L. GERSTNER chart *Kiplinger's Personal Finance* v71 no3 p43 Mr 2017

Consumer education

See also

Investment education

Research: Missing Product Information Doesn't Bother Consumers as Much as It Should S. Sah and D. Read *Harvard Business Review Digital Articles* p2 S 28 2017

When Hidden Algorithms Lead to Higher Prices M. L. Tellado *Consumer Reports* v82 no7 p4 Jl 2017

Consumer fraud

See also

Credit card fraud

Consumer goods

Earplugs R. Berendsohn color *Popular Mechanics* p35 S 2017

Ethylene J. Kaskey and L. Doan color *Bloomberg Businessweek* no4537 p21 S 11 2017

How Target Is Taking Sustainable Products Mainstream A. Winston *Harvard Business Review Digital Articles* p2 Ag 4 2015

Our Personal Best List J. Bodnar *Kiplinger's Personal Finance* v70 no12 p8 D 2016

PETRIFIED FOREST L. H. Lapham *Lapham's Quarterly* v10 no3 p12 Summ 2017

Why New Consumer Brands Must Scale Faster E. Yoon and S. Hughes *Harvard Business Review Digital Articles* p2 Jl 8 2016

Consumer goods—Maintenance & repair

CENTURY marks *Christian Century* v134 no7 p8 Mr 29 2017

Consumer goods—Sales & prices

THE PROBLEM WITH PRODUCT PROLIFERATION: INTERACTION M. MOCKER and J. W. ROSS color graph *Harvard Business Review* v95 no5 p16 S/O 2017

Consumer package goods

COME ON AND SHINE E. Griffith color *Fortune* v174 no6 p29 N 1 2016

Consumer price indexes

The 2018 revision of the Consumer Price Index geographic sample S. P. Paben, W. H. Johnson et al bibl chart color diag map *Monthly Labor Review* p1 O 2016

Going Cold Turkey J. Chatzky color *AARP: The Magazine* v59 no5A p30 Ag/S 2016

INTERNATIONAL STATISTICS *Economic Indicators* p35 Mr 2017

Consumer protection

See also

Product recall

Quality of products

Building a Better World, Together color *Consumer Reports* v82 no1 p8 Ja 2017

Consumer Warning Labels Aren't Working L. A. Robinson, W. K. Viscusi et al *Harvard Business Review Digital Articles* p2 N 30 2016

Data Monopolists Like Google Are Threatening the Economy K. Radinsky *Harvard Business Review Digital Articles* p2 Mr 2 2015

Empowering Consumers in a Digital World color *Consumer Reports* v82 no9 p5 S 2017

Fighting for Fairness on Every Front M. L. Tellado *Consumer Reports* v82 no8 p4 Ag 2017

Consumer protection—United States—Government policy

A Victory for Free Speech il *Consumer Reports* v82 no3 p8 Mr 2017

Consumer psychology

DON'T LAUNCH YOUR PRODUCT IN 2020 graph img *Harvard Business Review* v95 no3 p30 My/Je 2017

WHAT'S YOUR BEST INNOVATION BET? BY MAPPING A TECHNOLOGY'S PAST, YOU CAN PREDICT WHAT FUTURE CUSTOMERS WILL WANT M. SCHILLING bw chart color graph img *Harvard Business Review* v95 no4 p86 Jl/Ag 2017

Consumer purchasing services

THERE'S MORE TO THE MALL THAN SHOPPING K. PITSKER color *Kiplinger's Personal Finance* v70 no12 p13 D 2016

Consumer Reports (Periodical)

Consumer Reports' Surface Laptop flap is based on data from past Surface models M. HACHMAN color *PCWorld* v35 no9 p7 S 2017

Consumer research

See also

Psychographics

Building a Better World, Together color *Consumer Reports* v8

al bibl graph *Science* v354 no6310 p336 O 21 2016

Predicting the basis of convergent evolution J. T. Bridgham bibl color *Science* v354 no6310 p289 O 21 2016

Conversation

See also

Interviewing

3 Ways to Stay Calm When Conversations Get Intense A. J. Su *Harvard Business Review Digital Articles* p2 Je 9 2016

7 Things to Say When a Conversation Turns Negative K. K. Reardon *Harvard Business Review Digital Articles* p2 My 11 2016

8 Ways to Get a Difficult Conversation Back on Track M. Valcour *Harvard Business Review Digital Articles* p2 My 22 2017

ACADEMIC CONVERSATIONS S. Hamerla color *Literacy Today (2411-7862)* v34 no3 p30 N/D 2016

Bloody Thursday D. MENAKER color *Esquire* v166 no4 p13 N 2016

Create a Conversation, Not a Presentation J. Coleman *Harvard Business Review Digital Articles* p2 Jl 29 2015

A Game Plan for That Conversation You've Been Putting Off L. Davey *Harvard Business Review Digital Articles* p2 Ap 12 2017

GUEST LIST *Washingtonian Magazine* v52 no9 p26 Je 2017

Happiness hacks that really work color *Health* v31 no9 p16 N 2017

Having the Here's-What-I Want Conversation With Your Boss R. Shambaugh *Harvard Business Review Digital Articles* p2 N 20 2015

How to conduct difficult conversations N. Gold *People Management* p44 Ag 2017

How to Handle Difficult Conversations at Work R. Knight *Harvard Business Review Digital Articles* p2 Ja 9 2015

How to Have Difficult Conversations When You Don't Like Conflict J. Garfinkle *Harvard Business Review Digital Articles* p2 My 24 2017

How to Know If You Talk Too Much M. Goulston *Harvard Business Review Digital Articles* p2 Je 3 2015

How to Tell If Someone Wants to Stop Talking to You D. Clark *Harvard Business Review Digital Articles* p2 O 19 2015

Let's talk A. Scobey color *U.S. Catholic* v82 no3 p43 Mr 2017

Look Who's Talking S. Rushin color *Sports Illustrated* v126 no12 p60 My 1 2017

Meetings: When to Present and When to Converse N. Duarte *Harvard Business Review Digital Articles* p2 Mr 24 2015

oops *Parents* v92 no5 p62 My 2017

The Right Way to End a Meeting P. Axtell *Harvard Business Review Digital Articles* p2 Mr 11 2015

she sheds color *Parents* v92 no7 p97 Jl 2017

Talking About the Weather D. Bry *New York Times Magazine* p18 My 14 2017

You Just Had a Difficult Conversation at Work. Here's What to Do Next D. Bernardo *Harvard Business Review Digital Articles* p2 My 29 2017

Conversation—Management

The Work Conversations We Dread the Most, According to Research K. Jones *Harvard Business Review Digital Articles* p2 Ap 11 2016

Conversion (Religion)

EVER ANCIENT, EVER NEW E. Bruenig color *America* v217 no3 p18 Ag 7 2017

Facing discrimination, Dalit caste members are converting to Buddhism B. Dore color *Christian Century* v133 no24 p19 N 23 2016

Converters (Electronics)

Scott Sortor From Sebring, Florida, Asks… Does a TH350 Need a Kickdown Cable? M. Davis color diag *Hot Rod* v70 no4 p96 Ap 2017

Convertible automobiles

1989 Dodge Dakota Sport Convertible color *Popular Mechanics* p42 Jl 2017

Automotive Archaeology This Olds 442 Is Waiting to be Saved R. Brutt color *Hot Rod* v70 no1 p26 Ja 2017

THE MERCEDES-BENZ G-WAGEN B. Berk color *Car & Driver* v63 no2 p24 Ag 2017

Shortened 1957 Bel-Air Convertible R. Brutt color *Hot Rod* v70 no4 p18 Ap 2017

Convertible bonds

A Convertible Fund for the Risk-Averse R. ERMEY chart *Kip-*

linger's Personal Finance v71 no7 p61 Jl 2017

Convertible securities

See also

Convertible bonds

A Convertible Fund for the Risk-Averse R. ERMEY chart *Kiplinger's Personal Finance* v71 no7 p61 Jl 2017

Conviction (TV program)

Conviction D. Franich color *Entertainment Weekly* no1434 p48 O 7 2016

Convulsions—Case studies

The Test of a Lifetime A. Park color *Time* v190 no13 p52 O 2 2017

Conway, David J.

Resistance to malaria through structural variation of red blood cell invasion receptors diag *Science* v356 no6343 p1139 Je 16 2017

Conway, Kellyanne, 1967-

Comments img *New York* v50 no7 p8 Ap 3 2017

KELLY ANNE CONWAY IS A STAR O. NUZZI img *New York* v50 no6 p26 Mr 20 2017

KELLYANNE'S ALTERNATIVE UNIVERSE M. BALL color *Atlantic* v319 no3 p44 Ap 2017

The Long View R. LONG il *National Review* v69 no17 p34 S 11 2017

The Long View R. LONG il *National Review* v69 no6 p38 Ap 3 2017

MELANIA'S DIARY 1/21/2017 P. RUDNICK cartoon *New Yorker* v92 no48 p27 F 6 2017

OFF THE MARKET! The nuts and bolts of some of Washington's most expensive residential transactions *Washingtonian Magazine* v52 no11 p157 Ag 2017

"The Kellyanne Conway Show" R. LONG il *National Review* v69 no4 p34 Mr 6 2017

Conway, Stuart J.

Pyocyanin degradation by a tautomerizing demethylase inhibits Pseudomonas aeruginosa biofilms bibl diag graph *Science* v355 no6321 p1 Ja 13 2017

Conyers, Howard

CULINARY HERITAGE J. Benson color *Louisiana Life* v37 no6 p26 Jl/Ag 2017

Coogan, Steve

Steve Coogan If you were a critic, what would get four stars? D. WALTERS color *Bon Appetit* p154 S 2017

Coogan, Tim Pat

1916: 100 Years of Irish Independence, from the Easter Rising to the Present *Publishers Weekly* v263 no39 p79 S 26 2016

Coogler, Ryan, 1986-

BLACK PANTHER A. Breznican color *Entertainment Weekly* p20 Jl 24 2017

Cook, Andy

Strong unions are fighting against technology *People Management* p15 F 2017

Cook, Andy—Interviews

Strong unions are fighting against technology A. Cook *People Management* p15 F 2017

Cook, Bernie

FULL FRAME 2017: Twentieth Anniversary Retrospective *Film Quarterly* v71 no1 p91 Fall 2017

COOK, BILL

NORTHERN EXPOSURE color map *Sail* v48 no11 p40 N 2017

Cook, Blanche Wiesen

Eleanor in War and Love S. Dunn bw *New York Review of Books* v63 no19 p49 D 8 2016

First Lady to the World E. SHOWALTER *New York Times Book Review* p12 N 20 2016

Grande Dame M. K. BERAN bw color *National Review* v68 no21 p39 N 21 2016

Cook, Brian

DIGITAL COLLABORATORS color *Literacy Today (2411-7862)* v34 no4 p28 Ja/F 2017

Cook, Byron

The BEST & WORST LEGISLATORS 2017 R. G. RATCLIFFE *Texas Monthly* v45 no7 p82 Jl 2017

Cook, C. Jeffrey

None of the Above *Commentary* v141 no10 p1 D 2016

None of the Above *Commentary* v142 no5 p1 D 2016

Cook, Christopher D.

How Trump Can Unite the Left *Progressive* v81 no2 p8 F 2017

Trumping Labor cartoon *Progressive* v81 no3 p26 Mr 2017

Cook, Colin

Even a Shark Attack Can't Stop This Surfer J. RENDON color *Popular Science* v288 no6 p90 N/D 2016

COOK, DAVID

This Gravedigger Saves Lives color *Reader's Digest* v189 no1130 p10 My 2017

Cook, Elsa

CHARACTER *Christian Century* v134 no17 p22 Ag 16 2017

COOK, GARETH

JOSEPHINE DEL DEO *New York Times Magazine* p44 D 25 2016

'Old Is the New New' *New York Times Book Review* p12 N 27 2016

Cook, Gretchen

CHARACTER RECOGNITION: Private preschools are judging the "character" of applicants as well as their aptitude-even when children are as young as three *Washingtonian Magazine* v53 no1 p129 O 2017

HOW TO KEEP THE DOG-PARK PEACE *Washingtonian Magazine* v52 no9 p195 Je 2017

ROVER, COME HOME! *Washingtonian Magazine* v52 no5 p139 F 2017

Cook, James, 1728-1779—Medals

Tokens of friendship, tools of diplomacy: Presentation medals in the Age of Exploration R. M. Peck bw color *Magazine Antiques* v184 no5 p64 S/O 2017

Cook, Jane Hampton

THE BIG QUESTION cartoon *Atlantic* v318 no4 p112 N 2016

COOK, JENNY

Are These Remedies Safe? [Cover story] color *Prevention* v69 no6 p74 Je 2017

Cook, John

BEYOND ENDURANCE P. Garrison color *Flying* v144 no2 p80 F 2017

COOK, JOSEPH A.

Transformational Principles for NEON Sampling of Mammalian Parasites and Pathogens: A Response to Springer and Colleagues *BioScience* v66 no11 p917 N 1 2016

Cook, Kevin

The First Shock Jock *Smithsonian* v48 no3 p16 Je 2017

The Pyne Tree *Smithsonian* v48 no3 p18 Je 2017

Cook, Nicola J.

A supramolecular assembly mediates lentiviral DNA integration bibl color *Science* v355 no6320 p1 Ja 6 2017

Cook, Orbie

The Superfan R. Bragg color *Southern Living* v52 no9 p150 S 2017

Cook, Peter

A\J at 45 cartoon *Alternatives Journal (AJ) - Canada's Environmental Voice* v42 no2 p12 2016

Cook, Philip J.

Deadly force bibl color *Science* v355 no6327 p803 F 24 2017

Cook, Ramsay

In memoriam bw color *Maclean's* v129 no48/49 p82 D 5 2016

Cook, Robert

Commanders-in-chief *History Today* v67 no1 p62 Ja 2017

Cook, Roberta

The California Leafy Greens Industry Provides an Example of an Established Food Safety System *Amber Waves: The Economics of Food, Farming, Natural Resources, & Rural America* p43 Je 2017

Cook, Scott—Interviews

A CONVERSATION WITH INTUIT CHAIRMAN AND CO-FOUNDER SCOTT COOK [Cover story] D. CHAMPION color *Harvard Business Review* v95 no1 p62 Ja/F 2017

Cook, Stephen P.

The Bright One That Got Away: Fifty years ago this month, the author, then 16, came a hair's breadth from making a huge discovery *Sky & Telescope* v134 no1 p84 Jl 2017

Cook, Steven

O Brotherhood, Where Art Thou? *Foreign Affairs* v96 no2 p164 Mr/Ap 2017

Cook, Steven A.

Egypt's Nightmare bw *Foreign Affairs* v95 no6 p110 N/D 2016

Cook, Terri

Uncharted Territory color *Scientific American* v317 no1 p23 Jl

2017

Cook, Timothy D., 1960-

11 TIM COOK A. Lashinsky color *Fortune* v174 no7 p86 D 1 2016

7 highlights of Tim Cook's Q3 2017 financial call with analysts J. SNELL color *Macworld - Digital Edition* v34 no10 p7 O 2017

The Mother of All Early Days S. Ovide cartoon *Bloomberg Businessweek* no4514 p35 Mr 13 2017

TECH TRENDS CHANGING OUR WORLD S. Lynn, R. Leslie et al color *Black Enterprise* v47 no2 p46 S 2016

Tim Cook: Augmented reality will be an essential part of your daily life, like the iPhone O. RAYMUNDO color *Macworld - Digital Edition* p61 D 2016

Tim Cook reaffirms Apple's commitment to the Mac, in response to growing doubt C. McGARRY color *Macworld - Digital Edition* p7 F 2017

Titans color *Time* v189 no16/17 p94 My 1-8 2017

Why Tim Cook's Coming Out Matters for Apple, and Business D. Clark *Harvard Business Review Digital Articles* p2 O 30 2014

Cook, Timothy D., 1960—Interviews

APPLE FINDS ITS CORE A. Lashinsky color *Fortune* v176 no4 p112 S 15 2017

Tim Cook CEO, Apple: "I am so excited about it, I just want to yell out and scream" [Cover story] M. Murphy color *Bloomberg Businessweek* no4527 p52 Je 19 2017

Cook, Timothy D., 1960—Political & social views

Movers K. Stock bw cartoon color *Bloomberg Businessweek* no4497 p15 O 31 2016

Cookbooks

4 joyful and delicious home ideas color *Redbook* p148 D 2016

Comfort Food T. RAO *New York Times Book Review* p13 Jl 2 2017

The Complete Mediterranean Cookbook: 500 Vibrant, Kitchen-Tested Recipes for Living and Eating Well Every Day *Publishers Weekly* v263 no45 p55 N 7 2016

DONNA DAVIES J. BERG color *Chicago* v65 no11 p46 N 2016

A Few Good Deeds S. Evans color *Southern Living* v52 no10 p12 O 2017

HMH Looks for More in Culinary, Lifestyle C. Swanson color *Publishers Weekly* v264 no16 p6 Ap 17 2017

How We Love To Look P. KUH *Los Angeles Magazine* v61 no11 p64 N 2016

I Love My Library I. GARTEN color *House Beautiful* v159 no3 p124 Ap 2017

THE KITCHEN COOKBOOK color *Better Homes & Gardens* v95 no6 p146 Je 2017

Kitchen-Counter Couture color *Good Housekeeping* v264 no5 p57 My 2017

The Moosewood Restaurant Table *Publishers Weekly* v264 no32 p66 Ag 7 2017

TIMELESS M. True color *Sunset* v238 no2 p82 F 2017

THE ULTIMATE SOUTHERN THANKSGIVING COOKBOOK 2016 color *Southern Living* v51 no11 p95 N 2016

What is American food? J. BAINBRIDGE *Atlanta* v57 no6 p56 O 2017

Cookbooks—Evaluation

Harvesting the Bookshelf L. Feldman color *Time* v190 no12 p62 S 25 2017

Cookbooks—History

Back-to-Basics FRENCH BREAD W. Rubel *Mother Earth News* no279 p36 D/Ja 2017

Cook-Deegan, R.

Fostering reproducibility in industry-academia research color *Science* v357 no6353 p759 Ag 25 2017

Cooke, Bryce

Growing Organic Demand Provides High-Value Opportunities for Many Types of Producers *Amber Waves: The Economics of Food, Farming, Natural Resources, & Rural America* p51 F 2017

U.S. Agricultural Trade in 2016: Major Commodities and Trends *Amber Waves: The Economics of Food, Farming, Natural Resources, & Rural America* p1 My 2017

COOKE, CHARLES C. W.

France Votes *National Review* v69 no7 p30 Ap 17 2017

Hillary's Second Amendment Nonsense color *National Review* v68 no21 p20 N 21 2016

Magnificent Thrill Machines color *National Review* v69 no15 p24

Ag 14 2017

Points to Ponder *Reader's Digest* v189 no1128 p33 Mr 2017

Cooke, Sam, 1931-1964

Sam Cooke Had a Hammer F. Goodman bw color *American History* v52 no2 p56 Je 2017

Cooke, Sandra

DEVELOP A STRONG GALLOPING POSITION color *Practical Horseman* v45 no5 p38 My 2017

Cooke, Stefan

Barbara Newhall Follett: A Life in Letters color *Publishers Weekly* v263 no43 p50d O 24 2016

COOKE, STEVEN J.

Conserving Megafauna or Sacrificing Biodiversity? *BioScience* v67 no3 p193 Mr 2017

Envisioning the Future of Aquatic Animal Tracking: Technology, Science, and Application *BioScience* v67 no10 p884 O 2017

Cooke, Tim

CHIP SERVICE color *Golf Magazine* v59 no11 p44 N 2017

FINISH IN STYLE color *Golf Magazine* v59 no4 p62 Ap 2017

PUZZLED? color *Golf Magazine* v59 no9 p47 S 2017

STRETCH AWAY A SLICE color *Golf Magazine* v59 no7 p50 Jl 2017

THE THICK BLUE LINE color *Golf Magazine* v59 no6 p56 Je 2017

Cooke Aquaculture Inc.

Compliments for fishing C. MCINTYRE color *Maclean's* v130 no10 p48 N 2017

Cookie cutters

table talk D. SCHWARTZ color *Better Homes & Gardens* v95 no5 p14 My 2017

Cookie cutters—Evaluation

YOUR PANTRY color *Good Housekeeping* v263 no6 p153 D 2016

Cookie Monster (Fictitious character)

COOKIE MONSTER ON THE DOLE H. ALFORD cartoon *New Yorker* v93 no9 p29 Ap 17 2017

Cookies

See also

Bars (Desserts)

Biscotti

Chocolate chip cookies

All Tied Up C. SAFFITZ color *Bon Appetit* v61 no12 p85 D 2016 /Jan2017

ASK SUSAN S. WESTMORELAND color *Good Housekeeping* v264 no5 p112 My 2017

BHG GIFT GUIDE *Better Homes & Gardens* v94 no12 p10 D 2016

Candy Cottontail Cookies color *Good Housekeeping* v264 no4 p137 Ap 2017

CHRISTMAS COOKIES WITH A TWIST L. J. ANDREWS *South Dakota Magazine* v32 no4 p38 N/D 2016

Cooking with Coconut Oil J. Bessinger color *Amazing Wellness* v9 no2 p80 Spr 2017

CRIMSON CUTOUTS color *Better Homes & Gardens* v95 no2 p74 F 2016

Delicious Dunkers color *Good Housekeeping* v265 no5 p36 N 2017

Every Bite You Take [Cover story] H. BROWN color *Prevention* v68 no12 p30 D 2016

Flowerpot Cupcakes color *Good Housekeeping* v264 no5 p139 My 2017

Funny FiLL-IN C. PATEK *National Geographic Kids* no467 p36 F 2017

THE KITCHEN COOKBOOK *Better Homes & Gardens* v94 no12 p118 D 2016

the life C. Stern color *InStyle* v24 no10 p241 O 2017

MAKING WAVES L. TYRELL color *Martha Stewart Living* p86 O 2017

Mastering Design M. W. Spencer *New Orleans Homes & Lifestyles* v20 no4 p16 Aut 2017

Merry ... But Not Too Bright color diag *Consumer Reports* v82 no12 p67 D 2017

Mixing Bowl color *O, The Oprah Magazine* p148 F 2017

Red, White & Berry Bars D. Wise color *Southern Living* v52 no7 p124 Jl 2017

RISE. EAT. SHINE color *Better Homes & Gardens* v95 no9 p164

S 2017

Sandra Lee Favorites *TV Guide* p18 D 5 2016

SMART COOKIE cartoon *Bon Appetit* v61 no12 p167 D 2016 / Jan2017

THE SOUTHERN LIVING COOKIE COOKBOOK L. Cericola, K. Hammonds et al color *Southern Living* v51 no12 p190 D 2016

STROKES OF GENIUS E. N. GAGE color *Martha Stewart Living* no271 p19 Ja/F 2017

SUGAR RUSH! A. POSEY color *Bon Appetit* v61 no12 p136 D 2016 /Jan2017

Sugar & Spice L. REGE color *Martha Stewart Living* p66 My 2017

SUMMER SPECIAL color *Bon Appetit* v62 no7 p30 Jl 2017

SWEETS FOR YOUR SWEETIE G. LOFTS and S. DiGREGORIO color *Martha Stewart Living* no271 p90 Ja/F 2017

Unchosen Hardships L. Kosa color *Commonweal* v144 no6 p47 Mr 24 2017

What'S New, Cookie? D. GREENSPAN *Better Homes & Gardens* v94 no12 p112 D 2016

Cookies (Computer science)

HOW TO PROTECT YOUR DIGITAL SELF L. BÉNICHOU color *Wired* v25 no6 p36 Je 2017

Cookies—Evaluation

Cookie Town L. BALLA *Los Angeles Magazine* v61 no11 p130 N 2016

DIY RECIPE KITS L. Turner color *Amazing Wellness* v8 no6 p90 Early Winter2016

Cooking

See also

Appetizers

Baking

Breakfasts

Comfort food

Confectionery

Cooking (Bread)

Cooking (Chocolate)

Cooking (Coconut)

Cooking (Condiments)

Cooking (Eggs)

Cooking (Fruit)

Cooking (Herbs)

Cooking (Leftovers)

Cooking (Meat)

Cooking (Natural foods)

Cooking (Nuts)

Cooking (Olives)

Cooking (Pasta)

Cooking (Soft drinks)

Cooking (Vegetables)

Cooking (Vinegar)

Desserts

Fireplace cooking

Holiday cooking

Kitchens

Luncheons

Menus

Pancakes, waffles, etc.

Pizza

Pressure cooking

Recipe writing (Cooking)

Roasting (Cooking)

Salads

Sandwiches

Sauces

Side dishes (Cooking)

Smoking (Cooking)

Solar cooking

Soups

Stuffed foods (Cooking)

Stuffing (Cooking)

Tempura

Tortillas

17 Eat-Clean Secrets from Top Chefs J. Andriakos color *Health* v31 no3 p42 Ap 2017

21 ways to enjoy cooking with kids more K. CICERO color *Par-*

p102 2017 SpecialIssue

Low 'n Slow K. SHERWOOD *Nutrition Action Health Letter* v44 no2 p12 Mr 2017

MAGIC IN A JAR G. LOFTS color *Martha Stewart Living* p74 Jl/Ag 2017

make over your fridge K. CICERO *Parents* v91 no10 p110 O 2016

make thanksgiving in four hours E. CLARK *Parents* v91 no11 p112 N 2016

Making Healthy Meals with Minimal Fuss *Tufts University Health & Nutrition Letter* p1 S 2017 Supplement

Maple Syrup color *Vegetarian Today* no2 p14 Ap 2017

A Matter of Taste: Perfecting gazpacho beyond a recipe's instructions by learning to trust your own palate S. Nosrat *New York Times Magazine* p24 Jl 2 2017

Meal Kits Won't Start a Cooking Revolution-Yet A. Sifferlin color *Time* v190 no5 p18 Jl 31 2017

Mindful meals J. Iserloh color *Yoga Journal* no294 p38 S 2017

Mixing Bowl color *O, The Oprah Magazine* p146 N 2017

MOST EXPENNSIVE BRUNCH *Washingtonian Magazine* v52 no1 p92 O 2016

NANCY SILVERTON MAKES LOS ANGELES THAT MUCH SWEETER *Los Angeles Magazine* v61 no11 p131 N 2016

Nebraska cooks get cooking with Nebraska Kitchens Cookbook Vol. 3 color *Nebraska Life* v20 no6 p11 N/D 2016

Noodles Made Healthy color *Health* v31 no1 p107 Ja 2017

NUTRITION HOTLINE R. MANGELS *Vegetarian Journal* v35 no2 p2 2016

NUTRITION HOTLINE R. MANGELS *Vegetarian Journal* v36 no2 p2 2017

Olé, Four Ways color *Martha Stewart Living* p24 My 2017

one dough, six cookies K. TACK *Parents* p94 2015

One-Pan Wonders color *Health* v31 no2 p129 Mr 2017

PALEO BASICS V. TWEED color *Better Nutrition* v79 no10 p58 O 2017

The Paleo Vegan L. TURNER color *Better Nutrition* v78 no11 p78 N 2016

Party Time! R. Best color *Vegetarian Times* v43 no2 p52 N/D 2016

A Passion for Peas D. DANIELS-ZELLER *Vegetarian Journal* v35 no2 p22 2016

peeps show color *Parents* v92 no4 p68 Ap 2017

Pesto Perfection M. M. CHAPPEL color *Better Nutrition* v79 no4 p60 Ap 2017

The Pig That Changed My Life S. JENKINS color *Reader's Digest* v189 no1129 p74 Ap 2017

PLANT POWER! E. CLARK color *Parents* v92 no7 p106 Jl 2017

Portable & Affordable Vegan color *Better Nutrition* v79 no6 p60 Je 2017

PREP SCHOOL C. MOROCCO, A. STANEK et al bw color *Bon Appetit* v61 no11 p153 N 2016

Prime Rib img *New York* v50 no7 p69 Ap 3 2017

PURE AND SIMPLE A. RAPOPORT color *Bon Appetit* no8 p12 Ag 2017

Put More Garlic in Your Life V. TWEED color *Better Nutrition* v79 no1 p24 Ja 2017

Q&A: HOME-DELIVERED MEAL KITS *Tufts University Health & Nutrition Letter* p4 S 2017 Supplement

Quick Meals color *Vegetarian Today* no1 p42 F 2017

Raise the Crostini Bar color *Vegetarian Today* no2 p34 Ap 2017

THE RECIPES color *New York Times Magazine* p62 N 27 2016

resources *Parents* p140 2015

reviews. CROSSROADS D. Wasserman *Vegetarian Journal* v35 no4 p30 2016

Roast onions J. Iserloh color *Yoga Journal* no291 p34 My 2017

SCHOLARSHIP *Vegetarian Journal* v35 no1 p23 2016

SCRUMPTIOUS SAMPLER A. Wolfe color *Vegetarian Times* v43 no2 p80 N/D 2016

Short Rib Mole *Indianapolis Monthly* v40 no4 p58 D 2016

Should you try a subscription meal kit? *Harvard Health Letter* v42 no2 p7 D 2016

SL COOKING SCHOOL color *Southern Living* v52 no5 p150 My 2017

SL COOKING SCHOOL color *Southern Living* v52 no6 p140 Je 2017

SL cooking school K. Hammonds color *Southern Living* v52 no2 p142 F 2017

Socca Star A. Sullivan color *Bon Appetit* no1 p42 F 2017

solutions color *Parents* v92 no6 p110 Je 2017

soul FOOD L. Ladoceour and R. Rinaldi color *Yoga Journal* no288 p75 D 2016

Soup's On J. BOWDEN and J. BESSINGER color *Better Nutrition* v78 no11 p86 N 2016

Southern Veggie Burgers color *Vegetarian Today* no2 p24 Ap 2017

Spice It Up B. Lipton color *Health* v31 no2 p125 Mr 2017

Spring For Risotto color *Vegetarian Today* no2 p16 Ap 2017

SPRING FORWARD E. Graves *Martha Stewart Living* p8 Mr 2017

Spring PASTA PRIMER A. Hickman color *Health* v31 no3 p88 Ap 2017

Strawberry Cookies color *Vegetarian Today* no2 p46 Ap 2017

Strawberry Shortcake Bars color *Vegetarian Today* no2 p48 Ap 2017

Substituting Ingredients for Good Health *Tufts University Health & Nutrition Letter* v35 no1 p1 Mr 2017

SUMMERTIME + THE COOKING IS SLOW N. SIZEMORE color *Parents* v92 no6 p122 Je 2017

Super Salsas B. Lipton color *Health* v31 no6 p132 Jl 2017

Supper Is Solved! A. Goldfarb color *Parents* v92 no9 p138 S 2017

TASTES LIKE HOME *Southern Living* v52 no5 p96 My 2017

TEAM CURRY [Cover story] A. SHIPNUCK *Parents* v91 no6 p88 Je 2016

Thai-Style Curry color *Vegetarian Today* no2 p12 Ap 2017

THIS FRUIT IS PRETENDING TO BE MEAT color *Health* v31 no7 p18 S 2017

Time To Pig Out S. Evans color *Southern Living* v52 no6 p10 Je 2017

TOO HOT TO COOK? R. Bashinsky color *Health* v31 no6 p106 Jl 2017

Top-Tested Cooking Tips color *Good Housekeeping* v263 no5 p140 N 2016

TOP THAT M. MCLAUGHLIN *Indianapolis Monthly* v12 no40 p70 Ag 2017

Vegan Cooking Tips. Quick and Easy Taco Fillings N. Berkoff *Vegetarian Journal* v35 no1 p34 2016

Vegan Cooking Tips. Quick & Easy Tips for Working With Nutritional Yeast *Vegetarian Journal* v36 no3 p34 2017

Vegan Cooking Tips. QUINOA DISHES N. Berkoff *Vegetarian Journal* v36 no2 p32 2017

A Vegan in a Refugee Camp on the Thai-Burma Border Y. Radbod *Vegetarian Journal* v35 no2 p6 2016

Veganize Your Meal N. BRECHKA color *Better Nutrition* v79 no9 p60 S 2017

Veggie Nice! K. SHERWOOD *Nutrition Action Health Letter* v43 no9 p11 N 2016

VRG Catalog *Vegetarian Journal* v35 no2 p33 2016

Warm up to fall color *Health* v31 no9 p111 N 2017

Way Down South N. ZEVNIK color *Better Nutrition* v78 no11 p82 N 2016

Weeknight Warriors color *Vegetarian Today* no2 p42 Ap 2017

What's for Breakfast? color *Health* v31 no5 p115 Je 2017

What to Make with Yogurt J. Levy color *Health* v31 no3 p103 Ap 2017

what will the kids think? T. Brodesser-Akner bw *Bon Appetit* v62 no10 p48 O 2017

Which Cooking Methods Are Healthiest? J. Andriakos color *Health* v31 no6 p128 Jl 2017

Why I Have Takeout On Speed Dial D. THORNE color *Reader's Digest* v190 no1133 p16 S 2017

WINTER Warmer color *Vegetarian Times* v43 no2 p88 N/D 2016

a yard-to-table family *Parents* v91 no6 p124 Je 2016

Year of the Square img *New York* p66 F 9 2017

Your Complete Guide to Healthy Holidays *Tufts University Health & Nutrition Letter* v34 no9 p1 N 2016

Your Three-Course Fix *Tennis* v53 no3 p24 My/Je 2017

Cooking (Almonds)

CHERRY COBBLER WITH WHITE CHOCOLATE-ALMOND BISCUITS *Successful Farming* v115 no5 p63 Mid-Mr 2017

Chocolate Dream color *Amazing Wellness* v9 no3 p80 EarlySumm 2017

Have Your Cake C. SAFFITZ color *Bon Appetit* v62 no4 p48 Ap 2017

MMM...MORNING color *Good Housekeeping* v265 no5 p23 N

Cooking (Anchovies)

it's not Entertaining it's "having people over" A. ROMAN color *Bon Appetit* v62 no10 p78 O 2017

Cooking (Apple butter)

Apple Watch C. L. MUSIC color *Bon Appetit* v62 no10 p44 O 2017

Cooking (Apples)

See also

Cooking (Apple butter)

APPLE-CRANBERRY PIE *Successful Farming* v114 no10 p66 O 2016

Apple Watch C. L. MUSIC color *Bon Appetit* v62 no10 p44 O 2017

Next-Level SNACK HACKS L. SAXTON color *Seventeen* v76 no2 p90 Mr 2017

Rise and Shine color *American Cowboy* v23 no5 p68 F/Mr 2017

The Scoop on Cobbler L. Cericola and P. Lolley color *Southern Living* v52 no9 p142 S 2017

SINGULAR Sensation M. Kiesel color *O, The Oprah Magazine* p143 N 2017

Straight from the Orchard R. MARTINEZ color *Bon Appetit* p72 S 2017

What a Ham! color *Good Housekeeping* v263 no6 p150 D 2016

THE WORKBOOK color *Martha Stewart Living* p111 Mr 2017

Cooking (Apricots)

BETTER BAKING for the holidays M. GLISAN *Better Homes & Gardens* v94 no11 p74 N 2016

Easiest Ever THANKSGIVING [Cover story] D. Mazar and G. Corcos color *Good Housekeeping* v265 no5 p10 N 2017

MAKING FREEZER JAM M. GLISAN color *Better Homes & Gardens* v95 no6 p118 Je 2017

There's an App for That D. Lewon color *Backpacker* p38 My 2017

Cooking (Artichokes)

Skinny Artichoke Dipper *Saturday Evening Post* v289 no1 p27 Ja/F 2017

Cooking (Asparagus)

15-Minute All-Organic Meal Under $15 color *Prevention* v69 no4 p14 Ap 2017

Asparagus S. CASTLE color *Better Homes & Gardens* v95 no4 p132 Ap 2017

Buy 5, Drop 5 K. Glassman color *Women's Health* v14 no3 p116 Ap 2017

Easy, Fast, Healthy! [Cover story] K. HYMORE color *Prevention* v69 no4 p84 Ap 2017

GOOEY, GRILLED CRISPY, MELTY, AND CHEESE! GLORI-OUS color *O, The Oprah Magazine* p130 Mr 2017

THE KITCHEN COOKBOOK color *Better Homes & Gardens* v95 no4 p136 Ap 2017

PICKLE RECIPES for the Picking: Ferment or quick-pickle your harvest with this assortment of ideas from Mother Earth News bloggers K. Quillen, K. Shockey et al *Mother Earth News* no282 p56 Je/Jl 2017

ROASTED ASPARAGUS N. BROWN *Indianapolis Monthly* v12 no40 p76 Ag 2017

SL COOKING SCHOOL color *Southern Living* v52 no4 p146 Ap 2017

SUPER-SATISFYING SALADS color *Redbook* p118 Je 2017

Cooking (Avocado)

See also

Guacamole

4 small steps to a cheerier household color *Redbook* p130 Je 2017

AVOCADO TOAST J. Birdsall color *Bon Appetit* no8 p92 Ag 2017

A Game-Changing Dip J. Dady and J. Covert color *Men's Health* v32 no1 p24 Ja/F 2017

GUACAMOLE S. PUCKETT *Atlanta* v56 no9 p58 Ja 2017

Jenna Dewan Tatum P. KITA bw color *Men's Health* v32 no5 p36 Je 2017

Meet the Avo Bowl S. Dreisbach color *Glamour* v115 no7 p60 Jl 2017

Net Gain: Season For Crabs D. Curry color *New Orleans Magazine* v51 no10 p176 Ag 2017

NEW WAYS WITH AVOCADO M. GLISAN color *Better Homes & Gardens* v95 no8 p104 Ag 2017

Rainbow Rolls color *Good Housekeeping* v264 no6 p101 Je 2017

Sizzling Steak Tacos R. Melvin color *Southern Living* v52 no7 p112 Jl 2017

SUMMER QUICKIES K. Donnelly color *Women's Health* v14 no5 p92 Je 2017

Cooking (Bacon)

American Pie S. Sifton *New York Times Magazine* p32 Ja 15 2017

Bacon Bomb Potato Salad A. Larson *Idaho Magazine* v16 no10 p56 Jl 2017

Bacon Without Guilt S. Turow color *AARP: The Magazine* v60 no4A p58 Je/Jl 2017

BLT QUINOA BOWL color *Sking* p28 D 2016

cooking WITH CRAFT BEER E. HARE color *Cabin Living* p60 S 2017

Cook This Now: plums C. L. MUSIC color *Bon Appetit* p53 S 2017

A FESTIVE FEAST L. Cericola color *Southern Living* v51 no12 p142 D 2016

A GREAT MORNING STARTS HERE color *Redbook* p118 Ap 2017

LOW-MAINTENANCE MEALS L. TYRELL color *Martha Stewart Living* p76 Jl/Ag 2017

MMM...MORNING color *Good Housekeeping* v264 no2 p131 F 2017

Potato-Bacon Waffles *Idaho Magazine* v16 no6 p57 Mr 2017

Proud Mary L. Cericola and K. Rankin color *Southern Living* v52 no4 p138 Ap 2017

RECIPES A. Larson *Idaho Magazine* v16 no11 p56 Ag 2017

SPECTACULAR SIDES L. Cericola color *Southern Living* v51 no11 p100 N 2016

SPICE UP YOUR BLT M. HENNESSY color *Chicago* v66 no7 p42 Jl 2017

Super BOWLS [Cover story] K. HYMORE color *Prevention* v69 no2 p82 F 2017

Toast of the TOWN [Cover story] M. True and A. Brassinga color *Sunset* v237 no5 p70 N 2016

What a Ham! color *Good Housekeeping* v263 no6 p150 D 2016

Cooking (Bagels)

Buy 5, Drop 5 K. Glassman color *Women's Health* v14 no3 p116 Ap 2017

MMM...MORNING color *Good Housekeeping* v263 no6 p148 D 2016

Cooking (Bananas)

ALL RISE M. SHIH and G. LOFTS color *Martha Stewart Living* p110 O 2017

BANANA BREAD color *Washingtonian Magazine* v52 no7 p145 Ap 2017

BLOOD SUGAR BOOST color *Prevention* v68 no12 p14 D 2016

ONE BANANA BREAD 3 INGENIOUS TWISTS color *Redbook* p126 Ap 2017

Pro Bowl *Indianapolis Monthly* p42 F 2017

THIS IS BANANAS! Y. LEE color *Runner's World* v52 no3 p44 Ap 2017

Cooking (Basil)

home made PESTO color *Good Housekeeping* v265 no3 p116 S 2017

Cooking (Bass)

BASS AND HAM CAKES J. Miles color *Field & Stream* v122 no2 p28 Je/Jl 2017

Cooking (Beans)

Already Dressed A. STANEK color *Bon Appetit* v62 no2 p34 Mr 2017

Chicken Fight! D. Holzman, D. Huebschmann et al color *Men's Health* v32 no8 p88 O 2017

Cook Like a Texanist D. COURTNEY *Texas Monthly* v44 no12 p272 D 2016

Extreme Makeover: Breakfast Edition [Cover story] L. Sampedro color *Women's Health* v14 no1 p111 Ja/F 2017

FROM THE HEARTH L. TYRELL color *Martha Stewart Living* no271 p64 Ja/F 2017

LIMA BEAN LEGACY E. Kleiman color *Los Angeles Magazine* v62 no10 p18 O 2017

Pressure-Cooker Chili A. Hickman color *Southern Living* v52 no10 p126 O 2017

Simple, slimming sides L. Lillien color *Redbook* p98 O 2017

Skinny Artichoke Dipper *Saturday Evening Post* v289 no1 p27 Ja/F 2017

Slim and satisfying soups L. Lillien color *Redbook* p94 F 2017

Start With Beans L. REGE color *Martha Stewart Living* p66 Mr 2017

WEEKNIGHT COOKING A. Brassinga color *Sunset* v239 no3 p96 S 2017

Cooking (Bear meat)

BLACK & BLUE CHILI J. Miles color *Field & Stream* v122 no4 p24 S 2017

Cooking (Beef)

See also

Hamburgers

20-MINUTE MEALS color *Good Housekeeping* v264 no5 p121 My 2017

20-MINUTE MEALS color *Good Housekeeping* v265 no5 p25 N 2017

6 Dutch-Oven Recipes C. LAMM color *Trail Rider* v29 no3 p32 Ap 2017

6 Easy ONE-PAN SUPPERS [Cover story] K. Hymore color *Prevention* p84 Mr 2017

Asian Occasion D. Curry color *New Orleans Magazine* v51 no5 p92 Mr 2017

Aunt Betty's Corned Beef Bake *Idaho Magazine* v16 no6 p56 Mr 2017

Beet Chili at Wayward Sons C. DOWNES *D: The Magazine of Dallas* v43 no10 p80 O 2016

BETTER BURGERS, HOTTER DOGS B. P. KATZ and G. LOFTS color *Martha Stewart Living* no275 p67 Je 2017

Burger [Cover story] J. S. GOLUB color *Runner's World* v52 no6 p69 Jl 2017

CAST-IRON SKILLET CALZONE L. F. Prater *Successful Farming* v115 no3 p59 Mid-F 2017

CHEESEBURGER SOUP: MAKE A DOUBLE BATCH AND PACK LEFTOVERS IN LUNCHES FOR SCHOOL OR TO TAKE TO THE FIELD L. F. Prater *Successful Farming* v115 no11 p61 S 2017

A Cut Above [Cover story] M. D. Smith color *Amazing Wellness* v9 no6 p92 EarlyWint 2017

A CUT AbOVə ThE RƆST [Cover story] M. Sheraton color *Bon Appetit* p142 S 2017

DELICIOUS RECIPES POP THE HAPPIEST OF HOLIDAYS *Martha Stewart Living* no270 p14 D 2016

Dinner Tonight B. LEONE color *Bon Appetit* v62 no10 p33 O 2017

FAST & FRESH A. KOVEL color *Better Homes & Gardens* v95 no2 p76 F 2016

home made PIZZA DOUGH color *Good Housekeeping* v264 no3 p131 Mr 2017

how to cook CORNED BEEF M. GLISAN color *Better Homes & Gardens* v95 no3 p92 Mr 2017

IRISH STOUT BEEF & CABBAGE STIR FRY *Successful Farming* v115 no4 p65 Mr 2017

ITALIAN BEEF SANDWICHES: PUT INGREDIENTS INTO THE SLOW COOKER IN THE MORNING AND SUPPER WILL BE WAITING! *Successful Farming* v115 no12 p67 O 2017

Make a Chef-Designed Sandwich in Your Office Kitchen ... img *New York* v49 no20 p104 O 3 2016

Mince and Tatties S. Gutierrez *British Heritage Travel* v38 no3 p76 My/Je 2017

MMM...MORNING color *Good Housekeeping* v264 no2 p131 F 2017

Perfect Indoor Steak color *American Cowboy* v23 no6 p68 Ap/My 2017

The Power of 3 M. Kiesel color *O, The Oprah Magazine* p173 D 2016

Pressure-Cooker Chili A. Hickman color *Southern Living* v52 no10 p126 O 2017

Prime Time K. Squires color *Bloomberg Businessweek* no4510 p61 F 6 2017

Raise the Steaks T. Keith color *Sports Illustrated* v126 no16 p28 Je 5 2017

Shaking up the BURGER SCENE in Kearney S. KANSTEINER cartoon color *Nebraska Life* v20 no6 p30 N/D 2016

STEAK AU POIVRE color *AARP: The Magazine* v59 no5A p67 Ag/S 2016

STEAKHOUSE img *New York* p77 Mr 6 2017

STUFFED STEAK PINWHEELS: CELEBRATE NATIONAL BEEF MONTH WITH THIS TASTY DISH color *Successful Farming* v115 no7 p61 My 2017

super game, BETTER CHILI color *Better Homes & Gardens* v95 no2 p86 F 2016

TAXONOMY img *New York* p52 Ja 23 2017

THIN-POUNDED VENISON STEAKS J. Miles color *Field & Stream* v122 no3 p20 Ag 2017

TRAINING TABLE [Cover story] A. MacMillan bw color *Runner's World* v51 no10 p52 N 2016

WEEKNIGHT COOKING C. March color *Sunset* v238 no3 p80 Mr 2017

Cooking (Beef)—Evaluation

GOING DUTCH A. AHUJA *Cincinnati Magazine* v50 no3 p126 D 2016

Cooking (Beets)

Beauty of the Beets V. Willis color *Southern Living* v52 no3 p132 Mr 2017

Better, bolder hummus color *Redbook* p117 F 2017

CITRUS STARS L. TYRELL color *Martha Stewart Living* no271 p66 Ja/F 2017

fast, easy, fresh C. MOROCCO bw color *Bon Appetit* v61 no11 p47 N 2016

A Meal for Reuniting G. Hamilton *New York Times Magazine* p30 S 10 2017

Use Your Voodles S. BOCAR color *Martha Stewart Living* p74 S 2017

Cooking (Berries)

See also

Cooking (Blueberries)

Cooking (Cranberries)

BERRY GOOD SANGRÍA M. HENNESSY color *Chicago* v66 no8 p56 Ag 2017

EAT TO REMEMBER L. APPLEGATE color *Runner's World* v52 no2 p41 Mr 2017

SUPER BOTTLES S. Schneider color *Sunset* v237 no6 p100 D 2016

Cooking (Blackberries)

Lord Carnarvon's Boozy Bramble Pudding *British Heritage Travel* v38 no4 p47 Jl/Ag 2017

My Delicious Summer M. True color *Sunset* v238 no6 p64 Je 2017

r.s.v.p P. JACOBSEN, P. O'CAIN et al color *Bon Appetit* no8 p14 Ag 2017

Cooking (Blood)

SLAUGHTER SEASON E. S. Arnarsdóttir *Iceland Review* v54 no6 p86 N/D 2016

Cooking (Blueberries)

Better-for-You Blueberry Waffles *Saturday Evening Post* v289 no3 p23 My/Je 2017

Blueberry-Hazelnut Yogurt Bark color *Prevention* p17 Mr 2017

Blueberry Muffin Parfait color *Prevention* v69 no2 p17 F 2017

Eight Foods to Eat Now for Better Health color *Men's Health* v32 no7 p59 S 2017

Fried Delights D. Wise color *Southern Living* v52 no6 p134 Je 2017

Smooth Blends [Cover story] K. HYMORE color *Prevention* v69 no5 p76 My 2017

TANGLED UP IN BLUE[BERRIES] Y. LEE color *Runner's World* v52 no7 p18 Ag 2017

Cooking (Bourbon whiskey)

SIPPING FOR THE SEASON T. MCNALLY color *New Orleans Magazine* v51 no2 p90 D 2016

Cooking (Bread)

Back-to-Basics FRENCH BREAD W. Rubel *Mother Earth News* no279 p36 D/Ja 2017

BANANA BREAD color *Washingtonian Magazine* v52 no7 p145 Ap 2017

Buttered Up: Sweet and supple, kubaneh is shot through with fat to create a melting, airy bread T. Rao *New York Times Magazine* p30 Je 25 2017

DAILY BREADS W. Akin *Mother Earth News* no279 p30 D/Ja 2017

FAST & FRESH A. KOVEL color *Better Homes & Gardens* v95 no6 p102 Je 2017

HAIL TO THE CHEESE S. KROWIAK *Indianapolis Monthly* p47 N 2017

Joy's BIG EASY LUNCH J. BLACK color *Better Homes & Gardens* v95 no9 p126 S 2017

ONE BANANA BREAD 3 INGENIOUS TWISTS color *Redbook* p126 Ap 2017

Pan de Campo C. BOND *Texas Monthly* v44 no11 p42 N 2016

SPICE UP YOUR BLT M. HENNESSY color *Chicago* v66 no7 p42 Jl 2017

The Workbook color *Martha Stewart Living* p130 O 2017

Cooking (Broccoli)

Fiery Ideas J. WALDBIESER color *Women's Health* v14 no5 p146 Je 2017

FLAVOR EXPLOSION K. Soller color *Bon Appetit* v62 no6 p88 Je 2017

A FOOLPROOF FEAST A. Brassinga, E. Johnson et al color *Sunset* v237 no5 p81 N 2016

r.s.v.p A. CHRISTENSEN cartoon *Bon Appetit* no1 p10 F 2017

SUNNY SIDE UP C. MUIILKE color *Bon Appetit* v61 no12 p146 D 2016 /Jan2017

WEEKNIGHT COOKING color *Sunset* v238 no2 p86 F 2017

Cooking (Brussels sprouts)

THE KITCHEN COOKBOOK *Better Homes & Gardens* v94 no11 p138 N 2016

PERFECT SPROUTS M. HENNESSY color *Chicago* v65 no12 p64 D 2016

Winner, Winner, Turkey Dinner J. Bober color *InStyle* v23 no12 p283 N 2016

Cooking (Buffalo meat)

More treats, fewer calories L. Lillien color *Redbook* p85 Mr 2017

Cooking (Bulgur)

See also

   Tabbouleh

FAST & FRESH A. KOVEL *Better Homes & Gardens* v95 no1 p74 Ja 2017

Cooking (Butter)

Butter that does everything color *Redbook* p111 N 2017

CHEFFED-UP CASSEROLE M. HENNESSY color *Chicago* v66 no11 p52 N 2017

FIELDS OF GOLD: CELEBRATING THE SWEET CORN HARVEST IN THE BERKSHIRES AND BEYOND J. WALSH color map *Yankee* p44 Jl 2017

GRANDMA RIMARCHIK'S *Yankee* v80 no6 p37 N/D 2016

HOW TO MAKE THE WINNING LOBSTER ROLL A. TRAVERSO color *Yankee* p90 Jl 2017

LIQUID GOLD S. K. GILLINGHAM *Martha Stewart Living* no268 p122 O 2016

NEW OYSTER CULT P. HISE *Virginia Living* v15 no2 p38 F 2017

NEW WAYS WITH CELERY M. GLISAN color *Better Homes & Gardens* v95 no10 p108 O 2017

One-Skillet Suppers C. Saffitz color *Bon Appetit* v62 no4 p36 Ap 2017

the other kind of steak night Y. Ottolenghi color *Bon Appetit* v62 no4 p52 Ap 2017

ROASTED ASPARAGUS N. BROWN *Indianapolis Monthly* v12 no40 p76 Ag 2017

Roast Ham With a Latin Twist color *AARP: The Magazine* v60 no1A p57 D 2016/Ja 2017

Seaside Suppers P. S. York and K. Rankin color *Southern Living* v52 no7 p101 Jl 2017

Spatchcock a Turkey H. DUFOUR color *Popular Mechanics* p32 N 2017

The ultimate easy chicken dinner C. Hall color *Redbook* p22 Jl/Ag 2017

WINTER SOUPS TAKE ROOT C. Stone *Saturday Evening Post* v289 no1 p78 Ja/F 2017

The Wonder of Three Ingredients G. Hamilton *New York Times Magazine* p32 Mr 26 2017

Cooking (Cabbage)

Burn Your Vegetables: For this Mexican-style slaw, employ the power of fire and smoke S. Sifton color *New York Times Magazine* p26 Ag 6 2017

crank up the heat C. BOYD *Better Homes & Gardens* v94 no11 p102 N 2016

fast & fresh A. KOVEL color *Better Homes & Gardens* v95 no10 p114 O 2017

HOW TO SERVE SOUL *Atlanta* v56 no9 p77 Ja 2017

IRISH STOUT BEEF & CABBAGE STIR FRY *Successful Farming* v115 no4 p65 Mr 2017

new ways with RED CABBAGE M. XERAKIA *Better Homes & Gardens* v95 no1 p70 Ja 2017

Stir-Fry Shortcut color *Bon Appetit* v62 no4 p40 Ap 2017

WINTER SOUPS FROM THE CELLAR A. Chesman *Mother Earth News* no280 p50 F/Mr 2017

Cooking (Canola oil)

BISON TACOS color *Men's Health* v32 no3 p22 Ap 2017

Cooking (Caramel)

Cupcakes à la Mode D. Wise color *Southern Living* v52 no4 p144 Ap 2017

home made CARAMEL color *Good Housekeeping* v263 no6 p139 D 2016

SUGAR RUSH! A. POSEY color *Bon Appetit* v61 no12 p136 D 2016 /Jan2017

Cooking (Carrots)

AYESHA CURRY SCORES WITH HER TV SHOW & FOOD DELIVERY SERVICE S. E. JAMISON color *Ebony* v72 no11 p60 S 2017

CARROTS G. LUNA color *Better Homes & Gardens* v95 no6 p98 Je 2017

CARROTS S. PUCKETT *Atlanta* v56 no12 p62 Ap 2017

Delicious SUMMER FRUIT [Cover story] K. HYMORE color *Prevention* v69 no7 p84 Jl 2017

FEAST WITH BENEFITS [Cover story] L. Gnat and J. Albert color *O, The Oprah Magazine* p128 N 2017

it's going to be a / ROAST D. BOWEN *Martha Stewart Living* no268 p106 O 2016

THE KITCHEN COOKBOOK color *Better Homes & Gardens* v95 no3 p128 Mr 2017

THE LOVE color *Women's Health* v14 no6 p29 Jl 2017

THE MINI AND MERRY PATRY PLAN K. HYMORE color *Redbook* p126 D 2016

Soup's On S. BRILLS, J. WINBERG et al color *Backpacker* v45 no2 p36 Mr 2017

SPECTACULAR SIDES L. Cericola color *Southern Living* v51 no11 p100 N 2016

A TALE OF TWO TURKEYS L. Cericola color *Southern Living* v51 no11 p96 N 2016

Cooking (Cashew nuts)

BIRD IS THE WORD L. REGE color *Martha Stewart Living* p60 My 2017

NUTRITIONAL AND BREWER'S YEASTS V. Tweed color *Amazing Wellness* v9 no3 p24 EarlySumm 2017

Cooking (Cauliflower)

Cauliflower Is the New It Vegetable M. Gajanan color *Time* v190 no5 p28 Jl 31 2017

CRAZY FOR CAULIFLOWER C. Suddath color *Bloomberg Businessweek* no4521 p66 My 8 2017

FAST & FRESH A. KOVEL *Better Homes & Gardens* v94 no11 p92 N 2016

The frozen-meal makeover L. Lillien color *Redbook* p86 My 2017

Good To Go-To K. Massicot color *New Orleans Magazine* v51 no7 p36 My 2017

THE HANDBOOK *Martha Stewart Living* no268 p137 O 2016

the other kind of steak night Y. Ottolenghi color *Bon Appetit* v62 no4 p52 Ap 2017

THE PALEO VEGAN L. Turner and A. Nix color *Amazing Wellness* v8 no2 p84 Spr 2016

Sarah Michelle Gellar's Cauliflower Popcorn color *Entertainment Weekly* no1459 p18 Mr 31 2017

SINGULAR Sensation L. Pearson color *O, The Oprah Magazine* p107 Ja 2017

Toast of the TOWN [Cover story] M. True and A. Brassinga color *Sunset* v237 no5 p70 N 2016

Cooking (Celery)

Attitude T. McNally color *New Orleans Magazine* v51 no5 p94 Mr 2017

Joy's BIG EASY LUNCH J. BLACK color *Better Homes & Gardens* v95 no9 p126 S 2017

THE KITCHEN COOKBOOK color *Better Homes & Gardens* v95 no9 p134 S 2017

Lobster-and-Celery Rolls R. Kinane color *Entertainment Weekly* no1470 p16 Je 16 2017

THE NEW SOUTHERN SIDEBOARD L. Cericola color *South-*

ern Living v52 no11 p80 N 2017

NEW WAYS WITH CELERY M. GLISAN color *Better Homes & Gardens* v95 no10 p108 O 2017

Savory, Satisfying VENISON RECIPES: Learn the quirks of cooking with venison and use it in these flavorful preparations H. Shaw *Mother Earth News* no284 p28 O/N 2017

Cooking (Cereals)

    See also

        Cooking (Quinoa)

        Cooking (Rice)

        Polenta

Letters to the Editor L. Wilkinson, N. Willard et al color *Prevention* v69 no4 p4 Ap 2017

Cooking (Champagne)

On the Bubble T. BAIOCCHI color *Bon Appetit* v61 no12 p53 D 2016 /Jan2017

Cooking (Cheese)

AMERICA'S TRENDIEST COMFORT FOOD D. Joachim chart color *AARP: The Magazine* v59 no6A p10 O/N 2016

ASK SUSAN S. WESTMOREL color *Good Housekeeping* v264 no4 p112 Ap 2017

Aunt Betty's Corned Beef Bake *Idaho Magazine* v16 no6 p56 Mr 2017

A BRIGHT IDEA M. Sinclair color *O, The Oprah Magazine* p122 Ag 2017

CELERIAC S. SPUNGEN color *Rodale's Organic Life* v3 no1 p21 Ja 2017

CUT TO THE CAKES E. N. Hall, P. Lolley et al color *Southern Living* v51 no12 p156 D 2016

Fluff and Fold L. TYRELL color *Martha Stewart Living* p80 Jl/Ag 2017

HAIL TO THE CHEESE S. KROWIAK *Indianapolis Monthly* p47 N 2017

In the SUNSET KITCHEN E. Johnson color *Sunset* v237 no6 p98 D 2016

THE KITCHEN COOKBOOK color *Better Homes & Gardens* v95 no4 p136 Ap 2017

MAC AND CHEESE L. TYRELL color *Martha Stewart Living* p61 Mr 2017

Now Serving: Comfort and Joy K. O'SHEA-EVANS color *House Beautiful* v158 no10 p45 D 2016/Ja 2017

Popcorn-Cheddar Frico img *New York* v50 no15 p52 Jl 24 2017

Potent Protein color *Rodale's Organic Life* v3 no1 p89 Ja 2017

THE SOUTHERN LIVING CAST-IRON COOKBOOK E. N. Hall and L. Cericola color *Southern Living* v52 no9 p106 S 2017

SUNNY DELIGHTS [Cover story] H. Hayes color *Southern Living* v52 no2 p88 F 2017

The Sweetness of Fall S. Evans color *Southern Living* v52 no9 p12 S 2017

Tastes Like The WEEKEND color *Good Housekeeping* v264 no1 p62 Ja 1 2017

trail chef: Say Cheese N. COTE color *Backpacker* p34 S 2017

The Ultimate Comfort Food T. Rao *New York Times Magazine* p32 N 20 2016

WEEKNIGHT COOKING A. Brassinga color *Sunset* v237 no6 p96 D 2016

Zippy Grilled Cheese A. Larson *Idaho Magazine* v16 no5 p56 F 2017

Cooking (Cherries)

20-MINUTE SUPPERS A. Stewart color *Good Housekeeping* v265 no4 p117 O 2017

Dinner Tonight A. RAPOPORT color *Bon Appetit* no11 p43 N 2017

SORE-MUSCLE SOOTHER color *Prevention* v69 no8 p12 Ag 2017

Sweet Somethings J. MacCharles color *O, The Oprah Magazine* p38 D 2016

Cooking (Chicken)

    See also

        Fried chicken

15-Minute All-Organic Meal Under $15 color *Prevention* v69 no9 p14 O 2017

20-MINUTE MEALS [Cover story] color *Good Housekeeping* v265 no2 p118 Ag 2017

20-MINUTE SUPPERS color *Good Housekeeping* v264 no4 p120 Ap 2017

The Art of Uncooking S. Sifton *New York Times Magazine* p32 Ap 23 2017

BEYOND-EASY, COMPLETELY SURPRISING ITALIAN G. Corcos and D. Mazar color *Redbook* p144 O 2017

BIRD IS THE WORD L. REGE color *Martha Stewart Living* p60 My 2017

BRIGHT SPOTS N. Richardson and C. Morocco color *Bon Appetit* v62 no2 p86 Mr 2017

Buon Appetito! D. CURRY color *New Orleans Magazine* v51 no7 p72 My 2017

California Dreaming B. Ng color *Bon Appetit* v62 no7 p36 Jl 2017

Caprese with a Twist R. Melvin color *Southern Living* v52 no7 p122 Jl 2017

CELEBRATING THE SEASON M. J. Mateo color *Sunset* v237 no6 p88 D 2016

Chicken and Dumplings C. BOND *Texas Monthly* v45 no1 p32 Ja 2017

Chicken Fight! D. Holzman, D. Huebschmann et al color *Men's Health* v32 no8 p88 O 2017

Chicken Noodle Soup L. REGE color *Martha Stewart Living* no271 p61 Ja/F 2017

CHICKEN ON THE GRILL B. P. KATZ color *Martha Stewart Living* p71 Jl/Ag 2017

CHICKEN WINGS M. Michelson color *Skiing* p38 D 2016

Cinco de Mayo San Antonio Style P. Disbrowe and J. Hernandez color *Southern Living* v52 no5 p110 My 2017

Comforting dinners for cold, wintry nights color *Redbook* p136 D 2016

Cooking with Green Tea N. Zevnik color *Amazing Wellness* v9 no1 p84 Wint 2017

Dinner Tonight B. LEONE color *Bon Appetit* v62 no10 p33 O 2017

Dinner Tonight C. L. MUSIC color *Bon Appetit* no1 p29 F 2017

Dinner Tonight color *Bon Appetit* v62 no2 p29 Mr 2017

DON'T WORRY, EAT HAPPY C. L. MUSIC color *Bon Appetit* no1 p72 F 2017

Drumsticks, Please P. Grandjean color *Southern Living* v52 no5 p136 My 2017

Easy, Fast, Healthy! [Cover story] K. HYMORE color *Prevention* v69 no4 p84 Ap 2017

Easy No-Cook Dinners K. HYMORE color *Prevention* v69 no8 p86 Ag 2017

EAT LIKE a GREEK K. SOLLER color *Bon Appetit* no8 p84 Ag 2017

Eat Your Greens L. Cericola and R. Melvin color *Southern Living* v52 no4 p119 Ap 2017

EAT YOUR MEAT (AND FEEL BETTER ABOUT IT) A. STANEK and C. SAFFITZ cartoon color diag *Bon Appetit* no1 p88 F 2017

EXPANSIVE TASTE color *O, The Oprah Magazine* p138 S 2017

FAST & FRESH A. KOVEL color *Better Homes & Gardens* v95 no4 p98 Ap 2017

FAST & FRESH A. KOVEL color *Better Homes & Gardens* v95 no8 p124 Ag 2017

FEBRUARY RECIPES color *Southern Living* v52 no2 p8 F 2017

FILIPINO FOOD'S MOMENT E. Johnson color *Sunset* v238 no3 p73 Mr 2017

FRESH IN A FLASH S. CAREY color *Martha Stewart Living* p72 S 2017

FROM ROME WITH AMORE M. HENNESSY color *Chicago* v66 no3 p62 Mr 2017

Game on! *New Orleans Homes & Lifestyles* v20 no1 p24 Wint 2016

GLASS ACT N. Appleman color *Runner's World* v52 no2 p42 Mr 2017

GRILLED GOODNESS C. K. Jackson color *Essence* v48 no3 p109 Jl 2017

GRILLING 101 with Andy Husbands A. TRAVERSO, K. KELLER et al color *Yankee* p54 My/Je 2017

HEALTHY FOR THE HOLIDAYS L. TYRELL *Martha Stewart Living* no269 p80 N 2016

Here's the Rub A. Daniels color *AARP: The Magazine* v60 no2A p74 F/Mr 2017

HOW DOES YOUR LUNCH STACK UP? T. GINSBERG *Atlanta* v56 no7 p86 N 2016

How Not To Cook Like A Texan C. WALLACE *Texas Monthly*

v44 no12 p99 D 2016

how to cook CHICKEN WINGS M. GLISAN color *Better Homes & Gardens* v95 no6 p112 Je 2017

How to Grill Every Meal M. RUHLMAN bw color *Men's Health* v32 no5 p72 Je 2017

"I had no recipe for normal" H. SELLERS bw color *Good Housekeeping* v264 no5 p77 My 2017

Inside the Hot Mess Kitchen G. Moskowitz and M. Berman color *Glamour* v115 no9 p111 S 2017

In the Kitchen with James Whiteside C. ESCOYNE *Dance Magazine* v91 no6 p44 Je 2017

INTO THE BLUE I. Edwards color *Sunset* v239 no1 p8 Jl 2017

IRON CLAD S. PUCKETT color *Better Homes & Gardens* v95 no2 p106 F 2016

it's TOMATO season color *Good Housekeeping* v265 no3 p61 S 2017

JANUARY RECIPES color *Southern Living* v52 no1 p6 Ja 2017

Katsu Son A. Rapoport color *Bon Appetit* v62 no6 p38 Je 2017

THE KITCHEN COOKBOOK color *Better Homes & Gardens* v95 no2 p112 F 2016

THE KITCHEN COOKBOOK color *Better Homes & Gardens* v95 no9 p134 S 2017

LOW-MAINTENANCE MEALS L. TYRELL color *Martha Stewart Living* p76 Jl/Ag 2017

Make the Most of Your Meals K. HYMORE color *Prevention* v68 no11 p58 N 2016

Mixing Bowl color *O, The Oprah Magazine* p172 My 2017

A Month of Simple Suppers L. Cericola color *Southern Living* v52 no2 p117 F 2017

A New Spin on Succotash J. Levy color *Southern Living* v52 no6 p136 Je 2017

NOT-COOL CASSEROLE E. Passarella color *Southern Living* v52 no5 p97 My 2017

One Pot Cooking D. CURRY color *New Orleans Magazine* v52 no1 p108 S 2017

One-Skillet Suppers C. Saffitz color *Bon Appetit* v62 no4 p36 Ap 2017

PARTY ON THE GO A. Brassinga color *Sunset* v239 no4 p83 O 2017

A perfect (and easy!) pot pie C. Hall color *Redbook* p30 O 2017

PERFECTING THE... ROAST CHICKEN *Martha Stewart Living* no267 p71 S 2016

prep school N. RICHARDSON, C. MOROCCO et al bw color *Bon Appetit* v62 no7 p97 Jl 2017

r.s.v.p bw color *Bon Appetit* v61 no11 p14 N 2016

r.s.v.p L. WAHLER, H. SCHNEIDER et al bw *Bon Appetit* no11 p12 N 2017

Shamelessly French F. Lam color *New York Times Magazine* p26 D 4 2016

Silver PLATTERS [Cover story] J. WALDBIESER color *Women's Health* v14 no3 p140 Ap 2017

A Simple Roast Chicken C. MOROCCO and A. STANEK color *Bon Appetit* v62 no10 p64 O 2017

SIMPLY SUMMER: Take alfresco dining to the next level with light, must-try recipes from the celebrity chef and author C. Stone *Saturday Evening Post* v289 no4 p78 Jl/Ag 2017

SINGULAR Sensation L. Pearson color *O, The Oprah Magazine* p145 F 2017

SINGULAR Sensation M. Kiesel color *O, The Oprah Magazine* p135 S 2017

Skillet Wings P. Kita cartoon color *Men's Health* v32 no2 p31 Mr 2017

SLURRRRRRRP! C. GIDDINGS color *Bicycling* v58 no10 p20 N/D 2017

Smokin' With Love J. Passov color *Golf Magazine* v59 no11 p94 N 2017

SOUP SECRETS M. True color *Sunset* v238 no1 p82 Ja 2017

Soup's On! K. Rankin color *Southern Living* v52 no10 p109 O 2017

THE SOUTHERN LIVING COMFORT FOOD COOKBOOK [Cover story] L. Cericola color *Southern Living* v52 no1 p74 Ja 2017

SPECIAL PRESENTATION color *O, The Oprah Magazine* p138 F 2017

SPEEDY SUPPERS *Martha Stewart Living* no267 p76 S 2016

SPRING CHICKEN J. Waldbieser color *Women's Health* v14 no4

p101 My 2017

Spring Chicken! L. Cericola color *Southern Living* v52 no3 p119 Mr 2017

Spring Pasta A. BARAGHANI and N. Richardson color *Bon Appetit* v62 no4 p76 Ap 2017

Spring Slow-Cooker Soup P. Grandjean color *Southern Living* v52 no4 p132 Ap 2017

Super Dips L. Cericola color *Southern Living* v52 no2 p136 F 2017

#taco tuesday color *Good Housekeeping* v265 no2 p113 Ag 2017

Tastes like Fall [Cover story] color *Good Housekeeping* v265 no4 p109 O 2017

A TIME TO START E. Graves *Martha Stewart Living* no271 p8 Ja/F 2017

Tom Kitchin's Traditional Pot-Roasted Chicken S. Gutierrez color *British Heritage Travel* v38 no5 p74 S/O 2017

The ultimate easy chicken dinner C. Hall color *Redbook* p22 Jl/Ag 2017

A VERY MERRY CHRISMUKKAH M. YEH color *Rodale's Organic Life* v2 no7 p58 D 2016/Ja 2017

THE WEEK AHEAD [Cover story] E. Kopecky color *Runner's World* v52 no1 p52 Ja/F 2017

WEEKNIGHT COOKING color *Sunset* v238 no2 p86 F 2017

Weeknight Wonders L. Cericola and A. Dolge color *Southern Living* v52 no9 p123 S 2017

What I Know for Sure Oprah color *O, The Oprah Magazine* p112 Jl 2017

What We Really Eat G. Hamilton color *New York Times Magazine* p26 Ja 29 2017

When Too Much Is Just Enough S. Sifton *New York Times Magazine* p26 S 3 2017

WORLD OF FLAVOR E. Johnson color *Sunset* v239 no1 p74 Jl 2017

YOUR PANTRY color *Good Housekeeping* v264 no5 p131 My 2017

YOUR PANTRY color *Good Housekeeping* v265 no1 p112 Jl 2017

Your Three-Course Fix A. Friedman *Tennis* v53 no4 p26 Jl/Ag 2017

Cooking (Chickpeas)

15-Minute All-Organic Meal Under $15 color *Prevention* p12 Mr 2017

An American Classic Goes Low-Cal T. Mowry color *Entertainment Weekly* no1456 p20 Mr 10 2017

Cook Like a Pro: Summer Edition [Cover story] M. ROTHSTEIN, A. MASON et al bw color diag *Bon Appetit* v62 no7 p56 Jl 2017

Easy Okra V. Willis color *Southern Living* v52 no9 p138 S 2017

Go Whole Squash color *Bon Appetit* v62 no4 p42 Ap 2017

SWEET ON PEPPERS E. Johnson color *Sunset* v239 no3 p91 S 2017

Why I Love One-Pan Dinners S. Dreisbach and S. G. Levy color *Glamour* v115 no4 p128 Ap 2017

your weeknight GAME PLAN C. Ferreira color *Sunset* v238 no1 p60 Ja 2017

Cooking (Chives)

The Versatile Herb K. Hammonds color *Southern Living* v52 no4 p31 Ap 2017

Cooking (Chocolate)

See also

Cooking (Cocoa)

BREAK THE FAST I. Kirkland color *Essence* v48 no6 p123 O 2017

Chocolate Dream color *Amazing Wellness* v9 no3 p80 EarlySumm 2017

CHOCOLATE PARTY! E. Johnson color *Sunset* v238 no2 p77 F 2017

COLLEGE CAMPUS Cuisine color *Nebraska Life* v21 no1 p46 Ja/F 2017

Cupcakes à la Mode D. Wise color *Southern Living* v52 no4 p144 Ap 2017

DREAMING OF A White Chocolate CHEESECAKE color *Good Housekeeping* v263 no6 p31 D 2016

FOOD FOR THOUGHT [Cover story] C. KUZMA color *Runner's World* v52 no6 p30 Jl 2017

for the love of CHOCOLATE C. BOYD color *Better Homes & Gardens* v95 no4 p94 Ap 2017

Holiday Peppermint Bark *Saturday Evening Post* v288 no6 p27 N/D 2016

Holiday S'mores Rolls A. Larson *Idaho Magazine* v16 no3 p56 D 2016

homemade CHOCO-NUT SPREAD color *Good Housekeeping* v264 no2 p122 F 2017

Hot Chocolate Bar A. Larson *Idaho Magazine* v17 no1 p56 Ja 2017

Hot Chocolate *Martha Stewart Living* no270 p100 D 2016

How Sweet It Is! color *Amazing Wellness* p88 Fall 2017

In the SUNSET KITCHEN E. Johnson color *Sunset* v238 no4 p94 Ap 2017

Lee Cake J. Story *Idaho Magazine* v16 no1 p57 O 2016

matzo's makeover M. GLISAN color *Better Homes & Gardens* v95 no4 p106 Ap 2017

Reasons to have more chocolate L. Lillien color *Redbook* p85 S 2017

SINGULAR Sensation L. Pearson color *O, The Oprah Magazine* p145 F 2017

A SLICE ABOVE color *Better Homes & Gardens* v95 no11 p94 N 2017

Sugar & Spice L. REGE color *Martha Stewart Living* p66 My 2017

THE WORKBOOK color *Martha Stewart Living* no271 p111 Ja/F 2017

YOUR CHEAT SHEET TO... MAKING DELISH presents L. SAXTON color *Seventeen* v76 no12 p106 D 2016/Ja 2017

Cooking (Cinnamon)

Cinnamon twirl L. DELAP color *Maclean's* v129 no44 p72 N 7 2016

FULL OF SURPRISES M. SHIH color *Martha Stewart Living* p86 S 2017

MORNING GLORIES *Washingtonian Magazine* v52 no1 p86 O 2016

RECIPES A. Larson *Idaho Magazine* v16 no7 p56 Ap 2017

Roast Ham With a Latin Twist color *AARP: The Magazine* v60 no1A p57 D 2016/Ja 2017

Cooking (Citrus fruits)

    See also

        Cooking (Lemons)

GRAND OLD ICES color *Martha Stewart Living* p26 Jl/Ag 2017

MMM...MORNING color *Good Housekeeping* v265 no5 p23 N 2017

TURN OVER A NEW LEAF A. STANEK color *Bon Appetit* p110 S 2017

Cooking (Clams)

IN A FLASH E. PARKHURST *Virginia Living* v15 no1 p9 D 2016

RECIPES I. Newman *Virginia Living* v15 no1 p71 D 2016

Cooking (Cocoa)

Delicious Dunkers color *Good Housekeeping* v265 no5 p36 N 2017

Have Your Cake C. SAFFITZ color *Bon Appetit* v62 no4 p48 Ap 2017

Cooking (Coconut)

gourd almighty C. Morocco color *Bon Appetit* v61 no11 p68 N 2016

NO FLOUR, NO PROBLEM G. LOFTS color *Martha Stewart Living* p88 Ap 2017

SINGULAR Sensation M. Kiesel color *O, The Oprah Magazine* p106 Je 2017

SUMMER CRUSH C. March color *Sunset* v238 no6 p87 Je 2017

Wrap It Up: Discovering the wonders of a Parsi-style fish in banana leaves, cooked on the grill S. Nosrat *New York Times Magazine* p22 Jl 30 2017

Cooking (Codfish)

A Meal for Reuniting G. Hamilton *New York Times Magazine* p30 S 10 2017

Cooking (Coffee)

1951 COFFEE K. K. CONDON color *Better Homes & Gardens* v95 no5 p178 My 2017

Shaking up the BURGER SCENE in Kearney S. KANSTEINER cartoon color *Nebraska Life* v20 no6 p30 N/D 2016

THE TIPSY TEXAN'S COOK TAIL OF THE MONTH D. ALAN *Texas Monthly* v45 no2 p40 F 2017

WARM UP YOUR COOLDOWN L. APPLEGATE color *Runner's World* v51 no11 p50 D 2016

Cooking (Condensed milk)

Homemade Irish Cream color *Good Housekeeping* v264 no3 p115 Mr 2017

Cooking (Condiments)

    See also

        Cooking (Salad dressing)

it's not Entertaining it's "having people over" A. ROMAN color *Bon Appetit* v62 no10 p78 O 2017

Cooking (Coriander)

CAN'T TAKE THE HEAT? GET IN THE KITCHEN D. ZICKL color *Runner's World* v52 no7 p30 Ag 2017

WEEKNIGHT COOKING color *Sunset* v238 no6 p94 Je 2017

Cooking (Corn)

    See also

        Cooking (Popcorn)

        Corn bread

ALL EARS color *O, The Oprah Magazine* p112 Ag 2017

THE BETTER — THAN — EVER BREAKFAST GUIDE color *Redbook* p117 Ap 2017

BISON TACOS color *Men's Health* v32 no3 p22 Ap 2017

Ears to Mouth J. Gorant and T. Keith color *Sports Illustrated* v126 no15 p24 My 29 2017

Easy No-Cook Dinners K. HYMORE color *Prevention* v69 no8 p86 Ag 2017

FIELDS OF Gold: CELEBRATING THE SWEET CORN HARVEST IN THE BERKSHIRES AND BEYOND J. WALSH color map *Yankee* p44 Jl 2017

r.s.v.p cartoon *Bon Appetit* v62 no6 p10 Je 2017

The Soup of Summer P. Grandjean color *Southern Living* v52 no7 p120 Jl 2017

Street Corn at home *Saturday Evening Post* v289 no4 p25 Jl/Ag 2017

Summer Seafood Feast bw cartoon color *Men's Health* v32 no5 p30 Je 2017

Sweet Corn Gazpacho L. POWERS and K. O'SHEA-EVANS color *House Beautiful* p47 Jl 2017

Waffle On A. RAMPE color *Bon Appetit* p76 S 2017

Cooking (Cottage cheese)

SMOOTH MOVE M. KADEY color *Runner's World* v52 no7 p22 Ag 2017

Cooking (Cowpeas)

THE KITCHEN COOKBOOK V. Howard color *Better Homes & Gardens* v95 no11 p130 N 2017

Cooking (Crabs)

Catch Your FANCY C. Stone color *O, The Oprah Magazine* p110 Jl 2017

FOOD *Virginia Living* v15 no3 p55 Ap 2017

Home Entertainment *GQ: Gentlemen's Quarterly* v86 no11 p48 N 2016

THE KITCHEN COOKBOOK V. Howard color *Better Homes & Gardens* v95 no11 p130 N 2017

Net Gain: Season For Crabs D. Curry color *New Orleans Magazine* v51 no10 p176 Ag 2017

PENNY'S NEW FAVE color *Chicago* v66 no7 p40 Jl 2017

Race Fare T. Keith color *Sports Illustrated* v126 no14 p26 My 15-22 2017

SUMMER FAVORITES S. Dry color *Louisiana Life* v37 no6 p54 Jl/Ag 2017

WEEKNIGHT COOKING A. Brassinga color *Sunset* v237 no6 p96 D 2016

Cooking (Cranberries)

APPLE-CRANBERRY PIE *Successful Farming* v114 no10 p66 O 2016

Basecamp Thanksgiving K. KARLSON color *Backpacker* p32 N 2017

Bowling for Breakfast color *Men's Health* v32 no1 p60 Ja/F 2017

Coffeeless Coffeecakes: No caffeine required color *Nebraska Life* v21 no5 p46 S/O 2017

DREAMING OF A White Chocolate CHEESECAKE color *Good Housekeeping* v263 no6 p31 D 2016

LIFE AT LULU'S: A Seasonal "Sneeky" K. O'SHEA-EVANS color *House Beautiful* v159 no9 p62 N 2017

Cooking (Crawfish)

COOKING CREOLE D. CURRY color *New Orleans Magazine* v51 no3 p116 Ja 2017

Cooking (Cucumbers)

Already Dressed A. STANEK color *Bon Appetit* v62 no2 p34 Mr 2017

Dinner Tonight A. STANEK color *Bon Appetit* no8 p33 Ag 2017

FRESH FOR DINNER [Cover story] J. Seinfeld color *Redbook* p144 My 2017

SWEET ON PEPPERS E. Johnson color *Sunset* v239 no3 p91 S 2017

WELL ROUNDED M. Kadey color *Women's Health* v14 no3 p100 Ap 2017

Cooking (Curry)

HEADS ABOVE Y. LEE color *Runner's World* v52 no9 p42 O 2017

One Pot Cooking D. CURRY color *New Orleans Magazine* v52 no1 p108 S 2017

Cooking (Dairy products)

See also

Cooking (Butter)

Cooking (Cheese)

Cooking (Milk)

Cooking (Sour cream & milk)

Cooking (Yogurt)

Cooking (Dill)

DAFT ABOUT DILL M. Allan, Á. Snorradóttir et al *Iceland Review* v55 no3 p46 My/Je 2017

Dill Pickle Dip A. Larson *Idaho Magazine* v16 no3 p57 D 2016

Cooking (Duck)

HAPPY MEAL T. E. Nickens color *Field & Stream* v121 no8 p38 F/Mr 2017

Screw the Turkey! P. KITA cartoon color *Men's Health* v32 no9 p57 N 2017

SLOW vs FAST S. CASTLE *Better Homes & Gardens* v95 no1 p100 Ja 2017

Sportsman's Paradise *New Orleans Homes & Lifestyles* v20 no2 p24 Spr 2017

Cooking (Eggplant)

Eggplant and Zucchini Lasagna P. KITA color *Men's Health* v32 no7 p30 S 2017

HARVEST FEAST C. Stone *Saturday Evening Post* v289 no5 p76 S/O 2017

YOUR PANTRY color *Good Housekeeping* v265 no3 p128 S 2017

Cooking (Eggs)

See also

Soufflés

10-Minute Clean Meals color *Prevention* v69 no1 p58 Ja 2017

A CAROLINA CHRISTMAS L. Cericola and V. Howard color *Southern Living* v51 no12 p170 D 2016

EARTHLY TREASURES J. Waldbieser color *Women's Health* v14 no8 p93 O 2017

The easiest crowd-pleasing brunch C. Hall color *Redbook* p28 Ap 2017

Eggs on a Roll R. PATRONITE and R. RAISFELD img *New York* v50 no8 p112 Ap 17 2017

Egg & Tomato Breakfast Sandwich P. KITA color *Men's Health* v32 no8 p38 O 2017

A GREAT MORNING STARTS HERE color *Redbook* p118 Ap 2017

How to Grill Every Meal M. RUHLMAN bw color *Men's Health* v32 no5 p72 Je 2017

In the SUNSET KITCHEN E. Johnson color *Sunset* v239 no4 p92 O 2017

Katsu Son A. Rapoport color *Bon Appetit* v62 no6 p38 Je 2017

MEAL OF THE MONTH color *Prevention* v69 no4 p17 Ap 2017

Meet the Avo Bowl S. Dreisbach color *Glamour* v115 no7 p60 Jl 2017

Merle Dandridge J. ZAMBRANO color *O, The Oprah Magazine* p24 Mr 2017

Mixing Bowl color *O, The Oprah Magazine* p176 D 2016

MMM...MORNING color *Good Housekeeping* v263 no6 p148 D 2016

MMM... MORNING color *Good Housekeeping* v264 no3 p143 Mr 2017

MMM...MORNING color *Good Housekeeping* v264 no5 p129 My 2017

power up with BREAKFAST M. GLISAN color *Better Homes & Gardens* v95 no8 p116 Ag 2017

PUT AN EGG ON IT [Cover story] C. MOROCCO and A. STANEK color *Bon Appetit* v62 no4 p66 Ap 2017

r.s.v.p A. CHRISTENSEN cartoon *Bon Appetit* no1 p10 F 2017

Sausage, Egg, and Garlicky Greens [Cover story] cartoon color *Men's Health* v32 no4 p26 My 2017

SLURRRRRRRP! C. GIDDINGS color *Bicycling* v58 no10 p20 N/D 2017

Sopaipillas C. BOND *Texas Monthly* v45 no3 p42 Mr 2017

SPRINGTIME IN THE SOUTHLAND V. Howard color *Bon Appetit* v62 no4 p96 Ap 2017

Sun Surf & Sumac A. STANEK bw color *Bon Appetit* no8 p68 Ag 2017

TABLE FOR ONE C. K. Jackson color *Essence* v47 no11 p111 Mr 2017

TAPPED POTENTIAL S. Collins and S. Bocar color *Martha Stewart Living* p82 My 2017

TINY BUT MIGHTY B. Andrews color *Rodale's Organic Life* v2 no7 p92 D 2016/Ja 2017

WELL ROUNDED M. Kadey color *Women's Health* v14 no3 p100 Ap 2017

WHERE IT ALL BEGINS A. RAPOPORT color *Bon Appetit* v62 no4 p8 Ap 2017

Cooking (Fish)

See also

Cooking (Anchovies)

Cooking (Codfish)

Cooking (Salmon)

Cooking (Sardines)

Cooking (Trout)

THE CAN-DO SAUCE M. HENNESSY color *Chicago* v66 no5 p68 My 2017

Dinner's done ON THE GRILL! [Cover story] color *Redbook* p116 Jl/Ag 2017

DISH OF THE MONTH A. LIMPERT color *Washingtonian Magazine* v52 no7 p144 Ap 2017

ШELCOMэ TO CUTLET COUИTRЧ E. WARTZMAN color *Bon Appetit* p124 S 2017

FISH FRY s. collins and s. carey color *Martha Stewart Living* p86 Jl/Ag 2017

Fresh Perspective: Inspired by flavors of her heritage, Chef Diana Chauvin Galle puts a Thai twist on a local favorite *New Orleans Homes & Lifestyles* v20 no3 p24 Summ 2017

Fried Fish Lettuce Wraps img *New York* p59 F 20 2017

HEAD TO TAIL E. SIGURÐARDÓTTIR and Z. ROBRET *Iceland Review* v55 no2 p26 Mr/Ap 2017

Hit the Grill Mark S. MULLEN color *Bon Appetit* no8 p46 Ag 2017

THE KITCHEN COOKBOOK color *Better Homes & Gardens* v95 no2 p112 F 2016

OCEAn TO TABLE C. Leschin-Hoar color *Sunset* v238 no2 p68 F 2017

Sun Surf & Sumac A. STANEK bw color *Bon Appetit* no8 p68 Ag 2017

THE WORKBOOK color *Martha Stewart Living* p114 Jl/Ag 2017

Wrap It Up: Discovering the wonders of a Parsi-style fish in banana leaves, cooked on the grill S. Nosrat *New York Times Magazine* p22 Jl 30 2017

Cooking (Flowers)

SL COOKING SCHOOL color *Southern Living* v52 no3 p136 Mr 2017

Cooking (Fruit)

See also

Cooking (Apples)

Cooking (Apricots)

Cooking (Avocado)

Cooking (Bananas)

Cooking (Berries)

Cooking (Cherries)

Cooking (Citrus fruits)

Cooking (Peaches)

Cooking (Plums)

Cooking (Pomegranates)

Cooking (Pumpkin)

Char a Different Course M. Bittman color *GQ: Gentlemen's Quarterly* v97 no7 p64 Jl 2017

Dazzle Them! K. O'SHEA-EVANS color *House Beautiful* v159

no8 p60 O 2017

EASY AS PIE ACTUALLY, EASIER A. Cayne color *Redbook* p154 My 2017

Cooking (Garlic)

Lickety-Split Shrimp J. Levy color *Southern Living* v52 no4 p142 Ap 2017

THE RECIPES color *New York Times Magazine* p62 N 27 2016

SECOND ACT M. GLISAN color *Better Homes & Gardens* v95 no11 p86 N 2017

Spring Awakening A. Baraghani color *Bon Appetit* v62 no2 p38 Mr 2017

The Taste of Regret: How you should—and should not—cook with garlic S. Nosrat *New York Times Magazine* p26 O 1 2017

WILD TURKEY TONNATO J. Miles cartoon color *Field & Stream* v122 no1 p20 My 2017

Your ultimate busy-night meal C. Hall color *Redbook* p34 D 2016

Cooking (Ginger)

BETTER BAKING for the holidays M. GLISAN *Better Homes & Gardens* v94 no11 p74 N 2016

THE CAN-DO SAUCE M. HENNESSY color *Chicago* v66 no5 p68 My 2017

STICK TO THE RIBS M. Driskill color *Southern Living* v52 no6 p98 Je 2017

Cooking (Goat cheese)

SIMMER ALL DAY, PARTY ALL NIGHT T. B. M. Boyer and A. Shaya color *Southern Living* v52 no2 p110 F 2017

Cooking (Grapefruit)

CITRUS STARS L. TYRELL color *Martha Stewart Living* no271 p66 Ja/F 2017

ORANGES B. ANDREWS color *Rodale's Organic Life* v2 no7 p45 D 2016/Ja 2017

Cooking (Grapes)

COLD SUMMER SOUPS A. Sussman color *Sunset* v239 no1 p89 Jl 2017

Cooking (Ground meat)

cooking WITH CRAFT BEER E. HARE color *Cabin Living* p60 S 2017

Cooking (Ham)

BASS AND HAM CAKES J. Miles color *Field & Stream* v122 no2 p28 Je/Jl 2017

The Chew's Surefire Party-Starters color *Entertainment Weekly* no1443 p24 D 9 2016

... Or Just Buy Your Lunch From a Sandwich-Construction Specialist img *New York* v49 no20 p105 O 3 2016

Rex's Potato and Ham Soup A. Larson *Idaho Magazine* v16 no1 p56 O 2016

SL COOKING SCHOOL color *Southern Living* v52 no4 p146 Ap 2017

Cooking (Hazelnuts)

Blueberry-Hazelnut Yogurt Bark color *Prevention* p17 Mr 2017

homemade CHOCO-NUT SPREAD color *Good Housekeeping* v264 no2 p122 F 2017

Cooking (Herbs)

See also

Cooking (Basil)

Cooking (Garlic)

Butter that does everything color *Redbook* p111 N 2017

how to cook HERB SALSA M. GLISAN color *Better Homes & Gardens* v95 no4 p88 Ap 2017

LOVAGE color *Better Homes & Gardens* v95 no5 p120 My 2017

Cooking (Honey)

Hive to Table M. Taylor color *Women's Health* v14 no3 p91 Ap 2017

new ways with SWEET POTATOES M. GLISAN *Better Homes & Gardens* v94 no11 p88 N 2016

SWEET ON SWEET POTATOES A. Mcgreger color *Southern Living* v51 no11 p116 N 2016

Sweet Somethings J. MacCharles color *O, The Oprah Magazine* p38 D 2016

Cooking (Hot peppers)

See also

Cooking (Jalapeño)

Beet Chili at Wayward Sons C. DOWNES *D: The Magazine of Dallas* v43 no10 p80 O 2016

MAKE YOUR OWN HOT SAUCE IN THREE STEPS J. Finlayson cartoon *Men's Health* v32 no4 p114 My 2017

Cooking (Jalapeño)

MAKE YOUR OWN HOT SAUCE IN THREE STEPS J. Finlayson cartoon *Men's Health* v32 no4 p114 My 2017

Roasted Texas Caviar color *American Cowboy* v24 no1 p68 Je/Jl 2017

Cooking (Jam)

MAKING FREEZER JAM M. GLISAN color *Better Homes & Gardens* v95 no6 p118 Je 2017

Cooking (Kale)

15-Minute All-Organic Meal under $15 color *Prevention* v68 no12 p16 D 2016

FAST & FRESH A. KOVEL color *Better Homes & Gardens* v95 no4 p98 Ap 2017

NUTRITIONAL AND BREWER'S YEASTS V. Tweed color *Amazing Wellness* v9 no3 p24 EarlySumm 2017

Cooking (Kiwifruit)

Hive to Table M. Taylor color *Women's Health* v14 no3 p91 Ap 2017

Cooking (Lamb & mutton)

A Cut Above [Cover story] M. D. Smith color *Amazing Wellness* v9 no6 p92 EarlyWint 2017

FLAVOR EXPLOSION K. Soller color *Bon Appetit* v62 no6 p88 Je 2017

FULL OF SURPRISES M. SHIH color *Martha Stewart Living* p86 S 2017

IN PRAISE OF PECANS V. Willis color *Southern Living* v51 no11 p150 N 2016

LAMB SPICES & SHEEP PELTS *South Dakota Magazine* v33 no3 p30 S/O 2017

Now Serving: Comfort and Joy K. O'SHEA-EVANS color *House Beautiful* v158 no10 p45 D 2016/Ja 2017

Vroom Service T. Keith color *Sports Illustrated* v126 no18 p18 Je 26 2017

WEEKNIGHT COOKING C. March color *Sunset* v239 no4 p90 O 2017

Cooking (Leeks)

A LAID-BACK Easter Lunch M. C. Cairns color *Southern Living* v52 no4 p100 Ap 2017

WEEKNIGHT COOKING color *Sunset* v238 no4 p90 Ap 2017

WINTER SOUPS FROM THE CELLAR A. Chesman *Mother Earth News* no280 p50 F/Mr 2017

Cooking (Leftovers)

LEFTOVER RICE B. PORTER KATZ and G. LOFTS color *Martha Stewart Living* p69 S 2017

THE LEFTOVERS A. BARAGHANI color *Bon Appetit* v61 no11 p138 N 2016

Cooking (Lemons)

All Men Must Dine R. Kinane color *Entertainment Weekly* no1480 p44 S 1 2017

Aussie Invasion S. Dreisbach color *Glamour* no8 p102 Ag 2017

BRIGHT SPOTS N. Richardson and C. Morocco color *Bon Appetit* v62 no2 p86 Mr 2017

Bringing It All Back Home J. Centeno color *Bon Appetit* p56 S 2017

PEAR POWER C. March and E. Johnson color *Sunset* v238 no1 p77 Ja 2017

The Queens of KING C. Saffitz color *Bon Appetit* v62 no2 p78 Mr 2017

r.s.v.p A. MASON, J. RODIL et al bw *Bon Appetit* v62 no4 p10 Ap 2017

TINY BUT MIGHTY B. Andrews color *Rodale's Organic Life* v2 no7 p92 D 2016/Ja 2017

Cooking (Lentils)

EAT LIKE a GREEK K. SOLLER color *Bon Appetit* no8 p84 Ag 2017

NOT YOUR AVERAGE NOODLE S. KLEIN color *Runner's World* v52 no9 p39 O 2017

Yellow Lentil Salad color *Prevention* v69 no5 p17 My 2017

Cooking (Limes)

Attitude T. McNally color *New Orleans Magazine* v51 no5 p94 Mr 2017

Cooking (Liquors)

Drink the World color *Conde Nast Traveler* v52 no7 p82 Ag 2017

Cooking (Liver)

SLAUGHTER SEASON E. S. Arnarsdóttir *Iceland Review* v54 no6 p86 N/D 2016

Cooking (Lobsters)

HOW TO COOK A LOBSTER THE McLOONS WAY color *Yankee* p93 Jl 2017

HOW TO MAKE THE WINNING LOBSTER ROLL A. TRAVERSO color *Yankee* p90 Jl 2017

Lobster-and-Celery Rolls R. Kinane color *Entertainment Weekly* no1470 p16 Je 16 2017

A shellfish display A. HUTCHINS color *Maclean's* v130 no8 p12 S 2017

SHELL GAME T. Keith and S. Kwak color *Sports Illustrated* v127 no7 p26 S 4 2017

Cooking (Mackerel)

THE WORKBOOK color *Martha Stewart Living* p124 Ap 2017

Cooking (Mangos)

Dive In! color *Amazing Wellness* v9 no4 p80 Summ 2017

r.s.v.p A. MASON, J. RODIL et al bw *Bon Appetit* v62 no4 p10 Ap 2017

Cooking (Maple sugar & syrup)

Maple Dumplings (Grandpères) A. TRAVERSO color *Yankee* p64 Mr 2017

A NEW LEAF color *Women's Health* v14 no7 p38 S 2017

THE SOUTH'S MOST STORIED PIES M. A. Perry color *Southern Living* v51 no11 p132 N 2016

Wake to Cake E. HARE color *Cabin Living* p66 Mr 2017

Cooking (Marijuana)

HIGH CUISINE L. WIDDICOMBE cartoon color *New Yorker* v93 no10 p48 Ap 24 2017

Cooking (Marshmallow)

Fire Cones *Idaho Magazine* v16 no9 p57 Je 2017

Holiday S'mores Rolls A. Larson *Idaho Magazine* v16 no3 p56 D 2016

home made MARSHMALLOWS color *Good Housekeeping* v264 no5 p68M My 2017

POWER PUFFS color *Rodale's Organic Life* v2 no7 p30 D 2016/Ja 2017

Cooking (Meat)

See also

　Chili con carne

　Cooking (Beef)

　Cooking (Ground meat)

　Cooking (Lamb & mutton)

　Cooking (Pork)

　Cooking (Sausages)

　Meatballs

AYESHA CURRY SCORES WITH HER TV SHOW & FOOD DELIVERY SERVICE S. E. JAMISON color *Ebony* v72 no11 p60 S 2017

ballers C. MOROCCO color *Bon Appetit* v62 no10 p90 O 2017

The Burger, Perfectly Done cartoon chart color *Men's Health* v32 no6 p63 Ag 2017

COLD CUTS color *Women's Health* v14 no6 p32 Jl 2017

Curve Balls J. WALDBIESER color *Women's Health* v14 no9 p81 N 2017

Garne Guisada C. BOND *Texas Monthly* v45 no2 p36 F 2017

GOOD TO THE BONE color *Bon Appetit* v62 no6 p8 Je 2017

Hot Boudin! D. CURRY color *New Orleans Magazine* v51 no12 p114 O 2017

HOW TO COOK A LOBSTER THE McLOONS WAY color *Yankee* p93 Jl 2017

How to Make a... JERKY F. MAROUKIAN and T. AIAZZI color *Popular Mechanics* v193 no7 p80 S 2016

How to Sear a Steak C. PALMER color *Esquire* p141 BigBlackBook

A Middle Eastern Layer Cake for Dinner F. Lam *New York Times Magazine* p22 Ja 8 2017

SINGULAR Sensation M. Kiesel color *O, The Oprah Magazine* p135 S 2017

SL cooking school K. Hammonds color *Southern Living* v52 no1 p130 Ja 2017

starters A. MASON, A. STANEK et al color *Bon Appetit* v62 no6 p17 Je 2017

The Swedish Season S. Sifton *New York Times Magazine* p26 Mr 5 2017

THE TWO WAYS TO COOK MEAT F. MAROUKIAN color *Popular Mechanics* p68 S 2017

Cooking (Meringue)

Juicy Little Gems V. Willis color *Southern Living* v52 no5 p138 My 2017

Cooking (Milk)

See also

　Cooking (Condensed milk)

6 Dutch-Oven Recipes C. LAMM color *Trail Rider* v29 no3 p32 Ap 2017

The Art of Uncooking S. Sifton *New York Times Magazine* p32 Ap 23 2017

Desserts for the two of you color *Redbook* p126 F 2017

George Washington's Eggnog F. MAROUKIAN color *Popular Mechanics* p22 D 2016/Ja 2017

THE GOLDEN TOUCH color *Rodale's Organic Life* v2 no7 p89 D 2016/Ja 2017

Cooking (Mint)

Quick, healthy, filling pudding! K. HYMORE color *Redbook* p125 Ap 2017

Cooking (Miso)

Will It Miso? A. STANEK color *Bon Appetit* v62 no7 p34 Jl 2017

Cooking (Molasses)

How to Make... JERKY F. MAROUKIAN and T. AIAZZI color *Popular Mechanics* v193 no7 p80 S 2016

Sugar, Spice & Everything Nice: Grandma's molasses cookies are the stuff of memories for pastry chef Jeremy Fogg *New Orleans Homes & Lifestyles* v20 no4 p24 Aut 2017

Cooking (Mushrooms)

CORNUCOPIA STUFFED SQUASH *Successful Farming* v114 no11 p65 N 2016

EARTHLY TREASURES J. Waldbieser color *Women's Health* v14 no8 p93 O 2017

FAST & FRESH A. KOVEL color *Better Homes & Gardens* v95 no2 p76 F 2016

fully functional L. Turner and L. E. Frank color *Amazing Wellness* v9 no1 p62 Wint 2017

HARVEST FEAST C. Stone *Saturday Evening Post* v289 no5 p76 S/O 2017

KING TRUMPET MUSHROOM *South Dakota Magazine* v33 no3 p36 S/O 2017

SINGULAR Sensation M. Kiesel color *O, The Oprah Magazine* p135 O 2017

Three For the Tray D. Curry color *New Orleans Magazine* v51 no4 p88 F 2017

WEEKNIGHT COOKING color *Sunset* v238 no1 p88 Ja 2017

Cooking (Mussels)

Ciao Time! [Cover story] J. Waldbieser color *Women's Health* v13 no10 p89 D 2016

MUSSELS, REBOOTED M. HENNESSY color *Chicago* v65 no11 p60 N 2016

Cooking (Mustard)

FANCY THAT! A. REDDING and M. DANZER color *Bon Appetit* v61 no11 p104 N 2016

THE LEFTOVERS A. BARAGHANI color *Bon Appetit* v61 no11 p138 N 2016

Spring Fling color *Bon Appetit* v62 no4 p38 Ap 2017

Cooking (Natural foods)

Health Food You Can Love G. Hamilton *New York Times Magazine* p20 Ag 13 2017

Cooking (Nuts)

See also

　Cooking (Almonds)

　Cooking (Peanuts)

Fancy Fried Nuts P. Grandjean color *Southern Living* v52 no9 p146 S 2017

A SLICE ABOVE color *Better Homes & Gardens* v95 no11 p94 N 2017

Cooking (Oats)

See also

　Oatmeal

Crunch TIME J. Koslow color *O, The Oprah Magazine* p112 Ja 2017

Eight Foods to Eat Now for Better Health color *Men's Health* v32 no7 p59 S 2017

How Sweet It Is! color *Amazing Wellness* p88 Fall 2017

Make the Most of Your Meals K. HYMORE color *Prevention* v68 no11 p58 N 2016

Mince and Tatties S. Gutierrez *British Heritage Travel* v38 no3 p76 My/Je 2017

MMM...MORNING color *Good Housekeeping* v264 no6 p118 Je 2017

OATMEAL SOUFFLÉ: How to make the Hay-Adams hotel's genius breakfast confection *Washingtonian Magazine* v53 no1 p151 O 2017

PB & J Oatmeal Cup [Cover story] color *Prevention* v69 no6 p17 Je 2017

The Search for Simple and Good M. Goodman color *AARP: The Magazine* v60 no5A p58 Ag/S 2017

Cooking (Okra)

Easy Okra V. Willis color *Southern Living* v52 no9 p138 S 2017

NEW WAYS WITH OKRA G. LUNA color *Better Homes & Gardens* v95 no7 p104 Jl 2017

Cooking (Olive oil)

Comfort-Food Makeovers L. Turner color *Amazing Wellness* p90 Fall 2017

Game on! *New Orleans Homes & Lifestyles* v20 no1 p24 Wint 2016

HOME PLATE J. Benson color *Louisiana Life* v37 no5 p52 My/Je 2017

Liquid Gold C. SAFFITZ and B. CUSHING color *Bon Appetit* no11 p60 N 2017

SPICE IT UP color *Better Homes & Gardens* v95 no9 p141 S 2017

TABLE FOR ONE C. K. Jackson color *Essence* v47 no11 p111 Mr 2017

VENISON POYHA J. Miles *Field & Stream* v121 no7 p34 D 2016/Ja 2017

YOUR PANTRY color *Good Housekeeping* v265 no1 p112 Jl 2017

Cooking (Olives)

See also

Cooking (Olive oil)

20-MINUTE MEALS color *Good Housekeeping* v265 no5 p25 N 2017

RECIPES *Bon Appetit* v61 no12 p99 D 2016 /Jan2017

Cooking (Onions)

15-Minute All-Organic Meal Under $15 color *Prevention* v69 no7 p16 Jl 2017

5 quick & cute household tricks color *Redbook* p158 My 2017

ALL EARS color *O, The Oprah Magazine* p112 Ag 2017

BEYOND-EASY, COMPLETELY SURPRISING ITALIAN G. Corcos and D. Mazar color *Redbook* p144 O 2017

BIDWLL WINNING BURGER *Washingtonian Magazine* v52 no1 p152 O 2016

CHEFFED-UP CASSEROLE M. HENNESSY color *Chicago* v66 no11 p52 N 2017

Comfort-Food Makeovers L. Turner color *Amazing Wellness* p90 Fall 2017

FILIPINO FOOD'S MOMENT E. Johnson color *Sunset* v238 no3 p73 Mr 2017

Golden! C. SAFFITZ color *Bon Appetit* no8 p40 Ag 2017

MAC AND CHEESE E. McNamara color *Women's Health* v14 no5 p36 Je 2017

More treats, fewer calories L. Lillien color *Redbook* p85 Mr 2017

Outside-In Burgers: Reviving a family recipe with a tip for anyone seeking perfection A. TRAVERSO color *Yankee* p54 Jl 2017

Paleo-Friendly BBQ M. Hartwig color *Amazing Wellness* v9 no3 p82 EarlySumm 2017

r.s.v.p bw *Bon Appetit* v62 no10 p14 O 2017

SOUP SECRETS M. True color *Sunset* v238 no1 p82 Ja 2017

Tamales C. BOND *Texas Monthly* v44 no12 p44 D 2016

Cooking (Oranges)

BLOOD ORANGES M. XERAKIA *Better Homes & Gardens* v95 no1 p63 Ja 2017

ORANGES B. ANDREWS color *Rodale's Organic Life* v2 no7 p45 D 2016/Ja 2017

ROLL PUNCHES WITH THE color *O, The Oprah Magazine* p158 D 2016

Upgrade Your Ride Fuel color *Bicycling* v58 no1 p56 Ja/F 2017

Cooking (Oysters)

Home Shucked N. RICHARDSON, A. STANEK et al color *Bon Appetit* no11 p36 N 2017

KNIVES OUT C. Bond, A. Johnston et al *Texas Monthly* v44 no12 p90 D 2016

NEW OYSTER CULT P. HISE *Virginia Living* v15 no2 p38 F 2017

Oh Shucks! S. Dry color *Louisiana Life* v37 no4 p46 Mr/Ap 2017

OYSTER CASSEROLE L. Cericola, K. Hammonds et al color *Southern Living* v51 no12 p188 D 2016

OYSTER FEST S. DRY color *Louisiana Life* v37 no2 p24 N/D 2016

Oysters: A Love Story T. Rao *New York Times Magazine* p24 Ag 20 2017

SEAFOOD STEW FOR TWO D. ROSE img *New York* v49 no22 p88 O 31 2016

Three For the Tray D. Curry color *New Orleans Magazine* v51 no4 p88 F 2017

Cooking (Passion fruit)

CAN'T TAKE THE HEAT? GET IN THE KITCHEN D. ZICKL color *Runner's World* v52 no7 p30 Ag 2017

Cooking (Pasta)

See also

Lasagna

Ramen

AMERICA'S TRENDIEST COMFORT FOOD D. Joachim chart color *AARP: The Magazine* v59 no6A p10 O/N 2016

Caprese with a Twist R. Melvin color *Southern Living* v52 no7 p122 Jl 2017

CHEAP EATS! *Atlanta* v56 no12 p71 Ap 2017

CLEAN YOUR PLATE color *Women's Health* v14 no7 p162 S 2017

FAMILY NIGHTS color *Good Housekeeping* v263 no6 p143 D 2016

FLAVOR-PACKED PASTAS *Martha Stewart Living* no270 p94 D 2016

FROM ROME WITH AMORE M. HENNESSY color *Chicago* v66 no3 p62 Mr 2017

Garden-Fresh Pastas color *Martha Stewart Living* no275 p13 Je 2017

how to cook PASTA M. GLISAN *Better Homes & Gardens* v95 no1 p64 Ja 2017

Lasagna With Meat, 3 Cheeses, Eggplant, Asparagus and Peas T. SCALICI color *AARP: The Magazine* v59 no1A p50 D 2015/Ja 2016

Light Pasta with a Kick L. Cericola color *Southern Living* v52 no1 p124 Ja 2017

Meet your new favorite vegetable C. Hall color *Redbook* p22 Je 2017

PASTA NIGHT MAGIC C. HENRY color *Redbook* p120 Mr 2017

Pasta Night! R. Melvin color *Southern Living* v52 no5 p123 My 2017

RAMEN EMPIRE color *Women's Health* v14 no1 p44 Ja/F 2017

Salmon Pesto Pasta J. Covert color *Men's Health* v32 no1 p28 Ja/F 2017

THE SLOWER LANE S. ORR *Better Homes & Gardens* v95 no1 p2 Ja 2017

trail chef: Say Cheese N. COTE color *Backpacker* p34 S 2017

Weeknight Wonders L. Cericola and A. Dolge color *Southern Living* v52 no9 p123 S 2017

Your Three-Course Fix *Tennis* v53 no3 p24 My/Je 2017

Cooking (Pawpaw)

PAWPAW MEAD: Foraged fruit + fermentation = funky firewater A. Moore *Mother Earth News* no283 p28 Ag/S 2017

Cooking (Peaches)

BERRY GOOD SANGRÍA M. HENNESSY color *Chicago* v66 no8 p56 Ag 2017

Easy as Peach Pie D. Wise color *Southern Living* v52 no6 p138 Je 2017

THE KITCHEN COOKBOOK color *Better Homes & Gardens* v95 no6 p146 Je 2017

MAKE JAMS WITH LESS SUGAR: These recipes and tips offer a variety of options for preserving low-sugar jams without commercial pectin A. Chesman *Mother Earth News* no283 p16 Ag/S 2017

Peach Ice Cream C. BOND *Texas Monthly* v45 no6 p28 Je 2017

Cooking (Peanut butter)

ICE CREAM DREAM C. K. Jackson color *Essence* v48 no2 p105 Je 2017

'What is big jelly hiding from us?' S. FESCHUK color *Maclean's* v129 no48/49 p81 D 5 2016

Cooking (Peanuts)

ALL GROWN UP *Martha Stewart Living* no267 p84 S 2016

EVERY DAY I'M BRUSSELIN' M. Bittman color *Runner's World* v52 no1 p54 Ja/F 2017

Fancy Fried Nuts P. Grandjean color *Southern Living* v52 no9 p146 S 2017

The No-Bake Marvel L. Davis color *Bon Appetit* v62 no10 p40 O 2017

THE SOUTH'S MOST STORIED PIES M. A. Perry color *Southern Living* v51 no11 p132 N 2016

Cooking (Pears)

crank up the heat C. BOYD *Better Homes & Gardens* v94 no11 p102 N 2016

fully functional L. Turner and L. E. Frank color *Amazing Wellness* v9 no1 p62 Wint 2017

PEAR POWER C. March and E. Johnson color *Sunset* v238 no1 p77 Ja 2017

Cooking (Peas)

JUST ADD GREENS S. CAREY color *Martha Stewart Living* p84 Ap 2017

THE KITCHEN COOKBOOK S. Peacock color *Better Homes & Gardens* v95 no10 p160 O 2017

MMM... MORNING color *Good Housekeeping* v264 no1 p124 Ja 1 2017

One Potato, Two Potato color *Southern Living* v52 no3 p130 Mr 2017

Peas With Prosciutto, Tomatoes and Onion color *AARP: The Magazine* v59 no2A p71 F/Mr 2016

Spring Fling color *Bon Appetit* v62 no4 p38 Ap 2017

Spring Pasta A. BARAGHANI and N. Richardson color *Bon Appetit* v62 no4 p76 Ap 2017

Whole-Grain Goodness P. Grandjean color *Southern Living* v52 no5 p144 My 2017

WORLD OF FLAVOR E. Johnson color *Sunset* v239 no1 p74 Jl 2017

Cooking (Pecans)

A CAROLINA CHRISTMAS L. Cericola and V. Howard color *Southern Living* v51 no12 p170 D 2016

GRANDMA RIMARCHIK'S *Yankee* v80 no6 p37 N/D 2016

IN PRAISE OF PECANS V. Willis color *Southern Living* v51 no11 p150 N 2016

SIMMER ALL DAY, PARTY ALL NIGHT T. B. M. Boyer and A. Shaya color *Southern Living* v52 no2 p110 F 2017

Sportsman's Paradise *New Orleans Homes & Lifestyles* v20 no2 p24 Spr 2017

Cooking (Peppers)

BLACK & BLUE CHILI J. Miles color *Field & Stream* v122 no4 p24 S 2017

FAST & FRESH A. KOVEL *Better Homes & Gardens* v94 no11 p92 N 2016

FIERY FERMENTS to Preserve Your Peppers: Unlike store-bought condiments, these spicy concoctions are rich with nutrients and flavor developed through the process of lacto-fermentation K. K. Shockey *Mother Earth News* no283 p22 Ag/S 2017

Full of Flavor L. Cericola and A. Hickman color *Southern Living* v52 no6 p123 Je 2017

GREEN GIANT J. DRILLING *Cincinnati Magazine* v50 no6 p66 Mr 2017

SALAD DAYS M. HENNESSY color *Chicago* v66 no10 p50 O 2017

super game, BETTER CHILI color *Better Homes & Gardens* v95 no2 p86 F 2016

What's for Lunch? color *Amazing Wellness* v9 no1 p86 Wint 2017

Cooking (Persimmon)

Anniversary Punch K. O'SHEA-EVANS color *House Beautiful* v158 no9 p106 N 2016

Cooking (Pineapples)

Paleo-Friendly BBQ M. Hartwig color *Amazing Wellness* v9 no3 p82 EarlySumm 2017

Smooth Blends [Cover story] K. HYMORE color *Prevention* v69 no5 p76 My 2017

Cooking (Pistachios)

6 Easy ONE-PAN SUPPERS [Cover story] K. Hymore color *Prevention* p84 Mr 2017

Turkish "Disco" Pistachios img *New York* v49 no21 p77 O 17 2016

Cooking (Plums)

Cook This Now: plums C. L. MUSIC color *Bon Appetit* p53 S 2017

Cooking (Poem)

The New Super Bowls R. Meltzer Warren chart color *Consumer Reports* v82 no10 p42 O 2017

Cooking (Pomegranates)

Christmas DELUXE A. Baraghani color *Bon Appetit* v61 no12 p126 D 2016 /Jan2017

DINNER, UNDRESSED A. Fritch color *Women's Health* v14 no7 p99 S 2017

HEALTHY HOLIDAY DESSERTS K. HYMORE color *Prevention* v68 no12 p40 D 2016

IT'S THE BOMB *Martha Stewart Living* no270 p96 D 2016

ROLL PUNCHES WITH THE color *O, The Oprah Magazine* p158 D 2016

SHORTCUT BAKING M. GLISAN color *Better Homes & Gardens* v95 no11 p100 N 2017

SOUPING IS THE NEW JUICING D. Joachim color *AARP: The Magazine* v60 no2A p12 F/Mr 2017

Cooking (Popcorn)

KID STUFF C. BOERS color *Chicago* v66 no7 p38 Jl 2017

Popcorn-Cheddar Frico img *New York* v50 no15 p52 Jl 24 2017

SPICE IT UP color *Better Homes & Gardens* v95 no9 p141 S 2017

THE WORKBOOK color *Martha Stewart Living* no271 p111 Ja/F 2017

YOUR CHEAT SHEET TO... MAKING DELISH presents L. SAXTON color *Seventeen* v76 no12 p106 D 2016/Ja 2017

Cooking (Pork)

See also

Cooking (Bacon)

20-MINUTE SUPPERS color *Good Housekeeping* v264 no3 p135 Mr 2017

BANH MI BREAKDOWN E. MAH *Atlanta* v56 no7 p88 N 2016

Curve Balls J. WALDBIESER color *Women's Health* v14 no9 p81 N 2017

Dinner's done ON THE GRILL! [Cover story] color *Redbook* p116 Jl/Ag 2017

DON'T WORRY, EAT HAPPY C. L. MUSIC color *Bon Appetit* no1 p72 F 2017

FAST & FRESH A. KOVEL *Better Homes & Gardens* v95 no1 p74 Ja 2017

fast & fresh A. KOVEL color *Better Homes & Gardens* v95 no10 p114 O 2017

FEBRUARY RECIPES color *Southern Living* v52 no2 p8 F 2017

FROM THE HEARTH L. TYRELL color *Martha Stewart Living* no271 p64 Ja/F 2017

A Gyro From Down Under S. Sifton *New York Times Magazine* p28 Je 11 2017

Home Entertainment *GQ: Gentlemen's Quarterly* v86 no11 p48 N 2016

HOME PLATE J. Benson color *Louisiana Life* v37 no5 p52 My/Je 2017

Hot Boudin! D. CURRY color *New Orleans Magazine* v51 no12 p114 O 2017

HOW TO SERVE SOUL *Atlanta* v56 no9 p77 Ja 2017

JANUARY RECIPES color *Southern Living* v52 no1 p6 Ja 2017

LASAGNA BY THE LAYERS M. True color *Sunset* v238 no4 p87 Ap 2017

the life C. Stern color *InStyle* v24 no10 p241 O 2017

LIFE'S A PICNIC S. BOCAR and M. SHIH color *Martha Stewart Living* no275 p78 Je 2017

MIRACULOUS, MULTITASKING RECIPES D. Hay color *Redbook* p130 S 2017

NACHO NIRVANA M. HENNESSY color *Chicago* v66 no2 p52 F 2017

NEW WAYS WITH RADISHES M. GLISAN color *Better Homes & Gardens* v95 no4 p84 Ap 2017

NEW WAYS WITH WALNUTS M. GLISAN and J. LUST color *Better Homes & Gardens* v95 no3 p88 Mr 2017

PARTY HEARTY! S. DRY color *Louisiana Life* v37 no3 p22 Ja/F 2017

THE PERFECT BITE: PORK BELLY WITH FAVA LEAF MOLE color *Los Angeles Magazine* v62 no7 p94 Jl 2017

THE PERFECT BITE *Texas Monthly* v45 no6 p106 Je 2017

2017

Cooking (Rhubarb)

Strawberry-Rhubarb Coffee Cake A. TRAVERSO, M. FLEMING et al color *Yankee* p68 My/Je 2017

Cooking (Rice)

See also

Sushi

20-MINUTE MEALS [Cover story] color *Good Housekeeping* v265 no2 p118 Ag 2017

CELEBRATING THE SEASON M. J. Mateo color *Sunset* v237 no6 p88 D 2016

CLEAN YOUR PLATE color *Women's Health* v14 no7 p162 S 2017

EAT THIS NOW GOCHUJANG M. GUSAN *Better Homes & Gardens* v94 no11 p73 N 2016

Go Gourmet on Game Day cartoon color *Men's Health* v32 no9 p28 N 2017

THE KITCHEN COOKBOOK S. Peacock color *Better Homes & Gardens* v95 no10 p160 O 2017

LEFTOVER RICE B. PORTER KATZ and G. LOFTS color *Martha Stewart Living* p69 S 2017

A Month of Simple Suppers L. Cericola color *Southern Living* v52 no2 p117 F 2017

NOT YOUR AVERAGE NOODLE S. KLEIN color *Runner's World* v52 no9 p39 O 2017

Spring Awakening A. Baraghani color *Bon Appetit* v62 no2 p38 Mr 2017

TRADE KALE FOR COLLARDS V. Willis color *Southern Living* v52 no11 p126 N 2017

What We Really Eat G. Hamilton color *New York Times Magazine* p26 Ja 29 2017

Cooking (Rosemary)

ROAST GUINEA HEN FOR NINE G. FARKAS img *New York* v49 no22 p82 O 31 2016

Cooking (Rum)

REDBEARD COCKTAIL J. Sidman *Washingtonian Magazine* v52 no4 p184 Ja 2017

Cooking (Rye whiskey)

A BIG BATCH OF CHEER F. MAROUKIAN color *Popular Mechanics* p34 N 2017

Cooking (Sage)

The Queens of KING C. Saffitz color *Bon Appetit* v62 no2 p78 Mr 2017

Cooking (Salad dressing)

Dress Appropriately C. SAFFITZ color *Bon Appetit* v62 no10 p42 O 2017

Fresh, Homemade SALAD DRESSINGS K. Quillen, M. Wick et al *Mother Earth News* no281 p36 Ap/My 2017

HEADS ABOVE Y. LEE color *Runner's World* v52 no9 p42 O 2017

IN THE KITCHEN M. HENNESSY color *Chicago* v66 no6 p50 Je 2017

SINGULAR Sensation M. Kiesel color *O, The Oprah Magazine* p118 Ag 2017

Cooking (Salmon)

15-Minute All-Organic Meal Under $15 color *Prevention* v69 no7 p16 Jl 2017

Asparagus S. CASTLE color *Better Homes & Gardens* v95 no4 p132 Ap 2017

Catch OF the Day E. HARE color *Cabin Living* p60 Ap 2017

COOKING WITH FIRE L. TYRELL color *Martha Stewart Living* no275 p72 Je 2017

EASY WEEKNIGHTS color *Good Housekeeping* v263 no5 p181 N 2016

ENCORE! M. GLISAN *Better Homes & Gardens* v94 no11 p134 N 2016

FAST & FRESH M. XERAKIA and A. KOVEL color *Better Homes & Gardens* v95 no3 p98 Mr 2017

FRESH FOR DINNER [Cover story] J. Seinfeld color *Redbook* p144 My 2017

FRESH IN A FLASH S. CAREY color *Martha Stewart Living* p72 S 2017

HEALTHY FOR THE HOLIDAYS L. TYRELL *Martha Stewart Living* no269 p80 N 2016

LIQUID GOLD S. K. GILLINGHAM *Martha Stewart Living* no268 p122 O 2016

New Year's Bagel Fest color *Good Housekeeping* v264 no1 p113 Ja 1 2017

The Power of 3 M. Kiesel color *O, The Oprah Magazine* p173 D 2016

Salmon Pesto Pasta J. Covert color *Men's Health* v32 no1 p28 Ja/F 2017

SLOW vs FAST S. CASTLE *Better Homes & Gardens* v95 no1 p100 Ja 2017

SUNNY SIDE UP C. MUHLKE color *Bon Appetit* v61 no12 p146 D 2016 /Jan2017

THERE'S AN APP FOR THAT! color *Good Housekeeping* v263 no6 p135 D 2016

WEEKNIGHT COOKING color *Sunset* v238 no6 p94 Je 2017

WILD ABOUT SALMON! C. Stone *Saturday Evening Post* v289 no3 p76 My/Je 2017

Cooking (Sardines)

The Slice Is Right A. BARAGHANI color *Bon Appetit* p78 S 2017

Cooking (Sausages)

Brats Amore T. Keith color *Sports Illustrated* v126 no17 p24 Je 19 2017

Easy Oktoberfest Feast color *Good Housekeeping* v265 no4 p103 O 2017

Elk Valley Shrimp Boil *Idaho Magazine* v16 no12 p56 S 2017

Hot Potatoes J. Levy color *Southern Living* v52 no10 p128 O 2017

Sausage, Egg, and Garlicky Greens [Cover story] cartoon color *Men's Health* v32 no4 p26 My 2017

THE SOUTHERN LIVING COMFORT FOOD COOKBOOK [Cover story] L. Cericola color *Southern Living* v52 no1 p74 Ja 2017

Stir-Fry Shortcut color *Bon Appetit* v62 no4 p40 Ap 2017

THE WORKBOOK color *Martha Stewart Living* p114 Jl/Ag 2017

Cooking (Seafood)

See also

Cooking (Fish)

EATING WELL S. Dry color *Louisiana Life* v37 no2 p82 N/D 2016

Cooking (Sesame)

A VERY MERRY CHRISMUKKAH M. YEH color *Rodale's Organic Life* v2 no7 p58 D 2016/Ja 2017

Cooking (Shrimp)

15-Minute All-Organic Meal Under $15 color *Prevention* v69 no8 p14 Ag 2017

Asian Occasion D. Curry color *New Orleans Magazine* v51 no5 p92 Mr 2017

CHEERS to MOM P. S. York and S. Castle color *Southern Living* v52 no5 p90 My 2017

DEEP DIVE M. BUSICO *Los Angeles Magazine* v62 no6 p38 Je 2017

Elk Valley Shrimp Boil *Idaho Magazine* v16 no12 p56 S 2017

Go Gourmet on Game Day cartoon color *Men's Health* v32 no9 p28 N 2017

A Great Pot of Gumbo L. Cericola and P. Lolley color *Southern Living* v52 no3 p126 Mr 2017

GRITS S. PUCKETT *Atlanta* v56 no7 p64 N 2016

How Not To Cook Like A Texan C. WALLACE *Texas Monthly* v44 no12 p99 D 2016

Lickety-Split Shrimp J. Levy color *Southern Living* v52 no4 p142 Ap 2017

THE MINI AND MERRY PATRY PLAN K. HYMORE color *Redbook* p126 D 2016

the new CASSEROLE M. GLISAN color *Better Homes & Gardens* v95 no8 p110 Ag 2017

POKE 1-2-3 A. BARAGHANI color *Bon Appetit* no1 p56 F 2017

SUPER BOWLS L. REGE color *Martha Stewart Living* no271 p70 Ja/F 2017

THERE'S AN APP FOR THAT! color *Good Housekeeping* v263 no6 p135 D 2016

THIS IS BANANAS! Y. LEE color *Runner's World* v52 no3 p44 Ap 2017

TORTILLAS TONIGHT L. Cericola and R. Melvin color *Southern Living* v52 no1 p115 Ja 2017

WEEKNIGHT COOKING color *Sunset* v238 no5 p92 My 2017

YOUR PANTRY color *Good Housekeeping* v264 no6 p120 Je 2017

Cooking (Soft drinks)

ALL-STAR PITCHERS L. TYRELL color *Martha Stewart Living*

p58 My 2017

Blueberry Hill T. MCNALLY color *New Orleans Magazine* v52 no1 p110 S 2017

Cooking (Sour cream & milk)

Buttermilk Biscuit G. LOFTS color *Martha Stewart Living* p79 Ap 2017

BUTTERMILK PANCAKES B. PORTER KATZ color *Martha Stewart Living* p55 My 2017

Here's the dessert that bakes itself! C. Hall color *Redbook* p23 Mr 2017

Hit the Sweet Spot L. Cericola color *Southern Living* v52 no2 p140 F 2017

how to cook CHICKEN WINGS M. GLISAN color *Better Homes & Gardens* v95 no6 p112 Je 2017

It's All in the Hands: So much of the pleasure of baking is tied to touch D. Greenspan *New York Times Magazine* p28 Ap 30 2017

RETURN TO GLAMOUR M. True color *Sunset* v239 no3 p80 S 2017

WILD RABBIT RAGOUT C. ELEY *Indianapolis Monthly* v12 no40 p74 Ag 2017

Cooking (Soy sauce)

VENISON LOK LAK J. Miles color *Field & Stream* v121 no8 p26 F/Mr 2017

Cooking (Soybeans)

See also

Cooking (Soy sauce)

Cooking (Tofu)

EAT THIS NOW GOCHUJANG M. GUSAN *Better Homes & Gardens* v94 no11 p73 N 2016

Cooking (Spaghetti squash)

"This Is Amazing! What's In It?" J. Waldbieser color *Women's Health* v14 no2 p95 Mr 2017

Cooking (Spices)

See also

Cooking (Cinnamon)

Cooking (Ginger)

Cooking (Turmeric)

prep school N. RICHARDSON, C. MOROCCO et al bw color *Bon Appetit* v62 no7 p97 Jl 2017

Cooking (Spinach)

15-Minute All-Organic Meal Under $15 color *Prevention* p12 Mr 2017

Eat Your Greens L. Cericola and R. Melvin color *Southern Living* v52 no4 p119 Ap 2017

First the Vegetables D. Curry color *New Orleans Magazine* v51 no6 p88 Ap 2017

The Four Best Power Shakes for Men bw color *Men's Health* v32 no6 p70 Ag 2017

GREEN FUEL L. TYRELL color *Martha Stewart Living* p68 Mr 2017

GREEN GIANT J. DRILLING *Cincinnati Magazine* v50 no6 p66 Mr 2017

INTO THE SPOTLIGHT S. BOCAR color *Martha Stewart Living* p62 My 2017

JUST ADD GREENS S. CAREY color *Martha Stewart Living* p84 Ap 2017

LASAGNA BY THE LAYERS M. True color *Sunset* v238 no4 p87 Ap 2017

LIFE'S A PICNIC S. BOCAR and M. SHIH color *Martha Stewart Living* no275 p78 Je 2017

MMM... MORNING color *Good Housekeeping* v264 no1 p124 Ja 1 2017

Oh Shucks! S. Dry color *Louisiana Life* v37 no4 p46 Mr/Ap 2017

PARTY ON THE GO A. Brassinga color *Sunset* v239 no4 p83 O 2017

PASTA NIGHT MAGIC C. HENRY color *Redbook* p120 Mr 2017

SUPER BOWLS L. REGE color *Martha Stewart Living* no271 p70 Ja/F 2017

The Thrifty Girl's Guide to Brunch S. Sampson and S. G. Levy color *Glamour* v115 no3 p127 Mr 2017

Cooking (Sprouts)

EVERY DAY I'M BRUSSELIN' M. Bittman color *Runner's World* v52 no1 p54 Ja/F 2017

Mixing Bowl color *O, The Oprah Magazine* p137 S 2017

A Taste for Sprouts V. Willis color *Southern Living* v52 no1 p126 Ja 2017

Cooking (Squash)

See also

Cooking (Pumpkin)

Cooking (Zucchini)

20-MINUTE MEALS color *Good Housekeeping* v265 no1 p105 Jl 2017

5-minute PIE CRUST G. Vigoreaux color *Good Housekeeping* v265 no5 p33 N 2017

BRIGHT YOUNG THINGS J. Waldbieser color *Women's Health* v14 no5 p85 Je 2017

CORNUCOPIA STUFFED SQUASH *Successful Farming* v114 no11 p65 N 2016

DINNER TONIGHT C. Morocco color *Bon Appetit* v62 no6 p40 Je 2017

Drumsticks, Please P. Grandjean color *Southern Living* v52 no5 p136 My 2017

gourd almighty C. Morocco color *Bon Appetit* v61 no11 p68 N 2016

Go Whole Squash color *Bon Appetit* v62 no4 p42 Ap 2017

r.s.v.p bw color *Bon Appetit* v61 no11 p14 N 2016

SPEEDY SUPPERS *Martha Stewart Living* no267 p76 S 2016

THANKSGIVING SIDES D. CURRY color *New Orleans Magazine* v51 no1 p116 N 2016

Use Your Voodles S. BOCAR color *Martha Stewart Living* p74 S 2017

Cooking (Strawberries)

In the SUNSET KITCHEN E. Johnson color *Sunset* v238 no4 p94 Ap 2017

A LAID-BACK Easter Lunch M. C. Cairns color *Southern Living* v52 no4 p100 Ap 2017

Make the Perfect Summer Drink J. Momose color *Chicago* v66 no7 p62 Jl 2017

The New Art of Dessert B. HALLOCK color *Los Angeles Magazine* v61 no11 p124 N 2016

Stellar, surprising salsas C. Hall color *Redbook* p30 My 2017

Strawberry-Rhubarb Coffee Cake A. TRAVERSO, M. FLEMING et al color *Yankee* p68 My/Je 2017

Upgrade Your Ride Fuel color *Bicycling* v58 no1 p56 Ja/F 2017

WEIGHT LOSS WINNER color *Prevention* v69 no5 p14 My 2017

Cooking (Sugar)

See also

Cooking (Caramel)

Cooking (Maple sugar & syrup)

Cooking (Marshmallow)

Hot Chocolate *Martha Stewart Living* no270 p100 D 2016

Mixing Bowl color *O, The Oprah Magazine* p176 D 2016

r.s.v.p L. JOHNSON and J. KRAMER cartoon *Bon Appetit* v62 no2 p14 Mr 2017

Cooking (Sunflower seeds)

Crunch TIME J. Koslow color *O, The Oprah Magazine* p112 Ja 2017

Eat these for healthier eyes M. TAYLOR color *Redbook* p82 S 2017

Cooking (Sweet potatoes)

15-Minute All-Organic Meal Under $15 S. WILLIAMS color *Prevention* v69 no11 p14 N 2017

ART OF THE TART S. PUCKET and N. W. HOPKINS color *Better Homes & Gardens* v95 no3 p124 Mr 2017

Autumn HARVEST E. HARE color *Cabin Living* p58 O 2017

FAMILY NIGHTS color *Good Housekeeping* v263 no6 p143 D 2016

FAST & FRESH M. XERAKIA and A. KOVEL color *Better Homes & Gardens* v95 no3 p98 Mr 2017

A Man, a Pan, a Plan color *Men's Health* v31 no10 p34 D 2016

new ways with SWEET POTATOES M. GLISAN *Better Homes & Gardens* v94 no11 p88 N 2016

No Small Potatoes N. COTE color *Backpacker* p30 O 2017

THE PALEO VEGAN L. Turner and A. Nix color *Amazing Wellness* v8 no2 p84 Spr 2016

r.s.v.p bw *Bon Appetit* v62 no10 p14 O 2017

THE SPICE IS RIGHT L. L. Sercarz and M. GLISAN color *Better Homes & Gardens* v95 no9 p94 S 2017

SWEET ON SWEET POTATOES A. Mcgreger color *Southern Living* v51 no11 p116 N 2016

"This Is Amazing! What's In It?" J. Waldbieser color *Women's*

Health v14 no2 p95 Mr 2017

TRADE KALE FOR COLLARDS V. Willis color *Southern Living* v52 no11 p126 N 2017

Your Favorite Fall Foods, Hacked! S. Dreisbach and S. G. Levy color *Glamour* v114 no11 p113 N 2016

YOUR PANTRY color *Good Housekeeping* v265 no3 p128 S 2017

Cooking (Swordfish)

Mother Knows Best G. Hamilton *New York Times Magazine* p24 F 26 2017

Cooking (Tahini)

Cook Like a Pro: Summer Edition [Cover story] M. ROTHSTEIN, A. MASON et al bw color diag *Bon Appetit* v62 no7 p56 Jl 2017

THE NORMAN A. SUSSMAN color *Conde Nast Traveler* v52 no9 p34 O 2017

Why I Love One-Pan Dinners S. Dreisbach and S. G. Levy color *Glamour* v115 no4 p128 Ap 2017

Cooking (Tea)

A Grandmother's Secret Prescription T. Rao *New York Times Magazine* p24 Ja 22 2017

Green Party! V. Veteto color *Women's Health* v14 no1 p120 Ja/F 2017

THE HANDBOOK *Martha Stewart Living* no269 p127 N 2016

LET'S GET HEALTHY-ISH A. RAPOPORT color *Bon Appetit* no1 p8 F 2017

TEA TIME L. REGE color *Martha Stewart Living* p78 Jl/Ag 2017

Cooking (Tequila)

RAISE A GLASS C. K. Jackson color *Essence* v47 no10 p105 F 2017

Cooking (Thyme)

SIPPING FOR THE SEASON T. MCNALLY color *New Orleans Magazine* v51 no2 p90 D 2016

Spring Slow-Cooker Soup P. Grandjean color *Southern Living* v52 no4 p132 Ap 2017

Cooking (Tofu)

15-Minute All-Organic Meal under $15 color *Prevention* v68 no11 p14 N 2016

FAST & FRESH A. KOVEL color *Better Homes & Gardens* v95 no7 p114 Jl 2017

Not All Ragùs Are Italian S. Sifton *New York Times Magazine* p28 N 6 2016

WEEKNIGHT COOKING A. Brassinga color *Sunset* v239 no3 p96 S 2017

WEEKNIGHT MEALS [Cover story] color *Good Housekeeping* v265 no3 p121 S 2017

Cooking (Tomatoes)

15-Minute All-Organic Meal Under $15 color *Prevention* v69 no5 p13 My 2017

BRIGHT YOUNG THINGS J. Waldbieser color *Women's Health* v14 no5 p85 Je 2017

Bringing It All Back Home J. Centeno color *Bon Appetit* p56 S 2017

Char a Different Course M. Bittman color *GQ: Gentlemen's Quarterly* v97 no7 p64 Jl 2017

COOKING WITH FIRE L. TYRELL color *Martha Stewart Living* no275 p72 Je 2017

Cream of the Crop color *Martha Stewart Living* p29 S 2017

The easiest crowd-pleasing brunch C. Hall color *Redbook* p28 Ap 2017

Egg & Tomato Breakfast Sandwich P. KITA color *Men's Health* v32 no8 p38 O 2017

Fiery Ideas J. WALDBIESER color *Women's Health* v14 no5 p146 Je 2017

Fresh & Easy FROM THE FARMERS' MARKET K. HYMORE color *Prevention* v69 no9 p86 O 2017

A Gyro From Down Under S. Sifton *New York Times Magazine* p28 Je 11 2017

Hit the Grill Mark S. MULLEN color *Bon Appetit* no8 p46 Ag 2017

it's TOMATO season color *Good Housekeeping* v265 no3 p61 S 2017

LIMA BEAN LEGACY E. Kleiman color *Los Angeles Magazine* v62 no10 p18 O 2017

MAC AND CHEESE L. TYRELL color *Martha Stewart Living* p61 Mr 2017

THE NORMAN A. SUSSMAN color *Conde Nast Traveler* v52

no9 p34 O 2017

SHOW-ME Flavor color *Missouri Life* v44 no5 p72 Ag 2017

SIMPLY FRESH S. Dry bw color *Louisiana Life* v37 no5 p54 My/Je 2017

SINGULAR Sensation L. Pearson color *O, The Oprah Magazine* p107 Ja 2017

SINGULAR Sensation M. Kiesel color *O, The Oprah Magazine* p118 Ag 2017

SUMMER on a PLATE R. Martinez color *Bon Appetit* no8 p82 Ag 2017

summer on the side Y. Ottolenghi color *Bon Appetit* v62 no7 p50 Jl 2017

Tastes Like The WEEKEND color *Good Housekeeping* v264 no1 p62 Ja 1 2017

WE SAY TOMATOES B. P. KATZ color *Martha Stewart Living* p102 Jl/Ag 2017

What My Chinese Mother Made F. Lam *New York Times Magazine* p22 F 5 2017

your weeknight GAME PLAN C. Ferreira color *Sunset* v238 no1 p60 Ja 2017

Cooking (Trout)

Baked Trout with Mango Salsa S. Evans color *Missouri Life* v44 no6 p72 S 2017

FOOD FOR THOUGHT [Cover story] C. KUZMA color *Runner's World* v52 no6 p30 Jl 2017

PASTRAMI TROUT J. Miles color *Field & Stream* v121 no9 p20 Ap 2017

Cooking (Tuna)

FAST & FRESH A. KOVEL color *Better Homes & Gardens* v95 no8 p124 Ag 2017

home made PICKLES color *Good Housekeeping* v263 no5 p177 N 2016

POWER LUNCHES *Martha Stewart Living* no267 p78 S 2016

SPECIAL PRESENTATION color *O, The Oprah Magazine* p138 F 2017

What's for Dinner? R. HILMANTEL *Scholastic Choices* v32 no3 p12 N/D 2016

What's for Lunch? color *Amazing Wellness* v9 no1 p86 Wint 2017

Cooking (Turkey)

15-Minute All-Organic Meal Under $15 S. WILLIAMS color *Prevention* v69 no11 p14 N 2017

36 HOURS [Cover story] C. SAFFITZ and A. STANEK color *Bon Appetit* v61 no11 p130 N 2016

Basecamp Thanksgiving K. KARLSON color *Backpacker* p32 N 2017

BEST OF WHAT'S LEFT L. Cericola color *Southern Living* v51 no11 p156 N 2016

Easiest Ever THANKSGIVING [Cover story] D. Mazar and G. Corcos color *Good Housekeeping* v265 no5 p10 N 2017

Eat YOUR HEART OUT O. Manno color *Dance Spirit* v20 no9 p32 N 2016

FESTIVE FEAST 3 WAYS color *Good Housekeeping* v263 no6 p130 D 2016

Flipping the Bird *Martha Stewart Living* no269 p82 N 2016

THE HANDBOOK *Martha Stewart Living* no269 p127 N 2016

HOLIDAY GAME PLAN P. Perry *Saturday Evening Post* v288 no6 p82 N/D 2016

THE KITCHEN COOKBOOK *Better Homes & Gardens* v94 no11 p138 N 2016

a place at the table S. ORR *Better Homes & Gardens* v94 no11 p4 N 2016

Sandra Lee Favorites *TV Guide* v64 no48 p14 N 21 2016

SECOND ACT M. GLISAN color *Better Homes & Gardens* v95 no11 p86 N 2017

Spatchcock a Turkey H. DUFOUR color *Popular Mechanics* p32 N 2017

A TALE OF TWO TURKEYS L. Cericola color *Southern Living* v51 no11 p96 N 2016

Thanksgiving Road Trips S. Evans color *Southern Living* v52 no11 p12 N 2017

TOP 5: ... Healthy Ways to Cook Thanksgiving Turkey L. McGLASHAN color *Muscle & Performance* v9 no11 p66 N 2017

UP IN SMOKE BOURGEOIS color *Field & Stream* v122 no2 p66 Je/Jl 2017

WILD TURKEY TONNATO J. Miles cartoon color *Field & Stream* v122 no1 p20 My 2017

Cooking (Turkey)—Safety measures

YOUR BODY ON THANKSGIVING color *Prevention* v69 no11 p13 N 2017

Cooking (Turmeric)

THE GOLDEN TOUCH color *Rodale's Organic Life* v2 no7 p89 D 2016/Ja 2017

A Grandmother's Secret Prescription T. Rao *New York Times Magazine* p24 Ja 22 2017

Lighten Up, New York M. YOUNG color *Bon Appetit* v62 no7 p46 Jl 2017

Spice of Life P. MOLINE color *Rodale's Organic Life* v2 no7 p38 D 2016/Ja 2017

YOU'VE GOT TO TRY Turmeric K. Rockwood color diag *O, The Oprah Magazine* p98 Mr 2017

Cooking (Turnips)

SPRINGTIME IN THE SOUTHLAND V. Howard color *Bon Appetit* v62 no4 p96 Ap 2017

Cooking (Vanilla)

Cold, Creamy GOODNESS E. HARE color *Cabin Living* p58 Ag 2017

SORE-MUSCLE SOOTHER color *Prevention* v69 no8 p12 Ag 2017

Cooking (Vegetables)

See also

Cooking (Beans)
Cooking (Beets)
Cooking (Cabbage)
Cooking (Carrots)
Cooking (Cauliflower)
Cooking (Celery)
Cooking (Corn)
Cooking (Cowpeas)
Cooking (Cucumbers)
Cooking (Eggplant)
Cooking (Okra)
Cooking (Olives)
Cooking (Onions)
Cooking (Peas)
Cooking (Peppers)
Cooking (Potatoes)
Cooking (Radishes)
Cooking (Sprouts)
Cooking (Squash)
Cooking (Tomatoes)
Vegetable soup

The Autumnal Table Throw a dinner party Featuring the hearty bounty of the season M. HERMANSON *Virginia Living* v15 no6 p68 O 2017

Garden-Fresh Pastas color *Martha Stewart Living* no275 p13 Je 2017

GOd bLESS RED SAUCe AMeRiCA N. RICHARDSON color *Bon Appetit* p126 S 2017

GUACAMOLE S. PUCKETT *Atlanta* v56 no9 p58 Ja 2017

HOLIDAY GAME PLAN P. Perry *Saturday Evening Post* v288 no6 p82 N/D 2016

HOW TO GO GREEN [Cover story] S. Jurek cartoon color *Runner's World* v52 no2 p38 Mr 2017

A Middle Eastern Layer Cake for Dinner F. Lam *New York Times Magazine* p22 Ja 8 2017

NEW WAYS WITH OKRA G. LUNA color *Better Homes & Gardens* v95 no7 p104 Jl 2017

Pasta Night! R. Melvin color *Southern Living* v52 no5 p123 My 2017

Potatoes *Martha Stewart Living* no268 p16 O 2016

POWER LUNCHES *Martha Stewart Living* no267 p78 S 2016

Provence in a Bowl T. Rao *New York Times Magazine* p30 Ap 30 2017

SOUPING IS THE NEW JUICING D. Joachim color *AARP: The Magazine* v60 no2A p12 F/Mr 2017

Street Corn at home *Saturday Evening Post* v289 no4 p25 Jl/Ag 2017

THANKSGIVING SIDES D. CURRY color *New Orleans Magazine* v51 no1 p116 N 2016

Ugly but Good: Cooking your vegetables long past 'done' yields a deliriously sweet and rich version S. Nosrat *New York Times Magazine* p28 Ag 27 2017

YOUR PANTRY color *Good Housekeeping* v264 no4 p127 Ap 2017

Cooking (Vegetables)—Evaluation

Telling Tales J. DRILLING *Cincinnati Magazine* v50 no3 p132 D 2016

Cooking (Venison)

THE DEER STANDWICH J. Miles color *Field & Stream* v121 no6 p20 N 2016

HUNGER FLAMES D. DRAPER color *Field & Stream* v121 no8 p56 F/Mr 2017

Savory, Satisfying VENISON RECIPES: Learn the quirks of cooking with venison and use it in these flavorful preparations H. Shaw *Mother Earth News* no284 p28 O/N 2017

VENISON LOK LAK J. Miles color *Field & Stream* v121 no8 p26 F/Mr 2017

VENISON POYHA J. Miles *Field & Stream* v121 no7 p34 D 2016/Ja 2017

Cooking (Vinegar)

GRILLED SWEET POTATOES C. SALAZAR *Indianapolis Monthly* v12 no40 p69 Ag 2017

Hot-Weather Comfort Food: Cold pork noodles dressed in vinegar, from the East Village by way of Yunnan T. Rao *New York Times Magazine* p28 Jl 23 2017

WEEKNIGHT COOKING color *Sunset* v238 no5 p92 My 2017

Cooking (Walnuts)

home made CARAMEL color *Good Housekeeping* v263 no6 p139 D 2016

NEW WAYS WITH WALNUTS M. GLISAN and J. LUST color *Better Homes & Gardens* v95 no3 p88 Mr 2017

Cooking (Watermelons)

Delicious SUMMER FRUIT [Cover story] K. HYMORE color *Prevention* v69 no7 p84 Jl 2017

Punch Up Your Summer N. RICHARDSON color *Bon Appetit* no8 p42 Ag 2017

SINGULAR Sensation M. Kiesel color *O, The Oprah Magazine* p106 Jl 2017

Cooking (Whale meat)

50, 100 & 150 YEARS AGO bw color *Scientific American* v316 no3 p79 Mr 2017

Cooking (Wheat)

Bowling for Breakfast color *Men's Health* v32 no1 p60 Ja/F 2017

Happy, healthy pizza night L. Lillien color *Redbook* p87 N 2017

Cooking (Whiskey)

See also

Cooking (Bourbon whiskey)

BROWN LIQUOR FRIDAYS S. Schneider color *Sunset* v237 no5 p93 N 2016

Cooking (Wine)

ADD ONE OUNCE SCIENCE J. DETWILER and F. MAROUKIAN color *Popular Mechanics* p74 S 2017

Cooking (Yogurt)

BREAK THE FAST I. Kirkland color *Essence* v48 no6 p123 O 2017

Summer Yogurt Dishes color *Backpacker* p38 Ag 2017

WEEKNIGHT COOKING C. March color *Sunset* v239 no4 p90 O 2017

Your HEALTHY, FRESH, DELICIOUS meal plan [Cover story] M. LIPPERT color *Redbook* p120 F 2017

Cooking (Zucchini)

Eggplant and Zucchini Lasagna P. KITA color *Men's Health* v32 no7 p30 S 2017

First the Vegetables D. Curry color *New Orleans Magazine* v51 no6 p88 Ap 2017

GRILLING 101 with Andy Husbands A. TRAVERSO, K. KELLER et al color *Yankee* p54 My/Je 2017

THE KITCHEN COOKBOOK color *Better Homes & Gardens* v95 no8 p152 Ag 2017

MAC'S ZUCCHINI-CRUST PIZZA bw color *Skiing* p22 Wint 2017

Petal Pushers P. Hise color *Virginia Living* v15 no5 p46 Ag 2017

SIMPLY SUMMER: Take alfresco dining to the next level with light, must-try recipes from the celebrity chef and author C. Stone *Saturday Evening Post* v289 no4 p78 Jl/Ag 2017

Toss Like a Boss R. Kinane color *Entertainment Weekly* no1484 p50 S 29 2017

Using All That Squash V. Willis color *Southern Living* v52 no7 p114 Jl 2017

Viva ZUCCHINI D. MARCHETTI color *Better Homes & Gardens* v95 no8 p148 Ag 2017

Cooking competitions

Out & About: Yankee's favorite events this season *Yankee* v81 no5 p82 S/O 2017

Cooking education

Sam & Louis *Scholastic Choices* v33 no1 p24 S 2017

what will the kids think? T. Brodesser-Akner bw *Bon Appetit* v62 no10 p48 O 2017

Cooking equipment

See also
Kitchen appliances
Kitchen equipment
Kitchen utensils
Stoves

Countertop Intelligence K. Janeway chart color graph *Consumer Reports* v82 no11 p34 N 2017

GOOD HOUSEKEEPING REGISTRY WISH LIST N. SAPORITA color *Good Housekeeping* v264 no6 p49 Je 2017

How to Make a... ROCKET STOVE color *Popular Mechanics* v193 no7 p74 S 2016

KITCHEN WHISPERER B. Gold color *Good Housekeeping* v265 no1 p8 Jl 2017

Making Healthy Meals with Minimal Fuss *Tufts University Health & Nutrition Letter* p1 S 2017 Supplement

THE ONE-POT COOKER cartoon color *Men's Health* v32 no8 p86 O 2017

SERVICE CHECK J. Gordinier bw color *Esquire* p34 O 2017

Cooking equipment—Evaluation

See also
Kitchen appliances—Evaluation

WAFFLE MAKER color *Good Housekeeping* v265 no3 p148 S 2017

Cooking schools

PITMASTER TUFFY STONE: THE ZEN OF BARBECUE C. Kettlewell *Virginia Living* p28 2017 Smoke & Salt

Cooking—Computer network resources

Beware of cookery 'science' J. RICHLER color *Maclean's* p59 Je 2017

Cooking—Economic aspects

NEWS BITES [Cover story] *Tufts University Health & Nutrition Letter* v35 no3 p1 My 2017

Cooking—Equipment & supplies

See also
Kitchen utensils
Kitchens—Equipment & supplies
Outdoor cooking—Equipment & supplies

BEYOND SMOOTHIES T. Masters chart color *Yoga Journal* no289 p72 F 2017

The Cheap Man's Guide to a Better Kitchen D. Chang cartoon *GQ: Gentlemen's Quarterly* v97 no4 p54 Ap 2017

A Cut Above J. BAINBRIDGE and N. Pomeroy color *Bon Appetit* v61 no11 p38 N 2016

get in gear color *Bon Appetit* v61 no11 p72 N 2016

JUST ASK color *Vegetarian Today* no2 p6 Ap 2017

Mini Kitchen Makeover V. TWEED color *Better Nutrition* v79 no1 p10 Ja 2017

Modern Metals E. GAUKEL *Treasures* v6 no2 p10 O/N 2016

slow cooker vs. pressure cooker F. DURAND *Parents* v92 no2 p88 F 2017

SPRING CLEAN your kitchen H. Gray color *Better Nutrition* v79 no3 p16 Mr 2017

What's cooking? color *Backpacker* v45 no1 p50 Ja 2017

Cooking—Equipment & supplies—Evaluation

See also
Kitchen appliances—Evaluation

BIOLITE CAMPSTOVE K. Dupzyk color *Popular Mechanics* p18 Ap 2017

Field Notes color *Climbing* no353 p44 My/Je 2017

Cooking—Evaluation

baked GOOD R. Asbell color *Yoga Journal* no288 p85 D 2016

Beans & Rice! K. SHERWOOD *Nutrition Action Health Letter* v43 no10 p12 D 2016

LITTLE EFFORT, BIG FLAVOR B. Lipton color *Health* v31 no2 p110 Mr 2017

Cooking—Exhibitions

What's Cookin'? L. Hartman bw color *Publishers Weekly* v263 no44 p(Sp)14 O 31 2016

Cooking—Louisiana—New Orleans

Mike Gulotta [Cover story] T. McNally color *New Orleans Magazine* v51 no2 p64 D 2016

Cooking—Methodology

Lee Cake J. Story *Idaho Magazine* v16 no1 p57 O 2016

THE OTHER F-WORD J. Sidman *Washingtonian Magazine* v52 no6 p150 Mr 2017

Cooking—Physiological effect

AND NOW FOR THE NEXT COURSE A. WHITING *Washingtonian Magazine* v52 no1 p10 O 2016

Cooking—Psychological aspects

ANNA THOMAS N. Gregory color *Vegetarian Times* v43 no2 p86 N/D 2016

Cooking—Research

Americans Spend an Average of 37 Minutes a Day Preparing and Serving Food and Cleaning Up K. Hamrick *Amber Waves: The Economics of Food, Farming, Natural Resources, & Rural America* p26 N 2016

Cooking—Social aspects

ROLL CALL: Reporting for duty: I tracked down a long-lost IM recipe M. RUBINO *Indianapolis Monthly* v12 no40 p73 Ag 2017

Cooking—Software

COOKED DATA A. Kleeman cartoon *New Yorker* v92 no39 p76 N 28 2016

Cooking—Study & teaching

CENTER YOUR VISION WEDDING WORKSHOP *Cincinnati Magazine* v50 no7 p36 Ap 2017

Steaking His Claim S. KROWIAK *Indianapolis Monthly* v40 no7 p42 Mr 2017

Cooks

See also
Celebrity chefs
Pastry chefs
Women cooks

1983-2016 Jonathan Robert Sobol E. SENGER color *Maclean's* v129 no41 p62 O 17 2016

24 HOURS AT LAMBSTOCK P. HISE *Virginia Living* v15 no1 p66 D 2016

70 WAYS TO BE FASTER, HAPPIER, AND MORE CONFIDENT IN THE KITCHEN color *Redbook* p117 S 2017

Charlie Trotter Is Alive And Well C. SCHEDLER bw color *Chicago* v66 no8 p98 Ag 2017

THE Chef of the Future MARES ONLY ONE DISH CRAB BISQUE à la robot D. MARCHESE img *New York* p40 F 9 2017

Fast Hands! color *AARP: The Magazine* v60 no3A p66 Ap/My 2017

Feed Your Soul J. Lindsey color *Bicycling* v58 no6 p26 Jl 2017

From Dinner Failure to Mealtime Maven M. Santos color *Working Mother* v40 no4 p10 O/N 2017

FROM THE SOUL A. McLellan color *Louisiana Life* v37 no6 p52 Jl/Ag 2017

Funny FiLL-IN C. PATEK *National Geographic Kids* no467 p36 F 2017

GHETTO GASTRO M. MULLEN *Interview* v46 no8 p42 O 2016

Good Chops T. KIRTS *Indianapolis Monthly* p44 My 2017

How One Chef Created THE WORLD'S BEST BOWL OF RAMEN E. Lin color *Los Angeles Magazine* v62 no10 p4 O 2017

How We Love To Look P. KUH *Los Angeles Magazine* v61 no11 p64 N 2016

An Ideal Sundae: Like many of life's great things, ice cream concoctions are best when governed by rules D. Greenspan *New York Times Magazine* p34 S 10 2017

"I Love Being on an Airplane. It's Like Going to the Spa for Six Hours." H. GARVEY color *Conde Nast Traveler* v52 no9 p20 O 2017

IT'S THE PITS C. SAFFITZ color *Bon Appetit* v62 no6 p105 Je 2017

José Andrés M. Ruhlman *Humanities* v37 no4 p1 Fall 2016

Little Italy: Authentic Italian cuisine is among the last things you'd expect to find in Gila Bend, but Little Italy is the real deal. Even Prince Harry says it serves "the best pizza in the world" N. AUSTIN *Arizona Highways* v93 no6 p12 Je 2017

LOCAL FLAVOR A. McLellan color *Louisiana Life* v38 no1 p52 S/O 2017

LOUISIANA PROUD M. SIMONEAUX color *Louisiana Life* v37 no2 p20 N/D 2016

MAGICAL INGREDIENTS CHEFS LOVE color *Redbook* p118 S 2017

MAN of the WORLD O. Strand color *Vogue* v206 no11 p236 N 2016

My Dinner Party with GRANT C. Schedler color *Chicago* v66 no10 p98 O 2017

NEXT GENERATION color *Bon Appetit* v62 no2 p58 Mr 2017

The Next Generation: MEET THE CHEFS BROADENING L.A.'S DEFINITION OF JAPANESE FOOD G. SNYDER *Los Angeles Magazine* v62 no9 p110 S 2017

SECOND COURSE T. KIRTS *Indianapolis Monthly* v40 no4 p50 D 2016

SNOWED IN C. SAFFITZ bw color *Bon Appetit* v61 no12 p108 D 2016 /Jan2017

Taste MAKERS L. REGENSDORF, M. HOLGATE et al color *Vogue* v207 no3 p334 Mr 2017

TOOLS THEY USE color *Popular Mechanics* p112 D 2016/Ja 2017

Ugly but Good: Cooking your vegetables long past 'done' yields a deliriously sweet and rich version S. Nosrat *New York Times Magazine* p28 Ag 27 2017

Vivian Howard J. Crelin color *Current Biography* v78 no8 p49 Ag 2017

Cooks interviews

AARÓN SÁNCHEZ M. LOGAN *TV Guide* v65 no31 p11 Jl 24 2017

GREAT DANE J. DRILLING *Cincinnati Magazine* v50 no10 p122 Jl 2017

Michael Vinegar A. FLANGO *Cincinnati Magazine* v50 no6 p40 Mr 2017

Cooks—New York (State)—New York

Change Thy Ways: A LITTLE FRIENDLY ADVICE FOR NEW YORK CHEFS OPENING OUTPOSTS HERE J. STEIN color *Los Angeles Magazine* v62 no7 p33 Jl 2017

COOKSON, KAREN

CLASH OF THE TITANS cartoon *Vanity Fair* p84 Hollywood 2017 Supplement

Cooks—United States

See also

African American cooks

THE CHEF LOSES IT B. Martin bw color *GQ: Gentlemen's Quarterly* v86 no12 p208 D 2016

CULINARY HERITAGE J. Benson color *Louisiana Life* v37 no6 p26 Jl/Ag 2017

FORTY UNDER FORTY color *Washingtonian Magazine* v52 no7 p58 Ap 2017

Noah Sandoval C. SCHEDLER color *Chicago* v66 no6 p88 Je 2017

A ROUND FOR THE COOKS J. SIDMAN *Washingtonian Magazine* v52 no6 p17 Mr 2017

A Sugar High P. KUH *Los Angeles Magazine* p50 Ap 2017

Cookware

See also

Cast-iron cookware

Food steamers

Grill pans

Pots

Skillets

The Cheap Man's Guide to a Better Kitchen D. Chang cartoon *GQ: Gentlemen's Quarterly* v97 no4 p54 Ap 2017

Cookware 101 color *Prevention* v69 no6 p15 Je 2017

The French Are Coming! A. KNOWLTON, N. RICHARDSON et al bw color *Bon Appetit* v62 no4 p15 Ap 2017

HOW TO CHOOSE THE BEST COOKWARE color *Good Housekeeping* v265 no4 p64f O 2017

Just Throw It on the Grill B. LEONE color *Bon Appetit* v62 no6 p50 Je 2017

STOCK THE PANTRY J. Goodman color *Bloomberg Businessweek* no4500 p70 N 21 2016

Where new meets Old E. Gaukel *Treasures* v5 no5 p4 Ap/My 2016

Cookware—Evaluation

See also

Baking pans—Evaluation

The All-Clad Prep & Cook color *Bloomberg Businessweek* no4528 p75 Je 26 2017

the global gourmand color *House Beautiful* v159 no8 p68 O 2017

ONE-POT WONDERS color *Good Housekeeping* v264 no2 p121 F 2017

Simmer In Style N. STOFFREGEN color *Treasures* v5 no5 p38 Ap/My 2016

SKILLETS color *Good Housekeeping* v264 no3 p128 Mr 2017

table talk D. SCHWARTZ color *Better Homes & Gardens* v95 no5 p14 My 2017

Cool (The concept)

Google Glass Failed Because It Just Wasn't Cool U. Haque *Harvard Business Review Digital Articles* p2 Ja 30 2015

CoolAid (Company)

SOLUTIONS M. Vogt chart color *Horse & Rider* v56 no5 p24 My 2017

Coolants

DUALS ON DIESELS R. Bohacz *Successful Farming* v115 no5 p24 Mid-Mr 2017

Cooldown

6 Rules of Recovery A. HEFFERNAN color *Men's Health* v32 no5 p54 Je 2017

Coolen, Marco J. L.

The formation of peak rings in large impact craters bibl color graph *Science* v354 no6314 p878 N 18 2016

Cooley, Alexander

Dictators Without Borders: Power and Money in Central Asia R. Legvold *Foreign Affairs* v96 no3 p169 My/Je 2017

Cooley, Denton A., 1920-2016

Denton A. Cooley, 1920-2016 M. SWARTZ *Texas Monthly* v45 no1 p54 Ja 2017

Cooley, Matthew

DINNER AND A SHOW [Cover story] A. Young color *Sunset* v238 no6 p58 Je 2017

Coolidge, Calvin, 1872-1933

Getting Out the Vote M. Allen bw *Yankee* v80 no6 p168 N/D 2016

Coolidge, John

All in the (Presidential) Family P. TERZIAN color *Weekly Standard* v22 no44 p15 Jl 31 2017

Cooling of water

Supercooled water survives in no-man's-land A. G. Smart *Physics Today* v70 no2 p18 F 2017

Cooling systems

See also

Refrigeration & refrigerating machinery

HOMESTEAD HACKS: Our readers share clever projects that will help you live a self-sufficient life in the country, the suburbs, or the city R. D. Copeland *Mother Earth News* no282 p72 Je/Jl 2017

Passive cooling doesn't cost the planet J. Miller *Physics Today* v70 no4 p16 Ap 2017

Temperature Check R. THIEL color *Power & Motoryacht* v32 no11 p46 N 2016

Cooling systems—Design & construction

Highly efficient electrocaloric cooling with electrostatic actuation R. Ma, Z. Zhang et al bw diag *Science* v357 no6356 p1130 S 15 2017

Cooling systems—Evaluation

DOCK BOX *Sea Magazine* v108 no8 p24 Ag 2016

HVAC color *Architectural Record* v204 no12 p124 D 2016

Cooling—Equipment & supplies—Software

EVGA's sensor-laden iCX technology revolutionizes graphics card cooling B. CHACOS color graph *PCWorld* p102 Mr 2017

Coombe, Duncan

Can You Really Power an Organization with Love? *Harvard Business Review Digital Articles* p2 Ag 1 2016

"Don't Take It Personally" Is Terrible Work Advice *Harvard Business Review Digital Articles* p2 Mr 29 2017

See Colleagues as They Are, Not as They Were *Harvard Business Review Digital Articles* p2 Ja 14 2016

Coomes, David A.

Positive biodiversity-productivity relationship predominant in global forests bibl chart graph map *Science* v354 no6309 paaf8957-1 O 14 2016

Coon, Carl

Diamond's Space *Humanist* v77 no1 p5 Ja/F 2017

Coon, Carrie, 1981-
Post-Ingénue M. Schulman color *New Yorker* v93 no29 p12 S 25 2017

Coon, Carrie, 1981---Interviews
The Left overs J. Russell *TV Guide* v65 no14 p38 Ap 3 2017

COON, JOE
BRINGING BANDAR HOME color *Reason* v49 no6 p26 N 2017

Coon hunting
A DOG IN THE HUNT B. Heavey cartoon *Field & Stream* v122 no1 p46 My 2017

Cooney, Samantha
Celebrating Firsts color *Time* v190 no12 p6 S 25 2017
Six Poignant Novels for Young Readers color *Time* v190 no12 p61 S 25 2017

Coons, Chris, 1963-
CENTURY marks bw graph *Christian Century* v134 no19 p8 S 13 2017

Coons, Christopher
Scientists can't be silent color *Science* v357 no6350 p431 Ag 4 2017

Coonts, Stephen, 1946-
Armageddon File *Publishers Weekly* v264 no38 p56 S 18 2017

Coontz, Stephanie
THE BIG QUESTION cartoon *Atlantic* v320 no4 p124 N 2017

COOPER, AARON
Conservative Judaism and Its Discontents *Commentary* v143 no6 p4 Je 2017

Cooper, Anderson, 1967-
THE DOUBLE LIFE OF AHMAD OBALI B. SMITH bw color map *Chicago* v65 no11 p104 N 2016

Cooper, Anderson, 1967---Interviews
Anderson Cooper S. STALL *Indianapolis Monthly* v40 no7 p25 Mr 2017

COOPER, ANDREA
The Apostate *Sierra* v101 no6 p34 N/D 2016

Cooper, Andrew
Dialogue Across Difference color *Tricycle: The Buddhist Review* v26 no4 p48 Summ 2017

Cooper, Andrew Scott
THE BIG QUESTION cartoon *Atlantic* v318 no4 p112 N 2016

COOPER, ANTONIA T.
Assessing National Biodiversity Trends for Rocky and Coral Reefs through the Integration of Citizen Science and Scientific Monitoring Programs *BioScience* v67 no2 p134 F 2017

Cooper, Becky
Augustine color *New Yorker* v93 no7 p27 Ap 3 2017
Mermaid Spa color *New Yorker* v93 no3 p19 Mr 6 2017
Monroe color *New Yorker* v93 no13 p28 My 15 2017
Olmsted color *New Yorker* v92 no32 p31 O 10 2016
Sunday in Brooklyn color *New Yorker* v92 no46 p15 Ja 23 2017
Sunken Hundred color *New Yorker* v92 no41 p21 D 12 2016
Take Root color *New Yorker* v92 no37 p29 N 14 2016

COOPER, BILL
THE DISH ON THE SPOONS color *Outdoor Life* v224 no3 p64 Ap 2017

COOPER, BOB
SOMETHING OLD, SOMETHING NEW [Cover story] cartoon *Runner's World* v51 no10 p78 N 2016

COOPER, BRADLEY
LUKE GRIMES *Interview* v46 no8 p108 O 2016

Cooper, Breanna
CHANGE the CITY *Indianapolis Monthly* p55 Ap 2017
Hot on the TRAILS: A ROAD-FREE GUIDE TO EXPLORING CENTRAL INDIANA *Indianapolis Monthly* v40 no10 p59 Je 2017
My Live-Work Loft color *Indianapolis Monthly* p33 Ap 2017
Pot Stuff *Indianapolis Monthly* p27 My 2017

Cooper, Brittny
WRITERS' FEAST color *Christian Century* v134 no10 p30 My 10 2017

Cooper, Brittney C.
Feminism Cranked Up N. SHAWL *Ms.* v27 no1 p44 Spr 2017

Cooper, Carol Bradley
Chatter *Indianapolis Monthly* v40 no10 p13 Je 2017

Cooper, Clay O'Brien
COUNTING THE BIG BUCKS: Yes or No? color *Team Roping Journal* p50 O 2017
DON'T OVERTHINK THINGS K. Santos color *Spin to Win Rodeo* v21 no3 p46 My 2017
GETTING INTO THE SWING OF THINGS K. Santos color *Spin to Win Rodeo* v21 no1 p46 Mr 2017
GETTING THE MOST OUT OF EVERY HORSE color *Spin to Win Rodeo* v21 no2 p46 Ap 2017
STRAIT Chemistry J. Mankin color *Spin to Win Rodeo* v21 no3 p60 My 2017

Cooper, Craig
WORK, WIN, REPEAT T. Foster color *Men's Health* v31 no10 p20 D 2016

Cooper, Dennis, 1953-
Dennis Cooper's Change of Heart: As a novelist, he's been called the "most dangerous writer in America." But what kind of filmmaker will he be? J. McBride img *New York* v50 no16 p104 Ag 7 2017

Cooper, Dominic
Preacher A. D'Arminio *TV Guide* v65 no25 p37 Je 2017
TALK TO ME: PEAK TV HAS BROUGHT A FLOOD OF GLOBAL ACTING TALENT TO HOLLYWOOD. IT'S THE JOB OF DIALECT COACHES LIKE SAMARA BAY TO HELP THEM ALL SOUND RIGHT R. BRADLEY *New York Times Magazine* p32 Jl 23 2017

Cooper, Helene
Call Her Madame P. H. Bass color *Essence* v47 no12 p73 Ap 2017
Iron Lady P. SCULLY *Ms.* v27 no1 p45 Spr 2017
Madame President: The Extraordinary Journey of Ellen Johnson Sirleaf N. van de Walle *Foreign Affairs* v96 no3 p175 My/Je 2017
Routine Horrors color *New York Review of Books* v64 no16 p53 O 26 2017
A Woman in Charge J. MOORE *New York Times Book Review* p20 Mr 19 2017

Cooper, Jake
AMERICAN DREAM color *Spin to Win Rodeo* v20 no10 p20 D 2016

Cooper, James
Odysseys in Skepticism *Skeptical Inquirer* v41 no2 p65 Mr/Ap 2017

Cooper, Jim
ADD A STORAGE BUILDING color *Cabin Living* p65 O 2017
cabin maintenance ELASTO-WHAT? color *Cabin Living* p69 S 2017
Coping with Steep Slopes color *Cabin Living* p64 Ap 2017
IS DIY RIGHT FOR YOU? color *Cabin Living* p67 S 2017
PEACE OF MIND [Cover story] color *Cabin Living* p68 O 2017
Restoring a Log Finish color *Cabin Living* p14 Ag 2017

Cooper, Kari M.
Rapid cooling and cold storage in a silicic magma reservoir recorded in individual crystals color diag graph *Science* v356 no6343 p1154 Je 16 2017

Cooper, Keith
Hunting the Galaxy Killer *Sky & Telescope* v134 no1 p22 Jl 2017

Cooper, Kimberly L.
Decoding the evolution of species color *Science* v356 no6341 p904 Je 1 2017

Cooper, Lydia R.
Companion to James Welch's "The Heartsong of Charging Elk." *American Indian Quarterly* v41 no2 p182 Spr 2017

Cooper, M. J.
Observation of a large-scale anisotropy in the arrival directions of cosmic rays above 8×1018 eV *Science* v357 no6357 p1266 S 22 2017

Cooper, Marla
Dying on the Vine *Publishers Weekly* v264 no9 p77 F 27 2017

Cooper, Mary Ann
On the Job M. Branom color map *Weatherwise* v70 no4 p32 Jl/Ag 2017

Cooper, Matthew
Obama's Considerable, if Shaky, Legacy *Washington Monthly* p11 Ja/F 2017
Schoolhouse Rock Won't Stop Fascism J. Naureckas *Extra!* v29 no10 p4 D 2016
Thinking Again About Crime bw *Washington Monthly* v49 no3-5

p56 Mr-My 2017

Cooper, Matthew A.

Clonal hematopoiesis associated with TET2 deficiency accelerates atherosclerosis development in mice bibl diag *Science* v355 no6327 p842 F 24 2017

Cooper, Patrick G.

Loretta Devine color *Current Biography* v78 no5 p23 My 2017

Tyrese Gibson *Current Biography* v78 no6 p47 Je 2017

Cooper, R. L.

Observation of coherent elastic neutrino-nucleus scattering diag *Science* v357 no6356 p1123 S 15 2017

Cooper, Rachel

SEASON TICKETS *Washingtonian Magazine* v52 no3 p96 D 2016

Cooper, Rand Richards

Confessions of an Interloper bw color *Commonweal* v114 no14 p15 S 8 2017

The Fundamentals color *Commonweal* v144 no12 p28 Jl 7 2017

A Hillbilly Heist color *Commonweal* v144 no16 p27 O 6 2017

Only Connect color *Commonweal* v144 no8 p30 My 5 2017

Sighs, Tears, and Jogging color *Commonweal* v143 no19 p24 D 2 2016

Sold Out: A writer and his artist wife come to regret their choices *New York Times Book Review* p21 Ag 20 2017

Song and Solitude *Commonweal* v144 no2 p22 Ja 27 2017

TONI ERDMANN color *Commonweal* v144 no5 p26 Mr 10 2017

Trials of Faith color *Commonweal* v144 no2 p8 Ja 27 2017

TRUMP'S ANTENNAE color *Commonweal* v143 no20 p8 D 16 2016

Cooper, Richard N.

Basic Income: A Radical Proposal for a Free Society and a Sane Economy/Basic Income: A Guide for the Open-Minded *Foreign Affairs* v96 no6 p154 N/D 2017

Beating the Odds: Jump-Starting Developing Countries *Foreign Affairs* v96 no6 p153 N/D 2017

Capital Offenses: Business Crime and Punishment in America's Corporate Age *Foreign Affairs* v96 no1 p158 Ja/F 2017

Capital Without Borders: Wealth Managers and the One Percent *Foreign Affairs* v95 no6 p175 N/D 2016

The Curse of Cash *Foreign Affairs* v96 no3 p156 My/Je 2017

Dirty Secrets: How Tax Havens Destroy the Economy/A Fine Mess: A Global Quest for a Simpler, Fairer, and More Efficient Tax System *Foreign Affairs* v96 no3 p157 My/Je 2017

Faithonomics: Religion and the Free Market *Foreign Affairs* v96 no2 p170 Mr/Ap 2017

Global Trends: Paradox of Progress/World on the Move: Consumption Patterns in a More Equal Global Economy *Foreign Affairs* v96 no3 p156 My/Je 2017

The Industries of the Future *Foreign Affairs* v96 no1 p159 Ja/F 2017

The Innovation Illusion: How So Little Is Created by So Many Working So Hard *Foreign Affairs* v96 no2 p169 Mr/Ap 2017

The Language of Global Success: How a Common Tongue Transforms Multinational Organizations *Foreign Affairs* v96 no6 p154 N/D 2017

The Man Who Knew: The Life and Times of Alan Greenspan *Foreign Affairs* v95 no6 p174 N/D 2016

Robert McNamara's Other War: The World Bank and International Development *Foreign Affairs* v96 no6 p153 N/D 2017

Shadow Courts: The Tribunals That Rule Global Trade *Foreign Affairs* v96 no1 p158 Ja/F 2017

Taxing the Rich: A History of Fiscal Fairness in the United States and Europe *Foreign Affairs* v95 no6 p175 N/D 2016

Trans-Pacific Partnership: An Assessment *Foreign Affairs* v95 no6 p174 N/D 2016

Cooper, Roy, 1957-

For the Record color *Time* v189 no14 p6 Ap 17 2017

What the Nation Can Learn from North Carolina K. Ross color *Progressive* v81 no4 p34 Ap/My 2017

Whose Law Is It? *Governing* v30 no11 p12 Ag 2017

Cooper, Ryan

THE LAST POPULIST bw *Nation* v305 no5 p27 Ag 28 2017

One for the Money *Washington Monthly* p5 N/D 2016

Cooper, Scott

Tortured Souls *Foreign Affairs* v96 no3 p116 My/Je 2017

Cooper, Steven

Desert Remains: A Gus Parker and Alex Mills Novel *Publishers Weekly* v264 no32 p51 Ag 7 2017

Cooper, Sunny Chermé

The Last Prairie color *American Cowboy* v24 no1 p28 Je/Jl 2017

Cooper, Tim

A Framework for Strategists Assessing Emerging Markets *Harvard Business Review Digital Articles* p2 Jl 2 2015

If Data Is Money, Why Don't Businesses Keep It Secure? *Harvard Business Review Digital Articles* p2 F 10 2015

Cooper, Zachary A.

Potential role of intratumor bacteria in mediating tumor resistance to the chemotherapeutic drug gemcitabine diag *Science* v357 no6356 p1156 S 15 2017

Thinking clearly about China's layered Indo-Pacific strategy bibl *Bulletin of the Atomic Scientists* v73 no5 p305 2017

Cooper pair (Physics)

The fragility of distant Cooper pairs K. Behnia bibl diag *Science* v355 no6320 p26 Ja 6 2017

Cooperation

See also

Industrial cooperation

Public-private sector cooperation

5 Ways to Get Better at Asking for Help W. Baker *Harvard Business Review Digital Articles* p2 D 18 2014

Collaboration, from the Wright Brothers to Robots M. Schrage *Harvard Business Review Digital Articles* p2 Mr 23 2015

What It Takes to Innovate Within Large Corporations S. Ahuja *Harvard Business Review Digital Articles* p2 Je 15 2016

Cooperative agriculture—United States

CO-OP FARMSTANDS for Backyard Gardeners: Yard to Market Co-op has created an adaptable model for even the smallestscale growers to sell extra produce--from a bundle of herbs to dozens of eggs K. Quillen *Mother Earth News* no283 p36 Ag/S 2017

Cooperative research

Business backs the basics S. Suresh and R. A. Bradway color *Science* v354 no6309 p151 O 14 2016

GETTING YOUR STARS TO COLLABORATE H. K. GARDNER color *Harvard Business Review* v95 no1 p100 Ja/F 2017

It's the Partnership, Stupid B. SHNEIDERMAN and J. HENDLER *Issues in Science & Technology* v33 no4 p37 Summ 2017

A Scientist-Fisherman Partnership: COLLABORATION SPURS MUTUAL BENEFITS FOR RESEARCH AND INDUSTRY V. LaCapra *Oceanus* v52 no2 p4 Spr 2017

Cooperative societies

HOW COMMUNISTS AND CATHOLICS BUILT A COMMONWEALTH N. Schneider color *America* v217 no6 p18 S 18 2017

Cooperative societies—United States

Energy Cooperatives Make 'Solar Gardens' Bloom L. Noyes *Mother Earth News* no283 p8 Ag/S 2017

Greenbelt Earns Its Cooperative Stripes A. N. IFATEYO *In These Times* v41 no8 p8 Ag 2017

Cooperrider, Kensy

Making the rounds color *Science* v356 no6341 p914 Je 1 2017

Cooper's hawk

Cooper's Hawks N. Austin *Arizona Highways* v93 no10 p13 O 2017

Cooperstown (N.Y.)—Description & travel

Dad Trippers J. Passov color *Golf Magazine* v59 no6 p102 Je 2017

Cooray, A.

iPTF16geu: A multiply imaged, gravitationally lensed type Ia supernova color diag graph *Science* v356 no6335 p291 Ap 21 2017

Coordination compounds

Ammonia activation at a metal J. Hoover bibl diag *Science* v354 no6313 p707 N 11 2016

Coordination-induced weakening of ammonia,water, and hydrazine X–H bonds in a molybdenum complex M. J. Bezdek, Sheng Guo et al bibl diag *Science* v354 no6313 p730 N 11 2016

Coordinators (Human services)

How I found my outreach niche M. Wheeler-Dubas color *Science* v357 no6353 p837 Ag 25 2017

Coots, John Frederick

SANTA'S SURVEILLANCE R. MARR *Missouri Life* v43 no7 p65 D 2016/Ja 2017

Coover, Robert

The Hanging of the Schoolmarm cartoon *New Yorker* v92 no39

p80 N 28 2016

Twain's Men R. POWERS *New York Times Book Review* p11 Ja 22 2017

Copaken, Deborah

SEASONS FLEETING color *O, The Oprah Magazine* p35 S 2017

Copan, Lil

#24 Freud's Last Words: Dreams Follow the Mouth *Christian Century* v134 no12 p47 Je 7 2017

Angels Speaking Hebrew color *Christian Century* v133 no22 p47 O 26 2016

Daughter of an Irish Catholic and Bengali Muslim, by Liz Hingley color *Christian Century* v134 no4 p63 F 15 2017

Disrupting the Cradle to Prison Pipeline, by Ndume Olatushani color *Christian Century* v134 no8 p1 Ap 12 2017

Door Project artists from The Learning Tree, Derek Tuder and Astoshia Young color *Christian Century* v134 no10 p63 My 10 2017

The Fire Within; Sky Steps color *Christian Century* v134 no22 p47 O 25 2017

Gospel Feelings (gospelfeelings.com) color *Christian Century* v134 no2 p47 Ja 18 2017

Moses Caring for the Lost Lamb in Front of the Burning Bush; the book Maftir Yonah; Caleb Quieted the People color *Christian Century* v134 no20 p47 S 27 2017

Mural at Zaatari Syrian refugee camp, Jordan, 2013 color *Christian Century* v134 no6 p47 Mr 15 2017

ON Art *Christian Century* v134 no16 p39 Ag 2 2017

The Return color *Christian Century* v134 no18 p47 Ag 30 2017

Copayments (Insurance)

Five Minutes to PrEP Z. ZANE color *Advocate* no1090 p55 Ap 2017

Cope, Leslie

Mismatch repair deficiency predicts response of solid tumors to PD-1 blockade chart graph *Science* v357 no6349 p409 Jl 28 2017

Copel, Laurence

THE BUNGALOW BOOK LADY D. RUTH WILSON color *New Orleans Magazine* v51 no2 p34 D 2016

Copeland, Bryan

Copeland Taps Cosmic Vibes for Aardvarks' Disc K. Micallef color *Downbeat* v84 no8 p16 Ag 2017

Copeland, Drew

Being There bw color *Climbing* no355 p22 Ag 2017

Farm City color *Alternatives Journal (AJ) - Canada's Environmental Voice* v42 no2 p70 2016

Copeland, Edmund

Thomas Walter Bannerman Kibble *Physics Today* v69 no12 p68 D 2016

Copeland, Misty, 1982——Interviews

PEG + CAT M. LOGAN cartoon color *TV Guide* v64 no42 p46 O 10 2016

This Is What a Beauty Icon Looks Like Y. Chu color *Glamour* v115 no10 p87 O 2017

Copeland, Robert D.

DIY WIND GENERATOR *Mother Earth News* no281 p74 Ap/My 2017

HOMESTEAD HACKS: Our readers share clever projects that will help you live a self-sufficient life in the country, the suburbs, or the city *Mother Earth News* no282 p72 Je/Jl 2017

Copenhagen (Denmark)

Elegant Finish H. PEARMAN *Architectural Record* v205 no7 p99 Jl 2017

Copenhagen (Denmark)—Description & travel

THE DANISH GIRL E. FLORIO color *Conde Nast Traveler* v52 no4 p20 Ap 2017

Copepoda

Copepods Against Aedes Mosquitoes: A Very Risky Strategy P. N. COELHO and R. HENRY *BioScience* v67 no6 p489 Je 2017

Copepoda—Ecology

Journey Into the Ocean's Microbiomes A. A. Almada color *Oceanus* v51 no2 p68 Wint 2016

Copper

The Bottom Line J. Seidel color *Sail* v48 no4 p60 Ap 2017

Copper Canteen (Music)

'COPPER CANTEEN' R. GRAHAM bw *New York Times Magazine* p47 Mr 12 2017

Copper ions

Dynamic multinuclear sites formed by mobilized copper ions in NOx selective catalytic reduction C. Paolucci, I. Khurana et al bw color diag graph *Science* v357 no6354 p898 S 1 2017

Copper miners

Clayton Kenneth Cassidy A. A. DAVIS color *Maclean's* v130 no7 p66 Ag 2017

Copper mines & mining—History

Copper Queen Mine: Over the course of nearly 100 years, the Copper Queen Mine produced billions of pounds of copper. The mining operation closed in 1975, but the mine itself is still open to tourists who aren't afraid to take a train 1,500 feet into... N. AUSTIN *Arizona Highways* v93 no6 p8 Je 2017

Copper oxide

Active sites for CO2 hydrogenation to methanol on Cu/ZnO catalysts S. Kattel, P. J. Ramírez et al bibl graph *Science* v355 no6331 p1296 Mr 24 2017

Selective anaerobic oxidation of methane enables direct synthesis of methanol V. L. Sushkevich, D. Palagin et al diag graph *Science* v356 no6337 p523 My 5 2017

Copper wire

ASK OLD HOUSE JOURNAL M. E. Polson color *Old House Journal* v45 no3 p60 My 2017

Copperfield, David, 1956——Interviews

DAVID COPPERFIELD J. APATOW *Interview* v47 no1 p84 F 2017

Copperwork

ANDEAN COPPER AGE E. A. POWELL color *Archaeology* v70 no5 p20 S/O 2017

COPPER BRACELETS N. MOREAU color *Popular Mechanics* p97 Mr 2017

Copping, Ryan

The Promise and Challenge of Big Data for Pharma *Harvard Business Review Digital Articles* p2 N 29 2016

Coppins, McKay

The Defector cartoon *Atlantic* v320 no1 p20 Jl/Ag 2017

The Gentleman From Arizona color *Atlantic* v320 no2 p18 S 2017

What if the right-wing media wins? bw color *Columbia Journalism Review* v56 no2 p52 Fall 2017

Coppock, Mike

It Happened Here: Palo Duro Canyon color *American Cowboy* p65 LEGENDS OF TEXAS Special Issue 2017

Coppola, Eleanor

Paris Can Wait L. Greenblatt color *Entertainment Weekly* no1466 p44 My 19 2017

Coppola, Gabrielle

Deal Snapshot Intel + Mobileye diag graph *Bloomberg Businessweek* no4515 p21 Mr 20 2017

It's happening again color graph *Bloomberg Businessweek* no4531 p23 Jl 24 2017

Patience You Must Have, My Young Investors color *Bloomberg Businessweek* no4503 p27 D 12 2016

Coppola, Gia

Black, White & Right E. Wilson color *InStyle* v24 no7 p48 Jl 2017

COPPOLA, JOSEPH

Politicking and Emergent Media: US Presidential Elections of the 1890s *Film Quarterly* v71 no1 p123 Fall 2017

Coppola, Shawna

THE POWER OF REVISION color *Literacy Today (2411-7862)* v34 no5 p40 Mr/Ap 2017

Coppola, Sofia, 1971-

THE BEGUILED D. Coggan color *Entertainment Weekly* no1463/1464 p56 Ap/My 2017

The Beguiled Explores the Dark Side of Female Desire S. Zacharek color *Time* v190 no1 p51 Jl 3 2017

Best Director S. Zacharek color *Time* v189 no24 p40 Je 26 2017

EN PLEIN AIR D. GILMORE color *Vanity Fair* v59 no9 p145 S 2017

Love Is a Battlefield P. Travers color *Rolling Stone* no1290 p55 Je 29 2017

Coppola, Sophia

SOFIA COPPOLA'S THE BEGUILED D. Coggan color *Entertainment Weekly* no1453 p46 F 17 2017

COPPOLILLO, ROB

Fast, Safe, and Easy Anchoring color *Climbing* no355 p50 Ag 2017

The LSD Lower color *Climbing* no353 p50 My/Je 2017

Protect Your Belay, Protect Your Belayer color *Climbing* no354 p42 Jl 2017

Coptic Church

Egyptian Copts finally fulfilling dream of Jerusalem pilgrimage J. Wirtschafter and M. Nader color *Christian Century* v134 no9 p15 Ap 26 2017

Coptic Church—Egypt

Egypt's Copts face rising fears, divisions J. Wirtschafter, M. Nader et al color *Christian Century* v134 no10 p14 My 10 2017

Copus, Nick

Arrow D. Holbrook *TV Guide* v64 no48 p40 N 21 2016

Copying

UNKNOWN MAKERS A. Provan *Art in America* v104 no9 p138 O 2016

Copyright

Battle for Access E. BETZ color *Discover* v38 no1 p34 Ja/F 2017

Deals R. DEAHL color *Publishers Weekly* v264 no17 p12 Ap 24 2017

Obama Deal Sparks $65 Million Mystery J. Milliot, R. Deahl et al *Publishers Weekly* v264 no10 p8 Mr 6 2017

A Way to Make the National Digital Library Work: An Exchange M. Rasenberger bw *New York Review of Books* v63 no20 p101 D 22 2016

Copyright infringement lawsuits

AROUND THE WORLD *Science* v356 no6345 p1314 Je 30 2017

Copyright infringement—Canada

STUDENT DOWNLOADERS BEWARE M. ROBINSON color *Maclean's* v129 no44 p56 N 7 2016

Copyright lawsuits

Free the Copyright Office M. RASENBERGER *Publishers Weekly* v264 no19 p64 My 8 2017

Copyright licenses

Deals R. DEAHL bw color *Publishers Weekly* v264 no38 p13 S 18 2017

Copyright of digital media

See also

Digital rights management

The Weird Rules Governing What We Download K. Wiens *Harvard Business Review Digital Articles* p2 N 3 2015

Copyright—News briefs

Deals D. LEFFERTS color *Publishers Weekly* v263 no48 p12 N 28 2014

Deals R. DEAHL color *Publishers Weekly* v264 no10 p7 Mr 6 2017

Copyright—United States

Copyright Reform Is Never Happening A. R. Albanese *Publishers Weekly* v264 no16 p21 Ap 17 2017

Coquelle, Nicolas

The cytotoxic Staphylococcus aureus PSMα3 reveals a cross-α amyloid-like fibril bibl color diag graph *Science* v355 no6327 p831 F 24 2017

Coquina

Old Town N. Moreland bw cartoon color *Old House Journal* v45 no2 p34 Ap 2017

Coral bleaching

EYES IN THE DEEP J. Fischman color diag *Scientific American* v315 no6 p80 D 2016

Persistent Heat Decimates Coral Reefs D. FOX color *Discover* v38 no1 p23 Ja/F 2017

REBUILDING Reefs A. McDermott cartoon color *Science News* v190 no9 p18 O 29 2016

Coral reef ecology

See also

Coral bleaching

Coral Crusader H. Barkley color *Oceanus* v51 no2 p28 Wint 2016

Hidden Battles Reefs T. DeCarlo color *Oceanus* v51 no2 p32 Wint 2016

Ultrasounds for Coral Reefs? M. Kaplan color *Oceanus* v51 no2 p36 Wint 2016

Coral reef fishes—Physiology

The better to eat you with, my dear H. Thompson color *Science News* v191 no13 p44 Jl 8 2017

Coral reef restoration

REBUILDING Reefs A. McDermott cartoon color *Science News* v190 no9 p18 O 29 2016

Coral reefs & islands

Can deep reefs rescue shallow ones? K. R. Weiss *Science* v355 no6328 p903 Mr 3 2017

Can We Save Coral Reefs? C. Manfrino *UN Chronicle* v54 no1/2 p1 2017

Corrigendum: Assessing National Biodiversity Trends for Rocky and Coral Reefs through the Integration of Citizen Science and Scientific Monitoring Programs *BioScience* v67 no8 p774 Ag 2017

FINDINGS *Harper's Magazine* v333 no1998 p96 N 2016

More Floods and Faster-Rising Sea Levels: GEOLOGICAL RECORDS HELP FORECAST ESCALATING COASTAL HAZARDS L. Lippsett *Oceanus* v52 no2 p8 Spr 2017

Refilling the coral reef glass D. Obura color *Science* v357 no6357 p1215 S 22 2017

TheMap K. Wiles *History Today* v66 no11 p32 N 2016

Coral reefs & islands—Australia

See also

Great Barrier Reef

Australia needs a wake-up call N. Shumway, M. Maron et al bibl color *Science* v355 no6328 p918 Mr 3 2017

Coral reefs & islands—Caribbean Sea

See also

Mesoamerican Reef

Coral reefs & islands—Environmental conditions

21st-century rise in anthropogenic nitrogen deposition on a remote coral reef H. Ren, Chen et al diag graph *Science* v356 no6339 p749 My 19 2017

Coral reefs & islands—Mexico

BACK FROM THE DEAD P. RAINS *Sea Magazine* v108 no10 p18 O 2016

Coral Sea

Protecting the Coral Sea-the Cradle to the Great Barrier Reef A. Pedder *UN Chronicle* v54 no1/2 p1 2017

Coral reefs & islands—Mexico, Gulf of

Murky WATERS P. BEACH *Texas Monthly* v44 no12 p55 D 2016

Coralroots

SHE HAS AMAZING FOCUS *Arizona Highways* v93 no9 p44 S 2017

Corals

Can deep reefs rescue shallow ones? K. R. Weiss *Science* v355 no6328 p903 Mr 3 2017

Corals tie stronger El Niños to climate change C. Pala color *Science* v354 no6317 p1210 D 9 2016

Hermit crab takes shelter in corals M. QUINTANILLA color *Science News* v192 no7 p14 O 28 2017

Refilling the coral reef glass D. Obura color *Science* v357 no6357 p1215 S 22 2017

RESEARCH color *Science* v356 no6341 p918 Je 1 2017

Corals—Ecology

BACK FROM THE DEAD P. RAINS *Sea Magazine* v108 no10 p18 O 2016

Corals—Mortality

Great Barrier Reef sees worst coral die-off ever color *Science* v354 no6316 p1082 D 2 2016

Corals—Research

Coral Coring L. Lippsett *Oceanus* v52 no1 p7 Summ 2016

CORBETT, HOLLY

Are You Following the Herd? *Scholastic Choices* v32 no8 p16 My 2017

passport to pretty *Parents* v92 no2 p66 F 2017

Corbett, Jim, 1875-1955

JUNGLE LORE Redux A. MCKEAN bw color *Outdoor Life* v224 no2 p58 F/Mr 2017

Corbett, John

Cherry–Sakura color *Downbeat* v84 no5 p49 My 2017

The Hot Box chart *Downbeat* v84 no2 p71 F 2017

The Hot Box chart *Downbeat* v84 no5 p51 My 2017

The Hot Box chart *Downbeat* v84 no7 p49 Jl 2017

Walk Against Wind color *Downbeat* v84 no6 p61 Je 2017

CORBETT, RACHEL

GOTTSCHEE QUESTION cartoon *New Yorker* v93 no19 p20 Jl 3 2017

WHAT MAKES PROTEST ART GOOD? img *New York* v50 no8 p66 Ap 17 2017

CORBETT, SARA

RUTH HUBBARD *New York Times Magazine* p46 D 25 2016

Corbett, Sue

Jason Reynolds: The Hardest-Working Man in Washington color *Publishers Weekly* v264 no29 p28 Jl 17 2017

Jason Reynolds: Writing as Fast as He Can color *Publishers Weekly* v264 no11 p22 Mr 13 2017

MARTIN STEWART color *Publishers Weekly* v263 no52 p67 D 19 2016

The Prose of Cons color *Publishers Weekly* v264 no19 p25 My 8 2017

Spring 2017 Flying Starts color *Publishers Weekly* v264 no27 p36 Jl 3 2017

The Steads: Reconstructing Mark Twain's Only Picture Book bw color *Publishers Weekly* v264 no11 p23 Mr 13 2017

SURVIVAL STORIES color *Publishers Weekly* v264 no5 p24 Ja 30 2017

Corbett National Park (India)

Cutting Edges A. MCKEAN and N. KREBS *Outdoor Life* v224 no2 p11 F/Mr 2017

Corbyn, Jeremy, 1949-

Jeremy Corbyn's Judgment Day J. MILLER *In These Times* v41 no6 p41 Je 2017

Labour's Corbyn Faced Media Attacks From Right and Center--on Both Sides of Atlantic B. Norton *Extra!* v30 no6 p3 Jl/Ag 2017

Corbyn, Jeremy, 1949---Interviews

Jeremy Corbyn M. Leftly color *Time* v188 no16/17 p96 O 24 2016

Corcoran, Barbara, 1949-

I Love My Rope Swing color *House Beautiful* v159 no7 p124 S 2017

Corcoran, Heather

Long Road for NYC Public Projects color *Architectural Record* v205 no5 p26 My 2017

Perkins+Will *Architectural Record* v205 no4 p124 Ap 2017

Skidmore, Owings & Merrill *Architectural Record* v205 no4 p112 Ap 2017

Corcoran, Max—Interviews

Max Corcoran: 'Not Just the Groom' T. Conahan color *Practical Horseman* v45 no1 p24 Ja 2017

Corcoran, Michael

Healthcare Debate Has Room for Critics From the Right Only *Extra!* v30 no4 p3 My 2017

Corcos, Gabriele

Awesome Olives color *Good Housekeeping* v265 no5 p9 N 2017

BEYOND-EASY, COMPLETELY SURPRISING ITALIAN color *Redbook* p144 O 2017

Easiest Ever THANKSGIVING [Cover story] color *Good Housekeeping* v265 no5 p10 N 2017

CORD, ANNA F.

Harmonizing Biodiversity Conservation and Productivity in the Context of Increasing Demands on Landscapes graph *BioScience* v66 no10 p890 O 1 2016

Cord blood

Young human plasma renews old mice L. SANDERS color *Science News* v191 no9 p7 My 13 2017

Cordage

CORDAGE F. Tkaczyk *Mother Earth News* no279 p50 D/Ja 2017

Cordaro, James F.

BUILD A SINGLE-POINT TURNOUT [Cover story] color *Model Railroader* v84 no7 p48 Jl 2017

Corddry, Rob, 1971-

SOUL CHECK *Harper's Magazine* v334 no2001 p19 F 2017

CORDELL, DARCY

SCIENCE JOURNALISM color *Scientific American* v316 no2 p5 F 2017

Cordell, Susan

Plant diversity increases with the strength of negative density dependence at the global scale diag *Science* v356 no6345 p1389 Je 30 2017

Corden, James, 1978-

The 59th Annual Grammy Awards M. Roffman *TV Guide* v65 no6 p40 Ja 30 2017

James Corden M. Rich color *Current Biography* v78 no2 p21 F 2017

Sound Bites color *Entertainment Weekly* no1459 p7 Mr 31 2017

THE YEAR IN CHEERS & JEERS D. HOLBROOK *TV Guide* p34 D 19 2016

Corden, James, 1978—Interviews

This Host Is on Fire! N. Feeney color *Entertainment Weekly* no1451/1452 p28 F 3-10 2017

Corder, Stuartt A.

Spiral density waves in a young protoplanetary disk bibl graph *Science* v353 no6307 p1519 S 30 2016

CORDES, KELLY

Double Vision color *Climbing* no355 p26 Ag 2017

Cordes, Ron—Finance

KEEPING CHARITY IN THE FAMILY R. Derousseau color *Fortune* v174 no8 p54 D 15 2016

Cordiner, Kay

A Simple Way to Involve Frontline Clinicians in Managing Costs *Harvard Business Review Digital Articles* p2 O 11 2017

Cordova, Jon

On a Question of the Day color *Black Belt* v55 no6 p16 O/N 2017

Cordova, Sirena

Q: If you had an extra hour in your day, what would you do with it? color *O, The Oprah Magazine* p18 O 2017

Cordray, Richard, 1959-

Consumer Bureau at Risk *Congressional Digest* v96 no2 p11 F 1 2017

Corduroy

All in for Fall! color *Glamour* v115 no9 p47 S 2017

Cordyceps

Fungus for Fuel and Muscle Growth A. GONZALEZ color *Muscle & Performance* v9 no10 p30 O 2017

Core, Ericson

POINT BREAK C. Gunnestad color *Sound & Vision* v81 no9 p68 N 2016

CORE, LEOPOLDINE

Risk and Reward *New York Times Book Review* p25 My 7 2017

Core competencies

See also

Job skills

The Core Incompetencies of the Corporation G. Hamel *Harvard Business Review Digital Articles* p2 O 31 2014

Do You Have What It Takes to Help Your Team Be Creative? R. Epstein *Harvard Business Review Digital Articles* p2 D 8 2015

Making Matrix Organizations Actually Work H. Vantrappen and F. Wirtz *Harvard Business Review Digital Articles* p2 Mr 1 2016

Corea, Chick, 1941-

Birthday Milestone: Corea Relives Davis Years at Blue Note T. Panken color *Downbeat* v84 no1 p13 Ja 2017

GOINGS ON ABOUT TOWN color *New Yorker* v92 no34 p7 O 24 2016

The Musician H. Mandel color *Downbeat* v84 no8 p71 Ag 2017

Corel Corp.

COREL PAINTER 2018: PAINTING APP ADD TOOLS TO UNLEASH YOUR ARTISTIC POTENTIAL J. DOVE color *Macworld - Digital Edition* v34 no10 p95 O 2017

Corelli

LIGHT ON YOUR FEET color *Field & Stream* v121 no9 p74 Ap 2017

COREN, MICHAEL

Saviour-in-Chief color *Walrus* v14 no3 p16 Ap 2017

COREN, STANLEY

Conversing with Canines: THINK CAT IN THE HAT FOR TALKING TO DOGS *Psychology Today* v50 no5 p73 S/O 2017

Coreno, Annie

Art, Architecture & Photography bw color *Publishers Weekly* v263 no51 p19 D 12 2016

Art, Architecture & Photography bw color *Publishers Weekly* v264 no26 p21 Je 26 2017

BEST AUDIOBOOKS OF 2016 color *Publishers Weekly* v264 no2 p20 Ja 9 2017

'Hamilton' Named Audiobook Of the Year color *Publishers Weekly* v264 no24 p24 Je 12 2017

History bw color *Publishers Weekly* v263 no51 p51 D 12 2016

History bw color *Publishers Weekly* v264 no26 p54 Je 26 2017

COREY, JAMES S. A.

THE HUNGER AFTER YOU'RE FED cartoon *Wired* v25 no1 p56 Ja 2017

Corey, Lawrence

Broadly neutralizing antibodies to prevent HIV-1 diag *Science*

v357 no6359 p46 O 6 2017

Corgan, Billy
Random Notes color *Rolling Stone* no1278/1279 p26 Ja 12 2017

Corgel, Stefanie
THE LOOP ANNIE, D. CRAIG chart color *Runner's World* v52 no3 p12 Ap 2017

Coriander
how to cook CORNED BEEF M. GLISAN color *Better Homes & Gardens* v95 no3 p92 Mr 2017
Top with Cilantro K. Hammonds color *Southern Living* v52 no2 p34 F 2017

Corinthian Colleges Inc.
Defrauded For-Profit Grads Seek Relief S. Nasiripour bw color *Bloomberg Businessweek* no4505 p30 D 26 2016

Coriolis force
Elastic-wave propagation and the Coriolis force R. Snieder, C. Sens-Schönfelder et al *Physics Today* v69 no12 p90 D 2016

Cork (Ireland : County)
Ballymaloe House, County Cork, Ireland D. PRIOR color *Conde Nast Traveler* v52 no2 p46 F 2017

Cork flooring
FLOORING color *Old House Journal* v44 p65 2016 Design Center source Book
FLOORING *Design Center Sourcebook* p65 2016

Corker, Bob, 1952-
Milestones color *Time* v190 no14 p12 O 9 2017
A Senator Takes Charge In the Qatar Mess *Bloomberg Businessweek* no4529 p12 Jl 3 2017
A War of Words With Senator Bob Corker Endangers the President's Agenda P. Elliott color *Time* v190 no16/17 p11 O 23 2017

Corkill, Jade
BUCKLE UP C. Toy color *Spin to Win Rodeo* v21 no4 p17 Je 2017
CORKILL'S SAN ANTONIO ROSE C. Toy color diag *Spin to Win Rodeo* v21 no2 p52 Ap 2017
ELITE HARDWARE C. TOY color *Spin to Win Rodeo* v20 no11 p42 Ja 2017

Corkscrews
The Crucial Difference Between Christmas and a Trip to the Store K. Van Ogtrop color *Time* v188 no24 p71 D 12 2016
Here comes the sun color *House Beautiful* p88 Ag 2017

Corkscrews—Evaluation
PARTY DOWHN *Cincinnati Magazine* v50 no2 p30 N 2016

Corkum, Paul B.
Leonid Keldysh *Physics Today* v70 no6 p75 Je 2017
Tailored semiconductors for high-harmonic optoelectronics graph *Science* v357 no6348 p303 Jl 21 2017

Corlett, P. R.
Pavlovian conditioning–induced hallucinations result from overweighting of perceptual priors diag *Science* v357 no6351 p596 Ag 11 2017

Corlett, Richard T.
The broad footprint of climate change from genes to biomes to people bibl chart color *Science* v354 no6313 paaf7671-1 N 11 2016
Conserving the World's Megafauna and Biodiversity: The Fierce Urgency of Now *BioScience* v67 no3 p197 Mr 2017
Saving the World's Terrestrial Megafauna color *BioScience* v66 no10 p807 O 1 2016

CORLEY, ELIZABETH A.
Mapping the Landscape of Public Attitudes on Synthetic Biology *BioScience* v67 no3 p290 Mr 2017

Corma, Avelino
"Ab initio" synthesis of zeolites for preestablished catalytic reactions bibl chart diag *Science* v355 no6329 p1051 Mr 10 2017

Cormier, David
Teach College Students and Pay It Forward color *Black Belt* v55 no5 p74 Ag/S 2017

Cormorants
The Birds in the Hand color *Canadian Wildlife* v22 no5 p7 N/D 2016
DROP SHOT W. LATHAM and N. KREBS cartoon color *Outdoor Life* v224 no4 p12 My 2017
A genetic signature of the evolution of loss of flight in the Galapagos cormorant A. Burga, W. Wang et al color diag *Science* v356 no6341 p921 Je 1 2017

Corn
See also
Popcorn
Catching ancient maize domestication in the act J. Boddy color *Science* v354 no6315 p953 N 25 2016
A COMFORTABLY LARGE FARM SHOP A. McConnell *Successful Farming* v115 no5 p25 Mid-Mr 2017
Roasted Texas Caviar color *American Cowboy* v24 no1 p68 Je/Jl 2017
UPPER CRUST [Cover story] J. MURPHY color *Runner's World* v52 no4 p28 My 2017
WHEAT BEATS ANOTHER RETREAT *Successful Farming* v115 no5 p11 Mid-Mr 2017

Corn, David
BEE NOT AFRAID *Mother Jones* v42 no3 p62 My/Je 2017
THE RUSSIAN CONNECTION color *Mother Jones* v42 no4 p16 Jl/Ag 2017

Corn bread
CHAMPION CORNBREAD E. Wallace color *Southern Living* v52 no5 p99 My 2017
THE NEW SOUTHERN SIDEBOARD L. Cericola color *Southern Living* v52 no11 p80 N 2017
A perfect (and easy!) pot pie C. Hall color *Redbook* p30 O 2017

Corn diseases & pests
SILENT ALARMS: Look closely. Your corn might be trying to tell you something. Watch for signs of the following 5 nutrient deficiencies K. Birchmier *Successful Farming* v115 no11 p38 S 2017

Corn farming
CORNBOY VS. THE BILLION-DOLLAR BUG [Cover story] H. Nordhaus color *Scientific American* v316 no3 p64 Mr 2017
Genomic estimation of complex traits reveals ancient maize adaptation to temperate North America K. Swarts, R. M. Gutaker et al diag *Science* v357 no6350 p512 Ag 4 2017

Corn flowering
Unlocking a key to maize's amazing success E. Pennisi color *Science* v357 no6348 p240 Jl 21 2017

Corn industry—United States
GLOBAL GRAIN FUNDAMENTALS BEGIN TO IMPROVE: IS THE FIVE-YEAR BEAR MARKET FINALLY OVER? A. KLUIS *Successful Farming* v115 no9 p22 Ag 2017
ONE BIG FIELD M. McGinnis *Successful Farming* v114 no10 p22 O 2016

Corn prices
CORN REVENUE MOVES LOWER: A LONG-TERM LOW IS DUE IN 2017 A. Kluis *Successful Farming* v115 no12 p22 O 2017

Corn seeds
15-Minute All-Organic Meal Under $15 [Cover story] color *Prevention* v69 no6 p12 Je 2017

Corn stover as fuel
Of Corn Cribs and Soybean Sandals color *Weekly Standard* v22 no46 p2 Ag 14 2017
Why-o-fuel? D. Slater *Sierra* v102 no1 p20 Ja/F 2017

Corn yields
NUDGE YIELDS WITH NARROW ROWS J. Dietz and G. Gullickson *Successful Farming* v115 no4 p54 Mr 2017
PROVE IT ON THE FARM: ON-FARM TEST PLOTS HAVE LED TO SUCCESSFUL PRACTICE ADOPTION ON THIS FARM G. Gullickson *Successful Farming* v115 no11 p43 S 2017

Cornea diseases
Common Ailments of the Common Skier M. Hansen color *Powder* v46 no2 p40 O 2017

Cornec, Jean-Luc
TribuT color *Art in America* v104 no10 p167 N 2016

Cornejo, Maria
Zero to Hero N. REMSEN color *Vogue* v207 no11 p128 N 2017

Cornelius, Victoria
Resistance to malaria through structural variation of red blood cell invasion receptors diag *Science* v356 no6343 p1139 Je 16 2017

Cornell, Chris, 1964-2017
Chris Cornell 1964-2017 [Cover story] D. Fricke, K. Grow et al bw color *Rolling Stone* no1289 p40 Je 15 2017
Chris Cornell N. Feeney color *Entertainment Weekly* no1468/1469 p20 Je 2-9 2017

Cornell, David A.
Fracking and the future of fuels *Physics Today* v70 no2 p10 F 2017

Cornell, Jimmy
WHERE DO ALL THE BOATS GO? color map *Sail* v48 no2 p36 F 2017

Cornell University
5 small steps to better health color *Redbook* p96 D 2016

Cornett, Chester
The Chair Maker B. COLEMAN *Cincinnati Magazine* v50 no5 p84 F 2017

Cornett, Mick
Government's Plumbers M. Funkhouser *Governing* v30 no8 p4 My 2017

Cornfield, Gene
Focus on Keeping Up with Your Customers, Not Your Competitors *Harvard Business Review Digital Articles* p2 Ap 28 2016
There Are 4 Futures for CMOs (Some Better Than Others) *Harvard Business Review Digital Articles* p2 S 8 2017

Cornforth, Jon
Aloha Adventure J. Chen color *Popular Photography* v80 no11 p48 D 2016
Hot Spots *Popular Photography* v80 no11 p54 D 2016

Corngold, Noel
Energy from Nuclear Fission An Introduction *Physics Today* v70 no3 p61 Mr 2017

Corn—Government policy
CALIFORNIA TRADE JUSTICE COALITION: Hope for a New Trade Agenda A. LEHMER-CHANG color *Earth Island Journal* v32 no2 p15 Summ 2017

Corn—Health
KERNELS OF STRENGTH color *Women's Health* v13 no10 p31 D 2016

Corning, Beth
Truthiness color *Dance Magazine* v91 no3 p12 Mr 2017

Corning Inc.
Apple invests $200 million in Corning to innovate on Gorilla Glass C. McGARRY color *Macworld - Digital Edition* p46 Je 13 2017
INSIDE THE FAR-OUT GLASS LAB K. Bourzac bw color *MIT Technology Review* v120 no2 p100 Mr/Ap 2017

Cornish, Leah
The Superhero We've Been Waiting For color *Glamour* v115 no6 p110 Je 2017

Cornish College of the Arts (Seattle, Wash.)
Cornish College of the Arts Focuses on the Technical Side *Stage Directions* v30 no3 p52 Mr 2017

Cornoyer, Paul, 1864-1923
Washington Square in Winter color *Magazine Antiques* v183 no6 p31 N/D 2016

Corn—Planting
NUDGE YIELDS WITH NARROW ROWS J. Dietz and G. Gullickson *Successful Farming* v115 no4 p54 Mr 2017

Corn—Sales & prices
ODDS FAVOR HIGHER PRICES FOR 2017 M. McGinnis *Successful Farming* v115 no4 p18 Mr 2017
WHEN WILL TRENDS CHANGE? A. Kluis *Successful Farming* v115 no5 p18 Mid-Mr 2017

Cornuault, Jeffrey K.
Inflammation boosts bacteriophage transfer between Salmonella spp bibl diag *Science* v355 no6330 p1211 Mr 17 2017

Cornwall (England : County)—Description & travel
The Great British Day Off C. MUHLKE color *Bon Appetit* v62 no7 p70 Jl 2017

Cornwall, Courtney
THE NEW RELIGION R. Nelson *Virginia Living* v15 no3 p5 Ap 2017

Cornwall, Gaia
Jabari Jumps *Publishers Weekly* v264 no12 p71 Mr 20 2017

Cornwall, Warren
AGAINST THE GRAIN bw color map *Science* v357 no6359 p24 O 6 2017
THE BURNING QUESTION color *Science* v355 no6320 p18 Ja 6 2017
Can U.S. states and cities overcome Paris exit? graph *Science* v356 no6342 p1000 Je 9 2017

Demise of stream rule won't revitalize coal industry color *Science* v355 no6326 p674 F 17 2017
How a figure key to new HFC pact was born graph *Science* v354 no6311 p402 O 28 2016
RULES OF EVIDENCE color *Science* v355 no6325 p564 F 10 2017
Scientists hope risky winter voyage yields icy rewards color graph *Science* v356 no6335 p234 Ap 21 2017
Sea ice shrinks in step with carbon emissions color map *Science* v354 no6312 p533 N 4 2016
Trump targets environmental science for cuts color graph *Science* v355 no6329 p1000 Mr 10 2017
Trump team targets key climate metric color *Science* v354 no6318 p1364 D 16 2016
U.S.-Mexico water pact aims for a greener Colorado delta color *Science* v357 no6352 p635 Ag 18 2017

Cornwell, Don
What's Your One Shining Moment? I. Boudway cartoon *Bloomberg Businessweek* no4514 p73 Mr 13 2017

CORNWELL, JOHN
LESSONS LEARNED? *Commonweal* v144 no7 p2 Ap 14 2017

Cornwell, Patricia Daniels, 1956-
Chaos *Publishers Weekly* v263 no39 p66 S 26 2016

Corona, Leslie
Hello, Color! color *Parents* v92 no9 p129 S 2017

Corona del Mar (Newport Beach, Calif.)
CORONA DEL MAR, CA R. Jones color map *Sunset* v238 no2 p28 F 2017

Coronado, E. N. H.
Persistent effects of pre-Columbian plant domestication on Amazonian forest composition bibl chart graph map *Science* v355 no6328 p925 Mr 3 2017

Coronado, Shawna
IT HAPPENED AT THE FAIR *Mother Earth News* no284 p68 O/N 2017

Coronado National Memorial (Ariz.)
JOE'S CANYON TRAIL: Of the five trails in Coronado National Memorial, the best is arguably Joe's Canyon, which winds through waves of grama grasses that dispel stereotypes and come alive with the summer rains R. STIEVE *Arizona Highways* v93 no8 p54 Ag 2017

Coronary artery stenosis—Prevention
NEW CARDIOVASCULAR PROCEDURE V. Prevish *Cincinnati Magazine* v50 no12 p80 S 2017

Coronary heart disease diagnosis
Women and heart disease [Cover story] *Mayo Clinic Health Letter* v35 no7 p1 Jl 2017

Coronary heart disease risk factors
What we learn when two killers, heart disease and cancer, collide and reveal a common root S. Mukherjee *New York Times Magazine* p14 O 1 2017

Corporate bankruptcy
Why Bad Things Happen to Clean-Energy Startups J. Temple il *MIT Technology Review* v120 no4 p92 Jl/Ag 2017

Corporate bonds
See also
Junk bonds

Corporate capitalism
Speed, Wealth and Power T. Hauer *Society* v54 no2 p150 Ap 2017
TALKIN' 'BOUT AN ECOLOGICAL REVOLUTION *In These Times* v41 no8 p38 Ag 2017

Corporate communications
The Essential Guide to Crafting a Work Email G. Gavett *Harvard Business Review Digital Articles* p2 Jl 24 2015

Corporate corruption
DEPT. OF SHELL COMPANIES CLANDESTINE ACCOUNTS, & BRIBERY M. SMITH, S. VALLE et al cartoon color *Bloomberg Businessweek* no4526 p46 Je 12 2017

Corporate culture
3 Things Are Holding Back Your Analytics, and Technology Isn't One of Them T. Clark and D. Wiesenfeld *Harvard Business Review Digital Articles* p2 Je 8 2017
The 5 Elements of a Strong Leadership Pipeline J. Bersin *Harvard Business Review Digital Articles* p2 O 6 2016
5 Mistakes Employees Make When Challenging the Status Quo L. Kelly and C. Medina *Harvard Business Review Digital Articles*

2016

Corporate investment in communities

NO MARGIN, NO MISSION C. Leaf color *Fortune* v176 no4 p12 S 15 2017

Corporate lawyers

Why Lawyers Make Good Early-Stage Startup Hires D. Doktori and S. Reed *Harvard Business Review Digital Articles* p2 My 2 2016

Why Your Innovation Team Needs a Lawyer E. Dhawan *Harvard Business Review Digital Articles* p2 Jl 21 2016

Corporate lawyers—Congresses

Legalio Password? G. Farrell and K. Geiger color *Bloomberg Businessweek* no4495 p30 O 17 2016

Corporate meetings

CEOs Can't Give Feedback Only to Their Direct Reports D. R. Conant *Harvard Business Review Digital Articles* p2 Ag 24 2015

Don't Let Inexperience Stop You from Participating in Meetings A. Molinsky and M. Hahn color *Harvard Business Review Digital Articles* p2 Ja 4 2017

How to Design Meetings Your Team Will Want to Attend P. Axtell color *Harvard Business Review Digital Articles* p2 Ap 5 2017

How to Finally Kill the Useless, Recurring Meeting R. Fuller *Harvard Business Review Digital Articles* p2 Mr 17 2015

How to Make Your One-on-Ones with Employees More Productive R. Knight *Harvard Business Review Digital Articles* p2 Ag 8 2016

Corporate power

Carla Harris's 'Pearls' of Power S. Hill and A. GUMBS color *Black Enterprise* v47 no3 p35 O 2016

Corporate presidents

34 MINUTES WITH...Jeff Zucker G. SHERMAN img *New York* p12 Ja 23 2017

MEET 'MR. WINGONOMICS' MARK A. WINGO D. PRESSLEY color *Black Enterprise* v47 no5 p34 Ja/F 2017

New ABA President Outlines Priorities E. Nawotka chart color *Publishers Weekly* v264 no36 p12 S 4 2017

Stephanie Klasky-Gamer M. WAKIM *Los Angeles Magazine* v62 no9 p96 S 2017

USING ENGINEERED PLASTICS INSTEAD OF GLASS, A NEW GENERATION OF SPORTING OPTICS WILL BE LIGHTER, CLEARER, AND STRONGER A. McKEAN color *Outdoor Life* v224 no2 p48 F/Mr 2017

Winning Wireless C. Crowley color *Sound & Vision* v81 no10 p16 D 2016

Corporate presidents—Interviews

DON'T OVERSHARE YOUR MOBILE NUMBER R. STINSON color *Kiplinger's Personal Finance* v71 no10 p12 O 2017

Income Inequality, by Chance or by Choice D. McGinn *Harvard Business Review Digital Articles* p2 Mr 28 2017

Q&A L. BEDORD *Successful Farming* v114 no12 p56 Mid-N 2016

Corporate profits

See also

Price-earnings ratio

8 Reasons Companies Don't Capture More Value S. Michel *Harvard Business Review Digital Articles* p2 Ap 8 2015

APPENDIX B STATISTICAL TABLES RELATING TO INCOME, EMPLOYMENT, AND PRODUCTION *Economic Indicators* p395 S 2016

Barack Obama, By the Numbers B. LUEDERS *Progressive* p14 D 2016/Ja 2017

Bluetooth Headphones: You're Killing Me K. C. POHLMANN color *Sound & Vision* v81 no10 p30 D 2016

Corporate Inequality Is the Defining Fact of Business Today W. Frick *Harvard Business Review Digital Articles* p2 My 11 2016

HOW SHORT-TERM QUOTAS AFFECT PROFITS *Harvard Business Review* v95 no3 p32 My/Je 2017

It Was the Year of March at Diamond Book Distributors C. Reid color *Publishers Weekly* v264 no7 p6 F 13 2017

Publishers See Third-Quarter Bounce J. Milliot chart *Publishers Weekly* v263 no46 p4 N 14 2016

Stop Letting Quarterly Numbers Dictate Your Strategy D. Hersh *Harvard Business Review Digital Articles* p2 D 13 2016

To Manage a Platform, Think of It as a Micromarket U. Haque *Harvard Business Review Digital Articles* p2 Ap 13 2016

We Shouldn't Be Dazzled by Apple's Earnings Report J. P. Vazquez Sampere *Harvard Business Review Digital Articles* p2 F 4 2015

What Apple Should Do with Its Massive Piles of Money W. Lazonick *Harvard Business Review Digital Articles* p2 O 20 2014

X-Ray: Wells Fargo R. Derousseau diag *Money* v45 no11 p47 D 2016

Corporate purchasing

A Better Way for Employers to Procure Health Care R. S. Mecklenburg *Harvard Business Review Digital Articles* p2 N 17 2016

Corporate ratings

AMERICA'S TOP 50 COMPANIES 1917-2017 M. NOER and J. KAUFLIN chart graph *Forbes* v200 no3 p38 S 28 2017

Corporate reform

Government 'taking aim at Britain's boardrooms' GEORGIGYTON *People Management* p8 D 2016/Ja 2017

Corporate reorganizations

See also

Consolidation & merger of corporations—Economic aspects

Corporate divestiture

Can Nokia Reinvent Itself Again? R. G. McGrath *Harvard Business Review Digital Articles* p2 Ap 16 2015

The Example Larry and Sergey Should Follow (It's Not Buffett) T. R. Eisenmann *Harvard Business Review Digital Articles* p2 Ag 12 2015

Getting Reorgs Right S. Heidari-Robinson and S. Heywood diag *Harvard Business Review* v94 no11 p84 N 2016

How to (Gradually) Become a Different Company H. Vantrappen and D. Deneffe *Harvard Business Review Digital Articles* p2 O 15 2014

What Intel Needs to Remember About Marketing N. Dawar *Harvard Business Review Digital Articles* p2 Ap 25 2016

What to Do and Say After a Tough Reorganization R. Knight *Harvard Business Review Digital Articles* p2 O 23 2015

Why Google Became Alphabet T. Zenger *Harvard Business Review Digital Articles* p2 Ag 11 2015

A Yahoo Break-Up Could Be the Start of Lots of Splits B. Gomes-Casseres *Harvard Business Review Digital Articles* p2 D 3 2015

Corporate reorganizations—Great Britain

"We don't talk a corporate language - neither should our colleagues": The Co-op is back from the brink of disaster, and its staff are re-energised thanks to a huge series of immersive roadshows *People Management* p22 Je 2017

Corporate reorganizations—Management

A 5-Step Process for Reorganizing After a Merger S. Heidari-Robinson, S. Heywood et al *Harvard Business Review Digital Articles* p2 D 21 2016

Corporate reorganizations—Research

RESTRUCTURE OR RECONFIGURE? S. J. G. GIROD and S. KARIM *Harvard Business Review* v95 no2 p128 Mr/Ap 2017

Corporate resolutions

Make Your Work Resolutions Stick R. Knight *Harvard Business Review Digital Articles* p2 D 29 2014

Corporate sponsorship

Brands Pump Up the Volume in Pakistan C. Kay and F. Mangi color graph *Bloomberg Businessweek* no4530 p34 Jl 17 2017

Ford Motor Company Fund Supports Featured Document Exhibit *Prologue* v49 no1 p71 Spr 2017

Racing to Run A Two-Hour Marathon R. Penty and R. Weiss color graph *Bloomberg Businessweek* no4538 p18 S 18 2017

Corporate tax laws—United States

Trump vows to cut the corporate tax rate from 35% to 15%. Suppose Republicans could raise $2 trillion to pay for cuts (not an easy task). That would require hiking other taxes or ending popular deductions. And it can't all go to corporate giants, so... S. Kapur and P. Coy *Bloomberg Businessweek* no4538 p34 S 18 2017

Corporate taxes

Bad Apples A. GOLDHAMMER *Nation* v303 no19 p6 N 7 2016

A Brief Guide to U.S. Corporate Tax Reform W. Frick *Harvard Business Review Digital Articles* p2 S 7 2017

It's the Corporate Tax Rate, Stupid T. MECIA graph *Weekly Standard* v23 no4 p10 O 2 2017

ON THE BOOKS L. FARMER *Governing* v30 no2 p52 N 2016

Our Misguided Obsession with the Tax Code J. Fox *Harvard Busi-*

Je 17 2016

Midsize Companies Shouldn't Confuse Growth with Scaling R. Carucci *Harvard Business Review Digital Articles* p2 Jl 25 2016

The New Rules for Growing Outside Your Core Business C. Zook *Harvard Business Review Digital Articles* p2 My 4 2015

Using M&A to Increase Your Capacity for Growth M. Reeves, J. Harnoss et al *Harvard Business Review Digital Articles* p2 Jl 13 2016

When Large Companies Are Better at Entrepreneurship than Start-ups C. Zook *Harvard Business Review Digital Articles* p2 D 27 2016

Corporations—Growth—Management

3 Terrible Strategies for Companies Seeking Growth U. Haque *Harvard Business Review Digital Articles* p2 O 6 2014

Why Leaders Are Still So Hesitant to Invest in New Business Models B. Libert, M. Beck et al *Harvard Business Review Digital Articles* p2 D 21 2016

Corporations—Headquarters

Apple set to open new headquarters in April C. McGarry color *Macworld - Digital Edition* p4 Ap 2017

Corporations—Headquarters—Design & construction

The Art of the Deal M. SITZ *Architectural Record* v204 no10 p78 O 2016

Arts and Crafts L. RASKIN *Architectural Record* v204 no10 p37 O 2016

LAVA C. Foges color *Architectural Record* v205 no2 p120 F 2017

LEGACY BUILDING S. COCHRAN color *Architectural Digest* v74 no1 p232 Ja 2017

Corporations—Headquarters—Design & construction—Evaluation

Apple's New Digs J. Zorthian color *Time* v189 no9 p23 Mr 13 2017

Corporations—News briefs

Movers K. Stock color *Bloomberg Businessweek* no4508 p11 Ja 23 2017

Corporations—Political activity

A Board Member's Guide to Corporate Political Spending C. E. Bagley, B. Freed et al *Harvard Business Review Digital Articles* p2 O 30 2015

Lobbying Is Not Enough to Build Influence Among U.S. Law-makers M. D. Gottlieb and E. Gurney *Harvard Business Review Digital Articles* p2 D 28 2016

Corporations—Political activity—United States

ALEC's War on Local Control J. HIGHTOWER color *Progressive* v81 no7 p70 O/N 2017

Large Employers Are Key to Reforming Health Care R. S. Mecklenburg and L. A. Martin *Harvard Business Review Digital Articles* p2 Jl 27 2016

Progressivism in the Boardroom [Cover story] K. D. WILLIAMSON il *National Review* v69 no4 p24 Mr 6 2017

Corporations—Public relations

See also

Corporate image

Corporate sponsorship

Naming rights

Companies Fare Worse When the Press Exposes Their Problems Before They Do Claeys, V. Cauberghe et al *Harvard Business Review Digital Articles* p2 Ag 22 2016

CONSUMERS FLEX THEIR POLITICAL MUSCLE E. Fry *Fortune* v175 no3 p10 Mr 1 2017

How Companies Use Strategically Timed Announcements to Confuse the Market S. D. Graffin and S. Boivie *Harvard Business Review Digital Articles* p2 Ap 26 2016

NATION ON THE TAKE R. L. FISCHER *USA Today Magazine* v145 no2858 p20 N 2016

When Public Opinion Shifts, How Should Your Company Respond? P. G. Audia *Harvard Business Review Digital Articles* p2 S 29 2015

Your Company Should Be Helping Customers on Social M. Masri, D. Esber et al *Harvard Business Review Digital Articles* p2 Jl 15 2015

Corporations—Ratings & rankings

BREAKTHROUGH BRANDS 2017 L. Gallagher, A. Nusca et al color diag *Fortune* v75 no1 p64 Ja 1 2017

Corporations—Sociological aspects

See also

Corporate culture

The Intangible Things Employees Want from Employers A. B. Thompson *Harvard Business Review Digital Articles* p2 D 3 2015

Corporations—United States

THE BEST SMALL AND MEDIUM-SIZE COMPANIES TO WORK FOR J. Alsever color map *Fortune* v174 no6 p51 N 1 2016

Corporate Inequality Is the Defining Fact of Business Today W. Frick *Harvard Business Review Digital Articles* p2 My 11 2016

THE JUST 100: AMERICA'S BEST CORPORATE CITIZENS S. SCHAEFER color *Forbes* v198 no8 p82 D 20 2016

Corporations—Valuation

Investors Today Prefer Companies with Fewer Physical As sets B. Libert, M. Beck et al *Harvard Business Review Digital Articles* p2 S 29 2016

Making Sense of Uber's $40 Billion Valuation M. Wessel *Harvard Business Review Digital Articles* p2 D 10 2014

Tesla's Electric Shock M. Vella color *Time* v189 no15 p13 Ap 24 2017

CORRAL, EDUARDO C.

Border Patrol Agent *New Republic* v247 no11 p59 N 2016

CORREA, ARMANDO LUCAS

No Safe Haven *Publishers Weekly* v263 no40 p128 O 3 2016

Correa, Armando Lucas—Interviews

ARMANDO LUCAS CORREA I. Biedenharn color *Entertainment Weekly* no1436/1437 p103 O 21 2016

Correa-Baena, Juan-Pablo

Improving efficiency and stability of perovskite solar cells with photocurable fluoropolymers bibl chart graph *Science* v354 no6309 p203 O 14 2016

Incorporation of rubidium cations into perovskite solar cells improves photovoltaic performance bibl graph *Science* v354 no6309 p206 O 14 2016

Correctional institutions

See also

Detention facilities

Prisons

Mindfulness goes mainstream color *Yoga Journal* p24 2016 Special Issue

Corrections (Criminal justice administration)—Contracting out

Closing Doors at Private Prisons A. Greenblatt *Governing* v30 no2 p9 N 2016

Private Prisons Fail S. FREED WESSLER color *Nation* v304 no3 p6 Ja 30 2017

TRUMP SETS PRIVATE PRISONS FREE J. Surowiecki cartoon *New Yorker* v92 no40 p26 D 5 2016

Corrections (Criminal justice administration)—Contracting out—Economic aspects

Private Prisons Get A Boost From Trump M. Stroud and Z. R. Mider color *Bloomberg Businessweek* no4500 p28 N 21 2016

Corrections (Criminal justice administration)—Contracting out—Government policy

Payday for Private Prisons? *America* v216 no6 p9 Mr 20 2017

Corrections (Criminal justice administration)—United States

PRISON BREAK D. SLATER color *Mother Jones* v42 no4 p42 Jl/Ag 2017

Correll, Shelley

Research: Vague Feedback Is Holding Women Back *Harvard Business Review Digital Articles* p2 Ap 29 2016

To Succeed in Tech, Women Need More Visibility *Harvard Business Review Digital Articles* p2 S 13 2016

Corria, Gabrielle

Who I am *People Management* p51 Je 2017

CORRIGAN, KELLY

A MATTER OF LIFE AND BREAST *O, The Oprah Magazine* p84 O 2017

Points to Ponder color *Reader's Digest* v190 no1134 p35 O 2017

CORRIGAN, KEVIN

Arabian Nights color *Climbing* no357 p48 N 2017

A Climber's Guide to Food color *Climbing* no350 p36 D 2016/Ja 2017

Climbr: Climbing Partner Reviews *Climbing* no356 p32 S/O 2017

Goodbye to Unbelayvable *Climbing* no354 p17 Jl 2017

How to Lie Your Way to the Top color *Climbing* no351 p40 F/Mr 2017

How to Not Train color *Climbing* no353 p38 My/Je 2017
It's Not a Free Solo, It's a Highball, DAD! color *Climbing* no354 p35 Jl 2017
Sending Snacks color *Climbing* no350 p42 D 2016/Ja 2017
THANKS, VOLCANOES color *Climbing* no349 p69 N 2016
Van Mouse color *Climbing* no351 p24 F/Mr 2017
Welcome to Sendhaus™: America's Hippest New Climbing Gym color *Climbing* no355 p38 Ag 2017

Corris, Peter
Win, Lose or Draw *Publishers Weekly* v264 no29 p200 Jl 17 2017

Corrosion & anti-corrosives
See also
Seawater corrosion
Q + A *Boating World* v38 no4 p22 Ap 2017

Corrosion & anti-corrosives—Prevention
Procrastination Doesn't Pay C. Caswell *Boating World* v37 no9 p12 N/D 2016

Corrupt practices in college athlete recruitment
CARDINALS' SINS T. Layden color *Sports Illustrated* v127 no11 p26 O 9 2017
SHOESTORM [Cover story] A. Staples color *Sports Illustrated* v127 no11 p22 O 9 2017

Corrupt practices in college sports
See also
Corrupt practices in college athlete recruitment
A Corruption Probe Into College Hoops Exposes More Than Shady Deals S. Gregory color *Time* v190 no15 p17 O 16 2017

Corrupt practices in elections
The GOP Quest to Find Voter Fraud Draws Backlash A. Altman color *Time* v190 no4 p7 Jl 24 2017
Will Bob Mueller Separate Fact from Fiction? [Cover story] D. V. Drehle, T. Berenson et al color *Time* v190 no1 p24 Jl 3 2017

Corrupt practices in the banking industry
CAN WELLS FARGO GET WELL? G. Colvin chart color diag *Fortune* v175 no8 p138 Je 15 2017

Corruption
After Netanyahu N. ROGACHEVSKY color *Weekly Standard* v23 no6 p32 O 16 2017
Early Lessons from India's Demonetization Experiment B. Chakravorti *Harvard Business Review Digital Articles* p2 Mr 14 2017
FONTGATE R. Arbes cartoon *New Yorker* v93 no22 p20 Jl 31 2017
Is the third time the charm for Mexico's 'eternal candidate'? Hootsen color *America* v216 no10 p17 My 1 2017
The Price Isn't Right: Premium ticket costs mean that Broadway shows are increasingly the province of tourists with deep pockets W. SMITH *American Scholar* v86 no4 p101 Aut 2017

Corruption—Prevention
How to fight corruption R. Fisman and M. Golden color *Science* v356 no6340 p803 My 26 2017

Corruption—Russia
The Acid Test of Dissent in Russia B. PARKER color *Weekly Standard* v22 no40 p15 Je 26 2017

Corsair (Company)
Meet the Corsair One, Corsair's 'category-defying' gaming PC debut B. CHACOS color *PCWorld* p27 Mr 2017

CORSELLO, ANDREW
JOHN ELWAY CAN'T BE STOPPED color *GQ: Gentlemen's Quarterly* v86 no12 p186 D 2016
The Kid Is Alright color *AARP: The Magazine* v60 no3A p44 Ap/My 2017
The Revenge of the Happy Warrior color *GQ: Gentlemen's Quarterly* v97 no5 p80 My 2017

Corsello, Jason
Want to Be More Productive? Sit Next to Someone Who Is *Harvard Business Review Digital Articles* p2 F 14 2017

Corsets
THE EVOLUTION OF THE "IDEAL" BODY *Scholastic Choices* v32 no3 p4 N/D 2016
Waist Not, Want Not E. ELWICK-BATES bw color *Vogue* v206 no12 p156 D 2016

Corson, Francis
Self-organized Notch dynamics generate stereotyped sensory organ patterns in Drosophila color *Science* v356 no6337 p501 My 5 2017

CORSON, TREVOR
The Hidden Power of Funky Foods color *Men's Health* v32 no4 p65 My 2017

Corstange, Daniel
What Syrians Want *Hoover Digest: Research & Opinion on Public Policy* no1 p136 Wint 2017

Cort, Adam
100 years OF BOATS [Cover story] color *Sail* v48 no8 p30 Ag 2017
2017 PITTMAN INNOVATION AWARDS color *Sail* v48 no2 p58 F 2017
Another Vendée War of Attrition color *Sail* v48 no2 p20 F 2017
Back to Monohulls for the Cup color *Sail* v48 no11 p17 N 2017
BEST BOATS 2017 color *Sail* v47 no12 p24 D 2016
CAKEWALK TO NOVA SCOTIA color map *Sail* v48 no11 p44 N 2017
CLOSE to the Madding Crowd [Cover story] color *Sail* v48 no10 p36 O 2017
Dragonfly 28 Performance color *Sail* v48 no4 p28 Ap 2017
Elan E4 cartoon color *Sail* v48 no2 p30 F 2017
HOME IS WHERE THE BOAT IS color map *Sail* v48 no3 p38 Mr 2017
J/112e cartoon color diag *Sail* v48 no4 p26 Ap 2017
Jeanneau 51 color *Sail* v48 no7 p24 Jl 2017
Lionheart Wins Worlds color *Sail* v48 no11 p16 N 2017
Sage 15 color *Sail* v48 no3 p27 Mr 2017
A Season for the Record Books color *Sail* v48 no7 p16 Jl 2017
Setting Sail for the Cup color *Sail* v48 no4 p18 Ap 2017
SUN, SURF AND SWANS color *Sail* v48 no7 p30 Jl 2017
Three U.S. Medals at Youth Sailing Worlds color *Sail* v48 no3 p16 Mr 2017
Tiwal Cup Bigger than Ever color *Sail* v48 no9 p22 S 2017
U.S. Sonar Crew Scores Paralympic Silver color *Sail* v47 no12 p18 D 2016
Veterans Aiming for 2020 Games color *Sail* v48 no6 p16 Je 2017
Xcat color *Sail* v48 no11 p22 N 2017
A Young Foiler on the Go color *Sail* v48 no1 p20 Ja 2017

Cort, Adam—Awards
2017 PITTMAN INNOVATION AWARDS A. CORT, C. J. DOANE et al color *Sail* v48 no2 p58 F 2017

Cortazar, Esteban
Comme les COLOMBIENS L. RAMZI color *Vogue* v207 no7 p42 Jl 2017

Cortés, Clara
Cosas que escribiste sobre el fuego/Things You Wrote About the Fire *Publishers Weekly* v263 no46 p25 N 14 2016

Cortés, Hernán, 1485-1547
MASTER OF THE CONQUEST J. D. Lyons *Military History* v33 no6 p30 Mr 2017

CORTES, IVANA
BABY ON BOARD *USA Today Magazine* v145 no2858 p68 N 2016

Cortes-Ciriano, Isidro
Intersection of diverse neuronal genomes and neuropsychiatric disease: The Brain Somatic Mosaicism Network color *Science* v356 no6336 p395 Ap 28 2017

Cortes Gomez, Eduardo
Rb1 and Trp53 cooperate to suppress prostate cancer lineage plasticity, metastasis, and antiandrogen resistance bibl graph *Science* v355 no6320 p1 Ja 6 2017

Cortés-Ledesma, Felipe
ZATT (ZNF451)–mediated resolution of topoisomerase 2 DNA-protein cross-links diag *Science* v357 no6358 p1412 S 29 2017

Cortez, Jose
How to Defy Your Genes S. Mahoney color *AARP: The Magazine* v59 no4A p46 Je/Jl 2016

CORTEZ, MEGHAN BOGARDUS
25 People Who Bust the Myths color *AARP: The Magazine* v59 no4A p42 Je/Jl 2016
Kite Runner color *AARP: The Magazine* v59 no4A p66 Je/Jl 2016

Cortez, Michelle
For Diabetics, the Power of Knowing color graph *Bloomberg Businessweek* no4515 p40 Mr 20 2017
Innovation bw color *Bloomberg Businessweek* no4502 p43 D 5 2016
Nice Stent If You Can Get It color diag *Bloomberg Businessweek*

no4518 p34 Ap 10 2017

Cortez, Victor S.

Lactobacillus reuteri induces gut intraepithelial CD4+CD8αα+ T cells diag graph *Science* v357 no6353 p806 Ag 25 2017

Cortez Masto, Catherine, 1964-

SENATOR-ELECT CATHERINE CORTEZ MASTO C. L. RADELOFF *Ms.* v26 no3 p8 Fall 2016

Cortijo, Sandra

Phytochromes function as thermosensors in Arabidopsis bibl graph *Science* v354 no6314 p886 N 18 2016

Cortina, Gloria

PRIDE OF PLACE M. SLENSKE color *Architectural Digest* v73 no11 p64 N 2016

Cortina, Miguel

BIG. HEAVY. CAPABLE chart color *Motor Trend* v69 no5 p74 My 2017

BIG TIG color *Motor Trend* v69 no10 p92 O 2017

KING IN THE NORTH chart color map *Motor Trend* v69 no10 p68 O 2017

Corton, Christine L.

City in the Dark F. MacCarthy cartoon *New York Review of Books* v64 no2 p32 F 9 2017

Cortright, David

"A BOOK I'D LIKE MY ELECTED OFFICIALS TO READ" color *Christian Century* v133 no21 p28 O 12 2016

Dear Trump: The Iran Deal Worked. Apply The Same Approach To North Korea *NPQ: New Perspectives Quarterly* v34 no3 p19 Jl 2017

Corvette automobile

AMERICAN GLADIATOR J. BARUTH color *Road & Track* v69 no4 p88 N 2017

Are Exhaust Headers a Waste of Money on the Street? M. Davis chart color graph *Hot Rod* v70 no9 p104 S 2017

BLACK BULLION S. Lachenaur color *Hot Rod* v70 no2 p60 F 2017

Buried Treasure in Backyard R. Brutt color *Hot Rod* v70 no9 p22 S 2017

The Corvette Curse T. Taylor bw *Hot Rod* v70 no11 p8 N 2017

DODGE VIPER J. Jacquot color graph *Car & Driver* v63 no5 p26 N 2017

Dream Test E. J. Smith color *Hot Rod* v70 no10 p54 O 2017

EDITOR'S LETTER K. WOLFKILL *Road & Track* v69 no4 p20 N 2017

Corvette automobile—Evaluation

FIRST DRIVE "1963" Superformance Corvette Grand Sport C. Walton color *Motor Trend* v68 no12 p46 D 2016

FRATERNAL TWINS [Cover story] S. Evans chart color *Motor Trend* v68 no12 p42 D 2016

MANO A MANO T. Quiroga cartoon color *Car & Driver* v62 no7 p70 Ja 2017

Corvette automobile—Exhibitions

Old Iron Shows *South Dakota Magazine* v33 no2 p13 Jl/Ag 2017

Corvette automobile—History

The Corvette at 65 M. SOLOMON bw color *Forbes* v199 no6 p26 Je 13 2017

Corvidae—Behavior

A raven's memories are for the future M. Boeckle and N. S. Clayton color *Science* v357 no6347 p126 Jl 14 2017

Ravens parallel great apes in flexible planning for tool-use and bartering C. Kabadayi and M. Osvath chart graph *Science* v357 no6347 p202 Jl 14 2017

Corvino, John

Agreeing on How to Disagree R. K. Vischer color *Commonweal* v144 no16 p33 O 6 2017

Preserving Pluralism A. DeSANCTIS *National Review* v69 no15 p41 Ag 14 2017

Respecting Religion A. T. WALKER *Weekly Standard* v22 no45 p31 Ag 7 2017

Corvus corax—Behavior

Ravens parallel great apes in flexible planning for tool-use and bartering C. Kabadayi and M. Osvath chart graph *Science* v357 no6347 p202 Jl 14 2017

Corwin, Miles

A Moving Ministry *Los Angeles Magazine* p10 Ap 2017

The Sister & The Lifers *Los Angeles Magazine* p105 F 2017

Coryell, Larry, 1943-2017

Chords & Discords L. Coryell, A. Michie et al color *Downbeat* v84 no4 p10 Ap 2017

In Memoriam: Versatile Guitarist Larry Coryell bw *Downbeat* v84 no5 p22 My 2017

LARRY CORYELL BACK FROM THE BRINK [Cover story] B. MILKOWSKI color *Downbeat* v84 no2 p34 F 2017

Tribute to a Maestro B. MILKOWSKI color *Downbeat* v84 no5 p8 My 2017

Cosacchi, Daniel

BROTHERLY LOVE J. O'GRADY *America* v215 no18 p34 D 5 2016

Cosby, Bill, 1937-

Cosby's Accusers On the Mistrial: "We wanted to stand witness." N. Malone img *New York* v50 no13 p10 Je 26 2017

Coscolla, Mireia

Reversion of antibiotic resistance in Mycobacterium tuberculosis by spiroisoxazoline SMARt-420 bibl diag *Science* v355 no6330 p1206 Mr 17 2017

Coscos, Louie

Bumblebees show cognitive flexibility by improving on an observed complex behavior bibl diag *Science* v355 no6327 p833 F 24 2017

Cosell, Howard

REEXAMINING ALI R. LINN bw *Chicago* v66 no10 p26 O 2017

COSGROVE, ALWYN

Abs Made Easy color *Men's Health* v32 no5 p50 Je 2017

COSGROVE, BEN

The Sound of 6 Million Acres *Orion Magazine* v36 no2 p13 Mr/Ap 2017

Cosgrove, Delos

14 DELOS "TOBY" COSGROVE C. Leaf color *Fortune* v174 no7 p88 D 1 2016

Cosgrove, Jim

COMMON SCENTS M. W. SCHWARTZ color *Missouri Life* v44 no3 p18 My 2017

Cosgrove, Joanna

DRUG-FREE COLD & FLU RELIEF [Cover story] color *Amazing Wellness* v9 no6 p62 EarlyWint 2017

Cosgrove, Toby

SEEING TOMORROW C. Leaf color *Fortune* v175 no6 p4 My 1 2017

Così Fan Tutte (Theatrical production)

Così Fan Tutte S. J. Mudge *Opera News* v81 no10 p41 Ap 2017

COSIER, SUSAN

A Cleansing Fire *Audubon* v119 no2 p14 Summ 2017

Cosindas, Marie, 1923-2017

With color photography of a dreamlike lushness, Marie Cosindas pioneered a magic all her own T. Cole *New York Times Magazine* p16 S 10 2017

Cosino, Abril

Smells Like Teen Spirit D. B. Tyx *Sierra* v101 no5 p62 S/O 2016

Cosino, Ariss

Smells Like Teen Spirit D. B. Tyx *Sierra* v101 no5 p62 S/O 2016

Coskun, Ali

Highly elastic binders integrating polyrotaxanes for silicon microparticle anodes in lithium ion batteries diag *Science* v357 no6348 p279 Jl 21 2017

Cosmetic bags—Evaluation

MOTHERLY LOVE color *Martha Stewart Living* p48 My 2017

Off the Wall L. BAILEY *Indianapolis Monthly* v40 no7 p29 Mr 2017

Cosmetic dentistry

BEST DENTISTS *Washingtonian Magazine* v52 no9 p124 Je 2017

Cosmetic dermatology

See also

Facelift

Wrinkle treatment

CHINS UP: More Washington men are getting cosmetic injections to create stronger jawlines. What's behind the trend? C. Cunningham *Washingtonian Magazine* v53 no1 p113 O 2017

Services *Virginia Living* p107 2017 Best 20of Virginia

SKINFESSIONS K. Nichols color *Women's Health* v14 no1 p61 Ja/F 2017

Cosmetics

See also

no2 p74 Mr 2017

Our fave superfoods for your face L. Desantis color *Health* v31 no8 p33 O 2017

OVER THE RAINBOW M. Schulman color *New Yorker* v93 no29 p78 S 25 2017

pack light, look gorgeous color *Parents* v92 no8 p87 Ag 2017

Plum Crazy S. HOLLAND-MURPHY *D: The Magazine of Dallas* v43 no10 p63 O 2016

THE POPULAR KOREAN: QUICK-FIX GROOMING: TREND YOU'LL WANT TO KEEP ON HAND O. J. WILLIAMS color *Ebony* v72/73 no12/1 p54 O/N 2017

PROVEN ANTI-AGERS color *Good Housekeeping* v263 no5 p30 N 2016

put on your brights *Parents* v91 no11 p75 N 2016

red alert *Parents* v92 no2 p65 F 2017

Refresh Your Chest color *Health* v30 no10 p12 D 2016

Rose-Marie Swift K. Diamond color *InStyle* v24 no4 p150 Ap 2017

the RUN-DOWN N. Spradley color *Essence* v47 no11 p33 Mr 2017

RUNWAY REPORT Guarnieri color *Harper's Bazaar* no3650 p113 F 2017

SAVE FACE E. L. FOLEY and FEIFEI SUN *Atlanta* v57 no1 p38 My 2017

Scoring the Looks You Loved I. Biedenharn and C. Ciammaichelli color *Entertainment Weekly* no1435 p16 O 14 2016

the secret to lush lashes M. R. CHADWICK color *Better Homes & Gardens* v95 no11 p26 N 2017

Self-Made Women A. FINNEY color *Women's Health* v14 no9 p50 N 2017

Shelf Awareness J. W. Blaschke cartoon *O, The Oprah Magazine* p63 Ap 2017

Skin Guards A. Aguillard color *Southern Living* v52 no6 p50 Je 2017

Slick Days L. REGENSDORF color *Vogue* v207 no7 p54 Jl 2017

SMELLS LIKE TRUMP SPIRIT J. Black color *Esquire* p45 Ap 2017

Special Beauty Issue N. Brechka color *Better Nutrition* v79 no4 p6 Ap 2017

Spice Up Your Skin Care L. Desantis color *Health* v30 no10 p32 D 2016

SPOT Check M. Fuhrer *Dance Spirit* v21 no3 p58 Mr 2017

Stem Sell color *Vogue* v207 no7 p114 Jl 2017

Stop Wrestling with Your Razor S. STRAUSFOGEL color *Better Nutrition* v79 no6 p52 Je 2017

Strokes of Genius N. Spradley color *Essence* v47 no8 p45 D 2016

Sunset Eyes Are So Hot color *Health* v31 no8 p14 O 2017

Super Natural A. FINNEY color *Women's Health* v14 no8 p138 O 2017

swipe right! T. PEREZ color *Parents* v92 no3 p64 Mr 2017

There's a Mist for That color *Health* v31 no8 p10 O 2017

This is how you put on blush M. Roncal color *Redbook* p20 Je 2017

The trick that makes you glow M. Roncal color *Redbook* p20b S 2017

THE TRUTH ABOUT SUNSCREEN A. FRANZINO color *Good Housekeeping* v264 no6 p24 Je 2017

UNCHARTED WATERS K. D. HODES color *Women's Health* v14 no6 p144 Jl 2017

Vacation Items You'll Almost Always Regret Packing J. LABIANCA *Reader's Digest* v188 no1126 p52 D 2016/Ja 2017

The Very Best in Drugstore Lip Picks L. Desantis color *Health* v31 no3 p30 Ap 2017

virtual vacation T. PEREZ *Parents* v91 no6 p78 Je 2016

Volcanic Ash Is the New Charcoal color *Health* v31 no7 p18 S 2017

Warming Trends color *Better Nutrition* v79 no4 p22 Ap 2017

What's Hot in Natural Beauty T. T. Canel color *Health* v31 no3 p27 Ap 2017

What's Hot Now for Brows *Parents* v91 no12 p70 D 2016

WHERE TO BUY *Harper's Bazaar* no3651 p450 Mr 2017

Words with Friends color *Women's Health* v14 no2 p54 Mr 2017

Your Happiest Summer Hair C. T. Burns color *Health* v31 no6 p112 Jl 2017

You Were the Judge! color *Parents* v92 no9 p93 S 2017

Cosmetics equipment

See also

Eyelash curlers

BEAUTY UNDER $25 color *Redbook* p36 O 2017

The Best Makeup Bags color *Health* v31 no7 p20 S 2017

Cosmetics for men

Dark Beauty N. Walker color *Ebony* v72 no9 p45 Jl/Ag 2017

Cosmetics industry

GIRL BOSSES in the Glam Biz K. FOSTER color *Seventeen* v75 no11 p46 N 2016

HOW TO SHOP FOR MAKEUP... If You Can't Try It On K. FOSTER color *Seventeen* v76 no4 p32 Jl/Ag 2017

In Style: Beauty Brands With Social Media Cred S. Wong color *Bloomberg Businessweek* no4516 p18 Mr 27 2017

When Beauty Is Your 9-to-5 J. Militare and R. Nussbaum color *Glamour* v115 no10 p108 O 2017

Cosmetics industry—Equipment & supplies

At First Blush color *InStyle* v24 no4 p174 Ap 2017

Cosmetics industry—News briefs

Beauty for the Future S. Kitchens color *Glamour* v115 no5 p80 My 2017

Cosmetics industry—United States

A Great Foundation M. S. Eddy *Stage Directions* v30 no8 p12 Ag 2017

Cosmetics stores

Going Hollywood L. REGENSDORF and C. ELLENBERG color *Vogue* v207 no9 p444 S 2017

Cosmetics—Color

COLOR Coded M. Fuhrer *Dance Spirit* v21 no7 p98 S 2017

Cosmetics—Congresses

A SLEIGHFUL OF SANTAS, SURVEYED P. Edmonds color *National Geographic* v230 no6 p12 D 2016

Cosmetics—Economic aspects

FRESHER THAN EVER: VITAMIN C FOR YOUR SKIN color *Health* v31 no9 p14 N 2017

Cosmetics—Equipment & supplies

See also

Make-up brushes

batting above average color *Parents* v92 no4 p83 Ap 2017

NOT-SO-BASIC BRUSHES A. Jordan color *Essence* v47 no9 p34 Ja 2017

The Ultimate Beauty How-tos... F. Valdesolo, S. Kitchens et al color *Glamour* v115 no4 p204 Ap 2017

Cosmetics—Equipment & supplies—Evaluation

BEAUTY NEWS color *Harper's Bazaar* no3649 p264 D 2016/Ja 2017

day-to-night makeup color *Good Housekeeping* v263 no6 p46 D 2016

face savers color *Good Housekeeping* v263 no6 p34 D 2016

LADYLIKE & FEMININE color *Harper's Bazaar* no3648 p212 N 2016

LUXE & LAVISH color *Harper's Bazaar* no3648 p214 N 2016

MODERN & CHIC color *Harper's Bazaar* no3648 p214 N 2016

Cosmetics—Evaluation

150 BEAUTY MUST HAVES color *Harper's Bazaar* no3653 p214 My 2017

15 INSTANT SKIN FIXES Guarnieri color *Harper's Bazaar* no3652 p177 Ap 2017

2017 Readers' Choice K. D. Hodes color *InStyle* v24 no10 p154 O 2017

30-second MAKEOVER color *Good Housekeeping* v265 no2 p20 Ag 2017

42 new ALL-STAR PRODUCTS of the year [Cover story] G. WAY, T. HALL et al color *Redbook* p27 Jl/Ag 2017

5 beauty tricks I just learned V. Kirby color *Redbook* p42 Je 2017

5 beauty tricks I just learned V. Kirby color *Redbook* p48 Mr 2017

6 ways to revolutionize your beauty routine *Redbook* pC1 Mr 2017

Ace Your FOUNDATION K. FOSTER color *Seventeen* v76 no5 p40 S 2017

All Night Long S. Kitchens color *Glamour* v115 no7 p84 Jl 2017

At First Blush color *InStyle* v24 no4 p174 Ap 2017

AWASH WITH WONDER A. Finney color *Women's Health* v14 no7 p56 S 2017

BEAUTIFUL CHOICES L. Turner color *Amazing Wellness* p74 Fall 2017

BEAUTY BUYS from $4 color *Good Housekeeping* v264 no4 p30 Ap 2017

BEAUTY BUYS from $4 color *Good Housekeeping* v265 no5 p20 N 2017

BEAUTY BUYS from $5 color *Good Housekeeping* v264 no6 p23 Je 2017

BEAUTY BUYS from $7 color *Good Housekeeping* v265 no4 p20 O 2017

BEAUTY BUYS UNDER $25 color *Good Housekeeping* v264 no3 p22 Mr 2017

BEAUTY DIARIES Guarnieri color *Harper's Bazaar* no3651 p322 Mr 2017

Beauty for the Anime-Obsessed J. Mulrow and Ying Chu cartoon color *Glamour* v115 no2 p58 F 2017

BEAUTY NEWS A. Parnass color *Harper's Bazaar* no3651 p330 Mr 2017

BEAUTY NEWS A. Parnass color *Harper's Bazaar* no3654 p112 Je/Jl 2017

beauty NEWSFEED K. CASTAÑON color *Seventeen* v75 no11 p54 N 2016

beauty NEWSFEED K. FOSTER color *Seventeen* v76 no2 p72 Mr 2017

beauty NEWSFEED K. FOSTER color *Seventeen* v76 no5 p60 S 2017

Beauty S. GRINNELL bw color *Vanity Fair* v59 no7 p47 Summ 2017

BEAUTY'S NEW EXPERIMENT A. SYNNOTT color *Women's Health* v14 no9 p124 N 2017

Beauty & the Beach color *InStyle* v24 no6 p84 Je 2017

BEAUTY UNDER $25 color *Redbook* p28 Je 2017

BEAUTY UNDER $25 color *Redbook* p28 Mr 2017

BEAUTY UNDER $25 color *Redbook* p36 O 2017

BEAUTY UNDER $25 color *Redbook* p46 F 2017

Best. Beauty Gifts. Ever S. Kitchens cartoon color *Glamour* v114 no12 p128 D 2016

The Best Body Moisturizers color *InStyle* v23 no13 p200 D 2016

Black Is Beautiful color *Essence* v47 no10 p40 F 2017

BLOOM BOOM color *Women's Health* v14 no3 p(Sp)14 Ap 2017

BOHO & FLIRTY color *Harper's Bazaar* no3648 p216 N 2016

Bring some wine to your lips color *Redbook* p29 S 2017

But First, SKIN CARE A. Kallor color *Women's Health* v14 no1 p54 Ja/F 2017

the buzz color *InStyle* v24 no10 p194 O 2017

the buzz color *InStyle* v24 no3 p295 Mr 2017

the buzz color *InStyle* v24 no6 p110 Je 2017

CHARLOTTE TILBURY'S Magic Touch A. Serrano color *InStyle* v24 no10 p171 O 2017

cheap THRILLS E. STOVALL color *Seventeen* v76 no2 p84 Mr 2017

cheap THRILLS K. FOSTER color *Seventeen* v75 no11 p50 N 2016

CHIC easy PIECES L. Armstrong bw color *Harper's Bazaar* no3651 p420 Mr 2017

COLLAR ME PRETTY color *InStyle* v24 no9 p296 S 2017

Color POWER COUPLES K. FOSTER color *Seventeen* p108 Ja 1 2017

coming up ROSES S. BRICKELL color *Better Homes & Gardens* v95 no2 p16 F 2016

the COMPACT J. Wilson color *Essence* v48 no2 p46 Je 2017

the COMPACT J. Wilson color *Essence* v48 no5 p46 S 2017

the COMPACT N. Spradley color *Essence* v47 no11 p44 Mr 2017

COUNTER INTELLIGENCE M. M. GOLDSTEIN color *Martha Stewart Living* p46 Mr 2017

The customized plan for younger eyes A. HERTZIG color *Redbook* p45 S 2017

Cute for CLASS M. ABERMAN color *Seventeen* v76 no5 p48 S 2017

DARE TO WEAR COLOR Guarnieri color *Harper's Bazaar* no3653 p286 My 2017

THE DIGITAL AGE M. M. GOLDSTEIN color *Martha Stewart Living* p44 Jl/Ag 2017

digital directory color *InStyle* v24 no10 p26 O 2017

Does It Really Work? color *InStyle* v24 no5 p156 My 2017

Does It Really Work? color *InStyle* v24 no6 p99 Je 2017

DOPE STUFF ON MY DESK J. Wilson color *Essence* v47 no11 p26 Mr 2017

DOPE STUFF ON MY DESK J. Wilson color *Essence* v48 no2 p24 Je 2017

Double-Tap This E. Reimel and Ying Chu color *Glamour* v115 no3 p102 Mr 2017

Eau So Lovely color *Essence* v48 no6 p50 O 2017

ELIXIR, ELEVATED J. MOAZAMI bw color *Chicago* v66 no11 p46 N 2017

erica explores CONCEALERS E. Metzger color *Better Homes & Gardens* v95 no7 p18 Jl 2017

erica explores MICELLAR WATER E. Metzger color *Better Homes & Gardens* v95 no9 p24 S 2017

The Evening Suit S. P. Nadella color *Glamour* v114 no12 p94 D 2016

EYE CANDY color *Harper's Bazaar* no3651 p430 Mr 2017

Eye Shadow color *InStyle* v23 no13 p194 D 2016

Fab Fall Launches color *Essence* v48 no5 p48 S 2017

Face Scrubs to Leave You Glowing S. STRAUSFOGEL color *Better Nutrition* p30 My 2017

Fara Homidi color *InStyle* v24 no10 p190 O 2017

Fashion Does Fragrance E. Reimel and Y. Chu color *Glamour* v114 no11 p106 N 2016

Fast Beauty FIXES color *InStyle* v23 no13 p175 D 2016

Find Your Dream Mask L. Desantis color *Health* v31 no2 p38 Mr 2017

Find Your SPF OTP E. STOVALL color diag *Seventeen* v76 no3 p62 My 2017

FLORAL FAVORITES color *Harper's Bazaar* no3653 p142 My 2017

For best results, wait... how long? L. BALSAMO color *Redbook* p38 Jl/Ag 2017

FUN & FESTIVE STREET STYLE color *Seventeen* v76 no12 p92 D 2016/Ja 2017

GET CHEEKY A. Jordan color *Essence* v48 no3 p36 Jl 2017

GET THE GLOW color *Harper's Bazaar* no3654 p42 Je/Jl 2017

getting ready with DALLAS SHAW color *Better Homes & Gardens* v95 no9 p29 S 2017

GLITTER FOR GROWN-UPS A. Kallor cartoon *Harper's Bazaar* no3651 p418 Mr 2017

Glow Getters color *InStyle* v24 no5 p148 My 2017

Glow Up E. Reimel color *Glamour* v115 no10 p94 O 2017

Glow your own way M. OLIVA color *Redbook* p36 Je 2017

Going Out color *Seventeen* v76 no3 p46 My 2017

GOOD AT LOOKING BAD *Stage Directions* v30 no5 p23 My 2017

Guido Palau color *InStyle* v24 no11 p148 N 2017

HAVE A beautiful WINTER M. OLIVA color *Redbook* p38 N 2017

THE HEALING POWER OF LIPSTICK F. Valdesolo color *Women's Health* v14 no3 p(Sp)6 Ap 2017

HEALTHY SKIN WINS E. METZGER color *Better Homes & Gardens* v95 no10 p28 O 2017

HOLIDAY #HAIRGOALS color *Ebony* v72 no3 p58 D 2016/Ja 2017

Hot-weather-proof your skin V. KIRBY color *Redbook* p39 Je 2017

How to Repent for YOUR SKIN SINS color *InStyle* v24 no1 p62 Ja 2017

I Can't Live Without My ... color *InStyle* v24 no9 p331 S 2017

"I love looking a little disheveled" M. Deem color *Glamour* v115 no5 p74 My 2017

InSTYLE September 2017 color *InStyle* v24 no9 p365 S 2017

International RELATIONS color *Vogue* v207 no10 p206 O 2017

IN THE BUFF M. BOBO color *Ebony* v72 no4 p50 F 2017

I Tested Every Natural Deodorant on God's Green Earth... A. GOBLE color *GQ: Gentlemen's Quarterly* v97 no9 p94 S 2017

join the charcoal party! L. BALSAMO color *Seventeen* v76 no3 p100 My 2017

KELSEY & KENDRA A. Jordan color *Essence* v48 no2 p38 Je 2017

the life C. Stern color *InStyle* v24 no9 p425 S 2017

Lily Aldridge K. B. Brown color *InStyle* v24 no10 p187 O 2017

Lipsticks that flatter everyone color *Redbook* p14 My 2017

LUXE BEAUTY color *Harper's Bazaar* no3649 p174 D 2016/Ja 2017

Made for Me K. Erickson and Ying Chu color *Glamour* v115 no3 p104 Mr 2017

MAKEUP BRUSHES color *InStyle* v23 no13 p211 D 2016

MAKEUP MAGIC M. OLIVA color *Redbook* p42 O 2017

Cosmetics—Religious aspects

Cosmetics—Social aspects

Cosmetics—Testing

Cosmetologists

Cosmetology

See also

Cosmetologists
Hairdressing
Manicuring

Cosmic background radiation

See also

Cosmic ripples

Cosmic dust

Cosmic Hallelujah (Music)

Cosmic rays

See also

Ultra-high energy cosmic rays

COSMIC CAN-DO J. KELLY *Scientific American* v316 no6 p6 Je 2017

Cosmic ray catcher will probe supernovae from new perch E. Hand color *Science* v357 no6350 p437 Ag 4 2017

Muon surplus may reveal new physics E. CONOVER *Science News* v190 no11 p15 N 26 2016

New angle on cosmic rays J. S. I. Gallagher and F. Halzen color *Science* v357 no6357 p1240 S 22 2017

Cosmic rays—Research

DEEP-SPACE DEAL BREAKER C. L. Limoli color diag *Scientific American* v316 no2 p54 F 2017

From Workouts to Far Out M. DiChristina color *Scientific American* v316 no2 p4 F 2017

Cosmic ripples

European detector 'sees' space ripples color *Science* v357 no6359 p14 O 6 2017

Cosmological constants

GALACTIC CENSUS REAFFIRMS STANDARD MODEL OF COSMOLOGY *Physics Today* v70 no9 p22 S 2017

Cosmological distances

LET THE COUNTDOWN TO 2024 BEGIN M. E. Bakich map *Astronomy* v45 no8 p74 Ag 2017

Cosmology

See also

Big bang theory

Cosmic background radiation

Dark energy (Astronomy)

Origin of planets

Baking a Universe B. Skuse *Sky & Telescope* v133 no5 p34 My 2017

Charting the Unseen Sky L. SCHLEY color *Discover* v38 no9 p19 N 2017

A COSMIC CONTROVERSY A. H. GUTH, D. I. KAISER et al color *Scientific American* v317 no1 p5 Jl 2017

Mapping the galaxy one star at a time K. Haynes color diag *Astronomy* v45 no6 p31 Je 2017

New data fuel further debate on universe's expansion rate E. Conover *Science News* v191 no4 p18 Mr 4 2017

SHOCKING COLLISIONS of Cosmological Proportions A. Parker *Science & Technology Review* p20 Jl/Ag 2017

SPACE JAM C. COX *Atlanta* v57 no2 p34 Je 2017

Supersonic gas streams enhance the formation of massive black holes in the early universe S. Hirano, T. Hosokawa et al diag graph *Science* v357 no6358 p1375 S 29 2017

Cosmology—Bibliographies

BOOKS REVIEWED *Physics Today* v69 no12 p86 D 2016

Cosmopolitanism

In Defense of Cosmopolitanism G. Petriglieri *Harvard Business Review Digital Articles* p2 D 15 2016

A Shrinking Island K. GHATTAS color *Foreign Policy* no226 p67 S/O 2017

Cosmos (Film)

The best posters of 2016 A. Curry color *Film Comment* v53 no1 p96 Ja/F 2017

Coso Range (Calif.)

For the Good of the People M. Jacobs color *Black Belt* v55 no6 p74 O/N 2017

Cosplay

DON'T MISS THIS *Atlanta* v57 no5 p34 S 2017

COSS, STEPHEN

FRANKLIN'S SECRET HEARTACHE: HISTORIANS HAVE LONG DEBATED WHY BELOVED FOUNDER BENJAMIN FRANKLIN TREATED HIS WIFE SO SHABBILY. OUR WRITER HAS A STUNNING NEW THEORY [Cover story] *Smithsonian* v48 no5 p68 S 2017

Cossavella, Brianna

BABACOMARI: 50 Years Later *Arizona Highways* v93 no4 p43 Ap 2017

Desert Bighorn Sheep *Arizona Highways* v92 no7 p13 Jl 2016

Frank Lloyd Wright *Arizona Highways* v93 no4 p8 Ap 2017

THE LION KING *Arizona Highways* v93 no1 p48 Ja 2017

Stan's Barber Shop *Arizona Highways* v93 no2 p6 F 2017

Cossey, Caroline

RIGHT PLACE, RIGHT TIME S. Fairyington *Advocate* no1088 p20 D 2016/Ja 2017

Cost

See also

Cost effectiveness

Bad Math Props Up Border Wall K. Kakaes diag graph il *MIT Technology Review* v119 no6 p18 N/D 2016

FIVE BASICMED MYTHS DEBUNKED S. Pope color *Flying* v144 no7 p8 Jl 2017

INDOORS VERSUS OUTDOORS S. HELD *Indianapolis Monthly* v40 no7 p94 Mr 2017

Cost & standard of living

See also

Food consumption

Food prices

THE HUNGRY TIDE J. N. LOMAX *Texas Monthly* v45 no5 p80 My 2017

THE JUGGLE IS REAL D. Cunha cartoon *Parents* v92 no9 p112 S 2017

Percent of Income Spent on Food Falls as Income Rises C. Tuttle and A. Kuhns *Amber Waves: The Economics of Food, Farming, Natural Resources, & Rural America* p31 S 2016

THE PRICE OF THE GOOD LIFE A. MURPHY color graph *Forbes* v200 no5 p32 N 14 2017

THE THOUSAND DOLLAR PAGE M. Thakor and L. Khalfani-Cox bw color *Men's Health* v32 no7 p42 S 2017

Cost & standard of living—Canada

WHY WE ALL NEED TO HYGGE [Cover story] A. KINGSTON color *Maclean's* v129 no51/52 p50 D 26 2016

Cost & standard of living—United States

COASTS OF LIVING B. O'keefe map *Fortune* v176 no4 p176 S 15 2017

Don't Poor Lives Matter? H. I. Miller *Hoover Digest: Research & Opinion on Public Policy* no1 p72 Wint 2017

The Good Life on $40,000 a year S. MAHONEY color map *AARP: The Magazine* v59 no6A p58 O/N 2016

The Problem with the U.S. Economy Isn't Something Politicians Can Fix M. Levinson *Harvard Business Review Digital Articles* p2 N 29 2016

WHERE A $100K SALARY WILL TAKE YOU THE FARTHEST map *Fortune* v176 no2 p15 Ag 1 2017

Work Long and Prosper C. Blahous *Hoover Digest: Research & Opinion on Public Policy* no1 p57 Wint 2017

Cost, Fidel

CRYSTAL CLOCKS J. Rosen color diag *Science* v354 no6314 p822 N 18 2016

Cost, Jay

Are We Up to the Job? color *Weekly Standard* v22 no26 p18 Mr 13 2017

Bringing the Senate to Heel color *Weekly Standard* v23 no1 p15 S 11 2017

The Butcher's Bill cartoon *Weekly Standard* v22 no13 p13 D 5 2016

Corruption as a Way of Life color map *Weekly Standard* v22 no38 p18 Je 12 2017

A Debt to Posterity cartoon *Weekly Standard* v22 no29 p17 Ap 3 2017

Diagnosis: Heartburn color *Weekly Standard* v22 no47 p17 Ag 21 2017

The Disintegrating Obama Coalition color *Weekly Standard* v22 no11 p13 N 21 2016

The Doctor Is In color *Weekly Standard* v22 no20 p5 Ja 30 2017

Down-Ballot Blues *Weekly Standard* v22 no8 p9 O 31 2016

Entitled to Spend color *Weekly Standard* v22 no22 p18 F 13 2017

Everybody's Fault color *Weekly Standard* v22 no30 p10 Ap 10 2017

Filibusted color *Weekly Standard* v22 no31 p6 Ap 17 2017

Forecast: Gridlock color *Weekly Standard* v23 no2 p16 S 18 2017

Foundering Fathers color *Weekly Standard* v22 no39 p21 Je 19 2017

Founders' Keepers color *Weekly Standard* v22 no36 p13 My 29 2017

Getting Riled Up Over the Knee Jerk color *Weekly Standard* v23 no5 p18 O 9 2017

It's Frustrating at the Top color *Weekly Standard* v22 no16 p9 D 26 2016

Left, Right, Reverse *Weekly Standard* v22 no33 p20 My 8 2017

Loyal Opposition color *Weekly Standard* v22 no41 p10 Jl 3 2017

A Midterm Forecast color *National Review* v69 no19 p15 O 16 2017

Nullifying Calhoun *Weekly Standard* v22 no24 p16 F 27 2017

Obamacare Doings and Undoings color *Weekly Standard* v22 no28 p12 Mr 27 2017

Of Course Court Fights Are Bitter color *Weekly Standard* v22 no23 p14 F 20 2017

The Old Electoral College Try color *Weekly Standard* v22 no12 p18 N 28 2016

Orders of Merit *Weekly Standard* v22 no17 p32 Ja 2 2017

The Perils of Hyperbole color *Weekly Standard* v22 no17 p12 Ja 2 2017

The Prognostication Follies *Weekly Standard* v22 no5 p12 O 10 2016

Reagan Reconsidered bw *Weekly Standard* v22 no44 p30 Jl 31 2017

The Road to Statism... color *Weekly Standard* v22 no45 p11 Ag 7 2017

That's Infotainment *Weekly Standard* v22 no24 p36 F 27 2017

Trump's New Enemy cartoon *Weekly Standard* v22 no25 p19 Mr 6 2017

Unprecedented? color *Weekly Standard* v22 no37 p19 Je 5 2017

The Untouchables color *Weekly Standard* v23 no4 p16 O 2 2017

The Vision Thing color *Weekly Standard* v22 no44 p13 Jl 31 2017

What Goes Up... cartoon *Weekly Standard* v22 no19 p12 Ja 23 2017

You're Mired! color *Weekly Standard* v22 no34 p10 My 15 2017

Cost control

See also

Budget cuts

Technological innovations—Economic aspects

4 Ways to Cut Your Medical Bills E. O'Brien color *Money* v46 no6 p22 Jl 2017

Holding Down the Costs of the Cloud O. Kharif *Bloomberg Businessweek* no4508 p29 Ja 23 2017

How to Better Manage Your Company's Utility Bills J. Mandel, M. Dyson et al *Harvard Business Review Digital Articles* p2 N 24 2015

How to Cut Costs More Strategically P. Leinwand and V. Couto color *Harvard Business Review Digital Articles* p2 Mr 10 2017

How to Cut the Costs of Going Solar V. Aggarwal *Mother Earth News* no280 p77 F/Mr 2017

How to have a Linux home server on the cheap A. CAMPBELL color *PCWorld* v35 no5 p191 My 2017

Oilfield Cleanup Tools D. Wethe chart *Bloomberg Businessweek* no4503 p31 D 12 2016

Privateers on the Jersey Shore K. ARONOFF *In These Times* v41 no7 p10 Jl 2017

Save Money T. Stanger, J. Blyskal et al il *Consumer Reports* v82 no3 p30 Mr 2017

Sometimes Cutting R&D Spending Can Yield More Innovation R. Mudambi, T. Swift et al *Harvard Business Review Digital Articles* p2 Ja 8 2015

The World's Housing Crisis Doesn't Need a Revolutionary Solution J. Woetzel, J. Mischke et al *Harvard Business Review Digital Articles* p2 D 25 2014

Cost control—Methodology

5 Things to Know About Renovating Your Bathroom J. Garskof color *Money* v46 no2 p33 Mr 2017

Cost effectiveness

Cleaning up coal—cost-effectively R. F. Service color *Science* v356 no6340 p798 My 26 2017

YOU: THE INSTANT EXPERT color *Women's Health* v14 no4 p172 My 2017

Cost effectiveness of energy consumption

Purchasing Power: A new collaboration helped Minnesota double its solar capacity E. Daigneau *Governing* v30 no9 p20 Je 2017

Cost effectiveness of environmental policy

Rethinking the Social Cost of Carbon Dioxide: The standard benefit-cost methodology that is used to calculate marginal costs of environmental regulations should not be used for long-lasting greenhouse gases M. G. MORGAN, P. VAISHNAV et al *Issues in Science & Technology* v33 no4 p43 Summ 2017

Cost per thousand

The High Price of Low-Cost CPMs L. O'Shaughnessy *Harvard Business Review Digital Articles* p2 Ag 10 2016

Costa, Alessandro

A supramolecular assembly mediates lentiviral DNA integration bibl color *Science* v355 no6320 p1 Ja 6 2017

Costa, Fidel

Rapid cooling and cold storage in a silicic magma reservoir recorded in individual crystals color diag graph *Science* v356 no6343 p1154 Je 16 2017

Costa, Flavia R. C.

Forest conservation: Humans' handprints bibl color *Science* v355 no6324 p466 F 3 2017

Persistent effects of pre-Columbian plant domestication on Amazonian forest composition bibl chart graph map *Science* v355 no6328 p925 Mr 3 2017

Costa, James T.

Darwin, the crowdsourcer C. Kemp color *Science* v357 no6356 p1104 S 15 2017

Costa, Kyle C.

Pyocyanin degradation by a tautomerizing demethylase inhibits Pseudomonas aeruginosa biofilms bibl diag graph *Science* v355 no6321 p1 Ja 13 2017

Costa, Maria

Crystal structures of a group II intron lariat primed for reverse splicing color diag *Science* v354 no6316 paaf9258-1 D 2 2016

Costa, Pedro

SAYING 'YES' TO THE AVANT-GARDE P. Lutz color *Downbeat* v84 no3 p50 Mr 2017

Costa, Sofia Horta e

One Very Important Footnote bw *Bloomberg Businessweek* no4493 p51 O 3 2016

Costa Del Mar Sunglasses Inc.

Bright Future L. BECKETT color *Power & Motoryacht* v33 no2 p58 F 2017

Costa Rica

16 BEST YOGA ESCAPES [Cover story] M. Rabbitt color *Yoga Journal* no290 p19 Mr 2017

INTERNATIONAL *Sierra* v101 no6 p58 N/D 2016

Costantino, David A.

Zika virus produces noncoding RNAs using a multi-pseudoknot structure that confounds a cellular exonuclease bibl color graph *Science* v354 no6316 p1148 D 2 2016

Costanzo, Michael

Exploring genetic suppression interactions on a global scale diag *Science* v354 no6312 p599 N 4 2016

Costa-Pereira, Raul

Scientists need social media influencers *Science* v357 no6354 p880 S 1 2017

Costas, Bob, 1952-

Bob Costas J. Saraceno color *AARP: The Magazine* v59 no5A p13 Ag/S 2016

Costco Wholesale Corp.

COSTCO D. G. Herbert cartoon *Atlantic* v320 no4 p24 N 2017

News Roundup V. HAFSTAÐ *Iceland Review* v55 no4 p8 Jl/Ag 2017

A New Way to Rate Retailers on Providing Good Jobs Z. Ton *Harvard Business Review Digital Articles* p2 S 3 2015

Stock X-Ray: Costco Wholesale T. Tepper color diag *Money* v46 no8 p40 S 2017

Surviving Amazon D. FONDA color *Kiplinger's Personal Finance* v71 no7 p60 Jl 2017

Why Costco Is Lagging Online J. E. Ellis graph *Bloomberg Businessweek* no4535 p14 Ag 28 2017

Costco Wholesale Corp.—Finance

THE MAGIC IN THE WAREHOUSE N. Gabler color diag *Fortune* v174 no8 p182 D 15 2016

Coste, Xavier

Egon Schiele: His Life and Death *Publishers Weekly* v264 no34 p98 Ag 21 2017

Costello, Annette

From One Horse Parent To Another color *Dressage Today* v24 no2 p60 N 2017

Costello, Elvis, 1954-

NIGHT LIFE *New Yorker* v93 no17 p15 Je 19 2017

Paul and Elvis: The Fab Two B. HIATT bw *Rolling Stone* no1283 p16 Mr 23 2017

Costello, Elvis, 1954——Interviews

Elvis Costello [Cover story] B. HIATT *Rolling Stone* no1289 p22

Je 15 2017

Costello, Nikki
A home practice for powerful legs color *Yoga Journal* p98 2017 SpecialIssue

Costello, Roisin A.
THE BIG QUESTION cartoon *Atlantic* v320 no4 p124 N 2017

Costello, Scarlett
Scarlett COSTELLO *Interview* v47 no2 p94 Mr 2017

Coster, Gideon
Bidirectional eukaryotic DNA replication is established by quasi-symmetrical helicase loading graph *Science* v357 no6348 p314 Jl 21 2017

Coster-Waldau, Nikolaj, 1970-
Jaime Lannister's Rules for Survival N. Coster-Waldau color *GQ: Gentlemen's Quarterly* v97 no7 p102 Jl 2017
The Simpsons A. Bacle, D. Coggan et al color *Entertainment Weekly* no1482/1483 p34 S 22 2017

Costes, Léa M. M.
Reovirus infection triggers inflammatory responses to dietary antigens and development of celiac disease color diag *Science* v356 no6333 p44 Ap 7 2017

Costner, Kevin, 1955-
Limits of a feel-good movie L. H. Moses *Christian Century* v134 no4 p10 F 15 2017

Costs (Law)
TRIBUNAL FEES ARE FINISHED - and here's what happens next: Should employers brace themselves for a tsunami of claims? And will the government reintroduce fees in a different form? H. KIRTON *People Management* p8 S 2017

Cost & standard of living—Charts, diagrams, etc.
The Expense of Exclusive Living A. BROWN and A. MURPHY color graph *Forbes* v198 no5 p46 O 25 2016

Costume
See also
Cosmetics
Dance costume
Film costume
Halloween costumes
Theatrical costume
Costumes, Makeup & Wigs *Stage Directions* v30 no7 p20 Jl 1 2017
FIESTA Gown A. FULKERSON *Texas Monthly* v44 no11 p108 N 2016
In the Spirit: Step right up to Costumes Etc, Atlanta's 17,000-square-foot dress-up box G. CHAPMAN *Atlanta* v57 no6 p43 O 2017
Showstoppers S. FRISCIA *Dance Magazine* v90 no11 p40 N 2016
WHICH FICTIONAL CHARACTER'S WARDROBE DO YOU COVET THE MOST? C. M. Smith color *Entertainment Weekly* no1449 p18 Ja 20 2017

Costume design
ANGEL'S SANTA DRAG J. Derschowitz color *Entertainment Weekly* no1460/1461 p65 Ap 7-17 2017
BELLE OF THE BALL C. Collis color *Entertainment Weekly* no1439 p34 N 11 2016
THE BUNNY SUIT D. Coggan color *Entertainment Weekly* no1460/1461 p99 Ap 7-17 2017
Curating the Character's Closet J. Kucharski *Stage Directions* v30 no8 p20 Ag 2017
Digital Weaving J. Kucharski *Stage Directions* v30 no5 p18 My 2017
DOUBLET TROUBLE L. Vaccariello *Cincinnati Magazine* v50 no12 p59 S 2017
Friends with a Needle and Thread can Save a Marriage M. S. Eddy *Stage Directions* v30 no8 p2 Ag 2017
INSIDE THE HANDMAID'S STUDIO C. Brody color *Entertainment Weekly* no1467 p50 My 26 2017
Making The Knight of Mirrors J. S. Wood *Stage Directions* v29 no11 p44 N 2016
Mary Poppins Returns M. Snetiker color *Entertainment Weekly* no1457/1458 p22 Mr 17 2017
The Sex and the City Opening Credits C. Brody color *Entertainment Weekly* no1460/1461 p72 Ap 7-17 2017
Wild Things E. N. GAGE color *Martha Stewart Living* p31 O 2017

Costume designers

Digital Weaving J. Kucharski *Stage Directions* v30 no5 p18 My 2017
Do You Know These Labels? N. Silverstein, E. Velluto et al bw color *Glamour* v115 no3 p86 Mr 2017
THE MAN BEHIND THE MASKS A. D. LITTLE *Cincinnati Magazine* v50 no10 p28 Jl 2017
Quick Change: Costume Designer Paloma Young takes us back to the 1940s M. S. Eddy *Stage Directions* v30 no6 p22 Je 2017
Surviving a Home-Based Costume Craft Studio E. Flauto *Stage Directions* v30 no8 p8 Ag 2017

Costume designers—Interviews
Meet the crew... D. Holbrook *TV Guide* v65 no35 p7 Ag 21 2017

Costume—Competitions
Reining by the Bay color map *Horse & Rider* v56 no7 p28 Jl 2017

Costume—Exhibitions
SIMON STARLING C. M. Schultz color *Art in America* v105 no3 p125 Mr 2017

Costume—Sales & prices
The Costumer Is Thriving At 100 Years Young L. Mulcahy *Stage Directions* v30 no8 p23 Ag 2017

Cota, Isabella
Dollar So Ripped, It Might Actually Rip color *Bloomberg Businessweek* no4506 p12 Ja 9 2017
No Wall to Stop Migrant Cash From Going South color *Bloomberg Businessweek* no4502 p23 D 5 2016
Trump Hurts the Peso. That Helps Mexicans color graph *Bloomberg Businessweek* no4494 p20 O 10 2016
We Found Your Last Smartphone, Next to Your Old VCR color diag *Bloomberg Businessweek* no4499 p56 N 14 2016

Cote, Allison
Mitotic transcription and waves of gene reactivation during mitotic exit color graph *Science* v357 no6359 p119 O 6 2017

Cote, Atina
Exploring genetic suppression interactions on a global scale diag *Science* v354 no6312 p599 N 4 2016

Cote, David
20. Hear Three Way *New York* v50 no12 p116 Je 12 2017

COTE, JACQUELINE BURT
control freaks *Parents* v91 no9 p166 S 2016

Coté, Matt
AFTER THE FLOOD bw color *Bike Magazine* v24 no4 p58 Je 2017
FLY-IN FORT bw color *Skiing* p24 Wint 2017
The Gear Hacking Legends of Skiing color *Powder* p35 S 2017
HIGH COUNTRY HUSTLE bw color *Bike Magazine* v24 no3 p86 My 2017
man-made machine bw color *Bike Magazine* v24 no5 p38 Jl 2017

COTE, NICK
No Small Potatoes color *Backpacker* p30 O 2017
trail chef: Say Cheese color *Backpacker* p34 S 2017

Côté, Robin
Synthesis of mixed hypermetallic oxide BaOCa+ from laser-cooled reagents in an atom-ion hybrid trap diag graph *Science* v357 no6358 p1370 S 29 2017

Côte d'Ivoire—Description & travel
Smart Girls J. LICHTBLAU *American Scholar* v86 no1 p6 Wint 2017

COTHERN, MIKE
THE LAST TREK? *Idaho Magazine* v16 no12 p48 S 2017

COTHRAN, SHANNON
EAT YOUR HART OUT color *Missouri Life* v44 no4 p66 Je 2017

Cotillions
MRS. BELT'S COTILLION J. KENT-DOOLAN color *Indianapolis Monthly* v41 no2 p20 S 2017

Cotillo, Mary
PUTTING BOOKS TO WORK: Create lessons based on children's and YA books, side by side with the authors themselves, at ILA 2017 color *Literacy Today (2411-7862)* v34 no6 p30 My/Je 2017

Cotsarelis, George
Regeneration of fat cells from myofibroblasts during wound healing bibl color graph *Science* v355 no6326 p748 F 17 2017

Cott, Jonathan
THERE'S A MYSTERY THERE: THE PRIMAL VISION OF MAURICE SENDAK C. Smallwood *Harper's Magazine* v334 no2004 p79 My 2017

Cottage design & construction
SPRING DESIGN: ART W. GOODMAN img *New York* v50 no8
p81 Ap 17 2017
Cottage gardens
A GARDEN IN Montgomery S. GROSS and S. DALEY color
diag *Arts & Crafts Homes & the Revival* v12 no4 p59 Fall 2017
NATIVE ROSES ARE FOR THE BIRDS J. L. Baker color *Cabin
Living* p9 Ag 2017
Cottages
COTTAGE INDUSTRY K. FRANZMAN color *Indianapolis
Monthly* v41 no2 p82 S 2017
The First Rule of Book Club Is . . B. RAWLENCE color *New York
Times Book Review* p25 Ja 29 2017
glamping cabin *Cabin Living* p25 O 2017
Instant Classic K. Owen color *Southern Living* v52 no6 p13 Je
2017
The No-Mortgage NATURAL COTTAGE C. McClellan *Mother
Earth News* no281 p42 Ap/My 2017
Plane-Spotting at Edgar's E. CLARK color *Yankee* p14 Mr 2017
A Residence Fit for a President [Cover story] T. WATSON color
Archaeology v70 no4 p34 Je-Ag 2017
SMALL HOUSE, BIG LIFE D. McGLYNN color *O, The Oprah
Magazine* p26 Jl 2017
YOU CAN GO HOME AGAIN V. Rains color *Southern Living*
v52 no9 p92 S 2017
You Only Get What You Give D. PEAK color *Log Home Living*
v33 no9 p8 D 2016
Cottages—Conservation & restoration
The Beauty Within D. PEAK *Log Home Living* v33 no7 p8 S 2016
Cottages—Design & construction
HOLIDAY OPEN HOUSE J. Farmer color *Southern Living* v51
no12 p23 D 2016
LADY OF THE LAKE K. RENDA color *House Beautiful* v159
no4 p116 My 2017
vernacular to a fare-thee-well B. D. COLEMAN color *Arts &
Crafts Homes & the Revival* v11 no5 p56 Wint 2017
Cottages—Evaluation
FACE VALUE K. BARNES color *Better Homes & Gardens* v95
no5 p66 My 2017
HOME R. D'AGOSTINO color *Popular Mechanics* p6 D 2016/
Ja 2017
A House by the Lake T. CHIARELLA bw color *Popular Mechan-
ics* p88 D 2016/Ja 2017
Cottages—History
1830 HOUSE IN ROSLYN R. COLE color *Old House Journal*
v45 no4 p22 Je 2017
Cottages—Interior decoration
Big Dream, Tiny Cottage Z. Gowen color *Southern Living* v52
no3 p82 Mr 2017
A Fresh Coat of Paint S. Evans color *Southern Living* v52 no3
p8 Mr 2017
THE FUTURE IS HERE N. Farrell, C. Lamers et al color diag
Sunset v238 no4 p54 Ap 2017
into the light A. MAZE color *Better Homes & Gardens* v95 no3
p30 Mr 2017
scandinavian STORYBOOK B. D. Coleman color *Old House
Journal* v45 no3 p14 My 2017
Cottages—Maintenance & repair
from SOMETHING OLD to SOMETHING new C. HEITGER-
EWING color diag *Cabin Living* p34 Mr 2017
Living the Lake Life C. Wood color diag *Log Home Living* v33
no9 p56 D 2016
Cottages—Remodeling
In Transition V. Hart *New Orleans Homes & Lifestyles* v20 no1
p54 Wint 2016
Cotte de Saint-Brelade Site (Jersey)
A TRADITIONAL NEANDERTHAL HOME Z. ZORICH color
Archaeology v70 no2 p23 Mr/Ap 2017
Cotter, Jennifer A.
Extensive migration of young neurons into the infant human fron-
tal lobe color diag graph *Science* v354 no6308 paaf7073-1 O
7 2016
COTTLE, MICHELLE
A Bigger Seat at the Table: Are the new megadonors distorting
American society? *New York Times Magazine* p19 Ap 30 2017
SALLY QUINN'S NEXT ACT *Washingtonian Magazine* v52

no12 p72 S 2017
Cottom, Tressie McMillan
My President Was Black *Atlantic* v319 no2 p8 Mr 2017
Who Goes There? D. GOLDSTEIN *New York Times Book Review*
p10 Mr 12 2017
Cotton
Cotton Fields in Scottsdale K. MONTGOMERY *Arizona High-
ways* v93 no2 p8 F 2017
Cotton, Ben
When Spotting a Hack Doesn't Help You P. M. Barrett *Bloomberg
Businessweek* no4497 p36 O 31 2016
Cotton, Billy
Quiet Riot M. RUS color *Architectural Digest* v74 no2 p40 F 2017
Cotton, Deb
Deb Cotton, Now and Forever: The Final Goodbye J. Berry color
New Orleans Magazine v51 no10 p64 Ag 2017
Cotton, James, 1935-2017
Remembering James Cotton J. Johnson bw *Downbeat* v84 no6
p25 Je 2017
Cotton, Katie
The Road Home *Publishers Weekly* v264 no3 p57 Ja 16 2017
Cotton, Richard D.
Coping with the Effects of Emotionally Difficult Work *Harvard
Business Review Digital Articles* p2 Ag 16 2016
Cotton, Tom, 1977-
Notes on a Disaster J. Podhoretz *Commentary* v140 no2 p27 S
2015
The Pros and Cons of the President's Immigrant Travel Ban *Con-
gressional Digest* v96 no3 p12 Mr 2017
Senator on the Rise F. BARNES color *Weekly Standard* v22 no31
p12 Ap 17 2017
Cotton bolls
CAROLINE YOUNGBLOOD J. R. Kemp color *Louisiana Life*
v37 no5 p20 My/Je 2017
Cotton exports & imports
U.S. Upland Cotton Exports and Mill Use Projected To Improve F.
Badau *Amber Waves: The Economics of Food, Farming, Natu-
ral Resources, & Rural America* p34 Ag 2017
Cotton fibers
Biological fabrication of cellulose fibers with tailored properties
F. Natalio, R. Fuchs et al color *Science* v357 no6356 p1118 S
15 2017
Cotton growing
Dwight B. Heard: Although his legacy lives on in a world-re-
nowned museum that bears his name, Dwight Bancroft Heard
made a name for himself as a newspaper publisher, cattle baron
and political ally of Teddy Roosevelt R. SANTISTEVAN *Ari-
zona Highways* v93 no10 p8 O 2017
THE RING BEARER E. N. GAGE *Martha Stewart Living* no269
p35 N 2016
Cotton textiles—Environmental aspects
SUSTAINABLE COTTON D. Kessenides color *Bloomberg Busi-
nessweek* no4496 p62 O 24 2016
Cotton textiles—Evaluation
In Stitches color *House Beautiful* v159 no8 p48 O 2017
Cotton trade
See also
Cotton exports & imports
Toiling for King Cotton M. KRESE *In These Times* v41 no4 p22
Ap 2017
U.S. Upland Cotton Exports and Mill Use Projected To Improve F.
Badau *Amber Waves: The Economics of Food, Farming, Natu-
ral Resources, & Rural America* p34 Ag 2017
Cottonwood
Marceline R. S. Jefferson bw color *Missouri Life* v44 no6 p44
S 2017
Nebraska's long love affair with Trees color *Nebraska Life* v21
no4 p32 Jl/Ag 2017
Under the shade of a thirsty cottonwood C. Amundson *Nebraska
Life* v21 no4 p9 Jl/Ag 2017
Cottrell, Michael
How Utilities Are Using Blockchain to Modernize the Grid *Har-
vard Business Review Digital Articles* p2 Mr 23 2017
Cottrell, Robert
Russia, NATO, Trump: The Shadow World color *New York Re-
view of Books* v63 no20 p97 D 22 2016

Coty Inc.
How Coty Reinvigorated Its Supply Chain T. Halton and K. Perlman *Harvard Business Review Digital Articles* p2 My 19 2016

Couceiro, José R.
De novo design of a biologically active amyloid bibl graph *Science* v354 no6313 paah4949-1 N 11 2016

Couetil, Laurent L.
CONSULTANTS color *Equus* no475 p81 Ap 2017

Coufal, Nicole G.
An environment-dependent transcriptional network specifies human microglia identity color *Science* v356 no6344 p1248 Je 23 2017

Cough
What's That Cough? A. Macmillan color *Health* v30 no9 p86 N 2016
Why You Cough J. Stewart color *Men's Health* v31 no10 p86 D 2016

Cough treatment
6 WAYS TO SUCK IT UP WHEN COUGH, COLD, OR FLU STRIKE K. Donohue color *Maclean's* v129 no40 p70 O 10 2016
Chronic cough: Finding the cause *Mayo Clinic Health Letter* v35 no11 p7 N 2017
YOGI HEAL THYSELF S. WADYKA color *Yoga Journal* p106 2017 SpecialIssue

Coughlin, Joseph F.
The Longevity Economy: Inside the World's Fastest-Growing, Most Misunderstood Market *Publishers Weekly* v264 no35 p118 Ag 28 2017

Coughlin, Natalie
"We Always Want to Win" S. Dreisbach color *Glamour* v114 no7 p104 Jl 2016

Coughlin, Tom (Thomas Richard), 1946-
Rebounders T. Keith color diag *Sports Illustrated* v126 no1 p14 Ja 9 2017

Cough—Prevention
Fall Favorites color *Better Nutrition* v79 no10 p24 O 2017
Quiet Your Cough G. FERRER and B. LENNIHAN color *Better Nutrition* v78 no12 p26 D 2016

Coulber, Sarah
Gardens of Delight color *Canadian Wildlife* v23 no1 p32 Mr/Ap 2017

Coulier, Dave
TGIF A. D'ARMINIO *TV Guide* v65 no39 p63 S 18 2017

Coulson, Tim
Precipitation drives global variation in natural selection bibl chart diag map *Science* v355 no6328 p959 Mr 3 2017

Coulter, Audrey
Longines FEI World Cup™ North American League News color *Practical Horseman* v44 no12 p66 D 2016

Coulter, Chris
Emergence and spread of a human-transmissible multidrug-resistant nontuberculous mycobacterium bibl diag graph *Science* v354 no6313 p751 N 11 2016

Coulter, Kristi
"8 things I learned in my first year of being sober" *Glamour* v115 no1 p50 Ja 2017

Coulthurst, Audrey
AUDREY COULTHURST K. NIIDS HOLM color *Publishers Weekly* v263 no52 p68 D 19 2016

Council, Erika
GRANDMA USED TO MAKE P. MALKUS *Atlanta* v56 no9 p76 Ja 2017

Council of Economic Advisers (U.S.)
THE 70TH ANNIVERSARY OF THE COUNCIL OF ECONOMIC ADVISERS *Economic Indicators* p291 S 2016
CHAPTER 7 THE 70TH ANNIVERSARY OF THE COUNCIL OF ECONOMIC ADVISERS *Economic Indicators* p291 O 2016
APPENDIX A REPORT TO THE PRESIDENT ON THE ACTIVITIES OF THE COUNCIL OF ECONOMIC ADVISERS DURING 2015 *Economic Indicators* p381 S 2016

Council of Fashion Designers of America
In (and Out of) Fashion G. Doré color *InStyle* v24 no9 p261 S 2017

Counseling

See also
Educational counseling
Marriage counseling
Mentoring
Vocational guidance
The Accidental Career Coach M. NEMKO *Psychology Today* v49 no5 p48 S/O 2016
editor's note. On wanting more for others than they want for themselves K. Perina *Psychology Today* v49 no5 p4 S/O 2016
Hot for Teachers T. Toch color *Washington Monthly* v49 no6-8 p47 Je-Ag 2017
meaningful MUDRAS M. RABBITT color *Yoga Journal* no287 p31 N 2016
NIH's mentoring makes progress J. Vishwanatha, C. Pfund et al bibl *Science* v354 no6314 p840 N 18 2016
When sex hurts *Mayo Clinic Health Letter* v358 no8 p6 Ag 2017
Worried about the weight room? K. Canning color *Health* v31 no8 p55 O 2017

Counselor, The (Film)
ACCORDING TO: Donald Glover J. DUBOFF color *Vanity Fair* v58 no11 p98 N 2016

Counselors
Clutter counselor S. Wells *Christian Century* v134 no11 p35 My 24 2017

COUNTER, ROSEMARY
Deadline trauma color *Maclean's* v130 no2 p64 Mr 2017
Extreme art color *Maclean's* v129 no45 p46 N 14 2016
Fowl play on campus color *Maclean's* p11 Je 2017
Helping moose get it on color *Maclean's* v130 no4 p16 My 2017
Louvre of Arabia color *Maclean's* v129 no51/52 p71 D 26 2016
The most intimate of ubers color *Maclean's* v129 no41 p53 O 17 2016
The wolf of Juan de Fuca color *Maclean's* v130 no3 p13 Ap 2017

Counterarguments
What to Do When a "Devil's Advocate" Tries to Derail Your Project J. Cleaver *Harvard Business Review Digital Articles* p2 Ja 18 2016

Counterculture
How to Take Back the Counterculture M. Hirschorn *New York* v49 no24 p34 N 28 2016

Counterfactuals (Logic)
The Discontents of Counterfactualism P. Dukes *History Today* v67 no1 p72 Ja 2017
Use Failure as Fuel S. Weinman color *Men's Health* v31 no10 p36 D 2016

Counterfeits & counterfeiting—China
China's Bond Market Has a Forgery Problem *Bloomberg Businessweek* no4509 p36 Ja 30 2017

Counterinsurgency
See also
Special forces (Military science)

Counterproductivity (Labor)
Quash Your Bad Habits by Knowing What Triggers Them P. Bregman *Harvard Business Review Digital Articles* p2 O 8 2015

Counterrevolutions
The Long March to Bedlam R. J. BRESLER *USA Today Magazine* v146 no2866 p13 Jl 2017

Countertenors
Present in His Grace K. Massinger color *Commonweal* v144 no8 p32 My 5 2017

Counterterrorism
See also
War on Terrorism, 2001-2009
Are We Winning the Battle Against Terrorism? T. MOCKAITIS and J. ALTERMAN *New York Times Upfront* v149 no7 p22 Ja 9 2017
Concert Security's New Frontier S. KNOPPER color *Rolling Stone* no1293 p16 Ag 10 2017
The Fighters In the Battle for Mosul J. Malsin color *Time* v188 no18 p10 O 31 2016
Losing Hearts and Minds B. POWERS *New Republic* v248 no10 p8 O 2017
The War on Terror vs. the War on Poverty W. Easterly bw graph *New York Review of Books* v63 no18 p64 N 24 2016

Counterterrorism laws
Arizona's Manufactured Terrorism Threat B. Hodai color *Pro-*

gressive v81 no5 p51 Je/Jl 2017

Counterterrorism—Government policy

After the Bombs Have Fallen R. Ratnesar, C. Simpson et al color *Bloomberg Businessweek* no4531 p34 Jl 24 2017

How to Hunt a Lone Wolf D. Byman cartoon *Foreign Affairs* v96 no2 p96 Mr/Ap 2017

Counterterrorism—Government policy—United States

Bring Back Containment R. Joseph color *Weekly Standard* v22 no47 p18 Ag 21 2017

How Not to Fight Terrorism H. HURLBURT *New Republic* v248 no5 p8 My 2017

Trump and Terrorism H. Brands and P. Feaver color *Foreign Affairs* v96 no2 p28 Mr/Ap 2017

Counterterrorism—Government policy—United States—History—21st century

THIS MONTH: The U.S. Is Bombing at Least Six Countries. How Can the Anti-War Movement Step Up? P. BENNIS, V. PRASHAD et al *In These Times* v41 no10 p14 O 2017

Counterterrorism—History—21st century

Preventing the Next Attack L. Monaco color *Foreign Affairs* v96 no6 p23 N/D 2017

Counterterrorism—International cooperation

AFTER THE ISLAMIC STATE R. WRIGHT cartoon *New Yorker* v92 no41 p30 D 12 2016

The Former Head of the CIA on Managing the Hunt for Bin Laden L. E. Panetta and J. Bash *Harvard Business Review Digital Articles* p2 My 2 2016

Counterterrorism—Management

THE PARTY PLANNERS M. WARREN bw color diag map *Popular Mechanics* p82 Ap 2017

Counterterrorism—United States

Are We Any Safer? S. Weart, D. N. Blair et al color *Atlantic* v318 no4 p14 N 2016

Battling Lone-Wolf Terrorists at Home N. Rasmussen color *Time* v188 no16/17 p34 O 24 2016

Don't Follow the Money P. R. Neumann color *Foreign Affairs* v96 no4 p93 Jl/Ag 2017

The Other Forever War J. Goldsmith and M. C. Waxman *Hoover Digest: Research & Opinion on Public Policy* no1 p92 Wint 2017

Preventing the Next Attack L. Monaco color *Foreign Affairs* v96 no6 p23 N/D 2017

U.S.-Russia Tensions Reach Dangerous New Level M. Calabresi, S. Shuster et al color *Time* v188 no16/17 p5 O 24 2016

Winning the 9/11 Wars [Cover story] S. F. Hayes color *Weekly Standard* v22 no37 p6 Je 5 2017

Countesses

La Vita Brandolini J. REGINATO bw color *Vanity Fair* v59 no7 p128 Summ 2017

Counties

DUNDY COUNTY Road Trip A. J. BARTELS color *Nebraska Life* v20 no6 p40 N/D 2016

SOUTH DAKOTA TRIVIA *South Dakota Magazine* v32 no6 p16 Mr/Ap 2017

Counting Crows (Performer)

NIGHT LIFE *New Yorker* v93 no26 p15 S 4 2017

Countries

COUNTRIES CLOSEST IN SIZE TO EACH PROVINCE J. KIRBY map *Maclean's* v130 no2 p15 Mr 2017

Going the Extra Mile: Why a rural New England ramble always takes a bit longer than you'd think *Yankee* v81 no5 p26 S/O 2017

Country homes

Pretty farmhouse near Brady color *Nebraska Life* v21 no6 p20 N/D 2017

Country homes—Conservation & restoration

Restoration Possible color *Log Home Living* v33 no7 p21 S 2016

Country homes—England

Social Media color *Architectural Digest* v73 no11 p50 N 2016

Country life

Dinner with Arnold: And Burying the Sail-Cats S. CARR *Idaho Magazine* v16 no7 p54 Ap 2017

PEARL R. CUNNINGHAM *Idaho Magazine* v16 no5 p32 F 2017

Country life—Religious aspects

CATHOLIC BETWEEN THE COASTS W. Massey color *America* v216 no5 p24 Mr 6 2017

Country life—United States

Faith Matters C. Zaleski *Christian Century* v134 no2 p36 Ja 18 2017

Country music

See also

Alternative country music

AFTER DARK—ON THE STRIP color *Horse & Rider* v56 no11 p76 N 2017

Lost in the Stars D. SHIFLETT *Weekly Standard* v22 no4 p36 O 3 2016

Country Music Association (U.S)—Awards

Brad Paisley: The CMA's Stand-up Guy M. Vain color *Entertainment Weekly* no1438 p21 N 4 2016

Nashville Toasts the CMAs at 50 E. Finan color *Entertainment Weekly* no1434 p18 O 7 2016

What to Watch R. Rahman, J. Hibberd et al color *Entertainment Weekly* no1442 p53 D 2 2016 Rebellious Special Issue

Country music concerts

Legendary Texans color *American Cowboy* p18 LEGENDS OF TEXAS Special Issue 2017

Country music—Exhibitions

ROCK THIS COUNTRY *USA Today Magazine* v146 no2868 p58 S 2017

Country musicians

Glen Campbell J. Kluger color *Time* v190 no7 p13 Ag 21 2017

Country musicians—Interviews

The Fighting Side of Sturgill Simpson D. RITZ color *Rolling Stone* no1272 p22 O 20 2016

Country musicians—United States

AFTER DARK—ON THE STRIP color *Horse & Rider* v56 no11 p76 N 2017

Glen Campbell J. Bernstein color *Entertainment Weekly* no1478 / 1479 p105 Ag 18-25 2017

MERLE HAGGARD L. Lynn and M. Vain color *Entertainment Weekly* no1446/1447 p93 D 2016/Ja 2017

Rhinestone Superstar P. DOYLE and W. HERMES bw color *Rolling Stone* no1295 p16 S 7 2017

Country of origin (Immigrants)

The Butcher's Wife color *New York Times Magazine* p26 F 12 2017

Country Travel Discoveries LLC

Go West YOUNG MEN! (and women, too) color *Nebraska Life* v20 no6 p68 N/D 2016

Country Blues, The (Music)

Trailblazers and Hybrids HADLEY color *Downbeat* v83 no12 p76 D 2016

Country music—2011-2020—Reviews

Back in the Old Country M. Vain color *Entertainment Weekly* no1478 / 1479 p104 Ag 18-25 2017

HOT | NOT T. Keith color *Sports Illustrated* v125 no16 p20 N 14 2016

KELSEA BALLERINI M. Vain *Entertainment Weekly* no1446/1447 p76 D 2016/Ja 2017

SHANIA TWAIN K. O'Donnell color *Entertainment Weekly* no1446/1447 p72 D 2016/Ja 2017

Coup d'état, Iran, 1953

The Myths of 1953 R. TAKEYH bw *Weekly Standard* v22 no43 p21 Jl 24 2017

Coup d'état, Mali, 2012

Mali's Enduring Crisis S. D. WING *Current History* v116 no790 p189 My 2017

COUPLAND, DANIEL

The 'Dual Life' of Beatrix Potter bw color *National Review* v69 no6 p45 Ap 3 2017

Coupland, Douglas, 1961-

Generation X *Maclean's* v129 no42 p44 O 24 2016

Couple-owned business enterprises

That Magic Formula: GLAMGLOW FOUNDERS GLENN AND SHANNON DELLIMORE BUILT A FAST FORTUNE WITH A QUICK ACTING FACIAL MUD. AS THEY RAMP UP FOR THEIR NEXT MOVE, THE BEAUTY WORLD IS WATCHING I. SCHMIDT *Los Angeles Magazine* p64 Ag 2017

Couplers (Railroad cars)—Evaluation

Micro-Trains True-Scale couplers color *Model Railroader* v84 no3 p70 Mr 2017

Couples

See also
Gay couples
Infidelity (Couples)
Married people

86 the Tasting Menu? J. GORDINIER color *Esquire* v167 no1 p26 F 2017

THE BIG QUESTION L. Grunwald, J. Eugenides et al cartoon *Atlantic* v320 no4 p124 N 2017

THE CALLING OF THE INFERTILE WHO HOPE M. L. ANDERSON color *Christianity Today* v61 no4 p48 My 2017

The Case of the Disputed Lottery Ticket V. GLEMBOCKI color *Reader's Digest* v190 no1134 p29 O 2017

CONSCIOUS COUPLING B. Langmann bw color *Esquire* p116 N 2017

Finger Licking Good N. REEDER and D. POINTDUJOUR color *Ebony* v72 no4 p62 F 2017

GAYLE KING and FRANK EDWARDS color *AARP: The Magazine* v59 no2A p50 F/Mr 2016

How Couples (and Throuples!) Do Money J. Eidelson, E. Holland et al color *Bloomberg Businessweek* no4502 p74 D 5 2016

How to Be Yourself in Love and Sex J. Doll color *Glamour* v115 no3 p137 Mr 2017

In Defense of Emotional Cheating A. Breslaw color *Glamour* v115 no3 p140 Mr 2017

INK-STAINED HEARTS A. Breznican color *Entertainment Weekly* no1434 p61 O 7 2016

Invest in Mutual Fun B. Risher and J. Covert cartoon *Men's Health* v32 no1 p30 Ja/F 2017

JANICE RUDE and PRENTISS WILLSON color *AARP: The Magazine* v59 no2A p48 F/Mr 2016

JARED & IVANKA'S GUIDE TO MINDFUL MARRIAGE P. RUDNICK cartoon *New Yorker* v93 no17 p29 Je 19 2017

The Lovebirds G. MUNROE color *Walrus* v14 no7 p62 S 2017

The Loving Legacy A. Haglage and E. Mahaney bw color *Glamour* v114 no11 p141 N 2016

My boyfriend of four years doesn't want to move in together K. Van Kirk, H. Havrilesky et al color *Glamour* v115 no3 p144 Mr 2017

Our Relationship, in Pictures A. Kassem bw color *Glamour* v115 no3 p142 Mr 2017

REUNITED S. Koslow color *AARP: The Magazine* v59 no2A p46 F/Mr 2016

the Separation R. K. JOHNSON cartoon *New Yorker* v93 no7 p76 Ap 3 2017

Sing the Hero: A Hole in the Boat, And Ice in the Water K. WIDNER *Idaho Magazine* v16 no7 p21 Ap 2017

Umbrellas: The iPhones of the Victorian Age V. POSTREL bw *Reason* v48 no10 p8 Mr 2017

Wait, Maybe True Love Does Exist M. Mertens color *Glamour* v115 no9 p121 S 2017

WHEN I KNEW I FOUND THE ONE J. SPYRA cartoon *New Yorker* v92 no38 p41 N 21 2016

Which state has the happiest couples? color *Women's Health* v14 no4 p34 My 2017

YOU'RE YOUNGER. HE'S OLDER. WHY DO PEOPLE STILL CARE? R. Oltuski color *Women's Health* v14 no5 p108 Je 2017

Couples, Fred
Freddie Digs Deep J. Marksbury color *Golf Magazine* v59 no4 p78 Ap 2017

THE WINNING LOOK Linksoul and C. Barrett color *Golf Magazine* v59 no8 p38 Ag 2017

Couples on television
TV's HOTTEST COUPLES S. Malcom, I. Ratledge et al *TV Guide* v64 no15 p28 Ap 4 2016

Who Is the Best TV Couple? M. Z. Seitz img *New York* v49 no22 p100 O 31 2016

Couples therapy
CRUISE CONTROL H. ESTROFF MARANO *Psychology Today* v50 no5 p22 S/O 2017

Valley Girl G. DOYLE MELTON color *O, The Oprah Magazine* p36 Je 2017

Couples—Attitudes
I Love You—Now Go Home C. Drell and S. T. Brown color *Glamour* v115 no11 p105 N 2017

Couples—Finance
Your Retirement: A Team Effort color *Money* v45 no10 p12 N 2016

Couples—Legal status, laws, etc.
Can I Pretend to Be A Lesbian to Get a Couples Discount? K. A. Appiah *New York Times Magazine* p26 O 16 2016

Coupling reactions (Chemistry)
Snap deconvolution: An informatics approach to high-throughput discovery of catalytic reactions K. Troshin and J. F. Hartwig color *Science* v357 no6347 p175 Jl 14 2017

Coups d'état
Creeping Autocracy: The greatest risk to democracy? Not the prospect of a coup or a junta but the self-aggrandizement of "strong leaders" L. Diamond *Hoover Digest: Research & Opinion on Public Policy* no3 p55 Summ 2017

QUEEN'S RANSOM [Cover story] P. X. Rutz bw color map *Military History* v34 no4 p62 N 2017

Turkey's Reichstag Fire *Commentary* v142 no2 p1 S 2016

Coups d'état—Turkey
See also
Turkey—History—Attempted coup, 2016

Breakdowns of the year color *Science* v354 no6319 p1525 D 23 2016

Turkey and the Economics of Coups E. Meyersson *Harvard Business Review Digital Articles* p2 Jl 22 2016

Courage
See also
Moral courage

50 Reasons to Love Being 50+ M. Morris color *AARP: The Magazine* v30 no6A p63 O/N 2017

All the Gallant Men D. STRATTON and K. GIRE *Reader's Digest* v188 no1126 p82 D 2016/Ja 2017

Bringing a Hero Home M. Thompson color *Time* v188 no24 p50 D 12 2016

Dear 23-Year-Old Me color *AARP: The Magazine* v60 no2A p70 F/Mr 2017

It's Your Job to Tell the Hard Truths P. Bregman *Harvard Business Review Digital Articles* p2 O 17 2014

Points to Ponder color *Reader's Digest* v189 no1129 p31 Ap 2017

SHE'S GOT THE POWER S. Cristobal color *Harper's Bazaar* no3648 p244 N 2016

WOMEN WHO DARE bw color *Harper's Bazaar* no3648 p246 N 2016

You Have to Be Fast to Be Seen as a Great Leader J. Zenger and J. Folkman *Harvard Business Review Digital Articles* p2 F 26 2015

Courage—Religious aspects
The Faces of Courage R. A. SCHROTH color *America* v215 no18 p20 D 5 2016

Courchesne, Eric
Intersection of diverse neuronal genomes and neuropsychiatric disease: The Brain Somatic Mosaicism Network color *Science* v356 no6336 p395 Ap 28 2017

Couric, Katie
Icons color *Time* v189 no16/17 p122 My 1-8 2017

THE IMPORTANCE OF ASKING Questions color *InStyle* v24 no9 p204 S 2017

COURT, BEN
20 ESSENTIAL FIT-FLUENCERS bw color *Men's Health* v32 no9 p108 N 2017

ACTIVE STYLE AWARDS bw color *Men's Health* v32 no7 p(Sp)17 S 2017

BUILD YOUR BRAND color *Men's Health* v32 no7 p(Sp)6 S 2017

Nothing in Moderation color *Men's Health* v32 no7 p10 S 2017

Priyanka Chopra color *Men's Health* v32 no1 p34 Ja/F 2017

RECODE YOUR HEALTH color *Men's Health* v32 no7 p118 S 2017

SPECIAL OPS FITNESS SECRETS [Cover story] cartoon color *Men's Health* v32 no4 p94 My 2017

Court of Justice of the European Union
ECJ rules employers can ban religious clothing: But it would be 'foolhardy' to change dress codes based on this case, experts warn *People Management* p16 Ap 2017

Court rules—Wisconsin
Contempt for Democracy R. CONNIFF bw *Progressive* v81 no6 p6 Ag/S 2017

Courtesy

ALL IN A Day's Work L. HARRIS and S. THOMAS cartoon color *Reader's Digest* v190 no1134 p54 O 2017

CAN WE TALK? D. Slater color *Mother Jones* v42 no6 p59 N/D 2017

An Education in Civility N. M. Gorsuch *Weekly Standard* v23 no5 p9 O 9 2017

Offices Can Be Bastions of Civility in an Uncivil Time L. Gaines-Ross *Harvard Business Review Digital Articles* p2 Jl 14 2017

Paying Our Respects Y. N. DURFIELD, J. McKINNON et al color *O, The Oprah Magazine* p15 Je 2017

The Question S. GILDER, M. MURPHY et al *O, The Oprah Magazine* p16 Ap 2017

Safe Spaces and the Spiritual Exercises *America* v216 no7 p8 Ap 3 2017

UNCOMMON COURTESIES bw color *O, The Oprah Magazine* p102 Ap 2017

What I Know for Sure Oprah color *O, The Oprah Magazine* p140 Ap 2017

Courtesy—Social aspects

THE AGE OF RUDENESS *New York Times Magazine* p38 F 19 2017

Courthouses—Design & construction

Day in Court C. MCGUIGAN color diag *Architectural Record* v205 no3 p92 Mr 2017

Courthouses—History

CHEROKEE COUNTY HISTORIC COURTHOUSE CANTON 40 MILES NORTH OF ATLANTA J. GREEN *Atlanta* v56 no9 p170 Ja 2017

Courthouses—Missouri

COURT APPEAL J. BENNER *Missouri Life* v43 no6 p34 O/N 2016

COURTNEY, DAVID

The Beach Boys *Texas Monthly* v45 no5 p224 My 2017

Calling Dr. Chilton: GETTING TO THE BOTTOM OF THE BAFFLING BACKSTORY OF LUBBOCK'S LEGENDARY LEMONY LIBATION-ONE REFRESHING SIP AT A TIME *Texas Monthly* v45 no7 p168 Jl 2017

Cook Like a Texanist *Texas Monthly* v44 no12 p272 D 2016

FAN ADVICE FROM THE TEXANIST *Texas Monthly* v45 no9 p66 S 2017

Happy Texas Week, Y'all! *Texas Monthly* v45 no3 p212 Mr 2017

Just the Facts *Texas Monthly* v45 no6 p288 Je 2017

Low Stakes on the High Seas *Texas Monthly* v45 no1 p151 Ja 2017

Read Before Burning *Texas Monthly* v45 no2 p154 F 2017

The Return of Jefferson Davis *Texas Monthly* v45 no6 p48 Je 2017

Save Muny *Texas Monthly* v45 no4 p204 Ap 2017

The Spirit of '76 *Texas Monthly* v44 no11 p220 N 2016

Courtney, Jai

The Society PAGE *Interview* v46 no8 p60 O 2016

COURTNEY, SHAUN

DC HAS ITS BEST SHOT AT BRIDGING THE EAST/WEST-OF-THE-RIVER DIVIDE *Washingtonian Magazine* v52 no7 p106 Ap 2017

Courtneys, The (Performer)

NIGHT LIFE *New Yorker* v93 no32 p10 O 16 2017

Courts

Aren't Anglicans Protestant? T. C. MORGAN *Christianity Today* p19 Mr 2017

Courts-martial & courts of inquiry

Guantánamo lawyer: Military tribunals are built on American apartheid [Cover story] M. Paradis *America* v216 no10 p10 My 1 2017

Courts—Design & construction

Grounds for Justice H. PEARMAN color diag *Architectural Record* v205 no3 p106 Mr 2017

Courtship

See also
Dating (Social customs)

Financial Intimacy: Is Your Relationship Ready? A. Edmond Jr. and Z. D. Green color *Black Enterprise* v47 no3 p24 O 2016

Courtship in birds

Romancing the Water D. Walters color *Audubon* v119 no3 p49 Fall 2017

Courtship in fishes

Melatonin makes the midshipman hum S. Milius color *Science*
News v190 no9 p4 O 29 2016

Courts—New York (State)

Defense with Dignity D. C. Vock *Governing* v30 no6 p50 Mr 2017

Courts—United States

Fateful Dive into 'Closed' Park Pond J. C. Kozlowski *Parks & Recreation* v51 no12 p20 D 2016

Of Course Court Fights Are Bitter J. Cost color *Weekly Standard* v22 no23 p14 F 20 2017

Utilize the Courts A. NABAUM *New Republic* v248 no3 p36 Mr 2017

Why You Won't Get Your Day in Court J. S. Rakoff bw cartoon *New York Review of Books* v63 no18 p4 N 24 2016

Courtyard gardens

French Court A. Aguillard color *Southern Living* v52 no5 p15 My 2017

Coury, Lance

SLIPSTREAM color *Cycle World* v55 no10 p66 N 2016

Cousins

Pop Chart M. Mccluskey color *Time* v190 no16/17 p110 O 23 2017

Cousins, DeMarcus

NOVEMBER Blues B. Golliver color *Sports Illustrated* v125 no17 p88 N 21 2016 Double Issue

Cousins, Kirk, 1988-

Dying on the Vine T. Keith color *Sports Illustrated* v125 no15 p22 N 7 2016

Kirk Cousins C. Cullen color *Current Biography* v77 no11 p30 N 2016

Cousteau, Jacques, 1910-1997

BREATHE color *Prevention* v69 no8 p36 Ag 2017

Couté, Yohann

An algal photoenzyme converts fatty acids to hydrocarbons color graph *Science* v357 no6354 p903 S 1 2017

Couto, Vinay

How to Cut Costs More Strategically color *Harvard Business Review Digital Articles* p2 Mr 10 2017

COUTTS, IAN

TITANS of the Great Lakes color map *Canadian Geographic* v137 no4 p34 Jl/Ag 2017

Coutts, Marion, ca. 1965-

Marion Coutts M. Hagan *Current Biography* v78 no8 p26 Ag 2017

Coutu, Diane

High-Pressure Jobs and Mental Illness *Harvard Business Review Digital Articles* p2 Ap 2 2015

When You've Made Enough Money to Cause Family Tension *Harvard Business Review Digital Articles* p2 Ja 8 2016

Coutu, S.

Observation of a large-scale anisotropy in the arrival directions of cosmic rays above 8×10^{18} eV *Science* v357 no6357 p1266 S 22 2017

Couturier, Andy

The Abundance of Less: Lessons in Simple Living from Rural Japan *Publishers Weekly* v264 no24 p58 Je 12 2017

BOOKS IN BRIEF M. SCARLES color *Tricycle: The Buddhist Review* v27 no1 p100 Fall 2017

Couturier, Lydie

Self-organized Notch dynamics generate stereotyped sensory organ patterns in Drosophila color *Science* v356 no6337 p501 My 5 2017

COUZENS, E. D.

International Wildlife Law: Understanding and Enhancing Its Role in Conservation *BioScience* v67 no9 p784 S 2017

Couzin-Frankel, Jennifer

Anti-inflammatory prevents heart attacks color *Science* v357 no6354 p855 S 1 2017

BATTLING BIAS color *Science* v356 no6339 p686 My 19 2017

Call to halt heart trial raises vexing questions color *Science* v357 no6351 p538 Ag 11 2017

FATEFUL IMPRINTS color diag *Science* v355 no6321 p122 Ja 13 2017

Mission aims to salvage what's left of Nimrud color map *Science* v357 no6358 p1340 S 29 2017

Publication ban upends NIH lab, collaborators color *Science* v355 no6327 p783 F 24 2017

Supply of promising T cell therapy is strained color *Science* v356

no6343 p1112 Je 16 2017

Worries, confusion after cancer trial deaths color *Science* v354 no6317 p1211 D 9 2016

Cova, Corey

16 Ways to Hack Your Hoagie R. RAISFELD and R. PATRONITE img *New York* v49 no20 p102 O 3 2016

Coval, Kevin

Visual Artist Paul Branton L. CROSS color *Ebony* v72 no6 p20 Ap/My 2017

WHAT THE WHITE BOY WANTS M. POLLOCK color *Chicago* v66 no4 p90 Ap 2017

Covalent bonds (Chemistry)

Carbon can exceed four-bond limit L. HAMERS diag *Science News* v191 no2 p9 F 4 2017

Experimentally realized mechanochemistry distinct from force-accelerated scission of loaded bonds S. Akbulatov, Y. Tian et al diag graph *Science* v357 no6348 p299 Jl 21 2017

Two-dimensional sp2 carbon–conjugated covalent organic frameworks E. Jin, M. Asada et al diag graph *Science* v357 no6352 p673 Ag 18 2017

Covas, Rita

Extreme bird nests bring comforts, catastrophe S. Milius color *Science News* v190 no8 p4 O 15 2016

Covault, C. E.

Observation of a large-scale anisotropy in the arrival directions of cosmic rays above 8 × 1018 eV *Science* v357 no6357 p1266 S 22 2017

Cove, The (Film)

The Messenger J. Hahn *Sierra* v102 no1 p11 Ja/F 2017

Covenants not to compete

Stop Trying to Control How Ex-Employees Use Their Knowledge O. Lobel and J. Bessen *Harvard Business Review Digital Articles* p2 O 9 2014

Coventry, David

The Invisible Mile *Publishers Weekly* v264 no12 p50 Mr 20 2017

Cover crops

5 Expert-Recommended TOOLS FOR NO-TILL PLOTS J. Poncavage *Mother Earth News* no279 p43 D/Ja 2017

COVER CROPS CREATE SAVINGS: UTILIZING COVER CROPS CAN BOOST SOIL HEALTH, REDUCE PESTS, AND CYCLE NUTRIENTS D. Goerge *Successful Farming* v115 no6 p41 Ap 2017

COVER CROPS RENOVATE GRASSLAND R. Nickel *Successful Farming* v115 no5 p48 Mid-Mr 2017

A PATH TO SOIL HEALTH B. Spiegel *Successful Farming* v115 no3 p38 Mid-F 2017

SIDEDRESS AND SEED COVER CROPS A. McConnell and L. Bedord *Successful Farming* v115 no1 p32 Ja 2017

Cover crops—Environmental aspects

RUN FOR COVER T. PHILPOTT color *Mother Jones* v42 no4 p68 Jl/Ag 2017

Cover versions

RYAN ADAMS L. Greenblatt color *Entertainment Weekly* no1454/1455 p94 F 24 2017

Coverlets—Evaluation

Red, White and You color *Log Home Living* v33 no7 p40 S 2016

Covert, Bryce

Back to Work color *New Republic* v248 no8/9 p16 Ag/S 2017

Beyond Affirmative Action *Nation* v305 no6 p5 S 11 2017

Deadbeat Democrats *New Republic* v248 no10 p14 O 2017

EXIT LEFT bw color *Nation* v304 no16 p16 My 22 2017

Imaginary Inner Cities il *Nation* v303 no22 p5 N 28 2016

Jobs for a Few graph *Nation* v304 no6 p5 F 27 2017

Liberalism's Half-Life color graph *Nation* v304 no1 p14 Ja 2 2017 The Obama Years

Naming Names diag graph *Nation* v304 no15 p5 My 8 2017

Soaring Prices *Nation* v305 no2 p5 Jl 17 2017

Trump the Job Killer il *New Republic* v248 no6 p8 Je 2017

Covert, Jerilyn

The Burnout Quiz color *Men's Health* v32 no1 p31 Ja/F 2017

Conquer Any Obstacle cartoon color *Men's Health* v32 no4 p23 My 2017

Doughy No More color *Men's Health* v32 no1 p32 Ja/F 2017

Feel Great After a Bad Night of Sleep cartoon *Men's Health* v32 no4 p80 My 2017

A Game-Changing Dip color *Men's Health* v32 no1 p24 Ja/F 2017

How Caffeine Works cartoon color *Men's Health* v32 no4 p72 My 2017

Invest in Mutual Fun cartoon *Men's Health* v32 no1 p30 Ja/F 2017

Salmon Pesto Pasta color *Men's Health* v32 no1 p28 Ja/F 2017

Shore Up Your Shoulders cartoon color *Men's Health* v32 no1 p26 Ja/F 2017

Start Your ADVENTURE color *Men's Health* v32 no1 p20 Ja/F 2017

Sweat: The Details bw graph *Men's Health* v32 no6 p92 Ag 2017

WELCOME TO THE GOLDEN AGE OF SEX cartoon chart color *Men's Health* v32 no2 p102 Mr 2017

Coves (Valleys)

Made in Montauk B. COLACELLO color *Vanity Fair* v59 no8 p96 Ag 2017

An Unlikely Embrace W. SMITH *Sierra* v102 no3 p72 My/Je 2017

Covey, Douglas F.

Lysosomal cholesterol activates mTORC1 via an SLC38A9–Niemann-Pick C1 signaling complex bibl diag graph *Science* v355 no6331 p1306 Mr 24 2017

Covey, Stephen M. R.

The Connection Between Employee Trust and Financial Performance *Harvard Business Review Digital Articles* p2 Jl 18 2016

Coville, Frenchman Thomas

Records Tumble in Southern Ocean color *Sail* v48 no3 p20 Mr 2017

Coville, Thomas

Round-the-World Records Tumble color *Sail* v48 no4 p20 Ap 2017

Covington, Dennis

One Nation Under God *American Scholar* v86 no2 p117 Spr 2017

COVRETT, DONNA

ENCYCLOPEDIA CINCINNATI bw cartoon color *Cincinnati Magazine* v51 no1 p42 O 2017

Cowan, Amber

The Fine Tint C. Keller color *O, The Oprah Magazine* p30 O 2017

Tender Tribute J. Lovelace bw color *American Craft* v77 no2 p28 Ap/My 2017

COWAN, DAVID

Leonard Cohen's Life of Poetry and Song bw *American Conservative* v16 no1 p54 Ja/F 2017

Cowan, Diane

CRUSTACEAN ASSIGNATION P. Edmonds color *National Geographic* v232 no1 p29 Jl 2017

Cowan, Matthew

NRPA Aquatics Update *Parks & Recreation* p6 Aquatics Guide 2017

Cowan, N. B.

Zones, spots, and planetary-scale waves beating in brown dwarf atmospheres color graph *Science* v357 no6352 p683 Ag 18 2017

Cowan, Robert—Interviews

What a Headache S. WYKES *USA Today Magazine* v145 no2858 p33 N 2016

Coward of the County (Music)

EASY CHAIR R. Solnit *Harper's Magazine* v334 no2004 p4 My 2017

Cowboy boots

The Question S. BUTLER, B. CLEVENGER et al *O, The Oprah Magazine* p12 Mr 2017

Cowboy boots—Evaluation

Flashback Fashion color *American Cowboy* v23 no5 p53 F/Mr 2017

Save or Splurge? color *Horse & Rider* v55 no11 p22 N 2016

Cowboy Magic (Company)

Tame His Mane color *Horse & Rider* v56 no9 p34 S 2017

Cowboy poetry

The GRAND DAME of Cowboy Poetry C. Vaughan cartoon color *American Cowboy* v23 no5 p58 F/Mr 2017

Salute to Service B. Welch color *American Cowboy* v23 no5 p8 F/Mr 2017

Cowboys

175 WAYS TO GET WESTERN G. R. Schiavino cartoon color *American Cowboy* v23 no5 p26 F/Mr 2017

The ALL-NEW RACE for the ULTIMATE CROWN in Cowboy Town [Cover story] K. SANTOS color *Spin to Win Rodeo* v20 no10 p62 D 2016

ALMOST A Calamity C. WHITE *Idaho Magazine* v16 no5 p48 F 2017

At Home With... B. Welch color *American Cowboy* v24 no1 p16 Je/Jl 2017

The Boss Lady's View bw *American Cowboy* v23 no5 p10 F/Mr 2017

BUCKLE UP C. Toy color *Spin to Win Rodeo* v21 no5 p15 Jl 2017

A CITY SLICKER in the PANHANDLE J. SALAMON *Texas Monthly* v45 no8 p6 Ag 2017

Classic Cowpunchers bw color *American Cowboy* v24 no1 p10 Je/Jl 2017

Cowboy Christmas Power Hours color *American Cowboy* v23 no4 p76 D 2016/Ja 2017

Cowboy Up: Backhand Slip Catch color *American Cowboy* v23 no6 p65 Ap/My 2017

Cowboy Up: Dutch Oven Camp Cooking L. FELDMAN color *American Cowboy* v24 no1 p64 Je/Jl 2017

DON'T OVERTHINK THINGS K. Santos color *Spin to Win Rodeo* v21 no3 p46 My 2017

Family-Style B. Welch bw *Horse & Rider* v56 no8 p17 Ag 2017

The Heart of Cowboy Camp J. Young bw color *American Cowboy* v23 no6 p48 Ap/My 2017

Home on the Range bw *Popular Photography* v80 no11 p8 D 2016

Less Me, More We B. Welch color *Horse & Rider* v56 no9 p17 S 2017

Let Fly the Loop S. BUTCHER *Texas Monthly* v44 no11 p70 N 2016

Lost Skills J. Young cartoon *American Cowboy* v23 no5 p66 F/Mr 2017

Must-Haves M. Sanders color *American Cowboy* v23 no4 p87 D 2016/Ja 2017

NFR by the Numbers bw color *American Cowboy* v23 no4 p88 D 2016/Ja 2017

The Right Step L. Feldman color *American Cowboy* v24 no1 p48 Je/Jl 2017

Salute to Service B. Welch color *American Cowboy* v23 no5 p8 F/Mr 2017

SUBURBAN COWBOY E. O'NEILL color *Missouri Life* v44 no5 p26 Ag 2017

Thoughts on previous issues R. Reuck, S. Emmen-Outen et al color *American Cowboy* v24 no1 p24 Je/Jl 2017

True Champion N. Reid color *American Cowboy* v23 no4 p80 D 2016/Ja 2017

THE X FACTOR C. Toy color *Spin to Win Rodeo* v21 no5 p48 Jl 2017

YOUTH MOVEMENT N. Reid bw cartoon *American Cowboy* v23 no4 p72 D 2016/Ja 2017

Cowboys as artists

By Chance L. Feldman bw color *American Cowboy* v23 no5 p54 F/Mr 2017

The Greatest color *American Cowboy* v23 no5 p67 F/Mr 2017

Cowboys—Collectibles

My Collection color *Horse & Rider* v56 no8 p104 Ag 2017

That Old Time Feeling B. Welch color *American Cowboy* v23 no6 p38 Ap/My 2017

Cowboys—Competitions

The Cinch Timed Event Championship of the World C. Toy color *American Cowboy* v23 no5 p29 F/Mr 2017

ROPING IN THE THOMAS & MACK ...ANYTHING BUT AVERAGE K. SANTOS bw color *Spin to Win Rodeo* v20 no12 p66 F 2017

Cowboys—Congresses

CELEBRATING COWBOYS color *American Cowboy* v24 no1 p26 Je/Jl 2017

IT'S ALL HERE! color *Horse & Rider* v56 no11 p64 N 2017

Cowboys—Equipment & supplies

Day Help color *American Cowboy* v23 no5 p46 F/Mr 2017

Riding for the Brand color *American Cowboy* v23 no5 p48 F/Mr 2017

Cowboys—History

Northern Nevada's Cowboy Culture G. R. SCHIAVINO map *American Cowboy* v23 no5 p45 F/Mr 2017

Cowboys—Social life & customs

Take Me Away! E. O'NEILL color *Missouri Life* v44 no3 p32 My 2017

A Trip West bw color *American Cowboy* v23 no6 p10 Ap/My 2017

Cowboys—United States

Bigger Picture B. Welch color *American Cowboy* v23 no4 p8 D 2016/Ja 2017

Life and Land color *American Cowboy* v23 no4 p10 D 2016/Ja 2017

Magic Show T. Groneberg bw *American Cowboy* v23 no6 p21 Ap/My 2017

PLEASE PASS THE DZ R. Wiltz *South Dakota Magazine* v33 no3 p96 S/O 2017

Thoughts on previous issues R. Trotman, C. S. Underwood et al color *American Cowboy* v23 no4 p26 D 2016/Ja 2017

Cowee, Liza

Small Ant Workshop B. MARTIN color *American Craft* v76 no6 p14 D 2016-Ja 2017

Cowell, Stanley

NIGHT LIFE cartoon *New Yorker* v93 no6 p9 Mr 27 2017

Cowen, Brian, 1960-

Leadership Is About the Exercise of Judgment: AS TAOISEACH, I WAS ACUTELY AWARE THAT THE BUCK STOPPED WITH ME *Vital Speeches of the Day* v83 no9 p245 S 2017

Cowen, Tyler

AMERICA THE LETHARGIC color *Fortune* v175 no3 p14 Mr 1 2017

The Complacent Class: The Self-Defeating Quest for the American Dream W. R. Mead *Foreign Affairs* v96 no2 p175 Mr/Ap 2017

Immobility In America D. FRENCH color *National Review* v69 no8 p36 My 2017

Rested and Ready? J. Marks color *Weekly Standard* v22 no37 p35 Je 5 2017

Cowen, Tyler—Interviews

How America Gave Up on Change W. Frick color *Harvard Business Review Digital Articles* p2 Mr 3 2017

Cowgirls

Branch Dancing: One Shot Deserves Another C. WHITE *Idaho Magazine* v16 no7 p16 Ap 2017

Cowgirl Flair G. R. Schiavino bw color *American Cowboy* v23 no6 p40 Ap/My 2017

THOROUGHLY. MODERN. COWGIRL J. F. Meyer color *Horse & Rider* v56 no7 p60 Jl 2017

Cowie, Jefferson

The Great White Nope color *Foreign Affairs* v95 no6 p147 N/D 2016

COWLES, GREGORY

Inside the List *New York Times Book Review* p28 S 24 2017

Take the Money and Run, Mom: In this debut novel, the antiheroine makes off with a bundle of other people's cash *New York Times Book Review* p12 S 24 2017

COWLEY, PAUL D.

Envisioning the Future of Aquatic Animal Tracking: Technology, Science, and Application *BioScience* v67 no10 p884 O 2017

Cowley, S. W. H.

Jupiter's magnetosphere and aurorae observed by the Juno spacecraft during its first polar orbits diag graph *Science* v356 no6340 p826 My 26 2017

Cowley, Steven

Necessary and sufficient conditions for practical fusion power *Physics Today* v70 no10 p13 O 2017

Coworker relationships

3 Ways to Encourage Smarter Teamwork J. Whitehurst *Harvard Business Review Digital Articles* p2 S 7 2015

The Benefits of Saying Nice Things About Your Colleagues J. E. Dutton and J. Lee *Harvard Business Review Digital Articles* p2 Ag 1 2017

Calling Dr. Chilton: GETTING TO THE BOTTOM OF THE BAFFLING BACKSTORY OF LUBBOCK'S LEGENDARY LEMONY LIBATION-ONE REFRESHING SIP AT A TIME D. COURTNEY *Texas Monthly* v45 no7 p168 Jl 2017

Case Study: Should You Rehire Someone Who Left for a Competitor? J. Bhatnagar and N. Gupta bw color il *Harvard Business Review* v94 no12 p103 D 2016

Former Colleagues Are More Valuable than You Think D. Burkus *Harvard Business Review Digital Articles* p2 Ja 13 2016

Get Rid of Unhealthy Competition on Your Team A. C. Edmondson *Harvard Business Review Digital Articles* p2 Je 26 2015

Global Teams Should Have Office Visits, Not Offsites P. Hinds

Harvard Business Review Digital Articles p2 Mr 3 2016

Happy Workplaces Can Also Be Candid Workplaces E. Seppala and K. Cameron Harvard Business Review Digital Articles p2 My 31 2016

Help Your Team Agree on How They'll Collaborate M. Shapiro Harvard Business Review Digital Articles p2 S 8 2015

How Managers Can Avoid Playing Favorites R. Knight Harvard Business Review Digital Articles p2 Mr 15 2017

How to Build the Social Ties You Need at Work A. Gallo Harvard Business Review Digital Articles p2 S 23 2015

How to Deal with a Passive-Aggressive Colleague A. Gallo Harvard Business Review Digital Articles p2 Ja 11 2016

How to Handle a Colleague Who's a Jerk When the Boss Isn't Around Amy Jen Su Harvard Business Review Digital Articles p2 N 22 2016

How to Quit Your Job Without Burning Bridges R. Knight Harvard Business Review Digital Articles p2 D 4 2014

How to Tell a Coworker They're Annoying You C. Webb Harvard Business Review Digital Articles p2 Mr 10 2016

In the Age of Loneliness, Connections at Work Matter T. Leberecht Harvard Business Review Digital Articles p2 S 18 2015

Is Collegiality a Weapon or a Shield? R. E. Cipriano and J. L. Buller Change v49 no1 p54 Ja/F 2017

KICK IT WITH YOUR COLLEAGUES A. Cohen, M. Koester et al color Bloomberg Businessweek no4525 p55 Je 5 2017

Managing Up Without Sucking Up W. Johnson Harvard Business Review Digital Articles p2 D 15 2014

Outsmart Your Next Angry Outburst P. Bregman Harvard Business Review Digital Articles p2 My 6 2016

Research: Love-Hate Relationships at Work Might Be Good for You S. Melwani and N. Rothman Harvard Business Review Digital Articles p2 Ja 20 2015

Signs You Might Be a Toxic Colleague H. G. Halvorson Harvard Business Review Digital Articles p2 Mr 2 2016

The Underlying Psychology of Office Politics T. Chamorro-Premuzic Harvard Business Review Digital Articles p2 D 25 2014

We Learn More When We Learn Together J. E. Dutton and E. Heaphy Harvard Business Review Digital Articles p2 Ja 12 2016

What to Do When Your Boss Has a Favorite (and It's Not You) R. Knight Harvard Business Review Digital Articles p2 Je 16 2016

When an Argument Gets Too Heated, Here's What to Say L. Davey Harvard Business Review Digital Articles p2 Mr 3 2016

When It's Tough to Speak Up, Get Help from Your Coworkers J. R. Detert and E. R. Burris Harvard Business Review Digital Articles p2 Mr 4 2016

When Not to Treat a Colleague as You'd Want to Be Treated A. Wittenberg-Cox Harvard Business Review Digital Articles p2 Mr 3 2015

Cows

BULLS AT THE WIRE D. Hurteau color Field & Stream v121 no6 p34 N 2016

COW SAVVY: QUIET HANDLING AND STRATEGIC PRESSURE HELP CATTLE CHOOSE THE RIGHT DIRECTION R. Nickel Successful Farming v115 no6 p55 Ap 2017

$100 MORE PER COW! G. Johnston Successful Farming v115 no5 p60 Mid-Mr 2017

Cowsik, Ram

M. G. K. Menon (1928–2016) color Science v355 no6325 p586 F 10 2017

Cowtan, Kevin

Stay Out of Scientists' E-mails Scientific American v316 no4 p12 Ap 2017

Cox, Ana Marie

Aasif Mandvi Knows How To Make America Great Again color New York Times Magazine p86 O 9 2016

Ana Navarro Wants the G.O.P. to Stand Up to Trump New York Times Magazine p62 O 2 2016

Andy Slavitt Wants to Unite America on Health Care New York Times Magazine p50 Ag 13 2017

Billie Jean King Understands Colin Kaepernick New York Times Magazine p70 S 17 2017

Billy Eichner Wants You to Know He's Mainstream New York Times Magazine p58 S 10 2017

Bozoma Saint John Wants To Humanize Uber New York Times Magazine p58 S 3 2017

Carla Hayden Thinks Libraries Are a Key to Freedom New York

Times Magazine p66 Ja 22 2017

Carly Zakin And Danielle Weisberg Want You to Get The News New York Times Magazine p66 Ap 30 2017

Charlie Sykes Is Unsure About The Future Of the G.O.P New York Times Magazine p66 Ag 27 2017

Chuck Todd Thinks It's Important to Stay Neutral New York Times Magazine p70 O 8 2017

David Sedaris Wants You to Read His Diary New York Times Magazine p54 Jl 2 2017

Evan McMullin Is Very Concerned New York Times Magazine p62 Mr 5 2017

Franklin Leonard Wants To Diversify The Box Office New York Times Magazine p62 O 1 2017

Glenn Beck Is Sorry About All That color New York Times Magazine p70 N 27 2016

Heather Ann Thompson Thinks the Justice System Is Unfair New York Times Magazine p62 My 14 2017

Jenny Slate Hates Being Oversimplified New York Times Magazine p54 Jl 16 2017

Joe Buck Knows Why You Hate Him New York Times Magazine p50 F 5 2017

John Legend Can't Pretend Times Are Normal New York Times Magazine p66 F 26 2017

Joy Reid Has Never Heard a Good Argument For Trump color New York Times Magazine p54 Ja 29 2017

Marc Maron Is Coming Around to Being Famous New York Times Magazine p62 Je 11 2017

Maxine Waters Is Learning From Millennials New York Times Magazine p58 Jl 23 2017

Michael Eric Dyson Believes In Individual Reparations New York Times Magazine p50 Ja 8 2017

Nicolle Wallace Thinks White House Staffers Need to Have a Limit color New York Times Magazine p54 Ag 6 2017

Omarosa Manigault Changed Parties For Trump New York Times Magazine p78 O 30 2016

Rashida Jones Changed Her Mind About Porn New York Times Magazine p54 Jl 30 2017

Rebecca Skloot Feels Indebted To Henrietta Lacks New York Times Magazine p74 Ap 23 2017

Reza Aslan Thinks TV Can End Bigotry New York Times Magazine p94 Mr 26 2017

Russell Moore Can't Support Either Candidate New York Times Magazine p66 O 16 2016

Sue Fulton Thinks Equal Rights Make The Military Stronger New York Times Magazine p58 Ja 15 2017

Tiffany Haddish Doesn't Think Comedy Is a Game New York Times Magazine p54 Ag 20 2017

Trevor Noah Wasn't Expecting Liberal Hatred New York Times Magazine p58 N 6 2016

Vivek Murthy Thinks We Need to Learn How to Deal With Stress New York Times Magazine p58 Ja 1 2017

Willie J. Parker Changed His Mind About Abortion color New York Times Magazine p66 F 12 2017

Cox, Brian

A tribute to Stephen Hawking D. J. Eicher color Astronomy v45 no1 p54 Ja 2017

COX, CARL

GENE FITTING Scientific American v317 no3 p7 S 2017

Cox, Caroline

BEST OF ATLANTA Atlanta v56 no8 p106 D 2016

THE GOODS Atlanta v56 no9 p41 Ja 2017

Move It Atlanta v57 no6 p78 O 2017

A NEW CHAPTER Atlanta v56 no7 p48 N 2016

RURAL ARTSCAPE Atlanta v56 no7 p34 N 2016

SPACE JAM Atlanta v57 no2 p34 Je 2017

Your Fall To-Do List: Mark your calendars for these can't-miss artsy autumn events Atlanta v57 no6 p83 O 2017

Cox, Charlie

Marvel's The Defenders M. Roffman TV Guide v65 no25 p23 Je 2017

'The Defenders': Three and a Half Superheroes R. SHEFFIELD color Rolling Stone no1294 p24 Ag 24 2017

Cox, Christopher

DISPLACED Orion Magazine v35 no3 p18 My/Je 2016

Fossil Record Orion Magazine v35 no4/5 p32 Jl-O 2016

COX, DANIEL T. C.

Doses of Neighborhood Nature: The Benefits for Mental Health of Living with Nature *BioScience* v67 no2 p147 F 2017

COX, EMILY

IT PAYS TO INCREASE YOUR Word Power *Reader's Digest* v189 no1127 p132 F 2017

IT PAYS TO INCREASE YOUR Word Power *Reader's Digest* v189 no1128 p131 Mr 2017

IT PAYS TO INCREASE YOUR Word Power *Reader's Digest* v189 no1129 p133 Ap 2017

IT PAYS TO INCREASE YOUR Word Power *Reader's Digest* v190 no1134 p133 O 2017

Word Power *Reader's Digest* v188 no1124 p139 O 2016

Cox, Gary

Dark Intellect B. C. ANDERSON color *National Review* v69 no2 p38 F 6 2017

Cox, Harvey

The Market as God P. Hefner *Christian Century* v134 no15 p41 Jl 19 2017

When the market is God S. Paulsell *Christian Century* v134 no12 p35 Je 7 2017

COX, HEATHER

AHEAD OF THE CURRENT color *Indianapolis Monthly* v41 no2 p68 S 2017

Broad RIPPLE color map *Indianapolis Monthly* v41 no2 p66 S 2017

CAN YOU DIG IT? diag *Indianapolis Monthly* v41 no2 p72 S 2017

A DAM SHAME *Indianapolis Monthly* v41 no2 p64 S 2017

Downtown color map *Indianapolis Monthly* v41 no2 p73 S 2017

Farther Downstream color map *Indianapolis Monthly* v41 no2 p77 S 2017

GM STAMPING PLANT color map *Indianapolis Monthly* v41 no2 p75 S 2017

Hamilton COUNTY color map *Indianapolis Monthly* v41 no2 p63 S 2017

MAKING A SPLASH color *Indianapolis Monthly* v41 no2 p76 S 2017

Mounds STATE PARK color map *Indianapolis Monthly* v41 no2 p60 S 2017

Our Tech Office color *Indianapolis Monthly* v42 no2 p34 O 2017

Riverside PARK color map *Indianapolis Monthly* v41 no2 p68 S 2017

TOUR OF DOODY diag *Indianapolis Monthly* v41 no2 p65 S 2017

WHERE THE WILD THINGS ARE color *Indianapolis Monthly* v41 no2 p62 S 2017

THE White RIVER diag *Indianapolis Monthly* v41 no2 p59 S 2017

Cox, Jamieson

The 10 Best Albums color *Time* v188 no25-26 p152 D 19 2016 Double Issue

The 10 Best Songs color *Time* v188 no25-26 p154 D 19 2016 Double Issue

Hip-Hop's Secret Weapon Steps Into the Spotlight color *Time* v189 no5 p51 F 13 2017

Kehlani Turns Candor Into Virtue color *Time* v189 no6 p51 F 20 2017

Rap's Middle-Aged Everymen Return, Trash Talk In Tow color *Time* v189 no4 p53 Ja 23 2017

R&B's New Wave Is Embracing Creative Destruction color *Time* v189 no14 p49 Ap 17 2017

Tyler, the Creator Opens Up color *Time* v190 no6 p55 Ag 7 2017

Cox, Janice

AFTER-SUN CARE for Skin and Hair: After spending time in the sun, try these recipes for cooling masks, mists, bath soaks, gels, and more *Mother Earth News* no283 p32 Ag/S 2017

NATURAL INSECT REPELLENTS: Don't get bugged out—follow these simple DIY recipes to keep pests at bay *Mother Earth News* no282 p53 Je/Jl 2017

Cox, Jennifer

Parks, Recreation and Resilience *Parks & Recreation* v51 no12 p26 D 2016

Cox, Kendall

10 TIPS FROM U.S. OLYMPIAN LISA WILCOX color *Dressage Today* p44 My 2017

COX, KRISTA

MADE IN CHINA *Humanist* v77 no4 p35 Jl/Ag 2017

Cox, Laverne, 1984-

Laverne Cox's Horror Story T. Stack color *Entertainment Weekly* no1435 p48 O 14 2016

RED-CARPET INTELLIGENCE Emmys Edition C. Sosenko, J. Heyman et al color *Entertainment Weekly* no1484 p22 S 29 2017

Cox, Laverne, 1984—Interviews

I AM THAT GIRL Laverne Cox color *InStyle* v23 no12 p294 N 2016

Might As Well ... Jump S. Cristobal and S. Simon color *InStyle* v24 no7 p124 Jl 2017

COX, LOGAN

r.s.v.p bw color *Bon Appetit* v62 no7 p12 Jl 2017

Cox, Matthew

Chiaroscuro: The Mouse and the Candle *Publishers Weekly* v264 no9 p66a F 27 2017

COX, NANCY J.

In Flew Enza color *Natural History* v125 no9 p16 S 2017

COX, SAM

The Skis of the Year color *Powder* p82 S 2017

Cox, Shea

How to Treat Canine Snakebites *Mother Earth News* no282 p89 Je/Jl 2017

Cox, Stephen J.

Active sites in heterogeneous ice nucleation—the example of K-rich feldspars bibl bw diag *Science* v355 no6323 p367 Ja 27 2017

Cox, Stu

Lift Rises to Customers' Expectations *Stage Directions* v30 no9 p26 S 2017

Touring with Stage Automation – Part 2 *Stage Directions* v29 no12 p18 D 2016

Touring with Stage Automation *Stage Directions* v29 no11 p18 N 2016

Cox, Tim

THE BIG QUESTION cartoon *Atlantic* v319 no2 p100 Mr 2017

Cox, Tim—Interviews

At Home With... B. Welch color *American Cowboy* v24 no1 p16 Je/Jl 2017

Cox, Whitney

The Wonderful Allure of Tamil color *New York Review of Books* v64 no5 p51 Mr 23 2017

Coxhead, Gabriel

AMIE SIEGEL color *Art in America* v105 no4 p122 Ap 2017

DAVID HOCKNEY color *Art in America* v105 no5 p121 My 2017

For the People bw color *Art in America* p35 O 2017

KEN PRICE color *Art in America* v105 no3 p138 Mr 2017

LUKE WILLIS THOMPSON bw *Art in America* v105 no8 p131 S 2017

MARY HEILMANN *Art in America* v104 no9 p161 O 2016

URIEL ORLOW cartoon *Art in America* v104 no11 p129 D 2016

Coy, Peter

Anatomy of a Bad Marriage color *Bloomberg Businessweek* no4541 p10 O 9 2017

A BEAUTIFUL FRIENDSHIP cartoon *Bloomberg Businessweek* no4503 p70 D 12 2016

BEWARE OF SHARKS cartoon *Bloomberg Businessweek* no4518 p75 Ap 10 2017

The Deficits in Trump's Future graph *Bloomberg Businessweek* no4514 p8 Mr 13 2017

Dollar So Ripped, It Might Actually Rip color *Bloomberg Businessweek* no4506 p12 Ja 9 2017

Donald and The Dollar *Bloomberg Businessweek* no4503 p15 D 12 2016

DROP SOME KNOWLEDGE color *Bloomberg Businessweek* no4500 p80 N 21 2016

Exit the Old Elite *Bloomberg Businessweek* no4499 p26 N 14 2016

The Fed Is Driving Blind color graph *Bloomberg Businessweek* no4527 p43 Je 19 2017

The Game Putin Plays color *Bloomberg Businessweek* no4506 p6 Ja 9 2017

Hard Rain and Hard Lessons bw map *Bloomberg Businessweek* no4536 p12 S 4 2017

Heavenly Tax Reform color graph *Bloomberg Businessweek*

no4503 p6 D 12 2016

How Much Room to Grow? color *Bloomberg Businessweek* no4511 p8 F 13 2017

How to Manage The Sprawl map *Bloomberg Businessweek* no4534 p8 Ag 14 2017

The Human Mind Is Overrated cartoon color *Bloomberg Businessweek* no4529 p78 Jl 3 2017

If Not Dodd-Frank, Then … What? color graph *Bloomberg Businessweek* no4513 p40 Mr 6 2017

The Importance of Being Idle color *Bloomberg Businessweek* no4532 p8 Jl 31 2017

Is Anybody in Charge Here? chart color graph *Bloomberg Businessweek* no4496 p10 O 24 2016

Is There a Better Way to Take Aim at Inflation? *Bloomberg Businessweek* no4525 p13 Je 5 2017

Lies, Damn Lies, and Financial Statistics cartoon *Bloomberg Businessweek* no4518 p8 Ap 10 2017

Middle-Aged Productivity Heroes graph *Bloomberg Businessweek* no4498 p23 N 7 2016

The Mystery of Tepid Wage Growth graph *Bloomberg Businessweek* no4523 p17 My 22 2017

Now It's Revamp, Not Replace color graph *Bloomberg Businessweek* no4531 p29 Jl 24 2017

PETER NAVARRO, TRADE WARRIOR color *Bloomberg Businessweek* no4521 p54 My 8 2017

Politics/Policy color *Bloomberg Businessweek* no4505 p27 D 26 2016

Politics/Policy color graph *Bloomberg Businessweek* no4524 p27 My 29 2017

The Push and Pull Of Politics cartoon *Bloomberg Businessweek* no4493 p22 O 3 2016

Reviving Keystone XL Is No Sure Thing *Bloomberg Businessweek* no4510 p23 F 6 2017

THE ROBOTS ARE COMING (But You'll Still Need to Work) *Bloomberg Businessweek* no4528 p8 Je 26 2017

THE ROOTS OF OUR RAGE cartoon *Bloomberg Businessweek* no4510 p62 F 6 2017

A Safe Choice to Regulate Banks color *Bloomberg Businessweek* no4519 p35 Ap 24 2017

Show Us Your Tax Reforms color *Bloomberg Businessweek* no4517 p8 Ap 3 2017

THE SLO-MO ECONOMY color *Bloomberg Businessweek* no4498 p86 N 7 2016

So You Want to Be Like Silicon Valley? *Bloomberg Businessweek* no4537 p48 S 11 2017

Sunny Side Trump [Cover story] color graph *Bloomberg Businessweek* no4500 p8 N 21 2016

Tax Cuts. As Easy As … *Bloomberg Businessweek* no4521 p24 My 8 2017

Taxing Mexico. Or Not diag *Bloomberg Businessweek* no4510 p12 F 6 2017

Trump And Yellen: Besties? color *Bloomberg Businessweek* no4502 p12 D 5 2016

Trump Meets Reality graph *Bloomberg Businessweek* no4499 p28 N 14 2016

Trump's Uncertainty Principle color *Bloomberg Businessweek* no4509 p6 Ja 30 2017

Trump vows to cut the corporate tax rate from 35% to 15%. Suppose Republicans could raise $2 trillion to pay for cuts (not an easy task). That would require hiking other taxes or ending popular deductions. And it can't all go to corporate giants, so… *Bloomberg Businessweek* no4538 p34 S 18 2017

UHMM…CARE *Bloomberg Businessweek* no4506 p20 Ja 9 2017

Wanted: Forklift Driver color graph *Bloomberg Businessweek* no4504 p13 D 19 2016

Wharton's Policy Tool Isn't Just for Wonks color *Bloomberg Businessweek* no4522 p52 My 15 2017

Where the Next Crisis Will Come From color graph *Bloomberg Businessweek* no4496 p44 O 24 2016

Who's Afraid of Low Volatility? cartoon graph *Bloomberg Businessweek* no4533 p23 Ag 7 2017

WILL THE TRUMP BUMP GO THUNK? graph *Bloomberg Businessweek* no4520 p16 My 1 2017

COYNE, ANDREW

Back to Basics color *Walrus* v14 no4 p32 My 2017

COYNE, CHRISTOPHER J.

Digital Growth [Cover story] color *America* v215 no11 p19 O 17 2016

COYNE, JOHN R., JR.

Buchanan on Nixon: Triumph and Tragedy *American Conservative* v16 no3 p48 My/Je 2017

The Buckley Legacy In Voice and Print il *American Conservative* v16 no1 p48 Ja/F 2017

Coyne, Marley

THE NEW ESTABLISHMENT 2017 bw color *Vanity Fair* v59 no11 p87 N 2017

NEW ESTABLISHMENT bw cartoon color *Vanity Fair* v58 no11 p124 N 2016

Coyne, Wayne—Interviews

THE FLAMING LIPS' WAYNE COYNE E. R. Brown color *Entertainment Weekly* no1449 p58 Ja 20 2017

Coyote

BOOM OR BUST: Fireworks stores, Indiana roller coasters, and urban coyotes. Ask the Hoosierist S. STALL *Indianapolis Monthly* v40 no11 p15 Jl 2017

Coyotes K. Vaughn *Arizona Highways* v93 no2 p13 F 2017

DAMAGE CONTROL J. R. Sullivan color *Field & Stream* v121 no8 p40 F/Mr 2017

OLD FLAMES G. Kendall, J. Kacena et al color *Field & Stream* v122 no1 p10 My 2017

Coyote (Poem)

COYOTE M. Cadnum *Commonweal* v144 no7 p26 Ap 14 2017

Coyote trapping

COYOTE NATION T. CARPENTER color *Outdoor Life* v224 no1 p74 D 2016/Ja 2017

THE COYOTE SCALE T. WALRATH and A. McKEAN color *Outdoor Life* v224 no2 p78 F/Mr 2017

Coyote—Reproduction

Coyote Nation C. MacCarald color *National Wildlife (World Edition)* v55 no1 p40 D/Ja 2016

Coyote—Research

Coyote Nation C. MacCarald color *National Wildlife (World Edition)* v55 no1 p40 D/Ja 2016

Coypu

CAJUN COUNTRY J. FROIS color *Louisiana Life* v37 no3 p100 Ja/F 2017

Cozzens, Peter

Fair and Balanced J. Koster *American History* v52 no2 p12 Je 2017

Grant's Uncivil War *Smithsonian* v47 no7 p46 N 2016

Indian Country T. KAVULLA bw color *National Review* v69 no1 p38 Ja 23 2017

Unbury My Heart at Wounded Knee D. BRINKLEY *New York Times Book Review* p16 N 13 2016

Westward, Oh J. M. BANNER JR. cartoon *Weekly Standard* v22 no12 p37 N 28 2016

Cozzens, Peter—Interviews

ELUSIVE BALANCE N. TAPPAN *American History* v51 no6 p12 F 2017

Cozzolino, Pasquale

Doughy No More J. Covert color *Men's Health* v32 no1 p32 Ja/F 2017

CPG nucleotides

Integration of CpG-free DNA induces de novo methylation of CpG islands in pluripotent stem cells Y. Takahashi, J. Wu et al diag *Science* v356 no6337 p503 My 5 2017

CPR (First aid)

CPR Training P. C. Baker *New York Times Magazine* p26 S 10 2017

Did You Call 911? S. LOPEZ *Reader's Digest* v189 no1128 p8 Mr 2017

Crab meat

Race Fare T. Keith color *Sports Illustrated* v126 no14 p26 My 15-22 2017

Crab Nebula

A new look at the Crab Nebula color *Astronomy* v45 no9 p18 S 2017

Stars Explode in Earthly Skies K. HAYNES color *Discover* v38 no3 p12 Ap 2017

Crabapple, Molly

THE WALL C. Shafaieh cartoon *New Yorker* v93 no26 p21 S 4 2017

Crabb, Charles

The Thread color *New York Times Magazine* p14 O 9 2016

Crabbe, Barb

Building Your First-Aid Kit *Dressage Today* p18 My 2017

GASTRIC ULCERS: THE TRUE STORY color *Horse & Rider* v56 no8 p78 Ag 2017

The LONG HAUL cartoon *Horse & Rider* v56 no7 p94 Jl 2017

Meds or Management? [Cover story] cartoon *Horse & Rider* v56 no1 p36 Ja 2017

Playing the Hay Odds color *Horse & Rider* v56 no11 p102 N 2017

Prepare for the Worst color *Horse & Rider* v56 no9 p80 S 2017

READING RADIOGRAPHS color *Horse & Rider* v56 no2 p46 F 2017

Slow Medicine cartoon color *Horse & Rider* v56 no3 p52 Mr 2017

Take the 'One Health' Challenge [Cover story] cartoon *Horse & Rider* v56 no5 p52 My 2017

TO BREED OR NOT TO BREED? bw color *Horse & Rider* v56 no4 p56 Ap 2017

TOP 10 BLOOD TESTS color *Horse & Rider* v55 no11 p50 N 2016

VET'S TOP MUD TIPS color *Horse & Rider* v55 no12 p48 D 2016

Your Best First-Aid Kit color *Horse & Rider* v55 no12 p19 D 2016

Your Horse's Lumps & Bumps color *Horse & Rider* v56 no10 p86 O 2017

Crabbing

Lessons Learned D. J. Harding color *Power & Motoryacht* v34 no7 p16 Jl 2017

Crabs

Dividing the Spoils K. Moore color *Natural History* v125 no5 p7 My 2017

What in the World? color *National Geographic Kids* no470 p29 My 2017

CRABTREE, JOHN

Indigenous Empowerment in Evo Morales's Bolivia *Current History* v116 no787 p55 F 2017

Crack (Short story)

CRACK M. MCDONOUGH *Saturday Evening Post* v289 no1 p62 Ja/F 2017

Crack-Up (Music)

CRACK-UP A. Christenson *U.S. Catholic* v82 no10 p40 O 2017

Fleet Foxes' New Harmony [Cover story] J. WEINER color *Rolling Stone* no1289 p18 Je 15 2017

Three Alt-Country Stars Align With New Albums M. Ayers color *Time* v189 no24 p51 Je 26 2017

Crackers

GOOD THINGS color *Martha Stewart Living* p28 S 2017

Roll with It C. SAFFITZ color *Bon Appetit* no11 p58 N 2017

What Can I Bring? E. Heiskell color *Southern Living* v52 no10 p124 O 2017

Cracknell, Steven

Why Leaders Are Still So Hesitant to Invest in New Business Models *Harvard Business Review Digital Articles* p2 D 21 2016

Cracks (Poem)

Cracks S. Teresa color *U.S. Catholic* v82 no8 p11 Ag 2017

Craft, Joseph E.

Macrophage function in tissue repair and remodeling requires IL-4 or IL-13 with apoptotic cells diag *Science* v356 no6342 p1072 Je 9 2017

Craft, Kristen

Video Metrics Every Marketer Should Be Watching *Harvard Business Review Digital Articles* p2 Ap 24 2015

Craft beer

99 Cans Of Beer On the Wall J. M. VERIVE *Los Angeles Magazine* p48 Ja 2017

A Better Brew M. WALTHER color *National Review* v69 no6 p23 Ap 3 2017

Drink Local, Buy Global J. Kell color map *Fortune* v176 no1 p13 Jl 1 2017

HIGHWOOD J. REESE color *Chicago* v66 no10 p32 O 2017

Pride of Place—Sort of color *Weekly Standard* v22 no26 p4 Mr 13 2017

Something's Brewing J. BLITZER color *Esquire* v166 no4 p42 N 2016

Welcome M. J. Posey *Cincinnati Magazine* v50 no8 p82 My 2017

Craft beer—Economic aspects

Is Craft Beer All Froth? J. Kell color diag *Fortune* v175 no6 p15 My 1 2017

Craft beer—Equipment & supplies

The Bavarian beer purity law is adopted *History Today* v67 no4 p9 Ap 2017

Craft beer—Evaluation

Cheers! K. Hansen color *Cabin Living* p12 S 2017

HOMEGROWN HOPS J. CARRUTHERS color *Chicago* v66 no8 p54 Ag 2017

Craft festivals

EVENTS + EXHIBITS *Arts & Crafts Homes & the Revival* v12 no3 p18 Summ 2017

Craft shops

The Future Perfect D. DANIEL color *American Craft* v76 no6 p28 D 2016-Ja 2017

Crafts, Hannah

ON THE RUN *Lapham's Quarterly* v10 no3 p174 Summ 2017

Crafts, Nicholas

REFRAMING THE GREAT DIVERGENCE: A detailed study of the Enlightenment and the Great Divergence displays admirable depth of knowledge and subtlety of argument *History Today* v67 no6 p102 Je 2017

Crafty Apes (Company)

THIS STUDIO HAS A SPECIAL EFFECT ON MOVIES T. J. Huddleston color *Fortune* v175 no3 p26 Mr 1 2017

Cragun, Shane

Embracing Change Means Disrupting Your Day *Harvard Business Review Digital Articles* p2 Jl 22 2016

Craiciu, Ioana

Nanophotonic rare-earth quantum memory with optically controlled retrieval diag graph *Science* v357 no6358 p1392 S 29 2017

Craig, Cameron

What I Learned From 10 Years of Doing PR for Apple *Harvard Business Review Digital Articles* p2 Jl 27 2016

Craig, Carl

GOINGS ON ABOUT TOWN bw *New Yorker* v93 no4 p5 Mr 13 2017

Craig, Charmaine

Trust and Trauma E. LARKIN *New York Times Book Review* p18 My 28 2017

Craig, Daniel, 1968-

A Hillbilly 'Ocean's 11' P. Travers color *Rolling Stone* no1295 p56 S 7 2017

Honest Iago M. Schulman cartoon *New Yorker* v92 no39 p22 N 28 2016

Craig, David

After Simeon *America* v216 no1 p39 Ja 2 2017

After Simeon D. CRAIG *America* v216 no1 p39 Ja 2 2017

CRAIG, DON

THE LOOP chart color *Runner's World* v52 no3 p12 Ap 2017

Craig, Elise

GENERATION EXCELLENT bw *Wired* v24 no11 p58 N 2016

The Home Health Aide *New York Times Magazine* p38 F 26 2017

NOT-SO-FINE ART cartoon *Wired* v24 no12 p38 D 2016

Craig, George

Beckett Plays Beckett F. O'Toole bw *New York Review of Books* v63 no18 p37 N 24 2016

CRAIG, GWENDOLYN

A Homecoming on the Lake color *Audubon* v119 no3 p12 Fall 2017

CRAIG, JEANNE

The Natural color *Power & Motoryacht* v33 no1 p66 Ja 2017

Craig, Jeffrey M.

A twin tale to keep you up at night color *Science* v357 no6352 p653 Ag 18 2017

Craig, Kelly Fremon, 1980-

Kelly Fremon Craig J. Johnson color *Current Biography* v78 no9 p13 S 2017

The Edge of Seventeen L. Greenblatt color *Entertainment Weekly* no1441 p42 N 25 2016

Craig, Nancy

Not just Salk color *Science* v357 no6356 p1105 S 15 2017

Craig, Nate

Shutting Down Stores Doesn't Have to Be Bad for Business *Har-*

How Much Cranking Compression Is Safe on Pump Gas? M. Davis color *Hot Rod* v70 no5 p90 My 2017

WHY LEFT? P. Garrison color *Flying* v144 no4 p88 Ap 2017

Cranley, John

PARTY LINES A. KONERMANN color *Cincinnati Magazine* v51 no1 p24 O 2017

TOP OF THE CLASS J. WILLIAMS *Cincinnati Magazine* v50 no3 p34 D 2016

Cranshaw, Justin

How We Built a Virtual Scheduling Assistant at Microsoft *Harvard Business Review Digital Articles* p1 Jl 28 2017

CRANSTON, BRYAN

The Year in Reading [Cover story] *New York Times Book Review* p8 D 25 2016

Cranston, Bryan, 1956-

CRANSTON COMES ALIVE [Cover story] J. PRESSLER bw color *Esquire* p80 N 2017

FIRST LOOKS: Cranston in Charge I. Rudolph *TV Guide* v65 no2 p12 Ja 2 2017

A Life in Parts *Publishers Weekly* v264 no5 p198 Ja 30 2017

WATCH THIS/SORRY ABOUT THAT L. Rice color *Entertainment Weekly* no1450 p51 Ja 27 2017

Cranston, Carey—Interviews

A Museum for the People Behind the Volumes *American Scholar* v86 no1 p16 Wint 2017

Crappie

THE SLAB HARVEST J. Cermele cartoon color *Field & Stream* v121 no6 p59 N 2016

Crappie fishing

Cheers & Jeers T. Gilbert, B. Paty et al color *Field & Stream* v121 no8 p12 F/Mr 2017

Craps (Game)

Craps F. Kamer *New York Times Magazine* p28 O 16 2016

Crash (Film)

HOW TO CRASH THE OSCARS S. W. HUNT img *New York* v49 no24 p134 N 28 2016

Crashing (TV program)

Crashing J. Russell color *TV Guide* v65 no7 p38 F 13 2017

CRASH LANDING A. Marantz cartoon *New Yorker* v92 no47 p21 Ja 30 2017

The / MUST LIST color *Entertainment Weekly* no1460/1461 p3 Ap 7-17 2017

A Young Comic's Hope-Filled Crash D. D'Addario color *Time* v189 no7/8 p103 F 27 2017

Crate, Lisa

Fake News vs. Real News *Education Digest* v83 no1 p4 S 2017

CRATE, SUSAN

Climate Change Adaptation and Traditional Cultures in Northern Russia *Current History* v116 no792 p277 O 2017

Crater Lake (Or.)

Land of Lakes D. Hanson color *Sunset* v239 no1 p66 Jl 2017

Cratons

A seismic shift in continental tectonic plates B. Savage color *Science* v357 no6351 p549 Ag 11 2017

Cravatt, Benjamin F.

Activity-based protein profiling reveals off-target proteins of the FAAH inhibitor BIA 10-2474 chart color graph *Science* v356 no6342 p1084 Je 9 2017

Cravatts, Sara

BIKE BLUR color *Popular Photography* v80 no11 p24 D 2016

EN ROUTE color *Popular Photography* v80 no11 p86 D 2016

TOUR DE FORT bw color *Popular Photography* v80 no11 p26 D 2016

A WINNING YEAR [Cover story] bw color *Popular Photography* v81 no2 p50 Mr/Ap 2017

Craven, Morgan

KEEPING KIDS IN CLASS J. Thompson color *Essence* v48 no5 p74 S 2017

CRAVEN, PHILIP

The Paralympic Games and the Promotion of the Rights of Persons with Disabilities *UN Chronicle* v53 no2 p10 2016

Craven, Wes, 1939-2015

THE HILLS HAVE EYES C. Chiarella color *Sound & Vision* v82 no2 p70 F/Mr 2017

Crawford (Neb.)

Behemoth 'Coffee Burger' Rides Again in Sioux County N. Buck color *Nebraska Life* v21 no1 p15 Ja/F 2017

CRAWFORD, ALAN PELL

Snow Country: A journey through Japan reveals a country where modern and ancient create a haunting harmony *Virginia Living* v15 no4 p52 Je 2017

Crawford, Amy

Altered State: Taking to the sky to show how industry shapes the earth *Smithsonian* v48 no2 p12 My 2017

Flaunting It *Smithsonian* v48 no1 p14 Ap 2017

FORBIDDEN FLICKS: The U.S. export ban didn't keep Cubans from watching movies they loved *Smithsonian* v48 no4 p12 Jl/Ag 2017

Guiding Light color *Smithsonian* v47 no10 p12 Mr 2017

LAUNCHED INTO MEMORY *Smithsonian* v48 no3 p14 Je 2017

MISSISSIPPI MARTYR: Recalling a lynching that shocked America and galvanized the civil rights movement *Smithsonian* v48 no6 p16 O 2017

PROPHET MOTIVE: Decades later, Jean-Michel Basquiat's complex works are increasingly prescient--and valuable *Smithsonian* v48 no5 p12 S 2017

Seeing Red *Smithsonian* v47 no7 p14 N 2016

Crawford, Caroline V.

The labor supply of veterans with disabilities, 1995-2014 bibl chart color graph *Monthly Labor Review* p1 O 2016

Crawford, Charly, 1978-

Cowboy Cred J. Mankin color *Spin to Win Rodeo* v21 no5 p56 Jl 2017

Crawford, Cindy, 1966-

Cindy Crawford C. Ianzito color *AARP: The Magazine* v59 no2A p84 F/Mr 2016

My LIST: 24 hours with Cindy Crawford N. Silva-Jelly color *Harper's Bazaar* no3657 p126 O 2017

Crawford, Clayne

Lethal Showdown J. Halterman *TV Guide* v64 no48 p11 N 21 2016

Lethal Weapon J. Halterman *TV Guide* p41 D 5 2016

Lethal Weapon J. Halterman *TV Guide* v65 no4 p40 Ja 16 2017

Lethal Weapon N. Abrams, A. Bacle et al color *Entertainment Weekly* no1482/1483 p60 S 22 2017

Crawford, Douglas L.

The genomic landscape of rapid repeated evolutionary adaptation to toxic pollution in wild fish bibl graph *Science* v354 no6317 p1305 D 9 2016

Crawford, George

NAME GAME L. MURTHA *Cincinnati Magazine* v50 no6 p42 Mr 2017

Crawford, Ilse

Ett Hem Stockholm color *Conde Nast Traveler* v52 no8 p48 S 2017

Crawford, Jackie

BUCKLE UP J. Harrison and K. Gustave color *Team Roping Journal* p16 O 2017

Crawford Dominates WPRA Finals color *Spin to Win Rodeo* v20 no11 p16 Ja 2017

Crawford, Joan, 1908-1977

Mother's Day R. Brody color *New Yorker* v93 no16 p26 Je 5 2017

Crawford, Kate

LETTER TO SILICON VALLEY *Harper's Magazine* v334 no2001 p36 F 2017

CRAWFORD, MATTHEW B.

WORLD'S FUNNIEST WOODWORKER TELLS ALL color *Popular Mechanics* p64 S 2017

WORLD'S FUNNIEST WOODWORKER TELLS ALL color *Popular Mechanics* v193 no7 p64 S 2016

You Can't Say That! color *Weekly Standard* v22 no47 p38 Ag 21 2017

Crawford, Robert J.

How One Company Reduced Email by 64% *Harvard Business Review Digital Articles* p2 Je 18 2015

Crawford, Robert W.

In Recognition of Excellence *Parks & Recreation* v51 no11 p42 N 2016

Crawford, Susan

Governing the Smart, Connected City *Harvard Business Review Digital Articles* p2 O 31 2014

Crawford Peyton, Eve

Get More Actionable Ideas from Your Employees T. Wedell-Wedellsborg and P. Miller *Harvard Business Review Digital Articles* p2 N 25 2014

How Senior Executives Find Time to Be Creative E. Seppala *Harvard Business Review Digital Articles* p2 S 14 2016

How Spotify Balances Employee Autonomy and Accountability M. Mankins and E. Garton color *Harvard Business Review Digital Articles* p2 F 9 2017

How to Free Your Innate Creativity A. McKee *Harvard Business Review Digital Articles* p2 D 11 2015

How to Nourish Your Team's Creativity R. Carucci *Harvard Business Review Digital Articles* p2 My 9 2017

How to Rebrand Yourself as Creative When You're Not Perceived That Way D. Clark *Harvard Business Review Digital Articles* p2 My 25 2017

How to Work with Colleagues Who Are Less Creative than You K. D. Elsbach, B. Brown-Saracino et al *Harvard Business Review Digital Articles* p2 S 16 2015

The Inescapable Paradox of Managing Creativity L. A. Hill, G. Brandeau et al *Harvard Business Review Digital Articles* p2 D 12 2014

Innovation Leadership Lessons from the Marshmallow Challenge S. Anthony *Harvard Business Review Digital Articles* p2 D 9 2014

The Innovative Mindset Your Company Can't Afford to Lose S. Ahuja *Harvard Business Review Digital Articles* p2 O 13 2015

Is Innovation More About People or Process? A. Ovans *Harvard Business Review Digital Articles* p2 F 27 2015

Leaders Can Turn Creativity into a Competitive Advantage T. Brown *Harvard Business Review Digital Articles* p2 N 2 2016

Leading Digital Transformation Is Like Urban Planning P. Beswick *Harvard Business Review Digital Articles* p2 Ag 2 2017

Let Data Ask Questions, Not Just Answer Them M. Schrage *Harvard Business Review Digital Articles* p2 O 8 2014

Maybe Your Team Doesn't Need to Be More Creative T. Chamorro-Premuzic *Harvard Business Review Digital Articles* p2 N 27 2015

Measure Your Team's Intellectual Diversity *Harvard Business Review Digital Articles* p2 My 21 2015

The Productivity Payoff of Mobile Apps at Work J. Panepinto *Harvard Business Review Digital Articles* p2 N 13 2014

Resolving the Paradox of Group Creativity A. Walton *Harvard Business Review Digital Articles* p2 Ja 25 2016

THE SOUL IN THE MACHINE W. ISAACSON color *Vanity Fair* v59 no11 p110 N 2017

A Study Shows How to Find New Ideas Inside and Outside the Company L. Dahlander and S. O'Mahony *Harvard Business Review Digital Articles* p2 Jl 18 2017

To Be More Creative, Schedule Your Breaks J. G. Lu, M. Akinola et al *Harvard Business Review Digital Articles* p2 My 10 2017

To Get More Creative, Become Less Productive A. Markman *Harvard Business Review Digital Articles* p2 N 30 2015

Two Words That Kill Innovation R. L. Martin *Harvard Business Review Digital Articles* p2 D 9 2014

What the Research Tells Us About Team Creativity and Innovation R. Schwarz *Harvard Business Review Digital Articles* p2 D 15 2015

Creative ability in technology
See also
   Technological innovations
The Difference a Century Makes *Change* v82 no3 p3 Mr 2017
FLUX CAPACITOR A. FLANGO *Cincinnati Magazine* p39 Je 2017

Creative ability in technology—Congresses
THE INNOVATION ECONOMY: FOSTERING BUSINESS IN-VESTMENT AND TALENT IN LOS ANGELES *Los Angeles Magazine* p151 D 2016

Creative ability—Psychological aspects
Make any day more vibrant color *Redbook* p99 Ap 2017

Creative ability—Social aspects
It's OK If Going to a Conference Doesn't Feel Like Real Work K. Dillon *Harvard Business Review Digital Articles* p2 O 7 2015

Creative activities & seat work
jump in! by the pool T. G. HOPE color *Better Homes & Gardens* v95 no8 p168 Ag 2017

Creative Conners Inc.

Creative Conners, Inc *Stage Directions* v30 no3 p5 Mr 2017
Lift Rises to Customers' Expectations S. Cox *Stage Directions* v30 no9 p26 S 2017

Creative directors (Mass media industry)
Four Questions for Scott Brown *Texas Monthly* v45 no2 p6 F 2017
The Future of Humanitarianism [Cover story] M. J. MOONEY bw color *Popular Mechanics* v193 no7 p13 S 2016

Creative Sound Corp.
Creative Sound BlasterX Katana: The soundbar finally makes its way to PCs H. DINGMAN color *PCWorld* v35 no4 p91 Ap 2017

Creative thinking
4 Steps to Having More "Aha" Moments D. Rock and J. Davis color *Harvard Business Review Digital Articles* p2 O 12 2016
A Cognitive Trick for Solving Problems Creatively T. Scaltsas *Harvard Business Review Digital Articles* p2 My 4 2016
Don't Ask for New Ideas If You're Not Ready to Act on Them R. Ashkenas *Harvard Business Review Digital Articles* p2 F 2 2015
How to Do Walking Meetings Right R. Clayton, C. Thomas et al *Harvard Business Review Digital Articles* p2 Ag 5 2015
Leading a Brainstorming Session with a Cross-Cultural Team D. Livermore *Harvard Business Review Digital Articles* p2 My 27 2016
letter from the editors color *Foreign Policy* no221 p13 N/D 2016
You Can Teach Someone to Be More Creative T. Chamorro-Premuzic *Harvard Business Review Digital Articles* p2 F 23 2015

Creative thinking in children
How Thinking Like a Kid Can Spur Creativity P. Himmelman *Time* v188 no16/17 p15 O 24 2016

Creative writing
See also
   Poetry writing
Did she hide radical messages in her books? M. FORBES *Weekly Standard* v22 no42 p28 Jl 17 2017
The First Rule of Book Club Is . . . B. RAWLENCE color *New York Times Book Review* p25 Ja 29 2017
International Literature T. Parks *New York Times Book Review* p35 O 23 2016
Literature by Degree B. MARKOVITS *New York Times Book Review* p15 Mr 12 2017
Telling the Truth W. Mason *New York Times Magazine* p50 Mr 5 2017
To Get Over Something, Write About It M. F. R. Kets de Vries *Harvard Business Review Digital Articles* p2 N 26 2014
Who Needs An Outline? E. RASKIN color *Publishers Weekly* v264 no25 p116 Je 19 2017
Writer, Writer, Pants on Fire A. SOLOMON *New York Times Book Review* p33 O 23 2016

Creative writing—Study & teaching
Plot Twist S. STANKORB *Cincinnati Magazine* v50 no5 p52 F 2017

Creativity for Kids (Company)
BEST TOY AWARDS 2016 cartoon color *Good Housekeeping* v263 no5 p121 N 2016

Credentialism
Online Platforms Are Leveling the Playing Field for Global Job Seekers M. Tran *Harvard Business Review Digital Articles* p2 Je 11 2015

Credgington, Dan
High-performance light-emitting diodes based on carbene-metal-amides chart graph *Science* v356 no6334 p159 Ap 14 2017

Credi, Alberto
Gearing up molecular rotary motors color *Science* v356 no6341 p906 Je 1 2017

Credibility of the press
The decline of trust and truth S. GILMORE color *Maclean's* v130 no8 p8 S 2017

Credit
See also
   Agricultural credit
   Consumer credit
CORRECTION *House Beautiful* v158 no9 p168 N 2016
MONEY, CREDIT, AND SECURITY MARKETS *Economic Indicators* p26 Mr 2017

Credit Acceptance Corp.
E-Z Auto Loans Are A Tough Business T. Metcalf color graph

tainment Weekly no1472 p28 Je 30 2017

CREGAN, LISA

READY, FETE, GO ! color *House Beautiful* v158 no10 p92 D 2016/Ja 2017

WHAT TO DO WITH A WHITE BOX color *House Beautiful* v159 no1 p84 F 2017

Cregger, Zach

Wrecked J. Russell *TV Guide* v65 no35 p31 Ag 21 2017

Creighton, Ian

GET BACK AT IT! M. Gainsburg color *Women's Health* v14 no4 p84 My 2017

Six Simple Moves for Total-Body Strength color *Men's Health* v32 no6 p16 Ag 2017

Crelin, Joy

Al Horford color *Current Biography* v78 no9 p37 S 2017

Angel McCoughtry color *Current Biography* v78 no6 p64 Je 2017

Azéde Jean-Pierre color *Current Biography* v78 no6 p50 Je 2017

Ben Mendelsohn color *Current Biography* v78 no2 p48 F 2017

Ben Zobrist color *Current Biography* v78 no8 p91 Ag 2017

Brad Stevens color *Current Biography* v77 no11 p82 N 2016

Bruce Bochy color *Current Biography* v77 no10 p10 O 2016

Carli Lloyd color *Current Biography* v78 no2 p44 F 2017

Chen Man *Current Biography* v78 no9 p53 S 2017

Chloe Kim color *Current Biography* v78 no1 p32 Ja 2017

Daisy Ridley color *Current Biography* v77 no11 p73 N 2016

David Adjaye color *Current Biography* v78 no5 p3 My 2017

Dianne Newman color *Current Biography* v78 no6 p68 Je 2017

Elaine Welteroth color *Current Biography* v78 no2 p83 F 2017

Elle Fanning color *Current Biography* v78 no8 p33 Ag 2017

Eniola Aluko color *Current Biography* v77 no10 p3 O 2016

Eva Green color *Current Biography* v77 no10 p39 O 2016

Gugu Mbatha-Raw color *Current Biography* v78 no5 p58 My 2017

Heather Ann Thompson color *Current Biography* v78 no9 p90 S 2017

Issa Rae color *Current Biography* v78 no4 p68 Ap 2017

Jacob Hooker color *Current Biography* v78 no8 p44 Ag 2017

Jason Day color *Current Biography* v78 no3 p20 Mr 2017

Junya Watanabe *Current Biography* v78 no5 p92 My 2017

Kayvon Beykpour color *Current Biography* v78 no2 p12 F 2017

Laurie Hernandez color *Current Biography* v78 no2 p31 F 2017

Lisa Lucas color *Current Biography* v78 no3 p40 Mr 2017

Lori Wallach color *Current Biography* v78 no3 p86 Mr 2017

Luke Evans color *Current Biography* v78 no9 p18 S 2017

Maisie Williams color *Current Biography* v78 no3 p91 Mr 2017

Max Verstappen color *Current Biography* v78 no8 p86 Ag 2017

Meg Urry color *Current Biography* v78 no5 p87 My 2017

Mirga Gražinytė-Tyla color *Current Biography* v78 no4 p25 Ap 2017

Noah Syndergaard color *Current Biography* v78 no9 p85 S 2017

Pamela Adlon color *Current Biography* v78 no1 p3 Ja 2017

Penny Pritzker color *Current Biography* v77 no11 p63 N 2016

Pete Wells *Current Biography* v78 no1 p91 Ja 2017

Riz Ahmed color *Current Biography* v78 no4 p3 Ap 2017

Rob Delaney color *Current Biography* v77 no10 p21 O 2016

Ross Richie color *Current Biography* v77 no11 p68 N 2016

Sadiq Khan color *Current Biography* v77 no10 p72 O 2016

Sam Altman color *Current Biography* v78 no4 p7 Ap 2017

Sara Goldrick-Rab color *Current Biography* v78 no1 p13 Ja 2017

Sofia Boutella color *Current Biography* v78 no9 p3 S 2017

Susanna Mälkki color *Current Biography* v78 no5 p53 My 2017

Tituss Burgess color *Current Biography* v78 no3 p3 Mr 2017

Tracee Ellis Ross color *Current Biography* v78 no1 p74 Ja 2017

Vera Brosgol *Current Biography* v78 no8 p13 Ag 2017

Victoria Orphan color *Current Biography* v78 no4 p63 Ap 2017

Vivian Howard color *Current Biography* v78 no8 p49 Ag 2017

Yoshinori Ohsumi color *Current Biography* v78 no6 p78 Je 2017

Cremation

THE BURNING QUESTION L. BROWN cartoon color *Men's Health* v32 no5 p142 Je 2017

Cremation—Religious aspects—Christianity

Don't Scatter the Ashes—or Wear Them R. Ferrone color *Commonweal* v143 no20 p6 D 16 2016

Crematogaster

HIGH-WIRE ACT *Natural History* v125 no2 p2 F 2017

Cremen, Nanci

A JACK-OF-ALL-TRADES color *Literacy Today (2411-7862)* v34 no4 p12 Ja/F 2017

Cremonese, G.

Rosetta's comet 67P/Churyumov-Gerasimenko sheds its dusty mantle to reveal its icy nature bibl graph *Science* v354 no6319 p1566 D 23 2016

Surface changes on comet 67P/Churyumov-Gerasimenko suggest a more active past bw graph *Science* v355 no6332 p1392 Mr 31 2017

CRENSHAW, MARTHA

Transnational Jihadism & Civil Wars *Daedalus* v146 no4 p59 Fall 2017

Creole cooking

COOKING CREOLE D. CURRY color *New Orleans Magazine* v51 no3 p116 Ja 2017

Creoles

CALENDAR *New Orleans Magazine* v51 no3 p24 Ja 2017

Crépin, Anne-Sophie

Social norms as solutions bibl color *Science* v354 no6308 p42 O 7 2016

Crescent (Symbol)

A Super-Young Crescent Moon *Sky & Telescope* v133 no4 p51 Ap 2017

Crespi, Gabriella

Italian Modern Table color *Treasures* v5 no5 p11 Ap/My 2016

Crespo, Hiram

Live Well, Die Well: Does Neil Gorsuch Understand Epicurus? *Humanist* v77 no3 p6 My/Je 2017

Cressman, Natalie

NATALIE CRESSMAN & MIKE BONO K. Micallef color *Downbeat* v84 no1 p24 Ja 2017

Crest (Company)

Crest III 250 SLC *Boating World* v38 no1 p58 Ja 2017

Crested Butte (Colo.)—Description & travel

COMFORT ZONES S. Renner chart color *Sunset* v239 no4 p21 O 2017

Creswell, Robyn

The Seal of the Poets color *New York Review of Books* v64 no16 p24 O 26 2017

Tripoli Nights with a Master of Arabic color *New York Review of Books* v64 no4 p29 Mr 9 2017

Creton, Costantino

Molecular stitches for enhanced recycling of packaging bibl diag *Science* v355 no6327 p797 F 24 2017

Cretton, Destin Daniel

The Glass Castle J. McGovern color *Entertainment Weekly* no1478 / 1479 p84 Ag 18-25 2017

Creuzot, Cheryl

BUILDING BLACK FAMILY WEALTH D. Hamilton color *Ebony* v72 no9 p88 Jl/Ag 2017

Crewe, Jamie

Jamie Crewe P. Epps color *Art in America* v105 no3 p29 Mr 2017

Crews, Craig M.

Waste disposal–An attractive strategy for cancer therapy bibl chart diag *Science* v355 no6330 p1163 Mr 17 2017

Crews, Frederick

The Death Of Freud E. F. TORREY color *National Review* v69 no17 p35 S 11 2017

The Doctor's Discontents: A harshly critical new biography of the father of psychotherapy M. Edmundson *American Scholar* v86 no4 p124 Aut 2017

Freud's Clay Feet L. Appignanesi color *New York Review of Books* v64 no16 p36 O 26 2017

Freud: What's Left? bw *New York Review of Books* v64 no3 p6 F 23 2017

Our Freudian Complex [Cover story] G. Prochnik *New York Times Book Review* p1 Ag 20 2017

Crews, Terry, 1968-

TIM FERRISS TIM cartoon *Men's Health* v32 no9 p36 N 2017

Crichlow, Warren

BALDWIN'S RENDEZVOUS WITH THE TWENTY-FIRST CENTURY: I AM NOT YOUR NEGRO *Film Quarterly* v70 no4 p9 Summ 2017

Crichton, Michael, 1942-2008

THE HIT MAN S. KASHNER bw color *Vanity Fair* p172 Hollywood 2017 Supplement

Crick, Karen

Cincinnati Waldorf School *Cincinnati Magazine* v51 no1 p108 O 2017

Cricket (Sport)

See also

Twenty20 cricket

Cricket (Sport)—United States

Wicked Googly A. Fenwick and T. Keith color *Sports Illustrated* v125 no12 p22 O 10 2016

Crickets (Insect)

Does it taste good? D. GOLDMAN chart color *Popular Mechanics* p23 My 2017

Ground-Up Insects Could Nourish Millions J. DETWILER color *Popular Mechanics* p22 My 2017

Your True Stories IN 100 WORDS color *Reader's Digest* v190 no1133 p20 S 2017

Crickets (Insect)—Physiology

TRILLING INTRUDER M. A. Ronconi color *New York State Conservationist* v71 no2 p22 O 2016

CRIDER, JEFF

The Amateur's Guide to Africa's Highest Peak color diag *Conde Nast Traveler* v52 no5 p64 My 2017

Cries From Syria (Film)

Sundance Film Festival's Focus on Syria L. Thielen *Film Quarterly* v70 no4 p109 Summ 2017

Crime

See also

Bootlegging

Conspiracy

Espionage

Felonies

Genocide

Harassment

Juvenile delinquency

Poor women—Crimes against

Smuggling

Swindlers & swindling

White collar crimes

Women—Crimes against

The Antisocial Network M. Mariani *Psychology Today* v49 no5 p80 S/O 2016

THE BIG QUESTION B. Percy, T. French et al cartoon *Atlantic* v320 no3 p100 O 2017

CARTOONS *In These Times* v41 no7 p32 Jl 2017

Crime and Immigration New Forms of Exclusion and Discrimination M. C. WATERS color *Issues in Science & Technology* v33 no1 p29 Fall 2016

Farebox Fairness *Governing* v30 no8 p10 My 2017

The General and the Refugee E. REIDY color *New Republic* v248 no4 p38 Ap 2017

THE MYSTERIOUS CASE OF THE SEVERED FOOT B. EGERTON *D: The Magazine of Dallas* v43 no10 p150 O 2016

SMOOTH CRIMINALS S. POLAN *Psychology Today* v50 no3 p19 My/Je 2017

WHAT COPS KNOW [Cover story] P. Nickeas color *Chicago* v66 no7 p78 Jl 2017

Crime films

HENRY: PORTRAIT OF A SERIAL KILLER C. Chiarella color *Sound & Vision* v82 no4 p69 My 2017

A Hillbilly Heist R. R. Cooper color *Commonweal* v144 no16 p27 O 6 2017

How to Steal a Million-and Then Some E. Dockterman color diag *Time* v190 no8 p49 Ag 28 2017

JOHN WICK – CHAPTER 2 D. Vaughn color *Sound & Vision* v82 no8 p67 O 2017

LAW AND DISORDER E. LANDAU bw *GQ: Gentlemen's Quarterly* v86 no12 p131 D 2016

THE MAGFINICENT SEVEN (2016) D. Vaughn color *Sound & Vision* v82 no4 p68 My 2017

Crime films—Reviews

HEAT J. Krebs color *Sound & Vision* v82 no8 p71 O 2017

Crime in literature

By the Book T. French *New York Times Book Review* p8 O 2 2016

Crime in motion pictures

Burning Questions: The team behind Zero Dark Thirty revisits torture--this time in 1960s Detroit D. EDELSTEIN img *New York* v50 no15 p68 Jl 24 2017

Crime laboratories—Corrupt practices

A ROGUES' GALLERY OF BAD FORENSICS LABS C. J. CIARAMELLA *Reason* v49 no4 p38 Ag/S 2017

Crime on television

IS TV NEWS TOO VIOLENT? I. RUDOLPH *TV Guide* v65 no25 p6 Je 2017

Crime prevention

See also

Drug traffic—Prevention

Hate crimes—Prevention

Juvenile delinquency—Prevention

Research: When a Retail Store Closes, Crime Increases Around It T. Y. Chang and M. Jacobson *Harvard Business Review Digital Articles* p2 Je 29 2017

Crime prevention—Equipment & supplies

Bulletproofing W. BRENNAN bw color *Atlantic* v319 no1 p26 Ja/F 2017

Crime prevention—United States

CRIME FORECASTERS M. Hvistendahl color diag *Science* v353 no6307 p1484 S 30 2016

Crime scene searches

A State of Grief A. ALMENDRAL color *National Geographic* v231 no6 p106 Je 2017

Crime scenes

MISSISSIPPI MARTYR: Recalling a lynching that shocked America and galvanized the civil rights movement A. Crawford *Smithsonian* v48 no6 p16 O 2017

Crime writing

Don Winslow *New York Times Book Review* p6 Jl 2 2017

Crimea (Ukraine)—Description & travel

Crimea Welcomes a Flood of Putin Patriots E. Popina cartoon color *Bloomberg Businessweek* no4497 p21 O 31 2016

Crimean War, 1853-1856

WAR IN STILL LIFE D. Stadtler bw *Military History* v34 no2 p48 Jl 2017

Crime—Canada

How safe is your province? T. CIOLFE map *Maclean's* v130 no8 p17 S 2017

Crime—Congresses

Criminal Minds S. Stall *Indianapolis Monthly* v40 no10 p15 Je 2017

Crime—France

France at the Epicenter S. McCONNELL diag *American Conservative* v16 no3 p12 My/Je 2017

Crime—Illinois—Chicago

THE HUNTING ACCIDENT N. PARSI bw color *Chicago* v66 no9 p124 S 2017

Crime—India

The Killer Wrote Code B. Crair bw color *Bloomberg Businessweek* no4512 p68 F 20 2017

Crime—Louisiana

Marching to City Hall A. J. Johnson color *New Orleans Magazine* v51 no5 p38 Mr 2017

Crime—Louisiana—New Orleans

The Longest Yard A. J. Johnson color *New Orleans Magazine* v51 no4 p36 F 2017

Crime—New York (State)—New York

MEET THE MAN WHO TOLD THE STORY OF NEW YORK CITY, ONE CRIME AT A TIME T. Donnellan color *America* v216 no9 p14 Ap 24 2017

UNDER CONSTRUCTION J. FRANZEN color *New Yorker* v93 no33 p50 O 23 2017

Crime—News briefs

BRICKBATS C. OLIVER cartoon *Reason* v49 no1 p72 My 2017

Crimes against African Americans

The Bullet, the Cop, the Boy J. D. WALSH img *New York* v50 no12 p46 Je 12 2017

License to Hate: The label of "hate crime" is used to score political points, not to end violence. It should be eliminated V. D. Hanson *Hoover Digest: Research & Opinion on Public Policy* no2 p143 Spr 2017

TRACING AN ATROCITY: How an Obscure Affidavit in the National Archives Unraveled a Historical Mystery J. DESANTIS *Prologue* v49 no2 p42 Summ 2017

When The Past Is Present K. JORDAN *Los Angeles Magazine*

v62 no7 p15 Jl 2017

Crimes against gay people
QUEER THEORY *Harper's Magazine* v334 no2004 p17 My 2017

Crimes against humanity
See also
　Human trafficking
　Murder
THE GENESIS OF 'GENOCIDE' J. Winter *MHQ: Quarterly Journal of Military History* v29 no3 p17 Spr 2017
PROTECTING VULNERABLE POPULATIONS FROM GENOCIDE A. DIENG *UN Chronicle* v54 no4 p9 2017

Crimes against LGBT people
See also
　Crimes against gay people
HATE IN THE AGE OF TRUMP: Are America's LGBT centers under attack? D. REYNOLDS color *Advocate* no1091 p19 Je/Jl 2017

Crime—United States
American Crime Story E. Epstein *Weekly Standard* v22 no27 p12 Mr 20 2017
RECOGNIZE, RESIST, REPORT J. REEVES cartoon *Reason* v49 no1 p38 My 2017
To the Extreme J. Hitt color *New York Times Magazine* p17 D 11 2016
TRAIL OF FEARS K. BAKER color *New Republic* v248 no7 p18 Jl 2017

Criminal (Film)
CRIMINAL J. Krebs color *Sound & Vision* v81 no10 p70 D 2016

Criminal defendants
THE DISAPPEARING SIXTH AMENDMENT C. J. CIARAMELLA color *Reason* v49 no2 p12 Je 2017

Criminal investigation
See also
　Rewards programs (Criminal investigation)
COMEY'S LAW B. McLEAN color *Vanity Fair* v59 no4 p166 Mr 2017
A Corruption Probe Into College Hoops Exposes More Than Shady Deals S. Gregory color *Time* v190 no15 p17 O 16 2017
CSI: CHINA: The 19th and 20th centuries saw a revolution in Chinese forensic science, when traditional techniques were replaced by new methods from the West. Today, the world confronts another moment of transformation in forensic science D. Asen *History Today* v67 no7 p54 Jl 2017
THE MYSTERIOUS CASE OF THE SEVERED FOOT B. EGERTON *D: The Magazine of Dallas* v43 no10 p150 O 2016
QUEER THEORY *Harper's Magazine* v334 no2004 p17 My 2017

Criminal investigation—Software
MURDER, HE CALCULATED R. Kolker color diag graph *Bloomberg Businessweek* no4511 p48 F 13 2017

Criminal justice administration
See also
　Clemency
　Imprisonment
　Law enforcement
　Pardon
　Police
　Pretrial release
　Prisons
　Prosecutors
BAIL OUT J. J. CLAYTON *USA Today Magazine* v145 no2858 p22 N 2016
THE CONFESSIONS OF CLEVELAND BYNUM A. WREN color *Indianapolis Monthly* v42 no2 p74 O 2017
THE JUSTICE MACHINE I. Lapowsky color *Wired* v24 no11 p68 N 2016
THE WALLS ARE BULGING S. MCCOMAS *USA Today Magazine* v145 no2858 p24 N 2016
Why I'm For Hillary Clinton [Cover story] V. KIM *New York Times Upfront* v149 no4 p12 O 31 2016
THE WRONG MAN B. TAUB cartoon color *New Yorker* v93 no22 p46 Jl 31 2017

Criminal justice administration & ethics
The Case for Mercy: Some of the Unlikeliest People Oppose the Death Penalty E. Gunn color *Progressive* v81 no7 p26 O/N 2017

Criminal justice administration—Canada
Someone else's problem B. HUTCHINSON *Maclean's* v130 no8

p16 S 2017
The wheels of injustice M. FRISCOLANTI color *Maclean's* v130 no3 p35 Ap 2017

Criminal justice administration—Georgia
JACKSON POLICE DEPARTMENT JACKSON 53 MILES SOUTHEAST OF ATLANTA J. GREEN *Atlanta* v57 no1 p144 My 2017

Criminal justice administration—Texas
Law and the New Order A. Greenblatt *Governing* v30 no7 p26 Ap 2017
THE TROUBLE WITH INNOCENCE M. Hall *Texas Monthly* v45 no4 p96 Ap 2017

Criminal justice administration—United States
Animal CSI [Cover story] J. Byrd and N. Whitling color *Scientific American* v316 no1 p56 Ja 2017
BAIL MEANS JAIL: DEBTOR'S PRISON FOR THE UNCONVICTED Y. GUNASEKERA color *Progressive* v81 no6 p56 Ag/S 2017
OUT OF PRISON. OUT OF WORK E. BOEHM *Reason* v49 no3 p12 Jl 2017
TRUMPED J. Amber color *Essence* v48 no5 p100 S 2017
WHAT DO CRIME VICTIMS WANT FROM CRIMINAL JUSTICE REFORM? J. Keisling cartoon graph *Reason* v48 no7 p8 D 2016

Criminal justice policy
Prison Reform Politics A. Greenblatt *Governing* v30 no5 p10 F 2017

Criminal law
See also
　Capital punishment
　Elections—Corrupt practices
The Zone of Death K. PETERSON *Idaho Magazine* v16 no5 p45 F 2017

Criminal law—California
CLEAN SLATE CLUB S. Michaels color *Mother Jones* v42 no6 p11 N/D 2017

Criminal law—United States
American Crime Story E. Epstein *Weekly Standard* v22 no27 p12 Mr 20 2017
KNOWN UNKNOWNS M. Ruth Stegman *Commonweal* v144 no4 p4 F 24 2017

Criminal liability
See also
　Entrapment (Criminal law)

Criminal Minds (TV program)
Criminal Minds A. D'Arminio *TV Guide* v65 no19 p29 My 1 2017
Criminal Minds *TV Guide* v65 no41 p31 O 2 2017

Criminal profilers
Unmasking the Mad Bomber M. CANNELL *Smithsonian* v48 no1 p25 Ap 2017

Criminal records
Does Ban-the-Box Do Any Good? M. Maciag *Governing* v30 no1 p56 O 2016
How banning boxes encourages discrimination G. Boone *Monthly Labor Review* p1 Ja 2017

Criminal statistics
See also
　Criminal records
　Homicide rates

Criminal statistics—Canada
How safe is your province? T. CIOLFE map *Maclean's* v130 no8 p17 S 2017

Criminal statistics—United States
The Mythology of Immigrant Crime M. Maciag *Governing* v30 no7 p56 Ap 2017

Criminals
See also
　Drug couriers
　Drug dealers
　Mentally ill criminals
　Murderers
　Outlaws
　Swindlers & swindling
　Thieves
　Violent criminals
APPOINTMENT WITH DEATH J. LASDUN cartoon color *New*

Yorker v93 no19 p30 Jl 3 2017

THE CONFESSIONS OF CLEVELAND BYNUM A. WREN color *Indianapolis Monthly* v42 no2 p74 O 2017

THE WALLS ARE BULGING S. MCCOMAS *USA Today Magazine* v145 no2858 p24 N 2016

Criminals—Identification

Who Was That Masked Man? E. Epstein color *Weekly Standard* v22 no23 p8 F 20 2017

Criminals—Rehabilitation

The Pipe Fitter C. Rotella *New York Times Magazine* p47 F 26 2017

Criminals—United States

Jailhouse Experiments *Governing* v30 no10 p11 Jl 2017

THE KILLER NEXT DOOR J. BOND color *Reader's Digest* v189 no1130 p122 My 2017

TRUMP'S 3 MILLION CRIMINALS S. F. WESSLER color *Nation* v303 no25/26 p16 D 19 2016

Crimp, Douglas

Our Kind of Memoir R. Atkins color *Art in America* v105 no5 p55 My 2017

Crimp, Douglas—Exhibitions

ART *New Yorker* v92 no30 p10 S 26 2016

Crimp, Douglas—Interviews

Q&A: Douglas Crimp D. S. PALMER bw color *ARTnews* v115 no4 p74 Wint 2016/2017

Crisafi, Denise

How Stable is the Condition of Family Homelessness? chart *Society* v54 no1 p46 F 2017

Criscuolo, Chiara

Productivity Is Soaring at Top Firms and Sluggish Everywhere Else *Harvard Business Review Digital Articles* p2 Ag 24 2015

A Study of 16 Countries Shows That the Most Productive Firms (and Their Employees) Are Pulling Away from Everyone Else *Harvard Business Review Digital Articles* p2 Jl 13 2017

Criscuolo, Paola

The Biases That Keep Good R&D Projects from Getting Funded *Harvard Business Review Digital Articles* p2 Mr 17 2017

Crises—Economic aspects

Me the People *Commentary* v142 no1 p1 Jl/Ag 2016

Crises—Social aspects

What Man, and Climate Change, Has Wrought A. Baker color *Time* v189 no11 p15 Mr 27 2017

Crisis communication

Managing nuclear risk in South Asia M. E. Carranza bibl *Bulletin of the Atomic Scientists* v73 no1 p64 Ja 2017

Crisis management

See also

    Disaster resilience

    Nuclear crisis control

HANDLING A CRISIS J. Scott color *Successful Farming* v115 no7 p13 My 2017

Managing nuclear risk in South Asia R. Akhtar bibl *Bulletin of the Atomic Scientists* v73 no1 p62 Ja 2017

Pepsi, United, and the Speed of Corporate Shame A. Winston *Harvard Business Review Digital Articles* p2 Ap 12 2017

To Recover from a Crisis, Retell Your Company's Story H. Hutson and M. Johnson *Harvard Business Review Digital Articles* p2 My 2 2017

What Harvey Is Teaching the Health Care Sector About Managing Disasters N. A. Gandhi and R. S. Dhillon *Harvard Business Review Digital Articles* p2 S 12 2017

What It Was Like to Be a Manager in Ukraine C. Tsolkas *Harvard Business Review Digital Articles* p2 Je 2 2015

What Would It Take to Disrupt a Platform Like Facebook? J. Gans *Harvard Business Review Digital Articles* p2 Mr 23 2016

Crisis management—Computer network resources

Facebook's Community Help lets you aid your neighbors in a crisis I. PAUL color *PCWorld* p45 Mr 2017

Crisis pregnancy centers

Beware Google Ads for 'Abortion Consultations' A. Hines color *Bloomberg Businessweek* no4516 p30 Mr 27 2017

Crisis Pregnancy Centers in Crisis J. D. J. HAGEN color *Weekly Standard* v23 no4 p26 O 2 2017

Crisis pregnancy centers—Social aspects

A Crisis for Crisis-Pregnancy Centers J. D. Hagen color *Commonweal* v144 no4 p7 F 24 2017

Crisp, Chelsey

Fresh Off the Boat N. Abrams, A. Bacle et al color *Entertainment Weekly* no1482/1483 p63 S 22 2017

Crisp, Oliver D.

Saving Calvinism: Expanding the Reformed Tradition color *Publishers Weekly* v263 no45 p25 N 7 2016

Crispin, Jessa

Feminist Fail color *New Republic* v248 no3 p16 Mr 2017

Gibberish, Maya-Style H. WILHELM *Commentary* v144 no3 p49 O 2017

Where Have All the Communes Gone? A case for radical social experimentation *In These Times* v41 no10 p36 O 2017

Why I Am Not a Feminist: A Feminist Manifesto *Publishers Weekly* v263 no43 p67 O 24 2016

Yes All Women M. DOHERTY color *New Republic* v248 no4 p58 Ap 2017

CRISPRs (Genetics)

THE BIRTH OF CRISPR INC J. Cohen chart color diag *Science* v355 no6326 p680 F 17 2017

Can CRISPR Save Ben Dupree? A. Regalado color *MIT Technology Review* v119 no6 p80 N/D 2016

China sprints ahead in CRISPR therapy race D. Normile chart color *Science* v357 no6359 p20 O 6 2017

The CRISPR Antidote E. BETZ color *Discover* v38 no10 p10 D 2017

CRISPR-Cas: Adapting to change S. A. Jackson, R. E. McKenzie et al color *Science* v356 no6333 p40 Ap 7 2017

The CRISPR Pioneers A. Park color *Time* v188 no25-26 p116 D 19 2016 Double Issue

CRISPR, surrogate licensing, and scientific discovery J. L. Contreras and J. S. Sherkow bibl diag *Science* v355 no6326 p698 F 17 2017

Crystal-clear memories of a bacterium R. Globus and U. Qimron diag *Science* v357 no6356 p1096 S 15 2017

A cyclic oligonucleotide signaling pathway in type III CRISPR-Cas systems M. Kazlauskiene, G. Kostiuk et al *Science* v357 no6351 p605 Ag 11 2017

Designer Genes R. JACOBSEN color *Mother Jones* v42 no5 p44 S/O 2017

Edible CRISPR Could Precisely Target Dangerous Germs E. Mullin color *MIT Technology Review* v120 no4 p23 Jl/Ag 2017

Embryo editing takes another step to clinic K. Servick bw *Science* v357 no6350 p436 Ag 4 2017

IN THE IMAGE OF OUR CHOOSING N. BARCZI diag *Christianity Today* p48 Mr 2017

Intracellular signaling in CRISPR-Cas defense G. Amitai and R. Sorek color *Science* v357 no6351 p550 Ag 11 2017

IT'S OK TO EDIT YOUR KIDS' GENES R. BAILEY color *Reason* v49 no6 p6 N 2017

Making the cut in the dark genome J. M. Einstein and G. W. Yeo bibl diag *Science* v354 no6313 p705 N 11 2016

MICE MADE EASY J. Cohen color *Science* v354 no6312 p539 N 4 2016

NEW PRODUCTS: NEUROTECHNIQUES color *Science* v354 no6312 p641 N 4 2016

The Original CRISPR [Cover story] R. Mestel color diag graph *Science News* v191 no7 p22 Ap 15 2017

Patent pools for CRISPR technology L. Horn, J. L. Contreras et al bibl color *Science* v355 no6331 p1274 Mr 24 2017

A reporter does CRISPR J. Cohen color *Science* v354 no6312 p541 N 4 2016

Structures of the CRISPR genome integration complex A. V. Wright, Liu et al color *Science* v357 no6356 p1113 S 15 2017

Systematic mapping of functional enhancer–promoter connections with CRISPR interference C. P. Fulco, M. Munschauer et al bibl graph *Science* v354 no6313 p769 N 11 2016

CRISPRs (Genetics)—Lawsuits & claims

CRISPR patent ruling leaves license holders scrambling J. Cohen color *Science* v355 no6327 p786 F 24 2017

CRISPRs (Genetics)—News briefs

Quick Hits map *Scientific American* v315 no3 p22 S 2016

CRIST, CAROLYN

TOP HOSPITALS *Atlanta* v56 no9 p128 Ja 2017

CRIST, EILEEN

An Ecoregion-Based Approach to Protecting Half the Terrestrial Realm *BioScience* v67 no6 p534 Je 2017

The interaction of human population, food production, and biodiversity protection color diag graph *Science* v356 no6335 p260 Ap 21 2017

Cristobal, Sarah

AM I TOO OLD FOR THIS? color *InStyle* v24 no9 p422 S 2017

CHLOE AND HALLE color *InStyle* v24 no6 p128 Je 2017

COACH'S DINO-MITE YEAR color *Harper's Bazaar* no3649 p322 D 2016/Ja 2017

Might As Well ... Jump color *InStyle* v24 no7 p124 Jl 2017

MILLIE BOBBY BROWN UPSIDE DOWN color *InStyle* v24 no11 p178 N 2017

My Brows color *InStyle* v24 no5 p226 My 2017

My Legs color *InStyle* v24 no10 p224 O 2017

My LIST 24 hours with Marina Abramović color *Harper's Bazaar* no3648 p120 N 2016

THE NEW BUZZ color *Harper's Bazaar* no3648 p266 N 2016

Peter Philips color *InStyle* v24 no8 p106 Ag 2017

Qué Bella [Cover story] color *InStyle* v24 no8 p130 Ag 2017

SHE'S GOT THE POWER color *Harper's Bazaar* no3648 p244 N 2016

Still the One color *InStyle* v24 no10 p118 O 2017

They're Here to Help color *InStyle* v24 no4 p102 Ap 2017

Cristol, Dan

THE LOST BIRDS P. GREENBERG color *Audubon* v119 no3 p38 Fall 2017

Critchfield, Sara

How to Push Your Team to Take Risks and Experiment color *Harvard Business Review Digital Articles* p2 Mr 9 2017

CRITCHLOW, DONALD T.

Rise to Dominance color *National Review* v69 no7 p44 Ap 17 2017

Critical care medicine—Study & teaching

Mapping Geography of Critical Care Training *USA Today Magazine* v145 no2861 p4 F 2017

Critical discourse analysis

A Discourse on Discourse Studies A. Berger color *Society* v53 no6 p597 D 2016

Critical thinking

All the Skeptic Ladies C. Ward *Skeptical Inquirer* v41 no3 p66 My/Je 2017

Breathing control center neurons that promote arousal in mice K. Yackle, L. A. Schwarz et al diag graph *Science* v355 no6332 p1411 Mr 31 2017

Can Data Literacy Protect Us from Misleading Political Ads? W. Frick *Harvard Business Review Digital Articles* p2 Ap 5 2016

CATCHING A CONSPIRACY R. DAVIS and C. PAVITT color *Scientific American* v317 no2 p5 Ag 2017

Cincinnati Waldorf School K. Crick *Cincinnati Magazine* v51 no1 p108 O 2017

Don't be bored P. W. Marty *Christian Century* v134 no20 p3 S 27 2017

EXECUTIVE-LEVEL THINKING: Teaching 21st-century skills for effective reading comprehension K. B. Cartwright color *Literacy Today (2411-7862)* v34 no6 p38 My/Je 2017

How to Regain the Lost Art of Reflection M. Reeves, R. Torres et al *Harvard Business Review Digital Articles* p2 S 25 2017

Humanities, Too: In New Study, History Courses in Critical Thinking Reduce Pseudoscientific Beliefs K. Frazier *Skeptical Inquirer* v41 no4 p11 Jl/Ag 2017

IT'S CRITICAL L. ELDER *USA Today Magazine* v145 no2860 p42 Ja 2017

LISTEN TO THIS M. Godsey color *Literacy Today (2411-7862)* v34 no3 p28 N/D 2016

More on 'WhySkepticism?' J. Clinger and W. Hodgins *Skeptical Inquirer* v41 no4 p63 Jl/Ag 2017

Points to Ponder *Reader's Digest* v189 no1127 p20 F 2017

Shopper's Guide: Purchasing managers are pushing to have critical thinking lead the buying process K. Barrett and R. Greene *Governing* v30 no9 p58 Je 2017

Teaching with evidence M. Crocco, Halvorsen et al diag *Phi Delta Kappan* v98 no7 p67 Ap 2017

Critical thinking—Study & teaching

MASTERS OF TECH J. Santiago color *Literacy Today (2411-7862)* v34 no3 p12 N/D 2016

Criticism

See also

Bible—Criticism, interpretation, etc.

Critics

Literature—History & criticism

Press criticism

Avoiding criticism harms workplace performance *People Management* p63 N 2016

Is Laughter the Best Medicine? J. Crane *History Today* v66 no11 p19 N 2016

Managing the Critical Voices Inside Your Head P. Bregman *Harvard Business Review Digital Articles* p2 Ap 6 2015

Mission Critical M. BECK color *O, The Oprah Magazine* p46 N 2017

Criticism—Psychological aspects

A DISCOURAGING WORD T. Pitock *Saturday Evening Post* v289 no3 p10 My/Je 2017

Critics

See also

Authors & critics

America's top TV critic Matt Roush answers your burning questions *TV Guide* v65 no43 p2 O 16 2017

Bookends T. Mallon and L. Schillinger *New York Times Book Review* p27 S 3 2017

Liu Xiaobo's Last Text L. Xiaobo bw *New York Review of Books* v64 no14 p8 S 28 2017

Managing the Critical Voices Inside Your Head P. Bregman *Harvard Business Review Digital Articles* p2 Ap 6 2015

Critics Choice Awards (TV program)

CRITICS' CHOICE AWARDS NOMINATIONS S. Li color *Entertainment Weekly* no1441 p13 N 25 2016

A Starry Night R. Kinane color *Entertainment Weekly* no1446/1447 p25 D 2016/Ja 2017

Critics in literature

The Hardest Lesson of a Liberal Democracy? How to Live With Critics A. Kirsch *New York Times Book Review* p21 Je 18 2017

CROATTO, PETE

THE BEST SEATS IN THE HOUSE color *Publishers Weekly* v264 no11 p43 Mr 13 2017

Crocco, Margaret

Teaching with evidence diag *Phi Delta Kappan* v98 no7 p67 Ap 2017

Croce, Roberta

The complex that conquered the land diag *Science* v357 no6353 p752 Ag 25 2017

Croce giottesca di San Felice (Panel painting)

Crucifixion H. J. Hornik and M. C. Parsons color *Christian Century* v134 no1 p47 Ja 4 2017

Crocenzi, Todd S.

Mismatch repair deficiency predicts response of solid tumors to PD-1 blockade chart graph *Science* v357 no6349 p409 Jl 28 2017

Crocetto, Leah, 1980-

Higher Power: Soprano Leah Crocetto views singing as a gift she is called to share F. Cohn *Opera News* v81 no12 p7 Je 2017

Crochet, J. J.

Extremely efficient internal exciton dissociation through edge states in layered 2D perovskites bibl graph *Science* v355 no6331 p1288 Mr 24 2017

Crocheting

Maria Molteni A. RANALLO color *American Craft* v77 no3 p12 Je/Jl 2017

Crocker, John

Following Fifi: My Adventures Among Wild Chimpanzees; Lessons from Our Closest Relatives color *Publishers Weekly* v264 no41 p56 O 9 2017

Crocker, Katherine C.

Scientists stand with Standing Rock bibl color *Science* v353 no6307 p1506 S 30 2016

Crockett, A. G.

Driving Home the Safety Discussion il *Consumer Reports* v82 no9 p6 S 2017

Crockett, Christopher

Age of Saturn's rings debated bw *Science News* v190 no10 p10 N 12 2016

Cassini spacecraft gets a proper send-off color *Science News* v192 no3 p26 S 2 2017

Closest known exoplanet 'just' 4.24 light-years away color *Sci-*

ence News v190 no13 p20 D 24 2016

Dark Galaxies cartoon color *Science News* v190 no12 p18 D 10 2016

Dawn spacecraft maps Ceres water color *Science News* v191 no1 p8 Ja 21 2017

Fast radio burst's home identified color *Science News* v191 no2 p10 F 4 2017

Gaia mission maps over 1 billion stars color *Science News* v190 no8 p16 O 15 2016

Gamma rays linked to fast radio burst color *Science News* v190 no12 p11 D 10 2016

Interactive map reveals universe's hidden details color *Science News* v190 no11 p29 N 26 2016

Lost star may be failed supernova *Science News* v190 no8 p8 O 15 2016

Milky Way's black hole may hurl galactic spitballs our way color *Science News* v191 no2 p11 F 4 2017

Nobels honor the small and exotic cartoon color *Science News* v190 no9 p6 O 29 2016

The Opportunity ZONE color diag graph *Science News* v191 no12 p18 Je 24 2017

The stellar shreds of supernovas color *Science News* v191 no3 p32 F 18 2017

The Stellar Storyteller color *Science News* v191 no3 p20 F 18 2017

X-ray mystery shrouds Pluto color *Science News* v190 no11 p15 N 26 2016

Crockett, Jim
the producers P. DICKEY color *Better Homes & Gardens* v95 no5 p136 My 2017

CROCKETT, JOHN
BIODIESEL POWER: HOW IDAHO RESEARCH CHANGED THE WORLD *Idaho Magazine* v16 no8 p12 My 2017

Crocodiles—Behavior
When croc babies become teenagers N. Strochlic color *National Geographic* v230 no4 p24 O 2016

Crocodiles—Mythology
ONE + ONE = FORTY-NINE J. A. LOBELL color *Archaeology* v70 no3 p42 My/Je 2017

Crocodiles—Physiology
THE CASE OF THE MACHO CROCS M. Leslie color map *Science* v357 no6354 p859 S 1 2017

CROFT, DARREN P.
Using Social Network Measures in Wildlife Disease Ecology, Epidemiology, and Management *BioScience* v67 no3 p245 Mr 2017

Croft, Romy Madley—Interviews
Hot Tracks L. Robinson color *Vanity Fair* v59 no2 p38 F 2017

Crofton, Ian
The Little Book of Big History: The Story of the Universe, Human Civilization, and Everything in Between *Publishers Weekly* v264 no20 p49 My 15 2017

CROFTS, PAULINE
Sign up now to become a mentor *People Management* p62 O 2016

Crohn's disease
The road to Crohn's disease A. Kaser and R. S. Blumberg diag *Science* v357 no6355 p976 S 8 2017

Cro-Mags, The (Performer)
Staying Sharp J. J. McGowan color *AARP: The Magazine* v30 no6A p65 O/N 2017

Croman, Steve
GET OUT S. VAN ZUYLEN-WOOD color *Bloomberg Businessweek* no4495 p50 O 17 2016

Cromartie, Michael, 1950-2017
Evangelist to the Press Corps F. BARNES color *Weekly Standard* v23 no1 p13 S 11 2017

Crombie, Deborah—Interviews
Disquiet in the Yard E. FOXWELL *Publishers Weekly* v263 no52 p98 D 19 2016

Cromer, Cheryl
AROMATHERAPY TRAVEL KIT color *Amazing Wellness* v9 no4 p70 Summ 2017

DETOXIFY WITH AROMATHERAPY color *Amazing Wellness* v9 no2 p68 Spr 2017

FESTIVE HOLIDAY SCENTS color *Amazing Wellness* v9 no6 p80 EarlyWint 2017

trendWATCH color *Better Nutrition* v78 no12 p10 D 2016

Cromer, David
A Little Night Music A. GREEN bw *Vogue* v207 no11 p165 N 2017

Cromwell, James, 1940-
DISOBEDIENT M. Schulman cartoon *New Yorker* v93 no25 p30 Ag 28 2017

Cromwell, James, 1940-—Interviews
The Young Pope A. D'Arminio *TV Guide* v65 no4 p41 Ja 16 2017

Cromwell, Oliver, 1599-1658
Imperial Designs: Cromwell's move on Jamaica transformed Britain's early empire C. G. Pestana *History Today* v67 no6 p8 Je 2016

Cronin, J.
Observation of a large-scale anisotropy in the arrival directions of cosmic rays above 8×1018 eV *Science* v357 no6357 p1266 S 22 2017

Cronin, James W., 1931-2016
James Watson Cronin H. J. Frisch, J. E. Pilcher et al *Physics Today* v70 no3 p72 Mr 2017

James W. Cronin (1931–2016) A. A. Watson bw *Science* v353 no6307 p1501 S 30 2016

CRONIN, JUSTIN
Red Versus Blue: A fictional (so far) history of the Second American Civil War cartoon *New York Times Book Review* p11 Ap 23 2017

Cronin, Mike
THE INVENTION OF ST. PATRICK'S DAY *Saturday Evening Post* v289 no2 p78 Mr/Ap 2017

Cronin, Patrick
Popular piety color *U.S. Catholic* v82 no2 p5 F 2017

Cronk, Imran
Why We Don't Trust Driverless Cars — Even When We Should *Harvard Business Review Digital Articles* p2 O 18 2016

Cronk, Jordan
DAMNED SUMMER color *Film Comment* v53 no5 p22 S/O 2017

THE DREAMED PATH color *Film Comment* v53 no1 p24 Ja/F 2017

Harmonium color *Film Comment* v53 no3 p67 My/Je 2017

RIFLE color *Film Comment* v53 no3 p24 My/Je 2017

Cronos (Film)
The Master of Highbrow Horror T. RAFFERTY cartoon *Atlantic* v318 no4 p48 N 2016

CRONQUIST, EVANIE
DRUG ADVERTISING color *Scientific American* v315 no3 p5 S 2016

Crony capitalism
Big-Bank Hegemony: They have seized control of their own regulators C. WHALEN *American Conservative* v16 no5 p25 S/O 2017

The Cronyism Primer: Corporate welfare goes back at least to the Boston Tea Party A. A. WINTERS *American Conservative* v16 no4 p34 Jl/Ag 2017

FRIENDS IN HIGH PLACES M. CAMPBELL color *Maclean's* p32 Je 2017

Cronyn, Susan
The Thread *New York Times Magazine* p9 F 5 2017

Crook, Geoff
Mitigating coastal landslide damage color *Science* v357 no6355 p981 S 8 2017

Crooks, Kevin
Noise pollution is pervasive in U.S. protected areas graph map *Science* v356 no6337 p531 My 5 2017

Crooks, Nathan
Faces of the Venezuelan Exodus color *Bloomberg Businessweek* no4522 p15 My 15 2017

Crop diversification
CATTLE AND COVER CROPS IMPROVE SOIL HEALTH D. Goerge *Successful Farming* v114 no13 p59 D 2016

GAIN FROM CROP DIVERSITY: INCREASE VARIETY IN CROP ROTATION TO BOOST THE OVERALL HEALTH OF YOUR FIELD K. Birchmier *Successful Farming* v115 no9 p53 Ag 2017

REBUILDING A FARM R. Nickel *Successful Farming* v115 no3 p42 Mid-F 2017

Crop insurance

Designed in Davos, Tested in Zimbabwe A. Bjerga color *Bloomberg Businessweek* no4507 p37 Ja 16 2017

FINE-TUNE YOUR 2017 MARKETING PLAN A. Kluis *Successful Farming* v115 no4 p22 Mr 2017

Crop insurance—United States

Changes in Farmers' Financial Status May Affect Crop Insurance Demand K. Farrin *Amber Waves: The Economics of Food, Farming, Natural Resources, & Rural America* p45 N 2016

Conservation Compliance in the Crop Insurance Era R. Claassen and M. Bowman *Amber Waves: The Economics of Food, Farming, Natural Resources, & Rural America* p29 Jl 2017

Crop losses

Evolution of the wheat blast fungus through functional losses in a host specificity determinant Y. Inoue, T. T. P. Vy et al diag map *Science* v357 no6346 p80 Jl 7 2017

Crop management

ADAPT NEW IDEAS! B. FREESE *Successful Farming* v114 no13 p42 D 2016

Crop rotation

10 UP & COMERS: JASON MAUCK A. McConnell *Successful Farming* v115 no8 p40 Je/Jl 2017

10 UP & COMERS: PEOPLE TO WATCH IN AGRICULTURE L. Bedord *Successful Farming* v115 no8 p32 Je/Jl 2017

AN EYE FOR NEW CROPS R. Nickel *Successful Farming* v114 no13 p37 D 2016

MANAGING PESTS K. Birchmier *Successful Farming* v115 no4 p52 Mr 2017

Crop science

THE SUCCESSFUL INTERVIEW K. Birchmier *Successful Farming* v115 no11 p10 S 2017

Crop yields

See also
Corn yields

Traits Under the Lens G. Gullickson *Successful Farming* v115 no2 p44 F 2017

WEATHERING THE STORM A. Kluis *Successful Farming* v114 no11 p21 N 2016

Cropper, Maureen

Looking backward to move regulations forward color *Science* v355 no6332 p1375 Mr 31 2017

Crops

See also
Energy crops
Field crops
Grain
Seed crops
Seeds

SEEING IS BELIEVING *Successful Farming* v115 no6 p5 Ap 2017

Crops & climate

Seed Catalogs W. Blackmore *New York Times Magazine* p20 F 5 2017

Crops—Nutrition

Although Small, Markets Have Been Expanding for GE Crops With Traits That Increase Nutrient Content or Improve Taste J. McFadden *Amber Waves: The Economics of Food, Farming, Natural Resources, & Rural America* p19 Ag 2017

Crops—Origin

UNITED STATES OF CORN C. Zuckerman color *National Geographic* v231 no2 p18 F 2017

Crops—Sales & prices

TIME TO STOCK UP AT THE GROCERY STORE L. GERSTNER color *Kiplinger's Personal Finance* v71 no1 p15 Ja 2017

Crops—Water requirements

but how much does food drink? M. Koziol cartoon *Popular Science* v289 no2 p16 Mr/Ap 2017

Croquet players

CROQUET DEVOTEES J. Vrabel *Indianapolis Monthly* v40 no10 p20 Je 2017

Croquet—Competitions

CROQUET DEVOTEES J. Vrabel *Indianapolis Monthly* v40 no10 p20 Je 2017

CROSBIE, LYNN

It Is I Who Styles Donald Trump; or, Chérie (de Melania Knauss-Trump) cartoon *Walrus* v14 no3 p48 Ap 2017

Crosbie, Martin

My Temporary Life *Publishers Weekly* v264 no13 p64b Mr 27 2017

Scouting Report color *Publishers Weekly* v264 no13 p48 Mr 27 2017

Crosby, Caresse, 1892-1970

WHAT'S NEW IN LINGERIE L. McCarthy color *Harper's Bazaar* no3650 p196 F 2017

Crosby, David

DAVID CROSBY color *AARP: The Magazine* v60 no1A p9 D 2016/Ja 2017

Crosby, Heather

Mixing Bowl color *O, The Oprah Magazine* p108 Je 2017

Crosby, Jeff

LEAF SPRINGS 101 J. HEADLEE color *Dirt Sports + Off-Road* v51 no9 p34 S 2017

CROSE, CEDRI

Savory Cycle Ride, Midway, Kentucky *Cincinnati Magazine* p63 Je 2017

Crosilla, Dillon

Hymns of the Western Peaks: Loose Change in India bw color *Snowboarder* v29 no2 p82 O 2016

CROSLEY, SLOANE

The Business of Casual color *InStyle* v24 no4 p100 Ap 2017

GOING PLACES color *Harper's Bazaar* no3657 p169 O 2017

Hot Type bw *Vanity Fair* v59 no4 p116 Mr 2017

Hot Type color *Vanity Fair* v58 no11 p96 N 2016

Hot Type color *Vanity Fair* v59 no10 p128 O 2017

Hot Type color *Vanity Fair* v59 no8 p48 Ag 2017

HUMORISTS ON HUMOR: CRACKING THE CODE ON WHAT CRACKS US UP R. WARREN *Saturday Evening Post* v289 no5 p38 S/O 2017

STAGE OF ENLIGHTENMENT color *Vanity Fair* v59 no6 p74 My 2017

Tales Out of School *New York Times Book Review* p16 Ja 22 2017

Crosley, Tom

2017 Education Highlights: The Golden Thread of Parks and Recreation *Parks & Recreation* v52 no8 p52 Ag 2017

More Leadership-Themed Sessions at Conference *Parks & Recreation* v52 no5 p64 My 2017

NRPA Update: More Health and Wellness Sessions Offered at Conference This Year *Parks & Recreation* v52 no6 p40 Je 2017

Cross, Elizabeth

Mapping "The Hunger Games": Using location quotients to find the Districts of Panem *Career Outlook* p3 F 2017

CROSS, JASON

Daydream View: Sparse content is all that stands between Google and VR greatness color *PCWorld* v35 no1 p145 Ja 2017

Moto Z Play: Long-lasting, affordable, and modular too color graph *PCWorld* p114 O 2016

Pixel XL review : Google's new phone isn't a Nexus—it's better color graph *PCWorld* v35 no11 p46 N 2016

CROSS, LATOYA

'90s till infinity: EN VOGUE color *Ebony* v72 no6 p82 Ap/My 2017

CLOSE UP WITH CONDOLA RASHAD color *Ebony* v72 no6 p22 Ap/My 2017

Corey Hawkins Takes the Lead in 24: Legacy color *Ebony* v72 no4 p39 F 2017

Dear America, James Baldwin Is Still 'Not Your Negro' bw color *Ebony* v72 no4 p22 F 2017

December! color *Ebony* v72 no3 p34 D 2016/Ja 2017

EBONY POWER 100 Celebrated Black Excellence, Community and Creativity color *Ebony* v72 no4 p26 F 2017

February! cartoon color *Ebony* v72 no4 p24 F 2017

FIRST LOOK: FENCES color *Ebony* v72 no3 p38 D 2016/Ja 2017

FIRST LOOK: FIST FIGHT color *Ebony* v72 no4 p40 F 2017

FIRST LOOK: SHOTS FIRED color *Ebony* v72 no5 p26 Mr 2017

FIRST LOOK: SLEIGHT color *Ebony* v72 no6 p24 Ap/My 2017

In Our Cities bw color *Ebony* v72 no4 p42 F 2017

In Our Cities bw color *Ebony* v72 no6 p32 Ap/My 2017

January! bw color *Ebony* v72 no3 p36 D 2016/Ja 2017

Kenyatta A.C. Hinkle color *Ebony* v72 no5 p31 Mr 2017

Logan Browning's Black Face in a White Place color *Ebony* v72 no6 p28 Ap/My 2017

Love Fearlessly color *Ebony* v72 no4 p36 F 2017

MATTIE JAMES color *Ebony* v72 no6 p27 Ap/My 2017

No Longer 'Hidden Figures' color *Ebony* v72 no3 p30 D 2016/Ja 2017

RADAR GIFT GUIDE color *Ebony* v72 no3 p46 D 2016/Ja 2017

Spotlight on Brittani "Brittsense" Sensabaugh color *Ebony* v72 no3 p43 D 2016/Ja 2017

TEYANA TAYLOR color *Ebony* v72 no3 p40 D 2016/Ja 2017

TRISTAN 'MACK' WILDS color *Ebony* v72 no4 p34 F 2017

The "Underdog" Rises color *Ebony* v72 no8 p28 Je 2017

Visual Artist Paul Branton color *Ebony* v72 no6 p20 Ap/My 2017

Write the Power! color *Ebony* v72 no3 p44 D 2016/Ja 2017

CROSS, MIRIAM

The Best Bank for You cartoon *Kiplinger's Personal Finance* v71 no7 p26 Jl 2017

Break the Cycle of Recurring Fees cartoon *Kiplinger's Personal Finance* v71 no1 p31 Ja 2017

BUYING A NEW CAR? CHECK THE RESALE VALUE color *Kiplinger's Personal Finance* v71 no10 p13 O 2017

Cut Car Insurance Rates color *Kiplinger's Personal Finance* v71 no5 p43 My 2017

Disaster Relief color *Kiplinger's Personal Finance* v71 no12 p24 D 2017

Hire a Pro to Plan Your Trip color *Kiplinger's Personal Finance* v71 no11 p70 N 2017

MONEY MADE SIMPLE [Cover story] color *Kiplinger's Personal Finance* v71 no5 p24 My 2017

MONEY MANNERS cartoon *Kiplinger's Personal Finance* v71 no4 p48 Ap 2017

MONEY MANNERS cartoon *Kiplinger's Personal Finance* v71 no7 p44 Jl 2017

MONEY MANNERS chart color *Kiplinger's Personal Finance* v70 no12 p41 D 2016

MONEY MANNERS color *Kiplinger's Personal Finance* v71 no12 p37 D 2017

A New Take on Shipshape color *Kiplinger's Personal Finance* v71 no3 p71 Mr 2017

The Nongambler's Guide to Vegas color *Kiplinger's Personal Finance* v71 no8 p34 Ag 2017

PLAYING YOUR CARDS RIGHT color *Kiplinger's Personal Finance* v71 no2 p46 F 2017

A TIERED APPROACH TO ECONOMY CLASS color *Kiplinger's Personal Finance* v71 no2 p16 F 2017

Travel Abroad for Low-Cost Care bw color *Kiplinger's Personal Finance* v71 no1 p62 Ja 2017

When It Pays to Bend the Rules color *Kiplinger's Personal Finance* v71 no10 p44 O 2017

The Worry-Free Way to Rent a Car color *Kiplinger's Personal Finance* v71 no8 p69 Ag 2017

Cross, Ryan

Elderly chimps may get Alzheimer's disease color *Science* v357 no6350 p440 Ag 4 2017

The inside story on 20,000 vertebrates color *Science* v357 no6353 p742 Ag 25 2017

'Scientific wellness' study divides researchers color *Science* v357 no6349 p345 Jl 28 2017

Cross, Sandy

Nurses We Love K. Cicero color *Prevention* v69 no5 p42 My 2017

Cross-country skiing—Competitions

Ice the Drought J. Fuchs and T. Keith color *Sports Illustrated* v126 no8 p26 Mr 20 2017

Cross-cultural communication

3 Situations Where Cross-Cultural Communication Breaks Down G. Toegel and Barsoux *Harvard Business Review Digital Articles* p2 Je 8 2016

Leading Across Cultures Requires Flexibility and Curiosity D. Rowland *Harvard Business Review Digital Articles* p2 My 30 2016

Learning the Language of Indirectness A. Molinsky and M. Hahn *Harvard Business Review Digital Articles* p2 My 6 2015

Cross-cultural counseling

Will That Cross-Cultural Coach Really Help Your Team? A. Molinsky and C. Höferle *Harvard Business Review Digital Articles* p2 Ap 29 2015

Cross-cultural differences

African farmers' kids ace willpower test B. BOWER *Science News* v192 no1 p13 Ag 5 2017

All Quiet(ed) on the Eastern Front A. WALDRON *Weekly Standard* v22 no5 p14 O 10 2016

BEING THE BOSS IN BRUSSELS, BOSTON, AND BEIJING: IF YOU WANT TO SUCCEED, YOU'LL NEED TO ADAPT E. MEYER color graph il img *Harvard Business Review* v95 no4 p70 Jl/Ag 2017

Bookends: What distinguishes cultural exchange from cultural appropriation? R. Galchen and A. Holmes *New York Times Book Review* p27 Je 11 2017

Cultural Differences Are More Complicated than What Country You're From A. Molinsky *Harvard Business Review Digital Articles* p2 Ja 14 2016

Emotional Intelligence Doesn't Translate Across Borders A. Molinsky *Harvard Business Review Digital Articles* p2 Ap 20 2015

Resolve a Fight with a Remote Colleague A. Gallo *Harvard Business Review Digital Articles* p2 N 30 2015

To Connect Across Cultures, Find Out What You Have in Common A. Molinsky and Sujin Jang *Harvard Business Review Digital Articles* p2 Ja 20 2016

When Cultural Differences Interfere with Your Time A. Molinsky *Harvard Business Review Digital Articles* p2 Ap 14 2015

Will That Cross-Cultural Coach Really Help Your Team? A. Molinsky and C. Höferle *Harvard Business Review Digital Articles* p2 Ap 29 2015

Cross-cultural orientation

The Mistake Most Managers Make with Cross-Cultural Training A. Molinsky *Harvard Business Review Digital Articles* p2 Ja 15 2015

To Develop Cultural Dexterity, Seek It Out B. Banks *Harvard Business Review Digital Articles* p2 Je 24 2016

Cross-functional teams

75% of Cross-Functional Teams Are Dysfunctional B. Tabrizi *Harvard Business Review Digital Articles* p2 Je 23 2015

Develop Your Company's Cross-Functional Capabilities P. Leinwand, C. Mainardi et al *Harvard Business Review Digital Articles* p2 F 2 2016

Social Media Is Too Important to Be Left to the Marketing Department K. A. Quesenberry *Harvard Business Review Digital Articles* p2 Ap 19 2016

Cross selling

5 Ways to Increase Your Cross-Selling J. Senior, T. Springer et al *Harvard Business Review Digital Articles* p2 N 22 2016

Cross-selling financial services

How Fancy Private Bankers Cross-Sell N. Weinberg graph *Bloomberg Businessweek* no4510 p35 F 6 2017

Cross Timbers (Okla. & Tex.)

The Cross Timbers J. GIFFORD *American Forests* v123 no1 p32 Wint/Spr 2017

Cross-training (Sports)

Find Your Fit N. Fyffe and J. Shepherd color *Dressage Today* v23 no5 p28 Ja 2017

Technique Rx A. FELLER *Dance Magazine* v91 no1 p96 Ja 2017

Crossan, Sarah

We Come Apart *Publishers Weekly* v264 no17 p94 Ap 24 2017

Crossbows

THE FINE PRINT B. HEAVEY color *Field & Stream* v122 no5 p90 O 2017

Crossbreeding

$100 MORE PER COW! G. Johnston *Successful Farming* v115 no5 p60 Mid-Mr 2017

The Science of Making Food Taste Better T. John color *Time* v189 no5 p12 F 13 2017

CrossFit Inc.

CROSS FAT GAIN OFF YOUR LIST J. WUEBBEN color *Muscle & Performance* v8 no12 p16 D 2016

Welcome to the Sufferfest [Cover story] T. DASWICK color *Men's Health* v32 no4 p10 My 2017

Crossing Fingers, Kissing Hands (Poem)

Crossing Fingers, Kissing Hands M. VINCENZ *Nation* v305 no6 p36 S 11 2017

Crossland, Cathy L.

Less is more diag graph *Phi Delta Kappan* v98 no7 p55 Ap 2017

CROSSMAN, C. A.

Tokens of Our Affection cartoon *O, The Oprah Magazine* p17 F 2017

Crossman, Matt

What's on the Mizzou Training Table? color *Missouri Life* v44 no6 p66 S 2017

Crossovers (Highway engineering)

The Perfect Crossing T. De Chant cartoon *Wired* v24 no11 p66 N 2016

Crossword puzzles

IT PAYS TO INCREASE YOUR Word Power E. COX and H. RATHVON *Reader's Digest* v188 no1125 p145 N 2016

Just for the Halibut S. SPADACCINI *AARP: The Magazine* v59 no4A p71 Je/Jl 2016

MY HOMETOWN PAPER: Don Gonyea D. Gonyea color *Columbia Journalism Review* v56 no1 p50 Spr 2017

Crotalus molossus

Black-Tailed Rattlesnakes N. Austin *Arizona Highways* v93 no1 p13 Ja 2017

Crothall, Heather

The Thread *New York Times Magazine* p7 Jl 2 2017

Croton (Genus)

AROUND THE GARDEN S. Bender color *Southern Living* v52 no11 p51 N 2017

Crouch, Andy

THE 2017 BOOK of the YEAR color *Christianity Today* v61 no1 p57 Ja/F 2017

Crouch, Blake

Dark Matter *Publishers Weekly* v263 no40 p118 O 3 2016

Crouch, Brock—Interviews

BROCK CROUCH P. Harrington color *Snowboarder* v29 no2 p44 O 2016

CROUCH, MICHELLE

13 Home Security Secrets You Should Know color *Reader's Digest* v189 no1130 p130 My 2017

13 Mind-Blowing Discoveries Scientists Made This Year color *Reader's Digest* v190 no1133 p130 S 2017

13 Things Cruise Lines Won't Tell You *Reader's Digest* v188 no1125 p138 N 2016

13 Things Garbage Collectors Want You to Know color *Reader's Digest* v190 no1134 p128 O 2017

13 Things Pet Stores Won't Tell You color *Reader's Digest* v189 no1131 p128 Je 2017

13 Things Your Dreams Reveal About You *Reader's Digest* v188 no1124 p132 O 2016

13 Things Your Pharmacist Won't Tell You color *Reader's Digest* v189 no1129 p124 Ap 2017

all the feels *Parents* v92 no8 p136 Ag 2017

ARE YOU GETTING $CAMMED? *Scholastic Choices* v32 no6 p16 Mr 2017

Farmers' Market [Cover story] color *Prevention* v69 no7 p20 Jl 2017

Generation Z Z Z Z Z Z Z Z img *Scholastic Choices* v33 no1 p10 S 2017

manage your kid's digital life *Parents* v91 no12 p42 D 2016

One Deadly Night *Scholastic Choices* v32 no7 p10 Ap 2017

raise a science lover *Parents* v92 no2 p56 F 2017

Scientists share 50 food facts to help you live longer (and lose weight too) [Cover story] *Reader's Digest* v189 no1127 p63 F 2017

THE SECRET LIFE of SCHOOL cartoon color *Parents* v92 no9 p66 S 2017

SECRETS of People with HIGHLY STRESSFUL JOBS cartoon *Prevention* v69 no2 p64 F 2017

THE SINISTER SCIENCE OF IRRESISTIBLE JUNK FOOD *Scholastic Choices* v32 no4 p6 Ja 2017

Crovisier, J.

Seasonal exposure of carbon dioxide ice on the nucleus of comet 67P/Churyumov-Gerasimenko bibl bw graph *Science* v354 no6319 p1563 D 23 2016

CROW, CODY

Change It Up! color *Horse & Rider* v56 no9 p55 S 2017

Crow, Sheryl, 1962-

JULY'S HOTTEST EVENTS *Indianapolis Monthly* v40 no11 p20 Jl 2017

Making Myself Heard L. B. Ray color *InStyle* v24 no7 p52 Jl 2017

Crow, Sheryl, 1962-—Interviews

How to choose a happy life, by Sheryl Crow M. Rollins color *Redbook* p103 Je 2017

Sheryl Crow B. HIATT cartoon *Rolling Stone* no1286 p82 My 4 2017

SHERYL CROW REBORN M. Vain color *Entertainment Weekly* no1462 p60 Ap 21 2017

Crowd funding

BRINGING HERITAGE TO LIFE color *Walrus* v14 no6 p26 Jl/Ag 2017

Crowdfunding American Protest J. MCCARTNEY bw color *Publishers Weekly* v264 no39 p59 S 25 2017

Don't Expect New Crowdfunding Rules to Create a Startup Boom W. Frick *Harvard Business Review Digital Articles* p2 My 16 2016

Expand innovation finance via crowdfunding O. Sorenson, V. Assenova et al bibl color graph map *Science* v354 no6319 p1526 D 23 2016

Group Effort W. YAN *Discover* v38 no8 p16 O 2017

Kazoo Magazine Aims to Encourage Girls in Science B. RADFORD *Skeptical Inquirer* v41 no3 p7 My/Je 2017

Kickstarter Publishing in 2016 C. Reid *Publishers Weekly* v264 no6 p7 F 6 2017

PEOPLE POWER FOR POSITIVE CHANGE S. DANIELS *Iceland Review* v55 no2 p46 Mr/Ap 2017

The Unique Value of Crowdfunding Is Not Money—It's Community E. Mollick *Harvard Business Review Digital Articles* p2 Ap 21 2016

Crowd funding—Computer network resources

FREE MARKET PHILANTHROPY S. ADAMS color *Forbes* v198 no6 p92 N 8 2016

Crowd out (Music)

GO J. FOUMBERG, J. HARDBERGER et al bw color *Chicago* v66 no10 p105 O 2017

Crowder, Bland

CH-CH-CH-CH-CHANGES *Virginia Living* v15 no3 p29 Ap 2017

FREE RANGE? An "old hen" found in Harrisonburg was caught before she could work her prohibited ways *Virginia Living* v15 no2 p23 F 2017

HOW DRY WE WERE: Exploring Prohibition at the Library of Virginia bw *Virginia Living* v15 no5 p27 Ag 2017

NOT UP TO SNUFF? Soldier wannabes turned away for illiteracy *Virginia Living* v15 no4 p27 Je 2017

SALES BLITZ: Ford revs up the pressure to buy in Princess Anne color *Virginia Living* v15 no5 p29 Ag 2017

Smart Plants: The Flora of Virginia's new mobile app is the 21st century version of the classic botany card *Virginia Living* v15 no6 p67 O 2017

TESTING? TESTING? *Virginia Living* v15 no1 p27 D 2016

Crowder, Larry B.

Committing to socially responsible seafood color *Science* v356 no6341 p912 Je 1 2017

Ocean Research Priorities: Similarities and Differences among Scientists, Policymakers, and Fishermen in the United States *BioScience* v67 no5 p418 My 2017

Science-based management in decline in the Southern Ocean bibl map *Science* v354 no6309 p185 O 14 2016

Crowder, Lucien

Editor's note *Bulletin of the Atomic Scientists* v72 no6 p359 N 2016

Editor's note *Bulletin of the Atomic Scientists* v73 no2 p127 Mr 2017

Editor's note *Bulletin of the Atomic Scientists* v73 no3 p196 My 2017

Crowdflash Ltd.

A Digital Fact-Checker Fights Fake News D. G. Herbert color *Bloomberg Businessweek* no4507 p27 Ja 16 2017

Crowds

 See also

 Demonstrations (Collective behavior)

Celebrating the 50th Anniversary of the SUMMER OF LOVE 1967-2017 R. LOVE *AARP: The Magazine* v60 no5A p29 Ag/S 2017

CLIMBING AT THE NEW cartoon *Climbing* no356 p18 S/O 2017

Crowdsourcing

4 Mistakes That Kill Crowdsourcing Efforts M. W. Van Alstyne, A. Di Fiore et al *Harvard Business Review Digital Articles* p2 Jl 21 2017

Can the World Be Your doctor? R. LALIBERTE cartoon *Men's Health* v32 no9 p119 N 2017

Crowdsourced Products Sell Better When They're Marketed That Way M. Schreier, H. Nishikawa et al *Harvard Business Review Digital Articles* p2 N 8 2016

THE MAGIC OF "CROWDSOURCING" il *Harvard Business Review* v95 no1 p28 Ja/F 2017

Something for Nothing C. DEDERER color *Rodale's Organic Life* v2 no7 p31 D 2016/Ja 2017

Strategies for Crowdsourcing Your Job Search L. Zoref *Harvard Business Review Digital Articles* p2 My 8 2015

Your Biggest Social Media Fans Might Not Be Your Best Customers A. Samuel *Harvard Business Review Digital Articles* p2 D 24 2014

Crowdsourcing—Economic aspects

PAYING FOR ONLINE REVIEWS CAN BACKFIRE *Harvard Business Review* v95 no5 p22 S/O 2017

Crowdsourcing—Methodology

Why Some Crowdsourcing Efforts Work and Others Don't L. Dahlander and H. Piezunka *Harvard Business Review Digital Articles* p2 F 21 2017

Crowe, Cameron, 1957-

Harry Styles' New Direction [Cover story] color *Rolling Stone* no1286 p20 My 4 2017

JERRY MAGUIRE F. Kaplan color *Sound & Vision* v82 no5 p70 Je 2017

Crowe, David

Lincoln in the Bardo: A Novel color *Christian Century* v134 no10 p37 My 10 2017

Crowe, James E., Jr.

A"Trojan horse" bispecific-antibody strategy for broad protection against ebolaviruses bibl graph *Science* v354 no6310 p350 O 21 2016

CROWE, NANCY

THE BRIDGE TO COLLEGE color *Indianapolis Monthly* v41 no2 p144 S 2017

GET SMART: WHEN DECIDING WHICH SCHOOL IS THE BEST FIT FOR YOUR FAMILY, THESE ARE JUST A FEW VARIABLES TO CONSIDER *Indianapolis Monthly* p102 N 2017

Crowe, Russell

Artists color *Time* v189 no16/17 p40 My 1-8 2017

CURTIS HANSON color *Entertainment Weekly* no1446/1447 p96 D 2016/Ja 2017

Crowe, Shani

Force of Nature M. Carlos color *Essence* v48 no3 p43 Jl 2017

How We Communicate Now C. de León, A. L. Greco et al bw color *Glamour* v115 no3 p52 Mr 2017

Crowe, Vance

VANCE CROWE: MEET THE MAN BUILDING A VAST NET-WORK THROUGH TRIBES TO RALLY AGAINST THE PSEUDOSCIENCE ATTACKING GMOS J. Scott *Successful Farming* v115 no9 p10 Ag 2017

CROWE, VICTORIA

SUMMER MOTORING color *House Beautiful* p156 Ag 2017

Crowell, Hannah

FAIRY-TALE ENDING L. O'KEEFFE cartoon color *Better Homes & Gardens* v95 no2 p90 F 2016

Crowell, Miranda

YOU'RE INVITED TO DINNER WITH FRIENDS color *Sunset* v239 no4 p54 O 2017

Crowley, Alex

Poetry bw color *Publishers Weekly* v263 no51 p86 D 12 2016

Poetry color *Publishers Weekly* v264 no26 p97 Je 26 2017

Science bw color *Publishers Weekly* v263 no51 p106 D 12 2016

Science bw color *Publishers Weekly* v264 no26 p115 Je 26 2017

Crowley, Chris

home & help img *New York* p96 Mr 6 2017

In Conversation: A Jewish Grandma and a Korean Grandma on Their Dumplings img *New York* v49 no25 p102 D 12 2016

Younger Next Year cartoon color *AARP: The Magazine* v59 no6A p32 O/N 2016

Crowley, Claire

The Art of Sound color *Sound & Vision* v81 no9 p20 N 2016

Bedazzled! color *Sound & Vision* v82 no6 p22 Jl/Ag 2017

Bone Records color *Sound & Vision* v81 no9 p26 N 2016

Charlie Daniels Explores the Sound Quality Trail on Night Hawk bw color *Sound & Vision* v82 no1 p22 Ja 2017

Class D-Mystified bw color *Sound & Vision* v82 no5 p16 Je 2017

Expanded Oscar Coverage color *Sound & Vision* v82 no6 p17 Jl/Ag 2017

The Future of Audio color *Sound & Vision* v81 no9 p16 N 2016

The Future of Fiber color *Sound & Vision* v82 no1 p16 Ja 2017

Gary Brooker and Procol Harum Fuse Sonic Shades of Both Past and Present With Novum color *Sound & Vision* v82 no6 p24 Jl/Ag 2017

Greg Lake and ELP Welcome Us Back to the Hi-Fi Show That Never Ends bw color *Sound & Vision* v81 no10 p24 D 2016

HDR Is Getting Support From color *Sound & Vision* v82 no2 p17 F/Mr 2017

Hearing Is Believing color *Sound & Vision* v82 no6 p18 Jl/Ag 2017

Jerry Seinfeld's color *Sound & Vision* v82 no5 p17 Je 2017

Lee Loughnane and Chicago Assert Their 4.0 Authority on Blu-ray bw color *Sound & Vision* v81 no9 p22 N 2016

LG's Channel Plus color *Sound & Vision* v81 no10 p17 D 2016

MQA Is Coming to NAD's color *Sound & Vision* v81 no9 p17 N 2016

The Neal Morse Band Progresses Into the Realization of a Fine Sonic Dream color *Sound & Vision* v82 no5 p24 Je 2017

New Gear color *Sound & Vision* v82 no2 p30 F/Mr 2017

Noise Cancellation Goes Blue color *Sound & Vision* v82 no2 p18 F/Mr 2017

Now Here This color *Sound & Vision* v81 no9 p18 N 2016

OLED Turns 30 color *Sound & Vision* v82 no6 p16 Jl/Ag 2017

Out of the Blue color *Sound & Vision* v82 no5 p22 Je 2017

Party Animal color *Sound & Vision* v82 no1 p18 Ja 2017

Rated XXX color *Sound & Vision* v82 no6 p20 Jl/Ag 2017

Retro Elegance color *Sound & Vision* v82 no5 p20 Je 2017

Sonic Boom color *Sound & Vision* v81 no10 p2 D 2016

Sony Spiffed Up PS4 Pro color *Sound & Vision* v82 no1 p17 Ja 2017

Storage Solutions color *Sound & Vision* v81 no9 p29 N 2016

The Sweet Spot color *Sound & Vision* v82 no2 p20 F/Mr 2017

Tell It Like It Is color *Sound & Vision* v81 no10 p18 D 2016

This One Goes to 99 color *Sound & Vision* v81 no9 p28 N 2016

This Year's Model color *Sound & Vision* v82 no5 p18 Je 2017

Vive la Différence! color *Sound & Vision* v82 no1 p20 Ja 2017

Watching Your DVR From Anywhere color *Sound & Vision* v81 no9 p24 N 2016

Winning Wireless color *Sound & Vision* v81 no10 p16 D 2016

Wireless Hi-Res color *Sound & Vision* v82 no2 p16 F/Mr 2017

Crowley, David

DEATH OF A DYSTOPIAN A. WILKINSON bw cartoon *New Yorker* v93 no8 p22 Ap 10 2017

Crowley, Dennis

LEARNING NOT TO LEAD P. Marinova color *Fortune* v176 no2 p38 Ag 1 2017

CROWN, JUDITH

CONAGRA'S NEXT ACT color *Chicago* v65 no12 p32 D 2016

THE MUNOZ WAY cartoon color *Chicago* v65 no11 p19 N 2016

OUTWARD BOUND cartoon graph *Chicago* v66 no2 p13 F 2017

THE RETURN OF LUXE LIVING color *Chicago* v65 no12 p27 D 2016

Crown, The (Film)

Nice Hat M. Z. SEITZ img *New York* v49 no23 p84 N 14 2016

Crown, The (TV program)

ANOTHER SIDE OF MATT SMITH S. Vilkomerson color *Entertainment Weekly* no1439 p24 N 11 2016

BEING JOHN LITHGOW J. RUSSELL *TV Guide* v65 no11 p26 Mr 6 2017

The Crown M. ROUSH *TV Guide* v64 no46 p12 N 7 2016

The CROWN SEASON 2 S. Perry color *Entertainment Weekly* no1478 / 1479 p24 Ag 18-25 2017

Director Stephen Daldry on The Crown S. GUTIERREZ *British Heritage Travel* v37 no6 p30 N/D 2016

THE GOLDEN GLOBES: Who Should Win? M. ROUSH *TV Guide* v65 no2 p8 Ja 2 2017

A Great Family Business J. Freedland color *New York Review of Books* v64 no5 p16 Mr 23 2017

The Must List color *Entertainment Weekly* no1439 p3 N 11 2016

Ripped From the History Books? C. Agard color *Entertainment*

Weekly no1473 p51 Jl 7 2017

The royal treatment P. TREBLE color *Maclean's* v129 no44 p111 N 7 2016

A Sprawling Drama About Elizabeth II Aims to Be Netflix's New Crown Jewel E. Dockterman color *Time* v188 no19 p53 N 7 2016

'They Are Not Themselves': The Lives of the English Queens A. A. O'Donnell color *America* v216 no7 p38 Ap 3 2017

What to Watch R. Rahman, K. P. Sullivan et al color *Entertainment Weekly* no1438 p55 N 4 2016

Crown glass (Optics)

BULL'S-EYE GLASS color *Old House Journal* v45 no4 p78 Je 2017

Crown Media Holdings Inc.

THE QUEEN OF CHRISTMAS M. Callahan color *Bloomberg Businessweek* no4499 p79 N 14 2016

Crown Resorts Ltd.

JAMES AND THE GIANT BREACH W. D. COHAN color *Vanity Fair* p114 Hollywood 2017 Supplement

Crownline Boats Inc.

Crown Jewel A. JONES *Boating World* v38 no5 p32 My 2017

Crows—Behavior

The Crow's Song B. HEINRICH color *Natural History* v125 no11 p10 N 2017

Crowson, Dan

READER GALLERY bw color *Astronomy* v45 no11 p72 N 2017

READER GALLERY color *Astronomy* v44 no12 p70 D 2016

Crowston, Jonathan

Relief for retinal neurons under pressure bibl diag *Science* v355 no6326 p688 F 17 2017

Crowther, Thomas W.

Forest value: More than commercial *Science* v354 no6319 p1541 D 23 2016

Positive biodiversity-productivity relationship predominant in global forests bibl chart graph map *Science* v354 no6309 paaf8957-1 O 14 2016

Croxton, Ryan—Interviews

Bivalve Revival V. HUBBARD *Virginia Living* p19 2017 Smoke & Salt

Croxton, Travis—Interviews

Bivalve Revival V. HUBBARD *Virginia Living* p19 2017 Smoke & Salt

Croy, Oliver

Small Victories M. Moses bw color *American Craft* v77 no3 p24 Je/Jl 2017

Crubézy, Eric

Ancient genomic changes associated with domestication of the horse color diag *Science* v356 no6336 p442 Ap 28 2017

Crucible, The (Theatrical production)

10 — THE CRUCIBLE M. Snetiker *Entertainment Weekly* no1444/1445 p118 D 16 2016

Cruciferae

See also

Arabidopsis

Veggies du jour R. Begun chart color *Yoga Journal* no289 p70 F 2017

Wild Mustard and the Way of Zen W. Johnson color *Tricycle: The Buddhist Review* v26 no4 p27 Summ 2017

Crucifixion in art

Crucifixion H. J. Hornik and M. C. Parsons color *Christian Century* v133 no23 p47 N 9 2016

Cruelty

See also

Torture

Cruickshank, Dan

LONDON'S BORDER COUNTRY: From a priory hospital in the fields, to the Huguenots, Jack the Ripper and the Kray twins, Spitalfields has always been considered a place apart R. McWilliam *History Today* v67 no7 p100 Jl 2017

Cruise, Tom, 1962-

THE ALL-TIME GREATEST TOM CRUISE PERFORMANCES C. Nashawaty color *Entertainment Weekly* no1485 p39 O 6 2017

Cruise industry

13 Things Cruise Lines Won't Tell You M. CROUCH *Reader's Digest* v188 no1125 p138 N 2016

Cruises Could Be Big Winners in Cuba C. Palmeri color graph *Bloomberg Businessweek* no4522 p23 My 15 2017

ON A DREAM VACATION YOU WOULD M. ORWOLL, P. BRADY et al bw color *Conde Nast Traveler* v52 no7 p48 Ag 2017

Cruise missiles

The ambiguity challenge: Why the world needs a multilateral nuclear cruise missile agreement C. Parthemore bibl *Bulletin of the Atomic Scientists* v73 no3 p154 My 2017

Cruise ships—Evaluation

DUFFIELD 58: TRADITIONAL LINES AND A DOUG ZURN DESIGN CREATE A COUPLES CRUISER WITH RANGE AND COMFORT M. WERLING color *Sea Magazine* v109 no6 p38 Je 2017

FULL THROTTLE TO FT. LAUDERDALE [Cover story] color *Power & Motoryacht* v34 no11 p104 N 2017

Rising Tides J. von Sothen color *Bon Appetit* no1 p46 F 2017

Viking 93 MY S. Murray color *Power & Motoryacht* v34 no11 p76 N 2017

Cruise ships—History

On the Waterfront: Millions of people live, work and play along New York's rivers and harbor. Here, a snapshot of the marine traffic on one recent day—March 22—shows the amazing range of activity H. HUSSEIN *Smithsonian* v48 no2 p36 My 2017

Cruise ships—Safety measures

The Hard Way B. Bleyer cartoon color *Sail* v47 no12 p12 D 2016

Cruisers (Warships)

Boat Porn M. PETERS color *Power & Motoryacht* v33 no3 p36 Mr 2017

Crunch Time B. PIKE *Power & Motoryacht* v33 no3 p118 Mr 2017

Cruisers Yachts (Company)

Cruisers 50 Cantius D. J. Harding color *Power & Motoryacht* v34 no6 p28 Je 2017

CRUISERS 60 CANTIUS FLYBRIDGE M. WERLING *Sea Magazine* v108 no10 p40 O 2016

Crum, Alia

Stress Can Be a Good Thing If You Know How to Use It *Harvard Business Review Digital Articles* p2 S 3 2015

Crum, Thomas

Stress Can Be a Good Thing If You Know How to Use It *Harvard Business Review Digital Articles* p2 S 3 2015

Crumbley, Anna M.

Industrial biomanufacturing: The future of chemical production bibl chart color diag graph *Science* v355 no6320 p1 Ja 6 2017

Crumlin, Ethan

Atomic-layered Au clusters on α-MoC as catalysts for the low-temperature water-gas shift reaction chart diag graph *Science* v357 no6349 p389 Jl 28 2017

Crump, James

Antonio LOPEZ *Interview* v47 no2 p84 Mr 2017

Crust vegetation

The Desert's Living Skin K. MAST color *Discover* v38 no6 p22 Jl/Ag 2017

Crustacea

Some herbivorous dinos ate critters C. GRAMLING color *Science News* v192 no7 p12 O 28 2017

TIPPING THE SCALES: A SALUTE TO SOME COLOSSAL CRUSTACEANS *Yankee* p98 Jl 2017

Underwater pollinators color *National Wildlife (World Edition)* v55 no4 p8 Je/Jl 2017

Crutchfield, Allison

Crutchfield Sisters J. PELLY color *Rolling Stone* no1295 p43 S 7 2017

Crutchfield, Katie

Crutchfield Sisters J. PELLY color *Rolling Stone* no1295 p43 S 7 2017

WAXAHATCHEE N. Feeney color *Entertainment Weekly* no1476 p61 Ag 4 2017

Crutchfield, Will

GOINGS ON ABOUT TOWN bw *New Yorker* v93 no20 p5 Jl 10 2017

Crute, Sheree

Missouri, Compromised color *Washington Monthly* v49 no3-5 p40 Mr-My 2017

Crux (Constellation)

Heterostructures
Nanocrystals
Semiconductors

THE CRYSTAL METHOD color *InStyle* v24 no3 p328 Mr 2017
Robust spin-polarized midgap states at step edges of topological crystalline insulators P. Sessi, D. Di Sante et al bibl graph *Science* v354 no6317 p1269 D 9 2016

Crystals—Evaluation

The Most Insane Items in the Goop Gift Guide* D. Coggan color *Entertainment Weekly* no1442 p12 D 2 2016 Rebellious Special Issue

Crystals—Therapeutic use

A MANI WITH CRYSTAL POWER color *Health* v31 no1 p14 Ja 2017

Csatari, Jeff

BE A BACKYARD BADASS color *Men's Health* v32 no6 p100 Ag 2017

THE ILLUSTRATOR'S APPRENTICE *Saturday Evening Post* v288 no6 p56 N/D 2016

Csatari, Joseph

THE ILLUSTRATOR'S APPRENTICE J. Csatari *Saturday Evening Post* v288 no6 p56 N/D 2016

Csere, Csaba

Bullet with Butterfly Wings color *Car & Driver* v63 no2 p90 Ag 2017

RUNWAY MODEL diag *Car & Driver* v62 no10 p20 Ap 2017

TURBO DOGS color *Car & Driver* v63 no4 p30 O 2017

Csi (Company)

Committee for Skeptical Inquiry Timeline, 2001-2016 K. Frazier *Skeptical Inquirer* v40 no6 p51 N/D 2016

CSI: Crime Scene Investigation (TV program)

2004 M. Snetiker color *Entertainment Weekly* no1435 p49 O 14 2016

Csicsvari, J.

Superficial layers of the medial entorhinal cortex replay independently of the hippocampus bibl graph *Science* v355 no6321 p1 Ja 13 2017

Csokas, Marton

Into the Badlands J. Russell *TV Guide* v65 no11 p43 Mr 6 2017

Csorba, Emerson

The Problem with Millennials? They're Way Too Hard on Themselves *Harvard Business Review Digital Articles* p2 My 2 2016

CST Group (Company)

Services *Virginia Living* p107 2017 Best 20of Virginia

Ctrl (Music)

The Must List color *Entertainment Weekly* no1470 p1 Je 16 2017

Cuarón, Alfonso, 1961-

Future Shock A. Riesman img *New York* v49 no26 p73 D 26 2016

Cuarón, Jonás, 1981-

Desierto C. Nashawaty color *Entertainment Weekly* no1436/1437 p84 O 21 2016

Cuba

Cuba Profile *Congressional Digest* v95 no10 p3 D 2016

IN SEARCH OF THE Cuban Paso Fino M. del Carmen Martínez color *Equus* no474 p51 Mr 2017

Off the Charts B. ELLISON color map *Power & Motoryacht* v33 no4 p32 Ap 2017

Cuba—Armed Forces

FLASHBACK *MHQ: Quarterly Journal of Military History* v29 no3 p4 Spr 2017

Cuba—Commerce—United States

The Potential and Pitfalls of Doing Business in Cuba P. G. Alonso and A. Lee *Harvard Business Review Digital Articles* p2 Mr 16 2016

Cuba—Description & travel

Cuba Libre A. Ellin color *Money* v45 no10 p100 N 2016

THE CUBA SHORT LIST color *Conde Nast Traveler* v51 no10 p36 N 2016

How You Should Really Do Cuba cartoon chart *Conde Nast Traveler* v52 no3 p100 Mr 2017

ISLAND HOP P. GUZMÁN color *Conde Nast Traveler* v51 no10 p34 N 2016

A Tale of Two Cubas [Cover story] R. RADOSH and A. RADOSH color *Weekly Standard* v22 no40 p17 Je 26 2017

Cuba—Economic conditions

What You Might Not Know About the Cuban Economy J. I.

Dominguez *Harvard Business Review Digital Articles* p2 Ag 17 2015

Cuba—Foreign economic relations

CUBA TANTALIZES U.S. INDUSTRY diag *Fortune* v174 no8 p16 D 15 2016

Cuba—Foreign relations—United States

Advice for Trump on Post-Fidel Cuba J. Bruno *Washington Monthly* p1 Ja/F 2017

Cuba and America, the Next Generation V. Garcia *Wilson Quarterly* v40 no4 p1 Fall 2016

The Cuban Litmus Test A. J. Stavridis *Time* v188 no24 p49 D 12 2016

Doing Business in a Post-Fidel Cuba P. G. Alonso and A. Lee *Harvard Business Review Digital Articles* p2 D 19 2016

How to Keep U.S.-Cuba Relations on Track bw *Bloomberg Businessweek* no4502 p14 D 5 2016

Legislative Background on the Cuba Embargo *Congressional Digest* v95 no10 p11 D 2016

President Obama's Cuba Policy *Congressional Digest* v95 no10 p6 D 2016

The Pros and Cons of the United States' Embargo Against Cuba *Congressional Digest* v95 no10 p14 D 2016

U.S.-Cuba Relations Timeline *Congressional Digest* v95 no10 p2 D 2016

U.S. Embargo on Cuba *Congressional Digest* v95 no10 p1 D 2016

Cuba—Foreign relations—United States—History—20th century

FORBIDDEN FLICKS: The U.S. export ban didn't keep Cubans from watching movies they loved A. Crawford *Smithsonian* v48 no4 p12 Jl/Ag 2017

Cuba—History

A New Day for Cuba? R. ZISSOU *New York Times Upfront* v149 no7 p12 Ja 9 2017

WHIPLASH AND BACKLASH IN THE REPUBLIC OF CUBA S. Slade color *Reason* v49 no5 p28 O 2017

Cuban, Mark, 1958-

CALL IT, FRIENDO J. FIELDEN color *Esquire* p18 My 2017

CUBAN REVOLUTION S. HOLLANDSWORTH *Texas Monthly* v45 no4 p110 Ap 2017

NeNe Leakes for President! M. Snetiker color *Entertainment Weekly* no1436/1437 p16 O 21 2016

Cuban, Mark, 1958-—Interviews

HOW TO GET TO $1 MILLION [Cover story] color *Money* v46 no8 p44 S 2017

JUST MY TYPE D. Patrick and T. Keith color *Sports Illustrated* v125 no12 p23 O 10 2016

Mark Cuban GETS LOUD A. GRANT color *Esquire* p64 My 2017

Cuban boa

Bats beware: Cuban boas hunt by the numbers color *National Wildlife (World Edition)* v55 no6 p9 O/N 2017

Cuban cooking

PICK-ME-UP ARTISTS A. Limpert color *Washingtonian Magazine* v52 no7 p141 Ap 2017

Cuban treefrog

THE NATURAL EXPLANATION J. SERRAO color *Natural History* v125 no10 p2 O 2017

Cubans

The 8,000-Mile Shortcut K. Vick color map *Time* v188 no16/17 p69 O 24 2016

Cubans—Attitudes

FROM THE ARCHIVES B. DOHERTY, M. WELCH et al cartoon *Reason* v49 no2 p70 Je 2017

Cubans—Social conditions

Hot Spot L. J. Wertheim and T. Keith color *Sports Illustrated* v126 no13 p16 My 8 2017

Cubans—United States

Cuba and America, the Next Generation V. Garcia *Wilson Quarterly* v40 no4 p1 Fall 2016

Cuba—Social life & customs

Inside Cuba A. Rademacher bibl *Science* v355 no6320 p34 Ja 6 2017

Cubcrafters (Company)

XCUB GETS NON-TSO'D AVIONICS color *Flying* v144 no9 p16 S 2017

Cubie, Doreen

Broader Role for Botanical Gardens color *National Wildlife (World Edition)* v55 no3 p12 Ap/My 2017

A Flight for Their Lives color *National Wildlife (World Edition)* v54 no6 p30 O/N 2016

Cubism

What Picasso inspired in Prague R. Pepall bw color *Magazine Antiques* v183 no6 p108 N/D 2016

CUCCINELLO, HAYLEY

America's Richest Celebrities color *Forbes* v198 no9 p18 D 30 2016

BOOKING IT color *Forbes* v200 no2 p22 S 5 2017

Cucinelli, Brunello

My Favorite Thing color *Esquire* p162 BigBlackBook

My Stuff bw color *Vanity Fair* v58 no11 p80 N 2016

Cuckoos

Greater Roadrunners E. Balli *Arizona Highways* v93 no9 p15 S 2017

Cucumbers

EXCESS BAGGAGE color *Esquire* p52 My 2017

THREE, TWO, ONE... APPS! E. N. GAGE color *Martha Stewart Living* no275 p19 Je 2017

Cuddehe, Mary

A MATTER OF LIFE *Harper's Magazine* v334 no2002 p59 Mr 2017

Cuddy, Amy

Power Poses: Plus or Bust? A. PATUREL color *Discover* v38 no2 p18 Mr 2017

Cudlitz, Michael

A Song for Abraham D. Ross color *Entertainment Weekly* no1438 p26 N 4 2016

Cuellar, Erika

Forest conservation: Remember Gran Chaco bibl color *Science* v355 no6324 p465 F 3 2017

Cuenca, W. P.

Persistent effects of pre-Columbian plant domestication on Amazonian forest composition bibl chart graph map *Science* v355 no6328 p925 Mr 3 2017

Cuesta, C.

Observation of coherent elastic neutrino-nucleus scattering diag *Science* v357 no6356 p1123 S 15 2017

Cuff bracelets—Evaluation

cuff love A. Syrett color *InStyle* v24 no2 p128 F 2017

The LIST color *Harper's Bazaar* no3649 p129 D 2016/Ja 2017

Cuff links

Together at the Seams: Baseball meets art in Sioux Falls *South Dakota Magazine* v33 no2 p68 Jl/Ag 2017

Cuff links—Evaluation

Parlez-VOUS VIDE Poche? color *Esquire* p74 2017 BigBlackBook

Cuffs (Clothing)—Evaluation

BEAUTY NEWS A. Parnass color *Harper's Bazaar* no3653 p238 My 2017

FEST FORWARD L. TUDOR color *New Orleans Magazine* v51 no6 p76 Ap 2017

Flowers, Girl S. P. Nadella color *Glamour* v115 no2 p32 F 2017

HIGH CONTRAST color *Harper's Bazaar* no3650 p102 F 2017

WHAT'S NEW color *Harper's Bazaar* no3649 p314 D 2016/Ja 2017

Cugnini, Aldo

FROM OUR READERS *Sky & Telescope* v134 no1 p6 Jl 2017

Cui, Longji

Quantized thermal transport in single-atom junctions bibl diag graph *Science* v355 no6330 p1192 Mr 17 2017

Cuiné, Stéphan

An algal photoenzyme converts fatty acids to hydrocarbons color graph *Science* v357 no6354 p903 S 1 2017

CUINN, CARRY

Above the Timberline color *Publishers Weekly* v264 no39 p90 S 25 2017

Cuisinart Inc.

BOIL BARONS S. Chodosh color *Popular Science* v289 no5 p28 S/O 2017

HANDY MIXERS M. XERAKIA color *Better Homes & Gardens* v95 no6 p124 Je 2017

MICROWAVE OVEN [Cover story] K. Dupzyk color *Popular Mechanics* p24 S 2017

MICROWAVE OVEN K. Dupzyk color *Popular Mechanics* v193 no7 p24 S 2016

Cujia, K. S.

Quantum sensing with arbitrary frequency resolution diag graph *Science* v356 no6340 p837 My 26 2017

CULBERTSON, CYNTHIA

The Arabian Horse *Arabian Horse World* v57 no3 p8 D 2016

Culex quinquefasciatus

Case builds for another Zika vector S. MILIUS *Science News* v190 no9 p13 O 29 2016

Culinary Workers Union (Organization)

The Hotel Cleaner A. Fortini *New York Times Magazine* p46 F 26 2017

Cullen, Chris

Damian Lillard color *Current Biography* v77 no11 p49 N 2016

Diplo bw *Current Biography* v77 no10 p25 O 2016

Garbiñe Muguruza color *Current Biography* v78 no1 p46 Ja 2017

José Eduardo Agualusa color *Current Biography* v77 no11 p3 N 2016

Jozy Altidore color *Current Biography* v77 no11 p7 N 2016

Katinka Hosszú color *Current Biography* v77 no10 p58 O 2016

Kirk Cousins color *Current Biography* v77 no11 p30 N 2016

Kyle Lowry color *Current Biography* v77 no10 p77 O 2016

Paul Goldschmidt color *Current Biography* v77 no10 p30 O 2016

Tyronn Lue color *Current Biography* v78 no3 p45 Mr 2017

Cullen, David A.

Direct atomic-level insight into the active sites of a high-performance PGM-free ORR catalyst diag graph *Science* v357 no6350 p479 Ag 4 2017

Cullen, Heidi

Ask anything [Cover story] color *Women's Health* v14 no1 p24 Ja/F 2017

THE BLAME CHANGER H. Rosner color *Popular Science* v289 no4 p24 Jl/Ag 2017

Cullen, John

MAVS-dependent host species range and pathogenicity of human hepatitis A virus bibl graph *Science* v353 no6307 p1541 S 30 2016

Mouse models of acute and chronic hepacivirus infection *Science* v357 no6347 p204 Jl 14 2017

Cullen, Mairi

Emergence and spread of a human-transmissible multidrug-resistant nontuberculous mycobacterium bibl diag graph *Science* v354 no6313 p751 N 11 2016

Cullen, Nathan

BEST ORATOR D. SMITH color *Maclean's* v129 no47 p22 N 28 2016

Cullen, Sharon

Bound to a Spy color *Publishers Weekly* v264 no39 p92 S 25 2017

Cullen, William G.

An on/off Berry phase switch in circular graphene resonators diag graph *Science* v356 no6340 p845 My 26 2017

Cullinan, Heidi

Enjoy the Dance: Dancing, Book 2 *Publishers Weekly* v264 no8 p72 F 20 2017

Cullinan, Renee

Run Meetings That Are Fair to Introverts, Women, and Remote Workers *Harvard Business Review Digital Articles* p2 Ap 29 2016

Culling of animals

THE CULLING I. PARKER cartoon color *New Yorker* v92 no45 p42 Ja 16 2017

Fowl play on campus R. COUNTER color *Maclean's* p11 Je 2017

Should We Kill Animals to Save Them? M. Paterniti bw color graph *National Geographic* v232 no4 p70 O 2017

Wolves, Lies & Logging E. C. ALBERTS color *Alternatives Journal (AJ) - Canada's Environmental Voice* v42 no2 p66 2016

Culliton, Emily

The Misfortune of Marion Palm L. Greenblatt color *Entertainment Weekly* no1478 / 1479 p107 Ag 18-25 2017

Take the Money and Run, Mom: In this debut novel, the antiheroine makes off with a bundle of other people's cash G. COWLES *New York Times Book Review* p12 S 24 2017

Cullors, Patrisse—Interviews

Black Lives Matter C. Meyerson color *Glamour* v114 no12 p218 D 2016

Cullum, Munro
THE CONCUSSION COUNT T. FOSTER *Texas Monthly* v45 no9 p60 S 2017

Culotta, Elizabeth
PEOPLE ON THE MOVE [Cover story] color *Science* v356 no6339 p676 My 19 2017
A single wave of migration from Africa peopled the globe color *Science* v354 no6319 p1522 D 23 2016

Culpepper, Phillip
EARLY BIRDS J. R. Sullivan cartoon chart *Field & Stream* v121 no8 p28 F/Mr 2017

Culpo, Olivia, 1992-
Pack Your Bags color *InStyle* v24 no7 p73 Jl 2017
STYLE CRUSH Olivia Culpo S. Simon color *InStyle* v23 no13 p116 D 2016

Cultivated plants
See also
House plants
Ornamental plants
Transgenic plants
Ancient peoples reshaped Amazon B. BOWER *Science News* v191 no6 p13 Ap 1 2017
Persistent effects of pre-Columbian plant domestication on Amazonian forest composition C. Levis, F. R. C. Costa et al bibl chart graph map *Science* v355 no6328 p925 Mr 3 2017
Saffron S. HUSEYNOV *Natural History* v125 no2 p28 F 2017

Cultivators
LATE-MODEL CULTIVATOR PRICES RISE D. Mowitz *Successful Farming* v115 no5 p21 Mid-Mr 2017
POCKET PRICE GUIDE: Dealer Prices on Late-Model Field Cultivators *Successful Farming* v115 no5 p23 Mid-Mr 2017

Cultivators—Evaluation
TILLERS R. BERENDSOHN color *Popular Mechanics* p28 Ap 2017

CULTON, STEVE
HOT BRONZE color *Field & Stream* v122 no3 p51 Ag 2017

Cults
See also
Vodou
BOOKSHOP *Psychology Today* v49 no6 p93 N/D 2016
VODOU AND THE RAINBOW B. AHMED *Advocate* no1088 p56 D 2016/Ja 2017

Cults—History
Druids' Temple R. Griffiths *History Today* v67 no4 p70 Ap 2017

Cultural activities
ABOVE & BEYOND cartoon *New Yorker* v93 no27 p17 S 11 2017
Camille Russell Love *Atlanta* v57 no2 p94 Je 2017

Cultural activities—News briefs
ABOVE & BEYOND bw *New Yorker* v93 no10 p32 Ap 24 2017

Cultural appropriation
Asking for a Friend L. Featherstone color *Nation* v304 no5 p5 F 20 2017
Cultural Approbation color *Weekly Standard* v22 no48 p2 S 4 2017
Foodie Feud J. LILEKS *National Review* v69 no11 p33 Je 12 2017
LOVE, HATE, AND CULTURE WARS O. B. AREWA color il *Phi Kappa Phi Forum* v97 no1 p26 Spr 2017
What Do Writers Have a Right to Write? D. BLUM *Publishers Weekly* v263 no50 p76 D 5 2016

Cultural awareness
Leading Across Cultures Requires Flexibility and Curiosity D. Rowland *Harvard Business Review Digital Articles* p2 My 30 2016
Righting Words R. HILL, G. CAZARES et al color *O, The Oprah Magazine* p17 Jl 2017

Cultural centers
Editor's Letter A. ASTLEY color *Architectural Digest* v73 no11 p48 N 2016

Cultural centers—Design & construction
THE FUN PALACE AT FIFTY S. Mathews *Art in America* v104 no9 p114 O 2016
On the Boards color *Architectural Record* v205 no2 p26 F 2017
White Hot B. BROOME color diag *Architectural Record* v204 no12 p90 D 2016

Cultural centers—Evaluation
HISTORY & CULTURE COME TO LIFE—The Seneca Art &

Culture Center at Ganondagan G. P. Jemison color *New York State Conservationist* v71 no2 p14 O 2016

Cultural competence
Building on Diversity T. G. MATHEWSON *America* v215 no13 p12 O 31 2016
Why More Hospitals Should Prioritize Cultural Competency O. Duhart *Harvard Business Review Digital Articles* p2 My 26 2017

Cultural districts
the arts district T. HARLANDER color *Los Angeles Magazine* v62 no7 p63 Jl 2017
Drawn Away B. D. SMITH *Indianapolis Monthly* p49 F 2017
RECREATION STATIONS color *Los Angeles Magazine* v62 no7 p67 Jl 2017

Cultural identity
See also
Cultural nationalism
It's the Culture, Stupid L. DRUTMAN il *New Republic* v248 no11 p14 N 2017
Shared Culture, Shared Beliefs P. Woodriff and M. LIND *National Review* v69 no18 p2 O 2 2017
The Uses and Abuses of Cultural Identity S. ENJETI and M. KOSLOFF *National Review* v69 no17 p17 S 11 2017
The World Needs More Canada E. NAWOTKA *Publishers Weekly* v263 no39 p3 S 26 2016

Cultural industries
See also
Motion picture industry
Music industry
Publishers & publishing
The Best of Everything This Year-So Far E. Berman, R. Bruner et al color *Time* v189 no21 p61 Je 5 2017
CHEERS & JEERS D. HOLBROOK *TV Guide* v65 no31 p76 Jl 24 2017
THE Showbiz ISSUE color *Bloomberg Businessweek* no4519 p55 Ap 24 2017

Cultural industries—Computer network resources
HAPPY HOLIDAYS color *Entertainment Weekly* no1444/1445 p8 D 16 2016

Cultural industries—Congresses
Entertainment WEEKLY POPFEST color *Entertainment Weekly* no1435 p7 O 14 2016
Entertainment WEEKLY POPFEST™ color *Entertainment Weekly* no1438 p16 N 4 2016
TED's Shift from Old to New Power J. Heimans and H. Timms *Harvard Business Review Digital Articles* p2 D 1 2014

Cultural industries—Economic aspects
FINANCIAL ADVICE FROM THE STARS J. YUAN color *Bloomberg Businessweek* no4519 p86 Ap 24 2017

Cultural industries—News briefs
The BULLSEYE M. Snetiker color *Entertainment Weekly* no1444/1445 p124 D 16 2016
The Bullseye M. Snetiker color *Entertainment Weekly* no1451/1452 p112 F 3-10 2017
The / Bullseye M. Snetiker color *Entertainment Weekly* no1460/1461 p102 Ap 7-17 2017
The Bullseye M. Snetiker color *Entertainment Weekly* no1473 p64 Jl 7 2017
The Bullseye M. Snetiker color *Entertainment Weekly* no1474/1475 p122 Jl 21-28 2017
The Entertainment Weekly Must List R. Kinane color *Entertainment Weekly* no1441 p4 N 25 2016
Pop Chart R. Bruner, C. Lang et al color *Time* v189 no23 p54 Je 19 2017
THERE'S NO EW WITHOUT U H. Goldblatt color *Entertainment Weekly* no1480 p2 S 1 2017

Cultural industries—United States
The Culture Business: Mark Harris img *New York* p14 Ja 23 2017
HOLLYWOOD GIVES BACK K. Hahn *TV Guide* v65 no39 p22 S 18 2017
THE NEW ESTABLISHMENT 2016 *Vanity Fair* v58 no11 p115 N 2016

Cultural landscapes
THIS TOO SHALL PASS R. MARR cartoon *Missouri Life* v44 no3 p66 My 2017

Cultural literacy

THE CHECKLIST *Texas Monthly* v44 no11 p64 N 2016
THE CHECK LIST *Texas Monthly* v45 no1 p58 Ja 2017

Cultural movements

Here We Go! Oprah color *O, The Oprah Magazine* p21 My 2017

Cultural nationalism

The Case for Cultural Nationalism M. LIND *National Review* v69 no17 p27 S 11 2017

Shared Culture, Shared Beliefs P. Woodriff and M. LIND *National Review* v69 no18 p2 O 2 2017

Cultural pluralism

ALL ABOARD THE ZANDWAGON: Rising agency reflects the diversity of beauty with queer, trans, Muslim, punk, and plus-size models Z. ZANE *Advocate* no1093 p9 O/N 2017

Bookselling in a Time of Political Upheaval J. Rosen color *Publishers Weekly* v264 no6 p5 F 6 2017

Caution Ahead W. Voegeli *Claremont Review of Books* v17 no3 p13 Summ 2017

DIVERSITY AND ITS DISCONTENTS W. Voegeli *Claremont Review of Books* v17 no3 p8 Summ 2017

How to Run a Meeting of People from Different Cultures R. Knight *Harvard Business Review Digital Articles* p2 D 4 2015

Misquoting Madison R. R. Reilly *Claremont Review of Books* v17 no3 p45 Summ 2017

United we practice C. Gorrell bw *Yoga Journal* no292 p10 Je 2017

Cultural pluralism—United States

Wall Street Diversifies Itself B. McLEAN color *Atlantic* v319 no2 p20 Mr 2017

Cultural prejudices

FORTY YEARS AGO T. TALIAFERRO *Texas Monthly* v45 no4 p16 Ap 2017

Semantics derived automatically from language corpora contain human-like biases A. Caliskan, J. J. Bryson et al chart graph *Science* v356 no6334 p183 Ap 14 2017

Cultural property

> *See also*
> Historic buildings
> Historic sites

And the Winning Photo Is... P. Peek *British Heritage Travel* v38 no3 p80 My/Je 2017

JULIAETTA: WHERE THERE IS THERE AGAIN S. PETTICORD *Idaho Magazine* v16 no7 p32 Ap 2017

Mission aims to salvage what's left of Nimrud J. Couzin-Frankel color map *Science* v357 no6358 p1340 S 29 2017

Tricentennial: The Montreal Influence E. Laborde *New Orleans Magazine* v51 no12 p16 O 2017

Cultural relations

Bookends: What distinguishes cultural exchange from cultural appropriation? R. Galchen and A. Holmes *New York Times Book Review* p27 Je 11 2017

Cultural relativism

How America Lost Its Mind R. L. Kelly, V. Finn et al color *Atlantic* v320 no4 p12 N 2017

Cultural rights

From International Law to Local Communities: The Role of the United Nations in the Realization of Human Rights M. KJAERUM *UN Chronicle* v54 no4 p34 2017

Cultural transmission

Indigenous Intergenerational Teachings J. BURNS ROSS bw chart il map *American Indian Quarterly* v40 no3 p216 Summ 2016

Cultural values

The gospel in a violent culture T. M. Muehlhoff and R. Langer *Christian Century* v134 no12 p30 Je 7 2017

Culturally competent medical care

Why More Hospitals Should Prioritize Cultural Competency O. Duhart *Harvard Business Review Digital Articles* p2 My 26 2017

Culture

> *See also*
> Art & culture
> Corporate culture
> Cultural appropriation
> Cultural pluralism
> Culture conflict
> Intellectual life
> Mass media & culture

Popular culture
Youth culture

Calendar: Culture M. Gajanan and E. Berman color *Time* v188 no27-28 p106 D 26 2016

A Case for Acculturation J. Paterson *Education Digest* v83 no1 p29 S 2017

The Cultured Life J. EPSTEIN bw color *Weekly Standard* v22 no27 p26 Mr 20 2017

David Kowalski *Atlanta* v57 no2 p42 Je 2017

First Taste of Japan C. CALDWELL color *Weekly Standard* v22 no36 p5 My 29 2017

THE LIBRARY IS NOT DEAD I. Collins *Saturday Evening Post* v289 no1 p10 Ja/F 2017

new orleAns' new Groove B. ANDREWS color *Rodale's Organic Life* v2 no7 p66 D 2016/Ja 2017

"Party-Hop" Around the World chart color *Good Housekeeping* v264 no1 p131 Ja 1 2017

Product Success Is Not About the Zeitgeist C. R. Sunstein *Harvard Business Review Digital Articles* p2 Je 22 2016

Puppy Love D. Paul *Indianapolis Monthly* v40 no7 p144 Mr 2017

THE REAL NARCISSISTS [Cover story] R. WEBBER *Psychology Today* v49 no5 p52 S/O 2016

Research: The Biggest Culture Gaps Are Within Countries, Not Between Them B. Kirkman, V. Taras et al *Harvard Business Review Digital Articles* p2 My 18 2016

State of the City R. WHITCOMB color *Weekly Standard* v22 no39 p38 Je 19 2017

The terrible American turn toward illiberalism S. AHMARI *Commentary* v144 no3 p13 O 2017

A Tiny Village By Little Tokyo J. CARREIRO *Los Angeles Magazine* v61 no11 p24 N 2016

Vietnam color *National Geographic* v231 no6 pC11 Je 2017

William F. Buckley: El Hablo Espanol *American History* v51 no6 p8 F 2017

Culture (Music)

The Fastest Mouths in the South cartoon color *Rolling Stone* no1280 p53 F 9 2017

Culture conflict

THE RISE OF POLITICAL CORRECTNESS A. M. Codevilla *Claremont Review of Books* v16 no4 p37 Fall 2016

Culture conflict—United States

Dreamers in a Culture War K. Wright bw diag *Nation* v304 no8 p10 Mr 13 2017

How to Win the Culture War L. Lalami il *Nation* v305 no5 p10 Ag 28 2017

The terrible American turn toward illiberalism S. AHMARI *Commentary* v144 no3 p13 O 2017

Culture in art

Consumed Culture R. Aima color *Art in America* v105 no1 p29 Ja 2017

Cultured milk

GOOD FOR WHAT AILS YOU? L. MOYER *Nutrition Action Health Letter* v44 no2 p8 Mr 2017

Culture—History

A Nation of Regions: Modern Britain is dominated economically, culturally and politically by London, its capital city. It was not always the way, as an examination of medieval texts reveals E. Parker *History Today* v67 no7 p106 Jl 2017

No Island is an Island S. Lipscomb *History Today* v67 no2 p31 F 2017

Culture—Moral & ethical aspects

REMAKING OURSELVES M. WERNER *Humanist* v77 no2 p38 Mr/Ap 2017

Culture—Societies, etc.

FOXFIRE AT 50 S. HANSELL *Atlanta* v56 no8 p27 D 2016

Columber, Zachary W.

Swimming in polluted waters bibl diag *Science* v354 no6317 p1232 D 9 2016

Culver, Stuart

The Delivery Driver J. Lowe *New York Times Magazine* p42 F 26 2017

Culver City (Calif.)

THE HOT LIST color *Los Angeles Magazine* v62 no10 p160 O 2017

Culyer, Richard

BOTH SIDES THEN color *American History* v52 no3 p66 Ag

2017

CONFLICTED OVER COMBAT *American History* v52 no1 p66 Ap 2017

LBJ'S DEVIOUS DANCE *American History* v51 no6 p68 F 2017

READING WASHINGTON LIKE A BOOK color *American History* v52 no4 p69 O 2017

SECRET AGENT MEN bw color *American History* v52 no2 p66 Je 2017

Cumagun, Christian J. R.

Evolution of the wheat blast fungus through functional losses in a host specificity determinant diag map *Science* v357 no6346 p80 Jl 7 2017

Cumberbatch, Benedict, 1976-

BENEDICT CUMBERBATCH D. Franich color *Entertainment Weekly* no1444/1445 p28 D 16 2016

Doctor Strange: The Curious Case of Two Teasers D. Franich color *Entertainment Weekly* no1440 p14 N 18 2016

The Doctor Will See You Now [Cover story] C. Collis color *Entertainment Weekly* no1436/1437 p34 O 21 2016

He's One Weird Dude P. Travers color *Rolling Stone* no1274 p60 N 17 2016

The Hollow Crown: The Wars of the Roses J. Russell *TV Guide* p42 D 5 2016

The Mind-Bending Mr. Cumberbatch M. SCHULMAN bw color *Vanity Fair* v58 no11 p146 N 2016

Sherlock A. D'Arminio *TV Guide* p40 D 19 2016

TOM HIDDLESTON *Interview* v46 no8 p62 O 2016

Cumbers, Bob

TALK TO US color graph *Chicago* v66 no11 p16 N 2017

Cumbres & Toltec Scenic Railroad

The Charms of Chama K. Krone and C. Krone color *Trail Rider* v29 no2 p32 Mr 2017

Where the 21st century meets the 19th J. Dziedzic *Model Railroader* v84 no10 p68 O 2017

Cumenal, Frederic

EXECUTIVE SUMMARIES MARCH–APRIL 2017 color *Harvard Business Review* v95 no2 p158 Mr/Ap 2017

TIFFANY'S CEO ON CREATING A SUSTAINABLE SUPPLY CHAIN color graph img *Harvard Business Review* v95 no2 p41 Mr/Ap 2017

CUMINGS, BRUCE

Korean War Drums *Nation* v304 no12 p5 Ap 10 2017

Cumming, Alan, 1965—Interviews

Open to Possibilities B. Levine bw *Publishers Weekly* v263 no44 p(Sp)18 O 31 2016

Cumming, Charles

A Divided Spy *Publishers Weekly* v264 no14 p71 Ap 3, 2017

CUMMING, GRAEME S.

When, Where, and How Nature Matters for Ecosystem Services: Challenges for the Next Generation of Ecosystem Service Models *BioScience* v67 no9 p820 S 2017

Cummings, Derek A. T.

Dengue diversity across spatial and temporal scales: Local structure and the effect of host population size bibl graph *Science* v355 no6331 p1302 Mr 24 2017

Cummings, Earle

WORD EXCHANGE *Natural History* v125 no2 p9 F 2017

Cummings, Homer S. (Homer Stille), 1870-1956

SALVATION K. ARMSTRONG *Smithsonian* v47 no9 p70 Ja/F 2017

CUMMINGS, KELSEY

Dying in Full Detail: Mortality and Digital Documentary *Film Quarterly* v71 no1 p113 Fall 2017

Cummings, Lindsay

Empire Building J. MCCARTNEY color *Publishers Weekly* v264 no21 p45 My 22 2017

Cummings, Mathew

A Porch Long Missing M. E. Polson color diag *Arts & Crafts Homes & the Revival* v12 no3 p34 Summ 2017

Cummins, Claudia

Do the Twist color *Yoga Journal* p74 2017 Special Issue

Cummins, Eleanor

departing the waters cartoon *Popular Science* v289 no4 p84 Jl/Ag 2017

inside a smog dome color *Popular Science* v289 no4 p20 Jl/Ag 2017

I WISH SOMEONE WOULD INVENT... cartoon *Popular Science* v289 no4 p102 Jl/Ag 2017

Cummins Inc.

CUMMINS TO OFFER CRATE ENGINES color *Dirt Sports + Off-Road* v51 no3 p8 Mr 2017

Cumulonimbus

ATMOSPHERIC ELECTRICAL PHENOMENA: A Pilot's View G. J. Mulvey, J. F. Miller et al il *Weatherwise* v70 no5 p32 S/O 2017

Cuna (Central American people)

THE DREAM ISLANDS M. STOUT and R. STOUT color map *Sail* v48 no1 p30 Ja 2017

Cunanan, Tom

FORTY UNDER FORTY color *Washingtonian Magazine* v52 no7 p58 Ap 2017

Cundiff, Steven T.

Frequency combs enable rapid and high-resolution multidimensional coherent spectroscopy diag graph *Science* v357 no6358 p1389 S 29 2017

Cúneo, N. Rubén

Eocene lantern fruits from Gondwanan Patagonia and the early origins of Solanaceae bibl color diag *Science* v355 no6320 p1 Ja 6 2017

Cunha, Darlena

THE JUGGLE IS REAL cartoon *Parents* v92 no9 p112 S 2017

CUNHA, STEPHEN

POSTHOLE color *Powder* v46 no2 p94 O 2017

Cunliffe, Bill

KEYBOARD SCHOOL: THE MELDING OF CLASSICAL PIANO & BIG BAND JAZZ bw color *Downbeat* v84 no9 p82 S 2017

Cunliffe, Tom

CRUISING TIPS color *Sail* v47 no12 p16 D 2016

CRUISING TIPS color *Sail* v48 no11 p54 N 2017

CRUISING TIPS color *Sail* v48 no6 p48 Je 2017

CRUISING TIPS T. Cunliffe bw color *Sail* v48 no8 p55 Ag 2017

SCHOONERMEN in the CARIBBEAN 600 color map *Sail* v48 no6 p32 Je 2017

Cunningham, Aimee

Access Denied cartoon color diag graph *Science News* v192 no3 p20 S 2 2017

Access to quality health care has improved in most places map *Science News* v191 no12 p5 Je 24 2017

Antibodies defeat HIV by ganging up *Science News* v192 no6 p8 O 14 2017

Cows make powerful HIV antibodies color graph *Science News* v192 no2 p7 Ag 19 2017

Data back ban of artificial trans fats *Science News* v191 no9 p8 My 13 2017

Dengue may stoke Zika infections graph *Science News* v191 no8 p14 Ap 29 2017

Genetic risk of second cancer tallied *Science News* v191 no8 p12 Ap 29 2017

Lyme diagnostics could get an upgrade *Science News* v192 no4 p8 S 16 2017

New 'rules' for finding antibiotics *Science News* v191 no11 p8 Je 10 2017

New views snag science Nobels bw *Science News* v192 no7 p6 O 28 2017

No autism link to antidepressants graph *Science News* v191 no9 p9 My 13 2017

Parasites fight for nutrients color *Science News* v192 no6 p16 O 14 2017

Parkinson's may provoke T cells *Science News* v192 no1 p14 Ag 5 2017

Patch could someday replace flu shot color *Science News* v192 no1 p8 Ag 5 2017

Spread of bad proteins tied to diabetes color *Science News* v192 no3 p9 S 2 2017

Sunless tanner could protect skin color *Science News* v191 no13 p11 Jl 8 2017

Vaginal microbes hamper HIV drug *Science News* v191 no13 p8 Jl 8 2017

Cunningham, Bill, 1929-2016

BILL CUNNINGHAM *New York Times Magazine* p66 D 25 2016

Bill Cunningham Saw It All img *New York* v49 no25 p56 D 12

2016

Cunningham, Caroline

THE AGONY OF THE FEET *Washingtonian Magazine* v52 no1 p123 O 2016

BABY BOOM: Shady Grove Fertility is the largest fertility clinic in the country. How it got that way involved business innovation as well as science *Washingtonian Magazine* v52 no8 p119 My 2017

CHINS UP: More Washington men are getting cosmetic injections to create stronger jawlines. What's behind the trend? *Washingtonian Magazine* v53 no1 p113 O 2017

DC, WHERE POLITICAL ADS NEVER END *Washingtonian Magazine* v52 no5 p24 F 2017

Destination: The Airports *Washingtonian Magazine* v52 no2 p80 N 2016

DESTINATION WASHINGTON *Washingtonian Magazine* v52 no5 p22 F 2017

EIGHT PEOPLE TO WHIP YOU INTO SHAPE *Washingtonian Magazine* v52 no4 p108 Ja 2017

FIGHTING WORDS *Washingtonian Magazine* v52 no2 p230 N 2016

GENTLE DENTAL *Washingtonian Magazine* v52 no6 p103 Mr 2017

GIFT GUIDE 2016 *Washingtonian Magazine* v52 no3 p84 D 2016

THE GOOD WITH THE BAAAD: Not tempted by traditional yoga? Perhaps you'd enjoy trying it with goats *Washingtonian Magazine* v52 no11 p17 Ag 2017

HEAD REST: Nap rooms, self-care seminars-the art of slowing down is a fast-growing business. The latest: meditation boutiques. We tested three new meditation-only centers. Here's how they compare *Washingtonian Magazine* v52 no12 p109 S 2017

A LEAGUE OF HER OWN *Cincinnati Magazine* v50 no7 p68 Ap 2017

REALITY CHECK: Will your next surgery be done with virtual reality? More area hospitals are employing this cutting-edge technology *Washingtonian Magazine* v52 no12 p115 S 2017

SETTING THE PACE *Washingtonian Magazine* v52 no4 p114 Ja 2017

WIRED FOR SUCCESS *Washingtonian Magazine* v52 no9 p119 Je 2017

Cunningham, Caroline M.

Good Fortune color *Southern Living* v52 no2 p43 F 2017

Cunningham, Cindy Michelle

Wage and job-skill distributions in the National Compensation Survey bibl chart color graph *Monthly Labor Review* p1 F 2017

CUNNINGHAM, DEE

Chords & Discords color *Downbeat* v83 no11 p10 N 2016

Cunningham, Evan

Unemployment holds steady for much of 2016 but edges down in the fourth quarter bibl chart color graph *Monthly Labor Review* p1 Mr 2017

Cunningham, Jackson

Popular piety color *U.S. Catholic* v82 no2 p5 F 2017

Cunningham, Merce, 1919-2009

Bird Song J. Acocella cartoon *New Yorker* v93 no5 p20 Mr 20 2017

Time Flies J. Acocella cartoon *New Yorker* v92 no38 p10 N 21 2016

Cunningham, Philip A.

Is the Pope 'Anti-Jewish'? color *Commonweal* v144 no9 p19 My 19 2017

Cunningham, Rebecca

Changing How Patients and Doctors Talk About Death *Harvard Business Review Digital Articles* p2 D 1 2016

CUNNINGHAM, ROCHELLE

PEARL *Idaho Magazine* v16 no5 p32 F 2017

Cunningham, Saul A.

Ten policies for pollinators bibl color *Science* v354 no6315 p975 N 25 2016

CUNNINGHAM, VINSON

AFTER THE FLOOD cartoon *New Yorker* v93 no27 p69 S 11 2017

GHOST STORY cartoon *New Yorker* v92 no32 p102 O 10 2016

HOLLAND-DOZIER-HOLLAND *New Yorker* v92 no42 p76 D 19 2016

MAKING GOD FAMOUS cartoon color *New Yorker* v92 no45

p26 Ja 16 2017

THE PROTEST CANDIDATE cartoon color *New Yorker* v93 no2 p34 F 27 2017

YOU DON'T UNDERSTAND cartoon color *New Yorker* v93 no13 p85 My 15 2017

Cunningham, Zandra

GIRL BOSSES in the Glam Biz K. FOSTER color *Seventeen* v75 no11 p46 N 2016

CUNNINGHAM-COOK, MATTHEW

The Battle for the Soul of Black Politics *In These Times* v41 no5 p15 My 2017

Cunnington, Havilah

Stronger Than the Struggle: Uncomplicating Your Spiritual Battle *Publishers Weekly* v264 no41 p60 O 9 2017

Čuntova, Žanetá

MUSICIANS' GEAR GUIDE BEST OF THE 2017 NAMM SHOW color *Downbeat* v84 no4 p70 Ap 2017

Cuoco, Kaley, 1985-

HOT YOGA HOT BOD [Cover story] L. Majewski cartoon color *Women's Health* v13 no10 p65 D 2016

Cuomo, Alessandro

Reticulon 3-dependent ER-PM contact sites control EGFR non-clathrin endocytosis color diag graph *Science* v356 no6338 p617 My 12 2017

Cuomo, Andrew Mark, 1957-

10 THINGS WE'RE TALKING ABOUT T. A. Christian color diag *Essence* v47 no12 p75 Ap 2017

ANDREW THE UNLOVED: Based on his long list of accomplishments, New York's governor ought to be held up by progressives as a national leader. So why don't they like him? A. Greenblatt *Governing* v30 no10 p42 Jl 2017

Constitutional Inertia A. Greenblatt *Governing* v30 no4 p12 Ja 2017

For the Record color *Time* v189 no3 p4 Ja 16 2017

Powering Down *Earth Island Journal* v32 no1 p6 Spr 2017

Cuomo, Chris

Q: Who Is the Worst Leader of All Time? color *Atlantic* v319 no1 p100 Ja/F 2017

Cuong Nguyen

A chemical genetic roadmap to improved tomato flavor bibl graph *Science* v355 no6323 p391 Ja 27 2017

Cupboards

Clean It Like You Mean It A. ANDREWS color *Martha Stewart Living* no271 p30 Ja/F 2017

Cupcakes

Flowerpot Cupcakes color *Good Housekeeping* v264 no5 p139 My 2017

Lighten up C. BOYD color *Better Homes & Gardens* v95 no6 p134 Je 2017

MAGIC IN A JAR G. LOFTS color *Martha Stewart Living* p74 Jl/Ag 2017

Sandra Lee Favorites color *TV Guide* v64 no42 p14 O 10 2016

STEM SKILLS E. N. GAGE cartoon color *Martha Stewart Living* p19 Mr 2017

Cupich, Blase J., 1949-

America's New Cardinals T. John color *Time* v188 no16/17 p6 O 24 2016

Cupich Calls Church to Promote Solidarity After Trump Victory color *America* v215 p9 N 28 2016

Leaders color *Time* v189 no16/17 p64 My 1-8 2017

Signs of the Times [Cover story] color *Commonweal* v144 no10 p12 Je 2 2017

Cupp, S. E.

Is It Safe to Talk Politics Yet? bw color *Glamour* v115 no2 p77 F 2017

Curacao (Netherlands Antilles)

Curaçao color *Sports Illustrated* v126 no6 p150 F 20 2017

Curacao (Netherlands Antilles)—Description & travel

TRAVEL Curaçao color *Sports Illustrated* v126 no6 p166 F 20 2017

Curative medicine

How Much Is a Miracle Worth? C. Chen color *Bloomberg Businessweek* no4518 p21 Ap 10 2017

Curato, Nicole

Twelve Key Findings in Deliberative Democracy Research *Daedalus* v146 no3 p28 Summ 2017

The Plastic Inevitable T. PRODANOVICH color *Surfer* v58 no1 p28 Ap 2017

Current assets

A Refresher on Current Ratio A. Gallo *Harvard Business Review Digital Articles* p2 S 14 2015

Current events education

The 2017 Quiz on News-to-Be color *Time* v188 no27-28 p122 D 26 2016

Current good manufacturing practices

Kilogram-scale prexasertib monolactate monohydrate synthesis under continuous-flow CGMP conditions K. P. Cole, J. McClary Groh et al chart diag *Science* v356 no6343 p1144 Je 16 2017

Current ratio

A Refresher on Current Ratio A. Gallo *Harvard Business Review Digital Articles* p2 S 14 2015

Currey & Co.

Home Stretch color *House Beautiful* v159 no5 p48 Je 2017

Curricula (Courses of study)

    See also

      Curriculum planning

      Women's studies

Berkeley Goes Offline color *Weekly Standard* v22 no27 p13 Mr 20 2017

Continuing Education: Achieving the Dream P. Last and J. Southerst color *Maclean's* v129 no51/52 p58 D 26 2016

Engaging with Our Trials and Tribulations A. KARIM *Islamic Horizons* v46 no1 p19 Ja/F 2017

A FIVE-MINUTE GUIDE TO FIVE MILLENNIA OF HUMAN HISTORY K. Andersen cartoon *Esquire* p123 S 2017

Visual immersion for cultural understanding and multimodal literacy C. Smilan bibl color *Arts Education Policy Review* v118 no4 p220 2017

Curricula (Courses of study)—Law & legislation

The past and future of PHYSICS EDUCATION REFORM V. K. Otero and D. E. Meltzer *Physics Today* v70 no5 p50 My 2017

Curriculum planning

    See also

      Interdisciplinary approach in education

No Soft Spots J. Epstein *Claremont Review of Books* v17 no3 p66 Summ 2017

Curriculum planning—Congresses

Rejuvenation through Nature [Cover story] FAWZIA MAI TUNG *Islamic Horizons* v46 no2 p36 Mr/Ap 2017

Curriculum planning—United States

THE PATH TO EXEMPLARY E. Center, K. Bailey et al color *Literacy Today (2411-7862)* v34 no4 p34 Ja/F 2017

Currid-Halkett, Elizabeth

The New Conspicuous Consumption S. Begley color *Time* v189 no20 p18 My 29 2017

The Self-Indulgence of Today's New Elite B. SCHWARZ *American Conservative* v16 no5 p52 S/O 2017

Currie, Christopher J.

#trailchat color *Backpacker* p8 My 2017

CURRIE, CHUCK

Chords & Discords color *Downbeat* v84 no8 p10 Ag 2017

Currie, Melissa A.

Public Spaces and Social Equity *Parks & Recreation* v52 no3 p34 Mr 2017

Currie, Paul

Foyles CEO Paul Currie: Melding Bookselling and Mindfulness E. NAWOTKA color *Publishers Weekly* v264 no3 p16 Ja 16 2017

CURRIE, RACHEL

In the Arena bw *National Review* v69 no12 p40 Je 26 2017

CURRIE-KNIGHT, KEVIN

Dirty Words cartoon color *Reason* v48 no8 p56 Ja 2017

CURRIN, AMY M.

Q: What did you let go of that changed your life? color *O, The Oprah Magazine* p16 Ag 2017

Curry, Adrian

AL HIRSCHFELD color *Film Comment* v53 no2 p80 Mr/Ap 2017

ANDRZEJ KLIMOWSKI color *Film Comment* v53 no4 p80 Jl/Ag 2017

The best posters of 2016 color *Film Comment* v53 no1 p96 Ja/F 2017

GRAPHIC DETAIL color *Film Comment* v53 no3 p80 My/Je 2017

WIKTOR GÓRKA cartoon *Film Comment* v52 no6 p96 N/D 2016

Curry, Andrew

A 9,000-Year Love Affair cartoon color graph map *National Geographic* v231 no2 p30 F 2017

'Green hell' has long been home for humans color *Science* v354 no6310 p268 O 21 2016

The Road Almost Taken color *Archaeology* v70 no2 p32 Mr/Ap 2017

SANCTUARY color *Bicycling* v58 no6 p48 Jl 2017

SCIENCE IN A POST-BREXIT WORLD color *Discover* v38 no1 p28 Ja/F 2017

WHAT LIES BENEATH color *Atlantic* v320 no3 p52 O 2017

Curry, Dale

Asian Occasion color *New Orleans Magazine* v51 no5 p92 Mr 2017

Buon Appetito! color *New Orleans Magazine* v51 no7 p72 My 2017

CHRISTMAS CREATIONS color *New Orleans Magazine* v51 no2 p88 D 2016

COOKING CREOLE color *New Orleans Magazine* v51 no3 p116 Ja 2017

Eating Local color *New Orleans Magazine* v51 no9 p84 Jl 2017

First the Vegetables color *New Orleans Magazine* v51 no6 p88 Ap 2017

Hot Boudin! color *New Orleans Magazine* v51 no12 p114 O 2017

Net Gain: Season For Crabs color *New Orleans Magazine* v51 no10 p176 Ag 2017

One Pot Cooking color *New Orleans Magazine* v52 no1 p108 S 2017

Southern Cooking color *New Orleans Magazine* v51 no7 p70 My 2017

Summer Kitchen color *New Orleans Magazine* v51 no8 p104 Je 2017

THANKSGIVING SIDES color *New Orleans Magazine* v51 no1 p116 N 2016

Three For the Tray color *New Orleans Magazine* v51 no4 p88 F 2017

Curry, Dell

Flashback D. Kahn and T. Keith color *Sports Illustrated* v126 no18 p12 Je 26 2017

Curry, Helen Anne

Crops on demand L. Campos bw *Science* v354 no6313 p713 N 11 2016

Curry, Jack

"IT'S FOR YOU, JACKIE" *Washingtonian Magazine* v52 no2 p312 N 2016

NOT JUST DOG-PADDLING: Pups are getting into the pool for help with arthritis, chronic pain, and other ailments *Washingtonian Magazine* v52 no12 p163 S 2017

Curry, John Steuart, 1897-1946

THE ART OF WAR *MHQ: Quarterly Journal of Military History* v29 no2 p34 Wint 2017

Curry, Leonard

Thinking with trans diag *Christian Century* v134 no2 p34 Ja 18 2017

Curry, Stephen, 1988-

The Revenge of the Happy Warrior A. CORSELLO color *GQ: Gentlemen's Quarterly* v97 no5 p80 My 2017

Curry, Stephen, 1988——Interviews

SI NOW M. Gray color *Sports Illustrated* v126 no9 p4 Mr 27 2017

CURRY, TYLER

DEAR GAY MEN, AN OPEN LETTER color *Advocate* no1089 p27 F/Mr 2017

How Running Toward HIV Can Save Your Life: Taking meds can be easy. Learning how to breathe is the tricky part color *Advocate* no1091 p41 Je/Jl 2017

Take a Deep Breath: Living with HIV is Like Learning to hold your breath under water *Advocate* no1093 p23 O/N 2017

Curry, William T.

Decoupling genetics, lineages, and microenvironment in IDH-mutant gliomas by single-cell RNA-seq diag *Science* v355 no6332 p1391 Mr 31 2017

Curse of the Bahia Emerald, The (Short story)

The Curse of the Bahia Emerald E. WEIL and B. BORRELL cartoon *Wired* v25 no3 p84 Mr 2017

Curtain walls

q&a color *Timber Home Living* v27 no4 p26 Ag 2017

Curtin, David

HIDDEN WORLDS of fundamental particles *Physics Today* v70 no6 p46 Je 2017

Curtin, Jane

Pioneers [Cover story] color *Time* v189 no16/17 p14 My 1-8 2017

Curtis & Davis (Company)

LAKEFRONT LEGACY L. Cutrone color *Louisiana Life* v37 no6 p20 Jl/Ag 2017

Curtis, Adam, 1955-

Adam Curtis C. Mari color *Current Biography* v78 no4 p17 Ap 2017

IT ALL CONNECTS J. Lethem *New York Times Magazine* p60 O 30 2016

Curtis, Chris

WHAT'S LOCAL ANYWAY? M. Quinn *Governing* v30 no7 p50 Ap 2017

Curtis, Christina

Teach Your Team to Expect Success *Harvard Business Review Digital Articles* p2 Je 9 2016

Curtis, Cyrus Hermann Kotzschmar, 1850-1933

AMERICA'S MAGAZINE S. Slon *Saturday Evening Post* v289 no2 p4 Mr/Ap 2017

Curtis, Edward S., 1868-1952

Lulu and the Shadow Catcher C. Mott and J. A. Hayner bw color *Magazine Antiques* v184 no3 p82 My/Je 2017

Curtis, Nancy

a machine that pulls water from thin air. literally S. Fecht cartoon *Popular Science* v289 no2 p20 Mr/Ap 2017

CURTIS, RICHARD

Ho Ho Ho *Publishers Weekly* v263 no52 p128 D 19 2016

LOVE ACTUALLY J. McGovern color *Entertainment Weekly* no1460/1461 p86 Ap 7-17 2017

Curtis, Simon

GOODBYE CHRISTOPHER ROBIN I. Biedenharn color *Entertainment Weekly* no1478 / 1479 p54 Ag 18-25 2017

CURTIS, WAYNE

Decommissioning Lee: The controversial removal of a prominent New Orleans statue *American Scholar* v86 no4 p97 Aut 2017

THE EDUCATION OF RAJ BHAKTA color *Yankee* p126 Jl 2017

MR. DAVIS & HIS FANTASTIC RUM ACCELERATOR color diag *Wired* v25 no6 p68 Je 2017

A PLACE TO GET AWAY color *Yankee* p92 My/Je 2017

Curtis Cos.

CURTIS PORCHWORK B. Sullivan cartoon *Arts & Crafts Homes & the Revival* v12 no3 p72 Summ 2017

Curtis-Bey, Linda

What does it take to sustain a productive partnership in education? color *Phi Delta Kappan* v99 no1 p15 S 2017

Curtius, Joachim

Global atmospheric particle formation from CERN CLOUD measurements bibl graph map *Science* v354 no6316 p1119 D 2 2016

Curvature

Get Board S. O'BRIEN *Boating World* v38 no1 p12 Ja 2017

Curvy Widow (Theatrical production)

THE THEATRE color *New Yorker* v93 no23 p12 Ag 7 2017

Cusac, Anne-Marie

Jerusalem: A Cookbook/Cuba!: Recipes and Stories from the Cuban Kitchen/Taste of Persia: A Cook's Travels Through Armenia, Azerbaijan, Georgia, Iran, and Kurdistan... color *Progressive* p60 D 2016/Ja 2017

Cusack, John

Leaders color *Time* v189 no16/17 p64 My 1-8 2017

Cusanovich, Darren A.

Comprehensive single-cell transcriptional profiling of a multicellular organism diag *Science* v357 no6352 p661 Ag 18 2017

CUSHING, BELLE

The French Are Coming! bw color *Bon Appetit* v62 no4 p15 Ap 2017

Liquid Gold color *Bon Appetit* no11 p60 N 2017

ШЭ'LL HAVə WiNE, ИATURALLY color *Bon Appetit* p118 S 2017

r.s.v.p.: BEST NEW RESTAURANTS EDITION bw color *Bon Appetit* p16 S 2017

starters color *Bon Appetit* v62 no6 p17 Je 2017

The Urbanist: Chefs Search Out the Best Street Food img *New York* v49 no19 p24 S 19 2016

CUSHING, COREY

Riding With a Hackamore color *Horse & Rider* v56 no11 p41 N 2017

Cushioning materials

Innovation Fill-Air Flow E. Pfanner and M. Scaturro diag *Bloomberg Businessweek* no4495 p28 O 17 2016

Cushions—Evaluation

CASCADE CREEK color *Canoe & Kayak Magazine* v45 no1 p67 Wint 2017

COME RAIN OR SHINE color *House Beautiful* p19 Ag 2017

The cure for a bland sofa S. J. SHELTON color *Redbook* p136 Ap 2017

ROLL CALL color *Martha Stewart Living* p36 Jl/Ag 2017

Velvet for All Seasons H. BROWN color *House Beautiful* v159 no3 p36 Ap 2017

Cushman, Fiery

When We Don't Blame People for Their Bad Deeds *Harvard Business Review Digital Articles* p2 F 16 2016

Cusick, Marie

Pennsylvania nuns sue federal agency over natural gas pipeline color *Christian Century* v134 no18 p15 Ag 30 2017

Cusk, Rachel

By the Book *New York Times Book Review* p8 Ja 8 2017

Choose Your Own Rachel Cusk H. Fulavits img *New York* p101 Mr 6 2017

Fierce, She Got Outside the Moment C. Messud color *New York Review of Books* v64 no5 p28 Mr 23 2017

In the Name of Love color *Conde Nast Traveler* v52 no2 p60 F 2017

A Room Of Her Own [Cover story] M. Ali color *New York Times Book Review* p1 Ja 29 2017

THE SAD FACT *Harper's Magazine* v334 no2000 p25 Ja 2017

THE SAD FACT R. Cusk *Harper's Magazine* v334 no2000 p25 Ja 2017

TRANSIT H. AKLER color *Maclean's* no1 p61 F 17 2017

The Uncoupling R. FRANKLIN color *Atlantic* v319 no1 p37 Ja/F 2017

When Less Plot Is Actually More S. Begley color *Time* v189 no3 p58 Ja 16 2017

WORLD OF INTERIORS J. THURMAN cartoon color *New Yorker* v93 no23 p48 Ag 7 2017

Cussler, Clive, 1931-

The Cutthroat: An Isaac Bell Adventure *Publishers Weekly* v264 no5 p176 Ja 30 2017

H.L. HUNLEY SUBMARINERS' DEATHS STILL A MYSTERY B. Manley color *Military History* v34 no5 p10 Ja 2018

Nighthawk: A Novel from the Numa Files color *Publishers Weekly* v264 no11 p57 Mr 13 2017

Odessa Sea *Publishers Weekly* v263 no40 p100 O 3 2016

Custards

Apple Custard Cake: Re-creating a recipe from memory ... when the memory isnt yours A. TRAVERSO *Yankee* v81 no5 p68 S/O 2017

Custer, Anne

VEGAN Meat ALTERNATIVES *Vegetarian Journal* v35 no1 p24 2016

Vegetarian Action. Molly McBride, RD, LD Promoting Veganismm in the Corporate World *Vegetarian Journal* v35 no1 p35 2016

Custer, George A. (George Armstrong), 1839-1876

Custer at Mardi Gras E. Laborde bw *New Orleans Magazine* v51 no4 p144 F 2017

Custer State Park (S.D.)

SCUFFLE IN THE LOOP C. Begeman *South Dakota Magazine* v33 no3 p94 S/O 2017

Walking South Dakota: Rollie Noem saw the state one step at a time *South Dakota Magazine* v33 no2 p18 Jl/Ag 2017

Wildlife in Winter *South Dakota Magazine* v32 no4 p107 N/D 2016

Custom-designed houses

Back to Nature color *Timber Home Living* v27 no6 p12 D 2017

Custom Home Builders Directory *Washingtonian Magazine* v52 no11 p150 Ag 2017

ticles p2 D 28 2016

Research: Are Clients Loyal to Your Firm, or the People in It? J. Raffiee color *Harvard Business Review Digital Articles* p2 Ja 31 2017

Using Data to Strengthen Your Connections to Customers N. Harrison and D. O'Neill *Harvard Business Review Digital Articles* p2 Ag 25 2016

What Airbnb Understands About Customers' "Jobs to Be Done" K. Dillon *Harvard Business Review Digital Articles* p2 Ag 18 2016

What If You Could Learn Design from Apple? M. Bonchek *Harvard Business Review Digital Articles* p2 S 14 2016

Whole Foods Needs a More Consistent Pricing Message R. Mohammed *Harvard Business Review Digital Articles* p2 Ag 20 2015

Why User Experience Always Has to Come First M. Schrage *Harvard Business Review Digital Articles* p2 S 8 2016

Win Over Executives by Proving Customers Support Your Idea R. Ashkenas and D. Dworkin *Harvard Business Review Digital Articles* p2 Jl 14 2015

Customer relations—Management—Software

Too Many Executives Are Missing the Most Important Part of CRM C. Brown *Harvard Business Review Digital Articles* p2 Ag 24 2016

Using Digital Exhaust to Improve Sales M. Kovac *Harvard Business Review Digital Articles* p2 Jl 8 2016

Customer retention

Listen to Your Employees, Not Just Your Customers B. Benjamin *Harvard Business Review Digital Articles* p2 Ag 15 2016

The Value of Keeping the Right Customers A. Gallo *Harvard Business Review Digital Articles* p2 O 29 2014

Why Companies Are Advertising Their Master Brand D. L. Yohn *Harvard Business Review Digital Articles* p2 Mr 28 2016

Customer satisfaction

(I DON'T WANT NO) SATISFACTION SURVEY E. Dwyer *Saturday Evening Post* v289 no5 p28 S/O 2017

Just Don't Ask B. LUTZ *Road & Track* v69 no4 p100 N 2017

KICK-ASS CUSTOMER SERVICE: INTERACTION S. Davis, W. Johnson et al color *Harvard Business Review* v95 no3 p16 My/Je 2017

Missy Hammond Casino Dealer: The longtime French Lick Resort employee is something of a card L. WRIGHT *Indianapolis Monthly* v12 no40 p48 Ag 2017

My home insurer is offering identity-theft coverage. Is it worth buying? color *Consumer Reports* v82 no2 p15 F 2017

Rituals: The Last Pastrami J. D. Stein and J. Rothman img *New York* p18 F 9 2017

Track Customer Experience, but Don't Forget the Financials B. Fotsch *Harvard Business Review Digital Articles* p2 O 27 2014

The Two Sides of Employee Engagement S. Graber *Harvard Business Review Digital Articles* p2 D 4 2015

When Do Regulators Become More Important than Customers? M. Schrage *Harvard Business Review Digital Articles* p2 Ja 26 2015

Customer satisfaction surveys

Cars That Owners Love and Hate M. Monticello chart color *Consumer Reports* v82 no2 p46 F 2017

THE POWER OF POSITIVE SURVEYING bw *Harvard Business Review* v95 no1 p22 Ja/F 2017

Customer service management

MR. KNOW-IT-ALL J. MOOALLEM cartoon *Wired* v25 no10 p40 O 2017

Customer services

The 3 Elements of a Strong Corporate Identity P. Leinwand and C. Mainardi *Harvard Business Review Digital Articles* p2 D 9 2014

5 Questions That Will Help You Stay Ahead of Your Disruptors M. Schrage *Harvard Business Review Digital Articles* p2 My 5 2016

The Best Luxury Services Are Customized, Not Standardized A. Brant *Harvard Business Review Digital Articles* p2 Mr 2 2016

A Better Way to Manage Corporate Alliances A. Shipilov *Harvard Business Review Digital Articles* p2 D 2 2014

Companies Like United Need to Cultivate Good Judgment, and Free Their Employees to Use It J. Deighton *Harvard Business Review Digital Articles* p2 Ap 14 2017

The Curious Downside of an Owner's Mindset J. Allen *Harvard*

Business Review Digital Articles p2 Je 7 2016

Customer Care & FAQs *Missouri Life* v44 no2 p8 Ap 2017

Customer Service Needs to Be Either More or Less Robotic R. Sagarin *Harvard Business Review Digital Articles* p2 N 24 2014

Customers Like Self- Service, Unless It Undermines Customer Support M. Schrage *Harvard Business Review Digital Articles* p2 Jl 28 2015

Design Your Employee Experience as Thoughtfully as You Design Your Customer Experience D. L. Yohn *Harvard Business Review Digital Articles* p2 D 8 2016

The Internet of Things Changes the Company-Customer Relationship P. Weichselbaum *Harvard Business Review Digital Articles* p2 Je 29 2015

Keeping Customers Continuously Infatuated G. G. Burt *Harvard Business Review Digital Articles* p2 Ag 9 2016

KICK-ASS CUSTOMER SERVICE: INTERACTION S. Davis, W. Johnson et al color *Harvard Business Review* v95 no3 p16 My/Je 2017

KICK-ASS CUSTOMER SERVICE M. Dixon, L. Ponomareff et al chart color graph il img *Harvard Business Review* v95 no1 p110 Ja/F 2017

Scaling Customer Service as Your Startup Grows M. Redbord *Harvard Business Review Digital Articles* p2 S 11 2017

To Persuade Others, Give Them Options S. Martin *Harvard Business Review Digital Articles* p2 D 2 2014

Use Big Data to Create Value for Customers, Not Just Target Them N. Dawar *Harvard Business Review Digital Articles* p2 Ag 16 2016

What a Great Digital Customer Experience Actually Looks Like C. Borowski *Harvard Business Review Digital Articles* p2 N 9 2015

What Marketers Need to Understand About Augmented Reality A. Javornik *Harvard Business Review Digital Articles* p2 Ap 18 2016

What We Can Learn from One of the World's Most-Mocked Cars G. G. Burt *Harvard Business Review Digital Articles* p2 Ap 22 2016

When to Offer Fewer Customer Service Channels C. J. Grimm *Harvard Business Review Digital Articles* p2 My 19 2015

Why Facebook Messenger Is a Big Deal for Customer Service J. Gans *Harvard Business Review Digital Articles* p2 My 6 2016

Women Rule R. REISNER *Publishers Weekly* v264 no23 p56 Je 5 2017

Working with Strong Service Providers to Address the Urban Water and Sanitation Challenge S. Ramanantsoa *UN Chronicle* v53 no3 p28 2016

Customer services—Evaluation

See also

Mystery shopping

Everyone Says They Listen to Their Customers— Here's How to Really Do It A. Brant *Harvard Business Review Digital Articles* p2 O 28 2015

Customer services—Management

How to Know Which Digital Trends Are Worth Chasing R. Haslehurst, C. Randall et al *Harvard Business Review Digital Articles* p2 Jl 7 2016

Customer services—Software

Great UX Doesn't Guarantee a Great Customer Experience A. Richardson *Harvard Business Review Digital Articles* p2 Ag 12 2015

Customer services—United States

Bring Your Smartphone Shopping E. AMBROSE color *AARP: The Magazine* v59 no6A p23 O/N 2016

Customization

ADVENTURE BOUND [Cover story] M. EMERY color *Dirt Sports + Off-Road* v51 no1 p44 Ja 2017

Candy Crush color *Vogue* v206 no12 p160 D 2016

FAMILY TRADITION M. EMERY color *Dirt Sports + Off-Road* v51 no8 p40 Ag 2017

HOW OL'S WILDCAT CAME TO DOMINATE LONG-RANGE PRECISION-RIFLE SHOOTING J. B. SNOW color graph *Outdoor Life* v224 no2 p36 F/Mr 2017

THE NUCLEAR MARSHMALLOW M. EMERY color *Dirt Sports + Off-Road* v51 no8 p54 Ag 2017

Vicious B. Gillogly color *Hot Rod* v70 no8 p32 Ag 2017

Customizing of automobiles

CONTROL FREAK [Cover story] M. EMERY color *Dirt Sports + Off-Road* v51 no12 p54 D 2017

The Electric, Hydraulic, Mostly American Truck E. DYER bw color *Popular Mechanics* p15 N 2017

How to Skin a Cat R. D'AGOSTINO *Popular Mechanics* p8 N 2017

ONE OF THE GOOD GUYS M. EMERY color *Dirt Sports + Off-Road* v51 no9 p52 S 2017

RUNNING WILD [Cover story] D. SCANLON and M. EMERY color *Dirt Sports + Off-Road* v51 no12 p40 D 2017

Thom On Design: Whatever Happened to Customizing? T. Taylor color *Hot Rod* v70 no12 p92 D 2017

TRANSFORMED color *Road & Track* v69 no2 p16 S 2017

Cut flower industry

GROWN AT HOME L. M. Roberts color *National Geographic* v232 no5 p18 N 2017

Cut flowers

From Our Editor S. Donelson color *House Beautiful* v159 no4 p10 My 2017

Cut to the Feeling (Music)

HOW CARLY RAE JEPSEN AND LEAP! GAVE US SUMMER'S BEST POP ANTHEM M. Snetiker color *Entertainment Weekly* no1480 p50 S 1 2017

Cuthill, Innes C.

The biology of color color *Science* v357 no6350 p470 Ag 4 2017

Cutillo, Bob

CURING OUR MISPLACED FAITH IN MEDICINE R. Moll color *Christianity Today* v60 no8 p79 O 2016

Cutler, Anne

Hearing from you C. Day *Physics Today* v70 no4 p8 Ap 2017

Cutler, David M.

How the U.S. Can Reduce Waste in Health Care Spending by $1 Trillion *Harvard Business Review Digital Articles* p2 O 13 2015

CUTLER, G. CHRISTOPHER

Bee Ecotoxicology and Data Veracity: Appreciating the GLP Process *BioScience* v66 no12 p1066 D 1 2016

Cutlery

    See also

    Knives

Looking Sharp A. GARDNER *Indianapolis Monthly* p33 N 2017

MEN OF STEEL B. HEAVEY *Field & Stream* v121 no8 p110 F/Mr 2017

Cutlip, Kimbra

On the Job color *Weatherwise* v69 no6 p40 N-D 2016

On The Job: Marshall Shepherd *Weatherwise* v70 no2 p29 Mr/Ap 2017

On the Job: Tim Garrett *Weatherwise* v70 no1 p40 Ja/F 2017

Weather Front color *Weatherwise* v69 no6 p6 N-D 2016

CUTOLO, MORGAN

Conserve Your Cell Data (and Your Money) color *Reader's Digest* v189 no1130 p46 My 2017

Cutrone, Lee

As you are: logan killen interiors renews northshore house to reflect couples personalities and lifestyle *New Orleans Homes & Lifestyles* v20 no3 p46 Summ 2017

BACK AT THE RANCH color *Louisiana Life* v37 no4 p28 Mr/Ap 2017

Bonnie Maygarden *New Orleans Homes & Lifestyles* v20 no3 p22 Summ 2017

Bright Spot color *New Orleans Magazine* v51 no8 p54 Je 2017

design masters *New Orleans Homes & Lifestyles* v20 no4 p70 Aut 2017

ELEGANT GEOMETRY color *Louisiana Life* v37 no3 p26 Ja/F 2017

Family Friendly color *New Orleans Magazine* v51 no6 p54 Ap 2017

Family Tradition color *New Orleans Magazine* v51 no9 p52 Jl 2017

Grand Finale color *New Orleans Magazine* v52 no1 p62 S 2017

Industrial Lite: Designer Shauna Leftwich softens industrial edges of warehouse district condo *New Orleans Homes & Lifestyles* v20 no4 p65 Aut 2017

Joan Griswold *New Orleans Homes & Lifestyles* v20 no4 p22 Aut 2017

LABOR OF LOVE color *Louisiana Life* v37 no2 p28 N/D 2016

LAKEFRONT LEGACY color *Louisiana Life* v37 no6 p20 Jl/Ag 2017

LIVING HISTORY color *Louisiana Life* v37 no5 p24 My/Je 2017

NEW BUILD OF THE YEAR: Kendall Winingder and Patrick Schindler combine their talents with a who's team of experts to build their dream home *New Orleans Homes & Lifestyles* v20 no4 p42 Aut 2017

Prime of Their Lives: Retiring in style on St. Charles Avenue color *New Orleans Magazine* v51 no10 p66 Ag 2017

Rachel David *New Orleans Homes & Lifestyles* v20 no1 p20 Wint 2016

Saving Grace color *New Orleans Magazine* v51 no7 p56 My 2017

Scott Andresen *New Orleans Homes & Lifestyles* v20 no2 p20 Spr 2017

SITE SPECIFIC color *Louisiana Life* v38 no1 p26 S/O 2017

Time & Again *New Orleans Homes & Lifestyles* v20 no1 p42 Wint 2016

Well-Aged color *Louisiana Life* v37 no5 p41 My/Je 2017

Well Schooled color *New Orleans Magazine* v51 no12 p64 O 2017

Cutter, Susan L.

THE PERILOUS NATURE OF FOOD SUPPLIES: Natural Hazards, Social Vulnerability, and Disaster Resilience chart color graph map *Environment* v59 no1 p4 2017

Cutting (Materials)

SHOP TIPS J. KOPYCINSKI color *Dirt Sports + Off-Road* v51 no10 p66 O 2017

Cutting away (Poem)

Cutting away P. C. Hansel *Christian Century* v134 no22 p11 O 25 2017

Cutting horses

GOOD NEWS ABOUT CUTTING HORSE INJURIES C. Barakat and M. McCluskey color *Equus* no482 p12 N 2017

Cutting machines—Evaluation

WELDING INNOVATIONS D. Mowitz *Successful Farming* v115 no9 p36 Ag 2017

Cutting tools

A GOOD CLIP F. VIGNA *Martha Stewart Living* no270 p166 D 2016

Cutting tools—Evaluation

Circular Saws R. ROMANSKI color *Popular Mechanics* p26 F 2017

High-Tension Hacksaws color *Popular Mechanics* p42 D 2016/Ja 2017

The Next Generation of Multitools bw *Popular Mechanics* p42 Mr 2017

Wire Strippers color *Popular Mechanics* p36 Mr 2017

Cutwater Boats (Company)

Cutwater 242 Open *Sea Magazine* v108 no12 p53 D 2016

Cutwater 302 Sport Coupe B. Pike color *Power & Motoryacht* v33 no2 p42 F 2017

CUTWATER: 302 SPORT COUPE THIS OUTBOARD-POWERED CRUISER CAN HIT 50 MPH AND HOST A DOCKSIDE SUNSET DINNER M. WERLING color *Sea Magazine* v109 no6 p34 Je 2017

Cuy, José Esparza Chong

JOSÉ ESPARZA CHONG CUY H. MITCHELL color *Chicago* v66 no10 p44 O 2017

Cvitanović, Predrag

David Ritz Finkelstein *Physics Today* v70 no2 p68 F 2017

CVS/Pharmacy Inc.

Summer SURVIVAL GUIDE N. SAPORITA color *Good Housekeeping* v264 no6 p69 Je 2017

Cyanobacteria

The Dead Zone M. MANN color diag map *Walrus* v14 no6 p38 Jl/Ag 2017

How Cyanobacteria went green R. E. Blankenship color *Science* v355 no6332 p1372 Mr 31 2017

RESEARCH color *Science* v355 no6330 p1169 Mr 17 2017

Cyanobacterial blooms

A plankton bloom shifts as the ocean warms A. Z. Worden and S. Wilken bibl color diag *Science* v354 no6310 p287 O 21 2016

protect your watershed S. Moen color *Cabin Living* p13 Ag 2017

Cyanobacteria—Physiology

On the origins of oxygenic photosynthesis and aerobic respiration in Cyanobacteria R. M. Soo, J. Hemp et al chart diag *Science* v355 no6332 p1436 Mr 31 2017

Cyberbullying

Cyberbullying and its Implications for Human Rights L. Hackett *UN Chronicle* v53 no4 p1 2016

Cyberbullying and Its Implications for Human Rights L. HACKETT *UN Chronicle* v54 no4 p41 2017

The Modern Bully *USA Today Magazine* v145 no2860 p35 Ja 2017

The Reason Twitter's Losing Active Users U. Haque *Harvard Business Review Digital Articles* p2 F 12 2016

RIGHT UNDER YOUR NOSE A. BAIR *USA Today Magazine* v145 no2860 p32 Ja 2017

Secret's Problem Wasn't Trolls L. Laurenson *Harvard Business Review Digital Articles* p2 My 20 2015

Cyberbullying—Lawsuits & claims

The Case Of the Facebook Bully V. GLEMBOCKI color *Reader's Digest* v189 no1130 p29 My 2017

Cybercriminals

The Hackers M. Vella color diag *Time* v188 no25-26 p102 D 19 2016 Double Issue

Cyberinfrastructure

Envisioning the Future of Aquatic Animal Tracking: Technology, Science, and Application R. J. LENNOX, K. AARESTRUP et al *BioScience* v67 no10 p884 O 2017

A Shocking Internet Attack Shows America's Vulnerability H. S. Edwards and M. Vella color diag *Time* v188 no19 p7 N 7 2016

Cybernetics

TREKKIE TECH C. HARRINGTON color *Wired* v25 no10 p32 O 2017

Cyberspace

Red Herring J. Lewis *Harper's Magazine* v334 no2001 p2 F 2017

The Seductions of the Infosphere C. Handy *Harvard Business Review Digital Articles* p2 Jl 15 2015

Cyberspace operations (Military science)

ARE WE PREPARED FOR CYBERWAR? A. GREENBERG cartoon *Wired* v25 no9 p77 S 2017

"Netwar": The unwelcome militarization of the Internet has arrived J. Zittrain bibl *Bulletin of the Atomic Scientists* v73 no5 p300 2017

Why We Need Cyberwar Rules of Engagement Now L. Bershidsky *Bloomberg Businessweek* no4531 p40 Jl 24 2017

Cyberterrorism

The C-Suite and IT Need to Get on the Same Page on Cybersecurity C. McKinty *Harvard Business Review Digital Articles* p2 Ap 26 2017

Cyberwars: We Must Prepare Ourselves for the Wars of the Future E. Schmidt and J. Cohen *Time* v188 no27-28 p25 D 26 2016

The Hacking Bear A. I. KLEIN il *National Review* v68 no21 p33 N 21 2016

Recent WordPress vulnerability used to deface 1.5 million pages L. CONSTANTIN color *PCWorld* p47 Mr 2017

Russia Sanctions *Congressional Digest* v96 no3 p31 Mr 2017

A Safer, Smarter Grid B. Walsh color *Time* v189 no13 p30 Ap 10 2017

Safe Shopping in Cyberspace T. J. DONOHUE *Weekly Standard* v22 no17 p14 Ja 2 2017

Sci-Hub briefly shutters *Science* v357 no6356 p1079 S 15 2017

Your Money Or Your Data! D. Lawrence and J. Robertson color *Bloomberg Businessweek* no4523 p15 My 22 2017

Cyberterrorism prevention

As Cyber Threats Mount, Businesses Mount a Defense T. J. DONOHUE *Weekly Standard* v22 no38 p21 Je 12 2017

Cyber-Regulating Banks T. Newcombe *Governing* v30 no3 p62 D 2016

Good Cybersecurity Doesn't Try to Prevent Every Attack G. Bell *Harvard Business Review Digital Articles* p2 O 25 2016

Limit Cyberattacks with a System-Wide Safe Mode C. Herbolzheimer *Harvard Business Review Digital Articles* p2 My 17 2017

Preparing for a Black Swan Cyberattack C. Herbolzheimer *Harvard Business Review Digital Articles* p2 S 14 2016

Preparing for the Cyberattack That Will Knock Out U.S. Power Grids S. Madnick *Harvard Business Review Digital Articles* p2 My 10 2017

To Guard Against Cybercrime, Follow the Money M. Gardiner *Harvard Business Review Digital Articles* p2 My 26 2017

Cyberterrorism—Government policy

Cyber-Regulating Banks T. Newcombe *Governing* v30 no3 p62 D 2016

Cyberterrorism—History

LIGHTS OUT A. GREENBERG color map *Wired* v25 no7 p52 Jl 2017

Cyborg Nest (Company)

Do-It-Yourself Transhumanism A. Popescu bw color *Bloomberg Businessweek* no4512 p34 F 20 2017

Cyborgs

Your Next Assistant: A Cyborg C. O'CONNOR color *Forbes* v199 no4 p48 Ap 25 2017

Cyclades (Greece)

MILOS'S MOMENT E. N. Gage color *Conde Nast Traveler* v52 no5 p108 My 2017

Cycles

See also

Business cycles
Geological cycles
Rain & rainfall periodicity

Don't blame aliens for star's flickering L. GROSSMAN *Science News* v192 no5 p11 S 30 2017

Cyclic-AMP-dependent protein kinase

Local protein kinase A action proceeds through intact holoenzymes F. Donelson Smith, J. L. Esseltine et al color diag graph *Science* v356 no6344 p1288 Je 23 2017

Cycling

See also

Bicycle commuting
Cycling competitions
Motorcycling
Mountain biking

2018 INTERNATIONAL TRIPS (PLUS WINTER DOMESTIC TRIPS) *Sierra* v102 no5 p48 St/O 2017

all-american bike parade [Cover story] color *Parents* v92 no7 p52 Jl 2017

THE ART OF COOL S. GEARHART color *Bicycling* v58 no4 p18 My 2017

BEST OF THE WEST color *Sunset* v239 no1 p11 Jl 2017

THE BIG EMPTY A. FRANKEL color *Bike Magazine* v24 no3 p70 My 2017

BUILD A BETTER BIKE *Saturday Evening Post* v289 no2 p21 Mr/Ap 2017

BUZZ bw color *Bike Magazine* v24 no5 p24 Jl 2017

CORYN RIVERA IS NOT LIKE THE REST OF US G. LIU color *Bicycling* v58 no10 p32 N/D 2017

a cross to air: EL BRUC, SPAIN | MAY 14, 2017 | 3:01 P.M n. formosa cartoon *Bike Magazine* v24 no8 p34 N 2017

THE DIRT with Lani Dickinson color *Dance Spirit* v21 no8 p36 O 2017

The EDDY MERCKX Alphabet cartoon color *Bicycling* v58 no1 p40 Ja/F 2017

Escape the Gym K. Canning color *Health* v31 no5 p39 Je 2017

Fast and Happy R. Missel, J. Lindsey et al cartoon color *Bicycling* v58 no8 p24 S 2017

Find your exercise fit! *Harvard Health Letter* v42 no5 p4 Mr 2017

FIVE PLACES YOU HAVE TO RIDE BEFORE THEY CHANGE FOREVER E. SPENCE color *Bicycling* v58 no7 p36 Ag 2017

From Darkness to Light M. BRINKMAN *Idaho Magazine* v16 no2 p24 N 2016

hart-shaped trails: MEET THE FUTURE OF FEDERAL LAND MANAGEMENT k. gensheimer bw color *Bike Magazine* v24 no8 p32 N 2017

HIGH COUNTRY HUSTLE M. COTÉ bw color *Bike Magazine* v24 no3 p86 My 2017

I BATHE IN A RIVER AND DON'T GIVE A SHIT J. KYLE WHALEN color *Bicycling* v58 no7 p45 Ag 2017

I'M 44 AND I WANT TO GET RAD J. LINDSEY color *Bicycling* v58 no9 p48 O 2017

INTERNATIONAL *Sierra* v101 no6 p58 N/D 2016

JOIN THE RIDE L. FLICKINGER bw color *Bicycling* v58 no7 p20 Ag 2017

JOIN THE RIDE L. FLICKINGER bw color *Bicycling* v58 no8 p14 S 2017

Keep It Fresh J. Sumner color *Bicycling* v58 no6 p30 Jl 2017

let go: AND SURRENDER TO THE NOW m. ferrentino color

no1 p106 O 2017

Cyclins

Cyclin A2 is an RNA binding protein that controls Mre11 mRNA translation A. Kanakkanthara, K. B. Jeganathan et al bibl graph *Science* v353 no6307 p1549 S 30 2016

Cyclist physiology

ONE LAST SHOT I. DILLE color *Bicycling* v58 no10 p40 N/D 2017

Cyclists

the breakeway R. K. JOHNSON cartoon *New Yorker* v93 no7 p64 Ap 3 2017

GO AHEAD, OVERTHINK IT B. BROUDY color *Bicycling* v58 no8 p32 S 2017

Go Wild! color *Bicycling* v58 no6 p40 Jl 2017

GRIME AND PUNISHMENT *Los Angeles Magazine* p172 Ja 2017

JOIN THE RIDE L. FLICKINGER color *Bicycling* v58 no10 p10 N/D 2017

MEET THE MESSENGER C. GIDDINGS color *Bicycling* v58 no6 p46 Jl 2017

Mmm, Poke! color *Bicycling* v58 no6 p32 Jl 2017

OFF LINE color *Bike Magazine* v24 no8 p82 N 2017

RUNNING HOME [Cover story] M. REMY cartoon color *Runner's World* v52 no5 p74 Je 2017

SANCTUARY A. CURRY color *Bicycling* v58 no6 p48 Jl 2017

THE SELECTION B. STRICKLAND *Bicycling* v58 no4 p12 My 2017

THE SELECTION B. STRICKLAND cartoon color *Bicycling* v58 no1 p10 Ja/F 2017

SO ICONIC! C. SIDWELLS bw color *Bicycling* v58 no6 p17 Jl 2017

STRAIGHT TO THE BIG TIME M. HURFORD color *Bicycling* v58 no6 p42 Jl 2017

THANKS FOR THE RIDE C. RAMIREZ, R. MASONER et al color *Bicycling* v58 no10 p15 N/D 2017

THE THING THAT CHANGED IT ALL color *Bicycling* v58 no7 p23 Ag 2017

THE THING THAT CHANGED IT ALL L. ETHRIDGE color *Bicycling* v58 no10 p13 N/D 2017

THIS GRANDMOTHER CLIMBED ALPE D'HUEZ EIGHT TIMES IN ONE DAY! J. See color *Bicycling* v58 no6 p22 Jl 2017

THOSE LEGS! G. LIU bw *Bicycling* v58 no8 p39 S 2017

TO THE STARS THROUGH DIFFICULTIES C. GIDDINGS bw *Bicycling* v58 no10 p22 N/D 2017

Who Owns the Air? J. Servaas *Saturday Evening Post* v289 no1 p27 Ja/F 2017

YOU SHOULD KNOW cartoon *Bicycling* v58 no1 p12 Ja/F 2017

YOU SHOULD KNOW cartoon *Bicycling* v58 no8 p76 S 2017

Cyclists—Awards

aspirations of mediocrity k. butcher color *Bike Magazine* v24 no7 p48 S 2017

Cyclists—Clothing

ALMOST NAKED! J. LINDSEY color *Bicycling* v58 no7 p72 Ag 2017

ANDORRA DRIRELEASE MERINO ¾ JERSEY color *Bike Magazine* v24 no4 p106 Je 2017

DISTRICT HENLEY R. Palmer color *Bike Magazine* v24 no4 p102 Je 2017

KIAH TEE N. Formosa color *Bike Magazine* v24 no4 p104 Je 2017

ULTRAFINE MERINO T-SHIRT color *Bike Magazine* v24 no4 p104 Je 2017

Cyclists—Equipment & supplies

CAMELBAK K.U.D.U. PROTECTOR 10 R. Koch color *Bicycling* v58 no9 p70 O 2017

Cyclists—Nutrition

BREAD IS NOT THE ENEMY J. Stout color *Bicycling* v58 no8 p36 S 2017

Keep It Fresh J. Sumner color *Bicycling* v58 no6 p30 Jl 2017

Cyclists—Training of

Fast and Happy R. Missel, J. Lindsey et al cartoon color *Bicycling* v58 no8 p24 S 2017

How 1% Performance Improvements Led to Olympic Gold E. Harrell *Harvard Business Review Digital Articles* p2 O 30 2015

Cyclists—Travel

no free rides b. minnigh color *Bike Magazine* v23 no9 p19 D 2016

Cyclists—United States

Our Two-Wheel Transformation A. Marshall *Governing* v30 no1 p22 O 2016

Savory Cycle Ride, Midway, Kentucky C. CROSE *Cincinnati Magazine* p63 Je 2017

Cyclodextrins

Battle over rare disease drug ensnares NIH M. Wadman color *Science* v354 no6308 p18 O 7 2016

Cyclohexadiene

Femtosecond x-ray spectroscopy of an electrocyclic ring-opening reaction A. R. Attar, A. Bhattacherjee et al diag graph *Science* v356 no6333 p54 Ap 7 2017

Cyclones—Tropics

See also

Tropical storms

THE MOST KNOWN UNKNOWN J. (. c. Wilson color *Surfing Magazine* v53 no2 p32 F 2017

Cyclones—United States

A Cyclone for All Seasons J. B. Halverson *Weatherwise* v70 no5 p44 S/O 2017

Cyclosporine—Therapeutic use

Dry eyes? Try this! *Harvard Health Letter* v42 no6 p7 Ap 2017

Cygnus A

Second black hole spotted in famous galaxy color *Astronomy* v45 no9 p13 S 2017

Cyler, R. J.

RJ CYLER *Interview* v47 no5 p64 Je/Jl 2017

Cymbals—Evaluation

Crescent by Sabian Stanton Moore Collection M. Kern color *Downbeat* v83 no12 p108 D 2016

Sabian Artisan Elites M. Kern color *Downbeat* v84 no6 p86 Je 2017

Cymbeline (Play : Shakespeare)

Professor Shakespeare *Lapham's Quarterly* v10 no2 p114 Spr 2017

Cymru, Sinfonia

Jenkins: Cantata Memoria S. F. Vasta *Opera News* v81 no10 p55 Ap 2017

Cynicism

Ethics in Astrophotography: Seeing isn't always believing in the digital age J. Lodriguss *Sky & Telescope* v134 no3 p66 S 2017

Superstition Masquerading as Science R. AMMIRATI, S. O. LILIENFELD et al *Skeptical Inquirer* v40 no6 p14 N/D 2016

Cypress Cay (Company)

Cypress Cay Cabana 220 *Boating World* v38 no1 p59 Ja 2017

Cyprinidae

CAT HACKS K. SUTTON color *Outdoor Life* v224 no6 p35 Ag 2017

Cyprus—Economic conditions

Why Greece and Cyprus May Be Better Off Without the Euro L. Heracleous *Harvard Business Review Digital Articles* p2 Mr 10 2015

Cypseloides niger

Nest Quest R. Shivni color *Audubon* v119 no3 p46 Fall 2017

Cyrano de Bergerac (Theatrical production)

CLASSICAL MUSIC *New Yorker* v93 no13 p8 My 15 2017

Cyrille, Andrew

Cyrille's Brilliant Gamesmanship K. Micallef color *Downbeat* v84 no1 p17 Ja 2017

Cyrus, Kurt

Billions of Bricks color *Publishers Weekly* v263 no49 p19 D 7 2016

Cyrus, Miley, 1992-

Miley Cyrus L. Greenblatt color *Entertainment Weekly* no1485 p58 O 6 2017

MILEY'S SUMMER OF Love J. Pressler color *Harper's Bazaar* no3655 p146 Ag 2017

Sound Bites color *Entertainment Weekly* no1441 p5 N 25 2016

Cyrus, Noah—Interviews

17 Questions With Noah Cyrus color *Seventeen* v76 no3 p16 My 2017

Cysteine

Redox-based reagents for chemoselective methionine bioconjugation S. Lin, X. Yang et al bibl diag graph *Science* v355 no6325 p597 F 10 2017

Cysteine proteinases
NEW DEWORMING AGENT SHOWS PROMISE C. Barakat and M. McCluskey color *Equus* no473 p11 F 2017

Cystic fibrosis treatment
THE PRICE OF INSPIRATION M. HERPER chart color *Forbes* v200 no2 p84 S 5 2017

Cystisoma
Vanishing Act E. UNDERWOOD *Smithsonian* v47 no9 p16 Ja/F 2017

Cytech (Company)
When Spotting a Hack Doesn't Help You P. M. Barrett *Bloomberg Businessweek* no4497 p36 O 31 2016

Cytochrome c
Directed evolution of cytochrome c for carbon–silicon bond formation: Bringing silicon to life S. B. J. Kan, R. D. Lewis et al bibl diag graph *Science* v354 no6315 p1048 N 25 2016
Enzyme links up carbon and silicon L. HAMERS color *Science News* v190 no13 p11 D 24 2016
Locked and loaded for apoptosis K. L. Bren and E. L. Raven diag *Science* v356 no6344 p1236 Je 23 2017
Teaching nature the unnatural H. F. T. Klare and M. Oestreich bibl diag *Science* v354 no6315 p970 N 25 2016

Cytogenetics
CRISPRi-based genome-scale identification of functional long noncoding RNA loci in human cells M. A. Horlbeck, S. J. Liu et al bibl graph *Science* v355 no6320 p1 Ja 6 2017

Cytokines
See also
Growth factors
Anti-inflammatory effect of IL-10 mediated by metabolic reprogramming of macrophages W. K. Eddie Ip, N. Hoshi et al diag *Science* v356 no6337 p513 My 5 2017

Cytological research
RESEARCH color *Science* v357 no6350 p467 Ag 4 2017

Cytology
The CELL Atlas S. CONNOR bw color *MIT Technology Review* v120 no2 p58 Mr/Ap 2017
Whole cell maps chart a course for 21st-century cell biology R. Horwitz and G. T. Johnson color *Science* v356 no6340 p806 My 26 2017

Cytology—Abstracts
Coupling organelle inheritance with mitosis to balance growth and differentiation A. Asare, J. Levorse et al diag *Science* v355 no6324 p493 F 3 2017

Cytosine
Impact of cytosine methylation on DNA binding specificities of human transcription factors Y. Yin, E. Morgunova et al diag *Science* v356 no6337 p502 My 5 2017

CYWIŃSKI, PIOTR
The Rise of the Dwarf *American Conservative* v16 no2 p36 Mr/Ap 2017

Czarkowski, James
you may be right chart *U.S. Catholic* v82 no9 p5 S 2017

Czech Republic
ROAD TO RYCHLEB Y G. AVERILL bw color map *Bike Magazine* v24 no8 p48 N 2017

Czeisler, Charles A.
Reset Your Internal Clock to Fight Jet Lag color *Kiplinger's Personal Finance* v71 no5 p70 My 2017

Czerneda, Julie E.
Nebula Awards Showcase 2017 *Publishers Weekly* v264 no13 p86 Mr 27 2017

Czernowin, Chaya
CATACLYSM A. ROSS color *New Yorker* v93 no13 p92 My 15 2017

Czerski, Helen
Mysteries of the mundane M. Engel color *Science* v355 no6320 p33 Ja 6 2017
Storm in a Teacup: The Physics of Everyday Life B. Halfpap *Physics Today* v70 no8 p59 Ag 2017

Czinger, Kevin
RETOOLING THE SYSTEM M. PRINCE color *Road & Track* v69 no4 p58 N 2017

Czuczka, Tony
An Establishment Firebrand in Germany color *Bloomberg Businessweek* no4514 p28 Mr 13 2017

D

D & M Holdings Inc.
Denon AVR-X4200W A/V Receiver D. Kumin chart color graph *Sound & Vision* v81 no9 p58 N 2016

D & W Lounge (Company)
D&W LOUNGE *Texas Monthly* v45 no1 p101 Ja 2017

Da Wei
Uncle Sam in Midlife Crisis? *Wilson Quarterly* p6 Spr 2017

Daalder, Ivo H.
Responding to Russia's Resurgence color *Foreign Affairs* v96 no6 p30 N/D 2017

Dabanka, Afua
MOSAIC OF CULTURES M. STREET color *Ebony* v72 no8 p42 Je 2017

Dabis, François
We still need to beat HIV color *Science* v357 no6349 p335 Jl 28 2017

Dabney, Christina
Not Your Average Joe chart color *Consumer Reports* v82 no10 p8 O 2017

Dabney, R. S.
The Soul Mender color *Publishers Weekly* v263 no47 p76c N 21 2016

Dacey, Patrick
The Outer Cape *Publishers Weekly* v264 no14 p46 Ap 3, 2017

Dachs, Bernhard
Research: Arab Inventors Make the U.S. More Innovative *Harvard Business Review Digital Articles* p2 F 23 2017

Dachshunds
A Dog's Life T. Flanagan color *Sail* v48 no8 p12 Ag 2017
RACING WIENER DOGS S. BAHR color *Indianapolis Monthly* v42 no2 p16 O 2017

DA COSTA, CASSIE
The Florida Project color *Film Comment* v53 no5 p72 S/O 2017

Dacus, Lucy
NIGHT LIFE *New Yorker* v93 no27 p8 S 11 2017

D'Addario & Co
D'Addario Select Jazz Tenor Saxophone Mouthpiece J. Bowes color *Downbeat* v84 no5 p86 My 2017
Evans Calftone Drum Heads S. Hawk color *Downbeat* v83 no11 p81 N 2016

Daddario, Alexandra
AT LAST, SHE SPEAKS! C. Connors color *Women's Health* v14 no5 p142 Je 2017

D'Addario, Brian
Glam Rock M. GUIDUCCI color *Vogue* v207 no4 p184 Ap 2017

D'addario, Daniel
The 10 Best Episodes color *Time* v188 no25-26 p140 D 19 2016 Double Issue
The 10 Best Shows color *Time* v188 no25-26 p138 D 19 2016 Double Issue
Alan Thicke color *Time* v188 no27-28 p17 D 26 2016
All Happy Families, Alike color *Time* v190 no14 p48 O 9 2017
Amazon Tries to Complete F. Scott Fitzgerald's Unfinished Novel color *Time* v190 no5 p60 Jl 31 2017
American Horror Story Is Frightfully Good With Secrets color *Time* v188 no19 p55 N 7 2016
Antiheroines Are Resplendent In Harlots color *Time* v189 no12 p55 Ap 3 2017
Archie and the Gang Come Back to a Much Darker World color *Time* v189 no4 p47 F 6 2017
As Television Expands, the Emmys Are Becoming a Battlefield color *Time* v190 no10/11 p30 S 18 2017
Bad Boys (and Girls) Return to Fox In Shots Fired color *Time* v189 no12 p53 Ap 3 2017
Bateman's Stab at High Drama color *Time* v190 no5 p61 Jl 31 2017
The Best of Everything This Year-So Far color *Time* v189 no21 p61 Je 5 2017
Budget Wrestling Lights Up the Screen In Glow color *Time* v190 no2/3 p93 Jl 10-17 2017
Cards Returns With a Thud color *Time* v189 no21 p63 Je 5 2017
Darkness Under the Sun on USA's Gripping Drama the Sinner color *Time* v190 no6 p51 Ag 7 2017
Darkness Visible In 13 Reasons Why color *Time* v189 no13 p51

Ap 10 2017

Edie Falco As an Attorney Ripped from the Headlines color *Time* v190 no10/11 p108 S 18 2017

Edith Windsor color *Time* v190 no12 p15 S 25 2017

E!'s Teen Queen of Screens color *Time* v190 no6 p52 Ag 7 2017

Everyday People, Extraordinary Books color *Time* v190 no7 p53 Ag 21 2017

A Family Story With a Son on the Spectrum color *Time* v190 no7 p52 Ag 21 2017

Florence Henderson 1934-2016 color *Time* v188 no24 p70 D 12 2016

FX's Exploration of the Crack Epidemic Falters color *Time* v190 no2/3 p92 Jl 10-17 2017

Hairspray Live! Promises Retro Fun With Little Risk color *Time* v188 no24 p68 D 12 2016

Haters Back Off Takes a Star from YouTube to TV color *Time* v188 no16/17 p92 O 24 2016

HBO Offers a West-Ward Expansion of the Mind color *Time* v188 no14 p61 O 10 2016

Heigl's Star Quality Comes Through In the Courtroom color *Time* v189 no7/8 p103 F 27 2017

How They Make the Greatest Show on Earth [Cover story] color *Time* v190 no2/3 p66 Jl 10-17 2017

Issa Rae's Insecure Is the Sharpest Comedy of the Year color *Time* v190 no4 p50 Jl 24 2017

The Keepers Avoids True Crime's Ghastliest Pitfalls color *Time* v189 no21 p63 Je 5 2017

Lady Gaga, Brought Low color *Time* v190 no14 p54 O 9 2017

Larry David As the Social Critic Still In the Right color *Time* v190 no10/11 p104 S 18 2017

Laurie's New Healing Sleuth Takes a Dubious Chance color *Time* v188 no18 p45 O 31 2016

Make-Believe color *Time* v188 no25-26 p36 D 19 2016 Double Issue

Mary Tyler Moore color *Time* v189 no4 p13 F 6 2017

Megyn Kelly, Queen of TV Sparring, Meets Her Match color *Time* v189 no23 p53 Je 19 2017

Musical Theater and Misanthropy color *Time* v190 no7 p52 Ag 21 2017

Naomi Watts' Deceptive Therapist Just Can't Help Herself on Gypsy color *Time* v190 no1 p53 Jl 3 2017

Natalie Portman color *Time* v188 no22-23 p112 N/D 2016

Network TV's Calorie-Free Take on American Patriotism color *Time* v190 no13 p63 O 2 2017

A New Class of Hard-Ass Heroes color *Time* v188 no27-28 p109 D 26 2016

No Break for Orange's Prisoners color *Time* v189 no23 p53 Je 19 2017

Oilmen and Indians In a Saga of American West color *Time* v189 no14 p52 Ap 17 2017

On Amazon, a Troubled Letter-Writing Campaign from the Heart color *Time* v189 no19 p49 My 22 2017

On FX, a Bonfire of the Vain Biddies color *Time* v189 no9 p52 Mr 13 2017

On HBO, a Tyrannical New Pope Lusts for Power color *Time* v189 no3 p53 Ja 16 2017

An Onscreen Family, Raising Cane color *Time* v190 no1 p52 Jl 3 2017

On TNT's New Soap, Utopia Among the Manicurists color *Time* v189 no24 p49 Je 26 2017

Porn, Prostitutes and Heart on HBO's The Deuce color *Time* v190 no14 p47 O 9 2017

Racing the Clock In the ISIS Era color *Time* v188 no27-28 p108 D 26 2016

Radicals In Love Go Guerrilla color *Time* v189 no15 p52 Ap 24 2017

Sarah Jessica Parker color *Time* v188 no14 p64 O 10 2016

Sedgwick As a Tormented Hard-Ass *Time* v190 no15 p57 O 16 2017

So Far, Twin Peaks' Mysteries Remain Unsatisfying color *Time* v189 no21 p62 Je 5 2017

Speechless Gets Real About Families Affected by Disability color *Time* v188 no15 p56 O 17 2016

Streaming Now: Two Sets of Subversive Heroes color *Time* v190 no8 p51 Ag 28 2017

Television Manages to Put a New Twist on the California State of

Mind color *Time* v189 no6 p47 F 20 2017

This Is Us Metes Out Darkness In Search of a Moment's Delight color *Time* v189 no3 p49 Ja 30 2017

The Trouble With the Bachelorette (This Time) color *Time* v189 no24 p47 Je 26 2017

Trump Learned Lessons About Reality TV That The Apprentice Hasn't color *Time* v189 no4 p47 Ja 23 2017

A TV Legend's Unremarkable Return color *Time* v188 no15 p54 O 17 2016

TV's Great New Heroine Is Born In The Handmaid's Tale color *Time* v189 no18 p53 My 15 2017

TV's Real Mother of Draggin' color *Time* v190 no1 p53 Jl 3 2017

TV's Silly Season: A Guide color *Time* v189 no24 p48 Je 26 2017

A TV Traditionalist With a Weird Streak color *Time* v189 no14 p56 Ap 17 2017

The Uncanny Catharsis of Saturday Night Live color *Time* v189 no7/8 p23 F 27 2017

When the Most Human Human Isn't Actually Human color *Time* v189 no7/8 p104 F 27 2017

Will & Grace Hasn't Changed Much. And That's Just Fine color *Time* v190 no15 p57 O 16 2017

Will Has a Famous Name, but It Lacks Light-Footed Grace color *Time* v190 no4 p51 Jl 24 2017

With Mindhunter, Fincher Perfects the Art of Darkness color *Time* v190 no16/17 p99 O 23 2017

A Young Comic's Hope-Filled Crash color *Time* v189 no7/8 p103 F 27 2017

D'Addario, Michael

Glam Rock M. GUIDUCCI color *Vogue* v207 no4 p184 Ap 2017

D'Addario, Robert—Interviews

The Future of Fiber C. Crowley color *Sound & Vision* v82 no1 p16 Ja 2017

Daddy Longlegs (Film)

URBAN LEGENDS E. Hynes bw color *Film Comment* v53 no4 p22 Jl/Ag 2017

Daddy's Home 2 (Film)

ALSO PLAYING D. Heching color *Entertainment Weekly* no1478 / 1479 p69 Ag 18-25 2017

Daddy's Little Girls (Film)

GROWING UP NICELY C. Murray color *Essence* v48 no3 p52 Jl 2017

Daddy Yankee, 1977-

The New Science of the Truly Unstoppable, Impossible-to-Resist Summer Jam R. Bruner color *Time* v190 no9 p53 S 4 2017

Da Deppo, V.

Rosetta's comet 67P/Churyumov-Gerasimenko sheds its dusty mantle to reveal its icy nature bibl graph *Science* v354 no6319 p1566 D 23 2016

Surface changes on comet 67P/Churyumov-Gerasimenko suggest a more active past bw graph *Science* v355 no6332 p1392 Mr 31 2017

DADICH, SCOTT

BARACK OBAMA, NEURAL NETS, SELF-DRIVING CARS, AND THE FUTURE OF THE WORLD color *Wired* v24 no11 p124 N 2016

THE HAND OFF color *Wired* v25 no3 p12 Mr 2017

HOW TO SEE THE WORLD color map *Wired* v24 no12 p16 D 2016

THE POWER OF SCIENCE FICTION *Wired* v25 no1 p3 Ja 2017

Dadin, Ildar

To Protest In Russia J. NORDLINGER color *National Review* v69 no2 p22 F 6 2017

Dad's Journey Home- for Antone Pressler 1916-1990 (Poem)

Dad's Journey Home—for Antone Pressler 1916-1990 J. Redlin *South Dakota Magazine* v33 no2 p90 Jl/Ag 2017

Dady, Jason

A Game-Changing Dip color *Men's Health* v32 no1 p24 Ja/F 2017

Dae Ryun Chang

AlphaGo and the Limits of Machine Intuition *Harvard Business Review Digital Articles* p2 Mr 18 2016

Samsung Pay's Older Technology Could Be an Advantage *Harvard Business Review Digital Articles* p2 Jl 27 2015

Daewoong Nam

A three-dimensional movie of structural changes in bacteriorhodopsin bibl diag graph *Science* v354 no6319 p1552 D 23 2016

Daffodils

THE GRUMPY GARDENER S. Bender color *Southern Living* v52 no5 p58 My 2017

Dafforn, Timothy R.

Characterization of a dynamic metabolon producing the defense compound dhurrin in sorghum bibl graph *Science* v354 no6314 p890 N 18 2016

DAFNY, LEEMORE S.

Health Care Needs Real Competition color diag graph img *Harvard Business Review* v94 no12 p76 D 2016

The Risks of Health Insurance Company Mergers *Harvard Business Review Digital Articles* p2 S 24 2015

What the Trump Administration Needs to Do About Health Care *Harvard Business Review Digital Articles* p2 N 10 2016

Dagan, David

How Do You Get Ideologues to Change Their Minds? H. Schoenfeld *Washington Monthly* p1 S/O 2016

D'Agata, John

THE CONVERSATION T. L. Cox, R. Moss et al color *Atlantic* v319 no3 p12 Ap 2017

In DEFENSE of FACTS W. DERESIEWICZ color *Atlantic* v319 no1 p90 Ja/F 2017

Dagdeviren, Canan

The Body Electric S. ORNES color diag *Discover* v38 no6 p94 Jl/Ag 2017

The future of bionic dynamos bibl color *Science* v354 no6316 p1109-A D 2 2016

Dagen, Allison Swan

EMBRACING A LEADING ROLE: A look at the schoolwide impact of reading specialists *Literacy Today (2411-7862)* v35 no2 p22 S/O 2017

Daggers

awes8me Wicked Weapons J. AGRESTA color *National Geographic Kids* no465 p11 N 2016

King Tut's dagger J. HESTER color *Astronomy* v45 no8 p82 Ag 2017

Dagliya, Onur

Engineering extrinsic disorder to control protein activity in living cells bibl color *Science* v354 no6318 p1441 D 16 2016

D'Agostino, Abbey, 1992-

Olympic Recovery J. Fuchs and T. Keith color *Sports Illustrated* v127 no3 p18 Jl 24 2017

D'Agostino, Daniele

An accreting pulsar with extreme properties drives an ultraluminous x-ray source in NGC 5907 bibl chart graph *Science* v355 no6327 p817 F 24 2017

D'Agostino, Kris

The Antiques *Publishers Weekly* v263 no43 p52 O 24 2016

D'AGOSTINO, RYAN

A CLEAN, WELL-LIGHTED WORKROOM cartoon color *Popular Mechanics* p103 D 2016/Ja 2017

THE HELP REFLEX color *Popular Mechanics* p6 Mr 2017

HOME color *Popular Mechanics* p6 D 2016/Ja 2017

HOW TO BUY RECORDS color *Popular Mechanics* p38 My 2017

How to Skin a Cat *Popular Mechanics* p8 N 2017

THE NEW SELF-SUFFICIENCY *Popular Mechanics* p4 F 2017

The Personality-Driven Garden Fence color *Popular Mechanics* p99 Je 2017

Progress *Popular Mechanics* p6 S 2017

Safety and Freedom and Magazines *Popular Mechanics* p4 Ap 2017

THE STORY TELLER color *Popular Mechanics* p68 O 2017

Dah-Ning Yuan

Gravity field of the Orientale basin from the Gravity Recovery and Interior Laboratory Mission bibl graph *Science* v354 no6311 p438 O 28 2016

Dahai Luo

Crystal structure of unlinked NS2B-NS3 protease from Zika virus bibl color graph *Science* v354 no6319 p1597 D 23 2016

Dahill, Lisa E.

The Doubled Life of Dietrich Bonhoeffer: Women, Sexuality, and Nazi Germany *Christian Century* v134 no5 p38 Mr 1 2017

Eco-Reformation: Grace and Hope for a Planet in Peril L. D. Schade *Christian Century* v134 no16 p33 Ag 2 2017

Dahl, J. A.

Permanent human occupation of the central Tibetan Plateau in the early Holocene bibl bw color diag *Science* v355 no6320 p1 Ja 6 2017

DAHL, MELISSA

When Everything Is "Mine!" color *Parents* v92 no11 p38 N 2017

Dahl, Phoebe

Raise Your Voice [Cover story] i. T. Wright color *Glamour* v115 no3 p184 Mr 2017

Dahl, Roald, 1916-1990

THE SCIENCE OF PERSUASION K. Kupferschmidt color *Science* v356 no6336 p366 Ap 28 2017

Dahlander, Linus

The Biases That Keep Good R&D Projects from Getting Funded *Harvard Business Review Digital Articles* p2 Mr 17 2017

A Study Shows How to Find New Ideas Inside and Outside the Company *Harvard Business Review Digital Articles* p2 Jl 18 2017

Why Some Crowdsourcing Efforts Work and Others Don't *Harvard Business Review Digital Articles* p2 F 21 2017

Dahlhoff, Denise

Why Sprint and Radio Shack Are Shacking Up *Harvard Business Review Digital Articles* p2 F 10 2015

Why Target's Canadian Expansion Failed *Harvard Business Review Digital Articles* p2 Ja 20 2015

Dahlias

Dahlias! [Cover story] D. PRINZING color *Better Homes & Gardens* v95 no8 p140 Ag 2017

DAHLIE, SCOTT

Out of Service *Weekly Standard* v22 no4 p37 O 3 2016

Dahlke, Helen

THE WATER BANKER M. B. Griggs color *Popular Science* v289 no2 p22 Mr/Ap 2017

Dahlonega (Ga.)

Pretty. Sweet Cuisine *Atlanta* v57 no5 p139 S 2017

Dahlstrom, S. J.

Buildings Like Bones color *American Cowboy* p62 LEGENDS OF TEXAS Special Issue 2017

Dahms, Fabian

Large-amplitude transfer motion of hydrated excess protons mapped by ultrafast 2D IR spectroscopy graph *Science* v357 no6350 p491 Ag 4 2017

Dahozy, Brooks

Dahozy and Duby Win Sisters, Ore color *Spin to Win Rodeo* v21 no6 p22 Ag 2017

Dai, Hongjiu

Synthesis, debugging, and effects of synthetic chromosome consolidation: synVI and beyond color *Science* v355 no6329 p1045 Mr 10 2017

Dai, Hui

Satellite-based entanglement distribution over 1200 kilometers diag graph *Science* v356 no6343 p1140 Je 16 2017

Dai, Junbiao

3D organization of synthetic and scrambled chromosomes diag *Science* v355 no6329 p1050 Mr 10 2017

Bug mapping and fitness testing of chemically synthesized chromosome X diag *Science* v355 no6329 p1048 Mr 10 2017

Deep functional analysis of synII, a 770-kilobase synthetic yeast chromosome diag *Science* v355 no6329 p1047 Mr 10 2017

Engineering the ribosomal DNA in a megabase synthetic chromosome diag *Science* v355 no6329 p1049 Mr 10 2017

Synthesis, debugging, and effects of synthetic chromosome consolidation: synVI and beyond color *Science* v355 no6329 p1045 Mr 10 2017

Dai, Jun-Jun

"Perfect" designer chromosome V and behavior of a ring derivative diag *Science* v355 no6329 p1046 Mr 10 2017

Daigneau, Elizabeth

Breaking It Down *Governing* v30 no2 p20 N 2016

Bridging the Green Divide *Governing* v30 no6 p20 Mr 2017

Cleaning Up: After a natural disaster, environmental agencies are among the first on the ground *Governing* v30 no8 p20 My 2017

Crossing the Red-Blue Divide: One Tennessee group has taken the politics out of renewable energy *Governing* v30 no12 p20 S 2017

Going After Big Climate *Governing* v30 no1 p20 O 2016

Green from the Get-Go: At 24, Atlanta's new sustainability director has already spent a lifetime in the field *Governing* v31 no1

p20 O 2017

Greenout *Governing* v30 no4 p20 Ja 2017

Is Recycling Broken? *Governing* v30 no9 p50 Je 2017

Last Look *Governing* v30 no2 p64 N 2016

Purchasing Power: A new collaboration helped Minnesota double its solar capacity *Governing* v30 no9 p20 Je 2017

Seeing Climate Change *Governing* v30 no5 p22 F 2017

Setting the PACE *Governing* v30 no7 p20 Ap 2017

Two Buzzwords, Same Meaning? 'Zero waste' and 'circular economy' are often used together *Governing* v30 no10 p20 Jl 2017

What's Sustainability, Anyhow? *Governing* v30 no3 p20 D 2016

Dailey, Jane

The politics of sexual assault [Cover story] color *Christian Century* v134 no22 p28 O 25 2017

Daily, Emily

A Sport of Leaders color *Practical Horseman* v45 no5 p8 My 2017

Daily, Gretchen

Social norms as solutions bibl color *Science* v354 no6308 p42 O 7 2016

When, Where, and How Nature Matters for Ecosystem Services: Challenges for the Next Generation of Ecosystem Service Models *BioScience* v67 no9 p820 S 2017

DAILY, SUMMER

Beard, Bath & Beyond *Indianapolis Monthly* v40 no5 p25 Ja 2017

CHANGE the CITY *Indianapolis Monthly* p55 Ap 2017

Flashback color *Indianapolis Monthly* v42 no2 p54 O 2017

Leap of Faith *Indianapolis Monthly* p52 My 2017

Daily Burn Inc.

SWIMSUIT SHAPE-UP color *Good Housekeeping* v264 no5 p102 My 2017

Daily Show With Trevor Noah, The (TV program)

THE DECIDERS AND THE DAMNED G. CARTER *Vanity Fair* v58 no12 p62 D 2016

THE Good Guy P. Robinson color *Glamour* v115 no10 p168 O 2017

Daimler, Melissa

Listening Is an Overlooked Leadership Tool *Harvard Business Review Digital Articles* p2 My 25 2016

Why Leadership Development Has to Happen on the Job *Harvard Business Review Digital Articles* p2 Mr 16 2016

Daimler AG

GREEN HELLION C. CHILTON color *Road & Track* v68 no7 p80 Mr/Ap 2017

GRIP AND GRIN J. DEMATIO color *Road & Track* v68 no8 p90 My 2017

Haymaker M. Sutton color *Car & Driver* v62 no8 p84 F 2017

Mercedes-Benz C300 Coupe 4Matic chart color *Motor Trend* v69 no1 p130 Ja 2017

Mercedes-Benz E300 chart color *Motor Trend* v69 no1 p131 Ja 2017

Mercedes-Benz Generation EQ Concept A. Priddle color *Motor Trend* v69 no1 p18 Ja 2017

Mercedes-Benz GLS-Class chart color *Motor Trend* v69 no1 p54 Ja 2017

Mercedes-Benz Vision Van Concept A. MacKenzie color *Motor Trend* v68 no12 p20 D 2016

Sketching a High-Voltage Future E. Behrmann color *Bloomberg Businessweek* no4494 p43 O 10 2016

Theater of the Absurd J. Zoellter bw color diag *Car & Driver* v62 no11 p106 My 2017

Zee Über Trück E. DYER cartoon color *Popular Mechanics* v193 no7 p47 S 2016

Daimler Trucks North America LLC

The Internet-Connected Engine Will Change Trucking G. Westerman *Harvard Business Review Digital Articles* p2 N 4 2014

Daims, Holger

Giant viruses with an expanded complement of translation system components diag *Science* v356 no6333 p82 Ap 7 2017

Daines, Steve, 1960——Political & social views

MONTANANS ARE BEST AT RUNNING MONTANA S. DAINES *Vital Speeches of the Day* v83 no4 p111 Ap 2017

Dainty, Suellen

The Housekeeper *Publishers Weekly* v263 no50 p50 D 5 2016

Dairou, Julien

Guanine glycation repair by DJ-1/Park7 and its bacterial homo-

logs chart color diag graph *Science* v357 no6347 p208 Jl 14 2017

Dairy farms

Dairy family raises COWS AND QUADRUPLETS S. OLSON and B. OLSON color *Nebraska Life* v21 no2 p44 Mr/Ap 2017

Dairy industry

HOW A PETRO STATE HANDLES AN EMBARGO E. Fry color *Fortune* v176 no1 p13 Jl 1 2017

Dairy industry—China

Selling China On Cheese color graph *Bloomberg Businessweek* no4514 p20 Mr 13 2017

Dairy industry—Economic aspects

THE MAD CHEESE SCIENTISTS C. Rainey color graph *Bloomberg Businessweek* no4531 p56 Jl 24 2017

Dairy industry—India

Changes in Herd Composition a Key to Indian Dairy Production M. Landes and J. Cessna *Amber Waves: The Economics of Food, Farming, Natural Resources, & Rural America* p5 Je 2017

Dairy industry—United States

Historical Analysis of MPP-Dairy Suggests Limited Impact on Average Margins but Considerable Potential for Risk Reduction J. Cessna, T. Mark et al *Amber Waves: The Economics of Food, Farming, Natural Resources, & Rural America* p7 F 2017

Dairy Management Inc.

THE MAD CHEESE SCIENTISTS C. Rainey color graph *Bloomberg Businessweek* no4531 p56 Jl 24 2017

Dairy mixes

Is Whole-Milk Yogurt a Whole Lot Better? J. Calderone chart color *Consumer Reports* v82 no8 p18 Ag 2017

Dairy products

See also

Cheese

Cream

Cultured milk

Milk

ASK TUFTS EXPERTS A. H. Lichtenstein *Tufts University Health & Nutrition Letter* v35 no1 p8 Mr 2017

FOOD FOR THOUGHT *Nutrition Action Health Letter* v44 no4 p16 My 2017

QUICK STUDIES *Nutrition Action Health Letter* v44 no3 p12 Ap 2017

Raising the Bar L. MOYER and B. LIEBMAN *Nutrition Action Health Letter* v44 no5 p13 Je 2017

Dairy products industry—Economic aspects

Historical Analysis of MPP-Dairy Suggests Limited Impact on Average Margins but Considerable Potential for Risk Reduction J. Cessna, T. Mark et al *Amber Waves: The Economics of Food, Farming, Natural Resources, & Rural America* p7 F 2017

Dairy products—Evaluation

BETTER BUTTER J. DRILLING *Cincinnati Magazine* v50 no6 p144 Mr 2017

Dairy waste

Have it your whey J. RICHLER color *Maclean's* v129 no51/52 p68 D 26 2016

DAISAKU IKEDA

On Hardship & Hope: Two teachings to instill inspiration when we feel paralyzed by despair color *Tricycle: The Buddhist Review* v27 no1 p36 Fall 2017

Daisies

Root Causes M. Gunch color *New Orleans Magazine* v51 no6 p44 Ap 2017

DAISLEY, STEPHEN

The Not-So-Darling Buds of Theresa May *Commentary* v143 no6 p20 Je 2017

Daisuke Mayumi

Methane production from coal by a single methanogen bibl graph *Science* v354 no6309 p222 O 14 2016

DAJER, TONY

No Relief color *Discover* v38 no7 p22 S 2017

Dakin, Brett

From Spying to Killing *Washington Monthly* p6 Ja/F 2017

Dakota (North American people)

See also

Lakota (North American people)

Dakota truck

HOT ROD D. Wallace color *Hot Rod* v69 no12 p14 D 2016

trated v127 no6 p16 Ag 28 2017

NFC + EAST color *Sports Illustrated* v126 no5 p48 F 13 2017

WHY THE 'BOYS ARE BACK D. SOLOMON *Texas Monthly* v45 no9 p64 S 2017

Dallas Cowboys (Football team)—Officials & employees

BREATH OF FRESH HEIR A. Murphy color *Sports Illustrated* v126 no2 p34 Ja 16 2017

Dallas Mavericks (Basketball team)

10 Mavericks R. Nadkarni, B. Golliver et al color *Sports Illustrated* v125 no14 p110 O 24-31 2016

12 MAVERICKS color *Sports Illustrated* v127 no12 p94 O 16 2017

Mark Cuban GETS LOUD A. GRANT color *Esquire* p64 My 2017

Dallas Museum of Art

Flat Broke P. SIMEK *D: The Magazine of Dallas* v43 no10 p88 O 2016

Salaam to the Keir Collection in Dallas color *Magazine Antiques* v184 no3 p32 My/Je 2017

Dallas Opera (Performer)

AROUND TOWN *D: The Magazine of Dallas* v43 no10 p287 O 2016

Dallas Sniper Attack, Dallas, Tex., 2016

David Brown B. Luscombe color *Time* v189 no23 p56 Je 19 2017

DALLAVALLE, NANCY

NOT GETTING 'GETTING RELIGION' *Commonweal* v144 no6 p4 Mr 24 2017

Our Man at Newsweek bw *Commonweal* v144 no3 p28 F 10 2017

DALLEK, ROBERT

History's FIRST DRAFT color *Vanity Fair* v59 no10 p158 O 2017

DALLEMULE, LEANDRO

What's Your Data Strategy? color diag img *Harvard Business Review* v95 no3 p112 My/Je 2017

Dallmeier, F.

Persistent effects of pre-Columbian plant domestication on Amazonian forest composition bibl chart graph map *Science* v355 no6328 p925 Mr 3 2017

Dalmatian dog

The BEST DOG for YOU T. DASWICK bw *Men's Health* v32 no6 p126 Ag 2017

DALME, JUSTIN

Frigid Embrace: A Backcountry Winter Introduction *Idaho Magazine* v16 no10 p49 Jl 2017

Dalmia, Shikha

AMERICA NEEDS HIGH-SKILLED FOREIGN WORKERS color *Reason* v49 no1 p17 My 2017

DEPORTATIONS UP UNDER TRUMP color *Reason* v49 no4 p16 Ag/S 2017

Two Immigrants Debate Immigration color *Reason* v48 no7 p28 D 2016

Daloz, Kate

American Communism B. Doherty bw color *Reason* v48 no7 p56 D 2016

DALPHONSE, SHERRI

50 GREAT PLACES TO WORK *Washingtonian Magazine* v52 no6 p84 Mr 2017

Celebrate the Occasion *Washingtonian Magazine* v52 no4 p104 Ja 2017

THE NEW WASHINGTON OFFICE *Washingtonian Magazine* v52 no6 p76 Mr 2017

Dalrymple, Theodore

MOBILITY AND NOBILITY *Claremont Review of Books* v17 no2 p17 Spr 2017

Dalrymple, William

The Beautiful, Magical World of Rajput Art cartoon *New York Review of Books* v63 no18 p32 N 24 2016

Dalton, Annie

A Study in Gold: An Oxford Dogwalkers' Mystery color *Publishers Weekly* v264 no28 p67 Jl 10 2017

Dalton, Melissa G.

How Iran's hybrid-war tactics help and hurt it bibl *Bulletin of the Atomic Scientists* v73 no5 p312 2017

DALTON, RICK

College and Career Readiness Starts With Essential Skills *Education Digest* v82 no9 p41 My 2017

Dalton, Sarah

Me, Myself, and I J. MCCARTNEY color *Publishers Weekly* v264 no17 p38 Ap 24 2017

Daly, Claire

THE MYSTIC bw *Downbeat* v83 no11 p40 N 2016

Daly, Colleen

GO ON STRIKE C. RUSHTON bw *Runner's World* v52 no7 p36 Ag 2017

Daly, D.

Persistent effects of pre-Columbian plant domestication on Amazonian forest composition bibl chart graph map *Science* v355 no6328 p925 Mr 3 2017

Daly, John, 1966-

HOT | NOT T. Keith color *Sports Illustrated* v125 no16 p20 N 14 2016

Daly, Natasha

CARL SAGAN IMAGINES MARS color *National Geographic* v232 no2 p20 Ag 2017

FINGER PAINTING color *National Geographic* v231 no6 p2 Je 2017

GIRLS, BOYS, AND GENDERED TOYS color *National Geographic* v231 no1 p17 Ja 2017

RECORDS OF REBELLION bw color *National Geographic* v231 no5 p16 My 2017

THE SOFTER SIDE OF ROBOTICS diag *National Geographic* v231 no5 p18 My 2017

SPOTS AND STRIPES ARE NOT SO BLACK-AND-WHITE bw color *National Geographic* v232 no4 p18 O 2017

YOU ON A CHIP color diag *National Geographic* v232 no3 p136 S 2017

Daly, Paula

The Trophy Child *Publishers Weekly* v264 no3 p40 Ja 16 2017

Daly, Tyne, 1946-—Interviews

Behind the Scenes: Liner Notes L. T. Guinther *Opera News* v81 no12 p5 Je 2017

Dam failures

Lightbox J. Sanburn color *Time* v189 no7/8 p20 F 27 2017

Dam maintenance & repair

A DAM SHAME R. Annis, S. Bahr et al *Indianapolis Monthly* v41 no2 p64 S 2017

DAMAGED VILLANELLE (Poem)

DAMAGED VILLANELLE C. Bracken *New Yorker* v93 no10 p62 Ap 24 2017

D'Amario, Elena

Elena d'Amario L. KAY *Dance Magazine* v91 no1 p118 Ja 2017

Damasco, G.

Persistent effects of pre-Columbian plant domestication on Amazonian forest composition bibl chart graph map *Science* v355 no6328 p925 Mr 3 2017

Damascus steel

BLADE OF GLORY T. E. Nickens color *Field & Stream* v122 no2 p24 Je/Jl 2017

Damasio, Antonio

An End to Suffering: Can Buddhism create healthier individuals and communities? *New York Times Book Review* p17 Ag 13 2017

Damaske, Sarah

How Trump's Tax Proposals Will Affect Single Working Mothers *Harvard Business Review Digital Articles* p2 D 22 2016

The Two Main Sources of Stress for High-Status Workers *Harvard Business Review Digital Articles* p2 Ap 25 2016

What Do Women's Career Paths Really Look Like? *Harvard Business Review Digital Articles* p2 Je 8 2016

Damato, Karen

Get Ready for the New Math color diag *Money* v46 no1 p37 Ja/F 2017

Who Will Care for You? [Cover story] chart color map *Consumer Reports* v82 no10 p28 O 2017

Your IRA Withdrawal May Be Reversible color *Money* v46 no6 p30 Jl 2017

Damerst, Jeff

Railway Post Office color *Model Railroader* v84 no10 p16 O 2017

Dames, Chris

Anomalously low electronic thermal conductivity in metallic vanadium dioxide bibl graph *Science* v355 no6323 p371 Ja 27 2017

DAMES, NICHOLAS

CRITICISM IN THE TWILIGHT bw *Nation* v303 no23/24 p27 D 5 2016

Jane Austen Is Everything color *Atlantic* v320 no2 p92 S 2017

The Stubborn Optimist color *Atlantic* v319 no3 p38 Ap 2017

D'Amico, S.

Observation of a large-scale anisotropy in the arrival directions of cosmic rays above 8 × 1018 eV *Science* v357 no6357 p1266 S 22 2017

Damm, Darlene

As Machines Take Jobs, Companies Need to Get Creative About Making New Ones *Harvard Business Review Digital Articles* p2 My 22 2017

Damn (Music)

THE BEST ALBUMS OF 2017 (SO FAR) A. Bacle, E. R. Brown et al color *Entertainment Weekly* no1468/1469 p98 Je 2-9 2017

LEGACY MEDIA HUA HSU color *New Yorker* v93 no11 p74 My 1 2017

The Must List color *Entertainment Weekly* no1463/1464 p2 Ap/My 2017

Damned Summer (Film)

DAMNED SUMMER J. Cronk color *Film Comment* v53 no5 p22 S/O 2017

Damon, Matt, 1970-

A look back at Emmy wins, big moments and most memorable guest stars *TV Guide* v65 no41 p18 O 2 2017

MATT DAMON'S WATER FIGHT D. Coggan color *Entertainment Weekly* no1467 p14 My 26 2017

NEW YORK COMIC CON'S GREATEST HITS S. Li color *Entertainment Weekly* no1436/1437 p18 O 21 2016

Damon, Matt, 1970-—Interviews

TALKING TOILETS WITH MATT DAMON S. Goldberg *National Geographic* v232 no2 p6 Ag 2017

Damon, William

In the Spirit of Friendship *Hoover Digest: Research & Opinion on Public Policy* no4 p185 Fall 2016

d'Amora, Delphine

SNAP JUDGMENT graph *Mother Jones* v41 no6 p14 N/D 2016

YOU WILL LOSE YOUR JOB TO A ROBOT color *Mother Jones* v42 no6 p38 N/D 2017

Dampers (Mechanical devices)

HARMONIC BALANCER REPAIR SLEEVE: MAKE IT A POINT TO CHECK THE BALANCER FOR WEAR R. Bohacz *Successful Farming* v115 no12 p40 O 2017

SPOOL SAMPLE K. C. Colwell color *Car & Driver* v63 no5 p20 N 2017

Sway solution N. Walker bw *Canadian Geographic* v137 no3 p28 My 2017

YAW DAMPER R. Mark diag *Flying* v144 no10 p24 O 2017

Dampness in buildings

STUFF WATER INFILTRATION SCREWED UP M. Burke and M. Burke cartoon *Old House Journal* v45 no2 p54 Ap 2017

Damrauer, Scott M.

"Pheno"menal value for human health bibl diag *Science* v354 no6319 p1534 D 23 2016

Dams

Greenhouse Gas Emissions from Reservoir Water Surfaces: A New Global Synthesis B. R. DEEMER, J. A. HARRISON et al *BioScience* v66 no11 p949 N 1 2016

Lessons from the Oroville dam F. Vahedifard, A. AghaKouchak et al bibl *Science* v355 no6330 p1139 Mr 17 2017

The Original Brexit L. SCHLEY color *Discover* v38 no7 p19 S 2017

Dams & the environment

Damming, Lost Connectivity, and the Historical Role of Anadromous Fish in Freshwater Ecosystem Dynamics S. MATTOCKS, C. J. HALL et al *BioScience* v67 no8 p713 Ag 2017

Dams—Arizona

See also

Glen Canyon Dam (Ariz.)

HUGE UNDERTAKING G. LADD bw *Arizona Highways* v93 no5 p32 My 2017

Dams—California—Design & construction

AN ENERGY-GENERATING BEAVER DAM J. Leslie *Harper's Magazine* v333 no1998 p72 N 2016

Dams—Design & construction

River of Change *Orion Magazine* v35 no3 p66 My/Je 2016

UP AND OVER D. Stone diag *National Geographic* v231 no3 p22 Mr 2017

Dams—History

NATIONAL GALLERY UGANDA R. Griffiths *History Today* v67 no7 p78 Jl 2017

Dams—India

A DAM SHAME R. Annis, S. Bahr et al *Indianapolis Monthly* v41 no2 p64 S 2017

Dams—Iraq

BEFORE THE FLOOD D. FILKINS bw cartoon *New Yorker* v92 no43 p22 Ja 2 2017

Dams—Maintenance & repair

PROTECTING LIVES AND PROPERTY--DEC's Dam Safety Program L. Mitchell and A. Dominitz *New York State Conservationist* v71 no5 p21 Ap 2017

Dams—Safety measures

PROTECTING LIVES AND PROPERTY--DEC's Dam Safety Program L. Mitchell and A. Dominitz *New York State Conservationist* v71 no5 p21 Ap 2017

Dams—United States

FREE AT LAST D. ARNOLD *Sierra* v102 no3 p52 My/Je 2017

Tear Down These Walls J. Mark *Sierra* v102 no3 p4 My/Je 2017

Dán, Ádám

Role for migratory wild birds in the global spread of avian influenza H5N8 bibl graph map *Science* v354 no6309 p213 O 14 2016

Dana, Elspeth—Interviews

LITTLE DYNAMITE J. KINDELA chart color *Muscle & Performance* v9 no4 p28 Ap 2017

Dana, MaryAnn McKibben

Today's radio dramas color *Christian Century* v133 no25 p43 D 7 2016

Dana-Farber Cancer Institute

GETTING YOUR STARS TO COLLABORATE H. K. GARDNER color *Harvard Business Review* v95 no1 p100 Ja/F 2017

Radiation Triage A. Griswold color *Scientific American* v316 no6 p19 Je 2017

Danant, Stéphane

Demisch-Danant H. MARTIN bw color *Architectural Digest* v74 no2 p16 F 2017

D'Anastasio, Elisabetta

Complex multifault rupture during the 2016 Mw 7.8 Kaikōura earthquake, New Zealand color map *Science* v356 no6334 p154 Ap 14 2017

Dance

See also

Aerial dance

Ballet

Choreography

Jazz dance

7 common questions about applying for college: Advice from parents, dancers, and directors A. RIVERS *Dance Magazine* p12 2016/2017

advice for dancers L. HAMILTON *Dance Magazine* v91 no10 p24 O 2017

Be Fearless J. Stahl *Dance Magazine* v91 no10 p10 O 2017

Bird Song J. Acocella cartoon *New Yorker* v93 no5 p20 Mr 20 2017

BREATHE color *Prevention* v68 no11 p40 N 2016

Cassandre Joseph: How the STREB member conditions her body to pull off "impossible" stunts J. PETERS *Dance Magazine* v91 no9 p48 S 2017

C'mon, Get Happy M. McNamara bw color *Dance Spirit* v20 no10 p44 D 2016

CONTRAST, COUPLED B. GOLDEN color *Chicago* v66 no11 p40 N 2017

DANCE *New Yorker* v92 no38 p12 N 21 2016

DANCE *New Yorker* v93 no14 p6 My 22 2017

DANCE *New Yorker* v93 no30 p13 O 2 2017

DANCE *New Yorker* v93 no5 p20 Mr 20 2017

EAST RIVER EVENTS *South Dakota Magazine* v32 no4 p100 N/D 2016

Evolution of Dance: Choreography's constantly shifting role on the Great White Way S. GOLD *Dance Magazine* v91 no7 p20 Jl 2017

THE FINALS COUNTDOWN H. Rolfe color *Dance Spirit* v21 no8 p60 O 2017

p111 2016/2017 Supplement College Guide

Valdosta State University *Dance Magazine* v90 p106 2016/2017 Supplement College Guide

Virginia Commonwealth University *Dance Magazine* v90 p107 2016/2017 Supplement College Guide

Washington University in St. Louis *Dance Magazine* v90 p122 2016/2017 Supplement College Guide

Wayne State University *Dance Magazine* v90 p108 2016/2017 Supplement College Guide

Webster University *Dance Magazine* v90 p108 2016/2017 Supplement College Guide

Western Michigan University *Dance Magazine* v90 p109 2016/2017 Supplement College Guide

Western Oregon University *Dance Magazine* v90 p109 2016/2017 Supplement College Guide

Wichita State University *Dance Magazine* v90 p110 2016/2017 Supplement College Guide

Youngstown State University *Dance Magazine* v90 p112 2016/2017 Supplement College Guide

Dance Exchange (Performer)

The More Things Change... L. Traiger *Dance Magazine* v90 no11 p16 N 2016

Dance festivals

DANCE *New Yorker* v92 no33 p15 O 17 2016

DANCE *New Yorker* v92 no48 p12 F 6 2017

The Hills Are Alive: The Berkshires make a spectacular setting for a variety of cultural offerings all summer long M. R. Mercado *Opera News* v81 no12 p60 Je 2017

NorCal Takeover *Dance Magazine* v91 no6 p14 Je 2017

On the Circuit K. SCHWAB *Dance Magazine* v90 no11 p54 N 2016

Pillow Power N. Wozny *Dance Magazine* v91 no6 p16 Je 2017

Showstoppers S. FRISCIA *Dance Magazine* v90 no11 p40 N 2016

Dance festivals—Hawaii

Hula H. Yanagihara color *Conde Nast Traveler* v52 no1 p102 Ja 2017

Dance festivals—Reviews

Hula H. Yanagihara color *Conde Nast Traveler* v52 no1 p102 Ja 2017

Dance festivals—United States

Dive In: Where to find the cool kids this summer festival season *Dance Magazine* v91 no7 p12 Jl 2017

Dance floors

All the World's a Stage K. Brady color *Dance Spirit* v21 no4 p40 Ap 2017

"I'm sold on Harlequin Floors D. Roberts *Dance Magazine* v91 no10 p5 O 2017

Dance halls—Evaluation

DRINKS and DANCE HALLS *Texas Monthly* v45 no3 p106 Mr 2017

Dance Heginbotham (Performer)

Pas de Deux L. REGENSDORF and C. SCHAMA color *Vogue* v207 no9 p612 S 2017

Dance Magazine Awards

THE 2016 DANCE MAGAZINE AWARDS color *Dance Magazine* v91 no3 p16 Mr 2017

Dance Moms (TV program)

Dance Moms *TV Guide* v65 no43 p33 O 16 2017

"I'm Still Kalani" R. Zar *Dance Spirit* v21 no7 p66 S 2017

Dance music

More Than Backup L. WINGENROTH *Dance Magazine* v91 no1 p78 Ja 2017

Dance parties

ALL THE FEELS A. Igneri color *Bloomberg Businessweek* no4515 p64 Mr 20 2017

EVENT CALENDAR *Washingtonian Magazine* v52 no9 p198 Je 2017

Dance photography

Capturing your BEST FIRST Arabesque H. FOSTER *Dance Magazine* p8 2016/2017

GOINGS ON ABOUT TOWN color *New Yorker* v93 no18 p6 Je 26 2017

PURE IMAGINATION *Dance Spirit* v20 no10 p5 D 2016

Dance production & direction

DANCE *New Yorker* v92 no36 p12 N 7 2016

ON STAGE *Dance Magazine* v91 no8 p12 Ag 2017

Dance schools

2017-18 DANCE MAGAZINE COMPETITION & CONVENTION GUIDE *Dance Magazine* v91 no10 p50 O 2017

2017 HIGHER ED GUIDE *Dance Spirit* v21 no7 p106 S 2017

30 Years Ago This Month *Dance Magazine* v91 no1 p211 Ja 2017

7 common questions about applying for college: Advice from parents, dancers, and directors A. RIVERS *Dance Magazine* v90 p12 2016/2017 Supplement College Guide

ACCEPTANCE Anxieties N. Zisa *Dance Spirit* v21 no3 p64 Mr 2017

advice for dancers L. HAMILTON *Dance Magazine* v91 no9 p28 S 2017

Break Time N. WOZNY *Dance Magazine* v91 no6 p42 Je 2017

A CAREER & LEARNING RESOURCE GUIDE *Dance Magazine* v91 no3 p60 Mr 2017

A CAREER & LEARNING RESOURCE GUIDE *Dance Magazine* v91 no8 p76 Ag 2017

Collaborative Learning C. BAUER *Dance Magazine* v91 no1 p136 Ja 2017

consider COMMUNITY COLLEGE: There are perks to starting small A. SMITH *Dance Magazine* v90 p16 2016/2017 Supplement College Guide

dance finder: A CAREER & LEARNING RESOURCE GUIDE *Dance Magazine* v91 no6 p76 Je 2017

dance finder *Dance Magazine* v90 no11 p60 N 2016

dancefinder *Dance Magazine* v90 no12 p116 D 2016

featured school *Dance Magazine* v90 no12 p117 D 2016

HEADLINERS *Dance Spirit* v20 no10 p16 D 2016

Home Away From Home *Dance Magazine* v90 no11 p61 N 2016

The Institute for American Musical Theatre *Dance Magazine* v90 p75 2016/2017 Supplement College Guide

Institute of the Arts Barcelona *Dance Magazine* v90 p76 2016/2017 Supplement College Guide

A New Home for Choreograpers: NCCAkron launches its first official residency this month S. Sucato *Dance Magazine* v91 no7 p16 Jl 2017

SCHOOL DIRECTORY *Dance Spirit* v20 no10 p70 D 2016

SCHOOL DIRECTORY *Dance Spirit* v21 no3 p68 Mr 2017

SUMMER STUDY GUIDE 2017 *Dance Magazine* v91 no1 p140 Ja 2017

Transatlantic TRAINING M. Mcnamara *Dance Spirit* v21 no7 p80 S 2017

WHAT'S NEXT J. Stahl and F. M. Seegal *Dance Magazine* v91 no1 p36 Ja 2017

Dance schools—Curricula

YOUR QUESTIONS ANSWERED: What to ask to find the right college dance program A. RIVERS *Dance Magazine* v90 p10 2016/2017 Supplement College Guide

Dance schools—England

Wayne's New World: Wayne McGregor isn't keeping his state-of-the-art space to himself L. Cappelle *Dance Magazine* v91 no7 p14 Jl 2017

Dance Spirit (Periodical)

Happy 20th Birthday, DANCESPIRIT *Dance Spirit* v21 no7 p36 S 2017

Dance students

From Studio to Summertime L. WINGENROTH *Dance Magazine* v91 no1 p122 Ja 2017

POST-ACCEPTANCE LETTER Hurdles N. Loeffler-Gladstone *Dance Spirit* v21 no4 p56 Ap 2017

Dance teachers

The MOST INFLUENTIAL PEOPLE IN DANCE TODAY: THE MOVERS, SHAKERS AND CHANGEMAKERS HAVING THE BIGGEST IMPACT ON DANCE RIGHT NOW B. Schaefer, J. Stahl et al *Dance Magazine* v91 no7 p27 Jl 2017

MY TOWN A. Whiting *Washingtonian Magazine* v52 no5 p156 F 2017

Dance teams

Strong and Spirited: What it takes to be a member of a college dance team M. MCFERRAN *Dance Magazine* v91 no10 p44 O 2017

Dance techniques

Dancehall 101 N. Loeffler-Gladstone color *Dance Spirit* v21 no4 p54 Ap 2017

Dear Katie *Dance Spirit* v21 no1 p30 Ja 2017

THE Flip SIDE A. Smith color *Dance Spirit* v21 no4 p52 Ap 2017

Happy 2017! *Dance Spirit* v21 no1 p18 Ja 2017

MASTERING Partnered PIROUETTES J. Diana *Dance Spirit* v21 no3 p60 Mr 2017

Old-School Style: Why classic modern techniques are still an essential part of training today L. WINGENROTH *Dance Magazine* v91 no7 p54 Jl 2017

Reach New Heights K. Holmes *Dance Spirit* v21 no7 p84 S 2017

Ready for Anything J. G. Sadan color *Dance Magazine* v91 no3 p46 Mr 2017

RESIST THE Rivalry A. Marks *Dance Spirit* v21 no3 p62 Mr 2017

Shahadi WRIGHT JOSEPH N. Loeffier-Giadstore *Dance Spirit* v21 no3 p71 Mr 2017

Summer Study Regrets: Five pros share what they wish they'd done differently as summer intensive students K. HOLMES *Dance Magazine* v91 no7 p52 Jl 2017

Technique Rx A. FELLER *Dance Magazine* v91 no1 p96 Ja 2017

Variation Variations K. McGuire *Dance Spirit* v21 no3 p48 Mr 2017

Dance therapy—Study & teaching

University of Wisconsin—Milwaukee *Dance Magazine* v90 p111 2016/2017 Supplement College Guide

Dance training & conditioning

Dear Katie *Dance Spirit* v21 no1 p30 Ja 2017

Stretch Yourself K. SCHWAB *Dance Magazine* v91 no1 p138 Ja 2017

Dance—Auditions—Charts, diagrams, etc.

THE audition prep TIMELINE j. Queuene color *Dance Spirit* v21 no2 p42 F 2017

Dance—Congresses

DANCES SPIRIT 2017-2018 *Dance Spirit* v21 no8 p98 O 2017

Dance—Equipment & supplies

See also

Dance floors

Dance SPIRIT 2017 Survival GUIDE *Dance Spirit* v21 no4 p58 Ap 2017

Pumped-Up KICKS H. Rolfe *Dance Spirit* v21 no4 p50 Ap 2017

Dance—Exhibitions

ON STAGE *Dance Magazine* v91 no8 p12 Ag 2017

Dance—Georgia

Move It C. COX *Atlanta* v57 no6 p78 O 2017

Dancehall music

Dancehall 101 N. Loeffler-Gladstone color *Dance Spirit* v21 no4 p54 Ap 2017

Dance—History

Learning From the Past M. Hanson *Dance Magazine* v90 no11 p52 N 2016

Dance—History—Study & teaching

University of Oklahoma *Dance Magazine* v90 p119 2016/2017 Supplement College Guide

Dance in motion pictures, television, etc.

Whorled Series R. Brody bw *New Yorker* v92 no41 p12 D 12 2016

Dancemakers Inc.

DANCEMAKERS INC *Dance Spirit* v20 no10 p14 D 2016

Dance—New York (State)—New York

DANCE *New Yorker* v92 no44 p10 Ja 9 2017

DANCE *New Yorker* v93 no9 p14 Ap 17 2017

Dance—Performance

65 GREAT THINGS TO DO THIS MONTH J. FOUMBERG, J. HARDBERGER et al color *Chicago* v65 no11 p115 N 2016

Alonzo King LINES Ballet Gets Musical color *Dance Spirit* v20 no9 p23 N 2016

Coker College *Dance Magazine* v90 p54 2016/2017 Supplement College Guide

DANCE *New Yorker* v92 no42 p38 D 19 2016

DANCE *New Yorker* v93 no13 p16 My 15 2017

DANCE *New Yorker* v93 no32 p16 O 16 2017

Events *Virginia Living* v15 no3 p43 Ap 2017

THE GUIDE / 01.17 M. WAKIM *Los Angeles Magazine* p58 Ja 2017

Kylling It *Dance Magazine* v90 no12 p24 D 2016

LET'S GO Team! color *Dance Spirit* v21 no4 p10 Ap 2017

Like No Place Else Z. WHITTENBURG *Dance Magazine* v90 no12 p102 D 2016

MAI: Lil Buck and Jon Boogz W. Perron *Dance Magazine* v91 no9 p13 S 2017

SAVE THE DATE color *Dance Spirit* v20 no9 p24 N 2016

Shyamali: Sprouting Words C. LeFevre *Dance Magazine* v91 no9 p12 S 2017

Winter Preview M. Harss cartoon *New Yorker* v92 no37 p22 N 14 2016

Dance—Performance—Reviews

DANCE *New Yorker* v92 no30 p10 S 26 2016

DANCE *New Yorker* v93 no18 p12 Je 26 2017

DANCE *New Yorker* v93 no28 p8 S 18 2017

DANCE *New Yorker* v93 no9 p14 Ap 17 2017

ETC M. Cameran color *New Orleans Magazine* v51 no7 p151 My 2017

STREET SCENES J. ACOCELLA cartoon *New Yorker* v92 no43 p74 Ja 2 2017

Dance—Periodicals

40 Years Ago This Month *Dance Magazine* v90 no12 p123 D 2016

Dance—Physiological aspects

Dance It Out M. Lappe and S. G. Levy color *Glamour* v115 no4 p132 Ap 2017

Find Your Best Burn M. Heid color *Time* v190 no4 p45 Jl 24 2017

why i dance S. Sturm *Dance Magazine* v91 no7 p72 Jl 2017

Dance—Psychological aspects

why i dance J. Whiteside *Dance Magazine* v90 no11 p72 N 2016

Dance—Reviews

DANCE *New Yorker* v93 no16 p30 Je 5 2017

From Screen to Stage *Dance Magazine* v90 no12 p25 D 2016

Making His Own Rules C. ESCOYNE *Dance Magazine* v90 no11 p37 N 2016

Movement, Amplified B. GOLDEN bw *Chicago* v66 no10 p76 O 2017

A New Nutcracker for the Joffrey W. Perron *Dance Magazine* v90 no12 p26 D 2016

Reimagining a Classic S. GOLD *Dance Magazine* v90 no11 p20 N 2016

Dancers

See also

Ballet dancers

Bharata natyam dancers

Tap dancers

25 to Watch *Dance Magazine* v91 no1 p50 Ja 2017

advice for dancers L. HAMILTON *Dance Magazine* v91 no8 p24 Ag 2017

ALL ABOUT Jade *Dance Spirit* v21 no1 p26 Ja 2017

Articulate Artists *Dance Magazine* v91 no9 p61 S 2017

Ashley Mayeux G. HENDERSON *Dance Magazine* v91 no6 p46 Je 2017

ASSESS Your Specialty K. Holmes color *Dance Spirit* v21 no1 p56 Ja 2017

back to school (again): Professional dancer Ida Saki on why she chose to return to college A. RIVERS *Dance Magazine* v90 p24 2016/2017 Supplement College Guide

BEST ALL AROUND C. Bowers *Dance Spirit* v20 no10 p24 D 2016

Both Sides of the Curtain G. HENDERSON *Dance Magazine* v91 no8 p50 Ag 2017

Break Time N. WOZNY *Dance Magazine* v91 no6 p42 Je 2017

Can't Stop the Beat C. Bowers *Dance Spirit* v20 no10 p19 D 2016

Cassandre Joseph: How the STREB member conditions her body to pull off "impossible" stunts J. PETERS *Dance Magazine* v91 no9 p48 S 2017

Companion Pieces G. Santoro bw color *AARP: The Magazine* v60 no3A p64 Ap/My 2017

connect color *Dance Spirit* v21 no8 p38 O 2017

Dancing Through Language Barriers G. HENDERSON *Dance Magazine* v91 no6 p48 Je 2017

Dear Diary C. Bowers *Dance Spirit* v21 no3 p15 Mr 2017

THE DIRT C. Bowers *Dance Spirit* v21 no1 p24 Ja 2017

DIY Ballet: Five former Atlanta Ballet dancers have taken their careers into their own hands C. Thompson *Dance Magazine* v91 no10 p14 O 2017

Easton PAYNE H. Rolfe bw *Dance Spirit* v21 no8 p119 O 2017

Freelance Nation A. CASTRO *Dance Magazine* v91 no9 p34 S 2017

From BFA to Broadway L. WINGENROTH *Dance Magazine* v91 no8 p48 Ag 2017

FROM Comps To Campus L. D. Silva color *Dance Spirit* v21 no8

p96 O 2017

GET Her Look H. Rolfe color *Dance Spirit* v21 no1 p54 Ja 2017

GOINGS ON ABOUT TOWN color *New Yorker* v92 no46 p5 Ja 23 2017

Golden Girl J. J. Donatelli color *Dance Spirit* v21 no1 p34 Ja 2017

Happy 2017! *Dance Spirit* v21 no1 p18 Ja 2017

Happy Feet: What are your foot-care must-haves? A. RIVERS *Dance Magazine* v91 no10 p36 O 2017

Help! I'm Too K. Holmes color *Dance Spirit* v21 no4 p36 Ap 2017

HELP! I'm Too Short! K. Holmes color *Dance Spirit* v21 no4 p38 Ap 2017

HOW TO NAIL YOUR AUDITION VIDEO J. Diana color *Dance Spirit* v21 no1 p39 Ja 2017

Hubbard Street Dance Chicago's Season of Premieres color *Dance Spirit* v20 no9 p23 N 2016

I DON'T COMPETE. Madison Warnick color *Dance Spirit* v21 no8 p67 O 2017

An International Degree L. WINGENROTH *Dance Magazine* v91 no6 p50 Je 2017

KEVIN IEGA JEFF J. BERG color *Chicago* v66 no2 p32 F 2017

KIDA K. Holmes color *Dance Spirit* v20 no10 p36 D 2016

LET'S HEAR IT for the Boys *Dance Spirit* v21 no3 p10 Mr 2017

Lonely at the Top K. SCHWAB *Dance Magazine* v90 no11 p50 N 2016

Marketing Mistakes Z. WHITTENBURG *Dance Magazine* v91 no6 p52 Je 2017

The MOST INFLUENTIAL PEOPLE IN DANCE TODAY: THE MOVERS, SHAKERS AND CHANGEMAKERS HAVING THE BIGGEST IMPACT ON DANCE RIGHT NOW B. Schaefer, J. Stahl et al *Dance Magazine* v91 no7 p27 Jl 2017

The Musicality Question G. BERARDI *Dance Magazine* v91 no8 p30 Ag 2017

NETWORKING 101 M. B. JAMIN color *Dance Spirit* v21 no8 p68 O 2017

The new meaning of new media V. Vara color *Columbia Journalism Review* v56 no1 p104 Spr 2017

no average day K. BRADY *Dance Magazine* p18 2016/2017

AN ODE TO Comp Kids color *Dance Spirit* v21 no8 p30 O 2017

PORT DE Bras O. Manno *Dance Spirit* v21 no1 p32 Ja 2017

RESIST THE Rivalry A. Marks *Dance Spirit* v21 no3 p62 Mr 2017

The Road to Assistant: What conventions look for when choosing student assistants R. ZAR *Dance Magazine* v91 no10 p49 O 2017

Shelby Colona G. M. GARRETT *Dance Magazine* v91 no10 p22 O 2017

She's got the shakes in her elbow N. SAYEJ color *Maclean's* v129 no45 p55 N 14 2016

Shyamali: Sprouting Words C. LeFevre *Dance Magazine* v91 no9 p12 S 2017

Side Gig Woes G. HENDERSON *Dance Magazine* v91 no1 p114 Ja 2017

Sofiane Sylve: San Francisco Ballet's enigmatic ballerina opens up C. BAUER *Dance Magazine* v91 no9 p30 S 2017

Stage Mom Trauma L. HAMILTON *Dance Magazine* v90 no11 p24 N 2016

Summer Study BESTIES R. Zar bw color *Dance Spirit* v21 no1 p42 Ja 2017

TAKING THE Radio City STAGE L. Jakowenko and C. Bowers color *Dance Spirit* v20 no10 p30 D 2016

TALKIN' PARTIES with LIL BUCK J. Harman color *Glamour* v115 no1 p97 Ja 2017

#TeamHipHop *Dance Spirit* v20 no10 p22 D 2016

Train Trendy: Boutique fitness classes are popular--but are they right for your cross-training? L. WINGENROTH *Dance Magazine* v91 no9 p44 S 2017

Val CHMERKOVSKIY C. Bowers *Dance Spirit* v21 no3 p22 Mr 2017

Variation Variations K. McGuire *Dance Spirit* v21 no3 p48 Mr 2017

Vernard J. GILMOR C. Bowers bw *Dance Spirit* v20 no10 p24 D 2016

What Is Countertechnique? The method that wants to change how you think about dancing G. HENDERSON *Dance Magazine* v91 no9 p50 S 2017

What's on Your Mind? color *Dance Magazine* v91 no3 p6 Mr

2017

Who's Your Leading Man? *Dance Spirit* v21 no3 p20 Mr 2017

why i dance F. Chung *Dance Magazine* v91 no8 p88 Ag 2017

why i dance S. Sturm *Dance Magazine* v91 no7 p72 Jl 2017

Xiao Nan Yu: The National Ballet of Canada principal knows that flexibility isn't always a blessing J. STAHL *Dance Magazine* v91 no7 p50 Jl 2017

Dancers—Attitudes

Against All Odds L. Cappelle color *Dance Magazine* v91 no3 p52 Mr 2017

CAUTION: Toxic! K. Holmes *Dance Spirit* v20 no10 p58 D 2016

Ready for Anything J. G. Sadan color *Dance Magazine* v91 no3 p46 Mr 2017

READY, SET—PLACES! J. Ouellette color *Dance Spirit* v20 no10 p46 D 2016

Dancers—Education

See also

Education of ballet dancers

back to school (again) A. RIVERS *Dance Magazine* p24 2016/2017

PART-TIME POST-GRAD A. Brandt *Dance Magazine* p27 2016/2017

tackling two A. SMITH *Dance Magazine* p22 2016/2017

What's in a Diploma? S. WROTH *Dance Magazine* v91 no8 p33 Ag 2017

Dancers—Employment

The 2017 Jobs Guide *Dance Magazine* v91 no3 p54 Mr 2017

Dancers—Health

Ache, Throb, Hurt A. Stafford *Dance Magazine* v91 no1 p83 Ja 2017

Comfort Food Swaps E. C. HARRISON *Dance Magazine* v90 no11 p48 N 2016

Dear Katie K. Morgan *Dance Spirit* v20 no10 p26 D 2016

Elena d'Amario L. KAY *Dance Magazine* v91 no1 p118 Ja 2017

FIGHTING Fatigue N. Loeffler-Gladstone *Dance Spirit* v20 no10 p34 D 2016

Post-Performance Done Right K. HOLMES *Dance Magazine* v91 no4 p48 Ap 2017

Resolutions Nutritionists Wish You'd Make K. BRADY *Dance Magazine* v91 no1 p116 Ja 2017

SUGAR, SPICE AND Everything Nice O. Manno *Dance Spirit* v20 no10 p32 D 2016

Sweet Tooth Strategies C. Bauer color *Dance Spirit* v91 no3 p42 Mr 2017

Dancers—Interviews

Extra! C. Bowers color *Dance Spirit* v21 no2 p17 F 2017

FEET FIRST M. Fuhrer *Dance Spirit* v21 no3 p44 Mr 2017

Dancers—Mental health

Old-School Style: Why classic modern techniques are still an essential part of training today L. WINGENROTH *Dance Magazine* v91 no7 p54 Jl 2017

What's on Your Mind? *Dance Magazine* v91 no10 p6 O 2017

Dancers—Nutrition

Comfort Food Swaps E. C. HARRISON *Dance Magazine* v90 no11 p48 N 2016

Home Alone L. Hamilton color *Dance Magazine* v91 no3 p24 Mr 2017

Post-Performance Done Right K. HOLMES *Dance Magazine* v91 no4 p48 Ap 2017

SUGAR, SPICE AND Everything Nice O. Manno *Dance Spirit* v20 no10 p32 D 2016

Dancers—Physiology

Move It C. COX *Atlanta* v57 no6 p78 O 2017

Dancers—Psychology

Tackling Depression K. MCGUIRE *Dance Magazine* v90 no11 p46 N 2016

Dancers—Retirement

Home Alone L. Hamilton color *Dance Magazine* v91 no3 p24 Mr 2017

Dancers—Taxation

The Tax-Season Dance J. Peters color *Dance Magazine* v91 no3 p50 Mr 2017

Dancers—Training of

Summer Study Regrets: Five pros share what they wish they'd done differently as summer intensive students K. HOLMES *Dance Magazine* v91 no7 p52 Jl 2017

Dancers—United States

DANCERS AT EL CHISPAS K. GOODRICH *Indianapolis Monthly* v40 no11 p18 Jl 2017

Kennadi BOESE H. Rolfe *Dance Spirit* v21 no7 p119 S 2017

Dance—Social aspects

DANCIN' IN THE STREET [Cover story] M. PACKARD color *New Orleans Magazine* v51 no4 p58 F 2017

THE EVOLUTION OF DANCE T. Singer color *Scientific American* v317 no1 p66 Jl 2017

Dance—Study & teaching

See also

Ballet—Study & teaching

Dance—Study & teaching (Higher)

Dance camps

ABOVE & BEYOND cartoon *New Yorker* v92 no48 p12 F 6 2017

BEATING Senioritis N. Loeffler-Gladstone *Dance Spirit* v21 no1 p90 Ja 2017

Beyond Anatomy L. Wingenroth *Dance Magazine* v90 no12 p106 D 2016

Collaborative Learning C. BAUER *Dance Magazine* v91 no1 p136 Ja 2017

Dance It Out M. Lappe and S. G. Levy color *Glamour* v115 no4 p132 Ap 2017

Editor's Letter L. POLLOCK color *Art in America* v105 no3 p14 Mr 2017

featured school *Dance Magazine* v90 no12 p117 D 2016

HOLLYWOOD VIBE *Dance Spirit* v20 no10 p18 D 2016

Home Away From Home *Dance Magazine* v90 no11 p61 N 2016

Learning From the Past M. Hanson *Dance Magazine* v90 no11 p52 N 2016

LET'S GO Team! color *Dance Spirit* v21 no4 p10 Ap 2017

Merging movements: Diverse dance practices in postsecondary education K. Schupp bibl *Arts Education Policy Review* v118 no2 p104 2017

SCHOOL DIRECTORY *Dance Spirit* v21 no3 p68 Mr 2017

Dance—Study & teaching (Higher)

A CAREER & LEARNING RESOURCE GUIDE *Dance Magazine* v91 no4 p60 Ap 2017

Network to Success L. WINGENROTH *Dance Magazine* v91 no4 p54 Ap 2017

Dance—Terminology

MUST-KNOW Commercial DANCE TERMS M. Benjamin color *Dance Spirit* v20 no10 p60 D 2016

Dance—United States

Let's Dance! C. A. Inaba bw color *AARP: The Magazine* v59 no6A p52 O/N 2016

Dancing injuries

Pain POINTERS H. Rolfe color *Dance Spirit* v21 no8 p48 O 2017

Dancing injuries—Treatment

Moving THE Needle N. Loeffier-Gladstone *Dance Spirit* v21 no7 p58 S 2017

Dancing With the Stars (TV program)

17 Things That Will Definitely Maybe Happen in 2017, According to Real Science M. Snetiker color *Entertainment Weekly* no1448 p11 Ja 13 2017

CHARO CHA-CHAS ONTO DWTS L. Rice color *Entertainment Weekly* no1456 p18 Mr 10 2017

CHEERS & JEERS D. HOLBROOK color *TV Guide* v64 no42 p88 O 10 2016

Dance Card T. Keith chart color *Sports Illustrated* v126 no16 p30 Je 5 2017

Dancing King J. RUSSELL *TV Guide* v64 no40 p40 O 3 2016

Dancing With the Stars N. Abrams, C. Holub et al *Entertainment Weekly* no1482/1483 p48 S 22 2017

Dancing With the Stars THE COUPLES TO WATCH E. ASLANIAN *TV Guide* v65 no14 p6 Ap 3 2017

The Kids Are Alright: Why networks are betting on junior versions of top competition series J. RUSSELL *TV Guide* v65 no35 p4 Ag 21 2017

Let's Dance! C. A. Inaba bw color *AARP: The Magazine* v59 no6A p52 O/N 2016

PRIME TIME EASTERN *TV Guide* v64 no48 p50 N 21 2016

Tonight's Highlights *TV Guide* v64 no15 p56E Ap 4 2016

D'Andrea, Megan

How My Horse De-Stresses Me color *Horse & Rider* v55 no12 p72 D 2016

Dandridge, Merle

Merle Dandridge J. ZAMBRANO color *O, The Oprah Magazine* p24 Mr 2017

Dandruff—Prevention

FAST FIXES FOR FLAKES J. Martin color *Amazing Wellness* p24 Fall 2017

Dandruff—Treatment

Save Your Scalp [Cover story] A. Weil color *Prevention* v69 no6 p24 Je 2017

Dane, Eric

The Last Ship's Captain Takes a Break I. Rudolph *TV Guide* v65 no21 p11 My 15 2017

Daneils-Zeller, Debra

Modern Vegan Comfort Food *Vegetarian Journal* v35 no1 p18 2016

Danes, Claire, 1979-

Homeland I. Rudolph *TV Guide* v65 no2 p24 Ja 2 2017

Homeland J. Jensen color *Entertainment Weekly* no1449 p48 Ja 20 2017

DANESI, MARCEL

Stay Sharp color *Prevention* v69 no11 p96 N 2017

DANFORD, NATALIE

DINNER IS SERVED color *Publishers Weekly* v264 no10 p34 Mr 6 2017

Danforth, John C.

"A BOOK I'D LIKE MY ELECTED OFFICIALS TO READ" color *Christian Century* v133 no21 p28 O 12 2016

Danger Mouse (Performer)

Danger Mouse's 30th Century Vision E. R. Brown color *Entertainment Weekly* no1438 p60 N 4 2016

AN ECLECTIC SONIC SQUAD E. R. Brown color *Entertainment Weekly* no1438 p60 N 4 2016

Dangl, Jeffery L.

Intracellular innate immune surveillance devices in plants and animals chart color diag graph *Science* v354 no6316 paaf6395-1 D 2 2016

Danhua Shen

Gene expression profiling–guided clinical precision treatment for patients with endometrial carcinoma bibl color diag *Science* v354 no6319 p33 D 23 2016

Dani, Keshav

Pursuing science across nationalities and disciplines *Physics Today* v70 no6 p10 Je 2017

Danica Seafood Ltd.

WORLD-CLASS SEAFOOD DISTRIBUTION *Iceland Review* v54 no6 p124 N/D 2016

DANIEL, ALEX

The Indie E-Books Evolution *Publishers Weekly* v263 no39 p48 S 26 2016

THE Real Worlds color *Publishers Weekly* v263 no43 p26 O 24 2016

Self-Publishing in 2017 color *Publishers Weekly* v264 no4 p40 Ja 23 2017

Standing Out from the Pack color *Publishers Weekly* v263 no47 p60 N 21 2016

Daniel, B.

Observation of a large-scale anisotropy in the arrival directions of cosmic rays above 8×10^{18} eV *Science* v357 no6357 p1266 S 22 2017

Daniel, Diane

American Skillet Co color map *American Craft* v77 no3 p14 Je/Jl 2017

The Bright Side color *American Craft* v77 no2 p58 Ap/My 2017

Finder Not Keeper color *American Craft* v77 no2 p14 Ap/My 2017

The Future Perfect color *American Craft* v76 no6 p28 D 2016-Ja 2017

Game Theory color *American Craft* v77 no3 p64 Je/Jl 2017

Daniel, Jason

Pretty Pots of Spring Color L. M. Minor color *Southern Living* v52 no4 p18 Ap 2017

Daniel, John

A Changing World: Expectations of Higher Education *Change* v49 no4 p8 Jl/Ag 2017

Gifted *Publishers Weekly* v264 no8 p57 F 20 2017

Daniel, Lillian

A Colony in a Nation *Christian Century* v134 no16 p31 Ag 2 2017

Waking up the working class color *Christian Century* v133 no23 p36 N 9 2016

Daniel, Michael

Driving Home the Safety Discussion il *Consumer Reports* v82 no9 p6 S 2017

Why Is Cybersecurity So Hard? *Harvard Business Review Digital Articles* p2 My 22 2017

Daniel Berrigan prays the rosary at a supermarket: in July (Poem)

Daniel Berrigan prays the rosary at a supermarket: in July J. A. Brown *America* v216 no10 p45 My 1 2017

Daniel Boone National Forest (Ky.)

America's Original Frontier E. BENICH color *Backpacker* v45 no2 p28 Mr 2017

IN BLUEGRASS COUNTRY K. Dobie *Harper's Magazine* v333 no1998 p61 N 2016

Danielewicz, Kyle

I'm the Son of a Sailor color *Sail* v48 no2 p10 F 2017

Monster at Midnight color *Sail* v48 no7 p14 Jl 2017

Danielle, Britni

Dear America, James Baldwin Is Still 'Not Your Negro' bw color *Ebony* v72 no4 p22 F 2017

In Our Cities bw color *Ebony* v72 no5 p32 Mr 2017

RADAR GIFT GUIDE color *Ebony* v72 no3 p46 D 2016/Ja 2017

TASHA'S TIME color *Essence* v48 no5 p62 S 2017

THEN AND NOW Drama Queens color *Essence* v48 no5 p64 S 2017

Trap Karaoke Lets Fans Take Center Stage color *Ebony* v72 no9 p22 Jl/Ag 2017

WHO IS RUSSELL WESTBROOK? color *Ebony* v72 no6 p76 Ap/My 2017

Daniels, Alex

Here's the Rub color *AARP: The Magazine* v60 no2A p74 F/Mr 2017

Daniels, Anthony

Anthony Daniels, Good and Evil in the Garden of Art: Discrimination as the Guarantor of Civilization G. Vaughan *Society* v54 no4 p375 Ag 2017

KENNY BAKER color *Entertainment Weekly* no1446/1447 p91 D 2016/Ja 2017

Daniels, Charles Meldrum, 1885-1973

Pool Pals E. Brady and T. Keith chart color *Sports Illustrated* v127 no3 p24 Jl 24 2017

Daniels, Charlie

Thoughts on previous issues D. Bruce and J. Freeman color *American Cowboy* v23 no5 p24 F/Mr 2017

Daniels, Charlie—Interviews

At Home With... B. Welch color *American Cowboy* v23 no4 p16 D 2016/Ja 2017

Charlie Daniels Explores the Sound Quality Trail on Night Hawk M. METTLER and C. Crowley bw color *Sound & Vision* v82 no1 p22 Ja 2017

DANIELS, CHRIS

r.s.v.p bw color *Bon Appetit* v62 no7 p12 Jl 2017

Daniels, Craig

The Craig Daniels Dogson Telescope J. Oltion *Sky & Telescope* v133 no2 p70 F 2017

Daniels, Gary

32! THAT'S HOW MANY CLUB CHAMPIONSHIPS THIS READER HAS WON. HERE'S HIS SECRET D. DeNunzio color *Golf Magazine* v59 no9 p64 S 2017

Daniels, Harvey "Smokey"

IDENTITY, EMPATHY, AND INQUIRY color *Literacy Today (2411-7862)* v34 no5 p44 Mr/Ap 2017

DANIELS, J. D.

SIGNS and WONDERS color *Esquire* p107 My 2017

Daniels, Jay

Branch-specific plasticity of a bifunctional dopamine circuit encodes protein hunger graph *Science* v356 no6337 p534 My 5 2017

DANIELS, KARU F.

Genius at Work color *Ebony* v72 no4 p80 F 2017

Daniels, Katie

The Most Catholic of Families color *Commonweal* v144 no13 p29 Ag 11 2017

An Ordinary Sunday [Cover story] color *Commonweal* v144 no15 p11 S 22 2017

Daniels, Kevin

Research: How Incentive Pay Affects Employee Engagement, Satisfaction, and Trust *Harvard Business Review Digital Articles* p2 Mr 15 2017

Daniels, Lee, 1959-

Lee Daniels color *Vanity Fair* p163 Hollywood 2017 Supplement

Daniels, Robin

Spirituality that makes sense N. King *America* v216 no11 p54 My 15 2017

DANIELS, SAM

PEOPLE POWER FOR POSITIVE CHANGE *Iceland Review* v55 no2 p46 Mr/Ap 2017

Daniels, Symone

CROWNED jewels S. T. Brown color *Ebony* v72 no6 p90 Ap/My 2017

Daniels, Thomas

Emergence and spread of a human-transmissible multidrug-resistant nontuberculous mycobacterium bibl diag graph *Science* v354 no6313 p751 N 11 2016

DANIELS, VANESSA

Provoking Thoughts color *O, The Oprah Magazine* p18 N 2017

Daniels-Butler, Leah—Interviews

Leah Daniels-Butler, Casting Director, Empire M. Logan color *TV Guide* v64 no42 p13 O 10 2016

Danielsen, Finn

Biodiversity redistribution under climate change: Impacts on ecosystems and human well-being color *Science* v355 no6332 p1389 Mr 31 2017

Danielsson, Frida

A subcellular map of the human proteome color *Science* v356 no6340 p820 My 26 2017

Daniels-Zeller, Debra

Healthy Vegan Dishes on a BUDGET *Vegetarian Journal* v36 no3 p23 2017

A Passion for Peas *Vegetarian Journal* v35 no2 p22 2016

DANIELY, MARIE

The Question color *O, The Oprah Magazine* p14 N 2017

DANILOFF, CALEB

The RUNNER'S HIGH [Cover story] color diag *Runner's World* v52 no3 p68 Ap 2017

Danilo Norata, Giuseppe

mTORC1 activity repression by late endosomal phosphatidylinositol 3,4-bisphosphate diag *Science* v356 no6341 p968 Je 1 2017

Danilova, Ludmila

Mismatch repair deficiency predicts response of solid tumors to PD-1 blockade chart graph *Science* v357 no6349 p409 Jl 28 2017

Danino, Tal

Potential role of intratumor bacteria in mediating tumor resistance to the chemotherapeutic drug gemcitabine diag *Science* v357 no6356 p1156 S 15 2017

DANKER, RICH

Trump's Winning White House Bet color *Weekly Standard* v22 no12 p22 N 28 2016

Dankert, Christoph

Personalized Technology Will Upend the Doctor-Patient Relationship *Harvard Business Review Digital Articles* p2 Je 19 2015

Danler, Stephanie

THE BIG QUESTION cartoon *Atlantic* v319 no5 p96 Je 2017

EAT, DRINK & BE FRIENDLY cartoon *O, The Oprah Magazine* p100 Ap 2017

Danler, Stephanie Mannatt

That FIRST WARM DAY color *Esquire* p78 My 2017

Danler, Stephanie—Interviews

N.Y.C.: Tales of the City—A Reading from Three Novels L. Hartman bw *Publishers Weekly* v263 no44 p(Sp)24 O 31 2016

Dann, Kevin

Cosmic Explorer J. KAAG *New York Times Book Review* p13 Ja 15 2017

DANN, MOSHE

I Hear You Say *Commentary* v142 no3 p25 O 2016

Dannals, Robert F.

Chemogenetics revealed: DREADD occupancy and activation via converted clozapine graph *Science* v357 no6350 p503 Ag

4 2017

Dannenberg, Astrid

Social norms as solutions bibl color *Science* v354 no6308 p42 O 7 2016

Danner, Blythe

Blythe Danner L. Lynch color *AARP: The Magazine* v59 no1A p13 D 2015/Ja 2016

Danner, Mark

The Real Trump color *New York Review of Books* v63 no20 p8 D 22 2016

Robert B. Silvers (1929–2017) [Cover story] bw color *New York Review of Books* v64 no8 p31 My 11 2017

What He Could Do [Cover story] color *New York Review of Books* v64 no5 p4 Mr 23 2017

Danner Inc.

TREK STAR VOYAGERS J. BROWN color *Popular Science* p11 Ja/F 2017

Dannerbauer, H.

Molecular gas in the halo fuels the growth of a massive cluster galaxy at high redshift bibl graph *Science* v354 no6316 p1128 D 2 2016

D'Annibale, Amy Synnott

WRITTEN ALL OVER YOUR FACE [Cover story] color *Women's Health* v14 no5 p45 Je 2017

Dano, Paul, 1984-

Ben Stiller's True Crime J. McGovern color *Entertainment Weekly* no1486 p50 O 13 2017

DANON, DANNY

BDS Beat Down *USA Today Magazine* v145 no2860 p53 Ja 2017

Danon, Jonathan J.

Braiding a molecular knot with eight crossings bibl diag graph *Science* v355 no6321 p1 Ja 13 2017

Majorana bound state in a coupled quantum-dot hybrid-nanowire system bibl graph *Science* v354 no6319 p1557 D 23 2016

Danovaro, R.

An ecosystem-based deep-ocean strategy bibl color map *Science* v355 no6324 p452 F 3 2017

Dansk Inc.

Simmer In Style N. STOFFREGEN color *Treasures* v5 no5 p38 Ap/My 2016

Danson, Ted

THE GOOD PLACE D. Snierson color *Entertainment Weekly* no1477 p29 Ag 11 2017

HOW TED DANSON FOUND HIS Balance D. HOCHMAN color *AARP: The Magazine* v30 no6A p54 O/N 2017

Danta, Ron

Expanding Opportunities for Derby and Green Hunters *In Stride* v12 no5 p6 S 2017

Dante Alighieri, 1265-1321

BETWEEN HEAVEN AND HELL *Claremont Review of Books* v17 no2 p52 Spr 2017

Danticat, Edwidge, 1969-

EDWIDGE DANTICAT AT THE BORDER *Lapham's Quarterly* v10 no3 p128 Summ 2017

Giving Grief Its Due V. Sayers color *Commonweal* v114 no14 p29 S 8 2017

MIAMI *Harper's Magazine* p34 O 2017

SUNRISE, SUNSET E. Danticat cartoon *New Yorker* v93 no28 p54 S 18 2017

Touring the Dark Side: Edwidge Danticat surveys death in its many guises W. Grimes *New York Times Book Review* p21 Ag 13 2017

D'Antonio, Michael

Barack Obama and the Limits of Optimism J. Berry color *America* v216 no9 p25 Ap 24 2017

Danube River

A Cruise for All Reasons R. LOVE color *AARP: The Magazine* v59 no2A p38 F/Mr 2016

Danyi, Csaba

Hungarian Jazz Showcase: 10 Years in the Spotlight H. Mandel color *Downbeat* v84 no5 p14 My 2017

DANYLCHUK, ANDY J.

What's That Buzzing Noise? Public Opinion on the Use of Drones for Conservation Science *BioScience* v67 no4 p382 Ap 2017

Danylko, Kathryn

Whispers in the Windstorm: A Journey of God's Blessed Assur-

ance During My Year with Breast Cancer *Publishers Weekly* v264 no17 p58e Ap 24 2017

Danza, Tony, 1951—Interviews

WHO'S THE BOSS? 1984-1992 S. Vilkomerson color *Entertainment Weekly* no1434 p34 O 7 2016

DANZER, MATT

FANCY THAT! color *Bon Appetit* v61 no11 p104 N 2016

Danziger, Eric

TRUMP HOTELS' WEIRD PITCH A. Davidson color *New Yorker* v93 no18 p21 Je 26 2017

Danziger, Meryl

Sing it! A Biography of Pete Seeger color *Publishers Weekly* v263 no49 p85 D 7 2016

Dao, David

Calibrate Your Care D. FOSTER *National Review* v69 no8 p44 My 2017

Dao Wen Wang

Quality management for precision medicine clinical applications: A consensus from the China Precision Medicine Clinical Research and Application Association bibl *Science* v354 no6319 p11 D 23 2016

D'Apice, Raquel

10 ways to prepare your first-time-parent friends cartoon *Parents* v92 no3 p116 Mr 2017

3 Adult Tantrums I Would Like to Have color *Working Mother* v40 no4 p98 O/N 2017

advice every new mom needs [Cover story] color *Parents* v92 no7 p32 Jl 2017

I Am a Toddler, Ask Me Anything color *Parents* v92 no9 p62 S 2017

a letter to my child about growing up in the dark ages *Parents* v92 no1 p38 Ja 2017

A TEN-MONTH-OLD'S Letter to Santa *Reader's Digest* v188 no1126 p92 D 2016/Ja 2017

Dapper, Sven

LET THE LEG YIELD WORK FOR YOU color *Dressage Today* v23 no6 p22 F 2017

DaPra, Gloria

WHY FACEBOOK IS KEEPING PERFORMANCE REVIEWS: INTERACTION color *Harvard Business Review* v95 no1 p18 Ja/F 2017

D'APRILE, JASON

TADO SMART AC REMOTE color *Macworld - Digital Edition* v34 no11 p37 N 2017

Darack, Ed

Coast Mountains of British Columbia—Wilderness of Sky and Ice *Weatherwise* v70 no5 p8 S/O 2017

Weatherscapes: Denver, Colorado — The "Mile High City" color *Weatherwise* v70 no4 p8 Jl/Ag 2017

Weatherscapes: Singapore – The Diamond Island City-State *Weatherwise* v70 no1 p8 Ja/F 2017

Weatherscapes: The Grand Canyon of the Colorado River – Earth's Dynamic Past Opened by the Sky *Weatherwise* v70 no2 p8 Mr/Ap 2017

Weatherscapes: The Snowy Range – Hidden Alpine Gem *Weatherwise* v69 no6 p8 N-D 2016

Daramus, Iancu S.

Liability and Precaution bibl *Environment* v59 no5 p48 S/O 2017

Darbo, Patrika—Interviews

THE BOLD AND THE BEAUTIFUL M. Logan color *TV Guide* v65 no7 p46 F 13 2017

Darby, Brandon

THE RABBLE-ROUSER *Texas Monthly* v45 no2 p90 F 2017

Darby, Graham

KERENSKY IN HINDSIGHT: Alexander Kerensky, the last Russian premier before the Bolsheviks took power, decided to continue the war with Germany. He and his country would pay the price *History Today* v67 no7 p48 Jl 2017

Radetzky's march into obscurity *History Today* v66 no12 p28 D 2016

Darby, Robbie Ann

Street Style: FITNESS EDITION color *Women's Health* v14 no5 p18 Je 2017

Darby, Seyward

THE RISE OF THE VALKYRIES: In the alt-right, women are the future, and the problem *Harper's Magazine* p25 S 2017

Darcy James Argue's Secret Society (Performer)
Chords & Discords T. HUDAK, S. ROWE et al bw *Downbeat* v83 no12 p10 D 2016

Darden, Keith A.
Russian Revanche: External Threats & Regime Reactions *Daedalus* v146 no2 p128 Spr 2017

Darden, Shani
The Girl with the Magic Hands K. Diamond color *InStyle* v24 no3 p262 Mr 2017

Dardenne, Luc
The Outsider C. LORENTZEN *New Republic* v248 no10 p60 O 2017

Daredevil (Fictitious character)
NO. 16 DAREDEVIL D. Franich color *Entertainment Weekly* no1436/1437 p58 O 21 2016

Dargemont, Catherine
New developments for protein quality control diag *Science* v357 no6350 p450 Ag 4 2017

DARGIS, MANOHLA
CAN WE TALK? *New York Times Book Review* p16 D 4 2016

Dargusch, Paul
China must lead on emissions trading *Science* v357 no6356 p1106 S 15 2017

Daria (TV program)
Daria: 20 Years Later C. Brody color *Entertainment Weekly* no1460/1461 p68 Ap 7-17 2017

DARIMONT, CHRIS T.
Conserving the World's Megafauna and Biodiversity: The Fierce Urgency of Now *BioScience* v67 no3 p197 Mr 2017
Saving the World's Terrestrial Megafauna color *BioScience* v66 no10 p807 O 1 2016
Society Is Ready for a New Kind of Science--Is Academia? *BioScience* v67 no7 p591 Jl 2017

Daringer, Nichole M.
Nucleic acid detection with CRISPR-Cas13a/C2c2 color diag *Science* v356 no6336 p438 Ap 28 2017

Darity, William A., Jr.
My President Was Black *Atlantic* v319 no2 p8 Mr 2017

Darity, William, Jr.
EXIT LEFT bw color *Nation* v304 no16 p16 My 22 2017

Dark, Dan
ON A FIRST DATE *Indianapolis Monthly* p65 F 2017

Dark, David
The Unbearable Lightness Of Being U2 bw color *America* v217 no4 p38 Ag 21 2017
WHAT DO YOU DO WITH THE MAD THAT YOU FEEL? [Cover story] color *America* v216 no10 p26 My 1 2017

Dark Angel (TV program)
Dark Angel J. Russell *TV Guide* v65 no21 p34 My 15 2017

Dark energy (Astronomy)
The Dark Universe A. HADHAZY color diag graph *Discover* v38 no6 p76 Jl/Ag 2017
Extragalactic survey aims to shed light on dark energy T. Feder *Physics Today* v69 no10 p28 O 2016
GALACTIC CENSUS REAFFIRMS STANDARD MODEL OF COSMOLOGY *Physics Today* v70 no9 p22 S 2017
NOTHING REALLY MATTERS A. HADHAZY bw color *Discover* v27 no10 p46 D 2016
Survey finds galaxy clumps stirred up by dark energy D. Clery color *Science* v357 no6351 p537 Ag 11 2017

Dark matter (Astronomy)
BLACK HOLES from the Beginning of Time J. García-Bellido and S. Clesse color graph *Scientific American* v317 no1 p38 Jl 2017
Can dark matter vanquish controversial rival theory? A. Cho color *Science* v355 no6323 p337 Ja 27 2017
CAN TONS OF XENON FINALLY FIND DARK MATTER? J. Wenz color *Astronomy* v45 no7 p12 Jl 2017
Charting the dark side of the universe E. Conover color map *Science News* v192 no3 p32 S 2 2017
Dark matter hunters raise the bar color *Science* v356 no6340 p786 My 26 2017
A Dark Milky Way L. KRUESI color *Discover* v38 no1 p78 Ja/F 2017
The Dark Universe A. HADHAZY color diag graph *Discover* v38 no6 p76 Jl/Ag 2017

Debate heats up over black holes as dark matter A. Cho color *Science* v355 no6325 p560 F 10 2017
Distant galaxies may lack dark matter A. YEAGER *Science News* v191 no7 p10 Ap 15 2017
Double Darkness [Cover story] T. Siegfried color *Science News* v190 no13 p30 D 24 2016
Extragalactic survey aims to shed light on dark energy T. Feder *Physics Today* v69 no10 p28 O 2016
FROM OUR READERS D. Britz, M. Swanson et al color *Sky & Telescope* v134 no2 p6 Ag 2017
In search for unseen matter, physicists turn to dark sector A. Cho color diag *Science* v355 no6331 p1251 Mr 24 2017
In the Dark About Dark Matter L. Moustakas color diag graph *Sky & Telescope* v134 no2 p28 Ag 2017
Less Dark Matter in Young Galaxies? M. YOUNG *Sky & Telescope* v134 no1 p13 Jl 2017
Milky Way satellite distribution explained color *Astronomy* v45 no8 p17 Ag 2017
NOTHING REALLY MATTERS A. HADHAZY bw color *Discover* v27 no10 p46 D 2016
Probing the frontiers of particle physics with tabletop-scale experiments D. DeMille, J. M. Doyle et al color graph *Science* v357 no6355 p990 S 8 2017
Vera Rubin's Universe A. Yeager bw color graph *Sky & Telescope* v134 no2 p36 Ag 2017
Why we need dark matter F. Reddy color *Astronomy* v45 no11 p30 N 2017
X-ray 'bump' hints at dark matter E. CONOVER color *Science News* v191 no4 p8 Mr 4 2017

Dark matter (Astronomy)—Research
Dark matter searches come up empty E. CONOVER color *Science News* v190 no10 p14 N 12 2016
Hunting dark matter with GPS data color *Science* v355 no6324 p438 F 3 2017
A LARGE GALAXY MADE ALMOST ENTIRELY OF DARK MATTER *Physics Today* v69 no11 p24 N 2016

Dark Matter (Music)
HIGH CEILINGS J. Seabrook cartoon *New Yorker* v93 no24 p17 Ag 21 2017
Randy Newman Makes Irony Great Again J. DOLAN color *Rolling Stone* no1293 p54 Ag 10 2017

Dark Night (Film)
SHINY THINGS A. LANE cartoon *New Yorker* v92 no48 p80 F 6 2017

Dark pools (Economics)
Everybody Into The Dark Pool A. Massa color *Bloomberg Businessweek* no4519 p45 Ap 24 2017

Darkest Hour (Film)
ALSO PLAYING D. Heching color *Entertainment Weekly* no1478 / 1479 p69 Ag 18-25 2017

Darkest Minds, The (Film)
Harris DICKINSON *Interview* v47 no5 p61 Je/Jl 2017

Darkness & Light (Music)
A *Atlanta* v57 no1 p30 My 2017
John Legend L. B. Ray color *InStyle* v24 no2 p64 F 2017
John Legend Shows His Soul N. Feeney color *Entertainment Weekly* no1443 p58 D 9 2016
John Legend's Light Shines Even Brighter S. Lansky color *Time* v188 no24 p65 D 12 2016
The Playlist color *Rolling Stone* no1278/1279 p10 Ja 12 2017

Darknets (File sharing)
The Darknet: A Quick Introduction for Business Leaders A. Delamarter *Harvard Business Review Digital Articles* p2 D 9 2016

Dark Song, A (Film)
NOW PLAYING color *Entertainment Weekly* no1465 p45 My 12 2017

Darkspur (Short story)
Darkspur D. McFARLAND *American Scholar* v86 no2 p91 Spr 2017

Dark Tower, The (Film)
Summer Movie Preview: August S. Begley, E. Berman et al color *Time* v189 no20 p58 My 29 2017

Darkwah Oppong, N.
A Fermi-degenerate three-dimensional optical lattice clock color diag graph *Science* v357 no6359 p90 O 6 2017

Century v133 no25 p16 D 7 2016

DARRAGH, DAN

Chords & Discords color *Downbeat* v84 no5 p10 My 2017

Darre, Vincent

world of Vincent Darré M. OWENS color *Architectural Digest* no11 p40 N 1 2017

Darrell, Bracken

A Mouse (Maker) Roars At the Industry's Giants A. Ricadela color *Bloomberg Businessweek* no4515 p30 Mr 20 2017

DARRISAW, ARIS

WHERE ARE YOU GOING? color *O, The Oprah Magazine* p126 N 2017

Darrisaw, Michelle

Worth the Wait color *Southern Living* v52 no10 p44 O 2017

Darrow, Barb

THE 2017 Fortune Crystal Ball color diag *Fortune* v174 no7 p11 D 1 2016

CHANGE THE WORLD !!!! color diag map *Fortune* v176 no4 p74 S 15 2017

DREAM WEAVER color *Fortune* v176 no3 p74 S 1 2017

FORTY UNDER FORTY 2017 color *Fortune* v176 no3 p62 S 1 2017

MINING COMEDY GOLD color *Fortune* v176 no3 p70 S 1 2017

WORLD'S 50 GREATEST LEADERS [Cover story] color *Fortune* v175 no5 p46 Ap 1 2017

YOUTH REVOLT color *Fortune* v176 no3 p64 S 1 2017

Darrow, Clarence, 1857-1938

REASON IN BRONZE: CLARENCE DARROW to Reunite with WILLIAM JENNINGS BRYAN at Dayton Courthouse J. MELCHIOR *Humanist* v77 no4 p32 Jl/Ag 2017

Darrow, Joe

When Big Brother Parents img *New York* v50 no18 p34 S 4 2017

Darryl Carter Inc.

The New Classics color *House Beautiful* v159 no3 p31 Ap 2017

DARST, JEANNE

Dad, Interrupted color *Vogue* v206 no12 p102 D 2016

Darst, Seth A.

RNA polymerase motions during promoter melting color diag graph *Science* v356 no6340 p863 My 26 2017

Dartmouth College

Artificial intelligence, in so many words M. Hutson *Science* v357 no6346 p19 Jl 7 2017

Darviche, Shula Malkin

Do You Know Who Holds Your Office Together? *Harvard Business Review Digital Articles* p2 S 23 2015

Darvill, Arthur

DC's Legends of Tomorrow N. Abrams, A. Bacle et al color *Entertainment Weekly* no1482/1483 p66 S 22 2017

DARWALL, WILLIAM

Freshwater Megafauna: Flagships for Freshwater Biodiversity under Threat *BioScience* v67 no10 p919 O 2017

Darwin (N.T.)

ABORIGINAL QUEEN OF THE DESERT color *Advocate* no1091 p17 Je/Jl 2017

Darwin, Charles, 1809-1882

1849: Downe *Lapham's Quarterly* v10 no2 p127 Spr 2017

BODY LANGUAGE C. Darwin *Lapham's Quarterly* v10 no3 p49 Summ 2017

Charles Darwin N. SCHARPING color *Discover* v38 no4 p42 My 2017

Ivory Tower J. Ryerson *New York Times Book Review* p31 Mr 12 2017

The Scream Franchise *Lapham's Quarterly* v10 no3 p50 Summ 2017

Darzacq, Xavier

Mutations in the promoter of the telomerase gene TERT contribute to tumorigenesis by a two-step mechanism diag *Science* v357 no6358 p1416 S 29 2017

Das, Anshuman

MAVS-dependent host species range and pathogenicity of human hepatitis A virus bibl graph *Science* v353 no6307 p1541 S 30 2016

Das, Jishnu

The impact of training informal health care providers in India: A randomized controlled trial chart diag *Science* v354 no6308 paaf7384-1 O 7 2016

Das, Pratyush K.

Impact of cytosine methylation on DNA binding specificities of human transcription factors diag *Science* v356 no6337 p502 My 5 2017

Das, Sai Krupa

THE MESSY TRUTH ABOUT WEIGHT LOSS color graph *Scientific American* v316 no6 p36 Je 2017

Das, Saswato R.

Fossil Moon color *Scientific American* v317 no4 p18 O 2017

D.A.S. Audio SA

D.A.S. Audio Deployed at the Flying Monkey Movie House & Performance Center *Stage Directions* v30 no3 p18 Mr 2017

Das Rheingold (Music)

CLASSICAL MUSIC cartoon *New Yorker* v93 no16 p10 Je 5 2017

Das Rheingold (Theatrical production)

WAGNER WEEKEND A. ROSS cartoon *New Yorker* v92 no33 p104 O 17 2016

Dasgupta, Ani

How Mobile Apps Are Improving India's Rickshaws *Harvard Business Review Digital Articles* p1 Ja 13 2016

Dash, Catherine

BEST OF THE WEST color *Sunset* v237 no6 p11 D 2016

BEST OF THE WEST color *Sunset* v238 no3 p7 Mr 2017

BEST OF THE WEST color *Sunset* v238 no6 p9 Je 2017

the life color *InStyle* v24 no4 p215 Ap 2017

TOWN AND COUNTRY color *Sunset* v239 no3 p32 S 2017

Dash, Julie

Daughters of the Dust *New Yorker* v93 no5 p12 Mr 20 2017

Dash, Julie—Interviews

INVISIBLE SCRATCH LINES: AN INTERVIEW WITH JULIE DASH M. K. Holmes *Film Quarterly* v70 no2 p49 Wint 2016

Dashboards (Management information systems)

3 Ways Data Dashboards Can Mislead You J. Shapiro color graph *Harvard Business Review Digital Articles* p2 Ja 13 2017

What's Sustainability, Anyhow? E. Daigneau *Governing* v30 no3 p20 D 2016

Dashkova, Polina

Madness Treads Lightly *Publishers Weekly* v264 no31 p62 Jl 31 2017

Dashun Wang

Quantifying the evolution of individual scientific impact graph *Science* v354 no6312 p596 N 4 2016

DaSilva, Karen

How Atrius Health Is Making the Shift from Volume to Value *Harvard Business Review Digital Articles* p2 D 13 2016

da Silva, N. F.

Persistent effects of pre-Columbian plant domestication on Amazonian forest composition bibl chart graph map *Science* v355 no6328 p925 Mr 3 2017

da Silva, Peri

Will U.S. Upset the Apple Cart? *USA Today Magazine* v145 no2863 p5 Ap 2017

da Silva Guimarães, J. R.

Persistent effects of pre-Columbian plant domestication on Amazonian forest composition bibl chart graph map *Science* v355 no6328 p925 Mr 3 2017

Daskal, Jennifer

Public and Private Eyes cartoon *Foreign Affairs* v96 no6 p139 N/D 2017

Daskal, Lolly

Asking for a Raise When You're Afraid To *Harvard Business Review Digital Articles* p2 N 18 2015

Daskalakis, Demetre

THE LGBTQ HEALTH CARE BILL OF RIGHTS: New York City made an important step toward equality D. GUERRERO *Advocate* no1093 p60 O/N 2017

Dassault Aviation SA

FALCON 8X R. MARK chart color *Flying* v144 no5 p42 My 2017

Dassault Falcon (Jet transport)

POLISHING OFF THE RUST I. King color *Flying* v144 no9 p30 S 2017

Dassault Falcon (Jet transport)—Evaluation

FALCON 8X R. MARK chart color *Flying* v144 no5 p42 My 2017

Das Shrestha, Kashish

Merging paleobiology with conservation biology to guide the future of terrestrial ecosystems color *Science* v355 no6325 p594

Reader's Digest v189 no1130 p46 My 2017

Data protection

Feature: Security tips S. Ragan color *Macworld - Digital Edition* p59 Ja 2017

Feature: Your consumer rights this Christmas J. Martin bw color *Macworld - Digital Edition* p68 Ja 2017

If Data Is Money, Why Don't Businesses Keep It Secure? T. Cooper, R. LaSalle et al *Harvard Business Review Digital Articles* p2 F 10 2015

One Startup's Vision to Reinvent the Web for Better Privacy T. Simonite il *MIT Technology Review* v120 no2 p20 Mr/Ap 2017

Seven Ways to Protect Your Data S. Goldberg *Cincinnati Magazine* v50 no10 p72 Jl 2017

Data protection laws

New EU data rules 'should be an HR priority': Businesses urged to act swiftly, before legislation takes effect in the UK from May 2018 *People Management* p17 S 2017

Data quality

A 5-Step Process to Get More Out of Your Organization's Data J. M. Jachimowicz *Harvard Business Review Digital Articles* p2 Mr 16 2017

Assess Whether You Have a Data Quality Problem T. C. Redman *Harvard Business Review Digital Articles* p2 Jl 28 2016

Data Quality Should Be Everyone's Job T. C. Redman *Harvard Business Review Digital Articles* p2 My 20 2016

Only 3% of Companies' Data Meets Basic Quality Standards T. Nagle, T. C. Redman et al *Harvard Business Review Digital Articles* p2 S 11 2017

Stop Making Excuses for Your Flawed Data T. C. Redman *Harvard Business Review Digital Articles* p2 F 12 2015

Data recovery (Computer science)

Everything you need to know about Windows 10 recovery drives J. NOREM color *PCWorld* v35 no1 p188 Ja 2017

What Microsoft won't tell you about your Windows 10 recovery drive size J. NOREM color *PCWorld* p153 O 2016

Data recovery (Computer science)—Software—Evaluation

DISK DRILL 3: MAC UTILITY NOW RECOVERS DATA FROM iOS DEVICES, TOO J. R. BOOKWALTER cartoon color *Macworld - Digital Edition* p26 D 2016

Data removal (Computer science)—Software

Our favorite Mac cleanup tips color *Macworld - Digital Edition* v34 no4 p81 My 2017

Data science (Information science)

Academia's failure to retain data scientists F. Rodríguez-Sánchez, B. Marwick et al bibl *Science* v355 no6323 p357 Ja 27 2017

Assess Whether You Have a Data Quality Problem T. C. Redman *Harvard Business Review Digital Articles* p2 Jl 28 2016

The Best Data Scientists Get Out and Talk to People T. C. Redman color *Harvard Business Review Digital Articles* p2 Ja 26 2017

The Best Data Scientists Know How to Tell Stories M. Li *Harvard Business Review Digital Articles* p2 O 13 2015

Can We Quantify the Value of Connected Devices? S. Menon *Harvard Business Review Digital Articles* p2 O 20 2014

Can Your Data Be Trusted? T. C. Redman *Harvard Business Review Digital Articles* p2 O 29 2015

Data Scientists Don't Scale S. Frankel *Harvard Business Review Digital Articles* p2 My 22 2015

A Guide to Selecting an Analytics Vendor M. Redlon *Harvard Business Review Digital Articles* p2 O 23 2015

HOW DATA SCIENCE IS DISRUPTING THE JOB MARKET diag img *Harvard Business Review* v95 no5 p24 S/O 2017

Marketers Don't Need to Be Data Scientists D. Spitz *Harvard Business Review Digital Articles* p2 O 6 2014

Why You're Not Getting Value from Your Data Science K. Veeramachaneni *Harvard Business Review Digital Articles* p2 D 7 2016

Data security

See also

Data security failures

Artists, in their explorations of how tech companies violate our privacy, have begun to sound an alarm that we might not be ready to hear J. Wortham *New York Times Magazine* p12 Ja 1 2017

The Enemies of Data Security: Convenience and Collaboration C. S. Young *Harvard Business Review Digital Articles* p2 F 11 2015

Equifax, the Credit Reporting Industry, and What Congress Should Do Next M. Rotenberg *Harvard Business Review Digital Articles* p2 S 20 2017

The Ethics Conversation We're Not Having About Data K. Fung *Harvard Business Review Digital Articles* p2 N 12 2015

Feature: Security tips S. Ragan color *Macworld - Digital Edition* p59 Ja 2017

Feature: Your consumer rights this Christmas J. Martin bw color *Macworld - Digital Edition* p68 Ja 2017

Panel urges steps to boost evidence-based policy J. Mervis color *Science* v357 no6355 p959 S 8 2017

Welcome... *Macworld - Digital Edition* p3 Ja 2017

Data security failures

1 BILLION+ THE NUMBER OF ACCOUNTS COMPROMISED IN THE YAHOO HACK R. Hackett *Fortune* v75 no1 p16 Ja 1 2017

Can You Put a Dollar Amount on Your Company's Cyber Risk? L. Chacko, E. Sekeris et al *Harvard Business Review Digital Articles* p2 O 5 2016

Equifax and Why It's So Hard to Sue a Company for Losing Your Personal Information B. R. Sharton and D. S. Kantrowitz *Harvard Business Review Digital Articles* p2 S 22 2017

Equifax, the Credit Reporting Industry, and What Congress Should Do Next M. Rotenberg *Harvard Business Review Digital Articles* p2 S 20 2017

Thank You For Calling Equifax, Your Business Is Not Important to Us P. Regnier, S. Woolley et al *Bloomberg Businessweek* no4538 p38 S 18 2017

We're Here to Help *Kiplinger's Personal Finance* v71 no12 p4 D 2017

Your Biggest Cybersecurity Weakness Is Your Phone L. Dignan *Harvard Business Review Digital Articles* p2 S 22 2016

Your Equifax Defense L. GERSTNER color *Kiplinger's Personal Finance* v71 no12 p34 D 2017

Data security failures—History—21st century

Big Data Breaches T. John color *Time* v188 no14 p10 O 10 2016

Data security failures—Prevention

Your Company Needs a Communications Plan for Data Breaches H. Rollo and P. Tran *Harvard Business Review Digital Articles* p2 O 7 2016

Data security—Evaluation

A Data Breach You Can Smell J. Zorthian color *Time* v188 no18 p21 O 31 2016

Data transmission systems—Great Britain

BIG BROTHER IN THE U.K S. SHACKFORD *Reason* v48 no10 p9 Mr 2017

Data transmission systems—Law & legislation

BIG BROTHER IN THE U.K S. SHACKFORD *Reason* v48 no10 p9 Mr 2017

Data warehousing

See also

Cloud storage

Home Is Where The Data Is D. Bass graph *Bloomberg Businessweek* no4498 p54 N 7 2016

How to Spot Hidden Opportunities for Sales Growth A. A. Zoltners, P. K. Sinha et al *Harvard Business Review Digital Articles* p2 S 17 2015

My Five...: Tips for Staying Organized All Year Long J. Martinez *Literacy Today (2411-7862)* v35 no1 p4 Jl/Ag 2017

Database design

Growing pains for global monitoring of societal events R. Kennedy, D. Lazer et al bibl graph *Science* v353 no6307 p1502 S 30 2016

Database management

See also

Data integration (Computer science)

Data warehousing

Digital asset management

AI Can Comb Through Your Data to Create More Compelling Customer Experiences B. Morgan *Harvard Business Review Digital Articles* p2 Je 14 2017

Breaking Down Data Silos E. Wilder-James *Harvard Business Review Digital Articles* p2 D 5 2016

You Can Make Your Sales Data a Lot Better with a Little Discipline J. Fowler *Harvard Business Review Digital Articles* p2 Je 13 2017

Database security

How Safe Are Blockchains? It Depends A. Berke color *Harvard Business Review Digital Articles* p2 Mr 7 2017

Databases

See also

Electronic books

Electronic journals

Expanded Oscar Coverage M. Fleischmann and C. Crowley color *Sound & Vision* v82 no6 p17 Jl/Ag 2017

Genomic databases: A WHO affair S. E. Antonarakis, B. P. Koch et al *Science* v356 no6340 p812 My 26 2017

An interactive three-dimensional digital atlas and quantitative database of human development B. S. de Bakker, K. H. de Jong et al bibl color graph *Science* v354 no6315 paag0053-1 N 25 2016

WHO DECIDES? *New York* v50 no11 p56 My 29 2017

Data—Management

Data Quality Should Be Everyone's Job T. C. Redman *Harvard Business Review Digital Articles* p2 My 20 2016

The Dos and Don'ts of Working with Emerging-Market Data A. Rosenberg and L. Goodwin *Harvard Business Review Digital Articles* p2 Jl 8 2016

Got data? Now what? L. Bedord *Successful Farming* v114 no12 p10 Mid-N 2016

Nuclear Data Moves into the 21st Century A. Heller *Science & Technology Review* p12 S 2016

Prove It K. Birchmier *Successful Farming* v114 no12 p18 Mid-N 2016

What's Your Data Strategy? L. DALLEMULE and T. H. DAVENPORT color diag img *Harvard Business Review* v95 no3 p112 My/Je 2017

Data—Management—Research

Rapid data exchange helps keep a secret for 24 hours J. Miller *Physics Today* v69 no11 p19 N 2016

Data plans (Wireless telecommunication)—Charts, diagrams, etc.

THE MOBILE DATA SQUEEZE IS COMING A. Pressman diag *Fortune* v174 no8 p16 D 15 2016

Data—Social aspects

Using data wisely at the system level M. Lockwood, M. Dillman et al chart color *Phi Delta Kappan* v99 no1 p25 S 2017

Date rape

The Stories of Our Lives *Ms.* v27 no3 p40 Fall 2017

Dateline (TV program)

DATELINE DATE NIGHT color *Entertainment Weekly* no1457/1458 p56 Mr 17 2017

Dating (Social customs)

78 fun ways to spend less color *Redbook* p8 Je 2017

7 Habits That Will Save Your Long-Distance Relationship S. T. Brown color *Ebony* v72 no6 p68 Ap/My 2017

All the Rage L. Featherstone color *Nation* v305 no5 p5 Ag 28 2017

Am I the Last Romantic Millennial? L. Moore bw color *Glamour* v115 no5 p120 My 2017

ASKING FOR A FRIEND: TO BE INTERESTING TO OTHERS, BE INTERESTED IN THEM A. HIDDEN *Psychology Today* v50 no5 p20 S/O 2017

Bowl Her Over on a First Date K. FOX bw color diag *Men's Health* v32 no7 p71 S 2017

Crowdsource This color *Glamour* v114 no11 p126 N 2016

The Dating Game L. Featherstone il *Nation* v303 no17 p7 O 24 2016

Diary of a Working Mom's Date Night S. Heacock cartoon *Working Mother* v40 no3 p50 Ag/S 2017

HACKING CHIVALRY J. Black color *Esquire* p26 Ag 2017

Have the Best Date Ever (Seriously) C. THORP color *Seventeen* v76 no4 p56 Jl/Ag 2017

Kelsea Ballerini color *Health* v31 no9 p116 N 2017

Mating M. A. GREEN, L. LARSON et al bw color *GQ: Gentlemen's Quarterly* v86 no11 p58 N 2016

October, Whoa color *Glamour* v114 no12 p64 D 2016

Race & Dating: It's Complicated V. Carter color *Glamour* v115 no6 p91 Je 2017

Sex and the Single Girl, Puppy Love, Oy Vey L. KOGAN color *O, The Oprah Magazine* p38 Ag 2017

Sex, Super Likes & Five Years of Tinder C. Drell color *Glamour* v115 no5 p113 My 2017

THE THINKING MAN: ANSEL ELGORT M. Khidekel color *Women's Health* v14 no6 p118 Jl 2017

What comes after I. Kerner cartoon *Prevention* v69 no7 p26 Jl 2017

When the Ground Cracked *Psychology Today* v50 no5 p46 S/O 2017

The World Is Yours K. Kyles color *Ebony* v72 no6 p14 Ap/My 2017

You and Your Date Night B. GADDIS cartoon *Working Mother* p50 F/Mr 2017

Your Cheatin' Heart F. OGUNJINMI *USA Today Magazine* v145 no2862 p68 Mr 2017

Dating (Social customs)—Software

Confessions of a single mom on Tinder color *Redbook* p110 F 2017

HERE COMES EVERYBODY *Harper's Magazine* p19 O 2017

Why You Should Never Date Anyone You Meet IRL D. Schwartz color *Glamour* v115 no9 p126 S 2017

Dating services

Verify My Love J. Ganz color *Entertainment Weekly* no1477 p16 Ag 11 2017

Dating violence

Bad Romance S. DOLGOFF *Scholastic Choices* v32 no5 p16 F 2017

Datka, Jen

You Never Forget Your First Time diag il *Backpacker* v45 no2 p64 Mr 2017

Datsun automobile

1970-1973 DATSUN 240Z C. COMER color *Road & Track* v69 no2 p92 S 2017

FROM THE ROAD & TRACK ARCHIVES bw color *Road & Track* v69 no2 p94 S 2017

Dattilo, Bryan

DAYS OF OUR LIVES M. LOGAN *TV Guide* v65 no39 p64 S 18 2017

Dáttilo, Wesley

Higher predation risk for insect prey at low latitudes and elevations graph *Science* v356 no6339 p742 My 19 2017

Dattner, Ben

A CEO's Personality Can Undermine Succession Planning *Harvard Business Review Digital Articles* p2 S 15 2016

How Structured Debate Helps Your Team Grow *Harvard Business Review Digital Articles* p2 D 10 2015

How to Participate in Your Employee's Coaching *Harvard Business Review Digital Articles* p2 N 3 2014

How to Plan a Team Offsite That Actually Works *Harvard Business Review Digital Articles* p2 Je 25 2015

How to Turn an Interim Role into a Permanent Job color *Harvard Business Review Digital Articles* p2 Ja 16 2017

The Key to Performance Reviews Is Preparation *Harvard Business Review Digital Articles* p2 Je 21 2016

A Scorecard for Making Better Hiring Decisions *Harvard Business Review Digital Articles* p2 F 4 2016

When Coaching Finds That an Executive Isn't in the Right Role *Harvard Business Review Digital Articles* p2 Jl 31 2017

Why You Should Interview People Who Turn Down a Job with Your Company *Harvard Business Review Digital Articles* p2 Ag 1 2016

Dattner Architects (Company)

Our Snow-Salt Sheds Look Like Museums J. DAVIDSON img *New York* v49 no25 p76 D 12 2016

The Residences at P.S. 186 *Architectural Record* v205 no4 p196 Ap 2017

Daugaard, Dennis, 1953-

Dennis Daugaard B. Lightner color *Current Biography* v78 no3 p12 Mr 2017

Daugherty, Candace Z.

Rescue of exhausted CD8 T cells by PD-1–targeted therapies is CD28-dependent bw diag graph *Science* v355 no6332 p1423 Mr 31 2017

Daugherty, Jo Ann

Kawai ES110 Digital Piano color *Downbeat* v84 no9 p99 S 2017

Daugherty, Paul

5 Ways Product Design Needs to Evolve for the Internet of Things *Harvard Business Review Digital Articles* p2 N 14 2014

Gestures Will Be the Interface for the Internet of Things *Harvard*

Business Review Digital Articles p2 Jl 8 2015

How One Clothing Company Blends AI and Human Expertise *Harvard Business Review Digital Articles* p2 N 21 2016

When AI Becomes the New Face of Your Brand *Harvard Business Review Digital Articles* p2 Je 27 2017

Daughters

See also

Fathers & daughters

Mothers & daughters

THE BITE THAT CHANGED MY LIFE cartoon *Chicago* v66 no2 p78 F 2017

Born Trump M. BRENDAN DOUGHERTY il *National Review* v69 no12 p27 Je 26 2017

breaking binky A. KULP *Parents* v91 no10 p60 O 2016

How SHE-roes Raise Girls M. LaScala color *Parents* v92 no5 p17 My 2017

"MY DAD MADE ME FEEL BEAUTIFUL, teaching me to see the beauty beyond my disability." M. BLAKE color *Good Housekeeping* v264 no6 p63 Je 2017

THINGS I'M AFRAID MY DAUGHTER WILL BE DOING IN 2026 E. FLAKE cartoon *New Yorker* v93 no20 p54 Jl 10 2017

What Children Can Teach Us About Acceptance E. Bried *Parents* v91 no10 p16 O 2016

Zone DEFENSE M. BECK cartoon *O, The Oprah Magazine* p42 Ap 2017

Daughters of the Dust (Film)

Daughters of the Dust *New Yorker* v93 no5 p12 Mr 20 2017

Daughters—Psychology

HELENA, FALLING: And the human impulse, from the youngest age,to keep going D. Bratcher *Washingtonian Magazine* v52 no11 p176 Ag 2017

Daulton, Darren, 1962-2017

TRIBUTES T. Keith, J. Fuchs et al color *Sports Illustrated* v127 no5 p22 Ag 14 2017

Daum, Meghan

Egos: Memoir *New York Times Book Review* p27 My 28 2017

Egos: Memoirs *New York Times Book Review* p27 S 17 2017

Egos *New York Times Book Review* p27 Ap 2 2017

Egos *New York Times Book Review* p31 Jl 23 2017

Memoir *New York Times Book Review* p27 F 5 2017

Memoir *New York Times Book Review* p39 D 11 2016

ONLY CONNECT bw *Vogue* v207 no9 p680 S 2017

Daumiller, K.

Observation of a large-scale anisotropy in the arrival directions of cosmic rays above 8 × 1018 eV *Science* v357 no6357 p1266 S 22 2017

Dauphas, Nicolas

Titanium isotopic evidence for felsic crust and plate tectonics 3.5 billion years ago bw color graph *Science* v357 no6357 p1271 S 22 2017

Dauphin, Daniel

Loping 'Out Loud' bw color *Horse & Rider* v56 no7 p54 Jl 2017

Dautovich, Natalie

YOUR BODY ON TECH A. SHAFFER color *Better Homes & Gardens* v95 no4 p152 Ap 2017

Dauwels, Justin

Imaging the distribution of transient viscosity after the 2016 Mw 7.1 Kumamoto earthquake map *Science* v356 no6334 p163 Ap 14 2017

DÁVALOS, LILIANA M.

Deforestation and Coca Cultivation Rooted in Twentieth-Century Development Projects *BioScience* v66 no11 p974 N 1 2016

Davant, Meaghan Hannan

BONE TIRED *Washingtonian Magazine* v52 no5 p129 F 2017

Dave', Jagdish P.

TALK TO US color *Chicago* v66 no2 p11 F 2017

Dave, Kashyap

Impact of cytosine methylation on DNA binding specificities of human transcription factors diag *Science* v356 no6337 p502 My 5 2017

Dave Brubeck Quartet (Performer)

Chords & Discords J. R. VICKARY, T. GUILFOYLE et al bw color *Downbeat* v84 no6 p10 Je 2017

D'Aveni, Richard

3D Printing Will Revive Conglomerates *Harvard Business Review Digital Articles* p2 My 19 2015

Deals R. DEAHL bw color *Publishers Weekly* v264 no14 p7 Ap 3. 2017

Get Your Organization Ready for 3D Printing *Harvard Business Review Digital Articles* p2 Je 1 2015

The Time to Think About the 3D-Printed Future Is Now *Harvard Business Review Digital Articles* p2 My 6 2015

Davenport, Coral

How Trump Could Change America *New York Times Upfront* v149 no7 p8 Ja 9 2017

Davenport, David

Return of the "Forgotten Man" *Hoover Digest: Research & Opinion on Public Policy* no1 p33 Wint 2017

Rugged Individualism: Two of the gravest threats to this distinctively American value: nanny states and helicopter parents *Hoover Digest: Research & Opinion on Public Policy* no2 p42 Spr 2017

Davenport, Gary

DATA IS EVERYTHING color *Maclean's* v129 no51/52 p17 D 26 2016

Davenport, Julie

Patriotism in the pews color *U.S. Catholic* v82 no11 p5 N 2017

Davenport, Kelsey

Nuclear disarmament summits: A proposal to break the international impasse bibl *Bulletin of the Atomic Scientists* v73 no4 p264 Jl 2017

Davenport, Thomas H.

5 Essential Principles for Understanding Analytics *Harvard Business Review Digital Articles* p2 O 21 2015

7 Ways Microsoft Can Make LinkedIn Worth $26 Billion *Harvard Business Review Digital Articles* p2 Je 13 2016

Automation Won't Replace People as Your Competitive Advantage *Harvard Business Review Digital Articles* p2 Ag 10 2015

How Analytics Has Changed in the Last 10 Years (and How It's Stayed the Same) *Harvard Business Review Digital Articles* p1 Je 22 2017

How Machine Learning Is Helping Morgan Stanley Better Understand Client Needs *Harvard Business Review Digital Articles* p2 Ag 3 2017

How P&G and American Express Are Approaching AI *Harvard Business Review Digital Articles* p2 Mr 31 2017

The Knowledge Jobs Most Likely to Be Automated *Harvard Business Review Digital Articles* p2 Je 23 2016

Move Your Analytics Operation from Artisanal to Autonomous *Harvard Business Review Digital Articles* p2 D 2 2016

A New Way for Entrepreneurs to Think About IT *Harvard Business Review Digital Articles* p2 Je 28 2016

Setting Standards for the Internet of Things *Harvard Business Review Digital Articles* p2 N 21 2014

Wall Street Jobs Won't Be Spared from Automation *Harvard Business Review Digital Articles* p2 D 14 2016

What's Your Data Strategy? color diag img *Harvard Business Review* v95 no3 p112 My/Je 2017

Why Trump Doesn't Tweet About Automation color *Harvard Business Review Digital Articles* p2 Ja 12 2017

Will AI Companies Make Any Money? *Harvard Business Review Digital Articles* p2 Jl 12 2016

Davey, Justin

10 UP & COMERS: TYLER SCHNAITHMAN *Successful Farming* v115 no8 p34 Je/Jl 2017

MARK POESCHL: FFA CEO TALKS ABOUT THE ORGANIZATION'S UPS AND DOWNS, AND THE NEXT GENERATION OF AG LEADERS *Successful Farming* v115 no12 p10 O 2017

Davey, Liane

Deliver Feedback That Sticks *Harvard Business Review Digital Articles* p2 Ag 20 2015

Everyone's Network Should Provide Two Things *Harvard Business Review Digital Articles* p1 S 30 2016

A Game Plan for That Conversation You've Been Putting Off *Harvard Business Review Digital Articles* p2 Ap 12 2017

Handling Emotional Outbursts on Your Team *Harvard Business Review Digital Articles* p2 Ap 30 2015

Helping a Coworker Who's Stressed Out *Harvard Business Review Digital Articles* p2 S 10 2015

How to De-Escalate an Argument with a Coworker *Harvard Business Review Digital Articles* p2 Je 27 2017

p24 O 2017

Davidson, Bill

HELL, NO, WE WON'T GO! *Saturday Evening Post* v289 no4 p42 Jl/Ag 2017

Davidson, Cathy N., 1949-

Campus Choices C. CALHOUN *New York Times Book Review* p22 Ag 27 2017

Davidson, Chris

Oscar Billy Pippen Wright, 41 S. DOHERTY color *Surfer* v58 no6 p40 O 2017

What My Horse Wears on His Feet cartoon *Horse & Rider* v56 no5 p80 My 2017

Davidson, Christopher

Shadow Wars: The Secret Struggle for the Middle East J. Waterbury *Foreign Affairs* v96 no2 p185 Mr/Ap 2017

Davidson, Eileen—Interviews

THE YOUNG AND THE RESTLESS M. LOGAN *TV Guide* v65 no4 p44 Ja 16 2017

Davidson, Elijah

HOLLYWOOD AT PRAYER color *Christianity Today* v61 no6 p85 Jl/Ag 2017

Davidson, Gavin

ADVANCEMENTS IN THE TREATMENT OF PROSTATE CANCER GIVE HOPE TO PATIENTS color *Maclean's* v130 no6 p78 Jl 2017

CANADA LEADS GLOBAL HEALTH INITIATIVE color *Maclean's* v129 no50 p51 D 19 2016

From Doctor to Patient to Champion color *Maclean's* v130 no6 p75 Jl 2017

Davidson, Hugh

Nobodies J. Russell *TV Guide* p38 Ap 17 2017

Nobodies L. Greenblatt color *Entertainment Weekly* no1459 p52 Mr 31 2017

DAVIDSON, JOHN

STACE color *Idaho Magazine* v16 no1 p18 O 2016

DAVIDSON, JOHN DANIEL

A Failed Urbanism *National Review* v69 no9 p35 My 15 2017

Davidson, Justin

3 A Solar-Powered Adobe img *New York* v49 no21 p90 O 17 2016

6. See Der Rosenkavalier *New York* v50 no7 p88 Ap 3 2017

Avenue of the Idealists img *New York* v50 no7 p76 Ap 3 2017

DESIGNING TOMORROW *Smithsonian* v48 no3 p85 Je 2017

Drumming *New York* v49 no24 p154 N 28 2016

Flames of Contempt: The Grenfell Tower fire wasn't just a tragedy--it was the physical manifestation of political neglect img *New York* v50 no13 p80 Je 26 2017

Is Jane Jacobs Dead? img *New York* v49 no22 p110 O 31 2016

The Master img *New York* v50 no8 p115 Ap 17 2017

The Next New Astor Place img *New York* p83 F 9 2017

Our Snow-Salt Sheds Look Like Museums img *New York* v49 no25 p76 D 12 2016

OUR STREETS DEFY DICTATORS *New York* v49 no25 p47 D 12 2016

Revenge of the Trees img *New York* v49 no26 p80 D 26 2016

String Theory: Classical music needs new superfans. Nadia Sirota is doing her best to create them img *New York* v50 no15 p60 Jl 24 2017

The Ten Best Classical Music Performances of the Year img *New York* v49 no25 p130 D 12 2016

To Do img *New York* p78 F 20 2017

To Do: Twenty-five things to see, hear, watch, and read img *New York* v50 no10 p106 My 15 2017

Urbanities: Justin Davidson img *New York* v50 no8 p21 Ap 17 2017

Where the Top Notes Go img *New York* v49 no20 p114 O 3 2016

Davidson, Kendra

The Future of Genocide: International law changes, but human nature doesn't. Hoover fellow Norman M. Naimark on the ancient and persistent crime of genocide *Hoover Digest: Research & Opinion on Public Policy* no3 p164 Summ 2017

Davidson, Kristen

RIVER REBORN *New York State Conservationist* v71 no4 p10 F 2017

Davidson, Kristen L.

Design principles for new systems of assessment color *Phi Delta Kappan* v98 no6 p47 Mr 2017

Davidson, Laurie

'Will' explores the genesis of genius and Shakespeare's Catholic roots J. Anderson color *America* v217 no3 p48 Ag 7 2017

Davidson, Michael

A Fatal Mistake R. Slade color map *Yankee* v80 no6 p136 N/D 2016

Davidson, Morris—Exhibitions

At Vanderbilt: an influential artist and teacher remembered color *Magazine Antiques* v184 no4 p32 Jl/Ag 2017

DAVIDSON, OSHA GRAY

SUN BLOCKED *Sierra* v101 no5 p32 S/O 2016

Davidson, Robert

BREATHING NEW LIFE INTO IPF TREATMENTS I. Nath *Maclean's* v129 no47 p44 N 28 2016

Davidson, Rose

Drainage Pipe Lodge color *National Geographic Kids* no475 p7 N 2017

ELEPHANT "ASKS" FOR HELP *National Geographic Kids* no467 p13 F 2017

TOUCAN GETS NEW BEAK! *National Geographic Kids* no466 p12 D 2016/Ja 2017

Wild Vacation color *National Geographic Kids* no465 p6 N 2016

Wild Vacation *National Geographic Kids* no468 p11 Mr 2017

Davidson, Shelby

O TANNENBAUM color *Southern Living* v51 no12 p58 D 2016

DAVIDSON, TELLY

The New Republic's New Tilt: The magazine repudiates its 'neoliberal' past *American Conservative* v16 no5 p6 S/O 2017

Davidson, Varya

How Starbucks's Culture Brings Its Strategy to Life *Harvard Business Review Digital Articles* p2 D 30 2016

Davidson, Willie G.

AMERICAN FLAT-TRACK M. HOYER *Cycle World* v55 no11 p5 D 2016

Davidsson, B.

Rosetta's comet 67P/Churyumov-Gerasimenko sheds its dusty mantle to reveal its icy nature bibl graph *Science* v354 no6319 p1566 D 23 2016

Surface changes on comet 67P/Churyumov-Gerasimenko suggest a more active past bw graph *Science* v355 no6332 p1392 Mr 31 2017

Davidsson, Jan

A three-dimensional movie of structural changes in bacteriorhodopsin bibl diag graph *Science* v354 no6319 p1552 D 23 2016

David Sullivan, Robert

UNDOCUMENTED IN AMERICA chart color graph *America* v216 no4 p12 F 20 2017

Davie, Grace

Grace Davie, Religion in Britain: a Persistent Paradox R. Wallis *Society* v53 no6 p665 D 2016

DAVIES, ALEX

Drivers Not Wanted: An Oral History of the Darpa Grand Challenge bw color diag *Wired* v25 no8 p49 Ag 2017

GEARHEAD color *Wired* v25 no3 p34 Mr 2017

TAKE THE WHEEL: SELF-DRIVING CARS MUST CONNECT WITH HUMANS color *Wired* v25 no7 p13 Jl 2017

TOP THREE: ENJOY THE RIDE color *Wired* v25 no10 p48 O 2017

Davies, Anna

Family Is What You Make It *Parents* v91 no10 p24 O 2016

THE POWER OF ONE color *Women's Health* v14 no5 p101 Je 2017

THE UNITED STATES OF SEX color *Women's Health* v14 no2 p140 Mr 2017

DAVIES, BREESE

Boxed In bw *Walrus* p16 Ja\F 2017

Davies, Brian

How God Befriends Us bw *Commonweal* v143 no17 p36 O 21 2016

Davies, Brian A.

Cyclin A2 is an RNA binding protein that controls Mre11 mRNA translation bibl graph *Science* v353 no6307 p1549 S 30 2016

Davies, Catherine J.

Identification of single-site gold catalysis in acetylene hydrochlorination bw diag graph *Science* v355 no6332 p1399 Mr 31 2017

Davies, Chaz

FASTEST ON THE FLIPSIDE G. Ritchie color *Cycle World* v56 no3 p64 Ap 2017

Davies, Donna

DONNA DAVIES J. BERG color *Chicago* v65 no11 p46 N 2016

Davies, Ian W.

A multifunctional catalyst that stereoselectively assembles pro-drugs diag *Science* v356 no6336 p426 Ap 28 2017

Davies, John

WAR STORIES C. BELANGER bw *Chicago* v66 no11 p26 N 2017

Davies, John Clary

THE DARK AND THE LIGHT bw color *Powder* v45 no3 p94 N 2016

decay [Cover story] color *Powder* v45 no6 p66 F 2017

III: Just Go bw *Powder* v45 no3 p13 N 2016

IV: In Deep color *Powder* v45 no4 p13 D 2016

Siri: Alta, Utah color *Powder* p9 S 2017

A Skier's Must-Have: THE BIG DUMPS TI 5000 2 diag *Powder* p46 S 2017

Toni: Gora Mamay, Russia color *Powder* v46 no2 p9 O 2017

THE TOWER OF SUN color map *Powder* v46 no2 p52 O 2017

VI: The Good Life bw *Powder* v45 no6 p11 F 2017

V: Our Own Sense of Time bw *Powder* v45 no5 p11 Ja 2017

Davies, Kim

Surge in right whale deaths raises alarms E. Stokstad color map *Science* v357 no6353 p740 Ag 25 2017

Davies, Mark

IN QUOTES *People Management* p10 Je 2017

Davies, Nicola

Many: The Diversity of Life on Earth *Publishers Weekly* v264 no41 p70 O 9 2017

Davies, Paul

Many Planets, Not Much Life color *Scientific American* v315 no3 p8 S 2016

Davies, Ray, 1944-

Random Notes color *Rolling Stone* no1285 p20 Ap 20 2017

Davies, Ray, 1944-—Interviews

Ray Davies A. GREENE bw *Rolling Stone* no1284 p58 Ap 6 2017

Davies, Sophie

30 Adelaide Street Sydney *Architectural Record* v204 no10 p138 O 2016

Davies, Stuart J.

Plant diversity increases with the strength of negative density dependence at the global scale diag *Science* v356 no6345 p1389 Je 30 2017

Davies, Terence, 1945-

The Elusive Emily Dickinson M. ATKINSON *In These Times* v41 no5 p36 My 2017

Prometheus Unbound: Emily Dickinson comes confidently alive J. CHARYN *American Scholar* v86 no3 p104 Summ 2017

UNDER A BUSHEL R. Mead cartoon *New Yorker* v93 no12 p18 My 8 2017

Davies, W. J.

Improving global integration of crop research color *Science* v357 no6349 p359 Jl 28 2017

Davies, William

Science in litigation, the third branch of U.S. climate policy graph *Science* v357 no6355 p979 S 8 2017

Dávila, N.

Persistent effects of pre-Columbian plant domestication on Amazonian forest composition bibl chart graph map *Science* v355 no6328 p925 Mr 3 2017

Davis (Calif.)

DAVIS, CA C. Hall color map *Sunset* v238 no4 p36 Ap 2017

Davis, Alex

THE WHITE CITY REMAKE: HOW BOISE'S COLUMBIAN CLUB RECREATED THE 1893 WORLD'S FAIR J. S. DALE *Idaho Magazine* v16 no7 p8 Ap 2017

Davis, Alexander

Freelance Nation A. CASTRO *Dance Magazine* v91 no9 p34 S 2017

DAVIS, ALLISON P.

225 MINUTES WITH... Asahd Khaled: Touring the Children's Museum of Manhattan with the busiest baby in hip-hop img *New York* v50 no18 p18 S 4 2017

The Nicest Evil Girl in the World: Aubrey Plaza knows you want

her to be mean to you, and she's happy to oblige img *New York* v50 no15 p34 Jl 24 2017

Rachel Lindsay: Talking about whether America is ready for post-racial dating with the first-ever Bachelorette of color img *New York* v50 no12 p20 Je 12 2017

Davis, Amanda

How Subscriptions Are Creating Winners and Losers in Retail *Harvard Business Review Digital Articles* p2 Ja 8 2016

Davis, Angie

The Hate U Give L. Greenblatt color *Entertainment Weekly* no1454/1455 p102 F 24 2017

DAVIS, ANTHONY A.

Ahmoo Angeconeb color *Maclean's* v130 no8 p66 S 2017

Audrey Millicent van Zuiden color *Maclean's* no1 p66 F 17 2017

Betiana Namambwe Mubili: 1988 – 2017 color *Maclean's* v130 no10 p130 N 2017

Clayton Kenneth Cassidy color *Maclean's* v130 no7 p66 Ag 2017

Ellen Leah Isabel Watters color *Maclean's* v130 no2 p74 Mr 2017

Heather Anderson color *Maclean's* v130 no3 p74 Ap 2017

Ian Robert Lawson bw *Maclean's* v129 no40 p82 O 10 2016

Joseph Michael Howlett color *Maclean's* v130 no9 p82 O 2017

Mel Rocchio color *Maclean's* v130 no4 p74 My 2017

Riley Fullton Shannon color *Maclean's* p66 Je 2017

Scott David Leroux color *Maclean's* v129 no50 p66 D 19 2016

Tanner Brent Kaufmann color *Maclean's* v129 no42 p66 O 24 2016

Trevor Donald Sexsmith color *Maclean's* v129 no44 p118 N 7 2016

The walking man walks color *Maclean's* v129 no44 p62 N 7 2016

Davis, Antwon

Minding Our Business L. d. JOHNSON color *Ebony* v72 no3 p108 D 2016/Ja 2017

Davis, Arthur—Interviews

Trial & Erro's stunt double Arthur Davis J. Russell *TV Guide* p15 Ap 17 2017

Davis, Bebe

THE NORTH AMERICAN JUNIOR/YOUNG RIDER CHAMPI-ONSHIPS *Dressage Today* v24 no2 p14 N 2017

Davis, Benjamin G.

Posttranslational mutagenesis: A chemical strategy for exploring protein side-chain diversity diag *Science* v354 no6312 p597 N 4 2016

Davis, Betsy—Interviews

MEET BETSY DAVIS AND CHRISTINA COGAN S. SHIBATA *Sea Magazine* v108 no10 pPNW-1 O 2016

Davis, Bonnie

Horse Owner's Spring Notebook color *Trail Rider* v29 no4 p38 My 2017

PACK-AND-GO CHECKLISTS color *Trail Rider* v29 no3 p62 Ap 2017

Davis, Bryan

MR. DAVIS & HIS FANTASTIC RUM ACCELERATOR W. CURTIS color diag *Wired* v25 no6 p68 Je 2017

DAVIS, CAROLINE

Bach to Basics II: Using Melodies To Suggest Harmony [Cover story] bw color *Downbeat* v84 no5 p76 My 2017

DAVIS, CATHY DURBIN

Q: Who's your trusty sidekick for summer adventures, and why? color *O, The Oprah Magazine* p14 Je 2017

Davis, Charles

Green the Vote *Harper's Magazine* p2 O 2017

Davis, Charlotte

KONCHOG LHADREPA AND CHARLOTTE DAVIS color *Tricycle: The Buddhist Review* v26 no4 p19 Summ 2017

Davis, Chili—Interviews

BatLike a Lumberjack color *Popular Science* v288 no6 p62 N/D 2016

Davis, Clive, 1932-

NUMBER CRUNCH: BISEXUALITY chart *Advocate* no1088 p32 D 2016/Ja 2017

Davis, Clive, 1932-—Interviews

CLIVE DAVIS N. Maslow color *Entertainment Weekly* no1486 p59 O 13 2017

DAVIS, CRYSTAL

An Ecoregion-Based Approach to Protecting Half the Terrestrial Realm *BioScience* v67 no6 p534 Je 2017

Davis, Darryl
  Celebrating S&T's 75th Anniversary *Sky & Telescope* v133 no2 p6 F 2017

Davis, Daryl
  CENTURY marks bw graph *Christian Century* v134 no19 p8 S 13 2017
  Radical Reconciliation B. McGarvey *America* v216 no11 p62 My 15 2017

Davis, Dave
  The Thread *New York Times Magazine* p12 N 27 2016

DAVIS, DEBORAH
  Don't Leave Home Without It *Sierra* v102 no1 p18 Ja/F 2017

Davis, Dequandre
  She Was My Prosecutor T. HALLMAN *Reader's Digest* v188 no1124 p90 O 2016

DAVIS, DONNA
  Second Helpings *Sierra* v102 no2 p17 Mr/Ap 2017

Davis, Donny
  Donny Davis A. Gentry color *Spin to Win Rodeo* v21 no5 p20 Jl 2017

Davis, Dwight Filley
  The Man Behind the Cup N. Pantic *Tennis* v52 no6 p54 N/D 2016

Davis, Earl
  Recurring and triggered slow-slip events near the trench at the Nankai Trough subduction megathrust diag graph *Science* v356 no6343 p1157 Je 16 2017

Davis, Edward
  Merging paleobiology with conservation biology to guide the future of terrestrial ecosystems color *Science* v355 no6325 p594 F 10 2017

Davis, Ellen F.
  Abraham's radical trust *Christian Century* v133 no22 p29 O 26 2016

Davis, F. Daniel
  Distribution and clinical impact of functional variants in 50,726 whole-exome sequences from the DiscovEHR study chart graph *Science* v354 no6319 paaf6814-1 D 23 2016

Davis, Fiona
  The Dollhouse color *Publishers Weekly* v263 no44 p69 O 31 2016
  Location, Location J. R. ENSZER *Ms.* v27 no2 p44 Summ 2017

DAVIS, FRANK W.
  Synthesis Centers as Critical Research Infrastructure *BioScience* v67 no8 p750 Ag 2017

Davis, Garrick
  What to Make of T. S. Eliot? *Humanities* v37 no4 p1 Fall 2016

Davis, Garth
  DROP EVERYTHING J. POWERS bw color *Vogue* v206 no12 p270 D 2016
  Lion D. Franich color *Entertainment Weekly* no1442 p41 D 2 2016 Rebellious Special Issue

Davis, Geena, 1956——Interviews
  THE DEVIL AND MISS DAVIS D. HOLBROOK *TV Guide* v64 no46 p18 N 7 2016

Davis, George L.
  Boards Aren't as Global as Their Businesses *Harvard Business Review Digital Articles* p2 O 28 2014

Davis, Gerald F.
  80% of Companies Don't Know If Their Products Contain Conflict Minerals color *Harvard Business Review Digital Articles* p2 Ja 4 2017
  The Traits of Socially Innovative Companies *Harvard Business Review Digital Articles* p2 Ap 17 2015
  What Is Management Research Actually Good For? *Harvard Business Review Digital Articles* p2 My 28 2015

Davis, Heath Fogg
  The Case for Gender Anarchy E. N. BROWN color *Reason* v49 no4 p74 Ag/S 2017

Davis, Henry
  A Cut Above C. SORVINO color diag *Forbes* v200 no4 p92 O 24 2017

Davis, Jack E.
  Crude Awakening P. CONNORS *New York Times Book Review* p11 My 28 2017
  The Gulf: The Making of an American Sea color *Publishers Weekly* v264 no4 p73 Ja 23 2017
  Stone by Stone color *Orion Magazine* v36 no2 p8 Mr/Ap 2017

Davis, Jackie
  LONG DRIVE, SHORT HIKE color *Backpacker* v45 no1 p79 Ja 2017

Davis, Jeff
  The Fear and the Freedom: How the Second World War Changed Us *Military History* v34 no5 p71 Ja 2018

Davis, Jefferson, 1808-1889
  The People v. Jefferson Davis: A legal showdown 150 years ago laid bare the complexities of reuniting the States T. A. FRAIL *Smithsonian* v48 no2 p18 My 2017

Davis, Jennifer Pharr
  The First Steps *Backpacker* p71 Je 2017

Davis, Jeremy—Interviews
  Jeremy Davis A. Schell color *Sail* v48 no6 p12 Je 2017

DAVIS, JERRY W.
  Arnica City: Could the Dream Be Real? *Idaho Magazine* v16 no9 p51 Je 2017
  Flash of Gold: In the Flower Season *Idaho Magazine* v16 no7 p24 Ap 2017

DAVIS, JOE
  Wild Goose Chase *Idaho Magazine* v17 no1 p21 Ja 2017

Davis, Joel
  How moon dust will put a ring around MARS bw color diag *Astronomy* v44 no12 p46 D 2016

Davis, Joseph
  Rogers Brubaker, Trans: Gender and Race in an Age of Unsettled Identities *Society* v54 no1 p78 F 2017

Davis, Joseph F. Jr.
  The Risks and Benefits of Longeing color *Dressage Today* v24 no1 p20 O 2017

Davis, Josh
  4 Steps to Having More "Aha" Moments color *Harvard Business Review Digital Articles* p2 O 12 2016
  Teach Someone to Prioritize Using Psychological Distance *Harvard Business Review Digital Articles* p2 Mr 12 2015
  Zoning Out Can Make You More Productive *Harvard Business Review Digital Articles* p2 Je 5 2015

Davis, Joshua Clark
  The First 'Mission-Driven' Companies S. Begley color *Time* v190 no6 p22 Ag 7 2017

Davis, Josie
  WAR STORIES, THE SEQUEL color *Los Angeles Magazine* v62 no10 p132 O 2017

DAVIS, JOY LAWSON
  Joining Hands: Race, Social Justice, and Equal Opportunity in Your Classroom *Education Digest* v82 no4 p42 D 2016

DAVIS, JUDY LLOYD
  Your True Stories *Reader's Digest* v188 no1124 p22 O 2016

Davis, Justin
  Broc Cresta K. Santos color *Spin to Win Rodeo* v21 no5 p60 Jl 2017
  Golden Oldie C. Toy color *Spin to Win Rodeo* v21 no5 p46 Jl 2017
  Smith and Davis Surge color *Team Roping Journal* p34 O 2017

Davis, Katie
  How America Lost Its Mind color *Atlantic* v320 no4 p12 N 2017

Davis, Kenneth C.
  In the Shadow of Liberty: The Hidden History of Slavery, Four Presidents, and Five Black Lives color *Publishers Weekly* v263 no49 p84 D 7 2016

Davis, Kevin
  Brains Take the Stand C. CARR *New York Times Book Review* p19 Mr 12 2017

Davis, Kris
  KRIS DAVIS: 'Open To Surprise' B. Bambarger color *Downbeat* v84 no8 p51 Ag 2017

Davis, L. J.
  c. 1970: Brooklyn *Lapham's Quarterly* v10 no1 p179 Wint 2017

DAVIS, LAMAR M. II
  5 JEET KUNE DO FIGHTING PRINCIPLES color *Black Belt* v55 no4 p40 Je/Jl 2017

DAVIS, LIESEL
  The No-Bake Marvel color *Bon Appetit* v62 no10 p40 O 2017
  Thanksgiving LESSONS [Cover story] color *Bon Appetit* no11 p82 N 2017

Davis, Lindsey
  The Third Nero: A Flavia Alba Novel color *Publishers Weekly*

National Treasure *Opera News* v81 no5 p24 N 2016

Davis, Philip

How Mary Anne Became George T. Parks bw *New York Review of Books* v64 no17 p49 N 9 2017

So Long, Mary Ann T. L. JEFFERS *Commentary* v144 no3 p60 O 2017

Davis, Rachaell

WE ARE ONE color *Essence* v48 no3 p58 Jl 2017

Davis, Ray

What the Best Change Leaders Know, and Why They're So Hard to Copy B. Taylor *Harvard Business Review Digital Articles* p2 D 21 2016

DAVIS, RICH

CATCHING A CONSPIRACY color *Scientific American* v317 no2 p5 Ag 2017

Davis, Richard

Challenges in researching terrorism from the field bibl color *Science* v355 no6323 p352 Ja 27 2017

Supreme Democracy: The End of Elitism in Supreme Court Nominations *Publishers Weekly* v264 no17 p84 Ap 24 2017

Tactics for Asking Good Follow-Up Questions *Harvard Business Review Digital Articles* p2 N 7 2014

Davis, Roger J.

Multisite phosphorylation by MAPK bibl diag *Science* v354 no6309 p179 O 14 2016

Davis, Rufus

Posthole color *Powder* v45 no4 p146 D 2016

Davis, Sarah

The BEST & WORST LEGISLATORS 2017 R. G. RATCLIFFE *Texas Monthly* v45 no7 p82 Jl 2017

Davis, Seth

13 LOUISVILLE CARDINALS chart color *Sports Illustrated* v125 no15 p72 N 7 2016

14 INDIANA HOOSIERS chart color *Sports Illustrated* v125 no15 p73 N 7 2016

2017-18 TOP 10 color *Sports Illustrated* v126 no10 p40 Ap 10 2017

3 KENTUCKY WILDCATS chart color *Sports Illustrated* v125 no15 p62 N 7 2016

ALL-GLUE TEAM color *Sports Illustrated* v126 no8 p61 Mr 20 2017

The Case for ... Starting College Early color *Sports Illustrated* v126 no3 p19 Ja 23 2017

FACE OF A NATION color *Sports Illustrated* v125 no19 p86 D 12 2016

ONE TO CROW ON color *Sports Illustrated* v126 no9 p35 Mr 27 2017

Davis, Seth J.

Light-sensing phytochromes feel the heat bibl color *Science* v354 no6314 p832 N 18 2016

DAVIS, SHANNON

ISRAEL UPRISING color *Climbing* no349 p38 N 2016

Davis, Sierra

ALL OR NOTHING color *Powder* v45 no5 p106 Ja 2017

THE BEST DEAL IN SKIING color *Powder* v45 no3 p54 N 2016

CONNERY LUNDIN bw *Powder* p134 S 2017

Have Skis, Will Travel color *Powder* v45 no3 p44 N 2016

INSTAGRAM FOR SKIERS, 101 *Powder* v45 no5 p40 Ja 2017

LUCAS STÅL-MADISON color *Powder* v46 no2 p92 O 2017

A Mother's Nature bw color *Powder* v45 no4 p94 D 2016

The Skis of the Year color *Powder* p82 S 2017

Davis, Spencer

KICK-ASS CUSTOMER SERVICE: INTERACTION color *Harvard Business Review* v95 no3 p16 My/Je 2017

Davis, Stanley

SAVING THE BIG CHICKEN 1993 T. WHEATLEY *Atlanta* v57 no4 p128 Ag 2017

Davis, Steven J.

Chemtrails? In First Peer-Reviewed Published Survey, Atmospheric Scientists Say No K. FRAZIER *Skeptical Inquirer* v40 no6 p6 N/D 2016

Davis, Susan

An Approach to Ending Poverty That Works *Harvard Business Review Digital Articles* p2 Ja 22 2015

Davis, Tarik

STRANGE BANDFELLOWS J. KNAPP *Washingtonian Maga-*

zine v52 no5 p19 F 2017

Davis, Terrell

Hall Pass T. Rohan and T. Keith color *Sports Illustrated* v127 no4 p15 Ag 7 2017

Davis, Todd

Body of Water color *Orion Magazine* v35 no6 p58 N/D 2016

Window Left Open *Orion Magazine* v35 no3 p55 My/Je 2016

Davis, Tom

RUFF AND TUMBLE bw color *Field & Stream* v122 no6 p14 N 2017

Tom Davis: Cemetery Guide L. WRIGHT *Indianapolis Monthly* p54 N 2017

DAVIS, TOM R.

Assessing National Biodiversity Trends for Rocky and Coral Reefs through the Integration of Citizen Science and Scientific Monitoring Programs *BioScience* v67 no2 p134 F 2017

Davis, Trevor

DeepStack: Expert-level artificial intelligence in heads-up no-limit poker [Cover story] chart diag *Science* v356 no6337 p508 My 5 2017

Davis, Viola, 1965-

ACT OF GRACE J. LAHR cartoon color *New Yorker* v92 no42 p52 D 19 2016

Cause & Effect C. Shanahan color *InStyle* v23 no13 p72 D 2016

How to Get Away With Murder N. Abrams, B. L. Heldman et al *Entertainment Weekly* no1482/1483 p91 S 22 2017

Icons M. Streep, A. McQuade et al color *Time* v189 no16/17 p122 My 1-8 2017

Reconsidering August Wilson J. LEAF *National Review* v69 no5 p44 Mr 20 2017

Sound Bites color *Entertainment Weekly* no1456 p5 Mr 10 2017

SUPPORTING ACTRESS CONTENDER VIOLA DAVIS N. Sperling color *Entertainment Weekly* no1443 p46 D 9 2016

VIOLA DAVIS N. Sperling color *Entertainment Weekly* no1444/1445 p36 D 16 2016

Davis, Viola, 1965— Awards

The Bullseye M. Snetiker color *Entertainment Weekly* no1456 p72 Mr 10 2017

Pop Chart color *Time* v189 no9 p57 Mr 13 2017

A Starry Night R. Kinane color *Entertainment Weekly* no1446/1447 p25 D 2016/Ja 2017

DAVIS, WENDY

OBAMA'S AMERICA img *New York* v49 no20 p12 O 3 2016

Davis, Zac

John Oliver is good for the Republic. Or not color *America* v216 no6 p47 Mr 20 2017

Kanye, Kendrick, Chance & the Surprising Christian Language of Rap color *America* v216 no5 p34 Mr 6 2017

Davis Cup—History

The Man Behind the Cup N. Pantic *Tennis* v52 no6 p54 N/D 2016

Davis Frame Co.

COMPANY DIRECTORY color map *Timber Home Living* p89 2017 Annual Buyers

Davis Instruments Corp.

STORM BRAIN R. Verger color *Popular Science* v289 no4 p30 Jl/Ag 2017

Davis Museum & Cultural Center

A new look for the Davis at Wellesley E. H. Gustafson color *Magazine Antiques* v183 no6 p136 N/D 2016

DAVIS-GARDNER, ANGELA

The Gogol Notebook *American Scholar* v86 no1 p106 Wint 2017

Davison, Jillian

Dior and Me bw color *Glamour* no8 p66 Ag 2017

Davison, Jillian—Interviews

My Cuba Diary color *Glamour* v114 no11 p84 N 2016

Davison, Julia Collin

Cooking at Home with Bridget & Julia *Publishers Weekly* v264 no34 p105 Ag 21 2017

Davison, Kate

Something to Laugh About *History Today* v67 no3 p72 Mr 2017

Davoli, Teresa

Tumor aneuploidy correlates with markers of immune evasion and with reduced response to immunotherapy diag *Science* v355 no6322 p261 Ja 20 2017

Davydova, Angelina

Russia heightens defenses against climate change color *Science*

v357 no6357 p1221 S 22 2017

Dawar, Niraj

Has Google Finally Proven That Online Ads Cause Offline Purchases? *Harvard Business Review Digital Articles* p1 Je 1 2017

Labels Like "Millennial" and "Boomer" Are Obsolete *Harvard Business Review Digital Articles* p2 N 18 2016

A Simple Graph Explains the Complex Logic of the Big Beer Merger *Harvard Business Review Digital Articles* p2 O 20 2015

Use Big Data to Create Value for Customers, Not Just Target Them *Harvard Business Review Digital Articles* p2 Ag 16 2016

What Intel Needs to Remember About Marketing *Harvard Business Review Digital Articles* p2 Ap 25 2016

Why Localizing Marketing Doesn't Always Work *Harvard Business Review Digital Articles* p2 S 1 2016

Dawes, Laura

GOOD HEALTH AS THE FIRST LINE OF DEFENCE: Britain's wartime eff orts to maintain the nation's health received vital help from the Empire and the Americans V. Quirke *History Today* v67 no10 p102 O 2017

DAWES, NIC

How the Press Should Cover TRUMP color il *Nation* v304 no9 p22 Mr 20 2017

Dawg Yawp (Performer)

BIG WOOF C. ROSE *Cincinnati Magazine* v50 no5 p19 F 2017

DAWIDOFF, NICHOLAS

True Detective *New Republic* v248 no10 p56 O 2017

Dawidowski, M.

Inhibitors of PEX14 disrupt protein import into glycosomes and kill Trypanosoma parasites chart color diag graph *Science* v355 no6332 p1416 Mr 31 2017

Dawkins, Curtis

The Insiders J. CAROL OATES color *O, The Oprah Magazine* p82 Ag 2017

Dawkins, Richard, 1941-

Science Education, Communication on Display at CSICon S. Vyse *Skeptical Inquirer* v41 no2 p15 Mr/Ap 2017

Science in the Soul: Selected Writings of a Passionate Rationalist *Publishers Weekly* v264 no24 p56 Je 12 2017

SEEN & HEARD *Humanist* v76 no6 p7 N/D 2016

THE SELFISH GENE REVISITED *Skeptical Inquirer* v41 no2 p38 Mr/Ap 2017

Who Would You Believe? *USA Today Magazine* v145 no2860 p71 Ja 2017

Dawn (Performer)

Dawn Richard: Out of This World M. Vain color *Entertainment Weekly* no1441 p54 N 25 2016

Dawn (Space probe)

CERES HAS AN ABUNDANCE OF ICE J. Wenz color *Astronomy* v45 no4 p12 Ap 2017

Dawn of Discovery at Ceres M. D. Rayman *Sky & Telescope* v132 no6 p16 D 2016

Dawn Equipment Co.

JOE BASSETT J. Scott *Successful Farming* v115 no5 p8 Mid-Mr 2017

Dawodu, Mobolaji

Face Time P. BRADY color *Conde Nast Traveler* v52 no4 p102 Ap 2017

GQ STYLE FASHION DIRECTOR MOBOLAJI DAWODU A. WHITTLE color *Conde Nast Traveler* v52 no8 p30 S 2017

DAWSEY, CHASTITY PRATT

Michigan Shuts Down Bad Schools. Leading States Build Them Up *Education Digest* v82 no9 p34 My 2017

Dawsey, Holly

Fix That Beauty Oops color *Health* v30 no10 p29 D 2016

DAWSON, ANDREW

I SURVIVED color *Men's Health* v32 no6 p128 Ag 2017

The Thrill of Letting Go color *Men's Health* v32 no6 p12 Ag 2017

Dawson, Ashley

Facing the Flood D. SUBRAMANIAN bw *Publishers Weekly* v264 no36 p81 S 4 2017

Dawson, B. R.

Observation of a large-scale anisotropy in the arrival directions of cosmic rays above 8 × 1018 eV *Science* v357 no6357 p1266 S 22 2017

Dawson, Brett

Band Class Heroes B. ZIMMERMAN color *Downbeat* v84 no6 p8 Je 2017

DAWSON, FAITH

ANA ZORRILLA color *New Orleans Magazine* v51 no1 p30 N 2016

MICHAEL TISSERAND *New Orleans Magazine* v51 no3 p26 Ja 2017

REV. R. TONY RICARD color *New Orleans Magazine* v51 no2 p30 D 2016

Dawson, Jill

Full of Scotch and Self-Loathing: A novel uses the life of Patricia Highsmith to explore the territory between reality and fantasy H. LANE *New York Times Book Review* p17 Jl 30 2017

Dawson, Laura

The Bar Code Revolution *Publishers Weekly* v264 no21 p34 My 22 2017

A Different Kind of Bundle *Publishers Weekly* v264 no12 p24 Mr 20 2017

I Always Hated Keywords *Publishers Weekly* v264 no16 p23 Ap 17 2017

It's All About SKUs *Publishers Weekly* v264 no26 p19 Je 26 2017

Moving Beyond E-books *Publishers Weekly* v264 no38 p24 S 18 2017

The Next Steps in Digitization *Publishers Weekly* v264 no4 p20 Ja 23 2017

Taking a Positive View of the IDPF-W3C Merger *Publishers Weekly* v264 no9 p19 F 27 2017

A Watermarking Update *Publishers Weekly* v264 no30 p20 Jl 24 2017

Dawson, Mark A.

The cancer epigenome: Concepts, challenges, and therapeutic opportunities bibl diag *Science* v355 no6330 p1147 Mr 17 2017

Click chemistry enables preclinical evaluation of targeted epigenetic therapies diag *Science* v356 no6345 p1397 Je 30 2017

Dawson, Martin

ALL AROUND THE FARM® *Successful Farming* v115 no6 p77 Ap 2017

Dawson, Paul

FROM OUR READERS *Sky & Telescope* v133 no6 p6 Je 2017

Dawson, Sarah-Jane

Click chemistry enables preclinical evaluation of targeted epigenetic therapies diag *Science* v356 no6345 p1397 Je 30 2017

Dawson, Simon

Identification of single-site gold catalysis in acetylene hydrochlorination bw diag graph *Science* v355 no6332 p1399 Mr 31 2017

Dawson, Ted M.

A nuclease that mediates cell death induced by DNA damage and poly(ADP-ribose) polymerase-1 bw graph *Science* v354 no6308 paad6872-1 O 7 2016

Pathological α-synuclein transmission initiated by binding lymphocyte-activation gene 3 bibl graph *Science* v353 no6307 paah3374-1 S 30 2016

Dawson, Valina L.

A nuclease that mediates cell death induced by DNA damage and poly(ADP-ribose) polymerase-1 bw graph *Science* v354 no6308 paad6872-1 O 7 2016

Pathological α-synuclein transmission initiated by binding lymphocyte-activation gene 3 bibl graph *Science* v353 no6307 paah3374-1 S 30 2016

Dawson City: Frozen Time (Film)

Dawson City: Frozen Time *New Yorker* v93 no18 p13 Je 26 2017

Dax, Andreas

Buffer-gas cooling of antiprotonic helium to 1.5 to 1.7 K, and antiproton-to-electron mass ratio bibl chart diag graph *Science* v354 no6312 p610 N 4 2016

Day, Adrienne

HER SISTER'S KEEPER? color *O, The Oprah Magazine* p76 Je 2017

Day, Andra

'Ella 100' Celebrates First Lady of Song R. Musto color *Downbeat* v84 no1 p18 Ja 2017

The Summer Job I'll Never Forget color *Time* v190 no2/3 p55 Jl 10-17 2017

Day, Charles

Against the rising flood of information *Physics Today* v70 no9 p8 S 2017

Difficult decisions *Physics Today* v70 no10 p8 O 2017

Discoveries and explanations *Physics Today* v70 no3 p8 Mr 2017
From lab to clinic *Physics Today* v70 no8 p8 Ag 2017
Froth on the daydream *Physics Today* v69 no10 p8 O 2016
Hearing from you *Physics Today* v70 no4 p8 Ap 2017
Imaginary futures *Physics Today* v69 no12 p8 D 2016
Olive spoons and terrapin forks *Physics Today* v70 no2 p8 F 2017
Our new website *Physics Today* v70 no1 p8 Ja 2017
The state of open access *Physics Today* v70 no5 p8 My 2017
Transforming nature *Physics Today* v69 no11 p8 N 2016
Where's my flying car? *Physics Today* v70 no6 p8 Je 2017

Day, Dorothy, 1897-1980
A leap of fidelity M. Clark *U.S. Catholic* v82 no10 p10 O 2017

Day, Elizabeth
The Party *Publishers Weekly* v264 no25 p89 Je 19 2017
The Talented Mr. Gilmour: Elizabeth Day's psychological thriller, about an aristocrat's birthday party gone awry, updates Waugh, Highsmith and Fitzgerald C. JAMES *New York Times Book Review* p14 S 10 2017

Day, Jacki
SADDLE CHAT bw color graph *Horse & Rider* v56 no7 p21 Jl 2017

Day, James M. D.
Tungsten-182 heterogeneity in modern ocean island basalts chart diag *Science* v356 no6333 p66 Ap 7 2017

Day, Jason, 1987-
Jason Day J. Crelin color *Current Biography* v78 no3 p20 Mr 2017

Day, Je' Wesley
SOMETHING TO SIP ON N. H. REEDER and D. POINTDU-JOUR color *Ebony* v72 no6 p54 Ap/My 2017

DAY, PAUL B.
Assessing National Biodiversity Trends for Rocky and Coral Reefs through the Integration of Citizen Science and Scientific Monitoring Programs *BioScience* v67 no2 p134 F 2017

DAY, TERESA
BATON ROUGE color *Louisiana Life* v37 no4 p54 Mr/Ap 2017

Day Breaks (Music)
NORAH JONES N. Feeney color *Entertainment Weekly* no1434 p55 O 7 2016

Day care centers
WE NEED A DAYCARE REVOLUTION [Cover story] S. E. PFEFFER chart color *Working Mother* v40 no2 p52 Je/Jl 2017

Daya (Performer)
Best. Night. Ever color *Seventeen* p210 Ja 1 2017

Daya (Performer)—Interviews
17 Questions With Daya J. Abidor color *Seventeen* v76 no2 p20 Mr 2017

Day After, The (Film)
Keeping at It D. Lim bw color *Film Comment* v53 no4 p62 Jl/Ag 2017
Two from the Heart R. Brody color *New Yorker* v93 no30 p8 O 2 2017

DAYEN, DAVID
Club Fed color il *New Republic* v248 no11 p55 N 2017
Don't Get Met—It Pays *New Republic* v248 no7 p11 Jl 2017
The Forgotten Victims il *New Republic* v247 no12 p10 D 2016
Jamie Dimon and Other People's Money [Cover story] color *Nation* v305 no10 p12 O 23 2017
The Muck Starts Here *Nation* v303 no23/24 p4 D 5 2016
Taking Socialism to the Bank *In These Times* v41 no5 p27 My 2017

Daylight
START OF DARKNESS T. G. HOPE color *Better Homes & Gardens* v95 no11 p154 N 2017

Daylight Ghosts (Music)
CRAIG TABORN: 'GO INSIDE THE SOUND' [Cover story] K. MICALLEF color *Downbeat* v84 no3 p26 Mr 2017
Ghost Notes: Craig Taborn has become one of the best jazz pianists alive—by disappearing almost completely into his music A. Shatz *New York Times Magazine* p54 Je 25 2017

Daylight saving
The Original Point of Daylight Saving Time O. B. Waxman *Time* v189 no10 p21 Mr 20 2017

DAYRIT, JAY RUBEN
HOLD DEAR THE LAMPLIGHT cartoon *Wired* v25 no1 p82 Ja 2017

Days of Our Lives (TV program)
CHEERS & JEERS D. HOLBROOK *TV Guide* v65 no11 p92 Mr 6 2017
DAYS OF OUR LIVES M. LOGAN *TV Guide* v65 no25 p42 Je 2017
DAYS OF OUR LIVES M. LOGAN *TV Guide* v65 no39 p64 S 18 2017
DAY TIME M. LOGAN *TV Guide* v64 no48 p44 N 21 2016

Daystar Filters LLC
We put DayStar's Calcium Quark to the test T. Trusock bw color *Astronomy* v45 no2 p66 F 2017

Daytime Divas (TV program)
DAYTIME DIVAS C. Agard color *Entertainment Weekly* no1439 p12 N 11 2016
SCREEN GEMS color *Essence* v48 no3 p58 Jl 2017

Dayton, Jonathan
BATTLE OF THE SEXES D. Coggan color *Entertainment Weekly* no1478 / 1479 p42 Ag 18-25 2017
Chauvinist Racket J. PODHORETZ color *Weekly Standard* v23 no5 p46 O 9 2017
When King Was Queen S. E. ERICKSON bw color *Los Angeles Magazine* v62 no10 p94 O 2017

Dayton, Mark, 1947-
Capitol Hardball A. Greenblatt color *Governing* v30 no11 p9 Ag 2017

DAYTON, NATALIE
CAMP CHRISTMAS *Better Homes & Gardens* v94 no12 p96 D 2016
COLOR REGAL PURPLES *Better Homes & Gardens* v94 no11 p33 N 2016
FULL CIRCLE *Better Homes & Gardens* v94 no11 p124 N 2016
Let's get Cozy *Better Homes & Gardens* v95 no1 p88 Ja 2017
qenevieve GORDER *Better Homes & Gardens* v94 no11 p14 N 2016
we'll toast to that *Better Homes & Gardens* v94 no12 p20 D 2016

Dayton Audio (Company)
Line 'Em Up D. Kumin color graph *Sound & Vision* v82 no7 p36 S 2017

Daytona 500 (Automobile race)
Leading Off A. Lawrence color *Sports Illustrated* v126 no7 p6 Mr 6 2017

Daytona International Speedway (Daytona, Fla.)
FERRARI INVADES DAYTONA P. LERNER color *Road & Track* v68 no7 p8 Mr/Ap 2017

Daza, Riza
Comprehensive single-cell transcriptional profiling of a multicellular organism diag *Science* v357 no6352 p661 Ag 18 2017

DAZEY, STEPHANIE
Going Ape for Local Art: Thanks to a key hire, MailChimp has quietly become one of the city's biggest corporate supporters of local art *Atlanta* v57 no6 p77 O 2017

Dazieri, Sandrone
Kill the Father *Publishers Weekly* v263 no41 p56 O 10 2016

DC Comics Inc.
THE ULTIMATE SUPERHERO FACE-LIFT C. Holub color *Entertainment Weekly* no1456 p68 Mr 10 2017

DC Entertainment Inc.
DC Entertainment at New York Comic Con color *Publishers Weekly* v264 no38 p28 S 18 2017
DC Goes All-Out Marketing Rebirth Book Collections C. Reid color *Publishers Weekly* v264 no13 p11 Mr 27 2017

D.C. United (Soccer team)
HOW TO BE A BLEACHER-STOMPING, BEER-TOSSING D.C. UNITED FAN R. CARTAGENA, G. WEBER et al *Washingtonian Magazine* v52 no6 p70 Mr 2017

DC Universe
  See also
    Batman films
Supergirl D. Holbrook *TV Guide* v65 no6 p35 Ja 30 2017

D'CRUZE, NEIL
Some Animals Are More Equal than Others: Wild Animal Welfare in the Media *BioScience* v67 no1 p62 Ja 2017

De, Sandip
Passing epigenetic silence to the next generation diag *Science* v356 no6333 p28 Ap 7 2017

De Antonio Yachts (Company)

Open for Anything S. Shibata *Boating World* v37 no9 p8 N/D 2016

De cierta manera (Film)
The Seen and The Unseen B. R. Rich *Film Quarterly* v71 no1 p5 Fall 2017

de Abajo, F. J. García
Polaritons in van der Waals materials bibl chart color diag graph *Science* v354 no6309 paag1992-1 O 14 2016

Deabler, Alexandra
CALIFORNIA'S SONORA color map *Sunset* v239 no1 p28 Jl 2017

Deacons
Spring cleaning for the soul color *U.S. Catholic* v82 no3 p32 Mr 2017

Deacons—Catholic Church
A Neglected Order N. SCHNEIDER *America* v215 no11 p12 O 17 2016

Dead
See also
    Mummies
    Suicide victims
How to Be an Islander K. MALMO *Sierra* v102 no4 p60 Jl/Ag 2017
TALKING TO THE DEAD M. A. Ahmad *Saturday Evening Post* v289 no2 p10 Mr/Ap 2017
WHY MUMMIES? I. FRAZIER cartoon *New Yorker* v93 no2 p33 F 27 2017
Writing on Deadline D. Skinner color *Weekly Standard* v22 no24 p5 F 27 2017

Dead Air Armament (Company)
SILENCE, PLEASE J. Johnston color *Field & Stream* v122 no2 p34 Je/Jl 2017

Dead Calm (Film)
THE ESSENTIAL NICOLE KIDMAN L. Greenblatt color *Entertainment Weekly* no1472 p44 Je 30 2017

Dead lift (Weight lifting)
30 MUST-DO MOVES for 2017 L. McGLASHAN color *Muscle & Performance* v9 no1 p44 Ja 2017
All About the Deadlift L. BOYCE color *Muscle & Performance* v9 no8 p22 Ag 2017
Split-sational O. Manno *Dance Spirit* v21 no3 p34 Mr 2017

Dead Man Walking (Theatrical production)
Dead Man Walking A. Mellor *Opera News* v81 no10 p45 Ap 2017

Dead Sea scrolls
Cave that housed Dead Sea Scrolls found C. Wood color *Christian Century* v134 no6 p12 Mr 15 2017
SCROLL SEARCH D. WEISS color *Archaeology* v70 no3 p9 My/Je 2017

Dead 1904, The (Theatrical production)
THE UNDEAD T. Friend cartoon *New Yorker* v92 no38 p32 N 21 2016

Deadbeat (TV program)
Kal Penn Is a Deadbeat E. Maas *TV Guide* v64 no15 p15 Ap 4 2016

Dead—History
The Living Dead: BRUTALLY KILLED THOUSANDS OF YEARS AGO, EUROPE'S FAMED BOG BODIES ARE STARTING TO REVEAL THEIR SECRETS J. LEVINE *Smithsonian* v48 no2 p65 My 2017

Dead—Identification
RESEARCHERS SEEK TO ID MEXICAN WAR REMAINS B. Manley *Military History* v33 no6 p8 Mr 2017

Deadlines
4 Ways to Manage Deadlines on Cross-Cultural Teams E. G. Saunders *Harvard Business Review Digital Articles* p2 Je 10 2016
If You Dread Deadlines, You're Thinking About Them All Wrong E. G. Saunders *Harvard Business Review Digital Articles* p2 Mr 18 2016
LIMERICK LAUGHS *Saturday Evening Post* v288 no6 p112 N/D 2016
The Rapture or a Rupture? S. CARR *Idaho Magazine* v17 no1 p54 Ja 2017
Trade Imbalance B. Marks and T. Keith color *Sports Illustrated* v127 no4 p17 Ag 7 2017
What to Do If You Can't File Your Taxes on Time E. Stark color *Time* v189 no11 p18 Mr 27 2017

Deadpan (Film)
INDESTRUCTIBLE *Film Comment* v53 no2 p6 Mr/Ap 2017

Deadpool (Film)
4 — OPENING CREDITS J. McGovern *Entertainment Weekly* no1444/1445 p60 D 16 2016
Could Deadpool Get a Best Picture Nod? N. Sperling color *Entertainment Weekly* no1450 p16 Ja 27 2017
NO. 12 DEADPOOL J. McGovern color *Entertainment Weekly* no1436/1437 p54 O 21 2016
RYAN REYNOLDS T. Stack color *Entertainment Weekly* no1444/1445 p14 D 16 2016
THIS PICTURE IS PERFECT. BLAKE LIVELY IS NOT A. Morris color *Glamour* v115 no9 p188 S 2017
Zazie BEETZ D. Glover *Interview* v47 no5 p53 Je/Jl 2017

Deadringer (Music)
New Routes M. Trammell cartoon *New Yorker* v92 no44 p15 Ja 9 2017

Deaf & Blind (Short story)
DEAF AND BLIND L. VAPNYAR bw cartoon color *New Yorker* v93 no10 p82 Ap 24 2017

Deaf scientists
Building community for deaf scientists G. Buckley, S. Smith et al bibl color *Science* v355 no6322 p255 Ja 20 2017
Community network for deaf scientists H. J. Adler, K. L. Anbuhl et al color *Science* v356 no6336 p386 Ap 28 2017

Deafness
Now Hear This! C. Thorp color *Seventeen* v76 no4 p51 Jl/Ag 2017
PARDON? D. OWEN cartoon color *New Yorker* v93 no7 p38 Ap 3 2017
YOUR BODY ON... FIREWORKS [Cover story] J. Migala color *Women's Health* v14 no6 p84 Jl 2017

Deafness—Prevention
CAN YOU HEAR ME NOW? How to prevent—or deal with—hearing loss [Cover story] *Nutrition Action Health Letter* v43 no10 p3 D 2016
Fighting Hearing Loss C. Chen and D. Bloomfield cartoon chart *Bloomberg Businessweek* no4497 p37 O 31 2016

Deafness—Research
Hearing Loss Prevalence Declining in U.S *USA Today Magazine* v145 no2861 p3 F 2017

Deafness—Treatment
Dr. Weil [Cover story] A. Weil cartoon color *Prevention* p24 Mr 2017
What's holding you back from better hearing? *Harvard Health Letter* v42 no5 p3 Mr 2017

Deaf—Services for
Making Art Accessible L. Mulcahy *Stage Directions* v29 no10 p28 O 2016

Deahl, Rachel
Deals color *Publishers Weekly* v263 no44 p10 O 31 2016
Deals color *Publishers Weekly* v264 no11 p8 Mr 13 2017
Deals color *Publishers Weekly* v264 no17 p12 Ap 24 2017
Deals color *Publishers Weekly* v264 no30 p7 Jl 24 2017
Deals color *Publishers Weekly* v264 no35 p14 Ag 28 2017
Despite Some Editors' Weariness, Psychological Suspense Is Still Hot *Publishers Weekly* v263 no41 p5 O 10 2016
For Shari Lapena, Entering Crowded Category Proved An Asset color *Publishers Weekly* v264 no33 p6 Ag 14 2017
FRANKFURT BRIEFCASE 2016 *Publishers Weekly* v263 no39 p34 S 26 2016
FRANKFURT BRIEFCASE 2017 bw color *Publishers Weekly* v264 no39 p34 S 25 2017
Highlights from What American Agents Are Selling at the Fair bw cartoon color *Publishers Weekly* v264 no9 p21 F 27 2017
Is Mass Market Dying, Or Just Evolving—Again? color *Publishers Weekly* v264 no21 p4 My 22 2017
Is Publishing's Liberal Bias a Liability? color *Publishers Weekly* v264 no15 p8 Ap 10 2017
Obama Deal Sparks $65 Million Mystery *Publishers Weekly* v264 no10 p8 Mr 6 2017
Publishers Keep Calm And Carry On color *Publishers Weekly* v264 no12 p5 Mr 20 2017
TIME FOR A GOOD BOOK color *Publishers Weekly* v263 no46 p12 N 14 2016
Upstart D.C. Agents Making Waves in N.Y.C color *Publishers Weekly* v264 no36 p5 S 4 2017

World War II Books color *Publishers Weekly* v264 no30 p10 Jl 24 2017

de Almeida, R. M.

Observation of a large-scale anisotropy in the arrival directions of cosmic rays above 8 × 1018 eV *Science* v357 no6357 p1266 S 22 2017

de Almeida Matos, F. D.

Persistent effects of pre-Columbian plant domestication on Amazonian forest composition bibl chart graph map *Science* v355 no6328 p925 Mr 3 2017

Deals

The 7 Rules of Smarter Shopping D. Hochman color *AARP: The Magazine* v60 no2A p28 F/Mr 2017

Deals R. DEAHL bw color *Publishers Weekly* v264 no38 p13 S 18 2017

Obama Deal Sparks $65 Million Mystery J. Milliot, R. Deahl et al *Publishers Weekly* v264 no10 p8 Mr 6 2017

SNAP UP THESE DEALS color *Kiplinger's Personal Finance* v71 no6 p33 Je 2017

TAKEAWAY M. A. WOJNO cartoon *Kiplinger's Personal Finance* v71 no12 p72 D 2017

When You Shouldn't Try to Dominate a Negotiation S. Wiltermuth *Harvard Business Review Digital Articles* p2 Ag 27 2015

Deals—Charts, diagrams, etc.

Shark Tank's Toothless Deals E. CANAL, J. KAUFLIN et al color graph *Forbes* v198 no7 p24 N 29 2016

Deals—News briefs

Deals D. LEFFERTS color *Publishers Weekly* v264 no8 p8 F 20 2017

Deals R. DEAHL bw color *Publishers Weekly* v264 no23 p9 Je 5 2017

Deals R. DEAHL color *Publishers Weekly* v264 no31 p8 Jl 31 2017

Deals R. DEAHL *Publishers Weekly* v263 no39 p12 S 26 2016

Deamer, David W.

life springs [Cover story] color *Scientific American* v317 no2 p28 Ag 2017

Dean (Film)

Mary's Playing Our Song color *AARP: The Magazine* v60 no4A p9 Je/Jl 2017

Summer Movie Preview: June S. Begley, E. Berman et al color *Time* v189 no20 p50 My 29 2017

Dean, Andrew

Banding Together: New public-private partnerships may finally help bridge the digital divide D. C. Vock *Governing* v30 no8 p44 My 2017

Dean, Annie—Interviews

Want Your Boss to Say Yes to Flextime? W. Naugle color *Glamour* no8 p112 Ag 2017

Dean, Aria

Worry the Image bw color *Art in America* v105 no6 p41 Je/Jl 2017

Dean, Caroline

Distinct phases of Polycomb silencing to hold epigenetic memory of cold in Arabidopsis diag *Science* v357 no6356 p1142 S 15 2017

Dean, Christopher

The growth pattern of Neandertals, reconstructed from a juvenile skeleton from El Sidrón (Spain) color graph *Science* v357 no6357 p1282 S 22 2017

Dean, Cory R.

Electron optics with p-n junctions in ballistic graphene bibl graph *Science* v353 no6307 p1522 S 30 2016

Dean, D. J.

Observation of coherent elastic neutrino-nucleus scattering diag *Science* v357 no6356 p1123 S 15 2017

Dean, Eddie

AMERICA'S OLDEST LIVING DRUG ADVICE GOLUMNIST TELLS ALL *Washingtonian Magazine* v52 no11 p64 Ag 2017

DEAN, FLANNERY

How satire failed color *Maclean's* v129 no47 p56 N 28 2016

Dean, Geoffrey

Astrology's Bait of a Caring Cosmos J. Szimhart *Skeptical Inquirer* v40 no6 p62 N/D 2016

Tests of Astrology: A Critical Review of Hundreds of Studies I. W. KELLY *Skeptical Inquirer* v41 no3 p58 My/Je 2017

Dean, H.

Country-specific effects of neonicotinoid pesticides on honey bees and wild bees diag map *Science* v356 no6345 p1393 Je 30 2017

Dean, James

JOSEPH DIRAND color *Esquire* v167 no2 p80 Mr 2017

DEAN, JENNIFER

Room for All cartoon diag graph *Alternatives Journal (AJ) - Canada's Environmental Voice* v42 no2 p54 2016

Dean, John W. (John Wesley), 1938-—Interviews

John DEAN R. Perlstein bw *Esquire* p152 S 2017

Dean, Josh

AMERICA'S FITTEST CHEFS cartoon color *Men's Health* v32 no3 p104 Ap 2017

Are You There God? It's Me, the Pillow King color *Bloomberg Businessweek* no4507 p52 Ja 16 2017

BIG BOY *Men's Health* v32 no4 p111 My 2017

Decapitate And Chill bw *Bloomberg Businessweek* no4498 p64 N 7 2016

DRIVER AVAILABLE color *Bloomberg Businessweek* no4536 p58 S 4 2017

THE FAST AND THE FILTHY RICH color *Bloomberg Businessweek* no4510 p55 F 6 2017

GOING DEEP color *Sunset* v238 no5 p19 My 2017

How to Move a Town color *Bloomberg Businessweek* no4537 p68 S 11 2017

KING OF THE MOUNTAIN color *Sunset* v238 no2 p25 F 2017

Now Boarding For the Titanic Tour color *Bloomberg Businessweek* no4537 p54 S 11 2017

THE REAL MOST IMPORTANT MEAL OF THE DAY color *Bloomberg Businessweek* no4493 p82 O 3 2016

THIS IS THE STORY OF AMERICA'S FIRST PENIS TRANSPLANT cartoon color *Esquire* v167 no2 p122 Mr 2017

Your Boss Is Gonna Love Your New Drug Habit color *GQ: Gentlemen's Quarterly* v87 no1 p26 Ja 2017

Dean, Joshua T.

Cognitive science in the field: A preschool intervention durably enhances intuitive but not formal mathematics chart color diag graph *Science* v357 no6346 p47 Jl 7 2017

DEAN, KAREN

Q: What was the greatest summer read of your life? color *O, The Oprah Magazine* p16 Jl 2017

DEAN, MICHELLE

Don't Stop Believin' il *New Republic* v247 no12 p14 D 2016

HORROR SHOW: The nightmare logic of Twin Peaks *Harper's Magazine* p86 O 2017

The Search for Facts in a Post-Fact World color *Wired* v25 no10 p98 O 2017

THE SERENDIPITER'S JOURNEY color *Nation* v304 no11 p32 Ap 3 2017

SETTLING DOWN bw il *Nation* v303 no18 p33 O 31 2016

Sunken Pleasures color il *New Republic* v248 no11 p52 N 2017

The Talking Dead color *Walrus* v14 no8 p61 O 2017

Voices of America *New Republic* v248 no4 p56 Ap 2017

Dean, Michelle—Awards

Louise Erdrich, Matthew Desmond Win 2017 NBCC Awards C. Reid color *Publishers Weekly* v264 no12 p14 Mr 20 2017

Dean, Paul

SLATIN MOTOGEAR EZ-1 SUPERFABRIC MESH JACKET color *Cycle World* v55 no10 p18 N 2016

Dean, Sierra

Bayou Blues *Publishers Weekly* v264 no25 p97 Je 19 2017

DEAN, TAMARA

Good Neighbors *American Scholar* v86 no1 p60 Wint 2017

Dean, Will

The Business of Getting Dirty color *Fortune* v176 no5 p19 O 1 2017

de Anca, Celia

Our Emotional Attachment to Local Currencies *Harvard Business Review Digital Articles* p2 N 5 2014

To Foster Innovation, Connect Coworkers Who Share Aspirations *Harvard Business Review Digital Articles* p2 Jl 14 2016

Why Hiring for Cultural Fit Can Thwart Your Diversity Efforts *Harvard Business Review Digital Articles* p2 Ap 25 2016

de Andrade Lima Filho, D.

Persistent effects of pre-Columbian plant domestication on Amazonian forest composition bibl chart graph map *Science* v355 no6328 p925 Mr 3 2017

de Andrade Miranda, I. P.

Persistent effects of pre-Columbian plant domestication on Amazonian forest composition bibl chart graph map *Science* v355 no6328 p925 Mr 3 2017

Deane, Grant B.

Turbulence in breaking waves *Physics Today* v69 no10 p86 O 2016

DeAngelis, K. M.

Long-term pattern and magnitude of soil carbon feedback to the climate system in a warming world chart graph *Science* v357 no6359 p101 O 6 2017

Deans (Education)

Celebrating 35 Years of Tufts Health & Nutrition Letter: And the legacy of the newsletter's founder, Stanley N. Gershojf, PhD *Tufts University Health & Nutrition Letter* v35 no7 p6 S 2017

Dean Toste, F.

A catalytic fluoride-rebound mechanism for C(sp3)-CF3 bond formation diag *Science* v356 no6344 p1272 Je 23 2017

Dean/wolf Architects (Company)

To the Rescue M. SITZ color diag *Architectural Record* v205 no3 p118 Mr 2017

Deap Vally (Performer)

DEAP VALLY D. EHRLICH *Interview* v46 no8 p32 O 2016

Dear Angelica (Film)

Virtually There T. Burr bw *MIT Technology Review* v120 no2 p96 Mr/Ap 2017

Dear Evan Hansen (Theatrical Production)

7 — DEAR EVAN HANSEN M. R. Bernardo *Entertainment Weekly* no1444/1445 p118 D 16 2016

BEN PLATT M. Snetiker color *Entertainment Weekly* no1438 p69 N 4 2016

BULLIES H. ALS cartoon *New Yorker* v92 no42 p128 D 19 2016

Choreographing Cyberspace S. GOLD *Dance Magazine* v90 no12 p32 D 2016

Dear Evan Hansen, Thanks for Finding Us. We've Been Waiting for a Musical Like You S. Schrobsdorff color *Time* v189 no10 p59 Mr 20 2017

GOINGS ON ABOUT TOWN color *New Yorker* v92 no37 p11 N 14 2016

Hot Takes and Cold Shoulders M. Snetiker color *Entertainment Weekly* no1465 p10 My 12 2017

RISKY BUSINESS C. Brody, I. Biedenharn et al color *Entertainment Weekly* no1449 p38 Ja 20 2017

THE THEATRE *New Yorker* v92 no43 p7 Ja 2 2017

THE WORLD ACCORDING TO Gayle cartoon color *O, The Oprah Magazine* p34 My 2017

Dear White People (TV program)

DEAR IN THE SPOTLIGHT C. Agard color *Entertainment Weekly* no1472 p52 Je 30 2017

Dear White People J. Jensen color *Entertainment Weekly* no1463/1464 p93 Ap/My 2017

Logan Browning's Black Face in a White Place K. CHANEY and L. CROSS color *Ebony* v72 no6 p28 Ap/My 2017

Dearborn, Jenny

She Leads Learning B. Turvett color *Working Mother* p14 F/Mr 2017

Dearborn, Mary V.

Claims to Fame E. SHOWALTER *New York Times Book Review* p16 My 28 2017

EXTRAORDINARY ACTUALITY M. Bauerlein *Claremont Review of Books* v17 no3 p77 Summ 2017

Two Kinds Of People T. TEACHOUT bw *National Review* v69 no16 p41 Ag 28 2017

De Armas, Ana, 1988-

Looking Sharp J. POWERS and C. SCHAMA color *Vogue* v207 no9 p611 S 2017

A WOMAN OF INFLUENCE E. POENISCH bw color *Esquire* p120 O 2017

de Arquer, F. Pelayo Garc'a

Efficient and stable solution-processed planar perovskite solar cells via contact passivation bibl graph *Science* v355 no6326 p722 F 17 2017

Dearth, Gary

2016 Canadian Nationals *Arabian Horse World* v57 no2 p50 N 2016

ALL THE RIGHT PARTS *Arabian Horse World* v57 no5 p2 F 2017

ARABIAN HORSE WORLD'S TRAINERS ALMANAC *Arabian Horse World* v57 no1 p49 O 2016

Avonlea ARABIANS *Arabian Horse World* v57 no4 p1 Ja 2017

BECKER STABLES and Kheanne *Arabian Horse World* v57 no6 p1 Mr 2017

ELEANOR'S ARABIAN FARM *Arabian Horse World* v57 no10 p1 Jl 2017

EXPRESSAMO color *Arabian Horse World* v57 no7 p1 Ap 2017

In Memory of Sundance Kis V color *Arabian Horse World* v57 no7 p140 Ap 2017

OAK HAVEN FARMS *Arabian Horse World* v57 no12 p97 S 2017

Oran Van Crabbet *Arabian Horse World* v57 no1 p10 O 2016

THE PERFECT HORSE: A Conversation with Author Elizabeth Letts *Arabian Horse World* v57 no11 p154 Ag 2017

RGT MOZART *Arabian Horse World* v56 no12 p48 S 2016

Sarah Esqueda *Arabian Horse World* v57 no1 p65 O 2016

SCOTTSDALE 2017: The View from Center Ring color *Arabian Horse World* v57 no7 p104 Ap 2017

Stanley G. White Sr. July 31, 1936-April 3, 2017 *Arabian Horse World* v57 no8 p90 My 2017

Stanley White AND Harold Ray—ADVENTURES IN EGYPT ~1978~ *Arabian Horse World* v57 no8 p91 My 2017

Sur Teddy's Magna A Great One Retires *Arabian Horse World* v57 no1 p94 O 2016

U. S. Nationals AWPA Futurities *Arabian Horse World* v57 no3 p54 D 2016

The View from Center Ring *Arabian Horse World* v57 no1 p74 O 2016

Deary, Casey

Horse & Rider BEST QUOTES color *Horse & Rider* v55 no12 p39 D 2016

Stay Free in the Stop [Cover story] color *Horse & Rider* v56 no1 p25 Ja 2017

Deas, George T.

Martin Luther: hero, but no saint color *America* v216 no9 p44 Ap 24 2017

Dease, Michael

All These Hands J. Macnie color *Downbeat* v84 no3 p53 Mr 2017

Death

     See also

     Mortality

     Pets—Death

     Right to die

     Suicide

Back to Life S. SANDBERG cartoon color *O, The Oprah Magazine* p46 My 2017

Changing How Patients and Doctors Talk About Death J. Lakin, R. Bernacki et al *Harvard Business Review Digital Articles* p2 D 1 2016

Cooper's HEART R. GUMMERE cartoon color *O, The Oprah Magazine* p110 Ap 2017

Death of a caregiver I. S. Villegas *Christian Century* v134 no3 p10 F 2017

The Euphoria of the Dying J. McGowan color *Commonweal* v144 no7 p6 Ap 14 2017

"Her Father Lives in HER EYES" bw color *Good Housekeeping* v263 no5 p113 N 2016

In Her Wake: A few words about my mom, whom I wish were here to read them P. GULLEY *Indianapolis Monthly* p56 N 2017

Milestones *Time* v189 no18 p15 My 15 2017

TAKING A SHOT IN "TERROR" A. BLUE *USA Today Magazine* v145 no2860 p66 Ja 2017

The Things I Wish My Dad Knew About Me Before He Died S. B. LEWIS color *Reader's Digest* v189 no1131 p50 Je 2017

a trip to the other side R. Feltman cartoon *Popular Science* v289 no5 p76 S/O 2017

Woman Dies Searching for Monster B. RADFORD *Skeptical Inquirer* v40 no6 p12 N/D 2016

The year of Diana P. TREBLE color *Maclean's* v129 no51/52 p46 D 26 2016

Death care industry

     See also

     Cemeteries

Death certificates

A Better Reckoning color *Scientific American* v316 no4 p10 Ap 2017

ON THE RECORD E. COLLOFF *Scientific American* v317 no2 p6 Ag 2017

Death Dive to Saturn (TV program)

Cassini spacecraft gets a proper send-off C. Crockett color *Science News* v192 no3 p26 S 2 2017

Death Fighter (Film)

JOE LEWIS' LAST MOVIE RELEASED ON DVD, VOD color *Black Belt* v55 no6 p13 O/N 2017

Death Note (Film)

Death Note C. Nashawaty color *Entertainment Weekly* no1480 p35 S 1 2017

Death row inmates

DEATH ROW RUSH M. BLAU *Atlanta* v56 no12 p28 Ap 2017

Death threats

The Dangerous Ladies Affair: A Carpenter and Quincannon Mystery *Publishers Weekly* v263 no47 p92 N 21 2016

Death Valley (Calif. & Nev.)

BACK IN THE SADDLE J. BERLIN color *Flying* v144 no6 p60 Je 2017

EXTREME ATTRACTION M. JENKINS color map *Backpacker* p58 Ag 2017

Timbisha... M. Dolan color *American History* v52 no2 p72 Je 2017

Death Valley (Calif. & Nev.)—Description & travel

DESERT BLOOM A. ROSS cartoon color *New Yorker* v92 no37 p62 N 14 2016

THE OTHER SIDE OF DEATH VALLEY K. CLARK color *Dirt Sports + Off-Road* v51 no6 p36 Je 2017

Death Valley National Park (Calif. & Nev.)

DESERT BLOOM A. ROSS cartoon color *New Yorker* v92 no37 p62 N 14 2016

Death—Causes

See also

Suicide

Shot through the Eye and who's to Blame? M. Foys *History Today* v66 no10 p6 O 2016

Death—Law & legislation

Dispatches From the End of Life M. HUSTON *Psychology Today* v50 no1 p18 Ja/F 2017

Death of Louis XIV, The (Film)

The Inner Sanctum A. Serra bw color *Film Comment* v53 no1 p6 Ja/F 2017

THE LONG GOODBYE Y. TALU color *Film Comment* v53 no2 p27 Mr/Ap 2017

THE SETTING SUN Y. TALU color *Film Comment* v53 no2 p24 Mr/Ap 2017

Death—Religious aspects

A good death J. M. Griffith color *U.S. Catholic* v82 no1 p38 Ja 2017

Death—Risk factors

This Just In J. Zorthian *Time* v190 no9 p25 S 4 2017

Death—Social aspects

ALL TOO HUMAN H. Rosner color *Scientific American* v315 no3 p70 S 2016

Death—Social aspects—United States

"Your Story is OUR STORY" S. 1. Price color *Sports Illustrated* v125 no12 p38 O 10 2016

Deaton, Angus

THE THREAT OF INEQUALITY color graph *Scientific American* v315 no3 p48 S 2016

Well, No, But I Did Fly Over It Once cartoon *Weekly Standard* v22 no28 p2 Mr 27 2017

Deaton, Chris

100 Down... color *Weekly Standard* v22 no33 p6 My 8 2017

All Politics Are National color *Weekly Standard* v22 no39 p15 Je 19 2017

A Bipartisan Wall *Weekly Standard* v22 no19 p15 Ja 23 2017

Preexisting Suspicions color *Weekly Standard* v22 no32 p21 My 1 2017

Repeal, Replace, Regret cartoon *Weekly Standard* v22 no27 p16 Mr 20 2017

Swearing In *Weekly Standard* v22 no31 p8 Ap 17 2017

Washington Hasn't Changed cartoon *Weekly Standard* v22 no30 p6 Ap 10 2017

DEATON, DALE

Your True Stories IN 100 WORDS color *Reader's Digest* v189 no1130 p32 My 2017

Deaux, Joe

American Producers See an Election Boost color *Bloomberg Businessweek* no4500 p22 N 21 2016

Does Foreign Steel Threaten U.S. Security? color *Bloomberg Businessweek* no4524 p31 My 29 2017

How Does Tax Avoidance Play in Peoria? color *Bloomberg Businessweek* no4525 p42 Je 5 2017

U.S. Steel's Revitalization color *Bloomberg Businessweek* no4536 p42 S 4 2017

Will Trump Crush China Over Aluminum? color *Bloomberg Businessweek* no4510 p22 F 6 2017

DEAVEL, CATHERINE JACK

Preserving The Magic color *National Review* v69 no4 p45 Mr 6 2017

DEAVEL, DAVID P.

Preserving The Magic color *National Review* v69 no4 p45 Mr 6 2017

Deaver, Jeffrey

The Burial Hour: A Lincoln Rhyme Novel *Publishers Weekly* v264 no8 p64 F 20 2017

Deb, Siddhartha

Bookends: Do grants, professorships and other forms of institutional support help writers but hurt writing? *New York Times Book Review* p23 Jl 9 2017

Bookends *New York Times Book Review* p31 N 27 2016

Lonely Planet *New Republic* v248 no5 p63 My 2017

What's the best book, new or old, you read this year? *New York Times Book Review* p27 D 25 2016

DeBacco, Tom

island time color *Power & Motoryacht* v34 no10 p84 O 2017

DeBacker, Lori

LITTLE THINGS A. Gregory *Harper's Magazine* v334 no2001 p41 F 2017

de Bakker, Bernadette S.

An interactive three-dimensional digital atlas and quantitative database of human development bibl color graph *Science* v354 no6315 paag0053-1 N 25 2016

de Bakker, Paul I. W.

Negative selection in humans and fruit flies involves synergistic epistasis chart graph *Science* v356 no6337 p539 My 5 2017

De Ballaigue, Christopher

The transformation of Islam P. B. Ely *America* v217 no6 p54 S 18 2017

De Barros, Louis

Mega-earthquakes rupture flat megathrusts bibl graph *Science* v354 no6315 p1027 N 25 2016

de Barros, Paul

Flowers—Beautiful Life Vol. 2 color *Downbeat* v84 no7 p47 Jl 2017

The Hot Box chart *Downbeat* v84 no2 p71 F 2017

The Hot Box chart *Downbeat* v84 no5 p51 My 2017

The Hot Box *Downbeat* v84 no8 p69 Ag 2017

Madera Latino color *Downbeat* v84 no1 p65 Ja 2017

THE MAGIC TOUCH color *Downbeat* v84 no6 p126 Je 2017

OUTREACH YIELDS REWARDS IN VAIL color *Downbeat* v84 no6 p132 Je 2017

Rhythm Rules at PDX Jazz Fest color *Downbeat* v84 no5 p13 My 2017

Something Gold, Something Blue color *Downbeat* v83 no12 p63 D 2016

deBary, John

American Spirits color *Bloomberg Businessweek* no4528 p73 Je 26 2017

Debates & debating

See also

Political debates & debating

Editor's Note: Why We Let Underwhelming Colleges Host the Debates *Washington Monthly* p1 S/O 2016

For More than 100 Years, D.C. Has Drawn People to Protest A. Stern *Humanities* v37 no4 p1 Fall 2016

THE HOT SEAT M. HUSTON *Psychology Today* v49 no5 p9 S/O 2016

How Structured Debate Helps Your Team Grow B. Dattner *Har-*

vard Business Review Digital Articles p2 D 10 2015

The Loser W. Kristol *Weekly Standard* v22 no8 p6 O 31 2016

Public Debate, Scientific Skepticism, and Science Denial S. LEWANDOWSKY, M. E. MANN et al *Skeptical Inquirer* v41 no1 p40 Ja/F 2017

The Science Police: On highly charged issues, such as climate change and endangered species, peer review literature and public discourse are aggressively patrolled by self-appointed sheriffs in the scientific community K. KLOOR *Issues in Science & Technology* v33 no4 p78 Summ 2017

TUCKER CARLSON IS SORRY FOR BEING MEAN S. RODRICK color graph *GQ: Gentlemen's Quarterly* v97 no10 p84 O 2017

Debates & debating in mass media

A Lack of Ideas Has Consequences J. W. CEASER *Weekly Standard* v23 no3 p14 S 25 2017

Debates & debating—Social aspects

How Social Media Splits the Global Conversation N. Gardels and N. Berggruen *NPQ: New Perspectives Quarterly* v34 no1 p6 Ja 2017

Debatin, J.

Observation of a large-scale anisotropy in the arrival directions of cosmic rays above 8×10^{18} eV *Science* v357 no6357 p1266 S 22 2017

DeBaun, Morgon

Black News Matters C. Brooks Jr. color *Wired* v25 no3 p64 Mr 2017

DeBeau, Richard

How America Lost Its Mind color *Atlantic* v320 no4 p12 N 2017

Debei, S.

Rosetta's comet 67P/Churyumov-Gerasimenko sheds its dusty mantle to reveal its icy nature bibl graph *Science* v354 no6319 p1566 D 23 2016

Surface changes on comet 67P/Churyumov-Gerasimenko suggest a more active past bw graph *Science* v355 no6332 p1392 Mr 31 2017

De Bell, Matthew

Contingent valuation: Flawed logic? color *Science* v357 no6349 p363 Jl 28 2017

Putting a value on injuries to natural assets: The BP oil spill chart *Science* v356 no6335 p253 Ap 21 2017

de Bellaigue, Christopher

Iran: Still Waiting for Democracy color *New York Review of Books* v64 no12 p25 Jl 13 2017

OUR BETTER NATURES bw *Nation* v305 no7 p32 S 25 2017

DeBiasi, Frank

editor's letter color *Architectural Digest* v74 no1 p36 Ja 2017

Debigare, Adrienne

How Reddit the Business Lost Touch With Reddit the Culture *Harvard Business Review Digital Articles* p2 Jl 14 2015

Debit cards

Andrew Ross SORKIN M. Hainey color *Esquire* p68 My 2017

De Blasio, Bill, 1961-

DEFENDER OF THE COMMUNITY A. Feuer *Harper's Magazine* p41 Ap 2017

The Minimal Mayor [Cover story] K. SMITH color *National Review* v69 no18 p22 O 2 2017

New York Stands with Muslims *Islamic Horizons* v46 no3 p15 My/Je 2017

NYC vs. TRUMP [Cover story] J. MURPHY color *Nation* v304 no3 p12 Ja 30 2017

De Blasio, Bill, 1961—Interviews

IN CONVERSATION Bill de Blasio C. SMITH img *New York* v50 no18 p24 S 4 2017

DeBoer, Sherry

LEAVE USA STORY: We are in challenging times! We need your help *South Dakota Magazine* p6 S/O 2017 Supplement

Deboick, Sophia L.

The Friendly Recluse: Medieval hermits were the agony aunts of their day *History Today* v67 no7 p18 Jl 2017

DeBold, Jessica

Character Building: Carpenter and designer Matthew Holdren creates custom wood pieces with reclaimed materials *New Orleans Homes & Lifestyles* v20 no3 p30 Summ 2017

Floating in Space color *New Orleans Magazine* v51 no5 p150 Mr 2017

Found and Formed: Glass artist Mitchell Gaudet finds the extraordinary in the ordinary *New Orleans Homes & Lifestyles* v20 no4 p30 Aut 2017

Got Orange? color *New Orleans Magazine* v51 no7 p150 My 2017

Instyle Textiles *New Orleans Homes & Lifestyles* v20 no2 p30 Spr 2017

Laissez Les Bon Temps Roulez! color *New Orleans Magazine* v51 no4 p142 F 2017

De Brabander, Jef

An adipo-biliary-uridine axis that regulates energy homeostasis diag *Science* v355 no6330 p1173 Mr 17 2017

de Brantes, François

U.S. Health Care Is on the Cusp of Bundled Payments *Harvard Business Review Digital Articles* p2 D 11 2015

de Bree, Karel

An interactive three-dimensional digital atlas and quantitative database of human development bibl color graph *Science* v354 no6315 paag0053-1 N 25 2016

De Breuck, C.

Molecular gas in the halo fuels the growth of a massive cluster galaxy at high redshift bibl graph *Science* v354 no6316 p1128 D 2 2016

DeBrosse, Jim

WAITING FOR THE GREAT LEAP FORWARD *Cincinnati Magazine* v50 no8 p60 My 2017

A Writer's Story *Cincinnati Magazine* v50 no4 p50 Ja 2017

Debrow, Edwin

The PRISONER S. Hollandsworth *Texas Monthly* v45 no1 p92 Ja 2017

DeBruhl, Rick

Happy Campers color *AARP: The Magazine* v60 no4A p11 Je/Jl 2017

Debs, Eugene V. (Eugene Victor), 1855-1926

Before Bernie S. Richardson *American History* v52 no1 p34 Ap 2017

Debt

See also

External debts

Long-term debt

Student loan debt

ASK THE EXPERT S. Max, M. C. White et al diag *Money* v46 no2 p31 Mr 2017

FEDERAL FINANCE *Economic Indicators* p32 Ap 2017

FEDERAL FINANCE *Economic Indicators* p32 D 2016

FEDERAL FINANCE *Economic Indicators* p32 F 2017

Ray DALIO A. Carter color *Esquire* p62 O 2017

Smart ways to pay down debt N. Lapin color *Redbook* p43 F 2017

top 10 money to-dos of 2015 *Parents* p124 2015

Debt limit (Government)

Trump's New Deal R. PONNURU color *National Review* v69 no18 p13 O 2 2017

Debt management

See also

Debt relief

INVESTING AT EVERY AGE [Cover story] E. LEARY color *Kiplinger's Personal Finance* v71 no11 p48 N 2017

Debt relief

BORROWER'S REMORSE S. Burd color *Washington Monthly* v49 no9/10 p76 S/O 2017

Debt-to-equity ratio

A Refresher on Debt-to-Equity Ratio A. Gallo *Harvard Business Review Digital Articles* p2 Jl 13 2015

Debt-to-GDP ratio

The Courage Deficit S. F. Hayes color *Weekly Standard* v22 no26 p7 Mr 13 2017

The Once and Future Financial Crisis M. Schuman color *Bloomberg Businessweek* no4529 p10 Jl 3 2017

Debt—Canada

Maxed Out [Cover story] R. Robin color *Walrus* v14 no5 p28 Je 2017

Debt—Charts, diagrams, etc.

FEDERAL FINANCE *Economic Indicators* p32 Je 2017

Debt—Economic aspects

The World Owes Too Much Money A. Mayeda and S. Mohsin cartoon *Bloomberg Businessweek* no4495 p13 O 17 2016

Debugging in computer science

How to stop failing Windows Updates from bothering you I. PAUL color diag *PCWorld* v35 no11 p155 N 2016

Mac 911 G. FLEISHMAN color *Macworld - Digital Edition* v34 no9 p97 S 2017

Troubleshooting some nasty Safari malware J. Snell color diag *Macworld - Digital Edition* p51 Ap 2017

Debussy (Music)

Debussy/Orledge: Poe Operas W. R. Braun *Opera News* v81 no6 p52 D 2016

Debutante (Music)

POP ROCKS: Meet rock's next big thing: middle-aged, but still nerdy, trans girl Cait Brennan J. ANDERSON-MINSHALL *Advocate* no1093 p24 O/N 2017

Debutantes

How Is a Debut Novel Like Lizzy Bennet? K. A. FLYNN *New York Times Book Review* p29 Je 4 2017

De Cabrol, Milly

Pillow Talk color *Architectural Digest* v74 no4 p50 Ap 2017

de Cadenet, Amanda

Love Is Messy, and I'm Good With That color *Glamour* v115 no10 p128 O 2017

De Camilli, Pietro

Lipid transport by TMEM24 at ER-plasma membrane contacts regulates pulsatile insulin secretion diag *Science* v355 no6326 p709 F 17 2017

DeCamp, Stephen J.

Transition from turbulent to coherent flows in confined three-dimensional active fluids color *Science* v355 no6331 p1284 Mr 24 2017

De Candido, Rick

BUILDING A PORTABLE STAGING FIDDLE YARD color diag *Model Railroader* v84 no3 p38 Mr 2017

DeCarava, Roy, 1919-2009

Roy DeCarava wasn't photographing giants of jazz. He was photographing the people and places he knew and understood - an intimacy that produced jazz's seminal image *New York Times Magazine* p14 My 14 2017

De Cárdenas, Miguel Ángel

REMEMBERING A LEGEND D. E. Barber color *Dressage Today* v23 no11 p54 Ag 2017

De Cárdenas, Rafael

TWIST AND SHOUT S. COCHRAN color *Architectural Digest* no11 p138 N 1 2017

DeCarlo, Lauren

Los Angeles color map *Conde Nast Traveler* v51 no10 p64 N 2016

PACKING FOR THE ADIRONDACKS BRING ON THE KNITS AND HOT TODDYS color *Conde Nast Traveler* v52 no10 p46 N 2017

Decarlo, Scott

100 FASTEST-GROWING COMPANIES chart color diag map *Fortune* v176 no4 p157 S 15 2017

THE WORLD'S MOST ADMIRED COMPANIES color *Fortune* v175 no3 p113 Mr 1 2017

DeCarlo, Thomas M.

Hidden Battles Reefs color *Oceanus* v51 no2 p32 Wint 2016

21st-century rise in anthropogenic nitrogen deposition on a remote coral reef diag graph *Science* v356 no6339 p749 My 19 2017

DeCaro, James

Building community for deaf scientists bibl color *Science* v355 no6322 p255 Ja 20 2017

Decarre, Julieta

Forest conservation: Remember Gran Chaco bibl color *Science* v355 no6324 p465 F 3 2017

de Carvalho, W. Rodrigues

Observation of a large-scale anisotropy in the arrival directions of cosmic rays above 8 × 1018 eV *Science* v357 no6357 p1266 S 22 2017

De Castrique, Mark

Hidden Scars: A Sam Blackman Mystery *Publishers Weekly* v264 no30 p39 Jl 24 2017

Decathletes

THE BEAST OF WALL STREET [Cover story] J. KITA bw cartoon color *Men's Health* v32 no2 p80 Mr 2017

Decatur (Ga.)

Brush Sushi Izakaya J. ZYMAN *Atlanta* v56 no11 p66 Mr 2017

THE COMET PUB & LANES C. VAN DUSEN *Atlanta* v56 no7 p60 N 2016

Deccan traps

On the deep-mantle origin of the Deccan Traps P. Glišović and A. M. Forte bibl color *Science* v355 no6325 p613 F 10 2017

De Cecco, M.

Rosetta's comet 67P/Churyumov-Gerasimenko sheds its dusty mantle to reveal its icy nature bibl graph *Science* v354 no6319 p1566 D 23 2016

Surface changes on comet 67P/Churyumov-Gerasimenko suggest a more active past bw graph *Science* v355 no6332 p1392 Mr 31 2017

De Cegli, Rossella

Transcriptional activation of RagD GTPase controls mTORC1 and promotes cancer growth diag *Science* v356 no6343 p1188 Je 16 2017

DeCelles, Katherine

The Unintended Consequences of Diversity Statements *Harvard Business Review Digital Articles* p2 Mr 29 2016

December Bride, A (TV program)

COZY UP! IT'S YOUR HOLIDAY TV-MOVIE CHEAT SHEET D. Snierson color *Entertainment Weekly* no1443 p51 D 9 2016

Decentralization in government

Making climate science more relevant C. F. Kennel, S. Briggs et al bibl color *Science* v354 no6311 p421 O 28 2016

Decentralization in government—European Union countries

As Europe Devolves, America Centralizes M. Helprin *Claremont Review of Books* v16 no4 p90 Fall 2016

Decentralization in government—United States

As Europe Devolves, America Centralizes M. Helprin *Claremont Review of Books* v16 no4 p90 Fall 2016

Decentralization in management

An Organization-Wide Approach to Good Decision Making L. Neal and C. Spetzler *Harvard Business Review Digital Articles* p2 My 27 2015

Decentralization in management—Economic aspects

CASE STUDY: IS HOLACRACY FOR US? E. ROELOFSEN, T. YUE et al color il *Harvard Business Review* v95 no2 p151 Mr/Ap 2017

Deception

ARE YOU GETTING $CAMMED? M. CROUCH *Scholastic Choices* v32 no6 p16 Mr 2017

CHEATING TO KEEP A. SAMSON *Psychology Today* v50 no2 p19 Mr/Ap 2017

A Consistently Erroneous Technology J. RANDI *Skeptical Inquirer* v41 no5 p16 S/O 2017

The Great Pretender cartoon *Weekly Standard* v22 no30 p2 Ap 10 2017

pants on fire E. ZAMMETT RUDDY color graph *Parents* v92 no8 p56 Ag 2017

UNLOCKING THE VAULT [Cover story] C. FLORA *Psychology Today* v50 no2 p46 Mr/Ap 2017

What to Do If You Catch Your Boss in a Lie P. Meyer *Harvard Business Review Digital Articles* p2 Mr 28 2017

Deception—Prevention

hard truths J. DETZ *Parents* v92 no2 p106 F 2017

Deception—Psychological aspects

UNDER THE SKIN: THE NEGATIVE IMPACT OF SECRETS MAY STEM FROM THE WAY THEY LURK IN OUR MINDS M. HECK *Psychology Today* v50 no5 p17 S/O 2017

De Cervantes, Miguel

Rivka Galchen *New York Times Book Review* p27 F 19 2017

Dechambeau, Bryson

PLANE and SIMPLE [Cover story] D. Denunzio color *Golf Magazine* v59 no2 p70 F 2017

YOUNG GUN, OLD SOUL D. M. Clarke color *Golf Magazine* v59 no2 p10 F 2017

De Chant, Tim

The Perfect Crossing cartoon *Wired* v24 no11 p66 N 2016

Dechelle, Caitlin

CAITLIN DECHELLE color *Black Belt* v55 no5 p10 Ag/S 2017

Deciduous teeth

Baby Teeth Link Autism and Heavy Metals *USA Today Magazine* v146 no2869 p11 O 2017

Deciem Inc.

Northern Exposure K. MOLVAR color *Vogue* v207 no11 p152 N 2017

Decision making

3 Timeless Rules for Making Tough Decisions P. Bregman *Harvard Business Review Digital Articles* p2 N 2 2015

3 Ways to Make Less Biased Decisions H. J. Ross *Harvard Business Review Digital Articles* p2 Ap 16 2015

Advice and Credibility Go Hand-in-Hand for Managers D. A. Garvin and J. D. Margolis *Harvard Business Review Digital Articles* p2 Ja 13 2015

ASK A FLOWCHART R. CAPPS diag *Wired* v24 no12 p144 D 2016

Before You Agree to Take on New Work, Ask 3 Questions R. Walsh *Harvard Business Review Digital Articles* p2 My 23 2017

Beyond prediction: Using big data for policy problems S. Athey bibl color *Science* v355 no6324 p483 F 3 2017

Can TV Make You Slim? D. Bova color *Health* v31 no7 p55 S 2017

Decisions Are More Effective When More People Are Involved from the Start J. Whitehurst *Harvard Business Review Digital Articles* p2 Mr 15 2016

Decisions, Decisions, Decisions ... *USA Today Magazine* v146 no2867 p11 Ag 2017

The dishonest HONEST Act D. Michaels and T. Burke color *Science* v356 no6342 p989 Je 9 2017

Don't End a Meeting Without Doing These 3 Things B. Frisch and C. Greene *Harvard Business Review Digital Articles* p2 Ap 26 2016

Don't Let Outdated Management Structures Kill Your Company V. Nayar *Harvard Business Review Digital Articles* p2 F 10 2016

Downsize Your Stuff P. M. ESSWEIN cartoon *Kiplinger's Personal Finance* v71 no7 p36 Jl 2017

editor's note. ON SILENCE THAT IS DEAFENING *Psychology Today* v50 no2 p3 Mr/Ap 2017

Estimating the health benefits of environmental regulations A. McGartland, R. Revesz et al color *Science* v357 no6350 p457 Ag 4 2017

Go with your gut color *Yoga Journal* no295 p91 O 2017

Having Inside Information Leads to Worse Decisions S. Pillay *Harvard Business Review Digital Articles* p2 Ap 2 2015

Here's Why People Trust Human Judgment Over Algorithms W. Frick *Harvard Business Review Digital Articles* p2 F 27 2015

How AI Will Change the Way We Make Decisions A. Agrawal, J. Gans et al *Harvard Business Review Digital Articles* p2 Jl 26 2017

How Can I Make a... Tough Decision? *Scholastic Choices* v32 no8 p24 My 2017

How Leaders Can Let Go Without Losing Control M. Bonchek *Harvard Business Review Digital Articles* p2 Je 2 2016

How to Disagree with Your Boss J. Grenny *Harvard Business Review Digital Articles* p2 N 25 2014

HOW TO TRUST YOUR GUT color *Health* v31 no5 p10 Je 2017

How We Decide A. PIORE color diag *Discover* v38 no6 p34 Jl/Ag 2017

Identifying the Biases Behind Your Bad Decisions J. Beshears and F. Gino *Harvard Business Review Digital Articles* p2 O 31 2014

In Search of Answers M. Huston *Psychology Today* v50 no3 p10 My/Je 2017

Men Choose Differently When They Choose with Other Men H. Nikolova and C. Lamberton *Harvard Business Review Digital Articles* p2 S 14 2016

NICE GIRLS M. Gaitskill *Harper's Magazine* p38 Ap 2017

Nuclear War Should Require a Second Opinion color *Scientific American* v317 no2 p8 Ag 2017

Pour Out Light Unshadowed M. R. Simone *America* v216 no7 p52 Ap 3 2017

The Pros and Cons of Pros-and-Cons Lists C. Charyk color *Harvard Business Review Digital Articles* p2 Ja 6 2017

RADISHES S. PUCKETT *Atlanta* v56 no11 p62 Mr 2017

Reducing Noise in Decision Making: Interaction G. Berkooz, T. Mullie et al color *Harvard Business Review* v94 no12 p18 D 2016

Relearning the Art of Asking Questions T. Pohlmann and N. M. Thomas *Harvard Business Review Digital Articles* p2 Mr 27 2015

Robots Are Learning Complex Tasks Just by Watching Humans Do Them J. Shah *Harvard Business Review Digital Articles* p2

Je 21 2016

Slow Deciders Make Better Strategists M. Chussil *Harvard Business Review Digital Articles* p2 Jl 8 2016

Stop Playing the Victim with Your Time E. G. Saunders *Harvard Business Review Digital Articles* p2 Ja 21 2015

That's Outrageous! SOLUTIONS GONE WRONG *Reader's Digest* v189 no1127 p94 F 2017

This Quiz Will Save Your Waist J. Andriakos color *Health* v31 no7 p63 S 2017

To Change Everything, It Takes Everyone: The Sierra Club is part of a larger ecosystem of progressive change-makers M. BRUNE *Sierra* v102 no4 p6 Jl/Ag 2017

To Make Better Choices, Look at All Your Options Together S. Basu and K. Savani *Harvard Business Review Digital Articles* p2 Je 28 2017

Unsaturated Fat Best for Heart [Cover story] *Tufts University Health & Nutrition Letter* v35 no3 p1 My 2017

Using Data to Strengthen Your Connections to Customers N. Harrison and D. O'Neill *Harvard Business Review Digital Articles* p2 Ag 25 2016

Virtual doctor visits: A new kind of house call *Harvard Health Letter* v41 no12 p4 O 2016

What Generous People's Brains Do Differently N. Torres *Harvard Business Review Digital Articles* p2 O 1 2015

What Managers Really Need from Academics M. G. Jacobides *Harvard Business Review Digital Articles* p2 N 26 2014

When It's Safe to Rely on Intuition (and When It's Not) Connson Chou Locke *Harvard Business Review Digital Articles* p2 Ap 30 2015

When to Trust Robots with Decisions, and When Not To V. Dhar *Harvard Business Review Digital Articles* p2 My 17 2016

WHY BE AN AIRLINE PILOT? L. Abend color *Flying* v144 no9 p74 S 2017

Why That Risky Career Move Could Be a Safer Bet than You Think K. Firestone *Harvard Business Review Digital Articles* p2 Mr 11 2016

win your flextime fight K. ASHFORD color *Parents* v92 no7 p90 Jl 2017

Women Directors Change How Boards Work L. Liswood *Harvard Business Review Digital Articles* p2 F 17 2015

You Don't Need Charisma to Be an Inspiring Leader N. Tasler *Harvard Business Review Digital Articles* p2 O 27 2015

Decision making in business

A 10-Year Study Reveals What Great Executives Know and Do R. Carucci *Harvard Business Review Digital Articles* p2 Ja 19 2016

3 Ways Data Dashboards Can Mislead You J. Shapiro color graph *Harvard Business Review Digital Articles* p2 Ja 13 2017

4 Ways to Be More Effective at Execution J. Zenger and J. Folkman *Harvard Business Review Digital Articles* p2 My 23 2016

8 Ways Machine Learning Is Improving Companie's Work Processes D. Wellers, T. Elliott et al *Harvard Business Review Digital Articles* p2 My 31 2017

The Antidote to HiPPOs: Crowd Voting K. R. Lakhani *Harvard Business Review Digital Articles* p2 F 2 2016

Avoiding Decision Paralysis in the Face of Uncertainty P. Johnson *Harvard Business Review Digital Articles* p2 Mr 11 2015

Before You Make a Tough Decision, Imagine How You'll Have to Sell It J. L. Badaracco *Harvard Business Review Digital Articles* p2 Ag 29 2016

The Biases That Keep Good R&D Projects from Getting Funded P. Criscuolo, L. Dahlander et al *Harvard Business Review Digital Articles* p2 Mr 17 2017

Can Your Data Be Trusted? T. C. Redman *Harvard Business Review Digital Articles* p2 O 29 2015

A Checklist for Making Faster, Better Decisions E. Larson *Harvard Business Review Digital Articles* p2 Mr 7 2016

Companies Collect Competitive Intelligence, but Don't Use It B. Gilad *Harvard Business Review Digital Articles* p2 Jl 31 2015

How Decision Making Evolves as a Startup Grows B. Halligan *Harvard Business Review Digital Articles* p2 Mr 23 2016

How the Big Data Explosion Has Changed Decision Making M. Schrage *Harvard Business Review Digital Articles* p2 Ag 25 2016

How to Design (and Analyze) a Business Experiment O. Hauser and M. Luca *Harvard Business Review Digital Articles* p2 O

Fast exoskeleton optimization color graph *Science* v356 no6344 p1230 Je 23 2017

Decline & Fall (TV program)
Eva Goes Retro *TV Guide* v65 no19 p11 My 1 2017

DE COCK, KEVIN M.
HIV/AIDS—A History color *Natural History* v125 no9 p36 S 2017

DECOCQ, GUILLAUME
Combining Biodiversity Resurveys across Regions to Advance Global Change Research *BioScience* v67 no1 p73 Ja 2017

Decoders (Electronics)
Dual engines with a WOWSound decoder [Cover story] L. Puckett color *Model Railroader* v84 no7 p58 Jl 2017
Going Full Throttle with a LokSound decoder L. Puckett color *Model Railroader* v84 no4 p90 Ap 2017
Have clocks become too fast? J. Dziedzic color *Model Railroader* v84 no11 p72 N 2017
Not quite a DROP-IN DECODER E. White color diag *Model Railroader* v84 no11 p28 N 2017

Decoders (Electronics)—Design & construction
Getting the most from automatic functions L. Puckett color *Model Railroader* v84 no5 p58 My 2017

Decoders (Electronics)—Equipment & supplies
Getting the most from automatic functions L. Puckett color *Model Railroader* v84 no5 p58 My 2017

Decoders (Electronics)—Evaluation
ANE Model Lococruiser DCC decoder color *Model Railroader* v84 no1 p75 Ja 2017
Turnout control with accessory decoders L. Puckett color *Model Railroader* v84 no11 p60 N 2017

Decommunization
The Battle for Historical Memory in Postrevolutionary Ukraine O. SHEVEL *Current History* v115 no783 p258 O 2016

Decomposition (Chemistry)
See also
Biodegradation
The Odor of Death: An Overview of Current Knowledge on Characterization and Applications F. VERHEGGEN, K. A. PERRAULT et al *BioScience* v67 no7 p600 Jl 2017
Pyocyanin degradation by a tautomerizing demethylase inhibits Pseudomonas aeruginosa biofilms K. C. Costa, N. R. Glasser et al bibl diag graph *Science* v355 no6321 p1 Ja 13 2017

Deconstruction (Theatrical production)
Acts of Undermining I. TUTTLE *National Review* v69 no9 p38 My 15 2017

Deconvolution in spectrum analysis
Snap deconvolution: An informatics approach to high-throughput discovery of catalytic reactions K. Troshin and J. F. Hartwig color *Science* v357 no6347 p175 Jl 14 2017

Deconvolution of digital images
Restoring Detail with Deconvolution R. Brecher *Sky & Telescope* v134 no1 p68 Jl 2017

Decoration & ornament
See also
Exterior house decoration
Floral decorations
Flower arrangements
Glass painting & staining
Interior decoration
Interior decoration of chapels
Interior decoration of country homes
Mosaics (Art)
Mural painting & decoration
Ornamental moldings
Screens (Furniture)
Showrooms—Decoration
Table setting & decoration
Textile design
BOX SET F. VIGNA color *Martha Stewart Living* p120 Mr 2017
INSTANT ART *Martha Stewart Living* no267 p21 S 2016
Let it Glow color *Log Home Living* v34 no9 p54 D 2017
ORNAMENTAL C. HONG *Martha Stewart Living* no270 p122 D 2016
PLANT KINGDOM J. Silver color *Sunset* v238 no2 p60 F 2017
YOUR LIFE *USA Today Magazine* v145 no2860 p6 Ja 2017

Decoration & ornament—Evaluation

See also
Interior decoration—Evaluation
HOME RUN H. MARTIN color *Architectural Digest* v74 no7 p62 Jl 2017
HOME UNDER $150 color *Redbook* p114 Mr 2017
Spooktacular Decorating S. BOWER color *Good Housekeeping* v265 no4 p47 O 2017

Decoration & ornament—France
Making Waves H. MARTIN color *Architectural Digest* v74 no7 p22 Jl 2017

Decoration & ornament—Georgia (Republic)
Return TO GLORY B. BROWN color *House Beautiful* p48 Ag 2017

Decoration & ornament—Plant forms
Hotels in Full Bloom C. TATTOLI color *Conde Nast Traveler* v52 no2 p108 F 2017

Decoration & ornament—William & Mary style
William and Mary Carved crest leather back side chair with pierced front stretcher color *Magazine Antiques* v183 no6 p13 N/D 2016

Decoration of outdoor living spaces
Comfort & Curb Appeal L. Elliott color *Old House Journal* v45 no4 p48 Je 2017
Urban Oasis: Stylish New Orleans outdoor living spaces large, small and everything between V. Hart *New Orleans Homes & Lifestyles* v20 no3 p56 Summ 2017

Decorative arts
See also
Antiques
Carving (Decorative arts)
Costume
Decoration & ornament
Figurines
Furniture
Glass art
Jewelry
Mosaics (Art)
Porcelain
Scrolls (Decorative arts)
Textiles
Tiles
Woodwork
1968 CRAFTING SPACE K. K. CONDON color *Better Homes & Gardens* v95 no7 p172 Jl 2017
19th CENTURY MILLWORK: A RIOT OF EXTERIOR AND INTERIOR ORNAMENT IN WOOD color *Old House Journal* v45 no7 p22 O 2017
AN EXPLOSION OF COLORFUL TILE color *Old House Journal* v45 no7 p30 O 2017
A Few Great Show-Offs *Los Angeles Magazine* v61 no11 p74 N 2016
Good Fortune C. M. Cunningham color *Southern Living* v52 no2 p43 F 2017
GOOD THINGS E. N. GAGE *Martha Stewart Living* no268 p21 O 2016
IT'S GOURD SEASON E. Graves *Martha Stewart Living* no268 p8 O 2016
make sparks fly M. POLLITT color *Better Homes & Gardens* v95 no7 p68 Jl 2017
welcome P. POORE *Design Center Sourcebook* p9 2017

Decorative arts—Exhibitions
Tiffany Girl Power at the New-York Historical Society color *Magazine Antiques* v184 no4 p30 Jl/Ag 2017

Decorative arts—United States
CENTRHL REGIOFL *Virginia Living* p22 2017 Best 20of Virginia

Decorative arts—United States—Exhibitions
Last but not least E. H. Gustafson color *Magazine Antiques* v184 no2 p136 Mr/Ap 2017

Decorative paper
See also
Wallpaper
MARTYN LAWRENCE BULLARD ON CEILINGS K. O'SHEA-EVANS color *House Beautiful* v159 no7 p60 S 2017

Decorative plasterwork
ENRICHED & embellished: REVIVING ORNAMENTAL

PLASTERWORK M. E. POLSON color diag *Old House Journal* v45 no6 p40 S 2017

Decorator showhouses

The 2016 Magnolia Designer Show House B. Baribault, J. Rothman et al *Atlanta* v56 no7 p2 N 2016

FLOOR PLANS *Atlanta* v56 no7 p20 N 2016

MAGNOLIA DESIGN DETAILS *Atlanta* v56 no7 p44 N 2016

Decorators Supply Corp.

HOW TO BUILD CHARACTER E. Moody color *Martha Stewart Living* p76 My 2017

DeCotis, Ruth

BY SIMPLICITY SAVED bw color *Old House Journal* v45 no1 p32 F 2017

Decoy carvers

Shelf Life D. L. NG color *Field & Stream* v121 no6 p10 N 2016

Decoys (Hunting)

The Coot Surprise M. D. Johnson color *Field & Stream* v122 no5 pF8 O 2017

LIGHT AS A FEATHER color *Outdoor Life* v224 no7 pW10 S 2017

TWEAK THE DEKES T. CARPENTER color *Outdoor Life* v224 no7 pW9 S 2017

Decoys (Hunting)—Evaluation

ANGRY BIRDS W. BRANTLEY and D. HURTEAU bw cartoon color *Field & Stream* v121 no9 p47 Ap 2017

De Cremer, David

6 Traits That Predict Ethical Behavior at Work *Harvard Business Review Digital Articles* p2 N 22 2016

CC'ing the Boss on Email Makes Employees Feel Less Trusted *Harvard Business Review Digital Articles* p2 Ap 20 2017

Compliance Alone Won't Make Your Company Safe *Harvard Business Review Digital Articles* p2 My 18 2015

Cultural Stereotypes May Make You a Less Ethical Negotiator *Harvard Business Review Digital Articles* p2 Ja 8 2016

Huawei: A Case Study of When Profit Sharing Works *Harvard Business Review Digital Articles* p2 S 24 2015

Huawei's Culture Is the Key to Its Success *Harvard Business Review Digital Articles* p2 Je 11 2015

If You Feel Left Out at Work, Visualize Money *Harvard Business Review Digital Articles* p2 O 22 2015

Understanding Trust, In China and the West *Harvard Business Review Digital Articles* p2 F 11 2015

What China's Shift to a Service Economy Means for Its Managers *Harvard Business Review Digital Articles* p2 Jl 26 2016

When Transparency Backfires, and How to Prevent It *Harvard Business Review Digital Articles* p2 Jl 21 2016

Why Our Trust in Banks Hasn't Been Restored *Harvard Business Review Digital Articles* p2 Mr 3 2015

DeCURTIS, ANTHONY

GOLDEN OLDIES color *New York Times Book Review* p37 D 4 2016

Deczkowska, Aleksandra

Let's talk about language barriers color *Science* v356 no6341 p978 Je 1 2017

Dedeaux, Dawn

DAWN DEDEAUX J. R. Kemp bw color *Louisiana Life* v38 no1 p22 S/O 2017

De Decker, Kris

Warm Up to CHINESE GREENHOUSES *Mother Earth News* no281 p30 Ap/My 2017

Dederer, Claire

Love and Trouble: A Mid-Life Reckoning *Publishers Weekly* v264 no13 p94 Mr 27 2017

Neither Fight nor Flight color *Rodale's Organic Life* v3 no1 p40 Ja 2017

The Pie-Chart Review T. Jordan color diag *Entertainment Weekly* no1468/1469 p109 Je 2-9 2017

Something for Nothing color *Rodale's Organic Life* v2 no7 p31 D 2016/Ja 2017

Dederer, Verena

UBE2O remodels the proteome during terminal erythroid differentiation diag *Science* v357 no6350 p471 Ag 4 2017

Dedhia, Priya H.

Regeneration of fat cells from myofibroblasts during wound healing bibl color graph *Science* v355 no6326 p748 F 17 2017

DEDIĆ, JENNA AUTUORI

swim your way stronger [Cover story] chart color *Redbook* p77 Je 2017

Dedrick, Daniel

Exposing Unfair Pricing in Auto Insurance Rates color *Consumer Reports* v82 no5 p6 My 2017

Dee, Jonathan

THE LIVES OF OTHERS: Does the social novel have a future? *Harper's Magazine* p86 S 2017

The Outsider L. ROSENFELD *New York Times Book Review* p11 Ag 27 2017

Schlock and Awe color *New York Times Book Review* p14 S 25 2016

Dee, Mark

BETTER PLAYER DRIVERS color diag *Golf Magazine* v59 no3 p82 Mr 2017

BETTER PLAYER FAIRWAY WOODS color *Golf Magazine* v59 no5 p86 My 2017

BETTER PLAYER HYBRIDS color *Golf Magazine* v59 no5 p94 My 2017

BETTER PLAYER IRONS color *Golf Magazine* v59 no4 p112 Ap 2017

BLADE PUTTERS color *Golf Magazine* v59 no6 p84 Je 2017

GAME IMPROVEMENT DRIVERS color diag *Golf Magazine* v59 no3 p74 Mr 2017

GAME IMPROVEMENT FAIRWAY WOODS color *Golf Magazine* v59 no5 p82 My 2017

GAME IMPROVEMENT HYBRIDS color *Golf Magazine* v59 no5 p90 My 2017

GAME IMPROVEMENT IRONS color *Golf Magazine* v59 no4 p104 Ap 2017

LARGE MALLET PUTTERS color *Golf Magazine* v59 no6 p92 Je 2017

MAX GAME IMPROVEMENT DRIVERS color diag *Golf Magazine* v59 no3 p92 Mr 2017

MAX GAME IMPROVEMENT IRONS color *Golf Magazine* v59 no4 p117 Ap 2017

MIDSIZE MALLET PUTTERS color *Golf Magazine* v59 no6 p88 Je 2017

SWING SET color *Golf Magazine* v59 no3 p96 Mr 2017

THIS MONTH: DRIVERS color *Golf Magazine* v59 no3 p72 Mr 2017

THIS MONTH: Fairway Woods + Hybrids color *Golf Magazine* v59 no5 p81 My 2017

THIS MONTH: Irons! color *Golf Magazine* v59 no4 p103 Ap 2017

THIS MONTH: Putters + Wedges color *Golf Magazine* v59 no6 p83 Je 2017

WEDGES color *Golf Magazine* v59 no6 p98 Je 2017

DeeCee, Ravi

INDIAN AUTHORS AT SIBF bw color *Publishers Weekly* v263 no43 p(Sp)18 O 24 2016

Deeds Not Words (Short story)

DEEDS NOT WORDS T. HADLEY bw color *Atlantic* v319 no5 p88 Je 2017

Deedy, Carmen Agra

A LOVE ACQUIRED bw *Literacy Today (2411-7862)* v34 no5 p32 Mr/Ap 2017

Deek, Jasline

Wild emmer genome architecture and diversity elucidate wheat evolution and domestication color *Science* v357 no6346 p93 Jl 7 2017

Deeley, Cat

CAT HOUSE D. Keeps color *InStyle* p22 Home & Design 2016

Deelman, Ewa

Enhancing reproducibility for computational methods bibl color *Science* v354 no6317 p1240 D 9 2016

Deelman, P. W.

Strong coupling of a single electron in silicon to a microwave photon bibl graph *Science* v355 no6321 p1 Ja 13 2017

Deem, Megan

"I love looking a little disheveled" color *Glamour* v115 no5 p74 My 2017

SCENT OF STYLE color *O, The Oprah Magazine* p67 S 2017

DEEMER, BRIDGET R.

Greenhouse Gas Emissions from Reservoir Water Surfaces: A New Global Synthesis *BioScience* v66 no11 p949 N 1 2016

Deemyad, Shanti

Quantum and isotope effects in lithium metal color diag graph *Science* v356 no6344 p1254 Je 23 2017

Deen, Mark

Does Macron Hold the Key to Merkel's Heart? color *Bloomberg Businessweek* no4515 p26 Mr 20 2017

Give This Man A Party color *Bloomberg Businessweek* no4520 p27 My 1 2017

Thatcherism Redux in France bw color *Bloomberg Businessweek* no4502 p21 D 5 2016

Deen, Paula, 1947-

I Feel Bad About Paula Deen A. MACLIN *O, The Oprah Magazine* p145 My 2017

DEEN, SHULEM

Schemes for Living: An Isaac and Abraham reboot looks at a shady side of real estate *New York Times Book Review* p14 Jl 9 2017

Deep brain stimulation

Toward a targeted treatment for addiction M. C. Creed color diag *Science* v357 no6350 p464 Ag 4 2017

Deep diving

See also

Scuba diving

Deep Dive L. SCHLEY color *Discover* v38 no4 p14 My 2017

Not Breathing R. Bradley *New York Times Magazine* p16 Ja 1 2017

SNORKEL WITH SHARKS A. HALPERN color *Wired* v25 no10 p38 O 2017

Deep in the Heart of Texas (TV program)

Dave Chappelle's Stand-up Comedy Specials R. Rahman color *Entertainment Weekly* no1459 p53 Mr 31 2017

Deep learning (Machine learning)

Deep Driving C. Reiley *MIT Technology Review* v119 no6 p10 N/D 2016

Deep Learning Will Radically Change the Ways We Interact with Technology A. Singh bw color diag *Harvard Business Review Digital Articles* p2 Ja 30 2017

ENTREPRENEURS W. Knight, A. Regalado et al color il *MIT Technology Review* v120 no5 p48 S/O 2017

The Tech Trends You Can't Ignore in 2015 A. Webb *Harvard Business Review Digital Articles* p2 Ja 5 2015

WHAT'S EVERYBODY SO AFRAID OF? A. Teller color *Popular Mechanics* p72 N 2017

Deep-sea corals

Deep-sea corals feel the flow Yusuke Yokoyama and T. M. Esat bibl color *Science* v354 no6312 p550 N 4 2016

Deep-sea fisheries

A New Eye on Deep-Sea Fisheries L. Lippsett *Oceanus* v52 no1 p23 Summ 2016

Deep space

Seeking unexpected worlds L. Grossman color *Science News* v192 no6 p22 O 14 2017

Deep Space Industries Inc.

Luxembourg eyes asteroid mining *Science* v354 no6313 p686 N 11 2016

Deep Space Network

Deep Space Network glitches worry scientists P. Voosen color *Science* v353 no6307 p1477 S 30 2016

Deep Water (Film)

The SAILING SCENE E. Mulrain, S. Mergens et al color *Sail* v48 no7 p6 Jl 2017

Deep Water (TV program)

Murder Most Foul D. ANDERSON-MINSHALL color *Advocate* no1090 p57 Ap 2017

Deeper Understanding, A (Music)

SONGS FROM THE HEART D. Hyman cartoon color *Esquire* p45 S 2017

WHAT TO STREAM color *Entertainment Weekly* no1480 p49 S 1 2017

DeepMind Technologies Ltd.

Making AI Smarter, Faster W. Knight *MIT Technology Review* v120 no1 p22 Ja/F 2017

Deepwater Horizon (Film)

Blowed Up J. PODHORETZ color *Weekly Standard* v22 no7 p39 O 24 2016

Deepwater Horizon A. Lane *New Yorker* v92 no34 p15 O 24 2016

Deepwater Horizon Brings Life to Oil Tragedy S. Zacharek color *Time* v188 no14 p57 O 10 2016

DEEPWATER HORIZON D. Vaughn color *Sound & Vision* v82 no5 p65 Je 2017

IN DEEP A. LANE cartoon *New Yorker* v92 no32 p108 O 10 2016

Mark Wahlberg S. Lansky color *Time* v188 no14 p57 O 10 2016

THAT'S A WRAP L. LEBLANC-BERRY *Louisiana Life* v37 no2 p14 N/D 2016

Deepwater Wind LLC

Winds of Change color *Earth Island Journal* v32 no1 p5 Spr 2017

Deepwater Wind LLC—Officials & employees

WIND ON THE WATER B. Dumaine color diag map *Fortune* v175 no4 p184 Mr 15 2017

Deer

See also

Caribou

Stags (Deer)

Chew Velvet D. L. NG color *Field & Stream* v122 no3 p8 Ag 2017

FOOD-PLOT Rx NOCTURNAL BUCKS G. Almy color *Field & Stream* v122 no4 pW8 S 2017

in a snap color *Canadian Geographic* v136 no6 p19 D 2016

IN THE SHADOW OF DEATH E. Freedman color *Earth Island Journal* v32 no1 p42 Spr 2017

MAKE IT LAST T. HANSEN color *Outdoor Life* v224 no7 p28 S 2017

Stunted Growth G. Almy color *Field & Stream* v122 no5 pW5 O 2017

Watch: The Bachelorette A. WUNDERMAN color *Backpacker* p22 S 2017

Deer behavior

LUNAR BUCKS T. EDENFIELD and A. McKEAN color graph *Outdoor Life* v224 no5 p87 Je/Jl 2017

REAL-WORLD RUT [Cover story] M. KENYON color *Outdoor Life* v224 no9 p39 N 2017

Woods Rx: Overexposure G. Almy color *Field & Stream* v122 no3 pW9 Ag 2017

Deer control

Woods Rx: Overexposure G. Almy color *Field & Stream* v122 no3 pW9 Ag 2017

Deer farming

PISSED OFF A. Davidson color *New Yorker* v93 no29 p41 S 25 2017

Deer hunters

The Big Bully S. Bestul color *Field & Stream* v122 no3 pW1 Ag 2017

Busted! G. Almy color *Field & Stream* v122 no4 pW11 S 2017

Calling All Bucks T. J. Peterson color *Field & Stream* v122 no5 pW9 O 2017

Chase the Rut S. Bestul color *Field & Stream* v122 no5 pW11 O 2017

CRAZY FOR THE RUT M. Kenyon color *Outdoor Life* v223 no9 p44 N 2016

Fresh Takes S. Bestul color *Field & Stream* v122 no6 pW1 N 2017

Make a Mega Mock Scrape S. Bestul color *Field & Stream* v122 no5 pW7 O 2017

NO REGRETS W. Brantley color *Field & Stream* v122 no4 p30 S 2017

ON THE TRAIL B. Heavey cartoon *Field & Stream* v121 no7 p114 D 2016/Ja 2017

Small Wonders S. Bestul color *Field & Stream* v122 no3 pW5 Ag 2017

Stop That Buck! S. Bestul color *Field & Stream* v122 no6 pW4 N 2017

THE TAGGED-OUT DEER HUNTER'S GUIDE TO FALL [Cover story] W. Brantley, J. Cermele et al color *Field & Stream* v122 no6 p59 N 2017

Deer hunting

See also

Mule deer hunting

White-tailed deer hunting

84 Great Days A. Licata color *Field & Stream* v121 no6 p8 N 2016

AT HOME IN THE TIMBER H. BLOOD color *Outdoor Life* v224 no1 p42 D 2016/Ja 2017

THE BEST DAYS OF THE Rut [Cover story] S. BESTUL color *Field & Stream* v122 no6 p37 N 2017

The Big Bully S. Bestul color *Field & Stream* v122 no3 pW1 Ag

2017

BLOOD SWEAT & DEER [Cover story] S. Bestul and D. Hurteau color *Field & Stream* v121 no7 p44 D 2016/Ja 2017

BRIEFLY *New York State Conservationist* v72 no2 p28 O 2017

Busted! G. Almy color *Field & Stream* v122 no4 pW11 S 2017

Calling All Bucks T. J. Peterson color *Field & Stream* v122 no5 pW9 O 2017

The Call of the Wild D. Myers color *Field & Stream* v121 no7 p50 D 2016/Ja 2017

Chase the Rut S. Bestul color *Field & Stream* v122 no5 pW11 O 2017

Chew Velvet D. L. NG color *Field & Stream* v122 no3 p8 Ag 2017

DEER of the YEAR color *Outdoor Life* v224 no7 p49 S 2017

DEKE ATTACK D. HURTEAU bw color *Field & Stream* v122 no5 p16 O 2017

THE DISAPPEARING BACK FORTY--and Long Island's rising deer population A. Baio *New York State Conservationist* v72 no2 p17 O 2017

DOG DAYS color *Field & Stream* v122 no2 p83 Je/Jl 2017

DOUBLE TROUBLE M. SCOTT bw color *Outdoor Life* v224 no1 p44 D 2016/Ja 2017

DREAM LAND W. BRANTLEY color *Field & Stream* v122 no2 p92 Je/Jl 2017

EEB AND SCOOB J. ARTERBURN *Outdoor Life* v224 no3 p78 Ap 2017

Extreme Success G. Almy color *Field & Stream* v121 no6 pW1 N 2016

THE FAST TRACK R. STUART color *Outdoor Life* v224 no1 p46 D 2016/Ja 2017

THE FIXER B. HEAVEY color *Field & Stream* v122 no6 p90 N 2017

The Four-Day Deer Drive M. Hellickson cartoon color *Field & Stream* v121 no7 p52 D 2016/Ja 2017

FREE-RANGE A. McKEAN color *Outdoor Life* v224 no3 p43 Ap 2017

Halloween Treat S. Bestul color *Field & Stream* v122 no5 pW1 O 2017

HARD-EARNED BUCKS C. Kearns color *Field & Stream* v122 no4 p9 S 2017

Hard Times S. Bestul color *Field & Stream* v122 no4 pW1 S 2017

The Hill Workout J. Schefler cartoon color *Field & Stream* v121 no7 p46 D 2016/Ja 2017

Hone Sweet Hone S. Bestul color *Field & Stream* v122 no3 pB4 Ag 2017

Hot Spots G. Almy color *Field & Stream* v122 no3 pB1 Ag 2017

How to Be an Islander K. MALMO *Sierra* v102 no4 p60 Jl/Ag 2017

THE KNOCKDOWN MYTH R. SPOMER color *Outdoor Life* v224 no8 p26 O 2017

The Long (Cold!) Vigil G. Greenwalt bw color *Field & Stream* v121 no7 p54 D 2016/Ja 2017

Make a Mega Mock Scrape S. Bestul color *Field & Stream* v122 no5 pW7 O 2017

MAKE THIS YOUR FUNNEST DEER SEASON EVER T. HANSEN and D. McDOUGAL cartoon color *Outdoor Life* v224 no8 p35 O 2017

NO REGRETS W. Brantley color *Field & Stream* v122 no4 p30 S 2017

ONE BUCK, MANY LESSONS T. HANSEN color *Outdoor Life* v224 no8 p22 O 2017

THE ONES THAT GOT AWAY cartoon color *Outdoor Life* v223 no9 p54 N 2016

ON THE TRAIL B. Heavey cartoon *Field & Stream* v121 no7 p114 D 2016/Ja 2017

PARADISE FOUND A. McKEAN and A. ROBINSON color *Outdoor Life* v224 no1 p60 D 2016/Ja 2017

The Perfect-Plot Ambush J. Simpson bw cartoon *Field & Stream* v121 no7 p49 D 2016/Ja 2017

THE Perfect SHOOTER C. KEARNS color *Field & Stream* v121 no6 p67 N 2016

PRAIRIE PRIZE D. Draper cartoon *Field & Stream* v121 no6 p32 N 2016

Read the Beans S. Bestul color *Field & Stream* v122 no4 pW5 S 2017

SET THE STAGE T. Faulkner color *Outdoor Life* v223 no9 pH9 N 2016

Seven BEST DAYS of The Rut S. BESTUL color map *Field & Stream* v121 no6 p39 N 2016

Small Wonders S. Bestul color *Field & Stream* v122 no3 pW5 Ag 2017

STATE OF THE DEER RIFLE J. B. Snow color *Outdoor Life* v223 no9 p71 N 2016

Stop That Buck! S. Bestul color *Field & Stream* v122 no6 pW4 N 2017

THE TAGGED-OUT DEER HUNTER'S GUIDE TO FALL [Cover story] W. Brantley, J. Cermele et al color *Field & Stream* v122 no6 p59 N 2017

TARNISHED TROPHIES J. ARTERBURN *Outdoor Life* v224 no5 p102 Je/Jl 2017

Tornado Watch G. Almy color *Field & Stream* v122 no3 pW11 Ag 2017

The Track Attack R. Flannery color *Field & Stream* v121 no7 p47 D 2016/Ja 2017

TRACKS: How many lives intersect our own, just out of view? G. LEGLER color *Orion Magazine* v36 no1 p54 Ja/F 2017

TRANSITION SEASON T. HANSEN color *Outdoor Life* v224 no8 pB1 O 2017

THE TRUE North T. E. Nickens color *Field & Stream* v122 no5 p66 O 2017

THE VANISHING [Cover story] J. SULLIVAN color *Field & Stream* v122 no6 p64 N 2017

WHEN YOU SPOOK A BUCK B. VAZNIS color *Outdoor Life* v224 no8 pH13 O 2017

WHERE MONSTERS ROAR A. LICATA color *Field & Stream* v121 no7 p62 D 2016/Ja 2017

Deer hunting—Equipment & supplies

BOMBS AWAY BUCKS G. Bethge color *Outdoor Life* v223 no9 pH12 N 2016

BUCKS' BEDROOMS A. Mckean color *Outdoor Life* v223 no9 p34 N 2016

Deer hunting—Midwest (U.S.)

HOT CHOCOLATE J. Arterburn cartoon *Outdoor Life* v223 no9 p86 N 2016

Ionia County, MI color *Outdoor Life* v223 no9 p7 N 2016

Deer hunting—Psychological aspects

CRAZY FOR THE RUT M. Kenyon color *Outdoor Life* v223 no9 p44 N 2016

Deer hunting—Safety measures

TWO-TIMING WHITE TAILS D. HART color *Outdoor Life* v224 no8 pH8 O 2017

Deer populations

The Challenge of Suburban Deer Management S. Booth-Binczik *New York State Conservationist* v72 no2 p19 O 2017

THE DISAPPEARING BACK FORTY--and Long Island's rising deer population A. Baio *New York State Conservationist* v72 no2 p17 O 2017

YEAR OF THE GIANT S. Bestul color graph *Field & Stream* v122 no3 p30 Ag 2017

Deer Season (Short story)

DEER SEASON cartoon *New Yorker* v92 no32 p84 O 10 2016

Deer—Accidents

The Doe's Song L. TONINO color *Orion Magazine* v36 no1 p14 Ja/F 2017

Deer—Diseases

THE UNKNOWNS T. HANSEN color *Outdoor Life* v224 no2 p67 F/Mr 2017

Deere & Co.

LET'S MAKE A DEAL D. Mowitz *Successful Farming* v114 no13 p32 D 2016

POCKET PRICE GUIDE: Dealer Prices on Disk Rippers *Successful Farming* v115 no12 p39 O 2017

RECEIVER REBOOT A. McConnell and L. Bedord *Successful Farming* v115 no1 p32 Ja 2017

UNDERSTANDING WORKING FLUIDS: EVERYTHING GAS IS NOW RUNNING ON EFI SYSTEMS R. Bohacz *Successful Farming* v115 no11 p26 S 2017

Why John Deere Measures Employee Morale Every Two Weeks B. Power *Harvard Business Review Digital Articles* p2 My 24 2016

Deer—Food

Acorn Alternatives G. Almy color *Field & Stream* v122 no3 pW6 Ag 2017

Tornado Watch G. Almy color *Field & Stream* v122 no3 pW11 Ag 2017

Deerinck, Thomas J.

ChromEMT: Visualizing 3D chromatin structure and compaction in interphase and mitotic cells color *Science* v357 no6349 p370 Jl 28 2017

Deering, Chad

Rapid cooling and cold storage in a silicic magma reservoir recorded in individual crystals color diag graph *Science* v356 no6343 p1154 Je 16 2017

Deering, Kris

Breaking the 4K Barrier color graph *Sound & Vision* v82 no4 p34 My 2017

Deerman, Maddy

SHARP SHOOTING color *Spin to Win Rodeo* v21 no1 p15 Mr 2017

Deer—Population biology

Science for Sale B. LIVESEY color *Walrus* v14 no4 p24 My 2017

Deer—Wounds & injuries

The Doe's Song L. TONINO color *Orion Magazine* v36 no1 p14 Ja/F 2017

Deese, Brian

CLIMATE AND ENERGY POLICY, AT HOME AND ABROAD *Vital Speeches of the Day* v82 no12 p365 D 2016

Paris Isn't Burning color *Foreign Affairs* v96 no4 p83 Jl/Ag 2017

Deetz, Kelley Fanto

Bound to the Fire: How Virginia's Enslaved Cooks Helped Invent American Cuisine *Publishers Weekly* v264 no36 p79 S 4 2017

Dee Williams, Shannen

The lynching that shook the conscience of the world bw *America* v216 no12 p48 My 29 2017

Defa, Dustin Guy

Person to Person *New Yorker* v93 no23 p11 Ag 7 2017

Defecation

A Place to Go E. Royte color diag map *National Geographic* v232 no2 p94 Ag 2017

Defectors

THE TROUBLE WITH DEFECTORS S. Ritter *Harper's Magazine* v334 no2000 p30 Ja 2017

de Felice, Damiano

How Pharma Can Fix Its Reputation and Its Business at the Same Time color *Harvard Business Review Digital Articles* p2 F 3 2017

Defendants

No Jail Over Bail C. J. Ciaramella *Reason* v48 no7 p9 D 2016

Defender truck

The Electric, Hydraulic, Mostly American Truck E. DYER bw color *Popular Mechanics* p15 N 2017

Defenders, The (TV program : 2017)

616 PUBLiC ENEMiES DEFENDERS [Cover story] S. Li color *Entertainment Weekly* no1449 p26 Ja 20 2017

ALEXANDRA THE GREAT S. Li color *Entertainment Weekly* no1474/1475 p78 Jl 21-28 2017

Marvel's The Defenders M. Roffman *TV Guide* v65 no25 p23 Je 2017

Marvel's The Defenders M. ROUSH *TV Guide* v65 no35 p13 Ag 21 2017

Streaming Now: Two Sets of Subversive Heroes D. D'addario color *Time* v190 no8 p51 Ag 28 2017

'The Defenders': Three and a Half Superheroes R. SHEFFIELD color *Rolling Stone* no1294 p24 Ag 24 2017

Defenders of Wildlife (Organization)

THE PANTHER YOU WANT D. KUIPERS color *Orion Magazine* v35 no6 p49 N/D 2016

Defending Your Life (Film)

FEAR NOT *USA Today Magazine* v145 no2860 p64 Ja 2017

Defenouillère, Quentin

The cryo-EM structure of a ribosome–Ski2-Ski3-Ski8 helicase complex bibl color graph *Science* v354 no6318 p1431 D 16 2016

Defense attorneys

DEFENSE OF THE NERDS A. J. VICENS color *Mother Jones* v42 no6 p57 N/D 2017

The Lasting Legacy of a Life Devoted to Loving the Sinner D. V. Drehle color *Time* v190 no5 p31 Jl 31 2017

The Other Wall Trump Hasn't Built T. Schoenberg and S. Pet-

typiece color *Bloomberg Businessweek* no4534 p34 Ag 14 2017

Seeing Both Sides A. Engel *Publishers Weekly* v264 no10 p64 Mr 6 2017

Defense contracts—United States

OPENING ROUND color *MHQ: Quarterly Journal of Military History* v30 no1 p3 Aut 2017

Defense industries

NATO Makes It Rain R. Clough color graph *Bloomberg Businessweek* no4509 p12 Ja 30 2017

Defense industries—News briefs

News B. Manley color *Military History* v34 no5 p8 Ja 2018

Defense industries—United States

DEFENDING YOUR PORTFOLIO J. Wieczner color diag *Fortune* v175 no8 p78 Je 15 2017

Guns and Robots: We've paid too much attention to weapons of the future and too little to our forces today T. Donnelly *Hoover Digest: Research & Opinion on Public Policy* no3 p59 Summ 2017

LEARNING TO WORK THE NIGHT SHIFT: With the war effort, suddenly many more factories were working around the clock to fulfill their defense contracts G. Bijur and P. Martin *Saturday Evening Post* v289 no4 p96 Jl/Ag 2017

Defense industry mergers

THE BEST DEFENSE A. GARA color *Forbes* v199 no7 p30 Je 29 2017

Defense procurement

DANGER ZONE P. M. Barrett color diag *Bloomberg Businessweek* no4518 p50 Ap 10 2017

Defense procurement—Government policy

The Liberal Ideological Complex J. BERGNER color *Weekly Standard* v22 no16 p26 D 26 2016

Defensive backs (Football)

DEEP PURPLE B. Baskin color *Sports Illustrated* v125 no13 p30 O 17 2016

How to Win At the SLOTS T. Rohan color diag *Sports Illustrated* v125 no12 p32 O 10 2016

Leading Off color *Sports Illustrated* v125 no14 p10 O 24-31 2016

Defensive backs (Football)—Universities & colleges

SAFETY First A. Benoit color *Sports Illustrated* v126 no12 p38 My 1 2017

Defensive players

Position Change A. Staples and T. Keith color *Sports Illustrated* v126 no8 p20 Mr 20 2017

Deferred Action for Childhood Arrivals (U.S.)

BROKEN DREAMS W. Finnegan cartoon *New Yorker* v93 no28 p17 S 18 2017

Clock Is Ticking for DACA Solution T. J. DONOHUE *Weekly Standard* v23 no5 p14 O 9 2017

A DACA Deal R. VERBRUGGEN color *National Review* v69 no18 p26 O 2 2017

Did You Ever See a Dreamer Walking? B. SWAIM color *Weekly Standard* v23 no2 p9 S 18 2017

A Dream Derailed: Trump Revokes Young Immigrants' Protections M. Rhodan color *Time* v190 no10/11 p36 S 18 2017

Protecting unauthorized immigrant mothers improves their children's mental health J. Hainmueller, D. Lawrence et al diag *Science* v357 no6355 p1041 S 8 2017

Same Old, Same Old color *Weekly Standard* v23 no3 p10 S 25 2017

SANCTUARY CONUNDRUM A. MORETTI color *Phi Kappa Phi Forum* v97 no2 p8 Summ 2017

The Unmaking Of American Dreams S. Kapur, K. Mehrotra et al chart *Bloomberg Businessweek* no4537 p36 S 11 2017

DEFFNER, ELISABETH

Incredible Animal Friends color *National Geographic Kids* no470 p5 My 2017

Incredible Animal Friends *National Geographic Kids* no468 p5 Mr 2017

Defiant Ones, The (Film)

Dre and Jimmy's Excellent Adventure D. BROWNE bw *Rolling Stone* no1291/1292 p16 Jl 13 2017

JIMMY IOVINE Wants to Learn A. Grant color *Esquire* p72 Je/Jl 2017

Defibrillators

See also

Implantable cardioverter-defibrillators

S-ICD The Life-Saving Device That's Made to Last I. Nath color *Maclean's* v129 no40 p65 O 10 2016

Deficit financing

War Profiteering Ain't Physics L. C. GOODMAN *In These Times* v41 no6 p12 Je 2017

De Figueiredo, John M.

Will Federal Employees Work for a President They Disagree With? color graph *Harvard Business Review Digital Articles* p2 F 10 2017

De Filippi, Primavera

What Blockchain Means for the Sharing Economy *Harvard Business Review Digital Articles* p2 Mr 15 2017

Defined benefit pension plans

Rising Pension Liabilities K. Roth *Parks & Recreation* v52 no2 p12 F 2017

Definitions

A Way With Words color *Entertainment Weekly* no1440 p61 N 18 2016

What Is a Robot, Anyway? H. J. Wilson *Harvard Business Review Digital Articles* p2 Ap 15 2015

Deflation (Finance)

Fixing the Euro Zone and Reducing Inequality, Without Fleecing the Rich E. Lonergan and M. Blyth *Harvard Business Review Digital Articles* p2 Ja 9 2015

Defoe, Daniel, ca. 1661-1731

1659: Island of Despair D. Defoe *Lapham's Quarterly* v10 no1 p29 Wint 2017

DeFoe, Jennifer Kain

Solitude by the Seashore *Yankee* p89 Mr 2017

Deford, Frank, 1938-2017

CONFESSIONS OF A SPORTSWRITER F. Deford color *Sports Illustrated* v126 no16 p68 Je 5 2017

Frank Deford 1938-2017 A. Wolff and T. Keith color *Sports Illustrated* v126 no16 p19 Je 5 2017

Leading Off color *Sports Illustrated* v126 no16 p6 Je 5 2017

DEFORE, JOHN

THAT TIME RYAN ROSS DANCED WITH WINONA RYDER *Texas Monthly* v45 no2 p46 F 2017

Deforestation

Deforestation and Coca Cultivation Rooted in Twentieth-Century Development Projects L. M. DÁVALOS, K. M. SANCHEZ et al *BioScience* v66 no11 p974 N 1 2016

Who will watch the Amazon? E. Stokstad *Science* v356 no6338 p569 My 12 2017

Deformation of surfaces

Inflation-predictable behavior and co-eruption deformation at Axial Seamount S. L. Nooner and W. W. Chadwick Jr. bibl graph map *Science* v354 no6318 p1399 D 16 2016

DeFrancesco, Joey

JOEY DEFRANCESCO REJUVENATED MASTER [Cover story] D. OUELLETTE bw color *Downbeat* v84 no5 p40 My 2017

DeFRANCO, MICHELINE

A WRIGHT HOUSE IN ROCHESTER color *Old House Journal* v45 no3 p24 My 2017

DE FRENNE, PIETER

Combining Biodiversity Resurveys across Regions to Advance Global Change Research *BioScience* v67 no1 p73 Ja 2017

de Frey, Sheri R. Herrera

Why I Use Beneficial Insects For My Fly Control *Horse & Rider* v56 no4 p49 Ap 2017

DeFries, Ruth

Ecosystem management as a wicked problem chart color diag *Science* v356 no6335 p265 Ap 21 2017

A human-driven decline in global burned area chart graph map *Science* v356 no6345 p1356 Je 30 2017

De Fruyt, Filip

Too Much Charisma Can Make Leaders Look Less Effective *Harvard Business Review Digital Articles* p2 S 26 2017

Defy Ventures Inc.

When a Startup Means A Fresh Start A. Popescu color *Bloomberg Businessweek* no4507 p28 Ja 16 2017

de Galarce, Patricia Crain

Trauma and learning in America's classrooms chart color graph *Phi Delta Kappan* v98 no6 p35 Mr 2017

Degas, Edgar, 1834-1917

Degas' Other Woman N. SCHARPING cartoon *Discover* v38 no1

p91 Ja/F 2017

Life at the top S. Kelly cartoon *Magazine Antiques* v184 no1 p124 Ja/F 2017

Degel, Willie

NEW YORK STRIP M. Singer cartoon *New Yorker* v92 no45 p22 Ja 16 2017

DEGEN, BERND

Opportunities for Improved Transparency in the Timber Trade through Scientific Verification *BioScience* v66 no11 p990 N 1 2016

Degen, C. L.

Quantum sensing with arbitrary frequency resolution diag graph *Science* v356 no6340 p837 My 26 2017

DeGeneres, Ellen, 1958-

If You Build It, They Will Come M. BERG bw *Forbes* v199 no7 p102 Je 29 2017

INSIDE ELLEN'S COMING-OUT D. Snierson color *Entertainment Weekly* no1465 p49 My 12 2017

THE POWER OF POP CULTURE: ELLEN DEGENERES CHANGED EVERYTHING, BUT SHE DIDN'T DO IT ALONE D. ANDERSON-MINSHALL color *Advocate* no1091 p83 Je/Jl 2017

Quotable Quotes E. JONG, E. DEGENERES et al bw color *Reader's Digest* v190 no1132 p140 Jl/Ag 2017

Why it's COOL to be KIND [Cover story] E. BRIED color *Good Housekeeping* v265 no3 p85 S 2017

DeGeneres, Ellen, 1958-—Interviews

Ellen's Gone to the Dogs S. Bower color *Good Housekeeping* v265 no1 p122 Jl 2017

Degering, D.

Permanent human occupation of the central Tibetan Plateau in the early Holocene bibl bw color diag *Science* v355 no6320 p1 Ja 6 2017

De Giorgio, Francesco

HOW HORSES THINK bw cartoon color *Equus* no474 p59 Mr 2017

De Giorgio-Schoorl, José

HOW HORSES THINK bw cartoon color *Equus* no474 p59 Mr 2017

DEGIROLAMI, MARC O.

Fake Law color *Weekly Standard* v22 no34 p12 My 15 2017

Deglutition disorders

My husband often doesn't bother to put in his dentures when eating at home. Chunks of food get stuck in his throat from time to time. They eventually pass, but it's still worrisome. Is this dangerous? *Mayo Clinic Health Letter* v35 no5 p8 My 2017

Deglutition disorders—Diagnosis

Choking alert: Strategies for safe swallowing *Harvard Health Letter* v41 no12 p6 O 2016

Deglutition disorders—Risk factors

Choking alert: Strategies for safe swallowing *Harvard Health Letter* v41 no12 p6 O 2016

De Gouw, Jessica, 1988-

The Last Tycoon J. Halterman *TV Guide* v65 no25 p19 Je 2017

De Graaf, Reinier, 1964-—Interviews

Complexity and Candor in Architecture J. MINUTILLO *Architectural Record* v205 no10 p43 O 2017

Degrassi: Next Class (TV program)

DEGRASSI DOES IT AGAIN N. Serrao color *Entertainment Weekly* no1474/1475 p22 Jl 21-28 2017

De Grave, Kurt

Predicting human olfactory perception from chemical features of odor molecules bibl diag graph *Science* v355 no6327 p820 F 24 2017

DeGrazia, Ted, 1909-1982

The Mission in the Sun K. MONTGOMERY *Arizona Highways* v92 no11 p8 N 2016

de Groot, Jerome

Dignity, dance, passion and persecution aplenty *History Today* v67 no4 p61 Ap 2017

De Guerra Camero, Candido—Interviews

'I feel like I'm 20' CANDIDO [Cover story] M. Jackson color *Downbeat* v84 no5 p44 My 2017

DEHAAS, JOSH

BRIDGING THE EAST-WEST GAP [Cover story] color *Maclean's* v129 no44 p44 N 7 2016

De Hamel, Christopher

Antiquarian Dreams: Sometimes it's okay to judge history by its cover H. Hazen *American Scholar* v86 no4 p118 Aut 2017

Meetings with Remarkable Manuscripts: Twelve Journeys into the Medieval World *Publishers Weekly* v264 no32 p61 Ag 7 2017

de Haro, Guillermo

Meet the Teenagers Who Found Their Own Startups *Harvard Business Review Digital Articles* p2 D 5 2016

DeHart, Jason D.

Countering Students' Negative Narratives bw *Education Digest* v83 no3 p4 N 2017

Dehler Yachts GmbH

Dehler 34 Z. Prochazka cartoon color *Sail* v48 no1 p28 Ja 2017

Dehorning

DEHORNING dilemma K. JOHNSTON *Earth Island Journal* v32 no4 p33 Wint 2017

A Rise In Rhino Poaching? K. Samuelson color *Time* v189 no12 p16 Ap 3 2017

Dehouck, E.

Redox stratification of an ancient lake in Gale crater, Mars color *Science* v356 no6341 p922 Je 1 2017

Dehumanization

LIVING BY The Word *Christian Century* v134 no13 p18 Je 21 2017

Dehydration (Physiology)

Dehydration Generation color *Prevention* v69 no7 p8 Jl 2017

DRY RUN C. Barakat and M. Freckleton color *Equus* no476 p24 My 2017

Problem Solved Constipation R. LALIBERTE *Prevention* v69 no9 p24 O 2017

THIRST IS FIRST A. HUTCHINSON color *Runner's World* v52 no7 p20 Ag 2017

the thirsty body C. Maldarelli cartoon diag *Popular Science* v289 no2 p18 Mr/Ap 2017

Dehydration (Physiology)—Treatment

Pedialyte D. Brooks color *New York Times Magazine* p22 Ja 29 2017

Dehydration prevention

Dehydration Generation color *Prevention* v69 no7 p8 Jl 2017

HYDRATE your plate V. Clayton and A. Wolfe color *Yoga Journal* no293 p43 Ag 2017

Keep him well-watered bw color *Horse & Rider* v56 no7 p32 Jl 2017

your no-panic guide to fever K. BAYLESS *Parents* p58 2015

Deichmann, Dirk

Can 10 Minutes of Meditation Make You More Creative? *Harvard Business Review Digital Articles* p2 Ag 29 2017

How Design Thinking Turned One Hospital into a Bright and Comforting Place *Harvard Business Review Digital Articles* p2 D 2 2016

Deighton, John

Companies Like United Need to Cultivate Good Judgment, and Free Their Employees to Use It *Harvard Business Review Digital Articles* p2 Ap 14 2017

Deignan, Tom

Echoes of a Lost Faith color *Commonweal* v144 no8 p40 My 5 2017

A new path for unions color *America* v216 no11 p55 My 15 2017

WHITE TRASH color *America* v215 no12 p33 O 24 2016

DEIGNAN-SCHMIDT, STEVEN R.

A SOLID PLAN GONE AWRY color *Flying* v144 no7 p26 Jl 2017

Dein, Rachel

Natural Instincts H. MARTIN color *Architectural Digest* no6 p58 Je 1 2017

Deines, George

Aquatics Trends *Parks & Recreation* v51 no12 p50 D 2016

Deisseroth, Karl

The form and function of channelrhodopsin diag *Science* v357 no6356 p1111 S 15 2017

Gating of social reward by oxytocin in the ventral tegmental area color graph *Science* v357 no6358 p1406 S 29 2017

Thirst-associated preoptic neurons encode an aversive motivational drive diag *Science* v357 no6356 p1149 S 15 2017

Deitrick, Bernie

Get Healthier il *Consumer Reports* v82 no3 p25 Mr 2017

Deitsch, Richard

THE BEST ØF TELEVISION color *Sports Illustrated* v125 no18 p33 D 5 2016

HOW TO WATCH color *Sports Illustrated* v126 no8 p61 Mr 20 2017

MIKED VICK color *Sports Illustrated* v127 no7 p20 S 4 2017

New VIBRATIONS color *Sports Illustrated* v126 no10 p48 Ap 10 2017

Players Of the Year color *Sports Illustrated* v125 no20 p92 D 19 2016

Political Football color *Sports Illustrated* v125 no13 p18 O 17 2016

Shifting Center color *Sports Illustrated* v126 no5 p25 F 13 2017

VIEW SOME TWOSOME color *Sports Illustrated* v127 no11 p18 O 9 2017

Waiting on the Docs color *Sports Illustrated* v125 no20 p29 D 19 2016

WHO CAN BEAT UCONN? color *Sports Illustrated* v126 no8 p65 Mr 20 2017

DEITZ, PAULA

L'Orfeo Ascending color *Weekly Standard* v22 no30 p36 Ap 10 2017

DeJ Loaf (Performer)

FINALLY FREE E. Fluker color *Essence* v47 no11 p60 Mr 2017

De Jager, Philip L.

Single-cell RNA-seq reveals new types of human blood dendritic cells, monocytes, and progenitors color *Science* v356 no6335 p283 Ap 21 2017

Dejean, Ashley

HACKER, BANKER, SOLDIER, SPY bw color *Mother Jones* v42 no4 p19 Jl/Ag 2017

HACKS, LEAKS, AND TWEETS color *Mother Jones* v42 no4 p22 Jl/Ag 2017

THE KREMLIN'S GREMLINS color *Mother Jones* v42 no4 p20 Jl/Ag 2017

ON KOMPROMAT bw *Mother Jones* v42 no4 p24 Jl/Ag 2017

PUTIN'S LONG GAME color *Mother Jones* v42 no4 p26 Jl/Ag 2017

THE RUSSIAN CONNECTION color *Mother Jones* v42 no4 p16 Jl/Ag 2017

WIKILEAKS' ROLE *Mother Jones* v42 no4 p30 Jl/Ag 2017

YES SHE CAN: WOMEN ARE POWERING TEXAS' PROGRESSIVE COMEBACK *Mother Jones* v42 no5 p28 S/O 2017

de Jesus Sanchez-Gonzalez, Jose

Genomic estimation of complex traits reveals ancient maize adaptation to temperate North America diag *Science* v357 no6350 p512 Ag 4 2017

de Jesus Veiga Carim, M.

Persistent effects of pre-Columbian plant domestication on Amazonian forest composition bibl chart graph map *Science* v355 no6328 p925 Mr 3 2017

DeJong, David H.

American Indian Treaties: A Guide to Ratified and Unratified Colonial, United States, State, Foreign, and Intertribal Treaties and Agreements, 1607-1911 J. C. Jurss *American Indian Quarterly* v41 no2 p185 Spr 2017

DeJong, E.

Jupiter's interior and deep atmosphere: The initial pole-to-pole passes with the Juno spacecraft [Cover story] color graph *Science* v356 no6340 p821 My 26 2017

de Jong, Kees H.

An interactive three-dimensional digital atlas and quantitative database of human development bibl color graph *Science* v354 no6315 paag0053-1 N 25 2016

de Jong, S. J.

Observation of a large-scale anisotropy in the arrival directions of cosmic rays above 8 × 1018 eV *Science* v357 no6357 p1266 S 22 2017

DeJonge, Kendall

THIRSTY CROPS RUN A TEMP D. Mowitz *Successful Farming* v114 no10 p48 O 2016

de Jonge, Peter

THE NOTES OF PATRICK MODIANO *Harper's Magazine* v334 no2000 p77 Ja 2017

THE U.S. OPeN WONDeR YEAR [Cover story] *New York Times Magazine* p31 Ag 27 2017

Dejong-Hughes, Jodi

SOIL STEALER: TILLAGE IS A STEALTHY ERODER THAT ROBS YOUR PRECIOUS TOPSOIL. HERE'S HOW TO FIX IT G. GULLICKSON *Successful Farming* v115 no12 p44 O 2017

DeKalb County (Ga.)

MORE THAN MURALS D. Michaud *Atlanta* v57 no5 p28 S 2017

de Kanter, Froukje E. C.

An interactive three-dimensional digital atlas and quantitative database of human development bibl color graph *Science* v354 no6315 paag0053-1 N 25 2016

De Keersmaeker, Anne Teresa, 1960-

SOUND WAVES A. ROSS cartoon *New Yorker* v92 no35 p96 O 31 2016

De Keyser, J.

Xenon isotopes in 67P/Churyumov-Gerasimenko show that comets contributed to Earth's atmosphere diag *Science* v356 no6342 p1069 Je 9 2017

Dekker, Cees

Treadmilling by FtsZ filaments drives peptidoglycan synthesis and bacterial cell division bibl graph *Science* v355 no6326 p739 F 17 2017

Deklotz, Patricia

The Energizing Impact of Micro-Credentials in Kettle Moraine *Education Digest* v82 no9 p24 My 2017

De Koff, Derek

Waechter Architecture bw color *Architectural Record* v204 no12 p40 D 2016

Del Sol automobile

Revolutionary war [Cover story] J. Gall chart color diag *Car & Driver* v63 no2 p36 Ag 2017

de Laat, Joost

Cash for carbon: A randomized trial of payments for ecosystem services to reduce deforestation bw chart *Science* v357 no6348 p267 Jl 21 2017

De La Barrera, Rafael

Rapid development of a DNA vaccine for Zika virus bibl graph *Science* v354 no6309 p237 O 14 2016

De la Bédoyère, Guy

Praetorian: The Rise and Fall of Rome's Imperial Bodyguard R. A. Gabriel *Military History* v34 no2 p72 Jl 2017

De Laclos, Pierre Choderlos

Eternal Quadrangle C. YOUNG color *Weekly Standard* v22 no16 p37 D 26 2016

Delacroix, Kiara—Interviews

Sex, Power, and Posting L. Dunham color *Glamour* v115 no7 p89 Jl 2017

De la Cruz, Cesar

FREEZE FRAME WITH CESAR DE LA CUZ C. Toy color *Spin to Win Rodeo* v21 no3 p44 My 2017

De la Cruz, Jon

2017 KITCHEN OF THE YEAR K. Renda color *House Beautiful* v159 no8 p76 O 2017

DELAHAY, RICHARD J.

Using Social Network Measures in Wildlife Disease Ecology, Epidemiology, and Management *BioScience* v67 no3 p245 Mr 2017

Delahaye automobile

THE FALCONER DODICI B. Gillogly color *Hot Rod* v70 no1 p76 Ja 2017

Delaire, Olivier

Anomalously low electronic thermal conductivity in metallic vanadium dioxide bibl graph *Science* v355 no6323 p371 Ja 27 2017

Delamarter, Andrew

The Darknet: A Quick Introduction for Business Leaders *Harvard Business Review Digital Articles* p2 D 9 2016

de Lancie, John

INSPIRATION, SCI-FI, and the IMPORTANCE of Driving Your Own Bus *Humanist* v76 no6 p33 N/D 2016

DeLand, Lauren

AMALIE JAKOBSEN color *Art in America* v104 no10 p154 N 2016

Art Institute of Chicago color *Art in America* v105 no6 p140 Je/Jl 2017

KADER ATTIA color *Art in America* v105 no5 p134 My 2017

TANIA PÉREZ CÓRDOVA color *Art in America* p126 O 2017

DELANEY, REBECCA

bus behavior *Parents* v91 no9 p170 S 2016

Delaney, Rob, 1977-

Rob Delaney J. Crelin color *Current Biography* v77 no10 p21 O 2016

Delaney, Rob, 1977-—Interviews

CATASTROPHE A. D'Arminio *TV Guide* v64 no15 p48 Ap 4 2016

Delange, Titia

Not just Salk color *Science* v357 no6356 p1105 S 15 2017

de Langhe, Bart

Consumers Don't Understand the Relationship Between Time and Speed *Harvard Business Review Digital Articles* p2 N 3 2015

High Online User Ratings Don't Actually Mean You're Getting a Quality Product *Harvard Business Review Digital Articles* p2 Jl 4 2016

Linear Thinking in a Nonlinear World bw chart diag graph img *Harvard Business Review* v95 no3 p130 My/Je 2017

Delanoue, Renald

Drosophila insulin release is triggered by adipose Stunted ligand to brain Methuselah receptor bibl graph *Science* v353 no6307 p1553 S 30 2016

DELANY, ALEX

prep school bw color *Bon Appetit* v62 no10 p105 O 2017

prep school bw color *Bon Appetit* v62 no4 p112 Ap 2017

This Month in Beer color *Bon Appetit* no8 p24 Ag 2017

Delany, Dana

Dana Delany M. Rochlin color *AARP: The Magazine* v59 no6A p19 O/N 2016

de la O., Marsha

A NATURAL HISTORY OF LIGHT *New Yorker* v92 no41 p38 D 12 2016

DELAP, LEANNE

Cinnamon twirl color *Maclean's* v129 no44 p72 N 7 2016

Size matters color *Maclean's* v129 no44 p60 N 7 2016

Delap, Lucy

Who Had It So Good? *History Today* v67 no3 p56 Mr 2017

De la Peña, Matt

Matt de la Peña C. Mari color *Current Biography* v78 no6 p35 Je 2017

de la Rasilla, Marco

The growth pattern of Neandertals, reconstructed from a juvenile skeleton from El Sidrón (Spain) color graph *Science* v357 no6357 p1282 S 22 2017

Neandertal and Denisovan DNA from Pleistocene sediments bw color *Science* v356 no6338 p605 My 12 2017

de la Roche, Maike

Aging increases cell-to-cell transcriptional variability upon immune stimulation color diag graph *Science* v355 no6332 p1433 Mr 31 2017

De la Rosa, Swann—Interviews

AFTER THE BARRE J. KINDELA chart color *Muscle & Performance* v8 no12 p32 D 2016

DeLarverié, Stormé, 1920-2014

Club King H. Als cartoon *New Yorker* v92 no48 p6 F 6 2017

DE LA SANCHA, NOÉ U.

Getting Back to the Basics: Museum Collections and Satellite Imagery Are Critical to Analyzing Species Diversity *BioScience* v67 no5 p405 My 2017

De La Torre, Hector

How to Design a Corporate Wellness Plan That Actually Works *Harvard Business Review Digital Articles* p2 Mr 31 2016

DeLaunay, James

Gamma rays linked to fast radio burst C. CROCKETT color *Science News* v190 no12 p11 D 10 2016

Delauro, Rosa L., 1943-

Nevertheless, She Persisted R. BACON *Ms.* v27 no2 p45 Summ 2017

De Lavallade, Carmen

Companion Pieces G. Santoro bw color *AARP: The Magazine* v60 no3A p64 Ap/My 2017

Delaware

Paddys Day Tours America S. Andersen *Arabian Horse World* v57 no1 p147 O 2016

Delay of gratification

Cutest Advent Calendar color *Good Housekeeping* v263 no6 p163 D 2016

Delayed onset muscle soreness

How Sore Is TOO SORE? N. Clancy color *O, The Oprah Magazine* p72 Jl 2017

Delayed retirement

Age Boom D. ROTHKOPF cartoon *Foreign Policy* no222 p66 Ja/F 2017

Delbo, Marco

Identification of a primordial asteroid family constrains the original planetesimal population diag graph *Science* v357 no6355 p1026 S 8 2017

Delborne, Jason A.

Precaution and governance of emerging technologies bibl color *Science* v354 no6313 p710 N 11 2016

Delbourgo, James

Between Fable and Fact: A biography of a pioneering natural scientist B. BOUCHER *New York Times Book Review* p9 S 10 2017

Collecting for the Glory of God J. Uglow color *New York Review of Books* v64 no15 p34 O 12 2017

Del Carlo, John

JOHN DEL CARLO F. P. Driscoll *Opera News* v81 no7 p58 Ja 2017

del Carmen Martínez, María

IN SEARCH OF THE Cuban Paso Fino color *Equus* no474 p51 Mr 2017

Del Cerro Santamaria, Gerardo

PROFESSIONAL GRADE: Curious how the experts live? Take a look inside four kitchens belonging to people who design or work in them for a living J. Barger *Washingtonian Magazine* v53 no1 p161 O 2017

DEL-COLLE, ANDREW

Four Powerful Pickups cartoon color *Men's Health* v32 no4 p30 My 2017

del Coro Arizmendi, María

Ten policies for pollinators bibl color *Science* v354 no6315 p975 N 25 2016

Del Deo, Josephine, 1925-2016

JOSEPHINE DEL DEO G. COOK *New York Times Magazine* p44 D 25 2016

Delegated legislation

See also

Executive orders

War & emergency legislation

Gun Permittees Challenge Park Firearm Regulations J. C. Kozlowski *Parks & Recreation* v52 no3 p24 Mr 2017

Delegated legislation—United States

THE PEOPLE NOBODY WANTS F. J. Taylor *Saturday Evening Post* v289 no3 p34 My/Je 2017

Delegation of authority

See also

Employee empowerment

6 Myths About Empowering Employees D. Marquet *Harvard Business Review Digital Articles* p2 My 27 2015

Case Study: When You're Successful, Stretched Too Thin, and Indispensable A. Beard *Harvard Business Review Digital Articles* p2 Ag 9 2017

For Delegation to Work, It Has to Come with Coaching S. Nawaz *Harvard Business Review Digital Articles* p2 My 5 2016

Research: Delegating More Can Increase Your Earnings T. N. Hubbard *Harvard Business Review Digital Articles* p2 Ag 12 2016

Research on Delegating Shows How Uncomfortable We Are Making Choices for Others M. Steffel, E. F. Williams et al *Harvard Business Review Digital Articles* p2 Ag 30 2016

Startups Can't Revolve Around Their Founders If They Want to Succeed R. Gulati and A. DeSantola *Harvard Business Review Digital Articles* p2 Mr 4 2016

Superbosses Aren't Afraid to Delegate Their Biggest Decisions S. Finkelstein *Harvard Business Review Digital Articles* p2 Ag 24 2016

Why Delegating Tasks Before a Vacation Never Works C. A. Walker *Harvard Business Review Digital Articles* p2 Ag 2 2017

WHY WE PASS THE BUCK *Harvard Business Review* v94 no12 p26 D 2016

DE LEO, GIULIO

The Resilience of Marine Ecosystems to Climatic Disturbances *BioScience* v67 no3 p208 Mr 2017

de León, Concepción

31 Days of Giving chart color *Glamour* v114 no12 p192 D 2016

How I Found My Purpose color *Glamour* v114 no11 p138 N 2016

How to Flip Your Money Script color *Glamour* v115 no5 p124 My 2017

How We Communicate Now bw color *Glamour* v115 no3 p52 Mr 2017

Power Move color *Glamour* v114 no12 p63 D 2016

DeLeon, Jian

Vision Statements bw color *Conde Nast Traveler* v51 no11 p60 D 2016

De León, Kevin

BLUE REPUBLIC M. TINOCO *Mother Jones* v42 no4 p38 Jl/Ag 2017

Delerue, Fabien

Site-specific phosphorylation of tau inhibits amyloid-β toxicity in Alzheimer's mice bibl graph *Science* v354 no6314 p904 N 18 2016

de Léséleuc, Sylvain

An atom-by-atom assembler of defect-free arbitrary two-dimensional atomic arrays bibl bw diag graph *Science* v354 no6315 p1021 N 25 2016

Delevingne, Cara, 1992-

Bazaar's Best-Dressed LIST color *Harper's Bazaar* no3657 p124 O 2017

The Bullseye M. Snetiker color *Entertainment Weekly* no1457/1458 p108 Mr 17 2017

Cara Delevingne color *InStyle* v24 no1 p66 Ja 2017

CARA'S COMEBACK L. McCarthy color *Harper's Bazaar* no3651 p283 Mr 2017

Face of Change [Cover story] A. Aboah bw color *Glamour* no8 p124 Ag 2017

On Rebels and Role Models K. H. Biloxi, E. Wilson et al color *Glamour* v115 no10 p34 O 2017

The Society PAGE *Interview* v46 no8 p60 O 2016

Delevingne, Poppy

MODERN ENGLISH D. BLASBERG color *Architectural Digest* no11 p152 N 1 2017

Suit Yourself E. Wilson color *InStyle* v24 no6 p42 Je 2017

Deleyto, Celestino

Imagining Hollywood from the Outside In: A Conversation with Celestino Deleyto on From Tinseltown to Bordertown: Los Angeles on Film R. Longo *Film Quarterly* v70 no4 p118 Summ 2017

Delfs, Arne

It's Merkel 3, Schulz 0 In German Campaign color *Bloomberg Businessweek* no4523 p16 My 22 2017

Delftware

Robert D. Aronson H. MARTIN color *Architectural Digest* v74 no3 p30 Mr 2017

Delgadillo, Natalie

Discord: Can states and cities really uphold the Paris climate accord on their own? color *Governing* v30 no11 p20 Ag 2017

Delgado, Francisco

Contemporary Identities and Cultural Innovation *American Indian Quarterly* v40 no3 p283 Summ 2016

DELGADO, LUISA E.

Global Disparity in Ecological Science: A Complex Systems Perspective *BioScience* v67 no2 p105 F 2017

Human Well-Being and Historical Ecosystems: The Environmentalist's Paradox Revisited *BioScience* v67 no1 p5 Ja 2017

Delgado, Michael

Estimating economic damage from climate change in the United States color graph *Science* v356 no6345 p1362 Je 30 2017

Delgado, Sandra

HAVANA RESURRECTED B. GOLDEN color *Chicago* v66 no4 p42 Ap 2017

Delgado-Salinas, Alfonso

Forest conservation: Humans' handprints bibl color *Science* v355 no6324 p466 F 3 2017

Forest conservation: Remember Gran Chaco bibl color *Science* v355 no6324 p465 F 3 2017

Delgass, W. Nicholas

Dynamic multinuclear sites formed by mobilized copper ions in NOx selective catalytic reduction bw color diag graph *Science* v357 no6354 p898 S 1 2017

Delgaudio, Derek

Friends with a Needle and Thread can Save a Marriage M. S. Eddy *Stage Directions* v30 no8 p2 Ag 2017

DELGIUDICE, GLENN

An Unparalleled Opportunity for an Important Ecological Study *BioScience* v67 no10 p875 O 2017

DelGuidice, Mike

The Piano Man's Apprentice A. GREENE color *Rolling Stone* no1272 p24 O 20 2016

Delhomme, Benoît

Benoit DELHOMME M. MULLEN *Interview* v47 no2 p70 Mr 2017

DELHOMME, P. J.

BLADE CITY color *Outdoor Life* v224 no6 p58 Ag 2017

CHEAP ADVENTURES cartoon color *Outdoor Life* v224 no4 p30 My 2017

Deliberation

Authoritarian Deliberation in China Baogang He and M. E. Warren *Daedalus* v146 no3 p155 Summ 2017

Collusion in Restraint of Democracy: Against Political Deliberation I. Shapiro *Daedalus* v146 no3 p77 Summ 2017

Deliberation & the Challenge of Inequality A. Siu *Daedalus* v146 no3 p119 Summ 2017

Political Deliberation & the Adversarial Principle B. Manin *Daedalus* v146 no3 p39 Summ 2017

Deliberative democracy

Applying Deliberative Democracy in Africa: Uganda's First Deliberative Polls J. S. Fishkin, R. W. Mayega et al *Daedalus* v146 no3 p140 Summ 2017

Can Democracy be Deliberative & Participatory? The Democratic Case for Political Uses of Mini-Publics C. Lafont *Daedalus* v146 no3 p85 Summ 2017

Deliberative Citizens, (Non)Deliberative Politicians: A Rejoinder A. Bächtiger and S. Beste *Daedalus* v146 no3 p106 Summ 2017

Deliberative Democracy as Open, Not (Just) Representative Democracy H. Landemore *Daedalus* v146 no3 p51 Summ 2017

Deliberative Democracy in the Trenches C. R. Sunstein *Daedalus* v146 no3 p129 Summ 2017

Inequality is Always in the Room: Language & Power in Deliberative Democracy A. Lupia and A. Norton *Daedalus* v146 no3 p64 Summ 2017

Introduction J. S. Fishkin and J. Mansbridge *Daedalus* v146 no3 p6 Summ 2017

Twelve Key Findings in Deliberative Democracy Research N. Curato, J. S. Dryzek et al *Daedalus* v146 no3 p28 Summ 2017

DeLiberto, Thomas J.

Role for migratory wild birds in the global spread of avian influenza H5N8 bibl graph map *Science* v354 no6309 p213 O 14 2016

Delicatessens

Square Meal G. SNYDER *Los Angeles Magazine* v62 no9 p107 S 2017

Delight (Poem)

DELIGHT A. R. Ammons *Harper's Magazine* no2007 p75 Ag 2017

Deligny, O.

Observation of a large-scale anisotropy in the arrival directions of cosmic rays above 8×10^{18} eV *Science* v357 no6357 p1266 S 22 2017

DeLillo, Don, 1936-

Frozen Stiff A. GREENWALD *Commentary* v142 no1 p59 Jl/Ag 2016

THE ITCH D. DELILLO cartoon *New Yorker* v93 no23 p58 Ag 7 2017

De Lima, Leila

the challengers bw *Foreign Policy* no221 p58 N/D 2016

Duterte's Fiercest Critic Finds Herself In Jail N. Jenkins color *Time* v189 no9 p11 Mr 13 2017

Delinquent behavior

The Problem with Measuring Effects of Delinquent Peers in Education—and How to Get Around It T. AHN and J. TROGDON *Education Digest* v82 no9 p18 My 2017

Delirium

Disease sleuths unmask deadly encephalitis culprit P. Pulla color *Science* v357 no6349 p344 Jl 28 2017

DELISI, CHARLES

Notes from a Revolution: Lessons from the Human Genome Project *Issues in Science & Technology* v33 no3 p57 Spr 2017

DeLisi, Rick

KICK-ASS CUSTOMER SERVICE chart color graph il img *Harvard Business Review* v95 no1 p110 Ja/F 2017

Deliso, Chris

YUGOSLAVIA'S VERY SECRET SERVICE *History Today* v67 no8 p68 Ag 2017

Delivery (Obstetrics)

See also

Cesarean section

The Baby Spike M. Fischetti and Z. Armstrong diag *Scientific American* v317 no1 p76 Jl 2017

A Mother's Journey A. NADELLA color *Good Housekeeping* v265 no5 p62 N 2017

Delivery of goods

See also

Direct home delivery

Drone aircraft delivery

Big Food Swallows the Meal-Kit Hype J. Alsever color *Fortune* v176 no4 p27 S 15 2017

DINNER IN A BOX M. Leonhardt chart color *Money* v46 no8 p67 S 2017

New Meal Services That Deliver color *Men's Health* v32 no7 p66 S 2017

Delivery of goods (Law)

The Case of the Missing Comma V. GLEMBOCKI *Reader's Digest* v190 no1133 p18 S 2017

A SIX-WORD MY STERY SET IN 2049: THE LAST DELIVERY MAN'S LAST DELIVERY cartoon *Wired* v25 no10 p116 O 2017

Delivery of goods—Management

Wal-Mart Cracks the Whip on Suppliers M. Boyle *Bloomberg Businessweek* no4531 p14 Jl 24 2017

Delizonna, Laura

High-Performing Teams Need Psychological Safety. Here's How to Create It *Harvard Business Review Digital Articles* p2 2017

Dell, Michael, 1965-—Interviews

DELL'S NEW DESTINY R. KARLGAARD color *Forbes* v200 no2 p24 S 5 2017

Dell computers—Evaluation

Dell's futuristic Smart Desk PC will challenge Microsoft's Surface Studio I. PAUL color *PCWorld* p38 D 2016

Go PC! 5 killer MacBook Pro alternatives for disappointed Apple fans [Cover story] B. CHACOS color *PCWorld* p41 D 2016

Dell Inc.

Dell Inspiron 15 7000: A gaming laptop at a decidedly non-gaming price H. DINGMAN color graph *PCWorld* v35 no6 p84 Je 2017

Dell's wild 8K monitor goes on sale with a just-as-stunning price tag I. PAUL color *PCWorld* v35 no5 p41 My 2017

Dell XPS 13 Kaby Lake: Yes, this is the best one so far G. UNG color graph *PCWorld* v35 no1 p67 Ja 2017

What to Expect From the Dell-EMC Deal B. Gomes-Casseres *Harvard Business Review Digital Articles* p2 O 13 2015

Dell Inc.—Finance

DELL'S NEW DESTINY R. KARLGAARD color *Forbes* v200 no2 p24 S 5 2017

Dell Mitchell Architects (Company)

Island Girl T. Anderson and K. O'SHEA-EVANS color *House Beautiful* v159 no4 p43 My 2017

Dell Technologies Inc.

THE GAMBLERS BEHIND TECH'S BIGGEST DEAL EVER M. Lev-ram color *Fortune* v75 no1 p82 Ja 1 2017

DELL'ABATE, GARY

Always Watching color *Popular Mechanics* p38 Mr 2017

Cutting the Cord color *Popular Mechanics* p16 Ap 2017

MY VOICE — ACTIVATED HOUSE color *Popular Mechanics* p70 My 2017

THE ULTIMATE BACKYARD MOVIE SETUP color diag *Popular Mechanics* p97 Jl 2017

What I Learned AT MY Summer Job cartoon *Popular Mechanics* p64 Je 2017

Dellal, Gaby

3 Generations J. Mcgovern color *Entertainment Weekly* no1465

p41 My 12 2017

Dell'Amore, Christine

Shadow Cats color diag map *National Geographic* v231 no2 p104 F 2017

DellaSala, Dominick A.

A global map of roadless areas and their conservation status bibl color graph map *Science* v354 no6318 p1423 D 16 2016

Deller, Adam T.

Spiral density waves in a young protoplanetary disk bibl graph *Science* v353 no6307 p1519 S 30 2016

Deller, J.

Rosetta's comet 67P/Churyumov-Gerasimenko sheds its dusty mantle to reveal its icy nature bibl graph *Science* v354 no6319 p1566 D 23 2016

Surface changes on comet 67P/Churyumov-Gerasimenko suggest a more active past bw graph *Science* v355 no6332 p1392 Mr 31 2017

Delligatti, Jim

The Father of the Big Mac color *Weekly Standard* v22 no14 p3 D 12 2016

Dellner, Tom

Parks Using Technology to Engage and Inspire *Parks & Recreation* v52 no5 p42 My 2017

Reflections on a Career *Parks & Recreation* v52 no3 p44 Mr 2017

Delmarva Peninsula

Find an Empty Beach: There's no need to go far to find a deserted island--they're all along the Delmarva coast B. JENSEN *Washingtonian Magazine* v52 no11 p84 Ag 2017

Del Monte, William A.

WILLIAM A. DEL MONTE J. GERTNER *New York Times Magazine* p24 D 25 2016

Deloitte LLP

Where Minority-Worker Networks Are Passé J. Green color *Bloomberg Businessweek* no4531 p15 Jl 24 2017

DE LOMBAERDE, EMIEL

Combining Biodiversity Resurveys across Regions to Advance Global Change Research *BioScience* v67 no1 p73 Ja 2017

DeLong, David

When Learning at Work Becomes Overwhelming *Harvard Business Review Digital Articles* p2 Mr 20 2015

DeLong, Thomas J.

2 Myths About Engaging B-Players *Harvard Business Review Digital Articles* p2 N 28 2014

Delorme, Vincent

Reversion of antibiotic resistance in Mycobacterium tuberculosis by spiroisoxazoline SMARt-420 bibl diag *Science* v355 no6330 p1206 Mr 17 2017

De Los Santos Arias, Nelson Carlo

COCOTE N. Rapold color *Film Comment* v53 no5 p22 S/O 2017

Deloza, Lara

THE ROLE OF THE FAMILY color *Literacy Today (2411-7862)* v34 no5 p24 Mr/Ap 2017

DELPH, KATIE

What Causes a Thin Mane and Tail? [Cover story] *Horse & Rider* v56 no1 p14 Ja 2017

Delphian oracle

VESSELS OF THE GODS [Cover story] L. Ruffle *History Today* v67 no5 p50 My 2017

Delphinium

SOMETHING BORROWED, SOMETHING BLUE: A GREAT-AUNT'S LEGACY LIVES ON THROUGH A PACKET OF DELPHINIUM SEEDS J. SHIPLEY *Yankee* v81 no5 p126 S/O 2017

del-Pozo, Jorge

Red squirrels in the British Isles are infected with leprosy bacilli bibl color diag map *Science* v354 no6313 p744 N 11 2016

Delray Beach (Fla.)

Off script A. Kylie color *Canadian Geographic* v137 p6 2017 Travel

Del Rey, Lana, 1986-

NIGHT LIFE *New Yorker* v93 no33 p10 O 23 2017

REY OF LIGHT N. Feeney color *Entertainment Weekly* no1474/1475 p114 Jl 21-28 2017

del Rio, Carlos Martinez

Sweet relief for pollinators bibl color diag *Science* v355 no6326 p686 F 17 2017

Del Rosario, John

WHY MY GLOVES ARE NOT MADE IN THE U.S.A color *Popular Mechanics* p75 Jl 2017

Del Rosso, Steph

17. See Machinalia *New York* v50 no16 p113 Ag 7 2017

DELSONTRO, TONYA

Greenhouse Gas Emissions from Reservoir Water Surfaces: A New Global Synthesis *BioScience* v66 no11 p949 N 1 2016

Delstrac, Denis

Freightened: The Real Price of Shipping J. Fahrenkamp-Uppenbrink color *Science* v356 no6337 p484 My 5 2017

Delta Air Lines Inc.

A Fast-Track Promotion—With a Catch J. Johnsson and M. Schlangenstein diag *Bloomberg Businessweek* no4536 p19 S 4 2017

FLIGHT PATTERNS M. LOGAN BIKOFF *Atlanta* v56 no9 p28 Ja 2017

How to Really Do Cocktails at 35,000 Feet color *Conde Nast Traveler* v52 no4 p100 Ap 2017

Delta Air Lines Inc.—Finance

63 DELTA J. J. Roberts color *Fortune* v175 no4 p106 Mr 15 2017

Delta Powerboats (Company)

DELTA 88 CARBON SPORT YACHT *Sea Magazine* v109 no1 p42 Ja 2017

SPECIFICATIONS *Sea Magazine* v109 no1 p36 Ja 2017

Delta Region (Calif.)—Environmental conditions

Deep INTO THE Delta P. RAINS *Sea Magazine* v108 no9 p40 S 2016

Deltas—Environmental conditions

The Mission to Save Africa's Okavango Delta D. Quammen color map *National Geographic* v232 no5 p80 N 2017

De Luca, Andrea

An accreting pulsar with extreme properties drives an ultraluminous x-ray source in NGC 5907 bibl chart graph *Science* v355 no6327 p817 F 24 2017

De Luca, Vanessa K.

BACK TO SCHOOL color *Essence* v48 no5 p10 S 2017

BOYS TO MEN color *Essence* v48 no2 p8 Je 2017

LIFE LESSONS color *Essence* v47 no7 p4 N 2016

MY YEAR-END MESSAGE TO YOU color *Essence* v47 no8 p10 D 2016

SHOOT FOR THE STARS color *Essence* v47 no10 p14 F 2017

SIMPLE PLEASURES color *Essence* v47 no11 p14 Mr 2017

STRENGTH IN OUR STORY color *Essence* v47 no9 p8 Ja 2017

VACATION MODE color *Essence* v48 no3 p10 Jl 2017

WE MUST #PRESSON color *Essence* v47 no12 p10 Ap 2017

WOKE WONDERLAND color *Essence* v48 no6 p14 O 2017

de Lumley, Henry

Neandertal and Denisovan DNA from Pleistocene sediments bw color *Science* v356 no6338 p605 My 12 2017

De Luna, Tristan

FIRST SHIP BUILT IN NORTH AMERICA? B. Manley *Military History* v33 no6 p10 Mr 2017

Delury, John

Trump and North Korea color *Foreign Affairs* v96 no2 p46 Mr/Ap 2017

Delva, Wim

The transcontinental scientist color *Science* v355 no6322 p318 Ja 20 2017

Del Vecchio, G.

A nontoxic pain killer designed by modeling of pathological receptor conformations bibl diag graph *Science* v355 no6328 p966 Mr 3 2017

DELVES, JULIA

Performance Climbing Nutrition bw color graph *Climbing* no353 p48 My/Je 2017

Demacopoulos, George E.

HUMBLE AND HAUGHTY G. R. MURPHY *America* v215 no11 p36 O 17 2016

De Maigret, Caroline

America, C'est Chic color *InStyle* v24 no3 p176 Mr 2017

Demak, Richard

Actionable Offenses color diag *Sports Illustrated* v126 no7 p20 Mr 6 2017

Auto Pilots color *Sports Illustrated* v126 no7 p26 Mr 6 2017

Do You Speak Emoji? color *Sports Illustrated* v126 no7 p23 Mr 6 2017

FACES IN THE CROWD color *Sports Illustrated* v126 no7 p28 Mr 6 2017

HOT | NOT color *Sports Illustrated* v126 no7 p23 Mr 6 2017

No Exit color *Sports Illustrated* v126 no7 p30 Mr 6 2017

Protect and Serve color *Sports Illustrated* v126 no7 p17 Mr 6 2017

Test Prep color *Sports Illustrated* v126 no7 p24 Mr 6 2017

Wrestle Mania color *Sports Illustrated* v126 no7 p20 Mr 6 2017

Demand (Economic theory)

The More Climate Skeptics There Are, the Fewer Climate Entrepreneurs M. E. Kahn and D. Zhao *Harvard Business Review Digital Articles* p2 Mr 16 2017

The On-Demand Economy Is Growing, and Not Just for the Young and Wealthy C. Colby and K. Bell *Harvard Business Review Digital Articles* p2 Ap 14 2016

TO MAKE PETROLEUM USE MORE ACCEPTABLE AND MORE SUSTAINABLE *Vital Speeches of the Day* v83 no5 p158 My 2017

What America's Best BBQ Joint Can Teach You About Pricing R. Mohammed *Harvard Business Review Digital Articles* p2 N 12 2015

Where Predictive Analytics Is Having the Biggest Impact J. LaRiviere, P. McAfee et al *Harvard Business Review Digital Articles* p2 My 25 2016

de Manuel, Marc

Chimpanzee genomic diversity reveals ancient admixture with bonobos bibl diag graph map *Science* v354 no6311 p477 O 28 2016

Demarchelier, Patrick

STYLE with SUBSTANCE K. SMITH color *Vanity Fair* v59 no4 p96 Mr 2017

That Certain LOOK bw color *Vanity Fair* v59 no4 p174 Mr 2017

Demarchelier, Victor

THE NEW HUES color *Harper's Bazaar* no3651 p367 Mr 2017

Demarco (Performer)

NIGHT LIFE color *New Yorker* v93 no29 p18 S 25 2017

DeMarco, Emily

Acorn worms have a head for swimming color *Science News* v191 no2 p5 F 4 2017

Boning up on belly size cartoon *Science News* v190 no12 p32 D 10 2016

Disaster fuels geologic detective story color *Science News* v192 no4 p32 S 16 2017

Here's every total solar eclipse from now to 2040 map *Science News* v192 no1 p32 Ag 5 2017

How deep water surfaces around Antarctica color graph *Science News* v192 no4 p36 S 16 2017

How to make a (zebra)fish face color *Science News* v190 no10 p32 N 12 2016

Most penicillin allergies are off base color *Science News* v190 no13 p5 D 24 2016

New genes give mums the blues color *Science News* v192 no2 p12 Ag 19 2017

Nonstop sandpipers color map *Science News* v191 no3 p4 F 18 2017

A recurring rendezvous color *Science News* v191 no12 p32 Je 24 2017

Reusable rockets' red glare color *Science News* v190 no13 p44 D 24 2016

Surprising number of craters, splotches mark the moon bw *Science News* v190 no11 p32 N 26 2016

DeMarco, Mac, 1990-

Mac DeMarco D. Kiper color *Current Biography* v77 no11 p35 N 2016

DEMARCO, PETER

Thank You for Caring So Much color *Reader's Digest* v190 no1135 p42 N 2017

De Maria, Giorgio

Holy Horror W. Giraldi bw *Commonweal* v144 no3 p17 F 10 2017

De Martino, Alba

Tissue damage and senescence provide critical signals for cellular reprogramming in vivo bibl chart graph *Science* v354 no6315 paaf4445-1 N 25 2016

DEMARTINO, CRAIG

Family Values [Cover story] color *Climbing* no350 p20 D 2016/Ja 2017

DeMaso, Christina R.

Rapid development of a DNA vaccine for Zika virus bibl graph *Science* v354 no6309 p237 O 14 2016

De Massington, John

MIRACLE in the MARCHES I. Bass *History Today* v67 no3 p40 Mr 2017

De Massis, Alfredo

What Big Companies Can Learn from the Success of the Unicorns *Harvard Business Review Digital Articles* p2 Mr 14 2016

Demaster, Brian

How Life Insurers Can Bring Their Business into the 21st Century *Harvard Business Review Digital Articles* p2 Mr 25 2015

DEMATIO, JOE

GEOGRAPHY LESSONS color *Road & Track* v68 no5 p108 D 2016/Ja 2017

GRIP AND GRIN color *Road & Track* v68 no8 p90 My 2017

I CRASHED THE MCLAREN color *Road & Track* v68 no5 p58 D 2016/Ja 2017

de Matos Bonates, L. C.

Persistent effects of pre-Columbian plant domestication on Amazonian forest composition bibl chart graph map *Science* v355 no6328 p925 Mr 3 2017

De Matteo, Drea

The Sopranos Kiss Adriana Goodbye J. Hibberd color *Entertainment Weekly* no1470 p46 Je 16 2017

De Mauro, G.

Observation of a large-scale anisotropy in the arrival directions of cosmic rays above 8×1018 eV *Science* v357 no6357 p1266 S 22 2017

deMause, Neil

The Brooklyn Wars: The Stories Behind the Remaking of New York's Most Celebrated Borough *Publishers Weekly* v264 no24 p57 Je 12 2017

Coverage Skirts Hurricane's Outsized Impact on Poor *Extra!* v30 no8 p3 O 2017

Dembicki, Geoff

THE Timely DISAPPEARANCE of CLIMATE CHANGE DENIAL IN CHINA color *Foreign Policy* no224 p58 My/Je 2017

DEMBOSKI, JOHN R.

Transformational Principles for NEON Sampling of Mammalian Parasites and Pathogens: A Response to Springer and Colleagues *BioScience* v66 no11 p917 N 1 2016

De Meester, Luc

The broad footprint of climate change from genes to biomes to people bibl chart color *Science* v354 no6313 paaf7671-1 N 11 2016

de Mello Neto, J. R. T.

Observation of a large-scale anisotropy in the arrival directions of cosmic rays above 8×1018 eV *Science* v357 no6357 p1266 S 22 2017

DeMelo, Juno

"Don't Make My Love Mistake!" color *Women's Health* v14 no3 p119 Ap 2017

HOW TO AVOID A Travel Hangover color *O, The Oprah Magazine* p97 N 2017

Morning Glories color diag *Bon Appetit* v61 no11 p30 N 2016

Natural UPGRADES color *O, The Oprah Magazine* p100 Mr 2017

Photographic Memory color *O, The Oprah Magazine* p24 Jl 2017

Pinball Wizard color *O, The Oprah Magazine* p28 D 2016

Sweat: The Details bw graph *Men's Health* v32 no6 p92 Ag 2017

Taste the Rainbow color *Bon Appetit* v62 no7 p17 Jl 2017

True Colors color *Bon Appetit* v61 no12 p92 D 2016 /Jan2017

What experts tell their friends about EATING HEALTHY color *Redbook* p82 Ap 2017

What ob/gyns tell their friends cartoon *Redbook* p82 O 2017

Dementia

Be good to your heart and head color *Redbook* p77 S 2017

"I THOUGHT I HAD ALZHEIMER'S" M. COHEN color *Prevention* v69 no11 p54 N 2017

The Last Promise L. Penny color *AARP· The Magazine* v59 no6A p66 O/N 2016

Dementia patients

The Last Bursts of Memory J. VANOOSTING *American Scholar* v86 no1 p87 Wint 2017

Dementia patients—Care

REMEMBER WHEN? A. Cochran *Washingtonian Magazine* v52

no6 p167 Mr 2017

Time-Travel Therapy A. KOLSON HURLEY bw color *Atlantic* v319 no1 p28 Ja/F 2017

Two Ways to Better Care for Patients with Dementia S. H. Jain and J. Pratty *Harvard Business Review Digital Articles* p2 Ag 11 2015

Dementia prevention

6 ways yoga helps STOP THE CLOCK color *Yoga Journal* p8 2017 Special Issue

Caffeine D. SCHARDT *Nutrition Action Health Letter* v44 no1 p7 Ja/F 2017

Prevent and PROTECT J. Migala color *O, The Oprah Magazine* p74 Je 2017

A RARE SUCCESS AGAINST ALZHEIMER'S [Cover story] M. Kivipelto and K. Håkansson color graph *Scientific American* v316 no4 p32 Ap 2017

Remember When? E. A. KANE color *Better Nutrition* v79 no1 p32 Ja 2017

Stay Sharp J. TEITELBAUM color *Better Nutrition* v78 no11 p34 N 2016

Dementia—Genetic aspects

Solving the Alzheimer's PUZZLE K. Hobson color *O, The Oprah Magazine* p70 Je 2017

Dementia—Risk factors

Better Diet and Sleep Might Help Protect Your Brain [Cover story] *Tufts University Health & Nutrition Letter* v34 no9 p1 N 2016

DeMeo, Francesca

Meet the primordial asteroid family color diag *Science* v357 no6355 p972 S 8 2017

DeMers, Jayson

How to Craft an Agile Marketing Campaign *Harvard Business Review Digital Articles* p2 Ja 21 2015

Why No One's Reading Your Marketing Content *Harvard Business Review Digital Articles* p2 N 14 2014

Demetriadou, Angela

Single-molecule optomechanics in "picocavities" bibl graph *Science* v354 no6313 p726 N 11 2016

Demichelis, Francesca

SOX2 promotes lineage plasticity and antiandrogen resistance in TP53- and RB1-deficient prostate cancer bibl graph *Science* v355 no6320 p1 Ja 6 2017

de-Miguel, Sergio

Positive biodiversity-productivity relationship predominant in global forests bibl chart graph map *Science* v354 no6309 paaf8957-1 O 14 2016

De Mille, Agnes, 1905-1993

60 Years Ago This Month *Dance Magazine* v91 no4 p67 Ap 2017

Demille, Cecil B. (Cecil Blount), 1881-1959

Cecil B. DeMille Was Right M. Y. SOLOVEICHIK *Commentary* v143 no4 p11 Ap 2017

Moses and DeMille W. SCHIMMERLING *Commentary* v143 no6 p7 Je 2017

DeMille, David

Probing the frontiers of particle physics with tabletop-scale experiments color graph *Science* v357 no6355 p990 S 8 2017

Demin Zhou

Generation of influenza A viruses as live but replication-incompetent virus vaccines bibl graph *Science* v354 no6316 p1170 D 2 2016

Demineralization (Teeth)—Prevention

Teeth: an owner's manual J. CHEN color *Redbook* p77 Jl/Ag 2017

Deming, Drake

HAT-P-26b: A Neptune-mass exoplanet with a well-constrained heavy element abundance chart diag graph *Science* v356 no6338 p628 My 12 2017

Deming, Edwin Willard, 1860-1942

DEMING'S LAST STAND P. D. Toler *MHQ: Quarterly Journal of Military History* v29 no2 p87 Wint 2017

Deming, W. Edwards (William Edwards), 1900-1993

The Management Thinker We Should Never Have Forgotten J. Macht *Harvard Business Review Digital Articles* p2 Je 24 2016

DeMint, Jim, 1951-

Cracked Foundation J. MCCORMACK color *Weekly Standard* v22 no34 p8 My 15 2017

Demisch, Suzanne

Demisch Danant H. MARTIN bw color *Architectural Digest* v74

no2 p16 F 2017

De Mitri, I.

Observation of a large-scale anisotropy in the arrival directions of cosmic rays above 8×1018 eV *Science* v357 no6357 p1266 S 22 2017

Demler, Eugene

Bloch oscillations in the absence of a lattice graph *Science* v356 no6341 p945 Je 1 2017

Revealing hidden antiferromagnetic correlations in doped Hubbard chains via string correlators bw diag graph *Science* v357 no6350 p484 Ag 4 2017

Ultrafast many-body interferometry of impurities coupled to a Fermi sea bibl diag graph *Science* v354 no6308 p96 O 7 2016

Demme, Amanda

AVA DUVERNAY img *New York* v49 no19 p42 S 19 2016

Demme, Jonathan, 1944-2017

Jonathan Demme S. Zacharek color *Time* v189 no18 p15 My 15 2017

True Believer R. Horton color *Film Comment* v53 no4 p66 Jl/Ag 2017

Demme, Jonathan, 1944-—Interviews

Justin Timberlake and Jonathan Demme K. P. Sullivan color *Entertainment Weekly* no1435 p42 O 14 2016

Democracy

See also

Referendum

AMERICAN DEMOCRACY BESIEGED [Cover story] A. BERMAN color *Nation* v305 no3 p18 Jl 31 2017

As technology goes democratic, nations lose military control B. FitzGerald and J. Parziale bibl *Bulletin of the Atomic Scientists* v73 no2 p102 Mr 2017

Cardinal Bo on Myanmar's 'delicate' path to democracy G. O'Connell color *America* v217 no4 p16 Ag 21 2017

Cogs in the Machine R. R. Reilly *Claremont Review of Books* v17 no3 p48 Summ 2017

Collusion in Restraint of Democracy: Against Political Deliberation I. Shapiro *Daedalus* v146 no3 p77 Summ 2017

Correction Notice *Daedalus* v146 no4 p17 Fall 2017

DEMOCRACIES IN UPHEAVAL D. MALPASS *Forbes* v198 no9 p32 D 30 2016

Francis Fukuyama: Democracy Needs Elites A. Görlach and F. Fukuyama *NPQ: New Perspectives Quarterly* v34 no2 p9 My 2017

In Decline *Change* v82 no3 p16 Mr 2017

The infrastructure challenge A. CARSE *Issues in Science & Technology* v33 no3 p5 Spr 2017

The need for a translational science of democracy M. A. Neblo, W. Minozzi et al bibl color *Science* v355 no6328 p914 Mr 3 2017

Referendum vs. Institutionalized Deliberation: What Democratic Theorists Can Learn from the 2016 Brexit Decision C. Offe *Daedalus* v146 no3 p14 Summ 2017

The Road to Liberty W. Kristol *Weekly Standard* v22 no17 p7 Ja 2 2017

Russian Revanche: External Threats & Regime Reactions K. A. Darden *Daedalus* v146 no2 p128 Spr 2017

Steal the March W. Kristol *Weekly Standard* v22 no28 p8 Mr 27 2017

A Survival Guide for Democracies J. Kurlantzick color *Bloomberg Businessweek* no4535 p10 Ag 28 2017

There's a Waiter in My Soup J. EPSTEIN cartoon *Weekly Standard* v22 no28 p5 Mr 27 2017

WILL DONALD TRUMP DESTROY THE PRESIDENCY? J. GOLDSMITH color *Atlantic* v320 no3 p58 O 2017

Democracy & science

Too much democracy? N. STEHR and T. TAMURA *Issues in Science & Technology* v33 no1 p5 Fall 2016

Democracy—Brazil

THE APPROVAL MATRIX img *New York* v50 no6 p108 Mr 20 2017

Democracy—Europe

Liberal Democracy Is Eroding Right In Europe's Backyard I. Bremmer *Time* v190 no6 p16 Ag 7 2017

Democracy—European Union countries

The 'Trump Effect' [Cover story] D. GREEN color *Weekly Standard* v22 no16 p22 D 26 2016

Democracy—Germany

COME FOR THE GOULASH, STAY FOR THE DEMOCRACY
V. Silver color *Bloomberg Businessweek* no4529 p60 Jl 3 2017

Democracy—India
Democracy Besieged M. MIRZA *Islamic Horizons* v46 no2 p56 Mr/Ap 2017

Democracy—International cooperation
Visions of Democracy L. Diamond *Hoover Digest: Research & Opinion on Public Policy* no1 p14 Wint 2017

Democracy—Israel
Is Israeli Democracy in Danger? D. WAXMAN *Current History* v115 no785 p360 D 2016
There's Too Much Speech in Israel! M. CONTINETTI *Commentary* v142 no2 p72 S 2016

Democracy—Turkey
An Islamist Power Grab Derails Democracy in Turkey K. ÖKTEM *Current History* v115 no785 p331 D 2016

Democracy—United States
ALL TOGETHER NOW L. LESSIG *Sierra* v101 no5 p30 S/O 2016
The American Founders Entrusted Elites to Save Democracy from Itself N. Gardels *NPQ: New Perspectives Quarterly* v34 no2 p2 My 2017
Corporate Media Threatens Our Democracy B. SANDERS *In These Times* v41 no2 p28 F 2017
EASY CHAIR R. Solnit *Harper's Magazine* v334 no2002 p5 Mr 2017
How to Fix Democracy color *MIT Technology Review* v120 no1 p112 Ja/F 2017
How to Revive Democracy J. NICHOLS *Nation* v305 no3 p3 Jl 31 2017
Is It 1968? *Commentary* v142 no2 p1 S 2016
Koched-Up Economics C. LEHMANN *In These Times* v41 no8 p37 Ag 2017
Learning to Bargain M. T. KLARE bw *Nation* v304 no2 p15 Ja 16 2017
Renovating Democracy and Salvaging Globalization N. Gardels *NPQ: New Perspectives Quarterly* v34 no1 p2 Ja 2017
Rethinking the Vote A. Greenblatt *Governing* v30 no12 p10 S 2017
States of Confusion J. Yardley *New York Times Magazine* p34 N 6 2016
Too Much Democracy? J. Huffman *Hoover Digest: Research & Opinion on Public Policy* no4 p62 Fall 2016
Trump's Democracy Man J. LIFHITS color *Weekly Standard* v23 no3 p19 S 25 2017
Why We Must Focus Now on Maintaining Democracy, Civility and Perspective J. Klein color *Time* v188 no22-23 p22 N/D 2016
The Witch Is Dead E. Alterman diag *Nation* v304 no18 p6 Je 19 2017

Democracy—United States—Economic aspects
Shrinking the Gap Is Key for Democracy B. Obama color *Time* v188 no16/17 p36 O 24 2016

Democracy—United States—History
No Way Out But Up W. Kristol *Weekly Standard* v22 no5 p6 O 10 2016

Democracy—United States—Social aspects
As the Free World Turns G. R. SANDGREN, J. MAHONEY et al *Commentary* v144 no2 p4 S 2017
Is America Still Safe for Democracy? R. Mickey, S. Levitsky et al color *Foreign Affairs* v96 no3 p20 My/Je 2017
The Vulgar Manliness of Donald Trump: The Greeks and the Founders feared men like the president, and with good reason H. Mansfield *Commentary* v144 no2 p23 S 2017

Democracy—Venezuela
The Agony of Venezuela P. BARBIERI color *National Review* v69 no16 p30 Ag 28 2017

Democratic National Committee (U.S.)
The Battle for the DNC J. NICHOLS *Nation* v304 no9 p10 Mr 20 2017
Ellison's 3,143-County Strategy J. BLEIFUSS *In These Times* v41 no1 p5 Ja 2017
For Keith Ellison color *Nation* v304 no5 p3 F 20 2017
SURPRISE OUTCOMES TO THE MUELLER PROBE Y. BRENNER cartoon *New Yorker* v93 no20 p33 Jl 10 2017

Democratic National Convention
Democratic Party Platform: "We Are Stronger Together" *Congres-*

sional Digest v95 no8 p6 O 2016

Democratic Party (Ill.)
Battle of the Plutocrats J. MILLER *New Republic* v248 no11 p8 N 2017

Democratic Party (N.J.)—Elections
JOHN WISNIEWSKI'S INSURGENT CRUSADE B. DREYFUSS and B. DREYFUSS color il *Nation* v304 no8 p12 Mr 13 2017

Democratic Party (Neb.)
Lighting a Fire on the Prairie J. BLEIFUSS *In These Times* v41 no7 p30 Jl 2017

Democratic Party (Tex.)
HOUSTON, WE HAVE PROGRESS T. MURPHY color graph map *Mother Jones* v42 no5 p24 S/O 2017

Democratic Party (U.S.)
Are Republicans Mid-Terminal? [Cover story] F. BARNES color *Weekly Standard* v22 no36 p10 My 29 2017
THE BATTLE LINES HAVE BEEN DRAWN R. L. FISCHER *USA Today Magazine* v146 no2866 p14 Jl 2017
Beyond Resistance R. L. BOROSAGE *Nation* v304 no7 p4 Mr 6 2017
Both Sides Now M. HEMINGWAY color *Weekly Standard* v22 no46 p22 Ag 14 2017
CAN DEMOCRATS FIX THE PARTY? T. Dickinson color *Rolling Stone* no1290 p28 Je 29 2017
Core Dogma J. BOTTUM color *Weekly Standard* v22 no34 p16 My 15 2017
Defying the Dead Center *American Conservative* v15 no6 p5 N/D 2016
THE DEMOCRATIC PARTY'S IDENTITY CRISIS W. Voegeli *Claremont Review of Books* v17 no1 p30 Wint 2016/2017
Democrats And Plutocrats R. SALAM *National Review* v69 no18 p14 O 2 2017
The Democrats' Biggest Disaster N. NAREA and A. SHEPHARD color *New Republic* v248 no1/2 p8 Ja/F 2017
The Democrats' Dilemmas [Cover story] P. Elliott color diag map *Time* v190 no13 p36 O 2 2017
Democrats Must Become the Party of Freedom B. C. Lynn *Washington Monthly* p4 Ja/F 2017
How to Win Rural Voters Without Losing Liberal Values M. Longman *Washington Monthly* v49 no6-8 p9 Je-Ag 2017
How We Can Fight Trump R. L. BOROSAGE *Nation* v303 no23/24 p22 D 5 2016
Illiberalism: The Worldwide Crisis *Commentary* v142 no1 p1 Jl/Ag 2016
IT'S MY PARTY: The Democrats struggle to rise from the ashes A. Cockburn *Harper's Magazine* v335 no2006 p33 Jl 2017
Leftward March R. PONNURU il *National Review* v69 no12 p13 Je 26 2017
Litigating Politics K. D. WILLIAMSON color *National Review* v68 no23 p15 D 19 2016
The Luxury of Indecision J. THINDWA *In These Times* v40 no11 p7 N 2016
MAD LIBS color map *Mother Jones* v42 no3 p11 My/Je 2017
Minority Retort A. Kim *Washington Monthly* p9 Ja/F 2017
The Miseducation of Liberals D. RAVITCH il *New Republic* v248 no6 p16 Je 2017
THE NEXT BIG THING WILL BE A LOT OF... SMALL THINGS D. BOLLIER bw color *Nation* v305 no5 p16 Ag 28 2017
PIPELINE POPULISM: Out on the prairie, unlikely alliances may hold the key to transforming the Democratic Party K. ARONOFF *In These Times* v41 no10 p18 O 2017
The Resistance So Far M. Tomasky bw color *New York Review of Books* v64 no17 p42 N 9 2017
Revamp the Democratic Party A. NABAUM *New Republic* v248 no3 p35 Mr 2017
Should Democratic Socialists Be Democrats? *In These Times* v41 no5 p12 My 2017
The Swamp Suburb F. BARNES color *Weekly Standard* v22 no34 p14 My 15 2017
THERE ACTUALLY IS A WAY... S. TROBIANI *USA Today Magazine* v146 no2868 p20 S 2017
THERE'S NO OTHER DONALD TRUMP. THIS IS IT *Vital Speeches of the Day* v82 no10 p299 O 2016
Three Ideas to Check Trump and Revive the Democratic Party

DE NESNERA, KRISTIN L.

Long-Term Studies Contribute Disproportionately to Ecology and Policy *BioScience* v67 no3 p271 Mr 2017

De Neve, Jan-Emmanuel

Does Work Make You Happy? Evidence from the World Happiness Report *Harvard Business Review Digital Articles* p2 Mr 20 2017

Income Inequality Makes Whole Countries Less Happy *Harvard Business Review Digital Articles* p2 Ja 12 2016

Denevi, Brett

The new MOON *Physics Today* v70 no6 p38 Je 2017

Deng, Alex

To Really Help the Global Poor, Create Technology They'll Pay For *Harvard Business Review Digital Articles* p2 Ag 5 2015

Deng, Gejing

Trispecific broadly neutralizing HIV antibodies mediate potent SHIV protection in macaques color graph *Science* v357 no6359 p85 O 6 2017

Deng, Hui

Activity-based protein profiling reveals off-target proteins of the FAAH inhibitor BIA 10-2474 chart color graph *Science* v356 no6342 p1084 Je 9 2017

Deng, Juan

A central neural circuit for itch sensation color graph *Science* v357 no6352 p695 Ag 18 2017

Deng, M. T.

Majorana bound state in a coupled quantum-dot hybrid-nanowire system bibl graph *Science* v354 no6319 p1557 D 23 2016

Deng, X.

Breaking Lorentz reciprocity to overcome the time-bandwidth limit in physics and engineering bw diag graph *Science* v356 no6344 p1260 Je 23 2017

Deng, Ye-Xuan

"Perfect" designer chromosome V and behavior of a ring derivative diag *Science* v355 no6329 p1046 Mr 10 2017

Deng, Yingfeng

An adipo-biliary-uridine axis that regulates energy homeostasis diag *Science* v355 no6330 p1173 Mr 17 2017

Deng, Yiwen

Epigenetic regulation of antagonistic receptors confers rice blast resistance with yield balance bibl diag *Science* v355 no6328 p962 Mr 3 2017

DENG, ZHIQUN D.

Envisioning the Future of Aquatic Animal Tracking: Technology, Science, and Application *BioScience* v67 no10 p884 O 2017

Dengate, Jeff

ASK RW color *Runner's World* v52 no4 p35 My 2017

BOTTOMS UP color *Runner's World* v52 no5 p38 Je 2017

FALL SHOE GUIDE [Cover story] color graph *Runner's World* v52 no8 p59 S 2017

GEAR OF THE YEAR [Cover story] color *Runner's World* v51 no11 p56 D 2016

GROUND BREAKERS color *Runner's World* v52 no9 p71 O 2017

HAPPY TRAILS color *Runner's World* v52 no9 p78 O 2017

INSIDER TRAINING color *Runner's World* v52 no1 p90 Ja/F 2017

IT'S IN THE BAG color *Runner's World* v52 no2 p48 Mr 2017

ON A ROLL(ER) color *Runner's World* v52 no8 p32 S 2017

RISE OF THE MACHINES [Cover story] color *Runner's World* v51 no10 p60 N 2016

SOLID FOOTING cartoon color graph *Runner's World* v52 no3 p83 Ap 2017

SPEED RACERS color *Runner's World* v52 no5 p36 Je 2017

Spring SHOE GUIDE cartoon chart color diag *Runner's World* v52 no2 p71 Mr 2017

STORM STOPPERS color *Runner's World* v52 no3 p51 Ap 2017

STYLE FOR MILES bw color *Runner's World* v52 no6 p36 Jl 2017

TEST OF TIME color *Runner's World* v52 no4 p14 My 2017

VISION QUEST [Cover story] color *Runner's World* v52 no6 p34 Jl 2017

WHAT POSTRACE FOOD IS YOUR BIGGEST GUILTY PLEASURE? cartoon color *Runner's World* v52 no3 p14 Ap 2017

winter SHOE GUIDE cartoon chart color diag graph *Runner's*

World v51 no11 p87 D 2016

The WIRELESS RUNNER color *Runner's World* v52 no4 p1 My 2017

Dengue viruses

Dengue may stoke Zika infections A. CUNNINGHAM graph *Science News* v191 no8 p14 Ap 29 2017

IgG antibodies to dengue enhanced for FcγRIIIA binding determine disease severity T. T. Wang, J. Sewatanon et al bibl graph *Science* v355 no6323 p395 Ja 27 2017

One antibody for all and all antibodies for one *Science* v356 no6334 p149 Ap 14 2017

Dengue—Prevention

Dengue diversity across spatial and temporal scales: Local structure and the effect of host population size H. Salje, J. Lessler et al bibl graph *Science* v355 no6331 p1302 Mr 24 2017

Dengue—Transmission

Dengue diversity across spatial and temporal scales: Local structure and the effect of host population size H. Salje, J. Lessler et al bibl graph *Science* v355 no6331 p1302 Mr 24 2017

Dengue—Vaccination

Finally, a Vaccine for Dengue [Cover story] A. FAVREAU and C. MALDARELLI color *Popular Science* v288 no6 p36 N/D 2016

Denial (Film)

Denial L. Greenblatt color *Entertainment Weekly* no1434 p41 O 7 2016

Sighs, Tears, and Jogging R. R. Cooper color *Commonweal* v143 no19 p24 D 2 2016

Denial, Catherine J.

Making Marriage: Husbands, Wives, and the American State in Dakota and Ojibwe Country M. Cassidy *American Indian Quarterly* v40 no3 p288 Summ 2016

Denial of service attacks

BUT IS IT SAFE? A. GEORGE color *Popular Mechanics* p75 My 2017

HACKERS ARE GETTING BOLDER B. O'Keefe diag *Fortune* v75 no1 p100 Ja 1 2017

Risks Posed by Mobile Network Vulnerabilities *USA Today Magazine* v145 no2863 p8 Ap 2017

A Shocking Internet Attack Shows America's Vulnerability H. S. Edwards and M. Vella color diag *Time* v188 no19 p7 N 7 2016

De Nieves, Raúl—Exhibitions

RAÚL DE NIEVES S. Korman *Art in America* v104 no9 p155 O 2016

de Nijs, Bart

Single-molecule optomechanics in "picocavities" bibl graph *Science* v354 no6313 p726 N 11 2016

Denim

BEST BETS img *New York* v49 no20 p98 O 3 2016

DOUBLE THE DENIM M. JAMES color *Esquire* p54 My 2017

Three Writers. Three Sizes. Three Perfect Pairs of Jeans L. Chan color *Glamour* v115 no2 p38 F 2017

Denim—Evaluation

Adam's DENIM GUIDE A. Glassman bw color *O, The Oprah Magazine* p51 Ag 2017

Modern Fashion Meets Traditional Details [Cover story] color *Horse & Rider* v56 no8 p54 Ag 2017

Modern MOVES *Interview* v47 no2 p106 Mr 2017

NEW PRODUCTS color *Spin to Win Rodeo* v21 no1 p30 Mr 2017

De Niro, Robert, 1943-

EDITOR'S LETTER N. Rapold bw *Film Comment* v53 no3 p4 My/Je 2017

Even Greed Has a Price S. ERICKSON *Los Angeles Magazine* v62 no6 p56 Je 2017

FUNNY MONEY: Robert De Niro and Michelle Pfeiffer play Bernie and Ruth Madoff in HBO's film about how the scandal wrecked their infamous family J. HALTERMAN *TV Guide* v65 no21 p28 My 15 2017

A MAN APART M. HASKELL bw color *Film Comment* v53 no3 p26 My/Je 2017

Robert De Niro's Bronx Cheer J. Mcgovern color *Entertainment Weekly* no1438 p70 N 4 2016

What We Can & Cannot Fix J. Guhin bw *Commonweal* v144 no9 p22 My 19 2017

You Laughin' at Me? J. McGovern color *Entertainment Weekly* no1436/1437 p20 O 21 2016

De Niro, Robert, 1943——Interviews

GETTING ON WITH IT E. HYNES color *Film Comment* v53 no3 p31 My/Je 2017

You Talkin; to us? M. MURPHY color *Bloomberg Businessweek* no4519 p68 Ap 24 2017

Denis, Claire—Interviews

Parting the Clouds N. Rapold bw *Film Comment* v53 no4 p10 Jl/Ag 2017

DENIS, NELSON A.

Invisible Latinos *Publishers Weekly* v264 no4 p84 Ja 23 2017

Denise, Anika

Monster Trucks *Publishers Weekly* v263 no49 p60 D 7 2016

Denisenko, Andrej

Nanoscale nuclear magnetic resonance with chemical resolution diag *Science* v357 no6346 p67 Jl 7 2017

Denison, Maria

Media Engagement *Parks & Recreation* p12 Aquatics Guide 2017

Denison, Peter B.

We Need More Voters *Humanist* v77 no1 p47 Ja/F 2017

Denisovans

Close relative of Neandertals unearthed in China A. Gibbons color map *Science* v355 no6328 p899 Mr 3 2017

DECODING A DENISOVAN DEAD END? color diag map *Discover* v27 no10 p67 D 2016

Meet the Denisovans B. ALEX color map *Discover* v27 no10 p64 D 2016

DENIZET-LEWIS, BENOIT

The Thrill of Mass Intimacy *New York Times Book Review* p14 O 23 2016

ZERKA MORENO *New York Times Magazine* p32 D 25 2016

Denman, Keith

Posthole color *Powder* v45 no3 p148 N 2016

Denmeade, Samuel

Winning the Prostate Cancer War J. STEWART color *Men's Health* v32 no4 p75 My 2017

Denn, Neill

Publishers Keep Calm And Carry On color *Publishers Weekly* v264 no12 p5 Mr 20 2017

Denn, Rebekah

WASHINGTON'S OLYMPIA color map *Sunset* v238 no5 p34 My 2017

Denner, Joachim

Advances in organ transplant from pigs [Cover story] color *Science* v357 no6357 p1238 S 22 2017

Dennett, Daniel Clement, 1942-

Is Consciousness an Illusion? T. Nagel bw color *New York Review of Books* v64 no4 p32 Mr 9 2017

A SCIENCE OF THE SOUL J. ROTHMAN cartoon color *New Yorker* v93 no6 p46 Mr 27 2017

Transparency and Truth *NPQ: New Perspectives Quarterly* v34 no2 p44 My 2017

Denning, Courtney

Country Lore *Mother Earth News* no280 p85 F/Mr 2017

Denning, Steve

The Internet Is Finally Forcing Management to Care About People *Harvard Business Review Digital Articles* p2 My 5 2015

Dennis, Alison

The Carabiner color graph *Climbing* no350 p28 D 2016/Ja 2017

State of the Industry color *Climbing* no352 p14 Ap 2017

Dennis, Steven T.

Fired. But Not Finished bw *Bloomberg Businessweek* no4522 p30 My 15 2017

How Will They Know, And When Will They Know It? diag *Bloomberg Businessweek* no4518 p28 Ap 10 2017

To Pass Health Care, The Senate Needs Him color *Bloomberg Businessweek* no4524 p28 My 29 2017

DENNIS-BENN, NICOLE

MOURNING GLORY color *O, The Oprah Magazine* p84 Ag 2017

Dennison, Matthew

The 'Dual Life' of Beatrix Potter D. COUPLAND bw color *National Review* v69 no6 p45 Ap 3 2017

DENNISON, WILLIAM C.

Ecological Forecasting and the Science of Hypoxia in Chesapeake Bay *BioScience* v67 no7 p614 Jl 2017

Submersed Aquatic Vegetation in Chesapeake Bay: Sentinel Species in a Changing World *BioScience* v67 no8 p698 Ag 2017

Denny, Christine A.

Pcdhαc2 is required for axonal tiling and assembly of serotonergic circuitries in mice diag *Science* v356 no6336 p406 Ap 28 2017

DENNY, MARK

Geoengineering color *Natural History* v125 no6 p32 Je 2017

Denon (Company)

Fascia of the Future M. Fleischmann color *Sound & Vision* v82 no8 p54 O 2017

Density

Plant diversity increases with the strength of negative density dependence at the global scale C. V. S. Gunatilleke, F. He et al diag *Science* v356 no6345 p1389 Je 30 2017

Density functional theory

A conundrum for density functional theory S. Hammes-Schiffer bibl diag *Science* v355 no6320 p28 Ja 6 2017

Density functional theory is straying from the path toward the exact functional M. G. Medvedev, I. S. Bushmarinov et al bibl chart graph *Science* v355 no6320 p1 Ja 6 2017

Making the most of materials computations K. S. Thygesen and K. W. Jacobsen bibl diag *Science* v354 no6309 p180 O 14 2016

Density functionals

Revealing hidden antiferromagnetic correlations in doped Hubbard chains via string correlators T. A. Hilker, G. Salomon et al bw diag graph *Science* v357 no6350 p484 Ag 4 2017

Density wave theory

Spiral density waves in a young protoplanetary disk L. M. Pérez, J. M. Carpenter et al bibl graph *Science* v353 no6307 p1519 S 30 2016

Why do spiral galaxies spiral? D. J. Eicher color *Astronomy* v44 no12 p7 D 2016

Denson-Randolph, Nikkole—Interviews

Screen Saver Z. HUGHES color *Ebony* v72 no3 p106 D 2016/Ja 2017

Dental care

See also

Tooth care & hygiene

A Bad Bite Concerns More than Your Grin *USA Today Magazine* v146 no2869 p8 O 2017

GRIN & BEAR IT S. Shelley color *Virginia Living* v15 no5 p76 Ag 2017

Oral Health for Healthy Aging D. Scott color *Maclean's* v129 no40 p59 O 10 2016

This Just In J. Zorthian *Time* v188 no20 p19 N 14 2016

Dental care—United States

THE DENTAL DIVIDE M. OTTO cartoon *Mother Jones* v42 no5 p68 S/O 2017

Pediatric Patient Population Growing *USA Today Magazine* v146 no2869 p9 O 2017

Dental caries

brushing up T. REECE *Parents* v91 no12 p120 D 2016

A Mouthful of Answers J. Miller color *Parents* v92 no9 p30 S 2017

Pediatric Patient Population Growing *USA Today Magazine* v146 no2869 p9 O 2017

World of Medicine S. RIDEOUT *Reader's Digest* v188 no1126 p61 D 2016/Ja 2017

Dental floss

Flossing — What Is It Good For? B. ALEX bw color *Discover* v27 no10 p12 D 2016

GRIN & BEAR IT S. Shelley color *Virginia Living* v15 no5 p76 Ag 2017

To Floss or Not to Floss J. KEATS color *Discover* v38 no1 p88 Ja/F 2017

Dental hygiene

Love Them Longer S. ECKELKAMP color *Prevention* v69 no1 p94 Ja 2017

Dental instruments & apparatus

SOMETHING TO SMILE ABOUT L. ROBERTS *Indianapolis Monthly* v40 no11 p100 Jl 2017

A Tougher Tooth Thanks to Mussels *USA Today Magazine* v146 no2869 p7 O 2017

Dental laboratories

U.S. Dental Labs Are Gritting Their Teeth J. S. Hopkins color *Bloomberg Businessweek* no4519 p24 Ap 24 2017

Dental pulp

STEM CELLS MAY HELP HEAL SOFT-TISSUE INJURIES

AND ARTHRITIS C. Barakat and M. McCluskey color *Equus* no477 p16 Je 2017

Dentate gyrus

A disynaptic feedback network activated by experience promotes the integration of new granule cells D. D. Alvarez, D. Giacomini et al bibl graph *Science* v354 no6311 p459 O 28 2016

Dentifrices

See also

Toothpaste

hotBUYS. We Love It! color *Better Nutrition* v78 no12 p16 D 2016

SHAKE UP YOUR MORNING ROUTINE color *Prevention* v69 no4 p11 Ap 2017

Dentist & patient

GENTLE DENTAL C. Cunningham *Washingtonian Magazine* v52 no6 p103 Mr 2017

Dentistry

March highlights questions about benefits of science *Science News* v191 no9 p2 My 13 2017

Dentistry—Humor

ALL IN A Day's Work *Reader's Digest* v188 no1125 p84 N 2016

Dentists

2016 TOP DENTIST PROFILES *Indianapolis Monthly* v40 no4 p111 D 2016

APPOINTMENT WITH DEATH J. LASDUN cartoon color *New Yorker* v93 no19 p30 Jl 3 2017

Dentists Without Borders: A unique encounter with socialized medicine D. SEDARIS *Saturday Evening Post* v289 no5 p40 S/O 2017

FUNNY STUFF! S. Slon *Saturday Evening Post* v289 no5 p6 S/O 2017

Jennifer Plotnick H. GOLDFIELD img *New York* v50 no7 p18 Ap 3 2017

Sugar industry shifted health focus L. BEIL *Science News* v190 no8 p7 O 15 2016

TOP DENTISTS *Indianapolis Monthly* v40 no4 p105 D 2016

Dentists—United States

BEST DENTISTS *Washingtonian Magazine* v52 no2 p244 N 2016

BEST DENTISTS *Washingtonian Magazine* v52 no9 p124 Je 2017

VIRGINIA'S TOP DENTISTS *Virginia Living* v15 no5 p81 Ag 2017

Denton, Ally

What's the Password? Tech startups in Indianapolis are booming, but where are all the women founders? *Indianapolis Monthly* v40 no10 p53 Je 2017

DENTON, BARRY

HOLLYWOOD HORSEWOMAN bw color *Horse & Rider* v56 no10 p56 O 2017

Denton, Miles

Emergence and spread of a human-transmissible multidrug-resistant nontuberculous mycobacterium bibl diag graph *Science* v354 no6313 p751 N 11 2016

Denton, Nick

V.C. FOR VENDETTA D. MARGOLICK color *Vanity Fair* v59 no1 p108 Holiday 2017

Denton, Pat

HOLLYWOOD HORSEWOMAN B. DENTON bw color *Horse & Rider* v56 no10 p56 O 2017

D'Entremont, Susan

Popular piety color *U.S. Catholic* v82 no2 p5 F 2017

Dentures

My husband often doesn't bother to put in his dentures when eating at home. Chunks of food get stuck in his throat from time to time. They eventually pass, but it's still worrisome. Is this dangerous? *Mayo Clinic Health Letter* v35 no5 p8 My 2017

DeNunzio, David

32! THAT'S HOW MANY CLUB CHAMPIONSHIPS THIS READER HAS WON. HERE'S HIS SECRET color *Golf Magazine* v59 no9 p64 S 2017

5 WAYS TO GET A PERFECT READ color *Golf Magazine* v59 no8 p48 Ag 2017

5 WAYS TO SMOKE YOUR FAIRWAY WOODS color *Golf Magazine* v59 no10 p52 O 2017

82% color *Golf Magazine* v58 no11 p54 N 2016

83% THAT'S HOW MUCH THIS READER CUT HIS HANDI-CAP JUST BY USING HIS FEET color *Golf Magazine* v59 no6 p50 Je 2017

ACE OF FACE color *Golf Magazine* v59 no7 p48 Jl 2017

AID FOR WHAT AILS YOU color *Golf Magazine* v59 no1 p39 Ja 2017

ALTERNATE ROUTES color *Golf Magazine* v59 no6 p54 Je 2017

ATTACK MODE color *Golf Magazine* v59 no10 p42 O 2017

ATTACK THE BALL color diag *Golf Magazine* v59 no6 p52 Je 2017

ATTACK THE FLAG color *Golf Magazine* v59 no4 p52 Ap 2017

BASKET CASE color *Golf Magazine* v59 no10 p35 O 2017

BEAUTY SHOT color *Golf Magazine* v59 no8 p56 Ag 2017

BE Clutch HAVE Fun GO Low [Cover story] chart color *Golf Magazine* v58 no11 p61 N 2016

A BEND FOR BIG DRIVES color *Golf Magazine* v59 no1 p48 Ja 2017

Boom Times chart color *Golf Magazine* v59 no3 p55 Mr 2017

Brought to You by the Letter K color *Golf Magazine* v58 no11 p52 N 2016

BUILDING BLOCKS color *Golf Magazine* v59 no11 p52 N 2017

CHIP SERVICE color *Golf Magazine* v59 no11 p44 N 2017

CHIP SERVICE color *Golf Magazine* v59 no8 p46 Ag 2017

CHIP WITH YOUR 3-WOOD color *Golf Magazine* v59 no4 p60 Ap 2017

CLEAN CONTACT! color *Golf Magazine* v59 no4 p49 Ap 2017

CLOSE LIKE A CHAMP [Cover story] color *Golf Magazine* v59 no4 p96 Ap 2017

COURT ORDERS! color *Golf Magazine* v59 no9 p63 S 2017

CRACK THAT WHIP! color *Golf Magazine* v59 no11 p39 N 2017

CURVES AHEAD color *Golf Magazine* v59 no11 p57 N 2017

DO A HEAD CHECK color diag *Golf Magazine* v59 no11 p47 N 2017

DOUBLE PLAY color *Golf Magazine* v59 no1 p46 Ja 2017

DRIVE IT A MILE! color *Golf Magazine* v59 no8 p43 Ag 2017

DUKE OF HAZARDS color *Golf Magazine* v59 no9 p54 S 2017

EXIT SAND, MAN! color *Golf Magazine* v59 no5 p64 My 2017

A FAULT-FREE BACKSWING color *Golf Magazine* v59 no9 p50 S 2017

Find Your Personal Power Move color *Golf Magazine* v59 no7 p54 Jl 2017

FIND YOUR POWER RELEASE chart color *Golf Magazine* v59 no9 p56 S 2017

FINISH IN STYLE color *Golf Magazine* v59 no4 p62 Ap 2017

A FISTFUL OF SAND SAVES color diag *Golf Magazine* v59 no8 p58 Ag 2017

FIVE KEYS FOR SPEED [Cover story] color *Golf Magazine* v59 no7 p58 Jl 2017

Flight School color *Golf Magazine* v59 no1 p52 Ja 2017

Fringe Benefit color *Golf Magazine* v59 no2 p50 F 2017

GAME ON! color *Golf Magazine* v59 no2 p57 F 2017

GET A LEG UP ON THE TEE color *Golf Magazine* v59 no2 p56 F 2017

GET UP TO GO AROUND color *Golf Magazine* v59 no11 p56 N 2017

GIVE A SHORT STROKE THE FINGER color *Golf Magazine* v58 no11 p56 N 2016

GOLF Magazine's Top 100 Teachers in America color *Golf Magazine* v59 no3 p56 Mr 2017

GO LOW, GET FAST color *Golf Magazine* v59 no3 p52 Mr 2017

GO ON A BLENDER chart color *Golf Magazine* v59 no8 p55 Ag 2017

Go SPLAT! On the Tee Box color *Golf Magazine* v58 no12 p82 D 2016

GREEN MACHINE color *Golf Magazine* v59 no3 p50 Mr 2017

HAWAII'S 5-OH! color *Golf Magazine* v59 no1 p54 Ja 2017

High & Mighty color diag *Golf Magazine* v59 no3 p62 Mr 2017

HINGE TO WIN color *Golf Magazine* v59 no2 p55 F 2017

HIT A DRAW... RIGHT NOW! color diag *Golf Magazine* v58 no12 p80 D 2016

HIT LIKE A KID color *Golf Magazine* v59 no10 p38 O 2017

HIT ROPES OFF THE TEE color *Golf Magazine* v59 no2 p55 F 2017

HIT THE BRAKES AT IMPACT color *Golf Magazine* v59 no7 p46 Jl 2017

Ap 14 2017

De Nysschen, Johan—Interviews

What I'd Do Differently Johan de Nysschen, 57 J. PEARLEY HUFFMAN *Car & Driver* v63 no4 p108 O 2017

DENZINE, GYPSY

WHAT CHANGES, WHAT STAYS THE SAME il *Phi Kappa Phi Forum* v97 no2 p1 Summ 2017

Deodorants

help with hygiene T. CETTINA *Parents* v92 no8 p138 Ag 2017

Deodorants—Evaluation

Book Scents color *O, The Oprah Magazine* p70 F 2017

the buzz color *InStyle* v24 no4 p169 Ap 2017

Dark Beauty N. Walker color *Ebony* v72 no9 p45 Jl/Ag 2017

Great Innovators M. BOBO, J. LOVE et al color *Ebony* v72 no5 p44 Mr 2017

Gym color *Seventeen* v76 no3 p48 My 2017

Hot Stuff color *Amazing Wellness* v9 no4 p88 Summ 2017

I Tested Every Natural Deodorant on God's Green Earth... A. GOBLE color *GQ: Gentlemen's Quarterly* v97 no9 p94 S 2017

join the charcoal party! L. BALSAMO color *Seventeen* v76 no3 p100 My 2017

Master the New Mixology S. Nygaard color *Men's Health* v32 no3 p54 Ap 2017

DE OLIVEIRA, CLEUCI

The Many Shades of Maíra Mutti Araújo bw color *Foreign Policy* no225 p46 Jl/Ag 2017

de Oliveira, Felipe Fávaro

Nanoscale nuclear magnetic resonance with chemical resolution diag *Science* v357 no6346 p67 Jl 7 2017

de Oliveira, J.

Observation of a large-scale anisotropy in the arrival directions of cosmic rays above 8 × 1018 eV *Science* v357 no6357 p1266 S 22 2017

de Oliveira, M. A. Leigui

Observation of a large-scale anisotropy in the arrival directions of cosmic rays above 8 × 1018 eV *Science* v357 no6357 p1266 S 22 2017

Deoxyribose

See also

DNA

Mysterious unchanging DNA finds a purpose in life E. Pennisi *Science* v356 no6341 p892 Je 1 2017

De Paepe, Marianne

Inflammation boosts bacteriophage transfer between Salmonella spp bibl diag *Science* v355 no6330 p1211 Mr 17 2017

DePaoli, Michael

CAN NEUROSCIENCE HELP US UNDERSTAND TRUST AT WORK?: INTERACTION color *Harvard Business Review* v95 no2 p18 Mr/Ap 2017

DEPAOLO, MARK

ACUPUNCTURE A HOLISTIC TOOL FOR OPTIMUM HEALTH *Arabian Horse World* v57 no4 p182 Ja 2017

COMPLEMENTARY CARE *Arabian Horse World* v57 no5 p238 F 2017

TRAVEL TACTICS *Arabian Horse World* v57 no6 p156 Mr 2017

ULCERS PART ONE *Arabian Horse World* v57 no2 p138 N 2016

ULGERS PART TWO *Arabian Horse World* v57 no3 p286 D 2016

USING THE GLYCEMIC INDEX TO INCREASE HEALTH & PERFORMANCE *Arabian Horse World* v57 no1 p156 O 2016

DeParle, Jason

Feeling Their Pain color *New York Times Book Review* p16 S 25 2016

The Sea Swallows People color *New York Review of Books* v64 no3 p31 F 23 2017

Department stores

Shopping Spree L. Murtha *Cincinnati Magazine* v50 no5 p66 F 2017

Window Dressing T. B. BROWNE *Indianapolis Monthly* v40 no4 p26 D 2016

Department stores—History

Krauss E. Laborde bw *New Orleans Magazine* v51 no9 p136 Jl 2017

Department stores—United States

EVERYTHING MUST GO P. Wahba color diag *Fortune* v175 no3 p94 Mr 1 2017

Departments

See also

Personnel departments

There's a Difference Between Cooperation and Collaboration R. Ashkenas *Harvard Business Review Digital Articles* p2 Ap 20 2015

De Paula, Anne

Model Search Body Paint ANGUILLA color *Sports Illustrated* v126 no6 p140 F 20 2017

DE PAULA, MATTHEW

ELECTRIC YOUTH color *Road & Track* v69 no4 p60 N 2017

POWER RISING color *Road & Track* v69 no4 p84 N 2017

DEPAUW, LEEN

Combining Biodiversity Resurveys across Regions to Advance Global Change Research *BioScience* v67 no1 p73 Ja 2017

Depeche Mode (Performer)

DEPECHE MODE L. Greenblatt color *Entertainment Weekly* no1459 p58 Mr 31 2017

DEPECHE MODE L. Greenblatt *Entertainment Weekly* no1446/1447 p75 D 2016/Ja 2017

Dependency theory (International relations)

Rethinking 'Structural Violence' K. Hirschfeld *Society* v54 no2 p156 Ap 2017

Using the ERS County Economic Types To Explore Demographic and Economic Trends in Rural Areas L. Kusmin color graph *Amber Waves: The Economics of Food, Farming, Natural Resources, & Rural America* p1 D 2016

DePesa, Ryan

TALK TO US color *Chicago* v66 no2 p11 F 2017

Dépestre, René, 1926-

Hadriana in All My Dreams color *Publishers Weekly* v264 no10 p36 Mr 6 2017

De Petrocellis, Luciano

Activity-based protein profiling reveals off-target proteins of the FAAH inhibitor BIA 10-2474 chart color graph *Science* v356 no6342 p1084 Je 9 2017

DePew, Charlie

HOT NEW TV CRUSHES J. Abidor color *Seventeen* v76 no2 p18 Mr 2017

Deployment (Military strategy)

FIND TIME TO SERVE OTHERS J. STAVRIDIS *Vital Speeches of the Day* v83 no8 p244 Ag 2017

LOVE AND WAR C. Folsom color *Equus* no472 p44 Ja 2017

De Pontieu, B.

On the generation of solar spicules and Alfvénic waves diag *Science* v356 no6344 p1269 Je 23 2017

Deportation

My Parents Were Deported *New York Times Upfront* v149 no13 p9 My 15 2017

Deportation lawsuits

Trump: The New Deportation Threat J. Preston color *New York Review of Books* v64 no9 p8 My 25 2017

Deportation—Canada

Universally Undocumented T. MARLAN cartoon *Walrus* v14 no3 p20 Ap 2017

Deportation—Government policy

Trump: The New Deportation Threat J. Preston color *New York Review of Books* v64 no9 p8 My 25 2017

Deportation—Social aspects

THE BIG UNEASY R. WESTWOOD color *Maclean's* v130 no4 p42 My 2017

Deportation—United States

Cardinal Tobin calls on church leaders to 'put a face' on deportation crisis W. Massey color *America* v216 no13 p17 Je 12 2017

DEPORTATIONS UP UNDER TRUMP S. DALMIA color *Reason* v49 no4 p16 Ag/S 2017

El Paso bishop urges deportation halt until immigration is fixed M. J. O'Loughlin color *America* v217 no3 p16 Ag 7 2017

HANDBOOK FOR THE RESISTANCE *In These Times* v41 no1 p20 Ja 2017

More congregations become sanctuaries for immigrants under threat of deportation E. Evans, Y. Shimron et al *Christian Century* v133 no26 p18 D 21 2016

Sheriffs May Join President Trump's Deportation Force M. Rhodan color *Time* v189 no12 p18 Ap 3 2017

Threats to Deport Dreamers Are Cruel and Shortsighted *America*

v217 no3 p8 Ag 7 2017

White Out color *Weekly Standard* v22 no25 p2 Mr 6 2017

Who Belongs in America? L. Lalami il *Nation* v304 no9 p12 Mr 20 2017

Deportation—United States—Government policy

Bad neighbor policy? Mexico's President Peña Nieto struggles to respond to Trump administration Hootsen color *America* v216 no8 p16 Ap 17 2017

Deportees

CALLED AWAY J. BLITZER cartoon *New Yorker* v92 no46 p30 Ja 23 2017

Deposit accounts

Resolve Errors on Your Credit Card Bill L. GERSTNER chart *Kiplinger's Personal Finance* v71 no2 p51 F 2017

Deposit insurance—United States

Deposit Insurance Has Your Back L. GERSTNER chart *Kiplinger's Personal Finance* v71 no5 p49 My 2017

DePoy, Phillip

The English Agent *Publishers Weekly* v263 no51 p124 D 12 2016

Depp, Johnny, 1963-

DEPP FINANCING M. SEAL color *Vanity Fair* v59 no8 p110 Ag 2017

'Pirates 5' Scrapes the Franchise Bottom P. Travers color *Rolling Stone* no1289 p60 Je 15 2017

Depp, Lily-Rose, 1999-

BEAUTY'S NEW BALLER K. Diamond color *InStyle* v24 no5 p228 My 2017

HOORAY FOR Hollywood J. Ferrise, K. Peiffer et al color *InStyle* v23 no12 p252 N 2016

Depreciation

Selling Your Sewer's Story J. Marlowe *Governing* v30 no3 p63 D 2016

De Pree, Erin

Important factors in shaping physics identities *Physics Today* v70 no5 p12 My 2017

Depressed persons

FACING THE DARKNESS L. Entis color *Fortune* v174 no8 p64 D 15 2016

Depression in adolescence

The Kids Are Not All Right [Cover story] S. Schrobsdorff color diag *Time* v188 no19 p44 N 7 2016

Through the Motions N. BAZIS color *America* v215 p27 N 28 2016

What You Said About ... color map *Time* v188 no20 p5 N 14 2016

Depression in children

SAVE THE PAST LIFE FOR ME R. O'CONNOR cartoon *Chicago* v66 no1 p34 Ja 2017

Depression in men—Treatment

Good Girl A. Green color *Vogue* v207 no11 p96 N 2017

Depression in women

CASING the Joint E. GILBERT cartoon *O, The Oprah Magazine* p33 Mr 2017

Depressions (Economics)—1929

Yes We Did M. BRUNE *Sierra* v101 no6 p4 N/D 2016

Depressions (Economics)—1929—United States

How It Begins ... J. MEACHAM *New York Times Book Review* p14 Ja 22 2017

Déprez, Benoit

Reversion of antibiotic resistance in Mycobacterium tuberculosis by spiroisoxazoline SMARt-420 bibl diag *Science* v355 no6330 p1206 Mr 17 2017

Deprez, Esmé E.

Blue State AGs: The Dems' New Resistance bw *Bloomberg Businessweek* no4516 p25 Mr 27 2017

California's Dream color *Bloomberg Businessweek* no4500 p26 N 21 2016

Medical Journals Have a Problem color *Bloomberg Businessweek* no4536 p52 S 4 2017

SMOKE'EM OUT [Cover story] bw color *Bloomberg Businessweek* no4541 p40 O 9 2017

THIS ROBOTIC BABY MIGHT NEED CHANGING color *Bloomberg Businessweek* no4505 p64 D 26 2016

Trump Delays a Fight On Presidential Power color *Bloomberg Businessweek* no4520 p29 My 1 2017

Depth of field (Photography)

Understanding Aperture R. BURRESS *Arizona Highways* v93

no6 p9 Je 2017

De Quincey, Thomas, 1785-1859

The First Troll J. PARKER color *Atlantic* v318 no5 p28 D 2016

True Confessions D. HEITMAN color *Weekly Standard* v22 no18 p39 Ja 16 2017

Der, Channing J.

Drugging RAS: Know the enemy bibl diag *Science* v355 no6330 p1158 Mr 17 2017

Der Freischutz (Theatrical production)

Der Freischütz M. Wheeler *Opera News* v81 no7 p44 Ja 2017

Der Rosenkavalier (Theatrical production)

Der Rosenkavalier G. Hall *Opera News* v81 no9 p44 Mr 2017

THE PURSUIT OF THE ROSE J. S. MCMILLAN *Opera News* v81 no10 p36 Ap 2017

Renée FLEMING A. F. COLLINS color *Vanity Fair* v59 no5 p114 Ap 2017

Time Capsule R. Platt cartoon *New Yorker* v93 no9 p13 Ap 17 2017

Derailleurs

WHAT'S IN THE BOX? A SHIFT IN PERSPECTIVE t. engel color *Bike Magazine* v24 no6 p134 Ag 2017

Derailleurs—Evaluation

clutch move b. minnigh color *Bike Magazine* v24 no3 p54 My 2017

GET IN GEAR R. Palmer, T. Engel et al bw color *Bike Magazine* v24 no1 p122 Ja/F 2017

Derakshan, Hossein

A Smarter Web *MIT Technology Review* v120 no1 p12 Ja/F 2017

D'ERASMO, STACEY

His Past Discretions *New York Times Book Review* p12 N 13 2016

THOU SHALT NOT KILL color *O, The Oprah Magazine* p83 Ag 2017

Derby Cycle Werke GmbH

"WHERE DO I WANT TO RIDE? DUH, EVERYWHERE." J. Lindsey and B. STRICKLAND color *Bicycling* v58 no3 p48 Ap 2017

Derbyshire, John

DOESN'T ADD UP *Claremont Review of Books* v17 no2 p61 Spr 2017

Derbyshire, Keith M.

Intercellular communication and conjugation are mediated by ESX secretion systems in mycobacteria bibl diag graph *Science* v354 no6310 p347 O 21 2016

Derecho storms

A Retrospective on the Historical Derecho of June 29, 2012 J. B. Halverson *Weatherwise* v70 no5 p52 S/O 2017

Deregulation

The Taxi Industry Can Innovate, Too R. Mohammed *Harvard Business Review Digital Articles* p2 F 13 2015

Deregulation—United States

Deregulation Under Trump *Congressional Digest* v96 no4 p2 Ap 2017

Derek, Kevin—Interviews

Q&A WITH THE DIRECTOR OF "THE REAL MIYAGI" bw color *Black Belt* v55 no2 p39 F/Mr 2017

DERESIEWICZ, WILLIAM

In DEFENSE of FACTS color *Atlantic* v319 no1 p90 Ja/F 2017

A Jane Austen Kind of Guy: I GET IT THAT WOMEN FIND MY AFFINITY FOR THEIR WRITER INTRUSIVE, BUT HER WORLD HAS MUCH TO OFFER MEN, TOO *American Scholar* v86 no4 p84 Aut 2017

On Political Correctness *American Scholar* v86 no2 p30 Spr 2017

READY FOR PRIME TIME *Harper's Magazine* v333 no1998 p82 N 2016

Derevensky, Jeff

grab bags of awesome S. Dolgoff color *Good Housekeeping* v264 no5 p140 My 2017

Derevianko, Anatoly P.

Neandertal and Denisovan DNA from Pleistocene sediments bw color *Science* v356 no6338 p605 My 12 2017

Derfler-Rozin, Rellie

Does Doing the Same Work Over and Over Again Make You Less Ethical? *Harvard Business Review Digital Articles* p2 Mr 28 2017

De Rhodes, Alexandre

Mission in the vernacular P. Jenkins *Christian Century* v134 no4

p61 F 15 2017

DERING, CHERYL
The Question color *O, The Oprah Magazine* p14 N 2017

Derivative securities—Sales & prices
Dirty Deeds Hidden In a Mess of Data M. Leising *Bloomberg Businessweek* no4512 p38 F 20 2017

Der Ling, Princess
1903: Forbidden City P. D. Ling *Lapham's Quarterly* v10 no1 p162 Wint 2017

Dermatologic agents
See also
    Lip care preparations
    Sunscreens (Cosmetics)
Ace No-Makeup Makeup L. Desantis color *Health* v31 no2 p27 Mr 2017
Shiny, Healthy Hair for Less L. Desantis color *Health* v31 no2 p33 Mr 2017

Dermatologists
David Colbert A. Serrano color *InStyle* v24 no7 p94 Jl 2017
Yep, your skin needs a serum L. Desantis color *Health* v31 no9 p36 N 2017

Dermatology
BE HAPPIER IN YOUR SKIN G. WAY color *Redbook* p93 My 2017
TOP CANCER DOCTORS J. DUGDALE, J. HARDBERGER et al color *Chicago* v66 no1 p84 Ja 2017

Dermatophilosis
BENEATH THE SURFACE OF RAIN ROT L. Threlkeld color *Practical Horseman* v45 no6 p54 Je 2017

Dermody, Bill
No Ball Left Behind *Tennis* v52 no6 p76 N/D 2016

Dermody, Terence S.
Reovirus infection triggers inflammatory responses to dietary antigens and development of celiac disease color diag *Science* v356 no6333 p44 Ap 7 2017

Dern, Laura, 1967-
APOLOGIZER T. Friend cartoon *New Yorker* v92 no36 p17 N 7 2016
The Art of Science color *InStyle* v24 no11 p96 N 2017
THE DEADLIEST KLATCH B. HANDY bw *Vanity Fair* p170 Hollywood 2017 Supplement
FEEL THE Dern L. Hill color *InStyle* v24 no4 p200 Ap 2017
Hello! L. Brown color *InStyle* v24 no4 p24 Ap 2017
LAURA DERN D. Franich color *Entertainment Weekly* no1459 p34 Mr 31 2017
The Roush Review M. Roush color *TV Guide* v65 no7 p18 F 13 2017
Why I Love color *InStyle* v24 no2 p164 F 2017
Wild Women Do L. B. Ray color *InStyle* v24 no9 p208 S 2017

Dern, Laura, 1967—Interviews
Laura Dern D. WALTERS bw color *Conde Nast Traveler* v52 no6 p40 Je/Jl 2017

Dernavich, Drew
Esquipedia cartoon color graph *Esquire* p30 S 2017
I WAS MARRIED TO BANKSY cartoon *Esquire* p130 N 2017

De Robertis, Carolina
Baby, Behave! bw color *Weekly Standard* v22 no32 p3 My 1 2017
Clinton's Towering Fiasco color *Weekly Standard* v22 no32 p2 My 1 2017
Consensual Tools color *Weekly Standard* v22 no32 p2 My 1 2017

De Roffignac, Louis Philippe Joseph
Roffignac E. LABORDE cartoon *New Orleans Magazine* v51 no12 p168 O 2017

DeRogatis, Jim
The Lonely Crusade of Jim DeRogatis M. Caro color *Chicago* v66 no11 p90 N 2017

DeRousse, Edmond P.
Horsemanship, 60 & Over color *Horse & Rider* v55 no11 p12 N 2016

Derousseau, Ryan
AVOIDING A STEEP DESCENT color diag *Fortune* v175 no4 p44 Mr 15 2017
A BIG PAYOFF FOR CYBERCOP STOCKS color diag *Fortune* v176 no3 p28 S 1 2017
A COFFEE STOCK LOSES ITS BUZZ color diag *Fortune* v175 no3 p36 Mr 1 2017

KEEPING CHARITY IN THE FAMILY color *Fortune* v174 no8 p54 D 15 2016
A LEGACY WORTH WORKING FOR color *Fortune* v75 no1 p36 Ja 1 2017
RESISTING ACTIVISTS, AND WINNING color diag *Fortune* v176 no5 p38 O 1 2017
STOCKS THAT DODGE THE BUYBACK BLUES chart color diag *Fortune* v175 no6 p29 My 1 2017
STOCKS WITH A SHAKY FOUNDATION color diag *Fortune* v174 no6 p39 N 1 2016
WANTED: FRESH SOLUTIONS FOR AGE-OLD PROBLEMS color diag *Fortune* v175 no6 p68 My 1 2017
WHEN SHAREHOLDERS ARE SPECTATORS color diag *Fortune* v175 no2 p40 F 1 2017
X-Ray: Wells Fargo diag *Money* v45 no11 p47 D 2016

Deroy, Ophelia
The intelligent invertebrate color *Science* v354 no6316 p1110 D 2 2016

Derr, Seth
Old Dominion Granite color *Climbing* no353 p32 My/Je 2017

Derrible, Sybil
Street smart color *Science* v354 no6310 p293 O 21 2016

Derrickson, Scott
DOCTOR STRANGE B. A. DuHamel color *Sound & Vision* v82 no6 p70 Jl/Ag 2017
Doctor Strange C. Nashawaty color *Entertainment Weekly* no1439 p40 N 11 2016
Strange Interlude J. PODHORETZ *Weekly Standard* v22 no11 p43 N 21 2016

Derringer, Nancy
Addressing Low Reading Scores *Education Digest* v83 no1 p59 S 2017

DERROW, PAULA
DIABETES IN THE FAMILY color *Prevention* v68 no11 p86 N 2016
What Would You Do? cartoon *Women's Health* v14 no1 p141 Ja/F 2017

Der Sarkissian, Clio
Ancient genomic changes associated with domestication of the horse color diag *Science* v356 no6336 p442 Ap 28 2017

Derschowitz, Jessica
THE 25 MOST PATRIOTIC MOVIES OF ALL TIME color *Entertainment Weekly* no1472 p30 Je 30 2017
ANDREW RANNELLS REACHES THE HIGH NOTES IN FALSETTOS color *Entertainment Weekly* no1438 p70 N 4 2016
ANGEL'S SANTA DRAG color *Entertainment Weekly* no1460/1461 p65 Ap 7-17 2017
THE DEVIL IS IN THE D-FLAT color *Entertainment Weekly* no1454/1455 p41 F 24 2017
THE GREATEST DISNEY SONGS OF ALL TIME color *Entertainment Weekly* no1454/1455 p36 F 24 2017
ORPHAN BLACK A TO Z color *Entertainment Weekly* no1470 p24 Je 16 2017
The Tonys You Didn't See color *Entertainment Weekly* no1471 p16 Je 23 2017
What's Next for Hamilton's Breakout Stars? color *Entertainment Weekly* no1454/1455 p104 F 24 2017
WONDER WHEEL color *Entertainment Weekly* no1478 / 1479 p76 Ag 18-25 2017

Dershowitz, Alan, 1938—Political & social views
BALANCING ACT A. Marantz cartoon *New Yorker* v92 no41 p26 D 12 2016

De Rugy, Veronique
DEAR GOP: TAX CREDITS ARE NOT THE ANSWER *Reason* v49 no2 p13 Je 2017
FEDERAL INFRASTRUCTURE SPENDING IS A BAD DEAL *Reason* v48 no10 p14 Mr 2017
HEALTH CARE COSTS ARE THE REASON YOU'RE NOT GETTING A RAISE bw *Reason* v49 no5 p11 O 2017
New Zealand Has Pizza Delivery Drones *Reason* v48 no7 p16 D 2016
Since Obama Took Office, Debt Has Nearly Doubled graph *Reason* v48 no9 p15 F 2017
WHY ARE MARKETS REJOICING AT TRUMP'S WIN? *Reason* v48 no11 p10 Ap 2017
WHY STRONGER ECONOMIC GROWTH IS SO IMPOR-

TANT diag *Reason* v48 no8 p12 Ja 2017

Derujinsky, Gleb

Fashion Film Archives bw color *American History* v52 no3 p26 Ag 2017

Dervis, Kemal

Reflections on Progress: Essays on the Global Political Economy G. J. Ikenberry *Foreign Affairs* v96 no2 p167 Mr/Ap 2017

Derworiz, Colette

A trip to Lang Bay color *Maclean's* v130 no9 p15 O 2017

Why are grizzlies dying on Canada's railway tracks? color *Science* v355 no6325 p561 F 10 2017

DERY, MARK

The Eyes of The World Are Watching Now bw color *Publishers Weekly* v264 no15 p28 Ap 10 2017

Ghost Story bw color *Publishers Weekly* v264 no35 p96 Ag 28 2017

Deryabin, A.

Massive blow-out craters formed by hydrate-controlled methane expulsion from the Arctic seafloor graph map *Science* v356 no6341 p948 Je 1 2017

Desager, Matyas

De novo design of a biologically active amyloid bibl graph *Science* v354 no6313 paah4949-1 N 11 2016

Desai, Maya

Emergence and spread of a human-transmissible multidrug-resistant nontuberculous mycobacterium bibl diag graph *Science* v354 no6313 p751 N 11 2016

Desai, Mihir A.

The Debate on Corporate Tax Reform Just Started for Real *Harvard Business Review Digital Articles* p1 My 1 2017

Finance Can Be a Noble Profession (Yes, Really) *Harvard Business Review Digital Articles* p2 Jl 17 2017

Desai, Nirupa

The structure of the yeast mitochondrial ribosome bibl color *Science* v355 no6324 p528 F 3 2017

Desai, Saahil

COLLEGE ELECTORAL color *Washington Monthly* v49 no9/10 p58 S/O 2017

Desai, Sujay B.

MoS2 transistors with 1-nanometer gate lengths bibl color graph *Science* v354 no6308 p99 O 7 2016

Desai, Tariq

Chimpanzee genomic diversity reveals ancient admixture with bonobos bibl diag graph map *Science* v354 no6311 p477 O 28 2016

Desalvo, Mike

DeSalvo Builder Special M. YOZELL color *Bicycling* v58 no1 p76 Ja/F 2017

DeSalvo, Whitney

Mare Magic C. Toy color diag *Spin to Win Rodeo* v21 no3 p52 My 2017

Desan, Philippe

A LIFE BEYOND THE TOWER: While this new biography of Montaigne might include debatable interpretations of his Essays, it is an essential study of the writer's life N. Kenny *History Today* v67 no7 p94 Jl 2017

MIXED UP A. GOPNIK cartoon *New Yorker* v92 no45 p81 Ja 16 2017

A New Man D. GREEN diag *National Review* v69 no4 p39 Mr 6 2017

DeSANCTIS, ALEXANDRA

Preserving Pluralism *National Review* v69 no15 p41 Ag 14 2017

Religious Liberty after Obergefell color *National Review* v69 no11 p19 Je 12 2017

De Sanctis, Enzo

Energy from Nuclear Fission An Introduction N. Corngold *Physics Today* v70 no3 p61 Mr 2017

De Sanctis, M. C.

Localized aliphatic organic material on the surface of Ceres bibl graph *Science* v355 no6326 p719 F 17 2017

Seasonal exposure of carbon dioxide ice on the nucleus of comet 67P/Churyumov-Gerasimenko bibl bw graph *Science* v354 no6319 p1563 D 23 2016

DeSanctis, Marcia

Creature Comforts color *Vogue* v207 no3 p380 Mr 2017

THIGH Masters color *Vogue* v206 no12 p197a D 2016

De Santillana, Laura—Exhibitions

What Comes Next color *American Craft* v76 no6 p96 D 2016-Ja 2017

DeSANTIS, BALINDA

GIFTS that UPLIFT! cartoon *O, The Oprah Magazine* p148 D 2016

DESANTIS, JOHN

TRACING AN ATROCITY: How an Obscure Affidavit in the National Archives Unraveled a Historical Mystery *Prologue* v49 no2 p42 Summ 2017

Desantis, Lisa

Ace No-Makeup Makeup color *Health* v31 no2 p27 Mr 2017

BEAUTY'S NEXT BIG THINGS color *Health* v31 no7 p35 S 2017

Brow Growth Serums color *Health* v31 no2 p41 Mr 2017

Concealer game changer color diag *Health* v31 no8 p30 O 2017

Cover Up Anything color *Health* v31 no4 p27 My 2017

A Day at the Beach... color *Health* v31 no6 p34 Jl 2017

Does It Really Work? color *Health* v31 no5 p31 Je 2017

FIGHT THE FRIZZ AND WIN! color *Health* v31 no3 p94 Ap 2017

Find Your Dream Mask color *Health* v31 no2 p38 Mr 2017

FIND YOUR FRAGRANCE color *Health* v30 no9 p128 N 2016

GAME-CHANGING GIFTS color *Health* v30 no10 p116 D 2016

Get Lush Lips color *Health* v30 no9 p31 N 2016

I Want Her...Coral Lips color *Health* v31 no6 p32 Jl 2017

I Want Her... Lashes color *Health* v31 no4 p33 My 2017

I Want Her Polished Pony! color *Health* v31 no7 p50 S 2017

Our fave superfoods for your face color *Health* v31 no8 p33 O 2017

Power Ingredient: Gold! color *Health* v31 no1 p34 Ja 2017

Shiny, Healthy Hair for Less color *Health* v31 no2 p33 Mr 2017

Spice Up Your Skin Care color *Health* v30 no10 p32 D 2016

SUTTON FOSTER "Youthfulness Comes from Within" color *Health* v31 no4 p21 My 2017

UP YOUR BEAUTY GAME color *Health* v31 no1 p102 Ja 2017

The Very Best in Drugstore Lip Picks color *Health* v31 no3 p30 Ap 2017

Yep, your skin needs a serum color *Health* v31 no9 p36 N 2017

you REALLY can wear GLITTER after 30 color *Health* v31 no9 p88 N 2017

DeSantis, Marc G.

BEHIND THE LINES: TRAIN MAN color map *MHQ: Quarterly Journal of Military History* v30 no1 p24 Aut 2017

DESANTIS, MARISSA

Color Coordinated: At Paul Taylor Dance Company, its all about functional layers in colors that really pop *Dance Magazine* v91 no10 p33 O 2017

Millennial Pink: At New York City Ballet, the dancers add a bright twist to classic ballet pink *Dance Magazine* v91 no9 p40 S 2017

Desantis, Rachel

DRAFTING THE BACHELOR FANTASY LEAGUE color *Entertainment Weekly* no1446/1447 p26 D 2016/Ja 2017

DeSantola, Alicia

Startups Can't Revolve Around Their Founders If They Want to Succeed *Harvard Business Review Digital Articles* p2 Mr 4 2016

Des Barres, Pamela

Let It Bleed: How to Write a Rockin' Memoir *Publishers Weekly* v264 no7 p64 F 13 2017

Descartes, René, 1596-1650

HOW POVERTY KILLS wondeR and what we can do about it R. BELL *Humanist* v77 no5 p16 S/O 2017

Desch, Michael C.

The Soldier and the State: We thank you for your service--sucker! *American Conservative* v16 no5 p38 S/O 2017

The Unnamed Behemoth E. Miller bw *Commonweal* v144 no9 p32 My 19 2017

Desch, Steven

Radical idea could restore Arctic Ocean's sea ice S. Perkins color graph *Science News* v191 no9 p4 My 13 2017

De Schaepdrijver, Sophie

Under Germany's Thumb: An Englishwoman's journals shed new light on the occupation of Belgium during World War I M. SEYMOUR *New York Times Book Review* p20 Jl 2 2017

DESCHAMBEAULT, JOSETTE

2017

En Plein Derrière img *New York* v50 no15 p44 Jl 24 2017

The Father of Modern Powerboat Design M. PETERS color *Power & Motoryacht* v34 no6 p20 Je 2017

GREAT ODIN'S RAVEN! *Cincinnati Magazine* v50 no11 p31 Ag 2017

MILAN rising H. MARTIN bw color *Architectural Digest* v74 no8 p80 Ag 2017

Resources color *House Beautiful* v159 no3 p122 Ap 2017

THE RISK-TAKING, MOOD-MAKING MAGIC OF HAIDER ACKERMANN J. von Sothen color *Esquire* p126 S 2017

SPACE QUEST C. FOSTER color *House Beautiful* p116 Ag 2017

Style 100 J. Ferrise, E. Wilson et al color *InStyle* v23 no13 p79 D 2016

Designers—Exhibitions

Technicolor Dreams J. Tarmy color *Bloomberg Businessweek* no4532 p66 Jl 31 2017

Designers—Interviews

Eric Cesal M. SITZ *Architectural Record* v205 no1 p23 Ja 2017

Q&A WITH KEITH KREEGER *Texas Monthly* v45 no1 p26 Ja 2017

Designers—United States

Virgil Abloh J. K. DE VALLE color *Architectural Digest* v74 no3 p36 Mr 2017

Designing Women (TV program)

ROLE CALL JEAN SMART S. Vilkomerson color *Entertainment Weekly* no1449 p34 Ja 20 2017

Desiigner (Performer)—Interviews

DESIIGNER T. PUSHA *Interview* v46 no8 p34 O 2016

Desire

    See also

    Lust

CONSTANT CRAVINGS [Cover story] L. Turner color *Amazing Wellness* v9 no6 p44 EarlyWint 2017

LUST LESSONS A. Burroughs cartoon *Men's Health* v32 no3 p25 Ap 2017

THE NIGHT REPORT A. BARRODALE color *Tricycle: The Buddhist Review* v26 no2 p60 Wint 2016

Desired Things (Short story)

Desired Things A. McDermott *Commonweal* v143 no18 p24 N 11 2016

Desisa, Lelisa

A GOOD, LONG RUN color *Runner's World* v52 no6 p12 Jl 2017

MOONSHOT [Cover story] A. Hutchinson bw cartoon color map *Runner's World* v52 no5 p62 Je 2017

Desjardins, Jake

HOMESTEAD HACKS *Mother Earth News* no280 p66 F/Mr 2017

Deskey, Donald

MELTING POT MODERN S. D. Coffin cartoon color *Magazine Antiques* v184 no2 p110 Mr/Ap 2017

Desks

My Desk: DANIELLE STEEL color *Vanity Fair* v59 no10 p94 O 2017

Desks—Evaluation

Adam's Home STYLE SHEET color *O, The Oprah Magazine* p64 S 2017

HIGH or LOW? color *Good Housekeeping* v265 no3 p50 S 2017

Desktop environments (Computer interfaces)

How to use iCloud Drive's new Desktop and Documents access in macOS Sierra R. LOYOLA color *Macworld - Digital Edition* v33 no11 p135 N 2016

Desmarteau, Joel—Interviews

Small Breeders BIG RESULTS M. Moore *Arabian Horse World* v57 no4 p150 Ja 2017

De Smet, Frederik

De novo design of a biologically active amyloid bibl graph *Science* v354 no6313 paah4949-1 N 11 2016

Desmond, Howard

Lee Rubin: Our mentor and role model *Science* v355 no6327 p806 F 24 2017

Desmond, Kenneth

Kilogram-scale prexasertib monolactate monohydrate synthesis under continuous-flow CGMP conditions chart diag *Science* v356 no6343 p1144 Je 16 2017

Desmond, Matthew

HOUSE RULES: *New York Times Magazine* p48 My 14 2017

No. 10 EVICTED T. Jordan color *Entertainment Weekly* no1444/1445 p108 D 16 2016

Desmond, Paul

Kilogram-scale prexasertib monolactate monohydrate synthesis under continuous-flow CGMP conditions chart diag *Science* v356 no6343 p1144 Je 16 2017

Desmond-Hellmann, Susan, 1958-

SUE DESMOND-HELLMANN color *Bloomberg Businessweek* no4503 p76 D 12 2016

de Sousa Farias, E.

Persistent effects of pre-Columbian plant domestication on Amazonian forest composition bibl chart graph map *Science* v355 no6328 p925 Mr 3 2017

de Souza, F. C.

Persistent effects of pre-Columbian plant domestication on Amazonian forest composition bibl chart graph map *Science* v355 no6328 p925 Mr 3 2017

De Souza, João Pereira

Penguin and Human BFFs R. d. Janeiro and S. Schwartz color *National Geographic Kids* no465 p12 N 2016

DE SOUZA, NADIA

An Ecoregion-Based Approach to Protecting Half the Terrestrial Realm *BioScience* v67 no6 p534 Je 2017

de Souza, V.

Observation of a large-scale anisotropy in the arrival directions of cosmic rays above 8×10^{18} eV *Science* v357 no6357 p1266 S 22 2017

de Souza Coelho, L.

Persistent effects of pre-Columbian plant domestication on Amazonian forest composition bibl chart graph map *Science* v355 no6328 p925 Mr 3 2017

Despacito (Music)

THE BIGGEST SUMMER BREAKOUTS (SO FAR) E. R. Brown, D. Coggan et al color diag *Entertainment Weekly* no1474/1475 p15 Jl 21-28 2017

Two Latin Singers—and Justin Bieber—Hit No. 1 L. Shaw bw color *Bloomberg Businessweek* no4525 p21 Je 5 2017

WILL THIS MAN HAVE THE SONG OF SUMMER? M. Vain color *Entertainment Weekly* no1470 p12 Je 16 2017

Despair

Don't Give In to Despair A. NABAUM *New Republic* v248 no3 p37 Mr 2017

Despan, D.

Seasonal exposure of carbon dioxide ice on the nucleus of comet 67P/Churyumov-Gerasimenko bibl bw graph *Science* v354 no6319 p1563 D 23 2016

Despicable Me 3 (Film)

Despicable Me 3 L. Greenblatt color *Entertainment Weekly* no1473 p42 Jl 7 2017

MEET THE NEW MINION M. Snetiker color *Entertainment Weekly* no1467 p13 My 26 2017

Minions, Delightfully Relegated to Their Proper Place S. Zacharek color *Time* v190 no2/3 p90 Jl 10-17 2017

TREY PARKER'S DESPICABLE DEBUT M. Snetiker color *Entertainment Weekly* no1473 p14 Jl 7 2017

What's Hot Now J. Abidor color *Seventeen* v76 no3 p15 My 2017

Desplan, Claude

Glia relay differentiation cues to coordinate neuronal development in Drosophila color *Science* v357 no6354 p886 S 1 2017

Despommier, Dickson D., 1940-

My Nearest and Dearest Enemy J. MOORE *BioScience* v66 no10 p907 O 1 2016

Desportes, Alexandre-François, 1661-1743

Hungry for more J. Bleem color *U.S. Catholic* v82 no6 p50 Je 2017

Despotism

XU HONGCI E. Osnos cartoon *New Yorker* v92 no42 p94 D 19 2016

Desroses, Mathieu

Reversion of antibiotic resistance in Mycobacterium tuberculosis by spiroisoxazoline SMARt-420 bibl diag *Science* v355 no6330 p1206 Mr 17 2017

Dessay, Natalie, 1965-

CLASSICAL MUSIC *New Yorker* v93 no11 p5 My 1 2017

Dessen, Sarah, 1970-

Once and for All *Publishers Weekly* v264 no36 p89 S 4 2017

Dessert sauces—Evaluation

Enjoy Nebraska Spreadables color *Nebraska Life* v21 no1 p55 Ja/F 2017

Desserts

Bet you didn't know S. THOMPSON and J. SCHAFER color *National Geographic Kids* no465 p10 N 2016

BROWNIE POINTS S. CAREY *Martha Stewart Living* no269 p86 N 2016

Desserts for the two of you color *Redbook* p126 F 2017

Don't Have a Cow K. O'Reilly *Sierra* v102 no5 p8 St/O 2017

EDITOR'S LETTER M. Schaffer *Washingtonian Magazine* v52 no9 p14 Je 2017

Fresh & slimming snacks [Cover story] L. Lillien color *Redbook* p74 Je 2017

HALO-HALO REMIX L. BURUM *Los Angeles Magazine* v61 no11 p133 N 2016

Health Food You Can Love G. Hamilton *New York Times Magazine* p20 Ag 13 2017

ICE DREAMS [Cover story] J. R. FULLER color *Chicago* v66 no6 p45 Je 2017

Let Them Eat Cake! V. Hart *New Orleans Homes & Lifestyles* v20 no1 p66 Wint 2016

Lighten up C. BOYD color *Better Homes & Gardens* v95 no6 p134 Je 2017

Lord Carnarvon's Boozy Bramble Pudding *British Heritage Travel* v38 no4 p47 Jl/Ag 2017

The New Art of Dessert B. HALLOCK *Los Angeles Magazine* v61 no11 p124 N 2016

SL COOKING SCHOOL color *Southern Living* v52 no3 p136 Mr 2017

Soak It Up B. ESPARZA *Los Angeles Magazine* v61 no11 p129 N 2016

The Sweet Life *Los Angeles Magazine* v61 no11 p122 N 2016

SWEETS IN A FLASH color *Redbook* p127 Je 2017

A Tart to Remember: Some desserts from childhood never leave you D. Greenspan *New York Times Magazine* p22 Jl 2 2017

Tout Sweet *Los Angeles Magazine* p10 Ja 2017

Winterizing M. W. Spencer *New Orleans Homes & Lifestyles* v20 no1 p14 Wint 2016

Desserts—Charts, diagrams, etc.

IT'S PARTY TIME! WHERE'S THE CAKE? J. TRINH *Los Angeles Magazine* v61 no11 p128 N 2016

Desserts—Evaluation

Thank You Very Mochi G. SNYDER *Los Angeles Magazine* v62 no9 p116 S 2017

de Stanchina, Elisa

SOX2 promotes lineage plasticity and antiandrogen resistance in TP53- and RB1-deficient prostate cancer bibl graph *Science* v355 no6320 p1 Ja 6 2017

D'ESTE, CYNTHIA

AT WINTER *Humanist* v77 no1 p46 Ja/F 2017

DeSteno, David

2 Ways to Regain Your Boss's Trust *Harvard Business Review Digital Articles* p2 N 26 2014

The Connection Between Pride and Persistence *Harvard Business Review Digital Articles* p2 Ag 22 2016

To Make a Team More Effective, Find Their Commonalities *Harvard Business Review Digital Articles* p2 D 12 2016

Destination image (Tourism)

BUTCHART GARDENS D. HISLOP *Sea Magazine* v108 no10 pPNW-9 O 2016

CAPITOLA, CALIF *Sea Magazine* v108 no10 pCA-10 O 2016

MURAL TOWN D. HISLOP *Sea Magazine* v108 no10 pPNW-1 O 2016

RELAX YOURSELF IN LANGLEY D. HISLOP *Sea Magazine* v108 no10 pPNW-4 O 2016

Destiny, Ryan

Lenny Kravitz Gets Typecast on Star M. Logan *TV Guide* v64 no48 p10 N 21 2016

Star M. Logan *TV Guide* p44 D 5 2016

Destler, I. M.

America's Uneasy History with Free Trade *Harvard Business Review Digital Articles* p2 Ap 28 2016

De Strooper, Bart

De novo design of a biologically active amyloid bibl graph *Sci-*

ence v354 no6313 paah4949-1 N 11 2016

Destroyers (Warships)—Accidents

Lightbox K. Reilly color *Time* v190 no1 p14 Jl 3 2017

Destruction of cultural property

OUR HUMAN STORY J. Magness color *Archaeology* v70 no5 p6 S/O 2017

Desus & Mero (TV program)

Desus and Mero L. SCHWARTZBERG img *New York* v50 no6 p14 Mr 20 2017

HIGH RATINGS: DESUS & MERO JUDGE FALL TV M. YARM cartoon color *Wired* v25 no9 p30 S 2017

de Swaan, J. C.

Japan Is Counting on Shareholder Activism to Improve Its Economy *Harvard Business Review Digital Articles* p2 S 20 2017

de Tauzia-Moreau, Marie-Ludivine

The preprophase band of microtubules controls the robustness of division orientation in plants graph *Science* v356 no6334 p186 Ap 14 2017

Detavernier, Christophe

Super-dry reforming of methane intensifies CO_2 utilization via Le Chatelier's principle bibl diag graph *Science* v354 no6311 p449 O 28 2016

Detection of extrasolar planets

Exoplanet probe has focus problem color *Science* v357 no6350 p432 Ag 4 2017

Detective & mystery stories

See also

Ghost stories

Moving Beyond E-books L. Dawson *Publishers Weekly* v264 no38 p24 S 18 2017

MYSTERY NOVELS INSPIRED BY A CO-WORKING SPACE Z. KHALID cartoon *New Yorker* v93 no3 p33 Mr 6 2017

Ten Practical Tactics to Unravel the Uncanny M. POLIDORO *Skeptical Inquirer* v41 no1 p25 Ja/F 2017

Detective & mystery comic books, strips, etc.

CELL BLOCK GQ color *GQ: Gentlemen's Quarterly* v86 no12 p138 D 2016

Detective & mystery stories—Charts, diagrams, etc.

CATEGORY BESTSELLERS AUG. 29-SEPT. 25, 2016 *Publishers Weekly* v263 no41 p18 O 10 2016

CATEGORY BESTSELLERS chart *Publishers Weekly* v264 no33 p17 Ag 14 2017

CATEGORY BESTSELLERS C. JURIS chart *Publishers Weekly* v264 no7 p16 F 13 2017

Detectives

NOW HIRING: TEEN CIGARETTE NARCS J. STOOKSBERRY bw *Reason* v49 no6 p14 N 2017

Rescuing The Police A. STAPLETON color *Reader's Digest* v189 no1129 p12 Ap 2017

Detectives—United States

The Worst Case: Husband-and-wife private detectives work their saddest investigation yet: the murder of their own daughter A. WREN *Indianapolis Monthly* v40 no11 p52 Jl 2017

Detector design & construction

Exceptional points make for exceptional sensors J. Miller *Physics Today* v70 no10 p23 O 2017

Detector dogs

Safety and Freedom and Magazines R. D'AGOSTINO *Popular Mechanics* p4 Ap 2017

Detectors

See also

Fire detectors

Gunfire detection systems

Intelligent sensors

8 Tech Trends to Watch in 2016 A. Webb *Harvard Business Review Digital Articles* p2 D 8 2015

A JOLT TO THE SENSES R. MATHESON *USA Today Magazine* v145 no2860 p66 Ja 2017

Living technologies color *Natural History* v125 no5 p5 My 2017

New Synaptics fingerprint sensor sits under glass for smoother phone screens M. WILLIAMS color *PCWorld* v35 no1 p31 Ja 2017

Phytochrome B integrates light and temperature signals in Arabidopsis M. Legris, C. Klose et al bibl graph *Science* v354 no6314 p897 N 18 2016

Sensitive electromechanical sensors using viscoelastic graphene-polymer nanocomposites C. S. Boland, U. Khan et al bibl graph *Science* v354 no6317 p1257 D 9 2016

Startups Are Laser-Focused on Helping Self-Driving Cars See K. Steinmetz color *Time* v190 no9 p26 S 4 2017

Detectors—Design & construction

Roost Smart Water Leak and Freeze Detector: One feature short of perfection M. BROWN color *PCWorld* v35 no4 p98 Ap 2017

Detectors—Evaluation

new products: protein analysis color *Science* v356 no6341 p973 Je 1 2017

Roost Smart Water Leak and Freeze Detector: One feature short of perfection M. BROWN color *PCWorld* v35 no4 p98 Ap 2017

WIRELESS WATCHDOG A. McConnell and L. Bedord *Successful Farming* v115 no3 p25 Mid-F 2017

Detention facilities

See also

Prisons

Five Years of Vigils and Protests at the West County Detention Center D. BACON color *Progressive* v81 no2 p12 F 2017

Detention facilities—United States

Prisonville Could Soon Be Back in Business K. Mehrotra color *Bloomberg Businessweek* no4520 p18 My 1 2017

Detention of persons

See also

Concentration camps

Imprisonment

Prisons

1985: Turin *Lapham's Quarterly* v10 no1 p93 Wint 2017

Detergents

Clothes Quarters K. Janeway color *Consumer Reports* v82 no1 p12 Ja 2017

Detergents—Evaluation

SPRING CLEANING LAUNDRY SPECIAL C. FORTÉ and S. BOGDAN color *Good Housekeeping* v264 no5 p81 My 2017

Determination (Personality trait)

How to Break into Your CEO's Inner Circle J. Neatby *Harvard Business Review Digital Articles* p2 Ja 12 2015

How to meet your goals bw color *Redbook* p152 D 2016

Deterrence (Military strategy)

The Korean Missile Crisis S. D. Sagan color *Foreign Affairs* v96 no6 p72 N/D 2017

Nonstrategic nuclear weapons in Russia's evolving military doctrine K. Zysk bibl *Bulletin of the Atomic Scientists* v73 no5 p322 2017

Detert, James R.

Don't Let Your Brain's Defense Mechanisms Thwart Effective Feedback *Harvard Business Review Digital Articles* p2 Ag 18 2016

Nonverbal Cues Get Employees to Open Up—or Shut Down *Harvard Business Review Digital Articles* p2 D 11 2015

When It's Tough to Speak Up, Get Help from Your Coworkers *Harvard Business Review Digital Articles* p2 Mr 4 2016

Your Boss Won't Say Yes If Emotions Are Running High *Harvard Business Review Digital Articles* p2 D 19 2014

de Tezanos Pinto, Paula

The journey of a scientist mother color *Science* v356 no6339 p774 My 19 2017

Dethier, Dylan

THE LOW DOWN ON LEFT HAND LOW color *Golf Magazine* v59 no11 p72 N 2017

DeTienne, Kristen Bell

Ethics Allegations Will Hurt White House Staffers Even If They Turn Out to Be False bw *Harvard Business Review Digital Articles* p1 Je 2 2017

DETILLIO, SAMANTHA

Who is pushing the craft field forward? color *American Craft* v76 no6 p26 D 2016-Ja 2017

Detonation waves

NUKEMAP creator Alex Wellerstein puts nuclear risk on the radar E. Eaves color *Bulletin of the Atomic Scientists* v73 no4 p211 Jl 2017

Detonators

Detonation Science Blasts into a New Frontier H. Auten *Science & Technology Review* p12 Jl/Ag 2017

DE TORRE-CEIJAS, ROCÍO

New Zealand Shouldn't Ignore Feral Cats *BioScience* v67 no8

p686 Ag 2017

Detour, The (TV program)

The Detour D. Holbrook color *TV Guide* v65 no7 p41 F 13 2017

The Detour J. Russell *TV Guide* v65 no8 p35 F 27 2017

Detoxification (Alternative medicine)

DETOXIFY WITH AROMATHERAPY C. Cromer color *Amazing Wellness* v9 no2 p68 Spr 2017

Detoxing Foot Pads [Cover story] color *Prevention* v69 no2 p13 F 2017

Give Your Body a Break A. Reliford and B. B. Royall color *Essence* v47 no9 p86 Ja 2017

SPRING detox PLAN I. Eliaz color *Amazing Wellness* v9 no2 p46 Spr 2017

SPRING SWAG color *Amazing Wellness* v8 no2 p92 Spr 2016

Detoxification (Alternative medicine)—Equipment & supplies

how to do a BODY CLEANSE V. TWEED color *Better Nutrition* v79 no3 p38 Mr 2017

Detoxification (Alternative medicine)—Psychological aspects

THE panchakarma PRESCRIPTION E. Marglin color *Yoga Journal* no296 p32 N 2017

Detritus

Editor's Letter M. Hansche color *Rodale's Organic Life* v3 no1 p10 Ja 2017

Not Just Another Lovely Summer Day on the Water K. Madin *Oceanus* v52 no1 p30 Summ 2016

Detrixhe, John

Maybe the Flash Boys Are the Good Guys graph *Bloomberg Businessweek* no4498 p49 N 7 2016

Playtime for London's Fintech Companies cartoon *Bloomberg Businessweek* no4503 p33 D 12 2016

Detroit (Film)

American Horror Story P. Travers color *Rolling Stone* no1294 p56 Ag 24 2017

Burning Questions: The team behind Zero Dark Thirty revisits torture--this time in 1960s Detroit D. EDELSTEIN img *New York* v50 no15 p68 Jl 24 2017

Detroit L. Greenblatt color *Entertainment Weekly* no1476 p44 Ag 4 2017

The Must List color *Entertainment Weekly* no1477 p6 Ag 11 2017

The myth of white innocence K. Reklis color *Christian Century* v134 no19 p44 S 13 2017

NOW PLAYING color *Entertainment Weekly* no1478 / 1479 p87 Ag 18-25 2017

Reliving '67 Algiers Motel Incident A. Tinubu color *Ebony* v72 no9 p20 Jl/Ag 2017

TIMES OF TROUBLE A. LANE cartoon *New Yorker* v93 no23 p66 Ag 7 2017

Detroit (Mich.)

Detroit: The Remix C. MCGUIGAN *Architectural Record* v205 no4 p84 Ap 2017

Detroit (Mich.)—Description & travel

America's Most Adventurous Cities J. MESSIMER color *Men's Health* v32 no6 p42 Ag 2017

DON'T CALL IT A COMEBACK M. H. MILLER bw cartoon color *ARTnews* v115 no3 p118 Fall 2016

Tales From Motor City L. BERNSTEIN-MACHLAY *American Scholar* v86 no1 p82 Wint 2017

Detroit (Mich.)—Economic conditions

Detroit's Underground Economy V. V. PANNE *In These Times* v41 no7 p8 Jl 2017

MAKING A MOTOWN MIRACLE [Cover story] M. Heimer color *Fortune* v176 no4 p94 S 15 2017

POSTCARDS FROM THE PAST M. NOER color *Forbes* v200 no3 p76 S 28 2017

Detroit (Mich.)—Economic conditions—21st century

Dream Team J. KRAJESKI bw color *Nation* v305 no4 p20 Ag 14 2017

Detroit Free Press

MY HOMETOWN PAPER: Don Gonyea D. Gonyea color *Columbia Journalism Review* v56 no1 p50 Spr 2017

Detroit Lions (Football team)

4 Detroit Lions color *Sports Illustrated* v127 no7 p95 S 4 2017

NFC + NORTH color *Sports Illustrated* v126 no5 p49 F 13 2017

Detroit Lions (Football team)—History

JUST MY TYPE D. Patrick and T. Keith color *Sports Illustrated* v125 no20 p28 D 19 2016

Virgil Abloh color *Architectural Digest* v74 no3 p36 Mr 2017

What to Know NOW color *Glamour* v114 no11 p72 N 2016

Winter Is Coming [Cover story] color *Glamour* v114 no11 p53 N 2016

Devash, Meirav

MOST LIKELY TO NERD OUT bw color *Women's Health* v14 no6 p107 Jl 2017

The WH Menses Society [Cover story] cartoon color graph *Women's Health* v14 no1 p94 Ja/F 2017

Devault, Imai

MOST UNDERRATED color *Surfing Magazine* v53 no1 p52 Ja 2017

Devaux, Éloïse

Anti-coalescence of bosons on a lossy beam splitter bw chart diag graph *Science* v356 no6345 p1373 Je 30 2017

Deveau, Scott

Nelson Peltz Makes Nice bw *Bloomberg Businessweek* no4536 p30 S 4 2017

Developed countries—Social conditions—21st century

A TALE OF TWO WORLDS M. Hvistendahl color *Scientific American* v315 no3 p42 S 2016

Developing countries

MAPPING FRONTIER ECONOMIES [Cover story] A. MUSACCHIO and E. WERKER chart color diag graph il img *Harvard Business Review* v94 no12 p40 D 2016

Developing countries—Environmental conditions

Nature Museums and Botanical Gardens for Environmental Conservation in Developing Countries M. QUMSIYEH *BioScience* v67 no7 p589 Jl 2017

Developing countries—Foreign economic relations—United States

TRUMPING OBAMA ON CUBA J. A. NATHAN *USA Today Magazine* v145 no2862 p30 Mr 2017

Development leadership

ETHICAL LEADERSHIP—WINNING WITH INTEGRITY R. BERENBEIM *Vital Speeches of the Day* v83 no1 p22 Ja 2017

Developmental disabilities

See also

Autism

Down syndrome

Cynthia Frisina *Atlanta* v57 no2 p100 Je 2017

THE FARM IN THE DELL: THESE FARMS AND RANCHES GIVE ADULTS WITH DEVELOPMENTAL DISABILITIES A SENSE OF PURPOSE AND COMMUNITY L. F. Prater *Successful Farming* v115 no12 p64 O 2017

Developmental psychology

See also

Child psychology

Identity crises (Psychology)

Life change events

Executives, Protect Your Alone Time S. B. Kaufman and C. Gregoire *Harvard Business Review Digital Articles* p2 D 16 2015

TALKING TO OURSELVES C. Fernyhough color diag *Scientific American* v317 no2 p74 Ag 2017

Developmentally disabled—Services for

Better Service, Faster: A Design Thinking Case Study R. I. Sutton and D. Hoyt *Harvard Business Review Digital Articles* p2 Ja 6 2016

Devenski, Chris

5 FIREMEN IN THE HOLE S. Apstein color *Sports Illustrated* v126 no9 p47 Mr 27 2017

DeVere Group (Company)

Targeting the Nest Eggs Of U.K. Expats Z. Faux, B. Robertson et al *Bloomberg Businessweek* no4524 p39 My 29 2017

Devereaux, T. P.

Femtosecond electron-phonon lock-in by photoemission and x-ray free-electron laser chart diag *Science* v357 no6346 p71 Jl 7 2017

Devereux, Charlie

Argentina Finds Free Trade Is Hard to Do cartoon color graph *Bloomberg Businessweek* no4499 p40 N 14 2016

Latin America Drains Its Political Swamp bw *Bloomberg Businessweek* no4531 p38 Jl 24 2017

DeVesto, Tom

Dynamic Duo B. Ankosko color *Sound & Vision* v82 no3 p20 Ap 2017

Devey, Colin

COLIN DEVEY K. SHEIKH cartoon *Popular Science* p53 Ja/F 2017

De Vicenzo, Roberto

PENCIL WRECK J. Garrity color *Golf Magazine* v59 no4 p90 Ap 2017

De Vigan, Delphine, 1966-

Copycats and Confidantes: Friendship or identity theft? In a French best seller, it's hard to tell A. KUCZYNSKI *New York Times Book Review* p11 Jl 2 2017

Devil facial tumor disease

Benign Selection A. Braun *Natural History* v125 no1 p7 D 2016/Ja 2017

New cancer strikes Tasmanian devils color *Science* v357 no6347 p112 Jl 14 2017

Devil in motion pictures

2 — BLACK PHILLIP SPEAKS C. Collis *Entertainment Weekly* no1444/1445 p58 D 16 2016

DeVille, Abigail

LOST AND FOUND L. R. Frazier and J. Lowe *New York Times Magazine* p53 O 30 2016

Deville, Pierre

Quantifying the evolution of individual scientific impact graph *Science* v354 no6312 p596 N 4 2016

Devil Master, The (Film)

Home Invasion M. BARTON-FUMO color *Film Comment* v52 no6 p93 N/D 2016

Devils Hole (Nev.)

Response to Comments on "Reconciliation of the Devils Hole climate record with orbital forcing" G. E. Moseley, Y. V. Dublyansky et al bibl chart graph *Science* v354 no6310 p296-e O 21 2016

Devils Tower National Monument (Wyo.)

Pillars of the Earth L. LANCASTER color *Backpacker* p14 Je 2017

Devil's Candy, The (Film)

Hell Houses L. KERN color *Film Comment* v53 no3 p22 My/Je 2017

The Must List color *Entertainment Weekly* no1457/1458 p3 Mr 17 2017

Devil Wears Prada, The (Film)

THE DEVIL WEARS PRADA: A tyrannical boss is harming employee morale and her firm's reputation *People Management* p62 Ap 2017

Devinci Cycles (Company)

DOUBLE DUTY J. Weber, R. Palmer et al color *Bike Magazine* v24 no1 p88 Ja/F 2017

DeVine, Adam, 1984-—Interviews

ADAM DEVINE D. Franich color *Entertainment Weekly* no1465 p16 My 12 2017

Devine, Loretta

Loretta Devine P. G. Cooper color *Current Biography* v78 no5 p23 My 2017

de Visser, Karin E.

Neutrophils take a round-trip diag *Science* v357 no6359 p42 O 6 2017

de Vivo, Luisa

Ultrastructural evidence for synaptic scaling across the wake/sleep cycle bibl diag graph *Science* v355 no6324 p507 F 3 2017

de Vladar, Harold P.

Beyond Hamilton's rule color *Science* v356 no6337 p485 My 5 2017

Devlin, Paul

Upbeat Downbeat A. TEPPER color *Weekly Standard* v22 no13 p36 D 5 2016

Devlin, Teresa

The Historic New Orleans Collection: Teresa Devlin P. Marquis *New Orleans Homes & Lifestyles* v20 no3 p98 Summ 2017

DeVolpi, Alexander

Chernobyl nuclear-meltdown consequences *Physics Today* v69 no11 p13 N 2016

DEVON, NATASHA

Anatomy of a Panic Attack cartoon *Seventeen* v76 no12 p70 D 2016/Ja 2017

Devorkin, David

How to Make a... TELESCOPE J. NOBEL cartoon color *Popular*

Mechanics v193 no7 p72 S 2016

DeVos, Betsy, 1958-

BETSY DEVOS' HOLY WAR J. Reitman bw color *Rolling Stone* no1283 p26 Mr 23 2017

Betsy DeVos Takes Wrong Lesson from Obama's Education Reforms P. Greene color *Progressive* v81 no4 p33 Ap/My 2017

Betsy DeVos: The Investor Who Got a High Return J. Nichols color *Progressive* v81 no7 p57 O/N 2017

Campus Kangaroo Courts *Weekly Standard* v23 no3 p6 S 25 2017

A Chance for Choice: By appointing Betsy DeVos education secretary, President Trump shows he's listening to parents P. E. Peterson *Hoover Digest: Research & Opinion on Public Policy* no2 p152 Spr 2017

Choice for Secretary of Education M. FERGUSON color *Phi Delta Kappan* v98 no5 p74 F 2017

Does school choice create better choices? color *Christian Century* v134 no8 p1 Ap 12 2017

EDUCATION FOR SALE? L. DARLING-HAMMOND bw color *Nation* v304 no10 p16 Mr 27 2017

Fair hearings on campus cartoon color *Christian Century* v134 no22 p7 O 25 2017

Media Embrace of Ed 'Reform' Paved Way for Betsy DeVos M. Knefel *Extra!* v30 no2 p3 Mr 2017

The Media Wouldn't Look for the Union Label M. Continetti *Commentary* v143 no3 p64 Mr 2017

The Miseducation of Betsy DeVos D. RAVITCH *In These Times* v41 no2 p17 F 2017

MOST POWERFUL WOMEN: More than 100 of the area's most influential women in government, business, law, education, media, nonprofits, and the arts L. MILK *Washingtonian Magazine* v53 no1 p50 O 2017

MOTHERS OF THE WORLD, UNITE! S. DOYLE *In These Times* v41 no6 p44 Je 2017

An Odd Way to Discredit DeVos D. PAYA color *Weekly Standard* v22 no21 p12 F 6 2017

Overruled K. C. JOHNSON and S. J. TAYLOR color *Weekly Standard* v23 no5 p15 O 9 2017

The Pros and Cons of Federally Funded School Choice Programs *Congressional Digest* v96 no7 p12 S 2017

School choice and the common good *America* v216 no4 p8 F 20 2017

The Schoolyard Rebel H. S. Edwards color *Time* v188 no27-28 p64 D 26 2016

Segregation Now and Forever: Betsy DeVos and the Looting of Public Education S. Hutchinson *Humanist* v77 no1 p9 Ja/F 2017

Unworthy, Perhaps cartoon *Weekly Standard* v22 no19 p3 Ja 23 2017

Who Is Betsy DeVos? And how did she get to head of our schools? L. Miller img *New York* v50 no15 p28 Jl 24 2017

DeVos, Betsy, 1958——Religion

Heavens to Betsy K. RIZGA, J. Vélez et al cartoon chart map *Mother Jones* v42 no2 p30 Mr/Ap 2017

DEVOSS, DAVID

The Kurds Get Under Way color *Weekly Standard* v23 no5 p19 O 9 2017

So You Want to Be a (Social Media) Star color *Weekly Standard* v22 no46 p26 Ag 14 2017

Thailand's Royal Mess *Weekly Standard* v22 no8 p14 O 31 2016

This Land Is Their Land color *Weekly Standard* v22 no22 p20 F 13 2017

Devotion

A GREAT AND HARSH BEAUTY A. A. O'DONNELL *America* v215 no13 p33 O 31 2016

Lightbox color *Time* v189 no18 p18 My 15 2017

de Vré, Hank

The Virtuoso bw *Powder* v45 no5 p24 Ja 2017

Devries, Cisco

Setting the PACE E. Daigneau *Governing* v30 no7 p20 Ap 2017

de Vries, James

PepsiCo's Chief Design Officer on Creating an Organization Where Design Can Thrive *Harvard Business Review Digital Articles* p2 Ag 11 2015

de Vries, Manfred F. R. Kets

An Early Warning System for Your Team's Stress Level [Cover story] *Harvard Business Review Digital Articles* p2 Ap 26 2017

How to Manage Someone Who Can't Handle Ambiguity *Harvard*

Business Review Digital Articles p2 Mr 10 2015

Make Peace with Your Unlived Life *Harvard Business Review Digital Articles* p2 D 21 2016

DeVries, Ron

BOOM IN THE BURBS D. REISS color *Chicago* v66 no1 p26 Ja 2017

de Vrieze, Jop

Big studies clash over fetal growth rates graph *Science* v355 no6323 p336 Ja 27 2017

Funders groan under growing review burden color *Science* v357 no6349 p343 Jl 28 2017

de Vrij, Femke M. S.

Activity-based protein profiling reveals off-target proteins of the FAAH inhibitor BIA 10-2474 chart color graph *Science* v356 no6342 p1084 Je 9 2017

De Vynck, Gerrit

America's got NO Talent color graph *Bloomberg Businessweek* no4500 p32 N 21 2016

de Waal, Frans

Apes know what others believe bibl color *Science* v354 no6308 p39 O 7 2016

Dog Days, Cat Photos *New York Times Book Review* p10 N 13 2016

Human nature color *Science* v356 no6344 p1239 Je 23 2017

Dewaele, A.

Synthesis of FeH5: A layered structure with atomic hydrogen slabs diag graph *Science* v357 no6349 p382 Jl 28 2017

Dewald, Sarah

Sarah Dewald A. BROWNLEE *Cincinnati Magazine* v50 no11 p34 Ag 2017

DeWalt Industrial Tool Co.

DeWalt Demo Hammer color *Bloomberg Businessweek* no4529 p79 Jl 3 2017

Dewberry, John

THE EMPEROR OF EMPTY LOTS C. Pomorski bw color *Bloomberg Businessweek* no4538 p42 S 18 2017

DeWees, Amanda

Sea of Secrets *Publishers Weekly* v263 no41 p63 O 10 2016

With This Curse *Publishers Weekly* v263 no52 p90d D 19 2016

Dewerchin, Mieke

De novo design of a biologically active amyloid bibl graph *Science* v354 no6313 paah4949-1 N 11 2016

Dewey, Frederick E.

Distribution and clinical impact of functional variants in 50,726 whole-exome sequences from the DiscovEHR study chart graph *Science* v354 no6319 paaf6814-1 D 23 2016

Genetic identification of familial hypercholesterolemia within a single U.S. health care system chart graph *Science* v354 no6319 paaf7000-1 D 23 2016

Dewey, Kenneth

The Weather and Climate of Nebraska: The Heartland of Extremes bw chart color diag graph map *Weatherwise* v70 no4 p12 Jl/Ag 2017

Dewey, Samantha

Goal Oriented E. Laase and T. Keith color *Sports Illustrated* v127 no4 p20 Ag 7 2017

Dewhurst, David, 1945-

LESSONS OF UTAH BEACH ARE MORE IMPORTANT THAN EVER *Vital Speeches of the Day* v82 no12 p377 D 2016

Dewhurst, Steve

Building community for deaf scientists color *Science* v355 no6322 p255 Ja 20 2017

DeWille, Harry

WAYPOINT N. KREBS color *Outdoor Life* v224 no2 p7 F/Mr 2017

De Winne, Sophie

How to Allow Flexible Work Without Playing Favorites *Harvard Business Review Digital Articles* p2 2017

What to Do Before You Fire a Pivotal Employee *Harvard Business Review Digital Articles* p2 Ja 29 2016

DeWitt, Helen

Comments img *New York* v49 no15 p8 Jl 25 2016

DeWitt, John Lesesne

THE PEOPLE NOBODY WANTS F. J. Taylor *Saturday Evening Post* v289 no3 p34 My/Je 2017

DeWitt, Patricia

How America Lost Its Mind color *Atlantic* v320 no4 p12 N 2017

Dewitt, Robert

THE THROWBACK bw *Outdoor Life* v224 no6 p34 Ag 2017

A VANISHING LEGACY chart color *Outdoor Life* v224 no1 p48 D 2016/Ja 2017

Dewolf, John

Downtown Columbia M. M. KASHINO color *Washingtonian Magazine* v52 no7 p102 Ap 2017

DeWolfe, Chris, 1966-

Avenging MySpace K. CHAYKOWSKI color *Forbes* v199 no7 p46 Je 29 2017

DeWoody, Beth Rudin

COLLECTED WISDOM V. LOWRY color *Architectural Digest* v73 no12 p96 D 2016

DEWOODY, J. ANDREW

The Serengeti Rules: The Quest to Discover How Life Works and Why It Matters *BioScience* v66 no12 p1079 D 1 2016

Dexamethasone

Meds or Management? [Cover story] B. Crabbe cartoon *Horse & Rider* v56 no1 p36 Ja 2017

Dexheimer, Elizabeth

The Fall of Warren's CFPB? bw *Bloomberg Businessweek* no4500 p36 N 21 2016

Thank You For Calling Equifax, Your Business Is Not Important to Us *Bloomberg Businessweek* no4538 p38 S 18 2017

Dexter (TV program)

FOR THE BINGE TV VIEWER IN ALL OF US *USA Today Magazine* v145 no2860 p74 Ja 2017

Dexter, Eric

Research on a razor's edge *Science* v356 no6342 p1094 Je 9 2017

Dexter, Kyle G.

Forest conservation: Humans' handprints bibl color *Science* v355 no6324 p466 F 3 2017

Forest conservation: Remember Gran Chaco bibl color *Science* v355 no6324 p465 F 3 2017

Dexter, Mike

WATER BREAK K. MOORE color *Natural History* v125 no3 p2 Mr 2017

Dextrins

See also

Cyclodextrins

KERNELS OF STRENGTH color *Women's Health* v13 no10 p31 D 2016

Dey, Daniel—Interviews

Daniel Dey *American Forests* v122 no3 p4 Fall 2016

Dey, Matthew

Longitudinal data from the Occupational Employment Statistics survey bibl chart color graph *Monthly Labor Review* p1 O 2016

Dey, Rohini

NIGHT AND DEY H. MITCHELL color *Chicago* v66 no4 p63 Ap 2017

De Yoreo, James J.

Direction-specific van der Waals attraction between rutile TiO2 nanocrystals diag *Science* v356 no6336 p434 Ap 28 2017

DeYoung, Andrew

The Exo Project *Publishers Weekly* v264 no6 p68 F 6 2017

de Zeeuw, Aart

Social norms as solutions bibl color *Science* v354 no6308 p42 O 7 2016

De Zeeuw, Chris I.

Activity-based protein profiling reveals off-target proteins of the FAAH inhibitor BIA 10-2474 chart color graph *Science* v356 no6342 p1084 Je 9 2017

DEZIEL, SHANDA

It takes a village, actually color *Maclean's* p52 Je 2017

Unstoppable color *Maclean's* v130 no6 p60 Jl 2017

D.G. Yuengling & Son Inc.—Officials & employees

BOTTLE ROYALE C. PETERSON-WITHORN color graph *Forbes* v198 no5 p100 O 25 2016

Dhananjay, Siddharth

PARTY LINES S. Huver img *New York* v50 no17 p144 Ag 21 2017

DHANVANTARI, SUJAYA

TRANS color *Maclean's* v129 no50 p61 D 19 2016

Dhar, Ravi

How Google Optimized Healthy Office Snacks *Harvard Business*

Review Digital Articles p2 Mr 3 2016

Dhar, Vasant

When to Trust Robots with Decisions, and When Not To *Harvard Business Review Digital Articles* p2 My 17 2016

Dhar, Vilas

Impact Investing Needs Millennials *Harvard Business Review Digital Articles* p2 O 3 2014

Dharma

tricycle / ONLINE bw color *Tricycle: The Buddhist Review* v26 no4 p6 Summ 2017

Dharma (Buddhism)

The Buddha's Politics J. Shaheen *Tricycle: The Buddhist Review* v26 no3 p10 Spr 2017

A BUDDHIST BREXIT S. BATCHELOR color *Tricycle: The Buddhist Review* v26 no3 p68 Spr 2017

Is the Dharma Democratic? K. SPELLMEYER bw *Tricycle: The Buddhist Review* v26 no3 p62 Spr 2017

On Hardship & Hope: Two teachings to instill inspiration when we feel paralyzed by despair DAISAKU IKEDA color *Tricycle: The Buddhist Review* v27 no1 p36 Fall 2017

Oshin Liam Jennings M. Gesicki color *Tricycle: The Buddhist Review* v26 no2 p24 Wint 2016

Dharmarakshita

THUBTEN CHODRON *Tricycle: The Buddhist Review* v26 no2 p23 Wint 2016

Dharmawan, Dwiki

Dharmawan Promotes Indonesian Culture J. Ephland color *Downbeat* v84 no7 p21 Jl 2017

Dhawan, Erica

Recruiting Strategies for a Tight Talent Market *Harvard Business Review Digital Articles* p2 Ap 7 2016

Why Your Innovation Team Needs a Lawyer *Harvard Business Review Digital Articles* p2 Jl 21 2016

Dheur, Marie-Christine

Anti-coalescence of bosons on a lossy beam splitter bw chart diag graph *Science* v356 no6345 p1373 Je 30 2017

Dhillon, Ranu S.

The Fight Against Zika Can't Wait for a Vaccine *Harvard Business Review Digital Articles* p2 Ag 18 2016

To Fight the Zika Pandemic, Learn from Ebola *Harvard Business Review Digital Articles* p2 F 4 2016

What Harvey Is Teaching the Health Care Sector About Managing Disasters *Harvard Business Review Digital Articles* p2 S 12 2017

What We've Learned About Fighting Ebola *Harvard Business Review Digital Articles* p2 Jl 16 2015

The World Is Completely Unprepared for a Global Pandemic *Harvard Business Review Digital Articles* p2 Mr 15 2017

Dhingra, Sourabh

Sterilizing immunity in the lung relies on targeting fungal apoptosis-like programmed cell death color diag *Science* v357 no6355 p1037 S 8 2017

Dhingra, Swati

Salvaging Brexit color *Foreign Affairs* v95 no6 p90 N/D 2016

Dholakia, Utpal M.

Brands Are Behaving Like Organized Religions *Harvard Business Review Digital Articles* p2 F 18 2016

Everyone Hates Uber's Surge Pricing - Here's How to Fix It *Harvard Business Review Digital Articles* p2 D 21 2015

How Managers Should Judge Psychology Experiments *Harvard Business Review Digital Articles* p2 Ag 31 2015

The Perils of Algorithm- Based Marketing *Harvard Business Review Digital Articles* p2 Je 17 2015

A Quick Guide to Value-Based Pricing *Harvard Business Review Digital Articles* p2 Ag 9 2016

The Risks of Changing Your Prices Too Often *Harvard Business Review Digital Articles* p2 Jl 6 2015

A Study of 46,000 Shoppers Shows That Omnichannel Retailing Works color *Harvard Business Review Digital Articles* p2 Ja 3 2017

What to Do When Satisfied B2B Customers Refuse to Recommend You *Harvard Business Review Digital Articles* p2 Ag 13 2015

Why Nudging Your Customers Can Backfire *Harvard Business Review Digital Articles* p2 Ap 15 2016

Dhurandhar, Amit

Predicting human olfactory perception from chemical features of odor molecules bibl diag graph *Science* v355 no6327 p820 F 24 2017

d'Huy, Julien
THE EVOLUTION OF MYTHS color diag *Scientific American* v315 no6 p62 D 2016

Di, Dawei
High-performance light-emitting diodes based on carbene-metal-amides chart graph *Science* v356 no6334 p159 Ap 14 2017

Di, Jiangtao
Harvesting electrical energy from carbon nanotube yarn twist diag graph *Science* v357 no6353 p773 Ag 25 2017

Diabetes
See also
Non-insulin-dependent diabetes
All Yours B. O'Dair *Prevention* v68 no11 p3 N 2016
DIABETES IN THE FAMILY P. DERROW color *Prevention* v68 no11 p86 N 2016
Fighting Diabetes in the 21st Century L. R. Sørensen *Harvard Business Review Digital Articles* p2 D 29 2015
THE FRESH-FRUIT SOLUTION *Saturday Evening Post* v289 no4 p71 Jl/Ag 2017
Got Diabetes? What to Eat *Tufts University Health & Nutrition Letter* v34 no12 p4 F 2017
NEWS BITES *Tufts University Health & Nutrition Letter* v35 no1 p1 Mr 2017
The Slow-Motion Disaster M. Chan *Nutrition Action Health Letter* v44 no3 p7 Ap 2017
Sugarcoating THE TRUTH: As the battle over soda and obesity heats up, researchers say the sugar and beverage industries paid for dozens of studies that conclude their products don't pose health risks P. SMITH *New York Times Upfront* v149 no13 p10 My 15 2017

Diabetes prevention
3 More Reasons to Exercise V. Tweed color *Amazing Wellness* v8 no6 p12 Early Winter2016
better S. LIAO color *Better Homes & Gardens* v95 no11 p144 N 2017
THE BIG DIABETES IS AMERICA'S STEALTHY KILLER L. SCHULER cartoon color *Men's Health* v32 no2 p96 Mr 2017
DIABETES AWARENESS F. ESKER color *Louisiana Life* v37 no2 p12 N/D 2017
Healthy Fats Reduce Diabetes Risk *Tufts University Health & Nutrition Letter* v34 no9 p6 N 2016
I ♥ CHOCOLATE color *Prevention* v69 no2 p11 F 2017
LOOK YOUNG, FEEL EVEN YOUNGER [Cover story] J. STEWART cartoon color *Men's Health* v32 no1 p126 Ja/F 2017

Diabetes prevention—Computer network resources
Simple Digital Technologies Can Reduce Health Care Costs A. L. Fogel and J. C. Kvedar *Harvard Business Review Digital Articles* p2 N 14 2016

Diabetes risk factors
ASK THE DOCTOR A. L. KOMAROFF *Harvard Health Letter* v42 no1 p2 N 2016
QUICK STUDIES *Nutrition Action Health Letter* v44 no3 p12 Ap 2017
Stick With Your Doctor color *Prevention* v69 no6 p8 Je 2017

Diabetes—Diagnosis
HOW NEW CLOUD TECH IS CHANGING THE FACE OF DIABETES MANAGEMENT D. F. McCourt *Maclean's* v129 no48/49 p44 D 5 2016
LIVING WELL WITH DIABETES IS POSSIBLE R. Blickstead *Maclean's* v129 no48/49 p39 D 5 2016

Diabetes—Mortality
When the Sugar Ain't Sweet D. POINTDUJOUR color *Ebony* v72 no3 p88 D 2016/Ja 2017

Diabetes—Treatment
HOW NEW CLOUD TECH IS CHANGING THE FACE OF DIABETES MANAGEMENT D. F. McCourt *Maclean's* v129 no48/49 p44 D 5 2016

Diabetic neuropathies—Prevention
HAVE YOU HEARD C. DOW *Nutrition Action Health Letter* v44 no2 p6 Mr 2017

Diabetics
LIVING WELL WITH DIABETES IS POSSIBLE R. Blickstead *Maclean's* v129 no48/49 p39 D 5 2016

Diabetics—Attitudes
For Diabetics, the Power of Knowing M. Cortez color graph *Bloomberg Businessweek* no4515 p40 Mr 20 2017

Diablo Canyon Nuclear Powerplant (Calif.)
The Last Energy War: King CONG vs. Solartopia H. Wasserman cartoon *Progressive* p50 D 2016/Ja 2017

Diagnosis
See also
Catheterization
Diagnostic errors
Early diagnosis
Medical self-examination
Point-of-care testing
THE ALGORITHM WILL SEE YOU NOW S. MUKHERJEE cartoon *New Yorker* v93 no7 p46 Ap 3 2017
Can the World Be Your doctor? R. LALIBERTE cartoon *Men's Health* v32 no9 p119 N 2017
Check You Out! K. LAWLER and S. PERRINE cartoon *AARP: The Magazine* v60 no5A p20 Ag/S 2017
The Computer Will See You Now D. Fine Maron color *Scientific American* v317 no2 p24 Ag 2017
Expert consensus on point-of-care testing Xuezhong Yu, Huadong Zhu et al *Science* v354 no6319 p15 D 23 2016
IS YOUR CHILD SICK OR JUST FAKING IT? D. L. Hill color *Parents* v92 no9 p34 S 2017
Recommendations on the management and use of POCT in medical institutions (nosocomial) Xuezhong Yu, Huadong Zhu et al *Science* v354 no6319 p13 D 23 2016

Diagnosis methods
Probing for Parkinson's A. Pycha color *Scientific American* v316 no6 p14 Je 2017

Diagnosis of autism
OPENING DOORS FOR MY AUTISTIC SON J. NEWMAN color *Reader's Digest* v190 no1134 p78 O 2017

Diagnosis of autism in children
Living with Autism: Early intervention is critical to helping children diagnosed with autism reach their full potential I. MURTUZA *Islamic Horizons* v46 no3 p44 My/Je 2017

Diagnosis of diseases in cats
THE HOUSE-CAT MYSTERY E. Anthes color *New York Times Magazine* p54 My 21 2017

Diagnosis of diseases in horses
New Horse Headset Records EEGs S. Dulai Wenholz color *Practical Horseman* v45 no8 p68 Ag 2017

Diagnosis of edema
My legs sometimes become swollen, but they don't hurt and it doesn't feel like anything else is wrong. Why might this be happening? *Mayo Clinic Health Letter* v35 no7 p8 Jl 2017

Diagnosis of endometriosis
HOUGH HANGS TOUGH [Cover story] A. Prato color *Health* v31 no9 p82 N 2017

Diagnosis of food allergies
Are You Sure You Can't Eat That? color *Parents* v92 no8 p94 Ag 2017

Diagnosis of HIV infections
The Thread S. E. Bandele, D. Curtis et al *New York Times Magazine* p8 Je 25 2017

Diagnosis of mental depression
let's talk about your mood M. COHEN color *Parents* v92 no6 p94 Je 2017

Diagnosis—Equipment & supplies
Bad Diagnosis S. Nash color *Progressive* v81 no3 p34 Mr 2017

Diagnosis of attention-deficit hyperactivity disorder
let's talk about your mood M. COHEN color *Parents* v92 no6 p94 Je 2017

Diagnostic equipment industry
Needle Camera M. Belfiore bw color *Bloomberg Businessweek* no4512 p35 F 20 2017

Diagnostic errors
THE DEADLY MEDICAL MISTAKE YOU CAN AVOID P. Bergl color *Men's Health* v32 no2 p75 Mr 2017
How "Claire's Day" Began L. VACCARIELLO *Reader's Digest* v188 no1125 p35 N 2016
Is Your Doc Getting It Wrong? K. Mickle bw color *Glamour* v115 no9 p116 S 2017
Wrong! R. SHARPE cartoon *Prevention* v69 no7 p48 Jl 2017

Diagnostic errors—Prevention

Treatment options for obstructive sleep apnea *Harvard Health Letter* v42 no1 p6 N 2016

Diagnostic expert systems

Man vs. Machine: Dermatology M. Bergen color *Bloomberg Businessweek* no4529 p23 Jl 3 2017

Diagnostic imaging

See also

Brain imaging

Magnetic resonance imaging

I have a treadmill stress test scheduled to look for heart disease. I know this involves exercising, and I'm worried I'm not physically up to it. Is there another way to gather this information? *Mayo Clinic Health Letter* v35 no10 p8 O 2017

Diagnostic reagents & test kits—Evaluation

New At-Home Health Tests—Rated K. DOLD color *Men's Health* v32 no7 p86 S 2017

Dialectical theology

Me the People *Commentary* v142 no1 p1 Jl/Ag 2016

Dialectrical (Music)

Dialectrical/Port Bou B. Bambarger color *Downbeat* v84 no3 p59 Mr 2017

Diallo, Lili

LILI DIALLO M. B. EYERS color *Better Homes & Gardens* v95 no9 p20 S 2017

Dialogue coaches

TALK TO ME: PEAK TV HAS BROUGHT A FLOOD OF GLOBAL ACTING TALENT TO HOLLYWOOD. IT'S THE JOB OF DIALECT COACHES LIKE SAMARA BAY TO HELP THEM ALL SOUND RIGHT R. BRADLEY *New York Times Magazine* p32 Jl 23 2017

Diamant, Anita

The Jewish Wedding Now *Publishers Weekly* v264 no15 p69 Ap 10 2017

Diamond, Anna

Lights. Camera. Peacocks: A unique Smithsonian museum devoted to Asian arts reopens with an innovative new film that turns the building inside out *Smithsonian* v48 no6 p22 O 2017

Diamond, Jared

SCIENCE & RELIGION in the Rough *Humanist* v76 no6 p12 N/D 2016

Diamond, Kerry

BEAUTY'S NEW BALLER color *InStyle* v24 no5 p228 My 2017

Chris McMillan color *InStyle* v24 no3 p266 Mr 2017

The Girl with the Magic Hands color *InStyle* v24 no3 p262 Mr 2017

Model Beauty color *InStyle* v24 no3 p342 Mr 2017

Rose-Marie Swift color *InStyle* v24 no4 p150 Ap 2017

Diamond, Larry

Creeping Autocracy: The greatest risk to democracy? Not the prospect of a coup or a junta but the self-aggrandizement of "strong leaders" *Hoover Digest: Research & Opinion on Public Policy* no3 p55 Summ 2017

Visions of Democracy *Hoover Digest: Research & Opinion on Public Policy* no1 p14 Wint 2017

DIAMOND, LAUREN

Delicious Hydration Tips color *Reader's Digest* v189 no1131 p52 Je 2017

DIAMOND, MIKE

beach boys color *Architectural Digest* v74 no3 p108 Mr 2017

Diamond, Nell

IN FULL BLOOM M. GUIDUCCI, M. CARLOS et al color *Vogue* v207 no6 p114 Je 2017

DIAMOND, TIARA

Two Pulsars Blowing in the Wind *Sky & Telescope* v133 no6 p9 Je 2017

Diamond, Tina

THE OTHER (FAMOUS) FAMILY J. McGovern color *Entertainment Weekly* no1485 p37 O 6 2017

Diamond Aircraft Industries GmbH

DIAMOND LAUNCHES A FAMILY OF DA50 MODELS color *Flying* v144 no6 p17 Je 2017

Diamond Book Distributors Inc.

It Was the Year of March at Diamond Book Distributors C. Reid color *Publishers Weekly* v264 no7 p6 F 13 2017

Diamond industry

Diamond jewelry

Things M. McCluskey color *Time* v188 no25-26 p20 D 19 2016 Double Issue

Diamond jewelry—Evaluation

The BUY Jewelry color *Harper's Bazaar* no3648 p88 N 2016

Nice ICE color *Seventeen* p56 Ja 1 2017

Diamondback Bicycles (Company)

"I'VE GOT $3,000. CAN I GET A BIKE WITH NICE WHEELS?" L. Tanner and B. STRICKLAND color *Bicycling* v58 no3 p56 Ap 2017

Diamonds

How to... DESTROY ANYTHING color *Popular Mechanics* v193 no7 p83 S 2016

Large gem diamonds from metallic liquid in Earth's deep mantle E. M. Smith, S. B. Shirey et al bibl color *Science* v354 no6318 p1403 D 16 2016

Metallic hydrogen created in diamond vise R. F. Service color graph *Science* v355 no6323 p332 Ja 27 2017

What in the World? *National Geographic Kids* no467 p31 F 2017

Diamonds—Research

Diamonds from the deep *Physics Today* v70 no2 p80 F 2017

Diamont, Don—Interviews

DAYTIME M. LOGAN *TV Guide* v65 no37 p54 S 4 2017

Diana & the Paparazzi/Diana: The Day We Said Goodbye (TV program)

Diana and the Paparazzi/Diana: The Day We Said Goodbye I. Rudolph *TV Guide* v65 no35 p30 Ag 21 2017

DIANA, CARLA

Don't Blame the Robots; Blame Us color *Popular Science* v288 no6 p46 N/D 2016

Diana, Julie

HOW TO NAIL YOUR AUDITION VIDEO color *Dance Spirit* v21 no1 p39 Ja 2017

MASTERING Partnered PIROUETTES *Dance Spirit* v21 no3 p60 Mr 2017

Take Corrections, Correctly *Dance Magazine* v91 no4 p52 Ap 2017

Diana, Our Mother: Her Life & Legacy (Film)

The Princess Diaries color *Entertainment Weekly* no1476 p14 Ag 4 2017

Diana, Princess of Wales, 1961-1997

Dear Diana, You Still Rule. Love, Everyone J. Kantor and J. Harman color *Glamour* v115 no9 p42 S 2017

Diana, Princess of Wales (1961-1997) *British Heritage Travel* v38 no4 p10 Jl/Ag 2017

The Enduring Legacy of Diana R. Rahman and T. Stack color *Entertainment Weekly* no1476 p13 Ag 4 2017

How Diana Became Britain's 'Queen of the Heart' D. Stewart color *Time* v190 no9 p23 S 4 2017

Recalling the People's Princess T. BROWN bw color *Maclean's* v130 no7 p55 Ag 2017

REMEMBERING DIANA D. ARBITER, S. B. SMITH et al color *AARP: The Magazine* v60 no5A p50 Ag/S 2017

The year of Diana P. TREBLE color *Maclean's* v129 no51/52 p46 D 26 2016

Diana: Her True Story (TV program)

Diana and the Paparazzi/Diana: The Day We Said Goodbye I. Rudolph *TV Guide* v65 no35 p30 Ag 21 2017

Diane Von Furstenberg Studio LP

The Man Who Loves Women N. Silverstein, F. Kane et al color *Glamour* v115 no3 p94 Mr 2017

Prints Charming E. Wilson color *InStyle* v24 no3 p132 Mr 2017

Dianna, John

GONE, BUT NOT FORGOTTEN M. Emery *Dirt Sports + Off-Road* v51 no3 p6 Mr 2017

Diao, David

DAVID DIAO T. Istomina color *Art in America* v105 no5 p128 My 2017

Diao, Yixin

Global roadless areas: Consider terrain color *Science* v355 no6332 p1381 Mr 31 2017

Diapers

health news *Parents* v91 no6 p22 Je 2016

potty on! C. HWANG color *Parents* v92 no6 p40 Je 2017

CRYSTAL CLEAR PROVENANCE J. J. Roberts color *Fortune* v176 no4 p44 S 15 2017

Diapers—Evaluation

SAFE ECO STARS color *Good Housekeeping* v264 no4 p94 Ap 2017

Diaphragmatic hernia

Step out of the lab and engage G. Kardon color *Science* v355 no6330 p1234 Mr 17 2017

Diard, Médéric

Inflammation boosts bacteriophage transfer between Salmonella spp bibl diag *Science* v355 no6330 p1211 Mr 17 2017

Diarrhea

KNOW YOUR FLOW: A USER'S MANUAL H. Levine color *Health* v31 no3 p75 Ap 2017

Diarrhea Planet (Performer)

NIGHT LIFE *New Yorker* v92 no32 p26 O 10 2016

Diary (Literary form)

See also

Blogs

Fire on the Water: A newly discovered account of the biggest explosion of the pre-nuclear era surfaces after 100 years M. Wortman *Smithsonian* v48 no5 p15 S 2017

My Sleep Diary img *Scholastic Choices* pT7 S 2017 Supplement

Dias, Elizabeth

About 200 Americans Have Been Living In North Korea color *Time* v190 no9 p36 S 4 2017

The Angels of Irma [Cover story] color map *Time* v190 no12 p34 S 25 2017

The Art of the Hostage Deal color *Time* v190 no6 p30 Ag 7 2017

Ban Ki-moon color *Time* v188 no27-28 p70 D 26 2016

Emotional Divide color diag *Time* v189 no7/8 p38 F 27 2017

The God Squad color *Time* v189 no23 p36 Je 19 2017

The Heart Beat [Cover story] color *America* v215 no15 p15 N 14 2016

Houston After Harvey color *Time* v190 no10/11 p38 S 18 2017

How He Won color *Time* v188 no21 p48 N 21 2016

The Itsy-Bitsy, Teensy-Weensy, Tiny Fine Print That Can Allow Sexual Harassment to Go Unheard color *Time* v188 no18 p32 O 31 2016

Krista Tippett color *Time* v188 no24 p72 D 12 2016

The Lost Colony color *Time* v190 no15 p32 O 16 2017

Message Delivered [Cover story] color *Time* v188 no21 p28 N 21 2016

Moscow Cozies Up to the Right color *Time* v189 no10 p32 Mr 20 2017

Myanmar's Shame color *Time* v190 no13 p42 O 2 2017

The Other Side [Cover story] color diag *Time* v189 no4 p24 F 6 2017

The Person of the Year [Cover story] color diag map *Time* v188 no25-26 p46 D 19 2016 Double Issue

Sally Quinn color *Time* v190 no12 p68 S 25 2017

The Second Most Powerful Man In the World? [Cover story] color *Time* v189 no5 p24 F 13 2017

The Suite of Power [Cover story] color *Time* v189 no23 p22 Je 19 2017

Sybrina Fulton and Tracy Martin color *Time* v189 no4 p60 F 6 2017

The Terrible, Horrible, No Good, Very Bad Child-Care Problem color *Time* v188 no16/17 p38 O 24 2016

Trump Goes to War [Cover story] color *Time* v188 no16/17 p20 O 24 2016

Trump's Loyalty Test [Cover story] color *Time* v189 no20 p24 My 29 2017

The Utah Surprise color *Time* v188 no19 p11 N 7 2016

Dias, Marley

Where's My Story? C. GRISE *Scholastic Choices* v32 no4 p22 Ja 2017

Dias, Ranga P.

Observation of the Wigner-Huntington transition to metallic hydrogen bibl chart color graph *Science* v355 no6326 p715 F 17 2017

Dias, Sergio

Paradise Played M. Trammell cartoon *New Yorker* v93 no2 p10 F 27 2017

Dias, Yran Bartolomeu

What Makes Some Silicon Valley Companies So Successful *Harvard Business Review Digital Articles* p2 Ap 26 2016

Diaspora

See also

Chinese diaspora

Haitian diaspora

Muslim diaspora

Diasporas by the Numbers *Current History* v115 no784 p328 N 2016

The Growing Importance of Diaspora Politics F. B. ADAMSON *Current History* v115 no784 p291 N 2016

Diaspora—History

Diasporas' Impacts on Economic Development D. KAPUR *Current History* v115 no784 p298 N 2016

Diatchenko, Luda

miR-183 cluster scales mechanical pain sensitivity by regulating basal and neuropathic pain genes diag graph *Science* v356 no6343 p1168 Je 16 2017

Diaz, Alejandro

How Marketers Can Personalize at Scale *Harvard Business Review Digital Articles* p2 N 23 2015

Quantifying the Impact of Marketing Analytics *Harvard Business Review Digital Articles* p2 N 5 2015

Diaz, Cameron, 1972-

THE PERFECT HAIR CUT FINDER [Cover story] M. OLIVA bw color *Redbook* p36 Ap 2017

Diaz, David

Around here, developers don't just build buildings—they build entire neighborhoods M. M. KASHINO color *Washingtonian Magazine* v52 no7 p102 Ap 2017

Díaz, Dilys M. Vela

Plant diversity increases with the strength of negative density dependence at the global scale diag *Science* v356 no6345 p1389 Je 30 2017

Díaz, Junot

AFTERMATH bw cartoon *New Yorker* v92 no38 p48 N 21 2016

El Sueño Americano de Junot Díaz O. Segura bw color *America* v216 no12 p42 My 29 2017

'THE BRIEF WONDROUS LIFE OF OSCAR WAO' *New York Times Book Review* p30 Ja 8 2017

The Year in Reading [Cover story] *New York Times Book Review* p8 D 25 2016

Diaz, Lav

The Woman Who Left S. KLAWANS bw *Film Comment* v53 no3 p72 My/Je 2017

Diaz, Luis A. Jr.

Mismatch repair deficiency predicts response of solid tumors to PD-1 blockade chart graph *Science* v357 no6349 p409 Jl 28 2017

Diaz, Melonie

Room 104 J. Russell *TV Guide* v65 no31 p33 Jl 24 2017

Diaz, Natalie

Wolf OR-7 N. Diaz *Orion Magazine* v36 no1 p57 Ja/F 2017

Díaz, Sandra

Forest conservation: Remember Gran Chaco bibl color *Science* v355 no6324 p465 F 3 2017

Global climatic drivers of leaf size [Cover story] graph *Science* v357 no6354 p917 S 1 2017

DÍAZ, WENDY

Filling the Void in Spanish-language Islamic Material *Islamic Horizons* v46 no1 p40 Ja/F 2017

From Cuba to the Ka'ba: Yes, Cuba has a past, present, and future of Islam *Islamic Horizons* v46 no3 p52 My/Je 2017

Díaz Castro, M. L.

Observation of a large-scale anisotropy in the arrival directions of cosmic rays above 8×10^{18} eV *Science* v357 no6357 p1266 S 22 2017

DiBattista, Joseph

Precipitation drives global variation in natural selection bibl chart diag map *Science* v355 no6328 p959 Mr 3 2017

Di Benedetto, Antonio

A Great Writer We Should Know J. M. Coetzee bw cartoon *New York Review of Books* v64 no1 p59 Ja 19 2017

THE GUIDE DOG OF HERMOSILLA *Harper's Magazine* v334 no2004 p20 My 2017

VOYAGE TO THE INTERIOR B. KUNKEL color *New Yorker* v92 no46 p72 Ja 23 2017

DiBetta, Laura

Connecting People & Nature *New York State Conservationist* v72 no1 p15 Ag 2017

Diblock copolymers

Surprising states of order for linear diblock copolymers G. E. Stein diag *Science* v356 no6337 p487 My 5 2017

Thermal processing of diblock copolymer melts mimics metallurgy K. Kim, M. W. Schulze et al diag graph *Science* v356 no6337 p520 My 5 2017

DIBNER, PAULIE

HIGH-ALTITUDE TRAINING color *Conde Nast Traveler* v52 no9 p14 O 2017

Dibowski, Andreas

PRINCIPLES OF CROSS-COUNTRY RIDING L. Threlkeld color *Practical Horseman* v45 no3 p42 Mr 2017

Dicamba

7 MISSOURI DICAMBA-DAMAGE TAKEAWAYS G. Gullickson *Successful Farming* v115 no5 p42 Mid-Mr 2017

DiCaprio, Leonardo, 1974-

Citi Bike HQ Has a Wall of Fame, With Many Leos K. SCHNEIDER img *New York* v49 no25 p52 D 12 2016

Pioneers [Cover story] color *Time* v189 no16/17 p14 My 1-8 2017

Save a Whale, Save a Planet *UN Chronicle* v54 no1/2 p1 2017

DiCaprio, Leonardo, 1974—Interviews

Why the Climate Gets Top Billing color *National Geographic* v230 no5 p3 N 2016

DiCarlo, James E.

Design of a synthetic yeast genome bibl chart color graph *Science* v355 no6329 p1040 Mr 10 2017

Dice (Music)

For the Love of Jimi B. Milkowski color *Downbeat* v84 no9 p24 S 2017

Dice games

See also

Craps (Game)

Craps F. Kamer *New York Times Magazine* p28 O 16 2016

OBSESSED WITH GRAPHIC GAMES A. MAZE color *Better Homes & Gardens* v95 no8 p12 Ag 2017

DiChiera, David

Community Organizer *Opera News* v81 no9 p14 Mr 2017

DiChristina, Mariette

Dawn of Innovation color *Scientific American* v316 no5 p4 My 2017

Designing the City of Tomorrow Today color *Scientific American* v317 no1 p4 Jl 2017

From Science to Knowledge to Hope *Scientific American* v316 no6 p4 Je 2017

From Workouts to Far Out color *Scientific American* v316 no2 p4 F 2017

Ideas to Change the World color *Scientific American* v315 no6 p5 D 2016

In the Beginning color *Scientific American* v317 no2 p4 Ag 2017

Keeping the Future in Mind *Scientific American* v316 no4 p4 Ap 2017

Looking Forward color *Scientific American* v315 no3 p4 S 2016

Theory and Truth color *Scientific American* v315 no5 p4 N 2016

To Boldly Go color *Scientific American* v316 no3 p4 Mr 2017

Welcome to Everybody's Issue color *Scientific American* v317 no3 p6 S 2017

What's Next for Science? color *Scientific American* v316 no1 p3 Ja 2017

What the World Needs Now *Scientific American* v317 no4 p5 O 2017

Di Cicco, Dennis

Celestron's CGX Mount color *Sky & Telescope* v134 no5 p62 N 2017

Dick, Henry J. B.

The Quest for the Moho G. Schanker and L. Lippsett *Oceanus* v52 no1 p44 Summ 2016

Dick, Philip K., 1928-1982

PROP MASTER R. Goldberg color *Wired* v25 no10 p12 O 2017

DICK, R. J.

FIND YOUR CALLING color *Field & Stream* v122 no5 p50 O 2017

Dick Clark's New Year's Rockin' Eve With Ryan Seacrest (TV program)

Mariah Carey Sounds Off J. Hibberd color *Entertainment Weekly* no1448 p10 Ja 13 2017

New Year's Eve Roundup I. Ratledge *TV Guide* p41 D 19 2016

WHO WILL YOU SPEND NEW YEAR'S EVE WITH? M. Snetiker color *Entertainment Weekly* no1446/1447 p109 D 2016/Ja 2017

Dicke, Stacey Laird

Social Equity: Plays Key Role in New Braunfels' New Recreation Center *Parks & Recreation* v52 no10 p40 O 2017

Dickens, Charles, 1812-1870

BREATHE color *Prevention* v69 no7 p34 Jl 2017

MONTHS PAST JUNE *History Today* v67 no6 p22 Je 2016

A Timeless Observer/Writing With Sassigassity J. WILLIAMS *New York Times Book Review* p6 S 25 2016

A Victorian Toast R. Schaap color *New York Times Magazine* p42 D 11 2016

Dickens, Colin F.

Combining theory and experiment in electrocatalysis: Insights into materials design bibl color graph *Science* v355 no6321 p1 Ja 13 2017

Dickens, Kim

FEAR THE WALKING DEAD R. Moynihan *TV Guide* v64 no15 p51 Ap 4 2016

Fear the Walking Dead's Next Steps D. Ross color *Entertainment Weekly* no1468/1469 p93 Je 2-9 2017

Dickens, Rob

FIND YOUR COURSE TO SUCCESS T. Daswick cartoon color *Men's Health* v32 no3 p24 Ap 2017

DICKERSON, CAITLIN

HOW FAKE NEWS TURNED A SMALL TOWN UPSIDE DOWN: AT THE HEIGHT OF THE 2016 ELECTION, EXAGGERATED REPORTS OF A JUVENILE SEX CRIME BROUGHT A MEDIA MAELSTROM TO TWIN FALLS— ONE THE IDAHO CITY STILL HASN'T RECOVERED FROM *New York Times Magazine* p46 O 1 2017

Dickerson, Chad

LEAVE my ETSY ALONE M. Chafkin and J. Cao bw color *Bloomberg Businessweek* no4523 p48 My 22 2017

DICKEY, BRONWEN

CLIMB ABOARD, YE WHO SEEK THE TRUTH! color *Popular Mechanics* p84 S 2017

CLIMB ABOARD, YE WHO SEEK THE TRUTH! color *Popular Mechanics* v193 no7 p84 S 2016

Dickey, Colin

The Hidden Truth In Every Ghost Story S. Begley color *Time* v188 no18 p20 O 31 2016

THE NEW PARANOIA color *New Republic* v248 no7 p22 Jl 2017

Spooky T. MILES *New York Times Book Review* p12 O 30 2016

A View to a Kill color *New Republic* v248 no3 p54 Mr 2017

Dickey, Jack

13 THE REDS' BIG MACHINE color *Sports Illustrated* v126 no9 p66 Mr 27 2017

1 THE NEW TESTAMENT color *Sports Illustrated* v126 no9 p40 Mr 27 2017

4 A QUEST CALLED TRIBE color *Sports Illustrated* v126 no9 p46 Mr 27 2017

American Voices Sean Doolittle color *Sports Illustrated* v126 no8 p30 Mr 20 2017

The 'Boys Are Back color *Sports Illustrated* v126 no1 p12 Ja 9 2017

BUFFALOED color *Sports Illustrated* v126 no11 p60 Ap 17-24 2017

The Case for ... A Stadium-Funding Stiff-Arm color *Sports Illustrated* v126 no2 p20 Ja 16 2017

The Case for ... Banishing Beanballs color *Sports Illustrated* v126 no15 p26 My 29 2017

The Case for ... GIANCARLO STANTON color *Sports Illustrated* v127 no7 p30 S 4 2017

The Case for ... Killing TNF color *Sports Illustrated* v125 no18 p26 D 5 2016

Dawg Pounded color *Sports Illustrated* v125 no17 p22 N 21 2016 Double Issue

FLAG FOOTBALL chart color *Sports Illustrated* v125 no21 p46 D 26 2016

Garry KASPAROV color *Sports Illustrated* v127 no1 p78 Jl 3 2017

Ghostbusters [Cover story] color *Sports Illustrated* v125 no12 p24 O 10 2016

Gray Area color *Sports Illustrated* v126 no14 p20 My 15-22 2017

GRIMES AGAINST HUMANITY color *Sports Illustrated* v127 no2 p44 Jl 17 2017

NFL Playoffs: Choose Your Own Adventure color diag *Sports Illustrated* v126 no1 p64 Ja 9 2017

Roger Ailes color *Time* v189 no21 p14 Je 5 2017

Sane Old Story color *Sports Illustrated* v127 no6 p14 Ag 28 2017

Shock Jocks color *Sports Illustrated* v126 no5 p14 F 13 2017

Dickey, Page

Across the Pond color *Architectural Digest* v74 no1 p73 Ja 2017

the producers color *Better Homes & Gardens* v95 no5 p136 My 2017

Dickinson, Amy

Strangers Tend to Tell Me Things: A Memoir of Love, Loss, and Coming Home *Publishers Weekly* v264 no5 p194 Ja 30 2017

Dickinson, Amy—Interviews

ASK AMY ABOUT HERSELF ALREADY C. ZULKEY color *Chicago* v66 no3 p30 Mr 2017

DICKINSON, COLBY

DEATH OF A PHILOSOPHER color *America* v215 no16 p35 N 21 2016

Dickinson, David

Akatsuki Spies Massive Wave on Venus *Sky & Telescope* v133 no5 p8 My 2017

Cassini Finds Empty Space on First Finale Pass color *Sky & Telescope* v134 no2 p12 Ag 2017

Chinese FAST Opens for Business *Sky & Telescope* v133 no1 p11 Ja 2017

ExoMars Lander Fails, Orbiter Succeeds *Sky & Telescope* v133 no2 p10 F 2017

Huge "Gancedo" Found in Argentina *Sky & Telescope* v133 no1 p18 Ja 2017

Juno Will Stay in Current Orbit Around Jupiter *Sky & Telescope* v133 no6 p8 Je 2017

LHS 1140b: A Super-Earth in the Habitable Zone color *Sky & Telescope* v134 no2 p12 Ag 2017

NASA's Juno Makes First Science Pass *Sky & Telescope* v133 no1 p16 Ja 2017

Rosetta's Grand Finale *Sky & Telescope* v133 no1 p12 Ja 2017

DICKINSON, DIANA

CUTTING EDGE color *Better Homes & Gardens* v95 no9 p84 S 2017

IN GOOD SPIRITS color *Better Homes & Gardens* v95 no10 p140 O 2017

A MATTER OF TASTE chart color *Better Homes & Gardens* v95 no5 p98 My 2017

PARTY ON... THE CHEAP color *Better Homes & Gardens* v95 no6 p46 Je 2017

PHOTO ops color *Better Homes & Gardens* v95 no8 p74 Ag 2017

SIMPLY SHAKER color *Better Homes & Gardens* v95 no11 p112 N 2017

SMART HOME REBOOT *Better Homes & Gardens* v94 no12 p74 D 2016

smart SPEAKERS color *Better Homes & Gardens* v95 no6 p65 Je 2017

streaming devices color diag *Better Homes & Gardens* v95 no2 p68 F 2016

A TO Z GUIDE TO YOUR BEST NIGHT'S SLEEP *Better Homes & Gardens* v95 no1 p41 Ja 2017

WHAT MAKES YOUR GARDEN GROW? cartoon color *Better Homes & Gardens* v95 no3 p60 Mr 2017

Dickinson, Emily, 1830-1886

1862: Amherst, MA E. Dickinson *Lapham's Quarterly* v10 no2 p100 Spr 2017

EMILY DICKINSON J. Shipley *Yankee* p27 My/Je 2017

Emily Dickinson wrote poems R. STIEVE *Arizona Highways* v96 no7 p2 Jl 2017

OUT OF PRINT D. CHIASSON color *New Yorker* v92 no40 p77 D 5 2016

Raging Belle E. BLAKEMORE *Smithsonian* v48 no1 p16 Ap 2017

Toward Essentials M. ROBINSON *New York Times Book Review* p13 S 24 2017

Dickinson, Emily, 1830-1886—Exhibitions

Fame is a bee: Eyeing Emily Dickinson at the Morgan Library and on film E. Pochoda cartoon color *Magazine Antiques* v184

no1 p30 Ja/F 2017

An Unquiet Belle D. R. GOODMAN color *Weekly Standard* v22 no25 p42 Mr 6 2017

Dickinson, Harris

Harris Dickinson Makes Waves in Beach Rats J. McGovern color *Entertainment Weekly* no1480 p40 S 1 2017

New Wave N. HELLER and C. SCHAMA color *Vogue* v207 no9 p614 S 2017

Dickinson, John

Foot Fetish H. MARTIN bw color *Architectural Digest* no11 p30 N 1 2017

Dickinson, Lani

THE DIRT with Lani Dickinson color *Dance Spirit* v21 no8 p36 O 2017

Dickinson, Tim

ALL-AMERICAN KILLER color *Rolling Stone* no1275 p50 D 1 2016

THE BATTLE FOR MONTANA color *Rolling Stone* no1288 p26 Je 1 2017

CAN DEMOCRATS FIX THE PARTY? color *Rolling Stone* no1290 p28 Je 29 2017

Jerry Brown's California Dream bw color *Rolling Stone* no1298 p32 O 19 2017

RISE OF THE GRASSROOTS color *Rolling Stone* no1295 p31 S 7 2017

Taking On Guns color *Rolling Stone* no1294 p25 Ag 24 2017

WHAT THE PEOPLE REALLY WANT *Rolling Stone* no1281/1282 p30 F 23 2017

Dickler, Maura N.

PI3K pathway regulates ER-dependent transcription in breast cancer through the epigenetic regulator KMT2D bibl graph *Science* v355 no6331 p1324 Mr 24 2017

DICKMAN, AMY J.

Conserving the World's Megafauna and Biodiversity: The Fierce Urgency of Now *BioScience* v67 no3 p197 Mr 2017

Saving the World's Terrestrial Megafauna color *BioScience* v66 no10 p807 O 1 2016

DICKMAN, CHRISTOPHER R.

Making a New Dog? *BioScience* v67 no4 p374 Ap 2017

Dickman, Kyle

Pillar of fire color *Popular Science* v289 no4 p48 Jl/Ag 2017

Dickrell, Jill

pontoon mania color *Cabin Living* p60 Je 2017

Dicks, Lynn V.

Ten policies for pollinators bibl color *Science* v354 no6315 p975 N 25 2016

Dicks, Matthew

75 ways to be a grown-up *Parents* v91 no11 p95 N 2016

our cradle: it's ugly, but it rocks! color *Parents* v92 no8 p52 Ag 2017

What Am I Thinking? cartoon *Parents* v92 no9 p124 S 2017

Dickson, Amy L.

Injury-induced ctgfa directs glial bridging and spinal cord regeneration in zebrafish bibl graph *Science* v354 no6312 p630 N 4 2016

Dickson, Melissa

THOU SIMPLE TUBE *History Today* v67 no5 p66 My 2017

DiClerico, Daniel

Boost Your Health & Happiness at Home il *Consumer Reports* v82 no3 p22 Mr 2017

LET IT BLOW chart *Consumer Reports* v81 no12 p10 D 2016

Dictation (Educational method)—Software

NUANCE DRAGON PROFESSIONAL INDIVIDUAL FOR MAC 6.0: BETTER PERFORMANCE AND ACCURACY K. McELHEARN cartoon color *Macworld - Digital Edition* v33 no11 p43 N 2016

Dictators

Fidel Castro: Death of a Tyrant bw *National Review* v68 no23 p14 D 19 2016

KINGS OF COMMUNISM J. H. LEE bw color diag *Esquire* p94 S 2017

Dictatorship

Creeping Autocracy: The greatest risk to democracy? Not the prospect of a coup or a junta but the self-aggrandizement of "strong leaders" L. Diamond *Hoover Digest: Research & Opinion on Public Policy* no3 p55 Summ 2017

The Fate of Republics: Does the Roman story pose lessons for America? R. W. MERRY *American Conservative* v16 no4 p13 Jl/Ag 2017

THE RETURN OF THE CZAR [Cover story] A. Abel bw color *Maclean's* v130 no3 p40 Ap 2017

Dictators—Latin America

That's a Lot of Broken Eggs J. LILEKS *National Review* v68 no23 p33 D 19 2016

Dictator's Wife, The (Theatrical production)

The Dictator's Wife T. Smith *Opera News* v81 no10 p47 Ap 2017

Did You Wonder Who Fired the Gun? (Film)

Living Proof E. HYNES bw color *Film Comment* v53 no3 p16 My/Je 2017

Diddy, 1969—Interviews

Diddy Doesn't Like To Get Hot W. Staley *New York Times Magazine* p58 Jl 9 2017

Didi Chuxing (Company)

8 CHENG WEI S. Cendrowski color *Fortune* v174 no7 p85 D 1 2016

OUT-UBERING Uber How CHENG WEI, founder of China's DIDI, drove the Americans OFF THE ROAD in CHINA B. STONE and L. Y. CHEN color *Bloomberg Businessweek* no4494 p60 O 10 2016

What Uber's China Deal Says About the Limits of Platforms P. Ghemawat *Harvard Business Review Digital Articles* p2 Ag 10 2016

Didion, Joan, 1934-

JOAN DIDION *Interview* v47 no2 p263 Mr 2017

Joan Didion in the Deep South N. Rich bw *New York Review of Books* v64 no4 p8 Mr 9 2017

Robert B. Silvers (1929–2017) [Cover story] bw color *New York Review of Books* v64 no8 p31 My 11 2017

SLOUCHING TOWARDS BETHLEHEM *Saturday Evening Post* v289 no4 p38 Jl/Ag 2017

THE WHOLE WIDE WORLD OF JOAN DIDION I. Biedenharn color map *Entertainment Weekly* no1457/1458 p104 Mr 17 2017

A Writer's Life color *Vogue* v207 no10 p284 O 2017

Dido & Aeneas (Theatrical production)

Dido and Aeneas C. Hoile *Opera News* v81 no7 p40 Ja 2017

DiDomenico, Barbara

Finding Your Mind color *Prevention* v69 no9 p3 O 2017

DiDonato, Joyce, 1970-

BACKSTORY: Joyce DiDonato F. COHN *Opera News* v81 no6 p64 D 2016

Fall Preview R. Platt color *New Yorker* v93 no25 p8 Ag 28 2017

DiDonato, Tom

Changing an Organization's Culture, Without Resistance or Blame *Harvard Business Review Digital Articles* p2 Jl 15 2015

Die Hard (Film)

5 MOVIES FOR INSOMNIACS M. FELL *TV Guide* v65 no14 p45 Ap 3 2017

Die Königin von Saba (Music)

Goldmark: Die Konigin von Saba *Opera News* v81 no7 p51 Ja 2017

Die Meistersinger von Nuernberg (Theatrical production)

The Redneck Tenor M. HARDY *Texas Monthly* v44 no11 p82 N 2016

Die Walküre (Theatrical production)

Wagner: Die Walküre F. Cohn *Opera News* v81 no9 p51 Mr 2017

Die Zauberflöte (Theatrical production)

Dateline *Opera News* v81 no7 p10 Ja 2017

Die Zauberflöte M. T. Ketterson *Opera News* v81 no9 p38 Mr 2017

Diebold, Catrine—Interviews

THE LOOK BOOK A. SWERDLOFF img *New York* v49 no21 p75 O 17 2016

Diederich, Phillippe

Playing for the Devil's Fire color *Publishers Weekly* v263 no49 p100 D 7 2016

Diedricksen, Derek

Living Large By Living Small S. FITZ-GERALD *Los Angeles Magazine* p52 F 2017

Diehl, Elaine

THE PIES HAVE IT S. GOLDBERG color *Cincinnati Magazine* v51 no1 p82 O 2017

DIEHL, REBECCA M.

Applying Functional Traits to Ecogeomorphic Processes in Riparian Ecosystems *BioScience* v67 no8 p729 Ag 2017

Diehl, Travis

RAPHAEL MONTAÑEZ ORTIZ color *Art in America* v105 no8 p126 S 2017

Diehn, Scott H.

A selective insecticidal protein from Pseudomonas for controlling corn rootworms bibl chart graph *Science* v354 no6312 p634 N 4 2016

Diekhoff, Eric

GROWING PAINS FOR ILLINOIS CANNABIS FARM G. Johnston *Successful Farming* v115 no1 p56 Ja 2017

Diekman, Connie

advice every new mom needs [Cover story] color *Parents* v92 no7 p32 Jl 2017

Diekmann, Tom

THE FARM *Successful Farming* v115 no11 p75 S 2017

Dielectric devices—Evaluation

NEW PRODUCT SHOWCASE *Sky & Telescope* v133 no4 p64 Ap 2017

Dielectrics

Observation of Anderson localization in disordered nanophotonic structures H. Herzig Sheinfux, Y. Lumer et al diag graph *Science* v356 no6341 p953 Je 1 2017

Diener, Theodor O.

Stem Cell Research *Skeptical Inquirer* v41 no3 p63 My/Je 2017

Dieng, Adama

Protecting Vulnerable Populations from Genocide *UN Chronicle* v53 no4 p1 2016

PROTECTING VULNERABLE POPULATIONS FROM GENOCIDE *UN Chronicle* v54 no4 p9 2017

Diercks, Christian S.

The atom, the molecule, and the covalent organic framework diag *Science* v355 no6328 p923 Mr 3 2017

Dierdorff, Erich C.

Research: We're Not Very Self-Aware, Especially at Work *Harvard Business Review Digital Articles* p2 Mr 12 2015

Diering, Graham H.

Homer1a drives homeostatic scaling-down of excitatory synapses during sleep bibl graph *Science* v355 no6324 p511 F 3 2017

Diersen, Lisa

EQUUS Film Festival K. Brittle bw color *Dressage Today* v23 no7 p54 Mr 2017

Dies Miraculum (Poem)

DIES MIRACULUM B. Doyle *U.S. Catholic* v82 no8 p51 Ag 2017

Diesel, Vin, 1967-

BATTLE OF THE BALD, ETHNICALLY AMBIGUOUS ACTION HEROES chart color *Esquire* p25 Ap 2017

Sneak Peek at 2018 M. Fell *TV Guide* v65 no37 p45 S 4 2017

Diesel automobile emissions

Will Bosch Choke on VW's Exhaust? D. Lawrence, K. Mehrotra et al bw color *Bloomberg Businessweek* no4534 p12 Ag 14 2017

Diesel automobiles

Thank You, Mom M. Bean color *Men's Health* v32 no4 p4 My 2017

Diesel locomotives—Evaluation

Kato N scale SDP40F diesel locomotive C. Grivno color *Model Railroader* v84 no5 p65 My 2017

News & Products bw color *Model Railroader* v84 no9 p10 S 2017

News & Products color *Model Railroader* v84 no6 p10 Je 2017

Diesel locomotives—Maintenance & repair

DIGITALMR D. Kawala color *Model Railroader* v83 no12 p6 D 2016

Diesel motor exhaust gas

See also

Diesel automobile emissions

Dieselgate and Dollars M. Rechtin cartoon *Motor Trend* v68 no12 p28 D 2016

Your Say... G. FACKLER, J. ELLIOTT et al color *Motor Trend* v69 no3 p36 Mr 2017

Diesel motor exhaust gas—Prevention

IT'S A RECYCLING CENTER: UNDERSTANDING EXHAUST GAS RECIRCULATION R. Bohacz *Successful Farming* v115 no9 p33 Ag 2017

Diesel electric power-plants

DOCK BOX color *Sea Magazine* v109 no8 p32 Ag 2017

Dieser, Rodney B.

Building Better Cause-Marketing Relationships *Parks & Recreation* v52 no5 p60 My 2017

Diet

> *See also*
>
> Fasting
> Gastronomy
> Mediterranean diet
> Pork-free diet
> Reducing diets
> Vegetarianism

5 Little Ways to Detox Your Body A. Patz color *Health* v31 no7 p83 S 2017

6 burning workout questions—answered! J. Andriakos color *Health* v31 no9 p41 N 2017

An Anti-Aging Diet? [Cover story] B. LIEBMAN *Nutrition Action Health Letter* v44 no4 p3 My 2017

Are You Getting Enough Vitamin E from Your Diet? *Tufts University Health & Nutrition Letter* v35 no6 p3 Ag 2017

Ask Miles cartoon *Runner's World* v52 no4 p44 My 2017

Beach Body Boot Camp T. Anderson color *Health* v31 no6 p46 Jl 2017

Beyond Olive: Oils for Heart Health *Tufts University Health & Nutrition Letter* v35 no1 p3 Mr 2017

Brain-Healthy Diets J. GRAHAM color *Kiplinger's Personal Finance* v71 no7 p68 Jl 2017

Busting the Multivitamin Myth V. TWEED color *Better Nutrition* v79 no9 p8 S 2017

CAN ALZHEIMER'S DISEASE BE PREVENTED? E. A. Kane color *Amazing Wellness* v9 no3 p30 EarlySumm 2017

Can Food Help You Feel Better? A. STANLEY color *Seventeen* v75 no11 p62 N 2016

CHIN UP! J. Black bw *Esquire* p65 Ap 2017

Coming to Labels: Added Sugars *Tufts University Health & Nutrition Letter* v35 no3 p6 My 2017

Dietary Relief for Aching Joints *Tufts University Health & Nutrition Letter* v34 no12 p7 F 2017

DODGE DISEASE WITH DIET [Cover story] B. LIEBMAN *Nutrition Action Health Letter* v44 no5 p3 Je 2017

"Do I need to take a daily multi-vitamin and mineral in order to be healthy?" M. Binder *Vegetarian Journal* v35 no1 p14 2016

double the number of foods your kid likes! K. CICERO *Parents* v91 no11 p64 N 2016

EAT EARLY, STAY SLIM color *Health* v31 no8 p13 O 2017

Eating well—and loving it! C. McHugh color *Health* v31 no8 p6 O 2017

EAT LIKE A YOGI D. Macy color *Yoga Journal* p100 2017 Special Issue

Eat This, Not That! color *AARP: The Magazine* v59 no3A p32 Ap/My 2016

Eat What You Love Already color *Health* v30 no9 p14 N 2016

Eat your greens! B. Lipton color *Health* v31 no9 p107 N 2017

E-ssential! Vitamin E is as necessary as oxygen, but just how much we need is still up in the air H. ESTROFF MARANO *Psychology Today* v50 no2 p31 Mr/Ap 2017

The Everything Guide to Running A. Shaffer chart color *Health* v31 no3 p35 Ap 2017

FIT, FUN, FABULOUS [Cover story] A. Prato color *Health* v31 no2 p104 Mr 2017

The food swap that changed my body K. Canning color *Health* v31 no9 p51 N 2017

Get a Collagen Boost M. D. SMITH color *Better Nutrition* v79 no9 p62 S 2017

Getting slim with my sister A. Levi color *Health* v31 no8 p46 O 2017

GET YOUR BEST HAIR EVER S. Neibart color *Harper's Bazaar* no3656 p374 S 2017

Glow on the go R. S. Frazier color *Health* v31 no9 p54 N 2017

GO NATURAL IN 90 days color *Better Nutrition* v79 no7 p35 Jl 2017

Health Claims On Your Food *Tufts University Health & Nutrition Letter* v35 no1 p4 Mr 2017

HEALTH Q & A cartoon color *Good Housekeeping* v264 no2 p91 F 2017

Healthy Fats Reduce Diabetes Risk *Tufts University Health & Nutrition Letter* v34 no9 p6 N 2016

Heart problems tied to mom's diet L. BEIL cartoon *Science News* v190 no12 p14 D 10 2016

Homemade Dog Food M. Straus *Mother Earth News* no280 p78 F/Mr 2017

How I Found My Feel-Great Weight A. Levi color *Health* v31 no6 p48 Jl 2017

how to do a BODY CLEANSE V. TWEED color *Better Nutrition* v79 no3 p38 Mr 2017

HOW TO EAT P. SAGAL cartoon *Runner's World* v52 no2 p18 Mr 2017

Hungry for sleep V. Clayton color *Yoga Journal* no294 p41 S 2017

I'm hooked on taking care of my body A. Levi color *Health* v31 no9 p47 N 2017

Instagram Yourself Slim color *Health* v31 no7 p17 S 2017

JULIANNE HOUGH What I love color *Health* v31 no9 p29 N 2017

KELLY ROWLAND "You Have to Treat Yourself" J. Andriakos color *Health* v31 no2 p22 Mr 2017

Make healthy eating easy H. Powell color *Redbook* p95 O 2017

MANDY MOORE "I'm never going to deprive myself" J. Naftulin color *Health* v31 no9 p25 N 2017

Me, Minus 108 Pounds A. Levi color *Health* v31 no3 p44 Ap 2017

New Safe-Seafood Guidelines color *Parents* v92 no5 p68 My 2017

NEWSBITES [Cover story] *Tufts University Health & Nutrition Letter* v34 no8 p1 O 2016

nourish your practice *Yoga Journal* p110 2017 Special Issue

NUTRITION HOTLINE R. Mangels *Vegetarian Journal* v36 no3 p2 2017

OUR GH DO DIET PROMISE TO YOU J. LONDON color *Good Housekeeping* v264 no3 p99 Mr 2017

Penélope Cruz K. B. Brown color *InStyle* v24 no8 p111 Ag 2017

Please Pass the Algae H. ESTROFF MARANO *Psychology Today* v50 no2 p34 Mr/Ap 2017

Power up your diet with plant-based meals *Harvard Health Letter* v42 no6 p6 Ap 2017

Prioritizing good diets D. A. Cleveland bibl color *Science* v354 no6318 p1385 D 16 2016

Put Purple on Your Plate color *Health* v31 no6 p9 Jl 2017

The right (and wrong) ways to get a hot Hollywood bod J. Andriakos color *Health* v31 no8 p43 O 2017

Scale Stuck? J. Benjamin color *Health* v31 no3 p47 Ap 2017

Second opinion *Mayo Clinic Health Letter* v34 no11 p8 N 2016

Should you try a subscription meal kit? *Harvard Health Letter* v42 no2 p7 D 2016

Social Media Changed My Body A. Levi color *Health* v31 no7 p66 S 2017

sound bites L. Ladoceour color *Yoga Journal* p111 2017 Special Issue

STOP BEATING YOURSELF UP ABOUT FOOD V. Sole-smith color *Health* v31 no8 p112 O 2017

Stop the Weekend Weight Gain J. Andriakos color *Health* v31 no2 p45 Mr 2017

STRESS RELIEF TOOLKIT color *Better Nutrition* v79 no9 p38 S 2017

Strip Down J. DRILLING *Cincinnati Magazine* v50 no4 p148 Ja 2017

Substituting Ingredients for Good Health *Tufts University Health & Nutrition Letter* v35 no1 p1 Mr 2017

take OM HOME M. Rabbitt color *Yoga Journal* no288 p96 D 2016

Think Yourself Thin? K. Canning color *Health* v31 no6 p51 Jl 2017

This Diet May Help You Lose Weight./ This Diet May Help You Lose Weight [Cover story] A. Sifferlin color *Time* v189 no21 p48 Je 5 2017

THIS IS FASTING? M. Stacey color *Women's Health* v14 no8 p106 O 2017

This Quiz Will Save Your Waist J. Andriakos color *Health* v31 no7 p63 S 2017

U.S. Diets Still Out of Balance With Dietary Recommendations J. Bentley *Amber Waves: The Economics of Food, Farming, Natural Resources, & Rural America* p18 Jl 2017

Vegetarian Action. Scott Jurek: An Example for Vegan Athletes S. Lawrence *Vegetarian Journal* v36 no3 p35 2017

Supplement Strategy D. N. JACKSON color diag *Muscle & Performance* v9 no6 p57 Je 2017

Test Your Iron Smarts V. TWEED color *Better Nutrition* p64 My 2017

trend WATCH V. TWEED color *Better Nutrition* p10 My 2017

Vitamin D Essentials V. TWEED *Better Nutrition* v79 no1 p68 Ja 2017

WHAT'S YOUR SUPPLEMENT IQ? C. Barakat color *Equus* no472 p36 Ja 2017

YOUR SUPPLEMENT QUESTIONS, ANSWERED! T. Low Dog color *Amazing Wellness* p50 Fall 2017

Dietary supplements industry

TEST YOUR KNOWLEDGE D. N. JACKSON color *Muscle & Performance* v9 no9 p16 S 2017

Dietary supplements industry—Corrupt practices

How MusclePharm Went From Swole to Twig I. Boudway and Z. Faux bw color *Bloomberg Businessweek* no4497 p56 O 31 2016

Dietary supplements—Economic aspects

SUPPLEMENTAL KNOWLEDGE E. Marglin color *Yoga Journal* no293 p29 Ag 2017

Dietary supplements—Evaluation

AMINOS: ATHLETIC ASSETS D. N. JACKSON color diag *Muscle & Performance* v9 no11 p58 N 2017

ANAVITE R. GASPARI color *Muscle & Performance* v8 no12 p62 D 2016

Autumn Crush color *Amazing Wellness* p96 Fall 2017

Boost Your Performance color *Muscle & Performance* v9 no11 p62 N 2017

Building Bodies color *Muscle & Performance* v9 no8 p64 Ag 2017

Cheat Your Way to Lean! A. RIOS *Runner's World* v52 no3 p41 Ap 2017

customize YOUR HEALTH [Cover story] L. Turner color *Amazing Wellness* v9 no3 p54 EarlySumm 2017

Get to Know: Designer Protein J. SCHILDHOUSE color *Muscle & Performance* v9 no8 p32 Ag 2017

Grease Your Wheels L. McGLASHAN color *Muscle & Performance* v9 no8 p26 Ag 2017

Maximize Your Postworkout Recovery A. ATKINSON color *Muscle & Performance* v9 no11 p64 N 2017

Must-Haves color *Amazing Wellness* v9 no1 p92 Wint 2017

NOT YOUR FATHER'S FAT BURNER J. WUEBBEN color *Muscle & Performance* v8 no12 p14 D 2016

Plant-Based Power J. WUEBBEN color *Muscle & Performance* v9 no11 p33 N 2017

PREMIER PRODUCTS color *Muscle & Performance* v8 no12 p64 D 2016

PREWORKOUT 101 J. EDWARD color *Muscle & Performance* v9 no8 p59 Ag 2017

THE RIGHT STUFF color *Muscle & Performance* v9 no4 p64 Ap 2017

SMARTEN UP TO SHRINK YOUR GUT C. Hansen color *Men's Health* v32 no9 p73 N 2017

SPRING SWAG color *Amazing Wellness* v8 no2 p92 Spr 2016

TAKE HOME A WIN M. HANSEN color *Dressage Today* v23 no10 p15 Jl 2017

TEST YOUR KNOWLEDGE D. N. JACKSON color *Muscle & Performance* v9 no9 p16 S 2017

Warming Trends color *Amazing Wellness* v9 no2 p88 Spr 2017

Dietary supplements—Physiological aspects

ASHWAGANDHA: One Quality Supplement J. WUEBBEN color *Muscle & Performance* v9 no5 p11 My 2017

Mind Your Meds L. BEIL color *Prevention* v69 no2 p74 F 2017

Dietary supplements—Research

BRAIN-BOOSTING SUPPLEMENT COMBO J. WUEBBEN color *Muscle & Performance* v8 no12 p14 D 2016

Dietary supplements—Therapeutic use

7 COMMON NUTRIENT DEFICIENCIES L. TURNER color *Better Nutrition* v79 no3 p48 Mr 2017

allergy SURVIVAL GUIDE L. TURNER color *Better Nutrition* v79 no4 p56 Ap 2017

Anti-Aging Nutrition for Eyes *Tufts University Health & Nutrition Letter* v35 no5 p4 Jl 2017

A Cure for Everything? [Cover story] *Nutrition Action Health Letter* v43 no9 p5 N 2016

DIGESTION AND AGING M. T. Murray color *Amazing Wellness*

v8 no2 p64 Spr 2016

Gut Check C. DOW *Nutrition Action Health Letter* v44 no4 p9 My 2017

Magnesium: Superstar Rising V. TWEED chart color diag *Better Nutrition* v79 no4 p24 Ap 2017

Medical-Grade Collagen: 102 Million Dose, 35 Years, 4,700 Health Professionals J. Caras chart color diag *Better Nutrition* v79 no4 p20 Ap 2017

Diethylamine

Your Boss Is Gonna Love Your New Drug Habit J. DEAN color *GQ: Gentlemen's Quarterly* v87 no1 p26 Ja 2017

Dietitians

4 TIPS TO TELLING YOUR FARM'S STORY: NEBRASKA DIETITIAN AMBER PANKONIN SAYS WE CAN DO BETTER AT ENGAGING PASSIONATE CONSUMERS AND FOOD ACTIVISTS G. Johnston *Successful Farming* v115 no11 p16 S 2017

Dedicated Vegan Dietitian Dr. John Westerdahl H. Francis *Vegetarian Journal* v36 no1 p35 2017

June All-star color *Women's Health* v14 no5 p16 Je 2017

MAYE IN AUTUMN D. BLASBERG color *Vanity Fair* v59 no4 p172 Mr 2017

Vegetarian Action. Molly McBride, RD, LD Promoting Veganismm in the Corporate World A. Custer *Vegetarian Journal* v35 no1 p35 2016

Vegetarian Action. Vesanto Melina, Passionate Vegan Dietitian and Author C. Brown *Vegetarian Journal* v36 no2 p35 2017

Dietl, Gregory P.

Merging paleobiology with conservation biology to guide the future of terrestrial ecosystems color *Science* v355 no6325 p594 F 10 2017

Diet—Management

5 WAYS ...TO SURVIVE THE HOLIDAYS J. CONNOR cartoon *Muscle & Performance* v8 no12 p66 D 2016

7 TIPS FOR INDULGING THIS HOLIDAY SEASON J. SCHILDHOUSE color *Muscle & Performance* v8 no12 p28 D 2016

Diet—Physiological aspects

BEST BITES L. APPLEGATE color *Runner's World* v51 no10 p50 N 2016

NO EXCUSES J. SCHILDHOUSE color *Muscle & Performance* v9 no1 p28 Ja 2017

DIETRICH, ANDREA

the case of the cat-scented faucet cartoon *Popular Science* v289 no2 p82 Mr/Ap 2017

Dietrich, Carl

THINK VERTICAL B. BERK color *Road & Track* v69 no4 p68 N 2017

Dietrich, John

What's In The Name? ALL OF US: CELEBRATING A CENTURY OF HUMANISM L. L. SIMPSON *Humanist* v77 no5 p25 S/O 2017

Dietrich, Marlene, 1901-1992

Stage Fright *New Yorker* v93 no16 p29 Je 5 2017

Diet—United States

A Look at Calorie Sources in the American Diet S. Rehkamp color graph *Amber Waves: The Economics of Food, Farming, Natural Resources, & Rural America* p23 D 2016

Dietz, Brett William

Dietz: Headcase: Opera Introspective J. Rosenblum *Opera News* v81 no7 p50 Ja 2017

Dietz, Hendrik

Self-assembly of genetically encoded DNA-protein hybrid nanoscale shapes *Science* v355 no6331 p1283 Mr 24 2017

Dietz, John

NUDGE YIELDS WITH NARROW ROWS *Successful Farming* v115 no4 p54 Mr 2017

DIETZ, MATTHEW S.

Mapping Conservation Strategies under a Changing Climate *BioScience* v67 no6 p494 Je 2017

Dietz-LiVolsi, Danielle

Mother of Invention L. GOLDMAN color *Better Homes & Gardens* v95 no2 p134 F 2016

Dieulafoy, Jane

The TrowelBlazing women of ARCHAEOLOGY B. Hassett *History Today* v67 no2 p32 F 2017

Dieu Tu Uyen, Nguyen

Vietnam Shrugs Off the Loss of a Trade Pact *Bloomberg Business-week* no4512 p15 F 20 2017

Díez Muiño, Ricardo

Angular momentum–induced delays in solid-state photoemission enhanced by intra-atomic interactions chart color graph *Science* v357 no6357 p1274 S 22 2017

Diffee, Matt

15 QUESTIONS ABOUT BARBEQUE ANSWERED cartoon map *Esquire* p110 S 2017

The OCEAN IS SALTY bw cartoon color *Esquire* p106 O 2017

Differentiation (Developmental psychology)

LAUNCH color *Wired* v25 no7 p3 Jl 2017

Difficult People (TV program)

Difficult People A. D'Arminio *TV Guide* v65 no25 p23 Je 2017

Difficult People A. D'Arminio *TV Guide* v65 no35 p36 Ag 21 2017

Musical Theater and Misanthropy D. D'addario color *Time* v190 no7 p52 Ag 21 2017

A POP CULTURE LEXICON C. Agard color *Entertainment Weekly* no1468/1469 p41 Je 2-9 2017

Diffley, John F. X.

Bidirectional eukaryotic DNA replication is established by quasi-symmetrical helicase loading graph *Science* v357 no6348 p314 Jl 21 2017

Diffuse ionized gas (Astronomy)

Milky Way May Be Made with Swapped Gas C. M. CARLISLE color *Sky & Telescope* v134 no5 p10 N 2017

Diffusers (Fluid dynamics)

DADDY'S DAY GIFT GUIDE A. LUCAS color *Ebony* v72 no8 p46 Je 2017

ONE NIGHTSTAND M. Johns color *Popular Science* v289 no5 p34 S/O 2017

Diffusion of innovations

See also

Technology transfer

Navigating technology transfer issues A. G. Levine color *Science* v355 no6328 p975 Mr 3 2017

DI FILIPPO, PAUL

Things of Nature color *Weekly Standard* v22 no20 p37 Ja 30 2017

Di Fiore, A.

Persistent effects of pre-Columbian plant domestication on Amazonian forest composition bibl chart graph map *Science* v355 no6328 p925 Mr 3 2017

Di Fiore, Alessandro

4 Mistakes That Kill Crowdsourcing Efforts *Harvard Business Review Digital Articles* p2 Jl 21 2017

A Chief Innovation Officer's Actual Responsibilities *Harvard Business Review Digital Articles* p2 N 26 2014

How Corporate HQ Can Get More from Innovation Outposts *Harvard Business Review Digital Articles* p2 My 2 2017

Stop Treating B2B Customers Like Digital Novices *Harvard Business Review Digital Articles* p2 My 10 2016

Why B2B Companies Struggle with Collaborative Innovation *Harvard Business Review Digital Articles* p2 Mr 16 2016

Di Fiore, Pier Paolo

Reticulon 3–dependent ER-PM contact sites control EGFR non-clathrin endocytosis color diag graph *Science* v356 no6338 p617 My 12 2017

Digestion

See also

Intestinal absorption

4 STEPS TO BETTER DIGESTIVE HEALTH color *Good Housekeeping* v265 no3 p44 S 2017

Building a Better Gut E. A. KANE color *Better Nutrition* v78 no12 p32 D 2016

DIGESTION AND AGING M. T. Murray color *Amazing Wellness* v8 no2 p64 Spr 2016

FEELING THE BURN? J. Teitelbaum color *Amazing Wellness* v8 no6 p28 Early Winter2016

Our Doc Will See You Now R. Rajapaksa color *Health* v31 no7 p92 S 2017

What to do when your medication causes nausea *Harvard Health Letter* v42 no7 p7 My 2017

Digestion—Physiological aspects

Soothe Your Stomach T. Low Dog color *Prevention* v69 no11 p24 N 2017

Digestive enzymes

Mysteries of the Human Body EXPLAINED! K. LAWLER and C. SAGON cartoon color *AARP: The Magazine* v60 no3A p26 Ap/My 2017

Your Health *Saturday Evening Post* v289 no1 p71 Ja/F 2017

Digestive organs

love your BELLY K. ANSEL and M. KING color *Yoga Journal* p102 2017 SpecialIssue

Digestive system diseases

See also

Gastrointestinal diseases

Charcoal: A Go-To Remedy V. TWEED color *Better Nutrition* v78 no11 p24 N 2016

Digestive system diseases—Treatment

DIGESTION AND AGING M. T. Murray color *Amazing Wellness* v8 no2 p64 Spr 2016

Is 40 Years of Progress Enough? G. Attara cartoon *Maclean's* v129 no48/49 p76 D 5 2016

Diggs, Daveed, 1982-

DAVEED DIGGIN' I. Biedenharn color *Entertainment Weekly* no1470 p28 Je 16 2017

Daveed Diggs, Actor and Rapper E. Dockterman color *Time* v188 no15 p58 O 17 2016

Daveed Diggs' Dad-Chic A. LICATA color *Rolling Stone* no1273 p20 N 3 2016

Daveed Diggs J. Johnson color *Current Biography* v78 no2 p26 F 2017

SVU STAR POWER E. Aslanian *TV Guide* v65 no4 p21 Ja 16 2017

Diggs, Daveed, 1982——Interviews

Hot Tracks D. DIGGS color *Vanity Fair* v59 no1 p96 Holiday 2017

Di Giovannantonio, Luca G.

Transcriptional activation of RagD GTPase controls mTORC1 and promotes cancer growth diag *Science* v356 no6343 p1188 Je 16 2017

di Giovanni, Janine

Brave Hearts color *Vogue* v206 no11 p94 N 2016

Free Style color *Vogue* v207 no4 p218 Ap 2017

Three Stories of the Middle East *New York Times Book Review* p13 F 12 2017

Di Girolamo, Rocco

Combining polyethylene and polypropylene: Enhanced performance with PE/iPP multiblock polymers bibl chart graph *Science* v355 no6327 p814 F 24 2017

Digital asset management

Which Industries Are the Most Digital (and Why)? P. Gandhi, S. Khanna et al *Harvard Business Review Digital Articles* p2 Ap 1 2016

Digital audiobooks—Sales & prices

Getting the Measure of Downloadable Audio J. Milliot chart *Publishers Weekly* v264 no38 p5 S 18 2017

Digital audiotape recorders & recording

Take It to the Max D. SAX color *Esquire* v166 no5 p13 D 2016/Ja 2017

Digital badges in education

Microcredentials B. Berry, K. M. Airhart et al color il *Phi Delta Kappan* v98 no3 p34 N 2016

Digital cameras

See also

Camera phones

Digital single-lens reflex cameras

Coming to a Dashboard Near You M. Naranjo chart color *Consumer Reports* v82 no3 p58 Mr 2017

March Madness color *Consumer Reports* v82 no3 p67 Mr 2017

A wish list for the iPhone in 2017 J. SNELL color *Macworld - Digital Edition* p43 F 2017

Digital cameras—Design & construction

The Point- and-Shoot Reborn color *Bloomberg Businessweek* no4518 p71 Ap 10 2017

Digital cameras—Equipment & supplies

SCREEN GEMS P. Kolonia color *Popular Photography* v81 no2 p28 Mr/Ap 2017

Digital cameras—Evaluation

See also

Digital single-lens reflex cameras—Evaluation

For the Get Up and Go-Getter color *Consumer Reports* v81 no12 p46 D 2016

HEAD-TO-HEAD THE FINE PRINTS color *Wired* v25 no5 p54 My 2017

THE MAN IN THE BOX D. WINTERS color *Wired* v25 no5 p56 My 2017

ON-THE-GO GEAR L. Back color *Trail Rider* v29 no2 p56 Mr 2017

SLOW DOWN THE WORLD S. Horaczek color *Popular Science* v289 no5 p30 S/O 2017

TOP TOOLS color *Popular Photography* v81 no2 p14 Mr/Ap 2017

WHY WAIT? color *Popular Photography* v80 no11 p16 D 2016

Digital communications

THE ENEMIES OF EMPATHY R. A. SCHROTH *America* v215 no14 p36 N 7 2016

Is Technology Really Helping Us Get More Done? M. C. Mankins *Harvard Business Review Digital Articles* p2 F 25 2016

James Bond, Dunder Mifflin, and the Future of Product Placement L. Muzellec *Harvard Business Review Digital Articles* p2 Je 23 2016

Risks Posed by Mobile Network Vulnerabilities *USA Today Magazine* v145 no2863 p8 Ap 2017

Digital communications—Equipment & supplies

The Digital Cloud Is Underwater-and Vulnerable K. Vick and E. Barone color diag map *Time* v188 no15 p16 O 17 2016

Digital control systems

Making the DCC suitcase connection L. Puckett color diag *Model Railroader* v83 no12 p62 D 2016

Operating with Digital Command Control L. Puckett color *Model Railroader* v84 no2 p66 F 2017

Digital counters

Jump Start Data-Driven Parks Management *Parks & Recreation* v52 no5 p49 My 2017

Digital divide

Busing In Wi-Fi T. Newcombe *Governing* v30 no4 p60 Ja 2017

From the Editor *MIT Technology Review* v120 no1 p2 Ja/F 2017

Internet for All K. Vick color *Time* v189 no13 p34 Ap 10 2017

The Most Digital Companies Are Leaving All the Rest Behind J. Manyika, G. Pinkus et al *Harvard Business Review Digital Articles* p2 Ja 21 2016

Digital divide in education

Poor Students Face Digital Divide in How Teachers Learn to Use Tech B. Herold *Education Digest* v83 no3 p16 N 2017

Digital elevation models

A view of the Arctic in high relief bw *Science* v353 no6307 p1474 S 30 2016

Digital image watermarking

How to watermark multiple photos in Lightroom L. SNIDER color *Macworld - Digital Edition* p128 D 2016

Digital images

How to use Siri in macOS Sierra to find pictures in Photos on the fly L. SNIDER color *Macworld - Digital Edition* p125 F 2017

Digital images—Editing

How to use Photoshop Elements to combine images like a pro L. SNIDER color *Macworld - Digital Edition* p122 D 2016

Digital jukebox software

See also

iTunes (Digital music program)

Feature: Ask the iTunes Guy K. McElhearn cartoon color *Macworld - Digital Edition* p102 Ja 2017

Digital mammography

This Is Not Your Mother's Mammogram. It's a... 3-D Medical Breakthrough S. KLEIN bw *Prevention* v69 no2 p32 F 2017

Digital media

Can the digital revolution save Indian journalism? L. Chaudhry cartoon color *Columbia Journalism Review* p80 Fall/Wint 2016

Europe's Other Crisis: A Digital Recession B. Chakravorti and R. S. Chaturvedi *Harvard Business Review Digital Articles* p2 O 27 2015

OF MANY THINGS M. MALONE *America* v215 no11 p2 O 17 2016

Pokémon Go, Amazon Dash, and the Future of User Interaction M. Schrage *Harvard Business Review Digital Articles* p2 Jl 14 2016

Print is dead. Long live print M. Rosenwald cartoon *Columbia Journalism Review* p34 Fall/Wint 2016

The Revenge of the Real D. SAX *Columbia Journalism Review* p36 Fall/Wint 2016

SCHOOL OF JOURNALISM AND MASS COMMUNICATION TAKES DIGITAL MEDIA TO NEW HEIGHTS *Texas Monthly* v44 no11 p46 N 2016

When Silicon Valley Took Over Journalism F. Foer color *Atlantic* v320 no2 p28 S 2017

Digital media—Religious aspects

Digital Growth [Cover story] C. J. COYNE color *America* v215 no11 p19 O 17 2016

Word Files B. SHIRLEY color *America* v215 no11 p22 O 17 2016

Digital Object Identifiers

Background Screening Methodology: Is your methodology leading the way or a best practice in attracting risk? *Parks & Recreation* v52 no10 p46 O 2017

Digital photography

See also

Raw file formats (Digital photography)

Bonnie Maygarden L. Cutrone *New Orleans Homes & Lifestyles* v20 no3 p22 Summ 2017

PHOTO ops D. DICKINSON color *Better Homes & Gardens* v95 no8 p74 Ag 2017

Picture Perfect T. Bufete chart color diag graph *Consumer Reports* v82 no12 p14 D 2017

Secrets of Fake Photos Revealed J. KIFFEL-ALCHEH *National Geographic Kids* no469 p22 Ap 2017

Digital photography software

Mac 911 G. FLEISHMAN color *Macworld - Digital Edition* v34 no4 p111 My 2017

Digital projectors

IT'S SHOW TIME C. BOYD color *Better Homes & Gardens* v95 no8 p70 Ag 2017

Digital projectors—Evaluation

HEAD-TO-HEAD LIGHT HOUSES T. MOYNIHAN color *Wired* v25 no4 p38 Ap 2017

Optoma HD142X 3D DLP Projector A. Griffifin color graph *Sound & Vision* v81 no10 p62 D 2016

Digital Reasoning Systems Inc.

Wall Street's Robocop A. GARA and J. OBERWEIS color *Forbes* v199 no6 p62 Je 13 2017

Digital rights management

The Weird Rules Governing What We Download K. Wiens *Harvard Business Review Digital Articles* p2 N 3 2015

Digital sound recording

DIGGING UP DIGITAL MUSIC S. S. PATEL bw color *Archaeology* v70 no2 p9 Mr/Ap 2017

Digital sound recording—Research

This Just In J. Zorthian *Time* v188 no14 p23 O 10 2016

Digital storytelling

Hybrid Jobs Call for Hybrid Education J. E. Aoun *Harvard Business Review Digital Articles* p2 Ap 12 2016

Digital technology

See also

Digital media

3 Traps That Block Corporate Transformation V. Nayar *Harvard Business Review Digital Articles* p2 N 5 2014

The 5 Paradoxes of Digital Business Leadership T. Nielsen and P. Meehan *Harvard Business Review Digital Articles* p2 Jl 2 2015

60 Countries' Digital Competitiveness, Indexed B. Chakravorti, A. Bhalla et al *Harvard Business Review Digital Articles* p2 Jl 12 2017

6 Digital Strategies, and Why Some Work Better than Others J. Bughin and N. Van Zeebroeck *Harvard Business Review Digital Articles* p2 Jl 31 2017

7 Questions to Ask Before Your Next Digital Transformation B. Libert, M. Beck et al *Harvard Business Review Digital Articles* p2 Jl 14 2016

Access to Digital Technology Accelerates Global Gender Equality J. Sweet *Harvard Business Review Digital Articles* p2 My 17 2016

After 20 Years, It's Harder to Ignore the Digital Economy's Dark Side D. Tapscott *Harvard Business Review Digital Articles* p2 Mr 11 2016

Are You Accurately Measuring Your Company's Digital Strength? J. Maling, R. Fertig et al *Harvard Business Review Digital Ar-*

Digital technology—Economic aspects

Digital technology—Social aspects

RESTAURANTS' DIGITAL DILEMMA J. Kell color *Fortune* v175 no8 p57 Je 15 2017

THE STREAM TEAMS P. Thamel color *Sports Illustrated* v126 no4 p62 Ja 30 2017

Digital-to-analog converters

Meridian Audio Explorer2 USB DAC review: An inexpensive path to high-resolution audio M. BROWN color *Macworld - Digital Edition* p97 Je 13 2017

New Gear color *Sound & Vision* v82 no6 p26 Jl/Ag 2017

Digital-to-analog converters—Evaluation

Elac Element EA101EQ-G Integrated Amplifier/DAC D. Kumin chart color graph *Sound & Vision* v82 no3 p58 Ap 2017

Teac AI-503 USB DAC/Integrated Amplifier B. Ankosko color *Sound & Vision* v82 no7 p74 S 2017

Digital video recorders

Sony Projectors M. Fleischmann color *Sound & Vision* v82 no3 p17 Ap 2017

Storage Solutions A. GRIFFIN and C. Crowley color *Sound & Vision* v81 no9 p29 N 2016

Digital video recording

EVERY NIGHT PERFECT K. Dupzyk and J. Lynch bw color *Popular Mechanics* p84 O 2017

HOW TO DO EVERY THING WITH VIDEO M. Wilson and D. Dubno bw color diag *Popular Mechanics* p58 O 2017

MY GOPRO LIFE color *Popular Mechanics* p92 O 2017

Digital video recording—Equipment & supplies

How to turn your Mac into a digital video recorder for over-the-air TV G. FLEISHMAN color *Macworld - Digital Edition* v34 no6 p113 Je 2017

Digital single-lens reflex cameras

Pocket DSLR M. Belfiore bw color *Bloomberg Businessweek* no4508 p31 Ja 23 2017

Digital single-lens reflex cameras—Evaluation

ENTER HERE P. Ryan bw color graph *Popular Photography* v81 no1 p92 Ja/F 2017

For the Globetrotter color *Consumer Reports* v81 no12 p42 D 2016

NEW BOSS P. Ryan color graph *Popular Photography* v81 no2 p78 Mr/Ap 2017

Pentax's "Astro" DSLR A. Dyer *Sky & Telescope* v133 no2 p64 F 2017

Toy story S. Horaczek and A. Smith color *Popular Science* v289 no6 p44 N/D 2017

Digitization

6 Digital Strategies, and Why Some Work Better than Others J. Bughin and N. Van Zeebroeck *Harvard Business Review Digital Articles* p2 Jl 31 2017

Boards Can't Wait for CEOs to Prioritize Digital Change R. Charan *Harvard Business Review Digital Articles* p2 S 6 2017

Digital Transformation Doesn't Have to Leave Employees Behind Bouée *Harvard Business Review Digital Articles* p2 S 30 2015

How MIT and the Internet Archive Made Free E-books A. Green *Publishers Weekly* v264 no39 p10 S 25 2017

MAKE THE SWITCH F. LANIER *Sea Magazine* v109 no4 p28 Ap 2017

Prepare Your Workforce for the Automation Age C. Knoess, R. Harbour et al *Harvard Business Review Digital Articles* p2 N 23 2016

What to Do with All Those Cassettes D. Pogue color *Scientific American* v315 no3 p27 S 2016

Digitrax Inc.

Digitrax DCS240 advanced command station provides more power and upgrades L. Puckett diag *Model Railroader* v83 no12 p70 D 2016

Digitrax Evolution advanced DCC starter set L. Puckett color *Model Railroader* v84 no5 p62 My 2017

Di Giulio, C.

Observation of a large-scale anisotropy in the arrival directions of cosmic rays above 8×10^{18} eV *Science* v357 no6357 p1266 S 22 2017

Dignan, Larry

Your Biggest Cybersecurity Weakness Is Your Phone *Harvard Business Review Digital Articles* p2 S 22 2016

Dignelli, Andre

Andre Dignelli: "Life is a Competition" T. Conahan color *Practical Horseman* v45 no8 p22 Ag 2017

Dignity

The Dignity Deficit A. C. Brooks bw *Foreign Affairs* v96 no2 p106 Mr/Ap 2017

SLIPPERY SLOPE? DURKIN *Commonweal* v114 no14 p4 S 8 2017

you may be right T. Rinkoski, A. Dunn et al color *U.S. Catholic* v81 no12 p5 D 2016

D'IGNOTI, STEFANIA

Old World, Young Promise color *Forbes* v199 no1 p20 Ja 24 2017

DiGREGORIO, KATHLEEN

Q: What was the greatest summer read of your life? color *O, The Oprah Magazine* p16 Jl 2017

DIGREGORIO, SARAH

A ROUND OF APPLAUSE *Martha Stewart Living* no269 p90 N 2016

SWEETER BY THE DOZEN *Martha Stewart Living* no270 p136 D 2016

SWEETS FOR YOUR SWEETIE color *Martha Stewart Living* no271 p90 Ja/F 2017

THE TIME IS RIPE (TO BAKE WITH FRUIT) color *Martha Stewart Living* no275 p98 Je 2017

Di Iorio, John R.

Dynamic multinuclear sites formed by mobilized copper ions in NOx selective catalytic reduction bw color diag graph *Science* v357 no6354 p898 S 1 2017

Dijkgraaf, Robbert

Knowledge Is Infrastructure color *Scientific American* v316 no6 p8 Je 2017

Dijulia, Dom

GET UP TO GO AROUND color *Golf Magazine* v59 no11 p56 N 2017

Dike, Annie

Surgery Gone Bad color *Sail* v48 no1 p52 Ja 2017

Transat on a Fast Cat color *Sail* v48 no10 p14 O 2017

WIND CHICKEN GONE WILD color *Sail* v48 no7 p40 Jl 2017

Dildos

Hot Orgasmatron Teledildonics J. WAKEMAN color *Rolling Stone* no1274 p45 N 17 2016

Dilemma

Trump's Health-Care Dilemma D. F. Kettl *Governing* v30 no3 p16 D 2016

Dilenschneider, Robert L.

Caring for Aging Loved Ones color *Consumer Reports* v82 no12 p6 D 2017

Dilke, Lady

The Outcast Spirit *Publishers Weekly* v263 no39 p71 S 26 2016

Dill, David L.

Our Elections Are Not Secure color *Scientific American* v316 no3 p12 Mr 2017

Dill, Janette

The Entry-Level Health Care Jobs Men Are (and Are Not) Taking *Harvard Business Review Digital Articles* p2 F 24 2017

Dill, Joshua

From Russia with Dread color *Commonweal* v144 no1 p30 Ja 6 2017

DILL, KATHRYN

Body Parts on Demand color *Forbes* v198 no7 p56 N 29 2016

Dillard, J. D.

FIRST LOOK: SLEIGHT D. PHILYAW and L. CROSS color *Ebony* v72 no6 p24 Ap/My 2017

Dillard, Matt

You Never Forget Your First Time diag il *Backpacker* v45 no2 p64 Mr 2017

Dillard, Sarah

Research: How Female CEOs Actually Get to the Top *Harvard Business Review Digital Articles* p2 N 6 2014

Dillard, Stella

Always Use a Condiment J. LEDOUX *Atlanta* v56 no7 p84 N 2016

DILLE, IAN

ONE LAST SHOT color *Bicycling* v58 no10 p40 N/D 2017

Diller, Janelle

Changing the World, One Reader at a Time M. BURNETT color *Publishers Weekly* v264 no35 p60 Ag 28 2017

Diller, Phyllis, 1917-2012

Laugh Lines *Reader's Digest* v188 no1125 p119 N 2016

Diller Scofidio + Renfro (Company)

In the Heights J. GONCHAR *Architectural Record* v204 no11 p128 N 2016

Dillery, John

Alternate Exodus R. TADA bw *Weekly Standard* v22 no11 p37 N 21 2016

Dillin, Holly

WC CIAO PSYCHE *Arabian Horse World* v57 no9 p34 Je 2017

Dillman, Mary

Using data wisely at the system level chart color *Phi Delta Kappan* v99 no1 p25 S 2017

Dill-Marlow, Gari

December M. Moore *Arabian Horse World* v57 no3 p10 D 2016

Dillon, Asia Kate

Asia Kate DILION S. LaCAVA *Interview* v47 no6 p8 Ag 2017

BREAKING BILLIONS' BOYS' CLUB J. Hibberd color *Entertainment Weekly* no1454/1455 p20 F 24 2017

Yes, They Can J. Harman color *Glamour* v115 no9 p39 S 2017

Dillon, Asia Kate—Interviews

SHOWTIME'S FORAY INTO GENDERLESS TV D. ARTAVIA color *Advocate* no1090 p36 Ap 2017

Dillon, Eva

I Will Die a Russian: A marriage of convenience that yielded an intelligence bonanza *American Scholar* v86 no3 p123 Summ 2017

Dillon, Karen

Can You Be Friends With Your Boss? *Harvard Business Review Digital Articles* p2 N 28 2014

How to Handle 3 Types of Difficult Conversations *Harvard Business Review Digital Articles* p2 D 29 2014

How to Manage Your Team's Vacation Requests *Harvard Business Review Digital Articles* p2 Je 10 2015

How to Talk About Office Politics with a New Colleague *Harvard Business Review Digital Articles* p2 Je 17 2016

It's OK If Going to a Conference Doesn't Feel Like Real Work *Harvard Business Review Digital Articles* p2 O 7 2015

New Managers Should Focus on Helping Their Teams, Not Pleasing Their Bosses *Harvard Business Review Digital Articles* p2 Jl 7 2017

The Power of Designing Products for Customers You Don't Have Yet *Harvard Business Review Digital Articles* p2 Ag 31 2016

What Airbnb Understands About Customers' "Jobs to Be Done" *Harvard Business Review Digital Articles* p2 Ag 18 2016

What to Do If Your Boss Is a Control Freak *Harvard Business Review Digital Articles* p2 D 23 2014

What You Should (and Shouldn't) Focus on Before a Job Interview *Harvard Business Review Digital Articles* p2 Ag 28 2015

When a Private Message Ends Up in the Wrong Place *Harvard Business Review Digital Articles* p2 D 22 2014

Dillon, Mary

3 MARY DILLON P. Wahba color *Fortune* v174 no7 p75 D 1 2016

Dillon, Michael E.

Sweet relief for pollinators bibl color diag *Science* v355 no6326 p686 F 17 2017

Dillon, Moira R.

Cognitive science in the field: A preschool intervention durably enhances intuitive but not formal mathematics chart color diag graph *Science* v357 no6346 p47 Jl 7 2017

Dillon, Patrick

Rossini: L'Inganno Felice *Opera News* v81 no9 p53 Mr 2017

Verdi: I Due Foscari *Opera News* v81 no5 p56 N 2016

Dillow, Clay

AI WILL FIND ET *Popular Science* v288 no6 p30 N/D 2016

A Category 5 Business Problem color *Fortune* v176 no5 p13 O 1 2017

THE GREAT ROCKET RACE color *Fortune* v174 no6 p104 N 1 2016

JUST CALL IT SILICON COAST color *Fortune* v176 no2 p30 Ag 1 2017

SAFETY NET IN THE SKY color *Fortune* v174 no6 p24 N 1 2016

SUPERSONIC TRAVEL IS BOOMING color *Fortune* v174 no8 p34 D 15 2016

Tourists: China's New Political Weapon color *Fortune* v175 no8 p42 Je 15 2017

WAITING FOR THE EX-IM BANK *Fortune* v175 no6 p10 My 1 2017

A WHOLE LOT OF CORPORATE PLANES COULD SOON GET GROUNDED color *Fortune* v176 no2 p16 Ag 1 2017

WHY *FREE MONEY COULD BE THE FUTURE OF WORK color diag *Fortune* v176 no1 p68 Jl 1 2017

Dillwyn, David North

INSIDE OUT bw color *Conde Nast Traveler* v52 no5 p44 My 2017

Inside Out color *Architectural Digest* no5 p36 My 2017

WHAT LIES BENEATH color *Wired* v25 no5 p78 My 2017

DiLorenzo, Barbara

Renato and the Lion *Publishers Weekly* v264 no16 p66 Ap 17 2017

Di Luca, Massimiliano

Time Warp R. Li *Natural History* v124 no10 p7 N 2016

Di Luccia, Blanda

Lactobacillus reuteri induces gut intraepithelial $CD4+CD8\alpha\alpha+$ T cells diag graph *Science* v357 no6353 p806 Ag 25 2017

Dilworth, David

The SAILING SCENE color *Sail* v48 no7 p6 Jl 2017

DILWORTH, DIANNA

ALWAYS IN SEASON color *Publishers Weekly* v264 no16 p24 Ap 17 2017

FIFTY SHADES OF GREEN color *Publishers Weekly* v264 no12 p39 Mr 20 2017

Keeping the Spark Alive color *Publishers Weekly* v264 no23 p18 Je 5 2017

PREPARING FOR TAKE OFF color *Publishers Weekly* v264 no35 p29 Ag 28 2017

Urban Planning color *Publishers Weekly* v264 no35 p32 Ag 28 2017

Dim Sum (Poem)

Dim Sum M. Metivier color *U.S. Catholic* v82 no6 p11 Je 2017

DiMaggio, Joe, 1914-1999

BATTER, INTERRUPTED L. J. Wertheim and J. Feldman color *Sports Illustrated* v126 no11 p50 Ap 17-24 2017

Di Malta, Chiara

Transcriptional activation of RagD GTPase controls mTORC1 and promotes cancer growth diag *Science* v356 no6343 p1188 Je 16 2017

DiMarco, Chris

THE BALLAD OF A BIG CAT AND A GATOR M. Bamberger and J. Feldman color *Sports Illustrated* v126 no11 p64 Ap 17-24 2017

Di Marzo, Vincenzo

Activity-based protein profiling reveals off-target proteins of the FAAH inhibitor BIA 10-2474 chart color graph *Science* v356 no6342 p1084 Je 9 2017

Di Matteo, A.

Observation of a large-scale anisotropy in the arrival directions of cosmic rays above 8×10^{18} eV *Science* v357 no6357 p1266 S 22 2017

Dime

Broken Bow bricks hide buried treasure A. J. BARTELS color *Nebraska Life* v21 no4 p15 Jl/Ag 2017

DiMedio, Jason

Made in America *Harper's Magazine* v335 no2005 p2 Je 2017

Dimeo, Nate

Nate DiMeo's audio eruditionend E. H. Gustafson color *Magazine Antiques* v184 no5 p120 S/O 2017

Notes on an Imagined Plaque to Be Added to the Statue of General Nathan Bedford Forrest bw *Mother Jones* v42 no6 p62 N/D 2017

DIMERMAN, SARA

How Small Acts of Kindness Can GO A LONG WAY color *Maclean's* v129 no40 p69 O 10 2016

Dimers

The role of dimer asymmetry and protomer dynamics in enzyme catalysis T. Hun Kim, P. Mehrabi et al diag *Science* v355 no6322 p262 Ja 20 2017

Dimethyl sulfide

A Mighty & Mysterious Molecule W. Johnson color *Oceanus* v51 no2 p76 Wint 2016

Dimethyl sulfone—Therapeutic use

Treat TMJ Naturally J. Martin color *Amazing Wellness* v9 no1 p26

Wint 2017

Dimitrij (Theatrical production)
CLASSICAL MUSIC *New Yorker* v93 no22 p8 Jl 31 2017
Power Games R. Platt cartoon *New Yorker* v93 no22 p8 Jl 31 2017

DIMITROPOULOS, STAV
Trying to Lose My Religion bw *Discover* v38 no7 p26 S 2017

Dimmock, Jessica
Michigan *New York Times Magazine* p47 N 20 2016

Dimon, Jamie, 1956-
Why Isn't Jamie Dimon Telling Clients to Raise Wages Too? T. A.
Kochan *Harvard Business Review Digital Articles* p2 Jl 20 2016

Dimon, Jamie, 1956—Interviews
'If you can duplicate what they've done in Detroit around the
country, you're going to have a huge renaissance' M. Murphy
color *Bloomberg Businessweek* no4505 p46 D 26 2016

Dimopoulos, George
Changes in the microbiota cause genetically modified Anopheles
to spread in a population graph *Science* v357 no6358 p1396 S
29 2017

Dina (Film)
The Must List color *Entertainment Weekly* no1486 p9 O 13 2017

DINAN, KIM
SPECIAL DELIVERY *Cincinnati Magazine* v50 no4 p74 Ja 2017

DiNardo, Gina
Teach Safe Snuggling S. Bower color *Good Housekeeping* v264
no5 p142 My 2017

DiNardo, Kelly
21 HEALTH REASONS TO DO YOGA cartoon color *AARP: The
Magazine* v60 no3A p38 Ap/My 2017
Good Night, Toast cartoon *O, The Oprah Magazine* p103 My 2017
How to Escape Zombie Eating color *Health* v30 no9 p47 N 2016

Dine, Jim, 1935-
68 GREAT THINGS TO DO THIS MONTH J. FOUMBERG, J.
HARDBERGER et al color *Chicago* v66 no5 p119 My 2017

Dineen, Bob
Closing the Loop G. R. Schiavino color *Team Roping Journal* p94
S 2017
NTR Finals Cap Off Arizona Winter color *Spin to Win Rodeo* v21
no3 p18 My 2017

DINEEN, CARI WIRA
baby no. 2 *Parents* v91 no11 p90 N 2016
first teacher *Parents* v91 no9 p168 S 2016
HAPPY HOLIDAY SHOPPING *Better Homes & Gardens* v94
no12 p154 D 2016
Heat or Ice? color *Health* v30 no10 p65 D 2016

Diners (Restaurants)
Christmas Dinner at the Diner F. Flagg color *Southern Living* v51
no12 p131 D 2016
DEARLY DEPARTED M. Schulman cartoon *New Yorker* v93
no18 p20 Je 26 2017
DINING GUIDE *Cincinnati Magazine* p117 Je 2017
The Hot List P. POLLACK color *Chicago* v66 no11 p58 N 2017
THE OUT OF TOWNERS P. GIANOPULOS color *Chicago* v66
no11 p54 N 2017
Pinoy Power: AT LASA, TWO BROTHERS DELIVER FILI-
PINO COMFORT WITH CALIFORNIA STYLE G. SNYDER
Los Angeles Magazine v62 no9 p54 S 2017
WAYDOWN C. SCHEDLER color *Chicago* v66 no11 p56 N 2017

Diners (Restaurants)—Evaluation
CENTRAL J. FROIS color *Louisiana Life* v37 no2 p89 N/D 2016
THE DINING GUIDE *Atlanta* v57 no4 p123 Ag 2017
DINING GUIDE *New Orleans Magazine* v51 no1 p120 N 2016
GREATER NEW ORLEANS J. FROIS color *Louisiana Life* v37
no2 p92 N/D 2016
Kanpai Cool L. B. SUTER *Los Angeles Magazine* p41 My 2017
Lalo img *New York* v49 no23 p62 N 14 2016
Miami Heat E. S. BENN color *Bon Appetit* v62 no10 p56 O 2017
New Flame: With Stella, Neal Brown gets his groove back, qui-
etly serving rustic Southern European food cooked by open fire.
That's hot J. SPALDING color *Indianapolis Monthly* v41 no2
p44 S 2017
Performance Parties color *American Cowboy* v23 no4 p61 D
2016/Ja 2017
Purple Reign B. Smith color *Chicago* v66 no11 p74 N 2017
Sprouted Corn Cavatelli S. BAHR color *Indianapolis Monthly*
v41 no2 p46 S 2017

Telling Tales J. DRILLING *Cincinnati Magazine* v50 no3 p132
D 2016
URBAN COUNTRY CLUB P. POLLACK color *Chicago* v66
no11 p49 N 2017
Varuni Napoli C. LAUTERBACH *Atlanta* v57 no4 p44 Ag 2017
WITH A GROUP *Indianapolis Monthly* p60 F 2017
Zero Forks Given: Forget what your mother taught you and roll up
your sleeves; these dishesare meant to be eaten with nothing but
your hands M. VEGA *Atlanta* v57 no4 p35 Ag 2017

DINERSTEIN, ERIC
An Ecoregion-Based Approach to Protecting Half the Terrestrial
Realm *BioScience* v67 no6 p534 Je 2017

Dinerstein, Joel
How Cool Was That? J. EPSTEIN bw color *Weekly Standard* v22
no35 p30 My 22 2017

Ding, Mengning
Three-dimensional holey-graphene/niobia composite architectures for ultrahigh-rate energy storage color diag graph *Science*
v356 no6338 p599 My 12 2017

Ding, Ming-Zhu
Bug mapping and fitness testing of chemically synthesized chromosome X diag *Science* v355 no6329 p1048 Mr 10 2017
"Perfect" designer chromosome V and behavior of a ring derivative diag *Science* v355 no6329 p1046 Mr 10 2017

Ding, Wen-Qi
"Perfect" designer chromosome V and behavior of a ring derivative diag *Science* v355 no6329 p1046 Mr 10 2017

Dinghies
Comfort in the Cockpit D. Everitt cartoon *Sail* v48 no4 p58 Ap
2017
Tender Mercies C. J. Doane color *Sail* v48 no7 p80 Jl 2017

Dingle, Derek T.
50 BEST COMPANIES FOR DIVERSITY [Cover story] color
Black Enterprise v47 no3 p52 O 2016
BE 100s MILESTONES bw color *Black Enterprise* v47 no7 p76
My/Je 2017
Designing the Next Generation of Business Leaders color *Black
Enterprise* v47 no4 p24 N/D 2016
Developing Global Investment Strategies Post-Brexit color *Black
Enterprise* v47 no2 p19 S 2016
EVOLUTION color diag graph *Black Enterprise* v47 no7 p46
My/Je 2017
GRAND SLAM ENTREPRENEUR bw color *Black Enterprise*
v47 no8 p48 Jl/Ag 2017
Out From the Shadow of the Valley color *Black Enterprise* v47
no4 p18 N/D 2016
THE POWER BROKER *Black Enterprise* v47 no8 p50 Jl/Ag
2017
STRONG AS OAK color *Black Enterprise* v47 no7 p72 My/Je
2017
TAKE STEPS TO SECURE YOUR RETIREMENT NOW! graph
Black Enterprise v47 no3 p48 O 2016

Dingler, Felix A.
Of sizzling steaks and DNA repair diag *Science* v357 no6347 p130
Jl 14 2017

DINGMAN, HAYDEN
The 15 best new PC games of 2017, and their release dates color
PCWorld v35 no9 p70 S 2017
The $60 A10 headset is Astro's first budget-priced audio gear
color *PCWorld* v35 no7 p29 Jl 2017
9 REASONS WHY PC GAMING IS A BETTER VALUE THAN
CONSOLES bw color *PCWorld* p131 O 2016
Alienware 17 R4: Worth its weight in gold color graph *PCWorld*
v35 no9 p49 S 2017
The best PC games of 2017 (so far) color *PCWorld* v35 no8 p25
Ag 2017
Creative Sound BlasterX Katana: The soundbar finally makes its
way to PCs color *PCWorld* v35 no4 p91 Ap 2017
Dell Inspiron 15 7000: A gaming laptop at a decidedly non-gam-
ing price color graph *PCWorld* v35 no6 p84 Je 2017
Forza Horizon 3 (PC): Get ready to make your graphics card sweat
color *PCWorld* v35 no11 p114 N 2016
Gabe Newell's Reddit Q&A: on Half-Life 3, Steam support, and
more color *PCWorld* v35 no2 p25 F 2017
MSI's GT75VR Titan brings high-end HDR display tech to a gam-
ing laptop color *PCWorld* v35 no8 p102 Ag 2017

Nintendo Switch console details revealed color *PCWorld* v35 no2 p28 F 2017

Quern - Undying Thoughts: The closest we may ever come to a Riven sequel color *PCWorld* p120 Mr 2017

Razer Blade Pro (2016) review: Now this is how you do a 'Pro' laptop color graph *PCWorld* v35 no4 p80 Ap 2017

Razer Kraken V2: Two headsets, one leap forward color *PCWorld* v35 no2 p109 F 2017

Rock Band VR: Rock Band's roaring PC debut showcases Oculus Touch's potential color *PCWorld* v35 no5 p125 My 2017

Titanfall 2: Prepare for more mech-dropping, wall-running action color *PCWorld* p133 D 2016

'Torment: Tides of Numenera': The 'Planescape' successor you've been waiting for color *PCWorld* v35 no4 p103 Ap 2017

Total War Saga series focused on smaller 'powder-keg' moments in history color *PCWorld* v35 no8 p37 Ag 2017

Tyranny: Obsidian's RPG ponders the nature of evil color *PCWorld* v35 no1 p137 Ja 2017

Xbox One X: Everything you need to know about this powerful gaming console chart color *PCWorld* v35 no7 p32 Jl 2017

Dining room design & construction

Country Craftsman C. Johnson color *Timber Home Living* v27 no6 p42 D 2017

Dining room furniture—Evaluation

A COZIER DINING H. BROWN color *House Beautiful* v159 no8 p62 O 2017

SOFT FOCUS color *House Beautiful* p64 Ag 2017

Win this set! color *Sunset* v237 no5 p104 N 2016

Dining rooms

10 EASY WAYS TO REINVENT YOUR DINING ROOM cartoon color *Good Housekeeping* v263 no5 p66 N 2016

bolds & brights color *House Beautiful* v159 no7 p77 S 2017

FIND YOUR DINING ROOM STYLE color *Good Housekeeping* v263 no5 p74 N 2016

Mudroom, Pantry, and Kitchen All in a Row P. Poore color *Old House Journal* v45 no4 p74 Je 2017

Dining rooms—Equipment & supplies

A COZIER DINING H. BROWN color *House Beautiful* v159 no8 p62 O 2017

Dining rooms—Interior decoration

Room for Improvement cartoon color *House Beautiful* v159 no1 p22 F 2017

Dinneny, José R.

How plants hunt water S. Milius color *Science News* v192 no6 p24 O 14 2017

Dinner, The (Film)

THE DINNER J. McGovern color *Entertainment Weekly* no1463/1464 p34 Ap/My 2017

Dysfunction by the Plateful In The Dinner S. Zacharek color *Time* v189 no18 p55 My 15 2017

Dinner at Eight (Theatrical production)

Dinner Is Served J. ROBINSON *Opera News* v81 no9 p20 Mr 2017

Dinner theater—Evaluation

INTERNATIONAL color *Downbeat* v84 no2 p61 F 2017

Dinners & dining

See also

Food

Ready meals

Restaurant reviews

18.70 color *Horse & Rider* v56 no11 p30 N 2017

48 Hours in ...London D. POINTDUJOUR color *Ebony* v72 no3 p82 D 2016/Ja 2017

abcV C. Kormann color *New Yorker* v93 no15 p13 My 29 2017

Andrew Young: Politician, activist, national treasure J. BAINBRIDGE *Atlanta* v57 no3 p60 Jl 2017

ask REDBOOK color *Redbook* p28 F 2017

ASK SUSAN S. WESTMORELAND color *Good Housekeeping* v264 no3 p116 Mr 2017

BOTANICAL BEVERLY HILLS A. Preiser color *Sunset* v238 no5 p32 My 2017

Bread for the world B. Massingale color *U.S. Catholic* v82 no6 p10 Je 2017

Bucktown Nouveau [Cover story] J. FORMAN color *New Orleans Magazine* v52 no1 p102 S 2017

CHANGE IS AFOOT S. FENNESSY *Atlanta* v56 no8 p22 D 2016

CONNECTICUT *Yankee* p163 My/Je 2017

contagious kindness *Good Housekeeping* v263 no5 p12 N 2016

CULINARY SURPRISES S. Katzman and L. A. Addington color *Missouri Life* v44 no2 p92 Ap 2017

Dinner and a Show B. PHILLIPS *Texas Monthly* v45 no8 p20 Ag 2017

DINNER AND A SHOW [Cover story] A. Young color *Sunset* v238 no6 p58 Je 2017

Dinner with the Youngs: Our new column looks at how Atlantans dine--at home. This month politician Andrew Young, his son, and his grandchildren are "Home for Dinner" *Atlanta* v57 no3 p49 Jl 2017

eating img *New York* p68 Mr 6 2017

Events *Virginia Living* v15 no1 p39 D 2016

Extremely Fine And Incredibly Close G. FERGUSON *Los Angeles Magazine* v62 no9 p52 S 2017

Fire Fighter J. STEIN *Los Angeles Magazine* p48 Ap 2017

Food from the Heart P. Hise color *Virginia Living* v15 no5 p43 Ag 2017

FRENCH FLAIR V. LOWRY color *Architectural Digest* v73 no12 p56 D 2016

FRENCH, THREE WAYS G. DUFFY img *New York* v49 no22 p74 O 31 2016

From Our Editor S. Donelson color *House Beautiful* v158 no10 p2 D 2016/Ja 2017

The frozen-meal makeover L. Lillien color *Redbook* p86 My 2017

FUN! FOOD! FEST! [Cover story] F. ESKER color *New Orleans Magazine* v52 no1 p66 S 2017

Gran TORINO O. Thorisson bw color *Conde Nast Traveler* v52 no2 p84 F 2017

GRIND TIME J. DRILLING *Cincinnati Magazine* v50 no4 p150 Ja 2017

The Guide *D: The Magazine of Dallas* v43 no10 p270 O 2016

A Guide to Our New Dining Guide T. TALIAFERRO *Texas Monthly* v45 no9 p6 S 2017

HAMILTON A. KONERMANN *Cincinnati Magazine* p38 Je 2017

Hello, Darkness J. STEIN *Los Angeles Magazine* v62 no9 p49 S 2017

THE HOT LIST *Los Angeles Magazine* p132 F 2017

How black-ish Sets the Table color *Entertainment Weekly* no1441 p16 N 25 2016

How to Have a Grown-up Dinner Party (Without Feeling Too Grown-up) B. HANSEN-BUNDY cartoon *GQ: Gentlemen's Quarterly* v97 no5 p44 My 2017

ISLAND TIME: On Mackinac, clocks seem to run more slowly —that's why visitors rush there A. LYNCH color *Indianapolis Monthly* v41 no2 p37 S 2017

Joseph Guay & Tara Lee J. BAINBIDGE *Atlanta* v57 no6 p62 O 2017

The Last European Christmas M. O'Loughlin cartoon *Bon Appetit* v61 no12 p66 D 2016 /Jan2017

LET'S HAVE SUPPER S. Castle color *Southern Living* v52 no10 p96 O 2017

the life C. Stern color *InStyle* v24 no7 p131 Jl 2017

THE LOCALS' GUIDE TO FAR-FLUNG PLACES N. K. Hahn bw color *Chicago* v66 no1 p98 Ja 2017

Look Inward, ATL C. KUMMER *Atlanta* v56 no8 p82 D 2016

MAINE *Yankee* p108 My/Je 2017

A Mano C. LAUTERBACH *Atlanta* v57 no6 p60 O 2017

MASSACHUSETTS *Yankee* p146 My/Je 2017

A MERRY SOUTHERN CELEBRATION color *Southern Living* v51 no12 p141 D 2016

MOST OF THE COAST [Cover story] C. Coen color *New Orleans Magazine* v51 no5 p60 Mr 2017

NEW HAMPSHIRE *Yankee* p120 My/Je 2017

News From the Kitchen R. PEYTON color *New Orleans Magazine* v52 no1 p106 S 2017

"Not I," said the Cabin Guest C. HEITGER-EWING color *Cabin Living* p18 Ag 2017

Play Station J. DRILLING *Cincinnati Magazine* v50 no4 p146 Ja 2017

Pot Twist E. HILL-AGNUS *D: The Magazine of Dallas* v43 no10 p76 O 2016

Raising the Bar E. HILL-AGNUS *D: The Magazine of Dallas* v43 no10 p72 O 2016

The Really Hard Stuff M. Funkhouser *Governing* v30 no10 p4 Jl 2017

Restaurant GUIDE *Indianapolis Monthly* v40 no4 p139 D 2016

RHODE ISLAND *Yankee* p166 My/Je 2017

Rib Crib J. K. WOLFE *Cincinnati Magazine* v50 no4 p147 Ja 2017

Safari N. Niarchos color *New Yorker* v93 no26 p17 S 4 2017

Salad Daze A. BROWNLEE *Cincinnati Magazine* v50 no7 p152 Ap 2017

Sea Change T. NIEUWESTEEG *D: The Magazine of Dallas* v43 no10 p78 O 2016

A Side of Drama P. KUH *Los Angeles Magazine* p42 F 2017

A Slacker, a Sticky Situation, a Sensitive Subject L. KOGAN color *O, The Oprah Magazine* p30 Ja 2017

THE TEXANIST J. THOMAS *Texas Monthly* v45 no8 p148 Ag 2017

A Texas Fiesta J. B. Hager color *Southern Living* v52 no9 p17 S 2017

UKRAINE J. Lowe *New York Times Magazine* p22 S 24 2017

Unhappy Meal M. LABASH color *Weekly Standard* v22 no11 p5 N 21 2016

VERMONT *Yankee* p140 My/Je 2017

Victoria Camblin J. BAINBRIDGE *Atlanta* v57 no4 p46 Ag 2017

V: Our Own Sense of Time J. C. Davies bw *Powder* v45 no5 p11 Ja 2017

Washington, D.C M. Rosano color *Canadian Geographic* v137 p20 2017 Travel

WASHINGTON'S OLYMPIA R. Denn color map *Sunset* v238 no5 p34 My 2017

WE'RE GONNA PARTY LIKE WE'RE IN POST-SOVIET RUSSIA B. MORALES color *Bon Appetit* v62 no2 p64 Mr 2017

When the Commander in Chief Disrespects His Commanders J. Stavridis color *Time* v190 no16/17 p36 O 23 2017

Who's on First? D. Sanford *Parks & Recreation* v52 no3 p64 Mr 2017

WONDERFUL WESTFIELD S. HELD color *Indianapolis Monthly* v41 no2 p20 S 2017

Dinners & dining in the Bible
> *See also*
> Last Supper

A meal for many D. K. Hinman, G. Byerly et al color *U.S. Catholic* v82 no6 p5 Je 2017

Dinners & dining—Equipment & supplies

FANCY PICNICS color *Better Homes & Gardens* v95 no6 p12 Je 2017

Dinners & dining—Evaluation

THE HOT LIST B. HALLOCK and L. B. SUTER *Los Angeles Magazine* p132 D 2016

ONE TRIP, TWO WAYS: THAILAND D. Pointdujour color *Ebony* v72 no9 p56 Jl/Ag 2017

On Top of the World P. KUH *Los Angeles Magazine* p58 D 2016

Tratto K. VAUGHN *Arizona Highways* v92 no11 p12 N 2016

Dinners & dining—Physiological aspects

Beware the Late-Night Lag *Atlanta* v57 no6 p58 O 2017

Dinoflagellates

Strange creatures light up the polar 'twilight zone' color *Science* v354 no6313 p688 N 11 2016

Dinorah (Theatrical production)

Meyerbeer: Dinorah D. J. Baker *Opera News* v81 no5 p58 N 2016

Dinosaur anatomy

Dino fossils show some skin H. Thompson color diag *Science News* v191 no6 p32 Ap 1 2017

Head decor linked to bigger dinos H. Thompson graph *Science News* v191 no2 p32 F 4 2017

A Mesozoic aviary S. L. Brusatte bibl color diag *Science* v355 no6327 p792 F 24 2017

Missing Teeth L. E. Ogden color *Natural History* v125 no3 p7 Mr 2017

Skull Session A. ELBEIN *Smithsonian* v47 no8 p18 D 2016

Dinosaur extinction

Birds rebounded quickly after dinosaur mass extinction color *Science* v357 no6347 p114 Jl 14 2017

In Defense of Dinosaurs K. LACOVARA color *Natural History* v125 no11 p36 N 2017

Toxic algae may be culprit in mysterious dinosaur deaths C. Gramling *Science* v357 no6354 p857 S 1 2017

Dinosaur flight

A Mesozoic aviary S. L. Brusatte bibl color diag *Science* v355 no6327 p792 F 24 2017

Dinosaurs

6 FREQUENTLY ASKED QUESTIONS BY THE TIME-TRAVELING NATURE LOVER S. MUIR *Orion Magazine* v35 no6 p6 N/D 2016

7 Bite-size Facts About Dinosaurs color *National Geographic Kids* no475 p9 N 2017

Around the Country *Natural History* v125 no1 p34 D 2016/Ja 2017

Art Zone *National Geographic Kids* no467 p30 F 2017

Boning up on belly size E. DeMarco cartoon *Science News* v190 no12 p32 D 10 2016

Dinosaur family tree gets a makeover R. EHRENBERG diag *Science News* v191 no7 p7 Ap 15 2017

Dragon dinosaur met a muddy end M. Rosen cartoon *Science News* v190 no12 p5 D 10 2016

FIRE-BREATHING DINOSAURS? Physics, Fossils, and Functional Morphology vs. Pseudoscience P. J. SENTER *Skeptical Inquirer* v41 no4 p26 Jl/Ag 2017

Fleshing Out Dinosaurs A. Braun color *Natural History* v125 no6 p6 Je 2017

THE FOOTPRINTS OF GIANTS K. McLaughlin color map *Science* v356 no6344 p1224 Je 23 2017

Ma, where did they put T. rex? C. Gramling diag graph *Science* v355 no6331 p1249 Mr 24 2017

Researchers close in on ancient dinosaur proteins R. F. Service color *Science* v355 no6324 p441 F 3 2017

Smuggled dino eggs gave birth to 'baby dragons' color *Science* v356 no6338 p566 My 12 2017

Taking Wing [Cover story] S. Brusatte color *Scientific American* v316 no1 p48 Ja 2017

TWILIGHT IN DINOSAUR LAND: In Western Massachusetts, a family business unlike any other is in the hands of its last heir—a man who dutifully digs for dinosaur tracks as he ponders the end of an era J. SHATWELL color map *Yankee* p100 Jl 2017

What the Heck Is That Thing? S. Mirsky color *Scientific American* v317 no4 p90 O 2017

When Dinosaurs Went Bad G. TARLACH bw color *Discover* v38 no4 p66 My 2017

WORTH NOTING K. A. GAJEWSKI *Humanist* v77 no3 p48 My/Je 2017

Dinosaurs—Color

Averages can conceal how people and science learn E. Emerson *Science News* v190 no11 p2 N 26 2016

THE True Colors OF DINOSAURS [Cover story] J. Vinther color *Scientific American* v316 no3 p50 Mr 2017

Dinosaurs—Exhibitions

Around the Country color *Natural History* v125 no11 p40 N 2017

Dinosaurs—Extinction

ASTRO LETTERS S. Dacey, B. English et al color *Astronomy* v45 no6 p9 Je 2017

Dinosaurs—Food

Some herbivorous dinos ate critters C. GRAMLING color *Science News* v192 no7 p12 O 28 2017

Dinosaurs—Physiology
> *See also*
> Dinosaurs—Color

Missing Teeth L. E. Ogden color *Natural History* v125 no3 p7 Mr 2017

Dinosaurs—Research

Color Me Dino M. Rosen bw color diag *Science News* v190 no11 p24 N 26 2016

Di Novi, Denise—Interviews

Denise Di Novi W. J. Biddlecombe *Tricycle: The Buddhist Review* v26 no3 p22 Spr 2017

DINTER, PAUL E.

EXPANDING THE REAL *Commonweal* v144 no11 p2 Je 16 2017

Di Nunzio, Gildo

Metropolitan Opera M. MAZZARO *Opera News* v81 no9 p64 Mr 2017

Dioceses
> *See also*
> Cathedrals

Diogo, F.
Observation of a large-scale anisotropy in the arrival directions of cosmic rays above 8×1018 eV *Science* v357 no6357 p1266 S 22 2017

Dion, 1939-
Dion and the Disrupters R. Love color *AARP: The Magazine* v59 no2A p4 F/Mr 2016

Dion, Mark
MARK DION A. Rosenmeyer color *Art in America* v105 no5 p138 My 2017

Dion-Coté, Anne-Marie
Gene duplication can impart fragility, not robustness, in the yeast protein interaction network bibl color graph *Science* v355 no6325 p630 F 10 2017

Dione (Satellite)
Subsurface Ocean on Dione? C. M. CARLISLE *Sky & Telescope* v133 no2 p14 F 2017

Diones, Bruce
Miss Peregrine's Home for Peculiar Children *New Yorker* v92 no35 p24 O 31 2016

Dion Fletcher, Vanessa
THE STRENGTH OF WATER color *Art in America* p82 O 2017

Dionne, Danielle
Decoupling genetics, lineages, and microenvironment in IDH-mutant gliomas by single-cell RNA-seq diag *Science* v355 no6332 p1391 Mr 31 2017

Dionne, E. J. Jr.
Against Trumpian Triumphalism color *Commonweal* v143 no19 p8 D 2 2016
The Death of a Hero color *Commonweal* v144 no5 p8 Mr 10 2017
No Friend of the Worker bw *Commonweal* v144 no15 p7 S 22 2017
Obama's Post-Presidency color *Commonweal* v144 no2 p7 Ja 27 2017

Dionne, Jennifer
Visionary wrangles light E. Conover color *Science News* v192 no6 p23 O 14 2017

Dionne, Karen—Interviews
A Dark Fairy Tale O. H. COGDILL color *Publishers Weekly* v264 no15 p52 Ap 10 2017

Dionne, Rich
Weaving Conductive Threads *Stage Directions* v30 no1 p28 Ja 2017

Dionysus (Greek deity)
BACCHUS STORIES E. LABORDE bw *New Orleans Magazine* v51 no3 p168 Ja 2017

Diop, Anna
FRESH FACE: ANNA DIOP color *Essence* v47 no12 p38 Ap 2017

Dioramas—Design & construction
from our archives [April 1963] *Arizona Highways* v93 no2 p10 F 2017

Dioramas—Exhibitions
THE BATTLE OF SAN JACINTO DIORAMA A. GUSTAFSON and F. CURATOR *Texas Monthly* v44 no11 p100 N 2016

Dioxins—Analysis—Equipment & supplies
new products color *Science* v355 no6320 p96 Ja 6 2017

DIPACE, TOM
A Fitness Makeover color *Tennis* v53 no2 p60 Mr/Ap 2017

DiPalma, Elizabeth
The Thread *New York Times Magazine* p9 F 5 2017

Diphosphonates—Therapeutic use
Easy ways to build better bones *Harvard Health Letter* v42 no1 p4 N 2016

Diphtheria—Treatment
Life-saving diphtheria drug is running out K. Kupferschmidt bw *Science* v355 no6321 p118 Ja 13 2017

DiPiazza, Lillian
Lillian DiPiazza: Juggling her career and college, plus swimming and strength training J. STAHL *Dance Magazine* v91 no10 p40 O 2017

Diplo, 1978-
Diplo C. Cullen bw *Current Biography* v77 no10 p25 O 2016

Diplomacy
See also
Diplomatic protests

Intervention (International law)
Summit meetings
Current U.S.-Saudi Arabia Relationship *Congressional Digest* v95 no9 p3 N 2016
For a Concert of Powers S. H. BALCH *American Conservative* v15 no6 p23 N/D 2016
A New Strategy for Israeli Victory D. PIPES *Commentary* v143 no1 p13 Ja 2017
Steps to Hanoi G. O'CONNELL *America* v215 no16 p24 N 21 2016

Diplomacy—Study & teaching
Our people usually talk about foreign policy - not learning *People Management* p20 D 2016/Ja 2017

Diplomatic & consular service
CONFIRMATION B.S *Harper's Magazine* v335 no2005 p16 Je 2017

Diplomatic protests
You're Retired! cartoon color *Weekly Standard* v22 no46 p3 Ag 14 2017

Diplomats
See also
Ambassadors
Of Tribes and Terrorism L. SMITH color *Weekly Standard* v22 no39 p24 Je 19 2017
THE WOMAN WHO SAVED THE PLANET color *Scientific American* v317 no3 p86 S 2017

Diplomats—Interviews
The Envoy color *Foreign Affairs* v95 no6 p56 N/D 2016

Diplopia
She was 94, and all signs pointed to a stroke. But when tests came back negative, the doctors had to explore more unusual possibilities L. Sanders *New York Times Magazine* p20 O 1 2017

Dips (Appetizers)
See also
Guacamole
Cheesy dips for the win! color *Redbook* p150 O 2017
Super Dips L. Cericola color *Southern Living* v52 no2 p136 F 2017

Dipucchio, Kelly
Antoinette *Publishers Weekly* v263 no46 p54 N 14 2016

Dirand, Adrien
Soft Sell M. OWENS color *Architectural Digest* v74 no10 p48 O 1 2017

Dirand, Joseph
JOSEPH DIRAND color *Esquire* v167 no2 p80 Mr 2017

Dirda, Michael
Algernon Blackwood: The Master of the Supernatural bw *New York Review of Books* v63 no20 p92 D 22 2016
Fantasy Flashback bw *Weekly Standard* v23 no3 p33 S 25 2017
Ghostly Women bw *Weekly Standard* v22 no25 p38 Mr 6 2017
However Improbable bw *Weekly Standard* v22 no44 p34 Jl 31 2017
On to Atlantis! bw *Weekly Standard* v22 no38 p36 Je 12 2017

Direct currents
Electric Renaissance A. Sneed color *Scientific American* v316 no6 p20 Je 2017

Direct home delivery
Who's Using Meal Kits? M. Leonhardt chart *Money* v46 no8 p72 S 2017

Direct instruction
TEACHING A PEDAGOGY OF PEACE: Starting a dialogue by engaging one's differences A. O'Donnell *Literacy Today (2411-7862)* v35 no2 p38 S/O 2017

Direct marketing
See also
Direct e-marketing
Telemarketing
How Consumer Brands Can Connect with Customers in a Changing Retail Landscape R. Haslehurst, C. Randall et al *Harvard Business Review Digital Articles* p2 Ag 4 2017

Direct public offerings (Securities)
Direct listing (n.) *Bloomberg Businessweek* no4523 p39 My 22 2017

Direct selling
THE BUSINESS OF FRIENDSHIP M. STACEY color *Redbook* p108 D 2016

Direct e-marketing
> *See also*
>> Social media in marketing

Email Is the Best Way to Reach Millennials K. Naragon *Harvard Business Review Digital Articles* p2 N 12 2015

Email Marketing Best Practices *Parks & Recreation* v52 no5 p19 My 2017

How Consumer Brands Can Connect with Customers in a Changing Retail Landscape R. Haslehurst, C. Randall et al *Harvard Business Review Digital Articles* p2 Ag 4 2017

The Secret to Smartphone Marketing Is Still Email N. Mele *Harvard Business Review Digital Articles* p2 N 2 2015

Directors & directing
> *See also*
>> Motion picture producers & directors
>> Television producers & directors

CURTIS HANSON R. Crowe color *Entertainment Weekly* no1446/1447 p96 D 2016/Ja 2017

GARRY MARSHALL H. Winkler and D. Snierson color *Entertainment Weekly* no1446/1447 p86 D 2016/Ja 2017

Directors of corporations
> *See also*
>> Women directors of corporations

BECAUSE WE THINK RHETORIC IS IMPORTANT *Vital Speeches of the Day* v83 no9 p275 S 2017

The Board Directors You Need for a Digital Transformation T. Rickards and R. Grossman *Harvard Business Review Digital Articles* p2 Jl 13 2017

Decide Whether That Board Seat Is Right for You S. Smith *Harvard Business Review Digital Articles* p2 My 20 2015

How Boards Can Assess the Health of Their Companies C. Zook *Harvard Business Review Digital Articles* p2 N 2 2016

How Corporate Boards Connect, in Charts E. Heemskerk *Harvard Business Review Digital Articles* p2 Ap 21 2016

Improving the Way Boards, CEOs, and Shareholders Interact S. C. Y. Wong *Harvard Business Review Digital Articles* p2 Jl 28 2016

A MARKED MAN S. Zhang color *Wired* v24 no11 p46 N 2016

PASSION IN ACTION M. Hill color *Louisiana Life* v38 no1 p64 S/O 2017

POWER IN THE BOARDROOM bw color *Black Enterprise* v47 no8 p67 Jl/Ag 2017

Serving Shareholders Doesn't Mean Putting Profit Above All Else O. Hart and L. Zingales *Harvard Business Review Digital Articles* p2 O 12 2017

WITH BOARD SERVICE COMES RESPONSIBILITY E. G. S. Graves bw color *Black Enterprise* v47 no8 p6 Jl/Ag 2017

Directors of corporations—Interviews
Should You Talk About Race at Work? C. Leive color *Glamour* v114 no7 p98 Jl 2016

the STRATEGIC BOSS J. Thompson color *Essence* v48 no3 p80 Jl 2017

WHAT DO COLLEGE DANCE PROGRAMS really LOOK for? C. Bowers *Dance Spirit* v21 no7 p76 S 2017

Directors of corporations—Political activity
7 Charts Show How Political Affiliation Shapes U.S. Boards J. Cheng and B. Groysberg *Harvard Business Review Digital Articles* p2 Ag 23 2016

Directors of corporations—Psychology
Board Members Should Have to Take a Personality Test M. Schrage *Harvard Business Review Digital Articles* p2 N 10 2014

Directors of corporations—Selection & appointment
Boards Aren't as Global as Their Businesses G. L. Davis *Harvard Business Review Digital Articles* p2 O 28 2014

DIRNBÄCK, THOMAS
Combining Biodiversity Resurveys across Regions to Advance Global Change Research *BioScience* v67 no1 p73 Ja 2017

DiRocco, Daniel A.
A multifunctional catalyst that stereoselectively assembles prodrugs diag *Science* v356 no6336 p426 Ap 28 2017

Dirt roads
"I WANT TO GO ON DIRT-ROAD ADVENTURES." L. Tanner and B. STRICKLAND color *Bicycling* v58 no3 p42 Ap 2017

Dirty bombs
Dark Secrets, Dirty Bombs [Cover story] S. Shuster and Z. J. Miller color map *Time* v189 no14 p28 Ap 17 2017

Dirty Dancing (Film)
Dirty Dancing's Dynamic Duo A. D'Arminio *TV Guide* v65 no14 p9 Ap 3 2017

Dirty Dancing (TV program)
America's top TV critic Matt Roush answers your burning questions *TV Guide* v65 no25 p3 Je 2017

BABY'S BACK: The cast of ABC's reimagined Dirty Dancing gives the classic '80s film a musical lift A. D'ARMINIO *TV Guide* v65 no21 p26 My 15 2017

The Dirty Dancing Drinking Game S. Li color *Entertainment Weekly* no1467 p51 My 26 2017

Dirty Dancing: The Classic Story on Stage (Theatrical production)
"Dirty Dancing" brings Borscht Belt veteran full circle L. J. Green *Successful Farming* v115 no1 p43 Ja 2017

Dirty Money (Short story)
DIRTY MONEY Ihara Saikaku *Lapham's Quarterly* v10 no3 p63 Summ 2017

Dirty Projectors (Performer)
Dirty Projectors' Brave New Breakup Pop W. HERMES cartoon color *Rolling Stone* no1281/1282 p51 F 23 2017

Dirty Sexy Money (TV program)
I AM THAT GIRL Laverne Cox color *InStyle* v23 no12 p294 N 2016

TRANS BEAUTY SECRETS DAM color *Advocate* no1091 p76 Je/Jl 2017

Di Rupo, Elio
Elio Di Rupo E. E. Turner *Current Biography* v78 no8 p31 Ag 2017

DIRZO, RODOLFO
Conserving the World's Megafauna and Biodiversity: The Fierce Urgency of Now *BioScience* v67 no3 p197 Mr 2017

Merging paleobiology with conservation biology to guide the future of terrestrial ecosystems color *Science* v355 no6325 p594 F 10 2017

Saving the World's Terrestrial Megafauna color *BioScience* v66 no10 p807 O 1 2016

Disabilities
> *See also*
>> Developmental disabilities
>> Memory disorders
>> Mental illness
>> Vision disorders

The Charlie Gard case reveals a persistent bias against disability J. Bennett *America* v217 no3 p10 Ag 7 2017

FOREWORD M. Nasser *UN Chronicle* v53 no2 p4 2016

The Paralympic Games and the Promotion of the Rights of Persons with Disabilities P. CRAVEN *UN Chronicle* v53 no2 p10 2016

Stopping Stroke Karla, Rob et al color *Ebony* v72 no6 p64 Ap/My 2017

WELCOME TO MY WORLD: Living with a disability, I'm the one my peers call when their bodies start to fail. How sympathetic, or surprised, should I be? L. MILK *Washingtonian Magazine* v52 no12 p176 S 2017

Disability insurance
Social Security Cuts Target Trump Voters J. Green color map *Bloomberg Businessweek* no4525 p27 Je 5 2017

Why You Need Disability Coverage K. LANKFORD color *Kiplinger's Personal Finance* v71 no3 p38 Mr 2017

Disability insurance policies
Why You Need Disability Coverage K. LANKFORD color *Kiplinger's Personal Finance* v71 no3 p38 Mr 2017

Disability insurance—United States
An analysis of private long-term disability insurance access, cost, and trends P. Anand and D. Wittenburg bibl chart color *Monthly Labor Review* p1 Mr 2017

The Disabled American Worker B. Greeley graph map *Bloomberg Businessweek* no4504 p24 D 19 2016

Disabled veterans—Employment
The labor supply of veterans with disabilities, 1995-2014 M. S. Rutledge, G. T. Sanzenbacher et al bibl chart color graph *Monthly Labor Review* p1 O 2016

Disadvantaged schools
DIFFERENTIATED AND MEANINGFUL INSTRUCTION: Turning around districtwide performance by immersing stu-

dents in an engaging, literacy-rich environment L. Moody and J. Morrow *Literacy Today (2411-7862)* v35 no1 p18 Jl/Ag 2017

DISALVO, DANIEL

A Party of One *Commentary* v143 no2 p46 F 2017

The Treason of the Bureaucrats: The internal governmental revolt against Trump may backfire on 'the resistance' *Commentary* v143 no4 p23 Ap 2017

Di Sante, Domenico

Robust spin-polarized midgap states at step edges of topological crystalline insulators bibl graph *Science* v354 no6317 p1269 D 9 2016

DiSanti, Ben

Good Cybersecurity Can Be Good Marketing *Harvard Business Review Digital Articles* p2 S 23 2016

DISARE, MONICA

Linda Darling-Hammond on the Future of New York Education—and What She Makes of Betsy DeVos *Education Digest* v82 no8 p48 Ap 2017

Disarmament

See also

    Nuclear disarmament

SNAPSHOT OF THE PAST bw *In These Times* v40 no11 p23 N 2016

Disaster relief

See also

    Civilian evacuation

    Food relief

AFTER HARVEY'S RAGE ACROSS TEXAS, CATHOLIC CHARITIES RAMPS UP ITS RESPONSE K. Clarke color *America* v217 no6 p12 S 18 2017

Disaster Relief M. CROSS and K. LANKFORD color *Kiplinger's Personal Finance* v71 no12 p24 D 2017

THE GREAT FLOOD: AN ANNIVERSARY E. Laborde *Louisiana Life* v37 no4 p4 Mr/Ap 2017

Muslim agency joins disaster relief in the American South Y. Shimron color *Christian Century* v134 no20 p17 S 27 2017

Photostat: Mexico City Earthquake E. Martin and N. Cattan bw color *Bloomberg Businessweek* no4539 p38 S 25 2017

RELEASE NOTES cartoon color *Wired* v24 no12 p12 D 2016

We're Here to Help *Kiplinger's Personal Finance* v71 no12 p4 D 2017

When the Military Does Battle With Nature A. J. Stavridis color *Time* v190 no12 p45 S 25 2017

Disaster relief—Law & legislation—United States

The Gulf Opportunity Zone Helped Affected Counties Recover Economically After Hurricane Katrina J. Williamson and J. Pender *Amber Waves: The Economics of Food, Farming, Natural Resources, & Rural America* p1 O 2016

Disaster relief—United States

Hell and High Water S. MURRAY color *Power & Motoryacht* v34 no11 p46 N 2017

When Disaster Strikes, Businesses Step Up T. J. DONOHUE *Weekly Standard* v23 no3 p9 S 25 2017

Disaster resilience

America Is Not Ready for the Earthquakes Ahead K. Miles color map *Time* v190 no14 p21 O 9 2017

Disaster victims

See also

    Older disaster victims

How to Help Hurricane Victims Rebuild K. LANKFORD color *Kiplinger's Personal Finance* v71 no11 p18 N 2017

LAGUNDRI BAY NIAS, INDONESIA Z. MORTON color *Surfer* v58 no4 p56 Ag 2017

WILLIAM A. DEL MONTE J. GERTNER *New York Times Magazine* p24 D 25 2016

Disaster victims—Finance

The Kindness of Strangers M. Chan color *Time* v190 no12 p42 S 25 2017

Disaster victims—Government policy

The Lost Colony K. Vick, M. Calabresi et al color *Time* v190 no15 p32 O 16 2017

Disaster victims—Services for

Lessons from Boston's Experiment with The One Fund M. Weiss *Harvard Business Review Digital Articles* p2 Ja 22 2016

Disaster Artist, The (Film)

FUTURE FRANCO FILMS D. Coggan color *Entertainment*

Weekly no1454/1455 p82 F 24 2017

JAMES FRANCO IN The Disaster Artist C. Collis color *Entertainment Weekly* no1478 / 1479 p74 Ag 18-25 2017

Disasters

See also

    Famines

    Natural disasters

    Work-related injuries

GREAT UNKNOWNS cartoon *Popular Mechanics* p26 Mr 2017

LAST CHANCE: A classic board game gets a climate-change makeover J. BROWNING and S. BROWNING color *Orion Magazine* v36 no1 p32 Ja/F 2017

President Trump, There Is A Deal To Be Made With North Korea W. J. Perry *NPQ: New Perspectives Quarterly* v34 no2 p6 My 2017

Disasters in art—Exhibitions

Calamity and catharsis in Maine cartoon *Magazine Antiques* v184 no1 p47 Ja/F 2017

DISASTER AS DESTINY *USA Today Magazine* v146 no2866 p46 Jl 2017

Disasters—Environmental aspects

The Relevance of Soft Infrastructure in Disaster Management and Risk Reduction S. B. Ullberg and J. Warner *UN Chronicle* v53 no3 p20 2016

Disasters—Mexico

Aftermath E. GARRIDO color *Nation* v305 no9 p11 O 16 2017

Disasters—Press coverage

Eye of the Hurricane B. PIKE cartoon *Power & Motoryacht* v32 no12 p128 D 2016

Disasters—Religious aspects

THUBTEN CHODRON Dharmarakshita *Tricycle: The Buddhist Review* v26 no2 p23 Wint 2016

Disasters—Social aspects

Yemen's Humanitarian Nightmare A. Orkaby color *Foreign Affairs* v96 no6 p93 N/D 2017

Disbrowe, Paula

Cinco de Mayo San Antonio Style color *Southern Living* v52 no5 p110 My 2017

Seaside Greetings color *Southern Living* v51 no12 p79 D 2016

Disc brakes

See also

    Automobiles—Disc brakes

FLYWEIGHT FUELER [Cover story] D. Wallace color *Hot Rod* v70 no4 p62 Ap 2017

the little things m. ferrentino color *Bike Magazine* v24 no2 p48 Mr 2017

"SHOULD I GET A ROAD BIKE WITH DISC BRAKES? L. Flickinger and B. STRICKLAND color diag *Bicycling* v58 no3 p30 Ap 2017

Disc brakes—Evaluation

SUPERDIALED M. PHILLIPS color *Bicycling* v58 no4 p68 My 2017

Yokozuna Motoko Road Disc Brake M. Phillips color *Bicycling* v58 no4 p82 My 2017

Disc jockeys

As Is K. Sanneh cartoon *New Yorker* v93 no5 p24 Mr 20 2017

the life color *InStyle* v24 no2 p155 F 2017

Q+A J. BALL *Indianapolis Monthly* p46 My 2017

TOP-EARNING DJs color *Forbes* v200 no2 p26 S 5 2017

Disc jockeys—United States

Diplo C. Cullen bw *Current Biography* v77 no10 p25 O 2016

Discepolo, Valentina

Reovirus infection triggers inflammatory responses to dietary antigens and development of celiac disease color diag *Science* v356 no6333 p44 Ap 7 2017

Discernment (Christian theology)

Walk of life J. Molyneux *U.S. Catholic* v82 no8 p4 Ag 2017

Discharge of contracts

An Internet Whole and Free K. Raustiala color *Foreign Affairs* v96 no2 p140 Mr/Ap 2017

d'Ischia, Marco

From sequence to color diag *Science* v356 no6342 p1011 Je 9 2017

Disciples of Christ

April 30, Third Sunday of Easter J. M. Gallagher *Christian Century* v134 no8 p1 Ap 12 2017

Discipline

See also

Discipline of children

AFTER THE FALL J. Mervis color *Science* v354 no6311 p408 O 28 2016

CEASE AND DESIST, PLEASE R. W. Young color *Black Belt* v55 no3 p8 Ap/My 2017

A Healthier Approach to Business Travel P. Bregman *Harvard Business Review Digital Articles* p2 N 17 2015

Journaling: A Timeless Tool for Growth C. V. CLARKE color *Black Enterprise* v47 no2 p31 S 2016

Quotable Quotes *Reader's Digest* v188 no1124 p144 O 2016

Discipline of children

10 discipline mistakes L. GARISTO PFAFF chart color *Parents* v92 no6 p48 Je 2017

Solve My Screen-Time Skirmishes E. Z. Ruddy color graph *Parents* v92 no9 p56 S 2017

THE TROUBLE WITH TIME-OUTS A. BOWMAN color *Parents* v92 no4 p60 Ap 2017

Disclosure

How Running Toward HIV Can Save Your Life: Taking meds can be easy. Learning how to breathe is the tricky part T. CURRY color *Advocate* no1091 p41 Je/Jl 2017

Disclosure of information

See also

Financial disclosure

The Case Against Pay Transparency T. Zenger *Harvard Business Review Digital Articles* p1 S 30 2016

Cleaning Up Leaks Is a Messy Business P. M. Barrett *Bloomberg Businessweek* no4533 p35 Ag 7 2017

Companies Want to Disclose Employee Health Data to Shareholders, and It's a Bad Idea A. Lewis *Harvard Business Review Digital Articles* p2 Mr 4 2016

Enhancing reproducibility for computational methods V. Stodden, M. McNutt et al bibl color *Science* v354 no6317 p1240 D 9 2016

Having Inside Information Leads to Worse Decisions S. Pillay *Harvard Business Review Digital Articles* p2 Ap 2 2015

Disclosure of information lawsuits

He Objects C. Hannan bw *Bloomberg Businessweek* no4533 p25 Ag 7 2017

Disclosure of information—United States

Secrets the FBI May Not Want You to Know B. DREHER *Reader's Digest* v188 no1125 p144 N 2016

The Snowden Cure J. Goldsmith *Hoover Digest: Research & Opinion on Public Policy* no4 p133 Fall 2016

Discotheques

Boogie Wonderland M. GOLDBERG bw color *O, The Oprah Magazine* p21 Je 2017

Discount

5 Ways to Save Money on Amazon B. Tuttle color *Money* v46 no8 p21 S 2017

BYE-BYE, DISCOUNTS. HELLO, MARGINS P. Wahba color *Fortune* v176 no4 p30 S 15 2017

How to Cash In on Cash-Back Credit Cards A. Walker color graph *Consumer Reports* v82 no9 p46 S 2017

How to Stay in Premium Hotels Without Blowing Your Expense Account R. Mohammed *Harvard Business Review Digital Articles* p2 Ag 2 2016

Price-Sensitive Customers Will Tolerate Uncertainty R. Mohammed *Harvard Business Review Digital Articles* p2 Mr 26 2015

Sleuth Smarts color *Men's Health* v31 no10 p74 D 2016

Ticket Resellers M. EASTER cartoon *Men's Health* v32 no8 p30 O 2017

Discount houses (Retail trade)

MINIMALIST MAGIC H. Rolfe *Dance Spirit* v21 no7 p90 S 2017

Discounts for older people

Grab This $10 Parks Bargain ... Quick! J. Calfas color *Money* v46 no7 p26 Ag 2017

Discourse

Populism in Venezuela: When Discourse Derails Institutionalized Practice V. Rodner *Society* v53 no6 p629 D 2016

Discourse analysis

See also

Academic language

Critical discourse analysis

Written communication

A Discourse on Discourse Studies A. Berger color *Society* v53 no6 p597 D 2016

A HARROWING LINGUISTIC MOMENT A. KINGSTON *Maclean's* v129 no48/49 p10 D 5 2016

Discourse—Religious aspects

Advice for Conflict A. Olendzki *Tricycle: The Buddhist Review* v26 no4 p29 Summ 2017

Discoveries in archaeology

Archaeologists discover ancient Jewish artifacts, part of Jerusalem walls M. Chabin color *Christian Century* v133 no24 p16 N 23 2016

Cave that housed Dead Sea Scrolls found C. Wood color *Christian Century* v134 no6 p12 Mr 15 2017

CONNECTING TWO REALMS R. ATWOOD color *Archaeology* v70 no4 p55 Je-Ag 2017

DISCOVERING TERROR D. WEISS color *Archaeology* v70 no1 p14 Ja/F 2017

HUMAN WHYS AND WHEREFORES C. Valentino color *Archaeology* v70 no2 p4 Mr/Ap 2017

Looking Beyond the Hillforts [Cover story] J. URBANUS color *Archaeology* v70 no4 p38 Je-Ag 2017

Lucy had taller kin, footprints suggest B. BOWER color *Science News* v191 no1 p8 Ja 21 2017

Neolithic stone ring site holds new surprise: a buried square monument color *Science* v356 no6345 p1315 Je 30 2017

A Residence Fit for a President [Cover story] T. WATSON color *Archaeology* v70 no4 p34 Je-Ag 2017

SET IN STONE E. A. POWELL color *Archaeology* v70 no4 p44 Je-Ag 2017

THINKING BACK, LOOKING AHEAD cartoon *Archaeology* v70 no1 p6 Ja/F 2017

TOP 10 DISCOVERIES OF 2016 J. URBANUS, N. SWAMINATHAN et al bw cartoon color *Archaeology* v70 no1 p26 Ja/F 2017

Discoveries in geography

HOLES IN THE MAP S. CHODOSH map *Popular Science* p22 Ja/F 2017

A SINGLE MOMENT OF LIGHT J. Brown *Popular Science* p8 Ja/F 2017

Discoveries in geography—Equipment & supplies

The Modern Explorer's Survival Kit S. CHODOSH and P. HESS color *Popular Science* p80 Ja/F 2017

Discoveries in science

13 Mind-Blowing Discoveries Scientists Made This Year M. CROUCH color *Reader's Digest* v190 no1133 p130 S 2017

1823: Timisoara J. Bolyai *Lapham's Quarterly* v10 no2 p40 Spr 2017

2016 WORLD CHANGING IDEAS [Cover story] A. Sneed, J. Pavlus et al color *Scientific American* v315 no6 p32 D 2016

50, 100 & 150 YEARS AGO color *Scientific American* v316 no6 p77 Je 2017

Awesome universal chirp J. Berg color *Science* v354 no6319 p1507 D 23 2016

BACK TO THE FUTURE J. Brown color *Popular Science* v289 no6 p4 N/D 2017

BEST OF what's NEW 2017 [Cover story] *Popular Science* v289 no6 p7 N/D 2017

Data-driven predictions in the science of science A. Clauset, D. B. Larremore et al bibl color diag *Science* v355 no6324 p477 F 3 2017

Discoveries and explanations C. Day *Physics Today* v70 no3 p8 Mr 2017

Meet the World's 'Newest' Plants T. John color *Time* v189 no21 p12 Je 5 2017

The New Age of Discovery R. CONNIFF color *Smithsonian* v47 no10 p21 Mr 2017

Success in science depends on luck, plus much more *Science News* v192 no6 p2 O 14 2017

WAVE CATCHERS J. R. GRITZ *Smithsonian* v47 no8 p46 D 2016

What's Ahead in 2017 E. Quill bw *Science News* v190 no13 p36 D 24 2016

Discovery sport utility vehicle

ROCK SOLID M. PRINCE color *Road & Track* v68 no9 p78 Je

2017
Tested for you G. Buckley color *House Beautiful* p160 Ag 2017
Discovery sport utility vehicle—Evaluation
2017 Land Rover Discovery color *Motor Trend* v69 no3 p28 Mr 2017
DISCO IS BACK A. Priddle chart color *Motor Trend* v69 no6 p98 Je 2017
Exclusive Land Rover Discovery S. Evans color *Motor Trend* v68 no12 p18 D 2016
Discrimination
  See also
  Discrimination in employment
  Ethnic discrimination
  Race discrimination
  Sex discrimination
Joy Buolamwini A. Cohen color *Bloomberg Businessweek* no4529 p80 Jl 3 2017
Measuring and managing bias J. Berg color *Science* v357 no6354 p849 S 1 2017
The Perils of Pale S. Ager bw color diag *National Geographic* v231 no6 p70 Je 2017
PLAY IT FORWARD M. BOBENRIETH *UN Chronicle* v53 no2 p17 2016
Prejudgment call Han Lin color *Science* v355 no6320 p22 Ja 6 2017
Rising Fear *Change* v82 no3 p23 Mr 2017
STAY WELL, Raise Hell P. Rosen color *O, The Oprah Magazine* p65 Jl 2017
"What Are You?" L. BROCK, J. Bianchi et al *Scholastic Choices* v32 no7 p20 Ap 2017
Discrimination against overweight persons
Big, Bigger, Biggest *Change* v82 no3 p34 Mr 2017
Discrimination in education
  See also
  Race discrimination in education
Teachers Underrate Girls' Math Skills *USA Today Magazine* v145 no2859 p4 D 2016
Discrimination in employment
  See also
  Affirmative action programs
  Equal pay for equal work
  Sex discrimination in employment
43% of women have been asked to make tea in meetings *People Management* p32 My 2017
The Case of the Disqualifying Dreads V. GLEMBOCKI *Reader's Digest* v189 no1128 p25 Mr 2017
Hiring Discrimination Against Black Americans Hasn't Declined in 25 Years L. Quillian, D. Pager et al *Harvard Business Review Digital Articles* p2 O 11 2017
How banning boxes encourages discrimination G. Boone *Monthly Labor Review* p1 Ja 2017
How the Imagined "Rationality" of Engineering Is Hurting Diversity—and Engineering J. C. Williams and M. Multhaup *Harvard Business Review Digital Articles* p2 Ag 10 2017
Should Employers Fire Employees Who Attend White Supremacist Rallies? J. A. Clarke *Harvard Business Review Digital Articles* p2 S 19 2017
Stop Punishing the Family Man J. Levs *Harvard Business Review Digital Articles* p2 My 14 2015
What Facebook's Anti-Bias Training Program Gets Right F. Gino *Harvard Business Review Digital Articles* p2 Ag 24 2015
Why Subtle Bias Is So Often Worse than Blatant Discrimination E. King and K. Jones *Harvard Business Review Digital Articles* p2 Jl 13 2016
Discrimination in employment—Law & legislation—United States
Non-Discrimination Laws Make U.S. States More Innovative Huasheng Gao and Wei Zhang *Harvard Business Review Digital Articles* p2 Ag 17 2016
Discrimination in employment—Lawsuits & claims—Humor
That's Outrageous! SO SUE ME *Reader's Digest* v188 no1125 p137 N 2016
Discrimination in employment—Prevention
How to Speak Up If You See Bias at Work A. L. Williams color *Harvard Business Review Digital Articles* p2 Ja 20 2017
Discrimination prevention

Dare to Discipline (Again): The previous administration held that discipline amounted to discrimination. The new education secretary should reject this claim--if not in the name of common sense, then in the name of student achievement C. E. Finn *Hoover Digest: Research & Opinion on Public Policy* no3 p132 Summ 2017
STATE OF THE EUROPEAN UNION: AN "EXISTENTIAL CRISIS" JUNCKER *Vital Speeches of the Day* v82 no11 p328 N 2016
Discrimination—Canada
Celebrate Canada? Not yet S. WHITECLOUD-BRASS chart color *Maclean's* v130 no6 p21 Jl 2017
Discrimination—United States
Dare to Discipline (Again): The previous administration held that discipline amounted to discrimination. The new education secretary should reject this claim--if not in the name of common sense, then in the name of student achievement C. E. Finn *Hoover Digest: Research & Opinion on Public Policy* no3 p132 Summ 2017
Discussion in religious education
A God by any other name P. J. Kreeft *Christian Century* v134 no19 p24 S 13 2017
Disease management
Understanding Ascites in Cats A. Plotnick *Catnip* v24 no10 p5 O 2016
Disease prevalence
COPD CANADA'S EPIDEMIC D. F. McCourt *Maclean's* v129 no47 p46 N 28 2016
Doses of Neighborhood Nature: The Benefits for Mental Health of Living with Nature D. T. C. COX, D. F. SHANAHAN et al *BioScience* v67 no2 p147 F 2017
IT'S ALL ABOUT BREATHING D. Lynkowski color *Maclean's* v129 no47 p42 N 28 2016
Disease relapse—Prevention
Keep Cancer from Coming Back *Tufts University Health & Nutrition Letter* v35 no2 p6 2017
Preventing painful attacks *Mayo Clinic Health Letter* v35 no4 p4 Ap 2017
Urinary tract infections *Mayo Clinic Health Letter* v35 no6 p4 Je 2017
Disease research
BLOOD HEALTH & ORGAN TRANSPLANTS D. Wong-Rieger *Maclean's* v130 no9 p31 O 2017
Disease resistance of plants
Starving the enemy P. N. Dodds and E. S. Lagudah bibl diag *Science* v354 no6318 p1377 D 16 2016
Disease risk factors
  See also
  Cardiovascular diseases risk factors
  Heart disease risk factors
Short on Sleep? B. LIEBMAN *Nutrition Action Health Letter* v44 no5 p8 Je 2017
Disease susceptibility
health news *Parents* v91 no6 p22 Je 2016
Diseases
  See also
  Acute diseases
  Autism
  Brain diseases
  Cancer
  Cardiovascular diseases
  Chronic diseases
  Communicable diseases
  Disabilities
  Juvenile diseases
  Medical emergencies
  Mental illness
  Metabolic disorders
  Respiratory diseases
  Skin diseases
The End M. Fischetti graph *Scientific American* v317 no3 p96 S 2017
Go Ahead... Ask Us Anything M. Klein color *Popular Science* v288 no6 p102 N/D 2017
NOW FOR THE GOOD NEWS... *New York Times Upfront* p16 S 18 2017

Predict When You'll Get Sick color *Time* v189 no3 p22 Ja 30 2017

Worried Sick M. Rubino *Indianapolis Monthly* v40 no3 p12 N 2016

Diseases in men—Treatment

TOP THREE HERBS FOR MEN K. P. Singh Khalsa color *Amazing Wellness* v8 no2 p22 Spr 2016

Diseases in women—Risk factors

deserted [Cover story] M. W. Moyer color map *Women's Health* v14 no7 p150 S 2017

Diseases—Causes & theories of causation

See also

Health behavior

Parasitic worm may trigger mystery nodding syndrome G. Vogel color *Science* v355 no6326 p678 F 17 2017

Quantifying protein (dis)order C. Vogel bibl diag *Science* v355 no6327 p794 F 24 2017

Diseases—Mathematical models

Opportunities and challenges in modeling emerging infectious diseases C. J. E. Metcalf and J. Lessler diag graph *Science* v357 no6347 p149 Jl 14 2017

Diseases—Religious aspects—Christianity

How to live in hope C. R. Pinches color *Christian Century* v134 no15 p22 Jl 19 2017

Diseases—Risk factors

See also

Cardiovascular diseases—Risk factors

Heart diseases—Risk factors

Head CASE O. Manno *Dance Spirit* v21 no4 p26 Ap 2017

Take the 'One Health' Challenge [Cover story] B. Crabbe cartoon *Horse & Rider* v56 no5 p52 My 2017

What Your Family History Reveals J. Migala color diag *Health* v31 no3 p59 Ap 2017

Diseroad, William D.

Kilogram-scale prexasertib monolactate monohydrate synthesis under continuous-flow CGMP conditions chart diag *Science* v356 no6343 p1144 Je 16 2017

Dish Network Corp.

DISH Network *American Forests* v123 no1 p10 Wint/Spr 2017

Dish towels—Evaluation

BOTANY E. S. SOTO color *Better Homes & Gardens* v95 no5 p10 My 2017

Dishman, Eric

A MARKED MAN S. Zhang color *Wired* v24 no11 p46 N 2016

Dishwashers (Persons)

ASK CAROLYN [Cover story] C. FORTÉ bw color *Good Housekeeping* v264 no2 p57 F 2017

Cleans Up Real Nice B. Headley *Bon Appetit* v61 no12 p96 D 2016 /Jan2017

Dishwashing

THE BEST BET B. Doherty img *New York* v50 no10 p67 My 15 2017

Cleans Up Real Nice B. Headley *Bon Appetit* v61 no12 p96 D 2016 /Jan2017

Dishwashing machines

DISHWASHERS K. SELZER bw color *Better Homes & Gardens* v95 no11 p52 N 2017

LOAD THE DISHWASHER LIKE A GH BOSS color *Good Housekeeping* v265 no3 p94 S 2017

RAISING YOUR HOME'S IQ S. COLLINS and C. Sullivan color *Martha Stewart Living* p80 S 2017

Save Time and Add Convenience T. Bufete and C. Regan il *Consumer Reports* v82 no3 p24 Mr 2017

When to Get the Best Deals color graph *Consumer Reports* v82 no9 p40 S 2017

Dishwashing machines—Evaluation

GH'S KITCHEN of the FUTURE color *Good Housekeeping* v264 no6 p48K Je 2017

Disinfection & disinfectants

See also

Antiseptics

Infection—Prevention

Sterilization (Disinfection)

KEEPING IT CLEAN K. Donohue *Maclean's* v129 no40 p71 O 10 2016

Disjointed (TV program)

High Times: Kathy Bates lights up talking about her new comedy,

Disjointed I. RUDOLPH *TV Guide* v65 no35 p3 Ag 21 2017

STREAMING A. D'ARMINIO *TV Guide* v65 no35 p38 Ag 21 2017

Disks (Astrophysics)—Charts, diagrams, etc.

Planetary Almanac *Sky & Telescope* v132 no6 p44 D 2016

Dismal Swamp (N.C. & Va.)

The Dismal Swamp: One Road out of Slavery Took You Straight into the Boggiest Place You've Ever Been W. H. Funk *Humanities* v38 no2 p5 Spr 2017

Dismissal of employees

See also

Layoffs

Wrongful discharge

THE APPROVAL MATRIX: Our deliberately oversimplified guide to who falls where on our taste hierarchies img *New York* v50 no10 p118 My 15 2017

BOTS AT WORK MEN WILL LOSE THE MOST JOBS. THAT'S OK L. PENNY color *Wired* v25 no8 p14 Ag 2017

HIT THE ROAD, BILL T. BOSNIC *In These Times* v41 no6 p11 Je 2017

Mark Fields out as Ford CEO A. Priddle, A. MacKenzie et al color *Motor Trend* v69 no8 p24 Ag 2017

Should I Help an Unjustly Fired Co-Worker? K. A. Appiah *New York Times Magazine* p22 Je 25 2017

Turmoil imperils research university in Andes E. Rodríguez Mega color *Science* v357 no6349 p340 Jl 28 2017

"We'd like to make you an offer" H. KIRTON *People Management* p40 Je 2017

Dismondy, Maria

The Jelly Donut Difference: Sharing Kindness with the World *Publishers Weekly* v264 no35 p77f Ag 28 2017

Dismore, Jane

The Good Duchess *History Today* v66 no10 p4 O 2016

Disney, Walt, 1901-1966

Marceline R. S. Jefferson bw color *Missouri Life* v44 no6 p44 S 2017

Picket Lines in Paradise J. S. Friedman bw color *American History* v52 no2 p40 Je 2017

Disney films

A BOX OFFICE BEAUTY D. Coggan color *Entertainment Weekly* no1459 p10 Mr 31 2017

Disney Brings Good Things to Life D. Coggan color *Entertainment Weekly* no1459 p11 Mr 31 2017

THE GREATEST DISNEY SONGS OF ALL TIME K. P. Sullivan, M. Snetiker et al color *Entertainment Weekly* no1454/1455 p36 F 24 2017

YOUR TURN: What's the Best Disney Song Ever? color diag *Entertainment Weekly* no1454/1455 p42 F 24 2017

Disney Junior Worldwide (Company)

How Did I Get Here? N. KANTER bw color *Bloomberg Businessweek* no4504 p68 D 19 2016

Disparte, Dante

The Best Cybersecurity Investment You Can Make Is Better Training *Harvard Business Review Digital Articles* p2 My 16 2017

Blockchain Could Make the Insurance Industry Much More Transparent *Harvard Business Review Digital Articles* p2 Jl 12 2017

If You Think Fighting Climate Change Will Be Expensive, Calculate the Cost of Letting It Happen *Harvard Business Review Digital Articles* p2 Je 12 2017

Simple Ethics Rules for Better Risk Management *Harvard Business Review Digital Articles* p2 N 8 2016

Displaced workers—Training of

Business Leads Solutions to Workforce Challenges T. J. DONOHUE *Weekly Standard* v22 no13 p21 D 5 2016

Display of merchandise

Material World H. MARTIN color *Architectural Digest* v74 no9 p56 S 2017

Window Dressing T. B. BROWNE *Indianapolis Monthly* v40 no4 p26 D 2016

Display systems

See also

High Definition Multimedia Interface

Information display systems

Features, Features *Boating World* v38 no4 p50 Ap 2017

Mouthy MFD Z. PROCHAZKA *Boating World* v38 no4 p48 Ap

2017

PICTURE THIS: THE QUESTIONS THAT IMAGERY CAN HELP ANSWER ARE SIMPLE YET IMPORTANT L. Bedord *Successful Farming* v115 no11 p50 S 2017

TV Troubles A. GRIFFIN color *Sound & Vision* v82 no4 p19 My 2017

XCUB GETS NON-TSO'D AVIONICS color *Flying* v144 no9 p16 S 2017

Display systems—Evaluation

COMPUTER MONITORS A. GEORGE color *Popular Mechanics* p30 Ap 2017

Disposable income

What to EXPECT in Your 50s. HARRAR cartoon color *AARP: The Magazine* v60 no4A p28 Je/Jl 2017

Disposable tableware—Environmental aspects

THE WORST OF TINES J. LUNA color *Mother Jones* v42 no4 p66 Jl/Ag 2017

Dispute resolution (Law)

See also

Courts

LET'S NEGOTIATE E. L. FERNANDEZ *USA Today Magazine* v145 no2862 p72 Mr 2017

Disraeli, Benjamin, Earl of Beaconsfield, 1804-1881

The Enduring Lessons of Disraeli's Sybil P. GOTTFRIED *American Conservative* v16 no5 p62 S/O 2017

Disruptive technologies

3 Ways M&A Is Different When You're Acquiring a Digital Company A. Leroi *Harvard Business Review Digital Articles* p2 Jl 11 2017

Competing with Platforms That Ignore the Law B. Edelman and D. Geradin *Harvard Business Review Digital Articles* p2 Mr 25 2016

DO MILLENNIALS WANT TO LEARN TO FLY? *Flying* v144 no11 p10 N 2017

How Big Data Is Changing Disruptive Innovation M. Wessel *Harvard Business Review Digital Articles* p2 Ja 27 2016

How CEOs Can Manage Strategic Tensions J. Goddard and A. Pierre *Harvard Business Review Digital Articles* p2 D 19 2016

How Understanding Disruption Helps Strategists S. Anthony *Harvard Business Review Digital Articles* p2 N 18 2015

Ideas to Change the World M. DiChristina color *Scientific American* v315 no6 p5 D 2016

If Ford Wants to Beat Tesla, It Needs to Go All In J. Gans *Harvard Business Review Digital Articles* p2 Ap 20 2016

Let's Stop Arguing About Whether Disruption Is Good or Bad G. Satell *Harvard Business Review Digital Articles* p2 My 21 2015

We Need to Expand the Definition of Disruptive Innovation R. Chase *Harvard Business Review Digital Articles* p2 Ja 7 2016

What Do You Do Well That Others Don't? W. Johnson *Harvard Business Review Digital Articles* p2 O 6 2015

What Do You Really Mean by Business "Transformation"? S. Anthony *Harvard Business Review Digital Articles* p2 F 29 2016

What So Many Strategists Get Wrong About Digital Disruption F. Vermeulen color *Harvard Business Review Digital Articles* p2 Ja 3 2017

Where Disruptive Innovation Came From D. Sull *Harvard Business Review Digital Articles* p2 N 10 2015

Why Platform Disruption Is So Much Bigger than Product Disruption J. P. Vazquez Sampere *Harvard Business Review Digital Articles* p2 Ap 8 2016

Why Preventing Disruption in 2017 Is Harder Than It Was When Christensen Coined the Term M. Wessel *Harvard Business Review Digital Articles* p2 S 4 2017

Why Winner-Takes-All Thinking Doesn't Apply to the Platform Economy D. S. Evans and R. Schmalensee *Harvard Business Review Digital Articles* p2 My 4 2016

Disruptive technologies—Economic aspects

What We Know, Now, About the Internet's Disruptive Power A. Ovans *Harvard Business Review Digital Articles* p2 Ja 28 2015

Disruptive technologies—Management

The Board Directors You Need for a Digital Transformation T. Rickards and R. Grossman *Harvard Business Review Digital Articles* p2 Jl 13 2017

Diss, Guillaume

Gene duplication can impart fragility, not robustness, in the yeast protein interaction network bibl color graph *Science* v355 no6325 p630 F 10 2017

Dissenters

See also

Revolutionaries

In Case of Low Revenue B. Elgin, P. Robison et al cartoon *Bloomberg Businessweek* no4497 p50 O 31 2016

Distance (Poem)

Distance M. Nonaka *Christian Century* v134 no9 p28 Ap 26 2017

Distance education

At-Home Seminary A. C. EASTEP color *Christianity Today* v61 no4 p67 My 2017

FINDING A CLASSROOM, WHEREVER YOU ARE D. HEITMAN *Phi Kappa Phi Forum* v97 no2 p36 Summ 2017

NRPA Update *Parks & Recreation* v52 no3 p55 Mr 2017

Distefano, Anthony J.

KEEP THE MISSALETTES! *Commonweal* v144 no5 p2 Mr 10 2017

Distefano, Michael—Interviews

Hiring C-Suite Executives by Algorithm S. G. Carmichael *Harvard Business Review Digital Articles* p2 Ap 6 2015

Distelfeld, Assaf

Wild emmer genome architecture and diversity elucidate wheat evolution and domestication color *Science* v357 no6346 p93 Jl 7 2017

Distelhorst, Greg

Can Lean Manufacturing Put an End to Sweatshops? *Harvard Business Review Digital Articles* p2 My 26 2016

Distemper

6 Things you may not have known about Pigeon fever H. S. Thomas color *Equus* no470 p44 N 2016

Distillation apparatus

THE TOOLS THEY USE color *Popular Mechanics* p120 Ap 2017

Distilleries

BROWN LIQUOR FRIDAYS S. Schneider color *Sunset* v237 no5 p93 N 2016

Drink J. Sens color *Sunset* v237 no5 p62 N 2016

IT'S GOTTA BE THE WATER F. MAROUKIAN color *Popular Mechanics* p20 My 2017

Rum Country J. Neimark *Atlanta* v57 no5 p57 S 2017

SPIRITED AWAY J. Garibaldi chart color *Sunset* v239 no3 p24 S 2017

Distilleries—Equipment & supplies

THE TOOLS THEY USE color *Popular Mechanics* p120 Ap 2017

Distinto a Los Demas (Music)

Nicky Jam D. Kiper color *Current Biography* v78 no3 p36 Mr 2017

Distracted driving

See also

Text messaging & driving

Cartoons *New York Times Upfront* v149 no10 p24 Mr 13 2017

Don't Text and Drive, Grown-Ups color *Prevention* v69 no7 p11 Jl 2017

DRIVEN TO DISTRACTION P. SMITH, N. E. Bondette et al *New York Times Upfront* v149 no10 p10 Mr 13 2017

MEET THE TEXTALYZER P. Smith *New York Times Upfront* v149 no10 p13 Mr 13 2017

"My dad had a bucket list of 60 things. He'd only checked off 5 when his life was cut short." L. Carney bw color *Good Housekeeping* v264 no4 p81 Ap 2017

Distraction (Psychology)

Attention Deficit C. Chocano *New York Times Magazine* p11 O 1 2017

PRAYING ATTENTION G. DOYLE color *O, The Oprah Magazine* p34 Ag 2017

To Improve Your Focus, Notice How You Lose It M. Lipson *Harvard Business Review Digital Articles* p2 N 4 2015

TOSSING AND TURNING C. TRILLIN cartoon *New Yorker* v92 no45 p33 Ja 16 2017

Distress (Psychology)

GIVEN the EVIDENCE *Humanist* v77 no2 p8 Mr/Ap 2017

Mysteries of the Human Body EXPLAINED! K. LAWLER and C. SAGON cartoon color *AARP: The Magazine* v60 no3A p26 Ap/My 2017

Responding to Defiance in the Moment *Education Digest* v82 no7 p46 Mr 2017

Distributed computing

v144 no2 p7 S 2017

Diversity in the workplace

4 Ways Managers Can Be More Inclusive S. Finkelstein *Harvard Business Review Digital Articles* p2 Jl 13 2017

50 BEST WORKPLACES FOR DIVERSITY L. Entis, P. Marinova et al color *Fortune* v174 no8 p45 D 15 2016

The Biases That Punish Racially Diverse Teams K. W. Phillips, R. B. Lount Jr. et al *Harvard Business Review Digital Articles* p2 F 22 2016

Colorblind Diversity Efforts Don't Work J. Emerson *Harvard Business Review Digital Articles* p2 S 11 2017

Corporate Diversity Initiatives Should Include White Men A. Wittenberg-Cox *Harvard Business Review Digital Articles* p2 S 6 2016

Creating a Culture Where Employees Speak Up S. A. Hewlett *Harvard Business Review Digital Articles* p2 Ja 8 2016

Deloitte's Radical Attempt to Reframe Diversity A. Wittenberg-Cox *Harvard Business Review Digital Articles* p2 Ag 3 2017

Diverse Teams Feel Less Comfortable—and That's Why They Perform Better D. Rock, H. Grant et al *Harvard Business Review Digital Articles* p2 S 22 2016

Diversity Doesn't Stick Without Inclusion L. Sherbin and R. Rashid color *Harvard Business Review Digital Articles* p2 F 1 2017

Diversity in Publishing D. WACHTELL *Publishers Weekly* v263 no51 p152 D 12 2016

Diversity Policies Rarely Make Companies Fairer, and They Feel Threatening to White Men T. L. Dover, B. Major et al *Harvard Business Review Digital Articles* p2 Ja 4 2016

Don't Give Up on Unconscious Bias Training—Make It Better J. Emerson *Harvard Business Review Digital Articles* p2 Ap 28 2017

Firing James Damore Could Be a Setback for Google's Diversity Goals A. Wittenberg-Cox *Harvard Business Review Digital Articles* p2 Ag 10 2017

Global Teams Should Have Office Visits, Not Offsites P. Hinds *Harvard Business Review Digital Articles* p2 Mr 3 2016

How Managers Can Promote Healthy Discussions About Race K. H. Banks *Harvard Business Review Digital Articles* p2 Ja 7 2016

How "Neutral" Layoffs Disproportionately Affect Women and Minorities A. Kalev *Harvard Business Review Digital Articles* p2 Jl 26 2016

How Royal DSM Is Improving Its Geographic and Gender Diversity A. Wittenberg-Cox *Harvard Business Review Digital Articles* p2 Jl 21 2017

How the Imagined "Rationality" of Engineering Is Hurting Diversity—and Engineering J. C. Williams and M. Multhaup *Harvard Business Review Digital Articles* p2 Ag 10 2017

How to Build Trust on Your Cross-Cultural Team A. Molinsky and E. Gundling *Harvard Business Review Digital Articles* p2 Je 28 2016

How to Get Men Involved with Gender Parity Initiatives E. N. Sherf and S. Tangirala *Harvard Business Review Digital Articles* p2 S 13 2017

How to Signal That Your Company Cares About Diversity C. Romero *Harvard Business Review Digital Articles* p2 D 3 2015

I'LL TELL YOU SOMETHING ZAHIR IRANI: The rise of psychometric testing is harming workplace diversity *People Management* p18 Jl 2017

The Importance of Middle-Skill Jobs A. S. MODESTINO *Issues in Science & Technology* v33 no1 p41 Fall 2016

Lessons from Yelp's Empirical Approach to Diversity R. Williams, G. Subramani et al *Harvard Business Review Digital Articles* p2 S 20 2017

Meet 'Mr. Diversity' James E. Taylor T. Townsend and K. MEEKS chart color *Black Enterprise* v47 no3 p43 O 2016

Offices Can Be Bastions of Civility in an Uncivil Time L. Gaines-Ross *Harvard Business Review Digital Articles* p2 Jl 14 2017

People Suffer at Work When They Can't Discuss the Racial Bias They Face Outside of It S. A. Hewlett, M. Marshall et al *Harvard Business Review Digital Articles* p2 Jl 10 2017

Shut Up, They Explained A. Keiper color *Weekly Standard* v22 no47 p15 Ag 21 2017

Teams Solve Problems Faster When They're More Cognitively Diverse A. Reynolds and D. Lewis color graph *Harvard Business Review Digital Articles* p2 Mr 30 2017

To Understand Whether Your Company Is Inclusive, Map How Your Employees Interact B. Yamkovenko and S. Tavares *Harvard Business Review Digital Articles* p2 Jl 19 2017

We're Making the Wrong Case for Diversity in Silicon Valley T. L. Pittinsky *Harvard Business Review Digital Articles* p2 Ap 11 2016

What 11 CEOs Have Learned About Championing Diversity S. K. Johnson *Harvard Business Review Digital Articles* p2 2017

What It Will Take to Make the Tech Industry More Diverse S. Colby, H. Ma et al *Harvard Business Review Digital Articles* p2 Mr 15 2016

What We Learned from Improving Diversity Rates at Pinterest C. Morgan *Harvard Business Review Digital Articles* p2 Jl 11 2017

Why Brainstorming Works Better Online T. Chamorro-Premuzic *Harvard Business Review Digital Articles* p2 Ap 2 2015

Why Diverse Teams Are Smarter D. Rock and H. Grant *Harvard Business Review Digital Articles* p2 N 4 2016

Women and Minorities Are Penalized for Promoting Diversity S. K. Johnson and D. R. Hekman *Harvard Business Review Digital Articles* p2 Mr 23 2016

Diversity in the workplace—Great Britain

"We want to be the most diverse organisation on the planet": Why networks and targets aren't enough to meet the incredible ambition at Accenture *People Management* p20 Ap 2017

Diversity in the workplace—United States

50 BEST COMPANIES FOR DIVERSITY [Cover story] D. T. Dingle, L. Fraser et al color *Black Enterprise* v47 no3 p52 O 2016

Only 11% of Top Business School Case Studies Have a Female Protagonist L. Symons *Harvard Business Review Digital Articles* p2 Mr 9 2016

Slack Technologies E. Huet chart color *Bloomberg Businessweek* no4503 p42 D 12 2016

Why Your Diversity Program May Be Helping Women but Not Minorities (or Vice Versa) E. Apfelbaum *Harvard Business Review Digital Articles* p2 Ag 8 2016

Diversity training programs

Ending Gender Discrimination Requires More than a Training Program F. Gino *Harvard Business Review Digital Articles* p2 O 10 2014

Divers—Training of

becoming a navy master diver J. EMERSON and M. Koziol cartoon *Popular Science* v289 no2 p80 Mr/Ap 2017

Divide (Music)

A Global Hit Machine Scores Again S. Lansky color *Time* v189 no10 p53 Mr 20 2017

Dividend reinvestment

Make Stock Investing Affordable C. M. Brown color *Black Enterprise* v47 no4 p16 N/D 2016

Dividend yield

10 GREAT STOCKS FOR THE NEXT 10 YEARS D. FONDA color *Kiplinger's Personal Finance* v70 no12 p46 D 2016

Don't Dump Your Dividend Stocks J. R. KOSNETT *Kiplinger's Personal Finance* v71 no3 p60 Mr 2017

Dividends

Everyone's Jumping on the Yield Bandwagon M. Hobson color *Black Enterprise* v47 no2 p20 S 2016

INVESTOR'S MIDYEAR GUIDE J. Wieczner diag *Fortune* v175 no7 p49 Je 1 2017

Our Top Dividend Picks D. FONDA chart color *Kiplinger's Personal Finance* v71 no12 p50 D 2017

When Dividends Don't Pay J. Waggoner diag *Money* v46 no7 p34 Ag 2017

Dividends—Taxation

Taxing issues R. SPENCE color *Maclean's* no1 p50 F 17 2017

We Need to Raise Taxes for Shareholders and Cut Them for Companies E. Toder and A. D. Viard *Harvard Business Review Digital Articles* p2 N 1 2016

Divine Travels (Company)

CLIMB ABOARD, YE WHO SEEK THE TRUTH! B. DICKEY color *Popular Mechanics* v193 no7 p84 S 2016

Divine Comedy, The (Poem : Dante)

BETWEEN HEAVEN AND HELL *Claremont Review of Books* v17 no2 p52 Spr 2017

Divine Miss M, The (Music)

BETTE MIDLER K. O'Donnell color *Entertainment Weekly* no1436/1437 p100 O 21 2016

Diving

THE BEAUTY BELOW THE ICE L. BALLESTA color *National Geographic* v232 no1 p50 Jl 2017

Caymankind of Vacation *New York* v50 no17 p150 Ag 21 2017

Concrete Jungle S. Murray color *Power & Motoryacht* v34 no10 p68 O 2017

FLOATING TOWARD ECSTASY T. PITOCK *Saturday Evening Post* v289 no1 p56 Ja/F 2017

We Must Protect the Bounty and Beauty of the Sea E. Norton *UN Chronicle* v54 no1/2 p1 2017

WHERE HAVE ALL THE GOOD DIVES GONE? K. WOLFE *Cincinnati Magazine* v50 no2 p53 N 2016

Division of household labor

Are Chore Wars at Home Holding You Back at Work? R. Shambaugh color *Harvard Business Review Digital Articles* p2 Ja 19 2017

Division of labor

See also

Teams in the workplace

Make Sure Your Team's Workload Is Divided Fairly R. Knight *Harvard Business Review Digital Articles* p2 N 14 2016

Divorce

THE APPROVAL MATRIX img *New York* v49 no22 p136 O 31 2016

CASING the Joint E. GILBERT cartoon *O, The Oprah Magazine* p33 Mr 2017

CONFESSIONS OF DIVORCED MEN E. M. Brown color *Essence* v48 no6 p115 O 2017

does love end? M. BUSSOLA color *Parents* v92 no6 p106 Je 2017

Further Notes of a Recycled Housewife J. Rogers img *New York* v50 no11 p12 My 29 2017

How Pastors Perceive Domestic Violence chart *Christianity Today* p17 Mr 2017

Less Is More R. POLANECZKY color *Prevention* v68 no12 p34 D 2016

MAN OF LETTERS E. GREENWOOD color *O, The Oprah Magazine* p30 Ag 2017

No Stalemate R. Ferrone color *Commonweal* v114 no14 p8 S 8 2017

Out of Touch D. Nayeri *New York Times Magazine* p35 O 16 2016

PARENTAL GUIDANCE M. M. Kashino *Washingtonian Magazine* v52 no3 p122 D 2016

When the Ground Cracked *Psychology Today* v50 no5 p46 S/O 2017

When Your Paycheck Is Bigger Than His J. Baird and M. Mertens color *Glamour* v114 no12 p165 D 2016

Divorce (TV program)

Divorce *TV Guide* v64 no46 p33 N 7 2016

Sarah Jessica Parker Carries On A. D'ARMINIO *TV Guide* v64 no40 p24 O 3 2016

Sarah Jessica Parker D. D'addario color *Time* v188 no14 p64 O 10 2016

To Do J. GREEN, B. KACHKA et al img *New York* v49 no20 p136 O 3 2016

Divorce lawyers

WASHINGTON'S TOP DIVORCE LAWYERS *Washingtonian Magazine* v52 no3 p124 D 2016

Divorce—Costs

IT'S NOT JUST BRANGELINA C. Hymowitz *Bloomberg Businessweek* no4493 p53 O 3 2016

Divorced men

Can I Out My Ex-Husband To His Girlfriend? K. A. Appiah *New York Times Magazine* p20 Ja 8 2017

THE HALFWAY HOUSE J. C. Henriquez color *O, The Oprah Magazine* p25 Mr 2017

Divorced men—Psychology

Getting Over My Divorce? Studying the Numbers Helped C. Wilson color diag *Time* v189 no7/8 p115 F 27 2017

Divorced women

Forward Motion D. HOWARD color *Prevention* v69 no7 p76 Jl 2017

Divorce—Economic aspects

Divorce Doesn't Have to Derail Your Career A. Bassuk and J. Glickman *Harvard Business Review Digital Articles* p2 Ap 15 2015

Divorce—Psychological aspects

The Growing Case for Shared Parenting After Divorce B. Luscombe color *Time* v188 no14 p21 O 10 2016

Divorce—Religious aspects—Christianity

The End of Despair J. WATSON JR. il *America* v215 no19 p25 D 19 2016

Divorce—Research

IT'S NOT JUST BRANGELINA C. Hymowitz *Bloomberg Businessweek* no4493 p53 O 3 2016

Dixon, Akua

Akua Dixon: PLAYING WITH POWER D. Ouellette color *Downbeat* v84 no4 p44 Ap 2017

Strings in Jazz: Learning To Swing & Articulate in Style bw color *Downbeat* v84 no10 p186 O 2017

Dixon, David

Single-cell RNA-seq reveals new types of human blood dendritic cells, monocytes, and progenitors color *Science* v356 no6335 p283 Ap 21 2017

Dixon, Deborah

Deep exposures color *Science* v355 no6328 p916 Mr 3 2017

DIXON, LAURA

Bogotá, Colombia color *Foreign Policy* no224 p82 My/Je 2017

Dixon, Lucas

TROLL HUNTERS J. J. Roberts color *Fortune* v175 no2 p22 F 1 2017

Dixon, Matthew

KICK-ASS CUSTOMER SERVICE chart color graph il img *Harvard Business Review* v95 no1 p110 Ja/F 2017

Dixon, Nancy

Combining Virtual and Face-to-Face Work *Harvard Business Review Digital Articles* p2 Jl 1 2015

Dixon, Peter

Increased Demand for U.S. Agricultural Exports Would Likely Lead to More U.S. Jobs *Amber Waves: The Economics of Food, Farming, Natural Resources, & Rural America* p1 Je 2017

Dixon, Stephen

IN THIS ONE *Harper's Magazine* v333 no1998 p75 N 2016

Dixson, Danielle L.

LOST AT SEA color *Scientific American* v316 no6 p42 Je 2017

Dizaji, Nahid Borhani

Changes in the microbiota cause genetically modified Anopheles to spread in a population graph *Science* v357 no6358 p1396 S 29 2017

Dizziness—Diagnosis

WORKING OUT SAVED MY LIFE G. Graves color *Health* v31 no9 p92 N 2017

DJ Cavem Moetavation (Performer)

Dj Cavem H. Nordhaus bw *Rodale's Organic Life* v3 no1 p76 Ja 2017

DJ Khaled (Performer)

225 MINUTES WITH... Asahd Khaled: Touring the Children's Museum of Manhattan with the busiest baby in hip-hop A. P. DAVIS img *New York* v50 no18 p18 S 4 2017

HOW DJ KHALED ROLLS Z. O. GREENBURG color *Forbes* v200 no4 p58 O 24 2017

DJ Khaled (Performer)—Interviews

DJ KHALED cartoon *Vanity Fair* v59 no1 p192 Holiday 2017

DJ KHALED N. Feeney color *Entertainment Weekly* no1471 p60 Je 23 2017

Djaout, Kamel

Reversion of antibiotic resistance in Mycobacterium tuberculosis by spiroisoxazoline SMARt-420 bibl diag *Science* v355 no6330 p1206 Mr 17 2017

Djavadi, Négar

Unmaking the Persians L. Ermelino color *Publishers Weekly* v264 no34 p32 Ag 21 2017

Djerf, Warren

Theater Needs Tomorrow's Technicians Today *Stage Directions* v30 no10 p34 O 2017

DJI (Company)

Big Memories, Small Drone S. MURRAY color *Power & Motoryacht* v34 no10 p66 O 2017

FETISH: FLIGHT MANUAL A. PARDES color *Wired* v25 no9 p43 S 2017

Our Ultimate Holiday Wish List S. Silbert il *MIT Technology Re-*

view v119 no6 p25 N/D 2016

Djibouti—Description & travel

The Man Going Back D. Eggers bw *Foreign Policy* no221 p76 N/D 2016

Djokic, Tara

life springs [Cover story] color *Scientific American* v317 no2 p28 Ag 2017

Djokovic, Novak, 1987-

COURT of APPEALS R. GOOD *Tennis* v53 no1 p6 Ja/F 2017

Novak Djokovic *Tennis* v53 no1 p14 Ja/F 2017

THE TENNIS ROUNDTABLE chart *Tennis* v53 no1 p9 Ja/F 2017

Djureinovic, Dijana

A pathology atlas of the human cancer transcriptome diag *Science* v357 no6352 p660 Ag 18 2017

D-Link Corp.—Trials, litigation, etc.

Putting teeth into enforcing Internet of Things security G. FLEISHMAN color *Macworld - Digital Edition* p108 Mr 2017

Dlouhy, Jennifer A.

Carl 'I can' bw color graph *Bloomberg Businessweek* no4515 p23 Mr 20 2017

The Coming War On Gas color graph *Bloomberg Businessweek* no4519 p51 Ap 24 2017

How Climate Rules Might Fade Away color *Bloomberg Businessweek* no4504 p6 D 19 2016

The Little Think Tank Driving Trump's Policy *Bloomberg Businessweek* no4507 p24 Ja 16 2017

Pruitt Faces Fire on Climate Views bw *Bloomberg Businessweek* no4508 p25 Ja 23 2017

A Rush to Regulate Before Inauguration color diag *Bloomberg Businessweek* no4501 p24 N 28 2016

A Solar Trade Case Tailor-Made for Trump color graph *Bloomberg Businessweek* no4527 p49 Je 19 2017

Thanks to Ivanka, We May Always Have Paris color *Bloomberg Businessweek* no4519 p50 Ap 24 2017

Time for Going-Away Gifts? color *Bloomberg Businessweek* no4525 p6 Je 5 2017

Dmitrieva, Katia

Buffett's Bet on Canadian Real Estate bw *Bloomberg Businessweek* no4529 p27 Jl 3 2017

Chinese Buyers Move On From Vancouver chart *Bloomberg Businessweek* no4504 p37 D 19 2016

DNA

See also

Human DNA

Plant DNA

Ancient DNA B. ALEX color diag map *Discover* v38 no6 p52 Jl/Ag 2017

CAN A DNA TEST GIVE YOU A BETTER BODY? A. Kuczynski color *Harper's Bazaar* no3656 p468 S 2017

DECODING A DENISOVAN DEAD END? color diag map *Discover* v27 no10 p67 D 2016

De-extinction, nomenclature, and the law N. Wagner, A. Hochkirch et al color *Science* v356 no6342 p1016 Je 9 2017

Directing reconfigurable DNA nanoarrays Y. Yang and C. Lin color *Science* v357 no6349 p352 Jl 28 2017

DNA edits boost photosynthesis [Cover story] S. MILIUS color *Science News* v190 no13 p6 D 24 2016

DNA Fountain enables a robust and efficient storage architecture Y. Erlich and D. Zielinski bibl chart diag *Science* v355 no6328 p950 Mr 3 2017

DNA in seawater reveals shark numbers color *Science* v354 no6315 p949 N 25 2016

First Polynesians launched from East Asia to settle Pacific A. Gibbons color *Science* v354 no6308 p24 O 7 2016

GENE FITTING C. COX *Scientific American* v317 no3 p7 S 2017

The genome—seeing it clearly now D. R. Larson and T. Misteli diag *Science* v357 no6349 p354 Jl 28 2017

How to Defy Your Genes S. Mahoney color *AARP: The Magazine* v59 no4A p46 Je/Jl 2017

Imaging method catches DNA 'blinking' on R. Ehrenberg color *Science News* v191 no5 p16 Mr 18 2017

Message Control B. Borel color graph *Scientific American* v317 no4 p68 O 2017

Molecular force spectroscopy with a DNA origami–based nanoscopic force clamp P. C. Nickels, B. Wünsch et al bibl diag graph *Science* v354 no6310 p305 O 21 2016

Mysterious unchanging DNA finds a purpose in life E. Pennisi *Science* v356 no6341 p892 Je 1 2017

Neandertal genome reveals greater legacy in the living A. Gibbons *Science* v357 no6359 p21 O 6 2017

Neandertals mated early with modern humans A. Gibbons color *Science* v357 no6346 p14 Jl 7 2017

The Original CRISPR [Cover story] R. Mestel color diag graph *Science News* v191 no7 p22 Ap 15 2017

Passing epigenetic silence to the next generation S. De and J. A. Kassis diag *Science* v356 no6333 p28 Ap 7 2017

Reconfiguration of DNA molecular arrays driven by information relay J. Song, Z. Li et al diag *Science* v357 no6349 p371 Jl 28 2017

REWRITING THE CODE OF LIFE M. SPECTER cartoon *New Yorker* v92 no43 p34 Ja 2 2017

A supramolecular assembly mediates lentiviral DNA integration A. Ballandras-Colas, D. P. Maskell et al bibl color *Science* v355 no6320 p1 Ja 6 2017

Transgenerational inheritance: Models and mechanisms of non–DNA sequence–based inheritance E. A. Miska and A. C. Ferguson-Smith bibl color diag *Science* v354 no6308 p59 O 7 2016

Unspooling the Essential Code B. Lang *Discover* v38 no6 p6 Jl/Ag 2017

DNA-binding proteins

Transcription factors read epigenetics T. R. Hughes and S. A. Lambert diag *Science* v356 no6337 p489 My 5 2017

DNA copy number variations

β2-Adrenoreceptor is a regulator of the a-synuclein gene driving risk of Parkinson's disease S. Mittal, K. Bjørnevik et al cartoon chart graph *Science* v357 no6354 p891 S 1 2017

SCHIZOPHRENIA'S UNYIELDING MYSTERIES M. BALTER color diag *Scientific American* v316 no5 p54 My 2017

DNA damage

Bifurcating electron-transfer pathways in DNA photolyases determine the repair quantum yield Meng Zhang, Lijuan Wang et al bibl graph *Science* v354 no6309 p209 O 14 2016

Cigarettes cause telltale DNA damage R. EHRENBERG diag *Science News* v190 no11 p14 N 26 2016

The Problem With E-Cigarettes L. SCHLEY *Discover* v38 no10 p14 D 2017

DNA damage—Research

DNA damage is a pervasive cause of sequencing errors, directly confounding variant identification L. Chen, P. Liu et al bibl graph *Science* v355 no6326 p752 F 17 2017

DNA fingerprinting

Game-Changing Forensics Technique Uses Hair Proteins *Science & Technology Review* p2 Mr 2017

DNA folding

Archaea fold DNA like animals do M. TEMMING color *Science News* v192 no3 p14 S 2 2017

Self-assembly of genetically encoded DNA-protein hybrid nanoscale shapes F. Praetorius and H. Dietz *Science* v355 no6331 p1283 Mr 24 2017

DNA methylation

The DNA methyltransferase DNMT3C protects male germ cells from transposon activity J. Barau, A. Teissandier et al bibl diag graph *Science* v354 no6314 p909 N 18 2016

Impact of cytosine methylation on DNA binding specificities of human transcription factors Y. Yin, E. Morgunova et al diag *Science* v356 no6337 p502 My 5 2017

Integration of CpG-free DNA induces de novo methylation of CpG islands in pluripotent stem cells Y. Takahashi, J. Wu et al diag *Science* v356 no6337 p503 My 5 2017

DNA mutational analysis

DNA damage is a pervasive cause of sequencing errors, directly confounding variant identification L. Chen, P. Liu et al bibl graph *Science* v355 no6326 p752 F 17 2017

DNA nanotechnology

See also

DNA folding

DNA robots sort as they walk J. H. Reif diag *Science* v357 no6356 p1095 S 15 2017

DNA primase

The [4Fe4S] cluster of human DNA primase functions as a redox switch using DNA charge transport E. O'Brien, M. E. Holt et al color *Science* v355 no6327 p813 F 24 2017

DNA repair

DNA-PKcs structure suggests an allosteric mechanism modulating DNA double-strand break repair B. L. Sibanda, D. Y. Chirgadze et al bibl graph *Science* v355 no6324 p520 F 3 2017

Of sizzling steaks and DNA repair F. A. Dingler and K. J. Patel diag *Science* v357 no6347 p130 Jl 14 2017

ZATT (ZNF451)–mediated resolution of topoisomerase 2 DNA-protein cross-links M. J. Schellenberg, J. Ariel Lieberman et al diag *Science* v357 no6358 p1412 S 29 2017

DNA replication

Bidirectional eukaryotic DNA replication is established by quasi-symmetrical helicase loading G. Coster and J. F. X. Diffley graph *Science* v357 no6348 p314 Jl 21 2017

DNA replication–coupled histone modification maintains Polycomb gene silencing in plants D. Jiang and F. Berger diag *Science* v357 no6356 p1146 S 15 2017

DNA replication—Research

Mechanisms for initiating cellular DNA replication F. Bleichert, M. R. Botchan et al graph *Science* v355 no6327 p811 F 24 2017

DNA sequencing

Baby genome screening needs more time to gestate J. Kaiser color *Science* v354 no6311 p398 O 28 2016

Baby Genome Sequencing for Sale in China A. Regalado il *MIT Technology Review* v120 no5 p13 S/O 2017

China's policies regarding next-generation sequencing diagnostic tests Rui Zhang and Jinming Li *Science* v354 no6319 p9 D 23 2016

A composite window into human history N. N. Johannsen, G. Larson et al color map *Science* v356 no6343 p1118 Je 16 2017

DNA sequence-dependent epigenetic inheritance of gene silencing and histone H3K9 methylation X. Wang and D. Moazed diag *Science* v356 no6333 p88 Ap 7 2017

Gene–environment interplay J. Berg color *Science* v354 no6308 p15 O 7 2016

Growing Dependency L. E. Ogden color *Natural History* v125 no6 p7 Je 2017

THE ME PROJECT C. Neuhaus *Saturday Evening Post* v289 no2 p12 Mr/Ap 2017

New technologies boost genome quality E. Pennisi chart color *Science* v357 no6346 p10 Jl 7 2017

One brain, many genomes G. D. Evrony bibl color diag *Science* v354 no6312 p557 N 4 2016

Pinpointing HIV spread in Africa poses risks J. Cohen color *Science* v356 no6338 p568 My 12 2017

Pocket-sized sequencers start to pay off big E. Pennisi color *Science* v356 no6338 p572 My 12 2017

Protein structure determination using metagenome sequence data S. Ovchinnikov, H. Park et al bibl color graph *Science* v355 no6322 p294 Ja 20 2017

Qatar's genome effort slowly gears up J. Kaiser color *Science* v354 no6317 p1220 D 9 2016

'Scientific wellness' study divides researchers R. Cross color *Science* v357 no6349 p345 Jl 28 2017

Sequencers eye 10,000 plants color *Science* v357 no6350 p432 Ag 4 2017

Tardigrades aren't genetic mash-ups T. H. SAEY color *Science News* v192 no2 p13 Ag 19 2017

WE MAY KNOW WHAT WE KNOW WITHOUT UNDERSTANDING PRECISELY HOW WE KNOW IT W. R. BRODY *Vital Speeches of the Day* v83 no8 p237 Ag 2017

DNA sequencing—Equipment & supplies

Mining microbes: Creating genomic tools to fight disease A. Dance color *Science* v356 no6339 p761 My 19 2017

Oxford Nanopore A. Regalado color il *MIT Technology Review* v120 no4 p66 Jl/Ag 2017

DNA synthesis

See also
DNA replication

THE RISE OF SYNTHETIC DNA J. Alsever color *Fortune* v175 no2 p19 F 1 2017

DNA vaccines

DNA vaccines for Zika show promise M. ROSEN color diag *Science News* v191 no5 p12 Mr 18 2017

Do, Emi

Farm City D. COPELAND color *Alternatives Journal (AJ) - Canada's Environmental Voice* v42 no2 p70 2016

Do-it-yourself products industry

See also
Do-it-yourself work

Build Your Own INCUBATOR J. Gauthier *Mother Earth News* no280 p46 F/Mr 2017

Do-it-yourself work

ALL IN THE TIMING J. Smith chart color graph *Hot Rod* v70 no9 p70 S 2017

APPLY Yourself P. GUGLIELMETTI *Martha Stewart Living* no269 p106 N 2016

ASK CAROLYN C. FORTÉ color *Good Housekeeping* v264 no4 p58 Ap 2017

D.I.Y D. SPIOTTA cartoon *New Yorker* v93 no26 p42 S 4 2017

DIY Fall Skin Treats K. FOSTER color *Seventeen* v75 no11 p44 N 2016

DIY ICE RINK J. HARDBERGER color *Chicago* v65 no12 p30 D 2016

The Evolution of Home A. Gardon and P. Mastrovito color *Log Home Living* v34 no1 p38 F 2017

GREAT UNKNOWNS color *Popular Mechanics* v193 no7 p26 S 2016

i did it! K. SELZER *Better Homes & Gardens* v94 no12 p71 D 2016

IS DIY RIGHT FOR YOU? J. Cooper color *Cabin Living* p67 S 2017

JUST 3 MOVES A. Reliford color *Good Housekeeping* v265 no4 p100 O 2017

Making Room for Hobbies P. Reichard *New Orleans Homes & Lifestyles* v20 no1 p90 Wint 2016

Namaste Your Period Pain Away A. STANLEY color *Seventeen* v75 no11 p57 N 2016

ONE RING TO RULE THEM ALL E. Perkins chart color graph *Hot Rod* v70 no9 p80 S 2017

Score Your HAIR GOALS K. CASTAÑON cartoon color *Seventeen* v75 no11 p39 N 2016

Split-sational O. Manno *Dance Spirit* v21 no3 p34 Mr 2017

TIME TO SHINE K. CASTAÑON color *Seventeen* v75 no11 p86 N 2016

Do-it-yourself work—Computer network resources

'Primitive Technology' J. Kahn color *New York Times Magazine* p24 D 4 2016

do Amaral, D. D.

Persistent effects of pre-Columbian plant domestication on Amazonian forest composition bibl chart graph map *Science* v355 no6328 p925 Mr 3 2017

Doan, Lynn

Ethylene color *Bloomberg Businessweek* no4537 p21 S 11 2017

Doane, Charles J.

2017 PITTMAN INNOVATION AWARDS color *Sail* v48 no2 p58 F 2017

Allures 39.9 color diag *Sail* v48 no10 p28 O 2017

BEST BOATS 2017 color *Sail* v47 no12 p24 D 2016

Bigger Than the Cup color *Sail* v48 no1 p18 Ja 2017

The Bones of the Beast color *Sail* v48 no4 p96 Ap 2017

A Cruising Family Reunion color *Sail* v47 no12 p80 D 2016

Fareast 23R color *Sail* v48 no5 p22 My 2017

Haute Cuisine color *Sail* v48 no6 p80 Je 2017

In Defense of Larry Ellison color *Sail* v48 no10 p120 O 2017

Keeping Up with the Jones color *Sail* v48 no9 p96 S 2017

The King of Rum Row bw *Sail* v48 no1 p88 Ja 2017

Longue Route 2018 color *Sail* v48 no8 p88 Ag 2017

Lost and Found color *Sail* v48 no5 p80 My 2017

THE NEW FRONTIER color diag *Sail* v48 no4 p34 Ap 2017

Revenge of the Monomarans color *Sail* v48 no11 p80 N 2017

The SAILING SCENE color *Sail* v48 no7 p6 Jl 2017

Seascape 18 color *Sail* v48 no5 p23 My 2017

Self-Inflicted Wounds color *Sail* v48 no2 p96 F 2017

A Separate Reality color *Sail* v48 no3 p96 Mr 2017

Solaris 50 color *Sail* v48 no5 p20 My 2017

Tender Mercies color *Sail* v48 no7 p80 Jl 2017

UP A LAZY RIVER C. J. DOANE color *Sail* v48 no4 p44 Ap 2017

Xquisite X5 color *Sail* v48 no3 p24 Mr 2017

DOANE, KATHLEEN

MAGIC BATON *Cincinnati Magazine* v50 no10 p24 Jl 2017

PODCAST EARTH *Cincinnati Magazine* v50 no8 p18 My 2017

Q&A: Genevieve Janssens *Cincinnati Magazine* v50 no6 p118 Mr 2017

Doane, Nicki

LIVE JOY color *Yoga Journal* p66 2017 Special Issue

Dobbek, Holger

Playing marble run to make methane color diag *Science* v357 no6352 p642 Ag 18 2017

Dobbin, Frank

2016 HBR MCKINSEY AWARDS color *Harvard Business Review* v95 no3 p46 My/Je 2017

Research: Hiring Chief Risk Officers Led Banks to Take on Even More Risk *Harvard Business Review Digital Articles* p2 Jl 13 2017

Dobbins, Thomas A.

The Enduring Mystery of Luna 2: Amateur observers claimed to see its impact—but no trace of the crash site has ever been found *Sky & Telescope* v134 no3 p52 S 2017

Eyepieces for Planetary Observing *Sky & Telescope* v134 no1 p52 Jl 2017

Dobbs, Charlotte

How Self-Managed Companies Help People Learn on the Job *Harvard Business Review Digital Articles* p2 Ag 3 2016

DOBBS, CYNNAMON

Planning for the Future of Urban Biodiversity: A Global Review of City-Scale Initiatives *BioScience* v67 no4 p332 Ap 2017

Dobbs, David

Roundup: Science *New York Times Book Review* p22 S 24 2017

THE SMARTPHONE PSYCHIATRIST color *Atlantic* v320 no1 p78 Jl/Ag 2017

WAZED AND CONFUSED cartoon *Mother Jones* v41 no6 p53 N/D 2016

Dobbs, Jill

Financial Life color *Missouri Life* v44 no6 p78 S 2017

Dobbs, Richard

Emerging Demographics Are the New Emerging Markets *Harvard Business Review Digital Articles* p2 Jl 13 2016

The Productivity Challenge of an Aging Global Workforce *Harvard Business Review Digital Articles* p2 Ja 20 2015

Dobias, Devin T.

Ecological speciation of bacteriophage lambda in allopatry and sympatry bibl graph *Science* v354 no6317 p1301 D 9 2016

Dobie, Kathy

IN BLUEGRASS COUNTRY *Harper's Magazine* v333 no1998 p61 N 2016

Doblas, Verónica G.

Root diffusion barrier control by a vasculature-derived peptide binding to the SGN3 receptor color *Science* v355 no6322 p280 Ja 20 2017

Doblas-Reyes, Francisco J.

Using climate models to estimate the quality of global observational data sets bibl graph *Science* v354 no6311 p452 O 28 2016

Doble, Abner

Full Steam Ahead J. J. Geoghegan *American History* v52 no1 p26 Ap 2017

Doble steam automobiles

Doble Talk *American History* v52 no1 p31 Ap 2017

Full Steam Ahead J. J. Geoghegan *American History* v52 no1 p26 Ap 2017

Doblhoff-Dier, K.

Ultrafast electron diffraction imaging of bond breaking in di-ionized acetylene bibl graph *Science* v354 no6310 p308 O 21 2016

Döblin, Alfred, 1878-1957

1945: Los Angeles *Lapham's Quarterly* v10 no2 p177 Spr 2017

Doblmeier, Martin

Why Niebuhr mattered J. Byassee *Christian Century* v134 no7 p44 Mr 29 2017

DOBOSZ, JOHN

Class App color *Forbes* v199 no6 p50 Je 13 2017

Milking Your Stocks color *Forbes* v199 no7 p132 Je 29 2017

Peugeot on the Go color *Forbes* v200 no2 p48 S 5 2017

SMALL CAPS WITH BIG YIELDS chart color *Forbes* v198 no9 p98 D 30 2016

Dobrev, Nina, 1989-

GET THE COVER LOOK color *Harper's Bazaar* no3656 p350 S 2017

MUST HAVES color *Harper's Bazaar* no3656 p348 S 2017

My LIST: 24 hours with Nina Dobrev L. Christensen color *Harper's Bazaar* no3656 p336 S 2017

NINA'S GREATEST BEAUTY HITS color *Harper's Bazaar* no3656 p346 S 2017

NINA'S NIGHT OUT A. Gell color *Harper's Bazaar* no3656 p337 S 2017

THERE WILL BE TEARS S. Highfill color *Entertainment Weekly* no1454/1455 p54 F 24 2017

Dobrigkeit, C.

Observation of a large-scale anisotropy in the arrival directions of cosmic rays above 8 × 1018 eV *Science* v357 no6357 p1266 S 22 2017

Dobrosielski, Cris

7 REASONS YOU HAVE SORE MUSCLES V. Tweed color *Amazing Wellness* p78 Fall 2017

Dobrovic, Massimo

COMING OUT-OF THE COFFIN: Born on Halloween, actor MASSIMO DOBROVIC was destined to play the king of vampires, but "happily married gay man" may be his favorite role yet D. ANDERSON-MINSHALL *Advocate* no1093 p61 O/N 2017

DOBROWNER, MITCH

THE ONE DESN'T EVEN NEED A HEADLINE *Arizona Highways* v92 no11 p32 N 2016

Dobski, Bernard

Classical Regimes at War: Spartan Republicanism vs. Athenian Democracy *Society* v53 no6 p657 D 2016

DOBSON, ANDREW P.

Transformational Principles for NEON Sampling of Mammalian Parasites and Pathogens: A Response to Springer and Colleagues *BioScience* v66 no11 p917 N 1 2016

Dobson, James C., 1936-—Interviews

Donald Trump J. DOBSON color *Christianity Today* v60 no8 p58 O 2016

Doc McStuffins (TV program)

DAYTIME M. LOGAN *TV Guide* v65 no23 p42 My 29 2017

Dockery, Michelle, 1981-

Good Behavior A. Bacle, D. Coggan et al *Entertainment Weekly* no1482/1483 p39 S 22 2017

Good Behavior J. Jensen color *Entertainment Weekly* no1439 p50 N 11 2016

GOOD GIRL GONE BAD I. RUDOLPH *TV Guide* v64 no46 p22 N 7 2016

LADY IN RED L. Brown color *InStyle* v24 no3 p320 Mr 2017

Dockery, Michelle, 1981-—Interviews

Smooth Criminal S. Li color *Entertainment Weekly* no1440 p50 N 18 2016

Docking stations (Electronics)—Evaluation

HENGE DOCKS TETHERED DOCKING STATION R. LOYOLA color *Macworld - Digital Edition* p39 F 2017

Dockins, Chris

Estimating the health benefits of environmental regulations color *Science* v357 no6350 p457 Ag 4 2017

Docks

A RAIL-MARINE SHOWCASE [Cover story] H. R. Lloyd color *Model Railroader* v84 no7 p42 Jl 2017

Sorry, Mr Roboto! B. PIKE cartoon *Power & Motoryacht* v33 no3 p208 Mr 2017

Docks—Maintenance & repair

DOCKS BUILT TO LAST color *Cabin Living* p68 Ap 2017

Dockterman, David

Does stressing performance goals lead to too much, well, stress? color il *Phi Delta Kappan* v98 no6 p31 Mr 2017

Dockterman, Eliana

Anne Hathaway color *Time* v189 no10 p60 Mr 20 2017

The Best 25 Inventions of 2016 color *Time* v188 no22-23 p43 N/D 2016

The Best of Everything This Year-So Far color *Time* v189 no21 p61 Je 5 2017

Comics We Can't Wait For color *Time* v189 no5 p48 F 13 2017

Darren Aronofsky color *Time* v190 no13 p72 O 2 2017

Daveed Diggs, Actor and Rapper color *Time* v188 no15 p58 O 17 2016

Ellen Pao color *Time* v190 no14 p56 O 9 2017

Everything New Is Old Again color *Time* v189 no4 p49 F 6 2017

Fast & Furious: The Completist's Guide color *Time* v189 no14

p54 Ap 17 2017

A Game of Throne color diag *Time* v189 no3 p51 Ja 30 2017

Gina Prince-Bythewood, Filmmaker color *Time* v189 no10 p54 Mr 20 2017

The Handmaid's Tale, Retold color *Time* v189 no15 p45 Ap 24 2017

How to Steal a Million-and Then Some color diag *Time* v190 no8 p49 Ag 28 2017

How Twin Peaks Changed TV Forever color *Time* v189 no19 p51 My 22 2017

In a Quantum Leap, Star Trek Becomes a Female Enterprise color *Time* v190 no13 p59 O 2 2017

In the Gilmore Girls' Hometown, Things Are (Mostly) the Same color *Time* v188 no21 p69 N 21 2016

Is It Ethical to Have Sex With a Robot? *Time* v189 no7/8 p104 F 27 2017

The Itsy-Bitsy, Teensy-Weensy, Tiny Fine Print That Can Allow Sexual Harassment to Go Unheard color *Time* v188 no18 p32 O 31 2016

Lethally Blonde color *Time* v190 no6 p46 Ag 7 2017

Mapping the Girls Effect color diag *Time* v189 no6 p49 F 20 2017

Michelle Pfeiffer As a Nefarious House Guest color *Time* v190 no10/11 p102 S 18 2017

Naomi Watts color *Time* v190 no2/3 p93 Jl 10-17 2017

Neil Patrick Harris color *Time* v189 no3 p50 Ja 30 2017

Next Generation Leaders color *Time* v189 no9 p38 Mr 13 2017

Next Generation Leaders color *Time* v190 no16/17 p74 O 23 2017

The Podcast Finder color *Time* v189 no13 p52 Ap 10 2017

Pop Chart color *Time* v190 no6 p58 Ag 7 2017

The Real-Life Rebellion Behind Amazon's Good Girls Revolt color *Time* v188 no20 p56 N 14 2016

Returning TV That Deserves a Second Chance color *Time* v190 no14 p49 O 9 2017

Rewriting the Rules of Womanhood color *Time* v189 no11 p6 Mr 27 2017

Rogue One Rewinds-and Rewrites-the Star Wars Legacy color diag *Time* v188 no22-23 p100 N/D 2016

Sci-fi Evolves Into Disturbing Reality In Black Mirror and West-world color *Time* v188 no16/17 p90 O 24 2016

Show Me a Superhero color *Time* v189 no11 p60 Mr 27 2017

Spider-Man, Ranked color *Time* v190 no5 p59 Jl 31 2017

A Sprawling Drama About Elizabeth II Aims to Be Netflix's New Crown Jewel color *Time* v188 no19 p53 N 7 2016

Summer Movie Preview: August color *Time* v189 no20 p58 My 29 2017

Summer Movie Preview: July color *Time* v189 no20 p56 My 29 2017

Summer Movie Preview: June color *Time* v189 no20 p50 My 29 2017

Summer Movie Preview: May color *Time* v189 no20 p48 My 29 2017

Ta-Nehisi Coates Is Retooling America's Myth Factory color *Time* v189 no5 p47 F 13 2017

They Came to Slay color *Time* v189 no9 p56 Mr 13 2017

Tom Holland Swings In color *Time* v190 no2/3 p87 Jl 10-17 2017

The True Purpose of True Crime color *Time* v190 no16/17 p100 O 23 2017

When Writers Rule, TV Gets Wonderfully Weird color *Time* v189 no7/8 p102 F 27 2017

Why Wonder Woman Broke Through color *Time* v189 no23 p52 Je 19 2017

Wonder Woman Breaks Through color *Time* v188 no27-28 p98 D 26 2016

Zoe Saldana, Actor color *Time* v189 no3 p60 Ja 16 2017

Docosahexaenoic acid

RESEARCH FOCUSES ON PREVENTING PRETERM BIRTHS V. Prevish *Cincinnati Magazine* v50 no12 p82 S 2017

Doctor of philosophy degree

Lucking into science L. Yehia color *Science* v356 no6338 p654 My 12 2017

To Ph.D. or Not to Ph.D.? K. Kish *Parks & Recreation* v52 no9 p38 S 2017

Doctor Strange (Film)

10 — THE NYC CHASE K. P. Sullivan *Entertainment Weekly* no1444/1445 p61 D 16 2016

BENEDICT CUMBERBATCH D. Franich color *Entertainment*

Weekly no1444/1445 p28 D 16 2016

The Bullseye M. Snetiker color *Entertainment Weekly* no1439 p64 N 11 2016

Calling the Night Nurse C. Collis color *Entertainment Weekly* no1436/1437 p37 O 21 2016

THE CHECKLIST *Texas Monthly* v44 no11 p64 N 2016

Cover *Entertainment Weekly* no1436/1437 pC1 O 21 2016

The Cultural Saturation Chart D. GORDON and C. WEAVER bw color *GQ: Gentlemen's Quarterly* v86 no11 p72 N 2016

DOCTOR STRANGE B. A. DuHamel color *Sound & Vision* v82 no6 p70 Jl/Ag 2017

Doctor Strange C. Nashawaty color *Entertainment Weekly* no1439 p40 N 11 2016

Doctor Strange: The Curious Case of Two Teasers D. Franich color *Entertainment Weekly* no1440 p14 N 18 2016

The Doctor Will See You Now [Cover story] C. Collis color *Entertainment Weekly* no1436/1437 p34 O 21 2016

He's One Weird Dude P. Travers color *Rolling Stone* no1274 p60 N 17 2016

The Mind-Bending Mr. Cumberbatch M. SCHULMAN bw color *Vanity Fair* v58 no11 p146 N 2016

Strange Interlude J. PODHORETZ *Weekly Standard* v22 no11 p43 N 21 2016

Strange-r Danger: Mads Mikkelsen Evils Up C. Collis color *Entertainment Weekly* no1439 p41 N 11 2016

Doctor Who (TV program)

CHEERS & JEERS D. Holbrook color *TV Guide* v65 no7 p92 F 13-20 ?

DOCTOR WHO C. Collis color *Entertainment Weekly* p26 Jl 24 2017

A DOCTOR WHO CHARACTER COMES OUT OF THE TAR-DIS C. Collis color *Entertainment Weekly* no1462 p12 Ap 21 2017

Doctor Who Christmas Special A. D'Arminio *TV Guide* p38 D 19 2016

DOCTOR WHO CHRISTMAS SPECIAL C. Collis color *Entertainment Weekly* no1474/1475 p72 Jl 21-28 2017

MEET THE DOCTOR'S NEW COMPANION! PEARL MACK-IE C. Collis color *Entertainment Weekly* no1446/1447 p64 D 2016/Ja 2017

MOVIES AND SPECIALS *TV Guide* p31 D 5 2016

Doctoral degree

A bridge between undergraduate and doctoral degrees T. Hodapp and K. S. Woodle *Physics Today* v70 no2 p50 F 2017

Lucking into science L. Yehia color *Science* v356 no6338 p654 My 12 2017

Doctoral programs

Choosing the hard road K. Henke cartoon *Science* v355 no6321 p218 Ja 13 2017

Doctoral students

The art of triage E. White color *Science* v357 no6351 p618 Ag 11 2017

The transcontinental scientist W. Delva color *Science* v355 no6322 p318 Ja 20 2017

Doctoral students—Research

Using Longitudinal Data on Career Outcomes to Promote Improvements and Diversity in Graduate Education A. Mathur, A. L. Feig et al *Change* v48 no6 p42 N/D 2016

Doctoroff, Daniel L.

Dan Doctoroff C. SWANSON img *New York* v50 no17 p34 Ag 21 2017

Transforming the Metropolis D. Lind *Architectural Record* v205 no10 p51 O 2017

Doctorow, Cory

GIMME SHELTER cartoon *Wired* v25 no4 p15 Ap 2017

Greenfeld's "The Subprimes" and the Way Fiction Predicts the Present *Harvard Business Review Digital Articles* p2 My 15 2015

Mr. Robot Killed the Hollywood Hacker color *MIT Technology Review* v120 no1 p100 Ja/F 2017

TLA Program Highlights> bw color *Publishers Weekly* v264 no14 p24 Ap 3. 2017

Doctorow, Cory—Interviews

Cory Doctorow's 'FULLY AUTOMATED LUXURY COMMU-NIST CIVILIZATION' K. MANGU-WARD bw color *Reason* v49 no4 p54 Ag/S 2017

Doctrinal theology
See also
    Bible—Theology
    Dogma
    Grace (Theology)
    Holy Spirit
    Incarnation
    Jesus Christ
It is time to get past the snobbery against pastoral theologians J. Heft *America* v217 no2 p10 Jl 24 2017

Documenta
A Triumph Over Censorship J. Zorthian color *Time* v190 no6 p25 Ag 7 2017

Documentary filmmakers
BIG PLANS SMALL MINDS J. REICHERT color *Film Comment* v53 no1 p78 Ja/F 2017
IT ALL CONNECTS J. Lethem *New York Times Magazine* p60 O 30 2016

Documentary films
Cuban Documentary Retrospective at DocLisboa 2016 P. Aufderheide *Film Quarterly* v70 no3 p80 Spr 2017
Deals R. DEAHL color *Publishers Weekly* v264 no13 p10 Mr 27 2017
Film Brut T. Jeppesen bw color *Art in America* v104 no10 p41 N 2016
Film Chronicles Scott's Final Work B. Doerschuk color *Downbeat* v84 no3 p13 Mr 2017
FULL FRAME 2017: Twentieth Anniversary Retrospective B. Cook *Film Quarterly* v71 no1 p91 Fall 2017
HOW WE SHOW ALL SIDES OF WAR color *National Geographic* v231 no2 p6 F 2017
Memory Maker A. PATUREL color *Good Housekeeping* v264 no1 p69 Ja 1 2017
NEEDLE'S EYE MINISTRIES *Virginia Living* v15 no6 p43 O 2017
PAUL ALLEN PINPOINTS WRECK OF USS INDIANAPOLIS B. Manley bw *Military History* v34 no5 p8 Ja 2018
Polarities and Pyrotechnics: True/False Festival 2017 L. Du Graf *Film Quarterly* v71 no1 p87 Fall 2017
Q&A: Avicii S. VOZICK-LEVINSON *Rolling Stone* no1295 p23 S 7 2017
See Through Me E. HYNES color *Film Comment* v53 no2 p14 Mr/Ap 2017
Spielberg A. D'Arminio *TV Guide* v65 no41 p32 O 2 2017
STINK: THE REAL STORY OF TOXINS V. Tweed color *Amazing Wellness* v8 no2 p14 Spr 2016
TRUE NOTE B. Ratliff bw cartoon *Esquire* p33 Ap 2017

Documentary films—Production & direction
A Lens On the Psyche S. ERICKSON *Los Angeles Magazine* p94 Ap 2017

Documentary films—Reviews
THE 22-WORD REVIEW L. Greenblatt color *Entertainment Weekly* no1477 p38 Ag 11 2017
The Act of Documenting: Documentary Film in the 21st Century R. MUKHERJEE *Film Quarterly* v71 no1 p115 Fall 2017
DEAD RECKONING B. HANDY bw *Vanity Fair* v59 no6 p72 My 2017
A documentary on abortion that fails the women it portrays A. Mena color *America* v216 no10 p51 My 1 2017
THE EMPATHY MACHINE J. ANDERSONMINSHALL color *Advocate* no1090 p57 Ap 2017
The Nihilism of Julian Assange S. Halpern color *New York Review of Books* v64 no12 p13 Jl 13 2017
OFF THE RECORD: REENACTMENT AND INTIMACY IN CASTING JONBENET M. Francis and L. Hussein *Film Quarterly* v71 no1 p32 Fall 2017
Spielberg: Celebrating a life making movies that defined many moviegoers' lives M. ROUSH *TV Guide* v65 no41 p14 O 2 2017
Talk to ME color *Vogue* v206 no11 p180 N 2016
An unseen environmental disaster N. M. Flores *America* v217 no6 p57 S 18 2017

Documentary photography
Cover *Time* v188 no22-23 pC1 N/D 2016
EYE ON PARADISE R. Mercer *Iceland Review* v54 no6 p52 N/D 2016
Most Influential Photos [Cover story] B. Goldberger color *Time*
v188 no22-23 p66 N/D 2016

Documentary photography—United States
FINDING BEAUTY IN DECAY S. Dalati color *Magazine Antiques* v183 no6 p122 N/D 2016

Documentary television programs
ENTERTAINMENT WEEKLY'S PARTNERS IN CRIME H. Goldblatt color *Entertainment Weekly* no1472 p10 Je 30 2017

Documentary television programs—Reviews
HOLLYWOOD AT WAR! A. Breznican color *Entertainment Weekly* no1459 p38 Mr 31 2017

Documentation
See also
    Catalogs
    Libraries
THE REGISTERED MORGAN D. Bennett bw color *Equus* no471 p43 D 2016

DODD, C. KENNETH, JR.
Overcoming Challenges to the Recovery of Declining Amphibian Populations in the United States *BioScience* v67 no2 p156 F 2017

Dodd, Jake
Flash Frozen D. L. NG bw *Field & Stream* v121 no8 p10 F/Mr 2017

Dodd, Martina
AFTER "CHOCOLATE CITY" R. CARTAGENA *Washingtonian Magazine* v52 no8 p21 My 2017

Dodd, Meredith
Creating better stories color *Christian Century* v134 no20 p10 S 27 2017

Dodds, Klaus J.
Science-based management in decline in the Southern Ocean bibl map *Science* v354 no6309 p185 O 14 2016

Dodds, Peter N.
Starving the enemy bibl diag *Science* v354 no6318 p1377 D 16 2016

Dodge, Andrew
MODEL STOCK PENS along a fascia color *Model Railroader* v84 no5 p36 My 2017
Use natural soil and rocks in scenery color *Model Railroader* v84 no9 p52 S 2017

Dodge, Diana—Awards
Summer Champions Crowned *In Stride* v11 no6 p14 N 2016

Dodge, J. Steven
Lasers expose hidden electronic order diag *Science* v356 no6335 p246 Ap 21 2017

DODGE, NATT N.
THE CHIRICAHUA IS A STUDY IN ROCKS AND HISTORY *Arizona Highways* v93 no9 p36 S 2017
THE WILDERNESS OF unreality *Arizona Highways* v93 no3 p28 Mr 2017

Dodge, Samuel
Brexit Could Hurt the Most Here graph map *Bloomberg Businessweek* no4527 p20 Je 19 2017

Dodge automobile
See also
    Challenger automobile
    Dodge Charger automobile
    Dodge Demon automobile
    Dodge trucks
    Magnum automobile
    Viper automobile
1989 Dodge Dakota Sport Convertible color *Popular Mechanics* p42 Jl 2017
9.65 AT 140 [Cover story] D. R. Glad color *Hot Rod* v70 no7 p22 Jl 2017
Automotive Archaeology: The Bee in the Garage R. Brutt color *Hot Rod* v70 no12 p14 D 2017
DROP THE HAMMER T. L. Byrd color *Hot Rod* v70 no12 p32 D 2017

Dodge automobile—Evaluation
2018 Dodge Challenger SRT Demon C. Walton color *Motor Trend* v69 no10 p18 O 2017
GONE IN 2.3 SECONDS S. Horaczek color *Popular Science* v289 no5 p32 S/O 2017
More Traction, Less Satisfaction D. Beard color *Car & Driver* v62 no11 p112 My 2017

One Tool to Rule Them All K. C. Colwell color *Car & Driver* v63 no4 p96 O 2017

Dodge Charger automobile

Barn Full of Mopars! R. Brutt color *Hot Rod* v70 no2 p16 F 2017

GARAGE C. Clonts, J. Lieberman et al chart color diag *Motor Trend* v69 no10 p102 O 2017

Rutledge Wood's 1970 CHARGER B. Gillogly color *Hot Rod* v70 no11 p34 N 2017

SALT CHARGER B. Gillogly color *Hot Rod* v70 no2 p52 F 2017

Dodge Coronet automobile

Barn Full of Mopars! R. Brutt color *Hot Rod* v70 no2 p16 F 2017

Dodge Daytona automobile

The ghost of Bobby Isaac G. Stunkard color *Hot Rod* v70 no9 p62 S 2017

The Last Wing Car A. Rogers bw color *Hot Rod* v70 no6 p40 Je 2017

Dodge Demon automobile

Ezra Dyer E. Dyer color *Car & Driver* v63 no4 p36 O 2017

Knockout Punch E. Perkins color *Hot Rod* v70 no7 p8 Jl 2017

Dodge trucks

Automotive Archaeology: Mopars in the Trees R. Brutt color *Hot Rod* v70 no11 p16 N 2017

Macho Wagon Heading to New Home R. Brutt color *Hot Rod* v70 no6 p24 Je 2017

Dodge trucks—Evaluation

REVEALED: 2017 RAM POWER WAGON [Cover story] M. EMERY color *Dirt Sports + Off-Road* v51 no7 p28 Jl 2017

DODGEN, DAVID

SAILING AND SCUBA DIVING color *Sail* v48 no5 p36 My 2017

Dodger Stadium (Los Angeles, Calif.)

Go West, Young Men M. GOLDBERG bw color *Weekly Standard* v22 no34 p38 My 15 2017

Dodo

The life and times of dodos revealed S. MILIUS color *Science News* v192 no4 p6 S 16 2017

Dods, Robert

A three-dimensional movie of structural changes in bacteriorhodopsin bibl diag graph *Science* v354 no6319 p1552 D 23 2016

Dodson, Angela P.

How It All Began *USA Today Magazine* v146 no2866 p22 Jl 2017

Dodson, P. Claire

HIDING IN PLAIN SIGHT cartoon *O, The Oprah Magazine* p125 Mr 2017

Dodson, T. C.

Eye patches: Protein assembly of index-gradient squid lenses bw color graph *Science* v357 no6351 p564 Ag 11 2017

Dodson family

Preserving a Marsh for People and Wildlife: The Dotson Family Marsh A. M. Alvarez and E. Pfuehler *Parks & Recreation* v52 no2 p28 F 2017

Doe, Emily

From the beginning, I was told I was a best case scenario *Glamour* v114 no12 p215 D 2016

Doe, Jane—Trials, litigation, etc.

Criminal Background Checks for Youth Sport Coaches J. C. Kozlowski *Parks & Recreation* v52 no6 p20 Je 2017

Doe, Marcus

Orphaned by War color *Christianity Today* v60 no9 p95 N 2016

Doellman, Justin—Interviews

Cinnaticin kid: justin doellman J. COHEN *Cincinnati Magazine* v50 no6 p86 Mr 2017

DOERPER, VICTORIA

Showering with Spiders *Orion Magazine* v35 no6 p9 N/D 2016

Doerr, Anthony

Running Through Time *New York Times Book Review* p1 O 2 2016

Doerschuk, Bob

Cole Offers Exquisite Take on Standards color *Downbeat* v84 no10 p23 O 2017

Film Chronicles Scott's Final Work color *Downbeat* v84 no3 p13 Mr 2017

DOEST, JASPER

Snow Monkeys color map *National Geographic* v230 no4 p140 O 2017

Doetsch, Fiona

Hypothalamic regulation of regionally distinct adult neural stem cells and neurogenesis diag *Science* v356 no6345 p1383 Je 30 2017

Dog adoption

THE POWER OF PETS *Successful Farming* v115 no4 p64 Mr 2017

SEARCH AND RESCUE: At first, it seemed clear who needed whom the most W. SHEPPARD *Virginia Living* v15 no6 p25 O 2017

Urban Wild: IN SLOWLY GENTRIFYING DETROIT, YOU MIGHT SEE A FOX, OR EVEN A COYOTE, BUT WHERE HAVE ALL THE STRAY DOGS GONE? L. BERNSTEIN-MACHLAY *American Scholar* v86 no4 p76 Aut 2017

Dog attacks—Lawsuits & claims

The Case Of the Massive Guard Dogs V. GLEMBOCKI *Reader's Digest* v188 no1125 p29 N 2016

Dog barking

Small-Space Living N. B. McGough and P. S. York color *Southern Living* v52 no9 p33 S 2017

Dog behavior

BEWARE OF... HUGS? color *Women's Health* v14 no9 p29 N 2017

DECODING DOG-SPEAK E. BATTAGLIA *Martha Stewart Living* no267 p68 S 2016

Dog Behavior G. Paul *Skeptical Inquirer* v41 no1 p63 Ja/F 2017

A Dog's Life T. Flanagan color *Sail* v48 no8 p12 Ag 2017

Fear Aggression Usually Kicks In During Canine Adolescence *Your Dog (10780343)* v22 no10 p4 O 2016

GETTING INSIDE FIDO'S HEAD N. Strochlic color *National Geographic* v232 no4 p16 O 2017

pack mentality j. weber color *Bike Magazine* v24 no7 p44 S 2017

Teach Safe Snuggling S. Bower color *Good Housekeeping* v264 no5 p142 My 2017

Unleashed cartoon *National Geographic Kids* no472 p32 Ag 2017

Dog breeding

Siberia yields earliest evidence for dog breeding D. Grimm color *Science* v356 no6341 p896 Je 1 2017

The United States of Dogs G. Norman color *Weekly Standard* v22 no24 p30 F 27 2017

Dog breeding—History

The Dark Origins of Dog Breeding O. B. Waxman *Time* v189 no7/8 p27 F 27 2017

Dog breeds

See also

Bulldog

Terriers

The BEST DOG for YOU T. DASWICK bw color *Men's Health* v32 no6 p126 Ag 2017

GIANTS AMONG US: The city isn't built for extra-large dogs--but they're definitely built for the city M. D. G. Kaplan *Washingtonian Magazine* v52 no8 p207 My 2017

JE T'AIME FRENCHIES A. HEROLD *Los Angeles Magazine* p118 Mr 2017

MY DOGS R. VRABEL color *Popular Mechanics* p94 Ap 2017

Small-Space Living N. B. McGough and P. S. York color *Southern Living* v52 no9 p33 S 2017

Tree of dog breeds sheds light on canine history color *Science* v356 no6336 p355 Ap 28 2017

THE ULTIMATE MEN'S HEALTH DOG color *Men's Health* v32 no6 p120 Ag 2017

Dog collars—Evaluation

1939 PET GEAR L. HEDRICK color *Better Homes & Gardens* v95 no8 p184 Ag 2017

Accent the FURRY CREW *Sea Magazine* v108 no12 p43 D 2016

Dog day care

BEST OF HALL OF FAME *Washingtonian Magazine* v52 no11 p162 Ag 2017

Dog diseases

QUESTIONS OF DIGESTION J. Szabo color *Amazing Wellness* v9 no3 p76 EarlySumm 2017

Tree of dog breeds sheds light on canine history color *Science* v356 no6336 p355 Ap 28 2017

Dog equipment

Puppy love color *Equus* no481 p65 O 2017

Dog food

BONE APPÉTIT: Revery's chef-designed dog menu caters to a ruff crowd B. POWERS *Indianapolis Monthly* v40 no11 p39

Jl 2017
Canine care questions answered M. Freckleton color *Equus* no481 p62 O 2017

Dog genetics
DNA variants tied to dog sociability T. H. SAEY color *Science News* v190 no9 p12 O 29 2016
Early farmers expanded dogs' diet *Science* v354 no6313 p687 N 11 2016
'Friendliness' genes identified in dogs A. YEAGER *Science News* v192 no2 p8 Ag 19 2017

Dog genetics—Research
The Origins of Dogs G. TARLACH bw cartoon color graph map *Discover* v27 no10 p32 D 2016

Dog grooming industry—Equipment & supplies
Making Bath Time Better *Your Dog (10780343)* v22 no10 p11 O 2016

Dog industry
Rescue from the Meat Farm: Flying Dogs to Safety P. RORK *Idaho Magazine* v16 no11 p6 Ag 2017

Dog owners
See also
  Women dog owners
A COMMUNITY, UNLEASHED: The NoMa dog park opens this fall. It got built thanks to 400 neighbors who sneaked onto a vacant, muddy lot D. Bruno *Washingtonian Magazine* v53 no1 p213 O 2017
HOW TO KEEP THE DOG-PARK PEACE G. Cook *Washingtonian Magazine* v52 no9 p195 Je 2017
SEARCH AND RESCUE: At first, it seemed clear who needed whom the most W. SHEPPARD *Virginia Living* v15 no6 p25 O 2017
Where the Dogs Are *Your Dog (10780343)* v22 no10 p14 O 2016

Dog racing
RACING WIENER DOGS S. BAHR color *Indianapolis Monthly* v42 no2 p16 O 2017

Dog shows
DECK THE PAWS T. MALONE *Atlanta* v56 no8 p45 D 2016
Mardi Gras With Mavis color *AARP: The Magazine* v59 no2A p11 F/Mr 2016

Dog vaccination
Canine Campers N. B. McGough and P. S. York color *Southern Living* v52 no7 p35 Jl 2017

Dog walking
The Diplomacy of Dog Walking in Russia A. FERRIS-ROTMAN color *Foreign Policy* no225 p20 Jl/Ag 2017
LEASHED J. Torres color *New Yorker* v92 no32 p60 O 10 2016
Walk the Walk K. Stock color *Bloomberg Businessweek* no4503 p72 D 12 2016

Dogfighting
HOW TO KEEP THE DOG-PARK PEACE G. Cook *Washingtonian Magazine* v52 no9 p195 Je 2017
Lost and Found J. Fuchs and T. Keith color *Sports Illustrated* v126 no12 p20 My 1 2017

Dogfish
UNDER-DOGFISH J. Cermele color *Field & Stream* v121 no8 p20 F/Mr 2017

Dogfish Head Craft Brewery Inc.
The Founder of Dogfish Head on Flouting a 500- Year-Old Beer Law S. Calagione *Harvard Business Review Digital Articles* p2 My 5 2016

Doghouses
The Canine Cottage K. Owen color diag *Southern Living* v52 no5 p54 My 2017
IN THE DOG HOUSE R. Bacher color *Good Housekeeping* v263 no5 p208 N 2016
my night in the doghouse C. Alter *Washingtonian Magazine* v52 no11 p60 Ag 2017

Dogic, Zvonimir
Transition from turbulent to coherent flows in confined three-dimensional active fluids color *Science* v355 no6331 p1284 Mr 24 2017

Dogma
Present in Every Page R. E. Lauder *Commonweal* v144 no16 p39 O 6 2017

Dogs
See also

Dog breeds
Feral dogs
Beat the Heat A. Levi color *Health* v31 no5 p72 Je 2017
BEWARE OF... HUGS? color *Women's Health* v14 no9 p29 N 2017
Canis Sapiens E. GRAHAM *American Scholar* v86 no3 p15 Summ 2017
Conversing with Canines: THINK CAT IN THE HAT FOR TALKING TO DOGS S. COREN *Psychology Today* v50 no5 p73 S/O 2017
Decode Your Pet's Body Language L. Murray color *Health* v31 no3 p71 Ap 2017
Good Girl A. Green color *Vogue* v207 no11 p96 N 2017
The Gratitude Meter Z. Donaldson color *O, The Oprah Magazine* p26 S 2017
THE GRID: ANIMAL ANTICS *Saturday Evening Post* v289 no5 p26 S/O 2017
IN THE MINDS OF DOGS *Psychology Today* v50 no5 p70 S/O 2017
Leashed To the Here and Now: DO DOGS KNOW THAT WE KNOW THAT THEY'RE THINKING OF US? J. Bradshaw *Psychology Today* v50 no5 p90 S/O 2017
Man's Best Fiend T. D. Parry *History Today* v66 no12 p50 D 2016
MH WORLD color *Men's Health* v32 no4 p6 My 2017
Mutt Morality: DOGS KNOW HOW TO HAVE FUN, AND EN-CODED IN THEIR ANTICS IS A DEEP UNDERSTANDING OF FAIR PLAY M. BEKOFF *Psychology Today* v50 no5 p77 S/O 2017
Naughty PETS K. MILLER *National Geographic Kids* no466 p7 D 2016/Ja 2017
A New Case for Our First Friendship B. Lang *Discover* v27 no10 p6 D 2016
ONE IN FIVE color *Better Homes & Gardens* v95 no5 p156 My 2017
Posthole M. Grabijas, M. Englert et al color *Powder* v45 no4 p146 D 2016
Product Spotlights color *Better Nutrition* p63 My 2017
Puppy Love D. Paul *Indianapolis Monthly* v40 no7 p144 Mr 2017
Pups & Personal Space N. B. McGough and P. York color *Southern Living* v52 no3 p26 Mr 2017
ROVER, COME HOME! G. Cook *Washingtonian Magazine* v52 no5 p139 F 2017
#RWDOGRUN color *Runner's World* v52 no4 p12 My 2017
Secrets of the Canine Mind J. Kluger color *Time* v189 no19 p42 My 22 2017
THE SLOUGH A. McKEAN color *Outdoor Life* v224 no6 p48 Ag 2017
SURVIVAL OF THE CUTEST H. HERZOG *Psychology Today* v49 no6 p19 N/D 2016
Taking the IQ Test: ONE OF THE HARDEST TRICKS IS COM-ING UP WITH A WAY TO MEASURE DOG INTELLIGENCE R. ARDEN *Psychology Today* v50 no5 p74 S/O 2017
THIS HERO WEARS FUR T. DASWICK color *Men's Health* v32 no6 p122 Ag 2017
This Just In J. Zorthian *Time* v190 no4 p19 Jl 24 2017
Unleashed color *National Geographic Kids* no465 p38 N 2016
Water Dog M. PETERS color *Power & Motoryacht* v33 no4 p28 Ap 2017
WAYPOINT color *Outdoor Life* v224 no6 p7 Ag 2017
Why I Hate My Dog E. Egan color *Glamour* v114 no12 p174 D 2016
Winterproof Your Pup L. Murray color *Health* v31 no1 p70 Ja 2017
Your True Stories M. SUE LEEPER, L. ADAMS et al *Reader's Digest* v188 no1126 p30 D 2016/Ja 2017

Dogs Go Wolf (Short story)
DOGS GO WOLF L. Groff cartoon color *New Yorker* v93 no25 p68 Ag 28 2017

Dogs in motion pictures
NEWLY AVAILABLE MOVIES J. HOGAN *TV Guide* v65 no43 p40 O 16 2017
TORI THE DOG S. Li color *Entertainment Weekly* no1454/1455 p88 F 24 2017

Dogs' injuries
Canine care questions answered M. Freckleton color *Equus* no481 p62 O 2017

Dogs on television
JAGGER THE DOG N. Serrao color *Entertainment Weekly* no1466 p50 My 19 2017

Dogs—Competitions
DECK THE PAWS T. MALONE *Atlanta* v56 no8 p45 D 2016
FUN FESTIVALS IN CABIN COUNTRY color *Cabin Living* p14 Je 2017
Sweet Smell of Success D. HARVEY *Los Angeles Magazine* p24 Ap 2017

Dogs—Equipment & supplies
Welcome to My Doghouse color *InStyle* v23 no12 p290 N 2016

Dogs—Equipment & supplies—Evaluation
Accent the FURRY CREW *Sea Magazine* v108 no12 p43 D 2016

Dogs—Food
Breaking the Rules L. Lindner *Your Dog (10780343)* v22 no10 p2 O 2016
Going to the dogs color *Equus* no476 p65 My 2017
home & help S. Anderson, J. M. Bernstein et al img *New York* p96 Mr 6 2017
Homemade Dog Food M. Straus *Mother Earth News* no280 p78 F/Mr 2017

Dogs—Health
Beyond basic care L. Bonner color *Equus* no476 p62 My 2017
Breaking the Rules L. Lindner *Your Dog (10780343)* v22 no10 p2 O 2016
DOG DAYS OF WINTER E. BATTAGLIA *Martha Stewart Living* no270 p82 D 2016

Dogs—Humor
Laughter cartoon color diag *Reader's Digest* v190 no1132 p74 Jl/Ag 2017
SKETCHBOOK G. BOOTH cartoon *New Yorker* v92 no41 p59 D 12 2016

Dogsleds
TETHERED S. Mait and J. Queri color *Skiing* p36 D 2016

Dog's Purpose, A (Film)
A Dog's Purpose L. Greenblatt color *Entertainment Weekly* no1451/1452 p88 F 3-10 2017
Humans Give Meaning to A Dog's Purpose S. Zacharek color *Time* v189 no4 p52 F 6 2017
The New Boy Next Door D. Coggan color *Entertainment Weekly* no1450 p44 Ja 27 2017

Dogs—Services for
The Urbanist: The Best & Worst Cities to Be a Dog img *New York* v49 no15 p22 Jl 25 2016

Dogs—Social aspects
A Helping Paw M. W. Schwartz color *Missouri Life* v44 no2 p16 Ap 2017
WOMAN'S BEST FRIEND color *Women's Health* v14 no8 p56 O 2017

Dogs—Therapeutic use
happiness is a warm puppy S. Bower color *Good Housekeeping* v264 no3 p156 Mr 2017

Doherty, Bobby
ANT FARM TO TABLE img *New York* v49 no15 p36 Jl 25 2016
THE BEST BET img *New York* v50 no10 p67 My 15 2017
BEST BETS *New York* v49 no15 p63 Jl 25 2016
Be Your Own Magician img *New York* v49 no19 p86 S 19 2016
Brazilian for Breakfast img *New York* v49 no19 p77 S 19 2016
Games: Will Leitch img *New York* v50 no10 p30 My 15 2017
THE LOOK BOOK img *New York* v49 no15 p65 Jl 25 2016
The National Interest: Jonathan Chait img *New York* v50 no10 p17 My 15 2017
Pickled Napa Cabbage img *New York* v49 no15 p67 Jl 25 2016
Pistachio-Cherry Twice-Baked Croissants img *New York* v49 no19 p74 S 19 2016

Doherty, Brian
American Communism bw color *Reason* v48 no7 p56 D 2016
CASSANDRA OF THE CRASH color *Reason* v49 no3 p71 Jl 2017
DID THE LIBERTARIAN PARTY BLOW IT IN 2016? color *Reason* v48 no9 p44 F 2017
FIRE!!: THE ZORA NEALE HURSTON STORY color *Reason* v49 no3 p68 Jl 2017
FROM THE ARCHIVES cartoon *Reason* v49 no2 p70 Je 2017
The Great James Buchanan Conspiracy color *Reason* v49 no5 p66 O 2017

REVISITING RESTRICTIONS ON THE RIGHT TO BEAR ARMS *Reason* v48 no11 p15 Ap 2017
SEASTEADING IN PARADISE color diag map *Reason* v49 no2 p28 Je 2017
Selling the Silk Road Soap Opera color *Reason* v49 no4 p68 Ag/S 2017
'TO LIVE AND LET LIVE' color map *Reason* v49 no2 p36 Je 2017

DOHERTY, MAGGIE
BIG DISTURBANCES bw *Nation* v305 no2 p27 Jl 17 2017
Yes All Women color *New Republic* v248 no4 p58 Ap 2017

DOHERTY, MIKE
ALL OUR WRONG TODAYS color *Maclean's* v130 no2 p69 Mr 2017
THE ATTENTION MERCHANTS color *Maclean's* v129 no43 p61 O 31 2016
'Just lie on your back and write' color *Maclean's* v130 no4 p64 My 2017
THE MUSEUM AT THE END OF THE WORLD color *Maclean's* v129 no41 p57 O 17 2016

Doherty, Patrick
Lee Rubin: Our mentor and role model *Science* v355 no6327 p806 F 24 2017

Doherty, Rebecca
3 Ways Social Entrepreneurs Can Solve Their Talent Problem *Harvard Business Review Digital Articles* p2 Je 29 2016

DOHERTY, SEAN
HER BROTHER'S KEEPER color *Surfer* v58 no1 p58 Ap 2017
Oscar Billy Pippen Wright, 41 color *Surfer* v58 no6 p40 O 2017

DOHERTY, TIM S.
Making a New Dog? *BioScience* v67 no4 p374 Ap 2017

Doherty, Tom
Swimming in Sustainability in Loretto *Parks & Recreation* v51 no10 p40 O 2016

Dohle, Markus
THE FRANKFURT BOOK FAIR IS TRENDING UP A. R. ALBANESE color *Publishers Weekly* v264 no39 p32 S 25 2017

Dohlman, Erik
Historical Analysis of MPP-Dairy Suggests Limited Impact on Average Margins but Considerable Potential for Risk Reduction *Amber Waves: The Economics of Food, Farming, Natural Resources, & Rural America* p7 F 2017

Dohnalkova, Alice
Bottom-up construction of a superstructure in a porous uranium-organic crystal color graph *Science* v356 no6338 p624 My 12 2017

Dohrn, Walt
TROLLS T. J. Norton color *Sound & Vision* v82 no7 p69 S 2017

Dohyun Im
A three-dimensional movie of structural changes in bacteriorhodopsin bibl diag graph *Science* v354 no6319 p1552 D 23 2016

Doilies
Your New Summer Uniform: The Doily Dress A. Edwards Walker color *Glamour* v114 no7 p35 Jl 2016

DOKA, CHRISTINA
YOUR ONE WILD AND PRECIOUS SUMMER color *O, The Oprah Magazine* p86 Je 2017

Dokholyan, Nikolay V.
Engineering extrinsic disorder to control protein activity in living cells bibl color *Science* v354 no6318 p1441 D 16 2016

DOKKEN, TOM
THE UNDERDOG color *Outdoor Life* v224 no6 p46 Ag 2017

DOKTER, ADRIAAN M.
From Agricultural Benefits to Aviation Safety: Realizing the Potential of Continent-Wide Radar Networks *BioScience* v67 no10 p912 O 2017

Doktori, Daniel
Why Lawyers Make Good Early-Stage Startup Hires *Harvard Business Review Digital Articles* p2 My 2 2016

Do Kwon, Young
Trispecific broadly neutralizing HIV antibodies mediate potent SHIV protection in macaques color graph *Science* v357 no6359 p85 O 6 2017

DOLAN, JAY P.
A YEAR OF EXTREMES *America* v215 no15 p32 N 14 2016

DOLAN, JON

THE 50 GREATEST CONCERTS OF THE LAST 50 YEARS bw color *Rolling Stone* no1286 p30 My 4 2017

Essential Chuck color *Rolling Stone* no1285 p36 Ap 20 2017

Haim's Bright Retro-Pop Future color *Rolling Stone* no1291/1292 p63 Jl 13 2017

The Hits and Heartache of Jimmy Webb bw *Rolling Stone* no1285 p14 Ap 20 2017

Hot Band Lvl Up color *Rolling Stone* no1274 p36 N 17 2016

Making 'Hamilton' Even Greater Again color *Rolling Stone* no1276 p61 D 15 2016

Randy Newman Makes Irony Great Again color *Rolling Stone* no1293 p54 Ag 10 2017

The Real Lives of Rock Moms bw color *Rolling Stone* no1284 p19 Ap 6 2017

Ryan Adams Relives His Wonder Years color *Rolling Stone* no1281/1282 p52 F 23 2017

The Shins' New Adventures in Alt-Pop Romance color *Rolling Stone* no1283 p50 Mr 23 2017

Sting Makes a Surprise Return to Rock & Roll color *Rolling Stone* no1274 p58 N 17 2016

The xx's Dreamy Late-Night Rapture color *Rolling Stone* no1278/1279 p49 Ja 12 2017

Dolan, Kerry A.

BIG BET PHILANTHROPY color graph map *Forbes* v198 no8 p100 D 20 2016

China's Richest color map *Forbes* v198 no7 p28 N 29 2016

LESSONS AND IDEAS BY THE 100 GREATEST LIVING BUSINESS MINDS color *Forbes* v200 no3 p115 S 28 2017

THE WORLD'S BILLIONAIRES bw color diag graph map *Forbes* v199 no3 p84 Mr 28 2017

Dolan, Michael

AN AMERICAN PLACE *American History* v52 no1 p72 Ap 2017

DEPTH OF FIELD bw color *American History* v52 no4 p70 O 2017

The Dry Tortugas... color *American History* v52 no4 p72 O 2017

HE WASN'T ALL RIGHT AFTER ALL, JACK *American History* v52 no1 p70 Ap 2017

Timbisha... color *American History* v52 no2 p72 Je 2017

THE UNFORSAKEN bw color *American History* v52 no3 p70 Ag 2017

Dolan, Robert J.

Gun Manufacturers Need to Lead Change, Not Just Follow the Law *Harvard Business Review Digital Articles* p2 Mr 23 2016

Dolan, Sandi

The Customer-Service Rep E. Steuer *New York Times Magazine* p43 F 26 2017

Dolan-Leach, Caite

The Pie-Chart Review! I. Biedenharn color diag *Entertainment Weekly* no1454/1455 p103 F 24 2017

Dolby Laboratories Inc.

All About Atmos A. L. GRIFFIN diag *Sound & Vision* v82 no6 p19 Jl/Ag 2017

Dolce & Gabbana Srl

Dolce & Gabbana slides, $995 color *Vogue* v207 no6 p162 Je 2017

Gwen Stefani HER BEST EVER E. Wilson color *InStyle* v24 no3 p162 Mr 2017

Paint It Black N. R. POLLOCK *Architectural Record* v205 no4 p162 Ap 2017

Dolce, Joe

Reefer Gladness M. TAIBBI *New York Times Book Review* p11 D 18 2016

Dold, Kristen

DEFICIENCY NATION B12 color *Women's Health* v14 no7 p82 S 2017

END ON A HIGH NOTE color *Runner's World* v52 no9 p80 O 2017

Game Changers color *Women's Health* v14 no8 p122 O 2017

Get More for Your Co-Pay color *Men's Health* v31 no10 p88 D 2016

The Gut Diaries color *Women's Health* v13 no10 p78 D 2016

HAPPIER, HEALTHIER, WELLTHIER color *Women's Health* v14 no4 p89 My 2017

NEVER PAY FULL PRICE AGAIN color *Men's Health* v31 no10 p73 D 2016

New At-Home Health Tests—Rated color *Men's Health* v32 no7 p86 S 2017

PERPETUAL MOTION cartoon *Runner's World* v52 no1 p40 Ja/F 2017

PORTRAIT OF A Naked Woman chart color graph *Women's Health* v14 no7 p130 S 2017

The Snacking Diaries color *Women's Health* v14 no2 p106 Mr 2017

The Strength Secret Most Men Ignore bw color *Men's Health* v31 no10 p56 D 2016

TAKE THE PLUNGE color *Runner's World* v52 no7 p14 Ag 2017

THE WELLTHIEST CITIES IN AMERICA bw color *Women's Health* v14 no6 p120 Jl 2017

DOLE, ELIZABETH

REMEMBERING DIANA color *AARP: The Magazine* v60 no5A p50 Ag/S 2017

Dole, Robert J., 1923-

Can Bob Dole Make America Great Again? C. Bonanos img *New York* v49 no19 p12 S 19 2016

Dölen, Gül

Gating of social reward by oxytocin in the ventral tegmental area color graph *Science* v357 no6358 p1406 S 29 2017

Dolesh, Richard J.

Climate Change Is Changing the Face of Outdoor Recreation *Parks & Recreation* v52 no10 p30 O 2017

Climate Change, Parks and Health *Parks & Recreation* v52 no6 p30 Je 2017

Disasters! Are You Prepared? *Parks & Recreation* v51 no11 p48 N 2016

Endangered: The Rusty Patched Bumblebee *Parks & Recreation* v52 no3 p30 Mr 2017

The Gathering Pension Storm *Parks & Recreation* v52 no2 p34 F 2017

Green Infrastructure *Parks & Recreation* v52 no4 p42 Ap 2017

Green Workers Certification May Create New Training Opportunities *Parks & Recreation* v51 no10 p54 O 2016

In Appreciation of David Lose *Parks & Recreation* v52 no8 p64 Ag 2017

Monarchs Visit NRPA Waystation *Parks & Recreation* v51 no10 p96 O 2016

Our Disappearing Wildlife: What Parks Can Do About It *Parks & Recreation* v52 no1 p26 Ja 2017

What It Means to Serve on the NRPA Board of Directors *Parks & Recreation* v52 no10 p44 O 2017

Dolfman, Michael L.

Nursing and the Great Recession bibl *Monthly Labor Review* p1 Jl 2017

Dolge, Adam

Weeknight Wonders color *Southern Living* v52 no9 p123 S 2017

DOLGIN, REBECCA

COZY UP TO THIS *Martha Stewart Living* no268 p48 O 2016

HAPPY TO HOST color *Martha Stewart Living* no275 p28 Je 2017

Dolgoff, Stephanie

Bad Romance *Scholastic Choices* v32 no5 p16 F 2017

grab bags of awesome color *Good Housekeeping* v264 no5 p140 My 2017

is your kid destined for greatness? *Parents* v91 no11 p70 N 2016

The Real Reason I Work Out color *Health* v31 no2 p120 Mr 2017

teach your child to be a FORCE FOR GOOD color *Good Housekeeping* v264 no4 p138 Ap 2017

Dolgova, Evgenia

Can 10 Minutes of Meditation Make You More Creative? *Harvard Business Review Digital Articles* p2 Ag 29 2017

D'Olivo, J. C.

Observation of a large-scale anisotropy in the arrival directions of cosmic rays above 8 × 1018 eV *Science* v357 no6357 p1266 S 22 2017

Dolkos, Paul

Take your best shot bw color *Model Railroader* v84 no11 p46 N 2017

TRACKS IN THE STREET [Cover story] color *Model Railroader* v84 no10 p30 O 2017

Doll, Jen

Enough With the Total Honesty! color *Glamour* v115 no4 p142 Ap 2017

girl on top color *InStyle* v23 no13 p242 D 2016

How to Be Yourself in Love and Sex color *Glamour* v115 no3

p137 Mr 2017

Y.A. Realistic Fiction *New York Times Book Review* p34 N 13 2016

Dollar (United States currency)

Dollar So Ripped, It Might Actually Rip P. Coy, I. Cota et al color *Bloomberg Businessweek* no4506 p12 Ja 9 2017

Is the Dollar in a Trump Slump? L. Nguyen and L. C. McCormick graph *Bloomberg Businessweek* no4533 p30 Ag 7 2017

Mind-Blowing Facts About Your Money B. SPECKTOR *Reader's Digest* v189 no1128 p128 Mr 2017

Strong Dollar, Weak Thinking R. L. Martin *Harvard Business Review Digital Articles* p2 O 13 2015

WHAT A WEAKER DOLLAR MEANS TO YOU D. FONDA color *Kiplinger's Personal Finance* v71 no11 p10 N 2017

Dollar (United States currency)—History—20th century

How a Briton Created the Almighty Dollar R. Hurowitz *History Today* v67 no1 p6 Ja 2017

Dollar, Ellen Painter

Madness in Civilization: A Cultural History of Insanity, from the Bible to Freud, from the Madhouse to Modern Medicine/Madness: American Protestant Responses to Mental Illness color *Christian Century* v133 no21 p51 O 12 2016

Dollar cost averaging

Go Ahead—Invest Already W. Updegrave color diag *Money* v46 no4 p31 My 2017

Dollar Shave Club Inc.

Unilever's Big Strategic Bet on the Dollar Shave Club B. Chakravorti *Harvard Business Review Digital Articles* p2 Jl 28 2016

Dollase, Mark

BIG DEAL T. BRAND *Indianapolis Monthly* v40 no7 p32 Mr 2017

Doller, Trish

In a Perfect World *Publishers Weekly* v264 no14 p77 Ap 3. 2017

Dollinger, Sebastian

Beyond Basic T. Patterson bw color *Bloomberg Businessweek* no4541 p64 O 9 2017

Dolls

Yes, We Ken C. Weaver color *GQ: Gentlemen's Quarterly* v97 no7 p74 Jl 2017

Dolls—History

DOLLS THROUGH THE AGES C. KOLB bw *New Orleans Magazine* v51 no2 p42 D 2016

Doll's House, A (Theatrical production)

DIAL-A-FEMINIST M. Schulman cartoon *New Yorker* v93 no14 p32 My 22 2017

Home Free A. GREEN color *Vogue* v207 no4 p188 Ap 2017

THE IBSEN MYSTERY J. KELLY color *Vanity Fair* v59 no5 p94 Ap 2017

REWIND H. ALS cartoon *New Yorker* v93 no12 p74 My 8 2017

THE THEATRE *New Yorker* v93 no15 p11 My 29 2017

Dolly Sods (W. Va.)

Mountain Magic N. PIPENBERG map *Backpacker* p24 Je 2017

Dolman, Everett Carl

Can Science End War? B. R. Allenby color *Issues in Science & Technology* v33 no1 p91 Fall 2016

Dolnick, Ben

Cold Showers *New York Times Magazine* p26 Jl 23 2017

Dolnick, Edward

Baby Steps A. VERGHESE *New York Times Book Review* p16 Je 25 2017

Range Rovers *New York Times Book Review* p37 Je 4 2017

The Seeds of Life: From Aristotle to da Vinci, from Shark's Teeth to Frog's Pants, the Long and Strange Quest to Discover Where Babies Come From L. A. MARSCHALL color *Natural History* v125 no5 p46 My 2017

The Seeds of Life: From Aristotle to da Vinci, from Shark's Teeth to Frog's Pants, the Long and Strange Quest to Discover Where Babies Come From *Publishers Weekly* v264 no14 p65 Ap 3. 2017

The Seeds of Life S. Bay *Science* v356 no6342 p1009 Je 9 2017

Sex Cells J. S. GORDON *Commentary* v144 no2 p53 S 2017

DOLNICK, SAM

COCA CRYSTAL *New York Times Magazine* p59 D 25 2016

Dolomite Alps (Italy)—Description & travel

Peak Lunching J. MURPHY color *Conde Nast Traveler* v52 no2 p42 F 2017

Dolores (Film)

One Tough (Rebel, Activist, Feminist) Mother: The documentary Dolores shines a light on an overlooked hero of farmworkers' and women's rights L. BARCA *Ms.* v27 no3 p46 Fall 2017

Sundance 2017: Of Snow and Anguish B. R. Rich *Film Quarterly* v70 no4 p99 Summ 2017

DOLOWY, JOEY

THANKS FOR THE RIDE color *Bicycling* v58 no10 p15 N/D 2017

Dolphins

Dams threaten rare Mekong dolphins R. L. J. Brownell, R. R. Reeves et al bibl color *Science* v355 no6327 p805 F 24 2017

The Secret Language Of Dolphins C. BOYER color *National Geographic Kids* no471 p14 Je/Jl 2017

What Would Happen? C. BOYER cartoon *National Geographic Kids* no470 p7 My 2017

DOMANICK, JOE

A Change In the Force: A RUBBER-STAMP COMMITTEE NO MORE, THE LOS ANGELES POLICE COMMISSION HAS BEEN WORKING TO TRANSFORM LAPD POLICY. MATTHEW JOHNSON IS A BIG REASON WHY *Los Angeles Magazine* p68 Ag 2017

Domanski, Konrad

Incorporation of rubidium cations into perovskite solar cells improves photovoltaic performance bibl graph *Science* v354 no6309 p206 O 14 2016

Domar

advice every new mom needs [Cover story] color *Parents* v92 no7 p32 Jl 2017

Domar, Alice

advice every new mom needs [Cover story] color *Parents* v92 no7 p32 Jl 2017

Domart, Marie-Charlotte

A switch from canonical to noncanonical autophagy shapes B cell responses bibl graph *Science* v355 no6325 p641 F 10 2017

Dombrowski, Chris

Body of Water T. Davis color *Orion Magazine* v35 no6 p58 N/D 2016

DOMBROWSKI, LISA

Film Is Like a Battleground: Sam Fuller's War Movies *Film Quarterly* v70 no4 p130 Summ 2017

Domcke, Silvia

Impact of cytosine methylation on DNA binding specificities of human transcription factors diag *Science* v356 no6337 p502 My 5 2017

DOMENECH, BEN

Mythical President color *National Review* v69 no3 p43 F 20 2017

Domenech, Dan

A Look at the Educational Structure in Cuba *Education Digest* v83 no3 p57 N 2017

Domenech, Trystan

High-performance vitrimers from commodity thermoplastics through dioxaborolane metathesis color diag *Science* v356 no6333 p62 Ap 7 2017

Domes (Architecture)

Dome sweet dome M. Rosano color *Canadian Geographic* v137 no2 p26 Mr/Ap 2017

Domestic animals

See also

Cats

Dogs

Horses

Pets

CATS GONE WILD P. S. TAYLOR color *Maclean's* v130 no3 p50 Ap 2017

Dog Years color *Outdoor Life* v224 no6 p10 Ag 2017

ROVER, COME HOME! G. Cook *Washingtonian Magazine* v52 no5 p139 F 2017

Domestic architecture

See also

Apartment buildings

Beach houses

House construction

Log cabin design & construction

Ranch houses

Room layout (Dwellings)

AFFORDABLE CRAFTSMAN color *Arts & Crafts Homes & the Revival* v12 no2 p18 Spr 2017

Being There C. McGuigan *Architectural Record* v205 no6 p18 Je 2017

Boot Camp Beauty D. Peak color diag *Log Home Living* v34 no2 p70 Mr 2017

build color *Timber Home Living* p36 2017 Annual Buyers

COMFORT ZONE: Stately and elegant, Four Acres in Charlottesville is also a warm and welcoming family retreat V. HUBBARD *Virginia Living* v15 no4 p94 Je 2017

DETAIL YOUR DIGS S. Carlsen cartoon *Men's Health* v32 no3 p28 Ap 2017

Eye on Design S. BROWN *Timber Home Living* v27 no2 p6 Ap 2017

Facade-Off *Lapham's Quarterly* v10 no1 p82 Wint 2017

Family Friendly L. Cutrone color *New Orleans Magazine* v51 no6 p54 Ap 2017

FLOOR PLAN gallery color diag *Log Home Living* p96 2018 Annual Buyers Guide

GLOSSARY *Lapham's Quarterly* v10 no1 p220 Wint 2017

Great Old Capes color *Old House Journal* v45 no1 p36 F 2017

HANDCRAFTERS' gallery color diag *Log Home Living* p119 2018 Annual Buyers Guide

HEX APPEAL L. MURTHA *Cincinnati Magazine* v50 no8 p30 My 2017

Historic District / Old Wethersfield, Conn D. J. Silber bw color *Old House Journal* v45 no1 p34 F 2017

HISTORIC SPACES, MODERN FACES: New uses for rooms from bygone eras W. Sheppard *Virginia Living* v15 no4 p83 Je 2017

Home Loans *Lapham's Quarterly* v10 no1 p10 Wint 2017

HOME STRETCH: luxe outdoor living spaces create opportunities for gracious year-round entertaining V. Hubbard *Virginia Living* v15 no4 p81 Je 2017

HOT MOD M. LAWLER color *Chicago* v66 no5 p32 My 2017

A House Rescued Simplicity Restored B. D. Coleman color *Old House Journal* v45 no5 p14 Ag 2017

Lake Minded S. Logan color diag *Log Home Living* v34 no2 p24 Mr 2017

Let's Get Ready to Build color *Log Home Living* p60 2018 Annual Buyers Guide

Making History S. D. Albert color diag *Log Home Living* v34 no2 p58 Mr 2017

MY CHILDHOOD HOME J. Waters *Lapham's Quarterly* v10 no1 p206 Wint 2017

A New Old Farmhouse Melinda and David cartoon diag *Log Home Living* v34 no2 p40 Mr 2017

Old Town N. Moreland bw cartoon color *Old House Journal* v45 no2 p34 Ap 2017

ON THE MARKET *Virginia Living* v15 no4 p87 Je 2017

professional services *Design Center Sourcebook* p140 2016

Refining Rustic on the River cartoon color diag *Log Home Living* v33 no9 p42 D 2016

Remuddling color *Old House Journal* v45 no3 p88 My 2017

Resources *Old House Journal* v45 no5 p79 Ag 2017

Saratoga Springs/New York A. M. Strauss bw color *Old House Journal* v45 no5 p34 Ag 2017

Second Nature D. Peak color diag *Log Home Living* v34 no5 p26 Jl 2017

SITE SPECIFIC L. Cutrone color *Louisiana Life* v38 no1 p26 S/O 2017

Stack It Up color *Log Home Living* p68 2018 Annual Buyers Guide

Stick and Shingle color *Old House Journal* v45 no5 p36 Ag 2017

TREASURE ISLAND color *Vanity Fair* v59 no7 p49 Summ 2017

Domestic architecture—Design & construction
See also
Small houses—Design & construction
MAN OF THE HOUSE P. HALDEMAN *Los Angeles Magazine* v61 no11 p134 N 2016

SHIP TO SHORE D. THOMAS color *Architectural Digest* v74 no1 p196 Ja 2017

Domestic architecture—Designs & plans
Earth Tones A. HEROLD *Los Angeles Magazine* p36 F 2017

Living Large By Living Small S. FITZ-GERALD *Los Angeles Magazine* p52 F 2017

MASTER CLASS L. S. Rimini and R. Peregalli bw color *Architectural Digest* v74 no1 p176 Ja 2017

Domestic architecture—England
Home in On A. SESSA color *Conde Nast Traveler* v51 no11 p54 D 2016

Domestic architecture—Evaluation
beach boys M. DIAMOND color *Architectural Digest* v74 no3 p108 Mr 2017

Big Sky Beauty color *Timber Home Living* p38 2017 SpecialIssue

Coastal Charm color *Timber Home Living* p34 2017 SpecialIssue

Come Together color *Timber Home Living* p42 2017 SpecialIssue

THE FAB LIFE L. M. Labong color *Sunset* v238 no4 p50 Ap 2017

Get in the Mix color *Log Home Living* v34 no2 p8 Mr 2017

The Great Escape color *Timber Home Living* p54 2017 SpecialIssue

HISTORICAL REVISION A. SOLOMON color *Architectural Digest* v74 no3 p136 Mr 2017

A Home in an Orchard *Treasures* v6 no3 p17 D 2016/Ja 2017

Home in On A. SESSA color *Conde Nast Traveler* v51 no11 p54 D 2016

Hybrid Haven color *Timber Home Living* p50 2017 SpecialIssue

LIGHT FANTASTIC M. OWENS color *Architectural Digest* v74 no3 p98 Mr 2017

The Little Charmer K. Owen color diag *Southern Living* v52 no4 p42 Ap 2017

MCCOOK HAS THE WRIGHT LOOK M. MASICH color *Nebraska Life* v21 no2 p34 Mr/Ap 2017

Mountain Modern color *Timber Home Living* p46 2017 SpecialIssue

ode to beauty J. J. MARTIN bw color *Architectural Digest* v74 no3 p120 Mr 2017

Welcome Home color *Timber Home Living* p30 2017 SpecialIssue

Domestic architecture—Illinois
Lost & Found ... a restoration tale B. D. COLEMAN color *Old House Journal* v45 no7 p14 O 2017

Domestic architecture—Italy
A Lasting Memory M. MONDADORI SARTOGO color *Architectural Digest* v74 no10 p168 O 1 2017

Domestic architecture—New England
The Most Famous House in New Hampshire color *Yankee* p44 My/Je 2017

Domestic architecture—Southern States
The Little Charmer K. Owen color diag *Southern Living* v52 no4 p42 Ap 2017

Domestic architecture—United States
CASTLES IN AIR L. H. Lapham *Lapham's Quarterly* v10 no1 p12 Wint 2017

Domestic economic assistance
See also
Community development
Subsidies
Welfare recipients—Employment

Domestic fiction
"I Don't Know if He Knows How Lucky He Was" [Cover story] L. MILLER *Reader's Digest* v188 no1126 p67 D 2016/Ja 2017

Domestic relations
See also
Husband & wife
LAWYER PROFILES *Washingtonian Magazine* v52 no3 p125 D 2016

Domestic travel
2017 INTERNATIONAL TRIPS (PLUS WINTER DOMESTIC TRIPS) *Sierra* v101 no5 p48 S/O 2016

Domestication of animals
See also
Domestication of dogs
Domestication of horses
20 Things You Didn't Know About ... Animal Domestication G. TARLACH color *Discover* v38 no8 p82 O 2017

Dive deep to discover unexpected connections E. Quill *Science News* v191 no13 p2 Jl 8 2017

Making a New Dog? T. M. NEWSOME, P. J. S. FLEMING et al *BioScience* v67 no4 p374 Ap 2017

Domestication of animals—History
THE ROAD TO TAMENESS T. Hesman Saey and E. Engelhaupt color diag map *Science News* v191 no13 p20 Jl 8 2017

Domestication of dogs

A BOY'S BEST FRIEND HAS A SECRET PAST G. PAULSEN color *Reader's Digest* v190 no1134 p112 O 2017

HOW TO BUILD A DOG L. Trut and L. Alan Dugatkin color *Scientific American* v316 no5 p68 My 2017

Making a New Dog? T. M. NEWSOME, P. J. S. FLEMING et al *BioScience* v67 no4 p374 Ap 2017

Domestication of horses

DNA bucks tale of horse taming T. HESMAN SAEY color *Science News* v191 no10 p10 My 27 2017

HOW COAT COLOR PREFERENCES CHANGED THROUGH TIME C. Barakat and M. McCluskey color *Equus* no475 p24 Ap 2017

Learning life's lessons together N. J. Bailey color *Equus* no471 p64 D 2016

My Horse Minya S. Miller *Arabian Horse World* v57 no11 p39 Ag 2017

Domestication of plants

See also

Cultivated plants

Persistent effects of pre-Columbian plant domestication on Amazonian forest composition C. Levis, F. R. C. Costa et al bibl chart graph map *Science* v355 no6328 p925 Mr 3 2017

THE ROAD TO TAMENESS T. Hesman Saey and E. Engelhaupt color diag map *Science News* v191 no13 p20 Jl 8 2017

Domestico, Anthony

'A Kindly Presence of Mind' color *Commonweal* v144 no12 p14 Jl 7 2017

BOOKMARKS color *Commonweal* v144 no13 p35 Ag 11 2017

BOOKMARKS color *Commonweal* v144 no2 p28 Ja 27 2017

'Contrary by Temperament' bw *Commonweal* v144 no13 p10 Ag 11 2017

Double Focus bw *Commonweal* v144 no11 p37 Je 16 2017

The Freedoms of Fiction bw *Commonweal* v144 no8 p26 My 5 2017

Portrait of Our Time color *Commonweal* v144 no15 p34 S 22 2017

Scattered Lives *Commonweal* v144 no7 p36 Ap 14 2017

The World in Its Glory bw *Commonweal* v144 no4 p28 F 24 2017

Domet, Sarah

Leaving the Faith M. MELOY *New York Times Book Review* p15 O 16 2016

Domi, Max

MAX DOMI'S Success Depends on Accuracy R. Druzin bw *Maclean's* v129 no48/49 p40 D 5 2016

Domijan, Mirela

Phytochromes function as thermosensors in Arabidopsis bibl graph *Science* v354 no6314 p886 N 18 2016

Dominance (Psychology)

Good Bosses Switch Between Two Leadership Styles J. Maner *Harvard Business Review Digital Articles* p2 D 5 2016

History of winning remodels thalamo-PFC circuit to reinforce social dominance T. Zhou, H. Zhu et al color *Science* v357 no6347 p162 Jl 14 2017

Domingo, Plácido, 1941-

EURO STARS B. KIRCHNER *Opera News* v81 no7 p20 Ja 2017

Nabucco J. Malafronte *Opera News* v81 no9 p33 Mr 2017

Dominguez, Jorge I.

What You Might Not Know About the Cuban Economy *Harvard Business Review Digital Articles* p2 Ag 17 2015

Dominguez, Neidi—Interviews

First, Sheriff Joe. Next, President Trump C. BALLESTEROS *In These Times* v41 no3 p32 Mr 2017

Domínguez-Escalante Expedition (1776)

SALT OF THE EARTH E. Catino bw color *Skiing* p30 D 2016

Dominican Americans

'THE BRIEF WONDROUS LIFE OF OSCAR WAO' J. DIAZ, J. Aguirre et al *New York Times Book Review* p30 Ja 8 2017

Dominican sisters

In her shoes B. E. Reid *U.S. Catholic* v82 no1 p20 Ja 2017

Dominik, Martin

Relativistic deflection of background starlight measures the mass of a nearby white dwarf star chart color graph *Science* v356 no6342 p1046 Je 9 2017

Dominion Energy Inc.

A PIPELINE RUNS THROUGH IT R. DOUGHTEN *Sierra* v102 no3 p32 My/Je 2017

Dominitz, Alon

PROTECTING LIVES AND PROPERTY--DEC's Dam Safety Program *New York State Conservationist* v71 no5 p21 Ap 2017

Domino's Pizza Inc.

DELIVERING A $9 BILLION EMPIRE S. BERFIELD color *Bloomberg Businessweek* no4515 p42 Mr 20 2017

How Domino's Pizza Reinvented Itself B. Taylor *Harvard Business Review Digital Articles* p2 N 28 2016

When Pizza Saved a Life B. SPECKTOR *Reader's Digest* v188 no1124 p12 O 2016

Dominus, Susan

Hasan Minhaj Thinks Comedy Is for Weirdos *New York Times Magazine* p66 Je 25 2017

JUST ANOTHER DAY AT THE OFFICE color *Glamour* v115 no9 p194 S 2017

NOT JUST US: Is an open marriage a happier marriage? *New York Times Magazine* p34 My 14 2017

SIRDEANER WALKER *New York Times Magazine* p47 D 25 2016

Dominy, Anna

What My Horse Wears on His Feet cartoon *Horse & Rider* v56 no5 p80 My 2017

DOMINY, NATHANIEL J.

Frankenstein and the Horrors of Competitive Exclusion *BioScience* v67 no2 p107 F 2017

DOMISE, ANDRAY

ANOTHER DAY IN THE DEATH OF AMERICA color *Maclean's* v129 no44 p112 N 7 2016

The blackest man on council color *Maclean's* v129 no44 p20 N 7 2016

The candidates are out there *Maclean's* p10 Je 2017

The impulse to assimilate chart color *Maclean's* v130 no6 p13 Jl 2017

Into the abyss of black deaths cartoon color *Maclean's* v129 no46 p62 N 21 2016

VINE'S FATAL LESSON FOR THE TECH WORLD *Maclean's* v129 no45 p12 N 14 2016

WE WERE EIGHT YEARS IN POWER bw color *Maclean's* v130 no10 p124 N 2017

WHY FEAR AND DIVISION REMAIN UNDEFEATED color *Maclean's* v129 no41 p11 O 17 2016

Domitrovic, Brian

GOOD AS GOLD *Claremont Review of Books* v17 no1 p75 Wint 2016/2017

THE POWER OF MARKETS *Claremont Review of Books* v16 no4 p52 Fall 2016

Dommen, Josef

Global atmospheric particle formation from CERN CLOUD measurements bibl graph map *Science* v354 no6316 p1119 D 2 2016

Domnarski, William

Court Provocateur J. FABIAN WITT *New York Times Book Review* p27 O 9 2016

Domning, Daryl P.

WORD EXCHANGE *Natural History* v125 no2 p9 F 2017

Domoic acid

Toxic Mystery A. Mitchell color *Canadian Wildlife* v23 no2 p16 My/Je 2017

Toxic Ocean Condition Tied to Climate Shifts *USA Today Magazine* v145 no2865 p3 Je 2017

Don, Y.

Deterministic generation of a cluster state of entangled photons bibl diag graph *Science* v354 no6311 p434 O 28 2016

Don Giovanni (Theatrical production)

Summer Preview R. Platt cartoon *New Yorker* v93 no14 p12 My 22 2017

Don Quixote (Theatrical production)

Unflappable M. HARSS *Dance Magazine* v91 no10 p30 O 2017

DONADIO, RACHEL

Interlocking Pieces *New York Times Book Review* p10 Mr 26 2017

Donahue, Bill

CAN'T STOP NOW color *Backpacker* v45 no1 p70 Ja 2017

HIDDEN FROM VIEW color *Archaeology* v70 no2 p48 Mr/Ap 2017

Painting the Fence color *Yankee* p114 Mr 2017

TRAIL DAZE color *Backpacker* p62 O 2017

WHEN YONKERS WAS BONKERS bw color *Runner's World*

v51 no10 p82 N 2016

Donahue, Greg

Mitotic transcription and waves of gene reactivation during mitotic exit color graph *Science* v357 no6359 p119 O 6 2017

Donahue, Neil M.

Global atmospheric particle formation from CERN CLOUD measurements bibl graph map *Science* v354 no6316 p1119 D 2 2016

Donahue, Patrick

It's Merkel 3, Schulz 0 In German Campaign color *Bloomberg Businessweek* no4523 p16 My 22 2017

Donahue, William

Too Much Forgetting bw color *Commonweal* v144 no16 p22 O 6 2017

What 'America First' Means Here color *Commonweal* v144 no12 p10 Jl 7 2017

Donaker, Geoff

Lessons from Yelp's Empirical Approach to Diversity *Harvard Business Review Digital Articles* p2 S 20 2017

Donald, Ralph

Hollywood Enlists! Propaganda Films of World War II *Publishers Weekly* v264 no3 p52 Ja 16 2017

Donaldson, Amy

Profiles in Courage *Sierra* v102 no4 p4 Jl/Ag 2017

DONALDSON, EMILY

THE BURNING GIRL color *Maclean's* v130 no8 p62 S 2017

GRAVEYARD GOINGS-ON color *Maclean's* v130 no2 p68 Mr 2017

LOOKING FOR 'THE STRANGER' bw color *Maclean's* v129 no43 p62 O 31 2016

MANHATTAN BEACH color *Maclean's* v130 no9 p76 O 2017

MOONGLOW color *Maclean's* v129 no47 p60 N 28 2016

SOLITUDE: A SINGULAR LIFE IN A CROWDED WORLD color *Maclean's* v130 no4 p70 My 2017

SWING TIME *Maclean's* v129 no46 p62 N 21 2016

THE WITCHES OF NEW YORK color *Maclean's* v129 no44 p113 N 7 2016

Donaldson, Mark T.

Equine Fitness and Strength color *Dressage Today* v23 no5 p14 Ja 2017

Donaldson, Robin

A CALIFORNIA FIRM WORKS WITH AN INDUSTRIAL-DESIGNER CLIENT TO CREATE A CONTEMPORARY HOME IN THE SANTA BARBARA HILLS A. KLIMOSKI *Architectural Record* v205 no7 p41 Jl 2017

Donaldson, Zoe

For the Love of Henrietta bw color *O, The Oprah Magazine* p28 My 2017

GIFTS that UPLIFT! cartoon *O, The Oprah Magazine* p148 D 2016

The Gratitude Meter color *O, The Oprah Magazine* p20 Ja 2017

The Gratitude Meter color *O, The Oprah Magazine* p20 Je 2017

The Gratitude Meter color *O, The Oprah Magazine* p24 My 2017

The Gratitude Meter color *O, The Oprah Magazine* p26 O 2017

do Nascimento, J.-D. Jr.

Reconciling solar and stellar magnetic cycles with nonlinear dynamo simulations diag *Science* v357 no6347 p185 Jl 14 2017

Donatelli, Jen Jones

Golden Girl color *Dance Spirit* v21 no1 p34 Ja 2017

Donatelli, Tyler

Tyler Donatelli N. WOZNY *Dance Magazine* v91 no8 p22 Ag 2017

Donatiello, Nicholas

Why Is CEO Pay Rising? Maybe There Aren't Enough Good CEOs *Harvard Business Review Digital Articles* p2 O 5 2017

Donation of organs, tissues, etc.

The Gift That Keeps on Giving T. ANDERSON and D. POINTDUJOUR color *Ebony* v72 no6 p62 Ap/My 2017

HUMAN ORGANS FROM ANIMAL BODIES J. C. Izpisúa Belmonte cartoon color diag *Scientific American* v315 no5 p32 N 2016

My son's organ donation taught me death is not the last word E. Gregory il *America* v216 no13 p40 Je 12 2017

Donato, Flavio

Stellate cells drive maturation of the entorhinal-hippocampal circuit diag *Science* v355 no6330 p1172 Mr 17 2017

Donehower, Ross

Mismatch repair deficiency predicts response of solid tumors to PD-1 blockade chart graph *Science* v357 no6349 p409 Jl 28 2017

Donelson, Sophie

From Our Editor color *House Beautiful* v158 no9 p18 N 2016

From Our Editor color *House Beautiful* v159 no3 p8 Ap 2017

From Our Editor color *House Beautiful* v159 no9 p6 N 2017

From Our Editor *House Beautiful* v159 no5 p8 Je 2017

PURSUIT OF BEAUTY color *House Beautiful* v159 no3 p94 Ap 2017

Donelson Smith, F.

Local protein kinase A action proceeds through intact holoenzymes color diag graph *Science* v356 no6344 p1288 Je 23 2017

Dones, Luke

Worlds of Wonder *Sky & Telescope* v134 no3 p16 S 2017

Dong, Emma

Welcome to The Neighborhood color *Bloomberg Businessweek* no4525 p19 Je 5 2017

Dong, Junkai

Engineering the ribosomal DNA in a megabase synthetic chromosome diag *Science* v355 no6329 p1049 Mr 10 2017

Dong, Kang

Synthesis, debugging, and effects of synthetic chromosome consolidation: synVI and beyond color *Science* v355 no6329 p1045 Mr 10 2017

Dong, Ning

Global climatic drivers of leaf size [Cover story] graph *Science* v357 no6354 p917 S 1 2017

Dong, Suomeng

A paralogous decoy protects Phytophthora sojae apoplastic effector PsXEG1 from a host inhibitor bibl graph *Science* v355 no6326 p710 F 17 2017

Dong, Xianjun

β2-Adrenoreceptor is a regulator of the a-synuclein gene driving risk of Parkinson's disease cartoon chart graph *Science* v357 no6354 p891 S 1 2017

Dong, Xiu-Tao

Bug mapping and fitness testing of chemically synthesized chromosome X diag *Science* v355 no6329 p1048 Mr 10 2017

Dong, Yuemei

Changes in the microbiota cause genetically modified Anopheles to spread in a population graph *Science* v357 no6358 p1396 S 29 2017

Dong Gao

SOX2 promotes lineage plasticity and antiandrogen resistance in TP53- and RB1-deficient prostate cancer bibl graph *Science* v355 no6320 p1 Ja 6 2017

Dong-Hun Lee

Role for migratory wild birds in the global spread of avian influenza H5N8 bibl graph map *Science* v354 no6309 p213 O 14 2016

Dong Li

Increased spatiotemporal resolution reveals highly dynamic dense tubular matrices in the peripheral ER bibl bw color graph *Science* v354 no6311 paaf3928-1 O 28 2016

Dong Liu

Research: Shifting the Power Balance with an Abusive Boss *Harvard Business Review Digital Articles* p2 O 9 2017

Dong Lyu

The Conglomerate That Troubles China *Bloomberg Businessweek* no4533 p12 Ag 7 2017

Dong Su

Biaxially strained PtPb/Pt core/shell nanoplate boosts oxygen reduction catalysis bibl color graph *Science* v354 no6318 p1410 D 16 2016

Dong Zhenxiang

Grand Entrances img *New York* v50 no17 p76 Ag 21 2017

Donghia, Nina

Nucleic acid detection with CRISPR-Cas13a/C2c2 color diag *Science* v356 no6336 p438 Ap 28 2017

Donghoon Kim

Pathological α-synuclein transmission initiated by binding lymphocyte-activation gene 3 bibl graph *Science* v353 no6307 paah3374-1 S 30 2016

Dong-kyu, Kim

I Used to Be a Human Being img *New York* v49 no19 p32 S 19 2016

Donohue, Kether, 1985-
Lou Diamond Phillips: Worst Dad Ever? M. Roffman *TV Guide* v65 no43 p7 O 16 2017
Donohue, Mark, 1937-1975
THE GLORY OF PENSKE AND DONOHUE color *Road & Track* v68 no5 p18 D 2016/Ja 2017
DONOHUE, THOMAS J.
Americans Can Unify Around Economic Growth *Weekly Standard* v22 no11 p9 N 21 2016
As Cyber Threats Mount, Businesses Mount a Defense *Weekly Standard* v22 no38 p21 Je 12 2017
Bringing NAFTA Into the 21st Century *Weekly Standard* v22 no34 p23 My 15 2017
Building a 21st Century Workforce *Weekly Standard* v22 no48 p9 S 4 2017
Businesses Lead Solutions to Workforce Challenges *Weekly Standard* v22 no40 p7 Je 26 2017
Business Leads Solutions to Workforce Challenges *Weekly Standard* v22 no13 p21 D 5 2016
Capital Markets: Fueling Our Economic Growth *Weekly Standard* v22 no5 p22 O 10 2016
Clock Is Ticking for DACA Solution *Weekly Standard* v23 no5 p14 O 9 2017
Driving Another Decade of Energy Progress *Weekly Standard* v22 no41 p15 Jl 3 2017
Fighting Government's Fourth Branch *Weekly Standard* v22 no15 p9 D 19 2016
Four Decades of Court Battles and Counting *Weekly Standard* v22 no28 p9 Mr 27 2017
Getting Tax Reform Done—and Done Right *Weekly Standard* v22 no27 p25 Mr 20 2017
A Growth Agenda to Unite All Americans *Weekly Standard* v22 no18 p9 Ja 16 2017
A Historic Moment for U.S. Energy *Weekly Standard* v22 no30 p19 Ap 10 2017
An Important Trade Agreement You Haven't Heard Of *Weekly Standard* v22 no22 p19 F 13 2017
Innovation That's Out of This World *Weekly Standard* v22 no26 p25 Mr 13 2017
IP: The Roots of Innovation *Weekly Standard* v22 no23 p11 F 20 2017
It's Time to Build *Weekly Standard* v22 no35 p29 My 22 2017
A Lasting Solution to the Regulatory Nightmare *Weekly Standard* v22 no33 p35 My 8 2017
Leading Businesses Make a Difference *Weekly Standard* v22 no12 p21 N 28 2016
Let's Grow: Ideas to Get Our Economy Moving *Weekly Standard* v22 no19 p23 Ja 23 2017
Little-Known Law Makes a Big Difference *Weekly Standard* v22 no36 p9 My 29 2017
Meet Small Business Owners Who Depend on Trade *Weekly Standard* v22 no39 p31 Je 19 2017
NAFTA Modernization Moves Forward *Weekly Standard* v22 no44 p21 Jl 31 2017
Opportunity by the Truckload *Weekly Standard* v22 no16 p8 D 26 2016
Optimism Soars for Midsize Businesses *Weekly Standard* v22 no29 p9 Ap 3 2017
Progress on Limiting Health Insurance Costs Still Possible *Weekly Standard* v23 no2 p27 S 18 2017
Promoting Disability Employment Around the Globe *Weekly Standard* v22 no45 p19 Ag 7 2017
Protecting Consumers' Right to Arbitration *Weekly Standard* v22 no46 p29 Ag 14 2017
Protecting the Right to Take a Risk *Weekly Standard* v22 no42 p15 Jl 17 2017
Regulatory Relief Is on the Way *Weekly Standard* v22 no25 p9 Mr 6 2017
Remedies for Our Ailing Health Care System *Weekly Standard* v22 no7 p9 O 24 2016
Safe Shopping in Cyberspace *Weekly Standard* v22 no17 p14 Ja 2 2017
Seizing Our Energy Potential *Weekly Standard* v22 no14 p29 D 12 2016
Slow Confirmations Are Thwarting Progress *Weekly Standard* v23 no6 p9 O 16 2017

Small, Midsize Businesses Hold Key to Growth *Weekly Standard* v23 no4 p9 O 2 2017
Speaking Up for Free Speech *Weekly Standard* v22 no43 p8 Jl 24 2017
Taking DOL's Overtime Rule to Court *Weekly Standard* v22 no6 p11 O 17 2016
Tax Reform: Hard Work and High Stakes Ahead *Weekly Standard* v22 no47 p8 Ag 21 2017
Thank You, American Workers *Weekly Standard* v23 no1 p8 S 11 2017
Torts and Rules Can Stunt Tech Sector Growth *Weekly Standard* v22 no31 p13 Ap 17 2017
Trade and Growth Protect Against Global Turmoil *Weekly Standard* v22 no21 p19 F 6 2017
Trump's First 100 Days Bring Victories for Business *Weekly Standard* v22 no32 p17 My 1 2017
Vote for Jobs and Growth *Weekly Standard* v22 no10 p21 N 14 2016
Welcome to the Neighborhood, President Trump *Weekly Standard* v22 no20 p8 Ja 30 2017
When Disaster Strikes, Businesses Rise to Help *Weekly Standard* v22 no8 p19 O 31 2016
When Disaster Strikes, Businesses Step Up *Weekly Standard* v23 no3 p9 S 25 2017
Why Waste Our Energy? *Weekly Standard* v22 no24 p17 F 27 2017
Donor-advised funds
DONOR-ADVISED FUNDS SOAR ALONG WITH MARKETS E. Wine color *Forbes* v198 no7 p82 N 29 2016
Donor-Advised Funds: The Fastest-Growing Vehicle For Charitable Giving J. MULLICH color *Forbes* v200 no5 p88 N 14 2017
Q: My alma mater is offering a charitable gift annuity. Is that a good way to generate income? E. AMBROSE color *Kiplinger's Personal Finance* v71 no11 p46 N 2017
Donoso, David A.
Higher predation risk for insect prey at low latitudes and elevations graph *Science* v356 no6339 p742 My 19 2017
Donovan, Colleen
Contingent valuation: Flawed logic? color *Science* v357 no6349 p363 Jl 28 2017
Putting a value on injuries to natural assets: The BP oil spill chart *Science* v356 no6335 p253 Ap 21 2017
DONOVAN, E. CAROLINE
Ecological Forecasting and the Science of Hypoxia in Chesapeake Bay *BioScience* v67 no7 p614 Jl 2017
Donovan, Keith
PREDICTABLE PATTERNS AND SEXUAL ASSAULT A. KINGSTON *Maclean's* v129 no41 p10 O 17 2016
DONOVAN, MEGAN K.
LIFE BEFORE ROE color *Scientific American* v317 no3 p58 S 2017
Donovan, Tara
The Whole Is Greater color *American Craft* v77 no2 p96 Ap/My 2017
Donovan, Tristan
What's In a Board Game? S. Begley color *Time* v189 no22 p16 Je 12 2017
Donsa, S.
Observing the ultrafast buildup of a Fano resonance in the time domain bibl graph *Science* v354 no6313 p738 N 11 2016
Don't Give Up on Love (Music)
Deliberate Moves A. Cohen color *Downbeat* v84 no9 p27 S 2017
Don't Kill My Vibe (Music)
The Must List color *Entertainment Weekly* no1466 p3 My 19 2017
SIGRID N. Feeney color *Entertainment Weekly* no1465 p53 My 12 2017
Don't Think (Poem)
Don't Think K. CONNOLLY *Walrus* v14 no3 p43 Ap 2017
Dontoh, Ekow
Ghana Pays the Price Of Cheap Cocoa color *Bloomberg Businessweek* no4539 p28 S 25 2017
Dooley, Brian
People *Christian Century* v134 no12 p19 Je 7 2017
Dooley, Sarah
Ashes to Asheville *Publishers Weekly* v264 no8 p84 F 20 2017
Doolittle, Benjamin

POWER [Cover story] color *Christian Century* v134 no1 p22 Ja 4 2017

Doolittle, Lauren

Lauren Doolittle A. BRANDT *Cincinnati Magazine* p34 Je 2017

Doolittle, Sean—Interviews

American Voices Sean Doolittle J. Dickey and T. Keith color *Sports Illustrated* v126 no8 p30 Mr 20 2017

Doomsday Clock

Minutes to Midnight *Lapham's Quarterly* v10 no3 p117 Summ 2017

Doonan, Simon

BAZAAR THINGS color *Harper's Bazaar* no3656 p462 S 2017

Door County (Wis.)

Cape Calm M. Guerber color il *American Craft* v77 no2 p66 Ap/My 2017

Door design & construction

Front Door, Back Door AND DOORS INSIDE M. E. POLSON color diag *Old House Journal* v45 no5 p40 Ag 2017

Door fittings

BEDROOM DOORBELL! J. SCHADEWALD bw chart color *Popular Mechanics* v193 no7 p102 S 2016

HARDWARE & METALWORK color *Old House Journal* v44 p101 2016 Design Center source Book

Door industry

Renaissance Doors: Matthew Durish P. Marquis *New Orleans Homes & Lifestyles* v20 no3 p97 Summ 2017

Door knobs

Homecoming Season K. O'SHEA-EVANS and J. J. CONDON color *House Beautiful* v159 no7 p41 S 2017

Save, Repair, or Replace? M. E. POLSON color *Old House Journal* v44 no8 p44 D 2016

Secrets of a Weekend Lock Picker D. DUBNO cartoon color *Popular Mechanics* v193 no7 p29 S 2016

Door knobs—Evaluation

ALL ABOUT ALTITUDE R. Lengel bw *Flying* v144 no2 p28 F 2017

art + craft color *Arts & Crafts Homes & the Revival* v11 no5 p10 Wint 2017

Game Changer K. Sutton color *House Beautiful* v159 no2 p45 Mr 2017

HARDWARE color *Arts & Crafts Homes & the Revival* v12 no1 p48 2017 Resouce Guide

Door knockers—Evaluation

PUNCH list K. SELZER *Better Homes & Gardens* v94 no12 p64 D 2016

Door maintenance & repair

THE FORMAL FAÇADE IMPROVED R. Olsen color *Old House Journal* v45 no5 p32 Ag 2017

Doorbells

BEDROOM DOORBELL! J. SCHADEWALD bw chart color *Popular Mechanics* p102 S 2017

BEDROOM DOORBELL! J. SCHADEWALD chart color diag *Popular Mechanics* v193 no7 p102 S 2016

Grand Opening color *Log Home Living* v34 no7 p40 S 2017

Doorly, Henry

SUMMERTIME color *Nebraska Life* v21 no4 p18 Jl/Ag 2017

Doormats

THE NATURE OF ALL Things [Cover story] J. BREWSTER color *Cabin Living* p44 Ag 2017

Doormats—Evaluation

MEET AND GREET E. MOODY color *Martha Stewart Living* p28 My 2017

Doors

Just Take One color *Martha Stewart Living* p38 O 2017

Doors in art

Door Project artists from The Learning Tree, Derek Tuder and Astoshia Young L. Copan color *Christian Century* v134 no10 p63 My 10 2017

Doors—Evaluation

Aging in Place M. E. Polson color *Old House Journal* v45 no7 p74 O 2017

Entrance Exam K. L. Beamon *Architectural Record* v205 no10 p55 O 2017

Going Dutch color *Log Home Living* v34 no7 p20 S 2017

Grand Opening color *Log Home Living* v34 no7 p40 S 2017

Openings color *Architectural Record* v204 no12 p132 D 2016

Dop, Michiel

Mix and Match: Incerporating art and antiques with style and panache K. Wilburn *New Orleans Homes & Lifestyles* v20 no4 p102 Aut 2017

Dopamine

Disrupting Dopamine Dogma M. LOCKLEAR diag *Discover* v38 no1 p39 Ja/F 2017

Dopamine oxidation mediates mitochondrial and lysosomal dysfunction in Parkinson's disease L. F. Burbulla, P. Song et al graph *Science* v357 no6357 p1255 S 22 2017

Midbrain dopamine neurons control judgment of time S. Soares, B. V. Atallah et al bibl graph *Science* v354 no6317 p1273 D 9 2016

Rogue dopamine linked to Parkinson's L. SANDERS bw *Science News* v192 no5 p7 S 30 2017

Unexpected rewards induce dopamine-dependent positive emotion–like state changes in bumblebees C. J. Perry, L. Baciadonna et al bibl graph *Science* v353 no6307 p1529 S 30 2016

Why does time seem to fly when we're having fun? P. Simen and M. Matell bibl color *Science* v354 no6317 p1231 D 9 2016

Dopaminergic neurons

Dopamine neurons encode performance error in singing birds V. Gadagkar, P. A. Puzerey et al bibl graph *Science* v354 no6317 p1278 D 9 2016

Doping profiles (Semiconductors)

Photonic doping of epsilon-near-zero media I. Liberal, A. M. Mahmoud et al bibl diag *Science* v355 no6329 p1058 Mr 10 2017

Doppelt, Martin C.

Ancient Brews color *Science* v356 no6342 p1004 Je 9 2017

Doppler Labs Inc.

Now Here This M. Mettler and C. Crowley color *Sound & Vision* v81 no9 p18 N 2016

Dora, Yago

ON YAGO T. Paul color *Surfing Magazine* v53 no2 p66 F 2017

Dorado, Afrodita

What's the Biggest Risk You've Ever Taken? bw color *Glamour* no8 p26 Ag 2017

Doran, Anne

NO SHOW bw color *ARTnews* v116 no1 p84 Spr 2017

Rebel In the House *Los Angeles Magazine* v62 no6 p60 Je 2017

"R. H. Quaytman, Morning: Chapter 30" color *ARTnews* v115 no3 p33 Fall 2016

A Talk with Andrea Fraser color *ARTnews* v115 no4 p98 Wint 2016/2017

"Walker Evans: A Vernacular Style" *ARTnews* v116 no1 p16 Spr 2017

Doran, Kirk B.

Crossing borders along an endless frontier color *Science* v356 no6339 p694 My 19 2017

Doran, Michael

Getting In D. FRUM *New York Times Book Review* p16 O 16 2016

Ike's Gamble: America's Rise to Dominance in the Middle East S. YAQUB and J. Waterbury *Foreign Affairs* v96 no2 p185 Mr/Ap 2017

Middle East Misjudgment *Commentary* v141 no10 p1 D 2016

Middle East Misjudgment O. CEREN *Commentary* v142 no5 p41 D 2016

West of Suez R. TAKEYH bw *Weekly Standard* v22 no9 p36 N 7 2016

DORAN, PETER

The Impact of a Large-Scale Climate Event on Antarctic Ecosystem Processes chart graph *BioScience* v66 no10 p848 O 1 2016

Responses of Antarctic Marine and Freshwater Ecosystems to Changing Ice Conditions color graph *BioScience* v66 no10 p864 O 1 2016

Dorchester (England)

DORCHESTER *British Heritage Travel* v37 no6 p18 N/D 2016

Dore, Bhavya

Facing discrimination, Dalit caste members are converting to Buddhism color *Christian Century* v133 no24 p19 N 23 2016

In India, a legal group defends Muslims accused in terrorism cases color *Christian Century* v134 no7 p16 Mr 29 2017

Doré, Garance

In (and Out of) Fashion color *InStyle* v24 no9 p261 S 2017

Doremus, Holly

Merging paleobiology with conservation biology to guide the future of terrestrial ecosystems color *Science* v355 no6325 p594 F 10 2017

DORFMAN, ARIEL

The Truth That Set Her Free *New York Times Book Review* p18 D 25 2016

Dorfman, David—Interviews

David Dorfman K. SCHWAB *Dance Magazine* v91 no4 p18 Ap 2017

Dorfman, Elsa

Who's Asking? E. MORRIS color *Film Comment* v53 no3 p14 My/Je 2017

Dorfman, Kevin D.

Thermal processing of diblock copolymer melts mimics metallurgy diag graph *Science* v356 no6337 p520 My 5 2017

DORFMAN, LISA

ASK RW color *Runner's World* v52 no4 p35 My 2017

DORFMAN, MATT

The Best Book Covers of 2016 *New York Times Book Review* p18 D 11 2016

Doria-Rose, Nicole

Trispecific broadly neutralizing HIV antibodies mediate potent SHIV protection in macaques color graph *Science* v357 no6359 p85 O 6 2017

D'Orio, Wayne

Hamilton Goes to High School *Education Digest* v83 no2 p4 O 2017

Dorje, Ogyen Trinley, 1985-

Interconnected: Living Fully in a Global Society color *Publishers Weekly* v263 no51 p140 D 12 2016

DORLAND, STEVEN

Sensoriality and Wendat Steams *American Indian Quarterly* v41 no1 p1 Wint 2017

d'Orléans, Paul

ALL-NEW BROUGH SUPERIOR SS 100 bw color *Cycle World* v56 no1 p44 Ja/F 2017

CANNONBALLS DEEP *Cycle World* v56 no1 p21 Ja/F 2017

CRAZY IS THE NEW NORMAL [Cover story] color *Cycle World* v56 no6 p32 Jl 2017

HIGH-PERFORMANCE ATTACHÉ color *Cycle World* v56 no8 p48 S 2017

IN IT FOR THE MONEY *Cycle World* v56 no3 p26 Ap 2017

IT'S AN INDUSTRY THING *Cycle World* v56 no7 p26 Ag 2017

LOST IN THE SUPERMARKET color *Cycle World* v56 no5 p28 Je 2017

The New Café Racer Paradigm color *Cycle World* v55 no11 p42 D 2016

THE SAMURAI CODE color *Cycle World* v55 no11 p36 D 2016

A TALE OF TWO BIKERS bw *Cycle World* v55 no10 p22 N 2016

AN UN-SOUND FUTURE *Cycle World* v56 no9 p26 O 2017

Dorman, Isaiah

BLACK MAN AT THE LITTLE BIGHORN *South Dakota Magazine* v32 no4 p63 N/D 2016

Dorman, Sara Rich

Understanding Zimbabwe: From Liberation to Authoritarianism N. van de Walle *Foreign Affairs* v96 no3 p176 My/Je 2017

Dorment, Richard

Looking for 'Life Itself' [Cover story] J. Bell color *New York Review of Books* v64 no8 p42 My 11 2017

Dormers

Remuddling color *Old House Journal* v45 no3 p88 My 2017

Dormice

Blind climber color *Science* v355 no6322 p259 Ja 20 2017

Dorminey, Bruce

How high-speed stars escape the galaxy [Cover story] color *Astronomy* v45 no3 p22 Mr 2017

Dormitories

Code and Man at Yale bw *Weekly Standard* v22 no27 p4 Mr 20 2017

Dormitories—Design & construction

Floating Dorms J. Zorthian color *Time* v188 no14 p23 O 10 2016

DORMONTT, ELEANOR E.

Opportunities for Improved Transparency in the Timber Trade through Scientific Verification *BioScience* v66 no11 p990 N 1 2016

Dorna Sports SL

WHERE IS WORLD SUPERBIKE GOING? K. Cameron color *Cycle World* v56 no9 p50 O 2017

Dornfeld, Barry

When Your Company Has a Problem It Can't Ignore *Harvard Business Review Digital Articles* p2 O 7 2014

Dorosti, Q.

Observation of a large-scale anisotropy in the arrival directions of cosmic rays above 8 × 1018 eV *Science* v357 no6357 p1266 S 22 2017

Doroudi, Shayan

A cargo-sorting DNA robot color *Science* v357 no6356 p1112 S 15 2017

Dorough, Howie—Interviews

BACKSTREET'S BACK, ALL RIGHT! N. Feeney color *Entertainment Weekly* no1454/1455 p58 F 24 2017

DORRAM, SHARON

42 new ALL-STAR PRODUCTS of the year [Cover story] color *Redbook* p27 Jl/Ag 2017

Dorrance, Michelle

HAPPY FEET J. ACOCELLA cartoon *New Yorker* v92 no40 p82 D 5 2016

Dorrien, Gary

King & His Mentors bw *Commonweal* v144 no16 p17 O 6 2017

LESSONS FROM 20TH-CENTURY EUROPE: Saving democracy *Christian Century* v134 no13 p20 Je 21 2017

Dorris, Jesse

FIT TO BE tiled color *Martha Stewart Living* p122 O 2017

Dorsainvil, Aja—Interviews

Park and R.E.C.-reativity *Parks & Recreation* v51 no11 p52 N 2016

Dorset (England)—Description & Travel

DORCHESTER *British Heritage Travel* v37 no6 p18 N/D 2016

Dorsey, Avon

FE NOEL color *Essence* v48 no3 p22 Jl 2017

the HIT LIST color *Essence* v48 no5 p32 S 2017

SIMPLY AMAZING! color *Essence* v47 no11 p19 Mr 2017

STYLE YOUR GUY color *Essence* v48 no2 p28 Je 2017

STYLE YOUR GUY color *Essence* v48 no6 p36 O 2017

Dorsey, Chris

Reflections on the lectionary *Christian Century* v134 no18 p19 Ag 30 2017

Dorsey, Jack, 1976-

Jack Dorsey Is Losing Control of Twitter S. Frier and A. Sherman cartoon graph *Bloomberg Businessweek* no4495 p26 O 17 2016

DORSEY, NADIRI

The Question *O, The Oprah Magazine* p16 Ap 2017

Dorsey, Sandra

Ladies With Lassos: Four women known as the Cowgirls of Color have found a niche within the rodeo community L. PEOPLES img *New York* v50 no13 p46 Je 26 2017

Dorsey, Tim

Clownfish Blues *Publishers Weekly* v263 no48 p47 N 28 2016

Dos Cabezas Mountains (Ariz.)

Willcox Playa N. AUSTIN *Arizona Highways* v93 no8 p6 Ag 2017

Dosage of drugs

See also

Drug overdose

THE HANGOVER IS ... OVER M. Robin color *InStyle* v23 no13 p186 D 2016

Is your diet interfering with your medication regimen? *Harvard Health Letter* v42 no8 p4 Je 2017

Prescription bargain hunt *Harvard Health Letter* v42 no6 p1 Ap 2017

dos Anjos, R. C.

Observation of a large-scale anisotropy in the arrival directions of cosmic rays above 8 × 1018 eV *Science* v357 no6357 p1266 S 22 2017

Dose-response relationship (Biochemistry)

Eat Your Fruits and Vegetables to Help Fight Frailty *Tufts University Health & Nutrition Letter* v34 no8 p7 O 2016

Doshi, Neel

How Company Culture Shapes Employee Motivation *Harvard Business Review Digital Articles* p2 N 25 2015

There Are Two Types of Performance—but Most Organizations Only Focus on One *Harvard Business Review Digital Articles*

p2 O 10 2017

Dosman, Nicolás Alberto

Why music matters in urban school districts: The perspectives of students and parents of the Celia Cruz High School of Music, Bronx, New York bibl chart *Arts Education Policy Review* v118 no2 p67 2017

Dos Passos, John, 1896-1970

THOUGHTS ON: Work bw color *Forbes* v200 no4 p110 O 24 2017

Dos-Santos, André L. A.

Driving mosquito refractoriness to Plasmodium falciparum with engineered symbiotic bacteria color graph *Science* v357 no6358 p1399 S 29 2017

DOS SANTOS, MARCO A.

Greenhouse Gas Emissions from Reservoir Water Surfaces: A New Global Synthesis *BioScience* v66 no11 p949 N 1 2016

DOS SANTOS, ROBYN

Paying Our Respects color *O, The Oprah Magazine* p15 Je 2017

Dossena, Julien

PACO RABANNE Fashion CRUSH E. Wilson color *InStyle* v24 no8 p140 Ag 2017

Dossey, Larry

Pseudoscience versus science *Physics Today* v69 no11 p10 N 2016

Dostoyevsky, Fyodor, 1821-1881

TORMENT UNFORESEEN F. Dostoevsky *Lapham's Quarterly* v10 no3 p101 Summ 2017

DOTSON, CHAD

RED-LETTER DAYS *Cincinnati Magazine* v50 no8 p22 My 2017

Dotson-Renta, Lara

Points to Ponder *Reader's Digest* v188 no1125 p46 N 2016

Doty, Shaun

The Federal J. ZYMAN *Atlanta* v56 no12 p66 Ap 2017

Dou, Jiayi

Principles for designing proteins with cavities formed by curved β sheets bibl color graph *Science* v355 no6321 p1 Ja 13 2017

Double bassists

'GRAND SLAM' EVOLUTION D. Ouellette color *Downbeat* v84 no3 p45 Mr 2017

True Believer: Bass Soloman Howard's success is built on a foundation of faith that has seen him through some unusual challenges L. T. Guinther *Opera News* v81 no12 p65 Je 2017

Double Dutchess (Music)

The Bullseye M. Snetiker color *Entertainment Weekly* no1485 p64 O 6 2017

THE DUTCHESS REIGNS AGAIN M. Vain color *Entertainment Weekly* no1484 p56 S 29 2017

Double eagle (Coin)

The Case of the Double Eagle Gold Coins V. GLEMBOCKI color *Reader's Digest* v190 no1135 p23 N 2017

Double houses (Architecture)

house of the month J. MINUTILLO color diag *Architectural Record* v205 no2 p31 F 2017

Double majors (Education)

Doubling up J. LEWINGTON color *Maclean's* v130 no10 p77 N 2017

tacking two: Should you double-major? A. SMITH *Dance Magazine* v90 p22 2016/2017 Supplement College Guide

tackling two A. SMITH *Dance Magazine* p22 2016/2017

Double standard

Double Standards: Available In His and Hers S. Schrobsdorff color *Time* v188 no14 p63 O 10 2016

What's Up With the Orgasm Double Standard? S. M. Broom color *Glamour* v115 no7 p70 Jl 2017

Double-stranded RNA

Transgenerational transmission of environmental information in C. elegans A. Klosin, E. Casas et al diag *Science* v356 no6335 p320 Ap 21 2017

Double Take Comics (Company)

Using Graphic Novels, Bill Jemas Resurrects 'Night of the Living Dead' C. Reid *Publishers Weekly* v263 no40 p6 O 3 2016

Doubles tennis

Hold Strong G. Moran *Tennis* v53 no4 p72 Jl/Ag 2017

The most unorthodox doubles formations G. Fernandez bw color *Tennis* v53 no5 p76 S/O 2017

Strength IN NUMBERS A. FRIEDMAN *Tennis* v53 no4 p56 Jl/

Ag 2017

A Tradition Unlike Any Other E. McGrogan *Tennis* v53 no4 p58 Jl/Ag 2017

Doubt (TV program)

Beyond the LAW J. Halterman color *TV Guide* v65 no7 p32 F 13 2017

CHEERS & JEERS D. HOLBROOK *TV Guide* v65 no13 p88 Mr 20 2017

Heigl's Star Quality Comes Through In the Courtroom D. D'Addario color *Time* v189 no7/8 p103 F 27 2017

STAY TUNED L. Rice color *Entertainment Weekly* no1440 p13 N 18 2016

Doudna, Jennifer A.

COMING TO TERMS WITH CRISPR R. Kolker color *Bloomberg Businessweek* no4525 p62 Je 5 2017

A Crack in Creation: Gene Editing and the Unthinkable Power to Control Evolution *Publishers Weekly* v264 no15 p62 Ap 10 2017

A Crack in Creation K. Frischkorn color *Science* v356 no6342 p1005 Je 9 2017

Structures of the CRISPR genome integration complex color *Science* v357 no6356 p1113 S 15 2017

Dough

See also

Dumplings

Finger-Lickin' Biscuit Loaf color *Good Housekeeping* v264 no2 p107 F 2017

KNEAD TO KNOW J. RAY bw color *Wired* v25 no10 p26 O 2017

The NEW RULES of PIZZA cartoon color *Men's Health* v32 no8 p123 O 2017

Your Three-Course Fix color *Tennis* v53 no5 p18 S/O 2017

Dougherty, Debbie S.

The Omissions That Make So Many Sexual Harassment Policies Ineffective *Harvard Business Review Digital Articles* p2 My 31 2017

Dougherty, Emily

INDEPENDENT SPIRIT color *Redbook* p37 My 2017

IN WITH THE NOW color *O, The Oprah Magazine* p93 S 2017

Dougherty, Jim

5 Steps to Building Great Business Relationships *Harvard Business Review Digital Articles* p2 D 5 2014

The Two Traits Every Entrepreneur Needs *Harvard Business Review Digital Articles* p2 Mr 21 2016

Dougherty, Joseph D.

Pcdhαc2 is required for axonal tiling and assembly of serotonergic circuitries in mice diag *Science* v356 no6336 p406 Ap 28 2017

DOUGHERTY, MICHAEL B.

Born Trump il *National Review* v69 no12 p27 Je 26 2017

Chris BROCK *Interview* v47 no2 p66 Mr 2017

Illuminations color *National Review* v69 no17 p37 S 11 2017

Dougherty, Patrick

Ephemeral Is Beautiful J. Lovelace color *American Craft* v77 no3 p56 Je/Jl 2017

Doughnuts

THE DOUGHNUT KING J. RAUSA FULLER color *Chicago* v66 no11 p50 N 2017

Reasons to have more chocolate L. Lillien color *Redbook* p85 S 2017

Straight from the Orchard R. MARTINEZ color *Bon Appetit* p72 S 2017

THE WORKBOOK color *Martha Stewart Living* p111 Mr 2017

DOUGHTEN, REID

A PIPELINE RUNS THROUGH IT *Sierra* v102 no3 p32 My/Je 2017

DOUGHTIE, LYNNE

Inspiring Greatness: ADVANCING WOMEN LEADERS IN THE WORKPLACE color *Forbes* v199 no6 p74 Je 13 2017

Doughty, Louise

Along Came a Death Squad O. STEINHAUER *New York Times Book Review* p13 O 9 2016

DOUGLAS, ANN

Peer Review: Professor Ginsberg's notes on the Beat Generation, compiled over two decades of teaching bw *New York Times Book Review* p18 Ag 6 2017

DOUGLAS, ASHTYN

BATTLE FOR THE BAY color *Surfer* v58 no5 p62 S 2017

Billy "Mystic" Wilmot, 57 bw *Surfer* v58 no5 p40 S 2017

DEFENDING PARADISE bw color *Surfer* v57 no13 p40 Mr 2017

THE DROWNING ISLES color *Surfer* v58 no4 p76 Ag 2017

Going Off Script color *Surfer* v57 no12 p52 Ja/F 2017

AN ICY RESOLVE bw color *Surfer* v58 no2 p56 My 2017

Invasion of the Kelp Snatchers color *Surfer* v58 no1 p38 Ap 2017

Lisa Andersen color *Surfer* v58 no3 p28 Je 2017

Nat Young, 69 bw *Surfer* v58 no1 p40 Ap 2017

Saving San Miguel color *Surfer* v58 no2 p32 My 2017

TORREN MARTYN color *Surfer* v58 no3 p42 Je 2017

Douglas, Bruce

Brazilians Look for a Trump of Their Own cartoon *Bloomberg Businessweek* no4508 p15 Ja 23 2017

Douglas, Emma

A Season of You: A Cloud Bay Christmas Novel *Publishers Weekly* v264 no36 p75 S 4 2017

Douglas, Kelly Brown

"A BOOK I'D LIKE MY ELECTED OFFICIALS TO READ" color *Christian Century* v133 no21 p28 O 12 2016

Episcopal Divinity School to join Union Seminary, Brown Douglas named dean C. Kennel-Shank *Christian Century* v134 no13 p15 Je 21 2017

Douglas, Kirk

THOUGHTS FROM Our Readers bw *Forbes* v200 no3 p180 S 28 2017

Douglas, Leah

Made from Concentrate *Washington Monthly* p1 S/O 2016

Stolen Birthright color map *Nation* v305 no2 p18 Jl 17 2017

Douglas, Liza

The SAILING SCENE color *Sail* v48 no11 p6 N 2017

Douglas, Michael

The International Campaign to Abolish Nuclear Weapons *Time* v190 no16/17 p20 O 23 2017

Douglas, Michael, 1944-

To Life! [Cover story] D. HOCHMAN color *AARP: The Magazine* v59 no2A p56 F/Mr 2016

Douglas, Paul H.

The Supreme Court, the Senate and the Filibuster *America* v216 no10 p40 My 1 2017

DOUGLAS, SARAH

AROUND BASEL cartoon color *ARTnews* v115 no3 p138 Fall 2016

EDITOR'S LETTER color *ARTnews* v115 no4 p12 Wint 2016/2017

A Portrait of the Artist as a Collector color *ARTnews* v116 no1 p42 Spr 2017

DOUGLAS, SCOTT

THE FAST BREAK cartoon *Runner's World* v52 no2 p33 Mr 2017

MATT LLANO color *Runner's World* v51 no10 p32 N 2016

MOLLY HUDDLE cartoon color *Runner's World* v51 no11 p21 D 2016

STREAKER KING bw color *Runner's World* v51 no10 p46 N 2016

Douglas, Shawn M.

Bringing proteins into the fold [Cover story] bibl color *Science* v355 no6331 p1261 Mr 24 2017

DOUGLAS, SUSAN J.

Another War, Another Blitzerkrieg *In These Times* v41 no6 p13 Je 2017

The Antidote to Toxic Masculinity *In These Times* v41 no8 p13 Ag 2017

Arise, Ye Boomers of the Nation *In These Times* v41 no2 p16 F 2017

Cutting Off Your Base To Spite Your Foes *In These Times* v41 no5 p16 My 2017

If Nixon Could Tweet *In These Times* v41 no3 p18 Mr 2017

Our Loser President and His Sad Budget *In These Times* v41 no7 p13 Jl 2017

Trump's Anti-Mandate *In These Times* v41 no1 p18 Ja 2017

THE WOMAN WHO MIGHT HAVE BEEN PRESIDENT *In These Times* v40 no12 p44 D 2016

Douglas fir

last doug standing s. matthews bw *Bike Magazine* v23 no9 p46 D 2016

Douglass, Frederick, 1818-1895

FREDERICK DOUGLASS HATED SOCIALISM D. ROOT bw *Reason* v48 no11 p8 Ap 2017

DOUGLASS, JASON CODY

A New History of Animation *Film Quarterly* v70 no4 p128 Summ 2017

Doumanis, Nicholas

Europe at war and between the wars C. Baldoli *History Today* v66 no10 p62 O 2016

DOUNGLOMCHAN, KITSANA

When the Water Ran Cold *Reader's Digest* v189 no1128 p20 Mr 2017

DOUTHAT, ROSS

Ape Overload *National Review* v69 no15 p47 Ag 14 2017

Appetite for Creation color *National Review* v69 no19 p58 O 16 2017

Back to The Well color *National Review* v69 no7 p46 Ap 17 2017

Dark Journey color *National Review* v68 no24 p43 D 31 2016

Empire Builder color *National Review* v69 no4 p47 Mr 6 2017

Fear and Trembling color *National Review* v69 no3 p54 F 20 2017

Fear of a White Village color *National Review* v69 no8 p43 My 2017

Glittering Prizes color *National Review* v69 no6 p47 Ap 3 2017

Going Rogue color *National Review* v69 no1 p42 Ja 23 2017

Hollywood On Hollywood color *National Review* v69 no2 p47 F 6 2017

Jungle Fever color *National Review* v69 no9 p42 My 15 2017

Love and Its Complications color *National Review* v69 no17 p42 S 11 2017

Monster Mash color *National Review* v69 no11 p42 Je 12 2017

Not So Super color *National Review* v69 no5 p46 Mr 20 2017

Only Connect color *National Review* v68 no23 p42 D 19 2016

On the Beach color *National Review* v69 no16 p47 Ag 28 2017

A Strange Superman color *National Review* v68 no21 p47 N 21 2016

Sunlit Horror color *National Review* v69 no18 p43 O 2 2017

Today's Nat Turner bw *National Review* v68 no20 p46 N 7 2016

Troubled Genius color *National Review* v68 no19 p51 O 24 2016

Woker Woman color *National Review* v69 no12 p43 Je 26 2017

Dova, M. T.

Observation of a large-scale anisotropy in the arrival directions of cosmic rays above 8×10^{18} eV *Science* v357 no6357 p1266 S 22 2017

Dove, Alan

Agreeable antibodies: Antibody validation challenges and solutions color *Science* v357 no6356 p1165 S 15 2017

DOVE, JACKIE

Adobe Photoshop Elements 15 review: Image editor boosts its photo-manipulation features color *Macworld - Digital Edition* p111 D 2016

COREL PAINTER 2018: PAINTING APP ADD TOOLS TO UNLEASH YOUR ARTISTIC POTENTIAL color *Macworld - Digital Edition* v34 no10 p95 O 2017

Hands on with Setapp: Getting started with the Netflix of Mac apps color *Macworld - Digital Edition* p7 Mr 2017

How to create powerful presentations with Adobe Spark Video color *Macworld - Digital Edition* p99 F 2017

LUCIDCAM: STEREOSCOPIC 3D VR CREATION COMES TO THE MASSES color *Macworld - Digital Edition* v34 no10 p102 O 2017

LUMINAR: A SERIOUS CHALLENGER TO THE REIGNING PRO APPS FOR PHOTO EDITING MASTERY color *Macworld - Digital Edition* p25 F 2017

WACOM BAMBOO SLATE color *Macworld - Digital Edition* p44 D 2016

Dove, Rita

Titans color *Time* v189 no16/17 p94 My 1-8 2017

Dove, Tom

Bali 4.0 color *Sail* v48 no6 p28 Je 2017

BEST BOATS 2017 color *Sail* v47 no12 p24 D 2016

Nautitech 46 Fly [Cover story] color *Sail* v48 no8 p22 Ag 2017

Dover, L. P.

Blocked *Publishers Weekly* v264 no35 p111 Ag 28 2017

Dover, Robert

COMING HOME N. Jaffer color *Dressage Today* v23 no6 p58 F 2017

Dover, Tessa L.

Diversity Policies Rarely Make Companies Fairer, and They Feel Threatening to White Men *Harvard Business Review Digital Articles* p2 Ja 4 2016

DOVE-VIEBAHN, AVIVA

Hidden Figures: The American Dream and the Untold Story of the Black Women Mathematicians Who Helped Win the Space Race *Ms.* v26 no4 p41 Wint 2016

PEACE STRENGTH WISDOM WONDER *Ms.* v27 no3 p31 Fall 2017

Dovico, Adam

Making a S.P.E.C.I.A.L. first impression *Phi Delta Kappan* v98 no3 p55 N 2016

DOW, CAITLIN

The (Blood) Pressure's ON *Nutrition Action Health Letter* v43 no10 p7 D 2016

EXERCISE *Nutrition Action Health Letter* v44 no3 p9 Ap 2017

Gut Check *Nutrition Action Health Letter* v44 no4 p9 My 2017

HAVE YOU HEARD *Nutrition Action Health Letter* v44 no2 p6 Mr 2017

LOW-CAL SWEETENERS: Do low-calorie sweeteners like aspartame and sucralose cause cancer? Make you gain weight? Give you diabetes? Here's what the best evidence shows *Nutrition Action Health Letter* v44 no7 p7 S 2017

Probiotics: What's in a name? *Nutrition Action Health Letter* v44 no6 p8 Jl/Ag 2017

DOW, ROBERT LAFAYETTE

Humor in Uniform *Reader's Digest* v190 no1134 p136 O 2017

Dow, Ron

Oran Van Crabbet G. Dearth *Arabian Horse World* v57 no1 p10 O 2016

Dow Chemical Co.

THE BEST TIME TO BE AN ENGINEER J. FITTERLING *Vital Speeches of the Day* v83 no4 p125 Ap 2017

Doward, Anastasia

Still worried *U.S. Catholic* v82 no10 p5 O 2017

Dowd, Kimberly A.

Rapid development of a DNA vaccine for Zika virus bibl graph *Science* v354 no6309 p237 O 14 2016

DOWD, MAUREEN

DIANE VON FURSTENBERG color *Vogue* v207 no3 p414 Mr 2017

Elon Musk's FUTURE SHOCK bw color *Vanity Fair* v59 no5 p116 Ap 2017

Their Town *New York Times Magazine* p30 N 6 2016

Dowd, Maureen, 1952- Interviews

Post Election—Dowd Dishes C. Kirch color *Publishers Weekly* v263 no44 p(Sp)23 O 31 2016

Dowdle, Hillari

7 ideas to ignite your passion for practice color *Yoga Journal* p14 2017 Special Issue

Altogether Now cartoon *Yoga Journal* p108 2017 Special Issue

calm & bright color *Yoga Journal* no288 p58 D 2016

GEAR ESSENTIALS color *Yoga Journal* p18 2017 Special Issue

get back on the mat color *Yoga Journal* p8 2017 Special Issue

Pampering with Purpose color *Yoga Journal* p100 2017 Special Issue

POST-PRACTICE PAUSE color *Yoga Journal* p112 2017 Special Issue

TAP YOUR CORE POWER SOURCE color *Yoga Journal* p42 2017 Special Issue

ways of the Warrior bw color *Yoga Journal* p28 2017 Special Issue

Dowell, Anthony

50 Years Ago This Month *Dance Magazine* v91 no6 p83 Je 2017

Dow Jones industrial average—Charts, diagrams, etc.

WATCHING THE DOW LEAP J. Wieczner diag *Fortune* v175 no2 p84 F 1 2017

DOWLATABADI, HADI

Rethinking the Social Cost of Carbon Dioxide: The standard benefit-cost methodology that is used to calculate marginal costs of environmental regulations should not be used for long-lasting greenhouse gases *Issues in Science & Technology* v33 no4 p43 Summ 2017

DOWLE, JAYNE

HOMES by the sea color *House Beautiful* p62 Ag 2017

Owning a slice of the seaside color *House Beautiful* p61 Ag 2017

Dowling, Daisy Wademan

7 Simple Ways Working Parents Can Simultaneously Improve Their Careers, Their Families, and Themselves *Harvard Business Review Digital Articles* p2 Ja 4 2016

Balancing Parenting and Work Stress: A Guide bw *Harvard Business Review Digital Articles* p2 Mr 9 2017

The Best Ways Your Organization Can Support Working Parents bw *Harvard Business Review Digital Articles* p2 Ja 31 2017

Giving Effective Feedback When You're Short on Time *Harvard Business Review Digital Articles* p2 F 16 2015

How to Handle Work When Your Child Is Sick *Harvard Business Review Digital Articles* p2 Jl 18 2017

How to Work from Home When You Have Kids *Harvard Business Review Digital Articles* p2 S 14 2017

What the U.S. Military Can Teach Companies About Supporting Employees' Families *Harvard Business Review Digital Articles* p1 My 11 2017

When You're Leaving Your Job Because of Your Kids [Cover story] *Harvard Business Review Digital Articles* p2 Ap 11 2017

DOWLING, MICHAEL

SHARJAH INTERNATIONAL BOOK FAIR/AMERICAN LIBRARY ASSOCIATION LIBRARY CONFERENCE NOW IN ITS THIRD YEAR color *Publishers Weekly* v263 no43 p(Sp)6 O 24 2016

Down Beat Student Music Awards

DownBeat Celebrates 40 Years of SMAs F. Alkyer color *Downbeat* v84 no6 p97 Je 2017

Welcome to the 40th Annual DownBeat Student Music Awards B. Reed color *Downbeat* v84 no6 p94 Je 2017

Down syndrome

DOING HER BEST: HOW GROWING UP ON A FARM HELPED MY SISTER-IN-LAW LEARN TO LIVE INDEPENDENTLY *Successful Farming* v115 no12 p66 O 2017

No Smiling *Weekly Standard* v22 no13 p2 D 5 2016

Down syndrome—Patients—Services for

Act of Love J. NORDLINGER color *National Review* v69 no3 p27 F 20 2017

Down Under (Music)

1983 L. Greenblatt color *Entertainment Weekly* no1449 p59 Ja 20 2017

DOWNER, JOHN

THE FOOD ISSUE *New York Times Magazine* p37 O 9 2016

DOWNES, CATHERINE

Beet Chili at Wayward Sons *D: The Magazine of Dallas* v43 no10 p80 O 2016

Downes, Larry

A Brief Review of Hillary Clinton's Innovation Plan *Harvard Business Review Digital Articles* p2 Jl 15 2016

The Business Implications of the EU-U.S. "Privacy Shield" *Harvard Business Review Digital Articles* p2 F 10 2016

The Downside of the FCC's New Internet Privacy Rules *Harvard Business Review Digital Articles* p2 My 27 2016

How Europe Can Create Its Own Silicon Valley *Harvard Business Review Digital Articles* p2 Je 11 2015

How to Understand the EU-U.S. Digital Divide *Harvard Business Review Digital Articles* p2 O 19 2015

Is Tesla Really a Disruptor? (And Why the Answer Matters) *Harvard Business Review Digital Articles* p2 2017

The Right and Wrong Ways to Regulate Self-Driving Cars *Harvard Business Review Digital Articles* p2 D 6 2016

The Tangled Web of Net Neutrality and Regulation *Harvard Business Review Digital Articles* p2 Mr 31 2017

The U.S. Supreme Court Is Reining in Patent Trolls, Which Is a Win for Innovation color *Harvard Business Review Digital Articles* p1 Je 2 2017

What's Wrong with the FAA's New Drone Rules *Harvard Business Review Digital Articles* p2 Mr 2 2015

Why Congress Needs to Pass the Innovation Act This Time *Harvard Business Review Digital Articles* p2 Mr 9 2015

Why the Public Utility Model Is the Wrong Approach for Internet Regulation *Harvard Business Review Digital Articles* p2 N 11 2014

Downey, Brynna G.

Lifetime of the solar nebula constrained by meteorite paleomagnetism bibl graph *Science* v355 no6325 p623 F 10 2017

DOWNEY, JESSICA

fall out of TOUCH cartoon *Yoga Journal* no288 p45 D 2016

Downey, Laura J.
BEST OF ATLANTA *Atlanta* v56 no8 p106 D 2016
Downey, Robert, 1965-
Quotable Quotes color *Reader's Digest* v190 no1134 p140 O 2017
Downhill skiing—Competitions
Dope Runners [Cover story] D. Page color *Powder* v46 no2 p62 O 2017
Downie, Gordon, 1964-
Canadian Authors, Artists Collaborate To Honor Chanie Wenjack L. A. Williams color *Publishers Weekly* v263 no46 p5 N 14 2016
A farewell for the ages M. BARCLAY color *Maclean's* v129 no48/49 p70 D 5 2016
TRAGICALLY HIP ADDED TO THE SYLLABUS M. BARCLAY color *Maclean's* v129 no44 p50 N 7 2016
Downing, David, 1946-
Lenin's Roller Coaster *Publishers Weekly* v264 no5 p179 Ja 30 2017
Downing, Taylor
BOMBED INTO DEMOCRACY *History Today* v67 no8 p104 Ag 2017
Muddled thinking on the Western Front *History Today* v67 no1 p65 Ja 2017
Downing, Tyler
One hundred years of Current Employment Statistics: busting CES myths bibl chart color graph *Monthly Labor Review* p1 O 2016
DOWNS, FRANK W.
READERS' THOUGHTS ON PAST ISSUES color *Motor Trend* v69 no2 p26 F 2017
Downsizing (Film)
DOWNSIZING J. Nolfi color *Entertainment Weekly* no1478 / 1479 p79 Ag 18-25 2017
Downsizing of organizations
Coping with the Effects of Emotionally Difficult Work J. Clair, J. J. Ladge et al *Harvard Business Review Digital Articles* p2 Ag 16 2016
How "Neutral" Layoffs Disproportionately Affect Women and Minorities A. Kalev *Harvard Business Review Digital Articles* p2 Jl 26 2016
Is our redundancy process ageist? *People Management* p53 F 2017
What Intel Needs to Remember About Marketing N. Dawar *Harvard Business Review Digital Articles* p2 Ap 25 2016
Downstream Response to Imposed Flow Transformations
Understanding Set and Drift C. McBride graph *Sail* v47 no12 p44 D 2016
Downton Abbey (TV program)
The Bullseye M. Snetiker color *Entertainment Weekly* no1473 p64 Jl 7 2017
LADY IN RED L. Brown color *InStyle* v24 no3 p320 Mr 2017
NBA or BBC? T. Keith chart color *Sports Illustrated* v126 no18 p16 Je 26 2017
Downtown Boys (Performer)
NIGHT LIFE cartoon *New Yorker* v93 no6 p9 Mr 27 2017
Downward Dog (TV program)
America's top TV critic Matt Roush answers your burning questions *TV Guide* v65 no25 p3 Je 2017
Downward Dog: A tale (tail?) of two endearing underdogs M. ROUSH *TV Guide* v65 no23 p12 My 29 2017
Doxzen, Kevin W.
Structures of the CRISPR genome integration complex color *Science* v357 no6356 p1113 S 15 2017
Doya, David Malingha
The Race to Lead South Africa Is On color *Bloomberg Businessweek* no4524 p15 My 29 2017
Doyle, Amy
The Big Disconnect in Your Talent Strategy and How to Fix It *Harvard Business Review Digital Articles* p2 D 23 2016
Doyle, Arthur Conan, Sir, 1859-1930
Sherlock Out Loud: Stephen Fry narrates Arthur Conan Doyle's tales of a certain obsessive detective S. Callow *New York Times Book Review* p16 My 21 2017
Doyle, Brian, 1956-2017
The Adventures of John Carson in Several Quarters of the World: A Novel of Robert Louis Stevenson *Publishers Weekly* v264 no5 p174 Ja 30 2017

The Courage of His Convictions color *U.S. Catholic* v82 no11 p23 N 2017
DIES MIRACULUM B. Doyle *U.S. Catholic* v82 no8 p51 Ag 2017
A ferocious attention J. Hiskes *Christian Century* v134 no14 p10 Jl 5 2017
God, a note color *U.S. Catholic* v82 no1 p34 Ja 2017
Grace R. WILSON *American Scholar* v86 no2 p2 Spr 2017
Hall Mass color *U.S. Catholic* v82 no9 p36 S 2017
The Lightness of Errol Flynn *American Scholar* v86 no1 p100 Wint 2017
One afternoon in October *Christian Century* v133 no21 p11 O 12 2016
People C. Kennel-Shank *Christian Century* v134 no13 p17 Je 21 2017
Poem for a Quiet Lady at Saint Patrick's Church in Oregon color *U.S. Catholic* v82 no3 p11 Mr 2017
A Prayer For Our Daily Murder color *U.S. Catholic* v82 no2 p22 F 2017
Preamble H. E. Blake *Orion Magazine* v36 no1 p1 Ja/F 2017
The Requisite Darkness color *U.S. Catholic* v82 no4 p11 Ap 2017
Sanctuary color *U.S. Catholic* v82 no8 p29 Ag 2017
The Special Collection color *U.S. Catholic* v82 no5 p34 My 2017
Such Great Heights color *America* v215 p25 N 28 2016
THEIR IRREPRESSIBLE INNOCENCE color *Orion Magazine* v35 no6 p64 N/D 2016
Doyle, Diana
The Dry Tortugas color *Sail* v48 no6 p40 Je 2017
Doyle, Glennon
The Beauty Complex color *O, The Oprah Magazine* p39 N 2017
Come Out, Come Out, Whoever You Are color *O, The Oprah Magazine* p41 O 2017
A Mighty Mess color *O, The Oprah Magazine* p44 S 2017
Doyle, James E.
An occurrence at Oak Ridge: Morality in an age of nuclear peril bibl *Bulletin of the Atomic Scientists* v73 no2 p135 Mr 2017
Doyle, Jane
Interview Jane Doyle Recognizing WASPs [Cover story] bw color *Military History* v34 no4 p14 N 2017
Doyle, Jennifer
The Nation on its Honour *History Today* v67 no2 p3 F 2017
Doyle, John
Leicester City FC and the Benefits of an Underdog Brand *Harvard Business Review Digital Articles* p2 Ag 12 2016
Doyle, John M.
Probing the frontiers of particle physics with tabletop-scale experiments color graph *Science* v357 no6355 p990 S 8 2017
DOYLE, JULIE
home sweet cabin color *Cabin Living* p18 Ap 2017
Doyle, Kevin—Interviews
Environmental Career Forecasting S. Myrick *Parks & Recreation* v52 no4 p16 Ap 2017
Doyle, Mark
The Dry Tortugas color *Sail* v48 no6 p40 Je 2017
Doyle, Mike
DAN ABOUT TOWN: Party photographer Dan Swartz's monthly roundup of bashes, balls, and benefits *Washingtonian Magazine* v52 no11 p26 Ag 2017
DOYLE, PATRICK
THE 50 GREATEST CONCERTS OF THE LAST 50 YEARS bw color *Rolling Stone* no1286 p30 My 4 2017
Auerbach's Cheat Sheet bw color *Rolling Stone* no1290 p16 Je 29 2017
Benjamin Booker's L.A. Punk Chic bw color *Rolling Stone* no1287 p16 My 18 2017
Billy Joel [Cover story] bw *Rolling Stone* no1289 p62 Je 15 2017
Bonnie Raitt bw *Rolling Stone* no1287 p58 My 18 2017
Chuck Berry's Final Gift color *Rolling Stone* no1284 p16 Ap 6 2017
Dr. Hunter S. Thompson bw color *Rolling Stone* no1284 p24 Ap 6 2017
Eric Church bw *Rolling Stone* no1272 p58 O 20 2016
FALL ALBUM PREVIEW *Rolling Stone* no1297 p12 O 5 2017
Gary Clark Jr.'s Juke-Joint Couture color *Rolling Stone* no1278/1279 p16 Ja 12 2017
Hot Secret Weapon Rostam Batmanglij color *Rolling Stone*

no1274 p37 N 17 2016

Jack Antonoff's Therapy Rock color *Rolling Stone* no1290 p22 Je 29 2017

Judd Apatow bw *Rolling Stone* no1288 p58 Je 1 2017

The Legend Next Door bw color *Rolling Stone* no1278/1279 p38 Ja 12 2017

Phish's New Harmony bw color *Rolling Stone* no1273 p40 N 3 2016

The Photo Issue [Cover story] bw *Rolling Stone* no1299 p24 N 2 2017

Q&A: Jason Isbell color *Rolling Stone* no1293 p26 Ag 10 2017

Q&A: John Mayer color *Rolling Stone* no1291/1292 p30 Jl 13 2017

Q&A Robert Plant color *Rolling Stone* no1297 p19 O 5 2017

Rhinestone Superstar bw color *Rolling Stone* no1295 p16 S 7 2017

The Road Heats Up bw color *Rolling Stone* no1288 p11 Je 1 2017

Sam Smith's Raw Return bw color *Rolling Stone* no1298 p13 O 19 2017

Willie Nelson *Rolling Stone* no1288 p18 Je 1 2017

Doyle, Roddy, 1958-

All That Shite J. Walton bw color *New York Review of Books* v64 no17 p44 N 9 2017

WHEN THE PAST INTRUDES ON THE PRESENT W. SMITH color *Publishers Weekly* v264 no36 p59 S 4 2017

Doyle, Sabrina

Alone Across the Arctic map *Canadian Geographic* v137 no2 p30 Mr/Ap 2017

CALIFORNIA color map *Canadian Geographic* v135 no6 p32 D 2015

CITIZEN SCIENCE PROGRAMS color *Canadian Geographic* v135 no6 p80 D 2015

Cory Trépanier color *Canadian Geographic* v137 no1 p19 F 2017

DOWN TO EARTH color *Canadian Geographic* v137 no4 p58 Jl/Ag 2017

EXPLORER-IN-RESIDENCE SCHOOL VISITS color *Canadian Geographic* v136 no6 p77 D 2016

FEATURED FELLOW: SHELLEY AMBROSE color *Canadian Geographic* v137 no1 p78 F 2017

Marvellous Maine map *Canadian Geographic* v135 no6 p16 D 2015

ONE OCEAN EXPEDITIONS EXPANDS FLEET TO IN-CLUDE RCGS RESOLUTE color *Canadian Geographic* v137 no5 p75 S/O 2017

Robin Mazumder color *Canadian Geographic* v137 no3 p19 My 2017

DOYLE, SADY

The End of Roe as We Know It? *In These Times* v41 no1 p17 Ja 2017

MOTHERS OF THE WORLD, UNITE! *In These Times* v41 no6 p44 Je 2017

Trump Family Values *In These Times* v41 no5 p24 My 2017

Doyle, Thomas

DISCOVERING THEIR IDENTITY: Using gender nonconforming picture books in early education classrooms color *Literacy Today (2411-7862)* v34 no6 p20 My/Je 2017

Doyle, Tom

Captain Fantastic: Elton John's Stellar Trip Through the '70s *Publishers Weekly* v264 no4 p72 Ja 23 2017

D'oyley, Demetria Lucas

DeWanda Wise color *Essence* v47 no11 p42 Mr 2017

VANESSA + JILLIAN [Cover story] color *Essence* v47 no9 p58 Ja 2017

D'oyly Carte Opera Co. (Performer)

Obituaries *Opera News* v81 no6 p63 D 2016

Dozier, Lamont

HOLLAND-DOZIER-HOLLAND V. Cunningham *New Yorker* v92 no42 p76 D 19 2016

DPA Microphones (Company)

A history of precision and perfection continues to define DPA Microphones *Stage Directions* v30 no3 p15 Mr 2017

Dr. Brite (Company)

Winter Whites color *Prevention* v69 no1 p11 Ja 2017

Dr. Ken (TV program)

Dr. Ken J. Halterman *TV Guide* v64 no40 p58 O 3 2016

Dr. Wang Skincare LLC

breakthrough skin reliever color *Good Housekeeping* v264 no4

p92 Ap 2017

Drabble, Margaret, 1939-

CRACKING THE TEACUP A. M. WILSON color *Publishers Weekly* v264 no7 p42 F 13 2017

The Last Road Trip C. Ozick *New York Times Book Review* p1 F 19 2017

Dracunculiasis

THE RADICATOR B. YEOMAN *Atlanta* v57 no4 p66 Ag 2017

Draft (Military service)

See also

Draft registration

Draft registration

Should Women Have to Register for the Draft? J. SPEIER and E. DONNELLY *New York Times Upfront* v149 no11 p22 Ap 3 2017

Draft resisters

HELL, NO, WE WON'T GO! B. Davidson *Saturday Evening Post* v289 no4 p42 Jl/Ag 2017

Drafts (Authorship)—Exhibitions

A Treasure to Behold *USA Today Magazine* v146 no2866 p20 Jl 2017

Drag contests

ABORIGINAL QUEEN OF THE DESERT color *Advocate* no1091 p17 Je/Jl 2017

Drag queens

From Drag to Riches [Cover story] M. Snetiker color *Entertainment Weekly* no1471 p23 Je 23 2017

QUEENS FOR A DAY [Cover story] T. Manring color *Chicago* v66 no9 p112 S 2017

RuPaul Gets Political S. KORNHABER bw *Atlantic* v319 no5 p20 Je 2017

STORY TIME M. Meltzer cartoon *New Yorker* v92 no38 p33 N 21 2016

Drag Race (TV program)

Gaga Hitches a Ride on Drag Race J. Nolfi color *Entertainment Weekly* no1457/1458 p17 Mr 17 2017

Drag racing

2016 Pro Stock Problems, Solutions, and the Future T. Taylor color *Hot Rod* v70 no6 p60 Je 2017

BEAUTY BEYOND THE TWILIGHT ZONE T. Taylor bw color *Hot Rod* v70 no4 p30 Ap 2017

Bee Line Dragway N. AUSTIN *Arizona Highways* v93 no8 p8 Ag 2017

Brownsburg: Pit stops worth making in the west side's other racing town J. BURNHAM color diag *Indianapolis Monthly* v41 no2 p36 S 2017

The HOT ROD Archives D. Wallace color *Hot Rod* v70 no12 p10 D 2017

The HOT ROD Magazine Championship Drag Races T. Taylor bw *Hot Rod* v70 no2 p10 F 2017

Of missile bases and drag races M. Rechtin color *Motor Trend* v69 no11 p24 N 2017

Take 5 With CONNIE KALITTA T. Taylor bw color *Hot Rod* v70 no1 p20 Ja 2017

Until Next Time E. Perkins, B. Gillogly et al color *Hot Rod* v70 no12 p6 D 2017

Why the Rare Willys Was the Go-To Gasser T. Taylor color *Hot Rod* v70 no4 p84 Ap 2017

World's Greatest Drag Race E. Loh color graph *Motor Trend* v69 no11 p84 N 2017

Drag racing—Competitions

BIG K. Cameron color *Cycle World* v56 no5 p68 Je 2017

Drag racing—History

First Manufacturers Funny Car Championship T. Taylor bw *Hot Rod* v70 no12 p8 D 2017

Dragan, Lauren

Noise Cancellation Goes Blue color *Sound & Vision* v82 no2 p18 F/Mr 2017

Dragojevic, Katija

Berlioz: Roméo et Juliette J. Malafronte *Opera News* v81 no9 p52 Mr 2017

Dragonette (Performer)

DRAGONETTE DANCE THE PAIN AWAY N. Feeney color *Entertainment Weekly* no1440 p59 N 18 2016

Dragonflies

Bet you didn't know M. HARRIS color *National Geographic Kids*

Road Hawgs bw color *Field & Stream* v122 no2 p39 Je/Jl 2017

THE SHORE BOAR bw color *Field & Stream* v122 no1 p15 My 2017

SNOW BIRDS color *Field & Stream* v121 no6 p14 N 2016

Draper, Robert

Fragile Peace color map *National Geographic* v230 no5 p108 N 2016

HOW DONALD TRUMP'S OFF A CIVIL WAR WITHIN THE RIGHT-WING MEDIA *New York Times Magazine* p36 O 2 2016

How Hillary Became 'Hillary' *New York Times Magazine* p46 O 16 2016

OBAMA THE CARE OPERATION *New York Times Magazine* p32 F 19 2017

TRUMP VS. CONGRESS *New York Times Magazine* p30 Ap 2 2017

Draper, Ruth, 1884-1956

WHAT SHE SAID D. Owen cartoon *New Yorker* v92 no43 p21 Ja 2 2017

Draperies

Block Party [Cover story] color *Martha Stewart Living* p30 S 2017

CURTAINS TO CARPETS *Design Center Sourcebook* p83 2016

Drapery & Tracking *Stage Directions* v30 no7 p24 Jl 1 2017

Hanging Curtains & Drapery: 1900–1939 B. D. Coleman color *Arts & Crafts Homes & the Revival* v12 no4 p22 Fall 2017

Hanging Drapery B. D. Coleman bw color *Old House Journal* v45 no6 p52 S 2017

Spring Forward T. BROOKS and D. POINTDUJOUR color *Ebony* v72 no5 p53 Mr 2017

Draperies in interior decoration

backyard hideaway B. MOLLENKAMP color *Better Homes & Gardens* v95 no8 p84 Ag 2017

CURTAINS TO CARPETS color *Old House Journal* v44 p83 2016 Design Center source Book

Draperies—Equipment & supplies

Finishing Touches FOR WINDOWS & WALLS L. Elliott cartoon *Old House Journal* v45 no1 p48 F 2017

Draperies—Evaluation

As You Like It color *Martha Stewart Living* no275 p24 Je 2017

A DARLING SITTING ROOM K. Istomin and H. BROWN color *House Beautiful* v159 no1 p38 F 2017

Furnishings color *Architectural Record* v204 no12 p120 D 2016

Get the Look color *House Beautiful* v159 no1 p28 F 2017

TEXTILES cartoon color *Arts & Crafts Homes & the Revival* v12 no1 p14 2017 Resouce Guide

Drapery industry

The Evolving World of Fabrics and Soft Goods K. M. Mitchell *Stage Directions* v29 no11 p32 N 2016

Draut, Tamara

Waking up the working class L. Daniel color *Christian Century* v133 no23 p36 N 9 2016

Drawing

See also

Pencil drawing

ABOVE & BEYOND cartoon *New Yorker* v93 no14 p22 My 22 2017

Angels Speaking Hebrew L. Copan color *Christian Century* v133 no22 p47 O 26 2016

Drawing Center E. Buhe color *Art in America* v105 no1 p77 Ja 2017

Drawing connections J. McDermott color *Science* v356 no6343 p1202 Je 16 2017

The Drawing I Can't Stop Thinking About J. SALTZ img *New York* v50 no11 p112 My 29 2017

HOW DO YOU CREATE? *Missouri Life* v43 no6 p10 O/N 2016

Kepler near the terminator E. RIX bw color *Astronomy* v45 no11 p64 N 2017

Memory hooks E. RIX bw *Astronomy* v45 no2 p68 F 2017

Drawing equipment

IS THAT WHAT THEY SHOULD LOOK LIKE? T. Harris, B. Stoker et al bw color *Reader's Digest* v190 no1134 p98 O 2017

Drawing exhibitions

BENNY ANDREWS J. Kreimer color *Art in America* v105 no3 p128 Mr 2017

EXPLORATORY WORKS: DRAWINGS FROM THE DEPART-MENT OF TROPICAL RESEARCH FIELD EXPEDITIONS

Issues in Science & Technology v33 no4 p71 Summ 2017

GALLERIES AND MUSEUMS color *New York Review of Books* v64 no7 p63 Ap 20 2017

THE HERE AND THEN R. Kalina bw cartoon color *Art in America* v105 no4 p72 Ap 2017

SEEING JUSTICE DONE *USA Today Magazine* v145 no2864 p48 My 2017

TINO SEHGAL K. Green cartoon *Art in America* v105 no3 p139 Mr 2017

Drawing rooms

editor's note S. BROWN *Timber Home Living* p8 2017 SpecialIssue

Drawing software

Microsoft will save Microsoft Paint, making it a downloadable app M. HACHMAN color *PCWorld* v35 no9 p18 S 2017

DRAXLER, BREANNA

Dovekies Have a New Diet and Workout Plan *Audubon* v119 no2 p16 Summ 2017

Drayden, Nicky

THE ONE QUESTION INTERVIEW: NICKY DRAYDEN D. OYENIYI *Texas Monthly* v45 no6 p54 Je 2017

Drayton, Poppy

The Shannara Chronicles N. Abrams, B. L. Heldman et al *Entertainment Weekly* no1482/1483 p79 S 22 2017

Drdla-Schutting, R.

Gliogenic LTP spreads widely in nociceptive pathways bibl graph *Science* v354 no6316 p1144 D 2 2016

Dream of the Red Chamber (Theatrical production)

Dream of the Red Chamber R. M. Rinaldi *Opera News* v81 no6 p40 D 2016

Dreamcar (Performer)

DREAMCAR K. O'Donnell *Entertainment Weekly* no1446/1447 p77 D 2016/Ja 2017

Dreamed Path, The (Film)

THE DREAMED PATH J. Cronk color *Film Comment* v53 no1 p24 Ja/F 2017

Dreamer Is the Dream, The (Music)

CHRIS POTTER WAKING DREAMS T. Panken color *Downbeat* v84 no6 p42 Je 2017

Dreams

See also

Men's dreams

13 Things Your Dreams Reveal About You M. CROUCH *Reader's Digest* v188 no1124 p132 O 2016

Anxiety Dreams R. Lyster color *New York Times Magazine* p30 D 11 2016

DREAM CATCHERS N. Strochlic color *National Geographic* v231 no5 p22 My 2017

DREAMING VERSUS DOING S. Weigel bw color *Flying* v144 no8 p38 Ag 2017

God, a note B. Doyle color *U.S. Catholic* v82 no1 p34 Ja 2017

THE INTERPRETATION OF DREAMS B. PIKE bw *Power & Motoryacht* v34 no6 p144 Je 2017

Dreams (Music)

St. Patrick's Day Party Playlist color *Entertainment Weekly* no1457/1458 p24 Mr 17 2017

Dreams—Psychological aspects

Make Yourself Clear M. Beck color *O, The Oprah Magazine* p48 O 2017

NUDE NIGHTMARES bw *Women's Health* v14 no7 p42 S 2017

Dreezy (Performer)

7 HIP-HOP QUEENS TO HEAR NOW N. Feeney color *Entertainment Weekly* no1435 p57 O 14 2016

DREHER, BETH

Secrets the FBI May Not Want You to Know *Reader's Digest* v188 no1125 p144 N 2016

Dreher, Rob

Salt and Leaven P. WEHNER color *National Review* v69 no6 p40 Ap 3 2017

Dreher, Rod

Benedict Option I: Dreher's Plaintive Call B. P. MITCHELL bw *American Conservative* v16 no3 p44 My/Je 2017

Benedict Option II: The Jewish Example S. KAPLAN *American Conservative* v16 no3 p46 My/Je 2017

Deep roots, open doors S. Thorngate color *Christian Century* v134 no11 p22 My 24 2017

Detachment Plan P. Baumann color *Commonweal* v144 no7 p27 Ap 14 2017

Hillbilly Energy *American Conservative* v16 no1 p42 Ja/F 2017

The Idea of a Christian Village [Cover story] R. Dreher cartoon color *Christianity Today* p34 Mr 2017

Joy in the Mourning A. T. Walker *Weekly Standard* v22 no26 p36 Mr 13 2017

NAVIGATING the BENEDICT OPTION P. Gilger color *America* v216 no8 p18 Ap 17 2017

THE SEEKER J. ROTHMAN cartoon color *New Yorker* v93 no11 p46 My 1 2017

Dreher, Rod—Interviews

AN INTERVIEW WITH ROD DREHER B. MCCORMICK color *America* v216 no8 p24 Ap 17 2017

Dreibus, Tony

BLUE SKY IN AGRICULTURE *Successful Farming* v115 no1 p34 Ja 2017

Dreidel (Game)

THE BEST BET img *New York* v49 no25 p95 D 12 2016

Dreier, Lisa

No Company Can Solve a Massive Global Problem on Its Own *Harvard Business Review Digital Articles* p2 Ja 21 2016

Dreisbach, Shaun

50 States of Women bw chart color map *Glamour* v115 no9 p146 S 2017

Aussie Invasion color *Glamour* no8 p102 Ag 2017

By Women, for Women color *Glamour* v115 no2 p86 F 2017

The Cocktail Justification Matrix cartoon chart color *Glamour* v114 no12 p153 D 2016

Cooking the Pinterest Way color *Glamour* v115 no6 p88 Je 2017

Female Chefs Teach You to Cook color *Glamour* v115 no2 p66 F 2017

How Emma Stone Got Ripped color *Glamour* v115 no9 p114 S 2017

Meet the Avo Bowl color *Glamour* v115 no7 p60 Jl 2017

Simone BILES color *Glamour* v114 no12 p210 D 2016

Soup Is the New Juice color *Glamour* v114 no7 p89 Jl 2016

To Hell With Resolutions color *Glamour* v115 no1 p44 Ja 2017

"We Always Want to Win" color *Glamour* v114 no7 p104 Jl 2016

Why I Love One-Pan Dinners color *Glamour* v115 no4 p128 Ap 2017

Yoga That Will Kick Your Ass color *Glamour* v115 no11 p98 N 2017

Your Favorite Fall Foods, Hacked! color *Glamour* v114 no11 p113 N 2016

Dreismann, Alexander

Single-molecule optomechanics in "picocavities" bibl graph *Science* v354 no6313 p726 N 11 2016

Drell, Cady

I Love You—Now Go Home color *Glamour* v115 no11 p105 N 2017

Let's Get You Your Raise! cartoon *Glamour* v115 no11 p110 N 2017

Orgasm Pressure: Why?! cartoon color graph *Glamour* v115 no11 p108 N 2017

Sex, Super Likes & Five Years of Tinder color *Glamour* v115 no5 p113 My 2017

Drell, Sidney D. (Sidney David), 1926-2016

Book on Sakharov raises issues *Physics Today* v70 no2 p14 F 2017

Farewell to a Citizen-Scientist D. E. Hoffman *Hoover Digest: Research & Opinion on Public Policy* no2 p160 Spr 2017

Sidney David Drell J. D. Bjorken, R. L. Garwin et al *Physics Today* v70 no9 p69 S 2017

DREMAN, DAVID

GET READY FOR A BOND MELTDOWN *Forbes* v198 no8 p66 D 20 2016

The Last Video Chain color *Forbes* v199 no2 p52 F 28 2017

DRESCHER, ELIZABETH

A Virtual Faith color *America* v215 no10 p22 O 10 2016

Dresner, Alexander

Health Care Providers Need a Value Management Office *Harvard Business Review Digital Articles* p2 D 2 2015

Dresner, Amy

My Fair Junkie: A Memoir of Getting Dirty and Staying Clean *Publishers Weekly* v264 no26 p168 Je 26 2017

Dress code laws

Balance needed on dress codes *People Management* p6 Je 2017

Dress codes

See also

Dress codes in the workplace

Soup and Fishy color *Weekly Standard* v22 no44 p2 Jl 31 2017

The Style Guy M. A. Green cartoon color *GQ: Gentlemen's Quarterly* v97 no4 p50 Ap 2017

Dress codes in the workplace

The D.C. Working Man's True Power Suit S. Jefferies color *Washington Monthly* v49 no3-5 p6 Mr-My 2017

Is it time to ditch the dress code? ODUM *People Management* p44 N 2016

TRANS COMMUNITY AND SUMMER DRESS CODES [Cover story] *USA Today Magazine* v146 no2867 p1 Ag 2017

Dress codes in the workplace—Lawsuits & claims

ECJ rules employers can ban religious clothing: But it would be 'foolhardy' to change dress codes based on this case, experts warn *People Management* p16 Ap 2017

Dress codes—Great Britain

Balance needed on dress codes *People Management* p6 Je 2017

Dressage

See also

Dressage competitions

Riding aids

14 TRAINING TIPS FROM OLYMPIAN CARL HESTER [Cover story] K. F. Miller color *Practical Horseman* v45 no7 p42 Jl 2017

16 Questions with INGRID KLIMKE C. Wyllie color *Dressage Today* v23 no12 p52 S 2017

7 Things to Do in SEPTEMBER *Practical Horseman* v45 no9 p70 S 2017

Basic Horse Behavior for Dressage Success K. Dupont and A. Morris color *Dressage Today* v24 no1 p24 O 2017

Choose the Arabian Sporthorse J. Winkel color *Practical Horseman* v45 no1 p13 Ja 2017

Collection with THROUGHNESS and FORWARD DESIRE S. Hassler and B. Baumert color *Dressage Today* v24 no1 p28 O 2017

CREATING HARMONY AND EXPRESSION A. Carter color *Practical Horseman* v45 no2 p36 F 2017

DEVELOPING COLLECTION WITHOUT RESISTANCE K. Adams color *Practical Horseman* v45 no9 p46 S 2017

DRESSAGE AT DEVON 2016 *Dressage Today* v23 no5 p12 Ja 2017

DRESSAGE SNAPSHOT color *Dressage Today* v23 no9 p16 Je 2017

DRESSAGE SNAPSHOT color *Dressage Today* v24 no1 p16 O 2017

A FIRST LOOK AT COUNTER CANTER C. Foxley color diag *Dressage Today* v23 no4 p21 D 2016

Four Disciplines, Similar Themes S. Oliynyk color *Practical Horseman* v45 no7 p6 Jl 2017

Half Halts and Sliding Stops L. Mulvany color *Dressage Today* v23 no12 p62 S 2017

The Healing Power of Dressage T. Steward color *Dressage Today* v23 no9 p20 Je 2017

Here's How J. Jo Tate and C. Heleski color diag graph *Practical Horseman* v45 no9 p66 S 2017

Here's How J. J. TATE, S. LICO et al color *Practical Horseman* v45 no8 p56 Ag 2017

How can I keep my horse from jigging? color *Practical Horseman* v44 no12 p58 D 2016

Journey Through Germany J. Mellace *Dressage Today* v23 no7 p12 Mr 2017

LIPICA: The Original Home of the LIPIZZANER A. Morris color *Dressage Today* v23 no11 p44 Ag 2017

A New Meaning for "Never" S. Jacobsen color *Dressage Today* p62 My 2017

NEWS FROM THE DRESSAGE FOUNDATION color *Dressage Today* v24 no1 p14 O 2017

A Noble Champion Emerges J. Grossman color *Dressage Today* v23 no11 p62 Ag 2017

Praising the Horsey Parents J. Mellace *Dressage Today* v24 no2 p10 N 2017

PUSHING AWAY FROM THE BIT [Cover story] C. Traurig and B. Baumert color *Dressage Today* v23 no4 p24 D 2016

HIGHLIGHTS OF THE 2017 DRESSAGE4KIDS WEEKEND EQUESTRIAN PROGRAM *Dressage Today* v23 no8 p12 Ap 2017

Dressage—Awards

ISABELL WERTH TAKES TOP HONORS AT THE FEI WORLD CUP DRESSAGE FINAL OMAHA 2017 color *Dressage Today* v23 no9 p14 Je 2017

Three Cheers for the Coach of the Year K. Beaudoin color *Dressage Today* v23 no4 p66 D 2016

Dressage—Congresses

HIGHLIGHTS OF THE 2017 DRESSAGE4KIDS WEEKEND EQUESTRIAN PROGRAM *Dressage Today* v23 no8 p12 Ap 2017

INSIGHTS from Lilo Fore and Hans-Christian Matthiesen B. Baumert color graph *Dressage Today* v23 no8 p36 Ap 2017

Words of WISDOM from the West Coast L. Paulsen color *Dressage Today* v23 no8 p44 Ap 2017

Dressage—Equipment & supplies

emporium bw color *Dressage Today* v23 no11 p64 Ag 2017

emporium color *Dressage Today* v23 no6 p62 F 2017

Dressage—Societies, etc.

The IDA School Horse: A Breed of its Own K. Beaudoin color *Dressage Today* v23 no4 p36 D 2016

Dresselhaus, Mildred S., 1930-2017

Mildred S. Dresselhaus M. Endo, A. Jorio et al *Physics Today* v70 no6 p73 Je 2017

Dresses

BEST DRESS E. Wilson color *InStyle* v24 no11 p69 N 2017

BEST DRESS E. Wilson color *InStyle* v24 no8 p71 Ag 2017

BRIGHT YOUNG THINGS E. ELWICK-BATES and R. WALDMAN bw color *Vogue* v206 no11 p246 N 2016

THE CHIC SHEATH color *Vogue* v207 no9 p402 S 2017

CHILLI PEPPER B. Zehme cartoon *Chicago* v66 no1 p170 Ja 2017

Feel the BURN E. Wilson color *InStyle* v23 no12 p69 N 2016

Flowers in THE ATTIC *Interview* v46 no10 p114 D 2016/Ja 2017

HER 10 BEST EVER! Amy Adams E. Wilson color *InStyle* v23 no12 p74 N 2016

Kicking It color *Vogue* v207 no11 p172 N 2017

LET IT FLOW color *Essence* v47 no12 p17 Ap 2017

NINE NEW COLLABS: Coming soon img *New York* v49 no23 p52 N 14 2016

OFF THE SHOULDER bw color *Vogue* v207 no9 p400 S 2017

The Return of the Dynasty Dress color *Glamour* v115 no9 p216 S 2017

TOP OF THE ROCKS color *Vogue* v207 no11 p216 N 2017

TRAUMARAMA cartoon color *Seventeen* v76 no12 p108 D 2016/Ja 2017

Treasure ISLAND E. ELWICK-BATES color *Vogue* v207 no7 p126 Jl 2017

Under $50 Message Tees color *Seventeen* v76 no5 p32 S 2017

Dresses—Evaluation

$100 & Under color *Seventeen* p74 Ja 1 2017

4 dress-up & date-night solutions color *Redbook* p62 Je 2017

Adam's STYLE SHEET color *O, The Oprah Magazine* p64 My 2017

Amazing Lace S. P. Nadella color *Glamour* v114 no12 p96 D 2016

AMERICAN DAY DREAM color *Vogue* v207 no9 p684 S 2017

BEST DRESS E. Wilson color *InStyle* v24 no4 p73 Ap 2017

BOLD is what this season is all about. Look to GRAPHIC pieces that speak volumes and notice-me PRINTS that will turn heads color *Harper's Bazaar* no3650 p170 F 2017

BRIGHT SPOT color *Harper's Bazaar* no3650 p88 F 2017

THE CIRCLE GAME color *Vogue* v207 no3 p490 Mr 2017

COMFORT & JOY color *Women's Health* v14 no6 p148 Jl 2017

DANCING ON AIR color *Harper's Bazaar* no3648 p238 N 2016

FABULOUS at Every Age color *Harper's Bazaar* no3649 p239 D 2016/Ja 2017

THE Fan Girl C. Brody color *Glamour* v115 no10 p172 O 2017

FASHION UNDER $100 color *Redbook* p47 Je 2017

FASHION UNDER $100 S. AFFELT color *Redbook* p60 N 2017

Fighting Shape color *Glamour* v114 no7 p120 Jl 2016

Flower POWER color *Seventeen* v76 no2 p29 Mr 2017

THE FREE SPIRIT J. BLAKENEY color *Martha Stewart Living* p56 Jl/Ag 2017

FULL EFFECT J. Wilson color *Essence* v47 no11 p28 Mr 2017

THE GIRL Zoey Deutch E. Wilson color *InStyle* v24 no4 p89 Ap 2017

GREETINGS FROM CALIFORNIA color *Seventeen* p172 Ja 1 2017

her style color *InStyle* v24 no8 p32 Ag 2017

HVN color *Harper's Bazaar* no3648 p174 N 2016

instant style color *InStyle* v24 no4 p105 Ap 2017

InSTYLE June 2017 color *InStyle* v24 no6 p117 Je 2017

IN TO THE WILD C. ROITFELD color *Harper's Bazaar* no3649 p273 D 2016/Ja 2017

It's a Small World L. IMMEDIATO *Los Angeles Magazine* p31 Ap 2017

KHAKI, CLASS OF '17 color *Women's Health* v14 no3 p47 Ap 2017

THE LADY Sharon Stone E. Wilson color *InStyle* v24 no11 p84 N 2017

Major MINIS color *Seventeen* p88 Ja 1 2017

MATERIAL WORLD E. ELWICK-BATES color *Vogue* v207 no4 p254 Ap 2017

Mix & Match E. Wilson color *InStyle* v24 no2 p58 F 2017

THE MUST-HAVE color *Harper's Bazaar* no3648 p100 N 2016

"My goal is to find the easiest way to look effortless and unique." S. Schmitz bw color *Women's Health* v14 no3 p52 Ap 2017

THE NEW NEUTRALS color *Harper's Bazaar* no3650 p160 F 2017

Off to the Races J. B. Hager color *Southern Living* v52 no4 p62 Ap 2017

on demand color *InStyle* v24 no11 p61 N 2017

ON THE LINE color *Harper's Bazaar* no3657 p131 O 2017

Outfits for Days T. Nguyen color *Glamour* v115 no6 p42 Je 2017

pastels color *Good Housekeeping* v264 no5 p54 My 2017

PETAL PUSHERS color *Harper's Bazaar* no3652 p122 Ap 2017

PLAID TO THE BONE: A fall trend as versatile as it is classic E. STUART *Virginia Living* v15 no6 p37 O 2017

Putting on a Show N. REMSEN bw color *Vogue* v207 no10 p198 O 2017

ROCK SOLID color *Vogue* v207 no4 p228 Ap 2017

ROCK YOUR BODY color *Seventeen* p186 Ja 1 2017

RUNWAY REPORT color *Harper's Bazaar* no3650 p206 F 2017

Scoring the Looks You Loved I. Biedenharn and C. Ciammaichelli color *Entertainment Weekly* no1449 p20 Ja 20 2017

See the Light color *Seventeen* p200 Ja 1 2017

Shop Guide color *O, The Oprah Magazine* p173 My 2017

SHOP SPRING'S MUST-HAVE LOOKS color *Harper's Bazaar* no3650 p84 F 2017

STYLE CRUSH Anya Taylor-Joy S. Simon color *InStyle* v24 no4 p94 Ap 2017

THINK pink color *Harper's Bazaar* no3649 p298 D 2016/Ja 2017

Va-Va-Va Velvet S. P. Nadella color *Glamour* v114 no12 p92 D 2016

WAY OUT YONDER color *Vogue* v207 no9 p730 S 2017

What's Your PROM STYLE? color *Seventeen* p80 Ja 1 2017

WILD THINGS S. Zlotnick *Washingtonian Magazine* v52 no1 p107 O 2016

Dressing tables

DIMINUTIVE QUEEN ANNE CHERRY SCALLOPED TOP LOWBOY FROM THE CONNECTICUT RIVER VALLEY color *Magazine Antiques* v184 no3 p2 My/Je 2017

Hello! L. Brown color *InStyle* v24 no5 p18 My 2017

Dressmaking

FIESTA Gown A. FULKERSON *Texas Monthly* v44 no11 p108 N 2016

The Gilded Cage L. Mulcahy *Stage Directions* v29 no12 p28 D 2016

Dressner, Michelle A.

Hospital workers: an assessment of occupational injuries and illnesses bibl *Monthly Labor Review* p1 Je 2017

DREVITCH, GARY

All-American Angst *Psychology Today* v50 no1 p27 Ja/F 2017

Around the World in 2,557 Days... Paul Salopek *Psychology Today* v49 no6 p27 N/D 2016

The Bard of Self-Awareness *Psychology Today* v50 no4 p24 Ag 2017

Embrace Awkwardness *Psychology Today* v50 no3 p48 My/Je 2017

He Knows Where the Bodies Are Buried *Psychology Today* v50

no2 p27 Mr/Ap 2017

Massively Intelligent *Psychology Today* v50 no2 p44 Mr/Ap 2017

THE MYSTERY OF MOTIVATION *Psychology Today* v50 no1 p54 Ja/F 2017

The Risk Taker *Psychology Today* v50 no3 p27 My/Je 2017

The Seer of AI: Physicist MAX TEGMARK has borne witness to the rise of artificial intelligence and insists that we start thinking about what it means for humanity--before machines decide for us *Psychology Today* v50 no5 p27 S/O 2017

We Are Not Alone *Psychology Today* v49 no6 p47 N/D 2016

Drew, Dale

IS SOMEONE GOING TO HACK MY LIGHTBULB? D. DUBNO color *Popular Mechanics* p77 Mr 2017

Drew, Elizabeth

She's a Keeper A. FERGUSON *Commentary* v144 no3 p9 O 2017

Terrifying Trump color *New York Review of Books* v64 no4 p37 Mr 9 2017

Trump: The Presidency in Peril cartoon color *New York Review of Books* v64 no11 p59 Je 22 2017

Drew, Kimberly

KIMBERLY DREW J. Wilson color *Essence* v47 no11 p30 Mr 2017

RUJEKO HOCKLEY: Whitney Museum of American Art color *Vogue* v207 no10 p192 O 2017

Use Your Gift [Cover story] bw color *Glamour* v115 no3 p174 Mr 2017

Drew, Richard J.

Emergence and spread of a human-transmissible multidrug-resistant nontuberculous mycobacterium bibl diag graph *Science* v354 no6313 p751 N 11 2016

Drewes, Gerard

Click chemistry enables preclinical evaluation of targeted epigenetic therapies diag *Science* v356 no6345 p1397 Je 30 2017

Drexel, Katharine Mary, Saint, 1858-1955

Sanctifying the Acela K. J. Lopez color *America* v216 no8 p54 Ap 17 2017

Drexler, Clyde

CALLING ALL ENTREPRENEURS S. HILL color *Black Enterprise* v47 no8 p42 Jl/Ag 2017

Drexler, Rosalyn—Exhibitions

AROUND BOSTON S. ADAMS cartoon color *ARTnews* v115 no3 p147 Fall 2016

Dreyfus, Rachel J.

The Elements of Value: Interaction *Harvard Business Review* v94 no11 p18 N 2016

DREYFUSS, BARBARA

JOHN WISNIEWSKI'S INSURGENT CRUSADE color il *Nation* v304 no8 p12 Mr 13 2017

Dreyfuss, Bob

JOHN WISNIEWSKI'S INSURGENT CRUSADE color il *Nation* v304 no8 p12 Mr 13 2017

THE WEST WING'S PHONY FOREIGN-POLICY GURU color *Rolling Stone* no1294 p34 Ag 24 2017

Dreyfuss, Richard, 1947-

Shots Fired M. Roffman *TV Guide* v65 no13 p27 Mr 20 2017

Drezner, Daniel W.

Lives of the Mind T. TROY *Commentary* v143 no6 p49 Je 2017

The Rise of the Thought Leader D. SESSIONS bw *New Republic* v248 no7 p48 Jl 2017

The Shortlist *New York Times Book Review* p26 Ap 23 2017

What's the Big Idea? N. MILLMAN *New York Times Book Review* p26 My 7 2017

Dribbling (Basketball)

Pistol Pete's Homework Basketball B. Swanson *New York Times Magazine* p20 Ap 30 2017

Dried beef

How to Make... JERKY F. MAROUKIAN and T. AIAZZI color *Popular Mechanics* v193 no7 p80 S 2016

In the SUNSET KITCHEN color *Sunset* v239 no3 p100 S 2017

Dried flower arrangement

THE EVERLASTING GARDEN *Saturday Evening Post* v289 no3 p21 My/Je 2017

Dried fruit

Stocking Your Pantry Like a Pro K. O'SHEA-EVANS color *House Beautiful* v159 no2 p72 Mr 2017

Dried milk

Summer Yogurt Dishes color *Backpacker* p38 Ag 2017

Driftwood sculpture

CABIN art color *Cabin Living* p9 S 2017

Driggers, Kaleb

Driggers and Nogueira Roll Through July color *Team Roping Journal* p28 S 2017

Knowing How to Win color *Team Roping Journal* p74 O 2017

More of the Same B. Welch color *Spin to Win Rodeo* v21 no2 p70 Ap 2017

SOUTH BY SOUTHEAST color *Spin to Win Rodeo* v20 no9 p13 N 2016

YOU PICKED 'EM! [Cover story] B. WELCH and C. TOY color *Spin to Win Rodeo* v20 no12 p54 F 2017

Driggers, Kaleb—Interviews

Driggers Doesn't Let Roping Define Him K. Santos *Spin to Win Rodeo* v21 no1 p26 Mr 2017

Drijkoningen, Judith

Emergence and spread of a human-transmissible multidrug-resistant nontuberculous mycobacterium bibl diag graph *Science* v354 no6313 p751 N 11 2016

Drilling & boring

ASK ROY R. BERENDSOHN color *Popular Mechanics* p36 F 2017

Drilling Stainless Steel C. Lawson color *Sail* v48 no5 p49 My 2017

Revealing the dynamics of a large impact P. Barton bibl color *Science* v354 no6314 p836 N 18 2016

Drilling & boring machinery equipment

Know the Drill P. Hope color diag *Consumer Reports* v82 no12 p8 D 2017

Drilling & boring machinery—Evaluation

Know the Drill P. Hope color diag *Consumer Reports* v82 no12 p8 D 2017

Drilling & boring—Environmental aspects

THE FIGHT OVER FRACKING A. BARTH *New York Times Upfront* v149 no9 p10 F 20 2017

Drilling & boring—Equipment & supplies

Outfitting a Custom Toolkit J. SCIACCA color *Sound & Vision* v82 no8 p28 O 2017

UNDERWATER POWER TOOLS? D. DUBNO color *Popular Mechanics* p10 S 2017

Drilling & boring—Equipment & supplies—Evaluation

PRODUCT TEST TEAM D. MOWITZ *Successful Farming* v115 no2 p34 F 2017

Drilling, Joanne

BAKE ME HAPPY *Cincinnati Magazine* v50 no12 p102 S 2017

BETTER BUTTER *Cincinnati Magazine* v50 no6 p144 Mr 2017

Boho Bistro *Cincinnati Magazine* v50 no6 p142 Mr 2017

DOG DAZE *Cincinnati Magazine* v50 no10 p52 Jl 2017

Frankfort, 29 Kentucky *Cincinnati Magazine* p58 Je 2017

GOOD CHEMISTRY *Cincinnati Magazine* v50 no2 p60 N 2016

GREAT DANE *Cincinnati Magazine* v50 no10 p122 Jl 2017

GREEN GIANT *Cincinnati Magazine* v50 no6 p66 Mr 2017

GRIND TIME *Cincinnati Magazine* v50 no4 p150 Ja 2017

LOVIN' THE OVEN *Cincinnati Magazine* v50 no2 p122 N 2016

NEW KIDS ON THE BLOCK *Cincinnati Magazine* v50 no6 p81 Mr 2017

NIGHT MOVES *Cincinnati Magazine* v50 no8 p40 My 2017

PARTY CITY color *Cincinnati Magazine* v51 no1 p153 O 2017

Play Station *Cincinnati Magazine* v50 no4 p146 Ja 2017

PREMIER CRU CREW *Cincinnati Magazine* v50 no6 p72 Mr 2017

Pure Bar *Cincinnati Magazine* p114 Je 2017

Spice Island *Cincinnati Magazine* v50 no3 p130 D 2016

Strip Down *Cincinnati Magazine* v50 no4 p148 Ja 2017

SUNDRY SAMARITANS *Cincinnati Magazine* v50 no8 p106 My 2017

Telling Tales *Cincinnati Magazine* v50 no3 p132 D 2016

Tree House *Cincinnati Magazine* v50 no12 p103 S 2017

Turkish Delight color *Cincinnati Magazine* v51 no1 p157 O 2017

VINTAGE STOCK *Cincinnati Magazine* v50 no5 p160 F 2017

WONDER BREADS *Cincinnati Magazine* v50 no10 p124 Jl 2017

Drilling platforms

The Platform Paradox A. POPESCU *Los Angeles Magazine* p92 D 2016

Drills (Planting machinery)—Equipment & supplies

LAUNCHING A START-UP *Successful Farming* v115 no3 p32 Mid-F 2017

Drills (Practice)

Lead-Change Precision B. Avila and J. Paulson color *Horse & Rider* v56 no2 p26 F 2017

Open Up J. Paulson *Horse & Rider* v56 no8 p15 Ag 2017

POINT AND SHOOT G. Weir and D. DeNunzio color *Golf Magazine* v59 no4 p66 Ap 2017

DRIMMER, STEPHANIE WARREN

Are We Alone? color *National Geographic Kids* no474 p16 O 2017

Brain Bogglers color *National Geographic Kids* no470 p34 My 2017

Buried Secrets color map *National Geographic Kids* no470 p26 My 2017

Destination Space color *National Geographic Kids* no473 p8 S 2017

DESTINATION SPACE *National Geographic Kids* no469 p8 Ap 2017

MISSION to MARS bw color *National Geographic Kids* no465 p14 N 2016

THE SEARCH FOR PLANET NINE *National Geographic Kids* no468 p18 Mr 2017

Drinking (Physiology)

Give Your Body a Break A. Reliford and B. B. Royall color *Essence* v47 no9 p86 Ja 2017

Neurons that drive and quench thirst C. Gizowski and C. W. Bourque color diag *Science* v357 no6356 p1092 S 15 2017

Drinking behavior

See also

Drinking of alcoholic beverages

Taste

Break That Bad Habit—for Good J. Migala color *Health* v31 no1 p63 Ja 2017

DRINKING VINEGARS: HEALTHY OR HYPE? color *Health* v31 no5 p16 Je 2017

I'll Drink to That! B. HOWARD color *AARP: The Magazine* v59 no1A p20 D 2015/Ja 2016

Mocktail Hour B. Lipton color *Health* v31 no5 p120 Je 2017

Raise Alcohol Taxes, Reduce Violence K. Sobowale color *Scientific American* v317 no1 p10 Jl 2017

A Victorian Toast R. Schaap color *New York Times Magazine* p42 D 11 2016

Drinking cups

BIRD BY BIRD D. A. WOOD color *Missouri Life* v44 no3 p10 My 2017

FUN SIZE F. VIGNA color *Martha Stewart Living* p124 Jl/Ag 2017

Drinking cups—Evaluation

BOWL—ED OVER color *Bon Appetit* v62 no10 p74 O 2017

GARDEN PARTY color *Harper's Bazaar* no3649 p168 D 2016/Ja 2017

PARTY DOWHN *Cincinnati Magazine* v50 no2 p30 N 2016

Drinking customs—Great Britain

It's Always Time for Tea C. Hopley *British Heritage Travel* v38 no1 p68 Ja/F 2017

Drinking games

The Dirty Dancing Drinking Game S. Li color *Entertainment Weekly* no1467 p51 My 26 2017

Drinking glasses—Evaluation

going green color *Better Homes & Gardens* v95 no3 p50 Mr 2017

A HOLIDAY SOIREE H. BROWN color *House Beautiful* v158 no10 p36 D 2016/Ja 2017

Raise The Bar L. IMMEDIATO *Los Angeles Magazine* p38 My 2017

SPACE ODDITIES *Cincinnati Magazine* p32 Je 2017

Drinking of alcoholic beverages

See also

Controlled drinking

5 Myths About STRESS [Cover story] S. KLEIN cartoon *Prevention* v69 no5 p38 My 2017

A Happy Medium N. RONES and C. Bloom color *Martha Stewart Living* p66 Ap 2017

Jogging the Brain G. Reynolds color *New York Times Magazine* p28 N 27 2016

JULIANNE HOUGH What I love color *Health* v31 no9 p29 N 2017

Moderate Alcohol Intake May Help Preserve "Good" Cholesterol [Cover story] *Tufts University Health & Nutrition Letter* v35 no6 p1 Ag 2017

MY FATHER'S CELLAR J. SEABROOK cartoon color *New Yorker* v92 no46 p22 Ja 23 2017

prep school N. RICHARDSON, A. DELANY et al bw color *Bon Appetit* v62 no10 p105 O 2017

A Short History of My Long Drinking Life color *Bon Appetit* v62 no10 p96 O 2017

SOBER SATURDAY NIGHTS *Health* v31 no1 p14 Ja 2017

This Just In J. Zorthian *Time* v189 no13 p19 Ap 10 2017

This Just In J. Zorthian *Time* v190 no8 p21 Ag 28 2017

WE'LL HAVE WINE, NATURALLY B. CUSHING and M. A. ROSS color *Bon Appetit* p118 S 2017

What's your sleep IQ? color *Harvard Health Letter* v42 no9 p6 Jl 2017

Drinking of alcoholic beverages & psychology

The Ancient Art of Imbibing L. TONINO color *Tricycle: The Buddhist Review* v27 no1 p30 Fall 2017

Drinking of alcoholic beverages—Great Britain

LAST ORDERS FOR BOOZY LUNCHES? As Lloyd's of London bans daytime drinking, other businesses are reaching for the rule book rather than the pint glass D. LEWIS *People Management* p10 Ap 2017

Drinking of alcoholic beverages—Health aspects

KNOW YOUR RISKS K. ASP color *Better Homes & Gardens* v95 no10 p180 O 2017

NOT THE SPIRIT C. Cederquist color *Women's Health* v14 no2 p36 Mr 2017

Drinking of alcoholic beverages—History—18th century

HOW DRY WE WERE: Exploring Prohibition at the Library of Virginia B. Crowder bw *Virginia Living* v15 no5 p27 Ag 2017

Drinking of alcoholic beverages—Humor

Laughter: THE BEST MEDICINE color *Reader's Digest* v190 no1133 p92 S 2017

Drinking of alcoholic beverages—Research

Rethinking Drinking color *Prevention* v68 no11 p10 N 2016

Drinking of alcoholic beverages—Risk factors

HOW DRY WE WERE: Exploring Prohibition at the Library of Virginia B. Crowder bw *Virginia Living* v15 no5 p27 Ag 2017

Drinking water

CAN AMERICA AVOID ANOTHER FLINT? N. SCHARPING color *Discover* v38 no1 p18 Ja/F 2017

INFRASTRUCTURE SPENDING D. C. Vock *Governing* v30 no4 p33 Ja 2017

a machine that pulls water from thin air. literally S. Fecht cartoon *Popular Science* v289 no2 p20 Mr/Ap 2017

OUR SCHOOL: An Arctic community prepares its young people for the future L. MARKHAM color *Orion Magazine* v35 no6 p20 N/D 2016

Science News for Students K. Hulick, B. Brookshire et al color *Science News* v192 no4 p33 S 16 2017

Secrets of Nutritionists J. MIGALA color *Martha Stewart Living* p56 S 2017

SOLAR-POWERED PUMPS: Pump water with the power of the sun J. R. Yago *Mother Earth News* no284 p46 O/N 2017

Water—To Your Health! M. LALIBERTE and L. TIGAR color *Reader's Digest* v190 no1133 p33 S 2017

WATER WORKS: Can this 29-year-old gay man end the global water crisis? *Advocate* no1093 p48 O/N 2017

Drinking water quality

Bottled Water M. J. WEEDMAN img *New York* p56 F 9 2017

High-tech Hydration [Cover story] S. KLEIN color *Prevention* v69 no7 p28 Jl 2017

Drinking water—Equipment & supplies

New device harvests water from air T. SUMNER color *Science News* v191 no9 p10 My 13 2017

Drinking water—Lead content

Bill helps restore clean water to Flint, Michigan color *National Wildlife (World Edition)* v55 no3 p48 Ap/My 2017

A Year Later, Flint Still Can't Drink the Water J. Sanburn *Time* v189 no4 p12 Ja 23 2017

Drinking water—Societies, etc.

GET STARTED T. A. Christian *Essence* v47 no8 p117 D 2016

Drinot, Paulo

¡Viva Hobsbawm! *History Today* v67 no3 p63 Mr 2017

Driscoll, Clara

Tiffany Girl Power at the New-York Historical Society color *Magazine Antiques* v184 no4 p30 Jl/Ag 2017

Driscoll, F. Paul

American Classic *Opera News* v81 no9 p4 Mr 2017

Anniversary Celebration *Opera News* v81 no6 p4 D 2016

Classic Conversation *Opera News* v81 no7 p18 Ja 2017

DANIELA DESSÌ. GENOA, ITALY, MAY 14,1957-BRESCIA, ITALY, AUGUST 20, 2016 *Opera News* v81 no5 p62 N 2016

Diva Playlist *Opera News* v81 no5 p18 N 2016

JOHN DEL CARLO *Opera News* v81 no7 p58 Ja 2017

La Divina Redux *Opera News* v81 no9 p62 Mr 2017

Noteworthy & Now *Opera News* v81 no12 p13 Je 2017

OUT LATE: Jared Angle Talks Opera *Opera News* v81 no10 p16 Ap 2017

Patience Rewarded: Quinn Kelsey waited to sing the great Verdi baritone roles until the time was right. This month, he's San Francisco Opera's Rigoletto *Opera News* v81 no12 p45 Je 2017

A Picture of the Future *Opera News* v81 no7 p4 Ja 2017

ROBERT CARSEN *Opera News* v81 no10 p26 Ap 2017

Roméo et Juliette *Opera News* v81 no9 p33 Mr 2017

Scott Conner *Opera News* v81 no9 p10 Mr 2017

Sound Bites: Theo Hoffman: A native New Yorker returns to Missouri *Opera News* v81 no12 p58 Je 2017

Tristan und Isolde *Opera News* v81 no6 p38 D 2016

Variety Artist *Opera News* v81 no10 p6 Ap 2017

Driscoll's (Company)

STRAWBERRY VALLEY D. GOODYEAR cartoon *New Yorker* v93 no24 p30 Ag 21 2017

Driskill, Mark

STICK TO THE RIBS color *Southern Living* v52 no6 p98 Je 2017

Drive-in theaters

TIBBS DRIVE-IN THEATRE N. MONDAY *Indianapolis Monthly* v12 no40 p20 Ag 2017

Driver, Adam, 1983-

Bard on a Bus D. EDELSTEIN img *New York* v49 no26 p88 D 26 2016

Grounded R. Alleva color *Commonweal* v144 no6 p23 Mr 24 2017

SHAGADELIC, BABY! bw color *Esquire* p50 Je/Jl 2017

Driver, Adam, 1983—Interviews

Adam DRIVER N. BAUMBACH *Interview* v46 no10 p74 D 2016/Ja 2017

Driver, Christopher J.

Hardbarned: One Man's Quest for Meaningful Work in the American South *Publishers Weekly* v264 no17 p86 Ap 24 2017

Hardbarned! One Man's Quest for Meaningful Work in the American South *Publishers Weekly* v264 no21 p65c My 22 2017

DRIVER, MINNIE

I Love My Living Room color *House Beautiful* v159 no8 p128 O 2017

So Long, June Cleaver M. DRIVER *TV Guide* p16 Ap 17 2017

Speechless Gets Real About Families Affected by Disability D. D'addario color *Time* v188 no15 p56 O 17 2016

Speechless N. Abrams, B. L. Heldman et al color *Entertainment Weekly* no1482/1483 p75 S 22 2017

Driver assistance systems

Self-Driving-Car Safety color *Consumer Reports* v82 no2 p6 F 2017

D'RIVERA, PAQUITO

Chords & Discords color *Downbeat* v84 no5 p10 My 2017

Driveways

On the Road Again color *AARP: The Magazine* v60 no3A p48 Ap/My 2017

Driving ranges

Beyond Great color *Golf Magazine* v59 no1 p70 Ja 2017

DROBNITCH, SARAH T.

Long-Term Studies Contribute Disproportionately to Ecology and Policy *BioScience* v67 no3 p271 Mr 2017

Droddy, Noah

COOL (DUDE) RUNNING C. Kuzma color *Runner's World* v52 no1 p48 Ja/F 2017

Droege, Samuel

Words alone will not protect pollinators bibl color *Science* v355 no6323 p357 Ja 27 2017

Drogin, Ian

AEGEAN ODYSSEY color map *Sail* v48 no3 p44 Mr 2017

Droitcour, Brian

ANTONIO LOPEZ cartoon *Art in America* v104 no11 p120 D 2016

THE DIGITIZED MUSEUM *Art in America* v104 no9 p77 O 2016

GENERAL IDEA color *Art in America* v105 no4 p120 Ap 2017

JULIANA HUXTABLE color *Art in America* v105 no8 p124 S 2017

THE NATIONAL EXHIBITION color *Art in America* v105 no6 p128 Je/Jl 2017

SÃO PAULO BIENAL cartoon *Art in America* v104 no11 p128 D 2016

TERMINAL VELOCITY color *Art in America* v104 no10 p92 N 2016

VENICE Off Beat color *Art in America* v105 no8 p41 S 2017

Walter K. Scott color *Art in America* v105 no1 p23 Ja 2017

DROIT-VOLET, SYLVIE

WATCHING THE CLOCKS *Popular Science* v289 no5 p45 S/O 2017

Drollette, Dan

Pulitzer-winning author Tracy Kidder: Looking for the soul of the machine makers color *Bulletin of the Atomic Scientists* v73 no2 p74 Mr 2017

Taking stock: Steven Chu, former secretary of the Energy Department, on fracking, renewables, nuclear weapons, and his work, post-Nobel Prize color *Bulletin of the Atomic Scientists* v72 no6 p351 N 2016

Dromgoole, Dominic, 1963-

HAMLET GLOBE TO GLOBE: Two Years, 190,000 Miles, 197 Countries, One Play S. Greenblatt bw color *New York Times Book Review* p1 Ap 23 2017

Perchance to Dream C. ATAMIAN color *Weekly Standard* v22 no31 p43 Ap 17 2017

Drone aircraft

10 Ways Drones Are Changing Your World T. Foster color *Consumer Reports* v82 no1 p44 Ja 2017

8 drones that delighted us in 2016 color *PCWorld* v35 no1 p214 Ja 2017

Abuzz In the Drone Age P. LERNER *Los Angeles Magazine* p76 Ja 2017

ADVENTURES IN DRONE HORTICULTURE C. COLIN color *Popular Mechanics* p7 My 2017

Apple Is Bringing Drones to a Map Fight M. Gurman and A. Levin *Bloomberg Businessweek* no4503 p29 D 12 2016

BABY BOOMERS *Harper's Magazine* v334 no2004 p16 My 2017

DRONE ATTACK N. HONACHEFSKY color *Outdoor Life* v224 no7 p58 S 2017

The drone files S. Hepworth color *Columbia Journalism Review* p12 Fall/Wint 2016

DRONE RESPONSIBLY 7 LESSONS LEARNED THE HARD WAY A. POWELL color graph *Wired* v25 no5 p24 My 2017

THE DRUMBEAT FOR A PILOTLESS AIR TAXI CONTINUES color *Flying* v144 no4 p24 Ap 2017

FETISH: DIVER DOWN P. SARCONI color *Wired* v25 no7 p37 Jl 2017

Flying COWs and Other Drone Apps S. Berinato *Harvard Business Review Digital Articles* p2 My 17 2017

The Future of GETTING THERE is Almost Here- and WE'RE READY to GO cartoon *Conde Nast Traveler* v51 no11 p64 D 2016

Global Rush to Harness Drones Yields Ups and Downs J. CESSNA *BioScience* v67 no10 p944 O 2017

HIGH-FLYING HELP N. Strochlic color *National Geographic* v231 no6 p6 Je 2017

I flew combat drones... and I'm not a pilot K. D. Atherton color *Popular Science* v289 no6 p82 N/D 2017

iOS Accessories J. Mathis color *Macworld - Digital Edition* v34 no8 p80 Ag 2017

It's the U.S. Army Vs. the Drone Army D. Lawrence and S. Wang *Bloomberg Businessweek* no4536 p26 S 4 2017

LITTLE PIES IN THE SKY: THE FUTURE IS ALMOST HERE P. Garrison bw *Flying* v144 no10 p80 O 2017

Mad, Democrats? Blame the Iran Deal *Commentary* p1 Ja 2017

Mad, Democrats? Blame the Iran Deal *Commentary* v143 no1 p1

Ja 2017

Memorandum R. LONG il *National Review* v69 no5 p38 Mr 20 2017

no-fly zone [Cover story] R. Feltman color *Popular Science* v289 no6 p76 N/D 2017

Pollinator Drones N. Leiber bw color *Bloomberg Businessweek* no4516 p31 Mr 27 2017

POPULAR MACHINE EVERYWHERE color diag *Popular Mechanics* p14 D 2016/Ja 2017

The Response: A CREWLESS TRACKING SHIP color *Popular Mechanics* p76 Mr 2017

The Response: DRONES THAT CAN TAKE OFF FROM ANY-WHERE color *Popular Mechanics* p76 Mr 2017

The Response: RADAR SYSTEMS WITH BUILT-IN RF JAM-MERS color *Popular Mechanics* p74 Mr 2017

Sky Net D. STARR cartoon map *Wired* v25 no3 p38 Mr 2017

Unmanned Aerial Vehicles: Friend or Foe? M. FEENEY *USA Today Magazine* v145 no2862 p36 Mr 2017

The upside and downside of swarming drones I. Lachow bibl *Bulletin of the Atomic Scientists* v73 no2 p96 Mr 2017

What's That Buzzing Noise? Public Opinion on the Use of Drones for Conservation Science E. M. MARKOWITZ, M. C. NISBET et al *BioScience* v67 no4 p382 Ap 2017

What's Wrong with the FAA's New Drone Rules L. Downes *Harvard Business Review Digital Articles* p2 Mr 2 2015

WILDLIFE color *Canadian Geographic* v135 no6 p24 D 2015

ZIP LINE: Help from Above J. W. Rosen color *MIT Technology Review* v120 no4 p36 Jl/Ag 2017

Drone aircraft delivery

Drones to the Rescue B. Y. Lee *MIT Technology Review* v120 no4 p12 Jl/Ag 2017

New Zealand Has Pizza Delivery Drones V. de Rugy *Reason* v48 no7 p16 D 2016

Switzerland's New Medical Drones J. Zorthian color *Time* v190 no14 p23 O 9 2017

Drone aircraft equipment & supplies

DRONES D. SUPERTRAMP and R. FELNER chart color *Popular Mechanics* p78 O 2017

So You Crashed Your Drone color *Popular Mechanics* p37 D 2016/Ja 2017

Drone aircraft in agriculture

AFTER The Next Big Thing B. D. JOHNSON *Successful Farming* v114 no12 p78 Mid-N 2016

AG FROM ABOVE B. SPIEGEL *Successful Farming* v114 no12 p38 Mid-N 2016

The Bee Drone J. Zorthian color *Time* v189 no11 p27 Mr 27 2017

Drones can pollinate E. S. Eaton color *Science News* v191 no5 p4 Mr 18 2017

FLIGHT PLAN L. BEOORD *Successful Farming* v114 no12 p32 Mid-N 2016

Drone aircraft in business

See also

Drone aircraft delivery

Drone aircraft testing

DRONES ON MARS M. Golombek, A. Kehoe et al color *Astronomy* v45 no7 p34 Jl 2017

Drone aircraft—Design & construction

CRASH COURSE L. MURROW cartoon *Wired* v25 no6 p24 Je 2017

How Long Can DJI Rule the Sky? C. Larson color *Bloomberg Businessweek* no4518 p36 Ap 10 2017

Drone aircraft—Equipment & supplies—Evaluation

DRONE CHARGING STATION *Successful Farming* v114 no10 p30 O 2016

Drone aircraft—Evaluation

Big Memories, Small Drone S. MURRAY color *Power & Motoryacht* v34 no10 p66 O 2017

DJI SPARK: A FANTASTIC, AFFORDABLE DRONE THAT DEMANDS EXPENSIVE EXTRAS S. BELLAMY color *Macworld - Digital Edition* v34 no11 p73 N 2017

FETISH: FLIGHT MANUAL A. PARDES color *Wired* v25 no9 p43 S 2017

Innovation O. Kharif bw color *Bloomberg Businessweek* no4506 p28 Ja 9 2017

Our Ultimate Holiday Wish List S. Silbert il *MIT Technology Review* v119 no6 p25 N/D 2016

Zero-Casualty Mine Sweeping C. McDONALD cartoon color *Popular Science* p82 Ja/F 2017

Drone aircraft—France

Drone Hunters color *MIT Technology Review* v120 no3 p22 My/Je 2017

Drone aircraft—Government policy

NEW RULES FOR NEW FRONTIERS L. Entis color *Fortune* v174 no6 p80 N 1 2016

Drone aircraft—Law & legislation

2.5m A. Levin color *Bloomberg Businessweek* no4514 p29 Mr 13 2017

Ask a Drone Lawyer L. Amico *Harvard Business Review Digital Articles* p2 My 18 2017

The Debate Over Drone IDs A. Levin bw *Bloomberg Businessweek* no4534 p36 Ag 14 2017

New Zealand Has Pizza Delivery Drones V. de Rugy *Reason* v48 no7 p16 D 2016

Drone aircraft—Maintenance & repair

So You Crashed Your Drone color *Popular Mechanics* p37 D 2016/Ja 2017

Drone aircraft—Sales & prices

2.5m A. Levin color *Bloomberg Businessweek* no4514 p29 Mr 13 2017

Want a Drone of Your Own? M. Frank *Consumer Reports* v82 no1 p48 Ja 2017

Drone aircraft—Social aspects

Uber's Ad-Toting Drones Are Heckling Drivers Stuck in Traffic M. Reilly color *MIT Technology Review* v120 no1 p24 Ja/F 2017

Drone photography

GET THE PICTURE color *Wired* v25 no6 p8 Je 2017

Drone surveillance

Cetacean seeker A. Pope color graph *Canadian Geographic* v136 no6 p28 D 2016

Unmanned Aerial Vehicles: Friend or Foe? M. FEENEY *USA Today Magazine* v145 no2862 p36 Mr 2017

Drone warfare

Death from Above S. Shackford *Reason* v48 no7 p60 D 2016

Death from above: The perils of lethal drone strikes L. Calhoun bibl *Bulletin of the Atomic Scientists* v73 no2 p138 Mr 2017

Drone King, The (Short story)

THE DRONE KING K. VONNEGUT color *Atlantic* v320 no3 p88 O 2017

Drop Everything (Film)

CONNERY LUNDIN S. DAVIS bw *Powder* p134 S 2017

Dropbox Inc.

THE CLOUD 100 *Forbes* v200 no1 p81 Jl 27 2017

Eyeing a Dropbox IPO P. Burrows il *MIT Technology Review* v120 no2 p24 Mr/Ap 2017

Dropbox Inc.—Finance

Dropbox Gets Ready For the Road D. Bass and A. Barinka bw *Bloomberg Businessweek* no4534 p22 Ag 14 2017

Dropbox Inc.—Officials & employees

Dropbox's Drew Houston M. Chafkin and D. Bass color *Bloomberg Businessweek* no4526 p40 Je 12 2017

Dropinski, James

A multifunctional catalyst that stereoselectively assembles prodrugs diag *Science* v356 no6336 p426 Ap 28 2017

DRORBAUGH, VALLERIE

A Great Fall Makeover... in 5 Easy Steps *Better Homes & Gardens* v94 no11 p2 N 2016

Drosophila

Causal role for inheritance of H3K27me3 in maintaining the OFF state of a Drosophila HOX gene R. T. Coleman and G. Struhl diag *Science* v356 no6333 p41 Ap 7 2017

Drosophila insulin release is triggered by adipose Stunted ligand to brain Methuselah receptor R. Delanoue, E. Meschi et al bibl graph *Science* v353 no6307 p1553 S 30 2016

Glia relay differentiation cues to coordinate neuronal development in Drosophila V. M. Fernandes, Z. Chen et al color *Science* v357 no6354 p886 S 1 2017

Self-organized Notch dynamics generate stereotyped sensory organ patterns in Drosophila F. Corson, L. Couturier et al color *Science* v356 no6337 p501 My 5 2017

Drosophila melanogaster

Ring attractor dynamics in the Drosophila central brain S. S. Kim, H. Rouault et al diag graph *Science* v356 no6340 p849 My 26

2017

Drossart, P.

Seasonal exposure of carbon dioxide ice on the nucleus of comet 67P/Churyumov-Gerasimenko bibl bw graph *Science* v354 no6319 p1563 D 23 2016

Droste, Ed

Grizzly Bear's Vital New Tunes E. R. Brown and N. Feeney color *Entertainment Weekly* no1477 p57 Ag 11 2017

Drought management

As Drought Lets Up, California Faces New Water Struggles J. Worland *Time* v189 no3 p10 Ja 30 2017

Drought tolerance of plants

Dry Plants? Add Vinegar A. Braun color *Natural History* v125 no10 p8 O 2017

Droughts

The Pace — and Problems — of Climate Change Accelerate E. BETZ diag *Discover* v38 no1 p16 Ja/F 2017

Streets of Gold *Saturday Evening Post* v289 no4 p100 Jl/Ag 2017

Waiting for Water J. B. LITTLE *Audubon* v118 no6 p17 Wint 2016

Droughts—California

As Drought Lets Up, California Faces New Water Struggles J. Worland *Time* v189 no3 p10 Ja 30 2017

Dam Politics: The drought is over, but don't expect Sacramento to take any meaningful action to avert the next water crisis. That well is still bone dry V. D. Hanson *Hoover Digest: Research & Opinion on Public Policy* no3 p83 Summ 2017

Droughts—India

Bangalore was once the icon of a globalized, high tech future. Now it's the thirsty sign of a global catastrophe S. Subramanian color *Wired* v25 no5 p110 My 2017

Drouin, Roger

A Lift for Lichens color *Scientific American* v316 no4 p22 Ap 2017

Droujinski, Dimitry

The Fake Russian D. WISE *Smithsonian* v47 no7 p38 N 2016

Drouot, Alain

Edgefest Now Bigger Than Ever color *Downbeat* v83 no11 p95 N 2016

Jazz at the Limits: Avant Artists Convene at Edgefest color *Downbeat* v84 no2 p18 F 2017

Jazz on the French Riviera color *Downbeat* v84 no5 p132 My 2017

DROWN, JULE

Arizona Paradise color *Trail Rider* v29 no3 p54 Ap 2017

Drowning

Beacon of Strength: In troubled waters, it helps to remember the courage of a remarkable family friend E. CLARK *Yankee* v81 no5 p14 S/O 2017

Wave GOODBYE A. HANNAFORD *Texas Monthly* v45 no6 p35 Je 2017

WAYS TO PREVENT ELECTRIC SHOCK DROWNING [Cover story] *USA Today Magazine* v146 no2867 p1 Ag 2017

What Happens Next? After the Near Drowning S. CARR *Idaho Magazine* v16 no5 p54 F 2017

Drowning—Prevention

The Flip Turn M. BURKE color *Forbes* v199 no1 p100 Ja 24 2017

Drowning—Psychological aspects

DROWNING ON MY CUSHION K. LARRABEE bw *Tricycle: The Buddhist Review* v27 no1 p58 Fall 2017

Droz, PennElys

Design, Place and Indigenous Ways: Working with Local Communities *Parks & Recreation* v51 no12 p30 D 2016

Drozd, Pavel

Higher predation risk for insect prey at low latitudes and elevations graph *Science* v356 no6339 p742 My 19 2017

Drozdova, Katya

A Different "Special Relationship" *Hoover Digest: Research & Opinion on Public Policy* no1 p108 Wint 2017

Dr. Strangelove: Or, How I Learned to Stop Worrying & Love the Bomb (Film)

DR. STRANGELOVE F. Kaplan bw color *Sound & Vision* v81 no9 p71 N 2016

Drucker, Jesse

The Smart Person's Guide To Paying Taxes color *Bloomberg Businessweek* no4494 p10 O 10 2016

Drucker, Peter F. (Peter Ferdinand), 1909-2005

Clay Christensen on Peter Drucker J. Kirby *Harvard Business Review Digital Articles* p2 N 10 2014

THOUGHTS FROM Our Readers bw *Forbes* v200 no3 p180 S 28 2017

What Peter Drucker Had to Say About Automation R. Wartzman *Harvard Business Review Digital Articles* p2 N 2 2015

DRUCKER, STEPHEN

True to Form color *Architectural Digest* no11 p66 N 1 2017

Druckmann, Shaul

Ring attractor dynamics in the Drosophila central brain diag graph *Science* v356 no6340 p849 My 26 2017

Druffel, Barbara

ALL IN A ROW L. MURTHA *Cincinnati Magazine* v50 no7 p34 Ap 2017

Drug abuse

See also

Cocaine abuse

Drugs & sex

Opioid abuse

Bay Urea M. HEMINGWAY color *Weekly Standard* v23 no6 p6 O 16 2017

Chayce Doesn't Want to Be One of Them M. Mertens, W. Yakowicz et al color *Glamour* v115 no10 p149 O 2017

Christian recovery programs in Vancouver respond to opioid crisis A. Ambrosio color *Christian Century* v134 no15 p17 Jl 19 2017

INNOCENCE Is IRRELEVANT E. Yoffe bw *Atlantic* v320 no2 p66 S 2017

Mick Fleetwood A. GREENE bw *Rolling Stone* no1295 p58 S 7 2017

Shooting Up in Public Bathrooms Common *USA Today Magazine* v145 no2859 p12 D 2016

Drug abuse treatment

Kids Should Be Part of Mom's Treatment *USA Today Magazine* v146 no2867 p13 Ag 2017

Drug abuse—British Columbia

'Death, death—day in, day out' N. MACDONALD *Maclean's* no1 p12 F 17 2017

Needles in the trees B. HUTCHINSON color *Maclean's* v130 no7 p13 Ag 2017

Drug abuse—Canada

2,816 dead Canadians and counting P. Wells color *Maclean's* v130 no10 p20 N 2017

Drug abusers

See also

Drug addicts

WHAT AMERICA TAUGHT A MURDEROUS DRUG WARRIOR J. SULLUM color *Reason* v49 no4 p12 Ag/S 2017

Drug abuse—United States

The Drug Cascade H. S. Edwards color *Time* v190 no1 p32 Jl 3 2017

The Heroin Business Is Booming in America J. Smialek color *Bloomberg Businessweek* no4522 p32 My 15 2017

Heroin took over our town S. M. FERNÁNDEZ *Scholastic Choices* v32 no3 p6 N/D 2016

Drug accessibility

Children with cancer get more access to experimental drugs C. Schmidt color *Science* v357 no6351 p540 Ag 11 2017

How Pharma Can Fix Its Reputation and Its Business at the Same Time D. de Felice color *Harvard Business Review Digital Articles* p2 F 3 2017

Drug addiction

A Better Rx: States are making their much-criticized drug monitoring programs easier to use M. Quinn *Governing* v30 no8 p18 My 2017

Beyond Diagnostic Categories: Comprehensive Assessment of Psychopathology in Addiction and Mental Health Disorders V. Kumari *Psychology Today* v50 no3 p14 My/Je 2017

End the Epidemic color *America* v215 no13 p5 O 31 2016

THE FIGHT OF THEIR LIVES L. MURTHA *Cincinnati Magazine* v50 no2 p66 N 2016

What should doctors and drugmakers do to stop painkiller addiction? K. KIPLINGER color *Kiplinger's Personal Finance* v71 no5 p14 My 2017

YOUR BRAIN ON DRUGS C. MALDARELLI cartoon *Popular Science* p28 Ja/F 2017

Drug addiction—Psychological aspects

can v315 no6 p5 D 2016

THE LOOMING THREAT OF FACTORY — FARM SUPER-
BUGS M. Wenner Moyer color diag *Scientific American* v315
no6 p70 D 2016

New Weapon Against Bacteria *USA Today Magazine* v145
no2861 p11 F 2017

Prescribing a Predator E. S. Eaton bw color diag graph *Science
News* v191 no12 p22 Je 24 2017

WHO's dirty dozen microbes color *Science* v355 no6328 p890
Mr 3 2017

Why tolerance invites resistance K. Lewis and Y. Shan bibl diag
Science v355 no6327 p796 F 24 2017

Drug resistance in Escherichia coli

Scientists watch superbugs evolve L. HAMERS bw *Science News*
v190 no8 p11 O 15 2016

Drug resistance in microorganisms

See also

Drug resistance in bacteria

Emergence and spread of a human-transmissible multidrug-resistant nontuberculous mycobacterium J. M. Bryant, D. M. Grogono et al bibl diag graph *Science* v354 no6313 p751 N 11 2016

Launch your imagination with Science News stories *Science News*
v191 no12 p2 Je 24 2017

Drug resistance in microorganisms—International cooperation

U.N. declares war on superbugs *Science* v353 no6307 p1474 S
30 2016

Drug side effects

COULD YOU BE ADDICTED—AND NOT KNOW IT? V.
SOLE-SMITH color *Redbook* p88 N 2017

A Prescription for Better Health M. L. Tellado *Consumer Reports*
v82 no9 p4 S 2017

Too Many Meds? [Cover story] T. Carr, R. R. Peachman et al color
Consumer Reports v82 no9 p24 S 2017

YOU ON A CHIP N. Daly color diag *National Geographic* v232
no3 p136 S 2017

Drug therapy

See also

Administration of drugs

Antitussive agents

Chemotherapy (Cancer)

Should you increase HDL, and how? A. L. KOMAROFF *Harvard
Health Letter* v42 no9 p2 Jl 2017

THE UNBLINDING A. WREN *Indianapolis Monthly* v40 no3
p100 N 2016

What to do when medication makes you constipated *Harvard
Health Letter* v42 no10 p7 Ag 2017

What to do when your medication causes nausea *Harvard Health
Letter* v42 no7 p7 My 2017

Drug tolerance

Why tolerance invites resistance K. Lewis and Y. Shan bibl diag
Science v355 no6327 p796 F 24 2017

Drug traffic

THE DEA'S WARRANTLESS CASH GRAB C. J. CIARAMEL-
LA color *Reason* v49 no3 p13 Jl 2017

DRUG SMUGGLERS HAVE ALREADY BEATEN TRUMP'S
WALL T. C. BROWN color *Reason* v49 no1 p32 My 2017

hope riseS M. SZALAVITZ color *Women's Health* v14 no5 p154
Je 2017

Drug traffic—Mexico—Religious aspects

Priests killed in Mexico as drug violence spirals W. Williams color
Christian Century v133 no23 p14 N 9 2016

Drug traffic—Prevention

REFERENCES *Economic Indicators* p331 S 2016

Drug traffic—Social aspects

Priests killed in Mexico as drug violence spirals W. Williams color
Christian Century v133 no23 p14 N 9 2016

Drug traffic—United States—Lawsuits & claims

INDYCAP VICE L. J. Wertheim color *Sports Illustrated* v126 no2
p54 Ja 16 2017

Drug utilization

OPIOIDS M. Quinn *Governing* v30 no4 p35 Ja 2017

Drug withdrawal symptoms

It all started with partying D. McCarthy *Scholastic Choices* v32
no3 p10 N/D 2016

Drug abuse—Charts, diagrams, etc.

Tracking an Epidemic diag *Fortune* v176 no2 p15 Ag 1 2017

Drugged driving—Prevention

Doobs of hazard C. GILLIS color *Maclean's* v129 no41 p14 O
17 2016

Drugs

See also

AIDS (Disease)—Vaccination

Anti-infective agents

Drug accessibility

Drug overdose

Marijuana

Nonprescription drugs

Synthetic drugs

13 Things Your Pharmacist Won't Tell You M. CROUCH color
Reader's Digest v189 no1129 p124 Ap 2017

ADDERALL C. Schwartz *New York Times Magazine* p54 O 16
2016

Checkup for Your Medicine Cabinet R. WESTEN *AARP: The
Magazine* v59 no5A p20 Ag/S 2016

Easier cure for resistant TB J. Cohen color *Science* v355 no6326
p677 F 17 2017

Fighting Hearing Loss C. Chen and D. Bloomfield cartoon chart
Bloomberg Businessweek no4497 p37 O 31 2016

Multitask Better V. Tweed color *Amazing Wellness* v9 no1 p20
Wint 2017

The Side Effect A. ROBERT color *National Geographic* v231 no6
p128 Je 2017

Drugs & crime

See also

Drug traffic

A State of Grief A. ALMENDRAL color *National Geographic*
v231 no6 p106 Je 2017

Drugs & sex

BLURRED LINES: CHEMSEX & CONSENT: It's time to talk
about the elephant in the room Z. ZANE *Advocate* no1093 p58
O/N 2017

Drugs of abuse—Law & legislation

OPIATE OF THE MASSES J. HEARN *Humanist* v77 no1 p22
Ja/F 2017

Drugs—Economic aspects

Prescription bargain hunt *Harvard Health Letter* v42 no6 p1 Ap
2017

Drugs—Export & import trade

Cheap Drugs from Canada Won't Reduce U.S. Drug Prices R.
Mohammed *Harvard Business Review Digital Articles* p2 F 12
2016

Drugs—Physiological effect

See also

Antibiotics—Physiological effect

Drugs—Side effects

Effect of drugs on memory

EFFECTS OF DIET ON ULCER TREATMENT STUDIED C.
Barakat and M. McCluskey color *Equus* no472 p11 Ja 2017

Drugs—Prices

How Much Is a Miracle Worth? C. Chen color *Bloomberg Businessweek* no4518 p21 Ap 10 2017

It's Easier to Measure the Cost of Health Care than Its Value D.
Goldman, A. Chandra et al *Harvard Business Review Digital
Articles* p2 N 18 2014

Just the Medicine A. Mundy color *Washington Monthly* p4 N/D
2016

A New Way to Define Value in Drug Pricing P. B. Bach *Harvard
Business Review Digital Articles* p2 O 6 2015

Pushing Back on High Drug Prices color *Prevention* v68 no12 p12
D 2016

The Real Cost of "High- Priced" Drugs M. Rosenblatt *Harvard
Business Review Digital Articles* p2 N 17 2014

Remedies Beyond Reach F. QUIGLEY color *America* v215 no14
p14 N 7 2016

We Need More Transparency on the Cost of Specialty Drugs R.
Galvin and R. Longman *Harvard Business Review Digital Articles* p2 N 4 2014

Who Has the Power to Cut Drug Prices? Employers R. Galvin
and R. Longman *Harvard Business Review Digital Articles* p2
D 1 2015

Your Prescription Gets A Rebate—for Insurers R. Langreth
Bloomberg Businessweek no4494 p23 O 10 2016

Drugs—Prices—United States

4 Ways to Shoot Down Skyrocketing Drug Prices H. S. Edwards color *Time* v188 no16/17 p54 O 24 2016

Cheap Drugs from Canada Won't Reduce U.S. Drug Prices R. Mohammed *Harvard Business Review Digital Articles* p2 F 12 2016

Drug Costs Too High? Fire the Middleman N. Weinberg and R. Langreth *Bloomberg Businessweek* no4513 p28 Mr 6 2017

It's Time to Rein in Exorbitant Pharmaceutical Prices R. Mohammed *Harvard Business Review Digital Articles* p2 S 22 2015

Pharma's Worst Nightmare D. Bloomfield and H. Li cartoon *Bloomberg Businessweek* no4508 p18 Ja 23 2017

Price Gouging and the Dangerous New Breed of Pharma Companies A. G. Smith *Harvard Business Review Digital Articles* p2 Jl 6 2016

Drugs—Safety measures

See also

Drug disposal

Sharing the Medicine Chest *Your Dog (10780343)* v22 no10 p3 O 2016

Drugs—Side effects

Aspirin to Prevent Heart Attacks S. KLEIN *Prevention* v69 no4 p22 Ap 2017

Hidden Side Effects R. F. Mandelbaum color *Scientific American* v316 no1 p18 Ja 2017

Drugs—Social aspects

The Drug Chronicles D. BROWNE bw color *Rolling Stone* no1293 p28 Ag 10 2017

Drugstores

KEEPING SHOP IN MILLER M. KARST *South Dakota Magazine* v32 no4 p112 N/D 2016

Drugstores—Evaluation

Drugstore shopping is my therapy E. Seidman color *Health* v31 no9 p65 N 2017

Helpful High Street Shops *British Heritage Travel* v38 no4 p17 Jl/Ag 2017

Drugstores—United States

A Case for Why Health Systems Should Partner with Pharmacies W. H. Shrank *Harvard Business Review Digital Articles* p2 O 14 2015

Druids & druidism

Druids' Temple R. Griffiths *History Today* v67 no4 p70 Ap 2017

DRUM, KEVIN

Here's How to Save Obamacare *Mother Jones* v42 no1 p19 Ja/F 2017

LET'S MAKE SOME SAUSAGE AGAIN cartoon *Mother Jones* v42 no5 p12 S/O 2017

YOU WILL LOSE YOUR JOB TO A ROBOT color *Mother Jones* v42 no6 p38 N/D 2017

Drum music

Rhythmic Independence & Musicality on the Drum Set D. PRIETO color diag *Downbeat* v83 no11 p68 N 2016

Drum music—Instruction & study

Breaking 'The Medium Phenomenon' Condition R. MORGENSTEIN bw color *Downbeat* v84 no1 p100 Ja 2017

Drum set—Evaluation

GEAR BOX color *Downbeat* v83 no11 p82 N 2016

Yamaha Recording Custom Series M. Kern color *Downbeat* v83 no11 p81 N 2016

Drummers (Musicians)

BEAT MASTER R. J. SMITH *Cincinnati Magazine* v50 no8 p45 My 2017

Buddy Rich J. McDonough bw *Downbeat* v84 no1 p42 Ja 2017

Cyrille's Brilliant Gamesmanship K. Micallef color *Downbeat* v84 no1 p17 Ja 2017

DANIEL FREEDMAN T. Panken bw *Downbeat* v84 no3 p24 Mr 2017

MASTER OF CEREMONIES T. ADLER bw color *Vogue* v207 no6 p140 Je 2017

OLEG BUTMAN T. Panken color *Downbeat* v83 no12 p24 D 2016

Remembering Alphonse Mouzon B. Milkowski bw color *Downbeat* v84 no4 p18 Ap 2017

Sonic Portrait of Evans in '68 P. Lutz bw *Downbeat* v84 no10 p13 O 2017

TRAVIS BARKER D. M. Zepeda color *Runner's World* v52 no6

p96 Jl 2017

Drummers (Musicians)—Interviews

Lars Ulrich K. GROW cartoon *Rolling Stone* no1274 p62 N 17 2016

Drumming (Theatrical production)

Drumming J. DAVIDSON *New York* v49 no24 p154 N 28 2016

DRUMMOND, ANDREW

Go Big: Superhike map *Backpacker* p28 Ag 2017

DRUMMOND, SELBY

Paloma Elsesser color *Vogue* v207 no11 p126 N 2017

Drummy, Lawrence F.

Harvesting electrical energy from carbon nanotube yarn twist diag graph *Science* v357 no6353 p773 Ag 25 2017

Drums (Musical instruments)

The Indigenous Worship War M. LEE *Christianity Today* v61 no7 p20 S 2017

Drums (Musical instruments)—Equipment & supplies—Evaluation

GEAR BOX color *Downbeat* v83 no11 p82 N 2016

GEAR BOX color *Downbeat* v84 no6 p90 Je 2017

Drums (Musical instruments)—Evaluation

Evans Calftone Drum Heads S. Hawk color *Downbeat* v83 no11 p81 N 2016

GEAR BOX color *Downbeat* v84 no1 p108 Ja 2017

Drums (Musical instruments)—Performance

Breaking 'The Medium Phenomenon' Condition R. MORGENSTEIN bw color *Downbeat* v84 no1 p100 Ja 2017

Drumsticks (Musical instruments)

Vic Firth Modern Jazz Collection R. Bennett color *Downbeat* v84 no6 p86 Je 2017

Drunk (Music)

'It's Always Music First' THUNDERCAT J. Tangari color *Downbeat* v84 no6 p52 Je 2017

What to Stream color *Entertainment Weekly* no1454/1455 p96 F 24 2017

Drunk driving

You're Busted: And It's a Laugh C. WHITE *Idaho Magazine* v16 no8 p43 My 2017

Drunk History (TV program)

DRUNK HISTORY L. ACKEN *TV Guide* p49 D 5 2016

Druon, Maurice

Fantasy Flashback M. DIRDA bw *Weekly Standard* v23 no3 p33 S 25 2017

Druout, Alain

Vibes Legend Burton Bids Fond Farewell color *Downbeat* v84 no6 p13 Je 2017

Drury, Eleanor

Resistance to malaria through structural variation of red blood cell invasion receptors diag *Science* v356 no6343 p1139 Je 16 2017

Drutman, Lee

It's the Culture, Stupid il *New Republic* v248 no11 p14 N 2017

Tribalists and Ideologues color *Washington Monthly* v49 no6-8 p74 Je-Ag 2017

Trump's Supporters Revealed *Washington Monthly* p12 N/D 2016

Druzin, Randi

DO EVERYONE A FAVOUR CALL IN SICK color *Maclean's* v129 no40 p67 O 10 2016

GREENING YOUR HOME + BUSINESS color *Maclean's* v129 no50 p37 D 19 2016

HIV REMAINS A PREVALENT ISSUE IN CANADA *Maclean's* v129 no50 p52 D 19 2016

Is It Time to Fall Proof Your Parent's Home? color *Maclean's* v130 no3 p49 Ap 2017

MAX DOMI'S Success Depends on Accuracy bw *Maclean's* v129 no48/49 p40 D 5 2016

Dry, Sarah

Rain check color *Science* v355 no6331 p1272 Mr 24 2017

Dry, Stanley

CATCH OF THE DAY bw color *Louisiana Life* v38 no1 p54 S/O 2017

CREAM OF THE CROP color *Louisiana Life* v37 no4 p24 Mr/Ap 2017

EATING WELL color *Louisiana Life* v37 no2 p82 N/D 2016

Oh Shucks! color *Louisiana Life* v37 no4 p46 Mr/Ap 2017

OYSTER FEST color *Louisiana Life* v37 no2 p24 N/D 2016

PARTY HEARTY! color *Louisiana Life* v37 no3 p22 Ja/F 2017

SIMPLY FRESH bw color *Louisiana Life* v37 no5 p54 My/Je 2017

SUMMER FAVORITES color *Louisiana Life* v37 no6 p54 Jl/Ag 2017

Dry eye syndromes—Prevention

Dry Eyes R. LALIBERTE *Prevention* v69 no7 p18 Jl 2017

Dry eye syndromes—Risk factors

Dry Eyes R. LALIBERTE *Prevention* v69 no7 p18 Jl 2017

Dry eye syndromes—Treatment

Dry eyes? Try this! *Harvard Health Letter* v42 no6 p7 Ap 2017

Electronic screen alert: Avoid this vision risk *Harvard Health Letter* v42 no10 p3 Ag 2017

Second opinion *Mayo Clinic Health Letter* v35 no2 p8 F 2017

Dry Tortugas (Fla.)

The Dry Tortugas... M. Dolan color *American History* v52 no4 p72 O 2017

Imaging Adventure: Dry Tortugas R. S. Wright Jr. *Sky & Telescope* v133 no2 p32 F 2017

Dryden, Phylis

Q: What is the most significant fad of all time? color *Atlantic* v319 no3 p96 Ap 2017

Dryzek, John S.

Twelve Key Findings in Deliberative Democracy Research *Daedalus* v146 no3 p28 Summ 2017

D'Souza, David

Branch activities step up a gear: Webinars and walks among the new initiatives CIPD branches are embracing to support members *People Management* p60 Je 2017

D'Souza, Steven

Don't Get Surprised by Burnout *Harvard Business Review Digital Articles* p2 Je 17 2016

New Managers Don't Have to Have All the Answers *Harvard Business Review Digital Articles* p2 S 30 2015

Du, Chunhui

Control and local measurement of the spin chemical potential in a magnetic insulator bw diag *Science* v357 no6347 p195 Jl 14 2017

Du, Hao-Xing

"Perfect" designer chromosome V and behavior of a ring derivative diag *Science* v355 no6329 p1046 Mr 10 2017

Du, Juan

Cryo-EM structures of the triheteromeric NMDA receptor and its allosteric modulation graph *Science* v355 no6331 p1282 Mr 24 2017

Du, Peicheng

Tudor-SN–mediated endonucleolytic decay of human cell microRNAs promotes G1/S phase transition graph *Science* v356 no6340 p859 My 26 2017

Dua Lipa (Music)

What to Stream color *Entertainment Weekly* no1468/1469 p102 Je 2-9 2017

Dua Lipa (Performer)

10 ARTISTS WHO WILL RULE 2017 E. R. Brown, N. Feeney et al color *Entertainment Weekly* no1450 p56 Ja 27 2017

Dua LIPA: THE BRITISH SINGER SONGWRITER FUSES SOUL AND POP BY MAKING IT PERSONAL C. KELSEY *Interview* v47 no3 p22 Ap 2017

Dual-career families

Are Chore Wars at Home Holding You Back at Work? R. Shambaugh color *Harvard Business Review Digital Articles* p2 Ja 19 2017

Navigating Tradeoffs in a Dual-Career Marriage M. Valcour *Harvard Business Review Digital Articles* p2 Ap 14 2015

Dual diagnosis

A Connection to Caring: Phoenix House takes recovery to the next level B. Nordstrom *Psychology Today* v50 no5 p34 S/O 2017

Dual nationality

The Dual-Citizenship Crisis Rocking Politics Down Under R. Lewis color *Time* v190 no8 p11 Ag 28 2017

Dualism

See also

Mind & body

What (Real) Men (Really) Want D. T. PUTERBAUGH *USA Today Magazine* v145 no2862 p82 Mr 2017

Duan, Kaibo

Mapping the human DC lineage through the integration of high-dimensional techniques diag *Science* v356 no6342 p1044 Je 9 2017

Duan, Xiangfeng

Robust epitaxial growth of two-dimensional heterostructures, multiheterostructures, and superlattices color *Science* v357 no6353 p788 Ag 25 2017

Three-dimensional holey-graphene/niobia composite architectures for ultrahigh-rate energy storage color diag graph *Science* v356 no6338 p599 My 12 2017

Duan, Xidong

Robust epitaxial growth of two-dimensional heterostructures, multiheterostructures, and superlattices color *Science* v357 no6353 p788 Ag 25 2017

Duan Xu

Extensive migration of young neurons into the infant human frontal lobe color diag graph *Science* v354 no6308 paaf7073-1 O 7 2016

Duane, Daniel

IF YOU BUILD IT, WILL THEY COME? color *Bloomberg Businessweek* no4509 p59 Ja 30 2017

Duarte, Esteban

Anatomy of a Bad Marriage color *Bloomberg Businessweek* no4541 p10 O 9 2017

The Pressure Rises In Catalonia color *Bloomberg Businessweek* no4539 p36 S 25 2017

DUARTE, MATÍAS

WATCHING THE CLOCKS *Popular Science* v289 no5 p45 S/O 2017

Duarte, Nancy

Conquer Your Nerves Before Your Presentation *Harvard Business Review Digital Articles* p2 Ap 28 2015

Finding the Right Metaphor for Your Presentation *Harvard Business Review Digital Articles* p2 N 17 2014

How Experts Can Help a General Audience Understand Their Ideas *Harvard Business Review Digital Articles* p2 S 12 2016

Meetings: When to Present and When to Converse *Harvard Business Review Digital Articles* p2 Mr 24 2015

Successful Movements All Have 3 Acts *Harvard Business Review Digital Articles* p2 Mr 24 2016

To Win People Over, Speak to Their Wants and Needs *Harvard Business Review Digital Articles* p2 My 12 2015

Why I Write in PowerPoint *Harvard Business Review Digital Articles* p2 Jl 27 2015

Duarte, Paul A. P.

On a Question of the Day color *Black Belt* v55 no6 p16 O/N 2017

Duat (Theatrical production)

SHOWOFFS H. ALS cartoon *New Yorker* v92 no36 p80 N 7 2016

Dubai (United Arab Emirates)

All Roads Lead to Dubai C. AJUDUA color *Conde Nast Traveler* v51 no10 p52 N 2016

Residents and Residencies R. Aima *Art in America* v104 no9 p55 O 2016

Dubai (United Arab Emirates)—Description & travel

'Oh, DUBAI. I do not understand you' H. O'Neill color map *Canadian Geographic* v137 p30 2017 Travel

Dubansky, Katharine

BACKBONE FARM Growing Kids, Food, and Skills K. C. Compton *Mother Earth News* no280 p12 F/Mr 2017

Dubansky, Max—Interviews

BACKBONE FARM Growing Kids, Food, and Skills K. C. Compton *Mother Earth News* no280 p12 F/Mr 2017

Dubé, Deelee

Deelee Dubé Wins Sarah Vaughan Jazz Vocal Competition M. Barris color *Downbeat* v84 no2 p13 F 2017

Dube, Oeindrila

The dual components of mental health—Response bibl color *Science* v354 no6314 p840 N 18 2016

Dubin, Julie Weingardt

Handle a Sibling's Playdate *Parents* v92 no9 p169 S 2017

DUBIN, MINNA

9 parent click-bait headlines you never see online cartoon *Parents* v92 no7 p94 Jl 2017

Dubin, Steven C.

Ghosts of Apartheid color *Art in America* v105 no6 p61 Je/Jl 2017

Dubious Achievement Awards

Dubious Achievement Awards of 2016 color *Esquire* v166 no5

p50 D 2016/Ja 2017

Dublin (Ireland)—Description & travel

The Jet-Setters' Guide to Weekends N. K. HAHN color *Chicago* v66 no10 p92 O 2017

DUBLIN, HOLLY T.

Conserving the World's Megafauna and Biodiversity: The Fierce Urgency of Now *BioScience* v67 no3 p197 Mr 2017

Saving the World's Terrestrial Megafauna color *BioScience* v66 no10 p807 O 1 2016

Dublyansky, Yuri V.

Response to Comments on "Reconciliation of the Devils Hole climate record with orbital forcing" bibl chart graph *Science* v354 no6310 p296-e O 21 2016

DUBNO, DAN

ANYONE CAN BE SPIDER-MAN color *Popular Mechanics* p86 D 2016/Ja 2017

BETTER NUCLEAR POWER THROUGH PING PONG color diag *Popular Mechanics* p14 My 2017

The Camera That Makes Movies for You cartoon color *Popular Mechanics* p20 Ap 2017

HOW TO DO EVERY THING WITH VIDEO bw color diag *Popular Mechanics* p58 O 2017

HOW TO MAKE ANYTHING [Cover story] color diag *Popular Mechanics* p56 S 2017

IS SOMEONE GOING TO HACK MY LIGHTBULB? color *Popular Mechanics* p77 Mr 2017

Secrets of a Weekend Lock Picker [Cover story] color *Popular Mechanics* v193 no7 p29 S 2016

UNDERWATER POWER TOOLS? color *Popular Mechanics* p10 S 2017

WILL IT KILL YOU? bw color *Popular Mechanics* p88 Jl 2017

DUBNO, MICHAEL

HOW TO MAKE ANYTHING [Cover story] color diag *Popular Mechanics* p56 S 2017

Duboff, Josh

ACCORDING TO: Anna Kendrick bw *Vanity Fair* v59 no1 p100 Holiday 2017

ACCORDING TO: Donald Glover color *Vanity Fair* v58 no11 p98 N 2016

ACCORDING TO: Finn Wittrock bw *Vanity Fair* v59 no4 p118 Mr 2017

ACCORDING TO: Ilana Glazer color *Vanity Fair* v59 no8 p50 Ag 2017

ACCORDING TO: Kaitlin Olson bw *Vanity Fair* v59 no11 p72 N 2017

ACCORDING TO: Kyle Chandler color *Vanity Fair* v58 no12 p90 D 2016

AND THIS WAS BEFORE INSTAGRAM color *Vanity Fair* v59 no10 p197 O 2017

GIGI'S SPACE ODYSSEY [Cover story] color *Harper's Bazaar* no3654 p118 Je/Jl 2017

HIS OWN VERSION color *Vanity Fair* v59 no7 p107 Summ 2017

THE NEW ESTABLISHMENT 2017 bw color *Vanity Fair* v59 no11 p87 N 2017

NEW ESTABLISHMENT bw cartoon color *Vanity Fair* v58 no11 p124 N 2016

Dubois, David

The Two Big Ways Power Transforms a Person *Harvard Business Review Digital Articles* p2 F 26 2016

Du Bois, J.

Asymmetric synthesis of batrachotoxin: Enantiomeric toxins show functional divergence against NaV bibl diag graph *Science* v354 no6314 p865 N 18 2016

DUBOIS, LENA M.

The Odor of Death: An Overview of Current Knowledge on Characterization and Applications *BioScience* v67 no7 p600 Jl 2017

Du Boise, Simone

GREEN HOUSES B. RILEY *Atlanta* v56 no10 p28 F 2017

Dubreuil, Benjamin

Young phosphorylation is functionally silent bibl diag *Science* v354 no6309 p176 O 14 2016

Dubroff, Pati

42 new ALL-STAR PRODUCTS of the year [Cover story] color *Redbook* p27 Jl/Ag 2017

The New PASTELS cartoon *O, The Oprah Magazine* p62 Ap 2017

DUBROW, HENRY

A Bird in the Hand color graph *Kiplinger's Personal Finance* v71 no2 p6 F 2017

Dubs, Adolph, 1920-1979

EDITOR'S LETTER M. Schaffer *Washingtonian Magazine* v52 no9 p14 Je 2017

THE LAST AMBASSADOR W. GRUNEWALD *Washingtonian Magazine* v52 no9 p58 Je 2017

Dubuffet, Jean

$1 million Day *Treasures* v6 no2 p8 O/N 2016

DUCA, LAUREN

WHEN YOU ACHIEVE ALL OF YOUR GOALS, YOU STILL WAKE UP AS YOU *Vital Speeches of the Day* v83 no8 p226 Ag 2017

Ducasse, Alain, 1956——Interviews

10 Remarkable People on Having a Career That Matters *Harvard Business Review Digital Articles* p2 D 24 2014

Ducati motorcycle

2017 DUCATI 1299 SUPER-LEGGERA D. Canet color *Cycle World* v56 no7 p48 Ag 2017

2017 DUCATI DIAVEL DIESEL D. Canet color *Cycle World* v56 no7 p18 Ag 2017

SERVICE R. NIERLICH color *Cycle World* v56 no1 p54 Ja/F 2017

STUDYING ABROAD B. Adams color *Cycle World* v56 no1 p14 Ja/F 2017

THE TEN REST *Cycle World* v56 no10 p8 N 2017

Ducati motorcycle—Evaluation

2017 DUCATI MONSTER 1200 S S. MacDonald color *Cycle World* v56 no2 p10 Mr 2017

2017 DUCATI MULTISTRADA 950 N. Suesse color *Cycle World* v56 no2 p14 Mr 2017

2017 DUCATI SCRAMBLER DESERT SLED B. Adams bw color *Cycle World* v56 no1 p24 Ja/F 2017

2017 DUCATI SCRAMBLER DESERT SLED B. Adams color *Cycle World* v56 no3 p34 Ap 2017

2017 DUCATI SUPERSPORT AND SUPERSPORT S S. MacDonald color *Cycle World* v56 no4 p16 My 2017

Old Is the New New D. CURCURITO color *Popular Mechanics* p67 D 2016/Ja 2017

SCRAMBLER PARADOX color *Cycle World* v56 no3 p30 Ap 2017

Ducey, Doug, 1964-

The New Old Right M. Funkhouser *Governing* v30 no6 p4 Mr 2017

Ducey, Kenny

TROUT'S POND chart *Sports Illustrated* v126 no9 p45 Mr 27 2017

DUCHARME, JAMIE

THE LIGHT AT THE END OF THE RUN color *Women's Health* v14 no9 p118 N 2017

DUCHEN, JESSICA

360 DEGREES *Opera News* v81 no6 p34 D 2016

Duchesney, Ben

Flipping Genius color *Field & Stream* v122 no1 pF1 My 2017

Duchild, Alexander R.

Epitaxial lift-off of electrodeposited single-crystal gold foils for flexible electronics bibl bw diag *Science* v355 no6330 p1203 Mr 17 2017

Duchin, Faye

Climate optimism gets a road map color *Science* v356 no6340 p811 My 26 2017

Duchosal, Thibaud

WEATHER HOLD S. MAIT bw *Skiing* p8 Wint 2017

Duchovny, David, 1960-

CHECKING IN ON THE X-FILES K. Connolly color *Entertainment Weekly* no1485 p44 O 6 2017

THE RISE OF THE FAKE FAMOUS JACKASS NOVELIST J. LARSON img *New York* v50 no6 p80 Mr 20 2017

Duck behavior

PERHAPS THEY SLIPPED RIGHT BY YOU UNNOTICED WHEN YOU HAD color *Audubon* v119 no3 p48 Fall 2017

Duck Blind (Poem)

'DUCK BLIND' B. Collins bw *New York Times Book Review* p14 Ag 6 2017

Duck calls

THE RED ZONE B. Fitzpatrick color *Outdoor Life* v223 no9

pH11 N 2016

Duck migration

PERHAPS THEY SLIPPED RIGHT BY YOU UNNOTICED WHEN YOU HAD color *Audubon* v119 no3 p48 Fall 2017

Duck shooting

BO WHOOP COMES HOME W. BRANTLEY color *Field & Stream* v121 no6 p52 N 2016

¿CÓMO SE DICE CAST & BLAST? C. KEARNS cartoon color *Field & Stream* v121 no8 p83 F/Mr 2017

The Coot Surprise M. D. Johnson color *Field & Stream* v122 no5 pF8 O 2017

DUCKING THE GREAT SALT LAKE A. Mckean cartoon color *Outdoor Life* v223 no9 p31 N 2016

FIND YOUR CALLING D. Draper, B. ALLEN et al color *Field & Stream* v122 no5 p50 O 2017

FOWL PLAY T. E. NICKENS color *Field & Stream* v122 no2 p84 Je/Jl 2017

HALF HOUR OF GLORY T. E. Nickens bw color *Field & Stream* v122 no4 p26 S 2017

HERE THEY COME T. E. Nickens color *Field & Stream* v122 no5 p27 O 2017

The Imperfect Opener M. D. Johnson color *Field & Stream* v122 no4 pF1 S 2017

INCOMING GREENHEADS T. CARPENTER color *Outdoor Life* v224 no8 pW1 O 2017

THE JUMP-SHOOTER'S PLAYBOOK A. ROBINSON color *Outdoor Life* v224 no8 pW8 O 2017

Operation Black Duck M. D. Johnson color *Field & Stream* v122 no5 p80 O 2017

SOUTHERN COMFORT S. Evans color *Southern Living* v52 no1 p12 Ja 2017

STUDY ABROAD W. Brantley color *Field & Stream* v122 no6 p30 N 2017

THE TEAL ZONE T. CARPENTER color *Outdoor Life* v224 no7 pW5 S 2017

TWEAK THE DEKES T. CARPENTER color *Outdoor Life* v224 no7 pW9 S 2017

AN UNEXPECTED ALL-NIGHTER A. TRUDEL and N. KREBS cartoon color *Outdoor Life* v224 no2 p13 F/Mr 2017

DUCKLOW, HUGH W.

Microbial Community Dynamics in Two Polar Extremes: The Lakes of the McMurdo Dry Valleys and the West Antarctic Peninsula Marine Ecosystem chart color graph *BioScience* v66 no10 p829 O 1 2016

Responses of Antarctic Marine and Freshwater Ecosystems to Changing Ice Conditions color graph *BioScience* v66 no10 p864 O 1 2016

Duckor, Brent

Got grit? Maybe... color diag il *Phi Delta Kappan* v98 no7 p61 Ap 2017

Ducks

3 Strategies for Flocks N. Bahl *Audubon* v119 no3 p49 Fall 2017

AIM HIGH B. Zwiebel color *Audubon* v119 no3 p48 Fall 2017

OPEN-WATER DIVERS B. RUZZO color *Outdoor Life* v224 no1 p36 D 2016/Ja 2017

Sitting Ducks E. J. Peiker color *Audubon* v119 no3 p48 Fall 2017

Swamp Steward M. Bartels color *Audubon* v119 no3 p49 Fall 2017

TARGET: Bluebills M. D. Johnson color *Field & Stream* v122 no4 pF6 S 2017

DuckTales (TV program)

DuckTales for a New Generation M. Snetiker color *Entertainment Weekly* no1470 p10 Je 16 2017

Duckweeds

Mr. Rigolizzo and the amazing miracle weed that will save Sparta! (Or not.) S. Raviv *Atlanta* v57 no2 p84 Je 2017

Duckworth, Angela

Grit/Grit: The Power of Passion and Perseverance *Publishers Weekly* v264 no6 p18 F 6 2017

Duckworth, Jay

The Artists' Bugout Bag *Stage Directions* v30 no6 p36 Je 2017

But Will It Wash Off... *Stage Directions* v30 no8 p28 Ag 2017

I Ain't Got No Body: Need a dead body for a show? Get an intern and Saran Wrap *Stage Directions* v30 no9 p28 S 2017

Props has a Drinking Problem *Stage Directions* v30 no4 p28 Ap 2017

Props Still Has a Drinking Problem *Stage Directions* v30 no5 p28 My 2017

Duckworth, Tammy, 1968-

SENATOR-ELECT TAMMY DUCKWORTH J. R. ENSZER *Ms.* v26 no3 p7 Fall 2016

Sending a Message to Paul Ryan M. Ervin *Progressive* v81 no3 p24 Mr 2017

Ducournau, Julia

Girl, You'll Be a Cannibal Soon M. ATKINSON *In These Times* v41 no4 p52 Ap 2017

Healthy Appetite N. Rapold color *Film Comment* v52 no6 p8 N/D 2016

Raw C. Nashawaty color *Entertainment Weekly* no1457/1458 p74 Mr 17 2017

Raw *New Yorker* v93 no8 p10 Ap 10 2017

Ducournau, Julia—Interviews

PLEASURES OF THE FLESH M. BARTON-FUMO color *Film Comment* v53 no2 p42 Mr/Ap 2017

Duct tape

DUCT-TAPE DEFENSE J. HANSON color *Black Belt* v55 no6 p58 O/N 2017

WILD FIRES T. E. NICKENS color *Field & Stream* v121 no8 p44 F/Mr 2017

Ductility

High dislocation density–induced large ductility in deformed and partitioned steels B. B. He, B. Hu et al bw color diag *Science* v357 no6355 p1029 S 8 2017

Dudareva, Natalia

Emission of volatile organic compounds from petunia flowers is facilitated by an ABC transporter diag *Science* v356 no6345 p1386 Je 30 2017

Dudchenko, Olga

De novo assembly of the Aedes aegypti genome using Hi-C yields chromosome-length scaffolds chart color diag *Science* v356 no6333 p92 Ap 7 2017

Dude ranches—Montana

8 Great Gaited Getaways A. PAVIA color *Horse & Rider* v56 no10 p80 O 2017

Dudgeon, David

The broad footprint of climate change from genes to biomes to people bibl chart color *Science* v354 no6313 paaf7671-1 N 11 2016

DUDLEY, DAVID

Experts say Americans get an hour or two less shut-eye every night than we once did. What's keeping us up, and is there a way to make a restless nation go to bed? color *AARP: The Magazine* v59 no5A p54 Ag/S 2016

In Case of Blizzard, Do Nothing *Reader's Digest* v189 no1127 p16 F 2017

Last Band Standing color *AARP: The Magazine* v59 no4A p55 Je/Jl 2016

Surviving the '80s color *AARP: The Magazine* v59 no5A p47 Ag/S 2016

Dudley, Jessica

How Brigham & Women's Funds Health Care Innovation *Harvard Business Review Digital Articles* p2 O 15 2015

How One Hospital Turns Doctors into Leaders *Harvard Business Review Digital Articles* p2 D 12 2014

Dudman, Joshua T.

Deconstructing behavioral neuropharmacology with cellular specificity color *Science* v356 no6333 p42 Ap 7 2017

Dudok de Wit, Michael

The Red Turtle J. McGovern color *Entertainment Weekly* no1450 p44 Ja 27 2017

Dudy, L.

Bismuthene on a SiC substrate: A candidate for a high-temperature quantum spin Hall material diag graph *Science* v357 no6348 p287 Jl 21 2017

Due diligence

Before a Merger, Consider Company Cultures Along with Financials D. Fubini *Harvard Business Review Digital Articles* p2 D 26 2014

Dueck, Shannon

The Kindergarten Years D. K. Skvarla color *Dressage Today* v23 no5 p42 Ja 2017

The Value of Equine Education K. Beaudoin color *Dressage To-*

day v23 no4 p42 D 2016

Dueholm, Benjamin J.

But seriously, folks color *Christian Century* v134 no20 p36 S 27 2017

Liberalism and memory *Christian Century* v134 no19 p30 S 13 2017

Duehr, James

Enhancement of Zika virus pathogenesis by preexisting antiflavivirus immunity graph *Science* v356 no6334 p175 Ap 14 2017

Dueling—Law & legislation

On Your Honor J. GELERNTER *Weekly Standard* v22 no22 p38 F 13 2017

Dueño, José

Opposition to Óscar Romero's canonization was political color *America* v216 no8 p17 Ap 17 2017

Duesberg, Georg S.

All-printed thin-film transistors from networks of liquid-exfoliated nanosheets diag *Science* v356 no6333 p69 Ap 7 2017

Dufault, Renee Joy

Mind-Body Connection D. LEFFERTS color *Publishers Weekly* v264 no17 p28 Ap 24 2017

Duff, Hilary, 1987-

Younger M. Logan *TV Guide* v65 no27 p31 Je 26 2017

Duff, Hilary, 1987—Interviews

"I AM ENOUGH" [Cover story] A. SPENCER cartoon color *Redbook* p100 Ap 2017

Duff, Mike

ADD WATER TO DIRT AND YOU GET MUD. ADD BEER, WEED, AND 15,000 PEOPLE TO MUD AND YOU GET MICHIGAN MUD JAM color *Car & Driver* v63 no5 p106 N 2017

Aging Bull color *Car & Driver* v63 no5 p120 N 2017

CHARGE! color graph *Car & Driver* v62 no7 p78 Ja 2017

Crosshatch Patterns color *Car & Driver* v62 no10 p80 Ap 2017

THE FAST SHOW color *Car & Driver* v62 no11 p19 My 2017

Feel Lucky, Punk? [Cover story] color *Car & Driver* v63 no1 p36 Jl 2017

KING CUSH color *Car & Driver* v63 no4 p21 O 2017

McLaren's new 720S is the unknown and unexpected supercar revelation color *Car & Driver* v63 no1 p44 Jl 2017

Peter Schreyer, 63 cartoon *Car & Driver* v62 no10 p92 Ap 2017

RS KICKER color *Car & Driver* v62 no6 p21 D 2016

War can be fought with many things, sometimes even sandwiches color *Car & Driver* v62 no11 p70 My 2017

What I'd Do Differently: Walter Röhrl, 70 *Car & Driver* v63 no2 p104 Ag 2017

Duffel bags

AERIN LAUDER K. MOLVAR color *Conde Nast Traveler* v52 no7 p22 Ag 2017

Duffel bags—Evaluation

5 Gifts Your Grad Will Actually Use M. D. Harrington and L. Heffernan color *Money* v46 no5 p21 Je 2017

The latest word from our testers color *Backpacker* p54 My 2017

Money Bags color *GQ: Gentlemen's Quarterly* v86 no11 p122 N 2016

On a Roll color *AARP: The Magazine* v60 no5A p12 Ag/S 2017

Duffell, Joan C.

Madam Secretary, help us improve social-emotional learning color *Phi Delta Kappan* v98 no8 p64 My 2017

Duffer, Matt

That '80s Show S. LECKART bw color *Esquire* v166 no5 p144 D 2016/Ja 2017

Turned Upside Down A. STERNBERGH img *New York* v50 no17 p88 Ag 21 2017

Duffer, Matt—Interviews

THE DUFFER BROTHERS M. ROFFMAN *TV Guide* p16 D 19 2016

Duffer, Ross

That '80s Show S. LECKART bw color *Esquire* v166 no5 p144 D 2016/Ja 2017

Duffer, Ross—Interviews

THE DUFFER BROTHERS M. ROFFMAN *TV Guide* p16 D 19 2016

Duffield, Marshall

Duffield 58 S. Murray color *Power & Motoryacht* v34 no8 p28 Ag 2017

DUFFIELD, WENDELL

STUCK IN THE ORANGE WHALE *South Dakota Magazine* v32 no6 p96 Mr/Ap 2017

Duffield Yachts (Company)

DUFFIELD 58: TRADITIONAL LINES AND A DOUG ZURN DESIGN CREATE A COUPLES CRUISER WITH RANGE AND COMFORT M. WERLING color *Sea Magazine* v109 no6 p38 Je 2017

Duffin, Ruth

'THIS IS NO WAY TO LIVE' S. PROUDFOOT color *Maclean's* v129 no47 p14 N 28 2016

Duffner, Jordan Denari

What Catholics owe their Muslim brothers and sisters *America* v216 no3 p10 F 6 2017

Duffy, Austin G.

Mismatch repair deficiency predicts response of solid tumors to PD-1 blockade chart graph *Science* v357 no6349 p409 Jl 28 2017

Duffy, Eamon

The First Blood Libel Against the Jews cartoon *New York Review of Books* v63 no16 p51 O 27 2016

Secret Knowledge—or a Hoax? cartoon *New York Review of Books* v64 no7 p44 Ap 20 2017

DUFFY, GILLIAN

FRENCH, THREE WAYS img *New York* v49 no22 p74 O 31 2016

HOLIDAY FOOD img *New York* v49 no22 p71 O 31 2016

DUFFY, JACK

KENNEDY KILLING STILL A MYSTERY *USA Today Magazine* v145 no2858 p44 N 2016

Duffy, Jim

Thanks for the MEMORIES R. Sabin color *Sound & Vision* v82 no5 p30 Je 2017

Duffy, Michael

The Art of Warriors color *Time* v189 no9 p49 Mr 13 2017

Chief of Staff: Master of One color *Time* v189 no14 p56 Ap 17 2017

The Comey Misfire color *Time* v189 no19 p20 My 22 2017

Country First [Cover story] color *Time* v190 no7 p26 Ag 21 2017

Even Headstrong Generals Must Answer to Someone color *Time* v188 no18 p48 O 31 2016

Gwen Ifill color *Time* v188 no22-23 p13 N/D 2016

How Castro Will Be Trump's First Foreign Policy Test color *Time* v188 no24 p46 D 12 2016

How He Won color *Time* v188 no21 p48 N 21 2016

Klaus Schwab color *Time* v189 no4 p56 Ja 23 2017

Leaders color *Time* v189 no16/17 p64 My 1-8 2017

Life at 1600 [Cover story] color *Time* v189 no4 p26 Ja 23 2017

The Second Most Powerful Man In the World? [Cover story] color *Time* v189 no5 p24 F 13 2017

Special Counsel Named In Russia Probe color *Time* v189 no20 p29 My 29 2017

Will Bob Mueller Separate Fact from Fiction? [Cover story] color *Time* v190 no1 p24 Jl 3 2017

Duflo, Esther

Cognitive science in the field: A preschool intervention durably enhances intuitive but not formal mathematics chart color diag graph *Science* v357 no6346 p47 Jl 7 2017

DUFOUR, HUGUE

Spatchcock a Turkey color *Popular Mechanics* p32 N 2017

Dufour, Jeff

DAN ABOUT TOWN: Party photographer Dan Swartz's monthly roundup of bashes, balls, and benefits *Washingtonian Magazine* v52 no8 p30 My 2017

Dufour Yachts (Company)

The Kraken Awakes P. Nielsen color *Sail* v48 no11 p20 N 2017

Dufresne, Bethe

Never Forget bw color *Commonweal* v144 no7 p20 Ap 14 2017

Vodka on the Malecon color *Commonweal* v144 no1 p9 Ja 6 2017

Dufresne, Wylie

A CHEF'S TEST: THE AUTOMATIC OVEN color *Popular Mechanics* p77 My 2017

THE POPULAR MECHANICS GUIDE TO SELF-SUFFICIENCY [Cover story] color *Popular Mechanics* p55 F 2017

Steal Bill Telepan's Daughter's Lunch img *New York* v49 no20 p108 O 3 2016

Dufu, Tiffany

"My self-confidence was shattered overnight" bw color *Glamour* v115 no6 p108 Je 2017

Quotable Quotes E. JONG, E. DEGENERES et al bw color *Reader's Digest* v190 no1132 p140 Jl/Ag 2017

You Messed Up at Work. Now What? J. Thompson color *Essence* v48 no5 p77 S 2017

Dugan, Brandon

Release of mineral-bound water prior to subduction tied to shallow seismogenic slip off Sumatra graph *Science* v356 no6340 p841 My 26 2017

Dugatkin, Lee Alan

Fox and Friends M. ZUK *New York Times Book Review* p26 My 7 2017

HOW TO BUILD A DOG color *Scientific American* v316 no5 p68 My 2017

Scientists try to replay domestication T. H. Saey color *Science News* v191 no9 p29 My 13 2017

Dugdale, Julie

CHICAGOANS OF THE YEAR [Cover story] color *Chicago* v65 no12 p74 D 2016

CLASH OF THE TITANS color *Chicago* v66 no4 p26 Ap 2017

GET ON THE WATER color *Chicago* v66 no7 p60 Jl 2017

JUST FOR KICKS color *Chicago* v66 no8 p24 Ag 2017

TOP CANCER DOCTORS color *Chicago* v66 no1 p84 Ja 2017

THE TRUMP EFFECT color *Chicago* v66 no2 p18 F 2017

Duggan, Jennifer

A Portrait of the Prime Minister As a Young Man color *Time* v190 no4 p36 Jl 24 2017

Duggan, Jill

People and posts: Who's making HR headlines? *People Management* p50 Ag 2017

DUGGER, SHERRI

FIELD OF DREAMS: How a city girl-turned-accidental farmhand discovered heaven on earth *Indianapolis Monthly* v12 no40 p78 Ag 2017

The HOOSIER KITCHEN *Indianapolis Monthly* v12 no40 p60 Ag 2017

TOP PICKS *Indianapolis Monthly* v12 no40 p62 Ag 2017

Dugin, Aleksandr Gelyevich, 1962-

A Putin Fixer Claims Success With Turkey H. Meyer and O. Ant color *Bloomberg Businessweek* no4512 p15 F 20 2017

Dugoni, Robert

The Trapped Girl *Publishers Weekly* v263 no46 p34 N 14 2016

Dugoujon, Jean-Michel

Dispersals and genetic adaptation of Bantu-speaking populations in Africa and North America diag *Science* v356 no6337 p543 My 5 2017

Du Graf, Lauren

Polarities and Pyrotechnics: True/False Festival 2017 *Film Quarterly* v71 no1 p87 Fall 2017

Duhaime, Ann-Christine

Our Brains Love New Stuff, and It's Killing the Planet *Harvard Business Review Digital Articles* p2 Mr 17 2017

DuHamel, Brandon A.

BEAUTY AND THE BEAST color *Sound & Vision* v82 no8 p71 O 2017

CINEMA PARADISO color *Sound & Vision* v82 no5 p68 Je 2017

DOCTOR STRANGE color *Sound & Vision* v82 no6 p70 Jl/Ag 2017

GHOSTBUSTERS (2016) color *Sound & Vision* v82 no3 p67 Ap 2017

INDEPENDENCE DAY: RESURGENCE color *Sound & Vision* v82 no3 p68 Ap 2017

Moonlight chart color *Sound & Vision* v82 no6 p68 Jl/Ag 2017

PHANTASM: RAVAGER color *Sound & Vision* v82 no4 p71 My 2017

UNFORGIVEN color *Sound & Vision* v82 no8 p67 O 2017

WHISKEY TANGO FOXTROT color *Sound & Vision* v81 no9 p70 N 2016

Duhamel, Lauren

THIGH Masters M. DESANCTIS color *Vogue* v206 no12 p197a D 2016

Duhart, Olympia

Why More Hospitals Should Prioritize Cultural Competency *Harvard Business Review Digital Articles* p2 My 26 2017

Duhigg, Charles

From Beanie Babies to fidget spinners, the evolution of toy fads shows how technology has thrown the consumer economy into chaos *New York Times Magazine* p12 Ag 20 2017

Duivenvoorden, J. F.

Persistent effects of pre-Columbian plant domestication on Amazonian forest composition bibl chart graph map *Science* v355 no6328 p925 Mr 3 2017

Duke, Clifford S.

Toward a national, sustained U.S. ecosystem assessment bibl color *Science* v354 no6314 p838 N 18 2016

Duke, David Ernest, 1950-

WIZARD WATCH C. ROSE cartoon *New Orleans Magazine* v51 no1 p46 N 2016

Duke, Patty, 1946-2016

PATTY DUKE M. Gilbert and L. Rice color *Entertainment Weekly* no1446/1447 p92 D 2016/Ja 2017

DUKE, WINSTON L.

FROM THE ARCHIVES color *Reason* v49 no4 p78 Ag/S 2017

Duke Energy Corp.

State of Denial T. Korteti *Sierra* v101 no5 p22 S/O 2016

Duke University—Sports

1 DUKE BLUE DEVILS B. Hamilton chart color *Sports Illustrated* v125 no15 p60 N 7 2016

Dukes, Anthony

When It's Smart to Copy Your Competitor's Brand Promise *Harvard Business Review Digital Articles* p2 Mr 23 2017

Dukes, Paul

The Discontents of Counterfactualism *History Today* v67 no1 p72 Ja 2017

THE SAVAGE PUNISHMENT OF SIBERIAN EXILE: The wretched existence of those banished to Russia's freezing expanses east of the Urals is vividly described in this excellent study *History Today* v67 no6 p104 Je 2016

DUKOVIC, PARI

SHOWCASE color *New Yorker* v93 no11 p52 My 1 2017

Dulai Wenholz, Sushil

Enhancing Embryo-Transfer Effectiveness color *Practical Horseman* v45 no2 p69 F 2017

Genetic Test: Squamous Cell Carcinoma color *Practical Horseman* v45 no10 p68 O 2017

Season of Birth Can Affect Foal Size color *Practical Horseman* v45 no11 p68 N 2017

What Affects Heart Health in Event Horses? color *Practical Horseman* v45 no9 p76 S 2017

Dullemond, Cornelis P.

Spiral density waves in a young protoplanetary disk bibl graph *Science* v353 no6307 p1519 S 30 2016

DULLINGER, STEFAN

Scientific and Normative Foundations for the Valuation of Alien-Species Impacts: Thirteen Core Principles *BioScience* v67 no2 p166 F 2017

Duluth (Minn.)—Description & travel

AN AMERICAN PLACE M. Dolan *American History* v52 no1 p72 Ap 2017

Duluth (Minn.)—History

AN AMERICAN PLACE M. Dolan *American History* v52 no1 p72 Ap 2017

Dulwich Picture Gallery Enterprises Ltd.

English Visionary D. GREEN color *Weekly Standard* v22 no32 p41 My 1 2017

Duma, Miroslava—Interviews

CRACKING FASHION'S CODE R. Bhasin color *Harper's Bazaar* no3654 p142 Je/Jl 2017

Date with DIANE color *InStyle* v24 no3 p184 Mr 2017

DUMAIN, TERESA

Delete These E-mail Habits color *Reader's Digest* v189 no1131 p48 Je 2017

Pleasurable Health Hacks That Actually Work *Reader's Digest* v188 no1124 p60 O 2016

Dumaine, Brian

WIND ON THE WATER color diag map *Fortune* v175 no4 p184 Mr 15 2017

DUMAS, DANIEL

TIME FOR A MAN-CATION! color *Esquire* p114 O 2017

Dumbbells

Ascend & Deliver M. BERG chart color *Muscle & Performance*

v9 no10 p24 O 2017

Core Twist and Press chart *Men's Health* v32 no8 p60 O 2017

Establish Your Dominance L. McGLASHAN color *Muscle & Performance* v9 no9 p24 S 2017

FLAB-FREE ARMS S. Walter color *Good Housekeeping* v264 no6 p87 Je 2017

Gains of Thrones B. J. GADDOUR color *Men's Health* v32 no6 p34 Ag 2017

Get a Grip on the Farmer's Walk cartoon *Men's Health* v32 no9 p24 N 2017

Lift Light, Get Huge—Without Leaving Home! cartoon *Men's Health* v32 no8 p14 O 2017

THE NEXT FITNESS STAR WORKOUT [Cover story] M. GAINSBURG color *Women's Health* v14 no1 p156 Ja/F 2017

Dumont, Bruno, 1958-

Slack Bay *New Yorker* v93 no11 p11 My 1 2017

Dumont, Carl

Personalized Technology Will Upend the Doctor-Patient Relationship *Harvard Business Review Digital Articles* p2 Je 19 2015

Dumont, Emma

Breaking Big EMMA DUMONT S. Li, N. Abrams et al color *Entertainment Weekly* no1482/1483 p51 S 22 2017

THE X FACTOR J. RUSSELL *TV Guide* v65 no35 p14 Ag 21 2017

Dumplings

See also

Gnocchi

Building a Better Dumpling img *New York* v49 no25 p109 D 12 2016

Chicken and Dumplings C. BOND *Texas Monthly* v45 no1 p32 Ja 2017

A Dumpling Through the Digestive Tract A. MACMILLAN img *New York* v49 no25 p108 D 12 2016

How to Eat a Regular-Size Soup Dumpling H. GOLDFIELD img *New York* v49 no25 p106 D 12 2016

Maple Dumplings (Grandpères) A. TRAVERSO color *Yankee* p64 Mr 2017

OLD CHiNESE IS THE NEIII CHiNESə [Cover story] J. KRAMER and A. MASON color *Bon Appetit* p114 S 2017

Pork Dumplings *Indianapolis Monthly* v40 no10 p46 Je 2017

Dunant, Sarah

CYNICAL, DETERMINED, INTELLIGENT AND WITTY: A rich and complex portrait of the author of The Prince manages to combine scholarly analysis with the imagination of the historical novelist *History Today* v67 no10 p98 O 2017

In the Name of the Family *Publishers Weekly* v264 no6 p43 F 6 2017

New Narratives on Women's History *History Today* v67 no3 p65 Mr 2017

Princes of Darkness J. PARINI *New York Times Book Review* p19 Mr 19 2017

WARFARE, TERROR, MURDER AND BLOODSHED: A compelling narrative on the machinations of a Borgia pope and his offspring, with the added spice of Machiavelli's cool observations C. M. Richardson *History Today* v67 no7 p96 Jl 2017

WOMEN OF THRONES color *New York Times Book Review* p51 D 4 2016

DUNAVAN, CLAIRE PANOSIAN

Athlete, Interrupted color *Discover* v38 no4 p20 My 2017

Microbial Mystery bw color diag *Discover* v27 no10 p22 D 2016

Dunbar, Bonnie—Interviews

Interview with a ... Professor of aerospace engineering D. Angeles *Career Outlook* p1 Mr 2017

DUNBAR, ERICA ARMSTRONG

RINGING THE FREEDOM BELL color *Nation* v303 no25/26 p22 D 19 2016

Dunbar, George, b. 1927

ELEMENTS OF CHANCE color *Art in America* v104 no10 p45 N 2016

Dunbar, Mark

Choosing Your Fight: Political Correctness and Free Speech on Campus *Humanist* v77 no4 p9 Jl/Ag 2017

Kill All the Normies: Online Culture Wars From 4Chan And Tumblr To Trump And The Alt-Right *Humanist* v77 no5 p45 S/O 2017

To Be a Machine: Adventures Among Cyborgs, Utopians, Hackers, and the Futurists Solving the Modest Problem of Death *Humanist* v77 no3 p42 My/Je 2017

Dunbar, Robert B.

Science-based management in decline in the Southern Ocean bibl map *Science* v354 no6309 p185 O 14 2016

Duncan, Arne, 1964-

A BETTER CHANCE FOR NATIVE EDUCATION T. KOTES-KEY cartoon *Reason* v49 no1 p18 My 2017

Can Arne Duncan Save Chicago? L. Williamson color *Chicago* v65 no11 p86 N 2016

TALK TO US M. O'Connor, D. McGill et al color graph *Chicago* v65 no12 p24 D 2016

Duncan, Christopher M.

Summoned cartoon *Commonweal* v143 no17 p8 O 21 2016

Duncan, David S.

The 6 Most Common Innovation Mistakes Companies Make *Harvard Business Review Digital Articles* p2 Je 23 2015

Calculate How Much Your Company Should Invest in Innovation *Harvard Business Review Digital Articles* p2 D 17 2014

Innovation Isn't the Answer to All Your Problems *Harvard Business Review Digital Articles* p2 Je 2 2015

Zombie Projects: How to Find Them and Kill Them *Harvard Business Review Digital Articles* p2 Mr 4 2015

Duncan, Don

Frosting Flandreau: Two generations of bakers have cultivated the taste buds of Flandreau s citizenry for 88 years S. PERRY *South Dakota Magazine* v33 no2 p42 Jl/Ag 2017

Duncan, Elizabeth J.

Murder Is for Keeps: A Penny Brannigan Mystery *Publishers Weekly* v264 no9 p78 F 27 2017

Duncan, Eric

ERIC DUNCAN *Harper's Magazine* no2007 p17 Ag 2017

Duncan, Francis

Murder for Christmas color *Publishers Weekly* v264 no32 p54 Ag 7 2017

DUNCAN, GAYLE

Living Out Loud: On good food, great reads, and strong women color *O, The Oprah Magazine* p20 S 2017

Duncan, Jeff

The Case for Suppressor Technology *Time* v190 no15 p30 O 16 2017

Duncan, Melba—Interviews

What Executive Assistants Know About Managing Up N. Torres *Harvard Business Review Digital Articles* p2 D 23 2014

Duncan, William Lloyd

A PLACE TO GET AWAY color *Yankee* p92 My/Je 2017

Duncan-Jones, Katherine

Glimpses of Will B. SEITZ *Weekly Standard* v22 no22 p31 F 13 2017

Dundar, Can

Leaders color *Time* v189 no16/17 p64 My 1-8 2017

Dundas, Lawrence

the DUNDAS SOFA C. GERVAIS *Texas Monthly* v44 no11 p111 N 2016

Dundovic, A.

Observation of a large-scale anisotropy in the arrival directions of cosmic rays above 8 × 1018 eV *Science* v357 no6357 p1266 S 22 2017

Dune buggy racing

DUNE BUGGIES RACING ACROSS AMERICA J. OBER bw *Dirt Sports + Off-Road* v51 no6 p74 Je 2017

Duneier, Mitchell

Ghetto: The Invention of a Place, the History of an Idea H. W. Carter color *Christian Century* v133 no21 p42 O 12 2016

Dung beetles

The Indomitable Dung Beetle Plays Key Role in Parasite Regulation J. CESSNA *BioScience* v67 no6 p583 Je 2017

Dunham, Lena, 1986-

CHOP TO IT color *Vogue* v206 no11 p242 N 2016

Girl in Pants color *Glamour* v115 no5 p164 My 2017

Girls, Interrupted S. MARSHALL *New Republic* v248 no4 p50 Ap 2017

GIRL TALK C. MALLE color *Vogue* v207 no1 p76 Ja 2017

THE GOODBYE GIRLS S. Vilkomerson color *Entertainment Weekly* no1449 p22 Ja 20 2017

In Girls We Trust color *Glamour* v115 no2 p98 F 2017

LOUD MOUTH color *Vogue* v207 no6 p145 Je 2017

Mapping the Girls Effect E. Dockterman color diag *Time* v189 no6 p49 F 20 2017

My First Lilith color *Glamour* no8 p146 Ag 2017

The New Girls color *Glamour* v115 no2 p108 F 2017

On Fleek, C'est Chic? color *Vogue* v207 no4 p238 Ap 2017

Pioneers [Cover story] color *Time* v189 no16/17 p14 My 1-8 2017

RIDE OR DYE color *Vogue* v207 no9 p728 S 2017

Sex, Power, and Posting color *Glamour* v115 no7 p89 Jl 2017

WARNING: MAY BITE IF ASKED ABOUT FERTILITY color *Glamour* v115 no11 p100 N 2017

Dunham, Lena, 1986—Interviews

Girls I. Ratledge *TV Guide* v65 no14 p36 Ap 3 2017

Hannah and Her Sisters S. Vilkomerson color *Entertainment Weekly* no1463/1464 p95 Ap/My 2017

Later, Haters img *New York* p68 F 20 2017

Lena Dunham B. HIATT color *Rolling Stone* no1281/1282 p21 F 23 2017

Dunham, Maitreya J.

Evolution of protein phosphorylation across 18 fungal species bibl graph *Science* v354 no6309 p229 O 14 2016

Dunhill (Company)

GO LONG color *Esquire* p76 BigBlackBook

Dunietz, Jesse

Space Prospecting color *Scientific American* v317 no4 p14 O 2017

Dunigan, John

SNAP DECISION color *Golf Magazine* v59 no7 p50 Jl 2017

STOP YOUR CHOP! color *Golf Magazine* v59 no11 p54 N 2017

Dunkelman, Marc J.

How "Quality Time" Is Killing American Innovation *Harvard Business Review Digital Articles* p2 D 1 2014

Dunkin, Lacey

advice every new mom needs [Cover story] color *Parents* v92 no7 p32 Jl 2017

Dunkin' Donuts LLC

SCOOP DREAMS S. Rhimes color *New Yorker* v92 no32 p64 O 10 2016

What's In a (Brand) Name? K. Samuelson color *Time* v190 no7 p12 Ag 21 2017

Dunkirk (Film)

THE Anticipation Index *New York* v50 no6 p77 Mr 20 2017

THE BATTLE OF CHRISTOPHER NOLAN K. P. Sullivan color *Entertainment Weekly* no1474/1475 p56 Jl 21-28 2017

Christopher Nolan's Great War E. Berman color *Time* v190 no5 p53 Jl 31 2017

DUNKIRK K. P. Sullivan color *Entertainment Weekly* no1446/1447 p50 D 2016/Ja 2017

DUNKIRK K. P. Sullivan color *Entertainment Weekly* no1463/1464 p66 Ap/My 2017

Dunkirk Undone A. ROBERTS *Commentary* v144 no2 p51 S 2017

The Miracle of Dunkirk S. Zacharek color *Time* v190 no5 p48 Jl 31 2017

NOW PLAYING color *Entertainment Weekly* no1476 p48 Ag 4 2017

ON THE BEACH A. LANE color *New Yorker* v93 no22 p80 Jl 31 2017

Splendid Isolation [Cover story] M. Hastings bw color *New York Review of Books* v64 no15 p14 O 12 2017

Undone Dunkirk J. PODHORETZ color *Weekly Standard* v22 no45 p38 Ag 7 2017

Will Dunkirk Score Nolan His First Oscar? K. P. Sullivan color *Entertainment Weekly* no1476 p16 Ag 4 2017

Dunlap, Julie

Coming of Age at the End of Nature M. Landrigan *Orion Magazine* v36 no2 p59 Mr/Ap 2017

Dunleavey, M. P.

Got Cheap Genes? bw *AARP: The Magazine* v60 no2A p34 F/ Mr 2017

Dunlop, John

Frail of Mind, Human in Full M. LOFTUS color *Christianity Today* v61 no7 p82 S 2017

Dunlop, Michael

ISLE OF MAN TT M. Hoyer color *Cycle World* v56 no8 p54 S 2017

Dunn, Alexander R.

Vinculin forms a directionally asymmetric catch bond with F-actin chart color *Science* v357 no6352 p703 Ag 18 2017

Dunn, Bruce

Three-dimensional holey-graphene/niobia composite architectures for ultrahigh-rate energy storage color diag graph *Science* v356 no6338 p599 My 12 2017

Dunn, Daisy

2,500 Years in 30 Seconds *History Today* v67 no2 p58 F 2017

Dunn, Elizabeth G.

THE IMPOSSIBLE LIST bw cartoon color *Esquire* v167 no1 p70 F 2017

Ready to Rum-ble color *Bloomberg Businessweek* no4523 p64 My 22 2017

Dunn, Gabriel

Single-particle mapping of nonequilibrium nanocrystal transformations bibl bw graph *Science* v354 no6314 p874 N 18 2016

Dunn, Gaby

I Hate Everyone But You *Publishers Weekly* v264 no28 p90 Jl 10 2017

Dunn, Ian

Creating Safe Routes to Parks *Parks & Recreation* v52 no9 p46 S 2017

Dunn, Jancee

75 ways to be a grown-up *Parents* v91 no11 p95 N 2016

FACE ODYSSEY cartoon color *Vogue* v207 no1 p94 Ja 2017

Face ODYSSEY *Vogue* v207 no4 p172 Ap 2017

HOW I REBOOTED MY SEX LIFE color *Health* v31 no3 p98 Ap 2017

How to Bounce Back from Anything color *Health* v31 no7 p96 S 2017

The Real Reason I Work Out color *Health* v31 no2 p120 Mr 2017

Dunn, Jourdan, 1990-

MODEL MOMENT: JOURDAN DUNN color *Harper's Bazaar* no3653 p229 My 2017

Pack Your Bags color *InStyle* v24 no7 p73 Jl 2017

So What Do You Do, JOURDAN DUNN? color *InStyle* v24 no8 p114 Ag 2017

Dunn, Katherine, 1945-2016

KATHERINE DUNN C. ROPER *New York Times Magazine* p51 D 25 2016

A Portrait of the Artist as a Young Convict M. LAPOINTE color *Atlantic* v320 no3 p40 O 2017

Dunn, N. Ray

ELABELA deficiency promotes preeclampsia and cardiovascular malformations in mice color diag graph *Science* v357 no6352 p707 Ag 18 2017

Dunn, Rob

Never Out of Season: How Having the Food We Want When We Want It Threatens Our Food Supply and Our Future C. Moskowitz and A. Gawrylewski color *Scientific American* v316 no3 p76 Mr 2017

PLAY DIRTY bw color *Men's Health* v32 no2 p108 Mr 2017

Dunn, Sandra

In Canada, case spurs concern over misconduct secrecy A. Komnenic color *Science* v354 no6318 p1361 D 16 2016

Dunn, Sarah

The Arrangement *Publishers Weekly* v264 no2 p39 Ja 9 2017

The Pie-Chart Review! I. Biedenharn color diag *Entertainment Weekly* no1457/1458 p105 Mr 17 2017

DUNN, STAN

COMMUNICATION BREAKDOWN cartoon *Flying* v144 no3 p26 Mr 2017

MONTEREY EMERGENCY color *Flying* v144 no9 p24 S 2017

Dunn, Stephen, 1939-

THE INHERITANCE S. Dunn *New Yorker* v93 no26 p28 S 4 2017

Dunn, Susan

Eleanor in War and Love bw *New York Review of Books* v63 no19 p49 D 8 2016

An Icy Conquest bw color *New York Review of Books* v64 no17 p52 N 9 2017

Slaves in the White House color *New York Review of Books* v64 no8 p55 My 11 2017

Dunn, Tim

THE BANK *Texas Monthly* v45 no2 p92 F 2017

Dunne, Brenda Corey

Skin *Publishers Weekly* v264 no7 p78 F 13 2017

Dunne, Debbie
  MEET DEBBIE DUNNE color *Sea Magazine* v109 no8 pCA-8 Ag 2017

Dunne, Eimear M.
  Global atmospheric particle formation from CERN CLOUD measurements bibl graph map *Science* v354 no6316 p1119 D 2 2016

DUNNE, NATHAN
  BREAKING THE ICE bw *Film Comment* v53 no1 p72 Ja/F 2017

Dunne-Rite Performance Inc.
  TRAIL-READY TRUNK M. EMERY color *Dirt Sports + Off-Road* v51 no6 p50 Je 2017

Dunnett, Jane
  Mr. Smith Goes to Rome [Cover story] T. Parks bw color *New York Review of Books* v64 no15 p25 O 12 2017

Dunnett, Kaitlyn
  X Marks the Scot *Publishers Weekly* v264 no41 p46 O 9 2017

Dunning, Al
  Best Show-Halter Fit color *Horse & Rider* v56 no2 p32 F 2017
  Get Snaffle-Bit Smart color *Horse & Rider* v56 no8 p48 Ag 2017
  Mecate Tie Rope color *Horse & Rider* v56 no10 p50 O 2017
  Romal Reins color *Horse & Rider* v56 no6 p46 Je 2017
  Running Martingale color *Horse & Rider* v55 no12 p30 D 2016

DUNNING, BRAD
  Manual cartoon color *GQ: Gentlemen's Quarterly* v97 no7 p11 Jl 2017

Dunning-Kruger effect
  A Dunning-Kruger universe J. HESTER color *Astronomy* v45 no6 p14 Je 2017

Dunning School
  DEFENDING RECONSTRUCTION *Claremont Review of Books* v17 no2 p77 Spr 2017

DUNNUM, JONATHAN L.
  Transformational Principles for NEON Sampling of Mammalian Parasites and Pathogens: A Response to Springer and Colleagues *BioScience* v66 no11 p917 N 1 2016

Dunsker, Stewart B.
  The Thread bw cartoon *New York Times Magazine* p14 D 11 2016

Dunst, Kirsten, 1982-
  QUEEN OF THE WOOD NYMPHS: Who else but KIRSTEN DUNST could star in the Rodarte sisters' trippy first film? A. LAROCCA img *New York* v50 no16 p52 Ag 7 2017
  That Certain LOOK P. DEMARCHELIER bw color *Vanity Fair* v59 no4 p174 Mr 2017

Dunuwille, Mihindra
  Quantum and isotope effects in lithium metal color diag graph *Science* v356 no6344 p1254 Je 23 2017

Duopoly (Music)
  Chords & Discords J. BOWMAN, R. SOMMER et al bw *Downbeat* v84 no1 p10 Ja 2017

Dupanloup, Isabelle
  Chimpanzee genomic diversity reveals ancient admixture with bonobos bibl diag graph map *Science* v354 no6311 p477 O 28 2016

Du Pasquier, Nathalie
  NATHALIE DU PASQUIER K. Bellmann color *Art in America* v104 no10 p163 N 2016

Dupéré, Sébastien
  How Do You Waste Time at Work? K. Morell color *Bloomberg Businessweek* no4494 p70 O 10 2016

Dupin, Douglas
  HEART OF STONE *American History* v52 no1 p68 Ap 2017

DUPLASS, MARK
  Come Together. . *USA Today Magazine* v145 no2864 p21 My 2017

Duplex house design & construction
  Two of a Kind T. HENNIGAN *Architectural Record* v205 no6 p98 Je 2017

Duplex houses
        See also
    Double houses (Architecture)

Duplex houses—Interior decoration
  Second Home W. GOODMAN img *New York* p43 Ja 23 2017

Duplissy, Jonathan
  Global atmospheric particle formation from CERN CLOUD measurements bibl graph map *Science* v354 no6316 p1119 D 2 2016

Dupont, Kamila

Basic Horse Behavior for Dressage Success color *Dressage Today* v24 no1 p24 O 2017

Dupree, Benjamin
  Can CRISPR Save Ben Dupree? A. Regalado color *MIT Technology Review* v119 no6 p80 N/D 2016

Dupri, Jermaine
  Starcation: Atlanta O. RAYMOND and D. POINTDUJOUR color *Ebony* v72 no5 p59 Mr 2017
  STILL SO DEF M. SHAER *Atlanta* v57 no1 p84 My 2017

Dupuis, Éloïse
  Deadly devotion M. PATRIQUIN color *Maclean's* v129 no44 p24 N 7 2016

Dupuis, Sadie
  SAD 13 D. HYMAN *Interview* v46 no9 p24 N 2016

Dupzyk, Kevin
  AIR CONDITIONER color *Popular Mechanics* p18 Je 2017
  A BACKPACK WITH A COOLER color *Popular Mechanics* p83 D 2016/Ja 2017
  BIOLITE CAMPSTOVE color *Popular Mechanics* p18 Ap 2017
  BREAK THROUGH AWARDS 2017 [Cover story] bw color *Popular Mechanics* p56 N 2017
  EVERY NIGHT PERFECT bw color *Popular Mechanics* p84 O 2017
  Getting Started In... TRAIL RUNNING cartoon color *Popular Mechanics* v193 no7 p41 S 2016
  How the Coast Guard Reopened the Port of Houston color *Popular Mechanics* p13 N 2017
  How to Make... EXTINCT STEEL color *Popular Mechanics* p78 S 2017
  How to Make... EXTINCT STEEL color *Popular Mechanics* v193 no7 p78 S 2016
  HOW TO MAKE PLUTONIUM color *Popular Mechanics* p64 S 2017
  It's Not the Same as Running Around the Block color *Popular Mechanics* p41 S 2017
  It's Not the Same as Running Around the Block color *Popular Mechanics* v193 no7 p41 S 2016
  MADE in the USA color *Popular Mechanics* p64 Jl 2017
  MICROWAVE OVEN [Cover story] color *Popular Mechanics* p24 S 2017
  MICROWAVE OVEN [Cover story] color *Popular Mechanics* v193 no7 p24 S 2016
  SMART SPEAKER color *Popular Mechanics* p24 Mr 2017
  TELESCOPE color diag *Popular Mechanics* p18 F 2017
  the temple color *Popular Mechanics* p82 Jl 2017
  THINGS COME APART color *Popular Mechanics* p24 S 2017
  WATER HEATER color *Popular Mechanics* p30 D 2016/Ja 2017
  What's That, Deep in the Gulf of Mexico? cartoon color *Popular Mechanics* p8 Ap 2017
  What You Need color *Popular Mechanics* p42 S 2017
  What You Need color *Popular Mechanics* v193 no7 p42 S 2016
  Where to Run color *Popular Mechanics* p43 S 2017
  Where to Run color *Popular Mechanics* v193 no7 p43 S 2016
  WRIST WATCH color *Popular Mechanics* p76 Jl 2017

Duque, A.
  Persistent effects of pre-Columbian plant domestication on Amazonian forest composition bibl chart graph map *Science* v355 no6328 p925 Mr 3 2017

Duque, Lina
  How Academics and Researchers Can Get More Out of Social Media *Harvard Business Review Digital Articles* p2 Je 8 2016

DUR, PHILIP A.
  OFF-TARGET *Foreign Affairs* v95 no6 p196 N/D 2016

Dura-Europos (Extinct city)
  Moses and the Burning Bush, mural in Dura-Europos, Syria, ca. 239 CE *Christian Century* v134 no17 p47 Ag 16 2017

DURAK, TOMASZ
  Combining Biodiversity Resurveys across Regions to Advance Global Change Research *BioScience* v67 no1 p73 Ja 2017

Dural, Buckwheat, 1947-2016
  Milestones color *Time* v188 no14 p12 O 10 2016

DURAN, DAVID
  ALONE ON A ROMANTIC COUPLES GETAWAY color *Advocate* no1090 p48 Ap 2017

Durán, Diego, ca. 1537-ca. 1588
  FOR THE FEAR OF GOD D. Durán *Lapham's Quarterly* v10 no3

p169 Summ 2017

DURAN, MICHAEL

TAKE IT WITH YOU color *Wired* v24 no12 p84 D 2016

DURAND, FAITH

slow cooker vs. pressure cooker *Parents* v92 no2 p88 F 2017

Durand, Neva C.

De novo assembly of the Aedes aegypti genome using Hi-C yields chromosome-length scaffolds chart color diag *Science* v356 no6333 p92 Ap 7 2017

Durango, Julia

Here, There, Everywhere *Publishers Weekly* v264 no41 p67 O 9 2017

Durango Boot (Company)

Boots for Your Buckaroo color *Horse & Rider* v56 no9 p36 S 2017

Durango sport utility vehicle—Evaluation

Thunder(s)truck K. C. Colwell color *Car & Driver* v63 no4 p106 O 2017

Durant, Kevin, 1988-

HE'S THE ONE DURANT [Cover story] L. Jenkins color *Sports Illustrated* v126 no17 p32 Je 19 2017

The Liberation of Kevin Durant [Cover story] P. Solotaroff color *Rolling Stone* no1273 p34 N 3 2016

Durant, Sam—Exhibitions

SAM DURANT J. S. Li color *Art in America* v105 no3 p136 Mr 2017

DURANT, SARAH M.

Conserving the World's Megafauna and Biodiversity: The Fierce Urgency of Now *BioScience* v67 no3 p197 Mr 2017

Saving the World's Terrestrial Megafauna color *BioScience* v66 no10 p807 O 1 2016

Durante, D.

Jupiter's interior and deep atmosphere: The initial pole-to-pole passes with the Juno spacecraft [Cover story] color graph *Science* v356 no6340 p821 My 26 2017

DURBIN, GWENDOLYN

Q: What adventure would you love to share with your best friend? color *O, The Oprah Magazine* p12 Ja 2017

DURFIELD, YOLANDA N.

Paying Our Respects color *O, The Oprah Magazine* p15 Je 2017

Durham (England)—History

AFTER THE BATTLE D. WEISS bw color *Archaeology* v70 no3 p50 My/Je 2017

Durham, Jennifer N.

Mismatch repair deficiency predicts response of solid tumors to PD-1 blockade chart graph *Science* v357 no6349 p409 Jl 28 2017

Durham, Jimmie

ELEMENTS FROM THE ACTUAL WORLD J. Griffin color *Art in America* v105 no5 p76 My 2017

Durham, Jimmie—Exhibitions

Riots at the Museum J. Tarmy color *Bloomberg Businessweek* no4539 p72 S 25 2017

Durham, Monte

How to SHOP LIKE A BOSS J. ABIDOR color *Seventeen* p93 Ja 1 2017

DURKIN, MARY-CABRINI

SLIPPERY SLOPE? *Commonweal* v114 no14 p4 S 8 2017

Durland, Mark

A FISTFUL OF SAND SAVES color diag *Golf Magazine* v59 no8 p58 Ag 2017

PASS PARALLEL color diag *Golf Magazine* v59 no10 p47 O 2017

TIME FOR A CHANGE color diag *Golf Magazine* v59 no6 p39 Je 2017

TRY A "HINGE" STROKE color diag *Golf Magazine* v59 no9 p52 S 2017

Durmaz, V.

A nontoxic pain killer designed by modeling of pathological receptor conformations bibl diag graph *Science* v355 no6328 p966 Mr 3 2017

Duroc, Yann

The preprophase band of microtubules controls the robustness of division orientation in plants graph *Science* v356 no6334 p186 Ap 14 2017

DURÓN, MAXIMILÍANO

AROUND LOS ANGELES bw cartoon color *ARTnews* v115 no3

p154 Fall 2016

CONCRETE History [Cover story] bw cartoon color *ARTnews* v116 no1 p78 Spr 2017

HABITAT Moonlighting color *ARTnews* v115 no4 p38 Wint 2016/2017

Obsessions bw color *ARTnews* v115 no3 p54 Fall 2016

Durrani, Matin

Beyond Schrödinger's cat M. Kovac color *Science* v355 no6322 p253 Ja 20 2017

How animals exploit physical phenomena S. Perkins bw *Science News* v191 no1 p29 Ja 21 2017

DURRANI, SAJJAD

The Making of a Community *Islamic Horizons* v46 no2 p40 Mr/ Ap 2017

Durrant, MaryCay

The Mistakes PE Firms Make When They Pick CEOs for Portfolio Companies *Harvard Business Review Digital Articles* p2 S 6 2016

Durrett, Nekisha

BRINGING ART TO THE PUBLIC B. Andrews cartoon color *Black Enterprise* v47 no8 p102 Jl/Ag 2017

Durrett, Sylvana

Not So Junior LEAGUE P. GARCIA color *Vogue* v207 no4 p142 Ap 2017

DURSO, JIMI

Allan Holdsworth's Guitar Solo on 'Land Of The Bag Snake' bw *Downbeat* v84 no3 p112 Mr 2017

Applying 12-Tone Rows to Bass, Guitar color diag *Downbeat* v84 no7 p76 Jl 2017

David Krakauer's Clarinet Solos on 'Tribe Number Thirteen' bw *Downbeat* v83 no12 p104 D 2016

Donny McCaslin's Tenor Sax Solo on 'Faceplant' bw color *Downbeat* v84 no6 p84 Je 2017

Erik Friedlander's Cello Solo on '26 Gasoline Stations' bw color *Downbeat* v84 no1 p104 Ja 2017

Gary Smulyan's Baritone Sax Solo on 'Sassy Missy' bw color *Downbeat* v84 no10 p192 O 2017

George Garzone's Tenor Sax Solo on 'In Memory Of Leanne Nichols' [Cover story] bw color *Downbeat* v84 no5 p82 My 2017

Herbie Hancock's Synthesizer Solo on 'Chameleon' color *Downbeat* v84 no9 p96 S 2017

Howard Levy's Harmonica Solo on 'Seresta' bw color *Downbeat* v84 no8 p88 Ag 2017

Jane Ira Bloom's Soprano Saxophone Solo on 'Big Bill' bw color *Downbeat* v84 no2 p96 F 2017

Tomasz Stańko's Solo on 'Suspended Variation VI' bw color *Downbeat* v84 no4 p90 Ap 2017

Wolfgang Muthspiel's 5/4 Guitar Solo on 'Boogaloo' bw diag *Downbeat* v84 no7 p78 Jl 2017

Durst, Sarah Beth

Roar and Sparkles Go to School *Publishers Weekly* v264 no20 p53 My 15 2017

DURST, WILL

Bad Hair Daze cartoon *Progressive* v81 no5 p66 Je/Jl 2017

Bright Sides to a Trump Presidency cartoon *Progressive* p67 D 2016/Ja 2017

Executive Order Disorder color *Progressive* v81 no6 p66 Ag/S 2017

The Fake News President cartoon *Progressive* v81 no4 p66 Ap/ My 2017

How Trump's Fifth Avenue Shooting Plays Out cartoon *Progressive* v81 no7 p66 O/N 2017

Trump's First 100 Days *Progressive* v81 no3 p44 Mr 2017

Durtschi, Tim

A DESERT ISLAND J. Brown bw color *Powder* v45 no5 p28 Ja 2017

Dusa, Dan

Statin Denialism? *Skeptical Inquirer* v41 no5 p63 S/O 2017

Dusenbury, Linda

Social Emotional Learning in Elementary School: Preparation for Success *Education Digest* v83 no1 p36 S 2017

Dusinberre, Edward

All Together Now G. DALFONZO color *Weekly Standard* v22 no17 p30 Ja 2 2017

'There Is Only One Beethoven' L. Lockwood bw cartoon *New*

8 2016

Redefining Journalism In a Mobile World *Forbes* v199 no5 p12 My 16 2017

Rethinking the Way *Forbes* v198 no5 p26 O 25 2016

Seizing Our Brand's Destiny *Forbes* v198 no7 p16 N 29 2016

Speeding Our Way To Our New Mobile Future *Forbes* v199 no3 p22 Mr 28 2017

Storytelling Adapts To Media's New Era *Forbes* v199 no4 p10 Ap 25 2017

Why We Welcome the Seven-Year Itch *Forbes* v200 no4 p8 O 24 2017

Dwaileebe, Rati

FREE FOR ALL color *O, The Oprah Magazine* p20 O 2017

Dwarf planets

> See also
>
> Ceres (Dwarf planet)
>
> Pluto (Dwarf planet)

White dwarf mergers seen as antimatter source color *Astronomy* v45 no9 p19 S 2017

Dwarf stars

> See also
>
> Brown dwarf stars
>
> TRAPPIST-1
>
> White dwarf stars

7 Earth-Size Planets Orbit Dim Star C. M. Carlisle *Sky & Telescope* v133 no6 p12 Je 2017

Amateurs Track a DISINTEGRATING Planet M. Motta *Sky & Telescope* v133 no4 p66 Ap 2017

A centennial gift from Einstein T. D. Oswalt diag *Science* v356 no6342 p1015 Je 9 2017

Coming in from the Void? C. M. CARLISLE *Sky & Telescope* v133 no1 p12 Ja 2017

LHS 1140b: A Super-Earth in the Habitable Zone D. Dickinson color *Sky & Telescope* v134 no2 p12 Ag 2017

Like This World of Ours M. BARTUSIAK color *Natural History* v125 no5 p10 My 2017

The Opportunity ZONE C. Crockett color diag graph *Science News* v191 no12 p18 Je 24 2017

An unusual white dwarf star may be a surviving remnant of a sub-luminous Type Ia supernova S. Vennes, P. Nemeth et al chart diag *Science* v357 no6352 p680 Ag 18 2017

Dwarves (Mythological characters) in literature

The Secret Jews of The Hobbit *Commentary* v142 no2 p1 S 2016

Dweck, Carol

The Antidote to Our Anxious Times Is a Learning Mindset *Harvard Business Review Digital Articles* p2 Jl 28 2016

How Microsoft Uses a Growth Mindset to Develop Leaders *Harvard Business Review Digital Articles* p2 O 7 2016

What Having a "Growth Mindset" Actually Means *Harvard Business Review Digital Articles* p2 Ja 13 2016

Dwelling design & construction

> See also
>
> Apartment building design & construction
>
> Apartment design & construction
>
> Bungalow design & construction
>
> Condominium design & construction
>
> Farmhouse design & construction
>
> Home furnishings design & construction
>
> House construction
>
> Housing design & construction
>
> Public housing design & construction
>
> Vacation home design & construction
>
> Wooden-frame houses—Design & construction

Aging Gracefully K. Owen color *Southern Living* v52 no7 p15 Jl 2017

Amagansett Residence D. Sokol *Architectural Record* v205 no9 p146 S 2017

ANGLO FILE D. F. WOOD bw color *Architectural Digest* no6 p110 Je 1 2017

Being There C. McGuigan *Architectural Record* v205 no6 p18 Je 2017

Building Blocks A. MARTINS *Architectural Record* v205 no6 p68 Je 2017

Finding the Right Angle N. R. POLLOCK *Architectural Record* v205 no6 p80 Je 2017

Frame Time color diag *Timber Home Living* v27 no4 p10 Ag 2017

A Fresh Spin A. FIXSEN *Architectural Record* v205 no6 p42 Je 2017

house & garden details *Design Center Sourcebook* p108 2017

Into the Woods J. MINUTILLO *Architectural Record* v205 no6 p74 Je 2017

KEEPING IT REAL: Thanks to our historic housing stock, Cincinnati's rehabbed real estate market is the anti-anytown, usa A. BROWNLEE *Cincinnati Magazine* v50 no11 p74 Ag 2017

Knightsbridge Residence K. L. Beamon *Architectural Record* v205 no9 p148 S 2017

Lost & Found ... a restoration tale B. D. COLEMAN color *Old House Journal* v45 no7 p14 O 2017

Machine in the Garden S. STEPHENS *Architectural Record* v205 no6 p92 Je 2017

Mix it Up *Timber Home Living* v27 no6 p4 D 2017

THE MODERN EMPTY NEST K. Owen color *Southern Living* v52 no10 p88 O 2017

MULTIFAMILY HOUSING *Architectural Record* v205 no10 p83 O 2017

My Tiny House L. BAILEY *Indianapolis Monthly* v40 no11 p34 Jl 2017

NEW BUILD OF THE YEAR: Kendall Winingder and Patrick Schindler combine their talents with a who's team of experts to build their dream home L. CUTRONE *New Orleans Homes & Lifestyles* v20 no4 p42 Aut 2017

our happy place K. BLAYLOCK and J. BLAYLOCK color map *Cabin Living* p15 S 2017

Perfecting the Porch color *Timber Home Living* v27 no4 p16 Ag 2017

Playing (High-Design) House J. MURPHY color *Conde Nast Traveler* v52 no8 p44 S 2017

Recent History L. Postman color diag *Log Home Living* v34 no7 p54 S 2017

Relaxed Fit J. GONCHAR *Architectural Record* v205 no6 p106 Je 2017

Remuddling color *Old House Journal* v45 no7 p88 O 2017

Renovation Re-imagined [Cover story] S. Logan color *Log Home Living* v34 no7 p28 S 2017

Resources *Old House Journal* v45 no6 p87 S 2017

Steeling the Show J. GAUER *Architectural Record* v205 no6 p112 Je 2017

The Sum of Its Parts M. SITZ *Architectural Record* v205 no6 p86 Je 2017

two's better than one [Cover story] J. BREWSTER color diag *Cabin Living* p28 Ag 2017

Worth the Wait color *Timber Home Living* v27 no4 p30 Ag 2017

your house your way color diag *Timber Home Living* v27 no4 p50 Ag 2017

Dwelling maintenance & repair

Classic Country J. Borden color *Southern Living* v52 no11 p36 N 2017

DELETING A POOR ADDITION C. Neff color diag *Old House Journal* v45 no7 p32 O 2017

editor's letter color *Architectural Digest* no11 p28 N 1 2017

The Fix is In D. PEAK color *Log Home Living* v34 no7 p6 S 2017

Home Un-Wrecker: How adam Rayne restored a crumbling Walnut Hills Victorian to royal status A. KONERMANN *Cincinnati Magazine* v50 no11 p72 Ag 2017

KRISTEN & BEN WALTERS 2245 PARK AVE., WALNUT HILLS *Cincinnati Magazine* v50 no11 p75 Ag 2017

Maintaining the Dream color *Log Home Living* v34 no7 p25 S 2017

THE REBUILDING BOOM *Cincinnati Magazine* v50 no11 p70 Ag 2017

RYAN MESSER & JIMMY MUSURACA 992 MARION AVE., NORTH AVONDALE A. FLANGO *Cincinnati Magazine* v50 no11 p76 Ag 2017

You Are Now Entering the Money Pit A. KONERMANN *Cincinnati Magazine* v50 no11 p77 Ag 2017

Dwellings

> See also
>
> Animal habitations
>
> Apartment buildings
>
> Authors' homes & haunts
>
> Bungalows
>
> Cape Cod houses

Children's playhouses
Condominiums
Cottages
Country homes
Ecological houses
English authors—Homes & haunts
Farmhouses
Guesthouses
Haunted houses
Houseboats
Huts
Lean-tos (Dwellings)
Log cabins
Mansions
Parsonages
Ranch houses
Senior housing
Vacation homes
Wooden-frame houses

1188: Wales *Lapham's Quarterly* v10 no1 p78 Wint 2017

ALLEYS ARE BACK D. Reed *Washingtonian Magazine* v52 no6 p51 Mr 2017

At my house J. Francisco *Good Housekeeping* v264 no2 p8 F 2017

BLUES CLUES B. RILEY *Atlanta* v57 no6 p50 O 2017

Bumped Off C. CALDWELL cartoon *Weekly Standard* v22 no27 p9 Mr 20 2017

China color *National Geographic* v232 no1 p12 Jl 2017

Company's Coming! [Cover story] color *Good Housekeeping* v263 no5 p57 N 2016

COMPASS POINTS E. Pochoda color *Magazine Antiques* v184 no1 p130 Ja/F 2017

The Decorated Bathroom P. Poore color *Old House Journal* v44 no8 p72 D 2016

Detail Oriented color *Log Home Living* v34 no9 p8 D 2017

Facade-Off *Lapham's Quarterly* v10 no1 p82 Wint 2017

GLOSSARY *Lapham's Quarterly* v10 no1 p220 Wint 2017

Home (Be)Coming S. Murphy color *Log Home Living* v34 no7 p22 S 2017

HOME OF THE ANCIENTS *Arizona Highways* v93 no2 p40 F 2017

THE HOUSE MOVERS B. HUNHOFF *South Dakota Magazine* v32 no6 p69 Mr/Ap 2017

House Music *Lapham's Quarterly* v10 no1 p146 Wint 2017

Houses Needing Rescue color *Old House Journal* v44 no8 p40 D 2016

"I HAD TO WALK THROUGH FIRE for my kids" J. SMALL color *Good Housekeeping* v265 no1 p69 Jl 2017

INTO THE BLUE E. EICHINGER color *Chicago* v66 no4 p70 Ap 2017

It's About the Porch color *Old House Journal* v45 no4 p36 Je 2017

JUMP-START I. Edwards color *Sunset* v238 no1 p8 Ja 2017

LAKE OR POND... P. H. MILLER color *Cabin Living* p80 Ag 2017

Last Look E. Daigneau *Governing* v30 no2 p64 N 2016

Life After Combat color *Log Home Living* v33 no7 p53 S 2016

LIGHTING THE WAY J. TUNG *Martha Stewart Living* no267 p114 S 2016

MISCELLANY *Lapham's Quarterly* v10 no1 p212 Wint 2017

Morristown C. Bates bw color *Old House Journal* v44 no8 p38 D 2016

Moving In B. HEWITT and P. HEWITT color map *Yankee* p16 Mr 2017

MY CHILDHOOD HOME J. Waters *Lapham's Quarterly* v10 no1 p206 Wint 2017

The Pride of Shelburne Falls: This village in the Berkshire foothills has lots to be proud of—the famous Bridge of Flowers, for instance. But we recently discovered something else very special there M. Cohn color *Yankee* p40 Jl 2017

Remuddling color *Old House Journal* v44 no8 p96 D 2016

Save, Repair, or Replace? M. E. POLSON color *Old House Journal* v44 no8 p44 D 2016

Save Time and Add Convenience T. Bufete and C. Regan il *Consumer Reports* v82 no3 p24 Mr 2017

Sentimental Journey S. Murphy color diag *Log Home Living* v34 no9 p24 D 2017

The Space Issue S. BROWN *Timber Home Living* v27 no3 p10 Je 2017

SPINNING WOOLLEN T. BRAND *Indianapolis Monthly* p33 F 2017

Stay Safer C. Roberts il *Consumer Reports* v82 no3 p27 Mr 2017

Tenleytown/Washington, D.C J. C. Massey and S. Maxwell bw color *Old House Journal* v45 no3 p34 My 2017

Thanks for the MEMORIES R. Sabin color *Sound & Vision* v82 no5 p30 Je 2017

THIS OLD HOUSE A. Nash color *Southern Living* v52 no1 p104 Ja 2017

what feels fresh [Cover story] color *House Beautiful* v159 no9 p67 N 2017

Dwellings leasing & renting

For Rent D. Howland *Cabin Living* p15 Ag 2017

When It Pays to Bend the Rules M. CROSS color *Kiplinger's Personal Finance* v71 no10 p44 O 2017

Dwellings leasing & renting—Economic aspects

Make all rent checks payable to: WALL STREET P. Gopal graph *Bloomberg Businessweek* no4506 p30 Ja 9 2017

Dwellings leasing & renting—Social aspects

Make all rent checks payable to: WALL STREET P. Gopal graph *Bloomberg Businessweek* no4506 p30 Ja 9 2017

Dwellings—Air conditioning

Get Healthier J. Calderone and B. Deitrick il *Consumer Reports* v82 no3 p25 Mr 2017

Dwellings—California

Compound Interest C. NICHOLS color *Los Angeles Magazine* v62 no10 p128 O 2017

Fine Prints A. HEROLD *Los Angeles Magazine* v62 no6 p30 Je 2017

Hit or Miss *Los Angeles Magazine* v62 no6 p16 Je 2017

Zero Net Energy Ordinance *Mother Earth News* no283 p10 Ag/S 2017

Dwellings—California—Design & construction

MODERN VICTORIAN color diag *Sunset* v238 no5 p39 My 2017

Dwellings—California—Interior decoration

MODERN VICTORIAN color diag *Sunset* v238 no5 p39 My 2017

perch perfect A. FLEETWOOD color *Architectural Digest* v74 no4 p140 Ap 2017

Dwellings—Colorado

CURVES AHEAD L. MURTHA *Cincinnati Magazine* v50 no2 p34 N 2016

Dwellings—Conservation & restoration

Looking Sharpe B. Warren color *New Orleans Magazine* v51 no4 p54 F 2017

What to Expect in a Log Home Restoration color *Log Home Living* v33 no7 p64 S 2016

Dwellings—Design & construction

See also

Bungalows—Design & construction
Condominiums—Design & construction
Cottages—Design & construction
House construction
Houseboats—Design & construction
Housing—Design & construction
Vacation homes—Design & construction

3 A Solar-Powered Adobe J. Davidson img *New York* v49 no21 p90 O 17 2016

Down by the Riverside color *Yankee* p44 Mr 2017

editor's letter color *Architectural Digest* v74 no1 p36 Ja 2017

FULL HOUSE L. LIGHT color *Architectural Digest* v74 no1 p212 Ja 2017

FUN HOUSE K. R. KEGANS color *Better Homes & Gardens* v95 no4 p112 Ap 2017

Going From Door to Door D. KIPEN *Los Angeles Magazine* p18 F 2017

MAKING ROOM TO GROW H. G. Phillips *Washingtonian Magazine* v52 no6 p157 Mr 2017

Middle Ground V. Hart *New Orleans Homes & Lifestyles* v20 no2 p52 Spr 2017

The Old Grocery [Cover story] V. Hart *New Orleans Homes & Lifestyles* v20 no2 p42 Spr 2017

PALM BEACH STORY J. K. DE VALLE bw color *Architectural Digest* no5 p108 My 2017

Rhode Island B. Ulrich *New York Times Magazine* p45 N 20 2016

wright ON THE RIVER R. COLE color *Arts & Crafts Homes & the Revival* v12 no2 p50 Spr 2017

Young at Heart S. HARRELSON color *Architectural Digest* v74 no1 p160 Ja 2017

Dwellings—Design & construction—Evaluation

house of the month C. A. PEARSON color diag *Architectural Record* v204 no12 p25 D 2016

The Midcentury As Muse A. HEROLD *Los Angeles Magazine* p40 Ap 2017

Dwellings—Electric equipment

My Tiny House L. BAILEY *Indianapolis Monthly* v40 no11 p34 Jl 2017

Dwellings—Energy consumption

Tennessee Strong D. PEAK *Log Home Living* v34 no2 p6 Mr 2017

Dwellings—England

CHATSWORTH: THE PALACE OF THE PEAKS *British Heritage Travel* v38 no2 p60 Mr/Ap 2017

Garden District E. MacSweeney color *Vogue* v207 no11 p202 N 2017

Dwellings—Evaluation

FRESH HEIR T. BRAND color *Indianapolis Monthly* p34 Ap 2017

OFF THE MARKET! The nuts and bolts of some of Washington's most expensive residential transactions *Washingtonian Magazine* v52 no12 p149 S 2017

Dwellings—History

The Long Way Home K. Siber *National Parks* v91 no2 p32 Spr 2017

Postwar Challenges M. E. POLSON color *Old House Journal* v45 no3 p40 My 2017

Dwellings—India

ALL THE RAJ D. THOMAS color *Architectural Digest* v74 no4 p146 Ap 2017

Dwellings—Indiana

PILLAR OF WISDOM T. BRAND *Indianapolis Monthly* v40 no5 p22 Ja 2017

Dwellings—Interior decoration

A+ REVIVAL [Cover story] C. Lamers color *Sunset* v238 no4 p60 Ap 2017

Character study S. C. Kim color *Sunset* v238 no2 p38 F 2017

CURTAINS TO CARPETS color *Old House Journal* v44 p83 2016 Design Center source Book

design ideas that don't fade P. POORE color *Old House Journal* v44 p10 2016 Design Center source Book

ELEGANT GEOMETRY L. CUTRONE color *Louisiana Life* v37 no3 p26 Ja/F 2017

Hang some curtains! color *Redbook* p140 My 2017

HOME GROWN P. P. FISCHER color *Better Homes & Gardens* v95 no3 p112 Mr 2017

THE HOUSE THAT BLUE & WHITE BUILT K. O'SHEA-EVANS color *House Beautiful* v158 no9 p158 N 2016

Interior Decorating M. BECK cartoon *O, The Oprah Magazine* p42 Mr 2017

MEMPHIS Beat E. ELWICK-BATES color *Vogue* v206 no12 p164 D 2016

NEXT-LEVEL DESIGN C. Lamers color diag *Sunset* v237 no5 p31 N 2016

Roll the Tape K. O'SHEA-EVANS color *House Beautiful* v159 no1 p25 F 2017

Room for Improvement cartoon color *House Beautiful* v159 no1 p22 F 2017

Silver Linings B. Fishel color *Log Home Living* v33 no9 p28 D 2016

A Study in Good Taste B. Warren color *New Orleans Magazine* v51 no5 p56 Mr 2017

Worth the Wait K. Owen color *Southern Living* v52 no5 p28 My 2017

Dwellings—Lighting

HOME STYLE *Cincinnati Magazine* v50 no4 p36 Ja 2017

LIGHTING color *Old House Journal* v44 p91 2016 Design Center source Book

Dwellings—Louisiana

ELEGANT GEOMETRY L. CUTRONE color *Louisiana Life* v37 no3 p26 Ja/F 2017

JULIA STREET WITH POYDRAS THE PARROT J. STREET

bw *New Orleans Magazine* v51 no5 p22 Mr 2017

Prime of Their Lives: Retiring in style on St. Charles Avenue L. Cutrone color *New Orleans Magazine* v51 no10 p66 Ag 2017

Dwellings—Maintenance & repair

A Fresh Coat of Paint S. Evans color *Southern Living* v52 no3 p8 Mr 2017

Get Your House in Shape This Winter K. Close color *Money* v46 no1 p32 Ja/F 2017

LABOR OF LOVE M. Z. Roux color *Southern Living* v52 no3 p92 Mr 2017

Prevention, Procrastination & Woe P. Reichard *New Orleans Homes & Lifestyles* v20 no2 p82 Spr 2017

Readers' votes & editors' picks color *Old House Journal* v44 no8 p10 D 2016

Spring Fling M. Warner Spencer *New Orleans Homes & Lifestyles* v20 no2 p14 Spr 2017

Dwellings—Maintenance & repair—Costs

WHY BUYING A FIXER-UPPER MIGHT NOT BE WORTH IT K. Close color *Money* v45 no10 p21 N 2016

Dwellings—Montana

Mix it Up *Timber Home Living* v27 no6 p4 D 2017

Dwellings—New York (State)

Sleeping Beauty K. HACKETT color *Architectural Digest* v73 no11 p164 N 2016

Dwellings—Ohio

No Place Like Home L. MURTHA *Cincinnati Magazine* v50 no2 p40 N 2016

Dwellings—Oregon

Remaking History K. O'Shea-Evans bw color *House Beautiful* v158 no9 p112 N 2016

Dwellings—Remodeling for other use

The Greenhouse Effect J. L. HESTER bw cartoon color *Atlantic* v318 no4 p38 N 2016

Dwellings—Rhode Island

Rhode Island B. Ulrich *New York Times Magazine* p45 N 20 2016

Dwellings—Safety measures

Smart Homes' Top Job: Safety L. Eadicicco color *Time* v189 no7/8 p30 F 27 2017

There's No Place Like Home M. L. Tellado *Consumer Reports* v82 no3 p5 Mr 2017

Dwellings—Scotland

Whose Moors Are They? C. Newman color map *National Geographic* v231 no5 p84 My 2017

Dwellings—Tennessee—Design & construction

Southern Comfort H. MARTIN color *Architectural Digest* v74 no4 p43 Ap 2017

Dwellings—United States

Help Them Move K. D. WILLIAMSON *National Review* v69 no2 p20 F 6 2017

The House As a Home K. A. Brower color *Time* v189 no4 p37 Ja 23 2017

QUIET PLACES N. ABEBE *New York Times Magazine* p36 D 25 2016

Dwellings—Virginia

LUSH LIFE: An English-inspired oasis takes root in Vienna J. Sergent *Washingtonian Magazine* v52 no8 p172 My 2017

Dwellings—Washington (D.C.)

See also

  White House (Washington, D.C.)

HOUSES WITH HISTORY K. Randall *Washingtonian Magazine* v52 no9 p172 Je 2017

OFF THE MARKET! The nuts and bolts of some of Washington's most expensive residential transactions *Washingtonian Magazine* v52 no12 p149 S 2017

OFF THE MARKET!: The nuts and bolts of some of Washington's most expensive residential transactions *Washingtonian Magazine* v52 no8 p195 My 2017

Dworkin, Daniel

Leadership May Not Be the Problem with Your Innovation Team *Harvard Business Review Digital Articles* p2 Ag 25 2016

Win Over Executives by Proving Customers Support Your Idea *Harvard Business Review Digital Articles* p2 Jl 14 2015

Dworkin, Jennifer

Love & Diane N. DAVIS bw *Film Comment* v53 no1 p62 Ja/F 2017

Dwyer, Bernadette

NEW VICE PRESIDENT AND BOARD MEMBERS NAMED *Literacy Today (2411-7862)* v35 no1 p40 Jl/Ag 2017

Dwyer, Ed

BLESS IS MORE *Saturday Evening Post* v289 no4 p28 Jl/Ag 2017

THE FUNNY PAPERS *Saturday Evening Post* v288 no6 p36 N/D 2016

(I DON'T WANT NO) SATISFACTION SURVEY *Saturday Evening Post* v289 no5 p28 S/O 2017

DWYER, HUGO

Chords & Discords color *Downbeat* v84 no7 p10 Jl 2017

Dwyer, James

One church? *U.S. Catholic* v82 no7 p5 Jl 2017

DWYER, JIM

Without Hesitation *Reader's Digest* v188 no1126 p10 D 2016/Ja 2017

DWYER, LIZ

THE WAY FORWARD bw color *Ebony* v72 no4 p84 F 2017

DWYER, MARY

Measuring excellence color *Maclean's* v129 no44 p106 N 7 2016

Measuring excellence color *Maclean's* v130 no10 p108 N 2017

Dwyer, Matt

Front porch music sessions take center stage in Hastings E. CASE color *Nebraska Life* v21 no5 p76 S/O 2017

Dwyer, Olivia

Better in Winter color *Backpacker* p34 N 2017

Day DREAMING: The best dayhike in every state color *Backpacker* p52 S 2017

Left Behind *Backpacker* p20 N 2017

Oh, Crap! color *Backpacker* p21 Ag 2017

Summit Fever: MacIntyre Range, New York color *Backpacker* p26 S 2017

Dwyer, Paula

How About a Bit More Room For Competition? *Bloomberg Businessweek* no4531 p8 Jl 24 2017

Dy, Aaron J.

Nucleic acid detection with CRISPR-Cas13a/C2c2 color diag *Science* v356 no6336 p438 Ap 28 2017

Dyachuk, Vyacheslav

Multipotent peripheral glial cells generate neuroendocrine cells of the adrenal medulla color *Science* v357 no6346 p46 Jl 7 2017

Dyas, J.B.

Living the Dream color *Downbeat* v84 no1 p84 Ja 2017

DYBAS, CHERYL LYN

Counting Whales in the Seas, Trees in the Forests, and Mountain Lions on the Ridges *BioScience* v66 no12 p1013 D 1 2016

Dybkjaer, Gitte

Spending 10 Minutes a Day on Mindfulness Subtly Changes the Way You React to Everything color *Harvard Business Review Digital Articles* p2 Ja 18 2017

Dyck, Lillian

Home in the North A. WONG color *Alternatives Journal (AJ) - Canada's Environmental Voice* v42 no2 p60 2016

Dydio, P.

An artificial metalloenzyme with the kinetics of native enzymes bibl diag graph *Science* v354 no6308 p102 O 7 2016

Dye, John M.

A "Trojan horse" bispecific-antibody strategy for broad protection against ebolaviruses bibl graph *Science* v354 no6310 p350 O 21 2016

Dye, Pete

FINISH IN STYLE T. Cooke and D. DeNunzio color *Golf Magazine* v59 no4 p62 Ap 2017

Dyer, Alan

The 102-mm FCD100 Triplet APO Refractor *Sky & Telescope* v133 no6 p58 Je 2017

Pentax's "Astro" DSLR *Sky & Telescope* v133 no2 p64 F 2017

The Star Adventurer Mini Tracker: Sky-Watcher's newest Star Adventurer merges an astronomical tracker with a time-lapse motion controller *Sky & Telescope* v134 no6 p58 D 2017

Dyer, Buddy

Theme Park Bards color *Weekly Standard* v23 no1 p4 S 11 2017

DYER, CANDICE

TURTLES, EAGLES, AND BEAVERS, OH MY: Tucked among development and woods, the Chattahoochee Nature Center saves animals' lives *Atlanta* v57 no4 p52 Ag 2017

Dyer, Deidre

VISION STATEMENTS color *Bon Appetit* no1 p44 F 2017

Dyer, Elizabeth B.

Teacher self-captured video color il *Phi Delta Kappan* v98 no7 p49 Ap 2017

Dyer, Ezra

1991 BMW 325i color *Popular Mechanics* p60 Mr 2017

2017 Chevrolet Colorado ZR2 color *Popular Mechanics* p36 N 2017

2017 Chrysler Pacifica Hybrid color *Popular Mechanics* p37 Je 2017

2017 Land Rover Discovery color *Popular Mechanics* p43 S 2017

2018 Acura TLX color *Popular Mechanics* p43 S 2017

2018 Honda Odyssey color *Popular Mechanics* p40 S 2017

2018 Lexus LC 500 color *Popular Mechanics* p36 Je 2017

THE $60 INTERIOR REVIVAL color *Popular Mechanics* p42 Je 2017

BREAK THROUGH AWARDS 2017 [Cover story] bw color *Popular Mechanics* p56 N 2017

Dealer vs. Mechanic Showdown color *Popular Mechanics* p40 F 2017

The Desert Monster color *Popular Mechanics* p59 D 2016/Ja 2017

(Don't) DIY color *Popular Mechanics* p62 D 2016/Ja 2017

The Electric, Hydraulic, Mostly American Truck bw color *Popular Mechanics* p15 N 2017

Ezra Dyer *Car & Driver* v62 no8 p28 F 2017

Ezra Dyer color *Car & Driver* v62 no11 p33 My 2017

Ezra Dyer color *Car & Driver* v63 no1 p34 Jl 2017

Ezra Dyer color *Car & Driver* v63 no5 p32 N 2017

THE FALLACY OF THE SELF-PARKING CAR color *Popular Mechanics* p73 My 2017

The Guide to Car Options color *Popular Mechanics* p44 F 2017

HOW TO BLUETOOTH AN OLD CAR color *Popular Mechanics* p44 Jl 2017

How to Make a Great TV Show About Cars color *Popular Mechanics* p24 N 2017

How to Stick New Tech on an Old Car color *Popular Mechanics* p56 Mr 2017

The Least Distracting Distraction color *Popular Mechanics* p62 Mr 2017

THE MECHANICS OF FUN chart color *Popular Mechanics* p84 Mr 2017

The Miracle Material color *Popular Mechanics* p51 Mr 2017

The New Heathen Porsche bw color *Popular Mechanics* p38 F 2017

THE NEW, IMPROVED HYDROGEN CAR! color diag map *Popular Mechanics* p38 Jl 2017

The New Luxury Trucks color *Popular Mechanics* p50 S 2017

The New Luxury Trucks color *Popular Mechanics* v193 no7 p50 S 2016

The No-GPS Road Trip color *Popular Mechanics* p32 S 2017

Oh No! Your Car Got Scratched! color *Popular Mechanics* p52 S 2017

Oh No! Your Car Got Scratched! color *Popular Mechanics* v193 no7 p52 S 2016

Old Engine, New Tricks cartoon color *Popular Mechanics* p38 Je 2017

REVIEWS color *Popular Mechanics* p42 F 2017

REVIEWS color *Popular Mechanics* v193 no7 p54 S 2016

ROAD TESTED color *Popular Mechanics* p36 Ap 2017

ROAD TESTED color *Popular Mechanics* p46 Jl 2017

THINGS YOU NEED TO KNOW ABOUT FUEL bw chart color *Popular Mechanics* p29 Mr 2017

WAR REPORTER FOR A DAY color *Popular Mechanics* p24 O 2017

Zee Über Trück color *Popular Mechanics* p47 S 2017

Zee Über Trück color *Popular Mechanics* v193 no7 p47 S 2016

Dyer, Geoff

COURTSIDE CHRONiCLeS *New York Times Magazine* p50 Ag 27 2017

On Photography *New York Times Magazine* p14 Ja 8 2017

Something From Nothing: My obsession with the Necks, the greatest trio on earth *New York Times Magazine* p52 O 8 2017

Dyer, Heather

Magic in the City color *Publishers Weekly* v264 no5 p204 Ja 30 2017

Dyer, Jeff
  Choose the Right Innovation Method at the Right Time *Harvard Business Review Digital Articles* p2 D 31 2014
  To Make Money with Digital, Be an Innovator - Not a Strategist *Harvard Business Review Digital Articles* p2 Ja 8 2015
  Managing Multiparty Innovation color img *Harvard Business Review* v94 no11 p76 N 2016
Dyer, Justin
  NATURE IN THE DOCK *Claremont Review of Books* v16 no4 p31 Fall 2016
Dyer, Natalia
  THE Fresh Faces A. Rambharose color *Glamour* v115 no10 p178 O 2017
Dyer, Pamela N.
  Structure of histone-based chromatin in Archaea diag *Science* v357 no6351 p609 Ag 11 2017
Dyer, Serena
  BUYING BRITISH *History Today* v67 no8 p56 Ag 2017
Dyes & dyeing
      See also
        Indigo
        Natural dyes & dyeing
  COLOR US HAPPY *Better Homes & Gardens* v94 no11 p18 N 2016
  color your hair like a pro T. PEREZ *Parents* v91 no11 p78 N 2016
  HOMESTEAD HACKS: Our readers share clever projects that will help you live a self-sufficient life in the country, the suburbs, or the city S. Verberg *Mother Earth News* no283 p54 Ag/S 2017
  Platinum Power color *Health* v31 no6 p18 Jl 2017
  to dye for L. HEDRICK *Better Homes & Gardens* v94 no11 p16 N 2016
Dyes & dyeing—Leather
  DYE HARD J. KENT-DOOLAN color *Indianapolis Monthly* p30 Ap 2017
Dyes & dyeing—Textile fibers
  Oldest indigo-dyed fabric found B. BOWER color *Science News* v190 no8 p8 O 15 2016
Dying of the Light, The (Film)
  THE DYING OF THE LIGHT S. Guttenberg color *Sound & Vision* v82 no4 p71 My 2017
Dylan, Bob, 1941-
  ACCORDING TO: Finn Wittrock J. DUBOFF bw *Vanity Fair* v59 no4 p118 Mr 2017
  THE BAND M. Mettler bw color *Sound & Vision* v82 no3 p72 Ap 2017
  Bob Dylan, Nobelist A. FERGUSON cartoon *Weekly Standard* v22 no7 p11 O 24 2016
  BOB DYLAN, NOBEL LAUREATE D. T. MORAN *Humanist* v77 no1 p36 Ja/F 2017
  Bob the Bard D. HAJDU *Nation* v303 no19 p6 N 7 2016
  Bringing The Nobel Back Home L. THOMSON color *Publishers Weekly* v263 no43 p80 O 24 2016
  A corner turned D. D. Collum bw *U.S. Catholic* v82 no2 p38 F 2017
  Dylan, Deep in the Wee Small Hours M. GILMORE color *Rolling Stone* no1284 p51 Ap 6 2017
  DYLAN IN STOCKHOLM J. BERRY bw *New Orleans Magazine* v51 no2 p56 D 2016
  Dylan's Secret Archives A. GREENE bw color *Rolling Stone* no1291/1292 p11 Jl 13 2017
  Hitting the High(ish) Ones D. REILLY img *New York* v49 no20 p117 O 3 2016
  The Lyrics Laureate D. ORR *New York Times Book Review* p22 Mr 26 2017
  PARODY color *Weekly Standard* v22 no10 p40 N 14 2016
  Ring Them Bells A. GREENE bw color *Rolling Stone* no1274 p13 N 17 2016
  Tangled Up in Bob P. Candler color *Commonweal* v144 no10 p21 Je 2 2017
Dylan, Bob, 1941—Awards
  Knock, Knock, Knocking ... color *Weekly Standard* v22 no9 p4 N 7 2016
  News Briefs *Publishers Weekly* v263 no42 p10 O 17 2016
  The prize, it is a-changing J. J. WEINMAN bw *Maclean's* v129 no43 p59 O 31 2016

Dylan, Bob, 1941—Interviews
  Interviewing Dylan A. GREENE bw color *Rolling Stone* no1281/1282 p24 F 23 2017
Dylan, Levi
  Levi DYLAN G. SIEFF *Interview* v47 no1 p14 F 2017
Dylla, Doug
  Moving First-Time Buyers Off the Fence: Solving the Millennial Homebuyer Puzzle with Proven Online Solutions and Partnerships *Bridges (Federal Reserve Bank of St. Louis)* p6 Summ 2016
Dymatize Enterprises LLC
  PREWORKOUT 101 J. EDWARD color *Muscle & Performance* v9 no8 p59 Ag 2017
DYMOCK, EMILY
  Real Big Fish color *Idaho Magazine* v16 no1 p48 O 2016
Dymond, Jessica S.
  Design of a synthetic yeast genome bibl chart color graph *Science* v355 no6329 p1040 Mr 10 2017
Dynamics
      See also
        Fluid dynamics
  Helicity—invariant even in a viscous fluid H. Keith Moffatt color *Science* v357 no6350 p448 Ag 4 2017
Dynamiq (Company)
  ...SINCEREST FORM OF FLATTERY S. SHIBATA color *Sea Magazine* v109 no8 p8 Ag 2017
Dynasty (TV program)
  DYNASTY D. Holbrook *TV Guide* v65 no37 p34 S 4 2017
  My TV Motto: You Go High; I'll Go Low C. Brody color *Glamour* v115 no10 p40 O 2017
  The Return of the Dynasty Dress color *Glamour* v115 no9 p216 S 2017
Dynojet Research Inc.
  AN INTERESTING TWIST S. RICHARDS color diag *Dirt Sports + Off-Road* v51 no11 p62 N 2017
Dynon Avionics (Company)
  DYNON'S UPWARD PUSH color *Flying* v144 no10 p23 O 2017
Dyott, Thomas W.
  EMPIRE OF GLASS M. SHAKESPEARE bw color *Archaeology* v70 no2 p55 Mr/Ap 2017
Dysart, Joe
  Artificial Intelligence: Not Your Father's Toolbox: Some new artificial intelligence business tools to help park and rec agencies *Parks & Recreation* v52 no8 p72 Ag 2017
  Email Marketing: Still the killer app to beat for park and recreation agencies *Parks & Recreation* v52 no5 p18 My 2017
  Operations. The Digital Imposter: After penetrating your website, a hacker can do business as you *Parks & Recreation* v52 no6 p48 Je 2017
  Video Marketing: Now with a Bigger Bang for Park and Rec Agencies *Parks & Recreation* v51 no11 p18 N 2016
Dysmenorrhea
  Dietary Solutions for Menstrual Cramps M. D. SMITH color *Better Nutrition* p58 My 2017
  GOING TO the Gyno R. Zar color *Dance Spirit* v20 no9 p34 N 2016
Dysmenorrhea—Treatment
  Heat or Ice? C. W. Dineen color *Health* v30 no10 p65 D 2016
Dyson, James
  The Hair Dryer That Doesn't Get Hot A. GEORGE color *Popular Mechanics* v193 no7 p18 S 2016
Dyson, James, 1947-
  FLOWER POWER S. Larson cartoon *New Yorker* v92 no40 p25 D 5 2016
Dyson, Mark
  How to Better Manage Your Company's Utility Bills *Harvard Business Review Digital Articles* p2 N 24 2015
Dyson, Michael Eric
  A Cry From the Heart P. PHILLIPS *New York Times Book Review* p11 Ja 15 2017
  DEAR WHITE PEOPLE P. H. Bass color *Essence* v47 no11 p62 Mr 2017
  Taking white America to church E. J. Blum color *Christian Century* v134 no9 p32 Ap 26 2017
Dyson, Michael Eric—Interviews
  Michael Eric Dyson Believes In Individual Reparations A. M. Cox

New York Times Magazine p50 Ja 8 2017
Tough Love for White America N. Stockwell *Progressive* v81 no3 p38 Mr 2017

Dyson Direct Inc.
The Hair Dryer That Doesn't Get Hot A. GEORGE color diag *Popular Mechanics* v193 no7 p18 S 2016

Dyson Ltd.
THE SECRET TO GREAT HAIR? HOT AIR R. Kenneth Urken color *Esquire* p43 Ag 2017

Dyspareunia—Treatment
When sex hurts *Mayo Clinic Health Letter* v358 no8 p6 Ag 2017

Dysplasia—Prevention
CERVICAL DYSPLASIA & CERVICAL CANCER: NATU-RAL THERAPIES FOR TREATMENT & PREVENTION M. Schauch color *Better Nutrition* p41 My 2017

Dyspnea—Diagnosis
Gasping for Air R. Lloyd color *Scientific American* v316 no3 p26 Mr 2017

Dyspnea—Treatment
Gasping for Air R. Lloyd color *Scientific American* v316 no3 p26 Mr 2017

Dystonia
TALK TO US J. Hieshetter, N. Malitz et al bw *Chicago* v66 no3 p23 Mr 2017

Dystopias
GIMME SHELTER C. DOCTOROW cartoon *Wired* v25 no4 p15 Ap 2017

Dystopias in literature
The Dystopian Style in American Politics C. ROSEN *Commentary* v143 no6 p9 Je 2017
Survival is sacred N. Ripatrazone *Christian Century* v134 no16 p24 Ag 2 2017
With '1984' All the Rage, Is Dystopian Backlist a Publishing Utopia? J. Maher *Publishers Weekly* v264 no29 p3 Jl 17 2017

Dziak, Robert P.
Seismic constraints on caldera dynamics from the 2015 Axial Seamount eruption bibl color graph *Science* v354 no6318 p1395 D 16 2016

Dziawa, Piotr
Robust spin-polarized midgap states at step edges of topological crystalline insulators bibl graph *Science* v354 no6317 p1269 D 9 2016

Dziedzic, Jerry
Dispatching with track warrants chart *Model Railroader* v84 no8 p65 Ag 2017
Excursions and passenger specials color *Model Railroader* v84 no2 p76 F 2017
Fulfilling the role of conductor bw *Model Railroader* v84 no3 p71 Mr 2017
Have clocks become too fast? color *Model Railroader* v84 no11 p72 N 2017
Identifying which train just went by color *Model Railroader* v84 no6 p69 Je 2017
The poetry and purpose of operations color *Model Railroader* v84 no1 p76 Ja 2017
Put Rule 93 to work on your railroad color *Model Railroader* v84 no7 p67 Jl 2017
Time traveling via model railroads color *Model Railroader* v83 no12 p74 D 2016
Train Orders and Form D's chart color *Model Railroader* v84 no5 p57 My 2017
Was Al Kalmbach a railroader? color *Model Railroader* v84 no4 p100 Ap 2017
What's special about instructions? color *Model Railroader* v84 no9 p68 S 2017
Where the 21st century meets the 19th *Model Railroader* v84 no10 p68 O 2017

Dzugan, Laura C.
Spectroscopic snapshots of the proton-transfer mechanism in water bibl diag graph *Science* v354 no6316 p1131 D 2 2016

Dz-Wei Chow, Ryan
Promoting human rights through science color *Science* v357 no6359 p34 O 6 2017

Dzwons, Victoria
Being trans . . *Christian Century* v134 no5 p6 Mr 1 2017

E

E., Sheila
PRINCE color *Entertainment Weekly* no1446/1447 p87 D 2016/Ja 2017

E-Chiang Lee
Priming HIV-1 broadly neutralizing antibody precursors in human Ig loci transgenic mice bibl graph *Science* v353 no6307 p1557 S 30 2016

E. K. Blessing (Company)
Blessing BFH-1541 Flugelhorn B. Zimmerman color *Downbeat* v84 no8 p90 Ag 2017

E. Kahn's Sons Co.
LOST CITY A. Flango *Cincinnati Magazine* v50 no5 p58 F 2017

Eacker, Stephen M.
A nuclease that mediates cell death induced by DNA damage and poly(ADP-ribose) polymerase-1 bw graph *Science* v354 no6308 paad6872-1 O 7 2016

Eade, Philip
Addicted to alcohol and sex and haunted by God D. Leigh bw *America* v216 no3 p42 F 6 2017
Enfant Terrible D. PRYCE-JONES bw color *National Review* v68 no23 p37 D 19 2016
The Strange Genius of the Master J. Banville bw *New York Review of Books* v64 no2 p14 F 9 2017
WHITE MISCHIEF J. Epstein *Claremont Review of Books* v17 no2 p40 Spr 2017

EADES, JOHN
Project Greenglow: How Horizon Lost the Message in the Medium *Skeptical Inquirer* v41 no1 p52 Ja/F 2017

Eadicicco, Lisa
Artificial Intelligence Invades the Home ... In Toys color *Time* v188 no24 p20 D 12 2016
The Best 25 Inventions of 2016 color *Time* v188 no22-23 p43 N/D 2016
Calendar: Discovery color *Time* v188 no27-28 p84 D 26 2016
Equifax and the Perils of Password Protection color *Time* v190 no12 p21 S 25 2017
Google Searches for Its Voice color diag *Time* v190 no16/17 p68 O 23 2017
How AI Is Getting More Human color *Time* v188 no27-28 p96 D 26 2016
How the Internet Is Getting a Little Nicer, One Meme at a Time color *Time* v189 no23 p19 Je 19 2017
It's Getting Bot In the Kitchen color *Time* v189 no22 p18 Je 12 2017
Sleep, Thy Name Is Gadget color *Time* v189 no13 p20 Ap 10 2017
Smart Homes' Top Job: Safety color *Time* v189 no7/8 p30 F 27 2017
Streaming on a Shoestring color *Money* v46 no4 p15 My 2017
Track Action for Less color *Money* v46 no2 p23 Mr 2017
Uber Fail [Cover story] color diag *Time* v189 no24 p22 Je 26 2017
Why Amazon Bought Whole Foods color *Time* v190 no1 p11 Jl 3 2017
Why Is Rick and Morty So Fun? It's All About the References color *Time* v190 no6 p53 Ag 7 2017

Eads, George, 1967-—Interviews
MACGYVER I. Rudolph *TV Guide* v65 no39 p52 S 18 2017
MACGYVER'S DYNAMIC DUO I. RUDOLPH *TV Guide* v64 no46 p26 N 7 2016

Eagan, Daniel
Majority Rule bw *Film Comment* v53 no4 p77 Jl/Ag 2017

Eagan, James M.
Combining polyethylene and polypropylene: Enhanced performance with PE/iPP multiblock polymers bibl chart graph *Science* v355 no6327 p814 F 24 2017

Eagle behavior
Drone Hunters color *MIT Technology Review* v120 no3 p22 My/Je 2017

Eagle Nebula
MILKY WAY MEGAMOSAIC T. O'Donoghue *Sky & Telescope* v133 no6 p75 Je 2017

Eagle Scouts
Muslim Eagle Scouts Grow *Islamic Horizons* v46 no1 p14 Ja/F 2017

Eagle Creek (Boone County-Marion County, Ind.)

CLEARING THE AIR: Hookah-smoking, motorboating, and immigrants S. Stall *Indianapolis Monthly* v40 no10 p17 Je 2017

Eagle Huntress, The (Film)

The Eagle Huntress J. Nolfi color *Entertainment Weekly* no1438 p47 N 4 2016

Talk to ME color *Vogue* v206 no11 p180 N 2016

Eaglen, Mackenzie

A Military in Need color *Weekly Standard* v22 no32 p9 My 1 2017

Eagles (Performer)

Eagles vs. the Editors A. GREENE bw *Rolling Stone* no1287 p21 My 18 2017

Eagleton, Terry, 1943-

A man of many commitments M. Ross Romero color *America* v216 no13 p54 Je 12 2017

EAKIN, EMILY

Bury My Heart: Alexandra Fuller's deep dive into Lakota culture and history follows two reservation boys whose lives become fatefully intertwined *New York Times Book Review* p19 Jl 23 2017

Eakin, Hugh

The Swedish Kings of Cyberwar color map *New York Review of Books* v64 no1 p56 Ja 19 2017

Eapen, Zubin J.

Redesigning Care for High-Cost, High-Risk Patients color *Harvard Business Review Digital Articles* p2 F 7 2017

Ear

LAMB'S EAR S. Burt *New Yorker* v93 no14 p72 My 22 2017

Melodies in the Mind B. Lutz color *New Orleans Magazine* v51 no6 p34 Ap 2017

TRENDING M. BARNA chart color map *Discover* v38 no4 p12 My 2017

Ear anatomy

Outer ear infection *Mayo Clinic Health Letter* v34 no12 p4 D 2016

Ear canal—Physiology

ear infection 411 J. RAINEY MARQUEZ *Parents* v92 no4 p126 Ap 2017

Ear candling

Wax On, Wax Off color *Women's Health* v14 no8 p27 O 2017

Ear care & hygiene

SWIMMER'S EAR SOLUTIONS color *Prevention* v69 no7 p6 Jl 2017

Ear care & hygiene—Equipment & supplies

Can this trick help with ear problems? *Parents* v91 no6 p24 Je 2016

Ear diseases—Treatment

All Ears P. Mahaney color *Amazing Wellness* v9 no1 p82 Wint 2017

NOW HEAR THIS! L. Turner color *Amazing Wellness* v8 no6 p64 Early Winter2016

Ear plugs (Hearing protection)

Earplugs R. Berendsohn color *Popular Mechanics* p35 S 2017

Ear plugs (Hearing protection)—Evaluation

BATTLE LA BREEZE D. Canet color *Cycle World* v56 no3 p20 Ap 2017

Earplugs R. Berendsohn color *Popular Mechanics* v193 no7 p35 S 2016

Earache—Prevention

the night shift K. ROCKWOOD *Parents* v92 no1 p20 Ja 2017

Earbuds

Bedazzled! S. Guttenberg and C. Crowley color *Sound & Vision* v82 no6 p22 Jl/Ag 2017

Rated XXX S. Guttenberg and C. Crowley color *Sound & Vision* v82 no6 p20 Jl/Ag 2017

Earhart, Amelia, 1897-1937

History's Greatest Hits K. BOATNER and J. ROCCO color *National Geographic Kids* no465 p7 N 2016

Quotable Quotes *Reader's Digest* v188 no1125 p148 N 2016

RIHANNA TAKES FLIGHT bw color *Harper's Bazaar* no3651 p380 Mr 2017

The Yankee Flier: Amelia Earhart belonged to the nation and even the world. But she first made her name as a New Englander bw *Yankee* p144 Jl 2017

Earl Jean (Company)

4 EASY PIECES ENDLESS OUTFITS color *Good Housekeeping* v263 no5 p47 N 2016

Earle, Joe

Teaching by Numbers I. M. Stelzer color *Weekly Standard* v22 no29 p32 Ap 3 2017

Earle, Mason

THE DESCENT A. BURR color *Climbing* no356 p80 S/O 2017

THE DESCENT color *Climbing* no355 p80 Ag 2017

Earle, Sylvia A., 1935-

Celebrating Firsts S. Cooney color *Time* v190 no12 p6 S 25 2017

Firsts Women Who Are Changing the World [Cover story] N. Gibbs color *Time* v190 no10/11 p64 S 18 2017

She Favors Seas, He Prefers Stars N. DEGRASSE TYSON color *National Geographic* v232 no5 p24 N 2017

Sylvia Earle M. B. GRIGGS cartoon *Popular Science* p46 Ja/F 2017

Earley, Melissa

In the Not Quite Dark: Stories *Christian Century* v134 no4 p55 F 15 2017

Reflections on the lectionary *Christian Century* v133 no25 p21 D 7 2016

Earley, Seth

How Companies Are Benefiting from "Lite" Artificial Intelligence *Harvard Business Review Digital Articles* p2 Jl 19 2016

EARLY, GERALD

Indigo Man: Percival Everett's latest novel centers on a 56-year-old painter who has had an affair *New York Times Book Review* p8 Jl 30 2017

Early, Hank

Heaven's Crooked Finger: An Earl Marcus Mystery *Publishers Weekly* v264 no36 p66 S 4 2017

Early, Rosalind

Isabel Wilkerson *Humanities* v37 no4 p1 Fall 2016

Early, Steve

Richmond's Example to the Nation D. Helvarg color *Progressive* v81 no2 p40 F 2017

Top Cop S. Early *Washington Monthly* p11 N/D 2016

Early admission (School)

The Case for ... Starting College Early S. Davis and T. Keith color *Sports Illustrated* v126 no3 p19 Ja 23 2017

Early Americans (Music)

Jane Ira Bloom's Soprano Saxophone Solo on 'Big Bill' J. DURSO bw color *Downbeat* v84 no2 p96 F 2017

Early childhood education

See also

Kindergarten

College, Careers, and Kindergarten D. YAFFE *Education Digest* v82 no9 p44 My 2017

Dance and early childhood cognition: The Isadora Effect R. Faber bibl *Arts Education Policy Review* v118 no3 p172 2017

Defining quality in visual art education for young children: Building on the position statement of the Early Childhood Art Educators M. McClure, P. Tarr et al bibl *Arts Education Policy Review* v118 no3 p154 2017

Drama as a valuable learning medium in early childhood V. Brown bibl *Arts Education Policy Review* v118 no3 p164 2017

Powerful allies: Arts educators and early childhood educators joining forces on behalf of young children A. C. Baum bibl *Arts Education Policy Review* v118 no3 p183 2017

Early childhood education—United States

Early childhood arts education in the United States: A special issue of Arts Education Policy Review A. M. Reynolds and W. H. Valerio bibl *Arts Education Policy Review* v118 no3 p133 2017

Early Christian sculpture

The Good Shepherd, early fourth century, Museo Pio Cristiano, Vatican M. C. Parsons and H. J. Hornik color *Christian Century* v134 no9 p39 Ap 26 2017

Early diagnosis

Lyme diagnostics could get an upgrade A. CUNNINGHAM *Science News* v192 no4 p8 S 16 2017

Early intervention (Education)

CHANGING THEIR TRAJECTORY B. Wilson color *Literacy Today (2411-7862)* v34 no5 p48 Mr/Ap 2017

Early memories

BECOMING WILLARD W. SCOTT *Washingtonian Magazine* v52 no1 p224 O 2016

Child of Mine color *Vogue* v207 no10 p136 O 2017

Close Quarters M. A. Sternberg color *AARP: The Magazine* v60 no1A p54 D 2016/Ja 2017

FRACTURED MEMORIES S. WORLEY color *Chicago* v66 no9 p56 S 2017

Going Full Circle: In the Adult Diaper Aisle S. CARR *Idaho Magazine* v16 no10 p54 Jl 2017

Gordon Lightfoot N. Walker color *Canadian Geographic* v136 no6 p82 D 2016

Grandpa Ernie's Wool Jacket M. R. JOHNSON color *Cabin Living* p5 Ag 2017

Italian for Beginners H. Bering color *Weekly Standard* v22 no23 p5 F 20 2017

Join the Conversation *South Dakota Magazine* v33 no3 p19 S/O 2017

lake Love A. HASLETT bw color *Conde Nast Traveler* v52 no6 p90 Je/Jl 2017

Pikes and Pickerels *Commentary* v142 no1 p1 Jl/Ag 2016

Poor but Happy: The Wisdom of the Elders T. BRINKERHOFF *Idaho Magazine* v16 no9 p42 Je 2017

STUCK IN THE ORANGE WHALE W. DUFFIELD *South Dakota Magazine* v32 no6 p96 Mr/Ap 2017

Tamale Fest J. B. Hager color *Southern Living* v51 no12 p138 D 2016

WELL-SEASONED J. BARKER *Atlanta* v56 no7 p72 N 2016

Early modern history

ON THE SPOT: We ask 20 questions of leading historians on why their research matters, one book everyone should read and their views on the Tudors ... J. CHILDS *History Today* v67 no9 p112 S 2017

Early Modern Love Poem (Poem)

EARLY MODERN LOVE POEM O. Hazzard *Harper's Magazine* v335 no2006 p22 Jl 2017

Early retirement

ASK THE EXPERT E. O'brien, K. Mulhere et al chart *Money* v46 no1 p29 Ja/F 2017

RETIRE EARLY: HOW THEY CAN DO IT C. Weisser chart color diag *Money* v46 no3 p44 Ap 2017

RETIRE EARLY? YES YOU CAN [Cover story] E. O'brien color diag *Money* v46 no3 p34 Ap 2017

RETIRE WHEN YOU WANT J. B. CLARK color *Kiplinger's Personal Finance* v71 no3 p22 Mr 2017

Time to Rethink Early Retirement B. Steverman graph *Bloomberg Businessweek* no4516 p40 Mr 27 2017

We Retired Before 35 A. Breslaw color *Glamour* v115 no10 p136 O 2017

Early rising

Children of The Night R. BROOKHISER *National Review* v69 no15 p46 Ag 14 2017

Early voting

Black churches in North Carolina have responded to cutbacks in early voting by the Republican legislature by organizing "Souls to the Polls" marches after services J. Kelso color *Bloomberg Businessweek* no4498 p37 N 7 2016

Both Clinton and Trump are trying to win over Latinos in Florida, about 16 percent of all registered voters. Democrats have an advantage of 284,000 among them E. Larsen and J. Vidal color *Bloomberg Businessweek* no4498 p36 N 7 2016

In Utah, McMullin, a Mormon, is appealing to #NeverTrump voters, while Clinton is hoping a split GOP vote can give her a surprise win in a reliably red state M. Friberg color *Bloomberg Businessweek* no4498 p38 N 7 2016

Nevada voted twice for President Obama, but Republicans have spent millions trying to win its U.S. Senate seat—and perhaps the state I. Brekken color *Bloomberg Businessweek* no4498 p39 N 7 2016

The Polls Are Open A. Spear color *Bloomberg Businessweek* no4498 p34 N 7 2016

Early Women Filmmakers: An International Anthology 1902-1943 (Film)

Majority Rule D. Eagan bw *Film Comment* v53 no4 p77 Jl/Ag 2017

Early Years 1965-1972, The (Music)

PINK FLOYD M. Mettler bw color *Sound & Vision* v82 no2 p72 F/Mr 2017

Earmarking (Public finance)

LET'S MAKE SOME SAUSAGE AGAIN K. Drum cartoon *Mother Jones* v42 no5 p12 S/O 2017

Earned income tax credit

DEAR GOP: TAX CREDITS ARE NOT THE ANSWER V. DE RUGY *Reason* v49 no2 p13 Je 2017

Earnhardt, Dale, Jr., 1974-

Dale Earnhardt Jr S. Gregory color *Time* v189 no18 p15 My 15 2017

DALE JR.'S NASCAR COMEBACK R. Edelstein color *TV Guide* v65 no7 p50 F 13 2017

Earnhardt, Dale, Jr., 1974—Interviews

Take 5 With DALE EARNHARDT JR J. P. Huffman color *Hot Rod* v70 no11 p14 N 2017

Earnings forecasting

Everything You Need to Know About P/E Ratios P. J. Lim chart diag *Money* v46 no8 p36 S 2017

Earnings management

The Answer to Short-Termism Isn't Asking Investors to Be Patient A. Edmans *Harvard Business Review Digital Articles* p2 Jl 18 2017

Earnings

7 KEY PIECES J. HILLMAN color *Harper's Bazaar* no3656 p187 S 2017

BEST BETS img *New York* v49 no23 p56 N 14 2016

The BUY Jewelry color *Harper's Bazaar* no3656 p178 S 2017

CRYSTAL CLEAR color *Harper's Bazaar* no3656 p312 S 2017

Go Big, Girls I. Hwang color *Glamour* v114 no12 p58 D 2016

GRAPHIC CONTENT bw color *Harper's Bazaar* no3656 p262 S 2017

Hoop Dreams color *O, The Oprah Magazine* p63 N 2017

JUST ADD FRIENDS *Martha Stewart Living* no275 p8 Je 2017

Making Magic color *Vogue* v207 no7 p108 Jl 2017

The NEW STRONG *Interview* v46 no10 p90 D 2016/Ja 2017

PRETTY IS BACK A. Syrett color *InStyle* v24 no3 p354 Mr 2017

RED ZONE color *Harper's Bazaar* no3656 p314 S 2017

The STYLE FILE bw color *Harper's Bazaar* no3656 p335a S 2017

WHAT WE LOVE color *Harper's Bazaar* no3656 p97 S 2017

WHERE TO BUY color *Essence* v48 no3 p118 Jl 2017

WORK DOMINATION color *Women's Health* v14 no8 p54 O 2017

Earrings—Design & construction

MORE IS MORE color *Conde Nast Traveler* v52 no7 p24 Ag 2017

Earrings—Evaluation

27 Great Gifts *Atlanta* v56 no8 p55 D 2016

ALL DRESSED UP color *InStyle* v23 no13 p133 D 2016

Becoming Un-Obsessed S. Trong color *InStyle* v24 no9 p258 S 2017

Beyond the Boudoir color *Vogue* v207 no10 p304 O 2017

BLACK-TIE AFFAIR color *Harper's Bazaar* no3649 p192 D 2016/Ja 2017

BOHEMIAN RHAPSODY color *Harper's Bazaar* no3654 p92 Je/Jl 2017

Burn RUBBER *Interview* v47 no6 p28 Ag 2017

CADET CHIC color *Harper's Bazaar* no3651 p243 Mr 2017

Calvin Klein 205W39NYC earrings, $1,190 V. SMITH color *Vogue* v207 no10 p310 O 2017

center stage color *Seventeen* p160 Ja 1 2017

CHECK, PLEASE color *Harper's Bazaar* no3653 p112 My 2017

Clay Time M. L. BIKOFF *Atlanta* v56 no12 p48 Ap 2017

COLOR CODED color *Harper's Bazaar* no3651 p368 Mr 2017

the cover color *InStyle* v24 no11 p32 N 2017

DIAMONDS IN THE SKY color *Harper's Bazaar* no3653 p288 My 2017

DOPE STUFF ON MY DESK J. Wilson color *Essence* v47 no10 p28 F 2017

DOPE STUFF ON MY DESK J. Wilson color *Essence* v48 no5 p34 S 2017

Ear Candy E. Velluto color *Glamour* v115 no3 p71 Mr 2017

FABULOUS at Every Age color *Harper's Bazaar* no3648 p201 N 2016

FABULOUS at Every Age color *Harper's Bazaar* no3652 p163 Ap 2017

FASHION UNDER $100 [Cover story] color *Redbook* p63 My 2017

Feel confident in stripes B. Goreski color *Redbook* p22 Ap 2017

Fighting Shape color *Glamour* v114 no7 p120 Jl 2016

Fringe Festival color *Martha Stewart Living* no275 p22 Je 2017

getting ready with DR. KIM NICHOLS K. NICHOLS color *Better Homes & Gardens* v95 no3 p20 Mr 2017

THE GIRL Zendaya E. Wilson color *InStyle* v24 no6 p53 Je 2017

GOOD EVENING color *Harper's Bazaar* no3648 p92 N 2016

GREAT BUYS UNDER \$100 color *O, The Oprah Magazine* p104 D 2016

GREAT BUYS UNDER \$100: WOMAN OF THE WORLD color *O, The Oprah Magazine* p46 Jl 2017

Gucci earrings V. SMITH color *Vogue* v207 no4 p266 Ap 2017

GUEST LIST color *Harper's Bazaar* no3654 p94 Je/Jl 2017

HAVANA NIGHTS chart color *O, The Oprah Magazine* p64 Mr 2017

heartfelt L. Tudor color *New Orleans Magazine* v51 no4 p72 F 2017

her style color *InStyle* v24 no9 p108 S 2017

HIGH CONTRAST color *Harper's Bazaar* no3657 p176 O 2017

HOW ROUGE! Scarlet, crimson, ruby, fire-engine—whatever you call it, this season's hottest hue will have you seeing red S. STEVENSON color *Indianapolis Monthly* v42 no2 p30 O 2017

If You're Gearing Up for Date Night S. P. Nadella and A. Hou color *Glamour* v115 no9 p48 S 2017

The In/Out LIST color *Harper's Bazaar* no3650 p76 F 2017

The In/Out LIST color *Harper's Bazaar* no3653 p98 My 2017

It's UNCOMPLICATED *Interview* v47 no6 p29 Ag 2017

JEWEL TONES L. IMMEDIATO *Los Angeles Magazine* v62 no9 p29 S 2017

THE LADY Isabelle Huppert E. Wilson color *InStyle* v24 no6 p55 Je 2017

Lizzie Fortunato Earrings color *Bloomberg Businessweek* no4535 p71 Ag 28 2017

Lovely in La-La Land color *Essence* v48 no3 p88 Jl 2017

LUCY HALE A. Salazar color *InStyle* v24 no4 p57 Ap 2017

THE MAGIC OF A GREAT DRESS color *Redbook* p68 My 2017

MAKING WAVES: From dainty frills to major flounces, fashion is currently rife with ruffles S. STEVENSON bw color *Indianapolis Monthly* v41 no2 p30 S 2017

MODERN BRIDE color *Harper's Bazaar* no3654 p88 Je/Jl 2017

THE MUST-HAVE color *Harper's Bazaar* no3648 p100 N 2016

NEW WEAVE color *Harper's Bazaar* no3653 p129 My 2017

NOW TRENDING color *Seventeen* v76 no4 p20 Jl/Ag 2017

On Demand color *InStyle* v24 no1 p17 Ja 2017

ON THE SPOT color *Harper's Bazaar* no3654 p73 Je/Jl 2017

O'S SPRING FASHION LOOK BOOK color *O, The Oprah Magazine* p57 Mr 2017

Packing LIST A. Parnass color *Harper's Bazaar* no3653 p93 My 2017

POM SQUAD: Three cheers for summer's peppiest trend *Indianapolis Monthly* v40 no11 p26 Jl 2017

RED ALERT color *Harper's Bazaar* no3654 p74 Je/Jl 2017

RESORT REPORT bw color *Harper's Bazaar* no3657 p179 O 2017

RUN THE JEWELS *Atlanta* v57 no5 p48 S 2017

SADDLE UP color *Harper's Bazaar* no3650 p103 F 2017

The season's most flattering trend B. Goreski color *Redbook* p15 Je 2017

She Wears The Pants color *Glamour* v114 no7 p128 Jl 2016

Shoot for Some Hoops color *Glamour* v115 no10 p66 O 2017

Shop Guide color *O, The Oprah Magazine* p143 Mr 2017

SO BAZAAR color *Harper's Bazaar* no3650 p214 F 2017

SO BAZAAR color *Harper's Bazaar* no3654 p166 Je/Jl 2017

SOLDIER ON color *Harper's Bazaar* no3657 p141 O 2017

SPARKLE PLENTY *Cincinnati Magazine* v50 no5 p32 F 2017

STARS AND STRIPES color *Harper's Bazaar* no3653 p109 My 2017

the start color *InStyle* v24 no2 p31 F 2017

Stone AGE color *InStyle* v23 no13 p150 D 2016

The STYLE color *Harper's Bazaar* no3653 p123 My 2017

The STYLE color *Harper's Bazaar* no3655 p77 Ag 2017

STYLE STAR color *Harper's Bazaar* no3649 p184 D 2016/Ja 2017

Summer Scores color *InStyle* v24 no6 p71 Je 2017

Sun's Out Buns Out L. Balsamo color *Seventeen* v76 no3 p92 My 2017

TOP THAT! color *O, The Oprah Magazine* p63 Mr 2017

TOVE LOVE A. Salazar color *InStyle* v24 no1 p22 Ja 2017

Triple Threat color *Glamour* v115 no11 p142 N 2017

Wearable Sculpture M. L. BIKOFF *Atlanta* v56 no10 p43 F 2017

A WEEK OF Awesome Outfits S. Walter color *Good Housekeeping* v264 no4 p38 Ap 2017

Welcome to My Life color *InStyle* v23 no12 p144 N 2016

THE WELL-SPENT \$ DOLLAR bw *Harper's Bazaar* no3652 p124 Ap 2017

WHAT'S Next color *Harper's Bazaar* no3651 p390 Mr 2017

WHERE TO BUY color *Essence* v47 no10 p112 F 2017

WHERE TO BUY color *Essence* v48 no6 p128 O 2017

Wish List! color *Glamour* v114 no7 p62 Jl 2016

Work the LOOK color *Harper's Bazaar* no3652 p134 Ap 2017

Eartec Co. Inc.

Necessity--The Father of Innovation *Stage Directions* v30 no4 p9 Ap 2017

Earth (Film)

THE DISCOMFORTING LEGACY OF DEEPA MEHTA'S EARTH B. Qureshi *Film Quarterly* v70 no4 p77 Summ 2017

Earth (Music)

Matters of Experience B. MEYER color *Downbeat* v84 no1 p77 Ja 2017

Earth (Planet)

> *See also*
>
> Northern Hemisphere
> Water

75, 50 & 25 Years Ago R. W. Sinnott *Sky & Telescope* v132 no6 p7 D 2016

Check Out These Outrageous Facts J. WANDEL color *National Geographic Kids* no475 p4 N 2017

Closest known exoplanet 'just' 4.24 light-years away C. Crockett color *Science News* v190 no13 p20 D 24 2016

Conducive Atmosphere A. Hadhazy *Natural History* v124 no10 p6 N 2016

Earth's Surprise Neighbor Hints at Exoplanet Abundance E. BETZ color diag *Discover* v38 no1 p10 Ja/F 2017

The Geminids & the Ursids *Sky & Telescope* v132 no6 p48 D 2016

How Did Earth Gets Its Ocean? A. Sarafian color *Oceanus* v51 no2 p100 Wint 2016

How Earth Got its MOON T. Sumner color *Science News* v191 no7 p18 Ap 15 2017

January's top 10 targets G. CHAPLE color *Astronomy* v45 no1 p66 Ja 2017

Moon formation idea takes a violent turn color *Astronomy* v45 no1 p12 Ja 2017

My Rock of Ages: On being immortalized far out in the asteroid belt D. GRINSPOON *Sky & Telescope* v134 no3 p14 S 2017

The new MOON B. Denevi *Physics Today* v70 no6 p38 Je 2017

PLANETARY WEIGHT LOSS M. E. Bakich, R. Talcott et al color *Astronomy* v45 no4 p34 Ap 2017

Solar eclipse geometry M. E. Bakich color map *Astronomy* v45 no5 p34 My 2017

SPACESHIP EARTH W. LAWRENCE color map *Phi Kappa Phi Forum* v97 no1 p18 Spr 2017

STAR DOME/PATH OF THE PLANETS R. TALCOTT color diag *Astronomy* v45 no6 p38 Je 2017

Target open clusters P. HARRINGTON color *Astronomy* v45 no1 p69 Ja 2017

What Would Happen? C. BOYER cartoon *National Geographic Kids* no470 p7 My 2017

Earth (Planet)—Crust

> *See also*
>
> Earth (Planet)—Surface
> Regolith
> Slabs (Structural geology)

Earth's mantle is cooling fast T. SUMNER color *Science News* v191 no1 p14 Ja 21 2017

A HISTORY IN LAYERS [Cover story] J. Zalasiewicz and K. Peek color graph *Scientific American* v315 no3 p30 S 2016

A MAP OF EARTH'S VISCOUS CRUST *Physics Today* v69 no12 p24 D 2016

A measure of mantle melting P. D. Asimow bibl graph *Science* v355 no6328 p908 Mr 3 2017

Earth (Planet)—History

Impact ejecta at the Paleocene-Eocene boundary M. F. Schaller, M. K. Fung et al bibl bw graph *Science* v354 no6309 p225 O 14 2016

Earth (Planet)—Mantle

Earth's mantle is cooling fast T. SUMNER color *Science News* v191 no1 p14 Ja 21 2017

New tests reveal hotter mantle T. SUMNER color *Science News* v191 no6 p9 Ap 1 2017

On the deep-mantle origin of the Deccan Traps P. Glišović and A. M. Forte bibl color *Science* v355 no6325 p613 F 10 2017

Young, hot Earth kept gold in mantle A. WITZE *Science News* v190 no9 p10 O 29 2016

Earth (Planet)—Orbit

The smoking gun of the ice ages D. A. Hodell bibl diag *Science* v354 no6317 p1235 D 9 2016

Earth (Planet)—Photographs from space

Planet Earth to get a daily selfie M. Strauss color graph *Science* v355 no6327 p782 F 24 2017

Earth (Planet)—Rotation

Getting in Step J. RAO *Natural History* v125 no1 p38 D 2016/Ja 2017

A Saguaro's universe J. HESTER color *Astronomy* v45 no4 p20 Ap 2017

Earth (Planet)—Surface

Rocks retain bits of Earth's early crust T. SUMNER color *Science News* v191 no7 p8 Ap 15 2017

Searching for Life on the Newly Discovered Earthlike Planets J. Kluger color diag *Time* v189 no9 p24 Mr 13 2017

Earth Day

On eve of science march, planners look ahead L. Wessel color *Science* v356 no6334 p118 Ap 14 2017

ON THE SIDE OF SCIENCE S. Goldberg color *National Geographic* v231 no3 p4 Mr 2017

Earth gravitation

Death watch for climate probe P. Voosen color *Science* v357 no6357 p1225 S 22 2017

Earth movements

See also

Earthquakes

The hidden simplicity of subduction megathrust earthquakes Meier, J. P. Ampuero et al graph *Science* v357 no6357 p1277 S 22 2017

Mapping the future, of continents and batteries E. Emerson *Science News* v191 no1 p2 Ja 21 2017

Earth temperature

Climate Change cartoon color graph map *National Geographic* v231 no4 p30 Ap 2017

New tests reveal hotter mantle T. SUMNER color *Science News* v191 no6 p9 Ap 1 2017

Save Our Science, Save Our Planet M. Hamilton *Humanist* v77 no2 p6 Mr/Ap 2017

Earth topography

Global drainage patterns and the origins of topographic relief on Earth, Mars, and Titan B. A. Black, J. Taylor Perron et al diag graph *Science* v356 no6339 p727 My 19 2017

Earth (Planet)—Remote-sensing images

A new eye on Earth's atmosphere color *Science* v355 no6323 p331 Ja 27 2017

Earthquake damage

Another deadly quake rocks Mexico color *Science* v357 no6358 p1332 S 29 2017

Lightbox I. Grillo color *Time* v190 no13 p18 O 2 2017

New Zealand temblor points to threat of compound quakes B. Mason color map *Science* v355 no6331 p1250 Mr 24 2017

Earthquake magnitude

Coseismic rupturing stopped by Aso volcano during the 2016 Mw 7.1 Kumamoto earthquake, Japan A. Lin, T. Satsukawa et al bibl color graph *Science* v354 no6314 p869 N 18 2016

Unusual quake rattles Mexico L. Wade color map *Science* v357 no6356 p1084 S 15 2017

Earthquake prediction

Big quake hopscotched across faults T. SUMNER *Science News* v191 no8 p14 Ap 29 2017

Man-Made Solutions for Man-Made Quakes A. Kuchment color *Scientific American* v316 no2 p10 F 2017

Telltale Sounds of Tsunamis R. F. Mandelbaum color *Scientific American* v316 no4 p18 Ap 2017

Earthquake zones

Seismic array shifts to Alaska J. Rosen color *Science* v357 no6359 p22 O 6 2017

Earthquakes

See also

Earthquake magnitude

AFTER THE SKY FELL S. Armington color *Progressive* v81 no5 p22 Je/Jl 2017

Bad Moon Rising K. HAYNES color *Discover* v38 no1 p48 Ja/F 2017

Bangladesh Sits Atop Potential Major Quake Zone G. TARLACH color map *Discover* v38 no1 p22 Ja/F 2017

Coseismic rupturing stopped by Aso volcano during the 2016 Mw 7.1 Kumamoto earthquake, Japan A. Lin, T. Satsukawa et al bibl color graph *Science* v354 no6314 p869 N 18 2016

Earthquakes G. TARLACH color *Discover* v38 no4 p74 My 2017

The hidden simplicity of subduction megathrust earthquakes Meier, J. P. Ampuero et al graph *Science* v357 no6357 p1277 S 22 2017

Mega-earthquakes rupture flat megathrusts Q. Bletery, A. M. Thomas et al bibl graph *Science* v354 no6315 p1027 N 25 2016

Earthquakes—Alaska

Volcanic tremor and plume height hysteresis from Pavlof Volcano, Alaska A. R. Van Eaton, D. Fee et al bibl graph *Science* v355 no6320 p1 Ja 6 2017

Earthquakes—California

Seasonal water storage, stress modulation, and California seismicity C. W. Johnson, Y. Fu et al diag graph *Science* v356 no6343 p1161 Je 16 2017

Earthquakes—Indonesia—Sumatra

LAGUNDRI BAY NIAS, INDONESIA Z. MORTON color *Surfer* v58 no4 p56 Ag 2017

Earthquakes—Italy

Italy calls on Renzo Piano to Address Earthquake Resilience A. FIXSEN *Architectural Record* v204 no10 p26 O 2016

Earthquakes—Japan

See also

Sendai Earthquake, Japan, 2011

Imaging the distribution of transient viscosity after the 2016 Mw 7.1 Kumamoto earthquake J. D. P. Moore, H. Yu et al map *Science* v356 no6334 p163 Ap 14 2017

Tsunami debris spells trouble S. L. Chown map *Science* v357 no6358 p1356 S 29 2017

Earthquakes—Mexico

See also

Central Mexico Earthquake, 2017

Chiapas Earthquake, Mexico, 2017

Aftermath E. GARRIDO color *Nation* v305 no9 p11 O 16 2017

Unusual quake rattles Mexico L. Wade color map *Science* v357 no6356 p1084 S 15 2017

Earthquakes—Nepal

Vertically Challenged? color *Earth Island Journal* v32 no1 p6 Spr 2017

Earthquakes—New Zealand

Complex multifault rupture during the 2016 Mw 7.8 Kaikōura earthquake, New Zealand I. J. Hamling, S. Hreinsdóttir et al color map *Science* v356 no6334 p154 Ap 14 2017

Earthquakes—Oklahoma

Human Activity Shakes Up Geological Hazard Map M. BARNA color map *Discover* v38 no1 p64 Ja/F 2017

Shake, Rattle, and Sue: Oklahoma's oil industry ducks and covers to avoid taking responsibility for the state's earthquake boom D. Slater *Sierra* v102 no4 p20 Jl/Ag 2017

Earthquakes—United States

America Is Not Ready for the Earthquakes Ahead K. Miles color map *Time* v190 no14 p21 O 9 2017

Earthquakes—United States—Research

Man-Made Solutions for Man-Made Quakes A. Kuchment color *Scientific American* v316 no2 p10 F 2017

Earth's mantle

Seismic evidence for partial melting at the root of major hot spot plumes K. Yuan and B. Romanowicz diag graph *Science* v357 no6349 p393 Jl 28 2017

Earthshine

Cloudshine S. James O'meara color *Astronomy* v45 no7 p20 Jl 2017

Earwax

Wax On, Wax Off color *Women's Health* v14 no8 p27 O 2017

Eason, Tracy

Speak Your Truth bw color *Glamour* v115 no6 p22 Je 2017

East, Andrew
Perfectly BALANCED M. BERG bw color *Muscle & Performance* v9 no11 p44 N 2017

East Asian martial arts
See also
Hapkido
On Hapkido Functioning in All Four Ranges color *Black Belt* v55 no5 p17 Ag/S 2017

East Asian students
A Brief History of Imperial Examination and Its Influences K. Ko *Society* v54 no3 p272 Je 2017

East Asians—United States
Geographic Justice M. MULDER bw color *Christianity Today* v61 no1 p72 Ja/F 2017

East India Co.
India versus the East India Company J. Wilson *History Today* v67 no1 p7 Ja 2017

East Indian actors
THE WORLD'S HIS STAGE L. RAMZI bw *Vogue* v207 no6 p109 Je 2017

East Indian actors—Interviews
"Don't Be Afraid of Who You Are" M. Jacob color *Glamour* v115 no6 p116 Je 2017

East Indian American teenagers
BEE--BRAINED V. Vara *Harper's Magazine* v334 no2004 p54 My 2017

East Indian restaurants
Not Curry In a Hurry S. Marikar cartoon color *Bloomberg Businessweek* no4499 p84 N 14 2016

East Indian restaurants—Evaluation
BINDAAS A. Limpert *Washingtonian Magazine* v52 no2 p255 N 2016
NORTH J. FROIS color *Louisiana Life* v37 no3 p97 Ja/F 2017

East Indians—United States
Indians Reconsider Life in America S. Rai graph *Bloomberg Businessweek* no4516 p13 Mr 27 2017
SHOPPED AROUND N. SWAMINATHAN color *Mother Jones* v42 no5 p50 S/O 2017

East Indians—United States—Social conditions
Olathe, Kansas, became a global magnet for tech talent, thanks to plentiful jobs, cheap housing, and good schools. Then someone opened fire on a pair of Indian-born engineers [Cover story] R. Ratnesar color *Bloomberg Businessweek* no4522 p60 My 15 2017

EASTEP, AMANDA CLEARY
At-Home Seminary color *Christianity Today* v61 no4 p67 My 2017

Easter
A BUSHEL AND A PECK E. N. GAGE color *Martha Stewart Living* p23 Ap 2017
EASTER FEAST C. HONG and F. BOSWELL color *Martha Stewart Living* p100 Ap 2017
Egged On D. SKINNER color *Weekly Standard* v22 no32 p5 My 1 2017
HOP TO IT E. Graves *Martha Stewart Living* p10 Ap 2017
Print Sales Get an Easter Bump chart *Publishers Weekly* v264 no15 p9 Ap 10 2017
Who's the Wise One? Ask the Marshmallow Bunny S. CARR *Idaho Magazine* v16 no9 p54 Je 2017

Easter, Michael
The Guys Next Door color *Women's Health* v14 no1 p26 Ja/F 2017
HOW FAST COULD YOU RUN... HOW FAR COULD YOU GO... IF YOU TOOK OFF YOUR TRACKER AND RAN FREE? color *Women's Health* v14 no7 p168 S 2017
Muscle Secrets of NFL Vets color *Men's Health* v32 no8 p48 O 2017
MY BADASS MOM bw *Men's Health* v32 no4 p122 My 2017
SIX STEPS TO MAXIMUM FITNESS bw chart color *Men's Health* v32 no3 p39 Ap 2017
Ticket Resellers cartoon *Men's Health* v32 no8 p30 O 2017
WEIGHT FOR IT... color *Women's Health* v14 no5 p57 Je 2017
ZEN FOR MEN [Cover story] cartoon color *Men's Health* v32 no1 p118 Ja/F 2017

Easter, Zac
THE CTE Diaries R. Forgrave color *GQ: Gentlemen's Quarterly*

v87 no1 p88 Ja 2017

Easter cooking
Noodling Around C. Henry color *O, The Oprah Magazine* p135 Ap 2017
A Spring Feast color *Good Housekeeping* v264 no4 p114 Ap 2017

Easter egg hunts
Anna Silk A. Pope color *Canadian Geographic* v137 no3 p82 My 2017
Egged On D. SKINNER color *Weekly Standard* v22 no32 p5 My 1 2017

Easter eggs
CHIC EGGS P. GUGLIELMETTI color *Martha Stewart Living* p106 Ap 2017
egg-cellent new ideas for... EGGS chart color *Good Housekeeping* v264 no4 p65 Ap 2017
Elevate Your Easter Eggs K. Owen color *Southern Living* v52 no4 p33 Ap 2017
Where the Easter-Egg Tradition Comes From O. B. Waxman *Time* v189 no15 p19 Ap 24 2017

Easter—History
Where the Easter-Egg Tradition Comes From O. B. Waxman *Time* v189 no15 p19 Ap 24 2017

Easterly, William
The War on Terror vs. the War on Poverty bw graph *New York Review of Books* v63 no18 p64 N 24 2016

Eastern bluebird
BLUEBIRD COUNTRY J. Taylor *New York State Conservationist* v71 no5 p6 Ap 2017

Eastern Europe—Economic conditions
In Europe, Brain Drain Flows the Other Way Z. Simon *Bloomberg Businessweek* no4517 p16 Ap 3 2017

Eastern Europe—Politics & government—21st century
For Europe, More Tensions Grow in the East J. Micklethwait *Bloomberg Businessweek* no4541 p12 O 9 2017

Eastern Mennonite University
Virginia Leads the Way *Virginia Living* v15 no6 p83 O 2017

Eastern Nigeria
BIAFRA 50 YEARS ON: The civil war that resulted from the division of Nigeria was a major human disaster that should not be forgotten R. T. Howard *History Today* v67 no6 p36 Je 2016

Eastern rat snake
THE NATURAL EXPLANATION J. SERRAO color *Natural History* v125 no10 p2 O 2017

Eastern screech owl
Owls J. Rowen *New York State Conservationist* v71 no4 p32 F 2017

Eastern New Mexico University (Portales, N.M.)
PRIME PRACTICE PAYS PREMIUMS K. Santos color *Spin to Win Rodeo* v20 no9 p34 N 2016

Eastern Virginia Medical School (Norfolk, Va.)
Dynamic Duo *Virginia Living* v15 no1 p99 D 2016

Easter—Poetry
A villanelle for Easter Day *Christian Century* v134 no8 p1 Ap 12 2017

Eastes, Andrea N.
Transcriptional activation of RagD GTPase controls mTORC1 and promotes cancer growth diag *Science* v356 no6343 p1188 Je 16 2017

Eastland, Sam
Berlin Red: An Inspector Pekkala Novel of Suspense color *Publishers Weekly* v264 no14 p53 Ap 3. 2017

Eastland, Terry
Another Illegal Power Grab *Weekly Standard* v22 no5 p8 O 10 2016
A Great Scalia Successor *Weekly Standard* v22 no22 p8 F 13 2017
Investigations and Prosecutions color *Weekly Standard* v22 no35 p13 My 22 2017
Land of Disbelief color *Weekly Standard* v22 no28 p34 Mr 27 2017
A Most Fitting Tribute color *Weekly Standard* v22 no7 p12 O 24 2016
Recycling Religiously? color *Weekly Standard* v22 no10 p7 N 14 2016
The Senate Did Its Job *Weekly Standard* v22 no11 p8 N 21 2016
The Write Stuff *Weekly Standard* v22 no6 p5 O 17 2016

Eastman, Julius, 1940-1990

GUERRILLA MINIMALISM A. ROSS bw *New Yorker* v92 no46 p78 Ja 23 2017

Eastman Guitars (Company)
Eastman Custom Edition Guitars K. Baumann color *Downbeat* v84 no8 p91 Ag 2017

Eastman Music Co.
Eastman ETR824S Trumpet M. Stewart color *Downbeat* v84 no4 p93 Ap 2017

Eastmond, Peter J.
Fatty acids in arbuscular mycorrhizal fungi are synthesized by the host plant diag graph *Science* v356 no6343 p1175 Je 16 2017

Easton, Lois Brown
Strategic accountability is key to making PLCs effective chart il *Phi Delta Kappan* v98 no4 p43 D 2016/Ja 2017

Easton, Michael—Interviews
GENERAL HOSPITAL M. LOGAN *TV Guide* v64 no40 p62 O 3 2016

East Side High School (Cleveland, Mississippi)
OVERDUE ASSIGNMENTS color *Mother Jones* v42 no5 p16 S/O 2017

Eastwood, Clint, 1930-
How to Dramatize Heroism—and How Not To R. Alleva color *Commonweal* v143 no17 p27 O 21 2016
SULLY A. Greengart color *Sound & Vision* v82 no4 p67 My 2017
Sully *New Yorker* v92 no33 p14 O 17 2016

Eastwood, Scott, 1986-
Living by the Eastwood Code P. FLAX cartoon color *Men's Health* v32 no5 p27 Je 2017

Easun, Timothy
Adaptation *Science* v356 no6335 p243 Ap 21 2017

Easy (TV program)
CHARACTER STUDIES E. BLONDIAU color *America* v215 no13 p31 O 31 2016

Easy Chair: Occupied Territory (Short story)
EASY CHAIR: Occupied Territory R. Solnit *Harper's Magazine* v335 no2006 p5 Jl 2017

Eating disorders
See also
Compulsive eating
Hyperphagia
Damn, Demi! L. Donnenfeld color *Glamour* v115 no1 p12 Ja 2017
A Mighty Mess G. DOYLE color *O, The Oprah Magazine* p44 S 2017
Picky Eating: When to Worry *Parents* p56 2015
REST UP, CROSSFITTERS color *Muscle & Performance* v9 no1 p16 Ja 2017
Street Style: FITNESS EDITION R. A. Darby color *Women's Health* v14 no5 p18 Je 2017

Eating disorders in adolescence
Eating Disorder S. M. FERNANDEZ *Scholastic Choices* v32 no6 p10 Mr 2017

Eaton, Ben
Being a Bird L. TONINO *Orion Magazine* v36 no2 p7 Mr/Ap 2017

Eaton, Dana
Getting to Know Your Zone Committee Chairs K. Rover *In Stride* v12 no2 p39 Mr 2017

Eaton, David W.
Fault activation by hydraulic fracturing in western Canada bibl graph map *Science* v354 no6318 p1406 D 16 2016

EATON, ELIZABETH S.
Ancient marine reptile gave live birth color *Science News* v191 no5 p9 Mr 18 2017
Bacterial genes sterilize mosquitoes color *Science News* v191 no6 p10 Ap 1 2017
Drones can pollinate color *Science News* v191 no5 p4 Mr 18 2017
Finding beauty in a mouse wheel of life color *Science News* v191 no7 p32 Ap 15 2017
Immune cells give the heart a boost color *Science News* v191 no10 p8 My 27 2017
King snake's strength is in its squeeze color *Science News* v191 no7 p13 Ap 15 2017
Nerve cell miswiring tied to depression color *Science News* v191 no10 p12 My 27 2017
Organic compounds found on Ceres color *Science News* v191 no5 p8 Mr 18 2017

Prescribing a Predator bw color diag graph *Science News* v191 no12 p22 Je 24 2017
Seabirds negotiate parenting duties color *Science News* v191 no13 p16 Jl 8 2017

EATON, HILLARY
FAR OUT *Los Angeles Magazine* p52 Ap 2017
JONESING FOR CHOCOLATE... *Los Angeles Magazine* v61 no11 p125 N 2017
This Food Podcast Turns It Up to 11 *Los Angeles Magazine* p66 D 2016

EATON, JOE
All That Glitters ... color *AARP: The Magazine* v59 no5A p38 Ag/S 2016

Eaton, Ted
RESPECT YOUR ELDERS E. Perkins color *Hot Rod* v70 no3 p62 Mr 2017

Eau de Cologne
FALL'S TOP NOTES J. AMAY bw color *Ebony* v72/73 no12/1 p50 O/N 2017

Eau de Cologne—Evaluation
The 27-Year-Old Cologne Virgin C. Skipper bw *GQ: Gentlemen's Quarterly* v97 no5 p43 My 2017
Solar Power K. Erickson color *Glamour* v114 no7 p78 Jl 2016
THE TIP SHEET M. Hainey, N. Sullivan color *Esquire* p36 Ag 2017
You Smell Amazing E. Reimel color *Glamour* v115 no5 p76 My 2017

Eaves, Ali
THE EXCHANGE bw cartoon color *Men's Health* v32 no6 p18 Ag 2017
It Takes Two cartoon *Rodale's Organic Life* v3 no1 p30 Ja 2017

Eaves, Elisabeth
Can North America's advanced nuclear reactor companies help save the planet? bibl *Bulletin of the Atomic Scientists* v73 no1 p27 Ja 2017
Crusades of the clueless: Who will win the war on science? bibl *Bulletin of the Atomic Scientists* v72 no6 p418 N 2016
IARPA Director Jason Matheny advances tech tools for US espionage color *Bulletin of the Atomic Scientists* v73 no2 p67 Mr 2017
NUKEMAP creator Alex Wellerstein puts nuclear risk on the radar color *Bulletin of the Atomic Scientists* v73 no4 p211 Jl 2017

Eaves, L.
High-temperature quantum oscillations caused by recurring Bloch states in graphene superlattices color *Science* v357 no6347 p181 Jl 14 2017

Eaves, Paul
FIVE FLAT with Zane Bruce C. Toy color *Spin to Win Rodeo* v21 no6 p31 Ag 2017
FREEZE FRAME WITH PAUL EAVES C. Toy color *Spin to Win Rodeo* v21 no1 p44 Mr 2017
HEELIN' FEELIN' color *Team Roping Journal* p16 S 2017

EAYNS, LEWISH
MONEY SAVING GUIDE [Cover story] cartoon color *Good Housekeeping* v264 no2 p79 F 2017

eBay Inc.
The Cardinal Rules of Buying on eBay color *Esquire* p111 Big-BlackBook
Now on EBay: Russian Micro-Multinationals I. Khrennikov and S. Soper *Bloomberg Businessweek* no4515 p19 Mr 20 2017

eBay Inc.—Finance
EBay Tries to Push Past Its Tag-Sale Roots S. Soper bw graph *Bloomberg Businessweek* no4493 p42 O 3 2016

eBay Inc.—Officials & employees
EBay Tries to Push Past Its Tag-Sale Roots S. Soper bw graph *Bloomberg Businessweek* no4493 p42 O 3 2016

Ebeling, Ashlea
401(k) Interrupted color *Forbes* v199 no1 p58 Ja 24 2017
Blue State Blues map *Forbes* v199 no2 p102 F 28 2017
Child of the Pledge color *Forbes* v199 no5 p56 My 16 2017
FOOLPROOF FOUNDATIONS color *Forbes* v198 no9 p96 D 30 2016
IRAs Gone Wild color *Forbes* v198 no6 p62 N 8 2016
MONEY THERAPISTS color *Forbes* v200 no4 p104 O 24 2017

Ebell, Myron
Green Threat color *Earth Island Journal* v32 no1 p10 Spr 2017

Ebenezer Baptist Church (Atlanta, Ga.)
A MESSAGE OF PEACE J. RAINEY MARQUEZ *Atlanta* v56 no9 p31 Ja 2017

Eberhardt, A.
Observation of coherent elastic neutrino-nucleus scattering diag *Science* v357 no6356 p1123 S 15 2017

Eberhardt, Jennifer L. (Jennifer Lynn), 1965-
COP TALK: THE SOUND OF BIAS L. MURROW color *Wired* v25 no8 p20 Ag 2017

Eberhardt, Timothy C.
The Thread *New York Times Magazine* p10 Ja 15 2017

Eberl, Franziska
Releasing plant volatiles, as simple as ABC color *Science* v356 no6345 p1334 Je 30 2017

Ebersole, Christine—Interviews
KISS AND MAKEUP C. Collis color *Entertainment Weekly* no1459 p66 Mr 31 2017

EBERSOLE, RENE
MASS EXPOSURE color *Nation* v305 no11 p34 O 30 2017
TRUST YOUR GUT [Cover story] cartoon *Prevention* v69 no9 p60 O 2017

EBERSTADT, FERNANDA
Gone Guy *New York Times Book Review* p14 F 19 2017

Eberstadt, Mary
Boys Will Be... color *Weekly Standard* v22 no32 p39 My 1 2017
How the Abortion Debate Rocked Progressivism *Time* v189 no4 p32 F 6 2017
ONE NATION, UNDER GOD? G. V. Bradley *Claremont Review of Books* v17 no1 p46 Wint 2016/2017

Eberstadt, Nicholas
The Feminist Economy G. GILDER color *National Review* v69 no1 p36 Ja 23 2017
Men without Work *National Review* v68 no21 p31 N 21 2016

Ebert, Elizabeth
The GRAND DAME of Cowboy Poetry C. Vaughan cartoon color *American Cowboy* v23 no5 p58 F/Mr 2017

Ebert, R. W.
Jupiter's interior and deep atmosphere: The initial pole-to-pole passes with the Juno spacecraft [Cover story] color graph *Science* v356 no6340 p821 My 26 2017

Ebert, Roger, 1942-2013
A good critic. Film critic Roger Ebert made himself his own life project P. H. Nettleton color *U.S. Catholic* v82 no8 p45 Ag 2017

Ebner, David
COPD Treatment Takes Center Stage *Saturday Evening Post* v288 no6 p115 N/D 2016

Ebola virus
A "Trojan horse" bispecific-antibody strategy for broad protection against ebolaviruses A. Z. Wec, E. K. Nyakatura et al bibl graph *Science* v354 no6310 p350 O 21 2016
EPIDEMIC INSURANCE J. Cohen and J. Gerberding color graph *Science* v356 no6334 p125 Ap 14 2017
Hitting Ebola, to the power of two A. F. Labrijn and P. W. H. I. Parren bibl diag *Science* v354 no6310 p284 O 21 2016
Long Ago and Far Away V. Maestro color *Natural History* v125 no9 p2 S 2017
The World Is Completely Unprepared for a Global Pandemic R. S. Dhillon, D. Srikrishna et al *Harvard Business Review Digital Articles* p2 Mr 15 2017

Ebola virus disease
Are pigs involved in new Ebola outbreak? color *Science* v356 no6341 p888 Je 1 2017
BAT PATROL K. Kupferschmidt color *Science* v356 no6341 p901 Je 1 2017
Ebola reappears color *Science* v356 no6339 p668 My 19 2017
Fears of Ebola resurgence quickly dispelled in Liberia K. Kupferschmidt color *Science* v356 no6338 p575 My 12 2017
From Contamination to Containment [Cover story] C. E. M. COLTART, A. M. JOHNSON et al color *Natural History* v125 no9 p40 S 2017
New Ebola outbreak rings alarm bells early J. Cohen and G. Vogel color map *Science* v356 no6340 p788 My 26 2017
To Fight the Zika Pandemic, Learn from Ebola R. S. Dhillon, R. Glatter et al *Harvard Business Review Digital Articles* p2 F 4 2016
What We've Learned About Fighting Ebola R. S. Dhillon and D.

Srikrishna *Harvard Business Review Digital Articles* p2 Jl 16 2015

Ebola virus disease vaccination
Emergency Ebola vaccine backup *Science* v356 no6337 p468 My 5 2017

Ebola virus disease—Prevention
Why Top-Down Management Doesn't Work in the Fight Against Ebola A. C. Edmondson *Harvard Business Review Digital Articles* p2 D 16 2014

Ebola virus disease—Treatment
Fighting Ebola Means Managing Fear W. A. Fischer II and B. Fischer *Harvard Business Review Digital Articles* p2 O 2 2014
Salome Karwah A. Baker color *Time* v189 no9 p14 Mr 13 2017
To Fight Ebola, Stop Pointing Fingers B. Manville *Harvard Business Review Digital Articles* p2 O 21 2014

Ebony (Periodical)
In Our Cities A. V. WATSON, K. Kyles et al bw color *Ebony* v72 no4 p42 F 2017

Ebony, David
ANTHONY CARO color *Art in America* v105 no4 p111 Ap 2017
A.R. PENCK *Art in America* v104 no10 p148 N 2016
ASGER JORN *Art in America* v104 no9 p150 O 2016
Asia Society color *Art in America* v105 no1 p77 Ja 2017
BECKY SUSS: Jack Shainman color *Art in America* v105 no8 p119 S 2017
Inside the Concrete Bubble color *Art in America* p45 O 2017
A little off-center: The estimable outsider art collection of Audrey Heckler color *Magazine Antiques* v184 no4 p114 Jl/Ag 2017
MoMA PS1 and Foxy Production color *Art in America* v105 no6 p131 Je/Jl 2017
RADICAL DESTABILIZATION bw color *Art in America* v105 no3 p106 Mr 2017
RONALD LOCKETT color *Art in America* v104 no10 p150 N 2016
SANDRO CHIA color *Art in America* v105 no5 p127 My 2017
TAL R color *Art in America* v105 no3 p126 Mr 2017
WALTER ROBINSON cartoon *Art in America* v104 no11 p122 D 2016
Why the long face: The Jewish Museum explores Modigliani's lonely sense of self bw color *Magazine Antiques* v184 no5 p72 S/O 2017

Ebony, Team
DOWN BY THE SEA color *Ebony* v72 no9 p41 Jl/Ag 2017
Hello, and welcome to our Summer issue! color *Ebony* v72 no9 p14 Jl/Ag 2017
July/August color *Ebony* v72 no9 p18 Jl/Ag 2017
SNATCH That STYLE color *Ebony* v72 no9 p35 Jl/Ag 2017

Ebr, J.
Observation of a large-scale anisotropy in the arrival directions of cosmic rays above 8×10^{18} eV *Science* v357 no6357 p1266 S 22 2017

Ebrahim, Rafiq
Strangers on a Train *New York Times Magazine* p25 Mr 5 2017

Ebus, Bram
ARC OF DESPERATION color *Earth Island Journal* v32 no3 p25 Aut 2017

Eccentrics & eccentricities in art
Lehmann Maupin B. Augustine *Art in America* v105 no1 p80 Ja 2017

Eccles, Nigel
What's Your One Shining Moment? I. Boudway cartoon *Bloomberg Businessweek* no4514 p73 Mr 13 2017

Eccles, Robert G.—Interviews
How Accounting Can Help Build a Sustainable Economy E. Harrell *Harvard Business Review Digital Articles* p2 D 14 2015

Ecer, Ayperi Karabuda
High and Mighty K. CHAYKA color *New Republic* v248 no5 p66 My 2017

Echanis, Michael D.
MICHAEL D. ECHANIS HONORED POSTHUMOUSLY G. Walker color *Black Belt* v55 no5 p12 Ag/S 2017

Echelman, Janet
Sky Dance color *American Craft* v77 no3 p96 Je/Jl 2017

Echenique, Pedro M.
Angular momentum–induced delays in solid-state photoemission enhanced by intra-atomic interactions chart color graph *Science*

v357 no6357 p1274 S 22 2017

Echenoz, Jean

Special Envoy: A Spy Novel *Publishers Weekly* v264 no36 p65 S 4 2017

Echinacea (Plants)

Consider This color *Yoga Journal* no290 p14 Mr 2017

Echinacea (Plants)—Therapeutic use

10 Steps to Protect Yourself Against Colds and Flu *Tufts University Health & Nutrition Letter* v34 no8 p4 O 2016

DRUG-FREE COLD & FLU RELIEF [Cover story] J. Cosgrove color *Amazing Wellness* v9 no6 p62 EarlyWint 2017

Echoes of Silence (Film)

Color Box M. J. ROWIN bw *Film Comment* v53 no2 p77 Mr/Ap 2017

Echolocation in mammals

Blind climber color *Science* v355 no6322 p259 Ja 20 2017

How glass fronts deceive bats P. Stilz color diag *Science* v357 no6355 p977 S 8 2017

Echt, Maxx—Interviews

Maxx Echt: Huntington Botanical Department Systems Manager M. Branom *Weatherwise* v70 no5 p40 S/O 2017

ECK, ALIETA

OH, WHAT A TANGLED WEB WE WEAVE... *USA Today Magazine* v146 no2866 p18 Jl 2017

"Right" You Aren't *USA Today Magazine* v146 no2868 p17 S 2017

ROBBING THE MIDDLE CLASS *USA Today Magazine* v145 no2864 p26 My 2017

ECKEL, SARA

Divider-In-Chief *Psychology Today* v50 no3 p41 My/Je 2017

Listening to Jealousy [Cover story] *Psychology Today* v49 no6 p50 N/D 2016

ECKELBERRY, STEPHEN

An Amazing Year! *Parks & Recreation* v52 no8 p8 Ag 2017

'I Love Watching You Play' *Parks & Recreation* v52 no5 p8 My 2017

Innovation Labs: Opportunities to Share Ideas and Solutions *Parks & Recreation* v52 no3 p8 Mr 2017

Eckelkamp, Stephanie

Can Your Pet Skip the Shots? [Cover story] color *Prevention* v68 no11 p94 N 2016

Comfort Creatures color *Prevention* v68 no12 p94 D 2016

Love Them Longer color *Prevention* v69 no1 p94 Ja 2017

Plevention CLEANEST PACKAGED FOOD AWARDS 2017 [Cover story] color *Prevention* p60 Mr 2017

Eckels, Kenneth H.

Rapid development of a DNA vaccine for Zika virus bibl graph *Science* v354 no6309 p237 O 14 2016

Ecker, Joseph R.

Single-cell methylomes identify neuronal subtypes and regulatory elements in mammalian cortex diag *Science* v357 no6351 p600 Ag 11 2017

A transcription factor hierarchy defines an environmental stress response network diag *Science* v354 no6312 p598 N 4 2016

ECKERLIN, RALPH P.

Transformational Principles for NEON Sampling of Mammalian Parasites and Pathogens: A Response to Springer and Colleagues *BioScience* v66 no11 p917 N 1 2016

ECKERT, AMY S.

Heartland GETAWAYS color *AARP: The Magazine* v30 no6A p44 O/N 2017

Eckert, Carter J.

Park Chung Hee and Modern Korea: The Roots of Militarism A. J. Nathan *Foreign Affairs* v96 no1 p175 Ja/F 2017

Eckert, Jonathan

Backtalk *Phi Delta Kappan* v98 no3 p80 N 2016

Eckhardt, Giana M.

The Sharing Economy Isn't About Sharing at All *Harvard Business Review Digital Articles* p2 Ja 28 2015

Eckhardt, Jon

Making Business School Research More Relevant *Harvard Business Review Digital Articles* p2 D 24 2014

Eckhoff, Angela

Defining quality in visual art education for young children: Building on the position statement of the Early Childhood Art Educators bibl *Arts Education Policy Review* v118 no3 p154 2017

Eckhouse, Brian

Buffett Likes Solar, But Not the Price Tag bw *Bloomberg Businessweek* no4534 p26 Ag 14 2017

Liberal Nonprofits Ride The Anti-Trump Wave color *Bloomberg Businessweek* no4500 p30 N 21 2016

Raising Private Money For Public Projects *Bloomberg Businessweek* no4513 p46 Mr 6 2017

ROOFTOP SOLAR CLOUDS UP graph *Bloomberg Businessweek* no4496 p80 O 24 2016

A Shock From Cheap Gas color map *Bloomberg Businessweek* no4524 p38 My 29 2017

Eckleberry, Steve—Interviews

Get Yourself Outside This Winter *Parks & Recreation* v52 no1 p8 Ja 2017

Meet the New Chair *Parks & Recreation* v51 no10 p10 O 2016

The More We Learn, the More We Grow *Parks & Recreation* v51 no11 p6 N 2016

Eckley, Mike

A meal for many color *U.S. Catholic* v82 no6 p5 Je 2017

Eckstein, Arthur M.

In Circular Pursuit S. J. UNGAR bw *Weekly Standard* v22 no19 p33 Ja 23 2017

Moral Equivalence Run Amok R. RADOSH *Commentary* v143 no2 p39 F 2017

Eckstein, Bob

Everybody Falls Sometimes color *Publishers Weekly* v264 no40 p144 O 2 2017

GAME, SET...NAPTIME cartoon *Esquire* p46 S 2017

Shelf Lives *Publishers Weekly* v263 no39 p96 S 26 2016

Soapbox color *Publishers Weekly* v264 no17 p96 Ap 24 2017

Eckstrom, Lauren

Meet the force WITHIN YOU [Cover story] color *Yoga Journal* no294 p74 S 2017

Q: For stress relief, what is your go-to practice or pose? color *Yoga Journal* no294 p14 S 2017

Eclectic Home (Company)

BEST of HOME WINNERS *New Orleans Homes & Lifestyles* v20 no3 p76 Summ 2017

RESOURCES *New Orleans Homes & Lifestyles* v20 no1 p102 Wint 2016

Eclipsed (Theatrical production)

9 — ECLIPSED M. Snetiker color *Entertainment Weekly* no1444/1445 p118 D 16 2016

The Activist ARTIST L. Mulcahy *Stage Directions* v30 no3 p56 Mr 2017

Eclipses

See also

Lunar eclipses

Saros cycle

Solar eclipses

ALL AROUND Missouri color *Missouri Life* v44 no5 p85 Ag 2017

DANCING IN THE DARK E. WOOD bw chart color map *Missouri Life* v44 no5 p32 Ag 2017

DO YOU SPEAK "ECLIPSE"? M. E. Bakich color *Astronomy* v45 no8 p76 Ag 2017

Get ready for E-Day [Cover story] M. E. Bakich color map *Astronomy* v45 no8 p20 Ag 2017

THE GREAT AMERICAN ECLIPSE OF 2017 E. STEED cartoon *New Yorker* v93 no27 p65 S 11 2017

Have Sun, Will Travel J. R. Gritz *Smithsonian* v48 no4 p28 Jl/Ag 2017

Mind Melt S. SCOLES bw color *Discover* v38 no7 p30 S 2017

A short history of ECLIPSES R. Shubinski bw color *Astronomy* v45 no5 p49 My 2017

When the Day Dims B. Lang *Discover* v38 no7 p6 S 2017

Eclipsing binaries

RW Tauri, an Action-Packed Eclipser A. MacRobert *Sky & Telescope* v133 no1 p48 Ja 2017

Eco, Umberto, 1932-2016

1975: California U. Eco *Lapham's Quarterly* v10 no1 p80 Wint 2017

Chronicles of a Liquid Society bw *Publishers Weekly* v264 no33 p61 Ag 14 2017

École nationale supérieure des beaux-arts (France)

Buried Influence H. Aboul-Ela color *New York Times Magazine*

p34 O 9 2016

Ecological disturbances

Passing the point of no return D. Seekell bibl graph *Science* v354 no6316 p1109-C D 2 2016

Ecological disturbances—Mathematical models

Effects of network modularity on the spread of perturbation impact in experimental metapopulations L. J. Gilarranz, B. Rayfield et al diag graph *Science* v357 no6347 p199 Jl 14 2017

The importance of being modular M. Sales-Pardo diag *Science* v357 no6347 p128 Jl 14 2017

Ecological economics

See also

Ecosystem services

Pricing an ecosystem M. SAGOFF *Issues in Science & Technology* v33 no1 p11 Fall 2016

Ecological houses

Homebuyers Show Greater Interest in Green Living *Mother Earth News* no284 p7 O/N 2017

Winterize Your Home color *Good Housekeeping* v265 no5 p59 N 2017

Ecological impact

CUBA VERDE [Cover story] B. Weinberg color *Earth Island Journal* v32 no3 p18 Aut 2017

Dubai's Audacious Goal R. KUNZIG color map *National Geographic* v232 no4 p52 O 2017

UNCHARTED WATERS K. D. HODES color *Women's Health* v14 no6 p144 Jl 2017

Ecological regime shifts

When, Where, and How Nature Matters for Ecosystem Services: Challenges for the Next Generation of Ecosystem Service Models J. T. RIEB, R. CHAPLIN-KRAMER et al *BioScience* v67 no9 p820 S 2017

Ecological research

Australia to ax support for long-term ecology sites J. Pickrell color *Science* v357 no6352 p632 Ag 18 2017

Global Disparity in Ecological Science: A Complex Systems Perspective V. H. MARÍN and L. E. DELGADO *BioScience* v67 no2 p105 F 2017

Long-Term Studies Contribute Disproportionately to Ecology and Policy B. B. HUGHES, R. BEAS-LUNA et al *BioScience* v67 no3 p271 Mr 2017

Save Australia's ecological research D. Lindenmayer color *Science* v357 no6351 p557 Ag 11 2017

Ecological reserves

In the easternmost reaches of Canada, looking for where the cold waters of the Labrador Current and the warmth of the Gulf Stream create the foggiest place in the world color *New York Times Magazine* p24 D 11 2016

Ecological resilience

Build a More RESILIENT HOMESTEAD *Mother Earth News* no279 p18 D/Ja 2017

The Resilience of Marine Ecosystems to Climatic Disturbances J. K. O'LEARY, F. MICHELI et al *BioScience* v67 no3 p208 Mr 2017

Ecological Society of America—Congresses

Calendar of meetings *BioScience* v67 no8 p772 Ag 2017

Ecologists

A RARE SPECIES R. W. Goode color *Black Enterprise* v47 no8 p31 Jl/Ag 2017

Ecology

See also

Abiotic stress

Applied ecology

Ecological impact

Ecological regime shifts

Ecosystem health

Ecosystems

Global environmental change

Habitat (Ecology)

Human ecology

Life zones

Plant ecology

Predation (Biology)

Riparian ecology

Urban ecology (Biology)

Corrigendum : Long-Term Studies Contribute Disproportionately

to Ecology and Policy *BioScience* v67 no8 p775 Ag 2017

A DEEPER BOOM G. FERGUSON *Orion Magazine* v35 no4/5 p14 Jl-O 2016

Editorial S. L. COLLINS *BioScience* v67 no1 p3 Ja 2017

Mapping Conservation Strategies under a Changing Climate R. T. BELOTE, M. S. DIETZ et al *BioScience* v67 no6 p494 Je 2017

Noise pollution is pervasive in U.S. protected areas R. T. Buxton, M. F. McKenna et al graph map *Science* v356 no6337 p531 My 5 2017

Response from Livingston and Colleagues G. LIVINGSTON *BioScience* v67 no2 p105 F 2017

Saying goodbye to glaciers T. Moon color *Science* v356 no6338 p580 My 12 2017

Skills and Knowledge for Data-Intensive Environmental Research S. E. HAMPTON, M. B. JONES et al *BioScience* v67 no6 p546 Je 2017

Ecology—Exhibitions

Inside Cuba A. Rademacher bibl *Science* v355 no6320 p34 Ja 6 2017

Ecology—News briefs

BIRD FRIENDLY S. Stonebrook *Mother Earth News* no281 p10 Ap/My 2017

Ecology—Periodicals

ON THE SIDE OF SCIENCE S. Goldberg color *National Geographic* v231 no3 p4 Mr 2017

Ecology—Press coverage

Up to Speed: Two Months, One Page P. Rauber *Sierra* v102 no2 p22 Mr/Ap 2017

Economic activity

INTERNATIONAL STATISTICS *Economic Indicators* p35 My 2017

Economic activity—Corrupt practices

PRODUCTION AND BUSINESS ACTIVITY *Economic Indicators* p17 My 2017

Economic aspects of decision making

See also

Mental accounting (Economic theory)

How Our Company Learned to Make Better Predictions About Everything D. Hernandez *Harvard Business Review Digital Articles* p2 My 15 2017

Economic bubbles

China's Housing Bubble Wobble B. EINHORN *Bloomberg Businessweek* no4496 p52 O 24 2016

Tech Stocks Are Back ... in a Bubble P. J. Lim color diag *Money* v46 no9 p48 O 2017

Economic change

Corporations Weren't Designed to Run on Code D. Rushkoff *Harvard Business Review Digital Articles* p2 Mr 2 2016

Economic conditions in Africa

Mobile Carriers Start Hanging Up on Africa L. Prinsloo and J. Kew cartoon *Bloomberg Businessweek* no4530 p18 Jl 17 2017

Economic conditions in Asia—21st century

Asia K. Stock color map *Bloomberg Businessweek* no4536 p10 S 4 2017

Economic conditions in Brazil—21st century

Brazil's Great Leap Backward D. Biller, G. Shinohara et al diag *Bloomberg Businessweek* no4535 p30 Ag 28 2017

Economic conditions in Greece—21st century

Greece: A New Horizon color *Foreign Affairs* v96 no3 p86a My/Je 2017

Greece's Oldest Bank Sets the Benchmark color *Foreign Affairs* v96 no3 p86d My/Je 2017

Investment in Real Estate on the Rise color *Foreign Affairs* v96 no3 p86j My/Je 2017

Progressive Developments in Greek Trade and Industry color *Foreign Affairs* v96 no3 p86f My/Je 2017

Reigniting the Greek Economy color *Foreign Affairs* v96 no3 p86e My/Je 2017

Economic conditions in Iran—21st century

Iranian Voters Want a Share of the Wealth L. Nasseri and G. Motevalli color *Bloomberg Businessweek* no4521 p14 My 8 2017

Economic conditions in Italy

It's Time to Worry About Italian Debt G. Smith diag *Fortune* v176 no2 p17 Ag 1 2017

Economic conditions in the United States

CALCULATING CLIMATE COSTS *Earth Island Journal* v32

no3 p7 Aut 2017

If America's Economy Is Winner-Take-All, Why Are Some Smaller Businesses Thriving? K. Smith *Harvard Business Review Digital Articles* p2 S 1 2017

A Lasting Solution to the Regulatory Nightmare T. J. Donohue *Weekly Standard* v22 no33 p35 My 8 2017

Small, Midsize Businesses Hold Key to Growth T. J. DONOHUE *Weekly Standard* v23 no4 p9 O 2 2017

THE SMARTEST, MOST INTERESTING THING EVERY U.S. PRESIDENT EVER SAID ABOUT MONEY I. Salisbury color diag *Money* v46 no6 p51 Jl 2017

Economic conditions in the United States—21st century

KEVIN D. WILLIAMSON K. D. WILLIAMSON *Commentary* v142 no1 p38 Jl/Ag 2016

Economic conditions of older people

Hubris in the U.K A. Stuttaford color *Weekly Standard* v22 no37 p14 Je 5 2017

Economic conditions of students

MONEY MATTER$: Ways you can pay for school N. LOEFFLER-GLADSTONE *Dance Magazine* p20 2016/2017

Economic determinism

Bottom-up construction of a superstructure in a porous uranium-organic crystal P. Li, N. A. Vermeulen et al color graph *Science* v356 no6338 p624 My 12 2017

Economic development

See also

Business development
Infrastructure (Economics)
Stagnation (Economics)
Sustainable development

The Battle for the Boundary Waters S. Franson color *Progressive* v81 no5 p27 Je/Jl 2017

A Blueprint for More Inclusive Economic Growth A. Liu *Harvard Business Review Digital Articles* p2 Mr 3 2016

Capital Markets: Fueling Our Economic Growth T. J. Donohue *Weekly Standard* v22 no5 p22 O 10 2016

Consumer spending: past and present D. Scopelliti *Monthly Labor Review* p1 N 2016

Diasporas' Impacts on Economic Development D. KAPUR *Current History* v115 no784 p298 N 2016

Economic productivity in the air transportation industry: multifactor and labor productivity trends, 1990-2014 M. Russell bibl chart color diag graph *Monthly Labor Review* p1 Mr 2017

How Populism May Stifle Growth bw *Bloomberg Businessweek* no4520 p12 My 1 2017

How to fight corruption R. Fisman and M. Golden color *Science* v356 no6340 p803 My 26 2017

An Investment Model for the Arctic T. Vauraste color *Wilson Quarterly* p1 Summ 2017

Meaningful Work Should Not Be a Privilege of the Elite R. Straub and J. Kirby color *Harvard Business Review Digital Articles* p2 Ap 3 2017

Our Approach to Economic Growth Isn't Working R. D. Atkinson *Harvard Business Review Digital Articles* p2 F 16 2016

The Promise of a Truly Entrepreneurial Society R. Straub *Harvard Business Review Digital Articles* p2 Mr 25 2016

SELLING A FAIRER ECONOMY [Cover story] J. GEDDES color *Maclean's* v129 no51/52 p27 D 26 2016

Study Reveals How Witchcraft Harms Economies B. RADFORD *Skeptical Inquirer* v40 no6 p8 N/D 2016

To Really Help the Global Poor, Create Technology They'll Pay For A. Deng *Harvard Business Review Digital Articles* p2 Ag 5 2015

Trade and Growth Protect Against Global Turmoil T. J. DONOHUE *Weekly Standard* v22 no21 p19 F 6 2017

The Type of Innovation That Builds Nations B. Mezue *Harvard Business Review Digital Articles* p2 Ja 7 2015

Who Pays the Tax Bill? A progressive local tax is hard to find J. Marlowe *Governing* v30 no9 p63 Je 2017

Economic development projects—International cooperation

The Future Economy Project A. Ignatius *Harvard Business Review Digital Articles* p2 2017

Economic development projects—Management

Glaring Paradoxes: PROGRESS, BUT DISAPPOINTMENT *Vital Speeches of the Day* v83 no9 p265 S 2017

The New Markets Tax Credit O. Spurgeon III *Parks & Recreation*

v51 no11 p24 N 2016

Economic development—Africa

What Africa's Leaders Have Learned About Facing Huge Challenges J. Grenny *Harvard Business Review Digital Articles* p2 My 28 2015

Will Africa's Growth Help Africa's People? K. F. Nwanze *Harvard Business Review Digital Articles* p2 Jl 16 2015

Economic development—Brazil

Brazil's Great Leap Backward D. Biller, G. Shinohara et al diag *Bloomberg Businessweek* no4535 p30 Ag 28 2017

Economic development—China

China's Growth: A Brief History L. Yueh *Harvard Business Review Digital Articles* p2 D 9 2015

Contemplating Decline: China's challenge to America percolates on many fronts C. LAYNE *American Conservative* v16 no4 p29 Jl/Ag 2017

How Do You Say Déjà Vu in Chinese? M. Schuman bw color *Bloomberg Businessweek* no4498 p14 N 7 2016

Economic development—Finance

Economic Development's Bad Idea: Throwing money at businesses isn't the best approach M. Funkhouser *Governing* v30 no11 p59 Ag 2017

Economic development—Germany

The Latest German Model E. P. Lazear and S. Janssen *Hoover Digest: Research & Opinion on Public Policy* no1 p61 Wint 2017

Economic development—Government policy

Economic Development's Bad Idea: Throwing money at businesses isn't the best approach M. Funkhouser *Governing* v30 no11 p59 Ag 2017

Economic development—Greece

Greece: A New Horizon color *Foreign Affairs* v96 no3 p86a My/Je 2017

The Greek Pharmaceutical Industry: A Strong Contributor to its Economy color *Foreign Affairs* v96 no3 p86h My/Je 2017

Economic development—Laos

Financing the Country's Growth *Foreign Affairs* v95 no6 p(Sp)10 N/D 2016

LAOS color *Foreign Affairs* v95 no6 p(Sp)1 N/D 2016

Economic development—Nigeria

NIGERIA: TRANSFORMATION PRESENTS OPPORTUNITIES P. Trustfull color *Forbes* v200 no4 p(Sp)1 O 24 2017

Economic development—Palestinian Territories

Start-Up Palestine Y. Kaufmann color *Foreign Affairs* v96 no4 p113 Jl/Ag 2017

Economic development—Rwanda

RWANDA: REFORMS BOOST INVESTMENT P. Trustfull color *Forbes* v200 no3 p96 S 28 2017

Economic development—Texas

Oil and WATER R. G. RATCLIFFE *Texas Monthly* v45 no9 p27 S 2017

Economic development—United States

Americans Can Unify Around Economic Growth T. J. DONOHUE *Weekly Standard* v22 no11 p9 N 21 2016

APPENDIX A REPORT TO THE PRESIDENT ON THE ACTIVITIES OF THE COUNCIL OF ECONOMIC ADVISERS DURING 2015 *Economic Indicators* p381 O 2016

Back to Work B. COVERT color *New Republic* v248 no8/9 p16 Ag/S 2017

Cut the Payroll Tax J. C. CAPRETTA *National Review* v69 no19 p22 O 16 2017

THE ECONOMIC BENEFITS OF INVESTING IN U.S. INFRASTRUCTURE *Economic Indicators* p251 S 2016

Economic Growth Isn't Over, but It Doesn't Create Jobs Like It Used To M. Ford *Harvard Business Review Digital Articles* p2 Mr 14 2016

Economics is still struggling with its self-conception after the financial crisis — a disaster that economists were supposed to foresee but didn't J. Lanchester *New York Times Magazine* p14 F 12 2017

A Growth Agenda to Unite All Americans T. J. DONOHUE *Weekly Standard* v22 no18 p9 Ja 16 2017

HOW BAD IS THE GREAT AMERICAN SLOWDOWN? J. PETHOKOUKIS *Commentary* v142 no3 p12 O 2016

The irreversible momentum of clean energy B. Obama color *Science* v355 no6321 p126 Ja 13 2017

Let's Grow: Ideas to Get Our Economy Moving T. J. DONOHUE

and M. Luca *Harvard Business Review Digital Articles* p2 O 29 2015

Economics—News briefs

Americas K. Stock color *Bloomberg Businessweek* no4536 p10 S 4 2017

IN BRIEF K. Stock bw color graph *Bloomberg Businessweek* no4541 p8 O 9 2017

INDIA'S SICKENING AND IMMORAL MOVE S. FORBES *Forbes* v199 no1 p15 Ja 24 2017

Ups K. Stock color *Bloomberg Businessweek* no4494 p15 O 10 2016

Economics—Religious aspects—Buddhism

A More Mindful Economy C. BROWN *American Scholar* v86 no2 p14 Spr 2017

Economics—Statistical methods

See also

Economic indicators

Big-Data Gurus See What the Cadres Don't *Bloomberg Businessweek* no4502 p24 D 5 2016

REAL NUMBERS A. Davidson cartoon *New Yorker* v93 no7 p37 Ap 3 2017

Economics—United States

Pathways to Middle-Skill Allied Health Care Occupations B. K. FROGNER and S. M. SKILLMAN chart *Issues in Science & Technology* v33 no1 p52 Fall 2016

Economides, Aris

Distribution and clinical impact of functional variants in 50,726 whole-exome sequences from the DiscovEHR study chart graph *Science* v354 no6319 paaf6814-1 D 23 2016

Economists

50 Years Ago an Economist Worried About Unchecked Corporate Power. Here's What His Theory Got Wrong J. Gans *Harvard Business Review Digital Articles* p2 2017

Economics is still struggling with its self-conception after the financial crisis — a disaster that economists were supposed to foresee but didn't J. Lanchester *New York Times Magazine* p14 F 12 2017

AN ECONOMIST GOES TO SHANGHAI D. N. MCCLOSKEY color *Reason* v49 no2 p10 Je 2017

Leading in a 20-Year Winter M. Funkhouser *Governing* v30 no2 p59 N 2016

Economists—Attitudes

What Counts as Climate Consensus? D. Sylvan, P. Howard et al *National Review* v69 no11 p2 Je 12 2017

Economists—Political activity

PETER NAVARRO, TRADE WARRIOR P. COY, M. Jamrisko et al color *Bloomberg Businessweek* no4521 p54 My 8 2017

Economists—United States

The Architect of the Radical Right S. TANENHAUS color *Atlantic* v320 no1 p40 Jl/Ag 2017

CHINA'S CHILDHOOD EXPERIMENT D. Normile color diag *Science* v357 no6357 p1226 S 22 2017

Thomas Crombie Schelling (1921–2016) R. Zeckhauser color *Science* v355 no6327 p800 F 24 2017

Economy, Elizabeth C.

History With Chinese Characteristics color *Foreign Affairs* v96 no4 p141 Jl/Ag 2017

Economy travel

A TIERED APPROACH TO ECONOMY CLASS M. CROSS color *Kiplinger's Personal Finance* v71 no2 p16 F 2017

Ecosystem dynamics

Beyond the roots of human inaction: Fostering collective effort toward ecosystem conservation E. Amel, C. Manning et al color diag *Science* v356 no6335 p275 Ap 21 2017

ECOSYSTEM EARTH [Cover story] S. Vignieri and J. Fahrenkamp-Uppenbrink color *Science* v356 no6335 p258 Ap 21 2017

Ecosystem management as a wicked problem R. DeFries and H. Nagendra chart color diag *Science* v356 no6335 p265 Ap 21 2017

The interaction of human population, food production, and biodiversity protection E. Crist, C. Mora et al color diag graph *Science* v356 no6335 p260 Ap 21 2017

Passing the point of no return D. Seekell bibl graph *Science* v354 no6316 p1109-C D 2 2016

Ecosystem health

Beyond the roots of human inaction: Fostering collective effort

toward ecosystem conservation E. Amel, C. Manning et al color diag *Science* v356 no6335 p275 Ap 21 2017

Ecosystem management as a wicked problem R. DeFries and H. Nagendra chart color diag *Science* v356 no6335 p265 Ap 21 2017

Expert eavesdroppers occasionally catch a break E. Quill *Science News* v192 no1 p2 Ag 5 2017

Ecosystem management

ECOSYSTEM EARTH [Cover story] S. Vignieri and J. Fahrenkamp-Uppenbrink color *Science* v356 no6335 p258 Ap 21 2017

Expanding the Portfolio: Conserving Nature's Masterpieces in a Changing World R. J. HOBBS, E. S. HIGGS et al *BioScience* v67 no6 p568 Je 2017

The interaction of human population, food production, and biodiversity protection E. Crist, C. Mora et al color diag graph *Science* v356 no6335 p260 Ap 21 2017

National Ecosystem Assessments in Europe: A Review M. SCHRÖTER, C. BROWN et al chart *BioScience* v66 no10 p813 O 1 2016

Rebuilding the Home of the "People of the Forest" L. Seventko *American Forests* v122 no3 p7 Fall 2016

Why Earth Optimism? A. Balmford and N. Knowlton color *Science* v356 no6335 p225 Ap 21 2017

Ecosystem management—International cooperation

An ecosystem-based deep-ocean strategy R. Danovaro, J. Aguzzi et al bibl color map *Science* v355 no6324 p452 F 3 2017

Ecosystem services

See also

Payments for ecosystem services

Green accounting J. SALZMAN *Issues in Science & Technology* v33 no2 p16 Wint 2017

Human Well-Being and Historical Ecosystems: The Environmentalist's Paradox Revisited L. E. DELGADO and V. H. MARÍN *BioScience* v67 no1 p5 Ja 2017

Incorporating Sociocultural Phenomena into Ecosystem-Service Valuation: The Importance of Critical Pluralism C. J. VAN RIPER, A. C. LANDON et al *BioScience* v67 no3 p233 Mr 2017

National Ecosystem Assessments in Europe: A Review M. SCHRÖTER, C. BROWN et al chart *BioScience* v66 no10 p813 O 1 2016

Pricing an ecosystem M. SAGOFF *Issues in Science & Technology* v33 no1 p11 Fall 2016

Toward a national, sustained U.S. ecosystem assessment S. T. Jackson, C. S. Duke et al bibl color *Science* v354 no6314 p838 N 18 2016

When, Where, and How Nature Matters for Ecosystem Services: Challenges for the Next Generation of Ecosystem Service Models J. T. RIEB, R. CHAPLIN-KRAMER et al *BioScience* v67 no9 p820 S 2017

Ecosystems

9 PERMACULTURE PRACTICES: Apply permaculture to your land to nurture its natural features J. Bloom *Mother Earth News* no282 p22 Je/Jl 2017

Birthday Bioblitzes D. Ireland color *Canadian Wildlife* v23 no2 p30 My/Je 2017

Collaborative environmental governance: Achieving collective action in social-ecological systems Ö. Bodin color *Science* v357 no6352 p659 Ag 18 2017

High Consequences J. WHEELWRIGHT color map *Discover* v38 no7 p50 S 2017

How an Ecosystem Mindset Can Help People and Organizations Succeed J. Geraci *Harvard Business Review Digital Articles* p2 My 12 2016

I don't have a favorite place R. STIEVE *Arizona Highways* v93 no11 p2 N 2017

Merging paleobiology with conservation biology to guide the future of terrestrial ecosystems A. D. Barnosky, E. A. Hadly et al color *Science* v355 no6325 p594 F 10 2017

Opening Arctic passageways will shake up ecosystems S. Milius color *Science News* v190 no13 p23 D 24 2016

Positive biodiversity-productivity relationship predominant in global forests Jingjing Liang, T. W. Crowther et al bibl chart graph map *Science* v354 no6309 paaf8957-1 O 14 2016

Technology and the Great Outdoors: How an LED sign is aiding the fight against aquatic invasive species J. Bern *Parks & Recreation* v52 no5 p52 My 2017

Translating Regime Shifts in Shallow Lakes into Changes in Ecosystem Functions and Services S. HILT, S. BROTHERS et al *BioScience* v67 no10 p928 O 2017

Treating Arctic Ecosystems as Systems H. P. Huntington color *Environment* v59 no4 p34 Jl-Ag 2017

WHERE HAVE ALL THE INSECTS GONE? G. Vogel color graph *Science* v356 no6338 p576 My 12 2017

Ecstasy (Drug)

ENLISTING MARIJUANA AND MDMA TO FIGHT PTSD J. SULLUM color *Reason* v49 no6 p32 N 2017

Ecstasy (Drug)—Therapeutic use

Dance floor drug could treat PTSD color *Science* v357 no6354 p850 S 1 2017

Ecstasy (Psychology)

THE AGONY AND ECSTASY OF OT J. Niesen color *Sports Illustrated* v125 no16 p48 N 14 2016

Ecuador

A PIPELINE RUNS THROUGH IT T. CLYNES *Audubon* v118 no6 p18 Wint 2016

Ecuador—Environmental conditions

PACHAMAMA'S BLOOD G. Raygorodetsky color *Earth Island Journal* v32 no3 p34 Aut 2017

Eczema—Prevention

HEALING WATERS M. M. GOLDSTEIN color *Martha Stewart Living* no271 p36 Ja/F 2017

Eczema—Treatment

EASE ECZEMA A. Constantinides color *Amazing Wellness* v8 no6 p38 Early Winter2016

Eddaoudi, Mohamed

Hydrolytically stable fluorinated metal-organic frameworks for energy-efficient dehydration diag *Science* v356 no6339 p731 My 19 2017

Eddie Bauer Inc.

Keep 'Em Rollin' C. CASWELL *Boating World* v38 no3 p14 Mr 2017

A Pack Perfected M. GOULET cartoon *Popular Mechanics* p24 D 2016/Ja 2017

Eddie the Eagle (Film)

BEST OF FILM J. Fuchs color *Sports Illustrated* v125 no18 p46 D 5 2016

NEWLY AVAILABLE MOVIES M. FELL *TV Guide* v64 no48 p46 N 21 2016

Eddies

See also

Vortex motion

Leaf Swirls L. ALBANESE color *Backpacker* p35 O 2017

Eddings, Lexi

A Coldwater Warm Hearts Wedding *Publishers Weekly* v264 no14 p59 Ap 3. 2017

EDDY, MELISSA

Brave New World *New York Times Upfront* v149 no5 p12 N 21 2016

Eddy, Michael S.

Affecting Effects *Stage Directions* v30 no5 p2 My 2017

Another Opening... Finally!: Broadway's Oldest Theater, The Hudson, Returns as Broadway's Newest Space *Stage Directions* v30 no6 p30 Je 2017

Career is the Operative Word *Stage Directions* v30 no4 p2 Ap 2017

Creative Motion *Stage Directions* v30 no2 p22 F 2017

DESIGNING the undefinable *Stage Directions* v30 no8 p18 Ag 2017

Early Days *Stage Directions* v29 no10 p12 O 2016

Enter Stage Right . . *Stage Directions* v30 no3 p2 Mr 2017

Friends with a Needle and Thread can Save a Marriage *Stage Directions* v30 no8 p2 Ag 2017

A Great Foundation *Stage Directions* v30 no8 p12 Ag 2017

The Learning Curve of Theater *Stage Directions* v30 no10 p2 O 2017

managing the ephemeral *Stage Directions* v30 no10 p8 O 2017

Muslin, Paint and Light *Stage Directions* v30 no4 p18 Ap 2017

Production Partners *Stage Directions* v30 no7 p3 Jl 1 2017

Profile *Stage Directions* v30 no3 p20 Mr 2017

Projecting the Reflected Soul: San Francisco Opera's Mirror Solution for Don Giovanni *Stage Directions* v30 no9 p16 S 2017

Quick Change: Costume Designer Paloma Young takes us back to the 1940s *Stage Directions* v30 no6 p22 Je 2017

SOAR LIKE AN Eagle: Opera Theatre of St. Louis? production of Titus takes light *Stage Directions* v30 no9 p18 S 2017

Summer Catch-Up *Stage Directions* v30 no9 p2 S 2017

We Are Connected *Stage Directions* v30 no6 p2 Je 2017

Westward Journey *Stage Directions* v29 no11 p36 N 2016

Eddy, Norah

Decode the Fish Counter A. C. Shilton color *Men's Health* v32 no2 p58 Mr 2017

Edegran, Lars

Lured to New Orleans J. Berry color *New Orleans Magazine* v51 no6 p52 Ap 2017

Edelbrock, Vic, Jr., 1936-2017

A HOT RODDING Hero: THE LEGACY OF VIC EDELBROCK JR T. Taylor bw color *Hot Rod* v70 no11 p66 N 2017

Edelman, Benjamin

Competing with Platforms That Ignore the Law *Harvard Business Review Digital Articles* p2 Mr 25 2016

Digital Business Models Should Have to Follow the Law, Too *Harvard Business Review Digital Articles* p2 Ja 6 2015

The Online Ad Scams Every Marketer Should Watch Out For *Harvard Business Review Digital Articles* p2 O 13 2015

Uber Can't Be Fixed—It's Time for Regulators to Shut It Down *Harvard Business Review Digital Articles* p1 Je 21 2017

Edelman, David C.

A Step-by-Step Plan to Improve CMO-COO Collaboration *Harvard Business Review Digital Articles* p2 Ja 28 2015

EDELMAN, ERIC

Cheney Was Right color *Weekly Standard* v23 no5 p27 O 9 2017

Erdogan's Counter-Revolution [Cover story] color *Weekly Standard* v22 no32 p26 My 1 2017

Restoring Solvency color *Weekly Standard* v22 no25 p23 Mr 6 2017

Trump's Nuclear Tweets color *Weekly Standard* v22 no18 p24 Ja 16 2017

What Happened in Hamburg cartoon *Weekly Standard* v22 no43 p10 Jl 24 2017

Edelman, Ezra, 1974-

The Case of O.J. Simpson L. Moore bw color *New York Review of Books* v63 no16 p75 O 27 2016

Edelman, Gilad

All Criminal Justice Reform Is Local *Washington Monthly* p2 Ja/F 2017

Can the ACLU Stop Trump? color *Washington Monthly* v49 no3-5 p16 Mr-My 2017

A COLLEGE ADVISER IN EVERY SCHOOL color *Washington Monthly* v49 no9/10 p62 S/O 2017

The Sixteen Most Innovative People in Higher Education *Washington Monthly* p1 S/O 2016

Weak! cartoon color *Washington Monthly* v49 no6-8 p24 Je-Ag 2017

EDELSON, CHRIS

Don't Wait for Nuremberg *In These Times* v41 no4 p13 Ap 2017

Is Russia a Red Herring? *In These Times* v41 no3 p12 Mr 2017

EDELSTEIN, DAVID

7. See The Films of Martin Brest *New York* v50 no7 p88 Ap 3 2017

Bard on a Bus img *New York* v49 no26 p88 D 26 2016

Big Kill Hunting img *New York* v50 no18 p84 S 4 2017

Burning Questions: The team behind Zero Dark Thirty revisits torture--this time in 1960s Detroit img *New York* v50 no15 p68 Jl 24 2017

Dazed and Bereaved img *New York* v50 no8 p132 Ap 17 2017

Dead Man on Campus img *New York* v49 no15 p86 Jl 25 2016

Disrupting Widowhood: Dead loved ones come back as holograms in Marjorie Prime img *New York* v50 no16 p108 Ag 7 2017

Full Pardon img *New York* v49 no19 p94 S 19 2016

Gradations of Badness: The Exception pays little fealty to the history of Kaiser Wilhelm, but, oh, that glorious acting img *New York* v50 no11 p122 My 29 2017

Lovably Unlikable img *New York* v50 no6 p85 Mr 20 2017

Nat Turner's Confessions img *New York* v49 no20 p127 O 3 2016

Not Without My Mother img *New York* v49 no25 p132 D 12 2016

Slow Burn img *New York* v49 no23 p82 N 14 2016

The Ten Best Movies of the Year img *New York* v49 no25 p116 D 12 2016

To Do img *New York* p72 Ja 23 2017

To Do img *New York* v49 no20 p136 O 3 2016

To Do: Twenty-five things to see, hear, watch, and read img *New York* v50 no10 p106 My 15 2017

Trapped in History img *New York* p69 Ja 23 2017

The Umbrellas of Silver Lake img *New York* v49 no24 p148 N 28 2016

Universal Translator img *New York* v49 no22 p104 O 31 2016

Where Do Xenomorphs Come From? Alien: Covenant traces the origin of species img *New York* v50 no10 p96 My 15 2017

White Fright img *New York* p75 F 20 2017

Edelstein, Eve

Dr. Eve Edelstein A. FIXSEN *Architectural Record* v205 no7 p35 Jl 2017

EDELSTEIN, KEN

OUR RIVER *Atlanta* v57 no4 p58 Ag 2017

Edelstein, Lisa

Fitting a family together color *Redbook* p112 S 2017

Edelstein, Robert

DALE JR.'S NASCAR COMEBACK color *TV Guide* v65 no7 p50 F 13 2017

Edema

I wish I didn't feel so swell color *AARP: The Magazine* v30 no6A p12 O/N 2017

TAKING STOCK C. Barakat and M. Freckleton color *Equus* no473 p16 F 2017

Edema—Prevention

Compression stockings *Mayo Clinic Health Letter* v35 no2 p7 F 2017

Eden (TV program)

BACK TO THE GARDEN S. KNIGHT cartoon color *New Yorker* v93 no26 p24 S 4 2017

Eden, Cynthia

After the Dark *Publishers Weekly* v264 no7 p56 F 13 2017

Eden, Lynn

Editorial board *Bulletin of the Atomic Scientists* v72 no6 pebi N 2016

Eden, Max

School Discipline Reform and Disorder *Education Digest* v83 no1 p22 S 2017

Eden, Meg

NECK SCARVES *Commonweal* v144 no11 p10 Je 16 2017

Eden Creamery LLC

NO SCOOP NECESSARY C. Battan color *Bloomberg Businessweek* no4498 p90 N 7 2016

Eden McCallum Ltd.

What Happens When All Employees Work When They Feel Like It F. Vermeulen *Harvard Business Review Digital Articles* p2 D 17 2014

Edenborough, Frank

Emergence and spread of a human-transmissible multidrug-resistant nontuberculous mycobacterium bibl diag graph *Science* v354 no6313 p751 N 11 2016

Edenfield, Jim

The SAILING SCENE color *Sail* v48 no10 p8 O 2017

EDENFIELD, TANNER

LUNAR BUCKS color graph *Outdoor Life* v224 no5 p87 Je/Jl 2017

Eder, Derek

HACK ATTACK R. O'CONNOR cartoon *Chicago* v66 no3 p40 Mr 2017

Eder, Jacob S.

Holocaust Angst: The Federal Republic of Germany and American Holocaust Memory Since the 1970s A. Moravcsik *Foreign Affairs* v96 no2 p177 Mr/Ap 2017

Edfors, Fredrik

A pathology atlas of the human cancer transcriptome diag *Science* v357 no6352 p660 Ag 18 2017

EDGAR, GRAHAM J.

Assessing National Biodiversity Trends for Rocky and Coral Reefs through the Integration of Citizen Science and Scientific Monitoring Programs *BioScience* v67 no2 p134 F 2017

Edgar, Jolene

15 Things You Need to Know About Sun Protection color *Health* v31 no5 p25 Je 2017

what's the deal with K-BEAUTY? *Better Homes & Gardens* v95 no1 p21 Ja 2017

Edgar, Timothy H.

Beyond Snowden: Privacy, Mass Surveillance, and the Struggle to Reform the NSA bw *Publishers Weekly* v264 no17 p77 Ap 24 2017

Edgcomb, Virginia

Life Dwells Deep Within Earth's Crust G. Schanker *Oceanus* v52 no1 p48 Summ 2016

Edge, John T.

A History of Southern Food H. CARRIGAN color *Publishers Weekly* v264 no17 p78 Ap 24 2017

THE POTLIKKER PAPERS J. BAINBRIDGE *Atlanta* v57 no1 p62 My 2017

Edge of Forever, The (Music)

Pesacov: The Edge of Forever D. J. Baker *Opera News* v81 no5 p55 N 2016

Edge of Seventeen, The (Film)

The Edge of Seventeen L. Greenblatt color *Entertainment Weekly* no1441 p42 N 25 2016

The New Crush D. Coggan color *Entertainment Weekly* no1440 p18 N 18 2016

Teen Angst With a New Edge S. Begley color *Time* v188 no22-23 p104 N/D 2016

TOP of HER Class N. Sperling color *Entertainment Weekly* no1440 p38 N 18 2016

Edge of the Shoal, The (Short story)

The Edge of the Shoal C. Jones cartoon *New Yorker* v92 no33 p72 O 17 2016

Edgerton, Anna

In Congress, It's Do-or-Die Time for the GOP cartoon *Bloomberg Businessweek* no4530 p39 Jl 17 2017

Edgerton, Joel, 1974-

GOINGS ON ABOUT TOWN color *New Yorker* v92 no36 p4 N 7 2016

It Comes at Night and the High Art of the New Horror S. Zacharek color *Time* v189 no23 p49 Je 19 2017

JOEL EDGERTON Z. BARON bw color *GQ: Gentlemen's Quarterly* v86 no12 p218 D 2016

Loving *New Yorker* v92 no38 p23 N 21 2016

One Couple's 'Criminal' Marriage Y. VILLARREAL *Advocate* no1088 p17 D 2016/Ja 2017

Stay-at-Home Heroes R. Alleva color *Commonweal* v144 no1 p26 Ja 6 2017

Edges (Geometry)

GET TO THE POINT M. VINCENT and G. BETHGE cartoon *Outdoor Life* v224 no2 p32 F/Mr 2017

Edgette, Frieda

Mindfulness Can Improve Strategy, Too *Harvard Business Review Digital Articles* p2 My 2 2016

Edgewater (Chicago, Ill.)

EDGEWATER'S LUXE BOOM M. LAWLER color *Chicago* v66 no7 p16 Jl 2017

Edgington, Jane

RIVER REBORN *New York State Conservationist* v71 no4 p10 F 2017

Ediacaran fossils

LIFE ON THE EDGE T. Monmaney *Smithsonian* v48 no1 p56 Ap 2017

Edible fats & oils

See also

Butter

Food—Fat content

GOOD EGGS *Amazing Wellness* v8 no2 p8 Spr 2016

In the SUNSET KITCHEN color *Sunset* v238 no1 p90 Ja 2017

SMARTER FATS J. Bowden color *Amazing Wellness* v8 no2 p36 Spr 2016

Edible fats & oils—Health aspects

THE SKINNY ON FATS A. OGLETHORPE color *Better Homes & Gardens* v95 no4 p148 Ap 2017

Edible greens

BEYOND THE KALE M. Irvine and E. Johnson color *Sunset* v239 no4 p46 O 2017

green foods supplements V. Tweed color *Amazing Wellness* v8 no2 p12 Spr 2016

Little Big Time A. STANEK color *Bon Appetit* v62 no4 p28 Ap 2017

vegetable LOVE *Martha Stewart Living* no267 p106 S 2016

Edible insects

BURGER WITH FLIES T. PHILPOTT cartoon *Mother Jones* v42 no2 p64 Mr/Ap 2017

Ground-Up Insects Could Nourish Millions J. DETWILER color *Popular Mechanics* p22 My 2017

Edible landscaping

Good Enough to Eat E. Millard color *Log Home Living* v34 no4 p36 My 2017

Edible mushrooms

Hearty Italian Ragu color *Vegetarian Today* no2 p18 Ap 2017

SHOW-ME Flavor color *Missouri Life* v44 no3 p76 My 2017

Spring For Risotto color *Vegetarian Today* no2 p16 Ap 2017

Edible mushrooms—Therapeutic use

Fungus of Youth [Cover story] C. MIHELL color *Walrus* v14 no4 p20 My 2017

Edible plants

See also

Edible greens

Ancient Super Grain color *Vegetarian Today* no2 p28 Ap 2017

EDIBLE TREES J. V. TRAIL *American Forests* v123 no1 p16 Wint/Spr 2017

Go Green for Speed color *Health* v31 no1 p11 Ja 2017

power GREENS A. TUST color *Yoga Journal* no291 p21 My 2017

Super Supper Salads K. SHERWOOD *Nutrition Action Health Letter* v44 no6 p12 Jl/Ag 2017

Edie Parker (Company)

Brett Heyman color *Architectural Digest* v74 no4 p60 Ap 2017

Why I Love MY EDIE PARKER CLUTCH T. P. Henson color *InStyle* v24 no5 p262 My 2017

Edimax Technology Co. Ltd.

EDIMAX AC1200 DUAL BAND WI-FI USB ADAPTER G. FLEISHMAN color *Macworld - Digital Edition* v34 no6 p46 Je 2017

Edinburgh (Scotland)—Description & travel

Bonnie Scotland by Train *British Heritage Travel* v38 no2 p16 Mr/Ap 2017

EDINBURGH: Take a stroll around Auld Reekie, Scotland's photogenic capital city D. Huntley color *British Heritage Travel* v38 no5 p62 S/O 2017

Great British Holiday Traditions *British Heritage Travel* v37 no6 p14 N/D 2016

Edinger, Scott

Don't Obsess Over Getting Everything Done Before a Vacation *Harvard Business Review Digital Articles* p2 Je 9 2015

How to Get Your Salespeople to Execute Your Strategy *Harvard Business Review Digital Articles* p2 Mr 1 2016

Sales Reps, Stop Asking Leading Questions *Harvard Business Review Digital Articles* p2 Mr 17 2017

Sales Teams Need More (and Better) Coaching *Harvard Business Review Digital Articles* p2 My 8 2015

Edison, Emily

BEST FOODS FOR RUNNERS [Cover story] cartoon color *Runner's World* v52 no3 p54 Ap 2017

Edison, Thomas A. (Thomas Alva), 1847-1931

EDISONIAN DEMOCRACY A. Valiunas *Claremont Review of Books* v17 no1 p89 Wint 2016/2017

the new lighting HIGH TECH, HISTORICAL REVIVAL M. E. POLSON chart color *Old House Journal* v45 no1 p40 F 2017

THOUGHTS FROM Our Readers bw *Forbes* v200 no3 p180 S 28 2017

Editing

See also

Motion picture editing

Photographs—Editing

Style manuals for printing

Churchill Challenged *Commentary* v143 no4 p12 Ap 2017

Unknown Continents: A Conversation with Patricia Zimmermann and Scott MacDonald, authors of The Flaherty: Decades in the Cause of Independent Cinema G. Yue *Film Quarterly* v71 no1 p104 Fall 2017

Editing software

PDFPEN 9 AND PDFPENPRO 9: EDITING APPS GET SOLID ENHANCEMENTS OVER PREVIOUS VERSIONS G. FLEISHMAN color *Macworld - Digital Edition* v34 no6 p21 Je 2017

Éditions Barzakh (Company)

Algeria's New Imprint A. KAPLAN bw color *Nation* v304 no11 p20 Ap 3 2017

Editorial writing

INTRAMURAL POLITICS A. Beaujon *Washingtonian Magazine* v52 no2 p53 N 2016

Speak for Yourselves E. Alterman il *Nation* v303 no16 p6 O 17 2016

Editors

See also

Fashion editors

Periodical editors

Women editors

Celebrating 35 Years of Tufts Health & Nutrition Letter: And the legacy of the newsletter's founder, Stanley N. Gershojf, PhD *Tufts University Health & Nutrition Letter* v35 no7 p6 S 2017

Exit, Pursued by a Bear J. Coakley *Stage Directions* v30 no2 p2 F 2017

THE FERNDALE ENTERPRISE S. Hepworth bw *Columbia Journalism Review* v56 no1 p111 Spr 2017

An island moneymaker that knows everybody's secrets B. Wieners *Columbia Journalism Review* v56 no1 p80 Spr 2017

the kind of mom i am L. Vaccariello *Parents* v92 no2 p10 F 2017

MIDLIFE CRISIS DEPT.: FORE! D. Owen bw *New Yorker* v93 no33 p36 O 23 2017

a note from Kristen K. Bell *Parents* v91 no11 p8 N 2016

The Online Troll Patrol A. SIMMONS *Reader's Digest* v189 no1127 p12 F 2017

The poet editor of West Marin B. Tsui color *Columbia Journalism Review* v56 no1 p74 Spr 2017

Staying Alive L. PICKER color *Publishers Weekly* v263 no45 p34 N 7 2016

Victoria Camblin J. BAINBRIDGE *Atlanta* v57 no4 p46 Ag 2017

WAYPOINT: COLD BAY, AK color *Outdoor Life* v224 no9 p9 N 2017

WHY I OWE MY NEW JOB TO ELVIS B. RILEY *Atlanta* v57 no6 p18 O 2017

word play m. ferrentino color *Bike Magazine* v24 no4 p54 Je 2017

Editors—United States

BREITBART'S (OTHER) MAN IN THE WHITE HOUSE L. MULLINS *Washingtonian Magazine* v52 no9 p70 Je 2017

EDLEFSEN, JOYCE DRIGGS

NOT REALLY LOOKING TO GROW *Idaho Magazine* v16 no2 p33 N 2016

SUGAR CITY: SWEET TOWN, IDAHO *Idaho Magazine* v16 no11 p32 Ag 2017

Edmans, Alex

28 Years of Stock Market Data Shows a Link Between Employee Satisfaction and Long-Term Value *Harvard Business Review Digital Articles* p2 Mr 24 2016

The Answer to Short-Termism Isn't Asking Investors to Be Patient *Harvard Business Review Digital Articles* p2 Jl 18 2017

Performance-Based Pay for Executives Still Works *Harvard Business Review Digital Articles* p2 F 23 2016

Stop Making CEO Pay a Political Issue *Harvard Business Review Digital Articles* p2 Jl 18 2016

Edmond, Alfred, Jr.

3 Reality Checks You Must Face To Fix Your Finances color *Black Enterprise* v47 no4 p14 N/D 2016

Financial Intimacy: Is Your Relationship Ready? color *Black Enterprise* v47 no3 p24 O 2016

THE FIRST EVER BLACK MEN bw color *Black Enterprise* v47 no7 p40 My/Je 2017

PARENTS, PROTECT YOUR WEALTH [Cover story] cartoon color *Black Enterprise* v47 no3 p45 O 2016

Edmonds (Wash.)

Northwest Passage M. SITZ *Architectural Record* v205 no7 p104 Jl 2017

Edmonds, Patricia

All Moms, No Dads color *National Geographic* v230 no5 p30 N 2016

CRUSTACEAN ASSIGNATION color *National Geographic* v232 no1 p29 Jl 2017

DRY AS DEATH color *National Geographic* v231 no3 p130 Mr 2017

EXPLORER HONOR TO BRIAN SKERRY color *National Geographic* v232 no1 p24 Jl 2017

FISH'S FECUNDITY A BOON TO LABS color *National Geographic* v232 no3 p25 S 2017

GETTING A GRIP ON ADVENTURE color *National Geographic* v232 no1 p22 Jl 2017

IN SEARCH OF A RED-HOT LOVER color *National Geographic* v231 no6 p29 Je 2017

Made for Each Other color *National Geographic* v230 no4 p31 O 2016

A ONE-PARENT FAMILY, LITERALLY color *National Geographic* v232 no5 p29 N 2017

ONE PART HE, ONE PART SHE color *National Geographic* v231 no1 p26 Ja 2017

Parental Leave On Dads' Terms color *National Geographic* v231 no1 p104 Ja 2017

ROMANTIC ATTACHMENT color *National Geographic* v230 no6 p25 D 2016

SEX THAT WORKS UP A LATHER color *National Geographic* v231 no3 p29 Mr 2017

SHE MATES, HE INCUBATES color *National Geographic* v231 no5 p29 My 2017

A SLEIGHFUL OF SANTAS, SURVEYED color *National Geographic* v230 no6 p12 D 2016

THROWING HER WEIGHT AROUND color *National Geographic* v231 no2 p29 F 2017

WHEN SEX IS SO RIGHT (OR LEFT) color *National Geographic* v231 no4 p29 Ap 2017

Edmondson, Amy C.

Get Rid of Unhealthy Competition on Your Team *Harvard Business Review Digital Articles* p2 Je 26 2015

Improving On-the-Fly Teamwork in Health Care *Harvard Business Review Digital Articles* p2 N 30 2016

The Kinds of Teams Health Care Needs *Harvard Business Review Digital Articles* p2 D 16 2015

Why Top-Down Management Doesn't Work in the Fight Against Ebola *Harvard Business Review Digital Articles* p2 D 16 2014

Edmonstone-West, Barry

A 5-Step Process for Reorganizing After a Merger *Harvard Business Review Digital Articles* p2 D 21 2016

Edmonton Oilers (Hockey team)

The Arrival A. Prewitt color *Sports Illustrated* v126 no7 p70 Mr 6 2017

Division of net assets M. FRISCOLANTI color *Maclean's* v130 no10 p13 N 2017

Edmunds, Kristy

Master of Her Domain M. WAKIM *Los Angeles Magazine* p60 Ja 2017

Edmundson, Mark

The Doctor's Discontents: A harshly critical new biography of the father of psychotherapy *American Scholar* v86 no4 p124 Aut 2017

Edney, Anna

Is a Cigarette Without the Nicotine Still A Smoke? cartoon graph *Bloomberg Businessweek* no4533 p37 Ag 7 2017

Repeal and _____ *Bloomberg Businessweek* no4509 p22 Ja 30 2017

EDNIE, CAROLINE

Under Fyne skies color *House Beautiful* p66 Ag 2017

Ed Palermo Big Band, The (Performer)

The Great Un-American Songbook, Volumes I & II Hadley color *Downbeat* v84 no6 p68 Je 2017

Edqvist, Per-Henrik

A pathology atlas of the human cancer transcriptome diag *Science* v357 no6352 p660 Ag 18 2017

Edrioasteroidea

Ancient fossils feature tube feet L. HAMERS color *Science News* v192 no6 p12 O 14 2017

Edsall, Thomas Byrne

Soundbites *Extra!* v30 no7 p2 S 2017

Ed Sullivan Show, The (TV program)

Funny Never Gets Old R. Love color *AARP: The Magazine* v60 no4A p2 Je/Jl 2017

Eduardo Fairbairn, Carlos

READER GALLERY bw color *Astronomy* v45 no11 p72 N 2017

Education

See also

Aeronautics education

After school programs
Art education
Arts education
Career education
Catholic education
Community education
Consumer education
Continuing education
Cooking education
Creationism education
Curricula (Courses of study)
Dance education
Education of minorities
Educational equalization
Educational programs
Employment & education
Evolutionary theories study & teaching
General education
Group work in education
High technology & education
Higher education
Humanistic education
Humanities education
Internship programs
Learning
Literacy
Literacy education
Mass media & education
Mathematics education
Military education
Multilingual education
Music education
Occupational training
Picture books for children & education
Racism in education
Religious education
School choice
Science education
Secondary education
Social skills education
Special education
STEAM education
STEM education
Teachers
Technology education
Vocational education

5 ways to give the gift of health *Harvard Health Letter* v42 no1 p7 N 2016

BACK TO SCHOOL V. K. De Luca color *Essence* v48 no5 p10 S 2017

CHANGING THE WORLD KIDS SEE N. Strochlic color *National Geographic* v231 no3 p24 Mr 2017

CHAPTER 4 INEQUALITY IN EARLY CHILDHOOD AND EFFECTIVE PUBLIC POLICY INTERVENTIONS *Economic Indicators* p153 O 2016

DISRUPTION IN THE CLASSROOM R. Alrubail *Literacy Today (2411-7862)* v34 no5 p36 Mr/Ap 2017

Fall Back in Love With Your Job G. Roberts-Grey color *Essence* v47 no10 p71 F 2017

Few Women Run the Nation's School Districts. Why? D. R. SUPERVILLE *Education Digest* v82 no6 p14 F 2017

HANDING OVER THE PEN: Empowering students by encouraging them to write their own stories S. Jennis *Literacy Today (2411-7862)* v35 no1 p36 Jl/Ag 2017

LET'S START AT THE VERY BEGINNING S. HELD color *Indianapolis Monthly* v41 no2 p138 S 2017

LOST IN TRANSLATION H. MACGREGOR *Los Angeles Magazine* v61 no11 p140 N 2016

NETWORKING ISN'T JUST FOR WORK R. W. GOODE color *Black Enterprise* v47 no8 p34 Jl/Ag 2017

PLCs on steroids Moving teacher practice to the center of data teams M. J. Wasta chart il *Phi Delta Kappan* v98 no5 p67 F 2017

Potty Relief for Tired Trainers color *Parents* v92 no7 p30 Jl 2017

SCREEN BEE A. Gopnik cartoon *New Yorker* v92 no39 p70 N 28 2016

Teach the Children Well: Money lessons for the grandkids J. Chatzky and K. Hultgren cartoon color *AARP: The Magazine* v60 no5A p27 Ag/S 2017

Education & globalization

A ROAD MAP TO THE GLOBAL UNIVERSITY W. I. BRUSTEIN map *Phi Kappa Phi Forum* v97 no2 p16 Summ 2017

Education & politics—United States

Harvard's Shame J. NICHOLS *Nation* v305 no8 p4 O 9 2017

Education & state

See also

Endowments

School autonomy

Islamic Schools Face the Future: Independent schools are usually not required to adhere to education policy regulations if they receive no state or federal government funds S. BUKER *Islamic Horizons* v46 no3 p38 My/Je 2017

Education & state—Brazil

Brazil Has a School Problem F. Moura and J. Brice diag *Bloomberg Businessweek* no4513 p24 Mr 6 2017

Education & state—California

Standing against Islamophobia in California School Curricula M. THANGE *Islamic Horizons* v45 no6 p32 N/D 2016

Education & state—United States

Betsy DeVos: The Investor Who Got a High Return J. Nichols color *Progressive* v81 no7 p57 O/N 2017

Blending In L. Lalami color *New York Times Magazine* p11 Ag 6 2017

A Chance for Choice: By appointing Betsy DeVos education secretary, President Trump shows he's listening to parents P. E. Peterson *Hoover Digest: Research & Opinion on Public Policy* no2 p152 Spr 2017

The Core of a Just Society C. Phenicie *Hoover Digest: Research & Opinion on Public Policy* no2 p146 Spr 2017

Design principles for new systems of assessment L. A. Shepard, W. R. Penuel et al color *Phi Delta Kappan* v98 no6 p47 Mr 2017

The Editor's Note J. Richardson *Phi Delta Kappan* v98 no6 p4 Mr 2017

FROM THE ARCHIVES cartoon *Reason* v48 no9 p70 F 2017

HAIL THE (ED) WORK-AROUND A. SHLAES *Forbes* v199 no4 p32 Ap 25 2017

Madam Secretary, help us improve social-emotional learning M. J. Elias, S. J. Nayman et al color *Phi Delta Kappan* v98 no8 p64 My 2017

The Miseducation of Liberals D. RAVITCH il *New Republic* v248 no6 p16 Je 2017

Solving the teacher shortage B. Berry and P. M. Shields color *Phi Delta Kappan* v98 no8 p8 My 2017

Ten Priorities for Education Policy [Cover story] F. M. HESS color *National Review* v68 no19 p30 O 24 2016

Use Your Words--And Your Ideas: Arguments over education have divided America. Here's how reformers can swap acrimony for action M. J. Petrilli *Hoover Digest: Research & Opinion on Public Policy* no2 p155 Spr 2017

Washington View M. Ferguson *Phi Delta Kappan* v98 no8 p72 My 2017

Who Moved My Teachers? P. CALDWELL cartoon *Mother Jones* v42 no2 p36 Mr/Ap 2017

Who's Picking Up the Education Tab? H. S. Edwards color *Time* v188 no16/17 p76 O 24 2016

Education & state—United States—States

Sticky schools A. Podolsky, T. Kini et al color graph *Phi Delta Kappan* v98 no8 p19 My 2017

Education & the military

NOT UP TO SNUFF? Soldier wannabes turned away for illiteracy B. CROWDER *Virginia Living* v15 no4 p27 Je 2017

Education, An (Short story)

AN EDUCATION M. Szabó *Harper's Magazine* p18 S 2017

Education conferences

OUR ORLANDO FIVE: Favorite highlights from ILA 2017--or, some of the best of what you may have missed! *Literacy Today (2411-7862)* v35 no2 p8 S/O 2017

Education ministers

Heavens to Betsy K. RIZGA, J. Vélez et al cartoon chart map *Mother Jones* v42 no2 p30 Mr/Ap 2017

Education of African Americans

See also

Segregation in education—United States

DIVIDING LINES N. HANNAH-JONES *New York Times Magazine* p40 S 10 2017

Education of ballet dancers

What's in a Diploma? S. WROTH *Dance Magazine* v91 no8 p33 Ag 2017

Education of black people

See also

Black students

Education of African Americans

THE WAY TO SURVIVE IT WAS TO MAKE A's M. SECRET *New York Times Magazine* p56 S 10 2017

Education of farmers

Precision: PAIN POINTS L. Bedord *Successful Farming* v115 no9 p43 Ag 2017

Education of girls

Pop Chart R. Bruner, C. Lang et al color *Time* v190 no7 p54 Ag 21 2017

Education of minorities

Without inclusion, diversity initiatives may not be enough C. Puritty, L. R. Strickland et al color *Science* v357 no6356 p1101 S 15 2017

Education of rich people

DOCTORATE, DEGREE OR DROPOUT? D. CAM and A. AU-YEUNG diag graph *Forbes* v200 no5 p24 N 14 2017

Education of special education teachers

The Editor's Note J. Richardson *Phi Delta Kappan* v98 no8 p4 My 2017

Education of teachers' assistants

Putting paraeducators on the path to teacher certification J. Morrison and L. Lightner color *Phi Delta Kappan* v98 no8 p43 My 2017

Education research

Grading on an Invisible Curve M. J. Petrilli *Hoover Digest: Research & Opinion on Public Policy* no1 p150 Wint 2017

Opening your door to research M. Zoch and A. D. David color *Phi Delta Kappan* v98 no3 p28 N 2016

Paths to Engagement: PROVOKING INTELLECTUAL FERMENT through Pedagogies of Social Participation W. M. Sullivan *Change* v49 no3 p52 My/Je 2017

Education savings accounts

One Small Step to College J. B. Wogan *Governing* v30 no6 p38 Mr 2017

School Choice and Equitable Services: Disability and Income Status and Program Participation *Congressional Digest* v96 no7 p9 S 2017

Education theory

BUZZWORTHY J. H. NEWMAN, J. STALL et al *Indianapolis Monthly* p14 N 2017

Educational acceleration—United States

Three and Out P. Thamel and T. Keith color *Sports Illustrated* v125 no16 p16 N 14 2016

Educational accountability

The best of both worlds J. Schneider, J. Feldman et al color *Phi Delta Kappan* v98 no3 p60 N 2016

Strategic accountability is key to making PLCs effective L. B. Easton chart il *Phi Delta Kappan* v98 no4 p43 D 2016/Ja 2017

Educational accountability—United States

Leadership J. P. Starr il *Phi Delta Kappan* v98 no6 p70 Mr 2017

Educational attainment

Christians among higher educated, though not in U.S L. Markoe color *Christian Century* v134 no2 p14 Ja 18 2017

More Than Just a Job J. B. Wogan *Governing* v30 no1 p46 O 2016

SISTER ACT G. FREKING *Cincinnati Magazine* v50 no4 p24 Ja 2017

When a Fancy Degree Scares Employers Away M. Staton *Harvard Business Review Digital Articles* p2 Ja 6 2015

Educational attainment—United States

Boys with the Same Behavior Problems as Girls Tend to Complete Less Schooling *Education Digest* v82 no8 p63 Ap 2017

The Education Gap T. ALBERTA color *National Review* v68 no19 p14 O 24 2016

Educational change

Classroom: Lisa Miller img *New York* v49 no21 p22 O 17 2016

The Editor's Note J. Richardson *Phi Delta Kappan* v98 no7 p4 Ap 2017

Leadership J. P. Starr color *Phi Delta Kappan* v98 no8 p70 My 2017

Research: How the Best School Leaders Create Enduring Change A. Hill, L. Mellon et al *Harvard Business Review Digital Articles* p2 S 14 2017

Time for teacher learning, planning critical for school reform E. G. Merritt color *Phi Delta Kappan* v98 no4 p31 D 2016/Ja 2017

WHAT CHANGES, WHAT STAYS THE SAME G. DENZINE il *Phi Kappa Phi Forum* v97 no2 p1 Summ 2017

Educational change—Great Britain

How to Turn Around a Failing School A. Hill, L. Mellon et al *Harvard Business Review Digital Articles* p2 Ag 5 2016

Educational change—United States

Leadership J. P. Starr il *Phi Delta Kappan* v98 no6 p70 Mr 2017

Solidarity and Struggle R. CONNIFF *Progressive* v81 no2 p5 F 2017

Ten Priorities for Education Policy [Cover story] F. M. HESS color *National Review* v68 no19 p30 O 24 2016

Will Higher Education Reform Become Another Ideological War Zone? P. GLASTRIS *Washington Monthly* v49 no9/10 p14 S/O 2017

Educational change—United States—Government policy

EDUCATION FOR SALE? L. DARLING-HAMMOND bw color *Nation* v304 no10 p16 Mr 27 2017

Educational coaching

Coaching to Evaluate Teachers [Cover story] K. E. FOUAD *Islamic Horizons* v46 no2 p26 Mr/Ap 2017

Educational cooperation

See also

Partnerships in education

A better research-practice partnership E. Henrick, M. A. Munoz et al color *Phi Delta Kappan* v98 no3 p23 N 2016

Partnerships Between Schools and Communities Promote Reading Success A. A. Arnett and S. J. Gaither *Education Digest* v83 no2 p57 O 2017

Educational counseling

A COLLEGE ADVISER IN EVERY SCHOOL G. Edelman color *Washington Monthly* v49 no9/10 p62 S/O 2017

Educational equalization

Class Dismissed [Cover story] W. VOEGELI color *National Review* v69 no12 p24 Je 26 2017

How School Desegregation Unraveled L. HANCOCK bw color *Nation* v303 no19 p16 N 7 2016

Leadership J. P. Starr il *Phi Delta Kappan* v99 no2 p72 O 2017

When choice fosters inequality J. B. Ayscue, G. Siegel-Hawley et al chart color graph il *Phi Delta Kappan* v98 no4 p49 D 2016/Ja 2017

Educational equalization—United States

Achieving Equity Amid Poverty P. D. SMITH *Education Digest* v82 no8 p45 Ap 2017

The burden of inequity — AND WHAT SCHOOLS CAN DO ABOUT IT V. Mayfield color *Phi Delta Kappan* v98 no5 p8 F 2017

Learning from schools that close opportunity gaps S. E. LaCour, A. York et al *Phi Delta Kappan* v99 no1 p8 S 2017

Washington View M. Ferguson *Phi Delta Kappan* v98 no3 p74 N 2016

Educational evaluation

See also

Students—Rating of

Teacher evaluation

Building a better measure of school quality J. Schneider, R. Jacobsen et al color il *Phi Delta Kappan* v98 no7 p43 Ap 2017

The VALUE of Assessment: Transforming the Culture of Learning T. L. Rhodes *Change* v48 no5 p36 S/O 2016

Educational films

Engage Students' Creativity Through Animated Whiteboard Video Project M. O'SHEA *Education Digest* v82 no7 p61 Mr 2017

Educational finance

See also

Government aid to education

Higher education—Finance

Public education financing

Tuition

Illinois budget impasse damaging state universities D. Kramer *Physics Today* v70 no6 p32 Je 2017

Make this the best year for every kid J. PRESS color *Redbook* p110 S 2017

Educational fundraising

Should Parents Be Expected To Donate To a Public School? K. A. Appiah *New York Times Magazine* p34 N 27 2016

Educational games

From Angry Birds to Particle Physics J. Kahn color *Bloomberg Businessweek* no4508 p30 Ja 23 2017

Educational innovations

See also

Alternative education

Educators Share 10 Best Teaching, Technology Practices M. LEVITT *Education Digest* v82 no8 p56 Ap 2017

Educational innovations—Congresses

Takeaways from the 2016 Blended and Personalized Learning Conference J. F. FISHER and J. WHITE *Education Digest* v82 no6 p42 F 2017

Educational innovations—Software

Beyond Surfing D. HARRELL cartoon *Education Digest* v82 no7 p32 Mr 2017

Educational law & legislation—United States

See also

Every Student Succeeds Act of 2015 (United States)

United States. Education Amendments of 1972. Title IX

United States. Elementary & Secondary Education Act of 1965

United States. No Child Left Behind Act of 2001

Evolution Education and State Politics J. P. CARR *BioScience* v67 no8 p687 Ag 2017

Educational law cases

Under the Law J. Underwood *Phi Delta Kappan* v99 no1 p44 S 2017

Educational leadership

See also

Teacher leadership

Consensual Sex Under Title IX M. LISSACK *USA Today Magazine* v145 no2864 p67 My 2017

Leadership J. P. Starr color *Phi Delta Kappan* v98 no8 p70 My 2017

The power of reflective action to build teacher efficacy T. Awkard color *Phi Delta Kappan* v98 no6 p53 Mr 2017

Research: How the Best School Leaders Create Enduring Change A. Hill, L. Mellon et al *Harvard Business Review Digital Articles* p2 S 14 2017

Educational leadership—United States

Leadership J. P. Starr *Phi Delta Kappan* v99 no1 p40 S 2017

Positive school leadership J. Murphy, K. S. Louis et al color *Phi Delta Kappan* v99 no1 p21 S 2017

What Does It TAKE? *Literacy Today (2411-7862)* v35 no2 p43 S/O 2017

Educational planning

See also

School administration

From Dissemination to Propagation: A New Paradigm for Education Developers J. E. Froyd, C. Henderson et al *Change* v49 no4 p35 Jl/Ag 2017

Mahmoud Ayed Rashdan An Empowering Leader 1939 - 2017 *Islamic Horizons* v46 no3 p8 My/Je 2017

Transcending Apathy Towards Writing: A Love Letter to Henry David Thoreau C. O'Sullivan Sachar *Change* v49 no4 p55 Jl/Ag 2017

Educational programs

See also

Literacy programs

Non-school educational programs

ALL AROUND Missouri color *Missouri Life* v44 no5 p85 Ag 2017

CAMP AVID S. MaHan *Washingtonian Magazine* v52 no5 p117 F 2017

GETTING SCHOOLED E. Plott *Washingtonian Magazine* v52 no1 p129 O 2016

GROWING LEADERS S. HENRY *Sierra* v101 no5 p44 S/O 2016

STEAM-POWERED READERS R. B. Jackson color *Literacy Today (2411-7862)* v34 no4 p14 Ja/F 2017

The Torch Bearer C. SHMERLER *Tennis* v52 no6 p56 N/D 2016

Edwards, Irene

BEHIND THE SCENES color *Sunset* v239 no3 p8 S 2017

FIESTA TIME color *Sunset* v238 no3 p4 Mr 2017

FOOD + MEMORY color *Sunset* v237 no5 p8 N 2016

THE FOUR-DAY REBOOT color *Sunset* v238 no2 p15 F 2017

Gather color *Sunset* v237 no5 p54 N 2016

HOLIDAY SPIRIT color *Sunset* v237 no6 p8 D 2016

IN THE FIELD color *Sunset* v239 no4 p10 O 2017

INTO THE BLUE color *Sunset* v239 no1 p8 Jl 2017

JUMP-START color *Sunset* v238 no1 p8 Ja 2017

THE NEXT GREAT PLACE color *Sunset* v238 no2 p4 F 2017

PLUGGED IN color *Sunset* v238 no4 p14 Ap 2017

SHOW TIME color *Sunset* v238 no6 p6 Je 2017

WILD THINGS color *Sunset* v238 no5 p8 My 2017

Edwards, John Bel, 1966-

Payback, Louisiana Style A. Greenblatt *Governing* v30 no3 p9 D 2016

EDWARDS, KATE A.

Scientific Evidence for Fifty Percent? *BioScience* v67 no9 p781 S 2017

Edwards, Kimberly

Country Lore *Mother Earth News* no280 p85 F/Mr 2017

EDWARDS, KYLE

CANADIAN INJUSTICE color *Maclean's* v130 no10 p36 N 2017

Running from office *Maclean's* v130 no10 p16 N 2017

Tiny houses for a big battle color *Maclean's* v130 no10 p11 N 2017

Edwards, M.

Country-specific effects of neonicotinoid pesticides on honey bees and wild bees diag map *Science* v356 no6345 p1393 Je 30 2017

Edwards, Marc

the advocates bw *Foreign Policy* no221 p72 N/D 2016

WHISTLEBLOWERS J. MCQUAID *Smithsonian* v47 no8 p48 D 2016

Edwards, Marcus

Why Marcus? M. Bamberger color *Golf Magazine* v59 no3 p128 Mr 2017

Edwards, Martin

Continental Crimes *Publishers Weekly* v264 no23 p33 Je 5 2017

Edwards, Matt—Awards

Patents and Awards *Science & Technology Review* p24 D 2016

Edwards, Melvin—Exhibitions

DO SOMETHING WITH IT B. SCHWABSKY color *Nation* v305 no2 p35 Jl 17 2017

Edwards, Peter

Benefits of trees in tropical cities color *Science* v356 no6344 p1241 Je 23 2017

Edwards, R. Lawrence

Response to Comments on "Reconciliation of the Devils Hole climate record with orbital forcing" bibl chart graph *Science* v354 no6310 p296-e O 21 2016

Edwards, Richard—Interviews

Richard Edwards B. POWERS *Indianapolis Monthly* v42 no2 p23 O 2017

Edwards, Scott V.

Winter storms drive rapid phenotypic, regulatory, and genomic shifts in the green anole lizard graph *Science* v357 no6350 p495 Ag 4 2017

EDWARDS, YOLANDA

NORTHERN MOROCCO color map *Conde Nast Traveler* v52 no4 p64 Ap 2017

EDWORDS, FRED

The Kingstone Bible *Humanist* v77 no2 p44 Mr/Ap 2017

Eegeesiak, Okalik

The Arctic Ocean and the Sea Ice Is Our Nuna *UN Chronicle* v54 no1/2 p1 2017

Eel populations

Ottawa's slimiest problem M. CAMPBELL color *Maclean's* v130 no9 p18 O 2017

EELLS, JOSH

Life on Planet Mars bw color *Rolling Stone* no1274 p28 N 17 2016

THE NEXT-GENERATION NARCO color map *Rolling Stone* no1291/1292 p54 Jl 13 2017

Eels

THE ART OF THE EEL N. HONACHEFSKY and G. BETHGE color *Outdoor Life* v224 no4 p66 My 2017

The Vanishing Eels E. BETZ bw color map *Discover* v38 no8 p22 O 2017

Eels—Population biology—Research

A Slithery Ocean Mystery G. Schanker *Oceanus* v52 no1 p16 Summ 2016

Eero Inc.

Eero Home WiFi System 2 review: Beacons make this system even easier to install M. BROWN color diag graph *Macworld - Digital Edition* v34 no8 p98 Ag 2017

Eero Saarinen: The Architect Who Saw the Future (Film)

The Saarinens: Father and Son D. A. CIAMPAGLIA *Architectural Record* v205 no1 p38 Ja 2017

Effect of climate on biodiversity

Why the Revolution Will Not (but Must) Be Televised J. Naureckas *Extra!* v30 no7 p1 S 2017

Effect of climate on wildlife resources

VISIONS color *National Geographic* v232 no3 p10 S 2017

Effect of drought on plants

Farmers Employ Strategies To Reduce Risk of Drought Damages S. Wallander, E. Marshall et al *Amber Waves: The Economics of Food, Farming, Natural Resources, & Rural America* p57 Je 2017

Effect of drugs on memory

Dr. Weil [Cover story] A. Weil color *Prevention* v69 no1 p24 Ja 2017

I didn't know I was an addict J. Gellar *Scholastic Choices* v32 no3 p8 N/D 2016

Effect of earthquakes on buildings

Crowd Festivities Can Shake Richter Scale *USA Today Magazine* v145 no2865 p12 Je 2017

Effect of fires on plants

Using fire to promote biodiversity L. T. Kelly and L. Brotons bibl color *Science* v355 no6331 p1264 Mr 24 2017

Effect of herbicides on plants

WEED-CONTROL TECHNOLOGY UPDATE: NO TRULY NEW HERBICIDES ARE SLATED FOR 2017, BUT DICAMBA-TOLERANT SOYBEANS ARE READY TO COMPLETELY ROLL OUT THIS YEAR G. Gullickson color *Successful Farming* v115 no7 p36 My 2017

Effect of human beings on climate change

Climate Change: We Are What We Eat *USA Today Magazine* v145 no2865 p4 Je 2017

Effect of human beings on climatic changes

Disasters! Are You Prepared? R. J. Dolesh *Parks & Recreation* v51 no11 p48 N 2016

the long lens m. ferrentino bw color *Bike Magazine* v23 no9 p56 D 2016

Observed Arctic sea-ice loss directly follows anthropogenic CO2 emission D. Notz and J. Stroeve bibl graph *Science* v354 no6313 p747 N 11 2016

Our Brains Love New Stuff, and It's Killing the Planet Duhaime *Harvard Business Review Digital Articles* p2 Mr 17 2017

Effect of stress on animals

IS YOUR PET STRESSED OUT? J. Szabo color *Amazing Wellness* v9 no4 p76 Summ 2017

Effect of technological innovations on cities & towns

The Innovation Equation M. Funkhouser *Governing* v30 no1 p4 O 2016

Effect of technological innovations on financial institutions

Fintech Companies Could Give Billions of People More Banking Options J. Kendall color *Harvard Business Review Digital Articles* p2 Ja 20 2017

FinTech Is Weaving Charitable Giving into Everyday Transactions F. W. Paasche *Harvard Business Review Digital Articles* p2 Jl 11 2016

Playtime for London's Fintech Companies J. Detrixhe cartoon *Bloomberg Businessweek* no4503 p33 D 12 2016

The Rise of FinTech in Supply Chains D. Rogers, R. Leuschner et al *Harvard Business Review Digital Articles* p2 Je 22 2016

Effect of technological innovations on job vacancies

Leading Job Growth in the Digital Economy C. Fernández-Aráoz *Harvard Business Review Digital Articles* p2 Ag 5 2015

Effect of technological innovations on labor supply

How Leading Companies Build the Workforces They Need to Stay Ahead M. Mankins *Harvard Business Review Digital Articles* p2 S 6 2017

Effect of temperature on animals
Diet Change K. Moore color *Natural History* v125 no3 p6 Mr 2017
Effect of temperature on fishes
HOT HOLES B. RUZZO color *Outdoor Life* v224 no1 p102 D 2016/Ja 2017
Effect of temperature on plants
Phytochromes function as thermosensors in Arabidopsis Jae-Hoon Jung, M. Domijan et al bibl graph *Science* v354 no6314 p886 N 18 2016
Effect of volcanic eruptions on Earth temperature
Volcanic Eruptions Play a Large Part *USA Today Magazine* v145 no2865 p2 Je 2017
Effective teaching
Flipping Student Support Services to Improve Outcomes P. Whee-lan *Change* v48 no6 p36 N/D 2016
What a blind student taught me to see C. Caswell bw chart color diag *Phi Delta Kappan* v98 no3 p68 N 2016
Efficiency of sewage disposal plants
TOUR OF DOODY R. Annis, S. Bahr et al diag *Indianapolis Monthly* v41 no2 p65 S 2017
Efficiency wage theory
Do CEOs Really Have the Power to Raise Wages? W. Frick *Harvard Business Review Digital Articles* p2 Ap 23 2015
Efficient market theory
The Dark Side of Efficient Markets R. L. Martin *Harvard Business Review Digital Articles* p2 O 15 2014
Efflux (Microbiology)
Biased partitioning of the multidrug efflux pump AcrAB-TolC un-derlies long-lived phenotypic heterogeneity T. Bergmiller, A. M. C. Andersson et al diag *Science* v356 no6335 p311 Ap 21 2017
Effron, Marc
The Unsexy Fundamentals of Great HR *Harvard Business Review Digital Articles* p2 Ag 19 2015
Efremenko, Y.
Observation of coherent elastic neutrino-nucleus scattering diag *Science* v357 no6356 p1123 S 15 2017
Efron, Zac, 1987-
Artists color *Time* v189 no16/17 p40 My 1-8 2017
The Intersection color *Runner's World* v52 no6 p58 Jl 2017
Efroni, Sol
The linker histone H1.0 generates epigenetic and functional intra-tumor heterogeneity bibl graph *Science* v353 no6307 paaf1644-1 S 30 2016
Efstathiou, Christos
POLITICS BY CANDLELIGHT S. COLLINI color *Nation* v305 no1 p35 Jl 3 2017
EFSTATHIOU, GEORGE
A COSMIC CONTROVERSY color *Scientific American* v317 no1 p5 Jl 2017
Egan, Anthony
A Bananas Republic? *America* v215 no15 p12 N 14 2016
In South Africa, more calls for Zuma to go color *America* v216 no12 p15 My 29 2017
Egan, Casey
UNPLUGGING THE SELFIE GENERATION [Cover story] color graph map *National Geographic* v230 no4 p34 O 2016
Egan, Dan
The Death and Life of the Great Lakes C. Moskowitz and R. F. Mandelbaum color *Scientific American* v316 no3 p76 Mr 2017
A Deep Dive into Doleful Waters color *Canadian Wildlife* v23 no4 p40 S/O 2017
Five Alive R. MOOR *New York Times Book Review* p12 My 28 2017
THE GREAT LAKES: Present and Future Perils color graph map *Natural History* v125 no3 p24 Mr 2017
THE GREAT TAKEOVER color map *Discover* v38 no8 p56 O 2017
Invaders, climate change threaten Great Lakes C. Martin color *Science News* v191 no5 p30 Mr 18 2017
Troubled waters L. Danielle Jenkins color *Science* v355 no6328 p917 Mr 3 2017
Egan, Eleanor Franklin
TORPEDOED! color *MHQ: Quarterly Journal of Military History* v29 no4 p90 Summ 2017
Egan, Elisabeth

The Meaning of Michelle bw color *Glamour* v114 no12 p198 D 2016
The Optimist *New York Times Book Review* p20 O 9 2016
Read These and Weep color *Glamour* v115 no9 p40 S 2017
Why I Hate My Dog color *Glamour* v114 no12 p174 D 2016
You're Gonna Want to Read These... color *Glamour* v115 no10 p144 O 2017
Egan, Jennifer, 1962-
The City That Never Sleeps S. FOX color *Publishers Weekly* v264 no38 p44 S 18 2017
THE DINNER PARTY cartoon *New Yorker* v93 no16 p50 Je 5 2017
Diving Into the Wreck R. FRANKLIN color *Atlantic* v320 no4 p40 N 2017
A Heroine for Our Time S. Begley color *Time* v190 no15 p58 O 16 2017
The House by the Sea J. Egan color *Vogue* v207 no9 p284 S 2017
MANHATTAN BEACH E. DONALDSON color *Maclean's* v130 no9 p76 O 2017
ONCE UPON A TIME IN NEW YORK A. STYRON color *O, The Oprah Magazine* p107 N 2017
On the Waterfront A. Towles *New York Times Book Review* p1 O 8 2017
On the Wilder Shores of Brooklyn [Cover story] F. Prose bw *New York Review of Books* v64 no15 p28 O 12 2017
Sunken Pleasures M. DEAN color il *New Republic* v248 no11 p52 N 2017
Two Islands: Northern Ireland and Papua New Guinea don't seem so different in Nick Laird's new novel *New York Times Book Review* p8 Jl 2 2017
WATCH CLOSELY A. SCHWARTZ cartoon color map *New Yorker* v93 no32 p56 O 16 2017
Egan, Jennifer, 1962- —Interviews
Jennifer Egan *New York Times Book Review* p8 O 1 2017
Egan, Kerry
On Living J. Brown *Christian Century* v134 no4 p52 F 15 2017
OUR FIRST LOVE K. NORRIS *America* v216 no1 p38 Ja 2 2017
Quotable Quotes color *Reader's Digest* v189 no1129 p136 Ap 2017
TOUCHED BY AN ANGEL K. Egan *Saturday Evening Post* v288 no6 p20 N/D 2016
What Matters in the End H. LENDE *New York Times Book Review* p19 N 27 2016
Egan, Peter
THE FIVE-STROKE NORTON *Cycle World* v55 no10 p26 N 2016
Friends for Life color diag *Road & Track* v68 no10 p26 Jl 2017
ONCE MORE, INTO THE GREAT WIDE OPEN color *Road & Track* v68 no10 p88 Jl 2017
SOFTAILS color *Cycle World* v56 no9 p38 O 2017
TRIUMPH BONNEVILLE T120 bw chart color graph *Cycle World* v55 no11 p46 D 2016
The Very Long-Term Buell bw color *Cycle World* v55 no10 p48 N 2016
EGAN, SCOTT P.
The Web of Life, the Tangled Bank, and the Frequency of Genetic Exchange *BioScience* v67 no1 p91 Ja 2017
Egan, Timothy
UNPLUGGING THE SELFIE GENERATION [Cover story] color graph map *National Geographic* v230 no4 p34 O 2016
Egan, Tom
Mount Desert Island color *Sail* v48 no6 p38 Je 2017
Egana, Xabier
Sacred and secular unite on Basque church's walls R. Skirble color *Christian Century* v134 no2 p17 Ja 18 2017
Egeli, Sitki
Seeking a path toward missile nonproliferation bibl *Bulletin of the Atomic Scientists* v72 no6 p362 N 2016
Eger, Edith Eva
The Power to Heal: By helping patients uncover past trauma, a therapist and survivor of Auschwitz comes closer to understand-ing her own L. GOTTLIEB *New York Times Book Review* p19 O 8 2017
Eger, Isaac
The Pickup Artist *Los Angeles Magazine* v62 no6 p76 Je 2017
EGERTON, BROOKS

THE MYSTERIOUS CASE OF THE SEVERED FOOT *D: The Magazine of Dallas* v43 no10 p150 O 2016

Egerton, Jodi

Deals D. LEFFERTS color *Publishers Weekly* v264 no2 p12 Ja 9 2017

Egerton, Taron, 1989-

COLIN FIRTH & TARON EGERTON IN Kingsman: The Golden Circle J. McGovern color *Entertainment Weekly* no1478 / 1479 p44 Ag 18-25 2017

Kingsman: The Golden Circle C. Nashawaty color *Entertainment Weekly* no1484 p42 S 29 2017

Egg decoration

See also

Easter eggs

CHIC EGGS P. GUGLIELMETTI color *Martha Stewart Living* p106 Ap 2017

Egg industry

TOM THE EGG MAN *Washingtonian Magazine* v52 no1 p99 O 2016

Egg substitutes

Expiration Dates You Should Never Ignore T. GAGNON color *Reader's Digest* v189 no1129 p42 Ap 2017

Egg whites

WHERE IT ALL BEGINS A. RAPOPORT color *Bon Appetit* v62 no4 p8 Ap 2017

Egg yolk

FAFQ K. Patel and J. WUEBBEN color *Muscle & Performance* v9 no4 p12 Ap 2017

pick your finish *Martha Stewart Living* no269 p97 N 2016

Eggcups

NUFFIN BEATS A MUFFIN M. Kadey color *Runner's World* v52 no2 p40 Mr 2017

EGGE, SARAH

BERRY REDS *Better Homes & Gardens* v94 no12 p33 D 2016

GINKGO GREENS color *Better Homes & Gardens* v95 no3 p22 Mr 2017

Eggers, Dave, 1970-

DAVE EGGERS GETS POLITICAL J. Goodman color *Entertainment Weekly* no1436/1437 p16 O 21 2016

Death by Oil: After being driven off their land twice, Native Americans struck it rich in oil lands, only to be preyed upon by murderers *New York Times Book Review* p16 My 14 2017

FAREWELL cartoon *New Yorker* v92 no46 p20 Ja 23 2017

Jerry BROWN color *Vanity Fair* v59 no8 p76 Ag 2017

The Man Going Back bw *Foreign Policy* no221 p76 N/D 2016

Eggers, Dave, 1970—Interviews

TOO MUCH INFORMATION C. Thompson color *Mother Jones* v42 no3 p66 My/Je 2017

What Do Animals Think of the Greek Financial Crisis? In a new adult picture book, Ungrateful Mammals, the ever-inventive Dave Eggers pairs his whimsical drawings with quirky quotations K. Frischkorn *Smithsonian* v48 no6 p28 O 2017

Eggers, J. P.

Focus On the Customers You Want, Not the Ones You Have *Harvard Business Review Digital Articles* p2 Je 15 2015

Eggers, Kerry

INTERSTATE 5 KILLER color *Sports Illustrated* v125 no17 p108 N 21 2016 Double Issue

Egginton, William

Music key to a Cold War thaw L. A. Baglione color il *America* v216 no9 p46 Ap 24 2017

True Inventions R. BROOKHISER color *National Review* v69 no2 p44 F 6 2017

Eggleston, Mike

All Low- and Moderate-Income Areas Are Not Created Equal [Cover story] *Bridges (Federal Reserve Bank of St. Louis)* p1 Summ 2016

Eggnog

George Washington's Eggnog F. MAROUKIAN color *Popular Mechanics* p22 D 2016/Ja 2017

Eggold, Ryan

SPY GAME J. Russell color *TV Guide* v65 no7 p28 F 13 2017

Eggplant

Good Food eat to Beat inflammation P. O. BLUMBERG color *Prevention* v69 no9 p20 O 2017

'WICH CRAFT: Italian-sub lovers have reason to rejoice at Capo

---

Delicatessen A. Limpert *Washingtonian Magazine* v52 no11 p136 Ag 2017

Eggs

baked GOOD R. Asbell color *Yoga Journal* no288 p85 D 2016

EGGS BREAK OUT D. Wise color *Health* v31 no1 p92 Ja 2017

THE EXCHANGE W. C. WINTER and A. Nasir cartoon chart color graph *Men's Health* v32 no9 p16 N 2017

Fall fuel E. Brower color *Yoga Journal* no296 p22 N 2017

GATHER ROUNDS F. VIGNA color *Martha Stewart Living* p140 Ap 2017

GOOD EGGS *Amazing Wellness* v8 no2 p8 Spr 2016

Ham-Yam Quiche Dijon J. BOWDEN and J. BESSINGER color *Better Nutrition* v79 no4 p70 Ap 2017

How Do You Say "Yum" Around the World? J. PRESS *Scholastic Choices* p6 O 2017

Incredible Eggs color *Vegetarian Today* no2 p30 Ap 2017

Let's do brunch B. Risher color *Yoga Journal* no290 p78 Mr 2017

Salad DAYS [Cover story] K. Caldesi and G. Caldesi color *Yoga Journal* no292 p28 Je 2017

SINGULAR Sensation M. Kiesel cartoon color *O, The Oprah Magazine* p131 Ap 2017

SMARTER FATS J. Bowden color *Amazing Wellness* v8 no2 p36 Spr 2016

When mom has favorite, blame all the swimming S. Milius color *Science News* v190 no13 p4 D 24 2016

would you let your child eat 50 pounds of sugar? K. CICERO *Parents* v91 no6 p32 Je 2016

Eggs in art

egg-cellent new ideas for... EGGS chart color *Good Housekeeping* v264 no4 p65 Ap 2017

Eggs—Contamination

A Case of Chicken vs. Machine P. Ho and J. Gale cartoon color *Bloomberg Businessweek* no4507 p18 Ja 16 2017

Eggshells

Avian egg shape: Form, function, and evolution M. Caswell Stoddard, E. Hou Yong et al color diag *Science* v356 no6344 p1249 Je 23 2017

The most perfect thing, explained C. N. Spottiswoode diag *Science* v356 no6344 p1234 Je 23 2017

Eggs—Incubation

See also

Hatchability of eggs

Dinosaur eggs were slow to hatch L. Hamers color *Science News* v191 no2 p4 F 4 2017

HATCH A FLOCK O. H. Will III *Mother Earth News* no280 p42 F/Mr 2017

Egmont Group (Company)

Children's Fun Publishing Company color *Publishers Weekly* v264 no12 p14 Mr 20 2017

Ego (Psychology)

Ego Kills A. TOWER color *Climbing* no350 p30 D 2016/Ja 2017

Have We Been Thinking About Willpower the Wrong Way for 30 Years? N. Eyal *Harvard Business Review Digital Articles* p2 N 23 2016

How to Prevent Experts from Hoarding Knowledge D. Leonard *Harvard Business Review Digital Articles* p2 D 18 2014

Egret (Poem)

EGRET M. Cadnum *Commonweal* v144 no7 p26 Ap 14 2017

Egusquiza, Dustin

BUCKLE UP with Dustin Egusquiza C. Toy color *Spin to Win Rodeo* v21 no6 p19 Ag 2017

whatever IT Takes B. Welch color *Spin to Win Rodeo* v21 no1 p62 Mr 2017

Egypt

Being Vegan in Cairo Y. RADBOD *Vegetarian Journal* v35 no4 p24 2016

Egypt—Foreign relations—Israel

Mad, Democrats? Blame the Iran Deal *Commentary* p1 Ja 2017

Mad, Democrats? Blame the Iran Deal *Commentary* v143 no1 p1 Ja 2017

Egyptian antiquities

Buried Secrets S. W. DRIMMER color map *National Geographic Kids* no470 p26 My 2017

THE MYTH OF MUMMY WHEAT: Despite a total lack of evidence, the belief that grains of wheat found in Ancient Egyptian tombs could produce bountiful crops was surprisingly hardy G.

Moshenska *History Today* v67 no9 p36 S 2017
TO DIE LIKE AN EGYPTIAN M. BROWN color *Archaeology* v70 no5 p44 S/O 2017

Egyptian art
Akhenaten: EGYPT'S FIRST REVOLUTIONARY P. Hessler bw color diag map *National Geographic* v231 no5 p120 My 2017
Akhenaten P. Hessler bw color diag map *National Geographic* v231 no5 p120 My 2017

Egyptian authors
Portrait of the Author as a Historian A. Lee *History Today* v67 no1 p54 Ja 2017

Egyptian history
EGYPT'S FINAL REDOUBT IN CANAAN [Cover story] R. ATWOOD color *Archaeology* v70 no4 p26 Je-Ag 2017
NO PLACE LIKE HOME C. Valentino color *Archaeology* v70 no4 p4 Je-Ag 2017

Egyptian revolution, Egypt, 2011-
A DEATH IN CAIRO D. Walsh *New York Times Magazine* p26 Ag 20 2017

Egyptians
See **Egypt—Politics & government—2011-**
Egypt's Nightmare S. A. Cook bw *Foreign Affairs* v95 no6 p110 N/D 2016
O Brotherhood, Where Art Thou? A. A. Zeid and Cook *Foreign Affairs* v96 no2 p164 Mr/Ap 2017

Eha, Brian Patrick
CAN BITCOIN'S FIRST FELON HELP MAKE CRYPTOCURRENCY A TRILLION-DOLLAR MARKET? color diag *Fortune* v176 no1 p78 Jl 1 2017

Ehlers, Michael
Eremite Preserves Past, Shapes Future of Free-Jazz P. MARGASAK color *Downbeat* v84 no8 p18 Ag 2017

Ehlers, Vern, 1934-2017
First physicist in Congress dies D. Kramer *Physics Today* v70 no10 p38 O 2017

Ehlinger, Aaron C.
The [4Fe4S] cluster of human DNA primase functions as a redox switch using DNA charge transport color *Science* v355 no6327 p813 F 24 2017

Ehlmann, B. L.
Extensive water ice within Ceres' aqueously altered regolith: Evidence from nuclear spectroscopy bibl graph *Science* v355 no6320 p1 Ja 6 2017

Ehmke, Glenn
Publish openly but responsibly color *Science* v357 no6347 p141 Jl 14 2017

Ehmsen, Erika
BRITISH COLUMBIA'S EAST VANCOUVER color map *Sunset* v239 no3 p36 S 2017
PICK YOUR MEXICO PARADISE color *Sunset* v237 no5 p29 N 2016
UP ALL NIGHT color *Sunset* v237 no5 p25 N 2016

Ehning, Marcus
Winner's CIRCLE color *Practical Horseman* v44 no12 p64 D 2016

Ehrenberg, Rachel
Cigarettes cause telltale DNA damage diag *Science News* v190 no11 p14 N 26 2016
Common fungus may raise asthma risk *Science News* v191 no5 p16 Mr 18 2017
Dinosaur family tree gets a makeover diag *Science News* v191 no7 p7 Ap 15 2017
Imaging method catches DNA 'blinking' on color *Science News* v191 no5 p16 Mr 18 2017
Pain promoter also acts to relieve it *Science News* v191 no2 p6 F 4 2017
Protein detects when lungs fill with air *Science News* v191 no2 p7 F 4 2017
Scientists snoop to check on kelp *Science News* v192 no1 p10 Ag 5 2017
Social status alters immune system color *Science News* v190 no13 p7 D 24 2016
Strep B pigment attacks placenta bw *Science News* v190 no10 p8 N 12 2016
Synthetic cell may reveal what is necessary for life color *Science News* v190 no13 p26 D 24 2016

EHRENFELD, TEMMA
Character Counts cartoon *Weekly Standard* v22 no19 p35 Ja 23 2017
The Human Clock *Weekly Standard* v22 no41 p34 Jl 3 2017
Mind the Gap cartoon *Weekly Standard* v22 no14 p36 D 12 2016

Ehrenhalt, Alan
30 Years Later *Governing* v31 no1 p26 O 2017
Beyond Black and White *New York Times Book Review* p11 F 5 2017
Boulevard Dreams *Governing* v30 no3 p14 D 2016
Cities Inside and Out *Governing* v30 no5 p14 F 2017
The Democrats' Quandary: Can they find a winning formula and return to power? *Governing* v30 no12 p14 S 2017
Is Syracuse Necessary? Some want to save a fiscally challenged city by effectively abolishing it *Governing* v30 no8 p14 My 2017
The Legislative Time Machine *Governing* v30 no4 p14 Ja 2017
The Limits of Café Urbanism *Governing* v30 no6 p14 Mr 2017
Mayors, Promises and Reality *Governing* v30 no2 p14 N 2016
The Neighborhood Naming Game: What people call a community can have a big impact on its self-image *Governing* v31 no1 p14 O 2017
Next Stop: Anybody's Guess: There are no crystal balls in transportation. Some judges don't understand that color *Governing* v30 no11 p14 Ag 2017
Public Housing and Racial Reality *Governing* v30 no7 p14 Ap 2017
The Tea Party Centrists: A lot of the governors elected as hardliners in 2010 have surprised their states *Governing* v30 no9 p14 Je 2017
Walking the Walk: In creating walkable neighborhoods, a little audacity goes a long way *Governing* v30 no10 p14 Jl 2017
Welcome to Festival City *Governing* v30 no1 p14 O 2016

Ehrenreich, Alden, 1989-
3 — "WOULD THAT IT WERE SO SIMPLE" K. P. Sullivan color *Entertainment Weekly* no1444/1445 p58 D 16 2016
Alden EHRENREICH M. MARTIN *Interview* v46 no9 p86 N 2016

Ehrenreich, Barbara
CLASSIC HUMANIST *Humanist* v77 no1 p10 Ja/F 2017
NEW JOBS REQUIRE NEW IDEAS—AND NEW WAYS OF ORGANIZING *New York Times Magazine* p27 F 26 2017

Ehrensberger, Sebastian
Making Better Decisions in Your Family Business *Harvard Business Review Digital Articles* p2 S 8 2015

Ehrett, John
The Alt-Right Doesn't Care About the Constitution color *Washington Monthly* v49 no3-5 p8 Mr-My 2017

Ehrhart, Juliann
Systemic pan-AMPK activator MK-8722 improves glucose homeostasis but induces cardiac hypertrophy graph *Science* v357 no6350 p507 Ag 4 2017

Ehrhart, Sebastian
Global atmospheric particle formation from CERN CLOUD measurements bibl graph map *Science* v354 no6316 p1119 D 2 2016

EHRLICH, DIMITRI
DEAP VALLY *Interview* v46 no8 p32 O 2016

Ehrlich, Nikki
Twindergarten *Publishers Weekly* v264 no20 p55 My 15 2017

Ehrlich, Paul
Social norms as solutions bibl color *Science* v354 no6308 p42 O 7 2016

Ehrman, Fred
How Israel Wins *Commentary* v143 no3 p7 Mr 2017

E.I. du Pont de Nemours & Co.
THE C.E.O. OF H.I.V. C. GLAZEK *New York Times Magazine* p44 Ap 30 2017

Eibach Springs Inc.
SPRINGTIME FOR HITTING AND G-OUTS [Cover story] M. EMERY color *Dirt Sports + Off-Road* v51 no10 p36 O 2017

Eichelberger, Martin R.
advice every new mom needs [Cover story] color *Parents* v92 no7 p32 Jl 2017

Eichenbaum, Howard
Howard Eichenbaum (1947–2017) M. Hasselmo and C. Stern color *Science* v357 no6354 p875 S 1 2017

EICHENGREEN, BARRY

The Renminbi Goes Global color *Foreign Affairs* v96 no2 p157 Mr/Ap 2017

Where Did the Euro Go Wrong? *Current History* v116 no788 p116 Mr 2017

EICHENSEHER, TASHA

Ayurvedic TRANSFORMATION [Cover story] color *Yoga Journal* no287 p52 N 2016

ECLIPSE your fears color *Yoga Journal* no293 p51 Ag 2017

Goodnight, SLEEP ISSUES color *Yoga Journal* p102 2017 Special Issue

It's all ELEMENTAL [Cover story] color *Yoga Journal* no290 p64 Mr 2017

JUST ADD intensity [Cover story] color *Yoga Journal* no295 p74 O 2017

power by design color *Yoga Journal* no294 p17 S 2017

take OM HOME color *Yoga Journal* no289 p108 F 2017

take OM HOME color *Yoga Journal* no291 p86 My 2017

take OM HOME color *Yoga Journal* no292 p96 Je 2017

TAKE OM HOME color *Yoga Journal* no294 p96 S 2017

WHAT IT TAKES TO TEACH color *Yoga Journal* no287 p48 N 2016

Eicher, David

Deals R. DEAHL color *Publishers Weekly* v264 no26 p8 Je 26 2017

Eicher, David J.

The amazing William Herschel color *Astronomy* v45 no6 p8 Je 2017

America's observatory color *Astronomy* v45 no4 p6 Ap 2017

An astronomical workhorse *Astronomy* v45 no5 p6 My 2017

Collecting cosmic dust bw *Astronomy* v45 no4 p8 Ap 2017

Earth-mass vs. Earth-like color *Astronomy* v45 no1 p8 Ja 2017

Join me in Costa Rica color *Astronomy* v45 no8 p6 Ag 2017

Join us for a new solar eclipse trip! color *Astronomy* v45 no2 p6 F 2017

Let's hear it for abiogenesis color *Astronomy* v45 no9 p8 S 2017

Making light of galaxies color *Astronomy* v45 no11 p6 N 2017

Moonwalkers and women scientists highlighted at STARMUS IV color *Astronomy* v45 no6 p50 Je 2017

The mystery of quasars color *Astronomy* v45 no5 p8 My 2017

Portrait of a giant color *Astronomy* v45 no11 p8 N 2017

Reflections on Voyager color *Astronomy* v45 no10 p8 O 2017

See aurorae in beautiful Norway color *Astronomy* v45 no6 p6 Je 2017

Story of a supernova *Astronomy* v45 no3 p6 Mr 2017

A system of seven worlds color *Astronomy* v45 no7 p8 Jl 2017

A tribute to Stephen Hawking color *Astronomy* v45 no1 p54 Ja 2017

A universe with 10 times more galaxies color *Astronomy* v45 no3 p8 Mr 2017

Voyager's great legacy color *Astronomy* v45 no10 p6 O 2017

Water, water everywhere color *Astronomy* v45 no2 p8 F 2017

Whatever you do, just look color *Astronomy* v45 no8 p8 Ag 2017

Where has all the water gone? color *Astronomy* v45 no7 p6 Jl 2017

Why do spiral galaxies spiral? color *Astronomy* v44 no12 p7 D 2016

Year's biggest stories *Astronomy* v45 no1 p6 Ja 2017

Eichhorn, Kate

Copy That J. Stewart-Halevy bw *Art in America* v105 no3 p61 Mr 2017

Eichhorn, Tim

BARK + BITE M. Gearhart color *Hot Rod* v70 no8 p68 Ag 2017

EICHINGER, ELLE

INTO THE BLUE color *Chicago* v66 no4 p70 Ap 2017

OFF THE WALL color *Chicago* v66 no9 p92 S 2017

SPRING FORTH color *Chicago* v66 no4 p74 Ap 2017

(SUB)URBAN color *Chicago* v66 no9 p90 S 2017

EICHLER, GLENN

08:01:30 cartoon *New Yorker* v93 no8 p29 Ap 10 2017

Eichler, Tomá¿

A global brain state underlies C. elegans sleep behavior diag *Science* v356 no6344 p1247 Je 23 2017

Eichner, Billy, 1978-

BILLY EICHN ER R. Rahman color *Entertainment Weekly* no1441 p48 N 25 2016

Billy on How to Lighten Up C. LEE cartoon color *Men's Health*

v32 no9 p26 N 2017

BILLY TAKES A STAND C. Agard color *Entertainment Weekly* no1470 p50 Je 16 2017

THE CAREER MAKEOVER ISSUE WITH Billy Eichner [Cover story] K. Bahler color *Money* v46 no7 p38 Ag 2017

Difficult People A. D'Arminio *TV Guide* v65 no25 p23 Je 2017

A Modest Proposal color *GQ: Gentlemen's Quarterly* v97 no4 p56 Ap 2017

Musical Theater and Misanthropy D. D'addario color *Time* v190 no7 p52 Ag 21 2017

My Obsessions... *TV Guide* v65 no39 p14 S 18 2017

Sound Bites color *Entertainment Weekly* no1450 p9 Ja 27 2017

Sound Bites color *Entertainment Weekly* no1480 p4 S 1 2017

Eichner, Billy, 1978—Interviews

Billy Eichner Has a Few Questions img *New York* p66 Ja 23 2017

Billy Eichner Wants You to Know He's Mainstream A. M. Cox *New York Times Magazine* p78 S 10 2017

Man of the People C. Bagley color *InStyle* v24 no1 p88 Ja 2017

Eicosapentaenoic acid—Therapeutic use

Do omega-3s protect your thinking skills? *Harvard Health Letter* v42 no1 p3 N 2016

Eide, Stephen

Out of the Warehouse color *Weekly Standard* v22 no33 p45 My 8 2017

Eidelson, Josh

Changing Lanes color *Bloomberg Businessweek* no4528 p60 Je 26 2017

Exit the Old Elite *Bloomberg Businessweek* no4499 p26 N 14 2016

A Free Hand on Immigration graph *Bloomberg Businessweek* no4499 p32 N 14 2016

How Couples (and Throuples!) Do Money color *Bloomberg Businessweek* no4502 p74 D 5 2016

Immigrants Prepare For Life After Obama *Bloomberg Businessweek* no4501 p25 N 28 2016

Labor's Last Stand cartoon map *Bloomberg Businessweek* no4512 p25 F 20 2017

THE PREDICTION MATRIX bw color *Bloomberg Businessweek* no4496 p104 O 24 2016

Saru Jayaraman color *Bloomberg Businessweek* no4528 p76 Je 26 2017

Share This graph *Bloomberg Businessweek* no4530 p24 Jl 17 2017

A Texas Election Official Talks Like a Sheriff cartoon *Bloomberg Businessweek* no4493 p36 O 3 2016

Unions Want Hotels to Give ICE The Cold Shoulder bw *Bloomberg Businessweek* no4539 p44 S 25 2017

WORKERS OF SILICON VALLEY UNITE! *Bloomberg Businessweek* no4538 p22 S 18 2017

Eiermann, George

Systemic pan-AMPK activator MK-8722 improves glucose homeostasis but induces cardiac hypertrophy graph *Science* v357 no6350 p507 Ag 4 2017

Eifler, John

HOW TO PREPARE FOR A SENSITIVE RENOVATION color *Arts & Crafts Homes & the Revival* v12 no4 p58 Fall 2017

Eig, Jonathan

THE GREATEST PRICE color *Sports Illustrated* v127 no10 p54 O 2 2017

EIGEN, MICHAEL

Understanding the Victors *American Scholar* v86 no2 p3 Spr 2017

EIGENBROD, FELIX

When, Where, and How Nature Matters for Ecosystem Services: Challenges for the Next Generation of Ecosystem Service Models *BioScience* v67 no9 p820 S 2017

Eigenbrod, Ole

Fructose-driven glycolysis supports anoxia resistance in the naked mole-rat diag graph *Science* v356 no6335 p307 Ap 21 2017

Eigenbrode, J. L.

Redox stratification of an ancient lake in Gale crater, Mars color *Science* v356 no6341 p922 Je 1 2017

Eight Hours Don't Make a Day (TV program)

FELLOW FEELING A. MA color *Film Comment* v53 no3 p58 My/Je 2017

Eighteenth century

See also

Enlightenment

Cogs in the Machine R. R. Reilly *Claremont Review of Books* v17 no3 p48 Summ 2017

Eighty-Sixed (TV program)

Gazzie David: Riding the subway--and avoiding germs--with the highly neurotic television scion A. SWERDLOFF *New York* v50 no15 p12 Jl 24 2017

Eigner, V.

Hydrogen positions in single nanocrystals revealed by electron diffraction bibl color *Science* v355 no6321 p1 Ja 13 2017

Eiichi Mizohata

A three-dimensional movie of structural changes in bacteriorhodopsin bibl diag graph *Science* v354 no6319 p1552 D 23 2016

Eikelboom, J. A. J.

The impact of hunting on tropical mammal and bird populations graph map *Science* v356 no6334 p180 Ap 14 2017

Eikenberg, Darcy

Why People Quit Their Jobs: Interaction *Harvard Business Review* v94 no11 p18 N 2016

Eikenberry, Karl

Introduction *Daedalus* v146 no4 p6 Fall 2017

Eiko

More Self-Help Bestsellers Coming from Japan T. Tan color *Publishers Weekly* v264 no35 p17 Ag 28 2017

EIL, PHILIP

POST SCRIPT: HOW A SMALL-TIME CHICAGO DOCTOR CAME TO THE SOUTHEASTERN OHIO TOWN OF PORTSMOUTH AND HELPED SPUR AN EPIDEMIC *Cincinnati Magazine* v50 no10 p66 Jl 2017

Eilam, Tamar

Wild emmer genome architecture and diversity elucidate wheat evolution and domestication color *Science* v357 no6346 p93 Jl 7 2017

Eilers, Andreas

Lee Rubin: Our mentor and role model *Science* v355 no6327 p806 F 24 2017

Eilers, Yvan

Nanometer resolution imaging and tracking of fluorescent molecules with minimal photon fluxes bibl graph *Science* v355 no6325 p606 F 10 2017

EINARSDÓTTIR, GRÉTA SIGRÍDUR

MIDSUMMER NIGHT'S DREAM *Iceland Review* v55 no4 p86 Jl/Ag 2017

Einav, Liran

What the Cost of a Trip to the Vet Tells Us About Why Human Health Care Is So Expensive color *Harvard Business Review Digital Articles* p2 Ja 10 2017

Einhorn, Bruce

Beijing Is Mad About Thaad color *Bloomberg Businessweek* no4514 p16 Mr 13 2017

A Cash Crackdown Hits Gold Pawners color *Bloomberg Businessweek* no4502 p46 D 5 2016

The Cheap Phone Is Dead In China cartoon color *Bloomberg Businessweek* no4496 p36 O 24 2016

China's Bridge and Tunnel Addiction color *Bloomberg Businessweek* no4513 p47 Mr 6 2017

China's Foodmakers Try New Growth Recipes color diag *Bloomberg Businessweek* no4524 p22 My 29 2017

China's Housing Bubble Wobble *Bloomberg Businessweek* no4496 p52 O 24 2016

China—With Western Help—Finds Its Wings diag *Bloomberg Businessweek* no4522 p25 My 15 2017

The Chinese Rediscover Luxury color *Bloomberg Businessweek* no4509 p15 Ja 30 2017

Could Tesla Run Out of Gas in Hong Kong? *Bloomberg Businessweek* no4517 p25 Ap 3 2017

The Flu Shot's Chicken-And-Egg Problem color *Bloomberg Businessweek* no4493 p43 O 3 2016

For Chandon in China, a Kick From Champagne? graph *Bloomberg Businessweek* no4501 p21 N 28 2016

Global Trade Is Slowing color *Bloomberg Businessweek* no4500 p16 N 21 2016

India's Cash-Canceling Experiment color *Bloomberg Businessweek* no4501 p12 N 28 2016

India's Nuclear Industry Needs a Jolt color diag *Bloomberg Businessweek* no4526 p17 Je 12 2017

Japan's Big Bet color *Bloomberg Businessweek* no4505 p20 D 26 2016

LG Sees an Opening In the Smart Home *Bloomberg Businessweek* no4498 p44 N 7 2016

Philippine Casinos Are Cleaning Up color graph *Bloomberg Businessweek* no4521 p19 My 8 2017

Philippine Leader Scares Off Investors color *Bloomberg Businessweek* no4493 p23 O 3 2016

The Prenup That Didn't Stick chart color *Bloomberg Businessweek* no4498 p25 N 7 2016

Resources Water Fights color map *Bloomberg Businessweek* no4497 p19 O 31 2016

Russia, Japan, and China Fill the Trade Gap *Bloomberg Businessweek* no4502 p22 D 5 2016

Samsung's New Board Gets Back to Business color *Bloomberg Businessweek* no4513 p21 Mr 6 2017

A Scandal at Korea's Retirement Giant color *Bloomberg Businessweek* no4507 p31 Ja 16 2017

See Mario. See Mario Run color graph *Bloomberg Businessweek* no4503 p29 D 12 2016

Sony's Bet on Gamers Can't Get Much Bigger bw *Bloomberg Businessweek* no4499 p48 N 14 2016

South Korea's High-Value Targets *Bloomberg Businessweek* no4520 p17 My 1 2017

South Korea Tries to Curb the Chaebol color *Bloomberg Businessweek* no4504 p15 D 19 2016

Einloth, Barbara

Popular piety color *U.S. Catholic* v82 no2 p5 F 2017

Einstein, Albert, 1879-1955

1918: Berlin A. Einstein *Lapham's Quarterly* v10 no2 p125 Spr 2017

Albert Einstein M. BARNA color *Discover* v38 no4 p36 My 2017

GENIUS C. KALB bw color diag *National Geographic* v231 no5 p30 My 2017

GENIUS TAKES MANY FORMS S. Goldberg color *National Geographic* v231 no5 pC6 My 2017

Heroes of Science cartoon *Discover* v38 no4 p34 My 2017

PARODY *Weekly Standard* v22 no40 p40 Je 26 2017

PLAYING THE PART OF GENIUS color *National Geographic* v231 no4 p6 Ap 2017

When Heroics in Science Define Us B. Lang color *Discover* v38 no4 p6 My 2017

Einstein, Jaclyn M.

Making the cut in the dark genome bibl diag *Science* v354 no6313 p705 N 11 2016

Einstein, Maria

Content Confusion T. WU *New York Times Book Review* p21 N 27 2016

Einstein Group (Company)

CHARTER-ING A NEW COURSE D. Wilson color *New Orleans Magazine* v51 no8 p82 Je 2017

Eire, Carlos M. N., 1951-

CHARITY, PEACE, VITRIOL AND WAR: An ambitious survey of the 'Reformations' brilliantly conveys the drama of this convulsive period D. Gehring *History Today* v67 no10 p100 O 2017

Eiríksson, Ragnar

DAFT ABOUT DILL *Iceland Review* v55 no3 p46 My/Je 2017

Eiseley, Loren C., 1907-1977

1969: Philadelphia L. Eiseley *Lapham's Quarterly* v10 no2 p44 Spr 2017

Eiseman, Leatrice

MAKE OVER YOUR HOME WITH COLOR color *Redbook* p142 D 2016

EISEN, EMILY

r.s.v.p bw *Bon Appetit* v61 no12 p20 D 2016 /Jan2017

Eisen, Michael

Not just Salk color *Science* v357 no6356 p1105 S 15 2017

Eisen, Michael—Interviews

POPULAR MECHANICS color *Popular Mechanics* p14 Jl 2017

Eisen, Rich—Interviews

Rich Eisen J. Marksbury and J. Marksbury color *Golf Magazine* v59 no10 p32 O 2017

Eisenbarth, Stephanie C.

The DNA-sensing AIM2 inflammasome controls radiation-induced cell death and tissue injury bibl color graph *Science* v354 no6313 p765 N 11 2016

EISENBERG, DEBORAH

Robert B. Silvers (1929–2017) [Cover story] bw color *New York Review of Books* v64 no8 p31 My 11 2017

Eisenberg, Jesse, 1983-
YOU NEVER REALLY KNOW cartoon *New Yorker* v92 no46 p29 Ja 23 2017

Eisenberger, Peter
Roger Wolfe Cohen *Physics Today* v70 no8 p70 Ag 2017

Eisenbrand, Jochen
Nurtur&ing the spirit bw cartoon color *Magazine Antiques* v184 no1 p196 Ja/F 2017

Eisenbrandt, Matt
The manhunt for a martyr's killers K. Clarke *America* v216 no4 p49 F 20 2017

Eisenhauer, Wes
Extraordinary Encounter *South Dakota Magazine* v33 no3 p55 S/O 2017

Eisenhower, Dwight D. (Dwight David), 1890-1969
In Some Ways, He's a Bit Like Ike B. BAIER bw *Weekly Standard* v22 no20 p10 Ja 30 2017
Trivia T. TROY *Washingtonian Magazine* v52 no4 p104 Ja 2017
Where Our WWII Leaders Spent WWI J. WORSHAM *Prologue* v49 no2 p18 Summ 2017

Eisenman, Stephen F.
PAUL GAUGUIN color *Art in America* p127 O 2017

Eisenmann, Thomas R.
The Example Larry and Sergey Should Follow (It's Not Buffett) *Harvard Business Review Digital Articles* p2 Ag 12 2015
What Does an Aspiring Founder Need to Know? *Harvard Business Review Digital Articles* p1 Je 21 2017

Eisen-Martin, Tongo
WHERE WINDOWS SHOULD BE Tongo Eisen-Martin *Harper's Magazine* v334 no2001 p21 F 2017

Eisenstadt, Jill
Home Bodies: In Jill Eisenstadt's comic novel, a Manhattan family seeks safety in the Rockaways after 9/11 B. FISHMAN *New York Times Book Review* p8 Je 11 2017

Eisenstat, Russell
4 Ways CEOs Can Conquer Short-Termism *Harvard Business Review Digital Articles* p2 F 24 2017

Eisenstein, Sergei, 1898-1948
Notes for a General History of Cinema D. POLAN *Film Quarterly* v70 no2 p111 Wint 2016

Eisinger, Jesse
THE APPROVAL MATRIX img *New York* v50 no15 p88 Jl 24 2017
Club Fed D. DAYEN color il *New Republic* v248 no11 p55 N 2017
Crime and No Punishment T. Lavin cartoon color *Bloomberg Businessweek* no4530 p66 Jl 17 2017
Getting Away With It: Why America's top prosecutors no longer go after corporations or their executives J. KWAK *New York Times Book Review* p10 Jl 9 2017
Unjust Prosecution D. BAHNSEN color *National Review* v69 no17 p38 S 11 2017

Eisler, Kim
GAME PLAN *Washingtonian Magazine* v52 no11 p109 Ag 2017

Eisler, Matt
Matt Eisler and Kevin Heisner C. SCHEDLER color *Chicago* v66 no6 p80 Je 2017

EISNER, PETER
OUR MAN IN MANILA: HIS CLANDESTINE MISSIONS WERE VITAL TO MACARTHUR'S FAMED RETURN TO THE PHILIPPINES, YET THE FULL STORY OF CHICK PARSONS' DARING FEATS HAS NOT BEEN TOLD--UNTIL NOW *Smithsonian* v48 no5 p42 S 2017

Eitzen, Amy M.
Changing the Praxis of Retention in Higher Education: A Plan to TEACH All Learners *Change* v48 no6 p58 N/D 2016

Ek, Veronica
Hello, Ericsson. 'The Butcher' Is on the Line color *Bloomberg Businessweek* no4526 p35 Je 12 2017

Ekblaw, Ariel
The Potential for Blockchain to Transform Electronic Health Records bw *Harvard Business Review Digital Articles* p2 Mr 3 2017

Ekekwe, Ndubuisi
Africa's Maker Movement Offers Opportunity for Growth *Harvard Business Review Digital Articles* p2 My 29 2015
Bogus Audited Statements Are Holding Africa Back *Harvard Business Review Digital Articles* p2 Ag 22 2016
The Challenges Facing E-Commerce Start-ups in Africa *Harvard Business Review Digital Articles* p2 Mr 12 2015
How Digital Technology Is Changing Farming in Africa *Harvard Business Review Digital Articles* p2 My 18 2017
Improving Innovation in Africa *Harvard Business Review Digital Articles* p2 F 18 2015
What African Start-Ups Need to Do to Hire and Keep Great Talent *Harvard Business Review Digital Articles* p2 Ap 13 2015
What Africa's Banking Industry Needs to Do to Survive *Harvard Business Review Digital Articles* p2 Jl 28 2016
Why African Entrepreneurship Is Booming *Harvard Business Review Digital Articles* p2 Jl 11 2016

Ekerdt, David J. (David Joseph), 1949-
Letting Go P. Walsh color *Prevention* v69 no4 p54 Ap 2017

Ekers, R. D.
Molecular gas in the halo fuels the growth of a massive cluster galaxy at high redshift bibl graph *Science* v354 no6316 p1128 D 2 2016

Ekins, Dave
OFF-ROAD MOTORSPORTS HALL OF FAME 2017 INDUCTEES ANNOUNCED *Dirt Sports + Off-Road* v51 no12 p8 D 2017

Ekirch, A. Roger, 1950-
Mutiny and Identity J. M. J. BANNER color *Weekly Standard* v23 no1 p35 S 11 2017

Ekstein, Nikki
Crowned Jewels chart color *Bloomberg Businessweek* no4532 p65 Jl 31 2017
Game Changer: ANDREW ZOBLER color *Bloomberg Businessweek* no4534 p68 Ag 14 2017
A Haven for The Hunted color *Bloomberg Businessweek* no4532 p59 Jl 31 2017
How Much Is an Instagram Story Worth? color *Bloomberg Businessweek* no4513 p38 Mr 6 2017
WINTER WONDERLANDS color *Bloomberg Businessweek* no4541 p59 O 9 2017

El Cerrito (Calif.)
#NGM ADVANCES color *National Geographic* v231 no6 pC17 Je 2017

EL Marinero (Company)
Where to Eat Now *Texas Monthly* v45 no1 p110 Ja 2017

El Niño Current
Corals tie stronger El Niños to climate change C. Pala color *Science* v354 no6317 p1210 D 9 2016

El-P (Performer)
COMBAT RAP bw color *Rolling Stone* no1280 p40 F 9 2017
Vulgar prophecies A. Hearlson *Christian Century* v134 no6 p44 Mr 15 2017

El Paso (Tex.)—Description & travel
El Paso J. BREAL *Texas Monthly* v45 no5 p30 My 2017

El Paso (Tex.)—Social conditions
GET THE PICTURE? K. VINE *Texas Monthly* v45 no5 p88 My 2017

El Salvador—Social conditions
Churches in El Salvador help youths find life beyond gangs M. Legrain color *Christian Century* v134 no22 p16 O 25 2017

ELAC Electroacustic GmbH
Elac Uni-Fi UB5 Speaker System M. Fleischmann color graph *Sound & Vision* v82 no1 p60 Ja 2017

Elago Europe (Company)
ELAGO M4 STAND FOR iPHONE 7 J. MATHIS color *Macworld - Digital Edition* v34 no6 p45 Je 2017

Elahi, Mirza M.
Electron optics with p-n junctions in ballistic graphene bibl graph *Science* v353 no6307 p1522 S 30 2016

ELAHI, ROBIN
The Resilience of Marine Ecosystems to Climatic Disturbances *BioScience* v67 no3 p208 Mr 2017

El Aissami, Tareck
Meet Venezuela's New Iron-Fisted No. 2 A. Rosati, F. Zerpa et al color *Bloomberg Businessweek* no4511 p16 F 13 2017

El Akkad, Omar

American War L. Greenblatt color *Entertainment Weekly* no1462 p66 Ap 21 2017

THE IMPENDING CRISIS M. S. BELL *Nation* v305 no4 p36 Ag 14 2017

Red Versus Blue: A fictional (so far) history of the Second American Civil War J. CRONIN cartoon *New York Times Book Review* p11 Ap 23 2017

Elam, Deborah—Awards

Women of Excellence color *Working Mother* p48 F/Mr 2017

Elam, Douglas G.

100 FASTEST-GROWING COMPANIES chart color diag map *Fortune* v176 no4 p157 S 15 2017

El-Amin, Aaliyah

Critical consciousness A key to student achievement bw il *Phi Delta Kappan* v98 no5 p18 F 2017

Elan (Company)

Elan E4 A. Cort cartoon color *Sail* v48 no2 p30 F 2017

Elantra automobile—Evaluation

Hyundai Elantra chart color *Motor Trend* v69 no1 p126 Ja 2017

Little Feat J. Jacquot color graph *Car & Driver* v62 no7 p98 Ja 2017

Elastic scattering

Observation of coherent elastic neutrino-nucleus scattering D. Akimov, J. B. Albert et al diag *Science* v357 no6356 p1123 S 15 2017

Elastic waves

See also

Seismic waves

Apple seismology K. van Wijk and S. Hitchman *Physics Today* v70 no10 p94 O 2017

Elasticity (Economics)

See also

Engel's law

A Refresher on Price Elasticity A. Gallo *Harvard Business Review Digital Articles* p2 Ag 21 2015

Elastomers

cabin maintenance ELASTO-WHAT? J. Cooper color *Cabin Living* p69 S 2017

Elastomers—Evaluation

NEW PRODUCTS *Physics Today* v70 no10 p67 O 2017

Elazegui, Kate—Interviews

One Couple, Two Pregnancies, One Year Later A. Tsoulis-Reay img *New York* v49 no26 p10 D 26 2016

Elba, Idris, 1972-

The BEST OF Elba C. Nashawaty color *Entertainment Weekly* no1486 p30 O 13 2017

A MAN FOR ALL REASONS [Cover story] C. Nashawaty color *Entertainment Weekly* no1486 p26 O 13 2017

WE LOVE HEARING FROM YOU! color *Essence* v48 no6 p20 O 2017

Elba, Idris, 1972—Interviews

IDRIS ELBA: THE RIGHTS STUFF A. Wilkinson color *Entertainment Weekly* no1462 p52 Ap 21 2017

Elbadawi, Ibrahim

Democratic Transitions in the Arab World J. Waterbury *Foreign Affairs* v96 no6 p167 N/D 2017

Elbakyan, Alexandra

Sci-Hub briefly shutters *Science* v357 no6356 p1079 S 15 2017

Elbarbary, Reyad A.

Tudor-SN-mediated endonucleolytic decay of human cell microRNAs promotes G1/S phase transition graph *Science* v356 no6340 p859 My 26 2017

Elbaz, Netanel

Host cell attachment elicits posttranscriptional regulation in infecting enteropathogenic bacteria bibl graph *Science* v355 no6326 p735 F 17 2017

Elbe Sandstone Rocks (Czech Republic & Germany)

THE GERMAN WAY [Cover story] S. TROTTER color *Climbing* no349 p26 N 2016

ELBEIN, ASHER

Skull Session *Smithsonian* v47 no8 p18 D 2016

Elbein, Saul

A Final Fight for the Keystone Pipeline color *Rolling Stone* no1298 p24 O 19 2017

THE SEVENTH GENERATION *New York Times Magazine* p24 F 5 2017

United in Protest color map *National Geographic* v231 no5 p78 My 2017

Elby LP

"I WANT TO RIDE TO WORK EVERY DAY." color *Bicycling* v58 no3 p90 Ap 2017

Elder, Lee, 1934-

GLORY ON THE GREEN G. BLACK color *Ebony* v72 no4 p106 F 2017

ELDER, LINDA

IT'S CRITICAL *USA Today Magazine* v145 no2860 p42 Ja 2017

ELDER, ROBERT K.

The Great Migration img *New York Times Upfront* v149 no4 p16 O 31 2016

ELDER, SCOTT

Badger color *National Geographic Kids* no472 p26 Ag 2017

Bats color *National Geographic Kids* no474 p22 O 2017

FAKE LAKE *National Geographic Kids* no469 p20 Ap 2017

LOL Science cartoon *National Geographic Kids* no470 p24 My 2017

PENGUIN CITY *National Geographic Kids* no467 p14 F 2017

RACCOON *National Geographic Kids* no468 p20 Mr 2017

Surprise Party! cartoon color map *National Geographic Kids* no473 p16 S 2017

Elder care

Caring for Aging Loved Ones R. L. Dilenschneider, T. Allen et al color *Consumer Reports* v82 no12 p6 D 2017

The Delirium Diagnosis S. LONEY color *Walrus* v14 no9 p17 N 2017

Getting Help at Home P. Wang color *Consumer Reports* v82 no12 p40 D 2017

HOW SENIORS SUPPORT EACH OTHER D. Rosato color *Consumer Reports* v82 no12 p48 D 2017

Elder care—United States

To Grandmother's House We Go M. Boyle color *Bloomberg Businessweek* no4541 p15 O 9 2017

Elders (Plants)

WILD EDIBLES color *Missouri Life* v44 no4 p70 Je 2017

Eldorado automobile

TO MILL OR NOT TO MILL M. HOYER *Cycle World* v56 no1 p5 Ja/F 2017

Eldredge, Niles

Leveling up B. Autzen bibl color *Science* v353 no6307 p1505 S 30 2016

Eldredge, Richard L.

BEST OF ATLANTA *Atlanta* v56 no8 p106 D 2016

A BRILLIANT PAIRING *Atlanta* v56 no9 p78 Ja 2017

JANELLE MONÁE *Atlanta* v56 no9 p24 Ja 2017

Election Day

The Day America Stops Voting A. FERGUSON color *Weekly Standard* v22 no11 p22 N 21 2016

Martha's Month *Martha Stewart Living* no269 p4 N 2016

Voting for … Voting G. NORMAN bw color *Weekly Standard* v22 no11 p30 N 21 2016

With Smugness Toward None... A. SMARICK bw cartoon color *Weekly Standard* v22 no12 p26 N 28 2016

Election forecasting

Improving election prediction internationally R. Kennedy, S. Wojcik et al bibl graph *Science* v355 no6324 p515 F 3 2017

Election forecasting—Computer network resources

THE PULSE OF THE PEOPLE J. Bohannon color graph *Science* v355 no6324 p470 F 3 2017

Election law—United States

Legislative Background on the Electoral College *Congressional Digest* v96 no1 p15 Ja 2017

Real Representation: What if every voter in every election had the chance to cast a meaningful vote? L. YOUNG *Ms.* v27 no3 p8 Fall 2017

Election monitoring

More Poll Monitors May Mean More Trouble L. Etter and J. Hanna *Bloomberg Businessweek* no4495 p21 O 17 2016

Election recounts

INSIDE THE RECOUNT S. FRIESS bw color *New Republic* v248 no3 p46 Mr 2017

Jill Stein's Recounts Are Destructive to Democracy T. B. Olson *Time* v188 no24 p18 D 12 2016

Election security measures

Germany Builds An Election Firewall S. Nicola, C. Matlack et al *Bloomberg Businessweek* no4527 p48 Je 19 2017

Elections

> *See also*
> Campaign funds
> Contested elections
> Mayors—Elections
> Nominations for office
> Presidential elections

Fixin' for a Fight M. F. Jacobson *Nutrition Action Health Letter* v44 no1 p2 Ja/F 2017

OF MANY THINGS E. W. SCHMIDT *America* v215 no13 p2 O 31 2016

Results of the 2016 election of AAAS officers M. Jarvis *Science* v355 no6323 p360 Ja 27 2017

Sometimes a Deal Is Just a Deal M. CONTINETTI *Commentary* v144 no3 p64 O 2017

World Elections: Races to Watch T. John color *Time* v188 no27-28 p63 D 26 2016

Elections & international relations

THE KREMLIN'S GREMLINS A. Dejean, H. Levintova et al color *Mother Jones* v42 no4 p20 Jl/Ag 2017

Elections in mass media

SWAT TEAM [Cover story] T. Frank *Harper's Magazine* v333 no1998 p26 N 2016

Elections—Alabama

Moore Unmoored J. McCORMACK color *Weekly Standard* v23 no5 p12 O 9 2017

The Week color il *National Review* v69 no19 p4 O 16 2017

Elections—California

California's Woeful Republicans M. FLEMING *Weekly Standard* v22 no4 p18 O 3 2016

Elections—Corrupt practices

Against Russian Fever B. SHAPIRO *Nation* v304 no12 p4 Ap 10 2017

Paranoia Will Destroy Ya *Weekly Standard* v22 no13 p4 D 5 2016

The Real Election Fraud il *Nation* v303 no20 p3 N 14 2016

TAMPERING WITH THE HEART OF DEMOCRACY E. SOLOMON color *Maclean's* v129 no43 p11 O 31 2016

Elections—Corrupt practices—History—19th century

TESTING THE 15TH AMENDMENT H. Glasby *Prologue* v48 no4 p51 Wint 2016

Elections—Equipment & supplies

> *See also*
> Voting machines

Crappy, Buggy, Obsolete Voting Technology We Trust M. Riley, J. Robertson et al color *Bloomberg Businessweek* no4493 p60 O 3 2016

Elections—Europe

2017 Might Not Be Europe's 'Year of the Populist' After All I. Bremmer *Time* v189 no9 p12 Mr 13 2017

A continent divided C. Matlack and A. van der Schoot color *Bloomberg Businessweek* no4496 p20 O 24 2016

Elections—France

Après le Champagne, More Campaign G. Viscusi, H. Fouquet et al color graph *Bloomberg Businessweek* no4522 p34 My 15 2017

La Nostalgie et l'Oubli M. O. Steinfels bw *Commonweal* v144 no9 p7 My 19 2017

Movers C. Winter color graph *Bloomberg Businessweek* no4522 p13 My 15 2017

On the Stump for Macron—in Florida E. Schine and S. Rastello color *Bloomberg Businessweek* no4525 p12 Je 5 2017

SEEKING SIGNS OF A CATHOLIC REVIVAL IN FRANCE Gobry color *America* v216 no8 p26 Ap 17 2017

Elections—Georgia

A Georgia Election Is a TV Ad Bonanza M. Newkirk, J. McCormick et al bw *Bloomberg Businessweek* no4527 p50 Je 19 2017

Elections—Germany

Bot-hunters eye mischief in German election K. Kupferschmidt color *Science* v357 no6356 p1081 S 15 2017

Germany Stays in the Center M. Champion *Bloomberg Businessweek* no4538 p12 S 18 2017

It's Merkel 3, Schulz 0 In German Campaign A. Delfs, P. Donahue et al color *Bloomberg Businessweek* no4523 p16 My 22 2017

The Next Fake-News War S. Shuster and C. McDonald-gibson color *Time* v190 no10/11 p48 S 18 2017

Elections—Germany—History—21st century

Martin Schulz, Germany's Bernie Sanders T. John color diag *Time* v189 no12 p14 Ap 3 2017

Elections—Great Britain

Election Day in Liverpool: Victory for The Fab Four Party E. Laborde bw *New Orleans Magazine* v51 no10 p216 Ag 2017

Labour's Revival M. MARGARONIS diag *Nation* v305 no1 p3 Jl 3 2017

The Not-So-Darling Buds of Theresa May S. DAISLEY *Commentary* v143 no6 p20 Je 2017

Oh, Snap! R. Hutton, A. Morales et al color diag *Bloomberg Businessweek* no4519 p31 Ap 24 2017

One Tory's Story T. R. BROMUND color *Weekly Standard* v22 no40 p27 Je 26 2017

So Much for That Brexit Mandate G. Smith color *Fortune* v176 no1 p11 Jl 1 2017

Sorry, Tories J. MILLER *In These Times* v41 no8 p41 Ag 2017

Washington View M. Ferguson color *Phi Delta Kappan* v98 no6 p72 Mr 2017

Who's the best choice for the future of work? As Britain goes to the polls, the CIPD asks for legislation on zero hours and action on diversity H. KIRTON *People Management* p8 Je 2017

Elections—Great Britain—History—21st century

Election 2017: the key issues: Which battlegrounds will shape Britain's trip to the polls this June? *People Management* p15 My 2017

Elections—Iceland

The Pirate Party Sets Sail for Election Victory In Iceland T. John color *Time* v188 no19 p9 N 7 2016

Elections—Iran

Iranian Voters Want a Share of the Wealth L. Nasseri and G. Motevalli color *Bloomberg Businessweek* no4521 p14 My 8 2017

Table of Contents *NPQ: New Perspectives Quarterly* v34 no3 p1 Jl 2017

Elections—Kenya

Kenya Braces for Another Chaotic Election M. Cohen and F. Njini color *Bloomberg Businessweek* no4533 p28 Ag 7 2017

Elections—Liberia

As elections approach, a fragile peace holds in Liberia K. Clarke color *America* v216 no8 p15 Ap 17 2017

Elections—Minnesota

Will Minnesota Finally Go Red? B. CASSELMAN color *Weekly Standard* v22 no46 p24 Ag 14 2017

Elections—Morocco

Moroccan Rules U. LINDSEY color *Nation* v303 no22 p20 N 28 2016

Elections—Netherlands

Geert Goes Down color *Nation* v304 no12 p11 Ap 10 2017

Elections—Nevada

How to Win Congress With a Polar Bear Outfit, Cheez-Its, and a Bunch of iPads Z. Mider color *Bloomberg Businessweek* no4495 p20 O 17 2016

Elections—New York (State)

OF SCALES AND THUMBS R. BROOKHISER *American History* v52 no1 p18 Ap 2017

Elections—Ohio

PARTY LINES A. KONERMANN color *Cincinnati Magazine* v51 no1 p24 O 2017

Elections—Press coverage

Filling the void S. FESCHUK color *Maclean's* v129 no46 p65 N 21 2016

Trump's Path To Victory J. Green and S. Issenberg color *Bloomberg Businessweek* no4499 p20 N 14 2016

Elections—Psychological aspects

The Psychological Underpinnings of This Strange Political Summer T. Chamorro-Premuzic *Harvard Business Review Digital Articles* p2 Jl 14 2016

Elections—Social aspects

AFTERMATH G. Packer, A. Gawande et al bw cartoon *New Yorker* v92 no38 p48 N 21 2016

Elections—Texas

TEXAS IS THE FUTURE A. Cockburn *Harper's Magazine* v334 no2002 p26 Mr 2017

Elections—United States

AMERICAN DEMOCRACY BESIEGED [Cover story] A. BERMAN color *Nation* v305 no3 p18 Jl 31 2017

Are Republicans Mid-Terminal? [Cover story] F. BARNES color *Weekly Standard* v22 no36 p10 My 29 2017

The Balance of Power: Senate, House and State Races to Watch A. Altman color diag *Time* v188 no20 p36 N 14 2016

Bloc the Vote [Cover story] R. D. SULLIVAN color graph map *America* v215 no13 p16 O 31 2016

A Changed GOP Y. LEVIN il *National Review* v68 no22 p16 D 5 2016

Climate Change Affects Every Issue Voters Face R. Redford color *Time* v188 no16/17 p79 O 24 2016

COLLEGE ELECTORAL S. Desai color *Washington Monthly* v49 no9/10 p58 S/O 2017

Democrats' Geography Problem A. Greenblatt *Governing* v30 no4 p17 Ja 2017

Don't Mainstream The Alt-Right B. SHAPIRO *National Review* v68 no22 p41 D 5 2016

Don't Sweat the Primaries A. Greenblatt *Governing* v30 no2 p17 N 2016

EASY CHAIR W. Kirn *Harper's Magazine* v334 no2001 p5 F 2017

The Establishment Never Had a Chance F. Rich img *New York* v49 no23 p24 N 14 2016

Falling Apart at the Polls [Cover story] J. B. Wogan *Governing* v30 no2 p26 N 2016

Forecast: Gridlock J. COST color *Weekly Standard* v23 no2 p16 S 18 2017

How the Media Got Smarter About Calling Elections H. S. Edwards chart color *Time* v188 no20 p17 N 14 2016

How votes are wasted *Christian Century* v134 no17 p7 Ag 16 2017

I'M DOING MY PART, ARE YOU? H. KATZ *Humanist* v77 no3 p39 My/Je 2017

The Kids Will Be Fine H. WILHELM *National Review* v68 no22 p48 D 5 2016

Maine M. Paterniti *New York Times Magazine* p36 N 20 2016

A Midterm Forecast J. COST color *National Review* v69 no19 p15 O 16 2017

The New Red Scare bw color *Weekly Standard* v22 no16 p3 D 26 2016

NSA DOCUMENT EXTRACT 111016: 00:45GMT R. LONG *National Review* v68 no22 p50 D 5 2016

The Once And Future King County E. GRIEDER *Texas Monthly* v44 no11 p58 N 2016

POLITICS MATTER H. ARABADJIS *USA Today Magazine* v146 no2866 p26 Jl 2017

The Problem with 'Political Will' M. Funkhouser *Governing* v30 no5 p61 F 2017

The Pros and Cons of the Electoral College System *Congressional Digest* v96 no1 p18 Ja 2017

The Real Voter Fraud Z. ROTH color *New Republic* v248 no8/9 p10 Ag/S 2017

The Road to Victory in Virginia F. BARNES cartoon *Weekly Standard* v22 no38 p10 Je 12 2017

Shaken and Stirred J. W. Ceaser *Hoover Digest: Research & Opinion on Public Policy* no1 p9 Wint 2017

Those '60s Flashbacks C. MILORD, T. STRAKA et al *Commentary* v142 no4 p10 N 2016

Too Many Voters Lost in a Land of Clueless *USA Today Magazine* v145 no2859 p1 D 2016

TRUMP FILLS THE VACUUM: HE EXEMPLIFIES AND ACCELERATES THE DECLINE OF AMERICA'S INSTITUTIONS [Cover story] Y. LEVIN *Commentary* v142 no5 p16 D 2016

The Trump Voters Who'd Become My Friends M. Jacobson *New York* v49 no23 p23 N 14 2016

The Unpopular Populist [Cover story] color *Commonweal* v143 no19 p5 D 2 2016

Washington View M. Ferguson color *Phi Delta Kappan* v98 no6 p72 Mr 2017

The Week color il *National Review* v68 no22 p4 D 5 2016

WILL THE ELECTORAL COLLEGE EVER GO AWAY? J. MARKUSOFF color *Maclean's* v129 no47 p39 N 28 2016

Wrapped in an Enigma color *Weekly Standard* v22 no43 p6 Jl 24 2017

Elections—United States—Corrupt practices

How Real Are the Risks of a Rigged Election? H. S. Edwards color *Time* v188 no14 p36 O 10 2016

Elections—United States—History

"FEVER GRIPS THE ENTIRE NATION" A. GOLDHAMMER bw color il map *Nation* v303 no16 p10 O 17 2016

OF SCALES AND THUMBS R. BROOKHISER *American History* v52 no1 p18 Ap 2017

Elections—United States—History—21st century

TERMS OF ENGAGEMENT T. Barker *Harper's Magazine* v334 no2001 p28 F 2017

Elections—United States—Lawsuits & claims

Litigating Politics K. D. WILLIAMSON color *National Review* v68 no23 p15 D 19 2016

Elections—United States—Social aspects

Renovating Democracy and Salvaging Globalization N. Gardels *NPQ: New Perspectives Quarterly* v34 no1 p2 Ja 2017

Elections—West Bank

Hamas Takes a Step Away from Isolation J. Malsin color *Time* v190 no13 p15 O 2 2017

Elective surgery

4 Things to Do Before You Have Surgery color *Prevention* v69 no8 p8 Ag 2017

Electoral college

DEMOCRACY DENIED J. Nichols bw map *Progressive* p15 D 2016/Ja 2017

Drop the College J. NICHOLS color *Nation* v303 no25/26 p3 D 19 2016

The Electoral College Debate *Congressional Digest* v96 no1 p1 Ja 2017

Electoral College Reform *Congressional Digest* v96 no1 p8 Ja 2017

Electoral Masterpiece J. H. ANDERSON map *Weekly Standard* v22 no17 p10 Ja 2 2017

How the Electoral College System Works *Congressional Digest* v96 no1 p2 Ja 2017

How to Make the Electoral College Work for Everyone S. Silberstein graph map *Washington Monthly* v49 no3-5 p11 Mr-My 2017

Legislative Background on the Electoral College *Congressional Digest* v96 no1 p15 Ja 2017

A New Trade Consensus E. CONARD *National Review* v68 no22 p35 D 5 2016

The Old Electoral College Try J. COST color *Weekly Standard* v22 no12 p18 N 28 2016

The Pros and Cons of the Electoral College System *Congressional Digest* v96 no1 p18 Ja 2017

Whose Representative Government, Again? S. Richardson *American History* v52 no1 p6 Ap 2017

WILL THE ELECTORAL COLLEGE EVER GO AWAY? J. MARKUSOFF color *Maclean's* v129 no47 p39 N 28 2016

Electoral college—History

The Electoral College in History *Congressional Digest* v96 no1 p6 Ja 2017

Electoral reform

Canada Punts on Electoral Reform *America* v216 no5 p8 Mr 6 2017

Electoral College Reform *Congressional Digest* v96 no1 p8 Ja 2017

Reforming the reformers J. GEDDES color *Maclean's* v129 no42 p18 O 24 2016

Voting for Change D. C. Vock *Governing* v30 no1 p17 O 2016

Electric apparatus & appliances

See also

Hair dryers

Storage batteries

Transducers

Generators color *Popular Mechanics* v193 no7 p32 S 2016

Idle Power Hogs T. SCHLOSSBERG *Reader's Digest* v189 no1128 p41 Mr 2017

Electric apparatus & appliances—Evaluation

PUNCH LIST K. SELZER color *Better Homes & Gardens* v95 no2 p58 F 2016

STRANGE BREW G. Megroz color *Bloomberg Businessweek* no4514 p74 Mr 13 2017

Electric automobiles

See also

Solar cars

Tesla automobiles
The Inevitable EV color *MIT Technology Review* v120 no4 p100 Jl/Ag 2017
Sketching a High-Voltage Future E. Behrmann color *Bloomberg Businessweek* no494 p43 O 10 2016
A Small-Scale Power Solution Could Pay Big Dividends Across the U.S. J. Weiland color *Time* v190 no7 p22 Ag 21 2017
The Tesla of Buses A. OHNSMAN color *Forbes* v198 no8 p54 D 20 2016

Electric automobiles—Evaluation
0-60 MPH in 2.3 Seconds! F. Markus color graph *Motor Trend* v69 no5 p12 My 2017
2015 TESLA MODEL S P85D E. Tingwall bw color *Car & Driver* v62 no11 p12 Ap 2017
FIRST DRIVE Tesla Model 3 K. Reynolds and S. Evans color *Motor Trend* v69 no10 p16 O 2017
THE NEW BLOOD E. TINGWALL color *Car & Driver* v62 no7 p46 Ja 2017
People Management 10 BEST ECO FLEET CARS: The writing's on the wall for petrol and diesel cars - so what should your staff be driving? *People Management* p45 S 2017
STILL the BEST [Cover story] bw color *Popular Science* v289 no6 p70 N/D 2017
THUNDERSTRUCK D. ZENLEA color *Road & Track* v68 no9 p84 Je 2017

Electric automobiles—Sales & prices
The Everyman Ride For the Upper Half D. Hull, J. Butters et al bw *Bloomberg Businessweek* no4533 p14 Ag 7 2017
Why the Tesla model isn't replicable M. Rechtin color *Motor Trend* v69 no28 p28 Ap 2017

Electric batteries
See also
Fuel cells
Lithium cells
Better Batteries M. Sedacca color *Scientific American* v317 no4 p23 O 2017
The Perfect Battery S. ORNES color diag graph *Discover* v38 no6 p78 Jl 2017
Rechargeable nickel–3D zinc batteries: An energy-dense, safer alternative to lithium-ion J. F. Parker, C. N. Chervin et al bw chart diag g *Science* v356 no6336 p415 Ap 28 2017

Electric batteries—Evaluation
Focus on analytical equipment, sensors, and detectors A. Mandelis *Physics Today* v70 no2 p63 F 2017

Electric batteries—Maintenance & repair
Batteries and Boom G. Michal *Boating World* v37 no9 p28 N/D 2016

Electric batteries—Research
2016 WORLD CHANGING IDEAS [Cover story] A. Sneed, J. Pavlus et al color *Scientific American* v315 no6 p32 D 2016
Direct and continuous strain control of catalysts with tunable battery electrode materials Haotian Wang, Shicheng Xu et al bibl graph *Science* v354 no6315 p1031 N 25 2016

Electric bicycles—Evaluation
BOO YA! E-BIKES! color *Bicycling* v58 no8 p(Sp)2 S 2017
BULLS STURMVOGEL E EVO M. Yozell color *Bicycling* v58 no10 p0 N/D 2017
DOCKBOC GEAR, TOOLS AND TOYS color *Sea Magazine* v109 no26 Jl 2017
LOAD TOURING C. Giddings color *Bicycling* v58 no8 p(Sp)8 S 2017
QUICK NEO M. Yozell color *Bicycling* v58 no8 p(Sp)4 S 2017
SUPER COMMUTER+ 8S J. Sherry color *Bicycling* v58 no8 p(Sp)10 S 2017
TURBO EVO FSR COMP CARBON 6FATTIE R. Koch color *Bicycling* v58 no8 p(Sp)20 S 2017

Electric buses
Let the Light Shine In A. JONES color *Boating World* v38 no7 p38 Jl 2017
Platinum Upgrade: The Catalina series gets elevated styling and remains multitalented A. JONES color *Boating World* v38 no7 p42 Jl 2017

Electric cables
See also
Submarine cables
A TWELVE-MONTH-OLD'S Letter to Santa R. D'APICE *Reader's Digest* v188 no1126 p92 D 2016/Ja 2017

Electric cables—Evaluation
Old Tech, New Tech color *Old House Journal* v45 no2 p50 Ap 2017

Electric charge & distribution
the body electrician A. PIORE cartoon color *Popular Science* p64 Ja/F 2017

Electric conductivity
See also
Semiconductors
Superconductivity
Staying conductive in the stretch S. Napolitano bibl diag *Science* v355 no6320 p24 Ja 6 2017

Electric cooperatives
THE $164 BILLION CO-OPS YOU DON'T KNOW ABOUT N. SCHNEIDER color *Nation* v304 no16 p26 My 22 2017

Electric current measurement
Researcher goes all in to study eel electricity M. Quintanilla color graph *Science News* v192 no6 p4 O 14 2017

Electric eel
Researcher goes all in to study eel electricity M. Quintanilla color graph *Science News* v192 no6 p4 O 14 2017

Electric equipment in boats
CRUISING TIPS T. Cunliffe color *Sail* v48 no11 p54 N 2017
The Doctor Is In J. MOSER color *Power & Motoryacht* v34 no10 p44 O 2017
No Good Deed… G. MICHAL color *Boating World* v38 no7 p45 Jl 2017

Electric equipment in model railroads
News & Products color *Model Railroader* v84 no10 p10 O 2017

Electric equipment in motorcycles
GREAT EXPECTATIONS K. Cameron *Cycle World* v56 no9 p28 O 2017

Electric fences
Power an ELECTRIC FENCE with Solar: Easy to install and shockingly versatile, a solar electric fence will give you the Power to keep your animals in the pasture, even if you're off the grid J. R. Yago *Mother Earth News* no283 p44 Ag/S 2017
Small-Scale MOB GRAZING J. Salatin *Mother Earth News* no279 p72 D/Ja 2017

Electric fuses
DIY POWER MANAGEMENT [Cover story] J. KOPYCINSKI color *Dirt Sports + Off-Road* v51 no12 p66 D 2017

Electric generators—Alternating current
Engine Emergency: DOA! Part 1 M. SMITH color *Power & Motoryacht* v33 no3 p113 Mr 2017

Electric generators—Evaluation
Generators [Cover story] color *Popular Mechanics* p32 S 2017
Generators [Cover story] color *Popular Mechanics* v193 no7 p32 S 2016
Portable Hydropower O. Kharif cartoon color *Bloomberg Businessweek* no4493 p45 O 3 2016
POWER UP! B. Freese *Successful Farming* v115 no2 p50 F 2017

Electric impedance
Photonic doping tunes transparent media M. Wilson *Physics Today* v70 no5 p20 My 2017

Electric insulators & insulation
A twist on the Majorana fermion V. S. Pribiag graph *Science* v357 no6348 p252 Jl 21 2017

Electric Intercourse (Music)
THE 26-WORD REVIEW K. O'donnell color *Entertainment Weekly* no1465 p52 My 12 2017

Electric inverters
Solar Energy color *Cabin Living* p68 Ja/F 2017

Electric inverters—Evaluation
POWER UP! B. Freese *Successful Farming* v115 no2 p50 F 2017

Electric lamps
Vintage Lighting Restored M. ELLEN POLSON color *Arts & Crafts Homes & the Revival* v12 no4 p34 Fall 2017

Electric light fixtures
Rustic LIGHTING D. Howland color *Cabin Living* p9 Ja/F 2017
SAVING MONEY ON YOUR PROJECT color *Cabin Living* p11 Je 2017

Electric light fixtures—Evaluation
All the Right Moves J. Taraska color *Architectural Record* v205 no2 p124 F 2017

Bright Eyes S. COCHRAN color *Architectural Digest* v74 no3 p44 Mr 2017

Euroluce: The biennial lighting trade show, which took place alongside the Salone del Mobile last month, spanned four large pavilions at Milan's sprawling fairgrounds. Additional exhibitors showcased their introductions at off-site venues throughout... J. Minutillo color *Architectural Record* v205 no5 p137 My 2017

guiding lights W. T. Georgis color *Architectural Digest* v74 no4 p102 Ap 2017

Radiant Materials R. C. Orrell color *Architectural Record* v205 no5 p135 My 2017

Rustic Lighting M. R. JOHNSON color *Cabin Living* p38 Ja/F 2017

STUFF YOU WANT *Boating World* v38 no5 p30 My 2017

Electric lighting
See also
Electric light fixtures

A New Way to Think About Office Lighting I. Campbell, K. Calhoun et al *Harvard Business Review Digital Articles* p2 Je 27 2017

Electric lighting—Equipment & supplies
LIGHTING color *Old House Journal* v44 p91 2016 Design Center source Book

Electric lighting—Evaluation
HOME UNDER $100 color *Redbook* p106 Jl/Ag 2017

Electric locomotives
See also
Electro-diesel locomotives

Conquering Cajon in HO scale L. Illes color diag *Model Railroader* v84 no1 p46 Ja 2017

DIGITAL MR D. Kawala color diag *Model Railroader* v84 no1 p6 Ja 2017

Electric locomotives—Evaluation
ScaleTrains.com HO Union Pacific GTEL lives up to Museum Quality expectations D. Kawala color *Model Railroader* v84 no1 p68 Ja 2017

Electric locomotives—Maintenance & repair
Bringing engines back from the dead J. Kelly color *Model Railroader* v84 no1 p26 Ja 2017

Electric motorcycles
A Silent Road Warrior H. Elliott color *Bloomberg Businessweek* no4533 p59 Ag 7 2017

STUPID OR AMAZING? color *Popular Mechanics* p76 D 2016/Ja 2017

AN UN-SOUND FUTURE P. D'orléans *Cycle World* v56 no9 p26 O 2017

Electric power consumption
A Shock From Cheap Gas N. S. Malik and B. Eckhouse color map *Bloomberg Businessweek* no4524 p38 My 29 2017

Wind on the Upswing M. Hand *MIT Technology Review* v119 no6 p11 N/D 2016

Electric power distribution grids
A Fight Over the Electric Grid Could Reshape America's Green Power Boom J. Worland color *Time* v190 no2/3 p26 Jl 10-17 2017

NOT OFF THE GRID, BUT WE CAN SEE THE EDGE FROM HERE J. D. TUCCILLE color *Reason* v48 no10 p16 Mr 2017

A Small-Scale Power Solution Could Pay Big Dividends Across the U.S J. Worland color *Time* v190 no7 p22 Ag 21 2017

Electric power distribution grids—Security measures
Preparing for the Cyberattack That Will Knock Out U.S. Power Grids S. Madnick *Harvard Business Review Digital Articles* p2 My 10 2017

Electric power distribution—United States
THE $164 BILLION CO-OPS YOU DON'T KNOW ABOUT N. SCHNEIDER color *Nation* v304 no16 p26 My 22 2017

Electric power plants—European Union countries
THE BURNING QUESTION W. Cornwall color *Science* v355 no6320 p18 Ja 6 2017

Electric power production
Another Illegal Power Grab T. Eastland *Weekly Standard* v22 no5 p8 O 10 2016

Green Hydrogen M. C. Lott color *Scientific American* v316 no5 p21 My 2017

It's Electric—With the Right Mix A. Sneed color diag *Scientific American* v316 no3 p24 Mr 2017

Why Apple Is Getting into the Energy Business P. Fox-Penner *Harvard Business Review Digital Articles* p2 N 15 2016

Winds of Change J. Hsu color *Scientific American* v315 no5 p21 N 2016

Electric power production equipment—Evaluation
Generators [Cover story] color *Popular Mechanics* p32 S 2017

Electric power systems—Equipment & supplies
A Ceiling That Wirelessly Charges Devices J. Zorthian color *Time* v189 no3 p21 Ja 30 2017

Electric power—Africa
All of Africa Will Be Bright S. Butler *Sierra* v101 no5 p24 S/O 2016

Electric power—Asia
Powering Ahead: Turning Laos into ASEAN's 'Battery' *Foreign Affairs* v95 no6 p(Sp)6 N/D 2016

Electric properties of graphene
High-harmonic generation in graphene enhanced by elliptically polarized light excitation N. Yoshikawa, T. Tamaya et al color graph *Science* v356 no6339 p736 My 19 2017

High-temperature quantum oscillations caused by recurring Bloch states in graphene superlattices R. Krishna Kumar, X. Chen et al color *Science* v357 no6347 p181 Jl 14 2017

Plasmonic imaging is gaining momentum D. N. Basov and M. M. Fogler graph *Science* v357 no6347 p132 Jl 14 2017

Tuning quantum nonlocal effects in graphene plasmonics M. B. Lundeberg, Y. Gao et al bw diag *Science* v357 no6347 p187 Jl 14 2017

Electric railroads—Wires & wiring
BENCHWORK AND TRACK for the Beer Line addition E. White and C. Grivno color diag *Model Railroader* v84 no2 p36 F 2017

Build a WIRING HARNESS P. Birdsong color diag *Model Railroader* v84 no2 p54 F 2017

Electric shavers—Evaluation
Beard Be Gone M. STEFANOV bw color *Esquire* v167 no1 p46 F 2017

Electric shock
WAYS TO PREVENT ELECTRIC SHOCK DROWNING [Cover story] *USA Today Magazine* v146 no2867 p1 Ag 2017

Electric stimulation
See also
Cochlear implants

Electric switchgear
See also
Keyboards (Electronics)

SWITCH IT UP [Cover story] B. W. SMITH color *Dirt Sports + Off-Road* v51 no10 p48 O 2017

Electric switchgear—Equipment & supplies
SWITCH THE PLATES color *Old House Journal* v45 no3 p23 My 2017

Electric switchgear—Evaluation
ELGATO'S EVE HOMEKIT LIGHTSWITCH C. MCGARRY color *Macworld - Digital Edition* p45 D 2016

Nintendo Switch Launches This month *USA Today Magazine* v145 no2862 p80 Mr 2017

Electric toothbrushes
PACK A PUNCH H. Garrison Phillips *Washingtonian Magazine* v52 no9 p113 Je 2017

Electric utilities
How Utilities Are Using Blockchain to Modernize the Grid J. Basden and M. Cottrell *Harvard Business Review Digital Articles* p2 Mr 23 2017

Electric utilities—Rates
Building a Better World, Together color *Consumer Reports* v82 no1 p8 Ja 2017

Electric utilities—United States
A Shock From Cheap Gas N. S. Malik and B. Eckhouse color map *Bloomberg Businessweek* no4524 p38 My 29 2017

Why Apple Is Getting into the Energy Business P. Fox-Penner *Harvard Business Review Digital Articles* p2 N 15 2016

Electric vehicle design & construction
The New Nissan Leaf Is Fun. Can It Transform the Electric-Vehicle Market? J. Worland color *Time* v190 no13 p24 O 2 2017

Nissan Tries Turning Over a New Leaf Jie Ma and Masatsugu Horie *Bloomberg Businessweek* no4536 p18 S 4 2017

ctric vehicle industry forecasting

We're Going To Need More Lithium D. Merrill, J. Shankleman et al diag graph map *Bloomberg Businessweek* no4537 p60 S 11 2017

Electric vehicles

    See also

    Electric automobiles

    Electric motorcycles

BOOT SCOOT BOOGIE J. PEARLEY HUFFMAN chart color *Car & Driver* v63 no1 p64 Jl 2017

Build Your Own $500 Drift Trike D. Glad chart color *Hot Rod* v70 no10 p14 O 2017

Buses and Trucks Plug In for Power *Mother Earth News* no283 p9 Ag/S 2017

"Drive Clean" at a Discount *New York State Conservationist* v71 no6 p28 Je 2017

Electric Avenues Smart roads might serve as off-board EV range extenders F. Markus color *Motor Trend* v69 no9 p28 S 2017

Electric vehicle prospects L. E. ERICKSON *Issues in Science & Technology* v33 no3 p12 Spr 2017

The Existential Question Facing the Auto Industry M. L. Tushman *Harvard Business Review Digital Articles* p2 Ap 12 2016

The Future of Electric Vehicles Is Golf Carts, Not Tesla T. Bartman *Harvard Business Review Digital Articles* p2 My 14 2015

JUMP START E. HUMES *Sierra* v102 no5 p38 St/O 2017

Karma Revero Back to the future C. Walton color *Motor Trend* v69 no9 p18 S 2017

A Lot on the Line C. RITCHIE *Indianapolis Monthly* v40 no3 p68 N 2016

NEWS LETTERS M. Gaffney *Washingtonian Magazine* v52 no6 p199 Mr 2017

No Cars Go C. SYLVESTER color *Walrus* v14 no7 p18 S 2017

NOT SO FAST K. CAMERON *Cycle World* v56 no3 p28 Ap 2017

Things to Come E. Perkins color *Hot Rod* v70 no10 p8 O 2017

Electric vehicles—Environmental aspects

Electric Vehicles Climate Saviors, or Not? J. BARKENBUS chart color *Issues in Science & Technology* v33 no2 p55 Wint 2017

Electric vehicles—Evaluation

2017 EV BUYERS' GUIDE J. Motavalli *Sierra* v102 no5 p40 St/O 2017

Electric vehicles—Government policy

Norway Ditches The 'Fossil Car' M. Campbell and S. Sleire color *Bloomberg Businessweek* no4525 p31 Je 5 2017

Electric vehicles—Sales & prices

Electric Vehicles Are Here. Now We Need to Figure Out How to Charge Them J. Worland color *Time* v190 no16/17 p34 O 23 2017

Electric wire

    See also

    Electric fences

    Nanowires

Working with DCC cables color diag *Model Railroader* v84 no3 p62 Mr 2017

Electric wiring

Commons, grounds, and DCC L. Puckett color diag *Model Railroader* v84 no9 p56 S 2017

Electrical engineering—Bibliographies

NEW BOOKS *Physics Today* v69 no12 p60 D 2016

Electrical equipment wholesalers

Lighting & Electrical Equipment Manufacturers & Distributors *Stage Directions* v30 no7 p38 Jl 1 2017

Electrical injuries

THE HOUSE AT THE END OF THE WORLD J. Mooallem *New York Times Magazine* p38 Ja 8 2017

Electricity

    See also

    Hall effect

The 3 Stages of a Country Embracing Renewable Energy C. Burger and J. Weinmann *Harvard Business Review Digital Articles* p2 Ap 17 2017

ALL AROUND: THE FARM® P. Barbour *Successful Farming* v115 no12 p77 O 2017

BOOK LIGHT! J. SCHADEWALD color diag *Popular Mechanics* p96 N 2017

charging up a battery conference M. B. Griggs color *Popular Science* v289 no6 p80 N/D 2017

Going After Big Climate E. Daigneau *Governing* v30 no1 p20 O 2016

The search for MAGNETIC MONOPOLES A. Rajantie *Physics Today* v69 no10 p40 O 2016

Electro-diesel locomotives

TRACK SIDE PHOTOS color *Model Railroader* v84 no1 p78 Ja 2017

Electro-diesel locomotives—Evaluation

Accurately modeled HO EMD GP38-2 features powerful motor and sound S. Otte color *Model Railroader* v84 no1 p70 Ja 2017

Electrocatalysis

Combining theory and experiment in electrocatalysis: Insights into materials design Zhi Wei Seh, J. Kibsgaard et al bibl color graph *Science* v355 no6321 p1 Ja 13 2017

Electrodes

Charge delivery goes the distance Cheng and F. Li color *Science* v356 no6338 p582 My 12 2017

Colloidally prepared La-doped $BaSnO_3$ electrodes for efficient, photostable perovskite solar cells S. S. Shin, E. J. Yeom et al graph *Science* v356 no6334 p167 Ap 14 2017

Direct and continuous strain control of catalysts with tunable battery electrode materials Haotian Wang, Shicheng Xu et al bibl graph *Science* v354 no6315 p1031 N 25 2016

Electroencephalography

Getting Through *USA Today Magazine* v146 no2868 p36 S 2017

THE SQUISHY SCIENCE OF NEUROFEEDBACK P. A. Smith color *Bloomberg Businessweek* no4523 p30 My 22 2017

Electrolytes

Better Batteries M. Sedacca color *Scientific American* v317 no4 p23 O 2017

HOW CYCLING WORKS A. C. Shilton, S. Yeager et al cartoon diag *Bicycling* v58 no9 p21 O 2017

PASS THE SALT C. Barakat and M. Freckleton color *Equus* no478 p22 Jl 2017

WATER, BABY! color *Women's Health* v14 no5 p140 Je 2017

Electrolytic corrosion—Prevention

ALL ABOUT ANODES: WOULD A "ZINC" MADE OF AN-OTHER MATERIAL STILL WORK AS WELL? OR PER-HAPS BETTER? R. MCAFEE *Sea Magazine* v109 no5 p24 My 2017

Electromagnetic couplings

Long-distance operator for energy transfer F. J. Garcia-Vidal and J. Feist diag *Science* v357 no6358 p1357 S 29 2017

Electromagnetic fields

    See also

    Lorentz force

Can Electromagnetic Fields Create Ghosts? B. RADFORD *Skeptical Inquirer* v41 no3 p30 My/Je 2017

Electromagnetic therapy

THE ADDICTED BRAIN [Cover story] F. Smith color *National Geographic* v232 no3 p30 S 2017

Electromagnetism

    See also

    Electromagnetic fields

    Magnetic monopoles

Magnetic monopole search, past and present A. Scharff Goldhaber *Physics Today* v70 no6 p12 Je 2017

Electromechanical devices

Sensitive electromechanical sensors using viscoelastic graphene-polymer nanocomposites C. S. Boland, U. Khan et al bibl graph *Science* v354 no6317 p1257 D 9 2016

Electron configuration

    See also

    Electron spin states

Femtosecond electron-phonon lock-in by photoemission and x-ray free-electron laser S. Gerber, Yang et al chart diag *Science* v357 no6346 p71 Jl 7 2017

Electron density

A conundrum for density functional theory S. Hammes-Schiffer bibl diag *Science* v355 no6320 p28 Ja 6 2017

Electron diffraction

Electron diffraction and the hydrogen atom L. B. McCusker bibl diag *Science* v355 no6321 p136 Ja 13 2017

Electron diffraction sees hydrogen atoms J. Miller *Physics Today* v70 no3 p16 Mr 2017

Hydrogen positions in single nanocrystals revealed by electron

...action L. Palatinus, P. Brázda et al bibl color *Science* v355 no6321 p1 Ja 13 2017

Ultrafast electron diffraction imaging of bond breaking in di-ionized acetylene B. Wolter, M. G. Pullen et al bibl graph *Science* v354 no6310 p308 O 21 2016

Electron gas

A Fermi-degenerate three-dimensional optical lattice clock S. L. Campbell, R. B. Hutson et al color diag graph *Science* v357 no6359 p90 O 6 2017

Electron holography

Tracking the dynamics of electron expulsion C. Vozzi diag *Science* v356 no6343 p1126 Je 16 2017

Electron-ion collisions

A parity-breaking electronic nematic phase transition in the spin-orbit coupled metal Cd2Re2O7 J. W. Harter, Z. Y. Zhao et al diag *Science* v356 no6335 p295 Ap 21 2017

Electron microscopy

Clathrate colloidal crystals H. Lin, S. Lee et al bibl color *Science* v355 no6328 p931 Mr 3 2017

Imaging rotational dynamics of nanoparticles in liquid by 4D electron microscopy X. Fu, B. Chen et al bibl diag graph *Science* v355 no6324 p494 F 3 2017

Laser-driven nanoparticle motion in liquids P. Baum bibl color *Science* v355 no6324 p458 F 3 2017

LOOKING for TROUBLE on Optical Surfaces H. Auten *Science & Technology Review* p17 Ap/My 2017

RESEARCH color *Science* v355 no6324 p490 F 3 2017

RESOLVING SMALLER MOLECULES WITH CRYO-EM *Physics Today* v70 no9 p22 S 2017

Electron optics

Electron optics with p-n junctions in ballistic graphene M. M. Elahi, K. M. M. Habib et al bibl graph *Science* v353 no6307 p1522 S 30 2016

Electron-phonon interactions

Femtosecond electron-phonon lock-in by photoemission and x-ray free-electron laser S. Gerber, Yang et al chart diag *Science* v357 no6346 p71 Jl 7 2017

Electron research

Tuning quantum nonlocal effects in graphene plasmonics M. B. Lundeberg, Y. Gao et al bw diag *Science* v357 no6347 p187 Jl 14 2017

Electron spin

CONSTRAINING INTERPRETATIONS OF QUANTUM MECHANICS *Physics Today* v70 no2 p23 F 2017

A molecular spin-photovoltaic device X. Sun, S. Vélez et al color diag *Science* v357 no6352 p677 Ag 18 2017

Electron spin states

Addressing spin states with infrared light A. L. Falk bw *Science* v357 no6352 p649 Ag 18 2017

Classical-quantum sensors keep better time A. N. Jordan graph *Science* v356 no6340 p802 My 26 2017

Electronic address books

The Joys of Keeping An Address Book P. GOULD color *Reader's Digest* v190 no1133 p40 S 2017

Electronic amplifiers

See also

Audio amplifiers

Vintage 47's VA-185G Amplifier K. Baumann color *Downbeat* v84 no7 p80 Jl 2017

Electronic apparatus & appliances

See also

Automotive electronics

Electronic waste

Electronics for model railroads

Can We Quantify the Value of Connected Devices? S. Menon *Harvard Business Review Digital Articles* p2 O 20 2014

Forward Thinking J. Y. WOOD color *Power & Motoryacht* v34 no10 p50 O 2017

Ick! Clean Your Touch Screen! K. MURPHY *Reader's Digest* v188 no1125 p72 N 2016

Why We Need to Outsmart Our Smart Devices E. Bernstein *Harvard Business Review Digital Articles* p2 O 23 2014

Electronic apparatus & appliances—Evaluation

new products color *Science* v357 no6350 p516 Ag 4 2017

THE ULTIMATE GUIDE TO TECH @50+ STEPHANIE CHANG color *AARP: The Magazine* v59 no1A p34 D 2015/

Ja 2016

Electronic banking

See also

Electronic funds transfers

Internet banking

What Africa's Banking Industry Needs to Do to Survive N. Ekekwe *Harvard Business Review Digital Articles* p2 Jl 28 2016

Electronic book piracy

Digital Piracy L. SPENCER color *Publishers Weekly* v263 no45 p64 N 7 2016

Electronic book standards

Audiobook Publishing And Sales Take Off Up North E. NAWOTKA color *Publishers Weekly* v264 no41 p18 O 9 2017

Electronic books

At 25, Berrett-Koehler Looks Forward A. Gross color *Publishers Weekly* v264 no18 p12 My 1 2017

COMBINED PRINT AND E-BOOK BEST SELLERS *New York Times Book Review* p19 Jl 16 2017

COMBINED PRINT AND E-BOOK BEST SELLERS *New York Times Book Review* p23 F 26 2017

Content Discovery and Consumption Go Mobile B. F. O'Leary *Publishers Weekly* v263 no39 p25 S 26 2016

A Different Kind of Bundle L. Dawson *Publishers Weekly* v264 no12 p24 Mr 20 2017

How to Market Self-Published E-books to Libraries M. COKER *Publishers Weekly* v264 no13 p45 Mr 27 2017

iBook Bestsellers C. JURIS chart color *Publishers Weekly* v264 no12 p21 Mr 20 2017

iBOOKS AUDIO TOP 10 J. Maher and C. JURIS chart color *Publishers Weekly* v264 no28 p16 Jl 10 2017

iBooks Bestsellers chart color *Publishers Weekly* v263 no43 p17 O 24 2016

iBooks Bestsellers C. JURIS chart color *Publishers Weekly* v264 no39 p20 S 25 2017

The Indie E-Books Evolution A. DANIEL *Publishers Weekly* v263 no39 p48 S 26 2016

Taking a Look at Apple's and Amazon's E-book Bestsellers C. Reid chart *Publishers Weekly* v264 no29 p8 Jl 17 2017

Electronic books software

Serial Fiction on Tap J. D. BIERSDORFER *New York Times Book Review* p12 My 14 2017

Electronic books—Congresses

The Bad News About E-books J. Milliot graph *Publishers Weekly* v264 no4 p4 Ja 23 2017

Electronic books—Law & legislation

Digital Piracy L. SPENCER color *Publishers Weekly* v263 no45 p64 N 7 2016

Electronic books—Ratings & rankings

COMBINED PRINT AND E-BOOK BEST SELLERS *New York Times Book Review* p31 My 21 2017

Electronic books—Sales & prices

The Bad News About E-books J. Milliot graph *Publishers Weekly* v264 no4 p4 Ja 23 2017

Digital Fatigue A. WEINSTEIN *Publishers Weekly* v263 no42 p72 O 17 2016

'GOTT' Was Tops In 2016 J. Milliot *Publishers Weekly* v264 no33 p12 Ag 14 2017

Humble Bundle Reports $11 Million From E-book Bundles in 2016 C. Reid *Publishers Weekly* v264 no27 p11 Jl 3 2017

iBook Bestsellers chart color *Publishers Weekly* v264 no26 p16 Je 26 2017

iBooks Bestsellers chart color *Publishers Weekly* v264 no4 p15 Ja 23 2017

Electronic calendars—Computer network resources

How to get a shared family calendar with a Microsoft Account I. PAUL color diag *PCWorld* v35 no7 p188 Jl 2017

Electronic check conversion

Where Paper Checks Go—for Now R. Partington cartoon *Bloomberg Businessweek* no4497 p41 O 31 2016

Electronic cigarettes

Cartoons *New York Times Upfront* v149 no5 p24 N 21 2016

Do Less Harm E. LEHRER *Weekly Standard* v22 no5 p18 O 10 2016

The Problem With E-Cigarettes L. SCHLEY *Discover* v38 no10 p14 D 2017

Public health checkup C. Martin color *Science News* v190 no13

p18 D 24 2016

Smoke Signals C. STOFFERS *New York Times Upfront* v149 no5 p10 N 21 2016

Electronic commerce

See also
Internet auctions
Internet banking
Internet marketing

3 Ways to Get Your Own Digital Platform B. Libert, M. Beck et al *Harvard Business Review Digital Articles* p2 Jl 22 2016

AMAZON WON'T KNOW WHAT HIT 'EM! [Cover story] B. Stone, M. Boyle et al color graph *Bloomberg Businessweek* no4521 p42 My 8 2017

Big-Box Retailers Have Two Options If They Want to Survive D. L. Yohn *Harvard Business Review Digital Articles* p2 Je 22 2016

The Challenges Facing E-Commerce Start-ups in Africa N. Ekekwe *Harvard Business Review Digital Articles* p2 Mr 12 2015

Click and Spend K. Finn color *New Orleans Magazine* v51 no8 p32 Je 2017

Despite Dire Predictions, Salespeople Aren't Going Away A. A. Zoltners, P. K. Sinha et al *Harvard Business Review Digital Articles* p2 Mr 31 2016

Do You Want to Buy One Online? A comparison of the four major start-ups img *New York* v50 no9 p70 My 1 2017

DR. GWYNETH WILL SEE YOU S. Marikar cartoon *New Yorker* v93 no6 p16 Mr 27 2017

E-COMMERCE: BETTER LATE THAN NEVER P. Wahba color diag *Fortune* v176 no3 p18 S 1 2017

The ETSY Effect L. REGENSDORF and C. ELLENBERG color *Vogue* v207 no3 p374 Mr 2017

Exploring New E-commerce Opportunities K. RAUGUST color *Publishers Weekly* v264 no29 p25 Jl 17 2017

Good Cybersecurity Can Be Good Marketing J. Lucas, L. Minsky et al *Harvard Business Review Digital Articles* p2 S 23 2016

The Great Mall of China M. SCHUMAN and J. Ho chart color *Forbes* v198 no8 p48 D 20 2016

GROUP GIVING: THE MORE THE MERRIER J. Blyskal *Consumer Reports* v81 no12 p65 D 2016

High Online User Ratings Don't Actually Mean You're Getting a Quality Product B. de Langhe, P. Fernbach et al *Harvard Business Review Digital Articles* p2 Jl 4 2016

HOW E-COMMERCE IS MAKING STORES RELEVANT AGAIN P. Wahba color *Fortune* v175 no5 p24 Ap 1 2017

How Walmart Can Start Competing Online R. Mohammed *Harvard Business Review Digital Articles* p2 O 21 2015

Instagram Tries to Ease Users Into Shopping S. Frier cartoon *Bloomberg Businessweek* no4499 p49 N 14 2016

The Internet of "Stuff Your Mom Won't Do for You Anymore" R. Fisman and T. Sullivan *Harvard Business Review Digital Articles* p2 Jl 26 2016

Need more money? Read this [Cover story] N. Lapin color *Redbook* p34 My 2017

THE PERFECT POUR I. Frisch cartoon *Bloomberg Businessweek* no4499 p82 N 14 2016

Safe Shopping in Cyberspace T. J. DONOHUE *Weekly Standard* v22 no17 p14 Ja 2 2017

Shop Online With Confidence B. Braverman, A. Giorgianni et al graph il *Consumer Reports* v82 no12 p20 D 2017

Should You Compete with Amazon or Sell on Amazon? H. Schmid *Harvard Business Review Digital Articles* p2 My 23 2016

Will OpenBazaar Succeed Where Silk Road Failed? S. W. Malone color *Reason* v48 no7 p46 D 2016

Electronic commerce personnel

SOUQ.COM'S CEO ON BUILDING AN E-COMMERCE POWERHOUSE IN THE MIDDLE EAST: Winning trust in regions where payments are made in cash R. Mouchawar color *Harvard Business Review* v95 no5 p35 S/O 2017

Electronic commerce security measures

137% This Year's Spike in Online Fraud M. C. White color *Money* v45 no10 p19 N 2016

'Tis the Season for Stress-Free Shopping M. L. Tellado *Consumer Reports* v82 no12 p4 D 2017

Electronic commerce—Canada

THE INVISIBLE SELLING MACHINE S. M. Baldwin color *Fortune* v175 no4 p162 Mr 15 2017

Electronic commerce—China

China Gets Physical C. Larson color *Bloomberg Businessweek* no4499 p47 N 14 2016

Emerging Markets Find Their Mojo N. S. HUANG chart *Kiplinger's Personal Finance* v71 no12 p56 D 2017

Electronic commerce—Equipment & supplies—Evaluation

36 APPS THAT WILL SAVE YOU MONEY M. Leonhardt, K. Mulhere et al color *Money* v46 no4 p46 My 2017

Electronic commerce—Russia

Now on EBay: Russian Micro-Multinationals I. Khrennikov and S. Soper *Bloomberg Businessweek* no4515 p19 Mr 20 2017

Electronic commerce—Social aspects

FIXING DISCRIMINATION IN ONLINE MARKETPLACES R. FISMAN and M. LUCA color *Harvard Business Review* v94 no12 p88 D 2016

Electronic commerce—Software

Messaging Apps Are Changing How Companies Talk with Customers G. BenMark and D. Venkatachari *Harvard Business Review Digital Articles* p2 S 23 2016

Electronic controllers—Evaluation

TADO SMART AC REMOTE J. D'APRILE color *Macworld - Digital Edition* v34 no11 p37 N 2017

Electronic dance music

GOINGS ON ABOUT TOWN bw *New Yorker* v93 no4 p5 Mr 13 2017

Mason Gross School of the Arts at Rutgers University *Dance Magazine* v90 p82 2016/2017 Supplement College Guide

Electronic dance music—Religious aspects

WORSHIP WITH A DROP J. Neely color *Christianity Today* v61 no6 p50 Jl/Ag 2017

Electronic data processing

See also
Artificial intelligence
Computer programming
Computers in the health care industry
Data extraction
Data flow computing
Database management
Debugging in computer science
High performance computing
Natural language processing (Computer science)
Real-time computing
Remote computing

Extracting Insights from Vast Stores of Data R. Tobaccowala and S. Gupta *Harvard Business Review Digital Articles* p2 Ag 30 2016

Simplify Your Analytics Strategy N. Mulani *Harvard Business Review Digital Articles* p2 Je 15 2015

Today's Automation Anxiety Was Alive and Well in 1960 G. Gavett *Harvard Business Review Digital Articles* p2 F 8 2016

Electronic data processing equipment

SAILING INSTRUMENTS [Cover story] P. Gutowski color *Sail* v48 no8 p38 Ag 2017

Electronic death certificates

A Better Reckoning color *Scientific American* v316 no4 p10 Ap 2017

Electronic design automation—Congresses

Top CI Trends from CEDIA 2016 J. SCIACCA color *Sound & Vision* v82 no1 p19 Ja 2017

Electronic discussion groups

A biology journal provides a lesson in peer review R. E. Goldstein *Physics Today* v69 no12 p10 D 2016

THE MOVEMENT'S NEW VANGUARD IS TEENAGE "SHITLORDS." THE WORLD IS THEIR MESSAGE BOARD NOW M. READ img *New York* v50 no9 p34 My 1 2017

People Offer Better Ideas When They Can't See What Others Suggest A. Stephen, P. P. Zubcsek et al *Harvard Business Review Digital Articles* p2 Jl 24 2015

Electronic distribution of motion pictures

Netflix Zombies N. ROBEHMED bw *Forbes* v199 no7 p98 Je 29 2017

Electronic encyclopedias

IS WIKIPEDIA WOKE? D. KESSENIDES and M. CHAFKIN color *Bloomberg Businessweek* no4505 p70 D 26 2016

Electronic equipment enclosures—Evaluation

CASETIFY iPHONE 7 CASES AND COVERS S. J. PUREWAL

color *Macworld - Digital Edition* v34 no4 p42 My 2017
COOL IPAD CASE color *Flying* v144 no9 p13 S 2017
LIFEPROOF NÜÜD FOR THE 9.7-INCH iPAD PRO S. BEL-
LAMY color *Macworld - Digital Edition* p37 Mr 2017

Electronic equipment for guitars
ToneWoodAmp K. Baumann color *Downbeat* v84 no7 p81 Jl 2017

Electronic equipment in airplanes—Government policy
A WHOLE LOT OF CORPORATE PLANES COULD SOON
GET GROUNDED C. Dillow color *Fortune* v176 no2 p16 Ag
1 2017

Electronic fuel injection systems in automobiles
EFI FUEL PUMP PRIME STRATEGY: EVERYTHING GAS
IS NOW RUNING ON EFI SYSTEMS R. Bohacz *Successful
Farming* v115 no9 p32 Ag 2017

Electronic funds transfers
See also
Stored-value cards
Cash Comes Back in India A. Antony and S. Rai color *Bloomberg
Businessweek* no4529 p25 Jl 3 2017
CASHING OUT N. HELLER cartoon *New Yorker* v92 no32 p48
O 10 2016
The Countries That Would Profit Most from a Cashless World B.
Chakravorti, R. S. Chaturvedi et al *Harvard Business Review
Digital Articles* p2 My 31 2016
Give Well, Give Wisely F. TORABI cartoon color graph *O, The
Oprah Magazine* p56 D 2016
Online Bill Paying Isn't Foolproof L. GERSTNER chart *Kip-
linger's Personal Finance* v71 no7 p45 Jl 2017
TFW Your Country's Shredding Money And You Own a Payment
App S. Rai bw *Bloomberg Businessweek* no4507 p30 Ja 16 2017

Electronic games
See also
Computer games
Video games
Google makes the best Android apps easier to find with Android
Excellence M. SIMON color *PCWorld* v35 no7 p47 Jl 2017

Electronic games—Competitions
ROMANCING THE DRONE R. O'CONNOR color *Chicago* v66
no6 p30 Je 2017

Electronic games—Evaluation
The 15 best new PC games of 2017, and their release dates H.
DINGMAN color *PCWorld* v35 no9 p70 S 2017

Electronic government information
The Night Data Died A. FERGUSON *Commentary* v142 no5 p10
D 2016

Electronic health records
Are Doctors Finally Ready for Data? 'Health informatics' focuses
on delivering better medical outcomes M. Quinn *Governing* v31
no1 p18 O 2017
How the EMR Is Increasing Innovation and Creativity in Health
Care A. James Bender and R. S. Mecklenburg *Harvard Business
Review Digital Articles* p1 O 10 2017
How to Make Electronic Health Records an Asset Instead of a
Burden J. Butler and J. Fox *Harvard Business Review Digital
Articles* p2 D 8 2015
Making Predictive Analytics a Routine Part of Patient Care R. B.
Parikh, Z. Obermeyer et al *Harvard Business Review Digital
Articles* p2 Ap 21 2016
Patient-Reported Data Can Help People Make Better Health Care
Choices W. B. Weeks and J. N. Weinstein *Harvard Business Re-
view Digital Articles* p2 S 21 2015
"Pheno"menal value for human health D. J. Rader and S. M. Dam-
rauer bibl diag *Science* v354 no6319 p1534 D 23 2016
Tap Into Your Digital Health Records N. S. HUANG color *Kip-
linger's Personal Finance* v71 no2 p70 F 2017

Electronic health records—United States
Speeding Up the Digitization of American Health Care D. Blumenthal and A. Chopra *Harvard Business Review Digital Articles* p2 F 22 2016

Electronic industries—News briefs
LG's Channel Plus M. Fleischmann and C. Crowley color *Sound
& Vision* v81 no10 p17 D 2016

Electronic information resources
See also
Information storage & retrieval systems
DNA Fountain enables a robust and efficient storage architecture

Y. Erlich and D. Zielinski bibl chart diag *Science* v355 no6328
p950 Mr 3 2017
Teaching Digital Citizenship S. MAUGHAN color *Publishers
Weekly* v264 no34 p35 Ag 21 2017

Electronic instruments—Evaluation
IS IT TIME TO RETHINK INSTRUMENTATION? color *Flying*
v144 no1 p16 Ja 2017
new products color *Science* v357 no6354 p936 S 1 2017

Electronic journals
Digital color *Sports Illustrated* v126 no6 p14 F 20 2017
SOCIETY UPDATE color *Science News* v190 no8 p29 O15 2016
Speeding Our Way To Our New Mobile Future L. D'VORKIN
Forbes v199 no3 p22 Mr 28 2017

Electronic locking devices
See also
Smart locks
LOOK AGAIN P. ANTONELLI color *New York Times Magazine*
p50 N 13 2016

Electronic markets
See also
Business-to-business electronic markets
Stop Treating B2B Customers Like Digital Novices A. Di Fiore
and S. Schneider *Harvard Business Review Digital Articles* p2
My 10 2016

Electronic materials
Polymer-based transistors bring fully stretchable devices within
reach A. G. Smart *Physics Today* v70 no3 p14 Mr 2017

Electronic money
See also
Bitcoin
Cryptocurrencies
BLOCKCHAIN IN REAL LIFE J. J. Roberts *Fortune* v176 no3
p49 S 1 2017
CAN BITCOIN'S FIRST FELON HELP MAKE CRYPTOCUR-
RENCY A TRILLION-DOLLAR MARKET? B. P. Eha color
diag *Fortune* v176 no1 p78 Jl 1 2017
China's Central Bank Has Begun Cautiously Testing a Digital
Currency W. Knight color *MIT Technology Review* v120 no5
p22 S/O 2017
Electronic Money Is Too Easy color *MIT Technology Review* v120
no2 p108 Mr/Ap 2017
The Impact of the Blockchain Goes Beyond Financial Services
D. Tapscott and A. Tapscott *Harvard Business Review Digital
Articles* p2 My 10 2016
Paper Problem K. Rogoff *MIT Technology Review* v120 no2 p11
Mr/Ap 2017

Electronic money—Economic aspects
BLOCKCHAIN MANIA! [Cover story] R. Hackett color *Fortune*
v176 no3 p44 S 1 2017
Digital Currency Gets Its Biggest Test Yet R. Hackett color *Fortune* v176 no2 p13 Ag 1 2017

Electronic monitoring of parolees & probationers
WHEN 3M BOUGHT INTO THE ANKLE MONITOR BUSI-
NESS, IT ACQUIRED TROUBLE L. ETTER bw color diag
graph *Bloomberg Businessweek* no4518 p44 Ap 10 2017

Electronic music
See also
Synthesizer music

Electronic music—Reviews
Step Out M. Trammell cartoon *New Yorker* v93 no16 p22 Je 5
2017

Electronic newsletters
All the News That's Fit to Click M. Chafkin color *Bloomberg
Businessweek* no4498 p81 N 7 2016
FROM THE HILL chart *Issues in Science & Technology* v33 no1
p22 Fall 2016
The Triumphant Return of the Email Newsletter M. Aarons-Mele
Harvard Business Review Digital Articles p2 O 8 2015

Electronic publications
See also
Electronic books
Electronic encyclopedias
Electronic journals
Electronic newsletters
Electronic textbooks
Content Discovery and Consumption Go Mobile B. F. O'Leary

Publishers Weekly v263 no39 p25 S 26 2016

Electronic publishing

Challenges for Publishers in Uncertain Times R. Beardsley *Publishers Weekly* v263 no40 p12 O 3 2016

Electronic security systems—Moral & ethical aspects

the sorcerer's code m. hutson *Psychology Today* v49 no6 p78 N/D 2016

Electronic services

E-tailers Widen Bookselling Edge J. Milliot and E. Nawotka chart graph *Publishers Weekly* v264 no18 p4 My 1 2017

What a Great Digital Customer Experience Actually Looks Like C. Borowski *Harvard Business Review Digital Articles* p2 N 9 2015

Electronic Solutions Ulm GmbH & Co. KG

Going Full Throttle with a LokSound decoder L. Puckett color *Model Railroader* v84 no4 p90 Ap 2017

Electronic spreadsheets

7 Excel tips for huge spreadsheets: Split Screen, Freeze Panes, Format Painter and more J. D. SARTAIN color *PCWorld* v35 no8 p154 Ag 2017

Electronic spreadsheets—Software

Excel tips: 6 slick shortcuts, handy functions, and random-number generators J. D. SARTAIN diag *PCWorld* v35 no11 p148 N 2016

Electronic structure

See also

Fermi energy

Making the most of materials computations K. S. Thygesen and K. W. Jacobsen bibl diag *Science* v354 no6309 p180 O 14 2016

Electronic surveillance

See also

Video surveillance

Bigly Brother J. BAMFORD cartoon *Foreign Policy* no222 p68 Ja/F 2017

March 15, 1967: Tuned In to the Future A. BROWN bw color *Forbes* v198 no9 p26 D 30 2016

Opening Windows on Surveillance: the Scholarship of Gary Marx P. Regan *Society* v54 no4 p363 Ag 2017

Seeing a Bigger Picture K. Guzik *Society* v54 no4 p367 Ag 2017

SURVEILLANCE R. Hackett color *Fortune* v175 no4 p114 Mr 15 2017

Electronic surveillance—Social aspects

Even Bugs Will Be Bugged M. HUTSON color *Atlantic* v318 no4 p34 N 2016

Electronic surveillance—United States—Government policy

Microsoft's Civil Rights Crusader T. Simonite bw diag *MIT Technology Review* v119 no6 p13 N/D 2016

Electronic textbooks

SAVED BY THE DELL L. D. ROBERTS *Indianapolis Monthly* p79 F 2017

Student Aid A. Fraknoi color *Sky & Telescope* v134 no2 p84 Ag 2017

Electronic Theatre Controls Inc.

ETC Source Four Turns 25! *Stage Directions* v30 no9 p15 S 2017

Electronic ticketing

FINE DINING, FINE PRINT A. Spiegel *Washingtonian Magazine* v52 no2 p362 N 2016

Electronic toys—Evaluation

TAKE YOUR KID FOR A RIDE color *Men's Health* v31 no10 p(Sp)26 D 2016

Electronic trading of securities—Research

To slow or not? Challenges in subsecond networks N. F. Johnson bibl color graph *Science* v355 no6327 p801 F 24 2017

Electronic voting

Our Elections Are Not Secure D. L. Dill color *Scientific American* v316 no3 p12 Mr 2017

Electronic wallets

BREAKING THE BITCOIN BANK J. J. Roberts color *Fortune* v176 no5 p26 O 1 2017

Samsung Pay's Older Technology Could Be an Advantage Dae Ryun Chang *Harvard Business Review Digital Articles* p2 Jl 27 2015

Electronic wallets—Evaluation

Reinventions: Scrip J. Brustein color *Bloomberg Businessweek* no4494 p46 O 10 2016

Electronic waste

The New Gold Rush for Our e-Waste T. John color *Time* v190 no15 p10 O 16 2017

Electronic waste disposal

DEAD, BUT NOT FORGOTTEN R. Hackett color *Fortune* v176 no4 p38 S 15 2017

Electronic waste management

Recycling And Rehab J. HERBST *Los Angeles Magazine* v62 no6 p15 Je 2017

Electronic books—Charts, diagrams, etc.

COMBINED PRINT AND E-BOOK BEST SELLERS *New York Times Book Review* p23 F 12 2017

COMBINED PRINT AND E-BOOK BEST SELLERS *New York Times Book Review* p23 Je 25 2017

COMBINED PRINT AND E-BOOK BEST SELLERS *New York Times Book Review* p24 N 27 2016

iBook Bestsellers chart color *Publishers Weekly* v264 no32 p14 Ag 7 2017

iBook Bestsellers C. JURIS chart color *Publishers Weekly* v264 no19 p15 My 8 2017

iBooks Bestsellers chart color *Publishers Weekly* v264 no10 p17 Mr 6 2017

iBooks Bestsellers *Publishers Weekly* v263 no40 p18 O 3 2016

SMASHWORDS SELF-PUBLISHED BESTSELLERS LIST, SEPTEMBER 2016 chart color *Publishers Weekly* v263 no46 p20 N 14 2016

Electronics

See also

Cryoelectronics

Cybernetics

Electronic apparatus & appliances

Optoelectronics

Semiconductors

ARE BLUE LIGHT GLASSES LEGIT? color *Health* v31 no7 p22 S 2017

PACIFIC NORTHWEST EMPIRE J. Morse color *Model Railroader* v84 no6 p28 Je 2017

Electronics exhibitions

Betting the futureon artificial intelligence F. Markus color *Motor Trend* v69 no5 p22 My 2017

Electronics for model railroads

Adding sound to a vintage Kato locomotive [Cover story] L. Puckett color *Model Railroader* v84 no10 p56 O 2017

Build: DISPATCHER AND OPERATOR DESKS [Cover story] D. Ball color diag *Model Railroader* v84 no10 p45 O 2017

Have clocks become too fast? J. Dziedzic color *Model Railroader* v84 no11 p72 N 2017

How to build an operating switch stand [Cover story] G. Butts diag *Model Railroader* v84 no7 p52 Jl 2017

SIMPLE route selection P. LaGuardia color *Model Railroader* v84 no7 p39 Jl 2017

Turnout control with accessory decoders L. Puckett color *Model Railroader* v84 no11 p60 N 2017

Upgrading older turnouts [Cover story] T. Koester color *Model Railroader* v84 no7 p32 Jl 2017

Electronics on boats

FORMIDABLE FEATURES M. WERLING *Sea Magazine* v109 no7 p4 Jl 2017

The Modular Approach B. PIKE color *Power & Motoryacht* v34 no7 p74 Jl 2017

Pulling Back the Curtain J. Y. WOOD color *Power & Motoryacht* v34 no7 p26 Jl 2017

Q+A color *Boating World* v38 no7 p28 Jl 2017

Siren Marine MTC Boat-Monitoring System J. Y. WOOD color *Power & Motoryacht* v34 no7 p28 Jl 2017

STUFF YOU WANT color *Boating World* v38 no7 p32 Jl 2017

Electronics on boats—Evaluation

MFDs get OMGs *Sea Magazine* v109 no5 p48 My 2017

Electronics recycling

DEAD, BUT NOT FORGOTTEN R. Hackett color *Fortune* v176 no4 p38 S 15 2017

We Found Your Last Smartphone, Next to Your Old VCR M. Smith and I. Cota color diag *Bloomberg Businessweek* no4499 p56 N 14 2016

Electronics—Evaluation

NEW ELECTRONICS J. Y. WOOD color map *Power & Motoryacht* v32 no12 p26 D 2016

Electrons
> See also
>> Electron gas

Massive machine gears up to weigh nearly massless particles: An experiment in Germany looks for missing electron energy to infer neutrino rest mass T. Feder *Physics Today* v70 no8 p26 Ag 2017

Electrophoresis equipment

new products: dna/rna analysis color *Science* v357 no6357 p1317 S 22 2017

Electrophysiology
> See also
>> Electroencephalography
>> Neural circuitry

The Electric Touch J. KEATS color *Discover* v38 no9 p10 N 2017

Not-So-Gray Matter L. Pandell color *Wired* v24 no11 p44 N 2016

Electrostatic actuators

Highly efficient electrocaloric cooling with electrostatic actuation R. Ma, Z. Zhang et al bw diag *Science* v357 no6356 p1130 S 15 2017

ELEFTERIADES, JOHN

THE EXCHANGE cartoon color graph *Men's Health* v32 no8 p16 O 2017

Elemental diet

cheat, drink, & stil shrink A. Rios color *Yoga Journal* no293 p9 Ag 2017

Elementary (TV program)

Elementary I. Rudolph color *TV Guide* v64 no42 p40 O 10 2016

Elementary education—China

School Choice, Beijing Edition D. Roberts color *Bloomberg Businessweek* no4526 p15 Je 12 2017

Elementary school principals

PRINCIPLES FOR ELEMENTARY PRINCIPALS: Keys to remember when it comes to being a literacy leader T. Meidl and J. Lau *Literacy Today (2411-7862)* v35 no2 p24 S/O 2017

Elementary school teachers—Education

The Editor's Note J. Richardson *Phi Delta Kappan* v98 no8 p4 My 2017

Elementary schools
> See also
>> Kindergarten

CONNECT WITH YOUR CHILD'S CLASSROOM J. Hartshorn and J. Tahnk color *Parents* v92 no9 p86 S 2017

fickle friendships K. CICERO *Parents* v91 no10 p144 O 2016

THE SECRET LIFE OF SCHOOL M. Crouch cartoon color *Parents* v92 no9 p66 S 2017

Why Kids Need Recess A. WONG color *Atlantic* v318 no5 p22 D 2016

Elementary schools—United States

Connecting Kids with Nature M. BILLINGE color *Earth Island Journal* v32 no4 p15 Wint 2017

Finding Time for P.E *Parents* v91 no10 p36 O 2016

This Week in Trumpoplexy color *Weekly Standard* v22 no20 p3 Ja 30 2017

A WAVE OF GENEROSITY: Just one example of how the ILA network and book lovers everywhere helped restore libraries-- and hope T. Veazey color *Literacy Today (2411-7862)* v34 no6 p42 My/Je 2017

Elephant at the Mall Grand Opening (Poem)

ELEPHANT AT THE MALL GRAND OPENING M. Cadnum *Commonweal* v144 no16 p16 O 6 2017

Elephant behavior

How to Survive a Stampeding Elephant R. KARLGAARD color *Forbes* v199 no6 p28 Je 13 2017

Elephant care

Warriors to the Rescue A. VITALE color map *National Geographic* v232 no2 p76 Ag 2017

Elephant Crossing (Short story)

Elephant Crossing T. R. SHANKAR RAMAN *Orion Magazine* v35 no3 p6 My/Je 2016

Elephant seals

Lifetime experience #25 J. Jerabek color *Canadian Geographic* v137 no1 p27 F 2017

Elephants

Check Out These Outrageous Facts J. WANDEL color *National Geographic Kids* no475 p4 N 2017

Cohabitating with Elephants B. HEINRICH color *Natural History* v125 no5 p16 My 2017

ELEPHANT "ASKS" FOR HELP R. Davidson *National Geographic Kids* no467 p13 F 2017

Home Is Where They Make It J. R. Platt color diag *Scientific American* v315 no5 p20 N 2016

Hope for Elephants *Earth Island Journal* v32 no1 p9 Spr 2017

Points of State Pride color *Nebraska Life* v21 no6 p21 N/D 2017

Showing that every elephant—and every voice—counts color *National Wildlife (World Edition)* v55 no6 p48 O/N 2017

Elephants—Behavior

Lab tests aren't the answer for every science question E. Quill *Science News* v191 no6 p2 Ap 1 2017

Eler, Alicia

"You've got to break your back!" color *Glamour* v115 no4 p153 Ap 2017

El-Erian, Mohamed A., 1958-

How to Thrive as Market Cycles Return J. K. GLASSMAN color *Kiplinger's Personal Finance* v71 no6 p20 Je 2017

Prevent Your Star Performers from Losing Passion for Their Work M. E. Kibler *Harvard Business Review Digital Articles* p2 Ja 14 2015

Elevated highways

Cities Inside and Out A. Ehrenhalt *Governing* v30 no5 p14 F 2017

Elevator design & construction

Cutting-Edge Elevator Technology: Elevating architecture with destination dispatch controls C. C. Sullivan color *Architectural Record* v205 no8 p152 Ag 2017

PERIOD ELEVATORS color *Old House Journal* v45 no7 p76 O 2017

Elevators
> See also
>> Private residence elevators

Cutting-Edge Elevator Technology: Elevating architecture with destination dispatch controls C. C. Sullivan color *Architectural Record* v205 no8 p152 Ag 2017

Serapid - Lifting Expectations Everyday *Stage Directions* v30 no3 p64 Mr 2017

What Would Happen? C. BOYER *National Geographic Kids* no468 p7 Mr 2017

Elevators—Evaluation

Creative Conners, Inc *Stage Directions* v30 no3 p5 Mr 2017

Eleven Cages (Music)

Tepfer's Mathematical Ingenuity P. Lutz color *Downbeat* v84 no9 p14 S 2017

ELEY, CHRISTOPHER

WILD RABBIT RAGOUT *Indianapolis Monthly* v12 no40 p74 Ag 2017

Elf, Johan

Kinetics of dCas9 target search in Escherichia coli diag *Science* v357 no6358 p1420 S 29 2017

Nanometer resolution imaging and tracking of fluorescent molecules with minimal photon fluxes bibl graph *Science* v355 no6325 p606 F 10 2017

El-Faizy, Monique

Egypt's Copts face rising fears, divisions color *Christian Century* v134 no10 p14 My 10 2017

Elferink, Maarten

Global Demand for Food Is Rising. Can We Meet It? *Harvard Business Review Digital Articles* p2 Ap 7 2016

Elfman, Danny

PARTY LINES img *New York* v49 no21 p118 O 17 2016

ELGAR, MARK A.

PROMISCUOUS MEN, CHASTE WOMEN AND OTHER GENDER MYTHS color *Scientific American* v317 no3 p32 S 2017

Elgato Systems GmbH

ELGATO'S EVE HOMEKIT LIGHTSWITCH C. MCGARRY color *Macworld - Digital Edition* p45 D 2016

Elgin, Ben

How do you maximize the profits of a drug that treats a very rare disease? [Cover story] color *Bloomberg Businessweek* no4524 p42 My 29 2017

In Case of Low Revenue cartoon *Bloomberg Businessweek* no4497 p50 O 31 2016

THE PRICE OF A DIGITAL WORLD color *Bloomberg Business-*

week no4527 p58 Je 19 2017

Elgort, Ansel, 1994-
THE THINKING MAN: ANSEL ELGORT M. Khidekel color
Women's Health v14 no6 p118 Jl 2017

Elgort, Ansel, 1994—Interviews
The 3-Minute Interview J. Kantor and J. Harman bw *Glamour* no8
p40 Ag 2017
Ansel Elgort E. Berman color *Time* v190 no4 p48 Jl 24 2017

Eli Young Band (Performer)
THE ELI YOUNG BAND PLAYS THE GAME A. LANGER
Texas Monthly v45 no6 p48 Je 2017

Elia, Leandro
Why Mass Migration Is Good for Long-Term Economic Growth
Harvard Business Review Digital Articles p2 Ap 18 2017

Elias, Chad
EMERGENCY CINEMA AND THE DIGNIFIED IMAGE:
CELL PHONE ACTIVISM AND FILMMAKING IN SYRIA
Film Quarterly v71 no1 p18 Fall 2017

Elias, Eliane, 1960—Interviews
Eliane Elias Returns to Samba A. Morrison color *Downbeat* v84
no6 p18 Je 2017

Elias, Joshua E.
Seasonal cycling in the gut microbiome of the Hadza hunter-gatherers of Tanzania diag *Science* v357 no6353 p802 Ag 25 2017

Elias, Kimberly
Beyond the Transcript: The Need to Showcase More *Change* v49
no4 p14 Jl/Ag 2017

Elias, Maurice J.
Madam Secretary, help us improve social-emotional learning
color *Phi Delta Kappan* v98 no8 p64 My 2017

Eliaz, Isaac
BEYOND DIET AND EXERCISE *Amazing Wellness* v9 no1 p40
Wint 2017
HOMEOPATHIC STRESS RELIEF *Better Nutrition* v79 no9 p42
S 2017
JUST FOR MEN color *Better Nutrition* v79 no6 p41 Je 2017
MEN'S HEALTH GUIDE color *Amazing Wellness* v9 no3 p46
EarlySumm 2017
SPRING detox PLAN color *Amazing Wellness* v9 no2 p46 Spr
2017

Elie, Lolis Edward
Mourning a Friend, Losing a Hero E. C. Peyton color *New Orleans Magazine* v51 no8 p48 Je 2017

Elie, Michelle—Interviews
ART & CRAFT M. BOBO bw *Ebony* v72 no3 p62 D 2016/Ja
2017

ELIE, PAUL
REDEMPTION [Cover story] color *New York Times Magazine*
p44 N 27 2016
STRIKE UP THE BAND *New York Times Book Review* p66 D
4 2016

Elimelech, Menachem
Maximizing the right stuff: The trade-off between membrane permeability and selectivity color *Science* v356 no6343 p1137 Je
16 2017

Elinav, Eran
The DNA-sensing AIM2 inflammasome controls radiation-induced cell death and tissue injury bibl color graph *Science* v354
no6313 p765 N 11 2016

Eling, Nils
Aging increases cell-to-cell transcriptional variability upon im-
mune stimulation color diag graph *Science* v355 no6332 p1433
Mr 31 2017

Elion, Leandra
WE'RE IN THIS TOGETHER color *Literacy Today (2411-7862)*
v34 no4 p36 Ja/F 2017

Eliopoulos, Chris, 1967-
Cosmic Commandos *Publishers Weekly* v264 no22 p70 My 29
2017

Eliot, George, 1819-1880
Hovering over the deep S. Wells *Christian Century* v134 no17
p28 Ag 16 2017

Eliot, T. S. (Thomas Stearns), 1888-1965
Magic Lantern W. H. Pritchard bw *Weekly Standard* v22 no37 p33
Je 5 2017
What to Make of T. S. Eliot? G. Davis *Humanities* v37 no4 p1

Fall 2016

ELISCU, JENNY
Mayer's Heartbreak Diary bw *Rolling Stone* no1281/1282 p18 F
23 2017

Elite (Social sciences)
See also
Trend setters
Power Down *New York Times Magazine* p11 Ja 8 2017

Elite (Social sciences)—Canada
THE EDITORIAL *Maclean's* v129 no40 p5 O 10 2016

Elite (Social sciences)—History—21st century
The Financial World's Rotten Culture Is Still a Threat-to All of Us
R. Foroohar color *Time* v188 no16/17 p13 O 24 2016

Elite athletes
Gold-Medal Moms L. Krieger *Parents* v91 no9 p22 S 2016

EliteIron LLC
ELITE IRON REVOLUTION J. B. SNOW color *Outdoor Life*
v224 no5 pR6 Je/Jl 2017

Elitism
After Meritocracy F. Foer *New Republic* v248 no1/2 p4 Ja/F 2017
Masters of The Game K. D. WILLIAMSON *National Review* v68
no20 p34 N 7 2016

Elizabeth, Dorothy
THE ART of SIMPLICITY color *Bon Appetit* no8 p56 Ag 2017

ELIZABETH, JORDANNAH
An End to FGM: Nigeria joined 23 African countries in banning
female genital mutilation *Ms.* v27 no3 p17 Fall 2017

Elizabeth I, Queen of England, 1533-1603
Elizabethan Virtues M. Bayles *Claremont Review of Books* v17
no3 p85 Summ 2017

Elizabeth II, Queen of Great Britain, 1926-
A changing of the guard P. TREBLE color *Maclean's* v129
no48/49 p62 D 5 2016
Queen Elizabeth II, for 65 Years K. Samuelson color *Time* v189
no6 p13 F 20 2017
Regal Rides M. SOLOMON color *Forbes* v198 no7 p30 N 29
2016
Slacking, royally P. PATRICIA color graph *Maclean's* v129 no40
p49 O 10 2016

Elizabeth II, Queen of Great Britain, 1926-—Health
UNEASY LIES THE HEAD THAT WEARS THE CROWN P.
TREBLE color *Maclean's* no1 p58 F 17 2017

Elizondo, Eusebio
Still Welcoming the Stranger J. G. Young color *Commonweal*
v144 no5 p9 Mr 10 2017

Elk
King of the Hill D. L. NG color *Field & Stream* v122 no4 p10
S 2017

Elk hunting
7 WAYS TO TAKE TOUGH ELK T. Carpenter color *Outdoor Life*
v223 no9 pH1 N 2016
METHANE MOUNTAIN D. E. Petzal color *Field & Stream* v121
no7 p48 D 2016/Ja 2017
The Public's World Record *Outdoor Life* v224 no7 p10 S 2017
RECORD-BUSTING BULLS color *Outdoor Life* v224 no7 p12
S 2017
WAPITI WISDOM B. FITZPATRICK color *Outdoor Life* v224
no7 p26 S 2017
WORLD RECORD S. FELIX color *Outdoor Life* v224 no7 p34
S 2017

Elk hunting—Colorado
ALONE TOGETHER J. Babincsak color *Outdoor Life* v224 no5
p82 Je/Jl 2017
BULLS AT THE WIRE D. Hurteau color *Field & Stream* v121
no6 p34 N 2016

Elkabets, Moshe
PI3K pathway regulates ER-dependent transcription in breast cancer through the epigenetic regulator KMT2D bibl graph *Science*
v355 no6331 p1324 Mr 24 2017

Elkann, Lapo Edovard
John Phillips J. Phillips color *Car & Driver* v62 no10 p22 Ap 2017

El-Katiri, Laura
Oil's Fall Is a Challenge for Gulf Economies, but Also an Oppor-
tunity *Harvard Business Review Digital Articles* p2 Mr 7 2016
Saudi Arabia's Labor Market Challenge *Harvard Business Review
Digital Articles* p2 Jl 6 2016

FUNDING, RESEARCH, COMMUNICATION, AND POLICY E. SMITH *BioScience* v67 no10 p938 O 2017

Conceptions of Good Science in Our Data-Rich World chart *BioScience* v66 no10 p1 O 1 2016

ELLIOTT, LADELL

PRADAL SEREY bw color *Black Belt* v55 no5 p48 Ag/S 2017

Elliott, Lynn

Bedroom Basics cartoon *Old House Journal* v44 no8 p52 D 2016

Comfort & Curb Appeal color *Old House Journal* v45 no4 p48 Je 2017

Easy Fixes for your Furniture color *Old House Journal* v45 no6 p48 S 2017

Finishing Touches FOR WINDOWS & WALLS cartoon *Old House Journal* v45 no1 p48 F 2017

From Attic to the Basement color *Old House Journal* v45 no7 p46 O 2017

Kitchen Cleanups cartoon *Old House Journal* v45 no2 p48 Ap 2017

Make a Grand Entrance cartoon *Old House Journal* v45 no3 p48 My 2017

Projects for the Backyard color *Old House Journal* v45 no5 p50 Ag 2017

Elliott, Marianne, 1966-

ANGELS AND DEMONS O. EUSTIS color *Vanity Fair* v59 no5 p120 Ap 2017

Elliott, Miranda

"My boss was secretly filming me" color *Glamour* v115 no4 p156 Ap 2017

Elliott, Missy, 1971-

'I'm Better' J. E. SHEPHERD *New York Times Magazine* p21 Mr 12 2017

Elliott, Philip

After the Massacre [Cover story] color diag *Time* v190 no15 p22 O 16 2017

Beyond Repeal and Replace color diag map *Time* v190 no2/3 p30 Jl 10-17 2017

A Billionaire Resistance Targets President Trump from the Right color *Time* v189 no5 p31 F 13 2017

The Budget Battle Shows That Trump Needs to Read the Fine Print color *Time* v189 no18 p11 My 15 2017

Canada Welcomes Tech Companies That Are Spooked by Trump color *Time* v189 no14 p27 Ap 17 2017

Chaos Theory [Cover story] color *Time* v189 no7/8 p32 F 27 2017

Country First [Cover story] color *Time* v190 no7 p26 Ag 21 2017

The Democrats' Dilemmas [Cover story] color diag map *Time* v190 no13 p36 O 2 2017

Family First [Cover story] color *Time* v189 no22 p24 Je 12 2017

A GOP Revolt Threatens President Trump's Agenda color *Time* v189 no9 p9 Mr 13 2017

How President Trump Is Trampling Precedent color *Time* v189 no4 p9 F 6 2017

How She Lost color *Time* v188 no21 p58 N 21 2016

Inside Donald Trump's War Against the State [Cover story] color *Time* v189 no10 p26 Mr 20 2017

Kim Jong Un Isn't the Only Wild Card In the North Korea Crisis color *Time* v190 no10/11 p11 S 18 2017

The Lost Colony color *Time* v190 no15 p32 O 16 2017

Mike Pence Is No Ordinary Wingman color *Time* v188 no27-28 p52 D 26 2016

No Good Options on North Korea color *Time* v190 no4 p10 Jl 24 2017

The Persistent Passion of Vice President Mike Pence color *Time* v189 no21 p18 Je 5 2017

RIP, Repeal and Replace? The GOP Faces a New Crossroads color *Time* v190 no5 p13 Jl 31 2017

The Second Most Powerful Man In the World? [Cover story] color *Time* v189 no5 p24 F 13 2017

The Suite of Power [Cover story] color *Time* v189 no23 p22 Je 19 2017

The Trouble With Russia color map *Time* v189 no7/8 p44 F 27 2017

Trump Goes to War [Cover story] color *Time* v188 no16/17 p20 O 24 2016

Trump's Loyalty Test [Cover story] color *Time* v189 no20 p24 My 29 2017

Trump's Offensive Playbook [Cover story] color *Time* v190 no14

p32 O 9 2017

Trump Takes Over color *Time* v188 no22-23 p24 N/D 2016

Trump Tries Presidential, Before Reverting to Old Habits color *Time* v190 no9 p9 S 4 2017

The Truth Is Out There color *Time* v188 no15 p28 O 17 2016

A War of Words With Senator Bob Corker Endangers the President's Agenda color *Time* v190 no16/17 p11 O 23 2017

What Hillary Clinton's Insiders Know That Voters Don't-Yet color *Time* v188 no18 p14 O 31 2016

What It Will Take to Rebuild America [Cover story] color *Time* v189 no13 p22 Ap 10 2017

The White House Survival Guide color *Time* v189 no4 p30 Ja 23 2017

Why President Trump Is Struggling to Staff His Government color *Time* v189 no11 p9 Mr 27 2017

Why Stephen Bannon Doesn't Scare Washington Anymore color *Time* v190 no12 p11 S 25 2017

Will Bob Mueller Separate Fact from Fiction? [Cover story] color *Time* v190 no1 p24 Jl 3 2017

Zbigniew Brzezinski color *Time* v189 no22 p10 Je 12 2017

Elliott, Randy

Old School E. STIFLER WOLFE bw color *Powder* v46 no2 p48 O 2017

Elliott, Rebecca

STORMY WATERS: The fight over New York City's flood lines map *Harper's Magazine* v335 no2005 p46 Je 2017

Elliott, S. R.

Observation of coherent elastic neutrino-nucleus scattering diag *Science* v357 no6356 p1123 S 15 2017

Elliott, Sam—Interviews

Sam Elliott E. Berman *Time* v189 no23 p51 Je 19 2017

Elliott, Stephen

Sometimes I Think About It: Essays *Publishers Weekly* v264 no28 p75 Jl 10 2017

Elliott, Stewart—Interviews

Check, Please color *Timber Home Living* v27 no3 p14 Je 2017

Elliott, Timo

8 Ways Machine Learning Is Improving Companie's Work Processes *Harvard Business Review Digital Articles* p2 My 31 2017

Elliott, Vittoria

America's growing news deserts map *Columbia Journalism Review* v56 no1 p34 Spr 2017

Elliottsmith, Leslie

PARALLEL WORLDS J. R. KEMP bw color *Louisiana Life* v37 no3 p30 Ja/F 2017

Elliptical galaxies

See also

M87 (Galaxy)

GALAXIES ι Giant "Frankenstein" Spiral A. V. ACEVES *Sky & Telescope* v132 no6 p14 D 2016

READER GALLERY C. Eduardo Fairbairn, D. Crowson et al bw color *Astronomy* v45 no11 p72 N 2017

Elliptical orbits

1,000 YEARS OF SOLAR ECLIPSES M. Fischetti diag graph map *Scientific American* v317 no2 p62 Ag 2017

Elliptical trainers

Hot-Workout Alert S. G. Levy color *Glamour* v114 no11 p114 N 2016

Ellis, Allison M.

Your New Hires Won't Succeed Unless You Onboard Them Properly *Harvard Business Review Digital Articles* p2 Je 20 2017

Ellis, Benjamin

How CMOs and CROs Can Be Allies *Harvard Business Review Digital Articles* p2 Mr 26 2015

Ellis, Caitlin

The Other Invasion: The Anglo-Norman invasion of Ireland in 1167 sowed the seeds for centuries of tension between England and the Irish *History Today* v67 no9 p12 S 2017

ELLIS, DON

Chords & Discords color *Downbeat* v84 no5 p10 My 2017

Chords & Discords color *Downbeat* v84 no7 p10 Jl 2017

Ellis, Elaine Hirschl

Bespoke Tours for Serious Students P. Poore color *Arts & Crafts Homes & the Revival* v12 no2 p22 Spr 2017

Ellis, Emma Grey

THE LARGE HADRON COLLIDER: AN ORAL HISTORY bw

color *Wired* v25 no7 p20 Jl 2017

POPPING THE RED PILL color graph *Wired* v25 no10 p28 O 2017

THE TED TALK AN ORAL HISTORY bw diag *Wired* v25 no5 p26 My 2017

THE VIEW MASTERS color graph *Wired* v25 no4 p18 Ap 2017

WISH LIST 2016 color *Wired* v24 no12 p45 D 2016

ELLIS, ERLE C.

An Ecoregion-Based Approach to Protecting Half the Terrestrial Realm *BioScience* v67 no6 p534 Je 2017

Ellis, Grant

Along for the Ride color *Surfer* v57 no13 p14 Mr 2017

Ellis, James E.

CHINA'S ROBOT REVOLUTION color graph *Bloomberg Businessweek* no4520 p32 My 1 2017

How to Lose $6 Billion color graph *Bloomberg Businessweek* no4512 p19 F 20 2017

Music Festivals Have A Volume Problem color diag *Bloomberg Businessweek* no4512 p21 F 20 2017

VW's Latest Woe: A Reliance on Mexico *Bloomberg Businessweek* no4512 p20 F 20 2017

Why Costco Is Lagging Online graph *Bloomberg Businessweek* no4535 p14 Ag 28 2017

Why Japan's Idemitsu Isn't Feeling Blue color *Bloomberg Businessweek* no4520 p34 My 1 2017

Ellis, Janet

The Butcher's Hook *Publishers Weekly* v263 no46 p30 N 14 2016

Ellis, Jay

Insecure J. Jensen color *Entertainment Weekly* no1474/1475 p106 Jl 21-28 2017

Ellis, Jay—Interviews

BOYFRIEND MATERIAL C. Murray color *Essence* v47 no7 p48 N 2016

Insecure A. D'Arminio *TV Guide* v65 no35 p33 Ag 21 2017

Ellis, John

A Dedication to Health & Human Rights bw color graph *Popular Science* v289 no2 p84 Mr/Ap 2017

Ellis, John M.

MISSING THE POETRY *Claremont Review of Books* v16 no4 p73 Fall 2016

ELLIS, JOSEPH J.

The Year in Reading [Cover story] *New York Times Book Review* p8 D 25 2016

ELLIS, K. A.

Christianity Without an Adjective *Christianity Today* v61 no1 p28 Ja/F 2017

From 'Enemy of the People' to Friend *Christianity Today* v60 no9 p30 N 2016

God in Iran (Still) *Christianity Today* v61 no6 p26 Jl/Ag 2017

Revelation Versus Revolution *Christianity Today* p26 Ap 2017

UNDER DISCUSSION *Christianity Today* p17 Ap 2017

Ellis, Kimberly

RAGE AGAINST - THE - DEMOCRATIC MACHINE: A grass-roots revolt from the left is wresting control of the party away from the corporate establishment, one state at a time T. ANDERSON *In These Times* v41 no7 p18 Jl 2017

Ellis, Leigh

Rb1 and Trp53 cooperate to suppress prostate cancer lineage plasticity, metastasis, and antiandrogen resistance bibl graph *Science* v355 no6320 p1 Ja 6 2017

SOX2 promotes lineage plasticity and antiandrogen resistance in TP53- and RB1-deficient prostate cancer bibl graph *Science* v355 no6320 p1 Ja 6 2017

Ellis, Mary

NO HUSBAND NEEDED - I FLY A SPITFIRE: The memoir of a pioneering woman pilot who delivered vital fighter aircraft and bombers around Britain during the war C. Mulley *History Today* v67 no6 p100 Je 2016

Ellis, Nelsan, 1977-2017

Elementary I. Rudolph color *TV Guide* v64 no42 p40 O 10 2016

LAFAYETTE'S BON TEMPS R. Kinane color *Entertainment Weekly* no1474/1475 p20 Jl 21-28 2017

Milestones color *Time* v190 no4 p13 Jl 24 2017

Nelsan Ellis: 1977-2017 K. Hahn *TV Guide* v65 no31 p9 Jl 24 2017

Nelsan Ellis T. Stack color *Entertainment Weekly* no1474/1475

p20 Jl 21-28 2017

Ellis, Randall J.

Chemogenetics revealed: DREADD occupancy and activation via converted clozapine graph *Science* v357 no6350 p503 Ag 4 2017

Ellis, Scott

5 — SHE LOVES ME M. Snetiker *Entertainment Weekly* no1444/1445 p118 D 16 2016

Ellis, Siân

Gallivanting Gardens of the Cotswolds *British Heritage Travel* v38 no3 p30 My/Je 2017

KING COAL'S CASTLES *British Heritage Travel* v38 no2 p68 Mr/Ap 2017

THE MAIL COACH TO ABERYSTWYTH: Jolts and All: How to Journey in Style--as if It Were 1835 *British Heritage Travel* v38 no4 p38 Jl/Ag 2017

WALES IN THE YEAR OF LEGENDS *British Heritage Travel* v38 no3 p64 My/Je 2017

Ellis, Stephen

This Present Darkness: A History of Nigerian Organized Crime N. van de Walle *Foreign Affairs* v96 no1 p178 Ja/F 2017

Ellis, Terry

'90s till infinity: EN VOGUE L. CROSS color *Ebony* v72 no6 p82 Ap/My 2017

Ellis, Tom

Lucifer D. Holbrook *TV Guide* v65 no19 p32 My 1 2017

Lucifer N. Abrams, C. Holub et al *Entertainment Weekly* no1482/1483 p48 S 22 2017

Ellis-Ashburn, Hope

10 Tips for Traveling Solo with your horse bw color *Equus* no472 p54 Ja 2017

Another reason to ride color *Equus* no476 p96 My 2017

Return to Milky Way Farm color *Equus* no481 p71 O 2017

The second time around color *Equus* no473 p72 F 2017

WHAT YOU NEED TO KNOW ABOUT TRAILER TIRES color diag *Equus* no480 p50 S 2017

Ellisman, Mark H.

ChromEMT: Visualizing 3D chromatin structure and compaction in interphase and mitotic cells color *Science* v357 no6349 p370 Jl 28 2017

Ultrastructural evidence for synaptic scaling across the wake/sleep cycle bibl diag graph *Science* v355 no6324 p507 F 3 2017

ELLISON, AARON M.

Insights into Student Gains from Undergraduate Research Using Pre- and Post-Assessments *BioScience* v66 no12 p1070 D 1 2016

ELLISON, BEN

2017 PITTMAN INNOVATION AWARDS color *Sail* v48 no2 p58 F 2017

Darkness, Speed, and Bad Decisions color *Power & Motoryacht* v32 no12 p24 D 2016

Lost & Found [Cover story] color *Power & Motoryacht* v34 no6 p46 Je 2017

Off the Charts color map *Power & Motoryacht* v33 no4 p32 Ap 2017

Ellison, Frank

Finding ghosts in old layout photos K. Wills bw *Model Railroader* v84 no4 p33 Ap 2017

Ellison, Jesse

Why a Visa Crackdown Is Bad for Business color *Bloomberg Businessweek* no4528 p34 Je 26 2017

ELLISON, JULIE

Chamonix color *Climbing* no355 p34 Ag 2017

CLIMBING color *Backpacker* v45 no3 p120 Ap 2017

THE DESCENT color *Climbing* no352 p88 Ap 2017

Kodak Courage color *Climbing* no354 p18 Jl 2017

Latino Outdoors color *Climbing* no353 p20 My/Je 2017

Reality Check color *Climbing* no350 p15 D 2016/Ja 2017

Scarface color *Climbing* no354 p33 Jl 2017

Sending Snacks color *Climbing* no350 p42 D 2016/Ja 2017

TRANSITIONS color *Climbing* no356 p66 S/O 2017

What Inspires You? color *Climbing* no351 p17 F/Mr 2017

Ellison, Katherine

From Sand to Soil color *Discover* v38 no1 p82 Ja/F 2017

PRANK YOU VERY MUCH color *O, The Oprah Magazine* p30 Ap 2017

Ellison, Keith, 1963-
Ellison's 3,143-County Strategy J. BLEIFUSS *In These Times* v41 no1 p5 Ja 2017
For Keith Ellison color *Nation* v304 no5 p3 F 20 2017
THE PROTEST CANDIDATE V. CUNNINGHAM cartoon color *New Yorker* v93 no2 p34 F 27 2017
A Revolution Deferred C. STANGLER *In These Times* v41 no4 p19 Ap 2017
RULES FOR RADICALS T. MURPHY and R. Felton bw cartoon color *Mother Jones* v42 no2 p44 Mr/Ap 2017

ELLISON, SARAH
BLAND AMBITION color *Vanity Fair* v59 no10 p174 O 2017
THE ENABLERS color *Vanity Fair* v59 no8 p78 Ag 2017
IVANKA'S APPRENTICE color *Vanity Fair* v59 no2 p70 F 2017
THE NEW ESTABLISHMENT 2017 bw color *Vanity Fair* v59 no11 p87 N 2017
NEW ESTABLISHMENT bw cartoon color *Vanity Fair* v58 no11 p124 N 2016
THE PEACOCK THRONE color *Vanity Fair* v59 no4 p184 Mr 2017
ROGER, OVER AND OUT! cartoon *Vanity Fair* v58 no11 p104 N 2016
THE WESTEROS WING color *Vanity Fair* v59 no6 p84 My 2017

Ellison, Tisha Lewis
CLOSING THE FAMILIAL DIVIDE color *Literacy Today (2411-7862)* v34 no3 p16 N/D 2016

ELLMAN, BEN
The Urbanist: The Globalization of Local Radio img *New York* v49 no25 p32 D 12 2016

Ellner, Andy
Strong Patient-Provider Relationships Drive Healthier Outcomes *Harvard Business Review Digital Articles* p2 O 9 2015

Ellory, R. J.
A Dark and Broken Heart *Publishers Weekly* v264 no25 p92 Je 19 2017

ELLROY, JAMES
Buzz M For Murder bw color *Vanity Fair* v59 no11 p152 N 2017

Ellsberg, Daniel
THE OUTSIDE MAN M. GLADWELL cartoon color *New Yorker* v92 no42 p119 D 19 2016
PAPER PUSHERS *Harper's Magazine* v334 no2004 p37 My 2017

Ellsberg, Robert
SAINTS NOT SUPERHEROES [Cover story] color *America* v216 no6 p28 Mr 20 2017

Ellsworth, Loretta
Stars over Clear Lake color *Publishers Weekly* v264 no14 p50 Ap 3 2017

Ellul, P.
Improving global integration of crop research color *Science* v357 no6349 p359 Jl 28 2017

ELLWOOD, MARK
Rome bw chart color map *Conde Nast Traveler* v52 no3 p52 Mr 2017

El-Maarry, M. R.
Rosetta's comet 67P/Churyumov-Gerasimenko sheds its dusty mantle to reveal its icy nature bibl graph *Science* v354 no6319 p1566 D 23 2016

Elmaleh, Lisa
BERKELEY SPRINGS, WEST VIRGINIA *Harper's Magazine* p36 O 2017

Elmendorf, R. G.
The Reader Page color *Popular Mechanics* p8 D 2016/Ja 2017

Elmer, Jamie
A home practice to build a strong back color *Yoga Journal* no287 p45 N 2016
A home practice to build a strong back color *Yoga Journal* p57 2017 SpecialIssue

Elmer, John—Awards
Pants and Awards *Science & Technology Review* p23 S 2016

Elmer, Lon
Discussion *Smithsonian* v48 no4 p6 Jl/Ag 2017

Elmhurst (Ill.)
FIELD GUIDE: ELMHURST J. REESE color map *Chicago* v66 no9 p41 S 2017

Elmhurst College

50 Years of Greatness E. Enright bw color *Downbeat* v83 no11 p86 N 2016

Elmina Castle (Elmina, Ghana)
The Door of No Return R. Brown color *Commonweal* v144 no9 p39 My 19 2017

Elmore, Jack
CAITI & JACK V. HUBBARD *Virginia Living* v15 no2 p96 F 2017

Elmore, James R.
Distribution and clinical impact of functional variants in 50,726 whole-exome sequences from the DiscovEHR study chart graph *Science* v354 no6319 paaf6814-1 D 23 2016

El Moussa, Christina
Flip or Flop's Marital Flap L. Rice color *Entertainment Weekly* no1446/1447 p28 D 2016/Ja 2017

El Moussa, Tarek
Flip or Flop's Marital Flap L. Rice color *Entertainment Weekly* no1446/1447 p28 D 2016/Ja 2017

El Mozote Massacre, El Mozote, El Salvador, 1981
El Salvador's Ghost Town S. ESTHER MASLIN color *Nation* v304 no13 p20 Ap 17 2017

Elmquist, Joel K.
An adipo-biliary-uridine axis that regulates energy homeostasis diag *Science* v355 no6330 p1173 Mr 17 2017

El Rashidi, Yasmine
Caught Between Worlds color *New York Review of Books* v64 no7 p35 Ap 20 2017

Elrod, M.
Mars' atmospheric history derived from upper-atmosphere measurements of 38 Ar/36Ar diag *Science* v355 no6332 p1408 Mr 31 2017

Elrod, Susan
Increasing Student Success in STEM: Summary of A Guide to Systemic Institutional Change *Change* v49 no4 p26 Jl/Ag 2017

Els, Ernie, 1969-
THE BIG EASY, STILL DOING IT D. M. Clarke color *Golf Magazine* v59 no8 p9 Ag 2017
The Education of Samantha Els M. Bamberger color *Golf Magazine* v59 no10 p116 O 2017
MAN on a MISSION [Cover story] C. Barrett color *Golf Magazine* v59 no8 p62 Ag 2017
You're Up! color *Golf Magazine* v59 no10 p11 O 2017

Elsaesser, Thomas
Large-amplitude transfer motion of hydrated excess protons mapped by ultrafast 2D IR spectroscopy graph *Science* v357 no6350 p491 Ag 4 2017

ElSaffar, Amir
Not Two B. Meyer color *Downbeat* v84 no7 p63 Jl 2017

El-Sayed, Abdul
BELIEF IN A SHARED FUTURE: AN INTERVIEW WITH Abdul El-Sayed, MUSLIM-AMERICAN CANDIDATE FOR GOVERNOR OF MICHIGAN J. LEWIS BERG *Humanist* v77 no4 p28 Jl/Ag 2017

Elsbach, Kimberly D.
How to Work with Colleagues Who Are Less Creative than You *Harvard Business Review Digital Articles* p2 S 16 2015

Elsbrock, Tim
A WORD FROM OUR SPONSORS *Cincinnati Magazine* v50 no8 p4 My 2017

Elschner, Géraldine
The Three Kings: The Journey of the Magi *Publishers Weekly* v263 no39 p86 S 26 2016

Else, Jon
True South: Henry Hampton and 'Eyes on the Prize,' the Landmark Television Series That Reframed the Civil Rights Series *Publishers Weekly* v263 no45 p51 N 7 2016

Elsenhower, Susan
THE HUMANITY IN LARGE NUMBERS *Vital Speeches of the Day* v83 no2 p59 F 2017

Elsevier BV
Battle for Access E. BETZ color *Discover* v38 no1 p34 Ja/F 2017
Female researchers on the rise *Science* v355 no6330 p1104 Mr 17 2017
German researchers start 2017 without Elsevier journals G. Vogel color *Science* v355 no6320 p17 Ja 6 2017
Germany seeks 'big flip' in publishing model G. Vogel and K.

Kupferschmidt color graph *Science* v357 no6353 p744 Ag 25 2017

El-Showk, Sedeer

Small Gulf nation aims for big splash on Mars color *Science* v355 no6320 p12 Ja 6 2017

Elsie Green House & Home (Company)

french flair P. GUGLIELMETTI color *Better Homes & Gardens* v95 no10 p20 O 2017

El-Sisi, Abdel Fattah, 1954-

Egypt's Nightmare S. A. Cook bw *Foreign Affairs* v95 no6 p110 N/D 2016

Made-to-Please Religious Reforms: Egyptian strongman El-Sisi seeks ways to please Western supporters M. KOSABA *Islamic Horizons* v46 no4 p50 Jl/Ag 2017

THE SHADOW GENERAL P. HESSLER cartoon *New Yorker* v92 no43 p44 Ja 2 2017

El-Sisi, Abdel Fattah, 1954——Political & social views

Egypt's al-Sisi Finds a Kindred Spirit In President Trump I. Bremmer *Time* v189 no14 p14 Ap 17 2017

ELSNER, LYNN

Your True Stories *Reader's Digest* v188 no1124 p22 O 2016

ELSNER, STEPHANIE

SMART PEOPLE DO THE Dumbest THINGS! [Cover story] *Reader's Digest* v190 no1134 p62 O 2017

Elson & Co. Inc.

History Lesson M. OWENS color *Architectural Digest* no5 p48 My 2017

Elson, Karen

MY BEAUTY MARK... Karen Elson color *InStyle* v24 no3 p288 Mr 2017

Elson, Rachel F.

THE BEST PLACES TO LIVE IN AMERICA [Cover story] chart color map *Money* v46 no9 p54 O 2017

Elston, Ronald

LIFE AFTER LIFE S. Michaels color *Mother Jones* v42 no4 p10 Jl/Ag 2017

Elstrom, Peter

The Trump-Valley Fight Starts to Take Shape *Bloomberg Businessweek* no4510 p26 F 6 2017

When the Teacher Is An Ocean Away color graph *Bloomberg Businessweek* no4505 p22 D 26 2016

Elsworth, Derek

Understanding induced seismicity bibl color graph *Science* v354 no6318 p1380 D 16 2016

Elton, Catherine

Importing Business Lessons From El Norte diag *Bloomberg Businessweek* no4495 p38 O 17 2016

Elton, Jeff

Create a Strategy That Anticipates and Learns *Harvard Business Review Digital Articles* p2 O 6 2014

Predictive Medicine Depends on Analytics *Harvard Business Review Digital Articles* p2 O 23 2014

ELVERU, EMILY

funny finds color *Parents* v92 no6 p79 Je 2017

media to go color *Parents* v92 no8 p85 Ag 2017

Elves

LUXURY ELVES E. Allen cartoon *New Yorker* v92 no43 p19 Ja 2 2017

Elvira, 1951——Interviews

GHOUL TALK C. Collis color *Entertainment Weekly* no1436/1437 p104 O 21 2016

Elvis, Martin

The Crisis in Astronomy: One NASA flagship mission at a time hurts astrophysics and planetary science. Here's a solution *Sky & Telescope* v134 no3 p84 S 2017

Elway, John, 1960-

JOHN ELWAY CAN'T BE STOPPED A. CORSELLO color *GQ: Gentlemen's Quarterly* v86 no12 p186 D 2016

Elwell, Dick

50 years and 2 houses [Cover story] color map *Model Railroader* v84 no8 p40 Ag 2017

Layout names from a more playful era N. Besougloff color *Model Railroader* v84 no8 p8 Ag 2017

Elwick-Bates, Emma

BEST IN SHOE color *Vogue* v207 no1 p106 Ja 2017

BRIGHT YOUNG THINGS bw color *Vogue* v206 no11 p246 N 2016

Bulgari/Nicholas Kirkwood Bags color *Vogue* v207 no9 p368 S 2017

COAST to Coach color *Vogue* v207 no4 p134 Ap 2017

Country Club color *Vogue* v207 no11 p234 N 2017

Cover Story color *Vogue* v207 no9 p738 S 2017

CULTURE Club color *Vogue* v206 no12 p280 D 2016

Finding Her LEGS M. HOLGATE and M. GUIDUCCI color *Vogue* v207 no7 p40 Jl 2017

Heiress and GRACES color *Vogue* v206 no11 p114 N 2016

IN FULL BLOOM color *Vogue* v207 no6 p114 Je 2017

Le Click! color *Vogue* v207 no6 p62 Je 2017

MARY-KATE & ASHLEY OLSEN color *Vogue* v207 no3 p428 Mr 2017

MATERIAL WORLD color *Vogue* v207 no4 p254 Ap 2017

MEMPHIS Beat color *Vogue* v206 no12 p164 D 2016

Treasure Hunting color *Vogue* v207 no11 p120 N 2017

Treasure ISLAND color *Vogue* v207 no7 p126 Jl 2017

Waist Not, Want Not bw color *Vogue* v206 no12 p156 D 2016

WEIGHING In color *Vogue* v207 no3 p500 Mr 2017

Ely, Peter B.

The transformation of Islam *America* v217 no6 p54 S 18 2017

Elzein, Arijh

Regeneration of fat cells from myofibroblasts during wound healing bibl color graph *Science* v355 no6326 p748 F 17 2017

Email

See also

Spam (Email)

7 Email Problems, Solved A. Samuel *Harvard Business Review Digital Articles* p2 D 29 2016

Before You Respond to that Email, Pause A. K. Tjan *Harvard Business Review Digital Articles* p2 O 21 2014

CC'ing the Boss on Email Makes Employees Feel Less Trusted D. De Cremer *Harvard Business Review Digital Articles* p2 Ap 20 2017

Comey Discredits Himself color *Nation* v33 no21 p3 N 21 2016

Dear Readers M. Peyser *Reader's Digest* v189 no1129 p4 Ap 2017

Delete These E-mail Habits T. DUMAIN color *Reader's Digest* v189 no1131 p48 Je 2017

Dialogue *Los Angeles Magazine* v61 no11 p14 N 2016

Email and Calendar Data Are Helping Firms Understand How Employees Work M. L. Tushman, A. Kahn et al *Harvard Business Review Digital Articles* p2 Ag 28 2017

The Essential Guide to Crafting a Work Email G. Gavett *Harvard Business Review Digital Articles* p2 Jl 24 2015

How Can I ... Wow an Adult? *Scholastic Choices* v32 no6 p24 Mr 2017

How Donald Trump Jr.'s Emails Have Cranked Up the Heat on His Family [Cover story] D. V. Drehle, M. Calabresi et al color *Time* v190 no4 p22 Jl 24 2017

How to Give Negative Feedback Over Email J. K. Glei *Harvard Business Review Digital Articles* p2 O 7 2016

How to Make Sure Your Emails Give the Right Impression S. Harmon color *Harvard Business Review Digital Articles* p2 F 6 2017

How to Write Email with Military Precision K. Sehgal *Harvard Business Review Digital Articles* p2 N 22 2016

HUNGRY SOULS M. Bistline *Harper's Magazine* v333 no1999 p18 D 2016

Is Social Media Actually Helping Your Company's Bottom Line? F. V. Cespedes *Harvard Business Review Digital Articles* p2 Mr 3 2015

Mac 911 G. FLEISHMAN cartoon color *Macworld - Digital Edition* p123 Mr 2017

A Modest Proposal: Eliminate Email C. Newport *Harvard Business Review Digital Articles* p2 F 18 2016

MONEY MANNERS M. CROSS cartoon *Kiplinger's Personal Finance* v71 no4 p48 Ap 2017

Prevent Email Horror with a 2-Minute Send Delay K. S. Milway *Harvard Business Review Digital Articles* p2 Jl 23 2015

Scamming The Scammers J. VEITCH *Reader's Digest* v189 no1128 p15 Mr 2017

Scandal? What Scandal? M. HEMINGWAY *Weekly Standard* v22 no8 p28 O 31 2016

Some Companies Are Banning Email and Getting More Done D. Burkus *Harvard Business Review Digital Articles* p2 Je 8 2016

Stop Letting Email Control Your Work Day P. A. Argenti *Harvard Business Review Digital Articles* p2 S 7 2017

The Triumphant Return of the Email Newsletter M. Aarons-Mele *Harvard Business Review Digital Articles* p2 O 8 2015

What Email, IM, and the Phone Are Each Good For K. Decker and B. Decker *Harvard Business Review Digital Articles* p2 Jl 30 2015

What Work Email Can Reveal About Performance and Potential C. Nielsen *Harvard Business Review Digital Articles* p2 F 10 2016

When a Private Message Ends Up in the Wrong Place K. Dillon *Harvard Business Review Digital Articles* p2 D 22 2014

You Can Have Constructive Conflict Over Email J. Grenny *Harvard Business Review Digital Articles* p2 Mr 24 2015

Your Late-Night Emails Are Hurting Your Team M. Thomas *Harvard Business Review Digital Articles* p2 Mr 16 2015

Email & privacy—Law & legislation

Open Secrets A. Hess *New York Times Magazine* p11 My 14 2017

Email hacking

Your E-mail Password Will Never Be Safe D. Pogue color *Scientific American* v316 no1 p24 Ja 2017

Email hacking—Prevention

Yahoo's billion account breach: 5 things you should do to stay safe L. CONSTANTIN color *PCWorld* v35 no1 p41 Ja 2017

Email management

3 tools that easily unsubscribe you from emails M. ANSALDO color *PCWorld* v35 no6 p44 Je 2017

Actually, You Should Check Email First Thing in the Morning D. Clark *Harvard Business Review Digital Articles* p2 Mr 7 2016

How to replace 5 major Yahoo services and delete your Yahoo account I. PAUL color *PCWorld* v35 no1 p46 Ja 2017

I STINK AT EMAIL A. GEORGE *Popular Mechanics* p26 S 2017

Email software

6 more ways to make the most of Mail for iOS 10 B. PATTERSON color *Macworld - Digital Edition* p55 D 2016

Email systems

7 Email Problems, Solved A. Samuel *Harvard Business Review Digital Articles* p2 D 29 2016

Email Marketing: Still the killer app to beat for park and recreation agencies J. Dysart *Parks & Recreation* v52 no5 p18 My 2017

Fixing Our Unhealthy Obsession with Work Email M. Thomas *Harvard Business Review Digital Articles* p2 S 24 2015

How One Company Reduced Email by 64% A. Shipilov and R. J. Crawford *Harvard Business Review Digital Articles* p2 Je 18 2015

How to Keep Email from Ruining Your Vacation A. Huffington *Harvard Business Review Digital Articles* p2 2017

A Modest Proposal: Eliminate Email C. Newport *Harvard Business Review Digital Articles* p2 F 18 2016

Email—Government policy

Privacy legislation reintroduced for mail older than 180 days J. RIBEIRO color *PCWorld* v35 no2 p43 F 2017

Email—Humor

ALL IN A Day's Work *Reader's Digest* v188 no1125 p84 N 2016

Email—Security measures

Traveling for Work? You're a Prime Target for Hackers P. Everton *Harvard Business Review Digital Articles* p2 S 29 2016

Yahoo Mail stops automatic mail forwarding as privacy controversies swirl I. PAUL color *PCWorld* v35 no11 p42 N 2016

Your E-mail Password Will Never Be Safe D. Pogue color *Scientific American* v316 no1 p24 Ja 2017

Email—Social aspects

Why We're Addicted to Email-and How to Fix It J. K. Glei *Time* v188 no14 p23 O 10 2016

Emami, S. Noushin

A key malaria metabolite modulates vector blood seeking, feeding, and susceptibility to infection bibl chart diag *Science* v355 no6329 p1076 Mr 10 2017

Emanuel, Andy

Spot: MAYHEM 27.5+ 4-STAR BUILD color *Bike Magazine* v24 no8 p74 N 2017

Emanuel, Daniella

Local news on public airways graph *Columbia Journalism Review* v56 no1 p101 Spr 2017

Emanuel, Ezekiel J.

Tinkers and Tailors *New York Times Book Review* p17 Mr 19 2017

Who's Benefiting from MOOCs, and Why *Harvard Business Review Digital Articles* p2 S 22 2015

Emanuel, Kerry—Interviews

On the Job K. Cutlip color *Weatherwise* v69 no6 p40 N-D 2016

Emanuel, Rahm, 1959-

A BEE IN TRUMP'S BONNET E. McCLELLAND color *Chicago* v66 no5 p25 My 2017

IN CHICAGO, LET'S GET TO WORK R. EMANUEL *Vital Speeches of the Day* v82 no11 p335 N 2016

Leaders color *Time* v189 no16/17 p64 My 1-8 2017

Emanuel, Ryan E.

Flawed environmental justice analyses color *Science* v357 no6348 p260 Jl 21 2017

Embargo

The Power of a Good Example P. Rauber *Sierra* v102 no5 p22 St/O 2017

U.S. OIL'S $10 BILLION VENEZUELAN THREAT A. Nussbaum and S. Tobben color *Bloomberg Businessweek* no4534 p28 Ag 14 2017

Embargo—Cuba

U.S. Embargo on Cuba *Congressional Digest* v95 no10 p1 D 2016

Embarrassment

DON'T PANIC! G. Graves cartoon *O, The Oprah Magazine* p87 Mr 2017

SEX AGE MADONNA S. WELLER and J. NEWMAN cartoon color *AARP: The Magazine* v60 no2A p60 F/Mr 2017

TRAUMARAMA color *Seventeen* v75 no11 p104 N 2016

TRAUMARAMA color *Seventeen* v76 no5 p106 S 2017

Embarrassment in adolescence

MR. KNOW-IT-ALL C. NIEMANN cartoon *Wired* v25 no3 p26 Mr 2017

Embassy buildings

The Ambassador of Art C. MORGAN-FEIR color *Walrus* v14 no2 p17 Mr 2017

Embassy buildings—Design & construction

Diplomacy in Design C. MCGUIGAN and A. KLIMOSKI color *Architectural Record* v205 no3 p44 Mr 2017

Embezzlement investigation

THE APPROVAL MATRIX img *New York* v50 no6 p108 Mr 20 2017

Embiid, Joel

THE NEW NBA LEXICON B. Langmann bw color *Esquire* p20 N 2017

Embiid, Joel—Health

Embiid, Indiid L. Jenkins color *Sports Illustrated* v125 no16 p42 N 14 2016

Emblems in art

STANDARDS AND EMBLEMS OF THE BATTLE OF SEKIGAHARA E. SANO *Texas Monthly* v44 no11 p102 N 2016

EMBLETON, FIONA

Everything You Need to Know About... DRY SHAMPOO color *Seventeen* v76 no3 p58 My 2017

When Eating "Healthy" MESSES WITH YOUR SKIN color *Seventeen* v76 no4 p48 Jl/Ag 2017

Embracing the Homeless Woman Selling Papers (Poem)

Embracing the Homeless Woman Selling Papers *America* v216 no7 p43 Ap 3 2017

Embridge Inc.

Pushing Back on Pipelines S. Taylor and S. Luetmer color *Progressive* v81 no10 p24 N 2016

Tar Sands Are Coming to Wisconsin S. Taylor cartoon *Progressive* v81 no10 p28 N 2016

Embroidery—19th century

Outstanding New Hampshire Sampler by Harriet F. Hayden of Fitzwilliam color *Magazine Antiques* v183 no6 p20 N/D 2016

Embroidery—Design & construction

One Stitch at a Time M. OZAWA color *Martha Stewart Living* p34 My 2017

Embry, Ashley

The Keys to Running a Smooth Jog *In Stride* v12 no4 p31 Jl 2017

Embryo transplantation

Enhancing Embryo-Transfer Effectiveness S. Dulai Wenholz color *Practical Horseman* v45 no2 p69 F 2017

Embryology

See also

Embryos

Epigenesis
Fertilization (Biology)
Gametogenesis
Human embryology
Ovum
Placenta
Placodes

Assembly of embryonic and extraembryonic stem cells to mimic embryogenesis in vitro S. E. Harrison, B. Sozen et al diag *Science* v356 no6334 p153 Ap 14 2017

Ductal sex determination A. Swain diag *Science* v357 no6352 p648 Ag 18 2017

Embryogenesis in a dish M. Pera color *Science* v356 no6334 p137 Ap 14 2017

RETINOBLASTOMA RELATED1 mediates germline entry in Arabidopsis X. Zhao, J. Bramsiepe et al color diag *Science* v356 no6336 p396 Ap 28 2017

Embryology—Research

PUSHING THE LIMIT G. Vogel color *Science* v354 no6311 p404 O 28 2016

Embryonic stem cells

Are labmade human eggs coming soon? G. Vogel color *Science* v354 no6310 p272 O 21 2016

Assembly of embryonic and extraembryonic stem cells to mimic embryogenesis in vitro S. E. Harrison, B. Sozen et al diag *Science* v356 no6334 p153 Ap 14 2017

the body electrician A. PIORE cartoon color *Popular Science* p64 Ja/F 2017

PCGF3/5–PRC1 initiates Polycomb recruitment in X chromosome inactivation M. Almeida, G. Pintacuda et al color *Science* v356 no6342 p1081 Je 9 2017

Embryos

See also

Mammalian embryos

Elimination of the male reproductive tract in the female embryo is promoted by COUP-TFII in mice F. Zhao, H. L. Franco et al color graph *Science* v357 no6352 p717 Ag 18 2017

Female embryos dismantle male tissue T. HESMAN SAEY color *Science News* v192 no4 p10 S 16 2017

Smuggled dino eggs gave birth to 'baby dragons' color *Science* v356 no6338 p566 My 12 2017

Embryos—Research

Milestones color *Time* v189 no10 p12 Mr 20 2017

EMC Corp.

What to Expect From the Dell-EMC Deal B. Gomes-Casseres *Harvard Business Review Digital Articles* p2 O 13 2015

Emeagwali, Gloria

Acknowledging Africa color *Science* v357 no6348 p258 Jl 21 2017

Emerald City (TV program)

Emerald City J. Jensen color *Entertainment Weekly* no1446/1447 p108 D 2016/Ja 2017

Emerald City M. Logan *TV Guide* v65 no2 p30 Ja 2 2017

SHAUN CASSIDY M. Logan color *TV Guide* v65 no7 p11 F 13 2017

What to Watch WINTER TV EDITION color *Entertainment Weekly* no1448 p47 Ja 13 2017

Emergency housing—Design & construction

SHELTERING L. Collins cartoon *New Yorker* v92 no36 p18 N 7 2016

Emergency management

See also

Disaster relief

Fire drills

Hard Rain and Hard Lessons P. Coy and C. Flavelle bw map *Bloomberg Businessweek* no4536 p12 S 4 2017

The Relevance of Soft Infrastructure in Disaster Management and Risk Reduction S. B. Ullberg and J. Warner *UN Chronicle* v53 no3 p20 2016

What Harvey Is Teaching the Health Care Sector About Managing Disasters N. A. Gandhi and R. S. Dhillon *Harvard Business Review Digital Articles* p2 S 12 2017

When Disaster Strikes, Businesses Rise to Help T. J. Donohue *Weekly Standard* v22 no8 p19 O 31 2016

Emergency management—Equipment & supplies—Evaluation

It's the End of the World as We Know It I. Boudway color *Bloom-*

berg Businessweek no4510 p58 F 6 2017

Emergency management—United States

Unprepared for Disaster L. Lalami il *Nation* v305 no7 p10 S 25 2017

Emergency management—Washington (D.C.)

What If D.C. Is Next? [Cover story] J. NOBEL color *Rolling Stone* no1297 p26 O 5 2017

Emergency medical services

See also

Hospital emergency services

Recovery Will Take Long-term Effort K. CLARKE color *America* v215 no13 p10 O 31 2016

Emergency savings accounts

70 WAYS TO BUILD WEALTH color *Kiplinger's Personal Finance* v71 no4 p20 Ap 2017

Emergent literacy

CHANGING THEIR TRAJECTORY B. Wilson color *Literacy Today (2411-7862)* v34 no5 p48 Mr/Ap 2017

Emergent Vernacular Architecture (Company)

Rules of Engagement A. KLIMOSKI *Architectural Record* v204 no11 p47 N 2016

Emerging markets

The Dos and Don'ts of Working with Emerging-Market Data A. Rosenberg and L. Goodwin *Harvard Business Review Digital Articles* p2 Jl 8 2016

FAST-GROWING ECONOMIES, FOR CHEAP P. J. Lim and C. Bigda *Fortune* v174 no8 p115 D 15 2016

How U.S. Businesses Can Succeed in India in 2015 V. Govindarajan and G. Bagla *Harvard Business Review Digital Articles* p2 D 22 2014

MAPPING FRONTIER ECONOMIES [Cover story] A. MUSACCHIO and E. WERKER chart color diag graph il img *Harvard Business Review* v94 no12 p40 D 2016

Startup Accelerators Have Become More Popular in Emerging Markets—and They're Working P. Roberts and R. Kempner *Harvard Business Review Digital Articles* p2 O 2 2017

A Surprise Boost for Emerging Markets J. K. GLASSMAN color *Kiplinger's Personal Finance* v71 no2 p20 F 2017

The Trump Discount S. SCHAEFER color *Forbes* v199 no1 p60 Ja 24 2017

What Companies Have Learned from Losing Billions in Emerging Markets N. Hochberg, J. Klick et al *Harvard Business Review Digital Articles* p2 S 16 2015

What Engineering a Reverse Innovation Looks Like A. Winter and V. Govindarajan *Harvard Business Review Digital Articles* p2 N 4 2015

WHERE BULLS ARE CHINA-SHOPPING L. Shen color diag *Fortune* v176 no2 p23 Ag 1 2017

Where the Digital Economy Is Moving the Fastest B. Chakravorti, C. Tunnard et al *Harvard Business Review Digital Articles* p2 F 19 2015

Emerging markets—Charts, diagrams, etc.

Foreign Funds Stay on a Roll T. Tepper chart *Money* v46 no3 p77 Ap 2017

Emerson, Caryl

More things to read and watch and learn R. A. Schroth color *America* v216 no9 p6 Ap 24 2017

Emerson, Eva

Averages can conceal how people and science learn *Science News* v190 no11 p2 N 26 2016

Mapping the future, of continents and batteries *Science News* v191 no1 p2 Ja 21 2017

Sometimes failure is the springboard to success *Science News* v190 no8 p2 O 15 2016

EMERSON, JAMES

becoming a navy master diver cartoon *Popular Science* v289 no2 p80 Mr/Ap 2017

Emerson, Joelle

Colorblind Diversity Efforts Don't Work *Harvard Business Review Digital Articles* p2 S 11 2017

Don't Give Up on Unconscious Bias Training—Make It Better *Harvard Business Review Digital Articles* p2 Ap 28 2017

Emerson, Lake & Palmer (Music)

EMERSON, LAKE & PALMER M. Mettler color *Sound & Vision* v81 no10 p72 D 2016

Emerson, Mary Moody, 1774-1863

Mary Moody Emerson Was a Scholar, a Thinker, and an Inspiration N. A. Baker and S. H. Petrulionis *Humanities* v38 no1 p1 Wint 2017

Emerson, Michael

Person of Interest M. Roush *TV Guide* v64 no15 p8 Ap 4 2016

Emerson, Ralph Waldo, 1803-1882

BREATHE color *Prevention* v69 no11 p34 N 2017

Emerson College

Iliza Shlesinger M. Rich color *Current Biography* v78 no4 p72 Ap 2017

EMERY, CHRIS

HURRICANE PERCEPTION *USA Today Magazine* v146 no2868 p70 S 2017

Emery, Jodie

Sinking like stoners B. HUTCHINSON color *Maclean's* v130 no4 p11 My 2017

EMERY, LINDSEY

TATYANA MCFADDEN color *Runner's World* v52 no1 p86 Ja/F 2017

EMERY, MATT

THE 18TH ANNUAL SAND SPORTS SUPER SHOW color *Dirt Sports + Off-Road* v51 no2 p8 F 2017

2016 LUCAS OIL OFF-ROAD RACING SERIES FINISHES STRONG AT WILD HORSE PASS color *Dirt Sports + Off-Road* v51 no4 p34 Ap 2017

2017 UTV WORLD CHAMPIONSHIPS color *Dirt Sports + Off-Road* v51 no9 p10 S 2017

THE 50TH ANNUAL SEMA SHOW color *Dirt Sports + Off-Road* v51 no3 p24 Mr 2017

ADVENTURE BOUND [Cover story] color *Dirt Sports + Off-Road* v51 no1 p44 Ja 2017

ADVENTURE BOUND PART 2 color *Dirt Sports + Off-Road* v51 no2 p28 F 2017

BACK TO THE FUTURE *Dirt Sports + Off-Road* v51 no7 p6 Jl 2017

BIG FUN IN A LITTLE PACKAGE color *Dirt Sports + Off-Road* v51 no11 p18 N 2017

CAMPBELLS CRUSH IT AT KOH color *Dirt Sports + Off-Road* v51 no7 p12 Jl 2017

CAMP RZR WEST color *Dirt Sports + Off-Road* v51 no5 p10 My 2017

CLEANING UP color *Dirt Sports + Off-Road* v51 no10 p52 O 2017

CONSOLODATED POWER color *Dirt Sports + Off-Road* v51 no5 p34 My 2017

CONTROL FREAK [Cover story] color *Dirt Sports + Off-Road* v51 no12 p54 D 2017

DAYS OF FUTURE PAST *Dirt Sports + Off-Road* v51 no11 p6 N 2017

DESERT-READY HOT ROD color *Dirt Sports + Off-Road* v51 no7 p52 Jl 2017

FAMILY TRADITION color *Dirt Sports + Off-Road* v51 no8 p40 Ag 2017

FIRST LOOK: 2017 YAMAHA WOLVERINE R-SPEC EPS SPECIAL EDITION [Cover story] color *Dirt Sports + Off-Road* v51 no1 p16 Ja 2017

THE GALLOPING GHOST color *Dirt Sports + Off-Road* v51 no6 p42 Je 2017

GIVE THE PEOPLE WHAT THEY WANT color *Dirt Sports + Off-Road* v51 no5 p6 My 2017

GMZ UTV WINTER NATIONALS/BITD PARKER 250 color *Dirt Sports + Off-Road* v51 no5 p28 My 2017

GONE, BUT NOT FORGOTTEN *Dirt Sports + Off-Road* v51 no3 p6 Mr 2017

HAPPY WANDERERS UNITE IN FLAGSTAFF color *Dirt Sports + Off-Road* v51 no2 p42 F 2017

IN THE WORKS color *Dirt Sports + Off-Road* v51 no12 p18 D 2017

LUCAS OIL OFF-ROAD EXPO color *Dirt Sports + Off-Road* v51 no3 p10 Mr 2017

MCKILLER color *Dirt Sports + Off-Road* v51 no4 p38 Ap 2017

THE NUCLEAR MARSHMALLOW color *Dirt Sports + Off-Road* v51 no8 p54 Ag 2017

ONE-HOUR WONDER BURN OUT color *Dirt Sports + Off-Road* v51 no4 p46 Ap 2017

ONE-HOUR WONDERS color *Dirt Sports + Off-Road* v51 no3

p44 Mr 2017

ONE OF THE GOOD GUYS color *Dirt Sports + Off-Road* v51 no9 p52 S 2017

ONE OF THOSE THINGS color *Dirt Sports + Off-Road* v51 no2 p60 F 2017

PRACTICE HOW YOU PLAY [Cover story] color *Dirt Sports + Off-Road* v51 no2 p36 F 2017

PROTECTION PLUS color *Dirt Sports + Off-Road* v51 no4 p58 Ap 2017

PUFF DADDY color *Dirt Sports + Off-Road* v51 no1 p56 Ja 2017

RAM RUNNER [Cover story] color *Dirt Sports + Off-Road* v51 no1 p24 Ja 2017

REVEALED: 2017 RAM POWER WAGON [Cover story] color *Dirt Sports + Off-Road* v51 no7 p28 Jl 2017

ROB MACCACHREN color *Dirt Sports + Off-Road* v51 no9 p20 S 2017

ROB MAC: DRIVER OF THE YEAR color *Dirt Sports + Off-Road* v51 no9 p6 S 2017

ROB MAC RIPS TO THREE-PEAT BAJA 1000 OVERALL color *Dirt Sports + Off-Road* v51 no4 p10 Ap 2017

RUNNING WILD color *Dirt Sports + Off-Road* v51 no8 p6 Ag 2017

RUNNING WILD [Cover story] color *Dirt Sports + Off-Road* v51 no12 p40 D 2017

RUNNING WITH THE DEVIL color *Dirt Sports + Off-Road* v51 no3 p18 Mr 2017

SEMA NEW PRODUCTS 2016 color *Dirt Sports + Off-Road* v51 no4 p52 Ap 2017

SHAPE SHIFTER color *Dirt Sports + Off-Road* v51 no3 p46 Mr 2017

SPRINGTIME FOR HITTING AND G-OUTS [Cover story] color *Dirt Sports + Off-Road* v51 no10 p36 O 2017

T100 SALVATION color *Dirt Sports + Off-Road* v51 no11 p54 N 2017

TIME HAS COME color *Dirt Sports + Off-Road* v51 no2 p4 F 2017

TO EVERYTHING—TURN, TURN, TURN *Dirt Sports + Off-Road* v51 no6 p4 Je 2017

TRAIL-READY TRUNK color *Dirt Sports + Off-Road* v51 no6 p50 Je 2017

A TUN OF FUN color *Dirt Sports + Off-Road* v51 no5 p40 My 2017

WILD WEST SHOWOFF color *Dirt Sports + Off-Road* v51 no2 p22 F 2017

WORKINGMAN'S BLUE color *Dirt Sports + Off-Road* v51 no6 p16 Je 2017

WORLD DOMINATION color *Dirt Sports + Off-Road* v51 no10 p20 O 2017

THE YEAR THAT WAS *Dirt Sports + Off-Road* v51 no4 p6 Ap 2017

Emery, Nathan

Bird Brains or Avian Einsteins? KEN YASUKAWA *BioScience* v67 no7 p672 Jl 2017

EMERY, NOEMIE

Always in Vogue color *Weekly Standard* v22 no15 p17 D 19 2016

Good Luck With Your Predictions *Weekly Standard* v22 no5 p26 O 10 2016

The Soap Opera Comes to an End color *Weekly Standard* v22 no20 p23 Ja 30 2017

Tearing Up color *Weekly Standard* v22 no12 p11 N 28 2016

Why Hillary Failed bw color *Weekly Standard* v23 no4 p30 O 2 2017

EMI Group Ltd.

ALISON SUDOL K. SMITH color *Vanity Fair* v58 no12 p73 D 2016

Emigrant remittances

Changing the Way Cash Is Sent Home E. Robinson color graph *Bloomberg Businessweek* no4522 p44 My 15 2017

No Wall to Stop Migrant Cash From Going South N. Cattan and I. Cota color *Bloomberg Businessweek* no4502 p23 D 5 2016

Emigrant Wilderness (Calif.)

Sierra Solitude M. HORJUS color graph map *Backpacker* p20 Je 2017

Emigration & immigration

See also

     Human migrations

The Playlist bw *Rolling Stone* no1299 p11 N 2 2017

Eminent domain—United States

The Wall Needs the Consent of Many L. Etter and J. Sink map *Bloomberg Businessweek* no4510 p13 F 6 2017

Eming, Sabine A.

Inflammation and metabolism in tissue repair and regeneration diag *Science* v356 no6342 p1026 Je 9 2017

Emirates (Company)

Down and Out in FIRST CLASS D. Garner color *Esquire* p56 N 2017

TRIP OF A LIFETIME [Cover story] N. Saporita color *Good Housekeeping* v265 no3 p146 S 2017

THE WORLD IS NOT ENOUGH [Cover story] M. Campbell and D. Kamel color *Bloomberg Businessweek* no4506 p34 Ja 9 2017

YOU ARE AWESOME! *Good Housekeeping* v265 no3 p12 S 2017

Emirates Team New Zealand

Back to Monohulls for the Cup A. Cort color *Sail* v48 no11 p17 N 2017

A Dramatic Pause color *Sail* v48 no3 p17 Mr 2017

Emission control

Strengthening the Precautionary Principle in the Post-Paris Climate Regime A. Boswell bibl *Environment* v59 no5 p26 S/O 2017

Emission control—Government policy

Senate upholds methane control rule color *Science* v356 no6339 p668 My 19 2017

Emission control—International cooperation

A roadmap for rapid decarbonization J. Rockström, O. Gaffney et al bibl color graph *Science* v355 no6331 p1269 Mr 24 2017

The U.S.-China Climate Goals Should be More Aggressive A. Winston *Harvard Business Review Digital Articles* p2 N 12 2014

Emissions (Air pollution)

The promise of negative emissions K. S. Lackner bibl color *Science* v354 no6313 p714 N 11 2016

Research Digest *Alternatives Journal (AJ) - Canada's Environmental Voice* v42 no2 p11 2016

Emissions (Air pollution)—Government policy

Quick Hits map *Scientific American* v316 no1 p20 Ja 2017

Emissions (Air pollution)—Standards

Assessing the Sins of Volkswagen, Toyota, and General Motors J. Liker *Harvard Business Review Digital Articles* p2 S 24 2015

Emissions trading—China

China must lead on emissions trading P. Dargusch *Science* v357 no6356 p1106 S 15 2017

Emma, Queen, consort of Canute I, King of England

The Queen's Encomium E. Parker *History Today* v67 no5 p106 My 2017

Emmanouilidis, L.

Inhibitors of PEX14 disrupt protein import into glycosomes and kill Trypanosoma parasites chart color diag graph *Science* v355 no6332 p1416 Mr 31 2017

EMMANUEL, ADESHINA

THE GRIDIRON AND SOCIAL JUSTICE bw color *Ebony* v72 no4 p100 F 2017

HIP-HOP AND HYPERMASCULINITY color *Ebony* v72 no8 p67 Je 2017

IMPUNITY IN THE FINE PRINT: Chicago's police union contract ensures that abuses remain in the shadows *In These Times* v41 no7 p24 Jl 2017

REBIRTHED AFTER A LIFE IN THE SEX TRADE color *Ebony* v72 no6 p86 Ap/My 2017

EMMANUEL, GREG

The Earbud Revolution color *Rolling Stone* no1274 p16 N 17 2016

Emmaus (Israel : Extinct city)

"Incredible Things Today" M. R. Simone *America* v216 no8 p52 Ap 17 2017

Emmen-Outen, Stephanie

Thoughts on previous issues color *American Cowboy* v24 no1 p24 Je/Jl 2017

Emmer wheat

Austin *Texas Monthly* v45 no3 p129 Mr 2017

Emmerich, Roland

INDEPENDENCE DAY: RESURGENCE B. A. DuHamel color *Sound & Vision* v82 no3 p68 Ap 2017

Emmett, Jonathan

Prince Ribbit *Publishers Weekly* v264 no2 p65 Ja 9 2017

Emmett, Rik—Interviews

Rik Emmett on the Allied Forces Behind the Sound of RESolution9 M. METTLER bw color *Sound & Vision* v82 no2 p22 F/Mr 2017

EMMETT DUFFY, J.

Assessing National Biodiversity Trends for Rocky and Coral Reefs through the Integration of Citizen Science and Scientific Monitoring Programs *BioScience* v67 no2 p134 F 2017

Emmich, Val

VAL EMMICH I. Biedenharn color *Entertainment Weekly* no1468/1469 p110 Je 2-9 2017

Emmons, William R.

Does College Level the Playing Field? *Bridges (Federal Reserve Bank of St. Louis)* p7 Spr 2017

Emmott, Bill

Fixing the capitalist system J. Matteson *America* v217 no3 p47 Ag 7 2017

Macron's Victory Does Not Mean Liberalism Is Safe *NPQ: New Perspectives Quarterly* v34 no3 p43 Jl 2017

Emmy Awards

As Television Expands, the Emmys Are Becoming a Battlefield D. D'addario color *Time* v190 no10/11 p30 S 18 2017

CHEERS & JEERS D. HOLBROOK *TV Guide* v65 no41 p80 O 2 2017

A DATE WITH Niecy C. K. Jackson color *Essence* v48 no5 p84 S 2017

Emmy Spotlight color *Essence* v48 no5 p64 S 2017

A HISTORIC NIGHT AT THE EMMYS M. Roush *TV Guide* v64 no40 p12 O 3 2016

A NIGHT of FIRSTS L. Rice, D. Snierson et al color *Entertainment Weekly* no1484 p18 S 29 2017

Off to the Races! M. Roush *TV Guide* v65 no31 p4 Jl 24 2017

PARTY IN THE USA* (AND CANADA!) H. Goldblatt color *Entertainment Weekly* no1484 p6 S 29 2017

PRIME-TIME HUNGER GAMES R. KEEGAN color *Vanity Fair* v59 no7 p61 Summ 2017

SOMETHING NEW T. S. Young color *Essence* v48 no2 p76 Je 2017

Emo music

ALL THE FEELS A. Igneri color *Bloomberg Businessweek* no4515 p64 Mr 20 2017

Emoji Movie, The (Film)

THE EMOJI MOVIE D. Snierson color *Entertainment Weekly* no1463/1464 p70 Ap/My 2017

Emonts, B. H. C.

Molecular gas in the halo fuels the growth of a massive cluster galaxy at high redshift bibl graph *Science* v354 no6316 p1128 D 2 2016

EMORD, JONATHAN W.

The Administrative State on the Chopping Block *USA Today Magazine* v145 no2864 p18 My 2017

Back on Top *USA Today Magazine* v146 no2866 p30 Jl 2017

The Clinton Rule of Thumb *USA Today Magazine* v145 no2858 p16 N 2016

From Bias to Disruption for New Administration *USA Today Magazine* v145 no2863 p1 Ap 2017

THE GREAT UNRAVELING *USA Today Magazine* v145 no2862 p16 Mr 2017

Lincoln's Killer Is Killed *USA Today Magazine* v145 no2862 p19 Mr 2017

Repeal but not Replace *USA Today Magazine* v146 no2868 p18 S 2017

Russian Roulette *USA Today Magazine* v145 no2860 p21 Ja 2017

SANCTUARY . . . NOT! *USA Today Magazine* v145 no2860 p14 Ja 2017

Why the Left Curses Cursive *USA Today Magazine* v146 no2868 p40 S 2017

Emory & Henry College

Virginia Leads the Way *Virginia Living* v15 no6 p83 O 2017

Emory University—Curricula

Emory University *Dance Magazine* v90 p59 2016/2017 Supplement College Guide

Emoticons & emoji

Are Emojis Making Us Lazy? *Scholastic Choices* v32 no6 p2 Mr

2017

better S. LIAO color *Better Homes & Gardens* v95 no3 p134 Mr 2017

Do Real Men Emoji? D. MAGARY color *GQ: Gentlemen's Quarterly* v97 no5 p66 My 2017

Do You Speak Emoji? A. Ross, T. Keith et al color *Sports Illustrated* v126 no7 p23 Mr 6 2017

EMOJIS THAT CONFUSE ANNA FARIS D. Snierson color *Entertainment Weekly* no1476 p46 Ag 4 2017

Is This How You Use the Poo Emoji? K. SINTUMUANG color *Esquire* v166 no4 p30 N 2016

MASCARA made easy K. FOSTER color *Seventeen* v76 no12 p50 D 2016/Ja 2017

NONBINARY CODE M. MOLTENI cartoon *Wired* v25 no6 p20 Je 2017

Pop Chart R. Bruner, C. Lang et al color *Time* v188 no20 p57 N 14 2016

THE SECRET LIFE OF ANIMALS E. RYLAN, P. CHANDLEE et al cartoon *Reader's Digest* v190 no1134 p38 O 2017

This Just In J. Zorthian *Time* v190 no9 p25 S 4 2017

Emotional competence

Social Emotional Learning in Elementary School: Preparation for Success L. Dusenbury and R. P. Weissberg *Education Digest* v83 no1 p36 S 2017

Emotional eating

NEWS FROM THE World of Medicine S. RIDEOUT color *Reader's Digest* v189 no1129 p56 Ap 2017

Emotional intelligence

The Best Managers Are Boring Managers T. Chamorro-Premuzic *Harvard Business Review Digital Articles* p2 S 28 2015

The Downsides of Being Very Emotionally Intelligent T. Chamorro-Premuzic and A. Yearsley color *Harvard Business Review Digital Articles* p2 Ja 12 2017

The Emotional Impulses That Poison Healthy Teams A. McKee *Harvard Business Review Digital Articles* p2 Jl 16 2015

Emotional Intelligence Has 12 Elements. Which Do You Need to Work On? D. Goleman and R. E. Boyatzis color graph *Harvard Business Review Digital Articles* p2 F 6 2017

Get in the Right State of Mind for Any Negotiation M. Wheeler *Harvard Business Review Digital Articles* p2 My 5 2015

How Emotional Intelligence Became a Key Leadership Skill A. Ovans *Harvard Business Review Digital Articles* p2 Ap 28 2015

How New Managers Can Send the Right Leadership Signals A. Jen Su *Harvard Business Review Digital Articles* p2 Ag 8 2017

How to Help Someone Develop Emotional Intelligence A. McKee *Harvard Business Review Digital Articles* p2 Ap 24 2015

How to Hire for Emotional Intelligence A. McKee *Harvard Business Review Digital Articles* p2 F 5 2016

How to Look for Emotional Intelligence on Your Team C. Fernández-Aráoz *Harvard Business Review Digital Articles* p2 Ap 29 2015

How to Work with People Who Aren't Good at Working with People T. Chamorro-Premuzic *Harvard Business Review Digital Articles* p2 My 26 2015

Ignore Emotional Intelligence at Your Own Risk C. Fernández-Aráoz *Harvard Business Review Digital Articles* p2 O 22 2014

LONG LIVE THE BOOKWORM! *Saturday Evening Post* v289 no1 p71 Ja/F 2017

Recovering from an Emotional Outburst at Work S. David *Harvard Business Review Digital Articles* p2 My 8 2015

Returning to Work When You're Grieving [Cover story] S. Nawaz *Harvard Business Review Digital Articles* p2 Ap 28 2017

Signs That You Lack Emotional Intelligence M. M. Wilkins *Harvard Business Review Digital Articles* p2 D 31 2014

Teaching Teenagers to Develop Their Emotional Intelligence M. Brackett, D. Divecha et al *Harvard Business Review Digital Articles* p2 My 19 2015

What to Do When You're the Target of a Hurtful Office Rumor E. Seppala *Harvard Business Review Digital Articles* p2 D 2 2016

Why Certain Managers Thrive in Tough New Jobs While Others Get Fed Up Yuntao Dong, Myeong-Gu Seo et al *Harvard Business Review Digital Articles* p2 Ap 22 2015

Why Young Bankers, Lawyers, and Consultants Need Emotional Intelligence J. Runde *Harvard Business Review Digital Articles* p2 S 26 2016

You Can't Manage Emotions Without Knowing What They Really

Are A. Markman *Harvard Business Review Digital Articles* p2 D 23 2015

Your Employees' Emotions Are Clues to What Motivates Them A. Markman *Harvard Business Review Digital Articles* p2 My 18 2015

Emotional intelligence—Research

Read a Novel: It's Just What the Doctor Ordered S. Begley color *Time* v188 no19 p58 N 7 2016

Emotional labor

Care and FEEDING E. GILBERT color *O, The Oprah Magazine* p29 Je 2017

Emotional maturity

Executives, Protect Your Alone Time S. B. Kaufman and C. Gregoire *Harvard Business Review Digital Articles* p2 D 16 2015

Emotional stability

4 Steps to Dispel a Bad Mood A. Caillet, J. Hirshberg et al *Harvard Business Review Digital Articles* p2 Ap 6 2015

Emotional trauma

How Refugee Diasporas Respond to Trauma M. KOINOVA *Current History* v115 no784 p322 N 2016

VALERIE MASON-JOHN cartoon *Tricycle: The Buddhist Review* v26 no3 p20 Spr 2017

Emotional trauma in children

Trauma and learning in America's classrooms S. Terrasi and P. C. de Galarce chart color graph *Phi Delta Kappan* v98 no6 p35 Mr 2017

Emotions (Philosophy)

Emotions Are Cognitive, not Innate *USA Today Magazine* v146 no2867 p10 Ag 2017

Emotions Per Mile P. SAGAL cartoon *Runner's World* v52 no4 p42 My 2017

Emotions (Psychology)

See also

Anger

Belief & doubt

Bereavement

Burnout (Psychology)

Calmness

Character tests

Control (Psychology)

Desire

Embarrassment

Empathy

Enthusiasm

Fear

Gratitude

Happiness

Horror

Intimacy (Psychology)

Joy

Love

Mood (Psychology)

Nostalgia

Pain

Prejudices

Rejection (Psychology)

Resentment

Self-confidence

Shame

Stress (Psychology)

Sympathy

3 Ways to Better Understand Your Emotions S. David *Harvard Business Review Digital Articles* p2 N 10 2016

4 Ways to Control Your Emotions in Tense Moments J. Grenny *Harvard Business Review Digital Articles* p2 D 21 2016

AI's Real Risk M. Schrage *Harvard Business Review Digital Articles* p2 D 16 2015

back talk boot camp V. GLEMBOCKI *Parents* p72 2015

The Bare Issue bw color *Glamour* v115 no6 p115 Je 2017

BEAUTIFUL ORTHODOXY [Cover story] M. GALLI bw color *Christianity Today* v60 no8 p34 O 2016

The Behavioral Economics of Recycling R. Trudel *Harvard Business Review Digital Articles* p2 O 7 2016

Being a Good Boss in Dark Times J. Porter *Harvard Business Review Digital Articles* p2 Jl 5 2016

BE THE CHANGE [Cover story] K. Fowler color *Yoga Journal*

no296 p74 N 2017

Bumblebees exhibit signs of emotions E. UNDERWOOD *Science News* v190 no9 p12 O 29 2016

Closing the door: And opening another one [Cover story] C. Rose color *New Orleans Magazine* v51 no10 p54 Ag 2017

Conquering the Divided Self: ONE QUESTION FOR WEIKE WANG N. PELUSI *Psychology Today* v50 no5 p96 S/O 2017

CRUISE CONTROL H. ESTROFF MARANO *Psychology Today* v50 no5 p22 S/O 2017

Direction Finder P. J. RYAN color *America* v215 no13 p28 O 31 2016

The Dos and Don'ts of Work Email, from Emojis to Typos A. Brodsky *Harvard Business Review Digital Articles* p2 Ap 23 2015

Emotional Intelligence Doesn't Translate Across Borders A. Molinsky *Harvard Business Review Digital Articles* p2 Ap 20 2015

The Emotions That Make Us More Creative S. B. Kaufman *Harvard Business Review Digital Articles* p2 Ag 12 2015

EYE TO EYE: A BOND BETWEEN MINDS MAY SHOW ITSELF IN OUR PUPILS K. GOLDYNIA *Psychology Today* v50 no4 p20 Ag 2017

FEARS FOUNDED AND UNFOUNDED S. Freud *Lapham's Quarterly* v10 no3 p114 Summ 2017

A FOUR-LETTER FAN M. HUSTON *Psychology Today* v49 no5 p14 S/O 2016

Handling Emotional Outbursts on Your Team L. Davey *Harvard Business Review Digital Articles* p2 Ap 30 2015

How to Help Your Team Bounce Back from Failure A. Gallo *Harvard Business Review Digital Articles* p2 F 27 2015

How to Manage Your Emotions Without Fighting Them S. David *Harvard Business Review Digital Articles* p2 N 28 2016

How to (Safely) Let Off Steam *Saturday Evening Post* v289 no2 p72 Mr/Ap 2017

How We'll Really Feel if Robots Take Our Jobs G. Gavett *Harvard Business Review Digital Articles* p2 Ja 16 2015

I Got Fired: Rebuild your career after you've been shown the door K. BRADY *Dance Magazine* v91 no7 p56 Jl 2017

Lauren's Confessions L. Morgan color *Parents* v92 no7 p36 Jl 2017

Learn to listen to your emotions R. Miller *Yoga Journal* no287 p26 N 2016

Love IN THE YOGA STUDIO S. Herrington color *Yoga Journal* no296 p40 N 2017

Magic Words J. BIRCH *Psychology Today* v49 no5 p40 S/O 2016

Make Yourself Immune to Secondhand Stress S. Achor and M. Gielan *Harvard Business Review Digital Articles* p2 S 2 2015

Managing the Hidden Stress of Emotional Labor S. David *Harvard Business Review Digital Articles* p2 S 8 2016

Navigating the Emotional Side of a Career Transition R. Ashkenas *Harvard Business Review Digital Articles* p2 Ap 5 2016

The Others W. Morris *New York Times Magazine* p15 N 20 2016

a parent's musical powers color *Parents* v92 no7 p21 Jl 2017

A Playground Hug Means Everything M. M. Brown color *Parents* v92 no7 p18 Jl 2017

Play Without Feeling A. FOX color *Tennis* v53 no2 p70 Mr/Ap 2017

THE POWER (AND PERIL) OF PRIDE E. SILBER *Psychology Today* v49 no5 p10 S/O 2016

Research: Sleep-Deprived Leaders Are Less Inspiring C. M. Barnes *Harvard Business Review Digital Articles* p2 Je 15 2016

The Secret to Negotiating Is Reading People's Faces K. Wezowski *Harvard Business Review Digital Articles* p2 Je 16 2016

SIGHTS UNSEEN J. BREAL *Texas Monthly* v45 no3 p100 Mr 2017

STICK IT TO ME K. Massicot color *New Orleans Magazine* v51 no2 p38 D 2016

Still Wilderness: WHAT ARE WE FEELING WHEN WE ARE FEELING JOY? AND WHERE INSIDE US DOES THAT FEELING RESIDE? C. WIMAN *American Scholar* v86 no4 p36 Aut 2017

Sunshine outside the ivory tower A. Welch, C. Helena et al bw *Science* v357 no6357 p1322 S 22 2017

Tend and Defend C. BADCOCK and J. BLEYER *Psychology Today* v50 no2 p38 Mr/Ap 2017

This Just In J. Zorthian *Time* v189 no18 p25 My 15 2017

This Just In J. Zorthian *Time* v190 no13 p23 O 2 2017

TOXICITY AS A STEALTH TEACHER *Psychology Today* v50 no3 p4 My/Je 2017

What Are You Afraid Of? R. MAURER *Psychology Today* v49 no5 p50 S/O 2016

When Things Aren't 'OK' A. TILLERY and D. POINTDUJOUR color *Ebony* v72 no3 p90 D 2016/Ja 2017

When to Sell with Facts and Figures, and When to Appeal to Emotions M. D. Harris *Harvard Business Review Digital Articles* p2 Ja 26 2015

Woeful Words S. POLAN *Psychology Today* v50 no2 p21 Mr/Ap 2017

The Writing Cure M. MATOUSEK *Saturday Evening Post* v289 no1 p48 Ja/F 2017

Your Boss Won't Say Yes If Emotions Are Running High J. R. Detert and S. J. Ashford *Harvard Business Review Digital Articles* p2 D 19 2014

Your High-Intensity Feelings May Be Tiring You Out E. Seppala *Harvard Business Review Digital Articles* p2 F 1 2016

Emotions (Psychology) in children

powerful emotions L. GARISTO PFAFF *Parents* v91 no11 p144 N 2016

Emotions (Psychology) in literature

Novel Math M. Fischetti graph *Scientific American* v316 no2 p76 F 2017

Emotions (Psychology)—Economic aspects

Dealing with the Emotional Fallout of Selling Your Business J. Giesea *Harvard Business Review Digital Articles* p2 S 1 2015

Emotions (Psychology)—Physiological aspects

Ask anything V. Vlachonis, J. Blackburn et al bw color *Women's Health* v14 no4 p18 My 2017

Emotions (Psychology)—Research

An Auditory Component to Autism A. Pycha color *Scientific American* v315 no3 p16 S 2016

Emotions in animals

SO THAT'S WHY THE LONG FACE J. Berlin color *National Geographic* v232 no4 p26 O 2017

Emotiva Audio Corp.

Emotiva Airmotiv 5CH Speaker System D. Kumin color graph *Sound & Vision* v82 no1 p42 Ja 2017

Empathy

3 Ways to Show "Mumpathy" S. James *Parents* v91 no6 p13 Je 2016

50 Companies That Get Twitter - and 50 That Don't B. Parmar *Harvard Business Review Digital Articles* p2 Ap 27 2015

Automation Won't Replace People as Your Competitive Advantage T. H. Davenport and J. Kirby *Harvard Business Review Digital Articles* p2 Ag 10 2015

Compassion in action M. KORN bw *Yoga Journal* p18 2016 Special Issue

Corporate Empathy Is Not an Oxymoron B. Parmar *Harvard Business Review Digital Articles* p2 Ja 8 2015

Empathy Is Key to a Great Meeting A. McKee *Harvard Business Review Digital Articles* p2 Mr 23 2015

Empathy Is Still Lacking in the Leaders Who Need It Most E. J. Wilson III *Harvard Business Review Digital Articles* p2 S 21 2015

focus on feelings B. THORKELSON *Parents* v91 no6 p142 Je 2016

For Any Product to be Successful, Empathy Is Key J. Kolko *Harvard Business Review Digital Articles* p2 N 20 2014

How Great Coaches Ask, Listen, and Empathize E. Batista *Harvard Business Review Digital Articles* p2 F 18 2015

How Small Acts of Kindness Can GO A LONG WAY S. DIMERMAN color *Maclean's* v129 no40 p69 O 10 2016

If You Can't Empathize with Your Employees, You'd Better Learn To A. McKee *Harvard Business Review Digital Articles* p2 N 16 2016

It's Harder to Empathize with People If You've Been in Their Shoes R. Ruttan, McDonnell et al *Harvard Business Review Digital Articles* p2 O 20 2015

It Takes a Disaster to Remind Us of Our Common Humanity. Let's Not Forget That Too Soon S. Schrobsdorff color *Time* v190 no10/11 p115 S 18 2017

Let there be peace M. Murphy-Gill *U.S. Catholic* v82 no2 p4 F 2017

making sense T. REECE *Parents* v91 no9 p165 S 2016

MEDITATE in the moment M. RABBITT color *Yoga Journal* no291 p47 My 2017

Meet the force WITHIN YOU [Cover story] L. Eckstrom color *Yoga Journal* no294 p74 S 2017

On My Obsession with Sherwood Anderson: Revisiting Winesburg, Ohio again and again B. Falconer *Humanities* v38 no4 p1 Fall 2017

Our Empathy Problem R. WRIGHT color *Nation* v304 no2 p16 Ja 16 2017

A Process for Empathetic Product Design J. Kolko *Harvard Business Review Digital Articles* p2 Ap 23 2015

To Make a Team More Effective, Find Their Commonalities D. DeSteno *Harvard Business Review Digital Articles* p2 D 12 2016

To Win People Over, Speak to Their Wants and Needs N. Duarte *Harvard Business Review Digital Articles* p2 My 12 2015

The True Purpose of True Crime E. Dockterman color *Time* v190 no16/17 p100 O 23 2017

When a Prototype Isn't Enough, Use Theatrical Tricks to Sell Your Idea A. Boynton *Harvard Business Review Digital Articles* p2 Je 16 2017

Why Your Brain Loves Good Storytelling P. J. Zak *Harvard Business Review Digital Articles* p2 O 28 2014

Your Top Stresses, Handled G. Saltz color *Health* v30 no9 p82 N 2016

Your Unlearning Report S. VYSE *Skeptical Inquirer* v41 no3 p27 My/Je 2017

Empathy—Social aspects

Rules aren't enough C. Zulkey color *U.S. Catholic* v82 no2 p12 F 2017

Touching Base A. Hess color *New York Times Magazine* p15 D 4 2016

Empathy—Study & teaching

Rules aren't enough C. Zulkey color *U.S. Catholic* v82 no2 p12 F 2017

Emperor Jones, The (Theatrical production)

THE FALL GUYS H. ALS color *New Yorker* v93 no8 p74 Ap 10 2017

THE THEATRE *New Yorker* v93 no9 p6 Ap 17 2017

Empfield, Rob

Linear Lighting Frenzy: The lighting industry continues to seek inventive ways to make light more efficient and ultimately more appealing to vastly improve the user experience color diag *Architectural Record* v205 no8 p148 Ag 2017

Empire (TV program)

DEMI MOORE OF Empire T. Stack, N. Abrams et al color *Entertainment Weekly* no1482/1483 p78 S 22 2017

Empire M. Logan *TV Guide* v64 no46 p34 N 7 2016

Empire's Latest Rumer *TV Guide* v65 no13 p13 Mr 20 2017

EMPIRE/STAR CROSSOVER M. Logan *TV Guide* v65 no39 p45 S 18 2017

The Latest Empire Hitmaker M. Logan *TV Guide* v65 no41 p7 O 2 2017

Season Finale Shockers! I. Rudolph, M. Logan et al *TV Guide* v65 no25 p4 Je 2017

Empire Beauty Group (Company)

Bryshere "Yazz" Gray & Serayah color *Seventeen* v76 no12 p8 D 2016/Ja 2017

Empire State Building (New York, N.Y.)

First Drafts of History B. SPECKTOR bw *Reader's Digest* v190 no1132 p130 Jl/Ag 2017

Empiricism

Shared history E. D. Maier and F. R. Beardsley *Science* v356 no6338 p591 My 12 2017

Empiricus, Sextus

c. 200: Rome *Lapham's Quarterly* v10 no2 p123 Spr 2017

Employability

The Talent Curse J. PETERIGLIERI and G. PETERIGLIERI il *Harvard Business Review* v95 no3 p88 My/Je 2017

TRAINING FOR YOUR NEXT JOB, THE ONE THAT MIGHT NOT EXIST YET diag *Fortune* v175 no6 p9 My 1 2017

Wanted: Soft skills for today's jobs B. J. Hirsch il *Phi Delta Kappan* v98 no5 p12 F 2017

Employee affinity groups

Where Minority-Worker Networks Are Passé J. Green color *Bloomberg Businessweek* no4531 p15 Jl 24 2017

Employee assistance programs

WHO ARE YOUR STAFF CONFIDING IN? Almost all business offer EAPs to support their employees, but the numbers using them remain troublingly low *People Management* p36 Jl 2017

Employee attitude surveys

BORED AT WORK? YOU'RE NOT ALONE color *Fortune* v175 no4 p18 Mr 15 2017

The Most Desirable Employee Benefits K. Jones *Harvard Business Review Digital Articles* p2 F 15 2017

An update on SOII undercount research activities M. M. Gunter bibl chart color graph *Monthly Labor Review* p1 S 2016

Employee attitudes

See also

Job involvement

Job satisfaction

5 Questions to Help Your Employees Find Their Inner Purpose K. Hedges *Harvard Business Review Digital Articles* p2 2017

How to Help an Employee Who Rubs People the Wrong Way R. Knight *Harvard Business Review Digital Articles* p2 S 21 2017

Employee competitive behavior

How to Find Meaning in a Job That Isn't Your "True Calling" E. E. Smith *Harvard Business Review Digital Articles* p2 Ag 3 2017

The Pros and Cons of Competition Among Employees A. Steinhage, D. Cable et al *Harvard Business Review Digital Articles* p2 Mr 20 2017

Employee empowerment

6 Myths About Empowering Employees D. Marquet *Harvard Business Review Digital Articles* p2 My 27 2015

The Benefits of Peer-to-Peer Praise at Work S. Achor *Harvard Business Review Digital Articles* p2 F 19 2016

Build a Great Company Culture with Help from Technology A. Goldsmith and L. Levensaler *Harvard Business Review Digital Articles* p2 F 24 2016

Don't Ask for New Ideas If You're Not Ready to Act on Them R. Ashkenas *Harvard Business Review Digital Articles* p2 F 2 2015

Engagement Is a Means, Not an End M. Schrage *Harvard Business Review Digital Articles* p2 F 22 2016

For Delegation to Work, It Has to Come with Coaching S. Nawaz *Harvard Business Review Digital Articles* p2 My 5 2016

How to Decide Which Tasks to Delegate J. Blake *Harvard Business Review Digital Articles* p2 Jl 26 2017

The Problem with Saying "Don't Bring Me Problems, Bring Me Solutions" S. Nawaz *Harvard Business Review Digital Articles* p2 S 1 2017

Technology Isn't Enough to Empower Employees, Even in a Digital World D. A. Marchand and J. Peppard *Harvard Business Review Digital Articles* p2 F 17 2016

Employee empowerment—Case studies

Case Study: Is Holacracy for Us? E. Roelofsen and Tao Yue *Harvard Business Review Digital Articles* p2 D 8 2016

Employee fringe benefits

See also

Bonuses (Employee fringe benefits)

Employee vacations

Employer-supported day care

Flexible spending accounts

Cash In on Your Good Health K. LANKFORD color *Kiplinger's Personal Finance* v70 no12 p62 D 2016

Google Adds Benefits, Walmart Cuts Them; Oddly, the Logic Is the Same P. Cappelli *Harvard Business Review Digital Articles* p2 N 7 2014

Lots of Employees Get Misclassified as Contractors. Here's Why It Matters D. Weil *Harvard Business Review Digital Articles* p2 Jl 5 2017

Make It Easier for Your Boss to Say Yes to a Vacation Request H. Weeks *Harvard Business Review Digital Articles* p2 Je 3 2015

Meaningful Work Beats Over-the-Top Perks Every Time P. McCord *Harvard Business Review Digital Articles* p2 F 18 2016

The Most Desirable Employee Benefits K. Jones *Harvard Business Review Digital Articles* p2 F 15 2017

Research Shows That Organizations Benefit When Employees Take Sabbaticals D. Burkus *Harvard Business Review Digital Articles* p2 Ag 10 2017

To Hire Great Coders, Offer Learning, Not Just Money W. Frick

Harvard Business Review Digital Articles p2 Ja 27 2016

Vacation Policy in Corporate America Is Broken M. Thomas *Harvard Business Review Digital Articles* p2 Je 26 2015

Why Won't My Employees Admit They're Going on Vacation? K. Firestone *Harvard Business Review Digital Articles* p2 Ag 28 2015

Why Your Company Culture Should Match Your Brand D. L. Yohn *Harvard Business Review Digital Articles* p2 Je 26 2017

Employee fringe benefits—Government policy
The end of employee benefits? *People Management* p44 My 2017

Employee fringe benefits—Great Britain
The end of employee benefits? *People Management* p44 My 2017

Employee fringe benefits—United States
YOUR NEXT PAY RAISE WILL LOOK FAMILIAR S. BLOCK *Kiplinger's Personal Finance* v71 no11 p9 N 2017

Employee health promotion
Corporate Wellness Programs Lose Money A. Lewis and V. Khanna *Harvard Business Review Digital Articles* p2 O 15 2015

Employers Need to Recognize That Our Wellness Starts at Work J. Purcell *Harvard Business Review Digital Articles* p2 N 15 2016

Employers Should Offer Free Screenings for Depression D. Jacobs *Harvard Business Review Digital Articles* p2 D 11 2015

FIT FOR WORK V. MATTHEWS *People Management* p48 N 2016

How to Design a Corporate Wellness Plan That Actually Works H. De La Torre and R. Goetzel *Harvard Business Review Digital Articles* p2 Mr 31 2016

Meet the Wellness Programs That Save Companies Money J. Purcell *Harvard Business Review Digital Articles* p2 Ap 20 2016

Promoting a Culture of Health and Well-Being in the Workplace S. BURNELL color *Forbes* v200 no3 p46 S 28 2017

There Are Risks to Mindfulness at Work D. Brendel *Harvard Business Review Digital Articles* p2 F 11 2015

THE TIES THAT BIND AT LEVI'S E. Fry color map *Fortune* v176 no4 p104 S 15 2017

Why You Should Tell Your Team to Take a Break and Go Outside E. Seppala and J. Berlin *Harvard Business Review Digital Articles* p2 Je 26 2017

Workplace Wellness Programs Could Be Putting Your Health Data at Risk I. Ajunwa color *Harvard Business Review Digital Articles* p2 Ja 19 2017

Employee health promotion—Law & legislation
The GOP's Wellness Bill Would Give Employers Too Much Power A. Lewis *Harvard Business Review Digital Articles* p2 Mr 15 2017

Employee health promotion—Social aspects
CORPORATE WELLNESS PROGRAMS: HEALTHY ... OR HOKEY? E. Fry color *Fortune* v175 no4 p99 Mr 15 2017

Employee misconduct
FLIGHT OF THE CONCHORDS *People Management* p66 O 2016

Employee morale
   See also
   Employee competitive behavior
   Incentives in industry
The Easiest Thing You Can Do to Be a Great Boss D. Sturt *Harvard Business Review Digital Articles* p2 N 9 2015

Help Your Employees Be Themselves at Work D. Clark and C. Smith *Harvard Business Review Digital Articles* p2 N 3 2014

How Luxury Brands Can Motivate Service Employees E. Mady *Harvard Business Review Digital Articles* p2 N 2 2015

How to Fall Back in Love with Your Job C. O'Hara *Harvard Business Review Digital Articles* p2 Jl 23 2015

How to Motivate Employees to Go Beyond Their Jobs M. C. Bolino and A. C. Klotz *Harvard Business Review Digital Articles* p2 S 15 2017

How to Motivate Yourself When Your Boss Doesn't J. Mosow *Harvard Business Review Digital Articles* p2 N 14 2014

Manage Your Stress by Monitoring Your Body's Reactions to It E. A. Fox *Harvard Business Review Digital Articles* p2 O 2 2017

Research: Insecure Managers Don't Want Your Suggestions N. J. Fast, E. R. Burris et al *Harvard Business Review Digital Articles* p2 N 24 2014

Sentiment Analysis Can Do More than Prevent Fraud and Turnover M. Schrage *Harvard Business Review Digital Articles* p2 Ja 5 2016

Why Your Company Needs More Ceremonies P. Sanchez *Harvard Business Review Digital Articles* p2 Jl 27 2016

You Can Deliver Bad News to Your Team Without Crushing Them M. Gielan *Harvard Business Review Digital Articles* p2 Mr 21 2016

Employee morale—Management
To Motivate Employees, Show Them How They're Helping Customers F. Gino color *Harvard Business Review Digital Articles* p2 Mr 6 2017

Employee motivation
   See also
   Employee competitive behavior
   Incentives in industry
2 Myths About Engaging B-Players T. J. DeLong and V. Vijayaraghavan *Harvard Business Review Digital Articles* p2 N 28 2014

7 Things Leaders Do to Help People Change J. Zenger and J. Folkman *Harvard Business Review Digital Articles* p2 Jl 20 2015

Are You Trying to Solve the Wrong Problem? P. Bregman *Harvard Business Review Digital Articles* p2 D 7 2015

A Company's Good Deeds Can Energize Employees C. Lueneburger *Harvard Business Review Digital Articles* p2 D 3 2014

Developing Employees Who Think for Themselves F. Gino and B. Staats *Harvard Business Review Digital Articles* p2 Je 3 2015

Don't Underestimate the Power of Lateral Career Moves for Professional Growth K. Helvey *Harvard Business Review Digital Articles* p2 My 10 2016

Do You Know Who Holds Your Office Together? M. Ertman and S. M. Darviche *Harvard Business Review Digital Articles* p2 S 23 2015

FINISH STRONG B. Zeitlin color *Women's Health* v14 no8 p32 O 2017

Get Buy-In for Your Crazy Idea D. Burkus *Harvard Business Review Digital Articles* p2 Je 3 2015

Help Your Employees Be Themselves at Work D. Clark and C. Smith *Harvard Business Review Digital Articles* p2 N 3 2014

How a Fast Casual Chain Shows Employees Their Work Matters J. Olinto *Harvard Business Review Digital Articles* p2 N 19 2015

How Company Culture Shapes Employee Motivation L. McGregor and N. Doshi *Harvard Business Review Digital Articles* p2 N 25 2015

How Leaders Can Push Employees Without Stressing Them Out K. Firestone *Harvard Business Review Digital Articles* p2 My 23 2017

How Luxury Brands Can Motivate Service Employees E. Mady *Harvard Business Review Digital Articles* p2 N 2 2015

How to Build a Passionate Company J. Whitehurst *Harvard Business Review Digital Articles* p2 F 15 2016

How to Find Meaning in a Job That Isn't Your "True Calling" E. E. Smith *Harvard Business Review Digital Articles* p2 Ag 3 2017

How to Get an Employee to Work Faster C. O'Hara color *Harvard Business Review Digital Articles* p2 Ja 3 2017

How to Get Employees Excited to Do Their Work K. Decker and B. Decker *Harvard Business Review Digital Articles* p2 My 18 2015

How to Help Someone Discover Work That Excites Them A. Jen Su *Harvard Business Review Digital Articles* p2 S 13 2017

How to Make Work More Meaningful for Your Team L. Garrad and T. Chamorro-Premuzic *Harvard Business Review Digital Articles* p2 Ag 9 2017

How to Motivate Employees to Go Beyond Their Jobs M. C. Bolino and A. C. Klotz *Harvard Business Review Digital Articles* p2 S 15 2017

How to Motivate Someone You Don't Like L. Davey *Harvard Business Review Digital Articles* p2 N 4 2014

How to Motivate Yourself When Your Boss Doesn't J. Mosow *Harvard Business Review Digital Articles* p2 N 14 2014

How to Stay Motivated When Everyone Else Is on Vacation D. Clark *Harvard Business Review Digital Articles* p2 Ag 8 2016

How to Work Remotely Without Losing Motivation A. Buckholtz *Harvard Business Review Digital Articles* p2 S 22 2016

THE MODERN WORKPLACE graph *Vanity Fair* v59 no1 p82 Holiday 2017

Motivating Employees Is Not About Carrots or Sticks L. Lai *Harvard Business Review Digital Articles* p2 Je 27 2017

OFFICE SPACE: A programmer's apathy and lack of motivation are harming his productivity *People Management* p58 Ag 2017

PIONEERS, DRIVERS, INTEGRATORS, AND GUARDIANS: INTERACTION S. M. J. VICKBERG and K. CHRISTFORT color *Harvard Business Review* v95 no4 p18 Jl/Ag 2017

Recognizing Employees Is the Simplest Way to Improve Morale D. Novak *Harvard Business Review Digital Articles* p2 My 9 2016

Retaining Your Data Scientists M. Li *Harvard Business Review Digital Articles* p2 N 20 2014

The Right Way to Hold People Accountable *Harvard Business Review Digital Articles* p2 Ja 11 2016

Sales Bonuses Are Supposed to Motivate, So Don't Waste Them on Easy Targets A. A. Zoltners, P. K. Sinha et al *Harvard Business Review Digital Articles* p2 S 14 2017

THE SCIENCE OF PEP TALKS: TO FIRE UP YOUR TEAM, DRAW ON A RESEARCH-PROVEN, THREE-PART FORMULA D. MCGINN il *Harvard Business Review* v95 no4 p133 Jl/Ag 2017

Stop Calling People Out J. Giesea *Harvard Business Review Digital Articles* p2 O 24 2014

Stop Mindlessly Going Through Your Work Day L. Weiss *Harvard Business Review Digital Articles* p2 Mr 23 2017

The Surprising Persuasiveness of a Sticky Note K. Hogan *Harvard Business Review Digital Articles* p2 My 26 2015

Thinking Clearly About Your Company's Purpose G. Kenny *Harvard Business Review Digital Articles* p2 S 8 2016

To Encourage Innovation, Make It a Competition A. Rathi *Harvard Business Review Digital Articles* p2 N 19 2014

To Motivate Employees, Do 3 Things Well E. Seppala *Harvard Business Review Digital Articles* p2 Ja 4 2016

To Motivate Employees, Help Them Do Their Jobs Better T. Chamorro-Premuzic *Harvard Business Review Digital Articles* p2 N 12 2014

To Motivate Employees, Show Them How They're Helping Customers F. Gino color *Harvard Business Review Digital Articles* p2 Mr 6 2017

We Don't Shun Unethical Coworkers If They're High Performers R. L. Greenbaum and M. J. Quade *Harvard Business Review Digital Articles* p2 My 25 2016

What Motivates Employees More: Rewards or Punishments? T. Sharot *Harvard Business Review Digital Articles* p2 S 26 2017

What's the Right Kind of Bonus to Motivate Your Sales Force? D. J. Chung and D. Narayandas *Harvard Business Review Digital Articles* p2 S 12 2017

What to Do When People Don't Support Your Next Career Move D. Clark *Harvard Business Review Digital Articles* p2 Ag 26 2016

Why John Deere Measures Employee Morale Every Two Weeks B. Power *Harvard Business Review Digital Articles* p2 My 24 2016

Why Two Financial Targets Can Be Better than One S. Whitbread and M. Rosenbaum *Harvard Business Review Digital Articles* p2 D 20 2016

Why You Need an Imaginary Scapegoat N. Eyal bw *Harvard Business Review Digital Articles* p2 F 6 2017

Why You Should Watch Out for Your 5-Year Job Anniversary J. Zenger and J. Folkman *Harvard Business Review Digital Articles* p2 Ap 10 2015

Your Desire to Get Things Done Can Undermine Your Effectiveness F. Gino and B. Staats *Harvard Business Review Digital Articles* p2 Mr 22 2016

Your Employees' Emotions Are Clues to What Motivates Them A. Markman *Harvard Business Review Digital Articles* p2 My 18 2015

Employee orientation

Internal Hires Need Orientation Too L. Sterling *Harvard Business Review Digital Articles* p2 N 4 2016

What to Do When You're Returning to a Company You Used to Work For R. Knight *Harvard Business Review Digital Articles* p2 Ag 4 2017

Employee ownership

Treat Employees Like Business Owners J. Case *Harvard Business Review Digital Articles* p2 D 8 2015

Employee psychology

ANOTHER ARGUMENT FOR COGNITIVE DIVERSITY diag il img *Harvard Business Review* v95 no4 p32 Jl/Ag 2017

Employee recruitment

See also

Skilled labor recruitment

Teacher recruitment

3 Emerging Alternatives to Traditional Hiring Methods T. Chamorro-Premuzic *Harvard Business Review Digital Articles* p2 Je 26 2015

6 Ways to Recruit Superstar Talent to Your New Company B. Bergmann *Harvard Business Review Digital Articles* p2 F 17 2016

7 Practical Ways to Reduce Bias in Your Hiring Process R. Knight *Harvard Business Review Digital Articles* p2 Je 12 2017

As Your Company Evolves, What Happens to Employees Who Don't? R. Glazer *Harvard Business Review Digital Articles* p2 S 13 2017

The Best Ways to Hire Salespeople F. V. Cespedes and D. Weinfurter *Harvard Business Review Digital Articles* p2 N 2 2015

The Best Way to Hire from Inside Your Company J. R. Keller *Harvard Business Review Digital Articles* p2 Je 1 2015

Bob SCHIEFFER color *Vanity Fair* v59 no10 p216 O 2017

The Container Store's CEO on Finding and Keeping Front-Line Talent K. Tindell *Harvard Business Review Digital Articles* p2 N 19 2014

Digital Companies Need More Liberal Arts Majors T. Perrault *Harvard Business Review Digital Articles* p2 Ja 29 2016

Firms Are Wasting Millions Recruiting on Only a Few Campuses L. Rivera *Harvard Business Review Digital Articles* p2 O 23 2015

Fixing the Recruiting and Retention Problems in Britain's NHS A. Kaidi and R. Atun *Harvard Business Review Digital Articles* p2 2017

The Gap Between What Leaders Want and What Recruiters Deliver S. Marks *Harvard Business Review Digital Articles* p2 F 16 2016

Hiring Algorithms Are Not Neutral G. Mann and C. O'Neil *Harvard Business Review Digital Articles* p2 D 9 2016

Hiring and Managing in Turbulent Times C. Fernández-Aráoz *Harvard Business Review Digital Articles* p2 D 12 2016

How Companies Are Using Simulations, Competitions, and Analytics to Hire D. Carey and M. Smith *Harvard Business Review Digital Articles* p2 Ap 22 2016

How Geography Affects Where Elite Consulting Firms Recruit J. M. Olejarz *Harvard Business Review Digital Articles* p2 Jl 5 2016

How I Hired an Entirely Remote Workforce K. Shalev *Harvard Business Review Digital Articles* p2 Ap 14 2016

How to Avoid Hiring a Toxic Employee C. Porath *Harvard Business Review Digital Articles* p2 F 3 2016

How to Hire Like a Superboss S. Finkelstein *Harvard Business Review Digital Articles* p2 F 9 2016

How to Hire Without Getting Fooled by First Impressions T. Menon and L. Thompson *Harvard Business Review Digital Articles* p2 F 15 2016

How to Select the Right Freelancer for the Work J. Younger, T. Viale et al *Harvard Business Review Digital Articles* p2 F 23 2016

I still can't find my strategic HR genius *People Management* p55 Je 2017

Meaningful Work Beats Over-the-Top Perks Every Time P. McCord *Harvard Business Review Digital Articles* p2 F 18 2016

Recruiting Strategies for a Tight Talent Market E. Dhawan *Harvard Business Review Digital Articles* p2 Ap 7 2016

The Rise of the Rude Hiring Manager A. Kreamer *Harvard Business Review Digital Articles* p2 N 3 2014

Simple Online Tools to Make Hiring Easier D. Spinellis *Harvard Business Review Digital Articles* p2 My 4 2015

To Hire Great Coders, Offer Learning, Not Just Money W. Frick *Harvard Business Review Digital Articles* p2 Ja 27 2016

Tongal, cLance, and Topcoder Will Change How You Compete D. Creelman, J. Boudreau et al *Harvard Business Review Digital Articles* p2 N 7 2014

the truth about selling from home V. SOLE-SMITH *Parents* v91 no6 p96 Je 2016

What African Start-Ups Need to Do to Hire and Keep Great Talent N. Ekekwe *Harvard Business Review Digital Articles* p2 Ap

How to Select the Right Freelancer for the Work J. Younger, T. Viale et al *Harvard Business Review Digital Articles* p2 F 23 2016

If There's Only One Woman in Your Candidate Pool, There's Statistically No Chance She'll Be Hired S. K. Johnson, D. R. Hekman et al *Harvard Business Review Digital Articles* p2 Ap 26 2016

Interview Techniques That Get Beyond Canned Responses A. Bassuk and J. Glickman *Harvard Business Review Digital Articles* p2 F 19 2016

Is it acceptable to hire your sister? *People Management* p53 My 2017

IT'S GETTING HARDER TO HIRE B. O'Keefe diag *Fortune* v175 no5 p92 Ap 1 2017

"I used to spend half my time on candidates' complaints": How the charity revamped its applicant experience as part of an ambitious HR transformation project *People Management* p22 S 2017

PENNY MORDAUNT: Employing disabled people is about more than a moral imperative *People Management* p17 Ag 2017

Prejudgment call Yuka Takemon *Science* v355 no6320 p22 Ja 6 2017

What I Look for in Candidates Interviewing at My Startup C. Maio *Harvard Business Review Digital Articles* p2 N 15 2016

What People Analytics Can't Capture D. Goleman *Harvard Business Review Digital Articles* p2 Jl 7 2015

WHERE DOES THE ALGORITHM SEE YOU IN 10 YEARS? J. Alsever color *Fortune* v175 no7 p74 Je 1 2017

Employee selection—Methodology

How to Write a Résumé That Stands Out A. Gallo *Harvard Business Review Digital Articles* p2 D 19 2014

Employee selection—News briefs

News Briefs *Publishers Weekly* v264 no31 p8 Jl 31 2017

Employee services

　　See also

　　Employee assistance programs

WHO ARE YOUR STAFF CONFIDING IN? Almost all business offer EAPs to support their employees, but the numbers using them remain troublingly low *People Management* p36 Jl 2017

Employee stock options

Letting Workers Have a Share A. Melin and M. Mittelman bw color *Bloomberg Businessweek* no4527 p37 Je 19 2017

When Paper Beats Cash W. BALDWIN color *Forbes* v199 no7 p142 Je 29 2017

Employee surveillance

The Long-Term Effects of Tracking Employee Behavior G. Gavett *Harvard Business Review Digital Articles* p2 Jl 18 2016

Employee training

　　See also

　　Apprenticeship programs

　　Employee orientation

　　Internship programs

The 3 Things That Make Technical Training Worthwhile M. Li *Harvard Business Review Digital Articles* p2 Mr 18 2016

7 Ways to Improve Employee Development Programs K. Ferrazzi *Harvard Business Review Digital Articles* p2 Jl 31 2015

Analytics Training Isn't Enough to Create a Data-Driven Workforce A. Sweetwood *Harvard Business Review Digital Articles* p2 Ag 3 2017

The Best Cybersecurity Investment You Can Make Is Better Training D. Disparte and C. Furlow *Harvard Business Review Digital Articles* p2 My 16 2017

Businesses Lead Solutions to Workforce Challenges T. J. DONOHUE *Weekly Standard* v22 no40 p7 Je 26 2017

Coworkers Should Be Like Neighbors, Not Like Family A. Markman *Harvard Business Review Digital Articles* p2 O 31 2014

Help Employees Create Knowledge—Not Just Share It J. Hagel III and J. S. Brown *Harvard Business Review Digital Articles* p2 2017

How to Design Work Projects for Maximum Learning J. M. Stearn *Harvard Business Review Digital Articles* p2 Jl 22 2015

How to Get a New Employee Up to Speed S. Stibitz *Harvard Business Review Digital Articles* p2 My 22 2015

How to Manage Your Star Employee R. Knight *Harvard Business Review Digital Articles* p2 Je 30 2017

The Mistake Most Managers Make with Cross-Cultural Training

A. Molinsky *Harvard Business Review Digital Articles* p2 Ja 15 2015

A NEW MIND-SET H. Clancy color *Fortune* v75 no1 p30 Ja 1 2017

THE PROBLEM: HOW CAN PAY BE USED TO LEAD AND KEEP VALUED EMPLOYEES? D. J. Jonovic color *Successful Farming* v115 no7 p56 My 2017

Time Management Training Doesn't Work M. Thomas *Harvard Business Review Digital Articles* p2 Ap 22 2015

To Better Train Workers, Figure Out Where They Struggle A. Jaffer and M. Mourshed *Harvard Business Review Digital Articles* p2 Je 30 2017

Using Design Thinking to Embed Learning in Our Jobs J. Bersin *Harvard Business Review Digital Articles* p2 Jl 25 2016

What Facebook's Anti-Bias Training Program Gets Right F. Gino *Harvard Business Review Digital Articles* p2 Ag 24 2015

What Science Says About Identifying High-Potential Employees T. Chamorro-Premuzic, S. Adler et al *Harvard Business Review Digital Articles* p2 O 3 2017

When and Why to Part Ways with a Customer L. Arussy *Harvard Business Review Digital Articles* p2 F 13 2015

When Learning at Work Becomes Overwhelming D. DeLong *Harvard Business Review Digital Articles* p2 Mr 20 2015

Why Do We Spend So Much Developing Senior Leaders and So Little Training New Managers? V. Lipman *Harvard Business Review Digital Articles* p2 Je 28 2016

Employee training costs

To Better Train Workers, Figure Out Where They Struggle A. Jaffer and M. Mourshed *Harvard Business Review Digital Articles* p2 Je 30 2017

Employee training—Finance

There Is No Shortage of Leaders G. Petriglieri *Harvard Business Review Digital Articles* p2 D 15 2014

Employee training—Great Britain

Employees are hungrier to learn: Why ditching tick-box L&D made a fish factory a better place to work *People Management* p25 My 2017

Employee training—Japan

I'LL TELL YOU SOMETHING NADEEM KARBHARI N. KARBHARI *People Management* p18 F 2017

Employee training—Methodology

DO NOT READ THIS ARTICLE: Delivering learning exactly when it's needed isn't just common sense - it's a revolution for the L&D department M. CALNAN *People Management* p46 Ap 2017

Employee training—Software

We get our coaching expertise through an app G. GYTON *People Management* p25 F 2017

Employee training—United States

Stop Waiting for Governments to Close the Skills Gap J. Streur and G. Serafeim color *Harvard Business Review Digital Articles* p2 Ja 11 2017

Employee training—Vocational guidance

The next step: We help you to help your career *People Management* p56 Je 2017

Employee vacations

Are the People Who Take Vacations the Ones Who Get Promoted? S. Achor *Harvard Business Review Digital Articles* p2 Je 12 2015

Are We More Productive When We Have More Time Off? J. Zenger and J. Folkman *Harvard Business Review Digital Articles* p2 Je 17 2015

Dear Boss: Your Team Wants You to Go on Vacation R. Friedman *Harvard Business Review Digital Articles* p2 Je 18 2015

Employee's time off is adding up S. Sales *People Management* p53 F 2017

EMPLOYERS EXPAND PAID FAMILY LEAVE S. BLOCK color *Kiplinger's Personal Finance* v70 no12 p15 D 2016

Going on Vacation Doesn't Have to Stress You Out at Work E. G. Saunders *Harvard Business Review Digital Articles* p2 Je 2 2015

How to Be a Pro-Vacation Manager in a High-Pressure Industry L. J. Waitz *Harvard Business Review Digital Articles* p2 Je 22 2015

How to Make Unlimited Vacation Time Work at Your Company D. Burkus *Harvard Business Review Digital Articles* p2 Je 15

2015

How to Negotiate for Vacation Time D. M. Kolb and S. M. Brady *Harvard Business Review Digital Articles* p2 Je 19 2015

If You Can't Take a Vacation, Get the Most Out of Minibreaks E. Seppala *Harvard Business Review Digital Articles* p2 Jl 14 2015

Monetizing Lost Vacation Time A. Melin and B. Steverman color *Bloomberg Businessweek* no4495 p33 O 17 2016

Research Shows That Organizations Benefit When Employees Take Sabbaticals D. Burkus *Harvard Business Review Digital Articles* p2 Ag 10 2017

The Ripple Effects of Parents Not Using Their Vacation Time S. G. Carmichael *Harvard Business Review Digital Articles* p2 O 12 2015

VACATION MODE V. K. De Luca color *Essence* v48 no3 p10 Jl 2017

What One Company Learned from Forcing Employees to Use Their Vacation Time N. Pasricha *Harvard Business Review Digital Articles* p2 Ag 11 2017

Why Delegating Tasks Before a Vacation Never Works C. A. Walker *Harvard Business Review Digital Articles* p2 Ag 2 2017

Why Some of Us Dread Going on Vacation A. Markman *Harvard Business Review Digital Articles* p2 Je 16 2015

Employee vacations—Great Britain

"Unlimited holiday works because of our culture": Why a defence SME did away with leave limits *People Management* p23 Ag 2017

Employee vacations—Lawsuits & claims

Warning over huge holiday bill for workers: Paid leave or compensation may be due to those unable to take leave, says EU opinion *People Management* p17 Jl 2017

Employee vacations—Management

How to Manage Your Team's Vacation Requests K. Dillon *Harvard Business Review Digital Articles* p2 Je 10 2015

Managing Vacations When Your Team Is Global M. Hahn and A. Molinsky *Harvard Business Review Digital Articles* p2 S 25 2015

Employees

> *See also*
>
> Contract labor
> Electronic commerce personnel
> Employment of older people
> Employment of people with disabilities
> Equality in the workplace
> Home labor
> Medical personnel
> Models (Persons)
> Private police
> Problem employees
> Sanitation workers
> Women employees

Advice for Dealing with a Long-Winded Leader J. McCormack *Harvard Business Review Digital Articles* p2 Ja 9 2015

Bookends S. Deb and D. Stevens *New York Times Book Review* p31 N 27 2016

The Curious Science of When Multitasking Works W. Frick *Harvard Business Review Digital Articles* p2 Ja 6 2015

Don't Set Process Without Input from Frontline Workers S. New *Harvard Business Review Digital Articles* p2 Je 26 2015

Ethics Allegations Will Hurt White House Staffers Even If They Turn Out to Be False K. B. DeTienne bw *Harvard Business Review Digital Articles* p1 Je 2 2017

Graying America in Search of a Solution B. MCPHERSON *USA Today Magazine* v145 no2860 p30 Ja 2017

Help Employees Innovate By Giving Them the Right Challenge A. Imber *Harvard Business Review Digital Articles* p2 O 17 2016

How to Establish a Meeting-Free Day Each Week E. G. Saunders color *Harvard Business Review Digital Articles* p2 F 28 2017

How to Help Someone Develop Emotional Intelligence A. McKee *Harvard Business Review Digital Articles* p2 Ap 24 2015

How to Make Learning More Automatic G. Rubin *Harvard Business Review Digital Articles* p2 Ja 6 2016

How to Manage a Needy Employee R. Knight color *Harvard Business Review Digital Articles* p2 Je 5 2017

The Humans Working Behind the AI Curtain M. L. Gray and S. Suri bw *Harvard Business Review Digital Articles* p2 Ja 9 2017

"I Can't Unplug from Work, and It' Affecting My Colleague's Job" M. Santos cartoon color *Working Mother* v40 no3 p8 Ag/S 2017

Is Your Company Using Employee Data Ethically? Kon Leong *Harvard Business Review Digital Articles* p2 Mr 13 2017

"Office Housework" Gets in Women's Way D. M. Kolb and J. L. Porter *Harvard Business Review Digital Articles* p2 Ap 16 2015

Should employers be barred from asking job applicants what they earn? K. KIPLINGER *Kiplinger's Personal Finance* v71 no8 p14 Ag 2017

Stop Trying to Control How Ex-Employees Use Their Knowledge O. Lobel and J. Bessen *Harvard Business Review Digital Articles* p2 O 9 2014

Transforming Today's Bad Jobs into Tomorrow's Good Jobs Z. Ton and S. Kalloch *Harvard Business Review Digital Articles* p2 Je 12 2017

We Learn More When We Learn Together J. E. Dutton and E. Heaphy *Harvard Business Review Digital Articles* p2 Ja 12 2016

What Matters More to Your Workforce than Money A. Chamberlain color *Harvard Business Review Digital Articles* p2 Ja 17 2017

What Science Says About Identifying High-Potential Employees T. Chamorro-Premuzic, S. Adler et al *Harvard Business Review Digital Articles* p2 O 3 2017

What to Do When You Inherit a Team That Isn't Working Hard Enough J. Grenny bw *Harvard Business Review Digital Articles* p1 Je 2 2017

When You Feel Pressured to Do the Wrong Thing at Work J. L. Badaracco *Harvard Business Review Digital Articles* p2 N 2 2016

When You're the Person Your Colleagues Always Vent To S. L. Robinson and K. Schabram *Harvard Business Review Digital Articles* p2 N 30 2016

When You Should Worry About Failure, and When You Shouldn't A. Markman *Harvard Business Review Digital Articles* p2 Ja 5 2016

Why People Quit Their Jobs: Interaction L. Viar, D. Eikenberg et al *Harvard Business Review* v94 no11 p18 N 2016

You Really Can Change Your Reputation at Work C. O'Hara *Harvard Business Review Digital Articles* p2 S 11 2015

You're Never Done Finding Purpose at Work [Cover story] D. Pontefract *Harvard Business Review Digital Articles* p2 Mr 20 2016

Employees' workload

5 Ways to Focus Your Energy During a Work Crunch A. Jen Su *Harvard Business Review Digital Articles* p2 S 22 2017

7 Tricky Work Situations, and How to Respond to Them A. Bassuk *Harvard Business Review Digital Articles* p2 O 11 2017

Accomplish More by Committing to Less E. G. Saunders *Harvard Business Review Digital Articles* p2 Ja 30 2015

How to Say No to Taking on More Work R. Knight *Harvard Business Review Digital Articles* p2 D 29 2015

How to Tell Your Boss You Have Too Much Work R. Knight color *Harvard Business Review Digital Articles* p2 Ja 13 2017

If You Want to Motivate Employees, Stop Trusting Your Instincts T. Chamorro-Premuzic and L. Garrad color *Harvard Business Review Digital Articles* p2 F 8 2017

The Research Is Clear: Long Hours Backfire for People and for Companies S. G. Carmichael *Harvard Business Review Digital Articles* p2 Ag 19 2015

Employees—Alcohol use

LAST ORDERS FOR BOOZY LUNCHES? As Lloyd's of London bans daytime drinking, other businesses are reaching for the rule book rather than the pint glass D. LEWIS *People Management* p10 Ap 2017

What Should I Do About A Co-Worker Who Drinks On the Job? K. A. Appiah *New York Times Magazine* p18 F 5 2017

Working Long Hours Makes Us Drink More S. G. Carmichael *Harvard Business Review Digital Articles* p2 Ap 10 2015

Employees—Attitudes

> *See also*
>
> Job involvement
> Job satisfaction

2 Myths About Engaging B-Players T. J. DeLong and V. Vijayaraghavan *Harvard Business Review Digital Articles* p2 N 28 2014

Research: How Incentive Pay Affects Employee Engagement, Satisfaction, and Trust C. Ogbonnaya, K. Daniels et al *Harvard Business Review Digital Articles* p2 Mr 15 2017

A Simple Yet Powerful Way to Handle a Stress Episode M. Valcour *Harvard Business Review Digital Articles* p2 Ag 27 2015

Use Behavioral Economics to Achieve Wellness Goals D. A. Asch and K. G. Volpp *Harvard Business Review Digital Articles* p2 D 1 2014

When Treating Workers Well Leads to More Innovation W. Frick *Harvard Business Review Digital Articles* p2 N 3 2015

Employer-sponsored health insurance

A Better Way for Employers to Procure Health Care R. S. Mecklenburg *Harvard Business Review Digital Articles* p2 N 17 2016

Don't Bother Complaining About High-Deductible Health Plans L. Binder *Harvard Business Review Digital Articles* p2 N 13 2014

Navigating Health Care's Transition to Private Exchanges R. Birhanzel, S. Brown et al *Harvard Business Review Digital Articles* p2 N 7 2014

What to Do When Health Care Costs Start to Rise Again J. Antos *Harvard Business Review Digital Articles* p2 N 28 2014

Why GE, Boeing, Lowe's, and Walmart Are Directly Buying Health Care for Employees J. R. Slotkin, O. A. Ross et al *Harvard Business Review Digital Articles* p2 Je 9 2017

Employer-supported day care

DAYCARE MADE SIMPLE C. MCINTYRE color *Maclean's* v130 no7 p50 Ag 2017

Employers

189,245 graduates. 19,732 vacancies E. BURT *People Management* p44 F 2017

Does Ban-the-Box Do Any Good? M. Maciag *Governing* v30 no1 p56 O 2016

Employer-led Quality Assurance J. A. Tyszko *Change* v49 no1 p26 Ja/F 2017

EMPLOYERS HELP WITH COLLEGE SAVING K. PITSKER color *Kiplinger's Personal Finance* v71 no5 p13 My 2017

How to Tell Someone They're Being Laid Off R. Knight *Harvard Business Review Digital Articles* p2 Je 26 2015

Research: Why Employer Support Is So Important for Transgender Employees C. Thoroughgood and K. Sawyer *Harvard Business Review Digital Articles* p2 O 3 2017

What Employers Can Do to Accelerate Health Care Reform R. S. Mecklenburg *Harvard Business Review Digital Articles* p2 O 16 2015

Who Has the Power to Cut Drug Prices? Employers R. Galvin and R. Longman *Harvard Business Review Digital Articles* p2 D 1 2015

Employers—Corrupt practices

"My boss was secretly filming me" M. Elliott color *Glamour* v115 no4 p156 Ap 2017

Employers—Legal status, laws, etc.

Change is in the air for employers *People Management* p6 My 2017

Employment & education

Employment trends by typical entry-level education requirement bibl *Monthly Labor Review* p1 S 2017

Employment (Economic theory)

See also

    Discrimination in employment
    Employment in foreign countries
    Employment of Americans
    Employment of men
    Employment of mothers
    Employment of older people
    Employment of people with disabilities
    Employment of retirees
    Employment of the mentally ill
    Employment of undocumented immigrants
    Employment of veterans
    Employment tenure
    Job vacancies
    Sex discrimination in employment
    Unemployment

DARK FACTORY S. KOLHATKAR bw color *New Yorker* v93 no33 p70 O 23 2017

Donald and The Dollar P. Coy *Bloomberg Businessweek* no4503 p15 D 12 2016

EMPLOYMENT, UNEMPLOYMENT, AND WAGES *Economic Indicators* p11 Mr 2017

FINDING INSPIRATION IN THE TRADES K. Donohue color *Maclean's* v130 no3 p62 Ap 2017

The Gig Economy Is Real If You Know Where to Look I. Hathaway *Harvard Business Review Digital Articles* p2 Ag 13 2015

Girl Runs Away, Joins Circus K. Finley and M. Mertens color *Glamour* v114 no12 p180 D 2016

Hiring Discrimination Against Black Americans Hasn't Declined in 25 Years L. Quillian, D. Pager et al *Harvard Business Review Digital Articles* p2 O 11 2017

In Defense Of Robots R. D. ATKINSON *National Review* v69 no7 p35 Ap 17 2017

IS THIS ROBOT A FRIEND—OR A FOE? J. Alsever color diag *Fortune* v175 no4 p22 Mr 15 2017

Leading Job Growth in the Digital Economy C. Fernández-Aráoz *Harvard Business Review Digital Articles* p2 Ag 5 2015

We've got too many graduates *People Management* p6 N 2016

Employment (Economic theory)—Asia

The Asian Jobs Ladder Is Broken K. Hamlin, D. Roberts et al *Bloomberg Businessweek* no4528 p58 Je 26 2017

Employment (Economic theory)—California

Why California Is Such a Talent Magnet O. Lobel *Harvard Business Review Digital Articles* p2 Ja 19 2016

Employment (Economic theory)—Canada

The Habs, Poutine, Jobs: Welcome to Quebec S. Rastello and F. Tomesco graph *Bloomberg Businessweek* no4508 p16 Ja 23 2017

Employment (Economic theory)—Great Britain

Is this the end of agency work? The Taylor review included some radical ideas for the future of flexible working, potentially placing agencies in the firing line H. KIRTON *People Management* p8 Ag 2017

Employment (Economic theory)—United States

APPENDIX B STATISTICAL TABLES RELATING TO INCOME, EMPLOYMENT, AND PRODUCTION *Economic Indicators* p395 O 2016

DAYS OF FUTURE PAST M. Emery *Dirt Sports + Off-Road* v51 no11 p6 N 2017

Economy in recovery: How selected industries have fared since the Great Recession K. Green *Career Outlook* p1 S 2017

Employment expansion continues but at a slower pace M. Calvillo bibl *Monthly Labor Review* p1 Ap 2017

Employment trends by typical entry-level education requirement bibl *Monthly Labor Review* p1 S 2017

Establishment, firm, or enterprise: does the unit of analysis matter? bibl chart color graph *Monthly Labor Review* p1 N 2016

A GOOD JOB IS HARD TO FIND R. Lu color *America* v217 no4 p26 Ag 21 2017

The impact of technology on labor markets R. Works *Monthly Labor Review* p1 Je 2017

IT'S GETTING HARDER TO HIRE B. O'Keefe diag *Fortune* v175 no5 p92 Ap 1 2017

LETTER OF TRANSMITTAL J. Furman, S. E. Black et al *Economic Indicators* p9 O 2016

Multiple jobholding in states in 2015 S. Campolongo bibl chart color map *Monthly Labor Review* p1 F 2017

NAFTA Modernization Moves Forward T. J. DONOHUE *Weekly Standard* v22 no44 p21 Jl 31 2017

Occupational choices of the elderly F. Pryor bibl chart color *Monthly Labor Review* p1 F 2017

Occupational Requirements Survey: results from a job observation pilot test bibl chart color graph *Monthly Labor Review* p1 N 2016

Still worried F. Lesko, F. Koob et al *U.S. Catholic* v82 no10 p5 O 2017

Summer employment: A snapshot of teen workers D. Angeles *Career Outlook* p2 Je 2017

Top industries for job openings, July 2016 graph *Career Outlook* p1 S 2016

The Truth About the Gig Economy J. Fox graph *Bloomberg Businessweek* no4528 p14 Je 26 2017

Where Good Jobs Come From: Better policies could accomplish a lot M. Funkhouser *Governing* v30 no10 p59 Jl 2017

Employment agencies

How to Get Back in the Game K. Bahler *Money* v46 no1 p31 Ja/F 2017

What It's Like When a Stay-at-Home Dad Goes Back to Work W. Johnson *Harvard Business Review Digital Articles* p2 Ap 19 2016

Why Some People Intentionally Take a Pay Cut When Resuming Their Careers C. F. Cohen *Harvard Business Review Digital Articles* p2 Ja 28 2016

Employment reentry—History—20th century

February 1, 1935: America's Secret Strength A. BROWN color *Forbes* v198 no7 p34 N 29 2016

Employment references

How to Choose the Right References R. Knight *Harvard Business Review Digital Articles* p2 O 21 2014

How to Get the Most Out of Reference Checks P. Claman *Harvard Business Review Digital Articles* p2 Mr 10 2016

References Should Come from a Candidate's Coworkers, Not Just Their Boss D. Rupayana, C. A. Hedricks et al *Harvard Business Review Digital Articles* p2 2017

The Right Way to Check a Reference C. Fernández-Aráoz *Harvard Business Review Digital Articles* p2 F 11 2016

The Right Way to Check Someone's References R. Knight *Harvard Business Review Digital Articles* p2 Jl 29 2016

ROOM FOR IMPROVEMENT img *Harvard Business Review* v94 no11 p28 N 2016

When Someone Asks You for a Reference R. Knight *Harvard Business Review Digital Articles* p2 O 30 2015

Employment references—Research

The 20 Most Common Things That Come Up During Reference Checks C. A. Hedricks *Harvard Business Review Digital Articles* p2 Ag 4 2016

Employment statistics

See also

Unemployment—Statistics

Employment expansion continues but at a slower pace M. Calvillo bibl *Monthly Labor Review* p1 Ap 2017

Longitudinal data from the Occupational Employment Statistics survey M. Dey and E. W. Handwerker bibl chart color graph *Monthly Labor Review* p1 O 2016

One hundred years of Current Employment Statistics: busting CES myths M. Calvillo and T. Downing bibl chart color graph *Monthly Labor Review* p1 O 2016

Reconstruction of CES time series: implementing the 2010 OMB metropolitan area delineations S. M. Mance and J. R. Stewart bibl chart color graph *Monthly Labor Review* p1 O 2016

Wage and employment fluctuations during the housing market cycle R. Meharenna *Monthly Labor Review* p1 D 2016

Workforce growth in community-based care: meeting the needs of an aging population K. Sullivan *Monthly Labor Review* p1 D 2016

Employment tenure

An Experiment in Enlivening Stagnant Teams P. Wadors *Harvard Business Review Digital Articles* p2 Jl 3 2015

Whither the Faculty? M. J. Finkelstein, V. M. Conley et al *Change* v49 no4 p43 Jl/Ag 2017

WHY CMOs NEVER LAST AND WHAT TO DO ABOUT IT K. A. WHITLER and N. MORGAN chart color graph img *Harvard Business Review* v95 no4 p46 Jl/Ag 2017

Employment (Economic theory)—Charts, diagrams, etc.

Charts to watch in 2017 [Cover story] graph *Maclean's* v129 no51/52 p49 D 26 2016

EMPLOYMENT, UNEMPLOYMENT, AND WAGES *Economic Indicators* p11 F 2017

EMPLOYMENT, UNEMPLOYMENT, AND WAGES *Economic Indicators* p11 My 2017

EMPLOYMENT, UNEMPLOYMENT, AND WAGES *Economic Indicators* p11 S 2016

Summer employment: A snapshot of teen workers D. Angeles *Career Outlook* p2 Je 2017

Emporio Armani Srl

My LIST N. Vinson color *Harper's Bazaar* no3649 p144 D 2016/Ja 2017

Empson, William, 1906-1984

The Buddha and the Pantocrator C. Zaleski *Christian Century* v134 no2 p33 Ja 18 2017

EMRE, MERVE

The Eye of the Beholder *New Republic* v248 no3 p63 Mr 2017

Emre Arolat Architects (Company)

The Ripple Effect: Concealing a straightforward office tower within, a curvilinear exterior commands attention, S. MORENO color map *Architectural Record* v205 no5 p98 My 2017

EMRICH, OLIVER

WHAT'S THE VALUE OF A LIKE? color *Harvard Business Review* v95 no2 p108 Mr/Ap 2017

Emrys, Ruthanna

Winter Tide *Publishers Weekly* v263 no48 p51 N 28 2016

Emsley, Clive

MAKING AN IMPACT ON VIOLENCE *History Today* v67 no5 p102 My 2017

EMSLIE, SARA

MAKE IT LIGHTER, BRIGHTER, BIGGER color *House Beautiful* p70 Ag 2017

Emspak, Jesse

Nuclear Ghosts bw *Scientific American* v316 no5 p12 My 2017

Emtricitabine-tenofovir (Drug)

Five Minutes to PrEP Z. ZANE color *Advocate* no1090 p55 Ap 2017

THE NEW GAY SEXUAL REVOLUTION: PrEP, TasP, and fearless sex remind us we can't advance social justice without including sex in the equation J. ANDERSON-MINSHALL color *Advocate* no1091 p115 Je/Jl 2017

Emulators (Computer programs)

Mac emulators C. Grannell color *Macworld - Digital Edition* p61 Ap 2017

En Vogue (Performer)

'90s till infinity: EN VOGUE L. CROSS color *Ebony* v72 no6 p82 Ap/My 2017

Enamorado, Miguel

ANDY'S CANDY *Interview* v46 no8 p46 O 2016

Enard, Mathias

IN THE ZONE J. MCCARTHY color *Nation* v305 no6 p27 S 11 2017

West Meets East: A prize-winning French novelist presents a Viennese musicologist lost in dreams of a Levantine past J. COHEN *New York Times Book Review* p17 Jl 2 2017

Enberg, Dick

HOT | NOT T. Keith color *Sports Illustrated* v125 no12 p19 O 10 2016

Enbo Zhu

Ultrafine jagged platinum nanowires enable ultrahigh mass activity for the oxygen reduction reaction bibl chart graph *Science* v354 no6318 p1414 D 16 2016

Encarnación, Omar G.

Homage to Catalonia? color *New York Review of Books* v64 no17 p37 N 9 2017

Enceladus (Satellite)

Detecting molecular hydrogen on Enceladus J. S. Seewald color *Science* v356 no6334 p132 Ap 14 2017

Enceladus's Hydrothermal Heating, Europa's Leaks C. M. Carlisle color *Sky & Telescope* v134 no2 p10 Ag 2017

Food for microbes abundant on Enceladus P. Voosen bw *Science* v356 no6334 p121 Ap 14 2017

Encephalitis viruses

The Bugs of Summer color *Prevention* v69 no8 p9 Ag 2017

Enchanted Desna, The (Film)

Family Business R. Brody color *New Yorker* v93 no24 p6 Ag 21 2017

Enchiladas

TORTILLAS TONIGHT L. Cericola and R. Melvin color *Southern Living* v52 no1 p115 Ja 2017

Encina, Paz

PERSONAL THOUGHTS ON MY DAYS IN THE ARCHIVES *Film Quarterly* v70 no4 p47 Summ 2017

A SENSE OF PLACE: PAZ ENCINA'S RADICAL POETICS N. Brizuela *Film Quarterly* v70 no4 p49 Summ 2017

Under Duress B. R. Rich *Film Quarterly* v70 no4 p5 Summ 2017

Encrenaz, T.

Seasonal exposure of carbon dioxide ice on the nucleus of comet 67P/Churyumov-Gerasimenko bibl bw graph *Science* v354 no6319 p1563 D 23 2016

Encryption protocols

The risks of browsing online with Tor G. Fleishman cartoon diag

Macworld - Digital Edition p46 Ap 2017

Encyclopedias & dictionaries

BOOKS OF KNOWLEDGE C. Neuhaus *Saturday Evening Post* v289 no5 p14 S/O 2017

c. 950: Basra *Lapham's Quarterly* v10 no1 p39 Wint 2017

End of the world

A World Ever at Its End D. Penick bw diag *Tricycle: The Buddhist Review* v26 no4 p60 Summ 2017

End of the world—Humor

The odds on a Trumpocalypse S. FESCHUK color *Maclean's* v129 no47 p65 N 28 2016

Endangered plants

The Extinction Risk and Conservation Status of Most National Plants Are Unknown K. J. FEELEY *BioScience* v67 no9 p782 S 2017

Pangolins to get more protection color *Science* v354 no6309 p152 O 14 2016

Sharing Our Spaces E. BANKS RUSBY color *Earth Island Journal* v32 no3 p27 Aut 2017

Endangered species

See also

Endangered plants

BIGFOOT AS BIG MYTH: 7 PHASES OF MYTHMAKING: During its history, the hairy man-best has evolved though at least seven mythical embodiments J. NICKELL *Skeptical Inquirer* v41 no5 p52 S/O 2017

Bigfoot on Four Paws A. TESAR cartoon *Walrus* v14 no2 p22 Mr 2017

Do not publish D. Lindenmayer and B. Scheele color diag *Science* v356 no6340 p800 My 26 2017

Easter Island's Last Endemics Flirt With Extinction [Cover story] N. SCHARPING color *Discover* v38 no4 p24 My 2017

ENDANGERED! B. Banks color *Canadian Wildlife* v23 no1 p26 Mr/Ap 2017

Lost then Loved: The Case of the Tasmanian Tiger S. B. Gmelch and M. Z. Gmelch bw color map *Natural History* v125 no4 p36 Ap 2017

New Zealand's endemic dolphins are hanging by a thread C. Pala *Science* v355 no6325 p559 F 10 2017

Pangolins to get more protection color *Science* v354 no6309 p152 O 14 2016

Premature downgrade of panda's status Dongwei Kang and Junqing Li color *Science* v354 no6310 p295 O 21 2016

Response to "Listing Foreign Species Under the Endangered Species Act" J. VAN NORMAN, H. J. LYNCH et al *BioScience* v67 no10 p873 O 2017

Sharing Our Spaces E. BANKS RUSBY color *Earth Island Journal* v32 no3 p27 Aut 2017

Endangered species delisting

Yellowstone's grizzlies off endangered list color *Science* v356 no6345 p1314 Je 30 2017

Endangered species laws—United States

Time to Count the Costs--And Adapt: Environmental activists must quit playing politics and begin to practice one of the fundamental disciplines of good governance: weighing benefits against costs G. D. Libecap *Hoover Digest: Research & Opinion on Public Policy* no2 p127 Spr 2017

Endangered species listing

Quantify endangered species listings T. David Male and S. A. Temple color *Science* v356 no6345 p1342 Je 30 2017

Endangered species—Mexico

World's most endangered marine mammal down to 30 V. Morell color graph *Science* v355 no6325 p558 F 10 2017

Endangered species—United States

THE FUTURE OF YELLOWSTONE'S GRIZZLIES *Sierra* v102 no1 p40 Ja/F 2017

Endeavour (TV program)

Murder in Paradise A. JACOBS *American Conservative* v15 no6 p42 N/D 2016

Endemic plants

10 Plants WE SHOULD KNOW K. HUNHOFF *South Dakota Magazine* v33 no2 p27 Jl/Ag 2017

BIRDING T. Winston *Audubon* v119 no1 p44 Spr 2017

the dirt M. HUGHES *Better Homes & Gardens* v94 no11 p68 N 2016

Here Comes the Sun M. JANNOT *Audubon* v119 no1 p7 Spr 2017

NATIVE AQUATIC PLANT ALTERNATIVES *New York State Conservationist* v71 no5 p35 Ap 2017

Nine Brilliant Birds to Bring to Your Yard This Spring *Audubon* v119 no1 p44 Spr 2017

Work With What You've Got cartoon *Canadian Wildlife* v22 no5 p38 N/D 2016

Enders, Albrecht

What BMW's Corporate VC Offers That Regular Investors Can't *Harvard Business Review Digital Articles* p2 Jl 27 2017

Endersby, Jim

Floral History A. Henderson color *Weekly Standard* v22 no23 p32 F 20 2017

ENDICOTT, MARINA

Lynch Law color *Walrus* v14 no9 p62 N 2017

Endless Caverns (Va.)

What Lies Beneath: THE VALLEY'S BEAUTY ISN'T ALL ABOVE GROUND D. Leatherman *Washingtonian Magazine* v53 no1 p102 O 2017

Endo, Masayuki

Holliday junction resolvases mediate chloroplast nucleoid segregation diag *Science* v356 no6338 p631 My 12 2017

Endo, Morinobu

Mildred S. Dresselhaus *Physics Today* v70 no6 p73 Je 2017

Endocrine system physiology

Are Chemicals Contributing to the Obesity Epidemic? Although there is growing concern that everyday chemicals may contribute to weight woes, more research is needed *Tufts University Health & Nutrition Letter* v35 no7 p7 S 2017

Endogamy & exogamy

WHEN DNA AND CULTURE CLASH J. Kaiser color map *Science* v354 no6317 p1217 D 9 2016

Endometrial tumors—Diagnosis

Endometrial cancer *Mayo Clinic Health Letter* v35 no5 p4 My 2017

Endometrial tumors—Risk factors

Endometrial cancer *Mayo Clinic Health Letter* v35 no5 p4 My 2017

Endometriosis

Our Doc Will See You Now R. Rajapaksa color *Health* v30 no9 p103 N 2016

padma heat up [Cover story] A. Prato color *Health* v31 no8 p96 O 2017

WARNING: MAY BITE IF ASKED ABOUT FERTILITY L. Dunham color *Glamour* v115 no11 p100 N 2017

Endonucleases

Tudor-SN–mediated endonucleolytic decay of human cell microRNAs promotes G1/S phase transition R. A. Elbarbary, K. Miyoshi et al graph *Science* v356 no6340 p859 My 26 2017

Endoplasmic reticulum

Biggest organelle gets image update L. HAMERS color *Science News* v190 no11 p10 N 26 2016

A finer look at a fine cellular meshwork M. Terasaki bibl color *Science* v354 no6311 p415 O 28 2016

Increased spatiotemporal resolution reveals highly dynamic dense tubular matrices in the peripheral ER J. Nixon-Abell, C. J. Obara et al bibl bw color graph *Science* v354 no6311 paaf3928-1 O 28 2016

Lipid transport by TMEM24 at ER-plasma membrane contacts regulates pulsatile insulin secretion J. A. Lees, M. Messa et al diag *Science* v355 no6326 p709 F 17 2017

Reticulon 3–dependent ER-PM contact sites control EGFR non-clathrin endocytosis G. Caldieri, E. Barbieri et al color diag graph *Science* v356 no6338 p617 My 12 2017

Endorphin receptors

A nontoxic pain killer designed by modeling of pathological receptor conformations V. Spahn, G. Del Vecchio et al bibl diag graph *Science* v355 no6328 p966 Mr 3 2017

Endorphins

Friendship Tune-Up! C. Thorp color *Seventeen* v76 no5 p71 S 2017

Endorsements in advertising

See also

Athletes as advertising spokespersons

Stage Mom Trauma L. HAMILTON *Dance Magazine* v90 no11 p24 N 2016

The Wheaties Box and the Why of Celebrity Endorsements A.

Beard *Harvard Business Review Digital Articles* p2 Ap 5 2016

Endothelial cells

Organotypic vasculature: From descriptive heterogeneity to functional pathophysiology H. G. Augustin and G. Young Koh color *Science* v357 no6353 p771 Ag 25 2017

Endowment effect (Economics)

Behavior management L. Cingl, L. Wang et al color *Science* v356 no6335 p244 Ap 21 2017

Endowment of research

See also

Scholarships

Technology & state

Architectural Record Traveling Fellowships Awarded to Lea Oxenhandler and Benjamin Halpern D. COHEN color *Architectural Record* v205 no8 p20 Ag 2017

Conflict Resolution M. F. Jacobson *Nutrition Action Health Letter* v44 no2 p2 Mr 2017

Endowments

See also

Endowment of research

Family foundations

Don't Let A Drought Hit The Progressive! L. Johnson color *Progressive* v81 no5 p37 Je/Jl 2017

Forget About Grants! N. A. Schaumleffel *Parks & Recreation* v52 no2 p38 F 2017

IVY LEAGUE ENDOWMENTS UNDER FIRE A. Kim color *Washington Monthly* v49 no9/10 p67 S/O 2017

Things Go Better With 67 Million Coke Shares J. Lorin color *Bloomberg Businessweek* no4519 p46 Ap 24 2017

When Getting the Gear Isn't a Given S. MAHONEY color *Parents* v92 no11 p92 N 2017

Why Buyers and Sellers Inherently Disagree on What Things Are Worth C. K. Morewedge *Harvard Business Review Digital Articles* p2 My 13 2016

Endowments—United States

Love Lessons A. Fenwick and T. Keith color *Sports Illustrated* v125 no20 p26 D 19 2016

No Use for Old School Ties M. McDonald and J. Brustein color *Bloomberg Businessweek* no4526 p32 Je 12 2017

Why Major Philanthropists Are Giving More Money to Just One Cause W. Foster and A. Powell color *Harvard Business Review Digital Articles* p2 Ja 19 2017

Endowments—Universities & colleges

The College Endowment Gap K. Smith *Bloomberg Businessweek* no4531 p25 Jl 24 2017

A GOP Plan to Tax Gifts For Wealthy Schools J. Lorin *Bloomberg Businessweek* no4506 p23 Ja 9 2017

Endres, John C.

BOOKS ON THE BIBLE color *America* v216 no9 p28 Ap 24 2017

Endres, Manuel

Atom-by-atom assembly of defect-free one-dimensional cold atom arrays bibl diag graph *Science* v354 no6315 p1024 N 25 2016

Endurance riding (Horsemanship)

See also

Tevis Cup Ride

The 62nd, Tevis Cup G. STEWART-SPEARS *Arabian Horse World* v57 no12 p128 S 2017

Biltmore Challenge Endurance Rides: What's happening in the world of Arabian horses G. Stewart-Spears *Arabian Horse World* v57 no10 p104 Jl 2017

ENDURANCE at marbach: The 2016 ZSAA Endurance Event and German National Endurance Championships B. Finke *Arabian Horse World* v56 no12 p184 S 2016

enduring partners—Stagg and Cheryl Newman G. Stewart-Spears *Arabian Horse World* v57 no8 p122 My 2017

If Adversity Builds Character I Have Plenty D. WHYTE *Arabian Horse World* v57 no12 p146 S 2017

Miles to go J. Woehr color *Equus* no478 p68 Jl 2017

Miniature Horse Completes Endurance Ride color *Trail Rider* v29 no1 p12 Ja/F 2017

OLD DOMINION: Endurance Race G. STEWART-SPEARS *Arabian Horse World* v57 no11 p142 Ag 2017

Endurance riding (Horsemanship)—West (U.S.)

See also

Tevis Cup Ride

TEVIS CUP G. Stewart-Spears *Arabian Horse World* v56 no12 p164 S 2016

Endurance sports

Keep calm and carry on B. J. Lieberman color *Equus* no470 p72 N 2016

RACING TO BUILD AN ENDURANCE SPORTS EMPIRE P. Wahba color diag *Fortune* v176 no5 p116 O 1 2017

Vegetarian Action. Scott Jurek: An Example for Vegan Athletes S. Lawrence *Vegetarian Journal* v36 no3 p35 2017

Endurance sports—Competitions

Biltmore Challenge Endurance Rides: What's happening in the world of Arabian horses G. Stewart-Spears *Arabian Horse World* v57 no10 p104 Jl 2017

Enduraplas (Company)

ATV SPRAYERS: THESE UNITS WILL GO WHERE LARGER SPRAYERS CAN'T ENTER G. Gullickson color *Successful Farming* v115 no7 p28 My 2017

Endy, Timothy

Dengue diversity across spatial and temporal scales: Local structure and the effect of host population size bibl graph *Science* v355 no6331 p1302 Mr 24 2017

ENELOW, SHONNI

The Kid Slays in the Picture color *Film Comment* v53 no5 p20 S/O 2017

STRONGER TOGETHER bw color *Film Comment* v53 no5 p50 S/O 2017

Enemark, Christian

Biodefense in the 21st century G. Kwik Gronvall color *Science* v356 no6338 p588 My 12 2017

Enemies—Religious aspects

ENEMY K. Ward, B. Simmons et al color *Christian Century* v134 no5 p20 Mr 1 2017

LIVING BY The word *Christian Century* v133 no22 p20 O 26 2016

Enemy Swim Lake (S.D.)

enjoying lake life C. LOESCHKE color *Cabin Living* p16 Mr 2017

Energiewende

Inside the Energiewende C. STURM color *Issues in Science & Technology* v33 no2 p41 Wint 2017

Energy auditing

ENERGY STRATEGY FOR THE C-SUITE A. WINSTON, G. FAVALORO et al color graph img *Harvard Business Review* v95 no1 p138 Ja/F 2017

Energy bars (Food)

BATTLE OF THE Bars H. Rolfe *Dance Spirit* v21 no7 p54 S 2017

power play: FUEL FOR A NEW CATEGORY t. engel color *Bike Magazine* v24 no8 p36 N 2017

Energy bars (Food)—Evaluation

EXPIRES NEVER K. Bastone cartoon color *Runner's World* v51 no10 p48 N 2016

The Modern Explorer's Survival Kit S. CHODOSH and P. HESS color *Popular Science* p80 Ja/F 2017

Energy conservation

DIM-WITTED E. LANGSTON cartoon *Mother Jones* v41 no6 p61 N/D 2016

Energy-Saving $avings S. FRANKE color *Good Housekeeping* v264 no4 p87 Ap 2017

Hey Mr. Green! What's the greenest way to weatherize? B. Schildgen *Sierra* v102 no5 p12 St/O 2017

How to Overcome the Midday Slump C. O'Hara *Harvard Business Review Digital Articles* p2 Jl 1 2015

It's Time for Companies to Be Strategic About Energy A. Winston *Harvard Business Review Digital Articles* p2 Je 14 2016

PUT YOUR POWER USE UNDER THE MICROSCOPE L. BEDORD *Successful Farming* v114 no10 p50 O 2016

Energy consumption

Crossing the Red-Blue Divide: One Tennessee group has taken the politics out of renewable energy E. Daigneau *Governing* v30 no12 p20 S 2017

Energy efficiency M. BESSOUDO color *Issues in Science & Technology* v33 no1 p12 Fall 2016

The Energy Rebound Battle: An embattled economist's research shows that energy efficiency cant solve climate change. But it is an important contributor to human progress T. NORDHAUS

Issues in Science & Technology v33 no4 p51 Summ 2017

Idle Power Hogs T. SCHLOSSBERG *Reader's Digest* v189 no1128 p41 Mr 2017

Marder, Patzek, and Tinker reply M. Marder, T. Patzek et al *Physics Today* v70 no2 p13 F 2017

The Original Point of Daylight Saving Time O. B. Waxman *Time* v189 no10 p21 Mr 20 2017

Energy consumption of buildings

Enter Here: Easy, routine TLC for your doors and windows F. Esker *New Orleans Homes & Lifestyles* v20 no4 p98 Aut 2017

Energy consumption—Canada

USING ENERGY EFFICIENTLY IN THE FIGHT AGAINST CLIMATE CHANGE J. Carr color *Maclean's* v129 no50 p38 D 19 2016

Energy consumption—Law & legislation

Santa Monica to Adopt Ambitious Zero Net Energy Requirements D. S. GLENN color *Architectural Record* v204 no12 p18 D 2016

Energy consumption—Statistics

NOT SO FAST K. CAMERON *Cycle World* v56 no3 p28 Ap 2017

Energy consumption—United States

Energy Consumption and Production in Agriculture C. Hitaj *Amber Waves: The Economics of Food, Farming, Natural Resources, & Rural America* p15 F 2017

Energy Efficiency: Still Low-hanging Fruit: There are still plenty of ways we can use energy more efficiently. Simple changes would produce large effects J. L. Sweeney *Hoover Digest: Research & Opinion on Public Policy* no2 p121 Spr 2017

The Relationship Between Energy Prices and Food-Related Energy Use in the United States P. Canning and S. Rehkamp *Amber Waves: The Economics of Food, Farming, Natural Resources, & Rural America* p17 Je 2017

Energy crops

Cellulosic biofuel contributions to a sustainable energy future: Choices and outcomes G. P. Robertson, S. K. Hamilton et al color *Science* v356 no6345 p1349 Je 30 2017

Dedicating Agricultural Land to Energy Crops Would Shift Land Use R. Sands and S. Malcolm *Amber Waves: The Economics of Food, Farming, Natural Resources, & Rural America* p33 Ap 2017

Energy density

A Powerful Petawatt Laser for Experimental Science W. H. Goldstein *Science & Technology Review* p3 Jl/Ag 2017

Energy economics

ENERGY STRATEGY FOR THE C-SUITE A. WINSTON, G. FAVALORO et al color graph img *Harvard Business Review* v95 no1 p138 Ja/F 2017

Thirst for Fuel Drives Competition *Foreign Affairs* v95 no6 p(Sp)8 N/D 2016

Energy harvesting

Harvesting electrical energy from carbon nanotube yarn twist S. Hyeong Kim, C. S. Haines et al diag graph *Science* v357 no6353 p773 Ag 25 2017

A low-loss origami plasmonic waveguide F. Vetrone and F. Rosei diag *Science* v357 no6350 p452 Ag 4 2017

RESEARCH color *Science* v357 no6353 p768 Ag 25 2017

Energy industries

See also

Clean energy industries

Petroleum—Export & import trade

Petroleum industry

Solar energy industries

Cost of carbon capture drops, but does anyone want it? R. F. Service color graph *Science* v354 no6318 p1362 D 16 2016

Energy industries—Export & import trade

Driving Another Decade of Energy Progress T. J. DONOHUE *Weekly Standard* v22 no41 p15 Jl 3 2017

Energy industries—Social aspects

The Next Energy Revolution D. G. Victor and K. Yanosek color *Foreign Affairs* v96 no4 p124 Jl/Ag 2017

Energy industries—United States

Big Oil Roars Back L. STEFFY *Texas Monthly* v45 no2 p60 F 2017

Driving Another Decade of Energy Progress T. J. DONOHUE *Weekly Standard* v22 no41 p15 Jl 3 2017

A Historic Moment for U.S. Energy T. J. DONOHUE *Weekly*

Standard v22 no30 p19 Ap 10 2017

Safety first: The future of nuclear energy outside the United States M. M. May bibl *Bulletin of the Atomic Scientists* v73 no1 p38 Ja 2017

Unexpected Hikes in Energy Prices Increase the Likelihood of Food Insecurity C. Tuttle *Amber Waves: The Economics of Food, Farming, Natural Resources, & Rural America* p9 Jl 2017

Why Your Power Company Wants to Sell You More Than Electricity J. Worland color *Time* v189 no20 p20 My 29 2017

Energy levels (Quantum mechanics)

MANIPULATING ULTRACOLD MATTER [Cover story] J. Stajic, E. Hand et al color *Science* v357 no6355 p984 S 8 2017

Energy metabolism

See also

Bacteriorhodopsin

Basal metabolism

BEYOND SMOOTHIES T. Masters chart color *Yoga Journal* no289 p72 F 2017

Energy policy

See also

Solar energy policy

For whose benefit? K. Clarke color *U.S. Catholic* v82 no1 p42 Ja 2017

Energy policy & the environment

THE GLOBAL WARMING WILD CARD V. Sivaram bw color *Scientific American* v316 no5 p48 My 2017

Energy policy—European Union countries

Will climate-change efforts affect EU–Russian relations? (Probably not.) R. S. Salzman bibl *Bulletin of the Atomic Scientists* v72 no6 p384 N 2016

Energy policy—India

THE GLOBAL WARMING WILD CARD V. Sivaram bw color *Scientific American* v316 no5 p48 My 2017

Energy policy—International cooperation

An Oily Reset in U.S.-Russia Relations M. Philips graph *Bloomberg Businessweek* no4507 p38 Ja 16 2017

Energy policy—Mexico

U.S.-Mexico Energy and Climate Collaboration D. Wood *Wilson Quarterly* p1 Wint 2017

Energy policy—United States

Clinton and Trump: Where do they stand on science? D. Kramer *Physics Today* v69 no10 p24 O 2016

The Return of 'Drill, Baby, Drill' T. Berenson color *Time* v188 no22-23 p33 N/D 2016

Untapped Revenue S. Moore and J. Coleman color *Weekly Standard* v22 no29 p16 Ap 3 2017

Energy policy—United States—History—21st century

The Little Think Tank Driving Trump's Policy J. A. Dlouhy *Bloomberg Businessweek* no4507 p24 Ja 16 2017

Energy research—United States

The Inevitable EV color *MIT Technology Review* v120 no4 p100 Jl/Ag 2017

Energy security

Trump's First 100 Days Bring Victories for Business T. J. DONOHUE *Weekly Standard* v22 no32 p17 My 1 2017

Energy security—United States

A Historic Moment for U.S. Energy T. J. DONOHUE *Weekly Standard* v22 no30 p19 Ap 10 2017

Energy shortages

Solving the Twin Crises of Energy and Water Scarcity K. Moss and D. Frodl *Harvard Business Review Digital Articles* p2 Ja 25 2016

Energy storage

See also

Compressed air

Charged Up: Batteries Are the Next Target In China's Clean-Energy Conquest J. Worland color *Time* v190 no15 p20 O 16 2017

Three-dimensional holey-graphene/niobia composite architectures for ultrahigh-rate energy storage H. Sun, L. Mei et al color diag graph *Science* v356 no6338 p599 My 12 2017

Energy storage equipment

Liquefied gas electrolytes for electrochemical energy storage devices C. S. Rustomji, Y. Yang et al graph *Science* v356 no6345 p1351 Je 30 2017

Energy Transfer Partners LP

Bury Their Future at Standing Rock: The truth about the shutdown of the Dakota Pipeline N. Schaefer Riley *Commentary* v143 no1 p29 Ja 2017

Standing Their Ground M. K. FRANK *New York Times Upfront* v149 no4 p6 O 31 2016

Energynet.com (Company)

Why You Need the Internet to Drill M. Frazier *Bloomberg Businessweek* no4512 p33 F 20 2017

Enfield, N. J.

Junk cognition color *Science* v357 no6358 p1361 S 29 2017

ENFIELD, SUSAN

THE DOCTOR WILL OM WITH YOU NOW color *Yoga Journal* p10 2017 SpecialIssue

Eng, Dinah

BEFORE HE WAS A SHARK color *Fortune* v174 no7 p34 D 1 2016

DESIGNING A WORLD INSIDE color *Fortune* v175 no5 p26 Ap 1 2017

FIGHTING HIS WAY OUT OF A PAPER BAG color *Fortune* v176 no4 p40 S 15 2017

FOR WHICH WICH, SUCCESS IS IN THE BAG color *Fortune* v175 no6 p17 My 1 2017

MAN OF PROPERTIES color *Fortune* v175 no2 p30 F 1 2017

The Rise of the Ninja Gym color *Fortune* v75 no1 p24 Ja 1 2017

SAVED BY BARBECUE CHICKEN PIZZA color *Fortune* v174 no8 p58 D 15 2016

'THE HARDER I FALL, THE HIGHER THE BOUNCE' color *Fortune* v175 no8 p72 Je 15 2017

Engagement (Philosophy)

For the Common Good cartoon diag graph *Alternatives Journal (A.J) - Canada's Environmental Voice* v42 no3 p20 2016

RULES OF ENGAGEMENT L. BAYER *O, The Oprah Magazine* p100 Ap 2017

Engagements (Theatrical production)

To Do img *New York* v49 no15 p91 Jl 25 2016

Engber, Daniel

BODY, HEAL THYSELF color *Popular Science* v289 no6 p16 N/D 2017

The Sugar Wars bw color *Atlantic* v319 no1 p40 Ja/F 2017

WHEN THE LAB RAT IS A SNAKE color *New York Times Magazine* p65 My 21 2017

ENGE, KEVIN M.

Overcoming Challenges to the Recovery of Declining Amphibian Populations in the United States *BioScience* v67 no2 p156 F 2017

Engel, Amy

Seeing Both Sides *Publishers Weekly* v264 no10 p64 Mr 6 2017

Engel, J.

Persistent effects of pre-Columbian plant domestication on Amazonian forest composition bibl chart graph map *Science* v355 no6328 p925 Mr 3 2017

Engel, Katherine

A Single Mom Plans Her Next Act K. LANKFORD color *Kiplinger's Personal Finance* v71 no8 p72 Ag 2017

ENGEL, KELSEY

an unexpected gift color map *Cabin Living* p14 S 2017

Engel, Megan

Mysteries of the mundane color *Science* v355 no6320 p33 Ja 6 2017

Engel, Michael

Clathrate colloidal crystals bibl color *Science* v355 no6328 p931 Mr 3 2017

Engel, R.

Observation of a large-scale anisotropy in the arrival directions of cosmic rays above 8 × 1018 eV *Science* v357 no6357 p1266 S 22 2017

Engel, Tatiana A.

Selective modulation of cortical state during spatial attention bibl graph *Science* v354 no6316 p1140 D 2 2016

Engel, Travis

9POINT8 FALL LINE color *Bike Magazine* v24 no2 p84 Mr 2017

AGNOSTIC AGGRESSION color *Bike Magazine* v24 no1 p106 Ja/F 2017

BEATDOWN color *Bike Magazine* v24 no5 p102 Jl 2017

chromag color *Bike Magazine* v24 no2 p78 Mr 2017

DOUBLE DUTY color *Bike Magazine* v24 no1 p88 Ja/F 2017

Ellsworth color *Bike Magazine* v24 no7 p104 S 2017

EVEN FLOW bw color *Bike Magazine* v24 no1 p94 Ja/F 2017

EVIL'S THE FOLLOWING color *Bike Magazine* v23 no9 p94 D 2016

GET IN GEAR bw color *Bike Magazine* v24 no1 p122 Ja/F 2017

niner jet 9 color *Bike Magazine* v24 no3 p104 My 2017

power play: FUEL FOR A NEW CATEGORY color *Bike Magazine* v24 no8 p36 N 2017

Scott color *Bike Magazine* v24 no4 p90 Je 2017

Spot: MAYHEM 27.5+ 4-STAR BUILD color *Bike Magazine* v24 no8 p74 N 2017

WEAR WITHOUT TEAR: A TWO-YEAR THRASHING OF THE SPECIALIZED 2F0S color *Bike Magazine* v24 no8 p80 N 2017

WHAT'S IN THE BOX? A SHIFT IN PERSPECTIVE color *Bike Magazine* v24 no6 p134 Ag 2017

Engel v. Vitale (Supreme Court case)

PRAYING FOR CLARITY D. B. MOSKOWITZ bw *American History* v52 no2 p26 Je 2017

Engeland, Anders

β2-Adrenoreceptor is a regulator of the a-synuclein gene driving risk of Parkinson's disease cartoon chart graph *Science* v357 no6354 p891 S 1 2017

Engelbert, Catherine

Looking for Answers to the World's Biggest Challenges In the Eternal City color *Time* v188 no24 p31 D 12 2016

Engelbert, Giovanna Battaglia, 1979-

Living Large J. K. DE VALLE color *Architectural Digest* no11 p37 N 1 2017

ENGELBOURG, SETH I.

What's That Buzzing Noise? Public Opinion on the Use of Drones for Conservation Science *BioScience* v67 no4 p382 Ap 2017

ENGELHARD, MICHAEL

Wool Gathering *Sierra* v101 no6 p64 N/D 2016

Engelhardt, Trudy

PARODY color *Weekly Standard* v22 no7 p40 O 24 2016

ENGELHART, KATIE

League of nationalists color *Maclean's* v130 no2 p35 Mr 2017

Engelhaupt, Erika

ARTIFICIAL WOMB FOR PREEMIES? color *National Geographic* v232 no3 p24 S 2017

Every breath contains a molecule of history color *Science News* v191 no13 p38 Jl 8 2017

How science has fed female stereotypes color *Science News* v192 no3 p27 S 2 2017

THE ROAD TO TAMENESS color diag map *Science News* v191 no13 p20 Jl 8 2017

ENGELKING, CARL

CULTIVATING COMMON SENSE cartoon color graph *Discover* v38 no3 p32 Ap 2017

Dark Wings Decoded color *Discover* v38 no1 p65 Ja/F 2017

Go, Go AlphaGo color *Discover* v38 no1 p37 Ja/F 2017

Our Personal Favorites bw *Discover* v38 no4 p44 My 2017

Yeast bw color *Discover* v38 no6 p74 Jl/Ag 2017

Engelman, Alan N.

A supramolecular assembly mediates lentiviral DNA integration bibl color *Science* v355 no6320 p1 Ja 6 2017

Engelman, Dendy E.

3 experts on... SMILE LINES color *Good Housekeeping* v265 no5 p22 N 2017

DITCH THAT ITCH color *Good Housekeeping* v264 no3 p32 Mr 2017 winter skin SURVIVAL E. METZGER *Better Homes & Gardens* v94 no12 p22 D 2016

Engelman, Robert

The interaction of human population, food production, and biodiversity protection color diag graph *Science* v356 no6335 p260 Ap 21 2017

Engel's law

Percent of Income Spent on Food Falls as Income Rises C. Tuttle and A. Kuhns *Amber Waves: The Economics of Food, Farming, Natural Resources, & Rural America* p31 S 2016

Enger Auto Service & Tire Inc.

END OF THE ROAD B. Coleman *Cincinnati Magazine* v50 no5 p66 F 2017

Engesser, Taylor

HIGH STAKES color *Spin to Win Rodeo* v21 no5 p11 Jl 2017

Engheta, Nader

Photonic doping of epsilon-near-zero media bibl diag *Science* v355 no6329 p1058 Mr 10 2017

Engine design & construction

    See also

      Automobile engine design & construction

MICROMANAGEMENT E. Tingwall diag graph *Car & Driver* v63 no2 p28 Ag 2017

Engine equipment

PARTS & STUFF color *Hot Rod* v70 no11 p124 N 2017

Engine houses (Railroads)

PLANS FOR A DISTINCTIVE TRACKSIDE SHED H. W. Russell bw diag *Model Railroader* v84 no1 p60 Ja 2017

Where Credit Is Due bw color *Architectural Record* v205 no2 p16 F 2017

Engine maintenance & repair

The Halon Tragedy B. PIKE bw *Power & Motoryacht* v34 no11 p264 N 2017

Engine valve manufacturing

Take 5 With BILLY GODBOLD J. Pearley Huffman color diag *Hot Rod* v70 no7 p16 Jl 2017

Engineered Floors LLC

The Carpet Whisperer L. O'leary *New York Times Magazine* p45 F 26 2017

Engineering

    See also

      Automotive engineering

      Electronics

      Environmental engineering

      Installation of equipment

      Joints (Engineering)

      Pneumatics

      Robotics

      Synthetic biology

Building the future D. Riley bibl color *Science* v355 no6326 p702 F 17 2017

Conspiring with engineers helps make science great E. Quill *Science News* v192 no7 p2 O 28 2017

that's so cool! S. R. MURPHY *Parents* v92 no1 p32 Ja 2017

Engineering software—Evaluation

Autopilot E. J. Wallace color *Virginia Living* v15 no5 p37 Ag 2017

Engineering students

No, the Best Science Students Aren't Becoming Financiers N. Torres *Harvard Business Review Digital Articles* p2 D 22 2015

Engineering students—Attitudes

Why Do So Many Women Who Study Engineering Leave the Field? S. S. Silbey *Harvard Business Review Digital Articles* p2 Ag 23 2016

Engineering—Canada

Old Growth, New Shoots A. MANDEL-CAMPBELL cartoon *Walrus* v13 no10 p44 D 2016

Engineering—China

3 Myths about Engineering Talent in China and India V. Govindarajan and G. Bagla *Harvard Business Review Digital Articles* p2 D 9 2014

Engineers

    See also

      Automobile engineers

      Locomotive engineers

      Software engineers

26 MILES ABOVE EARTH L. PARKER color *Atlantic* v319 no5 p54 Je 2017

Big-Project Engineers Have to Deal with Too Much Red Tape S. Whitbread and N. D. Greene *Harvard Business Review Digital Articles* p2 Ja 14 2016

CLIPPERS, YACHTS, and the false promise of the wave line: John Scott Russell's 19th-century theory of ship design promised speed and delivered elegance. But, ultimately, it didn't hold water L. D. Ferreiro and A. Pollara *Physics Today* v70 no7 p52 Jl 2017

He's Got Nerve G. C. Orsak *D: The Magazine of Dallas* v43 no10 p122 O 2016

MAY@GH bw color *Good Housekeeping* v264 no5 p13 My 2017

TURBO DOGS C. Csere color *Car & Driver* v63 no4 p30 O 2017

WHAT TECHNOLOGY SHOULD I USE TO ENSURE MY LEGACY LIVES ON? R. CAPPS diag *Wired* v25 no8 p96 Ag 2017

Engineers—India

3 Myths about Engineering Talent in China and India V. Govindarajan and G. Bagla *Harvard Business Review Digital Articles* p2 D 9 2014

Engineers—United States

HOW to STOP the WIND B. HARGROVE color *Popular Mechanics* p86 S 2017

Engines

    See also

      Pumping machinery

      Tractors

Danish Treat S. SHIBATA color *Boating World* v38 no7 p6 Jl 2017

Forever Oil G. MICHAL *Boating World* v38 no3 p47 Mr 2017

GM'S HEI MODULE DWELL: THIS PRIMER WILL HELP YOU ADJUST THE DWELL ON ALL ENGINE TYPES R. Bohacz *Successful Farming* v115 no6 p26 Ap 2017

POWER PROGRESSION G. MICHAL *Boating World* v38 no2 p48 F 2017

Service R. NIERLICH and K. Cameron color *Cycle World* v56 no10 p66 N 2017

Engines—Evaluation

Centurion A. JONES *Boating World* v38 no1 p24 Ja 2017

CUMMINS TO OFFER CRATE ENGINES color *Dirt Sports + Off-Road* v51 no3 p8 Mr 2017

DIFFERENT STROKES color *Road & Track* v68 no6 p90 F 2017

A SECOND LOOK Z. PROCHAZKA *Boating World* v38 no5 p48 My 2017

England

Moments in Time B. FINKE *Arabian Horse World* v56 no12 p78 S 2016

England Is Mine (Film)

England Is Mine L. Greenblatt color *Entertainment Weekly* no1480 p40 S 1 2017

England Lost (Music)

The Playlist bw color *Rolling Stone* no1294 p10 Ag 24 2017

England—Description & travel

HIe THee TO HULL! D. Huntley *British Heritage Travel* v38 no1 p40 Ja/F 2017

In Search of Lorna Doone *British Heritage Travel* v37 no6 p44 N/D 2016

In Search of Middle England *British Heritage Travel* v38 no1 p18 Ja/F 2017

LEEDS R. Gardner color *British Heritage Travel* v38 no5 p58 S/O 2017

THE MAIL COACH TO ABERYSTWYTH: Jolts and All: How to Journey in Style--as if It Were 1835 S. Ellis *British Heritage Travel* v38 no4 p38 Jl/Ag 2017

Plymouth and Boston Illuminate for Thanksgiving *British Heritage Travel* v37 no6 p6 N/D 2016

Regal Echoes in Royal Greenwich S. Lawrence *British Heritage Travel* v38 no1 p26 Ja/F 2017

SOUTHAMPTON: Take the QEII Mile Through the Sea City *British Heritage Travel* v38 no4 p24 Jl/Ag 2017

Spring Breezes on the Open Road *British Heritage Travel* v38 no4 p28 Jl/Ag 2017

To the Great Beyond and North Yorkshire E. D. Huntley *British Heritage Travel* v38 no1 p28 Ja/F 2017

Touring the Welsh Marches: Land of Cider Apples, Offa's Dyke and Ancient Battles *British Heritage Travel* v38 no4 p21 Jl/Ag 2017

England—Economic conditions—21st century

Brexit Could Hurt the Most Here A. Tartar, J. Scott Diamond et al graph map *Bloomberg Businessweek* no4527 p20 Je 19 2017

Englander, Nathan

Chelsea Boy bw color *Vogue* v207 no11 p104 N 2017

'The Great British Baking Show' *New York Times Magazine* p40 O 8 2017

England—Religion—History

THE RITUAL LANDSCAPE color *Archaeology* v70 no3 p35 My/Je 2017

Engle, Randall—Interviews

CAN YOU MAKE YOURSELF SMARTER? J. RAINEY MARQUEZ *Atlanta* v56 no9 p115 Ja 2017

Engledow, Dave

The Little Girl Who Didn't Want to Go to Bed *Publishers Weekly* v264 no31 p85 Jl 31 2017

Englert, Matt
Posthole color *Powder* v45 no4 p146 D 2016

Englis, Jeannine
Can Crowdfunding Help Solve Our Health Issues? *AARP: The Magazine* v59 no2A p81 F/Mr 2016

English, Bill
Leaders color *Time* v189 no16/17 p64 My 1-8 2017

English, Bill (Simon William), 1961-
New Zealand's Rising Star Puts Election In Play T. John color *Time* v190 no10/11 p13 S 18 2017

English, Chantell
THE GUN EXCHANGE L. Miller img *New York* v49 no26 p22 D 26 2016

English, Charlie
From Here to Timbuktu T. ZOELLNER *New York Times Book Review* p48 Je 4 2017

English, Earl F.
TINTYPE TRICK? *Popular Photography* v81 no2 p27 Mr/Ap 2017

English, Jeannine
Palliative Care: A Key to Living With Dignity *AARP: The Magazine* v59 no1A p61 D 2015/Ja 2016
We Can Do More *AARP: The Magazine* v59 no3A p91 Ap/My 2016

English, Justin
Evolutionary drivers of thermoadaptation in enzyme catalysis [Cover story] bibl color graph *Science* v355 no6322 p289 Ja 20 2017

ENGLISH, MARY
Surviving a Pisces *USA Today Magazine* v145 no2862 p70 Mr 2017

English abbreviations
Life IN THESE UNITED STATES color *Reader's Digest* v190 no1133 p30 S 2017

English authors
A 21st-Century Agatha Christie L. PICKER color *Publishers Weekly* v264 no25 p84 Je 19 2017
Historic Literary Homes color *British Heritage Travel* v38 no5 p16 S/O 2017

English authors—Homes & haunts
Celebrating Jane Austen 2017 S. Lawrence color *British Heritage Travel* v38 no5 p28 S/O 2017
Kent: For a Festive Holiday in the Garden *British Heritage Travel* v37 no6 p20 N/D 2016

English Channel
The Original Brexit L. SCHLEY color *Discover* v38 no7 p19 S 2017

English etymology
Logophile Heaven! B. SPECKTOR color *Reader's Digest* v190 no1133 p78 S 2017

English gardens
Across the Pond P. Dickey color *Architectural Digest* v74 no1 p73 Ja 2017
BEYOND THE GARDEN GATE M. OZAWA *Martha Stewart Living* no267 p94 S 2016

English grammar
Funny FiLL-IN A. SHAW *National Geographic Kids* no469 p31 Ap 2017

English language
Countries with High English Proficiency Are More Innovative M. Tran *Harvard Business Review Digital Articles* p2 N 17 2015
FAKE I.D S. JIMENEZ bw *O, The Oprah Magazine* p138 My 2017
Funny FiLL-IN M. J. KRAUSS *National Geographic Kids* no468 p30 Mr 2017
PLEASE DON'T SAY THAT! *Saturday Evening Post* v289 no1 p30 Ja/F 2017
Rating the English Proficiency of Countries and Industries Around the World M. Tran and P. Burman *Harvard Business Review Digital Articles* p2 N 21 2016
The Scariest Word C. TRILLIN *New York Times Book Review* p29 N 27 2016
Speaking Freely M. Helprin *Claremont Review of Books* v17 no2 p98 Spr 2017
Why English, Not Mandarin, Is the Language of Innovation B. Fisher *Harvard Business Review Digital Articles* p2 Ja 12 2015

English language terms & phrases
GIFT WORDS L. Collins cartoon *New Yorker* v93 no9 p21 Ap 17 2017
IT PAYS TO INCREASE YOUR Word Power E. COX and H. RATHVON *Reader's Digest* v190 no1132 p135 Jl/Ag 2017

English language—Acquisition
Mariachi and Spanish speaking English learners: District initiatives, models, and education policy M. M. Neel bibl graph *Arts Education Policy Review* v118 no4 p208 2017

English language—Canada
Cross-Canada spell check T. CIOLFE map *Maclean's* v130 no7 p17 Ag 2017

English language—Composition & exercises
See also
English grammar
Funny FiLL-IN A. SHAW *National Geographic Kids* no469 p31 Ap 2017

English language—Composition & exercises—Study & teaching
THINKING LIKE A HISTORIAN: Developing disciplinary literacy in history among middle school struggling readers E. B. Claravall *Literacy Today (2411-7862)* v35 no1 p32 Jl/Ag 2017

English language—Study & teaching
California's Bilingual-Ed Mistake J. J. MILLER il *National Review* v69 no6 p19 Ap 3 2017

English language—Study & teaching—Immersion method
California's Bilingual-Ed Mistake J. J. MILLER il *National Review* v69 no6 p19 Ap 3 2017

English language—Usage
Logophile Heaven! B. SPECKTOR color *Reader's Digest* v190 no1133 p78 S 2017

English male authors
Have You Met Miss Jane?: Test your Austen I.Q.—from family scandals to a wet-shirted Colin Firth J. Schuessler and M. J. Murphy *New York Times Book Review* p15 Jl 16 2017

English mythology
WHITE HORSE OF THE SUN E. A. POWELL color *Archaeology* v70 no5 p9 S/O 2017

English orthography & spelling
Cross-Canada spell check T. CIOLFE map *Maclean's* v130 no7 p17 Ag 2017

English people
Audrey Millicent van Zuiden A. A. DAVIS color *Maclean's* no1 p66 F 17 2017

English pleasure horse classes
RGT MOZART G. DEARTH *Arabian Horse World* v56 no12 p48 S 2016
VERACITY KSB k. S. Buford *Arabian Horse World* v56 no12 p62 S 2016

English teachers
Backtalk L. Porosoff *Phi Delta Kappan* v99 no2 p80 O 2017

Engone-Obiang, Nestor L.
Positive biodiversity-productivity relationship predominant in global forests bibl chart graph map *Science* v354 no6309 paaf8957-1 O 14 2016

Engraving
AURIGNACIAN SCHOOL OF ART Z. ZORICH color *Archaeology* v70 no3 p16 My/Je 2017
The First Art: The Earliest Hominin Engraving C. KEMP bw color diag *Natural History* v125 no10 p34 O 2017
HEART ATTACK! *MHQ: Quarterly Journal of Military History* v29 no3 p20 Spr 2017

Engraving—Exhibitions
Charlotte Potter was browsing for inspiration, looking for the first steps in another dance with her *Virginia Living* v15 no1 p17 D 2016

Engreitz, Jesse M.
Systematic mapping of functional enhancer–promoter connections with CRISPR interference bibl graph *Science* v354 no6313 p769 N 11 2016

Engstrom, David M.
SILVER IS THE NEW OIL graph *Kiplinger's Personal Finance* v71 no4 p43 Ap 2017

Engvold, Oddbjørn
WHY IS THE SUN'S CORONA SO HOT? WHY ARE PROMINENCES SO COOL? *Physics Today* v70 no8 p35 Ag 2017

Enigma cipher system
Time Machines And War Machines A. BROWN color *Forbes* v199 no6 p20 Je 13 2017

ENJETI, ANJALI

no1 p18 Spr 2017

EYE ON 45 color *Science* v355 no6332 p1355 Mr 31 2017

Green the Vote C. Davis and T. A. Wildermuth *Harper's Magazine* p2 O 2017

Opportunities Lost? R. E. GROPP. *BioScience* v67 no8 p683 Ag 2017

The Shifting Politics of Taxing Carbon C. Flavelle *Bloomberg Businessweek* no4519 p52 Ap 24 2017

Time for Going-Away Gifts? E. Roston and J. A. Dlouhy color *Bloomberg Businessweek* no4525 p6 Je 5 2017

Trump and the Environment F. Krupp color *Foreign Affairs* v96 no4 p73 Jl/Ag 2017

TRUMP V. THE EARTH A. Davidson cartoon *New Yorker* v93 no8 p17 Ap 10 2017

U.S. off track for climate goal *Science* v353 no6307 p1475 S 30 2016

Words alone will not protect pollinators D. Inouye, S. Droege et al bibl color *Science* v355 no6323 p357 Ja 27 2017

Environmental protection

   See also

     Agriculture & the environment

     Biosecurity

     Climate change mitigation

     Environmental law

Conservation Begins With Your Boots On The Ground D. IRVIN *American Forests* v123 no2 p46 Summ 2017

Deciphering dueling analyses of clean water regulations K. J. Boyle, M. J. Kotchen et al color *Science* v357 no6359 p49 O 6 2017

DOING GOOD S. Pulia color *InStyle* v24 no9 p168 S 2017

Expanding the Portfolio: Conserving Nature's Masterpieces in a Changing World R. J. HOBBS, E. S. HIGGS et al *BioScience* v67 no6 p568 Je 2017

From Farm to Trash: Every year, billions of pounds of food end up in U.S. landfills. Can reducing the amount we throw away help end hunger—and protect the environment? L. ANASTASIA *New York Times Upfront* v149 no12 p14 Ap 24 2017

A Globally Rare eco system A. Abugattas, S. Archer et al *Parks & Recreation* v52 no4 p38 Ap 2017

GREENING YOUR HOME + BUSINESS R. Druzin color *Maclean's* v129 no50 p37 D 19 2016

Indigenous peoples: Conservation paradox P. O'B. Lyver and J. M. Tylianakis color *Science* v357 no6347 p142 Jl 14 2017

INTO THE FIELD A. GIRACCA *Orion Magazine* v35 no3 p46 My/Je 2016

Making Paris Work S. Herz bibl color map *Environment* v59 no2 p29 Mr/Ap 2017

New Deal on Pollutants Caps Good Year for Climate Action J. Worland color *Time* v188 no18 p11 O 31 2016

NEW LIFE FOR DEAD BATTERIES P. Constantakes and V. Minocha *New York State Conservationist* v71 no3 p26 D 2016

On Patrol L. Bobsein and S. Scherry *New York State Conservationist* v71 no3 p25 D 2016

THE Radically INTERNATIONAL History of AMERICA'S BEST IDEA T. Murphy color *Foreign Policy* no224 p66 My/Je 2017

SAVING THE WORLD'S OCEANS M. FRANK *New York Times Upfront* v149 no8 p12 Ja 30 2017

The Soil Depletion Crisis A. Richardson-Price *History Today* v66 no12 p4 D 2016

TEST YOUR ECO IQ *National Geographic Kids* no469 p30 Ap 2017

What's the damage from climate change? W. A. Pizer *Science* v356 no6345 p1330 Je 30 2017

When Less Means More: Conservation and protecting the environment adds to the blessings of Ramadan and one's year-round worship M. A. SHAH *Islamic Horizons* v46 no3 p46 My/Je 2017

Environmental protection—Canada

THE HAMMER DROPS ON CARBON S. PROUDFOOT color *Maclean's* v129 no42 p20 O 24 2016

A plan comes together F. LOS color map *Canadian Geographic* v135 no6 p60 D 2015

Treasured ISLANDS S. DONALD CAMERON color map *Canadian Geographic* v135 no6 p44 D 2015

Environmental protection—Cost effectiveness

Clear findings, smoggy debate color *Science* v355 no6325 p567 F 10 2017

Environmental protection—Economic aspects

A False Choice D. YARNOLD *Audubon* v119 no2 p8 Summ 2017

Environmental protection—Finance

PLUGGING THE PAST C. McKelvey and K. Martindale *New York State Conservationist* v71 no3 p18 D 2016

Treasured ISLANDS S. DONALD CAMERON color map *Canadian Geographic* v135 no6 p44 D 2015

Environmental protection—International cooperation

Climate change: The 2015 Paris Agreement thresholds and Mediterranean basin ecosystems J. Guiot and W. Cramer bibl *Science* v354 no6311 p465 O 28 2016

Environmental protection—Mexico

Saving San Miguel A. DOUGLAS color *Surfer* v58 no2 p32 My 2017

Environmental protection—New York (State)

On Patrol L. Bobseine and S. Scherry *New York State Conservationist* v71 no4 p27 F 2017

Program Highlights *New York State Conservationist* v71 no3 p21 D 2016

Environmental protection—News briefs

BRIEFLY *New York State Conservationist* v71 no3 p28 D 2016

Environmental protection—United States

Audubon, Now More Than Ever D. YARNOLD *Audubon* v119 no1 p8 Spr 2017

Environmental regulations

CLEAN ENERGY D. C. Vock *Governing* v30 no4 p36 Ja 2017

Environmental regulations—Research

Looking backward to move regulations forward M. Cropper, A. Fraas et al color *Science* v355 no6332 p1375 Mr 31 2017

Environmental remediation

Cleanup on Isle Nine J. Greenspan color *Scientific American* v315 no3 p20 S 2016

Environmental research

Skills and Knowledge for Data-Intensive Environmental Research S. E. HAMPTON, M. B. JONES et al *BioScience* v67 no6 p546 Je 2017

Environmental research—Arctic regions

The Arctic Environment in the Age of Man R. A. Virginia color *Wilson Quarterly* p1 Summ 2017

Environmental responsibility—Congresses

THE BUSINESS OF HUMANITY C. Leaf color *Fortune* v75 no1 p9 Ja 1 2017

Environmental risk assessment

Identifying the policy space for climate loss and damage R. Mechler and T. Schinko bibl color diag *Science* v354 no6310 p290 O 21 2016

Environmental television programs

PLANET EARTH II D. Vaughn color *Sound & Vision* v82 no7 p71 S 2017

Environmental toxicology

After Chile's fires, reforest private land M. J. Martinez-Harms, H. Caceres et al color *Science* v356 no6334 p147 Ap 14 2017

Europe's insufficient pollutant remediation R. J. Law and P. D. Jepson color *Science* v356 no6334 p148 Ap 14 2017

Environmentalism

   See also

     Environmental activism

Enemy of Humanity M. HERTSGAARD *Nation* v305 no1 p10 Jl 3 2017

A False Choice D. YARNOLD *Audubon* v119 no2 p8 Summ 2017

Greens Make Green T. NASSIF *Weekly Standard* v22 no5 p21 O 10 2016

Green Threat color *Earth Island Journal* v32 no1 p10 Spr 2017

Unboxing Environmentalism *Earth Island Journal* v32 no1 p2 Spr 2017

United in the Fight for Conservation C. O'MARA color *National Wildlife (World Edition)* v55 no5 p6 Ag/S 2017

Working Lands as Wild Lands M. Cimitile color *National Wildlife (World Edition)* v55 no5 p40 Ag/S 2017

Environmentalism in mass media

Covering the Climate J. GOODELL color *Rolling Stone* no1297 p22 O 5 2017

Environmentalism in motion pictures

An Inconvenient Truth sequel: Hope for a clean energy future color *National Wildlife (World Edition)* v55 no5 p46 Ag/S 2017

Environmentalism—Awards

ARCHIVES Events *Prologue* v48 no3 p66 Fall 2016

Environmentalism—Psychological aspects

Make Earth Great Again C. Caruso graph *Scientific American* v316 no3 p20 Mr 2017

Environmentalism—United States

An Opportunity for Environmentalists I. M. Stelzer color *Weekly Standard* v22 no26 p16 Mr 13 2017

Environmentalists

100 BEST Climate Solutions—And Why They're Going to Work S. Mowe color *Tricycle: The Buddhist Review* v26 no4 p44 Summ 2017

Demise of stream rule won't revitalize coal industry W. Cornwall color *Science* v355 no6326 p674 F 17 2017

Getting to YIMBY J. Hahn *Sierra* v102 no5 p18 St/O 2017

John Sheppard: Supporting the "TEAM" Improving our Air Quality *New York State Conservationist* v72 no1 p29 Ag 2017

Terry Hershey: 'A Force of Nature for Nature' S. Myrick *Parks & Recreation* v52 no3 p50 Mr 2017

The war in the Walbran A. Findlay color map *Canadian Geographic* v136 no6 p26 D 2016

Environmentalists—Interviews

Paul Hawken: "Game on" for global warming D. Stover bibl color *Bulletin of the Atomic Scientists* v73 no3 p145 My 2017

Student, Hiker, Sprogger W. Becktold *Sierra* v102 no5 p63 St/O 2017

"We're All in the Same Boat" Z. LOFTUS-FARREN color *Earth Island Journal* v32 no3 p46 Aut 2017

Environmental protection—Societies, etc.

A battle over the 'best science' D. Malakoff color *Science* v355 no6330 p1108 Mr 17 2017

Envy—Psychological aspects

Slaying the Green-Eyed Monster B. WARNER color *Publishers Weekly* v264 no17 p41 Ap 24 2017

Enxuto, João

VIEWER POSITIONING SYSTEM *Art in America* v104 no9 p122 O 2016

Enzensberg, Hans Magnus

Where Have All the Communes Gone? A case for radical social experimentation J. CRISPIN *In These Times* v41 no10 p36 O 2017

EnZinc (Company)

Breakthrough battery hinged on funding from program in Trump's crosshairs D. Kramer *Physics Today* v70 no6 p34 Je 2017

ENZINNA, WES

CRUDE AWAKENING color *Mother Jones* v42 no1 p32 Ja/F 2017

GUERRILLA GO PROS color *Mother Jones* v42 no4 p40 Jl/Ag 2017

"THIS IS A WAR AND WE INTEND TO WIN" bw color *Mother Jones* v42 no3 p14 My/Je 2017

Enzyme inhibitors

An algal photoenzyme converts fatty acids to hydrocarbons D. Sorigué, B. Légeret et al color graph *Science* v357 no6354 p903 S 1 2017

Enzymes

See also
Hybrid enzymes
Polymerases
Reductases

Characterization of a dynamic metabolon producing the defense compound dhurrin in sorghum T. Laursen, J. Borch et al bibl graph *Science* v354 no6314 p890 N 18 2016

Enzymes at work are enzymes in motion T. Saleh and C. G. Kalodimos bibl diag *Science* v355 no6322 p247 Ja 20 2017

Enzymes make light work of hydrocarbon production N. S. Scrutton diag *Science* v357 no6354 p872 S 1 2017

Evolutionary drivers of thermoadaptation in enzyme catalysis [Cover story] V. Nguyen, C. Wilson et al bibl color graph *Science* v355 no6322 p289 Ja 20 2017

Local protein kinase A action proceeds through intact holoenzymes F. Donelson Smith, J. L. Esseltine et al color diag graph *Science* v356 no6344 p1288 Je 23 2017

New developments for protein quality control R. Y. Hampton and C. Dargemont diag *Science* v357 no6350 p450 Ag 4 2017

A prominent glycyl radical enzyme in human gut microbiomes metabolizes trans-4-hydroxy-L-proline B. J. Levin, Y. Y. Huang et al diag *Science* v355 no6325 p595 F 10 2017

Quiet Your Cough G. FERRER and B. LENNIHAN color *Better Nutrition* v78 no12 p26 D 2016

The role of dimer asymmetry and protomer dynamics in enzyme catalysis T. Hun Kim, P. Mehrabi et al diag *Science* v355 no6322 p262 Ja 20 2017

Teaching nature the unnatural H. F. T. Klare and M. Oestreich bibl diag *Science* v354 no6315 p970 N 25 2016

Vital enzyme adapted to cooling Earth L. HAMERS *Science News* v191 no2 p8 F 4 2017

Enzymes—Industrial applications

Enzymes offer waste-to-energy solution M. Peplow diag *Science* v355 no6332 p1360 Mr 31 2017

Enzymology

Finding enzymes in the gut metagenome M. E. Glasner color *Science* v355 no6325 p577 F 10 2017

EO Products (Company)

Beauty for the Future S. Kitchens color *Glamour* v115 no5 p80 My 2017

Eocene paleobotany

Eocene lantern fruits from Gondwanan Patagonia and the early origins of Solanaceae P. Wilf, M. R. Carvalho et al bibl color diag *Science* v355 no6320 p1 Ja 6 2017

Eom, Dae Seok

A macrophage relay for long-distance signaling during postembryonic tissue remodeling bibl color graph *Science* v355 no6331 p1317 Mr 24 2017

Eom, Tae-Yeon

Restoring auditory cortex plasticity in adult mice by restricting thalamic adenosine signaling graph *Science* v356 no6345 p1352 Je 30 2017

Eötvös, Peter, 1944-

Eotvos: Paradise Reloaded (Lilith) J. Cadagin *Opera News* v81 no7 p47 Ja 2017

Eperon, Giles E.

Perovskite-perovskite tandem photovoltaics with optimized band gaps bibl chart graph *Science* v354 no6314 p861 N 18 2016

Ephemeral streams

The Big Pictures: SANTA CATALINA MOUNTAINS J. KIDA *Arizona Highways* v93 no6 p16 Je 2017

Ephippidae

Halloween Under The Sea B. F. SUMMERS color *National Geographic Kids* no474 p26 O 2017

Ephland, John

ARCHIE SHEPP PROUD PIONEER [Cover story] bw color *Downbeat* v84 no5 p36 My 2017

Dharmawan Promotes Indonesian Culture color *Downbeat* v84 no7 p21 Jl 2017

ELLEN ANDERSSON Leaving Spaces color *Downbeat* v84 no2 p23 F 2017

Fasching Fosters Creativity color *Downbeat* v84 no2 p60 F 2017

Following WISE MEN color *Downbeat* v83 no12 p54 D 2016

Java Jazz Provides Sonic Travelogue color *Downbeat* v84 no6 p14 Je 2017

JON BALKE bw *Downbeat* v84 no4 p24 Ap 2017

Kaiser Dives into Intriguing Waters color *Downbeat* v84 no3 p17 Mr 2017

Legends & Legacies color *Downbeat* v83 no12 p88 D 2016

Lloyd Marks Milestone at Oslo Fest color *Downbeat* v83 no11 p22 N 2016

Making Every Second Count bw *Downbeat* v83 no12 p78 D 2016

MOKSHA color *Downbeat* v84 no1 p25 Ja 2017

Ozella's Northern Stars color *Downbeat* v84 no10 p60 O 2017

PETER ASPLUND color *Downbeat* v84 no4 p20 Ap 2017

The Stone House color *Downbeat* v84 no7 p51 Jl 2017

Studio Cuts: Tales of the Tape bw *Downbeat* v83 no11 p61 N 2016

Towner's Pianistic Approach to Guitar bw *Downbeat* v84 no4 p16 Ap 2017

VIKTORIA TOLSTOY color *Downbeat* v84 no3 p25 Mr 2017

Ephrins

Ephrin B1–mediated repulsion and signaling control germinal center T cell territoriality and function P. Lu, C. Shih et al color *Science* v356 no6339 p716 My 19 2017

Repulsive behavior in germinal centers G. Leandros Moschovakis and R. Förster diag *Science* v356 no6339 p703 My 19 2017

EPHRON, DAN

Jerusalem Revisited *New York Times Book Review* p29 D 11 2016

Ephrussi, Anne

RNA localization feeds translation color *Science* v357 no6357 p1235 S 22 2017

Epict Inc.

WATCHAIR SMART ANTENNA M. BROWN color *Macworld - Digital Edition* p40 F 2017

Epictetus, ca. 55-135

BALANCE OF POWER Epictetus *Lapham's Quarterly* v10 no3 p24 Summ 2017

C. 108: Nicopolis *Lapham's Quarterly* v10 no1 p139 Wint 2017

EPICTETUS E. Batuman *New Yorker* v92 no42 p84 D 19 2016

Philosophers Who Like Stuff: Their case against frugality E. Westacott *Humanities* v38 no4 p1 Fall 2017

Epidemic chorea

Mass Panics *Lapham's Quarterly* v10 no3 p87 Summ 2017

Epidemics

See also

Influenza Epidemic, 1918-1919

Pandemics

CITYWIDE EPIDEMIC J. WUEBBEN color *Muscle & Performance* v9 no10 p19 O 2017

Contagions Make a Comeback [Cover story] S. Shah color *Science News* v190 no13 p32 D 24 2016

Ex–CDC head leads health drive *Science* v357 no6357 p1217 S 22 2017

For the Record color *Time* v190 no8 p7 Ag 28 2017

Long Ago and Far Away V. Maestro color *Natural History* v125 no9 p2 S 2017

Mosquitoes on the move J. R. Powell bibl color map *Science* v354 no6315 p971 N 25 2016

OUTBREAK [Cover story] C. Ash color *Science* v357 no6347 p144 Jl 14 2017

What We've Learned About Fighting Ebola R. S. Dhillon and D. Srikrishna *Harvard Business Review Digital Articles* p2 Jl 16 2015

Where has all the Zika gone? J. Cohen color graph *Science* v357 no6352 p631 Ag 18 2017

Epidemics—Prevention

A half-billion-dollar bid to head off emerging diseases J. Cohen color *Science* v355 no6322 p237 Ja 20 2017

Epidemics—United States

Our National Pain R. Chapman color *Sports Illustrated* v126 no17 p72 Je 19 2017

To Increase Vaccination Rates, Share Information on Disease Outbreaks A. B. Jena and D. Khullar *Harvard Business Review Digital Articles* p2 F 22 2017

Epidemiology

See also

Disease prevalence

Hypertension—Epidemiology

Pandemics

HANGOVER B. LUTZ color *New Orleans Magazine* v51 no2 p36 D 2016

Maternal antibodies' role in immunity H. Lemke, K. M. Gostic et al bibl color *Science* v355 no6326 p704 F 17 2017

Epidermal growth factor receptors

Keeping in touch with the ER network X. Tan and R. A. Anderson color *Science* v356 no6338 p584 My 12 2017

RESEARCH color *Science* v356 no6338 p594 My 12 2017

Epigenesis

Epigenetic plasticity and the hallmarks of cancer W. A. Flavahan, E. Gaskell et al diag *Science* v357 no6348 p266 Jl 21 2017

Epigenetics

See also

Animal epigenetics

Battling the Physical Symptoms of Stress P. Pal *Harvard Business Review Digital Articles* p2 Je 23 2016

The cancer epigenome: Concepts, challenges, and therapeutic opportunities M. A. Dawson bibl diag *Science* v355 no6330 p1147 Mr 17 2017

Causal role for inheritance of H3K27me3 in maintaining the OFF state of a Drosophila HOX gene R. T. Coleman and G. Struhl diag *Science* v356 no6333 p41 Ap 7 2017

The epigenetic landscape of T cell exhaustion D. R. Sen, J. Kaminski et al bibl graph *Science* v354 no6316 p1165 D 2 2016

Epigenetic regulation of antagonistic receptors confers rice blast resistance with yield balance Y. Deng, K. Zhai et al bibl diag *Science* v355 no6328 p962 Mr 3 2017

Epigenetics and the evolution of instincts G. E. Robinson and A. B. Barron color diag *Science* v356 no6333 p26 Ap 7 2017

Epigenetic stability of exhausted T cells limits durability of reinvigoration by PD-1 blockade K. E. Pauken, M. A. Sammons et al bibl graph *Science* v354 no6316 p1160 D 2 2016

GENES UNDER PRESSURE L. M. Zahn and B. A. Purnell color *Science* v354 no6308 p52 O 7 2016

The linker histone H1.0 generates epigenetic and functional intratumor heterogeneity C. Morales Torres, A. Biran et al bibl graph *Science* v353 no6307 paaf1644-1 S 30 2016

Passing epigenetic silence to the next generation S. De and J. A. Kassis diag *Science* v356 no6333 p28 Ap 7 2017

Epigenomics

Single-cell epigenomics: Recording the past and predicting the future G. Kelsey, O. Stegle et al diag *Science* v357 no6359 p69 O 6 2017

Single-cell methylomes identify neuronal subtypes and regulatory elements in mammalian cortex C. Luo, C. L. Keown et al diag *Science* v357 no6351 p600 Ag 11 2017

Epilepsy

JOAN OF ARC'S 'VOICES': INSPIRED OR EPILEPTIC? *Military History* v33 no5 p12 Ja 2017

Epilepsy—Surgery

The Epilepsy Dilemma D. Noonan color *Scientific American* v316 no4 p28 Ap 2017

Epilepsy—Treatment

The Epilepsy Dilemma D. Noonan color *Scientific American* v316 no4 p28 Ap 2017

Epilobium angustifolium

Fireweed color *Canadian Wildlife* v22 no5 p37 N/D 2016

Epinephrine autoinjectors

Don't Leave Home Without It D. DAVIS *Sierra* v102 no1 p18 Ja/F 2017

Full Disclosure A. BEATTIE *American Scholar* v86 no2 p18 Spr 2017

Pushing Back on High Drug Prices color *Prevention* v68 no12 p12 D 2016

You'll Feel a Little Pinch M. W. O'Reilly color *Commonweal* v143 no17 p6 O 21 2016

Epinephrine autoinjectors—Sales & prices

EPIPEN PANIC J. Wieczner color *Fortune* v174 no8 p21 D 15 2016

Epiphany

The Age of Misinformation B. j. Gould, D. W. Briggs et al *Skeptical Inquirer* v41 no5 p63 S/O 2017

WILD at HEART H. Bowles color *Vogue* v207 no1 p88 Ja 2017

Episcopal Church

Karen refugees revitalize two mainline churches, inspire film All Saints A. Sowder and H. Hahn color *Christian Century* v134 no20 p15 S 27 2017

St. Louis Episcopalians act against gun violence as homicide rate spikes D. Paulsen color *Christian Century* v134 no9 p14 Ap 26 2017

Episcopal clergy

People *Christian Century* v133 no24 p20 N 23 2016

Episcopal Divinity School (Cambridge, Mass.)

Episcopal Divinity School to affiliate with Union Theological in New York C. Kennel-Shank *Christian Century* v134 no7 p13 Mr 29 2017

Episcopalian theological seminaries

Forming priests among the people C. Kennel-Shank color *Christian Century* v134 no4 p30 F 15 2017

Episcopalians

What to Measure If You're Mission Driven Z. First *Harvard Business Review Digital Articles* p2 Jl 9 2015

Epistasis (Genetics)

Negative selection in humans and fruit flies involves synergistic epistasis M. Sohai, O. A. Vakhrusheva et al chart graph *Science* v356 no6337 p539 My 5 2017

Epitaxy

See also

Liquid phase epitaxy
Robust epitaxial growth of two-dimensional heterostructures, multiheterostructures, and superlattices Z. Zhang, P. Chen et al color *Science* v357 no6353 p788 Ag 25 2017

Epithelial cells
new products color *Science* v357 no6346 p98 Jl 7 2017
Spatiotemporal antagonism in mesenchymal-epithelial signaling in sweat versus hair fate decision C. P. Lu, L. Polak et al graph *Science* v354 no6319 paah6102-1 D 23 2016

Epithelium
Global mRNA polarization regulates translation efficiency in the intestinal epithelium A. E. Moor, M. Golan et al diag *Science* v357 no6357 p1299 S 22 2017

Epley, Nicholas
The Science of Sounding Smart *Harvard Business Review Digital Articles* p2 O 7 2015

Epoxy coatings—Evaluation
Gear P. Nielsen color *Sail* v48 no9 p28 S 2017

Eppinger, Laura
A new frontier color *U.S. Catholic* v81 no12 p45 D 2016

Epps, Omar
Shooter I. Ratledge *TV Guide* p43 D 5 2016

Epps, Philomena
Jamie Crewe color *Art in America* v105 no3 p29 Mr 2017

Epshteyn, Boris
THE REVOLUTION WILL BE TELEVISED (IT'LL JUST HAVE LOW PRODUCTION VALUES) [Cover story] F. GILLETTE bw color map *Bloomberg Businessweek* no4531 p44 Jl 24 2017

Epson America Inc.
SWEET 17 A. Ryder color *Popular Photography* v81 no2 p16 Mr/Ap 2017

Epson printers—Evaluation
SWEET 17 A. Ryder color *Popular Photography* v81 no2 p16 Mr/Ap 2017

Epson Singapore Pte Ltd.
Epson Home Cinema 3700 LCD Projector A. Griffin color graph *Sound & Vision* v82 no6 p46 Jl/Ag 2017

EPSTEIN, ANDREW
His True Vocation: The biography of a shy boy who overcame a hostile culture to become one of the great poets of his age bw *New York Times Book Review* p12 Ag 6 2017

Epstein, Benjamin
FIFTY Favorites *Los Angeles Magazine* p8 Ap 2017

Epstein, Daniel Mark
A Family Riven by Revolution T. LEE SIMMONS *National Review* v69 no16 p44 Ag 28 2017

Epstein, Edward Jay
ALTERNATIVE FACTS S. HALPERN color *Nation* v304 no7 p27 Mr 6 2017
The Enigma Machine G. SCHOENFELD *Weekly Standard* v22 no22 p30 F 13 2017
Hero, Traitor Or Spy? [Cover story] N. Lemann *New York Times Book Review* p1 Ja 15 2017
Snowden Job *Commentary* v143 no3 p52 Mr 2017

Epstein, Ethan
American Crime Story *Weekly Standard* v22 no27 p12 Mr 20 2017
Craving Statehood color *Weekly Standard* v22 no41 p16 Jl 3 2017
Golfing Alone cartoon *Weekly Standard* v23 no3 p5 S 25 2017
Kill This Idea color *Weekly Standard* v22 no19 p6 Ja 23 2017
North Korea, Then and Now *Weekly Standard* v22 no33 p7 My 8 2017
An Outlaw State color *Weekly Standard* v22 no25 p9 Mr 6 2017
Pressuring North Korea color *Weekly Standard* v22 no42 p7 Jl 17 2017
Sand in the Gears *Weekly Standard* v22 no48 p10 S 4 2017
Taipei Calling cartoon *Weekly Standard* v22 no15 p6 D 19 2016
The Taiwan Strait Freezes *Weekly Standard* v22 no4 p16 O 3 2016
Troubled Seoul color *Weekly Standard* v22 no30 p22 Ap 10 2017
Unhealthy Agency color *Weekly Standard* v22 no38 p8 Je 12 2017
Who Was That Masked Man? color *Weekly Standard* v22 no23 p8 F 20 2017
Will They Roll the Dice with Him? color *Weekly Standard* v22 no9 p15 N 7 2016

EPSTEIN, GARY
Defining Jewish Conservatism *Commentary* v144 no1 p4 Jl/Ag

2017

Epstein, Helen, 1947-
Routine Horrors H. Cooper color *New York Review of Books* v64 no16 p53 O 26 2017

Epstein, Ian
OBAMA'S AMERICA img *New York* v49 no20 p12 O 3 2016

EPSTEIN, JASON
Robert B. Silvers (1929–2017) [Cover story] bw color *New York Review of Books* v64 no8 p31 My 11 2017

EPSTEIN, JENNIFER RICE
It's a Bit of A Fixer-Upper: L.A. COUNTY'S OLDEST HOUSE, GAGE MANSION, LIES MOLDERING AWAY IN A BELL GARDENS TRAILER PARK. PRESERVING THE PLACE WILL COST MONEY, AND THAT HAS LEFT RESIDENTS DIVIDED ABOUT WHETHER TO SAFEGUARD THE LANDMARK *Los Angeles Magazine* p14 Ag 2017

EPSTEIN, JIM
THE SECRET, DANGEROUS WORLD OF VENEZUELAN BITCOIN MINING *Reason* v48 no8 p27 Ja 2017

EPSTEIN, JOSEPH
Article Sins Of The Father J. H. Reynolds and J. Ting *Commentary* v140 no2 p4 S 2015
The Best of Scribblers *Commentary* v140 no2 p41 S 2015
The Best of Scribblers: Edward Gibbon and the importance of great writing to great history *Commentary* v140 no2 p48 S 2015
Colonel Lew Schlicter, Mercenary *Commentary* v142 no3 p35 O 2016
Confessions of a Short Attention Span Man: Boredom is the enemy, and fear of boredom the spur *Commentary* v144 no3 p41 O 2017
The Cultured Life bw color *Weekly Standard* v22 no27 p26 Mr 20 2017
Do Culture and Politics Mix? cartoon *Weekly Standard* v22 no34 p5 My 15 2017
Fading Humor color *Weekly Standard* v22 no39 p5 Je 19 2017
First-Name Basis cartoon *Weekly Standard* v22 no18 p5 Ja 16 2017
Genial Screw-Off *Claremont Review of Books* v17 no3 p64 Summ 2017
A Great Deal *Claremont Review of Books* v17 no3 p67 Summ 2017
Hitting Eighty cartoon *Weekly Standard* v22 no17 p18 Ja 2 2017
Hope I Die Before I Get Young *Commentary* v143 no2 p34 F 2017
How Cool Was That? bw color *Weekly Standard* v22 no35 p30 My 22 2017
Incorruptible, Uncritical Devotion color *Weekly Standard* v22 no9 p5 N 7 2016
Joy in Mudville [Cover story] bw color *Weekly Standard* v22 no10 p17 N 14 2016
Modest Cultural Literacy *Claremont Review of Books* v17 no3 p66 Summ 2017
Money Talks—in My Case Softly cartoon *Weekly Standard* v22 no29 p5 Ap 3 2017
No Soft Spots *Claremont Review of Books* v17 no3 p66 Summ 2017
Petty Cash cartoon *Weekly Standard* v22 no43 p5 Jl 24 2017
A Rage to Write bw color *Weekly Standard* v22 no14 p30 D 12 2016
Sisters' Boy *Commentary* v143 no6 p35 Je 2017
Scruffy Bohemianism *Claremont Review of Books* v17 no3 p65 Summ 2017
Shabby Chic color *Weekly Standard* v23 no1 p5 S 11 2017
There's a Waiter in My Soup cartoon *Weekly Standard* v22 no28 p5 Mr 27 2017
UNIVERSITY OF CHICAGO DAYS *Claremont Review of Books* v17 no3 p64 Summ 2017
What's the Story? *Weekly Standard* v23 no3 p27 S 25 2017
WHITE MISCHIEF *Claremont Review of Books* v17 no2 p40 Spr 2017

Epstein, Richard A.
Climate Wars Heat Up *Hoover Digest: Research & Opinion on Public Policy* no4 p150 Fall 2016
Home Is Where the Market Is: What we should do--and stop doing--in the quest for "affordable housing" *Hoover Digest: Research & Opinion on Public Policy* no3 p137 Summ 2017
Is free speech under threat IN THE UNITED STATES? WE RE-

CEIVED TWENTY-SEVEN RESPONSES. WE PUBLISH THEM HERE, IN ALPHABETICAL ORDER *Commentary* v144 no1 p13 Jl/Ag 2017

LAWLESS RULES *Claremont Review of Books* v17 no3 p54 Summ 2017

Progressively Poorer *Hoover Digest: Research & Opinion on Public Policy* no1 p65 Wint 2017

"The Power of the Thought":Contempt for freedom of speech reflects impoverished minds. Colleges that reject intellectual diversity are much to blame *Hoover Digest: Research & Opinion on Public Policy* no3 p120 Summ 2017

Epstein, Robert

Do You Have What It Takes to Help Your Team Be Creative? *Harvard Business Review Digital Articles* p2 D 8 2015

Epstein, Suzanne L.

First flu is forever bibl diag *Science* v354 no6313 p706 N 11 2016

Epstein, Theo

IT WAS NOT AN INSTINCT, IT WAS A CHOICE *Vital Speeches of the Day* v83 no8 p222 Ag 2017

The Rainmaker T. Verducci color *Sports Illustrated* v125 no20 p110 D 19 2016

WORLD'S 50 GREATEST LEADERS [Cover story] H. E. Fry, M. Heimer et al color *Fortune* v175 no5 p46 Ap 1 2017

Epstein, Yaffa

Europe's biodiversity avoids fatal setback color *Science* v355 no6321 p140 Ja 13 2017

International Wildlife Law: Understanding and Enhancing Its Role in Conservation *BioScience* v67 no9 p784 S 2017

Epworth (England)

At Home with the Wesleys *British Heritage Travel* v37 no6 p70 N/D 2016

Equal pay for equal work

13 down, 8,987 to go...: Organisations have been slow to report their gender pay gaps. But the real question is how they will explain them when they do G. GYTON *People Management* p8 Jl 2017

Equal Pay for Equal Play? C. STOFFERS and B. Rothenberg *New York Times Upfront* v149 no7 p16 Ja 9 2017

(The Big)Salary Reveal [Cover story] L. Brody, J. Militare et al bw color *Glamour* v115 no3 p146 Mr 2017

We Have So Much Power! A. Reign color *Essence* v47 no9 p94 Ja 2017

Equal pay for equal work laws

global: SHORT TAKES *Ms.* v27 no3 p19 Fall 2017

Equal rights

The Non-Virtue of Intolerance D. ZIRIN color *Progressive* v81 no6 p68 Ag/S 2017

Equal rights amendments—United States

Nevada Says ERA Yes!: Propelled by a record number of women lawmakers, the state becomes the 36th to ratify the Equal Rights Amendment--and the first in 40 years C. N. BAKER *Ms.* v27 no2 p8 Summ 2017

Equal rights—United States

Clueless and Condescending cartoon *Weekly Standard* v22 no13 p3 D 5 2016

Equality

　　See also
　　　Educational equalization
　　　Equality in the workplace
　　　Gender inequality
　　　Social injustice
　　　Social justice

Asking for a Friend L. Featherstone color *Nation* v33 no21 p5 N 21 2016

Black Like Me J. Sexton *Harper's Magazine* p2 S 2017

Deliberation & the Challenge of Inequality A. Siu *Daedalus* v146 no3 p119 Summ 2017

Determinants of Child Health Inequalities in Developing Countries: a New Perspective I. Amate-Fortes, A. Guarnido-Rueda et al chart diag *Society* v53 no6 p641 D 2016

Documenting decline in U.S. economic mobility L. F. Katz and A. B. Krueger graph *Science* v356 no6336 p382 Ap 28 2017

EXIT LEFT J. Gamble, P. Mason et al bw color *Nation* v304 no16 p16 My 22 2017

Fixing the Euro Zone and Reducing Inequality, Without Fleecing the Rich E. Lonergan and M. Blyth *Harvard Business Review*

Digital Articles p2 Ja 9 2015

For the People's Budget diag *Nation* v304 no18 p3 Je 19 2017

Growth and Inequality *Commentary* v141 no10 p1 D 2016

Growth and Inequality *Commentary* v142 no5 p1 D 2016

Inequality is Always in the Room: Language & Power in Deliberative Democracy A. Lupia and A. Norton *Daedalus* v146 no3 p64 Summ 2017

Introduction J. S. Fishkin and J. Mansbridge *Daedalus* v146 no3 p6 Summ 2017

Near and Far W. Voegeli *Claremont Review of Books* v17 no3 p11 Summ 2017

Why Inequality Is an Urgent Business Problem R. Henderson *Harvard Business Review Digital Articles* p2 Mr 29 2017

Women Strike Back K. Pollitt color *Nation* v303 no19 p10 N 7 2016

Equality in the workplace

Colorblind Diversity Efforts Don't Work J. Emerson *Harvard Business Review Digital Articles* p2 S 11 2017

Firing James Damore Could Be a Setback for Google's Diversity Goals A. Wittenberg-Cox *Harvard Business Review Digital Articles* p2 Ag 10 2017

Gender Initiatives Are Culture Change Initiatives A. Wittenberg-Cox *Harvard Business Review Digital Articles* p2 O 14 2015

Is It OK to Get Paid More for Being Lucky? I. Almas, A. W. Cappelen et al color graph *Harvard Business Review Digital Articles* p2 Mr 9 2017

The Men Who Mentor Women A. M. Valerio and K. Sawyer *Harvard Business Review Digital Articles* p2 D 7 2016

Newswomen in Revolt M. Whyte *History Today* v67 no5 p14 My 2017

When the Media Covers Gender Inequality, the CSuite Listens L. Gaines-Ross *Harvard Business Review Digital Articles* p2 O 21 2015

Equality Now (Organization)

POWER WRAP C. WINTER color *Bloomberg Businessweek* no4505 p74 D 26 2016

Equality—Religious aspects

The New Testament's Take on 'Equality' A. WILSON *Christianity Today* v60 no9 p28 N 2016

Equality—Social aspects

The New Testament's Take on 'Equality' A. WILSON *Christianity Today* v60 no9 p28 N 2016

THE THREAT OF INEQUALITY A. Deaton color graph *Scientific American* v315 no3 p48 S 2016

Equality—United States

THREE BIG IDEAS: TWO BAD, ONE GOOD D. N. MCCLOSKEY cartoon *Reason* v48 no9 p8 F 2017

Unequal Rights D. R. Wilson color *New Orleans Magazine* v51 no7 p32 My 2017

Whose religious freedom? [Cover story] T. Wenger color *Christian Century* v134 no22 p24 O 25 2017

Equality—United States—Economic aspects

Friedman on Freedom M. Friedman *Hoover Digest: Research & Opinion on Public Policy* no2 p23 Spr 2017

Equations of state

NEW INSIGHT INTO AN INTRIGUING MATERIAL A. Parker color graph *Science & Technology Review* p12 O/N 2016

Equatorial currents—Research

Coral - Current Connections A. Alpert color *Oceanus* v51 no2 p48 Wint 2016

Equestrian accidents

50 Reasons to Love Being 50+ S. O'Brien color *AARP: The Magazine* v59 no5A p65 Ag/S 2016

Equestrian artists

The Clinic: PHOTO CRITIQUES S. von Dietze color *Dressage Today* v23 no11 p20 Ag 2017

Equestrian centers

Horse Properties ACROSS THE NATION W. Tinker *Arabian Horse World* v57 no8 p146 My 2017

Horses and People *Arabian Horse World* v56 no12 p234 S 2016

Living & Recreation *Virginia Living* p119 2017 Best 20of Virginia

URBAN HORSEKEEPING A. Heintzberger color *Dressage Today* v23 no10 p30 Jl 2017

Where WORK is PLAY K. Sanchez color *Dressage Today* v24 no2 p46 N 2017

Equestrian centers—Design & construction

One Jump Ahead color *Log Home Living* v34 no2 p14 Mr 2017

Equifax Inc.

Accidental Advocates M. KONCZAL *Nation* v305 no8 p9 O 9 2017

Equifax and Why It's So Hard to Sue a Company for Losing Your Personal Information B. R. Sharton and D. S. Kantrowitz *Harvard Business Review Digital Articles* p2 S 22 2017

Equifax hack: How to know if you're affected B. CHACOS color *PCWorld* v35 no10 p7 O 2017

The Equifax Job M. Riley, J. Robertson et al bw graph *Bloomberg Businessweek* no4541 p26 O 9 2017

Thank You For Calling Equifax, Your Business Is Not Important to Us P. Regnier, S. Woolley et al *Bloomberg Businessweek* no4538 p38 S 18 2017

Your Equifax Defense L. GERSTNER color *Kiplinger's Personal Finance* v71 no12 p34 D 2017

Equilibrium

A Bit Tipsy H. Leifert map *Natural History* v125 no3 p7 Mr 2017

Equilibrium (Physiology)

The 4 most important types of exercise color *Harvard Health Letter* v42 no4 p4 F 2017

ARM YOURSELF J. Crandell color *Yoga Journal* p26 2017 Special Issue

between the lines color *Yoga Journal* p90 2017 Special Issue

Dear Katie K. Morgan *Dance Spirit* v21 no4 p22 Ap 2017

Get to know... your hips R. Long color *Yoga Journal* p68 2017 SpecialIssue

High and Dry T. MIKACICH *Boating World* v38 no3 p16 Mr 2017

A home practice for Better balance D. Burkman color *Yoga Journal* p57 2017 Special Issue

How to move from Shalabhasana to Mayurasana D. Swenson color *Yoga Journal* no296 p55 N 2017

IN THIS SECTION color *Yoga Journal* p52 2017 Special Issue

lightness of being color *Yoga Journal* p70 2017 Special Issue

THE LUMBAR LOWDOWN A. Bauman color *Yoga Journal* p84 2017 Special Issue

playing with power color *Yoga Journal* p74 2017 Special Issue

plumb Perfect R. Cole color *Yoga Journal* p34 2017 Special Issue

Poses of the month L. Arch color *Yoga Journal* no287 p33 N 2016

REVOLVE TO EVOLVE P. Sterios color *Yoga Journal* p90 2017 Special Issue

strong spirit color *Yoga Journal* p84 2017 Special Issue

take the leap! B. Birney color *Yoga Journal* p62 2017 Special Issue

TEO DRAKE color *Yoga Journal* no292 p18 Je 2017

turn up the torque color *Yoga Journal* p78 2017 Special Issue

Equilibrium (Physiology) disorders

Curing a Stumbler C. Anderson and J. F. Meyer color *Horse & Rider* v56 no4 p64 Ap 2017

Equine-assisted therapy

CLOSE ENCOUNTERS C. Siebert and H. Bateman color *New York Times Magazine* p48 My 21 2017

Equine herpesvirus 1

EHV-1 VIABILITY HAS IMPLICATIONS FOR BIOSECURITY C. Barakat and M. McCluskey color *Equus* no478 p16 Jl 2017

Equine herpesvirus diseases

DRUG SHOWS PROMISE IN PREVENTING NEUROLOGICAL COMPLICATION C. Barakat and M. McCluskey *Equus* no476 p20 My 2017

Equine infectious anemia virus

Your Horse's Coggins Test E. M. KELLON color *Trail Rider* v29 no3 p14 Ap 2017

Equine infectious anemia—Diagnosis

Your Horse's Coggins Test E. M. KELLON color *Trail Rider* v29 no3 p14 Ap 2017

Equine influenza

Basic Training Principles for Sport Horse Soundness C. Lönnell color *Practical Horseman* v45 no11 p52 N 2017

EVIDENCE SUGGESTS EQUINE INFLUENZA VIRUS IS ZOONOTIC C. Barakat and M. McCluskey color *Equus* no470 p18 N 2016

Equine metabolic syndrome

GLOSSARY *Equus* no473 p71 F 2017

Equine sports medicine

HERE YOU COME AGAIN J. Mankin color *Spin to Win Rodeo* v20 no11 p40 Ja 2017

Equipment & supplies

See also

Cooking equipment

Hairdressing equipment & supplies

Photographic equipment

Prosthesis

Telecommunication equipment & supplies

cool beans color *Parents* v92 no8 p112 Ag 2017

Take your yoga to go M. Clarke color *Yoga Journal* no293 p24 Ag 2017

Equipment & supplies—Economic aspects

fall out of TOUCH J. DOWNEY cartoon *Yoga Journal* no288 p45 D 2016

The gift of meditation E. Marglin color *Yoga Journal* no288 p17 D 2016

Equispirit Trailer Co.

Trailer Updates 2017 L. BACK bw color *Trail Rider* v29 no3 p8 Ap 2017

Equity

Starting My Journey as NRPA's Chair L. T. ANDREWS JR. *Parks & Recreation* v52 no10 p8 O 2017

Equity (Real property)

Divide Your Home S. SHARF color *Forbes* v199 no7 p136 Je 29 2017

Dream-School Debt color *Money* v45 no10 p22 N 2016

Equity—Charts, diagrams, etc.

Oil and Equity Prices Rally chart diag *Money* v45 no10 p94 N 2016

Equity (Real property)—Charts, diagrams, etc.

THE CASE FOR FOCUSING ON GROWTH, NOT PROFITABILITY graph img *Harvard Business Review* v95 no5 p30 S/O 2017

Equivalence principle (Physics)

Einstein principle passes quantum test E. CONOVER *Science News* v191 no10 p8 My 27 2017

Equus

See also

Donkeys

Horses

Przewalski's horse

WILD WILD HORSES P. WILLIAMS *Smithsonian* v47 no8 p56 D 2016

Erace, Adam

THE CITY OF BROAD SHOULDERS color *Fortune* v175 no4 p60 Mr 15 2017

THE CITY ON THE HARBOR color *Fortune* v175 no7 p28 Je 1 2017

A Cooler Wine Cooler color *Bloomberg Businessweek* no4515 p62 Mr 20 2017

DOING BUSINESS IN: BUENOS AIRES color *Fortune* v175 no6 p27 My 1 2017

DOING BUSINESS IN: FRANKFURT color *Fortune* v176 no1 p39 Jl 1 2017

THE GATHERING PLACE color *Fortune* v176 no4 p64 S 15 2017

ON THE GRAND LAKE color *Fortune* v175 no8 p90 Je 15 2017

Eramia, Bob

FROM OUR READERS *Sky & Telescope* v133 no4 p6 Ap 2017

Erard, S.

Seasonal exposure of carbon dioxide ice on the nucleus of comet 67P/Churyumov-Gerasimenko bibl bw graph *Science* v354 no6319 p1563 D 23 2016

ERB, KELLY PHILLIPS

Shrink Your Salary color *Forbes* v199 no7 p138 Je 29 2017

Erb, Marcella L.

Assembly of a nucleus-like structure during viral replication in bacteria bibl color graph *Science* v355 no6321 p1 Ja 13 2017

Erb, Tobias J.

A synthetic pathway for the fixation of carbon dioxide in vitro bibl graph *Science* v354 no6314 p900 N 18 2016

Erby, Kelly

BEANTOWN BAEDEKER C. Suellentrop bw color *American History* v52 no2 p68 Je 2017

Ercan, Selen A.

Twelve Key Findings in Deliberative Democracy Research *Daedalus* v146 no3 p28 Summ 2017

Ercius, Peter

Single-particle mapping of nonequilibrium nanocrystal transformations bibl bw graph *Science* v354 no6314 p874 N 18 2016

Erdbrink, Thomas

TRUMP'S TRAVEL BAN *New York Times Upfront* v149 no10 p6 Mr 13 2017

Erdich, Louise

All Undone: Future Home of the Living God J. PHILLIPS *Ms.* v27 no3 p52 Fall 2017

Erdmann, M.

Observation of a large-scale anisotropy in the arrival directions of cosmic rays above 8×1018 eV *Science* v357 no6357 p1266 S 22 2017

Erdmann, R.

Inhibitors of PEX14 disrupt protein import into glycosomes and kill Trypanosoma parasites chart color diag graph *Science* v355 no6332 p1416 Mr 31 2017

Erdogan, Berrin

Your New Hires Won't Succeed Unless You Onboard Them Properly *Harvard Business Review Digital Articles* p2 Je 20 2017

Erdoğan, Recep Tayyip, 1954-

The Dutch Give Up on Trumpism C. CALDWELL color *Weekly Standard* v22 no28 p24 Mr 27 2017

Enemies of the state A. R. KHAN color *Maclean's* p42 Je 2017

Erdogan's Counter-Revolution [Cover story] E. EDELMAN color *Weekly Standard* v22 no32 p26 My 1 2017

Erdogan's Journey H. Karaveli color *Foreign Affairs* v95 no6 p121 N/D 2017

In Turkey It's Purge, Then Splurge A. Kandemir *Bloomberg Businessweek* no4529 p31 Jl 3 2017

Recep Tayyip Erdogan J. Malsin color *Time* v188 no25-26 p106 D 19 2016 Double Issue

THE THIRTY-YEAR COUP D. FILKINS bw cartoon *New Yorker* v92 no33 p60 O 17 2016

Turkey's Coming Chaos M. RUBIN color *National Review* v69 no11 p27 Je 12 2017

Turkey's president builds an Islamic nationalism while amassing power S. Peterson *Christian Century* v134 no8 p1 Ap 12 2017

Turkey's Reichstag Fire *Commentary* v142 no2 p1 S 2016

Turkey's Reichstag Fire: Explaining Erdogan's long game M. Rubin *Commentary* v142 no2 p46 S 2016

Will Turkey Vote to Give Erdogan Even More Power? J. Malsin color *Time* v189 no4 p11 F 6 2017

Erdoğan, Recep Tayyip, 1954-—Political & social views

Erdogan's Empire State of Mind M. Champion and O. Ant color *Bloomberg Businessweek* no4511 p14 F 13 2017

Turkey's Erdogan Threatens a Breakup With the E.U I. Bremmer *Time* v189 no13 p10 Ap 10 2017

Erdrich, Heid E.

More than Words *South Dakota Magazine* p10 S/O 2017 Supplement

Erdrich, Louise, 1954-

No. 4 LAROSE I. Biedenharn color *Entertainment Weekly* no1444/1445 p104 D 16 2016

Erfani, M.

Observation of a large-scale anisotropy in the arrival directions of cosmic rays above 8×1018 eV *Science* v357 no6357 p1266 S 22 2017

Erganbright, Russell

Let the Stones Stand Again *Sky & Telescope* v133 no4 p84 Ap 2017

Ergonomics

See also

Human-machine systems

Ergonomically Correct J. S. HO *USA Today Magazine* v146 no2866 p25 Jl 2017

VERTICAL REALITY: PHONES HAVE TILTED OUR WORLDVIEW C. THOMPSON cartoon *Wired* v25 no9 p40 S 2017

WORKING AGAINST DISASTER R. G. SHAPIRO color *Phi Kappa Phi Forum* v97 no1 p16 Spr 2017

Erickson, Alan

Mr. Clean Is on the Scene J. LABIANCA color *Reader's Digest* v190 no1135 p12 N 2017

Erickson, Edwin

Faith and Science at a Crossroad *Sky & Telescope* v134 no3 p6

S 2017

Erickson, John R.

Buffalo Gnats cartoon *American Cowboy* v23 no5 p22 F/Mr 2017

On Being Texan color *American Cowboy* p8 LEGENDS OF TEXAS Special Issue 2017

Erickson, Julia

DIGGING DEEP K. McGuire color *Dance Spirit* v20 no9 p47 N 2016

Erickson, Katheryn

THE 2017 GLAMOUR BEAUTY AWARD color *Glamour* v115 no4 p81 Ap 2017

'80s Strong color *Glamour* v115 no2 p120 F 2017

Adult Acne, Still? color *Glamour* v115 no10 p102 O 2017

The Dos of Summer Hair color *Glamour* v114 no7 p80 Jl 2016

The Dry Shampoo Mania Continues color *Glamour* v115 no10 p106 O 2017

Hair Color, the 2017 Way [Cover story] color *Glamour* v115 no7 p45 Jl 2017

How to Look Less Tired bw color *Glamour* v115 no3 p120 Mr 2017

How We Communicate Now bw color *Glamour* v115 no3 p52 Mr 2017

In Defense of Body Hair color *Glamour* v115 no6 p60 Je 2017

Made for Me color *Glamour* v115 no3 p104 Mr 2017

Mask Mania! color *Glamour* v114 no12 p132 D 2016

The New Matte color *Glamour* v115 no1 p38 Ja 2017

Solar Power color *Glamour* v114 no7 p78 Jl 2016

The Ultimate Beauty How-tos... color *Glamour* v115 no4 p204 Ap 2017

Waves Like This [Cover story] bw color *Glamour* v114 no11 p97 N 2016

What Sunrise Smells Like color *Glamour* v115 no5 p82 My 2017

Your Hair This Summer color *Glamour* v115 no6 p55 Je 2017

ERICKSON, LARRY E.

Electric vehicle prospects *Issues in Science & Technology* v33 no3 p12 Spr 2017

Erickson, Paul

The Politics of Late-Night Comedy color *Atlantic* v320 no1 p10 Jl/Ag 2017

ERICKSON, ST EVE

Blues Dabblers *New York Times Book Review* p15 Ap 2 2017

Dead Or Alive *Los Angeles Magazine* v62 no7 p54 Jl 2017

Even Greed Has a Price *Los Angeles Magazine* v62 no6 p56 Je 2017

A Fierce Role Model *Los Angeles Magazine* v62 no9 p72 S 2017

From the Great Beyond: HOLLYWOOD HELPED DRIVE F. SCOTT FITZGERALD TO THE GRAVE, BUT THE AUTHOR'S GHOST HAUNTS AMAZON'S COMPELLING NEW SERIES THE LAST TYCOON *Los Angeles Magazine* p60 Ag 2017

Judging The Art And Not The Artist *Los Angeles Magazine* p86 D 2016

A Lens On the Psyche *Los Angeles Magazine* p94 Ap 2017

Out of Step with Movie History *Los Angeles Magazine* p66 F 2017

A Strait-Laced America *Los Angeles Magazine* p64 My 2017

Stranger Than Fiction *Los Angeles Magazine* p84 Mr 2017

When King Was Queen bw color *Los Angeles Magazine* v62 no10 p94 O 2017

With Camelot Behind Her *Los Angeles Magazine* p72 Ja 2017

Ericson, Steve

Name That Tune F. MAAZEL *New York Times Book Review* p18 F 12 2017

Erie (Pa.)—Description & travel

PRESQUE ISLE STATE PARK A. BROWNLEE color *Cincinnati Magazine* v51 no1 p34 O 2017

Erie, Lake

LAKESIDE LANDMARK color *Timber Home Living* v27 no3 p88 Je 2017

Erie Canal (N.Y.)—History

Last Look D. Kidd *Governing* v30 no10 p64 Jl 2017

Eriksson, Nicholas

Who's Benefiting from MOOCs, and Why *Harvard Business Review Digital Articles* p2 S 22 2015

ERIKSSON, OVE

Combining Biodiversity Resurveys across Regions to Advance Global Change Research *BioScience* v67 no1 p73 Ja 2017

Erion, Mark D.
Systemic pan-AMPK activator MK-8722 improves glucose homeostasis but induces cardiac hypertrophy graph *Science* v357 no6350 p507 Ag 4 2017

Erivo, Cynthia, 1987-
CYNTHIA ERIVO N. Weldon color *Runner's World* v51 no11 p108 D 2016
PICK UP HER CROWN L. J. S. Porter color *Essence* v48 no3 p122 Jl 2017

Erixon, Fredrik
The Innovation Illusion: How So Little Is Created by So Many Working So Hard R. N. Cooper *Foreign Affairs* v96 no2 p169 Mr/Ap 2017

Erkela, E. M.
Observation of coherent elastic neutrino-nucleus scattering diag *Science* v357 no6356 p1123 S 15 2017

Erkiletian, Lynda
DAN ABOUT TOWN: Party photographer Dan Swartz's monthly roundup of bashes, balls, and benefits *Washingtonian Magazine* v53 no1 p28 O 2017

Erlebacher, Adrian
BABY'S FIRST ORGAN color *Scientific American* v317 no4 p46 O 2017

ERLER, CATRIONA TUDOR
Nature's Industry *Virginia Living* v15 no3 p79 Ap 2017

ERLER, EDWARD J.
SELF-WILLED DELUSION *USA Today Magazine* v145 no2860 p50 Ja 2017

Erlich, Reese
Distorted News from Venezuela color *Progressive* v81 no7 p48 O/N 2017
What's Really Going Down in Venezuela color *Progressive* v81 no7 p45 O/N 2017

Erlich, Yaniv
DNA Fountain enables a robust and efficient storage architecture bibl chart diag *Science* v355 no6328 p950 Mr 3 2017

Erlich, Yaniv—Interviews
Three Qs *Science* v354 no6311 p395 O 28 2016

Ermeling, Bradley A.
Making teaching visible through learning opportunities color *Phi Delta Kappan* v98 no8 p54 My 2017

Ermelino, Louisa
Glastonbury color *Publishers Weekly* v264 no30 p18 Jl 24 2017
Literary Fiction color *Publishers Weekly* v263 no51 p64 D 12 2016
The Magnificent Adrienne Sharp color *Publishers Weekly* v264 no32 p22 Ag 7 2017
Memoirs & Biographies color *Publishers Weekly* v263 no51 p72 D 12 2016
Shanghaied bw color map *Publishers Weekly* v264 no41 p20 O 9 2017
SPRING 2017 ADULT ANNOUNCEMENTS color *Publishers Weekly* v263 no51 p18 D 12 2016
Under the California Sun color *Publishers Weekly* v264 no23 p24 Je 5 2017
Under the Sicilian Sun color *Publishers Weekly* v264 no38 p22 S 18 2017
Unmaking the Persians color *Publishers Weekly* v264 no34 p32 Ag 21 2017
When a Child Calls color *Publishers Weekly* v264 no36 p26 S 4 2017
When in Milan color *Publishers Weekly* v264 no28 p20 Jl 10 2017

ERMEY, RYAN
THE BEST ROUTE TO BARGAIN AIRFARES color *Kiplinger's Personal Finance* v71 no4 p10 Ap 2017
CALENDAR color *Kiplinger's Personal Finance* v71 no1 p17 Ja 2017
Cheap Shares, Plenty of Cash chart color *Kiplinger's Personal Finance* v71 no11 p58 N 2017
A Convertible Fund for the Risk-Averse chart *Kiplinger's Personal Finance* v71 no7 p61 Jl 2017
Get a 6.5% Yield With a Stew of Junk Bonds chart *Kiplinger's Personal Finance* v71 no1 p61 Ja 2017
Low Fees, Low Minimum, Big Return chart *Kiplinger's Personal Finance* v71 no6 p57 Je 2017
MONEY MADE SIMPLE [Cover story] color *Kiplinger's Per-*

sonal Finance v71 no5 p24 My 2017
Mother and Daughter Score With Micro Caps chart *Kiplinger's Personal Finance* v70 no12 p61 D 2016
Not Your Average Utility Fund chart *Kiplinger's Personal Finance* v71 no5 p63 My 2017
One Family, Two Foreign Fund Winners chart *Kiplinger's Personal Finance* v71 no4 p62 Ap 2017
Sized Right for Ample Returns chart *Kiplinger's Personal Finance* v71 no12 p57 D 2017
This Fund Banks on Bank Loans chart *Kiplinger's Personal Finance* v71 no10 p63 O 2017
Three Ways to Join in Europe's Recovery chart *Kiplinger's Personal Finance* v71 no8 p55 Ag 2017
A Value Fund Leaps Ahead of Its Rivals chart *Kiplinger's Personal Finance* v71 no2 p62 F 2017

Ermler, Ulrich
The methanogenic CO2 reducing-and-fixing enzyme is bifunctional and contains 46 [4Fe-4S] clusters bibl diag *Science* v354 no6308 p114 O 7 2016
Methanogenic heterodisulfide reductase (HdrABC-MvhAGD) uses two noncubane [4Fe-4S] clusters for reduction color *Science* v357 no6352 p699 Ag 18 2017

Ernest, Jordan D.
Reovirus infection triggers inflammatory responses to dietary antigens and development of celiac disease color diag *Science* v356 no6333 p44 Ap 7 2017

Ernest Shackleton Loves Me (Theatrical production)
THE THEATRE *New Yorker* v93 no12 p5 My 8 2017

Ernfors, Patrik
miR-183 cluster scales mechanical pain sensitivity by regulating basal and neuropathic pain genes diag graph *Science* v356 no6343 p1168 Je 16 2017
Multipotent peripheral glial cells generate neuroendocrine cells of the adrenal medulla color *Science* v357 no6346 p46 Jl 7 2017

Ernst & Young LLP
WORKING MOTHERS OF THE YEAR 2017 *Working Mother* v40 no4 p82 O/N 2017

Ernst, Henriette
POWER WRAP C. WINTER color *Bloomberg Businessweek* no4505 p74 D 26 2016

ERNST, ULI
A BEELINE INTO BEE-LINING color *BioScience* v66 no10 p908 O 1 2016

Eronen, Jussi T.
Merging paleobiology with conservation biology to guide the future of terrestrial ecosystems color *Science* v355 no6325 p594 F 10 2017

Erotic art—Exhibitions
AROUND LOS ANGELES M. DURÓN bw cartoon color *ARTnews* v115 no3 p154 Fall 2016

Erotica
The Sexual Almanac *New York* v50 no12 p33 Je 12 2017

Erpenbeck, Jenny
STRANGERS AMONG US J. WOOD cartoon *New Yorker* v93 no29 p92 S 25 2017

Errata (Publishing)
Rethinking the dreaded r-word M. Enserink *Science* v356 no6342 p998 Je 9 2017
The World's Costliest Typos T. John *Time* v189 no10 p10 Mr 20 2017

Errors
See also
Common fallacies
22 AVOIDABLE ON-THE-WATER MISTAKE D. T. CLARKE *Boating World* v38 no3 p54 Mr 2017
THE FIX P. Carlsen cartoon *Old House Journal* v45 no7 p52 O 2017
Is It You? Or Your Horse? B. AVILA and J. PAULSON color *Horse & Rider* v56 no8 p44 Ag 2017
New Gaffes for the New Year color *Consumer Reports* v82 no1 p63 Ja 2017
SEATED CALF RAISE J. WUEBBEN color *Muscle & Performance* v9 no4 p13 Ap 2017
The WRONG ENVELOPE: HOW IT HAPPENED N. Sperling color *Entertainment Weekly* no1456 p46 Mr 10 2017
You Messed Up at Work. Now What? J. Thompson color *Essence*

v48 no5 p77 S 2017

Erskine, Alistair R.

How an Early Adopter of Electronic Health Records Uses Big Data *Harvard Business Review Digital Articles* p2 D 15 2016

Why This Health System Offers Refunds to Dissatisfied Patients *Harvard Business Review Digital Articles* p2 N 16 2016

Erskine, Peter, 1954-

Second Opinion J. Potter color *Downbeat* v84 no5 p53 My 2017

Ertegun, Mica

Under Mica's Spell J. REGINATO color *Vanity Fair* v59 no6 p116 My 2017

Ertman, Martha

Do You Know Who Holds Your Office Together? *Harvard Business Review Digital Articles* p2 S 23 2015

Reclassifying Office "Housework" *Harvard Business Review Digital Articles* p2 Ag 17 2015

Ervin, Andrew

Bit by Bit: How Video Games Transformed Our World *Publishers Weekly* v264 no12 p64 Mr 20 2017

Tales of the Unhinged: The characters in these insightful stories are often unstable, possibly even deranged *New York Times Book Review* p18 Jl 30 2017

Ervin, Mike

Sending a Message to Paul Ryan *Progressive* v81 no3 p24 Mr 2017

Erwei Song

Quality management for precision medicine clinical applications: A consensus from the China Precision Medicine Clinical Research and Application Association bibl *Science* v354 no6319 p11 D 23 2016

Erwin, Jennifer A.

Intersection of diverse neuronal genomes and neuropsychiatric disease: The Brain Somatic Mosaicism Network color *Science* v356 no6336 p395 Ap 28 2017

Erwin, Tami

Employees Will Use Tools They Helped Build *Harvard Business Review Digital Articles* p3 Ap 22 2015

Erythrocytes

See also

Reticulocytes

New developments for protein quality control R. Y. Hampton and C. Dargemont diag *Science* v357 no6350 p450 Ag 4 2017

Erythroxylum

Deforestation and Coca Cultivation Rooted in Twentieth-Century Development Projects L. M. DÁVALOS, K. M. SANCHEZ et al *BioScience* v66 no11 p974 N 1 2016

Esat, Tezer M.

Deep-sea corals feel the flow bibl color *Science* v354 no6312 p550 N 4 2016

Esaulova, Ekaterina

The microbial metabolite desaminotyrosine protects from influenza through type I interferon graph *Science* v357 no6350 p498 Ag 4 2017

Esber, Dianne

Your Company Should Be Helping Customers on Social *Harvard Business Review Digital Articles* p2 Jl 15 2015

Escalade sport utility vehicle

THE ESCALADE DILEMMA A. MacKenzie color *Motor Trend* v69 no11 p120 N 2017

Escalante, Leah E.

Decoupling genetics, lineages, and microenvironment in IDH-mutant gliomas by single-cell RNA-seq diag *Science* v355 no6332 p1391 Mr 31 2017

Escalante River (Utah)

out alive: capsized J. Vonesh color *Backpacker* p39 S 2017

Escape at Dannemora (TV program)

Ben Stiller's True Crime J. McGovern color *Entertainment Weekly* no1486 p50 O 13 2017

Escape behavior in animals

On the trail of the Nance County bear E. Schwartz cartoon *Nebraska Life* v20 no6 p16 N/D 2016

Escape sport utility vehicle—Evaluation

Ford Escape chart color *Motor Trend* v69 no1 p46 Ja 2017

Escaped prisoners

THE ACCIDENTAL GETAWAY DRIVER P. KIX cartoon color *GQ: Gentlemen's Quarterly* v97 no5 p110 My 2017

Escarpment Blues (Music)

The Great Canadian Song Map: Road Trip Edition H. WILSON color map *Canadian Geographic* v137 no4 p32 Jl/Ag 2017

Eschatology

See also

Future life

Kingdom of God

Who is Jesus for Muslims? A. Frykholm *Christian Century* v134 no12 p32 Je 7 2017

Escherichia coli

Biased partitioning of the multidrug efflux pump AcrAB-TolC underlies long-lived phenotypic heterogeneity T. Bergmiller, A. M. C. Andersson et al diag *Science* v356 no6335 p311 Ap 21 2017

Host cell attachment elicits posttranscriptional regulation in infecting enteropathogenic bacteria N. Katsowich, N. Elbaz et al bibl graph *Science* v355 no6326 p735 F 17 2017

Kinetics of dCas9 target search in Escherichia coli D. Lawson Jones, P. Leroy et al diag *Science* v357 no6358 p1420 S 29 2017

Superbug Arrives in the U.S M. BARNA color *Discover* v38 no1 p41 Ja/F 2017

Escobar, C. O.

Observation of a large-scale anisotropy in the arrival directions of cosmic rays above 8×10^{18} eV *Science* v357 no6357 p1266 S 22 2017

Escobar, Herton

Brazil's 'doomsday' scenario color *Science* v355 no6323 p334 Ja 27 2017

Escobar, Ticio

THE CLEARING *Film Quarterly* v70 no4 p65 Summ 2017

Escobedo, Ernesto

American Voices Ernesto Escobedo J. Lisanti and T. Keith color *Sports Illustrated* v126 no12 p18 My 1 2017

Escola, Cole

Wigstock M. Schulman cartoon *New Yorker* v93 no28 p10 S 18 2017

ESCOYNE, COURTNEY

Between the Idea and the Reality: Inside a rehearsal of Daniil Simkin's Rotunda Project *Dance Magazine* v91 no9 p37 S 2017

In the Kitchen with James Whiteside *Dance Magazine* v91 no6 p44 Je 2017

Making His Own Rules *Dance Magazine* v90 no11 p37 N 2016

The MOST INFLUENTIAL PEOPLE IN DANCE TODAY: THE MOVERS, SHAKERS AND CHANGEMAKERS HAVING THE BIGGEST IMPACT ON DANCE RIGHT NOW *Dance Magazine* v91 no7 p27 Jl 2017

What's Not Okay to Ask a Dancer to Do? *Dance Magazine* v91 no4 p31 Ap 2017

Esden, Pat

Reach for You: Dark Heart, Book 3 *Publishers Weekly* v264 no18 p44 My 1 2017

Eshel, Neir

Trial and error bibl graph *Science* v354 no6316 p1108 D 2 2016

Eshleman, James R.

Mismatch repair deficiency predicts response of solid tumors to PD-1 blockade chart graph *Science* v357 no6349 p409 Jl 28 2017

Esker, Fritz

April Events color *New Orleans Magazine* v51 no6 p26 Ap 2017

August Events color *New Orleans Magazine* v51 no10 p38 Ag 2017

CALENDAR *New Orleans Magazine* v51 no4 p26 F 2017

C.C. Lockwood color *Louisiana Life* v37 no3 p62 Ja/F 2017

Coach Ed Orgeron color *Louisiana Life* v37 no3 p66 Ja/F 2017

DIABETES AWARENESS color *Louisiana Life* v37 no2 p12 N/D 2016

Dr. Larry Hollier color *Louisiana Life* v37 no3 p64 Ja/F 2017

Enter Here: Easy, routine TLC for your doors and windows *New Orleans Homes & Lifestyles* v20 no4 p98 Aut 2017

EYE OF THE BEHOLDER color *Louisiana Life* v37 no4 p10 Mr/Ap 2017

February Events color *New Orleans Magazine* v51 no4 p26 F 2017

FIVE FACTS: STROKE *Louisiana Life* v37 no5 p12 My/Je 2017

FUN! FOOD! FEST! [Cover story] color *New Orleans Magazine* v52 no1 p66 S 2017

HAPPY (HEALTHY) TRAILS *Louisiana Life* v37 no6 p11 Jl/Ag

2017

HEART HEALTH color *Louisiana Life* v37 no3 p10 Ja/F 2017

LIVING WELL color *Louisiana Life* v37 no2 p76 N/D 2016

L. Kasimu Harris color *Louisiana Life* v37 no3 p60 Ja/F 2017

LOCA VORE *Louisiana Life* v38 no1 p14 S/O 2017

March Events color *New Orleans Magazine* v51 no5 p26 Mr 2017

October color *New Orleans Magazine* v51 no12 p28 O 2017

OUR TOP PICKS color *New Orleans Magazine* v51 no2 p28 D 2016

September color *New Orleans Magazine* v52 no1 p26 S 2017

TOP PICKS color *New Orleans Magazine* v51 no8 p28 Je 2017

TORUK: The First Flight color *New Orleans Magazine* v51 no4 p27 F 2017

Esmail, Sam

Haute News color *Vanity Fair* v59 no7 p42 Summ 2017

Esmark, Carol

Your In-Store Customers Want More Privacy *Harvard Business Review Digital Articles* p2 D 28 2016

Esolen, Anthony

More hyperbole for the culture wars A. Uelmen *America* v216 no10 p48 My 1 2017

Esophagogastric junction

Problem Solved: Heartburn R. LALIBERTE *Prevention* v69 no8 p22 Ag 2017

Esophagus—Diseases

See also

Deglutition disorders

Gastroesophageal reflux

How to Deal with Choke H. W. Werner color *Dressage Today* v23 no8 p18 Ap 2017

Espada, Daniel

Additional Park and Recreation Mapping and Data Resources: A variety of tools to help in planning a new facility or assessing a community's recreation needs *Parks & Recreation* v52 no8 p12 Ag 2017

Espada, João Carlos, 1955-

Stand on Tradition M. BLITZ color *Weekly Standard* v22 no27 p38 Mr 20 2017

Espadanal, J.

Observation of a large-scale anisotropy in the arrival directions of cosmic rays above 8 × 1018 eV *Science* v357 no6357 p1266 S 22 2017

Espadrilles

Go everywhere in espadrilles color *Redbook* p45 Je 2017

JANELLE LANGFORD J. Wilson color *Essence* v48 no2 p26 Je 2017

Espadrilles—Evaluation

17 Ways to... SLAY SUMMER STYLE color *Seventeen* v76 no3 p32 My 2017

España, Carla

BILINGUAL MATTERS color *Literacy Today (2411-7862)* v34 no3 p26 N/D 2016

ESPARZA, BILL

Soak It Up *Los Angeles Magazine* v61 no11 p129 N 2016

SOME LIKE IT HOT *Los Angeles Magazine* p64 Mr 2017

Esparza, Gabriela

backstory color *New Republic* v248 no7 p68 Jl 2017

Esparza, Rafa

The One and Only Hillary Clinton Whitney Biennial J. SALTZ img *New York* v50 no6 p82 Mr 20 2017

Rafa Esparza E. Lyle color *Art in America* v105 no4 p23 Ap 2017

Esparza, Raúl, 1970-

Law & Order: SVU I. Rudolph *TV Guide* v65 no21 p39 My 15 2017

Espinosa, Patricia

Dealing with details in Marrakesh color *Science* v354 no6311 p393 O 28 2016

ESPINOSA, RAMON

Home Alone color *Nation* v305 no11 p13 O 30 2017

Espinosa Medina, I.

The sacral autonomic outflow is sympathetic bibl color diag *Science* v354 no6314 p893 N 18 2016

Espinoza, Erick

NEXT WAVE: Bright Young Thing color *House Beautiful* v159 no9 p39 N 2017

Espinoza, Mariana

Super Summer Chefs *Parks & Recreation* v51 no10 p56 O 2016

ESPINOZA, ROBERT E.

Teaching Biology in the Field: Importance, Challenges, and Solutions *BioScience* v67 no6 p558 Je 2017

Espionage

Everyday Business Travelers Are Easy Targets for Espionage L. Bencie *Harvard Business Review Digital Articles* p2 N 10 2015

Free Radical N. Heller color *Vogue* v207 no9 p714 S 2017

GLEANINGS *Christianity Today* p18 Ap 2017

How an Airplane Laptop Ban Would Expose Company Data to Espionage L. Bencie *Harvard Business Review Digital Articles* p2 My 25 2017

The Ministry of Preemption J. BAMFORD color *Foreign Policy* no224 p78 My/Je 2017

Uber, But for Melt downs: Sexual harassment, corporate-espionage charges, taking advantage of drivers: The company that practically courts bad PR has an even greater, more existential dilemma R. Wiedeman img *New York* v50 no11 p34 My 29 2017

Espionage—China

I-Spy in China: a revival of Mao-era paranoia? V. Yu color *America* v216 no12 p16 My 29 2017

Espionage—Equipment & supplies

A BRIEF HISTORY OF SURVEILLANCE color *Atlantic* v318 no4 p34 N 2016

Espionage—History—Charts, diagrams, etc.

A BRIEF HISTORY OF SURVEILLANCE color *Atlantic* v318 no4 p34 N 2016

Espionage—United States

Foreign Intrigue color *Weekly Standard* v23 no5 p3 O 9 2017

The NSA's foreign surveillance: 5 things to know G. GROSS color *PCWorld* v35 no4 p37 Ap 2017

ESPN (Television network)

CRASH COURSE L. MURROW cartoon *Wired* v25 no6 p24 Je 2017

NFL DRAFT T. WORGO *TV Guide* p48 Ap 17 2017

Political Hardball color *Weekly Standard* v22 no34 p34 p3 My 15 2017

ESPN Inc.—Finance

GOT ANY IDEAS? [Cover story] I. BOUDWAY and M. CHAFKIN color graph *Bloomberg Businessweek* no4517 p48 Ap 3 2017

Esports

COLLEGES RECRUIT A NEW KIND OF ATHLETE: VIDEO GAMERS C. Morris color *Fortune* v176 no5 p23 O 1 2017

Gamer Shape S. Apstein and T. Keith color *Sports Illustrated* v127 no6 p18 Ag 28 2017

HOT | NOT T. Keith color *Sports Illustrated* v125 no21 p24 D 26 2016

Japan Isn't Getting Its Share Of Gaming Gold Yuji Nakamura and Takako Taniguchi bw color *Bloomberg Businessweek* no4539 p23 S 25 2017

ESPOSITO, CAMERON

These Are Your Sexual Rights color *Glamour* v114 no7 p94 Jl 2016

Esposito, Cameron, 1981—Interviews

In Search Of Girls town? Keep on Looking M. WAKIM *Los Angeles Magazine* v62 no6 p83 Je 2017

Esposito, Giancarlo

RETURN OF THE KINGPIN D. Snierson color *Entertainment Weekly* no1462 p54 Ap 21 2017

Esposito, Giancarlo—Interviews

Lord of the Fring img *New York* v50 no6 p76 Mr 20 2017

Esposito, Jennifer, 1972-

Jennifer's Way Kitchen color *Publishers Weekly* v264 no38 p65 S 18 2017

Esposito, Mark

Companies Are Working with Consumers to Reduce Waste *Harvard Business Review Digital Articles* p2 Je 7 2016

How Businesses Can Support a Circular Economy *Harvard Business Review Digital Articles* p2 F 1 2016

Esposito, Paolo

An accreting pulsar with extreme properties drives an ultraluminous x-ray source in NGC 5907 bibl chart graph *Science* v355 no6327 p817 F 24 2017

ESPOZ, JUSTINE BAYOD

Defying Tradition *Dance Magazine* v90 no11 p58 N 2016

Espree Animal Products Inc.

Holidays GIFTS in Every Price Range V. Green-Gott color *Practical Horseman* v45 no11 p56 N 2017

Esqueda, Sarah

Sarah Esqueda G. DEARTH *Arabian Horse World* v57 no1 p65 O 2016

ESSA, SAMAN

The Power of Faith: Muslim Houstonians welcome ISNA with flair *Islamic Horizons* v46 no3 p20 My/Je 2017

Essay (Literary form)

Black Like Me J. Sexton *Harper's Magazine* p2 S 2017

THE SHAMING OF THE SHREW D. Ugrešić *Harper's Magazine* v334 no2000 p23 Ja 2017

Writer's Seat A. FERGUSON bw color *Weekly Standard* v23 no1 p30 S 11 2017

Essay (Literary form)—Collections

Skeptics' Odysseys and Star Trek's Voyages K. FRAZIER *Skeptical Inquirer* v40 no6 p4 N/D 2016

Essayists

Eve Ewing H. NYHART color *Chicago* v66 no6 p82 Je 2017

Louis Menand C. Lambert *Humanities* v37 no4 p1 Fall 2016

Thoreau and the Legacy of Wilderness D. Brinkley *New York Times Book Review* p12 Jl 9 2017

What to Make of T. S. Eliot? G. Davis *Humanities* v37 no4 p1 Fall 2016

Essayists—Interviews

The problem with men A. KINGSTON color *Maclean's* v130 no3 p66 Ap 2017

Essel, Elena

Neandertal and Denisovan DNA from Pleistocene sediments bw color *Science* v356 no6338 p605 My 12 2017

ESSELSTYN, JACOB

Transformational Principles for NEON Sampling of Mammalian Parasites and Pathogens: A Response to Springer and Colleagues *BioScience* v66 no11 p917 N 1 2016

Esseltine, Jessica L.

Local protein kinase A action proceeds through intact holoenzymes color diag graph *Science* v356 no6344 p1288 Je 23 2017

Essences & essential oils

See also

Perfumes

congrats, you just found time for a pedicure! M. MATTHEWS BROWN color *Parents* v92 no6 p84 Je 2017

Consider This color *Yoga Journal* no290 p14 Mr 2017

EXOTIC OILS [Cover story] L. Turner color *Amazing Wellness* v9 no6 p82 EarlyWint 2017

Healing stones Y. M. Alpert color *Yoga Journal* no295 p24 O 2017

the health nut A. Brightfield cartoon *Better Homes & Gardens* v95 no4 p150 Ap 2017

Keeping It Fresh color *Better Nutrition* v79 no3 p22 Mr 2017

Plant Oils: Are They All Good for You? V. TWEED color *Better Nutrition* v79 no4 p72 Ap 2017

Power Tools: Titans C. Alter color *Time* v189 no16/17 p118 My 1-8 2017

QUICK FIXES J. Rice color *Amazing Wellness* v8 no2 p40 Spr 2016

SOMETHING IN THE AIR R. MONROE bw cartoon *New Yorker* v93 no31 p32 O 9 2017

Essences & essential oils industry

SOMETHING IN THE AIR R. MONROE bw cartoon *New Yorker* v93 no31 p32 O 9 2017

Essences & essential oils—Evaluation

5 beauty tricks I just learned V. Kirby bw color *Redbook* p43 Jl/ Ag 2017

Absolutely Essential S. Strausfogel color *Amazing Wellness* v9 no1 p74 Wint 2017

Eau So DELICATE color *O, The Oprah Magazine* p68 S 2017

How to Smell Like a Wild Man D. MICHEL color *Men's Health* v32 no9 p78 N 2017

Essences & essential oils—Research

An Essential Weapon against Pollution color *Prevention* v68 no12 p11 D 2016

Essences & essential oils—Therapeutic use

See also

Aromatherapy

Absolutely Essential S. Strausfogel color *Amazing Wellness* v9 no1 p74 Wint 2017

Esser, Duane

CONFORMATION CLINIC color *Horse & Rider* v56 no3 p29 Mr 2017

ESSER, MELISSA

Excess Gas in a Horse With Heaves *Horse & Rider* v55 no11 p14 N 2016

Essex, Andrew

Advertising Is Dead; Long Live Advertising S. Begley color *Time* v190 no1 p18 Jl 3 2017

Essick, Peter

OH, CANADA! T. MALONE *Atlanta* v56 no11 p36 Mr 2017

Essie (Company)

Perfectly quiet polishes color *Redbook* p35 O 2017

ESSL, FRANZ

Scientific and Normative Foundations for the Valuation of Alien-Species Impacts: Thirteen Core Principles *BioScience* v67 no2 p166 F 2017

Essletzbichler, Patrick

Nucleic acid detection with CRISPR-Cas13a/C2c2 color diag *Science* v356 no6336 p438 Ap 28 2017

Essmann, Jeffrey

Where and who you are color *U.S. Catholic* v82 no1 p12 Ja 2017

ESSWEIN, PATRICIA MERTZ

The Beckers Make Their Move color *Kiplinger's Personal Finance* v70 no12 p72 D 2016

Best Places to Retire [Cover story] color *Kiplinger's Personal Finance* v71 no8 p56 Ag 2017

Betting on the Texas (Olive) Oil Boom color *Kiplinger's Personal Finance* v71 no10 p22 O 2017

Boomers Go Bionic color *Kiplinger's Personal Finance* v71 no5 p64 My 2017

Can Tidying Up Change Your Life? cartoon *Kiplinger's Personal Finance* v71 no7 p39 Jl 2017

Crafting Down-Home Brews color *Kiplinger's Personal Finance* v71 no2 p25 F 2017

Downsize Your Stuff cartoon *Kiplinger's Personal Finance* v71 no7 p36 Jl 2017

Finding the Green in Your Junk color *Kiplinger's Personal Finance* v71 no4 p14 Ap 2017

Fix-Ups Buyers Will Love chart color *Kiplinger's Personal Finance* v71 no3 p41 Mr 2017

For the Man Who Has Everything color *Kiplinger's Personal Finance* v70 no12 p22 D 2016

Get the Scoop in Seattle cartoon color *Kiplinger's Personal Finance* v71 no7 p22 Jl 2017

Headshots Are Their Gig color *Kiplinger's Personal Finance* v71 no6 p24 Je 2017

Her Headphones Lull You to Sleep color *Kiplinger's Personal Finance* v71 no3 p17 Mr 2017

Home Prices Keep Climbing cartoon chart *Kiplinger's Personal Finance* v71 no4 p40 Ap 2017

MORTGAGE HELP FOR DEBT-SADDLED GRADS color graph *Kiplinger's Personal Finance* v71 no8 p15 Ag 2017

MORTGAGE OUTLOOK: MOSTLY GOOD NEWS color *Kiplinger's Personal Finance* v71 no1 p14 Ja 2017

An Old Game Gets a Do-Over color *Kiplinger's Personal Finance* v71 no8 p20 Ag 2017

Renovations Done Right color *Kiplinger's Personal Finance* v71 no11 p64 N 2017

Sharing a Taste of the South color *Kiplinger's Personal Finance* v71 no5 p16 My 2017

She Helps Launch Future Leaders color *Kiplinger's Personal Finance* v71 no12 p18 D 2017

A Smarter Way to Heat and Cool Your Home color *Kiplinger's Personal Finance* v70 no12 p39 D 2016

Use Your Home to Get More Income [Cover story] color graph *Kiplinger's Personal Finance* v71 no10 p38 O 2017

Using Tech to Feed Hungry People color *Kiplinger's Personal Finance* v71 no1 p22 Ja 2017

Estalrrich, Almudena

The growth pattern of Neandertals, reconstructed from a juvenile skeleton from El Sidrón (Spain) color graph *Science* v357 no6357 p1282 S 22 2017

Estate planning

See also

Insurance

Estate Planning for Snowbirds K. LANKFORD *Kiplinger's Personal Finance* v71 no4 p49 Ap 2017

Financial Life J. Dobbs color *Missouri Life* v44 no6 p78 S 2017

PROBLEM: AFTER TRYING TO GET FAMILY INVOLVEMENT WITH OUR ESTATE PLANNING, EVERYTHING HAS TURNED BITTER, AND WE STILL DON'T HAVE A PLAN IN PLACE M. Friesen *Successful Farming* v115 no6 p66 Ap 2017

THE PROBLEM M. Friesen *Successful Farming* v115 no2 p68 F 2017

Estate planning—United States

CREATE AN ESTATE DIRECTORY: HAVING IMPORTANT INFORMATION IN ONE PLACE IS A GIFT TO HEIRS L. F. Prater *Successful Farming* v115 no9 p66 Ag 2017

Estates (Law)

How to Talk About Getting a Will K. A. Renzulli color *Money* v46 no6 p20 Jl 2017

Unequal Treatment color *Money* v46 no2 p22 Mr 2017

Estates (Law)—Lawsuits & claims

GHOST LAWYER D. Leonard color *Bloomberg Businessweek* no4510 p42 F 6 2017

Estates (Law)—Management

Where Dead Celebrities Go to Live L. Coleman-Lochner cartoon color *Bloomberg Businessweek* no4530 p16 Jl 17 2017

Esteban, Ruben

Single-molecule optomechanics in "picocavities" bibl graph *Science* v354 no6313 p726 N 11 2016

Estée Lauder Cos. Inc.

Find Your Celeb SCENTSPIRATION K. FOSTER color diag *Seventeen* v75 no11 p48 N 2016

It's not an HR thing - it's a business thing C. NFWRFRY *People Management* p20 F 2017

Northern Exposure K. MOLVAR color *Vogue* v207 no11 p152 N 2017

Estefan, Emily

Music Royalty's Next Generation E. R. Brown color *Entertainment Weekly* no1457/1458 p96 Mr 17 2017

Esterling, Kevin M.

The need for a translational science of democracy bibl color *Science* v355 no6328 p914 Mr 3 2017

ESTEROW, MILTON

THE MODIGLIANI CODE bw color *Vanity Fair* v59 no6 p110 My 2017

Palazzo Intrigue bw color *Vanity Fair* v59 no2 p90 F 2017

Esters

See also

Pyrethroids

A general, modular method for the catalytic asymmetric synthesis of alkylboronate esters J. Schmidt, Junwon Choi et al bibl color *Science* v354 no6317 p1265 D 9 2016

Estes, Cary

SOUTH'S BEST TAILGATE color *Southern Living* v52 no4 p98 Ap 2017

ESTES, DOUGLAS

THE LINGUISTIC ORIGINS OF THE QUESTION color *Christianity Today* v61 no7 p64 S 2017

Estes, Emily

Minerals Made by Microbes color *Oceanus* v51 no2 p72 Wint 2016

ESTES, JAMES A.

Conserving the World's Megafauna and Biodiversity: The Fierce Urgency of Now *BioScience* v67 no3 p197 Mr 2017

Saving the World's Terrestrial Megafauna color *BioScience* v66 no10 p807 O 1 2016

We Need a Biologically Sound North American Conservation Plan *BioScience* v67 no8 p685 Ag 2017

Estes, Tim

Wall Street's Robocop A. GARA and J. OBERWEIS color *Forbes* v199 no6 p62 Je 13 2017

Estes Park (Colo.)

BEST IN TRAVEL 2017 K. A. Renzulli, M. Leonhardt et al color *Money* v46 no3 p58 Ap 2017

WEEKEND GETAWAYS L. BLEIBERG cartoon *Better Homes & Gardens* v95 no7 p170 Jl 2017

Esteves, José

Meet the Teenagers Who Found Their Own Startups *Harvard Business Review Digital Articles* p2 D 5 2016

ESTÉVEZ, RODRIGO A.

Scientific and Normative Foundations for the Valuation of Alien-Species Impacts: Thirteen Core Principles *BioScience* v67 no2 p166 F 2017

Esther, Charles R.

Emergence and spread of a human-transmissible multidrug-resistant nontuberculous mycobacterium bibl diag graph *Science* v354 no6313 p751 N 11 2016

Estheticians (Skin care)

Beauty Adventures in Japan color *Glamour* no8 p90 Ag 2017

Estill, Jim

CENTURY marks cartoon *Christian Century* v134 no2 p8 Ja 18 2017

Estonia—Description & travel

ESTONIA *New York Times Magazine* p48 S 24 2017

Estonia—Social conditions—1991-

WELCOME TO TOMORROW LAND V. Walt color map *Fortune* v175 no6 p60 My 1 2017

Estrabao, Sinuhe

From Cuba, With Dreams E. Hayasaki bw *Glamour* v115 no5 p176 My 2017

ESTRADA, ANDREA

Does Pride Goeth Before...? *USA Today Magazine* v146 no2868 p27 S 2017

Estrada, Diego

American Dreamer C. KUZMA color *Runner's World* v52 no5 p47 Je 2017

Estrogen

Do You Have PERIOD BRAIN? L. SAXTON color *Seventeen* v76 no3 p66 My 2017

KNOW YOUR FLOW: A USER'S MANUAL H. Levine color *Health* v31 no3 p75 Ap 2017

KNOW YOUR MIGRAINE TRIGGERS A. Reliford color *Good Housekeeping* v265 no4 p88 O 2017

Estrogen receptors

PI3K pathway regulates ER-dependent transcription in breast cancer through the epigenetic regulator KMT2D E. Toska, H. U. Osmanbeyoglu et al bibl graph *Science* v355 no6331 p1324 Mr 24 2017

Estrogen replacement therapy

BIRTH CONTROL UPDATE. A USER'S MANUAL H. Levine color *Health* v31 no6 p95 Jl 2017

Estuaries

A new angle on streams color *Science* v355 no6331 p1278 Mr 24 2017

Estuarine ecology

The Otter, the Salmon, and the Bittern C. K. LONGSTRETH color *Natural History* v125 no4 p18 Ap 2017

The Water Keeper's Dilemma L. POPPICK *Audubon* v119 no3 p10 Fall 2017

Esvelt, Kevin M.

Precaution: Open gene drive research bibl *Science* v355 no6325 p589 F 10 2017

Unnatural Responsibilities color *Scientific American* v316 no4 p50 Ap 2017

Eswine, Zack

HOW TO PREACH AND TEACH THE OLD TESTAMENT FOR ALL ITS WORTH color *Christianity Today* v61 no1 p53 Ja/F 2017

Etchegoyen, A.

Observation of a large-scale anisotropy in the arrival directions of cosmic rays above 8×10^{18} eV *Science* v357 no6357 p1266 S 22 2017

Etching

Fore Shadowing K. Homma bw *Christian Century* v133 no24 p47 N 23 2016

Etching—Exhibitions

Darker Horizon J. GARDNER color *Weekly Standard* v22 no28 p41 Mr 27 2017

Etchings in Amber (Music)

NATALIE CRESSMAN & MIKE BONO K. Micallef color *Downbeat* v84 no1 p24 Ja 2017

Eternity

From Eternity To Here S. Rushin color *Sports Illustrated* v126 no10 p80 Ap 10 2017

Ethanol

A 9,000-Year Love Affair A. Curry cartoon color graph map *National Geographic* v231 no2 p30 F 2017

Ethanol—Environmental aspects

Why-o-fuel? D. Slater *Sierra* v102 no1 p20 Ja/F 2017

Ethanol—Law & legislation

A Low Blow In the Corn Belt M. Parker color map *Bloomberg Businessweek* no4532 p40 Jl 31 2017

Ethanol—Sales & prices

ETHANOL UNEASE ALTHOUGH OUTPUT IS SETTING RECORDS *Successful Farming* v115 no2 p13 F 2017

Ethelred II, King of England, ca. 968-1016

READY TO RULE L. Roach *History Today* v67 no5 p24 My 2017

ETHERINGTON-SMITH, MEREDITH

Gothic Revival color *Architectural Digest* v73 no11 p152 N 2016

Ethernet (Local area network system)

Configure a Time Capsule as an ethernet-only storage device G. Fleishman color diag *Macworld - Digital Edition* p122 Ap 2017

Ethical investments

The Challenge of Socially Responsible Investing T. Tepper color diag *Money* v46 no7 p31 Ag 2017

TIMES CHANGE, BUT 'GREEN' FUNDS KEEP GROWING C. Taylor color diag *Fortune* v176 no4 p48 S 15 2017

Ethicists

Baptist ethicist and commentator dies at age 63 A. M. Banks *Christian Century* v134 no8 p1 Ap 12 2017

Ethics

See also

Business ethics

Conduct of life

Confidence

Conflict of interests

Corruption

Humanity

Immorality

Justice

Power (Philosophy)

Probabilism

Professional ethics

Reputation (Sociology)

Student ethics

War & ethics

Work ethic

Code of the West, History vs. Hollywood R. Soodalter cartoon *American Cowboy* v24 no1 p22 Je/Jl 2017

CORRUPTION SET IN CONCRETE HARDING *USA Today Magazine* v145 no2860 p26 Ja 2017

Cultivate a steady mind color *Yoga Journal* p94 2016 Special Issue

David, We Hardly Knew Ye M. Y. SOLOVEICHIK *Commentary* v144 no1 p11 Jl/Ag 2017

Does Confining Deplorable Remarks to Your Home Make Them All Right? K. A. Appiah *New York Times Magazine* p28 Ap 23 2017

The Ethicist K. A. Appiah *New York Times Magazine* p22 S 3 2017

Ethics Allegations Will Hurt White House Staffers Even If They Turn Out to Be False K. B. DeTienne bw *Harvard Business Review Digital Articles* p1 Je 2 2017

High Horses J. Coaston *New York Times Magazine* p9 Ag 13 2017

In Arms Sales We Trust U. ABDULLAH *Islamic Horizons* v46 no1 p58 Ja/F 2017

Introduction: Into the aftermath J. Mecklin *Bulletin of the Atomic Scientists* v73 no4 p210 Jl 2017

Mutt Morality: DOGS KNOW HOW TO HAVE FUN, AND ENCODED IN THEIR ANTICS IS A DEEP UNDERSTANDING OF FAIR PLAY M. BEKOFF *Psychology Today* v50 no5 p77 S/O 2017

Organize a Moral Resistance A. NABAUM *New Republic* v248 no3 p36 Mr 2017

Seeing Both Sides A. Engel *Publishers Weekly* v264 no10 p64 Mr 6 2017

Should I Tell Someone That His Father-in-Law Is a Child Molester? K. A. Appiah *New York Times Magazine* p22 Jl 9 2017

WHAT CAN I DO? GLOBAL WARMING SEEMS MORE LIKE A MORAL ISSUE IF WE FEEL WE CAN FIGHT IT L. MC-CAFFREY *Psychology Today* v50 no3 p16 My/Je 2017

What I Wish I'd Known A. D. Barnett bw color *Glamour* v115 no11 p138 N 2017

What Should I Do About A Co-Worker Who Drinks On the Job? K. A. Appiah *New York Times Magazine* p18 F 5 2017

When politics trumps faith F. P. Keller color *U.S. Catholic* v81 no11 p23 N 2016

ETHIER, JEAN-MICHEL

POSTHOLE color *Powder* v46 no2 p94 O 2017

Ethington, Tommie

Deep in the Heart color *American Cowboy* v23 no6 p24 Ap/My 2017

ETHIOPIA—Description & travel

ETHIOPIA A. POSTMAN color *Conde Nast Traveler* v52 no4 p36 Ap 2017

Ethiopian cooking

Bunna Café N. Niarchos color *New Yorker* v93 no6 p13 Mr 27 2017

Ethiopia—Social conditions—1974-

Wave of Unrest Crashes on Ethiopia T. John color *Time* v188 no15 p6 O 17 2016

Ethnic conflict

backstory color *New Republic* v248 no11 p68 N 2017

Ethnic discrimination

Are you a spy? A. ABEL color *Maclean's* v130 no7 p46 Ag 2017

Ethnic foods

Keep Your Hands Off Our Collards T. R. TOWNSEND and D. POINTDUJOUR color *Ebony* v72 no4 p60 F 2017

Ethnic groups

See also

African Americans

Asians

Indigenous peoples

GENEALOGY BUG BITE: Alt-facts, fake news, obsession and wasted days in the land of the dead R. NELSON *Virginia Living* v15 no4 p112 Je 2017

Ethnic groups—United States

Gender Can Be a Bigger Factor than Race in Raise Negotiations K. Jones *Harvard Business Review Digital Articles* p2 S 1 2016

Ethnic neighborhoods—United States

Ben Carson Is Right H. Husock *Commentary* v143 no3 p34 Mr 2017

Ethnic restaurants

See also

Japanese restaurants

Korean restaurants

Thai restaurants

Vietnamese restaurants

Majestic Baja P. KUH *Los Angeles Magazine* v62 no6 p36 Je 2017

NORTHERN VIRGINIA *Virginia Living* p86 2017 Best 20of Virginia

The Pita Rising P. KUH *Los Angeles Magazine* v62 no6 p42 Je 2017

UPTOWN J. REESE cartoon color *Chicago* v66 no5 p37 My 2017

Ethnic restaurants—Evaluation

5 More Asian-Style Starts *Los Angeles Magazine* p110 Ap 2017

5 More Morning Mezes J. LURIE *Los Angeles Magazine* p108 Ap 2017

Ballymaloe House, County Cork, Ireland D. PRIOR color *Conde Nast Traveler* v52 no2 p46 F 2017

BELOVED BACKWARDNESS E. S. ARNARSDÓTTIR *Iceland Review* v55 no1 p38 Ja/F 2017

THE DINING GUIDE *Atlanta* v56 no8 p189 D 2016

FRESH ON THE SCENE C. LAUTERBACH *Atlanta* v56 no8 p80 D 2016

THE HOT LIST *Los Angeles Magazine* p116 Ag 2017

LATE NIGHT *Atlanta* v56 no12 p81 Ap 2017

NOON *Atlanta* v56 no12 p74 Ap 2017

Restaurant GUIDE *Indianapolis Monthly* v12 no40 p178 Ag 2017

RESTAURANTS E. S. ARNARSDÓTTIR color *Iceland Review* v54 no5 p113 S-O 2016

Spice Island J. DRILLING *Cincinnati Magazine* v50 no3 p130 D 2016

TAPABAR A. Limpert *Washingtonian Magazine* v52 no2 p259 N 2017

Ethnicity in music

THE MUSIC ISSUE N. Abebe color *New York Times Magazine*

p16 Mr 12 2017

Ethnikē Trapeza tēs Hellados—Finance

Greece's Oldest Bank Sets the Benchmark color *Foreign Affairs* v96 no3 p86d My/Je 2017

Ethnocentrism

See also

Racism

Move with God K. P. Considine color *U.S. Catholic* v82 no2 p36 F 2017

Ethnology

See also

Acculturation

Blacks

Ethnic groups

Hunting & gathering societies

Indigenous peoples

Kinship

Language & languages

Manners & customs

Tattooing

Whites

Use Your Customers as Ethnographers J. W. Schlack *Harvard Business Review Digital Articles* p2 Ag 17 2015

ETHRIDGE, LESLIE

THE THING THAT CHANGED IT ALL color *Bicycling* v58 no10 p13 N/D 2017

Ethylene

See also

Polyethylene

Ethylene J. Kaskey and L. Doan color *Bloomberg Businessweek* no4537 p21 S 11 2017

Etihad Airways PJSC—Finance

Long Reach, Big Problems C. Jasper and D. K. Yousef bw *Bloomberg Businessweek* no4523 p22 My 22 2017

Etiology of Alzheimer's disease

Solving the Alzheimer's PUZZLE K. Hobson color *O, The Oprah Magazine* p70 Je 2017

Etiquette

See also

Business etiquette

Compliments

Conversation

Courtesy

Dating (Social customs)

Dinners & dining

Etiquette for women

Hospitality

Salutations

The 10 Simple Rules of Gym Etiquette M. ZIMMERMAN cartoon *Men's Health* v32 no9 p46 N 2017

COMMON SENSE AND THE GOLDEN RULE GO A LONG WAY D. HISLOP *Sea Magazine* v109 no1 p46 Ja 2017

First-Name Basis J. EPSTEIN cartoon *Weekly Standard* v22 no18 p5 Ja 16 2017

GOLDEN OLDIES *O, The Oprah Magazine* p98 Ap 2017

Gracious Guests N. B. McGough and P. S. York color *Southern Living* v52 no11 p47 N 2017

KINDER, GENTLER cartoon *O, The Oprah Magazine* p96 Ap 2017

Technology and Decorum inside the Mosque S. MUBARAK *Islamic Horizons* v46 no1 p52 Ja/F 2017

What I Know for Sure Oprah color *O, The Oprah Magazine* p140 Ap 2017

WOULDN'T IT BE NICE? L. SCHILLINGER cartoon *O, The Oprah Magazine* p98 Ap 2017

Etiquette for women

A guide to modern manners color *Redbook* p136 N 2017

Etiquette—Study & teaching

That's Outrageous! color *Reader's Digest* v189 no1131 p84 Je 2017

Etkin, Jordan

When Multitasking Makes You Happy and When It Doesn't *Harvard Business Review Digital Articles* p2 F 26 2015

ETKIND, ALEXANDER

Who's to Blame for Putinism? *Current History* v115 no783 p280 O 2016

Eton (Company)

Beyond Basic T. Patterson bw color *Bloomberg Businessweek* no4541 p64 O 9 2017

Etsy Inc.

Arts and Crafts L. RASKIN *Architectural Record* v204 no10 p37 O 2016

The ETSY Effect L. REGENSDORF and C. ELLENBERG color *Vogue* v207 no3 p374 Mr 2017

LEAVE my ETSY ALONE M. Chafkin and J. Cao bw color *Bloomberg Businessweek* no4523 p48 My 22 2017

Ettema, Thijs J. G.

Genomic exploration of the diversity, ecology, and evolution of the archaeal domain of life color *Science* v357 no6351 p563 Ag 11 2017

Ettenson, Richard

Does Your Company Have What It Takes to Go Global? *Harvard Business Review Digital Articles* p2 Ap 11 2016

Etter, Lauren

Another Border Clash for Trump color *Bloomberg Businessweek* no4507 p22 Ja 16 2017

Big Meat Braces for A Labor Shortage color *Bloomberg Businessweek* no4511 p19 F 13 2017

The Border Patrol Wants to Buy American color *Bloomberg Businessweek* no4497 p31 O 31 2016

ICE Agents Go From Advocate to Adversary color *Bloomberg Businessweek* no4518 p30 Ap 10 2017

More Poll Monitors May Mean More Trouble *Bloomberg Businessweek* no4495 p21 O 17 2016

North of the Border, South of the Wall color *Bloomberg Businessweek* no4518 p62 Ap 10 2017

Refugees, immigrants, expatriates. For some politicians, they're scapegoats. For Western Union, they're customers color *Bloomberg Businessweek* no4527 p74 Je 19 2017

This Deflation Has Grocers Fed Up graph *Bloomberg Businessweek* no4493 p30 O 3 2016

The Wall Needs the Consent of Many map *Bloomberg Businessweek* no4510 p13 F 6 2017

WHEN 3M BOUGHT INTO THE ANKLE MONITOR BUSINESS, IT ACQUIRED TROUBLE bw color diag graph *Bloomberg Businessweek* no4518 p44 Ap 10 2017

E.T.: The Extra-Terrestrial (Film)

OUR TOP PICKS F. ESKER color *New Orleans Magazine* v51 no3 p24 Ja 2017

What Really Happened After This Kiss in E.T.? A. Breznican and D. Coggan color *Entertainment Weekly* no1460/1461 p46 Ap 7-17 2017

Ettus, Samantha

December @ GH color *Good Housekeeping* v263 no6 p18 D 2016

Ettwiller, Laurence M.

DNA damage is a pervasive cause of sequencing errors, directly confounding variant identification bibl graph *Science* v355 no6326 p752 F 17 2017

Etwok LLC

How to use NetSpot to map out your Wi-Fi network J. BATTERSBY color *Macworld - Digital Edition* p105 F 2017

Etymology

See also

Names

IT PAYS TO INCREASE YOUR Word Power E. COX and H. RATHVON *Reader's Digest* v189 no1128 p131 Mr 2017

Etymotic Research Inc.

No More Suffering in Silence? J. Calderone color graph il *Consumer Reports* v82 no3 p15 Mr 2017

Tell It Like It Is S. Guttenberg and C. Crowley color *Sound & Vision* v81 no10 p18 D 2016

Etzioni, Amitai

Communitarian Antidotes to Populism *Society* v54 no2 p95 Ap 2017

Should Artificial Intelligence Be Regulated? *Issues in Science & Technology* v33 no4 p32 Summ 2017

We Must Not Be Enemies *American Scholar* v86 no1 p20 Wint 2017

ETZIONI, OREN

Should Artificial Intelligence Be Regulated? *Issues in Science & Technology* v33 no4 p32 Summ 2017

Eucalyptus oil

Dr. Low Dog [Cover story] T. L. Dog color *Prevention* v69 no1 p26 Ja 2017

Eucalyptus—Diseases & pests

Pathogens on the Move: A 100-Year Global Experiment with Planted Eucalypts T. I. BURGESS and M. J. WINGFIELD *BioScience* v67 no1 p14 Ja 2017

Eudy, Joshua

A Cut Above V. Paynich *Parks & Recreation* v52 no1 p56 Ja 2017

Eudyptes

When mom has favorite, blame all the swimming S. Milius color *Science News* v190 no13 p4 D 24 2016

Eugene Onegin (Theatrical production)

CLASSICAL MUSIC *New Yorker* v93 no9 p14 Ap 17 2017

Eugene Onegin W. Spiegelman and G. Barnett *Opera News* v81 no7 p34 Ja 2017

Eugenics

The eugenics movement and its impact on art education in the United States T. Hunter-Doniger bibl *Arts Education Policy Review* v118 no2 p83 2017

Eugenides, Jeffrey

THE BIG QUESTION cartoon *Atlantic* v320 no4 p124 N 2017

Eukaryotes

See also

Animals

Ancient Algae K. Moore color *Natural History* v125 no6 p6 Je 2017

Fossils contain earliest signs of shells T. SUMNER color *Science News* v190 no9 p9 O 29 2016

Intracellular innate immune surveillance devices in plants and animals J. D. G. Jones, R. E. Vance et al chart color diag graph *Science* v354 no6316 paaf6395-1 D 2 2016

Structure of the complete elongation complex of RNA polymerase II with basal factors H. Ehara, T. Yokoyama et al map *Science* v357 no6354 p921 S 1 2017

Yeast C. ENGELKING bw color *Discover* v38 no6 p74 Jl/Ag 2017

Eukaryotic cells—Genetics—Research

Yeast genome, by design K. Kannan and D. G. Gibson bibl color *Science* v355 no6329 p1024 Mr 10 2017

Eumenides, The (Play : Aeschylus)

ORIGINAL INTENT Aeschylus *Lapham's Quarterly* v10 no3 p29 Summ 2017

EUN, EUNICE

STOP THE MEETING MADNESS: HOW TO FREE UP TIME FOR MEANINGFUL WORK chart color img *Harvard Business Review* v95 no4 p62 Jl/Ag 2017

Eun-Joo Ahn

Observatories and Telescopes of Modern Times: Ground-Based Optical and Radio Astronomy Facilities Since 1945 *Physics Today* v70 no10 p64 O 2017

Eun Sung Yang

Rapid development of a DNA vaccine for Zika virus bibl graph *Science* v354 no6309 p237 O 14 2016

Eungul Lee

Positive biodiversity-productivity relationship predominant in global forests bibl chart graph map *Science* v354 no6309 paaf8957-1 O 14 2016

Eunuchs

Being trans . . V. Dzwons *Christian Century* v134 no5 p6 Mr 1 2017

Eurich, Tasha

"YOU DON'T HAVE TO PRETEND TO KNOW EVERYTHING": Organisational psychologist Dr Tasha Eurich on the power of self-awareness—and why Uber is getting it badly wrong C. NEWBERY *People Management* p40 Jl 2017

Euripides, ca. 480 B.C.-406 B.C.

438 BC: Pherae Euripides *Lapham's Quarterly* v10 no1 p126 Wint 2017

Eurocentrism

Islamism Implacable C. Hill *Hoover Digest: Research & Opinion on Public Policy* no1 p98 Wint 2017

Europa (Satellite)

Europa Geysers Point to Subsurface Ocean J. K. BEATTY *Sky & Telescope* v133 no2 p14 F 2017

SAILING EUROPA'S SEAS E. MASTROIANNI color *Discover* v38 no2 p57 Mr 2017

Europa (Satellite)—Research

Hope Springs Eternal for Easy Access to Water on Europa L. Billings color *Scientific American* v315 no6 p20 D 2016

Inside the Historic Mission to Europa E. BETZ bw color *Discover* v38 no2 p58 Mr 2017

Europe

DEEPBACKGROUND P. GIRALDI *American Conservative* v15 no6 p17 N/D 2016

Hominid roots may go back to Europe B. BOWER color *Science News* v191 no12 p9 Je 24 2017

The River Overfloweth L. SCHLEY map *Discover* v38 no10 p15 D 2017

Trepidation About Trump in Europe *USA Today Magazine* v145 no2863 p4 Ap 2017

European Commission

At 10, Europe's 'excellence' fund ponders changes K. Kupferschmidt and E. Pain color graph *Science* v355 no6329 p1002 Mr 10 2017

Europe's biodiversity avoids fatal setback A. Trouwborst, G. Chapron et al color *Science* v355 no6321 p140 Ja 13 2017

European Commission—Officials & employees

The E.U.'s Chief Executive on Trump, Populism and Russia C. McDonald-Gibson color *Time* v189 no7/8 p19 F 27 2017

European Medicines Agency

Vying for medicines agency *Science* v355 no6323 p330 Ja 27 2017

European mink

'Safe spaces' may save the European mink K. Karáth color *Science* v357 no6352 p636 Ag 18 2017

European Organization for Nuclear Research

An electron- proton collider could bridge the gap between the LHC and its successor T. Feder *Physics Today* v70 no5 p29 My 2017

European politics & government

'Belt & Road' vs. Liberal Order H. Yafei *NPQ: New Perspectives Quarterly* v34 no3 p31 Jl 2017

Yes, Merkel Won Again. But the Fires of European Populism Are Still Raging I. Bremmer color *Time* v190 no14 p16 O 9 2017

European rabbit

See also

Rabbits

Incredible Animal Friends E. DEFFNER color *National Geographic Kids* no470 p5 My 2017

European Southern Observatory

Earth-mass vs. Earth-like D. J. Eicher color *Astronomy* v45 no1 p8 Ja 2017

European Space Agency

Anatomy of a COMET J. Parker *Sky & Telescope* v133 no5 p14 My 2017

Mars mission a go; asteroid lander killed bw *Science* v354 no6317 p1208 D 9 2016

Rosetta's last moments, in pictures bw *Science* v354 no6308 p16 O 7 2016

European Union

The Business Implications of the EU-U.S. "Privacy Shield" L. Downes *Harvard Business Review Digital Articles* p2 F 10 2016

ERC—the next 10 years H. Nowotny color *Science* v355 no6329 p997 Mr 10 2017

Europe *New York Times Upfront* p2 S 18 2017 Supplement Poster

Europe signs onto climate deal *Science* v354 no6309 p153 O 14 2016

The E.U.'s New Digs J. Zorthian color *Time* v189 no3 p19 Ja 16 2017

For Europe, More Tensions Grow in the East J. Micklethwait *Bloomberg Businessweek* no4541 p12 O 9 2017

Islamism Implacable C. Hill *Hoover Digest: Research & Opinion on Public Policy* no1 p98 Wint 2017

Italy Lashes Out As Flow of Migrants Surges T. John color *Time* v190 no4 p9 Jl 24 2017

A Marxist Manifesto J. LOCONTE *Weekly Standard* v22 no5 p20 O 10 2016

The Precautionary Principle Under Fire R. Read and T. O'Riordan bibl *Environment* v59 no5 p4 S/O 2017

A Pregnant Pause: Brexit is now certain, but the terms are not. Britain still has time to work with the EU, head off political strife, and minimize economic pain T. G. Ash *Hoover Digest: Research & Opinion on Public Policy* no3 p93 Summ 2017

Eustace, Alan
26 MILES ABOVE EARTH L. PARKER color *Atlantic* v319 no5 p54 Je 2017

Eusthenopteron
When We Left Water G. TARLACH bw color *Discover* v38 no6 p44 Jl/Ag 2017

EUSTIS, OSKAR
ANGELS AND DEMONS color *Vanity Fair* v59 no5 p120 Ap 2017

Euthanasia
Last Words M. J. Salter *American Scholar* v86 no3 p57 Summ 2017
QUESTIONS AT THE END H. W. BAILLIE and G. MEI-LAENDER color *Commonweal* v144 no15 p2 S 22 2017

Euthanasia of animals
"No-Kill" Versus "Kill" Shelters *Your Dog (10780343)* v22 no10 p10 O 2016

Euthanasia—Government policy
More Bathos than Pathos G. Meilaender color *Commonweal* v144 no13 p14 Ag 11 2017

Euthanasia—Law & legislation
To Live and Die in Colorado *Weekly Standard* v22 no5 p2 O 10 2016

Euthanasia—Religious aspects—Christianity
More Bathos than Pathos G. Meilaender color *Commonweal* v144 no13 p14 Ag 11 2017

Eutrophication
Ecological Forecasting and the Science of Hypoxia in Chesapeake Bay J. M. TESTA, J. B. CLARK et al *BioScience* v67 no7 p614 Jl 2017
Eutrophication will increase during the 21st century as a result of precipitation changes E. Sinha, A. M. Michalak et al map *Science* v357 no6349 p405 Jl 28 2017
Nitrogen stewardship in the Anthropocene S. P. Seitzinger and L. Phillips color *Science* v357 no6349 p350 Jl 28 2017

Evaluation of agricultural equipment
Mother's Product Picks *Mother Earth News* no282 p14 Je/Jl 2017

Evaluation of retail stores
BEARING FRUIT: In Bill Weghorst's world, one great Honeysmith always beats a bag full of garden-variety produce S. KROWIAK color *Indianapolis Monthly* v41 no2 p42 S 2017
Flex Appeal: The city's newest athleisure shop pushes style to the edge S. BAHR *Indianapolis Monthly* v12 no40 p34 Ag 2017
happy place P. GUGLIELMETTI color *Better Homes & Gardens* v95 no11 p18 N 2017
ONE SIZE FITS ALL A. Brandy *Cincinnati Magazine* v50 no12 p36 S 2017
Stores K. Schneider img *New York* v50 no17 p80 Ag 21 2017
WANNA BUY A WATCH? S. Watson color *Esquire* p46 Je/Jl 2017
Yes, Atlanta Has "Bodegas" G. CHAPMAN *Atlanta* v57 no2 p49 Je 2017

Evaluators, The (Short story)
THE EVALUATORS N. K. JEMISIN bw cartoon *Wired* v25 no1 p64 Ja 2017

Evancho, Jackie, 2000-—Interviews
Jackie Evancho *Indianapolis Monthly* p23 My 2017

Evangelical churches
Defending the Faith (of Others) K. SHELLNUTT *Christianity Today* v61 no5 p17 Je 2017
EVANGELICAL CHURCH SHOPPING, EXPLAINED graph *Christianity Today* v60 no10 p21 D 2016
the silence of the lambs K. JOYCE color *New Republic* v248 no7 p38 Jl 2017
That Loving Feeling graph *Christianity Today* v61 no4 p15 My 2017
What Would Jesus Disrupt? Entrepreneurs from Crossroads Church try to scale their startups without selling their souls M. Farzier color *Bloomberg Businessweek* no4518 p56 Ap 10 2017

Evangelical churches—Canada
Evangelically liberal J. Byassee color *Christian Century* v133 no23 p26 N 9 2016

Evangelical Lutheran Church—Congresses
ISNA OUTREACH *Islamic Horizons* v45 no6 p9 N/D 2016

Evangelicalism
Evangelist to the Press Corps F. BARNES color *Weekly Standard*

v23 no1 p13 S 11 2017

Evangelicalism—Social aspects
Evangelical Christian Discourse in South Korea on the LGBT: the Politics of Cross-Border Learning J. Yi, G. Jung et al *Society* v54 no1 p29 F 2017

Evangelicalism—Societies, etc.
NO COMMENT cartoon *Progressive* p9 D 2016/Ja 2017

Evangelicalism—United States
OUR FAVORITE HERESIES graph *Christianity Today* v60 no9 p19 N 2016

Evangelische Kirche in Deutschland
German Protestant church renounces mission aiming to convert Jewish people T. Heneghan color *Christian Century* v133 no26 p17 D 21 2016

Evangelista, Christine
CHRISTINE EVANGELISTA S. Highfill and A. Wilkinson color *Entertainment Weekly* no1456 p59 Mr 10 2017

Evangelista, Linda, 1965-
Model Beauty K. Diamond color *InStyle* v24 no3 p342 Mr 2017

Evangelista, Linda, 1965-—Interviews
Secrets of a 52-year-old beauty V. Kirby color *Redbook* p48 S 2017

Evangelistic work
Pastoral Accompaniment as Evangelization *America* v216 no13 p8 Je 12 2017

Evangelists
See also
Televangelists
Not My Will, But Yours M. R. Simone *America* v216 no7 p50 Ap 3 2017

Evans, Alison
For the Record color *Time* v189 no24 p4 Je 26 2017

Evans, Andrew
The Black Penguin *Publishers Weekly* v264 no11 p80 Mr 13 2017

Evans, Carly
The third offset strategy: A misleading slogan bibl *Bulletin of the Atomic Scientists* v73 no2 p92 Mr 2017

Evans, Cerith Wyn—Exhibitions
snapshot A. Klimoski color *Architectural Record* v205 no8 p168 Ag 2017

Evans, Chris, 1981-
big dog M. POTTER bw color *Esquire* p72 Ap 2017
Chris Evans Ties a Bow on Gifted S. Zacharek color *Time* v189 no14 p53 Ap 17 2017

EVANS, CHRISTINA OHLY
King Como color *Conde Nast Traveler* v52 no8 p52 S 2017

Evans, Christopher D.
Time for responsible peatland agriculture bibl *Science* v354 no6312 p562 N 4 2016

EVANS, DAVE
Get into Gear color *Esquire* v167 no1 p4 F 2017

Evans, David S.
The Best Retailers Combine Bricks and Clicks *Harvard Business Review Digital Articles* p2 My 30 2016
A Deep Look Inside Apple Pay's Matchmaker Economics *Harvard Business Review Digital Articles* p2 Je 17 2016
Some of the Most Successful Platforms Are Ones You've Never Heard Of *Harvard Business Review Digital Articles* p2 Mr 28 2016
What Platforms Do Differently than Traditional Businesses *Harvard Business Review Digital Articles* p2 My 11 2016
Why Winner-Takes-All Thinking Doesn't Apply to the Platform Economy *Harvard Business Review Digital Articles* p2 My 4 2016

Evans, Dayna
No Boys Allowed img *New York* v49 no21 p67 O 17 2016
The Return of a Grunge Goddess: Shirley Manson, lead singer of '90s band Garbage, heads back on the road with Blondie img *New York* v50 no11 p87 My 29 2017

EVANS, DEBRA E.
The Question *O, The Oprah Magazine* p12 Mr 2017

Evans, Elizabeth
More congregations become sanctuaries for immigrants under threat of deportation *Christian Century* v133 no26 p18 D 21 2016

EVANS, HAROLD

The Liberation Game *New York Times Book Review* p20 My 7 2017

The Man With the Red Pencil: Harold Evans, editor par excellence, explains why good writing is a moral issue J. Holt *New York Times Book Review* p24 My 21 2017

Evans, Harold—Interviews

Sir Harold Evans E. Felsenthal color *Time* v189 no22 p60 Je 12 2017

Evans, Jack

A (Frightening) Bird's Eye View R. R. RYDER *USA Today Magazine* v145 no2858 p41 N 2016

Evans, James

BLACK LOVE THROUGH THE AGES C. K. Jackson color *Essence* v47 no10 p97 F 2017

Evans, Jason

Emergence and spread of a human-transmissible multidrug-resistant nontuberculous mycobacterium bibl diag graph *Science* v354 no6313 p751 N 11 2016

EVANS, JOHN

TOWERS OF POWER color *Climbing* no353 p58 My/Je 2017

EVANS, JONATHAN

A Bird in the Hand color graph *Kiplinger's Personal Finance* v71 no2 p6 F 2017

EVANS, KARL L.

Biodiversity in the City: Fundamental Questions for Understanding the Ecology of Urban Green Spaces for Biodiversity Conservation *BioScience* v67 no9 p799 S 2017

EVANS, KEITH

RACK ATTACK cartoon color *Outdoor Life* v224 no6 p14 Ag 2017

Evans, Kenneth M.

Science advice in the Trump White House [Cover story] bibl color *Science* v355 no6325 p574 F 10 2017

Evans, Lara M.

SHARED AUTHORITY bw *Art in America* p76 O 2017

Evans, Layne

Scuff-Resistant Paint *Architectural Record* v205 no9 p164 S 2017

Evans, Linda, 1942-

LINDA EVANS C. Mann color *Amazing Wellness* v9 no6 p22 EarlyWint 2017

Evans, Lissa

The Ministry of Information: Parsing the Facts of Fiction A. Hastie *Film Quarterly* v71 no1 p65 Fall 2017

Evans, Luke, 1979-

BELLA E. POENISCH color *Esquire* p106 N 2017

The Great Train Robbery A. D'ARMINIO *TV Guide* v65 no14 p41 Ap 3 2017

Luke Evans J. Crelin color *Current Biography* v78 no9 p18 S 2017

Evans, Luke, 1979-—Interviews

Becoming Gaston M. Snetiker color *Entertainment Weekly* no1457/1458 p78 Mr 17 2017

Evans, Michael

BACK TO THE (DIGITAL) DRAWING BOARD N. UNDERWOOD bw color *Maclean's* v129 no42 p48 O 24 2016

EVANS, NICHOLAS

Boundaries for biosecurity *Issues in Science & Technology* v33 no4 p18 Summ 2017

Evans, R. E.

An integrated diamond nanophotonics platform for quantum-optical networks bibl graph *Science* v354 no6314 p847 N 18 2016

Evans, R. J. W.

A Liberal Empire? Ruled from the Spas? bw *New York Review of Books* v64 no5 p36 Mr 23 2017

Evans, Rachel

Short the Food Court color *Bloomberg Businessweek* no4515 p34 Mr 20 2017

Trying to Make Active Funds Cool Again cartoon diag *Bloomberg Businessweek* no4518 p40 Ap 10 2017

Evans, Richard J., 1947-

A continent on the brink D. Beer *History Today* v67 no1 p63 Ja 2017

The demons have come out J. Friedrich *Christian Century* v134 no19 p10 S 13 2017

Europe Transformed M. RAPPORT *New York Times Book Review* p13 D 18 2016

The Historian Who Was Not Baffled by the Nazis M. Mazower bw *New York Review of Books* v63 no20 p70 D 22 2016

The Pursuit of Power: Europe 1815–1914 A. Moravcsik *Foreign Affairs* v96 no3 p164 My/Je 2017

Rise to Dominance D. T. CRITCHLOW color *National Review* v69 no7 p44 Ap 17 2017

A WARNING FROM HISTORY bw *Nation* v304 no9 p43 Mr 20 2017

EVANS, SAM WEISS

Biosecurity Governance for the Real World *Issues in Science & Technology* v33 no1 p84 Fall 2016

Evans, Scott

2017 Volkswagen Golf Alltrack color *Motor Trend* v69 no2 p67 F 2017

THE BEST OF DETROIT AND CES color *Motor Trend* v69 no4 p20 Ap 2017

DIVINE DRIVES [Cover story] color diag graph map *Motor Trend* v69 no11 p34 N 2017

EXCLUSIVE FIRST LOOK 2018 LINCOLN NAVIGATOR color *Motor Trend* v69 no7 p16 Jl 2017

Exclusive Land Rover Discovery color *Motor Trend* v68 no12 p18 D 2016

FIRST DRIVE: Tesla Model 3 color *Motor Trend* v69 no10 p16 O 2017

FIRST LOOK: BMW Concept Z4 color *Motor Trend* v69 no11 p16 N 2017

FRATERNAL TWINS [Cover story] chart color *Motor Trend* v68 no12 p42 D 2016

GARAGE chart color diag *Motor Trend* v69 no10 p102 O 2017

GARAGE chart color diag *Motor Trend* v69 no8 p96 Ag 2017

GARRAGE cartoon chart color *Motor Trend* v69 no3 p86 Mr 2017

Geneva's Greatest Hits color *Motor Trend* v69 no6 p12 Je 2017

HEAD VS. HEART [Cover story] chart color *Motor Trend* v69 no8 p38 Ag 2017

HEAVY IS THE TRUCK THAT TAKES THE CROWN [Cover story] chart color *Motor Trend* v69 no1 p90 Ja 2017

IDENTITY CRISIS chart color *Motor Trend* v69 no6 p66 Je 2017

Kia Stinger GT Track Drive color *Motor Trend* v69 no9 p22 S 2017

KING IN THE NORTH chart color map *Motor Trend* v69 no10 p68 O 2017

the leftovers... [Cover story] chart color *Motor Trend* v69 no4 p36 Ap 2017

Mercedes-Maybach: Vision 6 Cabriolet color *Motor Trend* v69 no11 p17 N 2017

O TRESPASS SWEETLY URGED! chart color *Motor Trend* v69 no3 p60 Mr 2017

TREND color *Motor Trend* v69 no2 p15 F 2017

Viva La RIVOLUZIONE chart color *Motor Trend* v69 no5 p46 My 2017

WAGONS, HO! color *Motor Trend* v69 no2 p62 F 2017

Evans, Sebastian

Track Stars T. ANDERSON color *Ebony* v72 no8 p68 Je 2017

Evans, Shannon

WELCOMED HOME il *America* v216 no8 p32 Ap 17 2017

Evans, Sid

Cheers to the South's Best color *Southern Living* v52 no4 p12 Ap 2017

A Few Good Deeds color *Southern Living* v52 no10 p12 O 2017

FOR THE LOVE OF PIE color *Southern Living* v51 no11 p16 N 2016

A Fresh Coat of Paint color *Southern Living* v52 no3 p8 Mr 2017

Happy Grandmother's Day color *Southern Living* v52 no5 p12 My 2017

I'll See You at the Market color *Southern Living* v52 no7 p12 Jl 2017

POWERFUL MEMORIES color *Southern Living* v52 no2 p14 F 2017

A PUPPY FOR CHRISTMAS color *Southern Living* v51 no12 p16 D 2016

Room for Two color *Southern Living* v52 no3 p18 Mr 2017

SOUTHERN COMFORT color *Southern Living* v52 no1 p12 Ja 2017

The Sweetness of Fall color *Southern Living* v52 no9 p12 S 2017

Thanksgiving Road Trips color *Southern Living* v52 no11 p12 N 2017

Time To Pig Out color *Southern Living* v52 no6 p10 Je 2017

Evans, Stephen

Baked Trout with Mango Salsa color *Missouri Life* v44 no6 p72 S 2017

Evans, Susan

THE INVENTION OF THANKSGIVING *Saturday Evening Post* v288 no6 p86 N/D 2016

Evans, Suzanne

DISCOVERING THEIR IDENTITY: Using gender nonconforming picture books in early education classrooms color *Literacy Today (2411-7862)* v34 no6 p20 My/Je 2017

Evans, Thomas C., Jr.

DNA damage is a pervasive cause of sequencing errors, directly confounding variant identification bibl graph *Science* v355 no6326 p752 F 17 2017

Evans, Thomas M.

HAT-P-26b: A Neptune-mass exoplanet with a well-constrained heavy element abundance chart diag graph *Science* v356 no6338 p628 My 12 2017

Evans, Walker, 1903-1975—Exhibitions

LAND INHABITED J. R. MARQUEZ *Atlanta* v56 no7 p40 N 2016

"Walker Evans: A Vernacular Style" A. Doran *ARTnews* v116 no1 p16 Spr 2017

Evans, Willie

Willie Evans (1937-2017) J. Fuchs and T. Keith color *Sports Illustrated* v126 no3 p18 Ja 23 2017

Evansky, Rose

The Woman Behind the Blowout J. Harman bw color *Glamour* v115 no4 p42 Ap 2017

Evaporators

NEW PRODUCTS color *Science* v354 no6316 p1174 D 2 2016

Evaporators—Evaluation

new products: general lab equipment color *Science* v356 no6335 p334 Ap 21 2017

Evapotranspiration

Precipitation drives global variation in natural selection A. M. Siepielski, M. B. Morrissey et al bibl chart diag map *Science* v355 no6328 p959 Mr 3 2017

Eveleigh, Douglas

H. Boyd Woodruff (1917–2017) bw *Science* v356 no6336 p381 Ap 28 2017

Even, J.

Extremely efficient internal exciton dissociation through edge states in layered 2D perovskites bibl graph *Science* v355 no6331 p1288 Mr 24 2017

Even the Gods (Poem)

Even the Gods N. Sealey *New York Times Magazine* p20 S 10 2017

Evengård, Birgitta

Biodiversity redistribution under climate change: Impacts on ecosystems and human well-being color *Science* v355 no6332 p1389 Mr 31 2017

Evening gowns

How to SHOP LIKE A BOSS J. ABIDOR color *Seventeen* p93 Ja 1 2017

LONG, LEAN EVENING color *Vogue* v207 no9 p404 S 2017

Evening gowns—Evaluation

BEST DRESS E. Wilson color *InStyle* v24 no2 p55 F 2017

Evening primrose

How Does Your Garden Glow? Creating a moon garden is easy and affordable. The result is an unexpected delight on a balmy summer night E. Millard color *Log Home Living* v34 no5 p34 Jl 2017

Evening Wind (Poem)

EVENING WIND B. Collins *Atlantic* v318 no4 p96 N 2016

Evening With the Stars (Theatrical production)

BARRE ESSENTIALS J. VRABEL *Indianapolis Monthly* v40 no3 p29 N 2016

Evening Out, An (Short story)

AN EVENING OUT G. GREENWELL bw color *New Yorker* v93 no24 p62 Ag 21 2017

Event history analysis

Growing pains for global monitoring of societal events R. Kennedy, D. Lazer et al bibl graph *Science* v353 no6307 p1502 S 30 2016

Eventide Asset Management LLC

INVESTING IN THE KINGDOM J. HAANEN color *Christianity Today* v60 no10 p50 D 2016

Eventing (Horsemanship)

COLLEGIATE EVENTING COMES OF AGE K. F. Miller color *Practical Horseman* v44 no12 p24 D 2016

DEVELOP A STRONG GALLOPING POSITION C. Rutledge and S. Cooke color *Practical Horseman* v45 no5 p38 My 2017

For the Love of the Horse S. Allan and S. Taylor color *Practical Horseman* v45 no2 p72 F 2017

Make a Checklist J. Pierce *Practical Horseman* v44 no12 p8 D 2016

Everall, Isobel

Emergence and spread of a human-transmissible multidrug-resistant nontuberculous mycobacterium bibl diag graph *Science* v354 no6313 p751 N 11 2016

EVERATT, KRISTOFFER T.

Conserving the World's Megafauna and Biodiversity: The Fierce Urgency of Now *BioScience* v67 no3 p197 Mr 2017

Saving the World's Terrestrial Megafauna color *BioScience* v66 no10 p807 O 1 2016

Everdeen, Katniss (Fictitious character)

KATNISS EVERDEEN, WHITE HOUSE INTERN APPLICATION C. FRAZIER cartoon *New Yorker* v92 no42 p65 D 19 2016

Everest, Mount (China & Nepal)

For the most determined R. STIEVE *Arizona Highways* v93 no8 p2 Ag 2017

Into the Deep M. Synnott color map *National Geographic* v231 no3 p104 Mr 2017

EverestWorld.Co. Ltd.

Circle of Sound B. Ankosko color *Sound & Vision* v82 no4 p20 My 2017

Everett, Bridget

STARTED FROM THE BOTTOM NOW SHE'S HERE C. Sosenko color *Entertainment Weekly* no1480 p18 S 1 2017

Everett, Cristina

10 — SCIENCE VS *Entertainment Weekly* no1444/1445 p114 D 16 2016

39 Perfect Pop Culture Presents color *Entertainment Weekly* no1442 p31 D 2 2016 Rebellious Special Issue

7 — THE WEST WING WEEKLY *Entertainment Weekly* no1444/1445 p114 D 16 2016

9 — BEAUTIFUL STORIES FROM ANONYMOUS PEOPLE *Entertainment Weekly* no1444/1445 p114 D 16 2016

BEST TRUE-CRIME PODCASTS color *Entertainment Weekly* no1457/1458 p100 Mr 17 2017

Gadgets to Gift color *Entertainment Weekly* no1441 p15 N 25 2016

GOING IRL color *Entertainment Weekly* no1465 p57 My 12 2017

No. 1 ANNA FARIS IS UNQUALIFIED color *Entertainment Weekly* no1444/1445 p112 D 16 2016

REALITY BREAK color *Entertainment Weekly* no1454/1455 p98 F 24 2017

RICHARD, CAN YOU HEAR US? color *Entertainment Weekly* no1456 p71 Mr 10 2017

Still Missing Richard Simmons color *Entertainment Weekly* no1459 p12 Mr 31 2017

UNQUALIFIED CATCH-UP color *Entertainment Weekly* no1436/1437 p28 O 21 2016

Your Sunshiny, Stupendous, Seriously Spectacular SUMMER BUCKET LIST color *Entertainment Weekly* no1470 p32 Je 16 2017

Everett, Jenny

THE NEW MIND-BODY CURE color diag *Women's Health* v14 no6 p76 Jl 2017

Everett, Kevin

ASK THE EXPERTS color *Runner's World* v52 no3 p42 Ap 2017

Everett, Lily

Home at Last: Sanctuary Island, Book 6 *Publishers Weekly* v264 no5 p186 Ja 30 2017

Everett, Percival, 1956-

The Conundrum of Percival Everett: His fiction is major, his audience not C. LORENTZEN img *New York* v50 no11 p125 My 29 2017

Indigo Man: Percival Everett's latest novel centers on a 56-year-old painter who has had an affair G. EARLY *New York Times Book Review* p8 Jl 30 2017

WORKING THROUGH IDEAS WITH FICTION E. HOLLEY JR. bw *Publishers Weekly* v264 no24 p34 Je 12 2017

Everglade kite
Resurgence A. Opar *Audubon* v119 no1 p1 Spr 2017

Everglades National Park (Fla.)
Vulture Vandals N. BRULLIARD *National Parks* v91 no4 p24 Fall 2017

Evergreen: Canceled World (Music)
Mightier Than the Sword C. Wolff color *Downbeat* v84 no4 p55 Ap 2017

Evergreen State College
TOP 150 MASTER'S UNIVERSITIES chart *Washington Monthly* v49 no9/10 p108 S/O 2017

Everhart, Ruth
Ruined B. McCleneghan *Christian Century* v134 no7 p38 Mr 29 2017

EVERIST, JULIA
True Colors color *Bon Appetit* v61 no12 p92 D 2016 /Jan2017

Everitt, Dick
Anchor Locker Arrangement cartoon *Sail* v48 no6 p56 Je 2017
Bearings, blocks, and more color *Sail* v48 no8 p62 Ag 2017
Cabin Condensation cartoon *Sail* v48 no11 p58 N 2017
Comfort in the Cockpit cartoon *Sail* v48 no4 p58 Ap 2017
How to reeve a new halyard cartoon color *Sail* v48 no1 p56 Ja 2017
Ice Boxes & Refrigeration color *Sail* v48 no7 p47 Jl 2017
Lockers color *Sail* v48 no9 p64 S 2017
Looking after Halyards color *Sail* v48 no5 p52 My 2017
Seacocks color *Sail* v48 no10 p84 O 2017
Weather Cloths cartoon *Sail* v48 no2 p68 F 2017

Everlasting flowers
See also
Dried flower arrangement
THE EVERLASTING GARDEN *Saturday Evening Post* v289 no3 p21 My/Je 2017

Evernham, Ray
Ray Evernham color *Car & Driver* v62 no6 p38 D 2016

Evers, J.
Spectral narrowing of x-ray pulses for precision spectroscopy with nuclear resonances diag *Science* v357 no6349 p375 Jl 28 2017

Evers-Hood, Ken
The Irrational Jesus: Leading the Fully Human Church L. Wood *Christian Century* v134 no17 p39 Ag 16 2017

EVERSOLE, ROBERT
Celebrate Earth Day color *Trail Rider* v29 no3 p16 Ap 2017
Mark Twain Country color *Trail Rider* v29 no4 p22 My 2017
Saddle Up for Spring color *Trail Rider* v29 no2 p24 Mr 2017
Winter-Riding Opportunities color *Trail Rider* v29 no1 p22 Ja/F 2017

Evert, Chris
Finishing Strong *Tennis* v52 no6 p4 N/D 2016
Guessing Game *Tennis* v53 no4 p6 Jl/Ag 2017
Marquee Attraction bw color *Tennis* v53 no5 p4 S/O 2017
Second Chances *Tennis* v53 no3 p4 My/Je 2017
Sunny Forecast *Tennis* v53 no1 p4 Ja/F 2017
A Tennis Mecca bw color *Tennis* v53 no2 p2 Mr/Ap 2017

Everton, Paul
Traveling for Work? You're a Prime Target for Hackers *Harvard Business Review Digital Articles* p2 S 29 2016

Every Brilliant Thing (Theatrical production)
Every Brilliant Thing *New York* v49 no25 p143 D 12 2016

Every Country's Sun (Music)
Pop img *New York* v50 no17 p116 Ag 21 2017

Every Man Jack (Company)
Soap Opera M. STEFANOV color *Esquire* v166 no4 p70 N 2016

Every Student Succeeds Act of 2015 (United States)
The art of partnerships D. H. Bowen and B. Kisida color graph il *Phi Delta Kappan* v98 no7 p8 Ap 2017
Design principles for new systems of assessment L. A. Shepard, W. R. Penuel et al color *Phi Delta Kappan* v98 no6 p47 Mr 2017
Every Student Succeeds Act: Federal Elementary and Secondary Education Policy *Congressional Digest* v96 no7 p4 S 2017
Linda Darling-Hammond on the Future of New York Education—and What She Makes of Betsy DeVos M. DISARE *Education*

Digest v82 no8 p48 Ap 2017
Washington View M. Ferguson *Phi Delta Kappan* v98 no3 p74 N 2016

Everybody Loves Raymond (TV program)
DORIS ROBERTS R. Romano and L. Rice color *Entertainment Weekly* no1446/1447 p86 D 2016/Ja 2017

Everybody Wants Some!! (Film)
Everybody Wants Some!! M. Nelson *Film Comment* v53 no1 p52 Ja/F 2017

Everyday life
See also
Activities of daily living
BAD WRAP P. Gulley *Saturday Evening Post* v289 no1 p16 Ja/F 2017
Castro's Cuba Is the Only Way of Life Many Have Known R. Kushner *Time* v188 no24 p45 D 12 2016
How to Become a Morning Person A. Sifferlin color *Time* v189 no10 p24 Mr 20 2017
In praise of poetry P. W. Marty *Christian Century* v134 no9 p3 Ap 26 2017
My LIST 24 hours with Marina Abramović S. Cristobal color *Harper's Bazaar* no3648 p120 N 2016
On All Floors J. Berlin color *National Geographic* v232 no4 p130 O 2017
She Leads Learning B. Turvett color *Working Mother* p14 F/Mr 2017
TRAUMARAMA color *Seventeen* v76 no5 p106 S 2017
Would You Rather... color *Seventeen* v76 no5 p110 S 2017

Everyman (Theatrical production)
GOD ONLY KNOWS H. ALS cartoon *New Yorker* v93 no3 p80 Mr 6 2017

Everything, Everything (Film)
AMANDLA STENBERG A. Breznican color *Entertainment Weekly* no1463/1464 p34 Ap/My 2017

Everything Now (Music)
Arcade Fire E. R. Brown color *Entertainment Weekly* no1476 p59 Ag 4 2017
Arcade Fire Go Dancing in the Dark W. HERMES color *Rolling Stone* no1293 p53 Ag 10 2017
Arcade Fire looks for God in a material world T. Kroenert color *America* v217 no5 p50 S 4 2017
The Playlist bw color *Rolling Stone* no1290 p10 Je 29 2017

Evga Corp.
EVGA GTX 1060 3GB: A compelling $200 graphics card with a questionable future B. CHACOS color graph *PCWorld* p81 O 2016
EVGA GTX 1080 Ti SC2: A ferocious graphics card with a radical cooler B. CHACOS chart color graph *PCWorld* v35 no6 p55 Je 2017

Evgeniou, Theos
Run Field Experiments to Make Sense of Your Big Data *Harvard Business Review Digital Articles* p2 N 12 2015

Eviction
Cast Out OF EDEN L. REIGSTAD *Texas Monthly* v45 no3 p51 Mr 2017

Evidence
Teaching with evidence M. Crocco, Halvorsen et al diag *Phi Delta Kappan* v98 no7 p67 Ap 2017

Evidence (Law)
See also
Confidential communications
Testimony (Law)

Evidence (Law)—United States
Courtroom forensic evidence often lacks scientific validity, report finds T. Feder *Physics Today* v69 no11 p32 N 2016
Hand Over the Data graph *MIT Technology Review* v120 no2 p26 Mr/Ap 2017

Evidence-based education
BUILDING A COMMUNITY OF LIFELONG LEARNING T. McKAY color *Phi Kappa Phi Forum* v97 no2 p10 Summ 2017

Evidence-based management
Performance and the People Factor M. Funkhouser *Governing* v30 no4 p59 Ja 2017

Evidence-based psychology
WHAT YOUR THERAPIST DOESN'T KNOW T. ROUSMANIERE color *Atlantic* v319 no3 p50 Ap 2017

Evil Bikes (Company)
AGNOSTIC AGGRESSION A. Smith, R. Palmer et al color *Bike Magazine* v24 no1 p106 Ja/F 2017
EVIL'S THE FOLLOWING T. Engel color *Bike Magazine* v23 no9 p94 D 2016

Evil Bikes LLC
"I WANT TO TAKE MORE RISKS." L. Mazzante and B. STRICKLAND color *Bicycling* v58 no3 p70 Ap 2017

Evil Dead, The (Film : 1981)
Your Ultimate Halloween Watch Guide C. Collis color *Entertainment Weekly* no1436/1437 p86 O 21 2016

Eviner, Inci—Exhibitions
SIGHTLINES R. Simonini color *Art in America* v105 no3 p41 Mr 2017

Evinrude Outboard Motors (Company)
Monsters of the Midrange A. JONES *Boating World* v38 no3 p20 Mr 2017
Stick the Landing P. FREDERIKSEN color *Power & Motoryacht* v34 no9 p30 S 2017

Evo Yachts (Company)
MORE THAN MEETS THE EYE S. SHIBATA *Sea Magazine* v109 no1 p10 Ja 2017

Evolution (Biology)
See also
 Epigenesis
 Origin of life
 Primate evolution
5 THINGS WE KNOW TO BE TRUE M. SHERMER, H. HALL et al cartoon *Scientific American* v315 no5 p46 N 2016
Antibiotic tolerance facilitates the evolution of resistance I. Levin-Reisman, I. Ronin et al bibl bw chart diag graph *Science* v355 no6327 p826 F 24 2017
Charles Darwin N. SCHARPING color *Discover* v38 no4 p42 My 2017
Decoupled ecomorphological evolution and diversification in Neogene-Quaternary horses J. L. Cantalapiedra, J. L. Prado et al bibl graph *Science* v355 no6325 p627 F 10 2017
Early animal fossils at risk K. McLaughlin color *Science* v356 no6335 p230 Ap 21 2017
EVERYTHING YOU KNOW ABOUT SEX IS WRONG: PART 1: THE GENDER BINARY A. HAFER *Humanist* v77 no4 p24 Jl/Ag 2017
Evolution's Error: HOW HUMAN NATURE WENT AWRY R. GRIGG *Humanist* v77 no3 p30 My/Je 2017
Evolution with No Reason: A Neutral View on Epigenetic Changes, Genomic Variability, and Evolutionary Novelty C. GUERRERO-BOSAGNA *BioScience* v67 no5 p469 My 2017
GENE FITTING C. COX *Scientific American* v317 no3 p7 S 2017
He Knows Where the Bodies Are Buried G. DREVITCH *Psychology Today* v50 no2 p27 Mr/Ap 2017
Improbable Replications J. B. LOSOS color *Natural History* v125 no7 p16 Jl/Ag 2017
IN THE MINDS OF DOGS *Psychology Today* v50 no5 p70 S/O 2017
Life list C. Martin color *Science News* v190 no13 p29 D 24 2016
More Hobbitses, Precious! G. TARLACH color *Discover* v38 no1 p25 Ja/F 2017
Vital enzyme adapted to cooling Earth L. HAMERS *Science News* v191 no2 p8 F 4 2017
Watching speciation in action B. R. Grant and P. R. Grant bibl color *Science* v355 no6328 p910 Mr 3 2017
We Are Not Alone G. DREVITCH *Psychology Today* v49 no6 p47 N/D 2016

Evolution (Biology)—Environmental aspects
PROMISCUOUS MEN, CHASTE WOMEN AND OTHER GENDER MYTHS C. FINE and M. A. ELGAR color *Scientific American* v317 no3 p32 S 2017

Evolution research
Beyond Hamilton's rule H. P. de Vladar and E. Szathmáry color *Science* v356 no6337 p485 My 5 2017

Evolutionary algorithms
ANIMAL MATH [Cover story] S. Milius cartoon color graph *Science News* v190 no12 p22 D 10 2016

Evolutionary theories
See also
 Evolution (Biology)
 Galactic evolution
 Solar evolution
Attractive Advantage *Natural History* v125 no4 p5 Ap 2017
Evolution Blooms J. Wallace *Natural History* v124 no10 p34 N 2016
Evolution in the College Classroom Facilitating Conversations about Science and Religion M. NISBET *Skeptical Inquirer* v41 no5 p22 S/O 2017
FORCE OF CREATION E. S. ARNARSDÓTTIR *Iceland Review* v55 no3 p18 My/Je 2017
Home Sweet Dome K. Long color *Scientific American* v316 no5 p16 My 2017
Life list C. Martin color *Science News* v190 no13 p29 D 24 2016
THE SELFISH GENE REVISITED R. DAWKINS *Skeptical Inquirer* v41 no2 p38 Mr/Ap 2017

Evolutionary theories study & teaching
CFI, Richard Dawkins, Teachers Slam as 'Unconscionable' Turkey's Decision to Ban Teaching Evolution K. FRAZIER *Skeptical Inquirer* v41 no5 p7 S/O 2017
Dissent with Modification R. Lloyd diag *Scientific American* v316 no5 p14 My 2017

Evolve (Music)
IMAGINE DRAGONS' DAN REYNOLDS M. Vain color *Entertainment Weekly* no1472 p57 Je 30 2017

Evrony, Gilad D.
One brain, many genomes bibl color diag *Science* v354 no6312 p557 N 4 2016

Evs Sports (Company)
LIFT AIR BOSS color *Flying* v144 no6 p12 Je 2017

EWALT, DAVID M.
DISRUPTION MACHINE [Cover story] color *Forbes* v198 no7 p76 N 29 2016
How the West Was Won color *Forbes* v199 no6 p44 Je 13 2017

Ewan, Chris, 1976-
Long Time Lost *Publishers Weekly* v263 no51 p125 D 12 2016

Ewell, Lars
On the value of carbon-ion therapy *Physics Today* v69 no11 p14 N 2016

Ewers, Melissa
REFRAMING RESEARCH color *Literacy Today (2411-7862)* v34 no5 p12 Mr/Ap 2017

Ewing, Ella Kate
A Tale of Two Kates G. WOOD bw *Missouri Life* v44 no2 p122 Ap 2017

Ewing, Ethan—Interviews
Ethan Ewing color *Surfing Magazine* v53 no1 p22 Ja 2017

Ewing, Jack
Emissions of Guilt: At Volkswagen, unethical practices and the push to be a market leader ended in a costly scandal B. McLEAN *New York Times Book Review* p11 Je 11 2017

Ewing, Maura
'Hustlers Are Entrepreneurs Denied Opportunity' color *Bloomberg Businessweek* no4502 p82 D 5 2016

Ewing, Rod
Déjà vu for U.S. nuclear waste color *Science* v356 no6345 p1313 Je 30 2017
Editorial board *Bulletin of the Atomic Scientists* v72 no6 pebi N 2016

Ewing, Susan
Resurrecting the Shark: A Scientific Obsession and the Mavericks Who Solved the Mystery of a 270-Million-Year-Old Fossil *Publishers Weekly* v264 no7 p66 F 13 2017

Ewing Marion Kauffman Foundation
Making Your Business Marriage Work color *Ebony* v72 no9 p70 Jl/Ag 2017

Ex-convicts
'First you survive' G. McClure color *U.S. Catholic* v82 no11 p18 N 2017
'Hustlers Are Entrepreneurs Denied Opportunity' M. Ewing color *Bloomberg Businessweek* no4502 p82 D 5 2016

Ex-convicts—Education
OUT AND UP L. MACFARQUHAR cartoon *New Yorker* v92 no41 p54 D 12 2016

Ex-convicts—Suffrage
The Case for Re-Enfranchisement J. Lewis Berg *Humanist* v76 no6 p6 N/D 2016

Ending Civil Death R. D. SULLIVAN *America* v215 no11 p18 O 17 2016

Whose Representative Government, Again? S. Richardson *American History* v52 no1 p6 Ap 2017

Ex-convicts—United States

OUT OF PRISON. OUT OF WORK E. BOEHM *Reason* v49 no3 p12 Jl 2017

Ex-football players—Employment

YOUNG MONEY A. SHERMAN color *Bloomberg Businessweek* no4511 p54 F 13 2017

Ex-football players—Health

Man in the MIDDLE S. L. Price color *Sports Illustrated* v126 no14 p102 My 15-22 2017

Ex-football players—Interviews

JUST MY TYPE D. Patrick and T. Keith color *Sports Illustrated* v125 no18 p25 D 5 2016

Ex Libris: New York Public Library (Film)

BOOK RATS S. KLAWANS color *Nation* v305 no8 p36 O 9 2017

Books, Rats and Elegant Shoes S. Zacharek color *Time* v190 no14 p51 O 9 2017

Ex Libris: The New York Public Library N. RAPOLD color *Film Comment* v53 no5 p70 S/O 2017

Ex Nihilo (Company)

The Place Beyond the Pines M. STEFANOV color *Esquire* v166 no5 p70 D 2016/Ja 2017

Ex-presidents

The Death of Iran's Ultimate Political Insider Gives Hard-Liners an Edge K. Vick and K. A. Serjoie color *Time* v189 no4 p13 Ja 23 2017

Ex-presidents—Psychology

Can an Ex-President Be Happy? B. BRADLEY HAGERTY color *Atlantic* v319 no1 p22 Ja/F 2017

Ex-presidents—United States

The Butcher's Bill J. COST cartoon *Weekly Standard* v22 no13 p13 D 5 2016

Can an Ex-President Be Happy? B. BRADLEY HAGERTY color *Atlantic* v319 no1 p22 Ja/F 2017

Obama Goes From the White House To Wall Street M. Abelson *Bloomberg Businessweek* no4539 p42 S 25 2017

THE TWO ANDREW JACKSONS M. KAZIN il *Nation* v305 no5 p35 Ag 28 2017

Exa Corp.

A MIGHTY WIND J. Pearley Huffman and J. Gall color *Car & Driver* v62 no6 p24 D 2016

ExactRail LLC

ExactRail HO scale SP gondola C. Grivno *Model Railroader* v84 no11 p67 N 2017

Examination of the blood

BLOOD TEST HELPS MONITOR JOINT INFECTIONS C. Barakat and M. McCluskey color *Equus* no480 p16 S 2017

Radiation Triage A. Griswold color *Scientific American* v316 no6 p19 Je 2017

TOP 10 BLOOD TESTS B. Crabbe color *Horse & Rider* v55 no11 p50 N 2016

Examinations

See also

Intelligence tests

Multiple choice examinations

Psychological tests

Skin SMARTS color *O, The Oprah Magazine* p72 O 2017

What's Your Headache IQ? K. Rockwood color *O, The Oprah Magazine* p102 N 2017

Winner's CIRCLE color *Practical Horseman* v45 no2 p66 F 2017

Exanthemata

What's that rash? A quick guide to itchy skin *Mayo Clinic Health Letter* v35 no10 p6 O 2017

Exanthemata—Diagnosis

What's That Rash?! E. Seidman color *Health* v31 no1 p77 Ja 2017

Exanthemata—Risk factors

Skin fold rashes *Mayo Clinic Health Letter* v35 no3 p6 Mr 2017

Excavating machinery

DIGGING UP THE PAST R. Verger color *Popular Science* v289 no5 p26 S/O 2017

Excavation

ICING ABOVE R. M. HANRAHAN cartoon *Flying* v144 no2 p24 F 2017

Excavations (Archaeology)

HOUSE RULES M. BROWN color *Archaeology* v70 no4 p14 Je-Ag 2017

KA-CHING! D. WEISS color *Archaeology* v70 no4 p9 Je-Ag 2017

LATE PALEOLITHIC MASTERPIECES E. A. POWELL color *Archaeology* v70 no4 p20 Je-Ag 2017

Secrets of the Terra-Cotta Warriors A. R. Williams color *National Geographic* v230 no5 p23 N 2016

TAKE ME OUT TO THE BALL GAME [Cover story] J. URBANUS color *Archaeology* v70 no4 p16 Je-Ag 2017

The Temple Builders of Malta E. A. POWELL color *Archaeology* v69 no6 p38 N/D 2016

TOMB COUTURE D. WEISS color *Archaeology* v70 no4 p16 Je-Ag 2017

WORLD ROUNDUP J. URBANUS color map *Archaeology* v70 no4 p24 Je-Ag 2017

Excavations (Archaeology)—Alaska

RACING THE THAW A. R. Williams color map *National Geographic* v231 no4 p134 Ap 2017

Excavations (Archaeology)—Australia

Australia's interior colonized quickly B. BOWER color *Science News* v190 no11 p18 N 26 2016

Humans' arrival in Australia redated M. TEMMING color *Science News* v192 no2 p10 Ag 19 2017

Excavations (Archaeology)—Canada

Coast over Corridor Z. ZORICH color *Archaeology* v69 no6 p17 N/D 2016

Excavations (Archaeology)—Cyprus

And They're Off! J. A. LOBELL color *Archaeology* v69 no6 p20 N/D 2016

Excavations (Archaeology)—Evaluation

OFF THE GRID M. GRUNBERG BANYASZ color *Archaeology* v69 no6 p10 N/D 2016

Excavations (Archaeology)—France

A LAST DAY, RECLAIMED J. URBANUS bw color *Archaeology* v69 no6 p48 N/D 2016

OFF THE GRID M. GRUNBERG BANYASZ color *Archaeology* v69 no6 p10 N/D 2016

RENAISSANCE MELODY E. A. POWELL color *Archaeology* v70 no4 p15 Je-Ag 2017

Excavations (Archaeology)—Great Britain

8,000 Years of Human History in London *British Heritage Travel* v38 no3 p10 My/Je 2017

Excavations (Archaeology)—Greece

Murder on the Mountain? J. URBANUS bw color *Archaeology* v69 no6 p14 N/D 2016

Excavations (Archaeology)—Hawaii

Shifting Sands J. A. LOBELL color *Archaeology* v69 no6 p22 N/D 2016

Excavations (Archaeology)—History

A LAST DAY, RECLAIMED J. URBANUS bw color *Archaeology* v69 no6 p48 N/D 2016

Excavations (Archaeology)—Ireland

SAMHAIN REVIVAL E. MULLALLY color *Archaeology* v69 no6 p34 N/D 2016

Excavations (Archaeology)—Korea

Korea's Half Moon Palace KIM color *Archaeology* v69 no6 p44 N/D 2016

Excavations (Archaeology)—Middle East

OUR HUMAN STORY J. Magness color *Archaeology* v70 no5 p6 S/O 2017

Excavations (Archaeology)—Peru

NO LONGER LOST C. Valentino color *Archaeology* v70 no5 p4 S/O 2017

Painted Worlds [Cover story] J. A. LOBELL color *Archaeology* v70 no5 p26 S/O 2017

Excavations (Archaeology)—Scotland

LOST KINGDOM OF THE BRITONS D. WEISS color *Archaeology* v70 no5 p32 S/O 2017

Excavations (Archaeology)—West Bank

SCROLL SEARCH D. WEISS color *Archaeology* v70 no3 p9 My/Je 2017

Exception, The (Film)

Gradations of Badness: The Exception pays little fealty to the history of Kaiser Wilhelm, but, oh, that glorious acting D. EDEL-

STEIN img *New York* v50 no11 p122 My 29 2017

Exceptional children

    See also

    Children with disabilities

Exceptionalism (Political science)

Code Switch M. JOUET cartoon color graph *Mother Jones* v42 no1 p17 Ja/F 2017

From Destiny to Purpose P. LAWRENCE color *Nation* v304 no2 p14 Ja 16 2017

The Strange Career of American Exceptionalism G. GRANDIN color *Nation* v304 no1 p22 Ja 2 2017 The Obama Years

Exceptionalism (Political science)—History

Making ATHENS GREAT AGAIN R. NEWBERGER GOLD-STEIN *Atlantic* v319 no3 p86 Ap 2017

Exceptionalism (Political science)—United States

American Exceptionalism H. Clinton color *Time* v188 no16/17 p83 O 24 2016

Republican Party Platform: "Making America Great Again" *Congressional Digest* v95 no8 p7 O 2016

Whose Land? [Cover story] J. D. WILSEY color *America* v215 p20 N 28 2016

Excess profits tax—United States

How should I handle a tax windfall that I don't want? K. KIP-LINGER *Kiplinger's Personal Finance* v71 no3 p15 Mr 2017

Exchange of publications

U.S.-Iran science exchange G. Schweitzer color *Science* v357 no6359 p11 O 6 2017

Exchange traded funds

4 BIG TRENDS YOU CAN RIDE FOR YEARS J. Waggoner color diag *Money* v46 no1 p70 Ja/F 2017

THE 50 BEST FUNDS TO BUY AND HOLD C. Fried color diag *Money* v46 no1 p64 Ja/F 2017

A Cheap Way to Own Tech D. FONDA chart *Kiplinger's Personal Finance* v70 no12 p59 D 2016

ETFs Are Hot. So's 3D Printing... I Got an Idea! A. Massa color *Bloomberg Businessweek* no4497 p43 O 31 2016

Fee Wars Heat Up N. S. HUANG chart *Kiplinger's Personal Finance* v71 no1 p57 Ja 2017

A Financial Fund Heats Up D. FONDA chart *Kiplinger's Personal Finance* v71 no6 p56 Je 2017

Gold Is for Cranks? Not So Fast W. BALDWIN chart color *Forbes* v199 no7 p128 Je 29 2017

Hidden Assets D. FISHER color *Forbes* v198 no8 p62 D 20 2016

How to Get Good Advice J. Bodnar *Kiplinger's Personal Finance* v71 no5 p6 My 2017

How to Use ETFs to Pick Other ETFs J. Waggoner diag *Money* v46 no6 p40 Jl 2017

I Can Haz Make You Money? D. Burger color *Bloomberg Businessweek* no4525 p37 Je 5 2017

THE MONEY 50 chart *Money* v46 no1 p68 Ja/F 2017

Protect Yourself From Ugly Currencies W. BALDWIN chart color graph *Forbes* v199 no1 p62 Ja 24 2017

An Rx for Healthier Gains D. FONDA chart *Kiplinger's Personal Finance* v71 no12 p54 D 2017

Schwab's Cut-Rate ETFs Are Catching On C. Stein color graph *Bloomberg Businessweek* no4494 p39 O 10 2016

Trying to Make Active Funds Cool Again R. Evans and A. Massa cartoon diag *Bloomberg Businessweek* no4518 p40 Ap 10 2017

Wall Street Diversifies Itself B. McLEAN color *Atlantic* v319 no2 p20 Mr 2017

YOUR ETF, YOUR LIBERATOR W. BALDWIN *Forbes* v198 no8 p65 D 20 2016

Exchange traded funds—Economic aspects

AN ETF TAX HUSTLE W. BALDWIN color *Forbes* v198 no6 p67 N 8 2016

Exchange traded funds—History—21st century

AN ETF TAX HUSTLE W. BALDWIN color *Forbes* v198 no6 p67 N 8 2016

Exchange traded funds—Sales & prices

That ETF May Not Be as Cheap as You Think P. J. Lim diag *Money* v46 no5 p36 Je 2017

Exchange traded funds—Charts, diagrams, etc.

THE BEST PERFORMERS chart *Money* v46 no1 p110 Ja/F 2017

Infrastructure Wins Fans D. FONDA chart *Kiplinger's Personal Finance* v71 no1 p60 Ja 2017

Market Readies for a Rate Hike T. Tepper chart *Money* v45 no11

p89 D 2016

Excited state energies

WATCHING PEROVSKITE PHOTOEXCITATIONS, ATOM BY ATOM *Physics Today* v70 no3 p21 Mr 2017

Exclamations (Grammar)

Ask the Editer B. K. SARGENT *Publishers Weekly* v264 no13 p52 Mr 27 2017

CURB YOUR ENTHUSIASM! cartoon chart graph *Atlantic* v319 no2 p18 Mr 2017

Exclaves—Evaluation

CAJUN COUNTRY J. FROIS color map *Louisiana Life* v37 no4 p97 Mr/Ap 2017

Excoffier, Laurent

Chimpanzee genomic diversity reveals ancient admixture with bonobos bibl diag graph map *Science* v354 no6311 p477 O 28 2016

Excommunication (Music)

Tyler Glenn's Rebirth N. Feeney color *Entertainment Weekly* no1439 p58 N 11 2016

Excretion

    See also

    Urine

I Tried Going Diaper-Free. It Stunk B. Randall cartoon *Working Mother* p58 F/Mr 2017

Excursions (Travel)

BASKING IN THE GLOW *Iceland Review* v54 no6 p130 N/D 2016

Catch Fall COLOR A. PAVIA color *Horse & Rider* v56 no9 p72 S 2017

COZY COUNTRY HIDEAWAY *Iceland Review* v54 no6 p128 N/D 2016

Here We Go! Oprah color *O, The Oprah Magazine* p17 Ja 2017

PILGRIMAGE VS. HOLIDAY TOUR OF HOMES J. GREEN *Atlanta* v56 no8 p46 D 2016

Executions & executioners

Tortured by 'Moderates' K. Jane Torrance color *Weekly Standard* v22 no47 p34 Ag 21 2017

Executive ability (Management)

    See also

    Delegation of authority

    Planning

A 10-Year Study Reveals What Great Executives Know and Do R. Carucci *Harvard Business Review Digital Articles* p2 Ja 19 2016

3 Ways Managers Start Off On the Wrong Foot H. G. Halvorson *Harvard Business Review Digital Articles* p2 O 6 2015

4 Ways Leaders Fritter Their Power Away R. Carucci *Harvard Business Review Digital Articles* p2 O 29 2015

4 Ways to Be More Effective at Execution J. Zenger and J. Folkman *Harvard Business Review Digital Articles* p2 My 23 2016

After the Handshake D. CIAMPA color *Harvard Business Review* v94 no12 p60 D 2016

Being a Parent Made Me a Better Manager, and Vice Versa J. Zikic *Harvard Business Review Digital Articles* p2 My 9 2016

The Best Managers Are Boring Managers T. Chamorro-Premuzic *Harvard Business Review Digital Articles* p2 S 28 2015

Deliver Feedback That Sticks L. Davey *Harvard Business Review Digital Articles* p2 Ag 20 2015

Do Women Make Bolder Leaders than Men? J. Zenger and J. Folkman *Harvard Business Review Digital Articles* p2 Ap 27 2016

Games Can Make You a Better Strategist M. Reeves and G. Wittenburg *Harvard Business Review Digital Articles* p2 S 7 2015

Good Leaders Are Good Learners L. A. Keating, P. A. Heslin et al *Harvard Business Review Digital Articles* p2 Ag 10 2017

How CEOs Can Keep Their Analytics Programs from Being a Waste of Time C. McShea, D. Oakley et al *Harvard Business Review Digital Articles* p2 Jl 21 2016

How Managers Can See the Future More Clearly J. Pistrui *Harvard Business Review Digital Articles* p2 O 2 2015

How Managers Drive Results and Employee Engagement at the Same Time J. Zenger and J. Folkman *Harvard Business Review Digital Articles* p2 Je 19 2017

How Senior Executives Stay Passionate About Their Work J. Morgan *Harvard Business Review Digital Articles* p2 2017

How to Break into Your CEO's Inner Circle J. Neatby *Harvard*

2016

Cybersecurity Is Every Executive's Job B. Sweeney *Harvard Business Review Digital Articles* p2 S 13 2016

David St. Pierre T. C. FISHMAN color *Chicago* v66 no6 p90 Je 2017

Dispel Your Team's Fear of Data T. C. Redman *Harvard Business Review Digital Articles* p2 Jl 16 2015

Do Managers and Leaders Really Do Different Things? J. O'Leary *Harvard Business Review Digital Articles* p2 Je 20 2016

Don't Let Your Mistakes Go to Waste M. Chussil *Harvard Business Review Digital Articles* p2 Mr 1 2016

Do You Have a Manager's Mindset? K. Tynan *Harvard Business Review Digital Articles* p2 O 1 2015

Even Experienced Executives Avoid Conflict R. Ashkenas *Harvard Business Review Digital Articles* p2 Mr 8 2016

Executives Get the IT They Deserve J. Peppard *Harvard Business Review Digital Articles* p2 D 1 2015

Feeling Powerful at Work Makes Us Feel Worse When We Get Home T. A. Foulk and K. Lanaj *Harvard Business Review Digital Articles* p2 Je 13 2017

Followers Don't See Their Leaders as Real People N. T. Washburn and B. Galvin color *Harvard Business Review Digital Articles* p2 Ja 23 2017

FRIDAY NIGHT AT THE COLONNADE J. BAINBRIDGE *Atlanta* v57 no6 p94 O 2017

Higher and Higher We Go A. Wintour *Vogue* v207 no1 p24 Ja 2017

How a New Generation of Business Leaders Views Philanthropy P. Goldman *Harvard Business Review Digital Articles* p2 F 29 2016

How Artificial Intelligence Will Redefine Management V. Kolbjørnsrud, R. Amico et al *Harvard Business Review Digital Articles* p2 N 2 2016

How Leaders Can Focus on the Big Picture E. Johnson *Harvard Business Review Digital Articles* p2 N 9 2016

How Leaders Can Help Others Influence Them R. Schwarz *Harvard Business Review Digital Articles* p2 Ag 24 2016

How Managers Can Make Group Projects More Efficient A. J. Su color *Harvard Business Review Digital Articles* p2 Ja 17 2017

How Managers Can See the Future More Clearly J. Pistrui *Harvard Business Review Digital Articles* p2 O 2 2015

How Managers Should Judge Psychology Experiments U. M. Dholakia *Harvard Business Review Digital Articles* p2 Ag 31 2015

How the Best CEOs Differ from Average Ones D. Stamoulis *Harvard Business Review Digital Articles* p2 N 15 2016

How to Handle Underperformers on a Team You Inherit R. Ashkenas *Harvard Business Review Digital Articles* p2 Je 15 2017

How to Keep Support for Your Project from Evaporating A. Rimm *Harvard Business Review Digital Articles* p2 Ag 10 2015

How to Manage a Team of All-Stars M. Mankins bw *Harvard Business Review Digital Articles* p2 Je 6 2017

How to Spot a Bad Boss During an Interview S. Stibitz *Harvard Business Review Digital Articles* p2 D 21 2015

How to Steer Clear of Office Gossip V. Lipman *Harvard Business Review Digital Articles* p2 O 19 2016

How to Work Confidently with Numbers People R. Knight *Harvard Business Review Digital Articles* p2 S 2 2015

Identifying the Biases Behind Your Bad Decisions J. Beshears and F. Gino *Harvard Business Review Digital Articles* p2 O 31 2014

Katia Beauchamp J. Johnson color *Current Biography* v77 no11 p21 N 2016

Keeping Your Strategy Meetings Focused on the Long Term S. Nawaz *Harvard Business Review Digital Articles* p2 Jl 27 2017

Make Sure Your Employees Have Good Things to Say About You Behind Your Back N. T. Washburn and B. Galvin *Harvard Business Review Digital Articles* p2 S 22 2016

Managers Are More Connected, But Not For The Better H. Mintzberg *Harvard Business Review Digital Articles* p2 Jl 20 2015

Managing 3 Types of Bad Bosses V. Nayar *Harvard Business Review Digital Articles* p2 D 1 2014

Mindfulness Works but Only If You Work at It M. Reitz and M. Chaskalson *Harvard Business Review Digital Articles* p2 N 4 2016

Moo-Young Han W. T. Chu and Kwang-Je Kim *Physics Today* v69 no11 p70 N 2016

THE NEW ESTABLISHMENT 2017 N. BILTON, W. ISAACSON et al bw color *Vanity Fair* v59 no11 p87 N 2017

New Managers Don't Have to Have All the Answers S. D'Souza and D. Renner *Harvard Business Review Digital Articles* p2 S 30 2015

New Managers Shouldn't Be Afraid to Express Their Emotions K. Hedges *Harvard Business Review Digital Articles* p2 Je 1 2017

NEXT LIST 2017 A. GREENBERG, C. METZ et al bw graph *Wired* v25 no5 p63 My 2017

Northern Bounty C. Armstrong color *Alternatives Journal (AJ) - Canada's Environmental Voice* v42 no2 p14 2016

PPID Update J. von Geldern color *Horse & Rider* v56 no2 p42 F 2017

Proof That Good Managers Really Do Make a Difference W. Frick *Harvard Business Review Digital Articles* p2 Ap 11 2016

The Pros and Cons of Robot Managers T. Chamorro-Premuzic and G. Ahmetoglu *Harvard Business Review Digital Articles* p2 D 12 2016

Pyrotechnics Beyond Definition T. H. Freeman *Stage Directions* v30 no2 p7 F 2017

Research: Executives Who Flatter Their CEOs Are More Likely to Criticize Them to the Press G. Keeves, J. Westphal et al bw *Harvard Business Review Digital Articles* p2 Ap 5 2017

Stop Reading Lists of Things Successful People Do E. Soyer and R. M. Hogarth *Harvard Business Review Digital Articles* p2 Mr 13 2017

Stop Trying to Please Everyone R. Ashkenas and M. McCreight *Harvard Business Review Digital Articles* p2 Jl 29 2015

Superbosses Aren't Afraid to Delegate Their Biggest Decisions S. Finkelstein *Harvard Business Review Digital Articles* p2 Ag 24 2016

A Survey of How 1,000 CEOs Spend Their Day Reveals What Makes Leaders Successful O. Bandiera, S. Hansen et al *Harvard Business Review Digital Articles* p2 O 12 2017

Taking Longer to Reach the Top Has Its Benefits K. Firestone *Harvard Business Review Digital Articles* p2 D 30 2015

There Are Two Types of Performance—but Most Organizations Only Focus on One L. McGregor and N. Doshi *Harvard Business Review Digital Articles* p2 O 10 2017

To Be a Great Leader, You Have to Learn How to Delegate Well J. Sostrin *Harvard Business Review Digital Articles* p2 O 10 2017

To Grow as a Leader, Seek More Complex Assignments C. Fernández-Aráoz *Harvard Business Review Digital Articles* p2 Jl 20 2016

To Succeed as a First-Time Leader, Relax D. Brendel *Harvard Business Review Digital Articles* p1 S 30 2016

Using Social Media Without Jeopardizing Your Career A. Samuel *Harvard Business Review Digital Articles* p2 Jl 20 2015

Want to Be an Outstanding Leader? Keep a Journal N. J. Adler *Harvard Business Review Digital Articles* p2 Ja 13 2016

We Shouldn't Always Need a "Business Case" to Do the Right Thing A. Taylor *Harvard Business Review Digital Articles* p2 S 19 2017

What Artificial Intelligence Can and Can't Do Right Now A. Ng *Harvard Business Review Digital Articles* p2 N 9 2016

What Does an Aspiring Founder Need to Know? T. R. Eisenmann and R. Howe *Harvard Business Review Digital Articles* p1 Je 21 2017

What It Really Means to Be a Chief Innovation Officer T. Wedell-Wedellsborg *Harvard Business Review Digital Articles* p2 D 5 2014

What Leadership Looks Like in Different Cultures T. Chamorro-Premuzic and M. Sanger *Harvard Business Review Digital Articles* p2 My 6 2017

What VCs Can Teach Executives About What Drives Returns M. Wessel *Harvard Business Review Digital Articles* p2 Je 25 2015

What Younger Managers Should Know About How They're Perceived J. Zenger and J. Folkman *Harvard Business Review Digital Articles* p2 S 29 2015

When Cultural Differences Interfere with Your Time A. Molinsky *Harvard Business Review Digital Articles* p2 Ap 14 2015

When You Have to Fire Good People M. Altschuler color *Harvard Business Review Digital Articles* p2 Mr 3 2017

Who Needs Advisory Boards? R. SALAM *National Review* v69 no17 p13 S 11 2017

Why Wonder Woman Broke Through E. Dockterman color *Time*

v189 no23 p52 Je 19 2017

Worried by his wandering hands *People Management* p52 Jl 2017

The Write Stuff J. Johnson color *Yankee* p26 Jl 2017

You Just Got Promoted. Now What? W. Naugle bw *Glamour* v115 no6 p104 Je 2017

Your Company Is Full of Good Experiments (You Just Have to Recognize Them) O. Hauser and M. Luca *Harvard Business Review Digital Articles* p2 N 23 2015

You're Never Too Experienced to Fake It Till You Learn It H. Ibarra *Harvard Business Review Digital Articles* p2 Ja 8 2015

Executives' attitudes

The Dangers of Hiring a Nice CEO E. L. Botelho, D. Wang et al *Harvard Business Review Digital Articles* p2 Je 7 2016

Don't Wake Me Unless There's Snacks K. Morell *Bloomberg Businessweek* no4504 p63 D 19 2016

Empathy Is Still Lacking in the Leaders Who Need It Most E. J. Wilson III *Harvard Business Review Digital Articles* p2 S 21 2015

First-Time Managers, Don't Do Your Team's Work for Them R. Ashkenas *Harvard Business Review Digital Articles* p2 S 21 2015

Good Leaders Aren't Afraid to Be Nice J. Panepinto *Harvard Business Review Digital Articles* p2 Ap 8 2015

Great Innovators Create the Future, Manage the Present, and Selectively Forget the Past V. Govindarajan *Harvard Business Review Digital Articles* p2 Mr 31 2016

How to Be a Pro-Vacation Manager in a High-Pressure Industry L. J. Waitz *Harvard Business Review Digital Articles* p2 Je 22 2015

How to Deal with a Boss Who Behaves Unpredictably C. O'Hara *Harvard Business Review Digital Articles* p2 N 3 2016

How to Keep Your Team Focused and Productive During Uncertain Times A. Gallo bw *Harvard Business Review Digital Articles* p2 Mr 8 2017

How to Know If Someone Is Ready to Be a Manager A. Ranieri *Harvard Business Review Digital Articles* p2 Je 2 2016

How to Manage Someone Who Can't Handle Ambiguity M. F. R. K. de Vries *Harvard Business Review Digital Articles* p2 Mr 10 2015

How to Negotiate for Yourself When People Don't Expect You To D. M. Kolb and D. A. Noumair *Harvard Business Review Digital Articles* p2 Je 17 2016

How to Push Your Team to Take Risks and Experiment S. Critchfield color *Harvard Business Review Digital Articles* p2 Mr 9 2017

How to Work for a Narcissistic Boss R. Knight *Harvard Business Review Digital Articles* p2 Ap 1 2016

How Your Leadership Has to Change as Your Startup Scales J. W. Hull *Harvard Business Review Digital Articles* p2 My 20 2016

If You Can't Say What Your Meeting Will Accomplish, You Shouldn't Have It B. Frisch and C. Greene *Harvard Business Review Digital Articles* p2 Ap 18 2016

If Your Boss Tells You to Get a Coach, Don't Panic R. Ashkenas *Harvard Business Review Digital Articles* p2 F 26 2015

Is It OK to Get Paid More for Being Lucky? I. Almas, A. W. Cappelen et al color graph *Harvard Business Review Digital Articles* p2 Mr 9 2017

Learn to Become a Less Autocratic Manager J. W. Hull *Harvard Business Review Digital Articles* p2 Mr 6 2015

Manager's divorce is getting us down *People Management* p52 D 2016/Ja 2017

New Managers Should Focus on Helping Their Teams, Not Pleasing Their Bosses K. Dillon *Harvard Business Review Digital Articles* p2 Jl 7 2017

People Won't Grow If You Think They Can't Change M. Valcour *Harvard Business Review Digital Articles* p2 Ap 21 2016

The Problem with Saying "My Door Is Always Open" M. Reitz and J. Higgins color *Harvard Business Review Digital Articles* p2 Mr 9 2017

Research: Your Abusive Boss Is Probably an Insomniac C. M. Barnes *Harvard Business Review Digital Articles* p2 N 7 2014

Serving on Boards Helps Executives Get Promoted S. Boivie, S. D. Graffin et al *Harvard Business Review Digital Articles* p2 My 20 2016

STOP THE MEETING MADNESS: HOW TO FREE UP TIME FOR MEANINGFUL WORK L. A. PERLOW, C. N. HADLEY

et al chart color img *Harvard Business Review* v95 no4 p62 Jl/Ag 2017

Stop Trying to Find Your True Self at Work G. Petriglieri *Harvard Business Review Digital Articles* p2 Ap 3 2015

The Trickle-Down Effect of Good (and Bad) Leadership J. Zenger and J. Folkman *Harvard Business Review Digital Articles* p2 Ja 14 2016

True Leaders Believe Dissent Is an Obligation B. Taylor bw *Harvard Business Review Digital Articles* p2 Ja 12 2017

The Unexpected Influence of Stories Told at Work F. Gino *Harvard Business Review Digital Articles* p2 S 15 2015

We're All Capable of Being an Abusive Boss [Cover story] M. Mawritz, R. L. Greenbaum et al *Harvard Business Review Digital Articles* p2 O 14 2016

What If Management Ideas Actually Mattered? G. Petriglieri *Harvard Business Review Digital Articles* p2 N 5 2015

What to Do After a Bad Performance Review C. O'Hara *Harvard Business Review Digital Articles* p2 O 29 2014

What to Do If You Catch Your Boss in a Lie P. Meyer *Harvard Business Review Digital Articles* p2 Mr 28 2017

What to Do If Your Boss Is a Control Freak K. Dillon *Harvard Business Review Digital Articles* p2 D 23 2014

When a Public Mistake Requires an Old-Fashioned Apology R. Ashkenas *Harvard Business Review Digital Articles* p2 Ja 7 2015

Win Over the Person Blocking Your Deal P. V. Weinstein *Harvard Business Review Digital Articles* p2 N 4 2014

Executives—China

What China's Shift to a Service Economy Means for Its Managers D. De Cremer and J. D. Shaw *Harvard Business Review Digital Articles* p2 Jl 26 2016

Executives—Computer network resources

Machine Intelligence Will Let Us All Work Like CEOs S. Zilis *Harvard Business Review Digital Articles* p2 Je 13 2016

Executives—Conduct of life

Becoming a Manager in a New Country A. Molinsky *Harvard Business Review Digital Articles* p2 S 14 2015

What You Can Do to Improve Ethics at Your Company C. McLaverty and A. McKee *Harvard Business Review Digital Articles* p2 D 29 2016

Executives—Congresses

FORGING A NEW SOCIAL COMPACT C. Leaf color *Fortune* v174 no7 p8 D 1 2016

Executives—Dismissal of

BIG FOOD'S MASS CEO EXODUS B. Kowitt color *Fortune* v176 no4 p138 S 15 2017

Executives—Employment

4 Things That Sink New Executives, and How to Overcome Them R. Carucci *Harvard Business Review Digital Articles* p2 F 9 2016

More of Us Are Working in Big Bureaucratic Organizations than Ever Before G. Hamel and M. Zanini *Harvard Business Review Digital Articles* p2 Jl 5 2016

WHEN HIRING EXECS, CONTEXT MATTERS MOST bw *Harvard Business Review* v95 no5 p20 S/O 2017

Executives—Health

All the Doctors Will See You Now S. Grobart color diag *Bloomberg Businessweek* no4508 p55 Ja 23 2017

HEART OF A CHAMPION A. WALLACE *Los Angeles Magazine* p120 Ap 2017

Why Leaders Don't Brag About Successfully Managing Stress J. R. Bailey *Harvard Business Review Digital Articles* p2 O 29 2014

Executives—History

The Evolution of the CMO C. FLEIT color *Harvard Business Review* v95 no4 p60 Jl/Ag 2017

Executives—Interviews

3-D Printing: The Future of Climbing Holds? Z. GATES color *Climbing* no354 p16 Jl 2017

Betting on the Texas (Olive) Oil Boom P. M. ESSWEIN color *Kiplinger's Personal Finance* v71 no10 p22 O 2017

The New Orleans Shakespeare Festival at Tulane color *New Orleans Magazine* v51 no8 p29 Je 2017

Project Manage Your Life D. Rousmaniere *Harvard Business Review Digital Articles* p2 F 10 2015

Q&A *People Management* p13 D 2016/Ja 2017

Three Qs *Science* v356 no6341 p889 Je 1 2017

WHEEL AND DEAL *Harper's Magazine* no2007 p19 Ag 2017

Executives—Mental health

Why Middle Managers Are So Unhappy J. Zenger and J. Folkman *Harvard Business Review Digital Articles* p2 N 24 2014

Executives—Psychology

BEING THE BOSS IN BRUSSELS, BOSTON, AND BEIJING: IF YOU WANT TO SUCCEED, YOU'LL NEED TO ADAPT E. MEYER color graph il img *Harvard Business Review* v95 no4 p70 Jl/Ag 2017

Good Bosses Create More Wellness than Wellness Plans Do E. Seppala *Harvard Business Review Digital Articles* p2 Ap 8 2016

How to Overcome Executive Isolation R. Ashkenas color *Harvard Business Review Digital Articles* p2 F 2 2017

How to Practice Mindfulness Throughout Your Work Day R. Hougaard and J. Carter *Harvard Business Review Digital Articles* p2 Mr 4 2016

How Your State of Mind Affects Your Performance A. Caillet, J. Hirshberg et al *Harvard Business Review Digital Articles* p2 D 8 2014

New Managers: Embrace Your Rookie Status L. Wiseman *Harvard Business Review Digital Articles* p2 O 2 2015

Spending 10 Minutes a Day on Mindfulness Subtly Changes the Way You React to Everything R. Hougaard, J. Carter et al color *Harvard Business Review Digital Articles* p2 Ja 18 2017

Stop Worrying About How Much You Matter P. Bregman *Harvard Business Review Digital Articles* p2 Je 25 2015

When Joking with Your Employees Leads to Bad Behavior Kai Chi (Sam) Yam *Harvard Business Review Digital Articles* p2 Mr 17 2017

When Was the Last Time You Took On a New Challenge? K. Firestone *Harvard Business Review Digital Articles* p2 F 17 2017

Why Middle Managers Are So Unhappy J. Zenger and J. Folkman *Harvard Business Review Digital Articles* p2 N 24 2014

Why You Should Make Time for Self-Reflection (Even If You Hate Doing It) J. Porter *Harvard Business Review Digital Articles* p2 Mr 21 2017

Executives—Rating of

See also

Rating of chief executive officers

Rating of women executives

A 6-Part Structure for Giving Clear and Actionable Feedback M. Goldsmith *Harvard Business Review Digital Articles* p2 Ag 7 2015

How Cisco Gets Brutally Honest Feedback to Top Leaders C. Frangos *Harvard Business Review Digital Articles* p2 D 29 2015

Identifying Leaders Who Could Bypass the Typical Promotion Path C. Frangos *Harvard Business Review Digital Articles* p2 S 27 2016

Executives—Recruiting

See also

Executive succession

How to Take the Bias Out of Interviews I. Bohnet *Harvard Business Review Digital Articles* p2 Ap 18 2016

What the Best Cross-Cultural Managers Have in Common L. Brimm *Harvard Business Review Digital Articles* p2 Je 29 2016

Executives—Retirement

Welcome Freshmen! C. Hymowitz color *Bloomberg Businessweek* no4516 p39 Mr 27 2017

Executives—Sexual behavior

How do I rebuff his advances? *People Management* p56 O 2016

Executives—Sweden

Are Successful CEOs Just Lucky? W. Frick *Harvard Business Review Digital Articles* p2 N 16 2015

Executives—Training of

Board Members Benefit from Becoming Mentors D. F. Melcher and A. J. Procopio *Harvard Business Review Digital Articles* p2 D 16 2014

Fixing the Leadership Gap in Southeast Asia V. Ratanjee and A. Pyrka *Harvard Business Review Digital Articles* p2 My 27 2015

Executives—United States

Business Tycoons bw cartoon color *American Cowboy* p32 LEGENDS OF TEXAS Special Issue 2017

Executives—United States—Interviews

'If you're in a partnership, you're only as good as your weakest partners' M. Murphy color *Bloomberg Businessweek* no4522

p54 My 15 2017

Exelis Inc.

Board Members Benefit from Becoming Mentors D. F. Melcher and A. J. Procopio *Harvard Business Review Digital Articles* p2 D 16 2014

Exercise

See also

Abdominal exercises

Aerobic exercises

Anaerobic exercises

Breathing exercises

Exercise for men

Exercise for women

Gymnastics

Hand exercises

Kegel exercises

Leg exercises

Muscle strength

Running

Strength training

Yoga

THE 12-MINUTE HOTEL-ROOM WORKOUT cartoon color *Esquire* p68 S 2017

12 Ways to Blast Calories in a Hurry L. Leicht color *Health* v30 no10 p62 D 2016

15 MINUTE WORKOUT color *Women's Health* v14 no8 p76 O 2017

4 Simple Exercises to Keep You Toned Through the Holidays cartoon *Prevention* v68 no11 p13 N 2016

5 habits that feel so good color *Redbook* p100 My 2017

5 Moves to Reinvent Your Rear T. Anderson color *Health* v30 no10 p42 D 2016

5 Myths About Exercise B. MILLER color *Prevention* v69 no11 p30 N 2017

5 Signs You're Working Out Too Much A. Schlinger color *Health* v30 no9 p65 N 2016

5 WAYS... To Hit the Clute-Ham Tie-In K. LOREN color *Muscle & Performance* v9 no7 p66 Jl 2017

6 burning workout questions—answered! J. Andriakos color *Health* v31 no9 p41 N 2017

6 Surprising Things That May Improve Breast-Cancer Treatment A. Sifferlin color *Time* v190 no15 p45 O 16 2017

The 7 HABITS OF HIGHLY EFFECTIVE MARATHONERS B. Stulberg and S. Magness cartoon color *Runner's World* v52 no6 p62 Jl 2017

7 ideas to ignite your passion for practice H. Dowdle color *Yoga Journal* p14 2017 Special Issue

Abs Anywhere L. MCGLASHAN color *Muscle & Performance* v9 no11 p26 N 2017

The All-New 6-Move Quad Crusher J. Schaeffer bw color *Men's Health* v31 no10 p126 D 2016

All Your Likes cartoon color *Seventeen* v76 no2 p16 Mr 2017

Are You Ready for MetaShred Extreme? B. J. Gaddour bw color *Men's Health* v32 no1 p132 Ja/F 2017

Arm Yourself Like Robin Wright color *Health* v31 no8 p13 O 2017

Ascend & Deliver M. BERG chart color *Muscle & Performance* v9 no10 p24 O 2017

ask the experts K. Rowse and M. H. Bell color *Dressage Today* v23 no6 p64 F 2017

A Baller's Guide to Abs B. J. Gaddour cartoon color *Men's Health* v32 no2 p8 Mr 2017

BALLS TO THE WALL J. CONNOR color *Muscle & Performance* v9 no4 p24 Ap 2017

Band Bicycle cartoon *Prevention* p16 Mr 2017

The Bay-kini Workout E. Abbate color *Glamour* v115 no5 p110 My 2017

Beach Body Boot Camp T. Anderson color *Health* v31 no6 p46 Jl 2017

The Beach-Towel WORKOUT *Seventeen* v76 no4 p54 Jl/Ag 2017

THE BEGINNER'S GUIDE TO LOSING WEIGHT J. Detz cartoon chart *Men's Health* v32 no1 p70 Ja/F 2017

BEST DEAL ON HEALTH CARE: exercise V. TWEED color *Better Nutrition* v78 no11 p14 N 2016

The Best Reasons to EXERCISE OZ color *O, The Oprah Magazine* p67 Ja 2017

better S. LIAO color *Better Homes & Gardens* v95 no2 p123 F 2016

better S. LIAO color *Better Homes & Gardens* v95 no9 p142 S 2017

Be your own personal trainer J. Andriakos color *Health* v31 no8 p21 O 2017

Bharadvajasana II [Cover story] K. Paalman color *Yoga Journal* no292 p53 Je 2017

Birds don't need exercise to stay fit for epic flights E. Pennisi color *Science* v355 no6321 p121 Ja 13 2017

The "Body Kindness" Workout R. Scritchfield color *Amazing Wellness* v9 no1 p78 Wint 2017

Body of knowledge [Cover story] R. Long color *Yoga Journal* no289 p44 F 2017

Build a Body Like J.Lo T. Anderson color *Health* v30 no9 p59 N 2016

Build Muscle at Any Age—Like This Guy A. MCCARRON color *Men's Health* v32 no7 p52 S 2017

Build Muscle on the Sly color *Men's Health* v32 no9 p30 N 2017

BULK SEASON L. BOYCE chart color *Muscle & Performance* v8 no12 p38 D 2016

Call a Workout Audible cartoon chart color *Men's Health* v32 no8 p52 O 2017

CAN A DNA TEST GIVE YOU A BETTER BODY? A. Kuczynski color *Harper's Bazaar* no3656 p468 S 2017

Change It Up! C. CROW and J. F. MEYER color *Horse & Rider* v56 no9 p55 S 2017

Chisel Your Back B. Gaddour bw color *Men's Health* v31 no10 p40 D 2016

Chloë Grace Moretz S. Zuckerman color *InStyle* v23 no12 p200 N 2016

Core Moves You've Never Tried L. BOYCE color *Muscle & Performance* v9 no7 p41 Jl 2017

The Core Principles M. Barroso color *Men's Health* v32 no2 p50 Mr 2017

The Couch Crusher B. J. Gaddour cartoon color *Men's Health* v32 no3 p14 Ap 2017

CROSS FAT GAIN OFF YOUR LIST J. WUEBBEN color *Muscle & Performance* v8 no12 p16 D 2016

CROSSFIT V. Tweed color *Amazing Wellness* v8 no6 p86 Early Winter2016

Define & Conquer M. BERG chart color *Muscle & Performance* v9 no10 p22 O 2017

Don't let winter drag you down! [Cover story] A. Sweeney color *Redbook* p36 F 2017

Don't Sweat Out Stress color *Prevention* v69 no6 p14 Je 2017

Down you go C. BUHAY color *Backpacker* p29 S 2017

Easy ways to get stronger *Harvard Health Letter* v42 no6 p4 Ap 2017

EGREGIOUS ACTS OF EXERCISE N. TUMMINELLO color *Muscle & Performance* v9 no10 p46 O 2017

EIGHT PEOPLE TO WHIP YOU INTO SHAPE C. Cunningham *Washingtonian Magazine* v52 no4 p108 Ja 2017

EMILY SKYE A New Kind of Fit Chick J. Naftulin color *Health* v31 no1 p56 Ja 2017

Emily Skye P. KITA bw color *Men's Health* v32 no6 p40 Ag 2017

Endless Recess C. Ianzito color *AARP: The Magazine* v60 no5A p16 Ag/S 2017

Enter a Parallette Universe color *Men's Health* v32 no1 p46 Ja/F 2017

Escape the Gym K. Canning color *Health* v31 no5 p39 Je 2017

The Everything Guide to Running A. Shaffer chart color *Health* v31 no3 p35 Ap 2017

EXERCISE AND BONE HEALTH color *Harvard Health Letter* v42 no2 p5 D 2016

Exercise for Couch Potatoes color *Prevention* v69 no8 p16 Ag 2017

Exercise intervals *Mayo Clinic Health Letter* v35 no6 p7 Je 2017

Exercise your gray matter color *Good Housekeeping* v265 no2 p98 Ag 2017

EXTRA REPS A. HUTCHINSON color *Runner's World* v52 no4 p26 My 2017

FAST GAINS FROM FITNESS color *Prevention* v69 no11 p16 N 2017

Fast-Track Your Fat Loss [Cover story] bw color *Men's Health* v31 no10 p124 D 2016

Feel-Good Work for your Senior Horse [Cover story] J. Forsberg Meyer color *Horse & Rider* v56 no2 p34 F 2017

Find your exercise fit! *Harvard Health Letter* v42 no5 p4 Mr 2017

Fire Up Your Hustle Muscles bw color *Men's Health* v31 no10 p127 D 2016

FIT FOR FREE L. SCHOLZ *Atlanta* v57 no1 p40 My 2017

Fit for Life B. Howard color *AARP: The Magazine* v59 no3A p44 Ap/My 2016

FIT IN 15 core values A. SHAFFER *Better Homes & Gardens* v94 no11 p164 N 2016

Fitness News Young Brains Can Use S. SEA GOLD color *Parents* v92 no5 p20 My 2017

FLEX TIME M. Gainsburg chart color *Women's Health* v14 no8 p78 O 2017

Forge the Maximus Body B. Maximus bw *Men's Health* v32 no3 p40 Ap 2017

fresh STARTS J. Francisco color *Good Housekeeping* v264 no1 p4 Ja 1 2017

Gains of Thrones B. J. GADDOUR color *Men's Health* v32 no6 p34 Ag 2017

Gentle Moves A. FERRETTI color *Prevention* v69 no11 p64 N 2017

Get a Grip on the Farmer's Walk cartoon *Men's Health* v32 no9 p24 N 2017

Get buff like Wonder Woman color *Health* v31 no9 p16 N 2017

Get Fierce In 5! cartoon color *Seventeen* v76 no2 p87 Mr 2017

Get Fit Fast T. VANDERMOLEN il *Backpacker* p28 Je 2017

GET FIT WITH A FRENEMY *Health* v31 no2 p15 Mr 2017

Get Fit Without Working Out! C. THORP color *Seventeen* v76 no3 p64 My 2017

Get Real A. Nix *Amazing Wellness* v9 no1 p8 Wint 2017

Get Ripped on These 6 Trips T. GRAHAM color *Men's Health* v32 no6 p29 Ag 2017

Get to know... your glutes J. Miller color *Yoga Journal* p76 2017 SpecialIssue

go with the flow color *Yoga Journal* p58 2017 Special Issue

guts and glory [Cover story] A. Prato color *Health* v30 no10 p104 D 2016

HAMSTRING HELPERS B. SABIN color *Runner's World* v51 no11 p54 D 2016

HAVE A BALL color *Good Housekeeping* v265 no2 p100 Ag 2017

the health nut A. Brightfield *Better Homes & Gardens* v94 no11 p158 N 2016

HEART-HEALTH WAKE-UPCALL B. BRODY bw cartoon color *Better Homes & Gardens* v95 no2 p125 F 2016

Help Me Transform My Thighs! T. Anderson color *Health* v31 no3 p52 Ap 2017

Here's an Idea: Rethink Your Rest Day cartoon color *Men's Health* v32 no8 p50 O 2017

High and Dry T. MIKACICH *Boating World* v38 no3 p16 Mr 2017

Hips, Hopped M. Gainsburg bw diag *Women's Health* v14 no3 p55 Ap 2017

Hit the Playground! M. Anderson color *Parents* v92 no9 p104 S 2017

HITTING REFRESH D. WILLEY color *Runner's World* v52 no4 p10 My 2017

A home practice to Boost heart health S. Nardini color *Yoga Journal* p33 2017 Special Issue

A home practice to build a strong back J. Elmer color *Yoga Journal* no287 p45 N 2016

A home practice to re-energize and find greater joy A. Kaivalya color *Yoga Journal* no288 p55 D 2016

House of Cardio B. J. GADDOUR cartoon color *Men's Health* v32 no4 p34 My 2017

How Emma Stone Got Ripped S. Dreisbach color *Glamour* v115 no9 p114 S 2017

"HOW I DROPPED 62 lbs ...AND A BAD RELATIONSHIP" color *Good Housekeeping* v265 no1 p101 Jl 2017

How I Found My Feel-Great Weight A. Levi color *Health* v31 no6 p48 Jl 2017

How I Shed 72 Pounds L. Murray color *Health* v31 no2 p58 Mr 2017

How to Be Unbreakable L. LEICHT cartoon color *Women's Health* v14 no9 p68 N 2017

How to move from High Lunge to Dhanurasana J. Blumstein color

cle & Performance v9 no5 p40 My 2017

Sweat Out Your Blahs J. SAVIN and A. STANLEY color Seventeen v76 no12 p65 D 2016/Ja 2017

SWIMSUIT SHAPE-UP color Good Housekeeping v264 no5 p102 My 2017

TAKE IT OUTSIDE Atlanta v56 no11 p48 Mr 2017

TAKE THE PLUNGE K. DOLD color Runner's World v52 no7 p14 Ag 2017

This Is Your Body on Exercise K. Canning color Health v31 no7 p72 S 2017

THIS WORKOUT IS ALL WET color Health v31 no9 p20 N 2017

TONE YOUR TUSH A. Reliford color Good Housekeeping v265 no1 p92 Jl 2017

The Totally Trail-Ready Workout L. McGLASHAN chart color Muscle & Performance v9 no9 p20 S 2017

Tracy Anderson's Beautiful Body Secrets [Cover story] R. S. Frazier color Health v31 no4 p82 My 2017

Travel + Tone color Health v30 no10 p18 D 2016

The Triathlon Training Trifecta bw color Men's Health v32 no2 p114 Mr 2017

The Unboring Workout S. G. Levy color Glamour v114 no12 p154 D 2016

Wake Up and Work Out! K. Canning color Health v31 no6 p24 Jl 2017

Warm Up for Horsemanship B. Henry and J. Paulson color Horse & Rider v55 no11 p25 N 2016

Weekend Warriors = #Winning color Health v31 no4 p12 My 2017

Welcome to the Jungle Gym M. ARAGONCILLO color Men's Health v32 no6 p50 Ag 2017

wellness TRAILBLAZERS A. OGLETHORPE color Better Homes & Gardens v95 no9 p146 S 2017

WE LOVE HEARING FROM YOU! color diag Essence v48 no5 p24 S 2017

What You Said About ... L. Rothman Time v189 no21 p4 Je 5 2017

The WH Menses Society [Cover story] M. Devash cartoon color graph Women's Health v14 no1 p94 Ja/F 2017

Why Not...Jump into Shape! color Health v31 no3 p11 Ap 2017

Work It Out(side) K. Casteel color Missouri Life v44 no6 p76 S 2017

THE WORLD IS YOUR GYM A. McCARRON, L. ROSENBAUM et al bw color Men's Health v32 no6 p114 Ag 2017

WRISTS OF FURY S. Munroe and D. DeNunzio color Golf Magazine v58 no12 p83 D 2016

you * health news Parents v92 no2 p70 F 2017

YOUR BEST BODY [Cover story] J. B. Southerland and C. Kuzma color Prevention v69 no6 p40 Je 2017

Your Fit in 10 Plan cartoon Prevention v69 no2 p16 F 2017

Your Fit in 10 Plan color Prevention v69 no11 p15 N 2017

Your Fit in 10 Plan color Prevention v69 no8 p17 Ag 2017

Your glutes [Cover story] J. Miller color Yoga Journal no292 p62 Je 2017

Exercise equipment
 See also
 Medicine balls
 Resistance bands (Exercise equipment)
 Treadmills (Exercise equipment)

Your New Travel Workouts A. McCARRON cartoon chart color Men's Health v32 no9 p48 N 2017

Exercise equipment—Evaluation

Intense Supps color Muscle & Performance v9 no10 p62 O 2017

Exercise for men

BEST. EXERCISE. EVER cartoon chart color Men's Health v32 no5 p130 Je 2017

Finish Your Six-Pack in Just 10 Minutes bw color Men's Health v32 no2 p116 Mr 2017

No-Gear Total-Body Blast E. SAMUEL color Men's Health v32 no8 p46 O 2017

Exercise for older people

MAKE OVER YOUR Metabolism [Cover story] C. KUZMA cartoon color graph Prevention v69 no5 p66 My 2017

Exercise for women

15 MINUTE WORKOUT M. Gainsburg color Women's Health v14 no3 p60 Ap 2017

THE BAYWATCH BODY BURN cartoon Women's Health v14 no5 p143 Je 2017

BEST SHAPE OF YOUR LIFE [Cover story] M. Gainsburg color Women's Health v13 no10 p76 D 2016

BYE-BYE, BELLY color Good Housekeeping v264 no3 p105 Mr 2017

Easy exercises that keep you young H. Powell color Redbook p77 Mr 2017

FLAB-FREE ARMS S. Walter color Good Housekeeping v264 no6 p87 Je 2017

The Get-Glowing WORKOUT C. Innes cartoon color Seventeen p142 Ja 1 2017

HIRED GUNS! [Cover story] M. Gainsburg color Women's Health v14 no5 p66 Je 2017

One minute to a better butt A. Swan cartoon color Redbook p99 My 2017

PICK A MOVE! ANY MOVE! [Cover story] A. CAMPBELL bw Women's Health v13 no10 p140 D 2016

Simply Toned J. B. SOUTHERLAND color Prevention v69 no9 p74 O 2017

TIGHTER TUSH S. Walter color Good Housekeeping v264 no4 p103 Ap 2017

Your Fit in 10 Plan color Prevention v69 no9 p17 O 2017

Exercise-induced anaphylaxis

Addressing Hives in the Performance Horse L. Gray color Dressage Today v23 no11 p18 Ag 2017

Exercise intensity

HIIT TUNES color Health v31 no3 p14 Ap 2017

Exercise personnel

SPIN THE WHEEL color Women's Health v14 no7 p40 S 2017

Exercise physiology

4 little moves that work wonders A. Sweeney color Redbook p24 N 2017

6 More Reasons to Get Up and Move A. Macmillan, A. Park et al color Time v190 no4 p40 Jl 24 2017

better Better Homes & Gardens v94 no11 p149 N 2016

Burn More Fat with Yoga color Health v31 no5 p14 Je 2017

The Exercise Paradox [Cover story] H. Pontzer color graph Scientific American v316 no2 p26 F 2017

FINDING FITNESS: Incorporating exercise and wellness can increase years of happiness and health S. Walsh Washingtonian Magazine v52 no8 p146 My 2017

Find Your Best Burn M. Heid color Time v190 no4 p45 Jl 24 2017

From Obese to Ironman A. Levi color Health v31 no5 p51 Je 2017

From Workouts to Far Out M. DiChristina color Scientific American v316 no2 p4 F 2017

IN THE BEGINNING... L. MCGLASHAN color Muscle & Performance v9 no1 p30 Ja 2017

Let's Take This Outside M. Bean color Men's Health v32 no6 p8 Ag 2017

Making Moves L. REGENSDORF and C. ELLENBERG color Vogue v207 no9 p452 S 2017

Powerhouse Renovation G. Reynolds New York Times Magazine p22 Mr 26 2017

Regular Exercise Is Part of Your Job R. Friedman Harvard Business Review Digital Articles p2 O 3 2014

The #TBT Workout E. Abbate color Glamour v115 no7 p58 Jl 2017

This Is Your Body on Exercise K. Canning color Health v31 no7 p72 S 2017

We've Got Your Back! M. ANDERSON color Parents v92 no11 p84 N 2017

The Wherever Workout color AARP: The Magazine v59 no4A p62 Je/Jl 2016

Exercise therapy

getting physical T. REECE Parents v91 no11 p140 N 2016

reach for the STARS color Yoga Journal no291 p8 My 2017

Exercise videos

DANCE REVOLUTION R. SHELLABARGER Indianapolis Monthly p32 F 2017

Exercise—Charts, diagrams, etc.

How Sore Is TOO SORE? N. Clancy color O, The Oprah Magazine p72 Jl 2017

Exercise—Equipment & supplies
 See also
 Foam rollers (Exercise equipment)

Medicine balls
Resistance bands (Exercise equipment)
The 2017 Performance Gear Awards bw color *Men's Health* v32 no4 p39 My 2017
Choose the Right Machine for You bw *Kiplinger's Personal Finance* v71 no1 p70 Ja 2017
REAR-DELT MACHINE FLYE (AKA REVERSE PEC DECK) J. WUEBBEN cartoon *Muscle & Performance* v8 no12 p16 D 2016

Exercise—Equipment & supplies—Evaluation
INSIDER TRAINING J. DENGATE color *Runner's World* v52 no1 p90 Ja/F 2017
Tack Room color *Practical Horseman* v45 no2 p70 F 2017

Exercise—Evaluation
Are You Overtraining? color *Health* v31 no2 p6 Mr 2017
EXERCISE C. DOW *Nutrition Action Health Letter* v44 no3 p9 Ap 2017
Get into Fighting Shape Like Ruby Rose color *Health* v31 no1 p16 Ja 2017
LEA MICHELE'S BETTER-BUTT SECRET color *Health* v31 no2 p15 Mr 2017
New Year, New Arms T. Anderson color *Health* v31 no1 p58 Ja 2017
Power Days Start Here C. McHugh color *Health* v31 no2 p8 Mr 2017
Tighten Up with a Towel T. Anderson color *Health* v31 no2 p51 Mr 2017
Turn up your burn J. Andriakos color *Health* v31 no9 p26 N 2017
Yes, you can stick to an exercise regimen! *Harvard Health Letter* v42 no3 p1 Ja 2017

Exercise—Humor
Laugh Lines *Reader's Digest* v189 no1128 p93 Mr 2017

Exercise—Study & teaching
Help! I'm Too Tall! K. Holmes color *Dance Spirit* v21 no4 p36 Ap 2017
ON A Roll O. Manno *Dance Spirit* v21 no4 p28 Ap 2017

Exhaust gas recirculation
IT'S A RECYCLING CENTER: UNDERSTANDING EXHAUST GAS RECIRCULATION R. Bohacz *Successful Farming* v115 no9 p33 Ag 2017

Exhaust systems
How Do Tuned, Equal-Length Headers Work? M. Davis color *Hot Rod* v70 no10 p86 O 2017
Service R. NIERLICH and K. Cameron color *Cycle World* v56 no10 p66 N 2017
Service R. NIERLICH color *Cycle World* v56 no6 p62 Jl 2017

Exhaust systems—Equipment & supplies
A MIGHTY (QUIET) WIND R. Verger color *Popular Science* v289 no4 p26 Jl/Ag 2017

Exhibition buildings—Design & construction
AS+GG's Massive Astana Expo City Nears Completion A. FIXSEN color *Architectural Record* v205 no3 p23 Mr 2017

Exhibition buildings—Evaluation
BRINGING VIKING-ERA ICELAND TO LIFE color *Iceland Review* v54 no5 p106 S-O 2016

Exhibition reviews
Arbus, Unearthed: Eight rarely seen New York moments C. BONANOS img *New York* v50 no9 p84 My 1 2017
ART cartoon *New Yorker* v93 no27 p15 S 11 2017
Knocking It Off G. Adamson color *Magazine Antiques* v184 no4 p22 Jl/Ag 2017

Exhibitions
    See also
    Agricultural exhibitions
    Art exhibitions
    Education—Exhibitions
    Fashion shows
    Library exhibits
    Museum exhibits
    Outdoor exhibitions
    Photography exhibits
    Religion—Exhibitions
    Trade shows
Around the Country *Natural History* v125 no1 p34 D 2016/Ja 2017
dates&events *Architectural Record* v205 no6 p165 Je 2017

EVENTS + EXHIBITS color *Arts & Crafts Homes & the Revival* v12 no4 p20 Fall 2017
FEBRUARY'S COOLEST EVENTS *Indianapolis Monthly* p22 F 2017
GOINGS ON ABOUT TOWN color *New Yorker* v93 no29 p11 S 25 2017
THE GREAT WAR IS COMING—SOON *USA Today Magazine* v145 no2860 p76 Ja 2017
Of the world J. Bleem color *U.S. Catholic* v82 no3 p26 Mr 2017

Exhibitions—France
The 1900 World's Fair Helped Shape How We Talk About Tech Today A. MOLELLA *NPQ: New Perspectives Quarterly* v33 no4 p31 O 2016

Exhibitions—United States
ABOVE & BEYOND cartoon *New Yorker* v92 no41 p20 D 12 2016
ARCHIVES Events *Prologue* v49 no2 p66 Summ 2017
EVENTS K. Lanza color *Magazine Antiques* v184 no4 p122 Jl/Ag 2017

Exile & Lightning (Poem)
'EXILE AND LIGHTNING' R. Pinsky bw *New York Times Book Review* p16 Ag 6 2017

Exile (Film)
EXILE, WITHIN AND WITHOUT: NEWWORK IN TWO MODES FROM RITHY PANH D. Boyle *Film Quarterly* v71 no1 p10 Fall 2017

Exile (Punishment)
AMERICA IS BETTER THAN THIS E. G. J. Graves color *Black Enterprise* v47 no8 p8 Jl/Ag 2017
Someone else's problem B. HUTCHINSON *Maclean's* v130 no8 p16 S 2017

Exiles, The (Film : 1961)
Site Lines R. Brody color *New Yorker* v92 no39 p17 N 28 2016

Exiles—Legal status, laws, etc.
Denied Clemency, Snowden Remains Trapped In Putin's Game S. Shuster color *Time* v189 no3 p7 Ja 30 2017

Exit interviewing
Don't Lose Track of High Performers Who Take a Hiatus C. F. Cohen *Harvard Business Review Digital Articles* p2 Ja 5 2016

Exley, Christine
New Research: Women Who Don't Negotiate Might Have a Good Reason *Harvard Business Review Digital Articles* p2 Ap 12 2016

Exley, Zack
WELCOME TO THE RESISTANCE *In These Times* v40 no12 p14 D 2016

Exobiology on Mars program (European Space Agency)
ExoMars Lander Fails, Orbiter Succeeds D. DICKINSON *Sky & Telescope* v133 no2 p10 F 2017
Mars mission a go; asteroid lander killed bw *Science* v354 no6317 p1208 D 9 2016

Exomes
Distribution and clinical impact of functional variants in 50,726 whole-exome sequences from the DiscovEHR study F. E. Dewey, M. F. Murray et al chart graph *Science* v354 no6319 paaf6814-1 D 23 2016

Exoneration
EXONERATION M. SHAER *Smithsonian* v47 no9 p80 Ja/F 2017
LAW AND DISORDER *Smithsonian* v47 no9 p79 Ja/F 2017
MEMORIES OF A MURDER R. AVIV bw cartoon *New Yorker* v93 no17 p36 Je 19 2017

Exorcism
Battling the Devil color *Vanity Fair* v58 no12 p140 D 2016
Psychic Arrested in Exorcism Scam B. RADFORD *Skeptical Inquirer* v41 no1 p12 Ja/F 2017
This EXORCIST Is Real W. FRIEDKIN bw color *Reader's Digest* v190 no1134 p118 O 2017

Exorcist, The (TV program)
CHEERS & JEERS D. HOLBROOK *TV Guide* v64 no48 p88 N 21 2016
THE DEVIL AND MISS DAVIS D. HOLBROOK *TV Guide* v64 no46 p18 N 7 2016
The Exorcist S. Li, N. Abrams et al color *Entertainment Weekly* no1482/1483 p92 S 22 2017
John Cho E. Berman color *Time* v190 no7 p51 Ag 21 2017

Exoskeleton

Fast exoskeleton optimization P. Malcolm, S. Galle et al color graph *Science* v356 no6344 p1230 Je 23 2017

Human-in-the-loop optimization of exoskeleton assistance during walking J. Zhang, P. Fiers et al diag *Science* v356 no6344 p1280 Je 23 2017

Exotic animals

Escaped pets could save endangered species color *Science* v355 no6320 p11 Ja 6 2017

Expanding universe

Is the universe expanding faster than expected? color *Astronomy* v45 no5 p14 My 2017

SUPERVOID T. LUCKETT, J. J. CARROLL et al *Scientific American* v315 no6 p9 D 2016

Expanse, The (TV program)

The Best Sci-Fi Show You Aren't Watching D. Ross and R. Rahman color *Entertainment Weekly* no1453 p53 F 17 2017

Physics matters in "The Expanse." Sin does, too S. Sawyer and E. Sundrup color *America* v216 no3 p48 F 6 2017

What to Watch R. Rahman, S. Vilkomerson et al color *Entertainment Weekly* no1451/1452 p100 F 3-10 2017

Expansion (Business)

6 WAYS TO GET MEDIA COVERAGE FOR YOUR STARTUP K. Johnson color *Black Enterprise* v47 no8 p14 Jl/Ag 2017

Airbnb Inches Its Way Into China O. Zaleski and L. Y. Chen color *Bloomberg Businessweek* no4503 p30 D 12 2016

The Best Entrepreneurs Think Globally, Not Just Digitally M. Schrage *Harvard Business Review Digital Articles* p2 Mr 10 2016

BookWalker Offers Digital Manga And Light Novels in English B. Alverson *Publishers Weekly* v263 no46 p12 N 14 2016

Case Study: When You Have to Choose Between Core and New Customers: An extreme sports company considers a VIP tier M. BERTINI and N. TAVASSOLI il *Harvard Business Review* v95 no5 p143 S/O 2017

China's Twitter Returns From the Dead D. Ramli, T. Hall et al color graph *Bloomberg Businessweek* no4526 p28 Je 12 2017

COMPETING ON SOCIAL PURPOSE: BRANDS THAT WIN BY TYING MISSION TO GROWTH O. R. VIL&#193 and S. BHARADWAJ chart diag il img *Harvard Business Review* v95 no5 p94 S/O 2017

COSTCO D. G. Herbert cartoon *Atlantic* v320 no4 p24 N 2017

The Curious Downside of an Owner's Mindset J. Allen *Harvard Business Review Digital Articles* p2 Je 7 2016

Expanding the Reach of Primary Care in Developing Countries K. Mossman, O. Bhattacharyya et al color *Harvard Business Review Digital Articles* p2 Je 6 2017

Foxconned? J. MCCORMACK cartoon *Weekly Standard* v22 no48 p17 S 4 2017

A Framework for Strategists Assessing Emerging Markets T. Cooper and M. Purdy *Harvard Business Review Digital Articles* p2 Jl 2 2015

F. Ronstadt Hardware Co.: Although Linda Ronstadt is the most famous Ronstadt, it was her grandfather, Federico Jose Maria Ronstadt, w ho made the family name synonymous w ith Tucson, Arizona R. RUSSO *Arizona Highways* v96 no7 p8 Jl 2017

Game of Porcelain Thrones P. CARBONARA and W. BALDWIN color *Forbes* v200 no2 p37 S 5 2017

The Greatest Barriers to Growth, According to Executives C. Zook *Harvard Business Review Digital Articles* p2 My 17 2016

HC Eyes More Global Expansion, Physical Distribution J. Milliot chart *Publishers Weekly* v264 no33 p5 Ag 14 2017

How to Set More-Realistic Growth Targets R. G. McGrath and A. van Putten *Harvard Business Review Digital Articles* p2 Jl 12 2017

Is This Indigo's Moment? J. Milliot chart *Publishers Weekly* v264 no30 p4 Jl 24 2017

Keeping the Zeal of a Startup as You Scale J. Allen *Harvard Business Review Digital Articles* p2 Jl 5 2016

Letter From the Editor E. J. Pollock *Bloomberg Businessweek* no4496 p5 O 24 2016

Long Reach, Big Problems C. Jasper and D. K. Yousef bw *Bloomberg Businessweek* no4523 p22 My 22 2017

Millenial burger M. HEMMADI color *Maclean's* no1 p46 F 17 2017

NETFLIX PRESENTS BUILDING A WORLD OF BINGE-WATCHERS L. Shaw and F. Gillette color *Bloomberg Businessweek* no4507 p40 Ja 16 2017

The New Rules for Growing Outside Your Core Business C. Zook *Harvard Business Review Digital Articles* p2 My 4 2015

ONE OCEAN EXPEDITIONS EXPANDS FLEET TO INCLUDE RCGS RESOLUTE S. Doyle color *Canadian Geographic* v137 no5 p75 S/O 2017

Season to Stopover *New York* v50 no17 p148 Ag 21 2017

STORAGE WARS N. KÖHLER color *Maclean's* v130 no7 p52 Ag 2017

The Taming of a Teen Emporium R. Williams and A. Molin color *Bloomberg Businessweek* no4518 p26 Ap 10 2017

UBER'S BOLD MOVE [Cover story] M. HELFT, A. Ohnsman et al color *Forbes* v198 no9 p58 D 30 2016

We Three Kings County Booksellers color *Publishers Weekly* v264 no33 p84 Ag 14 2017

What Engineering a Reverse Innovation Looks Like A. Winter and V. Govindarajan *Harvard Business Review Digital Articles* p2 N 4 2015

Why Xiaomi Can't Succeed Without India A. Gupta and H. Wang *Harvard Business Review Digital Articles* p2 Je 29 2015

Your Business Is Going to Depend on Connected Spenders, So You'd Better Understand Who They Are L. Keely color *Harvard Business Review Digital Articles* p2 Je 29 2015

Your Organization Wastes Time. Here's How to Fix It E. Garton *Harvard Business Review Digital Articles* p2 Mr 13 2017

Expansion teams

HOT | NOT T. Keith color *Sports Illustrated* v125 no18 p20 D 5 2016

Expansion (Business)—Charts, diagrams, etc.

100 FASTEST-GROWING COMPANIES S. Decarlo, D. G. Elam et al chart color diag map *Fortune* v176 no4 p157 S 15 2017

THE CASE FOR FOCUSING ON GROWTH, NOT PROFITABILITY graph img *Harvard Business Review* v95 no5 p30 S/O 2017

The Fast Tech 25 color *Forbes* v199 no6 p48 Je 13 2017

Expectation (Psychology)

Great Expectations M. MARSHALL *Texas Monthly* v45 no2 p78 F 2017

Expectorants—Therapeutic use

What pediatricians tell their friends S. WOOD color *Redbook* p79 S 2017

Expedia Inc.

Dara Khosrowshahi color *Bloomberg Businessweek* no4522 p92 My 15 2017

Experian DataLabs (Company)

A Dedicated Team of Problem Solvers Can Help Big Companies Act Like Lean Startups G. Satell *Harvard Business Review Digital Articles* p2 Ag 24 2016

Experience

See also

Aesthetic experience

Experiential learning

Facts (Philosophy)

Life change events

Work experience (Employment)

The Accidental Career Coach M. NEMKO *Psychology Today* v49 no5 p48 S/O 2016

BEHIND THE SCENES C. AARON, M. HARVEY et al bw color *In These Times* v40 no11 p48 N 2016

Dance With a Demon L. O'DONNELL *Psychology Today* v50 no2 p40 Mr/Ap 2017

Double Take A. MEDRESS *Psychology Today* v50 no4 p36 Ag 2017

in focus color *Yoga Journal* no288 p95 D 2016

Is Mental Illness the Exception or the Rule? A LONG-TERM STUDY SUGGESTS THAT MOST PEOPLE STRUGGLE AT SOME POINT D. RETTEW *Psychology Today* v50 no4 p18 Ag 2017

LAST LOOK A. SCHWEITZER color *Yoga Journal* p112 2017 SpecialIssue

a letter to my child about growing up in the dark ages R. D'APICE *Parents* v92 no1 p38 Ja 2017

Love at First Touch T. Roberts color *Parents* v92 no6 p20 Je 2017

love shack, baby Liz color *Parents* v92 no6 p12 Je 2017

Meet your next teacher: Aadil Palkhivala [Cover story] color *Yoga Journal* no293 p90 Ag 2017

Meet your next teacher [Cover story] *Yoga Journal* no291 p75 My 2017

On the road again C. Gorrell color *Yoga Journal* no291 p12 My 2017

oops *Parents* v92 no6 p140 Je 2017

PILGRIMAGE TO INDIA [Cover story] M. RABBITT color *Yoga Journal* no290 p34 Mr 2017

reconnecting as a family J. WILSON *Parents* p86 2015

Relatable Days With Rebecca Minkoff J. Hartshorn color *Parents* v92 no9 p15 S 2017

THE SIZE OF THINGS S. SCHWEBLIN cartoon *New Yorker* v93 no15 p56 My 29 2017

Speak, Memory color *AARP: The Magazine* v59 no2A p74 F/Mr 2016

TRAUMARAMA color *Seventeen* v76 no4 p92 Jl/Ag 2017

We are one C. Gorrell color *Yoga Journal* no291 p16 My 2017

What My Music Teacher Taught Me About Money C. Kornelis color *Money* v46 no6 p80 Jl 2017

Why I Hate My Dog E. Egan color *Glamour* v114 no12 p174 D 2016

Why Your Late Twenties Is the Worst Time of Your Life R. Zilca *Harvard Business Review Digital Articles* p2 Mr 7 2016

Your True Stories *Reader's Digest* v188 no1125 p39 N 2016

Experience (Religion)

SAY AMEN TO GOOD HEALTH C. Stieg bw *Good Housekeeping* v263 no5 p150 N 2016

Experience—Psychological aspects

Being Experienced Doesn't Automatically Make You a Great Mentor A. Molinsky *Harvard Business Review Digital Articles* p2 Ja 28 2015

Experiential learning

    See also

    Service learning

Hootsuite's CEO on What He Learned from Getting Hacked on Social Media R. Holmes *Harvard Business Review Digital Articles* p2 O 6 2016

OUR PARENTS ARE OUR FUTURE C. FRAZIER color *New Yorker* v93 no29 p50 S 25 2017

What I've LEARNED *Esquire* p82 BigBlackBook

Experiment (Poem)

Experiment M. CALLANAN *Walrus* v13 no9 p34 N 2016

Experimental Aircraft Association

WHAT A SHOW color *Flying* v144 no10 p82 O 2017

Experimental architecture

Brick by Brick M. Cockram bw color *Architectural Record* v205 no2 p100 F 2017

Experimental automobiles

Knockout Punch E. Perkins color *Hot Rod* v70 no7 p8 Jl 2017

Shoestring Styling T. Taylor bw *Hot Rod* v70 no9 p90 S 2017

Experimental automobiles—Evaluation

THE BEST OF DETROIT AND CES S. Evans color *Motor Trend* v69 no4 p20 Ap 2017

CONCEPT CARS D. Pund color *Car & Driver* v62 no7 p24 Ja 2017

Geneva's Greatest Hits S. Evans color *Motor Trend* v69 no6 p12 Je 2017

Experimental embryology

Mouse eggs made in the lab G. Vogel color *Science* v354 no6319 p1520 D 23 2016

Experimental films

KIYOSHI AWAZU bw color *Film Comment* v53 no5 p80 S/O 2017

Experimental psychology

How Managers Should Judge Psychology Experiments U. M. Dholakia *Harvard Business Review Digital Articles* p2 Ag 31 2015

Experiments

LOL Science S. ELDER cartoon *National Geographic Kids* no470 p24 My 2017

Your Company Is Full of Good Experiments (You Just Have to Recognize Them) O. Hauser and M. Luca *Harvard Business Review Digital Articles* p2 N 23 2015

Expertise

ASSESS Your Specialty K. Holmes color *Dance Spirit* v21 no1 p56 Ja 2017

Breaking up exercise ... Canola oil ... Probiotics ... Roasting veg-

etables A. H. Lichtenstein *Tufts University Health & Nutrition Letter* v34 no11 p8 Ja 2017

The End of Expertise B. Fischer *Harvard Business Review Digital Articles* p2 O 19 2015

Establish Expertise Inside Your Company D. Clark *Harvard Business Review Digital Articles* p2 Ag 19 2015

The Expertocracy B. SWAIM color *Weekly Standard* v22 no35 p26 My 22 2017

Get People to Listen to You When You're Not Seen as an Expert D. Clark *Harvard Business Review Digital Articles* p2 My 13 2015

What You Need to Stand Out in a Noisy World D. Clark color *Harvard Business Review Digital Articles* p2 Ja 6 2017

WHEN TECHNICAL SKILL BEATS EMOTIONAL INTELLIGENCE *Harvard Business Review* v95 no3 p36 My/Je 2017

Expertise—Social aspects

The Danger of Having Too Many Experts N. Lovegrove *Time* v188 no19 p17 N 7 2016

Expiration

Checkup for Your Medicine Cabinet R. WESTEN *AARP: The Magazine* v59 no5A p20 Ag/S 2016

Explicit memory

Getting an Audience to Remember Your Presentation A. Markman *Harvard Business Review Digital Articles* p2 S 21 2015

Exploitation of humans

The Dating Game L. Featherstone il *Nation* v303 no17 p7 O 24 2016

Human Resource Exploitation Training Manual *Lapham's Quarterly* v10 no3 p210 Summ 2017

Exploration of Jupiter

Jupiter – From Earth to Juno J. H. Rogers color *Sky & Telescope* v134 no5 p52 N 2017

Jupiter Rediscovered F. Bagenal *Sky & Telescope* v134 no6 p14 D 2017

Jupiter's interior and deep atmosphere: The initial pole-to-pole passes with the Juno spacecraft [Cover story] S. J. Bolton, A. Adriani et al color graph *Science* v356 no6340 p821 My 26 2017

Jupiter's magnetosphere and aurorae observed by the Juno spacecraft during its first polar orbits J. E. P. Connerney, A. Adriani et al diag graph *Science* v356 no6340 p826 My 26 2017

Exploratory fishing

DEVIL'S IN THE DETAILS T. E. Nickens color *Field & Stream* v122 no3 p32 Ag 2017

Explore Scientific LLC

The 102-mm FCD100 Triplet APO Refractor A. Dyer *Sky & Telescope* v133 no6 p58 Je 2017

Explore Scientific's 92° Long Eye Relief Eyepieces S. Walker *Sky & Telescope* v133 no6 p61 Je 2017

Grab Explore Scientific's 80mm APO, and go! G. Chaple color *Astronomy* v45 no4 p64 Ap 2017

Explorer 1 (Artificial satellite)

Difficult decisions C. Day *Physics Today* v70 no10 p8 O 2017

Explorer satellites

Difficult decisions C. Day *Physics Today* v70 no10 p8 O 2017

Explorers

Celebrity, Politics and Francis Drake S. Bradley *History Today* v67 no3 p3 Mr 2017

Dare To Explore C. M. TOMLIN color *National Geographic Kids* no473 p28 S 2017

THE DEEP SEA SIX color *Popular Science* p45 Ja/F 2017

EXPLORER HONOR TO BRIAN SKERRY P. Edmonds color *National Geographic* v232 no1 p24 Jl 2017

History's Most Misleading Maps: Today's high-tech devices aren't the only tools leading voyagers astray. And some "mistakes" were made deliberately C. Thompson *Smithsonian* v48 no4 p18 Jl/Ag 2017

Explorers—United States

FIELD NOTES color *National Geographic* v230 no6 p17 D 2016

Who Named It? S. SHIBATA *Sea Magazine* v108 no8 p12 Ag 2016

Explosions

    See also

    Nuclear explosions

ECHOES OF THIOKOL: Survivors and their descendants seek a memorial to a forgotten tragedy on the Georgia coast J. GRILLO *Atlanta* v57 no4 p18 Ag 2017

THE LONG ROAD BACK B. CARPENTER *USA Today Maga-*

no474 p16 O 2017

Closest known exoplanet 'just' 4.24 light-years away C. Crockett color *Science News* v190 no13 p20 D 24 2016

Destination Space S. W. DRIMMER color *National Geographic Kids* no473 p8 S 2017

DESTINATION SPACE S. W. DRIMMER *National Geographic Kids* no469 p8 Ap 2017

The exoplanet next door D. Clery color *Science* v354 no6319 p1518 D 23 2016

Imagining Exoplanets A. Tesar color *Walrus* v14 no5 p59 Je 2017

TRAPPIST-1 and the Seven Exoplanets color *Discover* v38 no5 p17 Je 2017

Where are they? M. Livio and J. Silk *Physics Today* v70 no3 p50 Mr 2017

World Weary? The Best Is Yet to Come S. SCOLES color *Discover* v38 no3 p40 Ap 2017

Extrasolar planets—Detection

Seek Exoplanets From Your Backyard D. CONTI color diag *Discover* v38 no2 p64 Mr 2017

Extrasolar planets—Orbits

7 Earth-sized planets circle nearby star A. YEAGER chart *Science News* v191 no5 p6 Mr 18 2017

Extrasolar planets—Research

FOUND IN SPACE M. KOZIOL diag *Popular Science* p24 Ja/F 2017

Starshot has ESO telescope time *Science* v355 no6321 p113 Ja 13 2017

Extraterrestrial beings

16 TIMES WE DIDN'T FIND E.T. J. Wenz cartoon *Astronomy* v45 no9 p34 S 2017

1899: Colorado Springs N. Tesla *Lapham's Quarterly* v10 no2 p24 Spr 2017

Alien Contact S. SCOLES bw color diag graph *Discover* v38 no6 p58 Jl/Ag 2017

BIGFOOT AS BIG MYTH: 7 PHASES OF MYTHMAKING: During its history, the hairy man-best has evolved though at least seven mythical embodiments J. NICKELL *Skeptical Inquirer* v41 no5 p52 S/O 2017

The Cultural Saturation Chart D. GORDON and C. WEAVER bw color *GQ: Gentlemen's Quarterly* v86 no11 p72 N 2016

Finding aliens B. BERMAN color *Astronomy* v45 no9 p10 S 2017

Impact ejecta at the Paleocene-Eocene boundary M. F. Schaller, M. K. Fung et al bibl bw graph *Science* v354 no6309 p225 O 14 2016

LAST PAGE color *Wired* v25 no9 p96 S 2017

Revoltingly Real Cosplay M. GILES color *Popular Science* v288 no6 p92 N/D 2016

Extraterrestrial beings on television

YOU'RE NOT FROM AROUND HERE, ARE YOU? S. Li color *Entertainment Weekly* no1440 p49 N 18 2016

Extraterrestrial life

See also

Extraterrestrial beings

On Titan, possible life ingredient seen T. H. SAEY color *Science News* v192 no3 p12 S 2 2017

Searching a Trillion Stars for ET R. H. Gray *Sky & Telescope* v134 no3 p38 S 2017

Extreme environments—Microbiology

Mine crystals harbor bizarre microbes A. YEAGER color *Science News* v191 no5 p15 Mr 18 2017

Extreme Light Infrastructure (Organization)

Eastern Europe's laser centers will debut without a star E. Cartlidge color *Science* v355 no6327 p785 F 24 2017

Extreme Reach Inc.

EXTREME REACH M. RONEY color *Forbes* v198 no9 p30 D 30 2016

Extreme sports

awes8me EXTREME SPORTS J. AGRESTA *National Geographic Kids* no467 p9 F 2017

EXTREME ANNAPOLIS: A spurned action-sports starwoos his hometown A. WHITING *Washingtonian Magazine* v52 no12 p20 S 2017

Extremists

See also

Radicals

Persecution in Russia and Kazakhstan worsens for Jehovah's Wit-

nesses L. Markoe and F. Weir *Christian Century* v134 no13 p13 Je 21 2017

TWEETING TERROR A. NICODEMO *USA Today Magazine* v145 no2860 p46 Ja 2017

Extremities (Anatomy)

A Leg Up on Arachnid Evolution G. TARLACH color *Discover* v38 no1 p80 Ja/F 2017

Extroverts

5 Misconceptions About Networking H. Ibarra *Harvard Business Review Digital Articles* p2 Ap 18 2016

Design a Workspace that Gives Extroverts Privacy, Too *Harvard Business Review Digital Articles* p2 O 22 2014

Introverts, Extroverts, and the Complexities of Team Dynamics F. Gino *Harvard Business Review Digital Articles* p2 Mr 16 2015

Exurban regions

ST. MICHAEL, MINNESOTA color *Washington Monthly* v49 no3-5 p30 Mr-My 2017

Exxon Mobil Corp.

The Boy Scout Leading State R. Ratnesar color *Bloomberg Businessweek* no4513 p14 Mr 6 2017

ExxonMobil's Shareholder Vote Is a Tipping Point for Climate Issues G. Serafeim and S. Kotsantonis color *Harvard Business Review Digital Articles* p2 Je 7 2017

How Exxon Is Learning To Let Go J. Carroll and D. Wethe color *Bloomberg Businessweek* no4519 p49 Ap 24 2017

The Rockefeller Family Fund Takes on ExxonMobil D. Kaiser and L. Wasserman color *New York Review of Books* v63 no20 p60 D 22 2016

Tillerson's Got a Private State Department J. Carroll and A. Steel *Bloomberg Businessweek* no4505 p30 D 26 2016

Exxon Mobil Corp.—Trials, litigation, etc.

Change in the Legal Climate M. Hemingway *Weekly Standard* v22 no13 p8 D 5 2016

Eyal, Jonathan

Are We Any Safer? color *Atlantic* v318 no4 p14 N 2016

Eyal, Nir

Have We Been Thinking About Willpower the Wrong Way for 30 Years? *Harvard Business Review Digital Articles* p2 N 23 2016

How Customers Get Hooked on Products *Harvard Business Review Digital Articles* p2 N 12 2014

Improving vaccine trials in infectious disease emergencies graph *Science* v357 no6347 p153 Jl 14 2017

Why You Need an Imaginary Scapegoat bw *Harvard Business Review Digital Articles* p2 F 6 2017

Eye

See also

Crystalline lens

Sunset Eyes Are So Hot color *Health* v31 no8 p14 O 2017

Eye anatomy

MAKE YOUR EYES POP T. T. Canel color *Health* v31 no2 p116 Mr 2017

Eye care

Blind Spots A. PATZ bw color *Women's Health* v14 no9 p72 N 2017

EXCESS BAGGAGE color *Esquire* p52 My 2017

Good Food: Protect Your vision P. ORMONT BLUMBERG color *Prevention* v69 no8 p34 Ag 2017

INNER PEACE, OUTER BEAUTY N. Quistgard color *Yoga Journal* p94 2017 Special Issue

MY BEAUTY MARK ... Christina Ricci color *InStyle* v24 no7 p97 Jl 2017

NOT SO EASY ON THE EYES color *Women's Health* v14 no5 p138 Je 2017

We Need to Talk About Your Eye Bags G. MUNCE color *GQ: Gentlemen's Quarterly* v97 no5 p48 My 2017

Eye care—Equipment & supplies

Custom EYES B. Underwood color *O, The Oprah Magazine* p86 N 2017

Eye contact

Chris Gardner Shows How to Practice The Power of Acknowledging Others C. Gardner bw *Black Enterprise* v47 no2 p28 S 2016

Eye diseases—Prevention

Product Spotlights color *Better Nutrition* v79 no7 p63 Jl 2017

Eye in the Sky (Film)

EYE IN THE SKY J. Krebs color *Sound & Vision* v81 no9 p71 N 2016

Eye makeup

See also

Mascara

ALL NIGHT LONG color *Seventeen* v76 no2 p116 Mr 2017

ASK APRIL cartoon color *Good Housekeeping* v263 no5 p22 N 2016

BEST NEW MAKEUP LOOKS Guarnieri color *Harper's Bazaar* no3656 p367 S 2017

BOLD Makeup M. ABERMAN color *Seventeen* v76 no2 p64 Mr 2017

Ciara Demystifies Her Whole Beauty Approach S. Kitchens and Ying Chu color *Glamour* v115 no3 p114 Mr 2017

Eye-Makeup Lookbook J. Mulrow color *Glamour* v115 no5 p72 My 2017

EYES WIDE OPEN color *Women's Health* v14 no5 p34 Je 2017

HIGH BROW color *Vogue* v207 no9 p436 S 2017

Mermaid Eyes J. Mulrow and Y. Chu color *Glamour* v115 no1 p36 Ja 2017

On Fleek, C'est Chic? L. Dunham color *Vogue* v207 no4 p238 Ap 2017

Prettier, brighter eyes in a flash M. Roncal color *Redbook* p18 Mr 2017

Put on liner perfectly M. OLIVA cartoon *Redbook* p12 My 2017

the secret to lush lashes M. R. CHADWICK color *Better Homes & Gardens* v95 no11 p26 N 2017

two ways K. Foster color *Seventeen* p180 Ja 1 2017

Your Cat Eye, Customized E. Reimel and Ying Chu color *Glamour* v115 no3 p108 Mr 2017

YOUR ULTIMATE LOOK-GREAT MANUAL color *Redbook* p5 My 2017

Eye makeup—Equipment & supplies

day-to-night makeup color *Good Housekeeping* v263 no6 p46 D 2016

Double-Tap This E. Reimel and Ying Chu color *Glamour* v115 no3 p102 Mr 2017

Eye-Makeup Lookbook! color *Glamour* v114 no11 p100 N 2016

Fab Fall Launches color *Essence* v48 no5 p48 S 2017

Gifts Galore! color *Essence* v47 no8 p52 D 2016

Mermaid Eyes E. Reimel color *Glamour* v115 no9 p84 S 2017

Need a Makeup Refresh? E. Reimel and Ying Chu cartoon *Glamour* v115 no2 p52 F 2017

The New Matte K. Erickson and Y. Chu color *Glamour* v115 no1 p38 Ja 2017

The New PASTELS P. Dubroff cartoon *O, The Oprah Magazine* p62 Ap 2017

O, THE OPRAH MAGAZINE Fall BEAUTY O-WARDS 2017 color *O, The Oprah Magazine* pC5 S 2017

Smoky EYES D. Gluck color *InStyle* v23 no12 p223 N 2016

Strokes of Genius N. Spradley color *Essence* v47 no8 p45 D 2016

Eye makeup—Evaluation

5 beauty tricks I just learned V. Kirby color *Redbook* p42 Je 2017

5 beauty tricks I just learned V. Kirby color *Redbook* p52 S 2017

BEAUTY UNDER $25 color *Redbook* p28 Mr 2017

A Classic Reimagined A. Serrano color *InStyle* v24 no9 p325 S 2017

Color POWER COUPLES K. FOSTER color *Seventeen* p108 Ja 1 2017

The customized plan for younger eyes A. HERTZIG color *Redbook* p45 S 2017

digital directory color *InStyle* v24 no10 p26 O 2017

Eye Shadow color *InStyle* v23 no13 p194 D 2016

GAME ON! color *O, The Oprah Magazine* p59 Je 2017

GET THE GLOW color *Harper's Bazaar* no3654 p42 Je/Jl 2017

GET YOUNGER LOOKING EYES Guarnieri color *Harper's Bazaar* no3657 p189 O 2017

GLITTER FOR GROWN-UPS A. Kallor cartoon *Harper's Bazaar* no3651 p418 Mr 2017

Lash miracles! P. STABLES color *Redbook* p46 N 2017

MAKEUP MAGIC M. OLIVA color *Redbook* p42 O 2017

The Party Starts Here A. Serrano color *InStyle* v23 no13 p165 D 2016

The sheer joys of summer color *Redbook* p27 Je 2017

Skin-TERTAINMENT E. STOVALL color *Seventeen* v76 no4 p43 Jl/Ag 2017

Your Easiest Routine Ever M. M. GOLDSTEIN color *Martha Stewart Living* no275 p42 Je 2017

Eye protection

See also

Protective eyeglasses

A step-by-step guide to the Great American Eclipse R. Talcott bw color *Astronomy* v45 no8 p26 Ag 2017

Eye tracking

Pleasure Principal S. Barmak color *Walrus* v14 no5 p38 Je 2017

Eyebrow care

BROW WOW WOW K. Schaefer color *Bloomberg Businessweek* no4525 p59 Je 5 2017

HIGH BROW color *Vogue* v207 no9 p436 S 2017

Highbrow Eyebrows M. GUNCH color *New Orleans Magazine* v52 no1 p52 S 2017

School of Karl E. Wilson color *InStyle* v24 no9 p157 S 2017

Shortcut to better brows M. Roncal color *Redbook* p23 N 2017

Eyebrows

Brow Growth Serums L. Desantis color *Health* v31 no2 p41 Mr 2017

Give yourself better brows P. STABLES cartoon color *Redbook* p18 My 2017

On Fleek, C'est Chic? L. Dunham color *Vogue* v207 no4 p238 Ap 2017

RAISING AN EYEBROW K. Bennett *Washingtonian Magazine* v52 no3 p117 D 2016

the secret to BOLD BROWS N. JUDAR color *Better Homes & Gardens* v95 no5 p18 My 2017

Shortcut to better brows M. Roncal color *Redbook* p23 N 2017

WORTH EVERY CENT E. Listfield color *Harper's Bazaar* no3657 p234 O 2017

Eyebrows—Care & hygiene

Arches de Triumph A. Finney color *Women's Health* v14 no1 p49 Ja/F 2017

The Art of the Arch M. MILRAD GOLDSTEIN *Martha Stewart Living* no268 p58 O 2016

Eye-Makeup Lookbook J. Mulrow color *Glamour* v115 no5 p72 My 2017

My Brows B. Shields and S. Cristobal color *InStyle* v24 no5 p226 My 2017

Eye—Care & hygiene

CANADA'S ELITE VISION-IMPAIRED ATHLETES ARE RAISING AWARENESS FOR UNIVERSAL EYE HEALTH D. F. McCourt bw *Maclean's* v129 no42 p33 O 24 2016

How to Look Less Tired K. Erickson, T. Williams et al bw color *Glamour* v115 no3 p120 Mr 2017

Jennifer Aniston on Dry Eye: "I Was Addicted to Eye Drops" L. Lombardi color *Health* v30 no9 p80 N 2016

THE NEW CONTOUR N. Spradley color *Essence* v47 no7 p30 N 2016

Say Goodbye to Contact Lenses and Glasses with PiXLTM — the New Non-Invasive Vision Improvement Procedure M. Sponagle color *Maclean's* v129 no42 p36 O 24 2016

TRUE beauty N. Quistgard color *Yoga Journal* p94 2017 Special Issue

Eye—Diseases

See also

Eye—Inflammation

Glaucoma

5 EYE SYMPTOMS YOU SHOULDN'T IGNORE color *Prevention* v69 no2 p9 F 2017

Eye redness *Mayo Clinic Health Letter* v35 no5 p7 My 2017

IN THE DARK R. Wiedeman cartoon *New Yorker* v92 no42 p49 D 19 2016

Eye—Examination

EYE OF THE BEHOLDER F. ESKER color *Louisiana Life* v37 no4 p10 Mr/Ap 2017

Eyeglass cases

SHOP NOTES cartoon color *Popular Mechanics* p46 D 2016/Ja 2017

Eyeglass frames

The Joy of Specs A. Giorgianni chart color diag il *Consumer Reports* v82 no2 p7 F 2017

Eyeglass frames—Evaluation

MADE IN THE USA color *Martha Stewart Living* no271 p46 Ja/F 2017

Eyeglass industry—Equipment & supplies

Now You See Me color *AARP: The Magazine* v60 no2A p14 F/Mr 2017

Eyeglasses

ARE BLUE LIGHT GLASSES LEGIT? color *Health* v31 no7 p22 S 2017

say "cheese" for border security S. Chodosh color *Popular Science* v289 no6 p78 N/D 2017

Time to Ditch Your Glasses? color *Kiplinger's Personal Finance* v71 no3 p69 Mr 2017

Eyeglasses—Evaluation

360° Vision color *Esquire* v166 no5 p66 D 2016/Ja 2017

Adam's TOP FIT TIPS color *O, The Oprah Magazine* p56 Ap 2017

bollé cartoon color *Snowboarder* v29 no4 p112 D 2016

ESSENTIALS M. HORJUS, A. ROY et al bw color *Backpacker* p93 N 2017

It's Baaack color *Weekly Standard* v22 no46 p2 Ag 14 2017

Now You See Me color *AARP: The Magazine* v60 no2A p14 F/Mr 2017

Toy story S. Horaczek and A. Smith color *Popular Science* v289 no6 p44 N/D 2017

WHAT A SPECTACLE J. Wilson color *Essence* v47 no10 p24 F 2017

Eye—Inflammation

On guard against EYE INJURIES [Cover story] K. Elizabeth Baril color *Equus* no476 p42 My 2017

Eyelash curlers

Lash miracles! P. STABLES color *Redbook* p46 N 2017

Eyelashes

I Want Her Lashes L. Desantis color *Health* v31 no4 p33 My 2017

Put on liner perfectly M. OLIVA cartoon *Redbook* p12 My 2017

the secret to BOLD BROWS N. JUDAR color *Better Homes & Gardens* v95 no5 p18 My 2017

Simple EYELASH Hacks I. VAN LOTRINGEN color *Seventeen* v76 no12 p52 D 2016/Ja 2017

Eyer, Jonathan

Can America's Blue States Tackle Climate Change on Their Own? color *Harvard Business Review Digital Articles* p2 Je 6 2017

Eyers, Claire E.

Local protein kinase A action proceeds through intact holoenzymes color diag graph *Science* v356 no6344 p1288 Je 23 2017

EYERS, MONIKA BIEGLER

COLOR GOURD GREENS color *Better Homes & Gardens* v95 no10 p34 O 2017

DELFT BLUE color *Better Homes & Gardens* v95 no8 p26 Ag 2017

GOLDEN YELLOW color *Better Homes & Gardens* v95 no7 p24 Jl 2017

HARVEST HUES color *Better Homes & Gardens* v95 no11 p34 N 2017

KIM FICARO color *Better Homes & Gardens* v95 no9 p22 S 2017

LILI DIALLO color *Better Homes & Gardens* v95 no9 p20 S 2017

MAKING A PROPER BED color diag *Better Homes & Gardens* v95 no10 p38 O 2017

OBSESSED WITH HUNTER-GATHERERS color *Better Homes & Gardens* v95 no9 p16 S 2017

SARAH STORMS color *Better Homes & Gardens* v95 no9 p18 S 2017

SEA SHADES color *Better Homes & Gardens* v95 no6 p26 Je 2017

Eyers, Patrick A.

Local protein kinase A action proceeds through intact holoenzymes color diag graph *Science* v356 no6344 p1288 Je 23 2017

Eyes Wide Shut (Music)

Kidz Bop Z. Jason *New York Times Magazine* p24 Mr 26 2017

Eyes of My Mother, The (Film)

The Eyes of My Mother *New Yorker* v92 no40 p16 D 5 2016

Eyestrain—Treatment

RELIEVE EYE STRAIN J. Martin color *Amazing Wellness* v9 no3 p28 EarlySumm 2017

Eyewitness (TV program)

Eyewitness J. Russell color *TV Guide* v64 no42 p36 O 10 2016

So Good It's Criminal D. ANDERSON-MINSHALL *Advocate* no1088 p62 D 2016/Ja 2017

USA's New Look: Darker Skies color *TV Guide* v64 no42 p19 O 10 2016

Eye—Wounds & injuries

Teaching Rape Prevention L. "ILHAM" BARTO *Islamic Horizons*

v46 no1 p49 Ja/F 2017

Eyfjörð, Steingrímur—Exhibitions

ART IN THE HEART OF TOWN P. STEFÁNSSON *Iceland Review* v55 no2 p12 Mr/Ap 2017

EYMAN, SCOTT

The Good Fight bw color *Film Comment* v53 no2 p78 Mr/Ap 2017

Eyre, Chris

Spirituality and the Reclamation of Lakota Masculinity in Chris Eyre's Skins (2002) P. L. BAYERS *American Indian Quarterly* v40 no3 p191 Summ 2016

Eyring, Aleksandra D.

Mismatch repair deficiency predicts response of solid tumors to PD-1 blockade chart graph *Science* v357 no6349 p409 Jl 28 2017

Eyster, Chase

A Friend Indeed color *Money* v46 no4 p76 My 2017

EZ Dock system (Company)

Paddlecraft Racks D. ARMITAGE color *Cabin Living* p59 Ap 2017

EZ-Hoist (Company)

Control the Process *Stage Directions* v29 no10 p7 O 2016

eZ-Hoist Has a Clear Mission: Scenic Automation Domination *Stage Directions* v30 no3 p54 Mr 2017

Ezer, Daphne

Phytochromes function as thermosensors in Arabidopsis bibl graph *Science* v354 no6314 p886 N 18 2016

Ezop, Phyllis

CUSTOMER LOYALTY IS OVERRATED: INTERACTION color *Harvard Business Review* v95 no3 p18 My/Je 2017

Ezrachi, Ariel

Priceless B. Nalebuff color *Science* v354 no6312 p560 N 4 2016

F

F-35 (Military aircraft)—Sales & prices

DANGER ZONE P. M. Barrett color diag *Bloomberg Businessweek* no4518 p50 Ap 10 2017

F-actin

Vinculin forms a directionally asymmetric catch bond with F-actin D. L. Huang, N. A. Bax et al chart color *Science* v357 no6352 p703 Ag 18 2017

F. Schumacher & Co.

A ROOM OF HER OWN Y. Huh color *House Beautiful* v159 no5 p54 Je 2017

F-Secure Corp.

Little Flocker reincarnates as Xfence, a free beta from F-Secure G. FLEISHMAN color *Macworld - Digital Edition* v34 no6 p107 Je 2017

F.A. Premier League

GO FIGURE T. Keith color *Sports Illustrated* v126 no16 p24 Je 5 2017

Leicester City FC and the Benefits of an Underdog Brand R. Angell, P. Bottomley et al *Harvard Business Review Digital Articles* p2 Ag 12 2016

Over There G. Wahl and T. Keith chart color *Sports Illustrated* v125 no13 p18 O 17 2016

Faaele, Daniel

THINK BIG A. Staples color *Sports Illustrated* v126 no7 p56 Mr 6 2017

Faas, Horst

FRONTLINE FOCUS D. Stadtler *Military History* v33 no6 p56 Mr 2017

Faber, Franziska

Microbiota-activated PPAR-γ signaling inhibits dysbiotic Enterobacteriaceae expansion graph *Science* v357 no6351 p570 Ag 11 2017

Faber, Hylke

How Companies Escape the Traps of the Past *Harvard Business Review Digital Articles* p2 Ap 26 2016

To Win the Civil War, Lincoln Had to Change His Leadership *Harvard Business Review Digital Articles* p2 My 30 2016

What FDR Knew About Managing Fear in Times of Change *Harvard Business Review Digital Articles* p2 My 4 2016

Faber, Joanna—Interviews

Q&A WITH JOANNA FABER color *Publishers Weekly* v264 no2 p30 Ja 9 2017

Faber, Rima

Dance and early childhood cognition: The Isadora Effect bibl *Arts Education Policy Review* v118 no3 p172 2017

FABER, SEBASTIAAN

The Catalonia Question [Cover story] *Nation* v305 no10 p4 O 23 2017

Fabergé eggs

THE SHELL GAME A. BROWN color *Forbes* v200 no3 p84 S 28 2017

FABIANI, LOUISE

Working with Nature color *Earth Island Journal* v32 no3 p54 Aut 2017

Fabian-Wheeler, Eileen

Slag for dry lot rehab? *Equus* no473 p67 F 2017

Fabini, Luis

Home on the Range bw *Popular Photography* v80 no11 p8 D 2016

Fabric shops

CROSSED STITCHES *Texas Monthly* v44 no12 p108 D 2016

Fabrication (Manufacturing)

See also

Metal fabrication

How to Scale Up B. KITE color *Popular Mechanics* p37 S 2017

How to Scale Up B. KITE color *Popular Mechanics* v193 no7 p37 S 2016

Innovation O. Kharif color *Bloomberg Businessweek* no4513 p39 Mr 6 2017

Fabris, L.

Observation of coherent elastic neutrino-nucleus scattering diag *Science* v357 no6356 p1123 S 15 2017

Fabry, Merrill

Building a Nation *Time* v189 no13 p24 Ap 10 2017

A Cure for the Ages color *Time* v189 no7/8 p86 F 27 2017

Points of Origin map *Time* v189 no16/17 p12 My 1-8 2017

The Race to Zero color diag map *Time* v188 no22-23 p38 N/D 2016

The Surprisingly Peaceful Origins of Bastille Day *Time* v190 no4 p19 Jl 24 2017

Where Did America's Summer Jobs Go? color diag *Time* v190 no2/3 p52 Jl 10-17 2017

Fabulous Baron Munchausen, The (Film)

Adventure Time M. SRAGOW color *Film Comment* v53 no5 p74 S/O 2017

Facchini, Peter J.

Plant metabolons assembled on demand bibl color *Science* v354 no6314 p829 N 18 2016

Faccio, Daniele

Plasmons that won't stick diag *Science* v356 no6345 p1336 Je 30 2017

Faccioli, Primetta

Wild emmer genome architecture and diversity elucidate wheat evolution and domestication color *Science* v357 no6346 p93 Jl 7 2017

Face

See also

Beards

Eyebrows

Mustaches

new rules for cleansing color *Parents* v92 no6 p83 Je 2017

Powder Play color *Vogue* v206 no12 p197c D 2017

Face masks

Mask Mania! K. Erickson color *Glamour* v114 no12 p132 D 2016

Photostat: Krakow's Hottest Accessory D. Kessenides and M. Waldoch color *Bloomberg Businessweek* no4528 p30 Je 26 2017

PRACTICAL MAGIC A. Finney color *Women's Health* v14 no3 p(Sp)18 Ap 2017

Skin SMARTS color *O, The Oprah Magazine* p72 O 2017

Face masks—Evaluation

ANNAHSTASIA ENUKE J. Wilson color *Essence* v47 no12 p26 Ap 2017

FACE SAVERS M. M. GOLDSTEIN *Martha Stewart Living* no269 p46 N 2016

Face masks—Social aspects

THE MASKERADE M. Goldberg color *O, The Oprah Magazine* p69 O 2017

Face Off (TV program)

America's top TV critic Matt Roush answers your burning ques-

tions M. Roush *TV Guide* v65 no31 p2 Jl 24 2017

Face perception

Brains encode faces piece by piece L. HAMERS bw *Science News* v191 no13 p9 Jl 8 2017

Here, Kitty Kitty! H. KRISCHER *Reader's Digest* v190 no1134 p41 O 2017

Saving Face K. Sheikh bw color *Scientific American* v317 no2 p12 Ag 2017

Two areas for familiar face recognition in the primate brain S. M. Landi and W. A. Freiwald color graph *Science* v357 no6351 p591 Ag 11 2017

Face perception—Software

Our Panopticon, Ourselves P. J. Williams color *Nation* v33 no21 p12 N 21 2016

Face-to-face communication

Collaborating Online Is Sometimes Better than Face-to-Face A. Samuel *Harvard Business Review Digital Articles* p2 Ap 1 2015

Facebook (Web resource)

4 ways to block political posts on Facebook A. CAMPBELL color *PCWorld* v35 no2 p189 F 2017

America's relationship with Mark Zuckerberg is It's complicated M. Chafkin and S. Frier color graph *Bloomberg Businessweek* no4539 p50 S 25 2017

ASK A FLOWCHART R. CAPPS chart diag *Wired* v25 no3 p96 Mr 2017

A BACKPACK WITH A COOLER K. Dupzyk color *Popular Mechanics* p83 D 2016/Ja 2017

Being Professionally Personable on Facebook A. Samuel *Harvard Business Review Digital Articles* p2 Ag 14 2015

Case Study: Should He Be Fired for That Facebook Post? M. A. Watson and G. R. Lopiano *Harvard Business Review Digital Articles* p2 D 11 2015

Chin Losers N. WELDON color *Runner's World* v52 no9 p45 O 2017

Corrections & Clarifications *Bloomberg Businessweek* no4525 p4 Je 5 2017

Dislike: Are state ethics rules keeping up with social media? T. Newcombe *Governing* v30 no8 p60 My 2017

Do I Report A Teacher's Racist Facebook Post? K. A. Appiah *New York Times Magazine* p18 Jl 2 2017

DON'T LET HER HAUNT YOU [Cover story] J. VRABEL cartoon color *Men's Health* v32 no1 p114 Ja/F 2017

The easy way to save Facebook videos J. NOREM color *PCWorld* p190 D 2016

The Facebook rescue that wasn't E. Bell color graph *Columbia Journalism Review* v56 no1 p19 Spr 2017

The Honor Guard B. MOCKENHAUPT color *Atlantic* v318 no5 p20 D 2016

How Facebook Could Stop J. Kahn, S. Nicola et al bw color *Bloomberg Businessweek* no4524 p56 My 29 2017

How Facebook Uses Empathy to Keep User Data Safe M. Luu-Van *Harvard Business Review Digital Articles* p2 Ap 28 2016

How to encrypt your Facebook messages with Secret Conversations I. PAUL color diag *PCWorld* v35 no11 p144 N 2016

I Used to Be a Human Being A. Sullivan and K. Dong-kyu img *New York* v49 no19 p32 S 19 2016

LEARNING FROM HORROR C. Benson-Allott *Film Quarterly* v70 no2 p58 Wint 2016

Lessons from Facebook's Fumble in India B. Chakravorti *Harvard Business Review Digital Articles* p2 F 16 2016

On Technology J. Herrman *New York Times Magazine* p14 O 8 2017

Q: MY 7-YEAR-OLD TOOK PICTURES OF MY NAKED 3-YEAR-OLD AND ALMOST PUT THEM ON FACEBOOK. HOW DO I EXPLAIN THIS IS A BAD IDEA? J. MOOALLEM cartoon *Wired* v24 no12 p32 D 2016

Red Meat from an Unexpected Source color *Weekly Standard* v22 no7 p4 O 24 2016

Save the DATE! bw color *Seventeen* v76 no2 p14 Mr 2017

Screen, I Wish I Knew How to Quit You J. HOUSMAN cartoon color *Surfer* v57 no13 p30 Mr 2017

SMARTPHONE DENIERS C. Neuhaus *Saturday Evening Post* v289 no1 p14 Ja/F 2017

Sorry, Kids: We Made You This Way S. Koslow color *AARP: The Magazine* v59 no3A p55 Ap/My 2016

TALK TO US color *Dance Spirit* v20 no9 p20 N 2016

When a Facebook Page Matters to Facebook S. Frier color *Bloomberg Businessweek* no4508 p28 Ja 23 2017

Why Facebook Is a Lot Like Listerine M. Chwe *Harvard Business Review Digital Articles* p2 Ap 17 2015

Why You Click on Those Cat Videos D. Thompson color *Fortune* v175 no2 p17 F 1 2017

A WOMAN'S WORK J. TOLENTINO bw cartoon *New Yorker* v93 no30 p38 O 2 2017

YE OLDE IKEA SEX TRAFFICKERS L. SKENAZY color *Reason* v49 no6 p15 N 2017

Facebook (Web resource)—Social aspects

SAFE C. Metz color diag *Wired* v24 no12 p106 D 2016

Facebook Inc.

1 MARK ZUCKERBERG [Cover story] A. Lashinsky color diag *Fortune* v174 no7 p66 D 1 2016

Antitrust Facebook M. L. SIFRY *Nation* v305 no11 p4 O 30 2017

CNN Has Had Enough S. Frier and G. Smith color graph *Bloomberg Businessweek* no4528 p20 Je 26 2017

Corrections & Clarifications *Bloomberg Businessweek* no4525 p4 Je 5 2017

Facebook Live Is the Company's Newest Strategic Weapon J. Gans *Harvard Business Review Digital Articles* p2 Ap 8 2016

Facebook Won't Hire You for Its Data Center M. Frazier *Bloomberg Businessweek* no4540 p27 O 2 2017

INSIDE FACEBOOK'S AI WORKSHOP: At the social network behemoth, machine learning has become a platform for the platform S. Berinato *Harvard Business Review Digital Articles* p14 Jl 1 2017

Inside Facebook's Big VR Lawsuit color *Time* v189 no3 p8 Ja 30 2017

Let's Not Kill Performance Evaluations Yet L. Goler, J. Gale et al il *Harvard Business Review* v94 no11 p90 N 2016

The New Advertising, As Seen on TV V. Vara color *Bloomberg Businessweek* no4502 p41 D 5 2016

WE CHANGED THE WORLD! (OOPS.) E. Griffith color *Fortune* v175 no7 p32 Je 1 2017

What Would It Take to Disrupt a Platform Like Facebook? J. Gans *Harvard Business Review Digital Articles* p2 Mr 23 2016

WHY FACEBOOK IS KEEPING PERFORMANCE REVIEWS: INTERACTION F. Langness, N. Schultz et al color *Harvard Business Review* v95 no1 p18 Ja/F 2017

Facebook Inc.—Finance

Movers K. Stock bw color graph *Bloomberg Businessweek* no4498 p19 N 7 2016

Facebook Inc.—Officials & employees

FACEBOOK: ITERATING DIVERSITY? V. Zarya *Fortune* v175 no2 p55 F 1 2017

FACEBOOK'S SECRET WEAPON V. Zarya color diag *Fortune* v176 no2 p26 Ag 1 2017

An Inside Look at Facebook's Approach to Automation and Human Work J. Kirby *Harvard Business Review Digital Articles* p2 Je 12 2015

SURVIVAL of the SHARINGEST S. Frier bw *Bloomberg Businessweek* no4520 p60 My 1 2017

Face—Care & hygiene

17 HAPPY, HEALTHY CHOICES for 2017 [Cover story] B. BURKE color *Redbook* p13 F 2017

DIY SPA FACIAL L. Turner color *Amazing Wellness* v9 no3 p70 EarlySumm 2017

Face ODYSSEY J. DUNN *Vogue* v207 no4 p172 Ap 2017

THE GRAND GARDEN PARTY color *Harper's Bazaar* no3653 p144 My 2017

SAVE FACE E. L. FOLEY and FEIFEI SUN *Atlanta* v57 no1 p38 My 2017

Your shortcut to radiant skin M. Roncal color *Redbook* p35 F 2017

Face—Care & hygiene—Equipment & supplies

IN TREATMENT WITH Hannah Bronfman D. Mazzone color *InStyle* v24 no4 p146 Ap 2017

You, Unfiltered S. George color *InStyle* v24 no4 p141 Ap 2017

Face in the Crowd, A (Film)

Seeing Trump on the Silver Screen J. Walker bw *Reason* v48 no7 p40 D 2016

The Shadow of 1957 W. D. GEHRING *USA Today Magazine* v145 no2860 p62 Ja 2017

Face in the Crowd, A (Theatrical production)

Elvis Costello [Cover story] B. HIATT *Rolling Stone* no1289 p22

Je 15 2017

Facelift

CHIN UP! J. Black bw *Esquire* p65 Ap 2017

I GOT A FACE LIFT AT 35 L. Krieger color *Harper's Bazaar* no3648 p220 N 2016

THE POPULAR KOREAN: QUICK-FIX GROOMING: TREND YOU'LL WANT TO KEEP ON HAND O. J. WILLIAMS color *Ebony* v72/73 no12/1 p54 O/N 2017

Faces Places (Film)

Faces Places: Two Artists Hit the Road S. Zacharek color *Time* v190 no15 p56 O 16 2017

WE CAN BE HEROES WANG MUYAN color *Film Comment* v53 no5 p24 S/O 2017

Facet Studio (Company)

Facet Studio N. R. Pollock bw color *Architectural Record* v204 no12 p48 D 2016

Facial care

Face Off K. MASSICOT color *New Orleans Magazine* v52 no1 p166 S 2017

Fall Into Fresh M. M. GOLDSTEIN color *Martha Stewart Living* p56 O 2017

THE NEW BOTOX FACIAL E. Listfield color *Harper's Bazaar* no3656 p390 S 2017

This is how you put on blush M. Roncal color *Redbook* p20 Je 2017

TRY THIS AT HOME! color *O, The Oprah Magazine* p74 O 2017

Facial care—Equipment & supplies

BEAUTY UNDER $25 color *Redbook* p28 Je 2017

Glow your own way M. OLIVA color *Redbook* p36 Je 2017

Facial cleansers

Clear, Glowy SKIN—Now Z. NTLOKO and P. Stables color *Seventeen* v76 no5 p38 S 2017

My LIST L. McCarthy color *Harper's Bazaar* no3650 p80 F 2017

Natural Body-Mind Soothers color *Prevention* v69 no5 p11 My 2017

Softer skin for everyone G. WAY color *Redbook* p58 F 2017

Facial cleansers—Evaluation

Beach color *Seventeen* v76 no3 p44 My 2017

CHARCOAL cleansers color *Better Homes & Gardens* v95 no8 p20 Ag 2017

the COMPACT N. Spradley color *Essence* v47 no9 p30 Ja 2017

Hot-weather-proof your skin V. KIRBY color *Redbook* p39 Je 2017

MOISTURIZING MATTERS A. R. Williams color *Southern Living* v52 no1 p43 Ja 2017

Water Fall K. Massicot color *New Orleans Magazine* v51 no9 p36 Jl 2017

Facial creams (Cosmetics)

Fall Into Fresh M. M. GOLDSTEIN color *Martha Stewart Living* p56 O 2017

Spring Steals! color *Essence* v47 no11 p40 Mr 2017

Facial creams (Cosmetics)—Evaluation

100 BEST BEAUTY EDITION A. FRANZINO color *Good Housekeeping* v264 no5 p23 My 2017

BEAUTY BUYS from $4 color *Good Housekeeping* v265 no5 p20 N 2017

the buzz color *InStyle* v24 no2 p114 F 2017

the COMPACT N. Spradley color *Essence* v47 no9 p30 Ja 2017

Going Out color *Seventeen* v76 no3 p46 My 2017

How to Repent for YOUR SKIN SINS color *InStyle* v24 no1 p62 Ja 2017

Masks that fix everything M. OLIVA color *Redbook* p50 S 2017

The Right Kind of Shine A. Mangum color *Bloomberg Businessweek* no4512 p79 F 20 2017

Smoother skin in seconds M. OLIVA color *Redbook* p47 Mr 2017

While You Were Sleeping J. Wilson color *Essence* v48 no6 p39 O 2017

Facial expression

Are Facial Expressions Universal? T. BURRELL color *Discover* v38 no5 p18 Je 2017

The Big Picture: The snap judgments we make based on people's online photographs may predict how we act toward them in person S. M. BUCKLIN *Psychology Today* v50 no5 p43 S/O 2017

YOUR SMILE: A USER'S MANUAL H. Levine color *Health* v30 no10 p97 D 2016

Facial masks (Cosmetics)

BEST FACE MASKS B. Le Poer Trench color *Harper's Bazaar* no3650 p180 F 2017

BRING THE SPA HOME K. S. BOX cartoon *Better Homes & Gardens* v95 no2 p18 F 2016

Facial masks (Cosmetics)—Evaluation

GORGEOUS GLOWING SKIN color *Harper's Bazaar* no3657 p249 O 2017

How to Stress Less color *InStyle* v24 no4 p160 Ap 2017

STOCK YOUR SPA cartoon color *Better Homes & Gardens* v95 no2 p20 F 2016

Facial paralysis

Losing My Father's Smile H. GOLDEN *Reader's Digest* v188 no1124 p56 O 2016

Facilitated communication

The Farce Known as 'FC' J. RANDI *Skeptical Inquirer* v41 no4 p14 Jl/Ag 2017

Facilitation (Business)

The Right Way to Cut People Off in Meetings B. Frisch and C. Greene *Harvard Business Review Digital Articles* p2 Ap 8 2016

The Right Way to Start a Meeting L. Davey color *Harvard Business Review Digital Articles* p2 Mr 2 2017

Facilitators (Persons)

3 Reasons Your Strategy Meetings Irritate Your Team D. Sundheim *Harvard Business Review Digital Articles* p2 Mr 1 2016

Facilities

    See also
      Auditoriums
      Community centers
      Sports facilities

The Plot To End Homelessness J. HERBST *Los Angeles Magazine* p22 My 2017

Facos, Michelle

Pitter Patter A. LAMAN *Indianapolis Monthly* v40 no4 p38 D 2016

Fact checking in politics

Fact Checking the 'Fact Checkers' *Weekly Standard* v22 no6 p2 O 17 2016

NYT Values Reputation for 'Balance' More Than Health of Sick Kids J. Naureckas *Extra!* v30 no5 p4 Je 2017

Factionalism (Politics)

What Syrians Want D. Corstange *Hoover Digest: Research & Opinion on Public Policy* no1 p136 Wint 2017

Factor Bikes (Company)

FACTOR O2 DISC L. Tanner color *Bicycling* v58 no9 p76 O 2017

Factories

    See also
      Clothing factories
      Printing plants
      Steel mills

Factories—Design & construction

Sayne Foundry M. Pepchinski *Architectural Record* v204 no11 p143 N 2016

Factories—Environmental aspects

Top Air Polluters M. Fischetti map *Scientific American* v316 no1 p72 Ja 2017

Factories—Location

What You Won't Hear About Trade and Manufacturing on the Campaign Trail W. C. Shih *Harvard Business Review Digital Articles* p2 My 2 2016

Factories—Remodeling for other use

Drawing On Its Past M. SEGAL *Los Angeles Magazine* p26 Ap 2017

Factory farms

HOG HELL A. SKOLNICK and L. BARRETT *Sierra* v102 no2 p28 Mr/Ap 2017

Factory Five (Company)

VERSION 3.0 B. Gillogly color *Hot Rod* v70 no8 p54 Ag 2017

Facts (Philosophy)

Bet You Didn't Know E. WHITMER color map *National Geographic Kids* no472 p6 Ag 2017

Fact Finders J. Chait *New Republic* v248 no5 p4 My 2017

Facts VS. Alternative Facts color *Time* v189 no11 p10 Mr 27 2017

Living truthfully *Christian Century* v134 no1 p7 Ja 4 2017

The Search for Facts in a Post-Fact World M. Dean color *Wired* v25 no10 p98 O 2017

Weird But True! M. TERRELL color map *National Geographic*

Kids no472 p4 Ag 2017

When Facts Backfire M. Shermer color *Scientific American* v316 no1 p69 Ja 2017

Fade (Music)

'Fade' T. C. WILLIAMS *New York Times Magazine* p53 Mr 12 2017

Fade (Theatrical production)

Theater of the Real *Chicago* v66 no10 p81 O 2017

Fade creams (Cosmetics)—Evaluation

HOW TO BE DARING WITH YOUR BEAUTY ROUTINE color *Harper's Bazaar* no3648 p66 N 2016

Fadel, Charles—Interviews

Character Qualities in a 21st Century Curriculum C. M. RUBIN *Education Digest* v82 no5 p17 Ja 2017

Fader, Amanda N.

Mismatch repair deficiency predicts response of solid tumors to PD-1 blockade chart graph *Science* v357 no6349 p409 Jl 28 2017

Fads

Q: What is the most significant fad of all time? D. Sim, H. George-Warren et al color *Atlantic* v319 no3 p96 Ap 2017

FADY, BRUNO

Synthesis Centers as Critical Research Infrastructure *BioScience* v67 no8 p750 Ag 2017

Fagal, William

TINTYPE TRICK? *Popular Photography* v81 no2 p27 Mr/Ap 2017

Fagan, Brian

Fishing: How the Sea Fed Civilization L. A. MARSCHALL color *Natural History* v125 no10 p47 O 2017

FAGAN, KATHY

The Ghost on the Handle *Nation* v305 no9 p33 O 16 2017

No Meteor *New Republic* v247 no12 p73 D 2016

FAGER, JEFF

THEIR FINEST HOURS bw color *Vanity Fair* v59 no10 p192 O 2017

Fagerberg, Linn

A pathology atlas of the human cancer transcriptome diag *Science* v357 no6352 p660 Ag 18 2017

A subcellular map of the human proteome color *Science* v356 no6340 p820 My 26 2017

Fagerhag, Mats—Interviews

Mats Fägerhag A. MacKenzie color *Motor Trend* v69 no2 p24 F 2017

Fagerlund, Robert D.

CRISPR-Cas: Adapting to change color *Science* v356 no6333 p40 Ap 7 2017

Fages, Antoine

Ancient genomic changes associated with domestication of the horse color diag *Science* v356 no6336 p442 Ap 28 2017

Faggioli, Massimo

As I have loved you M. Murphy-Gill bw *U.S. Catholic* v82 no4 p45 Ap 2017

Movements of history D. Christiansen *America* v217 no5 p48 S 4 2017

Fagiani, Matias R.

Spectroscopic snapshots of the proton-transfer mechanism in water bibl diag graph *Science* v354 no6316 p1131 D 2 2016

Fago, Angela

Predictable convergence in hemoglobin function has unpredictable molecular underpinnings bibl graph *Science* v354 no6310 p336 O 21 2016

FAGONE, JASON

NIGHTMARE IN MCLEAN *Washingtonian Magazine* v52 no1 p66 O 2016

Fahima, Tzion

Wild emmer genome architecture and diversity elucidate wheat evolution and domestication color *Science* v357 no6346 p93 Jl 7 2017

Fahlen, Christina

Posthole color *Powder* v45 no4 p146 D 2016

Fahmy, Mohamed

Inside 'Scorpion block' B. BETHUNE color *Maclean's* v129 no46 p14 N 21 2016

Fahnøe, Ulrik

Mouse models of acute and chronic hepacivirus infection *Science* v357 no6347 p204 Jl 14 2017

Fahrenheit, Daniel Gabriel, 1686-1736

I Know That Name bw *Discover* v38 no4 p41 My 2017

Fahrenheit 451 (Film)

The Bullseye M. Snetiker color *Entertainment Weekly* no1465 p64 My 12 2017

Fahrenkamp-Uppenbrink, Julia

ECOSYSTEM EARTH [Cover story] color *Science* v356 no6335 p258 Ap 21 2017

Freightened: The Real Price of Shipping color *Science* v356 no6337 p484 My 5 2017

Fahrenthold, David, 1978-

David Fahrenthold M. Hagan *Current Biography* v78 no5 p26 My 2017

Fahrmeier, Lynn

Precision Decisions *Successful Farming* v115 no4 p44 Mr 2017

FAI, GHULAM NABI

A Road to Peace or Disaster? Isn't it time for the world powers to ask the Kashmiris what they really want? *Islamic Horizons* v46 no4 p54 Jl/Ag 2017

Failaka Island (Kuwait)

BRONZE AGE BLING M. BROWN color *Archaeology* v70 no3 p14 My/Je 2017

Failure (Psychology)

THE EVERYTHING GUIDE TO: Sucking at Stuff D. MARCHESE img *New York* v49 no23 p64 N 14 2016

The League of Extraordinary LOSERS [Cover story] J. PRESS *Scholastic Choices* v32 no5 p10 F 2017

Learning from rejections A. Tay color *Science* v355 no6331 p1342 Mr 24 2017

LIFE LESSONS V. K. De Luca color *Essence* v47 no7 p4 N 2016

This Just In J. Zorthian *Time* v190 no13 p23 O 2 2017

When the Race Wins J. BEVERLY color *Runner's World* v52 no9 p60 O 2017

When You Should Worry About Failure, and When You Shouldn't A. Markman *Harvard Business Review Digital Articles* p2 Ja 5 2016

Write a Failure Résumé to Learn What Makes You Succeed B. Taylor *Harvard Business Review Digital Articles* p2 My 3 2016

Fain, Kathleen

Readers Respond color *Publishers Weekly* v263 no51 pC4 D 12 2016

FAIR, C. CHRISTINE

Pakistan's Deadly Grip on Afghanistan *Current History* v116 no789 p136 Ap 2017

Fair, Eric

Consequence: A Memoir M. Oppenheim *Military History* v33 no5 p70 Ja 2017

Fair, J. Henry

Industrial Scars T. Brorby color *Orion Magazine* v35 no6 p62 N/D 2016

Fair Housing Act of 1968 (U.S.)

POWER TRIO G. BLACK bw *Ebony* v72 no3 p138 D 2016/Ja 2017

Fair Oaks Farms (Company)

New Crop: As the nation's largest agritourism site, Northwest Indiana'... J. VRABEL color *Indianapolis Monthly* v41 no2 p53 S 2017

Fair trade goods

Why Buyers and Sellers Inherently Disagree on What Things Are Worth C. K. Morewedge *Harvard Business Review Digital Articles* p2 My 13 2016

Fairbairn, Carlos Eduardo

READER GALLERY color *Astronomy* v44 no12 p70 D 2016

FAIRBANK, VIVIANE

Can We Leave Now? cartoon *Walrus* p18 Ja\F 2017

Fairbanks, Cassandra

BELLE A. Marantz cartoon *New Yorker* v92 no48 p16 F 6 2017

FAIRBANKS, EVE

THE LAST WHITE AFRICANS color *Foreign Policy* no222 p48 Ja/F 2017

Fairchild, Karen—Interviews

LITTLE BIG TOWN L. Rice color *Entertainment Weekly* no1456 p34 Mr 10 2017

Fairchild, Robert

Bobby Pins Come Loose J. Acocella cartoon *New Yorker* v93 no12

p11 My 8 2017

Fairén, A. G.

Redox stratification of an ancient lake in Gale crater, Mars color *Science* v356 no6341 p922 Je 1 2017

Fairfax County (Va.)—Politics & government

The Swamp Suburb F. BARNES color *Weekly Standard* v22 no34 p14 My 15 2017

Fairfield, Roy P.

CLASSIC HUMANIST *Humanist* v77 no1 p10 Ja/F 2017

Fairfield County (Conn.)—History

CARTOON COUNTY, U.S.A C. MURPHY bw cartoon color *Vanity Fair* v59 no9 p158 S 2017

Fair Grounds Race Course (New Orleans, La.)

ETC M. Cameran color *New Orleans Magazine* v51 no9 p135 Jl 2017

Fairies

The Return of the Fairies M. POLIDORO *Skeptical Inquirer* v41 no3 p21 My/Je 2017

Fairlane automobile

AMERICAN BEAUTIES color *Road & Track* v68 no8 p10 My 2017

Black Ops T. Taylor color *Hot Rod* v69 no12 p34 D 2016

SUNSET STRIP color *Road & Track* v68 no8 p16 My 2017

Fairline Boats Ltd.

Fairline Squadron 53 J. Y. Wood color *Power & Motoryacht* v33 no3 p56 Mr 2017

Fairness

See also

Social injustice

Fairouz, Mohammed, 1985-

CULTURAL DIPLOMACY J. Rosenblum and k. T. Garcia *Opera News* v81 no7 p28 Ja 2017

Fairs

See also

Agricultural exhibitions

Art fairs

Renaissance fairs

Trade shows

ABOVE & BEYOND cartoon *New Yorker* v92 no39 p28 N 28 2016

Scouting the Guatemala International Book Fair color *Publishers Weekly* v264 no32 p20 Ag 7 2017

SWITZERLAND D. Heimburger color *Christianity Today* v61 no7 p12 S 2017

Fairy circles (Arid plant formation)

Circles in the Sand T. SISKIND color *Natural History* v125 no10 p48 O 2017

Fairy circle origin stories may merge S. MILIUS color *Science News* v191 no3 p17 F 18 2017

Supernova story continues, just like science journalism *Science News* v191 no3 p2 F 18 2017

Termites and plants both shape fairy circles color *Science* v355 no6322 p229 Ja 20 2017

Fairyington, Stephanie

RIGHT PLACE, RIGHT TIME *Advocate* no1088 p20 D 2016/Ja 2017

Fairy's Kiss, The (Theatrical production)

Kiss and Tell J. Acocella cartoon *New Yorker* v92 no47 p6 Ja 30 2017

Faisal, Mustafa Abu

Icons color *Time* v189 no16/17 p122 My 1-8 2017

Faison, Jay

A Climate Hawk Among the Deniers Z. Mider color *Bloomberg Businessweek* no4498 p70 N 7 2016

A Conservative Takes on Climate Change S. F. Hayward color *Weekly Standard* v22 no29 p22 Ap 3 2017

Faith

See also

Faith (Christianity)

Acts of Faith M. Robinson, L. Kerr et al *Harper's Magazine* v333 no1998 p2 N 2016

A chronic issue A. Scobey color *U.S. Catholic* v82 no7 p29 Jl 2017

Clutter counselor S. Wells *Christian Century* v134 no11 p35 My 24 2017

Do I Have To Tell My Family I'm No Longer Religious? K. A. Appiah *New York Times Magazine* p24 O 2 2016

Ever Deeper Faith M. Simone *America* v217 no2 p52 Jl 24 2017

Faith in real life J. C. Tobin color *U.S. Catholic* v82 no7 p18 Jl 2017

Faith Matters C. Zaleski *Christian Century* v134 no17 p42 Ag 16 2017

Faith MATTERS M. C. Barnes *Christian Century* v133 no23 p35 N 9 2016

Faith Matters S. Paulsell *Christian Century* v134 no14 p32 Jl 5 2017

THE FUTURE OF BELIEF K. Tippett color *America* v216 no4 p32 F 20 2017

How did your faith change in college? graph *America* v217 no4 p6 Ag 21 2017

LIFE AS LITURGY J. TURNER *American Conservative* v15 no6 p4 N/D 2016

Life's work: Building the church takes everyone [Cover story] J. Mesman Griffith, J. Schueller et al color *U.S. Catholic* v82 no8 p22 Ag 2017

LIVING BY The Word *Christian Century* v134 no15 p20 Jl 19 2017

NOT GETTING 'GETTING RELIGION' K. L. WOODWARD and N. DALLAVALLE *Commonweal* v144 no6 p4 Mr 24 2017

Patriotism in the pews S. G. Lynch, T. Poelker et al color *U.S. Catholic* v82 no11 p5 N 2017

Pray about it A. Scobey color *U.S. Catholic* v82 no7 p43 Jl 2017

Studies reveal how faith counts in placing spiritual before material goods D. Briggs *Christian Century* v134 no1 p17 Ja 4 2017

Thank God for the stars M. Murphy-Gill *U.S. Catholic* v81 no11 p4 N 2016

'You Are the One!' M. Simone *America* v217 no4 p54 Ag 21 2017

Faith & reason—Christianity

OF MANY THINGS M. MALONE *America* v215 no12 p2 O 24 2016

Faith (Christianity)

CRADLE CHRISTIANS *Christianity Today* v61 no1 p19 Ja/F 2017

Faith Matters S. Wells *Christian Century* v134 no13 p2 Je 21 2017

Godly play with adults S. Wells *Christian Century* v134 no15 p35 Jl 19 2017

JACK T. CHICK D. BARRY *New York Times Magazine* p20 D 25 2016

Just Give Me Jesus chart *Christianity Today* v61 no5 p15 Je 2017

LOVING ALL TYPES OF SOJOURNERS M. GALLI color *Christianity Today* v61 no5 p19 Je 2017

The Magnanimity of the Gospel K. Alys Robinson color *America* v217 no5 p54 S 4 2017

'Perhaps It Is True After All' [Cover story] P. J. Ryan color *Commonweal* v143 no19 p20 D 2 2016

Tapped Out J. Wren color *Christianity Today* v61 no1 p96 Ja/F 2017

Varieties of Faith E. Heartney color *Art in America* v105 no4 p47 Ap 2017

Faith (Islam)—Qur'anic teaching

Cambodian Cham Muslims and the Quran: A shattered community continues to rebuild its foundations of faith S. NAZY *Islamic Horizons* v46 no4 p34 Jl/Ag 2017

'Perhaps It Is True After All' [Cover story] P. J. Ryan color *Commonweal* v143 no19 p20 D 2 2016

The Way to Hope and Guidance: Muslims have the Quran to lead them toward success E. ABDELKADER *Islamic Horizons* v46 no4 p30 Jl/Ag 2017

Faith (Music)

SONGS OF A LIFETIME L. Greenblatt color *Entertainment Weekly* no1448 p31 Ja 13 2017

Faith development

Faith Matters M. C. Barnes *Christian Century* v134 no12 p40 Je 7 2017

No Place for Islamophobia in America: Islamophobia has its roots in the history of Western Christianity J. S. HARRIS *Islamic Horizons* v46 no3 p30 My/Je 2017

Why I stay D. Thomas *Christian Century* v134 no14 p13 Jl 5 2017

Faith in literature

Beyond Genealogy: On the wealth of stories that family novels leave behind J. Lucas *New York Times Book Review* p18 S 3 2017

Saving Calvin from Clichés [Cover story] M. Sitman bw *Com-*

monweal v144 no17 p18 O 20 2017

Faith—Biblical teaching

Trading in my narrative G. Atkinson *Christian Century* v134 no7 p30 Mr 29 2017

Faith—Religious aspects

Faith in the balance A. Camille color *U.S. Catholic* v82 no7 p47 Jl 2017

From Scotland to Sicily [Cover story] W. Storrar color *Commonweal* v144 no17 p9 O 20 2017

MUSLIM-CHRISTIAN DIALOGUE *Islamic Horizons* v46 no3 p10 My/Je 2017

The Power of Faith: Muslim Houstonians welcome ISNA with flair S. ESSA *Islamic Horizons* v46 no3 p20 My/Je 2017

Falasca, Marco

mTORC1 activity repression by late endosomal phosphatidylinositol 3,4-bisphosphate diag *Science* v356 no6341 p968 Je 1 2017

Falcke, H.

Observation of a large-scale anisotropy in the arrival directions of cosmic rays above 8×10^{18} eV *Science* v357 no6357 p1266 S 22 2017

Falco, Edie, 1963-

Law & Order True Crime: The Menendez Murders D. Franich, N. Abrams et al color *Entertainment Weekly* no1482/1483 p62 S 22 2017

Falco, Edie, 1963—Interviews

Edie Falco As an Attorney Ripped from the Headlines D. D'addario color *Time* v190 no10/11 p108 S 18 2017

EDIE FALCO I. Rudolph *TV Guide* v65 no37 p28 S 4 2017

Falcone, Patricia

Celebrating Targeted Investments in Innovative Research *Science & Technology Review* p3 Ap/My 2017

A New Paradigm for Medical Research color *Science & Technology Review* p3 O/N 2016

Falcone, Philip A.

Phil Falcone's Last Resort M. CAMPBELL color *Bloomberg Businessweek* no4527 p66 Je 19 2017

Falconer, Bruce

On My Obsession with Sherwood Anderson: Revisiting Winesburg, Ohio again and again *Humanities* v38 no4 p1 Fall 2017

Falconi, Lorena

Biodiversity redistribution under climate change: Impacts on ecosystems and human well-being color *Science* v355 no6332 p1389 Mr 31 2017

Falcons in art

A Peaceable Kingdom J. Skelly color *Orion Magazine* v35 no6 p32 N/D 2016

Fales-hill, Susan

STAYING POWER color *Essence* v47 no12 p104 Ap 2017

Falk, Abram L.

Addressing spin states with infrared light bw *Science* v357 no6352 p649 Ag 18 2017

Falk, Angela

no average day: The busy lives of dancers at Juilliard, Indiana University and Harvard K. BRADY *Dance Magazine* v90 p18 2016/2017 Supplement College Guide

Falk, Jen

To The Editor color *American Craft* v76 no6 p10 D 2016-Ja 2017

Falk, Richard

Power Shift: On the New Global Order G. J. Ikenberry *Foreign Affairs* v95 no6 p173 N/D 2016

Falke (Company)

ANDY'S Candy E. BROWN *Interview* v47 no3 p37 Ap 2017

Falkenberg, Gail

Golden Opportunity T. Perrotta *Tennis* v52 no6 p10 N/D 2016

FALKI, JENN

42 new ALL-STAR PRODUCTS of the year [Cover story] color *Redbook* p27 Jl/Ag 2017

Fal'ko, V. I.

High-temperature quantum oscillations caused by recurring Bloch states in graphene superlattices color *Science* v357 no6347 p181 Jl 14 2017

Fal'ko, Vladimir I.

Ballistic miniband conduction in a graphene superlattice bibl graph *Science* v353 no6307 p1526 S 30 2016

Falkowski, Paul G.

Biological control of aragonite formation in stony corals bw color graph *Science* v356 no6341 p933 Je 1 2017

Fall, Jenny

A subcellular map of the human proteome color *Science* v356 no6340 p820 My 26 2017

Fall Creek (Ind.)

Fall Creek Place: A neighborhood once known as "Dodge City" thrives anew K. F. Wells *Indianapolis Monthly* v40 no10 p32 Je 2017

Fall foliage

DRESSAGE SNAPSHOT color *Dressage Today* v24 no1 p16 O 2017

Fall to Winter (Poem)

Fall to Winter C. Laden *South Dakota Magazine* v32 no4 p106 N/D 2016

Falling Water (TV program)

Falling Water J. Jensen color *Entertainment Weekly* no1435 p48 O 14 2016

USA's New Look: Darker Skies color *TV Guide* v64 no42 p19 O 10 2016

Fallingwater (Pa.)

DO THE WRIGHT THING K. FRANZMAN and V. RUHTEN-BERG color *Indianapolis Monthly* p36 Ap 2017

Fallon, Jimmy, 1974-

Laugh Lines color *Reader's Digest* v190 no1134 p127 O 2017

Sound Bites color *Entertainment Weekly* no1476 p6 Ag 4 2017

Fallon, John

4 CEOs Who Are Making Frugal Innovation Work N. Radjou and J. Prabhu *Harvard Business Review Digital Articles* p2 N 28 2014

FALLON, SARAH

PARENT TRAP: YOUR KIDS WILL SEE INTERNET PORN. DEAL WITH IT. A CONVERSATION WITH PEGGY OREN-STEIN cartoon *Wired* v25 no9 p78 S 2017

Fallopian tubes—Anatomy

Let's talk about birth control color *Health* v31 no9 p20 N 2017

FALLOWS, JAMES

CHINA'S GREAT LEAP BACKWARD [Cover story] color *Atlantic* v318 no5 p58 D 2016

Despair and Hope in the Age of Trump color *Atlantic* v319 no1 p13 Ja/F 2017

Falls (Accidents)

The Elderly at High Risk for Bathroom Injuries *USA Today Magazine* v146 no2867 p6 Ag 2017

First Aid for Your Pet L. Murray color *Health* v30 no9 p106 N 2016

frozen fun R. RABKIN PEACHMAN *Parents* p137 2015

Keep On Moving G. MULLINS-COHEN *Parks & Recreation* v52 no1 p10 Ja 2017

Falls (Accidents) in old age—Prevention

THE GATEWAY TO ACTIVE SENIORS S. Thoreson and M. Hart *Parks & Recreation* v52 no1 p32 Ja 2017

Falls (Accidents) in old age—Research

Injuries Differ for Outdoors and Indoors *USA Today Magazine* v145 no2861 p1 F 2017

Falls (Accidents)—Prevention

Is It Time to Fall Proof Your Parent's Home? R. DRUZIN color *Maclean's* v130 no3 p49 Ap 2017

protection plan V. BEISER *Parents* v91 no10 p136 O 2016

Quick fixes to keep you from falling *Harvard Health Letter* v42 no3 p4 Ja 2017

Falls, Robert, 1954-

ROBERT FALLS B. Zehme cartoon *Chicago* v66 no3 p148 Mr 2017

False advertising

A Buffett Company With Angry Customers N. Buhayar color *Bloomberg Businessweek* no4499 p53 N 14 2016

Realtors gone wild J. CASTALDO color *Maclean's* p14 Je 2017

False confession

DNA EVIDENCE FREES THE INNOCENT R. J. NORRIS color *Reason* v49 no4 p34 Ag/S 2017

False news (Social media)

All the News That Causes Fits *America* v215 no18 p5 D 5 2016

And that's the way it isn't G. Adamson bw cartoon color *Magazine Antiques* v184 no2 p24 Mr/Ap 2017

ASK A FLOWCHART R. CAPPS chart diag *Wired* v25 no3 p96 Mr 2017

BOTS BITE MAN A. WEBB color *Mother Jones* v42 no2 p51 Mr/Ap 2017

A B.S. IN B.S *Esquire* p120 S 2017

CARTOONS *In These Times* v41 no5 p32 My 2017

Cartoons *New York Times Upfront* v149 no7 p24 Ja 9 2017

Fake News and Fake Science in the Age of Misinformation K. FRAZIER *Skeptical Inquirer* v41 no3 p4 My/Je 2017

'Fake' News and the Victorian Gentleman M. CONTINETTI *Commentary* v143 no1 p64 Ja 2017

Fake News *Change* v82 no3 p19 Mr 2017

THE FAKE-NEWS FALLACY A. CHEN cartoon color *New Yorker* v93 no26 p78 S 4 2017

FAKE NEWS FOOLING MILLIONS! C. STOFFERS *New York Times Upfront* v149 no7 p6 Ja 9 2017

FAKE NEWS FREAKOUT J. E. USCINSKI bw *Reason* v48 no10 p54 Mr 2017

Fake News vs. Real News L. Crate *Education Digest* v83 no1 p4 S 2017

FIGHTING FAKE NEWS: Made-up stories are taking over the internet. Are tech companies doing enough to stop the spread? S. GROSSBART *New York Times Upfront* v150 no1 p12 S 4 2017

FIREWALL P. Williams cartoon *New Yorker* v93 no7 p35 Ap 3 2017

FIT TO PRINT T. McWilliam, S. Arnswald et al bw color *Wired* v25 no5 p14 My 2017

THE HAND OFF S. DADICH color *Wired* v25 no3 p12 Mr 2017

How can we discourage bogus news stories? K. KIPLINGER *Kiplinger's Personal Finance* v71 no2 p18 F 2017

HOW FAKE NEWS TURNED A SMALL TOWN UPSIDE DOWN: AT THE HEIGHT OF THE 2016 ELECTION, EXAGGERATED REPORTS OF A JUVENILE SEX CRIME BROUGHT A MEDIA MAELSTROM TO TWIN FALLS—ONE THE IDAHO CITY STILL HASN'T RECOVERED FROM C. DICKERSON *New York Times Magazine* p46 O 1 2017

How Russia Weaponizes Fake News L. RESTON il *New Republic* v248 no6 p6 Je 2017

How to Stamp Out Fake News D. Pogue color *Scientific American* v316 no2 p24 F 2017

In 2016, Lies, the Whole Lies and Nothing but the Lies J. Stein color *Time* v188 no25-26 p158 D 19 2016 Double Issue

INSIDE THE ECHO CHAMBER W. Quattrociocchi color *Scientific American* v316 no4 p60 Ap 2017

Listening to ELVIS CURES Foot Fungus [Cover story] color *Women's Health* v14 no3 p70 Ap 2017

MADE IN MACEDONIA color *Wired* v25 no3 p10 Mr 2017

Maybe the Internet Is Just Terrible After All M. Read *New York* v49 no24 p38 N 28 2016

Real confusion about fake news color *Phi Delta Kappan* v98 no5 p6 F 2017

Research: Being in a Group Makes Us Less Likely to Fact-Check R. Meng, Youjung Jun et al *Harvard Business Review Digital Articles* p2 Ag 1 2017

Save the Postal Service J. HIGHTOWER color *Progressive* v81 no5 p70 Je/Jl 2017

The Search for Facts in a Post-Fact World M. Dean color *Wired* v25 no10 p98 O 2017

SURVIVING THE MIS INFORMATION AGE D. J. HELFAND *Skeptical Inquirer* v41 no3 p34 My/Je 2017

Varieties of Ridiculous Experience D. FOSTER *National Review* v69 no1 p44 Ja 23 2017

The victims of fake news N. Berman color *Columbia Journalism Review* v56 no2 p62 Fall 2017

Welcome to Macedonia, Fake News Factory to the World S. Subramanian color graph *Wired* v25 no3 p68 Mr 2017

WHICH ONE IS #FAKENEWS?* S. M. FERNÁNDEZ *Scholastic Choices* v32 no8 p6 My 2017

Without Apology E. Alterman *Nation* v305 no9 p10 O 16 2017

Falsettos (Theatrical production)

2 — FALSETTOS M. R. Bernardo color *Entertainment Weekly* no1444/1445 p118 D 16 2016

ANDREW RANNELLS REACHES THE HIGH NOTES IN FALSETTOS J. Derschowitz color *Entertainment Weekly* no1438 p70 N 4 2016

The Old Normal M. Schulman cartoon *New Yorker* v92 no32 p18 O 10 2016

THEATER OF THE MOMENT R. WEINERT-KENDT color *America* v215 no18 p30 D 5 2016

Falstaff (Theatrical production)

CLASSICAL MUSIC *New Yorker* v93 no19 p8 Jl 3 2017

Faludi, Susan

In the Darkroom L. Neff color *Christian Century* v133 no21 p53 O 12 2016

Fame

Addicted to Fame: From the Greeks to Lady Gaga D. H. Blake *Humanities* v38 no4 p1 Fall 2017

Taking on the PC Crowd: A Canadian professor gains fame and followers B. ANDERSON *American Conservative* v16 no4 p41 Jl/Ag 2017

Familial behavior in animals

See also

Parental behavior in animals

Families

See also

Brothers & sisters

Children

Cousins

Daughters

Divorce

Family vacations

Fathers

Golfers' families

Grandparent & child

Mothers

Parent & child

Parenthood

Parents

Sons

Tribes

3 Adult Tantrums I Would Like to Have R. D'Apice color *Working Mother* v40 no4 p98 O/N 2017

6 New Attractions for Summer K. Cicero *Parents* v91 no6 p16 Je 2016

ALL IN THE FAMILY B. GREENBERG *USA Today Magazine* v145 no2864 p72 My 2017

All in the Family K. Andrews *Virginia Living* v15 no3 p72 Ap 2017

ARE YOU MY MOTHER? I. PARKER cartoon color *New Yorker* v93 no14 p46 My 22 2017

Back Home Again J. YOUNG *Indianapolis Monthly* p94 F 2017

beach towns with benefits K. CICERO color *Parents* v92 no8 p74 Ag 2017

BIG CREEK: A FAMILY RECALLS YEARS AT THE LODGE K. WIDNER *Idaho Magazine* v16 no10 p32 Jl 2017

Can We Get Real About Having It All? B. Hauser color *Health* v31 no6 p91 Jl 2017

Cousins, Tacos & Cover Babies color *Parents* v92 no9 p10 S 2017

Days of Our Lives A. Hood *Yankee* v81 no1 p116 Ja/F 2017

Dear Readers B. Kelley *Reader's Digest* v189 no1131 p4 Je 2017

Don't forget the kids S. Butler *U.S. Catholic* v82 no11 p4 N 2017

Faith Matters C. Zaleski *Christian Century* v134 no11 p38 My 24 2017

A Family FISHING AFFAIR T. Hughes *New York State Conservationist* v71 no6 p10 Je 2017

Family-friendly science A. Zellmer cartoon *Science* v354 no6315 p1070 N 25 2016

fun [Cover story] color *Parents* v92 no7 p51 Jl 2017

Get Together D. Grossman color *Popular Photography* v80 no11 p66 D 2016

Go Away Together! K. Cicero color *Parents* v92 no9 p152 S 2017

Hassle-Free Family Getaways [Cover story] M. Santos color *Working Mother* v40 no2 p56 Je/Jl 2017

the Holidays Seasons not-so-best kept Secret color *O, The Oprah Magazine* p96 D 2016

How Should You Spend Your HOLIDAY HANG TIME? H. VIGGIANI color *Seventeen* v75 no11 p68 N 2016

in focus color *Yoga Journal* no288 p95 D 2016

In the communion of saints P. Gallagher color *U.S. Catholic* v81 no12 p31 D 2016

John Shields Y. RADBOD *Vegetarian Journal* v35 no4 p12 2016

Last-Minute Spring Break Trips K. Cicero *Parents* v92 no2 p16 F 2017

A Lifesaving Golf Date with His Dad D. CHRISINGER color *Reader's Digest* v190 no1134 p48 O 2017

Live Your Best Life color *O, The Oprah Magazine* p25 D 2016

Living With Grandma? Don't Knock It Till You Try It *Parents* v91 no10 p18 O 2016

Making the right memories M. Rollins color *Redbook* p6 Je 2017

Memories on Ice R. Marshall color *Money* v46 no2 p88 Mr 2017

THE MISSING *Harper's Magazine* v335 no2005 p20 Je 2017

Mitch's Fault M. GUNCH cartoon *New Orleans Magazine* v51 no12 p54 O 2017

a movable feast *Parents* v91 no9 p27 S 2016

The Mudslide A. BARTHOLOMEW color *Reader's Digest* v190 no1134 p8 O 2017

A new family activism M. Walker color *U.S. Catholic* v82 no11 p12 N 2017

our weirdest family tradition is... *Parents* p144 2015

parents 2 parents S. James cartoon color graph *Parents* v92 no3 p9 Mr 2017

Paying It Forward M. SOLHEIM *Kiplinger's Personal Finance* v71 no11 p4 N 2017

PROBLEM: AFTER TRYING TO GET FAMILY INVOLVEMENT WITH OUR ESTATE PLANNING, EVERYTHING HAS TURNED BITTER, AND WE STILL DON'T HAVE A PLAN IN PLACE M. Friesen *Successful Farming* v115 no6 p66 Ap 2017

Q: What is the most interesting family in history? J. Moyes, H. Rothschild et al color *Atlantic* v318 no5 p96 D 2016

RAISING Alexander C. TURNER *Reader's Digest* v188 no1124 p124 O 2016

The Rest Stop Road Trip M. ROACH color *Reader's Digest* v189 no1131 p72 Je 2017

Rewind: Back-to-School Movies M. Lascala chart color *Parents* v92 no9 p16 S 2017

Silver Streak color *Missouri Life* v44 no4 p22 Je 2017

Snow Day J. Youngerman and L. A. Miller bw *Art in America* v105 no4 p55 Ap 2017

A SON'S QUEST TO GIVE HIS DYING FATHER ARTIFICIAL IMMORTALITY J. VLAHOS color *Wired* v25 no8 p56 Ag 2017

Summer service A. Scobey color *U.S. Catholic* v82 no6 p43 Je 2017

Take a break A. Scobey color *U.S. Catholic* v82 no5 p43 My 2017

Thank God for That Crazy Little Bird C. BLOOM and B. T. GREIVE *Audubon* v119 no1 p20 Spr 2017

"The moment that CHANGED OUR LIVES FOREVER" J. Francisco color *Good Housekeeping* v265 no5 p58 N 2017

Tough Act to Follow K. CHONG cartoon *Walrus* v14 no6 p64 Jl/Ag 2017

#trailchat color *Backpacker* p8 S 2017

the ultimate guide to a blissful family vacation C. BIRNBAUM *Parents* v91 no6 p42 Je 2016

Under Mica's Spell J. REGINATO color *Vanity Fair* v59 no6 p116 My 2017

The Unexpected Benefits of Ending Up at the Back of the Pack S. Schrobsdorff color *Time* v189 no3 p63 Ja 16 2017

WELCOME TO THE GREEN MACHINE J. N. LOMAX *Texas Monthly* v45 no6 p126 Je 2017

What Children Can Teach Us About Acceptance E. Bried *Parents* v91 no10 p16 O 2016

What Happens Next (or Doesn't) M. SILVER *New York Times Book Review* p15 F 26 2017

What your mom's body says about you H. Levine color *Health* v31 no9 p59 N 2017

WORK-LIFE BALANCE IS A SHAM A. BRESLAW cartoon diag *Women's Health* v14 no3 p146 Ap 2017

The yoga of give & take S. Kempton color *Yoga Journal* no288 p28 D 2016

Families—Asia

RETURN OF THE MISSING DAUGHTERS M. D. GUPTA color graph *Scientific American* v317 no3 p80 S 2017

Families—Cuba

Castro's Cuba Is the Only Way of Life Many Have Known R. Kushner *Time* v188 no24 p45 D 12 2016

Families—Economic aspects

stop fighting about money! M. LILES *Parents* v91 no9 p156 S 2016

Family Businesses Need One Person to Conquer and Another to Rule J. Baron and R. Lachenauer *Harvard Business Review Digital Articles* p2 D 3 2014

When You've Made Enough Money to Cause Family Tension J. Baron, R. Lachenauer et al *Harvard Business Review Digital Articles* p2 Ja 8 2016

Family-owned business enterprises—Succession

BOTTLE ROYALE C. PETERSON-WITHORN color graph *Forbes* v198 no5 p100 O 25 2016

A LEGACY WORTH WORKING FOR R. Derousseau color *Fortune* v75 no1 p36 Ja 1 2017

Why Family Firms in East Asia Struggle with Succession C. Fernández-Aráoz, S. Iqbal et al *Harvard Business Review Digital Articles* p2 Mr 24 2015

Family planning

See also

Birth control

CAN THEIR PROBLEM BE SOLVED? *Successful Farming* v114 no13 p80 D 2016

Family planning services

IF YOU DEFUND IT, THEY WON'T COME H. Levintova color *Mother Jones* v42 no5 p15 S/O 2017

Family portraits

PLEASE DON'T SAY CHEESE S. Zlotnick *Washingtonian Magazine* v52 no6 p97 Mr 2017

Family psychotherapy

Report and Command D. T. PUTERBAUGH *USA Today Magazine* v145 no2858 p82 N 2016

Family recreation

See also

Family vacations

CALENDAR OF EVENTS *Idaho Magazine* v16 no5 p58 F 2017

dad's legacy M. FURTMAN color *Cabin Living* p50 O 2017

weekend getaways: family *Washingtonian Magazine* v52 no11 p89 Ag 2017

Family relations

The Absence of Assorted Things: Where Nothing Is Everything E. LEE *Idaho Magazine* v16 no12 p12 S 2017

FAMILY AND FOOD *Successful Farming* v114 no10 p64 O 2016

Keep Your Home Life Sane when Work Gets Crazy S. Friedman *Harvard Business Review Digital Articles* p2 F 23 2015

Let's talk A. Scobey color *U.S. Catholic* v82 no3 p43 Mr 2017

Lola's Story A. TIZON bw color *Atlantic* v319 no5 p64 Je 2017

THE TROUBLE WITH MIA: At what point do our adult children cease to be the adoring babies we once knew? K. W. Reyes *Saturday Evening Post* v289 no5 p18 S/O 2017

We need to talk A. Scobey color *U.S. Catholic* v82 no1 p36 Ja 2017

Family relations—Physiological aspects

How Family Ties Keep You Going, In Sickness and In Health A. Sifferlin color *Time* v189 no5 p20 F 13 2017

Family relations—Social aspects

Lightbox color *Time* v188 no14 p18 O 10 2016

Family reunions

backstory color *New Republic* v248 no7 p68 Jl 2017

My incarcerated nephew, the guest of honor H. Neumark color *Christian Century* v134 no8 p1 Ap 12 2017

Family size—Social aspects

Big Viking families nurtured murder B. BOWER *Science News* v190 no10 p16 N 12 2016

Family systems theory

Report and Command D. T. PUTERBAUGH *USA Today Magazine* v145 no2858 p82 N 2016

Family traditions

Family Ties *Outdoor Life* v223 no9 p10 N 2016

HOME FOR THE HOLIDAY L. MYERS *Missouri Life* v43 no7 p67 D 2016/Ja 2017

Home for the Holidays *Martha Stewart Living* no270 p23 D 2016

Family travel

A HOME OF LAST RESORT S. SMITH *Texas Monthly* v45 no5 p81 My 2017

THE NO-FLY, ALL-FUN VACATION [Cover story] M. Rollins and K. VALENTINI color diag *Redbook* p97 Jl/Ag 2017

RED, WHITE & PEACHY P. P. FISCHER color *Better Homes & Gardens* v95 no7 p126 Jl 2017

Family vacations

FAMILY-VACATION BREAKDOWN J. SPYRA cartoon *New Yorker* v93 no25 p41 Ag 28 2017

MAKE SOME AMAZING MEMORIES A. BARTZ and J. Press color *Redbook* p88 Jl/Ag 2017

THE NO-FLY, ALL-FUN VACATION [Cover story] M. Rollins and K. VALENTINI color diag *Redbook* p97 Jl/Ag 2017

Party TIME L. READIE MAYER color *Cabin Living* p58 D 2016

The Road More Traveled M. Hornung color *Money* v46 no3 p80 Ap 2017

THE ULTIMATE FAMILY GETAWAY color *Good Housekeeping* v264 no4 p142 Ap 2017

Family values

FAMILY VALUES M. Gessen *Harper's Magazine* v334 no2002 p35 Mr 2017

Family Video (Company)

The Last Video Chain N. KIRSCH and D. DREMAN color *Forbes* v199 no2 p52 F 28 2017

Family violence

See also

Child abuse

A Disobedient Woman L. Schenkman *New York Times Magazine* p34 Mr 26 2017

How Pastors Perceive Domestic Violence chart *Christianity Today* p17 Mr 2017

Kiran Ebrahim *Atlanta* v57 no2 p108 Je 2017

Together we rise C. Gorrell color *Yoga Journal* no287 p10 N 2016

WOMEN ON THE RUN N. RABIN and R. BACON *Ms.* v27 no2 p18 Summ 2017

Family violence—Canada

The Place Where Happiness Dwelled C. CARSWELL *Sierra* v102 no5 p24 St/O 2017

Family violence—Prevention

patrick stewart will look great forever C. WEAVER bw color *GQ: Gentlemen's Quarterly* v97 no3 p146 Mr 2017

Family stability—Charts, diagrams, etc.

What is the biggest obstacle to forming stable families? graph *America* v216 no11 p6 My 15 2017

Famines

President Trump Steps Up to Fight Famine *America* v217 no2 p8 Jl 24 2017

Famines—Africa

One Meal a Day L. PALMER color *New Republic* v248 no7 p32 Jl 2017

Famines—History—21st century

What Man, and Climate Change, Has Wrought A. Baker color *Time* v189 no11 p15 Mr 27 2017

Famines—International cooperation

Pope Francis calls for action as famine declared in South Sudan K. Clarke color *America* v216 no6 p15 Mr 20 2017

Famines—Kenya

Severe drought brings starving Kenyans to church doorsteps F. Nzwili *Christian Century* v134 no5 p16 Mr 1 2017

Famines—Somalia

snapshot *In These Times* v41 no5 p7 My 2017

Somalia on the Verge of Famine As U.N. Pleads for Help T. John color *Time* v189 no7/8 p17 F 27 2017

Famuyide, Abimbola

How Mayo Clinic Is Simplifying Prenatal Care for Low-Risk Patients *Harvard Business Review Digital Articles* p2 Je 19 2017

Fan, Fengjia

Efficient and stable solution-processed planar perovskite solar cells via contact passivation bibl graph *Science* v355 no6326 p722 F 17 2017

Fan, James

Efficient and stable solution-processed planar perovskite solar cells via contact passivation bibl graph *Science* v355 no6326 p722 F 17 2017

Restored iron transport by a small molecule promotes absorption and hemoglobinization in animals color graph *Science* v356 no6338 p608 My 12 2017

Fan, Jiayang

ART'S SAKE: BRIGHT AND SHINY bw *New Yorker* v93 no33 p38 O 23 2017

Dokebi Bar & Grill color *New Yorker* v93 no4 p22 Mr 13 2017

Mettä color *New Yorker* v93 no27 p18 S 11 2017

Parental Controls *New York Times Book Review* p12 Je 11 2017

The Price of Prosperity *New York Times Book Review* p38 N 13 2016

SUPER FANS cartoon *New Yorker* v93 no16 p38 Je 5 2017

THE THIRD PERSON cartoon *New Yorker* v93 no18 p22 Je 26 2017

When Music Was Life and Death *New York Times Book Review* p21 N 6 2016

Fan, Linlin Z.

Optical control of cell signaling by single-chain photoswitchable kinases bibl diag *Science* v355 no6327 p836 F 24 2017

Fan, Wenxin

In Case of Low Revenue cartoon *Bloomberg Businessweek* no4497 p50 O 31 2016

ON CHINESE AQUACULTURE FARMS, THE FISH ARE PUMPED WITH ANTIBIOTICS, AS ARE THE PIGS, WHOSE WASTE FEEDS THE FISH. SO LET'S TALK ABOUT THAT SEAFOOD PLATTER [Cover story] color graph *Bloomberg Businessweek* no4504 p38 D 19 2016

SAVING THE SOUTH CHINA SEA color map *Bloomberg Businessweek* no4505 p78 D 26 2016

Fan, Yabin

Chiral Majorana fermion modes in a quantum anomalous Hall insulator–superconductor structure diag *Science* v357 no6348 p294 Jl 21 2017

Fan, Yanqun

Deep functional analysis of synII, a 770-kilobase synthetic yeast chromosome diag *Science* v355 no6329 p1047 Mr 10 2017

Fan, Zhengxiao

History of winning remodels thalamo-PFC circuit to reinforce social dominance color *Science* v357 no6347 p162 Jl 14 2017

Fan clubs

Chi Society M. Rosenberg color *Sports Illustrated* v126 no9 p116 Mr 27 2017

Fan Yang

Anomalously low electronic thermal conductivity in metallic vanadium dioxide bibl graph *Science* v355 no6323 p371 Ja 27 2017

Fanatics Inc.

GAME TIME DECISIONS E. NOVY-WILLIAMS color *Bloomberg Businessweek* no4515 p59 Mr 20 2017

Fancher, Hampton

NINE LIVES T. Friend cartoon *New Yorker* v93 no24 p19 Ag 21 2017

Fancher, Richard

Root of the Problem J. Servaas *Saturday Evening Post* v288 no6 p27 N/D 2016

Fancher, Sheryl Carle

ENEMY color *Christian Century* v134 no5 p20 Mr 1 2017

Fanconi's anemia

Running for Her Life [Cover story] J. Brant bw color *Runner's World* v52 no6 p82 Jl 2017

Fancy work

See also

Knitting

Stitches of change J. Bleem color *U.S. Catholic* v81 no11 p50 N 2016

Fanderl, Harald

A Step-by-Step Plan to Improve CMO-COO Collaboration *Harvard Business Review Digital Articles* p2 Ja 28 2015

Fandry (Film)

Dirt Beneath the Daydreams D. Girish color *Film Comment* v53 no4 p74 Jl/Ag 2017

Fane, B.

Hawkmoths use nectar sugar to reduce oxidative damage from flight bibl graph *Science* v355 no6326 p733 F 17 2017

Fanelli, E.

An ecosystem-based deep-ocean strategy bibl color map *Science* v355 no6324 p452 F 3 2017

Fang, S.

Magnetic resonance spectroscopy of an atomically thin material using a single-spin qubit bibl color diag graph *Science* v355 no6324 p503 F 3 2017

OH DADDY! *Virginia Living* v15 no1 p19 D 2016

What big fangs you have, little blenny S. Milius color *Science News* v191 no10 p4 My 27 2017

Fang, Shaoli

Harvesting electrical energy from carbon nanotube yarn twist diag graph *Science* v357 no6353 p773 Ag 25 2017

Fang, Yufeng

A paralogous decoy protects Phytophthora sojae apoplastic effector PsXEG1 from a host inhibitor bibl graph *Science* v355 no6326 p710 F 17 2017

Fange, David

Kinetics of dCas9 target search in Escherichia coli diag *Science* v357 no6358 p1420 S 29 2017

FANGJING, MA

Asia's Rising Stars color *Forbes* v199 no5 p20 My 16 2017

Fangping Zhao

Urgent need for implementation of precision medicine in gastric cancer in China bibl chart *Science* v354 no6319 p39 D 23 2016

Fangwen Lu

Research: How Leadership Experience Affects Students *Harvard Business Review Digital Articles* p2 F 21 2017

Fankhauser, Christian

A photoreceptor's on-off switch bibl diag *Science* v354 no6310 p282 O 21 2016

Fannie Mae

Fannie and Freddie's Many Happy Returns J. Light graph *Bloomberg Businessweek* no4520 p30 My 1 2017

HIDDEN TREASURES OR MONEY PITS? M. Celarier color diag *Fortune* v175 no5 p33 Ap 1 2017

FANNIN, REBECCA

Asia's Rising Stars color *Forbes* v199 no5 p20 My 16 2017

Fanning, Dakota, 1994-

Go Fluoro E. Wilson color *InStyle* v24 no9 p180 S 2017

Fanning, Elle, 1998-

Best-Dressed LIST L. McCarthy color *Harper's Bazaar* no3648 p118 N 2016

Elle Fanning J. Crelin color *Current Biography* v78 no8 p33 Ag 2017

Feathered Friends E. Wilson color *InStyle* v24 no8 p74 Ag 2017

From Strong Roots A. Wintour bw color *Vogue* v207 no6 p38 Je 2017

Swept Away N. Heller color *Vogue* v207 no6 p87 Je 2017

Fanning, Mick

BE HERE NOW color *Surfing Magazine* v53 no3 p12 Mr 2017

IRISH CROSS ROADS T. PAUL color *Surfing Magazine* v53 no3 p68 Mr 2017

THE SERPENTINE PACT A. GOGGANS color *Surfer* v58 no1 p90 Ap 2017

Fanning, Ronan

Ronan Fanning, Eamon de Valera: A Will to Power J. Rossi *Society* v54 no3 p310 Je 2017

Fanrong Kong

A brief overview of matrix-assisted laser desorption/ionization time-of-flight mass spectrometry (MALDI-TOF MS) applications in clinical microbiology in China *Science* v354 no6319 p55 D 23 2016

Fans (Fashion accessories)

CREATIVELY COOL J. von Geldern color *Horse & Rider* v56 no6 p57 Je 2017

Fans (Machinery)

A MIGHTY (QUIET) WIND R. Verger color *Popular Science* v289 no4 p26 Jl/Ag 2017

Fans (Machinery)—Evaluation

For the BOAT *Sea Magazine* v108 no12 p45 D 2016

Fans (Persons)

See also

Automobile racing fans

Sports spectators

BEST AND WORST CITIES FOR FOOTBALL ENTHUSIASTS *USA Today Magazine* v146 no2867 p15 Ag 2017

ON BEING A FAN K. Cameron color *Cycle World* v56 no1 p58 Ja/F 2017

Fans (Persons)—Political activity

Lightbox color *Time* v188 no19 p12 N 7 2016

Fanshawe, Simon—Interviews

"Diversity doesn't have to be burdensome - it's magic": Stonewall co-founder and D&I consultant Simon Fanshawe on how to bridge the gap between good intentions and real change *People Management* p15 S 2017

FANSLAU, JILL
Funny FiLL-IN cartoon *National Geographic Kids* no470 p30 My 2017
Funny FILL-IN *National Geographic Kids* no466 p34 D 2016/ Ja 2017

Fantas-Eyes Inc.
Sunny Sunnies color *Good Housekeeping* v264 no6 p13 Je 2017

Fantasizing About Being Black (Music)
Otis Taylor: 'TRIUMPH IS THE KEY' J. Johnson color *Downbeat* v84 no4 p40 Ap 2017

Fantastic Beasts & Where to Find Them (Film)
Eddie Redmayne Wants to Make You Believe In Magic Again M. McCluskey color *Time* v188 no22-23 p106 N/D 2016
Eddie Redmayne Works His Magic D. Coggan color *Entertainment Weekly* no1441 p13 N 25 2016
FANTASTIC BEASTS AND WHERE TO FIND THEM A. Greengart color *Sound & Vision* v82 no7 p67 S 2017
Fantastic Beasts and Where to Find Them C. Nashawaty color *Entertainment Weekly* no1441 p36 N 25 2016
A FIELD GUIDE TO FANTASTIC BEASTS J. Hibberd color *Entertainment Weekly* no1442 p8 D 2 2016 Rebellious Special Issue
FIGHTING DEMONS A. LANE cartoon *New Yorker* v92 no39 p96 N 28 2016
girl on top J. Doll color *InStyle* v23 no13 p242 D 2016
Hey, These Beasts Are Fantastic! K. P. Sullivan color *Entertainment Weekly* no1441 p37 N 25 2016
Not your daughter's Harry Potter P. TREBLE color *Maclean's* v129 no46 p61 N 21 2016
Preserving The Magic D. P. DEAVEL and C. J. DEAVEL color *National Review* v69 no4 p45 Mr 6 2017
Wizards in New York B. F. Jones color *Christian Century* v133 no26 p44 D 21 2016
Wonder World H. FREEMAN color *Vogue* v206 no12 p242 D 2016

Fantasy
FLIGHTS OF FANCY: A MIDSUMMER'S DAYDREAM S. Weigel color *Flying* v144 no10 p38 O 2017
LET YOUR MIND WANDER M. HARRIS color *Discover* v38 no5 p30 Je 2017
When the Mind Wanders J. PELINI color *Atlantic* v320 no3 p26 O 2017

Fantasy fiction
INTRODUCING A WORLD of ENDLESS MISADVENTURES M. Wild *Publishers Weekly* v264 no9 pC1 F 27 2017
Julia Vanishes color *Publishers Weekly* v263 no49 p108 D 7 2016

Fantasy films—Reviews
BEAUTY AND THE BEAST B. A. DuHamel color *Sound & Vision* v82 no8 p71 O 2017
THE LEGO BATMAN MOVIE C. Chiarella color *Sound & Vision* v82 no8 p68 O 2017

Fantasy television programs
GEEK IDOLS R. KEEGAN color *Vanity Fair* v59 no9 p147a S 2017
Is Your Favorite Show Safe? M. ROFFMAN *TV Guide* v65 no21 p6 My 15 2017

Faoro, Tyler—Interviews
NEVER LOOK BACK J. KINDELA color *Muscle & Performance* v9 no4 p30 Ap 2017

Faraday effect
Quantized Faraday and Kerr rotation and axion electrodynamics of a 3D topological insulator Liang Wu, M. Salehi et al bibl graph *Science* v354 no6316 p1124 D 2 2016

Farage, Nigel, 1964-
HELLO, AMERICAN J. Green and Z. Mider color *Bloomberg Businessweek* no4503 p50 D 12 2016
How People Power Is Splitting Europe S. Shuster and V. Walt color diag *Time* v188 no25-26 p80 D 19 2016 Double Issue
Very Special Relationship D. GREEN cartoon *Weekly Standard* v22 no13 p10 D 5 2016

FARAGHER, JO
Have executive headhunters had their day? Anyone can locate top talent with the help of technology - but that doesn't mean in-house recruitment of executives is easy *People Management* p40 Ag 2017
Help! Sharing personal problems at work is no longer taboo.

People Management examines what that means for employers - and how HR can help in eight key crises [Cover story] *People Management* p26 Jl 2017
IS THE NATIONAL LIVING WAGE A PAY RISE TOO FAR? *People Management* p48 O 2016
It'll cost you... *People Management* p27 S 2017
Mentoring: Who's looking after your career? When everyone from business moguls to music icons has a mentor, shouldn't HR professionals follow suit? *People Management* p42 Ap 2017
PAY GAP *People Management* p26 F 2017
WHAT'S NEXT? *People Management* p36 Mr 2017
WHY CAN'T BRITS DO ALL THE JOBS? [Cover story] *People Management* p26 Je 2017
You had one job... [Cover story] *People Management* p26 Ap 2017

Farah, Nuruddin, 1945-
2002: Mogadishu *Lapham's Quarterly* v10 no1 p169 Wint 2017

Faraj, Samer
How to Get Experts to Work Together Effectively *Harvard Business Review Digital Articles* p2 My 10 2017

Faraon, Andrei
Nanophotonic rare-earth quantum memory with optically controlled retrieval diag graph *Science* v357 no6358 p1392 S 29 2017

Farar-Griefer, Shannon
Should Stop. Must Stop. Can't Stop [Cover story] S. FRIEDMAN bw color *Runner's World* v52 no4 p62 My 2017

Farb, Nathan
Portraits from the Détente Era *Wilson Quarterly* v40 no4 p3 Fall 2016

Farber, Jim
THE ESSENTIAL CHUCK BERRY *Entertainment Weekly* no1459 p15 Mr 31 2017

Farber, Madeline
Proposal Keeps Two Key Benefits for Moms *Time* v189 no10 p15 Mr 20 2017

Farber, Michael
"GOD BLESS ERIK KARLSSON" chart color *Sports Illustrated* v126 no13 p46 My 8 2017

Farchy, Jack
Peak Oil Could Be Here Sooner Than You Think bw *Bloomberg Businessweek* no4530 p32 Jl 17 2017

Fareast USA (Company)
Fareast 23R C. J. Doane color *Sail* v48 no5 p22 My 2017

Fareed Zakaria GPS (TV program)
The Merit System C. MALCOLM color *Weekly Standard* v23 no1 p11 S 11 2017

Fareej, Mohammed
No Way Home color *Time* v189 no14 p34 Ap 17 2017

Farfan-Rios, W.
Persistent effects of pre-Columbian plant domestication on Amazonian forest composition bibl chart graph map *Science* v355 no6328 p925 Mr 3 2017

Fargo (TV program : 2014)
And Don't Miss... J. Russell *TV Guide* v65 no13 p37 Mr 20 2017
BLOOD BROTHERS: Ewan McGregor on his dual acting triumph in Fargo-and why they're the role(s) of a lifetime A. D'ARMINIO *TV Guide* v65 no25 p26 Je 2017
DOUBLE TROUBLE J. Hibberd color *Entertainment Weekly* no1462 p42 Ap 21 2017
Fargo A. D'Arminio *TV Guide* p36 Ap 17 2017
HEARTLAND OF DARKNESS J. Hibberd color *Entertainment Weekly* no1462 p38 Ap 21 2017
The Must List color *Entertainment Weekly* no1465 p1 My 12 2017
Wrath of the Showrunners M. ZOLLER SEITZ img *New York* v50 no8 p130 Ap 17 2017

Fargo (TV program)
The lords of no mercy K. Reklis *Christian Century* v134 no17 p44 Ag 16 2017

Farha, Omar K.
Bottom-up construction of a superstructure in a porous uranium-organic crystal color graph *Science* v356 no6338 p624 My 12 2017

Farhadi, Asghar, 1972-
The Filmmaker Banned By Trump M. ATKINSON *In These Times* v41 no3 p39 Mr 2017
The Salesman J. McGovern color *Entertainment Weekly*

no1451/1452 p91 F 3-10 2017

UNSEEN AND UNHEARD S. KLAWANS color *Nation* v304 no7 p36 Mr 6 2017

Farhadi, Asghar, 1972—Interviews

Tragedy Foretold M. K. Schilling img *New York* p60 Ja 23 2017

Farhang, Alexander R.

Dopamine neurons encode performance error in singing birds bibl graph *Science* v354 no6317 p1278 D 9 2016

FARIA, ELISE

r.s.v.p bw *Bon Appetit* v61 no12 p20 D 2016 /Jan2017

Faris, Anna, 1976-

The Bullseye M. Snetiker color *Entertainment Weekly* no1478 / 1479 p110 Ag 18-25 2017

Chris Pratt on Mom! M. Roffman *TV Guide* v65 no4 p10 Ja 16 2017

EMOJIS THAT CONFUSE ANNA FARIS D. Snierson color *Entertainment Weekly* no1476 p46 Ag 4 2017

Mom N. Abrams, B. L. Heldman et al color *Entertainment Weekly* no1482/1483 p85 S 22 2017

No. 1 ANNA FARIS IS UNQUALIFIED C. Everett color *Entertainment Weekly* no1444/1445 p112 D 16 2016

SEPARATION ANXIETY D. Franich, D. Coggan et al color *Entertainment Weekly* no1478 / 1479 p14 Ag 18-25 2017

TOP BANANA D. Franich color *Entertainment Weekly* no1436/1437 p26 O 21 2016

WHAT NOW? D. Coggan *Entertainment Weekly* no1478 / 1479 p16 Ag 18-25 2017

Faris, Anna, 1976-—Interviews

Drop The Mic M. WAKIM *Los Angeles Magazine* p54 F 2017

Faris, Justin D.

Wild emmer genome architecture and diversity elucidate wheat evolution and domestication color *Science* v357 no6346 p93 Jl 7 2017

Faris, Paula

Calm your life color *Redbook* p87 S 2017

FARIS, PETER

TRACKING MYTHS color *Scientific American* v316 no4 p6 Ap 2017

Faris, Ron

Market to Millennials by Getting Out of the Way *Harvard Business Review Digital Articles* p2 D 9 2015

Faris, Valerie

Battle of the Sexes L. Greenblatt color *Entertainment Weekly* no1484 p46 S 29 2017

FARKAS, GEORGETTE

ROAST GUINEA HEN FOR NINE img *New York* v49 no22 p82 O 31 2016

Farkas, Remy

FRESHMAN YEAR VS. SENIOR YEAR J. BARTOLOMEO and A. STANLEY color *Seventeen* v76 no3 p102 My 2017

FARKAS, TIMOTHY E.

GROUP SELECTION AT THE UNIVERSITY OF CHICAGO: A SCIENTIFIC MEMOIR TO CHALLENGE CONSENSUS *BioScience* v67 no4 p393 Ap 2017

Farkonas, John

Pat Minick and the Chi-Town Hustler T. Taylor color *Hot Rod* v70 no6 p10 Je 2017

Farley, Amy

MERRY TRANSIT color *Essence* v47 no8 p92 D 2016

STELLA'S PAINT *South Dakota Magazine* v32 no4 p14 N/D 2016

Farley, Ed

MY TOWN J. Sugarman color *Washingtonian Magazine* v52 no7 p159 Ap 2017

Farley, Silas

MUSE R. Mead cartoon *New Yorker* v92 no45 p24 Ja 16 2017

Farley, Tim

SKEPTICAL ANNIVERSARIES *Skeptical Inquirer* v40 no6 p66 N/D 2016

Farm income

Examining Farm Sector and Farm Household Income D. Prager, C. Burns et al *Amber Waves: The Economics of Food, Farming, Natural Resources, & Rural America* p23 Ag 2017

ON THE RISE: USDA FORECASTS FIRST UPTURN IN FARM INCOME IN FOUR YEARS. WILL IT LAST? *Successful Farming* v115 no12 p12 O 2017

WINDS OF CHANGE? *Successful Farming* v115 no2 p12 F 2017

Farm income—United States

GOING UP: FARMLAND HOLDS ITS VALUE DESPITE LOWER FARM INCOME *Successful Farming* v115 no11 p12 S 2017

The Number of Midsize Farms Declined From 1992 to 2012, But Their Household Finances Remain Strong C. Burns color graph *Amber Waves: The Economics of Food, Farming, Natural Resources, & Rural America* p19 D 2016

Farm life

BUILDING A DREAM P. SYKES color *Vogue* v206 no11 p228 N 2016

Farm management

See also

Agricultural productivity

CAN THEIR PROBLEM BE SOLVED? *Successful Farming* v114 no13 p80 D 2016

CAN THEIR PROBLEM SOLVED? D. J. Jonovic *Successful Farming* v114 no11 p67 N 2016

Case Study: How Would You Save This Farm? F. L. Reinhardt il *Harvard Business Review* v94 no11 p105 N 2016

CATTLE AND COVER CROPS IMPROVE SOIL HEALTH D. Goerge *Successful Farming* v114 no13 p59 D 2016

Farm Moneyball G. Johnston *Successful Farming* v114 no12 p24 Mid-N 2016

FIELD OF DREAMS: How a city girl-turned-accidental farm-hand discovered heaven on earth S. DUGGER *Indianapolis Monthly* v12 no40 p78 Ag 2017

FIVE TRENDS THAT COULD CHANGE YOUR FARM G. Johnston *Successful Farming* v114 no11 p54 N 2016

FROM FIGHTER TO FARMER J. Scott *Successful Farming* v114 no11 p50 N 2016

HANDLING A CRISIS J. Scott color *Successful Farming* v115 no7 p13 My 2017

IDEA OF THE MONTH P. Barbour *Successful Farming* v114 no11 p76 N 2016

Modern Maps G. Gullickson *Successful Farming* v114 no12 p16 Mid-N 2016

PUT DRAIN TILING UNDER THE FINANCIAL MICRO-SCOPE *Successful Farming* v114 no13 p18 D 2016

READY TO SEEK OUT A GROCERY PARTNER? *Successful Farming* v114 no11 p56 N 2016

SHARE WHAT YOU KNOW J. SCOTT *Successful Farming* v114 no13 p20 D 2016

Farm management—Records & correspondence

Defend The Bottom Line L. Bedord *Successful Farming* v114 no12 p14 Mid-N 2016

Farm management—Study & teaching

STARTING A WETLANDS B. Freese *Successful Farming* v114 no13 p66 D 2016

Farm ownership

CAN THEIR PROBLEM BE SOLVED? D. J. Jonovic *Successful Farming* v115 no3 p62 Mid-F 2017

Farm produce

PRESERVING HOMEGROWN PRODUCE: Putting up the garden bounty at Polyface Farms is a family affair J. Salatin *Mother Earth News* no284 p53 O/N 2017

Farm produce prices

Magic Greens K. Krader color *Bloomberg Businessweek* no4527 p88 Je 19 2017

RISK MANAGEMENT SAVES THE FARM A. Kluis *Successful Farming* v114 no10 p18 O 2016

WHAT'S THE BIG IDEA? *Successful Farming* v114 no10 p12 O 2016

Farm produce—Economic aspects

REWARDING THE MARKET: FACE VOLATILITY WITH DISCIPLINE M. McGinnis *Successful Farming* v115 no11 p45 S 2017

Farm produce—Evaluation

BEARING FRUIT: In Bill Weghorst's world, one great Honeysmith always beats a bag full of garden-variety produce S. KROWIAK color *Indianapolis Monthly* v41 no2 p42 S 2017

Farm produce—Sales & prices

CO-OP FARMSTANDS for Backyard Gardeners: Yard to Market Co-op has created an adaptable model for even the smallestscale growers to sell extra produce--from a bundle of herbs to dozens of eggs K. Quillen *Mother Earth News* no283 p36 Ag/S 2017

Households Purchase More Produce and Low-Fat Dairy at Supermarkets, Supercenters, and Warehouse Club Stores A. Kuhns *Amber Waves: The Economics of Food, Farming, Natural Resources, & Rural America* p1 My 2017

U.S. Agricultural Trade in 2016: Major Commodities and Trends B. Cooke, A. Melton et al *Amber Waves: The Economics of Food, Farming, Natural Resources, & Rural America* p1 My 2017

Farm produce—United States—Sales & prices

GRAIN DROPS TO BARGAIN-BASEMENT PRICES: EXPECT GLOBAL DEMAND TO SOAR A. Kluis *Successful Farming* v115 no11 p18 S 2017

Farm shops

See also

Agricultural equipment—Maintenance & repair

THOUGHTFULLY DESIGNED FARM SHOP A. McConnell *Successful Farming* v115 no2 p57 F 2017

Farm shops—Equipment & supplies

ALL AROUND THE FARM N. Lehman, C. Geiger et al *Successful Farming* v115 no2 p79 F 2017

Farm shops—Evaluation

SEPARATING CLEAN AND DIRTY A. McConnell *Successful Farming* v115 no4 p61 Mr 2017

Farm tractors—Evaluation

GOING ELECTRIC J. Scott *Successful Farming* v115 no4 p46 Mr 2017

Farman, Mark

Evolution of the wheat blast fungus through functional losses in a host specificity determinant diag map *Science* v357 no6346 p80 Jl 7 2017

Farman-Farma, Nathalie

Folk Revival H. MARTIN color *Architectural Digest* v74 no3 p40 Mr 2017

Farmer, Damon B.

Carbon nanotube transistors scaled to a 40-nanometer footprint color graph *Science* v356 no6345 p1369 Je 30 2017

Farmer, Geoffrey

Breaking Through C. MORGAN-FEIR color *Walrus* v14 no7 p58 S 2017

Farmer, James

HOLIDAY OPEN HOUSE color *Southern Living* v51 no12 p23 D 2016

Farmer, John Paul

The U.S. Government Needs to Hire More Geeks *Harvard Business Review Digital Articles* p2 S 3 2015

Farmer, Liz

BUDGETING INSIDE THE LINES: FOR THE PAST 25 YEARS, COLORADO'S TAXPAYER BILL OF RIGHTS HAS DEFINED SPENDING IN THE STATE *Governing* v31 no1 p44 O 2017

BUILDING BLOCKS: BLOCKCHAIN TECHNOLOGY COULD REMAKE GOVERNMENT SERVICES FROM THE GROUND UP *Governing* v30 no12 p44 S 2017

City Fixers: Some city managers live in constant quest of new places with new problems to fix *Governing* v30 no8 p40 My 2017

FINANCIAL STRESS *Governing* v30 no4 p31 Ja 2017

FOSTER CARE *Governing* v30 no4 p39 Ja 2017

How to Beat Teacher Burnout: With More Education bw *Education Digest* v83 no2 p13 O 2017

MARIJUANA *Governing* v30 no4 p34 Ja 2017

THE MOST HATED MAN IN PENSIONLAND *Governing* v30 no7 p38 Ap 2017

NO 401(K)? SOME STATES HAVE YOU COVERED color *Governing* v30 no11 p50 Ag 2017

ON THE BOOKS *Governing* v30 no2 p52 N 2016

OUT OF THE SHADOWS *Governing* v30 no4 p40 Ja 2017

PAYDAY MAYDAY *Governing* v30 no6 p32 Mr 2017

PUBLIC OFFICIALS OF THE YEAR *Governing* v30 no3 p26 D 2016

STARVING THE SCHOOLS *Governing* v30 no9 p44 Je 2017

Farmer, Nina—Interviews

POLISHING A JEWEL K. HACKETT color *House Beautiful* v159 no1 p92 F 2017

FARMER, ROBIN

Angela D. Sims: The Legacy of Lynching bw color *Publishers Weekly* v263 no45 p24 N 7 2016

As Racial Tensions Lead The News, Books Follow color *Publishers Weekly* v263 no45 p1 N 7 2016

David Gushee color *Publishers Weekly* v263 no45 p21 N 7 2016

Larry W. Hurtado bw color *Publishers Weekly* v263 no45 p22 N 7 2016

Farmerie, Paul

The SAILING SCENE color *Sail* v48 no11 p6 N 2017

Farmers

See also

Amish farmers

Tomato growers

Women farmers

10 CHALLENGES FOR YOUNG FARMERS B. Freese *Successful Farming* v115 no8 p54 Je/Jl 2017

Corny Comics *South Dakota Magazine* v32 no6 p13 Mr/Ap 2017

EASTER ANNIVERSARY: IT'S A TIME OF NEW BEGINNINGS AND A TIME TO REFLECT AND REMEMBER L. F. Prater *Successful Farming* v115 no6 p63 Ap 2017

FEED 9.75 BILLION PEOPLE? NOT AS HARD AS IT LOOKS *Successful Farming* v115 no6 p11 Ap 2017

FIELD OF SCREAMS S. STALL color *Indianapolis Monthly* v42 no2 p18 O 2017

FIGHTER TO FARMER: NOMINATE FARMER VETERANS YOU KNOW FOR THE 2017 CONTEST J. Scott *Successful Farming* v115 no6 p54 Ap 2017

Gathering Experimental Evidence To Improve the Design of Agricultural Programs L. Lynch, D. Hellerstein et al *Amber Waves: The Economics of Food, Farming, Natural Resources, & Rural America* p1 Ag 2017

THE GLORIES OF FENNEL *South Dakota Magazine* v33 no3 p32 S/O 2017

HOW BIKES BUILT OUR HIGHWAYS M. Guroff *Saturday Evening Post* v289 no1 p82 Ja/F 2017

Improve Your Flock with TRAPNESTS H. Ussery *Mother Earth News* no281 p58 Ap/My 2017

LOCA VORE F. Esker *Louisiana Life* v38 no1 p14 S/O 2017

The Market Gardener's Toolkit *Mother Earth News* no280 p9 F/Mr 2017

MEET THE FIGHTER TO FARMER RECIPIENTS J. Scott *Successful Farming* v114 no10 p58 O 2016

Palmer amaranth is bedeviling farmers like no other weed. Ultimately, though, tools exist to defeat it G. Gullickson *Successful Farming* v115 no5 p32 Mid-Mr 2017

PALMER PLAGUES CRP ACRES K. Birchmier *Successful Farming* v115 no5 p40 Mid-Mr 2017

Reflections on the lectionary J. H. Lee *Christian Century* v134 no13 p19 Je 21 2017

Remote sensing for analyzing smallholder farm yields color *Science* v355 no6330 p1170 Mr 17 2017

SEEING IS BELIEVING *Successful Farming* v115 no6 p5 Ap 2017

Share of Farm Businesses Receiving Lease and Royalty Income From Energy Production Varies Across Regions C. Hitaj *Amber Waves: The Economics of Food, Farming, Natural Resources, & Rural America* p37 N 2016

SLIM PICKINGS T. PHILPOTT color *Mother Jones* v42 no3 p72 My/Je 2017

TARGET PRACTICE K. BIRCHMIER *Successful Farming* v114 no12 p52 Mid-N 2016

WE CAN FEED 9 BILLION: HOW DOES AMERICAN AGRICULTURE HELP FEED THE POPULATION? LET'S DO THE MATH D. Kurns *Successful Farming* v115 no6 p2 Ap 2017

WORDS MATTER D. KURNS *Successful Farming* v115 no5 p4 Mid-Mr 2017

Farmers' associations

CALENDAR OF EVENTS color *Idaho Magazine* v16 no1 p61 O 2016

Farmers' markets

FARMERS MARKER DISCOVERIS: Plus other joyful life lessons learned at the farmers markets B. Hunhoff and K. Hunhoff *South Dakota Magazine* v33 no3 p27 S/O 2017

Farmers' Market [Cover story] M. CROUCH color *Prevention* v69 no7 p20 Jl 2017

Farms—Economic aspects

GOING UP: FARMLAND HOLDS ITS VALUE DESPITE LOWER FARM INCOME *Successful Farming* v115 no11 p12 S 2017

Farms—Evaluation

FRESH PICKINGS J. Benson color *Louisiana Life* v38 no1 p50 S/O 2017

Farms—Finance

WHAT IS YOUR CMV? A. Kluis *Successful Farming* v114 no13 p22 D 2016

Farms—Germany

A Holiday at HERMANN FARM *Missouri Life* v43 no7 p28 D 2016/Ja 2017

Farms—Maryland

From Revolution to Rhythm & Blues S. Richardson bw color *American History* v52 no3 p6 Ag 2017

Farms—Missouri

AMAZING MAIZE MAZES A. Stewart *Missouri Life* v43 no6 p50 O/N 2016

EAT YOUR HART OUT S. COTHRAN color *Missouri Life* v44 no4 p66 Je 2017

Farms—North Carolina

TRUE GRITS S. Castle and M. C. Cairns color *Southern Living* v52 no10 p78 O 2017

Farms—Oregon

SMALL FARM, REAL PROFIT: This inspiring half-acre urban farm in Oregon is proving that size doesn't matter when it comes to profitability J. Volk *Mother Earth News* no284 p40 O/N 2017

Farms—United States

THE FARM IN THE DELL: THESE FARMS AND RANCHES GIVE ADULTS WITH DEVELOPMENTAL DISABILITIES A SENSE OF PURPOSE AND COMMUNITY L. F. Prater *Successful Farming* v115 no12 p64 O 2017

For Beginning Farmers, Business Survival Rates Increase With Scale and With Direct Sales to Consumers N. Key *Amber Waves: The Economics of Food, Farming, Natural Resources, & Rural America* p14 S 2016

Keep It Simple J. SUGARMAN *Washingtonian Magazine* v52 no11 p88 Ag 2017

The Number of Midsize Farms Declined From 1992 to 2012, But Their Household Finances Remain Strong C. Burns color graph *Amber Waves: The Economics of Food, Farming, Natural Resources, & Rural America* p19 D 2016

THE PROBLEM: EVERYTHING SEEMS TO BE ROLLING ALONG PERFECTLY RIGHT NOW. I HEAR ABOUT ALL THESE PROBLEMS, BUT WE DON'T SEEM TO HAVE ANY. AM I MISSING SOMETHING? M. Friesen *Successful Farming* v115 no9 p68 Ag 2017

THE PROBLEM: MY WIFE AND I ARE EXPERIENCING A NEW LEVEL OF PROBLEMS IN PLANNING TO PASS THE FARM ON TO OUR GRANDSON M. Friesen *Successful Farming* v115 no12 p70 O 2017

Farms—Valuation

What's Your Land Worth? J. SCOTT and B. SPIEGEL *Successful Farming* v114 no12 p66 Mid-N 2016

Farms—Virginia

Whole Hog E. J. CURRAN *Virginia Living* p13 2017 Smoke & Salt

Farne Salmon & Trout (Company)

Employees are hungrier to learn: Why ditching tick-box L&D made a fish factory a better place to work *People Management* p25 My 2017

Farnell, Richard

How U.S. Army Basic Training Turns Diverse Groups into Teams *Harvard Business Review Digital Articles* p2 Jl 18 2016

Mentor People Who Aren't Like You *Harvard Business Review Digital Articles* p2 Ap 17 2017

Farneth, Molly

Endure or Resist? cartoon *Commonweal* v144 no3 p32 F 10 2017

Farnsworth, David

TARGETING HISTORY color *Publishers Weekly* v264 no30 p32 Jl 24 2017

Farnsworth, Eric

As Nafta II begins, Mexico shows cautious optimism Hootsen color *America* v217 no6 p15 S 18 2017

Farnsworth, Ward

RHETORICAL QUESTIONS R. A. Lanham *Claremont Review of Books* v17 no2 p44 Spr 2017

FARNSWORTH-LIVINGSTON, DERRALD

Flock to Fontenelle bw color *Nebraska Life* v21 no6 p72 N/D 2017

Faroe Islands—Politics & government—21st century

Where National Breakups Are In the Cards T. John color *Time* v189 no7/8 p18 F 27 2017

Farooq, Umar

Construction of mosque gives Greek Muslims hope of greater religious parity *Christian Century* v133 no25 p14 D 7 2016

Farquhar, Scott

The Wizards From Oz N. KIRSCH color *Forbes* v199 no6 p36 Je 13 2017

FARR, COOPER M.

Addressing the Gender Gap in Distinguished Speakers at Professional Ecology Conferences *BioScience* v67 no5 p464 My 2017

Farr, Michael K.

FINANCIAL FUTURE: Planning for retirement? Here's why your family and a professional should be involved *Washingtonian Magazine* v52 no8 p140 My 2017

FARRAND, LOUISE

HOW DO YOU CLOSE A GENDER PAY GAP? With organisations fearful of following in the BBC's footsteps, employers are being urged to take action to tackle inequality *People Management* p10 S 2017

MISTKAES COST MONEY: If you thought payroll ran itself, recent high-profile cases mean you might need to think again. How do you avoid an expensive error? *People Management* p36 Ag 2017

FARRAR, DONALD R.

Sex and the Single Gametophyte: Revising the Homosporous Vascular Plant Life Cycle in Light of Contemporary Research *BioScience* v66 no11 p928 N 1 2016

Farrar, G.

Observation of a large-scale anisotropy in the arrival directions of cosmic rays above 8×1018 eV *Science* v357 no6357 p1266 S 22 2017

Farrar, Maureen

POWER PLANTS color *Muscle & Performance* v9 no6 p30 Je 2017

TRACKING YOUR WEIGHT LOSS color *Muscle & Performance* v8 no12 p15 D 2016

A WHEY BETTER (BLEND) PROTEIN color *Muscle & Performance* v9 no6 p34 Je 2017

Farrell, Frank B.

Tuning In & Out [Cover story] color *Commonweal* v144 no17 p24 O 20 2017

Farrell, Greg

Deutsche Bank Is in a Bind Over Trump Debt color *Bloomberg Businessweek* no4517 p39 Ap 3 2017

Legalio Password? color *Bloomberg Businessweek* no4495 p30 O 17 2016

LEGAL JEOPARDY bw color *Bloomberg Businessweek* no4541 p35 O 9 2017

Farrell, Mary H. J.

Clearing the Air bw color graph *Consumer Reports* v82 no11 p8 N 2017

Secrets to a Great Night's sleep chart color *Consumer Reports* v82 no2 p16 F 2017

Farrell, Nena

BEST OF THE WEST color *Sunset* v238 no3 p7 Mr 2017

THE FUTURE IS HERE color diag *Sunset* v238 no4 p54 Ap 2017

GET SMART color *Sunset* v239 no3 p46 S 2017

Farrell, Perry

Lollapalooza Legends bw color *Rolling Stone* no1293 p14 Ag 10 2017

Farrell, Will

Will Ferrell and Amy Poehler Bet on The House N. Sperling color *Entertainment Weekly* no1453 p12 F 17 2017

FARRELLY, MATTHEW

TOP 5 Books More Christian High Schoolers Should Be Encouraged to Read color *Christianity Today* v61 no4 p65 My 2017

Farrer, Austin

Mirrors to God P. BAUER *Weekly Standard* v22 no22 p36 F 13

2017

FARRIMOND, JOYCE
  We Hear You color *Horse & Rider* v56 no5 p12 My 2017

Farrin, Katie
  Changes in Farmers' Financial Status May Affect Crop Insurance Demand *Amber Waves: The Economics of Food, Farming, Natural Resources, & Rural America* p45 N 2016

Farrington, Kent
  Longines FEI World Cup™ North American League News color *Practical Horseman* v44 no12 p66 D 2016

Farris, Hamilton
  Perception drives the evolution of observable traits bibl color *Science* v355 no6320 p25 Ja 6 2017

Farris, Pamela J.
  VALUING THEIR VOICES color *Literacy Today (2411-7862)* v34 no6 p14 My/Je 2017

Farris, Ron
  THE MODERN EMPTY NEST K. Owen color *Southern Living* v52 no10 p88 O 2017

Farrow & Ball Inc.
  NOBLE PURPLES D. SCHWARTZ color *Better Homes & Gardens* v95 no9 p34 S 2017

Farrow, John—Interviews
  Murderous Storms L. PICKER color *Publishers Weekly* v264 no13 p77 Mr 27 2017

FARROW, RONAN
  ABUSES OF POWER bw color *New Yorker* v93 no33 p42 O 23 2017

FARSAD, NEGIN
  JOKING WHILE MUSLIM cartoon *Wired* v25 no4 p75 Ap 2017

FARSON, PETER
  SPACE ODDITY *Scientific American* v315 no3 p5 S 2016

Farthest: Voyager in Space, The (TV program)
  Nostalgic documentary relives triumphs of the Voyager mission L. Grossman color *Science News* v192 no2 p26 Ag 19 2017

Farzier, Mya
  What Would Jesus Disrupt? Entrepreneurs from Crossroads Church try to scale their startups without selling their souls color *Bloomberg Businessweek* no4518 p56 Ap 10 2017

Fasani, Kimmy
  ELEMENTS color *Snowboarder* v29 no5 p70 Ja 2017

Fasching, Elesia C.
  The price of political power color *Monthly Labor Review* p1 S 2016

Fasching, Liana
  Intersection of diverse neuronal genomes and neuropsychiatric disease: The Brain Somatic Mosaicism Network color *Science* v356 no6336 p395 Ap 28 2017

Fasciae (Anatomy)
  THE Magic OF Massage A. P. Taylor color *Dance Spirit* v21 no2 p32 F 2017

Fascinated (Short story)
  Zen Master Raven Stories R. A. ROSHI bw *Tricycle: The Buddhist Review* v27 no1 p120 Fall 2017

Fascism
  See also
    Neo-Nazism
  THE RETURN OF FASCISM S. BENHABIB color *New Republic* v248 no11 p36 N 2017
  The Uses and Misuses of 'Fascism' P. Gottfried *Society* v54 no4 p315 Ag 2017

Fascism—Europe
  Signs of Fascism Rising R. Kroes *Society* v54 no3 p218 Je 2017

Fascism—Italy—History—20th century
  The pain behind the pleasure R. Bosworth *History Today* v67 no2 p47 F 2017

Fascism—Social aspects
  Populism Is Not Fascism S. Berman bw *Foreign Affairs* v95 no6 p39 N/D 2016

Fascism—United States
  It Can't Happen Here B. SWAIM color *Weekly Standard* v23 no1 p9 S 11 2017
  It Didn't Happen Here J. J. MILLER *National Review* v69 no1 p40 Ja 23 2017
  Signs of Fascism Rising R. Kroes *Society* v54 no3 p218 Je 2017

Fascists

THE CARROT, THE STICK, AND THE BUGGY WHIP K. MANGU-WARD *Reason* v48 no10 p4 Mr 2017
In Name Only M. Feldman and S. Fortunato *Harper's Magazine* v335 no2006 p2 Jl 2017

Fashion
  See also
    Fashion & music
    Fashion & the military
    Hairstyles
    Men's clothing
    Women's clothing
  13 Accomplishments That Are Bigger Than They Seem K. Bonnell and P. R. Satran color *Glamour* v115 no6 p147 Je 2017
  THE 1940S S. Mooallem bw color *Harper's Bazaar* no3652 p228 Ap 2017
  5 ways to be fearless in color color *Redbook* p55a S 2017
  Adam's Home STYLE SHEET: MAD FOR PLAID A. Glassman color *O, The Oprah Magazine* p70 N 2017
  Adam's STYLE SHEET color *O, The Oprah Magazine* p66 N 2017
  All in for Fall! color *Glamour* v115 no9 p47 S 2017
  All Together Now color *Glamour* v115 no2 p97 F 2017
  ...And this is what our judges say bw color *Redbook* p67 S 2017
  ask REDBOOK color *Redbook* p20 Ap 2017
  BACK to the Future C. ELLENBERG color *Vogue* v207 no3 p366 Mr 2017
  Bertille Sefolosha F. SUN *Atlanta* v56 no11 p46 Mr 2017
  BEST DRESS E. Wilson color *InStyle* v24 no10 p87 O 2017
  THE BIG '80S S. Mooallem bw color *Harper's Bazaar* no3656 p326 S 2017
  BIG RED BOOTS color *InStyle* v24 no9 p414 S 2017
  Bill Cunningham Saw It All img *New York* v49 no25 p56 D 12 2016
  BLOGGER AND DESIGNER MARLIEN RENTMEESTER A. WHITTLE color *Conde Nast Traveler* v52 no10 p38 N 2017
  BRIGHT YOUNG THINGS E. ELWICK-BATES and R. WALDMAN bw color *Vogue* v206 no11 p246 N 2016
  Brigitte Macron M. HOLGATE and M. GUIDUCCI color *Vogue* v207 no9 p358 S 2017
  CAN YOU CHANGE YOUR LIFE BY CHANGING YOUR PANTS? Z. BARON color *GQ: Gentlemen's Quarterly* v97 no4 p70 Ap 2017
  A Century of Style M. GOULET and J. Roth bw color *Esquire* p77 O 2017
  CHANGE IS BEAUTIFUL A. FINNEY color *Women's Health* v14 no2 p146 Mr 2017
  Chaos Theory color *Vogue* v207 no7 p61 Jl 2017
  CHARLIE WINFIELD J. Chen color *Bloomberg Businessweek* no4506 p67 Ja 9 2017
  THE CLOSET IN THE CLOUD N. LISS-SCHULTZ cartoon *Mother Jones* v42 no1 p61 Ja/F 2017
  Come In, Charlie R. Gay color *InStyle* v24 no4 p208 Ap 2017
  CONSCIOUS COUPLING B. Langmann bw color *Esquire* p116 N 2017
  Cover *InStyle* v23 no13 pC1 D 2016
  DAVID CASAVANT J. Roth color *Esquire* p54 Ap 2017
  digital directory color *InStyle* v24 no6 p18 Je 2017
  DOES YOUR Style MATCH YOUR Soul? color *O, The Oprah Magazine* p116 Mr 2017
  The Dos & Don'ts of Athleisure color *Glamour* v114 no7 p52 Jl 2016
  Dressing the Part color *InStyle* v24 no3 p182 Mr 2017
  Dress to Unimpress color *InStyle* v24 no3 p318 Mr 2017
  Drew Barrymore K. B. Brown color *InStyle* v24 no11 p145 N 2017
  Due CARE A. Wintour color *Vogue* v207 no7 p30 Jl 2017
  Earning His Stripes N. REMSEN color *Vogue* v206 no11 p112 N 2017
  Fashion Cares For Its Own A. RONAN img *New York* v49 no25 p84 D 12 2016
  A Fashion Empire's New Clothes R. Williams and C. Matlack color graph *Bloomberg Businessweek* no4535 p17 Ag 28 2017
  Fashion Month Throwback! color *Glamour* v115 no9 p64 S 2017
  Feedback color *InStyle* v23 no13 p32 D 2016
  for the Win N. Spradley color *Essence* v47 no12 p57 Ap 2017
  Freckles, Lace, and Curls C. CHOCANO img *New York* v50 no6

p49 Mr 20 2017

Gabi Lee G. CHAPMAN *Atlanta* v57 no6 p48 O 2017

Generation Y. Shahidi bw color *Glamour* v115 no11 p124 N 2017

GET YOUR FLAIR ON M. Hainey color *Esquire* p48 Ap 2017

The Good, the Dad, and the Ugly S. NYGAARD bw cartoon color *Men's Health* v32 no5 p59 Je 2017

The Grand Essentials *D: The Magazine of Dallas* v43 no10 p64 O 2016

HANNAH PARAMORE BREEN J. Chen color *Bloomberg Businessweek* no4525 p63 Je 5 2017

Happy Birthday, VOGUE! *Vogue* v207 no4 p193 Ap 2017

HEATHER HUBBS J. Chen color *Bloomberg Businessweek* no4503 p75 D 12 2016

Hello! L. Brown color *InStyle* v24 no2 p12 F 2017

Hello! L. Brown color *InStyle* v24 no3 p58 Mr 2017

Hello! L. Brown color *InStyle* v24 no6 p20 Je 2017

Hello! L. Brown color *InStyle* v24 no9 p76 S 2017

Her Style's in the Bag color *Working Mother* v40 no2 p18 Je/Jl 2017

Hey, Jenna! J. Lyons, J. K. de Valle et al color *Glamour* v114 no11 p70 N 2016

How I Got My Style MICHAEL B. JORDAN J. CHEN color *Esquire* v166 no4 p49 N 2016

THE IN CROWD color *Seventeen* v76 no5 p92 S 2017

INDEPENDENT SPIRIT L. Kamps, E. DOUGHERTY et al color *Redbook* p37 My 2017

InSTYLE November 2016 color *InStyle* v23 no12 p237 N 2016

IT HAPPENED IN 1967 S. WELLER bw color *Vanity Fair* v59 no4 p192 Mr 2017

KÉLA WALKER J. Wilson color *Essence* v48 no6 p34 O 2017

Kwaidan Editions M. HOLGATE color *Vogue* v207 no9 p354 S 2017

Lady in Red M. G. Silver cartoon *O, The Oprah Magazine* p124 Mr 2017

Lele Pons Is the Most Popular Girl in Hollywood: A day in the life of YouTube's reigning queen of teens A. JONES img *New York* v50 no9 p53 My 1 2017

Living Large J. K. DE VALLE color *Architectural Digest* no11 p37 N 1 2017

LONG, LEAN EVENING color *Vogue* v207 no9 p404 S 2017

LOOK BETTER INSTANTLY B. BOYÉ cartoon color *Men's Health* v32 no2 p(Sp)12 Mr 2017

Makeup Marvels A. Jordan color *Essence* v48 no5 p37 S 2017

Maria Korovilas *Los Angeles Magazine* p36 Ja 2017

Model BEHAVIOR R. Sullivan, M. HOLGATE et al color *Vogue* v207 no1 p30 Ja 2017

MY BEAUTY MARK ... Rita Ora color *InStyle* v24 no4 p164 Ap 2017

My Red Carpet Diary M. Mullally color *InStyle* v24 no9 p216 S 2017

NAOMIE Harris L. SATENSTEIN, M. HOLGATE et al color *Vogue* v207 no3 p322 Mr 2017

The NEWS color *Harper's Bazaar* no3656 p320 S 2017

NEW YEAR NEW YOU Guarnieri color *Harper's Bazaar* no3649 p256 D 2016/Ja 2017

NINA'S NIGHT OUT A. Gell color *Harper's Bazaar* no3656 p337 S 2017

NO COLLAR, NO PROBLEM color *Esquire* p53 Ap 2017

Outfits for Days M. Giudicelli color *Glamour* v115 no10 p70 O 2017

Parallel LINES F. Noyes bw color *Esquire* p136 S 2017

The Power of Bare J. Nelson color *Glamour* no8 p28 Ag 2017

POWER PUFF color *Vogue* v206 no11 p244 N 2016

Real Style ... color *InStyle* v23 no13 p34 D 2016

real style color *InStyle* v24 no11 p40 N 2017

real style color *InStyle* v24 no4 p28 Ap 2017

Representation Matters D. Meles, L. E. Gonzalez color *Glamour* v115 no11 p22 N 2017

SHE'S GOT THE LOOK J. AMBROSE, J. PATTERSON et al *O, The Oprah Magazine* p121 Mr 2017

Sparkles FLY S. Mower, M. HOLGATE et al color *Vogue* v207 no3 p314 Mr 2017

THE SQUARE-TOE SHOE MUST DIE! cartoon color *GQ: Gentlemen's Quarterly* v97 no4 p118 Ap 2017

STEVEN TRISTAN YOUNG J. Chen color *Bloomberg Businessweek* no4511 p67 F 13 2017

Strong Is Stylish. End of Story c. leive color *Glamour* v114 no7 p26 Jl 2016

THE STRUGGLE OF THE BLACK DESIGNER Q. SMITH-BRUNETEAU bw color *Ebony* v72 no11 p44 S 2017

Style 100 J. Ferrise, E. Wilson et al color *InStyle* v23 no13 p79 D 2016

The Style Guy M. A. Green cartoon color *GQ: Gentlemen's Quarterly* v97 no3 p66 Mr 2017

The Style Guy M. Anthony Green color *GQ: Gentlemen's Quarterly* v97 no11 p46 N 2017

Suit yourself S. Kennedy color *Bloomberg Businessweek* no4522 p85 My 15 2017

This + That A. LAROCCA img *New York* v49 no23 p49 N 14 2016

This woman is about to cut her hair off [Cover story] Y. Chu color *Glamour* no8 p136 Ag 2017

TNT color *Vogue* v206 no11 p134 N 2016

TRUE WEST N. Silva-Jelly bw color *Harper's Bazaar* no3656 p430 S 2017

UNDER ARMOR M. T. Goldman cartoon *O, The Oprah Magazine* p122 Mr 2017

THE VERY RED CARPET: And other trends that most caught our eye on the runways R. RAMSEY and I. BROWN img *New York* v50 no16 p58 Ag 7 2017

VESTING OPTIONS D. STEVENS color *GQ: Gentlemen's Quarterly* v97 no4 p106 Ap 2017

VISION OF LOVELINESS L. Godin color *O, The Oprah Magazine* p121 Mr 2017

WELCOME TO THE ISSUE color *Harper's Bazaar* no3651 p60 Mr 2017

WELCOME TO THE ISSUE color *InStyle* v23 no13 p1 D 2016

What beauty really means *Redbook* p6 Jl/Ag 2017

What I Wear to Work: DAVID ROSENBLATT A. Cohen color *Bloomberg Businessweek* no4497 p71 O 31 2016

What I Wear to Work J. Chen color *Bloomberg Businessweek* no4494 p75 O 10 2016

WHAT MEN THINK ABOUT WHAT WOMEN WEAR K. Hart and L. McCarthy color *Harper's Bazaar* no3648 p194 N 2016

What's Hot Now R. Mosely color *Seventeen* v76 no5 p16 S 2017

What's your superpower? M. Rollins color *Redbook* p10 My 2017

Why America's First Daughter Is a Hit In China C. Campbell color *Time* v190 no2/3 p36 Jl 10-17 2017

Why I Love MY BETTIE PAGE PUMPS D. Von Teese color *InStyle* v24 no6 p172 Je 2017

WILD HAIR J. FIELDEN color *Esquire* p20 Ap 2017

Would You Rather... chart color *Seventeen* v76 no3 p112 My 2017

Zoë Kravitz color *InStyle* v24 no9 p356 S 2017

Zoey Deutch color *Los Angeles Magazine* v62 no10 p30 O 2017

Fashion & music

Six Decades of Rock Style bw color *Rolling Stone* no1298 p40 O 19 2017

Fashion & politics

Red Vs. Pink: The Politics of Fashion and Why a Hat Is No Longer Just a Hat S. Schrobsdorff color *Time* v189 no6 p55 F 20 2017

Fashion & sex

"I like to fashion myself as the Walmart greeter of sex ed." color *Glamour* v115 no7 p93 Jl 2017

Fashion & technology

Have It YOUR WAY E. Wilson color *InStyle* v23 no12 p51 N 2016

INSTAGRAM KILLED THE RETAIL STAR I. Frisch color *Bloomberg Businessweek* no4517 p74 Ap 3 2017

Fashion & the military

Style Warriors E. Wilson color *InStyle* v24 no11 p70 N 2017

Fashion accessories

See also

Handbags

Jewelry

The 2017 Essentials S. P. Nadella and E. Velluto color *Glamour* v115 no1 p23 Ja 2017

$25 & Under Statement Jewelry color *Seventeen* v76 no12 p32 D 2016/Ja 2017

Add to Cart: Five bright accessories, served five ways img *New York* v50 no12 p57 Je 12 2017

BEST BETS img *New York* v50 p50 F 20 2017

BEST WEEK EVER color *Seventeen* v76 no5 p21 S 2017

BUTTER color *Good Housekeeping* v265 no2 p56B Ag 2017

#BUYBLACK T. A. Christian, C. Market et al color *Essence* v47

no8 p19 D 2016

Comfort JOY L. Conrad color *Good Housekeeping* v263 no6 p114 D 2016

The Cover color *InStyle* v24 no1 p8 Ja 2017

DENIM'S Besties color *Seventeen* v76 no5 p28 S 2017

DIVINE *Interview* v47 no6 p96 Ag 2017

DIY Celeb Style J. Radosevich color *Seventeen* v76 no12 p30 D 2016/Ja 2017

DOPE STUFF ON MY DESK J. Wilson color *Essence* v47 no12 p22 Ap 2017

Earthly Delights *Los Angeles Magazine* p37 Mr 2017

Folk TALES color *Vogue* v206 no11 p258 N 2016

Glenda Bailey on the past and the future of Harper's Bazaar G. Bailey color *Harper's Bazaar* no3651 p180 Mr 2017

Hello! L. Brown color *InStyle* v24 no1 p6 Ja 2017

JAMEEL MOHAMMED J. Wilson color *Essence* v47 no12 p24 Ap 2017

Maria, Soo Joo & Emily invite you to Glamour's 2017 Kickoff Party! bw color *Glamour* v115 no1 p64 Ja 2017

MINI BAGS color *Good Housekeeping* v264 no2 p18 F 2017

north by northwest C. FISHMAN cartoon color *Better Homes & Gardens* v95 no2 p14 F 2016

Renting Just Got Better N. Silverstein color *Glamour* v114 no12 p112 D 2016

SPARKLE & SHINE color *Essence* v47 no8 p64 D 2016

Start Here S. P. Nadella and E. Velluto color *Glamour* v115 no1 p24 Ja 2017

STONE COLD FOXES color *Conde Nast Traveler* v52 no5 p40 My 2017

STYLE CRUSH Haley Bennett S. Simon color *InStyle* v24 no9 p192 S 2017

Style Your Home T. A. Christian color *Essence* v48 no5 p114 S 2017

Tassels & Pom-Poms color *Good Housekeeping* v265 no2 p13 Ag 2017

A Thing for Bling D. ZICKL color *Runner's World* v52 no7 p46 Ag 2017

a week of AWESOME OUTFITS L. Benoit color *Good Housekeeping* v265 no4 p34 O 2017

WELCOME TO THE ISSUE color *Harper's Bazaar* no3654 p26 Je/Jl 2017

WHAT'S YOUR STYLE? color *Seventeen* v76 no2 p122 Mr 2017

What to wear B. Haile color *U.S. Catholic* v81 no11 p8 N 2016

Fashion accessories design

See also

Jewelry design

Break the Mold color *Martha Stewart Living* p20 My 2017

On Demand color *InStyle* v24 no1 p17 Ja 2017

Fashion accessories—Evaluation

$100 & Under color *Seventeen* p74 Ja 1 2017

15 WAYS TO DO PEACOCK color *Good Housekeeping* v264 no3 p52D Mr 2017

$50 & Under Postprom Party color *Seventeen* v76 no2 p58 Mr 2017

90 YEARS OF STYLE bw color *Harper's Bazaar* no3654 p44 Je/Jl 2017

The Accessories Face-Off color *Seventeen* v75 no11 p28 N 2016

Adam's STYLE SHEET color *O, The Oprah Magazine* p64 F 2017

ALL DRESSED UP color *InStyle* v23 no13 p133 D 2016

All the Ruffles S. P. Nadella and A. Hou color *Glamour* no8 p50 Ag 2017

Anatomy of a Do color *Glamour* v114 no7 p36 Jl 2016

...And Now Just Jeans color *Glamour* no8 p52 Ag 2017

Anything GOES! color *Seventeen* p41 Ja 1 2017

Arm Candy A. R. Williams color *Southern Living* v52 no2 p67 F 2017

ARTFUL ACCESSORIES color *Harper's Bazaar* no3650 p192 F 2017

ASHLEY GRAHAM'S PARTY PICKS color *InStyle* v23 no13 p146 D 2016

Athleisure Remix! color *Glamour* v115 no7 p24 Jl 2017

BASIC INSTINCT color *Harper's Bazaar* no3650 p91 F 2017

Beach Days color *Glamour* v115 no6 p38 Je 2017

Be Bold Ying Chu color *Glamour* v115 no3 p180 Mr 2017

Becoming Un-Obsessed S. Trong color *InStyle* v24 no9 p258 S 2017

Bergen On Bags color *InStyle* v24 no7 p68 Jl 2017

Better With Time J. LOVE and M. BOBO color *Ebony* v72 no4 p57 F 2017

Between the Lines color *Vogue* v207 no6 p148 Je 2017

Beyond the Boudoir color *Vogue* v207 no10 p304 O 2017

BIG, BOLD & BEAUTIFUL color *O, The Oprah Magazine* p118 O 2017

BLUE NOTE color *Harper's Bazaar* no3651 p280 Mr 2017

BOLD is what this season is all about. Look to GRAPHIC pieces that speak volumes and notice-me PRINTS that will turn heads color *Harper's Bazaar* no3650 p170 F 2017

BRIGHT SPOT color *Harper's Bazaar* no3650 p88 F 2017

the buzz color *InStyle* v24 no10 p194 O 2017

CADET CHIC color *Harper's Bazaar* no3651 p243 Mr 2017

CANDYLAND color *Harper's Bazaar* no3651 p278 Mr 2017

CAT WALKING DEAD M. Heyman color *Harper's Bazaar* no3651 p442 Mr 2017

center stage color *Seventeen* p160 Ja 1 2017

CHIC easy PIECES L. Armstrong bw color *Harper's Bazaar* no3651 p420 Mr 2017

Clemons' Time C. Whitney and K. Clemons color *InStyle* v24 no9 p221 S 2017

Color BALANCE *Interview* v47 no2 p108 Mr 2017

COLOR CODED color *Harper's Bazaar* no3651 p368 Mr 2017

CORNER OFFICE MATERIAL color *Esquire* p53 Je/Jl 2017

Country Chic [Cover story] color *Glamour* v114 no11 p60 N 2016

The Cover color *InStyle* v23 no12 p26 N 2016

THE CUT img *New York* v49 no24 p73 N 28 2016

Cut LOOSE *Interview* v47 no2 p208 Mr 2017

DAY TO NIGHT color *Redbook* p74 F 2017

DECKED OUT: Make a splash at your next pool party with these hot summer accessories *Indianapolis Monthly* v40 no10 p28 Je 2017

Denim Always [Cover story] color *Glamour* no8 p152 Ag 2017

DILONE J. Ferrise color *InStyle* v24 no9 p143 S 2017

DINING IN STYLE WITH SARA STORY B. Mazurek and G. ANDERSON color *Harper's Bazaar* no3654 p98 Je/Jl 2017

DOING GOOD S. Pulia color *InStyle* v24 no10 p76 O 2017

the DRAMA of SPRING color *Essence* v47 no11 p80 Mr 2017

Ear Candy E. Velluto color *Glamour* v115 no3 p71 Mr 2017

ELLIE BAMBER A. Syrett color *InStyle* v24 no3 p121 Mr 2017

FABULOUS at Every Age color *Harper's Bazaar* no3649 p239 D 2016/Ja 2017

FABULOUS at Every Age color *Harper's Bazaar* no3651 p299 Mr 2017

FABULOUS at Every Age color *Harper's Bazaar* no3654 p103 Je/Jl 2017

FACE-LIFT color *Harper's Bazaar* no3651 p400 Mr 2017

FALL FORWARD color *Essence* v48 no5 p27 S 2017

Fall's prettiest outfits B. Goreski color *Redbook* p21 O 2017

FASHION UNDER $100 [Cover story] color *Redbook* p69 F 2017

FRESH COATS bw color *Vogue* v207 no10 p296 O 2017

A Fresh Coat S. P. Nadella and A. Hou color *Glamour* no8 p48 Ag 2017

The Getaway Dress A. R. Williams color *Southern Living* v52 no7 p39 Jl 2017

The Get color *InStyle* v23 no12 p43 N 2016

The Get-It Guide *Glamour* v114 no11 p182 N 2016

The Get-It Guide *Glamour* v115 no3 p211 Mr 2017

GET THE LOOK color *Seventeen* p66 Ja 1 2017

Get the LOOK SPRINGS MUST-HAVES color *Harper's Bazaar* no3651 p271 Mr 2017

THE GIRL Kaia Gerber E. Wilson color *InStyle* v24 no11 p81 N 2017

THE GIRL Margot Robbie E. Wilson color *InStyle* v23 no13 p109 D 2016

THE GIRL Rihanna E. Wilson color *InStyle* v23 no12 p79 N 2016

THE GIRL Zoë Kravitz E. Wilson color *InStyle* v24 no10 p97 O 2017

GREETINGS FROM CALIFORNIA color *Seventeen* p172 Ja 1 2017

GUEST LIST color *Harper's Bazaar* no3654 p94 Je/Jl 2017

Hand SOME *Interview* v47 no2 p158 Mr 2017

Heat WAVE *Interview* v47 no2 p104 Mr 2017

her style color *InStyle* v24 no11 p34 N 2017

her style color *InStyle* v24 no3 p84 Mr 2017

HIGH CONTRAST color *Harper's Bazaar* no3650 p102 F 2017

the HIT LIST A. Dorsey color *Essence* v48 no5 p32 S 2017

HOLDING COURT *Interview* v47 no2 p98 Mr 2017

HOLIDAY GIFT GUIDE M. BOBO and J. AMAY color *Ebony* v72 no3 p51 D 2016/Ja 2017

HOLIDAY OUTFITS color *InStyle* v23 no13 p143 D 2016

Hood Game Strong [Cover story] color *Glamour* v114 no11 p56 N 2016

HORSE POWER S. Kneen, H. Leutwyler et al bw color *Esquire* p104 2017 BigBlackBook

HOW TO WEAR IT... anywhere! color *Good Housekeeping* v264 no4 p28 Ap 2017

The In/Out LIST color *Harper's Bazaar* no3650 p76 F 2017

The In Out LIST color *Harper's Bazaar* no3651 p214 Mr 2017

The In/Out LIST color *Harper's Bazaar* no3654 p62 Je/Jl 2017

instant style color *InStyle* v24 no10 p125 O 2017

instant style color *InStyle* v24 no2 p71 F 2017

instant style color *InStyle* v24 no3 p207 Mr 2017

Insta-Outfit color *InStyle* v24 no11 p115 N 2017

IN THE FRAME E. Wilson color *InStyle* v24 no11 p202 N 2017

IN THE PINK A. ALAGEM color *Harper's Bazaar* no3654 p78 Je/Jl 2017

In the Spirit M. CAMERAN color *New Orleans Magazine* v51 no12 p46 O 2017

Into the Wild color *Glamour* no8 p130 Ag 2017

The IRL Guide to Dries Van Noten color *Esquire* v166 no4 p55 N 2016

IT'S SPRING! GO BIG OR GO HOME color *Essence* v47 no12 p94 Ap 2017

JAM ROCK SWEETNESS bw color *Vogue* v207 no6 p150 Je 2017

KELSEY & KENDRA A. Jordan color *Essence* v48 no2 p38 Je 2017

THE LADY Diane Sawyer E. Wilson color *InStyle* v23 no12 p82 N 2016

THE LADY Goldie Hawn E. Wilson color *InStyle* v24 no10 p100 O 2017

THE LADY Robin Wright E. Wilson color *InStyle* v23 no13 p112 D 2016

THE LADY Sharon Stone E. Wilson color *InStyle* v24 no11 p84 N 2017

THE LADY Tilda Swinton E. Wilson color *InStyle* v24 no3 p168 Mr 2017

La Vie en Rose color *Conde Nast Traveler* v52 no2 p21 F 2017

Layer your way to more outfits B. Goreski color *Redbook* p30 F 2017

Leather Heads N. SULLIVAN color *Esquire* v166 no4 p52 N 2016

LET'S DO FALL IN VIRGINIA J. B. Hager color *Southern Living* v51 no11 p62 N 2016

LIFE'S RICH TAPESTRY color *InStyle* v24 no10 p228 O 2017

The LIST color *Harper's Bazaar* no3650 p73 F 2017

The LIST color *Harper's Bazaar* no3654 p57 Je/Jl 2017

LOOK CUTE ON YOUR COMMUTE S. Zlotnick *Washingtonian Magazine* v52 no5 p113 F 2017

The LOOK *Interview* v47 no2 p96 Mr 2017

LOUNGE HAPPY! color *Women's Health* v14 no1 p178 Ja/F 2017

LUST FOR LIFE J. ROTH cartoon color *Esquire* p110 2017 BigBlackBook

Major MINIS color *Seventeen* p88 Ja 1 2017

Market color *Vanity Fair* v59 no4 p102 Mr 2017

Market: FABULOUS 40S color *Vanity Fair* v59 no9 p116 S 2017

Market SIMPLY STRIPES color *Vanity Fair* v59 no6 p50 My 2017

Mary-Kate & Ashley Olsen E. Wilson color *InStyle* v24 no9 p187 S 2017

MILLIE BOBBY BROWN UPSIDE DOWN S. Cristobal color *InStyle* v24 no11 p178 N 2017

Miuccia Prada E. Wilson color *InStyle* v24 no9 p190 S 2017

Mod '60s color *Seventeen* v76 no2 p56 Mr 2017

Modern MOVES *Interview* v47 no2 p106 Mr 2017

MODERN ROMANCE J. MOAZAMI color *Chicago* v66 no2 p34 F 2017

The most versatile dress M. Handahu color *Redbook* p82 F 2017

My Style color *InStyle* v23 no13 p158 D 2016

my style color *InStyle* v24 no11 p108 N 2017

THE NEW NEUTRALS color *Harper's Bazaar* no3650 p160 F 2017

NEW ROMANTICS L. Clark color *Harper's Bazaar* no3654 p154 Je/Jl 2017

Nothing but Bags color *Glamour* v115 no6 p130 Je 2017

on demand color *InStyle* v24 no11 p61 N 2017

on demand color *InStyle* v24 no2 p39 F 2017

ONES TO WATCH color *Harper's Bazaar* no3651 p284 Mr 2017

On the Cover color *Vanity Fair* p191 Hollywood 2017 Supplement

ON THE SPOT color *Harper's Bazaar* no3654 p73 Je/Jl 2017

Our Fall Favorites F. Kane and E. Velluto color *Glamour* no8 p62 Ag 2017

Outdoor Adventure A. Hou and M. Mendal color *Glamour* v115 no6 p36 Je 2017

Out fits for Days color *Glamour* no8 p60 Ag 2017

OUTFITS FOR DAYS color *Redbook* p70 O 2017

PANTS ON FIRE color *Vogue* v207 no1 p98 Ja 2017

PANTSUIT NATION color *Harper's Bazaar* no3654 p75 Je/Jl 2017

PARTY ON M. Bobo color *Ebony* v72 no3 p56 D 2016/Ja 2017

PATTERN PLAY color *Harper's Bazaar* no3651 p246 Mr 2017

PEARL Crush color *InStyle* v23 no12 p136 N 2016

Pink Grapefruit K. RENDA color *House Beautiful* v159 no2 p23 Mr 2017

Play Time! color *Glamour* v114 no11 p178 N 2016

Pom-Tastic! color *Seventeen* v76 no2 p44 Mr 2017

Pool PARTY color *Vogue* v207 no6 p156 Je 2017

POWER MOVE bw color *Harper's Bazaar* no3657 p157 O 2017

PRETTY IN PINK color *Harper's Bazaar* no3651 p244 Mr 2017

Putting on a Show N. REMSEN bw color *Vogue* v207 no10 p198 O 2017

RAF SIMONS'S BRAVE NEW WORLD N. Silva-Jelly color *Harper's Bazaar* no3654 p96 Je/Jl 2017

REBOOT YOUR WARDROBE WITH FALL'S BEST JEANS color *Harper's Bazaar* no3657 p147 O 2017

RED ALERT color *Harper's Bazaar* no3654 p74 Je/Jl 2017

RED-HOT A. Alagem color *Harper's Bazaar* no3654 p126 Je/Jl 2017

ROCK YOUR BODY color *Seventeen* p186 Ja 1 2017

RUN THE JEWELS *Atlanta* v57 no5 p48 S 2017

RUNWAY REPORT color *Harper's Bazaar* no3650 p206 F 2017

SADDLE UP color *Harper's Bazaar* no3650 p103 F 2017

School of Karl E. Wilson color *InStyle* v24 no9 p157 S 2017

The SCORE color *InStyle* v23 no12 p139 N 2016

See the Light color *Seventeen* p200 Ja 1 2017

Shirt Tales color *Vogue* v207 no10 p266 O 2017

Shop & Do Good color *Seventeen* v75 no11 p34 N 2016

Shop Like an Editor color *InStyle* v23 no12 p151 N 2016

SHOP SPRING'S MUST-HAVE LOOKS color *Harper's Bazaar* no3650 p84 F 2017

SHOP THE COLLECTION M. Elie and M. BOBO color *Ebony* v72 no3 p62 D 2016/Ja 2017

SIMPLY AMAZING! A. Dorsey color *Essence* v47 no11 p19 Mr 2017

Sky's the LIMIT color *InStyle* v24 no9 p305 S 2017

The smartest, prettiest winter buy B. Goreski color *Redbook* p23 D 2016

SNATCH That STYLE: Breaking Down Looks of Lyrical Trendsetters M. STREET color *Ebony* v72 no8 p44 Je 2017

SO BAZAAR color *Harper's Bazaar* no3651 p454 Mr 2017

Sparkling '50s color *Seventeen* v76 no2 p54 Mr 2017

Sporty Spice [Cover story] color *Glamour* v114 no11 p54 N 2016

SPRING BREAK color *Seventeen* v76 no2 p30 Mr 2017

the start color *InStyle* v24 no11 p51 N 2017

the start color *InStyle* v24 no2 p31 F 2017

State of Undress A. Mali bw color *Glamour* v115 no6 p122 Je 2017

Stella McCartney E. Wilson color *InStyle* v24 no9 p188 S 2017

Strap Happy! E. Velluto color *Glamour* v114 no12 p98 D 2016

STREET WISE *Interview* v47 no2 p100 Mr 2017

STYLE STAR color *Harper's Bazaar* no3657 p155 O 2017

SUIT YOURSELF A. R. Williams color *Southern Living* v51 no11 p57 N 2016

Summer Weekend Checklist color *Glamour* v115 no6 p35 Je 2017

SUPER NATURAL SUMMER color *O, The Oprah Magazine* p106 Ag 2017

THANKSGIVING WITH A VIEW C. Stern color *InStyle* v24 no11 p211 N 2017

THERE'S A GIRL IN MY SWEATER D. WALTERS bw color *Esquire* v166 no4 p108 N 2016

Think Small E. Velluto color *Glamour* no8 p70 Ag 2017

TIMELESS TAN A. ALAGEM color *Harper's Bazaar* no3654 p80 Je/Jl 2017

Twice? Nice! S. P. Nadella color *Glamour* no8 p58 Ag 2017

Urban Planning color *Glamour* v115 no6 p40 Je 2017

Velvet Crush color *Vogue* v207 no10 p294 O 2017

Vintage PROM VIBES color *Seventeen* v76 no2 p52 Mr 2017

WEIGHING In E. ELWICK color *Vogue* v207 no3 p500 Mr 2017

Welcome to My Life color *InStyle* v23 no12 p144 N 2016

THE WELL-SPENT $ DOLLAR color *Harper's Bazaar* no3650 p92 F 2017

THE WELL-SPENT $ DOLLAR color *Harper's Bazaar* no3651 p248 Mr 2017

THE WELL-SPENT $ DOLLAR color *Harper's Bazaar* no3654 p76 Je/Jl 2017

western PROMISES E. STUART *Virginia Living* v15 no2 p29 F 2017

What Kiersey Loves color *InStyle* v24 no9 p228 S 2017

WHAT'S Next color *Harper's Bazaar* no3651 p390 Mr 2017

What's Your PROM STYLE? color *Seventeen* p80 Ja 1 2017

What to Know Now L. Chan color *Glamour* v115 no6 p52 Je 2017

WHAT WE LOVE color *Harper's Bazaar* no3650 p44 F 2017

WHAT WE LOVE color *Harper's Bazaar* no3651 p77 Mr 2017

WHAT WE LOVE color *Harper's Bazaar* no3654 p28 Je/Jl 2017

WHERE FASHION GETS PERSONAL color *Harper's Bazaar* no3650 p95 F 2017

WHERE FASHION GETS PERSONAL color *Harper's Bazaar* no3651 p259 Mr 2017

WHERE TO BUY color *Essence* v47 no12 p128 Ap 2017

WHERE TO BUY color *Harper's Bazaar* no3650 p212 F 2017

Wide-Leg Wonders S. P. Nadella and A. Hou color *Glamour* no8 p46 Ag 2017

WISH YOU WERE HERE color *Conde Nast Traveler* v52 no6 p21 Je/Jl 2017

THE WOMAN Chrissy Teigen E. Wilson color *InStyle* v23 no12 p80 N 2016

THE WOMAN Jessica Alba E. Wilson color *InStyle* v23 no13 p110 D 2016

THE WOMAN Priyanka Chopra E. Wilson color *InStyle* v24 no11 p82 N 2017

THE WOMAN Rashida Jones E. Wilson color *InStyle* v24 no10 p98 O 2017

THE WOMAN Ruth Negga E. Wilson color *InStyle* v24 no3 p166 Mr 2017

Fashion collecting

Our Favorite Designer Collections (as Worn by Our Favorite Human Collections) J. MOORE bw color *GQ: Gentlemen's Quarterly* v97 no11 p33 N 2017

Fashion design

See also
    Hat design & hat making
    Haute couture
    Women's clothing design

5 BIG fall LOOKS color *Ebony* v72 no11 p34 S 2017

ARMOR AND LINGERIE A. OKEOWO cartoon color *New Yorker* v93 no29 p52 S 25 2017

Art of Letting Loose L. IMMEDIATO color *Los Angeles Magazine* v62 no7 p28 Jl 2017

BARE Essential color *Seventeen* v76 no4 p13 Jl/Ag 2017

Bewitched L. GÖKSENIN color *Vogue* v207 no4 p160 Ap 2017

Black, White & Right E. Wilson color *InStyle* v24 no7 p48 Jl 2017

Booster Shots color *GQ: Gentlemen's Quarterly* v97 no5 p96 My 2017

Calling All Crop Top Lovers color *Glamour* v114 no7 p65 Jl 2016

Cara Delevingne color *InStyle* v24 no1 p66 Ja 2017

COLLABORATION NATION: Memorable mash-ups over the last 15 years img *New York* v49 no23 p51 N 14 2016

The CROWN *Interview* v47 no6 p45 Ag 2017

DIVINE *Interview* v47 no6 p96 Ag 2017

DRESSING THE DUCHESS OF CAMBRIDGE M. CAMPBELL color *Maclean's* v129 no40 p54 O 10 2016

EDITOR'S LETTER G. Cerio color *Magazine Antiques* v184 no2 p16 Mr/Ap 2017

Face Forward J. Wilson color *Essence* v48 no3 p29 Jl 2017

Fashion HOUSE H. Bowles bw color *Vogue* v207 no4 p212 Ap 2017

FEATHERED GLORY B. BILGER bw cartoon color *New Yorker* v93 no29 p68 S 25 2017

FENDI'S FAIRY TALE J. J. Martin color *Harper's Bazaar* no3648 p272 N 2016

Flowers in THE ATTIC *Interview* v46 no10 p114 D 2016/Ja 2017

HELLO! L. Brown color *InStyle* v23 no13 p30 D 2016

Here We Go! Oprah color *O, The Oprah Magazine* p17 Je 2017

High Time S. Mower bw *Vogue* v207 no11 p117 N 2017

How Bob Mackie's Dazzling Designs Connected the Stars I. Biedenharn color *Entertainment Weekly* no1460/1461 p20 Ap 7-17 2017

Keep the FAITH color *Vogue* v207 no6 p64 Je 2017

Memewear J. Fisher *New York Times Magazine* p22 Ag 20 2017

Paradise FOUND color *Vogue* v206 no11 p130 N 2016

The Power of Carolina E. Wilson color *InStyle* v24 no4 p196 Ap 2017

QUIET STORM *Interview* v47 no6 p78 Ag 2017

SAADA AHMED D. Hobdy-olibrice color *Essence* v48 no3 p24 Jl 2017

Six Decades of Rock Style bw color *Rolling Stone* no1298 p40 O 19 2017

SPRING Style Forecast color *InStyle* v24 no1 p26 Ja 2017

STILL SLAYED J. AMAY color *Ebony* v72/73 no12/1 p42 O/N 2017

STYLE CRUSH Barbara Palvin S. Simon color *InStyle* v24 no1 p34 Ja 2017

The Style Guy cartoon *GQ: Gentlemen's Quarterly* v97 no5 p34 My 2017

TRANSFORMER R. MEAD cartoon color *New Yorker* v93 no29 p42 S 25 2017

Two for One img *New York* v50 no17 p64 Ag 21 2017

WHAT'S THE 411? color *Ebony* v72 no11 p42 S 2017

WORK *Interview* v47 no1 p91 F 2017

Yes, We Ken C. Weaver color *GQ: Gentlemen's Quarterly* v97 no7 p74 Jl 2017

YOU WANT YOUR MTV? A. LUCAS color *Ebony* v72 no8 p35 Je 2017

Fashion design competitions

Meet Our Challenge Winner! color *Seventeen* v76 no2 p49 Mr 2017

Fashion design exhibitions

How Has One Designer Spent Decades Defining the Avant-Garde? Rei Kawakubo's Comme des Garçons gets a restrospective at the Met V. HYLAND img *New York* v50 no8 p74 Ap 17 2017

Fashion designers

See also
    Women fashion designers

ALWAYS on MY MIND bw color *Vogue* v207 no9 p320 S 2017

Belle CURVE L. YAEGER, M. HOLGATE et al color *Vogue* v207 no3 p346 Mr 2017

CAPTURING CALVIN KLEIN B. COLACELLO color *Vanity Fair* v59 no9 p218 S 2017

The Class of 2017: Seven new faces at New York Fashion Week S. Franklin img *New York* v50 no18 p49 S 4 2017

CRACKING FASHION'S CODE R. Bhasin color *Harper's Bazaar* no3654 p142 Je/Jl 2017

DIOR'S NEW GUARD J. Picardie color *Harper's Bazaar* no3651 p410 Mr 2017

DONATELLA VERSACE S. SINGER bw color *Vogue* v207 no3 p424 Mr 2017

Eastern Promises N. Remsen, M. HOLGATE et al color *Vogue* v207 no9 p346 S 2017

EDITOR'S LETTER Glenda color *Harper's Bazaar* no3654 p54 Je/Jl 2017

Fashion's Breakout Star J. K. de Valle color *Glamour* v114 no11 p158 N 2016

Fingers On the Prints L. Leitch color *Vogue* v207 no6 p134 Je 2017

Fit for a Fashion Pro K. NEITZ color *Runner's World* v52 no8

p41 S 2017

Four Truths About Dressing Your Shape L. Chan, J. K. de Valle et al color *Glamour* v114 no11 p90 N 2016

Francesco RAGAZZI M. MULLEN *Interview* v47 no1 p20 F 2017

FUTURE FASHION *Iceland Review* v55 no3 p6 My/Je 2017

GIVENCHY'S Giacomettis H. BOWLES, M. HOLGATE et al color *Vogue* v207 no3 p350 Mr 2017

GUCCI'S URBAN GARDEN B. McKeon color *Harper's Bazaar* no3655 p124 Ag 2017

INTERVIEW WITH THE MAESTRO J. Picardie color *Harper's Bazaar* no3657 p236 O 2017

Jonathan SAUNDERS C. KELSEY *Interview* v47 no2 p112 Mr 2017

Junichi ABE C. KELSEY *Interview* v47 no1 p32 F 2017

Junya Watanabe J. Crelin *Current Biography* v78 no5 p92 My 2017

Kwaidan Editions M. HOLGATE color *Vogue* v207 no9 p354 S 2017

Making HISTORY color *Vogue* v206 no11 p106 N 2016

Maria Grazia Chiuri E. Wilson color *InStyle* v24 no11 p90 N 2017

MEMORIES are MADE of THIS bw color *Vogue* v207 no3 p276 Mr 2017

Miuccia PRADA C. Leive color *Glamour* v114 no12 p208 D 2016

A New Mecca of Cool R. MCKNIGHT color *Esquire* v167 no1 p44 F 2017

NEW NEXT NEW YORK D. VON FURSTENBERG *Interview* v46 no9 p70 N 2016

THE NEXT BRITISH INVASION J. von Søthen bw color *Esquire* p62 S 2017

NIC GALWAY A. WANG *Interview* v47 no2 p246 Mr 2017

OBJECTS of their DESIRE R. SULLIVAN, M. HOLGATE et al color *Vogue* v207 no3 p326 Mr 2017

Olivier's TWIST L. YAEGER bw color *Vogue* v206 no12 p142 D 2016

The Power of an Outsider E. Mahaney and K. Branch color *Glamour* v115 no1 p62 Ja 2017

Rebel Yell E. Wilson color *InStyle* v24 no8 p65 Ag 2017

Rosie Assoulin A. Syrett color *InStyle* v24 no5 p98 My 2017

SAADA AHMED D. Hobdy-olibrice color *Essence* v48 no3 p24 Jl 2017

SARAH BURTON H. Bowles color *Vogue* v207 no3 p430 Mr 2017

SARAH NAKINTU J. Wilson color *Essence* v47 no8 p40 D 2016

SIMONE ROCHA L. YAEGER color *Vogue* v207 no3 p424 Mr 2017

SJP [Cover story] L. Brown color *InStyle* v24 no1 p76 Ja 2017

SONIA RYKIEL color *Harper's Bazaar* no3648 p98 N 2016

STATE OF MIND L. IMMEDIATO *Los Angeles Magazine* v62 no6 p28 Je 2017

Stella McCARTNEY *Interview* v46 no10 p56 D 2016/Ja 2017

VACCARELLO'S VISION C. Swanson bw color *Harper's Bazaar* no3655 p152 Ag 2017

VERA WANG N. PHELPS color *Vogue* v207 no3 p419 Mr 2017

VICTORIA BECKHAM L. ARMSTRONG color *Vogue* v207 no3 p422 Mr 2017

Vision Statements J. DeLeon bw color *Condé Nast Traveler* v51 no11 p60 D 2016

Wham GLAM L. YAEGER color *Vogue* v206 no11 p108 N 2016

What I've LEARNED *Esquire* p82 BigBlackBook

Fashion designers—France

Chanel's Costume Drama S. KASHNER bw color *Vanity Fair* p158 Hollywood 2017 Supplement

Fashion designers—Interviews

BALMAIN C. WALLACE *Interview* v47 no6 p62 Ag 2017

FE NOEL A. Dorsey color *Essence* v48 no3 p22 Jl 2017

Lauren Conrad color *Maclean's* v130 no3 p56 Ap 2017

TOM FORD OVER SEX, SEEKING EMOTION A. LAROCCA img *New York* v50 no16 p48 Ag 7 2017

Fashion designers—Japan

REI L. SHAPTON *New York Times Magazine* p50 Ap 30 2017

Fashion designers—United States

Art of Letting Loose L. IMMEDIATO color *Los Angeles Magazine* v62 no7 p28 Jl 2017

Joe FreshGoods M. RAYMER color *Chicago* v66 no6 p87 Je 2017

MOM-AND-POP SHOP E. ALLEN cartoon color *New Yorker*

v93 no5 p72 Mr 20 2017

TOM FORD'S WILD KINGDOM T. BRODESSER-AKNER color *GQ: Gentlemen's Quarterly* v86 no12 p178 D 2016

Fashion design—History

FASHION'S ATTICS D. T. Max cartoon color *New Yorker* v93 no5 p62 Mr 20 2017

Fashion editors

The Real Housewives of Orange County I. Ratledge *TV Guide* v65 no31 p32 Jl 24 2017

Fashion exhibitions

See also

Fashion shows

Haute couture—Exhibitions

Best Dress E. Wilson color *InStyle* v24 no1 p31 Ja 2017

Cat's Meow E. Wilson color *InStyle* v24 no1 p32 Ja 2017

Clothes That Don't Need You [Cover story] D. Salle bw color *New York Review of Books* v64 no14 p10 S 28 2017

CRISTOBAL CRAZE bw *Harper's Bazaar* no3653 p82 My 2017

HER BEST EVER! Sienna Miller E. Wilson color *InStyle* v24 no1 p36 Ja 2017

Matters of taste G. Adamson color *Magazine Antiques* v184 no1 p24 Ja/F 2017

On with the SHOWS H. BOWLES color *Vogue* v206 no11 p136 N 2016

SPRING Style Forecast color *InStyle* v24 no1 p26 Ja 2017

What Inspired the Summer of Love? J. PARKER cartoon *Atlantic* v320 no1 p32 Jl/Ag 2017

Fashion in Film (Film)

Fashion in Film V. Lucca bw *Film Comment* v52 no6 p94 N/D 2016

Fashion in literature

Zero to Hero N. REMSEN color *Vogue* v207 no11 p128 N 2017

Fashion merchandising

See also

Fashion Week (Special events)

Is Amazon Europe's Next Top Model? A. Ricadela color *Bloomberg Businessweek* no4505 p21 D 26 2016

KS$ K. Bhasin color graph *Bloomberg Businessweek* no4495 p16 O 17 2016

Fashion periodicals

ASTONISH ME S. Mooallem bw color *Harper's Bazaar* no3651 p436 Mr 2017

Bazaar GARDENS Glenda color *Harper's Bazaar* no3653 p132 My 2017

BAZAAR: THE DEFINITION OF FASHION S. Mooallem bw *Harper's Bazaar* no3653 p268 My 2017

EDITOR'S LETTER G. Bailey color *Harper's Bazaar* no3653 p78 My 2017

EDITOR'S LETTER G. Bailey *Harper's Bazaar* no3657 p114 O 2017

Hello, and welcome to our Summer issue! T. Ebony color *Ebony* v72 no9 p14 Jl/Ag 2017

POP GOES BAZAAR S. Mooallem color *Harper's Bazaar* no3654 p132 Je/Jl 2017

Fashion photography

THE 43-DAY FASHION SHOOT img *New York* v50 no16 p66 Ag 7 2017

AM I TOO OLD FOR THIS? S. Cristobal color *InStyle* v24 no9 p422 S 2017

Ave Maria A. Syrett color *InStyle* v24 no9 p394 S 2017

Chelsea Boy N. Englander bw color *Vogue* v207 no11 p104 N 2017

Good Jeans color *Vogue* v207 no9 p640 S 2017

If You Like to Rework the Classics S. P. Nadella and A. Hou color *Glamour* v115 no9 p54 S 2017

Katy Perry color *InStyle* v24 no10 p178 O 2017

MOONLIGHT & ROSES color *Vogue* v207 no6 p102 Je 2017

Sex color *Glamour* v115 no7 p77 Jl 2017

STAR AND STRIPES color *Vanity Fair* v59 no2 p37 F 2017

Two for One img *New York* v50 no17 p64 Ag 21 2017

The Woman of Many Faces [Cover story] L. B. Ray color *InStyle* v24 no10 p206 O 2017

Fashion photography—History

Fashion Film Archives bw color *American History* v52 no3 p26 Ag 2017

Fashion shows

2017 WASHINGTONIAN BRIDE & GROOM UNVEILED color *Washingtonian Magazine* v52 no7 p158 Ap 2017

ALAÏA'S RETURN color *Harper's Bazaar* no3656 p319 S 2017

AROUND the WORLD, ONE PARTY at a TIME bw color *Vanity Fair* v59 no4 p121 Mr 2017

Bag Lover's Dream! color *Glamour* v115 no10 p83 O 2017

THE BRIDE WORE BLUSH color *Harper's Bazaar* no3653 p147 My 2017

Cameos on the Catwalk K. Samuelson color *Time* v190 no15 p12 O 16 2017

COUTURE REPORT color *Harper's Bazaar* no3656 p320 S 2017

A CUT ABOVE bw color *Harper's Bazaar* no3652 p149 Ap 2017

EVENT CALENDAR color *Washingtonian Magazine* v52 no7 p188 Ap 2017

FUTURE FASHION *Iceland Review* v55 no3 p6 My/Je 2017

Kyoto Crush J. K. DE VALLE color *Architectural Digest* v74 no8 p21 Ag 2017

MARCH OF THE DESIGNERS E. S. ARMARSÓTTIR *Iceland Review* v55 no2 p10 Mr/Ap 2017

MEETING OF THE (FLORAL) MINDS bw color *Harper's Bazaar* no3653 p136 My 2017

Natalie Portman HER BEST EVER E. Wilson color *InStyle* v24 no6 p50 Je 2017

On with the SHOWS H. BOWLES color *Vogue* v206 no11 p136 N 2016

Royal Anniversary [Cover story] N. Silverstein color *Glamour* v114 no11 p50 N 2016

What to wear B. Haile color *U.S. Catholic* v81 no11 p8 N 2016

Fashion shows—Exhibitions

DARE TO WEAR COLOR L. McCarthy color *Harper's Bazaar* no3648 p146 N 2016

Fashion shows—France

Keep the FAITH color *Vogue* v207 no6 p64 Je 2017

Fashion shows—New York (State)—New York

Queen of Everything [Cover story] L. Chan bw color *Glamour* v115 no7 p78 Jl 2017

Fashion shows—United States

2016 WASHINGTONIAN STYLE SETTERS *Washingtonian Magazine* v52 no3 p116 D 2016

STYLE IS ETERNAL: Yves Saint Laurent exhibition makes only East Coast stop at VMFA E. Parkhurst *Virginia Living* v15 no4 p23 Je 2017

World of Wonder Life's a Drag A. Sakoui color *Bloomberg Businessweek* no4521 p22 My 8 2017

Fashion stylists

24 HOURS with JASON REMBERT O. J. WILLIAMS color *Ebony* v72 no11 p94 S 2017

Flying in Style E. Wilson color *InStyle* v23 no13 p65 D 2016

My Vanity G. Sidibe color *InStyle* v24 no5 p232 My 2017

ROBERT RABENSTEINER bw color *Esquire* v167 no1 p41 F 2017

Where the Red-Carpet Madness Begins [Cover story] J. Harman color *Glamour* v115 no3 p47 Mr 2017

ZEN AND THE ART OF CLOSET MAINTENANCE C. Battan color *Bloomberg Businessweek* no4524 p67 My 29 2017

Fashion Week (Special events)

The Back Story E. Wilson color *InStyle* v24 no5 p79 My 2017

BEST DRESS E. Wilson color *InStyle* v24 no5 p67 My 2017

FORD MODELS color *Vanity Fair* v58 no11 p63 N 2016

TNT color *Vogue* v206 no11 p134 N 2016

Fashion—Africa

HELLBANGERS color *Mother Jones* v42 no1 p51 Ja/F 2017

Fashion—Awards

50 BEST DRESSED LIST J. Ferrise, E. Wilson et al color *InStyle* v24 no11 p186 N 2017

In (and Out of) Fashion G. Doré color *InStyle* v24 no9 p261 S 2017

Fashion—Economic aspects

LESSONS FROM THE SUSHI CONVEYOR BELT il *Harvard Business Review* v95 no4 p28 Jl/Ag 2017

Fashion—News briefs

BEST BETS img *New York* v50 no16 p88 Ag 7 2017

The NEWS bw color *Harper's Bazaar* no3655 p80 Ag 2017

NEWS color *Harper's Bazaar* no3648 p188 N 2016

Fashion—Social aspects

FASHIONABLE 50 [Cover story] J. Lisanti and R. Nadkarni

color *Sports Illustrated* v127 no3 p26 Jl 24 2017

Fashion—United States

EDITOR'S LETTER E. PARKHURST *Virginia Living* p17 2017 Best 20of Virginia

FASHION FOR THE SIXTY-SEVEN PERCENT: A revolution in the plus-size market A. C. FORD img *New York* v50 no16 p38 Ag 7 2017

TURN A CORNER J. Roth color *Esquire* p37 N 2017

Fass, Paula S.

Parent Trap N. SCHAEFER RILEY *Commentary* v142 no2 p56 S 2016

Fassbender, Michael, 1977-

SOUND BITES color *Entertainment Weekly* p10 Jl 24 2017

THE SPARK A. PETRUSICH color *Esquire* v166 no5 p106 D 2016/Ja 2017

Fassbinder, Rainer Werner, 1945-1982

FELLOW FEELING A. MA color *Film Comment* v53 no3 p58 My/Je 2017

Fassler, David

advice every new mom needs [Cover story] color *Parents* v92 no7 p32 Jl 2017

Fast, Nathanael J.

How Powerful, Low-Status Jobs Lead to Conflict *Harvard Business Review Digital Articles* p2 F 11 2016

Research: Insecure Managers Don't Want Your Suggestions *Harvard Business Review Digital Articles* p2 N 24 2014

Fast food restaurants—Evaluation

THE FAST-»FOOD« REMEDY L. B. SUTER *Los Angeles Magazine* p98 Ja 2017

LATE NIGHT *Atlanta* v56 no12 p81 Ap 2017

WHERE SHOULD I GO? diag *Bloomberg Businessweek* no4493 p83 O 3 2016

Fast food restaurants—Research

Building a Better World, Together color *Consumer Reports* v81 no12 p8 D 2016

Fast food restaurants—United States

Fast Food's Urban Invasion *American Scholar* v86 no2 p16 Spr 2017

The Latest Shortage: Fast-Food Workers L. Patton cartoon graph *Bloomberg Businessweek* no4507 p21 Ja 16 2017

Fast Forward Labs (Company)

How AI Fits into Your Data Science Team H. Mason *Harvard Business Review Digital Articles* p2 Jl 21 2017

Fast reactors

See also

Breeder reactors

Closing Japan's Monju fast breeder reactor: The possible implications M. Takubo bibl *Bulletin of the Atomic Scientists* v73 no3 p182 My 2017

Fast Times at Ridgemont High (Film)

DREW BARRYMORE R. Rahman color *Entertainment Weekly* no1451/1452 p98 F 3-10 2017

Fasteners

See also

Brackets

Locks & keys

Zippers

Secrets of a Weekend Lock Picker [Cover story] D. DUBNO color *Popular Mechanics* p29 S 2017

Fasting

See also

Fasts & feasts

CAN FASTING BE GOOD FOR YOU? J. Andriakos color *Health* v31 no7 p86 S 2017

Ramadan in Scandinavia: Muslims face the choice between "excessive" and "moderate" fasting E. POLJAREVIC *Islamic Horizons* v46 no3 p48 My/Je 2017

Why Is Everybody Suddenly Fasting? (And How Can I Fast Better Than Them?) J. VRABEL color *GQ: Gentlemen's Quarterly* v97 no6 p38 Je 2017

Fasting (Christianity)

The fasts we choose T. Larsen *Christian Century* v134 no5 p10 Mr 1 2017

Fasting—Physiological aspects

THIS IS FASTING? M. Stacey color *Women's Health* v14 no8 p106 O 2017

Fasts & feasts

See also

Thanksgiving Day

30 Cool THINGS ABOUT HOLIDAYS J. BEER *National Geographic Kids* no466 p24 D 2016/Ja 2017

FOWL AND FAIR: Backyard birds, neverending Vonnegut stories, and dining out on Thanksgiving. Ask the Hoosierist S. STALL *Indianapolis Monthly* p22 N 2017

A REMOVABLE FEAST E. A. POWELL color *Archaeology* v70 no1 p20 Ja/F 2017

Fast & the Furious, The (Film)

BABY, YOU CAN FLY MY CAR D. Franich color *Entertainment Weekly* no1462 p11 Ap 21 2017

Fast & Furious: The Completist's Guide E. Dockterman and M. Vella color *Time* v189 no14 p54 Ap 17 2017

Fat

See also

Fat content of food

Burn 40 Pounds of Fat B. GREGORY color *Men's Health* v32 no7 p64 S 2017

Is It Better to Burn Carbs or Burn Fat? M. Rodriguez color *Black Belt* v55 no1 p18 D 2016/Ja 2017

PUT FAT AT A LOSS D. N. JACKS color *Muscle & Performance* v9 no5 p12 My 2017

SUMMER SHRED PROGRAM J. GRINNELL chart color *Muscle & Performance* v9 no5 p40 My 2017

THE ULTIMATE PHA FAT BLAST L. McGLASHAN chart color *Muscle & Performance* v9 no5 p16 My 2017

Fat cells

Adipocytes L. SCHLEY color *Discover* v38 no9 p20 N 2017

Regeneration of fat cells from myofibroblasts during wound healing M. V. Plikus, C. F. Guerrero-Juarez et al bibl color graph *Science* v355 no6326 p748 F 17 2017

Fat content of food

Go Ahead, Stop Counting Calories M. Oaklander color *Health* v31 no5 p45 Je 2017

Healthy Foods B. Liebman and J. Hurley *Nutrition Action Health Letter* v44 p1 Je 2017 Supplement

Our doc will see you now R. Rajapaksa color *Health* v31 no8 p70 O 2017

Raising the Bar L. MOYER and B. LIEBMAN *Nutrition Action Health Letter* v44 no5 p13 Je 2017

Fat content of meat

Meat Depressed color *Weekly Standard* v22 no41 p2 Jl 3 2017

Fat Joe (Performer)

FAT JOE & REMY MA GO "ALL THE WAY UP" N. Feeney color *Entertainment Weekly* no1454/1455 p96 F 24 2017

Fatal Attraction (Film)

Glenn Close on the Meaning of Alex D. Coggan color *Entertainment Weekly* no1484 p44 S 29 2017

Fate & fatalism

THE AUTHOR RESPONDS img *New York* v50 no15 p7 Jl 24 2017

Dear Readers B. Kelley *Reader's Digest* v188 no1126 p4 D 2016/Ja 2017

Fate G. Bakker *Skeptical Inquirer* v41 no1 p62 Ja/F 2017

OPEN YOUR EYES color *Essence* v47 no9 p88 Ja 2017

Fatemi, Hossein

They Can't Go Home Again A. P. Q. Wittmeyer and J. Chase-Lubitz color *Foreign Policy* no226 p16 S/O 2017

Fate of the Furious, The (Film)

THE FATEFUL EIGHTH D. Franich color *Entertainment Weekly* no1462 p10 Ap 21 2017

The Fate of the Furious L. Greenblatt color *Entertainment Weekly* no1462 p44 Ap 21 2017

Old Legends, Neo-Heroes and Modern Dragons C. D. Reid color *Black Belt* v55 no5 p28 Ag/S 2017

POETIC LICENSE A. LANE color *New Yorker* v93 no10 p102 Ap 24 2017

WHAT MAKES A BLOCKBUSTER ... IN CHINA? color *Fortune* v175 no7 p10 Je 1 2017

Father & child

See also

Fathers & daughters

Fathers & sons

20 Dad Hacks for Enjoying Dadhood D. GORDON, D. Wade et

al cartoon chart color *GQ: Gentlemen's Quarterly* v97 no7 p32 Jl 2017

bath bombs J. SMALL color *Parents* v92 no3 p48 Mr 2017

Ghosting M. Binyam bw *New York Times Magazine* p24 Ag 6 2017

Head Rush color *Vogue* v207 no10 p182 O 2017

Helping Dads Boost Their Styling Mojo M. LaScala *Parents* v92 no2 p20 F 2017

Let's Hear It for the Dads S. James color *Parents* v92 no6 p15 Je 2017

"MY DAD MADE ME FEEL BEAUTIFUL, teaching me to see the beauty beyond my disability." M. BLAKE color *Good Housekeeping* v264 no6 p63 Je 2017

SHOOTING MAGIC J. ARTERBURN cartoon *Outdoor Life* v224 no7 p78 S 2017

Father & child—Psychological aspects

Engaging Fathers in Parenting Intervention Improves Outcomes for Both Kids and Fathers *Education Digest* v82 no8 p25 Ap 2017

Father & child—Research

Engaging Fathers in Parenting Intervention Improves Outcomes for Both Kids and Fathers *Education Digest* v82 no8 p25 Ap 2017

Father John Misty (Performer)

The Beautiful, Bizarre Mind of Father John Misty E. R. Brown color *Entertainment Weekly* no1462 p62 Ap 21 2017

The Gospel of Father John Misty W. HERMES cartoon *Rolling Stone* no1285 p51 Ap 20 2017

the LOONY TUNES of FATHER JOHN MISTY S. BALL color *GQ: Gentlemen's Quarterly* v97 no6 p136 Je 2017

The Playlist bw color *Rolling Stone* no1281/1282 p10 F 23 2017

RAMBLING MAN N. PAUMGARTEN cartoon color *New Yorker* v93 no18 p36 Je 26 2017

Random Notes color *Rolling Stone* no1291/1292 p35 Jl 13 2017

Father John Misty (Performer)—Interviews

Q&A: Father John Misty A. GREENE *Rolling Stone* no1284 p20 Ap 6 2017

Fatherhood

Dads Across Decades bw color *Parents* v92 no6 p24 Je 2017

Fatherless families—Psychological aspects

Papa Was a Rolling Stone R. E. VATZ *USA Today Magazine* v146 no2868 p35 S 2017

Fathers

1823: Timisoara J. Bolyai *Lapham's Quarterly* v10 no2 p40 Spr 2017

Dad to Dad Gift Guide M. LaScala color *Parents* v92 no6 p22 Je 2017

The Fathers of Our Wisdom M. Bean bw color *Men's Health* v32 no5 p8 Je 2017

Let's Hear It for the Dads S. James color *Parents* v92 no6 p15 Je 2017

Losing My Father's Smile H. GOLDEN *Reader's Digest* v188 no1124 p56 O 2016

On Photography G. Dyer *New York Times Magazine* p14 Ja 8 2017

OUR FATHERS IN THEIR OWN WORDS G. Roberts-Grey, R. Carroll et al color *Essence* v48 no2 p94 Je 2017

REQUIEM FOR A LOOSE CANNON K. RYAN color *Men's Health* v32 no5 p96 Je 2017

RICH MELMAN B. Zehme *Chicago* v66 no7 p104 Jl 2017

A SON'S PRAYER T. Price color *America* v217 no6 p42 S 18 2017

A TYPEWRITER R. Gardiner color *Men's Health* v32 no5 p139 Je 2017

WAIT FOR IT J. Squance color *Rodale's Organic Life* v3 no1 p96 Ja 2017

Your True Stories *Reader's Digest* v188 no1125 p39 N 2016

Fathers & daughters

Dad, Interrupted J. DARST color *Vogue* v206 no12 p102 D 2016

A father's dilemma: Which baseball team will my baby daughter root for? J. C. Kang *New York Times Magazine* p14 Jl 2 2017

HELENA, FALLING: And the human impulse, from the youngest age, to keep going D. Bratcher *Washingtonian Magazine* v52 no11 p176 Ag 2017

HELP CREATE THE NEXT GENERATION OF BOATERS M. WERLING *Sea Magazine* v108 no8 p5 Ag 2016

MAN OF LETTERS E. GREENWOOD color *O, The Oprah*

Magazine p30 Ag 2017

A Match Made in Florida M. Sharapova and M. Ayers color *Money* v46 no9 p92 O 2017

Out of the Cult and into the Church A. LeBaron color *Christianity Today* p79 Ap 2017

Sophia Hears the Siren's Song A. JENKINS *Sea Magazine* v108 no8 p16 Ag 2016

The Things I Wish My Dad Knew About Me Before He Died S. B. LEWIS color *Reader's Digest* v189 no1131 p50 Je 2017

What Should I Do About A Physician Who May Be a Quack? K. A. Appiah *New York Times Magazine* p26 Ja 15 2017

Fathers & Daughters (TV program)

Fathers & Daughters E. Blair color *New York Review of Books* v64 no12 p4 Jl 13 2017

Fathers & daughters—United States

FATHER ISSUES A. ABEL color *Maclean's* p40 Je 2017

Fathers & sons

THE ACTING COACH S. Slon *Saturday Evening Post* v289 no3 p18 My/Je 2017

CAN THEIR PROBLEM BE SOLVED? J. Brown *Successful Farming* v115 no4 p68 Mr 2017

The Last Bursts of Memory J. VANOOSTING *American Scholar* v86 no1 p87 Wint 2017

MY FATHER'S CELLAR J. SEABROOK cartoon color *New Yorker* v92 no46 p22 Ja 23 2017

My Son, the Man of Tomorrow color *Men's Health* v32 no5 p119 Je 2017

No Business Down There: A Canyon and Its Lore L. ADDINGTON *Idaho Magazine* v16 no11 p28 Ag 2017

Out of Reach P. Quinn color *Commonweal* v144 no17 p11 O 20 2017

PROTECTING YOUR SON FROM ISLAMAPHOBIA color *Men's Health* v32 no5 p118 Je 2017

RAISING BOYS WHO'LL NEVER GROW UP color *Men's Health* v32 no5 p114 Je 2017

A SON'S QUEST TO GIVE HIS DYING FATHER ARTIFICIAL IMMORTALITY J. VLAHOS color *Wired* v25 no8 p56 Ag 2017

Such Great Heights B. DOYLE color *America* v215 p25 N 28 2016

SUPPORTING A CHILD WHO'S TRANSITIONED color *Men's Health* v32 no5 p116 Je 2017

That Time I Failed Miserably at Charming My Own Son J. Stein color *Time* v189 no20 p60 My 29 2017

THE TIME HAS COME C. Kearns color *Field & Stream* v122 no6 p8 N 2017

Tough Talk *Men's Health* v32 no5 p114 Je 2017

UNCONDITIONAL M. SAGER color *Men's Health* v32 no5 p112 Je 2017

What Kind of Father Lets His Son Play Football? L. ZALESKI color *GQ: Gentlemen's Quarterly* v97 no9 p132 S 2017

Your True Stories IN 100 WORDS A. ASHBY, P. RAE et al color *Reader's Digest* v189 no1131 p32 Je 2017

Fathers & sons—United States

My Son Doesn't Care About the Super Bowl. So I Brought In a Ringer J. Stein color *Time* v189 no4 p59 F 6 2017

STOP US IF YOU'VE HEARD THIS ... M. Piellucci color *Sports Illustrated* v127 no8 p60 S 18 2017

Fathers' attitudes

Quotable Quotes color *Reader's Digest* v189 no1131 p136 Je 2017

Father's Day

currents *Boating World* v38 no6 p10 Je 2017

GAME PLAN M. Zimmerman color graph *Men's Health* v32 no5 p10 Je 2017

Fathers—Competitions

NAME THE BOAT S. SHIBATA *Sea Magazine* v108 no8 p10 Ag 2016

Fathers—Death

LOSING STREAK K. SCHULZ cartoon *New Yorker* v92 no49 p66 F 13 2017

"My dad had a bucket list of 60 things. He'd only checked off 5 when his life was cut short." L. Carney bw color *Good Housekeeping* v264 no4 p81 Ap 2017

Fathers—Social aspects

Out of Touch D. Nayeri *New York Times Magazine* p35 O 16 2016

Fathers—United States—Psychology

... And There's an Invisible Workload That Drags Men Down Too J. Levs color *Money* v46 no4 p66 My 2017

Fatigue

See also

Chronic fatigue syndrome

Mental fatigue

Rest periods

The Burnout Quiz M. DiTrolio and J. Covert color *Men's Health* v32 no1 p31 Ja/F 2017

The Data-Driven Case for Vacation S. Achor and M. Gielan *Harvard Business Review Digital Articles* p2 Jl 13 2016

The Research Is Clear: Long Hours Backfire for People and for Companies S. G. Carmichael *Harvard Business Review Digital Articles* p2 Ag 19 2015

Fatigue prevention

Give Yourself an Energy Makeover! G. GRAVES cartoon color *Prevention* v69 no2 p44 F 2017

How to Look Less Tired K. Erickson, T. Williams et al bw color *Glamour* v115 no3 p120 Mr 2017

UNSTOPPABLE ENERGY: A USER'S MANUAL H. Levine color *Health* v31 no4 p75 My 2017

What to Eat When You're Tired [Cover story] P. O. BLUMBERG color *Prevention* v69 no6 p28 Je 2017

Your energy is flagging S. Kempton color *Yoga Journal* p48 2016 Special Issue

Fatigue—Treatment

What's Next for Kanye West? E. R. Brown, J. Rubenstein et al color *Entertainment Weekly* no1443 p17 D 9 2016

FATIMA, RISHAT

Ibtihaj Muhammad Redefining the Muslim American Image [Cover story] *Islamic Horizons* v45 no6 p28 N/D 2016

Fats & oils

See also

Ointments

Beyond Olive: Oils for Heart Health *Tufts University Health & Nutrition Letter* v35 no1 p3 Mr 2017

Change Your Oil color *Good Housekeeping* v265 no3 p103 S 2017

Liquid GOLD color *O, The Oprah Magazine* p78 Mr 2017

Fattah, Zainab

Gulf Rulers Try Fighting Deficits With Taxes cartoon *Bloomberg Businessweek* no4497 p18 O 31 2016

A Mideast Rivalry Leads to a Split color map *Bloomberg Businessweek* no4526 p23 Je 12 2017

The Plucky Little Emirate Vs. Old Foes color *Bloomberg Businessweek* no4535 p36 Ag 28 2017

Fatty acid oxidation

new products: metabolomics color *Science* v356 no6338 p649 My 12 2017

Fatty acid synthesis

Fatty acids in arbuscular mycorrhizal fungi are synthesized by the host plant L. H. Luginbuehl, G. N. Menard et al diag graph *Science* v356 no6343 p1175 Je 16 2017

Fatty acids

See also

Acetic acid

Butyric acid

Enzymes make light work of hydrocarbon production N. S. Scrutton diag *Science* v357 no6354 p872 S 1 2017

Fatty liver

Eating to Beat Belly Fat [Cover story] *Tufts University Health & Nutrition Letter* v34 no11 p1 Ja 2017

Faubus, Lillian

AGING GRACEFULLY on the Homestead *Mother Earth News* no280 p34 F/Mr 2017

Faucets—Equipment & supplies

EDGEWOOD HALL: Welcome to Edgewood Hall color *House Beautiful* v159 no9 p50 N 2017

Faucets—Evaluation

Beyond the Brita T. RAMI img *New York* p61 F 9 2017

In This Luxe Kitchen, Purple Reigns K. RENDA and B. REYNAERT color *House Beautiful* v159 no7 p38 S 2017

PUNCH LIST K. SELZER color *Better Homes & Gardens* v95 no5 p60 My 2017

Faucett, William A.

Distribution and clinical impact of functional variants in 50,726 whole-exome sequences from the DiscovEHR study chart graph

Science v354 no6319 paaf6814-1 D 23 2016

FAUCHEUX, RON

The Gubernatorial Stakes: Looking for clues in New Jersey and Virginia *American Conservative* v16 no4 p6 Jl/Ag 2017

Fauci, Anthony S.

Sustained virologic control in SIV+ macaques after antiretroviral and α4β7 antibody therapy bibl graph *Science* v354 no6309 p197 O 14 2016

Fauda (TV program)

OCCUPATIONAL HAZARDS D. REMNICK cartoon *New Yorker* v93 no26 p32 S 4 2017

A TV Bonanza From the Homeland of Homeland E. Bronner *Bloomberg Businessweek* no4526 p20 Je 12 2017

Faught, Josh—Exhibitions

HEAVEN SENT G. Adamson cartoon color *Art in America* v105 no4 p90 Ap 2017

Faulconer, Kevin, 1967-

IT NOW FALLS TO CALIFORNIA REPUBLICANS *Vital Speeches of the Day* v83 no10 p297 O 2017

FAULKNER, KATE RONEY

Tree-Climbing Foxes and Other Success Stories *Natural History* v125 no2 p18 F 2017

Faulkner, Richard S.

Pershing's Crusaders: The American Soldier in World War I W. WALKER *MHQ: Quarterly Journal of Military History* v29 no4 p92 Summ 2017

Faulkner, Sarah

Posttranslational mutagenesis: A chemical strategy for exploring protein side-chain diversity diag *Science* v354 no6312 p597 N 4 2016

Faulkner, Travis

REMOTE SCOUTING color *Outdoor Life* v224 no6 pH6 Ag 2017

SET THE STAGE color *Outdoor Life* v223 no9 pH9 N 2016

Faulkner, Valerie

Less is more diag graph *Phi Delta Kappan* v98 no7 p55 Ap 2017

Faulkner, William

SOUTHERN HARM diag *Harper's Magazine* v335 no2005 p39 Je 2017

Fauls, Bob

the WAY WE WERE *Arabian Horse World* v57 no8 p61 My 2017

Faultfinding

HOW TO BE FAULTLESS M. SHENG YEN color *Tricycle: The Buddhist Review* v26 no2 p34 Wint 2016

Faults (Geology)

Localized seismic deformation in the upper mantle revealed by dense seismic arrays A. Inbal, J. P. Ampuero et al bibl graph *Science* v354 no6308 p88 O 7 2016

Faults (Geology)—New Zealand

New Zealand temblor points to threat of compound quakes B. Mason color map *Science* v355 no6331 p1250 Mr 24 2017

Faus, Isabelle

FLASH color *Climbing* no350 p8 D 2016/Ja 2017

Fausset, Richard

Emmett Till Revisited img *New York Times Upfront* v149 no11 p16 Ap 3 2017

FAUST, DREW GILPIN

The Year in Reading [Cover story] *New York Times Book Review* p8 D 25 2016

Fauth, A. C.

Observation of a large-scale anisotropy in the arrival directions of cosmic rays above 8 × 1018 eV *Science* v357 no6357 p1266 S 22 2017

FAUTIN, DAPHNE G.

Fiction and Our Changing Climate *American Scholar* v86 no1 p3 Wint 2017

Faux, Zeke

How MusclePharm Went From Swole to Twig bw color *Bloomberg Businessweek* no4497 p56 O 31 2016

The Mystery of the 4,555 Percent Return graph *Bloomberg Businessweek* no4517 p40 Ap 3 2017

Patience You Must Have, My Young Investors color *Bloomberg Businessweek* no4503 p27 D 12 2016

Red Flags Abounded On Platinum Partners *Bloomberg Businessweek* no4506 p31 Ja 9 2017

Targeting the Nest Eggs Of U.K. Expats *Bloomberg Businessweek*

no4524 p39 My 29 2017

THERE'S MORE THAN ONE WAY TO WEAR A Wire bw color *Bloomberg Businessweek* no4516 p52 Mr 27 2017

Faux finishes (Decorative arts)

Elevate Your Easter Eggs K. Owen color *Southern Living* v52 no4 p33 Ap 2017

Fava bean

THE BEST BET img *New York* v49 no20 p97 O 3 2016

FAVA BEANS *South Dakota Magazine* v33 no3 p34 S/O 2017

FAVALORO, GEORGE

ENERGY STRATEGY FOR THE C-SUITE color graph img *Harvard Business Review* v95 no1 p138 Ja/F 2017

Favaro, Ken

A Brief History of the Ways Companies Compete *Harvard Business Review Digital Articles* p2 Ap 22 2015

Defining Strategy, Implementation, and Execution *Harvard Business Review Digital Articles* p2 Mr 31 2015

Don't Draft a Digital Strategy Just Because Everyone Else Is *Harvard Business Review Digital Articles* p2 Mr 16 2016

Favoritism (Personnel management)

Being the Boss's Favorite Is Great, Until It's Not L. Kislik *Harvard Business Review Digital Articles* p2 My 19 2017

Favors, Jim

Trailerblazing: One couple takes a small boat on big adventures — by land and by sea color *Sea Magazine* v109 no8 p18 Ag 2017

Favors, Lisa

Trailerblazing: One couple takes a small boat on big adventures — by land and by sea color *Sea Magazine* v109 no8 p18 Ag 2017

FAVREAU, ALYSSA

Finally, a Vaccine for Dengue [Cover story] color *Popular Science* v288 no6 p36 N/D 2016

Favreau, Jon, 1966-

3 — KEEPIN' IT 1600 J. Goodman *Entertainment Weekly* no1444/1445 p114 D 16 2016

THE JUNGLE BOOK C. Chiarella color *Sound & Vision* v81 no10 p71 D 2016

Favreau, Jon, 1966-—Interviews

Keepin' It 1600 With Jon Favreau & Dan Pfeiffer R. Rahman color *Entertainment Weekly* no1435 p12 O 14 2016

Fawcett, Alexander

Photoinduced decarboxylative borylation of carboxylic acids diag *Science* v357 no6348 p283 Jl 21 2017

FAWCETT, EDMUND

Princely Provocateur: An account of Niccolò Machiavelli traces the career of a tricky personality in a politically stormy era *New York Times Book Review* p12 Je 18 2017

FAWCETT, MAX

Pressure Test diag *Walrus* v14 no2 p14 Mr 2017

Fawkes, Ray

Johnny Canuck color *Canadian Geographic* v137 no4 p82 Jl/Ag 2017

Fax machines—Evaluation

Huge coaster, one thin rail M. B. Griggs and A. Rosenblum color diag *Popular Science* v289 no6 p24 N/D 2017

Fay, Kathleen

OUR CABIN SURVIVED A WILDFIRE color *Cabin Living* p69 Je 2017

Fay, Nathaniel

OUR CABIN SURVIVED A WILDFIRE color *Cabin Living* p69 Je 2017

Fayadh, Ashraf

Jailed Palestinian Poet's Work Gets New Life in Parallel Translation J. Maher chart color *Publishers Weekly* v263 no44 p11 O 31 2016

Faye, Ingrid

A key malaria metabolite modulates vector blood seeking, feeding, and susceptibility to infection bibl chart diag *Science* v355 no6329 p1076 Mr 10 2017

Fayhee, M. John

Hikes Gone Wrong: We all love the trail. Sometimes love hurts color il *Backpacker* p69 S 2017

Trail Fails D. LEWON color *Backpacker* p6 S 2017

Fazal, Ali

THE WORLD'S HIS STAGE L. RAMZI bw *Vogue* v207 no6 p109 Je 2017

Fazal, Tanisha M.

Rebellion, War Aims & the Laws of War *Daedalus* v146 no1 p71 Wint 2017

Fazio, Teresa

COMMENTS color *Wired* v25 no3 p16 Mr 2017

Fazio, Tom

King of Clubs J. Passov and C. Barrett color *Golf Magazine* v59 no7 p36 Jl 2017

FAZZARE, ELIZABETH

Czech Mate color *Architectural Digest* v74 no10 p64 O 1 2017

Fazzini, N.

Observation of a large-scale anisotropy in the arrival directions of cosmic rays above 8 × 1018 eV *Science* v357 no6357 p1266 S 22 2017

FCA US LLC

2017 Chrysler Pacifica Hybrid E. DYER color *Popular Mechanics* p37 Je 2017

BIG, HEAVY, CAPABLE M. Cortina chart color *Motor Trend* v69 no5 p74 My 2017

Chrysler Pacifica chart color *Motor Trend* v69 no1 p138 Ja 2017

EXTRA FINS FOR THIS FISH R. C. Johnson color *Hot Rod* v70 no12 p58 D 2017

Fiat 124 Spider chart color *Motor Trend* v69 no1 p123 Ja 2017

INSIDE OUT D. N. DILLWYN bw color *Conde Nast Traveler* v52 no5 p44 My 2017

JAMBOREE B. S. ANICH color *Road & Track* v69 no4 p80 N 2017

Jeep Grand Cherokee Trackhawk F. Markus and J. Udy color *Motor Trend* v69 no7 p20 Jl 2017

Jeep Yuntu concept E. Tahaney color *Motor Trend* v69 no8 p20 Ag 2017

Learning to LOVE the MINIVAN 2017 CHRYSLER PACIFICA color *Esquire* v166 no4 p81 N 2016

Lost in Last Place color *Consumer Reports* v82 no8 p59 Ag 2017

More Traction, Less Satisfaction D. Beard color *Car & Driver* v62 no11 p112 My 2017

Ram 2500/3500 HD chart color *Motor Trend* v69 no1 p88 Ja 2017

Ram Rebel TRX Concept S. Ogbac color *Motor Trend* v69 no1 p16 Ja 2017

RETURN OF THE T/A B. Iger color *Hot Rod* v70 no8 p48 Ag 2017

REVEALED: 2017 RAM POWER WAGON [Cover story] M. EMERY color *Dirt Sports + Off-Road* v51 no7 p28 Jl 2017

Rutledge Wood's 1970 CHARGER B. Gillogly color *Hot Rod* v70 no11 p34 N 2017

Thunder(s)truck K. C. Colwell color *Car & Driver* v63 no4 p106 O 2017

Fcazier, Kendrick

NEW AND NO TABLE *Skeptical Inquirer* v41 no3 p60 My/Je 2017

Fea, John

A Bible for everyone? diag *Christian Century* v133 no26 p26 D 21 2016

Feagin, Nancy

The Curated Image K. LAMBERT color *Climbing* no350 p38 D 2016/Ja 2017

Fear

    See also
      Hysteria (Social psychology)
      Phobias

The 2017 Fear Index N. Hopper color diag *Time* v188 no27-28 p68 D 26 2016

BALANCE OF POWER Epictetus *Lapham's Quarterly* v10 no3 p24 Summ 2017

Conquer Your Nerves Before Your Presentation N. Duarte *Harvard Business Review Digital Articles* p2 Ap 28 2015

Coping with Judgment J. Susser *Dressage Today* v23 no8 p16 Ap 2017

easily embarrassed T. REECE *Parents* v92 no6 p138 Je 2017

FEAR bw *Tricycle: The Buddhist Review* v27 no1 p48 Fall 2017

"Fear Itself," Itself *Lapham's Quarterly* v10 no3 p62 Summ 2017

Fighting Ebola Means Managing Fear W. A. Fischer II and B. Fischer *Harvard Business Review Digital Articles* p2 O 2 2014

THE GIFT OF FEAR D. BRAZIER bw *Tricycle: The Buddhist Review* v27 no1 p52 Fall 2017

GLOSSARY *Lapham's Quarterly* v10 no3 p218 Summ 2017

How to Manage People Who Are Smarter than You R. Knight

Harvard Business Review Digital Articles p2 Ag 6 2015

Land of the Free, Home of the Brave M. Hamid color *Time* v188 no16/17 p68 O 24 2016

LEARNING TO SPEAK THE TRUTH D. HERNÁNDEZ bw *Tricycle: The Buddhist Review* v27 no1 p55 Fall 2017

MISCELLANY *Lapham's Quarterly* v10 no3 p212 Summ 2017

New-Year Trump Fears J. LILEKS *National Review* v69 no1 p33 Ja 23 2017

Persuasion Depends Mostly on the Audience T. Chamorro-Premuzic *Harvard Business Review Digital Articles* p2 Je 2 2015

PETRIFIED FOREST L. H. Lapham *Lapham's Quarterly* v10 no3 p12 Summ 2017

Pour Out Light Unshadowed M. R. Simone *America* v216 no7 p52 Ap 3 2017

A prenatal sequence to Worry less and trust more A. Owens color *Yoga Journal* no294 p69 S 2017

Road Trip, Bad Romance, Future Fashionista L. KOGAN cartoon *O, The Oprah Magazine* p44 F 2017

A SAFE CONTAINER FOR FEAR: WHEN YOU EMBRACE YOUR EMOTIONAL EXPERIENCE, ANXIETY FADES AWAY J. KORDA bw *Tricycle: The Buddhist Review* v27 no1 p64 Fall 2017

Survey Shows Americans Fear Ghosts, the Government, and Each Other C. POPPY *Skeptical Inquirer* v41 no1 p16 Ja/F 2017

THOROUGHBREDS ARE MADE FOR EVENTING H. Payne Caravella and N. Jaffer color *Practical Horseman* v45 no2 p40 F 2017

What are you afraid of? *Redbook* p136 Mr 2017

What Are You Afraid Of? R. MAURER *Psychology Today* v49 no5 p50 S/O 2016

WHAT GREEN TARA CAN TEACH US ABOUT FEAR: A CALMING EXERCISE M. CLAVIJO bw *Tricycle: The Buddhist Review* v27 no1 p60 Fall 2017

You worry constantly K. Holcombe color *Yoga Journal* p46 2016 Special Issue

FEAR, DAVID

The Breakout Star of 'Atlanta' color *Rolling Stone* no1293 p22 Ag 10 2017

Hot Actor Joe Alwyn color *Rolling Stone* no1274 p41 N 17 2016

Hot Cringe Queen Phoebe Waller-Bridge color *Rolling Stone* no1274 p43 N 17 2016

Fear of clowns

America's New Clown Panic M. Chan color *Time* v188 no15 p9 O 17 2016

Fears of a Clown M. HEMINGWAY color *Weekly Standard* v22 no10 p5 N 14 2016

Return of the Phantom Clowns B. RADFORD *Skeptical Inquirer* v41 no1 p8 Ja/F 2017

Fear of contamination

Don't Take This Quiz Before Bed A. CLAYBOURNE color diag *National Geographic Kids* no474 p20 O 2017

From the publisher P. W. Marty *Christian Century* v134 no3 p3 F 2017

Fear the Walking Dead (TV program)

ALSO COMING... A. D'Arminio *TV Guide* v65 no23 p31 My 29 2017

FEAR THE WALKING DEAD R. Moynihan *TV Guide* v64 no15 p51 Ap 4 2016

Fear the Walking Dead's Next Steps D. Ross color *Entertainment Weekly* no1468/1469 p93 Je 2-9 2017

WHAT TO WATCH R. Rahman, A. Wilkinson et al color *Entertainment Weekly* no1468/1469 p68 Je 2-9 2017

Fear—Economic aspects

Why Deutsche Bank Is Spooking the Markets G. Smith color *Time* v188 no15 p7 O 17 2016

Fearnley-Whittingstall, Hugh

River Cottage A to Z: Our Favourite Ingredients and How to Cook Them *Publishers Weekly* v264 no1 p51 Ja 2 2017

Fearon, James D.

Civil War & the Current International System chart graph *Daedalus* v146 no4 p18 Fall 2017

Fearon Hay Architects Ltd.

Halo Effect B. CARTER *Architectural Record* v205 no10 p70 O 2017

Fear—Physiological aspects

Master Log (& Other) Obstacles C. ANDERSON and J. F. MEY-

ER color *Horse & Rider* v56 no11 p96 N 2017

SCARED TO DEATH W. Cannon *Lapham's Quarterly* v10 no3 p176 Summ 2017

Fear—Political aspects

STEVE BIKO WITH THE BRUTAL TRUTH *Lapham's Quarterly* v10 no3 p171 Summ 2017

THE VICTORY OF A FEARFUL AMERICA S. GILMORE color *Maclean's* v129 no46 p38 N 21 2016

Fear—Psychological aspects

FEARS FOUNDED AND UNFOUNDED S. Freud *Lapham's Quarterly* v10 no3 p114 Summ 2017

IN SEARCH OF FEAR P. Petit *Lapham's Quarterly* v10 no3 p214 Summ 2017

LAND OF DARKNESS Suki Kim *Lapham's Quarterly* v10 no3 p205 Summ 2017

Not an Act *Lapham's Quarterly* v10 no3 p216 Summ 2017

Fear—Religious aspects—Christianity

Fear Not! color *America* v215 no19 p5 D 19 2016

Hate confession? J. Martin *America* v216 no5 p70 Mr 6 2017

Reflections on the lectionary M. M. White *Christian Century* v134 no15 p21 Jl 19 2017

Fear—Research

THE AGE OF FEAR N. STRAUSS color *Rolling Stone* no1272 p42 O 20 2016

Fear—Social aspects

THE AGE OF FEAR N. STRAUSS color *Rolling Stone* no1272 p42 O 20 2016

Hate Incidents Sow Fear Across U.S C. Alter and J. Sanburn color *Time* v189 no9 p13 Mr 13 2017

A SUGAR CUBE BESIDE A GALLON OF COFFEE F. PELLE-TIER chart color *Maclean's* v130 no6 p17 Jl 2017

Feast of the Holy Innocents

In the communion of saints P. Gallagher color *U.S. Catholic* v81 no12 p31 D 2016

FEASTER, FELICIA

Art Watch: Three artists moving the Atlanta art scene forward *Atlanta* v57 no6 p76 O 2017

FASHION TO PHOTOS: Atlanta style icons Sid and Ann Mashburn shine a light on photography *Atlanta* v57 no6 p34 O 2017

Feathers

Emergent cellular self-organization and mechanosensation initiate follicle pattern in the avian skin A. E. Shyer, A. R. Rodrigues et al color *Science* v357 no6353 p811 Ag 25 2017

Photos from the Field *Mother Earth News* no280 p112 F/Mr 2017

Featherstone, Liza

All the Rage color *Nation* v305 no5 p5 Ag 28 2017

Asking for a Friend color *Nation* v304 no5 p5 F 20 2017

Asking for a Friend color *Nation* v33 no21 p5 N 21 2017

Bad at Doing Good color *Nation* v304 no16 p5 My 22 2017

BDS(M) Drama color il *Nation* v304 no3 p5 Ja 30 2017

The Dating Game il *Nation* v303 no17 p7 O 24 2016

Driving Lessons color *Nation* v305 no3 p5 Jl 31 2017

Hangover Politics diag *Nation* v305 no1 p5 Jl 3 2017

Lack of Means Doesn't Justify End color *Nation* v305 no10 p5 O 23 2017

Naming Names color *Nation* v304 no9 p5 Mr 20 2017

Party Rules il *Nation* v305 no7 p5 S 25 2017

FEATHERSTONE, STEVE

PROFESSOR CARNAGE color *New Republic* v248 no5 p20 My 2017

Feaver, Peter

Not Too Cold, Not Too Hot color *Weekly Standard* v23 no2 p10 S 18 2017

Saving Realism from the So-Called Realists: A foreign-policy approach based in security and pragmatism is now characterized by retrenchment and radicalism *Commentary* v144 no2 p15 S 2017

Should America Retrench? *Foreign Affairs* v95 no6 p164 N/D 2016

Trump and Terrorism color *Foreign Affairs* v96 no2 p28 Mr/Ap 2017

Febbraro, M.

Observation of coherent elastic neutrino-nucleus scattering diag *Science* v357 no6356 p1123 S 15 2017

FEBER, RUTH E.

Some Animals Are More Equal than Others: Wild Animal Welfare in the Media *BioScience* v67 no1 p62 Ja 2017

Febos, Melissa, 1980-

Tale of Two Fathers L. TANENBAUM *New York Times Book Review* p23 Mr 12 2017

Febos, Melissa, 1980—Interviews

There's a Reason We Don't Say Certain Things Out Loud J. Thomas-Kennedy color *Publishers Weekly* v263 no48 p58 N 28 2016

February (Month)

The Perils of an Early Spring J. Worland color *Time* v189 no10 p9 Mr 20 2017

February Revolution, Russia, 1917

KERENSKY IN HINDSIGHT: Alexander Kerensky, the last Russian premier before the Bolsheviks took power, decided to continue the war with Germany. He and his country would pay the price G. Darby *History Today* v67 no7 p48 Jl 2017

Feces

Go Ahead... Ask Us Anything M. Koziol cartoon *Popular Science* p90 Ja/F 2017

why poop changes N. PRENTIS *Parents* v92 no8 p130 Ag 2017

Feces examination

No Relief T. DAJER color *Discover* v38 no7 p22 S 2017

Fecher, Benedikt

A nod to public open access infrastructures *Science* v356 no6344 p1242 Je 23 2017

Fecht, Sarah

anatomy of a hurricane color *Popular Science* v289 no4 p12 Jl/Ag 2017

THE AQUANAUTS cartoon *Popular Science* v289 no2 p47 Mr/Ap 2017

The Drone Catcher color *Popular Science* v288 no6 p64 N/D 2016

a machine that pulls water from thin air. literally cartoon *Popular Science* v289 no2 p20 Mr/Ap 2017

on a space walk, flying blind cartoon *Popular Science* v289 no5 p78 S/O 2017

staring into Earth's past cartoon *Popular Science* v289 no5 p20 S/O 2017

Feder, Toni

Climate change research cut as Canada focuses on mitigation: Barring a reversal, government-academia research networks will lapse and facilities in the high Arctic will shut down *Physics Today* v70 no9 p28 S 2017

Climate-data rescue efforts gear up *Physics Today* v70 no3 p31 Mr 2017

College-level project-based learning gains popularity *Physics Today* v70 no6 p26 Je 2017

Courtroom forensic evidence often lacks scientific validity, report finds *Physics Today* v69 no11 p32 N 2016

Despite financial squeeze, Japan continues drive to globalize its science enterprise *Physics Today* v70 no1 p24 Ja 2017

An electron- proton collider could bridge the gap between the LHC and its successor *Physics Today* v70 no5 p29 My 2017

Extragalactic survey aims to shed light on dark energy *Physics Today* v69 no10 p28 O 2016

Fates of two big radio dishes hang in the balance *Physics Today* v70 no2 p26 F 2017

Hobby-Eberly Telescope eyes sky with new capabilities *Physics Today* v70 no6 p36 Je 2017

Massive machine gears up to weigh nearly massless particles: An experiment in Germany looks for missing electron energy to infer neutrino rest mass *Physics Today* v70 no8 p26 Ag 2017

Middle East synchrotron light source is set to start up *Physics Today* v69 no12 p32 D 2016

Patent work blends science, business, and law *Physics Today* v70 no10 p36 O 2017

Pulsar timing arrays are poised to reveal gravitational waves: Radio observatories are accumulating data to detect mergers of supermassive black holes *Physics Today* v70 no7 p26 Jl 2017

Theory institute opens residence hall for visitors *Physics Today* v70 no4 p32 Ap 2017

Turmoil in Turkey hits science *Physics Today* v69 no12 p30 D 2016

Two-year colleges teach physics to widening range of students *Physics Today* v69 no11 p26 N 2016

UK science mired in uncertainty about Brexit *Physics Today* v70 no3 p24 Mr 2017

Undergraduate labs lag in science and technology *Physics Today* v70 no4 p26 Ap 2017

US academic fusion researchers sound alarm *Physics Today* v70 no5 p32 My 2017

Federal aid
See also
Federal aid to libraries
Federal aid to research

Federal aid to agricultural research
BIG SHIFT IN RESEARCH *Successful Farming* v115 no4 p14 Mr 2017

Federal aid to early childhood education
INEQUALITY IN EARLY CHILDHOOD AND EFFECTIVE PUBLIC POLICY INTERVENTIONS *Economic Indicators* p153 S 2016

Federal aid to education—United States
The Pros and Cons of Federally Funded School Choice Programs B. DeVos, P. Murray et al *Congressional Digest* v96 no7 p12 S 2017

Federal aid to higher education
Brazil Has a School Problem F. Moura and J. Brice diag *Bloomberg Businessweek* no4513 p24 Mr 6 2017

Federal aid to libraries
Follow the (Grant) Money B. Kenney *Publishers Weekly* v263 no42 p21 O 17 2016

Federal aid to medical research
Critics challenge NIH finding that bigger labs aren't necessarily better J. Kaiser color *Science* v356 no6342 p997 Je 9 2017

Federal aid to medical research—United States
Congress votes on sweeping biomedical bill J. Kaiser, J. Mervis et al color *Science* v354 no6316 p1085 D 2 2016

Publish and Perish R. HARRIS *Issues in Science & Technology* v33 no4 p29 Summ 2017

Federal aid to research
Brazil scientists brace for harder times color *Science* v357 no6348 p232 Jl 21 2017

EYE ON 45 color *Science* v357 no6353 p739 Ag 25 2017

Federal share of basic research hits new low J. Mervis graph *Science* v355 no6329 p1005 Mr 10 2017

Priorities for Jumpstarting the U.S. Industrial Economy D. Barton and B. J. Katz *Harvard Business Review Digital Articles* p2 F 2 2015

Federal aid to science education
India marches for science color *Science* v357 no6352 p628 Ag 18 2017

Federal budgets
The Budget Battle Shows That Trump Needs to Read the Fine Print P. Elliott, S. Frizell et al color *Time* v189 no18 p11 My 15 2017

A Budget for the Rest of Us J. BLEIFUSS *In These Times* v41 no7 p5 Jl 2017

CHURCH LEADERS SCRUTINIZE BUDGET AND HEALTH CARE PRIORITIES K. Clarke color graph *America* v216 no13 p12 Je 12 2017

A Debt to Posterity J. Cost cartoon *Weekly Standard* v22 no29 p17 Ap 3 2017

The Federal Budget Should Be an Opportunity for Reconciliation *America* v216 no13 p8 Je 12 2017

Fund global health: Save lives and money A. P. Galvani, M. C. Fitzpatrick et al color *Science* v356 no6342 p1018 Je 9 2017

Life at Trump Pavilion M. PILON color *New Republic* v248 no7 p12 Jl 2017

Shortsighted priorities J. Berg color *Science* v356 no6341 p887 Je 1 2017

Trump Budget Renews Call to Eliminate Arts, Library Funding A. Albanese *Publishers Weekly* v264 no22 p14 My 29 2017

Federal government
See also
Confederation of states

The Most Important Work M. Funkhouser *Governing* v31 no1 p4 O 2017

Ready to Resist Miyoko Sakashita *Earth Island Journal* v32 no1 p56 Spr 2017

Research: Opposition to Federal Spending Is Driven by Racial Resentment K. Krimmel and K. Rader *Harvard Business Review Digital Articles* p2 S 1 2017

Schumer's Losing This One F. Barnes color *Weekly Standard* v22 no47 p14 Ag 21 2017

Federal government—Mexico
Mexico's ambiguous invasive species plan L. M. Ochoa-Ochoa, O. A. Flores-Villela et al bibl *Science* v355 no6329 p1033 Mr 10 2017

Federal government—United States
3 Big Economic Ideas in Waiting R. Litan *Harvard Business Review Digital Articles* p2 O 9 2014

Federal Rulemaking Process *Congressional Digest* v96 no4 p3 Ap 2017

Fractured Federalism: It's hard to tell who's in charge of what in American government these days P. A. Harkness *Governing* v30 no12 p16 S 2017

Modern Federalism's Big 3 Moments: There's been a sea change in the way levels of government deal with each other D. F. Kettl *Governing* v31 no1 p16 O 2017

WILL THERE BE AN INTERNAL REVOLT AGAINST TRUMP? T. Troy color *Commentary* v143 no2 p12 F 2017

Federal government—United States—History
30 Years Later A. Ehrenhalt *Governing* v31 no1 p26 O 2017

Federal judges
See also
Supreme Court justices (U.S.)

The Judiciary: Realigning the Courts P. M. Barrett graph *Bloomberg Businessweek* no4530 p41 Jl 17 2017

Federal Laboratory Consortium (U.S.)
Patents and Awards *Science & Technology Review* p24 Mr 2017

A Tradition of Technological Breakthroughs with Commercial Success *Science & Technology Review* p3 Je 2017

Federal law enforcement agents
PARODY color *Weekly Standard* v22 no26 p40 Mr 13 2017

Federal prosecutors
THIS TIME, IT'S PERSONAL J. Toobin cartoon *New Yorker* v93 no23 p19 Ag 7 2017

Federal Reserve Bank of Minneapolis—Officials & employees
Neel Kashkari M. Boesler and J. Smialek color *Bloomberg Businessweek* no4527 p92 Je 19 2017

Federal Reserve banks—Management
The Push and Pull Of Politics P. Coy cartoon *Bloomberg Businessweek* no4493 p22 O 3 2016

Federal Reserve monetary policy
Is There a Better Way to Take Aim at Inflation? P. Coy *Bloomberg Businessweek* no4525 p13 Je 5 2017

Federal aid to education—Charts, diagrams, etc.
Timeline of Federal Support for K-12 Education: Evolution of U.S. Elementary and Secondary Education Policy *Congressional Digest* v96 no7 p3 S 2017

Federalist Society for Law & Public Policy Studies (U.S.)
FULL-COURT PRESS J. TOOBIN cartoon color *New Yorker* v93 no9 p24 Ap 17 2017

Federer, Roger, 1981-
Artist IN RESIDENCE [Cover story] L. J. Wertheim color *Sports Illustrated* v127 no6 p32 Ag 28 2017

Eighth WONDER L. J. Wertheim color *Sports Illustrated* v127 no3 p58 Jl 24 2017

For the Record color *Time* v190 no5 p9 Jl 31 2017

HEART OF THE CITY: Roger Federer's connection to New York is unmistakable, both on and off the court A. Wintour, b. E. McGrogan et al color *Tennis* v53 no5 p42 S/O 2017

A Hero's Welcome *Tennis* v52 no6 p14 N/D 2016

Man Out of Time S. Gregory color diag *Time* v189 no5 p42 F 13 2017

Marquee Attraction C. Evert bw color *Tennis* v53 no5 p4 S/O 2017

PEAK FEDERER [Cover story] R. BALDWIN bw color *GQ: Gentlemen's Quarterly* v97 no4 p82 Ap 2017

POLAROIDS BY WARHOL color *GQ: Gentlemen's Quarterly* v97 no4 p138 Ap 2017

Roger's New Chapter S. TIGNOR *Tennis* v53 no4 p80 Jl/Ag 2017

Top of His Game T. PERROTTA color *Weekly Standard* v22 no44 p37 Jl 31 2017

THE U.S. OPEN WONDER YEAR [Cover story] P. de Jonge *New York Times Magazine* p31 Ag 27 2017

Federer, Roger, 1981——Awards
WON FOR THE AGED L. J. Wertheim color *Sports Illustrated* v126 no5 p60 F 13 2017

Federico, C.

Seasonal exposure of carbon dioxide ice on the nucleus of comet 67P/Churyumov-Gerasimenko bibl bw graph *Science* v354 no6319 p1563 D 23 2016

Federman, Adam

Good Appetite: For the influential culinary writer Patience Gray, the best recipes began with plants and fish and the seasons L. SHAPIRO *New York Times Book Review* p14 S 24 2017

FedEx Corp.

SCORECARD G. CHUNG color *Forbes* v198 no6 p30 N 8 2016

Fedin, Igor

Direct optical lithography of functional inorganic nanomaterials diag graph *Science* v357 no6349 p385 Jl 28 2017

Fedyk, Anastassia

How to Tell If Machine Learning Can Solve Your Business Problem *Harvard Business Review Digital Articles* p2 N 15 2016

Research: How Investors' Reading Habits Influence Stock Prices *Harvard Business Review Digital Articles* p2 S 2 2016

Fee, Brian

Cars 3 Makes Career Anxiety (Almost) Fun S. Zacharek color *Time* v189 no24 p50 Je 26 2017

CARS 3 M. Snetiker color *Entertainment Weekly* no1463/1464 p50 Ap/My 2017

Fee, David

Volcanic tremor and plume height hysteresis from Pavlof Volcano, Alaska bibl graph *Science* v355 no6320 p1 Ja 6 2017

Fee for service (Medical fees)

PRICE FIX A. Davidson cartoon *New Yorker* v93 no15 p19 My 29 2017

Feed the Beast (TV program)

David Schwimmer C. Ianzito color *AARP: The Magazine* v59 no6A p80 O/N 2016

Feedback (Psychology)

3 Situations Where Cross-Cultural Communication Breaks Down G. Toegel and Barsoux *Harvard Business Review Digital Articles* p2 Je 8 2016

Circles, figure numbers, and our buddy Lou N. Besougloff *Model Railroader* v84 no6 p8 Je 2017

The Difference Between Coaching Rookies and Veterans L. Wiseman *Harvard Business Review Digital Articles* p2 Mr 2 2015

Don't Let Your Brain's Defense Mechanisms Thwart Effective Feedback J. R. Detert and E. R. Burris *Harvard Business Review Digital Articles* p2 Ag 18 2016

Employee Suggestion Schemes Don't Have to Be Exercises in Futility E. R. Burris *Harvard Business Review Digital Articles* p2 Ja 26 2016

Feedback Without Measurement Won't Do Any Good M. Schrage *Harvard Business Review Digital Articles* p2 Ag 5 2015

The Gender Gap in Feedback and Self-Perception R. Mayo *Harvard Business Review Digital Articles* p2 Ag 31 2016

Give Your Team More-Effective Positive Feedback C. Porath *Harvard Business Review Digital Articles* p2 O 25 2016

Giving Effective Feedback When You're Short on Time D. W. Dowling *Harvard Business Review Digital Articles* p2 F 16 2015

Giving Feedback When You're Conflict Averse A. J. Su *Harvard Business Review Digital Articles* p2 Ag 13 2015

How to Ask for Feedback That Will Actually Help You P. Bregman *Harvard Business Review Digital Articles* p2 D 5 2014

How to Deliver Criticism So Employees Pay Attention D. Bright color *Harvard Business Review Digital Articles* p2 Ja 17 2017

How to Get Feedback as a Freelancer S. King *Harvard Business Review Digital Articles* p2 Ag 19 2015

How to Get Feedback When No One Is Volunteering It K. Willyerd and B. Mistick *Harvard Business Review Digital Articles* p2 Ag 14 2015

How to Get the Feedback You Need C. O'Hara *Harvard Business Review Digital Articles* p2 My 15 2015

How to Give an Employee Feedback About Their Appearance A. Gallo *Harvard Business Review Digital Articles* p2 My 26 2017

How to Give Feedback to People Who Cry, Yell, or Get Defensive Amy Jen Su *Harvard Business Review Digital Articles* p2 S 21 2016

How to Give Feedback to Someone Who Gets Crazy Defensive H. Weeks *Harvard Business Review Digital Articles* p2 Ag 12 2015

How to Give Negative Feedback Over Email J. K. Glei *Harvard Business Review Digital Articles* p2 O 7 2016

How to Give Negative Feedback When Your Organization Is "Nice" J. Porter *Harvard Business Review Digital Articles* p2 Mr 14 2016

How to Give Tough Feedback That Helps People Grow M. Valcour *Harvard Business Review Digital Articles* p2 Ag 11 2015

How to Handle Negative Feedback D. Grote *Harvard Business Review Digital Articles* p2 Ag 17 2015

How to Improve at Work When You're Not Getting Feedback J. Zenger and J. Folkman *Harvard Business Review Digital Articles* p2 My 9 2017

How to Make Feedback Feel Normal J. Grenny *Harvard Business Review Digital Articles* p2 Ag 19 2016

Is How You Deliver Feedback Doing More Harm than Good? T. Chamorro-Premuzic *Harvard Business Review Digital Articles* p2 Ag 10 2015

The Key to Giving and Receiving Negative Feedback J. Grenny *Harvard Business Review Digital Articles* p2 Ag 6 2015

Learning to walk in another's shoes H. Gehlbach color *Phi Delta Kappan* v98 no6 p8 Mr 2017

Make It OK for Employees to Challenge Your Ideas H. Gregersen *Harvard Business Review Digital Articles* p2 My 6 2015

Managing On-Demand Talent J. Younger and N. Smallwood *Harvard Business Review Digital Articles* p2 Ja 28 2016

Match Your Motivational Tactic to the Situation J. Schroeder and A. Fishbach *Harvard Business Review Digital Articles* p2 Ja 8 2016

No, That Meeting Could Not Have Been an Email D. Burkus *Harvard Business Review Digital Articles* p2 Ap 21 2015

Should CEOs Respond When Employees Complain About Them Online? S. Clayton color *Harvard Business Review Digital Articles* p2 Ap 3 2017

Understanding When to Give Feedback *Harvard Business Review Digital Articles* p2 D 4 2014

Use Subtle Cues to Encourage Better Meetings J. Cohen *Harvard Business Review Digital Articles* p2 S 12 2016

Using Harsh Feedback to Fuel Your Career W. Treseder color *Harvard Business Review Digital Articles* p2 O 12 2016

What to Do After a Bad Performance Review C. O'Hara *Harvard Business Review Digital Articles* p2 O 29 2014

WHAT WILL YOU BE DOING THIS WINTER? color *Seventeen* v76 no12 p12 D 2016/Ja 2017

When Giving Critical Feedback, Focus on Your Nonverbal Cues E. Seppala color *Harvard Business Review Digital Articles* p2 Ja 20 2017

When It's OK to Ignore Feedback D. Clark *Harvard Business Review Digital Articles* p2 Ag 4 2015

When to Give Feedback in a Group and When to Do It One-on-One R. Schwarz *Harvard Business Review Digital Articles* p2 Ag 19 2015

Feeding America (Organization)

LEIGHTON MEESTER FIGHTS HUNGER M. L. Lenker color *Entertainment Weekly* no1477 p17 Ag 11 2017

Feeding behavior in animals

See also

Predation (Biology)

Diet Does Matter In OCD Development S. Wenholz color *Practical Horseman* v45 no6 p76 Je 2017

FED UP K. MOORE color *Natural History* v125 no11 p2 N 2017

Lunch Breaks L. E. Ogden bw *Natural History* v125 no11 p8 N 2017

PHOTO OF LASTING INTEREST *Reader's Digest* v189 no1128 p28 Mr 2017

real vampires of planet earth [Cover story] S. Milius color graph *Science News* v192 no7 p22 O 28 2017

The Secret Lives of Birds R. KWOK *Audubon* v119 no2 p18 Summ 2017

WHALE CULTURE P. Hammond, S. Heinrich et al color graph *Natural History* v125 no11 p30 N 2017

Feeds

See also

Hay as feed

6 FREQUENTLY ASKED QUESTIONS BY THE TIME-TRAVELING NATURE LOVER S. MUIR *Orion Magazine* v35 no6 p6 N/D 2016

Bears G. TARLACH bw color *Discover* v38 no10 p74 D 2017

News BITS color *Practical Horseman* v45 no2 p64 F 2017

Feedstock

Turn Food Scraps Into POULTRY FEASTS J. Salatin *Mother Earth News* no281 p99 Ap/My 2017

Feehley, Taylor

Neonatal acquisition of Clostridia species protects against colonization by bacterial pathogens diag *Science* v356 no6335 p315 Ap 21 2017

Feek, Rory

Rory Feek color *Publishers Weekly* v264 no8 p9 F 20 2017

Feeley, Jef

The Lawsuits Keep Coming for J&J bw *Bloomberg Businessweek* no4514 p21 Mr 13 2017

St. Louis Loses Favor With Plaintiffs cartoon *Bloomberg Businessweek* no4532 p16 Jl 31 2017

FEELEY, KENNETH J.

The Extinction Risk and Conservation Status of Most National Plants Are Unknown *BioScience* v67 no9 p782 S 2017

Feeley, Mark

Posthole color *Powder* v45 no4 p146 D 2016

Feeley, Thomas W.

Health Care Providers Need a Value Management Office *Harvard Business Review Digital Articles* p2 D 2 2015

Feeney, Denis

Found in Translation G. Hays color *New York Review of Books* v64 no11 p56 Je 22 2017

FEENEY, MATTHEW

Protecting Privacy color *Weekly Standard* v22 no48 p40 S 4 2017

Unmanned Aerial Vehicles: Friend or Foe? *USA Today Magazine* v145 no2862 p36 Mr 2017

Feeney, Megan

Proposed Endangered Species Delisting of Yellowstone Grizzly Bears *American Forests* v122 no3 p15 Fall 2016

Feeney, Nolan

10 ARTISTS WHO WILL RULE 2017 color *Entertainment Weekly* no1450 p56 Ja 27 2017

1963 - 2016 GEORGE MICHAEL color *Entertainment Weekly* no1448 p28 Ja 13 2017

THE 25-WORD REVIEW color *Entertainment Weekly* no1463/1464 p104 Ap/My 2017

3 ROUNDS WITH HANSON color *Entertainment Weekly* no1467 p40 My 26 2017

4 THINGS YOU DIDN'T SEE AT THE GRAMMYS color *Entertainment Weekly* no1454/1455 p16 F 24 2017

7 HIP-HOP QUEENS TO HEAR NOW color *Entertainment Weekly* no1435 p57 O 14 2016

And the Winner Is... chart color *Entertainment Weekly* no1451/1452 p26 F 3-10 2017

BACKSTREET'S BACK, ALL RIGHT! color *Entertainment Weekly* no1454/1455 p58 F 24 2017

THE BEST ALBUMS OF 2017 (SO FAR) color *Entertainment Weekly* no1468/1469 p98 Je 2-9 2017

Bruno Mars color *Entertainment Weekly* no1441 p55 N 25 2016

CHARLI XCX *Entertainment Weekly* no1446/1447 p75 D 2016/Ja 2017

Chris Cornell color *Entertainment Weekly* no1468/1469 p20 Je 2-9 2017

COOL GIRL INTERRUPTED color *Entertainment Weekly* no1438 p28 N 4 2016

DJ KHALED color *Entertainment Weekly* no1471 p60 Je 23 2017

DRAGONETTE DANCE THE PAIN AWAY color *Entertainment Weekly* no1440 p59 N 18 2016

Emma Bunton color *Entertainment Weekly* no1472 p50 Je 30 2017

FAT JOE & REMY MA GO "ALL THE WAY UP" color *Entertainment Weekly* no1454/1455 p96 F 24 2017

Fifty Shades' Top 40 Freakfest color *Entertainment Weekly* no1453 p56 F 17 2017

THE GOLDEN AGE OF HAIM color *Entertainment Weekly* no1467 p32 My 26 2017

Grizzly Bear's Vital New Tunes color *Entertainment Weekly* no1477 p57 Ag 11 2017

HAIM color *Entertainment Weekly* no1446/1447 p70 D 2016/Ja 2017

THE HEIRS APPARENT color *Entertainment Weekly* no1471 p63 Je 23 2017

INSIDE LADY GAGA'S SUPER-SECRET SUPER BOWL SET color *Entertainment Weekly* no1451/1452 p14 F 3-10 2017

JENS LEKMAN *Entertainment Weekly* no1446/1447 p72 D 2016/ Ja 2017

John Legend Shows His Soul color *Entertainment Weekly* no1443 p58 D 9 2016

JUKEBOX JURY SONG OF THE SUMMER EDITION color *Entertainment Weekly* no1467 p38 My 26 2017

JULIA MICHAELS color *Entertainment Weekly* no1446/1447 p74 D 2016/Ja 2017

KELLY CLARKSON color *Entertainment Weekly* no1446/1447 p76 D 2016/Ja 2017

Kenny Chesney color *Entertainment Weekly* no1438 p59 N 4 2016

Khalid's Teenage Dream color *Entertainment Weekly* no1456 p65 Mr 10 2017

THE KILLERS' WONDERFUL RETURN color *Entertainment Weekly* no1472 p56 Je 30 2017

Kurt Cobain, Remembered color *Entertainment Weekly* no1454/1455 p97 F 24 2017

KYLE color *Entertainment Weekly* no1462 p61 Ap 21 2017

Lady Gaga COMES DOWN to EARTH color *Entertainment Weekly* no1434 p26 O 7 2016

Leonard Cohen 1934-2016 color *Entertainment Weekly* no1441 p12 N 25 2016

The LIBERATION of JOJO color *Entertainment Weekly* no1436/1437 p30 O 21 2016

Lizzo's Feel-Good Revolution color *Entertainment Weekly* no1435 p56 O 14 2016

Lorde color *Entertainment Weekly* no1471 p62 Je 23 2017

LORDE: POP'S REIGNING DRAMA QUEEN color *Entertainment Weekly* no1468/1469 p102 Je 2-9 2017

Lorde Returns With the Year's First Great Pop Anthem color *Entertainment Weekly* no1457/1458 p93 Mr 17 2017

MAGGIE ROGERS color *Entertainment Weekly* no1454/1455 p95 F 24 2017

MUSIC color *Entertainment Weekly* no1444/1445 p88 D 16 2016

NORAH JONES color *Entertainment Weekly* no1434 p55 O 7 2016

One Direction? Try 5 Directions color *Entertainment Weekly* no1477 p58 Ag 11 2017

THE RACE TO FIND THE NEXT ONE DIRECTION color *Entertainment Weekly* no1478 / 1479 p22 Ag 18-25 2017

Rekindle Your Crush on Jennifer Paige color *Entertainment Weekly* no1462 p62 Ap 21 2017

REY OF LIGHT color *Entertainment Weekly* no1474/1475 p114 Jl 21-28 2017

THE SECRET INGREDIENTS OF LITTLE MIX color *Entertainment Weekly* no1441 p55 N 25 2016

Sia's Acting Encore color *Entertainment Weekly* no1436/1437 p100 O 21 2016

SIGRID color *Entertainment Weekly* no1465 p53 My 12 2017

This Host Is on Fire! color *Entertainment Weekly* no1451/1452 p28 F 3-10 2017

Timbaland color *Entertainment Weekly* no1460/1461 p96 Ap 7-17 2017

THE TRANSFORMATION OF KATY PERRY color *Entertainment Weekly* no1467 p28 My 26 2017

TWO COURSES WITH Chrissy Teigen color *Entertainment Weekly* no1443 p40 D 9 2016

Two Rock Icons Hop on a Conference Call... color *Entertainment Weekly* no1473 p56 Jl 7 2017

Tyler Glenn's Rebirth color *Entertainment Weekly* no1439 p58 N 11 2016

THE ULTIMATE 2016 ALBUM SWAP color *Entertainment Weekly* no1446/1447 p116 D 2016/Ja 2017

THE ULTIMATE SUMMER SINGLES SWAP color *Entertainment Weekly* no1477 p54 Ag 11 2017

WAXAHATCHEE color *Entertainment Weekly* no1476 p61 Ag 4 2017

What to Stream color *Entertainment Weekly* no1477 p57 Ag 11 2017

WHO'S THAT GIRL? color *Entertainment Weekly* no1465 p54 My 12 2017

The xx color *Entertainment Weekly* no1449 p56 Ja 20 2017

Zara Larsson Is Wide A-Woke color *Entertainment Weekly* no1457/1458 p94 Mr 17 2017

Fehder, Dan

The Top 20 Start-Up Accelerators in the U.S *Harvard Business Review Digital Articles* p2 Mr 31 2015

Fehr Cab Interiors Co.
NEW LIFE FOR WORN CABS: REPLACE DILAPIDATED INTERIORS IN HOURS WITH PREFORMED KITS T. Gaines *Successful Farming* v115 no9 p34 Ag 2017

Fehrenbacher, Katie
THE 2017 Fortune Crystal Ball color diag *Fortune* v174 no7 p11 D 1 2016
THE REVOLUTION STARTS HERE color *Fortune* v174 no7 p26 D 1 2016
Warren Buffett's All-In Clean-Energy Bet color diag map *Fortune* v174 no8 p158 D 15 2016
Wind Is Getting Really, Really Cheap color diag *Fortune* v174 no6 p16 N 1 2016

FEHRMAN, CRAIG
"A VERY LIMITED PLAYER" *Cincinnati Magazine* v50 no12 p66 S 2017
The Best Words: A Hoosier author writes what may be the definitive account of the 2016 election color *Indianapolis Monthly* v41 no2 p25 S 2017
Black History *Indianapolis Monthly* p23 F 2017
Bloody Good: The reigning king of "grit lit," Hoosier author Frank Bill returns with his third novel, The Savage *Indianapolis Monthly* p29 N 2017
ENCYCLOPEDIA CINCINNATI bw cartoon color *Cincinnati Magazine* v51 no1 p42 O 2017
Home Court *Indianapolis Monthly* p60 N 2017
LOUD & CLEAR bw color *Cincinnati Magazine* v51 no1 p74 O 2017
MINT CONDITION *Cincinnati Magazine* v50 no4 p28 Ja 2017
Off-Court Issues *Indianapolis Monthly* v40 no7 p51 Mr 2017
THE OLD COLLEGE TRY *Cincinnati Magazine* v50 no2 p17 N 2016
PACKING HIS BAGGAGE *Indianapolis Monthly* v40 no5 p46 Ja 2017
PARTY OF ONE *Cincinnati Magazine* v50 no8 p17 My 2017
Roxane Gay *Indianapolis Monthly* v40 no5 p19 Ja 2017
SLING STATE *Cincinnati Magazine* v50 no2 p20 N 2016
SURVEY SAYS *Cincinnati Magazine* v50 no5 p20 F 2017

Fei, Huilong
Three-dimensional holey-graphene/niobia composite architectures for ultrahigh-rate energy storage color diag graph *Science* v356 no6338 p599 My 12 2017

Fei Yan
Suppressing relaxation in superconducting qubits by quasiparticle pumping bibl graph *Science* v354 no6319 p1573 D 23 2016

FEIEREISEN, SHARON
Pick the Right Food for Every Task color *Reader's Digest* v190 no1135 p35 N 2017

FEIFER, GREGORY
The Best-Laid Plans: A new history argues that the Bolshevik Revolution was largely a matter of chance *New York Times Book Review* p14 Je 11 2017

Feig, Andrew L.
Using Longitudinal Data on Career Outcomes to Promote Improvements and Diversity in Graduate Education *Change* v48 no6 p42 N/D 2016

Feig, Paul, 1962-
GHOSTBUSTERS (2016) B. A. DuHamel color *Sound & Vision* v82 no3 p67 Ap 2017
Swimming Upstream: The advent of streaming film and television has brought untold freedom and opportunity to creators--and an unprecedented chance to get lost in the Peak TV shuffle D. Marchese img *New York* v50 no11 p111 My 29 2017

Feig, Vivian R.
Highly stretchable polymer semiconductor films through the nanoconfinement effect bibl graph *Science* v355 no6320 p1 Ja 6 2017

Feigenbaum, Evan A.
China and the World color *Foreign Affairs* v96 no1 p33 Ja/F 2017

FEIGHERY, GLEN
FROM THE ARCHIVES cartoon *Reason* v48 no10 p66 Mr 2017

Feild, Lewis, 1956-2016
True Champion N. Reid color *American Cowboy* v23 no4 p80 D 2016/Ja 2017

Feiler, Bruce—Interviews
Bruce Feiler N. Hopper color *Time* v189 no12 p64 Ap 3 2017

Feiling, Yang
Global roadless areas: Consider terrain color *Science* v355 no6332 p1381 Mr 31 2017

Feinberg, Danielle
BORN THIS WAY L. SOROKANICH, K. MACDONALD et al color *Popular Mechanics* p88 My 2017

Feinberg, David T.
How an Early Adopter of Electronic Health Records Uses Big Data *Harvard Business Review Digital Articles* p2 D 15 2016
Why This Health System Offers Refunds to Dissatisfied Patients *Harvard Business Review Digital Articles* p2 N 16 2016

Feinberg, Kenneth R., 1945-
LIVING BY The Word *Christian Century* v134 no12 p20 Je 7 2017

Feinberg, Richard
Aspirational Power: Brazil on the Long Road to Global Influence *Foreign Affairs* v95 no6 p185 N/D 2016
Beyond the Scandals: The Changing Context of Corruption in Latin America *Foreign Affairs* v96 no3 p166 My/Je 2017
China's Strategic Partnerships in Latin America: Case Studies of China's Oil Diplomacy in Argentina, Brazil, Mexico, and Venezuela, 1991–2015 *Foreign Affairs* v96 no3 p165 My/Je 2017
Creating Charismatic Bonds in Argentina: Letters to Juan and Eva Perón *Foreign Affairs* v95 no6 p184 N/D 2016
Cuba: Portfolio of Opportunities for Foreign Investment, 2016-17 *Foreign Affairs* v96 no2 p180 Mr/Ap 2017
Four Seasons in Havana *Foreign Affairs* v96 no3 p166 My/Je 2017
The Harper Era in Canadian Foreign Policy: Parliament, Politics, and Canada's Global Posture/Beyond Afghanistan: An International Security Agenda for Canada *Foreign Affairs* v96 no1 p167 Ja/F 2017
Home—So Different, So Appealing *Foreign Affairs* v96 no6 p163 N/D 2017
Latin America and the Caribbean 2030: Future Scenarios *Foreign Affairs* v96 no2 p179 Mr/Ap 2017
Left Behind: Chronic Poverty in Latin America and the Caribbean *Foreign Affairs* v96 no3 p167 My/Je 2017
The Organization of American States as the Advocate and Guardian of Democracy *Foreign Affairs* v95 no6 p183 N/D 2016
Peru: Staying the Course of Economic Success *Foreign Affairs* v96 no1 p169 Ja/F 2017
The Political Economy of China-Latin America Relations in the New Millennium: Brave New World *Foreign Affairs* v96 no2 p179 Mr/Ap 2017
Rebel Mother: My Childhood Chasing the Revolution *Foreign Affairs* v96 no3 p165 My/Je 2017
Reflections on Memory and Democracy *Foreign Affairs* v95 no6 p184 N/D 2016
Social Policies and Decentralization in Cuba: Change in the Context of Twenty-First-Century Latin America/Voces de cambio en el sector no estatal cubano (Voices of Change in the Cuban Private Sector)/The Cuban Affair *Foreign Affairs* v96 no6 p162 N/D 2017
Sólo así: Por una agenda ciudadana independiente (The Only Way: Toward an Independent Citizen Agenda) *Foreign Affairs* v96 no2 p180 Mr/Ap 2017
Toussaint Louverture: A Revolutionary Life *Foreign Affairs* v96 no1 p168 Ja/F 2017

Feinberg, Stephen A., 1960-
BIG GUN'S BIG FAIL S. Witt img *New York* v49 no23 p42 N 14 2016

FEINGOLD, RUSS
Our Legitimacy Crisis *Nation* v304 no11 p4 Ap 3 2017

FEINMAN TODD, BARBARA
CONFESSION OF A WASHINGTON GHOSTWRITER *Washingtonian Magazine* v52 no5 p64 F 2017

Feinstein, Dianne, 1933-
THE LIONESS IN WINTER G. SHEEHY and M. Tinoco bw color *Mother Jones* v42 no3 p34 My/Je 2017
The Pros and Cons of the President's Immigrant Travel Ban *Congressional Digest* v96 no3 p13 Mr 2017

Feinstein, Rochelle
The Artist's Artist A Rauschenberg Symposium color *Art in Amer-*

ica v105 no1 p44 Ja 2017

Feinstein, Susan

AHEAD OF THE PACK color *Consumer Reports* v81 no12 p12 D 2016

FEIRSTEIN, BRUCE

TOP SECRET: CONFIDENTIAL color *Vanity Fair* v59 no9 p136 S 2017

Feist, Johannes

Long-distance operator for energy transfer diag *Science* v357 no6358 p1357 S 29 2017

Feist, Leslie, 1976-

FEIST L. Greenblatt color *Entertainment Weekly* no1463/1464 p104 Ap/My 2017

Feit, Mike

you may be right color *U.S. Catholic* v81 no11 p5 N 2016

Feit Co.

BOOT UP N. Sullivan color *Esquire* p60 S 2017

FEITH, DAVID

After the Miracle *Commentary* v143 no4 p42 Ap 2017

Feith, Douglas J.

The Department of Pay-for-Slay: How the Palestinian Authority not only incites terrorist murder—but supports it with U.S. tax dollars *Commentary* v143 no4 p19 Ap 2017

Fejer, M. M.

A fully programmable 100-spin coherent Ising machine with all-to-all connections bibl diag graph *Science* v354 no6312 p614 N 4 2016

Fejklowicz, Kasia

MUSICIANS' GEAR GUIDE BEST OF THE 2017 NAMM SHOW color *Downbeat* v84 no4 p70 Ap 2017

Feklistov, Andrey

RNA polymerase motions during promoter melting color diag graph *Science* v356 no6340 p863 My 26 2017

Felbab-Brown, Vanda

Organized Crime, Illicit Economies, Civil Violence & International Order: More Complex Than You Think *Daedalus* v146 no4 p98 Fall 2017

Feld, Brad

LEADERS WHO GET HOW TO GIVE C. NICKISCH *Harvard Business Review Digital Articles* p12 Ja 1 2017

Feld, Kenneth

Ringmaster of the Universe K. VINTON color *Forbes* v198 no8 p50 D 20 2016

Feld, Stuart P.

A William Henry Rinehart Leander comes to the surface bw color *Magazine Antiques* v184 no5 p54 S/O 2017

Felder, Rachel

home & help img *New York* p96 Mr 6 2017

Felder, Richard M.

Teaching and Learning STEM: A Practical Guide S. Chasteen *Physics Today* v70 no5 p57 My 2017

FELDHEIM, BENJAMIN

WHY We LOVE CHICAGO bw cartoon color *Chicago* v66 no3 p75 Mr 2017

FELDMAN, AMY

Brand Boys color *Forbes* v199 no2 p58 F 28 2017

Fresh Prince of Beverly Hills color *Forbes* v199 no4 p54 Ap 25 2017

"Go Get Your Elephant" color *Forbes* v199 no7 p56 Je 29 2017

HOME SHOPPING NETWORKERS cartoon color *Forbes* v198 no8 p94 D 20 2016

Mattress Missionaries color *Forbes* v199 no5 p50 My 16 2017

The Septuagenarian Whiz Kid color *Forbes* v198 no9 p44 D 30 2016

Feldman, Ben

Superstore M. Roffman *TV Guide* v64 no40 p59 O 3 2016

Feldman, Benjamin E.

Observation of a nematic quantum Hall liquid on the surface of bismuth bibl graph *Science* v354 no6310 p316 O 21 2016

FELDMAN, BRIAN

The Internet As You Know It Does Not Exist *New York* v49 no21 p54 O 17 2016

THE YEAR IN MEMES img *New York* v49 no26 p38 D 26 2016

Feldman, Brian S.

The Decline of Black Business bw color *Washington Monthly* v49 no3-5 p31 Mr-My 2017

Feldman, Bruce

SAQUON BARKLEY'S TOUGHEST COMPETITION IN THE HEISMAN RACE color *Sports Illustrated* v127 no3 p97 Jl 24 2017

Feldman, Cassi

Why Charter School Leader Eva Moskowitz Endorses Betsy DeVos *Education Digest* v83 no1 p15 S 2017

Feldman, Christina

Understand, Realize, Give Up, Develop D. Brazier color *Tricycle: The Buddhist Review* v27 no1 p44 Fall 2017

Feldman, David

Safety Pins For Slackers: Does the like button impede social change? *Psychology Today* v50 no4 p40 Ag 2017

Terawatt-scale photovoltaics: Trajectories and challenges chart graph *Science* v356 no6334 p141 Ap 14 2017

Feldman, Enrique C.

EMBRACING THE UNKNOWN [Cover story] C. P. Clark color *Literacy Today (2411-7862)* v34 no5 p28 Mr/Ap 2017

Feldman, Jack L.

Breathing control center neurons that promote arousal in mice diag graph *Science* v355 no6332 p1411 Mr 31 2017

Feldman, Jacob

American Voices Pierre Garçon color *Sports Illustrated* v125 no17 p26 N 21 2016 Double Issue

THE BALLAD OF A BIG CAT AND A GATOR color *Sports Illustrated* v126 no11 p64 Ap 17-24 2017

BATTER, INTERRUPTED color *Sports Illustrated* v126 no11 p50 Ap 17-24 2017

BROWN POWER color *Sports Illustrated* v126 no11 p62 Ap 17-24 2017

BUFFALOED color *Sports Illustrated* v126 no11 p60 Ap 17-24 2017

CSI: MIAMI color *Sports Illustrated* v126 no11 p52 Ap 17-24 2017

FRINGS BENEFIT color *Sports Illustrated* v126 no11 p56 Ap 17-24 2017

HOW WE WATCH FOOTBALL color *Sports Illustrated* v125 no18 p36 D 5 2016

JUST RELOCATE, BABY! color map *Sports Illustrated* v126 no11 p66 Ap 17-24 2017

LIVE STRONGISH color *Sports Illustrated* v126 no11 p54 Ap 17-24 2017

MARTAVIS BRYANT WILL ... color *Sports Illustrated* v127 no4 p44 Ag 7 2017

PEYTON'S (OTHER) PLACE color *Sports Illustrated* v126 no11 p48 Ap 17-24 2017

PUMP IT UP color *Sports Illustrated* v126 no11 p58 Ap 17-24 2017

Road to Joy color *Sports Illustrated* v126 no17 p26 Je 19 2017

Rush More [Cover story] color *Sports Illustrated* v127 no8 p30 S 18 2017

SAVE US, LEBRON! color *Sports Illustrated* v126 no11 p68 Ap 17-24 2017

WHAT IF? ... A JOURNEYMAN QB'S DESPERATE PASS HADN'T SHAPED THE 2004 NFL DRAFT? color *Sports Illustrated* v126 no11 p48 Ap 17-24 2017

WHAT IF? ... BABE RUTH HAD BEEN DEALT TO THE WHITE SOX—GASP!—INSTEAD OF TO THE YANKEES? color *Sports Illustrated* v126 no11 p57 Ap 17-24 2017

WHAT IF? ... GEORGE HALAS—AND THE NFL—HAD SUNK IN LAKE MICHIGAN? color *Sports Illustrated* v126 no11 p51 Ap 17-24 2017

WHAT IF? ... MICHAEL JORDAN HAD NEVER BAGGED IT? color *Sports Illustrated* v126 no11 p60 Ap 17-24 2017

WHAT IF? ... MUHAMMAD ALI HAD NEVER MET MALCOLM X? color *Sports Illustrated* v126 no11 p61 Ap 17-24 2017

WHAT IF? ... ONE PRESIDENT'S PROGENY HADN'T ALTERED FOOTBALL FOREVER? color *Sports Illustrated* v126 no11 p64 Ap 17-24 2017

WHAT IF? ... THE PLAYERS' UNION HADN'T REJECTED A-ROD'S 2003 TRADE TO THE RED SOX? color *Sports Illustrated* v126 no11 p55 Ap 17-24 2017

WHAT IF? ... THESE FIVE CAREERS HADN'T BEEN ALTERED BY INJURY? color *Sports Illustrated* v126 no11 p53 Ap 17-24 2017

Fellowes, Julian, 1949-
Julian Fellowes M. Hagan color *Current Biography* v77 no11 p44 N 2016

Fellowship
2016 AAAS Fellows approved by the AAAS Council *Science* v354 no6315 p981 N 25 2016

Backpack with a Stranger W. McGOUGH il *Backpacker* p28 O 2017

FEATURED FELLOW: JESSICA LINDSAY PHILLIPS J. Pearce color *Canadian Geographic* v137 no4 p78 Jl/Ag 2017

Fellowship (Music)
GLENN ZALESKI B. Zimmerman color *Downbeat* v84 no5 p27 My 2017

Fells Point Songs (Poem)
Fells Point Songs A. MOTION *American Scholar* v86 no4 p59 Aut 2017

FELNER, RYAN
DRONES chart color *Popular Mechanics* p78 O 2017

Felonies—Lawsuits & claims
REVISITING RESTRICTIONS ON THE RIGHT TO BEAR ARMS B. DOHERTY *Reason* v48 no11 p15 Ap 2017

Felons—Legal status, laws, etc.
Ending Civil Death R. D. SULLIVAN *America* v215 no11 p18 O 17 2016

FELSENTHAL, CAROL
Bridget Gainer color *Chicago* v66 no6 p84 Je 2017
FIVE THINGS: OBAMA WHISTLES CONSTANTLY color *Chicago* v66 no9 p38 S 2017
SPRINGFIELD OR BUST color *Chicago* v66 no11 p24 N 2017
TONI'S SODA TAX SPIRAL color *Chicago* v66 no10 p21 O 2017

Felsenthal, Edward
On Leaders color *Time* v190 no16/17 p4 O 23 2017
Sir Harold Evans color *Time* v189 no22 p60 Je 12 2017
TIME's Second Century color *Time* v190 no13 p6 O 2 2017

FELSENTHAL, JULIA
KATE AND LAURA MULLEAVY color *Vogue* v207 no3 p418 Mr 2017

Felsic rocks
Titanium isotopic evidence for felsic crust and plate tectonics 3.5 billion years ago N. D. Greber, N. Dauphas et al bw color graph *Science* v357 no6357 p1271 S 22 2017

Felson, David
ARTHRITIS: What works. What doesn't [Cover story] *Nutrition Action Health Letter* v44 no8 p3 O 2017

FELTEN, ERIC
Goldwater's Blowout cartoon *Weekly Standard* v22 no15 p5 D 19 2016
Infrastructure and Infra Dig Structures color *Weekly Standard* v22 no12 p14 N 28 2016
Out of Tune color *Weekly Standard* v22 no35 p5 My 22 2017
Pledging Allegiance color *Weekly Standard* v22 no33 p16 My 8 2017
Untruth and Consequences cartoon color *Weekly Standard* v22 no19 p20 Ja 23 2017

Felter, Joseph
Agility in the Arsenal: Technology makes for better weapons--but only until our foes catch up. Why the Pentagon needs to move faster *Hoover Digest: Research & Opinion on Public Policy* no3 p65 Summ 2017
Limiting Civilian Casualties as Part of a Winning Strategy: The Case of Courageous Restraint *Daedalus* v146 no1 p44 Wint 2017

Feltes, McKenna
Lysosomal cholesterol activates mTORC1 via an SLC38A9–Niemann-Pick C1 signaling complex bibl diag graph *Science* v355 no6331 p1306 Mr 24 2017

Feltham, Jennifer—Interviews
Q&A *Los Angeles Magazine* p92 Ja 2017

Feltman, Rachel
A botnet vaccine [Cover story] color *Popular Science* v289 no6 p49 N/D 2017
Flint: a day by the bottle color *Popular Science* v289 no2 p11 Mr/Ap 2017
the heat is on diag *Popular Science* v289 no4 p8 Jl/Ag 2017
no-fly zone [Cover story] color *Popular Science* v289 no6 p76

N/D 2017
not a weather girl cartoon *Popular Science* v289 no4 p81 Jl/Ag 2017
a trip to the other side cartoon *Popular Science* v289 no5 p76 S/O 2017
WHAT CAME BEFORE THE BIG BANG? color *Popular Science* v289 no5 p52 S/O 2017
WHAT'S IN A GLASS OF WATER? color *Popular Science* v289 no2 p56 Mr/Ap 2017

FELTON, EMMANUEL
THE SECESSION MOVEMENT IN EDUCATION bw color graph map *Nation* v305 no7 p12 S 25 2017

Felton, Ryan
RULES FOR RADICALS bw cartoon color *Mother Jones* v42 no2 p44 Mr/Ap 2017

Felzenberg, Alvin S.
All the Right Moves [Cover story] D. Linker *New York Times Book Review* p1 My 14 2017
Hail and Farewell *Weekly Standard* v22 no10 p36 N 14 2016
In the Arena R. CURRIE bw *National Review* v69 no12 p40 Je 26 2017
Mastering Disaster bw color *National Review* v68 no21 p43 N 21 2016

Female athlete triad (Syndrome)
Sugar High! A. C. Shilton color *Bicycling* v58 no6 p36 Jl 2017

Female condoms
CONDOMS color *Women's Health* v14 no6 p42 Jl 2017

Female genital mutilation (Islamic law)
IT HAPPENS HERE T. Raja color *Mother Jones* v42 no4 p13 Jl/Ag 2017
An End to FGM: Nigeria joined 23 African countries in banning female genital mutilation J. ELIZABETH *Ms.* v27 no3 p17 Fall 2017
Genital cutting case in Michigan will test limits of religious liberty T. Bach *Christian Century* v134 no18 p14 Ag 30 2017

Female high school athletes
Whit and Wisdom J. Fuchs and T. Keith color *Sports Illustrated* v126 no11 p28 Ap 17-24 2017

Female infertility—Social aspects
WARNING: MAY BITE IF ASKED ABOUT FERTILITY L. Dunham color *Glamour* v115 no11 p100 N 2017

Female nude in art
WHEN PLAYBOY MADE IT BIG L. SKENAZY *Reason* v48 no11 p6 Ap 2017

Female orgasm
ALL MY ORGASMS [Cover story] E. Sole color *Women's Health* v14 no3 p124 Ap 2017
Orgasm Pressure: Why?! C. Drell cartoon color graph *Glamour* v115 no11 p108 N 2017
Should You Try a Yoni Egg? L. Murphy color *Glamour* v115 no7 p67 Jl 2017
What Really Gets Women Off? [Cover story] E. Koenig color *Glamour* v115 no7 p66 Jl 2017

Female reproductive organ diseases—Psychological aspects
QUEST FOR FIRE: FEMALE DESIRE IS ONE OF THE MOST ELUSIVE FACETS OF HUMAN BEHAVIOR--AND ITS ABSENCE IS WOMEN'S MOST COMMON SEXUAL COMPLAINT. CAN SCIENCE FIGURE OUT HOW TO IGNITE IT? K. ROWLAND *Psychology Today* v50 no5 p62 S/O 2017

Female reproductive organs
Menstrual Cycle "on a Chip" D. Fine Maron color *Scientific American* v316 no6 p16 Je 2017

Female-to-male transsexuals
MY HEALTH CARE IS NOT COSMETIC: Trans folks are up against a tidal wave of ignorance in the insurance industry C. HAYES color *Advocate* no1091 p110 Je/Jl 2017

Feminine beauty (Aesthetics)
everyone has an opinion about a woman's BODY color *Women's Health* v14 no7 p140 S 2017
LEARNING CURVE C. Guthrie cartoon *O, The Oprah Magazine* p129 Mr 2017
LOSING IT P. Rao color *Women's Health* v14 no2 p43 Mr 2017
Spritz on some warmth color *Redbook* p33 N 2017

Feminine hygiene products
Protection. PERIOD W. L. Wilson color *Essence* v48 no5 p112 S 2017

Fences (Play)

Shallow Fences J. PODHORETZ *Weekly Standard* v22 no20 p39 Ja 30 2017

Fences in art

Ten Directions: Lori McDonough puts your passport on display A. Petry *Indianapolis Monthly* v40 no10 p30 Je 2017

Fences—Design & construction

POST DRIVERS K. Birchmier *Successful Farming* v115 no3 p44 Mid-F 2017

Fencing

CONSULTANTS A. P. Knight *Equus* no482 p68 N 2017

Fendi, Delfina Delettrez

Super Fine A. Syrett color *InStyle* v24 no10 p236 O 2017

Fendi Adele Srl

Cristina Celestino H. MARTIN color *Architectural Digest* v74 no1 p58 Ja 2017

Fendi Mini Peekaboo bag color *Vogue* v206 no12 p296 D 2016

Fendi Srl

Bright Ideas M. BOBO color *Ebony* v72 no5 p35 Mr 2017

Feng, Danqing

Systemic pan-AMPK activator MK-8722 improves glucose homeostasis but induces cardiac hypertrophy graph *Science* v357 no6350 p507 Ag 4 2017

Feng, Lujia

Imaging the distribution of transient viscosity after the 2016 Mw 7.1 Kumamoto earthquake map *Science* v356 no6334 p163 Ap 14 2017

Feng, Qi

"Perfect" designer chromosome V and behavior of a ring derivative diag *Science* v355 no6329 p1046 Mr 10 2017

Feng, Wen

Systemic pan-AMPK activator MK-8722 improves glucose homeostasis but induces cardiac hypertrophy graph *Science* v357 no6350 p507 Ag 4 2017

Feng Chen

Oral precision medicine: Identification of microbes from saliva by mass spectrometry bibl *Science* v354 no6319 p60 D 23 2016

Feng shui

Claims of Chi: Besting a Tai Chi Master J. NICKELL *Skeptical Inquirer* v41 no1 p20 Ja/F 2017

Feng Zhang

High-resolution interrogation of functional elements in the non-coding genome bibl graph *Science* v353 no6307 p1545 S 30 2016

Feng Zhu

How Wikipedia Keeps Political Discourse from Turning Ugly *Harvard Business Review Digital Articles* p2 N 7 2016

Microsoft's Bid to Make Outlook More than Email *Harvard Business Review Digital Articles* p2 Ag 18 2015

Fengcheng Wu

Observation of a nematic quantum Hall liquid on the surface of bismuth bibl graph *Science* v354 no6310 p316 O 21 2016

Fengyu Hu

MAVS-dependent host species range and pathogenicity of human hepatitis A virus bibl graph *Science* v353 no6307 p1541 S 30 2016

FENGZHI HE

Freshwater Megafauna: Flagships for Freshwater Biodiversity under Threat *BioScience* v67 no10 p919 O 2017

Fenn, Forrest

PLOT OF GOLD A. Abel color *Maclean's* v130 no10 p40 N 2017

FENNESSY, CHRISTINE

AMANDA CHARNEY color *Runner's World* v52 no1 p89 Ja/F 2017

RW 2016 COVER SEARCH [Cover story] color *Runner's World* v51 no11 p62 D 2016

FENNESSY, STEVE

99, 100, 101...FULL STOP *Atlanta* v57 no5 p18 S 2017

AMERICAN CATHEDRAL *Atlanta* v57 no5 p88 S 2017

BEST OF ATLANTA *Atlanta* v56 no8 p106 D 2016

CHANGE IS AFOOT *Atlanta* v56 no8 p22 D 2016

CIVICS 101 *Atlanta* v56 no10 p16 F 2017

COUNTERPOINTS *Atlanta* v56 no12 p16 Ap 2017

Flip Your Ride: Jaguar on Wednesday, Lexus on Thursday, Porsche on Friday--welcome to Clutch! *Atlanta* v57 no3 p44 Jl 2017

LET THEM EAT CAKE *Atlanta* v56 no9 p16 Ja 2017

THE NEW REALITY *Atlanta* v57 no1 p14 My 2017

OUR CIVIC DNA *Atlanta* v56 no11 p16 Mr 2017

THE PROGNOSIS *Atlanta* v57 no3 p20 Jl 2017

Q AND A WITH MARYN MCKENNA *Atlanta* v57 no5 p100 S 2017

A RIVER RUNS THROUGH IT *Atlanta* v57 no4 p12 Ag 2017

A STORY AT HOME *Atlanta* v56 no7 p20 N 2016

THE SYMMETRY OF 50 *Atlanta* v57 no2 p18 Je 2017

WITNESS TO DARKNESS *Atlanta* v57 no1 p22 My 2017

Fenno, Lief E.

Thirst-associated preoptic neurons encode an aversive motivational drive diag *Science* v357 no6356 p1149 S 15 2017

Fenoff, Lynne

Down by the Riverside color *Yankee* p44 Mr 2017

Fenske, Pascal

Loss of a mammalian circular RNA locus causes miRNA deregulation and affects brain function color *Science* v357 no6357 p1254 S 22 2017

Fenson, Brad

YOUR Wildest DREAMS color *Field & Stream* v122 no5 p38 O 2017

Fentanyl

Bad medicine J. GATEHOUSE color *Maclean's* no1 p30 F 17 2017

DEADLY CHEMISTRY K. McLaughlin color diag *Science* v355 no6332 p1364 Mr 31 2017

Fenton, Flavio H.

Dynamics of a human spiral wave *Physics Today* v70 no2 p78 F 2017

Fenton, James

The Disasters of War color *New York Review of Books* v64 no9 p13 My 25 2017

Duterte's Last Hurrah: On the Road to Martial Law color *New York Review of Books* v64 no3 p20 F 23 2017

Moses in Mexico [Cover story] color *New York Review of Books* v64 no15 p12 O 12 2017

Murderous Manila: On the Night Shift color *New York Review of Books* v64 no2 p22 F 9 2017

Fenton, Laura

15 Minutes to a Simpler Day color *Parents* v92 no9 p158 S 2017

big ideas for small spaces color *Parents* v92 no3 p86 Mr 2017

party on! (a budget) *Parents* v91 no9 p143 S 2016

shelf help color *Parents* v92 no8 p121 Ag 2017

space to create color *Parents* v92 no5 p94 My 2017

Fenton, Roger, 1819-1869

WAR IN STILL LIFE D. Stadtler bw *Military History* v34 no2 p48 Jl 2017

Fenu, F.

Observation of a large-scale anisotropy in the arrival directions of cosmic rays above 8 × 1018 eV *Science* v357 no6357 p1266 S 22 2017

Fenwick, Alexandra

Checkmate color *Sports Illustrated* v125 no19 p26 D 12 2016

Friendsgiving color *Sports Illustrated* v125 no18 p24 D 5 2016

Long May You Ride color *Sports Illustrated* v125 no14 p26 O 24-31 2016

Love Lessons color *Sports Illustrated* v125 no20 p26 D 19 2016

Original Miracle on Ice color *Sports Illustrated* v125 no13 p20 O 17 2016

Still Rolling color *Sports Illustrated* v125 no17 p28 N 21 2016 Double Issue

Talking Back color *Sports Illustrated* v125 no16 p22 N 14 2016

Teen Tragedy color *Sports Illustrated* v125 no15 p26 N 7 2016

Wicked Googly color *Sports Illustrated* v125 no12 p22 O 10 2016

Fenyö, David

Synthesis, debugging, and effects of synthetic chromosome consolidation: synVI and beyond color *Science* v355 no6329 p1045 Mr 10 2017

Feral cats

Friends, Foes, and Felines J. HERBST color *Los Angeles Magazine* v62 no10 p98 O 2017

New Zealand Shouldn't Ignore Feral Cats C. ROUCO, R. DE TORRE-CEIJAS et al *BioScience* v67 no8 p686 Ag 2017

Feral dogs

Important City Hall Story Z. CRAIN *D: The Magazine of Dallas*

v43 no10 p300 O 2016

LOVE IN A WAR ZONE C. COLIN bw color *Men's Health* v32 no6 p124 Ag 2017

Urban Wild: IN SLOWLY GENTRIFYING DETROIT, YOU MIGHT SEE A FOX, OR EVEN A COYOTE, BUT WHERE HAVE ALL THE STRAY DOGS GONE? L. BERNSTEIN-MACHLAY *American Scholar* v86 no4 p76 Aut 2017

Feral pigeons

Incredible Animal Friends E. DEFFNER color *National Geographic Kids* no470 p5 My 2017

Ferber, Taylor

PARTY LINES img *New York* v50 no12 p112 Je 12 2017

PARTY LINES img *New York* v50 no15 p73 Jl 24 2017

Ferdinand (Film)

FERDINAND D. Heching color *Entertainment Weekly* no1478 / 1479 p75 Ag 18-25 2017

Ferdinand I, King of the Two Sicilies, 1751-1825

CHINA SYNDROME M. OWENS color *Architectural Digest* v73 no11 p78 N 2016

FERDOWSI, BOBAK

A Humongous Rocket That Just Might Work color diag *Popular Mechanics* p12 S 2017

IT'S NOT JUST ROCKET SCIENCE C. Leu color *Wired* v24 no11 p138 N 2016

Ferejohn, John

Forged Through Fire: War, Peace, and the Democratic Bargain G. J. Ikenberry *Foreign Affairs* v96 no2 p167 Mr/Ap 2017

Ferenbach, David A.

Local amplifiers of IL-4Rα-mediated macrophage activation promote repair in lung and liver diag *Science* v356 no6342 p1076 Je 9 2017

Ferencik, Erica

The River at Night L. Greenblatt color *Entertainment Weekly* no1449 p60 Ja 20 2017

Fergie, 1975——Interviews

THE DUTCHESS REIGNS AGAIN M. Vain color *Entertainment Weekly* no1484 p56 S 29 2017

Fergus, Edward

Confronting colorblindness il *Phi Delta Kappan* v98 no5 p30 F 2017

Fergus, Jim

The Vengeance of Mothers: The Journals of Margaret Kelly & Molly McGill *Publishers Weekly* v264 no31 p60 Jl 31 2017

Ferguson & Shamanian Architects (Company)

The Classicists color *Architectural Digest* v74 no1 p98 Ja 2017

FERGUSON, ANDREW

The AP's Pronoun Decree color *Weekly Standard* v22 no31 p10 Ap 17 2017

Blue on Blue in Virginia color *Weekly Standard* v22 no35 p15 My 22 2017

Bob Dylan, Nobelist cartoon *Weekly Standard* v22 no7 p11 O 24 2016

Courtiers in Denial cartoon *Weekly Standard* v22 no18 p10 Ja 16 2017

The Day America Stops Voting color *Weekly Standard* v22 no11 p22 N 21 2016

'Everybody Says How Cool I Am' color *Commentary* v143 no2 p1 F 2017

'Everybody Says How Cool I Am' *Commentary* v143 no2 p1 F 2017

Falling In and Out of Love--Again--with John McCain *Commentary* v144 no2 p9 S 2017

Flowers in Their Hair [Cover story] bw color *Weekly Standard* v22 no47 p24 Ag 21 2017

Immerse Yourself in 1776 and All That color *Weekly Standard* v22 no32 p10 My 1 2017

The Kiss-Up That Wasn't color *Weekly Standard* v22 no40 p8 Je 26 2017

The Man Who Would Be Kempton color *Weekly Standard* v23 no6 p21 O 16 2017

Microaggression and Macrononsense color *Weekly Standard* v22 no25 p26 Mr 6 2017

The Night Data Died *Commentary* v142 no5 p10 D 2016

The Palace Intrigue Obsession *Commentary* v143 no6 p11 Je 2017

Save Our Bureaucrats! *Commentary* v144 no1 p9 Jl/Ag 2017

Scared Straight cartoon *Weekly Standard* v22 no17 p5 Ja 2 2017

She's a Keeper *Commentary* v144 no3 p9 O 2017

The. American. People *Commentary* v143 no3 p12 Mr 2017

The Trump Disruption *Commentary* v143 no1 p10 Ja 2017

Trump on the Menu *Commentary* v143 no4 p9 Ap 2017

Trump's Chumps color *Weekly Standard* v22 no14 p8 D 12 2016

We're Only Human *Commentary* v142 no4 p46 N 2016

What Trump Can Learn from Nixon bw *Weekly Standard* v22 no12 p9 N 28 2016

Where the Rubber Meets the Road color *Weekly Standard* v22 no9 p10 N 7 2016

Writer's Seat bw color *Weekly Standard* v23 no1 p30 S 11 2017

The Ziegfeld of Political Theater color *Weekly Standard* v22 no36 p12 My 29 2017

Ferguson, Bob

Trump's Aggressive Moves In a Sloppy Game of Political Chess May Be His Undoing color *Time* v189 no20 p23 My 29 2017

Ferguson, Buffy

BELGIAN BEAUTY L. MOWRY *Atlanta* v57 no1 p44 My 2017

FERGUSON, GARY

A DEEPER BOOM *Orion Magazine* v35 no4/5 p14 Jl-O 2016

FERGUSON, GILLIAN

Extremely Fine And Incredibly Close *Los Angeles Magazine* v62 no9 p52 S 2017

Ferguson, Margaret

Helping Primary Care Doctors Contain Costs *Harvard Business Review Digital Articles* p2 D 30 2015

Ferguson, Maria

Choice for Secretary of Education color *Phi Delta Kappan* v98 no5 p74 F 2017

Washington View diag *Phi Delta Kappan* v98 no4 p74 D 2016/ Ja 2017

Washington View il *Phi Delta Kappan* v98 no7 p74 Ap 2017

Washington View *Phi Delta Kappan* v98 no8 p72 My 2017

Washington View *Phi Delta Kappan* v99 no1 p42 S 2017

Ferguson, Niall

A More Imperfect Union: Britain's separation from the EU: not merely a new political and legal arrangement but a deep and permanent schism *Hoover Digest: Research & Opinion on Public Policy* no3 p88 Summ 2017

Past Is Prologue *Hoover Digest: Research & Opinion on Public Policy* no1 p175 Wint 2017

The Russia Question: American relations with Moscow have become a geopolitical mess--a mess, very largely, of our own making *Hoover Digest: Research & Opinion on Public Policy* no2 p76 Spr 2017

Ferguson, Otis

Beyond the Kael *Commentary* v142 no2 p1 S 2016

Ferguson, Robert

True North: A British expat takes a nuanced look at Scandinavian culture L. Abend *New York Times Book Review* p7 Jl 16 2017

What to Do If Your Boss Asks You to Break the Rules *Harvard Business Review Digital Articles* p2 Ja 7 2016

Ferguson, Roger Walton, 1951——Interviews

Q&A: Roger Ferguson, CEO of TIAA bw cartoon *Bloomberg Businessweek* no4496 p54 O 24 2016

FERGUSON, SARAH

Running the Asylum *New York Times Book Review* p19 O 2 2016

FERGUSON, TRACEY M.

ART WALK AT HOME WITH THE LAWSONS color *Ebony* v72/73 no12/1 p58 O/N 2017

BLACK INK CREW color *Ebony* v72/73 no12/1 p46 O/N 2017

EDITOR'S LETTER color *Ebony* v72/73 no12/1 p12 O/N 2017

HEAVY METAL color *Ebony* v72 no11 p48 S 2017

HOUSTON: THE AMERICAN CITY OF THE FUTURE color *Ebony* v72 no11 p30 S 2017

MILLENNIAL PINK: THE LASTING COLOR OF NOW color *Ebony* v72 no11 p40 S 2017

ONE WAYANS WAY color *Ebony* v72 no11 p58 S 2017

SAY HELLO TO THE NEW GIRL *Ebony* v72 no11 p12 S 2017

Ferguson, Wes

Circling the Drain *Texas Monthly* v45 no9 p38 S 2017

Gone Fishin'; Fishin' Gone *Texas Monthly* v45 no5 p52 My 2017

Let the river run the blanco river *Texas Monthly* v45 no1 p104 Ja 2017

Let the river run the blanco river W. Ferguson *Texas Monthly* v45 no1 p104 Ja 2017

SAVING THE CABINET OAK *Texas Monthly* v45 no7 p46 Jl 2017

Ferguson-Smith, Anne C.
Transgenerational inheritance: Models and mechanisms of non–DNA sequence–based inheritance bibl color diag *Science* v354 no6308 p59 O 7 2016

Feringa, Ben L.
Locked synchronous rotor motion in a molecular motor diag *Science* v356 no6341 p964 Je 1 2017

Feringa, Ben—Awards
Chemistry Nobel honors mechanical bonds, molecular machines J. Miller *Physics Today* v69 no12 p18 D 2016

Ferland-Beckham, Chantelle
The Monastery and the Microscope color *Science* v357 no6355 p968 S 8 2017

Ferlez, Bryan
Structure of a symmetric photosynthetic reaction center–photosystem color *Science* v357 no6355 p1021 S 8 2017

Fermaglich, Mollie
Brave New World color *Publishers Weekly* v264 no30 p64 Jl 24 2017

Fermentation
See also
Brewing
EASE GAS WITH HERBS K. P. S. Khalsa color *Amazing Wellness* v9 no6 p40 EarlyWint 2017
FOOD TECH'S NEW BUZZWORD: "FERMENTATION" B. Kowitt color *Fortune* v175 no5 p15 Ap 1 2017

Fermented beverages—Evaluation
Get Cultured Chelsea Leu *Sierra* v101 no5 p8 S/O 2016

Fermented foods—Evaluation
Sour Power S. KROWIAK color *Indianapolis Monthly* p41 Ap 2017

Fermi, Enrico, 1901-1954
Where are they? M. Livio and J. Silk *Physics Today* v70 no3 p50 Mr 2017

Fermi energy
Ultrafast many-body interferometry of impurities coupled to a Fermi sea M. Cetina, M. Jag et al bibl diag graph *Science* v354 no6308 p96 O 7 2016

Fermi National Accelerator Laboratory
Anniversaries for particle physics M. Mangano color *Science* v356 no6344 p1213 Je 23 2017
The Neutrino Puzzle [Cover story] C. Moskowitz color diag map *Scientific American* v317 no4 p32 O 2017

Fermions
Faux particle commits physics faux pas E. CONOVER *Science News* v191 no13 p14 Jl 8 2017

Fermor, Patrick Leigh
THE SEVEN-YEAR ITCH *Harper's Magazine* p16 S 2017

Fernandes, Verónica
Dispersals and genetic adaptation of Bantu-speaking populations in Africa and North America diag *Science* v356 no6337 p543 My 5 2017

Fernandes, Vilaiwan M.
Glia relay differentiation cues to coordinate neuronal development in Drosophila color *Science* v357 no6354 p886 S 1 2017

FERNÁNDEZ, DENNY S.
Skills and Knowledge for Data-Intensive Environmental Research *BioScience* v67 no6 p546 Je 2017

FERNANDEZ, ELDONNA LEWIS
LET'S NEGOTIATE *USA Today Magazine* v145 no2862 p72 Mr 2017

Fernandez, Fernando
4 Big Economic Questions Now Facing the EU *Harvard Business Review Digital Articles* p2 Je 28 2016

Fernandez, Gabriela
THE BEST PLACES TO LIVE IN AMERICA [Cover story] chart color map *Money* v46 no9 p54 O 2017

Fernandez, Gigi
Learn how to cover the lob—and ensure that your team will van the point bw color *Tennis* v53 no2 p76 Mr/Ap 2017
The most unorthodox doubles formations bw color *Tennis* v53 no5 p76 S/O 2017
Serving strategies while in formation *Tennis* v53 no4 p76 Jl/Ag 2017

Three ways your team can break serve *Tennis* v53 no3 p74 My/Je 2017

Fernandez, Guillermo E.
Systemic pan-AMPK activator MK-8722 improves glucose homeostasis but induces cardiac hypertrophy graph *Science* v357 no6350 p507 Ag 4 2017

Fernández, Ignacio C.
Chile unprepared for Ph.D. influx *Science* v356 no6343 p1131 Je 16 2017

Fernandez, Jayham
On a Question of the Day color *Black Belt* v55 no6 p16 O/N 2017

Fernandez, Jose, 1992-2016
Darkness, Speed, and Bad Decisions B. ELLISON color *Power & Motoryacht* v32 no12 p24 D 2016
"Your Story is OUR STORY" S. l. Price color *Sports Illustrated* v125 no12 p38 O 10 2016

Fernández, M. Hernández
Decoupled ecomorphological evolution and diversification in Neogene-Quaternary horses bibl graph *Science* v355 no6325 p627 F 10 2017

Fernandez, Megan
ABOVE AND BEYOND *Indianapolis Monthly* v40 no7 p72 Mr 2017
AHEAD OF THE CURRENT color *Indianapolis Monthly* v41 no2 p68 S 2017
best of Indy *Indianapolis Monthly* v40 no4 p73 D 2016
Broad RIPPLE color map *Indianapolis Monthly* v41 no2 p66 S 2017
CAN YOU DIG IT? diag *Indianapolis Monthly* v41 no2 p72 S 2017
CHOICE TREATMENTS: Central Indiana doctors share an elective or cutting-edge procedure in their field *Indianapolis Monthly* p80 N 2017
CONSUMED *Indianapolis Monthly* v40 no11 p72 Jl 2017
Cover Girl *Indianapolis Monthly* v40 no4 p20 D 2016
A DAM SHAME *Indianapolis Monthly* v41 no2 p64 S 2017
Downtown color map *Indianapolis Monthly* v41 no2 p73 S 2017
Farther Downstream color map *Indianapolis Monthly* v41 no2 p77 S 2017
GM STAMPING PLANT color map *Indianapolis Monthly* v41 no2 p75 S 2017
Hamilton COUNTY color map *Indianapolis Monthly* v41 no2 p63 S 2017
Hot on the TRAILS: A ROAD-FREE GUIDE TO EXPLORING CENTRAL INDIANA *Indianapolis Monthly* v40 no10 p59 Je 2017
MAKING A SPLASH color *Indianapolis Monthly* v41 no2 p76 S 2017
Mounds STATE PARK color map *Indianapolis Monthly* v41 no2 p60 S 2017
Riverside PARK color map *Indianapolis Monthly* v41 no2 p68 S 2017
SAND CASTLE: A new downtown home channels chic Florida beach style color *Indianapolis Monthly* v41 no2 p32 S 2017
TOUR OF DOODY diag *Indianapolis Monthly* v41 no2 p65 S 2017
WHERE THE WILD THINGS ARE color *Indianapolis Monthly* v41 no2 p62 S 2017
THE White RIVER diag *Indianapolis Monthly* v41 no2 p59 S 2017

Fernandez, Rich
5 Ways to Boost Your Resilience at Work *Harvard Business Review Digital Articles* p2 Je 27 2016
Help Your Team Manage Stress, Anxiety, and Burnout *Harvard Business Review Digital Articles* p2 Ja 21 2016

FERNÁNDEZ, SANDY M.
Eating Disorder *Scholastic Choices* v32 no6 p10 Mr 2017
Heroin took over our town *Scholastic Choices* v32 no3 p6 N/D 2016
"I Had Depression": About one in five teens grapple with symptoms of depression, anxiety, or other emotional health issues--yet few talk about it. These kids are dedicated to changing that *Scholastic Choices* p18 O 2017
Show your money some love color *Redbook* p97 Je 2017
THE ultimate guide to SAVING TIME & FEELING IN CONTROL color *Redbook* p99 S 2017

WHICH ONE IS #FAKENEWS?* *Scholastic Choices* v32 no8 p6 My 2017

Fernández-Aráoz, Claudio

5 Rules for a Vacation that's Truly Worth It *Harvard Business Review Digital Articles* p2 Je 5 2015

Are We Evaluating U.S. Presidential Hopefuls All Wrong? *Harvard Business Review Digital Articles* p2 Jl 1 2015

Hiring and Managing in Turbulent Times *Harvard Business Review Digital Articles* p2 D 12 2016

How to Look for Emotional Intelligence on Your Team *Harvard Business Review Digital Articles* p2 Ap 29 2015

How to Make a Team of Stars Work *Harvard Business Review Digital Articles* p2 Jl 17 2015

Ignore Emotional Intelligence at Your Own Risk *Harvard Business Review Digital Articles* p2 O 22 2014

Keep Employees from Leaving by Emphasizing Teamwork *Harvard Business Review Digital Articles* p2 N 7 2016

Leading Job Growth in the Digital Economy *Harvard Business Review Digital Articles* p2 Ag 5 2015

The Right Way to Check a Reference *Harvard Business Review Digital Articles* p2 F 11 2016

To Grow as a Leader, Seek More Complex Assignments *Harvard Business Review Digital Articles* p2 Jl 20 2016

Why Boards Get C-Suite Succession So Wrong *Harvard Business Review Digital Articles* p2 My 15 2015

Why Family Firms in East Asia Struggle with Succession *Harvard Business Review Digital Articles* p2 Mr 24 2015

FERNÁNDEZ-GALIANO, ELADIO

International Wildlife Law: Understanding and Enhancing Its Role in Conservation *BioScience* v67 no9 p784 S 2017

Fernandez-Marcos, Pablo J.

Tissue damage and senescence provide critical signals for cellular reprogramming in vivo bibl chart graph *Science* v354 no6315 paaf4445-1 N 25 2016

Fernandez-Mateo, Isabel

A Study of the Champagne Industry Shows That Women Have Stronger Networks, and Profit from Them *Harvard Business Review Digital Articles* p2 Jl 20 2017

Fernández-Morera, Darío

The 'Golden Age' Myth of Spain's Muslim Era A. BAKSHIAN JR. il *American Conservative* v16 no4 p57 Jl/Ag 2017

Fernández-Nieves, Alberto

Transition from turbulent to coherent flows in confined three-dimensional active fluids color *Science* v355 no6331 p1284 Mr 24 2017

Fernbach, Phil

High Online User Ratings Don't Actually Mean You're Getting a Quality Product *Harvard Business Review Digital Articles* p2 Jl 4 2016

Ferns

Martha's Month chart color *Martha Stewart Living* p4 Ap 2017

Fernyhough, Charles

TALKING TO OURSELVES color diag *Scientific American* v317 no2 p74 Ag 2017

THE VOICES IN OUR HEADS J. GROOPMAN cartoon *New Yorker* v92 no44 p70 Ja 9 2017

Your Inner Voices C. SCHWARTZ *New York Times Book Review* p25 O 23 2016

Ferragamo, James—Interviews

FILLING THE SHOES J. FERRAGAMO color *Esquire* p62 2017 BigBlackBook

Ferrando, Carlos

Folding Bike Helmet N. Leiber color *Bloomberg Businessweek* no4539 p48 S 25 2017

Ferrante, Elena, 1943-

Feel the Power of the Dark Side M. RUSSO *New York Times Book Review* p23 N 6 2016

Ferrante's World [Cover story] E. Blair *New York Times Book Review* p1 N 6 2016

Novelist, Interrupted A. CHEE bw color *New Republic* v247 no12 p56 D 2016

The Real Elena Ferrante Surfaces-In Books S. Begley color *Time* v188 no20 p54 N 14 2016

Ferrante, Elena, 1943—Interviews

PROSE BY ANY OTHER NAME *Harper's Magazine* v333 no1999 p16 D 2016

Ferrara, Annette

Your Presentation Needs a Punch Line *Harvard Business Review Digital Articles* p2 My 21 2015

Ferrari, Joseph

Can a parish ever have clutter? *U.S. Catholic* v82 no3 p35 Mr 2017

Ferrari, Joseph R.—Interviews

Spring cleaning for the soul color *U.S. Catholic* v82 no3 p32 Mr 2017

Ferrari 458 Italia automobile

GENTLEMEN'S PARADE color *Road & Track* v68 no7 p12 Mr/Ap 2017

Ferrari automobile

1976 Ferrari Dino 208 GT4 B. Price color *Popular Mechanics* p56 S 2017

1976 Ferrari Dino 208 GT4 B. Price color *Popular Mechanics* v193 no7 p56 S 2016

THE 2017 SUPERCAR BUYER'S GUIDE color *Popular Mechanics* p30 S 2017

FERRARI INVADES DAYTONA P. LERNER color *Road & Track* v68 no7 p8 Mr/Ap 2017

GENTLEMEN'S PARADE color *Road & Track* v68 no7 p12 Mr/Ap 2017

JUST LIKE YESTERDAY color *Road & Track* v68 no7 p10 Mr/Ap 2017

THE LONELIEST FERRARI S. SMITH color *Road & Track* v68 no9 p46 Je 2017

SHOOTING BRAKE J. Cammisa chart color *Motor Trend* v69 no7 p98 Jl 2017

SUPERFREAK M. PRINCE color *Road & Track* v69 no4 p74 N 2017

TRUTH IN ADVERTISING A. MacKenzie chart color *Motor Trend* v69 no11 p92 N 2017

Ferrari automobile—Evaluation

A Sedan with Sprezzatura K. SINTUMUANG color *Esquire* v167 no1 p22 F 2017

Ferrari SpA

1976 Ferrari Dino 208 GT4 color *Popular Mechanics* v193 no7 p56 S 2016

THE LONELIEST FERRARI S. SMITH color *Road & Track* v68 no9 p46 Je 2017

A Sedan with Sprezzatura K. SINTUMUANG color *Esquire* v167 no1 p22 F 2017

Sergio Marchionne: CEO, FERRARI AND FCA A. MacKenzie color *Motor Trend* v69 no9 p30 S 2017

SHOOTING BRAKE J. Cammisa chart color *Motor Trend* v69 no7 p98 Jl 2017

TRUTH IN ADVERTISING A. MacKenzie chart color *Motor Trend* v69 no11 p92 N 2017

Ferrari-Adler, Jofie

MIDLIFE CRISIS DEPT.: FORE! D. Owen bw *New Yorker* v93 no33 p36 O 23 2017

Ferrario, L.

An unusual white dwarf star may be a surviving remnant of a sub-luminous Type Ia supernova chart diag *Science* v357 no6352 p680 Ag 18 2017

FERRARO, KATHLEEN

Light Up Your Life color *Backpacker* v45 no1 p24 Ja 2017

Ferrás, Cristina

Actin divides to conquer color diag *Science* v357 no6353 p756 Ag 25 2017

Ferrato, Jacob

Kicks Meister D. Bishop color *American Craft* v77 no2 p26 Ap/My 2017

Ferrazzi, Keith

6 Ways to Turn Managers into Coaches Again *Harvard Business Review Digital Articles* p2 Ag 10 2015

7 Ways to Improve Employee Development Programs *Harvard Business Review Digital Articles* p2 Jl 31 2015

How to Run a Great Virtual Meeting *Harvard Business Review Digital Articles* p2 Mr 27 2015

Technology Can Save Onboarding from Itself *Harvard Business Review Digital Articles* p2 Mr 25 2015

Use Your Staff Meeting for Peer-to-Peer Coaching *Harvard Business Review Digital Articles* p2 F 24 2015

Working Smoothly with a Virtual Boss *Harvard Business Review*

book p66 Je 2017

Ferris, Marc
What makes a patriot? P. W. Marty *Christian Century* v134 no22 p3 O 25 2017

Ferris, Neal
Flint, Feather, and Other Material Selves *American Indian Quarterly* v41 no2 p125 Spr 2017

Ferris, Timothy
FANTASTIC VOYAGE color diag *National Geographic* v232 no2 p22 Ag 2017

Ferrise, Jennifer
50 BEST DRESSED LIST color *InStyle* v24 no11 p186 N 2017
DILONE color *InStyle* v24 no9 p143 S 2017
EYE OF THE BEHOLDER color *InStyle* v24 no5 p218 My 2017
Happy Birthday, Annie Hall color *InStyle* v24 no4 p186 Ap 2017
HOORAY FOR Hollywood color *InStyle* v23 no12 p252 N 2016
A Mother in Arms color *InStyle* v24 no6 p148 Je 2017
The Parties color *InStyle* v23 no12 p84 N 2016
Style 100 color *InStyle* v23 no13 p79 D 2016
STYLE CRUSH Laura Harrier color *InStyle* v24 no10 p110 O 2017
Who Won Fashion? color *InStyle* v24 no5 p82 My 2017

FERRIS-ROTMAN, AMIE
The Diplomacy of Dog Walking in Russia color *Foreign Policy* no225 p20 Jl/Ag 2017

Ferriss, Joe
AN EGYPTIAN PRINCESS TAKES THE CROWN IN VEGAS *Arabian Horse World* v57 no8 p62 My 2017

FERRISS, TIM
Aging? What's That? bw cartoon color *Men's Health* v32 no5 p34 Je 2017
DO LESS, EARN MORE color *Men's Health* v32 no7 p90 S 2017
Turn Fear into Fuel bw color *Men's Health* v32 no6 p38 Ag 2017
When a 130-Pound Girl Can Lift More Than You cartoon color *Men's Health* v32 no4 p28 My 2017
Win Any Battle cartoon *Men's Health* v32 no8 p41 O 2017

Ferriss, Tim—Interviews
PROBLEM SOLVING WITH TECH'S HOTTEST SELF-HELP GURU M. Lev-Ram color *Fortune* v174 no7 p40 D 1 2016

Ferritic steel
Direct observation of individual hydrogen atoms at trapping sites in a ferritic steel Y. -. Chen, D. Haley et al bibl diag *Science* v355 no6330 p1196 Mr 17 2017

Ferro, Bobby
FERRO'S FAVORITE RACE J. OBER bw *Dirt Sports + Off-Road* v51 no9 p74 S 2017

Ferro, Michael, 1967-
TRONC IF YOU WANT TO SAVE JOURNALISM [Cover story] F. Gillette and G. Smith color *Bloomberg Businessweek* no4498 p74 N 7 2016

Ferrone, Cristina R.
Potential role of intratumor bacteria in mediating tumor resistance to the chemotherapeutic drug gemcitabine diag *Science* v357 no6356 p1156 S 15 2017

Ferrone, Rita
Between Past & Future color *Commonweal* v144 no7 p7 Ap 14 2017
Cardinal Virtues color *Commonweal* v144 no11 p8 Je 16 2017
Don't Scatter the Ashes—or Wear Them color *Commonweal* v143 no20 p6 D 16 2016
No Stalemate color *Commonweal* v114 no14 p8 S 8 2017
Reform of the Reform *Commonweal* v144 no3 p6 F 10 2017

FERRY, DAVID
A Fresh Approach to Fighting MS color *AARP: The Magazine* v30 no6A p29 O/N 2017
IRON GIANT: GET READY TO ROBO-RUMBLE! color diag *Wired* v25 no8 p24 Ag 2017

Ferry-Rooney, Raechel
TALK TO US color *Chicago* v66 no4 p19 Ap 2017

Fertig, Rod
Are You Accurately Measuring Your Company's Digital Strength? *Harvard Business Review Digital Articles* p2 S 7 2017

Fertility
Potent Pigments E. A. KANE color *Better Nutrition* v79 no10 p30 O 2017

Fertility clinics

BABY BOOM: Shady Grove Fertility is the largest fertility clinic in the country. How it got that way involved business innovation as well as science C. Cunningham *Washingtonian Magazine* v52 no8 p119 My 2017

Fertilization (Biology)
The Kiwi Connection J. CAREY *Audubon* v118 no6 p16 Wint 2016
The Sanctity of Human Life Act: Politicians Playing God K. Burrows *Humanist* v77 no5 p9 S/O 2017

Fertilization in vitro
Can flu shots help women get pregnant? M. Leslie color *Science* v355 no6331 p1247 Mr 24 2017
DON'T WORRY—IVF DOES NOT CAUSE CANCER *Health* v30 no9 p16 N 2016
Stem Cell Research W. F. Vitulli and T. O. Diener *Skeptical Inquirer* v41 no3 p63 My/Je 2017
World of Medicine S. RIDEOUT *Reader's Digest* v189 no1127 p58 F 2017

Fertilization of plants
See also
   Pollination
   Pollinators
Does urinating in my yard help fertilize it? color *Popular Mechanics* p100 S 2017
Go Ahead... Ask Us Anything M. Koziol cartoon *Popular Science* p90 Ja/F 2017

Fertilizer equipment—Evaluation
NEW AND IMPROVED A. McConnell and L. Bedord *Successful Farming* v115 no3 p24 Mid-F 2017

Fertilizer spreaders—Evaluation
NEW AND IMPROVED A. McConnell and L. Bedord *Successful Farming* v115 no3 p24 Mid-F 2017

Fertilizers
See also
   Manures
AROUND THE GARDEN S. Bender color *Southern Living* v52 no9 p34 S 2017
FEEDING CROPS IN TOUGH TIMES: FRUGAL AND FERTILIZER ARE TWO WORDS THAT GO TOGETHER IN TODAY'S FARM ECONOMY G. Johnston *Successful Farming* v115 no12 p50 O 2017
Stunted Growth G. Almy color *Field & Stream* v122 no5 pW5 O 2017

Fertilizers & the environment
RUN FOR COVER T. PHILPOTT color *Mother Jones* v42 no4 p68 Jl/Ag 2017

Ferziger, Jonathan
Cigars, Bubbly, and Subs Haunt Netanyahu *Bloomberg Businessweek* no4540 p35 O 2 2017
Good Deals Make Good Neighbors color map *Bloomberg Businessweek* no4510 p36 F 6 2017
If You Build It, Will Peace Come? color *Bloomberg Businessweek* no4519 p19 Ap 24 2017
Room With a View (of a Wall and Barbed Wire) color *Bloomberg Businessweek* no4516 p14 Mr 27 2017

FESCHUK, SCOTT
Bringing up baby color *Maclean's* v130 no7 p64 Ag 2017
CANADA'S OWN TWO TINY TRUMPS color *Maclean's* v130 no2 p73 Mr 2017
A children's guide to parenting color *Maclean's* v130 no3 p72 Ap 2017
Filling the void color *Maclean's* v129 no46 p65 N 21 2016
Finally, the end of hockey color *Maclean's* v130 no4 p73 My 2017
Hot tips for Trump's next debate color *Maclean's* v129 no40 p81 O 10 2016
How to talk (down) to the town-hall voter color *Maclean's* v129 no41 p61 O 17 2016
Let's make this choice easier for you color *Maclean's* v129 no42 p65 O 24 2016
National anthems chart color *Maclean's* v130 no6 p14 Jl 2017
No one to blame but ... everybody else color *Maclean's* v129 no44 p117 N 7 2016
The oaf of office color *Maclean's* v129 no51/52 p73 D 26 2016
The odds on a Trumpocalypse color *Maclean's* v129 no47 p65 N 28 2016
On the run color *Maclean's* v130 no8 p65 S 2017

Rock these reboots around the tree color *Maclean's* v129 no45 p61 N 14 2016

Sexy as the Rock color *Maclean's* v129 no50 p65 D 19 2016

The Shape of Our Robo-Doom color *Maclean's* v130 no9 p81 O 2017

...The best concession speech ever color *Maclean's* v129 no43 p65 O 31 2016

Translating Trump color *Maclean's* v130 no10 p128 N 2017

Was the White House always gold? color *Maclean's* no1 p65 F 17 2017

'What is big jelly hiding from us?' color *Maclean's* v129 no48/49 p81 D 5 2016

Festivals

See also

    Art festivals

    Comedy festivals

    Drama festivals

    Flower festivals

    Folk festivals

    Food festivals

    LGBT pride celebrations

    Literary festivals

    Mid-autumn Festival

    Music festivals

    Parades

    Renaissance fairs

    Wine festivals

2017 CINCINNATI INTERNATIONAL *Cincinnati Magazine* v50 no6 p124 Mr 2017

ABOVE & BEYOND cartoon *New Yorker* v93 no15 p12 My 29 2017

ANCHORED IN A SMALL TOWN L. MYERS cartoon *Missouri Life* v44 no3 p68 My 2017

THE ATLANTA SCIENCE FESTIVAL IS BACK K. VIMAL *Atlanta* v56 no11 p148 Mr 2017

BEST OF THE FESTS L. Roberts color *Indianapolis Monthly* v41 no2 p92 S 2017

CELEBRATION IN THE OAKS color *New Orleans Magazine* v51 no1 p29 N 2016

DON'T MISS LIST AUGUST 2016 *Sea Magazine* v108 no8 pPNW-14 Ag 2016

DON'T MISS LIST JULY 2017 *Sea Magazine* v109 no7 pPNW-18 Jl 2017

DON'T MISS LIST MAY 2017 *Sea Magazine* v109 no5 pPNW-6 My 2017

DON'T MISS LIST NOVEMBER 2016 *Sea Magazine* v108 no10 pPNW-11 O 2016

DONT MISS LIST OCTOBER 2016 *Sea Magazine* v108 no10 pCA-7 O 2016

DON'T MISS LIST OCTOBER 2016 *Sea Magazine* v108 no10 pPNW-11 O 2016

EDITOR'S LETTER N. Rapold color *Film Comment* v53 no1 p4 Ja/F 2017

EVENT CALENDAR *Washingtonian Magazine* v52 no1 p207 O 2016

GOINGS ON ABOUT TOWN color *New Yorker* v93 no25 p5 Ag 28 2017

HOLI MOLEY *Atlanta* v57 no1 p20 My 2017

JAPAN *New York Times Magazine* p30 S 24 2017

Junkies get their fix at Junkstock festival O. SNOW color *Nebraska Life* v21 no5 p84 S/O 2017

NOVEMBER'S COOLEST EVENTS *Indianapolis Monthly* v40 no3 p28 N 2016

Old West Balloon Fest fills Panhandle skies R. HOLSINGER color *Nebraska Life* v21 no5 p80 S/O 2017

OUR TOP PICKS F. ESKER color *New Orleans Magazine* v51 no1 p28 N 2016

Out & About *Martha Stewart Living* no268 p10 O 2016

OVER THE RAINBOW M. Schulman color *New Yorker* v93 no29 p78 S 25 2017

Safe Haven: The U.S. premiere of Donizetti's Assedio di Calais at Glimmerglass fits the festival's "home and homeland" theme M. Sigman *Opera News* v81 no12 p54 Je 2017

SEPTEMBER/OCTOBER K. Massicot bw color *Louisiana Life* v38 no1 p62 S/O 2017

The Spirit of Ollokot L. B. BATEMAN *Idaho Magazine* v16 no6 p42 Mr 2017

Stamford Celebrates Its Golden Georgian Heritage color *British Heritage Travel* v38 no5 p11 S/O 2017

Summer Forecast S. KNOPPER color *Rolling Stone* no1291/1292 p28 Jl 13 2017

Summer Holiday: OPERA NEWS's spotlights the best of the U.S. Festival scene M. Mazzaro *Opera News* v81 no12 p27 Je 2017

The Ticket: NOVEMBER'S COOLEST EVENTS *Indianapolis Monthly* p28 N 2017

TOGETHERNESS P. STEFÁNSSON *Iceland Review* v55 no4 p6 Jl/Ag 2017

TOO MANY TO EAT! L. HECK color *Missouri Life* v44 no5 p68 Ag 2017

A tribute to Stephen Hawking D. J. Eicher color *Astronomy* v45 no1 p54 Ja 2017

WOKE WONDERLAND V. K. De Luca color *Essence* v48 no6 p14 O 2017

Festivals—California

Entertainment WEEKLY POPFEST color *Entertainment Weekly* no1435 p7 O 14 2016

Entertainment WEEKLY POPFEST™ color *Entertainment Weekly* no1438 p16 N 4 2016

Festivals—England

World's Festival City for 70 Years *British Heritage Travel* v38 no1 p7 Ja/F 2017

Festivals—Louisiana

NOVEMBER/DECEMBER K. MASSICOT color *Louisiana Life* v37 no2 p100 N/D 2016

ON THE RUN M. Romer color *Louisiana Life* v37 no3 p38 Ja/F 2017

THE QUIZ OF KINGS E. LABORDE color *Louisiana Life* v37 no3 p110 Ja/F 2017

San Fermin en Nueva Orleans color *New Orleans Magazine* v51 no9 p27 Jl 2017

TOP PICKS F. Esker color *New Orleans Magazine* v51 no8 p28 Je 2017

Festivals—Spain

Chicken Among Bulls T. MECIA color *Weekly Standard* v22 no45 p33 Ag 7 2017

Festivals—Switzerland

SWITZERLAND D. Heimburger color *Christianity Today* v61 no7 p12 S 2017

Festivals—Texas

5 Fantastic Festivals *Audubon* v119 no1 p46 Spr 2017

IF DOWNTOWN AUSTIN *Texas Monthly* v44 no12 p16 D 2016

Festivals—United States

65 GREAT THINGS TO DO THIS MONTH J. FOUMBERG, J. HARDBERGER et al color *Chicago* v65 no11 p115 N 2016

ABOVE & BEYOND cartoon *New Yorker* v93 no18 p14 Je 26 2017

CALENDAR *Treasures* v6 no2 p34 O/N 2016

Christmas in Brausou *Missouri Life* v43 no6 p29 O/N 2016

Dark Skies Over Nebraska A. J. BARTELS cartoon color *Nebraska Life* v21 no4 p80 Jl/Ag 2017

Fortune on the Global Stage K. Bellstrom and C. Zillman color *Fortune* v176 no1 p18 Jl 1 2017

GO J. FOUMBERG, J. HARDBERGER et al color *Chicago* v66 no4 p113 Ap 2017

Rhythm Rules at PDX Jazz Fest P. de Barros color *Downbeat* v84 no5 p13 My 2017

STATEWIDE EVENTS N. BUCK color *Nebraska Life* v21 no4 p85 Jl/Ag 2017

To Do: Twenty-five things to see, hear, watch, and read D. EDELSTEIN, M. Z. SEITZ et al img *New York* v50 no10 p106 My 15 2017

Festivals—Universities & colleges

Hampton Fest Spotlights Stars, Students J. Ross color *Downbeat* v84 no5 p15 My 2017

Festivals—Virginia

Events *Virginia Living* v15 no4 p39 Je 2017

Feta cheese

SUMMER B. HOSTETTER *Indianapolis Monthly* v12 no40 p64 Ag 2017

Fetal alcohol syndrome

TREATING ADDICTED WOMEN during pregnancy D. Gilbert *Psychology Today* v50 no3 p25 My/Je 2017

Fetal brain—Abnormalities
Pioneering study images activity in fetal brains G. Miller bw *Science* v355 no6321 p117 Ja 13 2017
Fetal development—Research
Big studies clash over fetal growth rates J. de Vrieze graph *Science* v355 no6323 p336 Ja 27 2017
Fetal growth disorders
The Coat-Hanger Rebellion S. HOWARD *Ms.* v26 no4 p18 Wint 2016
Fetal tissues—Research
Fetal Tissue Investigative Panel *Congressional Digest* v96 no1 p16 Ja 2017
Panel slams fetal tissue research *Science* v355 no6321 p112 Ja 13 2017
Fetal tissues—Sales & prices
Fetal Tissue Investigative Panel *Congressional Digest* v96 no1 p16 Ja 2017
Fetch Robotics (Company)
A Job Plan for Robots and Humans T. Simonite color *MIT Technology Review* v120 no4 p34 Jl/Ag 2017
Feteha, Ahmed
A Mideast Rivalry Leads to a Split color map *Bloomberg Businessweek* no4526 p23 Je 12 2017
Fetherston, Julia
Impact Investing Needs Millennials *Harvard Business Review Digital Articles* p2 O 3 2014
Fetherstonhaugh, Brian
Developing a Strategy for a Life of Meaningful Labor *Harvard Business Review Digital Articles* p2 S 5 2016
Fetterman, Mindy
New Hope at Stage 4 color *AARP: The Magazine* v30 no6A p27 O/N 2017
Fetterolf, Samantha N.
Distribution and clinical impact of functional variants in 50,726 whole-exome sequences from the DiscovEHR study chart graph *Science* v354 no6319 paaf6814-1 D 23 2016
Fetters, K. Aleisha
Banish Back Pain the Natural Way color *Men's Health* v32 no7 p75 S 2017
How a Song Brings Out Your Beast cartoon *Men's Health* v32 no8 p78 O 2017
HOW FIT ARE YOU REALLY? chart color *Women's Health* v14 no4 p68 My 2017
RECTUS THE RIGHT WAY chart color *Muscle & Performance* v8 no12 p24 D 2016
A SICK FINISH color *Runner's World* v51 no10 p33 N 2016
Sleep Gadgets: What Works, What Doesn't color *Men's Health* v32 no8 p76 O 2017
Fetus
BABY STEPS C. Zuckerman bw *National Geographic* v231 no6 pC21 Je 2017
Fetz, Eberhard
Help, hope, and hype: Ethical dimensions of neuroprosthetics color *Science* v356 no6345 p1338 Je 30 2017
Feud (TV program)
ALL ABOUT FEUD A. D'ARMINIO and J. Halterman *TV Guide* v65 no8 p8 F 27 2017
America's top TV critic Matt Roush answers your burning questions M. Roush *TV Guide* v65 no21 p5 My 15 2017
ARCH NEMESES E. NUSSBAUM cartoon *New Yorker* v93 no5 p98 Mr 20 2017
Season of the Bitch: Bette vs. Joan R. SHEFFIELD color *Rolling Stone* no1284 p22 Ap 6 2017
Feud: Bette & Joan (TV program)
CATHERINE THE GREAT A. D'ARMINIO *TV Guide* v65 no14 p24 Ap 3 2017
Feud: Bette and Joan J. Jensen color *Entertainment Weekly* no1454/1455 p84 F 24 2017
FIGHT CLUB [Cover story] J. Cagle color *Entertainment Weekly* no1450 p22 Ja 27 2017
Hollywood Horror Story img *New York* p124 Mr 6 2017
On FX, a Bonfire of the Vain Biddies D. D'Addario color *Time* v189 no9 p52 Mr 13 2017
Feudalism
TOWERS OF POWER D. C. Weinczok *History Today* v66 no11 p34 N 2016

Feuer, Alan
DEFENDER OF THE COMMUNITY *Harper's Magazine* p41 Ap 2017
Feuerherd, Peter
You invited me in [Cover story] color *U.S. Catholic* v81 no12 p12 D 2016
Feuerstein, Mark
9JKL M. Roffman *TV Guide* v65 no37 p26 S 4 2017
My Obsessions... *TV Guide* v65 no23 p8 My 29 2017
Feuillet, C.
Improving global integration of crop research color *Science* v357 no6349 p359 Jl 28 2017
Feuilletons
The Art of Thinking in Other People's Heads A. Stern *Humanities* v38 no1 p1 Wint 2017
Fever
      See also
   Malaria
He thought he was getting the same stomach bug that his co-worker had. But his symptoms wound up being completely different L. Sanders color *New York Times Magazine* p18 Ag 6 2017
The Mystery of Cocoliztli R. ACUÑA-SOTO bw color *Natural History* v125 no9 p21 S 2017
WILDER. CRAZIER. FASTER! A. MURPHY bw color *Men's Health* v32 no8 p116 O 2017
Fever—Prevention
your no-panic guide to fever K. BAYLESS *Parents* p58 2015
FEWELL, BRENT
The Best of Intentions *American Conservative* v16 no1 p23 Ja/F 2017
Fey, Tina
Artists color *Time* v189 no16/17 p40 My 1-8 2017
Out & About *TV Guide* p4 D 5 2016
Sound Bites color *Entertainment Weekly* no1450 p9 Ja 27 2017
Sound Bites color *Entertainment Weekly* no1480 p4 S 1 2017
Tina Fey Is a Bossypants D. Holbrook *TV Guide* v65 no37 p14 S 4 2017
WHISKEY TANGO FOXTROT B. A. DuHamel color *Sound & Vision* v81 no9 p70 N 2016
Who's the BOSS? D. HOLBROOK *TV Guide* v65 no41 p20 O 2 2017
Feynman, Richard Phillips, 1918-1988
Our Personal Favorites C. ENGELKING, E. NECKAR et al bw *Discover* v38 no4 p44 My 2017
Fezza, Filomena
Activity-based protein profiling reveals off-target proteins of the FAAH inhibitor BIA 10-2474 chart color graph *Science* v356 no6342 p1084 Je 9 2017
Fiala, Károly
Changing climate shifts timing of European floods color graph *Science* v357 no6351 p588 Ag 11 2017
Fiat 124 automobile
Miata, People S. SMITH cartoon *Road & Track* v68 no7 p26 Mr/Ap 2017
Fiat 124 automobile—Evaluation
Fiat 124 Spider chart color *Motor Trend* v69 no1 p123 Ja 2017
THE NEW BLOOD E. TINGWALL color *Car & Driver* v62 no7 p46 Ja 2017
Fiat Chrysler Automobiles NV
Go Lutz Yourself B. LUTZ color *Road & Track* v68 no5 p126 D 2016/Ja 2017
Fiber, Alexandra
My boyfriend of four years doesn't want to move in together color *Glamour* v115 no3 p144 Mr 2017
Fiber cement
SEA CHANGE S. SMITH color *House Beautiful* p34 Ag 2017
Fiber cement siding
MAGNOLIA DESIGN DETAILS *Atlanta* v56 no7 p44 N 2016
Fiber in human nutrition
THE BEST WEIGHT-LOSS ADVICE EVER! L. Rotchford color *Women's Health* v14 no1 p126 Ja/F 2017
Brothy Bowl color *Vegetarian Today* no1 p26 F 2017
Fiber Facts V. Tweed color *Better Nutrition* v79 no11 p80 N 2017
FIBER FOODS color *Muscle & Performance* v9 no9 p61 S 2017
Hungry for sleep V. Clayton color *Yoga Journal* no294 p41 S 2017
Peanut Butter Power Snack Dip J. BOWDEN and J. BESSINGER

color *Better Nutrition* v79 no7 p56 Jl 2017

THE REAL DEAL ON FIBER J. Bowden color *Amazing Wellness* v8 no6 p42 Early Winter2016

Vegetable Soup color *Vegetarian Today* no1 p12 F 2017

Fiber lasers

Spatiotemporal mode-locking in multimode fiber lasers L. G. Wright, D. N. Christodoulides et al color *Science* v357 no6359 p94 O 6 2017

Fiber optics

Toto, I've a Feeling We're Still In Kansas (or Missouri) S. McBride and M. Bergen color *Bloomberg Businessweek* no4514 p33 Mr 13 2017

Fiberglass boats

    See also

      Fiberglass canoes

6 Simple Steps to a Custom Track System R. Robertson *Boating World* v37 no9 p22 N/D 2016

Fiberglass boats—Maintenance & repair

Filling in the Gaps B. PIKE color *Power & Motoryacht* v32 no12 p72 D 2016

Fiberglass canoes

CLIPPER CANOES color *Canoe & Kayak Magazine* v45 no1 p71 Wint 2017

NOVA CRAFT CANOE color *Canoe & Kayak Magazine* v45 no1 p94 Wint 2017

Fibers

    See also

      Paper

The Secret Fuel Your Body Craves M. YOUNG color *Men's Health* v32 no8 p92 O 2017

Fibers—Evaluation

Peco charges into scenery market with static grass C. Grivno color *Model Railroader* v84 no2 p72 F 2017

Fibrillin

The cytotoxic Staphylococcus aureus PSMα3 reveals a cross-α amyloid-like fibril E. Tayeb-Fligelman, O. Tabachnikov et al bibl color diag graph *Science* v355 no6327 p831 F 24 2017

Fibroblasts

Eggs grown from mouse skin cells T. H. SAEY color *Science News* v190 no10 p6 N 12 2016

Fibromyalgia

Problem Solved! [Cover story] R. LALIBERTE cartoon *Prevention* v69 no1 p18 Ja 2017

Fibromyalgia—Patients

Hope for Fibromyalgia J. Bowden color *Amazing Wellness* v9 no1 p36 Wint 2017

Fibromyalgia—Treatment

Hope for Fibromyalgia J. Bowden color *Amazing Wellness* v9 no1 p36 Wint 2017

Ficaro, Kim

KIM FICARO M. B. EYERS color *Better Homes & Gardens* v95 no9 p22 S 2017

Fick, B.

Observation of a large-scale anisotropy in the arrival directions of cosmic rays above 8×1018 eV *Science* v357 no6357 p1266 S 22 2017

Fick, Nathaniel C.

See Your Company Through the Eyes of a Hacker *Harvard Business Review Digital Articles* p2 Mr 24 2015

FICKE, ROSE

Q: Who's your trusty sidekick for summer adventures, and why? color *O, The Oprah Magazine* p14 Je 2017

Fickell, Luke

NEW COACH, OLD DREAM G. Freking *Cincinnati Magazine* v50 no12 p23 S 2017

Fiction

    See also

      Allegory

      Detective & mystery stories

      Fiction genres

      Ghost stories

      Graphic novels

      Novels of manners

      Science fiction

      Short story (Literary form)

      Young adult fiction

Best Sellers *New York Times Book Review* p44 N 13 2016

A Big Week for Adult Fiction chart *Publishers Weekly* v264 no21 p5 My 22 2017

CHILDREN'S BESTSELLERS C. JURIS chart *Publishers Weekly* v264 no12 p19 Mr 20 2017

COMBINED PRINT AND E-BOOK BEST SELLERS *New York Times Book Review* p22 Ap 9 2017

Fiction Lovers Have More Feelings color *Prevention* v68 no12 p10 D 2016

Fran Lebowitz *New York Times Book Review* p7 Mr 26 2017

Funny FiLL-IN M. J. KRAUSS *National Geographic Kids* no468 p30 Mr 2017

The Missing Millennial Novel T. TULATHIMUTTE *New York Times Book Review* p37 D 11 2016

PEN PALS A. Tan bw color *O, The Oprah Magazine* p34 N 2017

PRINT/HARDCOVER BEST SELLERS *New York Times Book Review* p24 F 26 2017

Telling Overlooked Stories L. PICKER color *Publishers Weekly* v264 no35 p103 Ag 28 2017

Why it pays to increase your WORD POWER [Cover story] B. SPECKTOR color *Reader's Digest* v190 no1133 p66 S 2017

With '1984' All the Rage, Is Dystopian Backlist a Publishing Utopia? J. Maher *Publishers Weekly* v264 no29 p3 Jl 17 2017

Fiction genres

'Contrary by Temperament' A. Domestico bw *Commonweal* v144 no13 p10 Ag 11 2017

Fiction writing

First Lines color *Publishers Weekly* v264 no21 p54 My 22 2017

Mary GAITSKILL: ONE OF OUR MOST ORIGINAL FICTION WRITERS TURNS HER WIT AND WISDOM TOWARD THE REAL WORLD, RIGHT WHEN WE NEED IT MOST L. NAKADATE *Interview* v47 no3 p34 Ap 2017

Seen and Unseen R. ROSENBLATT *New York Times Book Review* p8 Ag 27 2017

Fiction writing techniques

    See also

      First person narrative

Who Needs An Outline? E. RASKIN color *Publishers Weekly* v264 no25 p116 Je 19 2017

Fiction—Authorship

Meet the Judges N. A. SPECTOR color *Publishers Weekly* v263 no47 p62 N 21 2016

They Could Be Heroes S. SACKS bw color *New Republic* v248 no4 p44 Ap 2017

Fiction—Bibliographies

Reviews Roundup *Publishers Weekly* v263 no52 p90 D 19 2016

Fiction—Charts, diagrams, etc.

BESTSELLERS chart color *Publishers Weekly* v264 no32 p11 Ag 7 2017

BESTSELLERS chart *Publishers Weekly* v264 no2 p14 Ja 9 2017

BESTSELLERS C. JURIS chart *Publishers Weekly* v264 no7 p12 F 13 2017

Best Sellers *New York Times Book Review* p23 Mr 19 2017

BESTSELLERS OCTOBER 17–23 2016 C. JURIS chart color *Publishers Weekly* v263 no44 p13 O 31 2016

BESTSELLERS SEPTEMBER 26-OCTOBER 2, 2016 C. JURIS *Publishers Weekly* v263 no41 p15 O 10 2016

iBooks Bestsellers chart color *Publishers Weekly* v263 no44 p17 O 31 2016

iBooks Bestsellers chart color *Publishers Weekly* v264 no8 p16 F 20 2017

Fiction—Technique

    See also

      First person narrative

Fictitious characters

    See also

      Aquaman (Fictitious character)

      Batgirl (Fictitious character)

      Black Panther (Fictitious character)

      Buffy the Vampire Slayer (Fictitious character)

      Bumppo, Natty (Fictitious character)

      Cage, Luke (Fictitious character)

      Calrissian, Lando (Fictitious character)

      Daredevil (Fictitious character)

      Deadpool (Fictitious character)

      Everdeen, Katniss (Fictitious character)

The No-Fuss Fig Tree K. Hammonds color *Southern Living* v51 no11 p53 N 2016

Figaro! (90201) (Theatrical production)
CLASSICAL MUSIC *New Yorker* v93 no9 p14 Ap 17 2017

Figes, Orlando
A Very Close Friend of the Family bw *New York Review of Books* v63 no19 p40 D 8 2016
The Wild Child of Russian Literature color *New York Review of Books* v64 no8 p57 My 11 2017

Figgis, Genieve—Exhibitions
Sweet SORROW color *Vogue* v206 no12 p150 D 2016

Fighter planes
See also
Jet fighter planes
In Plane View CHRIS *Los Angeles Magazine* v61 no11 p28 N 2016
The Iranian Express E. OTTOLENGHI color map *Weekly Standard* v22 no44 p22 Jl 31 2017

Figinski, Theodore F.
Research: Companies Are Less Likely to Hire Current Military Reservists *Harvard Business Review Digital Articles* p2 O 13 2017

Figueira, J. M.
Observation of a large-scale anisotropy in the arrival directions of cosmic rays above 8×10^{18} eV *Science* v357 no6357 p1266 S 22 2017

Figueiredo, F. O. G.
Persistent effects of pre-Columbian plant domestication on Amazonian forest composition bibl chart graph map *Science* v355 no6328 p925 Mr 3 2017

Figueiredo, Margarida
Click chemistry enables preclinical evaluation of targeted epigenetic therapies diag *Science* v356 no6345 p1397 Je 30 2017

Figueres, Christiana
THE WOMAN WHO SAVED THE PLANET color *Scientific American* v317 no3 p86 S 2017

Figueroa, Lucila
Protecting unauthorized immigrant mothers improves their children's mental health diag *Science* v357 no6355 p1041 S 8 2017

Figueroa, Mario E.
GQNZ0247 *Texas Monthly* v45 no4 p32 Ap 2017

Figueroa, Raul
Scouting the Guatemala International Book Fair color *Publishers Weekly* v264 no32 p20 Ag 7 2017

Figueroa, Reynaldo
Student, Hiker, Sprogger W. Becktold *Sierra* v102 no5 p63 St/O 2017

Figurative art
68 GREAT THINGS TO DO THIS MONTH J. FOUMBERG, J. HARDBERGER et al color *Chicago* v66 no5 p119 My 2017

Figure skating competitions
FIGURE SKATING K. ROSEN *TV Guide* v65 no4 p48 Ja 16 2017

Figurines
See also
Clay figurines
Survival of The Cutest E. GAUKEL *Treasures* v6 no2 p26 O/N 2016
Water works M. HEMMADI color *Maclean's* v130 no9 p20 O 2017

Figurines—Design & construction
COMPLETE SET D. Steinberg cartoon *New Yorker* v93 no3 p23 Mr 6 2017

Figurines—Marketing
Magic in Miniature T. SANCTON bw color *Vanity Fair* v59 no9 p98 S 2017

FIGURSKI, JARED D.
Long-Term Studies Contribute Disproportionately to Ecology and Policy *BioScience* v67 no3 p271 Mr 2017

Fiji
Fiji [Cover story] color *Sports Illustrated* v126 no6 p32 F 20 2017

Fiji—Description & travel
TRAVEL Fiji color *Sports Illustrated* v126 no6 p61 F 20 2017

Fikenscher, Sven-Eric
Amid high tensions, an urgent need for nuclear restraint bibl *Bulletin of the Atomic Scientists* v73 no4 p279 Jl 2017

Filacchione, G.

Seasonal exposure of carbon dioxide ice on the nucleus of comet 67P/Churyumov-Gerasimenko bibl bw graph *Science* v354 no6319 p1563 D 23 2016

FILARDO, THOMAS W.
MEDICAL USE VS. ABUSE *Scientific American* v316 no2 p5 F 2017

Filbin, Mariella G.
Decoupling genetics, lineages, and microenvironment in IDH-mutant gliomas by single-cell RNA-seq diag *Science* v355 no6332 p1391 Mr 31 2017

Filby, Andrew
Single-cell RNA-seq reveals new types of human blood dendritic cells, monocytes, and progenitors color *Science* v356 no6335 p283 Ap 21 2017

Fildes, Annette Guarisco
U.S. Health Care Reform Can't Wait for Quality Measures to Be Perfect *Harvard Business Review Digital Articles* p2 O 4 2017

File transfer (Computer science)—Software
TRANSMIT 5: FILE TRANSFER UTILITY EXPANDS SUPPORT FOR CLOUD SERVICES G. FLEISHMAN color *Macworld - Digital Edition* v34 no9 p21 S 2017

Filene's Basement Corp.
Markdown Memories: When the original Filene's Basement closed 10 years ago this fall, Boston lost a quirky shopping experience-and a kind of common ground J. Johnson *Yankee* v81 no5 p156 S/O 2017

FILERI, PAUL
Monstrous Wonder bw *Film Comment* v52 no6 p95 N/D 2016

FILGATE, MICHELE
THE END IS HERE cartoon color *O, The Oprah Magazine* p111 My 2017
WE ALL FALL DOWN cartoon color *O, The Oprah Magazine* p91 Ap 2017

Filho, José Alves
PSCORE *Arabian Horse World* v57 no9 p26 Je 2017

Filibusters (Adventurers)
IMPERIAL WALKER P. CARLSON bw color *American History* v52 no3 p16 Ag 2017

Filibusters (Political science)
Filibusted J. Cost color *Weekly Standard* v22 no31 p6 Ap 17 2017

Filipchyk, Andrei
Loss of a mammalian circular RNA locus causes miRNA deregulation and affects brain function color *Science* v357 no6357 p1254 S 22 2017

Filipovic, Jill
It's Always Men *Time* v190 no15 p29 O 16 2017
Shiny Unhappy People N. S. RILEY *Commentary* v144 no1 p54 Jl/Ag 2017
SIN OF OMISSION color *Foreign Policy* no223 p50 Mr/Ap 2017
What Weinstein's Downfall Means for Other Predators *Time* v190 no16/17 p29 O 23 2017

Filippetti Yacht Srl
ITALIAN COOKING S. SHIBATA *Sea Magazine* v108 no9 p10 S 2016

Filkins, Dexter
BEFORE THE FLOOD bw cartoon *New Yorker* v92 no43 p22 Ja 2 2017
THE BREAKING POINT cartoon *New Yorker* v93 no32 p42 O 16 2017
MY HOMETOWN PAPER: Dexter Filkins color *Columbia Journalism Review* v56 no1 p41 Spr 2017
On the Fringes of ISIS *New York Times Book Review* p13 Ja 22 2017
THE THIRTY-YEAR COUP bw cartoon *New Yorker* v92 no33 p60 O 17 2016
THE WARRIOR MONK cartoon *New Yorker* v93 no15 p34 My 29 2017

Filler, Martin
The Brutal Dreams That Came True color *New York Review of Books* v63 no20 p22 D 22 2016
A Mystic Monumentality color *New York Review of Books* v64 no11 p14 Je 22 2017
New York's Vast Flop color *New York Review of Books* v64 no4 p11 Mr 9 2017

Fillers (Materials)
Pillow Talk C. K. Lehrman color *Consumer Reports* v82 no2 p22

F 2017

Secrets to a Great Night's sleep M. H. J. Farrell chart color *Consumer Reports* v82 no2 p16 F 2017

Fillerup Clark, Amber

Instamom B. BOSKER cartoon *Atlantic* v319 no2 p16 Mr 2017

Fillion, Nathan, 1971-

Nathan Fillion Heads to Brooklyn D. Holbrook *TV Guide* v65 no11 p14 Mr 6 2017

TV's HOTTEST COUPLES S. Malcom, I. Ratledge et al *TV Guide* v64 no15 p28 Ap 4 2016

Fillon, François, 1954-

Fillon Falling C. CALDWELL *Weekly Standard* v22 no22 p14 F 13 2017

France's Battle Royale T. John color *Time* v189 no5 p9 F 13 2017

France's Man to Take on the Far Right T. John color *Time* v188 no24 p14 D 12 2016

France Votes C. C. W. COOKE *National Review* v69 no7 p30 Ap 17 2017

In France, an Election Veers Off the Rails G. Viscusi and C. Matlack graph *Bloomberg Businessweek* no4511 p17 F 13 2017

Thatcherism Redux in France C. Matlack, M. Deen et al bw color *Bloomberg Businessweek* no4502 p21 D 5 2016

Film & video installations (Art)—Exhibitions

DOUGLAS GORDON A. Rosenmeyer color *Art in America* v105 no4 p125 Ap 2017

Life on Mars C. SWANSON img *New York* p58 Ja 23 2017

Film adaptations

ESMÉ IN NEVERLAND J. LEPORE cartoon *New Yorker* v92 no38 p34 N 21 2016

Film archives

The Great Library D. GIRISH bw *Film Comment* v53 no1 p91 Ja/F 2017

Film composers

Meet the crew... E. Aslanian *TV Guide* v65 no43 p8 O 16 2017

Film costume

A Fine Cut C. LAVERTY bw cartoon *Film Comment* v53 no5 p16 S/O 2017

Film crews

See also

Cinematographers

Motion picture producers & directors

Sound designers & design

BIG BEAR, CALIFORNIA J. Miller bw color *Snowboarder* v29 no4 p96 D 2016

Film critics

The Critic AND THE STAR L. ANOLIK bw cartoon *Vanity Fair* p180 Hollywood 2017 Supplement

Film festivals

See also

Biennale di Venezia

Sundance Film Festival

Toronto International Film Festival (Toronto, Ont.)

ABOVE & BEYOND cartoon *New Yorker* v92 no30 p18 S 26 2016

ABOVE & BEYOND cartoon *New Yorker* v93 no27 p17 S 11 2017

ABOVE & BEYOND cartoon *New Yorker* v93 no5 p26 Mr 20 2017

The American Black Film Festival Celebrates 20 Years with #ABFF20 K. Wilder color *Black Enterprise* v47 no2 p42 S 2016

AUTUMN AMUSEMENTS E. S. ARNARSDÓTTIR color *Iceland Review* v54 no5 p8 S-O 2016

Cuban Documentary Retrospective at DocLisboa 2016 P. Aufderheide *Film Quarterly* v70 no3 p80 Spr 2017

ENVIRONMENTAL FILM FESTIVAL *Washingtonian Magazine* v52 no6 p29 Mr 2017

Flashback S. DAILY color *Indianapolis Monthly* v42 no2 p54 O 2017

INSIGHTS color *Science* v356 no6337 p480 My 5 2017

Keeping at It D. Lim bw color *Film Comment* v53 no4 p62 Jl/Ag 2017

KEEPING COOL A. LANE bw color *New Yorker* v93 no11 p70 My 1 2017

Out & About *TV Guide* v65 no23 p4 My 29 2017

PARTY LINES S. W. Hunt img *New York* v50 no9 p98 My 1 2017

Reporting the Start of a Season: Toronto International Film Festi-

val R. Rich *Film Quarterly* v70 no2 p81 Wint 2016

REVIVALS AND FESTIVALS color *New Yorker* v92 no32 p29 O 10 2016

SUN VALLEY FILM FEST J. Hibberd color *Entertainment Weekly* no1459 p48 Mr 31 2017

Time for Planet in Focus color *Alternatives Journal (AJ) - Canada's Environmental Voice* v42 no3 p12 2016

UNITED WE SIT E. HYNES color *Film Comment* v53 no1 p66 Ja/F 2017

Wide range of offerings at region's Jewish film festivals *Successful Farming* v115 no1 p23 Ja 2017

Yankees favorite events this season chart *Yankee* v81 no1 p78 Ja/F 2017

Film festivals—Canada

Ten Facts about National Canadian Film Day 150 bw color *Walrus* v14 no3 p1 Ap 2017

Film festivals—India

Hooray for Bollywood! R. BERFANGER *Indianapolis Monthly* v12 no40 p13 Ag 2017

Film festivals—Italy

Days of Heaven: II Cinema Ritrovato on Its Thirtieth Anniversary J. Ma *Film Quarterly* v70 no2 p68 Wint 2016

Film festivals—Netherlands

Rotterdam 46: Tremors from a Nervous World B. Harris *Film Quarterly* v70 no4 p113 Summ 2017

Film festivals—Reviews

A Six-Letter Word K. Jones bw color *Film Comment* v53 no4 p58 Jl/Ag 2017

Film festivals—Switzerland

Part Seminar, Part Something Else: The 69th Festival del Film, Locarno J. White *Film Quarterly* v70 no2 p74 Wint 2016

Film festivals—Utah

Sundance 2017: Of Snow and Anguish B. R. Rich *Film Quarterly* v70 no4 p99 Summ 2017

Sundance Film Festival's Focus on Syria L. Thielen *Film Quarterly* v70 no4 p109 Summ 2017

Film makeup

Margot Robbie's Gold-Medal Makeover C. M. Smith color *Entertainment Weekly* no1450 p16 Ja 27 2017

Film noir

THE GUIDE / 03.17 *Los Angeles Magazine* p74 Mr 2017

Film poster design

ANDRZEJ KLIMOWSKI A. Curry color *Film Comment* v53 no4 p80 Jl/Ag 2017

Film posters

The best posters of 2016 A. Curry color *Film Comment* v53 no1 p96 Ja/F 2017

Film revivals

The Reboot Playbook Expands E. Berman color *Time* v188 no27-28 p116 D 26 2016

Film scriptwriting

NINE LIVES T. Friend cartoon *New Yorker* v93 no24 p19 Ag 21 2017

Film sequels

The Bullseye M. Snetiker color *Entertainment Weekly* no1468/1469 p112 Je 2-9 2017

Ewan McGregor E. Berman color *Time* v189 no11 p59 Mr 27 2017

Love Actually Continues J. McGovern color *Entertainment Weekly* no1467 p48 My 26 2017

NOW (RE)PLAYING M. YARM cartoon graph *Wired* v25 no3 p20 Mr 2017

Sequel With a Cause J. McGovern color *Entertainment Weekly* no1460/1461 p92 Ap 7-17 2017

UP TO THE Highest HEIGHT [Cover story] M. Snetiker color *Entertainment Weekly* no1470 p18 Je 16 2017

Film series

See also

Film sequels

Guardians of the Galaxy Vol. 2 *New Yorker* v93 no15 p5 My 29 2017

Film series—Reviews

SATURDAY NIGHT FEVER DIRECTOR'S CUT M. Mettler color *Sound & Vision* v82 no8 p70 O 2017

Film soundtracks

The Agenda color *Men's Health* v31 no10 p8 D 2016

Boss Lady M. WAKIM *Los Angeles Magazine* p74 D 2016

The Galaxy's Hottest Mixtape B. HIATT bw color *Rolling Stone* no1286 p14 My 4 2017

If There's Pain In Fifty Shades, There's Pleasure In Its Soundtrack S. Lansky color *Time* v189 no6 p52 F 20 2017

Reality Bites B. L. Heldman color *Entertainment Weekly* no1460/1461 p82 Ap 7-17 2017

SOUNDTRACK SOUND-OFF: VOL. 2'S BEST TRACKS E. R. Brown color *Entertainment Weekly* no1465 p41 My 12 2017

Film trailers

THE LAST JEDI: LUKE BREAKS HIS SILENCE A. Breznican color *Entertainment Weekly* no1463/1464 p18 Ap/My 2017

Film Noir at Gallop Park, On the Edge (Poem)

Film Noir at Gallop Park, On the Edge M. WICKER *Nation* v303 no23/24 p37 D 5 2016

Filmographies (Motion pictures)

APPETITE FOR DESTRUCTION Y. TALU bw color *Film Comment* v53 no5 p62 S/O 2017

Filtering software—Evaluation

FOR THOSE TIRED OF TRUMP NEWS, THERE'S A PLUG-IN FOR THAT J. Alsever color *Fortune* v176 no1 p10 Jl 1 2017

Filters & filtration design & construction

POSITIVE FILTRATION: IOWA SELECT FARMS IS BUILDING HIGH-TECH SOW BARNS DESIGNED TO KEEP DISEASE OUT B. Freese color *Successful Farming* v115 no7 p45 My 2017

Filters & filtration—Equipment & supplies

Make a Solar Filter J. Oltion *Sky & Telescope* v133 no6 p38 Je 2017

Fimmel, Travis

VIKINGS' NEW ERA D. Franich color *Entertainment Weekly* no1448 p54 Ja 13 2017

Fimmel, Travis—Interviews

Travis Fimmel D. Franich color *Entertainment Weekly* no1448 p55 Ja 13 2017

Fin (Music)

SOLO STAR A. Solomon color *Essence* v47 no12 p67 Ap 2017

Fin Gourmet Foods (Company)

RED STATE VENTURE CAPITAL P. ROBISON color *Bloomberg Businessweek* no4508 p42 Ja 23 2017

Final Audio Design (Company)

Game Changer S. Guttenberg color *Sound & Vision* v82 no3 p26 Ap 2017

Final Draft Inc.

FINAL DRAFT 10: NEW WAYS TO PLOT YOUR NEXT OSCAR-WORTHY SCREENPLAY J. R. BOOKWALTER color *Macworld - Digital Edition* p31 F 2017

Finalex (Company)

GET TO KNOW: FINAFLEX J. SCHILDHOUSE color *Muscle & Performance* v9 no4 p32 Ap 2017

Final Problem, The (TV program)

Ask Matt *TV Guide* v65 no6 p5 Ja 30 2017

Finan, Christopher M.

Drunks: An American History bw *Publishers Weekly* v264 no15 p61 Ap 10 2017

THE DRUNK VOTE C. M. Finan color *Atlantic* v320 no3 p18 O 2017

Finan, Eileen

Nashville Toasts the CMAs at 50 color *Entertainment Weekly* no1434 p18 O 7 2016

Finance

    See also

    Arts—Finance

    Business revenue

    Campaign funds

    Debt

    Financial management

    Financial performance

    Financing of transportation

    Fundraising

    Grants (Money)

    Income

    Insurance

    Investments

    Loans

    Money

    Personal finance

    Profit

    Public finance

    Real property—Finance

GLEANINGS bw *Christianity Today* p18 Mr 2017

Our Personal Best List J. Bodnar *Kiplinger's Personal Finance* v70 no12 p8 D 2016

Tidy Up Your Files J. Chatzky and W. Konrad color *AARP: The Magazine* v59 no3A p26 Ap/My 2016

The World's Costliest Typos T. John *Time* v189 no10 p10 Mr 20 2017

YOUR CHEAT SHEET TO... College! Money! Jobs! C. THORP chart color *Seventeen* v76 no3 p72 My 2017

Finance education

Finance Can Be a Noble Profession (Yes, Really) M. A. Desai *Harvard Business Review Digital Articles* p2 Jl 17 2017

Finance ministers

A Bananas Republic? A. EGAN *America* v215 no15 p12 N 14 2016

Finance—Charts, diagrams, etc.

FEDERAL FINANCE *Economic Indicators* p32 S 2016

Movers K. Stock cartoon color graph *Bloomberg Businessweek* no4512 p11 F 20 2017

Finance—Congresses

Calendar *Bridges (Federal Reserve Bank of St. Louis)* p2 Summ 2016

Finance—Software

Let's Get Digital F. TORABI color *O, The Oprah Magazine* p33 Ja 2017

Finance—Study & teaching

THE EDITORIAL *Maclean's* v129 no48/49 p5 D 5 2016

Finance—United States

THE MONEY CHAMPIONS [Cover story] K. Clark, M. Leonhardt et al color *Money* v45 no11 p52 D 2016

Financial abuse of older people

THE TERRIFYING TRUE STORY OF A $1 MILLION SCAM M. Leonhardt color *Money* v46 no5 p68 Je 2017

Financial abuse of older people—Prevention

Self-Defense Can Ward Off Senior Financial Abuse M. Leonhardt color *Money* v46 no1 p20 Ja/F 2017

Financial accountability

WHEN HELPING HURTS THE HELPERS S. Eekhoff Zylstra color *Christianity Today* v61 no6 p13 Jl/Ag 2017

Financial Accounting Foundation. Governmental Accounting Standards Board

Selling Your Sewer's Story J. Marlowe *Governing* v30 no3 p63 D 2016

Financial aid

News Briefs *Publishers Weekly* v264 no36 p12 S 4 2017

Financial crises

Are We Safe Yet? T. F. Geithner color *Foreign Affairs* v96 no1 p54 Ja/F 2017

DeVos, Trump Make the Student Loan Crisis Worse S. Ross color *Progressive* v81 no6 p44 Ag/S 2017

The Republic of Broken Dreams J. Fenby *History Today* v66 no11 p27 N 2016

Sweat the Details: It's a great time to sell a boat. Here's how to get it ready G. MANSFIELD color *Sea Magazine* v109 no8 p52 Ag 2017

VENEZUELA'S DEEPENING CRISIS HAS GLOBAL TENTACLES A. Vandermey diag *Fortune* v176 no3 p17 S 1 2017

Financial crises—Economic aspects

Where the Next Crisis Will Come From P. COY color graph *Bloomberg Businessweek* no4496 p44 O 24 2016

Financial crises—Europe

A FOUR-STAR RESPONSE TO THE REFUGEE CRISIS P. STRICKLAND *In These Times* v41 no7 p44 Jl 2017

Financial crises—Greece

Greece and Its Misguided Champions M. G. Jacobides *Harvard Business Review Digital Articles* p2 Ag 24 2015

Financial crises—Social aspects

The Financial World's Rotten Culture Is Still a Threat-to All of Us R. Foroohar color *Time* v188 no16/17 p13 O 24 2016

Financial crises—United States

WEAPONS OF MATH DESTRUCTION C. O'NEIL *Saturday Evening Post* v289 no2 p40 Mr/Ap 2017

Financial databases

Seven Ways to Protect Your Data S. Goldberg *Cincinnati Magazine* v50 no10 p72 Jl 2017

Financial disclosure

WHAT'S ROSS WORTH? D. Alexander color *Forbes* v200 no5 p42 N 14 2017

Financial executives

See also

Chief financial officers

On Money J. Lanchester *New York Times Magazine* p18 N 6 2016

Financial institutions

See also

Insurance companies

What We Lose When Giant Investment Funds Run All Our Companies D. Pitt-Watson *Harvard Business Review Digital Articles* p2 Jl 19 2016

Financial institutions—Asia

Financing the Country's Growth *Foreign Affairs* v95 no6 p(Sp)10 N/D 2016

Financial institutions—Software

See also

Finance—Software

Financial instruments

What Initial Coin Offerings Are, and Why VC Firms Care R. Kastelein *Harvard Business Review Digital Articles* p2 Mr 24 2017

Financial literacy

12 Steps to Financial Success: Empowering At-Risk Adults B. Joergens *Bridges (Federal Reserve Bank of St. Louis)* p9 Wint 2016/2017

Classes for All Classes K. Bahler color *Money* v46 no3 p19 Ap 2017

THE EDITORIAL *Maclean's* v129 no48/49 p5 D 5 2016

Financial management

See also

Budget

Debt management

Endowments

Investment management

Portfolio management (Investments)

Am I Obliged To Support My Elderly Mother? K. A. Appiah *New York Times Magazine* p30 N 20 2016

BECOMING A CAREGIVER L. F. Prater *Successful Farming* v115 no2 p62 F 2017

THE BEST LIST [Cover story] bw color *Kiplinger's Personal Finance* v71 no12 p58 D 2017

Create Some Money Magic color *Health* v31 no4 p9 My 2017

Did We Say That? K. Barrett and R. Greene *Governing* v30 no4 p58 Ja 2017

GAME PLAN FOR 2017 J. Spiegel *Successful Farming* v115 no3 p55 Mid-F 2017

Go Green on a Budget *Parks & Recreation* v51 no11 p55 N 2016

How to Improve Your Finance Skills (Even If You Hate Numbers) R. Knight *Harvard Business Review Digital Articles* p2 Mr 31 2017

The MONEY Do List A. Cao color *Money* v46 no1 p19 Ja/F 2017

Money Help for Aging Parents E. AMBROSE and S. BLOCK color *Kiplinger's Personal Finance* v71 no11 p34 N 2017

Petty Cash J. EPSTEIN cartoon *Weekly Standard* v22 no43 p5 Jl 24 2017

The Question M. MASZTAK, M. HESSION et al *O, The Oprah Magazine* p16 D 2016

THE RIGHT ROBOT FOR YOUR MONEY M. Leonhardt chart color *Money* v46 no1 p86 Ja/F 2017

Save your way to zero stress [Cover story] L. FREEDMAN color *Redbook* p120 My 2017

Son, Here Is How You Save M. HOUSEL color *Reader's Digest* v189 no1129 p38 Ap 2017

THREE MOST IMPORTANT MONEY LESSONS C. M. Brown color *Black Enterprise* v47 no2 p18 S 2016

A Tribe's Bad Deal with Wall Street A. Ganesan color *Progressive* v81 no10 p14 N 2016

WHAT IS A CREDIT SCORE? THE COST OF BORROWING img *Scholastic Choices* p5 O 2017 Supplement

What Single Women Need to Know J. BODNAR color *Kiplinger's Personal Finance* v71 no11 p25 N 2017

When Less Is More Money F. TORABI cartoon *O, The Oprah Magazine* p40 Mr 2017

When Small Changes Can Earn You Big Bucks L. RICHARDS color *Reader's Digest* v190 no1134 p52 O 2017

Why Two Financial Targets Can Be Better than One S. Whitbread and M. Rosenbaum *Harvard Business Review Digital Articles* p2 D 20 2016

The Wisdom of Warren D. CAPLINGER color *AARP: The Magazine* v59 no4A p32 Je/Jl 2016

You have too much stuff V. Reiss color *Yoga Journal* p49 2016 Special Issue

Financial market reaction

MORE UPS THAN DOWNS A. GARA color graph *Forbes* v200 no3 p52 S 28 2017

NO TIME TO WAIT C. Leaf color *Fortune* v174 no8 p11 D 15 2016

Financial market reaction—Congresses

Where Should Investors Turn Now? M. Heimer color *Fortune* v174 no8 p96 D 15 2016

Financial performance

See also

Profitability

Rate of return

Are CEOs Overhyped and Overpaid? T. Chamorro-Premuzic *Harvard Business Review Digital Articles* p2 N 1 2016

How a Culture of Silence Eats Away at Your Company D. Maxfield *Harvard Business Review Digital Articles* p2 D 7 2016

How Do You Rank the World's Best CEOs? C. Fombrun *Harvard Business Review Digital Articles* p2 F 6 2015

Marcus Leaver: CEO, Quarto Group J. Milliot color *Publishers Weekly* v263 no52 p28 D 19 2016

The Most Common Mistake People Make In Calculating ROI J. Knight *Harvard Business Review Digital Articles* p2 Ap 9 2015

Worries About Short-Termism Are 40 Years Old, but Are They Overblown? W. Frick *Harvard Business Review Digital Articles* p2 2017

Financial planners

THE RIGHT PRICE FOR ADVICE N. S. HUANG cartoon diag *Kiplinger's Personal Finance* v71 no12 p44 D 2017

Solving Family Money Fights T. Stanger chart il *Consumer Reports* v82 no5 p44 My 2017

When Star CEOs and Star Analysts Disagree, the Market Trusts the Analysts S. Boivie, S. D. Graffin et al *Harvard Business Review Digital Articles* p2 Ap 18 2016

Financial planning

See also

Estate planning

Retirement planning

Robo-advisors (Financial planning)

10 THINGS THE FINANCIAL CRISIS TAUGHT US P. J. Lim and T. Tepper color diag *Money* v46 no1 p46 Ja/F 2017

3 Ways to Budget for a Windfall color *Black Enterprise* v47 no4 p15 N/D 2016

BECOMING A CAREGIVER L. F. Prater *Successful Farming* v115 no2 p62 F 2017

CROWDSOURCING *Kiplinger's Personal Finance* v71 no12 p20 D 2017

The Early-Bird Dividend K. Holland color diag *Money* v46 no1 p27 Ja/F 2017

Financial Intimacy: Is Your Relationship Ready? A. Edmond Jr. and Z. D. Green color *Black Enterprise* v47 no3 p24 O 2016

GAME PLAN FOR 2017 J. Spiegel *Successful Farming* v115 no3 p55 Mid-F 2017

Get Your Passion Project Moving Without Quitting Your Day Job R. Knight *Harvard Business Review Digital Articles* p2 F 19 2015

Money Matters S. Murphy color *Log Home Living* v33 no7 p22 S 2016

OTHER LESSONS FROM THE RICH P. J. Lim *Money* v46 no9 p37 O 2017

PARENTS, PROTECT YOUR WEALTH [Cover story] A. Edmond Jr. cartoon color *Black Enterprise* v47 no3 p45 O 2016

THE PROBLEM M. Friesen *Successful Farming* v115 no2 p68 F 2017

Solving Family Money Fights T. Stanger chart il *Consumer Reports* v82 no5 p44 My 2017

What Children Should Chip In K. Clark diag *Money* v46 no2 p35 Mr 2017

Financial planning industry
Services *Virginia Living* p51 2017 Best 20of Virginia

Financial planning—Methodology
True Confessions of a Money Man A. ROTH color graph *AARP: The Magazine* v59 no5A p28 Ag/S 2016

Financial risk
Questioning Claims That Are Too Good to Be True K. Firestone *Harvard Business Review Digital Articles* p2 S 7 2016
"RISK ON, RISK OFF" M. Heimer *Fortune* v175 no4 p19 Mr 15 2017

Financial risk management
Are You Betting Too Big on Trump? W. BALDWIN chart color graph *Forbes* v199 no2 p90 F 28 2017
How Much Risk Can You Stand? A. K. SMITH color *Kiplinger's Personal Finance* v71 no2 p24 F 2017
Read This Before You Cosign J. Chatzky *AARP: The Magazine* v59 no6A p27 O/N 2016

Financial security
70 WAYS TO BUILD WEALTH color *Kiplinger's Personal Finance* v71 no4 p20 Ap 2017
Money's too tight to mention P. Cheese *People Management* p5 F 2017
TAKE STEPS TO SECURE YOUR RETIREMENT NOW! D. T. Dingle graph *Black Enterprise* v47 no3 p48 O 2016

Financial services industry
See also
   Wealth management services
AI May Soon Replace Even the Most Elite Consultants B. Libert and M. Beck *Harvard Business Review Digital Articles* p2 Jl 24 2017
Does College Level the Playing Field? W. R. Emmons, L. R. Ricketts et al *Bridges (Federal Reserve Bank of St. Louis)* p7 Spr 2017
Dog Food, TP and Insurance? L. GERSTNER color *Kiplinger's Personal Finance* v71 no11 p40 N 2017
FINANCIAL 45 LISTS *Black Enterprise* v47 no7 p68 My/Je 2017
The Financial Services Industry's Untapped Market S. A. Hewlett and A. T. Moffitt *Harvard Business Review Digital Articles* p2 D 8 2014
How P&G and American Express Are Approaching AI T. H. Davenport and R. Bean *Harvard Business Review Digital Articles* p2 Mr 31 2017
Lies, Damn Lies, and Financial Statistics P. Coy, S. Kishan et al cartoon *Bloomberg Businessweek* no4518 p8 Ap 10 2017
Services *Virginia Living* p79 2017 Best 20of Virginia
Should a Robot Manage Your Money? J. GARSKOF cartoon *AARP: The Magazine* v60 no3A p22 Ap/My 2017
Why Women Aren't Making It to the Top of Financial Services Firms A. Jaekel and E. St-Onge *Harvard Business Review Digital Articles* p2 O 25 2016

Financial services industry—Computer network resources
Watchdog Lacks Bite? M. Leonhardt color *Money* v45 no11 p15 D 2016

Financial services industry—France
Paris and Frankfurt Vie For Brexit's Spoils F. B. Valentini, S. Arons et al *Bloomberg Businessweek* no4530 p30 Jl 17 2017

Financial services industry—Government policy
The Fall of Warren's CFPB? S. Woolley and E. Dexheimer bw *Bloomberg Businessweek* no4500 p36 N 21 2016

Financial services industry—Officials & employees
Watchdog Lacks Bite? M. Leonhardt color *Money* v45 no11 p15 D 2016

Financial services industry—United States
The Fintech 50 S. SHARF, L. SHIN et al color *Forbes* v198 no7 p90 N 29 2016
Five Stages of Trump Grief M. Abelson and D. Campbell *Bloomberg Businessweek* no4501 p32 N 28 2016
In Need of a Fix N. Prins cartoon *Progressive* p27 D 2016/Ja 2017
The Psychology of a Market Bubble A. KATES SMITH *Kiplinger's Personal Finance* v71 no11 p16 N 2017
Wall Street Jobs Won't Be Spared from Automation T. H. Davenport *Harvard Business Review Digital Articles* p2 D 14 2016
What Wall Street Is Really Pushing For % M. Abelson graph *Bloomberg Businessweek* no4535 p26 Ag 28 2017

Financial services industry—United States—Government policy
THE 2017 WASHINGTON WISH LIST K. Clark, M. Leonhardt et al color diag *Money* v46 no1 p96 Ja/F 2017
Fixing Finance, Still N. GELINAS color *National Review* v69 no4 p30 Mr 6 2017

Financial services industry—United States—Officials & employees
Trading Wall Street For Jacksonville J. Levin color *Bloomberg Businessweek* no4509 p34 Ja 30 2017

Financial statements
See also
   Cash flow statements
5 Ways to Increase Your Cross-Selling J. Senior, T. Springer et al *Harvard Business Review Digital Articles* p2 N 22 2016
How One Bad Year Can Wreck Results K. KRISTOF color *Kiplinger's Personal Finance* v71 no7 p57 Jl 2017
YOUR HANDY EARNINGS-CALL DRINKING GAME color *Fortune* v175 no7 p14 Je 1 2017

Financial stress
Even high-rollers feel the pinch *People Management* p6 F 2017
FINANCIAL STRESS L. Farmer *Governing* v30 no4 p31 Ja 2017
STRESSING OUT ABOUT MONEY WILL MAKE YOU LOOK OLDER A. Adamczyk color *Money* v45 no11 p15 D 2016

Financial performance—Charts, diagrams, etc.
THE WEEKLY SCORECARD chart *Publishers Weekly* v263 no46 p5 N 14 2016
THE WEEKLY SCORECARD chart *Publishers Weekly* v264 no8 p6 F 20 2017

Financial stress—Charts, diagrams, etc.
MID-YEAR FINANCIAL CHECKUP J. McKinney diag graph *Black Enterprise* v47 no8 p52 Jl/Ag 2017

Financing of charter schools
CATHOLIC SCHOOLS WAIT ON TRUMP SCHOOL CHOICE PROMISES M. O'Loughlin color graph *America* v217 no4 p12 Ag 21 2017

Financing of environmental protection
SCORCHED EARTH DAY? R. D. Sullivan color graph *America* v216 no8 p12 Ap 17 2017

Financing of federal aid to research
Contractions: Slowing Down Research C. Flavelle and P. Murphy chart graph *Bloomberg Businessweek* no4534 p39 Ag 14 2017

Financing of government agencies
Africa's CDC Can End Malaria C. Manlan color *Scientific American* v317 no3 p10 S 2017
Trump administration outlines budget shake-up M. Hourihan and D. Parkes *Issues in Science & Technology* v33 no3 p19 Spr 2017

Financing of new business enterprises
A BUMPER CROP OF FRUIT-PICKING BOTS A. VLASITS diag *Wired* v25 no9 p38 S 2017
Celebs Dabble in Weird Food J. Kell color *Fortune* v176 no1 p14 Jl 1 2017
Driven S. ADAMS and K. KAM color *Forbes* v199 no5 p46 My 16 2017
The Innovator Gap I. Gur *MIT Technology Review* v120 no4 p10 Jl/Ag 2017

Financing of research
See also
   Endowment of research
   Federal aid to research
Brazil scientists brace for harder times color *Science* v357 no6348 p232 Jl 21 2017
Congress trumps president in backing science J. Mervis chart color *Science* v356 no6337 p470 My 5 2017
DOE freezes millions in awards J. Mervis color *Science* v356 no6337 p471 My 5 2017
Mexico's basic science funding falls short E. Frixione and J. P. Laclette *Science* v357 no6348 p260 Jl 21 2017
Research integrity revisited M. McNutt and R. M. Nerem color *Science* v356 no6334 p115 Ap 14 2017

Financing of research—Government policy
How to Maintain America's Edge L. R. Reif color *Foreign Affairs* v96 no3 p95 My/Je 2017

Financing of transportation
Next Stop: Anybody's Guess: There are no crystal balls in transportation. Some judges don't understand that A. Ehrenhalt color *Governing* v30 no11 p14 Ag 2017

FINCH, CHARLES
THRILLERS *New York Times Book Review* p10 O 30 2016
Thrillers *New York Times Book Review* p20 Je 4 2017

Finch, David
RIGHT PLACE, RIGHT TIME S. Fairyington *Advocate* no1088 p20 D 2016/Ja 2017

Finch, Elizabeth
"My native continent" cartoon *Magazine Antiques* v184 no2 p100 Mr/Ap 2017

Finch, Gavin
Paris and Frankfurt Vie For Brexit's Spoils *Bloomberg Businessweek* no4530 p30 Jl 17 2017
What Brexit Means for Banks color *Bloomberg Businessweek* no4496 p50 O 24 2016

Finch, Robert
The Outer Beach: A Thousand-Mile Walk on Cape Cod's Atlantic Shore *Publishers Weekly* v264 no9 p88 F 27 2017
Sand Walker F. MONTAIGNE *New York Times Book Review* p52 Je 4 2017

Fincham, Laurie—Interviews
The Future of Audio C. Crowley color *Sound & Vision* v81 no9 p16 N 2016

Fincham, Susanna—Interviews
The Trauma of Saving Animals R. Nuwer color *Scientific American* v316 no2 p20 F 2017

Fincher, David, 1962-
The True Purpose of True Crime E. Dockterman color *Time* v190 no16/17 p100 O 23 2017

Fincher, David, 1962-—Interviews
Through a Lens, DARKLY A. Grant color *Esquire* p60 N 2017

FINCK, LIANA
MANSPREADERS OF THE YEAR cartoon chart *New Yorker* v93 no17 p40 Je 19 2017

FINDER, JOSEPH
A Boy Becomes a Writer *Publishers Weekly* v264 no21 p96 My 22 2017

Finding Dory (Film)
FINDING DORY C. Chiarella color *Sound & Vision* v82 no3 p70 Ap 2017
Finding Trump's Refugee Policy M. Kamal *Humanist* v77 no2 p9 Mr/Ap 2017
The YEAR THAT WAS color *Entertainment Weekly* no1444/1445 p12 D 16 2016

Finding Neverland (Theatrical production)
FINDING YOUR NERVE IN FINDING NEVERLAND J. Moore *Cincinnati Magazine* v50 no8 p8 My 2017

Findlay, Andrew
all access bw color *Bike Magazine* v24 no5 p70 Jl 2017
CANADA'S GRANDEST TRAVERSE color map *Skiing* p88 D 2016
The war in the Walbran color map *Canadian Geographic* v136 no6 p26 D 2016

Findlay, Jessica Brown, 1989-
Antiheroines Are Resplendent In Harlots D. D'Addario color *Time* v189 no12 p55 Ap 3 2017

Fine, Cordelia
Born this way? S. Berenbaum bibl color *Science* v355 no6322 p254 Ja 20 2017
Not From Venus, Not From Mars A. MURPHY PAUL *New York Times Book Review* p10 F 26 2017
PROMISCUOUS MEN, CHASTE WOMEN AND OTHER GENDER MYTHS color *Scientific American* v317 no3 p32 S 2017

Fine, Jason
The Salvation of Brian Wilson bw color *Rolling Stone* no1295 p48 S 7 2017

Fine, P. V. A.
Persistent effects of pre-Columbian plant domestication on Amazonian forest composition bibl chart graph map *Science* v355 no6328 p925 Mr 3 2017

Fine, Steven
POWER AND LIGHT M. INGALL *New York Times Book Review* p56 D 4 2016

Fine Gael
A New Face for the Republic of Ireland T. John color *Time* v189 no23 p13 Je 19 2017

FineHouse Ltd.
ADDITIONAL LISTINGS *Arts & Crafts Homes & the Revival* v12 no1 p62 2017 Resouce Guide

FINELLI, MARY
Fishes *Vegetarian Journal* v36 no2 p26 2017

Fineman, Meredith
How to Start Networking in a New City *Harvard Business Review Digital Articles* p2 S 23 2016
What Your Professional Bio Needs to Get Noticed *Harvard Business Review Digital Articles* p2 Mr 2 2015

Finér, Leena
Positive biodiversity-productivity relationship predominant in global forests bibl chart graph map *Science* v354 no6309 paaf8957-1 O 14 2016

Fineran, Peter C.
CRISPR-Cas: Adapting to change color *Science* v356 no6333 p40 Ap 7 2017

Fines (Penalties)
Book 'Em, Danno! color *Weekly Standard* v23 no1 p3 S 11 2017
BRICKBATS C. OLIVER cartoon *Reason* v49 no2 p72 Je 2017
Brighton, Rocked color *Weekly Standard* v23 no5 p2 O 9 2017
CALENDAR: 08/2017 R. ERMEY color *Kiplinger's Personal Finance* v71 no8 p16 Ag 2017
The Forgotten Victims D. DAYEN il *New Republic* v247 no12 p10 D 2016
ISRAEL DECRIMINALIZES POT POSSESSION J. SULLUM color *Reason* v49 no2 p8 Je 2017
Jamie Dimon and Other People's Money [Cover story] D. DAYEN color *Nation* v305 no10 p12 O 23 2017
Justice at Sea color *Earth Island Journal* v32 no3 p9 Aut 2017

Fines (Penalties)—United States
Fines Alone Won't Deter Corporate Crime bw *Bloomberg Businessweek* no4500 p12 N 21 2016

Finfer, Laura
Younger and Older Executives Need Different Things from Coaching *Harvard Business Review Digital Articles* p2 Jl 6 2017

FINGER, BOBBY
'Grigio Girls' *New York Times Magazine* p57 Mr 12 2017

Finger, Terrell
Missouri K. Grannan *New York Times Magazine* p40 N 20 2016

Finger diseases—Treatment
How to Fix Trigger Finger M. Gunch cartoon *New Orleans Magazine* v51 no7 p46 My 2017

Finger dislocation
THE EXCHANGE M. Wolff color graph *Men's Health* v32 no7 p16 S 2017

Finger Lakes (N.Y.)
Water to Wine P. Brady bw color diag *Conde Nast Traveler* v52 no7 p72 Ag 2017

Fingerhut, Benjamin P.
Large-amplitude transfer motion of hydrated excess protons mapped by ultrafast 2D IR spectroscopy graph *Science* v357 no6350 p491 Ag 4 2017

Fingerprints
CSI TOOL FROM ANCIENT EGYPT A. R. Williams color *National Geographic* v231 no5 p24 My 2017
Weird but true! J. SWAIN and A. E. HURT color map *National Geographic Kids* no470 p4 My 2017

Fingerprints (Music)
THE ELI YOUNG BAND PLAYS THE GAME A. LANGER *Texas Monthly* v45 no6 p48 Je 2017

Fingers
GIVE A SHORT STROKE THE FINGER D. Denunzio and C. Preisinger color *Golf Magazine* v58 no11 p56 N 2016

Finishes & finishing
See also
Faux finishes (Decorative arts)
Lacquer & lacquering
Paint
Stains & staining
Varnish & varnishing
finish color *Timber Home Living* p46 2017 Annual Buyers
FINISHING TOUCH color *Timber Home Living* v27 no3 p32 Je 2017

Finishes & finishing—Evaluation

Enduring Finish M. E. Polson color *Old House Journal* v45 no2 p76 Ap 2017

Gear P. Nielsen color *Sail* v48 no4 p32 Ap 2017

Inside Job color *Log Home Living* v33 no7 p15 S 2016

Inside Job J. Taraska color *Architectural Record* v205 no2 p48 F 2017

Fink, Anya Loukianova

What arguments motivate citizens to demand nuclear disarmament? bibl *Bulletin of the Atomic Scientists* v73 no4 p255 Jl 2017

Fink, Carly

The Comprehensive Business Case for Sustainability *Harvard Business Review Digital Articles* p2 O 21 2016

Fink, Greg

A New Heading cartoon color *Car & Driver* v62 no10 p88 Ap 2017

Fink, Larry, 1952-

19 LARRY FINK J. Wieczner color *Fortune* v174 no7 p89 D 1 2016

FINK, LEON

Fix the Global Economy, Don't Flee It *In These Times* v41 no1 p15 Ja 2017

Fink, Richard II

From Young Professional to Respected Leader: Navigating the park and recreation career ladder *Parks & Recreation* v52 no5 p34 My 2017

Fink, U.

Seasonal exposure of carbon dioxide ice on the nucleus of comet 67P/Churyumov-Gerasimenko bibl bw graph *Science* v354 no6319 p1563 D 23 2016

Finkbeiner, Ann

NEAR-LIGHT-SPEED MISSION TO ALPHA CENTAURI [Cover story] color *Scientific American* v316 no3 p30 Mr 2017

Finkbeiner, Elena M.

Committing to socially responsible seafood color *Science* v356 no6341 p912 Je 1 2017

Finke, Betty

2016 british nationals *Arabian Horse World* v57 no1 p128 O 2016

2016 egyption event europe *Arabian Horse World* v57 no1 p140 O 2016

2017 ströhen european c-show and international b-show *Arabian Horse World* v57 no11 p132 Ag 2017

all nations cup festival *Arabian Horse World* v57 no3 p244 D 2016

The Arab Horse Society National Show 2017 *Arabian Horse World* v57 no12 p166 S 2017

BACK TO HIS ROOTS MASTER DESIGN GA *Arabian Horse World* v57 no1 p122 O 2016

BAIRACTAR--A ROYAL HERITAGE *Arabian Horse World* v57 no5 p208 F 2017

ENDURANCE at marbach: The 2016 ZSAA Endurance Event and German National Endurance Championships *Arabian Horse World* v56 no12 p184 S 2016

GUEST EDITORIAL *Arabian Horse World* v57 no3 p36 D 2016

IMPERIAL MADHEEN *Arabian Horse World* v57 no3 p36 D 2016

JC KLYM TO FAME *Arabian Horse World* v56 no12 p66 S 2016

MARWAN AL SHAQAB *Arabian Horse World* v57 no2 p72 N 2016

Moments in Time: A Queen in Winter *Arabian Horse World* v57 no8 p28 My 2017

Moments in Time *Arabian Horse World* v56 no12 p78 S 2016

Moments in Time: A Royal Gift *Arabian Horse World* v57 no9 p132 Je 2017

Moments in Time A Walk IN THE Park *Arabian Horse World* v57 no3 p210 D 2016

Moments in Time First Contact *Arabian Horse World* v57 no5 p156 F 2017

Moments in Time Forgotten Hero *Arabian Horse World* v57 no1 p98 O 2016

Moments in Time: FROM SMALL Beginnings *Arabian Horse World* v57 no10 p90 Jl 2017

Moments in Time On THE Road *Arabian Horse World* v57 no4 p154 Ja 2017

Moments in Time The Polish Pioneers bw *Arabian Horse World* v57 no7 p26 Ap 2017

Moments in Time: THE Russian Year *Arabian Horse World* v57

no11 p92 Ag 2017

The Other Mare *Arabian Horse World* v57 no2 p132 N 2016

PADRONS PSYCHE *Arabian Horse World* v57 no9 p1 Je 2017

A PRINCE OF EGYPT *Arabian Horse World* v57 no12 p148 S 2017

Saving Kasyd *Arabian Horse World* v57 no6 p46 Mr 2017

SIRE LINE: KOHEILAN ADJUZE DB: PERFORMANCE POWER FROM HUNGARY *Arabian Horse World* v57 no9 p122 Je 2017

SIRE LINE: KRZYZYK DB THE ROOTS OF POLISH BREEDING *Arabian Horse World* v57 no8 p94 My 2017

SIRE LINE: SAKLAWI I - PART 2: A GIFT TO THE WORLD *Arabian Horse World* v57 no11 p72 Ag 2017

SIRE LINE: SAKLAWI I PART I: A TALE OF IWO BROTHERS *Arabian Horse World* v57 no10 p78 Jl 2017

Wadee Al Shaqab color *Arabian Horse World* v57 no7 p1 Ap 2017

A WORLDWIDE LEGACY *Arabian Horse World* v57 no8 p8 My 2017

ZOBEYNI SIRE LINE - PART 1 *Arabian Horse World* v57 no6 p36 Mr 2017

ZOBEYNI SIRE LINE - PART 2: MAHRUSS, RIJM, AND THE UNLIKELY BROTHERS bw chart color *Arabian Horse World* v57 no7 p58 Ap 2017

Finkel, Eli

Why Marriage Is Harder Than Ever-and Maybe Better Too B. Luscombe color *Time* v190 no12 p25 S 25 2017

Finkel, Isobel

In Turkey, New Powers Won't Fix Old Problems color *Bloomberg Businessweek* no4519 p17 Ap 24 2017

Finkel, Michael

Alone With a Book: Christopher Knight lived without human contact on burglary and literature in backcountry Maine J. TYRANGIEL color *New York Times Book Review* p19 Ap 23 2017

THE BIG QUESTION cartoon *Atlantic* v319 no5 p96 Je 2017

Finkelstein, Amy

Research: Perhaps Market Forces Do Work in Health Care After All *Harvard Business Review Digital Articles* p2 D 5 2016

What the Cost of a Trip to the Vet Tells Us About Why Human Health Care Is So Expensive color *Harvard Business Review Digital Articles* p2 Ja 10 2017

Finkelstein, Arseny

Vectorial representation of spatial goals in the hippocampus of bats bibl graph *Science* v355 no6321 p1 Ja 13 2017

Finkelstein, David Ritz

David Ritz Finkelstein P. Cvitanović and L. Susskind *Physics Today* v70 no2 p68 F 2017

Finkelstein, Martin J.

Whither the Faculty? *Change* v49 no4 p43 Jl/Ag 2017

Finkelstein, Sydney

4 Ways Managers Can Be More Inclusive *Harvard Business Review Digital Articles* p2 Jl 13 2017

How to Hire Like a Superboss *Harvard Business Review Digital Articles* p2 F 9 2016

Jon Stewart, Superboss *Harvard Business Review Digital Articles* p2 Jl 30 2015

Superbosses Aren't Afraid to Delegate Their Biggest Decisions *Harvard Business Review Digital Articles* p2 Ag 24 2016

What Amazing Bosses Do Differently *Harvard Business Review Digital Articles* p2 N 27 2015

Finken, Brian

GE's Real-Time Performance Development *Harvard Business Review Digital Articles* p2 Ag 12 2015

Finkl, Katja

Propagation of Polycomb-repressed chromatin requires sequence-specific recruitment to DNA diag *Science* v356 no6333 p85 Ap 7 2017

Finkler, Earl

FROM OUR READERS *Sky & Telescope* v133 no5 p6 My 2017

Finland

Finland KAKSLAUTTANEN color *Sports Illustrated* v126 no6 p92 F 20 2017

Finland—Description & travel

TRAVEL Finland color *Sports Illustrated* v126 no6 p100 F 20 2017

Finland—History

NATIONAL GALLERY FINLAND R. Griffiths *History Today* v67 no9 p78 S 2017

Finlay, Barbara

Letter from the Front *American History* v52 no1 p51 Ap 2017

Finlayson, Jonathan

JONATHAN FINLAYSON P. Lutz color *Downbeat* v84 no1 p46 Ja 2017

Finlayson, Judith

MAKE YOUR OWN HOT SAUCE IN THREE STEPS cartoon *Men's Health* v32 no4 p114 My 2017

Finley, Ben

Posthole color *Powder* v45 no5 p108 Ja 2017

Finley, Carmel

Sea change M. Goud Collins bibl color *Science* v355 no6329 p1030 Mr 10 2017

Finley, Daniel

UBE2O remodels the proteome during terminal erythroid differentiation diag *Science* v357 no6350 p471 Ag 4 2017

Finley, Karen

Trump Can Thank the Arts for His Wealth *Time* v189 no4 p29 F 6 2017

Finley, Kristin

Girl Runs Away, Joins Circus color *Glamour* v114 no12 p180 D 2016

Finley, W.

UNSOLICITED BETA *Climbing* no355 p14 Ag 2017

Finn, Chester E.

Dare to Discipline (Again): The previous administration held that discipline amounted to discrimination. The new education secretary should reject this claim--if not in the name of common sense, then in the name of student achievement *Hoover Digest: Research & Opinion on Public Policy* no3 p132 Summ 2017

Improve governance for charters *Phi Delta Kappan* v98 no6 p63 Mr 2017

School of Hard Knocks *Hoover Digest: Research & Opinion on Public Policy* no4 p142 Fall 2016

The Schools We Deserve *Hoover Digest: Research & Opinion on Public Policy* no1 p146 Wint 2017

Finn, Daniel K.

Recycling Isn't Enough color *Commonweal* v144 no8 p12 My 5 2017

FINN, ED

Algorithm of the Enlightenment *Issues in Science & Technology* v33 no3 p21 Spr 2017

Finn, Eoin

A home practice to find peace & possibility color *Yoga Journal* no292 p66 Je 2017

Finn, Kathy

BIG DEVELOPMENTS color *Louisiana Life* v37 no4 p8 Mr/Ap 2017

Brain Gain color *New Orleans Magazine* v51 no6 p30 Ap 2017

Click and Spend color *New Orleans Magazine* v51 no8 p32 Je 2017

DOMAIN IN THE SKYLINE color *New Orleans Magazine* v51 no1 p32 N 2016

GROWING STRONG color *Louisiana Life* v37 no2 p10 N/D 2016

Harrison Avenue Boom color *New Orleans Magazine* v51 no9 p30 Jl 2017

MIXING IT UP color *Louisiana Life* v37 no3 p8 Ja/F 2017

New in New Orleans Real Estate color *New Orleans Magazine* v52 no1 p34 S 2017

OFFSHORE BLUES color *New Orleans Magazine* v51 no2 p32 D 2016

Oil Boom and Bust color *New Orleans Magazine* v51 no7 p30 My 2017

Paying for college: Don't let financial fear thwart your child's future color *New Orleans Magazine* v51 no10 p42 Ag 2017

POISED FOR PROFIT color *New Orleans Magazine* v51 no3 p28 Ja 2017

Supermarket Dot Com color *New Orleans Magazine* v51 no12 p36 O 2017

Tour Score color *New Orleans Magazine* v51 no5 p30 Mr 2017

What's In a Name? color *New Orleans Magazine* v51 no4 p30 F 2017

Finn, Melanie

'The Most Honest Place' L. ZEIDNER *New York Times Book Review* p20 O 2 2016

Finn, Mindy

GUEST LIST *Washingtonian Magazine* v52 no3 p20 D 2016

Finn, Patrick

The Go-to-Market Approach Startups Need to Adopt *Harvard Business Review Digital Articles* p2 Je 10 2016

Finn, Richard

TOUR DE FORT S. Cravatts bw color *Popular Photography* v80 no11 p26 D 2016

Finn, Victoria

How America Lost Its Mind color *Atlantic* v320 no4 p12 N 2017

Finnegan, Erin

Luchador color *Publishers Weekly* v263 no43 p62 O 24 2016

FINNEGAN, LEAH

Don't Stop the Press! color *New Republic* v248 no4 p16 Ap 2017

Finnegan, Seth

Increase in predator-prey size ratios throughout the Phanerozoic history of marine ecosystems diag *Science* v356 no6343 p1178 Je 16 2017

Finnegan, William

BROKEN DREAMS cartoon *New Yorker* v93 no28 p17 S 18 2017

A FAILING STATE bw cartoon *New Yorker* v92 no37 p48 N 14 2016

Mr. Nick Baker Teaches Today—Listen color *New York Review of Books* v64 no5 p31 Mr 23 2017

A RIGHTEOUS CASE cartoon color *New Yorker* v93 no13 p66 My 15 2017

FINNERAN, KEVIN

Middle Class Muddle *Issues in Science & Technology* v33 no1 p39 Fall 2016

No Time for Rubbernecking *Issues in Science & Technology* v33 no4 p19 Summ 2017

Take a Deep Breath *Issues in Science & Technology* v33 no2 p17 Wint 2017

Finney, Ali

Arches de Triumph color *Women's Health* v14 no1 p49 Ja/F 2017

AWASH WITH WONDER color *Women's Health* v14 no7 p56 S 2017

CHANGE IS BEAUTIFUL color *Women's Health* v14 no2 p146 Mr 2017

Editors Tell All! bw color *Women's Health* v14 no2 p60 Mr 2017

MAKE PEACE WITH YOUR HAIR color *Women's Health* v14 no4 p152 My 2017

MESSAGE ON A BOTTLE bw color *Women's Health* v14 no3 p(Sp)22 Ap 2017

PRACTICAL MAGIC color *Women's Health* v14 no3 p(Sp)18 Ap 2017

Self-Made Women color *Women's Health* v14 no9 p50 N 2017

SHOULD I GET BANGS? color *Women's Health* v14 no1 p164 Ja/F 2017

Super Natural color *Women's Health* v14 no8 p138 O 2017

WE'VE GOT YOU COVERED *Women's Health* v14 no5 p138 Je 2017

THE WIND IN YOUR HAIR [Cover story] bw color *Women's Health* v14 no6 p45 Jl 2017

Women's Health 2017 BEAUTY AWARDS color graph *Women's Health* v14 no5 p116 Je 2017

FINNEY, CAROLYN

An Invitation *Orion Magazine* v35 no4/5 p46 Jl-O 2016

Finnican, Greg

SUCKER PUNCH E. Perkins color *Hot Rod* v70 no3 p60 Mr 2017

Finnigan, Dan

Robots and Automation May Not Take Your Desk Job After All *Harvard Business Review Digital Articles* p2 N 22 2016

FINNO, CARRIE

Promoting Weight Gain After Illness *Horse & Rider* v56 no3 p12 Mr 2017

Fins (Anatomy)

Tuna fin hydraulics inspire aquatic robotics [Cover story] M. S. Triantafyllou diag *Science* v357 no6348 p251 Jl 21 2017

Finsterbusch, J.

Interactions between brain and spinal cord mediate value effects in nocebo hyperalgesia color *Science* v357 no6359 p105 O 6 2017

Finz, Stacy

Need You *Publishers Weekly* v264 no25 p98 Je 19 2017

Finzer, Nick

Clarity: The Art Behind Artistry bw *Downbeat* v84 no4 p86 Ap 2017

Fiol, Shae

They're with the Banda M. GOLDBERG color *O, The Oprah Magazine* p23 Jl 2017

Fioravanti, Leo

BEST OVERALL bw color *Surfing Magazine* v53 no1 p60 Ja 2017

BIGGEST LADYKILLER color *Surfing Magazine* v53 no1 p58 Ja 2017

MOST POWERFUL color *Surfing Magazine* v53 no1 p46 Ja 2017

Fiordland penguin

Rebel Penguins J. KIFFEL-ALCHEH color map *National Geographic Kids* no473 p26 S 2017

FIORENTINI, FRANCESCA

America Is Finally Winning Again(TM)! color *Nation* v304 no9 p28 Mr 20 2017

Fiorenza, Evan A.

Seagrass ecosystems reduce exposure to bacterial pathogens of humans, fishes, and invertebrates bibl graph *Science* v355 no6326 p731 F 17 2017

Fiorenza, Raffaele

Friendship *Science* v354 no6308 p46 O 7 2016

Fiorina, Carly, 1954-

Carly Fiorina's Legacy as CEO of Hewlett Packard B. Tabrizi *Harvard Business Review Digital Articles* p2 S 25 2015

Fire

HOMESTEAD HACKS: Our readers share clever projects that will help you live a self-sufficient life in the country, the suburbs, or the city *Mother Earth News* no284 p66 O/N 2017

The Things She'll Carry: In the event of a house fire, some of my possessions must be saved—and my wife stands ready to haul them P. GULLEY color *Indianapolis Monthly* v41 no2 p50 S 2017

Fire (Music)

THE ULTIMATE SUMMER SINGLES SWAP N. Feeney color *Entertainment Weekly* no1477 p54 Ag 11 2017

Fire alarms

fireproof your family J. MONINGER *Parents* v92 no1 p62 Ja 2017

Fire ants—Research

FANCY FOOTWORK S. MORROW color *Discover* v38 no9 p9 N 2017

Fire at Sea (Film)

CRITICS' CHOICE chart color *Film Comment* v53 no1 p12 Ja/F 2017

The Sea Swallows People J. DeParle color *New York Review of Books* v64 no3 p31 F 23 2017

Fire damage to buildings

Flames of Contempt: The Grenfell Tower fire wasn't just a tragedy—it was the physical manifestation of political neglect J. DAVIDSON img *New York* v50 no13 p80 Je 26 2017

Fire department equipment

Fire alarm J. GEDDES color *Maclean's* v130 no4 p34 My 2017

Fire departments

Hot Wings Z. MATTHEW color *Los Angeles Magazine* v62 no10 p20 O 2017

Fire departments—United States

Firehouse Food: For first responders, a shared meal is more than simply fuel S. Sifton *New York Times Magazine* p20 O 8 2017

Fire detectors

Your True Stories IN 100 WORDS color *Reader's Digest* v190 no1133 p20 S 2017

Fire engines

50, 100 & 150 YEARS AGO bw color *Scientific American* v317 no3 p94 S 2017

Fire extinguishers

MIDSEASON PREVENTIVE MAINTENANCE: PERFORM SOME QUICK AND SIMPLE CHECKS FOR A CAREFREE BALANCE OF THE BOATING SEASON D. HISLOP bw color *Sea Magazine* v109 no8 p28 Ag 2017

Suckers and Cemeteries S. CARR *Idaho Magazine* v16 no2 p54 N 2016

Fire extinguishing agents

fireproof your family J. MONINGER *Parents* v92 no1 p62 Ja 2017

Fire fighters

Firehouse Clout A. Greenblatt *Governing* v30 no9 p9 Je 2017

Last Call J. SHIPLEY *Yankee* v81 no1 p124 Ja/F 2017

LETTING A Wildfire BURN OVER YOU B. MOCKENHAUPT color *Reader's Digest* v189 no1131 p112 Je 2017

Fire fighters—United States

Firehouse Food: For first responders, a shared meal is more than simply fuel S. Sifton *New York Times Magazine* p20 O 8 2017

Fire lookout stations

FINDING STATION 77—A piece of history is restored at Stillwater Mountain fire tower A. C. Pedrick color *New York State Conservationist* v71 no2 p18 O 2016

Fire management

AMANDA STAMPER color *Popular Mechanics* p35 Je 2017

Fire prevention

See also

Fire drills

Tall building fires & fire prevention

Wildfire prevention

ALL IN A Day's Work L. HARRIS and S. THOMAS cartoon color *Reader's Digest* v190 no1134 p54 O 2017

Read Before Burning D. COURTNEY *Texas Monthly* v45 no2 p154 F 2017

Fire prevention equipment

Space Age Firefighters M. Kaufman color *Scientific American* v316 no6 p14 Je 2017

Fire resistant plants

FIRE-RESISTANT PLANTS K. Preece color *Cabin Living* p73 Ap 2017

Fire—Accidents

CUT IT OUT! cartoon *Canoe & Kayak Magazine* v45 no1 p42 Wint 2017

THE SECOND BURNING OF ATLANTA R. Burns *Atlanta* v56 no10 p84 F 2017

Firearm safety—Law & legislation

Safe Gun Policy Doesn't Have to Mean No Guns—Or No Safety K. V. Ogtrop color *Time* v190 no16/17 p111 O 23 2017

Firearm sales & prices

What Happens to Gun Laws After a Mass Shooting E. Barone color diag *Time* v190 no16/17 p23 O 23 2017

Firearm sights

LIGHTS OUT FOR HOGS G. BETHGE color *Outdoor Life* v224 no8 p24 O 2017

PEAK GLASS D. Hurteau, R. Mann et al color *Field & Stream* v122 no4 p69 S 2017

PINS APLENTY T. HANSEN color *Outdoor Life* v224 no6 pB1 Ag 2017

Firearm sights—Evaluation

FIRST-PLANE REVOLUTION A. McKEAN chart color *Outdoor Life* v224 no5 p15 Je/Jl 2017

Firearms

See also

Gun control

Hunting guns

Machine guns

Revolvers

Rifles

Shotguns

Silencers (Firearms)

BO WHOOP COMES HOME W. BRANTLEY color *Field & Stream* v121 no6 p52 N 2016

DIY TURKEY GUN A. ROBINSON and J. B. SNOW color *Outdoor Life* v224 no2 p86 F/Mr 2017

DOUBLE VISION P. Bourjaily color *Field & Stream* v121 no8 p34 F/Mr 2017

FIRE DRILLS J. JOHNSTON and P. BOURJAILY bw color *Field & Stream* v121 no8 p64 F/Mr 2017

How to... DESTROY ANYTHING color *Popular Mechanics* v193 no7 p83 S 2016

PARENTS POLL *Parents* v92 no2 p18 F 2017

SOUTHERN SWING P. Bourjaily color *Field & Stream* v122 no2 p32 Je/Jl 2017

Firearms industry—United States

Gun Manufacturers Need to Lead Change, Not Just Follow the Law R. J. Dolan *Harvard Business Review Digital Articles* p2

Mr 23 2016

Firearms ownership

Gunning for the Guns G. NORMAN color *Weekly Standard* v22 no7 p24 O 24 2016

Inside the Fight Over Guns on Campus B. WOFFORD color *Rolling Stone* no1284 p28 Ap 6 2017

TRIGGER WARNING M. J. GRAY color *Ebony* v72 no8 p86 Je 2017

Firearms—Charts, diagrams, etc.

What Happens to Gun Laws After a Mass Shooting E. Barone color diag *Time* v190 no16/17 p23 O 23 2017

Firearms—Design & construction

SHOOT 2X2X2 B. M. TOWSLEY color *Outdoor Life* v224 no4 pP13 My 2017

Firearms—Evaluation

10-RINGERS [Cover story] W. Brantley color *Field & Stream* v122 no6 p77 N 2017

ANGRY BIRDS W. BRANTLEY and D. HURTEAU bw cartoon color *Field & Stream* v121 no9 p47 Ap 2017

CARRY ON W. Brantley color *Field & Stream* v122 no1 p52 My 2017

DREAM GUNS P. Bourjaily cartoon color *Field & Stream* v122 no1 p28 My 2017

GUNS FOR WOMEN L. HOLDING color *Outdoor Life* v224 no6 p67 Ag 2017

KIMBER SUPER JAGARE J. B. SNOW chart color *Outdoor Life* v224 no9 p68 N 2017

RIFLES 0N HORSEBACK D. AADLAND color *Outdoor Life* v224 no6 p70 Ag 2017

Firearms—Government policy

Bringing out the big guns A. HUTCHINS color *Maclean's* v130 no4 p13 My 2017

Firearms—History

The Responsible Parties W. Utley and R. S. Neyland *Archaeology* v69 no6 p8 N/D 2016

Firearms—Law & legislation

Shot in the Dark D. Paul *Indianapolis Monthly* v40 no4 p160 D 2016

Firearms—Law & legislation—United States

Enjoy the Silence K. D. WILLIAMSON *National Review* v69 no8 p16 My 2017

REVISITING RESTRICTIONS ON THE RIGHT TO BEAR ARMS B. DOHERTY *Reason* v48 no11 p15 Ap 2017

Firearms—Law & legislation—United States—Social aspects

One Nation, Up In Arms E. Barone color diag map *Time* v188 no16/17 p64 O 24 2016

Firearms—Sales & prices

An Expansive Embrace *Islamic Horizons* v45 no6 p6 N/D 2016

Firearms—Sights—Evaluation

NIGHTFORCE 4-16X42 F1 ATACR J. B. SNOW color *Outdoor Life* v224 no1 pR16 D 2016/Ja 2017

Fireball (Company)

Pants on Fireball color *Weekly Standard* v22 no25 p2 Mr 6 2017

Fireblade motorcycle—Evaluation

2017 HONDA CBR1000RR/SP D. Canet color *Cycle World* v56 no3 p10 Ap 2017

Fireboats—Evaluation

It's a Gusher S. SHIBATA *Sea Magazine* v108 no9 p14 S 2016

Fire fighters—Salaries, etc.

Firehouse Clout A. Greenblatt *Governing* v30 no9 p9 Je 2017

Fireflies

Bringing Back the Light L. Tangley color *National Wildlife (World Edition)* v55 no4 p12 Je/Jl 2017

Glowworms keep their fishing lines sticky with a surprising ingredient color *Science* v354 no6319 p1509 D 23 2016

THE GRUMPY GARDEN S. Bender color *Southern Living* v52 no3 p38 Mr 2017

Spectacle of Lights G. Versed *Sierra* v102 no4 p14 Jl/Ag 2017

Firefly (TV program)

Ron Glass 1945-2016 K. P. Sullivan color *Entertainment Weekly* no1443 p17 D 9 2016

Firemaking

THE MYSTERY OF FIRE B. HEAVEY color *Field & Stream* v122 no2 p114 Je/Jl 2017

Firemaking—Equipment & supplies

FIRE-STARTING TOOLS for Any Situation J. Williams *Mother*

Earth News no281 p67 Ap/My 2017

SURVIVE ANYWHERE C. ALLEN, T. MACWELCH et al bw cartoon color diag *Outdoor Life* v224 no3 p33 Ap 2017

Fireplace cooking

Smoke Over the Water D. VAUGHN *Texas Monthly* v45 no8 p26 Ag 2017

Fireplace design & construction

The Franklin File V. M. Parachin bw color *American History* v52 no4 p34 O 2017

UNDERSTANDING FIREPLACES M. E. POLSON color diag *Old House Journal* v45 no7 p38 O 2017

Fireplaces

See also

Mantels

DESIGNING a dream J. BREWSTER color diag *Cabin Living* p66 D 2016

Dining Out color *Timber Home Living* v27 no4 p22 Ag 2017

MAKE OVER your haven A. LONGOBUCCO color *Good Housekeeping* v264 no1 p54 Ja 1 2017

MANTELPIECE THEATER color *Timber Home Living* v27 no6 p24 D 2017

ROBERT COUTURIER ON FIRE! K. O'SHEA-EVANS color *House Beautiful* v158 no10 p34 D 2016/Ja 2017

Fireplaces—Design & construction

Light His Fire M. OWENS color *Architectural Digest* v74 no1 p62 Ja 2017

ROCK this WAY color *Cabin Living* p49 D 2016

Fireplaces—Evaluation

product spotlight color *Timber Home Living* p51 2017 Annual Buyers

Winter Hot Stuff color *Old House Journal* v45 no7 p48 O 2017

Firer, Susan

Repetition Works for the Moon *New York Times Magazine* p15 F 19 2017

Fires

See also

Effect of fires on plants

Fire prevention

Forest fires

Boom town revival color *Maclean's* p36 Je 2017

THE FIRE ISSUE color *Field & Stream* v121 no8 p42 F/Mr 2017

IN THE ASHES L. Vaccariello *Cincinnati Magazine* v50 no5 p70 F 2017

THE MYSTERY OF FIRE B. HEAVEY color *Field & Stream* v122 no2 p114 Je/Jl 2017

WITH POYDRAS THE PARROT J. STREET bw *New Orleans Magazine* v51 no8 p24 Je 2017

Fires & the environment

A human-driven decline in global burned area N. Andela, D. C. Morton et al chart graph map *Science* v356 no6345 p1356 Je 30 2017

When Cooking Kills M. NIJHUIS color map *National Geographic* v232 no3 p76 S 2017

Fire—Safety measures

Q+A J. Gilbert *Cincinnati Magazine* v50 no3 p38 D 2016

Fires—History

FIRE IN THE FENS J. URBANUS color *Archaeology* v70 no1 p34 Ja/F 2017

Fires—Texas

Read Before Burning D. COURTNEY *Texas Monthly* v45 no2 p154 F 2017

Firestone, Karen

Does Having Grandchildren Persuade Women to Retire Early? *Harvard Business Review Digital Articles* p2 My 19 2015

How Hard Do Company Founders Really Work? *Harvard Business Review Digital Articles* p2 D 17 2014

How Leaders Can Push Employees Without Stressing Them Out *Harvard Business Review Digital Articles* p2 My 23 2017

How to Handle Losing a Major Client *Harvard Business Review Digital Articles* p2 Ja 27 2015

New Hires Create More Anxiety at a Midsized Company *Harvard Business Review Digital Articles* p2 Ap 23 2015

Questioning Claims That Are Too Good to Be True *Harvard Business Review Digital Articles* p2 S 7 2016

Taking Longer to Reach the Top Has Its Benefits *Harvard Business Review Digital Articles* p2 D 30 2015

Think About Any Risk Like an Investor *Harvard Business Review Digital Articles* p2 My 3 2016

What I Didn't Know About Becoming a CEO *Harvard Business Review Digital Articles* p2 N 9 2015

When to Tell Your Employees to Stay Home *Harvard Business Review Digital Articles* p2 F 27 2015

When Was the Last Time You Took On a New Challenge? *Harvard Business Review Digital Articles* p2 F 17 2017

Why Is It So Hard for Us to Admit Our Mistakes? *Harvard Business Review Digital Articles* p2 Mr 28 2016

Why That Risky Career Move Could Be a Safer Bet than You Think *Harvard Business Review Digital Articles* p2 Mr 11 2016

Why Won't My Employees Admit They're Going on Vacation? *Harvard Business Review Digital Articles* p2 Ag 28 2015

Firestone Tire & Rubber Co.

GEARBOX color *Dirt Sports + Off-Road* v51 no11 p70 N 2017

Fireworks

> *See also*
>> Flares

BOOM OR BUST: Fireworks stores, Indiana roller coasters, and urban coyotes. Ask the Hoosierist S. STALL *Indianapolis Monthly* v40 no11 p15 Jl 2017

BURNING MEN S. Hely color *Esquire* p28 Je/Jl 2017

A Fourth of July Fireworks Roundup! J. Russell *TV Guide* v65 no27 p32 Je 26 2017

Sights and Sounds color *National Geographic* v230 no5 p14 N 2016

Snap Dynamite Fireworks Photos J. LABIANCA color *Reader's Digest* v190 no1132 p33 Jl/Ag 2017

YOUR BODY ON... FIREWORKS [Cover story] J. Migala color *Women's Health* v14 no6 p84 Jl 2017

Fireworks—Evaluation

Sparktacular A Piece of Technological History in the Making *Stage Directions* v30 no3 p48 Mr 2017

Fireworks—Psychological aspects

Ease Fireworks Anxiety color *Horse & Rider* v56 no7 p38 Jl 2017

First (Short story)

FIRST J. ROGERS cartoon *Wired* v25 no1 p30 Ja 2017

First, Zachary

The Benefits of Unplugging as a Team *Harvard Business Review Digital Articles* p2 Ap 8 2015

Rethinking the Corporate Love Affair with Change *Harvard Business Review Digital Articles* p2 Mr 20 2017

Technology Changes, Good Management Doesn't *Harvard Business Review Digital Articles* p2 Ap 7 2016

What to Measure If You're Mission Driven *Harvard Business Review Digital Articles* p2 Jl 9 2015

First aid for animals

911 ACTION PLAN E. Pascoe and M. Mudge color *Practical Horseman* v45 no11 p42 N 2017

First aid for animals—Equipment & supplies

5 First-Aid Kit Essentials E. M. Kellon color *Trail Rider* v29 no2 p22 Mr 2017

First aid in illness & injury

> *See also*
>> Resuscitation

BOATING MAINTENANCE color *Cabin Living* p70 Ap 2017

FIRST AID BASICS color *Women's Health* v14 no1 p188 Ja/F 2017

First Aid for Eye Ouches J. Chen *Parents* v92 no8 p33 Ag 2017

First aid in illness & injury—Equipment & supplies

> *See also*
>> First aid kits

5 Items for Your First-Aid Kit *Parents* v91 no11 p36 N 2016

kids * health news *Parents* v91 no11 p30 N 2016

First aid kits

Backcountry First Aid A. CHARMOZ *Climbing* no350 p47 D 2016/Ja 2017

Building Your First-Aid Kit B. Crabbe *Dressage Today* p18 My 2017

FIND YOUR INNER PREPPER R. Verger color *Popular Science* v289 no4 p32 Jl/Ag 2017

First Aid on the Go T. L. Dog color *Prevention* v69 no6 p26 Je 2017

FIRST-AID PURGE C. Barakat and M. Freckleton *Equus* no476 p26 My 2017

ON-TRAIL FIRST-AID KIT R. E. Smith and H. Melocco color *Trail Rider* v29 no3 p64 Ap 2017

Update Your First Aid Kit N. MONSON color *AARP: The Magazine* v60 no4A p18 Je/Jl 2017

First aid kits—Evaluation

It's the End of the World as We Know It I. Boudway color *Bloomberg Businessweek* no4510 p58 F 6 2017

First Amendment protections (United States Constitution)

> *See also*
>> Freedom of religion
>> Freedom of speech
>> Freedom of the press

The Common Sense of Oklahomans L. Granados *Humanist* v77 no1 p6 Ja/F 2017

The First Amendment vs. Trump D. COLE color *Nation* v304 no4 p20 F 6 2017

Is free speech under threat IN THE UNITED STATES? WE RECEIVED TWENTY-SEVEN RESPONSES. WE PUBLISH THEM HERE, IN ALPHABETICAL ORDER F. ABRAMS, A. H. ALI et al *Commentary* v144 no1 p13 Jl/Ag 2017

A Setback for Free Speech *National Review* v69 no1 p12 Ja 23 2017

Your First Amendment Rights *New York Times Upfront* p1 S 18 2017 Supplement Poster

First Amendment protections (United States Constitution)—History—20th century

WHEN THE GOVERNMENT DECLARED WAR ON THE FIRST AMENDMENT D. Root color *Reason* v49 no5 p18 O 2017

First-born children

The Year That Was . . *Texas Monthly* v45 no1 p6 Ja 2017

First contact of aboriginal peoples with Westerners

> *See also*
>> Taino (West Indian people)—First contact with Europeans

CHRISTOPHER WHO? C. Rogers *History Today* v67 no8 p38 Ag 2017

First Dates (TV program)

First Dates D. Holbrook *TV Guide* v65 no14 p34 Ap 3 2017

First day of school

Sketchbook Liniers *New York Times Book Review* p30 Ag 27 2017

First grade (Education)

Is Kindergarten the New First Grade? *USA Today Magazine* v146 no2867 p5 Ag 2017

First impression (Psychology)

How to Hire Without Getting Fooled by First Impressions T. Menon and L. Thompson *Harvard Business Review Digital Articles* p2 F 15 2016

How to Make a Great First Impression R. Knight *Harvard Business Review Digital Articles* p2 S 12 2016

Making a S.P.E.C.I.A.L. first impression A. Dovico *Phi Delta Kappan* v98 no3 p55 N 2016

First Internet Bank of Indiana (Company)

BANK ON IT J. YOUNG color *Indianapolis Monthly* v41 no2 p30 S 2017

First National Bank of Commerce (Company)

What's In a Name? K. Finn color *New Orleans Magazine* v51 no4 p30 F 2017

First Nations (Canada)—British Columbia

A First Nation For the 21st Century N. O. Pearson color *Bloomberg Businessweek* no4541 p30 O 9 2017

First Nations (Canada)—Crimes against

A RIVER OF TEARS [Cover story] N. Macdonald color *Maclean's* v130 no7 p38 Ag 2017

First Nations (Canada)—Education

Truth and education J. LEWINGTON color *Maclean's* v130 no10 p52 N 2017

First Nations (Canada)—Government relations

ABOUT THAT TATTOO N. MACDONALD color *Maclean's* v129 no44 p25 N 7 2016

First Nations (Canada)—Medical care

Jordan's Principle L. CHAMBERS and K. BURNETT *American Indian Quarterly* v41 no2 p101 Spr 2017

First Nations (Canada)—Ontario

'We were here first' K. PINCHIN color map *Canadian Geographic* v137 no3 p34 My 2017

First Nations (Canada)—Yukon

Industrialist vs. Indigenous R. RUSSELL color *Walrus* v14 no3 p24 Ap 2017

First Nations social conditions

THE INTERVIEW N. MACDONALD color *Maclean's* v130 no6 p24 Jl 2017

First person narrative

Athwart J. LILEKS *National Review* v69 no2 p33 F 6 2017

A Cinderella STORY N. Lopes *Dance Spirit* v21 no3 p26 Mr 2017

Conjuring God P. S. Hawkins *Christian Century* v134 no12 p12 Je 7 2017

The Family Telescope: Even though I'd conceived of and built it, who was I to consider it my instrument? J. Manney *Sky & Telescope* v134 no6 p84 D 2017

Flock to Fontenelle D. FARNSWORTH-LIVINGSTON bw color *Nebraska Life* v21 no6 p72 N/D 2017

In the Garden K. LAUR *Cincinnati Magazine* v50 no5 p44 F 2017

It's Been Over a Year, and I Still Can't Decide on a Mattress J. YUAN *New York* v50 no9 p73 My 1 2017

Making my own home F. Kaplan color *Science* v354 no6309 p254 O 14 2016

My Advice L. Graham bw color *Seventeen* v75 no11 p108 N 2016

One Lap of America D. Freiburger color *Hot Rod* v70 no9 p114 S 2017

Out-of-control ministry C. L. Howard *Christian Century* v134 no12 p10 Je 7 2017

Skishoe L. JHUNG il *Backpacker* p30 N 2017

SURPRISE S. Sorensen, W. H. Griffith et al *Christian Century* v134 no12 p22 Je 7 2017

Take your mark: Competition Hikes C. BUHAY *Backpacker* p22 N 2017

First-person shooters (Video games)

RACE, GENDER, AND GENRE IN SPEC OPS: THE LINE S. Murray *Film Quarterly* v70 no2 p38 Wint 2016

First-person shooters (Video games)—Evaluation

Titanfall 2: Prepare for more mech-dropping, wall-running action H. DINGMAN color *PCWorld* p133 D 2016

First responders

The Heat Is On: To succeed, a new first responder network needs most states to opt in T. Newcombe *Governing* v30 no12 p62 S 2017

AN UNRAVELING WEB J. Miller color *Earth Island Journal* v32 no3 p49 Aut 2017

First They Killed My Father (Film)

ALSO PLAYING D. Heching color *Entertainment Weekly* no1478 / 1479 p44 Ag 18-25 2017

A Child Survives the Khmer Rouge S. Zacharek color *Time* v190 no13 p65 O 2 2017

FirstGen (TV program)

YVONNE ORJI C. Brody color *Entertainment Weekly* no1441 p49 N 25 2016

FirstNet (Company)

The Heat Is On: To succeed, a new first responder network needs most states to opt in T. Newcombe *Governing* v30 no12 p62 S 2017

First Wives Club, The (Film)

Streaming D. Coggan color *Entertainment Weekly* no1472 p46 Je 30 2017

Firtash, Dmitry

THE OLIGARCH WAITS R. Kolker bw color *Bloomberg Businessweek* no4512 p56 F 20 2017

Firth, Andrew E.

Neurodevelopmental protein Musashi-1 interacts with the Zika genome and promotes viral replication diag *Science* v357 no6346 p83 Jl 7 2017

Firth, Colin, 1960-—Interviews

COLIN FIRTH & TARON EGERTON IN Kingsman: The Golden Circle J. McGovern color *Entertainment Weekly* no1478 / 1479 p44 Ag 18-25 2017

Fisanotti, John

READER GALLERY color *Astronomy* v44 no12 p70 D 2016

Fiscal policy

JOHN MAYNARD TRUMP B. GREELEY bw *Bloomberg Businessweek* no4500 p44 N 21 2016

The Untouchables J. COST color *Weekly Standard* v23 no4 p16 O 2 2017

Fiscal policy—United States

The Great Pretender M. Konczal *Nation* v304 no17 p5 Je 5 2017

NIH overhead plan draws fire J. Kaiser color *Science* v356 no6341 p893 Je 1 2017

A Technology-Based Growth Policy G. TASSEY graph *Issues in Science & Technology* v33 no2 p80 Wint 2017

Fiscal policy—United States—History—21st century

A Tale of Two Tax Plans E. Barone color diag *Time* v188 no16/17 p37 O 24 2016

Fiscal year

Fiscal Fakery bw *National Review* v69 no5 p14 Mr 20 2017

Fischbacher, Christian

Make the Cut color *House Beautiful* v159 no5 p44 Je 2017

Fischer, Bill

The End of Expertise *Harvard Business Review Digital Articles* p2 O 19 2015

Fighting Ebola Means Managing Fear *Harvard Business Review Digital Articles* p2 O 2 2014

How Chinese Companies Disrupt Through Business Model Innovation *Harvard Business Review Digital Articles* p2 Jl 8 2016

Unlock Employee Innovation That Fits with Your Strategy *Harvard Business Review Digital Articles* p2 O 27 2014

Fischer, Bobby, 1943-2008

The Ultimate Pawn Sacrifice J. NEUGEBOREN *American Scholar* v86 no2 p86 Spr 2017

Fischer, Conan

The Limits of Nationhood: In the interwar period, France and Germany worked towards an integrated Europe *History Today* v67 no6 p12 Je 2016

Fischer, D.

Structure, force balance, and topology of Earth's magnetopause diag graph *Science* v356 no6341 p960 Je 1 2017

Fischer, Jenna, 1974-

Who Is the Best TV Couple? M. Z. Seitz img *New York* v49 no22 p100 O 31 2016

Fischer, Julia

Monkey lives revealed B. Bower color *Science News* v191 no5 p30 Mr 18 2017

Fischer, Lucy

Cinema by Design: Art Nouveau, Modernism, and Film History D. Callahan color *Film Comment* v53 no3 p78 My/Je 2017

Fischer, Markus

Positive biodiversity-productivity relationship predominant in global forests bibl chart graph map *Science* v354 no6309 paaf8957-1 O 14 2016

Fischer, Michael

THE REBUILDING BOOM *Cincinnati Magazine* v50 no11 p70 Ag 2017

Those Old Houses: 8K Construction is out to save Cincinnati's historic fabric, one home at a time L. MURTHA *Cincinnati Magazine* v50 no11 p78 Ag 2017

FISCHER, MOLLY

Love and War: Camille Paglia Predicted 2017 img *New York* p24 Mr 6 2017

NO FOOL *Harper's Magazine* v334 no2002 p91 Mr 2017

OBAMA'S AMERICA img *New York* v49 no20 p12 O 3 2016

What Happens When Work Becomes a Nonstop Chat Room *New York* v50 no10 p40 My 15 2017

Fischer, Oliver J.

Synthesis of resveratrol tetramers via a stereoconvergent radical equilibrium bibl diag graph *Science* v354 no6317 p1260 D 9 2016

FISCHER, PAIGE PORTER

CASUAL FRIDAYS color *Better Homes & Gardens* v95 no6 p138 Je 2017

family matters color *Better Homes & Gardens* v95 no5 p46 My 2017

HOME GROWN color *Better Homes & Gardens* v95 no3 p112 Mr 2017

LET'S TALK TURKEY *Better Homes & Gardens* v94 no11 p116 N 2016

living HISTORY color *Better Homes & Gardens* v95 no11 p122 N 2017

pretty ENOUGH TO EAT color *Better Homes & Gardens* v95 no9 p114 S 2017

RED, WHITE & PEACHY color *Better Homes & Gardens* v95 no7 p126 Jl 2017 the storyteller color *Better Homes & Gardens* v95 no8 p132 Ag 2017

FISCHER, RAYMOND L.
ALTER EGOS: Hillary Clinton, Barack Obama, and the Twilight Struggle Over American Power *USA Today Magazine* v145 no2860 p80 Ja 2017
THE BATTLE LINES HAVE BEEN DRAWN *USA Today Magazine* v146 no2866 p14 Jl 2017
NATION ON THE TAKE *USA Today Magazine* v145 no2858 p20 N 2016
TGI (TPRM) *USA Today Magazine* v145 no2864 p16 My 2017

Fischer, Robert
Exposing Unfair Pricing in Auto Insurance Rates color *Consumer Reports* v82 no5 p6 My 2017

Fischer, W. W.
Redox stratification of an ancient lake in Gale crater, Mars color *Science* v356 no6341 p922 Je 1 2017

Fischer, Walter
The Devil and Miss Mansfield J. HOBERMAN bw *Film Comment* v53 no5 p79 S/O 2017

Fischer, William A. II
Fighting Ebola Means Managing Fear *Harvard Business Review Digital Articles* p2 O 2 2014

Fischer, Woodward W.
On the origins of oxygenic photosynthesis and aerobic respiration in Cyanobacteria chart diag *Science* v355 no6332 p1436 Mr 31 2017

Fischetti, Mark
1,000 YEARS OF SOLAR ECLIPSES diag graph map *Scientific American* v317 no2 p62 Ag 2017
The Baby Spike diag *Scientific American* v317 no1 p76 Jl 2017
The End graph *Scientific American* v317 no3 p96 S 2017
The Many Ways to Innovate diag *Scientific American* v315 no5 p80 N 2016
Novel Math graph *Scientific American* v316 no2 p76 F 2017
Opioid Deaths Soar graph *Scientific American* v317 no4 p96 O 2017
Reactors Reshuffled graph *Scientific American* v317 no2 p84 Ag 2017
Sounds Like Trouble diag graph *Scientific American* v316 no6 p78 Je 2017
Top Air Polluters map *Scientific American* v316 no1 p72 Ja 2017
Trillions of Insects Migrate color graph *Scientific American* v316 no4 p84 Ap 2017

Fischhoff, Baruch
Challenges in researching terrorism from the field bibl color *Science* v355 no6323 p352 Ja 27 2017

Fischl, Eric
Painting Late America J. SALTZ img *New York* v49 no26 p89 D 26 2016

Fischman, Josh
EYES IN THE DEEP color diag *Scientific American* v315 no6 p80 D 2016

Fish & game licenses
A STUDENT LOAN D. HART color map *Outdoor Life* v224 no6 pH9 Ag 2017

Fish, J. L.
THE SHARPEST TOOL IN THE SHED S. SALABERT color *Backpacker* p71 Ag 2017

Fish, Peter
BATTLE GROUND color *Sunset* v238 no5 p70 My 2017

Fish as food
CATCH OF THE DAY S. Dry bw color *Louisiana Life* v38 no1 p54 S/O 2017
Decode the Fish Counter A. C. Shilton color *Men's Health* v32 no2 p58 Mr 2017
WHERE THERE'S SMOKE ... C. MOROCCO color *Bon Appetit* no11 p127 N 2017

Fish as laboratory animals
Zebrafish larvae could help to personalize cancer treatments M. Leslie color *Science* v357 no6353 p745 Ag 25 2017

Fish carcasses
Research Digest *Alternatives Journal (AJ) - Canada's Environmental Voice* v42 no3 p11 2016

Fish conservation
A Drastic Decline of River Herring: TINY STONES IN FISH HOLD CLUES TO HELP RESTORE POPULATIONS K. Madin *Oceanus* v52 no2 p2 Spr 2017
Stewards of the Sea E. Vance color map *National Geographic* v232 no3 p56 S 2017

Fish conservation—Law & legislation
Status quo won't save salmon in the Columbia River Basin color *National Wildlife (World Edition)* v54 no6 p46 O/N 2016

Fish culture
See also
Fish culturists
A FISH OUT OF WATER M. Oatman color *Mother Jones* v42 no1 p44 Ja/F 2017
Raw Appeal C. Leu *Sierra* v101 no4 p8 Jl/Ag 2016

Fish culture—New Brunswick
Compliments for fishing C. MCINTYRE color *Maclean's* v130 no10 p48 N 2017

Fish declines
FORECASTING THE FUTURE OF FISH M. Wicks *Oceanus* v51 no2 p94 Wint 2016
IN HOT WATER A. Witze color graph map *Science News* v191 no9 p18 My 13 2017
Paradise Unwound T. Gibson color map *National Wildlife (World Edition)* v55 no2 p32 F/Mr 2017

Fish evolution
Fossil fishes challenge 'urban legend' of evolution E. Pennisi color *Science* v353 no6307 p1483 S 30 2016
Fossils shake up fish family tree V. Callier color *Science News* v192 no5 p5 S 30 2017

Fish fillets
Baked Trout with Mango Salsa S. Evans color *Missouri Life* v44 no6 p72 S 2017
Fresh Perspective: Inspired by flavors of her heritage, Chef Diana Chauvin Galle puts a Thai twist on a local favorite *New Orleans Homes & Lifestyles* v20 no3 p24 Summ 2017
A LOT OF FISH IN THE SEA C. MOROCCO color *Bon Appetit* no8 p101 Ag 2017

Fish industry—China
How China Maintains Large Catches *USA Today Magazine* v145 no2865 p9 Je 2017

Fish kills
The genomic landscape of rapid repeated evolutionary adaptation to toxic pollution in wild fish N. M. Reid, D. A. Proestou et al bibl graph *Science* v354 no6317 p1305 D 9 2016

Fish larvae
How Do Larvae Find a Place to Settle Down?: NOT WITH SOUND CUES, SURPRISED SCIENTISTS SAY L. Lippsett *Oceanus* v52 no2 p30 Spr 2017

Fish metabolism
HOT HOLES B. RUZZO color *Outdoor Life* v224 no1 p102 D 2016/Ja 2017

Fish oils
Blood Levels of 0mega-3s from Fish, Plants Linked to Lower Fatal Heart Risk *Tufts University Health & Nutrition Letter* v34 no8 p3 O 2016
Get to Know: Nordic Naturals J. SCHILDHOUSE color *Muscle & Performance* v9 no9 p34 S 2017
Our Doc Will See You Now R. Rajapaksa color *Health* v30 no9 p103 N 2017

Fish oils—Evaluation
HEALTH color *Horse & Rider* v56 no2 p17 F 2017
PREMIER PROVISIONS color *Muscle & Performance* v9 no5 p64 My 2017

Fish physiology
WHEN SEX IS SO RIGHT (OR LEFT) P. Edmonds color *National Geographic* v231 no4 p29 Ap 2017

Fish population estimates
Google Haul Out: Earth Observation Imagery and Digital Aerial Surveys in Coastal Wildlife Management and Abundance Estimation J. H. MOXLEY, A. BOGOMOLNI et al *BioScience* v67 no8 p760 Ag 2017

Fish populations
See also
Fish declines
Populations Smaller than Previously Thought *USA Today Magazine* v145 no2865 p8 Je 2017
Portugal and the Ocean Economy A. P. Vitorino *UN Chronicle* v54

no1/2 p1 2017

Fish research

FISH'S FECUNDITY A BOON TO LABS P. Edmonds color *National Geographic* v232 no3 p25 S 2017

Fish sounds

How Do Larvae Find a Place to Settle Down?: NOT WITH SOUND CUES, SURPRISED SCIENTISTS SAY L. Lippsett *Oceanus* v52 no2 p30 Spr 2017

Fish stocking

STOCKING FISH + SAVING A LIFE S. Robb *New York State Conservationist* v71 no5 p18 Ap 2017

Fish tagging

EXPOSURE S. Murray color *Power & Motoryacht* v34 no7 p40 Jl 2017

Tagging a Squishy Squid E. Koenig *Oceanus* v52 no1 p24 Summ 2016

Fishbach, Ayelet

Match Your Motivational Tactic to the Situation *Harvard Business Review Digital Articles* p2 Ja 8 2016

Fishbein, Greg

How to Quantify Sustainability's Impact on Your Bottom Line *Harvard Business Review Digital Articles* p2 S 13 2017

Fishburne, Laurence, 1961-

Laurence Lightens Up color *AARP: The Magazine* v30 no6A p11 O/N 2017

Fishel, Brooke

Beauty to Behold color diag *Log Home Living* v34 no4 p26 My 2017

Forging New Roads color diag *Log Home Living* v33 no7 p30 S 2016

Silver Linings color *Log Home Living* v33 no9 p28 D 2016

Fishell, Gord

Human brains teach us a surprising lesson bibl color *Science* v354 no6308 p38 O 7 2016

Fisher (Mammal)

REAPPEARING ACT K. SIBER *National Parks* v91 no2 p20 Spr 2017

FISHER, ALEXANDER W.

Ecological Forecasting and the Science of Hypoxia in Chesapeake Bay *BioScience* v67 no7 p614 Jl 2017

FISHER, ALLIE

UNITED WAYPOINTS *Wired* v24 no12 p90 D 2016

FISHER, AYNSLEY MILLER

CUSTOM OF THE COUNTRY *Virginia Living* v15 no3 p94 Ap 2017

Fisher, Bill

Why English, Not Mandarin, Is the Language of Innovation *Harvard Business Review Digital Articles* p2 Ja 12 2015

Fisher, Carl

The Emma Messing Story: The remarkable life of a rabbi's daughter from Indianapolis M. Lasswell *Commentary* v143 no4 p36 Ap 2017

Fisher, Carrie, 1956-2016

1956 - 2016 CARRIE FISHER [Cover story] A. Breznican color *Entertainment Weekly* no1448 p18 Ja 13 2017

CARRIE FISHER M. Roush *TV Guide* v65 no4 p14 Ja 16 2017

THE CARRIE I KNEW A. Breznican color *Entertainment Weekly* no1448 p22 Ja 13 2017

Cover *Entertainment Weekly* no1448 pC1 Ja 13 2017

For the Record color *Time* v188 no22-23 p8 N/D 2016

THE LAST OF LEIA A. Breznican color *Entertainment Weekly* no1478 / 1479 p35 Ag 18-25 2017

The Princess Diarist A. Breznican color *Entertainment Weekly* no1442 p60 D 2 2016 Rebellious Special Issue

STAR WARS J. D. BIERSDORFER *New York Times Book Review* p29 D 4 2016

Two Stars That Lived-and Shone-Orbiting Each Other S. Zacharek color *Time* v189 no3 p10 Ja 16 2017

Fisher, Carrie, 1956-2016—Interviews

Carrie Fisher A. GREENE bw *Rolling Stone* no1276 p70 D 15 2016

Fisher, Corinne

Everyone Calm Down About My Being Single, Please color *Glamour* v114 no11 p132 N 2016

FISHER, DANIEL

Father (and Son) Knows Best color *Forbes* v199 no5 p62 My 16

2017

Hardened Target chart color *Forbes* v199 no1 p36 Ja 24 2017

Hidden Assets color *Forbes* v198 no8 p62 D 20 2016

Peak Performance color graph *Forbes* v198 no8 p44 D 20 2016

THE WORLD'S BILLIONAIRES bw color diag graph map *Forbes* v199 no3 p84 Mr 28 2017

FISHER, DANIEL CLARKSON

The Teacher Racket bw *Tricycle: The Buddhist Review* v26 no2 p26 Wint 2016

Fisher, Douglas

Elevating the Profession *Literacy Today (2411-7862)* v35 no2 p6 S/O 2017

Get Involved With ILA *Literacy Today (2411-7862)* v34 no4 p6 Ja/F 2017

Fisher, George A.

Mismatch repair deficiency predicts response of solid tumors to PD-1 blockade chart graph *Science* v357 no6349 p409 Jl 28 2017

Fisher, Helen, 1942-

WELCOME TO THE GOLDEN AGE OF SEX E. Sherman and J. Covert cartoon chart color *Men's Health* v32 no2 p102 Mr 2017

Fisher, Helen, ca. 1947—Interviews

"IF YOU UNDERSTAND HOW THE BRAIN WORKS, YOU CAN REACH ANYONE" [Cover story] A. BEARD bw *Harvard Business Review* v95 no2 p60 Mr/Ap 2017

Fisher, Isla, 1976-

Fairground color *Vanity Fair* v59 no6 p57 My 2017

Fisher, Jamie

Memewear *New York Times Magazine* p22 Ag 20 2017

Fisher, Jennifer

CHAINS OF LOVE E. Wilson color *InStyle* p52 Home & Design 2016

Inside Jennifer Fisher's Fridge S. Gaynes Levy color *Glamour* v115 no10 p122 O 2017

My Stuff JENNIFER FISHER color *Vanity Fair* v59 no8 p42 Ag 2017

Fisher, Josef

A chemical genetic roadmap to improved tomato flavor bibl graph *Science* v355 no6323 p391 Ja 27 2017

Fisher, Jules

Jules Fisher's Work with Derek DelGaudio *Stage Directions* v30 no8 p19 Ag 2017

FISHER, JULIA FREELAND

Takeaways from the 2016 Blended and Personalized Learning Conference *Education Digest* v82 no6 p42 F 2017

Will Eliminating the 'F' Eliminate Bad School Design? *Education Digest* v82 no4 p47 D 2016

FISHER, KEN

HERE ARE FIVE STOCKS—TO BE HOPEFUL FOR *Forbes* v198 no7 p62 N 29 2016

TRUMP-IMPERVIOUS MARKET *Forbes* v198 no9 p100 D 30 2016

TRUMP OR HILLARY? color *Forbes* v198 no6 p66 N 8 2016

FISHER, LINDSAY

Buckeye Street: Get to know the darling of Kokomo's historic district *Indianapolis Monthly* v12 no40 p38 Ag 2017

Make Tracks *Indianapolis Monthly* v40 no4 p36 D 2016

Fisher, Louis

The Strongest Branch of Liberty K. R. Kosar and A. Chan *Washington Monthly* p10 N/D 2016

FISHER, MARSHALL

CURING THE ADDICTION TO GROWTH color graph il img *Harvard Business Review* v95 no1 p66 Ja/F 2017

Fisher, Michael

Looking Ahead color *Sail* v48 no6 p22 Je 2017

Fisher, Miles Ryan

WHEN ALL WAS LOST: A team of outmatched kids--and a bigger surprise than a win *Washingtonian Magazine* v52 no9 p208 Je 2017

Fisher, Peter H.

Anthony Philip French *Physics Today* v70 no6 p74 Je 2017

Fisher, Sharon

What's Your Most Awkward Team-Building Experience? K. Morell cartoon *Bloomberg Businessweek* no4518 p78 Ap 10 2017

Fisher, Shoshana—Interviews

What I Wear to Work: SHOSHANA FISHER J. Chen color

Bloomberg Businessweek no4514 p75 Mr 13 2017

Fisher, Simcha

I THOUGHT GOOD CATHOLICS DIDN'T NEED THERAPY. THEN I WENT color *America* v217 no2 p36 Jl 24 2017

Fisher, Susan J,

BABY'S FIRST ORGAN color *Scientific American* v317 no4 p46 O 2017

Fisheries

See also

Deep-sea fisheries

Achieving and Maintaining Sustainable Fisheries J. Rice *UN Chronicle* v54 no1/2 p1 2017

Know Your Ocean. Love Your Ocean E. Penn *UN Chronicle* v54 no1/2 p1 2017

Large benefits to marine fisheries of meeting the 1.5°C global warming target W. W. L. Cheung, G. Reygondeau et al bibl graph *Science* v354 no6319 p1591 D 23 2016

The Sacred Cod H. TOURGEE color *Yankee* v80 no6 p30 N/D 2016

THE SHIPPING EXPERT *Iceland Review* v54 no6 p122 N/D 2016

Fisheries—Asia

Dam-building threatens Mekong fisheries R. Stone color map *Science* v354 no6316 p1084 D 2 2016

Fisheries—Canada

WILDLIFE color *Canadian Geographic* v137 no2 p20 Mr/Ap 2017

Fisheries—China

How China Maintains Large Catches *USA Today Magazine* v145 no2865 p9 Je 2017

Fisheries—Congresses

TALKING ABOUT SUSTAINABILITY *Iceland Review* v54 no6 p119 N/D 2016

Fisheries—Export & import trade

Poor fisheries struggle with U.S. import rule A. F. Johnson, M. Caillat et al bibl color *Science* v355 no6329 p1031 Mr 10 2017

Fisheries—Iceland

PILLAR OF THE ECONOMY *Iceland Review* v54 no6 p118 N/D 2016

Fisheries—International cooperation

Nations agree to create world's largest marine reserve in Antarctica color *Science* v354 no6312 p530 N 4 2016

Fishers

See also

Fishing guides

Lobster fishers

THE CHAMPS B. RUZZO and G. BETHGE color *Outdoor Life* v224 no5 p34 Je/Jl 2017

Coam Over J. JOHNSON *Boating World* v38 no6 p24 Je 2017

Fact or Superstition? J. BROWNLEE color *Power & Motoryacht* v34 no9 p32 S 2017

A Family FISHING AFFAIR T. Hughes *New York State Conservationist* v71 no6 p10 Je 2017

GOING DEEP J. Dean color *Sunset* v238 no5 p19 My 2017

INDIANA FISHING LURES color *Indianapolis Monthly* v42 no2 p67 O 2017

Joseph Michael Howlett A. A. DAVIS color *Maclean's* v130 no9 p82 O 2017

MEET AARON BEAN color *Sea Magazine* v109 no6 pPNW-8 Je 2017

Work the Water Column T. CLARKE *Boating World* v38 no4 p16 Ap 2017

Fishers—Attitudes

Mel Rocchio A. A. DAVIS color *Maclean's* v130 no4 p74 My 2017

THIS LAND WAS YOUR LAND H. HERRING, J. R. SULLIVAN et al cartoon color diag map *Field & Stream* v122 no1 p40 My 2017

Fishers—Employment

News Roundup V. HAFSTAÐ *Iceland Review* v55 no2 p18 Mr/Ap 2017

Fishers—Equipment & supplies

Choose the Right Light- Tackle Rod: Know a little lingo and how a rod will be used before purchasing one D. T. CLARKE *Boating World* v38 no8 p18 S/O 2017

Lesson in Lingo: Before someone can make an informed decision,

he needs to know the lingo of fishing rods. Here are the important terms *Boating World* v38 no8 p18 S/O 2017

Fishers—United States

PUBLIC APPEAL color *Field & Stream* v122 no4 p15 S 2017

Fishery gear

See also

Fishing boats

Awash in Plastic J. Greenspan graph *Scientific American* v317 no2 p20 Ag 2017

Fishery law & legislation

See also

Fish & game licenses

Fish conservation—Law & legislation

China cracks down on coastal fisheries D. Normile color *Science* v356 no6338 p573 My 12 2017

FOREIGN FISHING P. RAINS color map *Sea Magazine* v109 no6 p18 Je 2017

Fishery management

Fisherwomen--The Uncounted Dimension in Fisheries Management L. E. OGDEN *BioScience* v67 no2 p111 F 2017

Fishy Business E. STRICKLAND color *Foreign Policy* no222 p24 Ja/F 2017

Stewards of the Sea E. Vance color map *National Geographic* v232 no3 p56 S 2017

Fishery processing—Congresses

TALKING ABOUT SUSTAINABILITY *Iceland Review* v54 no6 p119 N/D 2016

Fishes

See also

Freshwater fishes

China cracks down on coastal fisheries D. Normile color *Science* v356 no6338 p573 My 12 2017

Evaluating Science's open-data policy D. G. Roche *Science* v357 no6352 p654 Ag 18 2017

The Everything Guide to Seafood K. Canning color *Health* v31 no5 p111 Je 2017

FALSE TRUTHS S. SAUTNER color *Outdoor Life* v224 no7 p60 S 2017

Fishes M. FINELLI *Vegetarian Journal* v36 no2 p26 2017

FISH FRY s. collins and s. carey color *Martha Stewart Living* p86 Jl/Ag 2017

Fishing With Fire *New York Times Upfront* v149 no3 p2 O 10 2016

Go Fish: Ripe, juicy tomatoes and fresh fish--could it get any better? Don't have heirlooms? Use cherry or campari tomatoes K. SHERWOOD *Nutrition Action Health Letter* v44 no7 p13 S 2017

THE INSIDERS CALL IT PEFO R. STIEVE *Arizona Highways* v93 no2 p2 F 2017

In The Raw A. Roman color *Bon Appetit* v62 no7 p78 Jl 2017

Just for the Halibut S. SPADACCINI *AARP: The Magazine* v59 no4A p71 Je/Jl 2016

New Safe-Seafood Guidelines color *Parents* v92 no5 p68 My 2017

Nonnative Fish to Control Aedes Mosquitoes: A Controversial, Harmful Tool V. M. AZEVEDO-SANTOS, J. R. S. VITULE et al *BioScience* v67 no1 p84 Ja 2017

The Odyssey of the Great Frigatebird K. PEEK *Audubon* v118 no6 p14 Wint 2016

A quick-start guide to the latest food terminology *Harvard Health Letter* v42 no8 p3 Je 2017

SPEED KILLS R. ROBERTSON and G. BETHGE color *Outdoor Life* v224 no4 p68 My 2017

Spice It Up B. Lipton color *Health* v31 no2 p125 Mr 2017

Super Supper Salads K. SHERWOOD *Nutrition Action Health Letter* v44 no6 p12 Jl/Ag 2017

Tag, They're It L. SCHLEY color *Discover* v38 no4 p18 My 2017

THE TASTIEST WAY TO SAVE THE PLANET chart color *GQ: Gentlemen's Quarterly* v97 no3 p122 Mr 2017

Top that salmon I. Odom color *Health* v31 no8 p132 O 2017

Trout: The Perfect Catch J. BOWDEN and J. BESSINGER color *Better Nutrition* v79 no9 p70 S 2017

Fishes—Fertility

FORECASTING THE FUTURE OF FISH M. Wicks *Oceanus* v51 no2 p94 Wint 2016

Fishes—Reintroduction

SOUTH COAST HABITAT RESTORATION: If You Build It,

They Will Come: Bringing Steelhead Back to the Central Coast M. GOMEZ color *Earth Island Journal* v32 no4 p16 Wint 2017

Fishhooks

JAPAN'S EARLY ANGLERS Z. ZORICH color *Archaeology* v70 no1 p18 Ja/F 2017

WHAT'S THAT SMELL? M. Modoski color *Field & Stream* v122 no2 p30 Je/Jl 2017

Fishing

> *See also*
> Bait fishing
> Bass fishing
> Billfish fishing
> Bluegill fishing
> Brown trout fishing
> Casting (Fishing)
> Salmon fishing
> Steelhead fishing
> Trout fishing

6 Must-Haves to Turn Your Pontoon Into a Fishing Machine L. Whiteley color *Cabin Living* p12 Ag 2017

8 Safety Hacks T. KEER *Boating World* v38 no1 p20 Ja 2017

THE ABYSS S. HEITING and G. BETHGE color *Outdoor Life* v224 no3 pF1 Ap 2017

Against The Grain J. WOOLDRIDGE color *Power & Motoryacht* v34 no8 p70 Ag 2017

Amelia's Big Fish R. Redman *New York State Conservationist* v71 no5 p40 Ap 2017

APRIL ANGLING: RADIATING SUCCESS color *Cabin Living* p12 Ap 2017

Ask MR S. Otte bw color *Model Railroader* v84 no6 p20 Je 2017

At a Glance *Sea Magazine* v109 no9 p58 S 2017

Autumn isn't just the end of summertime, it's bonus time L. Whiteley color *Cabin Living* p13 S 2017

BASS OF A DIFFERENT STRIPE S. RYAN and G. BETHGE color *Outdoor Life* v224 no4 p64 My 2017

BET YOU DON'T KNOW SPORTFISHING BOATS T. SERIO *Sea Magazine* v109 no9 p54 S 2017

CALL OF THE WILD color *Sunset* v237 no5 p52 N 2016

CAST AWAY F. F. Van de Water *Harper's Magazine* v333 no1999 p73 D 2016

Catching Memories D. J. Harding color *Power & Motoryacht* v34 no7 p12 Jl 2017

¿CÓMO SE DICE CAST & BLAST? C. KEARNS cartoon color *Field & Stream* v121 no8 p83 F/Mr 2017

A Conch's Life J. BROWNLEE color *Power & Motoryacht* v34 no7 p64 Jl 2017

dad's legacy M. FURTMAN color *Cabin Living* p50 O 2017

THE DISH ON THE SPOONS B. COOPER and G. BETHGE color *Outdoor Life* v224 no3 p64 Ap 2017

Don't Ask, Don't Tell P. FREDERIKSEN color *Power & Motoryacht* v33 no1 p38 Ja 2017

DON'T MISS LIST: AUGUST 2017 *Sea Magazine* v109 no8 pCA-11 Ag 2017

DRONE ATTACK N. HONACHEFSKY color *Outdoor Life* v224 no7 p58 S 2017

DROP SHOT W. LATHAM and N. KREBS cartoon color *Outdoor Life* v224 no4 p12 My 2017

THE FAMILY GUIDE TO NOODLING W. BRANTLEY color *Field & Stream* v122 no2 p76 Je/Jl 2017

FEEDING THE COWS J. Cermele color *Field & Stream* v122 no6 p22 N 2017

FISHING FROM THE SKY D. WALTERS cartoon color *Popular Mechanics* p88 Mr 2017

Fishing is Good for your Health cartoon *Cabin Living* p14 Ja/F 2017

A Fishing Massacree M. PETERS color *Power & Motoryacht* v33 no1 p36 Ja 2017

fish out of water J. Kramer color *Bon Appetit* v62 no2 p50 Mr 2017

FOR YOUR 'EYES ONLY B. RUZZO and G. BETHGE color map *Outdoor Life* v224 no2 p30 F/Mr 2017

FROST BITES M. Modoski color *Field & Stream* v121 no7 p70 D 2016/Ja 2017

FUN IN THE SUN color *Field & Stream* v122 no2 p65 Je/Jl 2017

Go Big, or Go Small P. FREDERIKSEN color *Power & Motoryacht* v32 no12 p22 D 2016

Hemingway's Fishing Rod J. BEYL *Idaho Magazine* v16 no3 p24 D 2016

HIGHS AND LOW COUNTRY T. E. Nickens color *Field & Stream* v121 no9 p58 Ap 2017

hooked color *Women's Health* v14 no8 p150 O 2017

A House Divided A. McKEAN *Outdoor Life* v224 no1 p12 D 2016/Ja 2017

HUNTBNB D. HART color *Outdoor Life* v224 no6 pH15 Ag 2017

Illegal fishing on the Galápagos high seas J. José Alava and F. Paladines color *Science* v357 no6358 p1362 S 29 2017

INDIANA FISHING LURES color *Indianapolis Monthly* v42 no2 p67 O 2017

In Praise of Smallness: Fishing the Little Creeks L. TANNER *Idaho Magazine* v16 no8 p6 My 2017

IRREGULAR JOE J. ARTERBURN cartoon *Outdoor Life* v224 no4 p78 My 2017

LAND A LUNKER BASS! color diag *Men's Health* v32 no6 p105 Ag 2017

LCAC ATTACK M. GOFF cartoon *Canoe & Kayak Magazine* v45 no1 p40 Wint 2017

LOOK OUT BELOW S. PENNAZ and G. BETHGE color *Outdoor Life* v224 no5 p38 Je/Jl 2017

Monster at Midnight K. Danielewicz color *Sail* v48 no7 p14 Jl 2017

ODE TO THE SPOON A. McKEAN color *Outdoor Life* v224 no6 p29 Ag 2017

OLD FLAMES C. Kearns color *Field & Stream* v121 no8 p8 F/Mr 2017

Papa's Lost Treasure K. MCCAFFERTY *Publishers Weekly* v264 no22 p44 My 29 2017

PIMP YOUR SHRIMP D. A. BROWN and G. BETHGE diag *Outdoor Life* v224 no3 p66 Ap 2017

POND HOPPING E. Stegemann *New York State Conservationist* v72 no1 p6 Ag 2017

Requiem for the Vaquita E. Vance color map *Scientific American* v317 no2 p36 Ag 2017

RESTLESS NATIVES color *Outdoor Life* v224 no6 p32 Ag 2017

Road Hawgs D. DRAPER bw color *Field & Stream* v122 no2 p39 Je/Jl 2017

SEARCHING FOR SILVER J. R. Sullivan color *Field & Stream* v122 no2 p26 Je/Jl 2017

SING ABOUT SPRING R. Preall *New York State Conservationist* v71 no5 p2 Ap 2017

THE SLAB HARVEST J. Cermele cartoon color *Field & Stream* v121 no6 p59 N 2016

A Speck In the Sea J. ALDRIDGE and A. SOSINSKI bw color *Power & Motoryacht* v34 no7 p48 Jl 2017

THE STAKES A. FREEMAN color *Canoe & Kayak Magazine* v45 no1 p32 Wint 2017

Stayin' Alive A. JONES *Boating World* v38 no3 p18 Mr 2017

THRILL RIDES color *Field & Stream* v122 no2 p37 Je/Jl 2017

THE THROWBACK R. DEWITT bw *Outdoor Life* v224 no6 p34 Ag 2017

THE UGLY FISH M. VINCENT and G. BETHGE color *Outdoor Life* v224 no3 p62 Ap 2017

UNDER-DOGFISH J. Cermele color *Field & Stream* v121 no8 p20 F/Mr 2017

WEATHER STRIPPING J. CERMELE cartoon color *Field & Stream* v121 no9 p16 Ap 2017

WELCOME TO THE JUNGLE J. CERMELE bw color *Field & Stream* v122 no2 p51 Je/Jl 2017

What Am I Looking At? A. JONES *Boating World* v38 no6 p20 Je 2017

When Your Best Fish Story Is About Catching ... A Goat R. BRAGG color *Reader's Digest* v190 no1135 p17 N 2017

Where the Fish and the Fisher-People Are img *New York* v50 no13 p60 Je 26 2017

Work the Water Column T. CLARKE *Boating World* v38 no4 p16 Ap 2017

YOUR OWN BACK YARD J. L. Hester cartoon *New Yorker* v93 no30 p19 O 2 2017

Fishing accidents

THE SHIPWRECK OF SAN LEON J. R. Sullivan cartoon *Field & Stream* v121 no7 p56 D 2016/Ja 2017

Fishing baits

How to Make a... BAIT BARREL C. J. CHIVERS bw *Popular Mechanics* p77 S 2017

How to Make a... BAIT BARREL C. J. CHIVERS cartoon *Popular Mechanics* v193 no7 p77 S 2016

ODE TO THE SPOON A. McKEAN color *Outdoor Life* v224 no6 p29 Ag 2017

RELISH THE WEENIE J. Cermele color *Field & Stream* v122 no3 p22 Ag 2017

WAYNE'S WORLD J. JOHNSTON color *Outdoor Life* v224 no8 p69 O 2017

WHAT'S THAT SMELL? M. Modoski color *Field & Stream* v122 no2 p30 Je/Jl 2017

Fishing baits—Design & construction

How to Make a... BAIT BARREL C. J. CHIVERS bw *Popular Mechanics* v193 no7 p77 S 2016

Fishing baits—Evaluation

FRESH BAITS J. Cermele color *Field & Stream* v122 no1 p68 My 2017

Fishing boats

Boater Beware J. BROWNLEE color *Power & Motoryacht* v34 no11 p58 N 2017

Cross-Culture color *House Beautiful* v159 no3 p26 Ap 2017

Find your Center A. JONES *Boating World* v38 no3 p40 Mr 2017

Steady as She Goes Z. Prochazka color *Sea Magazine* v109 no8 p46 Ag 2017

Fishing boats—Design & construction

LOAD THE BOAT J. BRANDT and T. HANSEN color diag *Outdoor Life* v224 no4 p48 My 2017

Fishing boats—Equipment & supplies

6 Simple Steps to a Custom Track System R. Robertson *Boating World* v37 no9 p22 N/D 2016

After the Catch... : The trip back to the dock after a day of fishing should be used wisely, for cleaning up D. T. CLARKE color *Boating World* v38 no7 p20 Jl 2017

Fishing boats—Evaluation

Fishing Platform S. SHIBATA *Boating World* v38 no6 p6 Je 2017

G3 Angler V17 SF *Boating World* v38 no1 p66 Ja 2017

Key Largo 216 LX *Boating World* v38 no1 p67 Ja 2017

THE POWER 'YAK REVIEW R. BURNLEY chart color *Outdoor Life* v224 no4 p14 My 2017

PURSUIT S 328 *Sea Magazine* v109 no4 p36 Ap 2017

Ski, Fish, Cruise, Save: The flagship of Chaparral's H2O line has something never seen before: outboard power A. JONES *Boating World* v38 no8 p32 S/O 2017

ULTIMATE DRIFT BOAT J. B. SNOW diag *Outdoor Life* v224 no1 p104 D 2016/Ja 2017

Fishing boats—Maintenance & repair

After the Catch... : The trip back to the dock after a day of fishing should be used wisely, for cleaning up D. T. CLARKE color *Boating World* v38 no7 p20 Jl 2017

Fishing bobbers

Get the Drift D. L. NG color *Field & Stream* v122 no1 p8 My 2017

Fishing equipment

See also

Fishing baits

Forward Thinking J. Y. WOOD color *Power & Motoryacht* v34 no10 p50 O 2017

How to Make a... BAIT BARREL C. J. CHIVERS bw *Popular Mechanics* p77 S 2017

Fishing equipment—Evaluation

FRESH BAITS J. Cermele color *Field & Stream* v122 no1 p68 My 2017

HOT RODS 2017 M. Modoski and J. Cermele cartoon color *Field & Stream* v122 no1 p59 My 2017

Fishing guides

The art of Sight-Casting L. SMITH FORD *Texas Monthly* v45 no9 p16 S 2017

Fishing Holdings LLC

Fishing Platform S. SHIBATA *Boating World* v38 no6 p6 Je 2017

Fishing lines

ADVANCES IN FISHING LINE THAT WILL CHANGE THE WAY WE FISH T. KUHN color *Outdoor Life* v224 no2 p47 F/Mr 2017

Fishing lures

All Spun Up M. Modoski color *Field & Stream* v121 no9 pF5

Ap 2017

FIRE BUGS G. THOMAS color *Field & Stream* v121 no9 p53 Ap 2017

Mining for Bronze J. Cermele color *Field & Stream* v121 no9 pF7 Ap 2017

SUMMER SURFACE BASS D. A. BROWN and G. BETHGE color *Outdoor Life* v224 no5 p31 Je/Jl 2017

Fishing lures—Evaluation

ALIVE AND FISHING M. VINCENT and G. BETHGE color *Outdoor Life* v224 no3 p67 Ap 2017

New electronic lure may catch too many fish; one state bans it M. Butler color *Field & Stream* v121 no9 p29 Ap 2017

New electronic lure may catch too many fish; one state bans it M. Butler color *Field & Stream* v122 no2 p35 Je/Jl 2017

Fishing nets

Making Waves *Reader's Digest* v188 no1125 p40 N 2016

Performance with purpose K. C. Horning color *U.S. Catholic* v81 no11 p12 N 2016

Fishing reels—Evaluation

THE 2017 FISHING GEAR GUIDE color *Field & Stream* v121 no8 p89 F/Mr 2017

HELL ON REELS 2017 M. Modoski and J. Cermele color *Field & Stream* v121 no9 p67 Ap 2017

Fishing reels—Maintenance & repair

How to Tuck Your Tackle In D. T. Clarke *Boating World* v37 no9 p18 N/D 2016

Fishing rigs—Evaluation

THE GREATEST RIG EVER MADE J. BRANDT color *Outdoor Life* v224 no1 p97 D 2016/Ja 2017

Fishing rods

TACKLE TEST 2017 T. KUHN chart color *Outdoor Life* v224 no3 p14 Ap 2017

Fishing rods—Design & construction

Choose the Right Light- Tackle Rod: Know a little lingo and how a rod will be used before purchasing one D. T. CLARKE *Boating World* v38 no8 p18 S/O 2017

Lesson in Lingo: Before someone can make an informed decision, he needs to know the lingo of fishing rods. Here are the important terms *Boating World* v38 no8 p18 S/O 2017

Fishing rods—Evaluation

The Future of Fishing K. Stock color *Bloomberg Businessweek* no4531 p63 Jl 24 2017

HOT RODS 2017 M. Modoski and J. Cermele cartoon color *Field & Stream* v122 no1 p59 My 2017

Technologically Amazing Fly Rod of the Month J. GLUCK color *Popular Mechanics* p32 Ap 2017

Fishing rods—Maintenance & repair

How to Tuck Your Tackle In D. T. Clarke *Boating World* v37 no9 p18 N/D 2016

Fishing tackle—Evaluation

BURNING RUBBER J. CERMELE, M. MODOSKI et al cartoon color *Field & Stream* v121 no8 p72 F/Mr 2017

Fishing techniques

See also

Casting (Fishing)

APRIL ANGLING: RADIATING SUCCESS color *Cabin Living* p12 Ap 2017

Bow Hunting J. Cermele color *Field & Stream* v122 no1 pF4 My 2017

BREAK OUT! W. BRANTLEY, J. CERMELE et al cartoon color *Field & Stream* v121 no9 p35 Ap 2017

BRUISER BROWNS S. RYAN color *Outdoor Life* v224 no7 p55 S 2017

CAT NIP J. Cermele cartoon color *Field & Stream* v121 no7 p32 D 2016/Ja 2017

Current Trends J. Cermele color *Field & Stream* v122 no1 pF7 My 2017

DEVIL'S IN THE DETAILS T. E. Nickens color *Field & Stream* v122 no3 p32 Ag 2017

FIRE BUGS G. THOMAS color *Field & Stream* v121 no9 p53 Ap 2017

A Fishing Life J. Brownlee color *Power & Motoryacht* v34 no8 p20 Ag 2017

Flipping Genius B. Duchesney color *Field & Stream* v122 no1 pF1 My 2017

FROST BITES M. Modoski color *Field & Stream* v121 no7 p70

D 2016/Ja 2017

HOT BRONZE S. CULTON color *Field & Stream* v122 no3 p51 Ag 2017

Learn Minimalist Fly-Fishing C. GERARD il *Backpacker* p36 My 2017

LOAD THE BOAT J. BRANDT and T. HANSEN color diag *Outdoor Life* v224 no4 p48 My 2017

OUT OF MY LEAGUE B. HEAVEY *Field & Stream* v122 no3 p86 Ag 2017

PANFISH AND PALM REELS D. A. BROWN color *Outdoor Life* v224 no1 p100 D 2016/Ja 2017

PIMP YOUR SHRIMP D. A. BROWN and G. BETHGE diag *Outdoor Life* v224 no3 p66 Ap 2017

RESTLESS NATIVES color *Outdoor Life* v224 no6 p32 Ag 2017

RUNNING OF THE BULLS S. RYAN and G. BETHGE color *Outdoor Life* v224 no3 p59 Ap 2017

SLAB WORK M. Modoski color *Field & Stream* v122 no3 p24 Ag 2017

So Close, Yet... P. FREDERIKSEN color *Power & Motoryacht* v32 no11 p48 N 2016

THE THROWBACK R. DEWITT bw *Outdoor Life* v224 no6 p34 Ag 2017

Fishing—Arizona

from our archives [May 1967] *Arizona Highways* v93 no8 p10 Ag 2017

Fishing—Equipment & supplies

Great Ways to Celebrate the Holidays color *Cabin Living* p12 D 2016

look at this trove, treasures untold E. KELLY and P. Hess cartoon *Popular Science* v289 no2 p76 Mr/Ap 2017

PADDLING + fishing A WINNING COMBO D. ARMITAGE color *Cabin Living* p62 Mr 2017

THE SHIPWRECK OF SAN LEON J. R. Sullivan cartoon *Field & Stream* v121 no7 p56 D 2016/Ja 2017

SPEED KILLS R. ROBERTSON and G. BETHGE color *Outdoor Life* v224 no4 p68 My 2017

TACKLE TEST 2017 T. KUHN chart color *Outdoor Life* v224 no3 p14 Ap 2017

Fishing—Equipment & supplies—Evaluation

THE 2017 FISHING GEAR GUIDE color *Field & Stream* v121 no8 p89 F/Mr 2017

ABU GARCIA REVO MGXTREME BAITCASTER color *Field & Stream* v121 no8 p93 F/Mr 2017

BURNING RUBBER J. CERMELE, M. MODOSKI et al cartoon color *Field & Stream* v121 no8 p72 F/Mr 2017

GARMIN STRIKER color *Field & Stream* v121 no8 p94 F/Mr 2017

NEXT-GEN FISH FINDERS: ENHANCED CHIRP AND BEYOND J. RAGUSO graph *Outdoor Life* v224 no2 p46 F/Mr 2017

RAPALA SKITTER V P. B. Mathiesen color *Field & Stream* v121 no8 p92 F/Mr 2017

SURFACE SEDUCER DOUBLE BARREL POPPER BODIES J. Cermele color *Field & Stream* v121 no8 p90 F/Mr 2017

Technologically Amazing Fly Rod of the Month J. GLUCK color *Popular Mechanics* p32 Ap 2017

Fishing—Great Britain

SO SUBTLE A CATCH S. Parkin *Harper's Magazine* v333 no1999 p67 D 2016

Fishing—Idaho

Real Big Fish E. DYMOCK color *Idaho Magazine* v16 no1 p48 O 2016

Fishing—Mexico—Baja California (State)

The Beauty of Baja J. BROWNLEE color *Power & Motoryacht* v33 no2 p38 F 2017

Fishing—South Dakota

Rock Creek Snapper *South Dakota Magazine* v33 no2 p91 Jl/Ag 2017

Fishing—United States

CHEAP ADVENTURES J. BRANDT and P. J. DELHOMME cartoon color *Outdoor Life* v224 no4 p30 My 2017

PANFISH AND PALM REELS D. A. BROWN color *Outdoor Life* v224 no1 p100 D 2016/Ja 2017

Tangled Lines P. D. McQUADE *Idaho Magazine* v16 no2 p6 N 2016

THE WEATHER RULES B. RUZZO and G. BETHGE color *Outdoor Life* v224 no4 p67 My 2017

THE WEEKENDERS B. RUZZO and G. BETHGE color map *Outdoor Life* v224 no4 p59 My 2017

Fishkin, James S.

Applying Deliberative Democracy in Africa: Uganda's First Deliberative Polls *Daedalus* v146 no3 p140 Summ 2017

Introduction *Daedalus* v146 no3 p6 Summ 2017

Fishman, Bill

Skepticism Should Be Nonpartisan *Skeptical Inquirer* v41 no3 p63 My/Je 2017

FISHMAN, BORIS

Home Bodies: In Jill Eisenstadt's comic novel, a Manhattan family seeks safety in the Rockaways after 9/11 *New York Times Book Review* p8 Je 11 2017

FISHMAN, CHARLES

ROCKETEER *Smithsonian* v47 no8 p36 D 2016

UP IN THE AIR *Smithsonian* v48 no3 p32 Je 2017

FISHMAN, COURTNEY

north by northwest cartoon color *Better Homes & Gardens* v95 no2 p14 F 2016

Fishman, Edward

Even Smarter Sanctions color *Foreign Affairs* v96 no6 p102 N/D 2017

FISHMAN, ELLY

CHICAGOANS OF THE YEAR [Cover story] color *Chicago* v65 no12 p74 D 2016

CONVERGENCE color *Chicago* v65 no11 p92 N 2016

DREAM DUO bw *Chicago* v66 no9 p49 S 2017

HIGHBROW GIFT GUIDE bw color *Chicago* v65 no12 p52 D 2016

THE IMPROBABLE ENCORE bw color *Chicago* v66 no2 p72 F 2017

THE LIFE OF A CITY bw *Chicago* v66 no1 p39 Ja 2017

VOX: ART FOR THE PEOPLE color *Chicago* v66 no9 p54 S 2017

WELCOME TO REFUGEE HIGH [Cover story] color *Chicago* v66 no6 p64 Je 2017

Fishman, Louise

Line Drive color *ARTnews* v115 no4 p9 Wint 2016/2017

Fishman, Ted C.

COLUMBIA'S IDENTITY CRISIS bw color graph *Chicago* v66 no1 p110 Ja 2017

David St. Pierre color *Chicago* v66 no6 p90 Je 2017

THE SINKING OF SEARS color *Chicago* v66 no4 p28 Ap 2017

THE VISTA TOWER color *Chicago* v66 no10 p24 O 2017

WHY We LOVE CHICAGO bw cartoon color *Chicago* v66 no3 p75 Mr 2017

Woman on Fire [Cover story] color *Chicago* v66 no7 p64 Jl 2017

Fishman Acoustic Amplication (Company)

Fishman SA Performance Audio Systems K. Baumann *Downbeat* v84 no8 p90 Ag 2017

Fishskin

ARTIFICIAL SKIN FROM THE SEA L. Parshley color diag *Bloomberg Businessweek* no4529 p58 Jl 3 2017

FISK, AARON T.

Envisioning the Future of Aquatic Animal Tracking: Technology, Science, and Application *BioScience* v67 no10 p884 O 2017

Fisk, Margaret Cronin

Can You Say Class Action in German? Nein color *Bloomberg Businessweek* no4505 p39 D 26 2016

The Lawsuits Keep Coming for J&J bw *Bloomberg Businessweek* no4514 p21 Mr 13 2017

Plaintiffs' Lawyers ? St. Louis *Bloomberg Businessweek* no4493 p31 O 3 2016

St. Louis Loses Favor With Plaintiffs cartoon *Bloomberg Businessweek* no4532 p16 Jl 31 2017

Fisk, Peter C.

Appraising the performance of performance appraisals *Monthly Labor Review* p1 D 2016

Fiske, Brian

6 RULES OF RESTORATIVE SLEEP cartoon chart *Men's Health* v32 no8 p72 O 2017

HOW ADHD MADE ME A BETTER CEO bw color *Men's Health* v31 no10 p83 D 2016

STRENGTH SERVICE cartoon color *Men's Health* v32 no4 p116 My 2017

Fiske, Edward B.

Self-governing schools, parental choice, and the need to protect the public interest *Phi Delta Kappan* v99 no1 p31 S 2017

Fiske, Judy

Money Talks—in My Case Softly J. Epstein cartoon *Weekly Standard* v22 no29 p5 Ap 3 2017

Fisman, Ray

Everything We Know About Platforms We Learned from Medieval France *Harvard Business Review Digital Articles* p2 Mr 24 2016

FIXING DISCRIMINATION IN ONLINE MARKETPLACES color *Harvard Business Review* v94 no12 p88 D 2016

If Your Argument Is Based on Economics, You've Already Lost *Harvard Business Review Digital Articles* p2 Je 24 2016

The Internet of "Stuff Your Mom Won't Do for You Anymore" *Harvard Business Review Digital Articles* p2 Jl 26 2016

A Super Bowl Ad Is the Equivalent of Lighting Money on Fire (Which Can Be More Strategic Than It Sounds) color *Harvard Business Review Digital Articles* p2 F 3 2017

Fisman, Raymond

How to fight corruption color *Science* v356 no6340 p803 My 26 2017

Fist Fight (Film)

FIRST LOOK: FIST FIGHT N. PARKER and L. CROSS color *Ebony* v72 no4 p40 F 2017

Tracy Morgan What's your favorite restaurant in the world? S. Z. WEXLER cartoon color *Bon Appetit* v62 no2 p104 Mr 2017

Fistfight, Sacramento, August 1950 (Short story)

FISTFIGHT, SACRAMENTO, AUGUST 1950 D. Means *Harper's Magazine* p77 O 2017

Fit automobile—Evaluation

Best & Worst Lists chart *Consumer Reports* v82 no4 p30 Ap 2017

Used Car Winners & Losers chart color *Consumer Reports* v82 no4 p49 Ap 2017

Fitbit Inc.

6 RULES OF RESTORATIVE SLEEP B. FISKE cartoon chart *Men's Health* v32 no8 p72 O 2017

Track Action for Less L. Eadicicco color *Money* v46 no2 p23 Mr 2017

Fitbit Inc.—Finance

DATA WON'T MAKE YOU FIT L. Entis color *Fortune* v176 no2 p33 Ag 1 2017

Fitch, David E.

OLD, BORING WAYS OF DOING CHURCH B. MCCRACKEN cartoon color *Christianity Today* v61 no1 p69 Ja/F 2017

Fitflop Ltd.

"Every time I've had a really good idea, it was because I thought, I would so buy that." D. Kennedy and Ying Chu color *Glamour* v115 no4 p114 Ap 2017

Fitness walking

Letters to the Editor M. Halligan, U. Heidenreich et al color *Prevention* v69 no5 p4 My 2017

Fits, The (Film)

BODIES THAT MATTER: BLACK GIRLHOOD IN THE FITS P. White *Film Quarterly* v70 no3 p23 Spr 2017

Fitterling, Jim

THE BEST TIME TO BE AN ENGINEER J. FITTERLING *Vital Speeches of the Day* v83 no4 p125 Ap 2017

MAKING SMALL TALK: THE CASE FOR LGBT DIVERSITY AND INCLUSION *Vital Speeches of the Day* v82 no12 p384 D 2016

Fitting rooms

Mirror, Mirror, You're the Smartest of Them All M. Townsend color *Bloomberg Businessweek* no4512 p42 F 20 2017

FITTS, ALEXIS SOBEL

THE SPEECH WHISPERER *Washingtonian Magazine* v52 no1 p58 O 2016

Fitts, Joey

The Internet of Things Will Change Your Company, Not Just Your Products *Harvard Business Review Digital Articles* p2 O 24 2014

FITZ, CAITLIN

The Accidental Patriots bw color *Atlantic* v318 no5 p36 D 2016

FITZGERALD, ADAM

Worlds in a Cell: Jorie Graham, ambushed by illness, uses poetry to interweave personal and collective history bw *New York*

Times Book Review p13 Ag 6 2017

FitzGerald, Ben

As technology goes democratic, nations lose military control bibl *Bulletin of the Atomic Scientists* v73 no2 p102 Mr 2017

Fitzgerald, Brenda

NEWSMAKERS *Science* v357 no6347 p113 Jl 14 2017

Fitzgerald, Brendan

From school newsletter to nonprofit newsroom *Columbia Journalism Review* v56 no1 p57 Spr 2017

Fitzgerald, Ella, 1917-1996

Ella by Starlight T. Gioia bw *Weekly Standard* v22 no29 p30 Ap 3 2017

Ella Fitzgerald J. McDonough bw *Downbeat* v84 no1 p38 Ja 2017

A TOAST TO GREATNESS N. H. REEDER and D. POINTDUJOUR color *Ebony* v72 no5 p58 Mr 2017

Fitzgerald, F. Scott (Francis Scott), 1896-1940

The I.O.U F. S. FITZGERALD cartoon *New Yorker* v93 no5 p80 Mr 20 2017

THE JAZZ AGE bw color *Harper's Bazaar* no3650 p202 F 2017

Laugh Lines color *Reader's Digest* v189 no1129 p104 Ap 2017

Lost and Found B. BAILEY *New York Times Book Review* p22 Je 4 2017

WELCOME TO THE ISSUE *Harper's Bazaar* no3650 p36 F 2017

Fitzgerald, Father Allan

In guns we trust? color *U.S. Catholic* v82 no2 p24 F 2017

Fitzgerald, Frances, 1940-

The Evangelicals: The Struggle to Shape America color *Publishers Weekly* v264 no7 p71 F 13 2017

From Jonathan Edwards to Billy Graham L. Madaras *America* v217 no3 p46 Ag 7 2017

MASTERS OF SCHISM C. LEHMANN color *Nation* v304 no17 p38 Je 5 2017

One Nation Under God D. Covington *American Scholar* v86 no2 p117 Spr 2017

Pew Research J. SHARLET bw color il *New Republic* v248 no6 p50 Je 2017

Reading evangelical history with one eye closed *Christian Century* v134 no8 p1 Ap 12 2017

What Would Donald Do? S. Buntz color *Washington Monthly* v49 no9/10 p131 S/O 2017

Where Evangelicals Came From G. Wills bw color *New York Review of Books* v64 no7 p26 Ap 20 2017

With God on Their Side A. Wolfe *New York Times Book Review* p1 Ap 2 2017

Fitzgerald, Frances, 1940—Interviews

THE DEEPER ROOTS of the Christian Right H. W. Carter color *Christianity Today* v61 no6 p60 Jl/Ag 2017

FitzGerald, Garret A.

Time for nonaddictive relief of pain bibl color *Science* v355 no6329 p1026 Mr 10 2017

Fitzgerald, Katherine A.

The DNA-sensing AIM2 inflammasome controls radiation-induced cell death and tissue injury bibl color graph *Science* v354 no6313 p765 N 11 2016

Fitzgerald, Kathy

Discussion *Smithsonian* v48 no4 p6 Jl/Ag 2017

FITZGERALD, LEE A.

Incorporating Sociocultural Phenomena into Ecosystem-Service Valuation: The Importance of Critical Pluralism *BioScience* v67 no3 p233 Mr 2017

Fitzgerald, Manfred—Interviews

Manfred Fitzgerald: SENIOR VICE PRESIDENT, GENESIS M. Rechtin color *Motor Trend* v69 no11 p30 N 2017

Fitzgerald, Matt

Chasing beauty, finding grace color *Christian Century* v134 no3 p27 F 2017

FitzGerald, Meghan

The More Women Earn, the Less Healthy They Feel *Harvard Business Review Digital Articles* p2 Ja 13 2016

FITZ-GERALD, SEAN

Drama In the Streets *Los Angeles Magazine* p68 Mr 2017

Living Large By Living Small *Los Angeles Magazine* p52 F 2017

Rent the Runway *Los Angeles Magazine* p72 D 2016

Fitzgerald, Zelda, 1900-1948

The Meaning of Zelda E. STONE and C. SIGAL *Commentary*

v144 no1 p6 Jl/Ag 2017

Fitzharris, Lindsey
DANGEROUS MEDICINE color *Scientific American* v317 no4 p74 O 2017

Fitzharris, Tim
10 Frames color *Popular Photography* v81 no1 p54 Ja/F 2017

FITZHERBERT, EMILY
The Consequences of Internal Migration in Sub-Saharan Africa: A Case Study *BioScience* v67 no7 p664 Jl 2017

Fitzloff, Mark
THE REWARDS OF RISK T. Foster color *Men's Health* v32 no1 p40 Ja/F 2017

Fitzmaurice, Michael J.
Before the Fight: Sculpture captures Fitzmaurice's last night in Khe Sanh *South Dakota Magazine* v33 no3 p56 S/O 2017

Fitzpatrick, Alex
THE 2017 Fortune Crystal Ball color diag *Fortune* v174 no7 p11 D 1 2016
8 Travel Ideas for the Winter-Weary color *Time* v189 no7/8 p114 F 27 2017
The Best 25 Inventions of 2016 color *Time* v188 no22-23 p43 N/D 2016
The Cheap(er) Private Jet color *Time* v189 no23 p21 Je 19 2017
Hand Me That Wrench: Farmers and Apple Fight Over the Toolbox color *Time* v190 no1 p20 Jl 3 2017
The No-Frills, Full-Fun Snapshot Is Back color *Time* v190 no4 p52 Jl 24 2017
A Razor Built for Assisted Shaving color *Time* v190 no1 p19 Jl 3 2017

Fitzpatrick, Anna
Duolingo *New York Times Magazine* p20 Jl 30 2017

FITZPATRICK, BRAD
BARREL LENGTH WISDOM color *Outdoor Life* v224 no1 p92 D 2016/Ja 2017
BEAT THE WIND color *Outdoor Life* v224 no8 p28 O 2017
BOOK SMARTS color *Outdoor Life* v224 no2 p76 F/Mr 2017
BOUNTIES FOR BUCKS color *Outdoor Life* v223 no9 p36 N 2016
HARDSHIP HONKERS color *Outdoor Life* v224 no8 p43 O 2017
LACEY AND THE LION color *Outdoor Life* v224 no6 p53 Ag 2017
MAXED MUZZLELOADERS color *Outdoor Life* v224 no9 p63 N 2017
THE RED ZONE color *Outdoor Life* v223 no9 pH11 N 2016
SHOOT FASTER, SHOOT BETTER color *Outdoor Life* v224 no9 p66 N 2017
SKINNING KNIVES 101 color *Outdoor Life* v224 no8 pH15 O 2017
WAPITI WISDOM color *Outdoor Life* v224 no7 p26 S 2017

Fitzpatrick, Cameron, 1992——Interviews
CAM FITZPATRICK P. G. Strout cartoon color *Snowboarder* v29 no4 p48 D 2016

Fitzpatrick, Conor
An environment-dependent transcriptional network specifies human microglia identity color *Science* v356 no6344 p1248 Je 23 2017

Fitzpatrick, Jameson
"UGO RONDINONE: I ♥ JOHN GIORNO" color *Art in America* v105 no8 p117 S 2017

Fitzpatrick, Meagan C.
Fund global health: Save lives and money color *Science* v356 no6342 p1018 Je 9 2017

Fitzpatrick, Megan
To The Editor color *American Craft* v77 no3 p10 Je/Jl 2017

Fitzpatrick, Peg
The Art of Aggressive Social Sharing *Harvard Business Review Digital Articles* p2 D 5 2014

Fitzpatrick, Scott M.
VOYAGES OF OLD A. R. Williams color *National Geographic* v232 no1 p20 Jl 2017

Fitzpatrick, Sheila
TOMB RAIDERS: The afterlives of Lenin *Harper's Magazine* v335 no2006 p90 Jl 2017

FITZPATRICK, TONY
Reimagining John James Audubon's "Birds of America" *Audubon* v118 no6 p52 Wint 2016

WHY We LOVE CHICAGO bw cartoon color *Chicago* v66 no3 p75 Mr 2017

Fitzsimons, Declan
How Shared Leadership Changes Our Relationships at Work *Harvard Business Review Digital Articles* p2 My 12 2016
Shakespeare's Characters Show Us How Personal Growth Should Happen color *Harvard Business Review Digital Articles* p2 Ja 30 2017

Fitzsimons, Eleanor
DIVINE SALOMÉ: Wild yet chaste, impudent and ageless, Sarah Bernhardt was inescapably Oscar Wilde's Salomé, 'the most splendid creation' *History Today* v67 no7 p66 Jl 2017

F.I.V. Edoardo Bianchi SpA
"I WANT A BIANCHI." M. Yozell and B. STRICKLAND color *Bicycling* v58 no3 p98 Ap 2017

Five Awake (Film)
COMMON GROUND L. LEBLANC-BERRY color *Louisiana Life* v37 no3 p12 Ja/F 2017

Five Came Back (Film)
The Long Way Home S. MEARS bw color *Film Comment* v53 no3 p74 My/Je 2017
STREAMING A. D'ARMINIO *TV Guide* v65 no13 p42 Mr 20 2017
When the Film Greats Went to War S. Zacharek color *Time* v189 no13 p50 Ap 10 2017

Five Came Back (TV program)
HOLLYWOOD AT WAR! A. Breznican color *Entertainment Weekly* no1459 p38 Mr 31 2017

Five Guys Named Moe (Theatrical production)
5 Guys 2 Coasts *Stage Directions* v30 no9 p20 S 2017
Summer Catch-Up M. S. Eddy *Stage Directions* v30 no9 p2 S 2017

Five hundred meter Aperture Spherical Telescope
THE BIGGEST EAR D. Normile color *Science* v353 no6307 p1488 S 30 2016
Chinese FAST Opens for Business D. DICKINSON *Sky & Telescope* v133 no1 p11 Ja 2017

Five Star Professional (Company)
2017 CINCINNATI AWARD WINNERS color *Cincinnati Magazine* v51 no1 p1 O 2017

Fix This Kitchen (TV program)
THE NEW REALITY S. FENNESSY *Atlanta* v57 no1 p14 My 2017

Fixsen, Anna
2017 Pritzker Prize Goes to Rafael Aranda, Carme Pigem, and Ramon Vilalta *Architectural Record* v205 no4 p27 Ap 2017
America's Top Architecture Schools 2018 chart *Architectural Record* v205 no9 p72 S 2017
AS+GG's Massive Astana Expo City Nears Completion color *Architectural Record* v205 no3 p23 Mr 2017
BIG Reveals Hyperloop One Design color *Architectural Record* v204 no12 p15 D 2016
Cersaie 2016 *Architectural Record* v204 no11 p59 N 2016
Chicago Architecture Biennial Preview *Architectural Record* v205 no4 p32 Ap 2017
A Data-Driven Approach to Revitalizing the L.A. River *Architectural Record* v205 no4 p34 Ap 2017
Diébédo Francis Kéré *Architectural Record* v205 no6 p28 Je 2017
Dr. Eve Edelstein *Architectural Record* v205 no7 p35 Jl 2017
A Fresh Spin *Architectural Record* v205 no6 p42 Je 2017
Full Circle Swing *Architectural Record* v205 no4 p211 Ap 2017
FXFOWLE Museum Breaks Ground on Liberty Island *Architectural Record* v204 no11 p28 N 2016
Is Design to Blame When a School Underperforms? color *Architectural Record* v205 no5 p30 My 2017
Italy calls on Renzo Piano to Address Earthquake Resilience *Architectural Record* v204 no10 p26 O 2016
Mackintosh Debris Turned to Art color *Architectural Record* v205 no3 p24 Mr 2017
NYC Unveils AIDS Memorial *Architectural Record* v205 no1 p22 Ja 2017
Out of the Woods *Architectural Record* v205 no1 p84 Ja 2017
Parkside of Oldtown, Phase Mb *Architectural Record* v205 no4 p197 Ap 2017
Paul Revere Williams, Unsung Hero *Architectural Record* v205 no1 p21 Ja 2017

Secret Garden *Architectural Record* v205 no7 p120 Jl 2017

Tipping the Scales *Architectural Record* v204 no10 p33 O 2016

Wall to Wall color *Architectural Record* v205 no5 p33 My 2017

Young & Ayata bw color *Architectural Record* v204 no12 p54 D 2016

Fixson, Sebastian K.

The 4 Main Ways to Innovate in a Digital Economy *Harvard Business Review Digital Articles* p2 Je 2 2016

A Case Study of Crowdsourcing Gone Wrong *Harvard Business Review Digital Articles* p2 D 15 2016

Fjords—Iceland

ISLAND OF OPPORTUNITY E. S. ARNARSDÓTTIR color *Iceland Review* v54 no5 p52 S-O 2016

Fjords—Norway

NAKED & AFRAID K. Beekman color *Skiing* p44 D 2016

FKA Twigs (Performer)—Interviews

FKA twigs L. Robinson color *Vanity Fair* v58 no12 p88 D 2016

Flach, Carol

Biological control of aragonite formation in stony corals bw color graph *Science* v356 no6341 p933 Je 1 2017

Flach, Tim

Endangered A. Gawrylewski color *Scientific American* v317 no4 p86 O 2017

Flack, Roberta, 1937—Interviews

MY TOWN A. Whiting *Washingtonian Magazine* v52 no9 p174 Je 2017

Flagan, Richard C.

Global atmospheric particle formation from CERN CLOUD measurements bibl graph map *Science* v354 no6316 p1119 D 2 2016

Flagg, Fannie

Christmas Dinner at the Diner color *Southern Living* v51 no12 p131 D 2016

Flagg, William J.

A Gift for All I. A. LDRICH *Yankee* p99 Mr 2017

Flags

See also

Banners

SHOWCASE SHOTS color *Nebraska Life* v21 no4 p106 Jl/Ag 2017

Flags of convenience

Whose Convenience? A. MARLOWE color map *Weekly Standard* v22 no14 p27 D 12 2016

Flags—Design & construction

The Wild Standard L. SMITH FORD *Texas Monthly* v45 no6 p23 Je 2017

Flagship stores—Evaluation

Secret Ginza color *Conde Nast Traveler* v52 no1 p52 Ja 2017

Flagstaff (Ariz.)

Arizona's TIP TOP W. HEALD *Arizona Highways* v93 no8 p32 Ag 2017

Flags—United States

The Birth of America's Flag Obsession O. B. Waxman *Time* v189 no23 p21 Je 19 2017

Flags—United States—States

Fifty Flags J. J. MILLER color *National Review* v69 no12 p22 Je 26 2017

Flaherty, Keith T.

Potential role of intratumor bacteria in mediating tumor resistance to the chemotherapeutic drug gemcitabine diag *Science* v357 no6356 p1156 S 15 2017

Flaim, Kate

2016 GIFT GUIDE color *Fortune* v174 no7 p43 D 1 2016

Flake, Emily

COLOR SCHEME cartoon *New Yorker* v92 no39 p15 N 28 2016

THINGS I'M AFRAID MY DAUGHTER WILL BE DOING IN 2026 cartoon *New Yorker* v93 no20 p54 Jl 10 2017

Flake, Jeff, 1962-

Conservatism In the Desert L. CALDWELL color *National Review* v69 no17 p15 S 11 2017

The Gentleman From Arizona M. Coppins color *Atlantic* v320 no2 p18 S 2017

Goldwater Revisited J. COBB *Commentary* v144 no3 p53 O 2017

Flake, Jeff, 1962-—Interviews

Jeff Flake J. Brewster color *Time* v190 no7 p56 Ag 21 2017

Flake implements

Whose Tools Are These? K. Wong color *Scientific American* v316

no1 p10 Ja 2017

Flaming Lips (Performer)

THE FLAMING LIPS' WAYNE COYNE E. R. Brown color *Entertainment Weekly* no1449 p58 Ja 20 2017

Flamingo (Poem)

Flamingo J. LARKIN *Progressive* v81 no5 p69 Je/Jl 2017

Flamingos

Flamingo Road M. BARTELS *Audubon* v119 no2 p20 Summ 2017

Flamingos' bones favor one-leg stance S. MILIUS color *Science News* v191 no12 p15 Je 24 2017

A World of Beauty color *National Geographic* v230 no5 p15 N 2016

Flamini, E.

Seasonal exposure of carbon dioxide ice on the nucleus of comet 67P/Churyumov-Gerasimenko bibl bw graph *Science* v354 no6319 p1563 D 23 2016

FLAMINI, MICHAEL

Leaving the Flatiron bw *Publishers Weekly* v264 no35 p132 Ag 28 2017

Flammability

Clean Combustion K. Moore *Natural History* v124 no10 p8 N 2016

Flammer, Larry

The Age of Misinformation *Skeptical Inquirer* v41 no5 p63 S/O 2017

Flammia, Christine

The Wright Way to Keep Your Cool color *Men's Health* v32 no2 p25 Mr 2017

Your Flight Attendant color *Men's Health* v32 no7 p34 S 2017

Flanagan, Brian

READER COMMENTS *America* v216 no3 p7 F 6 2017

FLANAGAN, CAITLIN

Can MEGYN KELLY ESCAPE Her Past? cartoon color *Atlantic* v319 no2 p88 Mr 2017

The Confessionalist color *Atlantic* v320 no3 p30 O 2017

A DEATH AT PENN STATE color *Atlantic* v320 no4 p92 N 2017

The People's Princess img *New York* v50 no10 p46 My 15 2017

Warm Comfort: Four years after 'Lean In,' Sheryl Sandberg shares new perspectives gained from grief *New York Times Book Review* p14 My 14 2017

Flanagan, Joseph C.

Double-heterojunction nanorod light-responsive LEDs for display applications bibl color graph *Science* v355 no6325 p616 F 10 2017

Flanagan, Katherine

Fresh Faced A. R. Williams color *Southern Living* v52 no5 p65 My 2017

Flanagan, Shalane

MATT LLANO S. DOUGLAS color *Runner's World* v51 no10 p32 N 2016

Flanagan, Tara

A Dog's Life color *Sail* v48 no8 p12 Ag 2017

Flanders, Judith

2014: London *Lapham's Quarterly* v10 no1 p66 Wint 2017

Christmas: A Biography *Publishers Weekly* v264 no33 p71 Ag 14 2017

FLANDERS, LAURA

Are The Young Turks Progressive Media's Rising Stars? color *Nation* v304 no9 p38 Mr 20 2017

Flanders, Tony

Meade's LightBridge Mini Series *Sky & Telescope* v132 no6 p58 D 2016

The Zhumell Z130: This remarkably inexpensive tabletop Dob is an outstanding performer color *Sky & Telescope* v134 no2 p58 Ag 2017

FLANGO, ADAM

AIR CARE: How CVG shed its costly reputation *Cincinnati Magazine* v50 no11 p21 Ag 2017

AUSTIN, TEXAS *Cincinnati Magazine* v50 no6 p46 Mr 2017

DOG DAZE *Cincinnati Magazine* v50 no10 p52 Jl 2017

FLUX CAPACITOR *Cincinnati Magazine* p39 Je 2017

GETTING DARK *Cincinnati Magazine* v50 no3 p29 D 2016

HANNIBAL LECTURE *Cincinnati Magazine* v50 no2 p18 N 2016

INTO THE WOOD *Cincinnati Magazine* v50 no8 p34 My 2017

A Key West Road Trip *Cincinnati Magazine* p57 Je 2017

LOST CITY *Cincinnati Magazine* v50 no5 p58 F 2017

Michael Vinegar *Cincinnati Magazine* v50 no6 p40 Mr 2017

NIGHT MOVES *Cincinnati Magazine* v50 no8 p40 My 2017

Pittsburgh *Cincinnati Magazine* p62 Je 2017

RYAN MESSER & JIMMY MUSURACA 992 MARION AVE., NORTH AVONDALE *Cincinnati Magazine* v50 no11 p76 Ag 2017

Flanigan, Tim

Shared space color *U.S. Catholic* v82 no11 p28 N 2017

Flannery, Julian

Fifty English Steeples S. Bradley *History Today* v67 no2 p64 F 2017

Flannery, Randy

The Track Attack color *Field & Stream* v121 no7 p47 D 2016/ Ja 2017

FLANNERY, RUSSELL

THE WORLD'S BILLIONAIRES bw color diag graph map *Forbes* v199 no3 p84 Mr 28 2017

FLANNERY, THOMAS JR.

Defending Milo *Publishers Weekly* v264 no8 p88 F 20 2017

Flannery, Tim

Can We Bring Back the Passenger Pigeon? bw color *New York Review of Books* v64 no7 p58 Ap 20 2017

Extravagant, Aggressive Birds Down Under color *New York Review of Books* v64 no4 p27 Mr 9 2017

Gone Fishing color *New York Review of Books* v64 no14 p37 S 28 2017

In Praise of Sandstone color *New York Review of Books* v64 no11 p28 Je 22 2017

Flappers (Women)

The original "It" Girl: Flappers took the country by storm in the roaring '20s and then suddenly vanished. Or did they? L. Simon *Smithsonian* v48 no5 p9 S 2017

What Did Flappers Want? You May Want to Ask a Millennial: Not that today's hipsters flaunt cigarettes and dance the Charleston. But from their nifty gadgets to their prolonged adolescence, young cosmopolitan women are surprisingly close in... P. O'Donnell *Smithsonian* v48 no5 p11 S 2017

Flares

75, 50 & 25 Years Ago R. W. Sinnott *Sky & Telescope* v132 no6 p7 D 2016

Flasch, Diane A.

Intersection of diverse neuronal genomes and neuropsychiatric disease: The Brain Somatic Mosaicism Network color *Science* v356 no6336 p395 Ap 28 2017

Flash (Fictitious character)

NO. 10 THE FLASH N. Abrams color *Entertainment Weekly* no1436/1437 p52 O 21 2016

Flash, The (TV program)

CHEERS & JEERS D. HOLBROOK *TV Guide* v65 no14 p80 Ap 3 2017

The Flash N. Abrams, A. Bacle et al color *Entertainment Weekly* no1482/1483 p82 S 22 2017

A SUPER GLEE REUNION N. Abrams color *Entertainment Weekly* no1457/1458 p82 Mr 17 2017

Flash memories (Computers)

See also

USB flash drives

Flash photography—Equipment & supplies—Evaluation

OUR PICKS color *Popular Photography* v81 no1 p14 Ja/F 2017

Flashlights

A headlamp color *Backpacker* p46 Ag 2017

The Perfect Battery S. ORNES color diag graph *Discover* v38 no6 p78 Jl/Ag 2017

SELF-DEFENSE FLASH-LIGHTS R. MANN color *Outdoor Life* v224 no8 pP1 O 2017

SHOP NOTES D. Owen color *Popular Mechanics* p92 S 2017

Flashlights—Evaluation

Flash Forward S. MURRAY color *Power & Motoryacht* v34 no8 p36 Ag 2017

PARTS & STUFF color *Hot Rod* v70 no12 p108 D 2017

FLASHMAN, JOHANNA

"Cliff Camping": The Latest Bucket-List Tick color *Climbing* no355 p16 Ag 2017

Climbing (Re)Structures color *Climbing* no356 p20 S/O 2017

Next-Gen Visualization color *Climbing* no357 p16 N 2017

Flat-earth theory

Rounding Error T. Keith color *Sports Illustrated* v126 no9 p23 Mr 27 2017

Flat screen television sets—Evaluation

Gifts That Keep On Rocking color *Rolling Stone* no1275 p31 D 1 2016

Flatbreads

FEW THINGS BRING PEOPLE TOGETHER LIKE MAN'OUSHE R. ASSIL color *Bon Appetit* v62 no2 p61 Mr 2017

starters N. RICHARDSON, J. BAINBRIDGE et al bw color diag *Bon Appetit* v62 no2 p19 Mr 2017

Flatcars—Evaluation

Wheels of Time HO 62-foot bulkhead flatcar S. Otte color *Model Railroader* v84 no5 p64 My 2017

Flateau, D.

Zones, spots, and planetary-scale waves beating in brown dwarf atmospheres color graph *Science* v357 no6352 p683 Ag 18 2017

Flatfishes

A LOT OF FISH IN THE SEA C. MOROCCO color *Bon Appetit* no8 p101 Ag 2017

Flatliners (Film)

FLATLINERS J. Ganz color *Entertainment Weekly* no1478 / 1479 p41 Ag 18-25 2017

Flatt, Bruce

CONVERSATION A. WILSON color graph *Forbes* v199 no7 p38 Je 29 2017

The Toll Collector [Cover story] A. GARA color map *Forbes* v199 no5 p68 My 16 2017

Flatulence

Excess Gas in a Horse With Heaves M. ESSER *Horse & Rider* v55 no11 p14 N 2016

Flatulence—Prevention

tummy troubles K. ROCKWOOD *Parents* v92 no2 p98 F 2017

Flatware

See also

Forks

Knives

Olive spoons and terrapin forks C. Day *Physics Today* v70 no2 p8 F 2017

Flatware—Evaluation

ALL SET *Martha Stewart Living* no267 p50 S 2016

for 2018 [Cover story] C. SWANSON and K. RENDA color *House Beautiful* v159 no9 p29 N 2017

Flaum, J. P.

Improve Your Ability to Learn *Harvard Business Review Digital Articles* p2 Je 8 2015

Flaus, Andrew

Unlocking the nucleosome bibl diag *Science* v355 no6322 p245 Ja 20 2017

Flauto, Elizabeth

Surviving a Home-Based Costume Craft Studio *Stage Directions* v30 no8 p8 Ag 2017

Flavahan, William A.

Epigenetic plasticity and the hallmarks of cancer diag *Science* v357 no6348 p266 Jl 21 2017

Flavell, Richard A.

The DNA-sensing AIM2 inflammasome controls radiation-induced cell death and tissue injury bibl color graph *Science* v354 no6313 p765 N 11 2016

Macrophage function in tissue repair and remodeling requires IL-4 or IL-13 with apoptotic cells diag *Science* v356 no6342 p1072 Je 9 2017

A pathogenic role for T cell–derived IL-22BP in inflammatory bowel disease bibl graph *Science* v354 no6310 p358 O 21 2016

Flavelle, Christopher

Alaska's Big Problem With Warmer Winters color *Bloomberg Businessweek* no4514 p26 Mr 13 2017

Contractions: Slowing Down Research chart graph *Bloomberg Businessweek* no4534 p39 Ag 14 2017

Federal Agencies Play 'Not It' With Flood Insurance *Bloomberg Businessweek* no4538 p28 S 18 2017

Flood Insurance Had Problems Before Harvey color *Bloomberg Businessweek* no4536 p38 S 4 2017

Hard Rain and Hard Lessons bw map *Bloomberg Businessweek*

no4536 p12 S 4 2017

The Incredible Shrinking State color *Bloomberg Businessweek* no4509 p23 Ja 30 2017

New Jersey Builds Walls Against a Rising Tide color *Bloomberg Businessweek* no4521 p25 My 8 2017

The Shifting Politics of Taxing Carbon *Bloomberg Businessweek* no4519 p52 Ap 24 2017

When Nature Gets An Insurance Policy color *Bloomberg Businessweek* no4531 p26 Jl 24 2017

Your Country Is Flooding? Tough Luck color *Bloomberg Businessweek* no4526 p24 Je 12 2017

Flaviviral diseases
See also
Zika virus infections

One year later, Zika scientists prepare for a long war G. Vogel graph *Science* v354 no6316 p1088 D 2 2016

Flaviviral diseases—Prevention

The year in health and medicine *Harvard Health Letter* v42 no2 p1 D 2016

Flaviviruses
See also
Dengue viruses
West Nile virus
Zika virus

Why are neurons susceptible to Zika virus? D. E. Griffin diag *Science* v357 no6346 p33 Jl 7 2017

Flavonoids

SCIENTIFIC UPDATE R. Mangels *Vegetarian Journal* v36 no2 p10 2017

Flavor
See also
Fruit—Flavor & odor

On the Tip of My Tongue E. NORTON color *Publishers Weekly* v264 no11 p71 Mr 13 2017

FLAX, PETER

All Eyes On the Next Flight *Los Angeles Magazine* p14 My 2017

THE BOMB DETECTIVE color *Popular Mechanics* p104 Ap 2017

Living by the Eastwood Code cartoon color *Men's Health* v32 no5 p27 Je 2017

THE LONG ROUTE color *Sunset* v238 no6 p17 Je 2017

OUT-SMART THE SUPER-MARKET color *Prevention* v69 no8 p60 Ag 2017

Flay, Bobby, 1964-

MAGICAL INGREDIENTS CHEFS LOVE color *Redbook* p118 S 2017

Flea markets

SEPTEMBER 2017 color *Missouri Life* v44 no6 p81 S 2017

thrift like a pro P. PORTER color *Better Homes & Gardens* v95 no3 p38 Mr 2017

Vermont Charm E. GAUKEL *Treasures* v6 no3 p10 D 2016/Ja 2017

Flea markets—Social aspects

The Beauty of Imperfection R. Ashwell color *AARP: The Magazine* v59 no5A p72 Ag/S 2016

Fleabag (TV program)

DIRTY BIRD E. NUSSBAUM cartoon *New Yorker* v92 no30 p76 S 26 2016

Hot Cringe Queen Phoebe Waller-Bridge D. FEAR color *Rolling Stone* no1274 p43 N 17 2016

Fleas—Behavior

LOL Science S. ELDER cartoon *National Geographic Kids* no470 p24 My 2017

Fleas—Control

Dear Doctor *Your Dog (10780343)* v22 no10 p15 O 2016

Fleder, Rob

List Serve T. Keith color *Sports Illustrated* v126 no12 p16 My 1 2017

Fleece, Esther

No More Faking Fine: Ending the Pretending *Publishers Weekly* v263 no41 p73 O 10 2016

Fleet Foxes (Performer)

CRACK-UP A. Christenson *U.S. Catholic* v82 no10 p40 O 2017

FITZGERALD & ME M. Miller color *Esquire* p32 Je/Jl 2017

Fleet Foxes' New Harmony [Cover story] J. WEINER color *Rolling Stone* no1289 p18 Je 15 2017

FLEETWOOD, AMELIA

perch perfect color *Architectural Digest* v74 no4 p140 Ap 2017

FLEETWOOD, KELLY J.

Estimation of Relative Potency from Bioassay Data that Include Values below the Limit of Quantitation *BioScience* v66 no11 p983 N 1 2016

Fleetwood, Mick—Interviews

Mick Fleetwood A. GREENE bw *Rolling Stone* no1295 p58 S 7 2017

Fleetwood, Tommy

Watch + Learn B. Gathright and J. Marksbury color *Golf Magazine* v59 no9 p32 S 2017

Fleetwood Mac (Performer)

FLEETWOOD MAC'S RUMOURS TURNS 40 L. Greenblatt color *Entertainment Weekly* no1451/1452 p106 F 3-10 2017

Stevie Nicks A. GREENE bw *Rolling Stone* no1283 p58 Mr 23 2017

FLEGAL, JANE A.

Climate engineering *Issues in Science & Technology* v33 no4 p11 Summ 2017

Flegenheimer, Matt

Supreme BATTLE *New York Times Upfront* v149 no10 p14 Mr 13 2017

Fleischer-Camp, Dean

The Year of Living Publicly J. Yuan img *New York* v50 no6 p71 Mr 20 2017

Fleischman, Paul

First Light, First Life: A Worldwide Creation Story color *Publishers Weekly* v263 no49 p27 D 7 2016

Fleischmann, Mark

Audioengine HD3 Loudspeaker color graph *Sound & Vision* v82 no6 p64 Jl/Ag 2017

AudioQuest DragonFly Red and DragonFly Black Amp/DACs color *Sound & Vision* v81 no10 p66 D 2016

Big Box Meets Little Speakers chart color graph *Sound & Vision* v82 no4 p38 My 2017

Elac Uni-Fi UB5 Speaker System color graph *Sound & Vision* v82 no1 p60 Ja 2017

Expanded Oscar Coverage color *Sound & Vision* v82 no6 p17 Jl/Ag 2017

Fascia of the Future color *Sound & Vision* v82 no8 p54 O 2017

Focal Dôme Flax 5.1 Speaker System color graph *Sound & Vision* v82 no2 p64 F/Mr 2017

Focal Utopia Headphones color *Sound & Vision* v82 no6 p42 Jl/Ag 2017

HDR Is Getting Support From color *Sound & Vision* v82 no2 p17 F/Mr 2017

HiFiMan SuperMini Music Player color *Sound & Vision* v82 no1 p54 Ja 2017

Jerry Seinfeld's color *Sound & Vision* v82 no5 p17 Je 2017

Klipsch Reference Premiere RP-140SA Atmos Elevation Module color graph *Sound & Vision* v81 no9 p54 N 2016

LG's Channel Plus color *Sound & Vision* v81 no10 p17 D 2016

LG V20 Smartphone color *Sound & Vision* v82 no3 p52 Ap 2017

Making Wafes color graph *Sound & Vision* v82 no7 p54 S 2017

MQA Is Coming to NAD's color *Sound & Vision* v81 no9 p17 N 2016

Onkyo TX-RZ610 A/V Receiver chart color graph *Sound & Vision* v81 no9 p44 N 2016

Retro 5.1 Done Right color graph *Sound & Vision* v82 no7 p62 S 2017

Rotel A12 Integrated Amplifier chart color graph *Sound & Vision* v82 no3 p42 Ap 2017

Solus Audio Entré II Loudspeaker color graph *Sound & Vision* v82 no6 p62 Jl/Ag 2017

Sony CAS-1 Compact Audio System color *Sound & Vision* v82 no2 p58 F/Mr 2017

Sony Projectors color *Sound & Vision* v82 no3 p17 Ap 2017

Sony Spiffed Up PS4 Pro color *Sound & Vision* v82 no1 p17 Ja 2017

Sony Walkman NW-ZX100HN Hi-Res Music Player Bundle color *Sound & Vision* v81 no10 p54 D 2016

This Just In... color *Sound & Vision* v82 no4 p17 My 2017

This Just In... color *Sound & Vision* v82 no8 p19 O 2017

Yamaha Aventage RX-A3060 A/V Receiver chart color graph *Sound & Vision* v82 no1 p50 Ja 2017

Fleming, James R.

Carl-Gustaf Rossby *Physics Today* v70 no1 p50 Ja 2017

Fleming, Jason

Potential role of intratumor bacteria in mediating tumor resistance to the chemotherapeutic drug gemcitabine diag *Science* v357 no6356 p1156 S 15 2017

Fleming, Lee

Expand innovation finance via crowdfunding bibl color graph map *Science* v354 no6319 p1526 D 23 2016

FLEMING, LOUISE

Which Way to Go? *USA Today Magazine* v146 no2868 p19 S 2017

Fleming, Mark

THE AUDACITY OF LIZ PUTNAM bw color *Yankee* p86 My/Je 2017

Barnard General Store color *Yankee* p64 My/Je 2017

BEHIND THE SCENES AT TOP SFIELD FAIR: IT MAY TURN 200 NEXT YEAR, BUT ITS APPEAL NEVER GETS OLD *Yankee* v81 no5 p128 S/O 2017

A Farmer's Best Friend color *Yankee* p104 Mr 2017

THE ISLAND DOCTOR bw color *Yankee* p98 My/Je 2017

'Old Gray Ancients' color *Yankee* p41 My/Je 2017

Pictures Hidden in Wood color *Yankee* p40 Mr 2017

Strawberry-Rhubarb Coffee Cake color *Yankee* p68 My/Je 2017

"WEEKENDS" WARRIOR color *Yankee* p50 Mr 2017

Fleming, Mark D.

UBE2O remodels the proteome during terminal erythroid differentiation diag *Science* v357 no6350 p471 Ag 4 2017

FLEMING, MATTHEW

California's Woeful Republicans *Weekly Standard* v22 no4 p18 O 3 2016

The Fight of His Life color *Weekly Standard* v22 no7 p15 O 24 2016

Fleming, Melissa

Why IBM Gives Top Employees a Month to Do Service Abroad *Harvard Business Review Digital Articles* p2 N 5 2014

FLEMING, PETER J. S.

Making a New Dog? *BioScience* v67 no4 p374 Ap 2017

Fleming, Renée, 1959-

DEPARTURES AND ARRIVALS A. ROSS cartoon *New Yorker* v93 no19 p72 Jl 3 2017

Renée FLEMING A. F. COLLINS color *Vanity Fair* v59 no5 p114 Ap 2017

Spring Preview R. Platt cartoon *New Yorker* v93 no4 p12 Mr 13 2017

Fleming, Sean W.

To understand rivers, let physics be your guide L. Hamers color *Science News* v191 no6 p29 Ap 1 2017

FLEMING, THEODORE H.

Using Plant-Animal Interactions to Inform Tree Selection in Tree-Based Agroecosystems for Enhanced Biodiversity *BioScience* v66 no12 p1046 D 1 2016

Fleming, Thomas

MIRACLE ON THE VISTULA bw color map *MHQ: Quarterly Journal of Military History* v30 no1 p66 Aut 2017

Fleming Yachts (Company)

MEDITERRANEAN PASSAGE A. HARPER chart color *Power & Motoryacht* v33 no4 p68 Ap 2017

FLEMISTER, BEAU

Geiselman (There Are Two) color *Surfing Magazine* v53 no3 p32 Mr 2017

Ghost Wave color *Surfing Magazine* v53 no2 p26 F 2017

FLEMMING, JOANNA MILLS

Envisioning the Future of Aquatic Animal Tracking: Technology, Science, and Application *BioScience* v67 no10 p884 O 2017

Flemming, Rose—Interviews

'I'm Not Willing to Sacrifice Freedom of Expression on the Altar of Cultural Diversity' N. GILLESPIE color *Reason* v49 no1 p44 My 2017

Flensberg, K.

Majorana bound state in a coupled quantum-dot hybrid-nanowire system bibl graph *Science* v354 no6319 p1557 D 23 2016

Flesh & Bone (Music)

NOTES ON A NIGHTMARE M. GUARINO color *Chicago* v66 no8 p37 Ag 2017

Fletcher, Anthony

CHANGE the CITY *Indianapolis Monthly* p55 Ap 2017

A WIDE-ANGLED LONG VIEW OF THE BRITISH ISLES: An exceptional and timely study of the British landscape takes us from long before the first human impact to its modern despoilers *History Today* v67 no7 p98 Jl 2017

Fletcher, Aubrey

10 UP & COMERS: AUBREY FLETCHER L. Prater *Successful Farming* v115 no8 p50 Je/Jl 2017

Fletcher, Catherine

MURDER AT THE VATICAN: An unsolved Renaissance mystery casts light on the dark world of extortion, revenge and power politics at the heart of the Catholic Church *History Today* v67 no10 p56 O 2017

Fletcher, James

Single-cell RNA-seq reveals new types of human blood dendritic cells, monocytes, and progenitors color *Science* v356 no6335 p283 Ap 21 2017

Fletcher, Richard J.

Two- and three-body contacts in the unitary Bose gas bibl diag graph *Science* v355 no6323 p377 Ja 27 2017

Fleurke, Floor

Europe's biodiversity avoids fatal setback color *Science* v355 no6321 p140 Ja 13 2017

FLEURKE, FLOOR M.

International Wildlife Law: Understanding and Enhancing Its Role in Conservation *BioScience* v67 no9 p784 S 2017

Fleury, Larry

On the Magazine's Archives bw *Black Belt* v55 no4 p17 Je/Jl 2017

Fleury, Sylvie—Exhibitions

The Makeup Artist J. ORTVED color *Vogue* v207 no11 p136 N 2017

FLEXE Inc.

The Airbnb Of Warehousing S. Soper *Bloomberg Businessweek* no4523 p32 My 22 2017

Flexibility (Mechanics)

Highly stretchable polymer semiconductor films through the nanoconfinement effect Jie Xu, Sihong Wang et al bibl graph *Science* v355 no6320 p1 Ja 6 2017

Flexible spending accounts

CALENDAR R. ERMEY color *Kiplinger's Personal Finance* v71 no3 p16 Mr 2017

Charitable Giving Is a Family Affair K. LANKFORD *Kiplinger's Personal Finance* v71 no12 p41 D 2017

GAME PLAN S. BLOCK color *Kiplinger's Personal Finance* v71 no6 p39 Je 2017

Flexible work arrangements

See also

Telecommuting

Everyone Likes Flex Time, but We Punish Women Who Use It D. Burkus *Harvard Business Review Digital Articles* p2 F 20 2017

Flexible jobs give workers choices M. S. Hicks *Monthly Labor Review* p1 My 2017

Flex Time Doesn't Need to Be an HR Policy S. Behson *Harvard Business Review Digital Articles* p2 D 4 2014

How to Allow Flexible Work Without Playing Favorites E. Marescaux and S. De Winne *Harvard Business Review Digital Articles* p2 2017

A New Chapter S. Barry *Working Mother* p5 F/Mr 2017

Prioritize Your Life Before Your Manager Does It for You G. McKeown *Harvard Business Review Digital Articles* p2 Je 1 2015

Things to Buy, Download, or Do When Working Remotely A. Samuel *Harvard Business Review Digital Articles* p2 F 4 2015

Thinking About a "Work from Anywhere" Arrangement? Ask These Questions First D. Clark *Harvard Business Review Digital Articles* p2 S 26 2017

Flexner, Abraham, 1866-1959

1939: Princeton, NJ *Lapham's Quarterly* v10 no2 p115 Spr 2017

In defense of basic research C. A. Tovey color *Science* v355 no6327 p804 F 24 2017

Flextime

Flex Equity L. NARGI diag *Working Mother* v40 no3 p26 Ag/S 2017

How a Flex-Time Program at MIT Improved Productivity, Resilience, and Trust P. Hirst *Harvard Business Review Digital Articles* p2 Je 30 2016

Flextime—Lawsuits & claims

New mother wins flexhwork case *People Management* p19 O 2016

Flicker, Siggy

Sound Bites color *Entertainment Weekly* no1486 p2 O 13 2017

Flickinger, Leah

FI'ZI:K R1B UOMO color *Bicycling* v58 no4 p88 My 2017

JOIN THE RIDE color *Bicycling* v58 no6 p12 Jl 2017

JOIN THE RIDE color *Bicycling* v58 no9 p16 O 2017

Oooh... Cozy! color *Bicycling* v58 no1 p64 Ja/F 2017

"SHOULD I GET A ROAD BIKE WITH DISC BRAKES? color diag *Bicycling* v58 no3 p30 Ap 2017

SPECIALIZED WOMEN'S DIVERGE COMP color *Bicycling* v58 no9 p66 O 2017

Swoop Down Hills cartoon *Bicycling* v58 no4 p14 My 2017

Totally Worth It! color *Bicycling* v58 no4 p22 My 2017

"WHAT'S A GOOD FIRST ROAD BIKE?" color *Bicycling* v58 no3 p18 Ap 2017

Flickr (Web resource)

How Yahoo Betrayed Its Users by Doing What They Asked D. Weinberger *Harvard Business Review Digital Articles* p2 D 16 2014

Flierl, Adrian

β2-Adrenoreceptor is a regulator of the a-synuclein gene driving risk of Parkinson's disease cartoon chart graph *Science* v357 no6354 p891 S 1 2017

Flies

SUPER FLY: YOU'RE GONNA LARVA IT M. CHIU cartoon *Wired* v25 no8 p32 Ag 2017

Flies as carriers of disease

A danger in the water K. Henderson color *Equus* no478 p80 Jl 2017

Why I Use Beneficial Insects For My Fly Control S. R. H. de Frey *Trail Rider* v29 no3 p17 Ap 2017

Flies—Control

Why I Use Beneficial Insects For My Fly Control S. R. H. de Frey *Trail Rider* v29 no3 p17 Ap 2017

Flight

> See also
>
> Flying-machines

Acoustic mirrors as sensory traps for bats S. Greif, S. Zsebök et al diag *Science* v357 no6355 p1045 S 8 2017

FLIGHTS OF THE CONDOR M. Lunken color *Flying* v144 no5 p66 My 2017

FLYING THE BOSS D. Karl color *Flying* v144 no5 p70 My 2017

MAYDAY! MAYDAY! MAYDAY! D. HABER color *Flying* v144 no5 p24 My 2017

RECURRENT TRAINING WITH A FRIEND L. Abend color *Flying* v144 no5 p74 My 2017

Flight, Tim

The Wolf Must Be in the Woods: The real and mythical dangers of the wilderness *History Today* v67 no6 p18 Je 2016

Flight attendants

AIRING YOUR GRIEVANCES P. MARX color *O, The Oprah Magazine* p102 Ap 2017

The Way It Was G. Hamilton *New York Times Magazine* p24 O 23 2016

Your Flight Attendant C. FLAMMIA color *Men's Health* v32 no7 p34 S 2017

Flight crews

> See also
>
> Air pilots
>
> Flight attendants

BLAME IT ON THE BRUSSELS SPROUTS L. Abend color *Flying* v144 no3 p82 Mr 2017

Flight delays & cancellations (Airlines)

How I Spent 24 Hours at Dulles M. J. Gaynor *Washingtonian Magazine* v52 no2 p87 N 2016

MERRY TRANSIT A. Farley and C. K. Jackson color *Essence* v47 no8 p92 D 2016

Flight instructors

PRECISION FLYING IS CRITICAL map *Flying* v144 no5 p23 My 2017

Flight jackets

Adam's STYLE SHEET A. Glassman color *O, The Oprah Magazine* p64 O 2017

SNATCH That STYLE: Breaking Down Looks of Lyrical Trend-

setters M. STREET color *Ebony* v72 no8 p44 Je 2017

Flight jackets—Evaluation

FUNCTIONAL FASHION color *Flying* v144 no4 p15 Ap 2017

Get Personal L. IMMEDIATO *Los Angeles Magazine* p29 F 2017

Slip into the World's Richest Coat color *GQ: Gentlemen's Quarterly* v86 no11 p36 N 2016

These Jackets Are the Bomb S. Kennedy color *Bloomberg Businessweek* no4498 p88 N 7 2016

This Jacket Is the Bomb(er) color *Esquire* v166 no4 p56 N 2016

Flight Outfitters (Company)

BUSH PILOT BAG color *Flying* v144 no11 p15 N 2017

Flight overbooking (Airlines)

Airlines Like United Can Underpay Bumped Passengers Because of a Government Rule R. Mohammed *Harvard Business Review Digital Articles* p2 Ap 12 2017

What to Do if You Get Bumped M. Leonhardt color *Money* v46 no6 p19 Jl 2017

Your Rights on Flights K. PITSKER cartoon *Kiplinger's Personal Finance* v71 no7 p42 Jl 2017

Flight planning (Aeronautics)

YOU DON'T ALWAYS HAVE TO LEARN THE HARD WAY B. Koebbe color *Flying* v144 no4 p36 Ap 2017

Flight schools

THE RIGHT COLLEGE CAN GET YOUR AVIATION CAREER OFF TO A FLYING START D. Smith color *Flying* v144 no11 p64 N 2017

Flight simulators

VIRTUAL AIRPORTS OF MY DIGITAL DREAMS S. Weigel color *Flying* v144 no4 p44 Ap 2017

Flight testing of airplanes

GARMIN UNVEILS BIZJET HUD color *Flying* v144 no7 p18 Jl 2017

Flight training

FLIGHTSAFETY'S HONDAJET TRAINING P. BERGQVIST bw color *Flying* v144 no5 p52 My 2017

INCORPORATING TECHNOLOGY IN FLIGHT TRAINING J. Zimmerman color *Flying* v144 no10 p34 O 2017

IS THE FA A PULLING A FAST ONE? M. Lunken *Flying* v144 no10 p67 O 2017

LEARNING TO FLY THE ICON A5 P. BERGQVIST color *Flying* v144 no1 p38 Ja 2017

MONTEREY EMERGENCY S. DUNN color *Flying* v144 no9 p24 S 2017

The Short Flight From Clerk to Cockpit M. Schlangenstein *Bloomberg Businessweek* no4494 p25 O 10 2016

Flight training—Safety measures

The Go-Around R. Mark color *Flying* v143 no12 p56 D 2016

FlightSafety International Inc.

FLIGHTSAFETY'S HONDAJET TRAINING P. BERGQVIST bw color *Flying* v144 no5 p52 My 2017

Flight—Safety measures

YOU DON'T ALWAYS HAVE TO LEARN THE HARD WAY B. Koebbe color *Flying* v144 no4 p36 Ap 2017

Flimm, Jürgen

CLASSICAL MUSIC *New Yorker* v93 no8 p8 Ap 10 2017

Manon Lescaut A. J. Goldmann *Opera News* v81 no9 p45 Mr 2017

Flims (Switzerland)

bogged down n. formosa bw *Bike Magazine* v24 no3 p56 My 2017

Flinchbaugh, Barry L.—Interviews

THE SUCCESSFUL INTERVIEW B. Spiegel *Successful Farming* v114 no10 p9 O 2016

Flinders, Tim

In My Solitude D. HEITMAN color *Weekly Standard* v22 no21 p34 F 6 2017

Flinders Ranges (S. Aust.)

THE FIRST AUSTRALIANS [Cover story] K. RAVILIOUS color *Archaeology* v70 no4 p49 Je-Ag 2017

Flint (Film)

Flint I. Rudolph *TV Guide* v65 no43 p38 O 16 2017

Flint (Mich.)

Michigan J. Dimmock *New York Times Magazine* p47 N 20 2016

Flint, Emma

Little Deaths L. Greenblatt color *Entertainment Weekly* no1449 p62 Ja 20 2017

Flint, Jill

Bull N. Abrams, A. Bacle et al color *Entertainment Weekly* no1482/1483 p66 S 22 2017

Flint, Kevin

We're Number One! color *Backpacker* v45 no1 p8 Ja 2017

Flint, Sunshine

ON A DREAM VACATION YOU WOULD M. ORWOLL, P. BRADY et al bw color *Conde Nast Traveler* v52 no7 p48 Ag 2017

FLINT, TROY

Breaking the Silence *Education Digest* v82 no6 p4 F 2017

Flint water crisis, Flint, Michigan, 2014-

The Waterworks J. Sanburn color *Time* v189 no13 p36 Ap 10 2017

A Year Later, Flint Still Can't Drink the Water J. Sanburn *Time* v189 no4 p12 Ja 23 2017

Flip-flops (Sandals)

EXTREME WEIRDNESS A. SHAW *National Geographic Kids* no469 p9 Ap 2017

Flipo, Marion

Reversion of antibiotic resistance in Mycobacterium tuberculosis by spiroisoxazoline SMARt-420 bibl diag *Science* v355 no6330 p1206 Mr 17 2017

Flipped classrooms

CLASSROOM CHEMISTRY L. AGRBA color *Maclean's* v130 no2 p63 Mr 2017

Three Ways the Flipped Classroom Leads to Better Subject Mastery A. SAMS and J. AGLIO *Education Digest* v82 no5 p52 Ja 2017

Flipping (Real estate investment)

Think You Can Flip a House? J. BARGER color *Washingtonian Magazine* v52 no7 p95 Ap 2017

Flirting

HIIT ♥N ME color *Women's Health* v14 no2 p38 Mr 2017

Flo-Rite Products Co.

SEED FIRMERS, COVERS G. Gullickson *Successful Farming* v114 no13 p51 D 2016

Floating harbors

DON'T MISS LIST SEPTEMBER 2016 *Sea Magazine* v108 no9 pPNW-15 S 2016

Floating houses

SEASTEADING IN PARADISE B. DOHERTY color diag map *Reason* v49 no2 p28 Je 2017

Floating houses—Evaluation

Floating Dorms J. Zorthian color *Time* v188 no14 p23 O 10 2016

Floating rate notes

Get a Boost From a Floating-Rate Fund J. R. KOSNETT color *Kiplinger's Personal Finance* v70 no12 p58 D 2016

Floatplanes

SHELTER AT THE EDGE OF THE WORLD A. Scott color *Sunset* v239 no3 p62 S 2017

Flock, Elizabeth

The Heart Is a Shifting Sea: Love and Marriage in Mumbai *Publishers Weekly* v264 no41 p52 O 9 2017

Floerke, Victoria A.

Retrieval practice protects memory against acute stress bibl chart graph *Science* v354 no6315 p1046 N 25 2016

Flood, Curt, 1938-1997

Should professional athletes be allowed to use their status to talk about things more important than the games they play? J. C. Kang *New York Times Magazine* p12 F 19 2017

Flood, Don

Fine Prints A. HEROLD *Los Angeles Magazine* v62 no6 p30 Je 2017

Flood, followed by a rainbow (Poem)

Flood, followed by a rainbow H. Kobernick *Christian Century* v134 no3 p22 F 2017

FLOOD, SCOTT

Chatter color graph *Indianapolis Monthly* v42 no2 p11 O 2017

Flood control

FLOOD OF MONEY C. THOMPSON cartoon *Wired* v25 no4 p32 Ap 2017

Natural Hydrologists K. Spence *Natural History* v125 no1 p22 D 2016/Ja 2017

Flood control—United States

New Jersey Builds Walls Against a Rising Tide C. Flavelle color *Bloomberg Businessweek* no4521 p25 My 8 2017

Flood damage

See also
　Flood damage of bridges

THE FLOOD WASN'T A TALKING POINT IN THE GOVERNOR'S RACE INITIALLY, BUT IN THE FINAL DAYS, JUSTICE'S TEAM LEVERAGED IT WITH AN AD THAT PORTRAYED HIM AS A SAVIOR AMID THE WRECKAGE E. Plott *Washingtonian Magazine* v52 no8 p190 My 2017

WHEN THE RAIN CAME E. PLOTT *Washingtonian Magazine* v52 no8 p76 My 2017

Flood damage of bridges

THE LONG GOODBYE R. HANSEN bw color *Missouri Life* v44 no5 p52 Ag 2017

Flood insurance—United States

Federal Agencies Play 'Not It' With Flood Insurance C. Flavelle, H. Perlberg et al *Bloomberg Businessweek* no4538 p28 S 18 2017

FLOOD INSURANCE DEBT IS RISING diag *Fortune* v176 no4 p23 S 15 2017

Flood Insurance Had Problems Before Harvey C. Flavelle color *Bloomberg Businessweek* no4536 p38 S 4 2017

Flood risk

Giving New Yorkers a Real Feel For Flooding R. Walker color *Bloomberg Businessweek* no4539 p46 S 25 2017

Flood insurance—Charts, diagrams, etc.

FLOOD INSURANCE DEBT IS RISING diag *Fortune* v176 no4 p23 S 15 2017

Floods

departing the waters E. Cummins cartoon *Popular Science* v289 no4 p84 Jl/Ag 2017

Flood warning K. Clarke color *U.S. Catholic* v82 no11 p42 N 2017

the night we evacuated Oroville M. B. Griggs cartoon *Popular Science* v289 no4 p84 Jl/Ag 2017

Trip Tips J. Goodnight color *Trail Rider* v29 no4 p17 My 2017

The WATSON FILES L. Heaton bw color *Foreign Policy* no224 p46 My/Je 2017

Floods & the environment

Swell or High Water A. Reese color graph *Scientific American* v316 no6 p21 Je 2017

Floods—Alberta

AFTER THE FLOOD M. COTÉ bw color *Bike Magazine* v24 no4 p58 Je 2017

see the forest b. minnigh color *Bike Magazine* v24 no4 p19 Je 2017

Floods—Australia

Warming Ocean Drove Catastrophic Australian Floods V. LaCapra *Oceanus* v52 no1 p11 Summ 2016

Floods—Canada

backstory color *New Republic* v248 no6 p72 Je 2017

Floods—China

See also
　Floods—Yellow River (China)

Finding China's Great Flood B. ALEX color map *Discover* v38 no1 p31 Ja/F 2017

Floods—Computer network resources

Giving New Yorkers a Real Feel For Flooding R. Walker color *Bloomberg Businessweek* no4539 p46 S 25 2017

Floods—Economic aspects

Climate Change Could Dampen Argentina's Recovery J. Gilbert map *Bloomberg Businessweek* no4539 p35 S 25 2017

Floods—Europe

Changing climate shifts timing of European floods G. Blöschl, J. Hall et al color graph *Science* v357 no6351 p588 Ag 11 2017

Measuring the changing pulse of rivers L. J. Slater and R. L. Wilby color *Science* v357 no6351 p552 Ag 11 2017

Timing of Europe's river floods shifting L. HAMERS map *Science News* v192 no3 p14 S 2 2017

Floods—Florida

Hurricane Irma bw *Bloomberg Businessweek* no4538 p19 S 18 2017

Floods—Haiti

Lightbox color *Time* v188 no15 p10 O 17 2016

Floods—History

China's Legendary Flood D. WEISS color *Archaeology* v69 no6 p21 N/D 2016

Floods—Idaho

THE RAVAGES OF MARCH: A FAR-FLUNG FAMILY STRUCK BY FLOODS K. WRIGHT *Idaho Magazine* v16 no8 p48 My 2017

Floods—Missouri

THE LONG GOODBYE R. HANSEN bw color *Missouri Life* v44 no5 p52 Ag 2017

Floods—New York (State)

'Layout In A Weekend,' we hardly knew ye H. Miller *Model Railroader* v84 no11 p8 N 2017

Floods—Risk assessment

Rising Sea Levels Won't Doom U.S. Coastal Cities M. E. Kahn *Harvard Business Review Digital Articles* p2 Ja 20 2016

Floods—West Virginia

WHEN THE RAIN CAME E. PLOTT *Washingtonian Magazine* v52 no8 p76 My 2017

You're Up! color *Golf Magazine* v58 no11 p12 N 2016

Floods—Yellow River (China)

China's Legendary Flood D. WEISS color *Archaeology* v69 no6 p21 N/D 2016

Floor cloths

ART + CRAFT color *Arts & Crafts Homes & the Revival* v12 no4 p11 Fall 2017

Make a Grand Entrance L. Elliott cartoon *Old House Journal* v45 no3 p48 My 2017

REIMAGINE THE TRADITIONAL A. GRAVES *Yankee* v81 no1 p45 Ja/F 2017

TRADITIONAL PAINTED FLOORS P. Poore color *Old House Journal* v45 no2 p30 Ap 2017

Floor coverings

See also

Carpets

Floor cloths

Rugs

Look Out, Below! A. Kwun *Architectural Record* v205 no4 p99 Ap 2017

The Right Flooring for Every Room J. Garskof chart color diag *Consumer Reports* v82 no8 p44 Ag 2017

Floor coverings—Evaluation

LATEST LOOKS UPDATE H. GILBERT color *House Beautiful* p96 Ag 2017

WALLS & CEILINGS cartoon color *Arts & Crafts Homes & the Revival* v12 no1 p18 2017 Resonce Guide

Woven WORKS A. NEASON color *House Beautiful* p126 Ag 2017

Floor design & construction

BEST FLOORING color *Timber Home Living* p28 2017 Special-Issue

BLAST from the PAST K. Kendall *Indianapolis Monthly* v40 no10 p86 Je 2017

flooring *Design Center Sourcebook* p102 2017

Plan on It diag *Log Home Living* p52 2018 Annual Buyers Guide

Floor maintenance & repair

Low Key Floors M. Ellen Polson color *Arts & Crafts Homes & the Revival* v12 no5 p34 Wint 2018

Floor paint

TRADITIONAL PAINTED FLOORS P. Poore color *Old House Journal* v45 no2 p30 Ap 2017

Floor plans

4 Key Questions to Ask as You Plan Your Timber Home *Timber Home Living* p20 2017 Annual Buyers

design color map *Timber Home Living* p26 2017 Annual Buyers

floor plans color diag *Cabin Living* p71 S 2017

from SITE PLAN to FLOOR PLAN color diag *Timber Home Living* v27 no2 p46 Ap 2017

MY LATEST DIY PROJECT, COMPLETED M. Bristol bw color *Old House Journal* v45 no4 p32 Je 2017

Perfect Harmony S. D. Albert cartoon color *Log Home Living* v33 no9 p64 D 2016

Second-Home Plans color diag *Timber Home Living* v27 no3 p28 Je 2017

Floor tiles

WALL & FLOOR TILES color *Old House Journal* v44 p33 2016 Design Center source Book

WALL & FLOOR TILES *Design Center Sourcebook* p33 2016

Flooring

See also

Wood floors

Map Out a Plan D. PEAK *Log Home Living* v34 no6 p6 Ag 2017

On the Surface K. Wilburn *New Orleans Homes & Lifestyles* v20 no1 p96 Wint 2016

THE SECRETS TO Floor Plan Perfection D. Peak, C. Hills et al diag *Log Home Living* v34 no1 p44 F 2017

Style Standouts color *Log Home Living* p58 2018 Annual Buyers Guide

TRUE VINTAGE STYLE R. Wampler and M. Gill color *Old House Journal* v45 no2 p32 Ap 2017

Flooring equipment—Evaluation

Ups and Downs color *Log Home Living* v34 no6 p38 Ag 2017

Flooring—Equipment & supplies—Evaluation

Look Out, Below! A. Kwun *Architectural Record* v205 no4 p99 Ap 2017

Floors

See also

Dance floors

Flooring

EXTREME WEIRDNESS A. SHAW *National Geographic Kids* no469 p9 Ap 2017

Floor Plan S. Mirsky color *Scientific American* v316 no4 p80 Ap 2017

Floors—Design & construction

See also

Wood floors—Design & construction

13 TIPS FOR GETTING THE MOST FROM A COZY CABIN color *Cabin Living* p8 Mr 2017

Floors—Evaluation

LILAC, TAUPE & WHITE color *Martha Stewart Living* p38 Jl/Ag 2017

Flora, Carlin

DOWN WITH EXTREMES! HEALTH, WELL-BEING, AND SUCCESS REST ON ONE PRINCIPLE: IN ALL THINGS MODERATION *Psychology Today* v50 no4 p80 Ag 2017

THE FRAUD WHO ISN'T *Psychology Today* v49 no6 p70 N/D 2016

THE HARDEST WORD [Cover story] *Psychology Today* v50 no5 p52 S/O 2017

The Undepressing News About Depression color *O, The Oprah Magazine* p80 Ap 2017

UNLOCKING THE VAULT [Cover story] *Psychology Today* v50 no2 p46 Mr/Ap 2017

View from the Top *Psychology Today* v50 no1 p62 Ja/F 2017

YOUR BRAIN color *Redbook* p80 Mr 2017

Floral decorations

See also

Flower arrangements

Fall Color, Four Ways M. S. Wells color *Southern Living* v52 no10 p15 O 2017

FALL FORWARD K. C. FREDERICK *Better Homes & Gardens* v94 no11 p48 N 2016

FULL CIRCLE N. DAYTON *Better Homes & Gardens* v94 no11 p124 N 2016

Vintage Holiday Homemaking JOHNSON *Treasures* v6 no3 p28 D 2016/Ja 2017

Floral print textiles

My Look L. Walters *Indianapolis Monthly* v40 no10 p29 Je 2017

Floral products

Pick these flowers! color *Redbook* p61 My 2017

FLORCZYK, PIOTR

Found in Translation *American Scholar* v86 no2 p109 Spr 2017

Florea, Bogdan I.

Activity-based protein profiling reveals off-target proteins of the FAAH inhibitor BIA 10-2474 chart color graph *Science* v356 no6342 p1084 Je 9 2017

Florence, John—Interviews

CONFIRMATION Z. Morton color *Surfing Magazine* v53 no2 p18 F 2017

IN SESSION T. PRODANOVICH color *Surfer* v58 no1 p48 Ap 2017

Florence Foster Jenkins (Film)

NEWLY AVAILABLE MOVIES M. FELL *TV Guide* v65 no23 p40 My 29 2017

Florence (Italy)—History—1421-1737

Renaissance Florence Was a Better Model for Innovation than

Silicon Valley Is E. Weiner *Harvard Business Review Digital Articles* p2 Ja 25 2016

Florens, F. B. Vincent

Can we protect island flying foxes? color *Science* v355 no6332 p1368 Mr 31 2017

Florent-Treacy, Elizabeth

An Early Warning System for Your Team's Stress Level [Cover story] *Harvard Business Review Digital Articles* p2 Ap 26 2017

Florer-Bixler, Melissa

Holy crumbs color *Christian Century* v134 no1 p10 Ja 4 2017

Sparrows, swallows, and us *Christian Century* v134 no17 p12 Ag 16 2017

Flores, Carlos A.

What Do New Faculty Members Want From Their University? *Change* v49 no4 p52 Jl/Ag 2017

Flores, Jeremy

Character study S. C. Kim color *Sunset* v238 no2 p38 F 2017

Flores, Jessica

FLOUR GIRL: Head baker Jessica Flores is a rising star at Open Society Public House S. KROWIAK *Indianapolis Monthly* v40 no11 p40 Jl 2017

Flores, Nichole M.

IN JEFFERSON'S SHADOW color *America* v216 no12 p28 My 29 2017

An unseen environmental disaster *America* v217 no6 p57 S 18 2017

WHEN THE K.K.K. CAME TO CHARLOTTESVILLE HOW SHOULD CATHOLICS RESPOND TO THE SIN OF RACISM? [Cover story] color *America* v217 no5 p34 S 4 2017

Where and who you are color *U.S. Catholic* v82 no1 p12 Ja 2017

Flores man

Very Distant Relative N. Wilson color *Natural History* v125 no7 p8 Jl/Ag 2017

Flores-Villela, Oscar A.

Mexico's ambiguous invasive species plan bibl *Science* v355 no6329 p1033 Mr 10 2017

Flórez, Juan Diego, 1973-

Werther S. Hastings *Opera News* v81 no9 p42 Mr 2017

Flórez-Rodríguez, Alexander

An Anthropocene map of genetic diversity bibl graph map *Science* v353 no6307 p1532 S 30 2016

Florian, Douglas, 1950-

Leap, Frog, Leap! color *Publishers Weekly* v263 no49 p56 D 7 2016

Florian, Federico

"ALL WATCHED OVER BY MACHINES OF LOVING GRACE" color *Art in America* v105 no6 p146 Je/Jl 2017

GETA BRĂTESCU bw *Art in America* p130 O 2017

Floriculturists

The strange case of the orange petunias K. Servick color *Science* v356 no6340 p792 My 26 2017

Florida

IN THE DARK A. D. Sorkin bw *New Yorker* v93 no29 p37 S 25 2017

WILD ABANDON B. KEVIN *Audubon* v118 no6 p38 Wint 2016

Florida, Richard L., 1957-

Are the Super-Rich Really Ruining the World's Great Cities? *Harvard Business Review Digital Articles* p2 Je 9 2017

City Limits: The renewal of central cities has also made them more unequal and segregated, a new book argues N. GELINAS *New York Times Book Review* p10 Jl 2 2017

A Failed Urbanism J. D. DAVIDSON *National Review* v69 no9 p35 My 15 2017

Hip, Cool & Unaffordable chart color *Alternatives Journal (AJ) - Canada's Environmental Voice* v42 no2 p42 2016

A Second Look at the 'Creative Class' Issue A. M. RENN *American Conservative* v16 no4 p53 Jl/Ag 2017

TECH CRUNCH BUILD CITIES THAT WON'T TRASH THE WORKING CLASS color *Wired* v25 no5 p17 My 2017

Too Much of a Good Thing J. S. Russell *Architectural Record* v205 no6 p49 Je 2017

The Unaffordable Urban Paradise color il *MIT Technology Review* v120 no4 p88 Jl/Ag 2017

What Inclusive Urban Development Can Look Like *Harvard Business Review Digital Articles* p2 Jl 11 2017

Florida Georgia Line (Performer)

When Florida Georgia Line Met the Backstreet Boys M. Vain color *Entertainment Weekly* no1453 p12 F 17 2017

Florida Keys (Fla.)

What Am I Looking At? A. JONES *Boating World* v38 no6 p20 Je 2017

Florida largemouth bass

The Big Unit A. WHITCOMB *Boating World* v38 no2 p18 F 2017

Florida panther

THE PANTHER YOU WANT D. KUIPERS color *Orion Magazine* v35 no6 p49 N/D 2016

Florida State University

Beyond Anatomy L. Wingenroth *Dance Magazine* v90 no12 p106 D 2016

Florida State University *Dance Magazine* v90 p63 2016/2017 Supplement College Guide

Hovering Can Hinder Transition to Adulthood *USA Today Magazine* v145 no2859 p11 D 2016

Florida State University—Sports

2 Florida State color *Sports Illustrated* v127 no5 p90 Ag 14 2017

Florida Tourism Industry Marketing Corp.

Squabbling in the Sunshine A. Greenblatt *Governing* v30 no8 p9 My 2017

Florida—Description & travel

The Dry Tortugas... M. Dolan color *American History* v52 no4 p72 O 2017

Endless ADVENTURES *Atlanta* v57 no5 p69 S 2017

FLORIDA M. Rosano color map *Canadian Geographic* v135 no6 p24 D 2015

FLORIDA *New York Times Magazine* p74 Mr 26 2017

FLORIDA'S NATURAL WONDERS B. BROUDY *Sierra* v102 no3 p28 My/Je 2017

Florida's Unsung Beach Towns V. F. Luesse color map *Southern Living* v52 no6 p63 Je 2017

Seaside Greetings P. Disbrowe color *Southern Living* v51 no12 p79 D 2016

Splash in the Sunshine State C. MCFARLAND color *Trail Rider* v29 no3 p50 Ap 2017

Tee, Ball J. Passov and C. Barrett chart color *Golf Magazine* v59 no3 p40 Mr 2017

TRAVEL DESTINATIONS color *New Orleans Magazine* v51 no5 p108 Mr 2017

Florida—Economic conditions

Florida S. Burnell color *Forbes* v198 no9 p27 D 30 2016

RICHEST BY STATE A. BROWN bw map *Forbes* v199 no4 p22 Ap 25 2017

Florida Project, The (Film)

ALSO PLAYING color *Entertainment Weekly* no1478 / 1479 p55 Ag 18-25 2017

CRITICS' CHOICE bw chart color *Film Comment* v53 no5 p14 S/O 2017

The Florida Project C. DA COSTA color *Film Comment* v53 no5 p72 S/O 2017

NOW PLAYING color *Entertainment Weekly* no1486 p46 O 13 2017

A Slice of Childhood Heaven In the Sunshine State S. Zacharek color *Time* v190 no15 p56 O 16 2017

YOUNG AT HEART A. LANE color *New Yorker* v93 no31 p80 O 9 2017

FLORIO, ERIN

THE DANISH GIRL color *Conde Nast Traveler* v52 no4 p20 Ap 2017

Die Hard color *Conde Nast Traveler* v52 no1 p116 Ja 2017

A Facial Worth the Flight color map *Conde Nast Traveler* v52 no8 p50 S 2017

Getting Warmer color *Conde Nast Traveler* v52 no4 p14 Ap 2017

Goes Down Easy color *Conde Nast Traveler* v52 no2 p54 F 2017

It's All in the Name color *Conde Nast Traveler* v52 no8 p42 S 2017

Meet and Greet color *Conde Nast Traveler* v52 no3 p40 Mr 2017

Mountain Men color *Conde Nast Traveler* v51 no11 p130 D 2016

Permission to Leave the Airport cartoon *Conde Nast Traveler* v51 no11 p126 D 2016

Rome bw chart color map *Conde Nast Traveler* v52 no3 p52 Mr 2017

Sweet Georgia color *Conde Nast Traveler* v52 no9 p38 O 2017

WE'RE TURNING 30 bw chart color *Conde Nast Traveler* v52

no8 p55 S 2017

Where to Sleep It Off color *Conde Nast Traveler* v51 no10 p50 N 2016

WORLDLY ADVICE color *Conde Nast Traveler* v52 no6 p22 Je/Jl 2017

Florists

FLORISTS LOSE ON FREE EXPRESSION S. SHACKFORD color *Reason* v49 no2 p6 Je 2017

Pot Stuff B. COOPER *Indianapolis Monthly* p27 My 2017

Florrie

America's top TV critic Matt Roush answers your burning questions *TV Guide* p7 D 5 2016

Flory, Paul J., 1910-1985

The Crown Jewel of the Queen City *Tennis* v52 no6 p68 N/D 2016

Flos (Company)

THROWING SHADE color *Esquire* v167 no2 p42 Mr 2017

Floto, R. Andres

Emergence and spread of a human-transmissible multidrug-resistant nontuberculous mycobacterium bibl diag graph *Science* v354 no6313 p751 N 11 2016

Flour

a whole lot of wholesome B. P. KATZ color *Martha Stewart Living* p82 Mr 2017

Flour as food

CATCH OF THE DAY S. Dry bw color *Louisiana Life* v38 no1 p54 S/O 2017

Flournoy, Angela

Angela Flournoy C. Mari color *Current Biography* v78 no4 p21 Ap 2017

'F.U.B.U.' *New York Times Magazine* p51 Mr 12 2017

Mohsin Hamid's 'Exit West' *New York Times Magazine* p43 O 8 2017

Flournoy, Page

FREE FOR ALL color *O, The Oprah Magazine* p20 O 2017

Flow, Heather—Interviews

HEATHER FLOW J. Chen color *Bloomberg Businessweek* no4510 p63 F 6 2017

Flow Advisory LLC

HEATHER FLOW J. Chen color *Bloomberg Businessweek* no4510 p63 F 6 2017

Flow cytometry—Equipment & supplies

new products color *Science* v357 no6346 p98 Jl 7 2017

Flower, Alexa

THE DEADLY VALLEY bw color *Climbing* no356 p44 S/O 2017

Rap Smart color *Climbing* no356 p40 S/O 2017

Flower, Roger J.

Reform China's fisheries subsidies color *Science* v356 no6345 p1343 Je 30 2017

Flower arrangements

An Azalea Affair A. Aguillard color *Southern Living* v52 no3 p11 Mr 2017

Budding Artist G. Haynes color *Southern Living* v52 no5 p22 My 2017

Fall Color, Four Ways M. S. Wells color *Southern Living* v52 no10 p15 O 2017

FINDING BEAUTY IN THE BASICS S. ORR *Better Homes & Gardens* v95 no2 p4 F 2016

A FLORAL AFFAIR J. Silver color *Sunset* v238 no6 p39 Je 2017

THE NEW "SOLO" TRAVEL color *Conde Nast Traveler* v52 no3 p98 Mr 2017

STUNING MADE SIMPLE P. GUGLIELMETTI *Martha Stewart Living* no270 p114 D 2016

Flower Boy (Music)

Tyler, the Creator Opens Up J. Cox color *Time* v190 no6 p55 Ag 7 2017

Tyler, the Obfuscator: The Odd Future leader sends mixed messages on his best album so far C. JENKINS img *New York* v50 no16 p106 Ag 7 2017

Flower festivals

Waterfalls of Mums S. Bender color *Southern Living* v52 no10 p36 O 2017

Flower gardening

See also

Bedding plants

AROUND THE GARDEN S. Bender color *Southern Living* v52 no7 p36 Jl 2017

How Does Your Garden Glow? Creating a moon garden is easy and affordable. The result is an unexpected delight on a balmy summer night E. Millard color *Log Home Living* v34 no5 p34 Jl 2017

LUCIANO GIUBBILEI color *Harper's Bazaar* no3653 p140 My 2017

Timing is Everything P. Marquis *New Orleans Homes & Lifestyles* v20 no2 p64 Spr 2017

Tulip Time Martha color *Martha Stewart Living* p19 S 2017

Flower Hunters (Short story)

Flower Hunters L. Groff cartoon *New Yorker* v92 no38 p78 N 21 2016

Flower petals

Flower hosts its own war of the sexes S. MILIUS color *Science News* v192 no1 p10 Ag 5 2017

Petal Pushers P. Hise color *Virginia Living* v15 no5 p46 Ag 2017

Flower petals in art

SARAH MEYOHAS color *Harper's Bazaar* no3653 p140 My 2017

Flower vending

Flower Men K. HERMANN color map *National Geographic* v231 no5 p112 My 2017

Flowering shrubs

SHRUBS SHAPE-UP M. HUGHES color *Better Homes & Gardens* v95 no4 p82 Ap 2017

Flowerpots—Design & construction

Pimp My Office Plant R. Suqi and C. Tompkins color *Bloomberg Businessweek* no4525 p60 Je 5 2017

Flowerpots—Evaluation

In the SUNSET GARDEN color *Sunset* v238 no5 p54 My 2017

Flowers

See also

Bedding plants

Flower petals

Being a Member Has Its Perks! cartoon color *AARP: The Magazine* v60 no3A p70 Ap/My 2017

Dahlias! [Cover story] D. PRINZING color *Better Homes & Gardens* v95 no8 p140 Ag 2017

Flash of Gold: In the Flower Season J. W. DAVIS *Idaho Magazine* v16 no7 p24 Ap 2017

Flower Power M. Warner Spencer *New Orleans Homes & Lifestyles* v20 no2 p104 Spr 2017

Hardy Harbingers color *Canadian Wildlife* v23 no1 p38 Mr/Ap 2017

HARDY HIBISCUS M. ROSS color *Better Homes & Gardens* v95 no8 p100 Ag 2017

iOS Games: THAT YOU SHOULD BE PLAYING RIGHT NOW J. Mathis color *Macworld - Digital Edition* v34 no11 p80 N 2017

A Little Birdie *Arizona Highways* v93 no6 p5 Je 2017

Make a bouquet last and last color *Redbook* p131 My 2017

Nodding Onion M. WALWYN color *Canadian Wildlife* v23 no1 p37 Mr/Ap 2017

ONLY ON OUR WEBSITE *South Dakota Magazine* v32 no6 p19 Mr/Ap 2017

petal POWER D. KERN color *Yoga Journal* no293 p17 Ag 2017

Plant Now for Winter (Really!) E. Millard color *Log Home Living* v33 no7 p38 S 2016

Say It With Flowers Z. Gowen color *Southern Living* v52 no5 p44 My 2017

Flowers, Brandon, 1981-

IN TUNE color *New Orleans Magazine* v51 no12 p51 O 2017

Flowers as food

Flowers with Flavor K. Hammonds color *Southern Living* v52 no3 p36 Mr 2017

In the SUNSET GARDEN color *Sunset* v238 no3 p38 Mr 2017

Flowers: Beautiful Life (Music)

Flowers—Beautiful Life Vol. 2 P. de Barros color *Downbeat* v84 no7 p47 Jl 2017

Flowers in art

See also

Flower petals in art

FORCE OF NATURE J. K. DE VALLE color *Architectural Digest* v74 no3 p116 Mr 2017

Natural Instincts H. MARTIN color *Architectural Digest* no6 p58 Je 1 2017

Flowers in the Dirt (Music)
PAUL MCCARTNEY M. Mettler bw color *Sound & Vision* v82 no5 p72 Je 2017

Floyd, Lynna
Every Woman Needs These Breast Cancer Lessons bw color *Glamour* v115 no10 p117 O 2017

Floyd, Safon
30 DAYS TO YOUR DREAM JOB [Cover story] color *Black Enterprise* v47 no4 p34 N/D 2016
5 Signs Your Job is Completely Stressing You Out color *Black Enterprise* v47 no4 p29 N/D 2016
FINDING PURPOSE IN PLASTIC SURGERY color *Black Enterprise* v47 no5 p29 Ja/F 2017
THE MOST POWERFUL WOMEN IN BUSINESS [Cover story] color *Black Enterprise* v47 no5 p56 Ja/F 2017
Out From the Shadow of the Valley color *Black Enterprise* v47 no4 p18 N/D 2016
POWER IN LONGEVITY color *Black Enterprise* v47 no5 p16 Ja/F 2017

Floyd, Samuel A.
Transformers E. J. HOLLEY color *Downbeat* v84 no8 p83 Ag 2017

Flu vaccine efficacy
One and Done [Cover story] L. Beil color graph *Science News* v192 no7 p18 O 28 2017

Fluctuations (Physics)
Experimental measurement of binding energy, selectivity, and allostery using fluctuation theorems J. Camunas-Soler, A. Alemany et al bibl graph *Science* v355 no6323 p412 Ja 27 2017

Flue covers
STUFF WATER INFILTRATION SCREWED UP M. Burke and M. Burke cartoon *Old House Journal* v45 no2 p54 Ap 2017

FLUET-CHOUINARD, ETIENNE
A Global Assessment of Inland Wetland Conservation Status *BioScience* v67 no6 p523 Je 2017

Fluid dynamic measurements
Arresting soap-bubble flows *Physics Today* v69 no11 p88 N 2016

Fluid dynamics
See also
Bernoulli effect (Fluid dynamics)
Diffusers (Fluid dynamics)
Eddies
Pneumatics
Vortex motion
Taking the measure of water's whirl A. G. Smart *Physics Today* v70 no10 p20 O 2017
Transition from turbulent to coherent flows in confined three-dimensional active fluids Wu, J. Bernard Hishamunda et al color *Science* v355 no6331 p1284 Mr 24 2017
Will More Cylinder-Head Flow Always Make More Power? M. Davis bw color *Hot Rod* v70 no7 p98 Jl 2017

Fluid mechanics
See also
Fluid dynamics
Hydraulics
NEW BOOKS *Physics Today* v70 no8 p62 Ag 2017
The turbulent cascade in five dimensions J. I. Cardesa, A. Vela-Martín et al color *Science* v357 no6353 p782 Ag 25 2017

Fluid therapy
Roll Out color *Health* v31 no2 p15 Mr 2017

Fluke, Joanne
Banana Cream Pie Murder: A Hannah Swensen Mystery *Publishers Weekly* v264 no5 p177 Ja 30 2017

Fluker, Elayne
FINALLY FREE color *Essence* v47 no11 p60 Mr 2017

Fluker, Walter Earl
The Ground Has Shifted: The Future of the Black Church in Post-Racial America color *Publishers Weekly* v263 no45 p27 N 7 2016

Fluorescence
NEW PRODUCTS: GENOMICS color *Science* v354 no6308 p121 O 7 2016
Twilight of the fluorescent frogs S. Milius color *Science News* v191 no7 p4 Ap 15 2017

Fluorescence microscopy—Equipment & supplies
new products color *Science* v357 no6359 p123 O 6 2017

Fluorescent lighting
Pants and Awards *Science & Technology Review* p23 S 2016

Fluorides
A catalytic fluoride-rebound mechanism for C(sp3)-CF3 bond formation M. D. Levin, T. Q. Chen et al diag *Science* v356 no6344 p1272 Je 23 2017

Fluoxetine
My Teenage Patient's Mom Is Slipping Her Prozac. What Should I Do? K. A. Appiah *New York Times Magazine* p16 Jl 16 2017

Flurry, Rob—Interviews
Q & A WITH ROB FLURRY *Texas Monthly* v45 no5 p28 My 2017

Flute playing
DRAWN TO JAZZ Y. Kato color *Downbeat* v84 no6 p114 Je 2017
MIDSUMMER NIGHT'S DREAM G. S. EINARSDÓTTIR *Iceland Review* v55 no4 p86 Jl/Ag 2017

Fluxus (Group of artists)
THE MUSIC OF CHANCE B. Brown color *Art in America* v105 no1 p54 Ja 2017

Fly Already (Short story)
FLY ALREADY E. Keret color *New Yorker* v93 no13 p76 My 15 2017

Fly fishing
A FEW GOOD FINDS N. SULLIVAN color *Esquire* p58 Ap 2017
FLY-FISHING J. GLUCK cartoon color *Popular Mechanics* p29 Je 2017
PAIN, SUFFERING & MUSKIES D. KARCZYNSKI color *Outdoor Life* v224 no8 p63 O 2017

Fly fishing—Equipment & supplies
The Future of Fishing K. Stock color *Bloomberg Businessweek* no4531 p63 Jl 24 2017

Fly tying
SPEED BUGS J. Cermele color *Field & Stream* v121 no7 p26 D 2016/Ja 2017

Flyak, Andrew I.
A "Trojan horse" bispecific-antibody strategy for broad protection against ebolaviruses bibl graph *Science* v354 no6310 p350 O 21 2016

Fly Honey Show, The (Theatrical production)
THE HONEY HIVE B. GOLDEN color *Chicago* v66 no8 p44 Ag 2017

Flying (Periodical)
A SOLID PLAN GONE AWRY S. R. DEIGNAN-SCHMIDT color *Flying* v144 no7 p26 Jl 2017

Flying automobile design & construction
DRIVE IN THE SKY J. STEWART color *Wired* v25 no10 p54 O 2017

Flying automobiles
DRIVE IN THE SKY J. STEWART color *Wired* v25 no10 p54 O 2017
Roads? Where We're Going ... K. Samuelson color *Time* v189 no23 p14 Je 19 2017

Flying automobiles—History
50, 100 & 150 YEARS AGO bw color *Scientific American* v316 no3 p79 Mr 2017

Flying by Foy (Company)
Flight Time *Stage Directions* v30 no5 p6 My 2017
Flying By Foy - Love to See You Fly *Stage Directions* v30 no3 p8 Mr 2017

Flying discs (Game)
On Our Honour H. Roderique color *Walrus* v14 no5 p24 Je 2017

Flying Dog Brewing Co.
The NATION of FLYING DOG A. WHITING *Washingtonian Magazine* v52 no4 p68 Ja 2017

Flying foxes
Bats S. ELDER color *National Geographic Kids* no474 p22 O 2017
Can we protect island flying foxes? C. E. Vincenot, F. B. Vincent Florens et al color *Science* v355 no6332 p1368 Mr 31 2017

Flying Lotus (Performer)
Brainfeeder Showcase Fuses Enlightened Funk, Innovative Jazz S. J. O'Connell color *Downbeat* v83 no12 p19 D 2016

Flying-machines
See also
Aerial propellers
Airplanes

Drone aircraft
Flying automobiles
Rockets (Aeronautics)
10 Ways Drones Are Changing Your World T. Foster color *Consumer Reports* v82 no1 p44 Ja 2017
Captured! bw *Military History* v34 no4 p80 N 2017
Where's my flying car? C. Day *Physics Today* v70 no6 p8 Je 2017

Flying-machines—Design & construction
ALL YOUR FLYING CAR QUESTIONS, ANSWERED color *Fortune* v175 no7 p13 Je 1 2017
DJI SPARK: A FANTASTIC, AFFORDABLE DRONE THAT DEMANDS EXPENSIVE EXTRAS S. BELLAMY color *Macworld - Digital Edition* v34 no11 p73 N 2017

Flying Dutchman, The (Theatrical production)
CLASSICAL MUSIC *New Yorker* v93 no12 p8 My 8 2017
Senta's CHOICE P. KENNICOTT *Opera News* v81 no10 p32 Ap 2017

Flymen Fishing Co.
SURFACE SEDUCER DOUBLE BARREL POPPER BODIES J. Cermele color *Field & Stream* v121 no8 p90 F/Mr 2017

FLYNN, ALICE M.
BRAVERY AT THE BATTLE OF THE BULGE *USA Today Magazine* v145 no2864 p44 My 2017

Flynn, Alison
CLASSROOM CHEMISTRY L. AGRBA color *Maclean's* v130 no2 p63 Mr 2017

Flynn, Billy—Awards
BEST OF DAYTIME 2016 M. LOGAN *TV Guide* p44 D 19 2016

Flynn, C.
The magnetic field and turbulence of the cosmic web measured using a brilliant fast radio burst bibl chart graph *Science* v354 no6317 p1249 D 9 2016

Flynn, Channing
The Questions Executives Should Ask About 3D Printing *Harvard Business Review Digital Articles* p2 Ap 19 2016

Flynn, Erin
Weight List color *Sports Illustrated* v126 no10 p30 Ap 10 2017

Flynn, Errol, 1909-1959
The Lightness of Errol Flynn B. DOYLE *American Scholar* v86 no1 p100 Wint 2017
REJECTED! C. Barrett color *MHQ: Quarterly Journal of Military History* v29 no4 p17 Summ 2017

Flynn, Francis J.
How to Work with Colleagues Who Are Less Creative than You *Harvard Business Review Digital Articles* p2 S 16 2015

Flynn, Gillian
COSTUME DRAMA cartoon *New Yorker* v92 no32 p78 O 10 2016

Flynn, James E.
READER COMMENTS *America* v216 no3 p7 F 6 2017

Flynn, Jill
How Women Can Show Passion at Work Without Seeming "Emotional" *Harvard Business Review Digital Articles* p2 S 30 2015

Flynn, Johnny
Genius L. Acken *TV Guide* p39 Ap 17 2017

Flynn, Kathleen A.
How Is a Debut Novel Like Lizzy Bennet? *New York Times Book Review* p29 Je 4 2017
The Jane Austen Project *Publishers Weekly* v264 no12 p52 Mr 20 2017
Style and Substance: Can genius be graphed? The word choices that explain why Jane Austen's work survives and thrives *New York Times Book Review* p13 Jl 16 2017

Flynn, Larry
Last Losers chart color *Sports Illustrated* v125 no21 p22 D 26 2016
Past Perfect color *Sports Illustrated* v125 no14 p22 O 24-31 2016
Rallying For Grant color *Sports Illustrated* v125 no21 p25 D 26 2016

Flynn, Michael T., 1958-
The Flynn Affair S. F. Hayes and T. Joscelyn *Weekly Standard* v22 no24 p6 F 27 2017
It's a Conspiracy! B. LUEDERS color *Progressive* v81 no3 p12 Mr 2017
Overseeing What's Overheard J. LIFHITS color *Weekly Standard* v22 no28 p16 Mr 27 2017

The Scariest Trump Adviser Is Michael Flynn img *New York* v49 no26 p13 D 26 2016
"The Kellyanne Conway Show" R. LONG il *National Review* v69 no4 p34 Mr 6 2017
Trump Plays Six Degrees of the KGB D. Kocieniewski and P. Robison color *Bloomberg Businessweek* no4506 p22 Ja 9 2017
The Week il *National Review* v69 no4 p4 Mr 6 2017

Flynn, Michael T., 1958——Political & social views
GENERAL CHAOS N. SCHMIDLE cartoon *New Yorker* v93 no2 p40 F 27 2017

Flynn, Molly
Socratism as a Vocation *Society* v54 no1 p64 F 2017

Flynn, Peter
THE DYING OF THE LIGHT S. Guttenberg color *Sound & Vision* v82 no4 p71 My 2017

FLYNN, SARAH WASSNER
awesome 8 color *National Geographic Kids* no170 p6 My 2017
Awesome 8 color *National Geographic Kids* no475 p8 N 2017

Flynn, Sean
ORLANDO: THE DAY AFTER color *GQ: Gentlemen's Quarterly* v86 no12 p190 D 2016

Flynn, Thomas J.
BRAVERY AT THE BATTLE OF THE BULGE A. M. FLYNN *USA Today Magazine* v145 no2864 p44 My 2017

FLYNN, VICTORIA SANDBROOK
Mission Central color *Publishers Weekly* v264 no6 p44 F 6 2017
Mothers from the Past color *Publishers Weekly* v264 no13 p68 Mr 27 2017

Flynn-Evans, Erin
Bed and Beyond color *O, The Oprah Magazine* p22 Mr 2017

Flynt, Diane
CIDER HOUSE RULES: Foggy Ridge Cider founder Diane Flynt earns third nod from James Beard J. Tennis *Virginia Living* v15 no6 p21 O 2017

Fnscia, Suzannah
Dynamic Duo *Dance Magazine* v90 no12 p28 D 2016

Foal diseases
A greater good G. Blatchford and H. Arington color *Equus* no480 p27 S 2017

Foals
ANNUAL COLLECTION OF BABY PHOTOS *Arabian Horse World* v57 no12 p10 S 2017
Arabian Horse World's annual collection of BABY PHOTOS *Arabian Horse World* v56 no12 p10 S 2016
Getting Ready for the Coming Season C. Reich *Arabian Horse World* v57 no4 p186 Ja 2017
Parting is Bittersweet, But Essential C. Reich *Arabian Horse World* v57 no12 p186 S 2017
Season of Birth Can Affect Foal Size S. Dulai Wenholz color *Practical Horseman* v45 no11 p68 N 2017
SLEEP LIKE A BABY? C. Barakat and M. Freckleton color *Equus* no477 p22 Je 2017
STUDY CONFIRMS EFFECTIVENESS OF THE "SQUEEZE TECHNIQUE" C. Barakat and M. McCluskey color *Equus* no482 p13 N 2017

Foals—Diseases
ADVANCES MADE IN FOAL SURVIVAL RATES C. Barakat and M. McCluskey color *Equus* no475 p26 Ap 2017
STUD FARM DIARIES C. Reich *Arabian Horse World* v57 no2 p134 N 2016

Foals—Health
STUD FARM DIARIES: "On the Bottle"—Feeding the Orphan or Rejected Foal C. Reich *Arabian Horse World* v57 no10 p98 Jl 2017

Foam
Roll With It G. GRAVES color *Prevention* v68 no12 p78 D 2016

Foam rollers (Exercise equipment)
DYNAMIC RELIEF E. CALDERONE color *Muscle & Performance* v9 no6 p24 Je 2017
ON A Roll O. Manno *Dance Spirit* v21 no4 p28 Ap 2017

Focaccia
ALEXIS NIDO-RUSSO J. BERG cartoon color *Chicago* v66 no3 p56 Mr 2017

Focal (Company)
Focal Dôme Flax 5.1 Speaker System M. Fleischmann color graph *Sound & Vision* v82 no2 p64 F/Mr 2017

Focal Utopia Headphones M. Fleischmann color *Sound & Vision* v82 no6 p42 Jl/Ag 2017

Focal-JMlab SAS

Vive la Différence! S. Guttenberg and C. Crowley color *Sound & Vision* v82 no1 p20 Ja 2017

FOCANT, JEAN-FRANÇOIS

The Odor of Death: An Overview of Current Knowledge on Characterization and Applications *BioScience* v67 no7 p600 Jl 2017

FOCHT, BECKY

Long-Term Studies Contribute Disproportionately to Ecology and Policy *BioScience* v67 no3 p271 Mr 2017

Focke, Florens

CEOs Earn Less at More-Prestigious Firms color *Harvard Business Review Digital Articles* p2 F 2 2017

Focus automobile—Evaluation

American SPEED, Served TWO WAYS color *Esquire* v166 no4 p77 N 2016

Ford Focus RS chart color *Motor Trend* v69 no1 p124 Ja 2017

the leftovers... [Cover story] J. Lieberman, C. Seabaugh et al chart color *Motor Trend* v69 no4 p36 Ap 2017

Foden, Wendy B.

The broad footprint of climate change from genes to biomes to people bibl chart color *Science* v354 no6313 paaf7671-1 N 11 2016

Foderaro, Lisa W.

Too Young to Say 'I Do'? Underage teens can still get married in most states. But some lawmakers and advocacy groups are trying to change that *New York Times Upfront* v149 no12 p6 Ap 24 2017

FODOR, PAM

The Question color *O, The Oprah Magazine* p14 N 2017

FOEGE, WILLIAM H.

Stamping Out Smallpox bw *Natural History* v125 no9 p24 S 2017

Foegley, Dave

Good Chops T. KIRTS *Indianapolis Monthly* p44 My 2017

Foer, Franklin

After Meritocracy *New Republic* v248 no1/2 p4 Ja/F 2017

BRAKE THE INTERNET P. O'Donnell *Washingtonian Magazine* v52 no12 p43 S 2017

It's Putin's World cartoon color *Atlantic* v319 no2 p13 Mr 2017

OBAMA'S AMERICA img *New York* v49 no20 p12 O 3 2016

Trust Bust: A lament about Silicon Valley's 'knowledge monopoly' J. HERRMAN *New York Times Book Review* p13 O 8 2017

Voltaire at Davos *New York Times Book Review* p15 F 19 2017

WHAT'S WRONG WITH THE DEMOCRATS? color *Atlantic* v320 no1 p48 Jl/Ag 2017

When Silicon Valley Took Over Journalism color *Atlantic* v320 no2 p28 S 2017

Why Liberalism Disappoints color *Atlantic* v320 no2 p46 S 2017

Foer, Jonathan Safran, 1977-

Grave Matter: The desecration of Jewish cemeteries has a long history—one that has nothing to do with the election of Donald Trump S. Mandel *Commentary* v143 no4 p27 Ap 2017

Here I Am: A Novel E. Palmer *Christian Century* v133 no26 p41 D 21 2016

HERE I AM: A NOVEL J. HYNES color *Phi Kappa Phi Forum* v97 no1 p31 Spr 2017

Here I Am *Publishers Weekly* v263 no50 p68 D 5 2016

A Strange Way to the Promised Land L. Mishan color *New York Review of Books* v63 no18 p35 N 24 2016

Foer, Joshua

CARVED BY LAVA color diag map *National Geographic* v231 no6 p112 Je 2017

Foersterling, Jack

GLASS color *Powder* p12 S 2017

STACY BARE color *Skiing* p28 Wint 2017

Fog Creek Software Inc.

UNDER THE HOOD: MAKE CODE MORE TINKER-FRIENDLY C. THOMPSON cartoon *Wired* v25 no7 p34 Jl 2017

Fog in art

Misty Morning *Arizona Highways* v93 no2 p5 F 2017

Fogarty, Mignon

A Quick Guide to Avoiding Common Writing Errors *Harvard Business Review Digital Articles* p2 Jl 22 2015

Fogel, Alexander L.

Simple Digital Technologies Can Reduce Health Care Costs *Har-*

vard Business Review Digital Articles p2 N 14 2016

FOGEL, SUSANNA

YOUR FROZEN EGG HAS A QUESTION cartoon *New Yorker* v93 no14 p39 My 22 2017

Fogelman, Dan

The Story of Us [Cover story] D. Snierson color *Entertainment Weekly* no1435 p18 O 14 2016

THIS IS US I. Ratledge *TV Guide* p28 D 5 2016

This Is Us Metes Out Darkness In Search of a Moment's Delight D. D'Addario color *Time* v189 no3 p49 Ja 30 2017

Foges, Chris

Allies and Morrison *Architectural Record* v205 no4 p120 Ap 2017

A Bright Future *Architectural Record* v205 no1 p78 Ja 2017

Design Museum Redux *Architectural Record* v205 no1 p44 Ja 2017

The Fair's the Thing *Architectural Record* v204 no11 p39 N 2016

Green House Effect *Architectural Record* v205 no7 p109 Jl 2017

LAVA color *Architectural Record* v205 no2 p120 F 2017

Splendor in the Glass *Architectural Record* v205 no9 p104 S 2017

Summer Follies color *Architectural Record* v205 no8 p46 Ag 2017

Take Me to the River color *Architectural Record* v205 no8 p96 Ag 2017

York Theatre Royal *Architectural Record* v204 no11 p150 N 2016

Fogg, B. J.

THE ultimate guide to SAVING TIME & FEELING IN CONTROL S. M. FERNÁNDEZ color *Redbook* p99 S 2017

Fogg, Jeremy

Sugar, Spice & Everything Nice: Grandma's molasses cookies are the stuff of memories for pastry chef Jeremy Fogg *New Orleans Homes & Lifestyles* v20 no4 p24 Aut 2017

Foggy Bottom Association

From Vision to Reality A. PILLALAMARRI bw *American Conservative* v16 no2 p9 Mr/Ap 2017

Foggy Ridge Cider (Company)

CIDER HOUSE RULES: Foggy Ridge Cider founder Diane Flynt earns third nod from James Beard J. Tennis *Virginia Living* v15 no6 p21 O 2017

Fogh Rasmussen, Anders, 1953-

Rasmussen's Refrain: Let Uncle Sam Do It D. BANDOW *American Conservative* v16 no2 p50 Mr/Ap 2017

Fogler, M. M.

Plasmonic imaging is gaining momentum graph *Science* v357 no6347 p132 Jl 14 2017

Polaritons in van der Waals materials bibl chart color diag graph *Science* v354 no6309 paag1992-1 O 14 2016

Fohr, Haley

A FRINGE FANTASIA D. HYMAN color *Chicago* v66 no10 p77 O 2017

Fohrman, Ian

The Farmer color *Powder* v45 no4 p38 D 2016

FOHT, BRENDAN P.

Snob Rock color *Weekly Standard* v22 no42 p35 Jl 17 2017

Folan, Peter

Can Catholics dissent from Pope Francis' teaching on the family? Wrong question color *America* v216 no8 p36 Ap 17 2017

Folayan, Sabaah

Whose Streets? Is a Ragged, Bracing Protest Document S. Zacharek color *Time* v190 no7 p50 Ag 21 2017

Whose Streets? J. McGovern color *Entertainment Weekly* no1478 / 1479 p85 Ag 18-25 2017

Folb, Jonathan

Emergence and spread of a human-transmissible multidrug-resistant nontuberculous mycobacterium bibl diag graph *Science* v354 no6313 p751 N 11 2016

Folding chairs

STYLE *New Orleans Homes & Lifestyles* v20 no4 p18 Aut 2017

Folding chairs—Evaluation

BEST BETS L. Schwartzberg and B. Doherty *New York* v49 no15 p63 Jl 25 2016

Foles, Nick

HOT | NOT T. Keith color *Sports Illustrated* v126 no9 p24 Mr 27 2017

FOLEY, CATHERINE M.

Listing Foreign Species under the Endangered Species Act: A Primer for Conservation Biologists *BioScience* v67 no7 p627 Jl 2017

Response to "Listing Foreign Species Under the Endangered Species Act" *BioScience* v67 no10 p873 O 2017

Foley, Emily L.
BEST OF ATLANTA *Atlanta* v56 no8 p106 D 2016
SAVE FACE *Atlanta* v57 no1 p38 My 2017

Foley, Francis
HOLLYWOOD HORSEWOMAN B. DENTON bw color *Horse & Rider* v56 no10 p56 O 2017

Foley, Greg
To Do: Twenty-five things to see, hear, watch, and read img *New York* v50 no10 p106 My 15 2017

Foley, Jonathan
Living by the lessons of the planet color *Science* v356 no6335 p251 Ap 21 2017
The War on Facts Undermines Democracy color *Scientific American* v316 no5 p10 My 2017

Foley, Margaret
QUEST: BACKPACKING ACROSS WESTERN NEW YORK *New York State Conservationist* v71 no5 p14 Ap 2017

Foley, Red
JOLE BLON'S ANNIVERSARY E. Laborde *Louisiana Life* v38 no1 p6 S/O 2017

Foley, Sean
Watch + Learn color *Golf Magazine* v59 no6 p26 Je 2017

Folger, Tim
DARKNESS AT THE EDGE OF THE WORLD color map *Smithsonian* v47 no10 p28 Mr 2017
MASS HYSTERIA color diag *Scientific American* v316 no2 p46 F 2017
THE WAR OVER REALITY color *Discover* v38 no4 p28 My 2017

Folic acid
Nutritional yeast is having a moment color *Health* v31 no9 p14 N 2017

Folk art
EDITOR'S LETTER G. Cerio color *Magazine Antiques* v184 no4 p18 Jl/Ag 2017
Nurtur&ing the spirit J. Eisenbrand bw cartoon color *Magazine Antiques* v184 no1 p196 Ja/F 2017

Folk art sales & prices
Welcome Basket C. TATTOLI color *Conde Nast Traveler* v52 no6 p104 Je/Jl 2017

Folk art—Exhibitions
Revisiting The Art of the Common Man E. Stillinger bw cartoon *Magazine Antiques* v184 no1 p110 Ja/F 2017
SIGHTLINES color *Art in America* v105 no4 p35 Ap 2017

Folk artists
Thoroughly modern Moses: What did Grandma Moses have in common with the likes of Jackson Pollock? Arguably, plenty J. Franklin color *Magazine Antiques* v184 no4 p74 Jl/Ag 2017

Folk festivals
58 GREAT THINGS TO DO THIS MONTH J. FOUMBERG, J. HARDBERGER et al color *Chicago* v66 no2 p101 F 2017
TOGETHERNESS P. STEFÁNSSON *Iceland Review* v55 no4 p6 Jl/Ag 2017

Folk museums
TRAVEL BACK IN TIME *Iceland Review* v54 no6 p103 N/D 2016

Folk music
FITZGERALD & ME M. Miller color *Esquire* p32 Je/Jl 2017
SOUTHWEST REGION *Virginia Living* p114 2017 Best 20of Virginia

Folk musicians
See also
Folk-rock musicians
The Folk Singer vs. the Millionaire J. BULLINGTON *In These Times* v41 no6 p8 Je 2017

Folk-rock musicians
The Vague Christianity Of Folk Rock T. Donnellan color *America* v216 no8 p38 Ap 17 2017

Folke, Carl
Social norms as solutions bibl color *Science* v354 no6308 p42 O 7 2014

Folkertsma, Laura
Controlled growth and form of precipitating microsculptures bw color diag graph *Science* v355 no6332 p1395 Mr 31 2017

Folkestone (England)
MEET THE FOLKESTONES J. MILLER *In These Times* v41 no2 p42 F 2017

Folkman, Joseph
4 Ways to Be More Effective at Execution *Harvard Business Review Digital Articles* p2 My 23 2016
7 Things Leaders Do to Help People Change *Harvard Business Review Digital Articles* p2 Jl 20 2015
Are We More Productive When We Have More Time Off? *Harvard Business Review Digital Articles* p2 Je 17 2015
The Assumptions That Make Giving Tough Feedback Even Tougher *Harvard Business Review Digital Articles* p2 Ap 30 2015
Companies Are Bad at Identifying High-Potential Employees *Harvard Business Review Digital Articles* p2 F 20 2017
Do Women Make Bolder Leaders than Men? *Harvard Business Review Digital Articles* p2 Ap 27 2016
How Age and Gender Affect Self-Improvement *Harvard Business Review Digital Articles* p2 Ja 5 2016
How Managers Drive Results and Employee Engagement at the Same Time *Harvard Business Review Digital Articles* p2 Je 19 2017
How to Improve at Work When You're Not Getting Feedback *Harvard Business Review Digital Articles* p2 My 9 2017
If Your Boss Thinks You're Awesome, You Will Become More Awesome *Harvard Business Review Digital Articles* p2 Ja 27 2015
People Who Think They're Great Coaches Often Aren't *Harvard Business Review Digital Articles* p2 Je 23 2016
Research: 10 Traits of Innovative Leaders *Harvard Business Review Digital Articles* p2 D 15 2014
The Traits of Leaders Who Do Things Fast and Well *Harvard Business Review Digital Articles* p2 N 16 2016
The Trickle-Down Effect of Good (and Bad) Leadership *Harvard Business Review Digital Articles* p2 Ja 14 2016
We Like Leaders Who Underrate Themselves *Harvard Business Review Digital Articles* p2 N 10 2015
What Great Listeners Actually Do *Harvard Business Review Digital Articles* p2 Jl 14 2016
What Separates Great HR Leaders from the Rest *Harvard Business Review Digital Articles* p2 Ag 17 2015
What To Do When the Boss Gives You Baseless Feedback *Harvard Business Review Digital Articles* p2 Mr 4 2015
What Younger Managers Should Know About How They're Perceived *Harvard Business Review Digital Articles* p2 S 29 2015
Why Middle Managers Are So Unhappy *Harvard Business Review Digital Articles* p2 N 24 2014
Why You Should Watch Out for Your 5-Year Job Anniversary *Harvard Business Review Digital Articles* p2 Ap 10 2015
You Have to Be Fast to Be Seen as a Great Leader *Harvard Business Review Digital Articles* p2 F 26 2015

Folkman, Mark
You Never Forget Your First Time diag il *Backpacker* v45 no2 p64 Mr 2017

Folkner, W.
Jupiter's interior and deep atmosphere: The initial pole-to-pole passes with the Juno spacecraft [Cover story] color graph *Science* v356 no6340 p821 My 26 2017

Folks, Casey
CASEY FOLKS: RACER, BEST IN THE DESERT FOUNDER, AND DRIVING FORCE DIES color *Dirt Sports + Off-Road* v51 no6 p6 Je 2017
TO EVERYTHING—TURN, TURN, TURN M. Emery *Dirt Sports + Off-Road* v51 no6 p4 Je 2017

Follain, John
A Petri Dish of Populist Dissent cartoon *Bloomberg Businessweek* no4501 p14 N 28 2016
When La Dolce Vita Starts to Sour color *Bloomberg Businessweek* no4536 p33 S 4 2017

Follette, Kent
HANDS ON THE WHEEL J. ROEDEL color *Louisiana Life* v37 no3 p14 Ja/F 2017

Folliculitis—Diagnosis
Our Doc Will See You Now R. Rajapaksa color *Health* v31 no6 p71 Jl 2017

Follman, D.

Direct frequency comb measurement of OD + CO→DOCO kinetics bibl graph *Science* v354 no6311 p444 O 28 2016

Followership

Attitudes of Influential Leadership K. Sellars *Parks & Recreation* v52 no5 p65 My 2017

Sustaining Leadership Greatness B. Heller *Parks & Recreation* v52 no5 p54 My 2017

Folsom, Cate

LOVE AND WAR color *Equus* no472 p44 Ja 2017

Foltz, Bob

Adding onto a SECOND DECK color diag *Model Railroader* v84 no8 p48 Ag 2017

Folwell, Dale

The $90 Billion Investor Who Can't Shake Wall Street N. Weinberg color *Bloomberg Businessweek* no4518 p38 Ap 10 2017

Fombrun, Charles

How Do You Rank the World's Best CEOs? *Harvard Business Review Digital Articles* p2 F 6 2015

FONDA, DAREN

10 Great All-Weather Stocks chart color *Kiplinger's Personal Finance* v71 no2 p52 F 2017

10 GREAT STOCKS FOR THE NEXT 10 YEARS color *Kiplinger's Personal Finance* v70 no12 p46 D 2016

13 STOCKS FOR THE TECH REVOLUTION cartoon chart color *Kiplinger's Personal Finance* v71 no4 p52 Ap 2017

8 STOCKS TO BUY NOW color *Kiplinger's Personal Finance* v71 no1 p50 Ja 2017

... AND 5 TO SELL cartoon *Kiplinger's Personal Finance* v71 no1 p51 Ja 2017

Boost Your Income With Options color *Kiplinger's Personal Finance* v71 no6 p52 Je 2017

A Cheap Way to Own Tech chart *Kiplinger's Personal Finance* v70 no12 p59 D 2016

Earn Up to 10% cartoon *Kiplinger's Personal Finance* v71 no6 p42 Je 2017

Earn Up to 6% From Our Fund Portfolios cartoon chart *Kiplinger's Personal Finance* v71 no3 p50 Mr 2017

A Financial Fund Heats Up chart *Kiplinger's Personal Finance* v71 no6 p56 Je 2017

Get 5% or More From Preferreds color *Kiplinger's Personal Finance* v70 no12 p53 D 2016

Infrastructure Wins Fans chart *Kiplinger's Personal Finance* v71 no1 p60 Ja 2017

INVESTORS TAKE A SHINE TO WATSON color *Kiplinger's Personal Finance* v71 no4 p12 Ap 2017

Low on REITs, High on Returns chart *Kiplinger's Personal Finance* v71 no11 p63 N 2017

Our Top Dividend Picks chart color *Kiplinger's Personal Finance* v71 no12 p50 D 2017

An Rx for Healthier Gains chart *Kiplinger's Personal Finance* v71 no12 p54 D 2017

Surviving Amazon color *Kiplinger's Personal Finance* v71 no7 p60 Jl 2017

We Add a Real Estate Fund chart *Kiplinger's Personal Finance* v71 no3 p62 Mr 2017

We Pick the Best Online Brokers chart color *Kiplinger's Personal Finance* v71 no10 p48 O 2017

What 7 Top Pros Are Doing Now color *Kiplinger's Personal Finance* v71 no8 p42 Ag 2017

WHAT A WEAKER DOLLAR MEANS TO YOU color *Kiplinger's Personal Finance* v71 no11 p10 N 2017

Why Interest Rates Matter cartoon graph *Kiplinger's Personal Finance* v71 no2 p57 F 2017

WORRIED ABOUT THE STOCK MARKET? cartoon *Kiplinger's Personal Finance* v71 no6 p13 Je 2017

Fonda, Jane, 1937-

Grace and Frankie M. Logan *TV Guide* v65 no13 p24 Mr 20 2017

Leading Ladies M. Rochlin color *AARP: The Magazine* v59 no4A p38 Je/Jl 2016

Fondakowski, Leigh

Dramatizing Deepwater Horizon A. Rademacher color *Science* v356 no6335 p256 Ap 21 2017

Fondas, Nanette

Making Caregiving Compatible with Work *Harvard Business Review Digital Articles* p2 O 12 2015

Millennials Say They'll Relocate for Work-Life Flexibility *Har-*

vard Business Review Digital Articles p2 My 7 2015

Foner, Eric, 1943-

Battles for Freedom: The Use and Abuse of American History *Publishers Weekly* v264 no13 p92 Mr 27 2017

Evolutionary Wars *New York Times Book Review* p10 Ja 22 2017

The Making and the Breaking of Robert E. Lee E. Foner *New York Times Book Review* p19 S 17 2017

Teaching the History of Radicalism in the Age of Obama color *Nation* v304 no1 p76 Ja 2 2017 The Obama Years

Refugees Old and New *Nation* v304 no6 p4 F 27 2017

Foner, Eric, 1943—Interviews

A Usable Past A conversation on Politics & History with Eric Foner R. KREITNER color *Nation* v304 no15 p16 My 8 2017

Fonfara, Paul

Seven Secrets Of Snow B. Zimmerman color *Downbeat* v84 no2 p85 F 2017

Fonseca, Roberto

ABUC J. Hale color *Downbeat* v83 no12 p79 D 2016

Different Perspective B. Reed color *Downbeat* v84 no4 p8 Ap 2017

Fonseca Explores Cuban Styles J. Murph color *Downbeat* v84 no4 p14 Ap 2017

Fonsi, Luis

The New Science of the Truly Unstoppable, Impossible-to-Resist Summer Jam R. Bruner color *Time* v190 no9 p53 S 4 2017

Two Latin Singers—and Justin Bieber—Hit No. 1 L. Shaw bw color *Bloomberg Businessweek* no4525 p21 Je 5 2017

Fonsi, Luis—Interviews

WILL THIS MAN HAVE THE SONG OF SUMMER? M. Vain color *Entertainment Weekly* no1470 p12 Je 16 2017

Fontaine, Kathleen

RECOGNIZING WHAT STUDENTS WANT TO READ: The Florida Reading Association-Children's Book Award diag *Literacy Today (2411-7862)* v34 no6 p44 My/Je 2017

FONTAINE, RICHARD

Restraint and Its Discontents *National Review* v69 no1 p26 Ja 23 2017

Fontainebleau Resorts LLC

THE APPROVAL MATRIX img *New York* v49 no23 p112 N 14 2016

Fontana, Isabeli

PRETTY IS BACK A. Syrett color *InStyle* v24 no3 p354 Mr 2017

Fontana, Santino

America's top TV critic Matt Roush answers your burning questions Melissa, Florrie et al *TV Guide* p7 D 5 2016

Fontanillas, Pierre

High-resolution interrogation of functional elements in the noncoding genome bibl graph *Science* v353 no6307 p1545 S 30 2016

FONTE, JOHN

The Return Of National Sovereignty *National Review* v68 no22 p20 D 5 2016

Fonte, S.

Localized aliphatic organic material on the surface of Ceres bibl graph *Science* v355 no6326 p719 F 17 2017

Fonti, S.

Seasonal exposure of carbon dioxide ice on the nucleus of comet 67P/Churyumov-Gerasimenko bibl bw graph *Science* v354 no6319 p1563 D 23 2016

Fonts & typefaces

FONTGATE R. Arbes cartoon *New Yorker* v93 no22 p20 Jl 31 2017

LETTERS OF NOTE: The Cincinnati Type & Print Museum is looking to make the past present A. KONERMANN *Cincinnati Magazine* v50 no10 p30 Jl 2017

Mac 911 G. FLEISHMAN bw color *Macworld - Digital Edition* v34 no10 p109 O 2017

Foo Fighters (Performer)

Foo Fighters' All-Star Return K. GROW color *Rolling Stone* no1293 p11 Ag 10 2017

Food

See also

Beverages

Chocolate

Coloring matter in food

Convenience foods

Enriched foods

Farm produce

Fats & oils

Feeding behavior in animals

Flour as food

Fruit

Functional foods

Grain

Natural foods

Nuts

Photography of food

Processed foods

Snack foods

Soyfoods

Stuffed foods (Cooking)

Vegetables

Vegetarian foods

10 Hidden Sources of Gluten During the Holidays [Cover story] M. D. Smith color *Better Nutrition* v79 no11 p72 N 2017

7 Food Trends for 2017 K. Steinmetz color *Time* v188 no27-28 p86 D 26 2016

All Yours B. O'Dair *Prevention* v68 no11 p3 N 2016

Ancient Superfoods You Should Eat Now N. Frehsee color *Health* v30 no10 p94 D 2016

APRIL FOOLS L. MOYER and B. LIEBMAN *Nutrition Action Health Letter* v44 no3 p8 Ap 2017

Are These 'Healthy' Foods Really Good for You? A. Park and A. Sifferlin color *Time* v190 no10/11 p32 S 18 2017

Are You Wasting Food? V. TWEED color *Better Nutrition* v78 no11 p92 N 2016

Bean Good? *Nutrition Action Health Letter* v43 no10 p15 D 2016

Best Dressed B. Lipton color *Health* v31 no4 p118 My 2017

The Cheesecake Factory P. Kita color *Men's Health* v32 no3 p70 Ap 2017

Cinco de Mayo SPA CUISINE L. TURNER color *Better Nutrition* p46 My 2017

CLASS-CONFLICT CUISINE S. JONES bw *Nation* v305 no11 p28 O 30 2017

COMING TO AMERICA A. RAPOPORT bw *Bon Appetit* v62 no2 p12 Mr 2017

THE COUNTER JOINT AS COMMUNITY BOOSTER R. WILLIAMS bw *Bon Appetit* v62 no2 p70 Mr 2017

Critter Crudités color *Good Housekeeping* v264 no6 p129 Je 2017

Cuisine of L.A *Los Angeles Magazine* p43 F 2017

cupcakes in costume E. CLARK *Parents* v91 no10 p82 O 2016

Curry You Can Carry color *Vegetarian Today* no2 p10 Ap 2017

Easy Squeezy color *O, The Oprah Magazine* p146 N 2017

EAT, MEMORY D. Wong Louie *Harper's Magazine* no2007 p39 Ag 2017

Eat these to fight allergies M. TAYLOR cartoon *Redbook* p88 My 2017

Fall Fumbles color *Consumer Reports* v82 no10 p67 O 2017

FAMILY AND FOOD *Successful Farming* v114 no10 p64 O 2016

Famines, fasts, and feasts A. Camille il *U.S. Catholic* v82 no6 p47 Je 2017

Fat Fictions: Don't get fooled by the fads when it comes to this nutrient A. FELLER *Dance Magazine* v91 no9 p46 S 2017

The Fawning Over Avocado Toast *Los Angeles Magazine* v61 no11 p66 N 2016

feel-good feasts C. Nash color *Health* v30 no10 p110 D 2016

Feel-Good Foods L. TURNER color *Better Nutrition* v79 no1 p58 Ja 2017

FEW THINGS BRING PEOPLE TOGETHER LIKE MAN'OUSHE R. ASSIL color *Bon Appetit* v62 no2 p61 Mr 2017

FLAT BELLY INDULGENCE E. WADE, T. GIDUS et al *USA Today Magazine* v145 no2858 p70 N 2016

FOOD FOR THOUGHT *Nutrition Action Health Letter* v44 no4 p16 My 2017

Foodie Feud J. LILEKS *National Review* v69 no11 p33 Je 12 2017

Fresh, Fast, Fabulous color *Health* v30 no10 p125 D 2016

From Far and Wide P. SHARPE *Texas Monthly* v45 no8 p22 Ag 2017

Get The Lead Out M. MELTON *Los Angeles Magazine* v61 no11 p20 N 2016

Go On, Have Some Dessert color *Health* v31 no7 p14 S 2017

GROCERY SHOPPING MADE EASY J. London color *Good Housekeeping* v263 no5 p152 N 2016

GUEST LIST: A monthly roundup of people we'd like to have over for drinks, food, and conversation *Washingtonian Magazine* v52 no8 p26 My 2017

The Happiness Effect M. D. SMITH color *Better Nutrition* v79 no1 p62 Ja 2017

HEALING Spices [Cover story] J. Jibrin and M. Bharadwaj color *Yoga Journal* no290 p83 Mr 2017

holiday gift kits L. TURNER color *Better Nutrition* v78 no12 p45 D 2016

HOME for the HOLIDAYS *Good Housekeeping* v263 no6 p16 D 2016

How Do You Say "Yum" Around the World? J. PRESS *Scholastic Choices* p6 O 2017

IF I WANT TO EAT EVERYTHING color *Wired* v25 no5 p5 My 2017

IN YOUR FACE! Calories everywhere you look L. MOYER *Nutrition Action Health Letter* v44 no1 p11 Ja/F 2017

Is It Germier To...? K. KLOSS *Reader's Digest* v188 no1124 p48 O 2016

The Kids' Table color *Good Housekeeping* v263 no5 p201 N 2016

Land of plenty J. Parrott color *U.S. Catholic* v82 no6 p12 Je 2017

Late Night Craven *Nutrition Action Health Letter* v43 no10 p16 D 2016

Let Them Eat veGan Cake l. mcguiness *Vegetarian Journal* v35 no4 p16 2016

The LONG GAME R. Haskell color *Vogue* v207 no10 p292 O 2017

Love in a dumpling J. Yogis color *Yoga Journal* no296 p96 N 2017

meal mash -ups G. KO *Parents* v91 no10 p126 O 2016

Mexican Linguine color *Vegetarian Today* no2 p26 Ap 2017

Mini Kitchen Makeover V. TWEED color *Better Nutrition* v79 no1 p10 Ja 2017

Mixing Bowl color *O, The Oprah Magazine* p140 Mr 2017

M-m-mmus *Nutrition Action Health Letter* v43 no10 p16 D 2016

THE MYTH OF SUPERFOOD C. Weinberg color *Men's Health* v32 no2 p53 Mr 2017

Noodles Made Healthy color *Health* v31 no1 p107 Ja 2017

Our Vegan Polish Spot Is So Polish, Polish-Americans Don't Think It's Polish T. SKOWRONSKI color *Bon Appetit* v62 no2 p69 Mr 2017

PALEO BASICS V. TWEED color *Better Nutrition* v79 no10 p58 O 2017

party on! (a budget) L. FENTON *Parents* v91 no9 p143 S 2016

PIZZA PARTY *Nutrition Action Health Letter* v44 no3 p14 Ap 2017

Pop-Tarts for Dinner J. KAY *Walrus* v14 no4 p66 My 2017

A quick-start guide to the latest food terminology *Harvard Health Letter* v42 no8 p3 Je 2017

Radical hospitality E. Sanna *U.S. Catholic* v82 no6 p4 Je 2017

Skinny Dips B. Lipton color *Health* v31 no1 p120 Ja 2017

Slash Refined Carbs All Day J. Andriakos color *Health* v31 no4 p114 My 2017

Smart Provisioning Z. Prochazka color *Sail* v48 no4 p75 Ap 2017

SPRING FORWARD E. Graves *Martha Stewart Living* p8 Mr 2017

Spring PASTA PRIMER A. Hickman color *Health* v31 no3 p88 Ap 2017

Start with a Rotisserie Chicken A. Hickman color *Health* v31 no4 p103 My 2017

Summer Slim Down L. TURNER color *Better Nutrition* p54 My 2017

SUPERFOOD SWEETS D. Wise color *Health* v31 no9 p98 N 2017

sweet charity color *Parents* v92 no5 p19 My 2017

take OM HOME M. Rabbitt color *Yoga Journal* no288 p96 D 2016

Test Your Iron Smarts V. TWEED color *Better Nutrition* p64 My 2017

Three Ways to Walk Off the Weight K. Canning color *Health* v31 no4 p53 My 2017

Tourist Traps: Tricks for eating healthy on tour K. BRADY *Dance Magazine* v91 no10 p38 O 2017

UPDATES: VEGAN FOOD IN CHAIN RESTAURANTS *Vegetarian Journal* v36 no3 p7 2017

Vegan Cooking Tips. Quick & Easy Tips for Working With Nutritional Yeast *Vegetarian Journal* v36 no3 p34 2017

veggie bits. Chicken-less Legs S. Gendler *Vegetarian Journal* v35 no4 p29 2016

veggie bits *Vegetarian Journal* v36 no3 p30 2017

Warm up to fall color *Health* v31 no9 p111 N 2017

Weird Foods Worth Trying S. Byrne, J. Calderone et al color *Consumer Reports* v82 no7 p14 Jl 2017

Welcome M. J. Posey *Cincinnati Magazine* v50 no8 p82 My 2017

WE'RE GONNA PARTY LIKE WE'RE IN POST-SOVIET RUSSIA B. MORALES color *Bon Appetit* v62 no2 p64 Mr 2017

What I Know for Sure Oprah color *O, The Oprah Magazine* p112 Jl 2017

What Is Aquafaba? L. TURNER color *Better Nutrition* p60 My 2017

What's in that kibble? A. Levi color *Health* v31 no8 p86 O 2017

Where to Eat Now *Texas Monthly* v45 no8 p84 Ag 2017

"WHY I LOVE not dieting" K. Miller color *Good Housekeeping* v263 no5 p159 N 2016

Why You Can't Rely on the Glycemic Index for Healthy Eating *Tufts University Health & Nutrition Letter* v34 no10 p6 D 2016

YES, THIS IS HEALTHY J. Gordinier cartoon color *Esquire* p23 Ap 2017

Your New Beauty Meal Plan A. C. Bacon and Y. Chu color *Glamour* v114 no11 p108 N 2016

Food & Agriculture Organization of the United Nations

Achieving and Maintaining Sustainable Fisheries J. Rice *UN Chronicle* v54 no1/2 p1 2017

Forestry for a Low-Carbon Future: Integrating Forests and Wood Products Into Climate Change Strategies A. E. Russell and B. M. Kumar bibl color *Environment* v59 no2 p16 Mr/Ap 2017

Food & Water Watch (Organization)

Frack Attack F. Madeson color *Progressive* p48 D 2016/Ja 2017

Food & wine pairing

The Case for Cases M. A. ROSS color *Bon Appetit* no11 p34 N 2017

CATEGORY BESTSELLERS C. JURIS chart *Publishers Weekly* v264 no12 p20 Mr 20 2017

Food additives

See also

Dietary supplements

Evidence Matters M. F. Jacobson *Nutrition Action Health Letter* v44 no3 p2 Ap 2017

I Got the Powder C. KWAK color *Bon Appetit* v62 no4 p22 Ap 2017

THE INGREDIENT GAME *Nutrition Action Health Letter* v44 no2 p9 Mr 2017

Food additives—Evaluation

SMARTEN UP TO SHRINK YOUR GUT C. Hansen color *Men's Health* v32 no9 p73 N 2017

Food allergy

FOOD ALLERGY RESCUE M. T. Murray color *Amazing Wellness* p66 Fall 2017

THE PEANUT DOCTOR IS IN L. WILLIAMSON color *Chicago* v66 no10 p28 O 2017

This Cupcake Could Kill Me...But This One Won't! K. SCHUG and J. PRESS *Scholastic Choices* v32 no5 p20 F 2017

Food allergy—Diet therapy

See also

Gluten-free diet

Antihistamine Alternatives E. A. KANE color *Better Nutrition* p24 My 2017

Food allergy—Prevention

food free-for-all K. CICERO color *Parents* v92 no4 p42 Ap 2017

Food allergy—Risk factors

His + Hers Food Allergies color *Health* v31 no8 p13 O 2017

Food analysis

FLAVOR QUEST *Better Homes & Gardens* v95 no5 p4 My 2017

mothers' DAY J. YONAN color *Better Homes & Gardens* v95 no5 p122 My 2017

What is American food? J. BAINBRIDGE *Atlanta* v57 no6 p56 O 2017

Where the worst type of fat is hiding in supermarket foods chart *Harvard Health Letter* v42 no3 p5 Ja 2017

Which Cooking Methods Are Healthiest? J. Andriakos color *Health* v31 no6 p128 Jl 2017

Food as gifts

The Gift of Food J. BALL-TUFFORD *Reader's Digest* v188 no1126 p50 D 2016/Ja 2017

Food banks

SUNDRY SAMARITANS J. DRILLING *Cincinnati Magazine* v50 no8 p106 My 2017

Food biotechnology

STUPID or AMAZING? J. HIRSCH color *Popular Mechanics* v193 no7 p108 S 2016

Food consumption

ARE YOU A SAVVY HOLIDAY EATER? K. Asp color *O, The Oprah Magazine* p124 D 2016

ASK DR. OZ: How do I avoid a HOLIDAY FOOD "COMA"? M. OZ color *Good Housekeeping* v265 no5 p71 N 2017

The Clean-Plate Club V. MATUS *Weekly Standard* v22 no4 p5 O 3 2016

How to Eat As Much As Possible (ACCORDING TO SCIENCE) S. BUSHWICK color *Reader's Digest* v190 no1135 p128 N 2017

Party Smart M. DiTrolio color *Men's Health* v31 no10 p68 D 2016

The Reasons We Buy (and Eat) Too Much Food P. Chandon *Harvard Business Review Digital Articles* p2 D 20 2016

Shares of Food Commodities Purchased Away From Home Vary by Commodity Biing-Hwan Lin *Amber Waves: The Economics of Food, Farming, Natural Resources, & Rural America* p26 Ap 2017

Supplement Support For Your New Year's Resolutions D. N. JACKSON color *Muscle & Performance* v9 no1 p58 Ja 2017

YOU BETTER WATCH OUT A. Atkins cartoon *O, The Oprah Magazine* p121 D 2016

Food consumption—History

Sugar Rush: The unsavory history of an insatiable American craving J. R. GRITZ *Smithsonian* v48 no2 p16 My 2017

Food containers

See also

Lunchboxes

CASE STUDIES F. VIGNA color *Martha Stewart Living* p120 S 2017

Neat Eats: 6 Great Food-Container Tricks K. KLOSS *Reader's Digest* v189 no1127 p46 F 2017

Superhydrophobic L. SCHLEY cartoon *Discover* v38 no3 p14 Ap 2017

Food containers—Evaluation

Chill'n A. BENNETT color *Cabin Living* p87 Ja/F 2017

PACK IT UP, PACK IT IN M. Khemsurov color *Bloomberg Businessweek* no4493 p84 O 3 2016

Food contamination

Floor Plan S. Mirsky color *Scientific American* v316 no4 p80 Ap 2017

Food cooperatives

CANOVA *South Dakota Magazine* v33 no3 p40 S/O 2017

Food deserts

LOST IN THE SUPERMARKET S. T. PAULSEN cartoon *Mother Jones* v42 no1 p64 Ja/F 2017

Food festivals

Arts, Culture & Entertainment *Virginia Living* p60 2017 Best 20of Virginia

BREAKING ALL THE REUELS R. Reuel *Virginia Living* p60 2017 Best 20of Virginia

Can't-Miss Fall Food Festivals *Atlanta* v57 no5 p148 S 2017

DESTINATIONS *Atlanta* v57 no5 p147 S 2017

DON'T MISS LIST *Atlanta* v57 no3 p36 Jl 2017

DON'T MISS LIST NOVEMBER 2016 *Sea Magazine* v108 no10 pPNW-11 O 2016

DON'T MISS LIST OCTOBER 2016 *Sea Magazine* v108 no10 pPNW-11 O 2016

EVENTS *Virginia Living* p15 2017 Smoke & Salt

Food from the Heart P. Hise color *Virginia Living* v15 no5 p43 Ag 2017

Foodie Festivities E. JACKSON *Atlanta* v56 no8 p72 D 2016

FUN! FOOD! FEST! [Cover story] F. ESKER color *New Orleans Magazine* v52 no1 p66 S 2017

THE GUIDE / 06.17 M. WAKIM *Los Angeles Magazine* v62 no6 p54 Je 2017

THE GUIDE / 09.17: 12 CAN'T-MISS EVENTS IN SEPTEMBER M. WAKIM *Los Angeles Magazine* v62 no9 p66 S 2017

THE GUIDE M. WAKIM *Los Angeles Magazine* p88 Ap 2017

JULY/AUGUST K. Massicot color *Louisiana Life* v37 no6 p62 Jl/Ag 2017

October F. ESKER color *New Orleans Magazine* v51 no12 p28 O 2017

Out & About J. B. ills color *Yankee* p80 Mr 2017

Out & About *Martha Stewart Living* no268 p10 O 2016

Sonic Boom *Los Angeles Magazine* v62 no6 p52 Je 2017

TOP PICKS F. Esker color *New Orleans Magazine* v51 no8 p28 Je 2017

Food habits

6 Winning Super Bowl Snack Ideas *Tufts University Health & Nutrition Letter* v34 no12 p3 F 2017

A BETTER BARBECUE A. Hickman color *Health* v31 no5 p90 Je 2017

Building a Better Gut E. A. KANE color *Better Nutrition* v78 no12 p32 D 2016

CLASS-CONFLICT CUISINE S. JONES bw *Nation* v305 no11 p28 O 30 2017

The Clean-Plate Club V. MATUS *Weekly Standard* v22 no4 p5 O 3 2016

Clutter Control: Curbing disorder can radically boost your well-being S. KRAUSS WHITBOURNE *Psychology Today* v50 no5 p39 S/O 2017

Double Down on Your Veggie Efforts S. SEA GOLD color *Parents* v92 no5 p22 My 2017

Eat Well to Keep Mind Sharp [Cover story] *Tufts University Health & Nutrition Letter* v34 no12 p1 F 2017

EAT YOUR WAY TO BETTER HEALTH M. OZ color *O, The Oprah Magazine* p86 S 2017

eat your way to GORGEOUS M. MANNARINO color *Seventeen* p144 Ja 1 2017

The Everything Guide to Seafood K. Canning color *Health* v31 no5 p111 Je 2017

FEEDING ON FEAR L. Goldman color *Women's Health* v14 no6 p100 Jl 2017

FLAT BELLY INDULGENCE E. WADE, T. GIDUS et al *USA Today Magazine* v145 no2858 p70 N 2016

Ford Fry: Chef and mega-restaurateur J. Bainbridge *Atlanta* v57 no5 p66 S 2017

Go Ahead, Stop Counting Calories M. Oaklander color *Health* v31 no5 p45 Je 2017

Got Diabetes? What to Eat *Tufts University Health & Nutrition Letter* v34 no12 p4 F 2017

GREAT BEFORE, GREATER AFTER! A. K. LAIRD *Women's Health* v14 no1 p12 Ja/F 2017

HEALTHY LIVING MADE EASY color *Health* v31 no1 p12 Ja 2017

The HOOSIER KITCHEN J. BALL, S. DUGGER et al *Indianapolis Monthly* v12 no40 p60 Ag 2017

How to Escape Zombie Eating K. Dinardo color *Health* v30 no9 p47 N 2016

Instagram Yourself Slim color *Health* v31 no7 p17 S 2017

Issa Rae J. ZAMBRANO color *O, The Oprah Magazine* p28 Ag 2017

Joseph Guay & Tara Lee J. BAINBIDGE *Atlanta* v57 no6 p62 O 2017

Late Night Craven *Nutrition Action Health Letter* v43 no10 p16 D 2016

Losing Big Saved My Life L. Murray color *Health* v30 no9 p54 N 2016

MAKING THE CUT L. McGLASHAN chart color *Muscle & Performance* v9 no4 p34 Ap 2017

Mastering Portion Control *Tufts University Health & Nutrition Letter* v34 no11 p4 Ja 2017

ME VS. THE BOY J. KITA and P. KITA bw color graph map *Men's Health* v32 no8 p108 O 2017

The mindful diet M. RABBITT color *Yoga Journal* p110 2016 Special Issue

Modern Vegan Comfort Food D. Daneils-Zeller *Vegetarian Journal* v35 no1 p18 2016

MOST LIKELY TO NERD OUT M. Devash bw color *Women's Health* v14 no6 p107 Jl 2017

NOTE FROM THE COORDINATORS. NATURAL FOODS: UPSCALE OR DOWNSCALE? MANY ROLES FOR PROMOTING VEGANISM D. Wasserman and C. Stabler *Vegetar-*

ian Journal v35 no2 p4 2016

not picky [Cover story] S. KUZEMCHAK color *Parents* v92 no7 p44 Jl 2017

OFF LINE color *Bike Magazine* v24 no1 p146 Ja/F 2017

PHARM TO TABLE M. OATMAN color *Mother Jones* v42 no6 p72 N/D 2017

Picky Eating: When to Worry *Parents* p56 2015

The Reasons We Buy (and Eat) Too Much Food P. Chandon *Harvard Business Review Digital Articles* p2 D 20 2016

reviews. EATING EARTH D. Wasserman *Vegetarian Journal* v35 no4 p30 2016

RITUAL LIZE IT *Los Angeles Magazine* p118 Ap 2017

Scrounging for sustenance J. LORINC color graph *Maclean's* v129 no44 p64 N 7 2016

Talking to Kids about GMOs M. D. SMITH color *Better Nutrition* v79 no4 p66 Ap 2017

This Is You on Sugar A. Levi color *Health* v31 no3 p68 Ap 2017

U.S. Diets Still Out of Balance With Dietary Recommendations J. Bentley *Amber Waves: The Economics of Food, Farming, Natural Resources, & Rural America* p18 Jl 2017

Why Do People Eat Vegetarian and Vegan Meals When Dining Out? *Vegetarian Journal* v36 no1 p22 2017

You just broke a resolution M. S. Kraftsow color *Yoga Journal* p42 2016 Special Issue

Food habits—Evaluation

How I Shed 72 Pounds L. Murray color *Health* v31 no2 p58 Mr 2017

Food habits—Management

Body Weight Fell Following Mandatory Calorie-Labeling Laws for New York Restaurant Menus B. Restrepo *Amber Waves: The Economics of Food, Farming, Natural Resources, & Rural America* p11 F 2017

Food habits—Physiological aspects

Beware the Late-Night Lag *Atlanta* v57 no6 p58 O 2017

Food habits—United States

NEWSBITES [Cover story] *Tufts University Health & Nutrition Letter* v34 no8 p1 O 2016

Food habits—United States—History

Make America **eat Again C. CALDWELL cartoon *Weekly Standard* v22 no19 p5 Ja 23 2017

Food handling

30 Ways to EAT MORE VEGGIES [Cover story] L. Turner color *Better Nutrition* v79 no11 p60 N 2017

Good Food: Meat Without Meds J. BROWN color *Prevention* v69 no11 p28 N 2017

KITCHEN-TESTED TIPS J. Carson, M. Krajek et al color *Vegetarian Today* no2 p4 Ap 2017

Pack a Safe Lunch *Parents* v91 no10 p30 O 2016

warm up to winter fruit K. CICERO *Parents* v92 no1 p26 Ja 2017

Food in art

ARTISTIC LIBERTY AT THE TABLE N. Strochlic color *National Geographic* v231 no2 p16 F 2017

THE PANCAKE PICASSO E. O'NEILL *Missouri Life* v43 no6 p26 O/N 2017

Food in literature

CATEGORY BESTSELLERS chart *Publishers Weekly* v264 no20 p16 My 15 2017

Food industrial waste

FASHIONING FOOD WASTE C. Zuckerman color *National Geographic* v231 no5 p14 My 2017

Food industry

See also

Beverage industry

Food prices

Grocery industry

Snack food industry

2017: the Year of Plant-Based Meat? M. F. Jacobson *Nutrition Action Health Letter* v44 no5 p2 Je 2017

24 HOURS AT LAMBSTOCK P. HISE *Virginia Living* v15 no1 p66 D 2016

3D PRINTED FOOD L. SOROKANICH color *Popular Mechanics* p78 D 2016/Ja 2017

BIG FOOD'S MASS CEO EXODUS B. Kowitt color *Fortune* v176 no4 p138 S 15 2017

Big Food Swallows the Meal-Kit Hype J. Alsever color *Fortune* v176 no4 p27 S 15 2017

The Billion-Dollar Opportunity in Single-Serve Food E. Yoon and M. Stacy *Harvard Business Review Digital Articles* p2 O 23 2015

FOOD TECH'S NEW BUZZWORD: "FERMENTATION" B. Kowitt color *Fortune* v175 no5 p15 Ap 1 2017

THE FUTURE OF FOOD [Cover story] Z. Carpenter color *Nation* v305 no11 p14 O 30 2017

NOTHING BUT THE TRUTH? L. MOYER and B. LIEBMAN *Nutrition Action Health Letter* v44 no8 p8 O 2017

SECOND TO NONE [Cover story] J. KRAMER bw color *Bon Appetit* p134 S 2017

Watch what you eat K. Clarke color *U.S. Catholic* v82 no6 p42 Je 2017

Yes, Atlanta Has "Bodegas" G. CHAPMAN *Atlanta* v57 no2 p49 Je 2017

YO, YOGURT! M. MANNARINO color *Better Homes & Gardens* v95 no6 p166 Je 2017

Food industry—Canada

The best meat you don't eat J. RICHLER color *Maclean's* v130 no2 p70 Mr 2017

Food industry—China

China's Foodmakers Try New Growth Recipes B. Einhorn and R. Chang color diag *Bloomberg Businessweek* no4524 p22 My 29 2017

Food industry—Employees—Labor unions

A fair deal for food workers A. Frykholm color *Christian Century* v134 no2 p10 Ja 18 2017

Food industry—Mergers

Big Food Is Going to Get Even Bigger J. Kell color diag *Fortune* v175 no4 p11 Mr 15 2017

Run! It's 3G Capital! C. Giammona and N. Buhayar cartoon *Bloomberg Businessweek* no4510 p31 F 6 2017

Food industry—Moral & ethical aspects

NEWSBITES [Cover story] *Tufts University Health & Nutrition Letter* v34 no10 p1 D 2016

Food industry—Quality control

The Growing Fight Against Food Fraud A. Park color *Time* v189 no3 p15 Ja 16 2017

Food industry—United States

Big Food Is Going to Get Even Bigger J. Kell color diag *Fortune* v175 no4 p11 Mr 15 2017

ERS's Updated Food Access Research Atlas Shows an Increase in Low-Income and Low-Supermarket Access Areas in 2015 A. Rhone and M. Ver Ploeg *Amber Waves: The Economics of Food, Farming, Natural Resources, & Rural America* p1 F 2017

Good Food Rising A. Lappé color *Earth Island Journal* v32 no4 p13 Wint 2017

Land of plenty J. Parrott color *U.S. Catholic* v82 no6 p12 Je 2017

Low-Income Areas With Low Supermarket Access Increased in Urban Areas, But Not in Rural Areas, Between 2010 and 2015 A. Rhone *Amber Waves: The Economics of Food, Farming, Natural Resources, & Rural America* p22 Ap 2017

U.S. Per Capita Availability of Red Meat, Poultry, and Fish Lowest Since 1983 J. Bentley *Amber Waves: The Economics of Food, Farming, Natural Resources, & Rural America* p18 F 2017

Food industry—Waste

Turn Food Scraps Into POULTRY FEASTS J. Salatin *Mother Earth News* no281 p99 Ap/My 2017

Food industry—Waste—Management

THE CLIQUE THAT'S CHANGING HOW SCHOOLKIDS EAT C. LEU *Sierra* v101 no5 p46 S/O 2016

DIRT, CHEAP R. Martin *Mother Earth News* no279 p55 D/Ja 2017

Food labeling

    See also

    Shelf-life dating of food

BREAD WINNERS L. MOYER and B. LIEBMAN *Nutrition Action Health Letter* v44 no2 p13 Mr 2017

Chill Out & Get Healthy Nicole *Better Nutrition* v79 no6 p6 Je 2017

Choose a Healthier Cereal *Parents* v91 no12 p24 D 2016

A Diet of Good Information M. L. Tellado *Consumer Reports* v82 no11 p4 N 2017

D-NAME RATING *Nutrition Action Health Letter* v44 no2 p14 Mr 2017

Eat Smarter, Eat Healthier [Cover story] S. Wadyka, C. Roberts et

al color *Consumer Reports* v82 no11 p18 N 2017

The Food Industry's Urgent Question: What Is Milk? B. Kowitt color *Fortune* v176 no3 p17 S 1 2017

Health Claims On Your Food *Tufts University Health & Nutrition Letter* v35 no1 p4 Mr 2017

Help Create a Veggie World *Vegetarian Journal* v35 no1 p32 2016

THE INGREDIENT GAME *Nutrition Action Health Letter* v44 no2 p9 Mr 2017

Is your salad dressing hurting your healthy diet? Bottled dressings are often rich sources of saturated fat, calories, sodium, and added sugar chart *Harvard Health Letter* v42 no7 p5 My 2017

Keeping Up with the "Clean Label" Movement A. Winston *Harvard Business Review Digital Articles* p2 O 30 2015

Mashed Potatoes & Minced Words *Consumer Reports* v82 no11 p67 N 2017

NEWtrition Facts|Labels L. MOYER and B. LIEBMAN *Nutrition Action Health Letter* v44 no7 p10 S 2017

NOTHING BUT THE TRUTH? L. MOYER and B. LIEBMAN *Nutrition Action Health Letter* v44 no8 p8 O 2017

NUTRITION LABEL Breakdown O. Manno chart img *Dance Spirit* v21 no3 p28 Mr 2017

Talking to Kids about GMOs M. D. SMITH color *Better Nutrition* v79 no4 p66 Ap 2017

Voluntary Labeling of Chicken "Raised Without Antibiotics" Has Posed Challenges for Firms and Consumers M. Bowman and K. K. Marshall *Amber Waves: The Economics of Food, Farming, Natural Resources, & Rural America* p35 S 2016

We Deserve Better M. F. Jacobson *Nutrition Action Health Letter* v44 no6 p2 Jl/Ag 2017

What a Year! M. F. Jacobson *Nutrition Action Health Letter* v43 no10 p2 D 2016

Food labeling laws

NEWSBITES [Cover story] *Tufts University Health & Nutrition Letter* v35 no7 p1 S 2017

Food labeling—Law & legislation

Body Weight Fell Following Mandatory Calorie-Labeling Laws for New York Restaurant Menus B. Restrepo *Amber Waves: The Economics of Food, Farming, Natural Resources, & Rural America* p11 F 2017

National GMO Labeling Bill Signed Into Law S. Stonebrook *Mother Earth News* no279 p6 D/Ja 2017

Food labeling—Methodology

Voilà! France's Next Culinary Advance bw *Bloomberg Businessweek* no4494 p12 O 10 2016

Food labeling—Research

Voilà! France's Next Culinary Advance bw *Bloomberg Businessweek* no4494 p12 O 10 2016

Food labeling—Standards

Coming to Labels: Added Sugars *Tufts University Health & Nutrition Letter* v35 no3 p6 My 2017

Food law & legislation

Dig In: The Food Freedom Act L. Noyes *Mother Earth News* no282 p10 Je/Jl 2017

Food Network Star (TV program)

LOCAL FLAVOR A. McLellan color *Louisiana Life* v38 no1 p52 S/O 2017

Food packaging

Bean Good? *Nutrition Action Health Letter* v43 no10 p15 D 2016

Neat Eats: 6 Great Food-Container Tricks K. KLOSS *Reader's Digest* v189 no1127 p46 F 2017

Taking Out the Meal-Kit Trash A. Nova color *Money* v46 no8 p74 S 2017

Food poisoning prevention

Avoiding health risks at the farmers' market *Harvard Health Letter* v42 no11 p3 S 2017

Build a better cookout *Harvard Health Letter* v42 no9 p3 Jl 2017

Great Grilling L. MOYER *Nutrition Action Health Letter* v44 no6 p11 Jl/Ag 2017

Food poisoning—Risk factors

Recipe for Disaster B. Lutz color *New Orleans Magazine* v51 no9 p34 Jl 2017

Food poisoning—Treatment

RX FOR FOOD POISONING J. Martin color *Better Nutrition* v78 no11 p26 N 2016

Food portions

The Billion-Dollar Opportunity in Single-Serve Food E. Yoon

and M. Stacy *Harvard Business Review Digital Articles* p2 O 23 2015

The HOOSIER KITCHEN J. BALL, S. DUGGER et al *Indianapolis Monthly* v12 no40 p60 Ag 2017

The Simple Trick to Eating Less Dessert color *Health* v31 no4 p14 My 2017

Food preferences

ASK TUFTS EXPERTS A. H. Lichtenstein *Tufts University Health & Nutrition Letter* v34 no8 p8 O 2016

COMMUNITY color *Vegetarian Times* v43 no2 p10 N/D 2016

double the number of foods your kid likes! K. CICERO *Parents* v91 no11 p64 N 2016

Eat What You Love Already color *Health* v30 no9 p14 N 2016

FOOD TRENDS G. Johnston *Successful Farming* v114 no10 p60 O 2016

Healthy Food Fun V. TWEED color *Better Nutrition* v79 no6 p8 Je 2017

How Can I Get My Toddler to Eat Meat? *Parents* v92 no2 p28 F 2017

RITUAL LIZE IT *Los Angeles Magazine* p118 Ap 2017

Food presentation

ABOVE & BEYOND cartoon *New Yorker* v92 no48 p12 F 6 2017

Food prices

5 Cheap Things Restaurants Love to Overcharge You For J. Calfas color *Money* v46 no6 p15 Jl 2017

International Food Security Assessment, 2017-2027 B. Meade and K. Thome *Amber Waves: The Economics of Food, Farming, Natural Resources, & Rural America* p26 Je 2017

Since 2009, Restaurant Prices Have Generally Risen Faster Than Grocery Store Prices A. Kuhns and S. Rehkamp *Amber Waves: The Economics of Food, Farming, Natural Resources, & Rural America* p53 Ag 2017

Food processing machinery—Evaluation

TOP TOOLS color *Good Housekeeping* v265 no4 p64e O 2017

Food production

The Future of Food K. MAST bw color *Discover* v38 no6 p38 Jl/Ag 2017

Global Demand for Food Is Rising. Can We Meet It? M. Elferink and F. Schierhorn *Harvard Business Review Digital Articles* p2 Ap 7 2016

The Thread J. Eise, A. Reyes et al *New York Times Magazine* p10 O 23 2016

UNITED STATES OF CORN C. Zuckerman color *National Geographic* v231 no2 p18 F 2017

Food quality

Augie's K. MONTGOMERY *Arizona Highways* v93 no9 p14 S 2017

editor's letter A. RAPOPORT bw *Bon Appetit* p14 S 2017

RESTAURANT OF THE YEAR A. KNOWLTON color *Bon Appetit* p103 S 2017

THE TEXANIST *Texas Monthly* v45 no9 p152 S 2017

Food recall

Increased Consumer Sensitivity to Food Safety Raised Financial Costs of Ground Beef Recalls F. Kuchler and R. M. Morrison *Amber Waves: The Economics of Food, Farming, Natural Resources, & Rural America* p1 O 2016

Food relief

SNAP JUDGMENT D. d'Amora graph *Mother Jones* v41 no6 p14 N/D 2016

USDA's FoodAPS: Providing Insights Into U.S. Food Demand and Food Assistance Programs J. E. Todd, L. Tiehen et al *Amber Waves: The Economics of Food, Farming, Natural Resources, & Rural America* p42 Ag 2017

Food safety

Blowin' in the Wind T. NINTEMANN *USA Today Magazine* v146 no2868 p73 S 2017

The California Leafy Greens Industry Provides an Example of an Established Food Safety System L. Calvin, H. Jensen et al *Amber Waves: The Economics of Food, Farming, Natural Resources, & Rural America* p43 Je 2017

China's Foodmakers Try New Growth Recipes B. Einhorn and R. Chang color diag *Bloomberg Businessweek* no4524 p22 My 29 2017

Good Food: Meat Without Meds J. BROWN color *Prevention* v69 no11 p28 N 2017

Regulation, Market Signals, and the Provision of Food Safety in

Meat and Poultry M. Ollinger and M. Taylor Rhodes *Amber Waves: The Economics of Food, Farming, Natural Resources, & Rural America* p1 My 2017

Food safety—Lawsuits & claims

China Retailers' Latest Woe: Food Vigilantes color *Bloomberg Businessweek* no4535 p18 Ag 28 2017

Food sales & prices

LOST IN THE SUPERMARKET S. T. PAULSEN cartoon *Mother Jones* v42 no1 p64 Ja/F 2017

Purchases of Foods by Convenience Type Driven by Prices, Income, and Advertising A. Okrent *Amber Waves: The Economics of Food, Farming, Natural Resources, & Rural America* p33 N 2016

The Raw Deal M. H. LEE *Los Angeles Magazine* v62 no9 p111 S 2017

The Rise of the Ailment Shopper B. Kowitt diag *Fortune* v174 no6 p14 N 1 2016

Food science

See also

Food safety

ROLL CALL: Reporting for duty: I tracked down a long-lost IM recipe M. RUBINO *Indianapolis Monthly* v12 no40 p73 Ag 2017

Food security

10 UP & COMERS: NADIA SHAKOOR B. Freese *Successful Farming* v115 no8 p44 Je/Jl 2017

CALORIES COUNT K. Nowakowski diag *National Geographic* v232 no4 p8 O 2017

Election Fever A. H. McGowan *Environment* v59 no1 p2 2017

Food Insecurity Among Children Declined to Pre-Recession Levels in 2015 A. Coleman-Jensen and M. Smith *Amber Waves: The Economics of Food, Farming, Natural Resources, & Rural America* p41 N 2016

Genome editors take on crops A. Scheben and D. Edwards bibl diag *Science* v355 no6330 p1122 Mr 17 2017

International Food Security Assessment, 2017-2027 B. Meade and K. Thome *Amber Waves: The Economics of Food, Farming, Natural Resources, & Rural America* p26 Je 2017

THE PERILOUS NATURE OF FOOD SUPPLIES: Natural Hazards, Social Vulnerability, and Disaster Resilience S. L. Cutter chart color graph map *Environment* v59 no1 p4 2017

Rage Against the Dying of the Reefs D. Helvarg color *Progressive* v81 no5 p15 Je/Jl 2017

Remote sensing for analyzing smallholder farm yields color *Science* v355 no6330 p1170 Mr 17 2017

Unexpected Hikes in Energy Prices Increase the Likelihood of Food Insecurity C. Tuttle *Amber Waves: The Economics of Food, Farming, Natural Resources, & Rural America* p9 Jl 2017

Water and food security in a changing world Brian I.6Baker *Monthly Labor Review* p1 Mr 2017

Food service

See also

Cafeterias

Catering services

Mobile food services

Restaurants

Bean Counter J. K. WOLFE *Cincinnati Magazine* v50 no6 p145 Mr 2017

Cooks, Illustrated *Cincinnati Magazine* v50 no6 p82 Mr 2017

DINING GUIDE *Cincinnati Magazine* v50 no6 p146 Mr 2017

FEAST YOUR EYES A. BRANDT *Cincinnati Magazine* v50 no6 p65 Mr 2017

FOOD FOR THOUGHT *Nutrition Action Health Letter* v44 no6 p16 Jl/Ag 2017

Future World: Food K. DE SEVE color *National Geographic Kids* no472 p24 Ag 2017

The Grill N. Niarchos color *New Yorker* v93 no19 p15 Jl 3 2017

Malta Made Me Do It M. Peters color *Conde Nast Traveler* v52 no9 p45 O 2017

Meeting Place J. ANDREWS *South Dakota Magazine* v32 no6 p36 Mr/Ap 2017

Modern Diner A. TRAVERSO *Yankee* v81 no1 p62 Ja/F 2017

NEW KIDS ON THE BLOCK J. DRILLING *Cincinnati Magazine* v50 no6 p81 Mr 2017

Q&A: HOME-DELIVERED MEAL KITS *Tufts University Health & Nutrition Letter* p4 S 2017 Supplement

Sliced, Sealed, Delivered J. ZYMAN *Atlanta* v56 no9 p53 Ja 2017

Uber's Food Delivery Experiment in Barcelona J. P. V. Sampere *Harvard Business Review Digital Articles* p2 F 25 2015

WHERE TO EAT NOW *Cincinnati Magazine* v50 no6 p62 Mr 2017

Food service—Economic aspects

Selling China On Cheese color graph *Bloomberg Businessweek* no4514 p20 Mr 13 2017

Food service—Evaluation

Boho Bistro J. DRILLING *Cincinnati Magazine* v50 no6 p142 Mr 2017

Golden Girls L. B. SUTER *Los Angeles Magazine* p46 Ap 2017

MEXICAN EATS *Washingtonian Magazine* v52 no1 p95 O 2017

Restaurant GUIDE color map *Indianapolis Monthly* v41 no2 p154 S 2017

Food service—Government policy

HOW A TACO TRUCK GETS STALLED P. Marinova color *Fortune* v174 no6 p86 N 1 2016

Food service—Marketing

How a Food-Ordering App Broke into a Crowded Market B. Gilad *Harvard Business Review Digital Articles* p2 N 25 2015

Food shortages

How to Help Africa Feed Itself A. Bjerga and S. Gebre *Bloomberg Businessweek* no4520 p20 My 1 2017

One Meal a Day L. PALMER color *New Republic* v248 no7 p32 Jl 2017

Food spoilage prevention

Forage with the Falling Fruit Map *Mother Earth News* no284 p7 O/N 2017

Food stamps—United States

Amazon Goes After The Walmart Shopper S. Soper and C. Giammona *Bloomberg Businessweek* no4508 p19 Ja 23 2017

CODE CRACKING YIREN LU color *New York Times Magazine* p39 N 13 2016

Food standards

The Hidden Story of Tasteless Chicken V. TWEED color *Better Nutrition* v79 no10 p10 O 2017

Food steamers

Essentials diag *Backpacker* v45 no3 p97 Ap 2017

THE ONE-POT COOKER cartoon color *Men's Health* v32 no8 p86 O 2017

Steam Power C. CHAEY color *Bon Appetit* v62 no4 p46 Ap 2017

Food steamers—Evaluation

MARKET WATCH *Los Angeles Magazine* v62 no9 p112 S 2017

Food storage

Hearty Italian Ragu color *Vegetarian Today* no2 p18 Ap 2017

make over your fridge K. CICERO *Parents* v91 no10 p110 O 2016

Pick Your Own *Nutrition Action Health Letter* v44 no4 p15 My 2017

Food substitutes

The Food Industry's Urgent Question: What Is Milk? B. Kowitt color *Fortune* v176 no3 p17 S 1 2017

Food supply

See also

Famines

Food consumption

Global Demand for Food Is Rising. Can We Meet It? M. Elferink and F. Schierhorn *Harvard Business Review Digital Articles* p2 Ap 7 2016

THE PERILOUS NATURE OF FOOD SUPPLIES: Natural Hazards, Social Vulnerability, and Disaster Resilience S. L. Cutter chart color graph map *Environment* v59 no1 p4 2017

Why Sourcing Local Food Is So Hard for Restaurants N. Torres *Harvard Business Review Digital Articles* p2 Je 15 2016

Food supply—China

CHINA'S $43 BILLION BID FOR FOOD SECURITY G. Colvin color diag *Fortune* v175 no6 p78 My 1 2017

Food supply—Environmental aspects

The Climate-Change Diet J. Worland color *Time* v188 no27-28 p16 D 26 2016

Food supply—Great Britain

FEEDING THE ARMY color *Archaeology* v70 no3 p33 My/Je 2017

Food tourism

Bull City E. WARTZMAN color *Bon Appetit* no11 p74 N 2017

Food writers

Pete Wells J. Crelin *Current Biography* v78 no1 p91 Ja 2017

Foodborne diseases

The California Leafy Greens Industry Provides an Example of an Established Food Safety System L. Calvin, H. Jensen et al *Amber Waves: The Economics of Food, Farming, Natural Resources, & Rural America* p43 Je 2017

Trouble in Tropics K. Pitz color *Oceanus* v51 no2 p60 Wint 2016

Foodborne diseases—Risk factors

Roach Buster B. Lutz color *New Orleans Magazine* v51 no5 p34 Mr 2017

Food—Caloric content

ARE YOU A SAVVY HOLIDAY EATER? K. Asp color *O, The Oprah Magazine* p124 D 2016

A Climber's Guide to Food K. CORRIGAN color *Climbing* no350 p36 D 2016/Ja 2017

Eat This, Not That! color *AARP: The Magazine* v59 no3A p32 Ap/My 2016

The Exercise Paradox [Cover story] H. Pontzer color graph *Scientific American* v316 no2 p26 F 2017

Get the Party Started! R. Meltzer Warren color *Consumer Reports* v82 no1 p9 Ja 2017

Step Away From the Sticky Bun! T. Calvo chart color *Consumer Reports* v82 no3 p36 Mr 2017

Food—Carbohydrate content

ASK TUFTS EXPERTS A. H. Lichtenstein *Tufts University Health & Nutrition Letter* v34 no8 p8 O 2016

Slash Refined Carbs All Day J. Andriakos color *Health* v31 no4 p114 My 2017

Food—Charts, diagrams, etc.

OUR GUIDE TO THE FUTURE OF FOOD *Nation* v305 no11 p23 O 30 2017

Food—Composition

See also

Food—Carbohydrate content

Food—Fat content

Food—Sugar content

THE FOOD ISSUE J. DOWNER *New York Times Magazine* p37 O 9 2016

Food—Economic aspects

families, finances, and the future *Parents* v91 no10 p118 O 2016

NEWS BITES *Tufts University Health & Nutrition Letter* v35 no1 p1 Mr 2017

Food—Evaluation

See also

Canned foods—Evaluation

24 TOP MUSCLE FOODS P. KITA color *Men's Health* v32 no7 p108 S 2017

BREAKFAST/DRINKS/DINNER... A. JURRIES color *Backpacker* v45 no3 p106 Ap 2017

GET ON BOARD J. R. FULLER color *Chicago* v66 no10 p52 O 2017

Give Thanks by Giving Food *USA Today Magazine* v145 no2858 p72 N 2016

The New Super Bowls R. Meltzer Warren chart color *Consumer Reports* v82 no10 p42 O 2017

The O List color *O, The Oprah Magazine* p47 Ag 2017

The Six Smartest Fast-Food Lunches J. STEWART bw color *Men's Health* v32 no5 p94 Je 2017

The S'more, the Merrier color *Martha Stewart Living* p32 Jl/Ag 2017

SUPERMARKET HEROES color *Women's Health* v14 no9 p106 N 2017

Food—Export & import trade

Follow the Money *Earth Island Journal* v32 no4 p9 Wint 2017

Food—Fat content

Calories Count V. TWEED color *Better Nutrition* v79 no3 p72 Mr 2017

Peanut Love color *Better Nutrition* v79 no3 p58 Mr 2017

Plant Oils: Are They All Good for You? V. TWEED color *Better Nutrition* v79 no4 p72 Ap 2017

Smart Fat Choices Might Slow Arthritis Progression [Cover story] *Tufts University Health & Nutrition Letter* v34 no8 p1 O 2016

STUFF WE LOVE color *Yoga Journal* no291 p22 My 2017

Food—Fermentation

Sour Power *Atlanta* v56 no9 p56 Ja 2017

Food industry—Charts, diagrams, etc.

PROTEIN POWDERS: Certifications & Label Lingo V. Tweed chart color *Amazing Wellness* v9 no1 p14 Wint 2017

Food—Iron content

Iron Will L. Claverie *New Orleans Homes & Lifestyles* v20 no1 p28 Wint 2016

Food—News briefs

FOODSTUFFS J. ZYMAN, C. VAN DUSEN et al *Atlanta* v56 no9 p54 Ja 2017

Food—Physiological aspects

6 FOOD MYTHS YOU CAN FORGET J. SCHILDHOUSE color *Muscle & Performance* v9 no5 p26 My 2017

Fuel Injector J. Fuchs and T. Keith color *Sports Illustrated* v127 no2 p24 Jl 17 2017

it takes two H. LEVINE *Better Homes & Gardens* v94 no11 p156 N 2016

Staving Off Cravings color *Prevention* v69 no7 p10 Jl 2017

Your Deep-Sleep Diet B. RISHER chart color *Men's Health* v32 no7 p68 S 2017

Food—Political aspects

BIG FOOD STRIKES BACK M. POLLAN color *New York Times Magazine* p40 O 9 2016

Food—Psychological aspects

LET THEM EAT CAKE S. FENNESSY *Atlanta* v56 no9 p16 Ja 2017

Food—Quality—Evaluation

LITTLE EFFORT, BIG FLAVOR B. Lipton color *Health* v31 no2 p110 Mr 2017

Food—Safety measures

The Growing Fight Against Food Fraud A. Park color *Time* v189 no3 p15 Ja 16 2017

Pack a Safe Lunch *Parents* v91 no10 p30 O 2016

Food security—Charts, diagrams, etc.

What Is Very Low Food Security and Who Experiences It A. Coleman-Jensen and M. Smith color *Amber Waves: The Economics of Food, Farming, Natural Resources, & Rural America* p38 D 2016

Food—Sensory evaluation

See also

Wine tasting

Food—Sodium content

PIE IN THE SKY C. KUMMER *New York Times Magazine* p67 O 9 2016

Foodstirs (Company)

IN THE KITCHEN WITH SARAH MICHELLE GELLAR I. Biedenharn color *Entertainment Weekly* no1465 p60 My 12 2017

Food—Study & teaching

Why Teach Kids About Food V. Tweed color *Amazing Wellness* v9 no4 p16 Summ 2017

Food—Sugar content

the health nut A. Brightfield cartoon color *Better Homes & Gardens* v95 no3 p146 Mr 2017

THE TRUTH ABOUT Sugar N. Loeffler-Gladstone *Dance Spirit* v21 no3 p30 Mr 2017

Food—Taxation

Even a 14-Cent Food Tax Could Lead to Healthier Choices R. Khan, K. Misra et al *Harvard Business Review Digital Articles* p2 S 29 2016

Foody, Amanda

Daughter of the Burning City *Publishers Weekly* v264 no19 p62 My 8 2017

Fool for Love (Play : Shepard)

A MAN IN FULL J. Nolfi color *Entertainment Weekly* no1477 p14 Ag 11 2017

Foong Khong, Yuen

Mind Games color *Foreign Affairs* v96 no3 p139 My/Je 2017

Foosball (Game)

He Shoots! He Scores! D. SINGER *Texas Monthly* v45 no8 p36 Ag 2017

Foot abnormalities—Prevention

Put Your Best Foot Forward J. Stewart color *Men's Health* v32 no2 p78 Mr 2017

Foot anatomy

Foot health *Mayo Clinic Health Letter* v34 p1 N 2016 Special Report

Foot care

Happy Feet: What are your foot-care must-haves? A. RIVERS

Dance Magazine v91 no10 p36 O 2017

INNER PEACE, OUTER BEAUTY N. Quistgard color *Yoga Journal* p94 2017 Special Issue

Foot exercises

STAND AND DELIVER K. Smeltz and D. DeNunzio color *Golf Magazine* v59 no1 p48 Ja 2017

Foot movements

83% THAT'S HOW MUCH THIS READER CUT HIS HANDICAP JUST BY USING HIS FEET D. DeNunzio color *Golf Magazine* v59 no6 p50 Je 2017

Football

See also

College football

Minor league football

6 Winning Super Bowl Snack Ideas *Tufts University Health & Nutrition Letter* v34 no12 p3 F 2017

AMERICAN ARTISTS TACKLE THE GRIDIRON *USA Today Magazine* v146 no2868 p50 S 2017

Hard Knocks Revisited M. Graham *Cincinnati Magazine* v50 no12 p44 S 2017

THE LORDS OF LAMBEAU A. Smith *Harper's Magazine* v334 no2000 p50 Ja 2017

MH WORLD color *Men's Health* v32 no8 p4 O 2017

PICTURE POWER *Iceland Review* v55 no3 p64 My/Je 2017

VITAL SIGNS A. AHMED and S. TRAVIS *Texas Monthly* v45 no9 p62 S 2017

What Kind of Father Lets His Son Play Football? L. ZALESKI color *GQ: Gentlemen's Quarterly* v97 no9 p132 S 2017

WHY I LOVE R. Zellweger color *InStyle* v24 no11 p220 N 2017

Football attendance

College Football's Fumble: Empty Stands E. Novy-Williams color *Bloomberg Businessweek* no4506 p17 Ja 9 2017

WHY DO I FEEL SO EMPTY INSIDE? M. McKnight and S. Kwak color *Sports Illustrated* v127 no10 p16 O 2 2017

Football coaches

"A VERY LIMITED PLAYER" C. Fehrman *Cincinnati Magazine* v50 no12 p66 S 2017

Football coaches—Attitudes

FLAG FOOTBALL J. Dickey chart color *Sports Illustrated* v125 no21 p46 D 26 2016

Football coaches—United States

A GOOD DAY'S WORK A. Benoit color *Sports Illustrated* v126 no17 p58 Je 19 2017

Football draft

ALL-TIME DRAFT T. Layden chart color *Sports Illustrated* v127 no3 p64 Jl 24 2017

Football draft—History—21st century

THE CRAB WHO PULLS OTHERS UP P. Thamel color *Sports Illustrated* v126 no11 p30 Ap 17-24 2017

GOLD MINED P. King color *Sports Illustrated* v126 no13 p42 My 8 2017

Greener Pastures E. Kaplan and T. Keith color *Sports Illustrated* v126 no12 p14 My 1 2017

NO ONE TO NO. 1 A. Staples color *Sports Illustrated* v126 no14 p96 My 15-22 2017

Rocky Weekend T. Keith color *Sports Illustrated* v126 no12 p16 My 1 2017

T.J. Day T. Keith color *Sports Illustrated* v126 no13 p18 My 8 2017

WAIT FOR IT … G. Bishop color *Sports Illustrated* v126 no13 p36 My 8 2017

WHAT IF? … A JOURNEYMAN QB'S DESPERATE PASS HADN'T SHAPED THE 2004 NFL DRAFT? D. Greene and J. Feldman color *Sports Illustrated* v126 no11 p48 Ap 17-24 2017

Wiki Tweaks T. Keith color *Sports Illustrated* v126 no13 p19 My 8 2017

Football fans

Football Absorbs a Knockout Blow T. J. Huddleston color diag *Fortune* v176 no4 p21 S 15 2017

Sane Old Story J. Dickey and T. Keith color *Sports Illustrated* v127 no6 p14 Ag 28 2017

The Superfan R. Bragg color *Southern Living* v52 no9 p150 S 2017

Football fans—Attitudes

FADE TO BLACK? A. Murphy color *Sports Illustrated* v125 no17 p70 N 21 2016 Double Issue

HATERS GONNA FLUCTUATE P. King color *Sports Illustrated* v127 no7 p40 S 4 2017

WHY DO I FEEL SO EMPTY INSIDE? M. McKnight and S. Kwak color *Sports Illustrated* v127 no10 p16 O 2 2017

Football fans—Humor

I'm a Football Fan. I Just Didn't Know It J. Stein color *Time* v188 no15 p63 O 17 2016

Football injuries

Head Games C. P. Pierce color *Sports Illustrated* v127 no4 p68 Ag 7 2017

Football injuries—Treatment

GET-RIGHT DAY G. Bishop color *Sports Illustrated* v125 no19 p68 D 12 2016

Football on television

Politics [Cover story] F. Gillette, S. Banjo et al color graph *Bloomberg Businessweek* no4498 p60 N 7 2016

Football on television—History—21st century

Easy Listening J. Traina and T. Keith color *Sports Illustrated* v127 no6 p17 Ag 28 2017

HOW WE WATCH FOOTBALL J. Feldman color *Sports Illustrated* v125 no18 p36 D 5 2016

Football players

See also
Quarterbacks (Football)
Rookie football players
Running backs (Football)
Tight ends (Football)

American Gladiators *America* v217 no5 p8 S 4 2017

Dan Marino's Coaching Success color *AARP: The Magazine* v59 no4A p68 Je/Jl 2016

Finding Myself G. Bishop color *Sports Illustrated* v126 no16 p80 Je 5 2017

Head Games B. POPPLEWELL color *Walrus* v14 no7 p30 S 2017

Kirk Cousins C. Cullen color *Current Biography* v77 no11 p30 N 2016

THE NFL WORKOUT [Cover story] L. MCGLASHAN chart color *Muscle & Performance* v9 no11 p52 N 2017

Football players—Attitudes

Taking a Knee D. ZIRIN *Nation* v305 no9 p3 O 16 2017

Football players—Awards

Value Judgments J. Jones and T. Keith chart color *Sports Illustrated* v125 no19 p28 D 12 2016

Football players—Interviews

PAPA GRONK'S SECRETS FOR MONEY SMART KIDS A. K. SMITH color *Kiplinger's Personal Finance* v70 no12 p14 D 2016

What I'd Do Differently Bob Chandler, 75 J. PEARLEY HUFFMAN color *Car & Driver* v63 no1 p112 Jl 2017

Zach Strief: Brewing success, both on the field and off A. McLellan color *New Orleans Magazine* v51 no10 p40 Ag 2017

Football players—Political activity

AT ARM'S LENGTH J. Jones color *Sports Illustrated* v127 no10 p38 O 2 2017

BRING US TOGETHER S. Kerr and C. Ballard color *Sports Illustrated* v127 no10 p28 O 2 2017

Kaepernick's Legacy Lives On D. ZIRIN color *Progressive* v81 no7 p68 O/N 2017

Football players—Substance use

MARTAVIS BRYANT WILL ... J. Feldman color *Sports Illustrated* v127 no4 p44 Ag 7 2017

Football players—Training of

Test Prep T. Keith and R. Demak color *Sports Illustrated* v126 no7 p24 Mr 6 2017

Football players—United States

MOVING RIGHT ALONG ... A. Benoit color *Sports Illustrated* v126 no5 p42 F 13 2017

Taking a Knee D. ZIRIN *Nation* v305 no9 p3 O 16 2017

Von Miller M. Rich color *Current Biography* v78 no3 p68 Mr 2017

Y.A. Tittle S. Gregory color *Time* v190 no16/17 p20 O 23 2017

Football playoffs

NFL PLAYOFFS K. ROSEN *TV Guide* v65 no2 p48 Ja 2 2017

Football playoffs—Universities & colleges

CASE FOR ... ALABAMA A. Staples color *Sports Illustrated* v125 no19 p38 D 12 2016

The Case for ... Clarity C. Johnson and T. Keith color *Sports Illustrated* v126 no1 p19 Ja 9 2017

CASE FOR ... CLEMSON B. Hamilton color *Sports Illustrated* v125 no19 p40 D 12 2016

CASE FOR ... OHIO STATE P. Thamel color *Sports Illustrated* v125 no19 p41 D 12 2016

CASE FOR ... WASHINGTON L. Schnell color *Sports Illustrated* v125 no19 p39 D 12 2016

CHANGE FOR THE BETTER [Cover story] A. Staples color diag *Sports Illustrated* v125 no19 p42 D 12 2016

CHAOS THEORIES A. Staples color *Sports Illustrated* v125 no17 p82 N 21 2016 Double Issue

Cover *Sports Illustrated* v125 no19 pC1 D 12 2016

THE FOUR TOPS color *Sports Illustrated* v125 no19 p30 D 12 2016

LEARNING TO FLY [Cover story] B. Hamilton color *Sports Illustrated* v126 no2 p24 Ja 16 2017

RUN IT BACK A. Staples color *Sports Illustrated* v126 no1 p34 Ja 9 2017

Football stadiums

Meet the NFL's Newest Stadium L. SOROKANICH color *Popular Mechanics* p20 S 2017

Tee Shots & Tailgating J. Passov color *Golf Magazine* v59 no11 p90 N 2017

Football stadiums—Design & construction

Meet the NFL's Newest Stadium L. SOROKANICH color *Popular Mechanics* v193 no7 p20 S 2016

Football team owners

AT ARM'S LENGTH J. Jones color *Sports Illustrated* v127 no10 p38 O 2 2017

Football teams

BUTLER BLUE III, AKA TRIP M. WELCH *Indianapolis Monthly* p24 N 2017

CELEBRATING SOCCER SUCCESS Z. Robert color *Iceland Review* v54 no5 p32 S-O 2016

FOR THE LOVE OF THE GAME R. BASS *Texas Monthly* v45 no9 p68 S 2017

KSU FOOTBALL *Atlanta* v56 no7 p26 N 2016

REBOUND C. BETHEA *Atlanta* v56 no7 p37 N 2016

SPORTS K. ROSEN *TV Guide* p48 D 19 2016

Superstitious Huskers win with skill and a little luck J. BOSCHEN color *Nebraska Life* v21 no5 p16 S/O 2017

Football teams—Finance

The Case for ... Exercising Caution B. Baskin and T. Keith color *Sports Illustrated* v126 no8 p29 Mr 20 2017

Football teams—History—20th century

Past Perfect L. Flynn and T. Keith color *Sports Illustrated* v125 no14 p22 O 24-31 2016

Football techniques

Pats' Solutions C. CALDWELL color *Weekly Standard* v22 no21 p16 F 6 2017

Football tournaments

See also
Football playoffs

CHANGING THE GAME FOR YOUNG PEOPLE IN HEALTH AND DEVELOPMENT M. SIDIBE *UN Chronicle* v53 no2 p22 2016

Win GAME DAY C. CHASE color *Seventeen* v75 no11 p65 N 2016

Football uniforms

THE GREAT SUPER BOWL JERSEY CAPER R. Klemko and J. Vrentas color *Sports Illustrated* v126 no11 p98 Ap 17-24 2017

Football coaches—United States—Charts, diagrams, etc.

Raw Data T. Keith color diag *Sports Illustrated* v126 no2 p17 Ja 16 2017

Football—Competitions

Dominate Fake Football S. JOSEPH color diag *Men's Health* v32 no7 p38 S 2017

FOUNDERS' DAY A. BARRA *American History* v52 no1 p22 Ap 2017

Hall of Fame City Plays Host to Football Exhibit *USA Today Magazine* v146 no2867 p16 Ag 2017

High-School-Football Games D. Hill color *New York Times Magazine* p30 N 27 2016

Superstitious Huskers win with skill and a little luck J. BOSCHEN color *Nebraska Life* v21 no5 p16 S/O 2017

Football—Competitions—History—20th century

The Quiz T. BALAZO color *Maclean's* v129 no46 p64 N 21 2016

Football—Defense
How to Win At the SLOTS T. Rohan color diag *Sports Illustrated* v125 no12 p32 O 10 2016

Football—Humor
Laughter THE BEST MEDICINE *Reader's Digest* v188 no1125 p112 N 2016
Wiki Tweaks T. Keith color *Sports Illustrated* v126 no13 p19 My 8 2017

Football—Offense
See also
Touchdowns (Football)
OUT OF OPTIONS A. Breer color *Sports Illustrated* v127 no7 p112 S 4 2017
Rush More [Cover story] J. Feldman color *Sports Illustrated* v127 no8 p30 S 18 2017
The System Is the Star P. Thamel chart color *Sports Illustrated* v125 no14 p50 O 24-31 2016

Football players—Charts, diagrams, etc.
ALL-TIME DRAFT T. Layden chart color *Sports Illustrated* v127 no3 p64 Jl 24 2017
Survey Says R. Klemko and T. Keith diag *Sports Illustrated* v126 no18 p14 Je 26 2017

Football players—Salaries, wages, etc.
GRIDIRON GRIDLOCK N. SANTOS color *Ebony* v72/73 no12/1 p90 O/N 2017

Football playoffs—Charts, diagrams, etc.
NFL Playoffs: Choose Your Own Adventure J. Dickey color diag *Sports Illustrated* v126 no1 p64 Ja 9 2017
Raw Data T. Keith color diag *Sports Illustrated* v126 no2 p17 Ja 16 2017

Football—Records
BELL EPOCH A. Murphy color *Sports Illustrated* v126 no3 p30 Ja 23 2017
No-lose Situation T. Keith color *Sports Illustrated* v125 no15 p20 N 7 2016

Football—Rules—History—20th century
WHAT IF? ... ONE PRESIDENT'S PROGENY HADN'T ALTERED FOOTBALL FOREVER? J. Fuchs and J. Feldman color *Sports Illustrated* v126 no11 p64 Ap 17-24 2017

Football—Rules—History—21st century
THE GOOD BOOK S. Rushin color *Sports Illustrated* v125 no17 p76 N 21 2016 Double Issue

Footballs
Hardware Update Is Available K. SINTUMUANG color *Esquire* p74 BigBlackBook
My Shot color *National Geographic Kids* no465 p37 N 2016

Football—Safety measures
CAN FOOTBALL BE SAVED? N. SCHMIDLE cartoon color *New Yorker* v92 no44 p38 Ja 9 2017

Football—Scouting
THE UNAWARE OLYMPICS T. Taylor color *Sports Illustrated* v126 no7 p46 Mr 6 2017

Football teams—Charts, diagrams, etc.
The Most Valuable NFL Teams K. BADENHAUSEN, M. OZANIAN et al color graph *Forbes* v198 no5 p32 O 25 2016
NFL Playoffs: Choose Your Own Adventure J. Dickey color diag *Sports Illustrated* v126 no1 p64 Ja 9 2017

Football—United States
THE GRIDIRON AND SOCIAL JUSTICE A. EMMANUEL bw color *Ebony* v72 no4 p100 F 2017

Football—United States—Competitions
The Fix Was In G. NORMAN color *Weekly Standard* v22 no14 p14 D 12 2016

Football—United States—History
Friendsgiving A. Fenwick and T. Keith color *Sports Illustrated* v125 no18 p24 D 5 2016

Football—United States—History—21st century
Cover *Sports Illustrated* v125 no17 pC1 N 21 2016 Double Issue

Football—United States—Social aspects
FOOTBALL IN AMERICA [Cover story] G. Bishop and M. Mcknight color *Sports Illustrated* v125 no17 p40 N 21 2016 Double Issue

Footbridges
See also
Rope bridges

DC HAS ITS BEST SHOT AT BRIDGING THE EAST/WEST-OF-THE-RIVER DIVIDE S. COURTNEY *Washingtonian Magazine* v52 no7 p106 Ap 2017
Pedestrian Cross-ing bw *Weekly Standard* v22 no26 p2 Mr 13 2017
Walk a Thin Line T. DAVIDGE color *Architectural Record* v205 no8 p77 Ag 2017
World's Longest Suspension Footbridge J. Zorthian color *Time* v190 no8 p21 Ag 28 2017

Footbridges—Design & construction
CURVES AHEAD S. COCHRAN color *Architectural Digest* v74 no2 p106 F 2017

Foot—Care & hygiene
THE AGONY OF THE FEET C. Cunningham *Washingtonian Magazine* v52 no1 p123 O 2016
Be kind to body and mind V. LATONA color *Yoga Journal* p14 2016 Special Issue
TRUE beauty N. Quistgard color *Yoga Journal* p94 2017 Special Issue

Foot—Diseases—Prevention
Foot health *Mayo Clinic Health Letter* v34 p1 N 2016 Special Report
Good old-fashioned mobility insurance: Protecting your feet and ankles *Harvard Health Letter* v41 no12 p1 O 2016

Footlockers
THE WAR TRUNK J. DETWILER color *Popular Mechanics* v193 no7 p97 S 2016

Foot—Physiology
THE AGONY OF THE FEET C. Cunningham *Washingtonian Magazine* v52 no1 p123 O 2016

Footsteps (Company)
APOSTATES ANONYMOUS T. Brodesser-Akner *New York Times Magazine* p36 Ap 2 2017

Footwear
See also
Ballet slippers
Boots
Shoes
Slippers (Footwear)
All the World's a Stage K. Brady color *Dance Spirit* v21 no4 p40 Ap 2017
Boot Forecast color *InStyle* v23 no12 p148 N 2016
The BUY Fashion color *Harper's Bazaar* no3656 p172 S 2017
COZY UP *Indianapolis Monthly* v40 no4 p161 D 2016
Don't THINK PINK H. Rolfe *Dance Spirit* v21 no3 p56 Mr 2017
From Our Editor S. Donelson color *House Beautiful* v159 no9 p6 N 2017
Glass Slipper (But Hipper) [Cover story] J. Palermo color *Glamour* v115 no4 p45 Ap 2017
Sole Survivor: How I found myself at the special store for special people with broken-down feet requiring special footwear D. Paul *Indianapolis Monthly* v12 no40 p192 Ag 2017
SPARKLE & SHINE, TWINKLE TOES! C. WALTER color *Ebony* v72 no11 p41 S 2017
SURPRISE ME *Vogue* v207 no11 p171 N 2017

Footwear design
FLORENCE in Abundance M. HOLGATE color *Vogue* v207 no4 p150 Ap 2017
SNOWSHOEING J. LYNCH color *Popular Mechanics* p49 D 2016/Ja 2017

Footwear industry
HAPPY FEET L. GOLDMAN color *Better Homes & Gardens* v95 no6 p152 Je 2017

Footwear industry—Economic aspects
How Adidas Got Back In the Game A. Ricadela color graph *Bloomberg Businessweek* no4493 p32 O 3 2016

Footwear—Evaluation
2017 Approach Shoe Roundup color *Climbing* no355 p40 Ag 2017
5 easy routes to style happiness color *Redbook* p78 My 2017
Adam's STYLE SHEET Adam color *O, The Oprah Magazine* p43 Ja 2017
Adam's STYLE SHEET color *O, The Oprah Magazine* p64 F 2017
BOOT CAMP A. GARDNER *Indianapolis Monthly* p34 N 2017
CLIMBING J. ELLISON color *Backpacker* v45 no3 p120 Ap 2017

Dior kitten heels, $890 V. SMITH color *Vogue* v207 no1 p112 Ja 2017

FLATS vs. HEELS color *Harper's Bazaar* no3648 p205 N 2016

Footwear A. H. BIBLE color diag graph il *Backpacker* v45 no3 p43 Ap 2017

GREAT BUYS UNDER $100 color *O, The Oprah Magazine* p42 Ja 2017

If You Just Want the It Shoe E. Velluto color *Glamour* v115 no9 p61 S 2017

Let It SLIDE color *Seventeen* p58 Ja 1 2017

LET IT SLIDE color *Seventeen* v76 no4 p24 Jl/Ag 2017

The New Velcro Sneaker J. MOORE color *GQ: Gentlemen's Quarterly* v97 no4 p41 Ap 2017

The O List color *O, The Oprah Magazine* p49 Mr 2017

on demand color *InStyle* v24 no3 p113 Mr 2017

Panta SHOES *Interview* v47 no2 p102 Mr 2017

Party On (in Flats) E. Velluto color *Glamour* v115 no4 p68 Ap 2017

Silver Belles color *Good Housekeeping* v265 no4 p17 O 2017

SOLE OBSESSION J. Bingaman color *Men's Health* v32 no2 p(Sp)16 Mr 2017

STRIPED JOGGERS color *Good Housekeeping* v264 no1 p16 Ja 1 2017

Suit Yourself color *Glamour* v115 no11 p66 N 2017

FOPPICK, LAURA

Birds of a (Faux) Feather color *Audubon* v119 no3 p14 Fall 2017

For Esme: With Love & Squalor (Short story)

ESMÉ IN NEVERLAND J. LEPORE cartoon *New Yorker* v92 no38 p34 N 21 2016

For Leila Means Night & Night Is Beautiful to the Desert Mind (Poem)

For Leila Means Night and Night Is Beautiful to the Desert Mind P. Metres *America* v216 no4 p41 F 20 2017

For Me & My Gal (Film)

A Man in Motion bw *Weekly Standard* v22 no46 p30 Ag 14 2017

For Peete's Sake (TV program)

REALITY TV T. ANDERSON and D. POINTDUJOUR color *Ebony* v72 no5 p65 Mr 2017

For Peter Pan on Her 70th Birthday (Theatrical production)

First Star to the Right H. Als cartoon *New Yorker* v93 no27 p14 S 11 2017

For-profit schools

For-Profit Trade Schools Prove Costly for Disadvantaged Black Youth *Education Digest* v82 no6 p63 F 2017

Why For-Profit Education Fails J. A. KNEE color *Atlantic* v318 no4 p30 N 2016

For-profit universities & colleges

BORROWER'S REMORSE S. Burd color *Washington Monthly* v49 no9/10 p76 S/O 2017

Kaplan Sells Its College But Keeps Its Profits L. Colby *Bloomberg Businessweek* no4521 p23 My 8 2017

Forage fishes

Ensuring a Moveable Feast K. Olsen color *National Wildlife (World Edition)* v55 no2 p14 F/Mr 2017

Foraging behavior (Animals)

Berries and Eggs Won't Be Enough color *Canadian Wildlife* v22 no5 p9 N/D 2016

Foraminifera

Foraminifera Invade the Mediterranean T. GUY-HAIM bw color map *Natural History* v125 no10 p12 O 2017

Forbes (Periodical)

100 YEARS OF HITS AND FLOPS M. SCHIFRIN color *Forbes* v200 no3 p54 S 28 2017

Adding Rattlesnake To Our Journalism L. D'VORKIN *Forbes* v200 no2 p12 S 5 2017

BIRTH OF THE FORBES 400 C. PETERSON-WITHORN color *Forbes* v200 no3 p36 S 28 2017

BOND OF BROTHERS M. SCHIFRIN bw *Forbes* v200 no3 p78 S 28 2017

CONVERSATION A. WILSON color *Forbes* v200 no4 p32 O 24 2017

FAKE NEWSSTAND! M. SOLOMON color *Forbes* v200 no3 p92 S 28 2017

THE FEMINIST MYSTIQUE C. O'CONNOR color *Forbes* v200 no3 p68 S 28 2017

Following Us Into Our Next 100 Years L. D'VORKIN *Forbes* v200 no1 p8 Jl 27 2017

FORBES @ 100 A. BROWN bw *Forbes* v199 no6 p30 Je 13 2017

FORBES @ 100 A. BROWN color *Forbes* v199 no3 p38 Mr 28 2017

FORBES @ 100 bw color *Forbes* v200 no3 p31 S 28 2017

July 1, 1968: HOUSTON, WE'VE GOT YOUR BACK A. BROWN bw color *Forbes* v200 no2 p32 S 5 2017

JULY 15, 1931: DRIVING FORCE A. BROWN bw color *Forbes* v200 no1 p30 Jl 27 2017

JUNE 12, 1989: CYBER-SOVIETS A. BROWN bw color *Forbes* v199 no7 p36 Je 29 2017

LAUGHING MATTERS C. BUCKLEY *Forbes* v200 no3 p90 S 28 2017

LOGO-A-GO-GO C. O'CONNOR *Forbes* v200 no3 p88 S 28 2017

NINE ZEROS: OCTOBER 9, 2006 A. BROWN color *Forbes* v200 no5 p36 N 14 2017

OUR FIRST 100 YEARS bw color *Forbes* v200 no3 p23 S 28 2017

Our Mobile World At Lightning Speed L. D'VORKIN *Forbes* v198 no6 p20 N 8 2016

RHYMES WITH "FORBES" B. Z. O. GREENBURG color *Forbes* v200 no3 p100 S 28 2017

Steve Forbes Talks Shop N. GILLESPIE color *Reason* v49 no6 p79 N 2017

Storytelling Adapts To Media's New Era L. D'VORKIN *Forbes* v199 no4 p10 Ap 25 2017

THE SUN NEVER SETS ON FORBES M. SOLOMON color *Forbes* v200 no3 p104 S 28 2017

TRUMP: THE ART OF THE SPIEL D. ALEXANDER bw color *Forbes* v200 no3 p98 S 28 2017

TRUMP: THE EARLY TWEETS (1982-2000) D. ALEXANDER color *Forbes* v200 no3 p94 S 28 2017

Why We Welcome the Seven-Year Itch L. D'VORKIN *Forbes* v200 no4 p8 O 24 2017

FORBES, B. C.

THOUGHTS ON Conflict *Forbes* v199 no4 p112 Ap 25 2017

Forbes, Edward Waldo

Where science meets art R. Ploeger and A. Shugar bibl bw color *Science* v354 no6314 p826 N 18 2016

Forbes, Malcolm

Did she hide radical messages in her books? *Weekly Standard* v22 no42 p28 Jl 17 2017

How Swift Saw It *Weekly Standard* v22 no31 p41 Ap 17 2017

LIFE AS A PARTY A. BROWN color *Forbes* v200 no3 p80 S 28 2017

THE SHELL GAME A. BROWN color *Forbes* v200 no3 p84 S 28 2017

Sort of Life *Weekly Standard* v22 no6 p34 O 17 2016

THOUGHTS ON Property *Forbes* v199 no5 p124 My 16 2017

FORBES, SEÁNAN

What's On Tap? color *Rodale's Organic Life* v3 no1 p46 Ja 2017

FORBES, SHARI L.

The Odor of Death: An Overview of Current Knowledge on Characterization and Applications *BioScience* v67 no7 p600 Jl 2017

FORBES, STEVE

CIVIL WAR II? CALIFORNIA'S FEVERED FANTASIES *Forbes* v199 no2 p17 F 28 2017

THE COLLAPSE OF OBAMACARE WHAT TO DO NOW *Forbes* v198 no7 p19 N 29 2016

CRACKDOWN ON NORTH KOREA UNAVOIDABLE NOW color *Forbes* v200 no1 p11 Jl 27 2017

ETHICS--THE ESSENCE OF SUCCESSFUL CAPITALISM *Vital Speeches of the Day* v83 no4 p128 Ap 2017

THE FORBES 2016 ALL-STAR EATERIES IN NEW YORK color *Forbes* v198 no9 p12 D 30 2016

HOW TO MAKE HEALTH CARE BETTER AND CHEAPER color *Forbes* v199 no6 p11 Je 13 2017

INDIA'S SICKENING AND IMMORAL MOVE *Forbes* v199 no1 p15 Ja 24 2017

THE MEDICAID DISASTER WHAT THE GOP MUST DO NOW *Forbes* v199 no7 p15 Je 29 2017

OBAMA'S FEEBLE APOLOGIA FOR THE ECONOMY *Forbes* v198 no6 p23 N 8 2016

PLEA TO HIGH COURT: KNOW YOUR LIMITS color *Forbes* v200 no5 p17 N 14 2017

WHY DON'T WE HAVE MORE BILLIONAIRES? color *Forbes* v199 no3 p25 Mr 28 2017

WHY GOP-CARE LOST THE PUBLIC *Forbes* v200 no2 p15 S 5 2017

WHY THE TRUMP TAX CUT SHOULD BE BIG AND BOLD *Forbes* v198 no9 p11 D 30 2016

Forbes, Steve, 1947—Interviews
Steve Forbes Talks Shop N. GILLESPIE color *Reason* v49 no6 p79 N 2017

Forbes, Wallace
BOND OF BROTHERS M. SCHIFRIN bw *Forbes* v200 no3 p78 S 28 2017

Forbes Media LLC—Officials & employees
THE TITANS VS. THE UNICORNS *Vital Speeches of the Day* v83 no6 p179 Je 2017

FORBEY, JEN
Tough Choices for a Pygmy Rabbit color map *Natural History* v125 no3 p9 Mr 2017

Forbidden Dance, The (Music)
The Forbidden Dance/Óbvio B. Zimmerman color *Downbeat* v84 no1 p76 Ja 2017

Forbis, Judith
ANSATA HEJAZI—BORN TO RULE *Arabian Horse World* v57 no8 p5 My 2017

Greener Pastures N. Valaitham *Arabian Horse World* v57 no10 p107 Jl 2017

Force & energy
    See also
        Conservation of energy
        Dark energy (Astronomy)
        Energy density
        Energy harvesting
        Energy storage
        Nuclear energy
        Reaction forces

5 Steps to Investing Your Energy More Wisely P. Bregman *Harvard Business Review Digital Articles* p2 Mr 8 2016

Large-amplitude transfer motion of hydrated excess protons mapped by ultrafast 2D IR spectroscopy F. Dahms, B. P. Fingerhut et al graph *Science* v357 no6350 p491 Ag 4 2017

Force & energy—Measurement
Once-baffling success of granular resistive force theory explained Sung Chang *Physics Today* v69 no11 p22 N 2016

Forced marriage
It's Time to Change the Story About Child Marriage color *Maclean's* v130 no3 p61 Ap 2017

Forcelli, Peter
A SHOT TO THE HEART S. CLIFFORD cartoon *New Yorker* v92 no34 p26 O 24 2016

Force of Things: An Opera for Objects, The (Theatrical production)
CLASSICAL MUSIC *New Yorker* v93 no31 p13 O 9 2017

FORD, ADAM T.
Conserving Megafauna or Sacrificing Biodiversity? *BioScience* v67 no3 p193 Mr 2017

Ford, Alex
Global analysis of protein folding using massively parallel design, synthesis, and testing color diag *Science* v357 no6347 p168 Jl 14 2017

FORD, ALICIA
In the ROUND color *House Beautiful* p120 Ag 2017

FORD, ASHLEY C.
FASHION FOR THE SIXTY-SEVEN PERCENT: A revolution in the plus-size market img *New York* v50 no16 p38 Ag 7 2017

Ford, Courtney L.
A bioinspired iron catalyst for nitrate and perchlorate reduction bibl diag *Science* v354 no6313 p741 N 11 2016

Ford, Doug—Interviews
VINTAGE FORD S. Zak color *Golf Magazine* v59 no4 p94 Ap 2017

Ford, Emma
10 BLANKETING TIPS FROM EMMA FORD L. Threlkeld color *Practical Horseman* v45 no10 p60 O 2017

Ford, Gerald R., 1913-2006
The Circus Comes to America C. Bonanos img *New York* p8 Ja 23 2017

Ford, Gilbert
The Marvelous Thing That Came from a Spring: The Accidental Invention of the Toy That Swept the Nation color *Publishers Weekly* v263 no49 p48 D 7 2016

Ford, Glenn, 1949-2015
A prosecutor's shame P. W. Marty *Christian Century* v133 no21 p3 O 12 2016

Ford, Harrison, 1942-
THE LONG SOLO FLIGHT OF HARRISON FORD [Cover story] J. MOORE bw color *GQ: Gentlemen's Quarterly* v97 no10 p116 O 2017

Ford, Jeffrey
The Twilight Pariah color *Publishers Weekly* v264 no28 p70 Jl 10 2017

Ford, John
THE QUIET MAN C. Chiarella color *Sound & Vision* v82 no3 p67 Ap 2017

FORD, LAUREN SMITH
The art of Sight-Casting *Texas Monthly* v45 no9 p16 S 2017
Brad Pearce Glass *Texas Monthly* v44 no11 p35 N 2016
Fleur de Lis Forge *Texas Monthly* v45 no5 p27 My 2017
Guest Ranch Redefined: EVERYTHING OLD IS NEW AGAIN AT THIS HILL COUNTRY HIDEAWAY *Texas Monthly* v45 no9 p13 S 2017
Guten Co *Texas Monthly* v45 no8 p17 Ag 2017
Keith Kreeger Studios *Texas Monthly* v45 no1 p25 Ja 2017
Moon Rivers Naturals *Texas Monthly* v45 no7 p25 Jl 2017
Odin Leather Goods *Texas Monthly* v45 no2 p32 F 2017
Pastrana Studio *Texas Monthly* v45 no4 p29 Ap 2017
The QUEEN of COOL *Texas Monthly* v45 no8 p66 Ag 2017
The Wild Standard *Texas Monthly* v45 no6 p23 Je 2017

Ford, Mark
Derek Walcott: 'What the Twilight Says' bw color *New York Review of Books* v63 no17 p44 N 10 2016
Finding Hardy at Last M. Wood bw *New York Review of Books* v63 no20 p63 D 22 2016
Hardy the Londoner W. H. Pritchard bw *Weekly Standard* v22 no26 p32 Mr 13 2017
She Shampooed & Renewed Us bw *New York Review of Books* v64 no16 p57 O 26 2017
Why He Deserves It bw *New York Review of Books* v63 no19 p16 D 8 2016

Ford, Martin
Economic Growth Isn't Over, but It Doesn't Create Jobs Like It Used To *Harvard Business Review Digital Articles* p2 Mr 14 2016

FORD, MATT
INNOCENCE *Smithsonian* v47 no9 p98 Ja/F 2017

FORD, MERIDITH
FEEL-GOOD DISHES [Cover story] *Atlanta* v56 no9 p70 Ja 2017
TO-GO *Atlanta* v56 no9 p75 Ja 2017

FORD, PAUL
OBAMA'S AMERICA img *New York* v49 no20 p12 O 3 2016

Ford, Peter
Europe's Muslims ask: Is terrorism a community problem? *Christian Century* v134 no16 p14 Ag 2 2017

Ford, Richard
Between Them: Remembering My Parents *Publishers Weekly* v264 no8 p74 F 20 2017
MAKE-WORK cartoon *New Yorker* v93 no16 p58 Je 5 2017
Perilous Business color *Esquire* p104 Je/Jl 2017
Runaway American Dream color *New York Times Book Review* p1 S 25 2016
We Three C. STRAYED *New York Times Book Review* p16 My 7 2017

Ford, Robert S.
Keeping Out of Syria color *Foreign Affairs* v96 no6 p16 N/D 2017

Ford, Sam
The Benefits of Taking a Slower Approach to Innovation *Harvard Business Review Digital Articles* p2 Je 26 2017

Ford, Shaun B.
The Comets of Edgar Allan Poe *Sky & Telescope* v132 no6 p30 D 2016

Ford, Tanisha C.—Interviews
Adorned Beauty GABBARA and A. LUCAS color *Ebony* v72 no6 p40 Ap/My 2017

What Research Tells Us About Making Accurate Predictions W. Frick *Harvard Business Review Digital Articles* p2 F 2 2015

Will Parks and Recreation Predict 2017? D. Snierson color *Entertainment Weekly* no1449 p50 Ja 20 2017

Forecasting—Charts, diagrams, etc.

And the Winner Is... N. Feeney, K. O'Donnell et al chart color *Entertainment Weekly* no1451/1452 p26 F 3-10 2017

THE PREDICTION MATRIX J. Eidelson and M. Glassman bw color *Bloomberg Businessweek* no4496 p104 O 24 2016

Forecasting—Competitions

Bringing probability judgments into policy debates via forecasting tournaments P. E. Tetlock, B. A. Mellers et al bibl color *Science* v355 no6324 p481 F 3 2017

Forecasting—Computer network resources

Prediction and explanation in social systems J. M. Hofman, A. Sharma et al bibl diag graph *Science* v355 no6324 p486 F 3 2017

Forecasting—Humor

The 2018 Time 100 J. Stein color *Time* v189 no16/17 p151 My 1-8 2017

Forecasting—Mathematical models

Improving election prediction internationally R. Kennedy, S. Wojcik et al bibl graph *Science* v355 no6324 p515 F 3 2017

Using Algorithms to Predict the Next Outbreak K. Radinsky *Harvard Business Review Digital Articles* p2 N 5 2014

ForeFlight LLC

EASY, AND FREE color *Flying* v144 no10 p18 O 2017

Foreign aid (American)

Entrepreneurship Needs to Be a Bigger Part of U.S. Foreign Aid S. R. Koltai *Harvard Business Review Digital Articles* p2 Ag 15 2016

President Trump Steps Up to Fight Famine *America* v217 no2 p8 Jl 24 2017

Reproductive Health Services *Congressional Digest* v96 no3 p30 Mr 2017

Foreign aid (American)—Developing countries

Your Country Is Flooding? Tough Luck C. Flavelle color *Bloomberg Businessweek* no4526 p24 Je 12 2017

Foreign aid (American)—Soviet Union

The Hesitant U.S. Rescue of the Soviet Economy D. V. Negroponte *Wilson Quarterly* v40 no4 p4 Fall 2016

Foreign business enterprises

As European Banks Retreat from the World Stage, China Is Stepping Up S. Lund and E. Windhagen *Harvard Business Review Digital Articles* p2 S 25 2017

Becoming a Manager in a New Country A. Molinsky *Harvard Business Review Digital Articles* p2 S 14 2015

Doing Business in a Post-Fidel Cuba P. G. Alonso and A. Lee *Harvard Business Review Digital Articles* p2 D 19 2016

Foreign business enterprises—China

Chinese Cars May Lose Their Learner's Permits *Bloomberg Businessweek* no4519 p28 Ap 24 2017

Mark Zuckerberg's Long March to China E. Parker il *MIT Technology Review* v119 no6 p100 N/D 2016

Foreign corporations—Russia

Why Multinationals Are Doubling Down on Russia M. Bozadzhieva *Harvard Business Review Digital Articles* p2 Ap 4 2016

Foreign correspondents

No Refuge from Trump M. Lough color *Commonweal* v144 no11 p9 Je 16 2017

Foreign exchange

Is the Dollar in a Trump Slump? L. Nguyen and L. C. McCormick graph *Bloomberg Businessweek* no4533 p30 Ag 7 2017

Sub-Saharan Africa's Most and Least Resilient Economies A. Rosenberg *Harvard Business Review Digital Articles* p2 F 5 2016

Foreign exchange intervention (Monetary policy)

It's Hard to Label China A Currency Manipulator E. Curran, S. Mohsin et al *Bloomberg Businessweek* no4500 p17 N 21 2016

Foreign exchange reserves

Of Debt and Detriment B. STEIL and E. SMITH *Weekly Standard* v22 no22 p22 F 13 2017

Foreign films

See also

Latin American films

Spanish films

WHOSE LATIN AMERICAN CINEMA? M. Betancourt *Film Quarterly* v70 no2 p9 Wint 2016

Foreign fishing

FOREIGN FISHING P. RAINS color map *Sea Magazine* v109 no6 p18 Je 2017

Foreign Intelligence Service of the Russian Federation

The Spy Who Added Me on LinkedIn G. M. Graff color *Bloomberg Businessweek* no4500 p54 N 21 2016

Foreign investment visas

How 'Golden Visas' Work T. John color *Time* v189 no19 p10 My 22 2017

So you want to move to the U.S P. Robison, K. Weise et al color diag graph *Bloomberg Businessweek* no4538 p48 S 18 2017

Welcome to America! Here's How Your Investment Is Doing S. Berfield color *Bloomberg Businessweek* no4493 p74 O 3 2016

Foreign investments

See also

External debts

China Spreads the Wealth Around S. Cendrowski color map *Fortune* v174 no8 p138 D 15 2016

Protect Yourself From Ugly Currencies W. BALDWIN chart color graph *Forbes* v199 no1 p62 Ja 24 2017

What Chinese Companies Want from International Deals Li Ma, J. Brett et al *Harvard Business Review Digital Articles* p2 F 12 2015

Foreign investments—Africa

RWANDA: REFORMS BOOST INVESTMENT P. Trustfull color *Forbes* v200 no3 p96 S 28 2017

What Western Investors Want from African Entrepreneurs R. Klingebiel and C. Stadler *Harvard Business Review Digital Articles* p2 N 11 2014

Foreign investments—China

Hollywood Hunts for Its Next Pot of Gold A. Sakoui and J. Y. de Morel bw *Bloomberg Businessweek* no4540 p24 O 2 2017

Of Debt and Detriment B. STEIL and E. SMITH *Weekly Standard* v22 no22 p22 F 13 2017

Foreign investments—Cuba

Cuba: Portfolio of Opportunities for Foreign Investment, 2016-17 R. Feinberg *Foreign Affairs* v96 no2 p180 Mr/Ap 2017

Foreign investments—Cyprus

Corrections & Clarifications *Bloomberg Businessweek* no4524 p6 My 29 2017

How to Launder A Russian Y. Onaran and V. Silver graph *Bloomberg Businessweek* no4522 p17 My 15 2017

Foreign investments—Kuwait

KDIPA: Changing the business landscape in Kuwait M. J. Al Ahmad A. Al Sabah *Foreign Affairs* v95 no6 p120d N/D 2016

Foreign investments—Laos

Time for Investment *Foreign Affairs* v95 no6 p(Sp)4 N/D 2016

Foreign investments—Mexico

Build the Wall! Por Favor K. RAPOZA and M. CHAIKIN color *Forbes* v199 no6 p66 Je 13 2017

Foreign investments—Nigeria

NIGERIA: TRANSFORMATION PRESENTS OPPORTUNITIES P. Trustfull color *Forbes* v200 no4 p(Sp)1 O 24 2017

Foreign language education

See also

English language education

Language & languages—Ability

VERÖLD, THE HOUSE OF VIGDÍS V. HAFSTAÐ *Iceland Review* v55 no4 p82 Jl/Ag 2017

Foreign language education software

Duolingo A. Fitzpatrick *New York Times Magazine* p20 Jl 30 2017

Foreign military bases (International law)

The Nation-Building Straw Man E. ABRAMS cartoon color *Weekly Standard* v22 no48 p11 S 4 2017

Foreign ministers (Cabinet officers)

U.S. AND CANADA: SHARING A CONTINENT BY CHANCE; BUT FRIENDS AND ECONOMIC PARTNERS BY CHOICE *Vital Speeches of the Day* v83 no5 p147 My 2017

Foreign news—News briefs

AROUND THE WORLD *Science* v356 no6345 p1314 Je 30 2017

Foreign nurses—Employment

Are English tests for nurses fair? Experts make the case for and against new language quizzes said to be deterring applicants *People Management* p13 Ag 2017

FOREMAN, DAVID

We Need a Biologically Sound North American Conservation Plan *BioScience* v67 no8 p685 Ag 2017

Foreman, George

Laugh Lines *Reader's Digest* v188 no1125 p119 N 2016

Foreman, Jonathan

Lionel Shriver Is Out of Line: And thank God *Commentary* v142 no5 p31 D 2016

Terror and the Failure of the Liberal Imagination: Three attacks in Britain highlight the West's inability to see the threat clearly *Commentary* v144 no1 p34 Jl/Ag 2017

The Timothy Hunt Witch Hunt: A joke told, a reputation destroyed *Commentary* v140 no2 p41 S 2015

The Timothy Hunt Witch Hunt *Commentary* v140 no2 p56 S 2015

Forensic anthropology

AFTER THE VANISHING L. Wade bw color graph *Science* v354 no6318 p1369 D 16 2016

Forensic chemistry

TO CATCH A PREDATOR J. Thompson color *Essence* v47 no10 p66 F 2017

Forensic orations

Supreme Court 'Manterruption' J. Zorthian color *Time* v189 no22 p17 Je 12 2017

Forensic sciences

Catching a Criminal J. KEATS color diag *Discover* v38 no6 p40 Jl/Ag 2017

Forensic Science Must Be Scientific S. Sah color *Scientific American* v317 no4 p12 O 2017

Unspooling the Essential Code B. Lang *Discover* v38 no6 p6 Jl/Ag 2017

Forensic sciences—History

CSI: CHINA: The 19th and 20th centuries saw a revolution in Chinese forensic science, when traditional techniques were replaced by new methods from the West. Today, the world confronts another moment of transformation in forensic science D. Asen *History Today* v67 no7 p54 Jl 2017

Forerunner Ventures LLC—Finance

The Retail Whisperer C. O'CONNOR color *Forbes* v198 no7 p58 N 29 2016

Forest biodiversity

Airborne laser-guided imaging spectroscopy to map forest trait diversity and guide conservation G. P. Asner, R. E. Martin et al bibl chart graph *Science* v355 no6323 p385 Ja 27 2017

Colombia peace deal blow dismays ecologists L. Wade color *Science* v354 no6310 p271 O 21 2016

Forest biodiversity conservation

Seeing the forest through the trees V. Kapos bibl color *Science* v355 no6323 p347 Ja 27 2017

Forest canopies

Canopies of many colors L. Hamers color map *Science News* v191 no5 p32 Mr 18 2017

Ian Leahy, Director of Urban Forests Programs *American Forests* v123 no1 p8 Wint/Spr 2017

Forest conservation

See also

Forest reserves

Reforestation

Can the Spiritual Values of Forests Inspire Effective Conservation? M. D. LOWMAN and P. A. SINU *BioScience* v67 no8 p688 Ag 2017

FOREST GUARDIANS I. N. Pearlman color *Earth Island Journal* v32 no4 p48 Wint 2017

Planting Hope J. DALEY *American Forests* v123 no3 p2 Fall 2017

Rising from the Ashes: Restoring Kentucky's Appalachian Forests A. Wisniewski *American Forests* v123 no3 p6 Fall 2017

Forest conservation—Latin America

Forest conservation: Humans' handprints C. Levis, C. R. Clement et al bibl color *Science* v355 no6324 p466 F 3 2017

Forest degradation

Jungles are now carbon emitters C. GRAMLING *Science News* v192 no7 p9 O 28 2017

Forest ecology

See also

Tree growth

Combining Biodiversity Resurveys across Regions to Advance

Global Change Research K. VERHEYEN, P. DE FRENNE et al *BioScience* v67 no1 p73 Ja 2017

HOW IS YOUNG FOREST CREATED? color *New York State Conservationist* v71 no2 p6 O 2016

What is Young Forest? color *New York State Conservationist* v71 no2 p3 O 2016

Forest ecology—Massachusetts

From the Forest to the Sea J. Stringfellow *Yankee* p99 Mr 2017

Forest fire prevention & control

Blazes highlight fire science struggle color *Science* v356 no6344 p1214 Je 23 2017

Forest fires

TRENDING L. SCHLEY graph map *Discover* v38 no5 p16 Je 2017

WILD FIRES T. E. NICKENS color *Field & Stream* v121 no8 p44 F/Mr 2017

Forest fires—Montana

RAVALLI COUNTY, MONTANA C. T. Tobin *Harper's Magazine* p27 O 2017

Forest fires—Portugal

Blazes highlight fire science struggle color *Science* v356 no6344 p1214 Je 23 2017

Forest fires—United States

FEEL THE BURN T. WALRATH color *Outdoor Life* v224 no7 pH5 S 2017

Fires blaze in mountain forests color *Science* v354 no6317 p1208 D 9 2016

Forest landowners

Quotable Goodness color *Cabin Living* p5 O 2017

Forest management

See also

Forest conservation

Forest rangers

The Congressional Review Act: Congress Putting Our Forests in Jeopardy R. Turner *American Forests* v123 no2 p10 Summ 2017

forest TLC M. MYLCHREEST color *Cabin Living* p52 O 2017

On Patrol L. Bobseine and S. Scherry *New York State Conservationist* v71 no4 p27 F 2017

Why Yale Owns a Forest J. Lorin color *Bloomberg Businessweek* no4536 p28 S 4 2017

Forest management—Finance

Countering the President's Budget Proposal R. Turner *American Forests* v123 no3 p14 Fall 2017

Forest management—Study & teaching

The Making of a Leader in Forestry L. SLOAN *American Forests* v122 no3 p46 Fall 2016

Forest management—United States

Losing Ground J. LLOYD *American Forests* v123 no2 p12 Summ 2017

Saving Forest Habitat S. STEEN *American Forests* v123 no2 p2 Summ 2017

WILDLAMDS FOR WILDLIFE: Working to protect and restore forest habitat for at-risk wildlife across the United States E. SPRAGUE, J. HYNICKA et al *American Forests* v123 no2 p20 Summ 2017

Woodland Wildflowers on the Edge M. ADAMOVIC *American Forests* v123 no2 p32 Summ 2017

Forest productivity

Humanity for Habitat K. Moore *Natural History* v125 no1 p6 D 2016/Ja 2017

Forest products

See also

Timber

Wood products

Feeding Extinction color *Earth Island Journal* v32 no4 p6 Wint 2017

SIBERIAN WOOD P. STEFÁNSSON *Iceland Review* v55 no3 p92 My/Je 2017

Forest protection

FOREST GUARDIANS I. N. Pearlman color *Earth Island Journal* v32 no4 p48 Wint 2017

Forest rangers

COMMON GROUND A. ROBINSON color *Outdoor Life* v224 no5 p70 Je/Jl 2017

On Patrol L. Bobseine and S. Scherry color *New York State Con-*

servationist v71 no2 p17 O 2016

On Patrol L. Bobseine and S. Scherry *New York State Conservationist* v71 no5 p20 Ap 2017

On Patrol L. Bobseine and S. Scherry *New York State Conservationist* v71 no6 p25 Je 2017

On Patrol: Real stories from Conservation Officers and Forest Rangers in the field L. Bobseine and S. Scherry *New York State Conservationist* v72 no1 p33 Ag 2017

Forest reserves

See also

Forest rangers

Clues in the Forest--Archaeology at Florence Hill State Forest K. E. Primeau, S. A. Hoskinson et al *New York State Conservationist* v72 no1 p18 Ag 2017

On Patrol: Real stories from Conservation Officers and Forest Rangers in the field L. Bobseine and S. Scherry *New York State Conservationist* v72 no2 p16 O 2017

Portage Pass Trail: Chugach National Forest, Alaska diag *Backpacker* p80 O 2017

Forest reserves—Arizona

See also

Coconino National Forest (Ariz.)

PUMPHOUSE WASH R. STIEVE *Arizona Highways* v93 no10 p54 O 2017

Forest reserves—Ohio

Easy Living A. M. HALLIGAN map *Backpacker* p19 O 2017

Forest reserves—United States

REPLANTING OUR NATIONAL FORESTS *Log Home Living* v34 no3 p14 Ap 2017

Forest restoration

A Thousand Acres and Counting *American Forests* v123 no2 p8 Summ 2017

WILDLAMDS FOR WILDLIFE: Working to protect and restore forest habitat for at-risk wildlife across the United States E. SPRAGUE, J. HYNICKA et al *American Forests* v123 no2 p20 Summ 2017

Forest restoration—International cooperation

Restoring tropical forests from the bottom up K. D. Holl bibl color *Science* v355 no6324 p455 F 3 2017

Forest roads

SAN FRANCISCO PEAKS LOOP A. MCGIVNEY *Arizona Highways* v93 no10 p52 O 2017

Forester, Amanda

My Highland Rebel *Publishers Weekly* v263 no46 p39 N 14 2016

Forester sport utility vehicle

Ratings chart *Consumer Reports* v82 no8 p60 Ag 2017

Forest Park (Portland, Or.)

GET AWAY CLOSE TO HOME *Sierra* v102 no3 p45 My/Je 2017

Forestry engineers

Ian Robert Lawson A. A. DAVIS bw *Maclean's* v129 no40 p82 O 10 2016

Forestry extension

The extent of forest in dryland biomes [Cover story] Bastin, N. Berrahmouni et al chart map *Science* v356 no6338 p635 My 12 2017

Forestry law & legislation

Panama's impotent mangrove laws G. A. Castellanos-Galindo, L. C. Kluger et al bibl *Science* v355 no6328 p918 Mr 3 2017

Forests & forestry

See also

Forest management

Landscape gardening

Planting (Plant culture)

Pruning

Rain forests

Reforestation

Tree planting

Urban forestry

Arnica City: Could the Dream Be Real? J. W. DAVIS *Idaho Magazine* v16 no9 p51 Je 2017

CATHER PEOPLE A. ROSS bw cartoon *New Yorker* v93 no30 p32 O 2 2017

Daniel Dey *American Forests* v122 no3 p4 Fall 2016

editor's LETTER R. STIEVE *Arizona Highways* v93 no6 p2 Je 2017

The extent of forest in dryland biomes [Cover story] Bastin, N.

Berrahmouni et al chart map *Science* v356 no6338 p635 My 12 2017

Forests of the Future G. POPKIN color map *Discover* v27 no10 p28 D 2016

Forest value: More than commercial C. Paul and T. Knoke bibl color *Science* v354 no6319 p1541 D 23 2016

From the Community *American Forests* v123 no3 p12 Fall 2017

Frontiers of Citizen Science B. BAKER *BioScience* v66 no11 p921 N 1 2016

Holiday Hike: Stephens State Forest, Iowa K. PETERSON map *Backpacker* p15 N 2017

HOW IS YOUNG FOREST CREATED? color *New York State Conservationist* v71 no2 p6 O 2016

Jad Daley, Vice President of Conservation Programs *American Forests* v123 no3 p9 Fall 2017

A Long and Bright Future for Longleaf Pine M. Friedel *American Forests* v123 no3 p6 Fall 2017

MEET THE ANIMALS OF THE YOUNG FOREST color *New York State Conservationist* v71 no2 p4 O 2016

MONOCHROME *Popular Photography* v80 no11 p29 D 2016

Mysteries in the edgelands S. Paulsell *Christian Century* v134 no4 p45 F 15 2017

Richard Kabat *American Forests* v122 no3 p9 Fall 2016

Vibrant Cities Lab: A State-of-the-Art Platform to Connect Urban Forest Leaders I. LEAHY *American Forests* v123 no3 p40 Fall 2017

weekend getaways: woods *Washingtonian Magazine* v52 no11 p87 Ag 2017

What is Young Forest? color *New York State Conservationist* v71 no2 p3 O 2016

Forests & forestry—Appalachian Region

RETURN OF THE GIANTS: The once and future mighty American chestnut C. KETTLEWELL *Virginia Living* v15 no6 p17 O 2017

Forests & forestry—Australia

life springs [Cover story] M. J. Van Kranendonk, D. W. Deamer et al color *Scientific American* v317 no2 p28 Ag 2017

Forests & forestry—British Columbia

FOOTPRINT IN MOUTH LIND cartoon *Alternatives Journal (AJ) - Canada's Environmental Voice* v42 no2 p10 2016

Forests & forestry—Canada

The magnificent SEVEN H. TAMMEMAG color *Canadian Geographic* v136 no6 p54 D 2016

The war in the Walbran A. Findlay color map *Canadian Geographic* v136 no6 p26 D 2016

WILDLIFE color *Canadian Geographic* v136 no6 p22 D 2016

Forests & forestry—Climatic factors

Seeing the Forest Through the Trees E. STRICKLAND color *Foreign Policy* no221 p28 N/D 2016

Forests & forestry—Environmental aspects

SENTINELS OF FOREST HEALTH [Cover story] A. McDermott color graph map *Science News* v190 no11 p20 N 26 2016

Forests & forestry—France

Countering the President's Budget Proposal R. Turner *American Forests* v123 no3 p14 Fall 2017

Forests & forestry—Latin America

Forest conservation: Humans' handprints C. Levis, C. R. Clement et al bibl color *Science* v355 no6324 p466 F 3 2017

Forests & forestry—New York (State)

GIFTS OF A FOREST Devereux, Catherine et al *New York State Conservationist* v71 no5 p24 Ap 2017

Forests & forestry—Tropics

Restoring tropical forests from the bottom up K. D. Holl bibl color *Science* v355 no6324 p455 F 3 2017

Forests & forestry—Tropics—Research

Seeing the Forest Through the Trees E. STRICKLAND color *Foreign Policy* no221 p28 N/D 2016

Forever on the Stage (Film)

Country Music's Iron Man *South Dakota Magazine* v32 no4 p62 N/D 2016

Forfeiture

COURT of APPEALS WITH REBEL GOOD Bo-hae Yu, T. Lykins et al *Tennis* v52 no6 p6 N/D 2016

Forgery

See also

Painting—Forgeries

A Man I Know Faked His Academic Credentials. Should I Tell His Fiancée? K. A. Appiah *New York Times Magazine* p20 O 23 2016

FORGET, ANDRÉ

Ms. Lonelyhearts color *Walrus* p60 Ja\F 2017

Forgiveness

LIVING BY THE WORD *Christian Century* v134 no18 p18 Ag 30 2017

THE LUXURY OF FORGIVENESS S. KRAUSS WHITBOURNE *Psychology Today* v49 no6 p23 N/D 2016

My Father Was the BTK Killer R. WENZL *Reader's Digest* v188 no1126 p112 D 2016/Ja 2017

YOU CAN'T GIVE IN C. Ballard color *Sports Illustrated* v126 no10 p70 Ap 10 2017

Forgiveness of sin

See also
 Confession (Christianity)

Can every sin be forgiven? B. Haile *U.S. Catholic* v82 no9 p49 S 2017

Forgiveness—Psychological aspects

What is forgiveness? A. Frykholm color *Christian Century* v134 no7 p10 Mr 29 2017

Forgiveness—Religious aspects—Christianity

ENEMY K. Ward, B. Simmons et al color *Christian Century* v134 no5 p20 Mr 1 2017

Forgive and Be Forgiven M. Simone *America* v217 no5 p53 S 4 2017

Forgrave, Reid

THE CTE Diaries color *GQ: Gentlemen's Quarterly* v87 no1 p88 Ja 2017

MINNESOTA NICE color *Mother Jones* v42 no3 p7 My/Je 2017

Forklift trucks

THE APPEAL OF ROUGH-TERRAIN FORKLIFTS D. Mowitz *Successful Farming* v114 no11 p24 N 2016

Model a modern log-grasping lift A. Taylor color *Model Railroader* v84 no6 p53 Je 2017

Forks

Olive spoons and terrapin forks C. Day *Physics Today* v70 no2 p8 F 2017

What Champion Pitmasters Pack M. MILLS and A. MILLS cartoon color *Men's Health* v32 no5 p44 Je 2017

Forks—Evaluation

Sunset Orange K. RENDA and B. REYNAERT color *House Beautiful* p15 Jl 2017

Tools OF THE Trade: Everything you need to shuck it, slice it and smoke it S. GEROUX and A. HUNTER *Virginia Living* p46 2017 Smoke & Salt

YOUR VISION QUEST PACKING LIST R. KOCH color *Bicycling* v58 no1 p78 Ja/F 2017

Forlani, Claire

Hawaii Five-0 J. Halterman *TV Guide* v64 no40 p56 O 3 2016

Forlani, Paolo

Putting Canada on the map S. Nemis color map *Canadian Geographic* v137 no4 p24 Jl/Ag 2017

Forman, James

When Black America Was Pro-Police P. BUTLER bw *Atlantic* v319 no5 p37 Je 2017

FORMAN, JAMES, JR.

FORTRESS AMERICA bw *Nation* v303 no16 p35 O 17 2016

Forman, Jay

Acalli Chocolate color *New Orleans Magazine* v51 no2 p71 D 2016

Brasa Bound color *New Orleans Magazine* v51 no12 p110 O 2017

Bucktown Nouveau [Cover story] color *New Orleans Magazine* v52 no1 p102 S 2017

Caribbean Room color *New Orleans Magazine* v51 no2 p72 D 2016

Clean Eats: A new wave transforms health food from bland to bold [Cover story] color *New Orleans Magazine* v51 no10 p172 Ag 2017

The Company Burger color *New Orleans Magazine* v51 no2 p78 D 2016

Counter Culture color *New Orleans Magazine* v51 no6 p84 Ap 2017

EAT. DRINK. ENJOY color *New Orleans Magazine* v51 no9 p56 Jl 2017

Emeril Lagasse color *New Orleans Magazine* v51 no2 p68 D 2016

FOCUSING ON THE FUNDAMENTALS color *New Orleans Magazine* v51 no3 p112 Ja 2017

Jamaica Style color *New Orleans Magazine* v51 no9 p80 Jl 2017

Meat color *New Orleans Magazine* v51 no4 p84 F 2017

RISING TIDE color *New Orleans Magazine* v51 no1 p112 N 2016

Small Hotels, Big Restaurants color *New Orleans Magazine* v51 no5 p88 Mr 2017

SPECIAL SANDWICH color *New Orleans Magazine* v51 no2 p84 D 2016

Spice Trade color *New Orleans Magazine* v51 no7 p84 My 2017

State of the Market *New Orleans Magazine* v51 no2 p69 D 2016

Tchoup Yard color *New Orleans Magazine* v51 no2 p74 D 2016

Tujague's color *New Orleans Magazine* v51 no2 p70 D 2016

Variety on Piety color *New Orleans Magazine* v51 no8 p100 Je 2017

Format of periodicals

EDITOR'S LETTER M. Murphy *Bloomberg Businessweek* no4527 p6 Je 19 2017

Redefining Journalism In a Mobile World L. D'VORKIN *Forbes* v199 no5 p12 My 16 2017

Formation (Music)

The 10 Best Songs J. Cox color *Time* v188 no25-26 p154 D 19 2016 Double Issue

SINGLES OF THE YEAR R. SHEFFIELD color *Rolling Stone* no1276 p18 D 15 2016

Formica, Piero

The Innovative Coworking Spaces of 15th-Century Italy *Harvard Business Review Digital Articles* p2 Ap 27 2017

The Two Essential Entrepreneurial Types *Harvard Business Review Digital Articles* p2 Ag 5 2015

Why Innovators Should Study the Rise and Fall of the Venetian Empire color *Harvard Business Review Digital Articles* p2 Ja 17 2017

Formisano, M.

Localized aliphatic organic material on the surface of Ceres bibl graph *Science* v355 no6326 p719 F 17 2017

Seasonal exposure of carbon dioxide ice on the nucleus of comet 67P/Churyumov-Gerasimenko bibl bw graph *Science* v354 no6319 p1563 D 23 2016

Formosa, Nicole

bogged down bw *Bike Magazine* v24 no3 p56 My 2017

a cross to air: EL BRUC, SPAIN | MAY 14, 2017 | 3:01 P.M cartoon *Bike Magazine* v24 no8 p34 N 2017

Diamondback Clutch color *Bike Magazine* v24 no6 p122 Ag 2017

FORWARD MOMENTUM color *Bike Magazine* v24 no1 p116 Ja/F 2017

FOX TRANSFER PERFORMANCE color *Bike Magazine* v24 no2 p85 Mr 2017

front lines bw *Bike Magazine* v24 no7 p23 S 2017

GET IN GEAR bw color *Bike Magazine* v24 no1 p122 Ja/F 2017

home base: THE BEST TRAILS ARE NEVER FAR AWAY bw *Bike Magazine* v24 no8 p19 N 2017

KIAH TEE color *Bike Magazine* v24 no4 p104 Je 2017

light fall color *Bike Magazine* v24 no6 p34 Ag 2017

TREK FUEL EX 9.8 WOMEN'S color *Bike Magazine* v23 no9 p90 D 2016

an unpredicted journey color *Bike Magazine* v24 no3 p46 My 2017

valley of light bw color *Bike Magazine* v24 no5 p56 Jl 2017

WILD EAST bw color *Bike Magazine* v24 no7 p80 S 2017

Formula Boats (Company)

Flexible Formula: The 310 BR is a bowrider that can cruise to the sandbar ... or the Bahamas ... in style A. JONES *Boating World* v38 no8 p40 S/O 2017

Formula 310 Bowrider *Boating World* v38 no1 p42 Ja 2017

Formula One automobiles

Friends for Life P. EGAN color diag *Road & Track* v68 no10 p26 Jl 2017

Max Verstappen J. Crelin color *Current Biography* v78 no8 p86 Ag 2017

Formula One automobiles—Competitions

THE SPECIALISTS M. SCHIRMER color *Road & Track* v68 no6 p48 F 2017

Formula Three automobiles—Competitions

What's On Demand This Month? *Motor Trend* v69 no10 p12 O

Breeze On! chart color *Sail* v48 no11 p50 N 2017

Fortes-Lima, Cesar
Dispersals and genetic adaptation of Bantu-speaking populations in Africa and North America diag *Science* v356 no6337 p543 My 5 2017

Forti, Simone
A Gathering of Sages *Dance Magazine* v91 no10 p12 O 2017

Fortification
BLOW THE BLOODY PLACE UP! J. Rüger *History Today* v67 no8 p24 Ag 2017
THE BRITISH HERITAGE TRAVEL PUZZLER D. Kniffen, D. Kniffen et al *British Heritage Travel* v38 no3 p78 My/Je 2017
Three Qs color *Science* v357 no6353 p737 Ag 25 2017

Fortification—Scotland
LOST KINGDOM OF THE BRITONS D. WEISS color *Archaeology* v70 no5 p32 S/O 2017

Fortini, Amanda
Business Trip color *Esquire* v167 no1 p28 F 2017
The Hotel Cleaner *New York Times Magazine* p46 F 26 2017

Fortitude—History
The Faces of Courage R. A. SCHROTH color *America* v215 no18 p20 D 5 2016

Fort Mason (Mason, Tex.)
CULTURE SHOCK: FORT MASON IS A CULTURAL OASIS AMID SAN FRANCISCO BAY'S HUSTLE AND BUSTLE color map *Sea Magazine* v109 no8 pCA-1 Ag 2017

Fort McMurray Wildfire, Alta., 2016
Downsizing the dream J. MARKUSOFF color *Maclean's* v130 no4 p24 My 2017

Fortna, Benjamin C.
'The Turkish Lawrence of Arabia': The dramatic life of the outlaw and special agent Eşref Bey epitomises the end of the Ottoman Empire *History Today* v67 no9 p8 S 2017

Fortney, Jonathan J.
HAT-P-26b: A Neptune-mass exoplanet with a well-constrained heavy element abundance chart diag graph *Science* v356 no6338 p628 My 12 2017

Fortress of Care (Poem)
Fortress of Care L. RITLAND *Walrus* v14 no9 p76 N 2017

Fortunato, Stephen
In Name Only *Harper's Magazine* v335 no2006 p2 Jl 2017

Fortune
See also
Fate & fatalism
Success
8 ways people try to get good luck around the world E. WHITMER *National Geographic Kids* no468 p10 Mr 2017
Success in science depends on luck, plus much more *Science News* v192 no6 p2 O 14 2017

Fortune, Paul
keep it classic M. RUS color *Architectural Digest* v74 no10 p134 O 1 2017

Fortune 500 companies
The Fortune Global 500 Isn't All That Global P. Ghemawat and N. Pisani *Harvard Business Review Digital Articles* p2 N 4 2014
PILING UP CO[subscript 2] SAVINGS B. O'Keefe diag *Fortune* v175 no7 p88 Je 1 2017
Research: How Female CEOs Actually Get to the Top S. Dillard and V. Lipschitz *Harvard Business Review Digital Articles* p2 N 6 2014

Fortune cookies
The Fortune Cookie M. J. Salter *American Scholar* v86 no3 p55 Summ 2017

Fortune Cookie, The (Poem)
The Fortune Cookie M. J. Salter *American Scholar* v86 no3 p55 Summ 2017

Fortunelli, Alessandro
Ultrafine jagged platinum nanowires enable ultrahigh mass activity for the oxygen reduction reaction bibl chart graph *Science* v354 no6318 p1414 D 16 2016

Forums (Discussion & debate)
See also
Online comments
Workshops (Adult education)
Looking for Answers to the World's Biggest Challenges In the Eternal City R. Foroohar, C. D. Wuerl et al color *Time* v188

no24 p31 D 12 2016

Forwards (Basketball)—Universities & colleges
PROJECT BIGGIE L. Winn color *Sports Illustrated* v126 no5 p82 F 13 2017

Forzieri, Giovanni
Satellites reveal contrasting responses of regional climate to the widespread greening of Earth diag *Science* v356 no6343 p1180 Je 16 2017

FOSE, CEDRIC
ENCYCLOPEDIA CINCINNATI bw cartoon color *Cincinnati Magazine* v51 no1 p42 O 2017

Fossey, Dian
The Gorillas Dian Fossey Saved E. Royte color graph map *National Geographic* v232 no3 p110 S 2017

Fossil biomolecules
See also
Fossil DNA
Egyptian mummy DNA, at last L. Wade color *Science* v356 no6341 p894 Je 1 2017

Fossil birds
Ancient avian voice box unearthed M. ROSEN color *Science News* v190 no10 p7 N 12 2016

Fossil bones
The Oldest Homo sapiens? K. Wong color *Scientific American* v317 no3 p12 S 2017
Weirdest Wonders on Wings R. Conniff bw color diag *National Geographic* v232 no5 p60 N 2017

Fossil cephalopoda—Anatomy
Fossil Octopus Is a Jurassic Jewel B. Switek color *Scientific American* v316 no3 p21 Mr 2017

Fossil DNA
A composite window into human history N. N. Johannsen, G. Larson et al color map *Science* v356 no6343 p1118 Je 16 2017
Fossil DNA shakes up elephant history M. TEMMING bw color *Science News* v191 no13 p8 Jl 8 2017

Fossil echinodermata
Earliest Known Relative N. Wilson color *Natural History* v125 no5 p6 My 2017

Fossil elephants
See also
Mammoths
Fossil DNA shakes up elephant history M. TEMMING bw color *Science News* v191 no13 p8 Jl 8 2017

Fossil fuel industries
See also
Petroleum industry
Coastal Cities Are Increasingly Vulnerable, and So Is the Economy that Relies on Them G. Unruh *Harvard Business Review Digital Articles* p2 S 7 2017

Fossil fuel power plants
What role could nuclear power play in limiting climate change? R. Rosner and A. Hearn bibl *Bulletin of the Atomic Scientists* v73 no1 p2 Ja 2017

Fossil fuel subsidies
Reform China's fisheries subsidies H. Yang, M. Ma et al color *Science* v356 no6345 p1343 Je 30 2017

Fossil fuels
See also
Shale oils
Aaron Robinson A. Robinson *Car & Driver* v62 no8 p26 F 2017
Coastal Cities Are Increasingly Vulnerable, and So Is the Economy that Relies on Them G. Unruh *Harvard Business Review Digital Articles* p2 S 7 2017
Divestment Alone Won't Beat Climate Change G. Serafeim and M. Fulton *Harvard Business Review Digital Articles* p2 N 4 2014
Much More Methane color *Earth Island Journal* v32 no4 p11 Wint 2017
Point of No Return color *Earth Island Journal* v32 no4 p4 Wint 2017

Fossil Group Inc.
Day Glow color *Glamour* v115 no7 p26 Jl 2017

Fossil hominid genetics
DNA data point to unknown hominid T. H. SAEY *Science News* v190 no10 p13 N 12 2016

Fossil hominids

See also
Homo naledi
Neanderthals
Close relative of Neandertals unearthed in China A. Gibbons color map *Science* v355 no6328 p899 Mr 3 2017
Fossils push back origin of humans B. BOWER color *Science News* v191 no13 p6 Jl 8 2017
Late Pleistocene archaic human crania from Xuchang, China Li, Wu et al bibl color diag graph *Science* v355 no6328 p969 Mr 3 2017
Newest member of human family is surprisingly young A. Gibbons color *Science* v356 no6338 p571 My 12 2017
Our Cousin Neo K. Wong color *Scientific American* v317 no2 p46 Ag 2017

Fossil hominids—Greece
Hominid roots may go back to Europe B. BOWER color *Science News* v191 no12 p9 Je 24 2017

Fossil hominids—Research
PROTEINS SOLVE A HOMININ PUZZLE N. SWAMINATHAN color *Archaeology* v70 no1 p11 Ja/F 2017

Fossil insects
FINDINGS *Harper's Magazine* v333 no1998 p96 N 2016

Fossil leaves
Fossil leaves bear witness to ancient carbon dioxide levels E. Hand color graph *Science* v355 no6320 p14 Ja 6 2017

Fossil lizards
'Four-legged snake' may be ancient lizard instead C. Gramling color *Science* v354 no6312 p536 N 4 2016

Fossil microorganisms
Earliest Known Relative N. Wilson color *Natural History* v125 no5 p6 My 2017
Microbes quick to occupy impact site T. SUMNER *Science News* v191 no1 p15 Ja 21 2017
Tiny fossils could be oldest signs of life M. ROSEN color *Science News* v191 no6 p6 Ap 1 2017

Fossil osteichthyes
Fossil fishes challenge 'urban legend' of evolution E. Pennisi color *Science* v353 no6307 p1483 S 30 2016

Fossil primates
Dawning of the Planet of the Apes M. BARNA color map *Discover* v38 no1 p67 Ja/F 2017

Fossil Rim Wildlife Center (Company)
WEEKEND GETAWAYS L. BLEIBERG cartoon *Better Homes & Gardens* v95 no7 p170 Jl 2017

Fossil snakes
'Four-legged snake' may be ancient lizard instead C. Gramling color *Science* v354 no6312 p536 N 4 2016

Fossil spiders
A Leg Up on Arachnid Evolution G. TARLACH color *Discover* v38 no1 p80 Ja/F 2017

Fossil teeth
Ancient tales from teeth H. Thompson color *Science News* v192 no6 p18 O 14 2017
Chipped teeth hint at Homo naledi diet B. BOWER color graph *Science News* v192 no4 p12 S 16 2017

Fossil teeth—Research
Ancient Monkey Teeth Change Evolutionary Timeline G. TARLACH bw color diag *Discover* v38 no1 p76 Ja/F 2017

Fossil trees
Sunspot cycle may be ancient routine T. SUMNER color *Science News* v191 no3 p16 F 18 2017

Fossil whales
Fossil whale hints at baleen makeover L. HAMERS color *Science News* v191 no11 p12 Je 10 2017

Fossils
See also
Fossil microorganisms
awes8me FUNKY FOSSILS J. AGRESTA *National Geographic Kids* no466 p8 D 2016/Ja 2017
Beyond DNA G. TARLACH color *Discover* v38 no7 p64 S 2017
Built for Stability L. E. Ogden *Natural History* v124 no10 p8 N 2016
Fossils contain earliest signs of shells T. SUMNER color *Science News* v190 no9 p9 O 29 2016
Oldest members of our species discovered in Morocco A. Gibbons color map *Science* v356 no6342 p993 Je 9 2017

SHALE GAME L. ANTHONY color map *Canadian Geographic* v137 no1 p50 F 2017
Why We Still Love 'Lucy' L. Pyne *History Today* v66 no12 p7 D 2016

Fossils—Collection & preservation
The Significance and Magnificence of Jehol Biota L. M. Chiappe and M. Qingjin *Natural History* v124 no10 p20 N 2016

Fossils—Exhibitions
Around the Country *Natural History* v124 no10 p40 N 2016

Fossils—Study & teaching
Ma, where did they put T. rex? C. Gramling diag graph *Science* v355 no6331 p1249 Mr 24 2017

FOSTER, CAROLINE
SPACE QUEST color *House Beautiful* p116 Ag 2017

Foster, Charles
Opposing effects of Elk-1 multisite phosphorylation shape its response to ERK activation bibl graph *Science* v354 no6309 p233 O 14 2016

FOSTER, CRAIG A.
Skepticism, at Heart, Is Not Partisan *Skeptical Inquirer* v41 no1 p14 Ja/F 2017
Vaccines, Autism, and the Promotion of Irrelevant Research: A Science-Pseudoscience Analysis *Skeptical Inquirer* v41 no3 p44 My/Je 2017

FOSTER, DALE
Q: What was the greatest summer read of your life? color *O, The Oprah Magazine* p16 Jl 2017

Foster, Dan
ALL AROUND THE FARM® color *Successful Farming* v115 no7 p67 My 2017

FOSTER, DANIEL
Asymmetric Rhetorical Warfare *National Review* v68 no20 p48 N 7 2016
Calibrate Your Care *National Review* v69 no8 p44 My 2017
A Course on Cursing color *National Review* v68 no23 p35 D 19 2016
Everything All the Time color *National Review* v69 no19 p60 O 16 2017
Make Politics Boring Again *National Review* v69 no5 p48 Mr 20 2017
On Infighting and Real Fighting *National Review* v69 no15 p48 Ag 14 2017
Sheer Lunacy *National Review* v69 no3 p56 F 20 2017
Varieties of Ridiculous Experience *National Review* v69 no1 p44 Ja 23 2017

Foster, David, 1949-
The Real Ex-Husband of Beverly Hills E. KONIGSBERG color diag *Vanity Fair* p164 Hollywood 2017 Supplement

Foster, Fred—Awards
2017 Distinguished Achievement Winners *Stage Directions* v30 no3 p6 Mr 2017

Foster, Gregory A.
Enhancement of Zika virus pathogenesis by preexisting antiflavivirus immunity graph *Science* v356 no6334 p175 Ap 14 2017

FOSTER, HANNAH
Capturing your BEST FIRST Arabesque *Dance Magazine* p8 2016/2017
Capturing your BEST FIRST Arabesque: How to take top-notch audition photos *Dance Magazine* v90 p8 2016/2017 Supplement College Guide

Foster, Helen Currie
Ghost Cave *Publishers Weekly* v264 no26 p159 Je 26 2017

Foster, Jody J.
Problem Colleagues and How to Deal S. Begley color *Time* v189 no14 p22 Ap 17 2017

FOSTER, JORDAN
All the Shades of Guilt color *Publishers Weekly* v264 no12 p54 Mr 20 2017
Crime and Power color *Publishers Weekly* v264 no8 p65 F 20 2017
Dirty Blue Line: Police Corruption And Brutality in Crime Fiction color *Publishers Weekly* v263 no47 p22 N 21 2016
The Limitless Possibilities of Crime color *Publishers Weekly* v264 no21 p72 My 22 2017
Luck and Book Sales *Publishers Weekly* v264 no3 p41 Ja 16 2017
A Mortal Detective color *Publishers Weekly* v263 no48 p46 N 28

2017

DARK ARTS bw *Chicago* v66 no3 p50 Mr 2017

ECCENTRIC BEASTS cartoon *Chicago* v66 no2 p28 F 2017

GO: 69 GREAT THINGS TO DO THIS MONTH color *Chicago* v66 no11 p103 N 2017

GO bw color *Chicago* v66 no10 p105 O 2017

GO color *Chicago* v65 no12 p119 D 2016

GO color *Chicago* v66 no4 p113 Ap 2017

HEY, BIG SPENDERS bw color *Chicago* v65 no12 p50 D 2016

HOW TO BUY ART [Cover story] bw color *Chicago* v66 no9 p128 S 2017

IDENTITY ARTIST color *Chicago* v66 no10 p72 O 2017

THE LENS OF A DISSIDENT bw *Chicago* v66 no4 p37 Ap 2017

MIGHTY MURAKAMI color *Chicago* v66 no6 p38 Je 2017

NIGHTMARES REVISITED color *Chicago* v66 no7 p28 Jl 2017

SOUTH SIDE STORY color *Chicago* v66 no11 p42 N 2017

WATER WORKS cartoon *Chicago* v66 no8 p40 Ag 2017

WRITTEN IN THE STARS cartoon *Chicago* v65 no11 p44 N 2016

Found objects (Art)

AD visits: Change Agent S. RIEGLER color *Architectural Digest* no11 p46 N 1 2017

CHAOS THEORY H. MARTIN color *Architectural Digest* no11 p142 N 1 2017

Foundation (Cosmetics)

Flawless skin in a flash M. Roncal color *Redbook* p24 Ap 2017

FOUNDATION MASTER CLASS color *Martha Stewart Living* p54 O 2017

Fresh Face D. Mazzone color *InStyle* v24 no3 p259 Mr 2017

Liquid Courage color *Martha Stewart Living* p52 O 2017

the secret to FOUNDATION E. METZGER color *Better Homes & Gardens* v95 no9 p26 S 2017

Foundation (Cosmetics)—Evaluation

2017 Readers' Choice K. D. Hodes color *InStyle* v24 no10 p154 O 2017

Beach color *Seventeen* v76 no3 p44 My 2017

erica explores CONCEALERS E. Metzger color *Better Homes & Gardens* v95 no7 p18 Jl 2017

Good Lighting E. Reimel color *Glamour* v115 no6 p70 Je 2017

MATE GALLERY color *Better Homes & Gardens* v95 no7 p16 Jl 2017

MY BEAUTY MARK ... Sofia Vergara color *InStyle* v24 no9 p346 S 2017

My Mom, the Beauty Icon A. R. Williams color *Southern Living* v52 no2 p72 F 2017

My Sister, the Beauty Icon A. R. Williams color *Southern Living* v52 no5 p74 My 2017

New shortcuts to flawless skin M. OLIVA color *Redbook* p16 My 2017

Women's Health 2017 BEAUTY AWARDS A. FINNEY color graph *Women's Health* v14 no5 p116 Je 2017

Foundation garments—Evaluation

7 genius underwear updates color *Redbook* p74 S 2017

Foundations (Engineering)

See also

Compressed air

Stand Guard color *Log Home Living* p72 2018 Annual Buyers Guide

Foundations (Engineering)—Design & construction

Laying the Groundwork for Success D. Mitchell color *Log Home Living* v34 no3 p22 Ap 2017

Founder, The (Film)

Empire Builder R. DOUTHAT color *National Review* v69 no4 p47 Mr 6 2017

FAMILY PACKS A. LANE cartoon *New Yorker* v92 no45 p86 Ja 16 2017

Fast-Food Godfather P. Travers color *Rolling Stone* no1280 p56 F 9 2017

The Founder Finds Drama Under the Golden Arches S. Zacharek color *Time* v189 no3 p53 Ja 30 2017

The Founder L. Greenblatt color *Entertainment Weekly* no1450 p46 Ja 27 2017

The Founder V. LUCCA color *Film Comment* v53 no1 p83 Ja/F 2017

Missions Accomplished R. Alleva color *Commonweal* v144 no4 p20 F 24 2017

Potted Kroc J. PODHORETZ *Weekly Standard* v22 no21 p39 F 6 2017

Trapped in History D. EDELSTEIN img *New York* p69 Ja 23 2017

Founders Brewing Co.

Cheers! K. Hansen color *Cabin Living* p12 S 2017

Founders Fund LLC

How Did I Get Here? K. HARTZ color *Bloomberg Businessweek* no4494 p76 O 10 2016

Power Player A. KONRAD color diag *Forbes* v199 no4 p84 Ap 25 2017

Founders of nations

Founders' Keepers J. COST color *Weekly Standard* v22 no36 p13 My 29 2017

THE GREAT-GRAND-DAUGHTERS OF CONFEDERATION [Cover story] M. Campbell bw color *Maclean's* v130 no6 p46 Jl 2017

Founding Fathers of the United States

A fighting chance G. Adamson color *Magazine Antiques* v184 no3 p20 My/Je 2017

THIS MODERN WORLD T. TOMORROW *In These Times* v41 no1 p6 Ja 2017

Founding Fathers of the United States—Computer network resources

Founders' Keepers J. COST color *Weekly Standard* v22 no36 p13 My 29 2017

FOUNTAIN, ANDREW G.

The Impact of a Large-Scale Climate Event on Antarctic Ecosystem Processes chart graph *BioScience* v66 no10 p848 O 1 2016

Fountain, Ben—Interviews

BEN FOUNTAIN'S LONG HOLLYWOOD TALK S. HARRIGAN *Texas Monthly* v44 no11 p116 N 2016

Fountain, Henry

Disaster fuels geologic detective story E. DeMarco color *Science News* v192 no4 p32 S 16 2017

Fountain, Timothy

Learning as You Go *South Dakota Magazine* v33 no3 p58 S/O 2017

Fountain grass

color theory K. BARNES color *Better Homes & Gardens* v95 no4 p56 Ap 2017

Fountain pens—Design & construction

Masters of Link J. Thomas color *Bloomberg Businessweek* no4536 p63 S 4 2017

Fountaine Pajot Motor Yachts

FOUNTAINE PAJOT MY37 *Sea Magazine* v108 no10 p33 O 2016

Fountaine Pajot SA

CAT BE NIMBLE, CAT BE QUICK D. J. HARDING chart color *Power & Motoryacht* v34 no10 p100 O 2017

Fountains—Design & construction

Fountain Fancy L. Tudor *New Orleans Homes & Lifestyles* v20 no2 p33 Spr 2017

Fountains—Equipment & supplies

Sparktacular's Sparkular *Stage Directions* v30 no5 p26 My 2017

Fouqueau, Thomas

The architecture of transcription elongation diag *Science* v357 no6354 p871 S 1 2017

Fouquet, Helene

Après le Champagne, More Campaign color graph *Bloomberg Businessweek* no4522 p34 My 15 2017

France's Industrial Past Haunts Macron color *Bloomberg Businessweek* no4536 p44 S 4 2017

Give This Man A Party color *Bloomberg Businessweek* no4520 p27 My 1 2017

Thatcherism Redux in France bw color *Bloomberg Businessweek* no4502 p21 D 5 2016

Fouquieria

TRIPP CANYON ROAD N. AUSTIN *Arizona Highways* v93 no9 p52 S 2017

Four Devotional Poems (Poem)

FOUR DEVOTIONAL POEMS E. J. García *Commonweal* v144 no11 p28 Je 16 2017

Four-dimensional imaging

Imaging rotational dynamics of nanoparticles in liquid by 4D electron microscopy X. Fu, B. Chen et al bibl diag graph *Science* v355 no6324 p494 F 3 2017

Four Seasons Hotels Inc.

Crowned Jewels N. Ekstein chart color *Bloomberg Businessweek* no4532 p65 Jl 31 2017

Founder-Led Companies Outperform the Rest—Here's Why Chris Zook *Harvard Business Review Digital Articles* p2 Mr 24 2016

LOS CABOS, MEXICO color *Power & Motoryacht* v33 no1 p52 Ja 2017

What Have They Done to The Four Seasons? E. KONIGSBERG img *New York* p46 Mr 6 2017

Four Seasons in Havana (TV program)

Four Seasons in Havana R. Feinberg *Foreign Affairs* v96 no3 p166 My/Je 2017

Four-stroke cycle engines

TWO-STROKES LIVE ON K. CAMERON *Cycle World* v56 no4 p34 My 2017

Four-stroke cycle engines—Design & construction

WHAT IS THE FOUR-STROKE CYCLE? K. Cameron color *Cycle World* v56 no5 p30 Je 2017

Four-wheel drive trucks

Clowns to the Left of Me, Jokers to the Right D. Pund chart color *Car & Driver* v63 no1 p104 Jl 2017

Four-wheel drive vehicles

BACK TO THE FUTURE M. Emery *Dirt Sports + Off-Road* v51 no7 p6 Jl 2017

SUVOCABULARY M. Cantu bw *Motor Trend* v69 no10 p65 O 2017

Four-wheel drive vehicles—Evaluation

2017 SXS/UTV BUYER'S GUIDE [Cover story] E. MADERO color *Dirt Sports + Off-Road* v51 no1 p30 Ja 2017

BEAST MODES [Cover story] J. H. HARPER chart color diag graph *Road & Track* v68 no9 p24 Je 2017

Four Winns Boats LLC

FOUR WINNS HORIZON 350 M. WERLING *Sea Magazine* v108 no12 p28 D 2016

Fourcy, Thomas

A CONVRSATION with Thomas Fourcy Al Shaqab Racing-Ecurie Haras Bouquetot Sas S. Andersen and D. Hearst *Arabian Horse World* v57 no6 p56 Mr 2017

Fournette, Leonard, 1995-

A Basket of Deplora-Bowls G. NORMAN color *Weekly Standard* v22 no18 p21 Ja 16 2017

THE CRAB WHO PULLS OTHERS UP P. Thamel color *Sports Illustrated* v126 no11 p30 Ap 17-24 2017

Fournier, Joseph A.

Spectroscopic snapshots of the proton-transfer mechanism in water bibl diag graph *Science* v354 no6316 p1131 D 2 2016

Fournier, Karl

Statement Piece J. LEVINE color *Architectural Digest* v74 no9 p85p S 2017

Fournier, Ron—Interviews

RON FOURNIER A. Beaujon *Washingtonian Magazine* v52 no1 p43 O 2016

Fournier, Susan

To Get More Out of Social Media, Think Like an Anthropologist *Harvard Business Review Digital Articles* p2 Ag 17 2016

What Trump Understands About Using Social Media to Drive Attention color *Harvard Business Review Digital Articles* p2 Mr 1 2017

Fournier, V.

Chronic exposure to neonicotinoids reduces honey bee health near corn crops diag *Science* v356 no6345 p1395 Je 30 2017

Foursquare (Web resource)

LEARNING NOT TO LEAD P. Marinova color *Fortune* v176 no2 p38 Ag 1 2017

You Are Here (So Buy Something) J. Wise *Bloomberg Businessweek* no4536 p24 S 4 2017

Fourteenth Street (Washington, D.C.)

WHAT MAKES A GREAT STREET? D. Reed *Washingtonian Magazine* v52 no3 p51 D 2016

Fourth of July

America's 'Real' Independence Day Is Not July 4 O. B. Waxman *Time* v190 no2/3 p23 Jl 10-17 2017

CELEBRATING July 4th at the NATIONAL ARCHIVES *Prologue* v48 no3 p71 Fall 2016

DIGNITY AND THE FOURTH D. Remnick cartoon *New Yorker* v93 no20 p23 Jl 10 2017

RODEO A-GO-GO G. A. Warner color *Sunset* v239 no1 p38 Jl 2017

Fourth of July celebrations

A Fourth of July Fireworks Roundup! J. Russell *TV Guide* v65 no27 p32 Je 26 2017

Fourth Phase, The (Film)

COLDFRONT color *Snowboarder* v29 no2 p12 O 2016

THE POWDER AND THE GLORY B. BRADLEY color *Vanity Fair* v58 no11 p184 N 2016

Fouse, Quincy

Honor Roles J. VRABEL *Indianapolis Monthly* p17 F 2017

FOUST, GRAHAM

REMAINERS *Harper's Magazine* v334 no2001 p68 F 2017

TWENTY-FOUR HOURS FROM HOME *Nation* v303 no20 p32 N 14 2016

FOUST, MICHAEL

LUTHER'S MONEY REFORMATION cartoon *Christianity Today* p30 Mr 2017

Foust Prater, Lisa

FAMILY *Successful Farming* v114 no13 p75 D 2016

Fout, Alison R.

A bioinspired iron catalyst for nitrate and perchlorate reduction bibl diag *Science* v354 no6313 p741 N 11 2016

Fowle, Kyle

What to Watch color *Entertainment Weekly* no1476 p54 Ag 4 2017

Fowle, Trances

Mad Enchantment Claude Monet and the Painting of the Water Lilies *History Today* v67 no1 p57 Ja 2017

Fowler, Ann—Awards

Three Cheers for the Coach of the Year K. Beaudoin color *Dressage Today* v23 no4 p66 D 2016

Fowler, Brandi

THE HFPA AND INSTYLE KICK OFF THE 2017 GOLDEN GLOBE AWARDS SEASON color *InStyle* v24 no1 p42 Ja 2017

The Parties color *InStyle* v23 no12 p84 N 2016

SOLID GOLD color *InStyle* v24 no3 p153 Mr 2017

Fowler, Bree

Shop Online With Confidence graph il *Consumer Reports* v82 no12 p20 D 2017

Fowler, Cary

Seeds on Ice: Svalbard and the Global Seed Vault C. Moskowitz color *Scientific American* v315 no3 p86 S 2016

Fowler, Jermaine

JERMAINE FOWLER C. M. Smith color *Entertainment Weekly* no1451/1452 p97 F 3-10 2017

Fowler, Jim

You Can Make Your Sales Data a Lot Better with a Little Discipline *Harvard Business Review Digital Articles* p2 Je 13 2017

Fowler, Kat

BE THE CHANGE [Cover story] color *Yoga Journal* no296 p74 N 2017

Fowler, Micah, 1998-

My Obsessions? *TV Guide* v65 no6 p8 Ja 30 2017

Fowler, Paige

Eat Like an Animal color *Women's Health* v13 no10 p96 D 2016

FOWLER, RACHEL A.

The Arctic in the Twenty-First Century: Changing Biogeochemical Linkages across a Paraglacial Landscape of Greenland *BioScience* v67 no2 p118 F 2017

Fowler, Rickie, 1988-

Justin Thomas J. Marksbury and C. Barrett color *Golf Magazine* v59 no3 p42 Mr 2017

Fowler, Susan

What Maslow's Hierarchy Won't Tell You About Motivation *Harvard Business Review Digital Articles* p2 N 26 2014

Fowlie, Danny

RETURN OF THE PATRÓN A. GOGGANS bw color map *Surfer* v57 no11 p64 D 2016

Fowlie, Meredith

Reforming the U.S. coal leasing program color graph *Science* v354 no6316 p1096 D 2 2016

Fowling

See also

Bird trapping

Pigeon shooting

Turkey hunting

Waterfowl shooting
BIRD SEASON COUNTDOWN J. WILSON and J. B. SNOW color *Outdoor Life* v224 no4 p26 My 2017
HARDSHIP HONKERS B. FITZPATRICK and A. ROBINSON color *Outdoor Life* v224 no8 p43 O 2017
LIGHT UPLAND LOADS J. HAVILAND color *Outdoor Life* v224 no7 p68 S 2017
ONE, TWO PUNCH T. KEER chart color *Outdoor Life* v224 no6 p40 Ag 2017
OVERNIGHT FLIGHT P. Bourjaily color *Field & Stream* v122 no5 p30 O 2017
SCRATCH, THE UNKILLABLE S. LINDEN color *Outdoor Life* v224 no6 p51 Ag 2017
SNOW BIRDS D. DRAPER color *Field & Stream* v121 no6 p14 N 2016
SOUTHERN SWING P. Bourjaily color *Field & Stream* v122 no2 p32 Je/Jl 2017
THE TEAL ZONE T. CARPENTER color *Outdoor Life* v224 no7 pW5 S 2017
TOP SHOTS J. Taylor chart color *Outdoor Life* v223 no9 p77 N 2016
TURKEY RECOVERY G. BETHGE color *Outdoor Life* v224 no3 pT7 Ap 2017
WAYPOINT N. KREBS color *Outdoor Life* v224 no4 p5 My 2017
WHEN DOVES DON'T FLY M. PEARCE color *Outdoor Life* v224 no7 pH1 S 2017

Fox & His Friends (Film)
Fox and His Friends color *New Yorker* v93 no26 p10 S 4 2017

Fox, Allen
How to Play Like You Practice *Tennis* v53 no3 p10 My/Je 2017
Play Without Feeling color *Tennis* v53 no2 p70 Mr/Ap 2017
The Power of Focus *Tennis* v53 no4 p12 Jl/Ag 2017

FOX, ANTHONY D.
The Arctic in the Twenty-First Century: Changing Biogeochemical Linkages across a Paraglacial Landscape of Greenland *BioScience* v67 no2 p118 F 2017

Fox, Ashley M.
INVEST IN YOURSELF IN 2017 color *Black Enterprise* v47 no5 p46 Ja/F 2017

FOX, DANIELLE
HONOR ROLL color *Men's Health* v32 no7 p(Sp)9 S 2017

Fox, De'Aaron
FOX ON THE RUN A. Sharp color *Sports Illustrated* v126 no18 p30 Je 26 2017

Fox, Dorian
DEEP LISTENING *National Parks* v91 no1 p36 Wint 2017
GHOSTS OF THE GORGE: COAL, CULTURE AND THE TRANSFORMATION OF NEW RIVER GORGE NATIONAL RIVER *National Parks* v91 no3 p26 Summ 2017
Revolutionary Roles *National Parks* v91 no4 p10 Fall 2017

FOX, DOUGLAS
THE CRISIS ON THE ICE bw color map *National Geographic* v232 no1 p30 Jl 2017
The Day Warming Began bw cartoon color *Discover* v27 no10 p54 D 2016
Our Rocks, Ourselves color *Discover* v38 no5 p60 Je 2017
Persistent Heat Decimates Coral Reefs color *Discover* v38 no1 p23 Ja/F 2017

Fox, Emily Jane
IVANKA'S APPRENTICE color *Vanity Fair* v59 no2 p70 F 2017
THE NEW ESTABLISHMENT 2017 bw color *Vanity Fair* v59 no11 p87 N 2017
NEW ESTABLISHMENT bw cartoon color *Vanity Fair* v58 no11 p124 N 2016
She's Gotta Have Grit bw color *Vanity Fair* v59 no9 p174 S 2017

Fox, Erica Ariel
Manage Your Stress by Monitoring Your Body's Reactions to It *Harvard Business Review Digital Articles* p2 O 2 2017

FOX, FAYE
ALL NATURAL *Opera News* v81 no7 p22 Ja 2017

Fox, Jeremy
Green Giant P. KUH *Los Angeles Magazine* p44 My 2017

Fox, John
3 Keys to Shifting How We Pay for Health Care *Harvard Business Review Digital Articles* p2 S 25 2015
Bringing the Power of Platforms to Health Care *Harvard Business*

Review Digital Articles p2 N 10 2016
Giving Patients an Active Role in Their Health Care *Harvard Business Review Digital Articles* p2 N 21 2016
How to Make Electronic Health Records an Asset Instead of a Burden *Harvard Business Review Digital Articles* p2 D 8 2015
LETTER FROM THE EDITOR cartoon *Cincinnati Magazine* v51 no1 p14 O 2017

FOX, JOHN FRANCIS
STORIES WE TELL OURSELVES color *Vanity Fair* v58 no11 p88 N 2016

FOX, JULIA
Then There Were Three *USA Today Magazine* v145 no2860 p57 Ja 2017

Fox, Justin
Alan Shrugged *New York Times Book Review* p14 N 6 2016
At Amazon, It's All About Cash Flow *Harvard Business Review Digital Articles* p2 O 20 2014
Could a Four-Year-Old Do What Carl Icahn Does? *Harvard Business Review Digital Articles* p2 O 27 2014
The Economics of Knowledge Sharing *Harvard Business Review Digital Articles* p2 O 16 2014
The Freelance Economy Still Runs on Word of Mouth *Harvard Business Review Digital Articles* p2 O 9 2014
How the Market Ruined Twitter *Harvard Business Review Digital Articles* p2 O 31 2014
How to Tell if You've Made a Good Decision *Harvard Business Review Digital Articles* p2 N 21 2014
No One Actually Knows How to Regulate the Internet *Harvard Business Review Digital Articles* p2 N 18 2014
Our Misguided Obsession with the Tax Code *Harvard Business Review Digital Articles* p2 O 10 2014
PIRATES OF THE RUST BELT color *Bloomberg Businessweek* no4511 p63 F 13 2017
The Problem With Guilds, from Silversmiths to Taxi Drivers *Harvard Business Review Digital Articles* p2 D 4 2014
Strategy Lessons From Jean Tirole *Harvard Business Review Digital Articles* p2 O 15 2014
The Truth About the Gig Economy graph *Bloomberg Businessweek* no4528 p14 Je 26 2017
Uber's CEO Has a Little Bit of Vanderbilt in Him *Harvard Business Review Digital Articles* p2 N 25 2014
We Have Better Things to Do Than Prosecute Insider Trading *Harvard Business Review Digital Articles* p2 D 11 2014
What Still Makes Silicon Valley So Special *Harvard Business Review Digital Articles* p2 D 5 2014
When a Simple Rule of Thumb Beats a Fancy Algorithm *Harvard Business Review Digital Articles* p2 O 2 2014
When Stock Buybacks Are Not a Waste of Money *Harvard Business Review Digital Articles* p2 N 4 2014
Why Twitter's Mission Statement Matters *Harvard Business Review Digital Articles* p2 N 13 2014
The World Is Still Not Flat *Harvard Business Review Digital Articles* p2 N 3 2014

FOX, KIT
Bowl Her Over on a First Date bw color diag *Men's Health* v32 no7 p71 S 2017
BREAK THE TRANSCONTINENTAL RECORD! color *Runner's World* v52 no2 p22 Mr 2017
Fleet Geek color *Runner's World* v52 no4 p39 My 2017
KICKING IT OLD-SCHOOL color *Runner's World* v51 no10 p24 N 2016
NO DOGS ALLOWED color map *Runner's World* v52 no3 p76 Ap 2017
RUN AWAY! [Cover story] color *Runner's World* v52 no7 p54 Ag 2017
Runnerhood of the Traveling Singlet color *Runner's World* v52 no7 p50 Ag 2017
Runner's Digest color *Runner's World* v52 no8 p48 S 2017
RUNNERS WITH H(e)ART [Cover story] color map *Runner's World* v51 no10 p64 N 2016
RW 2016 COVER SEARCH [Cover story] color *Runner's World* v51 no11 p62 D 2016

Fox, Megan, 1986-
CHEERS & JEERS *TV Guide* v65 no4 p88 Ja 16 2017

Fox, Michael J., 1961-
The Kid Is Alright A. CORSELLO color *AARP: The Magazine*

v60 no3A p44 Ap/My 2017

Fox, Michael J., 1961——Interviews

Seth ROGEN cartoon *Vanity Fair* v59 no8 p132 Ag 2017

Fox, Porter

BETTER FOR IT bw *Powder* v45 no4 p36 D 2016

THE NEXT ERA color *Powder* v45 no6 p44 F 2017

Fox, Rose

Romance & Erotica color *Publishers Weekly* v263 no51 p101 D 12 2016

Romance & Erotica color *Publishers Weekly* v264 no26 p110 Je 26 2017

SF, Fantasy & Horror color *Publishers Weekly* v263 no51 p112 D 12 2016

SF, Fantasy & Horror color *Publishers Weekly* v264 no26 p122 Je 26 2017

Fox, Russell Arben

It Still Takes a Village color *Commonweal* v143 no17 p14 O 21 2016

FOX, SUZANNE

The City That Never Sleeps color *Publishers Weekly* v264 no38 p44 S 18 2017

Fox, Terry, 1958-1981

Trailblazers bw color *Maclean's* v130 no6 p64 Jl 2017

Fox, W.

Observation of coherent elastic neutrino-nucleus scattering diag *Science* v357 no6356 p1123 S 15 2017

Fox hunting

TRADERS POINT HUNT G. PALMIERI *Indianapolis Monthly* p20 F 2017

Fox News

FOX EATS CROW E. NUSSBAUM cartoon *New Yorker* v92 no36 p64 N 7 2016

FOX'S LIBERAL: Pundit Jessica Tarlov on playing the villain on America's most watched cable network A. Whiting *Washingtonian Magazine* v52 no8 p51 My 2017

How Fox News Created the War on Christmas D. Cassino *Harvard Business Review Digital Articles* p2 D 9 2016

How to Fight Fox and Friends M. HERTSGAARD color *Nation* v304 no9 p14 Mr 20 2017

Kafka Wouldn't Dare E. Alterman il *Nation* v304 no11 p6 Ap 3 2017

Power: Gabriel Sherman img *New York* v50 no10 p26 My 15 2017

THE RIGHT OVERSHADOWS THE LEFT *Nation* v304 no9 p17 Mr 20 2017

Fox News—Officials & employees

And Then There Was Hannity F. Gillette and A. Sakoui bw color *Bloomberg Businessweek* no4520 p54 My 1 2017

Fox Racing Shox (Company)

HANDY ADJUSTABILITY M. KAUSCH color *Dirt Sports + Off-Road* v51 no9 p62 S 2017

Fox Sports (Company)—Officials & employees

MIKED VICK R. Deitsch, T. Keith et al color *Sports Illustrated* v127 no7 p20 S 4 2017

Fox Valley Models (Company)

Fox Valley Models N scale 7-post boxcar C. Grivno *Model Railroader* v84 no7 p66 Jl 2017

FOX-BREWSTER, THOMAS

Old World, Young Promise color *Forbes* v199 no1 p20 Ja 24 2017

Foxconn Technology Group (Company)

Foxconned? J. MCCORMACK cartoon *Weekly Standard* v22 no48 p17 S 4 2017

Foxe, John, 1516-1587

Actes and Angels: Early Protestants were suspicious of the supernatural. Despite this, John Foxe's martyrology was replete with angels M. Spry *History Today* v67 no9 p18 S 2017

Foxley, Corinne

A FIRST LOOK AT COUNTER CANTER color diag *Dressage Today* v23 no4 p21 D 2016

ROUNDING OUT FIRST LEVEL color diag *Dressage Today* v23 no5 p22 Ja 2017

To get a feel for the aids that ask your horse to bend ... color *Dressage Today* v23 no4 p72 D 2016

Foxman, Simone

For Rich Families, A Change in Tax Plans *Bloomberg Businessweek* no4502 p45 D 5 2016

Mystery Deal *Bloomberg Businessweek* no4510 p33 F 6 2017

Passive Investing for The Social Activist color *Bloomberg Businessweek* no4511 p40 F 13 2017

Fox-Penner, Peter

Why Apple Is Getting into the Energy Business *Harvard Business Review Digital Articles* p2 N 15 2017

Foxwell, Elizabeth

Amelia Peabody's Last Hurrah color *Publishers Weekly* v264 no20 p38 My 15 2017

Disquiet in the Yard *Publishers Weekly* v263 no52 p98 D 19 2016

Foxwell-Barajas, Alanna

Manga Mania color *Christianity Today* v60 no8 p24 O 2016

Foxworth, Nicole E.

Vitamin B3 modulates mitochondrial vulnerability and prevents glaucoma in aged mice bibl graph *Science* v355 no6326 p756 F 17 2017

Foxx, Anthony, 1971-——Interviews

RIGHT OF WAY FOR ROBO-CARS X. HARDING color *Popular Science* p16 Ja/F 2017

Foxx, Jamie, 1967-

Beat Shazam M. Roffman *TV Guide* v65 no21 p38 My 15 2017

Foxx, Virginia

The GOP's Wellness Bill Would Give Employers Too Much Power A. Lewis *Harvard Business Review Digital Articles* p2 Mr 15 2017

Foy, Claire, 1984-

Claire Foy C. Mari color *Current Biography* v78 no5 p30 My 2017

The Crown M. ROUSH *TV Guide* v64 no46 p12 N 7 2016

Nice Hat M. Z. SEITZ img *New York* v49 no23 p84 N 14 2016

The royal treatment P. TREBLE color *Maclean's* v129 no44 p111 N 7 2016

A Sprawling Drama About Elizabeth II Aims to Be Netflix's New Crown Jewel E. Dockterman color *Time* v188 no19 p53 N 7 2016

Foy, Janet

IN THE DEAD ZONE I. Verzemnieks color *New York Times Magazine* p82 D 11 2016

Foye, Meghann

DEAR Younger mE *Scholastic Choices* v33 no1 p20 S 2017

Your Body Right Now! Is this weird? Is that normal? And perhaps most important—is that me I smell? Here, answers to a few of your most pressing puberty-related questions (ones you're maybe too afraid to ask!) *Scholastic Choices* v32 no5 p6 F 2017

Foys, Martin

Shot through the Eye and who's to Blame? *History Today* v66 no10 p6 O 2016

Foyt, A. J.—Interviews

What I'd Do Differently A.J. Foyt, 82 J. P. HUFFMAN cartoon *Car & Driver* v62 no8 p92 F 2017

Foytlin, Jayden

The Kids Are Not All Right M. BENNET *Audubon* v118 no6 p12 Wint 2016

Fraas, Arthur

Looking backward to move regulations forward color *Science* v355 no6332 p1375 Mr 31 2017

FRABA BV

When Safety Comes First *Stage Directions* v30 no3 p58 Mr 2017

Frable, Palma

Pennsylvania E. Bazelon *New York Times Magazine* p47 N 20 2016

Frac sand

Communities Take the Lead in Battling Frac Sand Mines E. Ness color *Progressive* v81 no5 p19 Je/Jl 2017

Frachetti, Michael

Herders helped shape Silk Road B. BOWER color *Science News* v191 no7 p9 Ap 15 2017

Fracking wastewater disposal

THE SMALL TOWN THAT FOUGHT FRACKING J. NOBEL color *Rolling Stone* no1288 p38 Je 1 2017

Fracture prevention

Bone Smarts... Bess Dawson-Hughes [Cover story] B. Liebman *Nutrition Action Health Letter* v44 no6 p3 Jl/Ag 2017

Calcium Myths and Facts [Cover story] V. Tweed chart color *Better Nutrition* v79 no11 p26 N 2017

Fractures—Risk factors

Easy ways to build better bones *Harvard Health Letter* v42 no1

p4 N 2016

Fraden, Seth

Transition from turbulent to coherent flows in confined three-dimensional active fluids color *Science* v355 no6331 p1284 Mr 24 2017

Fraenzer, Juergen-Theodor

Community network for deaf scientists color *Science* v356 no6336 p386 Ap 28 2017

Fragments of a Rainy Season (Music)

IN RETROSPECT A. PETRUSICH cartoon color *New Yorker* v92 no47 p64 Ja 30 2017

Fragonard, Jean-Honoré, 1732-1806—Exhibitions

Plus Ça Change P. Schjeldahl cartoon *New Yorker* v92 no35 p14 O 31 2016

Fragrance Lock (Company)

Does It REALLY Work? color *InStyle* v23 no12 p197 N 2016

Fragrance of flowers

Protein helps push petunia's scent out A. YEAGER color *Science News* v192 no1 p15 Ag 5 2017

Frahm, Nicole

The epigenetic landscape of T cell exhaustion bibl graph *Science* v354 no6316 p1165 D 2 2016

FRAIL, T. A.

BETWEEN HEAVEN AND EARTH: HIGH IN THE MOUNTAINS OF WESTERN ETHIOPIA, AN ISOLATED CHRISTIAN COMMUNITY CLINGS TO AN ANCIENT WAY OF LIFE *Smithsonian* v48 no4 p88 Jl/Ag 2017

Lost in Translation *Smithsonian* v47 no7 p68 N 2016

The People v. Jefferson Davis: A legal showdown 150 years ago laid bare the complexities of reuniting the States *Smithsonian* v48 no2 p18 My 2017

SUSPICION *Smithsonian* v47 no9 p88 Ja/F 2017

Fraillon, Zana

The Bone Sparrow color *Publishers Weekly* v263 no49 p70 D 7 2016

Fraizer, Andy

What Next? Succession Planning for Nonprofits *Bridges (Federal Reserve Bank of St. Louis)* p5 Fall 2016

Fraknoi, Andrew

Student Aid color *Sky & Telescope* v134 no2 p84 Ag 2017

Fralick, Pamela

Collaboration Is Essential to Revitalizing Health Care in Canada map *Maclean's* v130 no6 p58 Jl 2017

Frampton, Kenneth

A Long Look Back *Architectural Record* v205 no9 p59 S 2017

Framus (Company)

Framus Mayfield Pro 16-3106 C. Morrison color *Downbeat* v84 no7 p82 Jl 2017

Fran Silvestre Arquitectos (Company)

Blurring the Clean Lines of MODERNISM J. Tarmy color *Bloomberg Businessweek* no4533 p55 Ag 7 2017

Franaszek, Andrzej

Invincible Reason E. HIRSCH color *New Republic* v248 no7 p60 Jl 2017

POLE APART A. KIRSCH cartoon color *New Yorker* v93 no15 p67 My 29 2017

France

CARLA UNCENSORED M. Heyman bw *Harper's Bazaar* no3656 p325 S 2017

Comme les COLOMBIENS L. RAMZI color *Vogue* v207 no7 p42 Jl 2017

Dentists Without Borders: A unique encounter with socialized medicine D. SEDARIS *Saturday Evening Post* v289 no5 p40 S/O 2017

Hardware Char B1 bis J. Guttman color *Military History* v34 no4 p20 N 2017

A Travel Adventure Changed My Life R. S. Frazier color *Health* v31 no1 p49 Ja 2017

France, Cara

The Best Digital Strategists Don't Think in Terms of Either/Or *Harvard Business Review Digital Articles* p2 Je 16 2015

Build Your Brand as a Relationship *Harvard Business Review Digital Articles* p2 My 9 2016

A Cheat Sheet for Marketers on the Future of Digital Platforms *Harvard Business Review Digital Articles* p2 My 5 2015

What Creativity in Marketing Looks Like Today *Harvard Busi-*

ness Review Digital Articles p2 Mr 22 2017

France, David

Life in the plague years D. FRANCE img *New York* v49 no23 p36 N 14 2016

A Right to Live A. Sullivan *New York Times Book Review* p1 N 27 2016

FRANCE, KIM

What to Do About Getting Old img *New York* p32 Ja 23 2017

France. Armée. Grande Armée

THE GRAND ARMY DIET M. BROWN color *Archaeology* v70 no4 p22 Je-Ag 2017

France—Description & travel

Of Land and Sea K. Wheelock color map *Conde Nast Traveler* v52 no6 p60 Je/Jl 2017

France—Economic conditions

Macron, Le Terminator MOUTET color *Weekly Standard* v22 no39 p18 Je 19 2017

France—Economic policy—21st century

Macron Economics G. Smith color *Fortune* v175 no7 p13 Je 1 2017

France—Foreign relations—Germany

Does Macron Hold the Key to Merkel's Heart? C. Matlack and M. Deen color *Bloomberg Businessweek* no4515 p26 Mr 20 2017

The Limits of Nationhood: In the interwar period, France and Germany worked towards an integrated Europe C. Fischer *History Today* v67 no6 p12 Je 2016

France—Foreign relations—United States

HOMECOMING E. Osnos cartoon *New Yorker* v93 no19 p18 Jl 3 2017

France—Politics & government

After the Macron-Le Pen race, how will 'new Catholics' reshape French politics? Gobry color *America* v216 no13 p16 Je 12 2017

An Insider's Outsider C. Caldwell color *Weekly Standard* v22 no33 p8 My 8 2017

France—Politics & government—21st century

MACRON ON THE MARCH IN FRANCE A. GOLDHAMMER color *Nation* v305 no2 p22 Jl 17 2017

France—Politics & government—2012-

A BAD WIND L. Collins cartoon *New Yorker* v92 no39 p33 N 28 2016

Frances (Film)

Jessica Lange Can Finally Relax K. Miller color *AARP: The Magazine* v60 no5A p40 Ag/S 2017

Franceschini, Mark

you may be right chart *U.S. Catholic* v82 no9 p5 S 2017

Francfort, Henri-Paul

Ancient genomic changes associated with domestication of the horse color diag *Science* v356 no6336 p442 Ap 28 2017

Franchin, Alessandro

Global atmospheric particle formation from CERN CLOUD measurements bibl graph map *Science* v354 no6316 p1119 D 2 2016

Franchises (Retail trade)

Can a Franchise Make You Rich? J. Thompson color *Essence* v47 no12 p83 Ap 2017

Franchise Innovators M. RONEY *Forbes* v200 no3 p176 S 28 2017

Gottwals Books Turns 10, Adds 15th Store J. Rosen color *Publishers Weekly* v264 no10 p5 Mr 6 2017

Top Franchisers Provide Unique Opportunities for Vets M. RONEY *Forbes* v198 no9 p106 D 30 2016

We used to know all our colleagues - and their dogs *People Management* p24 D 2016/Ja 2017

Francioli, Laurent C.

Negative selection in humans and fruit flies involves synergistic epistasis chart graph *Science* v356 no6337 p539 My 5 2017

Francis (Film)

THE EMPATHY MACHINE J. ANDERSONMINSHALL color *Advocate* no1090 p57 Ap 2017

Francis, Clinton D.

Precipitation drives global variation in natural selection bibl chart diag map *Science* v355 no6328 p959 Mr 3 2017

Francis, Dania V.

Linking job loss, inequality, mental health, and education color *Science* v356 no6343 p1127 Je 16 2017

FRANCIS, DAVID

A NEAR MISS color map *Flying* v144 no10 p28 O 2017

FRANCIS, FRÉDÉRIC

The Odor of Death: An Overview of Current Knowledge on Characterization and Applications *BioScience* v67 no7 p600 Jl 2017

Francis, Heather

Dedicated Vegan Dietitian Dr. John Westerdahl *Vegetarian Journal* v36 no1 p35 2017

Veggie Meals in (or near!) National Parks *Vegetarian Journal* v36 no1 p25 2017

Where Are They Now? Catching Up with the Past VRG Interns and Scholarships Winners *Vegetarian Journal* v36 no3 p9 2017

Francis, Leah Gunning

"A BOOK I'D LIKE MY ELECTED OFFICIALS TO READ" color *Christian Century* v133 no21 p28 O 12 2016

Francis, Marc

OFF THE RECORD: REENACTMENT AND INTIMACY IN CASTING JONBENET *Film Quarterly* v71 no1 p32 Fall 2017

Francis, Mark—Interviews

From the ground up *U.S. Catholic* v81 no12 p22 D 2016

FRANCIS, MATTHEW R.

WHAT CAME BEFORE THE BIG BANG? color *Popular Science* v289 no5 p52 S/O 2017

Francis, of Assisi, Saint, 1182-1226

Upstart from Assisi: St. Francis is probably our most popular saint. But do we know who he really is? [Cover story] K. Manning color *U.S. Catholic* v82 no10 p12 O 2017

Francis, Penny

Eclectic Home P. Marquis *New Orleans Homes & Lifestyles* v20 no1 p94 Wint 2016

Francis, Pope, 1936-

THE APPROVAL MATRIX img *New York* v49 no25 p204 D 12 2016

At a time of real division, how can we help clear the air? First, breathe K. Weber *America* v216 no6 p3 Mr 20 2017

Blaise Pascal, blessed doubter C. Zaleski *Christian Century* v134 no18 p35 Ag 30 2017

Can Pope Francis help Venezuela step back from the edge? T. Padgett color *America* v217 no3 p15 Ag 7 2017

Cardinal Virtues R. Ferrone color *Commonweal* v144 no11 p8 Je 16 2017

The Dialogue of Fraternity J. L. Fredericks color *Commonweal* v144 no6 p10 Mr 24 2017

Discerning a New Role M. O'LOUGHLIN color *America* v215 no14 p8 N 7 2014

Doors of Mercy color *America* v215 no16 p5 N 21 2016

A drone for your thoughts color *U.S. Catholic* v81 no11 p10 N 2016

The Ecumenical Pope G. O'CONNELL *America* v215 p24 N 28 2016

FATHER PFLEGER B. Zehme color *Chicago* v65 no12 p152 D 2016

For the Record color *Time* v188 no20 p6 N 14 2016

For the Record color *Time* v190 no12 p8 S 25 2017

Francis for the Poor G. O'CONNELL *America* v215 no15 p26 N 14 2016

Francis' Heavy Lift H. Alvaré color *America* v216 no7 p54 Ap 3 2017

Francis the Preacher G. O'CONNELL *America* v215 no18 p24 D 5 2016

From roommates to riches: Christian tradition is clear about the way people should live together--and it doesn't include fine dining on the first floor J. Bazan color *U.S. Catholic* v82 no8 p18 Ag 2017

A Good Friday people M. Clark color *U.S. Catholic* v82 no4 p10 Ap 2017

Green works of mercy K. Clarke color *U.S. Catholic* v81 no11 p42 N 2016

Is the Pope 'Anti-Jewish'? P. A. Cunningham color *Commonweal* v144 no9 p19 My 19 2017

L.G.B.T. Catholics Should Be 'Accompanied,' Pope Francis Urges *America* v215 no11 p8 O 17 2016

The 'Madness' of Mercy *Commonweal* v143 no20 p5 D 16 2016

A More Pastoral Magisterium R. R. Gaillardetz color *Commonweal* v144 no2 p18 Ja 27 2017

MOTHER TERESA: LET US CARRY HER SMILE IN OUR HEARTS P. FRANCIS *Vital Speeches of the Day* v82 no11

p339 N 2016

No Stalemate R. Ferrone color *Commonweal* v114 no14 p8 S 8 2017

On Board With Peter G. O'CONNELL *America* v215 no14 p22 N 7 2016

Pastoral Accompaniment as Evangelization *America* v216 no13 p8 Je 12 2017

PEOPLE AND THE PLANET C. CARSWELL *Sierra* v101 no5 p25 S/O 2016

A Pope for the (Media) Masses R. A. Schroth color *America* v217 no4 p58 Ag 21 2017

Pope Francis says Vatican II liturgical reform is 'irreversible' G. O'Connell color *America* v217 no6 p17 S 18 2017

Pope visits Egypt to join imams, Coptic church in rejecting violence C. Lamb *Christian Century* v134 no12 p14 Je 7 2017

Reform of the Reform R. Ferrone *Commonweal* v144 no3 p6 F 10 2017

Springtime in Asia? G. O'CONNELL *America* v215 no13 p27 O 31 2016

There Has Been Too Much Hatred and Vengeance *Vital Speeches of the Day* v83 no10 p286 O 2017

Vatican Power Shift G. O'CONNELL *America* v215 no12 p26 O 24 2016

VOICES of 2016 cartoon *Christian Century* v133 no26 p8 D 21 2016

Why We Can't Stop Talking About Pope Francis J. Carroll *Harvard Business Review Digital Articles* p2 N 10 2014

Francis, Pope, 1936----Travel

No Slowing Down G. O'CONNELL *America* v216 no1 p28 Ja 2 2017

Pope Bashing *America* v217 no7 p8 O 2 2017

Pope Francis tells Colombians, 'Be slaves of peace' G. O'Connell color *America* v217 no7 p15 O 2 2017

Francis, Ray—Awards

Ray Francis: A True Friend and Horseman N. Jaffer *In Stride* v12 no1 p55 Ja 2017

Francis, Richard

Affable, He Convicted Salem Innocents S. Schiff color *New York Review of Books* v64 no4 p22 Mr 9 2017

Francis, Tony

Around the Campfire color *Trail Rider* v29 no1 p6 Ja/F 2017

Francis Albert Sinatra & Antonio Carlos Jobim (Music)

Revisiting Sinatra's Bossa Gems A. Morrison color *Downbeat* v84 no9 p13 S 2017

Francis Marion National Forest (S.C.)

Jeff Lerner, Vice President of Conservation Program *American Forests* v122 no3 p8 Fall 2016

Francisco, Jane

Always LEARNING color *Good Housekeeping* v265 no1 p10 Jl 2017

At my house *Good Housekeeping* v264 no2 p8 F 2017

fresh STARTS color *Good Housekeeping* v264 no1 p4 Ja 1 2017

FULL HEART color *Good Housekeeping* v265 no5 p10 N 2017

Getting OUTSIDE color *Good Housekeeping* v264 no6 p8 Je 2017

GOOD NIGHTS *Good Housekeeping* v265 no4 p14 O 2017

me to we *Good Housekeeping* v264 no3 p8 Mr 2017

silver linings *Good Housekeeping* v264 no4 p16 Ap 2017

Skin DEEP color *Good Housekeeping* v264 no5 p9 My 2017

"The moment that CHANGED OUR LIVES FOREVER" color *Good Housekeeping* v265 no5 p58 N 2017

Franck, Matthew J.

FRIENDS AND ENEMIES *Claremont Review of Books* v17 no2 p28 Spr 2017

Franco, Heather L.

Elimination of the male reproductive tract in the female embryo is promoted by COUP-TFII in mice color graph *Science* v357 no6352 p717 Ag 18 2017

Franco, James, 1978-

THE DEUCE IS WILD! K. P. Sullivan color *Entertainment Weekly* no1456 p18 Mr 10 2017

The Deuce K. P. Sullivan, A. Bacle et al color *Entertainment Weekly* no1482/1483 p29 S 22 2017

HOW I GOT MY STYLE: JAMES FRANCO J. Roth bw color *Esquire* p58 S 2017

In Dubious Battle L. Greenblatt color *Entertainment Weekly* no1454/1455 p82 F 24 2017

Mean Streets R. SYME color *New Republic* v248 no10 p54 O 2017

Porn, Prostitutes and Heart on HBO's The Deuce D. D'addario color *Time* v190 no14 p47 O 9 2017

Sleaze and the City R. SHEFFIELD color *Rolling Stone* no1297 p20 O 5 2017

That '70s Show M. Z. SEITZ img *New York* v50 no18 p83 S 4 2017

VICE SQUAD E. NUSSBAUM cartoon *New Yorker* v93 no29 p102 S 25 2017

Franco, James, 1978——Interviews

JAMES FRANCO IN The Disaster Artist C. Collis color *Entertainment Weekly* no1478 / 1479 p74 Ag 18-25 2017

Franco, Jill

Jill Franco A. BRANDT color *Cincinnati Magazine* v51 no1 p32 O 2017

Franco Ciccro, Catalina

Classes for All Classes K. Bahler color *Money* v46 no3 p19 Ap 2017

Francois, Willie Dwayne III

Reflections on the lectionary *Christian Century* v133 no21 p21 O 12 2016

Frandsen, Peter

Chimpanzee genomic diversity reveals ancient admixture with bonobos bibl diag graph map *Science* v354 no6311 p477 O 28 2016

Frangos, Cassandra

Hire the Best People, and Let Them Work from Wherever They Are *Harvard Business Review Digital Articles* p2 F 8 2016

How Cisco Gets Brutally Honest Feedback to Top Leaders *Harvard Business Review Digital Articles* p2 D 29 2015

How to Get on the Shortlist for the C-Suite color *Harvard Business Review Digital Articles* p2 Mr 2 2017

Identifying Leaders Who Could Bypass the Typical Promotion Path *Harvard Business Review Digital Articles* p2 S 27 2016

Franich, Darren

10 — NO MAN'S SKY color *Entertainment Weekly* no1444/1445 p123 D 16 2016

1926-2017 Harry Dean Stanton color *Entertainment Weekly* no1484 p17 S 29 2017

THE 25 MOST PATRIOTIC MOVIES OF ALL TIME color *Entertainment Weekly* no1472 p30 Je 30 2017

3 ROUNDS WITH INSECURE color *Entertainment Weekly* no1468/1469 p44 Je 2-9 2017

5 — FIREWATCH *Entertainment Weekly* no1444/1445 p122 D 16 2016

8 — THE WITNESS *Entertainment Weekly* no1444/1445 p122 D 16 2016

ADAM DEVINE color *Entertainment Weekly* no1465 p16 My 12 2017

After the Verdict color *Entertainment Weekly* no1482/1483 p62 S 22 2017

ALL ABOUT ALIA color *Entertainment Weekly* no1441 p30 N 25 2016

BABY, YOU CAN FLY MY CAR color *Entertainment Weekly* no1462 p11 Ap 21 2017

BEHIND THE DESIGN OKJA color *Entertainment Weekly* no1446/1447 p52 D 2016/Ja 2017

The Belko Experiment color *Entertainment Weekly* no1457/1458 p75 Mr 17 2017

BENEDICT CUMBERBATCH color *Entertainment Weekly* no1444/1445 p28 D 16 2016

BEST SUPPORTING ACTOR color diag *Entertainment Weekly* no1451/1452 p50 F 3-10 2017

BIGGER, RISKIER & STILL 100% UN COUTH color *Entertainment Weekly* no1435 p30 O 14 2016

BLOSSOM color *Entertainment Weekly* no1486 p36 O 13 2017

Breaking Big BRANDON MICHEAL HALL color *Entertainment Weekly* no1482/1483 p65 S 22 2017

BRIGHT color *Entertainment Weekly* no1478 / 1479 p78 Ag 18-25 2017

Chance color *Entertainment Weekly* no1436/1437 p90 O 21 2016

CHARACTER FLAWLESS color *Entertainment Weekly* no1484 p17 S 29 2017

Cobie Smulders' Guide to Getting Action color *Entertainment*

Weekly no1436/1437 p84 O 21 2016

Conviction color *Entertainment Weekly* no1434 p48 O 7 2016

Doctor Strange: The Curious Case of Two Teasers color *Entertainment Weekly* no1440 p14 N 18 2016

The Essential Paxton color *Entertainment Weekly* no1456 p14 Mr 10 2017

THE FATEFUL EIGHTH color *Entertainment Weekly* no1462 p10 Ap 21 2017

Fuller House *Entertainment Weekly* no1482/1483 p106 S 22 2017

FUTURE MAN color *Entertainment Weekly* no1474/1475 p68 Jl 21-28 2017

GARRY SHANDLING color *Entertainment Weekly* no1446/1447 p98 D 2016/Ja 2017

The Girlfriend Experience color *Entertainment Weekly* no1482/1483 p38 S 22 2017

GLOW color *Entertainment Weekly* no1471 p57 Je 23 2017

Gold color *Entertainment Weekly* no1451/1452 p89 F 3-10 2017

The Greatest Villains of All Time color *Entertainment Weekly* no1436/1437 p66 O 21 2016

HIGH ANXIETY'S OBSCENE PHONE CALL color *Entertainment Weekly* no1460/1461 p28 Ap 7-17 2017

JUSTICE LEAGUE color *Entertainment Weekly* p18 Jl 24 2017

KATE BECKINSALE & MILLA JOVOVICH RESIDENT QueenS of the UNDERWORLD color *Entertainment Weekly* no1450 p38 Ja 27 2017

KRYPTON color *Entertainment Weekly* p24 Jl 24 2017

LAURA DERN color *Entertainment Weekly* no1459 p34 Mr 31 2017

Law & Order True Crime: The Menendez Murders color *Entertainment Weekly* no1482/1483 p62 S 22 2017

Lion color *Entertainment Weekly* no1442 p41 D 2 2016 Rebellious Special Issue

Marvel's Inhumans color *Entertainment Weekly* no1484 p48 S 29 2017

Marvel's The Punisher color *Entertainment Weekly* no1482/1483 p106 S 22 2017

MICHAEL PEÑA color *Entertainment Weekly* no1459 p46 Mr 31 2017

Mindhunter color *Entertainment Weekly* no1482/1483 p107 S 22 2017

The Mindy Project *Entertainment Weekly* no1482/1483 p107 S 22 2017

THE MUMMY color *Entertainment Weekly* no1446/1447 p52 D 2016/Ja 2017

THE MUMMY color *Entertainment Weekly* no1463/1464 p48 Ap/ My 2017

NO. 16 DAREDEVIL color *Entertainment Weekly* no1436/1437 p58 O 21 2016

NO. 18 Batgirl/Oracle color *Entertainment Weekly* no1436/1437 p59 O 21 2016

No. 1 INSIDE color *Entertainment Weekly* no1444/1445 p120 D 16 2016

NO. 2 SPIDER-MAN color *Entertainment Weekly* no1436/1437 p45 O 21 2016

PICTURE color diag *Entertainment Weekly* no1451/1452 p70 F 3-10 2017

Pledging Allegiance color *Entertainment Weekly* no1448 p17 Ja 13 2017

THE PROS OF CON color *Entertainment Weekly* no1476 p32 Ag 4 2017

RE-PACKING HEAT color *Entertainment Weekly* no1466 p42 My 19 2017

Riviera color *Entertainment Weekly* no1482/1483 p106 S 22 2017

Ryan Hansen Solves Crimes on Television* *Entertainment Weekly* no1482/1483 p109 S 22 2017

SARAH SILVERMAN I Love You, America color *Entertainment Weekly* no1482/1483 p108 S 22 2017

SEPARATION ANXIETY color *Entertainment Weekly* no1478 / 1479 p14 Ag 18-25 2017

Star Trek Discovery color *Entertainment Weekly* no1482/1483 p104 S 22 2017

Star Trek: Discovery color *Entertainment Weekly* no1485 p46 O 6 2017

StartUp *Entertainment Weekly* no1482/1483 p109 S 22 2017

STAR WARS: MEET THE NEW LANDO color *Entertainment Weekly* no1438 p20 N 4 2016

STEVE ZAHN GOES APE color *Entertainment Weekly* no1471 p52 Je 23 2017

Stranger Things 2 color *Entertainment Weekly* no1482/1483 p100 S 22 2017

Taboo color *Entertainment Weekly* no1448 p54 Ja 13 2017

A Tale of Two Sheldons color *Entertainment Weekly* no1482/1483 p44 S 22 2017

A TIMELINE OF TREKS color *Entertainment Weekly* no1476 p28 Ag 4 2017

Tin Star *Entertainment Weekly* no1482/1483 p109 S 22 2017

TOP BANANA color *Entertainment Weekly* no1436/1437 p26 O 21 2016

Transparent color *Entertainment Weekly* no1482/1483 p109 S 22 2017

Travis Fimmel color *Entertainment Weekly* no1448 p55 Ja 13 2017

A True Texas Gentleman color *Entertainment Weekly* no1456 p12 Mr 10 2017

TRUMP TV: A LINEUP color *Entertainment Weekly* no1438 p19 N 4 2016

Two for the Road color *Entertainment Weekly* no1466 p13 My 19 2017

UNWRAPPING THE MUMMY color *Entertainment Weekly* no1470 p42 Je 16 2017

VIKINGS color *Entertainment Weekly* no1474/1475 p70 Jl 21-28 2017

VIKINGS' NEW ERA color *Entertainment Weekly* no1448 p54 Ja 13 2017

WAR FOR THE PLANET OF THE APES color *Entertainment Weekly* no1463/1464 p70 Ap/My 2017

What to Watch color *Entertainment Weekly* no1434 p50 O 7 2016

What to Watch color *Entertainment Weekly* no1459 p56 Mr 31 2017

What to Watch color *Entertainment Weekly* no1466 p53 My 19 2017

What to Watch color *Entertainment Weekly* no1478 / 1479 p97 Ag 18-25 2017

White Famous color *Entertainment Weekly* no1486 p48 O 13 2017

WORST POTENTIAL ROOM MATES color *Entertainment Weekly* no1436/1437 p50 O 21 2016

You Must Remember This color *Entertainment Weekly* no1451/1452 p16 F 3-10 2017

YOUR GUIDE TO (ALMOST) UNDERSTANDING TWIN PEAKS color *Entertainment Weekly* no1466 p32 My 19 2017

Your Sunshiny, Stupendous, Seriously Spectacular SUMMER BUCKET LIST color *Entertainment Weekly* no1470 p32 Je 16 2017

FRANK, AARON
Building the Third Offset *Commentary* v142 no3 p8 O 2016

Frank, Amy
How to Leverage Geocaching to Promote Park and Recreation Events *Parks & Recreation* v52 no10 p52 O 2017

Frank, B.
Revealing the subfemtosecond dynamics of orbital angular momentum in nanoplasmonic vortices bibl diag *Science* v355 no6330 p1187 Mr 17 2017

FRANK, BARNEY
The Year in Reading [Cover story] *New York Times Book Review* p8 D 25 2016

Frank, Eric
Lee Rubin: Our mentor and role model *Science* v355 no6327 p806 F 24 2017

Frank, Jacquelyn
Thirst color *Publishers Weekly* v263 no50 p57 D 5 2016

Frank, Jerome D.
FINAL EXAM *Lapham's Quarterly* v10 no3 p144 Summ 2017

Frank, Jon
Vastly Variable Veggies *Mother Earth News* no280 p10 F/Mr 2017

Frank, Josef—Exhibitions
Frankly Speaking C. HONG bw color *Architectural Digest* v74 no1 p40 Ja 2017

Frank, Lois Ellen
fully functional color *Amazing Wellness* v9 no1 p62 Wint 2017

Frank, Lydia
How the Gender Pay Gap Widens as Women Get Promoted *Harvard Business Review Digital Articles* p2 N 5 2015

Why Banning Questions About Salary History May Not Improve Pay Equity *Harvard Business Review Digital Articles* p1 S 5 2017

FRANK, MARY
SAVING THE WORLD'S OCEANS *New York Times Upfront* v149 no8 p12 Ja 30 2017

Standing Their Ground *New York Times Upfront* v149 no4 p6 O 31 2016

WALLED OFF [Cover story] *New York Times Upfront* v149 no11 p6 Ap 3 2017

Frank, Michael
The Mighty Franks: A Memoir *Publishers Weekly* v264 no9 p87 F 27 2017

SPEED DRAWING color *Road & Track* v69 no1 p100 Ag 2017

Want a Drone of Your Own? *Consumer Reports* v82 no1 p48 Ja 2017

Frank, Rebecca Morgan
Sometimes We're All Living in a Foreign Country *Publishers Weekly* v264 no38 p53 S 18 2017

Frank, Robert
Through a Glass Darkly N. PINKERTON bw *Film Comment* v52 no6 p90 N/D 2016

Frank, Sarah
BULL A. D'ARMINIO *TV Guide* v65 no8 p28 F 27 2017

Frank, Steven J.
Measuring and Communicating Health Care Value with Charts *Harvard Business Review Digital Articles* p2 O 26 2015

Frank, Ted
He Objects C. Hannan bw *Bloomberg Businessweek* no4533 p25 Ag 7 2017

Frank, Thomas
SWAT TEAM [Cover story] *Harper's Magazine* v333 no1998 p26 N 2016

Frank Body (Company)
BODY AND SOUL... SKIN LIKE THIS I. VALDESOLO bw color *Women's Health* v13 no10 p126 D 2016

Frank Smythson Ltd.
FORGET THE BAG color *Conde Nast Traveler* v52 no2 p28 F 2017

Frank Zimmermann
John Michael Julius Madey *Physics Today* v70 no1 p70 Ja 2017

Franke, Nikolaus
Sometimes the Best Ideas Come from Outside Your Industry *Harvard Business Review Digital Articles* p2 N 21 2014

FRANKE, SHARON
DO I NEED A SMART... color *Popular Mechanics* p76 My 2017

Energy-Saving $avings color *Good Housekeeping* v264 no4 p87 Ap 2017

FRANKEL, ALEX
THE BIG EMPTY color *Bike Magazine* v24 no3 p70 My 2017

Frankel, Bud
How You Make Decisions Is as Important as What You Decide L. Minsky and J. T. Peters *Harvard Business Review Digital Articles* p2 Ap 28 2015

Frankel, Glenn
THE UNFORSAKEN M. Dolan bw color *American History* v52 no3 p70 Ag 2017

Frankel, Glenn—Interviews
Of World Wars and Cold Wars and Hollywood Classics: Noah Isenberg onWe'll Always Have Casablanca: The Life, Legend, and Afterlife of Hollywood's Most Beloved Movie and Glenn Frankel on High Noon: The Hollywood Blacklist and the Making of an American... R. Longo *Film Quarterly* v70 no3 p84 Spr 2017

Frankel, Laurie
5 things that will fill you with hope color *Redbook* p115 F 2017

Poppy's Secret H. ROSIN *New York Times Book Review* p20 F 12 2017

Frankel, Nicholas
Oscar Wilde: The Unrepentant Years *Publishers Weekly* v264 no33 p67 Ag 14 2017

Frankel, Stuart
Bots That Can Talk Will Help Us Get More Value from Analytics *Harvard Business Review Digital Articles* p2 N 24 2016

Data Scientists Don't Scale *Harvard Business Review Digital Articles* p2 My 22 2015

Franken, Al, 1951-

The 'Al Franken moment' B. McGarvey color *America* v217 no4 p53 Ag 21 2017

But seriously, folks B. J. Dueholm color *Christian Century* v134 no20 p36 S 27 2017

The Happy Warrior [Cover story] M. Binelli bw color *Rolling Stone* no1289 p46 Je 15 2017

Ms. Katch Manages Up cartoon *Weekly Standard* v22 no38 p4 Je 12 2017

Save It for the Car: To succeed as a senator, Al Franken had to suppress his sense of humor. Until now M. BALL *New York Times Book Review* p10 Je 11 2017

Search Party J. Mahler *New York Times Magazine* p9 Ja 1 2017

The Senator Who Was Not Funny K. SMITH *National Review* v69 no15 p30 Ag 14 2017

Franken, Al, 1951—Interviews

Al FRANKEN color *Vanity Fair* v59 no7 p144 Summ 2017

LIVE FROM D.C.! C. P. Pierce color *Esquire* p30 Je/Jl 2017

Q&A J. Walsh il *Nation* v304 no18 p5 Je 19 2017

Frankenthaler, Helen

First Blizzard color *Art in America* v104 no10 p49 N 2016

Frankfort (Ky.)—History

Frankfort, 29 Kentucky J. DRILLING *Cincinnati Magazine* p58 Je 2017

Frankfurt am Main (Germany)

DOING BUSINESS IN: FRANKFURT A. Erace color *Fortune* v176 no1 p39 Jl 1 2017

Frankfurter Buchmesse

The Big Deal at the Frankfurt Book Fair: Free Speech A. Albanese and E. Nawotka color *Publishers Weekly* v263 no43 p4 O 24 2016

THE FRANKFURT BOOK FAIR IS TRENDING UP A. R. ALBANESE color *Publishers Weekly* v264 no39 p32 S 25 2017

Frankfurters (Sausages)

DOG DAYS J. BAINBRIDGE *Atlanta* v57 no1 p58 My 2017

DOG DAZE M. BRANDSTETTER, A. BRANDT et al *Cincinnati Magazine* v50 no10 p52 Jl 2017

AN ODE TO THE HOT DOG S. Rushin color *Sports Illustrated* v127 no1 p104 Jl 3 2017

Frankfurters (Sausages)—Sales & prices

OVER-THE-TOP DOGS B. Baskin color *Sports Illustrated* v127 no1 p108 Jl 3 2017

Franklin, Allan

The Rise and Fall of the Fifth Force: Discovery, Pursuit, and Justification in Modern Physics M. Riordan *Physics Today* v70 no4 p56 Ap 2017

Franklin, Aretha, 1942-

Firsts Women Who Are Changing the World [Cover story] N. Gibbs color *Time* v190 no10/11 p64 S 18 2017

Paying R-E-S-P-E-C-T to "Respect" J. Goodman color *Entertainment Weekly* no1453 p59 F 17 2017

Q + A *Cincinnati Magazine* p28 Je 2017

Franklin, Barbara Hackman

EXECUTIVE SUMMARIES MAY–JUNE 2017 color *Harvard Business Review* v95 no3 p170 My/Je 2017

Franklin, Barbara Hackman—Interviews

The Board View: Directors Must Balance All Interests S. CLIFFE color *Harvard Business Review* v95 no3 p64 My/Je 2017

Franklin, Benjamin, 1706-1790

Discussion *Smithsonian* v48 no6 p6 O 2017

The Franklin File V. M. Parachin bw color *American History* v52 no4 p34 O 2017

FRANKLIN'S SECRET HEARTACHE: HISTORIANS HAVE LONG DEBATED WHY BELOVED FOUNDER BENJAMIN FRANKLIN TREATED HIS WIFE SO SHABBILY. OUR WRITER HAS A STUNNING NEW THEORY [Cover story] S. COSS *Smithsonian* v48 no5 p68 S 2017

In the Spirit of Friendship W. Damon *Hoover Digest: Research & Opinion on Public Policy* no4 p185 Fall 2016

One Step Forward, Two Steps Back bw chart color *O, The Oprah Magazine* p143 My 2017

Franklin, Deborah Read Rogers, 1708-1774

FRANKLIN'S SECRET HEARTACHE: HISTORIANS HAVE LONG DEBATED WHY BELOVED FOUNDER BENJAMIN FRANKLIN TREATED HIS WIFE SO SHABBILY. OUR WRITER HAS A STUNNING NEW THEORY [Cover story] S.

COSS *Smithsonian* v48 no5 p68 S 2017

Franklin, Jamie

Thoroughly modern Moses: What did Grandma Moses have in common with the likes of Jackson Pollock? Arguably, plenty color *Magazine Antiques* v184 no4 p74 Jl/Ag 2017

Franklin, Jerry

AGAINST THE GRAIN W. Cornwall bw color map *Science* v357 no6359 p24 O 6 2017

FRANKLIN, JONATHAN

HOW TO BECOME AN INTERNATIONAL GOLD SMUGGLER color *Bloomberg Businessweek* no4514 p54 Mr 13 2017

Franklin, Kelly Scott

Stand & Wait cartoon *Commonweal* v144 no3 p39 F 10 2017

Franklin, Kirk, 1970-

MAKING GOD FAMOUS V. CUNNINGHAM cartoon color *New Yorker* v92 no45 p26 Ja 16 2017

Franklin, Mary Beth

SOCIAL SECURITY: The Real Crisis K. McCORMALLY cartoon graph *Kiplinger's Personal Finance* v71 no6 p26 Je 2017

Franklin, Pam

My Five Sisters: A Psychological Thriller Based on a True Story of Multiple Personalities *Publishers Weekly* v264 no20 p50 My 15 2017

Franklin, Rosalind, 1920-1958

Rosalind Franklin color *Discover* v38 no4 p50 My 2017

Franklin, Ruth

Absolutely Fabulist *New York Times Book Review* p16 Mr 26 2017

The Case for Shirley Jackson C. McGRATH *New York Times Book Review* p15 O 2 2016

A Deep American Horror Exposed bw color *New York Review of Books* v64 no5 p47 Mr 23 2017

Diving Into the Wreck color *Atlantic* v320 no4 p40 N 2017

THE ESCAPE ARTIST: Nicole Krauss and her precursors *Harper's Magazine* p90 S 2017

HAUNTED HOUSES Z. HELLER cartoon *New Yorker* v92 no33 p90 O 17 2016

THE HUNGER ARTIST *New York Times Magazine* p24 Ag 13 2017

The Joy and Terror of Shirley Jackson E. JUDD *American Conservative* v15 no6 p53 N/D 2016

'Just Make Sure You Don't Forget' color *New York Review of Books* v64 no8 p46 My 11 2017

LIFE AS FICTION bw *New Yorker* v93 no6 p73 Mr 27 2017

The Uncoupling color *Atlantic* v319 no1 p37 Ja/F 2017

Franklin, Sheree

4 Ways to Own Your Personal Power During Extremely Stressful Work Periods *Black Enterprise* v47 no4 p29 N/D 2016

Franklin, Solange

The Class of 2017: Seven new faces at New York Fashion Week img *New York* v50 no18 p49 S 4 2017

FRANKLIN, SOPHIA A.

The Courage to Continue *Idaho Magazine* v16 no6 p21 Mr 2017

Frankopan, Peter

Succession in the Silk Roads *History Today* v67 no1 p4 Ja 2017

FRANKOVICH, NICHOLAS

The Word And Its Words color *National Review* v69 no8 p38 My 2017

Franks, Paul W.

Exposing the exposures responsible for type 2 diabetes and obesity bibl diag *Science* v354 no6308 p69 O 7 2016

Frank Sinatra Collection: The Timex Shows, The (Music)

Sinatra Keeps on Ticking J. MCDONOUGH color *Downbeat* v84 no8 p79 Ag 2017

Franson, Sally

The Battle for the Boundary Waters color *Progressive* v81 no5 p27 Je/Jl 2017

Franta, Connor

TALKING ABOUT MY GENERATION: CONNOR FRANTA MADE MILLIONS OFF BEING HIMSELF, AND IT'S ONLY THE BEGINNING D. ARTAVIA color *Advocate* no1091 p78 Je/Jl 2017

Frantz (Film)

Frantz color *New Yorker* v93 no7 p22 Ap 3 2017

FRANTZ J. Christman *U.S. Catholic* v82 no10 p40 O 2017

THE LIVING DEAD A. LANE cartoon *New Yorker* v93 no5 p100 Mr 20 2017

Frantz, Alan C.

Faculty Expressions of (No) Confidence in Institutional Leadership *Change* v49 no1 p62 Ja/F 2017

Franze, Kristian

Brain's physical structure aids wiring L. SANDERS color *Science News* v190 no8 p12 O 15 2016

FRANZEN, BILL

SETTING THE RECORD STRAIGHT cartoon *New Yorker* v92 no41 p35 D 12 2016

FRANZEN, JONATHAN

Bad Sexpectations F. MOORE *Commentary* v140 no2 p69 S 2015

UNDER CONSTRUCTION color *New Yorker* v93 no33 p50 O 23 2017

Franzese, Bruce

How America Lost Its Mind color *Atlantic* v320 no4 p12 N 2017

Franz Ferdinand, Archduke of Austria, 1863-1914

When the World Went to War [Cover story] D. McMillen *Prologue* v49 no2 p6 Summ 2017

FRANZINO, APRIL

100 BEST BEAUTY EDITION color *Good Housekeeping* v264 no5 p23 My 2017

22 ways to get SUMMERLICIOUS color *Good Housekeeping* v265 no1 p21 Jl 2017

5 new ways to DEFY YOUR AGE color *Good Housekeeping* v264 no3 p27 Mr 2017

ASK APRIL color *Good Housekeeping* v264 no1 p20 Ja 1 2017

ASK APRIL color *Good Housekeeping* v264 no3 p25 Mr 2017

Beauty Sleep color *Good Housekeeping* v265 no4 p25 O 2017

drugstore beauty stars from $4 [Cover story] color *Good Housekeeping* v265 no3 p25 S 2017

GOOD HAIR DAYS guaranteed! color *Good Housekeeping* v265 no2 p25 Ag 2017

GREAT HAIR STARTS IN THE SHOWER [Cover story] bw chart color *Good Housekeeping* v265 no5 p43 N 2017

HOW TO winterize your skin color *Good Housekeeping* v264 no1 p25 Ja 1 2017

MONEY SAVING GUIDE [Cover story] cartoon color *Good Housekeeping* v264 no2 p79 F 2017

THE TRUTH ABOUT SUNSCREEN color *Good Housekeeping* v264 no6 p24 Je 2017

What are the best ANTI-AGING TRICKS? cartoon color *Good Housekeeping* v264 no2 p23 F 2017

your BEAUTY PROBLEMS solved! cartoon color *Good Housekeeping* v264 no4 p33 Ap 2017

FRANZMAN, KATE

Audubon Road color *Indianapolis Monthly* p32 Ap 2017

CHANGE the CITY *Indianapolis Monthly* p55 Ap 2017

COTTAGE INDUSTRY color *Indianapolis Monthly* v41 no2 p82 S 2017

DO THE WRIGHT THING color *Indianapolis Monthly* p36 Ap 2017

TOWN COUNTRY color *Indianapolis Monthly* v42 no2 p78 O 2017

WINNER'S CUP: A local potter sends fans on a hunt for free mugs around the city *Indianapolis Monthly* v12 no40 p36 Ag 2017

Franzoni, Chiara

Crossing borders along an endless frontier color *Science* v356 no6339 p694 My 19 2017

Franzosa, E. A.

A prominent glycyl radical enzyme in human gut microbiomes metabolizes trans-4-hydroxy-L-proline diag *Science* v355 no6325 p595 F 10 2017

Frappier, Steven

A Mass Shooting cartoon *Men's Health* v32 no4 p82 My 2017

Frase, Peter

The Left's Dreams & Nightmares F. Pasquale cartoon *Commonweal* v144 no5 p30 Mr 10 2017

Fraser, Andrea—Interviews

A Talk with Andrea Fraser A. DORAN color *ARTnews* v115 no4 p98 Wint 2016/2017

Fraser, Carole

Carole Fraser: All About Access *New York State Conservationist* v71 no3 p9 D 2016

Fraser, David

A LIFELONG LOVE OF YACHTS P. M. ROHIT *Sea Magazine*
v108 no10 pCA-6 O 2016

Fraser, Lisa

50 BEST COMPANIES FOR DIVERSITY [Cover story] color *Black Enterprise* v47 no3 p52 O 2016

EVOLUTION color diag graph *Black Enterprise* v47 no7 p46 My/Je 2017

THE MOST POWERFUL WOMEN IN BUSINESS [Cover story] color *Black Enterprise* v47 no5 p56 Ja/F 2017

Fraser, Mat—Health

Lifting Off S. Apstein and T. Keith color *Sports Illustrated* v126 no1 p16 Ja 9 2017

FRASER, WILLIAM

The Impact of a Large-Scale Climate Event on Antarctic Ecosystem Processes chart graph *BioScience* v66 no10 p848 O 1 2016

Fraser Yachts (Company)

A LIFELONG LOVE OF YACHTS P. M. ROHIT *Sea Magazine* v108 no10 pCA-6 O 2016

FRASER-CAVASSONI, NATASHA

GRECIAN FORMULA color *Architectural Digest* no5 p130 My 2017

Frassati, Pier Giorgio

Verso l'alto M. J. Rose bw *U.S. Catholic* v82 no11 p45 N 2017

Fratangelo, Bjorn

The Pride of Pittsburgh *Tennis* v52 no6 p69 N/D 2016

Fraternization

How Do You Handle an Office Romance? K. Morell color *Bloomberg Businessweek* no4511 p62 F 13 2017

Frattini, Federico

What Big Companies Can Learn from the Success of the Unicorns *Harvard Business Review Digital Articles* p2 Mr 14 2016

Fratu, O.

Observation of a large-scale anisotropy in the arrival directions of cosmic rays above 8×10^{18} eV *Science* v357 no6357 p1266 S 22 2017

Fratzke, Harold

ALL AROUND THE FARM® color *Successful Farming* v115 no7 p67 My 2017

Fraud

See also

Internet fraud

Investment fraud

Telemarketing fraud

Ticket fraud

And that's the way it isn't G. Adamson bw cartoon color *Magazine Antiques* v184 no2 p24 Mr/Ap 2017

False Front C. Chocano color *New York Times Magazine* p13 My 21 2017

Is VW's Fraud the End of Large-Scale Corporate Deception? M. Schrage *Harvard Business Review Digital Articles* p2 S 29 2015

Just the Facts color *Weekly Standard* v22 no15 p3 D 19 2016

ON FEELING FRAUDULENT *Psychology Today* v49 no6 p4 N/D 2016

Online Purchases Decrease After Fraud *USA Today Magazine* v145 no2859 p6 D 2016

Professional Identity and Dishonest Behavior P. Houdek *Society* v54 no3 p253 Je 2017

Fraud in science

AFTER THE FALL J. Mervis color *Science* v354 no6311 p408 O 28 2016

Misconduct found in fetal study fight color *Science* v354 no6311 p394 O 28 2016

Fraud lawsuits

Wheels of Justice M. McCann and T. Keith color *Sports Illustrated* v126 no15 p13 My 29 2017

Will Wall Street (or the Rest of Us) Ever Learn? B. Taylor *Harvard Business Review Digital Articles* p2 Ap 10 2017

Fraud prevention

See also

Prevention of fraud in science

India's Answer to Safe Payments A. Chaudhary color *Bloomberg Businessweek* no4514 p44 Mr 13 2017

When a Con Man Calls D. Shadel cartoon *AARP: The Magazine* v30 no6A p24 O/N 2017

Fraud—United States

All That Glitters ... D. SHADEL and J. EATON color *AARP: The Magazine* v59 no5A p38 Ag/S 2016

It's happening again G. Coppola and J. Butters color graph *Bloomberg Businessweek* no4531 p23 Jl 24 2017

The Leadership Blind Spots at Wells Fargo S. M. Ochs *Harvard Business Review Digital Articles* p2 O 6 2016

FRAZEE, LAUREN J.

Planning for the Future of Urban Biodiversity: A Global Review of City-Scale Initiatives *BioScience* v67 no4 p332 Ap 2017

Frazer, Greg

STACK THAT PATTY! color *Women's Health* v14 no4 p36 My 2017

FRAZIER, CORA

BREAKING UP WITH YOUR PARENTS cartoon *New Yorker* v92 no37 p43 N 14 2016

KATNISS EVERDEEN, WHITE HOUSE INTERN APPLICATION cartoon *New Yorker* v92 no42 p65 D 19 2016

OUR PARENTS ARE OUR FUTURE color *New Yorker* v93 no29 p50 S 25 2017

Frazier, Dai

Party-Hair Lookbook J. Mulrow color *Glamour* v114 no12 p142 D 2016

Frazier, Danny Wilcox

Cleveland: Four Days in Donald Trump's America img *New York* v49 no15 p13 Jl 25 2016

Frazier, David C.

American Interests and Obligations map *National Review* v68 no23 p2 D 19 2016

FRAZIER, IAN

DRIVE TIME cartoon color *New Yorker* v93 no25 p34 Ag 28 2017

EXTRA CREDIT cartoon *New Yorker* v93 no23 p21 Ag 7 2017

GOODBYE, MY FUNDING cartoon *New Yorker* v93 no13 p43 My 15 2017

GREETINGS, FRIENDS! *New Yorker* v92 no42 p91 D 19 2016

HIGH-RISE GREENS cartoon *New Yorker* v92 no44 p52 Ja 9 2017

HINDSIGHT cartoon *New Yorker* v93 no12 p17 My 8 2017

INCIDENT REVIEW cartoon *New Yorker* v92 no43 p29 Ja 2 2017

The Magic of the Oldest Pueblo bw *New York Review of Books* v63 no16 p58 O 27 2016

MR. "T" cartoon *New Yorker* v92 no39 p32 N 28 2016

UNBURIED cartoon *New Yorker* v92 no35 p41 O 31 2016

A Vast and Terrifying Saga bw cartoon *New York Review of Books* v64 no3 p22 F 23 2017

VICTOR LASZLO'S BLOG bw *New Yorker* v93 no28 p27 S 18 2017

WHAT EVER HAPPENED TO THE RUSSIAN REVOLUTION? We journey through Vladimir Putin's Russia to measure the aftershocks of the political explosion that rocked the world a century ago--an event that the nation itself is pointedly ignoring *Smithsonian* v48 no6 p48 O 2017

WHY MUMMIES? cartoon *New Yorker* v93 no2 p33 F 27 2017

Frazier, Jennifer Mckenzie

The New Dallas color *Southern Living* v51 no11 p73 N 2016

FRAZIER, KENDRICK

Academies Report Urges Bolstered Efforts to Protect Integrity of Science *Skeptical Inquirer* v41 no4 p5 Jl/Ag 2017

The Amazing Cosmos of Gravitational Waves *Skeptical Inquirer* v41 no2 p14 Mr/Ap 2017

Buzz Aldrin: What That Apollo 11 'UFO' Really Was, and Why He Punched That Moon-Landing Denier *Skeptical Inquirer* v41 no1 p5 Ja/F 2017

CFI, Richard Dawkins, Teachers Slam as 'Unconscionable' Turkey's Decision to Ban Teaching Evolution *Skeptical Inquirer* v41 no5 p7 S/O 2017

Chemtrails? In First Peer-Reviewed Published Survey, Atmospheric Scientists Say No *Skeptical Inquirer* v40 no6 p6 N/D 2016

Committee for Skeptical Inquiry Timeline, 2001-2016 *Skeptical Inquirer* v40 no6 p51 N/D 2016

CSICon in Limelight, The Selfish Gene Revisited *Skeptical Inquirer* v41 no2 p4 Mr/Ap 2017

Fake News and Fake Science in the Age of Misinformation *Skeptical Inquirer* v41 no3 p4 My/Je 2017

The Fires of Creationists, and Rallying for Science *Skeptical Inquirer* v41 no4 p4 Jl/Ag 2017

Humanities, Too: In New Study, History Courses in Critical Thinking Reduce Pseudoscientific Beliefs *Skeptical Inquirer*

NEW AND NOTABLE *Skeptical Inquirer* v41 no1 p60 Ja/F 2017

NEW AND NOTABLE *Skeptical Inquirer* v41 no5 p60 S/O 2017

Odysseys in Skepticism *Skeptical Inquirer* v41 no2 p65 Mr/Ap 2017

Over 150 Scientific Organizations, Sixty-Two Nobel Laureates Urge Repeal of Controversial Immigration Ban *Skeptical Inquirer* v41 no3 p5 My/Je 2017

Science, Public Trust, and CSICon 2016 *Skeptical Inquirer* v41 no1 p4 Ja/F 2017

Skeptics' Odysseys and Star Trek's Voyages *Skeptical Inquirer* v40 no6 p4 N/D 2016

The Spectrum of Skepticism *Skeptical Inquirer* v41 no5 p4 S/O 2017

Frazier, LaToya Ruby, 1982-

LATOYA RUBY FRAZIER L. N. Williams color map *Essence* v47 no9 p48 Ja 2017

LOST AND FOUND *New York Times Magazine* p53 O 30 2016

Frazier, Mya

Facebook Won't Hire You for Its Data Center *Bloomberg Businessweek* no4540 p27 O 2 2017

Why You Need the Internet to Drill *Bloomberg Businessweek* no4512 p33 F 20 2017

Frazier, Rozalynn S.

Celeb Labels You'll Love color *Health* v30 no10 p48 D 2016

GAME-CHANGING GIFTS color *Health* v30 no10 p116 D 2016

Glow on the go color *Health* v31 no9 p54 N 2017

Gone Glamping color *Health* v31 no5 p54 Je 2017

Knit to Be Tied color *Health* v31 no7 p77 S 2017

Learn to Layer color *Health* v31 no2 p54 Mr 2017

MISTY COPELAND "It is so amazing to be unique" color *Health* v31 no8 p16 O 2017

THE MOST FLATTERING SWIMSUITS of 2017 color *Health* v31 no4 p34 My 2017

Our Favorite Sports Bras Now color *Health* v31 no3 p54 Ap 2017

The perfect LBB color *Health* v31 no8 p52 O 2017

POWER UP YOUR CORE color *Health* v31 no7 p128 S 2017

Step It Up color *Health* v30 no9 p68 N 2016

Swimsuits for Every Sport color *Health* v31 no6 p54 Jl 2017

Tracy Anderson's Beautiful Body Secrets [Cover story] color *Health* v31 no4 p82 My 2017

A Travel Adventure Changed My Life color *Health* v31 no1 p49 Ja 2017

Frazier Associates Architects (Company)

Services *Virginia Living* p153 2017 Best 20of Virginia

Frazis, Harley

Employed workers leaving the labor force: an analysis of recent trends bibl *Monthly Labor Review* p1 My 2017

Freakley, Simon J.

Identification of single-site gold catalysis in acetylene hydrochlorination bw diag graph *Science* v355 no6332 p1399 Mr 31 2017

Frears, Stephen, 1941-

Director Stephen Frears on Victoria and Abdul, Judi and More S. Gutierrez color *British Heritage Travel* v38 no5 p66 S/O 2017

VICTORIA & ABDUL J. McGovern color *Entertainment Weekly* no1478 / 1479 p46 Ag 18-25 2017

Frebel, Anna

Searching for the Oldest Stars F. van den Bosch *Physics Today* v69 no10 p56 O 2016

Frech, Adrianne

What Do Women's Career Paths Really Look Like? *Harvard Business Review Digital Articles* p2 Je 8 2016

Frechette, Layne B.

Single-particle mapping of nonequilibrium nanocrystal transformations bibl bw graph *Science* v354 no6314 p874 N 18 2016

Freckleton, Melinda

BUILT-IN BUG CONTROL *Equus* no478 p22 Jl 2017

Canine care questions answered color *Equus* no481 p62 O 2017

DOWNTIME FEEDING color *Equus* no475 p30 Ap 2017

DRY RUN color *Equus* no476 p24 My 2017

FECAL SAMPLE 101 color *Equus* no475 p30 Ap 2017

FIRST-AID PURGE *Equus* no476 p26 My 2017

FUNDAMENTALS OF CONDITIONING color *Equus* no476 p24 My 2017

GET YOUR HORSE'S SHINE ON color *Equus* no478 p24 Jl 2017

HEAD OFF HAY SHORTAGES *Equus* no474 p14 Mr 2017

HEAVE-HO HAZARDS color *Equus* no473 p16 F 2017

HOT-TOWEL TECHNIQUES color *Equus* no472 p16 Ja 2017

HOW TO SUPPORT HEALTHY HOOF GROWTH color *Equus* no480 p20 S 2017

IDENTIFYING LEG "CRUD" *Equus* no477 p24 Je 2017

INVESTIGATING REPEAT HOOF ABSCESSES color *Equus* no470 p22 N 2016

MUD TROUBLES *Equus* no472 p14 Ja 2017

ORGAN ID *Equus* no478 p22 Jl 2017

PASS THE SALT color *Equus* no478 p22 Jl 2017

POP QUIZ: ALL EARS color *Equus* no480 p20 S 2017

POP QUIZ: ANATOMY color *Equus* no473 p16 F 2017

POP QUIZ cartoon *Equus* no472 p14 Ja 2017

POP QUIZ? color *Equus* no474 p14 Mr 2017

POP QUIZ color *Equus* no475 p30 Ap 2017

POP QUIZ color *Equus* no482 p16 N 2017

PREVENT WINTER WEIGHT LOSS color *Equus* no471 p14 D 2016

REMOVING GRASS STAINS *Equus* no475 p32 Ap 2017

SAFE RECOVERY FROM SEDATION *Equus* no482 p16 N 2017

SIGNS OF A HOOF ABSCESS *Equus* no481 p22 O 2017

SLEEP LIKE A BABY? color *Equus* no477 p22 Je 2017

STRAP SAFETY color *Equus* no472 p14 Ja 2017

TAKING STOCK color *Equus* no473 p16 F 2017

THE TOLL TRAVEL TAKES color *Equus* no477 p22 Je 2017

TWO WAYS TO SOAK HAY *Equus* no476 p24 My 2017

WATCH OUT FOR WASPS color *Equus* no481 p20 O 2017

WATCH WINTER WATER INTAKE *Equus* no473 p18 F 2017

WHAT INFECTION LOOKS LIKE color *Equus* no482 p16 N 2017

WHEN YOUR HORSE IS COLICKY *Equus* no480 p20 S 2017

WINTER BARN VENTILATION color *Equus* no470 p24 N 2016

Freddie Mac (Company)

Fannie and Freddie's Many Happy Returns J. Light graph *Bloomberg Businessweek* no4520 p30 My 1 2017

HIDDEN TREASURES OR MONEY PITS? M. Celarier color diag *Fortune* v175 no5 p33 Ap 1 2017

FRÉDÉRIC, EMMANUEL JEAN-MICHEL

I'LL DEFEND FRANCE. I'LL DEFEND EUROPE *Vital Speeches of the Day* v83 no7 p201 Jl 2017

Frederica Von Stade (Music)

Frederica von Stade: The Complete Columbia Recital Albums D. Shengold *Opera News* v81 no6 p55 D 2016

Frederick (Md.)—Description & travel

THE ITINERARY: FREDERICK J. Sugarman *Washingtonian Magazine* v52 no2 p237 N 2016

Frederick, Alyssa R.

From abalone to advocacy color *Science* v357 no6349 p422 Jl 28 2017

Frederick, Dennie T.

Potential role of intratumor bacteria in mediating tumor resistance to the chemotherapeutic drug gemcitabine diag *Science* v357 no6356 p1156 S 15 2017

FREDERICK, KATE CARTER

FALL FORWARD *Better Homes & Gardens* v94 no11 p48 N 2016

HELLEBORES color *Better Homes & Gardens* v95 no2 p64 F 2016

Fredericks, Dan

Q: Who Is the Worst Leader of All Time? color *Atlantic* v319 no1 p100 Ja/F 2017

Fredericks, James L.

The Dialogue of Fraternity color *Commonweal* v144 no6 p10 Mr 24 2017

Here All Along bw *Commonweal* v144 no6 p29 Mr 24 2017

Fredericks, Richie

THE HUSTLE M. HANSEN bw color *Powder* p72 S 2017

Fredericks, Sawyer

Winners' Club *TV Guide* v65 no19 p23 My 1 2017

Fredericksburg (Tex.)—Description & travel

RED, WHITE & PEACHY P. P. FISCHER color *Better Homes & Gardens* v95 no7 p126 Jl 2017

Frederico, Bruno

A switch from canonical to noncanonical autophagy shapes B cell responses bibl graph *Science* v355 no6325 p641 F 10 2017

Frederico, Carlos

Brazil's public universities in crisis color *Science* v356 no6340 p812 My 26 2017

Frederik, Marina C. G.

Release of mineral-bound water prior to subduction tied to shallow seismogenic slip off Sumatra graph *Science* v356 no6340 p841 My 26 2017

FREDERIKSEN, PETER

Don't Ask, Don't Tell color *Power & Motoryacht* v33 no1 p38 Ja 2017

Don't Get Hosed color *Power & Motoryacht* v34 no11 p56 N 2017

Go Big, or Go Small color *Power & Motoryacht* v32 no12 p22 D 2016

Making Sound Choices color *Power & Motoryacht* v34 no7 p22 Jl 2017

NEW TRADITIONS chart color *Power & Motoryacht* v34 no9 p72 S 2017

So Close, Yet… color *Power & Motoryacht* v32 no11 p48 N 2016

Stick the Landing color *Power & Motoryacht* v34 no9 p30 S 2017

Frederiksen, Peter—Interviews

Miami Bound J. WOOLDRIDGE color *Power & Motoryacht* v33 no2 p62 F 2017

Frederix, Pim W. J. M.

Polymeric peptide pigments with sequence-encoded properties color graph *Science* v356 no6342 p1064 Je 9 2017

FREDETTE, JENNIFER

The French State of Emergency *Current History* v116 no788 p101 Mr 2017

Fredlund, Beau

GRAVITY IN MIDDLE EARTH color *Skiing* p66 D 2016

Fredrick, Jules

How to Choose a Cruising Crew bw color *Sail* v48 no6 p10 Je 2017

Fredrickson, Jack

Hidden Graves: A Del Elstrom Mystery *Publishers Weekly* v263 no50 p52 D 5 2016

Fredriksen, Paula

Ancient Identities S. Ruden color *Commonweal* v144 no16 p31 O 6 2017

Free & Fair (Company)

Beat the Lines at the Polls R. F. MANDELBAUM color *Popular Science* v288 no6 p96 N/D 2016

Free agents (Sports)—Economic aspects

The Case for … Exercising Caution B. Baskin and T. Keith color *Sports Illustrated* v126 no8 p29 Mr 20 2017

Free agents (Sports)—History—21st century

The Class Of 2016 B. Reiter *Sports Illustrated* v125 no15 p36 N 7 2016

MOVING RIGHT ALONG … A. Benoit color *Sports Illustrated* v126 no5 p42 F 13 2017

TONY JEFFERSON'S Wild Ride A. Benoit color *Sports Illustrated* v126 no8 p68 Mr 20 2017

Free Application for Federal Student Aid (United States)

5 Things to Know About the New FAFSA K. Clark and K. Mulhere *Money* v45 no10 p37 N 2016

Free appropriate public education

Not So Special Ed M. SWARTZ *Texas Monthly* v45 no3 p26 Mr 2017

Free cash flow

At Amazon, It's All About Cash Flow J. Fox *Harvard Business Review Digital Articles* p2 O 20 2014

Free climbing

How to Lie Your Way to the Top K. CORRIGAN color *Climbing* no351 p40 F/Mr 2017

LEGAL FOR A DAY J. LUCAS color *Climbing* no350 p64 D 2016/Ja 2017

Free electron lasers

European XFEL to shine as brightest, fastest x-ray source E. Cartlidge chart color *Science* v354 no6308 p22 O 7 2016

Free electron lasers—Design & construction

Unique free electron laser laboratory opens in China D. Normile color *Science* v355 no6322 p235 Ja 20 2017

Free enterprise

Free-Market Folly C. Wilber color *Commonweal* v144 no9 p15 My 19 2017

ILLIBERALISM: THE WORLDWIDE CRISIS S. AHMARI *Commentary* v142 no1 p17 Jl/Ag 2016

PITY PARTY diag *Fortune* v75 no1 p15 Ja 1 2017

Protecting the Right to Take a Risk T. J. DONOHUE *Weekly Standard* v22 no42 p15 Jl 17 2017

'This Economy Kills' A. Annett color *Commonweal* v144 no11 p21 Je 16 2017

Free Fallin' (Music)

ESSENTIAL PETTY L. Greenblatt *Entertainment Weekly* no1486 p20 O 13 2017

Free Fire (Film)

Dazed and Bereaved D. EDELSTEIN img *New York* v50 no8 p132 Ap 17 2017

Free Fire C. Nashawaty color *Entertainment Weekly* no1463/1464 p89 Ap/My 2017

Free Fire N. PINKERTON color *Film Comment* v53 no2 p67 Mr/ Ap 2017

Free material

How making its iWork and iLife apps free could hurt Apple and its users D. MOREN color *Macworld - Digital Edition* v34 no6 p17 Je 2017

Is Mass Distribution of the Qur'an Useful? S. SYED *Islamic Horizons* v45 no6 p44 N/D 2016

WIN A GARDEN REVAMP! color *Sunset* v238 no3 p94 Mr 2017

Free radicals (Chemistry)

See also

Methyl radicals

Free Radicals & Antioxidants D. N. JACKSON chart color *Muscle & Performance* v9 no5 p58 My 2017

Free State of Jones (Film)

NEWLY AVAILABLE MOVIES M. FELL *TV Guide* v65 no23 p40 My 29 2017

Free throw (Basketball)

THE COMMON TOUCH D. Gardner color *Sports Illustrated* v126 no7 p60 Mr 6 2017

Free trade

China is no friend of ours T. GLAVIN *Maclean's* v130 no4 p10 My 2017

Protection Racket R. PONNURU color *National Review* v68 no24 p17 D 31 2016

Three Resolutions For 2017 R. LANE *Forbes* v198 no9 p8 D 30 2016

Free trade—Canada

BAD NEWS color *Maclean's* v129 no44 p9 N 7 2016

THE INTERVIEW J. KIRBY color *Maclean's* v130 no4 p20 My 2017

Free trade—United States

America's Uneasy History with Free Trade I. M. Destler *Harvard Business Review Digital Articles* p2 Ap 28 2016

As the Free World Turns G. R. SANDGREN, J. MAHONEY et al *Commentary* v144 no2 p4 S 2017

BAD NEWS color *Maclean's* v129 no48/49 p9 D 5 2016

Chilly Trade Winds J. McCORMACK color *Weekly Standard* v22 no21 p10 F 6 2017

GLOBALIZATION DOESN'T GIVE A DAMN B. GRULEY and R. CLOUGH color *Bloomberg Businessweek* no4517 p54 Ap 3 2017

The Human Side of Trade: In a dynamic economy, short-term pain is real. But over the longer term? Free trade leads to better, richer lives R. Roberts *Hoover Digest: Research & Opinion on Public Policy* no2 p13 Spr 2017

If Not Free Trade, Then What? C. J. WOLF color *Weekly Standard* v22 no10 p15 N 14 2016

Trump and Trade I. M. STELZER color *Weekly Standard* v22 no15 p27 D 19 2016

Freece, Brett

Shelter from the Storm B. PIKE color *Power & Motoryacht* v32 no12 p74 D 2016

Freed, Allan

Calculating the Market Value of Leadership *Harvard Business Review Digital Articles* p2 Ap 3 2015

Freed, Andrew M.

Formation of the Orientale lunar multiring basin bibl graph *Science* v354 no6311 p441 O 28 2016

Freed, Benjamin

19 THINGS YOU REALLY OUGHT TO OO THIS MONTH *Washingtonian Magazine* v52 no3 p31 D 2016

19 THINGS YOU REALLY OUGHT TO DO THIS MONTH *Washingtonian Magazine* v52 no1 p33 O 2016

AFTER SHOCK *Washingtonian Magazine* v52 no1 p28 O 2016

BALCONY POLITICS *Washingtonian Magazine* v52 no9 p51 Je 2017

THE CAT GAME BACK *Washingtonian Magazine* v52 no6 p13 Mr 2017

FULL ATTIC? *Washingtonian Magazine* v52 no2 p17 N 2016

HOBBLED HOTEL? *Washingtonian Magazine* v52 no1 p17 O 2016

HOW TO AVOID A BIDDING WAR: "CLOSE DOWN THE OPEN HOUSE" color *Washingtonian Magazine* v52 no7 p98 Ap 2017

IN DEFENSE OF 2016 *Washingtonian Magazine* v52 no3 p13 D 2016

OUR BRAND IS FINE *Washingtonian Magazine* v52 no8 p17 My 2017

THE PURLOINED LETTER *Washingtonian Magazine* v52 no6 p18 Mr 2017

THE REAL AND THE FAKE: DC has always had conspiracy theories. Now they have actual addresses *Washingtonian Magazine* v52 no12 p15 S 2017

RENT SEEKERS *Washingtonian Magazine* v52 no11 p13 Ag 2017

WHERE & WHEN: 17 THINGS YOU REALLY OUGHT TO DO THIS MONTH *Washingtonian Magazine* v53 no1 p31 O 2017

WHERE & WHEN: 18 THINGS YOU REALLY OUGHT TO DO THIS MONTH *Washingtonian Magazine* v52 no12 p29 S 2017

WHERE & WHEN *Washingtonian Magazine* v52 no8 p35 My 2017

WHO IS WEBSTER G. TARPLEY? *Washingtonian Magazine* v52 no2 p20 N 2016

Freed, Bruce

A Board Member's Guide to Corporate Political Spending *Harvard Business Review Digital Articles* p2 O 30 2015

Freed, Damon

IT'S ALL RELATIVE M. W. SCHWARTZ *Missouri Life* v43 no7 p26 D 2016/Ja 2017

Freed, Donald

Intersection of diverse neuronal genomes and neuropsychiatric disease: The Brain Somatic Mosaicism Network color *Science* v356 no6336 p395 Ap 28 2017

Freed, Douglass, 1944-

IT'S ALL RELATIVE M. W. SCHWARTZ *Missouri Life* v43 no7 p26 D 2016/Ja 2017

Freed, John B.

REDBEARD IN ITALY D. Abulafia *History Today* v67 no5 p92 My 2017

Freed, Lynn

Travels of a Lifetime H. Alford *New York Times Book Review* p1 Jl 30 2017

FREED, STACEY

Cost-effective OWNERSHIP color *Cabin Living* p32 Ja/F 2017

Pure & Simple color *Timber Home Living* v27 no2 p28 Ap 2017

sun power [Cover story] color *Cabin Living* p34 O 2017

Freedland, Jonathan

Dover and Out [Cover story] color *New York Review of Books* v64 no8 p22 My 11 2017

A Great Family Business color *New York Review of Books* v64 no5 p16 Mr 23 2017

Theresa May's Losing Gamble color *New York Review of Books* v64 no12 p42 Jl 13 2017

Freedman, Andrew

Marijuana Inc J. B. Wogan color *Governing* v30 no11 p24 Ag 2017

Freedman, Daniel

DANIEL FREEDMAN T. Panken bw *Downbeat* v84 no3 p24 Mr 2017

Freedman, David H.

IBM color il *MIT Technology Review* v120 no4 p72 Jl/Ag 2017

SELF-DRIVING Trucks color *MIT Technology Review* v120 no2 p62 Mr/Ap 2017

Freedman, Eric

IN THE SHADOW OF DEATH color *Earth Island Journal* v32 no1 p42 Spr 2017

Freedman, Harry

God's Wording E. M. YODER JR. cartoon *Weekly Standard* v22

no19 p36 Ja 23 2017

Freedman, Ilene White

Fresh, Homemade SALAD DRESSINGS *Mother Earth News* no281 p36 Ap/My 2017

Freedman, Josh

Higher Red color *Washington Monthly* p1 N/D 2016

Freedman, Lawrence D.

The Cold War They Made: The Strategic Legacy of Roberta and Albert Wohlstetter *Foreign Affairs* v96 no1 p160 Ja/F 2017

The Darkening Web: The War for Cyberspace/Understanding Cyber Conflict: Fourteen Analogies *Foreign Affairs* v96 no6 p156 N/D 2017

The Drone Revolution color *Foreign Affairs* v95 no6 p153 N/D 2016

Elvis's Army: Cold War GIs and the Atomic Battlefield *Foreign Affairs* v95 no6 p176 N/D 2016

The Evolution of Modern Grand Strategic Thought *Foreign Affairs* v96 no1 p161 Ja/F 2017

The Exile: The Stunning Inside Story of Osama bin Laden and Al Qaeda in Flight *Foreign Affairs* v96 no6 p155 N/D 2017

The General vs. the President: MacArthur and Truman at the Brink of Nuclear War *Foreign Affairs* v96 no2 p172 Mr/Ap 2017

How Everything Became War and the Military Became Everything: Tales From the Pentagon *Foreign Affairs* v96 no1 p160 Ja/F 2017

Pearl Harbor: From Infamy to Greatness *Foreign Affairs* v95 no6 p177 N/D 2016

Reporting War: How Foreign Correspondents Risked Capture, Torture, and Death to Cover World War II/The War Beat, Europe: The American Media at War Against Nazi Germany/Alamein *Foreign Affairs* v96 no3 p158 My/Je 2017

A Savage War: A Military History of the Civil War *Foreign Affairs* v96 no1 p162 Ja/F 2017

Unclear Physics: Why Iraq and Libya Failed to Build Nuclear Weapons *Foreign Affairs* v96 no2 p173 Mr/Ap 2017

Freedman, Leonard P.

On rigor and replication color *Science* v356 no6333 p34 Ap 7 2017

FREEDMAN, LISA

Family + money = happiness?! color *Redbook* p105 N 2017

Save your way to zero stress [Cover story] color *Redbook* p120 My 2017

Freedman, Marc

Aging Societies Should Make More of Mentorship *Harvard Business Review Digital Articles* p2 Jl 6 2016

FREEDMAN, SAMUEL G.

Battle Hymns of the Republic *New York Times Book Review* p13 O 16 2016

Freedman, Shalom

Article So Long Love Songs *Commentary* v140 no2 p5 S 2015

Freedman, Steve—Interviews

Pyrotechnics Beyond Definition T. H. Freeman *Stage Directions* v30 no2 p7 F 2017

Freedman, Wendy

HUBBLE TROUBLE J. Sokol bw color *Science* v355 no6329 p1010 Mr 10 2017

Freedom (TV program)

George Michael: Freedom I. Ratledge *TV Guide* v65 no43 p34 O 16 2017

Freedom Highway (Music)

The New Protest Singers W. HERMES color *Rolling Stone* no1283 p49 Mr 23 2017

Freedom Jazz Dance (Music)

Play All B. RATLIFF color *Esquire* v166 no4 p28 N 2016

Freedom Jazz Dance: The Bootleg (Music)

Making Every Second Count J. EPHLAND bw *Downbeat* v83 no12 p78 D 2016

Freedom Jazz Dance: The Bootleg Series (Music)

HISTORICAL ALBUM OF THE YEAR bw color *Downbeat* v84 no8 p40 Ag 2017

Freedom of expression

See also

Freedom of religion

Freedom of speech

Freedom of the press

The Art of Lying Taki *American Conservative* v16 no3 p58 My/

Je 2017

Ten Principles of Free Speech T. G. Ash *Hoover Digest: Research & Opinion on Public Policy* no4 p159 Fall 2016

The U.N., Hard at Work color *Weekly Standard* v22 no31 p3 Ap 17 2017

When the Nazis Came to Skokie *America* v217 no6 p40 S 18 2017

Freedom of expression—Social aspects

Nonpartisan Nonprofits Fight for Free Expression, Part 2 J. Maher *Publishers Weekly* v264 no14 p5 Ap 3. 2017

Freedom of movement

DEFINING MOMENTS *Phi Kappa Phi Forum* v96 no4 p5 Wint 2016

FREEDOM OF MOVEMENT S. KLAWANS bw color *Nation* v303 no19 p33 N 7 2016

Freedom of religion

Assessing Spinoza R. K. MASON *Commentary* v142 no2 p13 S 2016

THE OTHER CHRISTIANITY TODAY T. OLSEN *Christianity Today* v60 no8 p7 O 2016

Religious Liberty after Obergefell A. DESANCTIS color *National Review* v69 no11 p19 Je 12 2017

Religious liberty order draws mixed reviews D. Gibson *Christian Century* v134 no12 p14 Je 7 2017

The Week bw color il *National Review* v69 no17 p4 S 11 2017

Freedom of religion—Government policy

Reversing previous trend, worldwide restrictions on religion are up E. M. Miller *Christian Century* v134 no10 p15 My 10 2017

Freedom of religion—Russia

U.S. commission: Russia among worst violators of religious freedom L. Markoe *Christian Century* v134 no11 p15 My 24 2017

Freedom of religion—United States

Freedom to Serve color *America* v215 no10 p5 O 10 2016

Hobby Lobby on Steroids color *Nation* v304 no6 p3 F 27 2017

Keep Your Panic Dry W. Kristol cartoon *Weekly Standard* v22 no13 p7 D 5 2016

THE Never-Ending Pursuit of Religious Liberty S. Slade bw color *America* v216 no6 p18 Mr 20 2017

Religious Freedom Act also protects atheists K. Winston *Christian Century* v134 no2 p15 Ja 18 2017

Which religion's liberty is most threatened in the United States? graph *America* v216 no6 p6 Mr 20 2017

Whose religious freedom? [Cover story] T. Wenger color *Christian Century* v134 no22 p24 O 25 2017

Freedom of speech

See also

Student speech

The Art of Lying Taki *American Conservative* v16 no3 p58 My/ Je 2017

Blasphemy Laws Attack Free Expression—Can Freethought Hit Back? A. Bissell-Siders *Humanist* v76 no6 p9 N/D 2016

The Campus Culture Wars K. Steinmetz, C. Alter et al color *Time* v190 no16/17 p48 O 23 2017

Choosing Your Fight: Political Correctness and Free Speech on Campus M. Dunbar *Humanist* v77 no4 p9 Jl/Ag 2017

Counterprotesters greet "free speech rally" H. Gass and S. Hinckley *Christian Century* v134 no19 p13 S 13 2017

The Discomfitures of Academic Life J. Imber color *Society* v54 no4 p337 Ag 2017

Free Speech and Learning from Difference R. Muldoon *Society* v54 no4 p331 Ag 2017

GATEKEEPERS A. Marantz cartoon *New Yorker* v93 no25 p32 Ag 28 2017

Next Generation Leaders E. Dockterman, N. Kumar et al color *Time* v190 no16/17 p74 O 23 2017

Psychological Harm and Free Speech on Campus A. Cohen *Society* v54 no4 p320 Ag 2017

SHUT UP! K. A. STRASSEL *USA Today Magazine* v146 no2866 p10 Jl 2017

Ten Principles of Free Speech T. G. Ash *Hoover Digest: Research & Opinion on Public Policy* no4 p159 Fall 2016

Three Resolutions For 2017 R. LANE *Forbes* v198 no9 p8 D 30 2016

Under the Law J. Underwood color *Phi Delta Kappan* v98 no4 p76 D 2016/Ja 2017

WE MUST #PRESSON V. K. De Luca color *Essence* v47 no12 p10 Ap 2017

Why We Must Still Defend Free Speech D. Cole color *New York Review of Books* v64 no14 p61 S 28 2017

Words Matter S. NOSSEL *Publishers Weekly* v263 no48 p72 N 28 2016

Freedom of speech lawsuits

"The Power of the Thought":Contempt for freedom of speech reflects impoverished minds. Colleges that reject intellectual diversity are much to blame R. A. Epstein *Hoover Digest: Research & Opinion on Public Policy* no3 p120 Summ 2017

Freedom of speech—United States

The Bill of Rights *New York Times Upfront* p1 S 18 2017 Supplement

CLASSIC HUMANIST *Humanist* v76 no6 p10 N/D 2016

Don't Kick Neo-Nazis Off the Internet *Bloomberg Businessweek* no4537 p14 S 11 2017

Fighting Words K. Steinmetz color *Time* v189 no22 p32 Je 12 2017

Is free speech under threat IN THE UNITED STATES? WE RECEIVED TWENTY-SEVEN RESPONSES. WE PUBLISH THEM HERE, IN ALPHABETICAL ORDER F. ABRAMS, A. H. ALI et al *Commentary* v144 no1 p13 Jl/Ag 2017

One Campus Arena Where Free Speech Is Not Up for Debate: Law Schools H. Gerken color *Time* v190 no4 p20 Jl 24 2017

Sensitive Senate D. HARSANYI *National Review* v69 no4 p48 Mr 6 2017

Speaking Up for Free Speech T. J. DONOHUE *Weekly Standard* v22 no43 p8 Jl 24 2017

Freedom of speech—United States—Law & legislation

Free Speech Gave Us Trump K. Mangu-Ward *Reason* v48 no7 p2 D 2016

Religious Liberty *Congressional Digest* v96 no6 p30 Je 2017

Freedom of speech—United States—Universities & colleges

A 'Fractious' Feminist Decries the Ruthless Thought Police Stifling Free Speech on Campus C. Paglia color *Time* v189 no12 p28 Ap 3 2017

The Right to Speech Vs. the Right to Censor B. Walsh color *Time* v189 no9 p19 Mr 13 2017

Freedom of the press

A note from the editor K. Pope *Columbia Journalism Review* v56 no2 p8 Fall 2017

STATE OF THE FOURTH ESTATE Z. Robert *Iceland Review* v54 no6 p72 N/D 2016

Freedom of the press—India

Can the digital revolution save Indian journalism? L. Chaudhry cartoon color *Columbia Journalism Review* p80 Fall/Wint 2016

Freedom of the press—United States

How the Press Should Cover TRUMP N. DAWES color il *Nation* v304 no9 p22 Mr 20 2017

In Defense of an Open, Fair and Free Press N. Gibbs color *Time* v189 no9 p4 Mr 13 2017

President vs. Press S. A. Nelson *USA Today Magazine* v145 no2864 p14 My 2017

Freedom to Marry, The (Film)

The Freedom to Marry L. Greenblatt color *Entertainment Weekly* no1456 p56 Mr 10 2017

Freej, Mohammed

Children of No Nation [Cover story] color map *Time* v188 no27-28 p38 D 26 2016

FREEL, TYLER

KRYLON CAMO bw color *Outdoor Life* v224 no5 p94 Je/Jl 2017

Freelance journalism

A Ticket to Write J. Ullian color *Money* v46 no1 p140 Ja/F 2017

FREEMAN, AMY

THE STAKES color *Canoe & Kayak Magazine* v45 no1 p32 Wint 2017

Freeman, Arthur J.

Arthur J. Freeman S. Bader, B. Harmon et al *Physics Today* v69 no11 p69 N 2016

Freeman, Benny D.

Maximizing the right stuff: The trade-off between membrane permeability and selectivity color *Science* v356 no6343 p1137 Je 16 2017

Freeman, Burgess B. III

Restoring auditory cortex plasticity in adult mice by restricting thalamic adenosine signaling graph *Science* v356 no6345 p1352 Je 30 2017

Freeman, David

COLIC SURGERY [Cover story] S. D. Wenholz color *Practical Horseman* v45 no7 p52 Jl 2017

Freeman, Devonta

DIVIDE AND CONQUER G. Bishop color *Sports Illustrated* v126 no2 p40 Ja 16 2017

Freeman, Dori

WHERE I STOOD D. HARRISON *Virginia Living* v15 no2 p25 F 2017

Freeman, Frank

Hellscapes & Home Life cartoon *Commonweal* v144 no7 p30 Ap 14 2017

A Polish poet's 'Brave New World' color *America* v216 no8 p47 Ap 17 2017

Freeman, Gordon J.

Rescue of exhausted CD8 T cells by PD-1–targeted therapies is CD28-dependent bw diag graph *Science* v355 no6332 p1423 Mr 31 2017

Freeman, Hadley

Gold Standard bw *Vogue* v207 no6 p120 Je 2017

Wonder World color *Vogue* v206 no12 p242 D 2016

Freeman, John

Tales of Two Americas: Stories of Inequality in a Divided Nation *Publishers Weekly* v264 no22 p54 My 29 2017

Freeman, Julie

Thoughts on previous issues color *American Cowboy* v23 no5 p24 F/Mr 2017

Freeman, Kenneth W.

A Guide to Being Compassionate During Layoffs *Harvard Business Review Digital Articles* p2 F 25 2016

Freeman, Margaret

Margaret's Blog *Dressage Today* p14 My 2017

Freeman, Morgan, 1937-

Ageless Grace color *AARP: The Magazine* v60 no3A p2 Ap/My 2017

A Pictorial Toast TO The Celebrated Life AND Stellar Career OF THE ACTOR Morgan Freeman D. HOCHMAN bw color *AARP: The Magazine* v60 no2A p46 F/Mr 2017

Freeman, Morgan, 1937—Interviews

The Story of Us With Morgan Freeman K. Hahn *TV Guide* v65 no41 p35 O 2 2017

FREEMAN, NATE

DISOWNING IVANKA cartoon color *ARTnews* v116 no1 p98 Spr 2017

A HISTORY OF VIOLENCE bw color *ARTnews* v116 no1 p20 Spr 2017

HOUSE ARREST bw cartoon *ARTnews* v115 no3 p92 Fall 2016

Mom & Popped bw color *ARTnews* v115 no4 p116 Wint 2016/2017

FREEMAN, NEAL B.

Firing Line At 50 bw color *National Review* v68 no19 p44 O 24 2016

Freeman, Paul

At Archive Edition M. Ellen Polson color *Arts & Crafts Homes & the Revival* v12 no4 p50 Fall 2017

Freeman, Phil

Lavish Box Set Salutes Ornette bw *Downbeat* v84 no4 p13 Ap 2017

Freeman, R. Edward

Our Biases Undermine Our Colleagues' Attempts to Be Authentic *Harvard Business Review Digital Articles* p2 Jl 5 2017

Freeman, Richard

Crossing borders along an endless frontier color *Science* v356 no6339 p694 My 19 2017

Profit Sharing Boosts Employee Productivity and Satisfaction *Harvard Business Review Digital Articles* p2 D 13 2016

FREEMAN, RU

A Day in the Life of a Refugee *New York Times Book Review* p15 O 9 2016

Freeman, Samuel

The Headquarters of Neo-Marxism bw color *New York Review of Books* v64 no5 p63 Mr 23 2017

Freeman, Sarah

THE BOOZE SLEUTH color *Chicago* v66 no1 p60 Ja 2017

Thirsty? color diag *Chicago* v66 no2 p57 F 2017

Freeman, Tessa

Dancing Through the Dog Days K. HOLMES *Dance Magazine* v91 no1 p130 Ja 2017

Freeman, Thomas H.
A Moment and a Space *Stage Directions* v30 no1 p6 Ja 2017
Pyrotechnics Beyond Definition *Stage Directions* v30 no2 p7 F 2017

Freeman, Wills Crofts
The 12.30 from Croydon *Publishers Weekly* v263 no52 p101 D 19 2016

Freeman-Wilson, Karen—Interviews
DO MAYORS DO IT BETTER? E. KILGORE img *New York* v50 no18 p30 S 4 2017

Freemium business model
Apple, Spotify, and the Battle over Freemium Jingping Zhang *Harvard Business Review Digital Articles* p2 My 13 2015

Freer Gallery of Art
WHERE & WHEN: 17 THINGS YOU REALLY OUGHT TO DO THIS MONTH R. Cartagena, B. Freed et al *Washingtonian Magazine* v53 no1 p31 O 2017

Freese, Betsy
10 CHALLENGES FOR YOUNG FARMERS *Successful Farming* v115 no8 p54 Je/Jl 2017
10 SUCCESSFUL FARMERS: DALE REICKS *Successful Farming* v115 no8 p16 Je/Jl 2017
10 SUCCESSFUL FARMERS: JOHN SCHWARTZ *Successful Farming* v115 no8 p23 Je/Jl 2017
10 UP & COMERS: NADIA SHAKOOR *Successful Farming* v115 no8 p44 Je/Jl 2017
ADAPT NEW IDEAS! *Successful Farming* v114 no13 p42 D 2016
cut+paste *Successful Farming* v114 no12 p58 Mid-N 2016
FLEX-WING ROTARY CUTTERS: TACKLE TALL WEEDS WITH THESE VERSATILE MACHINES *Successful Farming* v115 no11 p34 S 2017
JEFF HANSEN: THE OWNER OF IOWA SELECT FARMS IS IN EXPANSION MODE color *Successful Farming* v115 no7 p48 My 2017
LAND HO! HERE ARE THE TOP 10 THINGS YOU NEED TO KNOW ABOUT FARMLAND *Successful Farming* v115 no8 p56 Je/Jl 2017
PIGS *Successful Farming* v114 no13 p54 D 2016
POSITIVE FILTRATION: IOWA SELECT FARMS IS BUILD-ING HIGH-TECH SOW BARNS DESIGNED TO KEEP DIS-EASE OUT color *Successful Farming* v115 no7 p45 My 2017
POWER UP! *Successful Farming* v115 no2 p50 F 2017
Q&A *Successful Farming* v114 no12 p64 Mid-N 2016
SOW PROLAPSE SYNDROME: AN INCREASE IN THIS MYSTERIOUS PROBLEM HAS THE INDUSTRY SEARCH-ING FOR ANSWERS *Successful Farming* v115 no6 p40 Ap 2017
STARTING A WETLANDS *Successful Farming* v114 no13 p66 D 2016
TERRY HOLTON *Successful Farming* v115 no1 p10 Ja 2017

Freese family
STARTING A WETLANDS B. Freese *Successful Farming* v114 no13 p66 D 2016

Freethinkers
GIVEN the EVIDENCE *Humanist* v77 no1 p8 Ja/F 2017

Freeware (Computer software)
Autoguiding with PHD2 *Sky & Telescope* v134 no6 p64 D 2017

Freeware (Computer software)—Evaluation
The best PC game recording software: 5 freeware capture tools compared I. PAUL color graph *PCWorld* v35 no10 p83 O 2017

Freeze, Kellie
APB *TV Guide* v65 no6 p39 Ja 30 2017
The Arrangement *TV Guide* v65 no8 p34 F 27 2017
Chesapeake Shores *TV Guide* v65 no31 p34 Jl 24 2017
The Gong Show *TV Guide* v65 no27 p30 Je 26 2017

Freezing
NOSH IN THE NEW YEAR A. STANEK and C. SAFFITZ car-toon color *Bon Appetit* v61 no12 p120 D 2016 /Jan2017

Frehsee, Nicole
Ancient Superfoods You Should Eat Now color *Health* v30 no10 p94 D 2016

Frei, Frances—Interviews
Yes, Your Uber Driver Is Judging You S. G. Carmichael *Harvard Business Review Digital Articles* p2 F 20 2015

Freiburger, David
Coolness: A Moving Target color *Hot Rod* v70 no10 p106 O 2017
The Dream Car color *Hot Rod* v70 no3 p106 Mr 2017
FINISH LINE color *Hot Rod* v70 no6 p122 Je 2017
The Hoarding Problem color *Hot Rod* v69 no12 p113 D 2016
Horsepower Shaming color *Hot Rod* v70 no7 p122 Jl 2017
I've Taken the Silver color *Hot Rod* v70 no2 p106 F 2017
Mission Creep in Media color *Hot Rod* v70 no11 p130 N 2017
Old Cars in New Time color *Hot Rod* v70 no12 p114 D 2017
One Lap of America color *Hot Rod* v70 no9 p114 S 2017
The Power of Just Driving Around color *Hot Rod* v70 no1 p114 Ja 2017
Road Tunes color *Hot Rod* v70 no8 p122 Ag 2017
So Much Love color *Hot Rod* v70 no4 p106 Ap 2017
V8 Anything color *Hot Rod* v70 no5 p114 My 2017

Freight & freightage
The Bertrand M. GARRIOTT bw cartoon color diag *Nebraska Life* v21 no1 p72 Ja/F 2017
INTO THE STORM T. KORTEN color map *GQ: Gentlemen's Quarterly* v86 no11 p140 N 2016

Freight car models
HO scale freight cars C. Grivno *Model Railroader* v84 no7 p11 Jl 2017
A little paint can improve N scale ready-to-run freight cars J. Kelly color *Model Railroader* v84 no9 p20 S 2017
Model a MOW BOXCAR M. R. Snell color diag *Model Railroad-er* v84 no8 p53 Ag 2017
News & Products color *Model Railroader* v84 no11 p10 N 2017
N scale freight cars C. Grivno color *Model Railroader* v84 no7 p15 Jl 2017
Trackside Photos color *Model Railroader* v84 no8 p66 Ag 2017

Freight cars—Evaluation
WalthersMainline HO 53-foot Thrall corrugated-side gondola S. Otte color *Model Railroader* v84 no2 p74 F 2017

Freight cars—Models
Model an aluminum billet load M. R. Snell color diag *Model Rail-roader* v84 no3 p35 Mr 2017

Freight cars—Models—Evaluation
Atlas N scale Norfolk Southern gondola C. Grivno color *Model Railroader* v84 no4 p99 Ap 2017
Atlas O Maxi-IV well cars pack a heavy punch E. White color *Model Railroader* v84 no3 p68 Mr 2017
MTH HO scale New York City subway cars E. White chart color *Model Railroader* v84 no4 p94 Ap 2017
News & Products color *Model Railroader* v84 no4 p10 Ap 2017
WalthersProto HO scale PRR BR70n RPO-baggage car S. Otte color *Model Railroader* v84 no4 p96 Ap 2017

Freightened: The Real Price of Shipping (Film)
Freightened: The Real Price of Shipping J. Fahrenkamp-Uppen-brink color *Science* v356 no6337 p484 My 5 2017

Freight trucking—Charts, diagrams, etc.
POCKET PRICE GUIDE: Action Prices On Class 7 Day Cab Semitrucks chart *Successful Farming* v115 no7 p19 My 2017

Freije, Catherine A.
Nucleic acid detection with CRISPR-Cas13a/C2c2 color diag *Science* v356 no6336 p438 Ap 28 2017

Freire, M. M.
Observation of a large-scale anisotropy in the arrival directions of cosmic rays above 8 × 1018 eV *Science* v357 no6357 p1266 S 22 2017

Freire, Olival, Jr.
John Stewart Bell and Twentieth-Century Physics Vision and In-tegrity *Physics Today* v70 no2 p57 F 2017

FREITAG, MONICA
Winter Wonderland WEEKEND bw color *Cabin Living* p88 D 2016

Freitas, Donna
NEVER LET THEM SEE YOU CRY A. ROOT cartoon color *Christianity Today* p57 Mr 2017
Sex and the Catholic college campus C. Camosy *America* v217 no6 p55 S 18 2017

Freitas, Gerson, Jr.
Will Bad Beef Taint Brazil's Meat Master? cartoon chart *Bloom-berg Businessweek* no4516 p20 Mr 27 2017

FREIWALD, JAN

Long-Term Studies Contribute Disproportionately to Ecology and Policy *BioScience* v67 no3 p271 Mr 2017

Freiwald, Winrich A.
A dedicated network for social interaction processing in the primate brain color diag *Science* v356 no6339 p745 My 19 2017
Two areas for familiar face recognition in the primate brain color graph *Science* v357 no6351 p591 Ag 11 2017

Freking, Grant
BOATASHORE *Cincinnati Magazine* v50 no3 p32 D 2016
NEW COACH, OLD DREAM *Cincinnati Magazine* v50 no12 p23 S 2017
NORTHERN LIGHTS *Cincinnati Magazine* v50 no5 p69 F 2017
SISTER ACT *Cincinnati Magazine* v50 no4 p24 Ja 2017
WARM WHEELS *Cincinnati Magazine* v50 no6 p30 Mr 2017

Freling, Ryan E.
How to Design a Return Policy *Harvard Business Review Digital Articles* p2 Ag 2 2016

Frelinghuysen, Suzy, 1911-1988
Old avant-garde G. Cerio color *Magazine Antiques* v184 no3 p124 My/Je 2017

Frémaux, Thierry
Gatekeeping Without Tears J. Romney color *Film Comment* v53 no4 p78 Jl/Ag 2017

Frémaux, Thierry—Interviews
In the Beginning N. Rapold bw color *Film Comment* v53 no3 p10 My/Je 2017

Fremling, C.
iPTF16geu: A multiply imaged, gravitationally lensed type Ia supernova color diag graph *Science* v356 no6335 p291 Ap 21 2017

French, Alex
FOR THE DEFENSE color *Esquire* p130 S 2017
HARD CORPS color *Esquire* v167 no2 p142 Mr 2017
NOT-SO-INTELLECTUAL PROPERTY *New York Times Magazine* p30 Jl 30 2017

French, Anthony Philip
Anthony Philip French P. H. Fisher and C. H. Holbrow *Physics Today* v70 no6 p74 Je 2017

FRENCH, ASHA
Love Fearlessly color *Ebony* v72 no4 p36 F 2017
Write the Power! color *Ebony* v72 no3 p44 D 2016/Ja 2017

FRENCH, CHRISTOPHER C.
From Tiny Acorns ... *Skeptical Inquirer* v40 no6 p39 N/D 2016
The John Maddox Prize Nomination for Elizabeth Loftus *Skeptical Inquirer* v41 no2 p20 Mr/Ap 2017

French, Christopher E.
Deep functional analysis of synII, a 770-kilobase synthetic yeast chromosome diag *Science* v355 no6329 p1047 Mr 10 2017

French, Dan
The best of both worlds color *Phi Delta Kappan* v98 no3 p60 N 2016

FRENCH, DAVID
The Celebrity We Need [Cover story] color *National Review* v69 no9 p21 My 15 2017
Congress and Campus color *National Review* v69 no19 p38 O 16 2017
Gun Culture in Black and White *National Review* v69 no3 p36 F 20 2017
Immobility In America color *National Review* v69 no8 p36 My 2017
Is free speech under threat IN THE UNITED STATES? WE RECEIVED TWENTY-SEVEN RESPONSES. WE PUBLISH THEM HERE, IN ALPHABETICAL ORDER *Commentary* v144 no1 p13 Jl/Ag 2017
Malign Marcuse il *National Review* v69 no7 p32 Ap 17 2017
The Myth of the Virtuous Poor *National Review* v69 no2 p30 F 6 2017
Prosecuting Politics color *National Review* v69 no16 p16 Ag 28 2017
A Second Chance in Iraq color *National Review* v68 no21 p26 N 21 2016
Trumpocalypse [Cover story] il *National Review* v68 no23 p26 D 19 2016

French, Howard W.
The Clash of Victimizations D. Kurtz-Phelan color *Washington Monthly* v49 no6-8 p63 Je-Ag 2017

Recreating China's Imagined Empire I. Johnson color map *New York Review of Books* v64 no7 p33 Ap 20 2017

French, John
John French Wins Wire-To-Wire in the WCHR Professional Finals T. Booker *In Stride* v11 no6 p22 N 2016

French, John—Interviews
John French: 'Try to Always Find the Good' T. Conahan color *Practical Horseman* v45 no2 p22 F 2017

French, Paul
Shanghaied L. Ermelino bw color map *Publishers Weekly* v264 no41 p20 O 9 2017

French, Sue
Doodles in the Sky *Sky & Telescope* v133 no6 p54 Je 2017
The Inconstant Star: The joys of observing variable stars are predictably wonderful *Sky & Telescope* v134 no4 p54 O 2017
It's All About the Ears *Sky & Telescope* v133 no2 p54 F 2017
The Lion-Guarded Gate *Sky & Telescope* v133 no4 p54 Ap 2017
M33 in a 10-inch Scope *Sky & Telescope* v132 no6 p54 D 2016
Overlooked Wonders of Summer: Take some time to explore these lesser-known deep-sky sights chart color *Sky & Telescope* v134 no2 p54 Ag 2017
The Queen's Finest: Look to Cassiopeia for her varied collection of celestial treasure *Sky & Telescope* v134 no6 p55 D 2017
Showpiece Doubles: Point your telescope toward these gems of the late-summer sky *Sky & Telescope* v134 no3 p54 S 2017
The Spring Goddess *Sky & Telescope* v133 no5 p54 My 2017
Square Galaxies: Spend some time roping this herd of faint fuzzies in the Great Square of Pegasus chart color *Sky & Telescope* v134 no5 p55 N 2017
Summer Highlights: Warm nights and dark skies are ideal for enjoying these classic beauties *Sky & Telescope* v134 no1 p54 Jl 2017

French, Tana
THE BIG QUESTION cartoon *Atlantic* v320 no3 p100 O 2017
Murder, She Wrote S. Begley color *Time* v188 no15 p61 O 17 2016

French, Tana—Interviews
By the Book T. French *New York Times Book Review* p8 O 2 2016

French authors
See also
French novelists
MICHEL BUTOR L. DAVIS *New York Times Magazine* p58 D 25 2016

French Broad River (N.C. & Tenn.)
THE WEEKENDERS B. RUZZO and G. BETHGE color map *Outdoor Life* v224 no4 p59 My 2017

French bulldog
JE T'AIME FRENCHIES A. HEROLD *Los Angeles Magazine* p118 Mr 2017

French-Canadians
Je M'Excuse J. KAY cartoon *Walrus* p71 Ja\F 2017

French cooking
FRENCH, THREE WAYS G. DUFFY img *New York* v49 no22 p74 O 31 2016
French vs. Italian E. Laborde *New Orleans Magazine* v51 no7 p14 My 2017
HOLIDAY FOOD G. DUFFY img *New York* v49 no22 p71 O 31 2016

French language—Translating
HOW to READ PROUST in the ORIGINAL L. Brown *New York Times Book Review* p23 Mr 5 2017

French novelists
THE NOTES OF PATRICK MODIANO P. de Jonge *Harper's Magazine* v334 no2000 p77 Ja 2017

French presidential elections
CAN THE CENTER HOLD? L. COLLINS bw cartoon *New Yorker* v93 no12 p20 My 8 2017
France's Battle Royale T. John color *Time* v189 no5 p9 F 13 2017
Give This Man A Party M. Champion, H. Fouquet et al color *Bloomberg Businessweek* no4520 p27 My 1 2017
In France, an Election Veers Off the Rails G. Viscusi and C. Matlack graph *Bloomberg Businessweek* no4511 p17 F 13 2017

French restaurants
Last call at Le Mas J. RICHLER color *Maclean's* v129 no40 p75 O 10 2016

French restaurants—Evaluation

AS GOOD AS IT GETS A. AHUJA *Cincinnati Magazine* v50 no4 p144 Ja 2017

COAST TO COAST J. Steingarten color *Vogue* v207 no11 p208 N 2017

DINING GUIDE *Cincinnati Magazine* v50 no4 p153 Ja 2017

DINING GUIDE color *New Orleans Magazine* v51 no9 p88 Jl 2017

FRENCH *Cincinnati Magazine* v50 no8 p120 My 2017

LA VIE EN ROSE A. WITCHEL color *Vanity Fair* v59 no9 p168 S 2017

PANCAKES *Washingtonian Magazine* v52 no1 p89 O 2016

SCENE STEALER A. RICHMA color *Esquire* v166 no4 p124 N 2016

French-speaking people

Je M'Excuse J. KAY cartoon *Walrus* p71 Ja\F 2017

French—Attitudes

French Catholics' political awakening color *Christian Century* v134 no8 p1 Ap 12 2017

French Open (Paris, France)

French Open Issue *Tennis* v53 no3 p36 My/Je 2017

A Grand Slump P. Bodo *Tennis* v53 no3 p6 My/Je 2017

Tour Guide E. D. McGROGAN chart *Tennis* v53 no3 p32 My/Je 2017

Frenette, Paul S.

Self-renewal of a purified Tie2+ hematopoietic stem cell population relies on mitochondrial clearance bibl graph *Science* v354 no6316 p1156 D 2 2016

Frequent flyer programs

When a Premium Card Pays Off T. Tepper diag *Money* v45 no10 p32 N 2016

Frere, Justin J.

Enhancement of Zika virus pathogenesis by preexisting antiflavivirus immunity graph *Science* v356 no6334 p175 Ap 14 2017

Fresco painting

Lasers reveal long-hidden catacomb frescoes that have biblical themes J. McKenna color *Christian Century* v134 no15 p16 Jl 19 2017

Frese, Michael

Teaching personal initiative beats traditional training in boosting small business in West Africa chart graph *Science* v357 no6357 p1287 S 22 2017

Fresh Air (Music)

Cream of the Crop HADLEY color *Downbeat* v84 no1 p73 Ja 2017

Fresh off the Boat (TV program)

Constance Wu's Crazy Success R. Rahman color *Entertainment Weekly* no1485 p50 O 6 2017

Fresh Off the Boat N. Abrams, A. Bacle et al color *Entertainment Weekly* no1482/1483 p63 S 22 2017

Fresh water

See also

Drinking water

THE ART OF THE EEL N. HONACHEFSKY and G. BETHGE color *Outdoor Life* v224 no4 p66 My 2017

LIFE at River Bottom A. G. Landis color *Earth Island Journal* v32 no1 p49 Spr 2017

Release of mineral-bound water prior to subduction tied to shallow seismogenic slip off Sumatra A. Hüpers, M. E. Torres et al graph *Science* v356 no6340 p841 My 26 2017

Fresh water—Government policy

Water strategies for the next administration P. H. Gleiek bibl graph *Science* v354 no6312 p555 N 4 2016

Fresh water—International cooperation

Resources Water Fights B. Einhorn color map *Bloomberg Businessweek* no4497 p19 O 31 2016

FreshBooks (Company)

STARTING OVER B. BURLINGHAM color *Forbes* v199 no5 p92 My 16 2017

Fresh Prince of Bel-Air, The (TV program)

THE FRESH PRINCE OF BEL-AIR THEME SONG R. Rahman color *Entertainment Weekly* no1460/1461 p74 Ap 7-17 2017

Freshwater biodiversity

Damming, Lost Connectivity, and the Historical Role of Anadromous Fish in Freshwater Ecosystem Dynamics S. MATTOCKS, C. J. HALL et al *BioScience* v67 no8 p713 Ag 2017

Freshwater Megafauna: Flagships for Freshwater Biodiversity under Threat S. F. CARRIZO, S. C. JÄHNIG et al *BioScience* v67 no10 p919 O 2017

Freshwater ecology

Responses of Antarctic Marine and Freshwater Ecosystems to Changing Ice Conditions M. K. OBRYK, S. E. STAMMER-JOHN et al color graph *BioScience* v66 no10 p864 O 1 2016

Freshwater fishes

FISH FOR THOUGHT C. Zuckerman color *National Geographic* v231 no4 p16 Ap 2017

PITCH-BLACK BRONZEBACKS J. Cermele color *Field & Stream* v122 no4 p36 S 2017

Freshwater mussels

The Complex Lives of Freshwater Mussels A. G. LANDIS color *Natural History* v125 no3 p30 Mr 2017

Fresu, Paolo

Truesdell & Fresu Channel Evans & Davis D. Ouellette color *Downbeat* v84 no10 p16 O 2017

Freud, Emma

What's My Age Again? color *InStyle* v24 no9 p206 S 2017

Freud, Sigmund, 1856-1939

FEARS FOUNDED AND UNFOUNDED *Lapham's Quarterly* v10 no3 p114 Summ 2017

Lie on Sigmund Freud's Couch ... Online *USA Today Magazine* v146 no2867 p11 Ag 2017

THE STONE GUEST L. MENAND cartoon *New Yorker* v93 no25 p75 Ag 28 2017

Why We Pick Leaders with Deceptively Simple Answers G. Petriglieri *Harvard Business Review Digital Articles* p2 My 9 2016

Freudberg, Frank

Find Virgil *Publishers Weekly* v263 no52 p90a D 19 2016

Frey, Darren

Faulty logic bw color *Science* v356 no6338 p589 My 12 2017

Frey, Glenn, 1948-2016

GLENN FREY B. Seger and C. Collis color *Entertainment Weekly* no1446/1447 p91 D 2016/Ja 2017

Frey, Raman

A Manager's Job Is Making Sure Employees Have a Life Outside Work *Harvard Business Review Digital Articles* p2 Mr 25 2016

Frey, S. D.

Long-term pattern and magnitude of soil carbon feedback to the climate system in a warming world chart graph *Science* v357 no6359 p101 O 6 2017

FREYHOF, JÖRG

Freshwater Megafauna: Flagships for Freshwater Biodiversity under Threat *BioScience* v67 no10 p919 O 2017

Friars—History

COMMON GROUND M. BROWN color *Archaeology* v70 no3 p18 My/Je 2017

Friberg, Michael

In Utah, McMullin, a Mormon, is appealing to #NeverTrump voters, while Clinton is hoping a split GOP vote can give her a surprise win in a reliably red state color *Bloomberg Businessweek* no4498 p38 N 7 2016

Utah *New York Times Magazine* p42 N 20 2016

Frick, Laurie

Laurie Frick A. Quinn color *Issues in Science & Technology* v33 no1 p6 Fall 2016

Frick, Walter

3 Ways to Use MOOCs to Advance Your Career *Harvard Business Review Digital Articles* p2 Jl 26 2016

Apple: Luxury Brand or Mass Marketer? *Harvard Business Review Digital Articles* p2 O 2 2014

Are Most CEOs Too Old to Innovate? *Harvard Business Review Digital Articles* p2 N 20 2014

Are Successful CEOs Just Lucky? *Harvard Business Review Digital Articles* p2 N 16 2015

The Best Part of Entrepreneurship? Giving Up and Getting a Job *Harvard Business Review Digital Articles* p2 F 17 2016

Big Companies Don't Pay as Well as They Used To *Harvard Business Review Digital Articles* p2 F 13 2017

A Brief Guide to U.S. Corporate Tax Reform *Harvard Business Review Digital Articles* p2 S 7 2017

Can Apple Attract Top Researchers If It Keeps Their Research Secret? *Harvard Business Review Digital Articles* p2 N 2 2015

Can Data Literacy Protect Us from Misleading Political Ads? *Harvard Business Review Digital Articles* p2 Ap 5 2016

Can Profit Sharing Address Income Inequality? *Harvard Business Review Digital Articles* p2 S 7 2015

Can You Predict a Startup's Success Based on the Concept Alone? *Harvard Business Review Digital Articles* p2 S 10 2015

Commerce Secretary Pritzker on the Economy, Worker Training, and Trade with Asia *Harvard Business Review Digital Articles* p2 Je 12 2015

Companies in Happy Cities Invest More for the Long Term *Harvard Business Review Digital Articles* p2 Je 9 2015

Competition Is on the Decline, and That's Fueling Inequality *Harvard Business Review Digital Articles* p2 Mr 24 2017

Corporate Inequality Is the Defining Fact of Business Today *Harvard Business Review Digital Articles* p2 My 11 2016

The Curious Science of When Multitasking Works *Harvard Business Review Digital Articles* p2 Ja 6 2015

Did Trade with China Make U.S. Manufacturing Less Innovative? *Harvard Business Review Digital Articles* p2 D 8 2016

Do CEOs Really Have the Power to Raise Wages? *Harvard Business Review Digital Articles* p2 Ap 23 2015

Does Silicon Valley Still Care About Climate Change? *Harvard Business Review Digital Articles* p2 My 30 2017

Does Stating What Your Company Stands for Affect Your Bottom Line? *Harvard Business Review Digital Articles* p2 Ag 3 2015

Don't Expect New Crowdfunding Rules to Create a Startup Boom *Harvard Business Review Digital Articles* p2 My 16 2016

Do Tech Companies Really Need All That User Data? *Harvard Business Review Digital Articles* p2 S 21 2017

Here's Why People Trust Human Judgment Over Algorithms *Harvard Business Review Digital Articles* p2 F 27 2015

How America Gave Up on Change color *Harvard Business Review Digital Articles* p2 Mr 3 2017

How Can Companies Compete with Amazon? Netflix Has the Answer *Harvard Business Review Digital Articles* p2 Je 19 2017

How France Used Unemployment Benefits to Kickstart Entrepreneurship *Harvard Business Review Digital Articles* p2 Ja 8 2015

How Jamie Dimon's Minimum Wage Hike Could Backfire *Harvard Business Review Digital Articles* p2 Jl 13 2016

How Startup "Joiners" Are (and Aren't) Like Founders *Harvard Business Review Digital Articles* p2 Jl 20 2015

How the Carl Icahns of the World Benefit Firms but Not Workers *Harvard Business Review Digital Articles* p2 O 9 2015

How the Rise of the Post Office Explains American Innovation *Harvard Business Review Digital Articles* p2 F 3 2016

Larry Summers on What Business Can Do to Save the Middle Class *Harvard Business Review Digital Articles* p2 F 9 2015

Making Sense of Our Very Competitive, Super Monopolistic Economy *Harvard Business Review Digital Articles* p1 Jl 25 2017

The Other Digital Divide color *Harvard Business Review* v95 no3 p160 My/Je 2017

Proof That Good Managers Really Do Make a Difference *Harvard Business Review Digital Articles* p2 Ap 11 2016

The Real Reason Superstar Firms Are Pulling Ahead *Harvard Business Review Digital Articles* p2 O 5 2017

Research: Want More Entrepreneurs? Make College Cheaper *Harvard Business Review Digital Articles* p2 Jl 7 2016

Robert Reich on Redefining Full-Time Work, Obamacare, and Employer Benefits *Harvard Business Review Digital Articles* p2 Ja 21 2015

Should Older CEOs Be Forced to Retire? *Harvard Business Review Digital Articles* p2 F 15 2016

Tesla, Autopilot, and the Challenge of Trusting Machines *Harvard Business Review Digital Articles* p2 Jl 11 2016

To Hire Great Coders, Offer Learning, Not Just Money *Harvard Business Review Digital Articles* p2 Ja 27 2016

Understanding the Debate Over Inequality, Skills, and the Rise of the 1% *Harvard Business Review Digital Articles* p2 D 21 2015

The U.S. Startup Economy Is in Both Better and Worse Shape than We Thought *Harvard Business Review Digital Articles* p2 Mr 11 2016

What British, European, and American Policymakers Need to Do Now *Harvard Business Review Digital Articles* p2 Je 24 2016

What Happens When an Interim CEO Takes Over? *Harvard Business Review Digital Articles* p2 Je 12 2015

What Research Shows About Talking Back to a Jerk Boss *Harvard Business Review Digital Articles* p2 Ap 9 2015

What Research Tells Us About Making Accurate Predictions *Harvard Business Review Digital Articles* p2 F 2 2015

What to Do When People Draw Different Conclusions From the Same Data *Harvard Business Review Digital Articles* p2 Mr 31 2015

What You Should Know About Dodd-Frank and What Happens If It's Rolled Back color *Harvard Business Review Digital Articles* p2 Mr 2 2017

When Treating Workers Well Leads to More Innovation *Harvard Business Review Digital Articles* p2 N 3 2015

WHY AI CAN'T WRITE THIS ARTICLE (YET) *Harvard Business Review Digital Articles* p24 Jl 1 2017

Why Overtime Pay Doesn't Change How Much We Work *Harvard Business Review Digital Articles* p2 Jl 1 2015

Wikipedia Is More Biased Than Britannica, but Don't Blame the Crowd *Harvard Business Review Digital Articles* p2 D 3 2014

Worries About Short-Termism Are 40 Years Old, but Are They Overblown? *Harvard Business Review Digital Articles* p2 2017

Frick Collection

Metal of honor B. Laurence Scherer color *Magazine Antiques* v184 no3 p42 My/Je 2017

Frick Collection—Exhibitions

A curious George at the Frick color *Magazine Antiques* v184 no4 p40 Jl/Ag 2017

Fricke, David

Chris Cornell 1964-2017 [Cover story] bw color *Rolling Stone* no1289 p40 Je 15 2017

Essential Allman *Rolling Stone* no1290 p49 Je 29 2017

Essential Paul Simon bw color *Rolling Stone* no1275 p62 D 1 2016

Gorillaz Rave to the Apocalypse color *Rolling Stone* no1287 p14 My 18 2017

The Heart of the Allmans bw *Rolling Stone* no1281/1282 p19 F 23 2017

Inside Lou Reed's Archives color *Rolling Stone* no1283 p13 Mr 23 2017

Jam's Working-Class Heroes color *Rolling Stone* no1293 p19 Ag 10 2017

Leon Russell bw *Rolling Stone* no1276 p28 D 15 2016

Punk's Blood Brothers color *Rolling Stone* no1281/1282 p20 F 23 2017

REISSUES OF THE YEAR bw *Rolling Stone* no1276 p20 D 15 2016

The Road Heats Up bw color *Rolling Stone* no1288 p11 Je 1 2017

Rock's All-Star Weekend color *Rolling Stone* no1273 p13 N 3 2016

Roger Waters' Fight color *Rolling Stone* no1295 p13 S 7 2017

Tom Petty: 1950-2017 bw *Rolling Stone* no1299 p12 N 2 2017

Fricke, Martin P.

Roger Wolfe Cohen *Physics Today* v70 no8 p70 Ag 2017

Friction

GET YOUR Head IN THE Game N. Loeffler-Gladstone color *Dance Spirit* v20 no9 p68 N 2016

Friday Night Lights (TV program)

FRIDAY NIGHT LIGHTS S. Highfill color *Entertainment Weekly* no1434 p48 O 7 2016

THE PLAYERS color *Entertainment Weekly* no1434 p48 O 7 2016

Fridlund, Emily

Innocent and Confused M. HUSTAD *New York Times Book Review* p20 Ja 8 2017

Our Town: Deborah E. Kennedy's first novel delves into a community's secrets and silences *New York Times Book Review* p18 Ag 13 2017

Frieberg, Dan

Farm Moneyball G. Johnston *Successful Farming* v114 no12 p24 Mid-N 2016

Fried, Carla

THE 50 BEST FUNDS TO BUY AND HOLD color diag *Money* v46 no1 p64 Ja/F 2017

Feeling Trapped? How to Sell in This Tricky Market color diag *Money* v46 no9 p43 O 2017

A Home for Now and Later chart color *Money* v45 no11 p37 D 2016

Replot Your Income Plan color diag *Money* v45 no10 p39 N 2016

Shift Your Bond Gears color diag *Money* v46 no2 p47 Mr 2017

Shop Online With Confidence graph il *Consumer Reports* v82 no12 p20 D 2017

Time for a Portfolio Pit Stop color diag *Money* v46 no6 p33 Jl 2017

Why a Lower Car Payment Can Be a Costly Mistake color graph *Consumer Reports* v82 no12 p60 D 2017

X-Ray: Janus Global Unconstrained diag *Money* v46 no3 p32 Ap 2017

FRIED, DAISY

Riffs and Displacements: Adam Zagajewski finds poetry a 'slight exaggeration, until we make our homes in it.' *New York Times Book Review* p25 Jl 23 2017

Fried, Johannes

CHARLEMAGNE B. BETHUNE color *Maclean's* v129 no47 p62 N 28 2016

Fried, Kaj

Multipotent peripheral glial cells generate neuroendocrine cells of the adrenal medulla color *Science* v357 no6346 p46 Jl 7 2017

Fried, Naomi

Innovating in a Highly Regulated Industry Like Health Care *Harvard Business Review Digital Articles* p2 Je 12 2017

FRIED, STEPHEN

SAVED BY THE BELL *Smithsonian* v48 no1 p36 Ap 2017

Fried chicken

THE DESCENT J. ELLISON color *Climbing* no352 p88 Ap 2017

KFC (Korean Fried Chicken) J. ZYMAN *Atlanta* v57 no6 p53 O 2017

SINGULAR Sensation M. Kiesel cartoon color *O, The Oprah Magazine* p169 My 2017

Friedan, Betty, 1921-2006

1963: Grandview, NY *Lapham's Quarterly* v10 no1 p106 Wint 2017

FRIEDBERG, CARLYN

Understanding Academic Language and Its Connection to School Success *Education Digest* v82 no6 p58 F 2017

Friedeberg, Pedro

Talk to the Hand H. MARTIN color *Architectural Digest* no5 p26 My 2017

Friedel, Melanie

A Long and Bright Future for Longleaf Pine *American Forests* v123 no3 p6 Fall 2017

Frieden, Tom

Ex–CDC head leads health drive *Science* v357 no6357 p1217 S 22 2017

Pioneers [Cover story] color *Time* v189 no16/17 p14 My 1-8 2017

Frieden, Tom—Interviews

Is the U.S. Ready for Future Disease Threats? D. Fine Maron color *Scientific American* v316 no4 p24 Ap 2017

FRIEDERICI, PETER

9 THINGS I CAN'T LOOK AWAY FROM *Orion Magazine* v36 no1 p6 Ja/F 2017

FRIEDERSDORF, CONOR

Making Up Is Hard to Do color *Atlantic* v318 no4 p19 N 2016

Friedkin, Noah E.

Network science on belief system dynamics under logic constraints bibl diag graph *Science* v354 no6310 p321 O 21 2016

FRIEDKIN, WILLIAM

This EXORCIST Is Real bw color *Reader's Digest* v190 no1134 p118 O 2017

FRIEDLAENDER, ARI S.

Responses of Antarctic Marine and Freshwater Ecosystems to Changing Ice Conditions color graph *BioScience* v66 no10 p864 O 1 2016

Friedlander, Blaine

Wonderful Wetlands *USA Today Magazine* v146 no2866 p68 Jl 2017

Friedlander, Erik

Erik Friedlander's Cello Solo on '26 Gasoline Stations' J. DURSO bw color *Downbeat* v84 no1 p104 Ja 2017

FRIEDLANDER, JOEL

11 Tips for Successfully Working With a Cover Designer *Publishers Weekly* v264 no9 p47 F 27 2017

Design Options for Self-Publishers *Publishers Weekly* v263 no43 p42 O 24 2016

The Three Pillars of Blog Traffic color *Publishers Weekly* v264 no26 p134 Je 26 2017

Friedlander, Lee, 1934-

The Power of Car Pictures B. Shapiro bw *Popular Mechanics* p19 My 2017

FRIEDLANDER, PAUL

LANIAKEA SUPERCLUSTER *Scientific American* v315 no5 p6 N 2016

Friedländer, Saul, 1932-

COLD SWEAT S. Friedlander *Lapham's Quarterly* v10 no3 p88 Summ 2017

History's Drift A. ALTMAN *New York Times Book Review* p15 N 27 2016

FRIEDMAN, ANDREW

A Fitness Makeover color *Tennis* v53 no2 p60 Mr/Ap 2017

Strength IN NUMBERS *Tennis* v53 no4 p56 Jl/Ag 2017

THE TENNIS CONVERSATION: French Open *Tennis* v53 no3 p38 My/Je 2017

THE TENNIS CONVERSATION: GEAR bw color *Tennis* v53 no2 p22 Mr/Ap 2017

THE TENNIS CONVERSATION: Wimbledon *Tennis* v53 no4 p38 Jl/Ag 2017

US Open Special bw color *Tennis* v53 no5 p30 S/O 2017

Your Three-Course Fix *Tennis* v53 no4 p26 Jl/Ag 2017

Friedman, Ann

THE Disruptor color *Glamour* v115 no10 p166 O 2017

GUEST LIST *Washingtonian Magazine* v52 no6 p22 Mr 2017

FRIEDMAN, AVI

A Slow Revolution color graph *Alternatives Journal (AJ) - Canada's Environmental Voice* v42 no2 p36 2016

Friedman, Barry

Is 'democratic policing' the answer to law enforcement abuses? M. P. O'Connor color *America* v216 no13 p50 Je 12 2017

Robocops and Robbers J. Leovy *American Scholar* v86 no2 p115 Spr 2017

Friedman, Benjamin M.

Born to Be Free bw color *New York Review of Books* v64 no15 p39 O 12 2017

FRIEDMAN, DANIEL J.

A Useful David *Commentary* v144 no3 p5 O 2017

Friedman, Danielle

Is Tech Making Our Sex Lives Better or Worse? color *Glamour* v115 no7 p71 Jl 2017

Friedman, Devin

FAST FASTER, FASTEST color *GQ: Gentlemen's Quarterly* v86 no12 p212 D 2016

Introducing the Man You've Been Listening to All Year color *GQ: Gentlemen's Quarterly* v86 no12 p104 D 2016

FRIEDMAN, HARRIS L.

Public Debate, Scientific Skepticism, and Science Denial *Skeptical Inquirer* v41 no1 p40 Ja/F 2017

FRIEDMAN, JACLYN

These Are Your Sexual Rights color *Glamour* v114 no7 p94 Jl 2016

Friedman, Jake S.

Picket Lines in Paradise bw color *American History* v52 no2 p40 Je 2017

FRIEDMAN, JANE

Fast, Cheap, and Good *Publishers Weekly* v264 no21 p50 My 22 2017

First Go Narrow, Then Go Wide *Publishers Weekly* v264 no39 p64 S 25 2017

Mastering Your Online Presence *Publishers Weekly* v263 no39 p50 S 26 2016

Ready to Launch color *Publishers Weekly* v264 no4 p42 Ja 23 2017

FRIEDMAN, JENA

A RECIPE cartoon *New Yorker* v92 no44 p31 Ja 9 2017

FRIEDMAN, JEREMY

The Revolutionary Roots of Russian Foreign Policy *Current History* v116 no792 p258 O 2017

Friedman, Jon

Pursuing big dreams, Halberstam started small bw color *Columbia Journalism Review* v56 no1 p48 Spr 2017

The White House briefing room gets its 15 minutes color *Columbia Journalism Review* v56 no2 p84 Fall 2017

Friedman, Josh

It's O.K. to Be a Coward About Cancer color *Time* v190 no6 p21

Ag 7 2017

Friedman, Lauren F.

Take Charge of Your Heart Health chart color il *Consumer Reports* v82 no5 p24 My 2017

FRIEDMAN, MAYA

Long-Term Studies Contribute Disproportionately to Ecology and Policy *BioScience* v67 no3 p271 Mr 2017

Friedman, Michelle

Work of Love: A Theological Reconstruction of the Communion of Saints *Christian Century* v134 no17 p36 Ag 16 2017

Friedman, Milton, 1912-2006

Friedman on Freedom M. Friedman *Hoover Digest: Research & Opinion on Public Policy* no2 p23 Spr 2017

Milton Friedman's Misadventures in China J. B. GEWIRTZ *American Scholar* v86 no1 p30 Wint 2017

FRIEDMAN, NATHANIEL

The Ten Who'll Be Next color *GQ: Gentlemen's Quarterly* v97 no11 p114 N 2017

Friedman, Patri

AHOY, CITIZENS! L. Lowe cartoon *Bloomberg Businessweek* no4515 p66 Mr 20 2017

SEASTEADING IN PARADISE B. DOHERTY color diag map *Reason* v49 no2 p28 Je 2017

Friedman, Peter

Coast to Coast for a Cause L. Threlkeld color *Practical Horseman* v45 no3 p72 Mr 2017

Friedman, Ron

5 Myths of Great Workplaces *Harvard Business Review Digital Articles* p2 Mr 5 2015

9 Productivity Tips from People Who Write About Productivity *Harvard Business Review Digital Articles* p2 D 31 2015

Dear Boss: Your Team Wants You to Go on Vacation *Harvard Business Review Digital Articles* p2 Je 18 2015

Defusing an Emotionally Charged Conversation with a Colleague *Harvard Business Review Digital Articles* p2 Ja 12 2016

How to Spend the Last 10 Minutes of Your Day *Harvard Business Review Digital Articles* p2 N 10 2014

How to Support Employee Health Instead of Sapping It *Harvard Business Review Digital Articles* p2 N 30 2015

Regular Exercise Is Part of Your Job *Harvard Business Review Digital Articles* p2 O 3 2014

Staying Motivated After a Major Achievement *Harvard Business Review Digital Articles* p2 F 3 2015

What You Eat Affects Your Productivity *Harvard Business Review Digital Articles* p2 O 17 2014

Why Work Should Get a Little Harder Every Day *Harvard Business Review Digital Articles* p2 D 16 2014

Working Too Hard Makes Leading More Difficult *Harvard Business Review Digital Articles* p2 D 30 2014

Friedman, Sonia

From Strong Roots A. Wintour bw color *Vogue* v207 no6 p38 Je 2017

Gold Standard H. Freeman bw *Vogue* v207 no6 p120 Je 2017

FRIEDMAN, STEVE

Late Bloomer color *AARP: The Magazine* v59 no2A p52 F/Mr 2016

Should Stop. Must Stop. Can't Stop [Cover story] bw color *Runner's World* v52 no4 p62 My 2017

The Walking Cure [Cover story] cartoon color *Prevention* p40 Mr 2017

Friedman, Stew

Get More Done by Focusing Less on Work *Harvard Business Review Digital Articles* p2 F 5 2015

Great Performers Make Their Personal Lives a Priority *Harvard Business Review Digital Articles* p2 O 6 2016

How to Get Your Team to Coach Each Other *Harvard Business Review Digital Articles* p2 Mr 13 2015

Keep Your Home Life Sane when Work Gets Crazy *Harvard Business Review Digital Articles* p2 F 23 2015

Most Resolutions Fail Because They're Not Important Enough *Harvard Business Review Digital Articles* p2 Ja 14 2016

What Successful Work and Life Integration Looks Like *Harvard Business Review Digital Articles* p2 O 7 2014

What to Do If Your Parents Are Causing You Career Angst *Harvard Business Review Digital Articles* p2 Ag 5 2016

When You Realize You'll Never Get Your Dream Job *Harvard Business Review Digital Articles* p2 Ap 1 2015

Why Paid Leave Matters for the Future of Business *Harvard Business Review Digital Articles* p2 S 16 2015

Friedman, Thomas L., 1953-

The Case for Optimism [Cover story] D. Rothkopf color *Foreign Policy* no221 p55 N/D 2016

THANK YOU FOR BEING LATE [Cover story] J. Micklethwait *New York Times Book Review* p1 D 18 2016

TO INFINITY AND BEYOND P. M. Barrett cartoon *Bloomberg Businessweek* no4499 p86 N 14 2016

Friedman, Thomas L., 1953----Interviews

PW Talks with Thomas L. Friedman A. Albanese color *Publishers Weekly* v263 no45 p12 N 7 2016

FRIEDMAN, VANESSA

CARDINAL SINS color *New York Times Book Review* p65 D 4 2016

Friedman Pharmacy, The (Short story)

The Friedman Pharmacy J. J. CLAYTON *Commentary* v142 no4 p33 N 2016

Friedrich, Eberhard

Bayreuth J. Leipsic *Opera News* v81 no5 p46 N 2016

Friedrich, Glenn A.

Priming HIV-1 broadly neutralizing antibody precursors in human Ig loci transgenic mice bibl graph *Science* v353 no6307 p1557 S 30 2016

Friedrich, Jim

The demons have come out *Christian Century* v134 no19 p10 S 13 2017

Friedrichsen, Debra

From Dissemination to Propagation: A New Paradigm for Education Developers *Change* v49 no4 p35 Jl/Ag 2017

Friedwald, Will

Voices of a Golden Age C. WOLFF color *Downbeat* v84 no10 p74 O 2017

Friel, Anna

The Girlfriend Experience D. Franich, A. Bacle et al color *Entertainment Weekly* no1482/1483 p38 S 22 2017

Friend, David

The Naughty Nineties Set the Stage for Our Reality-TV Presidency J. Meacham color *Time* v190 no12 p33 S 25 2017

Friend, Richard H.

High-performance light-emitting diodes based on carbene-metal-amides chart graph *Science* v356 no6334 p159 Ap 14 2017

Friend, Rupert

A Homeland Death in the Line of Duty J. Hibberd color *Entertainment Weekly* no1462 p16 Ap 21 2017

Friend, Tad

ADDING A ZERO cartoon *New Yorker* v92 no32 p68 O 10 2016

APOLOGIZER cartoon *New Yorker* v92 no36 p17 N 7 2016

BRAIN TRUST cartoon *New Yorker* v93 no22 p19 Jl 31 2017

CALIFORNIA DREAMIN' cartoon color *New Yorker* v92 no44 p32 Ja 9 2017

ENVY cartoon *New Yorker* v93 no28 p20 S 18 2017

THE GOD PILL cartoon color *New Yorker* v93 no7 p54 Ap 3 2017

HORROR SHOW cartoon *New Yorker* v93 no16 p40 Je 5 2017

INSPIRATION cartoon *New Yorker* v93 no15 p17 My 29 2017

THE MOM SLOT cartoon *New Yorker* v93 no20 p25 Jl 10 2017

NINE LIVES cartoon *New Yorker* v93 no24 p19 Ag 21 2017

OUT-GUTTING cartoon *New Yorker* v93 no14 p30 My 22 2017

POPE IN A SOAP cartoon *New Yorker* v92 no46 p19 Ja 23 2017

PULVERIZER cartoon *New Yorker* v93 no17 p21 Je 19 2017

ROGUE bw *New Yorker* v93 no29 p39 S 25 2017

TRAFFIC cartoon *New Yorker* v92 no45 p24 Ja 16 2017

THE UNDEAD cartoon *New Yorker* v92 no38 p32 N 21 2016

Friends (Music)

Grizzly Bear's Vital New Tunes E. R. Brown and N. Feeney color *Entertainment Weekly* no1477 p57 Ag 11 2017

Friends From College (TV program)

FRIENDS FROM COLLEGE S. Li color *Entertainment Weekly* no1468/1469 p40 Je 2-9 2017

KEEGAN-MICHAEL KEY'S NEW COURSE S. Li color *Entertainment Weekly* no1474/1475 p104 Jl 21-28 2017

SCREEN GEMS color *Essence* v48 no3 p58 Jl 2017

Friendship

See also

Fellowship

Male friendship

3 GIRLFRIEND GETAWAYS color *Health* v30 no9 p20 N 2016

Around the World in 2,557 Days... Paul Salopek G. DREVITCH *Psychology Today* v49 no6 p27 N/D 2016

ASKING FOR A FRIEND: TO BE INTERESTING TO OTHERS, BE INTERESTED IN THEM A. HIDDEN *Psychology Today* v50 no5 p20 S/O 2017

The Beautiful Game: Coming at UI from Everywhere R. MCFARLAND *Idaho Magazine* v16 no7 p48 Ap 2017

Being Too Busy for Friends Won't Help Your Career N. J. Roese *Harvard Business Review Digital Articles* p1 Jl 28 2017

Best Laid Plans, Straight Talk, Helicopter Daughter L. KOGAN cartoon *O, The Oprah Magazine* p39 Ap 2017

BET ON FRIENDSHIP M. BRADY *Psychology Today* v50 no4 p10 Ag 2017

"Call Back Anytime" L. VACCARIELLO *Reader's Digest* v188 no1126 p34 D 2016/Ja 2017

Can You Be Friends With Your Boss? K. Dillon *Harvard Business Review Digital Articles* p2 N 28 2014

Do I Get Involved When A Parent Treats a Child Badly? K. A. Appiah color *New York Times Magazine* p38 D 11 2016

Double Take A. MEDRESS *Psychology Today* v50 no4 p36 Ag 2017

FINDING YOUR CROWD *Psychology Today* v50 no4 p9 Ag 2017

First Harvest: Moving a homestead also means planting in new soil color *Yankee* p14 Jl 2017

Frenemies W. H. Pritchard bw *Commonweal* v143 no20 p24 D 16 2016

Friends for the Ages A. J. BAIME and G. M. GARRETT color *AARP: The Magazine* v60 no4A p42 Je/Jl 2017

FRIENDSHIP {decoded} C. THORP, R. CARDOZA et al color *Seventeen* v76 no4 p86 Jl/Ag 2017

Friendship Tune-Up! C. Thorp color *Seventeen* v76 no5 p71 S 2017

Fruitcake M. J. Salter *American Scholar* v86 no3 p60 Summ 2017

The gift of friendship T. Charney color *Equus* no477 p88 Je 2017

He Was a Lifelong Buddy B. KAUFFMAN *American Conservative* v16 no5 p45 S/O 2017

The Hosts of Pantsuit Politics A. D. Pollard *Parents* v91 no11 p16 N 2016

How to Take a Productive Yet Refreshing Vacation [Cover story] D. Clark *Harvard Business Review Digital Articles* p2 Je 4 2015

Lack of Means Doesn't Justify End L. Featherstone color *Nation* v305 no10 p5 O 23 2017

Life IN THESE UNITED STATES color *Reader's Digest* v189 no1130 p40 My 2017

Making the right memories M. Rollins color *Redbook* p6 Je 2017

My Millennial Friend L. Schillinger color *Vogue* v206 no11 p74 N 2016

Navigating the Transition from Friend to Boss B. Gentry *Harvard Business Review Digital Articles* p2 F 24 2015

Old Favorites M. Rubino *Indianapolis Monthly* v42 no2 p10 O 2017

The Perks of PDA *Parents* v91 no10 p34 O 2016

Research: You Have Fewer Friends than You Think A. ". Pentland *Harvard Business Review Digital Articles* p2 My 12 2016

A Slacker, a Sticky Situation, a Sensitive Subject L. KOGAN color *O, The Oprah Magazine* p30 Ja 2017

Someone to Talk To D. Frolovskiy *New York Times Magazine* p23 Ja 1 2017

Something Between Us C. Oduah color *New York Times Magazine* p48 D 11 2016

So Your Friend Is Now Your Boss... J. Thompson color *Glamour* v114 no11 p134 N 2016

Summer Study BESTIES R. Zar bw color *Dance Spirit* v21 no1 p42 Ja 2017

This Is What Friends Are For color *Reader's Digest* v189 no1130 p108 My 2017

'TRUTH' AND Consequences E. GILBERT color *O, The Oprah Magazine* p28 Ja 2017

WALKIN' ON SUNSHINE O. Manno color *Dance Spirit* v21 no8 p54 O 2017

WHO ASKED YOU? WE DID! *Parents* v91 no12 p16 D 2016

Work Friends Make Us More Productive (Except When They Stress Us Out) D. Burkus *Harvard Business Review Digital Articles* p2 My 26 2017

Friendship in youth

Win the SQUAD GIFT EXCHANGE color *Seventeen* v76 no12 p73 D 2016/Ja 2017

Friendship—Religious aspects—Christianity

Vows of Friendship E. Tushnet bw color *America* v216 no3 p24 F 6 2017

Friendship—Social aspects

You Are Not Alone M. JONES color *Reader's Digest* v189 no1131 p54 Je 2017

Friends University (Wichita, Kan.)

Friends University *Dance Magazine* v90 p64 2016/2017 Supplement College Guide

Frier, Sarah

America's relationship with Mark Zuckerberg is It's complicated color graph *Bloomberg Businessweek* no4539 p50 S 25 2017

Augmenting Snap's Financial Reality color *Bloomberg Businessweek* no4523 p33 My 22 2017

CNN Has Had Enough color graph *Bloomberg Businessweek* no4528 p20 Je 26 2017

Fun Filters Don't Make Good Neighbors color *Bloomberg Businessweek* no4513 p35 Mr 6 2017

The German Far Right Gets American Aid color *Bloomberg Businessweek* no4540 p42 O 2 2017

How Facebook Could Stop bw color *Bloomberg Businessweek* no4524 p56 My 29 2017

In Case of Low Revenue cartoon *Bloomberg Businessweek* no4497 p50 O 31 2016

Instagram Tries to Ease Users Into Shopping cartoon *Bloomberg Businessweek* no4499 p49 N 14 2016

Jack Dorsey Is Losing Control of Twitter cartoon graph *Bloomberg Businessweek* no4495 p26 O 17 2016

Snapchat Can't Keep It Private color *Bloomberg Businessweek* no4509 p27 Ja 30 2017

Snapchat vs. the 'Influencers' color *Bloomberg Businessweek* no4537 p24 S 11 2017

Snap Has a Different Angle on Mobile Ads color *Bloomberg Businessweek* no4512 p43 F 20 2017

SURVIVAL of the SHARINGEST bw *Bloomberg Businessweek* no4520 p60 My 1 2017

When a Facebook Page Matters to Facebook color *Bloomberg Businessweek* no4508 p28 Ja 23 2017

Friesen, Helena

Exploring genetic suppression interactions on a global scale diag *Science* v354 no6312 p599 N 4 2016

Friesen, Myron

CAN THEIR PROBLEM BE SOLVED? *Successful Farming* v114 no10 p69 O 2016

CAN THEIR PROBLEM BE SOLVED? *Successful Farming* v115 no5 p66 Mid-Mr 2017

PROBLEM: AFTER TRYING TO GET FAMILY INVOLVEMENT WITH OUR ESTATE PLANNING, EVERYTHING HAS TURNED BITTER, AND WE STILL DON'T HAVE A PLAN IN PLACE *Successful Farming* v115 no6 p66 Ap 2017

THE PROBLEM: EVERYTHING SEEMS TO BE ROLLING ALONG PERFECTLY RIGHT NOW. I HEAR ABOUT ALL THESE PROBLEMS, BUT WE DON'T SEEM TO HAVE ANY. AM I MISSING SOMETHING? *Successful Farming* v115 no9 p68 Ag 2017

THE PROBLEM: MY WIFE AND I ARE EXPERIENCING A NEW LEVEL OF PROBLEMS IN PLANNING TO PASS THE FARM ON TO OUR GRANDSON *Successful Farming* v115 no12 p70 O 2017

THE PROBLEM *Successful Farming* v115 no2 p68 F 2017

Friesike, Sascha

A nod to public open access infrastructures *Science* v356 no6344 p1242 Je 23 2017

Friess, Steve

Another Way to Tap the 1 Percent color *Bloomberg Businessweek* no4493 p39 O 3 2016

INSIDE THE RECOUNT bw color *New Republic* v248 no3 p46 Mr 2017

Frieze Art Fair (London, England)

THE BRIEF *Art in America* v104 no9 p21 O 2016

Friezes

HENRY BOSCH CO B. Sullivan cartoon *Arts & Crafts Homes &*

the Revival v11 no5 p72 Wint 2017

Frigate-birds

Birds Sleep During Flights, Too B. ALEX color *Discover* v38 no1 p49 Ja/F 2017

The Odyssey of the Great Frigatebird K. PEEK *Audubon* v118 no6 p14 Wint 2016

Frigate-birds—Behavior

The Genius of the Frigatebird W. Lynch color *Canadian Wildlife* v23 no4 p46 S/O 2017

Frigeri, A.

Localized aliphatic organic material on the surface of Ceres bibl graph *Science* v355 no6326 p719 F 17 2017

Seasonal exposure of carbon dioxide ice on the nucleus of comet 67P/Churyumov-Gerasimenko bibl bw graph *Science* v354 no6319 p1563 D 23 2016

Frigidaire Co.

AIR CONDITIONER K. Dupzyk color *Popular Mechanics* p18 Je 2017

Friis, Agnete

What My Body Remembers *Publishers Weekly* v264 no11 p58 Mr 13 2017

Frilot, Shari

VIRTUAL REALITY IN REAL TIME: A CONVERSATION *Film Quarterly* v71 no1 p51 Fall 2017

Frimpong, Jemima A.

When Health Care Providers Look at Problems from Multiple Perspectives, Patients Benefit *Harvard Business Review Digital Articles* p2 Je 23 2017

Frings, Torsten

FRINGS BENEFIT G. Wahl and J. Feldman color *Sports Illustrated* v126 no11 p56 Ap 17-24 2017

FRINT, HUNTER

Whip It Good color *Field & Stream* v122 no5 p10 O 2017

Frisbie, David

CONSULTANTS *Equus* no481 p74 O 2017

Frisch, Bob

Before a Meeting, Tell Your Team That Silence Denotes Agreement *Harvard Business Review Digital Articles* p2 F 3 2016

Don't End a Meeting Without Doing These 3 Things *Harvard Business Review Digital Articles* p2 Ap 26 2016

If You Can't Say What Your Meeting Will Accomplish, You Shouldn't Have It *Harvard Business Review Digital Articles* p2 Ap 18 2016

Meetings Need a Shot Clock *Harvard Business Review Digital Articles* p2 Mr 16 2016

The Right Way to Cut People Off in Meetings *Harvard Business Review Digital Articles* p2 Ap 8 2016

Stand-Up Meetings Don't Work for Everybody *Harvard Business Review Digital Articles* p2 My 27 2016

To Hold Someone Accountable, First Define What Accountable Means *Harvard Business Review Digital Articles* p2 Je 28 2016

Why Decisions Get Second-Guessed, and What to Do About It *Harvard Business Review Digital Articles* p2 F 25 2016

Frisch, Henry J.

James Watson Cronin *Physics Today* v70 no3 p72 Mr 2017

Frisch, Ian

The Generation Z Consultants color *Bloomberg Businessweek* no4502 p86 D 5 2016

INSTAGRAM KILLED THE RETAIL STAR color *Bloomberg Businessweek* no4517 p74 Ap 3 2017

THE PERFECT POUR cartoon *Bloomberg Businessweek* no4499 p82 N 14 2016

Frischkorn, Kyle

A Brief History of Improbably Large Produce *Smithsonian* v48 no6 p13 O 2017

A Crack in Creation color *Science* v356 no6342 p1005 Je 9 2017

Sailing through uncertainty color *Science* v355 no6328 p986 Mr 3 2017

What Do Animals Think of the Greek Financial Crisis? In a new adult picture book, Ungrateful Mammals, the ever-inventive Dave Eggers pairs his whimsical drawings with quirky quotations *Smithsonian* v48 no6 p28 O 2017

FRISCIA, SUZANNAH

All in the Details *Dance Magazine* v91 no1 p110 Ja 2017

Athleisure for Dancers: Sporty classwear at Hubbard Street Dance Chicago *Dance Magazine* v91 no7 p44 Jl 2017

City Chic *Dance Magazine* v91 no6 p40 Je 2017

Dare to Stand Out *Dance Magazine* v91 no4 p45 Ap 2017

Electric Brights *Dance Magazine* v91 no8 p38 Ag 2017

From Catlike to Classical color *Dance Magazine* v91 no3 p38 Mr 2017

The MOST INFLUENTIAL PEOPLE IN DANCE TODAY: THE MOVERS, SHAKERS AND CHANGEMAKERS HAVING THE BIGGEST IMPACT ON DANCE RIGHT NOW *Dance Magazine* v91 no7 p27 Jl 2017

POINTES ON PARADE *Dance Magazine* v91 no4 p43 Ap 2017

Pop Art *Dance Magazine* v90 no12 p86 D 2016

Showstoppers *Dance Magazine* v90 no11 p40 N 2016

The "So You Think You Can Dance" Effect *Dance Magazine* v91 no6 p34 Je 2017

Stellar Slippers *Dance Magazine* v91 no8 p36 Ag 2017

What's Not Okay to Ask a Dancer to Do? *Dance Magazine* v91 no4 p31 Ap 2017

Friscolanti, Michael

Division of net assets color *Maclean's* v130 no10 p13 N 2017

An elite school's dark past bw color *Maclean's* v130 no10 p32 N 2017

THE FIRST FLIGHT color *Maclean's* v129 no48/49 p14 D 5 2016

HOUSE OF SPIES [Cover story] color *Maclean's* v130 no8 p30 S 2017

A moment of painful truth color *Maclean's* v130 no2 p18 Mr 2017

THE OTHER RUNAWAYS bw color *Maclean's* v129 no43 p20 O 31 2016

PREPARING FOR 'MONTH 13' [Cover story] color *Maclean's* v129 no51/52 p34 D 26 2016

Sex offenders anonymous *Maclean's* v130 no3 p15 Ap 2017

Still-present dangers color *Maclean's* v129 no42 p22 O 24 2016

'Wanted,' one more time color *Maclean's* v130 no1 p13 F 17 2017

The wheels of injustice color *Maclean's* v130 no3 p35 Ap 2017

Frisell, Bill, 1951-

BILL FRISELL [Cover story] B. MILKOWSKI color *Downbeat* v84 no7 p28 Jl 2017

Friston, Karl

Who's influencing brain science? *Science* v354 no6314 p809 N 18 2016

Fristrup, Kurt

Noise pollution is pervasive in U.S. protected areas graph map *Science* v356 no6337 p531 My 5 2017

Frita, Rosangela

Reversion of antibiotic resistance in Mycobacterium tuberculosis by spiroisoxazoline SMARt-420 bibl diag *Science* v355 no6330 p1206 Mr 17 2017

Fritch, Amy

DINNER, UNDRESSED color *Women's Health* v14 no7 p99 S 2017

Fritsche, Isabella

Ultrafast many-body interferometry of impurities coupled to a Fermi sea bibl diag graph *Science* v354 no6308 p96 O 7 2016

Frittatas

15-Minute All-Organic Meal Under $15 color *Prevention* v69 no4 p14 Ap 2017

MMM... MORNING color *Good Housekeeping* v264 no4 p118 Ap 2017

SANTA'S LITTLE CHEFS C. K. Jackson color *Essence* v47 no8 p133 D 2016

Fritton, Nicole

THE HERO color *Harper's Bazaar* no3648 p74 N 2016

Packing LIST color *Harper's Bazaar* no3653 p92 My 2017

Wish LIST color *Harper's Bazaar* no3648 p110 N 2016

FRITTS, STEVEN H.

An Unparalleled Opportunity for an Important Ecological Study *BioScience* v67 no10 p875 O 2017

Fritz, Allan

Wild emmer genome architecture and diversity elucidate wheat evolution and domestication color *Science* v357 no6346 p93 Jl 7 2017

FRITZ, SHERILYN C.

The Arctic in the Twenty-First Century: Changing Biogeochemical Linkages across a Paraglacial Landscape of Greenland *BioScience* v67 no2 p118 F 2017

Fritze, Ronald H.

LIKE AN EGYPTIAN B. BOUCHER *New York Times Book Review* p23 D 4 2016

Fritz-Popovski, Gerhard
Biological fabrication of cellulose fibers with tailored properties color *Science* v357 no6356 p1118 S 15 2017

Fritzsche, Peter
Especially Those at Home T. SNYDER *New York Times Book Review* p14 N 27 2016
Jackboots on the Ground *New York Times Book Review* p21 Mr 12 2017

Fritzsche, Stephan
Angular momentum–induced delays in solid-state photoemission enhanced by intra-atomic interactions chart color graph *Science* v357 no6357 p1274 S 22 2017

Fritzshall, Fritzie
LIVING MEMORY E. KANG color *Chicago* v66 no10 p37 O 2017

Frixione, Eugenio
Mexico's basic science funding falls short *Science* v357 no6348 p260 Jl 21 2017

Frizell, Sam
The Budget Battle Shows That Trump Needs to Read the Fine Print color *Time* v189 no18 p11 My 15 2017
Can Trump Handle the Truth? [Cover story] color *Time* v189 no12 p32 Ap 3 2017
Chaos Theory [Cover story] color *Time* v189 no7/8 p32 F 27 2017
Democrats Are Winning the Battle to Expand Voting Access color *Time* v188 no15 p5 O 17 2016
Democrats Look for an Upside In Obamacare's Repeal color diag *Time* v189 no3 p5 Ja 16 2017
Elizabeth Warren color *Time* v189 no21 p68 Je 5 2017
The End of an Era color *Time* v188 no21 p62 N 21 2016
The Face of the Opposition [Cover story] color *Time* v189 no6 p26 F 20 2017
The First Steps to 'Drain the Swamp' color *Time* v188 no22-23 p31 N/D 2016
A GOP Revolt Threatens President Trump's Agenda color *Time* v189 no9 p9 Mr 13 2017
How She Lost color *Time* v188 no21 p58 N 21 2016
How the Health Care Debate Reveals the GOP's Divisions color diag *Time* v189 no11 p16 Mr 27 2017
The Incredible Shrinking Power of the President's Threats color *Time* v189 no14 p9 Ap 17 2017
Making Airports and Bridges Great Again color *Time* v188 no22-23 p33 N/D 2016
Message Delivered [Cover story] color *Time* v188 no21 p28 N 21 2016
The Other Side [Cover story] color diag *Time* v189 no4 p24 F 6 2017
Russia and the Trump Campaign color *Time* v189 no12 p36 Ap 3 2017
Trump Country Worries About Replacing Obamacare color *Time* v189 no10 p14 Mr 20 2017
Trump Goes to War [Cover story] color *Time* v188 no16/17 p20 O 24 2016
Trump's Loyalty Test [Cover story] color *Time* v189 no20 p24 My 29 2017
Trump's Supreme Court Pick Puts Democrats In a Bind color diag *Time* v189 no5 p10 F 13 2017
What Hillary Clinton's Insiders Know That Voters Don't-Yet color *Time* v188 no18 p14 O 31 2016
What It Will Take to Rebuild America [Cover story] color *Time* v189 no13 p22 Ap 10 2017
Why James Comey Couldn't Keep the FBI Above Politics color *Time* v188 no20 p7 N 14 2016

Frizzera, Lorenzo
Positive biodiversity-productivity relationship predominant in global forests bibl chart graph map *Science* v354 no6309 paaf8957-1 O 14 2016

FRODEMAN, ROBERT
Philosopher's Corner: The End of Puzzle Solving *Issues in Science & Technology* v33 no2 p19 Wint 2017

Frodl, Debora
Solving the Twin Crises of Energy and Water Scarcity *Harvard Business Review Digital Articles* p2 Ja 25 2016

Froemke, Susan

Rancher, Farmer, Fisherman C. Wolner color *Science* v356 no6337 p483 My 5 2017

Frog behavior
Surprise Party! S. ELDER cartoon color map *National Geographic Kids* no473 p16 S 2017

Froggatt, Joanne, 1980-
Dark Angel J. Russell *TV Guide* v65 no21 p34 My 15 2017
Dark Angel Star Joanne Froggatt on Playing England's First Serial Killer S. GUTIERREZ *British Heritage Travel* v38 no3 p58 My/Je 2017

FROGNER, BIANCA K.
Pathways to Middle-Skill Allied Health Care Occupations chart *Issues in Science & Technology* v33 no1 p52 Fall 2016

Frogs
See also
Glass frogs (Amphibians)
Frogs K. KUBE cartoon color *Discover* v27 no10 p74 D 2016
Laugh Out Loud color *National Geographic Kids* no465 p36 N 2016
My Shot color *National Geographic Kids* no471 p32 Je/Jl 2017
OUTSIDE THE LINES: An Adult Coloring Experience bw *GQ: Gentlemen's Quarterly* v86 no12 p234 D 2016
SEX THAT WORKS UP A LATHER P. Edmonds color *National Geographic* v231 no3 p29 Mr 2017
SPRING FESTIVALS C. JAY *Louisiana Life* v37 no4 p62 Mr/Ap 2017
weird but true! M. HARRIS and J. BEER *National Geographic Kids* no467 p4 F 2017

Frogs, The (Play : Aristophanes)
Fire Down Below *Lapham's Quarterly* v10 no3 p10 Summ 2017

Frogs—Anatomy
What gives frogs the gift of grab S. MILIUS color *Science News* v191 no4 p11 Mr 4 2017

Frogs—Physiology—Research
Twilight of the fluorescent frogs S. Milius color *Science News* v191 no7 p4 Ap 15 2017

Froguel, Philippe
Detection of human adaptation during the past 2000 years bibl graph *Science* v354 no6313 p760 N 11 2016

FROIS, JEANNE
CAJUN COUNTRY color *Louisiana Life* v37 no3 p100 Ja/F 2017
CAJUN COUNTRY color map *Louisiana Life* v37 no4 p97 Mr/Ap 2017
CENTRAL color *Louisiana Life* v37 no3 p98 Ja/F 2017
CENTRAL color map *Louisiana Life* v37 no4 p95 Mr/Ap 2017
GREATER NEW ORLEANS color *Louisiana Life* v37 no2 p92 N/D 2016
GREATER NEW ORLEANS color map *Louisiana Life* v37 no4 p98 Mr/Ap 2017
NORTH color *Louisiana Life* v37 no3 p97 Ja/F 2017
NORTH color map *Louisiana Life* v37 no4 p94 Mr/Ap 2017
PLANTATION COUNTRY color *Louisiana Life* v37 no3 p99 Ja/F 2017
PLANTATION COUNTRY color map *Louisiana Life* v37 no4 p96 Mr/Ap 2017

Froitzheim, Armin
Terawatt-scale photovoltaics: Trajectories and challenges chart graph *Science* v356 no6334 p141 Ap 14 2017

Frölicher, Thomas L.
Large benefits to marine fisheries of meeting the 1.5°C global warming target bibl graph *Science* v354 no6319 p1591 D 23 2016

Frolova, Natalia
Changing climate shifts timing of European floods color graph *Science* v357 no6351 p588 Ag 11 2017

Frolova-Walker, Marina
The People's Opera J. Melick *Opera News* v81 no6 p62 D 2016

Frolovskiy, Dmitriy
Rent Control *New York Times Magazine* p38 O 30 2016
Someone to Talk To *New York Times Magazine* p23 Ja 1 2017

From 'Whereas Statements' (Poem)
From "Whereas Statements" L. L. Soldier *New York Times Magazine* p21 D 4 2016

From a Room: Volume One (Music)
CHRIS STAPLETON'S TRUE GRIT M. Vain color *Entertainment Weekly* no1465 p52 My 12 2017

The Outlaw Soul of Chris Stapleton W. HERMES color *Rolling Stone* no1287 p53 My 18 2017

From Saturday to Sunday (Film)
Bohemian Rhapsody M. Nelson bw *Film Comment* v53 no3 p11 My/Je 2017

From the King (Poem)
FROM THE KING N. Makoha *New York Times Magazine* p15 Jl 16 2017

From the Yellow House (Poem)
From 'The Yellow House' Chiwan Choi *New York Times Magazine* p19 Ja 22 2017

Froman, Kyle
Capturing your BEST FIRST Arabesque: How to take topnotch audition photos H. FOSTER *Dance Magazine* v90 p8 2016/2017 Supplement College Guide

Froment, Alain
Dispersals and genetic adaptation of Bantu-speaking populations in Africa and North America diag *Science* v356 no6337 p543 My 5 2017

Fromme, Petra
SPLIT-SECOND REACTIONS color *Scientific American* v316 no5 p62 My 2017

Fromme, Raimund
Structure of a symmetric photosynthetic reaction center–photosystem color *Science* v357 no6355 p1021 S 8 2017

FROMMER, FREDERIC J.
THE MISFITS OF SUMMER *Washingtonian Magazine* v52 no8 p70 My 2017

Frommer, Pauline
PREPARING FOR TAKE OFF D. DILWORTH color *Publishers Weekly* v264 no35 p29 Ag 28 2017

Fromont-Racine, Micheline
The cryo-EM structure of a ribosome–Ski2-Ski3-Ski8 helicase complex bibl color graph *Science* v354 no6318 p1431 D 16 2016

FROMSON, DANIEL
THE STRANGE, SPECTACULAR CON OF BOBBY CHARLES THOMPSON *Washingtonian Magazine* v52 no6 p62 Mr 2017

From The Names of 1,001 Strangers (Poem)
FROM "THE NAMES OF 1,001 STRANGERS" D. Chiasson *New Yorker* v93 no11 p38 My 1 2017

Fronsdal, Gil
The Buddha Before Buddhism: Wisdom from the Early Teachings M. SCARLES color *Tricycle: The Buddhist Review* v26 no2 p90 Wint 2016

Front Door Fashion (Company)
The Lawyer, the Wife, and the Wardrobe K. WISE *D: The Magazine of Dallas* v43 no10 p68 O 2016

Front yards & backyards
9 Easy Eco-Friendly Backyard Tips R. LISKA color *Reader's Digest* v189 no1131 p45 Je 2017
CRUSH 'EM ALL! M. Zimmerman bw *Men's Health* v32 no6 p104 Ag 2017
DIG INTO SPRING color *Sunset* v238 no4 p41 Ap 2017
GALLERY IN THE GARDEN M. M. Kashino *Washingtonian Magazine* v52 no3 p164 D 2016
Garden Variety E. Millard color *Log Home Living* v34 no9 p34 D 2017
POUR KILL A BEER! bw color diag *Men's Health* v32 no6 p106 Ag 2017
Projects for the Backyard L. Elliott color *Old House Journal* v45 no5 p50 Ag 2017
RACE A RIDING MOWER bw cartoon chart color *Men's Health* v32 no6 p102 Ag 2017
THE ULTIMATE BACKYARD MOVIE SETUP T. Chiarella, G. DELL'ABATE et al color diag *Popular Mechanics* p97 Jl 2017

Front yards & backyards—Design & construction
Build a Backyard Retreat B. COCHRAN color *Timber Home Living* v27 no2 p8 Ap 2017
California ease B. D. COLEMAN color diag *Arts & Crafts Homes & the Revival* v12 no2 p58 Spr 2017
DRY by DESIGN K. BARNES *Better Homes & Gardens* v95 no1 pZ1 Ja 2017

Frontal lobes
Extensive migration of young neurons into the infant human frontal lobe M. F. Paredes, D. James et al color diag graph *Science*

v354 no6308 paaf7073-1 O 7 2016
Human brains teach us a surprising lesson M. McKenzie and G. Fishell bibl color *Science* v354 no6308 p38 O 7 2016

Frontera Foods Inc.
CONAGRA'S NEXT ACT J. CROWN color *Chicago* v65 no12 p32 D 2016

Frontier & pioneer life
Communications on a SASKATCHEWAN HOMESTEAD: Two remote homesteaders try a variety of methods to reach out to society R. Melchiore *Mother Earth News* no284 p10 O/N 2017
Country Lore Readers' Tips to Live By *Mother Earth News* no284 p59 O/N 2017
Editor's Note T. PRODANOVICH color *Surfer* v58 no2 p12 My 2017
HOMESTEAD HACKS K. Gleaves and A. Budd *Mother Earth News* no281 p78 Ap/My 2017
LIFE ON THE FRONTIER color *Archaeology* v70 no3 p34 My/Je 2017
The Significance of the Frontier in Surfing History J. HOUSMAN color *Surfer* v58 no2 p40 My 2017

Frontier & pioneer life—Safety measures
Build a More RESILIENT HOMESTEAD *Mother Earth News* no279 p18 D/Ja 2017

Frontier & pioneer life—West (U.S.)
Lost Skills of the frontier teacher L. FELDMAN bw color *American Cowboy* v23 no6 p66 Ap/My 2017

Frontier (TV program)
ALLAN HAWCO A. POPE color *Canadian Geographic* v136 no6 p21 D 2016

Frontier, Jean-Martin
The Market Gardener's Toolkit *Mother Earth News* no280 p9 F/Mr 2017

Frosch, Matthew P.
Decoupling genetics, lineages, and microenvironment in IDH-mutant gliomas by single-cell RNA-seq diag *Science* v355 no6332 p1391 Mr 31 2017

Frost
See also
Thawing
Apple-Picking Time R. BROOKHISER color il *National Review* v68 no20 p47 N 7 2016

Frost, Adam
CAT-tailing as a fail-safe mechanism for efficient degradation of stalled nascent polypeptides diag *Science* v357 no6349 p414 Jl 28 2017

Frost, Bryan-Paul
Christopher Lynch and Jonathan Marks, Eds., Principle and Prudence in Western Political Thought *Society* v54 no3 p303 Je 2017

Frost, Carrie Frederick
Not a Novelty color *Commonweal* v144 no10 p9 Je 2 2017

Frost, Emma—Interviews
The White Princess S. GUTIERREZ *British Heritage Travel* v38 no2 p28 Mr/Ap 2017

Frost, Kathleen
HOME RUN C. KUZMA color *Runner's World* v52 no3 p20 Ap 2017

FROST, KAYLA
Canyon de Chelly National Monument *Arizona Highways* v92 no7 p7 Jl 2016
Jerry Jacka *Arizona Highways* v92 no7 p10 Jl 2016
WHAT'S NEW? *Arizona Highways* v92 no8 p8 Ag 2016

Frost, Mark
The Secret History of Twin Peaks D. Coggan color *Entertainment Weekly* no1436/1437 p106 O 21 2016
Small-Town Noir A. Thirlwell color *New York Review of Books* v64 no17 p4 N 9 2017

Frost, Phillip
A BOUNTIFUL MIND M. SCHIFRIN bw color *Forbes* v199 no1 p94 Ja 24 2017

Frost, Pop
THE WILDERNESS OF unreality N. N. DODGE *Arizona Highways* v93 no3 p28 Mr 2017

Frost, Robert
Keep Warm color *Equus* no472 p26 Ja 2017

Froustey, Mathilde

Mathilde Froustey J. STAHL *Dance Magazine* v90 no12 p98 D 2016

Froyd, Jeffrey E.

From Dissemination to Propagation: A New Paradigm for Education Developers *Change* v49 no4 p35 Jl/Ag 2017

Frozen (Film : 2013)

FROZEN J. Hibberd color *Entertainment Weekly* no1460/1461 p97 Ap 7-17 2017

MR. ROBOT J. KEHE color *Wired* v24 no12 p30 D 2016

Frozen (Theatrical production)

Meet Broadway's Frozen Foursome M. Snetiker color *Entertainment Weekly* no1480 p59 S 1 2017

Frozen dessert stands

i did it! K. SELZER color *Better Homes & Gardens* v95 no8 p58 Ag 2017

Frozen desserts

See also

Ice cream, ices, etc.

Ice, Ice (Pops), Baby! R. Kinane color *Entertainment Weekly* no1472 p18 Je 30 2017

IT'S NATIONAL ICE CREAM DAY S. LIAO color *Better Homes & Gardens* v95 no7 p158 Jl 2017

POP ART C. BOYD and D. CENTONI color *Better Homes & Gardens* v95 no7 p108 Jl 2017

Frozen fish

Ask Men's Health color *Men's Health* v32 no1 p12 Ja/F 2017

Frozen foods

Ask anything M. Thakor, L. Nwadike et al bw color *Women's Health* v14 no2 p18 Mr 2017

Frozen ground—Thawing

What Lies Beneath S. Goudarzi color *Scientific American* v315 no5 p11 N 2016

Frozen peaches

SL COOKING SCHOOL color *Southern Living* v52 no7 p126 Jl 2017

Frozen pizza

PIE IN THE SKY C. KUMMER *New York Times Magazine* p67 O 9 2016

Frozen tissue sections

Beyond The Blender L. TURNER color *Better Nutrition* v79 no6 p26 Je 2017

Frozen vegetables—Sales & prices

Will Millennials Eat Their Frozen Veggies? C. Giammona color graph *Bloomberg Businessweek* no4497 p23 O 31 2016

Frozen yogurt—Sales & prices

COSTUME DRAMA G. Flynn cartoon *New Yorker* v92 no32 p78 O 10 2016

Fruit

See also

Berries

Candied fruit

Seed pods

2 weeks is all it takes to feel an energy boost after upping your intake of FRUITS & VEGGIES S. LIAO color *Better Homes & Gardens* v95 no6 p150 Je 2017

better S. LIAO color *Better Homes & Gardens* v95 no11 p144 N 2017

CHEAP EATS! *Atlanta* v56 no12 p71 Ap 2017

Country Lore *Mother Earth News* no283 p67 Ag/S 2017

Desserts That Love You Back color *Health* v30 no9 p139 N 2016

FOOD FOR THOUGHT *Nutrition Action Health Letter* v44 no5 p16 Je 2017

Foodie Fun in the Sun L. TURNER color *Better Nutrition* v79 no7 p58 Jl 2017

THE FRESH-FRUIT SOLUTION *Saturday Evening Post* v289 no4 p71 Jl/Ag 2017

The Fruit Case L. MOYER and B. LIEBMAN *Nutrition Action Health Letter* v44 no4 p13 My 2017

IT'S THE PITS C. SAFFITZ color *Bon Appetit* v62 no6 p105 Je 2017

Mexican Linguine color *Vegetarian Today* no2 p26 Ap 2017

Mindful meals J. Iserloh color *Yoga Journal* no294 p38 S 2017

My stay-slim faves color *Health* v31 no8 p122 O 2017

Pick Your Own *Nutrition Action Health Letter* v44 no4 p15 My 2017

Post-Holiday Fast Food J. Bowden and J. Bessinger color *Better*

Nutrition v79 no11 p78 N 2017

Score All Your Fruits and Vegetables cartoon chart *Men's Health* v32 no8 p56 O 2017

THIS FRUIT IS PRETENDING TO BE MEAT color *Health* v31 no7 p18 S 2017

warm up to winter fruit K. CICERO *Parents* v92 no1 p26 Ja 2017

Word Play [Cover story] color *Prevention* v69 no6 p96 Je 2017

Fruit growing

See also

Berry growing

Tomato farming

How I Started a BACKYARD FARM: This suburbanite transformed a patch of grass into food and established a lucrative farm M. Brown *Mother Earth News* no283 p12 Ag/S 2017

Fruit growing—Equipment & supplies

Eating Local D. Curry color *New Orleans Magazine* v51 no9 p84 Jl 2017

Fruit in art

Berry Pretty color *Good Housekeeping* v264 no5 p19 My 2017

Fruit industry & the environment

Not Far from the Tree color *Canadian Wildlife* v23 no4 p16 S/O 2017

Fruit juices

BEST OF WASHINGTON HALL OF FAME *Washingtonian Magazine* v52 no3 p182 D 2016

BODY SHOTS [Cover story] A. Young color *Women's Health* v14 no6 p96 Jl 2017

NEWSBITES [Cover story] *Tufts University Health & Nutrition Letter* v35 no6 p1 Ag 2017

Ready, Set, Blend! L. TYRELL color *Martha Stewart Living* p86 Ap 2017

Soup Is the New Juice S. Dreisbach color *Glamour* v114 no7 p89 Jl 2016

Fruit juices—Evaluation

ARONIA JUICE *South Dakota Magazine* v33 no3 p40 S/O 2017

Fruit of the vine (Poem)

Fruit of the vine E. Potter *Christian Century* v134 no11 p12 My 24 2017

Fruit salads

Summer Kitchen D. Curry color *New Orleans Magazine* v51 no8 p104 Je 2017

Fruit syrups

Slush Fun T. KIRTS *Indianapolis Monthly* p41 My 2017

Fruit trees

Making the Cuts color *Southern Living* v52 no2 p44 F 2017

Fruitcake

CAKES FOR any OCCASION [Cover story] B. PORTER KATZ, S. BOCAR et al color *Martha Stewart Living* p70 My 2017

GREAT UNKNOWNS cartoon *Popular Mechanics* p33 D 2016/ Ja 2017

Have Your Fruitcake R. MARTINEZ color *Bon Appetit* v61 no12 p94 D 2016 /Jan2017

Fruitcake (Poem)

Fruitcake M. J. Salter *American Scholar* v86 no3 p60 Summ 2017

Fruit—Flavor & odor

A chemical genetic roadmap to improved tomato flavor D. Tieman, M. F. R. Resende Jr. et al bibl graph *Science* v355 no6323 p391 Ja 27 2017

Fruit—Physiological aspects

Eat these for better sleep M. TAYLOR color *Redbook* p84 D 2016

World of Medicine S. RIDEOUT *Reader's Digest* v188 no1126 p61 D 2016/Ja 2017

Fruit—Preservation

You Say Tomato... *Martha Stewart Living* no267 p15 S 2016

Fruit—Therapeutic use

ASK THE DOCTOR A. L. KOMAROFF *Harvard Health Letter* v42 no1 p2 N 2016

Spotting whole grains at the grocery store *Harvard Health Letter* v42 no5 p5 Mr 2017

Frum, David

DAVID FRUM *Commentary* v142 no1 p36 Jl/Ag 2016

The Downside of Pragmatism: It served our 'maker' cities well for a long time. Now it holds them back A. M. Renn *Governing* v30 no8 p22 My 2017

Getting In *New York Times Book Review* p16 O 16 2016

HOW TO BUILD AN AUTOCRACY cartoon color *Atlantic* v319

no2 p48 Mr 2017

IS IT 1968? [Cover story] *Commentary* v142 no2 p15 S 2016

Kevin D. Williamson on Yuval Levin's 'The Fractured Republic' *Commentary* v142 no1 p1 Jl/Ag 2016

Matthew Continetti on Yuval Levin's 'The Fractured Republic' *Commentary* v142 no1 p1 Jl/Ag 2016

Meir Soloveichik on Yuval Levin's 'The Fractured Republic' *Commentary* v142 no1 p1 Jl/Ag 2016

Those '60s Flashbacks *Commentary* v142 no4 p10 N 2016

FRUMHOFF, PETER C.

Climate engineering *Issues in Science & Technology* v33 no4 p9 Summ 2017

Frumkes, Lewis Burke

Word Power E. COX and H. RATHVON *Reader's Digest* v188 no1126 p131 D 2016/Ja 2017

Frusher, Stewart

Biodiversity redistribution under climate change: Impacts on ecosystems and human well-being color *Science* v355 no6332 p1389 Mr 31 2017

Frustration

See also

Control (Psychology)

Comey v. Trump S. F. Hayes color *Weekly Standard* v22 no39 p7 Je 19 2017

focus on feelings B. THORKELSON *Parents* v91 no6 p142 Je 2016

THE UNITED STATES OF SEX A. DAVIES color *Women's Health* v14 no2 p140 Mr 2017

Fry, Erika

100 BEST COMPANIES TO WORK FOR 2017 [Cover story] color diag map *Fortune* v175 no4 p79 Mr 15 2017

THE 2017 Fortune Crystal Ball color diag *Fortune* v174 no7 p11 D 1 2016

Americans Are Traveling More map *Fortune* v75 no1 p15 Ja 1 2017

ARE "DREAMERS" WORTH BILLIONS TO STATES? map *Fortune* v175 no2 p11 F 1 2017

BRAZIL'S SPORTS, SCANDAL, AND MARKET RALLY diag *Fortune* v174 no8 p21 D 15 2016

BUSINESS RULEMAKING IN THE U.S.: A BRIEF HISTORY color *Fortune* v174 no6 p80 N 1 2016

CHANGE THE WORLD !!!! color diag map *Fortune* v176 no4 p74 S 15 2017

CONSUMERS FLEX THEIR POLITICAL MUSCLE *Fortune* v175 no3 p10 Mr 1 2017

Corporate Scientists Go to Washington color *Fortune* v175 no5 p13 Ap 1 2017

CORPORATE WELLNESS PROGRAMS: HEALTHY ... OR HOKEY? color *Fortune* v175 no4 p99 Mr 15 2017

COULD NEW TECH (FINALLY) DESTROY THE PILLBOX? color *Fortune* v176 no1 p12 Jl 1 2017

DREAM WEAVER color *Fortune* v176 no3 p74 S 1 2017

E=MC× EARTH FRIENDLY = MANUFACTURING × CONSCIENTIOUSNESS× color *Fortune* v176 no4 p120 S 15 2017

END OF THE LINE color *Fortune* v175 no2 p80 F 1 2017

FORTY UNDER FORTY 2017 color *Fortune* v176 no3 p62 S 1 2017

HOW A PETRO STATE HANDLES AN EMBARGO color *Fortune* v176 no1 p13 Jl 1 2017

How India Broke Its Economy Overnight (on Purpose) color *Fortune* v75 no1 p18 Ja 1 2017

A Lawsuit Deluge for Opioid Inc color *Fortune* v176 no5 p16 O 1 2017

McKESSON FEELS THE PAIN chart color diag map *Fortune* v175 no8 p170 Je 15 2017

MINING COMEDY GOLD color *Fortune* v176 no3 p70 S 1 2017

MOST POWERFUL WOMEN INTERNATIONAL color *Fortune* v176 no5 p111 O 1 2017

A Mutual Fund Giant Flexes Its Muscles color diag *Fortune* v174 no8 p126 D 15 2016

OHIO, OURSELVES map *Fortune* v174 no6 p10 N 1 2016

THE REVOLUTION STARTS HERE color *Fortune* v174 no7 p26 D 1 2016

Sorry, Coal. Solar Is Where the Jobs Are color *Fortune* v175 no3 p12 Mr 1 2017

THE TIES THAT BIND AT LEVI'S color map *Fortune* v176 no4

p104 S 15 2017

Trump's Travel Ban Could Hit Colleges color diag *Fortune* v175 no4 p14 Mr 15 2017

WORLD'S 50 GREATEST LEADERS [Cover story] color *Fortune* v175 no5 p46 Ap 1 2017

You're Already Good. Here's How to Step It Up color *Fortune* v174 no6 p18 N 1 2016

YOUTH REVOLT color *Fortune* v176 no3 p64 S 1 2017

Fry, Ford

DON'T MISS LIST *Atlanta* v57 no3 p36 Jl 2017

Ford Fry: Chef and mega-restaurateur J. Bainbridge *Atlanta* v57 no5 p66 S 2017

Fry, Gareth

(Re)Creating The Encounter [Cover story] B. Reesman *Stage Directions* v29 no12 p12 D 2016

Fry, Jeremy

DIRECTOR'S CUT M. PRINCE cartoon *Road & Track* v69 no4 p92 N 2017

Frydenvang, J.

Redox stratification of an ancient lake in Gale crater, Mars color *Science* v356 no6341 p922 Je 1 2017

FRYE, CATHY

LOST IN BIG BEND color map *Reader's Digest* v190 no1132 p88 Jl/Ag 2017

Frye, Channing

RESERVE AND PROTECT R. Nadkarni color *Sports Illustrated* v126 no12 p33 My 1 2017

Frye, Phyllis

COURT'S IN SESSION: THE COUNTRY'S FIRST TRANSGENDER JUDGE WAS ALWAYS A RABBLE ROUSER J. ANDERSON-MINSHALL bw *Advocate* no1091 p96 Je/Jl 2017

Frye Co.

IN THE BAG color *Harper's Bazaar* no3648 p95 N 2016

Frykholm, Amy

Actors on the inside color *Christian Century* v134 no1 p28 Ja 4 2017

The Beautiful Possible: A Novel *Christian Century* v134 no11 p42 My 24 2017

Deep Work: Rules for Focused Success in a Distracted World *Christian Century* v134 no3 p33 F 2017

A fair deal for food workers color *Christian Century* v134 no2 p10 Ja 18 2017

FROM NIGERIA TO AMERICA AND BACK *Christian Century* v133 no24 p33 N 23 2016

Language in black and white bw *Christian Century* v134 no9 p10 Ap 26 2017

Magdalene: Poems color *Christian Century* v134 no10 p57 My 10 2017

The Many Deaths of Jew Süss: The Notorious Trial and Execution of an Eighteenth-Century Court Jew color *Christian Century* v134 no18 p37 Ag 30 2017

Ninety-Nine Stories of God *Christian Century* v133 no22 p38 O 26 2016

Real books, fake store *Christian Century* v133 no21 p10 O 12 2016

Seeking refuge color *Christian Century* v134 no5 p32 Mr 1 2017

She Flies On: A White, Southern, Christian Debutante Wakes Up *Christian Century* v134 no19 p41 S 13 2017

Talking together about immigration *Christian Century* v134 no17 p10 Ag 16 2017

True evangelical faith bw *Christian Century* v133 no25 p28 D 7 2016

Welcome to Missoula color *Christian Century* v133 no26 p22 D 21 2016

What is forgiveness? color *Christian Century* v134 no7 p10 Mr 29 2017

Who is Jesus for Muslims? *Christian Century* v134 no12 p32 Je 7 2017

Writing to Save a Life: The Louis Till File *Christian Century* v134 no6 p39 Mr 15 2017

FTSZ protein

Treadmilling by FtsZ filaments drives peptidoglycan synthesis and bacterial cell division A. W. Bisson-Filho, Hsu et al bibl graph *Science* v355 no6326 p739 F 17 2017

Fu, Da-Wei

An organic-inorganic perovskite ferroelectric with large piezoelectric response graph *Science* v357 no6348 p306 Jl 21 2017

Fu, Gregory C.

A general, modular method for the catalytic asymmetric synthesis of alkylboronate esters bibl color *Science* v354 no6317 p1265 D 9 2016

Transition metal-catalyzed alkyl-alkyl bond formation: Another dimension in cross-coupling chemistry diag *Science* v356 no6334 p152 Ap 14 2017

Fu, Liang

Large, valley-exclusive Bloch-Siegert shift in monolayer WS2 bibl diag *Science* v355 no6329 p1066 Mr 10 2017

Fu, Lisa

WORLD'S LARGEST CORPORATIONS chart diag *Fortune* v176 no2 pF1 Ag 1 2017

Fu, Mei-Qing

"Perfect" designer chromosome V and behavior of a ring derivative diag *Science* v355 no6329 p1046 Mr 10 2017

Fu, Niankai

Metal-catalyzed electrochemical diazidation of alkenes diag *Science* v357 no6351 p575 Ag 11 2017

Fu, Roger R.

Lifetime of the solar nebula constrained by meteorite paleomagnetism bibl graph *Science* v355 no6325 p623 F 10 2017

Fu, Xuewen

Imaging rotational dynamics of nanoparticles in liquid by 4D electron microscopy bibl diag graph *Science* v355 no6324 p494 F 3 2017

Fu, Yuning

Seasonal water storage, stress modulation, and California seismicity diag graph *Science* v356 no6343 p1161 Je 16 2017

Fu, Z.

Observation of coherent elastic neutrino-nucleus scattering diag *Science* v357 no6356 p1123 S 15 2017

Fu Ying

A New Urgent Realism Is Making Negotiations With North Korea More Likely N. Gardels *NPQ: New Perspectives Quarterly* v34 no3 p6 Jl 2017

Fubini, David

Before a Merger, Consider Company Cultures Along with Financials *Harvard Business Review Digital Articles* p2 D 26 2014

F.U.B.U. (Music)

'F.U.B.U.' A. FLOURNOY *New York Times Magazine* p51 Mr 12 2017

FUCA, YUAN

11th SHANGHAI BIENNALE color *ARTnews* v116 no1 p122 Spr 2017

AROUND BEIJING color *ARTnews* v115 no4 p131 Wint 2016/2017

Fuchs, Christoph

Crowdsourced Products Sell Better When They're Marketed That Way *Harvard Business Review Digital Articles* p2 N 8 2016

Fuchs, Elaine

Coupling organelle inheritance with mitosis to balance growth and differentiation diag *Science* v355 no6324 p493 F 3 2017

Spatiotemporal antagonism in mesenchymal-epithelial signaling in sweat versus hair fate decision graph *Science* v354 no6319 paah6102-1 D 23 2016

Fuchs, Jeremy

11 PURDUE BOILERMAKERS chart color *Sports Illustrated* v125 no15 p70 N 7 2016

17 ICONIC MOMENTS IN NHL HISTORY color *Sports Illustrated* v126 no4 p56 Ja 30 2017

Anything You Can Do ... color *Sports Illustrated* v126 no2 p23 Ja 16 2017

Back at the Starting Line color *Sports Illustrated* v126 no1 p18 Ja 9 2017

Back to the Basket color *Sports Illustrated* v126 no14 p28 My 15-22 2017

BEST OF FILM color *Sports Illustrated* v125 no18 p46 D 5 2016

THE BIG BANG color *Sports Illustrated* v125 no12 p50 O 10 2016

The Case for ... JAROMIR JAGR color *Sports Illustrated* v127 no9 p19 S 25 2017

The Case for ... The White Sox color *Sports Illustrated* v126 no12 p21 My 1 2017

Catching Trout color *Sports Illustrated* v127 no1 p26 Jl 3 2017

DOWNWARD-FACING BULL color *Sports Illustrated* v127 no7 p24 S 4 2017

Fuel Injector color *Sports Illustrated* v127 no2 p24 Jl 17 2017

GATORADE Players Of the Year color diag *Sports Illustrated* v127 no1 p72 Jl 3 2017

GENE MICHAEL (1938-2017) color *Sports Illustrated* v127 no8 p22 S 18 2017

ICE FLOW color *Sports Illustrated* v127 no9 p16 S 25 2017

Ice the Drought color *Sports Illustrated* v126 no8 p26 Mr 20 2017

JAKE LAMOTTA (1922-2017) color *Sports Illustrated* v127 no10 p22 O 2 2017

Jimmy Snuka (1943-2017) color *Sports Illustrated* v126 no4 p22 Ja 30 2017

Keep on Moving color *Sports Illustrated* v127 no6 p20 Ag 28 2017

The Last Leap color *Sports Illustrated* v126 no18 p20 Je 26 2017

Lost and Found color *Sports Illustrated* v126 no12 p20 My 1 2017

Missouri Compromise color *Sports Illustrated* v126 no10 p32 Ap 10 2017

The New Marshall Plan color diag *Sports Illustrated* v125 no15 p20 N 7 2016

Olympic Recovery color *Sports Illustrated* v127 no3 p18 Jl 24 2017

Pool Cue color *Sports Illustrated* v126 no16 p26 Je 5 2017

Present Moment color *Sports Illustrated* v126 no13 p20 My 8 2017

Rise Up color *Sports Illustrated* v126 no17 p28 Je 19 2017

Robert H. Boyle (1928-2017) color *Sports Illustrated* v126 no16 p32 Je 5 2017

RUGBY UNION color *Sports Illustrated* v127 no8 p24 S 18 2017

Running to The Top color *Sports Illustrated* v126 no5 p24 F 13 2017

Short Circuit color *Sports Illustrated* v126 no13 p22 My 8 2017

Steven Holcomb (1980-2017) color *Sports Illustrated* v126 no15 p20 My 29 2017

Team Israel 2017-17 color *Sports Illustrated* v126 no9 p26 Mr 27 2017

TRIBUTES color *Sports Illustrated* v127 no5 p22 Ag 14 2017

WHAT IF? ... ONE PRESIDENT'S PROGENY HADN'T ALTERED FOOTBALL FOREVER? color *Sports Illustrated* v126 no11 p64 Ap 17-24 2017

WHAT IF? ... WAYNE GRETZKY HADN'T SKATED OUT WEST? color *Sports Illustrated* v126 no11 p59 Ap 17-24 2017

WHAT WILL TEAM USA LOOK LIKE AT THE OLYMPICS? color *Sports Illustrated* v127 no11 p44 O 9 2017

Whit and Wisdom color *Sports Illustrated* v126 no11 p28 Ap 17-24 2017

WHO CAN END THE PENGUINS' REIGN? color *Sports Illustrated* v127 no11 p43 O 9 2017

WHO IS THE NEXT BREAKOUT STAR? color *Sports Illustrated* v127 no11 p43 O 9 2017

WILL CANADA'S 24-YEAR DROUGHT END? color *Sports Illustrated* v127 no11 p45 O 9 2017

Willie Evans (1937-2017) color *Sports Illustrated* v126 no3 p18 Ja 23 2017

Fuchs, Regina

Biological fabrication of cellulose fibers with tailored properties color *Science* v357 no6356 p1118 S 15 2017

Fucus gardneri

THE ROCKWEED RUSH R. Jacobsen cartoon color *Mother Jones* v41 no6 p8 N/D 2016

Fudge

The Sweet Life *Los Angeles Magazine* v61 no11 p122 N 2016

Fudge, Erica

You Are What You Eat *History Today* v67 no2 p41 F 2017

FUDICKAR, ADAM

ON THE MOVE: ANIMAL MIGRATION IN THE 21ST CENTURY color *Phi Kappa Phi Forum* v96 no4 p26 Wint 2016

Fuel

See also

Fossil fuels

Waste products as fuel

Biology leads the race to turn sunlight into fuels D. Kramer *Physics Today* v70 no4 p30 Ap 2017

Fracking and the future of fuels D. A. Cornell *Physics Today* v70 no2 p10 F 2017

Fuel additives
  OILED UP J. Pearley Huffman color *Car & Driver* v63 no4 p28 O 2017

Fuel cell vehicles
  Toward sustainable fuel cells I. E. Lester Stephens, J. Rossmeisl et al bibl graph *Science* v354 no6318 p1378 D 16 2016

Fuel cells
  Mr. Toyoda, please bring back MR2 E. Loh *Motor Trend* v69 no7 p12 Jl 2017
  Score One, Finally, For Hydrogen J. Ryan and C. Martin color *Bloomberg Businessweek* no4533 p21 Ag 7 2017
  Toward sustainable fuel cells I. E. Lester Stephens, J. Rossmeisl et al bibl graph *Science* v354 no6318 p1378 D 16 2016

Fuel costs
  Count Our Blessings B. LUTZ color *Road & Track* v68 no10 p112 Jl 2017

Fuel filters
  Diesel Issues N. Calder color *Sail* v48 no3 p54 Mr 2017

Fuel injection systems in automobiles
    See also
    Electronic fuel injection systems in automobiles
  WEEKEND EFI E. Perkins color *Hot Rod* v70 no10 p46 O 2017

Fuel laws
  Emission Permission L. Laursen color *Scientific American* v317 no2 p17 Ag 2017

Fuel pumps
    See also
    Automobile fuel systems
  ALL AROUND: THE FARM® P. Barbour *Successful Farming* v115 no12 p77 O 2017
  MY FIRST RIDE: T-PAIN T. Confoy cartoon color *Esquire* v167 no2 p62 Mr 2017

Fuel systems—Maintenance & repair
  CLEAN FUEL, HAPPY BOAT F. LANIER *Sea Magazine* v108 no9 p48 S 2016

Fuel tanks
  THEN AND NOW K. CAMERON *Cycle World* v55 no10 p24 N 2016

Fuel tanks—Evaluation
  GEARBOX color *Dirt Sports + Off-Road* v51 no6 p68 Je 2017

Fuel testing
  Yamaha's Top 10 Maintenance Tips *Boating World* v38 no5 p58 My 2017

Fuel—Costs—Government policy
  TIME TO STOCK UP AT THE GROCERY STORE L. GERSTNER color *Kiplinger's Personal Finance* v71 no1 p15 Ja 2017

Fueling
  departing the waters E. Cummins cartoon *Popular Science* v289 no4 p84 Jl/Ag 2017

Fuelwood
  FOREST TO TABLE J. KRAMER bw color *Bon Appetit* v62 no6 p98 Je 2017
  SEASONING your firewood [Cover story] color *Cabin Living* p56 O 2017

Fuentes, A.
  Persistent effects of pre-Columbian plant domestication on Amazonian forest composition bibl chart graph map *Science* v355 no6328 p925 Mr 3 2017

Fuerst, Brad
  We're Number One! color *Backpacker* v45 no1 p8 Ja 2017

Fuerzas Armadas Revolucionarias de Colombia
  The Difficult Road to Peace in Colombia E. POSADA-CARBO *Current History* v116 no787 p74 F 2017
  Getting to Peace in Colombia J. NORDLINGER color *National Review* v68 no23 p30 D 19 2016
  OUT OF THE JUNGLE J. L. ANDERSON cartoon color *New Yorker* v93 no11 p28 My 1 2017
  South America *New York Times Upfront* v149 no7 p26 Ja 9 2017
  When the Résumé Reads: 'GUERRILLA (1964-2016)' J. Otis color *Bloomberg Businessweek* no4528 p54 Je 26 2017

Fueta, R.
  Coseismic rupturing stopped by Aso volcano during the 2016 Mw 7.1 Kumamoto earthquake, Japan bibl color graph *Science* v354 no6314 p869 N 18 2016

Fuge, Heidi
  Horn Hunting *New York State Conservationist* v71 no4 p17 F 2017

Fugitive, The (TV program)
  HOW THE FUGITIVE FINALE MADE TV BETTER D. Bianculli *TV Guide* v65 no35 p8 Ag 21 2017
  ordinary PEOPLE LIKE US D. J. Gladstone bw color *Missouri Life* v44 no6 p58 S 2017

Fugitives from justice
  'Wanted,' one more time M. FRISCOLANTI color *Maclean's* no1 p13 F 17 2017

Fuglie, Keith
  U.S. Agricultural R&D in an Era of Falling Public Funding *Amber Waves: The Economics of Food, Farming, Natural Resources, & Rural America* p1 N 2016

Fuhrer, Margaret
  All-Around arTiST color *Dance Spirit* v21 no1 p44 Ja 2017
  THE BOYS OF BALLET *Dance Spirit* v21 no3 p36 Mr 2017
  COLOR Coded *Dance Spirit* v21 no7 p98 S 2017
  FEET FIRST *Dance Spirit* v21 no3 p44 Mr 2017
  Living That #BalletLife *Dance Spirit* v21 no7 p88 S 2017
  SPOT Check *Dance Spirit* v21 no3 p58 Mr 2017

Fuji, Mount (Japan)—History
  THE MAGIC MOUNTAIN F. LIDZ *Smithsonian* v48 no2 p48 My 2017

Fuji Bikes (Company)
  "I WANT TO TRY CYCLOCROSS." J. Hart and B. STRICKLAND color *Bicycling* v58 no3 p66 Ap 2017

Fujifilm digital cameras—Evaluation
  Gear of the Year color *Popular Photography* v80 no11 p56 D 2016
  A STAR'S TURN M. Leuchter color *Popular Photography* v81 no1 p64 Ja/F 2017

Fujifilm Holdings Corp.
  HAPPY MEDIUM P. Ryan color *Popular Photography* v80 no11 p14 D 2016

Fujii, T.
  Observation of a large-scale anisotropy in the arrival directions of cosmic rays above 8×1018 eV *Science* v357 no6357 p1266 S 22 2017

Fujimoto, Sōsuke, 1971-
  Salone del Mobile 2017: With over 2,000 exhibitors and nearly 350,000 visitors last month, Milan's furniture fair still proves to be the best in the world J. Minutillo color *Architectural Record* v205 no5 p65 My 2017

Fujimura, Makoto
  Cultural Whistleblowers M. Fujimura color *Christianity Today* p62 Mr 2017

FUJITA, CAROLE A.
  Q: What adventure would you love to share with your best friend? color *O, The Oprah Magazine* p12 Ja 2017

Fujita, Satoshi
  Root diffusion barrier control by a vasculature-derived peptide binding to the SGN3 receptor bibl color *Science* v355 no6322 p280 Ja 20 2017

Fujitani, Tadahiro
  TECHNICAL COMMENT ABSTRACTS *Science* v357 no6354 p881 S 1 2017

Fujiwara, Thomas
  The Ambition-Marriage Trade-Off Too Many Single Women Face *Harvard Business Review Digital Articles* p2 My 8 2017

Fukada, Koji
  Harmonium J. CRONK color *Film Comment* v53 no3 p67 My/Je 2017

Fuks, Garold
  Potential role of intratumor bacteria in mediating tumor resistance to the chemotherapeutic drug gemcitabine diag *Science* v357 no6356 p1156 S 15 2017

Fukuda, Shinji
  Neonatal acquisition of Clostridia species protects against colonization by bacterial pathogens diag *Science* v356 no6335 p315 Ap 21 2017

Fukushima Nuclear Accident, Fukushima, Japan, 2011—Economic aspects
  At Fukushima, Still More Heat than Light: Six years after a tsunami struck the Honshu coast, the ruins of the nuclear power plant seethe and the Japanese still await honest answers Toshio Nishi *Hoover Digest: Research & Opinion on Public Policy* no3 p102 Summ 2017

Fukushima Nuclear Accident, Fukushima, Japan, 2011—Social

aspects

At Fukushima, Still More Heat than Light: Six years after a tsunami struck the Honshu coast, the ruins of the nuclear power plant seethe and the Japanese still await honest answers Toshio Nishi *Hoover Digest: Research & Opinion on Public Policy* no3 p102 Summ 2017

FUKUYAMA, FRANCIS

The Year in Reading [Cover story] *New York Times Book Review* p8 D 25 2016

Fukuyama, Francis, 1952-—Interviews

Francis Fukuyama: Democracy Needs Elites A. Görlach and F. Fukuyama *NPQ: New Perspectives Quarterly* v34 no2 p9 My 2017

Fukuzawa, Yukichi, 1835-1901

1854: Nagasaki Yukichi Fukuzawa *Lapham's Quarterly* v10 no2 p169 Spr 2017

Fulavits, Heidi

Choose Your Own Rachel Cusk img *New York* p101 Mr 6 2017

Fulcher, David D., 1964-

Life Coach J. A. MILLER *Cincinnati Magazine* v50 no4 p56 Ja 2017

Fulchignoni, M.

Seasonal exposure of carbon dioxide ice on the nucleus of comet 67P/Churyumov-Gerasimenko bibl bw graph *Science* v354 no6319 p1563 D 23 2016

Fulco, Charles

The Day the Sun Disappears color map *National Wildlife (World Edition)* v55 no4 p18 Je/Jl 2017

Systematic mapping of functional enhancer–promoter connections with CRISPR interference bibl graph *Science* v354 no6313 p769 N 11 2016

Fuld, Leonard M.

An Exercise to Get Your Team Thinking Differently About the Future *Harvard Business Review Digital Articles* p2 Ja 23 2015

Only Half of Companies Actually Use the Competitive Intelligence They Collect *Harvard Business Review Digital Articles* p2 Ja 26 2016

Fulfillment Center (Theatrical production)

THE THEATRE *New Yorker* v93 no19 p5 Jl 3 2017

Fulk, Ken

Have It Both Ways color *House Beautiful* v159 no4 p30 My 2017

In Mr. Fulk's Neighborhood H. MARTIN bw color *Architectural Digest* v73 no11 p186 N 2016

FULKERSON, AMY

FIESTA Gown *Texas Monthly* v44 no11 p108 N 2016

Full Circle (Music)

Country Strong A. Nash color *AARP: The Magazine* v59 no3A p62 Ap/My 2016

Full Compass Systems Ltd.

Full Compass - Contributing to Customers and Community via the Arts *Stage Directions* v30 no3 p16 Mr 2017

Full Frontal (TV program)

FULL FRONTAL FRIENDS color *TV Guide* v65 no7 p47 F 13 2017

Full Frontal With Samantha Bee (TV program)

FULL FRONTAL WITH SAMANTHA BEE J. RUSSELL *TV Guide* v64 no40 p63 O 3 2016

SAMANTHA BEE R. Rahman color *Entertainment Weekly* no1444/1445 p18 D 16 2016

TALK TV'S BREAKOUT STARS color *Essence* v48 no5 p62 S 2017

Full moon

BLACK AND BLUE MOON K. Haynes, J. Fuller et al color *Astronomy* v44 no12 p44 D 2016

Bright-Sky Imaging R. Brecher color *Sky & Telescope* v134 no5 p68 N 2017

Full service restaurants—Evaluation

HEY, SHORTY B. MCKIBBEN *Atlanta* v56 no12 p79 Ap 2017

Full Tank: The Complete Album Collection (Music)

FULL TANK: THE COMPLETE ALBUM COLLECTION M. Mettler color *Sound & Vision* v82 no8 p72 O 2017

Full-time employment

BAD NEWS color *Maclean's* v129 no51/52 p11 D 26 2016

Precarious Employment *Change* v82 no3 p31 Mr 2017

What Do Women's Career Paths Really Look Like? S. Damaske and A. Frech *Harvard Business Review Digital Articles* p2 Je 8 2016

Full-time employment—Law & legislation

Robert Reich on Redefining Full-Time Work, Obamacare, and Employer Benefits W. Frick *Harvard Business Review Digital Articles* p2 Ja 21 2015

Fullbright Co.

TACOMA: THE MAKERS OF GONE HOME UNSPOOL A MESMERIZING SCIENCE FICTION STORY N. ALDERMAN color *Macworld - Digital Edition* v34 no10 p31 O 2017

Fulle, M.

Rosetta's comet 67P/Churyumov-Gerasimenko sheds its dusty mantle to reveal its icy nature bibl graph *Science* v354 no6319 p1566 D 23 2016

Surface changes on comet 67P/Churyumov-Gerasimenko suggest a more active past bw graph *Science* v355 no6332 p1392 Mr 31 2017

Fuller, Alexandra, 1969-

Bury My Heart: Alexandra Fuller's deep dive into Lakota culture and history follows two reservation boys whose lives become fatefully intertwined E. EAKIN *New York Times Book Review* p19 Jl 23 2017

Quiet Until the Thaw *Publishers Weekly* v264 no17 p60 Ap 24 2017

Fuller, Bryan

THE SAMURAI CODE P. d 'Orléans color *Cycle World* v55 no11 p36 D 2016

Fuller, Casey

Fuller Family Wins Inaugural No. 12 High Desert Showdown color *Team Roping Journal* p42 S 2017

new products color *Team Roping Journal* p44 S 2017

Fuller, Claire

Swimming Lessons *Publishers Weekly* v263 no46 p28 N 14 2016

You Found What? *Publishers Weekly* v264 no11 p88 Mr 13 2017

FULLER, JANET RAUSA

A CAKE TO REMEMBER color *Chicago* v66 no4 p56 Ap 2017

CULINARY ARTS color *Chicago* v66 no2 p48 F 2017

THE DOUGHNUT KING color *Chicago* v66 no11 p50 N 2017

GET ON BOARD color *Chicago* v66 no10 p52 O 2017

ICE DREAMS [Cover story] color *Chicago* v66 no6 p45 Je 2017

AN INDONESIAN FEAST color *Chicago* v66 no7 p44 Jl 2017

The Insider's Guide to FARMERS' MARKETS [Cover story] color *Chicago* v66 no6 p72 Je 2017

MASTER OF FIRE color *Chicago* v66 no8 p51 Ag 2017

Fuller, Jim

BLACK AND BLUE MOON color *Astronomy* v44 no12 p44 D 2016

Fuller, Margaret T.

Blocking promiscuous activation at cryptic promoters directs cell type–specific gene expression diag *Science* v356 no6339 p717 My 19 2017

FULLER, MICHAEL M.

Triumphs and Tribulations: An Intimate Account of How Long-Term Funding Affects the Lives of Scientists *BioScience* v67 no5 p477 My 2017

Fuller, Randall, 1963-

The Book That Changed America: How Darwin's Theory of Evolution Ignited a Nation D. CHIVERS *Humanist* v77 no3 p46 My/Je 2017

Darwin's American ascendancy M. P. Sheldon color *Science* v355 no6323 p356 Ja 27 2017

Evolutionary Wars E. FONER *New York Times Book Review* p10 Ja 22 2017

Reading Charles Darwin Utterly Changed How Charles Loring Brace Thought about Social Reform *Humanities* v38 no1 p1 Wint 2017

Selective Memory C. IRMSCHER *American Scholar* v86 no1 p113 Wint 2017

Survival of the Pithiest S. MILLER color *Weekly Standard* v22 no30 p30 Ap 10 2017

FULLER, RICHARD A.

Doses of Neighborhood Nature: The Benefits for Mental Health of Living with Nature *BioScience* v67 no2 p147 F 2017

Fuller, Ryan

Being Engaged at Work Is Not the Same as Being Productive *Harvard Business Review Digital Articles* p2 F 16 2017

How to Finally Kill the Useless, Recurring Meeting *Harvard*

Business Review Digital Articles p2 Mr 17 2015

The Paradox of Workplace Productivity *Harvard Business Review Digital Articles* p2 Ap 19 2016

A Primer on Measuring Employee Engagement *Harvard Business Review Digital Articles* p2 N 17 2014

What Great Managers Do Daily *Harvard Business Review Digital Articles* p2 D 14 2016

What Makes Great Salespeople *Harvard Business Review Digital Articles* p2 Jl 8 2015

Fuller, Simon

Farewell Idol R. MOYNIHAN *TV Guide* v64 no15 p35 Ap 4 2016

FULLER, STEVE

Does This Pro-science Party Deserve Our Votes? *Issues in Science & Technology* v33 no3 p31 Spr 2017

Fuller, Thomas, 1608-1661

THE POWER OF Touch M. THOMAS and D. LINDEN color *AARP: The Magazine* v59 no1A p38 D 2015/Ja 2016

Fuller, Tim

Fuller Family Wins Inaugural No. 12 High Desert Showdown color *Team Roping Journal* p42 S 2017

new products color *Team Roping Journal* p44 S 2017

Fuller House (TV program)

America's top TV critic Matt Roush answers your burning questions M. Roush *TV Guide* v65 no2 p6 Ja 2 2017

Fuller House A. Bacle, K. Connolly et al *Entertainment Weekly* no1482/1483 p106 S 22 2017

FULLER HOUSE GETS FESTIVE A. D'ARMINIO *TV Guide* p24 D 5 2016

FULLERTON, AIMEE H.

Envisioning, Quantifying, and Managing Thermal Regimes on River Networks *BioScience* v67 no6 p506 Je 2017

Fullerton, Elizabeth

ETEL ADNAN color *Art in America* v104 no10 p161 N 2016

FRANCIS ALŸS color *Art in America* v104 no10 p160 N 2016

LUBAINA HIMID cartoon *Art in America* v105 no4 p122 Ap 2017

MICHAEL ARMITAGE color *Art in America* p131 O 2017

ROBERT RAUSCHENBERG color *Art in America* v105 no3 p123 Mr 2017

Royal Academy of Arts color *Art in America* v105 no1 p90 Ja 2017

RYAN GANDER color *Art in America* v105 no5 p110 My 2017

"SOUL OF A NATION: ART IN THE AGE OF BLACK POWER" color *Art in America* v105 no8 p129 S 2017

VENICE—Punta della Dogana and Palazzo Grassi color *Art in America* v105 no6 p147 Je/Jl 2017

FULLERTON, GENNY

photo school: Get Serial color *Backpacker* p36 S 2017

Tell Your Story color diag *Backpacker* v45 no1 p38 Ja 2017

Fullheart, Salsa

Thoughts on previous issues color *American Cowboy* v24 no1 p24 Je/Jl 2017

FULLMAN, TIMOTHY J.

Mapping Conservation Strategies under a Changing Climate *BioScience* v67 no6 p494 Je 2017

Fully autonomous automobile driving

THE AI DETECTIVES P. Voosen color diag *Science* v357 no6346 p22 Jl 7 2017

Are Driverless Cars a Good Idea? *New York Times Upfront* v149 no13 p22 My 15 2017

auto no mo' us M. Gladwell, T. Vanderbilt et al bw color diag graph *Car & Driver* v63 no5 p58 N 2017

BAD NEWS: THE GOVERNMENT WANTS TO 'HELP' DRIVERLESS CAR COMPANIES R. BAILEY bw *Reason* v48 no10 p13 Mr 2017

Changing Lanes M. Chafkin and J. Eidelson color *Bloomberg Businessweek* no4528 p60 Je 26 2017

COMPUTER ON WHEELS color *Popular Science* p17 Ja/F 2017

Deep Driving C. Reiley *MIT Technology Review* v119 no6 p10 N/D 2016

Don't Blame the Robots; Blame Us C. DIANA color *Popular Science* v288 no6 p46 N/D 2016

Driverless Cars: What Could Possibly Go Wrong? R. Hutchinson *Harvard Business Review Digital Articles* p2 Ja 15 2016

DRIVERLESS DELAY P. HEANEY *Scientific American* v315 no3 p6 S 2016

Drivers Not Wanted: An Oral History of the Darpa Grand Challenge A. DAVIES bw color diag *Wired* v25 no8 p49 Ag 2017

Driving Into the Future J. Plungis color map *Consumer Reports* v82 no4 p10 Ap 2017

THE EDITORIAL *Maclean's* v129 no47 p7 N 28 2016

Editor's Letter E. Alterman *Car & Driver* v63 no5 p12 N 2017

THE FALLACY OF THE SELF-PARKING CAR E. DYER color *Popular Mechanics* p73 My 2017

FROM PARKING LOT TO PARADISE C. Ratti and A. Biderman color diag *Scientific American* v317 no1 p54 Jl 2017

FUTURE WORLD: Transportation K. DE SEVE color *National Geographic Kids* no470 p20 My 2017

How a College Kid Made His Honda Civic Self-Driving for $700 T. Simonite il *MIT Technology Review* v120 no3 p13 My/Je 2017

John Phillips J. Phillips color *Car & Driver* v63 no2 p30 Ag 2017

A Little Common Sense, and Control B. Lang *Discover* v38 no3 p7 Ap 2017

Machines are getting much, much smarter D. Malakoff color *Science* v354 no6310 p278 O 21 2016

On the Move color *Los Angeles Magazine* v62 no7 p6 Jl 2017

Outfitting Robo Car M. ANTONOFF color graph *Sound & Vision* v82 no7 p21 S 2017

Queasy Street Riding in autonomous cars without losing our lunch F. Markus color *Motor Trend* v69 no6 p28 Je 2017

RIGHT OF WAY FOR ROBO-CARS X. HARDING color *Popular Science* p16 Ja/F 2017

A Right to Keep and Drive Cars? J. GELERNTER cartoon *Weekly Standard* v22 no7 p16 O 24 2016

SELF-DRIVING CARS ARE COOL, BUT THEY'RE NOT FOR EVERYONE J. D. Tuccille color *Reason* v49 no5 p12 O 2017

Self-Driving Cars' Spinning-Laser Problem T. Simonite color *MIT Technology Review* v120 no4 p27 Jl/Ag 2017

Self-Driving Cars will change local real estate M. J. GAYNOR color *Washingtonian Magazine* v52 no7 p96 Ap 2017

Self-Driving the Economy F. Shafroth *Governing* v30 no4 p62 Ja 2017

SELF-DRIVING Trucks D. H. FREEDMAN color *MIT Technology Review* v120 no2 p62 Mr/Ap 2017

TAKE THE WHEEL: SELF-DRIVING CARS MUST CONNECT WITH HUMANS A. DAVIES color *Wired* v25 no7 p13 Jl 2017

Tesla, Autopilot, and the Challenge of Trusting Machines W. Frick *Harvard Business Review Digital Articles* p2 Jl 11 2016

Traffic G. TARLACH color *Discover* v38 no7 p74 S 2017

Unsafe at Any Speed J. PELINI cartoon *Atlantic* v319 no2 p22 Mr 2017

WHAT HAPPENS TO AMERICAN MYTH WHEN YOU TAKE THE DRIVER OUT OF IT? R. MOOR *New York* v49 no21 p36 O 17 2016

When Driving Is Obsolete D. HARSANYI *National Review* v68 no23 p44 D 19 2016

WHERE WE'RE GOING, WE WON'T NEED ROADS J. BROWN color *Popular Science* v289 no6 p42 N/D 2017

Why We Don't Trust Driverless Cars — Even When We Should K. Hosanagar and I. Cronk *Harvard Business Review Digital Articles* p2 O 18 2016

Your Driverless Ride Is Arriving W. Knight color il *MIT Technology Review* v119 no6 p34 N/D 2016

Fully autonomous automobile driving—Government policy

NEW RULES FOR NEW FRONTIERS L. Entis color *Fortune* v174 no6 p80 N 1 2016

Fully autonomous automobile driving—Law & legislation

The Right and Wrong Ways to Regulate Self-Driving Cars L. Downes *Harvard Business Review Digital Articles* p2 D 6 2016

Fully autonomous automobile driving—Security measures

A Path to Safer Roadways color *Consumer Reports* v82 no12 p5 D 2017

Self-Driving-Car Safety color *Consumer Reports* v82 no2 p6 F 2017

Fully autonomous automobile driving—Social aspects

The Blind Community Has High Hopes for Self-Driving Cars E. Woyke il *MIT Technology Review* v120 no1 p20 Ja/F 2017

Policing Driverless Cars A. Rosenblum il *MIT Technology Review* v119 no6 p15 N/D 2016

Fully autonomous automobile driving—Software

How Grand Theft Auto Steers Driverless Cars D. Hull color *Bloomberg Businessweek* no4519 p23 Ap 24 2017

Fulmer, Ashley

Employees Who Trust Their Managers Are More Likely to Trust Their CEOs *Harvard Business Review Digital Articles* p2 Jl 6 2017

Fulmer, Michael, 1993-

Michael Fulmer M. Hagan color *Current Biography* v78 no6 p39 Je 2017

Fulmer, Michael, 1993——Awards

NO PIPE DREAM S. Apstein color *Sports Illustrated* v126 no3 p40 Ja 23 2017

Fulton, Elaine

The Flawed Reformer *History Today* v67 no1 p56 Ja 2017

Fulton, Elizabeth A.

A stitch in time saves nine…billion bibl color *Science* v354 no6319 p1530 D 23 2016

Fulton, Mark

Divestment Alone Won't Beat Climate Change *Harvard Business Review Digital Articles* p2 N 4 2014

FULTON, MAXFIELD

Never Done: A History of Women's Work in Media Production *Film Quarterly* v70 no3 p101 Spr 2017

Fulton, Sue

Sue Fulton Thinks Equal Rights Make The Military Stronger A. M. Cox *New York Times Magazine* p58 Ja 15 2017

Fulton, Sybrina, 1966-

A MOTHER ON A MISSION color *Essence* v47 no10 p116 F 2017

Fulton, Sybrina, 1966——Interviews

Sybrina Fulton and Tracy Martin E. Dias color *Time* v189 no4 p60 F 6 2017

Fulton, William

Are Cities Growing or Not? *Governing* v30 no1 p24 O 2016

Jammed Cities *Governing* v30 no5 p25 F 2017

The New Laboratories *Governing* v30 no7 p23 Ap 2017

Not-So-New Urbanism: City revival has ceased to be a radical idea *Governing* v31 no1 p25 O 2017

Side Effects of 'The Great Inversion': Low pay and long, pricey commutes often go hand in hand *Governing* v30 no9 p23 Je 2017

Split Personalities *Governing* v30 no3 p24 D 2016

The Sun Belt's Urban Reality: The region grapples with familiar issues that need unique solutions color *Governing* v30 no11 p23 Ag 2017

Fultz, Markelle

LINGO BINGO T. Keith color *Sports Illustrated* v127 no1 p18 Jl 3 2017

Fume hoods

new products color *Science* v356 no6336 p446 Ap 28 2017

Fumiaki Kitahara

Positive biodiversity-productivity relationship predominant in global forests bibl chart graph map *Science* v354 no6309 paaf8957-1 O 14 2016

Fumihiro Kano

Great apes anticipate that other individuals will act according to false beliefs bibl chart diag graph *Science* v354 no6308 p110 O 7 2016

Fumiki Yoshihara

Suppressing relaxation in superconducting qubits by quasiparticle pumping bibl graph *Science* v354 no6319 p1573 D 23 2016

Fumio Arai

Self-renewal of a purified Tie2+ hematopoietic stem cell population relies on mitochondrial clearance bibl graph *Science* v354 no6316 p1156 D 2 2016

Fun & Games for Everyone (Film)

Color Box M. J. ROWIN bw *Film Comment* v53 no2 p77 Mr/Ap 2017

Fun (Music)

The Must List color *Entertainment Weekly* no1453 p1 F 17 2017

Fun Express Inc.

Camp Season on a Budget *Parks & Recreation* v52 no4 p52 Ap 2017

Fun Home (Theatrical production)

WHERE & WHEN M. J. Gaynor, A. Beaujon et al color *Washingtonian Magazine* v52 no7 p31 Ap 2017

Funabashi, Yoichi

Asia: Trump's Shock Doctrine Will Make China Even Stronger color *Time* v188 no27-28 p26 D 26 2016

Functional beverages

    See also

    Kombucha tea

The Four Best Power Shakes for Men bw color *Men's Health* v32 no6 p70 Ag 2017

SMARTEN UP TO SHRINK YOUR GUT C. Hansen color *Men's Health* v32 no6 p69 Ag 2017

Functional foods

Delish dips A. Young color *Yoga Journal* no295 p26 O 2017

Functional foods——Evaluation

EXPIRES NEVER K. Bastone cartoon color *Runner's World* v51 no10 p48 N 2016

Functional magnetic resonance imaging

Frequent lying alters brain activity L. SANDERS *Science News* v190 no11 p12 N 26 2016

Marketers Should Pay Attention to fMRI U. R. Karmarkar, C. Yoon et al *Harvard Business Review Digital Articles* p2 N 3 2015

When Brain Imaging Goes Awry L. SCHLEY color *Discover* v38 no1 p72 Ja/F 2017

Functional training

    See also

    Self-defense instruction

THE TOP 10 BEST FUNCTIONAL EXERCISES M. Berg bw color *Muscle & Performance* v8 no12 p46 D 2016

Functionals (Mathematics)

Density functional theory is straying from the path toward the exact functional M. G. Medvedev, I. S. Bushmarinov et al bibl chart graph *Science* v355 no6320 p1 Ja 6 2017

FUND, JOHN

Cold War Redux color *National Review* v68 no20 p44 N 7 2016

Fund, Ken

The Independent Spirit Flourishes in the Pacific Northwest A. GROSS color *Publishers Weekly* v263 no47 p32 N 21 2016

Fundraisers (Persons)

Historic Alexandria Foundation *Virginia Living* v15 no3 p39 Ap 2017

Real Estate and The Art Of War A. SALAS *Los Angeles Magazine* p15 My 2017

Fundraising

    See also

    Campaign funds

    Crowd funding

15 MINUTES *Cincinnati Magazine* v50 no4 p45 Ja 2017

ABOUT TOWN *Virginia Living* v15 no1 p37 D 2016

BEAUTIFUL DREAMERS D. KAZANJIAN color *Vogue* v207 no7 p100 Jl 2017

Breakfast (and Dinner) of Champions P. CLAASSEN color *Climbing* no353 p29 My/Je 2017

Come Together. M. DUPLASS *USA Today Magazine* v145 no2864 p21 My 2017

DESTINATION WASHINGTON C. CUNNINGHAM *Washingtonian Magazine* v52 no5 p22 F 2017

DOING GOOD C. Shanahan color *InStyle* v24 no4 p70 Ap 2017

Drags to Riches C. ZEIGLER color *Indianapolis Monthly* v42 no2 p20 O 2017

THE ELEMENTS S. Larson cartoon *New Yorker* v93 no12 p19 My 8 2017

The Empty Bowls Soup Tale: How you can help fight hunger in New Orleans A. O'Neil and R. Wallace *Parks & Recreation* v52 no8 p36 Ag 2017

EVENT CALENDAR *Washingtonian Magazine* v52 no2 p303 N 2016

Forget About Grants! N. A. Schaumleffel *Parks & Recreation* v52 no2 p38 F 2017

Four Weeks to the Finish Line K. LOREN chart color *Muscle & Performance* v9 no9 p30 S 2017

Get more cash for what you care about N. Lapin color *Redbook* p33 Ap 2017

GIVE ATLANTA S. MCGINNIS *Atlanta* v57 no6 p20 O 2017

Growing Up P. LAFFOON IV color *Cincinnati Magazine* v51 no1 p38 O 2017

Historic Alexandria Foundation *Virginia Living* v15 no3 p39 Ap

2017

LA LIST *Los Angeles Magazine* v62 no6 p95 Je 2017

Less Is More R. POLANECZKY color *Prevention* v68 no12 p34 D 2016

MIGHTY MORPHIN POWER PLAYER A. KROLL cartoon *Mother Jones* v41 no6 p46 N/D 2016

Mixing Dollars and Sense L. D. JOHNSON and S. T. BROWN color *Ebony* v72 no5 p74 Mr 2017

Moving On: How--and why--company founders shut down their troupes N. WOZNY *Dance Magazine* v91 no10 p46 O 2017

Penguin Mixes Art, Books for a Cause J. Maher color *Publishers Weekly* v264 no24 p10 Je 12 2017

Septic Poem L. Donnellan color *Cabin Living* p71 Ja/F 2017

Show Me The Money E. KELSEY *Psychology Today* v49 no6 p35 N/D 2016

So Long, Summer! E. Beyers color *Missouri Life* v44 no6 p18 S 2017

UNCHARTED WATERS A. RAPOPORT color *Bon Appetit* v61 no11 p12 N 2016

VIRGINIA OPERA *Virginia Living* v15 no6 p41 O 2017

Walker Used Group to Snare Corporate Cash B. LUEDERS diag *Progressive* v81 no10 p12 N 2016

WHAT'S NEW *Sea Magazine* v109 no7 pCA-12 Jl 2017

WHEN ALL WAS LOST: A team of outmatched kids--and a bigger surprise than a win M. R. Fisher *Washingtonian Magazine* v52 no9 p208 Je 2017

Where Gustav Dreamed Big color *Arts & Crafts Homes & the Revival* v11 no5 p16 Wint 2017

Fundraising—News briefs

ABOUT TOWN color *Virginia Living* v15 no5 p35 Ag 2017

Fundraising—United States

America's Largest Charities W. P. BARRETT color *Forbes* v198 no9 p24 D 30 2016

EVENT CALENDAR *Washingtonian Magazine* v52 no8 p212 My 2017

HINDUS FOR TRUMP R. Ali cartoon *New Yorker* v92 no36 p16 N 7 2016

SWAN SONG T. B. BROWNE *Indianapolis Monthly* v40 no5 p16 Ja 2017

Funds-of-funds (Investments)

How to Use ETFs to Pick Other ETFs J. Waggoner diag *Money* v46 no6 p40 Jl 2017

Funeral homes

Comfort & Joy S. A. SMITH color *Missouri Life* v44 no4 p58 Je 2017

Funeral processions

THE QUEEN PASSED ON, BUT THE QUEEN LIVES ON D. J. JENNINGS bw color *Louisiana Life* v37 no2 p40 N/D 2016

Funeral service

DEAD WEIGHT J. LEPORE cartoon *New Yorker* v93 no32 p83 O 16 2017

a trip to the other side R. Feltman cartoon *Popular Science* v289 no5 p76 S/O 2017

Funerals

See also

Funeral service

THE BURNING QUESTION L. BROWN cartoon color *Men's Health* v32 no5 p142 Je 2017

Can Dad Bring His Second Wife to Mom's Funeral? K. A. Appiah *New York Times Magazine* p24 My 14 2017

The Cradle-to-Grave Coalition J. MILLER *In These Times* v41 no10 p41 O 2017

Q + A *Cincinnati Magazine* v50 no8 p24 My 2017

The temporary gift of marriage M. C. Barnes *Christian Century* v134 no13 p33 Je 21 2017

Fung, John J.

Thomas Earl Starzl (1926–2017) color *Science* v356 no6337 p491 My 5 2017

Fung, Kaiser

The Ethics Conversation We're Not Having About Data *Harvard Business Review Digital Articles* p2 N 12 2015

What Popular Baby Names Teach Us About Data Analytics *Harvard Business Review Digital Articles* p2 Ap 3 2015

Why Fraudulent Ad Networks Continue to Thrive *Harvard Business Review Digital Articles* p2 O 28 2015

Yes, A/B Testing Is Still Necessary *Harvard Business Review Digital Articles* p2 D 10 2014

Fung, Megan K.

Impact ejecta at the Paleocene-Eocene boundary bibl bw graph *Science* v354 no6309 p225 O 14 2016

Fungal chromosomes

3D organization of synthetic and scrambled chromosomes G. Mercy, J. Mozziconacci et al diag *Science* v355 no6329 p1050 Mr 10 2017

BUILDING ON NATURE'S DESIGN [Cover story] L. M. Zahn and G. Riddihough color *Science* v355 no6329 p1038 Mr 10 2017

Deep functional analysis of synII, a 770-kilobase synthetic yeast chromosome Y. Shen, Y. Wang et al diag *Science* v355 no6329 p1047 Mr 10 2017

"Perfect" designer chromosome V and behavior of a ring derivative Xie, Li et al diag *Science* v355 no6329 p1046 Mr 10 2017

Fungal ecology

Fungal Feedback A. Braun color *Natural History* v125 no3 p8 Mr 2017

Fungal enzymes

See also

Koji

Breaking the Mold A. STANEK bw color *Bon Appetit* v61 no11 p34 N 2016

Fungal genetics

A global view of meiotic double-strand break end resection E. P. Mimitou, Shintaro Yamada et al bibl graph *Science* v355 no6320 p1 Ja 6 2017

Fungal genomes—Research

Design of a synthetic yeast genome S. M. Richardson, L. A. Mitchell et al bibl chart color graph *Science* v355 no6329 p1040 Mr 10 2017

Fungi

See also

Mushrooms

Yeast fungi

A bacterial global regulator forms a prion A. Hochschild and A. H. Yuan bibl color diag graph *Science* v355 no6321 p1 Ja 13 2017

Fungicides

Subbing Materials for Wood R. Tschoepe diag *Old House Journal* v45 no3 p58 My 2017

Fungi—Research

From Sand to Soil K. ELLISON color *Discover* v38 no1 p82 Ja/F 2017

FUNK, MCKENZIE

OPEN CITY *New York Times Magazine* p31 O 23 2016

Funk, William H.

A BILLIONAIRE FOR THE BEARS *Sierra* v102 no1 p44 Ja/F 2017

The Dismal Swamp: One Road out of Slavery Took You Straight into the Boggiest Place You've Ever Been *Humanities* v38 no2 p5 Spr 2017

Funk music

IS DAYTON THE WORLD CAPITAL OF FUNK? R. J. SMITH *Cincinnati Magazine* p72 Je 2017

Funk musicians

IS DAYTON THE WORLD CAPITAL OF FUNK? R. J. SMITH *Cincinnati Magazine* p72 Je 2017

Funk Wav Bounces (Music)

What to Stream color *Entertainment Weekly* no1473 p55 Jl 7 2017

Funke, Evan

A Maestro Returns: AT FELIX IN VENICE, EVAN FUNKE ROLLS OUT SUBLIMELY REGIONAL ITALIAN FOOD P. KUH color *Los Angeles Magazine* v62 no7 p38 Jl 2017

Funkhouser, Mark

The Case for Density *Governing* v30 no12 p4 S 2017

The Complexity of Simplicity *Governing* v30 no6 p59 Mr 2017

Constraints and Community: To get things done, leaders need to focus on the bigger picture *Governing* v30 no12 p61 S 2017

The Costs We Will Bear *Governing* v30 no11 p4 Ag 2017

Double-Loop Government: It's a learning strategy that produces conflict--and innovation *Governing* v30 no9 p59 Je 2017

Economic Development's Bad Idea: Throwing money at businesses isn't the best approach *Governing* v30 no11 p59 Ag 2017

The Evil That Institutions Do: Preventing it is a dilemma for managers, but it can be done *Governing* v30 no8 p59 My 2017

Getting It Done *Governing* v30 no3 p4 D 2016

Government's Plumbers *Governing* v30 no8 p4 My 2017

The Innovation Equation *Governing* v30 no1 p4 O 2016

The Language of Government *Governing* v30 no3 p59 D 2016

Leading in a 20-Year Winter *Governing* v30 no2 p59 N 2016

The Most Important Work *Governing* v31 no1 p4 O 2017

New Hope for College Towns *Governing* v30 no7 p59 Ap 2017

The New Old Right *Governing* v30 no6 p4 Mr 2017

The Pension Hammer *Governing* v30 no7 p4 Ap 2017

Performance and the People Factor *Governing* v30 no4 p59 Ja 2017

The Power of a P3 *Governing* v30 no1 p61 O 2016

The Problem with 'Political Will' *Governing* v30 no5 p61 F 2017

The Really Hard Stuff *Governing* v30 no10 p4 Jl 2017

A Strategy for Conflict *Governing* v30 no4 p4 Ja 2017

Where Decency Resides *Governing* v30 no9 p4 Je 2017

Where Good Jobs Come From: Better policies could accomplish a lot *Governing* v30 no10 p59 Jl 2017

Where the Money Is *Governing* v30 no2 p4 N 2016

Why Our Policing Is So Ineffective: Racism results in misdirected resources. Technology could help *Governing* v31 no1 p59 O 2017

Women and Power *Governing* v30 no5 p4 F 2017

Funny cars

Pat Minick and the Chi-Town Hustler T. Taylor color *Hot Rod* v70 no6 p10 Je 2017

RON CAPPS T. Taylor color *Hot Rod* v70 no5 p16 My 2017

Thom On Design Stance, Proportion, and How to Mic-Drop Your Next Project T. Taylor bw *Hot Rod* v69 no12 p84 D 2016

Funny Girl (Film)

Barbra Streisand's 75th Birthday M. FELL *TV Guide* p47 Ap 17 2017

Funny Little Snake (Short story)

Funny Little Snake T. Hadley cartoon *New Yorker* v93 no32 p66 O 16 2017

Fur

SPOTS AND STRIPES ARE NOT SO BLACK-AND-WHITE N. Daly bw color *National Geographic* v232 no4 p18 O 2017

Fur-bearing animals

SPOTS AND STRIPES ARE NOT SO BLACK-AND-WHITE N. Daly bw color *National Geographic* v232 no4 p18 O 2017

Fur garments

Escape Artistry color *Vogue* v207 no11 p180 N 2017

Fur garments—Evaluation

THE BIG CHILL bw *Harper's Bazaar* no3648 p260 N 2016

CHARM SCHOOL M. BOBO color *Ebony* v72 no4 p45 F 2017

Doesn't Look Fake color *Women's Health* v14 no1 p70 Ja/F 2017

Puffer Coats L. Indvik color *InStyle* v23 no13 p205 D 2016

Furber, Laurie

french flair P. GUGLIELMETTI color *Better Homes & Gardens* v95 no10 p20 O 2017

Fure, Ashley

CLASSICAL MUSIC *New Yorker* v93 no31 p13 O 9 2017

Füredi, Frank

The Invention of Individual Freedom *History Today* v67 no4 p7 Ap 2017

RAGE OF THE SNOWFLAKES K. C. Johnson *Claremont Review of Books* v17 no3 p62 Summ 2017

FURFARO, HANNAH

Bird's-Eye View *Audubon* v119 no1 p12 Spr 2017

Furia, Emily

"I WANT TO DRINK MY COFFEE WHILE I RIDE TO WORK." color *Bicycling* v58 no3 p40 Ap 2017

"SHOULD I GET A DROP-BAR OR A FLAT-BAR ROAD BIKE?" color *Bicycling* v58 no3 p108 Ap 2017

Furl, Sharon Moe

Country Lore *Mother Earth News* no281 p84 Ap/My 2017

Furla SpA

MUSIC ICONS GET THEIR OWN IT BAG bw color *Harper's Bazaar* no3653 p150 My 2017

Furlan, Alessandro

miR-183 cluster scales mechanical pain sensitivity by regulating basal and neuropathic pain genes diag graph *Science* v356 no6343 p1168 Je 16 2017

Multipotent peripheral glial cells generate neuroendocrine cells of the adrenal medulla color *Science* v357 no6346 p46 Jl 7 2017

Furlan, Scott N.

Comprehensive single-cell transcriptional profiling of a multicellular organism diag *Science* v357 no6352 p661 Ag 18 2017

Furlanetto, Giovanna

MUSIC ICONS GET THEIR OWN IT BAG bw color *Harper's Bazaar* no3653 p150 My 2017

Furler, Sia, 1975-

Making 'Hamilton' Even Greater Again J. DOLAN color *Rolling Stone* no1276 p61 D 15 2016

Furlong, Rob

Kill Shot B. POPPLEWELL cartoon *Walrus* v14 no2 p42 Mr 2017

Furlow, Chris

The Best Cybersecurity Investment You Can Make Is Better Training *Harvard Business Review Digital Articles* p2 My 16 2017

Furman, Jason, 1970-—Interviews

Competition Is on the Decline, and That's Fueling Inequality W. Frick *Harvard Business Review Digital Articles* p2 Mr 24 2017

Furmanczyk-Winogron, Pauline

Giovanni (the Great) *Publishers Weekly* v264 no39 p80d S 25 2017

Furnish, David

Funding the Right Projects: Lessons from the Elton John AIDS Foundation *Harvard Business Review Digital Articles* p2 D 1 2015

Furniss, Maureen

A New History of Animation J. C. DOUGLASS *Film Quarterly* v70 no4 p128 Summ 2017

Furniss, Tucker J.

Plant diversity increases with the strength of negative density dependence at the global scale diag *Science* v356 no6345 p1389 Je 30 2017

Furniture

See also

Bars (Furniture)

Bedroom furniture

Built-in furniture

Cabinets (Furniture)

Chairs

Desks

Implements, utensils, etc.

Kitchen cabinets

Living room furniture

Seating (Furniture)

Sofas

Tables (Furniture)

Workbenches

7 rules for a great room G. Schafer color *Redbook* p132 O 2017

ADDITIONAL LISTINGS *Arts & Crafts Homes & the Revival* v12 no1 p30 2017 Resouce Guide

Colonial to Gothic Revival M. E. Polson color *Old House Journal* v44 no8 p75 D 2016

Colorblock Cubbies color *Good Housekeeping* v265 no3 p47 S 2017

COOL AND COLLECTED E. MOODY color *Martha Stewart Living* p40 Jl/Ag 2017

Cristina Celestino H. MARTIN color *Architectural Digest* v74 no1 p58 Ja 2017

DARK KNIGHT D. THOMAS bw color *Architectural Digest* v73 no12 p48 D 2016

Décor Fresh for Spring K. Wilburn *New Orleans Homes & Lifestyles* v20 no2 p88 Spr 2017

Draw Close A. HEROLD *Los Angeles Magazine* p52 Mr 2017

FURNITURE & ACCESSORIES *Design Center Sourcebook* p71 2016

furniture & art color *Arts & Crafts Homes & the Revival* v12 no1 p22 2017 Resouce Guide

furniture & decorative accessories *Design Center Sourcebook* p56 2017

furniture FOR THE PORCH M. E. POLSON color *Arts & Crafts Homes & the Revival* v12 no3 p28 Summ 2017

Go With the Grain E. MOODY chart color *Martha Stewart Living* p36 Mr 2017

Moving the Merchandise B. PAYNTER *Treasures* v6 no5 p12 Ap/My 2017

No Limits cartoon color *Architectural Digest* v74 no1 p51 Ja 2017

Pastrana Studio L. S. FORD *Texas Monthly* v45 no4 p29 Ap 2017

PRO BONO J. Blitzer cartoon *New Yorker* v93 no27 p24 S 11 2017

Furtado, Nelly, 1978-
3 REINVENTIONS WE CAN'T WAIT TO HEAR M. Vain and J. Goodman color *Entertainment Weekly* no1446/1447 p76 D 2016/Ja 2017

Furtak, Erin Marie
Backtalk color *Phi Delta Kappan* v98 no8 p80 My 2017

Furtman, Michael
dad's legacy color *Cabin Living* p50 O 2017
do you know your eagles? color *Cabin Living* p9 D 2016
Go Mobile color *Audubon* v119 no3 p49 Fall 2017

Furtmüller, Gerhard
Even Tiny Rewards Can Motivate People to Go the Extra Mile *Harvard Business Review Digital Articles* p2 Je 7 2016

Furtney, Isaac
Discussion *Smithsonian* v47 no7 p10 N 2016

Furukawa, Hiroyasu
Water harvesting from air with metal-organic frameworks powered by natural sunlight diag *Science* v356 no6336 p430 Ap 28 2017

Furuno USA Inc.
Furuno TZTouch2 Software Update 4.01 J. Y. WOOD color *Power & Motoryacht* v33 no3 p46 Mr 2017
NEW ELECTRONICS J. Y. WOOD color *Power & Motoryacht* v32 no11 p54 N 2016

Fury, Nick (Fictitious character)
NO. 31 NICK FURY A. Breznican color *Entertainment Weekly* no1436/1437 p69 O 21 2016

Fusao Kato
Overlapping memory trace indispensable for linking, but not recalling, individual memories bibl graph *Science* v355 no6323 p398 Ja 27 2017

Fusaro, Dario
Molto Bene S. COCHRAN color *Architectural Digest* v74 no7 p96 Jl 2017

Fusaro, Vincent A.
How should we define "low-wage" work? An analysis using the Current Population Survey bibl chart color graph *Monthly Labor Review* p1 O 2016

Fusco, Francesca J.
Ask anything [Cover story] cartoon color *Women's Health* v13 no10 p22 D 2016

Fusco, Mark
Burnout factories color il *Phi Delta Kappan* v98 no8 p26 My 2017

Fuselier, S. A.
Xenon isotopes in 67P/Churyumov-Gerasimenko show that comets contributed to Earth's atmosphere diag *Science* v356 no6342 p1069 Je 9 2017

Fusion automobile—Evaluation
2017 Ford Fusion Sport A. Priddle color *Motor Trend* v68 no12 p24 D 2016
How the Chaste Make Haste K. A. Wilson color *Car & Driver* v62 no6 p98 D 2016

Fusion cooking
THE OTHER F-WORD J. Sidman *Washingtonian Magazine* v52 no6 p150 Mr 2017

Fusion Entertainment Ltd.
Sounds Terrific J. Y. WOOD color *Power & Motoryacht* v33 no3 p42 Mr 2017

Fusion reactors—Design & construction
THE FUSION UNDERGROUND W. W. Gibbs color diag *Scientific American* v315 no5 p38 N 2016

Fussel, Paul
THE ROAD TAKEN D. Garner color *Esquire* v167 no1 p52 F 2017

Fussell, Chris
Make Your Team Less Hierarchical *Harvard Business Review Digital Articles* p2 Jl 15 2015
Why Special Ops Stopped Relying So Much on Top- Down Leadership *Harvard Business Review Digital Articles* p2 My 27 2015

Fussenegger, Martin
β-cell–mimetic designer cells provide closed-loop glycemic control bibl graph *Science* v354 no6317 p1296 D 9 2016

Fuster, A.
Observation of a large-scale anisotropy in the arrival directions of cosmic rays above 8 × 1018 eV *Science* v357 no6357 p1266 S 22 2017

Fuster, José J.
Clonal hematopoiesis associated with TET2 deficiency accelerates atherosclerosis development in mice bibl diag *Science* v355 no6327 p842 F 24 2017

Futbol Club Barcelona (Soccer team)
Pitch Ahead T. Taylor and T. Keith color *Sports Illustrated* v127 no4 p18 Ag 7 2017
What Makes FC Barcelona Such a Successful Business A. Hatum and L. Silvestri *Harvard Business Review Digital Articles* p2 Je 16 2015
Why European Soccer Is Coming To America E. Novy-Williams color *Bloomberg Businessweek* no4534 p15 Ag 14 2017

Future, 1985-
'MASK OFF' A. BARSHAD color *New York Times Magazine* p21 Mr 12 2017

Future, The
AI's Future Is Not So Scary W. Knight il *MIT Technology Review* v119 no6 p17 N/D 2016
Looking Forward M. DiChristina color *Scientific American* v315 no3 p4 S 2016
Tomorrow bw color *Forbes* v199 no1 p112 Ja 24 2017

Future, The—Social aspects
Even Bugs Will Be Bugged M. HUTSON color *Atlantic* v318 no4 p34 N 2016
A TALE OF TWO WORLDS M. Hvistendahl color *Scientific American* v315 no3 p42 S 2016

Future life
See also
Soul
Who Are You? M. Shermer color *Scientific American* v317 no1 p73 Jl 2017
Who Is My Neighbor? C. GONZÁLEZ-ANDRIEU color *America* v215 no13 p21 O 31 2016

Future Man (TV program)
ALSO COMING... I. Ratledge *TV Guide* v65 no37 p44 S 4 2017
Future Man A. Bacle, K. Connolly et al *Entertainment Weekly* no1482/1483 p106 S 22 2017
Television img *New York* v50 no17 p98 Ag 21 2017

Future Politics (Music)
AN EAR FOR THE MOMENT E. VANDERHOOF color *Nation* v304 no7 p35 Mr 6 2017

Future punishment
See also
Hell
Does hell exist? K. P. Considine color *U.S. Catholic* v82 no3 p49 Mr 2017

Futures—Government policy
Cristiano Ronaldo and the 'Volatile' Investments D. Griffin cartoon *Bloomberg Businessweek* no4539 p27 S 25 2017

Futurologists
What Research Tells Us About Making Accurate Predictions W. Frick *Harvard Business Review Digital Articles* p2 F 2 2015

Fuyang Shi (China)
The Good Earth C. A. PEARSON *Architectural Record* v205 no4 p134 Ap 2017

Fuyu Gong
Fixing carbon, unnaturally bibl diag *Science* v354 no6314 p830 N 18 2016

F Word, The (TV program)
Fired Up M. LOGAN *TV Guide* v65 no23 p16 My 29 2017

Fyffe, Nicholas
Find Your Fit color *Dressage Today* v23 no5 p28 Ja 2017

Fynn, Shaun
Chandigarh Revealed: Le Corbusier's City Today bw *Publishers Weekly* v264 no8 p74 F 20 2017

G

G., A. L.
"Your sexuality and your naked body are not shameful." color *Glamour* v115 no7 p92 Jl 2017

G Adventures Inc.
On the road to saving the world C. MCINTYRE color *Maclean's*

p48 Je 2017

G. Joannou Cycle Co. Inc.
JAMIS ICON ELITE M. YOZELL color *Bicycling* v58 no1 p68 Ja/F 2017
"WHY SHOULD I SPEND $5,000 ON A BIKE?" R. Koch and B. STRICKLAND color *Bicycling* v58 no3 p46 Ap 2017

G. Passier & Sohn GmbH
Tack Room color *Practical Horseman* v45 no7 p69 Jl 2017

G3 (Company)
G3 Angler V17 SF *Boating World* v38 no1 p66 Ja 2017

G3 Boats (Company)
Diamond Setting: The first-class cabin at G3 pontoons just got a lot more plush and stylish A. JONES *Boating World* v38 no8 p44 S/O 2017

Gabalda-Sagarra, Marçal
Coupling between distant biofilms and emergence of nutrient time-sharing bw color graph *Science* v356 no6338 p638 My 12 2017

Gabaldon, Diana, 1952-
Seven Stones to Stand or Fall: A Collection of Outlander Fiction S. Gutierrez *British Heritage Travel* v38 no3 p74 My/Je 2017

GABA—Therapeutic use
QUITTING TIME M. Burklund color *Better Nutrition* v79 no4 p50 Ap 2017
Time for a Brake S. POLAN *Psychology Today* v49 no5 p31 S/O 2016

GABBARA, PRINCESS
Adorned Beauty color *Ebony* v72 no6 p40 Ap/My 2017
Beauty Unwrapped color *Ebony* v72 no5 p43 Mr 2017
Twisted Sisters color *Ebony* v72 no8 p43 Je 2017

Gabel, Elyes, 1983-
SCORPION M. Roffman *TV Guide* v65 no39 p35 S 18 2017

Gabel, Martin
Magnificent Obsessive N. DAVIS bw *Film Comment* v53 no3 p20 My/Je 2017

Gabelli, Mario, 1942-
Hidden Assets D. FISHER color *Forbes* v198 no8 p62 D 20 2016

Gabilly, Stéphane T.
Improving photosynthesis and crop productivity by accelerating recovery from photoprotection bibl chart color graph *Science* v354 no6314 p857 N 18 2016

GABLER, NEAL
Hello, Gorgeous *Saturday Evening Post* v288 no6 p44 N/D 2016
THE MAGIC IN THE WAREHOUSE color diag *Fortune* v174 no8 p182 D 15 2016
The ORIGINAL KARDASHIANS *Los Angeles Magazine* p112 D 2016

Gabler, Neal—Interviews
The Magic of Barbra Streisand J. Wolf *Saturday Evening Post* v288 no6 p29 N/D 2016

Gábor, Zsa Zsa, 1917-2016
1917-2016 Zsa Zsa Gabor D. Coggan color *Entertainment Weekly* no1446/1447 p26 D 2016/Ja 2017

Gabriel, David
Muy Maravilloso color *Weekly Standard* v22 no31 p4 Ap 17 2017

Gabriel, Juan, 1950-2016
Letter from Mexico City: The Life and Death of Juan Gabriel P. J. Smith *Film Quarterly* v70 no3 p69 Spr 2017

Gabriel, Rachael
Valuing differences: color *Phi Delta Kappan* v98 no8 p59 My 2017

Gabriel, Richard A.
The Campaigns of Sargon II, King of Assyria, 721-705 BC *Military History* v33 no5 p69 Ja 2017
Hannibal's Oath: The Life and Wars of Rome's Greatest Enemy color *Military History* v34 no5 p72 Ja 2018
HIS OWN WORST ENEMY color *Military History* v34 no2 p30 Jl 2017
Praetorian: The Rise and Fall of Rome's Imperial Bodyguard *Military History* v34 no2 p72 Jl 2017

Gabriel, Thomas
Finding refuge J. Szweda Jordan color *U.S. Catholic* v82 no8 p12 Ag 2017

Gabriels: Election Year in the Life of One Family, The (Theatrical production)
The Ten Best Theater Events of the Year J. Green img *New York*

v49 no25 p126 D 12 2016

Gabritschevsky, Eugen, 1893-1979
Mad scientist: The strange, protean artistry of Eugen Gabritschevsky K. M. Minturn bw cartoon color *Magazine Antiques* v184 no2 p118 Mr/Ap 2017
The Master of Eglfing-Haar S. Schwartz color *New York Review of Books* v64 no16 p20 O 26 2017

Gacita, Anthony
Changes in the microbiota cause genetically modified Anopheles to spread in a population graph *Science* v357 no6358 p1396 S 29 2017

Gad, Josh, 1981-
A Frozen Treat M. Snetiker color *Entertainment Weekly* no1471 p18 Je 23 2017
What I'd Do with It cartoon *GQ: Gentlemen's Quarterly* v87 no1 p17 Ja 2017

Gadag, Ankitha
She had tried so hard to be Gouda *Texas Monthly* v45 no1 p91 Ja 2017

Gadagkar, Vikram
Dopamine neurons encode performance error in singing birds bibl graph *Science* v354 no6317 p1278 D 9 2016

GADDIS, BAILEY
10 New Ways to Afford Fertility Treatments color *Working Mother* v40 no3 p40 Ag/S 2017
You and Your Date Night cartoon *Working Mother* p50 F/Mr 2017

Gaddis, Dalia E.
Hematopoietic stem cells gone rogue bibl color diag *Science* v355 no6327 p798 F 24 2017

Gaddour, B. J.
Are You Ready for MetaShred Extreme? bw color *Men's Health* v32 no1 p132 Ja/F 2017
A Baller's Guide to Abs cartoon color *Men's Health* v32 no2 p8 Mr 2017
BUILD COVER GUY MUSCLE [Cover story] J. KITA bw cartoon chart color *Men's Health* v32 no1 p98 Ja/F 2017
Chisel Your Back bw color *Men's Health* v31 no10 p40 D 2016
The Couch Crusher cartoon color *Men's Health* v32 no3 p14 Ap 2017
Gains of Thrones color *Men's Health* v32 no6 p34 Ag 2017
House of Cardio cartoon color *Men's Health* v32 no4 p34 My 2017
Orange Is the New Jacked cartoon color *Men's Health* v32 no5 p38 Je 2017
Your Back Pain Prescription bw color *Men's Health* v32 no1 p137 Ja/F 2017

Gadgil, Ashok
Arthur Hinton Rosenfeld *Physics Today* v70 no9 p72 S 2017

Gadiesh, Orit
Companies Drain Women's Ambition After Only 2 Years *Harvard Business Review Digital Articles* p2 My 18 2015

Gadot, Gal, 1985-
THE BRIEF CRUSADE OF THE RED HAWK P. Higbee *South Dakota Magazine* v33 no3 p62 S/O 2017
THE BULLSEYE M. Snetiker color *Entertainment Weekly* p28 Jl 24 2017
Gal Gadot N. Sperling color *Entertainment Weekly* no1444/1445 p52 D 16 2016
PEACE STRENGTH WISDOM WONDER A. DOVE-VIEBAHN *Ms.* v27 no3 p31 Fall 2017
People of the Comic Book cartoon *Weekly Standard* v22 no38 p2 Je 12 2017
Woker Woman R. DOUTHAT color *National Review* v69 no12 p43 Je 26 2017
A woman at last: In Wonder Woman, accomplishment trumps beauty P. H. Nettleton color *U.S. Catholic* v82 no9 p38 S 2017
The Wonder of Gal Gadot [Cover story] A. Morris color *Rolling Stone* no1295 p36 S 7 2017
Wonder Woman: A Perfect Paradox for the Generation That Expects to Have It All S. Schrobsdorff color *Time* v189 no22 p58 Je 12 2017

Gaelic Athletic Association
GIVE IT A HURL D. Grove color *Virginia Living* v15 no5 p17 Ag 2017

Gaetani, Glenn A.
Experimental constraints on the damp peridotite solidus and

oceanic mantle potential temperature bibl diag *Science* v355 no6328 p942 Mr 3 2017

Gaetz, Matt

The Pros and Cons of the President's Immigrant Travel Ban *Congressional Digest* v96 no3 p14 Mr 2017

GAF Materials Corp.

Stellar Roofing color *Good Housekeeping* v265 no1 p86 Jl 2017

GAFFIGAN, JIM

Laughter THE BEST MEDICINE *Reader's Digest* v189 no1128 p78 Mr 2017

GAFFNEY, ADAM

The Teeth Gap color il *New Republic* v248 no6 p64 Je 2017

GAFFNEY, CHRIS

THE LOOP bw color *Runner's World* v51 no11 p18 D 2016

GAFFNEY, EDWARD McGLYNN

ENGAGING POLITICS color *America* v215 no19 p31 D 19 2016

Gaffney, Kelly J.

Metalloprotein entatic control of ligand-metal bonds quantified by ultrafast x-ray spectroscopy diag *Science* v356 no6344 p1276 Je 23 2017

Gaffney, Matt

NAVIGATE NORTHWARD *Washingtonian Magazine* v52 no8 p223 My 2017

NEWS LETTERS *Washingtonian Magazine* v52 no6 p199 Mr 2017

Gaffney, Owen

A roadmap for rapid decarbonization bibl color graph *Science* v355 no6331 p1269 Mr 24 2017

Gafni, Noa

Why So Many Millennials Aren't Into Protest Movements *Harvard Business Review Digital Articles* p2 O 22 2015

Gaga: Five Foot Two (Film)

Lady Gaga, Brought Low D. D'addario color *Time* v190 no14 p54 O 9 2017

The Must List color *Entertainment Weekly* no1482/1483 p12 S 22 2017

GAGE, BEVERLY

Book of Mormons *New York Times Book Review* p12 Ja 29 2017

... How It Ends *New York Times Book Review* p15 Ja 22 2017

Identity Bites: An intellectual historian urges liberals to overcome their differences *New York Times Book Review* p12 Ag 20 2017

Negative Energy *New York Times Magazine* p11 F 5 2017

Second Nature *New York Times Magazine* p11 Mr 26 2017

GAGE, ELENI N.

50 WAYS TO GET LOST IN SUMMER color *Martha Stewart Living* p83 Jl/Ag 2017

AND...FADE-OUT color *Martha Stewart Living* p19 My 2017

A BUSHEL AND A PECK color *Martha Stewart Living* p23 Ap 2017

GOOD THINGS *Martha Stewart Living* no268 p21 O 2016

INSTYLE [Loves] MIAMI color *InStyle* v23 no13 p217 D 2016

IT'S COCKTAIL O'CLOCK! *Martha Stewart Living* no270 p128 D 2016

A Little Night Magic color *Martha Stewart Living* p104 O 2017

MILOS'S MOMENT color *Conde Nast Traveler* v52 no5 p108 My 2017

NEW WAY TO EAT color *Martha Stewart Living* p92 Ap 2017

OUR HOLIDAY GIFT GUIDE *Martha Stewart Living* no270 p31 D 2016

THE RING BEARER *Martha Stewart Living* no269 p35 N 2016

RIPE FOR DECORATING color *Martha Stewart Living* p104 S 2017

SCREEN MAGIC color *Martha Stewart Living* p25 S 2017

SERVE CHILLED color *Martha Stewart Living* p25 Jl/Ag 2017

STEM SKILLS cartoon color *Martha Stewart Living* p19 Mr 2017

STROKES OF GENIUS color *Martha Stewart Living* no271 p19 Ja/F 2017

THREE, TWO, ONE... APPS! color *Martha Stewart Living* no275 p19 Je 2017

Wild Things color *Martha Stewart Living* p31 O 2017

Gage, Fred H.

An environment-dependent transcriptional network specifies human microglia identity color *Science* v356 no6344 p1248 Je 23 2017

Intersection of diverse neuronal genomes and neuropsychiatric disease: The Brain Somatic Mosaicism Network color *Science*

v356 no6336 p395 Ap 28 2017

Gage, Thomas, 1603?-1656

FROM THE EDITOR *History Today* v66 no10 p2 O 2016

Gagel, Robert

What doctors tell their friends about bones S. WOOD color *Redbook* p82 D 2016

Gaghan, Stephen, 1965-

Gold D. Franich color *Entertainment Weekly* no1451/1452 p89 F 3-10 2017

Gagliani, Andrea

A meal for many color *U.S. Catholic* v82 no6 p5 Je 2017

Gagliani, Nicola

Macrophage function in tissue repair and remodeling requires IL-4 or IL-13 with apoptotic cells diag *Science* v356 no6342 p1072 Je 9 2017

A pathogenic role for T cell–derived IL-22BP in inflammatory bowel disease bibl graph *Science* v354 no6310 p358 O 21 2016

Gagliano, Monica

Can Plants Hear? M. Zaraska color *Scientific American* v317 no1 p21 Jl 2017

Gagliardi, Carlo

Reimagining the Boardroom for an Age of Virtual Reality and AI *Harvard Business Review Digital Articles* p2 Ap 3 2015

What to Know Before You Sign a Payment-by-Results Contract *Harvard Business Review Digital Articles* p2 S 5 2016

Gaglione, Vincent

Is America great? graph *America* v216 no5 p6 Mr 6 2017

Gagne, Jake

READER INFORMATION color *Cycle World* v56 no8 p66 S 2017

Gagneux, Sebastien

Reversion of antibiotic resistance in Mycobacterium tuberculosis by spiroisoxazoline SMARt-420 bibl diag *Science* v355 no6330 p1206 Mr 17 2017

Gagnon, Dominic

OF DIGITAL SELVES AND DIGITAL SOVEREIGNTY: OF THE NORTH M. Stewart *Film Quarterly* v70 no4 p23 Summ 2017

Gagnon, Fred

POWER [Cover story] color *Christian Century* v134 no1 p22 Ja 4 2017

GAGNON, GEOFFREY

The Fifty Greatest Living Athletes bw color *GQ: Gentlemen's Quarterly* v97 no11 p96 N 2017

Gagnon, Oli

HARMONIC CONVERGENCE bw *Snowboarder* v29 no4 p14 D 2016

IN FOCUS color *Snowboarder* v29 no3 p66 N 2016

NEW YORK CITY, NY bw cartoon color *Snowboarder* v29 no5 p82 Ja 2017

OLI GAGNON SHOT C. Navin bw *Snowboarder* v29 no4 p12 D 2016

GAGNON, TIFFANY

Expiration Dates You Should Never Ignore color *Reader's Digest* v189 no1129 p42 Ap 2017

Gagnon-Arsenault, Isabelle

Gene duplication can impart fragility, not robustness, in the yeast protein interaction network bibl color graph *Science* v355 no6325 p630 F 10 2017

GAIA (Artificial satellite)

Gaia Maps a 1,000,000,000+ Stars J. HATTENBACH *Sky & Telescope* v133 no1 p10 Ja 2017

The Milky Way, Transformed S. Hall and S. Goudarzi color *Scientific American* v315 no6 p14 D 2016

Gaidos, Susan

Charging the Future bw color diag *Science News* v191 no1 p22 Ja 21 2017

Make it stick color *Science News* v192 no4 p30 S 16 2017

Gailes, Stephanie—Interviews

Member Spotlight: Stephanie Gailes *Parks & Recreation* v52 no1 p41 Ja 2017

Gaillard, Jérémie

Microtubules acquire resistance from mechanical breakage through intralumenal acetylation diag graph *Science* v356 no6335 p328 Ap 21 2017

Gaillardetz, Richard R.

A Church That Can & Did Change color *Commonweal* v144 no16 p29 O 6 2017

A More Pastoral Magisterium color *Commonweal* v144 no2 p18 Ja 27 2017

Gaiman, Neil, 1960-

Cinnamon *Publishers Weekly* v264 no9 p99 F 27 2017

Everything You Think You Know About Neil Gaiman Is Wrong *New York* v50 no9 p83 My 1 2017

Hammer Time: Neil Gaiman voices myths from the North L. Yuknavitch *New York Times Book Review* p19 My 21 2017

Gaiman, Neil, 1960——Interviews

NEIL GAIMAN N. Serrao color *Entertainment Weekly* no1454/1455 p101 F 24 2017

Gainer, Bridget

Bridget Gainer C. FELSENTHAL color *Chicago* v66 no6 p84 Je 2017

Gaines, Barbara

THE BARD'S YARD B. GOLDEN color *Chicago* v66 no9 p52 S 2017

Gaines, Chip

Gaines and Losses *Weekly Standard* v22 no14 p2 D 12 2016

Gaines, Ernest J., 1933-

Close Quarters M. A. Sternberg color *AARP: The Magazine* v60 no1A p54 D 2016/Ja 2017

Gaines, Joanna

a new season color *Better Homes & Gardens* v95 no3 p14 Mr 2017

Gaines, Steven D.

U.S. seafood import restriction presents opportunity and risk bibl color map *Science* v354 no6318 p1372 D 16 2016

Gaines, Tharran

DIESEL NATURAL GAS CONVERSION: DUAL-FUEL CONVERSION KITS SLASH LARRY URWILLER'S IRRIGATION FUEL COSTS BY 25% TO 30% *Successful Farming* v115 no6 p52 Ap 2017

GIVE-AND-TAKE IRRIGATION: TEXAS FARMER USES MULTIPLE PRACTICES TO EARN STRONG YIELDS ON MINIMAL ACRE-INCHES OF WATER *Successful Farming* v115 no11 p46 S 2017

INNOVATION IN IRRIGATION *Successful Farming* v115 no2 p58 F 2017

MOBILE PIVOT PAYOFF: TOWABLE SPRINKLERS ARE A LOWER INVESTMENT PER ACRE WHILE STILL OFFERING THE YIELD POTENTIAL FROM IRRIGATION *Successful Farming* v115 no12 p56 O 2017

NEW LIFE FOR WORN CABS: REPLACE DILAPIDATED INTERIORS IN HOURS WITH PREFORMED KITS *Successful Farming* v115 no9 p34 Ag 2017

PMDI SUCCESS *Successful Farming* v115 no4 p50 Mr 2017

SMART PIVOT CONTROLS *Successful Farming* v115 no4 p49 Mr 2017

Gaines, Timea——Interviews

Bouncing Back After Breast Cancer K. Johnson and A. GUMBS color *Black Enterprise* v47 no3 p69 O 2016

Gaines-Ross, Leslie

Is It Safe for CEOs to Voice Strong Political Opinions? *Harvard Business Review Digital Articles* p2 Je 23 2016

Offices Can Be Bastions of Civility in an Uncivil Time *Harvard Business Review Digital Articles* p2 Jl 14 2017

What CEO Activism Looks Like in the Trump Era *Harvard Business Review Digital Articles* p2 O 2 2017

What CEOs Have Learned About Social Media *Harvard Business Review Digital Articles* p2 My 18 2015

What CEOs Should Know About Speaking Up on Political Issues *Harvard Business Review Digital Articles* p2 F 17 2017

What Executives Value in Their CEOs *Harvard Business Review Digital Articles* p2 Mr 5 2015

When the Media Covers Gender Inequality, the CSuite Listens *Harvard Business Review Digital Articles* p2 O 21 2015

Gainsbourg, Charlotte, 1971-

Face Time L. IMMEDIATO *Los Angeles Magazine* v62 no6 p25 Je 2017

Real Talk L. REGENSDORF color *Vogue* v207 no4 p167 Ap 2017

Gainsbourg, Charlotte, 1971——Interviews

Hot Tracks: CHARLOTTE GAINSBOURG bw *Vanity Fair* v59 no10 p132 O 2017

Gainsburg, Marissa

15 MINUTE WORKOUT color *Women's Health* v14 no1 p90 Ja/F 2017

15 MINUTE WORKOUT color *Women's Health* v14 no3 p60 Ap 2017

BARE MINIMUM [Cover story] color *Women's Health* v14 no7 p73 S 2017

BEST SHAPE OF YOUR LIFE [Cover story] color *Women's Health* v13 no10 p76 D 2016

A BODY IN MOTION & A BODY AT REST [Cover story] color *Women's Health* v14 no4 p156 My 2017

BUMP WATCH bw cartoon *Women's Health* v13 no10 p72 D 2016

FLAT ABS AFTER BABY color *Women's Health* v14 no2 p76 Mr 2017

FLEX TIME chart color *Women's Health* v14 no8 p78 O 2017

GET BACK AT IT! color *Women's Health* v14 no4 p84 My 2017

THE GIRLS NEXT DOOR color diag *Men's Health* v32 no9 p82 N 2017

Hips, Hopped bw diag *Women's Health* v14 no3 p55 Ap 2017

HIRED GUNS! [Cover story] color *Women's Health* v14 no5 p66 Je 2017

NAMASTAY AWHILE bw color diag *Women's Health* v14 no4 p78 My 2017

NEVER SKIP LEG DAY [Cover story] color *Women's Health* v14 no6 p(Sp)20 Jl 2017

THE NEXT FITNESS STAR WORKOUT [Cover story] color *Women's Health* v14 no1 p156 Ja/F 2017

The Resistance (Band) Rises! color *Women's Health* v14 no9 p61 N 2017

RIP, Dreadmill cartoon chart color *Women's Health* v14 no1 p84 Ja/F 2017

RUNFESSIONS color *Women's Health* v14 no2 p67 Mr 2017

SWEATY, SANDY, SCULPTED color *Women's Health* v14 no5 p136 Je 2017

WHO WILL BE THE NEXT FITNESS STAR? [Cover story] color *Women's Health* v14 no6 p(Sp)2 Jl 2017

Women's Health 2017 SHOE GUIDE color *Women's Health* v14 no3 p62 Ap 2017

Gaior, R.

Observation of a large-scale anisotropy in the arrival directions of cosmic rays above 8×10^{18} eV *Science* v357 no6357 p1266 S 22 2017

Gait disorders

The Healing Power of Dressage T. Steward color *Dressage Today* v23 no9 p20 Je 2017

Gaither, Steven J.

Partnerships Between Schools and Communities Promote Reading Success *Education Digest* v83 no2 p57 O 2017

Gaitskill, Mary

NICE GIRLS *Harper's Magazine* p38 Ap 2017

Gaitskill, Mary——Interviews

Mary GAITSKILL: ONE OF OUR MOST ORIGINAL FICTION WRITERS TURNS HER WIT AND WISDOM TOWARD THE REAL WORLD, RIGHT WHEN WE NEED IT MOST L. NAKADATE *Interview* v47 no3 p34 Ap 2017

Gaja, Angelo

BARBARESCO J. McINERNEY bw color *Esquire* p32 2017 BigBlackBook

Gajanan, Mahita

Calendar: Culture color *Time* v188 no27-28 p106 D 26 2016

Cauliflower Is the New It Vegetable color *Time* v190 no5 p28 Jl 31 2017

Feuds color *Time* v188 no25-26 p34 D 19 2016 Double Issue

Mandy Moore color *Time* v189 no24 p50 Je 26 2017

GAJAWEERA, NALIKA

What's So Wrong with Mindfulness? color *Tricycle: The Buddhist Review* v26 no2 p27 Wint 2016

Gajendran, Ravi S.

Employees Leave Good Bosses Nearly as Often as Bad Ones *Harvard Business Review Digital Articles* p2 Mr 8 2016

GAJEWSKI, KAREN ANN

WORTH NOTING *Humanist* v76 no6 p46 N/D 2016

WORTH NOTING *Humanist* v77 no1 p48 Ja/F 2017

WORTH NOTING *Humanist* v77 no3 p48 My/Je 2017

WORTH NOTING *Humanist* v77 no4 p48 Jl/Ag 2017

WORTH NOTING *Humanist* v77 no5 p48 S/O 2017

Gajiwala, P. H.

Chronic exposure to neonicotinoids reduces honey bee health near corn crops diag *Science* v356 no6345 p1395 Je 30 2017

Gal, L.

Revealing the subfemtosecond dynamics of orbital angular momentum in nanoplasmonic vortices bibl diag *Science* v355 no6330 p1187 Mr 17 2017

Galactic dynamics

16 Pisces, Arp 284 & the Unexpected Quasar: A Story of Time and Distance H. Banich *Sky & Telescope* v134 no4 p62 O 2017

ATOM & COSMOS A. YEAGER color *Science News* v192 no2 p6 Ag 19 2017

Galactic evolution

75, 50 & 25 YEARS AGO R. W. Sinnott *Sky & Telescope* v133 no6 p7 Je 2017

NGC 5529 H. Banich *Sky & Telescope* v133 no5 p57 My 2017

One frame in the cosmic movie *Astronomy* v44 no12 p6 D 2016

Galactic halos

Molecular gas in the halo fuels the growth of a massive cluster galaxy at high redshift B. H. C. Emonts, M. D. Lehnert et al bibl graph *Science* v354 no6316 p1128 D 2 2016

Galactic magnitudes

The Silver Coin M. Wedel chart color *Sky & Telescope* v134 no5 p42 N 2017

Square Galaxies: Spend some time roping this herd of faint fuzzies in the Great Square of Pegasus S. French chart color *Sky & Telescope* v134 no5 p55 N 2017

Galagos

High Robot E. Biba graph *Scientific American* v316 no5 p21 My 2017

Galán, Nely, 1963-

Empowering Woman J. Caplin color *Money* v46 no1 p24 Ja/F 2017

Galan, Sébastien R. G.

Posttranslational mutagenesis: A chemical strategy for exploring protein side-chain diversity diag *Science* v354 no6312 p597 N 4 2016

Galante, Cecilia

Stealing Our Way Home *Publishers Weekly* v264 no18 p57 My 1 2017

Galapagos Islands

Life in the Balance C. Solomon chart color map *National Geographic* v231 no6 p52 Je 2017

THE MAGIC OF GALÁPAGOS: to visit these unspoiled islands is to be transported back through the eons S. SLON *Saturday Evening Post* v289 no5 p54 S/O 2017

Galapagos tortoise

GLIMPSES B. HURD bw color *Orion Magazine* v35 no6 p38 N/D 2016

GALAS, DAVID J.

Notes from a Revolution: Lessons from the Human Genome Project *Issues in Science & Technology* v33 no3 p57 Spr 2017

Galassi, Jonathan

The Illusion of Utter Transparency bw color *New York Review of Books* v64 no8 p26 My 11 2017

ORIENT EPITHALAMION *New Yorker* v92 no43 p40 Ja 2 2017

Galaxies

See also

Elliptical galaxies

Galaxy clusters

Magellanic clouds

Milky Way

Nebulae

Planetary systems

Stars

16 Pisces, Arp 284 & the Unexpected Quasar: A Story of Time and Distance H. Banich *Sky & Telescope* v134 no4 p62 O 2017

The biggest spiderweb in the universe color *Astronomy* v45 no4 p14 Ap 2017

Cause of cosmic makeover reassessed A. YEAGER *Science News* v191 no4 p10 Mr 4 2017

The Cheshire Cat M. BARTUSIAK *Natural History* v124 no10 p10 N 2016

A CLOSER LOOK AT A SUPERMASSIVE BLACK HOLE diag *Astronomy* v45 no8 p18 Ag 2017

A colorful crustacean color *Astronomy* v45 no10 p74 O 2017

Dark Galaxies C. Crockett cartoon color *Science News* v190 no12 p18 D 10 2016

Discover 10 weird emission nebulae S. J. O'Meara color *Astronomy* v45 no5 p44 My 2017

Distant galaxy setting star-formation record color *Astronomy* v45 no4 p16 Ap 2017

Distorted galaxies E. RIX color *Astronomy* v45 no3 p66 Mr 2017

Early galaxy lived fast and died young A. YEAGER color *Science News* v191 no8 p7 Ap 29 2017

FALL INTO AUTUMN GALAXIES S. James O'Meara color *Astronomy* v45 no11 p46 N 2017

The final frontier bw *Astronomy* v45 no11 p74 N 2017

FIRST LIGHT t MeerKAT Online A. V. ACEVES *Sky & Telescope* v132 no6 p15 D 2016

Float like a butterfly color *Astronomy* v45 no4 p74 Ap 2017

Gaia mission maps over 1 billion stars C. CROCKETT color *Science News* v190 no8 p16 O 15 2016

Galaxy formation through cosmic recycling N. Hatch color *Science* v354 no6316 p1102 D 2 2016

Galaxy with a twist color *Astronomy* v45 no7 p74 Jl 2017

A Herculean enigma color *Astronomy* v45 no1 p74 Ja 2017

Herschel's Ghosts M. Bartels *Sky & Telescope* v133 no4 p30 Ap 2017

HOW STARS VISIT THE SOLAR NEIGHBORHOOD *Physics Today* v70 no6 p24 Je 2017

Less Dark Matter in Young Galaxies? M. YOUNG *Sky & Telescope* v134 no1 p13 Jl 2017

Machines that make sense of the sky J. Sokol color *Science* v357 no6346 p26 Jl 7 2017

Making light of galaxies D. J. EICHER color *Astronomy* v45 no11 p6 N 2017

Missing Matter Found L. KRUESI color *Discover* v38 no7 p70 S 2017

Odd One Out M. Wedel and M. WEDEL *Sky & Telescope* v134 no3 p43 S 2017

Of Black Holes and Galaxies C. M. Carlisle *Sky & Telescope* v133 no2 p18 F 2017

On the Alert for Apparitions P. Tyson *Sky & Telescope* v133 no4 p4 Ap 2017

OUR NEXT BILLION YEARS M. TEGMARK color *Discover* v38 no9 p58 N 2017

Our trillion-galaxy universe [Cover story] C. J. Conselice and A. Klesman color *Astronomy* v45 no6 p18 Je 2017

Our universe just got a whole lot bigger color *Astronomy* v45 no2 p16 F 2017

READER GALLERY color *Astronomy* v45 no10 p70 O 2017

Scientific success depends on finding light in darkness *Science News* v190 no12 p2 D 10 2016

Skipping through the Virgo Cluster S. J. O'Meara color *Astronomy* v45 no4 p58 Ap 2017

Stellar Splendor: A deepest, darkest sky offers an extraordinary encounter with the stars F. Schaaf *Sky & Telescope* v134 no4 p45 O 2017

THIS IS YOUR UNIVERSE S. BUSHWICK color *Popular Science* p20 Ja/F 2017

TWO IMAGERS are better than one C. Temple and T. Temple color *Astronomy* v45 no1 p50 Ja 2017

Uncommon bino galaxies S. J. O'MEARA color *Astronomy* v45 no5 p20 My 2017

A universe with 10 times more galaxies D. J. Eicher color *Astronomy* v45 no3 p8 Mr 2017

What in the World? color *National Geographic Kids* no475 p29 N 2017

When Galaxies Become Cannibals M. WEST color *Discover* v38 no8 p70 O 2017

Galaxies—Clusters

See also

Local Group (Astronomy)

Superclusters

GALAXY CLUSTERS The universe's cosmic lenses L. Kruesi color diag graph *Astronomy* v45 no2 p28 F 2017

Hickson groups E. RIX diag *Astronomy* v45 no6 p66 Je 2017

LANIAKEA SUPERCLUSTER P. FRIEDLANDER *Scientific American* v315 no5 p6 N 2016

NGC 5529 H. Banich *Sky & Telescope* v133 no5 p57 My 2017

The Perseus Galaxy Cluster T. Forte *Sky & Telescope* v133 no1 p57 Ja 2017

Galaxies—Red shift

[C II] 158-μm emission from the host galaxies of damped Lyman-alpha systems M. Neeleman, N. Kanekar et al bibl color graph *Science* v355 no6331 p1285 Mr 24 2017

Molecular gas in the halo fuels the growth of a massive cluster galaxy at high redshift B. H. C. Emonts, M. D. Lehnert et al bibl graph *Science* v354 no6316 p1128 D 2 2016

Galaxies—Research

Supermassive Black Holes in Close Dance M. YOUNG *Sky & Telescope* v134 no4 p13 O 2017

Galaxy clusters

The cosmic bullies next door L. Kruesi color *Astronomy* v45 no7 p28 Jl 2017

Peering through a galaxy cluster color *Science* v356 no6338 p564 My 12 2017

Square Galaxies: Spend some time roping this herd of faint fuzzies in the Great Square of Pegasus S. French chart color *Sky & Telescope* v134 no5 p55 N 2017

A Whale of a Galaxy Cluster: Reel in the denizens of Abell 194 — if those autumn skies ever clear K. Hewitt-White color *Sky & Telescope* v134 no5 p58 N 2017

Galaxy formation

Four for the Road M. Wedel *Sky & Telescope* v134 no4 p42 O 2017

Hubble Spies Faint Galaxies in Early Universe G. SCHILLING *Sky & Telescope* v133 no6 p8 Je 2017

Hunting the Galaxy Killer K. Cooper *Sky & Telescope* v134 no1 p22 Jl 2017

In the Dark About Dark Matter L. Moustakas color diag graph *Sky & Telescope* v134 no2 p28 Ag 2017

Side-by-side spirals color *Astronomy* v45 no8 p90 Ag 2017

Galaxy mergers

EYES IN THE SKY J. Berlin color *National Geographic* v231 no2 p132 F 2017

Galaxies in Collision S. Gottlieb *Sky & Telescope* v133 no5 p28 My 2017

Galbraith, Derek—Interviews

SERENDIPITY IN ALASKA J. Brown color *Powder* v45 no6 p46 F 2017

GALBRAITH, JAMES K.

A New Deal for Europe color *Nation* v305 no10 p22 O 23 2017

GALBREATH, KURT E.

Transformational Principles for NEON Sampling of Mammalian Parasites and Pathogens: A Response to Springer and Colleagues *BioScience* v66 no11 p917 N 1 2016

Galchen, Rivka

Bookends *New York Times Book Review* p31 O 30 2016

Bookends: What distinguishes cultural exchange from cultural appropriation? *New York Times Book Review* p27 Je 11 2017

FAIL FUNNIER cartoon *New Yorker* v92 no48 p28 F 6 2017

Forever Young *New York Times Book Review* p9 Ag 27 2017

IMAGINE THAT *New York Times Magazine* p66 O 30 2016

KEEPING IT OFF cartoon *New Yorker* v92 no30 p32 S 26 2016

What's the best book, new or old, you read this year? *New York Times Book Review* p27 D 25 2016

Galchenyuk, Alex

An NHL Star's Insane Muscle Moves J. Nosek cartoon *Men's Health* v32 no3 p44 Ap 2017

Gale, Janelle

Let's Not Kill Performance Evaluations Yet il *Harvard Business Review* v94 no11 p90 N 2016

Gale, Jason

A Case of Chicken vs. Machine cartoon color *Bloomberg Businessweek* no4507 p18 Ja 16 2017

ON CHINESE AQUACULTURE FARMS, THE FISH ARE PUMPED WITH ANTIBIOTICS, AS ARE THE PIGS, WHOSE WASTE FEEDS THE FISH. SO LET'S TALK ABOUT THAT SEAFOOD PLATTER [Cover story] color graph *Bloomberg Businessweek* no4504 p38 D 19 2016

Gale, Jonathan E.

Community network for deaf scientists color *Science* v356 no6336 p386 Ap 28 2017

Gale, Zach

GARAGE chart color diag *Motor Trend* v69 no9 p104 S 2017

NEW CARS 2018-2019 [Cover story] chart color *Motor Trend* v69 no9 p34 S 2017

NEW SUVS & TRUCKS 2018-2019 [Cover story] color *Motor Trend* v69 no10 p32 O 2017

Galea, Sandro

Is the U.S. Ready for a Single-Payer Health Care System? *Harvard Business Review Digital Articles* p2 Jl 18 2017

Why It's Hard to Measure Improved Population Health *Harvard Business Review Digital Articles* p2 S 16 2015

Galeano, Eduardo, 1940-2015

Hunter of Stories bw *Publishers Weekly* v264 no29 p206 Jl 17 2017

GALEF, DANIEL

Thanks for Everything [Cover story] cartoon color *Prevention* v68 no11 p96 N 2016

Galeon Yachts (Company)

GALEON 420 FLY: THE POLISH BUILDER PREMIERES A SOLID BOAT WITH A FEW NEAT TRICKS UP ITS SLEEVE Z. PROCHAZKA *Sea Magazine* v109 no5 p40 My 2017

Galeoon Sp. z.o.o. Sp.K.

GALEON 445 HTS M. WERLING *Sea Magazine* v108 no8 p34 Ag 2016

Galeota, Jay

How Merck Is Trying to Keep Disrupters at Bay *Harvard Business Review Digital Articles* p2 Je 8 2015

Galera, Daniel

The Shape of Bones *Publishers Weekly* v264 no25 p86 Je 19 2017

Galetti, Luciano

Forest conservation: Remember Gran Chaco bibl color *Science* v355 no6324 p465 F 3 2017

Galetti, Mauro

Biodiversity losses and conservation responses in the Anthropocene color diag graph map *Science* v356 no6335 p270 Ap 21 2017

Conserving the World's Megafauna and Biodiversity: The Fierce Urgency of Now *BioScience* v67 no3 p197 Mr 2017

Saving the World's Terrestrial Megafauna color *BioScience* v66 no10 p807 O 1 2016

Scientists need social media influencers *Science* v357 no6354 p880 S 1 2017

Galetto, Leonardo

Ten policies for pollinators bibl color *Science* v354 no6315 p975 N 25 2016

Galford, Robert M.

Why Decisions Get Second-Guessed, and What to Do About It *Harvard Business Review Digital Articles* p2 F 25 2016

Galiano Island (B.C.)

SWEPT AWAY M. True color *Sunset* v238 no3 p56 Mr 2017

Galilee (Israel)—In the New Testament

A Life of Boldness M. R. Simone *America* v216 no13 p60 Je 12 2017

Galilei, Galileo, 1564-1642

1615: Florence *Lapham's Quarterly* v10 no2 p29 Spr 2017

Galileo Galilei color *Discover* v38 no4 p45 My 2017

Galindo, Sara

PW Talks with Sara Galindo L. Ahuile color *Publishers Weekly* v264 no23 p15 Je 5 2017

Galindo-Uribarri, A.

Observation of coherent elastic neutrino-nucleus scattering diag *Science* v357 no6356 p1123 S 15 2017

Galinsky, Adam D.

How Powerful, Low-Status Jobs Lead to Conflict *Harvard Business Review Digital Articles* p2 F 11 2016

The Link Between Income Inequality and Physical Pain *Harvard Business Review Digital Articles* p2 Mr 21 2016

Galinsky, Ellen

Why Citi Got Rid of Assigned Desks *Harvard Business Review Digital Articles* p2 N 12 2014

Gall, Carlotta

Afghanistan: Obama's Sad Legacy color *New York Review of Books* v64 no1 p31 Ja 19 2017

Gall, Chris

The Littlest Train *Publishers Weekly* v264 no25 p108 Je 19 2017

Gall, Jared

25 CARS WORTH WAITING FOR color *Car & Driver* v62 no10 p32 Ap 2017

auto no mo' us bw color diag graph *Car & Driver* v63 no5 p58 N 2017

AXLES TO GRIND color graph *Car & Driver* v62 no6 p28 D 2016

The Battle of the Off-Road Beaters bw chart color graph *Car & Driver* v62 no6 p84 D 2016

The Car and Driver Guide to Automotive Bullsh!t color *Car & Driver* v63 no1 p76 Jl 2017

Fleet Files color *Car & Driver* v63 no4 p90 O 2017

FOURS TO BE RECKONED WITH color graph *Car & Driver* v62 no7 p94 Ja 2017

HOG CALLING color *Car & Driver* v62 no10 p18 Ap 2017

It's a Hellcat Thing color *Car & Driver* v63 no5 p100 N 2017

A MIGHTY WIND color *Car & Driver* v62 no6 p24 D 2016

On the Shoulders of Giants color *Car & Driver* v62 no11 p118 My 2017

Poster Boy color *Car & Driver* v63 no1 p98 Jl 2017

Revolutionary war [Cover story] chart color diag *Car & Driver* v63 no2 p36 Ag 2017

TWISTY SISTER color graph *Car & Driver* v62 no8 p13 F 2017

Gallaghe, Melissa

COCO AND MISCHA FEIFEI SUN *Atlanta* v56 no10 p44 F 2017

GALLAGHER, AUSTIN J.

Extinction Risk and Conservation of the Earth's National Animal Symbols *BioScience* v67 no8 p744 Ag 2017

Gallagher, Carol

Cheer to Eternity A. Gray and T. Keith color *Sports Illustrated* v126 no9 p23 Mr 27 2017

Gallagher, David

Akin to Conrad in Colombia bw color *New York Review of Books* v63 no16 p68 O 27 2016

Gallagher, Ileen

MEMORY MOTEL J. Seabrook cartoon *New Yorker* v92 no41 p29 D 12 2016

Gallagher, Jeffrey M.

April 30, Third Sunday of Easter *Christian Century* v134 no8 p1 Ap 12 2017

GALLAGHER, JOHN

Not in Our Name color *America* v215 p16 N 28 2016

Gallagher, John Robert

Rapid development of a DNA vaccine for Zika virus bibl graph *Science* v354 no6309 p237 O 14 2016

Gallagher, John S. III

New angle on cosmic rays color *Science* v357 no6357 p1240 S 22 2017

GALLAGHER, KAIT

Incredible Animal Friends color *National Geographic Kids* no471 p9 Je/Jl 2017

Gallagher, Kate

READER COMMENTS *America* v216 no6 p7 Mr 20 2017

Gallagher, Leigh

BREAKTHROUGH BRANDS 2017 color diag *Fortune* v75 no1 p64 Ja 1 2017

DREAM WEAVER color *Fortune* v176 no3 p74 S 1 2017

FINDING AN 'OCEAN' FREE FROM RIVALS color *Fortune* v176 no5 p34 O 1 2017

FORTY UNDER FORTY 2017 color *Fortune* v176 no3 p62 S 1 2017

HOW AIRBNB FOUND A MISSION—AND A BRAND [Cover story] color *Fortune* v75 no1 p56 Ja 1 2017

MINING COMEDY GOLD color *Fortune* v176 no3 p70 S 1 2017

THE ORIGINAL HOSPITALITY DISRUPTER color *Fortune* v175 no8 p87 Je 15 2017

WORLD'S 50 GREATEST LEADERS [Cover story] color *Fortune* v175 no5 p46 Ap 1 2017

YOUTH REVOLT color *Fortune* v176 no3 p64 S 1 2017

Gallagher, Liam, 1972-

Liam Gallagher's Sweet Revenge B. HIATT color *Rolling Stone* no1298 p16 O 19 2017

Gallagher, Mary

NAME THE BOAT S. SHIBATA color *Sea Magazine* v109 no8 p10 Ag 2017

GALLAGHER, MATT

KNOW YOUR ENEMY cartoon *Wired* v25 no1 p22 Ja 2017

GALLAGHER, MICHAEL

THE NUCLEAR THIRD RAIL *Commonweal* v144 no16 p2 O 6 2017

GALLAGHER, NICHOLAS M.

Norma-tivity color *Weekly Standard* v23 no6 p39 O 16 2017

Gallagher, Noel, 1967-

Random Notes color *Rolling Stone* no1288 p24 Je 1 2017

Random Notes color *Rolling Stone* no1293 p30 Ag 10 2017

Gallagher, Patrick

Ballistic miniband conduction in a graphene superlattice bibl graph *Science* v353 no6307 p1526 S 30 2016

Did God bless America? Patriotic songs should be approached carefully at church color *U.S. Catholic* v82 no9 p31 S 2017

In the communion of saints color *U.S. Catholic* v81 no12 p31 D 2016

Pittsburgh myth, Paris reality color *Science* v356 no6343 p1103 Je 16 2017

Gallagher, Rachael V.

Global climatic drivers of leaf size [Cover story] graph *Science* v357 no6354 p917 S 1 2017

Gallagher, Tom

President-Elect Trump: Is the Past Prologue? *Society* v54 no1 p10 F 2017

Gallagher, Winifred

Q: What was the most important letter in history? color *Atlantic* v320 no2 p104 S 2017

Gallaher, Jason

Whobert Whover, Owl Detective *Publishers Weekly* v264 no21 p89 My 22 2017

Gallardo, Rodrigo

De novo design of a biologically active amyloid bibl graph *Science* v354 no6313 paah4949-1 N 11 2016

Gallatin National Forest (Mont.)

BIG SKY, MONTANA color *Runner's World* v52 no4 p8 My 2017

Gallbladder—Physiology

ASK TUFTS EXPERTS A. H. Lichtenstein *Tufts University Health & Nutrition Letter* v35 no2 p8 2017

Galle, Samuel

Fast exoskeleton optimization color graph *Science* v356 no6344 p1230 Je 23 2017

Gallego, Eva María

"Ab initio" synthesis of zeolites for preestablished catalytic reactions bibl chart diag *Science* v355 no6329 p1051 Mr 10 2017

Gallegos, Justin

JUSTIN GALLEGOS color *Runner's World* v52 no1 p86 Ja/F 2017

Gallegos, Oscar

#trailchat color il map *Backpacker* p6 Je 2017

Gallegos, Stanley

Stan's Barber Shop B. COSSAVELLA *Arizona Highways* v93 no2 p6 F 2017

Galleries (Architecture)

Out & About color *Martha Stewart Living* p16 O 2017

Galleries (Architecture)—Design & construction

WORK OF ART: A happy, light-filled space in Brookland proves that multifunctional doesn't have to mean cluttered and confused J. Sergent *Washingtonian Magazine* v52 no12 p137 S 2017

The Galley, LLC.

Top Chef color *Log Home Living* v34 no4 p38 My 2017

Galleys

SHOW US YOUR cabin creativity color *Log Home Living* v34 no3 p80 Ap 2017

Galli, Mark

BEAUTIFUL ORTHODOXY [Cover story] bw color *Christianity Today* v60 no8 p34 O 2016

THE CHURCH'S INTEGRITY IN THE TRUMP YEARS cartoon *Christianity Today* v61 no1 p23 Ja/F 2017

THE GRACE OF CHURCH DISCIPLINE color *Christianity Today* v60 no10 p27 D 2016

I WASTED MY TIME WITH THIS. So should you color *Christianity Today* v61 no6 p74 Jl/Ag 2017

LOVING ALL TYPES OF SOJOURNERS color *Christianity Today* v61 no5 p19 Je 2017

The Most Astonishing Easter Miracle [Cover story] bw *Christianity Today* p28 Ap 2017

A REAL OPTION *Christianity Today* p9 Mr 2017

Sola Scriptura bw *Christianity Today* v61 no5 p50 Je 2017

THE SPIRITUAL ACT OF SUBSCRIPTION color *Christianity Today* v60 no8 p29 O 2016

WHAT TO MAKE OF DONALD TRUMP'S SOUL color *Christianity Today* v61 no4 p27 My 2017

Gallim Dance (Performer)

connect color *Dance Spirit* v21 no2 p20 F 2017

The Gallim Dream K. Schwab and L. Chilczuk color *Dance Spirit* v21 no2 p34 F 2017

Gallimore, Ronald

Making teaching visible through learning opportunities color *Phi Delta Kappan* v98 no8 p54 My 2017

Gallium (Metal)

A droplet that won't freeze harbors a crystal that won't melt A. G. Smart *Physics Today* v69 no10 p18 O 2016

Gallman, Wayne

Leading Off color *Sports Illustrated* v126 no1 p4 Ja 9 2017

Gallo, Amy

7 Questions to Ask Yourself Before Going Freelance *Harvard Business Review Digital Articles* p2 Jl 14 2015

7 Tips for Managing Freelancers and Independent Contractors *Harvard Business Review Digital Articles* p2 Ag 17 2015

The 8 Self-Assessments You Need to Improve at Work This Year *Harvard Business Review Digital Articles* p2 Ja 20 2016

The Condensed Guide to Running Meetings *Harvard Business Review Digital Articles* p2 Jl 6 2015

Contribution Margin: What It Is, How to Calculate It, and Why You Need It *Harvard Business Review Digital Articles* p2 O 13 2017

Dealing with Loneliness While Traveling for Work *Harvard Business Review Digital Articles* p2 N 19 2015

HBR's Best on Saying No to More Work color *Harvard Business Review Digital Articles* p2 Ja 30 2017

How People with Different Conflict Styles Can Work Together *Harvard Business Review Digital Articles* p2 Jl 24 2017

How to Become a Successful Freelancer *Harvard Business Review Digital Articles* p2 Jl 20 2016

How to Build a Meaningful Career *Harvard Business Review Digital Articles* p2 F 4 2015

How to Build the Social Ties You Need at Work *Harvard Business Review Digital Articles* p2 S 23 2015

How to Deal with a Mean Colleague *Harvard Business Review Digital Articles* p2 O 16 2014

How to Deal with a Passive-Aggressive Colleague *Harvard Business Review Digital Articles* p2 Ja 11 2016

How to Deliver Bad News to Your Employees *Harvard Business Review Digital Articles* p2 Mr 30 2015

How to Disagree with Someone More Powerful than You *Harvard Business Review Digital Articles* p2 Mr 17 2016

How to Get Your Colleagues' Attention *Harvard Business Review Digital Articles* p2 My 14 2015

How to Give an Employee Feedback About Their Appearance *Harvard Business Review Digital Articles* p2 My 26 2017

How to Help Your Team Bounce Back from Failure *Harvard Business Review Digital Articles* p2 F 27 2015

How to Keep Your Team Focused and Productive During Uncertain Times bw *Harvard Business Review Digital Articles* p2 Mr 8 2017

How to Make Sure You're Heard in a Difficult Conversation *Harvard Business Review Digital Articles* p2 N 9 2015

How to Manage a Toxic Employee *Harvard Business Review Digital Articles* p2 O 3 2016

How to Manage Managers *Harvard Business Review Digital Articles* p2 Ag 29 2016

How to Mentally Prepare for a Difficult Conversation *Harvard Business Review Digital Articles* p2 Ap 4 2016

How to Navigate a Turf War at Work *Harvard Business Review Digital Articles* p2 S 27 2017

How to Respond to an Offensive Comment at Work color *Harvard Business Review Digital Articles* p2 F 8 2017

How to Respond When Someone Takes Credit for Your Work *Harvard Business Review Digital Articles* p2 Ap 29 2015

How to Respond When Your Employee Asks for a Raise *Harvard Business Review Digital Articles* p2 F 17 2016

How to Speak Up About Ethical Issues at Work *Harvard Business Review Digital Articles* p2 Je 4 2015

How to Tell Your Colleague You Dropped the Ball *Harvard Business Review Digital Articles* p2 Mr 11 2016

How to Turn a Bad Day Around *Harvard Business Review Digital Articles* p2 O 16 2015

How to Write a Résumé That Stands Out *Harvard Business Review Digital Articles* p2 D 19 2014

Overcoming the Toughest Common Coaching Challenges *Harvard Business Review Digital Articles* p2 Ap 15 2015

A Refresher on A/B Testing *Harvard Business Review Digital Articles* p2 Je 28 2017

A Refresher on Breakeven Quantity *Harvard Business Review Digital Articles* p2 Je 22 2015

A Refresher on Cost of Capital *Harvard Business Review Digital Articles* p2 Ap 30 2015

A Refresher on Current Ratio *Harvard Business Review Digital Articles* p2 S 14 2015

A Refresher on Debt-to-Equity Ratio *Harvard Business Review Digital Articles* p2 Jl 13 2015

A Refresher on Discovery-Driven Planning *Harvard Business Review Digital Articles* p2 F 13 2017

A Refresher on Economic Value to the Customer *Harvard Business Review Digital Articles* p2 My 7 2015

A Refresher on Internal Rate of Return *Harvard Business Review Digital Articles* p2 Mr 17 2016

A Refresher on Marketing Myopia *Harvard Business Review Digital Articles* p2 Ag 22 2016

A Refresher on Marketing ROI *Harvard Business Review Digital Articles* p1 Jl 25 2017

A Refresher on Net Present Value *Harvard Business Review Digital Articles* p2 N 19 2014

A Refresher on Payback Method *Harvard Business Review Digital Articles* p2 Ap 18 2016

A Refresher on Price Elasticity *Harvard Business Review Digital Articles* p2 Ag 21 2015

A Refresher on Randomized Controlled Experiments *Harvard Business Review Digital Articles* p2 Mr 30 2016

A Refresher on Regression Analysis *Harvard Business Review Digital Articles* p2 N 4 2015

A Refresher on Return on Assets and Return on Equity *Harvard Business Review Digital Articles* p2 Ap 4 2016

A Refresher on Statistical Significance *Harvard Business Review Digital Articles* p2 F 16 2016

Resolve a Fight with a Remote Colleague *Harvard Business Review Digital Articles* p2 N 30 2015

The Right Way to Bring a Problem to Your Boss *Harvard Business Review Digital Articles* p2 D 5 2014

Setting the Record Straight on Job Interviews *Harvard Business Review Digital Articles* p2 N 11 2014

Setting the Record Straight on Managing Your Boss *Harvard Business Review Digital Articles* p2 D 18 2014

Setting the Record Straight on Negotiating Your Salary *Harvard Business Review Digital Articles* p2 Mr 9 2015

Setting the Record Straight: Using an Outside Offer to Get a Raise *Harvard Business Review Digital Articles* p2 Jl 5 2016

The Value of Keeping the Right Customers *Harvard Business Review Digital Articles* p2 O 29 2014

What to Do If You're Smarter than Your Boss *Harvard Business Review Digital Articles* p2 D 12 2014

What to Do When a Coworker Goes Over Your Head *Harvard Business Review Digital Articles* p2 D 22 2016

What to Do When Your Peer Becomes Your Boss *Harvard Business Review Digital Articles* p2 O 24 2016

What to Say and Do When Your Employee Has Another Job Offer *Harvard Business Review Digital Articles* p2 My 31 2016

When You're Worried About a Colleague's Mental Health *Harvard Business Review Digital Articles* p2 D 18 2015

Gallo, David

It's All in the Details B. Reesman *Stage Directions* v30 no3 p42 Mr 2017

Gallo, Kelly

The Internet Shouldn't Run on Dirty Energy *Harvard Business Review Digital Articles* p2 D 17 2015

Gallo, Robert C.

Shock and kill with caution bibl color *Science* v354 no6309 p177 O 14 2016

GALLO, TRAVIS

Addressing the Gender Gap in Distinguished Speakers at Professional Ecology Conferences *BioScience* v67 no5 p464 My 2017

GALLOP, CINDY

What to Do About Getting Old img *New York* p32 Ja 23 2017

Galloping

DEVELOP A STRONG GALLOPING POSITION C. Rutledge and S. Cooke color *Practical Horseman* v45 no5 p38 My 2017

Gone Away! J. Wofford color *Practical Horseman* v45 no1 p16 Ja 2017

Galloway, Bob

The Roving Mechanic B. PIKE *Power & Motoryacht* v34 no6 p78 Je 2017

Galloway, Brigid Elsken

The Nature of Things: 24 Stories About Embracing Reality *Publishers Weekly* v264 no13 p64d Mr 27 2017

Galloway, Eden

Eden GALLOWAY N. Loeffler-Gladstone color *Dance Spirit* v20 no9 p80 N 2016

GALLOWAY, JEFF

DOUBLE DIGITS? SWEET! color *Runner's World* v52 no8 p14 S 2017

EAT, DRINK, AND BE SPEEDY color *Runner's World* v52 no9 p16 O 2017

FIND YOUR WAY BACK color *Runner's World* v52 no1 p42 Ja/F 2017

FIT AND JOLLY! cartoon *Runner's World* v51 no11 p36 D 2016

HEAR ME OUT cartoon *Runner's World* v52 no6 p26 Jl 2017

IF THEY CAN'T SAY SOMETHING NICE... color *Runner's World* v52 no7 p29 Ag 2017

JUST FIVE MINUTES [Cover story] cartoon *Runner's World* v52 no4 p24 My 2017

SECOND CHANCE [Cover story] cartoon *Runner's World* v52 no5 p24 Je 2017

THE STARTING LINE [Cover story] cartoon *Runner's World* v52 no2 p30 Mr 2017

STILL GOING STRONG [Cover story] cartoon *Runner's World* v51 no10 p42 N 2016

WEATHER THE WEATHER cartoon *Runner's World* v52 no3 p40 Ap 2017

Galloway, Steven

CanLit gets lit up B. BETHUNE color *Maclean's* v129 no48/49 p32 D 5 2016

L'Affaire Galloway K. GOLD cartoon *Walrus* v13 no9 p40 N 2016

Gallun, Frederick J.

Community network for deaf scientists color *Science* v356 no6336 p386 Ap 28 2017

GALPIN, SHANNON

PEDALING A REVOLUTION *UN Chronicle* v53 no2 p25 2016

Galston, William A.

How One Political Start-Up Is Trying to Fight Gridlock *Harvard Business Review Digital Articles* p2 N 11 2014

What Your Country Should Do for You color *Washington Monthly* v49 no9/10 p126 S/O 2017

Galsworthy, Mike

A plan for U.K. science after the European Union referendum bibl color *Science* v355 no6320 p31 Ja 6 2017

SCIENCE IN A POST-BREXIT WORLD A. CURRY color *Discover* v38 no1 p28 Ja/F 2017

Galt, Rosalind—Interviews

Queering the Globe: A conversation with Rosalind Galt and Karl Schoonover on Queer Cinema in the World R. Longo *Film Quarterly* v70 no2 p94 Wint 2016

GALT, VIRGINIA

Not just for super geniuses color *Maclean's* v130 no10 p68 N 2017

Galvani, Alison P.

Fund global health: Save lives and money color *Science* v356 no6342 p1018 Je 9 2017

Galvanometer

The Fakery of Electrodermal Screening: Souped-up galvanometers are being used to assess people's health and determine what they supposedly need. Tests expose them as preposterous, and government agencies should stop their use S. BARRETT *Skeptical Inquirer* v41 no5 p40 S/O 2017

Galveston (Tex.)—Description & travel

Galveston: NEITHER SHIFTING SANDS NOR FLUCTUATING FORTUNES CAN ERODE THIS ISLAND TOWN'S IN-

DOMITABLE SPIRIT J. BREAL *Texas Monthly* v45 no7 p28 Jl 2017

Galveston Island (Tex.)—Description & travel

Island Life in Galveston R. Walsh color *Southern Living* v52 no3 p69 Mr 2017

Galveston (Tex.) hurricane, 1900

12,000 MARKS FOR TEXAS R. C. GREINER *Prologue* v49 no1 p18 Spr 2017

Galvin, Benjamin

Followers Don't See Their Leaders as Real People color *Harvard Business Review Digital Articles* p2 Ja 23 2017

Make Sure Your Employees Have Good Things to Say About You Behind Your Back *Harvard Business Review Digital Articles* p2 S 22 2016

Galvin, Noah

THE REAL O'NEALS M. Roffman *TV Guide* p30 D 5 2016

Galvin, Robert

We Need More Transparency on the Cost of Specialty Drugs *Harvard Business Review Digital Articles* p2 N 4 2014

Who Has the Power to Cut Drug Prices? Employers *Harvard Business Review Digital Articles* p2 D 1 2015

Galvita, Vladimir V.

Super-dry reforming of methane intensifies CO_2 utilization via Le Chatelier's principle bibl diag graph *Science* v354 no6311 p449 O 28 2016

Galway, Nick—Interviews

NIC GALWAY A. WANG *Interview* v47 no2 p246 Mr 2017

Gamache, Tom

FRINGE BENEFITS M. JAFFE *Arizona Highways* v93 no1 p32 Ja 2017

Gamal, El Amin—Interviews

AMIN EL GAMAL D. Meltzer Zepeda bw *Runner's World* v52 no9 p96 O 2017

Gamalon Machine Intelligence (Company)

AI Speed-Reading For the Masses A. Vance cartoon *Bloomberg Businessweek* no4512 p33 F 20 2017

Gamarra, L. Valenzuela

Persistent effects of pre-Columbian plant domestication on Amazonian forest composition bibl chart graph map *Science* v355 no6328 p925 Mr 3 2017

Gamba, Cristina

Ancient genomic changes associated with domestication of the horse color diag *Science* v356 no6336 p442 Ap 28 2017

Gambelia sila

SEX APPEAL K. MOORE color *Natural History* v125 no4 p2 Ap 2017

Gambel's quail

Gambel's Quail K. Vaughn *Arizona Highways* v93 no3 p13 Mr 2017

Gambini, John

Betting on the Texas (Olive) Oil Boom P. M. ESSWEIN color *Kiplinger's Personal Finance* v71 no10 p22 O 2017

GAMBLE, JESSA

OUT OF SIGHT color map *Canadian Geographic* v137 no2 p38 Mr/Ap 2017

Gamble, Joelle

American Woman bw *Nation* v304 no1 p60 Ja 2 2017 The Obama Years

EXIT LEFT bw color *Nation* v304 no16 p16 My 22 2017

Gamble, Richard

Jeremy Beer, The Philanthropic Revolution: An Alternative History of American Charity *Society* v54 no3 p307 Je 2017

Gamblers

GAME PLAN K. Eisler *Washingtonian Magazine* v52 no11 p109 Ag 2017

Gambling

See also

Gamblers

Sports betting

GAME PLAN K. Eisler *Washingtonian Magazine* v52 no11 p109 Ag 2017

How to Bet Smarter *Kiplinger's Personal Finance* v71 no8 p35 Ag 2017

LOSING It ALL J. ROSENGREN color *Atlantic* v318 no5 p66 D 2016

PLACE YOUR BETS: WHAT TO KNOW ABOUT THE FOUR

AREA CASINOS *Washingtonian Magazine* v52 no11 p112 Ag 2017

SHOW HIM THE MONEY R. O'CONNOR color *Chicago* v65 no11 p32 N 2016

Gambling behavior

Low Stakes on the High Seas D. COURTNEY *Texas Monthly* v45 no1 p151 Ja 2017

Gambling industry—China—Macau (Special Administrative Region)

What Happens in Vegas Doesn't Stay There D. Wei and C. Palmeri color *Bloomberg Businessweek* no4497 p24 O 31 2016

Gambling industry—History—21st century

Japan's Big Bet B. Einhorn, G. Huang et al color *Bloomberg Businessweek* no4505 p20 D 26 2016

Gambling industry—Louisiana

Asserting Tribal Sovereignty through Compact Negotiations J. PRECHT *American Indian Quarterly* v41 no1 p67 Wint 2017

Gambling on Indian reservations

The Development of a Gaming Enterprise for the Navajo Nation S. F. CARDER *American Indian Quarterly* v40 no4 p295 Fall 2016

Gambling—Economic aspects

Australia Battles Its Gambling Addiction J. Scott cartoon *Bloomberg Businessweek* no4493 p24 O 3 2016

Gambling—Law & legislation

Australia Battles Its Gambling Addiction J. Scott cartoon *Bloomberg Businessweek* no4493 p24 O 3 2016

Gambling—Moral & ethical aspects

A Pool and Its Money color *Money* v46 no3 p16 Ap 2017

Gambling—United States

The Alligator Wrestler and the Casino Boss L. GENSLER bw color *Forbes* v198 no6 p104 N 8 2016

Gambrel, Steven

RECIPE FOR SUCCESS H. MARTIN color *Architectural Digest* v73 no11 p104 N 2016

Gambrell, Dorothy

How Screwed Is Your Job? diag *Bloomberg Businessweek* no4528 p50 Je 26 2017

So You Want to Be Like Silicon Valley? *Bloomberg Businessweek* no4537 p48 S 11 2017

Trade Give and Take diag *Bloomberg Businessweek* no4500 p18 N 21 2016

Game calling (Hunting)

AT HOME IN THE TIMBER H. BLOOD color *Outdoor Life* v224 no1 p42 D 2016/Ja 2017

RAPID RECOVERY N. KREBS *Outdoor Life* v224 no9 p32 N 2017

TURKEY TACTICS THROUGH THE AGES N. KREBS color *Outdoor Life* v224 no3 p10 Ap 2017

Game calling (Hunting)—Equipment & supplies

NEXT-LEVEL TURKEY CALLS J. ARTERBURN, S. Wagner et al color *Outdoor Life* v224 no3 p50 Ap 2017

The Redneck Stradivari N. KREBS color *Outdoor Life* v224 no3 p8 Ap 2017

Game of Silence (TV program)

GAME OF SILENCE *TV Guide* v64 no15 p55 Ap 4 2016

Game of Thrones (TV program)

BEST OF SUMMER 2017 *TV Guide* v65 no23 p15 My 29 2017

BIG BOY J. DEAN *Men's Health* v32 no4 p111 My 2017

The Bullseye M. Snetiker color *Entertainment Weekly* no1480 p60 S 1 2017

CHEERS & JEERS D. HOLBROOK *TV Guide* v65 no23 p84 My 29 2017

A CLASH OF QUEENS J. Hibberd color *Entertainment Weekly* no1474/1475 p62 Jl 21-28 2017

DRAGONS AND WOLVES AND RATINGS, OH MY! J. Hibberd color *Entertainment Weekly* no1477 p12 Ag 11 2017

Editor's Note H. Goldblatt color *Entertainment Weekly* no1468/1469 p10 Je 2-9 2017

Emmy Races to Watch M. ROUSH *TV Guide* v65 no37 p10 S 4 2017

GAME OF THRONES: Inside the bloody battles, gory greyscale and the power of perfect shoulder pads—intel on Season 7 and its shocking finale K. HAHN *TV Guide* v65 no35 p26 Ag 21 2017

Game of Thrones K. Hahn *TV Guide* v65 no23 p28 My 29 2017

A HOUSE UNDIVIDED [Cover story] J. Hibberd color *Entertainment Weekly* no1468/1469 p28 Je 2-9 2017

How the 'Game' Changed Everything R. Sheffield bw color *Rolling Stone* no1291/1292 p50 Jl 13 2017

How They Make the Greatest Show on Earth [Cover story] D. D'addario color *Time* v190 no2/3 p66 Jl 10-17 2017

I Can't Believe It's Not TV! K. VanArendonk img *New York* v50 no7 p80 Ap 3 2017

Jaime Lannister's Rules for Survival N. Coster-Waldau color *GQ: Gentlemen's Quarterly* v97 no7 p102 Jl 2017

KILL THE BoY... ...LET THE MaN BE BORN! [Cover story] L. Hill bw color *Esquire* p78 Je/Jl 2017

The Never-Ending Story? J. Hibberd color *Entertainment Weekly* no1466 p14 My 19 2017

The Queen of Dragons Tells All A. MORRIS color *Rolling Stone* no1291/1292 p46 Jl 13 2017

STARK BEAUTY C. Lee color *InStyle* v24 no6 p142 Je 2017

SUMMER TV PREVIEW color *Entertainment Weekly* no1468/1469 p27 Je 2-9 2017

Thrones of Their Own B. Marks and T. Keith color *Sports Illustrated* v127 no2 p22 Jl 17 2017

The Universe M. McCluskey color *Time* v190 no2/3 p76 Jl 10-17 2017

A WESTEROS TEST(EROS) R. Kinane color *Entertainment Weekly* no1480 p44 S 1 2017

WHAT YOUR TV CRUSH SAYS ABOUT YOU E. Spitznagel color *Men's Health* v32 no3 p83 Ap 2017

What You Said About ... color map *Time* v190 no4 p5 Jl 24 2017

Game reserves—South Africa

at the SHARP END A. Toon and S. Toon color diag *Earth Island Journal* v32 no4 p30 Wint 2017

Game wardens

THE HEROIC WORK OF THIN GREEN LINE GAME WARDENS J. A. SWAN *American Forests* v122 no3 p32 Fall 2016

This Is My Job K. Schmitt color *Glamour* v115 no10 p132 O 2017

Games

See also

Ball games

Board games

Card games

Computer games

Electronic games

Family recreation

Foosball (Game)

Gambling

Games on horseback

Outdoor games

Puzzles

Reading games

Roleplaying games

Targets (Sports)

Video games

Word games

bubbles for everyone color *Parents* v92 no4 p67 Ap 2017

Businesses With Heart S. SEA GOLD color *Parents* v92 no4 p28 Ap 2017

CRUSH 'EM ALL! M. Zimmerman bw *Men's Health* v32 no6 p104 Ag 2017

HARRY'S NEXT GAMES P. TREBLE color *Maclean's* v129 no51/52 p47 D 26 2016

Home (Be)Coming S. Murphy color *Log Home Living* v34 no7 p22 S 2017

is your kid destined for greatness? S. DOLGOFF *Parents* v91 no11 p70 N 2016

Mastering Your Mental Game... TANIA SACHDEV J. bleyer *Psychology Today* v50 no2 p96 Mr/Ap 2017

party on! (a budget) L. FENTON *Parents* v91 no9 p143 S 2016

What in the World? *National Geographic Kids* no469 p34 Ap 2017

Word Play [Cover story] color *Prevention* v69 no5 p96 My 2017

Games & technology

What Technology Companies Can Learn from Toy Makers A. Samuel *Harvard Business Review Digital Articles* p2 Mr 30 2016

Games for dogs

Sweet Smell of Success D. HARVEY *Los Angeles Magazine* p24

Ap 2017

Games in art

Game Theory D. Daniel color *American Craft* v77 no3 p64 Je/Jl 2017

Games on horseback

The Clinic PHOTO CRITIQUES S. von Dietze color *Dressage Today* v23 no12 p26 S 2017

Games—Congresses

Sorry Not Sorry M. Rubino *Indianapolis Monthly* v12 no40 p10 Ag 2017

Games—Evaluation

OBSESSED WITH GRAPHIC GAMES A. MAZE color *Better Homes & Gardens* v95 no8 p12 Ag 2017

Games—Rules

Cabin Fever? C. HEITGER-EWING color *Cabin Living* p18 D 2016

Gametogenesis

Germ line–inherited H3K27me3 restricts enhancer function during maternal-to-zygotic transition F. Zenk, E. Loeser et al diag *Science* v357 no6347 p212 Jl 14 2017

Gametophytes

Sex and the Single Gametophyte: Revising the Homosporous Vascular Plant Life Cycle in Light of Contemporary Research C. H. HAUFLER, K. M. PRYER et al *BioScience* v66 no11 p928 N 1 2016

Gamification

Gamification Can Help People Actually Use Analytics Tools L. Sherer *Harvard Business Review Digital Articles* p2 F 25 2015

Gamma rays

Gamma rays linked to fast radio burst C. CROCKETT color *Science News* v190 no12 p11 D 10 2016

The Origin of the Milky Way's Mysterious Gamma Rays M. Young *Sky & Telescope* v134 no4 p14 O 2017

X-ray sterilization with accelerators is viable in US C. Boulware *Physics Today* v70 no1 p11 Ja 2017

Gan

SIEGE MENTALITY *Lapham's Quarterly* v10 no3 p97 Summ 2017

Gan Li

China's Numbers Man D. Roberts and X. Pi color *Bloomberg Businessweek* no4516 p12 Mr 27 2017

Ganahl, Pat

Pat Ganahl T. Taylor bw color *Hot Rod* v70 no5 p58 My 2017

Ganapol, Barry D.

Paul Frederick Zweifel *Physics Today* v70 no8 p73 Ag 2017

Gance, Abel, 1889-1981

Man of Action F. S. NEHME bw *Film Comment* v53 no1 p88 Ja/F 2017

GANCH, SUSIE

What do you collect and why? color *American Craft* v77 no2 p20 Ap/My 2017

Gandel, Stephen

A STOCK TRADER LOSES IN COURT. IT'S NO REASON TO CELEBRATE color *Fortune* v174 no6 p14 N 1 2016

Warren Buffett's All-In Clean-Energy Bet color diag map *Fortune* v174 no8 p158 D 15 2016

WORLD'S 50 GREATEST LEADERS [Cover story] color *Fortune* v175 no5 p46 Ap 1 2017

Gander (N.L.)

PLANE PEOPLE M. Schulman cartoon *New Yorker* v93 no6 p19 Mr 27 2017

Gander, Ryan

Editor's Letter L. POLLOCK color *Art in America* v105 no5 p16 My 2017

RYAN GANDER E. Fullerton color *Art in America* v105 no5 p110 My 2017

Gandert, Sean

Lost in Arcadia color *Publishers Weekly* v264 no19 p41 My 8 2017

Gandhi, Linnea—Interviews

Managers Shouldn't Fear Algorithm-Based Decision Making E. Harrell *Harvard Business Review Digital Articles* p2 S 7 2016

Gandhi, Neil A.

What Harvey Is Teaching the Health Care Sector About Managing Disasters *Harvard Business Review Digital Articles* p2 S 12 2017

Gandhi, Prashant

Which Industries Are the Most Digital (and Why)? *Harvard Business Review Digital Articles* p2 Ap 1 2016

Gandhi, Rahul, 1970-

Best Excuses for Sleeping on the Job T. John color *Time* v189 no20 p11 My 29 2017

India at 70 *Vital Speeches of the Day* v83 no10 p281 O 2017

Gandini, Marcello—Interviews

What I'd Do Differently Marcello Gandini, 78 J. PEARLEY HUFFMAN color *Car & Driver* v62 no6 p108 D 2016

Gandolfo, María A.

Eocene lantern fruits from Gondwanan Patagonia and the early origins of Solanaceae bibl color diag *Science* v355 no6320 p1 Ja 6 2017

Ganek, David—Trials, litigation, etc.

PAYBACK TIME B. Mclean color *Fortune* v75 no1 p90 Ja 1 2017

Ganesan, Anurudh

This Teen Invented a Lifesaving Vehicle: More than a million children worldwide die every year from preventable diseases. One teen's invention could change that B. ROSS img *New York Times Upfront* v149 no12 p12 Ap 24 2017

Ganesan, Arvind

A Tribe's Bad Deal with Wall Street color *Progressive* v81 no10 p14 N 2016

Gang, Jeanne—Interviews

DREAM DUO E. FISHMAN bw *Chicago* v66 no9 p49 S 2017

Jeanne Gang J. GONCHAR color *Architectural Record* v205 no2 p22 F 2017

Gang Liu

Synthetic nacre by predesigned matrix-directed mineralization bibl bw diag graph *Science* v354 no6308 p107 O 7 2016

Gang Lu

Biaxially strained PtPb/Pt core/shell nanoplate boosts oxygen reduction catalysis bibl color graph *Science* v354 no6318 p1410 D 16 2016

Gang members

THE QUEEN OF FLORENCIA S. QUINONES bw color *Los Angeles Magazine* v62 no10 p134 O 2017

Gang members—Attitudes

I thought I could 'save' gang members. I was wrong G. Boyle bw *America* v216 no11 p41 My 15 2017

Gang members—Psychology

I thought I could 'save' gang members. I was wrong G. Boyle bw *America* v216 no11 p41 My 15 2017

Gang violence

The Wild BUNCH S. HOLLANDSWORTH *Texas Monthly* v45 no4 p47 Ap 2017

Gangarosa, Lisa

TUMMY TROUBLE TOOLBOX S. LIAO *Better Homes & Gardens* v94 no12 p144 D 2016

Gangemi, Joe

Red Oaks J. Russell *TV Guide* v64 no40 p34 O 3 2016

Ganges River Delta (Bangladesh & India)

CLIMATE CHANGE: IN FOCUS color *National Geographic* v231 no5 p2 My 2017

Gangnam Style (Music)

2017 Milestones L. Rothman color *Time* v188 no27-28 p118 D 26 2016

Gangrene—Prevention

Second opinion *Mayo Clinic Health Letter* v35 no9 p8 S 2017

Gangs

Knead to heal G. Boyle S.J. bw *U.S. Catholic* v82 no6 p18 Je 2017

Gangs—California—Los Angeles

THE QUEEN OF FLORENCIA S. QUINONES bw color *Los Angeles Magazine* v62 no10 p134 O 2017

Gangsters on television

OldFellas G. ANASTASIA color *AARP: The Magazine* v59 no1A p44 D 2015/Ja 2016

GANGULY, SUMIT

Brutal Realities of British Rule in India *Current History* v116 no789 p157 Ap 2017

Gannett Co. Inc.

Gannett and the last great local hope D. Uberti color map *Columbia Journalism Review* v56 no1 p64 Spr 2017

How local is the local news at Gannett? L. Bastien and S. Blaskey diag *Columbia Journalism Review* v56 no1 p69 Spr 2017

Gannon, Megan

ARCHAEOLOGY IN A DIVIDED LAND color map *Science* v357 no6359 p28 O 6 2017

Fruits for the Frozen color *Scientific American* v316 no2 p18 F 2017

Germany to probe Nazi-era medical science bw *Science* v355 no6320 p13 Ja 6 2017

Ganoderma lucidum

Fungi Fever color *Prevention* v69 no5 p12 My 2017

Ganondagan State Historic Site (N.Y.)

HISTORY & CULTURE COME TO LIFE—The Seneca Art & Culture Center at Ganondagan G. P. Jemison color *New York State Conservationist* v71 no2 p14 O 2016

Gans, Herbert

1958: Levittown, NJ *Lapham's Quarterly* v10 no1 p65 Wint 2017

Gans, Joshua

50 Years Ago an Economist Worried About Unchecked Corporate Power. Here's What His Theory Got Wrong *Harvard Business Review Digital Articles* p2 2017

Facebook Live Is the Company's Newest Strategic Weapon *Harvard Business Review Digital Articles* p2 Ap 8 2016

Google, Yelp, and the Future of Search *Harvard Business Review Digital Articles* p2 Jl 10 2015

How AI Will Change Strategy: A Thought Experiment *Harvard Business Review Digital Articles* p2 O 3 2017

How AI Will Change the Way We Make Decisions *Harvard Business Review Digital Articles* p2 Jl 26 2017

How Much Is Trump Really Disrupting Politics-as-Usual? *Harvard Business Review Digital Articles* p2 Mr 1 2016

If Ford Wants to Beat Tesla, It Needs to Go All In *Harvard Business Review Digital Articles* p2 Ap 20 2016

The Obama Administration's Roadmap for AI Policy *Harvard Business Review Digital Articles* p2 D 21 2016

The Simple Economics of Machine Intelligence *Harvard Business Review Digital Articles* p2 N 17 2016

The Trade-Off Every AI Company Will Face *Harvard Business Review Digital Articles* p2 Mr 28 2017

What Would It Take to Disrupt a Platform Like Facebook? *Harvard Business Review Digital Articles* p2 Mr 23 2016

Why Elon Musk's New Strategy Makes Sense *Harvard Business Review Digital Articles* p2 Jl 25 2016

Why Facebook Messenger Is a Big Deal for Customer Service *Harvard Business Review Digital Articles* p2 My 6 2016

Gans, Keri

The Snacking Diaries color *Women's Health* v14 no2 p106 Mr 2017

Ganscha, Stefan

Cell-wide analysis of protein thermal unfolding reveals determinants of thermostability color *Science* v355 no6327 p812 F 24 2017

Gans-Morse, Jordan

Property Rights in Post-Soviet Russia: Violence, Corruption, and the Demand for Law R. Legvold *Foreign Affairs* v96 no6 p165 N/D 2017

Gant, Andrew

O Sing unto the Lord: A History of English Church Music D. A. Hoekema *Christian Century* v134 no19 p37 S 13 2017

Gantenbein, Christoph

Pair of Aces F. A. BERNSTEIN bw color *Architectural Digest* v74 no3 p60 Mr 2017

GANTZ, JEREMY

BEHIND THE SCENES bw color *In These Times* v40 no11 p48 N 2016

Gantz, L.

Deterministic generation of a cluster state of entangled photons bibl diag graph *Science* v354 no6311 p434 O 28 2016

Ganz, Jami

ADAM SCOTT AND CRAIG ROBINSON color *Entertainment Weekly* no1482/1483 p42 S 22 2017

THE BIGGEST SUMMER BREAKOUTS (SO FAR) color diag *Entertainment Weekly* no1474/1475 p15 Jl 21-28 2017

Bob's Burgers *Entertainment Weekly* no1482/1483 p34 S 22 2017

Curb Your Enthusiasm color *Entertainment Weekly* no1482/1483 p40 S 22 2017

The Deuce color *Entertainment Weekly* no1482/1483 p29 S 22 2017

Family Guy *Entertainment Weekly* no1482/1483 p34 S 22 2017

FLATLINERS color *Entertainment Weekly* no1478 / 1479 p41 Ag 18-25 2017

The Girlfriend Experience color *Entertainment Weekly* no1482/1483 p38 S 22 2017

Good Behavior *Entertainment Weekly* no1482/1483 p39 S 22 2017

Madam Secretary color *Entertainment Weekly* no1482/1483 p39 S 22 2017

NCIS: Los Angeles *Entertainment Weekly* no1482/1483 p38 S 22 2017

Outlander color *Entertainment Weekly* no1482/1483 p26 S 22 2017

Poldark *Entertainment Weekly* no1482/1483 p38 S 22 2017

Shameless color *Entertainment Weekly* no1482/1483 p30 S 22 2017

The Simpsons color *Entertainment Weekly* no1482/1483 p34 S 22 2017

SMILF *Entertainment Weekly* no1482/1483 p43 S 22 2017

Ten Days in the Valley color *Entertainment Weekly* no1482/1483 p43 S 22 2017

Verify My Love color *Entertainment Weekly* no1477 p16 Ag 11 2017

The Walking Dead color *Entertainment Weekly* no1482/1483 p38 S 22 2017

What to Watch color *Entertainment Weekly* no1474/1475 p108 Jl 21-28 2017

White Famous color *Entertainment Weekly* no1482/1483 p36 S 22 2017

Wisdom of the Crowd color *Entertainment Weekly* no1482/1483 p34 S 22 2017

Ganz, Javier

Intersection of diverse neuronal genomes and neuropsychiatric disease: The Brain Somatic Mosaicism Network color *Science* v356 no6336 p395 Ap 28 2017

Gao, Enlai

Harvesting electrical energy from carbon nanotube yarn twist diag graph *Science* v357 no6353 p773 Ag 25 2017

Gao, Feng

Bug mapping and fitness testing of chemically synthesized chromosome X diag *Science* v355 no6329 p1048 Mr 10 2017

Deep functional analysis of synII, a 770-kilobase synthetic yeast chromosome diag *Science* v355 no6329 p1047 Mr 10 2017

Gao, Grace

A Hero's Daughter J. NORDLINGER color *National Review* v69 no12 p20 Je 26 2017

Gao, Guanyin

All-oxide–based synthetic antiferromagnets exhibiting layer-resolved magnetization reversal diag *Science* v357 no6347 p191 Jl 14 2017

Gao, Qin

Segregation-induced ordered superstructures at general grain boundaries in a nickel-bismuth alloy color *Science* v357 no6359 p97 O 6 2017

Gao, Rui

Atomic-layered Au clusters on α-MoC as catalysts for the low-temperature water-gas shift reaction chart diag graph *Science* v357 no6349 p389 Jl 28 2017

Gao, Song

An organic-inorganic perovskite ferroelectric with large piezoelectric response graph *Science* v357 no6348 p306 Jl 21 2017

Gao, Xing

Late Pleistocene archaic human crania from Xuchang, China bibl color diag graph *Science* v355 no6328 p969 Mr 3 2017

Gao, Yandong

Microbiota-activated PPAR-γ signaling inhibits dysbiotic Enterobacteriaceae expansion graph *Science* v357 no6351 p570 Ag 11 2017

Gao, Yuanda

Tuning quantum nonlocal effects in graphene plasmonics bw diag *Science* v357 no6347 p187 Jl 14 2017

Gao Hu

Mass seasonal bioflows of high-flying insect migrants bibl graph *Science* v354 no6319 p1584 D 23 2016

Gaohua Liu

Principles for designing proteins with cavities formed by curved β sheets bibl color graph *Science* v355 no6321 p1 Ja 13 2017

Gaoxingyu Huang

Structure of a yeast step II catalytically activated spliceosome bibl diag *Science* v355 no6321 p1 Ja 13 2017

Gap Inc.

GREAT GIFTS under $50 color *Redbook* p40 D 2016

Petites, We See You! color *Glamour* v115 no11 p64 N 2017

Gap Inc.—Officials & employees

Connecting Unemployed Youth with Organizations That Need Talent W. Seldon and K. S. Milway *Harvard Business Review Digital Articles* p2 N 3 2016

Gappah, Petina

A Short History of Zaka the Zulu cartoon color *New Yorker* v92 no30 p58 S 26 2016

A Short History of Zaka the Zulu P. Gappah cartoon color *New Yorker* v92 no30 p58 S 26 2016

GARA, ANTOINE

Amazon Woman color *Forbes* v200 no4 p52 O 24 2017

THE BEST DEFENSE color *Forbes* v199 no7 p30 Je 29 2017

The Fintech 50 color *Forbes* v198 no7 p90 N 29 2016

LESSONS AND IDEAS BY THE 100 GREATEST LIVING BUSINESS MINDS bw color *Forbes* v200 no3 p115 S 28 2017

MONEY THERAPISTS color *Forbes* v200 no4 p104 O 24 2017

MORE UPS THAN DOWNS color graph *Forbes* v200 no3 p52 S 28 2017

One for Mickey's Mantel color *Forbes* v199 no6 p24 Je 13 2017

Peering Into Peer-to-Peer Loans color *Forbes* v198 no7 p98 N 29 2016

A PIECE OF THE ROCK color *Forbes* v200 no1 p28 Jl 27 2017

SURVIVORS' GILT bw chart *Forbes* v200 no3 p48 S 28 2017

The Toll Collector [Cover story] color map *Forbes* v199 no5 p68 My 16 2017

The Unreformed Stock Picker color *Forbes* v200 no1 p56 Jl 27 2017

Wall Street's Robocop color *Forbes* v199 no6 p62 Je 13 2017

THE WORLD'S BILLIONAIRES bw color diag graph map *Forbes* v199 no3 p84 Mr 28 2017

Garabedian, Raffi

Terawatt-scale photovoltaics: Trajectories and challenges chart graph *Science* v356 no6334 p141 Ap 14 2017

Garafola, Lynn

LYNN GARAFOLA S. Burke *Dance Magazine* v90 no12 p52 D 2016

Garage door design & construction

GARAGE SALE color *Log Home Living* v34 no7 p21 S 2017

Garage sales

U.S. 127 Yard Sale A. B. WALTERS *Cincinnati Magazine* p58 Je 2017

Garages

CALIFORNIA CALLING M. JORDAN color *Road & Track* v68 no7 p92 Mr/Ap 2017

Fresh cuts, Old Good Bikes, coffee color *Popular Mechanics* p49 F 2017

Macho Wagon Heading to New Home R. Brutt color *Hot Rod* v70 no6 p24 Je 2017

NO HILLS, NO PROBLEM! E. Barton color *Bicycling* v58 no7 p42 Ag 2017

One Man's Junk T. Lee Byrd color *Hot Rod* v70 no4 p26 Ap 2017

Take 5 With RICHARD PETTY color *Hot Rod* v70 no9 p18 S 2017

Two of a Kind E. Perkins color *Hot Rod* v70 no3 p6 Mr 2017

Garages—Equipment & supplies—Evaluation

Garage Utility color *Old House Journal* v45 no1 p50 F 2017

Garanča, Elina

Elīna Garanča: Revive H. Keys *Opera News* v81 no10 p56 Ap 2017

Garaus, Christian

Even Tiny Rewards Can Motivate People to Go the Extra Mile *Harvard Business Review Digital Articles* p2 Je 7 2016

Garb, Margaret

Cancer Does Discriminate *In These Times* v40 no12 p40 D 2016

Squatters' 60-Year War Against Private Property: Around 1230 a.m. on August 7, 1988, a small army of police officers in riot gear covered their badges, raised their batons and charged on foot and on horseback into Tompkins Square Park on New York's... *In These Times* v41 no7 p34 Jl 2017

The Welfare We Forgot *In These Times* v41 no3 p36 Mr 2017

Garbage (Performer)

The Return of a Grunge Goddess: Shirley Manson, lead singer of '90s band Garbage, heads back on the road with Blondie D. Evans img *New York* v50 no11 p87 My 29 2017

Garbage disposal units

THE COMPOST KING E. ROYTE *New York Times Magazine* p44 F 19 2017

Kitchen Cleanups L. Elliott cartoon *Old House Journal* v45 no2 p48 Ap 2017

KITCHEN REMODELING J. Kneiszel color *Cabin Living* p68 Je 2017

Garber, Ken

In a major shift, cancer drugs go 'tissue-agnostic' chart color *Science* v356 no6343 p1111 Je 16 2017

Garber, Stephanie

Caraval color *Publishers Weekly* v263 no42 p68 O 17 2016

Garber, Victor, 1949-

LIFE ON THE BIG SCREEN WITH TYPE 1 DIABETES A. Yu color *Maclean's* v129 no48/49 p38 D 5 2016

GARBER-PAUL, ELISABETH

THE WEED WARRIORS color *Rolling Stone* no1295 p45 S 7 2017

Garbo, Sandro

SPEED DRAWING M. FRANK color *Road & Track* v69 no1 p100 Ag 2017

Garbus, Martin

America's Invisible Inferno color *New York Review of Books* v63 no19 p24 D 8 2017

GARCEAU, ALICIA

CLUB MED: At one Carmel doctor's new office, patients pay monthly dues for healthcare *Indianapolis Monthly* p79 N 2017

FATHER FIGURE: Franciscan Health's cancer center has a secret weapon: a medical director who knows what it's like to be the parent of a leukemia patient *Indianapolis Monthly* p76 N 2017

PERSONAL AID *Indianapolis Monthly* p71 N 2017

WHAT IS A MICROHOSPITAL? St. Vincent and Franciscan introduce a new type of treatment center *Indianapolis Monthly* p83 N 2017

Garcetti, Eric

Tom Hayden color *Time* v188 no19 p11 N 7 2016

Garcia, Antero

A NARRATIVE ACROSS PLATFORMS: Transmedia, politics, and encouraging youth authorship anywhere and anytime *Literacy Today (2411-7862)* v35 no2 p34 S/O 2017

GARCÍA, ANTONIO J.

Improvising over Contemporary Harmonies Using Common Tones bw color *Downbeat* v84 no1 p98 Ja 2017

Garcia, B.

Observation of a large-scale anisotropy in the arrival directions of cosmic rays above 8×10^{18} eV *Science* v357 no6357 p1266 S 22 2017

Garcia, Ben

SHARED AUTHORITY bw *Art in America* p76 O 2017

Garcia, Charles

Seismic constraints on caldera dynamics from the 2015 Axial Seamount eruption bibl color graph *Science* v354 no6318 p1395 D 16 2016

García, E. J.

FOUR DEVOTIONAL POEMS *Commonweal* v144 no11 p28 Je 16 2017

Garcia, Gillian

She's Bangin' N. Spradley color *Essence* v47 no7 p39 N 2016

Garcia, Greg

5 THINGS TO KNOW ABOUT. . . THE GUEST BOOK J. RUSSELL *TV Guide* v65 no31 p20 Jl 24 2017

Garcia, Jessica

oops *Parents* v92 no7 p132 Jl 2017

GARCIA, JOSHUA J.

Aligned Transitions *Education Digest* v82 no5 p12 Ja 2017

Garcia, Kami

Fast Cars & Bad Boys A. Breznican color *Entertainment Weekly* no1436/1437 p106 O 21 2016

Garcia, Katherine

Step Up to a Breakthrough color *Women's Health* v14 no9 p88 N 2017

Garcia, Kathleen
  How NASA Uses Telemedicine to Care for Astronauts in Space *Harvard Business Review Digital Articles* p2 Jl 6 2017
Garcia, Kevin Thomas
  CULTURAL DIPLOMACY *Opera News* v81 no7 p28 Ja 2017
Garcia, Laia
  "I feel my best in this dress" color *Glamour* v115 no4 p55 Ap 2017
Garcia, Mayte
  The Most Beautiful: My Life with Prince *Publishers Weekly* v264 no31 p83 Jl 31 2017
Garcia, Nicole M.
  HOW DO YOU HOLD TOGETHER YOUR TRANS IDENTITY AND YOUR LIFE OF FAITH? color *Christian Century* v134 no2 p22 Ja 18 2017
Garcia, Nina
  Sound Bites color *Entertainment Weekly* no1484 p3 S 29 2017
GARCIA, PATRICIA
  Not So Junior LEAGUE color *Vogue* v207 no4 p142 Ap 2017
Garcia, Raquel A.
  Biodiversity redistribution under climate change: Impacts on ecosystems and human well-being color *Science* v355 no6332 p1389 Mr 31 2017
Garcia, Robert
  Reducing Health Disparities and Promoting Health Equity *Parks & Recreation* v52 no5 p40 My 2017
  Whitewashing the Los Angeles River? Gente-fication not Gentrification; Green displacement threatens communities of color and low-income communities *Parks & Recreation* v52 no9 p50 S 2017
GARCIA, ROY
  ROAR OF THE CROWD *Texas Monthly* v45 no6 p10 Je 2017
Garcia, Sergio, 1980-
  Feels Like the First Time S. Zak color *Golf Magazine* v59 no4 p76 Ap 2017
  A First Major Tournament (Finally) for Sergio García S. Gregory color *Time* v189 no15 p13 Ap 24 2017
  Leading Off color *Sports Illustrated* v126 no11 p8 Ap 17-24 2017
  Major Pain M. Broadie chart color *Golf Magazine* v59 no8 p70 Ag 2017
  A Man in Full A. Shipnuck and C. Barrett color *Golf Magazine* v59 no7 p28 Jl 2017
  MASTERFUL SERGIO D. M. Clarke color *Golf Magazine* v59 no6 p15 Je 2017
  MASTER STROKES 4 shots to go low [Cover story] color *Golf Magazine* v59 no6 p75 Je 2017
  Title Fight A. Shipnuck and C. Barrett color *Golf Magazine* v59 no8 p30 Ag 2017
  VIVA, SERGIO [Cover story] A. Shipnuck color *Sports Illustrated* v126 no11 p70 Ap 17-24 2017
  You're Up! color *Golf Magazine* v59 no7 p16 Jl 2017
Garcia, Vanessa
  Cuba and America, the Next Generation *Wilson Quarterly* v40 no4 p1 Fall 2016
García-Bellido, Juan
  BLACK HOLES from the Beginning of Time color graph *Scientific American* v317 no1 p38 Jl 2017
García Bernal, Gael, 1978-
  Going for Impact N. Terrero color *Entertainment Weekly* no1436/1437 p22 O 21 2016
  LOLA color *InStyle* v24 no1 p92 Ja 2017
  Mozart in the Jungle M. ROUSH *TV Guide* p22 D 5 2016
GARCÍA-BERTHOU, EMILI
  Nonnative Fish to Control Aedes Mosquitoes: A Controversial, Harmful Tool *BioScience* v67 no1 p84 Ja 2017
Garcia-Cabrera, K.
  Persistent effects of pre-Columbian plant domestication on Amazonian forest composition bibl chart graph map *Science* v355 no6328 p925 Mr 3 2017
García-Fojeda, Belén
  Local amplifiers of IL-4Rα-mediated macrophage activation promote repair in lung and liver diag *Science* v356 no6342 p1076 Je 9 2017
GarciaLive (Music)
  What to Stream color *Entertainment Weekly* no1476 p60 Ag 4 2017

García Márquez, Gabriel, 1927-2014
  c. 1950: Aracataca G. G. Marquez *Lapham's Quarterly* v10 no1 p53 Wint 2017
García-Montero, Luis G.
  The extent of forest in dryland biomes [Cover story] chart map *Science* v356 no6338 p635 My 12 2017
Garcia-Ojalvo, Jordi
  Coupling between distant biofilms and emergence of nutrient time-sharing bw color graph *Science* v356 no6338 p638 My 12 2017
Garcia Perez, Laura
  A pathogenic role for T cell–derived IL-22BP in inflammatory bowel disease bibl graph *Science* v354 no6310 p358 O 21 2016
Garcia-Pinto, D.
  Observation of a large-scale anisotropy in the arrival directions of cosmic rays above 8 × 1018 eV *Science* v357 no6357 p1266 S 22 2017
Garcia-Rivera, Alejandro
  A Life Lived in God's Love C. González-Andrieu color *America* v216 no5 p18 Mr 6 2017
García-Sánchez, Miguel
  The Colombian Paradox: Peace Processes, Elite Divisions & Popular Plebiscites graph *Daedalus* v146 no4 p152 Fall 2017
García Sánchez, Sergio
  Sketchbook: 'Moby-Dick,' Part 2 *New York Times Book Review* p21 Je 11 2017
  Sketchbook *New York Times Book Review* p26 Ja 15 2017
García-Sastre, Adolfo
  Enhancement of Zika virus pathogenesis by preexisting antiflavivirus immunity graph *Science* v356 no6334 p175 Ap 14 2017
García-Tabernero, Antonio
  The growth pattern of Neandertals, reconstructed from a juvenile skeleton from El Sidrón (Spain) color graph *Science* v357 no6357 p1282 S 22 2017
Garcia-Verdugo, Jose-Manuel
  Extensive migration of young neurons into the infant human frontal lobe color diag graph *Science* v354 no6308 paaf7073-1 O 7 2016
García-Vidal, Francisco J.
  Long-distance operator for energy transfer diag *Science* v357 no6358 p1357 S 29 2017
García-Villacorta, R.
  Persistent effects of pre-Columbian plant domestication on Amazonian forest composition bibl chart graph map *Science* v355 no6328 p925 Mr 3 2017
Garcilazo, Tomas
  The Outgate color *American Cowboy* v23 no4 p90 D 2016/Ja 2017
Garçon, Pierre
  American Voices Pierre Garçon J. Feldman and T. Keith color *Sports Illustrated* v125 no17 p26 N 21 2016 Double Issue
Gardell, Christer
  Hello, Ericsson. 'The Butcher' Is on the Line N. Rolander, V. Ek et al color *Bloomberg Businessweek* no4526 p35 Je 12 2017
Gardels, Nathan
  The American Founders Entrusted Elites to Save Democracy from Itself *NPQ: New Perspectives Quarterly* v34 no2 p2 My 2017
  The Era of Post-Party Politics: New Institutions That Embrace Participation Without Populism *NPQ: New Perspectives Quarterly* v33 no4 p2 O 2016
  How Social Media Splits the Global Conversation *NPQ: New Perspectives Quarterly* v34 no1 p6 Ja 2017
  If You Don't Have Solid Borders, You Get Walls *NPQ: New Perspectives Quarterly* v34 no3 p2 Jl 2017
  New Institutions that Embrace Participation Without Populism *NPQ: New Perspectives Quarterly* v34 no1 p9 Ja 2017
  A New Urgent Realism Is Making Negotiations With North Korea More Likely *NPQ: New Perspectives Quarterly* v34 no3 p6 Jl 2017
  Renovating Democracy and Salvaging Globalization *NPQ: New Perspectives Quarterly* v34 no1 p2 Ja 2017
  Salvaging Globalization *NPQ: New Perspectives Quarterly* v34 no1 p67 Ja 2017
  What the Burqini Ban Reveals *NPQ: New Perspectives Quarterly* v33 no4 p28 O 2016
  Why China Fears a 'Color Revolution' Incited by the West *NPQ: New Perspectives Quarterly* v33 no4 p8 O 2016

Gardens—United States
Garden States color *House Beautiful* v159 no2 p32 Mr 2017
In Bloom E. WOOD color *Missouri Life* v44 no2 p56 Ap 2017
Unexpected Bounties A. Bolen color *National Wildlife (World Edition)* v55 no2 p18 F/Mr 2017

Gardens—Vermont
GREEN GIANT E. E. OGDEN color *Better Homes & Gardens* v95 no3 p118 Mr 2017

Gardinassi, Luiz
mTOR regulates metabolic adaptation of APCs in the lung and controls the outcome of allergic inflammation graph *Science* v357 no6355 p1014 S 8 2017

GARDINER, BRYAN
NO INTERACTION REQUIRED color *Popular Science* v289 no6 p68 N/D 2017
WATCHING THE CLOCKS *Popular Science* v289 no5 p45 S/O 2017

Gardiner, Matthew
To Guard Against Cybercrime, Follow the Money *Harvard Business Review Digital Articles* p2 My 26 2017

Gardiner, Ronan
A TYPEWRITER color *Men's Health* v32 no5 p139 Je 2017

Gardner, Abby
BOOT CAMP *Indianapolis Monthly* p34 N 2017
COUNTRY PRIDE: Selling a log cabin to a military couple didn't come down to price *Indianapolis Monthly* p42 N 2017
"I won't be defined by my hair choices" color *Glamour* v115 no4 p102 Ap 2017
Looking Sharp *Indianapolis Monthly* p33 N 2017
"My beauty standard is me" color *Glamour* v115 no10 p92 O 2017

Gardner, April W.
Beneath the Blackberry Moon: The Red Feather *Publishers Weekly* v264 no4 p66 Ja 23 2017

Gardner, Chris
Chris Gardner Shows How to Practice The Power of Acknowledging Others bw *Black Enterprise* v47 no2 p28 S 2016

Gardner, David
2 KANSAS JAYHAWKS chart color *Sports Illustrated* v125 no15 p61 N 7 2016
Austin Power color *Sports Illustrated* v125 no19 p22 D 12 2016
THE COMMON TOUCH color *Sports Illustrated* v126 no7 p60 Mr 6 2017

Gardner, Dawn-Lyen
An Onscreen Family, Raising Cane D. D'addario color *Time* v190 no1 p52 Jl 3 2017
Queen Sugar M. Logan *TV Guide* v65 no25 p39 Je 2017

Gardner, Don
FIELD GOALS A. BRANDT *Cincinnati Magazine* p26 Je 2017

Gardner, Erle Stanley, 1889-1970
The Case of the Stuttering Bishop *Publishers Weekly* v264 no9 p96 F 27 2017

Gardner, Heidi K.
Collaborating Well in Large Global Teams *Harvard Business Review Digital Articles* p2 Jl 1 2015
GETTING YOUR STARS TO COLLABORATE color *Harvard Business Review* v95 no1 p100 Ja/F 2017
How to Capture Value from Collaboration, Especially If You're Skeptical About It *Harvard Business Review Digital Articles* p2 My 2 2017
How to Get People to Collaborate When You Don't Control Their Salary bw graph *Harvard Business Review Digital Articles* p2 Ja 23 2017
THE OVERCOMMITTED ORGANIZATION: WHY IT'S HARD TO SHARE PEOPLE ACROSS MULTIPLE TEAMS—AND WHAT TO DO ABOUT IT [Cover story] chart graph il img *Harvard Business Review* v95 no5 p58 S/O 2017

Gardner, Howard
How America Lost Its Mind color *Atlantic* v320 no4 p12 N 2017

Gardner, Ian
No Victory in Valhalla: The Untold Story of 3rd Battalion, 506th Parachute Infantry Regiment, From Bastogne to Berchtesgaden A. Paletta *Military History* v34 no1 p72 My 2017

Gardner, James
Art on the Line color *Weekly Standard* v22 no15 p37 D 19 2016
Charmed circle: A new exhibition at the Guggenheim examines the supernatural symbolist artists of late nineteenth-century

France color *Magazine Antiques* v184 no4 p102 Jl/Ag 2017
Darker Horizon color *Weekly Standard* v22 no28 p41 Mr 27 2017
Dealers' choice color *Magazine Antiques* v183 no6 p102 N/D 2016
Empathetic Eye color *Weekly Standard* v22 no41 p31 Jl 3 2017
Getting Things Moving color *Weekly Standard* v23 no6 p43 O 16 2017
Glamour Shots bw color *Weekly Standard* v22 no43 p37 Jl 24 2017
The Invention of the American Art Museum: From Craft to Kulturgeschichte, 1870–1930 color *Magazine Antiques* v184 no3 p66 My/Je 2017
Man of distinction cartoon *Magazine Antiques* v184 no1 p174 Ja/F 2017
Naples color *Magazine Antiques* v184 no4 p54 Jl/Ag 2017
A New World Old Master: The Met rescues a seventeenth-century Mexican artist from obscurity color *Magazine Antiques* v184 no5 p102 S/O 2017
Of an artist dying young color *Magazine Antiques* v184 no3 p96 My/Je 2017
Of Saints and Vandals color *Weekly Standard* v22 no18 p41 Ja 16 2017
An old master, newly arrived color *Magazine Antiques* v183 no6 p116 N/D 2016
On books color *Magazine Antiques* v184 no5 p42 S/O 2017
Rebel's Reward bw color *Weekly Standard* v22 no46 p38 Ag 14 2017
SHATTERING EFFECT bw cartoon color *Magazine Antiques* v184 no2 p126 Mr/Ap 2017
Underground Art color *Weekly Standard* v22 no24 p39 F 27 2017

Gardner, Jonathan
JONATHAN GARDNER J. Wolkoff cartoon *Art in America* v104 no11 p124 D 2016

Gardner, Kevin J.
Building Jerusalem: Elegies on Parish Churches J. P. Baumgaertner *Christian Century* v134 no3 p35 F 2017

Gardner, Rebecca
God Save the King! - Gloucester crowns a young prince *British Heritage Travel* v37 no6 p8 N/D 2016
LEEDS color *British Heritage Travel* v38 no5 p58 S/O 2017

Gardner, Richard J.
Multiple mechanisms for memory replay? bibl diag *Science* v355 no6321 p131 Ja 13 2017

GARDNER, ROYAL
International Wildlife Law: Understanding and Enhancing Its Role in Conservation *BioScience* v67 no9 p784 S 2017

Gardner, Sally
The Door That Led to Where *Publishers Weekly* v263 no40 p124 O 3 2016

Gardner, Samantha
EVERYDAY HEROES color *Runner's World* v51 no11 p16 D 2016

GARDNER, SHELLEY
Opportunities for Improved Transparency in the Timber Trade through Scientific Verification *BioScience* v66 no11 p990 N 1 2016

Gardner, T.
Fostering reproducibility in industry-academia research color *Science* v357 no6353 p759 Ag 25 2017

GARDNER, WILLIAM
Should 'Ballot Box Selfies' Be Banned? *New York Times Upfront* v149 no4 p22 O 31 2016

Gardner-Webb University
Week 2 color *Sports Illustrated* v127 no5 p60 Ag 14 2017

Gardon, Anne
The Evolution of Home color *Log Home Living* v34 no1 p38 F 2017

Garelick, Jon
NEC TEACHES JAZZ BY EXAMPLE bw color *Downbeat* v84 no10 p82 O 2017
ONE FAN AT A TIME color *Downbeat* v84 no9 p50 S 2017

Garff, Joakim
Kierkegaard's Muse: The Mystery of Regine Olsen *Publishers Weekly* v264 no17 p82 Ap 24 2017

Garfield (Comic strip)
MY HOMETOWN PAPER: Erin Ailworth E. Ailworth color *Co-*

lumbia Journal Review v56 no1 p81 Spr 2017

Garfield, Andrew, 1983-
HACKSAW RIDGE S. SLADE color *Reason* v48 no10 p64 Mr 2017
How Andrew Garfield Learned to Suffer Like the Saints S. Lansky color *Time* v189 no4 p51 Ja 23 2017
LEAD ACTOR CONTENDER ANDREW GARFIELD N. Sperling color *Entertainment Weekly* no1439 p46 N 11 2016
Scorsese's Passion P. Travers color *Rolling Stone* no1278/1279 p52 Ja 12 2017
SPIRITED AWAY J. Powers color *Vogue* v206 no12 p254 D 2016

Garfield, Andrew, 1983-—Interviews
Andrew Garfield S. Lansky color *Time* v188 no19 p57 N 7 2016
READER COMMENTS J. McGlynn, M. Conk et al *America* v216 no3 p7 F 6 2017

Garfinkle, Joel
How to Have Difficult Conversations When You Don't Like Conflict *Harvard Business Review Digital Articles* p2 My 24 2017

Garg, Lavanya
An Experiment in India Shows How Much Companies Have to Gain by Investing in Their Employees *Harvard Business Review Digital Articles* p1 Jl 25 2017

Gargano, Angela
WHO WILL BE THE NEXT FITNESS STAR? [Cover story] M. Gainsburg color *Women's Health* v14 no6 p(Sp)2 Jl 2017

Garibaldi, Jennye
SPIRITED AWAY chart color *Sunset* v239 no3 p24 S 2017

Garland, Judy, 1922-1969
The Glitterati T. STACKPOLE *Smithsonian* v47 no7 p22 N 2016

Garland, Val
RUNWAY REPORT Guarnieri color *Harper's Bazaar* no3650 p113 F 2017

Garland, Val—Interviews
Bold Always Wins A. Steinherr bw color *Glamour* v115 no11 p150 N 2017

Garlic
Buy 5, Drop 5 K. Glassman color *Women's Health* v13 no10 p98 D 2016
garlic V. Tweed color *Amazing Wellness* v9 no2 p12 Spr 2017
Planting garlic T. Brockman color *Christian Century* v133 no26 p11 D 21 2016

Garlic growers
GROWING GARLIC B. Modersohn *Successful Farming* v114 no11 p48 N 2016

Garlic growing
GROWING GARLIC B. Modersohn *Successful Farming* v114 no11 p48 N 2016

Garlic—Therapeutic use
BLACK GOLD W. Sheppard *Virginia Living* v15 no3 p27 Ap 2017
Put More Garlic in Your Life V. TWEED color *Better Nutrition* v79 no1 p24 Ja 2017

Garlin, Jeff, 1962-
INSIDE PEEK color *Chicago* v66 no6 p16 Je 2017
JEFF GARLIN [Cover story] B. Zehme color *Chicago* v66 no6 p132 Je 2017

Garlin, Jeff, 1962-—Interviews
Jeff Garlin R. Bruner color *Time* v189 no19 p50 My 22 2017

Garling, Caleb
INVENTORS color il *MIT Technology Review* v120 no5 p56 S/O 2017
PIONEERS color il *MIT Technology Review* v120 no5 p50 S/O 2017

GARLOCK, JODY
DIY DRAMA color *Better Homes & Gardens* v95 no7 p31 Jl 2017
EURO STAR *Better Homes & Gardens* v94 no12 p108 D 2016
everyday adventure *Better Homes & Gardens* v94 no11 p36 N 2016
a happy medium color diag *Better Homes & Gardens* v95 no5 p30 My 2017
i did it! color *Better Homes & Gardens* v95 no4 p50 Ap 2017
outside in color *Better Homes & Gardens* v95 no8 p44 Ag 2017
PEONY PINKS color *Better Homes & Gardens* v95 no5 p24 My 2017

GARMAN, JERRY
Chords & Discords color *Downbeat* v84 no9 p10 S 2017

GARMESTANI, AHJOND S.
Ecology for the Shrinking City *BioScience* v66 no11 p965 N 1 2016

GARMEY, JANE
ANNUAL RETURN color *Architectural Digest* v74 no8 p74 Ag 2017

Garmin International Inc.
GPSMAP® 8622 *Sea Magazine* v108 no12 p54 D 2016

Garmin Ltd.
A 360-DEGREE VIEW color *Flying* v144 no8 p13 Ag 2017
ENGINEER A BETTER BODY color *Men's Health* v31 no10 p(Sp)10 D 2016
Face off r. palmer color *Bike Magazine* v24 no7 p112 S 2017
GARMIN AUTOPILOTS! color *Flying* v144 no9 p18 S 2017
GARMIN D2 CHARLIE color *Flying* v144 no10 p20 O 2017
Garmin Quatix 5 Marine GPS Smartwatch J. Y. WOOD color *Power & Motoryacht* v34 no7 p28 Jl 2017
GARMIN VIRB ULTRA 30 D. Canet color *Cycle World* v56 no7 p22 Ag 2017
Gear P. Nielsen color *Sail* v48 no8 p28 Ag 2017
Looking Ahead M. Fisher color *Sail* v48 no6 p22 Je 2017
PORTABLE WEATHER color *Flying* v144 no11 p16 N 2017
Star Quality L. BECKETT color *Power & Motoryacht* v33 no4 p46 Ap 2017
SUPERCOMPUTERS M. Phillips color *Bicycling* v58 no6 p64 Jl 2017
Watch and Learn J. Y. WOOD color *Power & Motoryacht* v34 no11 p68 N 2017
WE FLY G1000 NXI S. POPE color *Flying* v144 no2 p56 F 2017

Garner, Dwight
COLLECTIVE Might color *Esquire* p70 Je/Jl 2017
Down and Out in FIRST CLASS color *Esquire* p56 N 2017
DRINKING GAMES bw color *Esquire* v166 no4 p82 N 2016
Making a SPLASH in the CITY color *Esquire* p44 Ag 2017
My BIG Foot color *Esquire* p68 Ap 2017
NAME DROPPING cartoon color *Esquire* v166 no5 p92 D 2016/Ja 2017
THE ROAD TAKEN color *Esquire* v167 no1 p52 F 2017
Run SILENT, Run DEEP bw *Esquire* p58 O 2017
SPENT color *Esquire* p72 S 2017
The TIPPING Point color *Esquire* v167 no2 p82 Mr 2017
You DIDN'T HEAR IT from Me... color *Esquire* p62 My 2017

Garner, Ethan C.
Treadmilling by FtsZ filaments drives peptidoglycan synthesis and bacterial cell division bibl graph *Science* v355 no6326 p739 F 17 2017

Garner, Hannah
Neutrophils take a round-trip diag *Science* v357 no6359 p42 O 6 2017

Garner, Helen
SCRUTINY J. WOOD cartoon *New Yorker* v92 no41 p73 D 12 2016

Garner, Jennifer, 1973-
DOING GOOD S. Simon color *InStyle* v24 no5 p62 My 2017

Garner, Julia, 1994-
Julia Garner M. Rich color *Current Biography* v78 no6 p43 Je 2017

Garner, Troy
FIELD GUIDE *Atlanta* v56 no11 p92 Mr 2017

Garnes, Norman
Families BEHIND the BADGE G. M. GRAFF color *AARP: The Magazine* v60 no1A p38 D 2016/Ja 2017

Garnett, Richard W.
Church, State & Playgrounds color *Commonweal* v114 no14 p12 S 8 2017

Garnier, Eric
Plant Functional Diversity: Organism Traits, Community Structure, and Ecosystem Properties M. J. LECHOWICZ *BioScience* v66 no12 p1082 D 1 2016
Synthesis Centers as Critical Research Infrastructure *BioScience* v67 no8 p750 Ag 2017

Garofalo-Wright, Lynn M.
Health Care Providers Must Stop Wasting Patients' Time *Harvard Business Review Digital Articles* p2 My 24 2017

Garofolo, John
Photos from the front line G. L. Buckley *America* v217 no2 p47

Jl 24 2017

Garrad, Lewis

The Dark Side of High Employee Engagement *Harvard Business Review Digital Articles* p2 Ag 16 2016

How to Make Work More Meaningful for Your Team *Harvard Business Review Digital Articles* p2 Ag 9 2017

If You Want to Motivate Employees, Stop Trusting Your Instincts color *Harvard Business Review Digital Articles* p2 F 8 2017

Garreta, Anne

Not One Day *Publishers Weekly* v264 no9 p72 F 27 2017

Garrett, Byron V.

THE ROLE OF THE FAMILY L. Deloza color *Literacy Today (2411-7862)* v34 no5 p24 Mr/Ap 2017

Garrett, Giannella M.

Friends for the Ages color *AARP: The Magazine* v60 no4A p42 Je/Jl 2017

GIUSEPPE BAUSILIO color *Dance Magazine* v91 no3 p22 Mr 2017

Shelby Colona *Dance Magazine* v91 no10 p22 O 2017

Garrett, Howard

BEST ORGANIC FERTILIZERS [Cover story] *Mother Earth News* no281 p16 Ap/My 2017

Garrett, Kevin

RED BALL EXPRES B. W. SMITH color *Dirt Sports + Off-Road* v51 no2 p14 F 2017

Garrett, Lynn

Becoming Awake and Aware *Publishers Weekly* v263 no39 p26 S 26 2016

Bending Toward Justice color *Publishers Weekly* v264 no4 p16 Ja 23 2017

Books for a Clearer Life color *Publishers Weekly* v264 no39 p23 S 25 2017

Christian Fiction Keeps Its Allure color *Publishers Weekly* v264 no21 p21 My 22 2017

Inspiration Is Everywhere color *Publishers Weekly* v264 no17 p20 Ap 24 2017

Inspiring Lives: Biographers immortalize the teachers and others who shaped their faith bw color *Publishers Weekly* v264 no29 p17 Jl 17 2017

Losing Their Religion bw color *Publishers Weekly* v264 no13 p19 Mr 27 2017

NEW VOICES ON TIMELESS SUBJECTS color *Publishers Weekly* v264 no32 p24 Ag 7 2017

Remembering the Spirit color *Publishers Weekly* v264 no25 p23 Je 19 2017

The Revolution, Then and Now color *Publishers Weekly* v263 no45 p8 N 7 2016

'TIS THE SEASON FOR DEVOTIONALS *Publishers Weekly* v263 no40 p84 O 3 2016

Waiting in the Wings color *Publishers Weekly* v263 no48 p20 N 28 2016

Garrett, Scott

Scott Garrett Turns to Extremists for Votes J. Green color *Bloomberg Businessweek* no4494 p29 O 10 2016

Garrett, Steven L.

Understanding Acoustics: An Experimentalist's View of Acoustics and Vibration P. Joseph *Physics Today* v70 no10 p61 O 2017

Garrett, Tim—Interviews

On the Job: Tim Garrett K. Cutlip *Weatherwise* v70 no1 p40 Ja/F 2017

Garrett, Tina

DANCING WITH ART T. ANGEL bw color *Missouri Life* v44 no3 p24 My 2017

Garrett, Wendy S.

Potential role of intratumor bacteria in mediating tumor resistance to the chemotherapeutic drug gemcitabine diag *Science* v357 no6356 p1156 S 15 2017

GARRIDO, EDGARD

Aftermath color *Nation* v305 no9 p11 O 16 2017

GARRIOTT, MOLLY

The Bertrand bw cartoon color diag *Nebraska Life* v21 no1 p72 Ja/F 2017

GARRISON, KEITH

THE THING THAT CHANGED IT ALL color *Bicycling* v58 no9 p19 O 2017

Garrison, Mike

Toolset Promotes Carbon-Capture Solution color *Science & Technology Review* p14 Ja/F 2017

Garrison, Peter

ALMOST THERE *Flying* v144 no7 p36 Jl 2017

BEYOND ENDURANCE color *Flying* v144 no2 p80 F 2017

DROP TEST color *Flying* v143 no12 p80 D 2016

HIGH, HEAVY AND SLOW *Flying* v144 no8 p34 Ag 2017

HUMAN, ALL TOO HUMAN *Flying* v144 no6 p34 Je 2017

HURRY HOME *Flying* v143 no12 p30 D 2016

IN THE REGION OF REVERSED COMMANDS *Flying* v144 no9 p34 S 2017

LEARNING TO RIDE A TRIKE *Flying* v144 no1 p30 Ja 2017

LITTLE PIES IN THE SKY: THE FUTURE IS ALMOST HERE bw *Flying* v144 no10 p80 O 2017

MORE THAN HE COULD HANDLE *Flying* v144 no4 p40 Ap 2017

A QUESTION OF JUDGMENT *Flying* v144 no3 p36 Mr 2017

REMEMBER BARRY GOLDWATER? color *Flying* v144 no1 p72 Ja 2017

ROTARY RISING diag *Flying* v144 no8 p80 Ag 2017

A SHORT HOP *Flying* v144 no5 p34 My 2017

STRANGE WINGS bw color *Flying* v144 no5 p80 My 2017

THE SYNTHETIC AND THE REAL color *Flying* v144 no7 p80 Jl 2017

TWO BOBS bw *Flying* v144 no9 p80 S 2017

THE UNSEEN *Flying* v144 no11 p34 N 2017

UNSTABILIZED APPROACH *Flying* v144 no2 p32 F 2017

VECTORS TO ZMB *Flying* v144 no10 p36 O 2017

VTOL RIDES AGAIN color *Flying* v144 no11 p80 N 2017

WE'D JUST LIKE TO ASK YOU A FEW QUESTIONS color *Flying* v144 no3 p88 Mr 2017

WHAT WORKED AND WHAT DIDN'T color *Flying* v144 no6 p80 Je 2017

WHY LEFT? color *Flying* v144 no4 p88 Ap 2017

Garrison, Vanessa

WHEN THE GIVING IS GOOD J. Thompson color *Essence* v47 no8 p114 D 2016

Garrity, John

Justin LEONARD color *Sports Illustrated* v127 no1 p74 Jl 3 2017

PENCIL WRECK color *Golf Magazine* v59 no4 p90 Ap 2017

What a Journey, Man! color *Golf Magazine* v59 no1 p21 Ja 2017

Garrow, David J.

All the President's Exes S. Begley color *Time* v189 no19 p55 My 22 2017

Portrait of Obama as a Young Man: A biography presents the former president as subordinating crucial aspects of his life—even love—to political expedience B. Staples *New York Times Book Review* p14 My 21 2017

Garrow, Stephen D.

How CEOs Can Work with an Active Board *Harvard Business Review Digital Articles* p2 Ag 8 2017

Garroway, Colin

Uptown Squirrels C. Kimmett color *Walrus* v14 no5 p26 Je 2017

Garry, Robert F.

Structural basis for antibody-mediated neutralization of Lassa virus [Cover story] color diag *Science* v356 no6341 p923 Je 1 2017

Garscadden, Alan

Explaining a few discoveries *Physics Today* v70 no9 p12 S 2017

Garskof, Josh

5 Things to Know About Renovating Your Bathroom color *Money* v46 no2 p33 Mr 2017

Lunch Break Money Boosters color *AARP: The Magazine* v30 no6A p19 O/N 2017

Need That Insurance? color *AARP: The Magazine* v60 no1A p24 D 2016/Ja 2017

The Right Flooring for Every Room chart color diag *Consumer Reports* v82 no8 p44 Ag 2017

Should a Robot Manage Your Money? cartoon *AARP: The Magazine* v60 no3A p22 Ap/My 2017

Garst, Karen L.

Women Beyond Belief: Discovering Life without Religion A. RECORD *Humanist* v77 no2 p42 Mr/Ap 2017

Garten, Ina, 1948-

I Love My Library color *House Beautiful* v159 no3 p124 Ap 2017

Who's That Lady? bw color *O, The Oprah Magazine* p127 Mr

2017

Garten, Ina, 1948-—Interviews

Ina Garten S. Begley color *Time* v190 no2/3 p100 Jl 10-17 2017

Gartner, Jared J.

Landscape of immunogenic tumor antigens in successful immuno-therapy of virally induced epithelial cancer graph *Science* v356 no6334 p200 Ap 14 2017

Garton, Eric

Engaging Your Employees Is Good, but Don't Stop There *Harvard Business Review Digital Articles* p2 D 9 2015

How Spotify Balances Employee Autonomy and Accountability color *Harvard Business Review Digital Articles* p2 F 9 2017

How to Make Agile Work for the C-Suite *Harvard Business Review Digital Articles* p2 Jl 19 2017

HR's Vital Role in How Employees Spend Their Time, Talent, and Energy diag *Harvard Business Review Digital Articles* p2 Ja 30 2017

What If Companies Managed People as Carefully as They Manage Money? *Harvard Business Review Digital Articles* p2 My 24 2017

Your Organization Wastes Time. Here's How to Fix It *Harvard Business Review Digital Articles* p2 Mr 13 2017

Garton, Neil

Click chemistry enables preclinical evaluation of targeted epigenetic therapies diag *Science* v356 no6345 p1397 Je 30 2017

Garton Ash, Timothy

Is Europe Disintegrating? color *New York Review of Books* v64 no1 p24 Ja 19 2017

A Pregnant Pause: Brexit is now certain, but the terms are not. Britain still has time to work with the EU, head off political strife, and minimize economic pain *Hoover Digest: Research & Opinion on Public Policy* no3 p93 Summ 2017

Robert B. Silvers (1929–2017) [Cover story] bw color *New York Review of Books* v64 no8 p31 My 11 2017

SETTING THE WORLD'S AGENDA M. C. McCARTHY *America* v215 no15 p35 N 14 2016

Ten Principles of Free Speech *Hoover Digest: Research & Opinion on Public Policy* no4 p159 Fall 2016

Garton Ash, Timothy—Interviews

"We Have to Hold the Line" I. Chotiner *Hoover Digest: Research & Opinion on Public Policy* no4 p155 Fall 2016

Garutti, Randy

Shake Shack: Recipes & Stories color *Publishers Weekly* v264 no14 p68 Ap 3. 2017

Garvey, Ed, 1940-2017

The Essence of Ed Garvey J. HIGHTOWER cartoon *Progressive* v81 no4 p70 Ap/My 2017

GARVEY, HUGH

"I Love Being on an Airplane. It's Like Going to the Spa for Six Hours." color *Conde Nast Traveler* v52 no9 p20 O 2017

ROARING LYON THE REVITALIZED CITY GETS A SAVVY NEW DESIGN HOTEL *Conde Nast Traveler* v52 no10 p32 N 2017

Garvey, John

Hiring for Mission color *Commonweal* v144 no3 p10 F 10 2017

What should guide U.S. immigration policy: self-interest or charity? *America* v216 no7 p10 Ap 3 2017

GARVEY, MARK

Humor in Uniform *Reader's Digest* v189 no1128 p134 Mr 2017

Garvin, Alexander

The Right Strategies A. Cohen color *Architectural Record* v204 no12 p33 D 2016

Garvin, David

Advice and Credibility Go Hand-in-Hand for Managers *Harvard Business Review Digital Articles* p2 Ja 13 2015

Reflecting on David Garvin's Imprint on Management S. Cliffe *Harvard Business Review Digital Articles* p2 My 18 2017

Garvin, Robert

You Can't Avoid Failure Unless You Do Nothing color *MIT Technology Review* v120 no1 p8 Ja/F 2017

Garvin, Shaniqua

Look at Us NOW! M. Simms color *O, The Oprah Magazine* p67 Ap 2017

Garwin, Richard L.

Sidney David Drell *Physics Today* v70 no9 p69 S 2017

GARWOOD, BIANCA

CHICER THAN RAP: HIP-HOP'S MOST FORMIDABLE FASHION VENTURES color map *Ebony* v72 no11 p80 S 2017

NOW STREAMING! color *Ebony* v72/73 no12/1 p88 O/N 2017

Gary (Ind.)

ArtHouse: A Social Kitchen *Architectural Record* v205 no4 p185 Ap 2017

Gary, Amy

Bohemian Rhapsody A. HENDERSON bw *Weekly Standard* v22 no41 p40 Jl 3 2017

Gary, Codi

Don't Call Me Sweetheart: Something Borrowed, Book 1 *Publishers Weekly* v264 no27 p61 Jl 3 2017

Gary, Heather Grennan

Out of service color *U.S. Catholic* v82 no4 p26 Ap 2017

GARY, JUNEAU MAHAN

Sport Promoting Human Development and Well-Being: Psychological Components of Sustainability *UN Chronicle* v53 no2 p30 2016

Garza, Victoria J.

Metal-catalyzed reductive coupling of olefin-derived nucleophiles: Reinventing carbonyl addition diag *Science* v354 no6310 paah5133-1 O 21 2016

Garzilli, Joanna

Big Miracles: The 11 Spiritual Rules for Ultimate Success *Publishers Weekly* v263 no51 p142 D 12 2016

Garzone, George

George Garzone's Tenor Sax Solo on 'In Memory Of Leanne Nichols' [Cover story] J. DURSO bw color *Downbeat* v84 no5 p82 My 2017

NIGHT LIFE *New Yorker* v93 no12 p9 My 8 2017

Garzouzi, Nicolas

the LONG VIEW I. PHILLIPS color *Architectural Digest* no5 p152 My 2017

Garzuglia, Monica

The extent of forest in dryland biomes [Cover story] chart map *Science* v356 no6338 p635 My 12 2017

Gas appliances—Vents

STUFF THERMALS SCREWED UP G. Leigh cartoon *Old House Journal* v45 no1 p54 F 2017

Gas chromatography equipment

Focus on test, measurement, and analytical equipment A. Mandelis *Physics Today* v70 no8 p66 Ag 2017

Gas chromatography—Evaluation

NEW PRODUCTS color *Science* v354 no6318 p1445 D 16 2016

Gas fields

Life on the Edge G. Raygorodetsky bw color graph map *National Geographic* v232 no4 p108 O 2017

Gas grills

In the SUNSET KITCHEN color *Sunset* v239 no1 p98 Jl 2017

Gas industry & the environment

The Coming War On Gas J. A. Dlouhy, M. Chediak et al color graph *Bloomberg Businessweek* no4519 p51 Ap 24 2017

Gas industry—Officials & employees

THE OLIGARCH WAITS R. Kolker bw color *Bloomberg Businessweek* no4512 p56 F 20 2017

Gas industry—United States

The Coming War On Gas J. A. Dlouhy, M. Chediak et al color graph *Bloomberg Businessweek* no4519 p51 Ap 24 2017

The U.S. unleashes the full power of shale, as a wave of its LNG exports hits the market N. S. Malik color map *Bloomberg Businessweek* no4496 p76 O 24 2016

Gas light fixtures

Resources *Old House Journal* v44 no8 p95 D 2016

Gas phase reactions

Global atmospheric particle formation from CERN CLOUD measurements E. M. Dunne, H. Gordon et al bibl graph map *Science* v354 no6316 p1119 D 2 2016

Gas pipeline design & construction

Flawed environmental justice analyses R. E. Emanuel color *Science* v357 no6348 p260 Jl 21 2017

Gas pipelines

BERKELEY SPRINGS, WEST VIRGINIA L. Elmaleh *Harper's Magazine* p36 O 2017

Gas pipelines—Canada

Pipelines imperil Canada's ecosystem J. J. Alava and N. Calle *Science* v355 no6321 p140 Ja 13 2017

Gas pipelines—Mediterranean Region

Big Gas Finds, Bigger Political Problems D. Wainer map *Bloomberg Businessweek* no4511 p37 F 13 2017

Gas prices

Buy the Gas Your Car Deserves D. MUHLBAUM *Kiplinger's Personal Finance* v71 no11 p71 N 2017

SB 1 ENSURES A GAS HIKE IS COMING P. M. ROHIT color *Sea Magazine* v109 no8 pCA-9 Ag 2017

TRAVEL SMART A. CONNERY color *Better Homes & Gardens* v95 no8 p182 Ag 2017

Gas storage

Alabama's "Chemical Katrina" M. Smith *Sierra* v102 no3 p20 My/Je 2017

Gas stoves

Change of Pace M. Rubino *Indianapolis Monthly* p12 Ap 2017

Gas stoves—Evaluation

GAS RANGES B. GOLD color *Good Housekeeping* v263 no5 p137 N 2016

Gas wells

PLUGGING THE PAST C. McKelvey and K. Martindale *New York State Conservationist* v71 no3 p18 D 2016

Program Highlights *New York State Conservationist* v71 no3 p21 D 2016

Gasc, S.

Xenon isotopes in 67P/Churyumov-Gerasimenko show that comets contributed to Earth's atmosphere diag *Science* v356 no6342 p1069 Je 9 2017

Gascony (France)

Comme des Gascons P. Guzmán color *Conde Nast Traveler* v52 no3 p74 Mr 2017

Gaskell, Elizabeth

Epigenetic plasticity and the hallmarks of cancer diag *Science* v357 no6348 p266 Jl 21 2017

Gaskill, Nicholas

Anticancer sulfonamides target splicing by inducing RBM39 degradation via recruitment to DCAF15 color diag *Science* v356 no6336 p397 Ap 28 2017

Gaskins, Sadie

How I Solved My Horse's Problem cartoon *Horse & Rider* v56 no1 p72 Ja 2017

Gasoline

No Cars Go C. SYLVESTER color *Walrus* v14 no7 p18 S 2017

Gasoline industry

GREAT UNKNOWNS cartoon *Popular Mechanics* v193 no7 p26 S 2016

Gasoline taxes

LET'S MAKE SOME SAUSAGE AGAIN K. Drum cartoon *Mother Jones* v42 no5 p12 S/O 2017

STATE TAXES SPIRAL UPWARD S. BLOCK cartoon *Kiplinger's Personal Finance* v71 no1 p13 Ja 2017

Gasoline taxes—California

Becau$e That'$ Democracy, Baby color *Weekly Standard* v22 no33 p2 My 8 2017

SB 1 ENSURES A GAS HIKE IS COMING P. M. ROHIT color *Sea Magazine* v109 no8 pCA-9 Ag 2017

Gasoline—Anti-knock & anti-knock mixtures

AMERICANS' $2 BILLION GAS MISTAKE M. C. White color *Money* v45 no10 p20 N 2016

High-Octane The key to efficiency? F. Markus cartoon *Motor Trend* v69 no2 p22 F 2017

Gáspár, Imre

RNA localization feeds translation color *Science* v357 no6357 p1235 S 22 2017

GASPARI, RICH

ANAVITE color *Muscle & Performance* v8 no12 p62 D 2016

Gasparini, Blaz

A cirrus cloud climate dial? map *Science* v357 no6348 p248 Jl 21 2017

Gasparri, Ignacio

Forest conservation: Remember Gran Chaco bibl color *Science* v355 no6324 p465 F 3 2017

Gasparrini, Francesca

A switch from canonical to noncanonical autophagy shapes B cell responses bibl graph *Science* v355 no6325 p641 F 10 2017

Gass, Ali

VOX: ART FOR THE PEOPLE E. FISHMAN color *Chicago* v66 no9 p54 S 2017

Gass, Henry

Counterprotesters greet "free speech rally" *Christian Century* v134 no19 p13 S 13 2017

Native Americans press to keep Bears Ears land a national monument *Christian Century* v134 no12 p17 Je 7 2017

New protected area in Utah includes land that's sacred for Native Americans color *Christian Century* v134 no3 p13 F 2017

Refugee plan divides religious leaders color *Christian Century* v134 no5 p12 Mr 1 2017

Supreme Court allows parts of travel ban to proceed before hearing case *Christian Century* v134 no16 p13 Ag 2 2017

Gassman-Pines, Anna

Linking job loss, inequality, mental health, and education color *Science* v356 no6343 p1127 Je 16 2017

Gassner, Dennis

Replicating The Replicants M. WAKIM color *Los Angeles Magazine* v62 no10 p140 O 2017

Gassner, M.

Gliogenic LTP spreads widely in nociceptive pathways bibl graph *Science* v354 no6316 p1144 D 2 2016

Gassner, Peter

Big Pharma's Friend A. KONRAD color *Forbes* v199 no6 p46 Je 13 2017

Gast, Alice P.

Physicists without borders *Physics Today* v70 no1 p10 Ja 2017

Gast, Leon

MUHAMMAD ALI color *Entertainment Weekly* no1446/1447 p90 D 2016/Ja 2017

Gastel, Barbara

Living up to my mentors cartoon *Science* v354 no6318 p1494 D 16 2016

GASTON, KEVIN J.

Doses of Neighborhood Nature: The Benefits for Mental Health of Living with Nature *BioScience* v67 no2 p147 F 2017

Gaston, Labadie

A Conversation with Neto Soldani *Arabian Horse World* v56 no12 p104 S 2016

Gastrectomy

Dramatic Changes *Virginia Living* v15 no1 p101 D 2016

Gastric diseases

QUESTIONS OF DIGESTION J. Szabo color *Amazing Wellness* v9 no3 p76 EarlySumm 2017

Gastrin-releasing peptide

Molecular and neural basis of contagious itch behavior in mice Yu, D. M. Barry et al bibl diag *Science* v355 no6329 p1072 Mr 10 2017

Gastroesophageal reflux

Make your voice heard! *Harvard Health Letter* v42 no7 p4 My 2017

Gastroesophageal reflux—Prevention

How Diet and Lifestyle Can Fight Heartburn and GERD *Tufts University Health & Nutrition Letter* v34 no10 p4 D 2016

What to eat when you have chronic heartburn *Harvard Health Letter* v42 no4 p6 F 2017

Gastrointestinal diseases

See also

Flatulence

Got Tummy Troubles? A. Patz color diag *Health* v30 no10 p85 D 2016

Problem Solved! [Cover story] R. LALIBERTE cartoon *Prevention* v68 no11 p18 N 2016

Gastrointestinal gas

8 Things You Should Never Do on an Airplane J. LABIANCA color *Reader's Digest* v189 no1129 p52 Ap 2017

STUDY: GAS IS IMPORTANT SIGN IN SAND COLIC CASES C. Barakat and M. McCluskey *Equus* no481 p12 O 2017

Gastrointestinal hemorrhage

A Gutsy Call D. G. ADLER color *Discover* v38 no2 p20 Mr 2017

Gastrointestinal hormones

See also

Somatostatin

Layer-specific modulation of neocortical dendritic inhibition during active wakefulness W. Muñoz, R. Tremblay et al bibl diag *Science* v355 no6328 p954 Mr 3 2017

Gastrointestinal system

Gaudet, Mitchell

Found and Formed: Glass artist Mitchell Gaudet finds the extraordinary in the ordinary J. DeBold *New Orleans Homes & Lifestyles* v20 no4 p30 Aut 2017

Gaudet, Rob

Rob Gaudet W. KALEC color *Louisiana Life* v37 no3 p52 Ja/F 2017

Gaudiano, Paolo

The Best Approach to Decision Making Combines Data and Managers' Expertise *Harvard Business Review Digital Articles* p2 Je 20 2017

Gauer, James

An Authentic Argument color *Architectural Record* v205 no2 p41 F 2017

Frank Lloyd Wright's Unity Temple Restored *Architectural Record* v205 no7 p36 Jl 2017

Full House *Architectural Record* v204 no11 p104 N 2016

The Great Divide *Architectural Record* v205 no4 p77 Ap 2017

In Harmony *Architectural Record* v204 no11 p49 N 2016

The Obamas Unveil Preliminary Design for Presidential Center *Architectural Record* v205 no6 p23 Je 2017

Steeling the Show *Architectural Record* v205 no6 p112 Je 2017

Gaukel, Erich

10 Tips: for scoring the best finds and prices at summer and fall outdoor antique markets *Treasures* v6 no6 p11 Je/Jl 2017

All About Color *Treasures* v6 no3 p14 D 2016/Ja 2017

Designers We'll Miss *Treasures* v6 no4 p4 F/Mr 2017

Early Signs of modernism *Treasures* v6 no5 p4 Ap/My 2017

The French Connection *Treasures* v6 no2 p4 O/N 2016

A Frink Lloyd Wright Home Built in the 1950s *Treasures* v6 no3 p4 D 2016/Ja 2017

Get Ready - It's Show Time! *Treasures* v6 no6 p4 Je/Jl 2017

Glass Vases by Ettore Sotsass: The late Italian architect and designer, known as much for his product designs as his buildings, was a master of color and shape *Treasures* v6 no6 p40 Je/Jl 2017

I LOVE IT *Treasures* v6 no3 p48 D 2016/Ja 2017

Mile-High Modern color *Treasures* v5 no5 p14 Ap/My 2016

Modern Metals *Treasures* v6 no2 p10 O/N 2016

A Montréal Gem *Treasures* v6 no5 p48 Ap/My 2017

Moved By Color *Treasures* v6 no2 p56 O/N 2016

Pyrex and Pickle Jars *Treasures* v6 no2 p6 O/N 2016

Survival of The Cutest *Treasures* v6 no2 p26 O/N 2016

Trivets *Treasures* v6 no4 p48 F/Mr 2017

Vermont Charm *Treasures* v6 no3 p10 D 2016/Ja 2017

Where new meets Old *Treasures* v5 no5 p4 Ap/My 2016

WHY I LOVE IT color *Treasures* v5 no5 p64 Ap/My 2016

Gault, Ross

THE GOOD, BAD, AND UGLY OF GLOBE-TREKKING DRAG WEEK COMPETITORS T. Taylor color *Hot Rod* v70 no2 p32 F 2017

Gaulton, Kyle J.

Detection of human adaptation during the past 2000 years bibl graph *Science* v354 no6313 p760 N 11 2016

GAUME, LAURENCE

Pitcher Plants Shape Up color diag *Natural History* v125 no5 p12 My 2017

Gaunitz, Charleen

Ancient genomic changes associated with domestication of the horse color diag *Science* v356 no6336 p442 Ap 28 2017

Gaunt, Matthew J.

A general catalytic β-C–H carbonylation of aliphatic amines to β-lactams bibl diag *Science* v354 no6314 p851 N 18 2016

Gaunt, Robert

REWIRING THE SENSE OF TOUCH E. Conant color *National Geographic* v232 no3 p19 S 2017

GAUR, VISHAL

CURING THE ADDICTION TO GROWTH color graph il img *Harvard Business Review* v95 no1 p66 Ja/F 2017

Gausman, Mary Alice

A LEAGUE OF HER OWN C. CUNNINGHAM *Cincinnati Magazine* v50 no7 p68 Ap 2017

Gautama Buddha, ca. 560 B.C.-ca. 480 B.C.

Is the Dharma Democratic? K. SPELLMEYER bw *Tricycle: The Buddhist Review* v26 no3 p62 Spr 2017

TREADING THE PATH WITH CARE [Cover story] W. HIGGINS color *Tricycle: The Buddhist Review* v26 no2 p38 Wint 2016

The Wisdom of TREES C. NEWMAN color *National Geographic* v231 no3 p52 Mr 2017

Gautama Buddha, ca. 560 B.C.-ca. 480 B.C.—Enlightenment

The Wisdom of TREES C. NEWMAN color *National Geographic* v231 no3 p52 Mr 2017

Gauthier, A.

Femtosecond electron-phonon lock-in by photoemission and x-ray free-electron laser chart diag *Science* v357 no6346 p71 Jl 7 2017

Gauthier, Julie

Build Your Own INCUBATOR *Mother Earth News* no280 p46 F/Mr 2017

Gautier, D.

Jupiter's interior and deep atmosphere: The initial pole-to-pole passes with the Juno spacecraft [Cover story] color graph *Science* v356 no6340 p821 My 26 2017

Gautreaux, Tim

The literary genius of Cervantes D. S. Hendrickson *America* v216 no9 p48 Ap 24 2017

Southern Echoes R. LEE color *New York Times Book Review* p18 Ja 29 2017

GAVAGAN, ED

Home of the Brave cartoon *Reader's Digest* v190 no1132 p99 Jl/Ag 2017

Gavaghan, Victoria

Fructose-driven glycolysis supports anoxia resistance in the naked mole-rat diag graph *Science* v356 no6335 p307 Ap 21 2017

gavelda, ben

dreams of youth color *Bike Magazine* v23 no9 p44 D 2016

Gaventa, Bill

Diversity and disability . . *Christian Century* v134 no10 p6 My 10 2017

Gavert, Nancy

Potential role of intratumor bacteria in mediating tumor resistance to the chemotherapeutic drug gemcitabine diag *Science* v357 no6356 p1156 S 15 2017

Gavett, Gretchen

The Essential Guide to Crafting a Work Email *Harvard Business Review Digital Articles* p2 Jl 24 2015

The Factors That Lead to a Pay Premium for Women *Harvard Business Review Digital Articles* p2 My 9 2016

The Factors That Lead to High CEO Pay *Harvard Business Review Digital Articles* p2 My 22 2015

How Counseling About Work Reduces Depression *Harvard Business Review Digital Articles* p2 Mr 6 2015

How Self-Service Kiosks Are Changing Customer Behavior *Harvard Business Review Digital Articles* p2 Mr 11 2015

How We'll Really Feel if Robots Take Our Jobs *Harvard Business Review Digital Articles* p2 Ja 16 2015

The Long-Term Effects of Tracking Employee Behavior *Harvard Business Review Digital Articles* p2 Jl 18 2016

Research: Companies See a Stock Bump After Executives Visit the White House *Harvard Business Review Digital Articles* p2 Jl 5 2017

Today's Automation Anxiety Was Alive and Well in 1960 *Harvard Business Review Digital Articles* p2 F 8 2016

Who Has Paid Sick Leave, Who Doesn't, and What's Changing *Harvard Business Review Digital Articles* p2 Ja 21 2015

Why Do We Publicly Shame People Out of Their Jobs? *Harvard Business Review Digital Articles* p2 Ap 6 2015

Workers Are Bad at Filling Out Timesheets, and It Costs Billions a Day *Harvard Business Review Digital Articles* p2 Ja 12 2015

Gavialis gangeticus

GOINGS ON ABOUT TOWN color *New Yorker* v93 no13 p7 My 15 2017

Gavier-Pizarro, Gregorio

Forest conservation: Remember Gran Chaco bibl color *Science* v355 no6324 p465 F 3 2017

Gavin, Catherine

Seattle Children's Hospital, South Clinic *Architectural Record* v205 no4 p189 Ap 2017

GAVIN, JAMES

The Divine One: A classic jazz singer turned husbands into managers and listeners into fans *New York Times Book Review* p22 Jl 23 2017

Gaviria, César
　Leaders color *Time* v189 no16/17 p64 My 1-8 2017
Gawande, Atul
　AFTERMATH bw cartoon *New Yorker* v92 no38 p48 N 21 2016
　IS HEALTH CARE A RIGHT? cartoon *New Yorker* v93 no30 p48
　　O 2 2017
　Points to Ponder color *Reader's Digest* v190 no1133 p25 S 2017
　TELL ME WHERE IT HURTS cartoon *New Yorker* v92 no46 p36
　　Ja 23 2017
　TRUMPCARE cartoon *New Yorker* v93 no3 p21 Mr 6 2017
Gawker Media LLC
　Gawkermania M. CONTINETTI *Commentary* v142 no1 p64 Jl/
　　Ag 2016
Gawker Media LLC—Trials, litigation, etc.
　DOWN AND DIRTY M. Potter color *Esquire* v167 no1 p82 F
　　2017
Gawrylewski, Andrea
　Bugged: The Insects Who Rule the World and the People Ob-
　　sessed with Them color *Scientific American* v317 no1 p72 Jl
　　2017
　Endangered color *Scientific American* v317 no4 p86 O 2017
　Explorers' Sketchbooks: The Art of Discovery & Adventure color
　　Scientific American v316 no4 p76 Ap 2017
　Never Out of Season: How Having the Food We Want When We
　　Want It Threatens Our Food Supply and Our Future color *Scien-
　　tific American* v316 no3 p76 Mr 2017
　Where the Animals Go: Tracking Wildlife with Technology in 50
　　Maps and Graphics color map *Scientific American* v317 no3 p88
　　S 2017
　Woolly: The True Story of the Quest to Revive One of History's
　　Most Iconic Extinct Creatures color *Scientific American* v317
　　no2 p80 Ag 2017
Gay, Denise L.
　Regeneration of fat cells from myofibroblasts during wound heal-
　　ing bibl color graph *Science* v355 no6326 p748 F 17 2017
Gay, Jason
　On with the Show color *Vogue* v206 no11 p212 N 2016
　WITHOUT A NET color *Vogue* v207 no9 p630 S 2017
Gay, Mary-Louise
　Short Stories for Little Monsters *Publishers Weekly* v264 no4 p79
　　Ja 23 2017
Gay, Michael J.
　WHERE & WHEN *Washingtonian Magazine* v52 no5 p31 F 2017
Gay, Parker
　FROM OUR READERS *Archaeology* v70 no4 p8 Je-Ag 2017
Gay, Roxane
　Black Lives Imagined *New York Times Book Review* p10 O 16
　　2016
　CARELESS LANGUAGE, AND THE ELECTION *Vital Speech-
　　es of the Day* v83 no4 p115 Ap 2017
　Come In, Charlie color *InStyle* v24 no4 p208 Ap 2017
　CONSUMED M. FERNANDEZ *Indianapolis Monthly* v40 no11
　　p72 Jl 2017
　CONVERSATIONS WITH KEYNOTERS C. Kirch color *Pub-
　　lishers Weekly* v264 no3 p4 Ja 16 2017
　Hunger L. Greenblatt color *Entertainment Weekly* no1470 p62 Je
　　16 2017
　MADONNA bw *Harper's Bazaar* no3650 p148 F 2017
　The Meaning of Michelle bw color *Glamour* v114 no12 p198 D
　　2016
　Quenching Your Thirst color *InStyle* v24 no9 p214 S 2017
　ROXANE GAY color *Entertainment Weekly* no1449 p61 Ja 20
　　2017
　Wild at Heart G. SIEFF *New York Times Book Review* p18 Ja 8
　　2017
Gay, Roxane—Interviews
　Roxane Gay color *New York Times Book Review* p7 Ja 29 2017
Gay, Roxanne—Interviews
　Roxane Gay C. FEHRMAN *Indianapolis Monthly* v40 no5 p19
　　Ja 2017
Gay, Trinity
　THE INTERSECTION bw color *Runner's World* v51 no11 p25
　　D 2016
　THE LOVELY LONELINESS J. BEVERLY cartoon *Runner's
　　World* v51 no11 p26 D 2016
　Teen Tragedy A. Fenwick and T. Keith color *Sports Illustrated*

　v125 no15 p26 N 7 2016
Gay activists
　FORBIDDEN LIVES M. GESSEN cartoon color *New Yorker* v93
　　no19 p22 Jl 3 2017
Gay activists—Interviews
　50 YEARS AFTER THE HOMOSEXUALS B. CONNELLY bw
　　Advocate no1089 p12 F/Mr 2017
Gay actors
　52 MINUTES WITH ... Andrew Rannells E. A. JUNG img *New
　　York* v50 no8 p18 Ap 17 2017
Gay actors—Interviews
　COMING OUT-OF THE COFFIN: Born on Halloween, actor
　　MASSIMO DOBROVIC was destined to play the king of vam-
　　pires, but "happily married gay man" may be his favorite role
　　yet D. ANDERSON-MINSHALL *Advocate* no1093 p61 O/N
　　2017
Gay adoption laws
　Closing Options for Adoptions N. SCHAEFER RILEY color
　　Weekly Standard v22 no40 p12 Je 26 2017
Gay artists—Interviews
　MYSTERIOUS SKIN J. ANDERSON-MINSHALL *Advocate*
　　no1088 p32 D 2016/Ja 2017
Gay bars
　A Change of Venue N. MARTINEZ *Los Angeles Magazine* v62
　　no6 p85 Je 2017
　Drags to Riches C. ZEIGLER color *Indianapolis Monthly* v42 no2
　　p20 O 2017
　JULIA STREET | WITH POYDRAS THE PARROT J. STREET
　　bw *New Orleans Magazine* v51 no6 p22 Ap 2017
Gay bookstores
　Between the Lines J. THOMAS bw color *Advocate* no1089 p62
　　F/Mr 2017
Gay choreographers
　MR. JONES: THERE ARE FEW THINGS MORE INTEREST-
　　ING THAN WATCHING THIS DANCER/CHOREOGRA-
　　PHER MOVE HIS BODY S. ABADSIDIS color *Advocate*
　　no1091 p89 Je/Jl 2017
Gay community
　IS DC BECOMING THE GAY CAPITAL OF AMERICA? K.
　　OLSEN *Washingtonian Magazine* v53 no1 p10 O 2017
Gay couples
　5 THINGS I LEARNED FROM DATING A BI GUY: Lasting
　　lessons learned from a relationship with a bisexual man. BY-
　　ALEXENDERCHEVES *Advocate* no1093 p57 O/N 2017
　How Do I Deal With a Gun At a Relative's Home? K. A. Appiah
　　New York Times Magazine p16 Ag 13 2017
Gay employees
　　　　　See also
　　　Lesbian employees
　What a Study of French Auditors Shows About Homophobia at
　　Work T. Roulet and S. Stenger *Harvard Business Review Digital
　　Articles* p2 Mr 29 2017
Gay executives
　Why Tim Cook's Coming Out Matters for Apple, and Business D.
　　Clark *Harvard Business Review Digital Articles* p2 O 30 2014
Gay Lesbian & Straight Education Network Inc.
　HOLLYWOOD HONORS LGBTQ YOUTH ADVOCATES R.
　　Kinane color *Entertainment Weekly* no1438 p20 N 4 2016
Gay male activists
　Stuck in the Middle with You: A black gay activist ponders mid-
　　Life C. STEPHENS *Advocate* no1093 p51 O/N 2017
Gay male artists
　SOUL GATHERING C. Arnold color *Essence* v47 no12 p68 Ap
　　2017
Gay male executives
　WHAT ABOUT BOB? THE GAY CHAIRMAN OF NBC EN-
　　TERTAINMENT WANTS TO ENLIGHTEN AND ENTER-
　　TAIN AMERICA D. REYNOLDS *Advocate* no1093 p42 O/N
　　2017
Gay men on television
　THIRTYSOMETHING UNDER COVERS B. Keith color *Enter-
　　tainment Weekly* no1460/1461 p40 Ap 7-17 2017
Gay men—Sexual behavior
　MORE THAN 40% OF GAY AND BI MEN ARE HAVING
　　CONDOMLESS SEX J. ANDERSON-MINSHALL *Advocate*
　　no1088 p27 D 2016/Ja 2017

THE NEW GAY SEXUAL REVOLUTION: PrEP, TasP, and fearless sex remind us we can't advance social justice without including sex in the equation J. ANDERSON-MINSHALL color
Advocate no1091 p115 Je/Jl 2017

Gay men's bars
A Change of Venue N. MARTINEZ *Los Angeles Magazine* v62
no6 p85 Je 2017

Gay motion picture producers & directors—Interviews
WAKEFIELD POOLE A. CHEE *Interview* v47 no3 p28 My 2017

Gay people
See also
  Gay travelers
  Lesbians
My First Year K. Bonnell bw color *Glamour* v115 no1 p48 Ja 2017

Gay people—China
HIV infections are spiking among young gay Chinese K.
McLaughlin color graph *Science* v355 no6332 p1359 Mr 31
2017

Gay politicians
Elio Di Rupo E. E. Turner *Current Biography* v78 no8 p31 Ag
2017
Meet Chicago's Movement Politician D. D. GUTTENPLAN color
Nation v305 no3 p22 Jl 31 2017

Gay pornography
ONE IN FIVE STRAIGHT MEN WATCHES GAY SEX B. SHU-
CART color *Advocate* no1089 p17 F/Mr 2017

Gay Pride Day
DON'T MISS THIS: OUR TOP FIVE PICKS FOR OCTOBER
Atlanta v57 no6 p38 O 2017

Gay pride parades
THE COLORS OF PRIDE P. STEFÁNSSON color *Iceland Re-
view* v54 no5 p3 S-O 2016
From the Editor P. Stefánsson color *Iceland Review* v54 no5 p4
S-O 2016

Gay rights
keeping score *Ms.* v26 no4 p6 Wint 2016

Gay rights—Lawsuits & claims
A Cake Dispute Rises To the Highest Court G. Stohr color *Bloomberg Businessweek* no4539 p43 S 25 2017

Gay rights—Religious aspects—Christianity
Wicked Ways M. Hemingway color *Weekly Standard* v22 no45
p8 Ag 7 2017

Gay rights—United States
THE NUMBER THAT NO MAN COULD NUMBER A. Heilbut
Harper's Magazine v334 no2001 p60 F 2017
Religious Liberty after Obergefell A. DESANCTIS color *National
Review* v69 no11 p19 Je 12 2017
SIX THINGS WE MUST DO TO SURVIVE TRUMP'S AMERI-
CA M. J. STERN color *Advocate* no1089 p42 F/Mr 2017
TIME TO PANIC M. GESSEN color *Advocate* no1089 p38 F/Mr
2017

Gay seminarians
READ color *Advocate* no1091 p36 Je/Jl 2017

Gay travelers
Greenland: Singular, Spectacular, Surprising C. LISOTTA color
Advocate no1089 p50 F/Mr 2017

Gay websites
Can I Out My Ex-Husband To His Girlfriend? K. A. Appiah *New
York Times Magazine* p20 Ja 8 2017

Gaya, Mauro
A switch from canonical to noncanonical autophagy shapes B cell
responses bibl graph *Science* v355 no6325 p641 F 10 2017

Gayley, Holly
INSEPARABLE ACROSS LIFETIMES color *Tricycle: The Buddhist Review* v27 no1 p76 Fall 2017

Gaynes Levy, Sara
The Beginner's Guide to Standing on Your Head color *Glamour*
v114 no7 p90 Jl 2016

Gaynor, Kaitlin M.
Eating ecosystems color *Science* v356 no6334 p136 Ap 14 2017

Gaynor, Michael J.
19 THINGS YOU REALLY OUGHT TO 00 THIS MONTH
Washingtonian Magazine v52 no3 p31 D 2016
19 THINGS YOU REALLY OUGHT TO DO THIS MONTH
Washingtonian Magazine v52 no1 p33 O 2016
2017 TECH TITANS *Washingtonian Magazine* v52 no8 p59 My

2017
ARTS GUIDE: Among all the plays, exhibits, concerts, and other
arts events ahead, here are 12 we most want to see in the fall and
beyond *Washingtonian Magazine* v52 no12 p40 S 2017
Celebrate the Occasion *Washingtonian Magazine* v52 no4 p104
Ja 2017
Destination: The Airports *Washingtonian Magazine* v52 no2 p80
N 2016
FOTOWEEKDC *Washingtonian Magazine* v52 no2 p35 N 2016
How I Spent 24 Hours at Dulles *Washingtonian Magazine* v52
no2 p87 N 2016
THE NERDIEST GROUP HOUSE IN WASHINGTON *Washing-
tonian Magazine* v52 no2 p74 N 2016
Self-Driving Cars will change local real estate color *Washingto-
nian Magazine* v52 no7 p96 Ap 2017
WHERE & WHEN: 18 THINGS YOU REALLY OUGHT TO
DO THIS MONTH *Washingtonian Magazine* v52 no11 p31 Ag
2017
WHERE & WHEN color *Washingtonian Magazine* v52 no7 p31
Ap 2017
WHERE & WHEN *Washingtonian Magazine* v52 no8 p35 My
2017

Gazella, Karolyn
Potent Cancer Fighters *Amazing Wellness* v9 no1 p30 Wint 2017

Gazpacho
A Matter of Taste: Perfecting gazpacho beyond a recipe's instruc-
tions by learning to trust your own palate S. Nosrat *New York
Times Magazine* p24 Jl 2 2017
Sweet Corn Gazpacho L. POWERS and K. O'SHEA-EVANS
color *House Beautiful* p47 Jl 2017

Gazzaley, Adam
THE REVOLUTION STARTS HERE color *Fortune* v174 no7
p26 D 1 2016

Gbajabiamila, Akbar
COWBOY NINJA: THE RANCHER AS OBSTACLE RACER T.
T. MURRISON *Idaho Magazine* v16 no10 p6 Jl 2017

Gdula, Michal
PCGF3/5–PRC1 initiates Polycomb recruitment in X chromosome inactivation color *Science* v356 no6342 p1081 Je 9 2017

Ge, Chenghao
Notch-Jagged complex structure implicates a catch bond in tuning
ligand sensitivity bibl diag graph *Science* v355 no6331 p1320
Mr 24 2017

Ge, Preston
Pathological α-synuclein transmission initiated by binding lymphocyte-activation gene 3 bibl graph *Science* v353 no6307
paah3374-1 S 30 2016

GE Appliances (Company)
How GE Appliances Built an Innovation Lab to Rapidly Prototype
Products B. Kapoor, K. Nolan et al *Harvard Business Review
Digital Articles* p2 Jl 18 2017

Ge Fu
Generation of influenza A viruses as live but replication-incom-
petent virus vaccines bibl graph *Science* v354 no6316 p1170
D 2 2016

Gea-Mallorquí, Ester
Mapping the human DC lineage through the integration of high-
dimensional techniques diag *Science* v356 no6342 p1044 Je 9
2017

Gearhart, John
Managing cell and human identity cartoon *Science* v356 no6334
p139 Ap 14 2017

Gearhart, Mark
BARK + BITE color *Hot Rod* v70 no8 p68 Ag 2017
Boost-Ready color *Hot Rod* v70 no5 p20 My 2017
IRON SUPPLEMENT color *Hot Rod* v70 no6 p86 Je 2017
Upped Ante color diag graph *Hot Rod* v70 no7 p54 Jl 2017

Gearhart, Sarah
THE ART OF COOL color *Bicycling* v58 no4 p18 My 2017
BARCELONA SPAIN color *Runner's World* v52 no8 p85 S 2017

Gearing
See also
  Automobile transmission
  Helical gears
  Ratchets
REAREND REDUX S. RICHARDS color *Dirt Sports + Off-*

Road v51 no11 p26 N 2017

Save Money: Burn Less Fuel M. SMITH color *Power & Motory-acht* v33 no1 p98 Ja 2017

Gearing—Equipment & supplies

FOX TRANSFER PERFORMANCE N. Formosa color *Bike Magazine* v24 no2 p85 Mr 2017

Gebbia, Marinella

Exploring genetic suppression interactions on a global scale diag *Science* v354 no6312 p599 N 4 2016

Gebbie, Katharine Blodgett

Lens Crafter F. Krentcil bw *Glamour* v115 no3 p36 Mr 2017

Gebelein, Brian

Control of species-dependent cortico-motoneuronal connections underlying manual dexterity diag graph *Science* v357 no6349 p400 Jl 28 2017

Gebhards, Stacy

STACE J. DAVIDSON color *Idaho Magazine* v16 no1 p18 O 2016

Gebhardt, Catalina

The formation of peak rings in large impact craters bibl color graph *Science* v354 no6314 p878 N 18 2016

Gebien, Darryl

Bad medicine J. GATEHOUSE color *Maclean's* no1 p30 F 17 2017

Gebre, Samuel

How to Help Africa Feed Itself *Bloomberg Businessweek* no4520 p20 My 1 2017

Geckler, Megan—Interviews

Tape Player color *O, The Oprah Magazine* p26 Ag 2017

Geddes, Jane

See Jane Thrive M. Bamberger color *Golf Magazine* v59 no7 p112 Jl 2017

Geddes, Jennifer Kelly

"Bad Mommy" Guilt Busters cartoon color *Working Mother* p54 F/Mr 2017

wear with care *Parents* v92 no5 p116 My 2017

GEDDES, JOHN

AW SHUCKS. ME? LEADER? color *Maclean's* v130 no7 p32 Ag 2017

THE BUMPY ROAD AHEAD [Cover story] color *Maclean's* v129 no42 p14 O 24 2016

Engaging the third solitude *Maclean's* v130 no7 p14 Ag 2017

Fire alarm color *Maclean's* v130 no4 p34 My 2017

THE INTERVIEW color *Maclean's* v129 no43 p12 O 31 2016

The last lines of defence color *Maclean's* v130 no3 p22 Ap 2017

The Liberal lowlights color *Maclean's* p29 Je 2017

LIFETIME ACHIEVEMENT AWARD color *Maclean's* v129 no47 p24 N 28 2016

NEW LIFE LESSONS color *Maclean's* v130 no4 p35 My 2017

PARLIAMENTARIAN OF THE YEAR color *Maclean's* v129 no47 p18 N 28 2016

A pivot to the pragmatic color *Maclean's* v129 no42 p26 O 24 2016

Reforming the reformers color *Maclean's* v129 no42 p18 O 24 2016

SELLING A FAIRER ECONOMY [Cover story] color *Maclean's* v129 no51/52 p27 D 26 2016

'THE AMERICAN DREAM MOVED TO CANADA' color *Maclean's* v129 no47 p28 N 28 2016

'THE ONLY ONE SMILING WILL BE PUTIN' color *Maclean's* v129 no46 p40 N 21 2016

This one's on the house color *Maclean's* v129 no45 p22 N 14 2016

Geden, Oliver

Anchor Management color *Issues in Science & Technology* v33 no2 p91 Wint 2017

Gedik, Nuh

Large, valley-exclusive Bloch-Siegert shift in monolayer WS2 bibl diag *Science* v355 no6329 p1066 Mr 10 2017

GEDMIN, JEFFREY

Five-Alarm Fire color *Weekly Standard* v22 no16 p30 D 26 2016

Gedzelman, Stanley David

Book Review: Where Meteorology Meets Art G. Siscoe *Weatherwise* v70 no2 p37 Mr/Ap 2017

Is Global Warming Good, or Was Arrhenius Erroneous? *Weatherwise* v70 no1 p30 Ja/F 2017

Gee, Alastair

The Shortlist / L.G.B.T. Fiction *New York Times Book Review* p50 N 13 2016

Gee, Michael

The Talk About Racial Bias Companies Should Be Having *Harvard Business Review Digital Articles* p2 Ag 23 2016

Gee, Samantha

An Expert Opinion on Where to Recharge This Season bw chart *Conde Nast Traveler* v52 no1 p112 Ja 2017

Geels, Frank W.

Sociotechnical transitions for deep decarbonization color diag *Science* v357 no6357 p1242 S 22 2017

Geese

Make a Splash P. Bourjaily color *Field & Stream* v122 no4 pF5 S 2017

Gefen, Orit

Antibiotic tolerance facilitates the evolution of resistance bibl bw chart diag graph *Science* v355 no6327 p826 F 24 2017

Gefen, Tuvia

Submillihertz magnetic spectroscopy performed with a nanoscale quantum sensor diag *Science* v356 no6340 p832 My 26 2017

GEFFNER, MARCIE

Stopping Suicdes color *Publishers Weekly* v264 no25 p104 Je 19 2017

Geforce (Company)

GeForce GTX 970 settlement website opens, Nvidia will pay graphics card owners $30 B. CHACOS color *PCWorld* p32 O 2016

Geheb, Ben

How Industrial Systems Are Turning into Digital Services *Harvard Business Review Digital Articles* p2 Je 23 2015

Geher, Glenn

16 LIFE LESSONS *Psychology Today* v49 no5 p62 S/O 2016

Gehl, Katherine M.

WHY POLITICS IS FAILING AMERICA color *Fortune* v175 no4 p74 Mr 15 2017

Gehlbach, Hunter

Building a better measure of school quality color il *Phi Delta Kappan* v98 no7 p43 Ap 2017

Learning to walk in another's shoes color *Phi Delta Kappan* v98 no6 p8 Mr 2017

Gehrels, Neil, 1952-2017

Cornelis A. Gehrels S. B. Cenko and F. Reddy *Physics Today* v70 no10 p75 O 2017

How to Swallow a Sun color *Scientific American* v316 no4 p38 Ap 2017

Gehrenbeck, Rick

Roland FP-90 color *Downbeat* v84 no1 p107 Ja 2017

Yamaha MX88 color *Downbeat* v84 no9 p98 S 2017

Gehring, David

CHARITY, PEACE, VITRIOL AND WAR: An ambitious survey of the 'Reformations' brilliantly conveys the drama of this convulsive period *History Today* v67 no10 p100 O 2017

GEHRING, WES D.

Hitch onto TCM *USA Today Magazine* v146 no2866 p76 Jl 2017

The Shadow of 1957 *USA Today Magazine* v145 no2860 p62 Ja 2017

"Star Wars" Goes Rogue *USA Today Magazine* v145 no2858 p63 N 2016

Teaming Up to Be Funny *USA Today Magazine* v145 no2858 p61 N 2016

Words of Past Images *USA Today Magazine* v146 no2868 p49 S 2017

GEHRT, STANLEY D.

Modernization, Risk, and Conservation of the World's Largest Carnivores *BioScience* v67 no7 p646 Jl 2017

Gehry, Frank O., 1929-

Bilbao Now A. H. GRAHAM color *Conde Nast Traveler* v52 no7 p44 Ag 2017

Gehry Archive Goes to Getty A. KLIMOSKI color *Architectural Record* v205 no5 p28 My 2017

Geib, Glenn

The Priceless Car Loan M. LALIBERTE and A. LEWIS color *Reader's Digest* v189 no1131 p86 Je 2017

Geibert, Walter

Dissolved organic sulfur in the ocean: Biogeochemistry of a petagram inventory bibl chart diag graph *Science* v354 no6311

p456 O 28 2016

Genomic databases: A WHO affair *Science* v356 no6340 p812 My 26 2017

GEIER, KATHLEEN

Abortion's No Wedge. It's a Winning Issue *In These Times* v41 no7 p16 Jl 2017

Does the Left Bear Any Blame for Trump? *In These Times* v41 no2 p12 F 2017

Geiger, Beth

Ghostly glimpses of Earth's glacial past color *Science News* v191 no10 p32 My 27 2017

Science News for Students color *Science News* v192 no4 p33 S 16 2017

Geiger, Chris

ALL AROUND THE FARM *Successful Farming* v115 no2 p79 F 2017

GEIGER, JOHN

Prince Albert II color *Canadian Geographic* v137 no5 p17 S/O 2017

Geiger, Keri

Legalio Password? color *Bloomberg Businessweek* no4495 p30 O 17 2016

The Rich Refugees Who Saved Trump cartoon *Bloomberg Businessweek* no4515 p14 Mr 20 2017

Geiger, Tray

All sizzle and no steak color graph il *Phi Delta Kappan* v99 no2 p53 O 2017

Geikie, Sarah

Develop Your Feel and Find Harmony color *Dressage Today* v23 no10 p26 Jl 2017

Geim, A. K.

High-temperature quantum oscillations caused by recurring Bloch states in graphene superlattices color *Science* v357 no6347 p181 Jl 14 2017

Geisel, Pamela

HOW FIT ARE YOU REALLY? K. A. Fetters chart color *Women's Health* v14 no4 p68 My 2017

Geiselman, Eric, 1988-

Geiselman (There Are Two) B. FLEMISTER color *Surfing Magazine* v53 no3 p32 Mr 2017

Geishas

SPIRITED AWAY L. Schillinger color *Vogue* v207 no3 p476 Mr 2017

Geisinger Health System (Company)

How an Early Adopter of Electronic Health Records Uses Big Data A. R. Erskine, B. Karunakaran et al *Harvard Business Review Digital Articles* p2 D 15 2016

Why This Health System Offers Refunds to Dissatisfied Patients J. R. Slotkin, C. D. Wendling et al *Harvard Business Review Digital Articles* p2 N 16 2016

Geissler, Phillip L.

Single-particle mapping of nonequilibrium nanocrystal transformations bibl bw graph *Science* v354 no6314 p874 N 18 2016

Geisst, Charles

BEWARE OF SHARKS P. Coy cartoon *Bloomberg Businessweek* no4518 p75 Ap 10 2017

Geist, Edward Moore

(Automated) planning for tomorrow: Will artificial intelligence get smarter? bibl *Bulletin of the Atomic Scientists* v73 no2 p80 Mr 2017

The secret of the SOVIET HYDROGEN BOMB *Physics Today* v70 no4 p40 Ap 2017

Geithner, Timothy F., 1961-

Are We Safe Yet? T. F. Geithner color *Foreign Affairs* v96 no1 p54 Ja/F 2017

Gel permeation chromatography—Equipment & supplies

NEW PRODUCTS: PROTEIN ANALYSIS color *Science* v354 no6310 p373 O 21 2016

Geladaki, Aikaterini

A subcellular map of the human proteome color *Science* v356 no6340 p820 My 26 2017

Gelato

Churn and Burn B. Marks and T. Keith color *Sports Illustrated* v127 no2 p20 Jl 17 2017

Gelato (Poem)

GELATO G. Stern *New Yorker* v93 no8 p46 Ap 10 2017

Gelb, Arthur, 1924-2014

EUGENE O'NEILL J. McCARTER color *New York Times Book Review* p27 D 4 2016

Our Worst Great Playwright F. O'Toole bw *New York Review of Books* v64 no9 p4 My 25 2017

Gelb, Barbara

13. Read By Women Possessed *New York* v49 no21 p121 O 17 2016

Gelb, Betsy D.

An Unlikely Marketing Lesson from Patent Lawyers *Harvard Business Review Digital Articles* p2 N 25 2014

Gelb, Gabriel M.

An Unlikely Marketing Lesson from Patent Lawyers *Harvard Business Review Digital Articles* p2 N 25 2014

Gelder, Paul

Summer Storm Batters OSTAR color *Sail* v48 no8 p18 Ag 2017

Geldings

Aged Arabian Geldings color *Horse & Rider* v56 no9 p59 S 2017

Aged Quarter Horse Geldings J. BAGKEY color *Horse & Rider* v56 no8 p51 Ag 2017

ask the experts C. Coley, I. Norris et al color *Dressage Today* p66 My 2017

Choose the Best Jumper J. Winkel color *Practical Horseman* v45 no6 p11 Je 2017

CONFORMATION CLINIC K. Banister color *Horse & Rider* v56 no4 p39 Ap 2017

CONFORMATION CLINIC S. Curl color *Horse & Rider* v56 no1 p31 Ja 2017

Conformation Correction color *Horse & Rider* v56 no3 p11 Mr 2017

Coping with a "macho" gelding K. A. Houpt color *Equus* no476 p89 My 2017

DRESSAGE SNAPSHOTS color *Dressage Today* v23 no5 p13 Ja 2017

One horse's journey T. Boros color *Equus* no476 p85 My 2017

Promoting Weight Gain After Illness C. THUNES and C. FINNO *Horse & Rider* v56 no3 p12 Mr 2017

Senior Quarter Horse Geldings M. KAPUSHION color *Horse & Rider* v56 no10 p53 O 2017

What Causes a Thin Mane and Tail? [Cover story] K. DELPH *Horse & Rider* v56 no1 p14 Ja 2017

Geldings—Behavior

The Company You Keep N. Chirico color *Horse & Rider* v56 no4 p19 Ap 2017

Help for a Nervous Pattern Horse J. Mellott color *Horse & Rider* v56 no4 p73 Ap 2017

Geldner, Niko

Root diffusion barrier control by a vasculature-derived peptide binding to the SGN3 receptor color *Science* v355 no6322 p280 Ja 20 2017

GELERNTER, DANIEL

Startupworld color *Weekly Standard* v22 no28 p40 Mr 27 2017

GELERNTER, JOSH

Glenn the Good [Cover story] bw *National Review* v68 no24 p22 D 31 2016

On Your Honor *Weekly Standard* v22 no22 p38 F 13 2017

A Right to Keep and Drive Cars? cartoon *Weekly Standard* v22 no7 p16 O 24 2016

GELINAS, NICOLE

City Limits: The renewal of central cities has also made them more unequal and segregated, a new book argues *New York Times Book Review* p10 Jl 2 2017

Fixing Finance, Still color *National Review* v69 no4 p30 Mr 6 2017

Gell, Aaron

NINA'S NIGHT OUT color *Harper's Bazaar* no3656 p337 S 2017

Gellar, Hannah

I watched his addiction take hold *Scholastic Choices* v32 no3 p9 N/D 2016

Gellar, Justin

I didn't know I was an addict *Scholastic Choices* v32 no3 p8 N/D 2016

Gellar, Sarah Michelle, 1977—Interviews

Cooking With Love color *Good Housekeeping* v264 no4 p77 Ap 2017

IN THE KITCHEN WITH SARAH MICHELLE GELLAR I. Biedenharn color *Entertainment Weekly* no1465 p60 My 12 2017

Geller, Jonathan B.

Tsunami-driven rafting: Transoceanic species dispersal and implications for marine biogeography color graph *Science* v357 no6358 p1402 S 29 2017

Geller, Laura

3 experts on... SMILE LINES color *Good Housekeeping* v265 no5 p22 N 2017

Geller, Leore T.

Potential role of intratumor bacteria in mediating tumor resistance to the chemotherapeutic drug gemcitabine diag *Science* v357 no6356 p1156 S 15 2017

GELLER, PAMELA

Is free speech under threat IN THE UNITED STATES? WE RECEIVED TWENTY-SEVEN RESPONSES. WE PUBLISH THEM HERE, IN ALPHABETICAL ORDER *Commentary* v144 no1 p13 Jl/Ag 2017

Gellert, R.

Redox stratification of an ancient lake in Gale crater, Mars color *Science* v356 no6341 p922 Je 1 2017

Gellhorn, Martha, 1908-1998

Martha Gellhorn's Choice Words B. ANASTAS *New York Times Book Review* p17 My 28 2017

Gellner, Arrol

STORYBOOK STYLE: America's Whimsical Homes of the 1920s color *Arts & Crafts Homes & the Revival* v12 no4 p18 Fall 2017

Gelman, Andrew

Measurement error and the replication crisis bibl graph *Science* v355 no6325 p584 F 10 2017

Gelman, Audrey

my style color *InStyle* v24 no4 p120 Ap 2017

Gelman, Brett

Lemon *New Yorker* v93 no26 p12 S 4 2017

GELMAN, LAUREN

Surprisingly Ordinary Allergy Triggers color *Reader's Digest* v189 no1129 p54 Ap 2017

Gelman, Laurie

Class Act: A former '90s wild child satirizes suburban parenthood K. HEINY *New York Times Book Review* p23 S 10 2017

CLASS MOM color *Good Housekeeping* v265 no1 p66 Jl 2017

LAURIE GELMAN I. Biedenharn color *Entertainment Weekly* no1476 p65 Ag 4 2017

Gelman, Susan A.

How "you" makes meaning bibl diag graph *Science* v355 no6331 p1299 Mr 24 2017

Gels (Pharmacy)—Evaluation

STOCK & TRADE color *Equus* no473 p68 F 2017

GELTING, RICK

battling a waterborne plague cartoon *Popular Science* v289 no2 p78 Mr/Ap 2017

Geltinger, Gunther

Moor color *Publishers Weekly* v263 no42 p46 O 17 2016

Geminder, Emily

Dead Girls and Other Stories *Publishers Weekly* v264 no32 p48 Ag 7 2017

Gemini (Constellation)

Gemini City Sights K. Hewitt-White *Sky & Telescope* v133 no2 p58 F 2017

Geminids (Meteors)

Evening Entertainment: Go out early and stay out late to catch the best meteor shower of the year S. N. Johnson-Roehr *Sky & Telescope* v134 no6 p48 D 2017

The Geminids & the Ursids *Sky & Telescope* v132 no6 p48 D 2016

Gemmeke, H.

Observation of a large-scale anisotropy in the arrival directions of cosmic rays above 8×10^{18} eV *Science* v357 no6357 p1266 S 22 2017

GEMMELL, KATHLEEN

Your True Stories IN 100 WORDS color *Reader's Digest* v189 no1130 p32 My 2017

Gems & precious stones

See also

Diamonds

Jade

ALL THAT GLITTERS color *Harper's Bazaar* no3651 p250 Mr 2017

ICING ABOVE R. M. HANRAHAN cartoon *Flying* v144 no2 p24 F 2017

Large gem diamonds from metallic liquid in Earth's deep mantle E. M. Smith, S. B. Shirey et al bibl color *Science* v354 no6318 p1403 D 16 2016

Should You Try a Yoni Egg? L. Murphy color *Glamour* v115 no7 p67 Jl 2017

To Rome with Love J. K. DE VALLE color *Architectural Digest* v74 no1 p66 Ja 2017

Why I Love HEART STONES J. Hudson color *InStyle* v24 no4 p228 Ap 2017

Genack, Azriel Z.

Observation of Anderson localization in disordered nanophotonic structures diag graph *Science* v356 no6341 p953 Je 1 2017

Genç, Kaya

Under the Shadow: Rage and Revolution in Modern Turkey *Publishers Weekly* v263 no41 p68 O 10 2016

A Very American Endeavor color *New York Review of Books* v64 no17 p23 N 9 2017

Gender

See also

Femininity

Gender differences (Sociology)

Gender identity

Gender role

Masculinity

Against Solidarity: AS A WRITER, WITH A WRITER'S CHRONIC NEED FOR DETACHMENT, I HAVE AVOIDED THE IDEOLOGY OF GENDER E. F. GORDON *American Scholar* v86 no4 p61 Aut 2017

The Average Mid-Forties Male College Graduate Earns 55% More Than His Female Counterparts E. Barth, C. Goldin et al *Harvard Business Review Digital Articles* p2 Je 12 2017

DETACHING MONEY FROM MANHOOD L. BLADES and S. T. BROWN color *Ebony* v72 no5 p69 Mr 2017

The long-run poverty and gender impacts of mobile money T. Suri and W. Jack bibl chart graph *Science* v354 no6317 p1288 D 9 2016

SEXUAL RELATIVITY AND GENDER REVOLUTION N. CATALANO *Humanist* v77 no4 p42 Jl/Ag 2017

Why Are Some Whistleblowers Vilified and Others Celebrated? D. M. Mayer *Harvard Business Review Digital Articles* p2 S 1 2016

Gender differences (Psychology)

See also

Androgyny (Psychology)

Gender role

American Girl T. Rosenberg cartoon color *National Geographic* v231 no1 p110 Ja 2017

The Dangerous Lives of Girls A. Okeowo color *National Geographic* v231 no1 p130 Ja 2017

Do Women Make Bolder Leaders than Men? J. Zenger and J. Folkman *Harvard Business Review Digital Articles* p2 Ap 27 2016

It's Hard to Be Female: the Statistics cartoon *National Geographic* v231 no1 p128 Ja 2017

Making a Man C. Brown cartoon color *National Geographic* v231 no1 p74 Ja 2017

Our Evolving Sense of Self SLAUGHTER cartoon *National Geographic* v231 no1 p152 Ja 2017

Parental Leave On Dads' Terms P. EDMONDS color *National Geographic* v231 no1 p104 Ja 2017

Research: We Are Way Harder on Female Leaders Who Make Bad Calls T. Huston *Harvard Business Review Digital Articles* p2 Ap 21 2016

Sexes Differ in Evolved Mate Preferences *USA Today Magazine* v145 no2865 p12 Je 2017

Why Men Have More Help Getting to the C-Suite S. Charas, L. L. Griffeth et al *Harvard Business Review Digital Articles* p2 N 16 2015

You Can Charge Women More, but Should You? R. Mohammed *Harvard Business Review Digital Articles* p2 Ja 29 2016

Gender differences (Psychology)—Research

Born This Way M. Shermer color *Scientific American* v315 no6 p84 D 2016

Gender differences (Sociology)

The Gender Issue color *National Geographic* v231 no1 p12 Ja 2017

Get It, Girls! M. Stevens, A. Sanchez color *Glamour* v115 no4 p30 Ap 2017

HOW VAIN ARE YOU? color *GQ: Gentlemen's Quarterly* v97 no9 p202 S 2017

A PORTRAIT OF GENDER TODAY cartoon *National Geographic* v231 no1 p14 Ja 2017

THE POWER OF PEERS S. Sandberg *National Geographic* v231 no1 p10 Ja 2017

THE POWER OF SELF G. Steinem *National Geographic* v231 no1 p8 Ja 2017

REDEFINING GENDER *National Geographic* v231 no1 p14 Ja 2017

To Hold Women Back, Keep Treating Them Like Men A. Wittenberg-Cox *Harvard Business Review Digital Articles* p2 Jl 24 2015

WHAT IF ALL COULD THRIVE? S. Goldberg color *National Geographic* v231 no1 p4 Ja 2017

Why Beauty Matters C. Leive color *Glamour* v115 no4 p28 Ap 2017

The XX Factor *Commentary* v143 no4 p37 Ap 2017

THE XX FACTOR: WHEN GENDER DIFFERENCES ARE IGNORED IN HEALTH STUDIES, IT'S WOMEN WHO PAY THE PRICE [Cover story] C. LEHMANN *Commentary* v143 no4 p13 Ap 2017

Gender expression

Permeable savior J. Morris *Christian Century* v134 no2 p12 Ja 18 2017

Gender identity

Asia Kate DILION S. LaCAVA *Interview* v47 no6 p8 Ag 2017

BRICKBATS cartoon *Reason* v48 no8 p64 Ja 2017

CAN I TOUCH YOUR HAIR? WHY DO YOU DRESS LIKE A BOY IF YOU LIKE GIRLS? S. KIRK *In These Times* v41 no10 p24 O 2017

The Church & Transgender Identity D. Cloutier and L. T. Johnson cartoon *Commonweal* v144 no5 p15 Mr 10 2017

COLOR CODE C. Zuckerman color *National Geographic* v231 no1 p18 Ja 2017

GIRLS, BOYS, AND GENDERED TOYS N. Daly color *National Geographic* v231 no1 p17 Ja 2017

HELPING FAMILIES TALK ABOUT GENDER cartoon *National Geographic* v231 no1 p16 Ja 2017

Identity search P. W. Marty *Christian Century* v134 no2 p3 Ja 18 2017

Infinite Identities [Cover story] K. Steinmetz color *Time* v189 no11 p48 Mr 27 2017

ONE PART HE, ONE PART SHE P. Edmonds color *National Geographic* v231 no1 p26 Ja 2017

SEX, SHRINKS, AND THE STATE D. N. MCCLOSKEY bw *Reason* v48 no11 p12 Ap 2017

TOUGH FLUIDITY: Complex Considerations for Trans Youth D. J. GOEMANS *Humanist* v77 no4 p20 Jl/Ag 2017

WHO'S THE FAIREST? K. Nowakowski color graph *National Geographic* v231 no1 p24 Ja 2017

Gender identity in the workplace

What to Do When Your Colleague Comes Out as Transgender D. Clark *Harvard Business Review Digital Articles* p2 F 5 2015

Gender identity—Social aspects

DISCOVERING THEIR IDENTITY: Using gender nonconforming picture books in early education classrooms S. Evans, S. Gilbert et al color *Literacy Today (2411-7826)* v34 no6 p20 My/Je 2017

Gender in art

ART color *New Yorker* v93 no32 p14 O 16 2017

SAFE SPACE P. SCHJELDAHL color *New Yorker* v93 no31 p78 O 9 2017

Gender in motion pictures

When History Makes the Cut B. R. Rich *Film Quarterly* v70 no3 p6 Spr 2017

Gender inequality

Access to Digital Technology Accelerates Global Gender Equality J. Sweet *Harvard Business Review Digital Articles* p2 My 17 2016

"Any HR person working here will be out of their comfort zone":

An industry-leading ad agency needed bold thinking to address a drastic gender imbalance *People Management* p20 Ag 2017

At Work I'm the Only... L. Liebman color *Glamour* v115 no4 p148 Ap 2017

BEYOND XX AND XY A. Montañez diag *Scientific American* v317 no3 p50 S 2017

Do Conservative Managers Give Smaller Bonuses to Women? F. Briscoe and A. Joshi *Harvard Business Review Digital Articles* p2 D 2 2016

Ending Gender Discrimination Requires More than a Training Program F. Gino *Harvard Business Review Digital Articles* p2 O 10 2014

How CEOs Can Put Gender Balance on the Agenda at Their Companies A. Wittenberg-Cox *Harvard Business Review Digital Articles* p2 N 30 2016

HOW DO YOU CLOSE A GENDER PAY GAP? With organisations fearful of following in the BBC's footsteps, employers are being urged to take action to tackle inequality L. FARRAND *People Management* p10 S 2017

How Not to Advocate for a Woman at Work D. M. Mayer *Harvard Business Review Digital Articles* p2 Jl 26 2017

How Reducing Gender Inequality Could Boost U.S. GDP by $2.1 Trillion K. Ellingrud, J. Manyika et al *Harvard Business Review Digital Articles* p2 Ap 12 2016

How to Get Men Involved with Gender Parity Initiatives E. N. Sherf and S. Tangirala *Harvard Business Review Digital Articles* p2 S 13 2017

I Am Nine Years Old E. CONANT color *National Geographic* v231 no1 p30 Ja 2017

IS THERE A "FEMALE" BRAIN? L. DENWORTH color diag graph *Scientific American* v317 no3 p38 S 2017

Looking inward at gender issues J. Berg color *Science* v355 no6323 p329 Ja 27 2017

NOT JUST FOR MEN M. L. STEFANICK color diag graph *Scientific American* v317 no3 p52 S 2017

PEDALING A REVOLUTION S. GALPIN *UN Chronicle* v53 no2 p25 2016

THE POWER OF MENTORS AND SPONSORS A. Yu *Maclean's* v130 no3 p59 Ap 2017

PROMISCUOUS MEN, CHASTE WOMEN AND OTHER GENDER MYTHS C. FINE and M. A. ELGAR color *Scientific American* v317 no3 p32 S 2017

Rethinking Gender R. M. Henig cartoon chart color map *National Geographic* v231 no1 p48 Ja 2017

THIS IS NOT A WOMEN'S ISSUE *Scientific American* v317 no3 p30 S 2017

This Issue Was Brought to You by... Women C. Leive color *Glamour* v115 no2 p18 F 2017

To Hold Women Back, Keep Treating Them Like Men A. Wittenberg-Cox *Harvard Business Review Digital Articles* p2 Jl 24 2015

To Understand Your Company's Gender Imbalance, Make a Graph A. Wittenberg-Cox *Harvard Business Review Digital Articles* p2 Mr 8 2016

TURKISH WOMEN RISING S. JONES and C. ASQUITH *Ms.* v27 no1 p34 Spr 2017

WHAT IF ALL COULD THRIVE? S. Goldberg color *National Geographic* v231 no1 p4 Ja 2017

What is the point of pay? P. Cheese *People Management* p5 S 2017

What I Wish I'd Known A. D. Barnett bw color *Glamour* v115 no11 p138 N 2017

What the Science Actually Says About Gender Gaps in the Workplace S. K. Johnson *Harvard Business Review Digital Articles* p2 2017

WHERE IN THE WORLD ARE WOMEN AND MEN MOST—AND LEAST—EQUAL? K. Nowakowski graph *National Geographic* v231 no1 p28 Ja 2017

WHITHER THE WAGE GAP? diag *Fortune* v176 no5 p15 O 1 2017

Why Gender Balance Can't Wait M. Landel *Harvard Business Review Digital Articles* p2 Mr 8 2016

Women Strike Back K. Pollitt color *Nation* v303 no19 p10 N 7 2016

Gender role

See also

v120 no2 p48 Mr/Ap 2017

GENE THERAPY FOR LAMINITIS? C. Barakat and M. Mc-Cluskey color diag *Equus* no474 p10 Mr 2017

One Man's Quest to Hack His Own Genes A. Regalado color il *MIT Technology Review* v120 no2 p13 Mr/Ap 2017

Relief for retinal neurons under pressure J. Crowston and I. Trounce bibl diag *Science* v355 no6326 p688 F 17 2017

Gene therapy—History

50, 100 & 150 YEARS AGO bw color *Scientific American* v316 no2 p75 F 2017

Gene therapy—Research

50, 100 & 150 YEARS AGO bw color *Scientific American* v316 no2 p75 F 2017

Gene therapy—Sales & prices

Gene-Therapy Cure Has Money-Back Guarantee A. Regalado il *MIT Technology Review* v119 no6 p24 N/D 2016

Genealogy

See also

Jesse trees

THE GENEALOGY OF WASHINGTON RESTAURANTS A. LIMPERT *Washingtonian Magazine* v52 no1 p64 O 2016

Genealogy—Computer network resources—Evaluation

FREE WEBSITE REVEALS YOUR RELATIVES AND MORE V. Quezada color *Money* v46 no2 p21 Mr 2017

Genealogy—Congresses

Virtual Genealogy Fair Is October 26 and 27 *Prologue* v48 no3 p69 Fall 2016

General education

See also

Literacy

Think Globally, Act Locally D. C. Paris *Change* v49 no4 p4 Jl/Ag 2017

General Electric Capital Corp.

General Electric Co.

Artifact: General Electric Lightbulb R. Clough and A. Ricadela color *Bloomberg Businessweek* no4527 p25 Je 19 2017

Building a Software Start-Up Inside GE B. Power *Harvard Business Review Digital Articles* p2 Ja 29 2015

Chasing the MR&T J. ". Pete Jr. color map *Model Railroader* v84 no4 p40 Ap 2017

The Corporate HQ Is an Anachronism R. Krishnamoorthy *Harvard Business Review Digital Articles* p2 Mr 13 2015

Corporate Universities Should Reflect a Company's Ideals R. Krishnamoorthy *Harvard Business Review Digital Articles* p2 O 16 2014

GAS RANGES B. GOLD color *Good Housekeeping* v263 no5 p137 N 2016

General Electric E. Woyke bw color il *MIT Technology Review* v120 no4 p78 Jl/Ag 2017

GE's Culture Challenge After Welch and Immelt R. Krishnamoorthy *Harvard Business Review Digital Articles* p2 Ja 26 2015

GE'S GLOBAL GROWTH EXPERIMENT: THE COMPANY PUSHED CROSS-BUSINESS COLLABORATION R. GULATI *Harvard Business Review* v95 no5 p52 S/O 2017

How to Transform a Traditional Giant into a Digital One R. Charan *Harvard Business Review Digital Articles* p2 F 26 2016

IS GE DUE FOR A COMEBACK? color *Fortune* v176 no1 p11 Jl 1 2017

Is the End of GE Capital Good News for Ecomagination? A. Winston *Harvard Business Review Digital Articles* p2 Ap 22 2015

A MIGHTY WIND M. JANCER diag *Wired* v25 no6 p28 Je 2017

News & Products color *Model Railroader* v84 no5 p10 My 2017

Selling GE Capital Was Both a Brave and a Good Idea J. P. V. Sampere *Harvard Business Review Digital Articles* p2 Ap 28 2015

General Electric Co.—Management

FIVE TRANSFORMATIONS S. PROKESCH *Harvard Business Review* v95 no5 p47 S/O 2017

General Electric Co.—Officials & employees

GE's Jeff Immelt J. Micklethwait color *Bloomberg Businessweek* no4511 p22 F 13 2017

THE GREAT TRANSFORMER A. IGNATIUS bw img *Harvard Business Review* v95 no5 p10 S/O 2017

HOW I REMADE GE: AND WHAT I LEARNED ALONG THE WAY J. R. IMMELT color *Harvard Business Review* v95 no5 p42 S/O 2017

General Hospital (TV program)

CHEERS & JEERS D. Holbrook color *TV Guide* v65 no7 p92 F 13 2017

GENERAL HOSPITAL M. LOGAN *TV Guide* v65 no31 p42 Jl 24 2017

Last of a Vanishing Breed M. LOGAN *TV Guide* v64 no15 p19 Ap 4 2016

General Mills Inc.

Champion of Breakfasts C. Vernon bw color *Working Mother* v40 no2 p12 Je/Jl 2017

GENERAL MILLS LOSES THE CULTURE WARS J. Kell color diag *Fortune* v175 no7 p66 Je 1 2017

Gentle Giants *Sierra* v102 no2 p10 Mr/Ap 2017

How General Mills and Kellogg Are Tackling Greenhouse Gas Emissions A. Winston *Harvard Business Review Digital Articles* p2 Je 1 2016

How I Did It color *Men's Health* v32 no3 p36 Ap 2017

General Motors automobiles—Design & construction

IN THE WORKS M. EMERY color *Dirt Sports + Off-Road* v51 no12 p18 D 2017

General Motors automobiles—Evaluation

2018 GMC Terrain A. Priddle color *Motor Trend* v69 no3 p21 Mr 2017

General Motors Co.

12 MARY BARRA N. Varchaver color *Fortune* v174 no7 p86 D 1 2016

2017 CHEVY COLORADO ZR2 [Cover story] A. MANSOUR color *Dirt Sports + Off-Road* v51 no10 p42 O 2017

ALL ABOUT THE Benjamins D. Welch chart color *Bloomberg Businessweek* no4523 p20 My 22 2017

A Continental Retreat C. Thomas, D. Welch et al color map *Bloomberg Businessweek* no4514 p23 Mr 13 2017

THE END OF LABOR A. GOLDSTEIN bw color *Nation* v305 no6 p22 S 11 2017

THE 'FRIDGE' ENTERS THE KITCHEN *Saturday Evening Post* v289 no5 p97 S/O 2017

GAME THEORY A. MacKenzie color *Motor Trend* v69 no3 p98 Mr 2017

GMC Acadia All Terrain chart color *Motor Trend* v69 no1 p65 Ja 2017

GM'S HEI MODULE DWELL: THIS PRIMER WILL HELP YOU ADJUST THE DWELL ON ALL ENGINE TYPES R. Bohacz *Successful Farming* v115 no6 p26 Ap 2017

GM's Stock Buyback Is Bad for America and the Company W. Lazonick and M. Hopkins *Harvard Business Review Digital Articles* p2 Mr 11 2015

How GM Uses Social Media to Improve Cars and Customer Service A. Boler-Davis *Harvard Business Review Digital Articles* p2 F 12 2016

LIVE LARGE ON A SUBSCRIPTION PLAN T. H. BLANTON color *Kiplinger's Personal Finance* v71 no7 p15 Jl 2017

THE PRESIDENT AND THE FORGOTTEN MAN D. D. GUTTENPLAN bw color *Nation* v304 no10 p21 Mr 27 2017

RECALLS chart color *Consumer Reports* v82 no12 p12 D 2017

SLIPPED DISC J. Bryant color *Hot Rod* v70 no8 p84 Ag 2017

That Big Indian Sign J. GILBERT *Cincinnati Magazine* v50 no8 p36 My 2017

General Motors India Pvt. Ltd.

What U.S. CEOs Can Learn from GM's India Failure V. Govindarajan and G. Bagla *Harvard Business Review Digital Articles* p2 Je 15 2017

General Motors trucks

GEAR UP J. Bryant color *Hot Rod* v70 no7 p76 Jl 2017

IN THE WORKS M. EMERY color *Dirt Sports + Off-Road* v51 no12 p18 D 2017

General relativity (Physics)

See also

Gravitational waves

Physical cosmology

Quantum gravity

A centennial gift from Einstein T. D. Oswalt diag *Science* v356 no6342 p1015 Je 9 2017

iPTF16geu: A multiply imaged, gravitationally lensed type Ia supernova A. Goobar, R. Amanullah et al color diag graph *Science* v356 no6335 p291 Ap 21 2017

Relativistic deflection of background starlight measures the mass of a nearby white dwarf star K. C. Sahu, J. Anderson et al chart color graph *Science* v356 no6342 p1046 Je 9 2017

THIS IS YOUR UNIVERSE S. BUSHWICK color *Popular Science* p20 Ja/F 2017

General stores

DELI DELIGHTS M. W. Schwartz, D. Breshears et al color *Missouri Life* v44 no3 p72 My 2017

General stores—Evaluation

Barnard General Store A. TRAVERSO and M. FLEMING color *Yankee* p64 My/Je 2017

from groceries to gossip D. Breshears bw color *Missouri Life* v44 no6 p52 S 2017

Generals

MIRACLE ON THE VISTULA T. Fleming bw color map *MHQ: Quarterly Journal of Military History* v30 no1 p66 Aut 2017

Generals—United States

Tear Down This Colloseum! Taki *American Conservative* v16 no4 p66 Jl/Ag 2017

Generals—United States—Attitudes

He Has Returned *Commentary* v142 no1 p1 Jl/Ag 2016

Generate Capital (Company)

Greening Business, One Project at a Time C. Martin bw color *Bloomberg Businessweek* no4505 p34 D 26 2016

Generation gap

Hail! Hail! rock 'n' roll! A. G. ARONOWITZ *Saturday Evening Post* v289 no4 p40 Jl/Ag 2017

Happy Warrior A. STILES *National Review* v69 no6 p48 Ap 3 2017

Research: The Biggest Culture Gaps Are Within Countries, Not Between Them B. Kirkman, V. Taras et al *Harvard Business Review Digital Articles* p2 My 18 2016

When Your Boss Is Younger than You R. Knight *Harvard Business Review Digital Articles* p2 O 9 2015

Generation X

The Sun & the Moon & the Rolling Stones R. Cohen color *AARP: The Magazine* v59 no4A p52 Je/Jl 2016

Generation X—Attitudes

THE BESTEST GENERATION R. COHEN bw color *Vanity Fair* v59 no9 p152 S 2017

Generation Y

and the survey says *U.S. Catholic* v82 no10 p29 O 2017

Asia's Rising Stars A. BEHAL, M. FANGJING et al color *Forbes* v199 no5 p20 My 16 2017

Communicating in the Workplace *USA Today Magazine* v145 no2863 p13 Ap 2017

Every Generation Wants Meaningful Work—but Thinks Other Age Groups Are in It for the Money K. P. Weeks *Harvard Business Review Digital Articles* p2 Jl 31 2017

Impact Investing Needs Millennials V. Dhar and J. Fetherston *Harvard Business Review Digital Articles* p2 O 3 2014

It Used to Be So Easy *Money* v46 no4 p5 My 2017

KIDS THESE DAYS: IT'S TIME TO STEREOTYPE A NEW GENERATION H. GENDREAU color *Wired* v25 no9 p26 S 2017

Market to Millennials by Getting Out of the Way R. Faris *Harvard Business Review Digital Articles* p2 D 9 2015

Maxine Waters Is Learning From Millennials A. M. Cox *New York Times Magazine* p58 Jl 23 2017

Millennials Say They'll Relocate for Work-Life Flexibility N. Fondas *Harvard Business Review Digital Articles* p2 My 7 2015

The Missing Millennial Novel T. TULATHIMUTTE *New York Times Book Review* p37 D 11 2016

Motivating Millennials Takes More than Flexible Work Policies T. Benson *Harvard Business Review Digital Articles* p2 F 11 2016

Research: Millennials Think About Work Too Much R. Zilca *Harvard Business Review Digital Articles* p2 Jl 15 2016

Sophomores Shrugged cartoon *Weekly Standard* v22 no48 p3 S 4 2017

What You're Hiding from When You Constantly Check Your Phone C. Lieberman *Harvard Business Review Digital Articles* p2 Ja 19 2016

Young Are a Handy Scapegoat for Elders' Attraction to Trump A. Johnson *Extra!* v29 no9 p1 N 2016

Generation Y consumers

Email Is the Best Way to Reach Millennials K. Naragon *Harvard Business Review Digital Articles* p2 N 12 2015

Moving First-Time Buyers Off the Fence: Solving the Millennial Homebuyer Puzzle with Proven Online Solutions and Partnerships D. Dylla and D. Caldwell-Tautges *Bridges (Federal Reserve Bank of St. Louis)* p6 Summ 2016

Will Millennials Eat Their Frozen Veggies? C. Giammona color graph *Bloomberg Businessweek* no4497 p23 O 31 2016

Will millennials save the car business? M. Rechtin color *Motor Trend* v69 no5 p20 My 2017

You're Smelling Different Again S. Wong *Bloomberg Businessweek* no4495 p19 O 17 2016

Generation Y—Attitudes

Are U.S. Millennial Men Just as Sexist as Their Dads? A. S. Kramer and A. B. Harris *Harvard Business Review Digital Articles* p2 Je 15 2016

Lunch Is Dead J. Kell color *Fortune* v175 no5 p12 Ap 1 2017

MILLENNIALS ARE NOT MONOLITHIC G. Colvin color *Fortune* v174 no6 p48 N 1 2016

A RETURN TO TRADITION FOR MILLENNIALS A. KINGSTON chart color *Maclean's* v130 no6 p12 Jl 2017

Social Science and the Public Interest *Society* v54 no3 p213 Je 2017

What Did Flappers Want? You May Want to Ask a Millennial: Not that today's hipsters flaunt cigarettes and dance the Charleston. But from their nifty gadgets to their prolonged adolescence, young cosmopolitan women are surprisingly close in... P. O'Donnell *Smithsonian* v48 no5 p11 S 2017

What Millennials Want from a New Job B. Rigoni and A. Adkins *Harvard Business Review Digital Articles* p2 My 11 2016

What Millennials Want from Work, Charted Across the World H. Bresman *Harvard Business Review Digital Articles* p2 F 23 2015

Why So Many Millennials Aren't Into Protest Movements N. Gafni *Harvard Business Review Digital Articles* p2 O 22 2015

Generation Y—Canada

Those flighty millennials C. MCINTYRE color *Maclean's* v130 no8 p14 S 2017

Generation Y—Economic conditions

HOW MUCH YOUNG PEOPLE ARE MAKING map *Fortune* v175 no5 p11 Ap 1 2017

Will millennials save the car business? M. Rechtin color *Motor Trend* v69 no5 p20 My 2017

Generation Y—Education

TWO SIDES OF THE SAME COIN D. WINSTON color *Tricycle: The Buddhist Review* v26 no3 p60 Spr 2017

Generation Y—Employment

IN GOOD Company L. ROMNEY color *Forbes* v198 no9 p67 D 30 2016

MILLENNIALS ARE NOT MONOLITHIC G. Colvin color *Fortune* v174 no6 p48 N 1 2016

Millennials Want to Be Coached at Work K. Willyerd *Harvard Business Review Digital Articles* p2 F 27 2015

THE NEW ORGANIZATION MEN (AND WOMEN) graph img *Harvard Business Review* v95 no2 p30 Mr/Ap 2017

Research: Millennials Can't Afford to Job Hop S. A. Hewlett and J. S. Kuhl *Harvard Business Review Digital Articles* p2 Ag 31 2016

What Facebook Knows About Engaging Millennial Employees L. Goler *Harvard Business Review Digital Articles* p2 D 16 2015

"You can't attract the best young candidates with yesterday's methods": How offering 'gaming time' has engaged a ticketing firm's millennials *People Management* p25 Je 2017

Young people are just smarter *People Management* p26 D 2016/ Ja 2017

Generation Y—Finance

How Many Avocado Toasts It Takes to Buy a Home J. Calfas color *Money* v46 no7 p14 Ag 2017

How Millenials Manage Their Money C. M. Brown color *Black Enterprise* v47 no3 p23 O 2016

Generation Y—Political activity

When Millennials Rule C. Alter color *Time* v190 no16/17 p88 O 23 2017

Generation Y—Psychology

The Problem with Millennials? They're Way Too Hard on Themselves E. Csorba *Harvard Business Review Digital Articles* p2 My 2 2016

What Do Millennials Really Want at Work? The Same Things the

Rest of Us Do B. N. Pfau *Harvard Business Review Digital Articles* p2 Ap 7 2016

Generation Y—United States

HOW WE DID IT T. Tepper color diag *Money* v46 no4 p56 My 2017

Millennials Are Actually Workaholics, According to Research S. G. Carmichael *Harvard Business Review Digital Articles* p2 Ag 17 2016

Generation Z

KIDS THESE DAYS: IT'S TIME TO STEREOTYPE A NEW GENERATION H. GENDREAU color *Wired* v25 no9 p26 S 2017

MILLENNIALS, MOVE OVER. GEN Z IS COMING diag *Fortune* v176 no1 p9 Jl 1 2017

Online Student Orientation: Guerrilla Style D. Swett *Change* v48 no5 p26 S/O 2016

Generation Z consumers

How to Market to the iGeneration J. Schneider *Harvard Business Review Digital Articles* p2 My 6 2015

Generational marketing

Labels Like "Millennial" and "Boomer" Are Obsolete N. Dawar *Harvard Business Review Digital Articles* p2 N 18 2016

Generations

See also

Baby boom generation

Generation gap

Generation Y

Generation Z

From selfies to selfless: Managing multigenerational teams A. G. Levine color *Science* v357 no6356 p1170 S 15 2017

Generations—Charts, diagrams, etc.

MILLENNIALS, MOVE OVER. GEN Z IS COMING diag *Fortune* v176 no1 p9 Jl 1 2017

Generations—United States—Social aspects

THE BESTEST GENERATION R. COHEN bw color *Vanity Fair* v59 no9 p152 S 2017

Generic drugs—Sales & prices

The Bitterest Pill N. VARDI and N. KARMALI cartoon color *Forbes* v199 no4 p38 Ap 25 2017

Generosity

See also

Gifts

ADAM AND REB'S RECOMMENDED RESOURCES *Harvard Business Review Digital Articles* p23 Ja 1 2017

BEAT GENEROSITY BURNOUT A. GRANT and R. REBELE color *Harvard Business Review Digital Articles* p3 Ja 1 2017

A Flexible Way to Give to Charity K. LANKFORD color *Kiplinger's Personal Finance* v70 no12 p44 D 2016

GENEROSITY BURNOUT — ARE YOU AT RISK? graph *Harvard Business Review Digital Articles* p21 Ja 1 2017

GIFTS that UPLIFT! J. BISSEY, ". T. TSHIKORORO et al cartoon *O, The Oprah Magazine* p148 D 2016

HOW AND WHEN SELFLESSNESS AT WORK BACKFIRES graph *Harvard Business Review Digital Articles* p16 Ja 1 2017

LEADERS WHO GET HOW TO GIVE C. NICKISCH *Harvard Business Review Digital Articles* p12 Ja 1 2017

MANAGING COLLABORATIVE OVERLOAD color *Harvard Business Review Digital Articles* p17 Ja 1 2017

MORE ON BEING GENEROUS WITHOUT BEING A DOORMAT A. GRANT and R. REBELE color *Harvard Business Review Digital Articles* p18 Ja 1 2017

Ordinary People Giving in Extraordinary Ways [Cover story] *Reader's Digest* v188 no1125 p87 N 2016

What Generous People's Brains Do Differently N. Torres *Harvard Business Review Digital Articles* p2 O 1 2015

Generosity—Psychological aspects

Giving Proof: It turns out that generosity really can make us happier G. Reynolds *New York Times Magazine* p16 S 17 2017

More on Being Generous Without Being a Doormat A. Grant and R. Rebele *Harvard Business Review Digital Articles* p2 F 22 2017

Generosity—Social aspects

THE Nicest Places IN America [Cover story] J. GREENFIELD color map *Reader's Digest* v190 no1135 p59 N 2017

Genersch, E.

Country-specific effects of neonicotinoid pesticides on honey bees

and wild bees diag map *Science* v356 no6345 p1393 Je 30 2017

Genes

See also

Immediate-early genes

Circadian clocks: Not your grandfather's clock F. W. Turek bibl diag *Science* v354 no6315 p992 N 25 2016

A crossroad of neuronal diversity to build circuitry S. Yoshinaga and K. Nakajima color *Science* v356 no6336 p376 Ap 28 2017

Durable resistance to rice blast Wang and B. Valent bibl color *Science* v355 no6328 p906 Mr 3 2017

The genes that make seahorses so weird color *Science* v354 no6318 p1357 D 16 2016

Human knockouts provide drug clues T. H. SAEY graph *Science News* v191 no9 p10 My 13 2017

Male sex in houseflies is determined by Mdmd, a paralog of the generic splice factor gene CWC22 A. Sharma, S. D. Heinze et al bw color *Science* v356 no6338 p642 My 12 2017

Pcdhαc2 is required for axonal tiling and assembly of serotonergic circuitries in mice W. V. Chen, C. L. Nwakeze et al diag *Science* v356 no6336 p406 Ap 28 2017

Predicting Phenotypes in a Changing Climate C. BEANS *BioScience* v67 no7 p593 Jl 2017

RESEARCH color *Science* v357 no6348 p263 Jl 21 2017

Genes—Evaluation

An ethics code for studying the San color *Science* v355 no6331 p1244 Mr 24 2017

Genesis Motors (Company)

Genesis GV80 Concept A. Priddle color *Motor Trend* v69 no7 p24 Jl 2017

GEOGRAPHY LESSONS J. DEMATIO color *Road & Track* v68 no5 p108 D 2016/Ja 2017

POWER RISING M. DE PAULA color *Road & Track* v69 no4 p84 N 2017

Genest, Karen

Speak up color *U.S. Catholic* v82 no4 p5 Ap 2017

Geneste, G.

Synthesis of FeH5: A layered structure with atomic hydrogen slabs diag graph *Science* v357 no6349 p382 Jl 28 2017

Genetic code

See also

Stop codons

An Alternative to the RNA World C. W. CARTER, JR. *Natural History* v125 no1 p28 D 2016/Ja 2017

Translational termination without a stop codon N. R. James, A. Brown et al bibl color *Science* v354 no6318 p1437 D 16 2016

Genetic disorders

See also

Inborn errors of metabolism

Expert consensus on inborn errors of metabolism screening Chunhua Zhang bibl chart diag *Science* v354 no6319 p62 D 23 2016

The Inheritance cartoon *O, The Oprah Magazine* p134 F 2017

WHEN DNA AND CULTURE CLASH J. Kaiser color map *Science* v354 no6317 p1217 D 9 2016

Genetic disorders—Gene therapy

Human embryo editing yields results T. HESMAN SAEY color *Science News* v191 no7 p16 Ap 15 2017

Genetic disorders—Prevention

OK on mitochondrial replacement color *Science* v354 no6319 p1508 D 23 2016

U.S. panel backs human gene editing T. HESMAN SAEY *Science News* v191 no5 p7 Mr 18 2017

Genetic disorders—Psychological aspects

A DIAGNOSTIC DILEMMA H. ESTROFF MARANO *Psychology Today* v50 no2 p22 Mr/Ap 2017

a rare condition, a beautiful legacy M. ZUCKER *Parents* v92 no2 p80 F 2017

Genetic disorders—Treatment

Diagnosis and treatment of inherited metabolic diseases in China Zhi-Chun Feng, Yan Wang et al bibl *Science* v354 no6319 p52 D 23 2016

Genetic engineering

See also

Cloning

Gene drive (Genetic engineering)

Gene therapy

Genome editing

The Urban Wild color *Chicago* v66 no8 p90 Ag 2017

Genitalia

>*See also*
>
>Male reproductive organs

Elimination of the male reproductive tract in the female embryo is promoted by COUP-TFII in mice F. Zhao, H. L. Franco et al color graph *Science* v357 no6352 p717 Ag 18 2017

Genitalia physiology

THE CASE OF THE MACHO CROCS M. Leslie color map *Science* v357 no6354 p859 S 1 2017

Genius

THE BRILLIANCE TRAP A. CIMPIAN and LESLIE color graph *Scientific American* v317 no3 p60 S 2017

GENIUS C. KALB bw color diag *National Geographic* v231 no5 p30 My 2017

GENIUS TAKES MANY FORMS S. Goldberg color *National Geographic* v231 no5 pC6 My 2017

GENIUS W. McPhail color *Esquire* p29 O 2017

Genius (TV program)

Drama of Einstein's life unfolds in new series E. Conover color *Science News* v191 no8 p34 Ap 29 2017

Genius L. Acken *TV Guide* p39 Ap 17 2017

T.R. Knight Is J. Edgar Hoover M. Roffman *TV Guide* v65 no14 p8 Ap 3 2017

VANESSA WILLIAMS *TV Guide* v65 no27 p7 Je 26 2017

Gennari, John

Flavor and Soul: Italian America at Its African American Edge *Publishers Weekly* v264 no2 p56 Ja 9 2017

Genoa (Italy)

GENOA T. Adler bw color *Conde Nast Traveler* v52 no6 p70 Je/Jl 2017

Genocide

THE GENESIS OF 'GENOCIDE' J. Winter *MHQ: Quarterly Journal of Military History* v29 no3 p17 Spr 2017

PROTECTING VULNERABLE POPULATIONS FROM GENOCIDE A. DIENG *UN Chronicle* v54 no4 p9 2017

THE RESPONSIBILITY TO PROTECT I. ŠIMONOVIĆ *UN Chronicle* v54 no4 p18 2017

Too Much Forgetting W. C. Donahue bw color *Commonweal* v144 no16 p22 O 6 2017

Whitewash Interrupted color *Weekly Standard* v23 no2 p2 S 18 2017

Genocide prevention

The Future of Genocide: International law changes, but human nature doesn't. Hoover fellow Norman M. Naimark on the ancient and persistent crime of genocide K. Davidson *Hoover Digest: Research & Opinion on Public Policy* no3 p164 Summ 2017

The Responsibility to Protect I. Simonovic *UN Chronicle* v53 no4 p1 2016

Genocide—Guatemala

Secretary of Genocide E. Alterman bw *Nation* v304 no5 p6 F 20 2017

Genocide—News briefs

GOOD NEWS color *Maclean's* v129 no44 p8 N 7 2016

Genocide—Prevention—International cooperation

Protecting Vulnerable Populations from Genocide A. Dieng *UN Chronicle* v53 no4 p1 2016

Genocide—Rwanda

The Long Shadow of Genocide in Rwanda S. THOMSON *Current History* v116 no790 p183 My 2017

Genome editing

The CRISPR Antidote E. BETZ color *Discover* v38 no10 p10 D 2017

cut+paste B. Freese *Successful Farming* v114 no12 p58 Mid-N 2016

Do Not Fear Gene-Edited Food J. SCHWARTZ color *Popular Science* v288 no6 p82 N/D 2016

Edited embryos reveal gene's function T. H. SAEY bw *Science News* v192 no6 p8 O 14 2017

GENE GENIES A. VLASITS color *Wired* v25 no6 p18 Je 2017

Genome editors take on crops A. Scheben and D. Edwards bibl diag *Science* v355 no6330 p1122 Mr 17 2017

Heart mutation fixed in embryos T. H. SAEY bw *Science News* v192 no3 p6 S 2 2017

Is Caution Enough? G. Meilaender color *Commonweal* v144 no7 p12 Ap 14 2017

IT'S OK TO EDIT YOUR KIDS' GENES R. BAILEY color *Reason* v49 no6 p6 N 2017

MICE MADE EASY J. Cohen color *Science* v354 no6312 p539 N 4 2016

Q&A B. FREESE *Successful Farming* v114 no12 p64 Mid-N 2016

THE RED LINE S. S. Hall color diag *Scientific American* v315 no3 p54 S 2016

Regulating the Brave New World of Human Gene Editing P. SMAGLIK color diag *Discover* v38 no1 p30 Ja/F 2017

A reporter does CRISPR J. Cohen color *Science* v354 no6312 p541 N 4 2016

Rethinking biosecurity J. KUZMA diag *Issues in Science & Technology* v33 no2 p12 Wint 2017

Science journalists don't use the science of 'nudge' E. Quill *Science News* v191 no5 p2 Mr 18 2017

SCIENCE LESSONS FOR THE NEXT PRESIDENT D. Malakoff and J. Mervis *Science* v354 no6310 p274 O 21 2016

Tunnel Through the Alps S. PALUS and J. SCHWARTZ color *Popular Science* v288 no6 p78 N/D 2016

U.S. attitudes on human genome editing D. A. Scheufele, M. A. Xenos et al color graph *Science* v357 no6351 p553 Ag 11 2017

U.S. panel backs human gene editing T. HESMAN SAEY *Science News* v191 no5 p7 Mr 18 2017

Genome editing—Congresses

Evolving policy with science R. A. Charo and R. O. Hynes color *Science* v355 no6328 p889 Mr 3 2017

Genome editing—Methodology

Embryo editing takes another step to clinic K. Servick bw *Science* v357 no6350 p436 Ag 4 2017

Genome editing—Moral & ethical aspects

Designer Genes R. JACOBSEN color *Mother Jones* v42 no5 p44 S/O 2017

Genomes

>*See also*
>
>Genes
>
>Human genome

Advances in organ transplant from pigs [Cover story] J. Denner color *Science* v357 no6357 p1238 S 22 2017

Circadian time signatures of fitness and disease J. Bass and M. A. Lazar bibl diag map *Science* v354 no6315 p994 N 25 2016

Combing the genome for the roots of autism E. Pennisi color *Science* v357 no6346 p25 Jl 7 2017

Deriving genomic diagnoses without revealing patient genomes K. A. Jagadeesh, D. J. Wu et al chart *Science* v357 no6352 p692 Ag 18 2017

The DNA methyltransferase DNMT3C protects male germ cells from transposon activity J. Barau, A. Teissandier et al bibl diag graph *Science* v354 no6314 p909 N 18 2016

First Polynesians launched from East Asia to settle Pacific A. Gibbons color *Science* v354 no6308 p24 O 7 2016

Hints of high-altitude mutations in Tibetan genomes color *Science* v356 no6333 p8 Ap 7 2017

Mapping Life's NETWORKS L. Hamers cartoon chart graph *Science News* v190 no9 p24 O 29 2016

Mismatch repair deficiency predicts response of solid tumors to PD-1 blockade D. T. Le, J. N. Durham et al chart graph *Science* v357 no6349 p409 Jl 28 2017

New Genus of Bacteria Found in Fracking Wells *USA Today Magazine* v146 no2867 p8 Ag 2017

Qatar's genome effort slowly gears up J. Kaiser color *Science* v354 no6317 p1220 D 9 2016

THE SCIENTISTS' APPRENTICE [Cover story] T. Appenzeller color *Science* v357 no6346 p16 Jl 7 2017

Sequencing all life captivates biologists E. Pennisi chart color *Science* v355 no6328 p894 Mr 3 2017

SHAKING UP THE TREE OF LIFE E. Pennisi color diag *Science* v354 no6314 p817 N 18 2016

Genomic imprinting in mammals

FATEFUL IMPRINTS J. Couzin-Frankel color diag *Science* v355 no6321 p122 Ja 13 2017

Genomics

>*See also*
>
>Epigenomics
>
>Microbial genomics

Ancient genomic changes associated with domestication of

the horse P. Librado, C. Gamba et al color diag *Science* v356 no6336 p442 Ap 28 2017

Big data, big picture: Metabolomics meets systems biology M. May color *Science* v356 no6338 p646 My 12 2017

Evolution with No Reason: A Neutral View on Epigenetic Changes, Genomic Variability, and Evolutionary Novelty C. GUERRERO-BOSAGNA *BioScience* v67 no5 p469 My 2017

A FANTASTIC VOYAGE IN GENOMICS L. M. Zahn color *Science* v357 no6359 p56 O 6 2017

The genomic landscape of rapid repeated evolutionary adaptation to toxic pollution in wild fish N. M. Reid, D. A. Proestou et al bibl graph *Science* v354 no6317 p1305 D 9 2016

Going global by adapting local: A review of recent human adaptation Shaohua Fan, M. E. B. Hansen et al bibl diag graph *Science* v354 no6308 p54 O 7 2016

LOOKING UNDER THE HOOD G. Johnston *Successful Farming* v115 no3 p50 Mid-F 2017

NEW PRODUCTS: GENOMICS color *Science* v354 no6308 p121 O 7 2016

Single-cell whole-genome analyses by Linear Amplification via Transposon Insertion (LIANTI) C. Chen, D. Xing et al graph *Science* v356 no6334 p189 Ap 14 2017

Genomics—Equipment & supplies

new products: genomics color *Science* v355 no6321 p210 Ja 13 2017

Genomics—Research

Genomic estimation of complex traits reveals ancient maize adaptation to temperate North America K. Swarts, R. M. Gutaker et al diag *Science* v357 no6350 p512 Ag 4 2017

The Tree of Life Reconsidered C. POTERA *BioScience* v67 no3 p316 Mr 2017

Genotype

ECONOMICAL PRODUCTS G. Johnston *Successful Farming* v115 no5 p53 Mid-Mr 2017

Genoways, Ted

ARTLESS cartoon chart *Mother Jones* v42 no5 p60 S/O 2017

BRINGING IN THE BEANS: Harvest on an American family farm *Harper's Magazine* p53 S 2017

CLOSE TO THE BONE *New York Times Magazine* p59 O 9 2016

THE GREAT ABANDONMENT bw *New Republic* v248 no1/2 p42 Ja/F 2017

"The Only Good Muslim Is a Dead Muslim" color *New Republic* v248 no6 p30 Je 2017

Gensheimer, Kurt

hart-shaped trails: MEET THE FUTURE OF FEDERAL LAND MANAGEMENT bw color *Bike Magazine* v24 no8 p32 N 2017

TEMPTING THE TOIYABE bw color *Bike Magazine* v23 no9 p70 D 2016

Gensler (Company)

DESIGNING A WORLD INSIDE D. Eng color *Fortune* v175 no5 p26 Ap 1 2017

GENSLER, LAUREN

The Alligator Wrestler and the Casino Boss bw color *Forbes* v198 no6 p104 N 8 2016

The Fintech 50 color *Forbes* v198 no7 p90 N 29 2016

THE MIDDLEMAN OF MIDDLE AMERICA color *Forbes* v200 no2 p62 S 5 2017

MONEY THERAPISTS color *Forbes* v200 no4 p104 O 24 2017

No Car, No Problem color *Forbes* v199 no2 p99 F 28 2017

Sleazy Image, Smart Play color *Forbes* v199 no7 p126 Je 29 2017

Gent, Edd

HUMANITARIANS color il *MIT Technology Review* v120 no5 p62 S/O 2017

Gentilcore, Tony

HIRED GUNS! [Cover story] M. Gainsburg color *Women's Health* v14 no5 p66 Je 2017

Gentile, Guy

THERE'S MORE THAN ONE WAY TO WEAR A Wire Z. FAUX bw color *Bloomberg Businessweek* no4516 p52 Mr 27 2017

Gentile, Mary C.

Talking About Ethics Across Cultures *Harvard Business Review Digital Articles* p2 D 23 2016

Gentiles

Conservative synagogues can now officially accept non-Jews as members L. Markoe *Christian Century* v134 no8 p1 Ap 12 2017

Gentili, Steve

Hybrid Powerlifter J. KINDELA color *Muscle & Performance* v9 no7 p28 Jl 2017

Gentl, Andrea

Coming Into Focus F. Winston bw color *Conde Nast Traveler* v52 no3 p90 Mr 2017

Gentle, Paula

Complex multifault rupture during the 2016 Mw 7.8 Kaikōura earthquake, New Zealand color map *Science* v356 no6334 p154 Ap 14 2017

Gentle Creature, A (Film)

Catastrophes on Parade N. Rapold color *Film Comment* v53 no4 p64 Jl/Ag 2017

Ship of Fools N. Rapold bw color *Film Comment* v53 no5 p8 S/O 2017

Gentrification

EASY CHAIR R. Solnit *Harper's Magazine* v333 no1998 p5 N 2016

Gentry, Audra

Donny Davis color *Spin to Win Rodeo* v21 no5 p20 Jl 2017

Truman House color *Spin to Win Rodeo* v21 no3 p28 My 2017

Tyler Merrill: Weatherford, Texas color *Spin to Win Rodeo* v21 no6 p26 Ag 2017

WHAT'S YOUR NUMBER color *Spin to Win Rodeo* v20 no9 p22 N 2016

WHAT'S YOUR NUMBER? color *Spin to Win Rodeo* v21 no4 p26 Je 2017

WHAT'S YOUR NUMBER with LORIE PATTERSON color *Spin to Win Rodeo* v20 no10 p30 D 2016

Gentry, Bill

Navigating the Transition from Friend to Boss *Harvard Business Review Digital Articles* p2 F 24 2015

GENTRY, BRAD

Society Is Ready for a New Kind of Science--Is Academia? *BioScience* v67 no7 p591 Jl 2017

Gentry, Denny

THE USTRC NATIONAL FINALS REMIX *Team Roping Journal* p10 S 2017

Gentry, Dick

FROM OUR READERS *Sky & Telescope* v133 no6 p6 Je 2017

Gentry, Richard J.

Research: Board Directors Are More Likely to Leave When a Firm Is Getting Criticized *Harvard Business Review Digital Articles* p2 Ag 9 2017

When Star CEOs and Star Analysts Disagree, the Market Trusts the Analysts *Harvard Business Review Digital Articles* p2 Ap 18 2016

Gentzel, Thomas J.

The Pros and Cons of Federally Funded School Choice Programs *Congressional Digest* v96 no7 p12 S 2017

Genzel, Reinhard

Distant galaxies may lack dark matter A. YEAGER *Science News* v191 no7 p10 Ap 15 2017

Geo Tracker automobile—Evaluation

The Battle of the Off-Road Beaters J. Gall bw chart color graph *Car & Driver* v62 no6 p84 D 2016

Geochemistry

See also

Biogeochemistry

Dino fossils show some skin H. Thompson color diag *Science News* v191 no6 p32 Ap 1 2017

Geochronometry

Fossils shake up fish family tree V. Callier color *Science News* v192 no5 p5 S 30 2017

Homo naledi's age surprises scientists B. BOWER color *Science News* v191 no11 p6 Je 10 2017

The Significance and Magnificence of Jehol Biota L. M. Chiappe and M. Qingjin *Natural History* v124 no10 p20 N 2016

Geodesy

See also

Earth (Planet)— Rotation

Astronomy Tools Actions Set E. RIX color *Astronomy* v44 no12 p66 D 2016

Geoghegan, John J.

Full Steam Ahead *American History* v52 no1 p26 Ap 2017

Geographic mobility

STAYING PUT IN A MOBILE ERA R. D. Sullivan chart color

graph map *America* v217 no2 p12 Jl 24 2017

TEXAS IN-MIGRATION AND OUT-MIGRATION K. TASKER *Texas Monthly* v45 no2 p50 F 2017

Geographic names—Canada

WHERE'S THIS? color *Canadian Geographic* v136 no6 p73 D 2016

Geographical distribution of fishes

WORLD-CLASS SEAFOOD DISTRIBUTION *Iceland Review* v54 no6 p124 N/D 2016

Geography

See also

Lunar geography

Maps

Voyages & travels

The 2018 revision of the Consumer Price Index geographic sample S. P. Paben, W. H. Johnson et al bibl chart color diag map *Monthly Labor Review* p1 O 2016

Geography competitions

LONDON, ONT., STUDENT CROWNED CANADIAN GEOGRAPHIC CHALLENGE CHAMPION A. Pope color *Canadian Geographic* v137 no4 p77 Jl/Ag 2017

Geoinformatics

Knowledge keepers J. BENNETT color *Canadian Geographic* v137 no5 p29 S/O 2017

Geological cycles

WHERE DID IT ALL BEGIN? K. MCGOWAN color map *Popular Science* v289 no5 p38 S/O 2017

Geological mapping

THE NORTH POLE F. ROOTS map *Canadian Geographic* v137 no2 p46 Mr/Ap 2017

Geological maps

Great Migrations *Lapham's Quarterly* v10 no2 p10 Spr 2017

HOLES IN THE MAP S. CHODOSH map *Popular Science* p22 Ja/F 2017

You Say Tomato ... J. KATZ map *Reader's Digest* v190 no1132 p124 Jl/Ag 2017

Geological repositories

See also

Radioactive waste repositories

Death and succession among Finland's nuclear waste experts V. Ialenti *Physics Today* v70 no10 p48 O 2017

Geological Survey of Canada

BEST OF THE 2016 RCGS AWARDS AND FELLOWS DINNER A. Pope color *Canadian Geographic* v137 no1 p75 F 2017

Geologists

See also

Paleontologists

Attracted to Magnetics L. Lippsett *Oceanus* v52 no1 p52 Summ 2016

SUPERCONTINENT SUPERPUZZLE [Cover story] A. Witze color map *Science News* v191 no1 p18 Ja 21 2017

Geologists—Attitudes

Zealandia may be eighth continent T. SUMNER map *Science News* v191 no5 p11 Mr 18 2017

Geology

A SHOCKING IMPACT: DISGUISED BY VOLCANOES AND CHALLIS S. WILLSEY *Idaho Magazine* v16 no12 p18 S 2017

Geology—Iceland

EXPLORING THE SNOW DESERT: What better way to experience Europe's largest glacier than from the very top of it? *Iceland Review* v55 no3 p102 My/Je 2017

ICELAND FROM OLD TO NEW: NEW THINGS ARE AFOOT AT THE CULTURE HOUSE *Iceland Review* v55 no3 p119 My/Je 2017

RAUFARHÓLSHELUR: A Trip into Earth's Creation *Iceland Review* v55 no3 p101 My/Je 2017

Geomagnetism

See also

Magnetic fields

Magnetic storms

Geometric decoration & ornament

Pattern Play color *Architectural Digest* v74 no3 p33 Mr 2017

Geometric quantum phases

An on/off Berry phase switch in circular graphene resonators F. Ghahari, D. Walkup et al diag graph *Science* v356 no6340 p845 My 26 2017

Geometrical diffraction

Controlled growth and form of precipitating microsculptures C. Nadir Kaplan, W. L. Noorduin et al bw color diag graph *Science* v355 no6332 p1395 Mr 31 2017

Geometry

See also

Edges (Geometry)

Shapes

Mathematicians Find the Answers J. REHMEYER diag *Discover* v38 no1 p41 Ja/F 2017

Geooptics LLC

CubeSat networks hasten shift to commercial weather data E. Hand color *Science* v357 no6347 p118 Jl 14 2017

Geophysics

See also

Ice

Marine geophysics

Seismology

NEW BOOKS *Physics Today* v70 no8 p62 Ag 2017

Geopolitics

The complicated geopolitics of renewable energy S. Paltsev bibl *Bulletin of the Atomic Scientists* v72 no6 p390 N 2016

GEORGE, ALEXANDER

The Best of Technology 2016 color *Popular Mechanics* p17 D 2016/Ja 2017

THE BRITISH BRUISER color *Popular Mechanics* p41 Ap 2017

BUT IS IT SAFE? color *Popular Mechanics* p75 My 2017

COMPUTER MONITORS color *Popular Mechanics* p30 Ap 2017

Gadgets for the Edge of the World color *Popular Mechanics* p46 Mr 2017

A Garage Sale on Your Phone cartoon chart color *Popular Mechanics* p24 My 2017

The Hair Dryer That Doesn't Get Hot color *Popular Mechanics* p18 S 2017

The Hair Dryer That Doesn't Get Hot color *Popular Mechanics* v193 no7 p18 S 2016

I STINK AT EMAIL *Popular Mechanics* p26 S 2017

THE NEW, IMPROVED HYDROGEN CAR! color diag map *Popular Mechanics* p38 Jl 2017

A Side Table That Can Charge Your Phone color *Popular Mechanics* p110 Ap 2017

GEORGE, DANIEL

Trigger Trash *Idaho Magazine* v16 no6 p6 Mr 2017

George, Haydy

Inactivation of porcine endogenous retrovirus in pigs using CRISPR-Cas9 diag *Science* v357 no6357 p1303 S 22 2017

George, Henry, 1839-1897

CAPITALISM, BY GEORGE! M. KINSLEY color *Vanity Fair* v59 no10 p142 O 2017

GEORGE, JANEL

The War on Women's Health: Trumpcare leaves 23 million more people uninsured and slashes $834 billion from Medicaid, rewarding the wealthy while penalizing low-income women *Ms.* v27 no2 p36 Summ 2017

GEORGE, JASON

My Obsessions... *TV Guide* v64 no40 p13 O 3 2016

George, Kallie

The Lost Gift: A Christmas Story *Publishers Weekly* v263 no39 p90 S 26 2016

George, Katy

25% of CEOs' Time Is Spent on Tasks Machines Could Do color *Harvard Business Review Digital Articles* p2 F 3 2017

GEORGE, NELSON

Invisibly Black *New York Times Book Review* p14 Ja 15 2017

George, Paul

HOW OKC GOT ITS MAN L. Jenkins color *Sports Illustrated* v127 no3 p50 Jl 24 2017

George, Prince of Cambridge, 2013-

The little prince P. TREBLE color *Maclean's* v129 no40 p52 O 10 2016

George, Sheryl

You, Unfiltered color *InStyle* v24 no4 p141 Ap 2017

George, Terry

The Promise L. Greenblatt color *Entertainment Weekly* no1463/1464 p90 Ap/My 2017

George, Todd
  THE LAKE HOUSE cartoon *Cabin Living* p88 Mr 2017
George Crumb: Voice of the Whale (Film)
  Legends & Legacies J. EPHLAND color *Downbeat* v83 no12 p88 D 2016
George Mason University
  George Mason University *Dance Magazine* v90 p65 2016/2017 Supplement College Guide
  Sweet as Honey: UNIVERSITY OF RICHMOND AND GEORGE MASON UNIVERSITY ADD BEEHIVES TO THE CURRICULUM *Virginia Living* v15 no6 p87 O 2017
George Mason University. School of Law
  A Most Fitting Tribute T. EASTLAND color *Weekly Standard* v22 no7 p12 O 24 2016
George Washington University
  George Washington University *Dance Magazine* v90 p65 2016/2017 Supplement College Guide
Georges, Arthur
  Amphibians on the brink color map *Science* v357 no6350 p454 Ag 4 2017
Georges, Matt
  SOUTH OF THE BOARDERS cartoon color *Snowboarder* v29 no5 p64 Ja 2017
Georgetown University
  BEST BANG FOR THE BUCK SOUTHEAST COLLEGES chart *Washington Monthly* v49 no9/10 p54 S/O 2017
  Georgetown Steps Up J. CARR color *America* v215 no10 p14 O 10 2016
  Georgetown University apologizes for its role in historical slave trade A. M. Banks color *Christian Century* v134 no11 p16 My 24 2017
  A Painful Legacy C. STOFFERS *New York Times Upfront* v149 no8 p6 Ja 30 2017
George-Warren, Holly
  Q: What is the most significant fad of all time? color *Atlantic* v319 no3 p96 Ap 2017
George Washington Bridge (New York, N.Y.)
  FROZEN L. Widdicombe cartoon *New Yorker* v92 no32 p34 O 10 2016
Georgia
  THE DINING GUIDE *Atlanta* v56 no11 p225 Mr 2017
  FRESH ON THE SCENE C. LAUTERBACH *Atlanta* v56 no11 p64 Mr 2017
  ONE TEAM TO UNITE THEM ALL C. BETHEA *Atlanta* v56 no11 p100 Mr 2017
  Pretty. Sweet Cuisine *Atlanta* v57 no5 p139 S 2017
Georgia (Republic)—Description & travel
  Sweet Georgia E. FLORIO color *Conde Nast Traveler* v52 no9 p38 O 2017
Georgia Institute of Technology
  SOUNDS OF SCIENCE J. R. MARQUEZ *Atlanta* v56 no11 p34 Mr 2017
Georgia Public Broadcasting
  NOISES OFF C. PENDLEY *Atlanta* v56 no11 p28 Mr 2017
Georgia state history
  Nine ways to explore Georgia history *Atlanta* v57 no2 p72 Je 2017
Georgia State University
  ATLANTA MAGAZINE DIGITAL *Atlanta* v57 no2 p12 Je 2017
Georgia—Description & travel
  50 Things Every Georgian Must Do *Atlanta* v57 no2 p64 Je 2017
  DESTINATIONS *Atlanta* v57 no2 p145 Je 2017
  FIVE REASONS TO LOVE... MARIETTA L. MOWRY *Atlanta* v56 no8 p66 D 2016
  WELCOME TO CARTERSVILLE H. S. PHILBRICK *Atlanta* v56 no7 p18 N 2016
Georgia—History
  Sosebee Cove, Georgia R. H. MOHLENBROCK *Natural History* v124 no10 p42 N 2016
Georgian architecture (British)
  GEORGIAN BY CANDLELIGHT R. COLE color *Old House Journal* v45 no6 p24 S 2017
Georgian Court University (Lakewood, N.J.)
  Georgian Court University *Dance Magazine* v90 p66 2016/2017 Supplement College Guide
Georgia—Politics & government—1951-
  The Democrats Went Down to Georgia B. MASCHINOT *In These*

Times v41 no5 p8 My 2017
Georgiev, Georgio
  SHADES OF GREEN color *Popular Photography* v80 no11 p30 D 2016
Georgiou, Andreas—Trials, litigation, etc.
  Greece's Least Wanted Man Lives in Maryland R. Schmidt color *Bloomberg Businessweek* no4493 p25 O 3 2016
  The Scandalous Plight of A Greek Whistleblower *Bloomberg Businessweek* no4534 p10 Ag 14 2017
Georgis, William T.
  guiding lights color *Architectural Digest* v74 no4 p102 Ap 2017
Geostationary satellites
  Weather Front M. Branom *Weatherwise* v70 no2 p6 Mr/Ap 2017
Geothermal resources
  See also
    Hot springs
  Kenya's Energy Quandary R. C. Thurnett color map *Earth Island Journal* v32 no2 p39 Summ 2017
GeoXplor Corp.
  An Account of Clayton Valley and the Great Nevada LITHIUM RUSH P. Tullis color graph *Bloomberg Businessweek* no4517 p60 Ap 3 2017
Gephart, Dustin
  THE FARM *Successful Farming* v115 no11 p75 S 2017
Geraci, John
  How an Ecosystem Mindset Can Help People and Organizations Succeed *Harvard Business Review Digital Articles* p2 My 12 2016
  To Innovate, Think Like a 19th-Century Barn Raiser *Harvard Business Review Digital Articles* p2 Ag 4 2016
  What I Learned from Trying to Innovate at the New York Times *Harvard Business Review Digital Articles* p2 Ap 7 2016
  What Your Moonshot Can Learn from the Apollo Program *Harvard Business Review Digital Articles* p2 Ap 4 2017
Geraci, Ron
  Ancient Remedies for Modern Maladies color *Men's Health* v32 no5 p84 Je 2017
  THE FUTURE OF PROFITS, TODAY color *Bloomberg Businessweek* no4502 p2 D 5 2016
Geradin, Damien
  Competing with Platforms That Ignore the Law *Harvard Business Review Digital Articles* p2 Mr 25 2016
GERAGHTY, JIM
  The Normal One il *National Review* v69 no19 p13 O 16 2017
Geraniums
  DIG INTO SPRING color *Sunset* v238 no4 p41 Ap 2017
Gérard, Audrey
  Visualizing dynamic microvillar search and stabilization during ligand detection by T cells color *Science* v356 no6338 p598 My 12 2017
Gerard, Courtney
  COME ONE, COME ALL color *Backpacker* v45 no1 p64 Ja 2017
  Eat for Endurance color *Backpacker* v45 no1 p36 Ja 2017
  Find the Perfect Partner color *Backpacker* v45 no2 p31 Mr 2017
  Learn Minimalist Fly-Fishing il *Backpacker* p36 My 2017
  THE PATH LESS TRAVELED color *Backpacker* v45 no1 p86 Ja 2017
  Treat Aches and Pains diag *Backpacker* v45 no1 p32 Ja 2017
Gerard, J.-C.
  Jupiter's magnetosphere and aurorae observed by the Juno spacecraft during its first polar orbits diag graph *Science* v356 no6340 p826 My 26 2017
Gerbaldi, Claudio
  Improving efficiency and stability of perovskite solar cells with photocurable fluoropolymers bibl chart graph *Science* v354 no6309 p203 O 14 2016
Gerber, Julie A.
  Navigating Indieworld: A Beginner's Guide to Self-Publishing and Marketing Your Book color *Publishers Weekly* v263 no45 p54 N 7 2016
Gerber, Kaia
  "My Mom Taught Me Less Is More" K. Gerber and F. Valdesolo color *Glamour* v115 no5 p69 My 2017
Gerber, Leah R.
  Without inclusion, diversity initiatives may not be enough color *Science* v357 no6356 p1101 S 15 2017

Gerber, S.
Femtosecond electron-phonon lock-in by photoemission and x-ray free-electron laser chart diag *Science* v357 no6346 p71 Jl 7 2017

Gerber, Sander
The Department of Pay-for-Slay: How the Palestinian Authority not only incites terrorist murder—but supports it with U.S. tax dollars *Commentary* v143 no4 p19 Ap 2017

GERBER, TONY
Becoming Jane [Cover story] bw color map *National Geographic* v232 no4 p30 O 2017

Gerberding, Julie
EPIDEMIC INSURANCE color graph *Science* v356 no6334 p125 Ap 14 2017

GERBIC, SUSAN
How I Got Hooked on the Skeptical World *Skeptical Inquirer* v40 no6 p45 N/D 2016
Let Your Questioning Start with Wikipedia *Skeptical Inquirer* v41 no2 p24 Mr/Ap 2017
Philosopher and CSI Fellow Robert Carroll, Creator of Skeptics Dictionary, Dies at Seventy-One *Skeptical Inquirer* v41 no1 p11 Ja/F 2017

Gerdemann, Ulrike
The epigenetic landscape of T cell exhaustion bibl graph *Science* v354 no6316 p1165 D 2 2016

Gerdes, Kenn
Mechanisms of bacterial persistence during stress and antibiotic exposure bibl diag graph *Science* v354 no6318 paaf4268-1 D 16 2016

GERECHT, REUEL MARC
The CIA, Post-Obama color *Weekly Standard* v22 no15 p24 D 19 2016
The Face-Off [Cover story] color *Weekly Standard* v22 no24 p22 F 27 2017
No Easy Way Out color *Weekly Standard* v23 no6 p11 O 16 2017
Perfect Partners color *Weekly Standard* v23 no2 p29 S 18 2017
'Principled Realism' color *Weekly Standard* v22 no38 p24 Je 12 2017
Protecting Palestine color *Weekly Standard* v22 no18 p30 Ja 16 2017
Wellsprings of Violence *Hoover Digest: Research & Opinion on Public Policy* no4 p94 Fall 2016

Geremia, Lauren
NEXT-LEVEL DESIGN C. Lamers color diag *Sunset* v237 no5 p31 N 2016

Gergely, Fanni
Neurodevelopmental protein Musashi-1 interacts with the Zika genome and promotes viral replication diag *Science* v357 no6346 p83 Jl 7 2017

Gerges, Fawaz A.
ISIS: A History J. Waterbury *Foreign Affairs* v95 no6 p188 N/D 2016

Gerhaher, Christian
Berg: Wozzeck W. R. Braun *Opera News* v81 no10 p54 Ap 2017
Room for Interpretation A. WASSERMAN *Opera News* v81 no6 p22 D 2016

Gerhardstein, Al
ENCYCLOPEDIA CINCINNATI A. BROWNLEE, B. COLEMAN et al bw cartoon color *Cincinnati Magazine* v51 no1 p42 O 2017

Geriatric assessment
Gathering Around *Virginia Living* v15 no1 p103 D 2016

Geriatric nursing
COMPLICATED CARE W. RYAN *Commonweal* v114 no14 p2 S 8 2017

Geriner, Alex
Doorman Design P. Marquis *New Orleans Homes & Lifestyles* v20 no1 p93 Wint 2016

Gerken, Heather
One Campus Arena Where Free Speech Is Not Up for Debate: Law Schools color *Time* v190 no4 p20 Jl 24 2017

Gerkin, Richard C.
Predicting human olfactory perception from chemical features of odor molecules bibl diag graph *Science* v355 no6327 p820 F 24 2017

GERLACH, KENDRA

I Survived! [Cover story] *Reader's Digest* v189 no1128 p62 Mr 2017

Germ cells
IN THE IMAGE OF OUR CHOOSING N. BARCZI diag *Christianity Today* p48 Mr 2017
Linking stem cells to germ cells Vielle-Calzada color *Science* v356 no6336 p378 Ap 28 2017

Germ theory of disease
Morbid Curiosity D. BURCH color *Natural History* v125 no9 p3 S 2017

Germain, Thomas
Eat Smarter, Eat Healthier [Cover story] color *Consumer Reports* v82 no11 p18 N 2017
The New War on Obesity chart color diag *Consumer Reports* v82 no10 p48 O 2017
Shattered chart color diag graph *Consumer Reports* v82 no12 p30 D 2017

Germain, Wayne
Rubber Tub Captures Sawdust color *Popular Mechanics* p29 F 2017

German, Chris
Chris German K. GRAY cartoon *Popular Science* p49 Ja/F 2017

German, Gustavo
OUT OF BOUNDS A. McCook color *Science* v355 no6323 p339 Ja 27 2017

German, Lauren
CHICAGO FIRE I. Rudolph *TV Guide* v65 no39 p50 S 18 2017

German Americans
A YANK IN THE SS R. Soodalter *Military History* v33 no5 p40 Ja 2017

German art—Exhibitions
Martin Luther's Burning Questions [Cover story] I. D. Rowland color *New York Review of Books* v64 no10 p10 Je 8 2017

German authors
MR. BLITZED N. Paumgarten cartoon *New Yorker* v93 no5 p30 Mr 20 2017

German Frers (Company)
Hallberg-Rassy 40 Mk II Z. Prochazka color *Sail* v48 no8 p24 Ag 2017

German history
THAT SINKING FEELING B. Hogan color *MHQ: Quarterly Journal of Military History* v29 no4 p28 Summ 2017
A U-BOAT'S U-TURN [Cover story] W. Bernard bw color map *MHQ: Quarterly Journal of Military History* v29 no4 p40 Summ 2017

German military history
What's the Point? J. GUTTMAN color *MHQ: Quarterly Journal of Military History* v29 no4 p11 Summ 2017

German shepherd dog
FLYING THE CANINE HIGHWAY D. Karl color *Flying* v144 no4 p78 Ap 2017
GIANTS AMONG US: The city isn't built for extra-large dogs--but they're definitely built for the city M. D. G. Kaplan *Washingtonian Magazine* v52 no8 p207 My 2017
SIP! STAY! cartoon *Women's Health* v13 no10 p42 D 2016
THIS HERO WEARS FUR T. DASWICK color *Men's Health* v32 no6 p122 Ag 2017
Top Dog *Military History* v33 no6 p80 Mr 2017

German shorthaired pointer
SCRATCH, THE UNKILLABLE S. LINDEN color *Outdoor Life* v224 no6 p51 Ag 2017

Germanicus Caesar, 15 B.C.-19 A.D.
Tacitus' Perfect Man E. Southon *History Today* v67 no8 p18 Ag 2017

Germanus, Nicolaus
You Had To Be There C. TATTOLI color *Conde Nast Traveler* v52 no5 p132 My 2017

Germany. Bundesanstalt für Finanzdienstleistungsaufsicht
Preparing to Pop a Bubble, Just in Case S. Kahl and A. Blackman color *Bloomberg Businessweek* no4535 p29 Ag 28 2017

Germany—Armed Forces
Calls To Arms J. NORDLINGER color *National Review* v68 no24 p20 D 31 2016

Germany—Description & travel
DOING BUSINESS IN: FRANKFURT A. Erace color *Fortune* v176 no1 p39 Jl 1 2017

A JOURNEY Through Germany L. Paulsen color *Dressage Today* v23 no7 p32 Mr 2017

Germany—Economic policy—21st century

Germany Should Get With the 'Bad Bank' cartoon *Bloomberg Businessweek* no4514 p10 Mr 13 2017

Germany—Emigration & immigration

Germany's Maternity Wards Are Booked C. Matlack, N. Kresge et al color graph *Bloomberg Businessweek* no4504 p16 D 19 2016

Germany—Foreign relations

How evils wins S. Wells *Christian Century* v134 no7 p35 Mr 29 2017

Germany—Foreign relations—Great Britain

A Good Germany? K. Graham *History Today* v67 no7 p8 Jl 2017

Germany—Foreign relations—Turkey

This Just Got Awkward C. Thomas and R. Buergin color graph *Bloomberg Businessweek* no4532 p36 Jl 31 2017

Germany—Foreign relations—United States

What 'America First' Means Here W. Donahue color *Commonweal* v144 no12 p10 Jl 7 2017

Germany—Military policy—History—20th century

D-DAY THROUGH A GERMAN LENS R. M. Citino color *MHQ: Quarterly Journal of Military History* v29 no4 p68 Summ 2017

Germer, Christopher

To Recover from Failure, Try Some Self-Compassion color *Harvard Business Review Digital Articles* p2 Ja 5 2017

Germination

See also

Vernalization

Sterilizing immunity in the lung relies on targeting fungal apoptosis-like programmed cell death N. Shlezinger, H. Irmer et al color diag *Science* v357 no6355 p1037 S 8 2017

Germlat, Barb

Still worried *U.S. Catholic* v82 no10 p5 O 2017

Gero, Annette

A stitch in wartime: The American Folk Art Museum presents a fascinating collection of quilts made by men at arms bw color *Magazine Antiques* v184 no4 p92 Jl/Ag 2017

GEROMEL, RICARDO

THE WORLD'S BILLIONAIRES bw color diag graph map *Forbes* v199 no3 p84 Mr 28 2017

Gerontology

See also

Aging

Can Crowdfunding Help Solve Our Health Issues? J. Englis *AARP: The Magazine* v59 no2A p81 F/Mr 2016

GEROUX, SARAH

Tools OF THE Trade: Everything you need to shuck it, slice it and smoke it *Virginia Living* p46 2017 Smoke & Salt

Gerrard, Brian

Bae Watch A. TILLERY and S. TIABROWN color *Ebony* v72 no4 p82 F 2017

Gerrard, Justin

Bae Watch A. TILLERY and S. TIABROWN color *Ebony* v72 no4 p82 F 2017

Gerriets International (Company)

Flooring & Seating *Stage Directions* v30 no7 p34 Jl 1 2017

GERRISH, GRETCHEN A.

Teaching Biology in the Field: Importance, Challenges, and Solutions *BioScience* v67 no6 p558 Je 2017

GERRMANN, ERIC

The Skis of the Year color *Powder* p82 S 2017

Gerrymandering

Computers Made Gerrymandering Worse. Can They Fix It? E. Barone diag map *Time* v190 no14 p14 O 9 2017

Democracy vs. Math E. Bazelon *New York Times Magazine* p48 S 3 2017

The Future of the Gerrymander T. Helfman *Commentary* v143 no3 p9 Mr 2017

The Gerrymander Myth D. McLAUGHLIN color il *National Review* v69 no3 p16 F 20 2017

How Unfair Is the Map? A new measurement may identify gerrymandering A. Greenblatt *Governing* v30 no8 p17 My 2017

IN MATH WE TRUST HOW DATA CAN SAVE DEMOCRACY C. THOMPSON cartoon *Wired* v25 no5 p40 My 2017

Is the Gerrymander on Its Way Out? New court action may threaten a 200-year-old practice T. Helfman *Commentary* v143 no1 p34 Ja 2017

Mad, Democrats? Blame the Iran Deal *Commentary* p1 Ja 2017

Mad, Democrats? Blame the Iran Deal *Commentary* v143 no1 p1 Ja 2017

Gerrymandering lawsuits

PLEA TO HIGH COURT: KNOW YOUR LIMITS S. FORBES color *Forbes* v200 no5 p17 N 14 2017

Gershenson, Anna—Interviews

In Conversation: A Jewish Grandma and a Korean Grandma on Their Dumplings C. CROWLEY img *New York* v49 no25 p102 D 12 2016

Gershenzon, Jonathan

Releasing plant volatiles, as simple as ABC color *Science* v356 no6345 p1334 Je 30 2017

GERSHGORN, DAVE

The End of the Language Barrier color *Popular Science* v288 no6 p84 N/D 2016

The Internet of "Meh" color *Popular Science* v288 no6 p72 N/D 2016

Light Hammer Heavy Hitter color *Popular Science* v288 no6 p68 N/D 2016

SMART WATCHES, DISSECTED color *Popular Science* v288 no6 p20 N/D 2016

Gershoni, D.

Deterministic generation of a cluster state of entangled photons bibl diag graph *Science* v354 no6311 p434 O 28 2016

Gershwin, George, 1898-1937

GEORGE GERSHWIN: HERE TO STAY J. McDonough bw *Downbeat* v84 no8 p38 Ag 2017

Gerson, Jody—Interviews

JODY GERSON bw color *Bloomberg Businessweek* no4506 p68 Ja 9 2017

Gerson, Michael

The Politics of Late-Night Comedy color *Atlantic* v320 no1 p10 Jl/Ag 2017

Gerson, Stéphane

Grief and Reckoning M. THERNSTROM *New York Times Book Review* p16 F 5 2017

Gerstberger, Stefanie

Posttranslational mutagenesis: A chemical strategy for exploring protein side-chain diversity diag *Science* v354 no6312 p597 N 4 2016

Gerstein, Daniel M.

Glaring gaps: America needs a biodefense upgrade bibl *Bulletin of the Atomic Scientists* v73 no2 p86 Mr 2017

GERSTEIN, MARC

Mattress Missionaries color *Forbes* v199 no5 p50 My 16 2017

Gerstein, Suzy

EYES WIDE OPEN color *Women's Health* v14 no5 p34 Je 2017

Gerstl, S. S. A.

Direct observation of individual hydrogen atoms at trapping sites in a ferritic steel bibl diag *Science* v355 no6330 p1196 Mr 17 2017

GERSTNER, KATHARINA

Harmonizing Biodiversity Conservation and Productivity in the Context of Increasing Demands on Landscapes graph *BioScience* v66 no10 p890 O 1 2016

GERSTNER, LISA

Are Your Bank Accounts at Risk? chart *Kiplinger's Personal Finance* v71 no12 p42 D 2017

The Best Bank for You cartoon *Kiplinger's Personal Finance* v71 no7 p26 Jl 2017

Best Cards for College Students chart *Kiplinger's Personal Finance* v71 no10 p46 O 2017

THE BEST REWARDS CARD FOR YOU color graph *Kiplinger's Personal Finance* v71 no8 p22 Ag 2017

BOOMERS CASH OUT ART COLLECTIONS color *Kiplinger's Personal Finance* v71 no2 p14 F 2017

Budgeting Tools for Every Style cartoon *Kiplinger's Personal Finance* v71 no1 p34 Ja 2017

Credit, Debit or Cash? cartoon color *Kiplinger's Personal Finance* v71 no3 p32 Mr 2017

Deposit Insurance Has Your Back chart *Kiplinger's Personal Finance* v71 no5 p49 My 2017

Dog Food, TP and Insurance? color *Kiplinger's Personal Finance* v71 no11 p40 N 2017

FIGHTING THE INTERNET'S DARK SIDE *Kiplinger's Personal Finance* v71 no11 p12 N 2017

FOR NEWLYWEDS WHO HAVE EVERYTHING color *Kiplinger's Personal Finance* v71 no6 p15 Je 2017

How to Get Sweeter Card Rewards chart *Kiplinger's Personal Finance* v71 no6 p40 Je 2017

Learn From the Credit-Score Elite chart *Kiplinger's Personal Finance* v71 no3 p43 Mr 2017

Max Out Points for Holiday Shopping chart *Kiplinger's Personal Finance* v70 no12 p45 D 2016

Miles or Cash Back: Which Is Better? chart *Kiplinger's Personal Finance* v71 no8 p40 Ag 2017

Mobile Deposit: Give It a Shot chart *Kiplinger's Personal Finance* v71 no1 p41 Ja 2017

MONEY MADE SIMPLE [Cover story] color *Kiplinger's Personal Finance* v71 no5 p24 My 2017

Online Bill Paying Isn't Foolproof chart *Kiplinger's Personal Finance* v71 no7 p45 Jl 2017

A Payout for Credit Score Customers chart *Kiplinger's Personal Finance* v71 no4 p50 Ap 2017

A Premium Travel Card With a Catch chart *Kiplinger's Personal Finance* v71 no11 p47 N 2017

PROTECT POINTS AND MILES FROM THEFT color *Kiplinger's Personal Finance* v71 no3 p12 Mr 2017

Resolve Errors on Your Credit Card Bill chart *Kiplinger's Personal Finance* v71 no2 p51 F 2017

RETAILERS HAVE THEIR EYE ON YOU color *Kiplinger's Personal Finance* v71 no5 p12 My 2017

TIME TO STOCK UP AT THE GROCERY STORE color *Kiplinger's Personal Finance* v71 no1 p15 Ja 2017

Your Equifax Defense color *Kiplinger's Personal Finance* v71 no12 p34 D 2017

YOUR TV MIGHT BE SPYING ON YOU color *Kiplinger's Personal Finance* v71 no6 p14 Je 2017

Gerthsen, Dagmar

Active sites in heterogeneous ice nucleation—the example of K-rich feldspars bibl bw diag *Science* v355 no6323 p367 Ja 27 2017

Gertner, Jon

From Techie to Titan *New York Times Book Review* p20 O 16 2016

PANDORA'S UMBRELLA *New York Times Magazine* p58 Ap 23 2017

The View From Above: What do we lose when a research satellite goes dark? *New York Times Magazine* p54 S 17 2017

WILLIAM A. DEL MONTE *New York Times Magazine* p24 D 25 2016

GERVAIS, CHRISTINE

the DUNDAS SOFA *Texas Monthly* v44 no11 p111 N 2016

Gervais, Ricky, 1961-

PARTY LINES img *New York* v49 no23 p88 N 14 2016

Gervais, Ricky, 1961——Interviews

Ricky GERVAIS color *Vanity Fair* v59 no9 p247 S 2017

Gerver, Michael J.

Climate change scenarios and risks *Physics Today* v70 no9 p11 S 2017

Gerwarth, Robert

Neither War Nor Peace M. MACMILLAN *New York Times Book Review* p16 D 11 2016

GERWIG, GRETA

Annie BAKER: ON THE STAGE, THE PULITZER PRIZE-WINNING PLAYWRIGHT BUILDS DIORAMA-LIKE REALITIES. IN HER OWN LIFE, THINGS ARE MUCH MORE MYSTERIOUS *Interview* v47 no3 p24 Ap 2017

Gerwig, Greta, 1983——Interviews

"Kiss all the people you want to kiss" K. Branch and E. Mahaney color *Glamour* v115 no2 p82 F 2017

Gesicki, Matt

Oshin Liam Jennings color *Tricycle: The Buddhist Review* v26 no2 p24 Wint 2016

Gesselman, Amanda

Sometimes when I get incredibly horny color *Glamour* v114 no12 p172 D 2016

Gessen, Masha

Even President Trump Couldn't Turn Russia Into a Friend of the U.S color *Time* v188 no16/17 p35 O 24 2016

FAMILY VALUES *Harper's Magazine* v334 no2002 p35 Mr 2017

FORBIDDEN LIVES cartoon color *New Yorker* v93 no19 p22 Jl 3 2017

Masha Gessen P. NEIDL color *Rolling Stone* no1295 p46 S 7 2017

THE REICHSTAG FIRE NEXT TIME: The coming crackdown *Harper's Magazine* v335 no2006 p25 Jl 2017

The Sad Fate of Birobidzhan R. Pipes color *New York Review of Books* v63 no16 p66 O 27 2016

TIME TO PANIC color *Advocate* no1089 p38 F/Mr 2017

Gessen, Masha—Interviews

Outrage Is Not Optional Y. KUNICHOFF *In These Times* v41 no5 p30 My 2017

Gestational age

signs it's almost time M. COHEN *Parents* v92 no4 p124 Ap 2017

Gestational diabetes

complicating factors H. PEVZNER *Parents* p129 2015

second-trimester surprises L. SINGER MORAN *Parents* v92 no8 p128 Ag 2017

Gestrin, Albert

Ditch Rider F. A. LOOMIS *Idaho Magazine* v16 no1 p28 O 2016

Gesture

SYMBOLIC GESTURES R. SULLIVAN *Commonweal* v144 no13 p2 Ag 11 2017

What Ever Happened to the Romantic Gesture? L. LARSON color *GQ: Gentlemen's Quarterly* v97 no10 p78 O 2017

Gesture controlled interfaces (Computer systems)

Gestures Will Be the Interface for the Internet of Things P. Daugherty, O. Schybergson et al *Harvard Business Review Digital Articles* p2 Jl 8 2015

Get Down Tonight: The Disco Explosion (Music)

WYES-TV/CHANNEL 12 PROGRAM GUIDE color *New Orleans Magazine* v51 no2 p142 D 2016

Get Happy (Music)

John Abercrombie T. PANKEN color *Downbeat* v83 no12 p114 D 2016

Get Out (Film)

THE 10 BEST MOVIES OF THE YEAR SO FAR L. Greenblatt and C. Nashawaty color *Entertainment Weekly* no1472 p40 Je 30 2017

ATTACK OF THE KILLER WHITE PEOPLE K. P. Sullivan color *Entertainment Weekly* no1454/1455 p80 F 24 2017

Bigotry is the Monster in Jordan Peele's New Film K. KYLES color *Ebony* v72 no5 p20 Mr 2017

CHEAP THRILLS: FOR THE PRODUCER JASON BLUM, 'GET OUT' IS JUST THE LATEST HORROR BLOCKBUSTER IN AN EIGHT-YEAR RUN OF LEAN, INVENTIVE AND SCARILY PROFITABLE HITS R. Bradley *New York Times Magazine* p44 My 14 2017

Fear of a White Village R. DOUTHAT color *National Review* v69 no8 p43 My 2017

GET OUT BREAKS OUT J. Nolfi color *Entertainment Weekly* no1456 p16 Mr 10 2017

GETTING IN AND OUT: Who owns black pain? Z. Smith *Harper's Magazine* v335 no2006 p85 Jl 2017

HANG IN THERE, DUDE! B. Stephen color *Esquire* p96 Je/Jl 2017

Hollywood Signs: Mark Harris: The Get Out Effect Does Hollywood know what to do with a surprise success? img *New York* v50 no9 p13 My 1 2017

Jordan Peele Is Terrifying color *GQ: Gentlemen's Quarterly* v97 no3 p82 Mr 2017

Jordan Peele Made Us Seriously Laugh. Now He's Going to Scare Us Silly E. Berman color *Time* v189 no7/8 p108 F 27 2017

Lost Weekend J. PODHORETZ color *Weekly Standard* v22 no28 p43 Mr 27 2017

THE MUST LIST color *Entertainment Weekly* p2 Jl 24 2017

The Response to 'Get Out' D. Lindelof *New York Times Magazine* p41 O 8 2017

SCARY PLACES A. LANE cartoon *New Yorker* v93 no3 p84 Mr 6 2017

Timely Provocations R. Alleva color *Commonweal* v144 no7 p24 Ap 14 2017

White Fright D. EDELSTEIN img *New York* p75 F 20 2017

Get Shorty (TV program)

Get Shorty I. Ratledge *TV Guide* v65 no35 p37 Ag 21 2017

Get Shorty: This adaptation gets Elmore Leonard just right M. ROUSH *TV Guide* v65 no35 p12 Ag 21 2017

Shorty and Sweet I. Ratledge *TV Guide* v65 no23 p9 My 29 2017

Get Down, The (TV program)
WELCOME TO THE BOOGIE DOWN O. SEGURA *America* v215 no10 p42 O 10 2016

Gethard, Chris, 1980-
9 — BEAUTIFUL STORIES FROM ANONYMOUS PEOPLE C. Everett *Entertainment Weekly* no1444/1445 p114 D 16 2016

Gettle, Steve
Freeze Frame color *National Wildlife (World Edition)* v55 no2 p20 F/Mr 2017

Gettleman, Jeffrey
Foreign Correspondence: A journalist's account of his long fascination with Africa N. MOHAMED *New York Times Book Review* p17 Jl 9 2017

Getty, Keith—Interviews
Singing Isn't Just for Sunday S. GUTHRIE bw color *Christianity Today* v61 no7 p80 S 2017

Getty, Rosetta
"MY PACKING ADVICE? ROLL EVERYTHING AND BRING A DRY SHAMPOO" A. WHITTLE color *Conde Nast Traveler* v52 no4 p26 Ap 2017
Rosetta's THRONE E. Wilson color *InStyle* v24 no3 p344 Mr 2017

Getty, Sabine
MEMPHIS Beat E. ELWICK-BATES color *Vogue* v206 no12 p164 D 2016

Getty Research Institute
Gehry Archive Goes to Getty A. KLIMOSKI color *Architectural Record* v205 no5 p28 My 2017

Get Up, Stand Up (Music)
Hot Tracks L. ROBINSON color *Vanity Fair* v59 no5 p54 Ap 2017

Getz, Gad
Decoupling genetics, lineages, and microenvironment in IDH-mutant gliomas by single-cell RNA-seq diag *Science* v355 no6332 p1391 Mr 31 2017

GETZ, ISAAC
ISAAC GETZ: Hierarchies are unnatural - it's time for a liberating revolution *People Management* p16 Mr 2017

Getzels, Peter
MUSIC IS LIFE A. Whiting *Washingtonian Magazine* v52 no9 p22 Je 2017

Geuer, Jana K.
Dissolved organic sulfur in the ocean: Biogeochemistry of a petagram inventory bibl chart diag graph *Science* v354 no6311 p456 O 28 2016
Genomic databases: A WHO affair *Science* v356 no6340 p812 My 26 2017

Geum
GEUMS M. ROSS color *Better Homes & Gardens* v95 no4 p74 Ap 2017

Geun Ho Ahn
MoS2 transistors with 1-nanometer gate lengths bibl color graph *Science* v354 no6308 p99 O 7 2016

Geuter, S.
Interactions between brain and spinal cord mediate value effects in nocebo hyperalgesia color *Science* v357 no6359 p105 O 6 2017

Gevaert, Kris
De novo design of a biologically active amyloid bibl graph *Science* v354 no6313 paah4949-1 N 11 2016

Gevers, Dirk
Potential role of intratumor bacteria in mediating tumor resistance to the chemotherapeutic drug gemcitabine diag *Science* v357 no6356 p1156 S 15 2017

Gevinson, Tavi, 1996-
Kenneth LONERGAN *Interview* v46 no9 p40 N 2016
PARTY LINES S. Huver img *New York* v50 no17 p144 Ag 21 2017

Gewertz, Catherine
Where Career Plans Start Early *Education Digest* v83 no1 p54 S 2017

Gewirth, Andrew A.
Restored iron transport by a small molecule promotes absorption and hemoglobinization in animals color graph *Science* v356 no6338 p608 My 12 2017

Gewirtz, Julian Baird

The Cruise That Changed China bw *Foreign Affairs* v95 no6 p101 N/D 2016
Milton Friedman's Misadventures in China *American Scholar* v86 no1 p30 Wint 2017
Unlikely Partners: Chinese Reformers, Western Economists, and the Making of Global China color *Publishers Weekly* v263 no48 p63 N 28 2016

Geyser, Morgan
A Bogeyman Who Drove Kids to Attempt Murder M. Chan color *Time* v189 no4 p50 F 6 2017

Geysers
CROWNING GLORY E. Conant bw *National Geographic* v230 no6 p132 D 2016

Gezari, Vanessa M.
End note color *Columbia Journalism Review* v56 no2 p112 Fall 2017
VIEWFINDER color *Columbia Journalism Review* v56 no2 p40 Fall 2017
The view from Hollywood color *Columbia Journalism Review* p42 Fall/Wint 2016

Gezon, Lisa L.
The Health Benefits of a Bicycle-Pedestrian Trail *Parks & Recreation* v51 no12 p16 D 2016

Ghaferi, Amir A.
The Next Wave of Hospital Innovation to Make Patients Safer *Harvard Business Review Digital Articles* p2 Ag 8 2016

Ghahari, Fereshte
An on/off Berry phase switch in circular graphene resonators diag graph *Science* v356 no6340 p845 My 26 2017

Ghana—Officials & employees
The Commencement of the Free Senior High School Policy *Vital Speeches of the Day* v83 no10 p283 O 2017

Ghana—Social conditions—21st century
Ghana's Last Mile J. W. Rosen color map *MIT Technology Review* v120 no1 p74 Ja/F 2017

Ghana—Social life & customs
Ghana's Last Mile J. W. Rosen color map *MIT Technology Review* v120 no1 p74 Ja/F 2017

Ghanem, Khalil G.
A microbiome variable in the HIV-prevention equation color *Science* v356 no6341 p907 Je 1 2017

Ghani, Ashraf, 1949-
'Afghanistan Is the Front Line' N. Kumar and F. Shoaib color *Time* v189 no22 p38 Je 12 2017

Ghani, Mariam
MARIAM GHANI D. Markus color *Art in America* v104 no10 p151 N 2016

GHANSAH, RACHEL KAADZI
THE MAKING AND UNMAKING OF DYLANN ROOF bw color *GQ: Gentlemen's Quarterly* v97 no9 p186 S 2017

Ghastly Dreadfuls, The (Theatrical production)
A DREADFUL TIME T. MALONE *Atlanta* v57 no6 p36 O 2017

GHATTAS, KIM
A Shrinking Island color *Foreign Policy* no226 p67 S/O 2017

GHAZANFAR, SHAHINA A.
An Ecoregion-Based Approach to Protecting Half the Terrestrial Realm *BioScience* v67 no6 p534 Je 2017

Ghazzali, 1058-1111
Timeless Teachings for Young Readers G. HENRY *Islamic Horizons* v45 no6 p34 N/D 2016

Ghebreyesus, Tedros Adhanom
What the World Health Organization's New Leader Must Tackle A. Sifferlin color *Time* v189 no21 p11 Je 5 2017
WHO selects African leader *Science* v356 no6340 p786 My 26 2017

Ghemawat, Pankaj
As Brexit Negotiations Start, Companies Need Contingency Plans *Harvard Business Review Digital Articles* p2 Je 16 2017
The EU Needs to Make Sure Continental Countries Don't Exit *Harvard Business Review Digital Articles* p2 Je 28 2016
Figuring Out Which Companies and Industries Will Be Most Damaged by Brexit *Harvard Business Review Digital Articles* p2 Mr 29 2017
The Fortune Global 500 Isn't All That Global *Harvard Business Review Digital Articles* p2 N 4 2014
GLOBALIZATION IN THE AGE OF TRUMP: PROTECTION-

ISM WILL CHANGE HOW COMPANIES DO BUSINESS—BUT NOT IN THE WAYS YOU THINK [Cover story] color graph img *Harvard Business Review* v95 no4 p112 Jl/Ag 2017

If Trump Abandons the TPP, China Will Be the Biggest Winner *Harvard Business Review Digital Articles* p2 D 12 2016

MBAs Need to Stop Assuming That Markets Always Work *Harvard Business Review Digital Articles* p2 N 21 2014

People Are Angry About Globalization. Here's What to Do About It *Harvard Business Review Digital Articles* p2 N 4 2016

Trump, Globalization, and Trade's Uncertain Future *Harvard Business Review Digital Articles* p2 N 11 2016

What Economists Know That Managers Don't (and Vice Versa) *Harvard Business Review Digital Articles* p2 N 6 2014

What Uber's China Deal Says About the Limits of Platforms *Harvard Business Review Digital Articles* p2 Ag 10 2016

Gheorghe, Eliza

What arguments motivate citizens to demand nuclear disarmament? bibl *Bulletin of the Atomic Scientists* v73 no4 p255 Jl 2017

Gherghel-Lascu, A.

Observation of a large-scale anisotropy in the arrival directions of cosmic rays above 8 × 1018 eV *Science* v357 no6357 p1266 S 22 2017

Ghia, P. L.

Observation of a large-scale anisotropy in the arrival directions of cosmic rays above 8 × 1018 eV *Science* v357 no6357 p1266 S 22 2017

Ghirlando, Rodolfo

Cryo-EM structures and atomic model of the HIV-1 strand transfer complex intasome bibl color *Science* v355 no6320 p1 Ja 6 2017

Ghiso, María Paula

THE REAL SUMMER EXPERIENCE: Going beyond the vacation essay to foster deeper school-community relationships *Literacy Today (2411-7862)* v35 no1 p8 Jl/Ag 2017

Ghissi, Francescuccio, fl. 1359-ca. 1386—Exhibitions

Getting hitched: The St. John Altarpiece color *Magazine Antiques* v184 no3 p30 My/Je 2017

Ghobash, Omar Saif

Advice for Young Muslims color *Foreign Affairs* v96 no1 p96 Ja/F 2017

A father opens up the Islamic world T. Donnellan *America* v216 no3 p47 F 6 2017

Ghomeshi, Jian—Trials, litigation, etc.

THE YEAR IN PICTURES [Cover story] color *Maclean's* v129 no50 p21 D 19 2016

GHORASHI, HANNAH

Private Practices bw cartoon chart color *ARTnews* v115 no3 p84 Fall 2016

Ghose, Seve

CPRP Certification: The Key to Career Advancement *Parks & Recreation* v52 no1 p44 Ja 2017

Ghosh, Amitav, 1956-

1962: Calcutta *Lapham's Quarterly* v10 no1 p149 Wint 2017

Fiction and Our Changing Climate D. G. FAUTIN and G. HART *American Scholar* v86 no1 p3 Wint 2017

Waking up to the Anthropocene [Cover story] N. Wirzba color *Christian Century* v134 no20 p22 S 27 2017

Ghosh, Avik W.

Electron optics with p-n junctions in ballistic graphene bibl graph *Science* v353 no6307 p1522 S 30 2016

Ghosh, Sourav

Macrophage function in tissue repair and remodeling requires IL-4 or IL-13 with apoptotic cells diag *Science* v356 no6342 p1072 Je 9 2017

Ghoshal, Kalpana

Mouse models of acute and chronic hepacivirus infection *Science* v357 no6347 p204 Jl 14 2017

Ghosn, Carlos

Globalism Is Alive and Well: Just Ask Carlos Ghosn M. Reel, K. Inoue et al color *Bloomberg Businessweek* no4531 p50 Jl 24 2017

Ghost (Film)

Ghost's Clay Foreplay S. Vilkomerson color *Entertainment Weekly* no1460/1461 p81 Ap 7-17 2017

Ghost Hunting (Film)

Acting Out E. HYNES color *Film Comment* v53 no5 p18 S/O

2017

Ghost in the Shell (Film)

Ghost in the Shell *New Yorker* v93 no10 p24 Ap 24 2017

OUT OF HER SHELL J. Black color *Esquire* p36 Ap 2017

WONDER WOMEN A. LANE cartoon *New Yorker* v93 no8 p76 Ap 10 2017

Ghost Light (Theatrical production)

LCT's Associate PM Kevin Orzechowski talks integrating Ghost Light into the Claire Tow Theater *Stage Directions* v30 no10 p9 O 2017

managing the ephemeral M. S. Eddy *Stage Directions* v30 no10 p8 O 2017

THE THEATRE cartoon *New Yorker* v93 no16 p16 Je 5 2017

Ghost stories

Australia's Storied Ghosts J. NICKELL *Skeptical Inquirer* v41 no5 p12 S/O 2017

Bogeyman Hunt *Lapham's Quarterly* v10 no3 p178 Summ 2017

The Greatest of Ghost Stories N. CLARK bw *American Conservative* v15 no6 p55 N/D 2016

Murder by Darkness: Does Mammoth Caves Specter Harbor a Secret? J. NICKELL *Skeptical Inquirer* v41 no4 p12 Jl/Ag 2017

Ghost towns

Ghost on the Plain: The Rugged Serenity of Gilmore S. POWELL *Idaho Magazine* v16 no12 p44 S 2017

Ghost Wave (Performer)

Ghost Wave B. Flemister color *Surfing Magazine* v53 no2 p26 F 2017

Ghostbusters (Film : 1984)

SCENE STEALERS R. CHUN color *Wired* v25 no3 p78 Mr 2017

Surviving the '80s D. DUDLEY, M. GRANT et al color *AARP: The Magazine* v59 no5A p47 Ag/S 2016

Ghostbusters (Film : 2016)

5 — KEVIN'S INTERVIEW D. Rovenstine *Entertainment Weekly* no1444/1445 p60 D 16 2016

GHOSTBUSTERS (2016) B. A. DuHamel color *Sound & Vision* v82 no3 p67 Ap 2017

KATE McKINNON N. Sperling color *Entertainment Weekly* no1444/1445 p24 D 16 2016

Ghosted (TV program)

3 THINGS TO KNOW ABOUT GHOSTED M. Roffman *TV Guide* v65 no37 p42 S 4 2017

5 Loaded Questions for Adam Scott J. Harman color *Glamour* v115 no11 p44 N 2017

GHOSTED D. Snierson color *Entertainment Weekly* no1474/1475 p74 Jl 21-28 2017

Poets, Prophets, Ghosts color *Chicago* v66 no10 p70 O 2017

Ghost on the Handle, The (Poem)

The Ghost on the Handle K. FAGAN *Nation* v305 no9 p33 O 16 2017

Ghosts

Can Electromagnetic Fields Create Ghosts? B. RADFORD *Skeptical Inquirer* v41 no3 p30 My/Je 2017

'Ghostly' Image at Haunted Stanley Hotel B. RADFORD *Skeptical Inquirer* v40 no6 p9 N/D 2016

The Phoenix Driveway Ghost B. RADFORD *Skeptical Inquirer* v41 no4 p24 Jl/Ag 2017

Ghosts (Play : Ibsen)

1881: Norway H. Ibsen *Lapham's Quarterly* v10 no1 p142 Wint 2017

Ghosts in literature

Ghostly Women M. DIRDA bw *Weekly Standard* v22 no25 p38 Mr 6 2017

Ghosts in motion pictures

THE BEST GHOST STORIES OF ALL TIME color *Entertainment Weekly* no1473 p43 Jl 7 2017

Ghost Story, A (Film)

COME BACK A. LANE color *New Yorker* v93 no20 p92 Jl 10 2017

A Ghost of a Storyline M. ATKINSON *In These Times* v41 no7 p37 Jl 2017

A Ghost Story Chills-and Makes You Wonder S. Zacharek color *Time* v190 no4 p49 Jl 24 2017

A GHOST STORY K. P. Sullivan color *Entertainment Weekly* no1463/1464 p68 Ap/My 2017

Hauntingly Lovely T. MARKATOS color *Weekly Standard* v22 no44 p36 Jl 31 2017

Phantom Pains C. LORENTZEN *New Republic* v248 no8/9 p64 Ag/S 2017

SHEET MUSIC I. Sara Smith color *Film Comment* v53 no4 p36 Jl/Ag 2017

Summer Preview R. Brody cartoon *New Yorker* v93 no14 p20 My 22 2017

Ghostwriters

CONFESSION OF A WASHINGTON GHOSTWRITER B. FEINMAN TODD *Washingtonian Magazine* v52 no5 p64 F 2017

Houdini and the Cancer of Superstition M. POLIDORO *Skeptical Inquirer* v40 no6 p32 N/D 2016

Ghsmart (Company)

What 20 Years as a Remote Organization Has Taught Us About Managing Remote Teams R. Street, D. Wang et al *Harvard Business Review Digital Articles* p2 F 20 2017

Gi Xue

Highly stretchable polymer semiconductor films through the nanoconfinement effect bibl graph *Science* v355 no6320 p1 Ja 6 2017

Giaccari, U.

Observation of a large-scale anisotropy in the arrival directions of cosmic rays above 8 × 1018 eV *Science* v357 no6357 p1266 S 22 2017

Giacobbe, Alyssa

ATLAS OBSCURA BERBER LODGE IS A HIP OASIS HIDDEN AMONG OLIVE AND CITRUS GROVES NEAR THE MOUNTAINS OUTSIDE MARRAKECH color *Conde Nast Traveler* v52 no10 p30 N 2017

HOW TO FIND YOUR SELF color *Women's Health* v14 no6 p132 Jl 2017

LIVE Long AND PROSPER [Cover story] color *Women's Health* v14 no1 p170 Ja/F 2017

Giacometti, Alberto, 1901-1966

FACE TO FACE B. SCHWABSKY color *Nation* v305 no9 p35 O 16 2017

Giacomini, Damiana

A disynaptic feedback network activated by experience promotes the integration of new granule cells bibl graph *Science* v354 no6311 p459 O 28 2016

GIACOSA, GIUSEPPE

La Bohème *Opera News* v81 no7 p55 Ja 2017

Giago, Tim

Covering Standing Rock J. Monet color *Columbia Journalism Review* v56 no1 p86 Spr 2017

Giamatti, Paul, 1967-

Billions *TV Guide* v65 no19 p31 My 1 2017

Giambanco, Valentina

Blood and Bone color *Publishers Weekly* v263 no44 p52 O 31 2016

Giambrone, James

AGING GRACEFULLY on the Homestead *Mother Earth News* no280 p34 F/Mr 2017

Giammarchi, M.

Observation of a large-scale anisotropy in the arrival directions of cosmic rays above 8 × 1018 eV *Science* v357 no6357 p1266 S 22 2017

Giammona, Craig

Amazon Goes After The Walmart Shopper *Bloomberg Businessweek* no4508 p19 Ja 23 2017

Breitbart Advertisers Take Political Fire, Too color *Bloomberg Businessweek* no4502 p31 D 5 2016

Chobani Welcomes an Old Enemy to Its Dairy Case color *Bloomberg Businessweek* no4529 p16 Jl 3 2017

Halal's Rise From Street Carts to Whole Foods color *Bloomberg Businessweek* no4494 p24 O 10 2016

The Hatchet Men And the Hot Dog color diag *Bloomberg Businessweek* no4533 p50 Ag 7 2017

MEAT MARKETER [Cover story] color graph map *Bloomberg Businessweek* no4511 p42 F 13 2017

Packaging Salmon Jerky for the Masses color *Bloomberg Businessweek* no4495 p36 O 17 2016

Run! It's 3G Capital! cartoon *Bloomberg Businessweek* no4510 p31 F 6 2017

This Deflation Has Grocers Fed Up graph *Bloomberg Businessweek* no4493 p30 O 3 2016

WHOLE FOODS MARKET'S Identity Crisis color diag *Bloomberg Businessweek* no4519 p22 Ap 24 2017

Will Millennials Eat Their Frozen Veggies? color graph *Bloomberg Businessweek* no4497 p23 O 31 2016

Giandrea, Michael D.

Estimating the U.S. labor share bibl chart color graph *Monthly Labor Review* p1 F 2017

Gianelle, Damiano

Positive biodiversity-productivity relationship predominant in global forests bibl chart graph map *Science* v354 no6309 paaf8957-1 O 14 2016

Gianforte, Greg

The Banjo Player vs. the Billionaire D. D. GUTTENPLAN color *Nation* v304 no17 p12 Je 5 2017

Gianni Versace SpA

Statement Belts R. WALDMAN, M. HOLGATE et al color *Vogue* v207 no9 p382 S 2017

Giannulli, Mossimo

NO MORE PLAID PANTS J. Paskin color *Bloomberg Businessweek* no4497 p66 O 31 2016

Giannulli, Tom

How to Pay for Health Care/The Case for Capitation: Interaction *Harvard Business Review* v94 no11 p20 N 2016

Gianopulos, Jim

Movers K. Stock color *Bloomberg Businessweek* no4517 p13 Ap 3 2017

GIANOPULOS, PETER

BEST IN BIRD color *Chicago* v65 no11 p58 N 2016

BITE THEIR TONGUES color *Chicago* v66 no3 p66 Mr 2017

A NEW LEAF color *Chicago* v66 no4 p52 Ap 2017

THE OUT OF TOWNERS color *Chicago* v66 no11 p54 N 2017

WINTER WARMERS color *Chicago* v66 no2 p45 F 2017

Giant hogweed

Poisonous Plants C. RYAN diag map *Backpacker* p34 My 2017

Giant Manufacturing Co. Ltd.

GIANT ANTHEM ADVANCED PRO 29 0 R. Koch color *Bicycling* v58 no9 p68 O 2017

"I WANT A GOOD ROAD BIKE, BUT I DON'T WANT TO SPEND MORE THAN $1,000." T. Rojek and B. STRICKLAND color *Bicycling* v58 no3 p50 Ap 2017

TURBO LEVO FSR COMP CARBON 6FATTIE R. Koch color *Bicycling* v58 no8 p(Sp)20 S 2017

Giant panda

Premature downgrade of panda's status Dongwei Kang and Junqing Li color *Science* v354 no6310 p295 O 21 2016

Giant sequoia

Return of Giants Z. S. GEORGE color *Orion Magazine* v36 no1 p7 Ja/F 2017

SURVIVOR *Sierra* v102 no3 p2 My/Je 2017

Gianvito Rossi (Company)

The Style REPORT: FALL'S MUST-HAVES color *Harper's Bazaar* no3656 p288 S 2017

Giardina, Christian P.

Plant diversity increases with the strength of negative density dependence at the global scale diag *Science* v356 no6345 p1389 Je 30 2017

Giardino, M.

Localized aliphatic organic material on the surface of Ceres bibl graph *Science* v355 no6326 p719 F 17 2017

Giarrizzo, Tommaso

Fringe on the brink: Intertidal reefs at risk color *Science* v357 no6348 p261 Jl 21 2017

GIBB, TOM

A SECRET WAR IN THE AMERICAS color *America* v215 no19 p33 D 19 2016

Gibbens, Brendon

PEAKING bw color *Surfer* v58 no4 p106 Ag 2017

Gibbon, Edward, 1737-1794

AMBITION, STYLE AND SACRIFICE: The challenges that Edward Gibbon faced remain much the same for historians today P. Lay *History Today* v67 no6 p3 Je 2016

The Best of Scribblers: Edward Gibbon and the importance of great writing to great history J. Epstein *Commentary* v140 no2 p48 S 2015

The Best of Scribblers J. Epstein *Commentary* v140 no2 p41 S 2015

Gibson, Daniel G.
Yeast genome, by design bibl color *Science* v355 no6329 p1024 Mr 10 2017

Gibson, David
Landmark Luther exhibits explore his technological and theological legacy color *Christian Century* v133 no23 p16 N 9 2016
Religious liberty order draws mixed reviews *Christian Century* v134 no12 p14 Je 7 2017
SNAP leader resigns while group faces suit on legal practices color *Christian Century* v134 no5 p15 Mr 1 2017

Gibson, Debbie
Dancing With the Stars N. Abrams, C. Holub et al *Entertainment Weekly* no1482/1483 p48 S 22 2017

Gibson, Emma K.
Identification of single-site gold catalysis in acetylene hydrochlorination bw diag graph *Science* v355 no6332 p1399 Mr 31 2017

Gibson, Erin
THROWING SHADE LIKE A PRO A. Bacle color *Entertainment Weekly* no1450 p52 Ja 27 2017

Gibson, George
Deals R. DEAHL color *Publishers Weekly* v263 no44 p10 O 31 2016

Gibson, Janine
A crisis of relevance color *Columbia Journalism Review* v56 no2 p23 Fall 2017

Gibson, Mel, 1956-
Blood Father M. FELL *TV Guide* v65 no11 p48 Mr 6 2017
For Mel Gibson, War Is (Very Bloody) Hell D. REILLY img *New York* v49 no22 p96 O 31 2016
HACKSAW RIDGE D. Vaughn color *Sound & Vision* v82 no7 p67 S 2017
Hacksaw Ridge L. Greenblatt color *Entertainment Weekly* no1439 p47 N 11 2016
A Leading Man Saves Hacksaw Ridge from Hackdom S. Zacharek color *Time* v188 no19 p56 N 7 2016
Troubled Genius R. DOUTHAT color *National Review* v68 no19 p51 O 24 2016

Gibson, Mel, 1956-—Awards
Hacksaw Ridge *New Yorker* v92 no39 p18 N 28 2016

Gibson, Michael
Join Our Click bw color *Ebony* v72 no8 p12 Je 2017

Gibson, Patrick
Patrick GIBSON *Interview* v47 no5 p71 Je/Jl 2017

Gibson, Robert
Acceptable *Alternatives Journal (AJ) - Canada's Environmental Voice* v42 no3 p80 2016
FOOD *Alternatives Journal (AJ) - Canada's Environmental Voice* v42 no2 p80 2016

Gibson, Terry
Paradise Unwound color map *National Wildlife (World Edition)* v55 no2 p32 F/Mr 2017
THE SAILFISH COAST color map *Outdoor Life* v224 no2 p25 F/Mr 2017

Gibson, William
BACK IN TIME TO AN ICE AGE AND A GREAT FIRE *History Today* v67 no8 p98 Ag 2017

Gibson-Davis, Christina M.
Linking job loss, inequality, mental health, and education color *Science* v356 no6343 p1127 Je 16 2017

Giddings, Caitlin
"I QUIT MY JOB, AND I WANT TO RIDE ACROSS THE COUNTRY." color *Bicycling* v58 no3 p62 Ap 2017
"I WISH MY RIDES COULD GO ON FOREVER." color *Bicycling* v58 no3 p110 Ap 2017
LOAD TOURING color *Bicycling* v58 no8 p(Sp)8 S 2017
The Mechanic You Want in Your Corner bw color *Bicycling* v58 no1 p26 Ja/F 2017
MEET GISELLE, THE BIKE-PACKING PUP! color *Bicycling* v58 no4 p44 My 2017
MEET THE MESSENGER color *Bicycling* v58 no6 p46 Jl 2017
RUNNING. SERIOUSLY?! YES! color *Bicycling* v58 no9 p56 O 2017
SLURRRRRRRP! color *Bicycling* v58 no10 p20 N/D 2017
Totally Worth It! color *Bicycling* v58 no4 p22 My 2017
TO THE STARS THROUGH DIFFICULTIES bw *Bicycling* v58 no10 p22 N/D 2017

Giddings, Olivia
Emergence and spread of a human-transmissible multidrug-resistant nontuberculous mycobacterium bibl diag graph *Science* v354 no6313 p751 N 11 2016

Gidla, Sujatha
THE APPROVAL MATRIX img *New York* v50 no15 p88 Jl 24 2017

GIDUS, TARA
FLAT BELLY INDULGENCE *USA Today Magazine* v145 no2858 p70 N 2016

Gidwani, Nick
How to Support Employees' Learning Goals While Getting Day-to-Day Stuff Done *Harvard Business Review Digital Articles* p2 Ag 1 2017

Gidwitz, Adam
Saints and Sinners S. CHAINANI *New York Times Book Review* p19 O 9 2016

Gielan, Michelle
The Busier You Are, the More You Need Mindfulness *Harvard Business Review Digital Articles* p2 D 18 2015
Consuming Negative News Can Make You Less Effective at Work *Harvard Business Review Digital Articles* p2 S 14 2015
The Data-Driven Case for Vacation *Harvard Business Review Digital Articles* p2 Jl 13 2016
Make Yourself Immune to Secondhand Stress *Harvard Business Review Digital Articles* p2 S 2 2015
Optimists Are Better at Finding New Jobs *Harvard Business Review Digital Articles* p2 Ap 15 2016
Resilience Is About How You Recharge, Not How You Endure *Harvard Business Review Digital Articles* p2 Je 24 2016
You Can Deliver Bad News to Your Team Without Crushing Them *Harvard Business Review Digital Articles* p2 Mr 21 2016
You Can Improve Your Default Response to Stress bw *Harvard Business Review Digital Articles* p2 Ja 5 2017

GIERINGER, DALE H.
FROM THE ARCHIVES bw *Reason* v49 no1 p70 My 2017

Gies, Erica
The Meaning of Lichen color *Scientific American* v316 no6 p52 Je 2017

Giesea, Jeff
Dealing with the Emotional Fallout of Selling Your Business *Harvard Business Review Digital Articles* p2 S 1 2015
Design a Retirement That Excites You *Harvard Business Review Digital Articles* p2 N 17 2015
Stop Calling People Out *Harvard Business Review Digital Articles* p2 O 24 2014

Gieselmann, Marc A.
Selective modulation of cortical state during spatial attention bibl graph *Science* v354 no6316 p1140 D 2 2016

Giessen, H.
Revealing the subfemtosecond dynamics of orbital angular momentum in nanoplasmonic vortices bibl diag *Science* v355 no6330 p1187 Mr 17 2017

Giffard, Hermione
RETHINKING ROCKET SCIENCE: A study of the early history of jet engines transforms the way we should think about technological change J. A. Maiolo *History Today* v67 no9 p102 S 2017
Revolution, evolution or reinvention? *History Today* v66 no10 p58 O 2016

Giffin, Doc—Interviews
DOCTOR IN THE HOUSE J. McAlley color *Golf Magazine* v58 no12 p58 D 2016

Gifford, Bill
Hearts & Minds cartoon color *Men's Health* v32 no3 p112 Ap 2017
LIVING TO 120 color *Scientific American* v315 no3 p62 S 2016

GIFFORD, DANIEL
Golden Age of Postcards *Saturday Evening Post* v288 no6 p52 N/D 2016

GIFFORD, JOHN
The Cross Timbers *American Forests* v123 no1 p32 Wint/Spr 2017

Gifford lectures
From God-talk to God's work A. P. Pauw *Christian Century* v134 no14 p22 Jl 5 2017

Gifford Pinchot National Forest (Wash.)

Life Finds a Way: Gifford Pinchot National Forest, Washington L. LANCASTER color map *Backpacker* p22 S 2017

Gifford's Ice Cream & Candy Co.
DARK SIDE of an ICE CREAM EMPIRE A. Powers *Washingtonian Magazine* v53 no1 p78 O 2017

Gift books
BOOKS TO UNPLUG WITH A. GROSS color *Publishers Weekly* v264 no7 p28 F 13 2017

Gift certificates
Show Me the Money *Consumer Reports* v81 no12 p25 D 2016

Gift giving
Dad to Dad Gift Guide M. LaScala color *Parents* v92 no6 p22 Je 2017

Editor's Letter M. Hansche color *Rodale's Organic Life* v2 no7 p9 D 2016/Ja 2017

Something for Nothing C. DEDERER color *Rodale's Organic Life* v2 no7 p31 D 2016/Ja 2017

Gift giving—Management
How to (Shamelessly) Regift This Holiday Season J. LABIANCA *Reader's Digest* v188 no1126 p54 D 2016/Ja 2017

Gift registries
WRITE A BETTER WISH LIST A. Giorgianni color *Consumer Reports* v81 no12 p41 D 2016

Gift shops—Evaluation
BE OUR GUEST A. BRANDT *Cincinnati Magazine* v50 no6 p44 Mr 2017

Homes color *New Orleans Magazine* v51 no5 p118 Mr 2017

it's a colorful life S. BRICKELL cartoon color *Better Homes & Gardens* v95 no4 p10 Ap 2017

Gift wrapping
wrap party! J. PHILLIP color *Good Housekeeping* v263 no6 p36 D 2016

Gift wrapping—Equipment & supplies
Get a do-it-all organizer! J. Jones color *Redbook* p28 O 2017

Gifted (Film)
Chris Evans Ties a Bow on Gifted S. Zacharek color *Time* v189 no14 p53 Ap 17 2017

Gifted, The (TV program)
Breaking Big EMMA DUMONT S. Li, N. Abrams et al color *Entertainment Weekly* no1482/1483 p51 S 22 2017

The Gifted S. Li, N. Abrams et al color *Entertainment Weekly* no1482/1483 p50 S 22 2017

MARK YOUR CALENDAR! *TV Guide* v65 no37 p46 S 4 2017

THE X FACTOR J. RUSSELL *TV Guide* v65 no35 p14 Ag 21 2017

Gifted persons
Teen scientists already changing the world color *Science News* v191 no7 p29 Ap 15 2017

Gifts
See also
Charitable giving

Ask Martha Martha color *Martha Stewart Living* p50 My 2017

BUG throwback GOT YOU COVERED B. WENGERT *Better Homes & Gardens* v94 no12 p156 D 2016

Desperately Seeking Sweet Stop E. Crawford Peyton color *New Orleans Magazine* v51 no4 p46 F 2017

A GIFT FOR KIDS THAT PAYS DIVIDENDS T. Stanger *Consumer Reports* v81 no12 p31 D 2016

GIFTS THAT GO THE DISTANCE D. Rosato color *Consumer Reports* v81 no12 p45 D 2016

GIFTS that UPLIFT! J. BISSEY, ". T. TSHIKORORO et al cartoon *O, The Oprah Magazine* p148 D 2016

grab bags of awesome S. Dolgoff color *Good Housekeeping* v264 no5 p140 My 2017

A guide to modern manners color *Redbook* p136 N 2017

HERE COME THE BRIDE'S BASKETS! JOHNSON *Treasures* v6 no6 p30 Je/Jl 2017

Here We Go! color *O, The Oprah Magazine* p23 D 2016

How to choose the perfect leaving present: Row over Tate chief's boat gift shines a light on tricky area of office etiquette *People Management* p15 Je 2017

Humor in Uniform color *Reader's Digest* v190 no1135 p135 N 2017

Merry ... But Not Too Bright color diag *Consumer Reports* v82 no12 p67 D 2017

MY HOLIDAY WISH LIST *Missouri Life* v43 no7 p10 D 2016/

Ja 2017

Old and New Holiday Traditions D. Harris color *Money* v45 no11 p10 D 2016

The Question M. MASZTAK, M. HESSION et al *O, The Oprah Magazine* p16 D 2016

Win the SQUAD GIFT EXCHANGE color *Seventeen* v76 no12 p73 D 2016/Ja 2017

The Write Stuff color *Log Home Living* v34 no9 p16 D 2017

A Year of Celebration M. L. Tellado *Consumer Reports* v81 no12 p5 D 2016

Zen Palace A. Jones img *New York* p46 F 9 2017

Gifts for children
Shopping for Kids this Holiday Season L. PETERSON *Atlanta* v56 no7 p48 N 2016

Gifts in business
Esquire'S HOLIDAY GIFT GUIDE cartoon color *Esquire* v166 no5 p75 D 2016/Ja 2017

Gifts—Computer network resources
GROUP GIVING: THE MORE THE MERRIER J. Blyskal *Consumer Reports* v81 no12 p65 D 2016

Gifts—Evaluation
2016 Holiday GIFT GUIDE A. Vorrasi, M. Gleeson et al color *InStyle* v23 no13 p249 D 2016

5 amazing gifts that give back color *Redbook* p78 D 2016

DADDY'S DAY GIFT GUIDE A. LUCAS color *Ebony* v72 no8 p46 Je 2017

DAZZLE THEM color *House Beautiful* v158 no10 p21 D 2016/Ja 2017

DIY RECIPE KITS L. Turner color *Amazing Wellness* v8 no6 p90 Early Winter2016

Early Bird Gift Guide S. JEAN SHELTON color *Redbook* p112 N 2017

Gift Guide color *Vanity Fair* v59 no1 p68 Holiday 2017

GIFTS THAT GIVE S. T. BROWN color *Ebony* v72 no3 p92 D 2016/Ja 2017

GOOD-FOR-YOU gifts cartoon color *Amazing Wellness* v8 no6 p68 Early Winter2016

The O List color *O, The Oprah Magazine* p55 F 2017

Put a Great Spin on the Gift-Giving Season *USA Today Magazine* v145 no2858 p78 N 2017

RADAR GIFT GUIDE L. CROSS and B. DANIELLE color *Ebony* v72 no3 p46 D 2016/Ja 2017

Gig economy
Most gig economy workers 'want employment rights': But survey says few rely on platforms for their main income, and most are happy with pay *People Management* p15 Ap 2017

We're happy not to be in the gig economy: How a courier company's commitment to values is marking it out from the competition *People Management* p22 My 2017

Whitehall is gunning for 'gig' jobs *People Management* p6 Mr 2017

Who needs staff? *People Management* p26 My 2017

Gigabyte Technology Co. Ltd.
Brix Gaming UHD (GBBNi7HG4-950): A lot of performance in a little PC A. YEE color graph *PCWorld* v35 no1 p123 Ja 2017

Gigabyte Aero 15: A near-perfect power user's laptop G. MAHUNG color graph *PCWorld* v35 no8 p87 Ag 2017

Gigabyte PC (GB-GZ1DTi7-1070): A powerhouse PC diminished by noisy fans A. YEE color graph *PCWorld* v35 no2 p71 F 2017

Gigi (Theatrical production)
ONCE IN LOVE WITH GIGI L. JACOBS cartoon *Vanity Fair* v59 no4 p212 Mr 2017

Giglio, Karina
THE ITINERARY: LOUDOUN COUNTY *Washingtonian Magazine* v52 no1 p113 O 2016

Giglio, L.
A human-driven decline in global burned area chart graph map *Science* v356 no6345 p1356 Je 30 2017

Gikas, Mike
Have More Fun With Your Phone chart color il *Consumer Reports* v82 no3 p48 Mr 2017

Gil, Yolanda
Enhancing reproducibility for computational methods bibl color *Science* v354 no6317 p1240 D 9 2016

Gilad, Benjamin
Companies Collect Competitive Intelligence, but Don't Use It

Harvard Business Review Digital Articles p2 Jl 31 2015
"Competitive Intelligence" Shouldn't Just Be About Your Competitors *Harvard Business Review Digital Articles* p2 My 18 2015
How a Food-Ordering App Broke into a Crowded Market *Harvard Business Review Digital Articles* p2 N 25 2015
How to Actually Put Your Marketing Data to Use *Harvard Business Review Digital Articles* p2 O 27 2015
Only Half of Companies Actually Use the Competitive Intelligence They Collect *Harvard Business Review Digital Articles* p2 Ja 26 2016
The Right Way to Use Competitive Intelligence *Harvard Business Review Digital Articles* p2 Je 16 2016

Gilan, Omer
Click chemistry enables preclinical evaluation of targeted epigenetic therapies diag *Science* v356 no6345 p1397 Je 30 2017

Gilarranz, Luis J.
Effects of network modularity on the spread of perturbation impact in experimental metapopulations diag graph *Science* v357 no6347 p199 Jl 14 2017

Gilbane, Sara—Interviews
all in the family K. HACKETT color *House Beautiful* v159 no7 p112 S 2017

Gilbert, Alan, 1967-
Redefining the Gold Standard: As he winds down his New York Philharmonic tenure with Das Rheingold, Alan Gilbert looks forward to new beginnings H. Stewart *Opera News* v81 no12 p51 Je 2017

Gilbert, Dan
Dan of Letters M. Rosenberg color *Sports Illustrated* v127 no2 p64 Jl 17 2017

Gilbert, David
UNDERGROUND cartoon *New Yorker* v92 no48 p60 F 6 2017

Gilbert, Deja
College Students Experience High Rates of Alcohol Abuse, Mental Health issues *Psychology Today* v50 no5 p25 S/O 2017
TREATING ADDICTED WOMEN during pregnancy *Psychology Today* v50 no3 p25 My/Je 2017

Gilbert, Elizabeth, 1969-
Beyond Inspiration S. BALIN color *Publishers Weekly* v264 no27 p80 Jl 3 2017
Care and FEEDING color *O, The Oprah Magazine* p29 Je 2017
CASING the Joint cartoon *O, The Oprah Magazine* p33 Mr 2017
GIVE YOURSELF a Hand cartoon *O, The Oprah Magazine* p45 D 2016
Let's See How Alive We Can Be J. Pressler img *New York* v49 no24 p62 N 28 2016
SELF, CENTERED color *O, The Oprah Magazine* p39 S 2017
'TRUTH' AND Consequences color *O, The Oprah Magazine* p28 Ja 2017

Gilbert, Elizabeth, 1969—Interviews
No One Is Too Busy to Be Creative D. Rousmaniere *Harvard Business Review Digital Articles* p2 D 2 2015

GILBERT, HAYLEY
FINISHING TOUCHES color *House Beautiful* p108 Ag 2017
LATEST LOOKS UPDATE color *House Beautiful* p96 Ag 2017

GILBERT, JAMES R.
Google Haul Out: Earth Observation Imagery and Digital Aerial Surveys in Coastal Wildlife Management and Abundance Estimation *BioScience* v67 no8 p760 Ag 2017

Gilbert, Jay
Dirty Money: I FOUGHT THE LAW AND I WON. SORT OF *Cincinnati Magazine* v50 no10 p46 Jl 2017
ENCYCLOPEDIA CINCINNATI bw cartoon color *Cincinnati Magazine* v51 no1 p42 O 2017
JUNGLE LOVE: A brief history of Cincinnati's love affair with animals, from fat-rendered soap to Fiona the hippo *Cincinnati Magazine* v50 no10 p23 Jl 2017
NIGHT MOVES *Cincinnati Magazine* v50 no8 p40 My 2017
ONE CALLER HAS A TRUCK STOP NAMED AFTER HIM *Cincinnati Magazine* v50 no8 p44 My 2017
Q + A *Cincinnati Magazine* v50 no10 p32 Jl 2017
Q+A *Cincinnati Magazine* v50 no3 p38 D 2016
Q+A *Cincinnati Magazine* v50 no5 p28 F 2017
Rock of Aged *Cincinnati Magazine* v50 no12 p40 S 2017
That Big Indian Sign *Cincinnati Magazine* v50 no8 p36 My 2017

Gilbert, Jonathan
Climate Change Could Dampen Argentina's Recovery map *Bloomberg Businessweek* no4539 p35 S 25 2017

Gilbert, Kathy L.
People color *Christian Century* v134 no22 p20 O 25 2017
People color *Christian Century* v134 no6 p17 Mr 15 2017
UMC court rules against consecrating gay bishops color *Christian Century* v134 no11 p13 My 24 2017

Gilbert, Kenyatta R.
A Pursued Justice: Black Preaching from the Great Migration to Civil Rights R. Lischer *Christian Century* v134 no10 p42 My 10 2017

Gilbert, Luke A.
CRISPRi-based genome-scale identification of functional long noncoding RNA loci in human cells bibl graph *Science* v355 no6320 p1 Ja 6 2017

Gilbert, Marius
Reducing antimicrobial use in food animals color graph *Science* v357 no6358 p1350 S 29 2017
Role for migratory wild birds in the global spread of avian influenza H5N8 bibl graph map *Science* v354 no6309 p213 O 14 2016

Gilbert, Melissa
PATTY DUKE color *Entertainment Weekly* no1446/1447 p92 D 2016/Ja 2017

Gilbert, Paul
Good Governance *Parks & Recreation* v52 no2 p16 F 2017
A MONUMENTAL Decision: What to Do with Confederate Monuments? *Parks & Recreation* v52 no10 p36 O 2017

Gilbert, Sara, 1975-
Small Changes for a Big Difference color *Prevention* v69 no2 p4 F 2017

GILBERT, SOPHIE
Neglectful Bohemians *New York Times Book Review* p18 Ja 8 2017
Old Flames Die Hard: A sequel by Sylvia Brownrigg reunites former lovers two decades later *New York Times Book Review* p19 S 3 2017

Gilbert, Susan
DISCOVERING THEIR IDENTITY: Using gender nonconforming picture books in early education classrooms color *Literacy Today (2411-7862)* v34 no6 p20 My/Je 2017

Gilbert, Tim
Cheers & Jeers color *Field & Stream* v121 no8 p12 F/Mr 2017

Gilbert, Troy
Bringing a Hero Home M. Thompson color *Time* v188 no24 p50 D 12 2016

Gilbreath, Ashley
Living the Country Life A. Preiser color *Southern Living* v52 no4 p108 Ap 2017

Gilbreath, Evelyn
Dream Buddy on a Trail Ride cartoon *Horse & Rider* v56 no3 p72 Mr 2017
How I Solved My Horse's Problem cartoon *Horse & Rider* v56 no1 p72 Ja 2017
When I Was a Horse-Crazy Kid, I... color *Horse & Rider* v56 no2 p72 F 2017

Gilchrist, Chelsea
Empowering Older Adults to Age Out Loud! *Parks & Recreation* v52 no5 p38 My 2017

Gilchrist, Duncan
How Netflix's Content Strategy Is Reshaping Movie Culture *Harvard Business Review Digital Articles* p2 Ag 31 2017

Gilchrist, Jim
TRUMP'S TROOPS D. Neiwert, S. Posner et al *Mother Jones* v41 no6 p31 N/D 2016

Gilchrist, Keir
Keir GILCHRIST J. ORTVED *Interview* v47 no6 p10 Ag 2017

GILCHRIST, TRACY E.
DID HOLLYWOOD SABOTAGE MY MARRIAGE? Perhaps a lack of examples doomed me to fail in love *Advocate* no1093 p16 O/N 2017
REVEALING THE "THROUPLE" BEHIND WONDER WOMAN: Did you know the world's hottest superhero was inspired by a polyamorous relationship? *Advocate* no1093 p27 O/N 2017

Gilcreast, Aaron
Why Top Management Should Listen to Activist Investors *Har-*

vard Business Review Digital Articles p2 N 30 2016

Gilday Renovations (Company)
BUILDER PROFILES *Washingtonian Magazine* v52 no1 p170 O 2016

GILDEMEISTER, ALFREDO
Chalet C7 Hotel Portillo color *Conde Nast Traveler* v52 no9 p112 O 2017

GILDER, GEORGE
The Feminist Economy color *National Review* v69 no1 p36 Ja 23 2017

Gilder, Joshua
WHAT A COUNTRY! (AGAIN!): WHO'D HAVE THOUGHT THERE'D COME A TIME WHEN THE KING OF COLD WAR COMEDY, YAKOV SIMIRNOFF, JUST MIGHT MAKE A COMEBACK? AN ONLY-IN-AMERICA-RIGHT-NOW STORY L. MULLINS *Washingtonian Magazine* v52 no12 p64 S 2017

GILDER, SUSAN
The Question *O, The Oprah Magazine* p16 Ap 2017

Gilders
Gold Standard L. BAILEY *Indianapolis Monthly* v40 no3 p38 N 2016

Gilead Sciences Inc.
Can This Fallen Biotech Be Revived? K. KRISTOF *Kiplinger's Personal Finance* v71 no5 p61 My 2017
Why I'm Hanging On to a Loser K. KRISTOF *Kiplinger's Personal Finance* v71 no10 p62 O 2017

Gilens, Martin
The price of political power E. C. Fasching color *Monthly Labor Review* p1 S 2016

Giles, Alfred
COMPASS POINTS E. Pochoda color *Magazine Antiques* v184 no1 p130 Ja/F 2017

Giles, Jeff
Heartthrobs and Hellscapes S. Begley color *Time* v189 no4 p54 F 6 2017
Novel Inspiration color *Entertainment Weekly* no1451/1452 p111 F 3-10 2017
Y.A. Fantasy Fiction *New York Times Book Review* p35 N 13 2016

GILES, MADELEINE E.
The Arctic in the Twenty-First Century: Changing Biogeochemical Linkages across a Paraglacial Landscape of Greenland *BioScience* v67 no2 p118 F 2017

GILES, MATT
Revoltingly Real Cosplay color *Popular Science* v288 no6 p92 N/D 2016
Surprising History of the Ace of Cakes color *Popular Science* v288 no6 p94 N/D 2016

Giles, Sunnie
The Most Important Leadership Competencies, According to Leaders Around the World *Harvard Business Review Digital Articles* p2 Mr 15 2016

Gilfillan, Susan
Lactobacillus reuteri induces gut intraepithelial CD4+CD8$\alpha\alpha$+ T cells diag graph *Science* v357 no6353 p806 Ag 25 2017

Gilger, Kristin
St. Augustine's love life *America* v216 no7 p46 Ap 3 2017

Gilger, Patrick
NAVIGATING the BENEDICT OPTION color *America* v216 no8 p18 Ap 17 2017
Re-enchanting the World color *America* v215 no10 p16 O 10 2016

Gilkes, Rohan
Be Innclusive S. E. Jamison color *Ebony* v72 no9 p77 Jl/Ag 2017

Gill, John Freeman
The Pie-Chart Review I. Biedenharn color diag *Entertainment Weekly* no1459 p63 Mr 31 2017
To Do img *New York* v50 no6 p90 Mr 20 2017

Gill, Mark
England Is Mine L. Greenblatt color *Entertainment Weekly* no1480 p40 S 1 2017

Gill, Michael
TRUE VINTAGE STYLE color *Old House Journal* v45 no2 p32 Ap 2017

Gill, Noelle
Changing an Organization's Culture, Without Resistance or Blame *Harvard Business Review Digital Articles* p2 Jl 15 2015

Gill, Tim
THE QUIET CRUSADER A. Kroll color *Rolling Stone* no1291/1292 p38 Jl 13 2017

Gillen, Aiden, 1968-
A Handy Guide to HBO's Favorite Actors img *New York* v50 no18 p80 S 4 2017

GILLEO, MARGARET P.
BEYOND "JUST CAUSE" color *Commonweal* v144 no16 p4 O 6 2017

Giller, M.
Observation of a large-scale anisotropy in the arrival directions of cosmic rays above 8×1018 eV *Science* v357 no6357 p1266 S 22 2017

Gilles & Boissier (Company)
Gilles & Boissier Bardula Studio A. Klimoski color *Architectural Record* v205 no2 p109 F 2017

Gillespie, Dizzy, 1917-1993
DIZZY GILLESPIE T. Panken bw *Downbeat* v84 no1 p34 Ja 2017

Gillespie, Ed, 1961-
ED RECKONING: The Republican candidate for governor of Virginia comes straight from the national GOP establishment. Not long ago, his résumé could have been a plus. These days, it might be Ed Gillespie's biggest challenge S. van Zuylen-Wood *Washingtonian Magazine* v53 no1 p84 O 2017
The Road to Victory in Virginia F. BARNES cartoon *Weekly Standard* v22 no38 p10 Je 12 2017

Gillespie, James
Building a Better Robot: POTOMAC SCHOOL WINS NATIONAL CHAMPIONSHIP *Virginia Living* v15 no6 p101 O 2017

Gillespie, Lisa Jane
100 Steps for Science: Why It Works and How It Happened *Publishers Weekly* v264 no12 p72 Mr 20 2017

Gillespie, Michael Boyce
ONE STEP AHEAD: A CONVERSATION WITH BARRY JENKINS *Film Quarterly* v70 no3 p52 Spr 2017

GILLESPIE, NICK
'BUY AMERICAN' IS UN-AMERICAN *Reason* v49 no5 p18 O 2017
Documentarian Ken Burns on How Vietnam Explains the Current Political Moment color *Reason* v49 no5 p79 O 2017
Free Speech, No Shit color *Reason* v49 no3 p50 Jl 2017
FROM THE ARCHIVES bw cartoon *Reason* v48 no11 p70 Ap 2017
FROM THE ARCHIVES bw color *Reason* v49 no3 p70 Jl 2017
'I'm Not Willing to Sacrifice Freedom of Expression on the Altar of Cultural Diversity' color *Reason* v49 no1 p44 My 2017
P.J. O'Rourke: Things Are Going to Be Fine color *Reason* v49 no2 p38 Je 2017
Steve Forbes Talks Shop color *Reason* v49 no6 p79 N 2017

Gillespie, Shawn M.
Decoupling genetics, lineages, and microenvironment in IDH-mutant gliomas by single-cell RNA-seq diag *Science* v355 no6332 p1391 Mr 31 2017

GILLETTE, ALLISON
The Question *O, The Oprah Magazine* p16 D 2016

Gillette, Felix
29 Reasons Why BuzzFeed Is Getting Into the TV Game color *Bloomberg Businessweek* no4526 p60 Je 12 2017
And Then There Was Hannity bw color *Bloomberg Businessweek* no4520 p54 My 1 2017
Baby's First Virtual Assistant color *Bloomberg Businessweek* no4506 p27 Ja 9 2017
Everybody Must Get Streamed color *Bloomberg Businessweek* no4504 p30 D 19 2016
Marlboro color *Bloomberg Businessweek* no4514 p46 Mr 13 2017
THE MILLENNIAL CORD CUTTING SINGULARITY IS NIGH color *Bloomberg Businessweek* no4513 p56 Mr 6 2017
NETFLIX PRESENTS BUILDING A WORLD OF BINGE-WATCHERS color *Bloomberg Businessweek* no4507 p40 Ja 16 2017
Politics [Cover story] color graph *Bloomberg Businessweek* no4498 p60 N 7 2016
The Resurrection Drug color graph *Bloomberg Businessweek* no4499 p42 N 14 2016
THE REVOLUTION WILL BE TELEVISED (IT'LL JUST HAVE LOW PRODUCTION VALUES) [Cover story] bw color

map *Bloomberg Businessweek* no4531 p44 Jl 24 2017
TRONC IF YOU WANT TO SAVE JOURNALISM [Cover story] color *Bloomberg Businessweek* no4498 p74 N 7 2016
The Trump-Loving Lawyer Who Won't Stop Suing Fox News color *Bloomberg Businessweek* no4540 p60 O 2 2017

GILLIAM, FRANK S.
Combining Biodiversity Resurveys across Regions to Advance Global Change Research *BioScience* v67 no1 p73 Ja 2017

Gilliam, Jan
GROWING INTERESTS cartoon *Magazine Antiques* v184 no1 p118 Ja/F 2017

Gillian-Daniel, Donald L.
Promoting Student Academic Achievement Through Faculty Development about Inclusive Teaching *Change* v48 no5 p16 S/O 2016

Gillibrand, Kirsten, 1966-
BACK IN THE SPOTLIGHT *Successful Farming* v114 no13 p16 D 2016
Comments img *New York* v50 no8 p10 Ap 17 2017
THE CONTENDER J. Van Meter color *Vogue* v207 no11 p198 N 2017
KIRSTEN GILLIBRAND IS AN ENTHUSIASTIC NO R. TRAISTER img *New York* v50 no7 p32 Ap 3 2017
On the Verge A. WINTOUR color *Vogue* v207 no11 p74 N 2017
Pioneers [Cover story] color *Time* v189 no16/17 p14 My 1-8 2017

Gillibrand, Kirsten, 1966——Political & social views
Kirsten Gillibrand T. STUART color *Rolling Stone* no1295 p44 S 7 2017

Gilligan, Peter
Emergence and spread of a human-transmissible multidrug-resistant nontuberculous mycobacterium bibl diag graph *Science* v354 no6313 p751 N 11 2016

GILLIHAN, SETH J.
Depressed Without Knowing It: Even when we know what depression looks like, we can miss it in ourselves *Psychology Today* v50 no5 p50 S/O 2017

Gillilland, Merritt G.
Neonatal acquisition of Clostridia species protects against colonization by bacterial pathogens diag *Science* v356 no6335 p315 Ap 21 2017

Gillim, Hayden
MAN. VAN. PLAN M. Hoyer color *Cycle World* v55 no11 p60 D 2016

Gillingham, Kenneth
Reforming the U.S. coal leasing program color graph *Science* v354 no6316 p1096 D 2 2016

GILLINGHAM, SARA KATE
LIQUID GOLD *Martha Stewart Living* no268 p122 O 2016

Gillings, Michael
Microbial mass movements color *Science* v357 no6356 p1099 S 15 2017

Gillis, Anna Maria
Elaine Pagels *Humanities* v37 no4 p1 Fall 2016

Gillis, Betty
The Cre Run Oaks and Bob Magness Derby at Delaware Park S. Andersen *Arabian Horse World* v57 no12 p184 S 2017

GILLIS, CHARLIE
Absolutely some trespassing color *Maclean's* v129 no43 p26 O 31 2016
Doobs of hazard color *Maclean's* v129 no41 p14 O 17 2016
Fighting the beast color *Maclean's* v129 no48/49 p54 D 5 2016
HOW TO KILL A PIPELINE color *Maclean's* v129 no51/52 p20 D 26 2016
How to make a candidate color *Maclean's* no1 p26 F 17 2017
It could happen here [Cover story] color *Maclean's* v129 no47 p26 N 28 2016
A moment of painful truth color *Maclean's* v130 no2 p18 Mr 2017
MONEY CAN'T BUY HAPPY KIDS color *Maclean's* v129 no44 p21 N 7 2016
THE PIGEON TUNNEL color *Maclean's* v129 no41 p58 O 17 2016
RODEO'S NFL MOMENT color *Maclean's* v130 no2 p52 Mr 2017

Gillis, Joe
The Cre Run Oaks and Bob Magness Derby at Delaware Park S. Andersen *Arabian Horse World* v57 no12 p184 S 2017

Gilliver, Peter
LEXICON TOTIUS ANGLICITATIS J. Camplin *History Today* v67 no5 p96 My 2017

Gillogly, Brandan
2.5 HORSEPOWER PER CUBIC INCH! color *Hot Rod* v70 no4 p76 Ap 2017
The 50 Quickest Cars of Drag Week 2016 —and Then Some chart color *Hot Rod* v70 no2 p18 F 2017
850HP LS FORMULA color *Hot Rod* v70 no4 p78 Ap 2017
BACK TO THE SALT chart color *Hot Rod* v70 no1 p28 Ja 2017
THE FALCONER DODICI color *Hot Rod* v70 no1 p76 Ja 2017
FINDING FORGOTTEN HORSEPOWER color *Hot Rod* v70 no3 p64 Mr 2017
INFERNO [Cover story] color *Hot Rod* v70 no8 p24 Ag 2017
MENACE color *Hot Rod* v70 no7 p44 Jl 2017
More Doors, More Fun color *Hot Rod* v70 no5 p8 My 2017
Mothers 1959 SEDAN DELIVERY color *Hot Rod* v70 no11 p56 N 2017
MPG HEADS CHAMPION SMALL-BLOCK FORD color *Hot Rod* v70 no3 p58 Mr 2017
Mustang ROUSH P-51 color *Hot Rod* v70 no11 p30 N 2017
New Classes, New Winners, and New Recipes for Horsepower color *Hot Rod* v70 no3 p56 Mr 2017
A RECORD 48 YEARS IN THE MAKING color *Hot Rod* v70 no1 p34 Ja 2017
The Ringbrothers' G-Code Camaro BLUEPRINTED color *Hot Rod* v70 no6 p50 Je 2017
Roadster Shop's Widebody 1970 Camaro Track Weapoon RAMPAGE color *Hot Rod* v69 no12 p18 D 2016
Rutledge Wood's 1970 CHARGER color *Hot Rod* v70 no11 p34 N 2017
SALT CHARGER color *Hot Rod* v70 no2 p52 F 2017
STREETABLE 469CI BIG-BLOCK CHEVY color *Hot Rod* v70 no4 p74 Ap 2017
STREET MACHINE ELIMINATOR'S ELITE EIGHT color *Hot Rod* v70 no3 p80 Mr 2017
TESTED: TOTAL SEAL'S 110V RING FILER color *Hot Rod* v70 no2 p72 F 2017
TRIPLE THREAT color *Hot Rod* v70 no5 p64 My 2017
Tweaked Torino color *Hot Rod* v70 no12 p48 D 2017
Until Next Time color *Hot Rod* v70 no12 p6 D 2017
VERSION 3.0 color *Hot Rod* v70 no8 p54 Ag 2017
Vicious color *Hot Rod* v70 no8 p32 Ag 2017
Z/409: The '69 Camaro Chevrolet Should Have Built color *Hot Rod* v70 no10 p24 O 2017
ZR71 color *Hot Rod* v70 no5 p26 My 2017

Gilly's Bowl & Grille (Poem)
GILLY'S BOWL & GRILLE C. Van Landingham *New Yorker* v92 no45 p58 Ja 16 2017

Gilman, Charlotte Perkins, 1860-1935
WE WERE RIGHT ALL ALONG color *Yankee* p26 Mr 2017

Gilmor, Merideth
Rich Rituals B. KIZER, J. LEWIS et al color *O, The Oprah Magazine* p14 Ja 2017

GILMORE, DAN
A BOARDROOM OF ONE'S OWN color *Vanity Fair* v59 no7 p55 Summ 2017
DANCING IN THE MOONLIGHT color *Vanity Fair* v59 no5 p61 Ap 2017
EN PLEIN AIR color *Vanity Fair* v59 no9 p145 S 2017
TANGLED UP IN BLUE color *Vanity Fair* v59 no8 p52 Ag 2017

Gilmore, David
Chords & Discords A. CARTER-BEY, D. HAMILTON et al color *Downbeat* v83 no11 p10 N 2016

Gilmore, Eamon
the exchange E. GILMORE and S. HADDAD *Foreign Policy* no222 p26 Ja/F 2017

Gilmore, Mikal
Chuck Berry 1926-2017 bw color *Rolling Stone* no1285 p22 Ap 20 2017
Dylan, Deep in the Wee Small Hours color *Rolling Stone* no1284 p51 Ap 6 2017
The Last Brother: Gregg Allman 1947-2017 color *Rolling Stone* no1290 p44 Je 29 2017
LEONARD COHEN 1934-2016 bw color *Rolling Stone* no1276 p52 D 15 2016

A New Trip Through Pepper-Land color *Rolling Stone* no1288 p49 Je 1 2017

Gilmore, Nicholas

Hot on the TRAILS: A ROAD-FREE GUIDE TO EXPLORING CENTRAL INDIANA *Indianapolis Monthly* v40 no10 p59 Je 2017

GILMORE, SCOTT

52 months of torture and zero answers color *Maclean's* v129 no45 p20 N 14 2016

Canada's unspoken crisis color graph map *Maclean's* v129 no50 p12 D 19 2016

CONFESSIONS OF A SELF-LOATHING TORY color *Maclean's* v130 no4 p32 My 2017

The decline of trust and truth color *Maclean's* v130 no8 p8 S 2017

THE GRIEF OF SUSAN B. ANTHONY color *Maclean's* v129 no46 p39 N 21 2016

How the West is winning color *Maclean's* v129 no41 p32 O 17 2016

MISPLACED PRIDE color *Maclean's* v130 no6 p22 Jl 2017

THE MORNING AFTER DONALD TRUMP color *Maclean's* v129 no43 p32 O 31 2016

THE NOT–SO–CRAZY CASE AGAINST CLINTON color *Maclean's* v129 no44 p36 N 7 2016

OUTSIDE THE OTTAWA BUBBLE color *Maclean's* p28 Je 2017

Populist goes the world color *Maclean's* v130 no3 p25 Ap 2017

The terrorists on the right color *Maclean's* v130 no9 p12 O 2017

The Tories need to go gay color *Maclean's* v130 no7 p10 Ag 2017

THE TORIES WHO SHOULD NOT BE NAMED [Cover story] *Maclean's* v129 no51/52 p14 D 26 2016

Trudeau, 'Trump Whisperer' *Maclean's* v130 no2 p10 Mr 2017

TRUMP IS STILL STANDING BUT DOES IT MATTER? color *Maclean's* v129 no42 p43 O 24 2016

TRUMP'S NEW WORLD ORDER color *Maclean's* v129 no48/49 p26 D 5 2016

THE VICTORY OF A FEARFUL AMERICA color *Maclean's* v129 no46 p38 N 21 2016

When robots steal your job color *Maclean's* no1 p8 F 17 2017

WOULD TRUMP WIN THE TORY LEADERSHIP? color *Maclean's* v129 no47 p13 N 28 2016

Gilmore, Vernard J.

Vernard J. GILMOR C. Bowers bw *Dance Spirit* v20 no10 p24 D 2016

Gilmore, Woody

The Beginning of the End of the Rear-Engine Funny Car T. Taylor color *Hot Rod* v69 no12 p12 D 2016

Gilmore Girls (TV program)

America's top TV critic Matt Roush answers your burning questions Kristen, Jay et al *TV Guide* p6 D 19 2016

CHEERS & JEERS D. HOLBROOK *TV Guide* v65 no13 p88 Mr 20 2017

GILMORE GIRLS: ANOTHER YEAR IN THE LIFE?! S. Highfill color *Entertainment Weekly* no1457/1458 p18 Mr 17 2017

In the Gilmore Girls' Hometown, Things Are (Mostly) the Same E. Dockterman color *Time* v188 no21 p69 N 21 2016

Table for two P. H. Nettleton color *U.S. Catholic* v81 no12 p38 D 2016

Gilmore Girls: A Year in the Life (TV program)

THE FINAL FOUR CHAPTERS S. Highfill color *Entertainment Weekly* no1441 p24 N 25 2016

Gilmore Girls: A Year in the Life J. Jensen color *Entertainment Weekly* no1441 p47 N 25 2016

Gilmore Girls Revival Guide S. Highfill color *Entertainment Weekly* no1443 p14 D 9 2016

RETURN TO STARS HOLLOW I. RATLEDGE *TV Guide* v64 no48 p30 N 21 2016

Gilmour, Ana

ask the experts cartoon color *Dressage Today* v23 no5 p64 Ja 2017

Tune Your Riding Position to Put Your Horse into "Drive" [Cover story] color diag *Dressage Today* v24 no2 p26 N 2017

Gilpatrick, John

Bench Your Best chart color *Men's Health* v32 no1 p52 Ja/F 2017

Gil-Perotin, Sara

Extensive migration of young neurons into the infant human frontal lobe color diag graph *Science* v354 no6308 paaf7073-1 O 7 2016

Gilroy, Dan

FIGHT THE POWER A. Carter color *Esquire* p32 N 2017

Gilroy, Tony

The Bonfire of Humanity J. PARKER color *Atlantic* v320 no4 p32 N 2017

GILSDORF, ETHAN

Misfit Creatures: Anxious heroes navigate unfamiliar planets *New York Times Book Review* p13 S 17 2017

Players Gonna Play *New York Times Book Review* p16 O 2 2016

Gilsdorf, Mark

METALHEAD A. BRANDT *Cincinnati Magazine* v50 no4 p42 Ja 2017

Gilsinan, Kathy

THE CHURCH OF THE FLYING SPAGHETTI MONSTER cartoon *Atlantic* v318 no4 p23 N 2016

Gilson, Dave

WEST BLING *Mother Jones* v42 no2 p4 Mr/Ap 2017

Gilstrap, John

SPOTLIGHT ON John Gilstrap color *Publishers Weekly* v264 no11 p49 Mr 13 2017

Gilvarry, Alex, 1982-

Eastman Was Here *Publishers Weekly* v264 no27 p49 Jl 3 2017

Gimbals (Mechanical devices)—Evaluation

DRONES D. SUPERTRAMP and R. FELNER chart color *Popular Mechanics* p78 O 2017

Gimenez, Carlos

Miami's Mayor Climbs Aboard the Trump Train J. Levin and P. Murphy color *Bloomberg Businessweek* no4512 p28 F 20 2017

Gimenez, Rebecca

12 Trailering Myths: Busted! color *Trail Rider* v29 no2 p18 Mr 2017

3 Steps to Safe Winter Hauling color *Trail Rider* v29 no1 p34 Ja/F 2017

Aftermarket Accessories color *Trail Rider* v29 no4 p18 My 2017

Around the Campfire color *Trail Rider* v29 no2 p6 Mr 2017

Equine Traveling Papers color *Trail Rider* v29 no3 p10 Ap 2017

Horse Owner's Spring Notebook color *Trail Rider* v29 no4 p38 My 2017

How to Change a Trailer Tire color *Trail Rider* v29 no1 p18 Ja/F 2017

Gimlet Media (Company)

A Standalone Podcast Network, Just Maybe L. Shaw cartoon *Bloomberg Businessweek* no4499 p50 N 14 2016

Gimme Danger (Film)

A Heart Full of Napalm J. JARMUSCH *Los Angeles Magazine* v61 no11 p92 N 2016

In This Battle of the Bands, Oasis Beats Iggy I. Guzmán color *Time* v188 no20 p51 N 14 2016

Gimmy, Gregor

What BMW's Corporate VC Offers That Regular Investors Can't *Harvard Business Review Digital Articles* p2 Jl 27 2017

Gimson, Ernest

A Big Tent P. Poore *Arts & Crafts Homes & the Revival* v11 no5 p8 Wint 2017

vernacular to a fare-thee-well B. D. COLEMAN color *Arts & Crafts Homes & the Revival* v11 no5 p56 Wint 2017

Gin

Blueberry Hill T. MCNALLY color *New Orleans Magazine* v52 no1 p110 S 2017

By Any Measurement T. McNally color *New Orleans Magazine* v51 no4 p90 F 2017

Coming Around Again T. Mcnally color *New Orleans Magazine* v51 no9 p86 Jl 2017

NEXT GIN J. Kell color *Fortune* v175 no2 p28 F 1 2017

Gin—Evaluation

THE RICHEST POURS color *Forbes* v198 no9 p49 D 30 2016

That's the Spirit L. J. Solmonson *Sierra* v102 no3 p8 My/Je 2017

Ginger

Brothy Bowl color *Vegetarian Today* no1 p26 F 2017

SPICE things up color *Good Housekeeping* v265 no4 p87 O 2017

WINDOWSILL GINGER M. VILJOEN color *Better Homes & Gardens* v95 no2 p72 F 2016

Ginger beer

Real Ginger Beer F. MAROUKIAN color *Popular Mechanics* p22 Jl 2017

Gingerbread

Edd Kimber's Nanna's Gingerbread S. Gutierrez *British Heritage*

Travel v38 no2 p77 Mr/Ap 2017

Sandra Lee Favorites *TV Guide* p18 D 5 2016

TREE-MENDOUS GINGERBREAD color *Good Housekeeping* v263 no6 p113 D 2016

Gingerbread houses

winter wonderlands L. BLEIBERG *Better Homes & Gardens* v94 no11 p166 N 2016

Gingerich, Owen

Kepler and the Universe *Physics Today* v69 no10 p55 O 2016

Gingras, Anne-Claude

Exploring genetic suppression interactions on a global scale diag *Science* v354 no6312 p599 N 4 2016

GINGRAS, CALEB

#Climbing Training color *Climbing* no352 p9 Ap 2017

Gingras, Elizabeth

THE RIGHT CANTER FOR EVERY SITUATION [Cover story] bw chart color *Practical Horseman* v45 no10 p28 O 2017

Gingras, Yves

Peer review as conflict *Physics Today* v70 no10 p16 O 2017

Gingrich, Newt, 1943-

Details, Details F. BARNES cartoon *Weekly Standard* v23 no3 p11 S 25 2017

from the stacks *New Republic* v248 no10 p5 O 2017

Literary License D. Grann *New Republic* v248 no10 p5 O 2017

The Year in Reading [Cover story] *New York Times Book Review* p8 D 25 2016

Ginhoux, Florent

Mapping the human DC lineage through the integration of high-dimensional techniques diag *Science* v356 no6342 p1044 Je 9 2017

Ginn, DeWitt

NEW CLASSIC M. SIMONEAUX color *Louisiana Life* v37 no4 p20 Mr/Ap 2017

Ginno, Paul A.

Impact of cytosine methylation on DNA binding specificities of human transcription factors diag *Science* v356 no6337 p502 My 5 2017

Gino, Francesca

Antagonistic Mediators Can Make Resolving Disputes Easier *Harvard Business Review Digital Articles* p2 Ag 19 2016

Are You Too Stressed to Be Productive? Or Not Stressed Enough? *Harvard Business Review Digital Articles* p2 Ap 14 2016

Companies Like Amazon Need to Run More Tests on Workplace Practices *Harvard Business Review Digital Articles* p2 Ag 20 2015

Developing Employees Who Think for Themselves *Harvard Business Review Digital Articles* p2 Je 3 2015

Don't Let Emotions Screw Up Your Decisions *Harvard Business Review Digital Articles* p2 My 6 2015

Don't Make Important Decisions Late in the Day *Harvard Business Review Digital Articles* p2 F 23 2016

Ending Gender Discrimination Requires More than a Training Program *Harvard Business Review Digital Articles* p2 O 10 2014

Experiment with Organizational Change Before Going All In *Harvard Business Review Digital Articles* p2 O 13 2014

Explaining Gender Differences at the Top *Harvard Business Review Digital Articles* p2 S 23 2015

How to Handle Interrupting Colleagues *Harvard Business Review Digital Articles* p2 F 22 2017

How to Make Employees Feel Like They Own Their Work *Harvard Business Review Digital Articles* p2 D 7 2015

How to Make Networking at Conferences Feel Less Icky *Harvard Business Review Digital Articles* p2 O 12 2015

Identifying the Biases Behind Your Bad Decisions *Harvard Business Review Digital Articles* p2 O 31 2014

If You're Loyal to a Group, Does It Compromise Your Ethics? *Harvard Business Review Digital Articles* p2 Ja 6 2016

Introverts, Extroverts, and the Complexities of Team Dynamics *Harvard Business Review Digital Articles* p2 Mr 16 2015

It's the Weekend! Why Are You Working? *Harvard Business Review Digital Articles* p2 Ap 10 2015

The Powerful Way Onboarding Can Encourage Authenticity *Harvard Business Review Digital Articles* p2 N 26 2015

Radical Transparency Can Reduce Bias—but Only If It's Done Right *Harvard Business Review Digital Articles* p2 O 10 2017

Reclaim Your Commute color *Harvard Business Review* v95 no3 p149 My/Je 2017

The Remedy for Unproductive Busyness *Harvard Business Review Digital Articles* p2 Ap 24 2015

The Right Way to Brag About Yourself *Harvard Business Review Digital Articles* p2 My 20 2015

The Rise of Behavioral Economics and Its Influence on Organizations *Harvard Business Review Digital Articles* p2 O 10 2017

Small Measures Can Liberate Employees to Contribute Their Best *Harvard Business Review Digital Articles* p2 N 2 2016

Teams Who Share Personal Stories Are More Effective *Harvard Business Review Digital Articles* p2 Ap 25 2016

There's a Word for Using Truthful Facts to Deceive: Paltering *Harvard Business Review Digital Articles* p2 O 5 2016

To Motivate Employees, Show Them How They're Helping Customers color *Harvard Business Review Digital Articles* p2 Mr 6 2017

The Unexpected Influence of Stories Told at Work *Harvard Business Review Digital Articles* p2 S 15 2015

We're Unethical at Work Because We Forget Our Misdeeds *Harvard Business Review Digital Articles* p2 My 18 2016

What Facebook's Anti-Bias Training Program Gets Right *Harvard Business Review Digital Articles* p2 Ag 24 2015

What We Miss When We Judge a Decision by the Outcome *Harvard Business Review Digital Articles* p2 S 2 2016

When Networking, Being Yourself Really Does Work *Harvard Business Review Digital Articles* p2 S 27 2016

Why CEOs Can't Stay Silent in the Wake of Events Like Charlottesville *Harvard Business Review Digital Articles* p2 2017

Why the U.S. Government Is Embracing Behavioral Science *Harvard Business Review Digital Articles* p2 S 18 2015

Why We Are So Careless with the Things We Own *Harvard Business Review Digital Articles* p2 D 2 2016

Your Desire to Get Things Done Can Undermine Your Effectiveness *Harvard Business Review Digital Articles* p2 Mr 22 2016

Ginsberg, Allen, 1926-1997

Peer Review: Professor Ginsberg's notes on the Beat Generation, compiled over two decades of teaching A. DOUGLAS bw *New York Times Book Review* p18 Ag 6 2017

Ginsberg, Allen, 1926-1997—Interviews

FILIAL POETRY S. Braitman *Harper's Magazine* v334 no2002 p16 Mr 2017

GINSBERG, JANIE

The rise and rise of edtech color *Maclean's* v129 no44 p52 N 7 2016

Ginsberg, Louis—Interviews

FILIAL POETRY S. Braitman *Harper's Magazine* v334 no2002 p16 Mr 2017

GINSBERG, TODD

HOW DOES YOUR LUNCH STACK UP? *Atlanta* v56 no7 p86 N 2016

Ginsburg, Ruth Bader, 1933-

Fighting Words E. SHOWALTER bw color il *New Republic* v247 no11 p42 N 2016

A Love Supreme F. Allen color *AARP: The Magazine* v59 no1A p53 D 2015/Ja 2016

My Own Words R. C. BACON *Ms.* v26 no4 p39 Wint 2016

This Is How We Do R. Love color *AARP: The Magazine* v59 no1A p5 D 2015/Ja 2016

Ginsburg, Ruth Bader, 1933-—Interviews

Liner Notes: Ruth Bader Ginsburg L. T. GUINTHER *Opera News* v81 no10 p68 Ap 2017

Ginseng—Export & import trade

CASH CROP R. J. Smith *Cincinnati Magazine* v50 no12 p70 S 2017

Gintis, Herbert

Uniting the (Social) Sciences? L. BARRETT *BioScience* v67 no10 p937 O 2017

GINTY, MOLLY M.

Seeing Red: Periods Gone Public: Taking a Stand for Menstrual Equity *Ms.* v27 no3 p53 Fall 2017

Ginzburg, Rubén

Forest conservation: Remember Gran Chaco bibl color *Science* v355 no6324 p465 F 3 2017

Gioffre, Rosalba

Vegano Italiano *Publishers Weekly* v264 no27 p70 Jl 3 2017

Gioia, Dana
HEANEY IN HADES *Claremont Review of Books* v17 no2 p49 Spr 2017
Time to Plant Tears *American Scholar* v86 no2 p120 Spr 2017

Gioia, Paul
Publish openly but responsibly color *Science* v357 no6347 p141 Jl 14 2017

Gioia, Ted
Ella by Starlight bw *Weekly Standard* v22 no29 p30 Ap 3 2017

Giolito, Malin Persson
First-Person Shooter L. HAAS *New York Times Book Review* p8 Mr 26 2017
Quicksand *Publishers Weekly* v264 no4 p53 Ja 23 2017

Gioni, Massimiliano
THE ART NEWS ACCORD bw color *ARTnews* v116 no1 p32 Spr 2017

Gioni, Massimiliano—Interviews
THE ART NEWS ACCORD A. Heiss and M. Gioni bw color *ARTnews* v116 no1 p32 Spr 2017

Giordana (Company)
GIORDANA NX-G JACKET J. Sherry color *Bicycling* v58 no9 p88 O 2017

Giordano, Anthony J.
Forest conservation: Remember Gran Chaco bibl color *Science* v355 no6324 p465 F 3 2017

Giordano, Daniel
THE LOOK BOOK A. SWERDLOFF img *New York* v50 no16 p89 Ag 7 2017

Giordano, Mario
Under the Sicilian Sun L. Ermelino color *Publishers Weekly* v264 no38 p22 S 18 2017

Giordano, Vince—Interviews
Giordano's Future in the Past K. Micallef color *Downbeat* v83 no11 p20 N 2016

Giorgianni, Anthony
The Joy of Specs chart color diag il *Consumer Reports* v82 no2 p7 F 2017
Save Money il *Consumer Reports* v82 no3 p30 Mr 2017
Shop Online With Confidence graph il *Consumer Reports* v82 no12 p20 D 2017
A TRULY HEARTFELT GIFT color *Consumer Reports* v81 no12 p50 D 2016
WRITE A BETTER WISH LIST color *Consumer Reports* v81 no12 p41 D 2016

Giorgio Armani SpA
Anything to DECLARE? color *Esquire* p112 S 2017
Berry Lips color *InStyle* v24 no9 p336 S 2017
Market color *Vanity Fair* v59 no5 p46 Ap 2017
The Pick color *InStyle* v23 no12 p206 N 2016
THERE'S A GIRL IN MY SWEATER D. WALTERS bw color *Esquire* v166 no4 p108 N 2016
WELCOME TO THE ISSUE *Harper's Bazaar* no3657 p50 O 2017

GIORGIS, HANNAH
'OOOUUU' color *New York Times Magazine* p57 Mr 12 2017

Giovanni, Monica A.
Distribution and clinical impact of functional variants in 50,726 whole-exome sequences from the DiscovEHR study chart graph *Science* v354 no6319 paaf6814-1 D 23 2016
Genetic identification of familial hypercholesterolemia within a single U.S. health care system chart graph *Science* v354 no6319 paaf7000-1 D 23 2016

GIOVANNINI, JOSEPH
CLEAR INTENTIONS bw color *Architectural Digest* v74 no1 p202 Ja 2017
Out of the Ordinary color *Architectural Digest* v74 no2 p36 F 2017

Giphy Inc.
How to save your Vine videos right now I. PAUL color *PCWorld* p184 D 2016

GIRACCA, AMANDA
INTO THE FIELD *Orion Magazine* v35 no3 p46 My/Je 2016

Giraffe
MYSTERY ON THE SAVANNA [Cover story] A. SHOUMATOFF color map *Smithsonian* v47 no10 p53 Mr 2017
NINJA GIRAFFES D. BROWN *National Geographic Kids* no468

p24 Mr 2017
Up to Speed: Two Months, One Page P. Rauber *Sierra* v102 no3 p22 My/Je 2017

Giraffe, The (Poem)
THE GIRAFFE M. Cadnum *Commonweal* v144 no12 p25 Jl 7 2017

Giraffe—Reproduction
East Africa turmoil imperils giraffes J. Qiu color diag *Science* v356 no6344 p1220 Je 23 2017

GIRALDI, PHILIP
DEEPBACKGROUND *American Conservative* v15 no6 p17 N/D 2016
DEEP BACKGROUND *American Conservative* v16 no1 p36 Ja/F 2017
DEEP BACKGROUND *American Conservative* v16 no4 p44 Jl/Ag 2017
Exposing Shabby Intelligence bw *American Conservative* v16 no2 p6 Mr/Ap 2017

Giraldi, William
Holy Horror bw *Commonweal* v144 no3 p17 F 10 2017

Giraldo, L. E. Urrego
Persistent effects of pre-Columbian plant domestication on Amazonian forest composition bibl chart graph map *Science* v355 no6328 p925 Mr 3 2017

Girard, Alexander
Nurtur&ing the spirit J. Eisenbrand bw cartoon color *Magazine Antiques* v184 no1 p196 Ja/F 2017

Girard, Geoffrey
Truthers color *Publishers Weekly* v264 no23 p54 Je 5 2017

Girard, M.-E.
M-E Girard K. BAVER color *Publishers Weekly* v263 no52 p68 D 19 2016

Girard, Philippe
HAITI'S JACOBIN D. A. BELL color *Nation* v33 no21 p40 N 21 2016
The Insurrectionist P. BERMAN *New York Times Book Review* p30 D 11 2016

Girardi, Joe, 1964-
How to Coach, According to 5 Great Sports Coaches S. G. Carmichael *Harvard Business Review Digital Articles* p2 F 25 2015

Girdhar, Yogesh
A Smarter Undersea Robot color *Oceanus* v51 no2 p90 Wint 2016

GIRE, KEN
All the Gallant Men *Reader's Digest* v188 no1126 p82 D 2016/Ja 2017

Girish, Devika
Dirt Beneath the Daydreams color *Film Comment* v53 no4 p74 Jl/Ag 2017
The Great Library bw *Film Comment* v53 no1 p91 Ja/F 2017

Girl Scouts
Smart Cookie S. SHELLEY *Virginia Living* v15 no3 p49 Ap 2017

Girl Scouts of the United States of America
THE FUTURE FOR GIRL SCOUTS IN AMERICA AND ABROAD *Vital Speeches of the Day* v82 no10 p312 O 2016

Girlfriend Experience, The (TV program)
The Girlfriend Experience D. Franich, A. Bacle et al color *Entertainment Weekly* no1482/1483 p38 S 22 2017
Nothing Scares Louisa Krause J. Harman color *Glamour* v115 no11 p41 N 2017
The Ten Best TV Shows of the Year M. Z. Seitz img *New York* v49 no25 p120 D 12 2016

Girlfriends' Guide to Divorce (TV program)
Girlfriends' Guide to Divorce *TV Guide* v65 no4 p36 Ja 16 2017

Girlhood (Film)
SCENES OF HURT AND RAPTURE: CÉLINE SCIAMMA'S GIRLHOOD E. Wilson *Film Quarterly* v70 no3 p10 Spr 2017

Girl on the Train, The (Film)
The Art of Being Blunt [Cover story] A. Synnott color *InStyle* v23 no12 p238 N 2016
The Bullseye M. S. @marcsnetiker color *Entertainment Weekly* no1435 p64 O 14 2016
Emily Blunt's Girl on a Train In Vain S. Zacharek color *Time* v188 no15 p53 O 17 2016
Getting Back on Track C. Chiarella color *Sound & Vision* v82 no4 p66 My 2017
The Girl on the Train L. Greenblatt color *Entertainment Weekly*

no1435 p40 O 14 2016

SEEING THINGS A. LANE cartoon *New Yorker* v92 no33 p108 O 17 2016

Girls

See also

Fathers & daughters

Photography of girls

Teenage girls

10-Year-Old-Girl Powers We Should All Reclaim K. Bonnell and P. Redmond Satran color *Glamour* v115 no5 p195 My 2017

GIVING GIRLS A FUTURE color *Good Housekeeping* v263 no5 p99 N 2016

Girls (TV program)

The Bullseye M. Snetiker color *Entertainment Weekly* no1446/1447 p124 D 2016/Ja 2017

The Bullseye M. Snetiker color *Entertainment Weekly* no1463/1464 p114 Ap/My 2017

Do Endings Matter Anymore? Yes, but not nearly as much as they used to. TV is moving away from finale fever—which is making for better TV M. Z. Seitz *New York* v50 no12 p92 Je 12 2017

Girls, Interrupted S. MARSHALL *New Republic* v248 no4 p50 Ap 2017

Girls I. Ratledge color *TV Guide* v65 no7 p43 F 13 2017

THE GOODBYE GIRLS S. Vilkomerson color *Entertainment Weekly* no1449 p22 Ja 20 2017

Mapping the Girls Effect E. Dockterman color diag *Time* v189 no6 p49 F 20 2017

The Must List color *Entertainment Weekly* no1451/1452 p4 F 3-10 2017

RIZ AHMED: THE NEW BOY ON GIRLS S. Li and R. Rahman color *Entertainment Weekly* no1453 p52 F 17 2017

Girls' clothing

Keys to Prom Style Success J. ABIDOR color *Seventeen* v76 no2 p50 Mr 2017

Prom MONEY SAVERS L. SAXTON color *Seventeen* v76 no2 p98 Mr 2017

Girls' clothing—Evaluation

$50 & Under Postprom Party color *Seventeen* v76 no2 p58 Mr 2017

Vintage PROM VIBES color *Seventeen* v76 no2 p52 Mr 2017

Girls of the Golden West (Theatrical production)

CLASSICAL MUSIC color *New Yorker* v93 no29 p30 S 25 2017

Girls' pants—Evaluation

The Get-It Guide *Glamour* v115 no11 p157 N 2017

Girls Trip (Film)

The Bullseye M. Snetiker color *Entertainment Weekly* no1476 p68 Ag 4 2017

Buoyant, Breezy and Brassy, Girls Trip Never Trips Up S. Zacharek color *Time* v190 no5 p57 Jl 31 2017

Girls Trip *New Yorker* v93 no25 p17 Ag 28 2017

GIRL TRIPPING R. R. Robertson color *Essence* v48 no3 p82 Jl 2017

PELICAN BRIEFS L. LeBlanc-Berry color *Louisiana Life* v37 no6 p10 Jl/Ag 2017

Girls Who Code

Why We Should Be Excited About the Future L. SOROKANICH color *Popular Mechanics* p95 My 2017

Girls—Education

Thank You, FLOTUS! color *Glamour* v115 no1 p14 Ja 2017

Girls—Services for

Revolutionary Empowerment for Girls in Nepal E. Satow color *Maclean's* v130 no3 p65 Ap 2017

Girls—Social conditions

Smart Girls J. LICHTBLAU *American Scholar* v86 no1 p6 Wint 2017

Girls—United States

Girls in White Dresses G. T. LEMMON *Ms.* v27 no2 p31 Summ 2017

Girl With the Dragon Tattoo, The (Film)

Rooney on the Move [Cover story] N. Heller color *Vogue* v207 no10 p243 O 2017

Girma, Eden

Our galaxy's center creates planet-sized swarms of gas color *Astronomy* v45 no5 p21 My 2017

Giro (Company)

18 FOR 18 G. Liu color *Bicycling* v58 no9 p63 O 2017

Giro Sport Design (Company)

GIRO PROLIGHT TECHLACE M. Phillips color *Bicycling* v58 no10 p66 N/D 2017

GIROD, STÉPHANE J.G.

RESTRUCTURE OR RECONFIGURE? *Harvard Business Review* v95 no2 p128 Mr/Ap 2017

Gironde (France)—Description & travel

FRENCH FLAIR V. LOWRY color *Architectural Digest* v73 no12 p56 D 2016

Gisler, Sean

A Community for Growth: A Community for Growth At John Volken Academy, students gain skills for life and love *Psychology Today* v50 no5 p18 S/O 2017

Gisleson, Anne

Read 'Em and Weep: A book club leads the author deep into her sorrows E. F. GORDON *New York Times Book Review* p25 O 8 2017

Gisondi, Joe

The Bigfoot Obsession J. NICKELL *Skeptical Inquirer* v41 no4 p62 Jl/Ag 2017

Gisriel, Christopher

Structure of a symmetric photosynthetic reaction center–photosystem color *Science* v357 no6355 p1021 S 8 2017

Gist, Kimber

This Is My Job J. Militare color *Glamour* v114 no11 p137 N 2016

GISTARO, ERIN

Where Water Means Life *Ms.* v26 no4 p11 Wint 2016

Gitler, Aaron D.

Old moms say, no Sir bibl diag *Science* v355 no6330 p1126 Mr 17 2017

UNLOCKING THE MYSTERY OF ALS color *Scientific American* v316 no6 p46 Je 2017

Gitlin, Martin

Powerful Moments in Sports: The Most Significant Sporting Events in American History *Publishers Weekly* v264 no10 p53 Mr 6 2017

GITLIN, TODD

Throwing Anna Under the Train *New York Times Book Review* p49 N 13 2016

Gittelsohn, John

The Bond King Gets Lost in the Crowd bw *Bloomberg Business week* no4539 p29 S 25 2017

Dan Ivascyn *Bloomberg Businessweek* no4531 p72 Jl 24 2017

What Happened to the New Normal for Bonds? bw *Bloomberg Businessweek* no4504 p36 D 19 2016

Gittin, Vaughn, 1980-

ANATOMY OF A DRIFT CAR P. Thomas color *Hot Rod* v70 no8 p60 Ag 2017

GITTINGS, CHRIS

HIGH-SPEED RELOADING color *Outdoor Life* v224 no1 pR1 D 2016/Ja 2017

Gittins, Rob

Investigating Mr. Wakefield *Publishers Weekly* v263 no41 p59 O 10 2016

Gitzinger, Marc

Reversion of antibiotic resistance in Mycobacterium tuberculosis by spiroisoxazoline SMARt-420 bibl diag *Science* v355 no6330 p1206 Mr 17 2017

Giubbilei, Luciano

LUCIANO GIUBBILEI color *Harper's Bazaar* no3653 p140 My 2017

Giudicelli, Mari

Outfits for Days color *Glamour* v115 no10 p70 O 2017

Giuffra, Valentina

Ancient Remedies for Modern Maladies R. GERACI color *Men's Health* v32 no5 p84 Je 2017

Giulietti, Monica

Tesla Is Betting on Solar, Not Just Batteries *Harvard Business Review Digital Articles* p2 Jl 2 2015

Giulio Cesare (Theatrical production)

Pale Caesar A. Wasserman *Opera News* v81 no5 p54 N 2016

Giulivi, Cecilia

Microbiota-activated PPAR-γ signaling inhibits dysbiotic Enterobacteriaceae expansion graph *Science* v357 no6351 p570 Ag 11 2017

Giuntoli, David—Interviews

Grimm *TV Guide* v65 no2 p31 Ja 2 2017

Giuseppe Pelicci, Pier

Transcriptional activation of RagD GTPase controls mTORC1 and promotes cancer growth diag *Science* v356 no6343 p1188 Je 16 2017

Giusti, Kathy

A New Approach to Safely Sharing Cancer Patients' Data *Harvard Business Review Digital Articles* p1 Je 21 2017

One Obstacle to Curing Cancer: Patient Data Isn't Shared *Harvard Business Review Digital Articles* p2 N 28 2016

What Cancer Researchers Can Learn from Direct-to-Consumer Companies color *Harvard Business Review Digital Articles* p2 Ja 12 2017

Giustino, Feliciano

Perovskite-perovskite tandem photovoltaics with optimized band gaps bibl chart graph *Science* v354 no6314 p861 N 18 2016

Give More Love (Music)

Ringo Starr A. GREENE color *Rolling Stone* no1294 p20 Ag 24 2017

GIVEN, KATHRYN

MUSEUM–WORTHY color *Architectural Digest* v73 no12 p41 D 2016

GIVEN, SARA

10 quick and easy toddler-meal ideas, from toddlers *Parents* v92 no2 p108 F 2017

apps we wish existed color *Parents* v92 no4 p102 Ap 2017

If Parents Were Middle-Schoolers color *Parents* v92 no5 p12 My 2017

Givenchy, Hubert de, 1927-

GIVENCHY'S Giacomettis H. BOWLES, M. HOLGATE et al color *Vogue* v207 no3 p350 Mr 2017

Givhan, Jennifer

Protection Spell *Publishers Weekly* v264 no3 p38 Ja 16 2017

Givhan, Robin

Forever Tracy J. Wilson color *Essence* v48 no5 p96 S 2017

Gizowski, Claire

Neurons that drive and quench thirst color diag *Science* v357 no6356 p1092 S 15 2017

GJELTEN, TOM

ISLANDS IN THE SUN *New York Times Book Review* p45 D 4 2016

Gjerde, Kristina M.

An ecosystem-based deep-ocean strategy bibl color map *Science* v355 no6324 p452 F 3 2017

Science-based management in decline in the Southern Ocean bibl map *Science* v354 no6309 p185 O 14 2016

Gjoni, Eron

Zoë and the Trolls N. MALONE img *New York* v50 no15 p21 Jl 24 2017

GJRLEY, LAUREN KAORI

Jefferson County, U.S.A *In These Times* v41 no4 p60 Ap 2017

Glacial crevasses

SIX HUNDRED MILES WITH SKIS, KITES, AND WIND K. Long color *National Geographic* v231 no3 p14 Mr 2017

Glacial Decoy (Theatrical production)

When Worlds Collide J. Acocella bw *New Yorker* v92 no48 p11 F 6 2017

Glacial Epoch

2.7-million-year-old ice opens window on past P. Voosen color map *Science* v357 no6352 p630 Ag 18 2017

A World Ever at Its End D. Penick bw diag *Tricycle: The Buddhist Review* v26 no4 p60 Summ 2017

Glacial lakes

Melting glaciers: Hidden hazards Q. Zhang, F. Zhang et al color *Science* v356 no6337 p495 My 5 2017

Glacial lakes—Research

Chile's glacial lakes pose newly recognized flood threat J. Palmer color *Science* v355 no6329 p1004 Mr 10 2017

Glacial landforms

See also

Glacial lakes

Ghostly glimpses of Earth's glacial past B. Geiger color *Science News* v191 no10 p32 My 27 2017

Glacial melting

See also

Ice sheets—Thawing

Elegy Series color *Issues in Science & Technology* v33 no1 p96 Fall 2016

Melting glaciers: Hidden hazards Q. Zhang, F. Zhang et al color *Science* v356 no6337 p495 My 5 2017

Glacial melting—Research

Joint research push targets fast-melting Antarctic ice P. Voosen color *Science* v354 no6309 p159 O 14 2016

A Mooring in Iceberg Alley R. Jackson color *Oceanus* v51 no2 p16 Wint 2016

Glacier National Park (B.C.)

Uncertain Weather A. MALCHIK *Orion Magazine* v36 no1 p11 Ja/F 2017

Glaciers

THE DESCENT M. EARLE color *Climbing* no355 p80 Ag 2017

DROPPING INTO WORK E. MASTROIANNI color *Discover* v27 no10 p7 D 2016

FROZEN WORLD *National Geographic Kids* no466 p26 D 2016/Ja 2017

GLASS color *Powder* v45 no3 p26 N 2016

GREEN LAND P. STEFÁNSSON *Iceland Review* v55 no3 p24 My/Je 2017

How glaciers shaped the sea floor color *Science* v356 no6336 p354 Ap 28 2017

INTO THE GLACIER: Delving into the Ice *Iceland Review* v55 no3 p100 My/Je 2017

Is ice sheet collapse in West Antarctica unstoppable? C. Hulbe color map *Science* v356 no6341 p910 Je 1 2017

LOOK TWICE ... *Reader's Digest* v189 no1127 p128 F 2017

The Multitrophic Effects of Climate Change and Glacier Retreat in Mountain Rivers S. C. FELL, J. L. CARRIVICK et al *BioScience* v67 no10 p897 O 2017

OMG NASA! C. Armstrong color *Alternatives Journal (AJ) - Canada's Environmental Voice* v42 no2 p11 2016

Saying goodbye to glaciers T. Moon color *Science* v356 no6338 p580 My 12 2017

Glaciers & climate

New rift in Greenland glacier *Science* v356 no6335 p226 Ap 21 2017

Glaciers—Environmental conditions

MELTDOWN [Cover story] E. BETZ color diag map *Discover* v38 no5 p36 Je 2017

Studies in Solitude B. Lang *Discover* v38 no5 p6 Je 2017

Glaciers—Greenland

New rift in Greenland glacier *Science* v356 no6335 p226 Ap 21 2017

Glaciers—Himalaya Mountains

The Legal Rights of Nature T. John color *Time* v189 no14 p14 Ap 17 2017

Glaciers—Iceland

COLD CASE P. STEFÁNSSON *Iceland Review* v54 no6 p26 N/D 2016

ENVIRONMENTALLY SUSTAINABLE ADVENTURE *Iceland Review* v55 no3 p104 My/Je 2017

EXPLORING THE SNOW DESERT: What better way to experience Europe's largest glacier than from the very top of it? *Iceland Review* v55 no3 p102 My/Je 2017

FACE TO FACE WITH THE GLACIERS OF ICELAND *Iceland Review* v55 no3 p104 My/Je 2017

FROM THE EDITOR P. Stefánsson *Iceland Review* v55 no2 p4 Mr/Ap 2017

FROZEN P. STEFÁNSSON *Iceland Review* v55 no2 p32 Mr/Ap 2017

YOUR GUIDE TO THE BEST OUTDOOR ADVENTURES IN ICELAND *Iceland Review* v55 no3 p103 My/Je 2017

Glaciers—Pakistan

THE DESCENT A. BURR color *Climbing* no357 p72 N 2017

Glackens, Edith Dimock

"Miss Dimock is not orthodox at all": The life and career of Edith Dimock Glackens A. Berman bw cartoon color *Magazine Antiques* v184 no5 p84 S/O 2017

Glad, Douglas

9.65 AT 140 [Cover story] color *Hot Rod* v70 no7 p22 Jl 2017

Build Your Own $500 Drift Trike chart color *Hot Rod* v70 no10 p14 O 2017

Hot Rod Anything!: The Bomber R/C color *Hot Rod* v70 no4 p12 Ap 2017

Gladbach, Amadeus
Site-specific phosphorylation of tau inhibits amyloid-β toxicity in Alzheimer's mice bibl graph *Science* v354 no6314 p904 N 18 2016

Gladstone, Douglas J.
ordinary PEOPLE LIKE US bw color *Missouri Life* v44 no6 p58 S 2017

Gladstone, G. R.
Jupiter's magnetosphere and aurorae observed by the Juno spacecraft during its first polar orbits diag graph *Science* v356 no6340 p826 My 26 2017

Gladu, Marilyn
MOST COLLEGIAL S. NEMIS color *Maclean's* v129 no47 p23 N 28 2016

Gladwell, Malcolm
auto no mo' us bw color diag graph *Car & Driver* v63 no5 p58 N 2017
Brit MARLING [Cover story] *Interview* v47 no2 p118 Mr 2017
THE OUTSIDE MAN cartoon color *New Yorker* v92 no42 p119 D 19 2016

Glaenzer, Stefan
Will Britain Keep Investing in a Sex Offender's Venture Fund? A. Satariano, K. Wiggins et al *Bloomberg Businessweek* no4539 p22 S 25 2017

Glaeser, Edward L., 1967-
Infrastructure and Infra Dig Structures E. FELTEN color *Weekly Standard* v22 no12 p14 N 28 2016

Glafke, Michaela
What We Believe M. Halpin color *Glamour* v114 no12 p195 D 2016

GlamGlow (Company)
HEALTHY SKIN WINS E. METZGER color *Better Homes & Gardens* v95 no10 p28 O 2017
That Magic Formula: GLAMGLOW FOUNDERS GLENN AND SHANNON DELLIMORE BUILT A FAST FORTUNE WITH A QUICK ACTING FACIAL MUD. AS THEY RAMP UP FOR THEIR NEXT MOVE, THE BEAUTY WORLD IS WATCHING I. SCHMIDT *Los Angeles Magazine* p64 Ag 2017

Glamour (Periodical)
All Together Now color *Glamour* v115 no2 p97 F 2017
Wow. Just Wow color *Glamour* v114 no12 p201 D 2016

Glantz, Jen
How This 29-Year-Old Makes a Living as a Professional Bridesmaid K. Bahler color *Money* v46 no6 p10 Jl 2017

Glanzer, Joseph
ALL AROUND THE FARM® *Successful Farming* v115 no6 p77 Ap 2017

Glasberg, Gary, 1966-2016
Gary Glasberg A. D'Arminio color *TV Guide* v64 no42 p17 O 10 2016

Glasbrenner, Jeff
EVEREST PEAK Performer [Cover story] A. Murphy color *Sports Illustrated* v126 no13 p26 My 8 2017
Peak Season color *Sports Illustrated* v126 no13 p12 My 8 2017

Glasby, Heather
TESTING THE 15TH AMENDMENT *Prologue* v48 no4 p51 Wint 2016

GLASER, APRIL
STRONGER TOGETHER *Wired* v24 no12 p23 D 2016
WISH LIST 2016 color *Wired* v24 no12 p45 D 2016

Glaser, C.
Observation of a large-scale anisotropy in the arrival directions of cosmic rays above 8 × 1018 eV *Science* v357 no6357 p1266 S 22 2017

Glaser, Charles L.
Getting Out of the Gulf color *Foreign Affairs* v96 no1 p122 Ja/F 2017

Glaser, Jon
JON GLASER N. Weldon color *Runner's World* v52 no1 p112 Ja/F 2017

Glaser, Nikki
GET UP Stand Up [Cover story] A. Breslaw bw color *Women's Health* v13 no10 p103 D 2016
These Are Your Sexual Rights color *Glamour* v114 no7 p94 Jl 2016

GLASGOW, ZOEY

Sky's the Limit Festus color *Missouri Life* v44 no5 p14 Ag 2017
The Small Festival with a Big Heart color *Missouri Life* v44 no6 p24 S 2017
Through the Looking Glass bw *Missouri Life* v44 no6 p23 S 2017
TREASURE TROVE color *Missouri Life* v44 no5 p21 Ag 2017

Glasgow School of Art
Mackintosh Debris Turned to Art A. FIXSEN color *Architectural Record* v205 no3 p24 Mr 2017

Glasner, Margaret E.
Finding enzymes in the gut metagenome color *Science* v355 no6325 p577 F 10 2017

Glasper, Robert
Building Bridges B. ZIMMERMAN color *Downbeat* v84 no2 p8 F 2017
NO BARRIERS. NO LIMITS. NO FEAR [Cover story] P. Lutz color *Downbeat* v84 no2 p24 F 2017

Glaspy, Margaret
NIGHT LIFE *New Yorker* v93 no18 p12 Je 26 2017

Glass
See also
Glassware
8 ways people try to get good luck around the world E. WHITMER *National Geographic Kids* no468 p10 Mr 2017
A Colorful Welcome B. D. Coleman color *Old House Journal* v45 no7 p54 O 2017
Lens Crafter F. Krentcil bw *Glamour* v115 no3 p36 Mr 2017
MEETING NOTES B. Bower color *Science News* v190 no13 p9 D 24 2016
through the looking glass C. Maldarelli bw *Popular Science* v289 no2 p86 Mr/Ap 2017
WORTH THEIR WEIGHT F. VIGNA *Martha Stewart Living* no267 p132 S 2016

Glass, Bärbel
The structure and flexibility of conical HIV-1 capsids determined within intact virions bibl color *Science* v354 no6318 p1434 D 16 2016

Glass, Charles
ALL THE LAST WARS: Around the world with the Goya of conflict photography *Harper's Magazine* p45 S 2017
How Assad Is Winning color map *New York Review of Books* v64 no3 p15 F 23 2017
In the Horrorscape of Aleppo color *New York Review of Books* v64 no9 p18 My 25 2017

Glass, Christopher K.
An environment-dependent transcriptional network specifies human microglia identity color *Science* v356 no6344 p1248 Je 23 2017

Glass, Gary D.
Introducing a Psychotherapy for the Collective: A Paradigm Shift for College Mental Health *Change* v48 no6 p16 N/D 2016

Glass, Hugh
Wrong From Right B. HUNHOFF *South Dakota Magazine* v32 no4 p87 N/D 2016

Glass, Julia
Where the Willed Things Are: When a renowned children's book author dies, his longtime assistant must unravel his knotty legacy D. Leavitt *New York Times Book Review* p19 Ag 13 2017

Glass, Ron, 1945-2016
Ron Glass 1945-2016 K. P. Sullivan color *Entertainment Weekly* no1443 p17 D 9 2016

Glass, S.
Bismuthene on a SiC substrate: A candidate for a high-temperature quantum spin Hall material diag graph *Science* v357 no6348 p287 Jl 21 2017

Glass art
See also
Glass painting & staining
Glass sculpture
Glassware
Glass Act C. Kolb color *New Orleans Magazine* v51 no5 p40 Mr 2017
Through the Looking Glass Z. Glasgow bw *Missouri Life* v44 no6 p23 S 2017

Glass art—Exhibitions
What Comes Next color *American Craft* v76 no6 p96 D 2016-Ja 2017

Glass artists

Tender Tribute J. Lovelace bw color *American Craft* v77 no2 p28 Ap/My 2017

Glass beads

SEA SHADES M. B. EYERS color *Better Homes & Gardens* v95 no6 p26 Je 2017

Glass blowing & working

See also

Hot shops (Glass blowing & working)

GLASSBLOWER PATRICK CASANOVA'S color *Cabin Living* p11 Ap 2017

Glass bottles—Evaluation

BLENKO *Treasures* v6 no4 p14 F/Mr 2017

Glass chandeliers

TIME AND SPACE J. WOGAN color *Conde Nast Traveler* v52 no5 p42 My 2017

Glass cleaners (Compounds)—Evaluation

Gear P. Nielsen color *Sail* v48 no4 p32 Ap 2017

Glass construction

Chicken-wire Glass B. D. Coleman bw color *Old House Journal* v45 no1 p56 F 2017

INSIDE THE FAR-OUT GLASS LAB K. Bourzac bw color *MIT Technology Review* v120 no2 p100 Mr/Ap 2017

Last Look A. Greenblatt *Governing* v30 no9 p64 Je 2017

Glass construction—Evaluation

A New Addition to the Glass Jungle J. Zorthian color *Time* v189 no14 p23 Ap 17 2017

WASH AND GO C. RODRIGUES color *House Beautiful* p133 Ag 2017

Glass craft—Exhibitions

BONG SHOW N. Paumgarten cartoon *New Yorker* v93 no13 p36 My 15 2017

Glass factories—History—19th century

EMPIRE OF GLASS M. SHAKESPEARE bw color *Archaeology* v70 no2 p55 Mr/Ap 2017

Glass frogs (Amphibians)

Glass frog moms do care after all S. MILIUS color *Science News* v191 no8 p16 Ap 29 2017

Scientists find amazement in what's most familiar *Science News* v191 no8 p2 Ap 29 2017

Glass houses—Design & construction

CONSERVATORIES color *Old House Journal* v45 no6 p78 S 2017

Glass industry

See also

Glass blowing & working

Glass Act C. Kolb color *New Orleans Magazine* v51 no5 p40 Mr 2017

Glass industry—United States

PIRATES OF THE RUST BELT J. Fox color *Bloomberg Businessweek* no4511 p63 F 13 2017

Glass painting & staining

The Brilliance of Colored Light A. GRAVES and A. TUCKER color *Yankee* v80 no6 p38 N/D 2016

Hand-Painting Glass Gobos *Stage Directions* v30 no8 p14 Ag 2017

Glass sculpture

The Fine Tint C. Keller color *O, The Oprah Magazine* p30 O 2017

Glass tables

Bright Spot L. Cutrone color *New Orleans Magazine* v51 no8 p54 Je 2017

Glass Castle, The (Film)

The Glass Castle J. McGovern color *Entertainment Weekly* no1478 / 1479 p84 Ag 18-25 2017

Glassdoor Inc.

ROBERT HOHMAN color *Bloomberg Businessweek* no4509 p64 Ja 30 2017

Glasser, Nathaniel R.

Pyocyanin degradation by a tautomerizing demethylase inhibits Pseudomonas aeruginosa biofilms bibl diag graph *Science* v355 no6321 p1 Ja 13 2017

Glass—Evaluation

The Wild Things color *House Beautiful* v159 no2 p36 Mr 2017

Glass—Exhibitions

CALENDAR OF SHOWS *Magazine Antiques* v184 no1 p212 Ja/F 2017

Glass House (New Canaan, Conn.)

Skylights and Shadows: Philip Johnson's Sculpture Gallery at the Glass House shines once again M. SITZ bw color *Architectural Record* v205 no5 p49 My 2017

Glassman, Adam

Adam's DENIM GUIDE bw color *O, The Oprah Magazine* p51 Ag 2017

Adam's Home STYLE SHEET color *O, The Oprah Magazine* p52 Jl 2017

Adam's Home STYLE SHEET: MAD FOR PLAID color *O, The Oprah Magazine* p70 N 2017

Adam's STYLE SHEET color *O, The Oprah Magazine* p50 Jl 2017

Adam's STYLE SHEET color *O, The Oprah Magazine* p64 O 2017

Glassman, Bernie

NOW WHAT? E. Marko color *Tricycle: The Buddhist Review* v26 no4 p68 Summ 2017

Glassman, Bernie—Interviews

Nothing Solid B. Glassman *Tricycle: The Buddhist Review* v26 no4 p71 Summ 2017

GLASSMAN, JAMES K.

Best Ways to Invest in Bonds Now chart *Kiplinger's Personal Finance* v71 no3 p18 Mr 2017

Buy Retail Stocks at Wholesale Prices chart *Kiplinger's Personal Finance* v71 no5 p18 My 2017

A Dozen Ways to Cash In on China color *Kiplinger's Personal Finance* v71 no12 p14 D 2017

How to Thrive as Market Cycles Return color *Kiplinger's Personal Finance* v71 no6 p20 Je 2017

Investments You Can Do Without color *Kiplinger's Personal Finance* v71 no7 p18 Jl 2017

Join the Race to $1 Trillion Stocks chart color *Kiplinger's Personal Finance* v71 no10 p18 O 2017

My 10 Top Stock Picks for 2017 chart *Kiplinger's Personal Finance* v71 no1 p19 Ja 2017

THE NOT-SO-DISMAL SCIENCE *Washingtonian Magazine* v52 no6 p45 Mr 2017

Profit From Being a Patient Investor chart *Kiplinger's Personal Finance* v71 no8 p17 Ag 2017

Star Fund Managers Aren't Extinct chart *Kiplinger's Personal Finance* v71 no11 p22 N 2017

A Surprise Boost for Emerging Markets color *Kiplinger's Personal Finance* v71 no2 p20 F 2017

Want Growth? Focus on Sales color *Kiplinger's Personal Finance* v70 no12 p18 D 2016

Worrying About the Bear? Don't chart *Kiplinger's Personal Finance* v71 no4 p16 Ap 2017

Glassman, Keri

Ask anything [Cover story] color *Women's Health* v14 no1 p24 Ja/F 2017

Buy 5, Drop 5 color *Women's Health* v14 no1 p138 Ja/F 2017

BUY 5, DROP 5 color *Women's Health* v14 no6 p104 Jl 2017

Glassman, Mark

Hyperinflation graph *Bloomberg Businessweek* no4505 p19 D 26 2016

THE PREDICTION MATRIX bw color *Bloomberg Businessweek* no4496 p104 O 24 2016

Glassman, Peter

Readers Respond color *Publishers Weekly* v264 no3 p2 Ja 16 2017

Glassman, Sallie Ann—Interviews

A Free Spirit A. MCLELLAN color *New Orleans Magazine* v52 no1 p30 S 2017

Glass Menagerie, The (Theatrical production)

THE REVEALER S. WEISS *New York Times Magazine* p28 Mr 5 2017

THE THEATRE *New Yorker* v92 no48 p7 F 6 2017

Glassware

See also

Bohemian glass

Blakely Glassware bw *Arizona Highways* v93 no5 p8 My 2017

FULL CIRCLE M. OZAWA color *Martha Stewart Living* p60 O 2017

GIFT GUIDE 2016 M. Khemsurov color *Bloomberg Businessweek* no4500 p67 N 21 2016

LOAD THE DISHWASHER LIKE A GH BOSS color *Good*

Housekeeping v265 no3 p94 S 2017

MAKING THE CUT L. HEDRICK color *Better Homes & Gardens* v95 no11 p56 N 2017

On the Horizon M. Moses color *American Craft* v76 no6 p36 D 2016-Ja 2017

Pack a Wallop T. WILLEY color *Bon Appetit* v61 no12 p56 D 2016 /Jan2017

Glassware—Evaluation

BLENKO *Treasures* v6 no4 p14 F/Mr 2017

Spooktacular Decorating S. BOWER color *Good Housekeeping* v265 no4 p47 O 2017

Glassware—Italy—Venice

Glass House H. MARTIN color *Architectural Digest* v74 no9 p58 S 2017

Glastris, Paul

AMERICA'S BEST COLLEGES FOR ADULT LEARNERS *Washington Monthly* v49 no9/10 p25 S/O 2017

Call of Duty *Washington Monthly* v49 no3-5 p4 Mr-My 2017

Hillary Opens the Overton Window *Washington Monthly* p2 N/D 2016

Is Donald Trump America's Milosevic? *Washington Monthly* p8 Ja/F 2017

Obama's Top 50 Accomplishments, Revisited *Washington Monthly* p12 Ja/F 2017

Three Ideas to Check Trump and Revive the Democratic Party *Washington Monthly* v49 no6-8 p4 Je-Ag 2017

Will Higher Education Reform Become Another Ideological War Zone? *Washington Monthly* v49 no9/10 p14 S/O 2017

Glastron Boats (Company)

Glastron GS 259 *Boating World* v38 no1 p46 Ja 2017

Glatter, Robert

To Fight the Zika Pandemic, Learn from Ebola *Harvard Business Review Digital Articles* p2 F 4 2016

Glaubitz, Charles

Starseeds color *Publishers Weekly* v264 no2 p49 Ja 9 2017

Glaucoma

THE BRAIN OF BEN BARRES K. MILLER color diag *Discover* v38 no7 p58 S 2017

ON TENTERHOOKS D. Karl bw *Flying* v144 no8 p70 Ag 2017

Relief for retinal neurons under pressure J. Crowston and I. Trounce bibl diag *Science* v355 no6326 p688 F 17 2017

Glaucoma—Prevention

EYE OF THE BEHOLDER F. ESKER color *Louisiana Life* v37 no4 p10 Mr/Ap 2017

Glaucoma—Research

Vitamin B3 modulates mitochondrial vulnerability and prevents glaucoma in aged mice P. A. Williams, J. M. Harder et al bibl graph *Science* v355 no6326 p756 F 17 2017

Glaude, Eddie S.

Now What? color *Time* v188 no21 p42 N 21 2016

Glaude, Eddie S. Jr.

In the Debate Over Campus Free Speech, Who Are the Real Special Snowflakes? color *Time* v190 no14 p25 O 9 2017

What White America Must Do Next color *Time* v190 no8 p42 Ag 28 2017

Glaus, Florian

RNA polymerase motions during promoter melting color diag graph *Science* v356 no6340 p863 My 26 2017

Glauser, G.

A worldwide survey of neonicotinoids in honey graph *Science* v357 no6359 p109 O 6 2017

Glave, James

Stronger Together color *Alternatives Journal (AJ) - Canada's Environmental Voice* v42 no3 p48 2016

GLAVIN, TERRY

China is no friend of ours *Maclean's* v130 no4 p10 My 2017

Cool while it lasted bw color *Maclean's* v129 no50 p10 D 19 2016

One mother's brave choice color *Maclean's* v129 no40 p28 O 10 2016

THE PROBLEM WITH REFUGEES color *Maclean's* v130 no3 p34 Ap 2017

The time for brave things color *Maclean's* v130 no2 p9 Mr 2017

The true test of Canadianness chart color *Maclean's* v130 no6 p20 Jl 2017

GlaxoSmithKline

Gene-Therapy Cure Has Money-Back Guarantee A. Regalado il

MIT Technology Review v119 no6 p24 N/D 2016

Glažar, Petar

Loss of a mammalian circular RNA locus causes miRNA deregulation and affects brain function color *Science* v357 no6357 p1254 S 22 2017

Glazebrook, Karl

Early galaxy lived fast and died young A. YEAGER color *Science News* v191 no8 p7 Ap 29 2017

Glazek, Christopher

THE C.E.O. OF H.I.V *New York Times Magazine* p44 Ap 30 2017

House of Pain bw color *Esquire* p100 N 2017

JESSE WILLIAMS color *Esquire* v166 no5 p94 D 2016/Ja 2017

Glazer, Greer

A MESSAGE FROM THE DEAN *Cincinnati Magazine* v50 no8 p68 My 2017

Glazer, Ilana, 1987-

ACCORDING TO: Ilana Glazer J. DUBOFF color *Vanity Fair* v59 no8 p50 Ag 2017

Why I Love LAVENDER BATH SALTS color *InStyle* v24 no7 p142 Jl 2017

Glazer, Michele

SEEN *New Yorker* v93 no6 p63 Mr 27 2017

Glazer, Robert

As Your Company Evolves, What Happens to Employees Who Don't? *Harvard Business Review Digital Articles* p2 S 13 2017

Glazing (Food science)

Apple cider is amazing C. Hall color *Redbook* p28 N 2017

Gleason, James—Interviews

EVANGELISM Is Alive in Portland M. BINDER color *Christianity Today* p36 Ap 2017

Gleason, Robert

And into the Fire *Publishers Weekly* v264 no15 p54 Ap 10 2017

Gleaves, Kevin

HOMESTEAD HACKS *Mother Earth News* no281 p78 Ap/My 2017

Gleeson, Domhnall, 1983-

Domhnall Gleeson Proves (Once More) He Can Do Almost Anything K. Samuelson color *Time* v190 no16/17 p104 O 23 2017

PLAY ANYTHING A. Bilmes color *Esquire* p27 O 2017

Gleeson, Joseph G.

Intersection of diverse neuronal genomes and neuropsychiatric disease: The Brain Somatic Mosaicism Network color *Science* v356 no6336 p395 Ap 28 2017

Gleeson, Michael

2016 Holiday GIFT GUIDE color *InStyle* v23 no13 p249 D 2016

Glefke, Larry

USEF Agrees to Rehearing Request *Practical Horseman* v45 no5 p68 My 2017

Glei, Jocelyn K.

How to Give Negative Feedback Over Email *Harvard Business Review Digital Articles* p2 O 7 2016

Why We're Addicted to Email-and How to Fix It *Time* v188 no14 p23 O 10 2016

Gleich, Caroline

Time-Stop bw color *Powder* v45 no5 p62 Ja 2017

Gleick, James, 1954-

Can We Escape from Time? J. Lanchester bw color *New York Review of Books* v63 no18 p30 N 24 2016

OBAMA'S AMERICA img *New York* v49 no20 p12 O 3 2016

Running Through Time A. Doerr *New York Times Book Review* p1 O 2 2016

Time Travel: A History *Publishers Weekly* v263 no50 p69 D 5 2016

Time travel book tours a fascinating fiction T. Siegfried color *Science News* v191 no1 p29 Ja 21 2017

When They Came from Another World color diag *New York Review of Books* v64 no1 p28 Ja 19 2017

Gleiek, Peter H.

Water strategies for the next administration bibl graph *Science* v354 no6312 p555 N 4 2016

Glein, Christopher R.

Cassini finds molecular hydrogen in the Enceladus plume: Evidence for hydrothermal processes chart graph *Science* v356 no6334 p155 Ap 14 2017

Gleit, Naomi

FACEBOOK'S SECRET WEAPON V. Zarya color diag *Fortune*

v176 no2 p26 Ag 1 2017

GLEMBOCKI, VICKI

back talk boot camp *Parents* p72 2015

The Case of The Deadly Avalanche *Reader's Digest* v188 no1126 p21 D 2016/Ja 2017

The Case of the Disputed Lottery Ticket color *Reader's Digest* v190 no1134 p29 O 2017

The Case of the Disqualifying Dreads *Reader's Digest* v189 no1128 p25 Mr 2017

The Case of the Double Eagle Gold Coins color *Reader's Digest* v190 no1135 p23 N 2017

The Case Of the Facebook Bully color *Reader's Digest* v189 no1130 p29 My 2017

The Case of The Lousy Super Bowl Seats *Reader's Digest* v189 no1127 p35 F 2017

The Case Of the Massive Guard Dogs *Reader's Digest* v188 no1125 p29 N 2016

The Case of the Missing Comma *Reader's Digest* v190 no1133 p18 S 2017

The Case of the Ring and The Broken Engagement color *Reader's Digest* v189 no1131 p19 Je 2017

The Case Of the Terrifying Trail *Reader's Digest* v188 no1124 p27 O 2016

The Case of The Violent Rap Lyrics color *Reader's Digest* v189 no1129 p23 Ap 2017

how to raise an optimist color *Parents* v92 no4 p50 Ap 2017

Glen Canyon Dam (Ariz.)

HUGE UNDERTAKING G. LADD bw *Arizona Highways* v93 no5 p32 My 2017

Glencross, Andrew

Why the UK Voted for Brexit: David Cameron's Great Miscalculation A. Moravcsik *Foreign Affairs* v96 no3 p164 My/Je 2017

Glenn, Deborah Snoonian

Boston Public Library *Architectural Record* v205 no4 p180 Ap 2017

Santa Monica to Adopt Ambitious Zero Net Energy Requirements color *Architectural Record* v204 no12 p18 D 2016

Sixth Street Viaduct *Architectural Record* v205 no4 p207 Ap 2017

Spanning the Ages *Architectural Record* v205 no9 p48 S 2017

Glenn, John, 1921-2016

ASTRO NEWS *Astronomy* v45 no3 p14 Mr 2017

Glenn the Good [Cover story] J. GELERNTER bw *National Review* v68 no24 p22 D 31 2016

John Glenn J. Kluger color *Time* v188 no27-28 p17 D 26 2016

Glenn, Larry

BLUE SKY IN AGRICULTURE M. McGinnis, T. Dreibus et al *Successful Farming* v115 no1 p34 Ja 2017

Glenn, Tyler, 1983-

Tyler Glenn's Rebirth N. Feeney color *Entertainment Weekly* no1439 p58 N 11 2016

Glenn Cohen, I.

Influence, integrity, and the FDA: An ethical framework color *Science* v357 no6354 p876 S 1 2017

Glennie, Alexander

Never Forget B. Dufresne bw color *Commonweal* v144 no7 p20 Ap 14 2017

Glennon, Emma E.

Reducing antimicrobial use in food animals color graph *Science* v357 no6358 p1350 S 29 2017

Glennon, Michael

Secret Wars *Harper's Magazine* no2007 p3 Ag 2017

SECURITY BREACH: Trump's tussle with the bureaucratic state color *Harper's Magazine* v335 no2005 p40 Je 2017

Glick, Henry B.

Positive biodiversity-productivity relationship predominant in global forests bibl chart graph map *Science* v354 no6309 paaf8957-1 O 14 2016

Glick, Pam

PAM GLICK J. Kreimer *Art in America* v104 no9 p154 O 2016

Glick, Sam

Personalized Recommendation Engines Are Coming to Health Care *Harvard Business Review Digital Articles* p2 Jl 6 2016

GLICK, SHIMON

Conservative Judaism and Its Discontents *Commentary* v143 no6 p4 Je 2017

Glickman, Jodi

Divorce Doesn't Have to Derail Your Career *Harvard Business Review Digital Articles* p2 Ap 15 2015

Interview Techniques That Get Beyond Canned Responses *Harvard Business Review Digital Articles* p2 F 19 2016

When Should You Fire a "Good Enough" Employee? *Harvard Business Review Digital Articles* p2 My 25 2015

GLICKMAN, SUSAN

Laurentian Suite *Walrus* v14 no8 p58 O 2017

Glicksman, Marcie

β2-Adrenoreceptor is a regulator of the a-synuclein gene driving risk of Parkinson's disease cartoon chart graph *Science* v357 no6354 p891 S 1 2017

Lee Rubin: Our mentor and role model *Science* v355 no6327 p806 F 24 2017

Glicksman, Robert L.

Science in litigation, the third branch of U.S. climate policy graph *Science* v357 no6355 p979 S 8 2017

Gliders (Aeronautics)

Let Go: Gliding over the Tetons K. MILLGATE *Idaho Magazine* v16 no8 p40 My 2017

PERLAN GLIDER REACHES NEW HEIGHTS color *Flying* v144 no11 p18 N 2017

Vintage Weekend in Key Largo color *Flying* v144 no2 p82 F 2017

Gliding & soaring

Let Go: Gliding over the Tetons K. MILLGATE *Idaho Magazine* v16 no8 p40 My 2017

Glimcher, Andrea

DEALER'S CHOICE R. SULLIVAN color *Vogue* v207 no4 p124 Ap 2017

Glimelius, Bengt

A pathology atlas of the human cancer transcriptome diag *Science* v357 no6352 p660 Ag 18 2017

Glindmeier, Russ—Interviews

Q&A: Russ Glindmeier *Arizona Highways* v93 no1 p9 Ja 2017

Glinert, Lewis

Mark My Word D. WOLPE bw *Weekly Standard* v22 no25 p36 Mr 6 2017

GLISAN, MAGGIE

bake the season color *Better Homes & Gardens* v95 no10 p122 O 2017

BETTER BAKING for the holidays *Better Homes & Gardens* v94 no11 p74 N 2016

CROWD CONTROL color *Better Homes & Gardens* v95 no11 p72 N 2017

DROP-INS welcome *Better Homes & Gardens* v94 no12 p82 D 2016

ENCORE! *Better Homes & Gardens* v94 no11 p134 N 2016

FOOD GIFTS color *Better Homes & Gardens* v95 no11 p14 N 2017

how to cook CHICKEN WINGS color *Better Homes & Gardens* v95 no6 p112 Je 2017

how to cook CORNED BEEF color *Better Homes & Gardens* v95 no3 p92 Mr 2017

how to cook HERB SALSA color *Better Homes & Gardens* v95 no4 p88 Ap 2017

how to cook PASTA *Better Homes & Gardens* v95 no1 p64 Ja 2017

kick back & DRINK UP color *Better Homes & Gardens* v95 no7 p124 Jl 2017

MAKING FREEZER JAM color *Better Homes & Gardens* v95 no6 p118 Je 2017

matzo's makeover color *Better Homes & Gardens* v95 no4 p106 Ap 2017

the new CASSEROLE color *Better Homes & Gardens* v95 no8 p110 Ag 2017

NEW WAYS WITH AVOCADO color *Better Homes & Gardens* v95 no8 p104 Ag 2017

NEW WAYS WITH CELERY color *Better Homes & Gardens* v95 no10 p108 O 2017

NEW WAYS WITH RADISHES color *Better Homes & Gardens* v95 no4 p84 Ap 2017

new ways with SWEET POTATOES *Better Homes & Gardens* v94 no11 p88 N 2016

NEW WAYS WITH WALNUTS color *Better Homes & Gardens* v95 no3 p88 Mr 2017

power up with BREAKFAST color *Better Homes & Gardens* v95

2016 shattered Earth's heat record T. SUMNER map *Science News* v191 no3 p9 F 18 2017

Global Fund to Fight AIDS, Tuberculosis, & Malaria

Global Fund lessons for Sustainable Development Goals J. D. Sachs and G. Schmidt-Traub color *Science* v356 no6333 p32 Ap 7 2017

Venezuela's HIV drug crisis color *Science* v355 no6325 p552 F 10 2017

Globalization

The 4 Things It Takes to Succeed in the Digital Economy L. Anderson and I. Wladawsky-Berger *Harvard Business Review Digital Articles* p2 Mr 24 2016

Business Leads Solutions to Workforce Challenges T. J. DONOHUE *Weekly Standard* v22 no13 p21 D 5 2016

Business: Localization Can Help America Win Around the World J. Immelt color *Time* v188 no27-28 p32 D 26 2016

China's 'One Belt, One Road' Plan Marks The Next Phase Of Globalization Z. Bijian *NPQ: New Perspectives Quarterly* v34 no3 p27 Jl 2017

Despite financial squeeze, Japan continues drive to globalize its science enterprise T. Feder *Physics Today* v70 no1 p24 Ja 2017

The Fortune Global 500 Isn't All That Global P. Ghemawat and N. Pisani *Harvard Business Review Digital Articles* p2 N 4 2014

GLOBALIZATION DOESN'T GIVE A DAMN B. GRULEY and R. CLOUGH color *Bloomberg Businessweek* no4517 p54 Ap 3 2017

Globalization Is Becoming More About Data and Less About Stuff S. Lund, J. Manyika et al *Harvard Business Review Digital Articles* p2 Mr 14 2016

GLOBAL MOTORS A. MacKenzie color *Motor Trend* v69 no4 p98 Ap 2017

Learning from Local Building Cultures to Improve Housing Project Sustainability T. Joffroy *UN Chronicle* v53 no3 p11 2016

Multinationals Have a Bright Future, If You Know Where to Look A. Gupta and Haiyan Wang *Harvard Business Review Digital Articles* p2 Je 14 2017

People Are Angry About Globalization. Here's What to Do About It P. Ghemawat *Harvard Business Review Digital Articles* p2 N 4 2016

Physicists without borders A. P. Gast *Physics Today* v70 no1 p10 Ja 2017

Putting People before profit P. Cheese *People Management* p5 D 2016/Ja 2017

TRADING WITH AMERICA T. Newmyer diag *Fortune* v174 no6 p132 N 1 2016

What Happens After the Election T. Newmyer color *Fortune* v174 no6 p9 N 1 2016

The Winner-Take-All Economy A. M. Renn *Governing* v30 no4 p22 Ja 2017

World Order 2.0 R. Haass color *Foreign Affairs* v96 no1 p2 Ja/F 2017

Globalization—Congresses

Salvaging Globalization N. Gardels and N. Berggruen *NPQ: New Perspectives Quarterly* v34 no1 p67 Ja 2017

Globalization—Economic aspects

Alpine Disconnect M. Campbell and S. Kennedy cartoon *Bloomberg Businessweek* no4507 p35 Ja 16 2017

Has the World Reached Peak Trade? R. Foroohar color *Time* v188 no16/17 p44 O 24 2016

Steal the March W. Kristol *Weekly Standard* v22 no28 p8 Mr 27 2017

We Can't Undo Globalization, but We Can Improve It G. Pinkus, J. Manyika et al color *Harvard Business Review Digital Articles* p2 Ja 10 2017

Globalization—History—21st century

THE TRUTH ABOUT GLOBALIZATION A. IGNATIUS bw img *Harvard Business Review* v95 no4 p10 Jl/Ag 2017

Why Globalization Stalled F. Hu and M. Spence color *Foreign Affairs* v96 no4 p54 Jl/Ag 2017

Globalization—Social aspects

GLOBALIZATION IN THE AGE OF TRUMP: PROTECTIONISM WILL CHANGE HOW COMPANIES DO BUSINESS—BUT NOT IN THE WAYS YOU THINK [Cover story] P. GHEMAWAT color graph img *Harvard Business Review* v95 no4 p112 Jl/Ag 2017

Global Positioning System—Charts, diagrams, etc.

A BRIEF HISTORY OF GPS G. Barber and A. Sammon cartoon color *Mother Jones* v41 no6 p54 N/D 2016

Globes

Monumental Scottish Terrestrial Globe color *Magazine Antiques* v184 no3 p7 My/Je 2017

Saturn Has a Southern Apparition A. MacRobert *Sky & Telescope* v133 no5 p48 My 2017

Globes—Design & construction

World Processor Globes color *Bloomberg Businessweek* no4540 p79 O 2 2017

Globicephala

Voyages J. Lowe *New York Times Magazine* p16 F 26 2017

Globular clusters

CLUSTERS IN CONTRAST R. Brecher *Sky & Telescope* v133 no6 p74 Je 2017

Seeing Through the Dust: Turning to technology can improve your resolution of globular clusters E. Mihelich *Sky & Telescope* v134 no1 p57 Jl 2017

Globus, Rea

Crystal-clear memories of a bacterium diag *Science* v357 no6356 p1096 S 15 2017

Globus pallidus

Cognition, behavior, and the globus pallidus *Science* v354 no6312 p594 N 4 2016

GLOCK, ALLISON

EATING YOUR FEELINGS *Atlanta* v56 no9 p68 Ja 2017

Glock, Caspar

Activity-dependent spatially localized miRNA maturation in neuronal dendrites bibl graph *Science* v355 no6325 p634 F 10 2017

Glomb, Theresa M.

The Powerful Effect of Noticing Good Things at Work *Harvard Business Review Digital Articles* p2 S 4 2015

Gloria (Film)

The Kid Slays in the Picture S. ENELOW color *Film Comment* v53 no5 p20 S/O 2017

Gloria Dominguez-Bello, Maria

Seasonal cycling in the gut microbiome of the Hadza hunter-gatherers of Tanzania diag *Science* v357 no6353 p802 Ag 25 2017

Glorius, Frank

Hydrogenation of fluoroarenes: Direct access to all-cis-(multi)fluorinated cycloalkanes diag *Science* v357 no6354 p908 S 1 2017

Glory Days (Music)

THE SECRET INGREDIENTS OF LITTLE MIX N. Feeney color *Entertainment Weekly* no1441 p55 N 25 2016

THE ULTIMATE 2016 ALBUM SWAP E. R. Brown and N. Feeney color *Entertainment Weekly* no1446/1447 p116 D 2016/Ja 2017

Glory of Cities, The (Poem)

The Glory of Cities A. OSTRIKER *Progressive* v81 no10 p42 N 2016

GLOSE, BILL

APPALACHIAN SLY: Unfortunate characters suffer multiple miseries before attempting to turn calamity into good fortune *Virginia Living* v15 no6 p27 O 2017

HISTORY'S HUMAN FACE *Virginia Living* v15 no1 p29 D 2016

IN THE SPOTLIGHT *Virginia Living* v15 no3 p31 Ap 2017

SEARCH FOR THE DIVINE *Virginia Living* v15 no2 p19 F 2017

TARNISHED IDEALS: A young boy emerges from the dark shadow cast by his ne'er-do-well half-brother *Virginia Living* v15 no4 p29 Je 2017

Gloss, Ken

Caring for Books You Value J. BILLS and S. SHEFFIELD color *Yankee* v80 no6 p28 N/D 2016

Glosses & glossaries

GLOSSARY *History Today* v67 no5 p110 My 2017

MUST-KNOW Commercial DANCE TERMS M. Benjamin color *Dance Spirit* v20 no10 p60 D 2016

Glossier Inc.

Gloss Castle K. Branch color *Vogue* v207 no10 p219 O 2017

Glott, Florian

Robust spin-polarized midgap states at step edges of topological crystalline insulators bibl graph *Science* v354 no6317 p1269 D 9 2016

Glotzer, Sharon C.

Clathrate colloidal crystals bibl color *Science* v355 no6328 p931 Mr 3 2017

Gloucester Point (Va.)
BATTLE SCHEMES: BATTERY INCLUDED map *MHQ: Quarterly Journal of Military History* v30 no1 p20 Aut 2017

Glove industry—Employees
WHY MY GLOVES ARE NOT MADE IN THE U.S.A J. Del Rosario color *Popular Mechanics* p75 Jl 2017

Glover, Crispin—Interviews
The Outsiders bw color *GQ: Gentlemen's Quarterly* v87 no1 p76 Ja 2017

Glover, Dick
COMEDY BOOM B. RAFTERY color *Wired* v25 no4 p76 Ap 2017

Glover, Donald, 1983-
ACCORDING TO: Donald Glover J. DUBOFF color *Vanity Fair* v58 no11 p98 N 2016
THE DONALD GLOVER EXPERIMENT M. J. MOORE color *Nation* v304 no3 p37 Ja 30 2017
GET YOUR FLAIR ON M. Hainey color *Esquire* p48 Ap 2017
STAR WARS: MEET THE NEW LANDO D. Franich color *Entertainment Weekly* no1438 p20 N 4 2016
TRENDING NOW M. Mertyl, K. Hawlk et al color *Wired* v25 no4 p12 Ap 2017
WEIRD WAR C. BATTAN cartoon *New Yorker* v92 no41 p70 D 12 2016
Who (or What) Won 2016? R. Browne img *New York* v49 no26 p84 D 26 2016
Zazie BEETZ *Interview* v47 no5 p53 Je/Jl 2017

Glover, Julian
A CAST IRON LEGACY W. J. Ashworth *History Today* v67 no8 p100 Ag 2017

Glover, Scott
Hard Times At The L.A. Times E. LEIBOWITZ *Los Angeles Magazine* p104 Ja 2017

Glover-Cutter, Kira
Mitigating coastal landslide damage color *Science* v357 no6355 p981 S 8 2017

Gloves
fall CLEANING B. THORKELSON color *Better Homes & Gardens* v95 no10 p50 O 2017

Gloves—Design & construction
WHY MY GLOVES ARE NOT MADE IN THE U.S.A J. Del Rosario color *Popular Mechanics* p75 Jl 2017

Gloves—Evaluation
ALPINESTARS' ALL-NEW SUPERTECH GLOVE B. Adams color *Cycle World* v56 no1 p16 Ja/F 2017
apparel color *Climbing* no352 p49 Ap 2017
THE BEST BET B. Doherty img *New York* v50 no10 p67 My 15 2017
Boring Gloves Get the Finger color *GQ: Gentlemen's Quarterly* v86 no11 p40 N 2016
A CASE OF THE BLUES A. R. Williams color *Southern Living* v52 no1 p39 Ja 2017
emporium color *Dressage Today* v23 no10 p64 Jl 2017
ESSENTIAL GEAR color *Black Belt* v55 no2 p60 F/Mr 2017
Keep Warm R. Frost color *Equus* no472 p26 Ja 2017
The List color *O, The Oprah Magazine* p59 D 2016
POWDER 80'S P. Bridges color *Snowboarder* v29 no2 p138 O 2016
PRACTICAL PRODUCTS L. BACK color *Trail Rider* v29 no4 p52 My 2017
Quiet Storm color *Essence* v47 no8 p106 D 2016
RIDING GLOVES D. Canet color *Cycle World* v56 no4 p26 My 2017
SOLUTIONS L. Armstrong color *Horse & Rider* v56 no2 p18 F 2017
STOCK & TRADE color *Equus* no470 p64 N 2016
A Well-Oiled Machine S. WATSON color *Esquire* v167 no1 p38 F 2017

Glow (Music)
The Best Stocking Stuffers (And A Few Lumps Of Coal) E. R. Brown color *Entertainment Weekly* no1442 p56 D 2 2016 Rebellious Special Issue

Glow (TV program)
4 new ways to be thrilled and inspired color *Redbook* p104 Je 2017
AFTER GLOW K. Connolly and S. Vilkomerson color *Entertainment Weekly* no1473 p24 Jl 7 2017
BLING RING E. NUSSBAUM cartoon *New Yorker* v93 no19 p70 Jl 3 2017
Budget Wrestling Lights Up the Screen In Glow D. D'addario color *Time* v190 no2/3 p93 Jl 10-17 2017
The Bullseye M. Snetiker color *Entertainment Weekly* no1472 p64 Je 30 2017
Dead Or Alive S. ERICKSON *Los Angeles Magazine* v62 no7 p54 Jl 2017
GLOW S. Vilkomerson color *Entertainment Weekly* no1468/1469 p52 Je 2-9 2017
MARC MARON S. Vilkomerson color *Entertainment Weekly* no1468/1469 p53 Je 2-9 2017
NEXT UP IN THE RING! M. Snetiker color *Entertainment Weekly* no1473 p27 Jl 7 2017

GLOWCZEWSKA, KLARA
FINE CHINA bw color map *Harper's Bazaar* no3655 p95 Ag 2017

Glownia, James M.
Femtosecond electron-phonon lock-in by photoemission and x-ray free-electron laser chart diag *Science* v357 no6346 p71 Jl 7 2017
Metalloprotein entatic control of ligand-metal bonds quantified by ultrafast x-ray spectroscopy diag *Science* v356 no6344 p1276 Je 23 2017

Gloyd, Terri
Life Before and After All the High-Rises *New York* v50 no18 p68 S 4 2017

Gloyn, Liz
AT HOME WITH THE STOICS: Do Stoic philosophy and the family mix? The writings of Seneca show how the model Stoic, relying on nothing but his own mind, can still be a loving family man *History Today* v67 no9 p48 S 2017

Gluck, Didi
CAUSE & EFFECT color *InStyle* v24 no2 p52 F 2017
getting ready with SALMA HAYEK color *Better Homes & Gardens* v95 no4 p16 Ap 2017
Smoky EYES color *InStyle* v23 no12 p223 N 2016

Gluck, Dylan
Our Love Story, in One Picture A. L. Greco bw *Glamour* v115 no1 p54 Ja 2017

GLUCK, JON
FLY-FISHING cartoon color *Popular Mechanics* p29 Je 2017
Technologically Amazing Fly Rod of the Month color *Popular Mechanics* p32 Ap 2017

Glück, Louise, 1943-
Louise Glück S. Moyer *Humanities* v37 no4 p1 Fall 2016

GLUCK, MARISSA
Homes Under $950K color *Los Angeles Magazine* v62 no10 p122 O 2017
What Is Art Really Worth? *Los Angeles Magazine* p36 D 2016

Gluck, Sarah D.
Community network for deaf scientists color *Science* v356 no6336 p386 Ap 28 2017

Gluckman, Mark
Exposing Unfair Pricing in Auto Insurance Rates color *Consumer Reports* v82 no5 p6 My 2017

Glucocorticoids
REASSURING FINDINGS ABOUT PREDNISOLONE C. Barakat and M. McCluskey color *Equus* no476 p18 My 2017

Glucose carrier proteins
Regulation of sugar transporter activity for antibacterial defense in Arabidopsis K. Yamada, Yusuke Saijo et al bibl diag graph *Science* v354 no6318 p1427 D 16 2016

Glucose in the body—Measurement—Equipment & supplies
For Diabetics, the Power of Knowing M. Cortez color graph *Bloomberg Businessweek* no4515 p40 Mr 20 2017

Glue
ASK MR bw color *Model Railroader* v84 no3 p20 Mr 2017
How to Glue Anything color *Popular Mechanics* p44 Mr 2017
Investors Go Long on Slime J. Wieczner color *Fortune* v175 no7 p12 Je 1 2017
a timely Idea *Saturday Evening Post* v289 no5 p26 S/O 2017

Glunz, Stefan
Terawatt-scale photovoltaics: Trajectories and challenges chart graph *Science* v356 no6334 p141 Ap 14 2017

GLUSAC, ELAINE

Get Off The Loop color *Conde Nast Traveler* v52 no2 p36 F 2017

Glusman, John

Deals D. LEFFERTS color *Publishers Weekly* v263 no51 p5 D 12 2016

Glusman, Karl, 1988-

Zoë Kravitz and Karl Glusman L. RAMZI color *Vogue* v207 no6 p58 Je 2017

Gluteal muscles—Anatomy

Your glutes [Cover story] J. Miller color *Yoga Journal* no292 p62 Je 2017

Gluten

10 Hidden Sources of Gluten During the Holidays [Cover story] M. D. Smith color *Better Nutrition* v79 no11 p72 N 2017

Gluten-Free Desserts color *Health* v30 no9 p16 N 2016

KNEAD TO KNOW J. RAY bw color *Wired* v25 no10 p26 O 2017

Gluten-free cooking

Stealth Ways to EAT LEAN M. KADEY bw color *Muscle & Performance* v9 no1 p54 Ja 2017

Gluten-free diet

FAFQ (FREQUENTLY ASKED FOOD QUESTIONS) K. Patel and J. WUEBBEN color *Muscle & Performance* v9 no9 p18 S 2017

The host for most color *U.S. Catholic* v82 no8 p5 Ag 2017

JUST ASK color *Vegetarian Today* no1 p6 F 2017

NUTRITION HOTLINE R. MANGELS *Vegetarian Journal* v35 no2 p2 2016

The Paleo Vegan L. TURNER color *Better Nutrition* v78 no11 p78 N 2016

Should You Go Gluten-Free? *Parents* v91 no11 p32 N 2016

Stealth Ways to EAT LEAN M. KADEY bw color *Muscle & Performance* v9 no1 p54 Ja 2017

WHEN GOOD DIETS GO BAD D. Denunzio color *Golf Magazine* v59 no2 p56 F 2017

Gluten-free diet—Physiological aspects

NEWS FROM THE World of Medicine S. RIDEOUT color *Reader's Digest* v190 no1132 p51 Jl/Ag 2017

Gluten-free foods

Against the Grain S. KROWIAK *Indianapolis Monthly* v40 no7 p39 Mr 2017

Glycemic index

New Insights: Glycemic Index: The glycemic index may help predict the blood sugar effects of a food, but it doesn't tell the whole story, especially when combining foods *Tufts University Health & Nutrition Letter* v35 no7 p3 S 2017

USING THE GLYCEMIC INDEX TO INCREASE HEALTH & PERFORMANCE M. DEPAOLO *Arabian Horse World* v57 no1 p156 O 2016

Glycogen

HOLIDAY TRIMMINGS [Cover story] P. N. Bede cartoon color *Runner's World* v51 no11 p46 D 2016

Glycogenolysis

Systemic pan-AMPK activator MK-8722 improves glucose homeostasis but induces cardiac hypertrophy R. W. Myers, Guan et al graph *Science* v357 no6350 p507 Ag 4 2017

Glycols

Ruthenium-catalyzed insertion of adjacent diol carbon atoms into C-C bonds: Entry to type II polyketides M. Bender, B. W. H. Turnbull et al diag *Science* v357 no6353 p779 Ag 25 2017

Glycolysis

Aerobic glycolysis promotes T helper 1 cell differentiation through an epigenetic mechanism Min Peng, Na Yin et al bibl graph *Science* v354 no6311 p481 O 28 2016

Fructose-driven glycolysis supports anoxia resistance in the naked mole-rat T. J. Park, J. Reznick et al diag graph *Science* v356 no6335 p307 Ap 21 2017

Warburg meets epigenetics C. H. Patel and J. D. Powell bibl diag *Science* v354 no6311 p419 O 28 2016

Glycomics

Glycomics and its application potential in precision medicine Youxin Wang, E. Adua et al bibl diag *Science* v354 no6319 p36 D 23 2016

Glycosylation

Developing an HIV vaccine B. F. Haynes and D. R. Burton bibl diag *Science* v355 no6330 p1129 Mr 17 2017

Glynn, Liz

Dancing in the Streets M. SLENSKE bw color *Architectural Di-*

gest v74 no3 p62 Mr 2017

TAKE ME OUT TO THE BALLROOM A. M. HOMES color *Vanity Fair* v59 no4 p191 Mr 2017

Glyphosate—Environmental aspects

Science for Sale B. LIVESEY color *Walrus* v14 no4 p24 My 2017

Gmail (Web resource)

Gmail is dumping Windows XP and Vista, now what? I. PAUL color *PCWorld* p165 Mr 2017

You can now send and receive money right in the Android Gmail app M. SIMON color *PCWorld* v35 no4 p44 Ap 2017

Gmelch, Morgan Z.

Lost then Loved: The Case of the Tasmanian Tiger bw color map *Natural History* v125 no4 p36 Ap 2017

Gmelch, Sharon Bohn

Lost then Loved: The Case of the Tasmanian Tiger bw color map *Natural History* v125 no4 p36 Ap 2017

Gnanasambandam, Chandra

Innovation Is as Much About Finding Partners as Building Products *Harvard Business Review Digital Articles* p2 Jl 20 2017

Gnann, Christian

A subcellular map of the human proteome color *Science* v356 no6340 p820 My 26 2017

Gnat, Lisa

FEAST WITH BENEFITS [Cover story] color *O, The Oprah Magazine* p128 N 2017

Gnocchi

Fresh & Easy FROM THE FARMERS' MARKET K. HYMORE color *Prevention* v69 no9 p86 O 2017

One Potato, Two Potato color *Southern Living* v52 no3 p130 Mr 2017

Gnus

Drowned wildebeest provide ecological feast E. Pennisi color diag *Science* v356 no6344 p1217 Je 23 2017

LONG WAY HOME *Phi Kappa Phi Forum* v96 no4 p5 Wint 2016

Go (Game)

Artificial intelligence ups its game J. Bohannon color *Science* v354 no6319 p1518 D 23 2016

Computer defeats master at ancient Chinese game T. Sumner color *Science News* v190 no13 p28 D 24 2016

Go, Go AlphaGo C. ENGELKING color *Discover* v38 no1 p37 Ja/F 2017

Go Count the First Seven Stars (Poem)

Ditch the City and Go Country: How to Master the Art of Rural Life from a Former City Dweller color *Publishers Weekly* v264 no25 p107 Je 19 2017

Goa (India : State)—Religion

Goa, Rome of the East P. Jenkins color *Christian Century* v134 no18 p44 Ag 30 2017

Goa (India : State)—Social life & customs

Goa, Rome of the East P. Jenkins color *Christian Century* v134 no18 p44 Ag 30 2017

Goal (Psychology)

3 Popular Goal-Setting Techniques Managers Should Avoid D. Grote color *Harvard Business Review Digital Articles* p2 Ja 2 2017

3 Productivity Tips You Can Start Using Today D. Clark *Harvard Business Review Digital Articles* p2 Mr 2 2016

Does stressing performance goals lead to too much, well, stress? D. Dockterman and C. Weber color il *Phi Delta Kappan* v98 no6 p31 Mr 2017

Do this to meet your goals A. Sweeney color *Redbook* p19 S 2017

Downsize Your Stuff P. M. ESSWEIN cartoon *Kiplinger's Personal Finance* v71 no7 p36 Jl 2017

Failure to Launch S. Tia Brown color *Ebony* v72 no8 p66 Je 2017

Fallon Taylor's Best Advice for Any Rider F. TAYLOR and N. CHIRICO color *Horse & Rider* v56 no11 p118 N 2017

THE FOUR PILLARS OF MORAL LEADERSHIP D. Seidman and C. Leaf color *Fortune* v176 no4 p90 S 15 2017

Go On, Have Some Dessert color *Health* v31 no7 p14 S 2017

How to Say No to Things You Want to Do D. Clark *Harvard Business Review Digital Articles* p2 Ja 4 2016

LIVE YOUR DREAM H. LEVINE color *Yoga Journal* p28 2016 Special Issue

The One-Item To-Do List color *Health* v30 no10 p18 D 2016

Points to Ponder *Reader's Digest* v189 no1127 p20 F 2017

power by design T. EICHENSEHER color *Yoga Journal* no294

p17 S 2017

The Stretch Goal Paradox S. B. SITKIN, C. C. MILLER et al color diag il img *Harvard Business Review* v95 no1 p92 Ja/F 2017

To Achieve a Major Goal, First Tackle a Few Small Ones A. Markman *Harvard Business Review Digital Articles* p2 F 24 2017

Vegetarian Action. Vegan in the Army: Specialist Brianna Kearney S. Gendler *Vegetarian Journal* v35 no2 p35 2016

Your Future: Dear Younger Me *Scholastic Choices* pT9 S 2017 Supplement

Goal setting in personnel management

7 Things Leaders Do to Help People Change J. Zenger and J. Folkman *Harvard Business Review Digital Articles* p2 Jl 20 2015

When to Set Rigid Goals, and When to Be Flexible S. Martin and H. Mankin bw *Harvard Business Review Digital Articles* p2 Ja 27 2017

Goat cheese

tastes like SUMMER bw cartoon color *Good Housekeeping* v264 no6 p104 Je 2017

Goat cheese—Evaluation

EDITORS' CHOICE FOOD AWARDS 2016 A. Traverso and K. Liebenson-Morse color *Yankee* v80 no6 p73 N/D 2016

Goat meat

The best meat you don't eat J. RICHLER color *Maclean's* v130 no2 p70 Mr 2017

Goat milk

GOAT MILK SOAP *South Dakota Magazine* v33 no3 p39 S/O 2017

Goats

Instant Cattle-Panel Cage R. Hackenberg *Mother Earth News* no282 p86 Je/Jl 2017

Lightbox color *Time* v190 no2/3 p16 Jl 10-17 2017

Nanny State L. VACCARIELLO *Cincinnati Magazine* v50 no10 p132 Jl 2017

The Unchosen R. J. Kern color *National Geographic* v232 no5 p104 N 2017

Goats—Wounds & injuries

When Your Best Fish Story Is About Catching ... A Goat R. BRAGG color *Reader's Digest* v190 no1135 p17 N 2017

Goban, A.

A Fermi-degenerate three-dimensional optical lattice clock color diag graph *Science* v357 no6359 p90 O 6 2017

GOBLE, ANDREW

GQ'S 2016 Grooming Awards color *GQ: Gentlemen's Quarterly* v86 no11 p130 N 2016

GQ's 2017: GROOMING AWARDS bw color *GQ: Gentlemen's Quarterly* v97 no1 p56 N 2017

I Tested Every Natural Deodorant on God's Green Earth... color *GQ: Gentlemen's Quarterly* v97 no9 p94 S 2017

Manual cartoon color *GQ: Gentlemen's Quarterly* v97 no7 p11 Jl 2017

Mating bw color *GQ: Gentlemen's Quarterly* v86 no11 p58 N 2016

Goble, Steve

The Bloody Black Flag: A Spider John Mystery *Publishers Weekly* v264 no29 p198 Jl 17 2017

Goblet, Dominique

Life Studies S. HETI *New York Times Book Review* p11 F 26 2017

Gobos (Lighting)

Hand-Painting Glass Gobos *Stage Directions* v30 no8 p14 Ag 2017

Gobry, Pascal-Emmanuel

After the Macron-Le Pen race, how will 'new Catholics' reshape French politics? color *America* v216 no13 p16 Je 12 2017

SEEKING SIGNS OF A CATHOLIC REVIVAL IN FRANCE color *America* v216 no8 p26 Ap 17 2017

God

See also

God (Christianity)

Holy Spirit

Jesus Christ

Theology

Answering Our Daughters H. ALVARÉ *America* v215 no15 p14 N 14 2016

Bearing with the Patience of God D. RISHMAWY *Christianity Today* p28 Mr 2017

Bonfire Buddha L. TONINO cartoon color *Tricycle: The Buddhist*

Review v26 no3 p24 Spr 2017

Bowie brought us together S. Johnson *U.S. Catholic* v82 no1 p4 Ja 2017

A Critical Care Surgeon Meets the Great Physician K. L. Butler color *Christianity Today* p80 Mr 2017

God, a note B. Doyle color *U.S. Catholic* v82 no1 p34 Ja 2017

Great Chain of Contempt F. H. BUCKLEY *American Conservative* v15 no6 p27 N/D 2016

Hallowing the Gaps R. M. Pennoyer II color *Commonweal* v144 no11 p26 Je 16 2017

Kingdom of the Son J. W. MARTENS *America* v215 no15 p38 N 14 2016

Life's work: Building the church takes everyone [Cover story] J. Mesman Griffith, J. Schueller et al color *U.S. Catholic* v82 no8 p22 Ag 2017

LIVING BY The Word *Christian Century* v134 no14 p20 Jl 5 2017

May 7, Fourth Sunday of Easter *Christian Century* v134 no8 p1 Ap 12 2017

OPEN MY HEART color *Essence* v47 no10 p108 F 2017

Out of the ordinary A. Scobey color *U.S. Catholic* v82 no11 p43 N 2017

Prayer without answers color *Christian Century* v134 no8 p1 Ap 12 2017

Reflections on the lectionary T. D. Anderson *Christian Century* v134 no1 p21 Ja 4 2017

SAVED THROUGH CHILD-BEARING W. ALSUP color *Christianity Today* v60 no10 p54 D 2016

VASTER THAN THE ANCIENTS IMAGINED C. MEEKS color *Christianity Today* v60 no8 p70 O 2016

WHEN GOD DOES THE UNEXPECTED K. KANDIAH color *Christianity Today* p52 Mr 2017

Wrestling with Eternity F. A. JAMES III *Christianity Today* v60 no10 p58 D 2016

God (Christianity)

See also

Holy Spirit

DO YOU KNOW THIS SONG? T. OLSEN *Christianity Today* p7 Ap 2017

Grace stet OR Grace ALONE? B. R. BARRON and R. E. OLSON bw *Christianity Today* p42 Ap 2017

HOW DID JESUS FIND ME IN PARAGUAY? ES COMPLICADO. (BUT NOT REALLY.) P. JOHNSON color *Christianity Today* p52 Ap 2017

LIVING BY The Word *Christian Century* v134 no20 p20 S 27 2017

The OLDER TESTAMENT: An Origin Story A. Gregory cartoon *Esquire* p136 O 2017

Out of the Cult and into the Church A. LeBaron color *Christianity Today* p79 Ap 2017

The Presence M. S. J. Simone *America* v216 no11 p58 My 15 2017

Tapped Out J. Wren color *Christianity Today* v61 no1 p96 Ja/F 2017

Tune Out the Noise M. Simone *America* v217 no3 p50 Ag 7 2017

God (Christianity)—Fatherhood

The Freedom of the Father's Children M. R. Simone *America* v216 no3 p52 F 6 2017

God (Christianity)—Simplicity

Life is Complex. God Is Not D. Rishmawy *Christianity Today* v61 no6 p24 Jl/Ag 2017

God of Vengeance (Theatrical production)

14. See God of Vengeance *New York* p131 Mr 6 2017

God of War (Film)

Woman of Wonder, God of War, Shortcomings of Yoga and Hero of India C. D. Reid color *Black Belt* v55 no6 p28 O/N 2017

Godbold, Billy—Interviews

Take 5 With BILLY GODBOLD J. Pearley Huffman color diag *Hot Rod* v70 no7 p16 Jl 2017

Godbout, Greg—Interviews

Advice on Running a Government Agency Like a Startup, from Someone Who's Tried It M. Hoch *Harvard Business Review Digital Articles* p2 Ap 12 2017

Goddard, Bob

Asymmetrical Riding cartoon *Trail Rider* v29 no1 p72 Ja/F 2017

Mounting Blocks color *Trail Rider* v29 no2 p72 Mr 2017

Oskar the Invisible Horse color *Trail Rider* v29 no4 p72 My 2017

Goddard, John

How CEOs Can Manage Strategic Tensions *Harvard Business Review Digital Articles* p2 D 19 2016

Goddard, Jules

How to Turn Around a Failing School *Harvard Business Review Digital Articles* p2 Ag 5 2016

The One Type of Leader Who Can Turn Around a Failing School bw color *Harvard Business Review Digital Articles* p2 O 20 2016

Research: How the Best School Leaders Create Enduring Change *Harvard Business Review Digital Articles* p2 S 14 2017

GODDARD, MARK A.

Biodiversity in the City: Fundamental Questions for Understanding the Ecology of Urban Green Spaces for Biodiversity Conservation *BioScience* v67 no9 p799 S 2017

Planning for the Future of Urban Biodiversity: A Global Review of City-Scale Initiatives *BioScience* v67 no4 p332 Ap 2017

Goddard, Molly

STYLE CRUSH Jenna Coleman S. Simon color *InStyle* v24 no6 p56 Je 2017

Goddard, Sophie

How to DUMP SOMEONE color *Seventeen* v76 no12 p74 D 2016/Ja 2017

Goddard, William A. III

Ultrafine jagged platinum nanowires enable ultrahigh mass activity for the oxygen reduction reaction bibl chart graph *Science* v354 no6318 p1414 D 16 2016

Goddu, Krystyna Poray

Spring 2017 Flying Starts color *Publishers Weekly* v264 no27 p36 Jl 3 2017

Godec, Jernej

The epigenetic landscape of T cell exhaustion bibl graph *Science* v354 no6316 p1165 D 2 2016

Epigenetic stability of exhausted T cells limits durability of reinvigoration by PD-1 blockade bibl graph *Science* v354 no6316 p1160 D 2 2016

God—Faithfulness

Witnesses to Life J. W. MARTENS color *America* v215 no13 p39 O 31 2016

Godfrey (Company)

Sweetwater 2286 SB *Boating World* v38 no1 p64 Ja 2017

GODFREY, GAVIN

ATLANTA *Atlanta* v56 no10 p70 F 2017

THE MORTUARY MOGUL: Willie Watkins will bury you in style--its his calling *Atlanta* v57 no6 p23 O 2017

THE NEXT NAPSTER? Major record labels take on Spinrilla, an Atlanta music streaming service *Atlanta* v57 no2 p28 Je 2017

"THE MAGIC NEGRO" *Atlanta* v56 no11 p40 Mr 2017

GODFREY-JUNE, JEAN

GWYNERGY! color *Women's Health* v14 no3 p(Sp)2 Ap 2017

Godfrey-Smith, Peter

The intelligent invertebrate O. Deroy color *Science* v354 no6316 p1110 D 2 2016

Other Minds: The Octopus, The Sea, and the Deep Origins of Consciousness L. A. MARSCHALL color *Natural History* v125 no3 p46 Mr 2017

Thinking in the Deep C. SAFINA *New York Times Book Review* p9 Ja 1 2017

What the Octopus Knows O. JUDSON color *Atlantic* v319 no1 p34 Ja/F 2017

GODIN, BENOÎT

Measuring research benefits *Issues in Science & Technology* v33 no4 p14 Summ 2017

Godin, Leona

VISION OF LOVELINESS color *O, The Oprah Magazine* p121 Mr 2017

God—Promises

Not Settling for Less [Cover story] P. J. WADELL color *America* v215 no16 p20 N 21 2016

Godsey, Mike

LISTEN TO THIS color *Literacy Today (2411-7826)* v34 no3 p28 N/D 2016

GODUTO, DIANA

STORIES WE TELL OURSELVES color *Vanity Fair* v58 no11 p88 N 2016

Godwin, Ian

All-printed thin-film transistors from networks of liquid-exfoliated nanosheets diag *Science* v356 no6333 p69 Ap 7 2017

Godwin, Jimmy

A Veteran's Son Goes to VIETNAM G. SHELBY *Reader's Digest* v188 no1125 p114 N 2016

God—Wrath

From the publisher P. W. Marty *Christian Century* v134 no13 p3 Je 21 2017

Goehring, April

Cryo-EM structures of the triheteromeric NMDA receptor and its allosteric modulation graph *Science* v355 no6331 p1282 Mr 24 2017

Goeltl, F.

Selective oxidative dehydrogenation of propane to propene using boron nitride catalysts bibl diag graph *Science* v354 no6319 p1570 D 23 2016

GOEMANS, DEBORAH JUNE

TOUGH FLUIDITY: Complex Considerations for Trans Youth *Humanist* v77 no4 p20 Jl/Ag 2017

GOENS, GEORGE A.

The Role of the School *USA Today Magazine* v145 no2864 p56 My 2017

Goerge, Dee

CATTLE AND COVER CROPS IMPROVE SOIL HEALTH *Successful Farming* v114 no13 p59 D 2016

COVER CROPS CREATE SAVINGS: UTILIZING COVER CROPS CAN BOOST SOIL HEALTH, REDUCE PESTS, AND CYCLE NUTRIENTS *Successful Farming* v115 no6 p41 Ap 2017

MATTRACKS SAVE SEED CROPS: WRESTLING WITH DOING FIELD OPERATIONS ON SOGGY SOILS? THESE RUBBER TRACKS CAN HELP *Successful Farming* v115 no12 p54 O 2017

Goerke, Christine

CHRISTINE GOERKE H. Stewart *Opera News* v81 no10 p28 Ap 2017

Goerttler, S.

Spectral narrowing of x-ray pulses for precision spectroscopy with nuclear resonances diag *Science* v357 no6349 p375 Jl 28 2017

GOES (Meteorological satellite)

A new eye on Earth's atmosphere color *Science* v355 no6323 p331 Ja 27 2017

Goes, Peter

Timeline: A Visual History of Our World color *Publishers Weekly* v263 no49 p86 D 7 2016

GOETHE, JOHANN WOLFGANG VON, 1749-1832

THOUGHTS ON Property *Forbes* v199 no5 p124 My 16 2017

Goetschel, Samira

City 40 C. Gramling *Science* v356 no6337 p482 My 5 2017

GOETTSCH, BÁRBARA

The Role of Botanical Gardens in the Conservation of Cactaceae *BioScience* v66 no12 p1057 D 1 2016

Goetzel, Ron

How to Design a Corporate Wellness Plan That Actually Works *Harvard Business Review Digital Articles* p2 Mr 31 2016

GOFF, MATTHEW

LCAC ATTACK cartoon *Canoe & Kayak Magazine* v45 no1 p40 Wint 2017

Goffee, Rob

Authentic Workplaces Don't Try to Make Everyone the Same *Harvard Business Review Digital Articles* p2 N 12 2015

Volkswagen and the End of Corporate Spin *Harvard Business Review Digital Articles* p2 O 28 2015

GoFundMe (Company)

FREE MARKET PHILANTHROPY S. ADAMS color *Forbes* v198 no6 p92 N 8 2016

GOGGANS, ASHTON

"All decisions, even those of a traveler roaming the world, require a compromise." color *Surfer* v58 no2 p38 My 2017

IN THE SHADOW OF GIANTS color *Surfer* v58 no5 p70 S 2017

LET THEM LOG bw color *Surfer* v57 no12 p62 Ja/F 2017

MATT CLARK bw color *Surfer* v57 no13 p62 Mr 2017

OUT OF BOUNDS color *Surfer* v57 no12 p74 Ja/F 2017

THE PROXIMITY TAPES bw color *Surfer* v58 no3 p56 Je 2017

RETURN OF THE PATRÓN bw color map *Surfer* v57 no11 p64

D 2016
THE SERPENTINE PACT color *Surfer* v58 no1 p90 Ap 2017
Shaper Hall of Fame color *Surfer* v58 no2 p40 My 2017
SHOWCASE color *Surfer* v58 no5 p78 S 2017
Sons of Sam color *Surfer* v58 no2 p34 My 2017
WARREN SMITH color *Surfer* v58 no3 p44 Je 2017

Goggins, Walton, 1971-
Six J. Jensen color *Entertainment Weekly* no1449 p50 Ja 20 2017

Gogh, Vincent van, 1853-1890
REACHING FOR THE STARS bw cartoon *ARTnews* v116 no1 p127 Spr 2017
Stolen Art That Made a Return T. John color *Time* v188 no15 p8 O 17 2016

Gogo Business Aviation LLC
FASTER AND BETTER: A LOOK AT THE NEXT-GENERA-TION NETWORK POWERING IN-FLIGHT ENTERTAIN-MENT T. VELOCCI color *Forbes* v200 no3 p72 S 28 2017

Goh, Evelyn
Rising China's Influence in Developing Asia A. J. Nathan *Foreign Affairs* v96 no6 p169 N/D 2017

Gohar, Laila
Nine Cool Girls L. Michael and R. RAMSEY img *New York* v50 no10 p60 My 15 2017
Secrets of the Foundation Free F. Valdesolo color *Glamour* v115 no6 p66 Je 2017

Gohara, Mona
42 new ALL-STAR PRODUCTS of the year [Cover story] color *Redbook* p27 Jl/Ag 2017
Bright On! color *O, The Oprah Magazine* p52 Ja 2017

GOHEEN, JACOB R.
Conserving Megafauna or Sacrificing Biodiversity? *BioScience* v67 no3 p193 Mr 2017

Going in Style (Film)
7. See The Films of Martin Brest D. EDELSTEIN *New York* v50 no7 p88 Ap 3 2017

Going public (Securities)
Eyeing a Dropbox IPO P. Burrows il *MIT Technology Review* v120 no2 p24 Mr/Ap 2017
Goodbye, Unicorns. Hello, IPOs! E. Griffith color *Fortune* v175 no6 p7 My 1 2017
HOW TO SNAG A STOCK TICKER J. Wieczner *Fortune* v75 no1 p20 Ja 1 2017
INVESTORS SEEK SWEET COIN J. J. Roberts diag *Fortune* v176 no1 p88 Jl 1 2017
THE IPO STATUS REPORT color *Fortune* v175 no6 p8 My 1 2017
Snapchat Can't Keep It Private S. Frier and A. Barinka color *Bloomberg Businessweek* no4509 p27 Ja 30 2017
SNAP JUDGMENT diag *Fortune* v175 no3 p11 Mr 1 2017
Stock X-Ray: Snap T. Tepper color diag *Money* v46 no5 p39 Je 2017
Tech IPOs Want to Get Ahead of Trump A. Barinka *Bloomberg Businessweek* no4500 p33 N 21 2016
WHERE HAVE ALL THE PUBLIC COMPANIES GONE? *Fortune* v175 no2 p17 F 1 2017

Going public (Securities)—History—21st century
Snapchat Faces the Public [Cover story] J. Stein color diag *Time* v189 no9 p26 Mr 13 2017
Snap's Audacious Wall Street Play J. Wieczner *Time* v189 no9 p30 Mr 13 2017

Going public (Securities)—Russia
Toys 'R' Russia? Retailer Detsky Mir Says, 'Da' C. Matlack and I. Khrennikov color *Bloomberg Businessweek* no4512 p23 F 20 2017

Going public (Securities)—Charts, diagrams, etc.
POSTAL SAVINGS BANK OF CHINA GOES BIG S. Cendrowski diag *Fortune* v174 no8 p24 D 15 2016

Gokce, Nusret
Grand Entrances img *New York* v50 no17 p76 Ag 21 2017

GÖKÇEK, MUSTAFA
From Abdulhamid II to Ataturk: Change or Continuity in Turkey's History *Islamic Horizons* v46 no3 p54 My/Je 2017

GÖKSENIN, LILI
Bewitched color *Vogue* v207 no4 p160 Ap 2017
Clean ESCAPES color *Vogue* v206 no12 p184 D 2016

Golan, David

Detection of human adaptation during the past 2000 years bibl graph *Science* v354 no6313 p760 N 11 2016

Golan, Guy
Wild emmer genome architecture and diversity elucidate wheat evolution and domestication color *Science* v357 no6346 p93 Jl 7 2017

Golan, Matan
Global mRNA polarization regulates translation efficiency in the intestinal epithelium diag *Science* v357 no6357 p1299 S 22 2017

Golan, Talia
Potential role of intratumor bacteria in mediating tumor resistance to the chemotherapeutic drug gemcitabine diag *Science* v357 no6356 p1156 S 15 2017

Golani, Ofra
Global mRNA polarization regulates translation efficiency in the intestinal epithelium diag *Science* v357 no6357 p1299 S 22 2017

Golbeck, John H.
Structure of a symmetric photosynthetic reaction center–photosystem color *Science* v357 no6355 p1021 S 8 2017

Gold
Epitaxial lift-off of electrodeposited single-crystal gold foils for flexible electronics N. K. Mahenderkar, Q. Chen et al bibl bw diag *Science* v355 no6330 p1203 Mr 17 2017
Power Ingredient: Gold! L. Desantis color *Health* v31 no1 p34 Ja 2017

Gold (Film)
Gold *New Yorker* v92 no49 p14 F 13 2017
SHINY THINGS A. LANE cartoon *New Yorker* v92 no48 p80 F 6 2017

GOLD, ADAM
Dua Lipa's Tough Love color *Rolling Stone* no1291/1292 p18 Jl 13 2017

Gold, Betty
GAS RANGES color *Good Housekeeping* v263 no5 p137 N 2016
KITCHEN WHISPERER color *Good Housekeeping* v265 no1 p8 Jl 2017
Save Time IN THE KITCHEN color *Good Housekeeping* v264 no3 p87 Mr 2017

GOLD, GLEN DAVID
ASSAUT SUR L'UNIVERS cartoon *Wired* v25 no1 p87 Ja 2017

Gold, Herbert
THE POSTER CRAZE: Freaky, funny, and fashionable, in the '60s, these were the signs of our times *Saturday Evening Post* v289 no4 p41 Jl/Ag 2017

Gold, Kerry
Is Trump Inc. the President's Greatest Vulnerability? A group of enterprising lawyers thinks it might be, whether all roads lead to Russia or not img *New York* v50 no12 p40 Je 12 2017
L'Affaire Galloway cartoon *Walrus* v13 no9 p40 N 2016

Gold, Nick
How to conduct difficult conversations *People Management* p44 Ag 2017

GOLD, RACHEL BENSON
LIFE BEFORE ROE color *Scientific American* v317 no3 p58 S 2017

Gold, Sam
Home Free A. GREEN color *Vogue* v207 no4 p188 Ap 2017
THE REVEALER S. WEISS *New York Times Magazine* p28 Mr 5 2017
REWIND H. ALS cartoon *New Yorker* v93 no12 p74 My 8 2017
We Are the Dane: Director Sam Gold and his star, Oscar Isaac, stage & Hamlet that's both theatrical and honest S. HOLDREN img *New York* v50 no15 p69 Jl 24 2017

Gold, Sunny Sea
Businesses With Heart color *Parents* v92 no4 p28 Ap 2017
Could this be the only diet you'll ever need? color diag *Health* v31 no8 p91 O 2017
THE CUT-OFF POINT color *O, The Oprah Magazine* p86 O 2017
Double Down on Your Veggie Efforts color *Parents* v92 no5 p22 My 2017
Fitness News Young Brains Can Use color *Parents* v92 no5 p20 My 2017
Get Her in the Zen Zone color *Parents* v92 no4 p30 Ap 2017
immunity now! *Parents* v91 no11 p38 N 2016

Keep Your Little Soccer Star Safe color *Parents* v92 no4 p26 Ap 2017

the pet & pollen connection color *Parents* v92 no4 p23 Ap 2017

The Power of Virtual Chemo color *Parents* v92 no5 p26 My 2017

PT for Potty Problems? Yup color *Parents* v92 no3 p16 Mr 2017

Rock On, Single Moms *Parents* v92 no1 p16 Ja 2017

Safety on the Martial-Arts Mat color *Parents* v92 no5 p28 My 2017

A Salve for the Shot color *Parents* v92 no4 p24 Ap 2017

Which DIY Health Tests Are Worth It? color *Health* v31 no2 p77 Mr 2017

Gold, Sylviane

17 Shows, 1 Legend *Dance Magazine* v91 no8 p20 Ag 2017

Broadway's Next Bets: The stars and stories hitting stages soon *Dance Magazine* v91 no9 p24 S 2017

Choreographing Cyberspace *Dance Magazine* v90 no12 p32 D 2016

Dancing in a Chair and in the Air: in the Air Katrina Lenk's Broadway gigs are wildly diverse. Her latest is The Bands visit *Dance Magazine* v91 no10 p20 O 2017

Dancing with the Stars color *Dance Magazine* v91 no3 p20 Mr 2017

Evolution of Dance: Choreography's constantly shifting role on the Great White Way *Dance Magazine* v91 no7 p20 Jl 2017

The Golden Ticket [Cover story] *Dance Magazine* v91 no4 p26 Ap 2017

A Place to Play *Dance Magazine* v91 no1 p46 Ja 2017

Reimagining a Classic *Dance Magazine* v90 no11 p20 N 2016

Spring Awakening *Dance Magazine* v91 no4 p20 Ap 2017

Gold, Tanya

CITY OF GILT *Harper's Magazine* v334 no2002 p67 Mr 2017

Gold coins

For the Record color *Time* v188 no24 p7 D 12 2016

Gold in art—Exhibitions

Treasures beyond gold: A new exhibition examines the luxury arts of the ancient Americas J. Pillsbury color *Magazine Antiques* v184 no5 p108 S/O 2017

Gold ingots

For the Record color *Time* v188 no24 p7 D 12 2016

Gold markets

Gold Gets Its Own Flash Crash S. Barton and E. van der Walt graph *Bloomberg Businessweek* no4529 p26 Jl 3 2017

Gold mines & mining

ARC OF DESPERATION B. Ebus color *Earth Island Journal* v32 no3 p25 Aut 2017

Deep in a mine, earthquake gold awaits P. Voosen color *Science* v356 no6341 p891 Je 1 2017

THE HAPPY MINER K. HUNHOFF *South Dakota Magazine* v32 no6 p65 Mr/Ap 2017

Gold mines & mining—Idaho

IDAHO'S POMPEII: A GOLD RUSH TOWN DROWNED R. McRAE *Idaho Magazine* v16 no7 p42 Ap 2017

Gold mines & mining—Mexico

A Gold Rush in Mexico's Deadly South E. Martin, B. Bain et al color *Bloomberg Businessweek* no4497 p20 O 31 2016

Gold mines & mining—South Dakota

PROSPECTING IN THE HILLS R. JENSEN *South Dakota Magazine* v32 no6 p60 Mr/Ap 2017

Gold panning

THE HAPPY MINER K. HUNHOFF *South Dakota Magazine* v32 no6 p65 Mr/Ap 2017

PROSPECTING IN THE HILLS R. JENSEN *South Dakota Magazine* v32 no6 p60 Mr/Ap 2017

Gold rings—Evaluation

FOREVER LINKED color *Harper's Bazaar* no3648 p112 N 2016

WHERE FASHION GETS PERSONAL G. MAHARY color *Harper's Bazaar* no3648 p139 N 2016

Gold smuggling

HOW TO BECOME AN INTERNATIONAL GOLD SMUGGLER M. SMITH and J. FRANKLIN color *Bloomberg Businessweek* no4514 p54 Mr 13 2017

GOLDBERG, ANDREW

SMART WATCHES, DISSECTED color *Popular Science* v288 no6 p20 N/D 2016

Goldberg, Carrie

TAKING TROLLS TO COURT M. TALBOT cartoon color *New Yorker* v92 no40 p56 D 5 2016

Goldberg, Daniel

Embodied inequality color *Science* v354 no6315 p978 N 25 2016

Goldberg, Elyssa

taking stockholm bw color *Bon Appetit* v61 no11 p84 N 2016

GOLDBERG, JEANNE

THE POLITICIZATION of Scientific Issues: Looking through Galileo's Lens or through the Imaginary Looking Glass *Skeptical Inquirer* v41 no5 p34 S/O 2017

Goldberg, Jeffrey

THE AUTOCRATIC ELEMENT color *Atlantic* v320 no3 p8 O 2017

A HALF A DOZEN BATTLES bw *Atlantic* v320 no4 p10 N 2017

THE LESSONS OF HENRY KISSINGER bw color *Atlantic* v318 no5 p50 D 2016

OBAMA, RACE, AND AMERICA'S FUTURE color *Atlantic* v319 no1 p8 Ja/F 2017

A REPORTER'S STORY bw *Atlantic* v319 no5 p8 Je 2017

Goldberg, Jesse H.

Dopamine neurons encode performance error in singing birds bibl graph *Science* v354 no6317 p1278 D 9 2016

GOLDBERG, JONAH

Is free speech under threat IN THE UNITED STATES? WE RECEIVED TWENTY-SEVEN RESPONSES. WE PUBLISH THEM HERE, IN ALPHABETICAL ORDER *Commentary* v144 no1 p13 Jl/Ag 2017

GOLDBERG, MARSHALL

Go West, Young Men bw color *Weekly Standard* v22 no34 p38 My 15 2017

Goldberg, Melissa

All the President's Pictures color *O, The Oprah Magazine* p30 N 2017

THE Beauty OF Giving color *O, The Oprah Magazine* p76 N 2017

Boogie Wonderland bw color *O, The Oprah Magazine* p21 Je 2017

DOUBLE HEADER color *O, The Oprah Magazine* p92 N 2017

high & MIGHTY color *O, The Oprah Magazine* p168 D 2016

HOW WELL DO YOU KNOW YOUR Hair? color *O, The Oprah Magazine* p59 Ag 2017

THE MASKERADE color *O, The Oprah Magazine* p69 O 2017

Pretty Awesome color *O, The Oprah Magazine* p26 My 2017

Spring BEAUTY O-WARDS 2017 color *O, The Oprah Magazine* p69 My 2017

Sweet Dreams Are Made of This color *O, The Oprah Magazine* p30 D 2016

They're with the Banda color *O, The Oprah Magazine* p23 Jl 2017

GOLDBERG, MICHELLE

College and Consent: A kaleidoscopic tour through the campus sexual assault controversy *New York Times Book Review* p11 S 17 2017

GOLDBERG, NANCY

THIS TOO SHALL PASS . . . *Sea Magazine* v108 no10 p20 O 2016

Goldberg, Richard M.

Mismatch repair deficiency predicts response of solid tumors to PD-1 blockade chart graph *Science* v357 no6349 p409 Jl 28 2017

Goldberg, Rob

THE LOOK BOOK A. SWERDLOFF img *New York* v49 no23 p57 N 14 2016

Goldberg, Robert

Managing a Family (and Cash Flow) K. LANKFORD color *Kiplinger's Personal Finance* v71 no10 p72 O 2017

Goldberg, Rube, 1883-1970

A Winter Lift *South Dakota Magazine* v32 no4 p18 N/D 2016

Goldberg, Ruby

PROP MASTER color *Wired* v25 no10 p12 O 2017

GOLDBERG, RYAN

the DRUG RUNNERS *Texas Monthly* v45 no8 p74 Ag 2017

Goldberg, Stephen B.

How to Handle a Disagreement on Your Team *Harvard Business Review Digital Articles* p2 Jl 10 2017

Goldberg, Sue

THE PIES HAVE IT color *Cincinnati Magazine* v51 no1 p82 O 2017

Q&A: A "See" Change *Cincinnati Magazine* v51 no1 p144 O

Golden Globe Awards

7 Things You Didn't See L. Rice, M. Snetiker et al color *Entertainment Weekly* no1449 p14 Ja 20 2017

editor's letter Glenda color *Harper's Bazaar* no3653 p162 My 2017

THE HFPA AND INSTYLE KICK OFF THE 2017 GOLDEN GLOBE AWARDS SEASON B. Fowler color *InStyle* v24 no1 p42 Ja 2017

January! T. PAYNE and L. CROSS bw color *Ebony* v72 no3 p36 D 2016/Ja 2017

To Do img *New York* v49 no26 p96 D 26 2016

Your Golden Globes Workout Plan E. Berman color diag *Time* v189 no3 p55 Ja 16 2017

Golden Goose (Company)

Golden Goose Sneakers J. MOORE *GQ: Gentlemen's Quarterly* v86 no11 p35 N 2016

Golden retriever

DOG NABS THIEF S. McCollum *National Geographic Kids* no467 p13 F 2017

SIP! STAY! cartoon *Women's Health* v13 no10 p42 D 2016

Golden State Warriors (Basketball team)

1 Warriors B. Golliver, R. Nadkarni et al color *Sports Illustrated* v125 no14 p96 O 24-31 2016

BALLERS I. BOUDWAY color *Bloomberg Businessweek* no4535 p44 Ag 28 2017

FEELING THE CRUNGH B. Golliver color *Sports Illustrated* v126 no3 p36 Ja 23 2017

The Golden State Warriors As 2017 NBA Champions S. Gregory color *Time* v189 no24 p11 Je 26 2017

Killer Crossover T. S. YOUNG and S. T. BROWN color *Ebony* v72 no6 p74 Ap/My 2017

Tom MESCHERY J. McCallum color *Sports Illustrated* v127 no1 p84 Jl 3 2017

Golden State Warriors (Basketball team)—History—21st century

1 WARRIORS color *Sports Illustrated* v127 no12 p78 O 16 2017

THE HUSTLE L. Jenkins color *Sports Illustrated* v126 no14 p32 My 15-22 2017

NO COACH, NO PROBLEM C. Ballard color *Sports Illustrated* v126 no15 p28 My 29 2017

Goldenberg, Jacob

People Offer Better Ideas When They Can't See What Others Suggest *Harvard Business Review Digital Articles* p2 Jl 24 2015

Goldenberg, Marni

Stay on Your Smartphone! *Parks & Recreation* v51 no11 p14 N 2016

Golden Cockerel, The (Theatrical production)

CLASSICAL MUSIC *New Yorker* v93 no14 p12 My 22 2017

GoldenEar Technology (Company)

GoldenEar Technology Triton Reference Loudspeaker A. Griffifin color graph *Sound & Vision* v82 no5 p36 Je 2017

Golden Eight, The (Music)

Ron Rambach's Music Matters Closes Shop K. Micallef color *Downbeat* v84 no4 p17 Ap 2017

Golden Gate Bridge (San Francisco, Calif.)

The Earth From Above color *Entertainment Weekly* no1462 p66 Ap 21 2017

SECRETS OF THE GOLDEN GATE BRIDGE K. JAZYNKA *National Geographic Kids* no467 p20 F 2017

Golden Girls, The (TV program)

The Golden Girls BINGE A. Wilkinson color *Entertainment Weekly* no1453 p40 F 17 2017

Pop Chart R. Bruner, C. Lang et al color *Time* v188 no16/17 p94 O 24 2016

Goldenrods

GOLDENRODS G. LOFTS color *Martha Stewart Living* p82 Ap 2017

Worth Their Weight in Gold M. Wexler color *National Wildlife (World Edition)* v55 no5 p12 Ag/S 2017

Golden Shovel Anthology, The (Poem)

Moon T. Yu *New York Times Magazine* p19 Ap 30 2017

Golden snub-nosed monkey

Snow Monkeys J. DOEST color map *National Geographic* v230 no4 p140 O 2016

GOLDET, ANTOINE

WHY DID THIS INNOCENT MAN PLEAD GUILTY? color

Reader's Digest v189 no1131 p118 Je 2017

Goldfarb, Avi

How AI Will Change Strategy: A Thought Experiment *Harvard Business Review Digital Articles* p2 O 3 2017

How AI Will Change the Way We Make Decisions *Harvard Business Review Digital Articles* p2 Jl 26 2017

The Obama Administration's Roadmap for AI Policy *Harvard Business Review Digital Articles* p2 D 21 2016

The Simple Economics of Machine Intelligence *Harvard Business Review Digital Articles* p2 N 17 2016

The Trade-Off Every AI Company Will Face *Harvard Business Review Digital Articles* p2 Mr 28 2017

Goldfarb, Aviva

Supper Is Solved! color *Parents* v92 no9 p138 S 2017

GOLDFARB, BEN

The Codfather color *Mother Jones* v42 no2 p38 Mr/Ap 2017

Teddy or Not *Audubon* v119 no2 p12 Summ 2017

GOLDFIELD, DAVID

Rebel Yells: How the Charleston elite brought on the American Civil War bw *New York Times Book Review* p22 Ap 23 2017

Goldfield, Hannah

home & help img *New York* p96 Mr 6 2017

How to Eat a Regular-Size Soup Dumpling img *New York* v49 no25 p106 D 12 2016

Jennifer Plotnick img *New York* v50 no7 p18 Ap 3 2017

You Are What You Eat: An exploration of women's lives through the food they consumed *New York Times Book Review* p25 O 8 2017

Goldfinches

Invasion of the Garden Snatcher and Other Tales of Suburban Apocalypse K. Van Ogtrop color *Time* v189 no23 p55 Je 19 2017

Goldfish

Goldfish Gone Wild *New York Times Upfront* v149 no10 p2 Mr 13 2017

Goldhaber, Alfred Scharff

Magnetic monopole search, past and present *Physics Today* v70 no6 p12 Je 2017

Goldhaber, Dan

Why make it hard for teachers to cross state borders? color il *Phi Delta Kappan* v98 no5 p55 F 2017

Goldhaber-Gordon, David

Ballistic miniband conduction in a graphene superlattice bibl graph *Science* v353 no6307 p1526 S 30 2016

Goldhagen, Sarah Williams

The Architectural Experience *Architectural Record* v205 no4 p67 Ap 2017

Minding the Gap *Architectural Record* v204 no11 p122 N 2016

URBAN PASTORALS bw color *Art in America* v105 no3 p88 Mr 2017

GOLDHAMMER, ARTHUR

Bad Apples *Nation* v303 no19 p6 N 7 2016

"FEVER GRIPS THE ENTIRE NATION" bw color il map *Nation* v303 no16 p10 O 17 2016

MACRON ON THE MARCH IN FRANCE color *Nation* v305 no2 p22 Jl 17 2017

Goldhill, Simon

Before Straight and Gay D. COHEN cartoon color *Atlantic* v319 no2 p40 Mr 2017

Goldin, Claudia

The Average Mid-Forties Male College Graduate Earns 55% More Than His Female Counterparts *Harvard Business Review Digital Articles* p2 Je 12 2017

GOLDIN, NAN

THE RAW, REAL, AND UTTERLY INSPIRING STORY OF A NEW YORK KID WHO MADE HIS OWN RULES FOR LIVING, 10 TILLETT WRIGHT'S NEW MEMOIR IS A TRIBAL CRY FOR A WHOLE GENERATION *Interview* v46 no8 p116 O 2016

Golding, Karen

Karen Golding Is a Steward for the Horse: This horse show icon believes that safeguarding equine welfare is her No. 1 priority as a steward R. Rover *In Stride* v12 no3 p37 My 2017

Golding, William, 1911-1993

'Lord of the Flies' 60 Years Later L. LOWRY *New York Times Book Review* p29 O 30 2016

GOLDMAN, ARI L.
Catholic Mission *New York Times Book Review* p19 N 27 2016

Goldman, Dana
It's Easier to Measure the Cost of Health Care than Its Value *Harvard Business Review Digital Articles* p2 N 18 2014
Understanding Health Care's Short-Termism Problem *Harvard Business Review Digital Articles* p2 S 28 2015

Goldman, David P.
American Civil Religion *Claremont Review of Books* v17 no3 p6 Summ 2017
American Civil Religion W. A. McDougall and D. P. Goldman *Claremont Review of Books* v17 no3 p6 Summ 2017
NEITHER AMERICAN, NOR CIVIL, NOR A RELIGION *Claremont Review of Books* v17 no2 p64 Spr 2017

GOLDMAN, DEVORAH
The Bee's Needs *Weekly Standard* v22 no4 p34 O 3 2016
Mother, May I? color *Weekly Standard* v22 no27 p40 Mr 20 2017

Goldman, Don
MEET THE filter guy color *Astronomy* v45 no11 p52 N 2017

GOLDMAN, DUFF
Does it taste good? chart color *Popular Mechanics* p23 My 2017

Goldman, Duff—Interviews
Surprising History of the Ace of Cakes M. GILES color *Popular Science* v288 no6 p94 N/D 2016

Goldman, Emma
THE MAZE *Harper's Magazine* v335 no2006 p31 Jl 2017

Goldman, Gretchen T.
Ensuring scientific integrity in the Age of Trump bibl cartoon *Science* v355 no6326 p696 F 17 2017

Goldman, Henry
Where Are All the Tourists? color diag *Bloomberg Businessweek* no4514 p15 Mr 13 2017

Goldman, Jason G.
The Brainy Big Cats color *Scientific American* v315 no6 p18 D 2016
One's True Nature color *Scientific American* v315 no6 p24 D 2016
The Remarkable Timing of Seals color *Scientific American* v316 no1 p17 Ja 2017
Scaredy-Cats color *Scientific American* v317 no4 p18 O 2017
Which One Is Mom Again? color *Scientific American* v316 no4 p18 Ap 2017

Goldman, Jeremy
Nearly Half of Companies Say They Don't Have the Digital Skills They Need *Harvard Business Review Digital Articles* p1 Jl 28 2017

Goldman, Leslie
CAREGIVER'S PREP GUIDE color *Better Homes & Gardens* v95 no11 p146 N 2017
FEATS OF THE MIND color *Women's Health* v14 no8 p86 O 2017
FEEDING ON FEAR color *Women's Health* v14 no6 p100 Jl 2017
HAPPY FEET color *Better Homes & Gardens* v95 no6 p152 Je 2017
HOW TO WIN AT Wellness color *O, The Oprah Magazine* p83 F 2017
THE JOY OF NOT COOKING color *Women's Health* v14 no2 p102 Mr 2017
Mother of Invention color *Better Homes & Gardens* v95 no2 p134 F 2016
PUT YOUR YEAR IN GEAR color *Better Homes & Gardens* v95 no9 p158 S 2017
SCREEN TIME RULES *Better Homes & Gardens* v95 no6 p165 Je 2017
the secret bunion society color *Parents* v92 no7 p84 Jl 2017
SKYE HIGH CONFIDENCE [Cover story] color *Women's Health* v14 no6 p63 Jl 2017
STAY WELL ON THE WAY color *Good Housekeeping* v264 no5 p101 My 2017
WHEN LESS IS MORE bw *O, The Oprah Magazine* p89 O 2017

Goldman, Marcia
happiness is a warm puppy S. Bower color *Good Housekeeping* v264 no3 p156 Mr 2017

GOLDMAN, MARTIN S.
Campus Chaos *Commentary* v142 no1 p14 Jl/Ag 2016

Goldman, Melissa T.
UNDER ARMOR cartoon *O, The Oprah Magazine* p122 Mr 2017

Goldman, Paula
How a New Generation of Business Leaders Views Philanthropy *Harvard Business Review Digital Articles* p2 F 29 2016

Goldman, Samuel
Easy for Him to Say color *Commonweal* v114 no14 p31 S 8 2017

GOLDMAN, TANYA
Matinee Melodrama: Playing with Formula in the Sound Serial *Film Quarterly* v70 no2 p106 Wint 2016

Goldman Sachs Group Inc.
Can Wall Street Save Trump From Himself? W. D. COHAN color *Atlantic* v319 no3 p22 Ap 2017
GOLDMAN SACHS D. Campbell color graph *Bloomberg Businessweek* no4505 p38 D 26 2016
IS GOLDMAN SACHS STILL NO. 1 ON WALL STREET? W. D. Cohan chart color diag *Fortune* v175 no8 p184 Je 15 2017
A Very Goldman White House W. D. COHAN color *Vanity Fair* v59 no8 p90 Ag 2017
New Lloyd D. Campbell color *Bloomberg Businessweek* no4530 p26 Jl 17 2017

Goldman Sachs Group Inc.—Finance
Goldman Sachs Embraces Automation, Leaving Many Behind N. Byrnes il *MIT Technology Review* v120 no3 p22 My/Je 2017
X-Ray: Goldman Sachs T. Tepper diag *Money* v46 no2 p50 Mr 2017

Goldmann, A. J.
Armide *Opera News* v81 no7 p42 Ja 2017
Hamburg *Opera News* v81 no10 p42 Ap 2017
King Arthur *Opera News* v81 no10 p42 Ap 2017
Manon Lescaut *Opera News* v81 no9 p45 Mr 2017
Salzburg *Opera News* v81 no5 p48 N 2016

Goldman Sachs & Co.—Trials, litigation, etc.
Will Wall Street (or the Rest of Us) Ever Learn? B. Taylor *Harvard Business Review Digital Articles* p2 Ap 10 2017

Goldmark, Karl
Goldmark: Die Konigin von Saba *Opera News* v81 no7 p51 Ja 2017

Goldratt, Eliyahu M., 1948-2011
Constraints and Community: To get things done, leaders need to focus on the bigger picture M. Funkhouser *Governing* v30 no12 p61 S 2017

Gold—Research
Identification of single-site gold catalysis in acetylene hydrochlorination G. Malta, S. A. Kondrat et al bw diag graph *Science* v355 no6332 p1399 Mr 31 2017
Long-standing gold mystery solved E. CONOVER *Science News* v191 no3 p11 F 18 2017

Goldrick-Rab, Sara, ca. 1977-
On Money G. Rivlin color *New York Times Magazine* p18 My 21 2017
Sara Goldrick-Rab J. Crelin color *Current Biography* v78 no1 p13 Ja 2017

Gold—Sales & prices
Hedging Inflation Without Gold J. Waggoner color diag *Money* v46 no4 p34 My 2017

Goldsborough, Robert
Murder, Stage Left: A Nero Wolfe Mystery *Publishers' Weekly* v264 no4 p58 Ja 23 2017

Goldschmidt, Elizabeth A.
Storing light in a tiny box diag *Science* v357 no6358 p1354 S 29 2017

Goldschmidt, Paul, 1987-
Paul Goldschmidt C. Cullen color *Current Biography* v77 no10 p30 O 2016

Goldshmidt-Tran, Orit
The cytotoxic Staphylococcus aureus PSMα3 reveals a cross-α amyloid-like fibril bibl color diag graph *Science* v355 no6327 p831 F 24 2017

Goldsleger, Cheryl
Indeterminate cartoon *Art in America* v104 no11 p47 D 2016

Goldsmith, Ashley
Build a Great Company Culture with Help from Technology *Harvard Business Review Digital Articles* p2 F 24 2016

Goldsmith, Jack
Beware the Temptations of Ever-Expanding Executive Powers color *Time* v188 no16/17 p81 O 24 2016
Leaders color *Time* v189 no16/17 p64 My 1-8 2017

Now What? color *Time* v188 no21 p42 N 21 2016

The Other Forever War *Hoover Digest: Research & Opinion on Public Policy* no1 p92 Wint 2017

The Snowden Cure *Hoover Digest: Research & Opinion on Public Policy* no4 p133 Fall 2016

WILL DONALD TRUMP DESTROY THE PRESIDENCY? color *Atlantic* v320 no3 p58 O 2017

Goldsmith, Jeff

How U.S. Hospitals and Health Systems Can Reverse Their Sliding Financial Performance *Harvard Business Review Digital Articles* p2 O 5 2017

Goldsmith, Marshall

A 6-Part Structure for Giving Clear and Actionable Feedback *Harvard Business Review Digital Articles* p2 Ag 7 2015

Goldsmith, Mike

Sound M. D. Greenfield *Physics Today* v70 no6 p64 Je 2017

Goldsmith, Tim

Crystal Visions P. LAFFOON IV *Cincinnati Magazine* v50 no6 p50 Mr 2017

Goldstein, Amy

The Book of Jobs J. D. VANCE *Commentary* v143 no6 p40 Je 2017

THE END OF LABOR bw color *Nation* v305 no6 p22 S 11 2017

GOLDSTEIN, BERNARD D.

New toxic chemical regulations bw *Issues in Science & Technology* v33 no2 p8 Wint 2017

Goldstein, Bill—Interviews

The Year that Created Modernism C. REID color *Publishers Weekly* v264 no29 p210 Jl 17 2017

GOLDSTEIN, DANA

The Education of Barack Obama bw color diag *Nation* v304 no1 p64 Ja 2 2017 The Obama Years

Who Goes There? *New York Times Book Review* p10 Mr 12 2017

Goldstein, David B.

Arthur Hinton Rosenfeld *Physics Today* v70 no9 p72 S 2017

Goldstein, Debbie

Responding to Feedback You Disagree With *Harvard Business Review Digital Articles* p2 Ap 14 2017

GOLDSTEIN, DR. EVAN

HOW TO BE A BETTER BOTTOM color *Advocate* no1090 p40 Ap 2017

Goldstein, Jennifer

IN WITH THE NOW color *O, The Oprah Magazine* p93 S 2017

Goldstein, Jessica M.

Are Arrogant Men Still Funny? color *Glamour* v115 no5 p152 My 2017

Fitness, According to Superheroes bw chart color *Glamour* v115 no2 p63 F 2017

How Pop Culture Depicts Mental Illness color *Glamour* v115 no4 p120 Ap 2017

Goldstein, Lisa S.

Backtalk diag *Phi Delta Kappan* v98 no6 p80 Mr 2017

Goldstein, Markus

Teaching personal initiative beats traditional training in boosting small business in West Africa chart graph *Science* v357 no6357 p1287 S 22 2017

Goldstein, Melissa

THE CHANGE MAKER color *Sunset* v238 no1 p17 Ja 2017

GOLDSTEIN, MELISSA MILRAD

All Systems Go color *Martha Stewart Living* p46 S 2017

The Art of the Arch *Martha Stewart Living* no268 p58 O 2016

Better Skin, Distilled *Martha Stewart Living* no267 p44 S 2016

COUNTER INTELLIGENCE color *Martha Stewart Living* p38 My 2017

COUNTER INTELLIGENCE color *Martha Stewart Living* p46 Mr 2017

COUNTER INTELLIGENCE color *Martha Stewart Living* p48 S 2017

COUNTER INTELLIGENCE *Martha Stewart Living* no268 p62 O 2016

COUNTER INTELLIGENCE *Martha Stewart Living* no269 p50 N 2016

THE DIGITAL AGE color *Martha Stewart Living* p44 Jl/Ag 2017

The Essential: Loafer color *Martha Stewart Living* p50 S 2017

The Essential: Raincoat color *Martha Stewart Living* p52 Ap 2017

FACE SAVERS *Martha Stewart Living* no269 p46 N 2016

Fall Into Fresh color *Martha Stewart Living* p56 O 2017

HEALING WATERS color *Martha Stewart Living* no271 p36 Ja/F 2017

MERRY AND BRIGHT *Martha Stewart Living* no270 p72 D 2016

PRESERVE AND PROTECT color *Martha Stewart Living* p36 My 2017

SMARTER SCREENS color *Martha Stewart Living* no275 p38 Je 2017

Super Naturals color *Martha Stewart Living* p60 Ap 2017

Your Easiest Routine Ever color *Martha Stewart Living* no275 p42 Je 2017

Goldstein, Norm

Tracks of a Traitor bw color map *American History* v52 no4 p56 O 2017

Goldstein, Raymond

A biology journal provides a lesson in peer review *Physics Today* v69 no12 p10 D 2016

Peer review as collaboration T. Shinbrot *Physics Today* v70 no10 p15 O 2017

GOLDSTEIN, REBECCA NEWBERGER

Making ATHENS GREAT AGAIN *Atlantic* v319 no3 p86 Ap 2017

GOLDSTEIN, RICHARD

MARIJUANA ON CAMPUS: By the '60s, this former street drug had become the sacrament of the youth generation. Here, a recent college graduate describes the phenomenon and the attraction *Saturday Evening Post* v289 no4 p42 Jl/Ag 2017

Goldstein, Robert

Censorship Tale B. KAUFFMAN *American Conservative* v16 no3 p43 My/Je 2017

GOLDSTEIN, SARAH

THE MAN IN MONO color *GQ: Gentlemen's Quarterly* v97 no9 p180 S 2017

Goldstein, Sophie

House of Women color *Publishers Weekly* v264 no28 p73 Jl 10 2017

Goldstein, William H.

A Powerful Petawatt Laser for Experimental Science *Science & Technology Review* p3 Jl/Ag 2017

GOLDSTON, DAVID

Not'Til the Fat Lady Sings TSCA's Next Act *Issues in Science & Technology* v33 no1 p73 Fall 2016

Goldstone, Brian

A PRAYER'S CHANGE B. Goldstone *Harper's Magazine* v334 no2004 p40 My 2017

A PRAYER'S CHANGE *Harper's Magazine* v334 no2004 p40 My 2017

Goldstone, Ilana—Interviews

Muslin, Paint and Light M. S. Eddy *Stage Directions* v30 no4 p18 Ap 2017

Goldstone, Lawrence

THE PIGBOAT'S ORIGINS M. Oppenheim color *American History* v52 no3 p67 Ag 2017

Goldstyn, Jacques

The Handbook *Publishers Weekly* v264 no29 p218 Jl 17 2017

Goldsworthy, Adrian

Devise and Conquer J. E. LENDON *Weekly Standard* v22 no36 p36 My 29 2017

Pax Romana J. Lacey *MHQ: Quarterly Journal of Military History* v29 no3 p92 Spr 2017

Pax Romana: War, Peace and Conquest in the Roman World T. Jones *Christian Century* v134 no11 p41 My 24 2017

Goldsworthy, Ray L.

Community network for deaf scientists color *Science* v356 no6336 p386 Ap 28 2017

Goldwasser, Edwin Leo

Edwin Leo Goldwasser R. A. Carrigan and R. O. Simmons *Physics Today* v70 no9 p70 S 2017

Goldwater, Barry M. (Barry Morris), 1909-1998

Goldwater's Blowout E. FELTEN cartoon *Weekly Standard* v22 no15 p5 D 19 2016

REMEMBER BARRY GOLDWATER? P. Garrison color *Flying* v144 no1 p72 Ja 2017

THE SILENT MAJORITY J. Toobin cartoon *New Yorker* v93 no14 p27 My 22 2017

Flight School S. Munroe and D. DeNunzio color *Golf Magazine* v59 no1 p52 Ja 2017

Funny FiLL-IN J. FANSLAU cartoon *National Geographic Kids* no470 p30 My 2017

High-Visibility Golf Balls D. Millard *New York Times Magazine* p24 S 3 2017

ROUGH CUTS K. Kirk and D. DeNunzio color *Golf Magazine* v59 no4 p65 Ap 2017

THE THICK BLUE LINE T. Cooke and D. DeNunzio color *Golf Magazine* v59 no6 p56 Je 2017

Why Do I Hit My Irons Thin? K. Sprecher and D. DeNunzio *Golf Magazine* v59 no8 p48 Ag 2017

Why Do My Putts Jump Off Line? S. Bosdosh and D. DeNunzio *Golf Magazine* v59 no4 p65 Ap 2017

Golf balls—Evaluation

Curtis Luck J. Marksbury color *Golf Magazine* v59 no11 p25 N 2017

Luke Donald C. Barrett color *Golf Magazine* v59 no2 p29 F 2017

ROCK IT & ROLL IT M. Chwasky and R. Sauerhaft color *Golf Magazine* v59 no3 p99 Mr 2017

Ryan Moore C. Barrett color *Golf Magazine* v59 no3 p29 Mr 2017

Golf carts

Santa Delivers...Advice M. DiTrolio color *Men's Health* v31 no10 p33 D 2016

Golf clubs (Associations)

BEAUTY SHOT D. DeNunzio color *Golf Magazine* v59 no8 p56 Ag 2017

Modern Love J. Passov and C. Barrett color *Golf Magazine* v58 no11 p36 N 2016

National Treasures J. Passov color *Golf Magazine* v59 no4 p120 Ap 2017

Save Muny D. COURTNEY *Texas Monthly* v45 no4 p204 Ap 2017

Soothe Moves J. Sens and J. Passov color *Golf Magazine* v59 no5 p103 My 2017

You're Up! color *Golf Magazine* v59 no11 p13 N 2017

Golf clubs (Associations)—Evaluation

Leaders in the Clubhouse J. Passov color *Golf Magazine* v58 no11 p94 N 2016

Lifestyles of the Top 100 J. Passov color *Golf Magazine* v59 no10 p88 O 2017

Living & Recreation *Virginia Living* p92 2017 Best 20of Virginia

Golf clubs (Sporting goods)

5 WAYS TO SMOKE YOUR FAIRWAY WOODS M. Hackett and D. Denunzio color *Golf Magazine* v59 no10 p52 O 2017

THE BEST GRIP IN THE GAME J. Miller color *Golf Magazine* v58 no12 p71 D 2016

CHIP SERVICE D. Abraham and D. DeNunzio color *Golf Magazine* v59 no8 p46 Ag 2017

CRACK THAT WHIP! D. Abraham and D. Denunzio color *Golf Magazine* v59 no11 p39 N 2017

Designated Drivers A. Shipnuck and C. Barrett color *Golf Magazine* v59 no3 p28 Mr 2017

FIT BITS R. Sauerhaft and R. Sauerhaft color *Golf Magazine* v59 no8 p90 Ag 2017

IT'S HY TIME M. Chwasky and D. Denunzio color *Golf Magazine* v58 no11 p56 N 2016

ONE LENGTH ONLY? R. Sauerhaft and R. Sauerhaft color *Golf Magazine* v58 no11 p86 N 2016

PLAYING FAVORITES R. Sauerhaft color *Golf Magazine* v59 no7 p86 Jl 2017

SEVEN HEAVEN D. Doniger and D. Denunzio color *Golf Magazine* v59 no11 p43 N 2017

SNAP DECISION J. Dunigan and D. DeNunzio color *Golf Magazine* v59 no7 p50 Jl 2017

THIS MONTH: Irons! M. Chwasky, M. Dee et al color *Golf Magazine* v59 no4 p103 Ap 2017

THE TINKERER M. Chwasky color *Golf Magazine* v58 no12 p62 D 2016

TRY THIS! CURVE BALLS D. Sargent and D. Denunzio color *Golf Magazine* v59 no10 p44 O 2017

You're Up! color *Golf Magazine* v59 no10 p11 O 2017

YOUR EXIT PLAN M. Jacobs and D. DeNunzio color *Golf Magazine* v59 no6 p50 Je 2017

Golf clubs (Sporting goods)—Evaluation

BETTER PLAYER FAIRWAY WOODS M. Chwasky, M. Dee et al color *Golf Magazine* v59 no5 p86 My 2017

BETTER PLAYER HYBRIDS M. Chwasky, M. Dee et al color *Golf Magazine* v59 no5 p94 My 2017

BETTER PLAYER IRONS M. Chwasky, M. Dee et al color *Golf Magazine* v59 no4 p112 Ap 2017

BOOM SERVICE A. Johnson and R. Sauerhaft color *Golf Magazine* v58 no11 p84 N 2016

COR Strength A. Johnson and R. Sauerhaft color *Golf Magazine* v59 no7 p82 Jl 2017

First Look STEALTH BOMBERS R. Sauerhaft and R. Sauerhaft color *Golf Magazine* v58 no11 p78 N 2016

GAME IMPROVEMENT FAIRWAY WOODS M. Chwasky, M. Dee et al color *Golf Magazine* v59 no5 p82 My 2017

GAME IMPROVEMENT HYBRIDS M. Chwasky, M. Dee et al color *Golf Magazine* v59 no5 p90 My 2017

GAME IMPROVEMENT IRONS M. Chwasky, M. Dee et al color *Golf Magazine* v59 no4 p104 Ap 2017

GET SMART M. Chwasky and R. Sauerhaft color *Golf Magazine* v59 no7 p85 Jl 2017

GO BIG OR GO HOME M. Chwasky and R. Sauerhaft color *Golf Magazine* v58 no11 p80 N 2016

GOOD WOOD M. Chwasky and R. Sauerhaft color *Golf Magazine* v59 no8 p86 Ag 2017

HELPING HANDS A. Johnson and R. Sauerhaft color *Golf Magazine* v58 no11 p82 N 2016

HIGH-END HAMMERS M. Chwasky and R. Sauerhaft color *Golf Magazine* v59 no7 p80 Jl 2017

HIGH FIVE A. Johnson and R. Sauerhaft color *Golf Magazine* v59 no2 p80 F 2017

Jon Rahm C. Barrett color *Golf Magazine* v59 no7 p29 Jl 2017

LONG-GAME CHANGERS M. Chwasky and R. Sauerhaft color *Golf Magazine* v59 no8 p89 Ag 2017

Lydia Ko J. Marksbury color *Golf Magazine* v59 no9 p29 S 2017

MATERIAL WORLD R. Sauerhaft and R. Sauerhaft color *Golf Magazine* v59 no2 p78 F 2017

THESE DRIVERS ARE EPIC M. Chwasky and R. Sauerhaft color *Golf Magazine* v59 no2 p82 F 2017

Weapons of Choice M. Chwasky color *Golf Magazine* v59 no10 p94 O 2017

Golf coaches

GETTING INTO THE SWING T. Wendel color *Washingtonian Magazine* v52 no7 p126 Ap 2017

Golf course architects

The 6th Annual Travelin' Joe AWARDS J. Passov and C. Barrett color *Golf Magazine* v59 no2 p38 F 2017

All Over the Map J. Passov color *Golf Magazine* v59 no10 p82 O 2017

GIL HANSE J. Passov color *Golf Magazine* v59 no1 p92 Ja 2017

Golf course design & construction

HOW WE RANK THEM chart *Golf Magazine* v59 no10 p8 O 2017

King of Clubs J. Passov and C. Barrett color *Golf Magazine* v59 no7 p36 Jl 2017

TEEING OFF color *Golf Magazine* v59 no10 p16 O 2017

Golf course maintenance

Damage Control D. Pelz and J. Marksbury color *Golf Magazine* v59 no10 p30 O 2017

Golf courses

See also

Holes (Golf)

COURSE RATER CONFIDENTIAL color *Golf Magazine* v59 no10 p78 O 2017

Dad Trippers J. Passov color *Golf Magazine* v59 no6 p102 Je 2017

Grains & Beauty J. Passov and C. Barrett color *Golf Magazine* v59 no5 p42 My 2017

It's All Fun and Gains D. Pelz and C. Barrett color *Golf Magazine* v59 no6 p30 Je 2017

LAND A LUNKER BASS! color diag *Men's Health* v32 no6 p105 Ag 2017

Paradise Island M. Bamberger color *Golf Magazine* v59 no11 p112 N 2017

A Perfect Read M. Bamberger color *Golf Magazine* v58 no11 p114 N 2016

A SALTY TREAT G. Peterson and D. Denunzio color *Golf Magazine* v59 no11 p42 N 2017

Tee, Ball J. Passov and C. Barrett chart color *Golf Magazine* v59

no3 p40 Mr 2017

TEEING OFF J. Passov color *Golf Magazine* v59 no1 p14 Ja 2017

While You're In the Neighborhood... A Top 100 Trip Planner J. Passov color *Golf Magazine* v59 no10 p92 O 2017

You're Up! color *Golf Magazine* v59 no6 p11 Je 2017

Your Ultimate Golf Bucket List J. Passov color *Golf Magazine* v59 no8 p92 Ag 2017

Golf courses—Arizona

Small Wonder J. Passov and C. Barrett color *Golf Magazine* v59 no4 p42 Ap 2017

Golf courses—California

North Star J. Passov and C. Barrett color *Golf Magazine* v59 no2 p40 F 2017

TEEING OFF J. Passov color *Golf Magazine* v59 no9 p16 S 2017

Golf courses—Canada

SHOCK OF THE NEW color *Golf Magazine* v59 no10 p70 O 2017

Golf courses—Colorado

Top Golf J. Passov color *Golf Magazine* v59 no9 p90 S 2017

Golf courses—Design & construction

The 6th Annual Travelin' Joe AWARDS J. Passov and C. Barrett color *Golf Magazine* v59 no2 p38 F 2017

HAWAII'S 5-OH! J. King and D. DeNunzio color *Golf Magazine* v59 no1 p54 Ja 2017

Mississippi Queen J. Passov and C. Barrett color *Golf Magazine* v59 no1 p36 Ja 2017

THE NINETEENTH HOLE J. Kersten cartoon *New Yorker* v92 no34 p25 O 24 2016

North Star J. Passov and C. Barrett color *Golf Magazine* v59 no2 p40 F 2017

Golf courses—Evaluation

Five to Watch color *Golf Magazine* v59 no10 p76 O 2017

Go Big & Go Home J. Passov color *Golf Magazine* v59 no3 p106 Mr 2017

The Golfer's Ultimate Guide Ireland J. Passov color *Golf Magazine* v59 no7 p90 Jl 2017

Island Fever J. Passov color *Golf Magazine* v59 no5 p100 My 2017

Kiwi's Big Adventure J. Passov color *Golf Magazine* v59 no1 p91 Ja 2017

The Long Game E. MATUSZEWSKI color *Forbes* v200 no1 p108 Jl 27 2017

Save Muny D. COURTNEY *Texas Monthly* v45 no4 p204 Ap 2017

SHOCK OF THE NEW color *Golf Magazine* v59 no10 p70 O 2017

Small Wonder J. Passov and C. Barrett color *Golf Magazine* v59 no4 p42 Ap 2017

Striking Gold—Again J. Passov and J. Marksbury color *Golf Magazine* v59 no9 p38 S 2017

TEEING OFF J. Passov color *Golf Magazine* v59 no9 p16 S 2017

TEE TIME IN TEXAS *Texas Monthly* v45 no3 p124 Mr 2017

Top Golf J. Passov color *Golf Magazine* v59 no9 p90 S 2017

Golf courses—Florida

Bet On Black J. Passov and J. Marksbury color *Golf Magazine* v59 no10 p27 O 2017

Golf courses—Georgia

DEAD AT AUGUSTA J. Passov color *Golf Magazine* v59 no4 p72 Ap 2017

Golf courses—Ireland

The Golfer's Ultimate Guide Ireland J. Passov color *Golf Magazine* v59 no7 p90 Jl 2017

Golf courses—New England

TEEING OFF color *Golf Magazine* v59 no10 p16 O 2017

Golf courses—New York (State)—Long Island

What About Bob? M. Bamberger color *Golf Magazine* v59 no2 p104 F 2017

Golf courses—North Carolina

Five to Watch color *Golf Magazine* v59 no10 p76 O 2017

Golf courses—South Carolina

The Long Game E. MATUSZEWSKI color *Forbes* v200 no1 p108 Jl 27 2017

Golf courses—Texas

Lone Star Links J. Passov and J. Marksbury color *Golf Magazine* v59 no11 p30 N 2017

Golf courses—United States

HOW WE RANK THEM chart *Golf Magazine* v59 no10 p8 O 2017

Ode to Joe D. Denunzio color *Golf Magazine* v59 no10 p8 O 2017

U.S. and the World Edition J. Passov chart color *Golf Magazine* v59 no10 p62 O 2017

Golf courses—Virginia

Striking Gold—Again J. Passov and J. Marksbury color *Golf Magazine* v59 no9 p38 S 2017

Golf courses—Wisconsin

COLLISION COURSE J. Sens color *Sports Illustrated* v126 no17 p62 Je 19 2017

Dream On J. Sens color *Golf Magazine* v59 no6 p62 Je 2017

Erin Go Ah J. Passov color *Golf Magazine* v59 no6 p70 Je 2017

Erin Go Par M. Bamberger and T. Keith color *Sports Illustrated* v126 no17 p15 Je 19 2017

Golf equipment

See also

Golf balls

Golf clubs (Sporting goods)

Curtis Luck J. Marksbury color *Golf Magazine* v59 no11 p25 N 2017

Daniel Summerhays J. Marksbury color *Golf Magazine* v59 no10 p25 O 2017

DISTANCE BLADES M. Chwasky color *Golf Magazine* v59 no11 p82 N 2017

G400 Drivers and Irons M. Chwasky color *Golf Magazine* v59 no9 p84 S 2017

Henrik Stenson C. Barrett color *Golf Magazine* v59 no8 p31 Ag 2017

THE KEEPERS OF THE GAME T. CHIARELLA color *Popular Mechanics* p48 Je 2017

LIGHT & LONG M. Chwasky color *Golf Magazine* v59 no11 p86 N 2017

LOOK SHARP M. Chwasky color *Golf Magazine* v59 no9 p86 S 2017

Lydia Ko J. Marksbury color *Golf Magazine* v59 no9 p29 S 2017

MINI-BOMBERS M. Chwasky and A. Johnson color *Golf Magazine* v59 no10 p96 O 2017

SMOOTH OPERATORS M. Chwasky color *Golf Magazine* v59 no11 p88 N 2017

Sole Mates A. Johnson color *Golf Magazine* v59 no10 p98 O 2017

SPIN TO WIN M. Chwasky and D. DeNunzio chart color *Golf Magazine* v59 no8 p59 Ag 2017

STUFF WE LOVE color *Golf Magazine* v59 no11 p64 N 2017

THIS MONTH: Putters + Wedges M. Chwasky, M. Dee et al color *Golf Magazine* v59 no6 p83 Je 2017

Golf equipment—Evaluation

BLADE PUTTERS M. Chwasky, M. Dee et al color *Golf Magazine* v59 no6 p84 Je 2017

Brendan Steele C. Barrett color *Golf Magazine* C v59 no6 p23 Je 2017

LARGE MALLET PUTTERS M. Chwasky, M. Dee et al color *Golf Magazine* v59 no6 p92 Je 2017

MIDSIZE MALLET PUTTERS M. Chwasky, M. Dee et al color *Golf Magazine* v59 no6 p88 Je 2017

Untie Him J. Passov color *Golf Magazine* v59 no6 p106 Je 2017

WEDGES M. Chwasky, M. Dee et al color *Golf Magazine* v59 no6 p98 Je 2017

Golf for children

It's Tome for a Change P. Kostis and C. Barrett color *Golf Magazine* v58 no11 p34 N 2016

Golf for women

See also

LPGA Tour (Golf)

See Jane Thrive M. Bamberger color *Golf Magazine* v59 no7 p112 Jl 2017

Golf handicapping

83% THAT'S HOW MUCH THIS READER CUT HIS HANDI-CAP JUST BY USING HIS FEET D. DeNunzio color *Golf Magazine* v59 no6 p50 Je 2017

Golf instruction

ATTACK THE FLAG M. Perpich and D. DeNunzio color *Golf Magazine* v59 no4 p52 Ap 2017

A BEND FOR BIG DRIVES B. O'Neal and D. DeNunzio color *Golf Magazine* v59 no1 p48 Ja 2017

CLEAN CONTACT! M. Chuck and D. DeNunzio color *Golf*

Magazine v59 no4 p49 Ap 2017

DOUBLE PLAY K. Weeks and D. DeNunzio color *Golf Magazine* v59 no1 p46 Ja 2017

A FAULT-FREE BACKSWING S. Munroe and D. DeNunzio color *Golf Magazine* v59 no9 p50 S 2017

FIND YOUR POWER RELEASE J. Hardy and D. DeNunzio chart color *Golf Magazine* v59 no9 p56 S 2017

GAME ON! E. Ibarguen, Durham et al color *Golf Magazine* v59 no2 p57 F 2017

HINGE TO WIN D. Denunzio color *Golf Magazine* v59 no2 p55 F 2017

HIT ROPES OFF THE TEE E. a. Tischler, O. Fields et al color *Golf Magazine* v59 no2 p55 F 2017

HOOK-PROOF YOUR SWING M. Blackburn, Birmingham et al color diag *Golf Magazine* v59 no2 p54 F 2017

Long-Distance Service D. Pelz and C. Barrett color *Golf Magazine* v59 no4 p40 Ap 2017

MIND YOUR MISS D. Denunzio and T. Stickney color *Golf Magazine* v59 no2 p49 F 2017

MORE POP, LESS POP-UP K. Sprecher and D. DeNunzio color diag *Golf Magazine* v59 no4 p54 Ap 2017

One for the Money M. Broadie and C. Barrett color *Golf Magazine* v59 no4 p38 Ap 2017

PATRICK READS K. Kirk and D. DeNunzio color *Golf Magazine* v59 no1 p44 Ja 2017

POSE A STRIKE M. Hackett and D. DeNunzio color *Golf Magazine* v59 no1 p42 Ja 2017

PRESS HERE! S. Mackenzie and D. DeNunzio color *Golf Magazine* v59 no8 p54 Ag 2017

private LESSONS color *Golf Magazine* v59 no9 p97 S 2017

SEE IT AND SPIETH IT! E. Johnson and D. DeNunzio color *Golf Magazine* v59 no1 p50 Ja 2017

STAND AND DELIVER K. Smeltz and D. DeNunzio color *Golf Magazine* v59 no1 p48 Ja 2017

TEE SHEET E. Ibarguen and D. DeNunzio color *Golf Magazine* v59 no1 p47 Ja 2017

THIS IS YOUR LAST SLICE D. Doniger, B. Hills et al color *Golf Magazine* v59 no2 p45 F 2017

TRY A "HINGE" STROKE M. Durland, N. Grande et al color diag *Golf Magazine* v59 no9 p52 S 2017

TRY THIS! Feast On the Green M. Jacobs and D. DeNunzio color *Golf Magazine* v59 no8 p59 Ag 2017

Watch + Learn J. Murphy and C. Barrett color *Golf Magazine* v59 no4 p36 Ap 2017

Why Can't I Hit Long Bunker Shots? B. Manzella, N. Orleans et al *Golf Magazine* v59 no2 p52 F 2017

Golf on television

ON COURSE FOR DRAMA R. A. BERENZ *TV Guide* v65 no25 p43 Je 2017

Sports Highlights *TV Guide* v64 no15 p51 Ap 4 2016

Golf records

The Case for ... The Career Slam M. Bamberger and T. Keith color *Sports Illustrated* v127 no4 p24 Ag 7 2017

Golf resorts—Evaluation

Grains & Beauty J. Passov and C. Barrett color *Golf Magazine* v59 no5 p42 My 2017

Soothe Moves J. Sens and J. Passov color *Golf Magazine* v59 no5 p103 My 2017

Golf rules

ASK THE RULES GUY R. Guy and C. Barrett color *Golf Magazine* v59 no1 p26 Ja 2017

ASK THE RULES GUY R. Guy and C. Barrett color *Golf Magazine* v59 no4 p34 Ap 2017

It's Tome for a Change P. Kostis and C. Barrett color *Golf Magazine* v58 no11 p34 N 2016

Peter's Parting Shot P. Kostis and C. Barrett color *Golf Magazine* v59 no1 p32 Ja 2017

Rules Aren't Made to Be Broken M. Bamberger color *Golf Magazine* v59 no6 p124 Je 2017

You're Up! color *Golf Magazine* v59 no1 p13 Ja 2017

You're Up! color *Golf Magazine* v59 no9 p11 S 2017

YOU SHOOT, YOU SCORE! D. DeNunzio and D. DeNunzio color *Golf Magazine* v59 no1 p50 Ja 2017

Golf shoes—Evaluation

SOLE PROV IDERS A. Johnson and R. Sauerhaft color *Golf Magazine* v59 no8 p84 Ag 2017

Golf techniques

See also

Pitching (Golf)

Putting (Golf)

Swing (Golf)

Wedge shot (Golf)

The 43% Solution R. Sauerhaft and C. Barrett chart color *Golf Magazine* v59 no6 p32 Je 2017

5 WAYS TO SMOKE YOUR FAIRWAY WOODS M. Hackett and D. Denunzio color *Golf Magazine* v59 no10 p52 O 2017

82% D. Denunzio color *Golf Magazine* v58 no11 p54 N 2016

ACE OF FACE V. J. Trolio and D. DeNunzio color *Golf Magazine* v59 no7 p48 Jl 2017

All Mixed Up M. Broadie and J. Marksbury color *Golf Magazine* v59 no9 p36 S 2017

ASK THE RULES GUY R. Guy and C. Barrett color *Golf Magazine* v59 no4 p34 Ap 2017

ATTACK MODE J. Leishman and D. Denunzio color *Golf Magazine* v59 no10 p42 O 2017

ATTACK THE BALL J. Plecker and D. DeNunzio color diag *Golf Magazine* v59 no6 p52 Je 2017

BASKET CASE J. Plecker and D. Denunzio color *Golf Magazine* v59 no10 p35 O 2017

BE Clutch HAVE Fun GO Low [Cover story] J. Rose and D. Denunzio chart color *Golf Magazine* v58 no11 p61 N 2016

THE BEST GRIP IN THE GAME J. Miller color *Golf Magazine* v58 no12 p71 D 2016

BUILDING BLOCKS C. Preisinger and D. Denunzio color *Golf Magazine* v59 no11 p52 N 2017

CHIP SERVICE T. Cooke and D. Denunzio color *Golf Magazine* v59 no11 p44 N 2017

CHIP WITH YOUR 3-WOOD S. Munroe and D. DeNunzio color *Golf Magazine* v59 no4 p60 Ap 2017

CLEAN CONTACT! M. Chuck and D. DeNunzio color *Golf Magazine* v59 no4 p49 Ap 2017

COURT ORDERS! J. Leishman and D. DeNunzio color *Golf Magazine* v59 no9 p63 S 2017

CRACK THAT WHIP! D. Abraham and D. Denunzio color *Golf Magazine* v59 no11 p39 N 2017

CURVES AHEAD M. Hunt and D. Denunzio color *Golf Magazine* v59 no11 p57 N 2017

DJ's Secret Sauce M. Broadie and C. Barrett color *Golf Magazine* v59 no6 p28 Je 2017

DO A HEAD CHECK D. Sargent and D. Denunzio color diag *Golf Magazine* v59 no11 p47 N 2017

DUKE OF HAZARDS J. Sieckmann and D. Denunzio color *Golf Magazine* v59 no9 p54 S 2017

EXIT SAND, MAN! M. Hackett and D. DeNunzio color *Golf Magazine* v59 no5 p64 My 2017

A FAULT-FREE BACKSWING S. Munroe and D. DeNunzio color *Golf Magazine* v59 no9 p50 S 2017

Find Your Personal Power Move M. Adams, B. Najar et al color *Golf Magazine* v59 no7 p54 Jl 2017

FIND YOUR POWER RELEASE J. Hardy and D. DeNunzio chart color *Golf Magazine* v59 no9 p56 S 2017

FIVE KEYS FOR SPEED [Cover story] J. Thomas and D. Denunzio color *Golf Magazine* v59 no7 p58 Jl 2017

Fly It High, Land It Softly D. Pelz and C. Barrett color *Golf Magazine* v59 no5 p40 My 2017

Fringe Benefit D. Denunzio, B. Riggs et al color *Golf Magazine* v59 no2 p50 F 2017

GET GOOD! DO IT FAST! [Cover story] L. Thompson and J. Ledesma color *Golf Magazine* v59 no11 p58 N 2017

GET UP TO GO AROUND D. Dijulia and D. Denunzio color *Golf Magazine* v59 no11 p56 N 2017

GO LOW, GET FAST M. Jacobs and D. DeNunzio color *Golf Magazine* v59 no3 p52 Mr 2017

Go the Distance M. Broadie and C. Barrett color *Golf Magazine* v58 no11 p32 N 2016

Have No Fear! D. Pelz and C. Barrett color *Golf Magazine* v59 no3 p38 Mr 2017

High & Mighty D. Doniger and D. DeNunzio color diag *Golf Magazine* v59 no3 p62 Mr 2017

HINGE TO WIN D. Denunzio evaluation *Golf Magazine* v59 no2 p55 F 2017

HIT A DRAW... RIGHT NOW! M. Blackburn and D. DeNunzio

color diag *Golf Magazine* v58 no12 p80 D 2016

HIT LIKE A KID M. Chuck and D. Denunzio color *Golf Magazine* v59 no10 p38 O 2017

HIT THE BRAKES AT IMPACT J. Sutton and D. DeNunzio color *Golf Magazine* v59 no7 p46 Jl 2017

HOW MUCH CAN YOU BITE OFF? E. Alpenfels and D. DeNunzio color *Golf Magazine* v59 no5 p67 My 2017

How to Build a Swing You Can Believe in K. Kirk color *Golf Magazine* v59 no9 p71 S 2017

It's All Fun and Gains D. Pelz and C. Barrett color *Golf Magazine* v59 no6 p30 Je 2017

JUST HIT! M. Bender and D. Denunzio color *Golf Magazine* v59 no2 p52 F 2017

LASER SHOW C. Harmon and D. DeNunzio color *Golf Magazine* v59 no6 p44 Je 2017

THE LOW DOWN ON LEFT HAND LOW M. Blackburn and D. Dethier color *Golf Magazine* v59 no11 p72 N 2017

MAKE LAYUPS A SLAM DUNK J. Plecker and D. DeNunzio color *Golf Magazine* v59 no7 p52 Jl 2017

MASTERFUL SERGIO D. M. Clarke color *Golf Magazine* v59 no6 p15 Je 2017

Master of None A. Shipnuck and J. Marksbury color *Golf Magazine* v59 no9 p28 S 2017

MASTER STROKES 4 shots to go low [Cover story] S. Garcia and S. Zak color *Golf Magazine* v59 no6 p75 Je 2017

MISSION: POSSIBLE! D. Phillips chart color *Golf Magazine* v59 no9 p76 S 2017

NIX YOUR CHILI-DIP M. Chuck and D. DeNunzio color *Golf Magazine* v59 no9 p64 S 2017

OH, SNAP! M. Hunt and D. DeNunzio color *Golf Magazine* v59 no9 p52 S 2017

PAINT A PERFECT SWING [Cover story] K. Chappell and D. DeNunzio color *Golf Magazine* v59 no5 p71 My 2017

PARADISE LOST J. King and D. Denunzio color *Golf Magazine* v59 no10 p51 O 2017

PASS PARALLEL M. Durland and D. Denunzio color diag *Golf Magazine* v59 no10 p47 O 2017

THE PERFECT CHIP J. Hallett and D. DeNunzio color *Golf Magazine* v59 no5 p49 My 2017

POINT & SHOOT D. Denunzio and J. Sieckmann color *Golf Magazine* v58 no11 p54 N 2016

POWER CORD T. Ruggiero and D. DeNunzio color *Golf Magazine* v59 no7 p44 Jl 2017

POWER: PURE & SIMPLE [Cover story] J. Rahm and J. Ledesma color *Golf Magazine* v59 no10 p55 O 2017

Practice Like a Pro [Cover story] D. Berger color *Golf Magazine* v59 no3 p65 Mr 2017

private LESSONS color *Golf Magazine* v59 no11 p97 N 2017

private LESSONS color *Golf Magazine* v59 no2 p89 F 2017

private LESSONS color *Golf Magazine* v59 no5 p105 My 2017

private LESSONS color *Golf Magazine* v59 no7 p99 Jl 2017

Pulling Out All the Flops D. Pelz and C. Barrett color *Golf Magazine* v59 no7 p35 Jl 2017

PURE GENIUS D. Denunzio and J. Murphy color *Golf Magazine* v58 no11 p50 N 2016

PUTT WITHOUT FEAR J. Sieckmann and D. DeNunzio color diag *Golf Magazine* v59 no5 p56 My 2017

PUZZLED? T. Cooke and D. DeNunzio color *Golf Magazine* v59 no9 p47 S 2017

READY? DRAW! M. Hunt and D. DeNunzio color *Golf Magazine* v59 no5 p54 My 2017

REALITY BITES B. Mccabe and D. DeNunzio color *Golf Magazine* v59 no4 p64 Ap 2017

(Really) Close Encounters D. Pelz and J. Marksbury color *Golf Magazine* v59 no9 p34 S 2017

ROUGH CUTS K. Kirk and D. DeNunzio color *Golf Magazine* v59 no4 p65 Ap 2017

Run It or Fly It K. Sprecher and D. DeNunzio color *Golf Magazine* v59 no3 p48 Mr 2017

SAVING PAR: GRIND OVER MATTER G. Weir and D. DeNunzio color *Golf Magazine* v59 no3 p45 Mr 2017

The Short Story M. Broadie and J. Marksbury chart color *Golf Magazine* v59 no10 p31 O 2017

SIGHT CLUB T. J. Tomasi and D. DeNunzio color *Golf Magazine* v59 no5 p62 My 2017

SNAP DECISION J. Dunigan and D. DeNunzio color *Golf Magazine* v59 no7 p50 Jl 2017

Split the Middle B. Riggs and D. DeNunzio color *Golf Magazine* v58 no12 p84 D 2016

STOP YOUR CHOP! J. Dunigan and D. Denunzio color *Golf Magazine* v59 no11 p54 N 2017

STOP YOUR DROP B. Mogg and D. DeNunzio color *Golf Magazine* v58 no12 p83 D 2016

STRETCH AWAY A SLICE T. Cooke and D. DeNunzio color *Golf Magazine* v59 no7 p50 Jl 2017

SURVIVAL TACTICS M. Jacobs and D. DeNunzio color *Golf Magazine* v59 no9 p60 S 2017

THE SWING OF A KING B. Brewer and D. DeNunzio color *Golf Magazine* v58 no12 p67 D 2016

TAPE-MEASURE TEE SHOTS! L. Mucklow and D. DeNunzio chart color *Golf Magazine* v58 no12 p75 D 2016

That Hits the Spot D. Pelz and C. Barrett color *Golf Magazine* v59 no2 p32 F 2017

THE THICK BLUE LINE T. Cooke and D. DeNunzio color *Golf Magazine* v59 no6 p56 Je 2017

THIS MONTH: Fairway Woods + Hybrids M. Chwasky, M. Dee et al color *Golf Magazine* v59 no5 p81 My 2017

THIS SWEET-SWINGING JUNIOR ADDED THIRTY YARDS ALMOST OVERNIGHT WITH A NEW FINISH. HERE'S HOW D. DeNunzio color *Golf Magazine* v59 no7 p46 Jl 2017

THOUGHT-FREE CHIPS K. Stenzel and D. Denunzio color *Golf Magazine* v59 no10 p40 O 2017

TOWER OF POWER B. Riggs, D. Denunzio color *Golf Magazine* v59 no11 p48 N 2017

TRY A "HINGE" STROKE M. Durland, N. Grande et al color diag *Golf Magazine* v59 no9 p52 S 2017

TRY THIS! CURVE BALLS D. Sargent and D. Denunzio color *Golf Magazine* v59 no10 p44 O 2017

TRY THIS! GRIP IT "N CHIP IT...IN! D. Doniger and D. DeNunzio color *Golf Magazine* v59 no6 p58 Je 2017

TURN STYLE K. Sprecher and D. DeNunzio color *Golf Magazine* v59 no6 p42 Je 2017

Watch + Learn C. O'connell and C. Barrett color *Golf Magazine* v58 no11 p30 N 2016

Watch + Learn J. Plecker and C. Barrett color *Golf Magazine* v59 no5 p36 My 2017

Watch + Learn J. Tattersall and C. Barrett color *Golf Magazine* v59 no7 p32 Jl 2017

Watch + Learn M. Perpich and J. Marksbury color *Golf Magazine* v59 no11 p28 N 2017

Why Can't I Hit Long Bunker Shots? B. Manzella, N. Orleans et al *Golf Magazine* v59 no2 p52 F 2017

Why Do My Putts Jump Off Line? S. Bosdosh and D. DeNunzio *Golf Magazine* v59 no4 p65 Ap 2017

Wrap Star M. Perpich and D. DeNunzio color *Golf Magazine* v59 no5 p58 My 2017

You're Up! color *Golf Magazine* v59 no7 p16 Jl 2017

You're Up! color *Golf Magazine* v59 no9 p11 S 2017

Your Lucky Number: 13 M. Broadie and C. Barrett color *Golf Magazine* v59 no7 p34 Jl 2017

ZEN AT WORK J. Sieckmann and D. DeNunzio color *Golf Magazine* v59 no7 p41 Jl 2017

Golf tees

ALTERNATE ROUTES B. Riggs and D. DeNunzio color *Golf Magazine* v59 no6 p54 Je 2017

Golf tournaments

See also

PGA Championship (Golf tournament)

PGA Tour (Association)

Presidents Cup

29TH DELTA JEWISH OPEN *Successful Farming* v115 no1 p19 Ja 2017

32! THAT'S HOW MANY CLUB CHAMPIONSHIPS THIS READER HAS WON. HERE'S HIS SECRET D. DeNunzio color *Golf Magazine* v59 no9 p64 S 2017

April Events F. Esker color *New Orleans Magazine* v51 no6 p26 Ap 2017

Best of the Rest E. D. McGROGAN *Tennis* v53 no1 p32 Ja/F 2017

THE BIG EASY, STILL DOING IT D. M. Clarke color *Golf Magazine* v59 no8 p9 Ag 2017

Bucking the Trend R. Asselta and J. Marksbury color *Golf Magazine* v59 no11 p21 N 2017

Let the Gains Begin M. Broadie and C. Barrett color *Golf Magazine* v59 no2 p36 F 2017

Living Larger A. Shipnuck and J. Marksbury color *Golf Magazine* v59 no10 p24 O 2017

Lone Star Links J. Passov and J. Marksbury color *Golf Magazine* v59 no11 p30 N 2017

Major Pain M. Broadie chart color *Golf Magazine* v59 no8 p70 Ag 2017

The New Queen Bee M. Washchyshyn and J. Marksbury color *Golf Magazine* v59 no10 p21 O 2017

PATRICK REED: WIN BIG [Cover story] D. DeNunzio color *Golf Magazine* v59 no9 p68 S 2017

PENCIL WRECK J. Garrity color *Golf Magazine* v59 no4 p90 Ap 2017

A SALTY TREAT G. Peterson and D. Denunzio color *Golf Magazine* v59 no11 p42 N 2017

Season's Readings M. Broadie and J. Marksbury chart color *Golf Magazine* v59 no11 p32 N 2017

Still Going Strong R. Asselta, A. Sports et al color *Golf Magazine* v59 no9 p25 S 2017

TEEING OFF color *Golf Magazine* v59 no2 p16 F 2017

TEEING OFF J. Sens color *Golf Magazine* v59 no5 p18 My 2017

Watch + Learn T. Sones and C. Barrett color *Golf Magazine* v59 no1 p30 Ja 2017

What in the World? M. Broadie and C. Barrett color *Golf Magazine* v59 no5 p38 My 2017

Golf tournaments—Management

EXECUTIVE ORDERS A. Shipnuck and S. Kwak color *Sports Illustrated* v127 no11 p18 O 9 2017

Golf training

Cover *Golf Magazine* v59 no9 pC1 S 2017

That Hits the Spot D. Pelz and C. Barrett color *Golf Magazine* v59 no2 p32 F 2017

TIME FOR A CHANGE M. Durland and D. DeNunzio color diag *Golf Magazine* v59 no6 p39 Je 2017

Golf—Betting

A FISTFUL OF SAND SAVES M. Durland and D. DeNunzio color diag *Golf Magazine* v59 no8 p58 Ag 2017

WAIT FOR IT... C. Preisinger and D. DeNunzio color *Golf Magazine* v59 no8 p57 Ag 2017

Golf—China

THE PGA TOUR TAKES ON CHinA S. Cendrowski color *Fortune* v174 no6 p116 N 1 2016

Golf—Coaching

GETTING INTO THE SWING T. Wendel color *Washingtonian Magazine* v52 no7 p126 Ap 2017

Golf—Competitions

THE 2017 MASTERS color *Golf Magazine* v59 no4 p71 Ap 2017

ASK THE RULES GUY R. Guy and C. Barrett color *Golf Magazine* v59 no5 p34 My 2017

REALITY BITES B. Mccabe and D. DeNunzio color *Golf Magazine* v59 no4 p64 Ap 2017

Golf courses—Charts, diagrams, etc.

U.S. and the World Edition J. Passov chart color *Golf Magazine* v59 no10 p62 O 2017

Golf—Drive

HIT A DRAW... RIGHT NOW! M. Blackburn and D. DeNunzio color diag *Golf Magazine* v58 no12 p80 D 2016

NO MORE CHIPPING HANG-UPS D. Rader and D. DeNunzio color *Golf Magazine* v58 no12 p81 D 2016

One for the Money M. Broadie and C. Barrett color *Golf Magazine* v59 no4 p38 Ap 2017

private LESSONS color *Golf Magazine* v59 no4 p125 Ap 2017

Split the Middle B. Riggs and D. DeNunzio color *Golf Magazine* v58 no12 p84 D 2016

STOP YOUR DROP B. Mogg and D. DeNunzio color *Golf Magazine* v58 no12 p83 D 2016

THE SWING OF A KING B. Brewer and D. DeNunzio color *Golf Magazine* v58 no12 p67 D 2016

TAPE-MEASURE TEE SHOTS! L. Mucklow and D. DeNunzio chart color *Golf Magazine* v58 no12 p75 D 2016

THIS IS YOUR LAST SLICE D. Doniger, B. Hills et al color *Golf Magazine* v59 no2 p45 F 2017

Golf—Drive—Equipment & supplies

COR Strength A. Johnson and R. Sauerhaft color *Golf Magazine* v59 no7 p82 Jl 2017

HIGH-END HAMMERS M. Chwasky and R. Sauerhaft color *Golf Magazine* v59 no7 p80 Jl 2017

MINI-BOMBERS M. Chwasky and A. Johnson color *Golf Magazine* v59 no10 p96 O 2017

William McGirt C. Barrett color *Golf Magazine* v58 no11 p27 N 2016

Golf—Equipment & supplies

See also
Golf balls
Golf clubs (Sporting goods)

Boom Times R. Sauerhaft and D. DeNunzio chart color *Golf Magazine* v59 no3 p55 Mr 2017

Going Once, Going Twice J. Passov color *Golf Magazine* v59 no4 p124 Ap 2017

NO MORE PLAID PANTS J. Paskin color *Bloomberg Businessweek* no4497 p66 O 31 2016

SWING SET M. Chwasky, M. Dee et al color *Golf Magazine* v59 no3 p96 Mr 2017

THIS MONTH: DRIVERS M. Chwasky, M. Dee et al color *Golf Magazine* v59 no3 p72 Mr 2017

TIP THE SCALES R. Sauerhaft and D. DeNunzio chart color *Golf Magazine* v59 no4 p58 Ap 2017

Golf—Equipment & supplies—Design & construction

THIS MONTH: Irons! M. Chwasky, M. Dee et al color *Golf Magazine* v59 no4 p103 Ap 2017

Golf—Equipment & supplies—Evaluation

BETTER PLAYER DRIVERS M. Chwasky, M. Dee et al color diag *Golf Magazine* v59 no3 p82 Mr 2017

BETTER PLAYER FAIRWAY WOODS M. Chwasky, M. Dee et al color *Golf Magazine* v59 no5 p86 My 2017

BETTER PLAYER HYBRIDS M. Chwasky, M. Dee et al color *Golf Magazine* v59 no5 p94 My 2017

BETTER PLAYER IRONS M. Chwasky, M. Dee et al color *Golf Magazine* v59 no4 p112 Ap 2017

BOOM SERVICE A. Johnson and R. Sauerhaft color *Golf Magazine* v58 no11 p84 N 2016

GAME IMPROVEMENT DRIVERS M. Chwasky, M. Dee et al color diag *Golf Magazine* v59 no3 p74 Mr 2017

GAME IMPROVEMENT FAIRWAY WOODS M. Chwasky, M. Dee et al color *Golf Magazine* v59 no5 p82 My 2017

GAME IMPROVEMENT HYBRIDS M. Chwasky, M. Dee et al color *Golf Magazine* v59 no5 p90 My 2017

GAME IMPROVEMENT IRONS M. Chwasky, M. Dee et al color *Golf Magazine* v59 no4 p104 Ap 2017

GO BIG OR GO HOME M. Chwasky and R. Sauerhaft color *Golf Magazine* v58 no11 p80 N 2016

GREAT LENGTHS A. Johnson and R. Sauerhaft color *Golf Magazine* v59 no1 p86 Ja 2017

HELPING HANDS A. Johnson and R. Sauerhaft color *Golf Magazine* v58 no11 p82 N 2016

HIGH FIVE A. Johnson and R. Sauerhaft color *Golf Magazine* v59 no2 p80 F 2017

J.B. Holmes C. Barrett color *Golf Magazine* v59 no5 p31 My 2017

Justin Thomas C. Barrett color *Golf Magazine* v59 no4 p33 Ap 2017

LONG SHOTS M. Chwasky and R. Sauerhaft color *Golf Magazine* v59 no1 p84 Ja 2017

Luke Donald C. Barrett color *Golf Magazine* v59 no2 p29 F 2017

MATERIAL WORLD R. Sauerhaft and R. Sauerhaft color *Golf Magazine* v59 no2 p78 F 2017

MAX GAME IMPROVEMENT DRIVERS M. Chwasky, M. Dee et al color diag *Golf Magazine* v59 no3 p92 Mr 2017

MAX GAME IMPROVEMENT IRONS M. Chwasky, M. Dee et al color *Golf Magazine* v59 no4 p117 Ap 2017

Patrick Reed C. Barrett color *Golf Magazine* v59 no1 p25 Ja 2017

ROCK IT & ROLL IT M. Chwasky and R. Sauerhaft color *Golf Magazine* v59 no3 p99 Mr 2017

Ryan Moore C. Barrett color *Golf Magazine* v59 no3 p29 Mr 2017

SMART MISSILES M. Chwasky, A. Johnson et al color *Golf Magazine* v59 no1 p82 Ja 2017

THESE DRIVERS ARE EPIC M. Chwasky and R. Sauerhaft color *Golf Magazine* v59 no2 p82 F 2017

Golfers

See also
Women golfers

Beyond Great color *Golf Magazine* v59 no1 p70 Ja 2017

The Big Breakthrough M. Broadie and C. Barrett color *Golf Magazine* v59 no1 p35 Ja 2017

Damage Control D. Pelz and J. Marksbury color *Golf Magazine* v59 no10 p30 O 2017

DRIVE IT A MILE! J. Sutton and D. DeNunzio color *Golf Magazine* v59 no8 p43 Ag 2017

Feels Like the First Time S. Zak color *Golf Magazine* v59 no4 p76 Ap 2017

Fly It High, Land It Softly D. Pelz and C. Barrett color *Golf Magazine* v59 no5 p40 My 2017

A GOLF MAGAZINE STUDY IT'S TIME TO CHANGE YOUR AIM B. Christina and E. Alpenfels color *Golf Magazine* v59 no11 p76 N 2017

Hats Off to Ollie P. Madden and C. Barrett color *Golf Magazine* v59 no5 p27 My 2017

It's a One-derful Life R. Reilly and C. Barrett color *Golf Magazine* v59 no1 p28 Ja 2017

Jordan Spieth B. Muteba color *Current Biography* v78 no5 p82 My 2017

Let the Gains Begin M. Broadie and C. Barrett color *Golf Magazine* v59 no2 p36 F 2017

No Gust, No Glory D. Pelz and C. Barrett color *Golf Magazine* v59 no1 p34 Ja 2017

PLANE and SIMPLE [Cover story] D. Denunzio color *Golf Magazine* v59 no2 p70 F 2017

PRESS HERE! S. Mackenzie and D. DeNunzio color *Golf Magazine* v59 no8 p54 Ag 2017

private LESSONS color *Golf Magazine* v58 no12 p89 D 2016

private LESSONS color *Golf Magazine* v59 no6 p109 Je 2017

(Really) Close Encounters D. Pelz and J. Marksbury color *Golf Magazine* v59 no9 p34 S 2017

SEE IT AND SPIETH IT! E. Johnson and D. DeNunzio color *Golf Magazine* v59 no1 p50 Ja 2017

A SHEEP IN WOLF'S CLOTHING D. DeNunzio color *Golf Magazine* v59 no9 p9 S 2017

Spanish Class P. Madden and C. Barrett color *Golf Magazine* v59 no2 p25 F 2017

SPIN TO WIN M. Chwasky and D. DeNunzio chart color *Golf Magazine* v59 no8 p59 Ag 2017

TAKE A CHANT! B. McCabe and D. Denunzio color *Golf Magazine* v59 no10 p44 O 2017

The Tao of Sam M. Bamberger color *Golf Magazine* v59 no5 p120 My 2017

"The Greatest Shot I Ever Saw" S. Zak color *Golf Magazine* v59 no2 p65 F 2017

Title Fight A. Shipnuck and C. Barrett color *Golf Magazine* v59 no8 p30 Ag 2017

TRY THIS! Feast On the Green M. Jacobs and D. DeNunzio color *Golf Magazine* v59 no8 p59 Ag 2017

What A Girl Wants A. Shipnuck and C. Barrett color *Golf Magazine* v59 no4 p32 Ap 2017

What in the World? M. Broadie and C. Barrett color *Golf Magazine* v59 no5 p38 My 2017

Wrap It Up! J. Passov color *Golf Magazine* v59 no1 p88 Ja 2017

WRISTS OF FURY S. Munroe and D. DeNunzio color *Golf Magazine* v58 no12 p83 D 2016

Golfers' families

The Education of Samantha Els M. Bamberger color *Golf Magazine* v59 no10 p116 O 2017

Golfers—Attitudes

Brutish Empire M. Broadie and C. Barrett color *Golf Magazine* v59 no3 p36 Mr 2017

The DJ Universe M. Chwasky color *Golf Magazine* v59 no1 p68 Ja 2017

DOUBLE PLAY K. Weeks and D. DeNunzio color *Golf Magazine* v59 no1 p46 Ja 2017

His Brother's Looper S. Zak color *Golf Magazine* v59 no1 p76 Ja 2017

"I Want to Make Them Proud" A. Shipnuck color *Golf Magazine* v59 no1 p58 Ja 2017

Morgan Hoffmann J. Marksbury and C. Barrett color *Golf Magazine* v59 no1 p37 Ja 2017

The Other Player of the Year M. Bamberger color *Golf Magazine* v59 no1 p108 Ja 2017

Peter's Parting Shot P. Kostis and C. Barrett color *Golf Magazine* v59 no1 p32 Ja 2017

THE ULTIMATE DRIVING MACHINE [Cover story] D. DeNunzio color *Golf Magazine* v59 no1 p78 Ja 2017

What a Journey, Man! C. Morfit, J. Garrity et al color *Golf Magazine* v59 no1 p21 Ja 2017

Golfers—Interviews

Grin to Win C. Barrett and S. Zak color *Golf Magazine* v58 no11 p23 N 2016

HE'S THE alpha dog C. Morfit color *Golf Magazine* v59 no2 p58 F 2017

Scott Piercy J. Marksbury and C. Barrett color *Golf Magazine* v59 no7 p38 Jl 2017

Golfers—Training of

You're Up! color *Golf Magazine* v59 no1 p13 Ja 2017

Golfers—United States

ACE IN THE CROWD R. Reilly color *Golf Magazine* v58 no12 p52 D 2016

Air Palmer M. Bamberger color *Golf Magazine* v58 no12 p104 D 2016

ARNIE ON JACK *Golf Magazine* v58 no12 p29 D 2016

Arnold Palmer D. Von Drehle color *Time* v188 no14 p12 O 10 2016

AUGUSTA ROYALTY K. Bense color *Golf Magazine* v58 no12 p34 D 2016

DOCTOR IN THE HOUSE J. McAlley color *Golf Magazine* v58 no12 p58 D 2016

THE DRIVE THAT CHANGED EVERYTHING J. Passov color *Golf Magazine* v58 no12 p46 D 2016

EMPIRE OF THE SON J. Passov color *Golf Magazine* v58 no12 p30 D 2016

FIRST GOLFER A. Shipnuck, M. Bamberger et al color *Sports Illustrated* v127 no4 p48 Ag 7 2017

GOLF'S KING OF COOL J. Sens color *Golf Magazine* v58 no12 p42 D 2016

THE HEARTBREAK KID P. Madden color *Golf Magazine* v58 no12 p49 D 2016

IN HIS OWN WORDS C. Barrett color *Golf Magazine* v58 no12 p20 D 2016

THE MEANING OF ARNIE [Cover story] A. Shipnuck color *Golf Magazine* v58 no12 p16 D 2016

PITCH HITTER M. Chwasky color *Golf Magazine* v58 no12 p65 D 2016

WHEN WE WERE KINGS D. M. Clarke color *Golf Magazine* v58 no12 p11 D 2016

You're Up! color *Golf Magazine* v59 no2 p12 F 2017

Golf—History

A BRIEF HISTORY OF LEISURE L. Smith bw color *Mother Jones* v42 no4 p59 Jl/Ag 2017

CHASING 62 M. Bamberger color diag *Sports Illustrated* v126 no10 p54 Ap 10 2017

THE PGA TOUR TAKES ON CHinA S. Cendrowski color *Fortune* v174 no6 p116 N 1 2016

Golf injuries—Charts, diagrams, etc.

He's Back T. Keith chart color *Sports Illustrated* v125 no18 p19 D 5 2016

Golf—News briefs

TEEING OFF color *Golf Magazine* v59 no2 p16 F 2017

Golf—Scorekeeping

The Big Breakthrough M. Broadie and C. Barrett color *Golf Magazine* v59 no1 p35 Ja 2017

CHASING 62 M. Bamberger color diag *Sports Illustrated* v126 no10 p54 Ap 10 2017

GOLFSelect (Company)

Kiwi's Big Adventure J. Passov color *Golf Magazine* v59 no1 p91 Ja 2017

Golf—Statistics

The Short Story M. Broadie and J. Marksbury chart color *Golf Magazine* v59 no10 p31 O 2017

Golf—Study & teaching

Reintroducing the Game of Golf J. R. Johnson *Parks & Recreation* v52 no1 p50 Ja 2017

Golf tournaments—Charts, diagrams, etc.

PAR EXCELLENCE T. Keith chart color *Sports Illustrated* v127 no8 p18 S 18 2017

Golf—United States

Leading Off A. Shipnuck color *Sports Illustrated* v125 no12 p8 O 10 2016

Goliath (TV program)
Goliath M. Roffman *TV Guide* v64 no40 p38 O 3 2016
A TV Legend's Unremarkable Return D. D'addario color *Time* v188 no15 p54 O 17 2016

Gollehon, Robin
Bits That Go Ouch! [Cover story] color *Horse & Rider* v56 no1 p44 Ja 2017

Gollin, Randi
Jussara Lee bw *Rodale's Organic Life* v3 no1 p54 Ja 2017

Golliver, Ben
10 Bucks color *Sports Illustrated* v125 no14 p84 O 24-31 2016
10 Mavericks color *Sports Illustrated* v125 no14 p110 O 24-31 2016
11 Bulls color *Sports Illustrated* v125 no14 p86 O 24-31 2016
11 Pelicans color *Sports Illustrated* v125 no14 p111 O 24-31 2016
12 Heat color *Sports Illustrated* v125 no14 p88 O 24-31 2016
12 Suns color *Sports Illustrated* v125 no14 p112 O 24-31 2016
13 Magic color *Sports Illustrated* v125 no14 p89 O 24-31 2016
13 Nuggets color *Sports Illustrated* v125 no14 p113 O 24-31 2016
14 76ers color *Sports Illustrated* v125 no14 p90 O 24-31 2016
14 Kings color *Sports Illustrated* v125 no14 p114 O 24-31 2016
15 Lakers color *Sports Illustrated* v125 no14 p116 O 24-31 2016
15 Nets color *Sports Illustrated* v125 no14 p92 O 24-31 2016
1 Cavaliers color *Sports Illustrated* v125 no14 p72 O 24-31 2016
1 Warriors color *Sports Illustrated* v125 no14 p96 O 24-31 2016
2016-17 Viewers' Guide color *Sports Illustrated* v125 no14 p118 O 24-31 2016
2017-18 ENTERTAINMENT VALUE GUIDE color *Sports Illustrated* v127 no12 p76 O 16 2017
2 Celtics *Sports Illustrated* v125 no14 p74 O 24-31 2016
2 Spurs color *Sports Illustrated* v125 no14 p98 O 24-31 2016
3 Clippers color *Sports Illustrated* v125 no14 p99 O 24-31 2016
3 Raptors color *Sports Illustrated* v125 no14 p75 O 24-31 2016
4 Pistons color *Sports Illustrated* v125 no14 p76 O 24-31 2016
4 Trail Blazers color *Sports Illustrated* v125 no14 p100 O 24-31 2016
5 Hornets color *Sports Illustrated* v125 no14 p78 O 24-31 2016
5 Thunder color *Sports Illustrated* v125 no14 p102 O 24-31 2016
6 Hawks color *Sports Illustrated* v125 no14 p80 O 24-31 2016
6 Jazz color *Sports Illustrated* v125 no14 p103 O 24-31 2016
7 Grizzlies color *Sports Illustrated* v125 no14 p104 O 24-31 2016
7 Pacers color *Sports Illustrated* v125 no14 p81 O 24-31 2016
8 Rockets color *Sports Illustrated* v125 no14 p106 O 24-31 2016
8 Wizards color *Sports Illustrated* v125 no14 p82 O 24-31 2016
9 Knicks color *Sports Illustrated* v125 no14 p83 O 24-31 2016
9 Timberwolves color *Sports Illustrated* v125 no14 p108 O 24-31 2016
Care Taker color *Sports Illustrated* v126 no10 p26 Ap 10 2017
FEELING THE CRUNGH color *Sports Illustrated* v126 no3 p36 Ja 23 2017
L.A. Story color *Sports Illustrated* v125 no19 p106 D 12 2016
NOVEMBER Blues color *Sports Illustrated* v125 no17 p88 N 21 2016 Double Issue
Scouting Reports color *Sports Illustrated* v125 no14 p70 O 24-31 2016
Seven for The Road color *Sports Illustrated* v125 no20 p122 D 19 2016
SI's Top 100 color *Sports Illustrated* v125 no14 p94 O 24-31 2016
WHAT IF? ... WALTON AND ODEN AND ROY HAD STAYED HEALTHY? (DON'T EVEN START ON MJ) color *Sports Illustrated* v126 no11 p67 Ap 17-24 2017

Gollo, Nuria
GUARDIAN OF THE GIRL-CHILD S. O'GRADY color *Foreign Policy* no223 p36 Mr/Ap 2017

Golombek, Matthew
DRONES ON MARS color *Astronomy* v45 no7 p34 Jl 2017

GOLSBY-SMITH, TONY
MANAGEMENT IS MUCH MORE THAN A SCIENCE: THE LIMITS OF DATA-DRIVEN DECISION MAKING il *Harvard Business Review* v95 no5 p128 S/O 2017

Golson, Terry
The Soundtrack of Our Lives color *Dressage Today* v24 no1 p60 O 2017

Golston, Allan
Why Diversity Matters in Education E. G. J. Graves color *Black Enterprise* v47 no2 p8 S 2016

GOLUB, JOANNA SAYAGO
Burger [Cover story] color *Runner's World* v52 no6 p69 Jl 2017

Golub, Todd R.
Decoupling genetics, lineages, and microenvironment in IDH-mutant gliomas by single-cell RNA-seq diag *Science* v355 no6332 p1391 Mr 31 2017
Potential role of intratumor bacteria in mediating tumor resistance to the chemotherapeutic drug gemcitabine diag *Science* v357 no6356 p1156 S 15 2017

Golubov, Jordan
Mexico's invasive species plan in context bw *Science* v356 no6336 p386 Ap 28 2017

Golup, G.
Observation of a large-scale anisotropy in the arrival directions of cosmic rays above 8×1018 eV *Science* v357 no6357 p1266 S 22 2017

Golz, Paul
Interview Paul Golz A German View of D-Day L. Bradner bw *Military History* v34 no5 p14 Ja 2018

Gombe National Park (Tanzania)
The Trees of Gombe J. GOODALL and D. Rothkopf *Foreign Policy* no224 p84 My/Je 2017

Gombos, Andrew
THE BIG QUESTION cartoon *Atlantic* v318 no4 p112 N 2016
THE CONVERSATION color *Atlantic* v318 no5 p12 D 2016

Gombosi, T. I.
Xenon isotopes in 67P/Churyumov-Gerasimenko show that comets contributed to Earth's atmosphere diag *Science* v356 no6342 p1069 Je 9 2017

Gomer, Robert
Robert Gomer D. Menzel, M. C. Tringides et al *Physics Today* v70 no5 p67 My 2017

Gomes-Casseres, Benjamin
Don't Base Business Partnerships on Personal Chemistry *Harvard Business Review Digital Articles* p2 O 2 2015
Is the LinkedIn Acquisition Microsoft's Attempt to Build Its Own Alphabet? *Harvard Business Review Digital Articles* p2 Je 15 2016
Making Mergers, Acquisitions, and Other Business Combinations Work *Harvard Business Review Digital Articles* p2 Ag 6 2015
The Pfizer-Allergan Deal Shouldn't Be Just About Tax Inversion *Harvard Business Review Digital Articles* p2 N 24 2015
What Does Whole Foods Get from Amazon? Alexa, for Starters *Harvard Business Review Digital Articles* p2 Je 19 2017
What to Expect From the Dell-EMC Deal *Harvard Business Review Digital Articles* p2 O 13 2015
What We Can Learn from Merger Deals That Never Happened *Harvard Business Review Digital Articles* p2 Je 21 2016
A Yahoo Break-Up Could Be the Start of Lots of Splits *Harvard Business Review Digital Articles* p2 D 3 2015

GOMEZ, ANDRE
You've Never Seen a Pork Chop Like This color *Bon Appetit* v62 no2 p71 Mr 2017

Gomez, Carlos
THE YEAR IN BUM STEERS Sports *Texas Monthly* v45 no1 p90 Ja 2017

GOMEZ, CRISTINA
THE NEW SALES IMPERATIVE color diag il img *Harvard Business Review* v95 no2 p118 Mr/Ap 2017

Gomez, Isabella—Interviews
LATINA LESBIAN TAKES ON NEW MEANING IN TRUMP ERA Y. VILLARREAL color *Advocate* no1090 p58 Ap 2017

Gomez, Jesse
Microstructural proliferation in human cortex is coupled with the development of face processing bibl graph *Science* v355 no6320 p1 Ja 6 2017

Gomez, Juan L.
Chemogenetics revealed: DREADD occupancy and activation via converted clozapine graph *Science* v357 no6350 p503 Ag 4 2017

Gomez, Louis M.
The right network for the right problem color diag *Phi Delta Kappan* v98 no3 p8 N 2016

GOMEZ, MAURICIO
SOUTH COAST HABITAT RESTORATION: If You Build It, They Will Come: Bringing Steelhead Back to the Central Coast

color *Earth Island Journal* v32 no4 p16 Wint 2017

Gomez, Patrick

Survivor: an Outing and an Ousting color *Entertainment Weekly* no1463/1464 p21 Ap/My 2017

Gomez, Ramiro—Exhibitions

HOME AND AWAY P. SCHJELDAHL color *New Yorker* v93 no18 p72 Je 26 2017

Gomez, Selena, 1992-

All-in-Ones E. Wilson color *InStyle* v24 no5 p72 My 2017

Bazaar's Best-Dressed LIST color *Harper's Bazaar* no3657 p124 O 2017

BEST DRESS E. Wilson color *InStyle* v24 no4 p73 Ap 2017

Certain WOMEN A. Wintour color *Vogue* v207 no4 p84 Ap 2017

A FEMININE MYSTIQUE D. BLASBERG color *Vanity Fair* v59 no2 p88 F 2017

Hello! L. Brown color *InStyle* v24 no9 p76 S 2017

Hung Vanngo S. Zuckerman color *InStyle* v24 no9 p342 S 2017

On Her Own Terms [Cover story] R. Haskell color *Vogue* v207 no4 p194 Ap 2017

Team Players E. Wilson color *InStyle* v24 no10 p92 O 2017

Wizards of Waverly Place? color *Seventeen* v76 no3 p16 My 2017

Gomez, Selena, 1992—Interviews

Selena On Fire [Cover story] L. Brown color *InStyle* v24 no9 p366 S 2017

Gomez Berisso, M.

Observation of a large-scale anisotropy in the arrival directions of cosmic rays above 8×10^{18} eV *Science* v357 no6357 p1266 S 22 2017

Gómez-Gualdrón, Diego A.

Bottom-up construction of a superstructure in a porous uranium-organic crystal color graph *Science* v356 no6338 p624 My 12 2017

Gómez-López, Gonzalo

Tissue damage and senescence provide critical signals for cellular reprogramming in vivo bibl chart graph *Science* v354 no6315 paaf4445-1 N 25 2016

Gomez-Mejia, Luis R.

How Anxiety Affects CEO Decision Making *Harvard Business Review Digital Articles* p2 Jl 19 2016

Gomez Vitale, P. F.

Observation of a large-scale anisotropy in the arrival directions of cosmic rays above 8×10^{18} eV *Science* v357 no6357 p1266 S 22 2017

Gompers, Paul

What Private Equity Investors Think They Do for the Companies They Buy *Harvard Business Review Digital Articles* p2 Je 18 2015

Goncalves, Affonso

COMMON SENSE A. TAUBIN bw color *Film Comment* v52 no6 p32 N/D 2016

GONCHAR, JOANN

Command Performance color *Architectural Record* v205 no8 p109 Ag 2017

Factory Made *Architectural Record* v205 no7 p82 Jl 2017

In the Heights *Architectural Record* v204 no11 p128 N 2016

Jeanne Gang color *Architectural Record* v205 no2 p22 F 2017

Modern Reboot bw color *Architectural Record* v205 no2 p52 F 2017

Movable Feasts *Architectural Record* v204 no10 p119 O 2016

The Next Wave *Architectural Record* v205 no9 p131 S 2017

Record Hosts 19th Innovation Conference, in San Francisco *Architectural Record* v205 no7 p34 Jl 2017

Relaxed Fit *Architectural Record* v205 no6 p106 Je 2017

Second Avenue Subway *Architectural Record* v205 no4 p200 Ap 2017

Stacking the Deck: A New York residential tower presents a new take on the city's classic skyscrapers color map *Architectural Record* v205 no5 p91 My 2017

A Study in Materials *Architectural Record* v205 no1 p100 Ja 2017

A Thirst for More color diag *Architectural Record* v205 no3 p124 Mr 2017

Gonda, David D.

An environment-dependent transcriptional network specifies human microglia identity color *Science* v356 no6344 p1248 Je 23 2017

Gondolas

WISH YOU WEREN'T HERE! color *Powder* v45 no3 p142 N 2016

Gone Now (Music)

Jack Antonoff Shines a Light In the Dark S. Lansky color *Time* v189 no22 p56 Je 12 2017

Gong, Jianhui

Deep functional analysis of synII, a 770-kilobase synthetic yeast chromosome diag *Science* v355 no6329 p1047 Mr 10 2017

Engineering the ribosomal DNA in a megabase synthetic chromosome diag *Science* v355 no6329 p1049 Mr 10 2017

Gong, Xinyi

THE LOOK BOOK img *New York* v49 no26 p53 D 26 2016

Gong, Yun-Hong

Satellite-based entanglement distribution over 1200 kilometers diag graph *Science* v356 no6343 p1140 Je 16 2017

Gong Show, The (TV program)

The Gong Show K. Freeze *TV Guide* v65 no27 p30 Je 26 2017

Meet The Gong Show's New Host J. Russell *TV Guide* v65 no27 p4 Je 26 2017

Gonmadje, Christelle

Positive biodiversity-productivity relationship predominant in global forests bibl chart graph map *Science* v354 no6309 paaf8957-1 O 14 2016

GONNERMAN, JENNIFER

BRONX TALE cartoon color *New Yorker* v92 no41 p36 D 12 2016

NEIGHBORHOOD WATCHED bw cartoon *New Yorker* v93 no18 p30 Je 26 2017

Gonorrhea treatment

AROUND THE WORLD color *Science* v357 no6347 p112 Jl 14 2017

Gonsalves, Marie

I Wish My Horse's Mentor Could Be... color *Horse & Rider* v56 no6 p88 Je 2017

Gonyea, Don

MY HOMETOWN PAPER: Don Gonyea color *Columbia Journalism Review* v56 no1 p50 Spr 2017

Gonzaga University—Sports

9 GONZAGA BULLDOGS L. Schnell chart color *Sports Illustrated* v125 no15 p68 N 7 2016

OUTSIDE JOB L. Schnell color *Sports Illustrated* v126 no8 p46 Mr 20 2017

Gonzaga-Jauregui, Claudia

Distribution and clinical impact of functional variants in 50,726 whole-exome sequences from the DiscovEHR study chart graph *Science* v354 no6319 paaf6814-1 D 23 2016

Genetic identification of familial hypercholesterolemia within a single U.S. health care system chart graph *Science* v354 no6319 paaf7000-1 D 23 2016

Gonzales, Manuel

Sixth Sense and Sensibility: Daryl Gregory's novel features the conflicted members of a family of psychics *New York Times Book Review* p18 Ag 13 2017

Gonzales, Mark

Yo Soy Muslim: A Father's Letter to His Daughter *Publishers Weekly* v264 no22 p67 My 29 2017

GONZALES, MICHAEL A.

'90s TILL INFINITY: LEADERS OF THE NEW SCHOOL bw color *Ebony* v72 no8 p90 Je 2017

Gonzales, Shirley

COUNTING DOWN TO ZERO D. C. Vock *Governing* v30 no5 p38 F 2017

Gonzales, T.

Persistent effects of pre-Columbian plant domestication on Amazonian forest composition bibl chart graph map *Science* v355 no6328 p925 Mr 3 2017

GONZALEZ, ADAM

FACTORS FOR GROWTH color *Muscle & Performance* v9 no9 p50 S 2017

Five to Fight Fat color *Muscle & Performance* v9 no9 p28 S 2017

Fungus for Fuel and Muscle Growth color *Muscle & Performance* v9 no10 p30 O 2017

Gonzalez, Andrew

Effects of network modularity on the spread of perturbation impact in experimental metapopulations diag graph *Science* v357 no6347 p199 Jl 14 2017

Gonzalez, Anthony—Interviews
Anthony Gonzalez As an Explorer of the Afterlife S. Begley color *Time* v190 no10/11 p110 S 18 2017

Gonzalez, Barb
Roku Ultra Streaming Player color *Sound & Vision* v82 no2 p48 F/Mr 2017

Gonzalez, Carlos G.
Seasonal cycling in the gut microbiome of the Hadza hunter-gatherers of Tanzania diag *Science* v357 no6353 p802 Ag 25 2017

Gonzalez, Desi
THE PUBLIC AS PRODUCER *Art in America* v104 no9 p82 O 2016

Gonzalez, Eiza
Eiza GONZÁLEZ *Interview* v47 no5 p68 Je/Jl 2017

Gonzalez, Enrique
MAKING THEIR HORSES — AND THEIR MARK K. F. Miller color *Practical Horseman* v45 no3 p28 Mr 2017

González, Gabriela, 1965-
Gabriela González M. Hagan *Current Biography* v77 no10 p35 O 2016

Gonzalez, Inez
SAN IGNACIO DEL BABACOMARI F. C. BROPHY *Arizona Highways* v93 no4 p36 Ap 2017

Gonzalez, Joey—Interviews
What I Wear to Work J. Chen color *Bloomberg Businessweek* no4504 p67 D 19 2016

Gonzalez, Jorge
Jojo's Got the Mojo J. SCHILDHOUSE color *Muscle & Performance* v9 no9 p32 S 2017

GONZÁLEZ, JOSÉ G.
Estamos Aquí *Orion Magazine* v35 no4/5 p49 Jl-O 2016

González, Justo L.
Decline and rise C. Scharen color *Christian Century* v134 no4 p46 F 15 2017
The Evolution of Sunday M. BARRETT color *Christianity Today* v61 no5 p70 Je 2017
WRITERS' FEAST color *Christian Century* v134 no10 p30 My 10 2017

Gonzalez, Karina
Reframing the Climate Narrative *Earth Island Journal* v32 no4 p56 Wint 2017

GONZALEZ, KENNITH
Why I'm For Donald Trump [Cover story] *New York Times Upfront* v149 no4 p13 O 31 2016

Gonzalez, Luz E.
Representation Matters color *Glamour* v115 no11 p22 N 2017

Gonzalez, Maria
Your Car Commute Is a Chance to Practice Mindfulness *Harvard Business Review Digital Articles* p2 N 13 2014

GONZALEZ, MIKE
An Elegy for Venezuela's Revolution *In These Times* v41 no7 p15 Jl 2017

Gonzalez, N.
Observation of a large-scale anisotropy in the arrival directions of cosmic rays above 8 × 1018 eV *Science* v357 no6357 p1266 S 22 2017

Gonzalez, Patrick
Merging paleobiology with conservation biology to guide the future of terrestrial ecosystems color *Science* v355 no6325 p594 F 10 2017

Gonzalez, Ramon
Industrial biomanufacturing: The future of chemical production bibl chart color diag graph *Science* v355 no6320 p1 Ja 6 2017

González, Rigoberto
Rudolfo Anaya *Humanities* v37 no4 p1 Fall 2016

González Alonso, Pablo
When Should Multinationals Move Back into Venezuela? *Harvard Business Review Digital Articles* p2 S 1 2017

González-Andrieu, Cecilia
America, Be Beautiful *America* v217 no2 p54 Jl 24 2017
A Life Lived in God's Love color *America* v216 no5 p18 Mr 6 2017
Students of Color Face a Trump Presidency *America* v215 no18 p16 D 5 2016
Who Is My Neighbor? color *America* v215 no13 p21 O 31 2016

González-López, Olga

MAVS-dependent host species range and pathogenicity of human hepatitis A virus bibl graph *Science* v353 no6307 p1541 S 30 2016

Gonzalez Trotter, Dinko
Systemic pan-AMPK activator MK-8722 improves glucose homeostasis but induces cardiac hypertrophy graph *Science* v357 no6350 p507 Ag 4 2017

Goobar, A.
iPTF16geu: A multiply imaged, gravitationally lensed type Ia supernova color diag graph *Science* v356 no6335 p291 Ap 21 2017

Gooch, Brad
A Sufi's Second Act A. MOAVENI *New York Times Book Review* p18 Ja 22 2017

Gooche, Louise
LIVE Long AND PROSPER [Cover story] A. GIACOBBE and J. MIGALA color *Women's Health* v14 no1 p170 Ja/F 2017

Good & evil
See also
Guilt (Psychology)
Make today great again P. W. Marty *Christian Century* v133 no22 p3 O 26 2016

Good, Caroline
CAPTURING THE CAT: The arrival of big cats to 19th-century London forced a change in the image left by mythology and the Old Masters *History Today* v67 no10 p36 O 2017

Good, Gregory A.
Gathering the human stories of science *Physics Today* v70 no5 p74 My 2017

GOOD, REBEL
COURT of APPEALS color *Tennis* v53 no2 p8 Mr/Ap 2017
COURT of APPEALS *Tennis* v53 no1 p6 Ja/F 2017
COURT of APPEALS *Tennis* v53 no3 p12 My/Je 2017
In Box *Tennis* v53 no4 p14 Jl/Ag 2017

Good Behavior (TV program)
CHEERS & JEERS D. HOLBROOK *TV Guide* p96 D 5 2016
Good Behavior A. Bacle, D. Coggan et al *Entertainment Weekly* no1482/1483 p39 S 22 2017
Good Behavior J. Jensen color *Entertainment Weekly* no1439 p50 N 11 2016
GOOD GIRL GONE BAD I. RUDOLPH *TV Guide* v64 no46 p22 N 7 2016

Good Bones (TV program)
FIXER UPPER FILL-INS TO FLIP OVER D. Rovenstine color *Entertainment Weekly* no1486 p51 O 13 2017
NaILed IT J. Vrabel *Indianapolis Monthly* p70 F 2017

Good Earth (Company)
Earthly Pleasures N. BRARA color *Vogue* v207 no11 p166 N 2017

Good for You (Music)
What to Stream color *Entertainment Weekly* no1476 p60 Ag 4 2017

Good Friday
Homeless bodies J. McBride *Christian Century* v134 no6 p28 Mr 15 2017

Good Girls Revolt (TV program)
The Real-Life Rebellion Behind Amazon's Good Girls Revolt E. Dockterman color *Time* v188 no20 p56 N 14 2016
Women's work P. H. Nettleton color *U.S. Catholic* v82 no3 p38 Mr 2017

Good Life (Music)
Get Up, Stand Up for Reggae J. POET color *Downbeat* v84 no8 p77 Ag 2017

Good Morning America (TV program)
how to ORGANIZE EVERYTHING J. PHILLIP color *Good Housekeeping* v264 no3 p47 Mr 2017
THE WORLD ACCORDING TO Gayle color *O, The Oprah Magazine* p36 D 2016

Good Time (Film)
Caught in the Act R. Brody cartoon *New Yorker* v93 no23 p10 Ag 7 2017
DESPERADOES A. LANE color *New Yorker* v93 no24 p82 Ag 21 2017
Good Time K. P. Sullivan color *Entertainment Weekly* no1478 / 1479 p84 Ag 18-25 2017
Pattinson Packs a Punch In Good Time S. Zacharek color *Time* v190 no7 p51 Ag 21 2017

Good Will Hunting (Film)
GOOD WILL HUNTING J. Shipley *Yankee* p27 Mr 2017
Goodall, Amanda
If Your Boss Could Do Your Job, You're More Likely to Be Happy
  at Work *Harvard Business Review Digital Articles* p2 D 29 2016
Why The Best Hospitals Are Managed by Doctors *Harvard Busi-*
  ness Review Digital Articles p2 D 27 2016
Goodall, Jane, 1934-
Becoming Jane [Cover story] T. GERBER bw color map *National*
  Geographic v232 no4 p30 O 2017
The Trees of Gombe *Foreign Policy* no224 p84 My/Je 2017
Goodall, Jane, 1934---Interviews
Date with DIANE D. V. Furstenberg color *InStyle* v24 no9 p202
  S 2017
Goodall, Susie
Susie Goodall A. Schell color *Sail* v48 no10 p18 O 2017
Goodavage, Maria
America's Canine Protectors S. Begley color *Time* v188 no19 p16
  N 7 2016
Goodbye Christopher Robin (Film)
GOODBYE CHRISTOPHER ROBIN I. Biedenharn color *Enter-*
  tainment Weekly no1478 / 1479 p54 Ag 18-25 2017
Goodbye Yellow Brick Road (Music)
Essential Elton John R. Sheffield bw color *Rolling Stone* no1283
  p52 Mr 23 2017
Good Doctor, The (TV program)
FREDDIE HIGHMORE OF The Good Doctor N. Abrams, C.
  Holub et al color *Entertainment Weekly* no1482/1483 p54 S 22
  2017
THE GOOD DOCTOR I. Rudolph *TV Guide* v65 no37 p24 S 4
  2017
New Fall TV: Winners and Losers J. HALTERMAN *TV Guide*
  v65 no43 p4 O 16 2017
Television img *New York* v50 no17 p98 Ag 21 2017
Goode, Chris
How Juicing Changed My Life K. Wilder and A. GUMBS color
  Black Enterprise v47 no4 p46 N/D 2016
Goode, Robin White
Get to Know Your Campus Career Development Office color
  Black Enterprise v47 no3 p32 O 2016
THE GREAT CHARTER SCHOOL DEBATE color *Black Enter-*
  prise v47 no5 p32 Ja/F 2017
IN THE CHAMPION'S CIRCLE color graph *Black Enterprise*
  v47 no7 p64 My/Je 2017
NETWORKING ISN'T JUST FOR WORK color *Black Enter-*
  prise v47 no8 p34 Jl/Ag 2017
Out From the Shadow of the Valley color *Black Enterprise* v47
  no4 p18 N/D 2016
A RARE SPECIES color *Black Enterprise* v47 no8 p31 Jl/Ag
  2017
STANDING UP FOR OUR STUDENTS color *Black Enterprise*
  v47 no7 p28 My/Je 2017
Goodell, Jeff
Covering the Climate color *Rolling Stone* no1297 p22 O 5 2017
The Doomsday Glacier color *Rolling Stone* no1287 p44 My 18
  2017
The Governor's Superstorm color *Rolling Stone* no1297 p31 O
  5 2017
SCOTT PRUITT'S CRIMES AGAINST NATURE color *Rolling*
  Stone no1293 p44 Ag 10 2017
WILL WE MISS OUR LAST CHANCE? bw color *Rolling Stone*
  no1278/1279 p28 Ja 12 2017
Goodell, Roger, 1959-
Happily Ever After ... color *Sports Illustrated* v126 no5 p112 F
  13 2017
Goodell, Roger, 1959---Political & social views
CHIEF CONCERNS FOOTBALL IS... color *Sports Illustrated*
  v125 no17 p57 N 21 2016 Double Issue
Gooder, Lee
IDEA OF THE MONTH P. Barbour *Successful Farming* v114
  no13 p90 D 2016
Goodfellas (TV program)
LATE NIGHT L. ACKEN *TV Guide* v64 no48 p45 N 21 2016
Goodfellow, Ian
INVENTORS E. Beras, C. Garling et al color il *MIT Technology*
  Review v120 no5 p56 S/O 2017

Neurodevelopmental protein Musashi-1 interacts with the Zika
  genome and promotes viral replication diag *Science* v357
  no6346 p83 Jl 7 2017
Good Fight, The (Film)
Short Circuit J. Fuchs and T. Keith color *Sports Illustrated* v126
  no13 p22 My 8 2017
Good Fight, The (TV program)
The Good Fight J. Jensen color *Entertainment Weekly*
  no1454/1455 p85 F 24 2017
THE GOOD FIGHT L. Rice color *Entertainment Weekly*
  no1446/1447 p68 D 2016/Ja 2017
The GOOD LIFE I. Rudolph color *TV Guide* v65 no7 p30 F 13
  2017
GOOD NEWS L. Rice color *Entertainment Weekly* no1453 p28
  F 17 2017
Packing Even More Punch Into The Good Fight L. Rice color *En-*
  tertainment Weekly no1463/1464 p14 Ap/My 2017
GOODHAND, JONATHAN
The Tangled Politics of Postwar Justice in Sri Lanka *Current His-*
  tory v116 no789 p130 Ap 2017
Goodhart, David
Those Who Leave and Those Who Stay J. MILLER *In These*
  Times v41 no7 p41 Jl 2017
Goodhart, Pippa
My Very Own Space *Publishers Weekly* v264 no19 p58 My 8 2017
Goodheart, Eugene
Revolution: Removing its Halo *Society* v54 no2 p100 Ap 2017
Good Housekeeping Institute (New York, N.Y.)
TECH OF ALL TRADES S. Tedesco color *Good Housekeeping*
  v265 no2 p6 Ag 2017
GOODKIND, TERRY
THOUGHTS ON Conflict *Forbes* v199 no4 p112 Ap 25 2017
Goodknight, Joseph
Taking six-dimensional spectra in finite time diag *Science* v356
  no6345 p1333 Je 30 2017
Goodluck, Kalen
TRUMP'S TROOPS *Mother Jones* v41 no6 p31 N/D 2016
Goodman, Allan
Lifeline for refugee scholars color *Science* v354 no6317 p1207
  D 9 2016
GOODMAN, ALLEGRA
F.A.Q.s cartoon *New Yorker* v93 no27 p62 S 11 2017
Goodman, Allegra---Interviews
Allegra Goodman *New York Times Book Review* p6 Jl 16 2017
Goodman, Amy, 1957-
Speech Lessons L. RATNER *Nation* v303 no19 p4 N 7 2016
When Journalism Gets a Jail Threat, Most Media Respond With
  Silence [Cover story] J. Naureckas *Extra!* v29 no8 p1 O 2016
Goodman, Amy, 1957---Interviews
'This Country Is at a Tipping Point' N. Stockwell cartoon color
  Progressive v81 no10 p35 N 2016
Goodman, Carolyn
The Mayors Goodman J. Buntin *Governing* v30 no4 p46 Ja 2017
GOODMAN, DANIEL ROSS
An Unquiet Belle color *Weekly Standard* v22 no25 p42 Mr 6 2017
Goodman, Emma
Early life stress confers lifelong stress susceptibility in mice via
  ventral tegmental area OTX2 diag *Science* v356 no6343 p1185
  Je 16 2017
Goodman, Fred
Sam Cooke Had a Hammer bw color *American History* v52 no2
  p56 Je 2017
GOODMAN, JAMES
The Other 1 Percent *New York Times Book Review* p25 O 9 2016
Profiles in Caution: In the heart of the civil rights struggle, a poli-
  tician and an activist found common ground *New York Times*
  Book Review p9 Jl 2 2017
Goodman, Jessica
2 — MY FAVORITE MURDER color *Entertainment Weekly*
  no1444/1445 p114 D 16 2016
3 — KEEPIN' IT 1600 *Entertainment Weekly* no1444/1445 p114
  D 16 2016
3 REINVENTIONS WE CAN'T WAIT TO HEAR color *Enter-*
  tainment Weekly no1446/1447 p76 D 2016/Ja 2017
THE CHAINSMOKERS *Entertainment Weekly* no1446/1447 p76
  D 2016/Ja 2017

DAVE EGGERS GETS POLITICAL color *Entertainment Weekly* no1436/1437 p16 O 21 2016

EVANESCENCE'S AMY LEE color *Entertainment Weekly* no1443 p60 D 9 2016

FIFTH HARMONY HIT A SOUR NOTE color *Entertainment Weekly* no1446/1447 p28 D 2016/Ja 2017

Ginger Spice color *Entertainment Weekly* no1460/1461 p71 Ap 7-17 2017

Heartless color *Entertainment Weekly* no1440 p62 N 18 2016

AN ICON REMEMBERED color *Entertainment Weekly* no1448 p33 Ja 13 2017

MUSIC color *Entertainment Weekly* no1444/1445 p88 D 16 2016

NIALL HORAN *Entertainment Weekly* no1446/1447 p75 D 2016/ Ja 2017

Paying R-E-S-P-E-C-T to "Respect" color *Entertainment Weekly* no1453 p59 F 17 2017

WHO D.R.A.M color *Entertainment Weekly* no1439 p59 N 11 2016

Wild Writer Walks on Washington color *Entertainment Weekly* no1451/1452 p18 F 3-10 2017

Goodman, Jillian

PRIDE AND PROTOCOL color *Bloomberg Businessweek* no4523 p63 My 22 2017

STOCK THE PANTRY color *Bloomberg Businessweek* no4500 p70 N 21 2016

Goodman, Jo

A Touch of Frost *Publishers Weekly* v264 no16 p53 Ap 17 2017

Goodman, Joan F.

The shame of shaming color *Phi Delta Kappan* v99 no2 p26 O 2017

Goodman, Lauren

WISH LIST 2016 color *Wired* v24 no12 p45 D 2016

Goodman, Lenn

Listening and Hearing *Society* v54 no2 p163 Ap 2017

GOODMAN, LEONARD C.

War Profiteering Ain't Physics *In These Times* v41 no6 p12 Je 2017

We Have a Villain. We Need a Vision *In These Times* v41 no3 p16 Mr 2017

Goodman, Lizzy

Conor Oberst Goes Home img *New York* v49 no19 p88 S 19 2016

The Last Moment of the Last Great Rock Band img *New York* v50 no10 p86 My 15 2017

Love, Cleo img *New York* v49 no25 p89 D 12 2016

New York Stories A. GREENE color *Rolling Stone* no1290 p17 Je 29 2017

Goodman, Myra

The Search for Simple and Good color *AARP: The Magazine* v60 no5A p58 Ag/S 2017

Goodman, Oscar Baylin, 1939-

The Mayors Goodman J. Buntin *Governing* v30 no4 p46 Ja 2017

GOODMAN, PETER

A New Concept for Indie Bookstores *Publishers Weekly* v264 no20 p60 My 15 2017

Goodman, Robert M.

H. Boyd Woodruff (1917–2017) bw *Science* v356 no6336 p381 Ap 28 2017

Goodman, Sherri

Changing Climates for Arctic Security bw color *Wilson Quarterly* p1 Summ 2017

GOODMAN, WENDY

1 An Experiment in the Woods img *New York* v49 no21 p80 O 17 2016

2 Sleep With the Fishes img *New York* v49 no21 p86 O 17 2016

5 Forever Futuristic img *New York* v49 no21 p96 O 17 2016

A Camper on the Ceiling img *New York* v49 no19 p65 S 19 2016

Halloween All Year img *New York* v49 no15 p69 Jl 25 2016

"Interwar Technicolor Dream House" img *New York* v50 no7 p59 Ap 3 2017

Second Home img *New York* p43 Ja 23 2017

SPRING DESIGN: ART img *New York* v50 no8 p81 Ap 17 2017

This Old Boardinghouse: A once-abandoned Boerum Hill building got stripped down to its bones and built back up again img *New York* v50 no13 p63 Je 26 2017

Wonder Brothers: The Goethe-, Tolstoy-, and Melnikov-inspired Carroll Gardens apartment of two young siblings and business

partners img *New York* v50 no12 p78 Je 12 2017

Goodnight, Charles, 1836-1929

It Happened Here: Palo Duro Canyon M. Coppock color *American Cowboy* p65 LEGENDS OF TEXAS Special Issue 2017

It Happened Here: Weatherford bw map *American Cowboy* p70 LEGENDS OF TEXAS Special Issue 2017

TEXAS TITANS bw *American Cowboy* p58 LEGENDS OF TEXAS Special Issue 2017

Goodnight, Julie

Alone on the Trail color *Horse & Rider* v56 no11 p46 N 2017

Around the Campfire L. Ann Puana, T. Kincade et al color *Trail Rider* v29 no2 p6 Mr 2017

Be Trail-Tack Savvy color *Horse & Rider* v56 no9 p51 S 2017

Canter with Confidence color *Trail Rider* v29 no4 p44 My 2017

Chaps by Discipline K. Navarra color *Horse & Rider* v55 no12 p58 D 2016

Ground Work at Liberty color *Trail Rider* v29 no1 p40 Ja/F 2017

Open a Trail Gate color *Horse & Rider* v56 no8 p46 Ag 2017

Safety in Numbers color *Trail Rider* v29 no3 p24 Ap 2017

Settle Your Cinchy Horse color *Trail Rider* v29 no2 p42 Mr 2017

Take Charge color *Horse & Rider* v56 no7 p51 Jl 2017

Trip Tips color *Trail Rider* v29 no3 p6 Ap 2017

Turn Back for Safety color *Horse & Rider* v56 no10 p48 O 2017

Women's Riding and Wholeness Retreat color *Trail Rider* v29 no1 p14 Ja/F 2017

Good Place, The (TV program)

A GOOD MAN EMERGES D. Snierson color *Entertainment Weekly* no1471 p56 Je 23 2017

THE GOOD PLACE BREAKS BAD D. Snierson color *Entertainment Weekly* no1472 p14 Je 30 2017

THE GOOD PLACE J. Russell *TV Guide* v65 no39 p47 S 18 2017

HEAVEN HELP US J. McDERMOT color *America* v215 no14 p37 N 7 2016

I LOVE LUCIFER E. NUSSBAUM cartoon *New Yorker* v92 no48 p78 F 6 2017

The Must List color *Entertainment Weekly* no1484 p9 S 29 2017

Siri, Who's the Good Place Scene-Stealer? N. Abrams color *Entertainment Weekly* no1436/1437 p93 O 21 2016

Streaming S. Li color *Entertainment Weekly* no1477 p44 Ag 11 2017

What to Watch R. Rahman, D. Snierson et al color *Entertainment Weekly* no1449 p54 Ja 20 2017

Goodreads Inc.

Goodreads Marks 10 Years of Supporting Books, Reading C. Reid color *Publishers Weekly* v264 no39 p12 S 25 2017

Goodrich, David W.

Rb1 and Trp53 cooperate to suppress prostate cancer lineage plasticity, metastasis, and antiandrogen resistance bibl graph *Science* v355 no6320 p1 Ja 6 2017

SOX2 promotes lineage plasticity and antiandrogen resistance in TP53- and RB1-deficient prostate cancer bibl graph *Science* v355 no6320 p1 Ja 6 2017

GOODRICH, JANE

The House That Changed Everything bw color *Yankee* p30 Mr 2017

GOODRICH, KATIE

CHANGE the CITY *Indianapolis Monthly* p55 Ap 2017

DANCERS AT EL CHISPAS *Indianapolis Monthly* v40 no11 p18 Jl 2017

Hot on the TRAILS: A ROAD-FREE GUIDE TO EXPLORING CENTRAL INDIANA *Indianapolis Monthly* v40 no10 p59 Je 2017

Goodrich, Maxwell M.

Rb1 and Trp53 cooperate to suppress prostate cancer lineage plasticity, metastasis, and antiandrogen resistance bibl graph *Science* v355 no6320 p1 Ja 6 2017

Goodrich, Terry Lee

New Smithsonian museum aids Baylor's preservation of black gospel recordings *Christian Century* v133 no21 p18 O 12 2016

Goodrich, Zachary W.

Rb1 and Trp53 cooperate to suppress prostate cancer lineage plasticity, metastasis, and antiandrogen resistance bibl graph *Science* v355 no6320 p1 Ja 6 2017

GOODSON, LEELEE

'Ain't Doing Right': NO MATTER YOUR AGE, BEING OPEN TO NEW LOVE IS NEVER EASY color *Yankee* p122 Jl 2017

Good Wife, The (TV program)
Julianna Margulies C. Ianzito color *AARP: The Magazine* v59 no4A p76 Je/Jl 2016

Goodwin, A. H.
Celebrating S&T's 75th Anniversary *Sky & Telescope* v133 no2 p6 F 2017

Goodwin, Daisy
Daisy Goodwin on Victoria, Victoria and Victoria-The Queen, Novel and Show S. Gutierrez *British Heritage Travel* v38 no1 p38 Ja/F 2017
NEVERTHELESS, HER MAJESTY PERSISTED color *Foreign Policy* no223 p46 Mr/Ap 2017
Victoria: A Novel B. Patrick *British Heritage Travel* v37 no6 p78 N/D 2016
Victoria color *Publishers Weekly* v263 no45 p38 N 7 2016

Goodwin, Daisy—Interviews
DAISY GOODWIN T. Jordan color *Entertainment Weekly* no1451/1452 p110 F 3-10 2017

GOODWIN, DORIS KEARNS
OFFICE POLITICS bw color *Vanity Fair* v58 no11 p156 N 2016

Goodwin, Elizabeth
The Selfie, Medieval Style *History Today* v67 no2 p6 F 2017

Goodwin, George
DEPICTING REVOLUTION AND INDEPENDENCE *History Today* v67 no8 p102 Ag 2017
Flying a Kite with Franklin T. Stanley *History Today* v67 no2 p62 F 2017

Goodwin, Gordon
BIG PHAT PRODUCTION VALUES color *Downbeat* v84 no2 p88 F 2017

GOODWIN, JASON
Birth of the Modern Middle East: This account of the region's modernizers points to the complexity of Muslim identities *New York Times Book Review* p20 Jl 23 2017
QUEEN'S ISLAM *New York Times Book Review* p50 D 4 2016

Goodwin, John Noble, 1824-1887
Governor's Mansion N. AUSTIN *Arizona Highways* v93 no11 p6 N 2017

Goodwin, Julia
Welcome *House Beautiful* p3 Ag 2017

Goodwin, Lauren
The Dos and Don'ts of Working with Emerging-Market Data *Harvard Business Review Digital Articles* p2 Jl 8 2016

GOODWIN, MATTHEW
What Brexit Means for Britain *Current History* v116 no788 p107 Mr 2017

Goodwin, Matthew David
Latin@ Rising: An Anthology of Latin@ Science Fiction & Fantasy color *Publishers Weekly* v264 no1 p40 Ja 2 2017

Goodwin, Michael
The Collapse of Fair-Minded Journalism *USA Today Magazine* v146 no2868 p12 S 2017
The Myth of the Tech Whiz Who Quits College to Start a Company *Harvard Business Review Digital Articles* p2 Ja 9 2015

Goodwin, Shikha Jain
My lessons in mentorship color *Science* v356 no6344 p1302 Je 23 2017

Goodwin, Victoria M.
The microbial metabolite desaminotyrosine protects from influenza through type I interferon graph *Science* v357 no6350 p498 Ag 4 2017

Goodyear, Dana
DUNGEONS AND DRAGONS cartoon *New Yorker* v93 no15 p18 My 29 2017
IT HAPPENED HERE diag *New Yorker* v93 no29 p40 S 25 2017
STRAWBERRY VALLEY cartoon *New Yorker* v93 no24 p30 Ag 21 2017
VALLEY CATS cartoon color *New Yorker* v92 no49 p44 F 13 2017

Goodyear Corp.
GUMSHOES E. TINGWALL chart color *Car & Driver* v63 no2 p66 Ag 2017

Goodyear Tire & Rubber Co.
Ball Bearing Might autonomous cars be borne on airless basketballs? F. Markus color *Motor Trend* v69 no7 p28 Jl 2017

Google (Web resource)

4 REASONS WHY I SWITCHED FROM GOOGLE TO BING M. Hachman color *PCWorld* v35 no9 p83 S 2017
DISMISS the Dis G. D. MELTON cartoon *O, The Oprah Magazine* p37 My 2017
Google combats fake news with 'Fact Check' results in search and news I. PAUL color *PCWorld* v35 no5 p57 My 2017
Google, Yelp, and the Future of Search J. Gans *Harvard Business Review Digital Articles* p2 Jl 10 2015
Nicely Subversive R. Ward *Skeptical Inquirer* v41 no5 p65 S/O 2017
Your Most-Googled Summer Body Issues… M. Choi color *Glamour* v114 no7 p71 Jl 2016

Google AdWords (Web resource)
Google's Opioid Ad Addiction M. Smith, J. Levin et al color *Bloomberg Businessweek* no4540 p21 O 2 2017

Google Analytics (Web resource)
7 Marketing Technologies Every Company Must Use L. Gudema *Harvard Business Review Digital Articles* p2 N 3 2014

Google Calendar (Web resource)
The Tools You Need to Make Every Meeting More Productive A. Samuel *Harvard Business Review Digital Articles* p2 Mr 12 2015

Google Chrome (Computer software)
Gmail is dumping Windows XP and Vista, now what? I. PAUL color *PCWorld* p165 Mr 2017
Google Chrome will start blocking noisy autoplay videos in January B. CHACOS color *PCWorld* v35 no10 p14 O 2017
How to switch to Chrome's Material Design settings page for an easier experience I. PAUL color *PCWorld* p170 Mr 2017

Google Docs (Web resource)
The 8 Digital Productivity Tools Everyone Should Adopt A. Samuel *Harvard Business Review Digital Articles* p2 Je 20 2016

Google Fiber Inc.
Toto, I've a Feeling We're Still In Kansas (or Missouri) S. McBride and M. Bergen color *Bloomberg Businessweek* no4514 p33 Mr 13 2017

Google Glass
Google Glass Failed Because It Just Wasn't Cool U. Haque *Harvard Business Review Digital Articles* p2 Ja 30 2015

Google Home (Smart speaker)
HOME SMART HOME K. PITSKER bw color *Kiplinger's Personal Finance* v71 no10 p64 O 2017
Smart Speakers: Which Is the Best Buy? B. Tuttle color *Money* v46 no8 p14 S 2017

Google Inc.
9 free ways to get the most out of Google's Play Music app B. PATTERSON color *PCWorld* v35 no1 p201 Ja 2017
Beyond Surfing D. HARRELL cartoon *Education Digest* v82 no7 p32 Mr 2017
Commercial Overfishing map *Discover* v38 no2 p17 Mr 2017
The Conversation Google Killed W. SALETAN *Weekly Standard* v22 no48 p31 S 4 2017
Data Monopolists Like Google Are Threatening the Economy K. Radinsky *Harvard Business Review Digital Articles* p2 Mr 2 2015
Daydream View: Sparse content is all that stands between Google and VR greatness J. CROSS color *PCWorld* v35 no1 p145 Ja 2017
DISRUPTION IN THE CLASSROOM R. Alrubail *Literacy Today (2411-7862)* v34 no5 p36 Mr/Ap 2017
Feedback N. A. Smith color graph *MIT Technology Review* v119 no6 p8 N/D 2016
A Giant in Search, But a Wisp in the Cloud M. Bergen *Bloomberg Businessweek* no4498 p53 N 7 2016
Google Adds Benefits, Walmart Cuts Them; Oddly, the Logic Is the Same P. Cappelli *Harvard Business Review Digital Articles* p2 N 7 2014
GOOGLE ASSISTANT: 5 KILLER NEW FEATURES YOU SHOULD BE USING R. WHITWAM color *PCWorld* v35 no8 p121 Ag 2017
GOOGLE BACKUP AND SYNC: WORKS BEST FOR THOSE ALREADY TIED INTO GOOGLE'S ECOSYSTEM G. FLEISHMAN color *Macworld - Digital Edition* v34 no9 p17 S 2017
Google brands malicious websites with 'repeat offender' warnings I. PAUL color *PCWorld* v35 no1 p54 Ja 2017

Google Builds Operating System From Scratch S. ORNES bw diag *Discover* v38 no1 p52 Ja/F 2017

Google Couldn't Survive with One Strategy M. Reeves *Harvard Business Review Digital Articles* p2 Ag 18 2015

Google Drive dumps Windows XP and Vista, now what? I. PAUL color *PCWorld* p56 D 2016

Google Drive is being replaced by Backup and Sync: What to expect M. HACHMAN color *PCWorld* v35 no10 p10 O 2017

Google Home: Google puts its A.I. on a nightstand for the win J. PHILLIPS color *PCWorld* p115 D 2016

Google may slam the brakes on its self-driving car to partner with auto makers P. SAYER color *PCWorld* v35 no1 p33 Ja 2017

Google's $2.7 Billion Antitrust Fine T. John color *Time* v190 no2/3 p9 Jl 10-17 2017

Google Searches for Its Voice L. Eadicicco color diag *Time* v190 no16/17 p68 O 23 2017

GOOGLE'S ELITE HACKER SWAT TEAM VS. EVERYONE R. Hackett color *Fortune* v176 no1 p60 Jl 1 2017

Google's Fuchsia OS is out in the open and shrouded in mystery C. HOFFMAN color *PCWorld* p22 O 2016

Google's next wearable is a $350 Levi's jacket that controls music by brushing your sleeve M. SIMON color *PCWorld* v35 no4 p29 Ap 2017

Google's Quantum Leap T. Simonite color *MIT Technology Review* v120 no4 p22 Jl/Ag 2017

Google's Secret Formula for Management? Doing the Basics Well R. Sadun *Harvard Business Review Digital Articles* p2 2017

Google Wifi: Mesh networking made easy M. BROWN color graph *PCWorld* v35 no1 p59 Ja 2017

How I deleted Google from my life S. AXON color diag *PCWorld* v35 no7 p179 Jl 2017

In Ads We Trust A. Vance color *Bloomberg Businessweek* no4521 p6 My 8 2017

INSIDE GOOGLE'S MOONSHOT FACTORY D. Thompson cartoon color *Atlantic* v320 no4 p60 N 2017

It's Baaack color *Weekly Standard* v22 no46 p2 Ag 14 2017

Look familiar? M. Gurman color *Bloomberg Businessweek* no4494 p33 O 10 2016

Modified Limited Hangouts D. HARSANYI *National Review* v69 no18 p44 O 2 2017

Net Results color *Vogue* v207 no3 p254 Mr 2017

New Streaming Devices A. D'ARMINIO *TV Guide* p14 D 5 2016

Pixel XL review : Google's new phone isn't a Nexus—it's better J. CROSS color graph *PCWorld* v35 no11 p46 N 2016

Q&A WITH ALEXANDER BREGMAN color *Publishers Weekly* v263 no43 p(Sp)23 O 24 2016

Shut Up, They Explained A. Keiper color *Weekly Standard* v22 no47 p15 Ag 21 2017

Silicon Valley's Registry Problem img *New York* v49 no26 p17 D 26 2016

A Spotlight on Harassment at Google E. Huet and M. Bergen *Bloomberg Businessweek* no4525 p33 Je 5 2017

This AI flushes out trolls R. Verger and J. Will color *Popular Science* v289 no6 p65 N/D 2017

The Thread G. Chiu, K. Goldberg et al *New York Times Magazine* p7 Ja 1 2017

The timing is perfect for a new Chromebook Pixel M. SIMON color *PCWorld* v35 no10 p16 O 2017

Want to Do Corporate Innovation Right? Go Inside Google Brain G. Satell *Harvard Business Review Digital Articles* p2 Je 1 2016

WE HAVE SEEN THE LIGHT color *Men's Health* v31 no10 p(Sp)32 D 2016

Where the digital dollars have gone S. Hepworth, C. Spike et al graph *Columbia Journalism Review* p58 Fall/Wint 2016

Why Google Became Alphabet T. Zenger *Harvard Business Review Digital Articles* p2 Ag 11 2015

You can now send and receive money right in the Android Gmail app M. SIMON color *PCWorld* v35 no4 p44 Ap 2017

You Will Not Think Outside the Box C. ROSEN *Commentary* v144 no2 p7 S 2017

Google Inc.—Finance

Google Returns to Earth M. Chafkin and M. Bergen color *Bloomberg Businessweek* no4503 p44 D 12 2016

Google Inc.—Management

GOOGLE SEARCHES ITS SOUL E. McGirt color diag *Fortune* v175 no2 p48 F 1 2017

Google Inc.—Officials & employees

100 BEST COMPANIES TO WORK FOR 2017 [Cover story] M. C. Bush, S. Lewis-kulin et al color diag map *Fortune* v175 no4 p79 Mr 15 2017

Q+A: Jessica Brillhart J. Pontin color *MIT Technology Review* v120 no2 p28 Mr/Ap 2017

Google Maps

Google Maps tips color *PCWorld* v35 no9 p112 S 2017

The Sports Bar B. Gregory and P. Kita cartoon *Men's Health* v32 no2 p30 Mr 2017

Summer SURVIVAL GUIDE N. SAPORITA color *Good Housekeeping* v264 no6 p69 Je 2017

UNITED WAYPOINTS A. FISHER *Wired* v24 no12 p90 D 2016

Google Ngrams (Web resource)

A Quick Guide to Avoiding Common Writing Errors M. Fogarty *Harvard Business Review Digital Articles* p2 Jl 22 2015

Google Translate (Web resource)

US AND HIS KINGDOM OF THE FLUBBINGS OF SHADOWS J. SHANE cartoon color *Wired* v25 no10 p22 O 2017

Google Inc.—Trials, litigation, etc.

Google vs. the EU Explains the Digital Economy B. Iyer and U. S. Rangan *Harvard Business Review Digital Articles* p2 D 12 2016

Googling Ourselves (Poem)

GOOGLING OURSELVES P. Schultz *New Yorker* v93 no33 p76 O 23 2017

Goon (Performer)

The Playlist color *Rolling Stone* no1274 p10 N 17 2016

Goon: Last of the Enforcers (Film)

ALSO PLAYING color *Entertainment Weekly* no1478 / 1479 p41 Ag 18-25 2017

Goop Inc.

A symptom of a deeper problem A. KINGSTON color *Maclean's* v130 no7 p8 Ag 2017

The Wellness Epidemic A. LAROCCA img *New York* v50 no13 p38 Je 26 2017

Goose Island Beer Co.

CHINA'S NEW CRAFT-BEER BULLY S. Cendrowski color diag *Fortune* v175 no4 p152 Mr 15 2017

Goose migration

CHASING THE GHOSTS OF APRIL R. MARR color *Missouri Life* v44 no2 p62 Ap 2017

HARDSHIP HONKERS B. FITZPATRICK and A. ROBINSON color *Outdoor Life* v224 no8 p43 O 2017

Goose shooting

THE COLD OPEN C. KEARNS cartoon color *Field & Stream* v121 no7 p18 D 2016/Ja 2017

Down and Out (of Sight) T. E. Nickens color *Field & Stream* v122 no5 pF1 O 2017

FIND YOUR CALLING D. Draper, B. ALLEN et al color *Field & Stream* v122 no5 p50 O 2017

INCOMING GREENHEADS T. CARPENTER color *Outdoor Life* v224 no8 pW1 O 2017

LIGHT AS A FEATHER color *Outdoor Life* v224 no7 pW10 S 2017

GOOSEFF, MICHAEL

The Impact of a Large-Scale Climate Event on Antarctic Ecosystem Processes chart graph *BioScience* v66 no10 p848 O 1 2016

Responses of Antarctic Marine and Freshwater Ecosystems to Changing Ice Conditions color graph *BioScience* v66 no10 p864 O 1 2016

Goossens, Sander

Gravity field of the Orientale basin from the Gravity Recovery and Interior Laboratory Mission bibl graph *Science* v354 no6311 p438 O 28 2016

Gootenberg, Jonathan S.

Nucleic acid detection with CRISPR-Cas13a/C2c2 color diag *Science* v356 no6336 p438 Ap 28 2017

Gopal, Prashant

Apple's Way-Open House color *Bloomberg Businessweek* no4497 p34 O 31 2016

Cleaning up in the wake of hurricanes, tornadoes, and other catastrophes has become a lucrative business for companies such as Cavalry color *Bloomberg Businessweek* no4538 p17 S 18 2017

Homebuilders Look to Trump for a Mood Lift cartoon *Bloomberg Businessweek* no4508 p35 Ja 23 2017

The Housing Crunch Hits the Heartland cartoon *Bloomberg Busi-*

nessweek no4516 p36 Mr 27 2017

Houston and the Politics of Immigration color *Bloomberg Businessweek* no4537 p31 S 11 2017

Make all rent checks payable to: WALL STREET graph *Bloomberg Businessweek* no4506 p30 Ja 9 2017

Robots Will Build Your Next House color *Bloomberg Businessweek* no4519 p43 Ap 24 2017

Want a $1 Million Paycheck? Skip College and Go Work in A Lumberyard bw color graph *Bloomberg Businessweek* no4529 p32 Jl 3 2017

Gopalakrishnan, Shyam

An Anthropocene map of genetic diversity bibl graph map *Science* v353 no6307 p1532 S 30 2016

Gopalakrishnan, Vancheswaran

Potential role of intratumor bacteria in mediating tumor resistance to the chemotherapeutic drug gemcitabine diag *Science* v357 no6356 p1156 S 15 2017

GOPALAN, RADHAKRISHNAN

COMP TARGETS THAT WORK: HOW TO KEEP EXECUTIVES FROM GAMING THE SYSTEM color graph img *Harvard Business Review* v95 no5 p102 S/O 2017

Gopnik, Adam

AMERICANISMS cartoon *New Yorker* v92 no49 p29 F 13 2017

AMERICAN NIRVANA cartoon *New Yorker* v93 no23 p69 Ag 7 2017

BRUSH UP YOUR SHAKESPEARE cartoon *New Yorker* v92 no33 p85 O 17 2016

THE ILLIBERAL IMAGINATION cartoon *New Yorker* v93 no5 p88 Mr 20 2017

Magic in a Web *New York Times Book Review* p24 N 13 2016

MIXED UP cartoon *New Yorker* v92 no45 p81 Ja 16 2017

A NEW MAN cartoon color *New Yorker* v93 no19 p61 Jl 3 2017

NO CIGAR cartoon *New Yorker* v92 no47 p20 Ja 30 2017

Onward and Upward: In his new memoir, Adam Gopnik recounts a charmed decade in 1980s New York V. GORNICK *New York Times Book Review* p14 O 1 2017

RATTLING THE CAGE cartoon color *New Yorker* v93 no8 p71 Ap 10 2017

SHOT OF COURAGE cartoon *New Yorker* v93 no30 p64 O 2 2017

STREET CRED bw cartoon *New Yorker* v92 no30 p69 S 26 2016

Till Dinner Do Us Part A. GOPNIK color *Walrus* v14 no8 p36 O 2017

Till Dinner Do Us Part color *Walrus* v14 no8 p36 O 2017

WE COULD ALL HAVE BEEN CANADIANS cartoon *New Yorker* v93 no13 p79 My 15 2017

Gopnik, Alison

MAKING AI MORE HUMAN color *Scientific American* v316 no6 p60 Je 2017

SCREEN BEE cartoon *New Yorker* v92 no39 p70 N 28 2016

Why Be a Parent? M. Angell bw color *New York Review of Books* v63 no17 p8 N 10 2016

Goralski, Maria

Anticancer sulfonamides target splicing by inducing RBM39 degradation via recruitment to DCAF15 color diag *Science* v356 no6336 p397 Ap 28 2017

Gorant, Jim

The Case for ... Fewer Cowboys color *Sports Illustrated* v126 no11 p29 Ap 17-24 2017

DAWG DAYS color *Sports Illustrated* v127 no5 p28 Ag 14 2017

Ears to Mouth color *Sports Illustrated* v126 no15 p24 My 29 2017

Swing Shift color *Sports Illustrated* v126 no15 p22 My 29 2017

Gorbachev, Mikhail Sergeevich, 1931-

'It All Looks As If the World Is Preparing for War' color *Time* v189 no5 p22 F 13 2017

Leaders color *Time* v189 no16/17 p64 My 1-8 2017

The New Russia R. Legvold *Foreign Affairs* v95 no6 p186 N/D 2016

Gorbachova, Liudmyla

Changing climate shifts timing of European floods color graph *Science* v357 no6351 p588 Ag 11 2017

Gorbunova, Vera

A conserved NAD+ binding pocket that regulates protein-protein interactions during aging bibl graph *Science* v355 no6331 p1312 Mr 24 2017

Gordeliy, Valentin

Mechanism of transmembrane signaling by sensor histidine kinases color *Science* v356 no6342 p1043 Je 9 2017

Gorder, Genevieve

qenevieve GORDER N. DAYTON *Better Homes & Gardens* v94 no11 p14 N 2016

Gordham, Pravin

A Bananas Republic? A. EGAN *America* v215 no15 p12 N 14 2016

Gordillo, Ruth

An adipo-biliary-uridine axis that regulates energy homeostasis diag *Science* v355 no6330 p1173 Mr 17 2017

Gordimer, Nadine, 1923-2014

IT CAME N. Gordimer *Lapham's Quarterly* v10 no3 p34 Summ 2017

Gordinier, Jeff

86 the Tasting Menu? color *Esquire* v167 no1 p26 F 2017

The Best New RESTAURANTS IN AMERICA, 2017 bw color *Esquire* p62 N 2017

COOK BY NUMBERS bw color *Esquire* p22 Ag 2017

GENIE IN A BOTTLE cartoon color *Esquire* p42 S 2017

GO NATUREL IN PARIS color *Esquire* p100 My 2017

HOW TO SOUND LIKE A SERIOUS GASTRONOME cartoon *Esquire* p121 S 2017

I'M WITH STUPID color *Esquire* p15 Je/Jl 2017

IS THIS GUY THE MOST HATED RESTAURATEUR IN AMERICA? cartoon color *Esquire* v167 no2 p56 Mr 2017

MAKE AMERICA HAPPY AGAIN color *Esquire* v167 no1 p60 F 2017

Martini, Please, No BS color *Esquire* v166 no5 p46 D 2016/Ja 2017

THE NEXT MEAT MAESTROS color *Esquire* p20 Je/Jl 2017

Pacific Heights color *Esquire* v166 no4 p32 N 2016

THE PASSION OF DANIEL bw color *Esquire* v167 no2 p136 Mr 2017

RENÉ REDZEPI'S MEXICO color *Esquire* p28 My 2017

SERVICE CHECK bw color *Esquire* p34 O 2017

The Tao of Hosting bw color *Esquire* v166 no5 p33 D 2016/Ja 2017

TIME FOR A MAN-CATION! color *Esquire* p114 O 2017

WINE GONE WILD color *Esquire* p98 My 2017

YES, THIS IS HEALTHY cartoon color *Esquire* p23 Ap 2017

Gordis, Daniel

A Biography of Zion A. HERNROTH-ROTHSTEIN *Commentary* v142 no3 p44 O 2016

Making a Nation-State D. GREEN color *National Review* v68 no24 p36 D 31 2016

Gordiyenko, Yuliya

Translational termination without a stop codon bibl color *Science* v354 no6318 p1437 D 16 2016

Gordon, Alastair

Design as Salvation F. A. Bernstein *Architectural Record* v205 no1 p43 Ja 2017

GORDON, ASCELIN

Metaresearch for Evaluating Reproducibility in Ecology and Evolution *BioScience* v67 no3 p282 Mr 2017

Gordon, Avishag

Sleeping Beauties of Political Science: The Case of AF Bentley chart graph *Society* v54 no4 p355 Ag 2017

GORDON, BRUCE

Reading the Reformation in 2017 bw color *Christianity Today* v61 no1 p46 Ja/F 2017

Gordon, Daniel

'Civilization' and the Self-Critical Tradition *Society* v54 no2 p106 Ap 2017

Gordon, David N.

Rapid development of a DNA vaccine for Zika virus bibl graph *Science* v354 no6309 p237 O 14 2016

GORDON, DEBRA L.

Office De-stress Ideas color *Reader's Digest* v189 no1130 p49 My 2017

Gordon, Dee

Bad Girls from History: Wicked or Misunderstood? *Publishers Weekly* v264 no41 p55 O 9 2017

GORDON, DEVIN

20 Dad Hacks for Enjoying Dadhood cartoon chart color *GQ: Gentlemen's Quarterly* v97 no7 p32 Jl 2017

The Cultural Saturation Chart bw color *GQ: Gentlemen's Quarterly* v86 no11 p72 N 2016

The Ten Who'll Be Next color *GQ: Gentlemen's Quarterly* v97 no11 p114 N 2017

Gordon, Donald—Awards

Scotland stalwart given top accolade *People Management* p56 F 2017

GORDON, DORIA R.

Society Is Ready for a New Kind of Science--Is Academia? *BioScience* v67 no7 p591 Jl 2017

Gordon, Douglas—Exhibitions

DOUGLAS GORDON A. Rosenmeyer color *Art in America* v105 no4 p125 Ap 2017

Gordon, Ed

THE FIRST EVER BLACK MEN A. A. Edmond Jr. bw color *Black Enterprise* v47 no7 p40 My/Je 2017

Gordon, Edmund

Absolutely Fabulist R. FRANKLIN *New York Times Book Review* p16 Mr 26 2017

The Invention of Angela Carter *Publishers Weekly* v264 no2 p57 Ja 9 2017

METAMORPHOSES J. ACOCELLA cartoon color *New Yorker* v93 no4 p71 Mr 13 2017

She Escaped to Become Original A. Lurie bw *New York Review of Books* v64 no4 p16 Mr 9 2017

Gordon, Elizabeth

From Our Editor S. Donelson *House Beautiful* v159 no5 p8 Je 2017

GORDON, EMILY FOX

Against Solidarity: AS A WRITER, WITH A WRITER'S CHRONIC NEED FOR DETACHMENT, I HAVE AVOIDED THE IDEOLOGY OF GENDER *American Scholar* v86 no4 p61 Aut 2017

Read 'Em and Weep: A book club leads the author deep into her sorrows *New York Times Book Review* p25 O 8 2017

Gordon, Emily V.

The Romantic Comedian E. Berman color *Time* v190 no1 p49 Jl 3 2017

GORDON, EVELYN

Getting Settled *Commentary* v144 no2 p44 S 2017

Gordon, Evelyn J.

What Do New Faculty Members Want From Their University? *Change* v49 no4 p52 Jl/Ag 2017

Gordon, Hamish

Global atmospheric particle formation from CERN CLOUD measurements bibl graph map *Science* v354 no6316 p1119 D 2 2016

GORDON, JAMES

NO ARGUMENTS FOR NON-RENEWABLES color *Alternatives Journal (AJ) - Canada's Environmental Voice* v42 no2 p78 2016

Gordon, Jeffrey I.

Food and microbiota in the FDA regulatory framework color *Science* v357 no6346 p39 Jl 7 2017

Lactobacillus reuteri induces gut intraepithelial CD4+CD8αα+ T cells diag graph *Science* v357 no6353 p806 Ag 25 2017

Gordon, Jeremy

Fair-Weather Fandom *New York Times Magazine* p28 Ja 15 2017

GORDON, JOHN STEELE

Dispelling the Myths *Commentary* v143 no2 p42 F 2017

The Napoleon of Modesty *Commentary* v143 no1 p52 Ja 2017

Sacrifice on the Western Front *Commentary* v142 no1 p50 Jl/Ag 2016

Sex Cells *Commentary* v144 no2 p53 S 2017

Gordon, Joshua—Interviews

Mental health chief to stress neural circuits M. Wadman color *Science* v354 no6311 p405 O 28 2016

Gordon, Jullien

CELEBRATE C. K. Jackson color *Essence* v47 no8 p152 D 2016

GORDON, KAREN L.

A Rubric to Evaluate Citizen-Science Programs for Long-Term Ecological Monitoring *BioScience* v67 no9 p834 S 2017

Gordon, Ken

You Can Talk About Innovation Without Resorting to Cliches *Harvard Business Review Digital Articles* p2 F 4 2016

Gordon, Kim—Interviews

KIM GORDON K. O'Donnell color *Entertainment Weekly*

no1440 p59 N 18 2016

Gordon, Linda

The Second Coming of the KKK: The Ku Klux Klan of the 1920s and the American Political Tradition *Publishers Weekly* v264 no35 p119 Ag 28 2017

GORDON, MALCOLM S.

Anesthesia and Euthanasia of Amphibians and Reptiles Used in Scientific Research: Should Hypothermia and Freezing Be Prohibited? *BioScience* v67 no1 p53 Ja 2017

Gordon, Marsha

Film Is Like a Battleground: Sam Fuller's War Movies L. DOMBROWSKI *Film Quarterly* v70 no4 p130 Summ 2017

The Good Fight S. EYMAN bw color *Film Comment* v53 no2 p78 Mr/Ap 2017

GORDON, MARY

Echoes of a Lost Faith T. Deignan color *Commonweal* v144 no8 p40 My 5 2017

Mea Culpa: A Brooklyn convent provides a fragile refuge from a family's shame *New York Times Book Review* p11 O 8 2017

TENDER IS THE PAST H. CAIN color *O, The Oprah Magazine* p82 Je 2017

There Your Heart Lies *Publishers Weekly* v264 no12 p47 Mr 20 2017

GORDON, MERYL

Good Old New Journalism color *New York Times Book Review* p15 Ja 29 2017

WHEN JACKIE MET BUNNY color *Vanity Fair* v59 no10 p144 O 2017

GORDON, PETER E.

AFTER THE INFERNO color *Nation* v304 no7 p31 Mr 6 2017

Call Him Karl *New York Times Book Review* p24 O 23 2016

Kierkegaard's Rebellion bw color *New York Review of Books* v63 no17 p21 N 10 2016

Gordon, Philip

The Crisis in U.S.- Israeli Relations *Foreign Affairs* v95 no6 p132 N/D 2016

A Vision of Trump at War color *Foreign Affairs* v96 no3 p10 My/Je 2017

Gordon, Robby

THE 18TH ANNUAL SAND SPORTS SUPER SHOW M. EMERY color *Dirt Sports + Off-Road* v51 no2 p8 F 2017

GONE, BUT NOT FORGOTTEN M. Emery *Dirt Sports + Off-Road* v51 no3 p6 Mr 2017

Gordon, Robert J.

Productivity and progress *Monthly Labor Review* p1 S 2017

Gordon, Seth, 1976-

Baywatch C. Nashawaty color *Entertainment Weekly* no1468/1469 p88 Je 2-9 2017

BAYWATCH L. Rice color *Entertainment Weekly* no1446/1447 p56 D 2016/Ja 2017

Baywatch Proves There's Nothing Wrong With a Little Skin, Sand and Surf S. Zacharek color *Time* v189 no21 p57 Je 5 2017

Gordon, Stephen V.

Red squirrels in the British Isles are infected with leprosy bacilli bibl color diag map *Science* v354 no6313 p744 N 11 2016

Gordon, Tom

Nuclear Power and Risk Psychology *Skeptical Inquirer* v41 no2 p64 Mr/Ap 2017

Gordon, Vernita

Coupling and sharing when life is hard color *Science* v356 no6338 p583 My 12 2017

Gordon, Zachary

A bioinspired iron catalyst for nitrate and perchlorate reduction bibl diag *Science* v354 no6313 p741 N 11 2016

GORDON MAH UNG

AMD Threadripper grab: Dell's Alienware shuts out other major vendors for 2017 color *PCWorld* v35 no7 p19 Jl 2017

Intel revealed the Core i9 ship dates, but you won't like them chart color *PCWorld* v35 no7 p9 Jl 2017

Optane Memory: Why you may want Intel's futuristic cache in your PC color diag graph *PCWorld* v35 no7 p101 Jl 2017

Gordon Research Conferences

Gordon Research Conferences [Cover story] color *Science* v355 no6327 p848 F 24 2017

Gordon-Levitt, Joseph, 1981-

Snowden *New Yorker* v92 no30 p17 S 26 2016

On the road again color *Yoga Journal* no291 p12 My 2017

practice imperfect *Yoga Journal* p6 2017 Special Issue

Relief is here! *Yoga Journal* p3 2017 SpecialIssue

seekers WANTED color *Yoga Journal* no288 p15 D 2016

Together we rise color *Yoga Journal* no287 p10 N 2016

United we practice bw *Yoga Journal* no292 p10 Je 2017

We are one color *Yoga Journal* no291 p16 My 2017

What matters most color *Yoga Journal* no294 p12 S 2017

Why we practice *Yoga Journal* no290 p12 Mr 2017

YOU, EVEN STRONGER! *Yoga Journal* p6 2017 Special Issue

Younger every year *Yoga Journal* p4 2017 Special Issue

GORRIVAN, PHILIP

Have It Both Ways color *House Beautiful* v159 no4 p30 My 2017

Gorski, Philip

Becoming America *Christian Century* v134 no5 p28 Mr 1 2017

Gorsuch, Neil M., 1967-

Angling for a Supreme Pick F. BARNES *Weekly Standard* v22 no22 p10 F 13 2017

CASE STUDIES J. Toobin cartoon *New Yorker* v93 no7 p33 Ap 3 2017

The Democrats v. Gorsuch color *National Review* v69 no7 p13 Ap 17 2017

An Education in Civility N. M. Gorsuch *Weekly Standard* v23 no5 p9 O 9 2017

For the Record color *Time* v189 no5 p6 F 13 2017

A Great Scalia Successor T. Eastland *Weekly Standard* v22 no22 p8 F 13 2017

Higher Justice [Cover story] A. J. White color *Weekly Standard* v22 no23 p20 F 20 2017

How Neil Gorsuch Is Shaking Up the Supreme Court T. Berenson color *Time* v190 no15 p9 O 16 2017

Neil Gorsuch M. Rich color *Current Biography* v78 no9 p23 S 2017

Patriotic Gorsuch *Commentary* v143 no3 p23 Mr 2017

Soundbites *Extra!* v30 no2 p2 Mr 2017

Supreme BATTLE P. SMITH, D. Victor et al *New York Times Upfront* v149 no10 p14 Mr 13 2017

Supreme Extremism *America* v216 no6 p8 Mr 20 2017

Trump's Supreme Court Pick Puts Democrats In a Bind T. Berenson and S. Frizell color diag *Time* v189 no5 p10 F 13 2017

Under the Law J. Underwood color *Phi Delta Kappan* v98 no7 p76 Ap 2017

The Value of Life M. Hemingway *Weekly Standard* v22 no22 p9 F 13 2017

Gorton, Jessica

You Never Forget Your First Time diag il *Backpacker* v45 no2 p64 Mr 2017

GORZELANY, JIM

THE FAST AND THE LUXURIOUS color *Forbes* v200 no4 p60 O 24 2017

TECH TO THE FUTURE color *Forbes* v198 no6 p74 N 8 2016

Gosalia, Nehal

Distribution and clinical impact of functional variants in 50,726 whole-exome sequences from the DiscovEHR study chart graph *Science* v354 no6319 paaf6814-1 D 23 2016

Goscha, Christopher

Vietnam before the War *History Today* v67 no2 p20 F 2017

Goshawk—Behavior

MURRAY M. TERRA-BERNS *Idaho Magazine* v16 no6 p32 Mr 2017

Goshen College

TOP 150 BACCALAUREATE COLLEGES chart *Washington Monthly* v49 no9/10 p114 S/O 2017

Gosling, Ryan, 1980-

Cover *Entertainment Weekly* no1446/1447 pC1 D 2016/Ja 2017

Disney Darlings Who Kill J. McGovern color *Entertainment Weekly* no1467 p16 My 26 2017

GOSLING'S FIRST LAW OF STYLE bw *GQ: Gentlemen's Quarterly* v87 no1 p100 Ja 2017

How to Replicate a Hit P. Travers color *Rolling Stone* no1298 p53 O 19 2017

La La Land, a Truly Modern Hollywood Musical, Strikes All the Best Chords R. Bruner color *Time* v188 no24 p61 D 12 2016

La La Land *New Yorker* v92 no42 p32 D 19 2016

LEADING MAN C. Heath bw color *GQ: Gentlemen's Quarterly* v87 no1 p40 Ja 2017

PROP MASTER R. Goldberg color *Wired* v25 no10 p12 O 2017

RYAN GOSLING HAS ANOTHER KILLER LOOK cartoon color *Esquire* p64 S 2017

Sound Bites color *Entertainment Weekly* no1449 p10 Ja 20 2017

A tonic for the times B. D. JOHNSON color *Maclean's* v129 no50 p56 D 19 2016

Gosling, Ryan, 1980—Interviews

RYAN GOSLING IN Blade Runner 2049 S. Vilkomerson color *Entertainment Weekly* no1478 / 1479 p52 Ag 18-25 2017

Gosnell, Greer

Virgin Atlantic Tested 3 Ways to Change Employee Behavior *Harvard Business Review Digital Articles* p2 Ag 1 2016

Gospel, The (Music)

The Playlist color *Rolling Stone* no1275 p8 D 1 2016

Gospel music

New Smithsonian museum aids Baylor's preservation of black gospel recordings T. L. Goodrich *Christian Century* v133 no21 p18 O 12 2016

Gospel singers—United States

MAKING GOD FAMOUS V. CUNNINGHAM cartoon color *New Yorker* v92 no45 p26 Ja 16 2017

Gossaert, Jan, ca. 1478-ca. 1532

Redefining family J. Bleem color *U.S. Catholic* v81 no12 p50 D 2016

Gosselaar, Mark-Paul

WATCH THIS/SORRY ABOUT THAT D. Snierson color *Entertainment Weekly* no1438 p51 N 4 2016

Gosselin, David

An environment-dependent transcriptional network specifies human microglia identity color *Science* v356 no6344 p1248 Je 23 2017

Gosseries, Olivia

Reactivation of latent working memories with transcranial magnetic stimulation bibl graph *Science* v354 no6316 p1136 D 2 2016

Gossett, Reina—Interviews

The New Girls L. Dunham and J. Konner color *Glamour* v115 no2 p108 F 2017

Gossip

How to Tell the Difference Between Venting and Office Gossip L. Davey *Harvard Business Review Digital Articles* p2 N 29 2016

How to Work for a Gossipy Boss R. Knight color *Harvard Business Review Digital Articles* p2 Ja 23 2017

The real truth about gossip *Redbook* p132 Je 2017

What You Can Do If You Have a Gossiping Boss J. Grenny *Harvard Business Review Digital Articles* p2 N 21 2016

Gossip Girl (TV program)

AND THIS WAS BEFORE INSTAGRAM J. DUBOFF color *Vanity Fair* v59 no10 p197 O 2017

Gossip in the workplace

The Antidote to Office Gossip A. Bassuk and C. Lew *Harvard Business Review Digital Articles* p2 N 11 2016

How to Steer Clear of Office Gossip V. Lipman *Harvard Business Review Digital Articles* p2 O 19 2016

Stop Enabling Gossip on Your Team J. Grenny *Harvard Business Review Digital Articles* p2 Ja 9 2015

Gostic, Katelyn M.

Maternal antibodies' role in immunity bibl color *Science* v355 no6326 p704 F 17 2017

Potent protection against H5N1 and H7N9 influenza via childhood hemagglutinin imprinting bibl chart graph *Science* v354 no6313 p722 N 11 2016

Gosudarstvennyi Ermitazh (Russia)

Blooming Genius M. OWENS color *Architectural Digest* v74 no10 p180 O 1 2017

Goswami, Amit

The Everything Answer Book: How Quantum Science Explains Love, Death, and the Meaning of Life *Publishers Weekly* v264 no7 p68 F 13 2017

Goswami, Sangeeta

Genetic biomarker for cancer immunotherapy diag *Science* v357 no6349 p358 Jl 28 2017

GOSWAMI, VARUN R.

Conserving the World's Megafauna and Biodiversity: The Fierce Urgency of Now *BioScience* v67 no3 p197 Mr 2017

Saving the World's Terrestrial Megafauna color *BioScience* v66

no10 p807 O 1 2016

Goszczko, Ilona
Greater role for Atlantic inflows on sea-ice loss in the Eurasian Basin of the Arctic Ocean chart diag graph *Science* v356 no6335 p285 Ap 21 2017

Gotanda, Kiyoko M.
Precipitation drives global variation in natural selection bibl chart diag map *Science* v355 no6328 p959 Mr 3 2017

Gotham (TV program)
CHEERS & JEERS D. HOLBROOK *TV Guide* v64 no40 p88 O 3 2016
Gotham N. Abrams, B. L. Heldman et al *Entertainment Weekly* no1482/1483 p84 S 22 2017
Our Reporter Heads to Gotham D. Holbrook *TV Guide* p8 Ap 17 2017

Gotham, Rich
How an NBA Team Thinks About Data, Talent, and Pricing D. Rousmaniere *Harvard Business Review Digital Articles* p2 Mr 23 2015

Gothelf, Jeff
Bring Agile to the Whole Organization *Harvard Business Review Digital Articles* p2 N 14 2014
How HR Can Become Agile (and Why It Needs To) *Harvard Business Review Digital Articles* p2 Je 19 2017
You Need to Manage Digital Projects for Outcomes, Not Outputs color *Harvard Business Review Digital Articles* p2 F 6 2017

Gothic revival (Architecture)
A Cottage Bathroom P. Poore bw color *Old House Journal* v45 no5 p66 Ag 2017
GOTHIC HORROR bw color *Old House Journal* v45 no4 p88 Je 2017
Gothic Revival M. ETHERINGTON-SMITH color *Architectural Digest* v73 no11 p152 N 2016

GOTO, STEPHANIE
Kitchens color *Architectural Digest* no11 p73 N 1 2017

Gott, Lisa M.
A Thirty-Something Girl *Publishers Weekly* v264 no21 p65b My 22 2017

Gottesman, Omri
Distribution and clinical impact of functional variants in 50,726 whole-exome sequences from the DiscovEHR study chart graph *Science* v354 no6319 paaf6814-1 D 23 2016
Genetic identification of familial hypercholesterolemia within a single U.S. health care system chart graph *Science* v354 no6319 paaf7000-1 D 23 2016

Gottesman, Susan
Not just Salk color *Science* v357 no6356 p1105 S 15 2017

GOTTFRIED, PAUL
The Enduring Lessons of Disraeli's Sybil *American Conservative* v16 no5 p62 S/O 2017
The Uses and Misuses of 'Fascism' *Society* v54 no4 p315 Ag 2017

Gottfried, Paul E.
MEN IN BLACK M. Ledeen *Claremont Review of Books* v17 no2 p39 Spr 2017

Gotthardt, Michael
Fructose-driven glycolysis supports anoxia resistance in the naked mole-rat diag graph *Science* v356 no6335 p307 Ap 21 2017

Gottlieb, Amy
The Beautiful Possible: A Novel A. Frykholm *Christian Century* v134 no11 p42 My 24 2017

Gottlieb, Andrew C.
Mythical River *Orion Magazine* v35 no4/5 p107 Jl-O 2016

GOTTLIEB, ANTHONY
The Rake's Progress *New York Times Book Review* p14 Ja 8 2017

GOTTLIEB, JENNA
COALITION CRISIS *Iceland Review* v55 no1 p72 Ja/F 2017
GEYSIR'R GRAPHIC DESIGNER *Iceland Review* v54 no6 p68 N/D 2016
HAILING HELICOPTER *Iceland Review* v55 no1 p10 Ja/F 2017
LIGHTING UP REYKJAVÍK *Iceland Review* v55 no2 p6 Mr/Ap 2017

GOTTLIEB, LORI
The Other Side of 40 *New York Times Book Review* p23 O 9 2016
The Power to Heal: By helping patients uncover past trauma, a therapist and survivor of Auschwitz comes closer to understanding her own *New York Times Book Review* p19 O 8 2017

Gottlieb, Michael D.
Lobbying Is Not Enough to Build Influence Among U.S. Lawmakers *Harvard Business Review Digital Articles* p2 D 28 2016

Gottlieb, Robert
Allegro Con Brio *New York Times Book Review* p1 Jl 2 2017
'A Monstrous Prodigy' R. Gottlieb bw *New York Review of Books* v63 no19 p27 D 8 2016
The Best of Words T. MALLON bw *New York Times Book Review* p17 S 25 2016
Brilliant, Touching, Tough bw color *New York Review of Books* v64 no5 p39 Mr 23 2017
In the Mood for Love *New York Times Book Review* p1 O 1 2017
The Long-Distance Reader C. Benfey bw *New York Review of Books* v63 no18 p21 N 24 2016
'Make 'Em Cry, Make 'Em Laugh, Make 'Em Wait' color *New York Review of Books* v64 no10 p25 Je 8 2017

Gottlieb, Scott
Is a Cigarette Without the Nicotine Still A Smoke? A. Edney and J. Kaplan cartoon graph *Bloomberg Businessweek* no4533 p37 Ag 7 2017
Needed: A Spine Transplant for the FDA: The new chief of the Food and Drug Administration must move fast, avoid politics, and confront overregulation H. I. Miller *Hoover Digest: Research & Opinion on Public Policy* no3 p45 Summ 2017

Gottlieb, Steve
Galaxies in Collision *Sky & Telescope* v133 no5 p28 My 2017
George Abell's Ethereal Bubbles *Sky & Telescope* v134 no1 p34 Jl 2017

Gottman, Julie Schwartz
The Good FIGHT A. Atkins cartoon *O, The Oprah Magazine* p92 F 2017

Gottschalk, Kurt
Art Ensemble Origin Story bw *Downbeat* v84 no6 p80 Je 2017
Rock 'n' Roll 'n' Romance at (le) Poisson Rouge color *Downbeat* v84 no2 p46 F 2017
Signs of Changing Times bw *Downbeat* v84 no10 p72 O 2017
Spiritual Awakenings color *Downbeat* v84 no7 p61 Jl 2017

Gottscheers
GOTTSCHEE QUESTION R. Corbett cartoon *New Yorker* v93 no19 p20 Jl 3 2017

Gottwald, Lukasz, 1973-
OUTSIDERS THE EXILE T. Brodesser-Akner *New York Times Magazine* p41 O 30 2016

Gouaux, Eric
Cryo-EM structures of the triheteromeric NMDA receptor and its allosteric modulation graph *Science* v355 no6331 p1282 Mr 24 2017

Goucher College
Goucher College *Dance Magazine* v90 p67 2016/2017 Supplement College Guide

Gouda cheese
GOOEY, GRILLED CRISPY, MELTY, AND CHEESE! GLORIOUS color *O, The Oprah Magazine* p130 Mr 2017

Goudarzi, Sara
The Milky Way, Transformed color *Scientific American* v315 no6 p14 D 2016
Unstacking the Deck *American Scholar* v86 no3 p14 Summ 2017
What Lies Beneath color *Scientific American* v315 no5 p11 N 2016

Goud Collins, Margaret
Sea change bibl color *Science* v355 no6329 p1030 Mr 10 2017

Goude, Ingrid
FEBRUARY 1960 H. Martin bw color *Popular Photography* v81 no1 p104 Ja/F 2017

Goudie, Adrew
SAVAGE NOBLES AND NOBLE SAVAGES R. Carver *History Today* v67 no8 p101 Ag 2017

Gough, Denise
REDEMPTION SONG A. GREEN color *Vogue* v207 no10 p288 O 2017

Goujard, Clothilde
Trade Fears Grip America's Northern Neighbor *Wilson Quarterly* p4 Spr 2017

Goukassian, Elena
19 THINGS YOU REALLY OUGHT TO 00 THIS MONTH *Washingtonian Magazine* v52 no3 p31 D 2016

performance audits? K. Barrett and R. Greene *Governing* v30 no12 p60 S 2017

Government agencies—United States—Officials & employees
Federal employees contemplate what would make them leave N. TABOR *New York* v50 no17 p50 Ag 21 2017

Government agency reorganization
DEEP BACKGROUND P. GIRALDI *American Conservative* v16 no1 p36 Ja/F 2017
Making Government Reorgs Work S. Heidari-Robinson color *Harvard Business Review Digital Articles* p2 Mr 30 2017

Government aid
See also
Government aid to education
Government aid to museums

Government aid to education
D.C. Opportunity Scholarship Program: Impacts of a Federally Funded School Voucher Program *Congressional Digest* v96 no7 p7 S 2017
Illinois budget impasse damaging state universities D. Kramer *Physics Today* v70 no6 p32 Je 2017

Government aid to education—New York (State)
Money for Class Trips *New York State Conservationist* v71 no4 p28 F 2017

Government aid to museums
Engaging the third solitude J. GEDDES *Maclean's* v130 no7 p14 Ag 2017

Government aid to religious education
WHAT CAN WE EXPECT FROM THE SUPREME COURT'S NEW TERM? E. K. BOEGEL color *America* v215 no12 p13 O 24 2016

Government aid to research
See also
Federal aid to research
Business backs the basics S. Suresh and R. A. Bradway color *Science* v354 no6309 p151 O 14 2016
Fund global health: Save lives and money A. P. Galvani, M. C. Fitzpatrick et al color *Science* v356 no6342 p1018 Je 9 2017
Global Disparity in Ecological Science: A Complex Systems Perspective V. H. MARÍN and L. E. DELGADO *BioScience* v67 no2 p105 F 2017
A top mathematician joins the Macron revolution E. Pain color *Science* v356 no6344 p1223 Je 23 2017

Government attorneys
See also
Public defenders

Government comptrollers
THE ACCOUNTANT *Texas Monthly* v45 no2 p90 F 2017

Government laboratories
Can a trusting relationship between DOE and its labs be restored? D. Kramer *Physics Today* v70 no3 p27 Mr 2017
TINY BUILDING BLOCKS OFFER OUTSIZED PROTECTION AND BREATHABILITY R. Hansen *Science & Technology Review* p20 D 2016

Government liability (International law)
U.S. Court Jurisdiction and Foreign States *Congressional Digest* v95 no9 p5 N 2016

Government Mule (Performer)
Jam's Working-Class Heroes D. FRICKE color *Rolling Stone* no1293 p19 Ag 10 2017

Government policy
See also
Emigration & immigration—Government policy
Environmental policy
CHALLENGING THE STATUS QUO WITH STEM CELLS C. Tompot *Saturday Evening Post* v289 no1 p70 Ja/F 2017
From abalone to advocacy A. R. Frederick color *Science* v357 no6349 p422 Jl 28 2017
FROM THE ARCHIVES V. POSTREL, T. W. HAZLETT et al cartoon *Reason* v48 no10 p66 Mr 2017
How to Design a Return Policy N. Janakıraman, H. Syrdal et al *Harvard Business Review Digital Articles* p2 Ag 2 2016
How to Produce Translational Research to Guide Arctic Policy A. H. FLEMING and N. D. PYENSON *BioScience* v67 no6 p490 Je 2017
Public Policy and Advocacy Outlook for 2017 D. Tyahla *Parks & Recreation* v52 no1 p18 Ja 2017

Why the U.S. Government Is Embracing Behavioral Science F. Gino *Harvard Business Review Digital Articles* p2 S 18 2015

Government policy on climate change
Lean In to Climate Change G. MCCARTHY color *Foreign Policy* no224 p76 My/Je 2017
THE NEW CLIMATE B. Latour *Harper's Magazine* v334 no2004 p13 My 2017
THE Timely DISAPPEARANCE of CLIMATE CHANGE DENIAL IN CHINA G. Dembicki color *Foreign Policy* no224 p58 My/Je 2017
The Wages of Sin Is the Death of the World D. ROTHKOPF color *Foreign Policy* no224 p74 My/Je 2017

Government policy on information technology
Disrupted Government: Florida wants to cut IT costs. But is the state going about it all wrong? T. Newcombe *Governing* v30 no9 p62 Je 2017

Government policy on renewable energy sources
States Lead the Way with Renewable Energy Policy *Mother Earth News* no284 p6 O/N 2017
The World United to Save the Earth: The global movement of serious investment in renewable energy continues, despite President Trump's campaign pledge to focus on the domestic coal and oil industries S. A. CATOVIC *Islamic Horizons* v46 no3 p42 My/Je 2017

Government policy—United States
INEQUALITY IN EARLY CHILDHOOD AND EFFECTIVE PUBLIC POLICY INTERVENTIONS *Economic Indicators* p153 S 2016
The Night Data Died A. FERGUSON *Commentary* v142 no5 p10 D 2016
PHOTO color *Reason* v48 no11 p7 Ap 2017
School Discipline Reform and Disorder M. Eden *Education Digest* v83 no1 p22 S 2017
SEDENTARY SENATE T. MCCLINTOCK *USA Today Magazine* v145 no2864 p22 My 2017
The West Coast Fights Back Against Trump S. ABRAMSKY color il *Nation* v304 no6 p16 F 27 2017

Government publications—Exhibitions
Ford Motor Company Fund Supports Featured Document Exhibit *Prologue* v49 no1 p71 Spr 2017

Government publications—United States
25th JFK Assassination Secrets Scheduled for 2017 Release J. Sanburn color *Time* v188 no27-28 p119 D 26 2016

Government regulation
See also
Trade regulation
A Rush to Regulate Before Inauguration J. A. Dlouhy color diag *Bloomberg Businessweek* no4501 p24 N 28 2016

Government regulation—Economic aspects
THE RED TAPE CONUNDRUM: HOW THE WRONG KIND OF REGULATION IS STRANGLING BUSINESS—AND WHAT TO DO ABOUT IT [Cover story] B. O'Keefe color diag *Fortune* v174 no6 p76 N 1 2016

Government regulation—History—21st century
THE RED TAPE CONUNDRUM: HOW THE WRONG KIND OF REGULATION IS STRANGLING BUSINESS—AND WHAT TO DO ABOUT IT [Cover story] B. O'Keefe color diag *Fortune* v174 no6 p76 N 1 2016

Government regulation—Social aspects
Trump's New Math On Regulations B. Greeley color *Bloomberg Businessweek* no4511 p24 F 13 2017

Government report writing
The Gathering Storms till looms D. Kramer *Physics Today* v69 no11 p29 N 2016

Government research
DATA FOR ALL? J. Mervis color *Science* v355 no6325 p573 F 10 2017
RULES OF EVIDENCE W. Cornwall color *Science* v355 no6325 p564 F 10 2017

Government revenue
Self-Driving the Economy F. Shafroth *Governing* v30 no4 p62 Ja 2017
A Strategy for Conflict M. Funkhouser *Governing* v30 no4 p4 Ja 2017
A THOUSAND CUTS M. Maciag and J. B. Wogan *Governing* v30 no5 p32 F 2017

Government securities
See also
Municipal bonds
GET READY FOR A BOND MELTDOWN D. DREMAN *Forbes* v198 no8 p66 D 20 2016
Grow your hard-earned cash N. Lapin color *Redbook* p24 Je 2017

Government securities—United States—Sales & prices
Mnuchin Ponders Locking in Low Rates L. Capo McCormick and S. Mohsin *Bloomberg Businessweek* no4521 p39 My 8 2017

Government spending policy
TRUMP'S BUDGET BLUFF J. Surowiecki cartoon *New Yorker* v92 no49 p34 F 13 2017

Government spending policy—United States
See also
Holman rule (U.S.)
Entitled to Spend J. COST color *Weekly Standard* v22 no22 p18 F 13 2017
Our Misguided Obsession with the Tax Code J. Fox *Harvard Business Review Digital Articles* p2 O 10 2014
The Redistribution Fallacy J. Piereson *Commentary* v140 no2 p51 S 2015

Government statistics
Trustworthy—Not Alternative—Statistics bw *Bloomberg Businessweek* no4513 p16 Mr 6 2017

Governmental investigations
See also
Antitrust investigations

Governmental investigations—Canada
Broken before it begins B. HUTCHINSON color *Maclean's* p34 Je 2017

Governmental investigations—United States
The Curious Case of the Disappearing Laptop A. C. McCARTHY *National Review* v69 no18 p16 O 2 2017
Defining Trumpism Down color *Weekly Standard* v22 no45 p6 Ag 7 2017
'Extremely Unfair' M. WARREN color *Weekly Standard* v22 no44 p12 Jl 31 2017
For the Record color *Time* v188 no27-28 p10 D 26 2016
LEGAL JEOPARDY T. Schoenberg, S. Pettypiece et al bw color *Bloomberg Businessweek* no4541 p35 O 9 2017

Government securities—Charts, diagrams, etc.
FEDERAL FINANCE *Economic Indicators* p32 My 2017

Governors
See also
Military governors
Extremists, 'X-Men,' and an Ex-Governor D. Pinault color *Commonweal* v144 no12 p12 Jl 7 2017
Hickenlooper's Fellows K. Barrett and R. Greene *Governing* v30 no2 p58 N 2016
INMATE NO. 40892-424 D. BERNSTEIN color *Chicago* v66 no10 p60 O 2017
LARRY HOGAN IS HAVING A GRAND OLD TIME AS GOVERNOR L. MULLINS *Washingtonian Magazine* v52 no5 p52 F 2017
The Philosopher King K. Steinmetz color *Time* v190 no10/11 p58 S 18 2017
Speed Read K. KENDALL *Indianapolis Monthly* v40 no3 p18 N 2016
Two Paths Diverged in the Midwest. Here's Where They Led T. ANDERSON *In These Times* v41 no8 p20 Ag 2017

Governors—California
CALIFORNIA IS NOT TURNING BACK. NOT NOW, NOT EVER J. BROWN *Vital Speeches of the Day* v83 no3 p79 Mr 2017

Governors—Dwellings
Governor's Mansion N. AUSTIN *Arizona Highways* v93 no11 p6 N 2017

Governors—Elections
SOCIAL ISSUES A. Greenblatt *Governing* v30 no4 p37 Ja 2017

Governors—Georgia
PERDUE AND AGRICULTURE, FRIENDS FROM THE START *Successful Farming* v115 no3 p12 Mid-F 2017

Governors—Interviews
Jerry Brown's California Dream T. Dickinson bw color *Rolling Stone* no1298 p32 O 19 2017

Governors—Nevada

SCHOOL CHOICE A. Greenblatt *Governing* v30 no4 p38 Ja 2017

Governors—Texas
W. LEE "PAPPY" O'DANIEL P. CARLSON bw color *American History* v52 no2 p18 Je 2017

Governors—United States
ANDREW THE UNLOVED: Based on his long list of accomplishments, New York's governor ought to be held up by progressives as a national leader. So why don't they like him? A. Greenblatt *Governing* v30 no10 p42 Jl 2017
Assistant Presidents D. F. Kettl *Governing* v30 no1 p16 O 2016
Chris Christie's Last Fight J. ZENGERLE bw color *GQ: Gentlemen's Quarterly* v97 no11 p74 N 2017
EDWIN EDWARDS AT 90 E. Laborde *Louisiana Life* v37 no5 p4 My/Je 2017
GETTING VETERANS BACK TO WORK E. BOEHM color *Reason* v49 no6 p38 N 2017
Smoke, Mirrors and Job Creation M. Maciag *Governing* v30 no6 p56 Mr 2017
The Virtue of Holdovers *Governing* v30 no6 p11 Mr 2017

Govind, Vidya
Fructose-driven glycolysis supports anoxia resistance in the naked mole-rat diag graph *Science* v356 no6335 p307 Ap 21 2017

Govindarajan, Tarunya
Why Unicorns Are Struggling *Harvard Business Review Digital Articles* p2 Ap 21 2016

Govindarajan, Vijay
3 Myths about Engineering Talent in China and India *Harvard Business Review Digital Articles* p2 D 9 2014
3 Ways Businesses Are Addressing Inequality in Emerging Markets *Harvard Business Review Digital Articles* p2 Ja 23 2015
Business Can Help End Child Labor *Harvard Business Review Digital Articles* p2 Ap 9 2015
Doing Business in India Requires a Mobile-First Strategy *Harvard Business Review Digital Articles* p2 D 23 2016
Great Innovators Create the Future, Manage the Present, and Selectively Forget the Past *Harvard Business Review Digital Articles* p2 Mr 31 2016
How Amazon Adapted Its Business Model to India *Harvard Business Review Digital Articles* p2 Jl 20 2016
How Companies Escape the Traps of the Past *Harvard Business Review Digital Articles* p2 Ap 26 2016
How Disney Found Its Way Back to Creative Success *Harvard Business Review Digital Articles* p2 Je 3 2016
How the U.S. and India Can Strengthen Their Business Ties *Harvard Business Review Digital Articles* p2 Ja 22 2015
How U.S. Businesses Can Succeed in India in 2015 *Harvard Business Review Digital Articles* p2 D 22 2014
Let Go of What Made Your Company Great *Harvard Business Review Digital Articles* p2 Ap 13 2016
Stop Saying Big Companies Can't Innovate *Harvard Business Review Digital Articles* p2 Je 6 2016
To Grow as a Person, Selectively Forget the Past *Harvard Business Review Digital Articles* p2 My 12 2016
To Win the Civil War, Lincoln Had to Change His Leadership *Harvard Business Review Digital Articles* p2 My 30 2016
Understanding the Rise of Manufacturing in India *Harvard Business Review Digital Articles* p2 S 18 2015
What Engineering a Reverse Innovation Looks Like *Harvard Business Review Digital Articles* p2 N 4 2015
What FDR Knew About Managing Fear in Times of Change *Harvard Business Review Digital Articles* p2 My 4 2016
What Innovative Companies Can Learn from Keurig's Highs and Lows *Harvard Business Review Digital Articles* p2 Je 20 2016
What Ruthless Innovators Can Learn from the New England Patriots *Harvard Business Review Digital Articles* p2 Mr 9 2016
What U.S. CEOs Can Learn from GM's India Failure *Harvard Business Review Digital Articles* p2 Je 15 2017
Which U.S. Companies Are Doing the Most R&D in China and India? *Harvard Business Review Digital Articles* p2 Mr 26 2015
Why Unicorns Are Struggling *Harvard Business Review Digital Articles* p2 Ap 21 2016

Głowacka, Katarzyna
Improving photosynthesis and crop productivity by accelerating recovery from photoprotection bibl chart color graph *Science* v354 no6314 p857 N 18 2016

Gowdy, Barbara

Body of Work M. LITTLE bw *Walrus* v14 no3 p63 Ap 2017

'Just lie on your back and write' M. DOHERTY color *Maclean's* v130 no4 p64 My 2017

Stormy Transports: Heavy weather catapults a woman into a stranger's body S. COKAL *New York Times Book Review* p11 Jl 2 2017

Gowen, Zoë

Big Dream, Tiny Cottage color *Southern Living* v52 no3 p82 Mr 2017

Cutest Garden Shed Ever color diag *Southern Living* v51 no11 p44 N 2016

Do Right with White color *Southern Living* v52 no1 p24 Ja 2017

The Elegance of Alliums color *Southern Living* v52 no5 p48 My 2017

Get Creative with Turkey Plates color *Southern Living* v52 no11 p15 N 2017

The More the Merrier color *Southern Living* v52 no5 p50 My 2017

Say It With Flowers color *Southern Living* v52 no5 p44 My 2017

Season Opener color *Southern Living* v52 no4 p34 Ap 2017

Gowran, Olivia

Kilogram-scale prexasertib monolactate monohydrate synthesis under continuous-flow CGMP conditions chart diag *Science* v356 no6343 p1144 Je 16 2017

Gowrinathan, Nimmi

TERRORIST AND ALIEN *Harper's Magazine* v334 no2001 p32 F 2017

Goya, Francisco, 1746-1828

EYEWITNESS TO HORROR P. D. Toler color *MHQ: Quarterly Journal of Military History* v29 no4 p86 Summ 2017

Goya, Jonathan

Systems-level analysis of mechanisms regulating yeast metabolic flux bibl diag graph *Science* v354 no6311 paaf2786-1 O 28 2016

GOYANES, CRISTINA

SECRET STRESS BUSTERS of the Stars *Scholastic Choices* v32 no7 p16 Ap 2017

Goydos, Paul—Interviews

Paul Goydos J. Marksbury and C. Barrett color *Golf Magazine* v59 no5 p45 My 2017

GP & J Baker Ltd.

INSTANT ROOM: A DAPPER FAMILY SALON M. Aiduss color *House Beautiful* v159 no9 p46 N 2017

GQ (Periodical)

GQ HQ color *GQ: Gentlemen's Quarterly* v97 no6 p20 Je 2017

Grab, D.

Best cost estimate of greenhouse gases *Science* v357 no6352 p655 Ag 18 2017

GRABELL, MICHAEL

CUT TO THE BONE cartoon *New Yorker* v93 no12 p46 My 8 2017

GRABER, CYNTHIA

The Disease Detectives color *New Republic* v248 no1/2 p10 Ja/F 2017

Graber, Sean

It's Not HR's Job to Be Strategic *Harvard Business Review Digital Articles* p2 O 31 2014

The Two Sides of Employee Engagement *Harvard Business Review Digital Articles* p2 D 4 2015

Why Remote Work Thrives in Some Companies and Fails in Others *Harvard Business Review Digital Articles* p2 Mr 20 2015

Grabijas, Marty

Posthole color *Powder* v45 no4 p146 D 2016

Grable, David W.

ONE FELL SWOOP cartoon *Outdoor Life* v223 no9 p16 N 2016

Grabowski, Norman

Where Did T-Buckets Come From? T. Taylor bw *Hot Rod* v70 no7 p10 Jl 2017

Grace & Frankie (TV program)

Grace and Frankie M. Logan *TV Guide* v65 no13 p24 Mr 20 2017

Out & About color *TV Guide* v65 no7 p4 F 13 2017

Grace (Theology)

See also

Spiritual gifts

Forgive and Be Forgiven M. Simone *America* v217 no5 p53 S 4 2017

JUST SAY NO TO SHAME [Cover story] T. KING cartoon color *Christianity Today* v60 no10 p34 D 2016

Our Spiritual Gifts Have an Expiration Date A. WILSON *Christianity Today* v61 no5 p22 Je 2017

Grace, Joshua B.

Scienceblind *Christian Century* v134 no19 p42 S 13 2017

Grace, Kate

KATE THE GREAT E. Strout color *Runner's World* v51 no11 p44 D 2016

Grace, Laura Jane

Tranny L. Greenblatt color *Entertainment Weekly* no1439 p63 N 11 2016

Graceffo, Antonio

Dropping Bombs, Kuntaw Style color *Black Belt* v55 no4 p22 Je/Jl 2017

Getting (Ka)Popped in Singapore color *Black Belt* v55 no2 p20 F/Mr 2017

Good Morning, Vietnam(ese Martial Artists)! color *Black Belt* v55 no3 p20 Ap/My 2017

Poverty vs. Professional Fighting in Southeast Asia color *Black Belt* v55 no6 p22 O/N 2017

Singapore, Part 2: Caught Up in Catch Wrestling color *Black Belt* v55 no5 p22 Ag/S 2017

Gracey, Michael

THE GREATEST SHOWMAN T. Stack color *Entertainment Weekly* no1478 / 1479 p70 Ag 18-25 2017

Graci, Chad

Southern Comforts color *House Beautiful* v158 no10 p31 D 2016/Ja 2017

Gracias, David H.

DNA sequence-directed shape change of photopatterned hydrogels via high-degree swelling color diag *Science* v357 no6356 p1126 S 15 2017

Grackles

THE BIG PICTURE *South Dakota Magazine* v33 no3 p50 S/O 2017

Grackles—Behavior

The Greatness of the Grackle N. NICHOLS *D: The Magazine of Dallas* v43 no10 p45 O 2016

Graczyk, Piotr

Lee Rubin: Our mentor and role model *Science* v355 no6327 p806 F 24 2017

Grade inflation

Making the Grade color diag *Weekly Standard* v22 no35 p3 My 22 2017

The Suicide of Meritocracy H. MANSFIELD bw *Weekly Standard* v22 no46 p12 Ag 14 2017

Grade point average

PUMPING IT UP? graph *Phi Kappa Phi Forum* v97 no2 p5 Summ 2017

Grade repetition—Law & legislation

The Wisdom of Mandatory Grade Retention B. A. JACOB *Education Digest* v82 no7 p29 Mr 2017

Grading & marking (Students)

The best of both worlds J. Schneider, J. Feldman et al color *Phi Delta Kappan* v98 no3 p60 N 2016

Making grades more meaningful C. Hochbein and M. Pollio chart color il *Phi Delta Kappan* v98 no3 p49 N 2016

Grading & marking (Students)—Social aspects

The Suicide of Meritocracy H. MANSFIELD bw *Weekly Standard* v22 no46 p12 Ag 14 2017

Gradney, Kristen

Feast. Fast. Repeat C. SAGON color *AARP: The Magazine* v60 no1A p14 D 2016/Ja 2017

Graduate education

Choose a program, have a life S. H. Jones color *Science* v357 no6355 p1058 S 8 2017

Graduate student mobility

PRO MOTION J. Niesen chart color *Sports Illustrated* v127 no5 p71 Ag 14 2017

Graduate students

See also

Doctoral students

Graduate students—Attitudes

MBAs Need to Stop Assuming That Markets Always Work P. Ghemawat *Harvard Business Review Digital Articles* p2 N 21 2014

Graduate students—United States—Employment

Trump the Union Buster M. RIVLIN-NADLER color *New Republic* v248 no7 p8 Jl 2017

Graduates

    See also

    College graduates

Graduation (Education)

Beyond the Transcript: The Need to Showcase More G. Wienhausen and K. Elias *Change* v49 no4 p14 Jl/Ag 2017

Graduation (Film)

Graduation *New Yorker* v93 no11 p10 My 1 2017

WONDER WOMEN A. LANE cartoon *New Yorker* v93 no8 p76 Ap 10 2017

Graduation gifts

5 Gifts Your Grad Will Actually Use M. D. Harrington and L. Heffernan color *Money* v46 no5 p21 Je 2017

Financial Gifts for New Graduates K. LANKFORD *Kiplinger's Personal Finance* v71 no6 p38 Je 2017

Graduation rate—Charts, diagrams, etc.

BEST BANG FOR THE BUCK WESTERN COLLEGES chart *Washington Monthly* v49 no9/10 p56 S/O 2017

TOP 150 MASTER'S UNIVERSITIES chart *Washington Monthly* v49 no9/10 p108 S/O 2017

Gradwell, Eileen

The No-Excuses Guide to Walking color *Prevention* v69 no7 p82 Jl 2017

Gradwohl, Carol

KITCHEN-TESTED TIPS color *Vegetarian Today* no2 p4 Ap 2017

Grady, Anne

Handle Your Stress Better by Knowing What Causes It *Harvard Business Review Digital Articles* p1 Je 21 2017

What to Do If Your Team Is Letting You Down *Harvard Business Review Digital Articles* p2 My 4 2015

Grady-White Boats Inc.

FAMILY FISHER S. SHIBATA *Boating World* v38 no5 p8 My 2017

Grady Gammage Memorial Auditorium (Tempe, Ariz.)

Frank Lloyd Wright B. COSSAVELLA *Arizona Highways* v93 no4 p8 Ap 2017

Graf, Courtney

What school horses taught me color *Equus* no481 p80 O 2017

Graf, Holger

SHAPE SHIFTERS L. IMMEDIATO color *Los Angeles Magazine* v62 no10 p32 O 2017

Gräf, Uta

The Stretch color *Dressage Today* v23 no4 p30 D 2016

Gräfe, S.

Ultrafast electron diffraction imaging of bond breaking in di-ionized acetylene bibl graph *Science* v354 no6310 p308 O 21 2016

GRAFF, E. J.

THEY PERSISTED color *Mother Jones* v42 no4 p34 Jl/Ag 2017

Graff, Garrett M.

CHASING THE PHANTOM map *Wired* v25 no4 p52 Ap 2017

The Deep State: What were the nation's plans to govern after a nuclear strike? J. VOGT *New York Times Book Review* p18 Je 18 2017

Families BEHIND the BADGE color *AARP: The Magazine* v60 no1A p38 D 2016/Ja 2017

THE INCONVENIENT COMRADE color *Esquire* p90 Je/Jl 2017

The Spy Who Added Me on LinkedIn color *Bloomberg Businessweek* no4500 p54 N 21 2016

TRUMP FORCE ONE bw color *Bloomberg Businessweek* no4515 p48 Mr 20 2017

WATCHING THE WATCHER bw *Wired* v24 no12 p132 D 2016

Graff, Jessie

Jessie Graff P. KITA cartoon color *Men's Health* v32 no8 p35 O 2017

The World Is Her Playground [Cover story] M. STACEY color *Women's Health* v14 no8 p130 O 2017

GRAFF, LISA

Trying to Fit In ... *New York Times Book Review* p25 Ag 27 2017

Graff, Lucile

Precursor processing for plant peptide hormone maturation by subtilisin-like serine proteinases bibl color graph *Science* v354 no6319 p1594 D 23 2016

Graffin, Scott D.

How Companies Use Strategically Timed Announcements to Confuse the Market *Harvard Business Review Digital Articles* p2 Ap 26 2016

Serving on Boards Helps Executives Get Promoted *Harvard Business Review Digital Articles* p2 My 20 2016

When Star CEOs and Star Analysts Disagree, the Market Trusts the Analysts *Harvard Business Review Digital Articles* p2 Ap 18 2016

Graffiti

But Will It Wash Off... J. Duckworth *Stage Directions* v30 no8 p28 Ag 2017

GQNZ0247 *Texas Monthly* v45 no4 p32 Ap 2017

Writing on the Wall *Arizona Highways* v96 no7 p56 Jl 2017

Graffiti artists

I WAS MARRIED TO BANKSY D. Dernavich cartoon *Esquire* p130 N 2017

Graffiti removal

Mr. Clean Is on the Scene J. LABIANCA color *Reader's Digest* v190 no1135 p12 N 2017

Graft rejection prevention

Harnessing Cellular Tools from Immune Systems to Help Prevent Graft Rejection M. Levings and L. J. West color *Maclean's* v130 no9 p34 O 2017

Grafting (Horticulture)

GRAFTING FRUIT TREES: Fuse stems with rootstocks to form fast-growing, fruit-bearing plants L. Reich *Mother Earth News* no282 p39 Je/Jl 2017

Gragg, Walt

Ordinary Soldiers in Extraordinary Circumstances A. Appel color *Publishers Weekly* v264 no13 p34 Mr 27 2017

GRAHAM, ADAM H.

Bilbao Now color *Conde Nast Traveler* v52 no7 p44 Ag 2017

mothers of pearl bw color map *Conde Nast Traveler* v52 no6 p78 Je/Jl 2017

Graham, Alex

Transatlantic Hound M. TAUBE cartoon *Weekly Standard* v22 no13 p38 D 5 2016

Graham, Ashley

21 Ways to Please Your SELF C. Leive color *Glamour* v115 no7 p12 Jl 2017

Ashley Graham DOES DENIM color *InStyle* v24 no2 p90 F 2017

FALL FASHION A. LAROCCA img *New York* v50 no16 p29 Ag 7 2017

Going Bare... color *Glamour* v115 no6 p138 Je 2017

Great Style Has No Size color *InStyle* v23 no12 p124 N 2016

If You Like to Rework the Classics S. P. Nadella and A. Hou color *Glamour* v115 no9 p54 S 2017

NOW, THIS IS A SUPERMODEL: ASHLEY GRAHAM ISN'T A SAMPLE SIZE.: Which is exactly why she's become the face of a movement J. YUAN img *New York* v50 no16 p30 Ag 7 2017

Our Bodies. No Shame S. Altopp-Miller, G. Thomas et al color *Glamour* v115 no9 p32 S 2017

Sex color *Glamour* v115 no7 p77 Jl 2017

Taking the Perfect Selfie color *InStyle* v24 no3 p186 Mr 2017

Graham, Ashley—Interviews

Ashley GRAHAM A. Prato color *Glamour* v114 no12 p222 D 2016

Queen of Everything [Cover story] L. Chan bw color *Glamour* v115 no7 p78 Jl 2017

Graham, Aubrey Drake

Who (or What) Won 2016? R. Browne img *New York* v49 no26 p84 D 26 2016

Graham, Barney S.

Rapid development of a DNA vaccine for Zika virus bibl graph *Science* v354 no6309 p237 O 14 2016

GRAHAM, BENJAMIN

Get Lost on Wyoming's Edge color *Backpacker* p14 S 2017

Graham, Billy, 1918-

What to Think of the Reverend Graham M. Malone *America* v216 no8 p3 Ap 17 2017

Graham, Brandon

Good for Nothing *Publishers Weekly* v263 no48 p42 N 28 2016

Graham, Chuck

SOARING UNDER THE RADAR *American Forests* v123 no2 p42 Summ 2017

Tour de California color *Backpacker* p12 My 2017

Tree-Climbing Foxes and Other Success Stories *Natural History* v125 no2 p18 F 2017

GRAHAM, DAVID A.

Red State, Blue City cartoon *Atlantic* v319 no2 p24 Mr 2017

Graham, Devonte'

TWO OF A KIND L. Winn color *Sports Illustrated* v126 no1 p48 Ja 9 2017

Graham, Drew Storm

To The Editor color *American Craft* v76 no6 p10 D 2016-Ja 2017

GRAHAM, ELYSE

Canis Sapiens *American Scholar* v86 no3 p15 Summ 2017

Spheres of Influence *American Scholar* v86 no2 p15 Spr 2017

Ulysses: The Video Game *American Scholar* v86 no1 p17 Wint 2017

Graham, Franklin, 1952-

What to Think of the Reverend Graham M. Malone *America* v216 no8 p3 Ap 17 2017

Graham, Heather

The Rising *Publishers Weekly* v263 no46 p33 N 14 2016

Graham, James

BREATHING LIFE BACK INTO THE PAST: The hobby of historical reenactment now has a deep history of its own. The Sealed Knot Society, the first reenactment society, was formed as long ago as 1968, the last year steam was used on British Railways *British Heritage Travel* v38 no4 p64 Jl/Ag 2017

The SAILING SCENE color *Sail* v48 no6 p6 Je 2017

Graham, Jorie, 1950-

WITH MOTHER IN THE KITCHEN J. Graham *New Yorker* v92 no41 p50 D 12 2016

Worlds in a Cell: Jorie Graham, ambushed by illness, uses poetry to interweave personal and collective history A. FITZGERALD bw *New York Times Book Review* p13 Ag 6 2017

GRAHAM, JUDITH

Brain-Healthy Diets color *Kiplinger's Personal Finance* v71 no7 p68 Jl 2017

Graham, Kat, 1989-

Pajama Party E. Wilson color *InStyle* v24 no7 p42 Jl 2017

Graham, Katharine, 1917-2001

Kay's Kind of Summer M. BLAIS color *Vanity Fair* v59 no7 p110 Summ 2017

Graham, Katrina

We're All Capable of Being an Abusive Boss [Cover story] *Harvard Business Review Digital Articles* p2 O 14 2016

Graham, Kevin

IMPUNITY IN THE FINE PRINT: Chicago's police union contract ensures that abuses remain in the shadows A. EMMANU-EL *In These Times* v41 no7 p24 Jl 2017

Graham, Kirk

A Good Germany? *History Today* v67 no7 p8 Jl 2017

Graham, Lauren, 1967-

THE FINAL FOUR CHAPTERS S. Highfill color *Entertainment Weekly* no1441 p24 N 25 2016

Gilmore Girls: A Year in the Life J. Jensen color *Entertainment Weekly* no1441 p47 N 25 2016

Gilmore Girls Revival Guide S. Highfill color *Entertainment Weekly* no1443 p14 D 9 2016

HOW TO BE HAPPY A. SPENCER color *Good Housekeeping* v264 no1 p75 Ja 1 2017

In the Gilmore Girls' Hometown, Things Are (Mostly) the Same E. Dockterman color *Time* v188 no21 p69 N 21 2016

My Advice bw color *Seventeen* v75 no11 p108 N 2016

RETURN TO STARS HOLLOW I. RATLEDGE *TV Guide* v64 no48 p30 N 21 2016

Talking as Fast as I Can I. Biedenharn color *Entertainment Weekly* no1442 p62 D 2 2016 Rebellious Special Issue

Graham, Lauren, 1967-—Interviews

The 3-Minute Interview J. Radloff and J. Harman color *Glamour* v114 no12 p82 D 2016

STARS HOLLOW HOMECOMING [Cover story] S. Highfill color *Entertainment Weekly* no1441 p18 N 25 2016

GRAHAM, LAWRENCE OTIS

Upwardly Minded *New York Times Book Review* p10 F 5 2017

Graham, Lindsey, 1955-

PHOTO color *Reason* v48 no11 p7 Ap 2017

Graham, Loren

Love Conquers All W. HERBERT bw *Weekly Standard* v22 no9 p30 N 7 2016

Graham, Martha, 1894-1991

On Their Feet C. ATAMIAN color *Weekly Standard* v22 no15 p35 D 19 2016

Graham, Matthew

PARK YOURSELF HERE color *Washingtonian Magazine* v52 no7 p116 Ap 2017

Graham, Michael

Hard Knocks Revisited *Cincinnati Magazine* v50 no12 p44 S 2017

Graham, Mike

JOLLY GOOD FELLAS J. Sugarman *Washingtonian Magazine* v52 no3 p94 D 2016

GRAHAM, NICHOLAS A. J.

The Resilience of Marine Ecosystems to Climatic Disturbances *BioScience* v67 no3 p208 Mr 2017

Graham, Ruth

ACTS OF FAITH *New York Times Magazine* p48 O 16 2016

'COPPER CANTEEN' bw *New York Times Magazine* p47 Mr 12 2017

MANY AMERICANS ARE OUT OF WORK, OR NEED BETTER JOBS. MANY EMPLOYERS HAVE GOOD JOBS THEY CAN'T FILL. CAN TRAINING PROGRAMS MORE INTELLIGENTLY MATCH THEM UP? *New York Times Magazine* p48 F 26 2017

A Second Chance at Choice *New York Times Magazine* p46 Jl 23 2017

Graham, Susan

BACKSTORY: Susan Graham F. COHN *Opera News* v81 no5 p64 N 2016

Graham, Todd R.

Exploring genetic suppression interactions on a global scale diag *Science* v354 no6312 p599 N 4 2016

GRAHAM, TYLER

Get Ripped on These 6 Trips color *Men's Health* v32 no6 p29 Ag 2017

UNLOCK YOUR STRENGTH color diag *Men's Health* v32 no7 p94 S 2017

Grahame Hardie, D.

Targeting an energy sensor to treat diabetes color *Science* v357 no6350 p455 Ag 4 2017

Graham-Felsen, Sam

The Pull-Up *New York Times Magazine* p20 Jl 2 2017

Graham-Leviss, Katherine

The 5 Skills That Innovative Leaders Have in Common *Harvard Business Review Digital Articles* p2 D 20 2016

Grail

c. 1225: France *Lapham's Quarterly* v10 no2 p57 Spr 2017

Grain

See also
Wheat

Against-the-Grain Holidays M. D. SMITH color *Better Nutrition* v78 no11 p88 N 2016

Ask Martha color diag *Martha Stewart Living* p72 Ap 2017

Bowl, PREP SCHOOL Salad, Sammy! J. Levy color *Health* v31 no7 p122 S 2017

Cereal Numbers *Nutrition Action Health Letter* v43 no9 p14 N 2016

Cereal Smarts L. MOYER and B. LIEBMAN *Nutrition Action Health Letter* v43 no9 p12 N 2016

Choose a Healthier Cereal *Parents* v91 no12 p24 D 2016

Fall fuel E. Brower color *Yoga Journal* no296 p22 N 2017

GOLDEN CHILD N. RICHARDSON color *Bon Appetit* v62 no2 p100 Mr 2017

GREAT GRAINS B. BRODY *Better Homes & Gardens* v94 no12 p152 D 2016

HACKING THE GRAIN M. OSTRANDER color *Nation* v305 no11 p18 O 30 2017

IDLE TALK: LARGE GRAIN STOCKS REVIVE THE DEBATE OVER U.S. LAND RETIREMENT *Successful Farming* v115 no6 p10 Ap 2017

It's Crunch Time B. Lipton color *Health* v31 no7 p154 S 2017

Muesli Magic N. Zevnik and V. TWEED color *Better Nutrition* v79 no9 p14 S 2017

Rock Your Morning B. Lipton color *Health* v30 no9 p148 N 2016

Summer-fresh pastas J. Iserloh color *Yoga Journal* no293 p40 Ag

2017
Vegan Cooking Tips. QUINOA DISHES N. Berkoff *Vegetarian Journal* v36 no2 p32 2017
Whole grains *Mayo Clinic Health Letter* v35 no1 p6 Ja 2017

Grain diseases & pests
WHAT'S YOUR BIN'S IQ? GROWERS PROTECT STORED GRAIN BY BOOSTING THEIR BIN'S BRAIN POWER L. Bedord color *Successful Farming* v115 no7 p40 My 2017

Grain orientation (Materials)
Segregation-induced ordered superstructures at general grain boundaries in a nickel-bismuth alloy Z. Yu, P. R. Cantwell et al color *Science* v357 no6359 p97 O 6 2017

Grain sales & prices
See also
Corn prices
Corny Comics *South Dakota Magazine* v32 no6 p13 Mr/Ap 2017
LATE-MODEL CULTIVATOR PRICES RISE D. Mowitz *Successful Farming* v115 no5 p21 Mid-Mr 2017
REWARDING THE MARKET: FACE VOLATILITY WITH DISCIPLINE M. McGinnis *Successful Farming* v115 no11 p45 S 2017
SEASONAL PRICE PATTERNS WORK AGAIN A. Kluis *Successful Farming* v115 no1 p18 Ja 2017
WEATHERING THE STORM A. Kluis *Successful Farming* v114 no11 p21 N 2016

Grain storage—Equipment & supplies
WHAT'S YOUR BIN'S IQ? GROWERS PROTECT STORED GRAIN BY BOOSTING THEIR BIN'S BRAIN POWER L. Bedord color *Successful Farming* v115 no7 p40 My 2017

Grain trade—United States
GLOBAL GRAIN FUNDAMENTALS BEGIN TO IMPROVE: IS THE FIVE-YEAR BEAR MARKET FINALLY OVER? A. KLUIS *Successful Farming* v115 no9 p22 Ag 2017

Grainger, Alan
The extent of forest in dryland biomes [Cover story] chart map *Science* v356 no6338 p635 My 12 2017

Grain—Marketing
ADD THIS MARKETING TOOL M. McGinnis *Successful Farming* v114 no11 p29 N 2016
BASIS MANAGEMENT M. McGinnis *Successful Farming* v115 no4 p25 Mr 2017
THE SUCCESSFUL INTERVIEW M. McGinnis *Successful Farming* v114 no11 p12 N 2016

Graizbord, Carlos
None of the Above *Commentary* v141 no10 p1 D 2016
None of the Above *Commentary* v142 no5 p6 D 2016

GRAJEK, GORDON
HOME ENTERTAINMENT color *Good Housekeeping* v263 no5 p144 N 2016
your PERSONAL GADGETS color diag *Good Housekeeping* v263 no6 p105 D 2016

Grajewski, Julian
FROM OUR READERS *Sky & Telescope* v133 no6 p6 Je 2017

GRAM, JOHN R.
Acting Out Assimilation *American Indian Quarterly* v40 no3 p251 Summ 2016

Gramling, Carolyn
City 40 *Science* v356 no6337 p482 My 5 2017
'Four-legged snake' may be ancient lizard instead color *Science* v354 no6312 p536 N 4 2016
Jungles are now carbon emitters *Science News* v192 no7 p9 O 28 2017
Ma, where did they put T. rex? diag graph *Science* v355 no6331 p1249 Mr 24 2017
New views snag science Nobels bw *Science News* v192 no7 p6 O 28 2017
Resurrection Science color *Science* v354 no6317 p1228 D 9 2016
Some herbivorous dinos ate critters color *Science News* v192 no7 p12 O 28 2017
Storm documentary proves timely color *Science News* v192 no7 p29 O 28 2017
Toxic algae may be culprit in mysterious dinosaur deaths *Science* v357 no6354 p857 S 1 2017

Grammarians
PLEASE DON'T SAY THAT! *Saturday Evening Post* v289 no1 p30 Ja/F 2017

Grammer, Kelsey, 1955-
AMAZON BETS ON THE LAST TYCOON T. Stack color *Entertainment Weekly* no1476 p53 Ag 4 2017

Grammy Awards
4 THINGS YOU DIDN'T SEE AT THE GRAMMYS N. Feeney color *Entertainment Weekly* no1454/1455 p16 F 24 2017
The 59th Annual Grammy Awards M. Roffman *TV Guide* v65 no6 p40 Ja 30 2017
THE ARTIST WAY C. Murray color *Essence* v48 no2 p57 Je 2017
Calendar FEBRUARY color *Popular Mechanics* p8 F 2017
EXAMINING THE GRAMMYS' RACE ISSUE E. R. Brown, K. O'Donnell et al color *Entertainment Weekly* no1454/1455 p13 F 24 2017
For the Record color *Time* v189 no7/8 p6 F 27 2017
For Your Consideration Grammys color *Entertainment Weekly* no1446/1447 p118 D 2016/Ja 2017
GQ HQ bw color *GQ: Gentlemen's Quarterly* v97 no4 p38 Ap 2017
KIND OF NEW F. KAPLAN bw cartoon *New Yorker* v93 no14 p34 My 22 2017
Predicting Pop's Big Night S. KNOPPER color *Rolling Stone* no1280 p18 F 9 2017
The Race Is On color *Entertainment Weekly* no1451/1452 p23 F 3-10 2017
Rock the Vote! color *Entertainment Weekly* no1451/1452 p24 F 3-10 2017
This Host Is on Fire! N. Feeney color *Entertainment Weekly* no1451/1452 p28 F 3-10 2017

Grammy Awards—Charts, diagrams, etc.
And the Winner Is... N. Feeney, K. O'Donnell et al chart color *Entertainment Weekly* no1451/1452 p26 F 3-10 2017

Gran Chaco
Forest conservation: Remember Gran Chaco T. Särkinen, T. Kuemmerle et al bibl color *Science* v355 no6324 p465 F 3 2017

Granada, Stephanie
BEST OF THE WEST color *Sunset* v238 no5 p11 My 2017
BEST OF THE WEST color *Sunset* v239 no3 p11 S 2017
GONE FOR A RIDE color *Sunset* v238 no3 p24 Mr 2017
Secrets of South Florida color map *Southern Living* v52 no1 p45 Ja 2017

Granados, Luis
The Common Sense of Oklahomans *Humanist* v77 no1 p6 Ja/F 2017

GRANADOS-CIFUENTES, CAMILA
Worm-snail Ships Out! bw color *Natural History* v125 no6 p10 Je 2017

Grand Banks Yachts Ltd.
COMMAND PERFORMANCE B. PIKE chart color diag *Power & Motoryacht* v33 no3 p84 Mr 2017
Whole New World B. PIKE chart color *Power & Motoryacht* v34 no8 p40 Ag 2017

Grand Canyon (Ariz.)
The Big Pictures: GRAND CANYON [Cover story] *Arizona Highways* v93 no1 p17 Ja 2017
Confluence T. Valtin *Sierra* v101 no4 p52 Jl/Ag 2016
GROWING, GROWING, GONE T. WILLIAMS *Arizona Highways* v93 no1 p44 Ja 2017
Here We Go! Oprah color *O, The Oprah Magazine* p17 Ja 2017
Muddying the Waters S. Mirsky cartoon *Scientific American* v315 no5 p78 N 2016
Sales is kind of like the Grand Canyon S. Anderson *New York Times Magazine* p14 S 10 2017
That Was Then *National Parks* v91 no4 p60 Fall 2017
What I Know for Sure Oprah color *O, The Oprah Magazine* p114 Ja 2017

Grand Canyon (Ariz.)—Description & travel
Jacob Lake Ranger Station N. AUSTIN *Arizona Highways* v96 no7 p6 Jl 2017
ROOM WITH A VIEW color *O, The Oprah Magazine* p113 Ja 2017

Grand Canyon National Park (Ariz.)
Built to Last *Arizona Highways* v93 no3 p56 Mr 2017
FRINGE BENEFITS M. JAFFE *Arizona Highways* v93 no1 p32 Ja 2017
from our archives [July 1946] *Arizona Highways* v93 no1 p10 Ja 2017

Let There Be Light *Arizona Highways* v96 no7 p5 Jl 2017

The View Is Made by Walking J. Mark *Sierra* v102 no2 p14 Mr/Ap 2017

Grand Canyon National Park (Ariz.)—Description & travel

CAPE ROYAL ROAD Cape Royal offers one of the best overlooks in Grand Canyon National Park. It's impressive, and so is the narrow, winding road that takes you there N. AUSTIN *Arizona Highways* v93 no6 p52 Je 2017

Grand Canyon University

Grand Canyon University *Dance Magazine* v90 p67 2016/2017 Supplement College Guide

Grand Central Publishing (Company)

Search Begins for Raab's Successor at Grand Central J. Milliot color *Publishers Weekly* v263 no52 p12 D 19 2016

Grand Designs (TV program)

FIXER UPPER FILL-INS TO FLIP OVER D. Rovenstine color *Entertainment Weekly* no1486 p51 O 13 2017

Grand Prix racing

    See also

        United States Grand Prix Race

EL GANADOR color *Cycle World* v56 no6 p74 Jl 2017

Start Your Engines! F. Seidel color *New York Review of Books* v64 no1 p16 Ja 19 2017

Tips From a World Cup Champion B. Baumert color *Dressage Today* v23 no9 p40 Je 2017

Grand Prix racing—History—21st century

Auto Pilots A. Lawrence, T. Keith et al color *Sports Illustrated* v126 no7 p26 Mr 6 2017

Grand Rounds Inc.—Officials & employees

Refer Madness M. HERPER color *Forbes* v198 no9 p78 D 30 2016

Grand strategy (Political science)

How to Succeed in the Networked World Slaughter color *Foreign Affairs* v95 no6 p76 N/D 2016

A New Truman Doctrine T. Kaine color *Foreign Affairs* v96 no4 p36 Jl/Ag 2017

Grand Teton National Park (Wyo.)

FINDING YOUR PERSONAL SUMMIT color *Powder* v45 no6 p92 F 2017

THE GALLERY color *Runner's World* v52 no9 p12 O 2017

Show Time M. JOHNSON-GROH color diag *Backpacker* p30 Ag 2017

Grand Theft Auto games

How Grand Theft Auto Steers Driverless Cars D. Hull color *Bloomberg Businessweek* no4519 p23 Ap 24 2017

Grandage, Michael, 1962-

Meet Broadway's Frozen Foursome M. Snetiker color *Entertainment Weekly* no1480 p59 S 1 2017

Grand Canyon-Parashant National Monument (Ariz.)

Desert Gator: The life and times of Clem of Grand Canyon-Parashant N. BRULLIARD *National Parks* v91 no3 p58 Summ 2017

Grandchildren

    See also

        Granddaughters

CROSSING OVER: Yes, I have cancer, but no treatment's needed--yet. And then? A. COCHRAN *Washingtonian Magazine* v52 no8 p224 My 2017

stories on sanibel L. Vaccariello bw *Parents* v92 no8 p8 Ag 2017

Granddaughters

THE GREAT-GRAND-DAUGHTERS OF CONFEDERATION [Cover story] M. Campbell bw color *Maclean's* v130 no6 p46 Jl 2017

Grande, Ariana, 1993-

For the Record color *Time* v189 no21 p7 Je 5 2017

Random Notes color *Rolling Stone* no1290 p26 Je 29 2017

'Side to Side' H. CILLS color *New York Times Magazine* p52 Mr 12 2017

Sound Bites color *Entertainment Weekly* no1470 p4 Je 16 2017

Grande, Lance

The Curator color *Natural History* v125 no11 p48 N 2017

Curators: Behind the Scenes of Natural History Museums C. Moskowitz color *Scientific American* v316 no3 p76 Mr 2017

Grande, Naples

TRY A "HINGE" STROKE color diag *Golf Magazine* v59 no9 p52 S 2017

Grande, Rutilio

Rutilio Grande: Is another saint on the way for El Salvador? il *America* v216 no7 p17 Ap 3 2017

Grandfathers

A Compass/Level J. Seger color *Men's Health* v32 no5 p138 Je 2017

IDAHO'S POMPEII: A GOLD RUSH TOWN DROWNED R. McRAE *Idaho Magazine* v16 no7 p42 Ap 2017

Pop and the Peanut Brittle K. Purvis color *Southern Living* v51 no12 p134 D 2016

Why I Love M. Kors color *InStyle* v24 no3 p378 Mr 2017

Grandi, Paola

Click chemistry enables preclinical evaluation of targeted epigenetic therapies diag *Science* v356 no6345 p1397 Je 30 2017

GRANDIN, GREG

The Strange Career of American Exceptionalism color *Nation* v304 no1 p22 Ja 2 2017 The Obama Years

Grandin Road (Company)

BACKYARD BONFIRES color *Timber Home Living* v27 no4 p28 Ag 2017

Grandinetti, Roberto

WAR STORIES color *Los Angeles Magazine* v62 no10 p123 O 2017

GRANDISON, BAIHLEY

GLOBE TROTTING: VENTURING AROUND THE WORLD FROM A COOL OTR SHOP *Cincinnati Magazine* v50 no10 p40 Jl 2017

Grandjean, Paige

Drumsticks, Please color *Southern Living* v52 no5 p136 My 2017

Fancy Fried Nuts color *Southern Living* v52 no9 p146 S 2017

How Fresh! color *Health* v31 no5 p105 Je 2017

The Soup of Summer color *Southern Living* v52 no7 p120 Jl 2017

Spring Slow-Cooker Soup color *Southern Living* v52 no4 p132 Ap 2017

Whole-Grain Goodness color *Southern Living* v52 no5 p144 My 2017

Grandmaster Flash (Performer)

NIGHT LIFE *New Yorker* v92 no32 p26 O 10 2016

Grandmothers

Days of Our Lives A. Hood *Yankee* v81 no1 p116 Ja/F 2017

A grandmother's death prompts a search for her in family snapshots. Photographs are our reservoirs of memory, our talismans of mourning T. Cole *New York Times Magazine* p12 Jl 16 2017

Lola's Story A. TIZON bw color *Atlantic* v319 no5 p64 Je 2017

Poor but Happy: The Wisdom of the Elders T. BRINKERHOFF *Idaho Magazine* v16 no9 p42 Je 2017

a strong tradition R. WALKER color map *Cabin Living* p17 Ag 2017

WELL-SEASONED J. BARKER *Atlanta* v56 no7 p72 N 2016

Grandparent & child

The Absence of Assorted Things: Where Nothing Is Everything E. LEE *Idaho Magazine* v16 no12 p12 S 2017

Passing a love of science through generations color *Science News* v191 no10 p30 My 27 2017

Grandparents

    See also

        Grandmothers

        Grandparent & child

South Carolina J. Woodson *New York Times Magazine* p58 N 20 2016

stories on sanibel L. Vaccariello bw *Parents* v92 no8 p8 Ag 2017

Teach the Children Well: Money lessons for the grandkids J. Chatzky and K. Hultgren cartoon color *AARP: The Magazine* v60 no5A p27 Ag/S 2017

When the Water Ran Cold K. DOUNGLOMCHAN *Reader's Digest* v189 no1128 p20 Mr 2017

Grand River Enterprises Six Nations Ltd.—Trials, litigation, etc.

These Cigarettes Are Smokin' D. Voreacos and A. Martin color graph *Bloomberg Businessweek* no4532 p14 Jl 31 2017

Granduciel, Adam

SONGS FROM THE HEART D. Hyman cartoon color *Esquire* p45 S 2017

THINK PIECES A. PETRUSICH cartoon *New Yorker* v93 no24 p78 Ag 21 2017

Grandy, A. S.

Long-term pattern and magnitude of soil carbon feedback to the climate system in a warming world chart graph *Science* v357 no6359 p101 O 6 2017

GRANEK, ELISE F.

Incorporating Sociocultural Phenomena into Ecosystem-Service Valuation: The Importance of Critical Pluralism *BioScience* v67 no3 p233 Mr 2017

Granell, Antonio

A chemical genetic roadmap to improved tomato flavor bibl graph *Science* v355 no6323 p391 Ja 27 2017

Graner, Magnus

THE ART OF FUN K. KRICHKO bw color *Powder* v45 no5 p92 Ja 2017

Graney, Pat

What's Not Okay to Ask a Dancer to Do? C. ESCOYNE, S. FRISCIA et al *Dance Magazine* v91 no4 p31 Ap 2017

Grange, Jacques

Light His Fire M. OWENS color *Architectural Digest* v74 no1 p62 Ja 2017

Granger, Courtney

HEARTFELT VOCALS A. WICKS color *Louisiana Life* v37 no3 p112 Ja/F 2017

GRANGER, DAVID

THE INCUMBENTS color diag *Car & Driver* v62 no7 p62 Ja 2017

GRANGER, DEREK

CLASH OF THE TITANS cartoon *Vanity Fair* p84 Hollywood 2017 Supplement

Granholm, Natasha

My brand: A "collaborative leader" fluent in two different cultures color *Working Mother* v40 no2 p2 Je/Jl 2017

Granite

NEWFOUND ROCKS MAY BE PROGENY OF PRIMORDIAL CRUST *Physics Today* v70 no5 p22 My 2017

Grann, David

Blood for Oil A. H. STURGIS bw color *Reason* v49 no6 p72 N 2017

By the Light of a Deadly Moon C. Howorth color *Time* v189 no15 p53 Ap 24 2017

Death by Oil: After being driven off their land twice, Native Americans struck it rich in oil lands, only to be preyed upon by murderers D. EGGERS *New York Times Book Review* p16 My 14 2017

Killers of the Flower Moon: The Osage Murders and the Birth of the FBI color *Publishers Weekly* v264 no22 p62 My 29 2017

Literary License *New Republic* v248 no10 p5 O 2017

THE MAN HOLLYWOOD CAN'T STOP READING K. P. Sullivan color *Entertainment Weekly* no1462 p64 Ap 21 2017

OIL AND WATER color *Mother Jones* v42 no3 p59 My/Je 2017

Grann, David—Interviews

David Grann *New York Times Book Review* p7 Ap 30 2017

Hidden HISTORY *Interview* v47 no3 p37 Ap 2017

Grannan, Katy

Missouri *New York Times Magazine* p40 N 20 2016

Grannell, Craig

Feature: Guide to System Preferences in Sierra color *Macworld - Digital Edition* p31 Ja 2017

Mac emulators color *Macworld - Digital Edition* p61 Ap 2017

Granof, Corinne

ALL TOGETHER bw color *Art in America* v105 no6 p82 Je/Jl 2017

Grant, Adam

Adam Grant M. Rich color *Current Biography* v78 no9 p27 S 2017

BEAT GENEROSITY BURNOUT color *Harvard Business Review Digital Articles* p3 Ja 1 2017

CHRISTOPHER NOLAN Wants You to Silence Your Phones color *Esquire* p48 Ag 2017

Every marriage needs... a meeting? color *Redbook* p110 Ap 2017

GENEROSITY BURNOUT color *Harvard Business Review* v95 no2 p162 Mr/Ap 2017

How to Talk to a Loved One Who Is Suffering color *Time* v189 no15 p43 Ap 24 2017

JIMMY IOVINE Wants to Learn color *Esquire* p72 Je/Jl 2017

Let's Not Kill Performance Evaluations Yet il *Harvard Business Review* v94 no11 p90 N 2016

Mark Cuban GETS LOUD color *Esquire* p64 My 2017

MORE ON BEING GENEROUS WITHOUT BEING A DOORMAT color *Harvard Business Review Digital Articles* p18 Ja 1 2017

More on Being Generous Without Being a Doormat *Harvard Business Review Digital Articles* p2 F 22 2017

NEW EYES on VIETNAM color *Esquire* p69 S 2017

RENAISSANCE Woman color *Esquire* p56 O 2017

Through a Lens, DARKLY color *Esquire* p60 N 2017

When the Worst Happens color *AARP: The Magazine* v60 no4A p52 Je/Jl 2017

Grant, Adam—Interviews

"Above All, Acknowledge the Pain" A. IGNATIUS color *Harvard Business Review* v95 no3 p142 My/Je 2017

Grant, Adam H.

Dar y recibir/Give and Take *Publishers Weekly* v263 no46 p20 N 14 2016

Grant, Alastair

Phytochromes function as thermosensors in Arabidopsis bibl graph *Science* v354 no6314 p886 N 18 2016

GRANT, ALLISON SWEET

Every marriage needs... a meeting? color *Redbook* p110 Ap 2017

Grant, B. Rosemary

Watching speciation in action bibl color *Science* v355 no6328 p910 Mr 3 2017

GRANT, BARRI LEINER

BOHO LOUNGE color *Chicago* v66 no4 p68 Ap 2017

bold & beautiful L. KOGAN color *Better Homes & Gardens* v95 no9 p106 S 2017

OFFICE UPGRADE: Work from home in style color *Chicago* v66 no9 p80 S 2017

Grant, Cheryl S.

I Survived! [Cover story] *Reader's Digest* v189 no1128 p62 Mr 2017

Why Am I Bleeding? [Cover story] color *Glamour* v114 no11 p116 N 2016

Grant, Christine

How to manage remote workers *People Management* p54 N 2016

Grant, Christopher

CHRISTOPHER GRANT *Dance Spirit* v21 no3 p39 Mr 2017

Grant, Conrad

How Systems Engineering Can Help Fix Health Care *Harvard Business Review Digital Articles* p2 F 9 2017

Grant, Daniel

'I Don't Want That Crap in My Gallery' cartoon *Commonweal* v144 no5 p24 Mr 10 2017

Outdoorsy Types color *Commonweal* v144 no1 p28 Ja 6 2017

Grant, Donna

OVER 50 AND FABULOUS G. Roberts-Grey color *Essence* v47 no8 p140 D 2016

Grant, Douglas

HOW LIES SPREAD color *Nation* v304 no9 p19 Mr 20 2017

Grant, Gregory R.

Mitotic transcription and waves of gene reactivation during mitotic exit color graph *Science* v357 no6359 p119 O 6 2017

Grant, Heidi

Diverse Teams Feel Less Comfortable—and That's Why They Perform Better *Harvard Business Review Digital Articles* p2 S 22 2016

Why Diverse Teams Are Smarter *Harvard Business Review Digital Articles* p2 N 4 2016

Grant, Hugh

Looking for Answers to the World's Biggest Challenges In the Eternal City color *Time* v188 no24 p31 D 12 2016

Grant, J. A.

Redox stratification of an ancient lake in Gale crater, Mars color *Science* v356 no6341 p922 Je 1 2017

Grant, J. T.

Selective oxidative dehydrogenation of propane to propene using boron nitride catalysts bibl diag graph *Science* v354 no6319 p1570 D 23 2016

Grant, Jeremy

8 Ways Governments Can Improve Their Cybersecurity [Cover story] *Harvard Business Review Digital Articles* p2 Ap 25 2017

COMMENTS color *Wired* v25 no3 p16 Mr 2017

Grant, Jon E.

Addicted to PICKING cartoon *O, The Oprah Magazine* p102 My 2017

Grant, June

Designing for Change H. Rae *Sierra* v102 no1 p26 Ja/F 2017

GRANT, KATHARINE

God Help the Queen *New York Times Book Review* p17 D 18 2016

On the Road to Nowhere: In the midst of the Irish famine, two children venture from home *New York Times Book Review* p16 S 3 2017

GRANT, MEG

Diane Keaton CAN'T STOP *AARP: The Magazine* v59 no1A p30 D 2015/Ja 2016

The Stunning Beauty of a Pacific Northwest Sea color *AARP: The Magazine* v60 no2A p44 F/Mr 2017

Surviving the '80s color *AARP: The Magazine* v59 no5A p47 Ag/S 2016

Grant, Mira, 1978-

Into the Drowning Deep *Publishers Weekly* v264 no40 p122 O 2 2017

Grant, Peter R.

Evolution, climate change, and extreme events color *Science* v357 no6350 p451 Ag 4 2017

Watching speciation in action bibl color *Science* v355 no6328 p910 Mr 3 2017

GRANT, RICHARD

THINGS THAT GO BOOM *Smithsonian* v47 no9 p54 Ja/F 2017

Grant, Richard, 1963-

Cave Dwellers *Publishers Weekly* v264 no9 p67 F 27 2017

Grant, Ulysses S. (Ulysses Simpson), 1822-1885

Grant's Uncivil War P. COZZENS *Smithsonian* v47 no7 p46 N 2016

Mad, Democrats? Blame the Iran Deal *Commentary* p1 Ja 2017

Mad, Democrats? Blame the Iran Deal *Commentary* v143 no1 p1 Ja 2017

Grant County (Ky.)

No Help from Noah *Governing* v30 no8 p11 My 2017

Grant Park Orchestra (Performer)

Waste No Weekend *Chicago* v66 no7 p51 Jl 2017

Grantchester (TV program)

Grantchester *TV Guide* v65 no27 p35 Je 26 2017

HIGHLIGHTS *TV Guide* v65 no31 p31 Jl 24 2017

GRANTHAM, MICHELE

The Question *O, The Oprah Magazine* p12 Mr 2017

Grants (Money)

See also

Scholarships

Betsy DeVos Takes Wrong Lesson from Obama's Education Reforms P. Greene color *Progressive* v81 no4 p33 Ap/My 2017

Bookends: Do grants, professorships and other forms of institutional support help writers but hurt writing? S. Deb and B. Moser *New York Times Book Review* p23 Jl 9 2017

CITIES GO ROGUE T. ANDERSON *In These Times* v41 no3 p24 Mr 2017

Funders groan under growing review burden J. de Vrieze color *Science* v357 no6349 p343 Jl 28 2017

Indianola Promise Community: Improving Academic Outcomes in the Delta D. Moore *Bridges (Federal Reserve Bank of St. Louis)* p1 Wint 2016/2017

NEWS FROM THE DRESSAGE FOUNDATION *Dressage Today* v23 no11 p12 Ag 2017

NIH to cap grants for well-funded investigators J. Kaiser graph *Science* v356 no6338 p574 My 12 2017

Pony Finals Dreams Come True *In Stride* v12 no5 p8 S 2017

Protecting the Delaware River Basin color *National Wildlife (World Edition)* v55 no5 p44 Ag/S 2017

Grants (Money)—History

GOODBYE, MY FUNDING I. FRAZIER cartoon *New Yorker* v93 no13 p43 My 15 2017

Grants (Money)—Management

GOODBYE, MY FUNDING I. FRAZIER cartoon *New Yorker* v93 no13 p43 My 15 2017

Grants in aid (Public finance)

See also

Block grants

Granular material testing

Forcing Failure in Granular Materials H. Auten *Science & Tech-*

nology Review p20 Mr 2017

A thermodynamic theory of granular material endures: Theorists have tested what seemed like an untestable conjecture: that all the possible arrangements of grains in a packing are equally probable A. G. Smart *Physics Today* v70 no9 p20 S 2017

Granule cells

A disynaptic feedback network activated by experience promotes the integration of new granule cells D. D. Alvarez, D. Giacomini et al bibl graph *Science* v354 no6311 p459 O 28 2016

Modular brain construction P. J. H color *Science* v354 no6308 p78 O 7 2016

Granulocytes

See also

Neutrophils

Neutrophils take a round-trip H. Garner and K. E. de Visser diag *Science* v357 no6359 p42 O 6 2017

Grapefruit

grapefruit color *Vegetarian Today* no1 p14 F 2017

NEWSBITES [Cover story] *Tufts University Health & Nutrition Letter* v34 no12 p1 F 2017

Grapefruit juice

YOU'RE INVITED TO DINNER WITH FRIENDS M. Crowell color *Sunset* v239 no4 p54 O 2017

Grapes

Fruits of Summer: The season's bounty in flavor-packed parcels M. W. Spencer *New Orleans Homes & Lifestyles* v20 no3 p112 Summ 2017

GOOD THINGS E. N. GAGE *Martha Stewart Living* no268 p21 O 2016

Grapes of Wrath (Theatrical production)

Noteworthy & Now F. P. Driscoll *Opera News* v81 no12 p13 Je 2017

Grapes—Physiology

Acorn Alternatives G. Almy color *Field & Stream* v122 no3 pW6 Ag 2017

Graphene

Ballistic miniband conduction in a graphene superlattice J. R. Wallbank, P. Gallagher et al bibl graph *Science* v353 no6307 p1526 S 30 2016

Graphene visualized *Physics Today* v70 no4 p72 Ap 2017

Plasmonic imaging is gaining momentum D. N. Basov and M. M. Fogler graph *Science* v357 no6347 p132 Jl 14 2017

Three-dimensional holey-graphene/niobia composite architectures for ultrahigh-rate energy storage H. Sun, L. Mei et al color diag graph *Science* v356 no6338 p599 My 12 2017

Graphic artists

BRINGING ART TO THE PUBLIC B. Andrews cartoon color *Black Enterprise* v47 no8 p102 Jl/Ag 2017

Graphic artists—Interviews

SPEED DRAWING M. FRANK color *Road & Track* v69 no1 p100 Ag 2017

Graphic arts

See also

Animated films

Information design

Painting

Picture books

The Loneliest Place color *Art in America* v105 no1 p36 Ja 2017

Sketchbook S. García Sánchez *New York Times Book Review* p26 Ja 15 2017

Graphic arts—Exhibitions

Holy Cities B. G. Prusak color *Commonweal* v143 no20 p20 D 16 2016

Graphic design

See also

Magazine cover design

Eric Rodenbeck A. Popescu color *Bloomberg Businessweek* no4539 p76 S 25 2017

Graphic designers

GEYSIR'R GRAPHIC DESIGNER J. GOTTLIEB *Iceland Review* v54 no6 p68 N/D 2016

GRAPHIC SCIENCE M. RHODES color *Wired* v25 no3 p30 Mr 2017

A NEW LOOK: Langford farmer develops lighter camouflage pattern *South Dakota Magazine* v33 no3 p14 S/O 2017

PRESSING IDEAS R. Mercer *Iceland Review* v54 no6 p24 N/D

2016

Graphic novels

Comics in Libraries and Schools at the New York Public Library color *Publishers Weekly* v264 no38 p33 S 18 2017

FROM THE EDITOR P. Lay *History Today* v66 no11 p2 N 2016

Graphic Novels Rise, Periodicals Struggle in 2016 S. O'LEARY color *Publishers Weekly* v264 no7 p36 F 13 2017

Insight Editions Launches Comics Imprint C. Reid color *Publishers Weekly* v263 no43 p10 O 24 2016

'Moby-Dick,' Part 3 S. G. Sánchez *New York Times Book Review* p22 Je 18 2017

New York Comic Con 2017 Adds Library Programming R. SHIVENER color *Publishers Weekly* v264 no38 p25 S 18 2017

Selling Graphic Novels to a Diverse Audience C. Reid color *Publishers Weekly* v264 no31 p4 Jl 31 2017

Graphic novels—Marketing

Library Demand for Graphic Novels Keeps Growing H. MAC-DONALD color *Publishers Weekly* v264 no20 p19 My 15 2017

Graphic novels—Publishing

The World Needs More Sheroes J. MCCARTNEY cartoon color *Publishers Weekly* v264 no9 p41 F 27 2017

Graphics processing units (Computers)

AMD, Nvidia coin-mining cards appear as gaming GPU shortage intensifies B. CHACOS color *PCWorld* v35 no8 p21 Ag 2017

AMD Radeon RX 550: A thrilling budget graphics card with a perplexing price B. CHACOS chart color graph *PCWorld* v35 no6 p74 Je 2017

AMD Radeon RX Vega: Vega 56, Vega 64, and liquid-cooled Vega 64 tested B. CHACOS chart color graph *PCWorld* v35 no10 p23 O 2017

Hands-on: AMD's Radeon Vega Frontier Edition vs Nvidia Titan Xp G. MAH UNG color *PCWorld* v35 no8 p105 Ag 2017

More high-end GPUs are now compatible with Dell's 8K monitor A. SHAH color *PCWorld* v35 no5 p43 My 2017

THE NEW INTEL A. TILLEY color graph *Forbes* v198 no8 p78 D 20 2016

Graphics processing units (Computers)—Evaluation

EVGA GTX 1060 3GB: A compelling $200 graphics card with a questionable future B. CHACOS color graph *PCWorld* p81 O 2016

EVGA's sensor-laden iCX technology revolutionizes graphics card cooling B. CHACOS color graph *PCWorld* p102 Mr 2017

Nvidia's GeForce GTX 1050 and GTX 1050 Ti can give prebuilt PCs a big boost B. CHACOS bw chart color *PCWorld* v35 no11 p13 N 2016

Grason, Greg

Introduction to the Theory of Soft Matter From Ideal Gases to Liquid Crystals *Physics Today* v69 no11 p60 N 2016

Grass, Günter, 1927-2015

The Lion in Winter M. Hofmann bw *New York Review of Books* v64 no10 p39 Je 8 2017

Of All That Ends bw *Publishers Weekly* v263 no44 p61 O 31 2016

Grassed waterways

BORDER BUNNIES A. McKEAN color *Outdoor Life* v224 no1 p34 D 2016/Ja 2017

Grasses

See also

Oats

Green Is Gold G. Marzorati bw color *Bloomberg Businessweek* no4529 p71 Jl 3 2017

Mobile MUTE specifies subsidiary cells to build physiologically improved grass stomata M. T. Raissig, J. L. Matos et al bibl diag *Science* v355 no6330 p1215 Mr 17 2017

Grasses—Genetics

Gene offers clues to grasses' success L. HAMERS color *Science News* v191 no7 p12 Ap 15 2017

Grasses—Varieties

FINDING A GRASSY PATCH color *Martha Stewart Living* p33 My 2017

Grasshopper sparrow

Safety Net M. JANNOT color *Audubon* v119 no3 p18 Fall 2017

Wake-Up Call M. JANNOT color *Audubon* v119 no3 p5 Fall 2017

Grassi, D.

Jupiter's interior and deep atmosphere: The initial pole-to-pole passes with the Juno spacecraft [Cover story] color graph *Science* v356 no6340 p821 My 26 2017

Seasonal exposure of carbon dioxide ice on the nucleus of comet 67P/Churyumov-Gerasimenko bibl bw graph *Science* v354 no6319 p1563 D 23 2016

Grassland birds

CHAIN REACTION E. Royte *Audubon* v119 no1 p38 Spr 2017

GRASSO, DAVIDE

DAVIDE GRASSO IS THE CEO OF CONVERSE *Harvard Business Review* v95 no3 p160 My/Je 2017

Grassroots movements

CARAVAN AGAINST FEAR S. ABRAMSKY color *Nation* v305 no3 p14 Jl 31 2017

A DOWN PAYMENT ON ENDING MASS INCARCERATION A. RICHARDS *In These Times* v41 no1 p11 Ja 2017

Not In Their Backyard G. KAHN *Los Angeles Magazine* p74 F 2017

OBAMA'S LOST ARMY [Cover story] M. L. SIFRY color *New Republic* v248 no3 p18 Mr 2017

Grateful (Music)

What to Stream color *Entertainment Weekly* no1472 p58 Je 30 2017

Grateful Dead (Performer)

Dark Side of the Dead D. BROWNE bw color *Rolling Stone* no1285 p11 Ap 20 2017

Lockn' Roll J. HOLT *Weekly Standard* v22 no6 p37 O 17 2016

Graters

tools of the trade B. HEADLEY color *Bon Appetit* p82 S 2017

Gratitude

7 Ways to Thank People in Your Network E. Baehr *Harvard Business Review Digital Articles* p2 D 1 2015

"Always be grateful" [Cover story] A. Morris color *Glamour* v115 no3 p192 Mr 2017

APPRECIATE C. K. Jackson color *Essence* v47 no7 p124 N 2016

Chris Gardner Shows How to Practice The Power of Acknowledging Others C. Gardner bw *Black Enterprise* v47 no2 p28 S 2016

EVERYDAY HEROES Raising Grateful Kids A. Reliford color *Good Housekeeping* v265 no5 p82 N 2017

FULL HEART J. Francisco color *Good Housekeeping* v265 no5 p10 N 2017

The Goodness of Gratitude L. FIELDS *Reader's Digest* v188 no1124 p42 O 2016

The Gratitude Meter Z. Donaldson bw color *O, The Oprah Magazine* p26 D 2016

Grow in gratitude A. Scobey color *U.S. Catholic* v81 no11 p43 N 2016

How Gratitude Can Help Your Career P. Bregman *Harvard Business Review Digital Articles* p2 O 1 2015

How to Eat As Much As Possible (ACCORDING TO SCIENCE) S. BUSHWICK color *Reader's Digest* v190 no1135 p128 N 2017

LET US GIVE THANKS R. Holtzmann *South Dakota Magazine* v32 no4 p46 N/D 2016

Life L. MARTIN, J. STEIN et al *Reader's Digest* v188 no1124 p40 O 2016

Missing Mama S. HUBBARD and D. POINTDUJOUR color *Ebony* v72 no6 p65 Ap/My 2017

MY YEAR-END MESSAGE TO YOU V. K. De Luca color *Essence* v47 no8 p10 D 2016

Spring for Hygge [Cover story] L. Tedesco color *Women's Health* v14 no3 p78 Ap 2017

Stop Making Gratitude All About You H. G. Halvorson *Harvard Business Review Digital Articles* p2 Je 29 2016

Why Customer Gratitude Trumps Loyalty M. Bonchek *Harvard Business Review Digital Articles* p2 O 19 2015

The "Write" Way to Show Gratitude L. M. Smith *USA Today Magazine* v145 no2862 p64 Mr 2017

Gratitude—Psychological aspects

Thanks for Everything [Cover story] D. GALEF cartoon color *Prevention* v68 no11 p96 N 2016

Gratton, Lynda

How Work Will Change When Most of Us Live to 100 *Harvard Business Review Digital Articles* p2 Je 27 2016

Our Assumptions About Old and Young Workers Are Wrong *Harvard Business Review Digital Articles* p2 N 14 2016

What Younger Workers Can Learn from Older Workers, and Vice Versa *Harvard Business Review Digital Articles* p2 N 18 2016

Grätzel, Michael

Improving efficiency and stability of perovskite solar cells with photocurable fluoropolymers bibl chart graph *Science* v354 no6309 p203 O 14 2016

Incorporation of rubidium cations into perovskite solar cells improves photovoltaic performance bibl graph *Science* v354 no6309 p206 O 14 2016

Grau, Daniel J.

Mutation of a nucleosome compaction region disrupts Polycomb-mediated axial patterning bibl chart diag *Science* v355 no6329 p1081 Mr 10 2017

Grau, H. Ricardo

Forest conservation: Remember Gran Chaco bibl color *Science* v355 no6324 p465 F 3 2017

GRAUBART, MICHAEL

A Sober (not Somber) Summer *USA Today Magazine* v146 no2866 p29 Jl 2017

GRAUDAL, LARS

An Ecoregion-Based Approach to Protecting Half the Terrestrial Realm *BioScience* v67 no6 p534 Je 2017

Graudin, Ryan

Invictus *Publishers Weekly* v264 no27 p78 Jl 3 2017

Grave goods

GUIDE TO THE AFTERLIFE KIM color *Archaeology* v70 no1 p16 Ja/F 2017

Gravediggers

This Gravedigger Saves Lives D. COOK color *Reader's Digest* v189 no1130 p10 My 2017

Gravel, Ryan

MAKE NO LITTLE PLANS T. WHEATLEY *Atlanta* v57 no1 p17 My 2017

Gravel, Tara

BLADE PUTTERS color *Golf Magazine* v59 no6 p84 Je 2017

LARGE MALLET PUTTERS color *Golf Magazine* v59 no6 p92 Je 2017

MIDSIZE MALLET PUTTERS color *Golf Magazine* v59 no6 p88 Je 2017

THIS MONTH: Putters + Wedges color *Golf Magazine* v59 no6 p83 Je 2017

WEDGES color *Golf Magazine* v59 no6 p98 Je 2017

Gravel roads—Design & construction

back at the lake D. ZIRBEL color map *Cabin Living* p14 O 2017

Graven, Heather D.

THE CARBON CYCLE in a changing climate *Physics Today* v69 no11 p48 N 2016

Graves (TV program)

Graves J. Halterman color *TV Guide* v64 no42 p37 O 10 2016

GRAVES, ANNIE

The Brilliance of Colored Light color *Yankee* v80 no6 p38 N/D 2016

Dreamscapes of Maine: Kathleen Buchanan's handmade prints reveal a misty world of islands, seabirds, and coastal sheep color *Yankee* p36 Jl 2017

Great Barrington, Massachusetts color *Yankee* v80 no6 p88 N/D 2016

HANOVER, NEW HAMPSHIRE *Yankee* v81 no1 p68 Ja/F 2017

AN IDEAL SETTING: JEWELRY ARTIST CAROLYN MORRIS BACH TRANSFORMS AN OVERGROWN 18TH-CENTURY CAPE INTO A POLISHED WORK-AND-LIVING SPACE *Yankee* v81 no5 p32 S/O 2017

Narragansett, Rhode Island: In this town, a mile-long beach is the local playground color map *Yankee* p56 Jl 2017

'Old Gray Ancients' color *Yankee* p41 My/Je 2017

Old Wethersfield, Connecticut color map *Yankee* p68 Mr 2017

Pictures Hidden in Wood color *Yankee* p40 Mr 2017

REIMAGINE THE TRADITIONAL *Yankee* v81 no1 p45 Ja/F 2017

A Respite from the Crowds color *Yankee* p86 Mr 2017

Salem, Massachusetts: Maritime history and witchy lore exist side by side in one of the most idiosyncratic towns in the country *Yankee* v81 no5 p70 S/O 2017

A Walk That Says Maine color *Yankee* p88 Mr 2017

Graves, Christopher

Is Insulting Your Rival's Supporters Ever a Good Idea? *Harvard Business Review Digital Articles* p2 O 7 2016

When Saying Something Nice Is the Only Way to Change Someone's Mind color *Harvard Business Review Digital Articles* p2

O 10 2016

Why Debunking Myths About Vaccines Hasn't Convinced Dubious Parents *Harvard Business Review Digital Articles* p2 F 20 2015

Why Every Ad Today Feels Political (Even If It Isn't) color *Harvard Business Review Digital Articles* p2 F 7 2017

Graves, Daren

Critical consciousness A key to student achievement bw il *Phi Delta Kappan* v98 no5 p18 F 2017

Graves, Earl G. Jr.

AMERICA IS BETTER THAN THIS color *Black Enterprise* v47 no8 p8 Jl/Ag 2017

THE BE 100s FOR A NEW GENERATION color *Black Enterprise* v47 no7 p8 My/Je 2017

Conscientious Consumerism: Making Black Dollars Matter color *Black Enterprise* v47 no2 p6 S 2016

Why Diversity Matters in Education color *Black Enterprise* v47 no2 p8 S 2016

Graves, Earl G. Sr.

BLACK MEN XCEL: CHANGING THE NARRATIVE OF MEN OF COLOR color *Black Enterprise* v47 no7 p6 My/Je 2017

WITH BOARD SERVICE COMES RESPONSIBILITY bw color *Black Enterprise* v47 no8 p6 Jl/Ag 2017

Graves, Elizabeth

About Face *Martha Stewart Living* p8 O 2017

ALWAYS A STUDENT color *Martha Stewart Living* p8 S 2017

HIT REFRESH *Martha Stewart Living* no267 p8 S 2016

HOP TO IT *Martha Stewart Living* p10 Ap 2017

IT'S GOURD SEASON *Martha Stewart Living* no268 p8 O 2016

LET'S DO THIS color *Martha Stewart Living* p6 My 2017

OPEN SEASON *Martha Stewart Living* p14 Jl/Ag 2017

A SLICE OF LIFE *Martha Stewart Living* no269 p8 N 2016

SPECIAL DELIVERY *Martha Stewart Living* no270 p10 D 2016

SPRING FORWARD *Martha Stewart Living* p8 Mr 2017

A TIME TO START *Martha Stewart Living* no271 p8 Ja/F 2017

Graves, Ginny

COMPOSITION Class color *Vogue* v207 no3 p382 Mr 2017

DON'T PANIC! cartoon *O, The Oprah Magazine* p87 Mr 2017

FIND A DEEPER HAPPINESS color *Health* v31 no5 p100 Je 2017

GETTING TO YES! YES! YES! cartoon *O, The Oprah Magazine* p128 D 2016

Give Yourself an Energy Makeover! cartoon color *Prevention* v69 no2 p44 F 2017

Good News About the "Bad" Cancers color *Health* v30 no9 p97 N 2016

Her Healing Garden color *Prevention* v69 no4 p30 Ap 2017

LITTLE BOY LOST... & FOUND color *Good Housekeeping* v263 no5 p105 N 2016

Rise of the Wellness Coach color *Women's Health* v14 no2 p121 Mr 2017

Roll With It color *Prevention* v68 no12 p78 D 2016

TAMING Migraines color *O, The Oprah Magazine* p83 Ap 2017

WORKING OUT SAVED MY LIFE color *Health* v31 no9 p92 N 2017

Graves, Kelsey

Nebraska Wineries and Breweries color *Nebraska Life* v21 no2 p64 Mr/Ap 2017

Graves, Lucas

Truth-Testing in the Post-Truth Era B. Lueders *Progressive* v81 no3 p40 Mr 2017

Graves, Tabitha

Uncertain Weather A. MALCHIK *Orion Magazine* v36 no1 p11 Ja/F 2017

Graves, Travis

Swing Consistency color *Team Roping Journal* p58 O 2017

Tryan and Graves Hit for $22K at RHR color *Spin to Win Rodeo* v21 no5 p16 Jl 2017

TWICE AS NICE color *Team Roping Journal* p14 S 2017

Graves' disease—Treatment

My thyroid went totally haywire W. Meer color *Health* v31 no9 p77 N 2017

Gravies

GENEROUS GRAVY S. Castle color *Southern Living* v52 no5 p104 My 2017

one-dish THANKS GIVING color *Good Housekeeping* v263 no5

Margaret's Blog *Dressage Today* v23 no10 p16 Jl 2017

Gray, Louise—Interviews

Louise Gray *Smithsonian* v47 no8 p18 D 2016

Gray, Lydia

Addressing Hives in the Performance Horse color *Dressage Today* v23 no11 p18 Ag 2017

Gray, Macy, 1967-

MACY GRAY S. J. O'Connell bw *Downbeat* v83 no12 p23 D 2016

GRAY, MADISON J.

TRIGGER WARNING color *Ebony* v72 no8 p86 Je 2017

Gray, Maggie

SI NOW color *Sports Illustrated* v125 no14 p6 O 24-31 2016

Gray, Mary L.

The Humans Working Behind the AI Curtain bw *Harvard Business Review Digital Articles* p2 Ja 9 2017

Gray, Maryann

ACCIDENTAL KILLERS A. GREGORY cartoon color *New Yorker* v93 no28 p28 S 18 2017

Gray, Myron, 1958-

IF EVER THERE WERE A TIME WHEN WE NEED TO WORK WITH AND THROUGH EACH OTHER, IT'S NOW *Vital Speeches of the Day* v83 no9 p270 S 2017

Gray, Robert H.

Searching a Trillion Stars for ET *Sky & Telescope* v134 no3 p38 S 2017

Gray, Shelley Shepard

Love Held Captive *Publishers Weekly* v264 no35 p112 Ag 28 2017

Gray, Thomas N. E.

Saving the saola from extinction color *Science* v357 no6357 p1248 S 22 2017

Wildlife-snaring crisis in Asian forests bibl color *Science* v355 no6322 p255 Ja 20 2017

Gray, Todd

MADE IN LA J. S. Li *Art in America* v104 no9 p158 O 2016

Gray, Todd A.

Intercellular communication and conjugation are mediated by ESX secretion systems in mycobacteria bibl diag graph *Science* v354 no6310 p347 O 21 2016

Gray fox

In the Wild color *Canadian Wildlife* v23 no4 p10 S/O 2017

Gray hair

Getting Over Gray W. KIRN *Reader's Digest* v188 no1125 p98 N 2016

Gray mouse lemur

Dawning of the Planet of the Apes M. BARNA color map *Discover* v38 no1 p67 Ja/F 2017

Gray Organschi Architecture LLC

A Study in Materials J. GONCHAR *Architectural Record* v205 no1 p100 Ja 2017

Gray seal

Gray Seals and White Sharks Meet Anew G. B. SKOMAL and S. A. WOOD color *Natural History* v125 no7 p22 Jl/Ag 2017

Gray seal—Behavior

Google Haul Out: Earth Observation Imagery and Digital Aerial Surveys in Coastal Wildlife Management and Abundance Estimation J. H. MOXLEY, A. BOGOMOLNI et al *BioScience* v67 no8 p760 Ag 2017

Gray whale

Join the herd diag *Backpacker* v45 no1 p14 Ja 2017

Grayling, A. C.

A necessary evil? P. Lauritzen color *America* v217 no4 p50 Ag 21 2017

Graynor, Ari

Funny Girl color *InStyle* v24 no6 p58 Je 2017

PARTY LINES T. Ferber and K. Van Syckle img *New York* v50 no12 p112 Je 12 2017

Graynor, Ari—Interviews

ARI GRAYNOR IS NO JOKE... C. Collis color *Entertainment Weekly* no1470 p48 Je 16 2017

Gray-Randle, Joanna

DRESSAGE AT DEVON 2016 *Dressage Today* v23 no5 p12 Ja 2017

Grazia, Maria

BEST DRESS E. Wilson color *InStyle* v24 no9 p177 S 2017

Grazia Malabarba, Maria

Reticulon 3–dependent ER-PM contact sites control EGFR non-clathrin endocytosis color diag graph *Science* v356 no6338 p617 My 12 2017

GRAZIANO, MICHAEL

MANAGING THE HUNGER MOOD *Saturday Evening Post* v289 no2 p46 Mr/Ap 2017

Grazing

See also

Rotational grazing

Beefing Up Bird Habitat P. SAHA *Audubon* v119 no1 p16 Spr 2017

MANAGE GRAZING BEHAVIOR: INFLUENCING THE GRAZING HABITS OF CATTLE CAN LEAD TO MORE UNIFORM FORAGE USE R. Nickel *Successful Farming* v115 no9 p58 Ag 2017

SAFEGUARDS FOR GRAZING ALFALFA: MANAGE THE RISK OF BLOAT WHEN HARVESTING ALFALFA BY GRAZING R. Nickel *Successful Farming* v115 no9 p62 Ag 2017

Grazing—Equipment & supplies

SOLUTIONS chart color *Horse & Rider* v56 no3 p18 Mr 2017

Grazing—Physiological aspects

Slow feeding is best color *Horse & Rider* v56 no10 p34 O 2017

Grazinyte-Tyla, Mirga

Baltic Baton R. Platt cartoon *New Yorker* v92 no30 p14 S 26 2016

Mirga Gražinytė-Tyla J. Crelin color *Current Biography* v78 no4 p25 Ap 2017

Greaney, Patrick

Costa's Conceptualism B. Ryan color *Art in America* v105 no1 p37 Ja 2017

Great Barrier Reef

Australia needs a wake-up call N. Shumway, M. Maron et al bibl color *Science* v355 no6328 p918 Mr 3 2017

Great Barrier Reef sees worst coral die-off ever color *Science* v354 no6316 p1082 D 2 2016

Persistent Heat Decimates Coral Reefs D. FOX color *Discover* v38 no1 p23 Ja/F 2017

Great Barrington (Mass.)

Great Barrington, Massachusetts A. GRAVES and J. BIDWELL color *Yankee* v80 no6 p88 N/D 2016

Great Basin National Park (Nev.)

Great Basin Getaway [Cover story] K. KRONE and C. KRONE color *Trail Rider* v29 no4 p32 My 2017

Great Basin—Description & travel

Great Basin Getaway [Cover story] K. KRONE and C. KRONE color *Trail Rider* v29 no4 p32 My 2017

Great Basin—History

Lost Skills J. Young cartoon *American Cowboy* v23 no5 p66 F/Mr 2017

Great blue heron

exposure color *Canadian Geographic* v137 no5 p12 S/O 2017

in a snap color *Canadian Geographic* v135 no6 p20 D 2015

Great Britain. Army

Sacrifice on the Western Front *Commentary* v142 no1 p1 Jl/Ag 2016

Valor The Fighting Parson F. Jastrzembski color *Military History* v34 no4 p16 N 2017

Great Britain. Dept. for International Development

BRITAIN UNITED, FOR THE GOOD OF THE WORLD *Vital Speeches of the Day* v83 no5 p151 My 2017

Great Britain. Financial Conduct Authority

Playtime for London's Fintech Companies J. Detrixhe cartoon *Bloomberg Businessweek* no4503 p33 D 12 2016

Why the U.K.'s Whistles Remain Mostly Unblown L. Vaughan color *Bloomberg Businessweek* no4525 p38 Je 5 2017

Great Britain. Foreign & Commonwealth Office—Officials & employees

Our people usually talk about foreign policy - not learning *People Management* p20 D 2016/Ja 2017

Great Britain. HM Revenue & Customs

Good Communication Requires Experimenting with Your Language M. Luca and O. Hauser *Harvard Business Review Digital Articles* p2 F 4 2016

MISTKAES COST MONEY: If you thought payroll ran itself, recent high-profile cases mean you might need to think again. How do you avoid an expensive error? L. FARRAND *People*

Management p36 Ag 2017

She only makes tea and sweeps the floors *People Management* p10 F 2017

Great Britain. National Health Service

Dearly Beloved color *Weekly Standard* v22 no36 p3 My 29 2017

Flexible working 'key to solving NHS brain drain': HR professionals say nurses prefer agency work *People Management* p10 Mr 2017

"People were sceptical but now we're delivering better patient care": Why an NHS Trust invested in upskilling middle managers as OD practitioners *People Management* p25 S 2017

Great Britain. Royal Air Force

Top Dog *Military History* v33 no6 p80 Mr 2017

Great Britain. Royal Navy

FATHER OF THE NAVY D. Harris bw color *Military History* v34 no5 p22 Ja 2018

LETTER FROM MHQ: SAILOR AND SAVIOR B. Hogan color *MHQ: Quarterly Journal of Military History* v30 no1 p28 Aut 2017

MASTERMIND OF DUNKIRK [Cover story] P. J. Kiger bw color map *MHQ: Quarterly Journal of Military History* v30 no1 p30 Aut 2017

Great Britain. Royal Navy. Women's Royal Naval Service

On the Cover C. Lindsey *Hoover Digest: Research & Opinion on Public Policy* no3 p200 Summ 2017

Great Britain. Royal Navy—History

THE BLOODY CODE J. A. Haymond *MHQ: Quarterly Journal of Military History* v29 no2 p14 Wint 2017

Great Britain—Colonies

Empire's Other Whites W. Jackson *History Today* v66 no12 p43 D 2016

Great Britain—Description & travel

THE BRITISH HERITAGE TRAVEL PUZZLER *British Heritage Travel* v37 no6 p87 N/D 2016

THE BRITISH HERITAGE TRAVEL PUZZLER *British Heritage Travel* v38 no4 p78 Jl/Ag 2017

English Channel *British Heritage Travel* v37 no6 p4 N/D 2016

Great British Holiday Traditions *British Heritage Travel* v37 no6 p14 N/D 2016

Journey into Secret Britain *British Heritage Travel* v37 no6 p43 N/D 2016

Living History at Open Air Museums S. Reeves *British Heritage Travel* v38 no1 p48 Ja/F 2017

Revealed: World's Best Travel Destination D. Huntley *British Heritage Travel* v38 no2 p24 Mr/Ap 2017

SOUTHWELL *British Heritage Travel* v38 no3 p24 My/Je 2017

Touring in the Lake District *British Heritage Travel* v38 no3 p20 My/Je 2017

Yes, You Can Travel on a Dime! T. E. Holmes color map *Essence* v48 no2 p71 Je 2017

Great Britain—Economic conditions

Europe After Brexit M. Matthijs color *Foreign Affairs* v96 no1 p85 Ja/F 2017

Great Britain—Foreign economic relations

Salvaging Brexit S. Dhingra color *Foreign Affairs* v95 no6 p90 N/D 2016

Great Britain—Foreign relations—21st century

The U.S.'s "Special Relationship" Is with Germany, Not Britain V. R. Berghahn *Harvard Business Review Digital Articles* p2 Je 29 2016

Great Britain—Foreign relations—United States

Britain's Bridge to Nowhere G. Younge il *Nation* v304 no6 p10 F 27 2017

Very Special Relationship D. GREEN cartoon *Weekly Standard* v22 no13 p10 D 5 2016

What Brexit Means for the Openness of the World Economy G. Mukunda *Harvard Business Review Digital Articles* p2 Je 24 2016

Great Britain—Foreign relations—United States—History

Entwined and Engaged *British Heritage Travel* v38 no3 p28 My/Je 2017

A Very Special Relationship J. O'SULLIVAN il *National Review* v69 no3 p38 F 20 2017

Great Britain—History

William the Wanderer N. Orme *History Today* v66 no12 p32 D 2016

Great Britain—History—11th Century

A century of CONQUEST K. Wiles *History Today* v66 no10 p11 O 2016

VALIANT LOSERS K. Weikert *History Today* v66 no10 p34 O 2016

Great Britain—Kings & rulers

Keep calm and adventure on P. TREBLE bw color *Maclean's* v129 no40 p56 O 10 2016

Queen Elizabeth II, for 65 Years K. Samuelson color *Time* v189 no6 p13 F 20 2017

Taking them on tour P. TREBLE bw color *Maclean's* v129 no40 p50 O 10 2016

Great Britain—Kings & rulers—Biography

King John dies in Newark R. Cavendish *History Today* v66 no10 p8 O 2016

Great Britain—Maps

English Channel *British Heritage Travel* v37 no6 p4 N/D 2016

Great Britain—Military history

THE DAY THE EARTH BLEW OPEH E. G. Lengel *MHQ: Quarterly Journal of Military History* v29 no2 p51 Wint 2017

Great Britain—Politics & government

Court of the Conscripts *History Today* v66 no11 p42 N 2016

If I was prime minister... *People Management* p42 Je 2017

Labour's Revival M. MARGARONIS diag *Nation* v305 no1 p3 Jl 3 2017

Thatcher's Jewish Brain Trust: The story of Britain's unknown neoconservatives R. Philpot *Commentary* v144 no2 p27 S 2017

Theresa May's Losing Gamble J. Freedland color *New York Review of Books* v64 no12 p42 Jl 13 2017

Great Britain—Politics & government—21st century

Britain Stumbles Toward Exit Talks With a Reinvigorated Europe D. Stewart color *Time* v189 no24 p7 Je 26 2017

Great Britain—Relations—United States

Hands Across the Sea D. Huntley *British Heritage Travel* v37 no6 p26 N/D 2016

Great Britain—Social life & customs

A Dish of Tea M. Kaufman *British Heritage Travel* v38 no4 p76 Jl/Ag 2017

Teatime at Christmas S. Lawrence *British Heritage Travel* v37 no6 p83 N/D 2016

Great Britain—Social life & customs—History

No Island is an Island S. Lipscomb *History Today* v67 no2 p31 F 2017

Great Dane

DOG EATS SOCKS K. Jazynka *National Geographic Kids* no466 p13 D 2016/Ja 2017

Great-grandmothers

The Second Coming of the Schnecken J. Kramer *Bon Appetit* v61 no12 p82 D 2016 /Jan2017

Great Lakes (Africa)

Oil extraction imperils Africa's Great Lakes E. Verheyen bibl color *Science* v354 no6312 p561 N 4 2016

Great Lakes (North America)

See also

Erie, Lake

Superior, Lake

CHOMPING AT NATURE'S BIT E. Knapp *New York State Conservationist* v71 no6 p7 Je 2017

THE GREAT LAKES: Present and Future Perils D. EGAN color graph map *Natural History* v125 no3 p24 Mr 2017

Great Lakes (North America)—Environmental conditions

Retrospect S. Potter bw map *Weatherwise* v69 no6 p10 N-D 2016

Great men & women

See also

Celebrities

Leaders

Louisianians of the Year M. W. SPENCER *Louisiana Life* v37 no3 p50 Ja/F 2017

A Note to Our Readers *Current Biography* v78 no5 p2 My 2017

Great News (TV program)

Great News J. Russell *TV Guide* p40 Ap 17 2017

Great News N. Abrams, B. L. Heldman et al color *Entertainment Weekly* no1482/1483 p88 S 22 2017

Tina Fey Is a Bossypants D. Holbrook *TV Guide* v65 no37 p14 S 4 2017

Who's the BOSS? D. HOLBROOK *TV Guide* v65 no41 p20 O

2 2017

Great Performances (TV program)
DECEMBER Programming Highlights color *New Orleans Magazine* v51 no2 p134 D 2016

Great Plains Manufacturing Inc.
SHOOT STARTER WITH SEED A. McConnell and L. Bedord *Successful Farming* v114 no10 p30 O 2016

Great powers (International relations)
The Era of American Global Leadership Is Over. Here's What Comes Next I. Bremmer color *Time* v188 no27-28 p21 D 26 2016
Responding to Russia's Resurgence I. H. Daalder color *Foreign Affairs* v96 no6 p30 N/D 2017
The Thucydides Trap G. ALLISON color *Foreign Policy* no224 p80 My/Je 2017
Will India Start Acting Like a Global Power? A. Ayres cartoon *Foreign Affairs* v96 no6 p83 N/D 2017

Great Pyramid (Egypt)
The Anti-Indiana Jones Measures the Pyramids N. Strochlic color *National Geographic* v230 no5 p27 N 2016

Great Pyrenees
Living a Good Life *Mother Earth News* no283 p5 Ag/S 2017

Great Sioux Reservation (N.D. & S.D.)
OIL AND WATER D. GRANN color *Mother Jones* v42 no3 p59 My/Je 2017

Great Smoky Mountains National Park (N.C. & Tenn.)
Get a new perspective color *Backpacker* p16 S 2017
Splash Zones *Atlanta* v57 no2 p150 Je 2017

Great Society
Once-Great Society D. F. Kettl *Governing* v30 no5 p18 F 2017

Great Sound (Bermuda Islands)
The 35th AMERICA'S CUP [Cover story] C. MUSELER color *Sail* v48 no5 p28 My 2017

Great Sphinx (Egypt)
Buried Secrets S. W. DRIMMER color map *National Geographic Kids* no470 p26 My 2017

Great Wall of China (China)
LAST BATTLE ON THE GREAT WALL Jiaxin Du *Military History* v33 no5 p30 Ja 2017

Great Western Railway (Great Britain)
GOD'S WONDERFUL RAILWAY S. Lawrence *British Heritage Travel* v38 no2 p38 Mr/Ap 2017
GWR ON DISPLAY D. Huntley color *British Heritage Travel* v38 no5 p38 S/O 2017

Great Britain—Church history—1066-1485
The Perils of PIETY K. Harvey *History Today* v67 no1 p11 Ja 2017

Great Britain—Economic conditions—1997-
The Harsh Reality of Brexit Sets In I. Bremmer *Time* v188 no16/17 p8 O 24 2016

Great Britain—History—Anglo-Saxon period, 449-1066
A century of CONQUEST K. Wiles *History Today* v66 no10 p11 O 2016

Great Britain—History—Civil War, 1642-1649
The Civil Wars' Troubled Waters R. Blakemore *History Today* v67 no2 p29 F 2017

Great Britain—History—Elizabeth, 1558-1603
BEHIND THE CURTAIN M. BROWN *Archaeology* v70 no2 p17 Mr/Ap 2017

Great Britain—History—Withdrawal from the European Union, 2016
4 Big Economic Questions Now Facing the EU F. Fernandez *Harvard Business Review Digital Articles* p2 Je 28 2016
BAD NEWS color *Maclean's* v129 no41 p9 O 17 2016
The Best Path to Brexit Is Painful for Both Sides bw *Bloomberg Businessweek* no4503 p8 D 12 2016
Brexit and the Triumph of Insularity D. Champion *Harvard Business Review Digital Articles* p2 Je 24 2016
The Brexit Door *Hoover Digest: Research & Opinion on Public Policy* no4 p33 Fall 2016
A Brief History of Britain's Relationship with Europe, Starting in 6000 BCE I. Morris *Harvard Business Review Digital Articles* p2 Je 24 2016
Bring on the lawyers M. Campbell and S. Baker color *Bloomberg Businessweek* no4496 p16 O 24 2016
Britain's 'Rock' In Spain Gets Caught In a Hard Place K. Samuel-

son color *Time* v189 no14 p11 Ap 17 2017
Business Leaders Have Abandoned the Middle Class U. Haque *Harvard Business Review Digital Articles* p2 Je 27 2016
A CEO's Guide to Navigating Brexit M. Reeves and P. Carlsson-Szlezak *Harvard Business Review Digital Articles* p2 Je 29 2016
Companies Shouldn't Wait to Prepare for the Post-Brexit World M. Reeves, P. Carlsson-Szlezak et al *Harvard Business Review Digital Articles* p2 N 3 2016
A Definitive Guide to the Brexit Negotiations D. Malhotra *Harvard Business Review Digital Articles* p2 Ag 5 2016
Developing Global Investment Strategies Post-Brexit D. T. Dingle color *Black Enterprise* v47 no2 p19 S 2016
The EU Needs to Make Sure Continental Countries Don't Exit P. Ghemawat *Harvard Business Review Digital Articles* p2 Je 28 2016
GOOD NEWS color *Maclean's* v129 no46 p8 N 21 2016
I don't know if I'll be allowed back in *People Management* p34 D 2016/Ja 2017
If Your Argument Is Based on Economics, You've Already Lost T. Sullivan and R. Fisman *Harvard Business Review Digital Articles* p2 Je 24 2016
May Spells Out Her Ambitious Wish List T. Ross *Bloomberg Businessweek* no4508 p14 Ja 23 2017
Plan forming for EU visas *People Management* p10 N 2016
A plan for U.K. science after the European Union referendum M. Galsworthy and M. McKee bibl color *Science* v355 no6320 p31 Ja 6 2017
Preparing for Brexit Just Got Harder T. Ross color *Bloomberg Businessweek* no4507 p15 Ja 16 2017
Roving Eye: International Literature T. Parks *New York Times Book Review* p27 D 18 2016
Salvaging Brexit S. Dhingra color *Foreign Affairs* v95 no6 p90 N/D 2016
SCIENCE IN A POST-BREXIT WORLD A. CURRY color *Discover* v38 no1 p28 Ja/F 2017
Theresa May and the EU Square Off Over Brexit T. Ross and I. Wishart color *Bloomberg Businessweek* no4515 p16 Mr 20 2017
UK science, post-Brexit J. Wilsdon color *Science* v355 no6331 p1243 Mr 24 2017
What Brexit is revealing S. Wells color *Christian Century* v133 no25 p35 D 7 2016
What Brexit Means for Banks G. Finch color *Bloomberg Businessweek* no4496 p50 O 24 2016
What Brexit Means for Britain M. GOODWIN *Current History* v116 no788 p107 Mr 2017
What Brexit Means for the Openness of the World Economy G. Mukunda *Harvard Business Review Digital Articles* p2 Je 24 2016
What British, European, and American Policymakers Need to Do Now W. Frick *Harvard Business Review Digital Articles* p2 Je 24 2016
Will They Really Leave, and How? K. Thomas cartoon *New York Review of Books* v63 no16 p40 O 27 2016
Will your best staff take flight? V. MATTHEWS *People Management* p32 D 2016/Ja 2017

Great Britain—Politics & government—1945-1964
Cold War Clem: Fiercely anti-Communist, Clement Attlee found Britain's intelligence agencies to be invaluable tools D. W. B. Lomas *History Today* v67 no9 p16 S 2017

Great Britain—Politics & government—2007-
See also
British withdrawal from the European Union, 2016-
BRITAIN'S MIDSUMMER FEVER DREAM J. Harris color *Nation* v305 no4 p16 Ag 14 2017
The Party of Left-Wing Anti-Semitism *Commentary* v141 no9 p1 N 2016
The Party of Left-Wing Anti-Semitism *Commentary* v142 no4 p1 N 2016
The Scrooges in Charge J. MILLER *In These Times* v41 no5 p41 My 2017

Great British Bake Off, The (TV program)
How the Cookie Crumbles D. Coggan color *Entertainment Weekly* no1434 p18 O 7 2016

Great British Baking Show, The (TV program)
HIGHLIGHTS *TV Guide* v65 no25 p33 Je 2017
'The Great British Baking Show' N. Englander *New York Times*

Magazine p40 O 8 2017

Great Divide, The (Film)

THE GREAT DIVIDE A. CHAN bw *Film Comment* v53 no1 p54 Ja/F 2017

Greater Omaha Packing Co Inc.

A Cut Above C. SORVINO color diag *Forbes* v200 no4 p92 O 24 2017

Greater scaup

TARGET: Bluebills M. D. Johnson color *Field & Stream* v122 no4 pF6 S 2017

Greater wax moth

Plastic-Eating Worms M. Sedacca color *Scientific American* v317 no2 p21 Ag 2017

Great Escape, The (Music)

Escape, Breathe, Fight R. Marech *National Parks* v91 no3 p4 Summ 2017

Greatest, The (Music)

Sia's Acting Encore N. Feeney color *Entertainment Weekly* no1436/1437 p100 O 21 2016

Greatest Showman, The (Film)

CIRCUS MAXIMUS H. BOWLES color *Vogue* v207 no9 p718 S 2017

THE GREATEST SHOWMAN T. Stack color *Entertainment Weekly* no1478 / 1479 p70 Ag 18-25 2017

Hugh Jackman in The Greatest Showman T. Stack color *Entertainment Weekly* no1467 p46 My 26 2017

ZENDAYA K. SMITH color *Vanity Fair* p87 Hollywood 2017 Supplement

Greathouse, T. K.

Jupiter's interior and deep atmosphere: The initial pole-to-pole passes with the Juno spacecraft [Cover story] color graph *Science* v356 no6340 p821 My 26 2017

Great Migration, 1910-1970

The Great Migration R. K. ELDER img *New York Times Upfront* v149 no4 p16 O 31 2016

Great Mississippi River Flood, 1927

THE GREAT FLOOD: AN ANNIVERSARY E. Laborde *Louisiana Life* v37 no4 p4 Mr/Ap 2017

Great Mosque (Mecca, Saudi Arabia)

NATIONAL GALLERY SAUDI ARABIA R. Griffiths *History Today* v67 no10 p78 O 2017

Great Recession, 2008-2013

AIR CARE: How CVG shed its costly reputation A. FLANGO *Cincinnati Magazine* v50 no11 p21 Ag 2017

Can Anything Save Us from Unintended Consequences? S. VYSE *Skeptical Inquirer* v41 no4 p20 Jl/Ag 2017

Economy in recovery: How selected industries have fared since the Great Recession K. Green *Career Outlook* p1 S 2017

HOW BAD IS THE GREAT AMERICAN SLOWDOWN? J. PETHOKOUKIS *Commentary* v142 no3 p12 O 2016

Great Train Robbery, The (TV program)

The Great Train Robbery A. D'ARMINIO *TV Guide* v65 no14 p41 Ap 3 2017

Great Un-American Songbook, The (Music)

The Great Un-American Songbook, Volumes I & II Hadley color *Downbeat* v84 no6 p68 Je 2017

Great Wall, The (Film)

Pop Chart R. Bruner, C. Lang et al color *Time* v189 no10 p58 Mr 20 2017

Wall and Polo and Wick - Oh, My! C. D. Reid color *Black Belt* v55 no4 p28 Je/Jl 2017

Great War, The (Film)

The Great War M. ROUSH *TV Guide* v65 no14 p18 Ap 3 2017

Greaves, Jane S.

Spiral density waves in a young protoplanetary disk bibl graph *Science* v353 no6307 p1519 S 30 2016

Grebe, Ronald

we asked you answered color *Cabin Living* p8 D 2016

Greber, Basil

Assembly principles and structure of a 6.5-MDa bacterial microcompartment shell color diag *Science* v356 no6344 p1293 Je 23 2017

Greber, Nicolas D.

Titanium isotopic evidence for felsic crust and plate tectonics 3.5 billion years ago bw color graph *Science* v357 no6357 p1271 S 22 2017

Greco, Alanna Lauren

A 10-Second Shoe Hack color *Glamour* v115 no7 p19 Jl 2017

"He saved my life" color *Glamour* v115 no4 p144 Ap 2017

How We Communicate Now bw color *Glamour* v115 no3 p52 Mr 2017

Our Love Story, in One Picture bw *Glamour* v115 no1 p54 Ja 2017

"People should be less scared of sex." [Cover story] color *Glamour* v115 no7 p88 Jl 2017

Regarding People Who Don't Have Period Sex color *Glamour* no8 p110 Ag 2017

Greco, Edwin F.

Dynamics of a human spiral wave *Physics Today* v70 no2 p78 F 2017

Grede, Emma—Interviews

"It's OK to be whatever size you are" L. Chan color *Glamour* v114 no12 p116 D 2016

Greece

Children of No Nation [Cover story] color map *Time* v188 no27-28 p38 D 26 2016

Greece—Economic conditions

As Hopelessness Sets In, Grexit May Be Inevitable L. Heracleous *Harvard Business Review Digital Articles* p2 S 1 2015

What Greece Has to Do Now: Fix Its Economy M. G. Jacobides *Harvard Business Review Digital Articles* p2 F 27 2015

Greece—Economic conditions—21st century

Grexit Would Be Even More Dangerous than Economists Realize M. G. Jacobides *Harvard Business Review Digital Articles* p2 Je 29 2015

Greece—Economic conditions—1974-

Greece's Least Wanted Man Lives in Maryland R. Schmidt color *Bloomberg Businessweek* no4493 p25 O 3 2016

Greece's Problem Is More Complicated than Austerity M. G. Jacobides *Harvard Business Review Digital Articles* p2 Jl 27 2015

If Greece Embraces Uncertainty, Innovation Will Follow G. Serafeim *Harvard Business Review Digital Articles* p2 Mr 13 2015

Why Greece and Cyprus May Be Better Off Without the Euro L. Heracleous *Harvard Business Review Digital Articles* p2 Mr 10 2015

Greece—Economic policy—1974-

If Greece Embraces Uncertainty, Innovation Will Follow G. Serafeim *Harvard Business Review Digital Articles* p2 Mr 13 2015

Greece—Foreign economic relations

Greece's Problem Is More Complicated than Austerity M. G. Jacobides *Harvard Business Review Digital Articles* p2 Jl 27 2015

Greece—History—Classical period, ca. 480 B.C.-323 B.C.

See also

Greece—History—Peloponnesian War, 431-404 B.C.

BEWARE THE FURIES T. Zacharis *Military History* v33 no6 p62 Mr 2017

Greece—History—Peloponnesian War, 431-404 B.C.

BEWARE THE FURIES T. Zacharis *Military History* v33 no6 p62 Mr 2017

Greece—Politics & government—1974-

Rocking the Cradle of Democracy J. PSAROPOULOS *American Scholar* v86 no2 p6 Spr 2017

Greek art—Exhibitions

Mad as Hellas at the Onassis Cultural Center C. Pappas color *Magazine Antiques* v184 no3 p28 My/Je 2017

Greek gods

See also

Dionysus (Greek deity)

BACCHUS STORIES E. LABORDE bw *New Orleans Magazine* v51 no3 p168 Ja 2017

Greek history

Greece: Beautiful but Broken *American Conservative* v16 no5 p66 S/O 2017

Greek inscriptions

When the Ancient Greeks Began to Write E. A. POWELL color *Archaeology* v70 no3 p44 My/Je 2017

Greek language

THE DREAD GORGON C. Alexander *Lapham's Quarterly* v10 no3 p186 Summ 2017

Greek language—Alphabet

SPEAKING VOLUMES C. Valentino *Archaeology* v70 no3 p4 My/Je 2017

When the Ancient Greeks Began to Write E. A. POWELL color

Archaeology v70 no3 p44 My/Je 2017

Greek letter societies

Cultural Approbation color *Weekly Standard* v22 no48 p2 S 4 2017

Why Fraternities and Sororities Have Houses O. B. Waxman *Time* v190 no10/11 p29 S 18 2017

Greek letter societies—United States

CHAPTER UPDATE K. WHITE color *Phi Kappa Phi Forum* v97 no2 p6 Summ 2017

LOOKING BACK AT PHI KAPPA PHI'S FELLOWS B. COL-VIN color *Phi Kappa Phi Forum* v97 no2 p24 Summ 2017

Greek revival (Architecture)

TALE OF A Charleston SINGLE HOUSE S. GROSS and S. DAL-EY color *Old House Journal* v45 no1 p24 F 2017

Greek yogurt

Chobani Welcomes an Old Enemy to Its Dairy Case C. Giammona color *Bloomberg Businessweek* no4529 p16 Jl 3 2017

Greeks

ARCHAEOLOGY IN A DIVIDED LAND M. Gannon color map *Science* v357 no6359 p28 O 6 2017

Greeley, Brendan

The Disabled American Worker graph map *Bloomberg Business-week* no4504 p24 D 19 2016

JOHN MAYNARD TRUMP bw *Bloomberg Businessweek* no4500 p44 N 21 2016

Trump's New Math On Regulations color *Bloomberg Business-week* no4511 p24 F 13 2017

Trump Threatens to Undo Nafta's Auto Alley bw graph *Bloom-berg Businessweek* no4509 p25 Ja 30 2017

Green, Adam

CENTER STAGE color *Vogue* v207 no6 p126 Je 2017

CHEKHOV MATES bw *Vogue* v206 no12 p252 D 2016

GIRL ON FIRE color *Vogue* v207 no3 p464 Mr 2017

Good Girl color *Vogue* v207 no11 p96 N 2017

Home Free color *Vogue* v207 no4 p188 Ap 2017

HOUSE OF SHADOWS color *Vogue* v207 no7 p96 Jl 2017

A Little Night Music bw *Vogue* v207 no11 p165 N 2017

Long RANGE bw *Vogue* v207 no1 p43 Ja 2017

On the Bright Side color *Vogue* v207 no3 p384 Mr 2017

REDEMPTION SONG color *Vogue* v207 no10 p288 O 2017

School of LIFE bw *Vogue* v206 no11 p222 N 2016

Time After Time color *Vogue* v207 no4 p240 Ap 2017

YOURS Truly color *Vogue* v206 no11 p182 N 2016

Green, Alex

For a Few Months, A Spanish-Language Bookstore in Boston color *Publishers Weekly* v264 no10 p18 Mr 6 2017

From MOOC to Bestseller color *Publishers Weekly* v264 no24 p6 Je 12 2017

How MIT and the Internet Archive Made Free E-books *Publishers Weekly* v264 no39 p10 S 25 2017

THE HUMAN SIDE OF WAR bw color *Publishers Weekly* v264 no30 p22 Jl 24 2017

On the Road with the Hachette Book Group chart color *Publishers Weekly* v264 no32 p8 Ag 7 2017

A Sea Change at America's Test Kitchen *Publishers Weekly* v264 no27 p10 Jl 3 2017

Welcoming Spaces color *Publishers Weekly* v264 no22 p23 My 29 2017

Green, Charles H.

CAN NEUROSCIENCE HELP US UNDERSTAND TRUST AT WORK?: INTERACTION color *Harvard Business Review* v95 no2 p18 Mr/Ap 2017

Green, David Gordon

Gyllenhaal Only Gets Stronger S. Zacharek color *Time* v190 no14 p50 O 9 2017

GREEN, DOMINIC

Art for App's Sake *Commentary* v142 no1 p61 Jl/Ag 2016

Banlieue Battles color *Weekly Standard* v22 no24 p19 F 27 2017

English Visionary color *Weekly Standard* v22 no32 p41 My 1 2017

Five Paths for the EU color *Weekly Standard* v22 no28 p14 Mr 27 2017

The Known Wolf color *Weekly Standard* v22 no38 p20 Je 12 2017

Making a Nation-State color *National Review* v68 no24 p36 D 31 2016

A New Man diag *National Review* v69 no4 p39 Mr 6 2017

Nothing Is Illuminated *Commentary* v142 no3 p53 O 2016

Object Lessons color *Weekly Standard* v22 no37 p37 Je 5 2017

Opposites Attract bw color *Weekly Standard* v22 no11 p34 N 21 2016

The Portrait of a Man color *Weekly Standard* v22 no47 p42 Ag 21 2017

The Prime Minister Goes All In color *Weekly Standard* v22 no20 p14 Ja 30 2017

Rattling the EU Cage color *Weekly Standard* v22 no15 p13 D 19 2016

So You Want to Write a Novel *Weekly Standard* v22 no4 p15 O 3 2016

A Specter Is Haunting Davos color *Weekly Standard* v22 no21 p14 F 6 2017

Trump Dominates This, Too bw *Weekly Standard* v22 no17 p13 Ja 2 2017

The 'Trump Effect' [Cover story] color *Weekly Standard* v22 no16 p22 D 26 2016

Untied Kingdom color map *Weekly Standard* v22 no30 p26 Ap 10 2017

Very Special Relationship cartoon *Weekly Standard* v22 no13 p10 D 5 2016

Water and Light color *Weekly Standard* v23 no5 p44 O 9 2017

Green, Duncan

From thought to action A. J. Brown color *America* v216 no5 p43 Mr 6 2017

Green, Emma

The Demagogues Move In *Hoover Digest: Research & Opinion on Public Policy* no4 p56 Fall 2016

Green, Eugène

The Son of Joseph Y. TALU color *Film Comment* v53 no1 p85 Ja/F 2017

Green, Eva, 1980-

Eva Green J. Crelin color *Current Biography* v77 no10 p39 O 2016

Green, Gerald, 1986-

GOING GREEN R. Nadkarni color *Sports Illustrated* v126 no12 p37 My 1 2017

Green, Henry, 1905-1974

EVERY DAY, EVERY YEAR A. THIRLWELL color *Nation* v304 no5 p32 F 20 2017

Green, Isaac

INVESTING IN THE TRUMP ERA J. McKinney color *Black En-terprise* v47 no5 p19 Ja/F 2017

Green, Jane—Interviews

Jane Green *New York Times Book Review* p7 Jl 30 2017

Green, Jay

KIERKEGAARD color *Christianity Today* v61 no1 p54 Ja/F 2017

Green, Jeff

Boardrooms of the Living Dead *Bloomberg Businessweek* no4534 p27 Ag 14 2017

Ford Has Some Catching Up to Do color diag *Bloomberg Busi-nessweek* no4524 p20 My 29 2017

Halal's Rise From Street Carts to Whole Foods color *Bloomberg Businessweek* no4494 p24 O 10 2016

Making Opioid Addiction Searchable *Bloomberg Businessweek* no4535 p22 Ag 28 2017

Uber Without the Smartphone color *Bloomberg Businessweek* no4530 p22 Jl 17 2017

Welcome to Pride Night color *Bloomberg Businessweek* no4493 p29 O 3 2016

Where Minority-Worker Networks Are Passé color *Bloomberg Businessweek* no4531 p15 Jl 24 2017

GREEN, JESSE

Canadian Nice: The Musical *New York* v50 no6 p86 Mr 20 2017

The King and His Wartime Consigliere img *New York* v49 no26 p91 D 26 2016

Real-Time Results *New York* v49 no23 p86 N 14 2016

Scattered Brushstrokes of Beauty img *New York* v50 no8 p134 Ap 17 2017

The Secret Lives of Edward Gorey *New York* v49 no25 p142 D 12 2016

The Ten Best Theater Events of the Year img *New York* v49 no25 p126 D 12 2016

To Do img *New York* p86 Ja 9 2017

To Do img *New York* v49 no20 p136 O 3 2016

GREEN, JOEY

My Tea Does What?! *Reader's Digest* v188 no1125 p140 N 2016

GREEN, JOHN

John Green R. Means *Current Biography* v78 no8 p38 Ag 2017

The Year in Reading [Cover story] *New York Times Book Review* p8 D 25 2016

Green, John Patrick

Hippopotamister *Publishers Weekly* v263 no49 p89 D 7 2016

Green, Jon

The need for a translational science of democracy bibl color *Science* v355 no6328 p914 Mr 3 2017

Green, Jonathan M.

Food and microbiota in the FDA regulatory framework color *Science* v357 no6346 p39 Jl 7 2017

GREEN, JOSH

50 YEARS OF SIX FLAGS *Atlanta* v57 no2 p32 Je 2017

ADULT SWIM *Atlanta* v56 no9 p108 Ja 2017

ATLANTA *Atlanta* v56 no10 p70 F 2017

The BRAVES' NEW WORLD *Atlanta* v56 no12 p84 Ap 2017

CHEROKEE COUNTY HISTORIC COURTHOUSE CANTON 40 MILES NORTH OF ATLANTA *Atlanta* v56 no9 p170 Ja 2017

COMMEMORATIVE AIR FORCE DIXIE WING PEACHTREE CITY 36 MILES SOUTHWEST OF ATLANTA *Atlanta* v56 no12 p144 Ap 2017

THE CONNECTOR *Atlanta* v56 no12 p19 Ap 2017

FOWLER PARK RECREATION CENTER CUMMING 35 MILES NORTH OF ATLANTA *Atlanta* v56 no8 p200 D 2016

GHOST TOWNE *Atlanta* v56 no11 p24 Mr 2017

HOME IMPROVEMENT? *Atlanta* v57 no1 p91 My 2017

JACKSON POLICE DEPARTMENT JACKSON 53 MILES SOUTHEAST OF ATLANTA *Atlanta* v57 no1 p144 My 2017

LAND: ATLANTA'S OUTDOOR RECREATION PLAYGROUND *Atlanta* v57 no4 p56 Ag 2017

MADISON DRUG CO. MADISON 59 MILES EAST OF ATLANTA *Atlanta* v56 no10 p144 F 2017

PEDAL POWER: Tech-savvy bike rental programs are rolling far beyond the BeltLine *Atlanta* v57 no3 p28 Jl 2017

PILGRIMAGE VS. HOLIDAY TOUR OF HOMES *Atlanta* v56 no8 p46 D 2016

PORTERDALE MILL LOFTS/PORTERDALE 35 MILES SOUTHEAST OF ATLANTA *Atlanta* v56 no11 p232 Mr 2017

SAVING PLACE *Atlanta* v56 no11 p35 Mr 2017

TANK TREATMENT *Atlanta* v56 no9 p19 Ja 2017

Their Goal: A Place on the Team *Atlanta* v56 no11 p101 Mr 2017

TOP DOCS 2017: Every year we present a roster of the best metro Atlanta doctors, as chosen by their peers. On the following pages, find 720 of the area's most trusted physicians--our biggest list ever *Atlanta* v57 no3 p65 Jl 2017

TROLLEY TROUBLE *Atlanta* v56 no7 p28 N 2016

WATER: CAST A LURE, GRAB A TUBE, AND PADDLE AN OAR *Atlanta* v57 no4 p51 Ag 2017

WINDOW WASHING BUCKHEAD 6 MILES NORTH OF DOWNTOWN *Atlanta* v56 no7 p236 N 2016

Green, Joshua

Chillary Clinton color *Bloomberg Businessweek* no4493 p35 O 3 2016

Enter the Bannon [Cover story] color *Bloomberg Businessweek* no4540 p40 O 2 2017

HELLO, AMERICAN color *Bloomberg Businessweek* no4503 p50 D 12 2016

ONE. HUNDRED. PERCENT. bw color *Bloomberg Businessweek* no4513 p50 Mr 6 2017

THE REMAKING OF DONALD TRUMP color *Bloomberg Businessweek* no4530 p48 Jl 17 2017

Scott Garrett Turns to Extremists for Votes color *Bloomberg Businessweek* no4494 p29 O 10 2016

Social Security Cuts Target Trump Voters color map *Bloomberg Businessweek* no4525 p27 Je 5 2017

THE TRUMP MACHINE IS BUILT TO LAST. BIGLY color map *Bloomberg Businessweek* no4497 p44 O 31 2016

Trump's K Street Office color *Bloomberg Businessweek* no4508 p22 Ja 23 2017

Trump's Path To Victory color *Bloomberg Businessweek* no4499 p20 N 14 2016

What if The President Loses His Party? bw *Bloomberg Businessweek* no4533 p8 Ag 7 2017

Green, Kate

TINO SEHGAL cartoon *Art in America* v105 no3 p139 Mr 2017

Green, Kathleen

Data on display: Senior shift: Activities change as we age *Career Outlook* p1 My 2017

Economy in recovery: How selected industries have fared since the Great Recession *Career Outlook* p1 S 2017

Interview with a ... color *Career Outlook* p1 O 2016

You're a what? Life coach *Career Outlook* p2 F 2017

Green, Kenneth Hart

Philosopher's Guide S. J. LENZNER *Weekly Standard* v22 no8 p39 O 31 2016

Green, Kirsten

A FORERUNNER IN VENTURE CAPITAL L. Rao color *Fortune* v176 no1 p36 Jl 1 2017

Green, Kitty

Casting JonBenét C. Nashawaty color *Entertainment Weekly* no1463/1464 p88 Ap/My 2017

Green, Laci

Crowdsource This color *Glamour* v115 no9 p124 S 2017\

Green, Lauren

Protect and Serve color *Sports Illustrated* v126 no7 p17 Mr 6 2017

Green, Lee J.

Cowboy Chicken *Successful Farming* v115 no1 p44 Ja 2017

"Dirty Dancing" brings Borscht Belt veteran full circle *Successful Farming* v115 no1 p43 Ja 2017

Millsaps starts Jewish studies minor, Professor James Bowley honored *Successful Farming* v115 no1 p37 Ja 2017

Green, Linda Mai

YUKI KIMURA color *Art in America* v105 no3 p137 Mr 2017

Green, Louise—Interviews

NO LIMITS T. ROJEK color *Bicycling* v58 no9 p34 O 2017

Green, M. P.

Observation of coherent elastic neutrino-nucleus scattering diag *Science* v357 no6356 p1123 S 15 2017

Green, Mark

Trump's Democracy Man J. LIFHITS color *Weekly Standard* v23 no3 p19 S 25 2017

Green, Mark Anthony

BLACK ATHLETES MATTER bw *GQ: Gentlemen's Quarterly* v86 no12 p184 D 2016

DONALD GLOVER color *GQ: Gentlemen's Quarterly* v86 no12 p188 D 2016

How the Style Guy Turns $1,000 into $3,000 color *GQ: Gentlemen's Quarterly* v87 no1 p10 Ja 2017

How to Be Vain: A Modern Man's Primer color *GQ: Gentlemen's Quarterly* v97 no9 p96 S 2017

I GOT YOU, BABE bw color *GQ: Gentlemen's Quarterly* v97 no6 p96 Je 2017

Manual cartoon color *GQ: Gentlemen's Quarterly* v97 no7 p11 Jl 2017

Mating bw color *GQ: Gentlemen's Quarterly* v86 no11 p58 N 2016

Sickest Collaborations on the Planet, Part 2 > Louis Vuitton x Supreme color *GQ: Gentlemen's Quarterly* v97 no6 p36 Je 2017

Starring The King [Cover story] color *GQ: Gentlemen's Quarterly* v97 no11 p86 N 2017

The Style Guy bw color *GQ: Gentlemen's Quarterly* v97 no9 p76 S 2017

The Style Guy cartoon color *GQ: Gentlemen's Quarterly* v97 no4 p50 Ap 2017

The Style Guy color *GQ: Gentlemen's Quarterly* v86 no12 p100 D 2016

Three Young Designers Bring Back Custom Suits—and They're Actually Affordable bw color *GQ: Gentlemen's Quarterly* v97 no4 p42 Ap 2017

Green, Martin

Terawatt-scale photovoltaics: Trajectories and challenges chart graph *Science* v356 no6334 p141 Ap 14 2017

GREEN, MELVYN

The First Lady of Reefer Madness cartoon *Walrus* p36 Ja\F 2017

Green, Michael

Why Americans Are So Angry Despite America's Strong Economy *Harvard Business Review Digital Articles* p2 Ag 2 2016

Green, Michael J.

Bibles and Ginseng G. G. Chang *New York Times Book Review* p19 Ap 9 2017

Green, Morgan
　Tell the World Who You Are [Cover story] bw *Glamour* v115 no3 p200 Mr 2017
GREEN, PATRICK
　Gunning For eSports Equality *Los Angeles Magazine* p26 Mr 2017
　Keeping His Fingers Crossed *Los Angeles Magazine* v61 no11 p30 N 2016
GREEN, PENELOPE
　20-Something *New York Times Book Review* p14 F 5 2017
Green, Peter
　The Art of Wrath H. Pelliccia color *New York Review of Books* v64 no15 p42 O 12 2017
　A Family Cruise color diag *New York Review of Books* v64 no16 p28 O 26 2017
Green, Rachel
　Not just Salk color *Science* v357 no6356 p1105 S 15 2017
　When stop makes sense bibl diag *Science* v354 no6316 p1106 D 2 2016
Green, Renée
　RENÉE GREEN M. Heddaya cartoon *Art in America* v104 no11 p131 D 2016
GREEN, RODNEY J.
　The Man Who Killed Quantrill bw cartoon *Missouri Life* v44 no3 p50 My 2017
Green, Sara Faye
　THIS COULD HAPPEN IN YOUR HOMETOWN bw color *Women's Health* v14 no7 p88 S 2017
GREEN, STEPHANIE
　I'm With Him *Washingtonian Magazine* v52 no4 p102 Ja 2017
Green, Thomas
　Perovskite-perovskite tandem photovoltaics with optimized band gaps bibl chart graph *Science* v354 no6314 p861 N 18 2016
Green, Yasmin
　Net Results color *Vogue* v207 no3 p254 Mr 2017
Green, Zara D.
　Financial Intimacy: Is Your Relationship Ready? color *Black Enterprise* v47 no3 p24 O 2016
　WE FOUND LOVE C. Penn color *Essence* v47 no9 p80 Ja 2017
Green Angels (Company)
　QUEENS OF THE Stoned Age cartoon color *GQ: Gentlemen's Quarterly* v97 no3 p116 Mr 2017
Green Arrow (Fictitious character)
　NO. 25 GREEN ARROW N. Abrams color *Entertainment Weekly* no1436/1437 p63 O 21 2016
Green Bay Packers (Football team)
　2 Green Bay Packers color *Sports Illustrated* v127 no7 p93 S 4 2017
　HOT | NOT T. Keith color *Sports Illustrated* v126 no1 p15 Ja 9 2017
　THE LORDS OF LAMBEAU A. Smith *Harper's Magazine* v334 no2000 p50 Ja 2017
　PACK IT UP, PACK IT IN G. Bishop color *Sports Illustrated* v126 no3 p33 Ja 23 2017
Green Bay Packers (Football team)—Officials & employees
　It's Not Easy Being Green A. Murphy color *Sports Illustrated* v125 no19 p60 D 12 2016
Green cards
　Should I Speak Up About a Green-Card Marriage? K. A. Appiah *New York Times Magazine* p24 Ja 29 2017
Green Creative LLC
　Lightbulb Moment J. KAUFLIN and J. D. MARKMAN color *Forbes* v199 no6 p58 Je 13 2017
Green Day (Performer)
　Green Day K. O'donnell color *Entertainment Weekly* no1435 p55 O 14 2016
　Green Day's New Fire A. GREENE color *Rolling Stone* no1284 p13 Ap 6 2017
Green diesel fuels
　Green Hydrogen M. C. Lott color *Scientific American* v316 no5 p21 My 2017
Green iguana
　Incredible Animal Friends E. DEFFNER *National Geographic Kids* no468 p5 Mr 2017
Green infrastructure (Economics)
　Green Infrastructure R. J. Dolesh *Parks & Recreation* v52 no4

p42 Ap 2017
　Quantifying Green Infrastructure's Stormwater Capture Potential S. Ozbenian *Parks & Recreation* v52 no9 p42 S 2017
Green Lantern (Fictitious character)
　NO. 17 Green Lantern C. Holub color *Entertainment Weekly* no1436/1437 p59 O 21 2016
Green Mountain National Forest (Vt.)
　Distance Dreaming R. WICHELNS color graph map *Backpacker* v45 no1 p26 Ja 2017
Green movement
　Seeds of Change V. Szostak cartoon *Alternatives Journal (AJ) - Canada's Environmental Voice* v42 no3 p54 2016
Green products
　Can Walmart Get Us to Buy Sustainable Products? A. Winston *Harvard Business Review Digital Articles* p2 F 24 2015
　Nature's best beauty secrets K. D. HODES color *Redbook* p48 Ap 2017
Green River (Ky. : River)
　PICTURE PERFECT *Saturday Evening Post* v288 no6 p116 N/D 2016
Green roofs (Gardening)
　Emerald City M. Ozawa color *Martha Stewart Living* p92 S 2017
Green roofs (Gardening)—Environmental aspects
　Bats in the Bronx K. Pierre-Louis color *Scientific American* v316 no1 p15 Ja 2017
Green tea
　THE BEST FOOD FOR MEN 2017 [Cover story] P. KITA cartoon color *Men's Health* v32 no1 p106 Ja/F 2017
　Cooking with Green Tea N. Zevnik color *Amazing Wellness* v9 no1 p84 Wint 2017
　FAFQ (FREQUENTLY ASKED FOOD QUESTIONS) K. Patel and J. WUEBBEN color *Muscle & Performance* v9 no10 p20 O 2017
　Five Foods to Fend Off Cancer M. YOUNG color *Men's Health* v32 no9 p64 N 2017
　Green Party! V. Veteto color *Women's Health* v14 no1 p120 Ja/F 2017
　ICED TEA color *Women's Health* v14 no5 p164 Je 2017
　Undo a Sugar Binge K. KLOSS *Reader's Digest* v188 no1124 p58 O 2016
Green Tea LLC
　WIN A TRIP TO MAUI! color *Sunset* v238 no2 p98 F 2017
Green tea—Therapeutic use
　30 Superfoods for a Healthier Life K. KLOSS color *Prevention* v69 no11 p44 N 2017
　The gift of meditation E. Marglin color *Yoga Journal* no288 p17 D 2016
Green technology
　　　See also
　　　Clean coal technologies
　GREEN LEADERSHIP GROWING AMONG CANADIAN BUSINESSES D. F. McCourt color *Maclean's* v129 no50 p40 D 19 2016
Green Wave (Company)
　Calling for kelp J. RICHLER color *Maclean's* no1 p63 F 17 2017
GREENBAUM, DANIELLA J.
　Immoral Equivalence *Commentary* v144 no1 p50 Jl/Ag 2017
Greenbaum, Dov
　Matters of life and death color *Science* v355 no6329 p1029 Mr 10 2017
Greenbaum, Rebecca L.
　We Don't Shun Unethical Coworkers If They're High Performers *Harvard Business Review Digital Articles* p2 My 25 2016
　We're All Capable of Being an Abusive Boss [Cover story] *Harvard Business Review Digital Articles* p2 O 14 2016
Greenbaum, Steven G.
　Polymeric peptide pigments with sequence-encoded properties color graph *Science* v356 no6342 p1064 Je 9 2017
Greenbelt, Stephen
　Feast of Eden: A look at humanity's most famous star-crossed couple S. Ruden *American Scholar* v86 no4 p122 Aut 2017
Greenbelts—Research
　The Health Benefits of a Bicycle-Pedestrian Trail L. L. Gezon, E. McKendry-Smith et al *Parks & Recreation* v51 no12 p16 D 2016
Greenberg, Andy

ARE WE PREPARED FOR CYBERWAR? cartoon *Wired* v25 no9 p77 S 2017

LIGHTS OUT color map *Wired* v25 no7 p52 Jl 2017

NEXT LIST 2017 bw graph *Wired* v25 no5 p63 My 2017

Reporters Need Edward Snowden cartoon *Wired* v25 no3 p66 Mr 2017

GREENBERG, BRIAN

ALL IN THE FAMILY *USA Today Magazine* v145 no2864 p72 My 2017

Greenberg, David

A Consequential Presidency color *Washington Monthly* v49 no3-5 p58 Mr-My 2017

Hail to the Chief Doodles B. SPECKTOR *Reader's Digest* v189 no1127 p126 F 2017

The War That Never Ends: Vietnam divided Americans 50 years ago. It continues to divide us today *New York Times Book Review* p16 S 17 2017

Greenberg, Gary

50 Reasons to Love Being 50+ color *AARP: The Magazine* v60 no5A p57 Ag/S 2017

SAFETY IN NUMBERS? The mathematics of predicting war chart color *Harper's Magazine* v335 no2005 p67 Je 2017

WILD THINGS *Harper's Magazine* v334 no2000 p94 Ja 2017

Greenberg, Jeff

A TV Casting Titan Tells All D. Snierson color *Entertainment Weekly* no1462 p55 Ap 21 2017

Greenberg, Joel

Is it religious freedom or noise disturbance? Israelis debate call to prayer color *Christian Century* v134 no10 p17 My 10 2017

GREENBERG, JOSH

Celebrity science color *Issues in Science & Technology* v33 no1 p19 Fall 2016

GREENBERG, KAREN J.

SKIN IN THE GAME color *Nation* v304 no12 p34 Ap 10 2017

Greenberg, Mike

Mike and ... Still Mike? T. Keith color *Sports Illustrated* v126 no3 p17 Ja 23 2017

GREENBERG, PAUL

THE LOST BIRDS color *Audubon* v119 no3 p38 Fall 2017

Greenberg, Richard, 1958-

His Inner Contrarian A. WITCHEL *New York Times Book Review* p16 O 23 2016

Greenberg, Ted

In the Shadow Of a Bear J. Tarmy color *Bloomberg Businessweek* no4541 p66 O 9 2017

Greenberg, Will

"NONE OF US IS ENTIRELY INNOCENT" bw *Mother Jones* v42 no2 p24 Mr/Ap 2017

Greenberger, Alex

AROUND NEW YORK color *ARTnews* v116 no1 p110 Spr 2017

EDITORS' PICKS color *ARTnews* v115 no4 p26 Wint 2016/2017

"INVISIBLE ADVERSARIES" color *ARTnews* v115 no4 p134 Wint 2016/2017

A New Future from the Passed color *ARTnews* v116 no1 p66 Spr 2017

Private Practices bw cartoon chart color *ARTnews* v115 no3 p84 Fall 2016

Wait-What Was That?! bw color *ARTnews* v116 no1 p96 Spr 2017

Greenblatt, Alan

Above the Fray *Governing* v30 no6 p17 Mr 2017

Abroad in America: Once a rich resource for state colleges, international students may leave U.S. universities high and dry *Governing* v30 no8 p32 My 2017

ACROSS THE AISLE *Governing* v30 no7 p12 Ap 2017

All or Nothing: Democrats need to win this year's governors' races *Governing* v30 no9 p17 Je 2017

ANDREW THE UNLOVED: Based on his long list of accomplishments, New York's governor ought to be held up by progressives as a national leader. So why don't they like him? *Governing* v30 no10 p42 Jl 2017

BACK TO BASICS *Governing* v30 no6 p26 Mr 2017

Barber Poles and Red Tape *Governing* v31 no1 p10 O 2017

Block Grant Jitters *Governing* v30 no7 p10 Ap 2017

Bluegrass Blood Feud *Governing* v30 no1 p9 O 2016

Board of Confusion *Governing* v30 no10 p9 Jl 2017

Burying Bad News *Governing* v30 no4 p11 Ja 2017

Capitol Hardball color *Governing* v30 no11 p9 Ag 2017

Changing Course *Governing* v30 no3 p17 D 2016

Closing Doors at Private Prisons *Governing* v30 no2 p9 N 2016

Clumsy Reform *Governing* v30 no3 p10 D 2016

Constitutional Inertia *Governing* v30 no4 p12 Ja 2017

Dangerous Liaisons: In the current climate, violence is seeping into politics *Governing* v30 no10 p17 Jl 2017

The Decline of the Shrug *Governing* v30 no12 p11 S 2017

Deficit in Dallas *Governing* v30 no7 p11 Ap 2017

Democrats' Geography Problem *Governing* v30 no4 p17 Ja 2017

DeVos vs. Denver *Governing* v30 no9 p10 Je 2017

Don't Sweat the Primaries *Governing* v30 no2 p17 N 2016

Ensuring Representation *Governing* v30 no7 p17 Ap 2017

Exiting Academe *Governing* v30 no3 p12 D 2016

Firehouse Clout *Governing* v30 no9 p9 Je 2017

Fizzcal Responsibility *Governing* v30 no4 p9 Ja 2017

Fracking and Reality *Governing* v30 no5 p11 F 2017

Governing in the Dark *Governing* v30 no9 p10 Je 2017

Home from the Capitol *Governing* v30 no5 p12 F 2017

Household Names *Governing* v30 no5 p19 F 2017

How Unfair Is the Map? A new measurement may identify gerrymandering *Governing* v30 no8 p17 My 2017

Indictment? What Indictment? *Governing* v31 no1 p11 O 2017

IN THE DARK *Governing* v30 no1 p26 O 2016

Last Look *Governing* v30 no9 p64 Je 2017

Law and the New Order *Governing* v30 no7 p26 Ap 2017

Leaving Money on the Table *Governing* v30 no7 p9 Ap 2017

LIFE AFTER COAL *Governing* v30 no3 p44 D 2016

Lone Star Legal Show color *Governing* v30 no11 p38 Ag 2017

Mayoral Roller Coaster: Why can't Seattle find leaders it wants to keep? *Governing* v31 no1 p17 O 2017

A Maze Called Workers' Comp *Governing* v30 no3 p11 D 2016

MUSEUM WARS *Governing* v30 no6 p9 Mr 2017

None of the Above: Have 2016's candidates made room for third parties? *Governing* v30 no12 p17 S 2017

No Urge to Merge *Governing* v31 no1 p12 O 2017

Nuclear Withdrawal *Governing* v30 no9 p12 Je 2017

Off-Limits *Governing* v30 no12 p12 S 2017

On the Defensive *Governing* v31 no1 p9 O 2017

A Party in POWER *Governing* v30 no4 p26 Ja 2017

Payback, Louisiana Style *Governing* v30 no3 p9 D 2016

Playing by New Rules: The democratic process is under siege in the states, just as it is in Washington *Governing* v30 no9 p24 Je 2017

Prison Reform Politics *Governing* v30 no5 p10 F 2017

The Pruitt Backlash *Governing* v30 no5 p9 F 2017

PUBLIC OFFICIALS OF THE YEAR *Governing* v30 no3 p26 D 2016

A Push to the Left color *Governing* v30 no11 p17 Ag 2017

Rethinking the Vote *Governing* v30 no12 p10 S 2017

RICHER AND POORER: How could the nation's wealthiest state become a fiscal basket case? *Governing* v30 no12 p30 S 2017

SCHOOL CHOICE *Governing* v30 no4 p38 Ja 2017

SHADY POLITICS *Governing* v30 no1 p11 O 2016

SOCIAL ISSUES *Governing* v30 no4 p37 Ja 2017

Squabbling in the Sunshine *Governing* v30 no8 p9 My 2017

Suburban Liberties *Governing* v30 no4 p10 Ja 2017

THE TWO ATLANTAS: Things are looking up right now in the city. Well, at least part of it *Governing* v31 no1 p36 O 2017

Uncommon Cooperation *Governing* v30 no12 p9 S 2017

The URBAN OPPOSITION *Governing* v30 no5 p26 F 2017

When Is a Judge Too Old? *Governing* v30 no1 p10 O 2016

Winning the Permit Game *Governing* v30 no1 p12 O 2016

Greenblatt, Bob

WHAT ABOUT BOB? THE GAY CHAIRMAN OF NBC ENTERTAINMENT WANTS TO ENLIGHTEN AND ENTERTAIN AMERICA D. REYNOLDS *Advocate* no1093 p42 O/N 2017

Greenblatt, Leah

THE 10 BEST BOOKS OF THE YEAR SO FAR color *Entertainment Weekly* no1470 p60 Je 16 2017

THE 10 BEST MOVIES OF THE YEAR SO FAR color *Entertainment Weekly* no1472 p40 Je 30 2017

1983 color *Entertainment Weekly* no1449 p59 Ja 20 2017

1984 color *Entertainment Weekly* no1456 p66 Mr 10 2017

1985 color *Entertainment Weekly* no1434 p57 O 7 2016

1985 color *Entertainment Weekly* no1470 p59 Je 16 2017

1987 color *Entertainment Weekly* no1486 p59 O 13 2017

1990 color *Entertainment Weekly* no1476 p60 Ag 4 2017

1994 color *Entertainment Weekly* no1466 p58 My 19 2017

20th Century Women color *Entertainment Weekly* no1446/1447 p105 D 2016/Ja 2017

THE 22-WORD REVIEW color *Entertainment Weekly* no1477 p38 Ag 11 2017

THE 25 MOST PATRIOTIC MOVIES OF ALL TIME color *Entertainment Weekly* no1472 p30 Je 30 2017

9 — "MOVES LIKE FIENNES" *Entertainment Weekly* no1444/1445 p61 D 16 2016

The Accountant color *Entertainment Weekly* no1436/1437 p83 O 21 2016

American Honey color *Entertainment Weekly* no1434 p44 O 7 2016

American War color *Entertainment Weekly* no1462 p66 Ap 21 2017

Another Day in the Death of America color *Entertainment Weekly* no1435 p59 O 14 2016

ARCADE FIRE'S WIN BUTLER color *Entertainment Weekly* no1476 p58 Ag 4 2017

Arrival color *Entertainment Weekly* no1440 p42 N 18 2016

AYELET WALDMAN color *Entertainment Weekly* no1448 p62 Ja 13 2017

The Bad Batch color *Entertainment Weekly* no1472 p43 Je 30 2017

Battle of the Sexes color *Entertainment Weekly* no1484 p46 S 29 2017

The Beguiled color *Entertainment Weekly* no1472 p44 Je 30 2017

THE BEST ALBUMS OF 2017 (SO FAR) color *Entertainment Weekly* no1468/1469 p98 Je 2-9 2017

THE BIGGEST SUMMER BREAKOUTS (SO FAR) color diag *Entertainment Weekly* no1474/1475 p15 Jl 21-28 2017

The Birth of a Nation color *Entertainment Weekly* no1435 p44 O 14 2016

Blade Runner 2049 color *Entertainment Weekly* no1486 p42 O 13 2017

A Book of American Martyrs color *Entertainment Weekly* no1451/1452 p109 F 3-10 2017

Cars 3 color *Entertainment Weekly* no1471 p48 Je 23 2017

CHART FLASHBACK 1989 color *Entertainment Weekly* no1439 p58 N 11 2016

Chemistry color *Entertainment Weekly* no1468/1469 p107 Je 2-9 2017

The Child color *Entertainment Weekly* no1471 p66 Je 23 2017

Christine color *Entertainment Weekly* no1436/1437 p85 O 21 2016

Confessions of a Mad Animator color *Entertainment Weekly* no1463/1464 p107 Ap/My 2017

DAVID BOWIE color *Entertainment Weekly* no1446/1447 p88 D 2016/Ja 2017

Dear Friend, From My Life I Write to You in Your Life color *Entertainment Weekly* no1454/1455 p103 F 24 2017

Deepwater Horizon color *Entertainment Weekly* no1434 p40 O 7 2016

Denial color *Entertainment Weekly* no1434 p41 O 7 2016

DEPECHE MODE color *Entertainment Weekly* no1459 p58 Mr 31 2017

DEPECHE MODE *Entertainment Weekly* no1446/1447 p75 D 2016/Ja 2017

Despicable Me 3 color *Entertainment Weekly* no1473 p42 Jl 7 2017

Detroit color *Entertainment Weekly* no1476 p44 Ag 4 2017

A Dog's Purpose color *Entertainment Weekly* no1451/1452 p88 F 3-10 2017

Do Not Become Alarmed color *Entertainment Weekly* no1468/1469 p108 Je 2-9 2017

The Edge of Seventeen color *Entertainment Weekly* no1441 p42 N 25 2016

England Is Mine color *Entertainment Weekly* no1480 p40 S 1 2017

THE ESSENTIAL NICOLE KIDMAN color *Entertainment Weekly* no1472 p44 Je 30 2017

ESSENTIAL PETTY *Entertainment Weekly* no1486 p20 O 13 2017

Exit West color *Entertainment Weekly* no1457/1458 p103 Mr 17 2017

The Fate of the Furious color *Entertainment Weekly* no1462 p44 Ap 21 2017

FEIST color *Entertainment Weekly* no1463/1464 p104 Ap/My 2017

FLEETWOOD MAC'S RUMOURS TURNS 40 color *Entertainment Weekly* no1451/1452 p106 F 3-10 2017

The Founder color *Entertainment Weekly* no1450 p46 Ja 27 2017

The Freedom to Marry color *Entertainment Weekly* no1456 p56 Mr 10 2017

A GAY Old Timeline color diag *Entertainment Weekly* no1471 p32 Je 23 2017

The Girl on the Train color *Entertainment Weekly* no1435 p40 O 14 2016

Gorillaz in Our Midst color *Entertainment Weekly* no1463/1464 p107 Ap/My 2017

GUNS N' ROSES' APPETITE FOR DESTRUCTION color *Entertainment Weekly* no1474/1475 p116 Jl 21-28 2017

Hacksaw Ridge color *Entertainment Weekly* no1439 p47 N 11 2016

Harry Styles color *Entertainment Weekly* no1466 p57 My 19 2017

The Hate U Give color *Entertainment Weekly* no1454/1455 p102 F 24 2017

The Hearts of Men color *Entertainment Weekly* no1459 p65 Mr 31 2017

Hidden Figures color *Entertainment Weekly* no1448 p48 Ja 13 2017

The Hitman's Bodyguard color *Entertainment Weekly* no1478 / 1479 p86 Ag 18-25 2017

Hunger color *Entertainment Weekly* no1470 p62 Je 16 2017

In Dubious Battle color *Entertainment Weekly* no1454/1455 p82 F 24 2017

Ingrid Goes West color *Entertainment Weekly* no1478 / 1479 p83 Ag 18-25 2017

Jackie color *Entertainment Weekly* no1443 p47 D 9 2016

Kevin Hart color *Entertainment Weekly* no1444/1445 p22 D 16 2016

Landline color *Entertainment Weekly* no1474/1475 p99 Jl 21-28 2017

LCD Soundsystem color *Entertainment Weekly* no1480 p53 S 1 2017

LEONARD COHEN color *Entertainment Weekly* no1446/1447 p98 D 2016/Ja 2017

Life in Code color *Entertainment Weekly* no1478 / 1479 p108 Ag 18-25 2017

Lincoln in the Bardo color *Entertainment Weekly* no1453 p60 F 17 2017

Little Deaths color *Entertainment Weekly* no1449 p62 Ja 20 2017

Live by Night color *Entertainment Weekly* no1446/1447 p101 D 2016/Ja 2017

Made for Love *Entertainment Weekly* no1474/1475 p119 Jl 21-28 2017

Manhattan Beach color *Entertainment Weekly* no1485 p60 O 6 2017

Miley Cyrus color *Entertainment Weekly* no1485 p58 O 6 2017

Miranda Lambert color *Entertainment Weekly* no1441 p52 N 25 2016

The Misfortune of Marion Palm color *Entertainment Weekly* no1478 / 1479 p107 Ag 18-25 2017

Moonglow color *Entertainment Weekly* no1441 p62 N 25 2016

The Mothers color *Entertainment Weekly* no1438 p62 N 4 2016

MUSIC color *Entertainment Weekly* no1444/1445 p88 D 16 2016

No. 1 LA LA LAND color *Entertainment Weekly* no1444/1445 p48 D 16 2016

No. 1 THE FOOD ORGY color *Entertainment Weekly* no1444/1445 p58 D 16 2016

No. 1 THE NIX color *Entertainment Weekly* no1444/1445 p102 D 16 2016

No. 2 MOONLIGHT color *Entertainment Weekly* no1444/1445 p50 D 16 2016

No. 2 WHEN BREATH BECOMES AIR color *Entertainment Weekly* no1444/1445 p104 D 16 2016

No. 3 HOMEGOING color *Entertainment Weekly* no1444/1445 p104 D 16 2016

No. 3 MANCHESTER BY THE SEA color *Entertainment Weekly* no1444/1445 p51 D 16 2016

No. 6 THE HANDMAIDEN color *Entertainment Weekly* no1444/1445 p54 D 16 2016

No. 6 THE VEGETARIAN color *Entertainment Weekly* no1444/1445 p104 D 16 2016

No. 7 MIDNIGHT SPECIAL color *Entertainment Weekly* no1444/1445 p55 D 16 2016

No. 7 THE GIRLS color *Entertainment Weekly* no1444/1445 p106 D 16 2016

No. 9 LAB GIRL color *Entertainment Weekly* no1444/1445 p108 D 16 2016

No. 9 SING STREET color *Entertainment Weekly* no1444/1445 p56 D 16 2016

Nobodies color *Entertainment Weekly* no1459 p52 Mr 31 2017

Nocturnal Animals color *Entertainment Weekly* no1441 p38 N 25 2016

ORAL HISTORY THE FIFTH ELEMENT color *Entertainment Weekly* no1474/1475 p80 Jl 21-28 2017

Our Souls at Night color *Entertainment Weekly* no1485 p39 O 6 2017

Paris Can Wait color *Entertainment Weekly* no1466 p44 My 19 2017

Perfect Little World color *Entertainment Weekly* no1450 p60 Ja 27 2017

Personal Shopper color *Entertainment Weekly* no1457/1458 p73 Mr 17 2017

The Promise color *Entertainment Weekly* no1463/1464 p90 Ap/ My 2017

The River at Night color *Entertainment Weekly* no1449 p60 Ja 20 2017

Rough Night color *Entertainment Weekly* no1471 p51 Je 23 2017

The Rules Do Not Apply color *Entertainment Weekly* no1457/1458 p105 Mr 17 2017

Rules Don't Apply color *Entertainment Weekly* no1442 p42 D 2 2016 Rebellious Special Issue

RYAN ADAMS color *Entertainment Weekly* no1454/1455 p94 F 24 2017

Silence color *Entertainment Weekly* no1446/1447 p105 D 2016/ Ja 2017

Snatched color *Entertainment Weekly* no1466 p42 My 19 2017

SONGS OF A LIFETIME color *Entertainment Weekly* no1448 p31 Ja 13 2017

Split color *Entertainment Weekly* no1450 p42 Ja 27 2017

SUMMER'S CHILLIEST THRILLERS color *Entertainment Weekly* no1473 p60 Jl 7 2017

Swing Time color *Entertainment Weekly* no1440 p60 N 18 2016

Today Will Be Different color *Entertainment Weekly* no1434 p59 O 7 2016

To the Bone color *Entertainment Weekly* no1474/1475 p98 Jl 21-28 2017

Tranny color *Entertainment Weekly* no1439 p63 N 11 2016

Transformers: The Last Knight color *Entertainment Weekly* no1472 p42 Je 30 2017

Trolls color *Entertainment Weekly* no1439 p44 N 11 2016

Una color *Entertainment Weekly* no1486 p43 O 13 2017

A United Kingdom color *Entertainment Weekly* no1453 p48 F 17 2017

The Unkillable Lizzie Borden color *Entertainment Weekly* no1477 p60 Ag 11 2017

The Wangs vs. the World color *Entertainment Weekly* no1436/1437 p102 O 21 2016

WarReN BEAtty An ORAL HISTORY color *Entertainment Weekly* no1440 p30 N 18 2016

We Were Eight Years in Power color *Entertainment Weekly* no1485 p62 O 6 2017

What to Watch color *Entertainment Weekly* no1434 p50 O 7 2016

What to Watch color *Entertainment Weekly* no1451/1452 p100 F 3-10 2017

What to Watch color *Entertainment Weekly* no1466 p53 My 19 2017

What to Watch color *Entertainment Weekly* no1484 p53 S 29 2017

Wind River color *Entertainment Weekly* no1477 p38 Ag 11 2017

Greenblatt, Stephen

Almost Paradise: A cultural history that traces the path of the first man and woman M. ROBINSON *New York Times Book Review* p18 O 8 2017

Can We Ever Master King Lear? cartoon color *New York Review of Books* v64 no3 p34 F 23 2017

HAMLET GLOBE TO GLOBE: Two Years, 190,000 Miles, 197 Countries, One Play bw color *New York Times Book Review* p1 Ap 23 2017

IF YOU PRICK US cartoon color *New Yorker* v93 no20 p34 Jl 10 2017

THE INVENTION OF SEX cartoon color *New Yorker* v93 no17 p24 Je 19 2017

The King of the Bitter Laugh bw *New York Review of Books* v64 no7 p46 Ap 20 2017

Legends of the Fall [Cover story] M. Warner bw color *New York Review of Books* v64 no14 p22 S 28 2017

GreenBlender Inc.

Smoothies at Your Service K. Schaefer color *Bloomberg Businessweek* no4520 p70 My 1 2017

GREENBURG, ZACK O'MALLEY

America's Richest Celebrities color *Forbes* v198 no9 p18 D 30 2016

Google Slayer color *Forbes* v199 no6 p54 Je 13 2017

HOW DJ KHALED ROLLS color *Forbes* v200 no4 p58 O 24 2017

LESSONS AND IDEAS BY THE 100 GREATEST LIVING BUSINESS MINDS bw color *Forbes* v200 no3 p115 S 28 2017

Music Goes Freemium bw *Forbes* v199 no7 p96 Je 29 2017

RHYMES WITH "FORBES" color *Forbes* v200 no3 p100 S 28 2017

We Knew Them When color *Forbes* v199 no1 p22 Ja 24 2017

Greenburger, Francis

MAN OF PROPERTIES D. Eng color *Fortune* v175 no2 p30 F 1 2017

GREENE, ANDY

THE 50 GREATEST CONCERTS OF THE LAST 50 YEARS bw color *Rolling Stone* no1286 p30 My 4 2017

Another Side of Paul Simon bw *Rolling Stone* no1272 p16 O 20 2016

The Battle of Standing Rock color *Rolling Stone* no1275 p23 D 1 2016

Beck's Hard Road to Happy Songs bw *Rolling Stone* no1294 p19 Ag 24 2017

Bowie's Touring Alumni Say Goodbye color *Rolling Stone* no1280 p14 F 9 2017

Carrie Fisher bw *Rolling Stone* no1276 p70 D 15 2016

David Bowie's Parting Gift color *Rolling Stone* no1273 p16 N 3 2016

Dylan's Secret Archives bw color *Rolling Stone* no1291/1292 p11 Jl 13 2017

Eagles vs. the Editors bw *Rolling Stone* no1287 p21 My 18 2017

The Early Scoops bw color *Rolling Stone* no1283 p20 Mr 23 2017

FALL ALBUM PREVIEW *Rolling Stone* no1297 p12 O 5 2017

Fred Armisen color *Rolling Stone* no1272 p28 O 20 2016

Gene Simmons bw *Rolling Stone* no1297 p58 O 5 2017

Green Day's New Fire color *Rolling Stone* no1284 p13 Ap 6 2017

How U2 Got Back to 'The Joshua Tree' bw *Rolling Stone* no1280 p11 F 9 2017

Iggy Pop bw *Rolling Stone* no1278/1279 p58 Ja 12 2017

Interviewing Dylan bw color *Rolling Stone* no1281/1282 p24 F 23 2017

Jake Tapper bw *Rolling Stone* no1294 p62 Ag 24 2017

Joe Walsh bw *Rolling Stone* no1293 p58 Ag 10 2017

Lennon Revealed bw color *Rolling Stone* no1291/1292 p32 Jl 13 2017

Leonard Cohen's Golden Hour color *Rolling Stone* no1274 p15 N 17 2016

Machine Gun Kelly color *Rolling Stone* no1285 p16 Ap 20 2017

Making the First Issue bw color *Rolling Stone* no1278/1279 p24 Ja 12 2017

Marilyn Manson bw *Rolling Stone* no1298 p55 O 19 2017

Mick Fleetwood bw *Rolling Stone* no1295 p58 S 7 2017

New York Stories color *Rolling Stone* no1290 p17 Je 29 2017

Petty's 'Last Big One'? color *Rolling Stone* no1278/1279 p13 Ja 12 2017

Phil Collins bw *Rolling Stone* no1275 p70 D 1 2016

The Photo Issue [Cover story] bw *Rolling Stone* no1299 p24 N 2 2017

The Piano Man's Apprentice color *Rolling Stone* no1272 p24 O 20 2016

Q&A: Demi Lovato color *Rolling Stone* no1298 p18 O 19 2017

Q&A: Father John Misty *Rolling Stone* no1284 p20 Ap 6 2017

Q&A: Lil Yachty color *Rolling Stone* no1290 p24 Je 29 2017

RADIOHEAD'S GENIUS & PARANOIA [Cover story] bw color *Rolling Stone* no1289 p34 Je 15 2017

Ray Davies bw *Rolling Stone* no1284 p58 Ap 6 2017

The Resuscitation of Sum 41 color *Rolling Stone* no1273 p17 N 3 2016

Ringo Starr color *Rolling Stone* no1294 p20 Ag 24 2017

Ring Them Bells bw color *Rolling Stone* no1274 p13 N 17 2016

The Road Heats Up bw color *Rolling Stone* no1288 p11 Je 1 2017

Rock Hall's Epic Night color *Rolling Stone* no1286 p9 My 4 2017

Sammy Hagar color *Rolling Stone* no1290 p58 Je 29 2017

Shania's Hard Road Back color *Rolling Stone* no1281/1282 p15 F 23 2017

The Smiths' Sad Saga bw color *Rolling Stone* no1275 p14 D 1 2016

Stevie Nicks bw *Rolling Stone* no1283 p58 Mr 23 2017

The Summer of Bad Blood bw color *Rolling Stone* no1295 p22 S 7 2017

Talking to Power bw color *Rolling Stone* no1288 p20 Je 1 2017

The Ties That Bind bw color *Rolling Stone* no1298 p20 O 19 2017

Tim Kaine's Top Five color *Rolling Stone* no1273 p15 N 3 2016

U2 Reinvent 'The Joshua Tree' [Cover story] bw color *Rolling Stone* no1289 p16 Je 15 2017

U2's New Fire [Cover story] color *Rolling Stone* no1297 p11 O 5 2017

Greene, Cary

Before a Meeting, Tell Your Team That Silence Denotes Agreement *Harvard Business Review Digital Articles* p2 F 3 2016

Don't End a Meeting Without Doing These 3 Things *Harvard Business Review Digital Articles* p2 Ap 26 2016

If You Can't Say What Your Meeting Will Accomplish, You Shouldn't Have It *Harvard Business Review Digital Articles* p2 Ap 18 2016

Meetings Need a Shot Clock *Harvard Business Review Digital Articles* p2 Mr 16 2016

The Right Way to Cut People Off in Meetings *Harvard Business Review Digital Articles* p2 Ap 8 2016

To Hold Someone Accountable, First Define What Accountable Means *Harvard Business Review Digital Articles* p2 Je 28 2016

Why Decisions Get Second-Guessed, and What to Do About It *Harvard Business Review Digital Articles* p2 F 25 2016

Greene, Catherine

Growing Organic Demand Provides High-Value Opportunities for Many Types of Producers *Amber Waves: The Economics of Food, Farming, Natural Resources, & Rural America* p51 F 2017

Greene, Dan

12 XAVIER MUSKETEERS chart color *Sports Illustrated* v125 no15 p71 N 7 2016

5 MINUTE GUIDE color *Sports Illustrated* v126 no8 p58 Mr 20 2017

5 VILLANOVA WILDCATS chart color *Sports Illustrated* v125 no15 p64 N 7 2016

7 VIRGINIA CAVALIERS chart color *Sports Illustrated* v125 no15 p66 N 7 2016

American Voices Nneka Ogwumike color *Sports Illustrated* v125 no12 p20 O 10 2016

THE BEST AND BRIGHTEST [Cover story] color *Sports Illustrated* v127 no2 p28 Jl 17 2017

Big SHOTS color *Sports Illustrated* v126 no8 p32 Mr 20 2017

THE BRACKETS *Sports Illustrated* v126 no8 p40 Mr 20 2017

Broga? color *Sports Illustrated* v126 no14 p24 My 15-22 2017

The Case for ... CHANGING THE TRANSFER RULE color *Sports Illustrated* v127 no8 p26 S 18 2017

Class Rank color *Sports Illustrated* v126 no8 p17 Mr 20 2017

COWBOY DOWN color *Sports Illustrated* v126 no1 p54 Ja 9 2017

KEENESANITY color *Sports Illustrated* v126 no4 p52 Ja 30 2017

LOCAL HERO color *Sports Illustrated* v126 no9 p39 Mr 27 2017

NBA JAM color *Sports Illustrated* v127 no1 p90 Jl 3 2017

Slam Bunk color *Sports Illustrated* v127 no5 p19 Ag 14 2017

TRAVIS KELCE DOES A VERY TRAVIS KELCE THING color *Sports Illustrated* v127 no12 p26 O 16 2017

WHAT IF? ... A JOURNEYMAN QB'S DESPERATE PASS HADN'T SHAPED THE 2004 NFL DRAFT? color *Sports Illustrated* v126 no11 p48 Ap 17-24 2017

WHAT IF? ... BABE RUTH HAD BEEN DEALT TO THE WHITE SOX—GASP!—INSTEAD OF TO THE YANKEES? color *Sports Illustrated* v126 no11 p57 Ap 17-24 2017

Greene, David

THE EXPEDITIONS color map *Canadian Geographic* v137 no4 p49 Jl/Ag 2017

GREENE, DEBORAH

An Open Letter To the Shoppers Who Consoled Me [Cover story] *Reader's Digest* v188 no1125 p94 N 2016

Greene, Erin

Our Bodies. No Shame color *Glamour* v115 no9 p32 S 2017

Greene, Francis J.

Research: Writing a Business Plan Makes Your Startup More Likely to Succeed *Harvard Business Review Digital Articles* p2 Jl 14 2017

Greene, Greta

Knopf to Publish Memoir of a Father's Loss J. Maher color *Publishers Weekly* v264 no7 p5 F 13 2017

Greene, Harry W.

Merging paleobiology with conservation biology to guide the future of terrestrial ecosystems color *Science* v355 no6325 p594 F 10 2017

Teaching Biology in the Field: Importance, Challenges, and Solutions *BioScience* v67 no6 p558 Je 2017

Greene, Hunter

HUNTER GREENE IS EXACTLY WHAT BASEBALL NEEDS [Cover story] L. Jenkins color *Sports Illustrated* v126 no12 p22 My 1 2017

IT'S ALIVE! THE SLASHER COULD BE MAKING A Comeback B. Reiter color *Sports Illustrated* v126 no12 p29 My 1 2017

Greene, Jayson

Knopf to Publish Memoir of a Father's Loss J. Maher color *Publishers Weekly* v264 no7 p5 F 13 2017

Greene, Jeremey A.

When Television Was a Medical Device *Humanities* v38 no2 p6 Spr 2017

Greene, Jimmy

Flowers—Beautiful Life Vol. 2 P. de Barros color *Downbeat* v84 no7 p47 Jl 2017

Jimmy Greene T. PANKEN color *Downbeat* v84 no6 p138 Je 2017

Greene, Joshua—Interviews

Three's Company K. HACKETT color *House Beautiful* v159 no5 p92 Je 2017

Greene, Mark I.

Peter C. Nowell (1928–2016) color *Science* v355 no6328 p913 Mr 3 2017

Greene, Nathaniel D.

Big-Project Engineers Have to Deal with Too Much Red Tape *Harvard Business Review Digital Articles* p2 Ja 14 2016

Greene, Peter

Betsy DeVos Takes Wrong Lesson from Obama's Education Reforms color *Progressive* v81 no4 p33 Ap/My 2017

Greene, Richard

Big Little Lies: Ten ways public officials fool some of the people most of the time *Governing* v30 no8 p58 My 2017

Collective Edge *Governing* v30 no3 p58 D 2016

Did We Say That? *Governing* v30 no4 p58 Ja 2017

Does Business Know Best? You can't run a public agency like a private company, but you can borrow ideas *Governing* v30 no10 p58 Jl 2017

Flipping the Safety Switch *Governing* v30 no5 p60 F 2017

Hickenlooper's Fellows *Governing* v30 no2 p58 N 2016

Informally Grading the States *Governing* v30 no7 p58 Ap 2017

Keeping It In-House *Governing* v30 no1 p60 O 2016

Managing Expectations for 2047: Here are the five trends we predict will unfold over the next three decades *Governing* v31 no1 p58 O 2017

Open Wide: Why can't legislative websites be less opaque? color *Governing* v30 no11 p58 Ag 2017

Operating Room *Governing* v30 no6 p58 Mr 2017

Shopper's Guide: Purchasing managers are pushing to have critical thinking lead the buying process *Governing* v30 no9 p58

Je 2017

Watchdog, Undone: Will budget cuts and political ire endanger performance audits? *Governing* v30 no12 p60 S 2017

GREENE, ROBERT II

WHITE SUPREMACIST VIOLENCE IS ALL TOO AMERICAN *In These Times* v41 no10 p26 O 2017

Greene, Samuel A.

From Boom to Bust: Hardship, Mobilization & Russia's Social Contract chart graph *Daedalus* v146 no2 p113 Spr 2017

Greenfeld, Karl Taro, 1964-

Greenfeld's "The Subprimes" and the Way Fiction Predicts the Present C. Doctorow *Harvard Business Review Digital Articles* p2 My 15 2015

GREENFIELD, JEREMY

THE Nicest Places IN America [Cover story] color map *Reader's Digest* v190 no1135 p59 N 2017

Greenfield, Lauren

Flaunting It A. CRAWFORD *Smithsonian* v48 no1 p14 Ap 2017

Greenfield, Michael D.

Sound *Physics Today* v70 no6 p64 Je 2017

Greenfield, Nathan

The ones the war forgot P. TREBLE color *Maclean's* v129 no43 p45 O 31 2016

Greenfield, Rebecca

THE IMPOSSIBLE CLIMB cartoon *Bloomberg Businessweek* no4508 p59 Ja 23 2017

Nothing to Wear To Work color *Bloomberg Businessweek* no4535 p68 Ag 28 2017

SENSORY OVERLOAD color *Bloomberg Businessweek* no4512 p82 F 20 2017

Greengart, Avi

10 Cloverfield Lane chart color *Sound & Vision* v81 no9 p66 N 2016

FANTASTIC BEASTS AND WHERE TO FIND THEM color *Sound & Vision* v82 no7 p67 S 2017

ROGUE ONE: A STAR WARS STORY color *Sound & Vision* v82 no7 p70 S 2017

SULLY color *Sound & Vision* v82 no4 p67 My 2017

Green-Gott, Veronica

Holidays GIFTS in Every Price Range color *Practical Horseman* v45 no11 p56 N 2017

Stay Positive color *Practical Horseman* v45 no11 p72 N 2017

Greenhorns, The (Film)

SeveRine von Tscharner Fleming bw *Rodale's Organic Life* v3 no1 p62 Ja 2017

Greenhouse, Linda

How Smart Women Got the Chance bw *New York Review of Books* v64 no6 p21 Ap 6 2017

Who Killed the ERA? [Cover story] bw color *New York Review of Books* v64 no15 p6 O 12 2017

Greenhouse effect (Atmosphere)

See also

Greenhouse gases

Greenhouse gardening

Garden Variety E. Millard color *Log Home Living* v34 no9 p34 D 2017

Greenhouse gas mitigation

Can America's Blue States Tackle Climate Change on Their Own? J. Eyer and M. E. Kahn color *Harvard Business Review Digital Articles* p2 Je 6 2017

China must lead on emissions trading P. Dargusch *Science* v357 no6356 p1106 S 15 2017

Curbing Aviation Emissions *Congressional Digest* v95 no10 p13 D 2016

Ditching Dirty Cars color *Earth Island Journal* v32 no3 p8 Aut 2017

Estimating economic damage from climate change in the United States S. Hsiang, R. Kopp et al color graph *Science* v356 no6345 p1362 Je 30 2017

Why carbon capture is not enough J. LOVERING and A. TREMBATH *Issues in Science & Technology* v33 no4 p12 Summ 2017

Will climate-change efforts affect EU–Russian relations? (Probably not.) R. S. Salzman bibl *Bulletin of the Atomic Scientists* v72 no6 p384 N 2016

Greenhouse gas mitigation—Government policy

Electric Vehicles Climate Saviors, or Not? J. BARKENBUS chart

color *Issues in Science & Technology* v33 no2 p55 Wint 2017

How Climate Rules Might Fade Away M. Philips, M. Drajem et al color *Bloomberg Businessweek* no4504 p6 D 19 2016

Greenhouse gas mitigation—International cooperation

The U.S.-China Climate Goals Should be More Aggressive A. Winston *Harvard Business Review Digital Articles* p2 N 12 2014

What Business Leaders Need to Know About the Paris Climate Conference A. Winston *Harvard Business Review Digital Articles* p2 D 1 2015

Greenhouse gases

See also

Carbon dioxide

Best cost estimate of greenhouse gases R. Revesz, M. Greenstone et al *Science* v357 no6352 p655 Ag 18 2017

Coordinated Action Against Climate Change A New World Symphony J. C. S. LONG *Issues in Science & Technology* v33 no3 p78 Spr 2017

Electric vehicle prospects L. E. ERICKSON *Issues in Science & Technology* v33 no3 p12 Spr 2017

The Energy Rebound Battle: An embattled economist's research shows that energy efficiency cant solve climate change. But it is an important contributor to human progress T. NORDHAUS *Issues in Science & Technology* v33 no4 p51 Summ 2017

Reframing the Climate Narrative K. Gonzalez *Earth Island Journal* v32 no4 p56 Wint 2017

What Carbon Really Costs E. BETZ color *Discover* v38 no6 p10 Jl/Ag 2017

What's the Beef? Do the Math E. Malter and J. Mark *Sierra* v102 no2 p38 Mr/Ap 2017

Greenhouse gases—Environmental aspects

THE HEAT IS ON P. L. WARD *USA Today Magazine* v145 no2862 p56 Mr 2017

Greenhouse gases—Government policy

Will the Climate Treaty Get the Money It Needs? chart graph *MIT Technology Review* v120 no1 p26 Ja/F 2017

Greenhouse gases—International cooperation

U.S. off track for climate goal *Science* v353 no6307 p1475 S 30 2016

Greenhouse gases—Management

ASK WHAT YOU CAN DO FOR YOUR CLIMATE C. MURN *Humanist* v77 no3 p25 My/Je 2017

Greenhouse management

WINTER FRESH color *Sunset* v237 no6 p46 D 2016

Greenhouses

See also

Greenhouse gardening

The Greenhouse Effect J. L. HESTER bw cartoon color *Atlantic* v318 no4 p38 N 2016

Greenhouse Gas Emissions from Reservoir Water Surfaces: A New Global Synthesis B. R. DEEMER, J. A. HARRISON et al *BioScience* v66 no11 p949 N 1 2016

SHOVELING BLOSSOMS G. KLEINER color *Orion Magazine* v36 no1 p64 Ja/F 2017

SPRING MEANS VINTAGE HILL D. A. WOOD color *Missouri Life* v44 no2 p10 Ap 2017

Warm Up to CHINESE GREENHOUSES K. De Decker *Mother Earth News* no281 p30 Ap/My 2017

Greenhouses—Design & construction

Fruits for the Frozen M. Gannon color *Scientific American* v316 no2 p18 F 2017

Greenhut, Barry

Acoustics of Musical Instruments *Physics Today* v70 no4 p58 Ap 2017

Greenidge, Kaitlyn

Beauty is Strength color *Glamour* v115 no6 p134 Je 2017

Invitation to a Killing *New York Times Book Review* p19 F 12 2017

Greening, Justine, 1969-

Apprenticeship pressure piles on *People Management* p6 Ag 2017

Greenland shark—Research

Greenland Sharks Can Live 500 Years and Counting B. ALEX color *Discover* v38 no1 p79 Ja/F 2017

Greenland—Antiquities

THE LOST NORSE E. Kintisch color graph map *Science* v354 no6313 p696 N 11 2016

Greenland—Description & travel

ADVENTURES OF A LIFETIME color *Iceland Review* v54 no5 p109 S-O 2016

Greenland: Singular, Spectacular, Surprising C. LISOTTA color *Advocate* no1089 p50 F/Mr 2017

Greenland—Environmental conditions

MELTDOWN E. Kintisch color diag graph *Science* v355 no6327 p788 F 24 2017

A SONG OF ICE E. KOLBERT cartoon color map *New Yorker* v92 no34 p50 O 24 2016

Greenlaw, Linda, 1960-

Shiver Hitch color *Publishers Weekly* v264 no16 p47 Ap 17 2017

Greenman, Ben

Long Live the Prince: A fan's appreciation takes the musical measure of Prince, the man and symbol J. WILLIAMS *New York Times Book Review* p9 Ap 30 2017

Greenow, Linda

Follow the Birds *New York State Conservationist* v71 no3 p32 D 2016

Greenpeace International

Banner Week for Bores color *Weekly Standard* v22 no21 p3 F 6 2017

Publishers Find Themselves Enmeshed in Greenpeace–Paper Company Fight J. Milliot *Publishers Weekly* v264 no25 p6 Je 19 2017

GreenSky LLC

THE MIDDLEMAN OF MIDDLE AMERICA L. GENSLER color *Forbes* v200 no2 p62 S 5 2017

Greenspan, Alan, 1926-

Charlie Rose talks to... Sebastian Mallaby A. Greenspan bw *Bloomberg Businessweek* no4501 p16 N 28 2016

Greenspan, Dorie

bake the season color *Better Homes & Gardens* v95 no10 p122 O 2017

Homemade Chic *New York Times Magazine* p22 Ag 13 2017

An Ideal Sundae: Like many of life's great things, ice cream concoctions are best when governed by rules *New York Times Magazine* p34 S 10 2017

It's All in the Hands: So much of the pleasure of baking is tied to touch *New York Times Magazine* p28 Ap 30 2017

On the Road: A cake you can take with you anywhere *New York Times Magazine* p24 O 8 2017

A Tart to Remember: Some desserts from childhood never leave you *New York Times Magazine* p22 Jl 2 2017

What'S New, Cookie? *Better Homes & Gardens* v94 no12 p112 D 2016

Greenspan, Jesse

Awash in Plastic graph *Scientific American* v317 no2 p20 Ag 2017

Cleanup on Isle Nine color *Scientific American* v315 no3 p20 S 2016

GREENSPAN, KAREN

THE LILA OF THE GNAWA bw color *Natural History* v125 no3 p34 Mr 2017

Greenspan, Michael

How to Launch a Successful Portfolio Career *Harvard Business Review Digital Articles* p2 My 4 2017

Greenspun, Lawrence

What Business Can Learn from Government *Harvard Business Review Digital Articles* p2 Ja 12 2015

Greenstein, Shane

How Wikipedia Keeps Political Discourse from Turning Ugly *Harvard Business Review Digital Articles* p2 N 7 2016

Net Neutrality Rules Will Make Winners and Losers Out of Businesses *Harvard Business Review Digital Articles* p2 Je 27 2016

Greenstone, Michael

Best cost estimate of greenhouse gases *Science* v357 no6352 p655 Ag 18 2017

Reforming the U.S. coal leasing program color graph *Science* v354 no6316 p1096 D 2 2016

Green—Symbolic aspects

The Political History of St. Patrick's Day Green O. B. Waxman *Time* v189 no11 p27 Mr 27 2017

Greenville (S.C.)—Economic conditions—21st century

Learning to Prosper in a Factory Town N. Byrnes color map *MIT Technology Review* v119 no6 p64 N/D 2016

Greenwald, Abe

As the Free World Turns *Commentary* v144 no2 p4 S 2017

CLEANING UP OBAMA'S FOREIGN POLICY MESS *Commentary* v142 no4 p15 N 2016

Fair Is Foul and Foul Is Fair color *Commentary* v143 no2 p1 F 2017

FAIR IS FOUL AND FOUL IS FAIR *Commentary* v143 no2 p24 F 2017

Frozen Stiff *Commentary* v142 no1 p59 Jl/Ag 2016

Is This the End of the 'Free World'? *Commentary* v143 no6 p15 Je 2017

Greenwald, Alexandra

Border: A Journey to the Edge of Europe *Christian Century* v134 no18 p39 Ag 30 2017

Greenwald, Anthony G.

An AI stereotype catcher color *Science* v356 no6334 p133 Ap 14 2017

Greenwald, Noah F.

Artificial intelligence in research color *Science* v357 no6346 p28 Jl 7 2017

Greenwalt, David

Grimm Says Goodbye M. Logan *TV Guide* v65 no13 p12 Mr 20 2017

Greenwalt, Garry

The Long (Cold!) Vigil bw color *Field & Stream* v121 no7 p54 D 2016/Ja 2017

GREENWELL, GARTH

AN EVENING OUT G. GREENWELL bw color *New Yorker* v93 no24 p62 Ag 21 2017

Garth Greenwell M. Hagan bw *Current Biography* v78 no3 p24 Mr 2017

GET OUT OF TOWN color *New Yorker* v93 no12 p62 My 8 2017

Wandering Men *New York Times Book Review* p16 O 9 2016

Greenwich (London, England)

Regal Echoes in Royal Greenwich S. Lawrence *British Heritage Travel* v38 no1 p26 Ja/F 2017

Greenwood, Adrian

Victoria's Scottish Lion: The Life of Colin Campbell, Lord Clyde R. Guttman *Military History* v33 no5 p70 Ja 2017

Greenwood, Brian

Stay on Your Smartphone! *Parks & Recreation* v51 no11 p14 N 2016

GREENWOOD, ELIZABETH

MAN OF LETTERS color *O, The Oprah Magazine* p30 Ag 2017

Greenwood, Jerusha

Stay on Your Smartphone! *Parks & Recreation* v51 no11 p14 N 2016

Greenwood, Veronique

do bacteria make it rain? color *Popular Science* v289 no4 p22 Jl/Ag 2017

Night Owl Genes color *Scientific American* v317 no3 p21 S 2017

Green-Wood Cemetery (New York, N.Y.)

GOINGS ON ABOUT TOWN color *New Yorker* v93 no11 p4 My 1 2017

"Said to Be" S. CAREY color *Natural History* v125 no9 p48 S 2017

Greer, Andrew Sean

It's a Summer Day color *New Yorker* v93 no17 p54 Je 19 2017

Love Boat color *Sunset* v238 no6 p78 Je 2017

Mom's Dinner Party Diaries *Reader's Digest* v188 no1125 p62 N 2016

OFF TO SEE THE WIZARDS color *New York Times Book Review* p69 D 4 2016

Travels of a Lifetime C. Buckley *New York Times Book Review* p1 Jl 30 2017

GREER, BETSY

Who is pushing the craft field forward? color *American Craft* v76 no6 p26 D 2016-Ja 2017

Greer, Judy

I'm Sexy and I Know It? color *InStyle* v24 no7 p116 Jl 2017

Greer, Lindred—Interviews

"Leadership Qualities" vs. Competence: Which Matters More? S. Cliffe *Harvard Business Review Digital Articles* p2 N 5 2015

GREER, MICHAEL

A Case for Multimedia Storytelling *Publishers Weekly* v264 no26 p184 Je 26 2017

Greer, Nick

OLDIES AND GOODIES C. R. JOYNT *Washingtonian Maga-*

zine v52 no3 p26 D 2016

Greer, Tasha

PICKLE RECIPES for the Picking: Ferment or quick-pickle your harvest with this assortment of ideas from Mother Earth News bloggers *Mother Earth News* no282 p56 Je/Jl 2017

Greeting cards

See also

Christmas cards

Valentines

the SURPRISE inside color *Better Homes & Gardens* v95 no2 p46 F 2016

Greeting cards—Evaluation

Fabulous Finds S. M. MULLINS *Cincinnati Magazine* v50 no2 pH4 N 2016

Greetings, Friends! (Poem)

GREETINGS, FRIENDS! I. FRAZIER *New Yorker* v92 no42 p91 D 19 2016

Greffet, Jean-Jacques

Anti-coalescence of bosons on a lossy beam splitter bw chart diag graph *Science* v356 no6345 p1373 Je 30 2017

Gregersen, Hal

BURSTING THE CEO BUBBLE color *Harvard Business Review* v95 no2 p76 Mr/Ap 2017

Make It OK for Employees to Challenge Your Ideas *Harvard Business Review Digital Articles* p2 My 6 2015

When Was the Last Time You Asked, "Why Are We Doing It This Way?" *Harvard Business Review Digital Articles* p2 Ap 1 2016

Gregg, A. J.

PERPETUAL MOTION K. Dold cartoon *Runner's World* v52 no1 p40 Ja/F 2017

Gregg, Brian

How CMOs and CROs Can Be Allies *Harvard Business Review Digital Articles* p2 Mr 26 2015

Gregg, Gabi

Makeup Marvels A. Jordan color *Essence* v48 no5 p37 S 2017

Grego, Angela

Sensory Development Playgrounds for Parks, Schools *Parks & Recreation* p8 2017 Supplement Field Guide - Supplier and Resource Directory

Gregoire, Carolyn

Executives, Protect Your Alone Time *Harvard Business Review Digital Articles* p2 D 16 2015

Your Mindful Day [Cover story] color *Prevention* v69 no9 p80 O 2017

GREGOIRE, CHARLIE

OSHKOSH OR BUST color *Flying* v144 no11 p50 N 2017

Gregoire, Lauren J.

Ocean mixing and ice-sheet control of seawater 234U/238U during the last deglaciation bibl graph *Science* v354 no6312 p626 N 4 2016

Gregoratti, Leonardo

LOST TREASURE RECAPTURED IN WORDS: The destruction of Palmyra robbed us of one of antiquity's great trading cities. A slim but evocative study reminds us of its importance *History Today* v67 no10 p96 O 2017

Gregorek, Jerzy

TIM FERRISS TIM cartoon *Men's Health* v32 no9 p36 N 2017

Gregorian calendar

Early Spring J. RAO color *Natural History* v125 no3 p45 Mr 2017

Gregory, Alex

The OLDER TESTAMENT: An Origin Story cartoon *Esquire* p136 O 2017

Gregory, Alice

ACCIDENTAL KILLERS cartoon color *New Yorker* v93 no28 p28 S 18 2017

Good Press: A tale of plot twists and publicists in midcentury New York *New York Times Book Review* p15 S 10 2017

LITTLE THINGS *Harper's Magazine* v334 no2001 p41 F 2017

What's the best book, new or old, you read this year? *New York Times Book Review* p27 D 25 2016

Gregory, Andy—Interviews

MEET ANDY GREGORY color *Sea Magazine* v109 no7 pPNW-8 Jl 2017

Gregory, Brielle

400 Years of Wisdom bw *Men's Health* v32 no5 p12 Je 2017

Am I Going to Post This, or Are You? cartoon graph *Men's Health*

v32 no9 p80 N 2017

Burn 40 Pounds of Fat color *Men's Health* v32 no7 p64 S 2017

FROM THIN TO FAT AND BACK color *Men's Health* v32 no3 p66 Ap 2017

How to Lose Those 10 Dang Pounds color *Men's Health* v32 no8 p90 O 2017

"I LOST 285 POUNDS" color *Men's Health* v31 no10 p24 D 2016

The Sports Bar cartoon *Men's Health* v32 no2 p30 Mr 2017

TAX PRO TRICKS bw cartoon *Men's Health* v32 no3 p34 Ap 2017

World-Class Fat-Blasting Secrets color map *Men's Health* v32 no5 p89 Je 2017

GREGORY, CHRIS

Best Shoeing Method for Low Heels? *Horse & Rider* v56 no5 p16 My 2017

Gregory, Cynthia, 1946-

40 Years Ago This Month *Dance Magazine* v90 no12 p123 D 2016

Gregory, Danny

Let's get rid of art education in schools color *Phi Delta Kappan* v98 no7 p21 Ap 2017

Gregory, Daryl

Sixth Sense and Sensibility: Daryl Gregory's novel features the conflicted members of a family of psychics M. Gonzales *New York Times Book Review* p18 Ag 13 2017

SPOONBENDERS B. J. GRUBISIC color *Maclean's* v130 no7 p60 Ag 2017

GREGORY, DAVID

You Shall Tell Your Child: A journalist celebrates a year of Jewish holidays *New York Times Magazine* p8 Ap 30 2017

Gregory, Dick, 1932-2017

Dick Gregory T. Smiley color *Time* v190 no9 p17 S 4 2017

Gregory, Eric

My son's organ donation taught me death is not the last word il *America* v216 no13 p40 Je 12 2017

Gregory, Ernesto

Privacy concerns prompt protests in California G. Hodgson *Physics Today* v69 no12 p46 D 2016

Gregory, Hamilton

McNAMARA'S BOYS *MHQ: Quarterly Journal of Military History* v29 no3 p70 Spr 2017

Gregory, Nicole

ANNA THOMAS color *Vegetarian Times* v43 no2 p86 N/D 2016

Gregory, Paul R.

Can Trump Handle Putin? *Hoover Digest: Research & Opinion on Public Policy* no1 p103 Wint 2017

The Infrastructure Myth *Hoover Digest: Research & Opinion on Public Policy* no1 p28 Wint 2017

"It's Best Not to Mess with Us": The nuclear poker game with Moscow has already begun--or, rather, resumed *Hoover Digest: Research & Opinion on Public Policy* no2 p97 Spr 2017

The Walking Dead *Hoover Digest: Research & Opinion on Public Policy* no4 p66 Fall 2016

Gregory, Philippa, 1954-—Interviews

Philippa Gregory *New York Times Book Review* p6 Ag 13 2017

Gregory, Richard

Click chemistry enables preclinical evaluation of targeted epigenetic therapies diag *Science* v356 no6345 p1397 Je 30 2017

Gregory, Sean

Aaron Judge Sizes Up As Baseball's Best New Hope color *Time* v190 no8 p22 Ag 28 2017

After the Massacre [Cover story] color diag *Time* v190 no15 p22 O 16 2017

America's Cup color *Time* v190 no2/3 p11 Jl 10-17 2017

Atlanta's Patriot Way color *Time* v190 no4 p55 F 6 2017

Boycotts and Brain Damage Cast a Dark Shadow Over Football Season color *Time* v190 no10/11 p25 S 18 2017

The Chicago Cubs and Their Unlikely Ace Could Make History color *Time* v188 no18 p50 O 31 2016

A Corruption Probe Into College Hoops Exposes More Than Shady Deals color *Time* v190 no15 p17 O 16 2017

Dale Earnhardt Jr color *Time* v189 no18 p15 My 15 2017

The Fastest Man on Wheels color *Time* v188 no27-28 p74 D 26 2016

A First Major Tournament (Finally) for Sergio García color *Time* v189 no15 p13 Ap 24 2017

Garbiñe Muguruza color *Time* v190 no9 p64 S 4 2017

The Golden State Warriors As 2017 NBA Champions color *Time* v189 no24 p11 Je 26 2017

How Female Athletes Can Help Advance the Fight for Fair Pay color *Time* v189 no12 p23 Ap 3 2017

The Jobs That Weren't Saved color *Time* v189 no20 p36 My 29 2017

Jordan Spieth color *Time* v190 no6 p17 Ag 7 2017

The Joy of Sharing color *Time* v189 no7/8 p62 F 27 2017

Kid Sports Inc [Cover story] color diag *Time* v190 no9 p42 S 4 2017

Lightbox color *Time* v189 no24 p14 Je 26 2017

Lightbox color *Time* v190 no12 p18 S 25 2017

The Making of a Cynical Sporting Spectacle In the Desert color *Time* v190 no8 p54 Ag 28 2017

Man Out of Time color diag *Time* v189 no5 p42 F 13 2017

Meet the Class of 2016 color *Time* v188 no18 p22 O 31 2016

Next Generation Leaders color *Time* v190 no16/17 p74 O 23 2017

The Shoddy Science Behind Fidget Spinners color *Time* v189 no19 p17 My 22 2017

Tom Brady color *Time* v189 no6 p13 F 20 2017

Tom Brady's Payback Play color *Time* v189 no4 p55 F 6 2017

Trump's Offensive Playbook [Cover story] color *Time* v190 no14 p32 O 9 2017

Tunnel Out of Danger color *Time* v189 no13 p37 Ap 10 2017

Usain Bolt color *Time* v190 no7 p13 Ag 21 2017

What It Takes to Win It All color diag *Time* v188 no14 p24 O 10 2016

Why There Is Crying In Baseball, and Tennis, and Golf, and Soccer ... color *Time* v190 no5 p25 Jl 31 2017

Y.A. Tittle color *Time* v190 no16/17 p20 O 23 2017

Gregory, Susanna
The Habit of Murder: The Twenty-Third Chronicle of Matthew Bartholomew *Publishers Weekly* v264 no35 p107 Ag 28 2017

Gregory, Vanessa
SOUTH'S BEST MUSEUM color *Southern Living* v52 no4 p84 Ap 2017

Gregory County (S.D.)
Join the Conversation *South Dakota Magazine* v33 no3 p19 S/O 2017

Greider, Carol
Not just Salk color *Science* v357 no6356 p1105 S 15 2017

GREIDER, WILLIAM
The Debate We Need *Nation* v303 no17 p6 O 24 2016

GREIF, MARK
OBAMA'S AMERICA img *New York* v49 no20 p12 O 3 2016

Philosophers and Other Lovers *New York Times Book Review* p11 N 6 2016

Greif, Michael
BULLIES H. ALS cartoon *New Yorker* v92 no42 p128 D 19 2016

Greif, Stefan
Acoustic mirrors as sensory traps for bats diag *Science* v357 no6355 p1045 S 8 2017

Greilsammer, David
GOINGS ON ABOUT TOWN color *New Yorker* v93 no8 p4 Ap 10 2017

GREIMAN, STEPHEN E.
Transformational Principles for NEON Sampling of Mammalian Parasites and Pathogens: A Response to Springer and Colleagues *BioScience* v66 no11 p917 N 1 2016

Greiner, Jochen
An accreting pulsar with extreme properties drives an ultraluminous x-ray source in NGC 5907 bibl chart graph *Science* v355 no6327 p817 F 24 2017

Greiner, Lori
Advice Worth Taking color *AARP: The Magazine* v59 no2A p30 F/Mr 2016

Greiner, Markus
Atom-by-atom assembly of defect-free one-dimensional cold atom arrays bibl diag graph *Science* v354 no6315 p1024 N 25 2016

GREINER, ROBERT C.
12,000 MARKS FOR TEXAS *Prologue* v49 no1 p18 Spr 2017

GREISINGER, RALPH
Life cartoon *Reader's Digest* v190 no1132 p30 Jl/Ag 2017

Greitens, Eric, 1974-
Governing in the Dark A. Greenblatt *Governing* v30 no9 p10 Je

2017

Greiter, Martin
Robust spin-polarized midgap states at step edges of topological crystalline insulators bibl graph *Science* v354 no6317 p1269 D 9 2016

Greive, Bradley Trevor
Readers Respond bw *Publishers Weekly* v264 no2 p3 Ja 9 2017

Thank God for That Crazy Little Bird *Audubon* v119 no1 p20 Spr 2017

Gremer, Lothar
Fibril structure of amyloid-β(1–42) by cryo–electron microscopy color diag *Science* v357 no6359 p116 O 6 2017

Grenada—History—American Invasion, 1983
Striking Back Against Empire F. BERRIGAN bw color *In These Times* v40 no11 p33 N 2016

Grenades
DISCUS HAND GRENADE C. McNab *MHQ: Quarterly Journal of Military History* v29 no3 p25 Spr 2017

Grenfell, Bryan T.
Reducing antimicrobial use in food animals color graph *Science* v357 no6358 p1350 S 29 2017

Grenier, Jean-Christophe
Social status alters immune regulation and response to infection in macaques bibl graph *Science* v354 no6315 p1041 N 25 2016

Grenier, Melinda
The Real Cause of the U.S. Car Slide: SUVs diag *Bloomberg Businessweek* no4518 p24 Ap 10 2017

GRENIER, PAUL
Legitimate Differences *American Conservative* v16 no1 p33 Ja/F 2017

Grennon, Jillian
i did it! K. SELZER *Better Homes & Gardens* v94 no12 p71 D 2016

Grenny, Joseph
A 3-Step Plan for Turning Weaknesses into Strengths color *Harvard Business Review Digital Articles* p2 Ja 26 2017

4 Ways to Control Your Emotions in Tense Moments *Harvard Business Review Digital Articles* p2 D 21 2016

5 Ways to Minimize Office Distractions *Harvard Business Review Digital Articles* p2 D 17 2015

6 Ways to Reduce the Stress of Presenting *Harvard Business Review Digital Articles* p2 Ag 31 2015

7 Ways to Stop a Meeting from Dragging On *Harvard Business Review Digital Articles* p2 Ap 25 2016

Almost All Managers Have at Least One Career-Limiting Habit *Harvard Business Review Digital Articles* p2 Jl 5 2016

Are You Sure You Want to Be a Manager? *Harvard Business Review Digital Articles* p2 S 22 2015

How to Deal with the Irrational Parts of a Negotiation *Harvard Business Review Digital Articles* p2 Je 6 2016

How to Disagree with Your Boss *Harvard Business Review Digital Articles* p2 N 25 2014

How to Get Work Done on the Road *Harvard Business Review Digital Articles* p2 N 9 2015

How to Make Feedback Feel Normal *Harvard Business Review Digital Articles* p2 Ag 19 2016

How to Raise Sensitive Issues During a Virtual Meeting *Harvard Business Review Digital Articles* p2 Mr 14 2017

How to React to Biased Comments at Work *Harvard Business Review Digital Articles* p2 My 3 2017

How to Talk Politics at Work Without Alienating People *Harvard Business Review Digital Articles* p2 S 14 2016

The Key to Giving and Receiving Negative Feedback *Harvard Business Review Digital Articles* p2 Ag 6 2015

Signs Your Team Is Too Strong for Its Own Good *Harvard Business Review Digital Articles* p2 Je 29 2015

Stop Enabling Gossip on Your Team *Harvard Business Review Digital Articles* p2 Ja 9 2015

Trick Yourself into Breaking a Bad Habit *Harvard Business Review Digital Articles* p2 Ja 18 2016

What Africa's Leaders Have Learned About Facing Huge Challenges *Harvard Business Review Digital Articles* p2 My 28 2015

What to Do About Mediocrity on Your Team *Harvard Business Review Digital Articles* p2 Ap 20 2017

What to Do If a Conversation Is Turning Loud and Aggressive *Harvard Business Review Digital Articles* p2 Mr 17 2016

What to Do When You Inherit a Team That Isn't Working Hard Enough bw *Harvard Business Review Digital Articles* p1 Je 2 2017

What You Can Do If You Have a Gossiping Boss *Harvard Business Review Digital Articles* p2 N 21 2016

When to Solve Your Team's Problems, and When to Let Them Sort It Out *Harvard Business Review Digital Articles* p2 Jl 20 2017

You Can Have Constructive Conflict Over Email *Harvard Business Review Digital Articles* p2 Mr 24 2015

You Might Be the Reason Your Employees Aren't Changing *Harvard Business Review Digital Articles* p2 F 17 2015

Grensing, Gina Chiodi

25 years in the making color diag *Cabin Living* p48 Ja/F 2017

making the connection [Cover story] color diag *Cabin Living* p38 O 2017

PREVENT ICE DAMS color *Cabin Living* p66 O 2017

a real charmer color diag *Cabin Living* p36 Je 2017

strength in numbers color *Cabin Living* p26 D 2016

Greshko, Michael

HOW VERTEBRATES GOT THEIR COATS color *National Geographic* v232 no4 p14 O 2017

Turned to Stone color *National Geographic* v231 no6 p92 Je 2017

GRESSEL, MADDIE

OFF the BEATEN PATH color *GQ: Gentlemen's Quarterly* v97 no9 p154 S 2017

GRESSITT, KIT-BACON

Can We Talk About Trump? *Publishers Weekly* v264 no39 p112 S 25 2017

Greten, Tim F.

Mismatch repair deficiency predicts response of solid tumors to PD-1 blockade chart graph *Science* v357 no6349 p409 Jl 28 2017

Gretler, Corinne

Halal's Rise From Street Carts to Whole Foods color *Bloomberg Businessweek* no4494 p24 O 10 2016

Pins and Needles in The Heart of the Alps color *Bloomberg Businessweek* no4531 p31 Jl 24 2017

Gretzky, Wayne, 1961-

WHAT IF? ... WAYNE GRETZKY HADN'T SKATED OUT WEST? J. Fuchs and J. Feldman color *Sports Illustrated* v126 no11 p59 Ap 17-24 2017

Gretzky, Wayne, 1961—Interviews

THE INTERVIEW J. GATEHOUSE color *Maclean's* v129 no41 p12 O 17 2016

Grewal, Dhruv

When Upbeat Commercials Backfire *Harvard Business Review Digital Articles* p2 O 23 2015

Grey, Jacqui

Diverse Teams Feel Less Comfortable—and That's Why They Perform Better *Harvard Business Review Digital Articles* p2 S 22 2016

Grey, Stella

Mid-Life Ex Wife: A Diary of Divorce, Online Dating, and Second Chances *Publishers Weekly* v264 no11 p73 Mr 13 2017

GREY, TOBIAS

Songs From the Barricades *New York Times Book Review* p13 Ap 2 2017

Grey, Zane, 1872-1939

BOLT FROM THE BLUE G. Hodges color map *National Geographic* v232 no2 p120 Ag 2017

THE LEGEND OF PEARL GREY E. H. PEPLOW JR. *Arizona Highways* v92 no7 p34 Jl 2016

Greycork (Company)

Greycork A. RANALLO color *American Craft* v77 no2 p12 Ap/My 2017

Grey's Anatomy (TV program)

America's top TV critic Matt Roush answers your burning questions *TV Guide* v65 no41 p3 O 2 2017

The Cast of Grey's Anatomy H. Goldblatt, A. Writing et al color *Entertainment Weekly* no1439 p23 N 11 2016

GOING OUT WITH A BANG N. Abrams, B. L. Heldman et al color *Entertainment Weekly* no1463/1464 p10 Ap/My 2017

Grey's Anatomy M. Logan *TV Guide* v65 no11 p40 Mr 6 2017

Grey's Anatomy M. Logan *TV Guide* v65 no19 p29 My 1 2017

GREY'S ANATOMY M. Logan *TV Guide* v65 no39 p48 S 18

2017

Grey's Anatomy: The Body Bomb L. Rice color *Entertainment Weekly* no1460/1461 p98 Ap 7-17 2017

Patrick Dempsey C. Ianzito color *AARP: The Magazine* v59 no1A p64 D 2015/Ja 2016

Greyson, Maeve

Sadie's Highlander: Highland Protector *Publishers Weekly* v264 no28 p71 Jl 10 2017

Gribble, Cody

The New Kids are All Right A. Shipnuck and C. Barrett color *Golf Magazine* v59 no2 p28 F 2017

Gribble, David

SAPPHO and her brothers *History Today* v66 no10 p46 O 2016

Gribel, R.

Persistent effects of pre-Columbian plant domestication on Amazonian forest composition bibl chart graph map *Science* v355 no6328 p925 Mr 3 2017

Gribetz, Uriel E.

Hunts Point *Publishers Weekly* v264 no14 p56 Ap 3, 2017

Gridley, Janet

SETTING THE SCENE M. Feldman color *House Beautiful* v159 no8 p86 O 2017

GRIEDER, ERICA

California Should Be More Like Texas color *Reason* v48 no8 p58 Ja 2017

The Once And Future King County *Texas Monthly* v44 no11 p58 N 2016

Grief

Cover *Time* v189 no15 pC1 Ap 24 2017

Grieving with Brahms R. Miska color *U.S. Catholic* v82 no3 p19 Mr 2017

How to Handle Shared Grief at Work A. Ranieri *Harvard Business Review Digital Articles* p2 My 26 2015

How to Offer Support to a Grieving Colleague S. Nawaz bw *Harvard Business Review Digital Articles* p2 Ap 3 2017

"I've Come to Clean Your Shoes" M. HARRAH color *Reader's Digest* v189 no1130 p52 My 2017

Life After Death [Cover story] B. Luscombe color *Time* v189 no15 p38 Ap 24 2017

Making Your Workplace Safe for Grief J. Moss color *Harvard Business Review Digital Articles* p2 Je 6 2017

Mourning Becomes Her K. BOLONIK color *Prevention* v68 no11 p34 N 2016

One afternoon in October B. DOYLE *Christian Century* v133 no21 p11 O 12 2016

Open up to love color *Yoga Journal* p70 2016 Special Issue

Sing a new song E. Sanna *U.S. Catholic* v82 no3 p4 Mr 2017

What You Said About ... color *Time* v189 no18 p6 My 15 2017

why i dance J. Whiteside *Dance Magazine* v90 no11 p72 N 2016

Grief therapy

WASHING MY BOY'S BODY F. Ostaseski color *Tricycle: The Buddhist Review* v26 no4 p74 Summ 2017

Grief—Religious aspects—Christianity

LIVING BY The Word *Christian Century* v134 no7 p20 Mr 29 2017

Grienberger, Christine

Behavioral time scale synaptic plasticity underlies CA1 place fields diag *Science* v357 no6355 p1033 S 8 2017

Grier, Laura

Wild Alaska *Saturday Evening Post* v289 no2 p54 Mr/Ap 2017

Grier, Peter

Supreme Court allows parts of travel ban to proceed before hearing case *Christian Century* v134 no16 p13 Ag 2 2017

GRIERSON, BRUCE

How Could You? cartoon *Walrus* v13 no10 p15 D 2016

GRIERSON, TIM

THE APES ARE COMING color *Popular Mechanics* p12 Jl 2017

THE INCREDIBLY SPECIAL EFFECTS AWARDS bw color *Popular Mechanics* p75 F 2017

Griesbeck, Morgane

Single-cell RNA-seq reveals new types of human blood dendritic cells, monocytes, and progenitors color *Science* v356 no6335 p283 Ap 21 2017

Griesser, Markus

Synthesis of resveratrol tetramers via a stereoconvergent radical equilibrium bibl diag graph *Science* v354 no6317 p1260 D 9

2016

Grievance procedures

Anger Management J. Lustig *New York Times Magazine* p15 O 30 2016

Coping with the Loss of an Equine Partner J. Susser color *Dressage Today* v23 no12 p16 S 2017

No one will challenge this bully S. Sales *People Management* p53 S 2017

PARODY color *Weekly Standard* v22 no26 p40 Mr 13 2017

Grieve, Andrew

#trailchat A. Grieve, J. Wells et al color *Backpacker* v45 no2 p10 Mr 2017

#trailchat color *Backpacker* v45 no2 p10 Mr 2017

Griffen, Wendell

People B. Allen color *Christian Century* v134 no11 p18 My 24 2017

Griffeth, Lauren L.

Why Men Have More Help Getting to the C-Suite *Harvard Business Review Digital Articles* p2 N 16 2015

Griffey, Randall R.

"My native continent" cartoon *Magazine Antiques* v184 no2 p100 Mr/Ap 2017

Griffin, Al

All About Atmos diag *Sound & Vision* v82 no6 p19 Jl/Ag 2017

AVR Advice color *Sound & Vision* v82 no1 p26 Ja 2017

The Big Short [Cover story] color graph *Sound & Vision* v82 no8 p36 O 2017

Connection Conundrums color *Sound & Vision* v82 no2 p26 F/Mr 2017

Contrast and Color bw color graph *Sound & Vision* v82 no4 p62 My 2017

Epson Home Cinema 3700 LCD Projector color graph *Sound & Vision* v82 no6 p46 Jl/Ag 2017

GoldenEar Technology Triton Reference Loudspeaker color graph *Sound & Vision* v82 no5 p36 Je 2017

HDMI Anxiety color *Sound & Vision* v82 no7 p24 S 2017

Hi-Res Streams color *Sound & Vision* v82 no5 p19 Je 2017

Hisense 50H8C LCD Ultra HDTV color graph *Sound & Vision* v81 no9 p40 N 2016

HOW TO BUY AN ULTRA HDTV color *Sound & Vision* v82 no1 p32 Ja 2017

MQA Explained color *Sound & Vision* v82 no8 p24 O 2017

Optoma HD142X 3D DLP Projector color graph *Sound & Vision* v81 no10 p62 D 2016

Panasonic DMP-UB900 Ultra HD Blu-ray Player color *Sound & Vision* v82 no2 p40 F/Mr 2017

Sharp Aquos LC-75N8000U LCD Ultra HDTV color graph *Sound & Vision* v82 no1 p52 Ja 2017

Sony UBP-X800 Ultra HD Blu-ray Player color *Sound & Vision* v82 no6 p38 Jl/Ag 2017

Soundbar Shortcomings color *Sound & Vision* v81 no10 p22 D 2016

Storage Solutions color *Sound & Vision* v81 no9 p29 N 2016

TV Troubles color *Sound & Vision* v82 no4 p19 My 2017

VApex PRO Fixed Frame Screen chart color *Sound & Vision* v81 no10 p64 D 2016

Vizio M65-D0 Ultra HD Display color graph *Sound & Vision* v81 no10 p56 D 2016

What's the Frequency? color *Sound & Vision* v82 no3 p23 Ap 2017

X Marks the Spot color graph *Sound & Vision* v82 no4 p58 My 2017

Griffin, Ashley

Through our eyes Perspectives from black teachers color *Phi Delta Kappan* v98 no5 p36 F 2017

Griffin, Aurora

Girl Uncorrupted E. K. Cahill color *Commonweal* v144 no3 p25 F 10 2017

Griffin, Becki

LIGHT WORK L. HOWARD *Better Homes & Gardens* v95 no1 pN2 Ja 2017

Griffin, Diane E.

Why are neurons susceptible to Zika virus? diag *Science* v357 no6346 p33 Jl 7 2017

Griffin, Donal

Cristiano Ronaldo and the 'Volatile' Investments cartoon *Bloom-*

berg Businessweek no4539 p27 S 25 2017

HOW TO MAKE A €367 MILLION LOSS DISAPPEAR *Bloomberg Businessweek* no4508 p36 Ja 23 2017

Griffin, Emilie

From empathy to action *America* v217 no6 p54 S 18 2017

Griffin, Gale

BRICKBATS cartoon *Reason* v48 no10 p68 Mr 2017

Griffin, Jared

How the City of Keller, Texas, Built a Dog Agility Course S. Myrick *Parks & Recreation* v52 no2 p49 F 2017

Griffin, Jonathan

ELEMENTS FROM THE ACTUAL WORLD color *Art in America* v105 no5 p76 My 2017

Ethnic Fraud and Art *Art in America* v105 no8 p22 S 2017

PENTTI MONKKONEN *Art in America* v104 no9 p160 O 2016

Redcat color *Art in America* v105 no1 p88 Ja 2017

SITElines color *Art in America* v104 no10 p157 N 2016

Griffin, Kiana

Eliminating Grade Levels M. Jo Madda *Education Digest* v83 no2 p61 O 2017

Griffin, Maggie

CREATIVE CORNER L. MOWRY *Atlanta* v56 no7 p54 N 2016

Griffin, Nora

YEVGENIYA BARAS cartoon *Art in America* v104 no11 p121 D 2016

Griffin, Patrick

The Townshend Moment: The Making of Empire and Revolution in the Eighteenth Century *Publishers Weekly* v264 no41 p58 O 9 2017

Griffin, Scott

The Case Of the Terrifying Trail V. GLEMBOCKI *Reader's Digest* v188 no1124 p27 O 2016

Griffini, Gianmarco

Improving efficiency and stability of perovskite solar cells with photocurable fluoropolymers bibl chart graph *Science* v354 no6309 p203 O 14 2016

Griffis, Roger B.

Biodiversity redistribution under climate change: Impacts on ecosystems and human well-being color *Science* v355 no6332 p1389 Mr 31 2017

Griffith, Andy, 1926-2012

The Shadow of 1957 W. D. GEHRING *USA Today Magazine* v145 no2860 p62 Ja 2017

Griffith, Brittany

Gypsy Kitchen J. Lucas color *Climbing* no356 p28 S/O 2017

Griffith, Erin

AGE OF DISSONANCE color *Fortune* v174 no7 p49 D 1 2016

APPLE REBOOTS IN CHINA color *Fortune* v176 no5 p106 O 1 2017

THE BLACK CEILING color *Fortune* v176 no5 p94 O 1 2017

A BLIND EYE TO THE TRUTH color *Fortune* v176 no2 p46 Ag 1 2017

BOXED IN color diag *Fortune* v176 no5 p86 O 1 2017

BRINGING 'HARD SCIENCE' TO THE MASSES color *Fortune* v176 no4 p35 S 15 2017

CHASING RAINBOWS color *Fortune* v175 no5 p39 Ap 1 2017

COME ON AND SHINE color *Fortune* v174 no6 p29 N 1 2016

DREAM WEAVER color *Fortune* v176 no3 p74 S 1 2017

FORTY UNDER FORTY 2017 color *Fortune* v176 no3 p62 S 1 2017

FROM BOOM TO DOOM color *Fortune* v176 no4 p68 S 15 2017

Get Ready for Fast Furniture color *Fortune* v175 no8 p40 Je 15 2017

Goodbye, Unicorns. Hello, IPOs! color *Fortune* v175 no6 p7 My 1 2017

IN TRUMP TECH (MUST) TRUST color *Fortune* v75 no1 p52 Ja 1 2017

IT'S TIME TO TAKE AI SERIOUSLY color *Fortune* v175 no3 p51 Mr 1 2017

IT WAS BUZZ AT FIRST SIGHT color *Fortune* v174 no8 p81 D 15 2016

LESSONS IN UBER'S ROUGH RIDE color *Fortune* v175 no6 p32 My 1 2017

MANAGING L'ORÉAL'S 'ORGANIZED CHAOS' color *Fortune* v175 no4 p26 Mr 15 2017

MINING COMEDY GOLD color *Fortune* v176 no3 p70 S 1 2017

MOST POWERFUL WOMEN color *Fortune* v176 no5 p54 O 1 2017

MOST POWERFUL WOMEN INTERNATIONAL color *Fortune* v176 no5 p111 O 1 2017

OF VICE AND MEN color *Fortune* v175 no4 p71 Mr 15 2017

ONCE CODDLED, NOW CURBED color *Fortune* v176 no3 p40 S 1 2017

ON MESSAGE, OFF TARGET color *Fortune* v176 no1 p44 Jl 1 2017

THE QUEEN OF POP [Cover story] color diag *Fortune* v176 no5 p70 O 1 2017

TECH TAKEOVER IN TOYLAND color diag *Fortune* v176 no5 p76 O 1 2017

THE UGLY UNETHICAL UNDERSIDE OF SILICON VALLEY color *Fortune* v75 no1 p72 Ja 1 2017

(VIRTUAL) REALITY BITES color *Fortune* v175 no2 p45 F 1 2017

WE CHANGED THE WORLD! (OOPS.) color *Fortune* v175 no7 p32 Je 1 2017

What Uber Means for the Valley color *Fortune* v176 no1 p12 Jl 1 2017

YOU'LL LAUGH! CRY! (MAYBE BUY.) color *Fortune* v175 no8 p94 Je 15 2017

YOUTH REVOLT color *Fortune* v176 no3 p64 S 1 2017

Griffith, Jessica Mesman

A good death color *U.S. Catholic* v82 no1 p38 Ja 2017

Healing presence *U.S. Catholic* v82 no4 p38 Ap 2017

The middle ages color *U.S. Catholic* v82 no7 p38 Jl 2017

A new kind of music color *U.S. Catholic* v82 no3 p45 Mr 2017

Our bad habit: The recent film that fixates on nuns having fun isn't all that funny color *U.S. Catholic* v82 no10 p38 O 2017

Tea service color *U.S. Catholic* v82 no6 p45 Je 2017

Griffith, Logan—Interviews

AV CLUB Davidaisy bw *Snowboarder* v29 no4 p34 D 2016

Griffith, Mike

Almost Too Much Music color *New Orleans Magazine* v51 no7 p50 My 2017

AULD ACQUAINTANCES color *New Orleans Magazine* v51 no3 p46 Ja 2017

Carnival Clash bw *New Orleans Magazine* v51 no4 p48 F 2017

CHRISTMAS PRESENTS bw *New Orleans Magazine* v51 no2 p52 D 2016

GROOVE color *New Orleans Magazine* v51 no8 p58 Je 2017

Hot Weather, Cool Concerts: Escape the heat with great live music color *New Orleans Magazine* v51 no10 p60 Ag 2017

July Jammin' color *New Orleans Magazine* v51 no9 p46 Jl 2017

March Forth color *New Orleans Magazine* v51 no5 p50 Mr 2017

Music's Best Month color *New Orleans Magazine* v51 no6 p48 Ap 2017

POP RULES color *New Orleans Magazine* v51 no1 p52 N 2016

Two Festivals to Watch color *New Orleans Magazine* v51 no12 p58 O 2017

Griffith, Mimi

A life with loss color *U.S. Catholic* v82 no1 p5 Ja 2017

Griffith, Reade

Hedge Fund Resurrection N. VARDI color *Forbes* v198 no8 p58 D 20 2016

Griffith, William H.

SURPRISE *Christian Century* v134 no12 p22 Je 7 2017

Griffiths, Andrew D.

Transient compartmentalization of RNA replicators prevents extinction due to parasites bibl chart graph *Science* v354 no6317 p1293 D 9 2016

GRIFFITHS, KATE D.

Female Privilege *Nation* v304 no10 p4 Mr 27 2017

Griffiths, Paul

Who I am *People Management* p49 D 2016/Ja 2017

Griffiths, Paul J.

To the University, with Love color *Commonweal* v144 no11 p39 Je 16 2017

Griffiths, Rhys

African Renaissance Monument *History Today* v66 no10 p70 O 2016

The Count's Temple *History Today* v67 no3 p70 Mr 2017

Druids' Temple *History Today* v67 no4 p70 Ap 2017

The Grave of Ferdinando Palaiologos *History Today* v67 no1 p70

Ja 2017

Hotel Castel Dracula *History Today* v67 no2 p70 F 2017

NATIONAL GALLERY BOLIVIA *History Today* v67 no8 p76 Ag 2017

NATIONAL GALLERY CAMBODIA *History Today* v67 no5 p78 My 2017

NATIONAL GALLERY FINLAND *History Today* v67 no9 p78 S 2017

NATIONAL GALLERY SAUDI ARABIA *History Today* v67 no10 p78 O 2017

NATIONAL GALLERY UGANDA *History Today* v67 no7 p78 Jl 2017

GRIFFITHS, ROB

Hackintosh: Build a DIY Mac for gaming color graph *Macworld - Digital Edition* v34 no8 p11 Ag 2017

Hackintosh: Should you build one? color *Macworld - Digital Edition* v34 no8 p7 Ag 2017

Griffon Brands (Company)

BOXED VODKA JUST WANTS TO BE LOVED J. Miller cartoon *Bloomberg Businessweek* no4507 p64 Ja 16 2017

GRIGG, RICHARD

Evolution's Error: HOW HUMAN NATURE WENT AWRY *Humanist* v77 no3 p30 My/Je 2017

Griggs, Mary Beth

charging up a battery conference color *Popular Science* v289 no6 p80 N/D 2017

Exposed color *Popular Science* v289 no4 p70 Jl/Ag 2017

Huge coaster, one thin rail color diag *Popular Science* v289 no6 p24 N/D 2017

the night we evacuated Oroville cartoon *Popular Science* v289 no4 p84 Jl/Ag 2017

Road-Ready Garden diag *Popular Science* p86 Ja/F 2017

Robert Ballard cartoon *Popular Science* p50 Ja/F 2017

so you want to terraform Mars color *Popular Science* v289 no4 p14 Jl/Ag 2017

stressed out: gauging global water worries map *Popular Science* v289 no2 p8 Mr/Ap 2017

Sylvia Earle cartoon *Popular Science* p46 Ja/F 2017

THE WATER BANKER color *Popular Science* v289 no2 p22 Mr/Ap 2017

which way to tomorrow? color *Popular Science* v289 no5 p11 S/O 2017

Griggs, Murray

Back-Through Gate color *Horse & Rider* v56 no6 p35 Je 2017

Precise Circles color *Horse & Rider* v56 no2 p23 F 2017

Grigio Girls (Music)

'Grigio Girls' B. FINGER *New York Times Magazine* p57 Mr 12 2017

Grigolia-Rosenbaum, Jacob

The Good Fight K. M. Mitchell *Stage Directions* v30 no10 p12 O 2017

Grigolo, Vittorio, 1977-

Bravura STYLE J. MELICK *Opera News* v81 no6 p24 D 2016

Grigoriadis, Vanessa

College and Consent: A kaleidoscopic tour through the campus sexual assault controversy M. GOLDBERG *New York Times Book Review* p11 S 17 2017

Rape on Campus color *Glamour* v115 no9 p139 S 2017

Grigoriev, I. V.

High-temperature quantum oscillations caused by recurring Bloch states in graphene superlattices color *Science* v357 no6347 p181 Jl 14 2017

Grigsby, John

When America Was Most Innovative, and Why bw graph *Harvard Business Review Digital Articles* p2 Mr 6 2017

GRIJALVA, RAÚL

Wonder Beyond Words *Sierra* v101 no4 p68 Jl/Ag 2016

Grijalva, Raul M., 1948-

The Pros and Cons of the Obama Era Federal Lands Policy: Should Congress Repeal the Obama Administration's Public Land Management Rule? *Congressional Digest* v96 no6 p10 Je 2017

Grill, Stephan W.

The mechanics of positioning skin follicles color *Science* v357 no6353 p750 Ag 25 2017

Grill, William

The Wolves of Currumpaw *Publishers Weekly* v263 no49 p18 D
　7 2016
Grill pans
　ROASTING PANS M. XERAKIA color *Better Homes & Gardens*
　　v95 no11 p142 N 2017
Grilli, Ricardo
　1954 B. Milkowski color *Downbeat* v84 no3 p65 Mr 2017
Grilling (Cooking)
　13 Ways To Ensure BBQ Success J. Irons color *Sail* v48 no7 p10
　　Jl 2017
　FIRE UP YOUR WEEK C. Morocco color diag *Bon Appetit* v62
　　no6 p64 Je 2017
　GOOD TO THE BONE color *Bon Appetit* v62 no6 p8 Je 2017
　GRILLED GOODNESS C. K. Jackson color *Essence* v48 no3
　　p109 Jl 2017
　In the SUNSET KITCHEN color *Sunset* v238 no6 p98 Je 2017
　Just Throw It on the Grill B. LEONE color *Bon Appetit* v62 no6
　　p50 Je 2017
　Level Up Your Grilling Game C. BOERS color *Chicago* v66 no7
　　p54 Jl 2017
　License to GRILL A. Sánchez color *O, The Oprah Magazine* p109
　　Je 2017
　MAN VS. WILD BOAR R. O'CONNOR color *Chicago* v66 no7
　　p22 Jl 2017
　RETURN OF THE KING S. Schneider color *Sunset* v239 no1
　　p102 Jl 2017
　SMOKE RING: The litmus test for good barbecue, tender, no-
　　nonsense beef brisket represents low, slow food at its best J.
　　SPALDING *Indianapolis Monthly* v12 no40 p45 Ag 2017
　SPRING CHICKEN J. Waldbieser color *Women's Health* v14 no4
　　p101 My 2017
　THE ULTIMATE TAILGATE GRILL TEST M. SULA color
　　Popular Mechanics p34 Jl 2017
　Vroom Service T. Keith color *Sports Illustrated* v126 no18 p18
　　Je 26 2017
　Zippy Grilled Cheese A. Larson *Idaho Magazine* v16 no5 p56 F
　　2017
Grillo, A. F.
　Observation of a large-scale anisotropy in the arrival directions
　　of cosmic rays above 8×10^{18} eV *Science* v357 no6357 p1266
　　S 22 2017
Grillo, Anthony S.
　Restored iron transport by a small molecule promotes absorption
　　and hemoglobinization in animals color graph *Science* v356
　　no6338 p608 My 12 2017
Grillo, Emiliano
　Watch + Learn V. J. Trolio and C. Barrett color *Golf Magazine* v59
　　no8 p34 Ag 2017
Grillo, Ioan
　Blood Brothers: Two siblings—a bricklayer in Texas and a drug
　　cartel boss in Mexico—get involved in money laundering at the
　　racetrack *New York Times Book Review* p23 S 24 2017
　Lightbox color *Time* v190 no13 p18 O 2 2017
　Next Generation Leaders color *Time* v189 no9 p38 Mr 13 2017
Grillo, Jerry
　ECHOES OF THIOKOL: Survivors and their descendants seek
　　a memorial to a forgotten tragedy on the Georgia coast *Atlanta*
　　v57 no4 p18 Ag 2017
　MEET JOE J. GRILLO *Atlanta* v56 no7 p98 N 2016
　A STORY AT HOME S. FENNESSY *Atlanta* v56 no7 p20 N 2016
Grillo, Kelly J.
　Changing the Praxis of Retention in Higher Education: A Plan to
　　TEACH All Learners *Change* v48 no6 p58 N/D 2016
Grills (Cooking)
　13 Ways To Ensure BBQ Success J. Irons color *Sail* v48 no7 p10
　　Jl 2017
　BEST NEW RESTAURANTS J. Bainbridge, C. Lauterbach et al
　　Atlanta v57 no5 p78 S 2017
　WIN A HIGH-TECH GRILL! T. Enriquez color *Sunset* v238 no6
　　p108 Je 2017
Grills (Cooking)—Equipment & supplies
　In the SUNSET KITCHEN color *Sunset* v239 no1 p98 Jl 2017
Grills (Cooking)—Evaluation
　5 high-tech gadgets for an outdoor cookout color *PCWorld* p168
　　O 2016
　Bar Excellence J. K. WOLFE *Cincinnati Magazine* v50 no3 p128

　D 2016
Grill-Spector, Kalanit
　Microstructural proliferation in human cortex is coupled with the
　　development of face processing bibl graph *Science* v355 no6320
　　p1 Ja 6 2017
Grimaldi, Richard D.
　Sexual Stimulation *Humanist* v77 no5 p5 S/O 2017
Grimes, Brent
　GRIMES AGAINST HUMANITY J. Dickey color *Sports Illus-
　　trated* v127 no2 p44 Jl 17 2017
GRIMES, D. SABELA
　STREET TO STAGE *Dance Magazine* v91 no7 p42 Jl 2017
Grimes, Jacob
　Cassini finds molecular hydrogen in the Enceladus plume: Evi-
　　dence for hydrothermal processes chart graph *Science* v356
　　no6334 p155 Ap 14 2017
Grimes, Jared
　by Jared Grimes Tap dancer *Dance Magazine* v91 no10 p80 O
　　2017
Grimes, Luke—Interviews
　LUKE GRIMES B. COOPER *Interview* v46 no8 p108 O 2016
Grimes, Miko
　GRIMES AGAINST HUMANITY J. Dickey color *Sports Illus-
　　trated* v127 no2 p44 Jl 17 2017
Grimes, Nikki
　Garvey's Choice color *Publishers Weekly* v263 no49 p72 D 7 2016
Grimes, Tiffany
　Show Up. Be You color *Glamour* v115 no5 p18 My 2017
　"We keep choosing each other" L. Brody bw color *Glamour* v115
　　no3 p159 Mr 2017
Grimes, William
　Touring the Dark Side: Edwidge Danticat surveys death in its
　　many guises *New York Times Book Review* p21 Ag 13 2017
Grimm (TV program)
　Grimm Says Goodbye M. Logan *TV Guide* v65 no13 p12 Mr 20
　　2017
　Grimm *TV Guide* v65 no2 p31 Ja 2 2017
Grimm, Cynthia J.
　When to Offer Fewer Customer Service Channels *Harvard Busi-
　　ness Review Digital Articles* p2 My 19 2015
Grimm, David
　CHIMPS IN WAITING color *Science* v356 no6343 p1114 Je 16
　　2017
　PETA targets early-career wildlife researcher color *Science* v357
　　no6356 p1087 S 15 2017
　Siberia yields earliest evidence for dog breeding color *Science*
　　v356 no6341 p896 Je 1 2017
Grimm, Gavin
　For the Record color *Time* v189 no10 p4 Mr 20 2017
GRIMM, MARIA
　FOR THOSE LEFT BEHIND *USA Today Magazine* v145 no2858
　　p38 N 2016
Grimm, Rudolf
　Ultrafast many-body interferometry of impurities coupled to a
　　Fermi sea bibl diag graph *Science* v354 no6308 p96 O 7 2016
GRIMM, VOLKER
　When, Where, and How Nature Matters for Ecosystem Services:
　　Challenges for the Next Generation of Ecosystem Service Mod-
　　els *BioScience* v67 no9 p820 S 2017
Grimmer, Nick
　KITTEN ON BOARD S. Schwartz *National Geographic Kids*
　　no469 p13 Ap 2017
Grimsley, Shane
　Resistance to malaria through structural variation of red blood cell
　　invasion receptors diag *Science* v356 no6343 p1139 Je 16 2017
Grímsson, Aron Már Ingham
　MUSIC IN HER WORDS *Iceland Review* v55 no1 p14 Ja/F 2017
　ON PAR WITH NONE *Iceland Review* v55 no2 p14 Mr/Ap 2017
　PUNK FINDS A HOME *Iceland Review* v55 no1 p8 Ja/F 2017
Grimwood, Jack
　More Russian Reads color *Publishers Weekly* v264 no13 p30 Mr
　　27 2017
GRINBERG, MARAT
　Russian, Jew, American *Commentary* v144 no1 p61 Jl/Ag 2017
Grinding & polishing
　CORDAGE F. Tkaczyk *Mother Earth News* no279 p50 D/Ja 2017

Grinding & polishing equipment—Evaluation
UNDERWATER POWER TOOLS? D. DUBNO color *Popular Mechanics* p10 S 2017

Grinding machines—Evaluation
MEAT EATERS A. ROBINSON color *Outdoor Life* v224 no1 p21 D 2016/Ja 2017
TOP TOOL PICKS FOR CHRISTMAS *Successful Farming* v114 no13 p74 D 2016

GRINDLE, ABE
AUDACIOUS PHILANTHROPY: LESSONS FROM 15 WORLD-CHANGING INITIATIVES chart img *Harvard Business Review* v95 no5 p110 S/O 2017

Grindle, Douglas
How We Won and Lost the War in Afghanistan: Two Years in the Pashtun Homeland *Publishers Weekly* v264 no39 p99 S 25 2017

Grindle, Merilee S.
Reflections on Memory and Democracy R. Feinberg *Foreign Affairs* v95 no6 p184 N/D 2016

GRINDLEY, LUCAS
THE BIGGEST HOMOPHOBES: THE LGBT RIGHTS MOVEMENT HAS HAD ITS SHARE OF VILLAINS color *Advocate* no1091 p102 Je/Jl 2017

Grinin, Alexey
The Rydberg constant and proton size from atomic hydrogen bw chart color diag graph *Science* v357 no6359 p79 O 6 2017

Grinnell, Joseph, 1877-1939
Charting a Century of Climate Change A. MURDOCK *USA Today Magazine* v145 no2860 p72 Ja 2017

GRINNELL, JUSTIN
Load of Doggcrapp chart color *Muscle & Performance* v9 no11 p30 N 2017
SUMMER SHRED PROGRAM chart color *Muscle & Performance* v9 no5 p40 My 2017

GRINNELL, SUNHEE
Beauty bw color *Vanity Fair* v59 no7 p47 Summ 2017
Beauty cartoon color *Vanity Fair* p94 Hollywood 2017 Supplement
JET — SET SPAE SCAPES color map *Vanity Fair* v58 no12 p81 D 2016

Grinnell College
BEING A FISH OUT OF WATER IS TOUGH, BUT IT'S HOW YOU EVOLVE K. NANJIANI *Vital Speeches of the Day* v83 no8 p234 Ag 2017

Grinspoon, David
Chasing the Elusive 2014 MU69 color *Sky & Telescope* v134 no5 p12 N 2017
DEEP TIME, DEEP SURVIVAL color *Scientific American* v315 no3 p76 S 2016
Earth in Human Hands: Shaping Our Planet's Future *Publishers Weekly* v263 no41 p70 O 10 2016
Life Outside the Habitable Zone *Sky & Telescope* v134 no1 p14 Jl 2017
Mars and Our Expectations *Sky & Telescope* v133 no1 p20 Ja 2017
My Rock of Ages: On being immortalized far out in the asteroid belt *Sky & Telescope* v134 no3 p14 S 2017
Not Venus Again *Sky & Telescope* v133 no5 p12 My 2017

Grint, Rupert, 1988-
GROWN-UP GRINT C. Collis color *Entertainment Weekly* no1457/1458 p60 Mr 17 2017
Snatch A. D'ARMINIO *TV Guide* v65 no11 p44 Mr 6 2017

Grip (Golf)
GIVE A SHORT STROKE THE FINGER D. Denunzio and C. Preisinger color *Golf Magazine* v58 no11 p56 N 2016
TRY THIS! GRIP IT "N CHIP IT...IN! D. Doniger and D. DeNunzio color *Golf Magazine* v59 no6 p58 Je 2017

Grip strength
Don't shake hands with this crab S. Milius color *Science News* v191 no4 p4 Mr 4 2017

Grippando, James
Most Dangerous Place: A Jack Swyteck Novel *Publishers Weekly* v263 no48 p44 N 28 2016

Grise, Chrisanne
Could His Hip-Hop Save the Earth? *Scholastic Choices* v32 no6 p22 Mr 2017
the right workout for you *Parents* v92 no1 p48 Ja 2017
The Summer of Change *Scholastic Choices* v32 no8 p20 My 2017

Where's My Story? *Scholastic Choices* v32 no4 p22 Ja 2017
Winter-Break Entertainment *Parents* p22 2015

Grisetti, Joshua Steven
God in My Head: The True Story of an Ex-Christian Who Accidentally Met God *Publishers Weekly* v264 no9 p66h F 27 2017

Grisham, John, 1955-
A Town Violated color *Time* v190 no8 p44 Ag 28 2017
First Editions: Stolen Fitzgerald manuscripts jump-start John Grisham's thriller K. TUCKER *New York Times Book Review* p18 Je 18 2017
John Grisham J. MASLIN *New York Times Book Review* p30 Je 4 2017

Grisham, Therese
Director: Her Art and Resilience in Times of Transition C. RICKEY *Film Quarterly* v70 no4 p124 Summ 2017

Grisly Hand, The (Performer)
HAND JIVE A. BURGER *Missouri Life* v43 no7 p25 D 2016/Ja 2017

Grissom, Eric
The Mark *Publishers Weekly* v264 no31 p58d Jl 31 2017

Gristwood, Sarah
WOMEN OF THRONES S. DUNANT color *New York Times Book Review* p51 D 4 2016

Griswold, Ann
Radiation Triage color *Scientific American* v316 no6 p19 Je 2017

Griswold, Eliza
Lives Among the Ruins *New York Times Book Review* p1 Jl 23 2017
Nadia MURAD color *Glamour* v114 no12 p206 D 2016
UNDERMINED cartoon color *New Yorker* v93 no19 p48 Jl 3 2017
What Little Act of Courage Inspired You This Year? bw color *Glamour* v114 no12 p52 D 2016

Griswold, Frank
TURNING POINTS P. LERNER color *Road & Track* v68 no10 p98 Jl 2017

Griswold, Joan
Joan Griswold L. Cutrone *New Orleans Homes & Lifestyles* v20 no4 p22 Aut 2017

Griswold v. Connecticut (Supreme Court case)
A MATTER OF PRIVACY D. B. MOSKOWITZ bw *American History* v52 no3 p22 Ag 2017

Grit Grease & Tears (Music)
Empowerment HADLEY color *Downbeat* v84 no2 p76 F 2017

Grits
GRITS S. PUCKETT *Atlanta* v56 no7 p64 N 2016

GRITTON, BARB
The Question *O, The Oprah Magazine* p12 Mr 2017

Gritz, Jennie Rothenberg
Have Sun, Will Travel *Smithsonian* v48 no4 p28 Jl/Ag 2017
PEACEMAKER *Smithsonian* v47 no8 p50 D 2016
Sugar Rush: The unsavory history of an insatiable American craving *Smithsonian* v48 no2 p16 My 2017
WAVE CATCHERS *Smithsonian* v47 no8 p46 D 2016

Grivno, Cody
Atlas HO scale FMC 5347 boxcar color *Model Railroader* v84 no9 p62 S 2017
Atlas N Dry-Flo covered hopper *Model Railroader* v84 no6 p68 Je 2017
Atlas N scale Norfolk Southern gondola color *Model Railroader* v84 no4 p99 Ap 2017
BENCHWORK AND TRACK for the Beer Line addition color diag *Model Railroader* v84 no2 p36 F 2017
Electro-Motive Division SD40-2 diesel locomotive color *Model Railroader* v84 no7 p10 Jl 2017
ExactRail HO scale SP gondola *Model Railroader* v84 no11 p67 N 2017
Fox Valley Models N scale 7-post boxcar *Model Railroader* v84 no7 p66 Jl 2017
HO scale details and accessories color *Model Railroader* v84 no7 p14 Jl 2017
HO scale freight cars *Model Railroader* v84 no7 p11 Jl 2017
HO scale locomotives color *Model Railroader* v84 no7 p10 Jl 2017
How to customize a Quonset hut color *Model Railroader* v84 no1 p28 Ja 2017

How to model a BIG INDUSTRY color diag *Model Railroader* v84 no4 p78 Ap 2017

InterMountain HO scale GP10 diesel color *Model Railroader* v84 no10 p60 O 2017

Kato N scale SDP40F diesel locomotive color *Model Railroader* v84 no5 p65 My 2017

Make a hill from foam peanuts color *Model Railroader* v84 no10 p22 O 2017

Menards HO scale Red Owl grocery store color *Model Railroader* v84 no8 p64 Ag 2017

Micro-Trains N scale Airslide hopper color *Model Railroader* v84 no3 p69 Mr 2017

Moloco HO General American 50-foot insulated boxcar color *Model Railroader* v83 no12 p72 D 2016

NEWS & PRODUCTS color *Model Railroader* v83 no12 p10 D 2016

News & Products color *Model Railroader* v84 no8 p10 Ag 2017

N scale freight cars color *Model Railroader* v84 no7 p15 Jl 2017

Paint, decal, and weather a locomotive color diag *Model Railroader* v83 no12 p28 D 2016

Peco charges into scenery market with static grass color *Model Railroader* v84 no2 p72 F 2017

Replace warped handrails on an HO scale diesel color diag *Model Railroader* v84 no5 p22 My 2017

Rivarossi HO scale 50-foot boxcar color *Model Railroader* v84 no1 p74 Ja 2017

Showcase color *Model Railroader* v84 no7 p13 Jl 2017

Tangent HO 40-foot Mini Hy-Cube boxcar *Model Railroader* v84 no9 p63 S 2017

Upgrade a Varney gondola kit [Cover story] color *Model Railroader* v84 no7 p24 Jl 2017

WalthersMainline HO covered hopper color *Model Railroader* v84 no7 p64 Jl 2017

Z scale locomotives color *Model Railroader* v84 no7 p16 Jl 2017

Grizzly bear

big picture bw color *Canadian Geographic* v137 no1 p12 F 2017

The Griz is Good for Ya E. SHAW il *Backpacker* p18 S 2017

in a snap color *Canadian Geographic* v137 no4 p16 Jl/Ag 2017

Proposed Endangered Species Delisting of Yellowstone Grizzly Bears R. Turner and M. Feeney *American Forests* v122 no3 p15 Fall 2016

THE RETURN OF THE GRIZZLY A. TEASDALE *Sierra* v102 no1 p38 Ja/F 2017

Why are grizzlies dying on Canada's railway tracks? C. Derworiz color *Science* v355 no6325 p561 F 10 2017

Yellowstone's grizzlies off endangered list color *Science* v356 no6345 p1314 Je 30 2017

Grizzly bear populations

LOST BEARS: WILL GRIZZLY BEARS RETURN TO THE NORTH CASCADES? K. SIBER *National Parks* v91 no3 p36 Summ 2017

Grizzly bear—Government policy

THE FUTURE OF YELLOWSTONE'S GRIZZLIES *Sierra* v102 no1 p40 Ja/F 2017

Grobart, Sam

All the Doctors Will See You Now color diag *Bloomberg Businessweek* no4508 p55 Ja 23 2017

Catch Him If You Can color *Bloomberg Businessweek* no4504 p62 D 19 2016

Headphone Hall of Fame color *Bloomberg Businessweek* no4511 p64 F 13 2017

TECH THE HALLS color *Bloomberg Businessweek* no4500 p78 N 21 2016

Grobler, Anneke

Vaginal bacteria modify HIV tenofovir microbicide efficacy in African women chart graph *Science* v356 no6341 p938 Je 1 2017

Groc, Isabelle

The Two Sides of Sea Otters Sea otters color *Canadian Wildlife* v22 no5 p24 N/D 2016

Groceries

Consumers Paid Less for Grocery Store Foods in 2016 Than in 2015 A. Kuhns and D. Levin *Amber Waves: The Economics of Food, Farming, Natural Resources, & Rural America* p8 Mr 2017

Dirty Secrets color *Prevention* v69 no7 p12 Jl 2017

Turkey Day Countdown! *Reader's Digest* v188 no1125 p66 N

2016

Groceries—Evaluation

from groceries to gossip D. Breshears bw color *Missouri Life* v44 no6 p52 S 2017

A pantry that stays organized J. Jones color *Redbook* p30 Ap 2017

Groceries—Management

A pantry that stays organized J. Jones color *Redbook* p30 Ap 2017

Groceries—Sales & prices

I'll See You at the Market S. Evans color *Southern Living* v52 no7 p12 Jl 2017

THE MANY EFFECTS OF OIL'S BIG BUST diag *Fortune* v174 no6 p11 N 1 2016

Grocers—Economic aspects

This Deflation Has Grocers Fed Up C. Giammona and L. Etter graph *Bloomberg Businessweek* no4493 p30 O 3 2016

Grocers—History—21st century

This Deflation Has Grocers Fed Up C. Giammona and L. Etter graph *Bloomberg Businessweek* no4493 p30 O 3 2016

Grocery industry

See also

Delicatessens

Food cooperatives

Being a Member Has Its Perks! cartoon color *AARP: The Magazine* v60 no3A p70 Ap/My 2017

CHIP SHOT M. BRANDSTETTER *Cincinnati Magazine* v50 no7 p154 Ap 2017

Consumers Paid Less for Grocery Store Foods in 2016 Than in 2015 A. Kuhns and D. Levin *Amber Waves: The Economics of Food, Farming, Natural Resources, & Rural America* p8 Mr 2017

The Grocery Industry Confronts a New Problem: Only 10% of Americans Love Cooking E. Yoon *Harvard Business Review Digital Articles* p2 S 22 2017

Since 2009, Restaurant Prices Have Generally Risen Faster Than Grocery Store Prices A. Kuhns and S. Rehkamp *Amber Waves: The Economics of Food, Farming, Natural Resources, & Rural America* p53 Ag 2017

Yes, for You, Ann-Margret color *AARP: The Magazine* v60 no3A p7 Ap/My 2017

Grocery industry—Illinois

The Goodness of Grain color *Log Home Living* v33 no9 p16 D 2016

Grocery industry—Missouri

DELI DELIGHTS M. W. Schwartz, D. Breshears et al color *Missouri Life* v44 no3 p72 My 2017

Grocery industry—United States

Shares of Food Commodities Purchased Away From Home Vary by Commodity Biing-Hwan Lin *Amber Waves: The Economics of Food, Farming, Natural Resources, & Rural America* p26 Ap 2017

Grocery shopping

The Cereal Aisle R. M. WARREN chart color *Men's Health* v32 no5 p78 Je 2017

Target Slips Up M. Boyle color graph *Bloomberg Businessweek* no4528 p13 Je 26 2017

Whole Foods Is Becoming Amazon's Brick-and-Mortar Pricing Lab H. Simon *Harvard Business Review Digital Articles* p2 S 12 2017

Grochowski, Sara

Spring 2017 Flying Starts color *Publishers Weekly* v264 no27 p36 Jl 3 2017

Traci Chee color *Publishers Weekly* v263 no52 p70 D 19 2016

Grodent, D.

Jupiter's magnetosphere and aurorae observed by the Juno spacecraft during its first polar orbits diag graph *Science* v356 no6340 p826 My 26 2017

GRODINSKY, PEGGY

Tour de Maine: An unforgettable bike trip into the heart of a famous landscape and the lives of its people *Yankee* v81 no5 p20 S/O 2017

Grodman, Craig

ALL AROUND THE FARM *Successful Farming* v115 no2 p79 F 2017

Grodner, Allison—Interviews

Big Brother M. Logan *TV Guide* v65 no35 p32 Ag 21 2017

Grodsky, Teresa

Senior Games: Everybody Can Play *Parks & Recreation* v52 no1 p16 Ja 2017

Grodstein, Lauren
Dad Drops In B. Anastas *New York Times Book Review* p17 Ap 9 2017

GROEN, DANIELLE
Woman of the Wand cartoon *Walrus* p44 Ja\F 2017

Groen, Hendrik
The Secret Diary of Hendrik Groen, 83 1/4 Years Old *Publishers Weekly* v264 no22 p41 My 29 2017

Groenewald, Dawie—Trials, litigation, etc.
DEADLY TRADE B. CHRISTY bw color graph map *National Geographic* v230 no4 p56 O 2016

GROFF, JONATHAN
Tree Huggers, Unite! A Guide to Sustainable Style color *GQ: Gentlemen's Quarterly* v97 no10 p59 O 2017

Groff, Jonathan, 1985-
Mindhunter T. Stack, A. Bacle et al color *Entertainment Weekly* no1482/1483 p107 S 22 2017

Groff, Lauren, 1978-
DOGS GO WOLF L. Groff cartoon color *New Yorker* v93 no25 p68 Ag 28 2017
Flower Hunters cartoon *New Yorker* v92 no38 p78 N 21 2016

Grogono, Dorothy M.
Emergence and spread of a human-transmissible multidrug-resistant nontuberculous mycobacterium bibl diag graph *Science* v354 no6313 p751 N 11 2016

Groh, Joann
Senior LIVING R. Bird *Cincinnati Magazine* v50 no7 p73 Ap 2017

Grohl, David, 1969-
ROCK STAR MOM S. COLL *Washingtonian Magazine* v52 no8 p84 My 2017

Grohl, Virginia Hanlon
The Real Lives of Rock Moms J. DOLAN bw color *Rolling Stone* no1284 p19 Ap 6 2017

Grohmann, Dina
Molecular force spectroscopy with a DNA origami–based nanoscopic force clamp bibl diag graph *Science* v354 no6310 p305 O 21 2016

Grohsjean, Thorsten
The Biases That Keep Good R&D Projects from Getting Funded *Harvard Business Review Digital Articles* p2 Mr 17 2017

Groin—Wounds & injuries
CLOSING THE (THIGH) GAP N. TUMMINELLO cartoon *Muscle & Performance* v9 no5 p22 My 2017

Grolleau, Fabien
Flights of Fancy C. RO color *Earth Island Journal* v32 no2 p54 Summ 2017

Grollemund, Rebecca
Dispersals and genetic adaptation of Bantu-speaking populations in Africa and North America diag *Science* v356 no6337 p543 My 5 2017

Groneberg, Tom
Magic Show bw *American Cowboy* v23 no6 p21 Ap/My 2017

Gronkowski, Gordon, 1959-
PAPA GRONK'S SECRETS FOR MONEY SMART KIDS A. K. SMITH color *Kiplinger's Personal Finance* v70 no12 p14 D 2016

GRONSKI, SCOTT
Deep State of Affairs *Commentary* v143 no4 p4 Ap 2017

Gronvall, Gigi Kwik
Biodefense in the 21st century color *Science* v356 no6338 p588 My 12 2017

Groom, Gloria
GLORIA GROOM J. BERG color *Chicago* v66 no6 p40 Je 2017

GROOM, WINSTON
Still Life with Corn *Weekly Standard* v22 no41 p29 Jl 3 2017

Grooming behavior in animals
Seabirds negotiate parenting duties E. S. EATON color *Science News* v191 no13 p16 Jl 8 2017
TURTLES GROOM WARTHOG Park and A. Shaw color *National Geographic Kids* no465 p13 N 2016
You missed a spot, bee M. Temming color *Science News* v192 no5 p32 S 30 2017

Grooming for men

See also
Men's clothing
Frozen Assets J. ROTH color *Esquire* p72 BigBlackBook
Look Your Best B. BOYÉ, S. NYGAARD et al color *Men's Health* v32 no5 p99 Je 2017
SPIC AND SPAN B. BOYÉ color *Men's Health* v32 no5 p108 Je 2017
THIS STORY MAKES NO SCENTS M. Stefanov cartoon color *Esquire* p66 Ap 2017
True Masculinity Is Grooming Your Elbows T. J. MILLER color *GQ: Gentlemen's Quarterly* v86 no11 p66 N 2016
Why It's Time to Go Back to the Mall J. VRABEL cartoon *GQ: Gentlemen's Quarterly* v97 no3 p74 Mr 2017
YOUR GUIDE TO WINNING MOVEMBER F. Katz cartoon *Esquire* p30 N 2017

Grooming for men—Equipment & supplies
BEARDED MEN DISCOVER BEAUTY PRODUCTS J. J. Roberts diag *Fortune* v75 no1 p24 Ja 1 2017
Date Ready! M. BOBO color *Ebony* v72 no4 p58 F 2017
GQ'S 2016 Grooming Awards A. GOBLE color *GQ: Gentlemen's Quarterly* v86 no11 p130 N 2016
GQ's 2017: GROOMING AWARDS A. HURLY, C. WOLF et al bw color *GQ: Gentlemen's Quarterly* v97 no11 p56 N 2017
The Perfect Dopp Kit… color *Esquire* p138 BigBlackBook

Grooming for women
NEW SKIN NO DOWNTIME L. Schaffner color *Harper's Bazaar* no3649 p330 D 2016/Ja 2017

Grooms, Amanda
THE 2017 GLAMOUR BEAUTY AWARD color *Glamour* v115 no4 p81 Ap 2017

Groopman, Jerome
FOOD FIGHTS cartoon color *New Yorker* v93 no7 p92 Ap 3 2017
Putting Profits Ahead of Patients bw color *New York Review of Books* v64 no12 p47 Jl 13 2017
THE SECRET OF SLEEP bw color *New Yorker* v93 no33 p88 O 23 2017
Sick But Not Sick bw cartoon *New York Review of Books* v64 no2 p30 F 9 2017
THE VOICES IN OUR HEADS cartoon *New Yorker* v92 no44 p70 Ja 9 2017

Groot, Nikée
The extent of forest in dryland biomes [Cover story] chart map *Science* v356 no6338 p635 My 12 2017

Grootenboer, Hanneke
The Reinvention of Seeing *History Today* v67 no2 p60 F 2017

GROPP, ROBERT E.
Advancing Team Research for Science and Society *BioScience* v67 no2 p103 F 2017
Applying Science *BioScience* v67 no9 p779 S 2017
BioScience®: A Forum for Integrating the Life Sciences *BioScience* v67 no5 p403 My 2017
From Politics to Science: The Way Forward *BioScience* v66 no12 p1007 D 1 2016
NSF: Time for Big Ideas *BioScience* v66 no11 p920 N 1 2016
Opportunities Lost? *BioScience* v67 no8 p683 Ag 2017
Telling the Story of Science *BioScience* v67 no4 p319 Ap 2017
Time for Collective Action *BioScience* v67 no7 p587 Jl 2017

GRORUD-COLVERT, KIRSTEN
Long-Term Studies Contribute Disproportionately to Ecology and Policy *BioScience* v67 no3 p271 Mr 2017

Gros Morne National Park (N.L.)
WHAT A BILLION LOOKS LIKE color *Canadian Wildlife* v22 no5 p10 N/D 2016

Grosek, Gerald
A life with loss color *U.S. Catholic* v82 no1 p5 Ja 2017
Speak up color *U.S. Catholic* v82 no4 p5 Ap 2017
you may be right color *U.S. Catholic* v81 no12 p5 D 2016

Gross, Andrew
The Saboteur *Publishers Weekly* v264 no25 p91 Je 19 2017

Gross, Anisse
At 25, Berrett-Koehler Looks Forward color *Publishers Weekly* v264 no18 p12 My 1 2017
B.C. Presses Broaden Their Reach and Band Together color *Publishers Weekly* v263 no47 p44 N 21 2016
Bookstores of Every Kind color *Publishers Weekly* v263 no47 p50 N 21 2016

BOOKS TO UNPLUG WITH color *Publishers Weekly* v264 no7 p28 F 13 2017

The Eternal Town Square color *Publishers Weekly* v264 no28 p62 Jl 10 2017

Happy Holidays for Indies in 2016 color *Publishers Weekly* v264 no2 p6 Ja 9 2017

HEAD OF THE HOUSE bw color *Publishers Weekly* v264 no18 p22 My 1 2017

How to Be a Kickass Boss, with Kim Scott color *Publishers Weekly* v264 no3 p8 Ja 16 2017

An Immigrant Experience color *Publishers Weekly* v263 no50 p41 D 5 2016

The Independent Spirit Flourishes in the Pacific Northwest color *Publishers Weekly* v263 no47 p32 N 21 2016

Indie Booksellers See Early Holiday Boost color *Publishers Weekly* v263 no50 p4 D 5 2016

Power-Couple Breakfast, with Lesley Stahl and Ann Patchett color *Publishers Weekly* v264 no3 p6 Ja 16 2017

Gross, Christian

Quantum simulations with ultracold atoms in optical lattices cartoon color diag *Science* v357 no6355 p995 S 8 2017

Revealing hidden antiferromagnetic correlations in doped Hubbard chains via string correlators bw diag graph *Science* v357 no6350 p484 Ag 4 2017

Gross, Dennis

Look Your Best B. BOYÉ, S. NYGAARD et al color *Men's Health* v32 no5 p99 Je 2017

Gross, Elana Lyn

Let's Get You Your Raise! cartoon *Glamour* v115 no11 p110 N 2017

Gross, Gerhard P.

The Myth and Reality of German Warfare: Operational Thinking From Moltke the Elder to Heusinger R. Guttman bw *Military History* v34 no1 p74 My 2017

GROSS, GRANT

The NSA's foreign surveillance: 5 things to know color *PCWorld* v35 no4 p37 Ap 2017

Gross, H. R. (Harold Royce), 1899-1987

He Was One of a Kind, Alas F. BARNES *Weekly Standard* v22 no10 p9 N 14 2016

Gross, Hannah

Hannah GROSS *Interview* v47 no5 p67 Je/Jl 2017

Gross, James

Can Your Mobile Customers Afford to Watch Your Ads? *Harvard Business Review Digital Articles* p2 D 8 2015

Gross, Joann

Around the Campfire color *Trail Rider* v29 no2 p6 Mr 2017

Gross, John D.

Distortion of histone octamer core promotes nucleosome mobilization by a chromatin remodeler diag *Science* v355 no6322 p263 Ja 20 2017

Gross, Juliane

Biological control of aragonite formation in stony corals bw color graph *Science* v356 no6341 p933 Je 1 2017

GROSS, KELSEY BLINDT

THE LOOP bw color *Runner's World* v51 no11 p18 D 2016

Gross, Liza

From Field and Stream to Table color *National Wildlife (World Edition)* v54 no6 p16 O/N 2016

GROSS, LOUIS J.

Skills and Knowledge for Data-Intensive Environmental Research *BioScience* v67 no6 p546 Je 2017

Synthesis Centers as Critical Research Infrastructure *BioScience* v67 no8 p750 Ag 2017

Gross, Matt

WE RUN THE STREETS [Cover story] color *Runner's World* v52 no9 p62 O 2017

Gross, Nzingah

IT'S NOT JUST ROCKET SCIENCE C. Leu color *Wired* v24 no11 p138 N 2016

GROSS, STEVE

A GARDEN IN Montgomery color diag *Arts & Crafts Homes & the Revival* v12 no4 p59 Fall 2017

TALE OF A Charleston SINGLE HOUSE color *Old House Journal* v45 no1 p24 F 2017

Gross, Tal

Air Pollution Is Making Office Workers Less Productive *Harvard Business Review Digital Articles* p2 S 29 2016

Gross, Terry

Terry Gross A. Lifson *Humanities* v37 no4 p1 Fall 2016

Gross, William H. (William Hunt), 1944-

The Bond King Gets Lost in the Crowd J. Gittelsohn bw *Bloomberg Businessweek* no4539 p29 S 25 2017

X-Ray: Janus Global Unconstrained C. Fried diag *Money* v46 no3 p32 Ap 2017

Gross, William H. (William Hunt), 1944——Political & social views

Movers K. Stock color *Bloomberg Businessweek* no4500 p15 N 21 2016

Gross, Yann

Modern Amazonia color map *National Geographic* v231 no2 p120 F 2017

Gross domestic product

APPENDIX B STATISTICAL TABLES RELATING TO INCOME, EMPLOYMENT, AND PRODUCTION *Economic Indicators* p395 S 2016

The fading American dream: Trends in absolute income mobility since 1940 R. Chetty, D. Grusky et al bw graph *Science* v356 no6336 p398 Ap 28 2017

The Forecasting Sweet Spot Between Micro and Macro E. Yoon, J. Bartlow et al *Harvard Business Review Digital Articles* p2 Ag 26 2016

GDP Is a Wildly Flawed Measure for the Digital Age B. Libert and M. Beck *Harvard Business Review Digital Articles* p2 Jl 28 2016

The Industry Bottom Line A. JONES *Boating World* v38 no2 p4 F 2017

The Price Is Right P. LAAKMANN *National Review* v69 no19 p18 O 16 2017

TOTAL OUTPUT, INCOME, AND SPENDING *Economic Indicators* p1 Mr 2017

Gross domestic product—Australia

The Price of Australia's Complacency M. Heath and K. Painter color *Bloomberg Businessweek* no4541 p33 O 9 2017

Gross domestic product—Canada

Canadian Mining's Dark Heart R. POPLAK color *Walrus* v13 no9 p26 N 2016

Eye for Talent J. TEPPERMAN cartoon *Walrus* v13 no9 p54 N 2016

Gross domestic product—China

Corrections & Clarifications *Bloomberg Businessweek* no4511 p6 F 13 2017

WHO'S ON TOP? diag *Fortune* v175 no3 p11 Mr 1 2017

Gross domestic product—United States

CHAPTER 2 THE YEAR IN REVIEW AND THE YEARS AHEAD *Economic Indicators* p51 O 2016

THE COST OF CARRYING DEBT P. SUDERMAN *Reason* v48 no11 p9 Ap 2017

How Reducing Gender Inequality Could Boost U.S. GDP by $2.1 Trillion K. Ellingrud, J. Manyika et al *Harvard Business Review Digital Articles* p2 Ap 12 2016

Gross income—Taxation

Hide Cash From the IRS—Legally W. BALDWIN diag *Forbes* v199 no2 p94 F 28 2017

Gross margins

Gun Manufacturers Need to Lead Change, Not Just Follow the Law R. J. Dolan *Harvard Business Review Digital Articles* p2 Mr 23 2016

Gross national product

See also

   Gross domestic product

GDP Is a Wildly Flawed Measure for the Digital Age B. Libert and M. Beck *Harvard Business Review Digital Articles* p2 Jl 28 2016

Gross state product

RICHEST BY STATE A. BROWN bw map *Forbes* v199 no4 p22 Ap 25 2017

GROSSBART, SARAH

FIGHTING FAKE NEWS: Made-up stories are taking over the internet. Are tech companies doing enough to stop the spread? *New York Times Upfront* v150 no1 p12 S 4 2017

Gross domestic product—Charts, diagrams, etc.

Is Anybody in Charge Here? P. Coy chart color graph *Bloomberg Businessweek* no4496 p10 O 24 2016
TOTAL OUTPUT, INCOME, AND SPENDING *Economic Indicators* p1 Ag 2017
TOTAL OUTPUT, INCOME, AND SPENDING *Economic Indicators* p1 My 2017

Gross domestic product—United States—Charts, diagrams, etc.
TOTAL OUTPUT, INCOME, AND SPENDING *Economic Indicators* p1 D 2016
TOTAL OUTPUT, INCOME, AND SPENDING *Economic Indicators* p1 F 2017
TOTAL OUTPUT, INCOME, AND SPENDING *Economic Indicators* p1 S 2016

Grosse, Katharina
PAINT THE TOWN J. L. BELCOVE color *Architectural Digest* v74 no2 p68 F 2017

Grosse, Katharina—Exhibitions
KATHARINA GROSSE R. Wetzler cartoon *Art in America* v105 no4 p112 Ap 2017

Grossenbacher, Brian
Surf Bashed D. L. NG color *Field & Stream* v122 no6 p10 N 2017

Grosser, Tilo
Time for nonaddictive relief of pain bibl color *Science* v355 no6329 p1026 Mr 10 2017

Grossman, Dave
PROFESSOR CARNAGE S. FEATHERSTONE color *New Republic* v248 no5 p20 My 2017

Grossman, David
Blood, Sweat and Laughs [Cover story] G. Shteyngart *New York Times Book Review* p1 Mr 5 2017
KILLER INSTINCTS B. SCHATZ *Mother Jones* v42 no2 p28 Mr/Ap 2017
The King of the Bitter Laugh S. Greenblatt bw *New York Review of Books* v64 no7 p46 Ap 20 2017

Grossman, Debbie
DEEP BLACK AND WHITE color *Popular Photography* v81 no2 p36 Mr/Ap 2017
FACE FACTS color *Popular Photography* v81 no1 p46 Ja/F 2017
FLEETING GRACE color *Popular Photography* v81 no2 p32 Mr/Ap 2017
Get Together color *Popular Photography* v80 no11 p66 D 2016

Grossman, Gene
What Trade Deals Are Good For *Harvard Business Review Digital Articles* p2 My 24 2016

Grossman, Jennifer
A Noble Champion Emerges color *Dressage Today* v23 no11 p62 Ag 2017

Grossman, Jeremiah—Interviews
YOUR TV MIGHT BE SPYING ON YOU L. GERSTNER color *Kiplinger's Personal Finance* v71 no6 p14 Je 2017

Grossman, Joanna L.
Understanding Your Legal Options If You've Been Sexually Harassed *Harvard Business Review Digital Articles* p1 Je 22 2017

Grossman, Joshua M.
Important factors in shaping physics identities *Physics Today* v70 no5 p12 My 2017

Grossman, Judi Mills
INTO THE BLUE E. EICHINGER color *Chicago* v66 no4 p70 Ap 2017

Grossman, Lev
Resistance Is Futile *New York Times Book Review* p1 Je 25 2017

Grossman, Lisa
All eyes on the eclipse color *Science News* v192 no1 p4 Ag 5 2017
CASSINI'S Curtain Call bw color *Science News* v192 no3 p16 S 2 2017
Cosmic lens sees black hole's burps color graph *Science News* v192 no4 p16 S 16 2017
Cosmic rays raid the Milky Way color *Science News* v192 no6 p7 O 14 2017
Don't blame aliens for star's flickering *Science News* v192 no5 p11 S 30 2017
Flares hold clues to solar mystery color *Science News* v192 no5 p6 S 30 2017
Light-bending by distant star seen color *Science News* v191 no13 p10 Jl 8 2017
Metallic air may have swaddled moon *Science News* v192 no1

p7 Ag 5 2017
New views snag science Nobels bw *Science News* v192 no7 p6 O 28 2017
Nostalgic documentary relives triumphs of the Voyager mission color *Science News* v192 no2 p26 Ag 19 2017
Seeking unexpected worlds color *Science News* v192 no6 p22 O 14 2017
Solar system birthed Jupiter early on color *Science News* v191 no13 p18 Jl 8 2017
Spacecraft finds no rings around Pluto [Cover story] color *Science News* v192 no7 p15 O 28 2017

Grossman, Rhys
The Board Directors You Need for a Digital Transformation *Harvard Business Review Digital Articles* p2 Jl 13 2017
The Industries That Are Being Disrupted the Most by Digital *Harvard Business Review Digital Articles* p2 Mr 21 2016

Grossman, Sharon R.
Systematic mapping of functional enhancer–promoter connections with CRISPR interference bibl graph *Science* v354 no6313 p769 N 11 2016

GROSSMAN, WENDY
Spreading Skepticism *Skeptical Inquirer* v40 no6 p41 N/D 2016

Grossniklaus, Ueli
RETINOBLASTOMA RELATED1 mediates germline entry in Arabidopsis color diag *Science* v356 no6336 p396 Ap 28 2017

Grote, Dick
3 Popular Goal-Setting Techniques Managers Should Avoid color *Harvard Business Review Digital Articles* p2 Ja 2 2017
Every Manager Needs to Practice Two Types of Coaching *Harvard Business Review Digital Articles* p1 S 30 2016
How to Handle Negative Feedback *Harvard Business Review Digital Articles* p2 Ag 17 2015
A Step-by-Step Guide to Firing Someone *Harvard Business Review Digital Articles* p2 F 17 2016
What to Do When You Think Your Performance Review Is Wrong bw *Harvard Business Review Digital Articles* p2 Mr 7 2017

Grotius, Hugo, 1583-1645
LAWS OF WAR: FOUNDING FATHERS J. A. Haymond color *MHQ: Quarterly Journal of Military History* v30 no1 p16 Aut 2017

Grotz, Jennifer
Window Left Open T. Davis *Orion Magazine* v35 no3 p55 My/Je 2016

Grotzinger, J. P.
Redox stratification of an ancient lake in Gale crater, Mars color *Science* v356 no6341 p922 Je 1 2017

Ground-effect machines
See also
Vertically rising aircraft
THE FLOATING WORLD M. BRANDSTETTER *Cincinnati Magazine* v50 no5 p24 F 2017

Ground meat
Easy Oktoberfest Feast color *Good Housekeeping* v265 no4 p103 O 2017

Groundhog Day
CAJUN COUNTRY J. FROIS color *Louisiana Life* v37 no3 p100 Ja/F 2017

Groundhog Day (Film)
When Every Day Is Groundhog Day S. I. Rosenbaum img *New York* v50 no7 p71 Ap 3 2017

Groundhog Day (Theatrical production)
ET TU, MURRAY? A. Carter cartoon *Esquire* v167 no2 p58 Mr 2017
On Broadway, It's Déjà Vu All Over-and Not Just for Groundhog Day E. Berman color *Time* v189 no18 p51 My 15 2017

Groundwater
Pingo L. SCHLEY *Discover* v38 no7 p12 S 2017
The Quest for H2O D. Mitchell color *Log Home Living* v34 no5 p24 Jl 2017

Groundwater pollution
Pollution reaches old groundwater T. SUMNER *Science News* v191 no10 p12 My 27 2017

Groundwater—Arsenic content
Global Arsenic Contamination: Living With the Poison Nectar S. K. Singh and E. A. Stern bibl color map *Environment* v59 no2 p24 Mr/Ap 2017

Group decision making

Is Your Team Coordinating Too Much, or Not Enough? R. Schwarz *Harvard Business Review Digital Articles* p2 Mr 23 2017

Group identity

See also

Cultural identity

Klaus Schwab M. Duffy color *Time* v189 no4 p56 Ja 23 2017

The Problem with Rewarding Individual Performers J. Van Bavel and D. Packer *Harvard Business Review Digital Articles* p2 D 27 2016

Group medical practice

See also

Health maintenance organizations

What the Trump Administration Needs to Do About Health Care L. S. Dafny and T. H. Lee *Harvard Business Review Digital Articles* p2 N 10 2016

Group of Seven (Organization)

For the Record color *Time* v189 no23 p8 Je 19 2017

Group of Twenty countries—Congresses

The Biggest Absence at This Year's G-20? Moral Authority S. Shuster color *Time* v190 no4 p12 Jl 24 2017

Group problem solving

See also

Brainstorming

The Problem-Solving Process That Prevents Groupthink A. Markman *Harvard Business Review Digital Articles* p2 N 25 2015

Group sex in motion pictures

No. 1 THE FOOD ORGY L. Greenblatt color *Entertainment Weekly* no1444/1445 p58 D 16 2016

Group work in education

See also

Workshops (Adult education)

Ready for a New Year D. Barone *Literacy Today (2411-7862)* v35 no1 p6 Jl/Ag 2017

Groupe PSA (Company)

Peugeot on the Go J. MULLER and J. DOBOSZ color *Forbes* v200 no2 p48 S 5 2017

Groups

See also

Hate groups

Musical groups

Tribes

Grouse shooting

RUFF AND TUMBLE T. DAVIS bw color *Field & Stream* v122 no6 p14 N 2017

THE TRUE North T. E. Nickens color *Field & Stream* v122 no5 p66 O 2017

Groussin, O.

Rosetta's comet 67P/Churyumov-Gerasimenko sheds its dusty mantle to reveal its icy nature bibl graph *Science* v354 no6319 p1566 D 23 2016

Surface changes on comet 67P/Churyumov-Gerasimenko suggest a more active past bw graph *Science* v355 no6332 p1392 Mr 31 2017

Grout, Cyrus

Why make it hard for teachers to cross state borders? color il *Phi Delta Kappan* v98 no5 p55 F 2017

Grove, Andrew S., 1936-2016

Remembering Andy Grove, the Teacher R. A. Burgelman *Harvard Business Review Digital Articles* p2 Mr 23 2016

TRUST NONE, FEAR ALL A. Grove *Lapham's Quarterly* v10 no3 p125 Summ 2017

Grove, Daryl

GIVE IT A HURL color *Virginia Living* v15 no5 p17 Ag 2017

Grove, Lloyd

Best press he's ever had bw cartoon color *Columbia Journalism Review* v56 no2 p68 Fall 2017

Groves, Alexander

Studio Swine H. MARTIN bw color *Architectural Digest* v74 no10 p100 O 1 2017

Groves, Maria Noel

HERBAL HEART TONICS: Incorporate these five delicious herbs into your daily routine to strengthen and gladden your heart *Mother Earth News* no284 p14 O/N 2017

GROVIER, N. K.

FROM THE ARCHIVES color *Reason* v49 no4 p78 Ag/S 2017

GROW, KORY

THE 50 GREATEST CONCERTS OF THE LAST 50 YEARS bw color *Rolling Stone* no1286 p30 My 4 2017

Chester's Last Days color *Rolling Stone* no1294 p13 Ag 24 2017

Chris Cornell 1964-2017 [Cover story] bw color *Rolling Stone* no1289 p40 Je 15 2017

Essential Chuck color *Rolling Stone* no1285 p36 Ap 20 2017

FALL ALBUM PREVIEW *Rolling Stone* no1297 p12 O 5 2017

Foo Fighters' All-Star Return color *Rolling Stone* no1293 p11 Ag 10 2017

Jack Johnson's New Wave bw color *Rolling Stone* no1291/1292 p20 Jl 13 2017

Josh Homme's Desert Dance Party bw *Rolling Stone* no1291/1292 p14 Jl 13 2017

Lars Ulrich cartoon *Rolling Stone* no1274 p62 N 17 2016

McCartney Shares His Touring Secrets color *Rolling Stone* no1291/1292 p26 Jl 13 2017

Metallica's Monster Summer color *Rolling Stone* no1290 p13 Je 29 2017

The Road Heats Up bw color *Rolling Stone* no1288 p11 Je 1 2017

Roger Waters Returns to Rock color *Rolling Stone* no1283 p11 Mr 23 2017

Spoon's Secret Influences bw color *Rolling Stone* no1284 p18 Ap 6 2017

The Who's Big Plans bw color *Rolling Stone* no1275 p11 D 1 2016

Growing season (Agriculture)

KEY SUMMER MAINTENANCE CHORES R. Bohacz *Successful Farming* v115 no8 p52 Je/Jl 2017

Grown Ass Woman (Music)

Trouble Free Hadley color *Downbeat* v84 no4 p59 Ap 2017

Growth factors

COSMETIC PROCEDURES S. HELD color *Indianapolis Monthly* p89 Ap 2017

mTORC1 activity repression by late endosomal phosphatidylinositol 3,4-bisphosphate A. L. Marat, A. Wallroth et al diag *Science* v356 no6341 p968 Je 1 2017

Groysberg, Boris

The 3 Things CEOs Worry About the Most *Harvard Business Review Digital Articles* p2 Mr 16 2015

7 Charts Show How Political Affiliation Shapes U.S. Boards *Harvard Business Review Digital Articles* p2 Ag 23 2016

How to Survive a Company Scandal You Had Nothing to Do With *Harvard Business Review Digital Articles* p2 Ag 31 2016

The Political Issues Board Directors Care Most About *Harvard Business Review Digital Articles* p2 F 16 2016

Grubb, Flora

A Garden of Her Own J. CHAI *Martha Stewart Living* no268 p52 O 2016

SITTING PRETTY M. OZAWA color *Martha Stewart Living* no275 p32 Je 2017

Grubb, T. D.

Observation of a large-scale anisotropy in the arrival directions of cosmic rays above 8×1018 eV *Science* v357 no6357 p1266 S 22 2017

Grubbly Farms (Company)

FOODSTUFFS *Atlanta* v56 no12 p58 Ap 2017

Grubbs, Steve—Interviews

PPID Update J. von Geldern color *Horse & Rider* v56 no2 p42 F 2017

Gruben, Maureen

Art at the edge B. A. Jordan color map *Canadian Geographic* v137 no2 p24 Mr/Ap 2017

Gruber, David

UNDER THE WAVES color *National Geographic* v232 no4 p138 O 2017

GRUBISIC, BRETT JOSEF

THE DAD DIALOGUES color *Maclean's* v129 no42 p60 O 24 2016

DYSTOPIAS AND ARTY DOGS color *Maclean's* v130 no3 p68 Ap 2017

MISTER MONKEY color *Maclean's* v129 no45 p56 N 14 2016

SPOONBENDERS color *Maclean's* v130 no7 p60 Ag 2017

SUCH A LOVELY LITTLE WAR color *Maclean's* v129 no50 p60 D 19 2016

Grubman, Bonnie

Children's Galleys to Grab color *Publishers Weekly* v264 no20 p(Sp)46 My 15 2017

Grudinin, Sergei

Mechanism of transmembrane signaling by sensor histidine kinases color *Science* v356 no6342 p1043 Je 9 2017

Grudova, Camilla

The Doll's Alphabet *Publishers Weekly* v264 no35 p98 Ag 28 2017

Whose Reality Is It? E. ALTER color *Publishers Weekly* v264 no35 p101 Ag 28 2017

Grühn, Bastian

Research: How a New CEO Can Make a Firm More Entrepreneurial *Harvard Business Review Digital Articles* p2 N 17 2016

Gruia, Ronald

DATA IS EVERYTHING color *Maclean's* v129 no51/52 p17 D 26 2016

Gruley, Bryan

GLOBALIZATION DOESN'T GIVE A DAMN color *Bloomberg Businessweek* no4517 p54 Ap 3 2017

The Hatchet Men And the Hot Dog color diag *Bloomberg Businessweek* no4533 p50 Ag 7 2017

How Does Tax Avoidance Play in Peoria? color *Bloomberg Businessweek* no4525 p42 Je 5 2017

IS KRATOM A DEADLY DRUG Or A Life-Saving Medicine? cartoon color *Bloomberg Businessweek* no4503 p54 D 12 2016

Grumet, Robert S.

First Manhattans: A History of the Indians of Greater New York B. Rindfleisch *American Indian Quarterly* v40 no4 p382 Fall 2016

GRUMMAN BENDER, RACHEL

skin solutions *Parents* v91 no9 p161 S 2016

GRUNBERG-BANYASZ, MALIN

OFF THE GRID color *Archaeology* v70 no4 p10 Je-Ag 2017

OFF THE GRID color *Archaeology* v70 no5 p10 S/O 2017

Grundberg, Ida

Single-cell RNA-seq reveals new types of human blood dendritic cells, monocytes, and progenitors color *Science* v356 no6335 p283 Ap 21 2017

Gruneberg, Ulrike

Organelle inheritance—what players have skin in the game? bibl color *Science* v355 no6324 p459 F 3 2017

Grunewald, Gabriele

ATHLETE GETS CANCER. ATHLETE FIGHTS CANCER. REPEAT, AGAIN & AGAIN ... T. Layden color *Sports Illustrated* v127 no2 p54 Jl 17 2017

Grünewald, Matthias, 16th century Isenheim Altar

Crucifixion H. J. Hornik and M. C. Parsons color *Christian Century* v134 no1 p47 Ja 4 2017

GRUNEWALD, WILL

THE LAST AMBASSADOR *Washingtonian Magazine* v52 no9 p58 Je 2017

Grunwald, Lisa

THE BIG QUESTION cartoon *Atlantic* v320 no4 p124 N 2017

Grusdt, Fabian

Revealing hidden antiferromagnetic correlations in doped Hubbard chains via string correlators bw diag graph *Science* v357 no6350 p484 Ag 4 2017

Grusky, David

The fading American dream: Trends in absolute income mobility since 1940 bw graph *Science* v356 no6336 p398 Ap 28 2017

Gruson, V.

Attosecond dynamics through a Fano resonance: Monitoring the birth of a photoelectron bibl graph *Science* v354 no6313 p734 N 11 2016

Grutter, K. E.

Quantum correlations from a room-temperature optomechanical cavity color diag graph *Science* v356 no6344 p1265 Je 23 2017

GRYBAUSKAS, TIMOTHY

#Climbing Training color *Climbing* no352 p9 Ap 2017

Gryphon Online Safety (Company)

Gryphon Router M. Belfiore bw color *Bloomberg Businessweek* no4499 p51 N 14 2016

Grypshon Industries (Company)

STICKY MAT FOR TOOLS color *Flying* v144 no4 p16 Ap 2017

Grzelczak, Marek

Growing anisotropic crystals at the nanoscale color diag *Science* v356 no6343 p1120 Je 16 2017

GSK Consumer Healthcare (Company)

Leading Businesses Make a Difference T. J. DONOHUE *Weekly Standard* v22 no12 p21 N 28 2016

Gstaad (Switzerland)

TNT E. TNT color *Vogue* v207 no4 p162 Ap 2017

GTO automobile

One of None J. Machaqueiro color *Hot Rod* v70 no10 p36 O 2017

GTPase-activating protein—Research

GTPase activity-coupled treadmilling of the bacterial tubulin FtsZ organizes septal cell wall synthesis X. Yang, Z. Lyu et al bibl graph *Science* v355 no6326 p744 F 17 2017

Gu, Lin

Atomic-layered Au clusters on α-MoC as catalysts for the low-temperature water-gas shift reaction chart diag graph *Science* v357 no6349 p389 Jl 28 2017

Gu, Zirong

Control of species-dependent cortico-motoneuronal connections underlying manual dexterity diag graph *Science* v357 no6349 p400 Jl 28 2017

Guacamole

Dazzle Them! K. O'SHEA-EVANS color *House Beautiful* v159 no8 p60 O 2017

Jenna Dewan Tatum P. KITA bw color *Men's Health* v32 no5 p36 Je 2017

Olé, Four Ways color *Martha Stewart Living* p24 My 2017

Guadagnino, Luca, 1971-

CALL ME BY YOUR NAME J. Nolfi color *Entertainment Weekly* no1478 / 1479 p63 Ag 18-25 2017

A Summer Place bw color *Film Comment* v53 no5 p6 S/O 2017

Guadalupe River (Tex.)

The Great Guadalupe J. C. Smith color *Southern Living* v52 no7 p45 Jl 2017

Guajardo, Mario—Interviews

Q & A WITH MARIO GUAJARDO *Texas Monthly* v45 no3 p34 Mr 2017

Guam

The U.S. Territory In the Line of North Korea's 'Enveloping Fire' color *Time* v190 no8 p14 Ag 28 2017

Guam—Social conditions

Craving Statehood E. EPSTEIN color *Weekly Standard* v22 no41 p16 Jl 3 2017

Guan, Frank

Is Culture Borrowing Always Theft? img *New York* v49 no15 p75 Jl 25 2016

So...Rock Is Dead? img *New York* v50 no10 p91 My 15 2017

WHY EVER STOP PLAYING VIDEO GAMES img *New York* p28 F 20 2017

Guan, Hong-Ping

Systemic pan-AMPK activator MK-8722 improves glucose homeostasis but induces cardiac hypertrophy graph *Science* v357 no6350 p507 Ag 4 2017

Guan, Yonsheng

RETINOBLASTOMA RELATED1 mediates germline entry in Arabidopsis color diag *Science* v356 no6336 p396 Ap 28 2017

Guan, Yuanfang

Predicting human olfactory perception from chemical features of odor molecules bibl diag graph *Science* v355 no6327 p820 F 24 2017

Guan-Cheng Li

Expand innovation finance via crowdfunding bibl color graph map *Science* v354 no6319 p1526 D 23 2016

Guandalini, Stefano

Reovirus infection triggers inflammatory responses to dietary antigens and development of celiac disease color diag *Science* v356 no6333 p44 Ap 7 2017

Guangchun, Lei

Biodiversity losses and conservation responses in the Anthropocene color diag graph map *Science* v356 no6335 p270 Ap 21 2017

Guangtao Zhu

A chemical genetic roadmap to improved tomato flavor bibl graph *Science* v355 no6323 p391 Ja 27 2017

Guangzhong Liu

Expert consensus on point-of-care testing *Science* v354 no6319 p15 D 23 2016

Recommendations on the management and use of POCT in medical institutions (nosocomial) *Science* v354 no6319 p13 D 23

2016

Guangzhou Automobile Group Co. Ltd.

Is China's Trumpchi Coming to America? color *Bloomberg Businessweek* no4509 p19 Ja 30 2017

Winter of Discontent B. LUTZ color *Road & Track* v68 no7 p104 Mr/Ap 2017

Guanosine triphosphatase

Transcriptional activation of RagD GTPase controls mTORC1 and promotes cancer growth C. Di Malta, D. Siciliano et al diag *Science* v356 no6343 p1188 Je 16 2017

Guantanamo Bay Detention Camp

Guantánamo lawyer: Military tribunals are built on American apartheid [Cover story] M. Paradis *America* v216 no10 p10 My 1 2017

Reflections on a Great and Disappointing President S. MUWAKKIL *In These Times* v41 no2 p44 F 2017

Guarana

Energy Patches color *Prevention* v68 no11 p16 N 2016

Guarana, Cristiano

Research: Sleep Deprivation Can Make It Harder to Stay Calm at Work *Harvard Business Review Digital Articles* p2 2017

Guaranteed annual income

The Free Banquet G. Scialabba color *Commonweal* v144 no8 p19 My 5 2017

The Indestructible IDEA of the Basic INCOME J. WALKER color *Reason* v49 no3 p32 Jl 2017

No Strings Attached Z. Patton color *Governing* v30 no11 p32 Ag 2017

A Utopian Idea Whose Time May Finally Have Arrived M. Vella color *Time* v189 no15 p17 Ap 24 2017

WHY *FREE MONEY COULD BE THE FUTURE OF WORK C. Dillow and B. Rainwater color diag *Fortune* v176 no1 p68 Jl 1 2017

Guaranteed annual income—Social aspects

AS GLOBAL INEQUALITY GROWS, SOME SILICON VALLEY EXECUTIVES THINK A UNIVERSAL INCOME WILL BE THE ANSWER—AND THE BETA TEST IS HAPPENING IN KENYA A. Lowrey *New York Times Magazine* p52 F 26 2017

Guaranty funds

Obamacare's Days Dwindle Down *Weekly Standard* v22 no6 p3 O 17 2016

Guard cells (Plant anatomy)

Making more of your stomata color *Science* v355 no6330 p1169 Mr 17 2017

Mobile MUTE specifies subsidiary cells to build physiologically improved grass stomata M. T. Raissig, J. L. Matos et al bibl diag *Science* v355 no6330 p1215 Mr 17 2017

Guard duty

MY DOGS R. VRABEL color *Popular Mechanics* p94 Ap 2017

Guardado-Sanchez, Elmer

Spin-imbalance in a 2D Fermi-Hubbard system diag graph *Science* v357 no6358 p1385 S 29 2017

Guardia, Ciera

The Risks and Benefits of Turnout for Dressage Horses [Cover story] color *Dressage Today* v24 no2 p18 N 2017

Guardians of Peace (Film)

The Sony Hack Shows How Lawless the Internet Really Is M. Schrage *Harvard Business Review Digital Articles* p2 D 17 2014

Guardians of the Galaxy Vol.2 (Film)

CALENDAR color *Entertainment Weekly* no1463/1464 p74 Ap/My 2017

Gamora the Merrier C. Collis color *Entertainment Weekly* no1465 p20 My 12 2017

Go With It J. PODHORETZ *Weekly Standard* v22 no35 p39 My 22 2017

GUARDIANS OF THE GALAXY VOL.2 C. Nashawaty color *Entertainment Weekly* no1465 p40 My 12 2017

Guardians of the Galaxy Vol. 2 *New Yorker* v93 no15 p5 My 29 2017

The Guardians Return P. Travers color *Rolling Stone* no1287 p56 My 18 2017

Guardians Vol. 2 Laughs It Up, Self-Indulgently S. Zacharek color *Time* v189 no18 p54 My 15 2017

TO INFINITY WAR AND BEYOND! C. Collis color *Entertainment Weekly* no1466 p12 My 19 2017

Two for the Road D. Franich color *Entertainment Weekly* no1466 p13 My 19 2017

WE ARE FAMILY A. LANE cartoon *New Yorker* v93 no13 p94 My 15 2017

Guardians of the Galaxy: Awesome Mix (Music)

The Galaxy's Hottest Mixtape B. HIATT bw color *Rolling Stone* no1286 p14 My 4 2017

Guardiola, Herizen

Herizen GUARDIOLA S. LACAVA *Interview* v46 no9 p20 N 2016

Guardtime (Company)

Cloud Armor That's Not Quite So Fluffy D. Lawrence *Bloomberg Businessweek* no4504 p32 D 19 2016

Guarecuco, Rohiverth

Fabrication of fillable microparticles and other complex 3D microstructures color diag *Science* v357 no6356 p1138 S 15 2017

Guarino, F.

Observation of a large-scale anisotropy in the arrival directions of cosmic rays above 8×1018 eV *Science* v357 no6357 p1266 S 22 2017

GUARINO, MARK

NOTES ON A NIGHTMARE color *Chicago* v66 no8 p37 Ag 2017

Guarino, Tammy

DESIGN MOTIFS FOR A KITCHEN color *Old House Journal* v45 no6 p32 S 2017

Guarnaschelli, Alex

Tiers of JOY color *O, The Oprah Magazine* p140 O 2017

Guarnido-Rueda, Almundena

Determinants of Child Health Inequalities in Developing Countries: a New Perspective chart diag *Society* v53 no6 p641 D 2016

Guarnieri, Anne-Marie

15 INSTANT SKIN FIXES color *Harper's Bazaar* no3652 p177 Ap 2017

BEAUTY DIARIES color *Harper's Bazaar* no3651 p322 Mr 2017

BEST NEW MAKEUP LOOKS color *Harper's Bazaar* no3656 p367 S 2017

DARE TO WEAR COLOR color *Harper's Bazaar* no3653 p286 My 2017

GET GORGEOUS SKIN color *Harper's Bazaar* no3649 p262 D 2016/Ja 2017

GET MAJOR VOLUME color *Harper's Bazaar* no3648 p209 N 2016

GET YOUNGER LOOKING EYES color *Harper's Bazaar* no3657 p189 O 2017

GLAM BY TONIGHT color *Harper's Bazaar* no3649 p251 D 2016/Ja 2017

HALEYBENNETT'S BEAUTY DIARY color *Harper's Bazaar* no3657 p192 O 2017

NEW YEAR NEW YOU color *Harper's Bazaar* no3649 p256 D 2016/Ja 2017

RADIANT SKIN color *Harper's Bazaar* no3651 p314 Mr 2017

RUNWAY REPORT color *Harper's Bazaar* no3650 p113 F 2017

RUNWAY REPORT color *Harper's Bazaar* no3654 p107 Je/Jl 2017

SUMMER BEAUTY ESSENTIALS color *Harper's Bazaar* no3653 p234 My 2017

UPDATE YOUR LOOK color *Harper's Bazaar* no3651 p311 Mr 2017

UPDATE YOUR LOOK color *Harper's Bazaar* no3655 p89 Ag 2017

GUASPARI, DAVID

Resolved to Play *Weekly Standard* v22 no5 p41 O 10 2016

Room at the Top color *Weekly Standard* v22 no21 p36 F 6 2017

Gubar, Susan, 1944-

Reading and Writing Cancer: How Words Heal K. Saupe *Christian Century* v133 no26 p42 D 21 2016

Gubernatorial elections

Is Virginia for Populists? G. ZORNICK color *Nation* v304 no17 p19 Je 5 2017

Gubernatorial elections—Maryland

Why I'm Running H. Kelly color *Glamour* v115 no10 p146 O 2017

Gubernatorial elections—New Jersey

All or Nothing: Democrats need to win this year's governors' races A. Greenblatt *Governing* v30 no9 p17 Je 2017

The Gubernatorial Stakes: Looking for clues in New Jersey and Virginia R. FAUCHEUX *American Conservative* v16 no4 p6 Jl/Ag 2017

Gubernatorial elections—Virginia

All or Nothing: Democrats need to win this year's governors' races A. Greenblatt *Governing* v30 no9 p17 Je 2017

The Gubernatorial Stakes: Looking for clues in New Jersey and Virginia R. FAUCHEUX *American Conservative* v16 no4 p6 Jl/Ag 2017

The Normal One J. GERAGHTY il *National Review* v69 no19 p13 O 16 2017

Gucci (Company)

Bazaar's Best-Dressed LIST color *Harper's Bazaar* no3654 p64 Je/Jl 2017

BEST DRESS E. Wilson color *InStyle* v24 no3 p141 Mr 2017

BOLD AND SEXY, color *Harper's Bazaar* no3648 p90 N 2016

Cat Ladies, Unite! [Cover story] J. Lance color *Glamour* v114 no11 p45 N 2016

A FANTASTIC BEAST... ...And where to FIND it J. Roth color *Esquire* p40 O 2017

GUCCI, do better M. HARRIS color *Ebony* v72 no11 p27 S 2017

Gucci earrings V. SMITH color *Vogue* v207 no4 p266 Ap 2017

GUCCI'S MAIN MAN Z. BARON color *GQ: Gentlemen's Quarterly* v86 no12 p216 D 2016

The Loafer Steps Out T. Patterson color *Bloomberg Businessweek* no4532 p64 Jl 31 2017

MAGIC HOUR color *Conde Nast Traveler* v52 no10 p29 N 2017

Sparkles FLY S. Mower, M. HOLGATE et al color *Vogue* v207 no3 p314 Mr 2017

The Superhero Sweater J. CHEN color *Esquire* v166 no5 p55 D 2016/Ja 2017

Wait, Platform Sneakers Are Back? [Cover story] F. Krentcil and J. Harman color *Glamour* no8 p35 Ag 2017

Wild Things color *Architectural Digest* v74 no9 p60 S 2017

Gucci Mane, 1980-

Spring Preview M. Trammell cartoon *New Yorker* v93 no4 p10 Mr 13 2017

Guccio Gucci SpA

IT'S PERSONAL *Interview* v47 no5 p94 Je/Jl 2017

Gudauskas, Dane

AN ICY RESOLVE A. DOUGLAS bw color *Surfer* v58 no2 p56 My 2017

SPIRIT ANIMAL K. TAYLOR bw color *Surfer* v57 no11 p54 D 2016

Welcome to the Pizote House T. Prodanovich color *Surfer* v57 no11 p12 D 2016

Gude, Olivia—Interviews

An interview with Olivia Gude about connecting school and community arts practice J. Berglin *Arts Education Policy Review* v118 no1 p60 2017

Gudema, Louis

7 Marketing Technologies Every Company Must Use *Harvard Business Review Digital Articles* p2 N 3 2014

Gudenkauf, Heather

Not a Sound *Publishers Weekly* v264 no12 p55 Mr 20 2017

Gudipati, M. S.

Seasonal exposure of carbon dioxide ice on the nucleus of comet 67P/Churyumov-Gerasimenko bibl bw graph *Science* v354 no6319 p1563 D 23 2016

Gudjónsdóttir, Brynhildur—Interviews

THE FEMALE VOICE OF NJÁLL V. HAFSTAÐ *Iceland Review* v54 no5 p14 S-O 2016

Gudlaugsson, E.

Massive blow-out craters formed by hydrate-controlled methane expulsion from the Arctic seafloor graph map *Science* v356 no6341 p948 Je 1 2017

Gudmestad, Julie

Get to know... your hamstrings color *Yoga Journal* p90 2017 SpecialIssue

Gudmundsen, Geir—Interviews

Test Prep T. Keith and R. Demak color *Sports Illustrated* v126 no7 p24 Mr 6 2017

Guedes, G. P.

Observation of a large-scale anisotropy in the arrival directions of cosmic rays above 8×10^{18} eV *Science* v357 no6357 p1266 S 22 2017

Gueissaz, Eric

Out of the ORDINARY M. JAFFE *Arizona Highways* v92 no7 p42 Jl 2016

Güell, Marc

Inactivation of porcine endogenous retrovirus in pigs using CRISPR-Cas9 diag *Science* v357 no6357 p1303 S 22 2017

Guelzo, Allen

Allen C. Guelzo, Redeeming the Great Emancipator D. Schaub *Society* v54 no2 p196 Ap 2017

Lincoln's Forgotten Middle Years color *Washington Monthly* v49 no6-8 p65 Je-Ag 2017

The Enigma of Ulysses S. Grant *Washington Monthly* p8 N/D 2016

Guemas, Virginie

Using climate models to estimate the quality of global observational data sets bibl graph *Science* v354 no6311 p452 O 28 2016

Guenez, Ghizlan

EVERY WHICH WAY BUT LOOSE S. Azam color *Vogue* v207 no7 p93 Jl 2017

Guerber, Megan

Cape Calm color il *American Craft* v77 no2 p66 Ap/My 2017

Mergers color *American Craft* v76 no6 p38 D 2016-Ja 2017

The Subterranean Scene color il *American Craft* v77 no3 p80 Je/Jl 2017

Guercino, 1591-1666

Christ and the Woman of Samaria at the Well by Guercino (Giovanni Francesco Barbieri) H. J. Hornik and M. C. Parsons color *Christian Century* v134 no5 p47 Mr 1 2017

Guerilla (TV program)

Radicals In Love Go Guerrilla D. D'Addario color *Time* v189 no15 p52 Ap 24 2017

Guèrin, Gilles

Release of mineral-bound water prior to subduction tied to shallow seismogenic slip off Sumatra graph *Science* v356 no6340 p841 My 26 2017

Guerin, Greg

The extent of forest in dryland biomes [Cover story] chart map *Science* v356 no6338 p635 My 12 2017

GUERRA, PIA

COMICS *In These Times* v41 no10 p46 O 2017

Guerrero (Mexico : State)—Environmental conditions

A Gold Rush in Mexico's Deadly South E. Martin, B. Bain et al color *Bloomberg Businessweek* no4497 p20 O 31 2016

GUERRERO, DESIREE

50 FOR 50: EVERY STATE HAS ITS OWN LGBT LEADERS AND HEROES. 50 CURRENT LGBT LEADERS SHARE THEIR STATE'S HEROES map *Advocate* no1091 p98 Je/Jl 2017

BECOMING MY OWN WARRIOR: HE WASN'T EVEN OUT TO HIS PARENTS YET, BUT JOSHUA THOMAS HAD TO TELL THEM HE WAS HIV-POSITIVE. HE SURVIVED AND TELLS OTHERS HOW YOU CAN, TOO *Advocate* no1093 p33 O/N 2017

BLAQUE OUT: BEING OUTED AS TRANS DIDN'T RUIN THIS YOUTUBE STAR. IT GAVE HER MORE FREEDOM color graph *Advocate* no1091 p78 Je/Jl 2017

COACHELLA IS HELLA QUEER THIS YEAR color *Advocate* no1090 p51 Ap 2017

Does a Bare Bush Increase Your Risk for STIs? color *Advocate* no1090 p42 Ap 2017

Gyno Paps Aren't Just for Cis Women *Advocate* no1090 p47 Ap 2017

THE LGBTQ HEALTH CARE BILL OF RIGHTS: New York City made an important step toward equality *Advocate* no1093 p60 O/N 2017

MAINTAINING BISEXUAL SEXUAL HEALTH AND WELLNESS bw *Advocate* no1090 p46 Ap 2017

MORE LEADING HEALTH EXPERTS AND ORGANIZATIONS ENDORSE UNDETECTABLE = UNTRANSMITTABLE: WHEN IS THERE ZERO RISK OF TRANSMITTING HIV? *Advocate* no1093 p33 O/N 2017

THE MOTHER OF PRIDE: THE FIRST PRIDE WAS ORGANIZED BY A BISEXUAL WOMAN bw *Advocate* no1091 p120 Je/Jl 2017

SAY HER NAME: As one murder case is closed, another begins, marking 16 trans women killed before August *Advocate* no1093

p8 O/N 2017
SHE'S ALL THAT: LESBIAN SENSATION GIGI GORGEOUS IS ALSO A MODEL, SPOKESPERSON, ACTIVIST, AND A TRANS WOMAN IN LOVE color *Advocate* no1091 p77 Je/Jl 2017

Victorian Lust color *Advocate* no1091 p30 Je/Jl 2017

GUERRERO-BOSAGNA, CARLOS

Evolution with No Reason: A Neutral View on Epigenetic Changes, Genomic Variability, and Evolutionary Novelty *BioScience* v67 no5 p469 My 2017

Guerrero-Juarez, Christian F.

Regeneration of fat cells from myofibroblasts during wound healing bibl color graph *Science* v355 no6326 p748 F 17 2017

Guerrilla (TV program)

Guerrilla Chic E. JONES *In These Times* v41 no6 p38 Je 2017

IDRIS ELBA: THE RIGHTS STUFF A. Wilkinson color *Entertainment Weekly* no1462 p52 Ap 21 2017

Guerrillas

Lasting Images color *Time* v190 no12 p50 S 25 2017

Guerrillas—Social conditions

OUT OF THE JUNGLE J. L. ANDERSON cartoon color *New Yorker* v93 no11 p28 My 1 2017

Guerrini, Christi J.

Myriad take two: Can genomic databases remain secret? color *Science* v356 no6338 p586 My 12 2017

GUERRY, ANNE D.

Society Is Ready for a New Kind of Science—Is Academia? *BioScience* v67 no7 p591 Jl 2017

Guers, John J.

Minority investigators lack NIH funding color *Science* v356 no6342 p1018 Je 9 2017

Guest, Christopher, 1948-

Mascots D. Coggan color *Entertainment Weekly* no1435 p44 O 14 2016

Seriously funny and funnily serious J. SEMLEY color *Maclean's* v129 no42 p63 O 24 2016

Under the Giant Heads of Mascots Live Absurd Humans Just Like Us E. Berman color *Time* v188 no16/17 p85 O 24 2016

Guest rooms

Going the Distance K. RENDA and B. REYNAERT color *House Beautiful* p18 Jl 2017

How to Freshen Up a Guest Room, Fast! color *Good Housekeeping* v263 no5 p60 N 2016

The Inn at Castle Rock: Like so many things in Bisbee, this old hotel has its quirks, including 14 funky guest rooms with names such as Crying Shame and Last Chance, a "Ghost Book" and a "moat." K. MONTGOMERY *Arizona Highways* v93 no11 p14 N 2017

Guesthouses

1 An Experiment in the Woods W. GOODMAN img *New York* v49 no21 p80 O 17 2016

ATLAS OBSCURA BERBER LODGE IS A HIP OASIS HIDDEN AMONG OLIVE AND CITRUS GROVES NEAR THE MOUNTAINS OUTSIDE MARRAKECH A. GIACOBBE color *Conde Nast Traveler* v52 no10 p30 N 2017

Wild Vacation R. DAVIDSON color *National Geographic Kids* no465 p6 N 2016

Guesthouses—Design & construction

CLEAR INTENTIONS J. GIOVANNINI bw color *Architectural Digest* v74 no1 p202 Ja 2017

WARM WELCOME D. NETTO color *Architectural Digest* v73 no11 p182 N 2016

Guesthouses—Evaluation

KAUAI'S NEXT WAVE [Cover story] C. Roth color *Sunset* v238 no3 p44 Mr 2017

Theory institute opens residence hall for visitors T. Feder *Physics Today* v70 no4 p32 Ap 2017

Guests of the Ayatollah: The First Battle in America's War With Militant Islam (Book)

444 DAYS IN HELL R. Soodalter *Military History* v33 no6 p18 Mr 2017

Guet, Călin C.

Biased partitioning of the multidrug efflux pump AcrAB-TolC underlies long-lived phenotypic heterogeneity diag *Science* v356 no6335 p311 Ap 21 2017

Guetta, David, 1967-

David Guetta M. Hagan color *Current Biography* v78 no1 p18 Ja 2017

Guevara, J. E.

Persistent effects of pre-Columbian plant domestication on Amazonian forest composition bibl chart graph map *Science* v355 no6328 p925 Mr 3 2017

Guggenheim, Peggy, 1898-1979

Palazzo Intrigue M. ESTEROW bw color *Vanity Fair* v59 no2 p90 F 2017

Guggenheim Museum Bilbao (Spain)

Bilbao Now A. H. GRAHAM color *Conde Nast Traveler* v52 no7 p44 Ag 2017

Guggenmos, A.

Soft x-ray excitonics bw diag *Science* v357 no6356 p1134 S 15 2017

Gugino, Carla, 1971-

Orange You Glad? E. Wilson color *InStyle* v24 no6 p44 Je 2017

Guglielmetti, Petra

APPLY Yourself *Martha Stewart Living* no269 p106 N 2016

CHIC EGGS color *Martha Stewart Living* p106 Ap 2017

Crowned Beauties color *Southern Living* v52 no11 p61 N 2017

french flair color *Better Homes & Gardens* v95 no10 p20 O 2017

happy place color *Better Homes & Gardens* v95 no11 p18 N 2017

kids' stuff color *Better Homes & Gardens* v95 no8 p16 Ag 2017

OBSESSED WITH TRIM & TASSELS color *Better Homes & Gardens* v95 no10 p16 O 2017

STUNING MADE SIMPLE *Martha Stewart Living* no270 p114 D 2016

what's your HANG-UP? color *Better Homes & Gardens* v95 no9 p50 S 2017

Guha, Roneeta

The power and potential of teacher residencies color graph *Phi Delta Kappan* v98 no8 p31 My 2017

The Teacher Residency *Education Digest* v83 no2 p38 O 2017

Guhin, Jeff

What We Can & Cannot Fix bw *Commonweal* v144 no9 p22 My 19 2017

Guibert, Hervé, 1955-1991

AMOUR FOU H. Guibert color *Harper's Magazine* v335 no2005 p23 Je 2017

Guida, Alessandro

Transcriptional activation of RagD GTPase controls mTORC1 and promotes cancer growth diag *Science* v356 no6343 p1188 Je 16 2017

Guida, Roberto

Global atmospheric particle formation from CERN CLOUD measurements bibl graph map *Science* v354 no6316 p1119 D 2 2016

Guide dogs

"He saved my life" A. L. Greco color *Glamour* v115 no4 p144 Ap 2017

Guidebooks

In Focus color *Publishers Weekly* v264 no35 p34 Ag 28 2017

PREPARING FOR TAKE OFF D. DILWORTH color *Publishers Weekly* v264 no35 p29 Ag 28 2017

Urban Planning D. Dilworth color *Publishers Weekly* v264 no35 p32 Ag 28 2017

Guided missile bases

    See also

Intercontinental ballistic missile bases

Guided missile testing

    See also

Ballistic missile testing

Guided missiles

    See also

Ballistic missiles

Editor's note L. Crowder *Bulletin of the Atomic Scientists* v72 no6 p359 N 2016

Guided missiles—Korea (North)

Where a Bad World Means Good Business J. Mattingly and A. Sharp color *Bloomberg Businessweek* no4533 p16 Ag 7 2017

Guide Dog of Hermosilla, The (Short story)

THE GUIDE DOG OF HERMOSILLA A. di Benedetto *Harper's Magazine* v334 no2004 p20 My 2017

Guidelines

GO NUTS S. Shelley *Virginia Living* v15 no3 p9 Ap 2017

Guidi, Jennifer

Get into the Groove M. RUS color *Architectural Digest* v74 no4 p72 Ap 2017

Guido, Guadalupe

The Carpet Whisperer L. O'leary *New York Times Magazine* p45 F 26 2017

Guidotti, Maria

AMERICAN EXPORT color *Cycle World* v56 no6 p68 Jl 2017

GUIDUCCI, MARK

Babe RUTH color *Vogue* v207 no3 p348 Mr 2017

Belle CURVE color *Vogue* v207 no3 p346 Mr 2017

Brigitte Macron color *Vogue* v207 no9 p358 S 2017

Bulgari/Nicholas Kirkwood Bags color *Vogue* v207 no9 p368 S 2017

Eastern Promises color *Vogue* v207 no9 p346 S 2017

Finding Her LEGS color *Vogue* v207 no7 p40 Jl 2017

FORCES TO RECKON WITH bw color *Vogue* v207 no3 p357 Mr 2017

FULL ENGLISH bw color *Vogue* v207 no10 p252 O 2017

GIVENCHY'S Giacomettis color *Vogue* v207 no3 p350 Mr 2017

Glam Rock color *Vogue* v207 no4 p184 Ap 2017

GLOBAL Warmth color *Vogue* v207 no1 p34 Ja 2017

Heart and Sole color *Vogue* v207 no9 p388 S 2017

Hey, Lady! color *Vogue* v207 no7 p58 Jl 2017

IN FULL BLOOM color *Vogue* v207 no6 p114 Je 2017

JENNY SCHLENZKA: Performance Space 122 color *Vogue* v207 no10 p192 O 2017

LEG Work color *Vogue* v207 no3 p338 Mr 2017

Making a Name color *Vogue* v207 no11 p168 N 2017

Mansur Gavriel Coats color *Vogue* v207 no9 p386 S 2017

Model BEHAVIOR color *Vogue* v207 no1 p30 Ja 2017

NAOMIE Harris color *Vogue* v207 no3 p322 Mr 2017

NIEVES Zuberbühler color *Vogue* v207 no4 p156 Ap 2017

OBJECTS of their DESIRE color *Vogue* v207 no3 p326 Mr 2017

Off the Menu color *Vogue* v207 no9 p380 S 2017

Paint It Black color *Vogue* v207 no9 p366 S 2017

Queen of the Jungle color *Vogue* v207 no9 p396 S 2017

Riley Keough color *Vogue* v207 no9 p372 S 2017

Sasha LANE color *Vogue* v206 no12 p138 D 2016

Sies Marjan Shoes color *Vogue* v207 no9 p362 S 2017

Sparkles FLY color *Vogue* v207 no3 p314 Mr 2017

Spot ON color *Vogue* v207 no1 p34 Ja 2017

Statement Belts color *Vogue* v207 no9 p382 S 2017

Taste MAKERS color *Vogue* v207 no3 p334 Mr 2017

TNT cartoon color *Vogue* v207 no3 p342 Mr 2017

TNT color *Vogue* v207 no9 p392 S 2017

Guild DeArmond Rhythm (Company)

Guild DeArmond Rhythm Chief Reissue Pickups K. Baumann color *Downbeat* v84 no3 p115 Mr 2017

Guilds—History

The Problem With Guilds, from Silversmiths to Taxi Drivers J. Fox *Harvard Business Review Digital Articles* p2 D 4 2014

GUILFOYLE, TOM

Chords & Discords bw color *Downbeat* v84 no6 p10 Je 2017

Guiliana, Mark

Jersey J. Murph color *Downbeat* v84 no10 p55 O 2017

Guilickson, Gil

KNOW NOZZLES *Successful Farming* v115 no2 p41 F 2017

Guillain-Barré syndrome—Treatment

A Bridge Back to Life K. RIDDERBUSCH *Atlanta* v56 no7 p214 N 2016

Guillamat-Prats, Raquel

Local amplifiers of IL-4Rα-mediated macrophage activation promote repair in lung and liver diag *Science* v356 no6342 p1076 Je 9 2017

Guillard, P.

Molecular gas in the halo fuels the growth of a massive cluster galaxy at high redshift bibl graph *Science* v354 no6316 p1128 D 2 2016

Guillaume Tell (Theatrical production)

Guillaume Tell *Opera News* v81 no9 p59 Mr 2017

Hitting the Mark W. R. Braun and D. Shengold *Opera News* v81 no7 p32 Ja 2017

A SUDDEN SHADOW A. ROSS cartoon *New Yorker* v92 no36 p76 N 7 2016

Guillaumet, J.-L.

Persistent effects of pre-Columbian plant domestication on Ama-

zonian forest composition bibl chart graph map *Science* v355 no6328 p925 Mr 3 2017

Guillemot, Yves—Interviews

UBISOFT'S CEO ISN'T PLAYING GAMES C. Morris color *Fortune* v176 no3 p21 S 1 2017

GUILLERMOPRIETO, ALMA

Robert B. Silvers (1929–2017) [Cover story] bw color *New York Review of Books* v64 no8 p31 My 11 2017

Guilliams, Martin

Macrophage, a long-distance middleman bibl color *Science* v355 no6331 p1258 Mr 24 2017

Guillot, T.

Jupiter's interior and deep atmosphere: The initial pole-to-pole passes with the Juno spacecraft [Cover story] color graph *Science* v356 no6340 p821 My 26 2017

Guillou, Florian

The DNA methyltransferase DNMT3C protects male germ cells from transposon activity bibl diag graph *Science* v354 no6314 p909 N 18 2016

Guilt (Psychology)

balance is BS C. BIRNBAUM *Parents* v91 no9 p126 S 2016

i don't feel guilty about not feeling guilty B. PAESEL color *Parents* v92 no5 p84 My 2017

Let Go of Guilt J. Andriakos color *Health* v30 no10 p26 D 2016

Guimaraes, Helder

Be Your Own Magician B. Doherty img *New York* v49 no19 p86 S 19 2016

Guinan, Mary Louise Cecilia, 1884-1933

T FOR TEXAS, G FOR A GOOD TIME P. CARLSON bw color *American History* v52 no4 p18 O 2017

Guinard, Morgane

The Poisoned Will of Jean Meslier: A French priest's shocking attack on religion called for the fall of altars and the heads of kings *History Today* v67 no10 p12 O 2017

Guinea

GUINEA *New York Times Magazine* p54 S 24 2017

Guinn, Jeff

Keep Them Poor & Tired K. Massinger color *Commonweal* v144 no15 p41 S 22 2017

Guinther, Louise T.

Behind the Scenes: Liner Notes *Opera News* v81 no12 p5 Je 2017

FREDERICA VON STADE *Opera News* v81 no10 p22 Ap 2017

Liner Notes: Ruth Bader Ginsburg *Opera News* v81 no10 p68 Ap 2017

True Believer: Bass Soloman Howard's success is built on a foundation of faith that has seen him through some unusual challenges *Opera News* v81 no12 p65 Je 2017

Guiot, Joel

Climate change: The 2015 Paris Agreement thresholds and Mediterranean basin ecosystems bibl *Science* v354 no6311 p465 O 28 2016

Guitar

See also

Ukulele

GEARHEAD: ROCK GROUP D. PIERCE color *Wired* v25 no8 p42 Ag 2017

Guitar music (Jazz)

Towner's Pianistic Approach to Guitar J. Ephland bw *Downbeat* v84 no4 p16 Ap 2017

Guitar picks—Evaluation

Guild DeArmond Rhythm Chief Reissue Pickups K. Baumann color *Downbeat* v84 no3 p115 Mr 2017

Guitar—Electronic equipment—Evaluation

T-Rex Replicator K. Baumann color *Downbeat* v84 no1 p107 Ja 2017

Guitar—Equipment & supplies

ToneWoodAmp K. Baumann color *Downbeat* v84 no7 p81 Jl 2017

Vintage Sounds J. Weir *Missouri Life* v43 no6 p17 O/N 2016

Guitar—Evaluation

Campellone Deluxe Series Archtop K. Baumann color *Downbeat* v84 no10 p194 O 2017

Eastman Custom Edition Guitars K. Baumann color *Downbeat* v84 no8 p91 Ag 2017

Framus Mayfield Pro 16-3106 C. Morrison color *Downbeat* v84 no7 p82 Jl 2017

GEAR BOX color *Downbeat* v84 no7 p84 Jl 2017

GEAR color *Downbeat* v83 no12 p96 D 2016

Heritage KB Groove Master Archtop K. Baumann color *Downbeat* v83 no12 p106 D 2016

Santa Cruz Guitar Co. FS Model C. Morrison color *Downbeat* v84 no7 p80 Jl 2017

Guitarists

See also

Bass guitarists

BALLER FROM THE HOLLER: JEAN DOWELL WAS A GROUND-BREAKING ATHLETE and collegiate basketball coach. Now, with an unlikely second act (and a guitar), she is bringing it all back home J. BURHAN *Cincinnati Magazine* v50 no11 p82 Ag 2017

CHUCK BERRY K. O'Donnell color *Entertainment Weekly* no1459 p14 Mr 31 2017

Holt County's Christmas Lesson P. B. KARO cartoon *Nebraska Life* v20 no6 p48 N/D 2016

In Memoriam: Versatile Guitarist Larry Coryell bw *Downbeat* v84 no5 p22 My 2017

Joel Harrison D. OUELLETTE color *Downbeat* v84 no2 p106 F 2017

Kurt Rosenwinkel Goes DIY, Forms New Label B. Milkowski color *Downbeat* v83 no12 p15 D 2016

LARRY CORYELL BACK FROM THE BRINK [Cover story] B. MILKOWSKI color *Downbeat* v84 no2 p34 F 2017

A Quick Lesson in Rock Herstory F. Krentcil color *Glamour* no8 p33 Ag 2017

Remembering Allan Holdsworth B. Milkowski bw *Downbeat* v84 no7 p22 Jl 2017

STEPPIN' OUT E. J. Wallace *Virginia Living* v15 no3 p25 Ap 2017

Tribute to a Maestro B. MILKOWSKI color *Downbeat* v84 no5 p8 My 2017

Why Ladies Pick Guitar Players E. Spitznagel bw *Men's Health* v31 no10 p42 D 2016

YOTAM SILBERSTEIN Burning Brightly B. Milkowski color *Downbeat* v84 no2 p20 F 2017

Guitarists—Interviews

Bob Weir D. BROWNE bw *Rolling Stone* no1273 p58 N 3 2016

Guiteau, Charles Julius, 1841-1882

A Stalwart of Stalwarts J. Bellamy *Prologue* v48 no3 p36 Fall 2016

Gujarat (India)—Economic conditions

A Slowdown in Modi's Backyard B. Pradhan and I. Marlow color *Bloomberg Businessweek* no4541 p36 O 9 2017

Gujarat (India)—Politics & government—21st century

A Slowdown in Modi's Backyard B. Pradhan and I. Marlow color *Bloomberg Businessweek* no4541 p36 O 9 2017

Gül, Ali

Changing climate shifts timing of European floods color graph *Science* v357 no6351 p588 Ag 11 2017

Gulati, Ranjay

GE'S GLOBAL GROWTH EXPERIMENT: THE COMPANY PUSHED CROSS-BUSINESS COLLABORATION *Harvard Business Review* v95 no5 p52 S/O 2017

Startups Can't Revolve Around Their Founders If They Want to Succeed *Harvard Business Review Digital Articles* p2 Mr 4 2016

Gülen movement

Turkey's Witch Hunt T. Michel color *Commonweal* v143 no18 p10 N 11 2016

Guleserian, Kris

Close to Her Heart B. Hargrove *D: The Magazine of Dallas* v43 no10 p116 O 2016

Gulf Coast (U.S.)

Bud and Friends E. Laborde *New Orleans Magazine* v51 no5 p14 Mr 2017

Gulf Cooperation Council

How Iran's hybrid-war tactics help and hurt it M. G. Dalton bibl *Bulletin of the Atomic Scientists* v73 no5 p312 2017

Residents and Residencies R. Aima *Art in America* v104 no9 p55 O 2016

Gulf Stream—Environmental conditions

Oceanic Highway I. L. Bras color *Oceanus* v51 no2 p40 Wint 2016

Gulfstream Aerospace Corp.

FIRST LOOK: GULFSTREAM G500 [Cover story] S. POPE chart color *Flying* v143 no12 p40 D 2016

SOARING ABOVE THE REST T. VELOCCI color *Forbes* v198 no5 p34 O 25 2016

Gulfstream airplanes—Evaluation

SOARING ABOVE THE REST T. VELOCCI color *Forbes* v198 no5 p34 O 25 2016

Gulfstream Yachts (Company)

Gulfstream 52 D. HARDING JR. color *Power & Motoryacht* v32 no12 p34 D 2016

Guliani, Neema Singh

They're Here to Help S. Cristobal color *InStyle* v24 no4 p102 Ap 2017

Gulick, Sean P. S.

The formation of peak rings in large impact craters bibl color graph *Science* v354 no6314 p878 N 18 2016

Gulkis, S.

Jupiter's interior and deep atmosphere: The initial pole-to-pole passes with the Juno spacecraft [Cover story] color graph *Science* v356 no6340 p821 My 26 2017

Gullberg, B.

Molecular gas in the halo fuels the growth of a massive cluster galaxy at high redshift bibl graph *Science* v354 no6316 p1128 D 2 2016

GULLETTE, WILLIAM T.

CLASH OF THE TITANS cartoon *Vanity Fair* p84 Hollywood 2017 Supplement

GULLEY, AARON

COLOMBIA RISING color *Bicycling* v58 no7 p54 Ag 2017

AN IMPROBABLE CONVERGENCE color *Bicycling* v58 no1 p44 Ja/F 2017

Gulley, Philip

BAD WRAP *Saturday Evening Post* v289 no1 p16 Ja/F 2017

DON'T HAVE A COW: It seemed like a bright idea to raise cattle, but the average cow is a disaster waiting to happen *Saturday Evening Post* v289 no5 p16 S/O 2017

Idol Minds *Indianapolis Monthly* v40 no7 p48 Mr 2017

I'M ALL FOR BEING NICE *Saturday Evening Post* v288 no6 p19 N/D 2016

In Her Wake: A few words about my mom, whom I wish were here to read them *Indianapolis Monthly* p56 N 2017

Live and Learn: As kids return to school, here's a lesson on education: A lot of it happens during summer, and theory has nothing to do with it *Indianapolis Monthly* v12 no40 p50 Ag 2017

Made in the Shade cartoon *Indianapolis Monthly* v42 no2 p51 O 2017

MARCH BADNESS *Saturday Evening Post* v289 no2 p14 Mr/Ap 2017

No Cause for Alarm *Indianapolis Monthly* p48 My 2017

No Picnic: Nothing is as good in real life as it is in theory *Indianapolis Monthly* v40 no10 p50 Je 2017

Nothing New *Indianapolis Monthly* p46 F 2017

Over It color *Indianapolis Monthly* p52 Ap 2017

A Pledge to Bullies *Indianapolis Monthly* v40 no5 p42 Ja 2017

Sick and Tired *Indianapolis Monthly* v40 no4 p63 D 2016

The Silver Lining *Indianapolis Monthly* v40 no3 p64 N 2016

SPRING CLEANING *Saturday Evening Post* v289 no3 p16 My/Je 2017

A Step Up: I first met Governor Holcomb on the Statehouse stairs. Both he and Indiana were ascending *Indianapolis Monthly* v40 no11 p48 Jl 2017

The Things She'll Carry: In the event of a house fire, some of my possessions must be saved—and my wife stands ready to haul them color *Indianapolis Monthly* v41 no2 p50 S 2017

Gullickson, Gil

7 MISSOURI DICAMBA-DAMAGE TAKEAWAYS *Successful Farming* v115 no5 p42 Mid-Mr 2017

ABBEY WICK: SOIL HEALTH SPECIALIST KNOWS HOW TO CONNECT WITH FARMERS bw *Successful Farming* v115 no7 p5 My 2017

ATV SPRAYERS: THESE UNITS WILL GO WHERE LARGER SPRAYERS CAN'T ENTER color *Successful Farming* v115 no7 p28 My 2017

BEHIND THE NUMBERS: WHAT YOU CAN GLEAN FROM YIELD CONTESTS *Successful Farming* v115 no9 p48 Ag 2017

BLUE SKY IN AGRICULTURE *Successful Farming* v115 no1

p34 Ja 2017

BUGS IN A JUG *Successful Farming* v114 no12 p48 Mid-N 2016

HAY MOISTURE TESTERS *Successful Farming* v115 no4 p57 Mr 2017

HOW TO SORT SOIL FERTILITY CLAIMS *Successful Farming* v114 no10 p14 O 2016

HOW TO WEATHERPROOF YOUR FARM (SORT OF) [Cover story] *Successful Farming* v114 no11 p30 N 2016

MEET METABOLIC RESISTANCE *Successful Farming* v115 no5 p44 Mid-Mr 2017

Modern Maps *Successful Farming* v114 no12 p16 Mid-N 2016

NUDGE YIELDS WITH NARROW ROWS *Successful Farming* v115 no4 p54 Mr 2017

Palmer amaranth is bedeviling farmers like no other weed. Ultimately, though, tools exist to defeat it *Successful Farming* v115 no5 p32 Mid-Mr 2017

PROVE IT ON THE FARM: ON-FARM TEST PLOTS HAVE LED TO SUCCESSFUL PRACTICE ADOPTION ON THIS FARM *Successful Farming* v115 no11 p43 S 2017

SEED FIRMERS, COVERS *Successful Farming* v114 no13 p51 D 2016

SOIL STEALER: TILLAGE IS A STEALTHY ERODER THAT ROBS YOUR PRECIOUS TOPSOIL. HERE'S HOW TO FIX IT *Successful Farming* v115 no12 p44 O 2017

Traits Under the Lens *Successful Farming* v115 no2 p44 F 2017

WEED-CONTROL TECHNOLOGY UPDATE: NO TRULY NEW HERBICIDES ARE SLATED FOR 2017, BUT DICAMBA-TOLERANT SOYBEANS ARE READY TO COMPLETELY ROLL OUT THIS YEAR color *Successful Farming* v115 no7 p36 My 2017

WHERE DICAMBA STANDS FOR 2017 *Successful Farming* v115 no1 p16 Ja 2017

Gullickson, Gill

10 SUCCESSFUL FARMERS: BRYAN JORGENSEN *Successful Farming* v115 no8 p22 Je/Jl 2017

10 UP & COMERS: CASEY HOOK *Successful Farming* v115 no8 p46 Je/Jl 2017

10 UP & COMERS: MEAGHAN ANDERSON *Successful Farming* v115 no8 p36 Je/Jl 2017

BARRY DUNN: SOUTH DAKOTA STATE UNIVERSITY'S NEW PRESIDENT TACKLES RESTRUCTURING WITH WEB-BASED TOOL AND AIMS TO EXTEND THE LAND-GRANT MISSION *Successful Farming* v115 no6 p10 Ap 2017

GULLIVER, KATRINA

Call It Sleep *Weekly Standard* v22 no35 p35 My 22 2017

Gulls

Almost Spring on Craigville Beach K. WHOULEY color *Yankee* p92 Mr 2017

Waiting for Water J. B. LITTLE *Audubon* v118 no6 p17 Wint 2016

Gulls—Research

Northern exposure J. BENNETT color *Canadian Geographic* v135 no6 p33 D 2015

Gulotta, Michael

Mike Gulotta [Cover story] T. McNally color *New Orleans Magazine* v51 no2 p64 D 2016

GULSBY, ALEX

pass fail: Summit at Sunset il *Backpacker* p32 S 2017

Gum disease—Prevention

Problem Solved: Gum Disease R. LALIBERTE *Prevention* v69 no6 p18 Je 2017

Gum disease—Treatment

Problem Solved: Gum Disease R. LALIBERTE *Prevention* v69 no6 p18 Je 2017

Gumber, Sanjeev

Sustained virologic control in SIV+ macaques after antiretroviral and $\alpha4\beta7$ antibody therapy bibl graph *Science* v354 no6309 p197 O 14 2016

Gumbo (Soup)

A Great Pot of Gumbo L. Cericola and P. Lolley color *Southern Living* v52 no3 p126 Mr 2017

Gumbs, Alisa

4 Ways to Own Your Personal Power During Extremely Stressful Work Periods *Black Enterprise* v47 no4 p29 N/D 2016

5 Signs Your Job is Completely Stressing You Out color *Black Enterprise* v47 no4 p29 N/D 2016

Bouncing Back After Breast Cancer color *Black Enterprise* v47

no3 p69 O 2016

Carla Harris's 'Pearls' of Power color *Black Enterprise* v47 no3 p35 O 2016

FINDING PURPOSE IN PLASTIC SURGERY color *Black Enterprise* v47 no5 p29 Ja/F 2017

How Juicing Changed My Life color *Black Enterprise* v47 no4 p46 N/D 2016

PENNEY WISE color *Black Enterprise* v47 no2 p34 S 2016

SURPRISE, SURPRISE WOMEN ARE OUTPERFORMING MEN graph *Black Enterprise* v47 no7 p18 My/Je 2017

Work Grind Killing You? color *Black Enterprise* v47 no4 p28 N/D 2016

Gummer, Grace, 1986-

AMAZING GRACE N. Silva-Jelly color *Harper's Bazaar* no3657 p244 O 2017

GUMMERE, REBECCA

Cooper's HEART cartoon color *O, The Oprah Magazine* p110 Ap 2017

Gums & resins

new products color *Science* v357 no6351 p613 Ag 11 2017

Guðmundsson, Birgir—Interviews

STATE OF THE FOURTH ESTATE Z. Robert *Iceland Review* v54 no6 p72 N/D 2016

Gun control

Comments img *New York* p8 Ja 9 2017

HOLSTER IT RIGHT R. MANN color *Outdoor Life* v224 no4 pP8 My 2017

NIH quietly shelves gun research program M. Wadman *Science* v357 no6356 p1082 S 15 2017

Shot in the Dark D. Paul *Indianapolis Monthly* v40 no4 p160 D 2016

Gun control—Maryland

WHY DID A CONSERVATIVE JUDGE UPHOLD AN ASSAULT WEAPONS BAN? D. ROOT color *Reason* v49 no3 p6 Jl 2017

Gun control—United States

DEAR ITT IDEOLOGIST P. KARMAN *In These Times* v40 no12 p7 D 2016

Self-Inflicted Carnage G. Orfalea color *Commonweal* v144 no13 p17 Ag 11 2017

Taking On Guns T. DICKINSON color *Rolling Stone* no1294 p25 Ag 24 2017

Under the Law J. Underwood il *Phi Delta Kappan* v98 no6 p74 Mr 2017

WHY THE GUN-CONTROL MOVEMENT FAILS G. YOUNGE color *Nation* v303 no19 p12 N 7 2016

Gun control—United States—Law & legislation

Don't Silence the Sound of Gunfire *Bloomberg Businessweek* no4539 p14 S 25 2017

Gun exchange programs

Comments img *New York* p8 F 9 2017

Gun laws—United States

Guns on campus: Is that physics? D. A. Roberts *Physics Today* v70 no6 p15 Je 2017

Let's Have a Real Gun Debate color *Weekly Standard* v23 no6 p7 O 16 2017

Safe Gun Policy Doesn't Have to Mean No Guns—Or No Safety K. V. Ogtrop color *Time* v190 no16/17 p111 O 23 2017

Gun laws—United States—States

SHOULD YOU TELL THE COPS YOU HAVE A GUN? J. Sullum color graph *Reason* v49 no5 p7 O 2017

Gunadie, Andrew

Bright lights, big history color *Canadian Geographic* v137 no3 p26 My 2017

GUNARATANA, BHANTE

OVERCOMING ILL WILL color *Tricycle: The Buddhist Review* v26 no3 p38 Spr 2017

GUNASEKERA, YOUSHA

BAIL MEANS JAIL: DEBTOR'S PRISON FOR THE UNCONVICTED color *Progressive* v81 no6 p56 Ag/S 2017

Gunatilleke, C. V. Savitri

Plant diversity increases with the strength of negative density dependence at the global scale diag *Science* v356 no6345 p1389 Je 30 2017

Gunatilleke, I. A. U. Nimal

Plant diversity increases with the strength of negative density dependence at the global scale diag *Science* v356 no6345 p1389 Je 30 2017

Gunawan, Merry

Mapping the human DC lineage through the integration of high-dimensional techniques diag *Science* v356 no6342 p1044 Je 9 2017

Gunch, Modine

Bless her, Father: For she has sinned (sort of) color *New Orleans Magazine* v51 no10 p56 Ag 2017

Codebreakers cartoon *New Orleans Magazine* v51 no9 p42 Jl 2017

THE FRIGHT BEFORE CHRISTMAS color *New Orleans Magazine* v51 no2 p48 D 2016

Highbrow Eyebrows color *New Orleans Magazine* v52 no1 p52 S 2017

How to Fix Trigger Finger cartoon *New Orleans Magazine* v51 no7 p46 My 2017

HOW TO SAVE A CAT color *New Orleans Magazine* v51 no3 p42 Ja 2017

Masking Like a Baby Cake color *New Orleans Magazine* v51 no4 p44 F 2017

Mitch's Fault cartoon *New Orleans Magazine* v51 no12 p54 O 2017

The Price of Fear cartoon *New Orleans Magazine* v51 no8 p46 Je 2017

Root Causes color *New Orleans Magazine* v51 no6 p44 Ap 2017

Snow Me Something color *New Orleans Magazine* v51 no5 p46 Mr 2017

TOFURKEY IN THE OVEN cartoon *New Orleans Magazine* v51 no1 p48 N 2016

Gundar-Goshen, Ayelet

Hit and Run A. TSABARI *New York Times Book Review* p22 Mr 19 2017

Gunderman, Nicole

Nicole Gunderman A. BRANDT *Cincinnati Magazine* v50 no3 p44 D 2016

Gundersen, Edna

Bruce Springsteen bw *AARP: The Magazine* v60 no1A p13 D 2016/Ja 2017

John Mellencamp color *AARP: The Magazine* v60 no4A p15 Je/Jl 2017

Plan the Perfect Vacation cartoon color *AARP: The Magazine* v59 no6A p46 O/N 2016

Gundersen, Gregory

Boiling it down color *Bloomberg Businessweek* no4526 p76 Je 12 2017

Gunderson, Grant

HOLD, PLEASE S. MAIT color *Skiing* p16 D 2016

Gundlach, Heidrun

Wild emmer genome architecture and diversity elucidate wheat evolution and domestication color *Science* v357 no6346 p93 Jl 7 2017

Gundlach, Jeffrey E., 1959-

Earn Up to 6% From Our Fund Portfolios D. FONDA cartoon chart *Kiplinger's Personal Finance* v71 no3 p50 Mr 2017

Gundling, Ernest

How to Build Trust on Your Cross-Cultural Team *Harvard Business Review Digital Articles* p2 Je 28 2016

Gunfire detection systems

Shots Fired J. Sanburn color *Time* v190 no13 p48 O 2 2017

Gunhus, Jeff

Resurrection America color *Publishers Weekly* v264 no30 p4 Jl 24 2017

Guðni Th. Jóhannesson, 1968-

News Roundup E. S. ARNARSDÓTTIR color *Iceland Review* v54 no5 p18 S-O 2016

Gunn, Dwyer

INTERNAL AFFAIRS *Psychology Today* v50 no2 p64 Mr/Ap 2017

Gunn, Erik

The Case for Mercy: Some of the Unlikeliest People Oppose the Death Penalty color *Progressive* v81 no7 p26 O/N 2017

How David Clarke Became the American Right's Sheriff color *Progressive* v81 no3 p32 D 2016/Ja 2017

The Little School District That Could bw color *Progressive* v81 no3 p20 Mr 2017

Gunn, George

ALL AROUND THE FARM *Successful Farming* v115 no2 p79 F 2017

THE FARM *Successful Farming* v115 no11 p75 S 2017

Gunn, James

Go With It J. PODHORETZ *Weekly Standard* v22 no35 p39 My 22 2017

GUARDIANS OF THE GALAXY VOL. 2 [Cover story] C. Collis color *Entertainment Weekly* no1463/1464 p24 Ap/My 2017

Guardians Vol. 2 Laughs It Up, Self-Indulgently S. Zacharek color *Time* v189 no18 p54 My 15 2017

Gunn, Tim, 1953-

What beauty really means *Redbook* p6 Jl/Ag 2017

Gunnestad, Corey

ASSASSIN'S CREED color *Sound & Vision* v82 no7 p68 S 2017

HARDCORE HENRY color *Sound & Vision* v82 no4 p70 My 2017

JACK REACHER: NEVER GO BACK color *Sound & Vision* v82 no5 p65 Je 2017

JASON BOURNE color *Sound & Vision* v82 no4 p69 My 2017

KEANU color *Sound & Vision* v81 no10 p70 D 2016

THE LEGEND OF TARZAN color *Sound & Vision* v82 no3 p68 Ap 2017

THE NICE GUYS color *Sound & Vision* v82 no1 p71 Ja 2017

POINT BREAK color *Sound & Vision* v81 no9 p68 N 2016

RESIDENT EVIL: THE FINAL CHAPTER color *Sound & Vision* v82 no8 p68 O 2017

TEENAGE MUTANT NINJA TURTLES: OUT OF THE SHADOWS color *Sound & Vision* v82 no2 p71 F/Mr 2017

WARCRAFT color *Sound & Vision* v82 no2 p69 F/Mr 2017

Gunning, Sally Cabot

HISTORY'S HUMAN FACE B. GLOSE *Virginia Living* v15 no1 p29 D 2016

Gunnison (Colo.)

home base: THE BEST TRAILS ARE NEVER FAR AWAY n. formosa bw *Bike Magazine* v24 no8 p19 N 2017

Gunnlaugsson, Sigmundur David, 1975-

A STRANGE CALM - EXIT THE RABBLE-ROUSERS H. Lárusson color *Iceland Review* v54 no5 p58 S-O 2016

Gunpowder

ROUND DOWN J. von Benedikt color *Field & Stream* v122 no5 p25 O 2017

Guns n' Roses (Performer)

GUNS N' ROSES' APPETITE FOR DESTRUCTION L. Greenblatt color *Entertainment Weekly* no1474/1475 p116 Jl 21-28 2017

Gunsmoke (TV program)

TV'S BEST WESTERNS M. ROUSH *TV Guide* v65 no14 p23 Ap 3 2017

Gunstocks

FIT AND SHIM P. Bourjaily color *Field & Stream* v122 no3 p28 Ag 2017

Gunter, Matthew M.

An update on SOII undercount research activities bibl chart color graph *Monthly Labor Review* p1 S 2016

Günther, Patrick

Mapping the human DC lineage through the integration of high-dimensional techniques diag *Science* v356 no6342 p1044 Je 9 2017

Gunzer, Matthias

Visualizing the function and fate of neutrophils in sterile injury and repair color graph *Science* v357 no6359 p111 O 6 2017

Guo, Aibing

Will Beijing Also Have A Friend at State? bw *Bloomberg Businessweek* no4504 p26 D 19 2016

Guo, Amy

Regeneration of fat cells from myofibroblasts during wound healing bibl color graph *Science* v355 no6326 p748 F 17 2017

Guo, Jinghua

Atomic-layered Au clusters on α-MoC as catalysts for the low-temperature water-gas shift reaction chart diag graph *Science* v357 no6349 p389 Jl 28 2017

Guo, Jingkai

DNA sequence-directed shape change of photopatterned hydrogels via high-degree swelling color diag *Science* v357 no6356 p1126 S 15 2017

Guo, Rui
"Perfect" designer chromosome V and behavior of a ring derivative diag *Science* v355 no6329 p1046 Mr 10 2017

Guo, Wei-Min
A central neural circuit for itch sensation color graph *Science* v357 no6352 p695 Ag 18 2017

Guo, Xue-Jiao
"Perfect" designer chromosome V and behavior of a ring derivative diag *Science* v355 no6329 p1046 Mr 10 2017

Guo, Yakun
Engineering the ribosomal DNA in a megabase synthetic chromosome diag *Science* v355 no6329 p1049 Mr 10 2017

Guo, Zhi
Long-range hot-carrier transport in hybrid perovskites visualized by ultrafast microscopy diag graph *Science* v356 no6333 p59 Ap 7 2017

Guo, Zhuang
All-oxide–based synthetic antiferromagnets exhibiting layer-resolved magnetization reversal diag *Science* v357 no6347 p191 Jl 14 2017

Guo-li Ming
A nuclease that mediates cell death induced by DNA damage and poly(ADP-ribose) polymerase-1 bw graph *Science* v354 no6308 paad6872-1 O 7 2016

Guojun Zhang
Recommendations on the management and use of POCT in medical institutions (nosocomial) *Science* v354 no6319 p13 D 23 2016

Guomundsdottir, Maria Helga
ON A QUEST I. R. Björnsdottir *Iceland Review* v54 no6 p76 N/D 2016

Guppies—Reproduction
Brainpower aids guppy mate choice S. MILIUS *Science News* v191 no7 p12 Ap 15 2017

Guppies—Sexual behavior
Brainpower aids guppy mate choice S. MILIUS *Science News* v191 no7 p12 Ap 15 2017

Guppta, Kavi
Don't Let Your Company Culture Just Happen *Harvard Business Review Digital Articles* p2 Jl 7 2016

Gupta, Anil
How China's Government Helps—and Hinders—Innovation *Harvard Business Review Digital Articles* p2 N 16 2016
Multinationals Have a Bright Future, If You Know Where to Look *Harvard Business Review Digital Articles* p2 Je 14 2017
The Reason Silicon Valley Beat Out Boston for VC Dominance *Harvard Business Review Digital Articles* p2 N 15 2016
Why Xiaomi Can't Succeed Without India *Harvard Business Review Digital Articles* p2 Je 29 2015

Gupta, Animesh
Ecological speciation of bacteriophage lambda in allopatry and sympatry bibl graph *Science* v354 no6317 p1301 D 9 2016

Gupta, Arun
The Crackdown Has Begun color *Progressive* v81 no4 p56 Ap/My 2017
The Scary New Normal for Immigrants color *Progressive* v81 no5 p55 Je/Jl 2017

GUPTA, MONICA DAS
RETURN OF THE MISSING DAUGHTERS color graph *Scientific American* v317 no3 p80 S 2017

Gupta, Nakul
Case Study: Should You Rehire Someone Who Left for a Competitor? bw color il *Harvard Business Review* v94 no12 p103 D 2016

Gupta, Narayani
Delhi, the Forever City *UN Chronicle* v53 no3 p3 2016

Gupta, Raj
Overcome Your Biases and Build a Great Team *Harvard Business Review Digital Articles* p2 D 25 2014

Gupta, Rana K.
Regeneration of fat cells from myofibroblasts during wound healing bibl color graph *Science* v355 no6326 p748 F 17 2017

Gupta, Ravi
RUNNING ON HOPE [Cover story] B. AUSTEN color *New Republic* v248 no10 p18 O 2017

Gupta, Ruchi

THE PEANUT DOCTOR IS IN L. WILLIAMSON color *Chicago* v66 no10 p28 O 2017

Gupta, S.
Redox stratification of an ancient lake in Gale crater, Mars color *Science* v356 no6341 p922 Je 1 2017

Gupta, Sunil
Extracting Insights from Vast Stores of Data *Harvard Business Review Digital Articles* p2 Ag 30 2016
In Mobile Advertising, Timing Is Everything *Harvard Business Review Digital Articles* p2 N 4 2015

GUPTA, TANVI
Asia's Rising Stars color *Forbes* v199 no5 p20 My 16 2017

Gupta, Vanita, 1974-
Vanita Gupta J. Johnson color *Current Biography* v78 no1 p22 Ja 2017

Gupta, Vinay
A Brief History of Blockchain bw *Harvard Business Review Digital Articles* p2 F 28 2017
How Blockchain Could Help Emerging Markets Leap Ahead *Harvard Business Review Digital Articles* p2 My 17 2017
The Promise of Blockchain Is a World Without Middlemen color *Harvard Business Review Digital Articles* p2 Mr 6 2017

Gur, Ilan
The Innovator Gap *MIT Technology Review* v120 no4 p10 Jl/Ag 2017

Gura, Philip E.
THE ROMANCE OF REFORM B. WINEAPPLE bw *Nation* v304 no15 p32 My 8 2017

Gurbatri, Candice
Potential role of intratumor bacteria in mediating tumor resistance to the chemotherapeutic drug gemcitabine diag *Science* v357 no6356 p1156 S 15 2017

Gurbaxani, Vijay
You Don't Have to Be a Software Company to Think Like One *Harvard Business Review Digital Articles* p2 Ap 20 2016

GURBISZ, CASSIE
Submersed Aquatic Vegetation in Chesapeake Bay: Sentinel Species in a Changing World *BioScience* v67 no8 p698 Ag 2017

GUREVITCH, JESSICA
Harmonizing Biodiversity Conservation and Productivity in the Context of Increasing Demands on Landscapes graph *BioScience* v66 no10 p890 O 1 2016

GURGANUS, ALLAN
Trading Mazes *New York Times Book Review* p18 O 2 2016

Gurib, Ameenah, 1959-
Ameenah Gurib B. Lightner *Current Biography* v78 no4 p30 Ap 2017

GURIEL, JASON
No Strength in Numbers cartoon *Walrus* v14 no6 p15 Jl/Ag 2017

Gurira, Danai, 1978-
Danai Gurira B. Muteba color *Current Biography* v77 no10 p44 O 2016
THE KINGDOM & THE POWER [Cover story] A. Breznican color *Entertainment Weekly* no1474/1475 p30 Jl 21-28 2017

GURLEY, GABRIELLE
A Veteran's Odyssey *Publishers Weekly* v264 no23 p42 Je 5 2017

Gurley, Todd
HOT | NOT S. Kwak color *Sports Illustrated* v127 no10 p17 O 2 2017
Leading Off color *Sports Illustrated* v127 no9 p4 S 25 2017

Gurman, Adrienne
Summer Catch-Up M. S. Eddy *Stage Directions* v30 no9 p2 S 2017

Gurman, Mark
Apple Is Bringing Drones to a Map Fight *Bloomberg Businessweek* no4503 p29 D 12 2016
Apple's Alternative to Virtual Reality color *Bloomberg Businessweek* no4516 p29 Mr 27 2017
Look familiar? color *Bloomberg Businessweek* no4494 p33 O 10 2016
Mac Pro Users Want Updates? color *Bloomberg Businessweek* no4505 p33 D 26 2016
Microsoft Surfaces color graph *Bloomberg Businessweek* no4521 p31 My 8 2017
Samsung Would Love to Talk About This Phone color *Bloomberg Businessweek* no4517 p36 Ap 3 2017

Your Next Phone Will Probably Cost $1,000 graph *Bloomberg Businessweek* no4538 p24 S 18 2017

Gurnah, Abdulrazak

Gravel Heart color *Publishers Weekly* v264 no24 p38 Je 12 2017

Gurney, Dan

FORWARD MOMENTUM M. PRINCE bw *Road & Track* v69 no4 p64 N 2017

Gurney, Elise

Lobbying Is Not Enough to Build Influence Among U.S. Lawmakers *Harvard Business Review Digital Articles* p2 D 28 2016

Guroff, Margaret

HOW BIKES BUILT OUR HIGHWAYS *Saturday Evening Post* v289 no1 p82 Ja/F 2017

Gursky, Andreas

Media Market color *Art in America* v104 no10 p170 N 2016

GURU, SIDDESWARA M.

Publish openly but responsibly color *Science* v357 no6347 p141 Jl 14 2017

Synthesis Centers as Critical Research Infrastructure *BioScience* v67 no8 p750 Ag 2017

Gurun, Umit G.

Patent Trolling Isn't Dead—It's Just Moving to Delaware *Harvard Business Review Digital Articles* p2 Je 28 2017

Gurung, Prabal, 1979-

Belle CURVE L. YAEGER, M. HOLGATE et al color *Vogue* v207 no3 p346 Mr 2017

Gurus

Namaste Now try my herbal toothpaste P. R. Sanjai and B. Pradhan color graph *Bloomberg Businessweek* no4502 p27 D 5 2016

Gurvitz, David

The Two Worlds of a Soviet Spy bw *Commentary* v143 no3 p27 Mr 2017

Gurwitch, Annabelle

GROWING PAINS N. BEACH cartoon color *O, The Oprah Magazine* p110 My 2017

Just Say Thanks cartoon *Prevention* p28 Mr 2017

Off-Key but In Sync cartoon *Prevention* v69 no1 p34 Ja 2017

Piece of Cake [Cover story] cartoon *Prevention* v68 no11 p26 N 2016

Gurwitch Products LLC

LAURA MERCIER bw color *Harper's Bazaar* no3656 p269 S 2017

Gus Wüstemann Architects (Company)

The Past Laid Bare H. PEARMAN *Architectural Record* v205 no10 p90 O 2017

GUSAN, MAGGIE

EAT THIS NOW GOCHUJANG *Better Homes & Gardens* v94 no11 p73 N 2016

Gush, Simon—Exhibitions

"RECENT HISTORIES" E. IDUMA bw color *ARTnews* v116 no1 p115 Spr 2017

Gushchin, Ivan

Mechanism of transmembrane signaling by sensor histidine kinases color *Science* v356 no6342 p1043 Je 9 2017

Gushee, David P.

David Gushee R. Farmer color *Publishers Weekly* v263 no45 p21 N 7 2016

Gusher, Traci

How to Integrate Data and Analytics into Every Part of Your Organization *Harvard Business Review Digital Articles* p2 Je 23 2017

Gušić, Ivan

Neandertal and Denisovan DNA from Pleistocene sediments bw color *Science* v356 no6338 p605 My 12 2017

GUSKEY, JORDAN

No Dumb Luck color diag *Indianapolis Monthly* v41 no2 p17 S 2017

Gusovsky, Fabian

Lee Rubin: Our mentor and role model *Science* v355 no6327 p806 F 24 2017

GUSTAFSON, ANDREW

THE BATTLE OF SAN JACINTO DIORAMA *Texas Monthly* v44 no11 p100 N 2016

GUSTAFSON, DAVID I.

MAKING THE CASE FOR US AGRICULTURAL RESEARCH *BioScience* v67 no3 p311 Mr 2017

Gustafson, Eleanor H.

History lessonend color *Magazine Antiques* v184 no4 p128 Jl/Ag 2017

Last but not least color *Magazine Antiques* v184 no2 p136 Mr/Ap 2017

Masterful mixing at the Hammer color *Magazine Antiques* v184 no3 p136 My/Je 2017

Nate DiMeo's audio eruditionend color *Magazine Antiques* v184 no5 p120 S/O 2017

A new look for the Davis at Wellesley color *Magazine Antiques* v183 no6 p136 N/D 2016

The origins of caller ID? color *Magazine Antiques* v184 no1 p216 Ja/F 2017

Gustafson, Joseph

2017 BMW R nineT SCRAMBLER color *Cycle World* v56 no1 p8 Ja/F 2017

2017 HARLEY-DAVIDSON STREET GLIDE SPECIAL color *Cycle World* v55 no11 p8 D 2016

2017 KAWASAKI NINJA 1000 ABS color *Cycle World* v56 no7 p14 Ag 2017

2018 YAMAHA STAR VENTURE TOURER bw color *Cycle World* v56 no9 p14 O 2017

Little Bike, Big Promise color *Cycle World* v55 no11 p44 D 2016

LOW AND SLOW THROUGH FLYOVER COUNTRY color *Cycle World* v56 no4 p50 My 2017

Gustafsson, Torgny

Biological control of aragonite formation in stony corals bw color graph *Science* v356 no6341 p933 Je 1 2017

Gustave, Kaitlin

Brown and Nogueira Split $11K at Windy Ryon color *Spin to Win Rodeo* v21 no6 p20 Ag 2017

BUCKLE UP color *Team Roping Journal* p16 O 2017

BUCKLE UP with Clint Summers color *Team Roping Journal* p22 S 2017

Freeze Frame color *Team Roping Journal* p74 S 2017

FREEZE FRAME WITH WHITNEY DESALVO color *Spin to Win Rodeo* v21 no6 p42 Ag 2017

IVY AND HAWKINS GET A GRIPP chart color *Team Roping Journal* p18 O 2017

Gustavsson, Simon

Suppressing relaxation in superconducting qubits by quasiparticle pumping bibl graph *Science* v354 no6319 p1573 D 23 2016

Gustavus Adolphus College

Gustavus Adolphus College *Dance Magazine* v90 p68 2016/2017 Supplement College Guide

Gustin, Grant, 1990-

The Flash N. Abrams, A. Bacle et al color *Entertainment Weekly* no1482/1483 p66 S 22 2017

A SUPER GLEE REUNION N. Abrams color *Entertainment Weekly* no1457/1458 p82 Mr 17 2017

Gustings, Paul

Paul Gustings T. McNally color *New Orleans Magazine* v51 no2 p76 D 2016

Gusui Wu

A selective insecticidal protein from Pseudomonas for controlling corn rootworms bibl chart graph *Science* v354 no6312 p634 N 4 2016

Gut, Ivo

Chimpanzee genomic diversity reveals ancient admixture with bonobos bibl diag graph map *Science* v354 no6311 p477 O 28 2016

Gut, Marta

Chimpanzee genomic diversity reveals ancient admixture with bonobos bibl diag graph map *Science* v354 no6311 p477 O 28 2016

Gut microbiome

Chemical transformation of xenobiotics by the human gut microbiota N. Koppel, V. Maini Rekdal et al diag *Science* v356 no6344 p1246 Je 23 2017

Food and microbiota in the FDA regulatory framework J. M. Green, M. J. Barratt et al color *Science* v357 no6346 p39 Jl 7 2017

Gut cell metabolism shapes the microbiome P. D. Cani color *Science* v357 no6351 p548 Ag 11 2017

How gut bacteria may affect anxiety M. TEMMING *Science News* v192 no5 p12 S 30 2017

Microbiota-activated PPAR-γ signaling inhibits dysbiotic Entero-bacteriaceae expansion M. X. Byndloss, E. E. Olsan et al graph *Science* v357 no6351 p570 Ag 11 2017

Seasonal change in the gut [Cover story] S. Peddada color *Science* v357 no6353 p754 Ag 25 2017

Seasonal cycling in the gut microbiome of the Hadza hunter-gath-erers of Tanzania S. A. Smits, J. Leach et al diag *Science* v357 no6353 p802 Ag 25 2017

Gutaker, Rafal M.

Genomic estimation of complex traits reveals ancient maize ad-aptation to temperate North America diag *Science* v357 no6350 p512 Ag 4 2017

Guten Co.

Q&A S. SAUER *Texas Monthly* v45 no8 p18 Ag 2017

Guterl, Fred

Is Fusion in Our Future? color *Scientific American* v316 no3 p17 Mr 2017

Guterres, António, 1949-

AT THE TOP OF THE LIST A. GUTERRES *Vital Speeches of the Day* v83 no7 p197 Jl 2017

global *Ms.* v26 no4 p18 Wint 2016

The World's New Diplomat In Chief T. John color *Time* v188 no27-28 p13 D 26 2016

Gutfreund, Hanoch

Einstein's magnum opus A. Robinson color *Science* v357 no6353 p763 Ag 25 2017

Ivory Tower J. Ryerson *New York Times Book Review* p35 Ag 27 2017

GUTH, ALAN H.

A COSMIC CONTROVERSY color *Scientific American* v317 no1 p5 Jl 2017

Guthörl, Daniela

RETINOBLASTOMA RELATED1 mediates germline entry in Arabidopsis color diag *Science* v356 no6336 p396 Ap 28 2017

Guthrie, Catherine

FEEL YOUR BEST color *Yoga Journal* p12 2017 Special Issue

I'M FLAT AND I'M PROUD bw color *O, The Oprah Magazine* p90 O 2017

LEARNING CURVE cartoon *O, The Oprah Magazine* p129 Mr 2017

Guthrie, John

Greater role for Atlantic inflows on sea-ice loss in the Eurasian Basin of the Arctic Ocean chart diag graph *Science* v356 no6335 p285 Ap 21 2017

Guthrie, Julian

How to Make a Spaceship M. J. Neufeld *Physics Today* v70 no6 p62 Je 2017

XPRIZE launched new kind of space race M. Rosen color *Science News* v190 no8 p28 O 15 2016

Guthrie, Mitch

2017 RZR FACTORY RACING ROSTER *Dirt Sports + Off-Road* v51 no7 p8 Jl 2017

Guthrie, Savannah, 1971——Interviews

My Obsessions... *TV Guide* v65 no37 p15 S 4 2017

GUTHRIE, STEVE

Singing Isn't Just for Sunday bw color *Christianity Today* v61 no7 p80 S 2017

Guthrie, Suzanne

Learning to love Thérèse *Christian Century* v133 no25 p10 D 7 2016

Gutiérrez, Christopher

An on/off Berry phase switch in circular graphene resonators diag graph *Science* v356 no6340 p845 My 26 2017

Gutiérrez, Eliécer E.

Specimen collection crucial to taxonomy bibl *Science* v355 no6331 p1275 Mr 24 2017

GUTIÉRREZ, LUCI

SUBWAY SUBSTITUTES cartoon *New Yorker* v93 no23 p53 Ag 7 2017

Gutierrez, Luis

Corruption as a Way of Life J. COST color map *Weekly Standard* v22 no38 p18 Je 12 2017

Patriotism in the pews color *U.S. Catholic* v82 no11 p5 N 2017

The Pros and Cons of the President's Immigrant Travel Ban *Congressional Digest* v96 no3 p23 Mr 2017

Gutierrez, P. J.

Rosetta's comet 67P/Churyumov-Gerasimenko sheds its dusty mantle to reveal its icy nature bibl graph *Science* v354 no6319 p1566 D 23 2016

Surface changes on comet 67P/Churyumov-Gerasimenko suggest a more active past bw graph *Science* v355 no6332 p1392 Mr 31 2017

Gutierrez, Steve

ANGLO-FILE *British Heritage Travel* v38 no2 p74 Mr/Ap 2017

ANGLO-FILE *British Heritage Travel* v38 no3 p12 My/Je 2017

Annalena McAfee, Author of Hame, on Her Love Letter to Scot-land color *British Heritage Travel* v38 no5 p71 S/O 2017

Biking the Legends of Wales *British Heritage Travel* v38 no1 p10 Ja/F 2017

BOOK REPORT *British Heritage Travel* v38 no2 p72 Mr/Ap 2017

THE BRITISH HERITAGE TRAVEL INTERVIEW Lady Car-narvon of Highclere *British Heritage Travel* v38 no4 p42 Jl/Ag 2017

Daisy Goodwin on Victoria, Victoria and Victoria-The Queen, Novel and Show *British Heritage Travel* v38 no1 p38 Ja/F 2017

Dark Angel Star Joanne Froggatt on Playing England's First Serial Killer *British Heritage Travel* v38 no3 p58 My/Je 2017

Director Stephen Daldry on The Crown *British Heritage Travel* v37 no6 p30 N/D 2016

Director Stephen Frears on Victoria and Abdul, Judi and More color *British Heritage Travel* v38 no5 p66 S/O 2017

Edd Kimber's Nanna's Gingerbread *British Heritage Travel* v38 no2 p77 Mr/Ap 2017

Fruity Teatime Sweets *British Heritage Travel* v38 no4 p74 Jl/Ag 2017

LIFE ON LONDON'S WATERWAYS *British Heritage Travel* v37 no6 p36 N/D 2016

Mince and Tatties *British Heritage Travel* v38 no3 p76 My/Je 2017

Out of the Highlands: Outlander stars Sam Heughan and Caitriona Balfe and writer Matthew B. Roberts on season three, post-Culloden Scotland and the resilient, far-reaching Scots culture color *British Heritage Travel* v38 no5 p42 S/O 2017

POLDARK'S HEIDA REED color *British Heritage Travel* v38 no5 p48 S/O 2017

ROYAL PAIN: King Charles III *British Heritage Travel* v38 no3 p70 My/Je 2017

Seven Stones to Stand or Fall: A Collection of Outlander Fiction *British Heritage Travel* v38 no3 p74 My/Je 2017

THE TEES THAT BIND *British Heritage Travel* v38 no2 p34 Mr/Ap 2017

Tom Kitchin's Traditional Pot-Roasted Chicken color *British Heritage Travel* v38 no5 p74 S/O 2017

Victoria: The Queen *British Heritage Travel* v37 no6 p12 N/D 2016

The White Princess *British Heritage Travel* v38 no2 p28 Mr/Ap 2017

Gutowski, Phil

Cover Up color diag *Sail* v48 no10 p80 O 2017

Fuel's Paradise color diag *Sail* v48 no2 p64 F 2017

Keeping Your Cool color diag *Sail* v48 no4 p64 Ap 2017

SAILING INSTRUMENTS [Cover story] color *Sail* v48 no8 p38 Ag 2017

Güttel, Wolfgang H.

Even Tiny Rewards Can Motivate People to Go the Extra Mile *Harvard Business Review Digital Articles* p2 Je 7 2016

Guttenberg, Steve

The Art of Sound color *Sound & Vision* v81 no9 p20 N 2016

Bedazzled color *Sound & Vision* v82 no4 p22 My 2017

Bedazzled! color *Sound & Vision* v82 no6 p22 Jl/Ag 2017

Both Sides Now color *Sound & Vision* v82 no3 p24 Ap 2017

Come Fly With Me color *Sound & Vision* v82 no3 p22 Ap 2017

THE DYING OF THE LIGHT color *Sound & Vision* v82 no4 p71 My 2017

Game Changer color *Sound & Vision* v82 no3 p26 Ap 2017

Hearing Is Believing color *Sound & Vision* v82 no6 p18 Jl/Ag 2017

Jewels for the Ear color *Sound & Vision* v82 no7 p20 S 2017

The Joy of Sound color *Sound & Vision* v82 no3 p18 Ap 2017

Looking Good color *Sound & Vision* v82 no7 p22 S 2017

MrSpeakers Aeon Headphones color *Sound & Vision* v82 no8 p20

O 2017

NO MORE MR. NICE GUY: On HBO's Ballers, good egg Steve Guttenberg breaks bad--and puts Dwayne Johnson between a rock and a hard place M. LOGAN *TV Guide* v65 no31 p22 Jl 24 2017

Out of the Blue color *Sound & Vision* v82 no5 p22 Je 2017

Rated XXX color *Sound & Vision* v82 no6 p20 Jl/Ag 2017

The Shock of the New color *Sound & Vision* v82 no4 p18 My 2017

Sony MDR-Z1R Headphones color *Sound & Vision* v82 no3 p62 Ap 2017

Steve Guttenberg Joins Ballers I. Ratledge *TV Guide* v65 no25 p8 Je 2017

The Sweet Spot color *Sound & Vision* v82 no2 p20 F/Mr 2017

Take It Easy color *Sound & Vision* v82 no4 p24 My 2017

Tell It Like It Is color *Sound & Vision* v81 no10 p18 D 2016

This One Goes to 99 color *Sound & Vision* v81 no9 p28 N 2016

This Year's Model color *Sound & Vision* v82 no5 p18 Je 2017

Vive la Différence! color *Sound & Vision* v82 no1 p20 Ja 2017

GUTTENPLAN, D. D.

The Banjo Player vs. the Billionaire color *Nation* v304 no17 p12 Je 5 2017

Meet Chicago's Movement Politician color *Nation* v305 no3 p22 Jl 31 2017

Mourn, Resist, Organize il *Nation* v303 no22 p3 N 28 2016

A Party for the People color *Nation* v305 no1 p4 Jl 3 2017

A PEOPLE'S REVOLT color *Nation* v303 no23/24 p10 D 5 2016

POWER PLAYERS bw color *Nation* v304 no6 p21 F 27 2017

THE PRESIDENT AND THE FORGOTTEN MAN bw color *Nation* v304 no10 p21 Mr 27 2017

TROUBLE IN OHIO color *Nation* v303 no18 p18 O 31 2016

Weapons of Mass Distraction color *Nation* v304 no6 p8 F 27 2017

Gutterson, Neal—Interviews

Q&A B. FREESE *Successful Farming* v114 no12 p64 Mid-N 2016

Guttfield, Laura

Who I am *People Management* p51 Mr 2017

Gutting, Elizabeth Word

Abraham Verghese *Humanities* v37 no4 p1 Fall 2016

Gutting, Gary

More than Animals color *Commonweal* v144 no9 p28 My 19 2017

Volunteers or Conscripts? G. D. O'Brien color *Commonweal* v144 no1 p36 Ja 6 2017

What Videos Can't Show color *Commonweal* v143 no18 p12 N 11 2016

Güttler, C.

Rosetta's comet 67P/Churyumov-Gerasimenko sheds its dusty mantle to reveal its icy nature bibl graph *Science* v354 no6319 p1566 D 23 2016

Surface changes on comet 67P/Churyumov-Gerasimenko suggest a more active past bw graph *Science* v355 no6332 p1392 Mr 31 2017

Guttman, Jon

Death Battalions *MHQ: Quarterly Journal of Military History* v29 no3 p11 Spr 2017

Hardware AH-64D Apachen Longbow *Military History* v33 no6 p16 Mr 2017

Hardware Char B1 bis color *Military History* v34 no4 p20 N 2017

Hardware Krupp 28 cm K5(E) Railway Gun color *Military History* v34 no2 p20 Jl 2017

Hardware R621 Gruppenstand color *Military History* v34 no5 p20 Ja 2018

Hardware Type 94 Infantry Mortar *Military History* v33 no5 p20 Ja 2017

MAORI MARTIAL ARTS *Military History* v33 no5 p48 Ja 2017

Norse Knarr cartoon *Military History* v34 no1 p20 My 2017

Valor The Selfless Survivor bw color *Military History* v34 no1 p16 My 2017

What's the Point? color *MHQ: Quarterly Journal of Military History* v29 no4 p11 Summ 2017

Guttman, Mitchell

Xist recruits the X chromosome to the nuclear lamina to enable chromosome-wide silencing bibl graph *Science* v354 no6311 p468 O 28 2016

Guttman, Robert

The Fleet at Flood Tide: America at Total War in the Pacific, 1944-

45 *Military History* v33 no6 p74 Mr 2017

The Myth and Reality of German Warfare: Operational Thinking From Moltke the Elder to Heusinger bw *Military History* v34 no1 p74 My 2017

Operation Agreement: Jewish Commandos and the Raid on Tobruk *Military History* v33 no5 p72 Ja 2017

Victoria's Scottish Lion: The Life of Colin Campbell, Lord Clyde *Military History* v33 no5 p70 Ja 2017

Guy, Donna J.

Creating Charismatic Bonds in Argentina: Letters to Juan and Eva Perón R. Feinberg *Foreign Affairs* v95 no6 p184 N/D 2016

Guy, Eddie

MEET THE NEW (ISH) GUY color *Wired* v25 no4 p8 Ap 2017

Guy, Jon

Far Out S. HELD *Indianapolis Monthly* p14 My 2017

Paradise Reimagined J. YOUNG *Indianapolis Monthly* p8 My 2017

Guy, Zac

History Repeats color *Log Home Living* v34 no2 p16 Mr 2017

Guyatt, Nicholas

Our Ruinous Betrayal of Indians and Black Americans D. S. Reynolds bw *New York Review of Books* v63 no20 p89 D 22 2016

GUY-HAIM, TAMAR

Foraminifera Invade the Mediterranean bw color map *Natural History* v125 no10 p12 O 2017

Guyler-Alaniz, Marji

FARMHERS ON FILM: LEARN MORE ABOUT THE FEMALE FARMERS AND RANCHERS IN THE FARMHER PROJECT *Successful Farming* v115 no12 p67 O 2017

Guyon, Bertrand

Look Who's Crashing COUTURE E. Wilson color *InStyle* v24 no4 p63 Ap 2017

GUYTON, GEORGI

READY OR NOT, HERE THEY COME: It could be the biggest shift in the way young people are trained for decades. But how businesses plan to put the upcoming payroll tax to use has yet to be seen *People Management* p34 Ap 2017

Guzei, Ilia A.

Enantioselective photochemistry through Lewis acid–catalyzed triplet energy transfer bibl chart diag graph *Science* v354 no6318 p1391 D 16 2016

GUZIK, HANNAH

State of Rebellion *In These Times* v41 no2 p8 F 2017

Guzik, Keith

Seeing a Bigger Picture *Society* v54 no4 p367 Ag 2017

Guzmán, Isaac

The Beach Boy and the Boss: Darkness on the Edge of Two Memoirs color *Time* v188 no14 p58 O 10 2016

In This Battle of the Bands, Oasis Beats Iggy color *Time* v188 no20 p51 N 14 2016

Leon Russell color *Time* v188 no22-23 p13 N/D 2016

Mike Love: Brian Took His T-Bird Away color *Time* v188 no14 p59 O 10 2016

Ryan Adams Offers His Opus of Despair color *Time* v189 no6 p51 F 20 2017

A Star-Studded Tribute to a Lovable Lensman color *Time* v188 no24 p64 D 12 2016

Guzman, Lina

Making Math Count More for Young Latinos bw *Education Digest* v83 no1 p8 S 2017

Guzmán, Pilar

Carbon Beach color *Conde Nast Traveler* v52 no7 p32 Ag 2017

Comme des Gascons color *Conde Nast Traveler* v52 no3 p74 Mr 2017

Dressing the Part bw *Conde Nast Traveler* v52 no3 p16 Mr 2017

Golden Rules bw *Conde Nast Traveler* v52 no1 p20 Ja 2017

Here, Here! color *Conde Nast Traveler* v52 no7 p14 Ag 2017

In Your Words color *Conde Nast Traveler* v52 no10 p20 N 2017

ISLAND HOP color *Conde Nast Traveler* v51 no10 p34 N 2016

A Love Letter to Zambia color *Conde Nast Traveler* v52 no2 p102 F 2017

MASTERS OF CEREMONY color *Conde Nast Traveler* v51 no10 p138 N 2016

New Comfort Zones bw *Conde Nast Traveler* v52 no4 p12 Ap 2017

OAXACA bw color *Conde Nast Traveler* v52 no8 p84 S 2017

An ODE to HOTELS on the Amalfi Coast color *Conde Nast Traveler* v52 no1 p74 Ja 2017

Playing Huis color *Conde Nast Traveler* v51 no11 p56 D 2016

Solo Flight color *Conde Nast Traveler* v51 no11 p20 D 2016

WHERE IN THE WORLD TO EAT cartoon color *Conde Nast Traveler* v52 no9 p53 O 2017

Where You Lead bw *Conde Nast Traveler* v52 no2 p12 F 2017

ZAMBIA + BOTSWANA color *Conde Nast Traveler* v52 no4 p44 Ap 2017

Guzmán Loera, Joaquin, 1957-

THE HUNT FOR EL CHAPO P. Solotaroff color *Rolling Stone* no1294 p44 Ag 24 2017

Gwathmey, Judith

Minority investigators lack NIH funding color *Science* v356 no6342 p1018 Je 9 2017

Gwatney, Sandy

Behind the Chutes A. Bohus color *American Cowboy* v24 no1 p69 Je/Jl 2017

Gwen, Martha

letter to my teenage self color *Dance Spirit* v21 no2 p24 F 2017

Gwin, Aaron

BIKE MAGAZINE PHOTO ANNUAL 2017 bw color *Bike Magazine* v24 no6 p72 Ag 2017

Gwin, Peter

The Burning Heart of Africa color map *National Geographic* v231 no5 p56 My 2017

Gwosch, Klaus C.

Nanometer resolution imaging and tracking of fluorescent molecules with minimal photon fluxes bibl graph *Science* v355 no6325 p606 F 10 2017

Gwynne, S. C.

Running on Empty M. NELSON color *Weekly Standard* v22 no13 p32 D 5 2016

Gyasi, Yaa

Homegoing: A Novel E. Brown *Christian Century* v133 no23 p41 N 9 2016

No. 3 HOMEGOING L. Greenblatt color *Entertainment Weekly* no1444/1445 p104 D 16 2016

Yaa Gyasi C. Mari color *Current Biography* v78 no8 p40 Ag 2017

Gyenis, András

Observation of a nematic quantum Hall liquid on the surface of bismuth bibl graph *Science* v354 no6310 p316 O 21 2016

Gygi, Steven P.

UBE2O remodels the proteome during terminal erythroid differentiation diag *Science* v357 no6350 p471 Ag 4 2017

Gyllenhaal, Jake, 1980-

In Life, the Blob from Mars Is Small and Very Scary S. Zacharek color *Time* v189 no12 p56 Ap 3 2017

Gyllenhaal, Jake, 1980—Interviews

JAKE GYLLENHAAL IN Stronger J. McGovern color *Entertainment Weekly* no1478 / 1479 p39 Ag 18-25 2017

Gyllenhaal, Maggie, 1977-

Laid Bare A. MORRIS img *New York* v50 no17 p94 Ag 21 2017

PROJECT RED LIGHT A. Carter bw color *Esquire* p37 S 2017

Gymnasiums—Equipment & supplies

Build a Home Gym You'll Actually Use bw *Kiplinger's Personal Finance* v71 no1 p70 Ja 2017

Gymnasiums—Evaluation

G Is for Gains J. UHL *Indianapolis Monthly* v40 no7 p34 Mr 2017

HARDER, BETTER, FASTER, STRONGER K. Schaefer color *Bloomberg Businessweek* no4511 p66 F 13 2017

Gymnasiums—Social aspects

HIIT ♥N ME color *Women's Health* v14 no2 p38 Mr 2017

Gymnastics

The Ethics of Watching Gymnastics M. O'ROURKE and A. Kudacki img *New York* v49 no15 p54 Jl 25 2016

"I HAVEN'T HAD THIS MUCH FUN SINCE I WAS A KID!" J. Ketteler color *Good Housekeeping* v264 no1 p109 Ja 1 2017

Ja, Ja — Muskeln Machen! J. CISSIK bw chart *Muscle & Performance* v9 no7 p18 Jl 2017

MISS VAL M. ANGELI color *Los Angeles Magazine* v62 no10 p142 O 2017

Gymnasts

See also

Women gymnasts

Simone BILES color *Vanity Fair* v59 no1 p129 Holiday 2017

Gynandromorphism

Gynandromorphism [Cover story] C. A. BUTLER color *Natural History* v125 no5 p20 My 2017

Gynecologists

What ob/gyns tell their friends J. DEMELO cartoon *Redbook* p82 O 2017

Gynecology

Rules Smart Gynos Break M. Masters color *Health* v31 no5 p57 Je 2017

Gynnå, Arvid H.

Nanometer resolution imaging and tracking of fluorescent molecules with minimal photon fluxes bibl graph *Science* v355 no6325 p606 F 10 2017

Gypsy (Music)

STEVIE NICKS' SHOW STARTER J. Nolfi color *Entertainment Weekly* no1472 p49 Je 30 2017

Gypsy (TV program)

Gypsy J. Jensen color *Entertainment Weekly* no1472 p48 Je 30 2017

The Must List color *Entertainment Weekly* no1473 p1 Jl 7 2017

Naomi Watts' Deceptive Therapist Just Can't Help Herself on Gypsy D. D'addario color *Time* v190 no1 p53 Jl 3 2017

Naomi Watts E. Dockterman color *Time* v190 no2/3 p93 Jl 10-17 2017

STEVIE NICKS' SHOW STARTER J. Nolfi color *Entertainment Weekly* no1472 p49 Je 30 2017

Gyroscopes

See also

Gyrostabilizers

Steady as She Goes Z. Prochazka color *Sea Magazine* v109 no8 p46 Ag 2017

Gyrostabilizers

At Sea With Seakeeper M. SMITH color *Power & Motoryacht* v34 no11 p141 N 2017

Stabilizing the Market J. Y. WOOD color *Power & Motoryacht* v32 no11 p146 N 2016

GYTON, GEORGI

13 down, 8,987 to go...: Organisations have been slow to report their gender pay gaps. But the real question is how they will explain them when they do *People Management* p8 Jl 2017

Government 'taking aim at Britain's boardrooms' *People Management* p8 D 2016/Ja 2017

These are the experts deciding the future of HR... ...shouldn't you know who they are? [Cover story] *People Management* p24 Ag 2017

They said we'd never get creatives to learn *People Management* p20 O 2016

We get our coaching expertise through an app *People Management* p25 F 2017

What does HARD BREXIT mean? Skilled and unskilled labour may be treated very differently when the UK leaves the single market - and that means many businesses are already concerned about talent *People Management* p8 Mr 2017

What volunteering did for me: HR professionals share their experiences of giving something back *People Management* p12 S 2017

"Without migrants, we don't have a business" *People Management* p34 Je 2017

"YOUR EMPLOYEES ARE THE PEOPLE WHO MAKE YOU WIN": Organisations are too focused on great players, says HR guru Dave Ulrich - it's time to start playing a team game *People Management* p40 Ap 2017

Gza (Performer)

NIGHT LIFE *New Yorker* v92 no39 p26 N 28 2016

H

H & H Marine Inc.

HH66 P. Nielsen cartoon color *Sail* v48 no2 p32 F 2017

H & M Hennes & Mauritz AB

The Taming of a Teen Emporium R. Williams and A. Molin color *Bloomberg Businessweek* no4518 p26 Ap 10 2017

H & R Block Inc.

BILL COBB color *Bloomberg Businessweek* no4518 p80 Ap 10 2017

H & R Block Inc.—Finance

Stock X-Ray: H&R Block I. Salisbury diag *Money* v46 no4 p36 My 2017

H. Huntsman & Sons (Company)

Savile Row Arrives Stateside T. Patterson bw color *Bloomberg Businessweek* no4530 p59 Jl 17 2017

Ha, Sura

A chemical biology route to site-specific authentic protein modifications bibl diag graph *Science* v354 no6312 p623 N 4 2016

Ha, Taekjip

Flipping nanoscopy on its head bibl diag graph *Science* v355 no6325 p582 F 10 2017

Notch-Jagged complex structure implicates a catch bond in tuning ligand sensitivity bibl diag graph *Science* v355 no6331 p1320 Mr 24 2017

Haag, Pamela

An amoral enterprise F. R. Herrmann color *America* v216 no13 p54 Je 12 2017

Haaker, Colton

CAMPBELLS CRUSH IT AT KOH M. EMERY and E. MILLER color *Dirt Sports + Off-Road* v51 no7 p12 Jl 2017

Haanaes, Knut

Navigating the Dozens of Different Strategy Options *Harvard Business Review Digital Articles* p2 Je 24 2015

HAANEN, JEFF

Do Smartphones Give Your Soul Cancer? A balanced, biblical take on the devices we can't seem to live without color *Christianity Today* v61 no4 p64 My 2017

INVESTING IN THE KINGDOM color *Christianity Today* v60 no10 p50 D 2016

Haarman, Susan

What God Demands bw *Commonweal* v143 no18 p43 N 11 2016

Haas, Brett

FLIGHT PLAN L. BEOORD *Successful Farming* v114 no12 p32 Mid-N 2016

Haas, Derek A.

Delivering Higher Value Care Means Spending More Time with Patients *Harvard Business Review Digital Articles* p2 D 26 2014

Getting Bundled Payments Right in Health Care *Harvard Business Review Digital Articles* p2 O 19 2015

Health Care Providers Need a Value Management Office *Harvard Business Review Digital Articles* p2 D 2 2015

The Mayo Clinic Model for Running a Value-Improvement Program *Harvard Business Review Digital Articles* p2 O 22 2015

Measuring and Communicating Health Care Value with Charts *Harvard Business Review Digital Articles* p2 O 26 2015

A Payment Model That Prevents Unnecessary Medical Treatment *Harvard Business Review Digital Articles* p2 D 19 2016

Haas, Kelsey M.

Evolution of protein phosphorylation across 18 fungal species bibl graph *Science* v354 no6309 p229 O 14 2016

HAAS, LIDIJA

The Escape Artist color *New Republic* v247 no12 p70 D 2016

First-Person Shooter *New York Times Book Review* p8 Mr 26 2017

HAAS, LIZ

Traverse of the Clods color *Climbing* no353 p36 My/Je 2017

HAAS, RICHARD C.

WHAT ABOUT TRUMP? color *Commonweal* v144 no2 p2 Ja 27 2017

Haas, Simon

Sacred Spaces W. ROBINSON color *Esquire* p126 BigBlackBook

HAAS, TANNI

Your True Stories IN 100 WORDS color *Reader's Digest* v189 no1131 p32 Je 2017

Haas, Tommy

A Tennis Tourney Moves Forward P. LERNER *Los Angeles Magazine* p24 Mr 2017

Haas, W. R.

Permanent human occupation of the central Tibetan Plateau in the early Holocene bibl bw color diag *Science* v355 no6320 p1 Ja 6 2017

Haase, Kerstin

Mutational signatures associated with tobacco smoking in human cancer bibl graph *Science* v354 no6312 p618 N 4 2016

Haass, Richard

Where to Go From Here [Cover story] color *Foreign Affairs* v96 no4 p2 Jl/Ag 2017

A World in Disarray: American Foreign Policy and the Crisis of the Old Order G. J. Ikenberry *Foreign Affairs* v96 no1 p156 Ja/F 2017

World Order 2.0 color *Foreign Affairs* v96 no1 p2 Ja/F 2017

Habanero

FIERY FERMENTS to Preserve Your Peppers: Unlike store-bought condiments, these spicy concoctions are rich with nutrients and flavor developed through the process of lacto-fermentation K. K. Shockey *Mother Earth News* no283 p22 Ag/S 2017

Habash, Gabe

Danger Position: An ambitious collegiate wrestler has one last shot at the title he seeks J. R. CLARK *New York Times Book Review* p18 Jl 23 2017

Literary Fiction color *Publishers Weekly* v264 no26 p72 Je 26 2017

Politics Was Front and Center At This Year's AWP Conference color *Publishers Weekly* v264 no8 p4 F 20 2017

Typewriters, Bombs, Jellyfish color *Publishers Weekly* v264 no11 p69 Mr 13 2017

Habegger, Lukas

Distribution and clinical impact of functional variants in 50,726 whole-exome sequences from the DiscovEHR study chart graph *Science* v354 no6319 paaf6814-1 D 23 2016

Haber, Allan—Interviews

Jail Break C. Menzel color *Powder* p42 S 2017

HABER, DENNIS

MAYDAY! MAYDAY! MAYDAY! color *Flying* v144 no5 p24 My 2017

Haber, Fritz, 1868-1934

THE KAISER'S GRIM REAPER W. Walker bw *MHQ: Quarterly Journal of Military History* v30 no1 p48 Aut 2017

Haber, J.

Spectral narrowing of x-ray pulses for precision spectroscopy with nuclear resonances diag *Science* v357 no6349 p375 Jl 28 2017

HABER, LEIGH

10 TITLES TO PICK UP NOW color *O, The Oprah Magazine* p110 N 2017

IT'S ALWAYS SUNNY in Everton, Massachusetts cartoon color *O, The Oprah Magazine* p104 Mr 2017

WHAT A BOOK CAN DO [Cover story] color *O, The Oprah Magazine* p76 Jl 2017

Haberkorn, Todd

Strange New Worlds B. R. REYNOLDS color *Los Angeles Magazine* v62 no10 p104 O 2017

Haberl, Frank

An accreting pulsar with extreme properties drives an ultraluminous x-ray source in NGC 5907 bibl chart graph *Science* v355 no6327 p817 F 24 2017

Habersham, Myrtle

Your AARP color *AARP: The Magazine* v59 no2A p80 F/Mr 2016

Habib, K. M. Masum

Electron optics with p-n junctions in ballistic graphene bibl graph *Science* v353 no6307 p1522 S 30 2016

HABIB, SAMRA

QUEERING ISLAM color *Advocate* no1089 p56 F/Mr 2017

Habig, Christopher

How to Pay for Health Care/The Case for Capitation: Interaction *Harvard Business Review* v94 no11 p20 N 2016

Habila, Helon

The Chibok Girls: The Boko Haram Kidnappings and Islamist Militancy in Nigeria *Publishers Weekly* v263 no40 p110 O 3 2016

Habit

See also

Food habits

Health behavior

Reading interests

AFTER THE SHOW C. Bowers *Dance Spirit* v21 no4 p42 Ap 2017

EXECUTIVE SUMMARIES color *Harvard Business Review* v95 no1 p166 Ja/F 2017

Habit forming P. W. Marty *Christian Century* v134 no4 p3 F 15 2017

HOW HABIT BEATS NOVELTY [Cover story] color diag *Harvard Business Review* v95 no1 p60 Ja/F 2017

I Make All Things New M. R. Simone *America* v216 no8 p50

Ap 17 2017

Naming Names L. Featherstone color *Nation* v304 no9 p5 Mr 20 2017

Q: What do you consistently do to boost happiness? J. Hanson Lasater, N. Rizopoulos et al color *Yoga Journal* no296 p12 N 2017

Ride Off the Rail W. WETHERELL and N. CHIRICO color *Horse & Rider* v56 no8 p92 Ag 2017

To Form Successful Habits, Know What Motivates You G. Rubin *Harvard Business Review Digital Articles* p2 Mr 17 2015

YOUR BRAIN C. FLORA color *Redbook* p80 Mr 2017

Habit breaking
See also
Smoking cessation

The Question T. NAPOLI, C. McCARTHY et al *O, The Oprah Magazine* p14 F 2017

Trick Yourself into Breaking a Bad Habit J. Grenny *Harvard Business Review Digital Articles* p2 Ja 18 2016

Why New Personal Productivity Efforts Don't Stick M. Thomas and S. Thomas *Harvard Business Review Digital Articles* p2 Ja 19 2016

Habit (Company)
BETTER DIETING THROUGH CHEMISTRY A. Cohen color *Bloomberg Businessweek* no4516 p70 Mr 27 2017

DIGITAL DIET J. Kell color *Fortune* v175 no4 p38 Mr 15 2017

Habitable planets
Life Outside the Habitable Zone D. Grinspoon *Sky & Telescope* v134 no1 p14 Jl 2017

Habitable planets—Research
Searching for Life on the Newly Discovered Earthlike Planets J. Kluger color diag *Time* v189 no9 p24 Mr 13 2017

Habitable zone (Outer space)
Life Outside the Habitable Zone D. Grinspoon *Sky & Telescope* v134 no1 p14 Jl 2017

The Opportunity ZONE C. Crockett color diag graph *Science News* v191 no12 p18 Je 24 2017

Habitat (Ecology)
See also
Artificial habitats

THE FOOTPRINTS OF GIANTS K. McLaughlin color map *Science* v356 no6344 p1224 Je 23 2017

In the Company of DINOSAURS W. S. Hoffman *New York State Conservationist* v71 no5 p28 Ap 2017

NWF names 100th certified community color *National Wildlife (World Edition)* v55 no3 p44 Ap/My 2017

Organic Slug Control S. Slape-Hoysagk *Mother Earth News* no282 p83 Je/Jl 2017

PENGUIN CITY S. ELDER *National Geographic Kids* no467 p14 F 2017

Turkey Trot E. LARK color *Yankee* v80 no6 p14 N/D 2016

URBAN PASTORALS S. W. Goldhagen bw color *Art in America* v105 no3 p88 Mr 2017

Habitat conservation
Connecting forest habitat for wildlife and people color *National Wildlife (World Edition)* v55 no2 p46 F/Mr 2017

Saving Forest Habitat S. STEEN *American Forests* v123 no2 p2 Summ 2017

Scientific Evidence for Fifty Percent? Y. F. WIERSMA, D. J. H. SLEEP et al *BioScience* v67 no9 p781 S 2017

We Need a Biologically Sound North American Conservation Plan D. JOHNS, J. TERBORGH et al *BioScience* v67 no8 p685 Ag 2017

Habitat destruction
Migratory birds under threat F. Bairlein bibl diag *Science* v354 no6312 p547 N 4 2016

Habito, Ruben L. F., 1947-
BE STILL & KNOW R. L. F. HABITO color *Tricycle: The Buddhist Review* v26 no3 p34 Spr 2017

Habit—Social aspects
OLD HABITS DIE HARD, BUT THEY DO DIE [Cover story] R. G. MCGRATH color *Harvard Business Review* v95 no1 p54 Ja/F 2017

Habtezghi, Nazenet
Simone Missick color *Essence* v47 no12 p44 Ap 2017

Hacaoglu, Selcan
In Turkey, New Powers Won't Fix Old Problems color *Bloomberg Businessweek* no4519 p17 Ap 24 2017

Hachette Book Group Inc.—Officials & employees
On the Road with the Hachette Book Group A. Green chart color *Publishers Weekly* v264 no32 p8 Ag 7 2017

Hachman, Mark
The 11 most intriguing Fall Creators Update features in Windows 10 Build 16215 color *PCWorld* v35 no7 p11 Jl 2017

4 REASONS WHY I SWITCHED FROM GOOGLE TO BING color *PCWorld* v35 no9 p83 S 2017

Adobe Flash will die by 2020, Adobe and browser makers say color *PCWorld* v35 no9 p23 S 2017

AMD shows how Zen—now renamed Ryzen—is its best chip family in a decade [Cover story] color *PCWorld* v35 no1 p9 Ja 2017

AMD Threadripper prices undercut Intel's Core i9 by as much as $1,000 chart color *PCWorld* v35 no8 p9 Ag 2017

The best consumer antivirus products of 2016 are Avira and Norton chart color *PCWorld* p33 Mr 2017

Comcast is the fastest ISP, and T-Mobile is the fastest wireless carrier, Ookla says color graph *PCWorld* v35 no10 p18 O 2017

Confirmed: Windows 10 may cut off devices with older CPUs color *PCWorld* v35 no9 p20 S 2017

Consumer Reports' Surface Laptop flap is based on data from past Surface models color *PCWorld* v35 no9 p7 S 2017

Google Drive is being replaced by Backup and Sync: What to expect color *PCWorld* v35 no10 p10 O 2017

Hands-on: Microsoft's Surface Studio is a Windows PC for the Mac crowd color *PCWorld* p28 D 2016

Hands-on: Paint 3D Preview remixes Paint for the HoloLens generation color *PCWorld* p32 D 2016

Here we go again: Microsoft's popping up ads from the Windows 10 taskbar color *PCWorld* p52 D 2016

How to remove ransomware: Use this battle plan to fight back color *PCWorld* v35 no4 p129 Ap 2017

HP Elite x3: This could be the last great Windows phone color graph *PCWorld* v35 no11 p68 N 2016

If you've ever owned a PC with a DVD drive, you may get a $10 settlement color *PCWorld* p38 Mr 2017

Intel demotes PCs, giving datacenter chips first crack at new technologies color *PCWorld* p22 Mr 2017

Lenovo's ThinkPad X1 Tablet modules add features but limit functionality color *PCWorld* p128 D 2016

Logitech Craft hands-on: This keyboard's mini-Surface Dial is truly innovative color *PCWorld* v35 no10 p67 O 2017

Meet Opera Neon, Opera's radical vision for the future of web browsers color *PCWorld* v35 no2 p17 F 2017

Microsoft announces Office 2019 for customers who don't want to pay forever for Office 365 color *Macworld - Digital Edition* v34 no11 p109 N 2017

Microsoft halts Minecraft updates for Windows 10 phones cartoon color *PCWorld* v35 no2 p14 F 2017

Microsoft seems ready to give up on Windows phones, if not Windows 10 Mobile color *PCWorld* p48 D 2016

Microsoft slips four more features into the Fall Creators Update with Build 16251 color *PCWorld* v35 no9 p14 S 2017

Microsoft Surface Pro (2017): More power for more money color graph *PCWorld* v35 no7 p57 Jl 2017

Microsoft Surface Studio: Creativity is a sublime, pricey experience color graph *PCWorld* v35 no7 p87 Jl 2017

Microsoft will save Microsoft Paint, making it a downloadable app color *PCWorld* v35 no9 p18 S 2017

Mozilla promises a next-gen Firefox engine that will deliver huge improvements color *PCWorld* p61 D 2016

A new Microsoft foldable device patent offers more grist for the Surface phone rumor mill cartoon *PCWorld* v35 no2 p11 F 2017

Samsung Galaxy Book: An excellent 2-in-1 for a good price color graph *PCWorld* v35 no7 p71 Jl 2017

Sunrise calendar is dead, and only some features live on in Outlook color *PCWorld* p26 O 2016

A Surface all-in-one PC may lead a Microsoft hardware refresh in October color *PCWorld* p16 O 2016

Surface Laptop: Microsoft's MacBook Air killer nails what students need color graph *PCWorld* v35 no8 p62 Ag 2017

Tech threats that scare the experts color *Macworld - Digital Edition* p41 Ap 2017

Wanawiki is the WannaCry fix that might save affected PCs color *PCWorld* v35 no6 p25 Je 2017

Windows 10 Build 16241 gives the best sneak peek yet at the Fall Creators Update color *PCWorld* v35 no8 p16 Ag 2017

Windows 10 Creators Update could ship March 31, and we're already worried about bugs color *PCWorld* p14 Mr 2017

Windows 10 Creators Update: Microsoft adds fun to its flagship OS color *PCWorld* v35 no5 p67 My 2017

Windows 10's Creators Update bug bash begins [Cover story] color *PCWorld* p11 Mr 2017

Windows 10's privacy settings will be simpler with Creators' Update color map *PCWorld* v35 no2 p36 F 2017

Windows Vista has just days to live color *PCWorld* v35 no4 p42 Ap 2017

Hacinli, Cynthia

THE ITINERARY: TYSONS *Washingtonian Magazine* v52 no3 p101 D 2016

Hackamores

Riding With a Hackamore C. CUSHING and J. PAULSON color *Horse & Rider* v56 no11 p41 N 2017

Hackathons

HACK YOUR DNA AND 19 OTHER WAYS TO BE YOUR OWN DOCTOR G. RUBENSTEIN cartoon color *Men's Health* v32 no9 p114 N 2017

Hackenberg, Robert

Instant Cattle-Panel Cage *Mother Earth News* no282 p86 Je/Jl 2017

HACKENMILLER, ALLISON

The Question color *O, The Oprah Magazine* p14 N 2017

Hacker, Jacob S.

AN AMERICAN SICKNESS *New York Times Book Review* p1 Ap 9 2017

THE BETTER DEAL L. COMPA color *America* v215 no10 p36 O 10 2016

HORSE AND RABBIT STEW I. Stelzer *Claremont Review of Books* v17 no1 p82 Wint 2016/2017

HACKETT, ISAAC

Cheers & Jeers color *Field & Stream* v122 no6 p12 N 2017

Hackett, Jim

Ford Finds a New Leader, By Design A. Lashinsky color *Fortune* v176 no4 p132 S 15 2017

Ford Has Some Catching Up to Do K. Naughton, J. Green et al color diag *Bloomberg Businessweek* no4524 p20 My 29 2017

HACKETT, KATHLEEN

all in the family color *House Beautiful* v159 no7 p112 S 2017

All Together Now color *House Beautiful* p68 Jl 2017

IF THESE WALLS COULD TALK... *Better Homes & Gardens* v95 no1 p94 Ja 2017

POLISHING A JEWEL color *House Beautiful* v159 no1 p92 F 2017

RUSTIC REVISITED color *Better Homes & Gardens* v95 no10 p132 O 2017

Sleeping Beauty color *Architectural Digest* v73 no11 p164 N 2016

Three's Company color *House Beautiful* v159 no5 p92 Je 2017

UNCOMMON THREADS color *Better Homes & Gardens* v95 no2 p102 F 2016

Hackett, Liam

Cyberbullying and its Implications for Human Rights *UN Chronicle* v53 no4 p1 2016

Cyberbullying and Its Implications for Human Rights *UN Chronicle* v54 no4 p41 2017

Hackett, Mark

5 WAYS TO SMOKE YOUR FAIRWAY WOODS color *Golf Magazine* v59 no10 p52 O 2017

EXIT SAND, MAN! color *Golf Magazine* v59 no5 p64 My 2017

POSE A STRIKE color *Golf Magazine* v59 no1 p42 Ja 2017

Hackett, Robert

100 FASTEST-GROWING COMPANIES chart color diag map *Fortune* v176 no4 p157 S 15 2017

1 BILLION+ THE NUMBER OF ACCOUNTS COMPROMISED IN THE YAHOO HACK *Fortune* v75 no1 p16 Ja 1 2017

THE 2017 Fortune Crystal Ball color diag *Fortune* v174 no7 p11 D 1 2016

BITCOIN INVESTORS ARE FEELING GOLDEN, FOR NOW diag *Fortune* v176 no5 p17 O 1 2017

BITCOIN IS BACK diag *Fortune* v175 no2 p11 F 1 2017

BLOCKCHAIN MANIA! [Cover story] color *Fortune* v176 no3 p44 S 1 2017

BREAKTHROUGH BRANDS 2017 color diag *Fortune* v75 no1 p64 Ja 1 2017

BUG BARONESS AND LUTA SECURITY CEO KATIE MOUSSOURIS EXPLAINS THE ECONOMY OF EXPLOITS color *Fortune* v176 no1 p65 Jl 1 2017

CHANGE THE WORLD !!!! color diag map *Fortune* v176 no4 p74 S 15 2017

China's Big Play for Small Chips color *Fortune* v175 no3 p16 Mr 1 2017

DEAD, BUT NOT FORGOTTEN color *Fortune* v176 no4 p38 S 15 2017

Digital Currency Gets Its Biggest Test Yet color *Fortune* v176 no2 p13 Ag 1 2017

DREAM WEAVER color *Fortune* v176 no3 p74 S 1 2017

THE FATHER OF THE INFORMATION AGE (FINALLY) GETS HIS OWN BOOK color *Fortune* v176 no2 p17 Ag 1 2017

FORTY UNDER FORTY 2017 color *Fortune* v176 no3 p62 S 1 2017

G IS FOR GRAVEYARD color *Fortune* v175 no4 p40 Mr 15 2017

GOOGLE'S ELITE HACKER SWAT TEAM VS. EVERYONE color *Fortune* v176 no1 p60 Jl 1 2017

IF SILICON VALLEY WENT TO WASHINGTON color *Fortune* v175 no2 p26 F 1 2017

The Latest Victim of Uber's Bold Disruption May Be Itself color *Time* v189 no10 p22 Mr 20 2017

MEET MARVEL'S CHIEF MYTHMAKER color *Fortune* v175 no3 p24 Mr 1 2017

MINING COMEDY GOLD color *Fortune* v176 no3 p70 S 1 2017

SURVEILLANCE color *Fortune* v175 no4 p114 Mr 15 2017

WANTED: FRESH SOLUTIONS FOR AGE-OLD PROBLEMS color diag *Fortune* v175 no6 p68 My 1 2017

What You Should Read This Spring color *Fortune* v175 no5 p16 Ap 1 2017

Why a Global Cyber Crisis Stalled-This Time color map *Time* v189 no20 p7 My 29 2017

WORLD'S 50 GREATEST LEADERS [Cover story] color *Fortune* v176 no5 p46 Ap 1 2017

THE WORLD'S MOST DANGEROUS HACKER GROUPS *Fortune* v176 no1 p55 Jl 1 2017

YOUTH REVOLT color *Fortune* v176 no3 p64 S 1 2017

Hackett, Sean R.

Systems-level analysis of mechanisms regulating yeast metabolic flux bibl diag graph *Science* v354 no6311 paaf2786-1 O 28 2016

Hackett, Troy A.

Restoring auditory cortex plasticity in adult mice by restricting thalamic adenosine signaling graph *Science* v356 no6345 p1352 Je 30 2017

Hacking (Computers)

Accidental Advocates M. KONCZAL *Nation* v305 no8 p9 O 9 2017

ASK A FLOWCHART R. CAPPS diag *Wired* v25 no4 p96 Ap 2017

Beware the Tricks and Traps of Donald Trump, News Manipulator In Chief J. Klein color *Time* v188 no27-28 p34 D 26 2016

THE @-BOMB M. Schwartz *New York Times Magazine* p30 Ja 8 2017

Cold-War Dangers color *Nation* v303 no19 p3 N 7 2016

CYBERKIDS C. Battan cartoon *New Yorker* v92 no44 p20 Ja 9 2017

Demo: Hacking a voting machine color *PCWorld* v35 no11 p162 N 2016

Do's and Don'ts Concerning Public Wi-Fi *USA Today Magazine* v146 no2867 p3 Ag 2017

Embracing the Hack Attack M. Brubaker *Parks & Recreation* v52 no5 p70 My 2017

Equifax and the Perils of Password Protection L. Eadicicco color *Time* v190 no12 p21 S 25 2017

The Equifax Job M. Riley, J. Robertson et al bw graph *Bloomberg Businessweek* no4541 p26 O 9 2017

HACKED [Cover story] J. J. Roberts and A. Lashinsky color diag *Fortune* v176 no1 p52 Jl 1 2017

The Hacking Bear A. I. KLEIN il *National Review* v68 no21 p33 N 21 2016

Hacking Myself Is the Most Surprisingly Humiliating Decision

I've Ever Made J. Stein color *Time* v189 no12 p63 Ap 3 2017

Hootsuite's CEO on What He Learned from Getting Hacked on Social Media R. Holmes *Harvard Business Review Digital Articles* p2 O 6 2016

Medical Systems Hacks Are Scary, but Medical Device Hacks Could Be Even Worse D. Nickelson *Harvard Business Review Digital Articles* p2 My 15 2017

North Korea Is Hacking Bitcoin N. Yuji and K. Sam *Bloomberg Businessweek* no4538 p29 S 18 2017

POPULAR MECHANICS EVERYWHERE color *Popular Mechanics* p8 S 2017

See Your Company Through the Eyes of a Hacker N. C. Fick *Harvard Business Review Digital Articles* p2 Mr 24 2015

The Sony Hack Shows How Lawless the Internet Really Is M. Schrage *Harvard Business Review Digital Articles* p2 D 17 2014

Wall Street Hillary *Weekly Standard* v22 no8 p2 O 31 2016

What's the likelihood that a national U.S. election could be hacked? color *Popular Mechanics* p104 N 2017

When Coders Become Stickup Artists D. Lepido, G. Turner et al color *Bloomberg Businessweek* no4517 p35 Ap 3 2017

Why Companies Shouldn't Try to Hack Their Hackers C. E. Thomas *Harvard Business Review Digital Articles* p2 My 24 2017

THE WORLD'S MOST DANGEROUS HACKER GROUPS R. Hackett *Fortune* v176 no1 p55 Jl 1 2017

Yahoo data breach affects at least 500 million users, company says M. KAN color *PCWorld* p48 O 2016

The Yahoo! Hack Goes From Bad to Worse J. Robertson *Bloomberg Businessweek* no4505 p36 D 26 2016

Hacking (Computers)—Competitions

Hacking the Need For a Full-Time Job L. Chapman cartoon *Bloomberg Businessweek* no4518 p33 Ap 10 2017

Hacking (Computers)—Economic aspects

A BIG PAYOFF FOR CYBERCOP STOCKS R. Derousseau color diag *Fortune* v176 no3 p28 S 1 2017

Hacking (Computers)—History—21st century

HACKERS ARE GETTING BOLDER B. O'Keefe diag *Fortune* v75 no1 p100 Ja 1 2017

Hacking (Computers)—Lawsuits & claims

DEFENSE OF THE NERDS A. J. VICENS color *Mother Jones* v42 no6 p57 N/D 2017

Hacking (Computers)—Social aspects

Operations. The Digital Imposter: After penetrating your website, a hacker can do business as you J. Dysart *Parks & Recreation* v52 no6 p48 Je 2017

Our Elections Are Not Secure D. L. Dill color *Scientific American* v316 no3 p12 Mr 2017

Hacking (Computers)—Software

Seriously, Beware the 'Shadow Brokers' D. Lawrence color *Bloomberg Businessweek* no4521 p34 My 8 2017

Hacking Team (Company)

THE @-BOMB M. Schwartz *New York Times Magazine* p30 Ja 8 2017

Hackman, Sarah

Down-to-Earth Decadence color *Missouri Life* v44 no4 p74 Je 2017

Hacko, Susan

Around the Campfire color *Trail Rider* v29 no4 p8 My 2017

Hacksaw Ridge (Film)

Andrew Garfield S. Lansky color *Time* v188 no19 p57 N 7 2016

For Mel Gibson, War Is (Very Bloody) Hell D. REILLY img *New York* v49 no22 p96 O 31 2016

GOOD FIGHTS A. LANE cartoon *New Yorker* v92 no36 p82 N 7 2016

HACKSAW RIDGE D. Vaughn color *Sound & Vision* v82 no7 p67 S 2017

Hacksaw Ridge L. Greenblatt color *Entertainment Weekly* no1439 p47 N 11 2016

A Leading Man Saves Hacksaw Ridge from Hackdom S. Zacharek color *Time* v188 no19 p56 N 7 2016

Universal Translator D. EDELSTEIN img *New York* v49 no22 p104 O 31 2016

Hacksaws

High-Tension Hacksaws color *Popular Mechanics* p42 D 2016/Ja 2017

Hacktivism

COME FOR THE GOULASH, STAY FOR THE DEMOCRACY V. Silver color *Bloomberg Businessweek* no4529 p60 Jl 3 2017

Hacohen, Nir

Single-cell RNA-seq reveals new types of human blood dendritic cells, monocytes, and progenitors color *Science* v356 no6335 p283 Ap 21 2017

HADAS, RACHEL

Waiting With Kipling *American Scholar* v86 no1 p18 Wint 2017

HADDAD, FANAR

Why 'Artificiality' Fails to Explain Iraq's Woes *Current History* v115 no785 p343 D 2016

Haddad, Georges

Minority investigators lack NIH funding color *Science* v356 no6342 p1018 Je 9 2017

Haddad, John

FIELD & MAIN *Virginia Living* v15 no1 p25 D 2016

HAPPY CAMPERS *Virginia Living* v15 no1 p23 D 2016

HADDAD, SALEEM

the exchange *Foreign Policy* no222 p26 Ja/F 2017

Haddish, Tiffany

Tiffany Haddish Doesn't Think Comedy Is a Game A. M. Cox *New York Times Magazine* p54 Ag 20 2017

Haddock, Laura

THE THINKING MAN SAM CLAFLIN M. Khidekel color *Women's Health* v14 no5 p106 Je 2017

Haddon, Dayle

Dayle Haddon E. PERETZ color *Vanity Fair* v58 no11 p183 N 2016

UPDATE YOUR LOOK Guarnieri color *Harper's Bazaar* no3651 p311 Mr 2017

Haden, Charlie, 1937-2014

CHARLIE HADEN: PURSUING LIBERATION J. WOODARD bw *Downbeat* v84 no3 p36 Mr 2017

Chords & Discords J. R. VICKARY, T. GUILFOYLE et al color *Downbeat* v84 no6 p10 Je 2017

Hader, Bill, 1978-

TELEVISION'S COMEDY AUTEURS S. Larson bw *New Yorker* v93 no26 p62 S 4 2017

HADERO, MERON

The Gift Elephant's Mouth: Hopping continents, moving through time, stories explore power's borders *New York Times Book Review* p18 Je 11 2017

Hadfield, Chris, 1959-

on a space walk, flying blind S. Fecht cartoon *Popular Science* v289 no5 p78 S/O 2017

Points to Ponder *Reader's Digest* v188 no1126 p23 D 2016/Ja 2017

Hadhazy, Adam

Arousing Performance bw *Natural History* v125 no11 p7 N 2017

Boom Box *Natural History* v125 no1 p8 D 2016/Ja 2017

Cardinal Rules color *Natural History* v125 no4 p6 Ap 2017

Conducive Atmosphere *Natural History* v124 no10 p6 N 2016

The Dark Universe color diag graph *Discover* v38 no6 p76 Jl/Ag 2017

Déjà Vu color *Natural History* v125 no7 p8 Jl/Ag 2017

Gut Check color *Natural History* v125 no6 p8 Je 2017

Layers of Hominin History color *Natural History* v125 no10 p8 O 2017

Light Activated color *Natural History* v125 no3 p8 Mr 2017

NOTHING REALLY MATTERS bw color *Discover* v27 no10 p46 D 2016

Road to Greener Pastures color *Natural History* v125 no5 p8 My 2017

A Tangled Food Web *Natural History* v125 no2 p7 F 2017

Hadian, K.

Inhibitors of PEX14 disrupt protein import into glycosomes and kill Trypanosoma parasites chart color diag graph *Science* v355 no6332 p1416 Mr 31 2017

Hadid, Bella, 1996-

All-in-Ones E. Wilson color *InStyle* v24 no5 p72 My 2017

Bazaar's Best-Dressed LIST N. Silva-Jelly color *Harper's Bazaar* no3656 p230 S 2017

Best Dress E. Wilson color *InStyle* v24 no1 p31 Ja 2017

the cover color *InStyle* v24 no8 p30 Ag 2017

Go Fluoro E. Wilson color *InStyle* v24 no9 p180 S 2017

Hello! L. Brown color *InStyle* v24 no8 p24 Ag 2017

My LIST L. McCarthy cartoon color *Harper's Bazaar* no3653 p102 My 2017

Qué Bella [Cover story] S. Cristobal color *InStyle* v24 no8 p130 Ag 2017

September Was Huge color *Glamour* v114 no11 p42 N 2016

Hadid, Bella, 1996——Interviews

Bella Hadid K. B. Brown color *InStyle* v24 no6 p102 Je 2017

Hadid, Gigi, 1995-

The A-LIST color *Harper's Bazaar* no3654 p58 Je/Jl 2017

THE APPROVAL MATRIX img *New York* v49 no24 p180 N 28 2016

Better to Gather color *Vogue* v207 no11 p138 N 2017

GIGI'S SPACE ODYSSEY [Cover story] J. Duboff color *Harper's Bazaar* no3654 p118 Je/Jl 2017

Mad Plaids E. Wilson color *InStyle* v24 no11 p72 N 2017

MODEL MOMENT: GIGI HADID color *Harper's Bazaar* no3651 p317 Mr 2017

The White–Sneaker Revolution N. Silverstein color *Glamour* v114 no7 p60 Jl 2016

Hadid, Zaha, 1950-2016

Star Ship H. PEARMAN *Architectural Record* v204 no11 p78 N 2016

Hadisiswoyo, Panut

Riding in a Rickshaw With a Hostage Orangutan D. Stone color *National Geographic* v230 no5 p25 N 2016

Hadjab, Saida

Multipotent peripheral glial cells generate neuroendocrine cells of the adrenal medulla color *Science* v357 no6346 p46 Jl 7 2017

Hadjer, David

David Hadjer H. MARTIN cartoon *Architectural Digest* v74 no4 p38 Ap 2017

HADLEY, CONSTANCE NOONAN

STOP THE MEETING MADNESS: HOW TO FREE UP TIME FOR MEANINGFUL WORK chart color img *Harvard Business Review* v95 no4 p62 Jl/Ag 2017

Hadley, Frank-John

Cream of the Crop color *Downbeat* v84 no1 p73 Ja 2017

Empowerment color *Downbeat* v84 no2 p76 F 2017

Good Deals color *Downbeat* v84 no5 p58 My 2017

The Great Un-American Songbook, Volumes I & II color *Downbeat* v84 no6 p68 Je 2017

International Studies color *Downbeat* v84 no9 p68 S 2017

The Late Shows color *Downbeat* v84 no10 p64 O 2017

Mercy, Mercy, Mercy! color *Downbeat* v83 no12 p72 D 2016

Personal Strains of the Blues color *Downbeat* v84 no3 p60 Mr 2017

Places To Go, People To See color *Downbeat* v84 no6 p70 Je 2017

Seeds Sown and Grown color *Downbeat* v84 no9 p66 S 2017

Shared Vision, Common Spirit bw *Downbeat* v84 no4 p61 Ap 2017

Singing on Solid Ground color *Downbeat* v83 no11 p56 N 2016

Sweeter Than Honey bw *Downbeat* v84 no8 p75 Ag 2017

Trailblazers and Hybrids color *Downbeat* v83 no12 p76 D 2016

Trouble Free color *Downbeat* v84 no4 p59 Ap 2017

Yuletide Joy color *Downbeat* v83 no12 p84 D 2016

Hadley, Tessa

Bad Dreams *Publishers Weekly* v264 no13 p65 Mr 27 2017

Bitter and Delicious: Tales that disclose the uncanny within the commonplace L. H. COHEN *New York Times Book Review* p12 Je 11 2017

DEEDS NOT WORDS T. HADLEY bw color *Atlantic* v319 no5 p88 Je 2017

Funny Little Snake cartoon *New Yorker* v93 no32 p66 O 16 2017

Hadly, Elizabeth A.

Merging paleobiology with conservation biology to guide the future of terrestrial ecosystems color *Science* v355 no6325 p594 F 10 2017

Hadrian, Emperor of Rome, 76-138

THE WALL AT THE END OF THE EMPIRE [Cover story] J. A. LOBELL color *Archaeology* v70 no3 p26 My/Je 2017

Hadrian's Wall (England)

DEFENSIVE STRATEGY AND THE CONSTRUCTION OF THE WALL color *Archaeology* v70 no3 p30 My/Je 2017

FEEDING THE ARMY color *Archaeology* v70 no3 p33 My/Je 2017

SPEAKING VOLUMES C. Valentino *Archaeology* v70 no3 p4

My/Je 2017

Hadrian's Wall (England)—History

THE WALL AT THE END OF THE EMPIRE [Cover story] J. A. LOBELL color *Archaeology* v70 no3 p26 My/Je 2017

Writing on the Walls V. D. Hanson *Hoover Digest: Research & Opinion on Public Policy* no4 p163 Fall 2016

Hadrosauridae

Fossil Record C. Cox *Orion Magazine* v35 no4/5 p32 Jl-O 2016

Hadt, Ryan G.

Metalloprotein entatic control of ligand-metal bonds quantified by ultrafast x-ray spectroscopy diag *Science* v356 no6344 p1276 Je 23 2017

Hadwin, Adam

Playing It Cool R. Asselta and C. Barrett color *Golf Magazine* v59 no8 p27 Ag 2017

Hadzibabic, Zoran

Two- and three-body contacts in the unitary Bose gas bibl diag graph *Science* v355 no6323 p377 Ja 27 2017

HAEFFELE-BALCH, STEFANIE

Disasters Should Be Dull color *Reason* v48 no9 p66 F 2017

Haefner, Rosemary

SKIRTING THE SALARY QUESTION K. PITSKER color *Kiplinger's Personal Finance* v71 no7 p14 Jl 2017

Haegel, Nancy M.

Terawatt-scale photovoltaics: Trajectories and challenges chart graph *Science* v356 no6334 p141 Ap 14 2017

Haemophilus influenzae

Autopsy of a Deadly Virus J. K. TAUBENBERGER bw color *Natural History* v125 no9 p14 S 2017

HAFER, ABBY

EVERYTHING YOU KNOW ABOUT SEX IS WRONG: PART 1: THE GENDER BINARY *Humanist* v77 no4 p24 Jl/Ag 2017

HAFIZ, SAMEERA

Deportations *In These Times* v41 no1 p25 Ja 2017

Hafner, Reese—Awards

DanceSPIRIT FutureSTAR 2016 N. Loeffler-Gladstone *Dance Spirit* v20 no10 p63 D 2016

Hafstad, Vala

THE FEMALE VOICE OF NJÁLL *Iceland Review* v54 no5 p14 S-O 2016

HEART FOR ART *Iceland Review* v55 no4 p18 Jl/Ag 2017

LOVE IN THE LAST CHAPTER *Iceland Review* v55 no4 p14 Jl/Ag 2017

MASTER OF ILLUSION color *Iceland Review* v54 no5 p12 S-O 2016

News Roundup *Iceland Review* v54 no6 p18 N/D 2016

News Roundup *Iceland Review* v55 no2 p18 Mr/Ap 2017

News Roundup *Iceland Review* v55 no3 p8 My/Je 2017

News Roundup *Iceland Review* v55 no4 p8 Jl/Ag 2017

OLD MURDER CASE REVIVED *Iceland Review* v55 no3 p10 My/Je 2017

POLLUTION IN PARADISE *Iceland Review* v55 no3 p70 My/Je 2017

THERMAL BLISS *Iceland Review* v55 no3 p106 My/Je 2017

TRUE COLORS *Iceland Review* v54 no6 p22 N/D 2016

VERÖLD, THE HOUSE OF VIGDÍS *Iceland Review* v55 no4 p82 Jl/Ag 2017

HAGAN, JOE

Between the Covers bw color *Vanity Fair* v59 no11 p144 N 2017

Hagan, Molly

Adam Pendleton color *Current Biography* v78 no9 p62 S 2017

A. G. Sulzberger color *Current Biography* v78 no9 p80 S 2017

Anderson .Paak color *Current Biography* v78 no6 p88 Je 2017

Andrew Kaczynski color *Current Biography* v78 no8 p59 Ag 2017

Angelique Kerber color *Current Biography* v78 no4 p42 Ap 2017

Ariya Jutanugarn color *Current Biography* v78 no6 p54 Je 2017

Bhaskar Sunkara *Current Biography* v77 no11 p86 N 2016

Brooke Henderson color *Current Biography* v78 no4 p38 Ap 2017

Conor McGregor color *Current Biography* v78 no3 p64 Mr 2017

Corey Hawkins color *Current Biography* v78 no9 p32 S 2017

Daniel Pemberton color *Current Biography* v78 no2 p62 F 2017

David Fahrenthold *Current Biography* v78 no5 p26 My 2017

David Guetta color *Current Biography* v78 no1 p18 Ja 2017

Denis Villeneuve color *Current Biography* v78 no4 p90 Ap 2017

Derek Cianfrance color *Current Biography* v78 no3 p15 Mr 2017

Gabriela González *Current Biography* v77 no10 p35 O 2016

Garth Greenwell bw *Current Biography* v78 no3 p24 Mr 2017

Gary Sánchez color *Current Biography* v78 no5 p77 My 2017

Giannis Antetokounmpo color *Current Biography* v78 no6 p3 Je 2017

Henry Threadgill color *Current Biography* v77 no10 p87 O 2016

Ibtihaj Muhammad color *Current Biography* v78 no1 p51 Ja 2017

Inbee Park color *Current Biography* v78 no2 p58 F 2017

Isaiah Thomas color *Current Biography* v78 no8 p82 Ag 2017

Issey Ogata color *Current Biography* v78 no8 p64 Ag 2017

Jamelle Bouie color *Current Biography* v77 no10 p14 O 2016

Jérôme Bel color *Current Biography* v78 no5 p12 My 2017

Johannes Öhman color *Current Biography* v78 no1 p55 Ja 2017

Julian Fellowes color *Current Biography* v77 no11 p44 N 2016

Julio Urias *Current Biography* v78 no4 p86 Ap 2017

Karan Mahajan color *Current Biography* v78 no1 p37 Ja 2017

Karl-Anthony Towns color *Current Biography* v78 no4 p82 Ap 2017

Lindsey Stirling color *Current Biography* v78 no9 p76 S 2017

Manuel Neuer color *Current Biography* v78 no5 p73 My 2017

Marcel Hirscher color *Current Biography* v78 no2 p35 F 2017

Marion Coutts *Current Biography* v78 no8 p26 Ag 2017

Martin Wolf *Current Biography* v78 no2 p88 F 2017

Mary Jepkosgei Keitany color *Current Biography* v78 no9 p48 S 2017

Michael Fulmer color *Current Biography* v78 no6 p39 Je 2017

Phillipa Soo color *Current Biography* v77 no11 p77 N 2016

Rachel Platten color *Current Biography* v77 no11 p59 N 2016

Sophie Turner color *Current Biography* v77 no10 p92 O 2016

Tatyana McFadden color *Current Biography* v78 no3 p59 Mr 2017

Tina Charles color *Current Biography* v78 no5 p18 My 2017

Zhang Zanbo *Current Biography* v78 no2 p92 F 2017

Hagan, Shelly

Fun Filters Don't Make Good Neighbors color *Bloomberg Businessweek* no4513 p35 Mr 6 2017

Hagan, Thomas

mTOR regulates metabolic adaptation of APCs in the lung and controls the outcome of allergic inflammation graph *Science* v357 no6355 p1014 S 8 2017

Hagar, Sammy, 1947—Interviews

Sammy Hagar A. GREENE color *Rolling Stone* no1290 p58 Je 29 2017

HAGE, MATT

ALASKA CROSSING color *Canoe & Kayak Magazine* v45 no1 p56 Wint 2017

Hagel, Chuck, 1946-

The third offset strategy: A misleading slogan L. J. Korb and C. Evans bibl *Bulletin of the Atomic Scientists* v73 no2 p92 Mr 2017

Hagel, John III

Finding the Money in the Internet of Things *Harvard Business Review Digital Articles* p2 N 11 2014

Great Businesses Scale Their Learning, Not Just Their Operations color *Harvard Business Review Digital Articles* p2 Je 7 2017

Help Employees Create Knowledge—Not Just Share It *Harvard Business Review Digital Articles* p2 2017

Technology Should Be About More than Efficiency *Harvard Business Review Digital Articles* p2 S 25 2015

Turn the Pressures of Technology into Potential *Harvard Business Review Digital Articles* p2 O 8 2014

We Need to Expand Our Definition of Entrepreneurship *Harvard Business Review Digital Articles* p2 S 28 2016

Hagen, Bill

MATTRACKS SAVE SEED CROPS: WRESTLING WITH DOING FIELD OPERATIONS ON SOGGY SOILS? THESE RUBBER TRACKS CAN HELP D. Goerge *Successful Farming* v115 no12 p54 O 2017

Hagen, John D.

A Crisis for Crisis-Pregnancy Centers color *Commonweal* v144 no4 p7 F 24 2017

HAGEN, JOHN D. JR.

Crisis Pregnancy Centers in Crisis color *Weekly Standard* v23 no4 p26 O 2 2017

Hagen, Wim J. H.

The structure and flexibility of conical HIV-1 capsids determined within intact virions bibl color *Science* v354 no6318 p1434 D 16 2016

Hager, Jenna Bush

Dear Sasha and Malia ... color *Time* v189 no4 p43 Ja 23 2017

LET'S DO FALL IN VIRGINIA color *Southern Living* v51 no11 p62 N 2016

Off to the Races color *Southern Living* v52 no4 p62 Ap 2017

Tamale Fest color *Southern Living* v51 no12 p138 D 2016

A Texas Fiesta color *Southern Living* v52 no9 p17 S 2017

Weekend in West Virginia color *Southern Living* v52 no2 p74 F 2017

HAGERTY, BARBARA BRADLEY

Can an Ex-President Be Happy? color *Atlantic* v319 no1 p22 Ja/F 2017

CROSSING THE WASTELAND OF FAITH color *Christianity Today* v60 no10 p44 D 2016

When Your Child Is a Psychopath color *Atlantic* v319 no5 p78 Je 2017

Hagest, Destiny

Country Lore *Mother Earth News* no280 p85 F/Mr 2017

Hagfeldt, Anders

Improving efficiency and stability of perovskite solar cells with photocurable fluoropolymers bibl chart graph *Science* v354 no6309 p203 O 14 2016

Incorporation of rubidium cations into perovskite solar cells improves photovoltaic performance bibl graph *Science* v354 no6309 p206 O 14 2016

Hagfishes

Unusually loose skin protects hagfish S. MILIUS color *Science News* v191 no2 p13 F 4 2017

Hagfishes—Behavior

Secrets of the Houdini-like hagfish color *Science* v355 no6321 p112 Ja 13 2017

Haggard, Merle, 1937-2016

MERLE HAGGARD L. Lynn and M. Vain color *Entertainment Weekly* no1446/1447 p93 D 2016/Ja 2017

Haggard, William H.

Weather in the Courtroom: Memoirs from a Career in Forensic Meteorology G. Henderson *Physics Today* v70 no10 p61 O 2017

Haggerty, Nicholas

Manifestations *Commonweal* v144 no15 p43 S 22 2017

Haggis, Paul, 1953-

HOW TO CRASH THE OSCARS S. W. HUNT img *New York* v49 no24 p134 N 28 2016

Hagiu, Andrei

Companies Need an Option Between Contractor and Employee *Harvard Business Review Digital Articles* p2 Ag 21 2015

The Dawning of the Age of Flex Labor *Harvard Business Review Digital Articles* p2 S 4 2015

FINDING THE PLATFORM IN YOUR PRODUCT: FOUR STRATEGIES THAT CAN REVEAL HIDDEN VALUE il *Harvard Business Review* v95 no4 p94 Jl/Ag 2017

Hagiwara, Yuki

Is Japan Ready To Abandon Pacifism? color *Bloomberg Businessweek* no4536 p37 S 4 2017

Haglage, Abby

How Did We Get Here? [Cover story] color *Glamour* v115 no7 p64 Jl 2017

The Loving Legacy bw color *Glamour* v114 no11 p141 N 2016

My Family Is Stuck in Aleppo color *Glamour* v115 no5 p149 My 2017

"The suffragettes would not back down" color *Glamour* v115 no2 p80 F 2017

Hagmann, Johannes-Geert

Mobilizing US physics in World War I *Physics Today* v70 no8 p44 Ag 2017

Hagner, Meredith

Search Party J. Jensen color *Entertainment Weekly* no1441 p46 N 25 2016

Hagoort, Jaco

An interactive three-dimensional digital atlas and quantitative database of human development bibl color graph *Science* v354 no6315 paag0053-1 N 25 2016

HAGUE, PATRICK

DOG DAZE *Cincinnati Magazine* v50 no10 p52 Jl 2017

Hague, Tim

BOXING SHADOWS A. HUTCHINS bw *Maclean's* v130 no9

Haikus By Don, Jr. (Poem)
HAIKUS BY DON, JR W. STEPHEN cartoon *New Yorker* v93 no32 p33 O 16 2017

Hail
Weather Front K. Cutlip color *Weatherwise* v69 no6 p6 N-D 2016

Hail, Caesar! (Film)
3 — "WOULD THAT IT WERE SO SIMPLE" K. P. Sullivan color *Entertainment Weekly* no1444/1445 p58 D 16 2016

Hail to the Chief (Music)
Hail to the Chieftain A. Tucker *Smithsonian* v47 no9 p11 Ja/F 2017

Haile, Beth
Addicted to piety color *U.S. Catholic* v82 no5 p10 My 2017
Can every sin be forgiven? *U.S. Catholic* v82 no9 p49 S 2017
A disarmament of the heart color *U.S. Catholic* v82 no2 p10 F 2017
Image of God color *U.S. Catholic* v82 no11 p10 N 2017
Is there a difference between mercy and compassion? color *U.S. Catholic* v82 no5 p49 My 2017
Social network color *U.S. Catholic* v82 no8 p10 Ag 2017
What is the common good? *U.S. Catholic* v82 no11 p49 N 2017
What to wear color *U.S. Catholic* v81 no11 p8 N 2016

Hailey, Leisha—Interviews
REunIons The L Word T. Stack color *Entertainment Weekly* no1471 p38 Je 23 2017

Haili Qian
Opportunities and advantages for the development of precision medicine in China *Science* v354 no6319 p6 D 23 2016

Hailwood, Mark
Pubs and Politics in Stuart England *History Today* v67 no1 p3 Ja 2017

Haim (Performer)
Face OF Bass R. SULLIVAN color *Vogue* v207 no7 p44 Jl 2017
THE GOLDEN AGE OF HAIM N. Feeney, A. Bacle et al color *Entertainment Weekly* no1467 p32 My 26 2017
Haim Doesn't Want to Be "Cool" J. Harman color *Glamour* no8 p38 Ag 2017
Haim J. Bernstein color *Entertainment Weekly* no1473 p57 Jl 7 2017
HAIM N. Feeney color *Entertainment Weekly* no1446/1447 p70 D 2016/Ja 2017
Haim's Bright Retro-Pop Future J. DOLAN color *Rolling Stone* no1291/1292 p63 Jl 13 2017
Sisters in Arms J. Weiner bw color *Rolling Stone* no1287 p40 My 18 2017

Haim, Alana
Haim Doesn't Want to Be "Cool" J. Harman color *Glamour* no8 p38 Ag 2017

Haim, Este
THE GOLDEN AGE OF HAIM N. Feeney, A. Bacle et al color *Entertainment Weekly* no1467 p32 My 26 2017

Hainan Sheng (China)
Can China Make Hainan A Medical Paradise? L. Hui and J. Y. de Morel *Bloomberg Businessweek* no4522 p20 My 15 2017

Haines (Alaska)
GLASS color *Powder* v45 no6 p18 F 2017

Haines, A.
A climate policy pathway for near- and long-term benefits color *Science* v356 no6337 p493 My 5 2017

Haines, Billy
SHENANDOAH VALLEY *Virginia Living* p138 2017 Best 20of Virginia
WILLIAM HAINES DESIGNS: The legacy of a silent film star *Virginia Living* p140 2017 Best 20of Virginia

Haines, Carter S.
Harvesting electrical energy from carbon nanotube yarn twist diag graph *Science* v357 no6353 p773 Ag 25 2017

HAINES, TOM
Sleeping with Oil *Orion Magazine* v35 no4/5 p8 Jl-O 2016

Hainey, Michael
100 YEARS OLD AND STILL A KNOCKOUT bw color *Esquire* p56 S 2017
Andrew Ross SORKIN color *Esquire* p68 My 2017
Artistic License [Cover story] color *Architectural Digest* v73 no11 p142 N 2016
Danny MEYER color *Esquire* p74 Je/Jl 2017

GET YOUR FLAIR ON color *Esquire* p48 Ap 2017
THE NATURAL [Cover story] bw color *Esquire* p92 O 2017
THREE WISE MEN bw color *Esquire* p88 2017 BigBlackBook
THE TIP SHEET color *Esquire* p36 Ag 2017
THE TIP SHEET color *Esquire* v167 no2 p74 Mr 2017

Haining, Richard
AROUND THE BEND N. Janowitz color *American Craft* v77 no2 p44 Ap/My 2017

Haining, W. Nicholas
The epigenetic landscape of T cell exhaustion bibl graph *Science* v354 no6316 p1165 D 2 2016
Epigenetic stability of exhausted T cells limits durability of reinvigoration by PD-1 blockade bibl graph *Science* v354 no6316 p1160 D 2 2016

Hainmueller, Jens
How economic, humanitarian, and religious concerns shape European attitudes toward asylum seekers bibl graph map *Science* v354 no6309 p217 O 14 2016
Protecting unauthorized immigrant mothers improves their children's mental health diag *Science* v357 no6355 p1041 S 8 2017

Hair
See also
Beards
Eyebrows
Crowning Glory color *Health* v30 no9 p20 N 2016
The Cut of the Year color *Health* v30 no10 p34 D 2016
fight the fade *Parents* v91 no6 p77 Je 2016
FIGHT THE FRIZZ AND WIN! L. Desantis color *Health* v31 no3 p94 Ap 2017
GET YOUR BEST HAIR EVER S. Neibart color *Harper's Bazaar* no3656 p374 S 2017
goodbye, frizz! color *Parents* v92 no7 p71 Jl 2017
Great Hair Starts in the Shower color *Health* v30 no9 p14 N 2016
Helping Dads Boost Their Styling Mojo M. LaScala *Parents* v92 no2 p20 F 2017
How to Talk So Your Stylist Will Listen C. T. Burns color *Health* v31 no8 p108 O 2017
IDENTIFYING LEG "CRUD" C. Barakat and M. Freckleton *Equus* no477 p24 Je 2017
My Hair M. Ryan color *InStyle* v24 no10 p222 O 2017
Our Doc Will See You Now R. Rajapaksa color *Health* v31 no5 p63 Je 2017
play with your ponytail K. SANDOVAL BOX color *Parents* v92 no8 p90 Ag 2017
Product Spotlights color *Better Nutrition* v79 no10 p79 O 2017
Toxin-Free Hair Care S. STRAUSFOGEL color *Better Nutrition* v78 no11 p38 N 2016
Your Happiest Summer Hair C. T. Burns color *Health* v31 no6 p112 Jl 2017

Hair (Theatrical production)
Let the Sunshine In H. Als color *New Yorker* v92 no46 p8 Ja 23 2017

Hair analysis
Game-Changing Forensics Technique Uses Hair Proteins *Science & Technology Review* p2 Mr 2017

Hair care & hygiene
2017 SUMMER HAIR Handbook color *O, The Oprah Magazine* p58 Jl 2017
AFTER-SUN CARE for Skin and Hair: After spending time in the sun, try these recipes for cooling masks, mists, bath soaks, gels, and more J. Cox *Mother Earth News* no283 p32 Ag/S 2017
ask REDBOOK color *Redbook* p16 D 2016
Curly Cues N. Spradley color *Essence* v47 no11 p47 Mr 2017
Fun 1st-Day STYLES E. STOVALL color *Seventeen* v76 no5 p42 S 2017
GET THE LOOK color *Harper's Bazaar* no3653 p180 My 2017
getting ready with MICHELLE BREYER color *Better Homes & Gardens* v95 no11 p29 N 2017
Great Hair—in Your Sleep! M. ABERMAN color *Seventeen* v76 no2 p61 Mr 2017
Growing PAINS J. THOMPSON color *O, The Oprah Magazine* p62 Je 2017
Happy HAIR DAYS! N. Mangrum color *O, The Oprah Magazine* p82 Mr 2017
HEALTHY SHINY HAIR color *Harper's Bazaar* no3652 p249 Ap 2017

healthy summer HAIR HABITS N. JUDAR cartoon color *Better Homes & Gardens* v95 no8 p22 Ag 2017

Here We Go! Oprah color *O, The Oprah Magazine* p19 Jl 2017

How to Win at Holiday Hair M. Choi color *Glamour* v114 no12 p138 D 2016

HOW WELL DO YOU KNOW YOUR Hair? M. Goldberg color *O, The Oprah Magazine* p59 Ag 2017

inside the GH BEAUTY LAB B. ARAL and M. OZ color *Good Housekeeping* v265 no3 p34 S 2017

The Itchy and Scratchy Show Z. SCHAEFFER color *Rodale's Organic Life* v2 no7 p90 D 2016/Ja 2017

"I won't be defined by my hair choices" A. Gardner and Ying Chu color *Glamour* v115 no4 p102 Ap 2017

KERATIN V. Tweed color *Amazing Wellness* v9 no4 p24 Summ 2017

Let's Talk Curly Hair S. Kitchens bw color *Glamour* v115 no5 p86 My 2017

MAKE PEACE WITH YOUR HAIR A. FINNEY color *Women's Health* v14 no4 p152 My 2017

My Blond D. Harry and L. B. Ray color *InStyle* v24 no5 p216 My 2017

My Hair M. Ryan color *InStyle* v24 no10 p222 O 2017

Problem Solved! R. LALIBERTE color *Prevention* v68 no12 p22 D 2016

Scalp Care 101 A. Jordan color *Essence* v48 no5 p50 S 2017

Secrets of a Southern Salon A. Roderique-jones color *Southern Living* v52 no9 p37 S 2017

She Air-Dried Her Hair This Morning S. Kitchens color *Glamour* v115 no11 p69 N 2017

Tame His Mane color *Horse & Rider* v56 no9 p34 S 2017

USE THIS MUCH for great hair M. OLIVA color *Redbook* p22 My 2017

WHIRLS AND HAIR WHORLS C. Barakat and M. McCluskey color *Equus* no470 p18 N 2016

Your Hair Lookbook J. Mulrow and Ying Chu color *Glamour* v115 no4 p104 Ap 2017

YOUR ULTIMATE LOOK-GREAT MANUAL color *Redbook* p5 My 2017

Hair care products

See also

Hair conditioners

Hair dyeing & bleaching

Hair spray

Shampoos

2017's top trends for moms T. PEREZ *Parents* v92 no1 p46 Ja 2017

30 ways to wow T. PEREZ and S. M. BAUER *Parents* v91 no9 p107 S 2016

5 Ways to Use Charcoal L. TURNER color *Better Nutrition* v79 no7 p30 Jl 2017

BEAUTY Q&A color *InStyle* v23 no12 p209 N 2016

Beauty Secrets of the Desert S. Strausfogel color *Better Nutrition* v79 no11 p38 N 2017

Beauty Tools S. STRAUSFOGEL color *Better Nutrition* v79 no4 p38 Ap 2017

a breath of fresh hair *Parents* v91 no12 p69 D 2016

CAN YOU POP PILLS FOR BETTER LOOKS? M. Munson color *Esquire* p52 N 2017

color your hair like a pro T. PEREZ *Parents* v91 no11 p78 N 2016

CURL power E. METZGER *Better Homes & Gardens* v94 no11 p24 N 2016

Everything You Need to Know About... DRY SHAMPOO F. EMBLETON color *Seventeen* v76 no3 p58 My 2017

fight the fade *Parents* v91 no6 p77 Je 2016

FIGHT THE FRIZZ AND WIN! L. Desantis color *Health* v31 no3 p94 Ap 2017

FLAWLESS BEAUTY K. CHANEY and A. LUCAS bw color *Ebony* v72 no6 p42 Ap/My 2017

goodbye, frizz! color *Parents* v92 no7 p71 Jl 2017

GOOD HAIR DAYS guaranteed! A. FRANZINO color *Good Housekeeping* v265 no2 p25 Ag 2017

Great Hair Starts in the Shower color *Health* v30 no9 p14 N 2016

GREAT HAIR STARTS IN THE SHOWER [Cover story] A. FRANZINO bw chart color *Good Housekeeping* v265 no5 p43 N 2017

HAVE A GOOD HAIR DAY J. Martin color *Amazing Wellness* v8

no2 p74 Spr 2016

Janelle Monáe Is Our Hair Hero color *Health* v31 no5 p14 Je 2017

The Latest Lice Advice color *Parents* v92 no3 p20 Mr 2017

MANE MATTERS J. AMAY color *Ebony* v72/73 no12/1 p52 O/N 2017

need a lift? color *Parents* v92 no3 p63 Mr 2017

PRESERVE AND PROTECT M. MILRAD GOLDSTEIN color *Martha Stewart Living* p36 My 2017

Product Spotlights color *Better Nutrition* v79 no11 p79 N 2017

Q&A: Gabrielle Union's inspiring advice V. Kirby color *Redbook* p48 N 2017

Sneaky strategies for better hair M. OLIVA *Redbook* p50 N 2017

STRAIGHT FROM THE SOURCE M. Stefanov color *Esquire* p66 S 2017

Summer Hair 101 A. Jordan color *Essence* v48 no2 p49 Je 2017

THERMAL BRUSH N. Spradley color *Essence* v47 no11 p55 Mr 2017

USE THIS MUCH for great hair M. OLIVA color *Redbook* p22 My 2017

WE'RE BUZZING OVER HONEY color *Better Homes & Gardens* v95 no11 p22 N 2017

Your Hair Lookbook J. Mulrow color *Glamour* v115 no6 p58 Je 2017

Hair care products—Evaluation

the COMPACT N. Spradley color *Essence* v47 no10 p42 F 2017

COUNTER INTELLIGENCE M. M. GOLDSTEIN *Martha Stewart Living* no270 p76 D 2016

Does It Really Work? color *InStyle* v24 no4 p166 Ap 2017

Does It Really Work? L. Desantis color *Health* v31 no5 p31 Je 2017

Frizz Fighters color *Good Housekeeping* v265 no2 p28 Ag 2017

GET MAJOR VOLUME Guarnieri color *Harper's Bazaar* no3648 p209 N 2016

HAIR REPAIR [Cover story] M. Oliva color *Redbook* p32 Je 2017

HEALTHY SHINY CURLS color *Harper's Bazaar* no3648 p279 N 2016

Little ways to boost your color M. OLIVA color *Redbook* p54 O 2017

MAKE YOUR HAIR easy hair M. OLIVA color *Redbook* p36 S 2017

Not Your Basic Braids L. BALSAMO color *Seventeen* v76 no4 p29 Jl/Ag 2017

PAMPER YOUR CURLS *Better Homes & Gardens* v94 no11 p27 N 2016

Platinum Power color *Health* v31 no6 p18 Jl 2017

Ready for the Summer? color *Amazing Wellness* v9 no3 p88 EarlySumm 2017

Scoring the Looks You Loved I. Biedenharn and C. Ciammaichelli color *Entertainment Weekly* no1453 p20 F 17 2017

Self-Care Sunday E. Reimel color *Glamour* v115 no11 p72 N 2017

Split Ends, Begone! E. Reimel color *Glamour* v115 no5 p78 My 2017

THE WIND IN YOUR HAIR [Cover story] A. Finney bw color *Women's Health* v14 no6 p45 Jl 2017

You: Weatherproofed! D. MICHEL color *Men's Health* v32 no6 p82 Ag 2017

Hair conditioners

MALAIKA CHANEY A. Jordan color *Essence* v48 no6 p46 O 2017

"SHAMPOOING" CONDITIONERS J. Thomas color *Good Housekeeping* v263 no5 p28 N 2016

STRAIGHT FROM THE SOURCE M. Stefanov color *Esquire* p66 S 2017

Hair conditioners—Evaluation

the COMPACT J. Wilson color *Essence* v48 no5 p46 S 2017

HEALTHY SHINY CURLS color *Harper's Bazaar* no3648 p279 N 2016

Hydrating Shampoos & Conditioners color *Good Housekeeping* v265 no5 p49 N 2017

PRESERVE AND PROTECT M. MILRAD GOLDSTEIN color *Martha Stewart Living* p36 My 2017

Hair dryers

17 hairstyles that slay E. STOVALL color *Seventeen* p112 Ja 1 2017

CHOOSE YOUR OWN ADVENTURE color *O, The Oprah Mag-*

DID YOU KNOW? O. Manno color *Dance Spirit* v20 no9 p32 N 2016

The Dry Shampoo Mania Continues K. Erickson color *Glamour* v115 no10 p106 O 2017

Everything You Need to Know About... DRY SHAMPOO F. EMBLETON color *Seventeen* v76 no3 p58 My 2017

healthy summer HAIR HABITS N. JUDAR cartoon color *Better Homes & Gardens* v95 no8 p22 Ag 2017

HOW TO BE A HAIRCOLOR GENIUS K. Bennett Demaio color *O, The Oprah Magazine* p128 O 2017

MAKE PEACE WITH YOUR HAIR A. FINNEY color *Women's Health* v14 no4 p152 My 2017

Hairspray Live! (TV program)

17 QUESTIONS WITH THE CAST OF Hairspray Live! color *Seventeen* v76 no12 p16 D 2016/Ja 2017

America's top TV critic Matt Roush answers your burning questions M. Roush *TV Guide* v65 no2 p6 Ja 2 2017

THE BEAT GOES ON J. HALTERMAN *TV Guide* p34 D 5 2016

COUCH CULTURE C. ZULKEY color *Chicago* v65 no12 p47 D 2016

Hairspray Live! Promises Retro Fun With Little Risk D. D'Addario color *Time* v188 no24 p68 D 12 2016

MADDIE BAILLIO M. Snetiker color *Entertainment Weekly* no1442 p51 D 2 2016 Rebellious Special Issue

You Can't Stop the Chic M. Snetiker color *Entertainment Weekly* no1442 p51 D 2 2016 Rebellious Special Issue

Hairstyles

17 hairstyles that slay E. STOVALL color *Seventeen* p112 Ja 1 2017

2017 SUMMER HAIR Handbook color *O, The Oprah Magazine* p58 Jl 2017

5 beauty tricks I just learned V. Kirby color *Redbook* p65 D 2016

Alicia Keys color *InStyle* v24 no4 p156 Ap 2017

The Bob SQUAD A. Serrano color *InStyle* v24 no6 p81 Je 2017

BowWow C. Malle and C. ELLENBERG color *Vogue* v207 no9 p450 S 2017

CURL power E. METZGER *Better Homes & Gardens* v94 no11 p24 N 2016

Curl POWER J. Thompson color *O, The Oprah Magazine* p78 O 2017

Curly Cues N. Spradley color *Essence* v47 no11 p47 Mr 2017

The Devil on My Shoulders T. PRODANOVICH color *Surfer* v58 no3 p94 Je 2017

The Dos of Summer Hair K. Erickson color *Glamour* v114 no7 p80 Jl 2016

double-duty dos K. Foster color *Seventeen* p194 Ja 1 2017

Dressed-up hair that's so simple P. STABLES color *Redbook* p60 D 2016

Friendship Ponies color *Glamour* v115 no7 p17 Jl 2017

Frizz Fighters color *Good Housekeeping* v265 no2 p28 Ag 2017

Fun 1st-Day STYLES E. STOVALL color *Seventeen* v76 no5 p42 S 2017

Gilty Treasure color *Good Housekeeping* v263 no5 p21 N 2016

GOOD HAIR DAYS guaranteed! A. FRANZINO color *Good Housekeeping* v265 no2 p25 Ag 2017

Great Hair—in Your Sleep! M. ABERMAN color *Seventeen* v76 no2 p61 Mr 2017

GREAT LENGTHS bw color *Vogue* v207 no9 p440 S 2017

Hair Horoscopes color *Essence* v47 no9 p36 Ja 2017

Hair Ribbons color *InStyle* v23 no13 p180 D 2016

HAIR TO BE DIFFERENT S. Kwak color *Sports Illustrated* v127 no12 p20 O 16 2017

HOLIDAY #HAIRGOALS color *Ebony* v72 no3 p58 D 2016/Ja 2017

INDEPENDENT SPIRIT L. Kamps, E. DOUGHERTY et al color *O, The Oprah Magazine* p113 My 2017

Let's Talk Curly Hair S. Kitchens bw color *Glamour* v115 no5 p86 My 2017

Merry Manes N. Spradley color *Essence* v47 no8 p61 D 2016

MET GALA MADNESS R. Kinane color *Entertainment Weekly* no1465 p12 My 12 2017

"My dreads gave me time" S. Kitchens and Ying Chu color *Glamour* v115 no3 p118 Mr 2017

Natural WOMAN J. Thompson color *O, The Oprah Magazine* p74 F 2017

Party-Hair Lookbook J. Mulrow color *Glamour* v114 no12 p142

D 2016

PARTY LINES [Cover story] img *New York* p85 Ja 9 2017

THE PERFECT HAIR CUT FINDER [Cover story] M. OLIVA bw color *Redbook* p36 Ap 2017

Score Your HAIR GOALS K. CASTAÑON cartoon color *Seventeen* v75 no11 p39 N 2016

Scoring the Looks You Loved I. Biedenharn and C. Ciammaichelli color *Entertainment Weekly* no1435 p16 O 14 2016

SHAGADELIC, BABY! bw color *Esquire* p50 Je/Jl 2017

She's Bangin' N. Spradley color *Essence* v47 no7 p39 N 2016

SHOULD I GET BANGS? A. FINNEY color *Women's Health* v14 no1 p164 Ja/F 2017

TAKE IT OFF [Cover story] M. Lynch color *Women's Health* v14 no7 p64 S 2017

TALKING HEADS color *O, The Oprah Magazine* p128 Ap 2017

This woman is about to cut her hair off [Cover story] Y. Chu color *Glamour* no8 p136 Ag 2017

Trending Tresses A. Jordan color *Essence* v48 no5 p53 S 2017

Waves Like This [Cover story] K. Erickson and Y. Chu bw color *Glamour* v114 no11 p97 N 2016

Which Legion Hairstyle Is Right for You? A. WEATHERFORD img *New York* v50 no8 p121 Ap 17 2017

The Year of the Detail J. Harman color *Glamour* v114 no12 p77 D 2016

YOUR CHEAT SHEET TO... The Perfect Prom Night M. MANNARINO color *Seventeen* p208 Ja 1 2017

Your Hair Lookbook J. Mulrow and Ying Chu color *Glamour* v115 no4 p104 Ap 2017

Your Hair Lookbook J. Mulrow color *Glamour* v115 no10 p90 O 2017

Your Hair Lookbook J. Mulrow color *Glamour* v115 no6 p58 Je 2017

Your Hair This Summer K. Erickson color *Glamour* v115 no6 p55 Je 2017

Hairstyles—Equipment & supplies

HOLD STEADY color *Vogue* v206 no12 p266 D 2016

Hairy Ape, The (Theatrical production)

Primal Edge H. Als cartoon *New Yorker* v93 no6 p6 Mr 27 2017

Haitian diaspora

New Respect for Haiti's Kamoken T. PADGETT *America* v215 p12 N 28 2016

Haitian refugees

Forsaken at the Border? J. McDERMOTT *America* v215 no11 p11 O 17 2016

Haitian Revolution, 1791-1804

What We Learned From... The Haitian Revolution J. Byrne color *Military History* v34 no5 p18 Ja 2018

Haitians—United States

MIAMI E. Danticat *Harper's Magazine* p34 O 2017

Haiti—Description & travel

5 Reasons to Visit the First Free Black Republic O. RAYMOND and D. POINTDUJOUR color *Ebony* v72 no4 p68 F 2017

Haiti Earthquake, Haiti, 2010

Haiti's 'Republic of NGOs' M. SCHULLER *Current History* v116 no787 p68 F 2017

Haiti—Economic conditions

HAITI IN CRISIS B. BROWN, P. SMITH et al *New York Times Upfront* v149 no6 p8 D 12 2016

Haiti—Politics & government—1986-

New Respect for Haiti's Kamoken T. PADGETT *America* v215 p12 N 28 2016

Haiti—Social conditions

Church Agencies Prepare Emergency Response in Haiti K. CLARKE color *America* v215 no12 p8 O 24 2016

Haiyan Wang

How China's Government Helps—and Hinders—Innovation *Harvard Business Review Digital Articles* p2 N 16 2016

Multinationals Have a Bright Future, If You Know Where to Look *Harvard Business Review Digital Articles* p2 Je 14 2017

The Reason Silicon Valley Beat Out Boston for VC Dominance *Harvard Business Review Digital Articles* p2 N 15 2016

Hajdu, David, 1955-

Bob the Bard *Nation* v303 no19 p6 N 7 2016

BOLD-SOUNDING THINGS *Nation* v304 no17 p42 Je 5 2017

CRUISING TO THE EDGE color *Nation* v305 no3 p35 Jl 31 2017

Missing Notes J. M. Wilson bw *Commonweal* v143 no18 p44 N

11 2016

Pop Music Is Smarter Than It Appears S. Begley color *Time* v188 no14 p22 O 10 2016

REDEMPTION SONG color *Nation* v303 no25/26 p36 D 19 2016

TOP OF THE POPS J. WINDOLF color *New York Times Book Review* p71 D 4 2016

Hájková, Anna

NEW AVENUES OF GERMANY'S PAST: As Holocaust survivors die, new approaches are required to tell their history, as shown in this unsentimental, emphatic account of the inhabitants of a Berlin street *History Today* v67 no7 p104 Jl 2017

Hakala, Jani

Global atmospheric particle formation from CERN CLOUD measurements bibl graph map *Science* v354 no6316 p1119 D 2 2016

HAKAMI, RAMZI

Predatory Journals: Write, Submit, and Publish the Next Day *Skeptical Inquirer* v41 no5 p32 S/O 2017

Håkansson, Krister

A RARE SUCCESS AGAINST ALZHEIMER'S [Cover story] color graph *Scientific American* v316 no4 p32 Ap 2017

Hakim, David

THE CREATIVE GENIUSES BEHIND "CARS" color *Hot Rod* v70 no8 p42 Ag 2017

Hakimpour, Paul

mTOR regulates metabolic adaptation of APCs in the lung and controls the outcome of allergic inflammation graph *Science* v357 no6355 p1014 S 8 2017

Halal food

Halal from Farm to Fork: To build trust, the halal meat certification system needs a tune-up M. ABDULLAH *Islamic Horizons* v46 no3 p32 My/Je 2017

Halal food industry—History

Halal's Rise From Street Carts to Whole Foods J. Green, C. Giammona et al color *Bloomberg Businessweek* no4494 p24 O 10 2016

Halamka, John D.

The Potential for Blockchain to Transform Electronic Health Records bw *Harvard Business Review Digital Articles* p2 Mr 3 2017

Using Big Data to Make Wiser Medical Decisions *Harvard Business Review Digital Articles* p2 D 14 2015

Halas, George, 1895-1983

WHAT IF? ... GEORGE HALAS—AND THE NFL—HAD SUNK IN LAKE MICHIGAN? K. Kahler and J. Feldman color *Sports Illustrated* v126 no11 p51 Ap 17-24 2017

Halberstam, David

ON MARTIN LUTHER KING *Harper's Magazine* v334 no2001 p39 F 2017

Halberstam, David, 1934-2007

Pursuing big dreams, Halberstam started small J. Friedman bw color *Columbia Journalism Review* v56 no1 p48 Spr 2017

Halbertal, Moshe

Saul and David's destructive powers W. Brueggemann *Christian Century* v134 no16 p30 Ag 2 2017

Haldane, Duncan—Awards

Foundational theories in topological physics garner Nobel Prize Sung Chang *Physics Today* v69 no12 p14 D 2016

Haldane, John

Evil to Good to God bw *Commonweal* v144 no5 p13 Mr 10 2017

HALDEMAN, PETER

MAN OF THE HOUSE *Los Angeles Magazine* v61 no11 p134 N 2016

Halderman, H. R.

NIXON'S S.O.B C. Whipple bw color *American History* v52 no4 p48 O 2017

Hale, Henry E.

Russian Patronal Politics Beyond Putin *Daedalus* v146 no2 p30 Spr 2017

Hale, Iago

Wild emmer genome architecture and diversity elucidate wheat evolution and domestication color *Science* v357 no6346 p93 Jl 7 2017

Hale, James

53rd Street color *Downbeat* v84 no2 p79 F 2017

ABUC color *Downbeat* v83 no12 p79 D 2016

ACT CELEBRATES 25 color *Downbeat* v84 no6 p59 Je 2017

CJA Sets Students on Positive Path with Music color *Downbeat* v84 no5 p142 My 2017

CJC EXPANDS SIZE, OFFERINGS color *Downbeat* v84 no10 p154 O 2017

Coker Fosters Customized Learning at New School color *Downbeat* v84 no7 p86 Jl 2017

CSULB Students Meet High Standards color *Downbeat* v84 no8 p94 Ag 2017

FOCUSYEAR BASEL GOES DEEP color *Downbeat* v84 no3 p105 Mr 2017

HERBIE NICHOLS: RIGHTFUL HONOR bw *Downbeat* v84 no8 p36 Ag 2017

'I HAVE EVERYTHING' bw *Downbeat* v83 no12 p46 D 2016

JANE IRA BLOOM: CHASING A MERCURIAL SOUND bw *Downbeat* v84 no8 p46 Ag 2017

JU Creates 'Holistic' Musicians color *Downbeat* v84 no10 p198 O 2017

LITCHFIELD FOSTERS 'LIFETIME CONNECTIONS' color *Downbeat* v84 no3 p72 Mr 2017

MAUREEN CHOI color *Downbeat* v84 no9 p25 S 2017

MSM Hires Harris for Jazz Program color *Downbeat* v84 no3 p118 Mr 2017

Revealing Liaisons bw *Downbeat* v84 no1 p32 Ja 2017

THELONIOUS MONK bw *Downbeat* v84 no1 p30 Ja 2017

Toronto Highlights Diversity color *Downbeat* v84 no5 p127 My 2017

Wayne State Faces Bright Future color *Downbeat* v84 no9 p102 S 2017

Hale, Jennifer

HACKER CRACK-UP color *Wired* v25 no6 p10 Je 2017

HALE, JOHN R.

TRACKING MYTHS color *Scientific American* v316 no4 p6 Ap 2017

HALE, KATHLEEN

Singled Out color *Vogue* v207 no11 p166 N 2017

Hale, Lucy, 1989——Interviews

PRETTY LITTLE LIARS S. Highfill color *Entertainment Weekly* no1468/1469 p56 Je 2-9 2017

Hale, Ronald

THE GREEN RUSH color *Earth Island Journal* v32 no4 p41 Wint 2017

Hale, Shannon

The Littlest Frenemies: Elementary-school social life has its perils in this middle-grade graphic memoir K. MESSNER *New York Times Book Review* p26 My 14 2017

Hale, Tom

TENDER CHOICES color *Sail* v48 no4 p50 Ap 2017

YARD CARE color *Sail* v48 no10 p72 O 2017

Hale, Tony

Parental Guidance M. Rubino *Indianapolis Monthly* v40 no4 p12 D 2016

Halep, Simona, 1991-

Simona Halep *Tennis* v53 no1 p50 Ja/F 2017

Halevy, I.

The geologic history of seawater pH bibl diag *Science* v355 no6329 p1069 Mr 10 2017

Halevy, Nir

How Powerful, Low-Status Jobs Lead to Conflict *Harvard Business Review Digital Articles* p2 F 11 2016

HALEY, BRENDAN

RECENT OUTINGS color *Advocate* no1090 p15 Ap 2017

Haley, Brett

A Cowboy Makes a Comeback In The Hero S. Zacharek color *Time* v189 no23 p51 Je 19 2017

Sam Elliott E. Berman *Time* v189 no23 p51 Je 19 2017

Haley, D.

Direct observation of individual hydrogen atoms at trapping sites in a ferritic steel bibl diag *Science* v355 no6330 p1196 Mr 17 2017

Haley, Garrett

My President Was Black *Atlantic* v319 no2 p8 Mr 2017

HALEY, HOSS

What's your favorite work of public art? color *American Craft* v77 no3 p16 Je/Jl 2017

Haley, Nikki, 1972——Interviews

The World Is Watching A. Parker color *Glamour* v115 no11 p115

N 2017

Half Dome (Calif.)
YOSEMITE NATIONAL PARK, CALIFORNIA color *Runner's World* v52 no7 p8 Ag 2017

Half-life (Nuclear physics)
Rarest nucleus reluctant to decay E. CONOVER *Science News* v190 no9 p11 O 29 2016

Half marathons (Running)
ASK THE EXPERTS H. North, M. Merlino et al color *Runner's World* v52 no2 p36 Mr 2017
CAPE COVE, OREGON color *Runner's World* v52 no6 p8 Jl 2017
CHUCK TODD C. Bethea color *Runner's World* v52 no2 p96 Mr 2017
Finding Grace C. MICHEL cartoon color *Runner's World* v52 no6 p52 Jl 2017
GET READY, GET SET... M. KITA chart color *Runner's World* v52 no7 p71 Ag 2017
A GOOD, LONG RUN color *Runner's World* v52 no6 p12 Jl 2017
RACE TO THE AFTER-PARTY [Cover story] A. C. SHILTON color *Runner's World* v52 no2 p86 Mr 2017

Half Waif (Performer)
Follow Ahead M. Trammell cartoon *New Yorker* v93 no8 p6 Ap 10 2017

Halfon, Robert—Interviews
"THIS ISN'T A STEALTH TAX": Skills minister Robert Halfon explains the thinking behind the apprenticeship levy R. Halfon *People Management* p37 Ap 2017

Halford, Macy
Higher Yearning C. BAUER *New York Times Book Review* p17 F 19 2017
My Utmost: A Devotional Memoir V. Weaver-Zercher color *Christian Century* v134 no10 p51 My 10 2017
O & I J. Wilson color *Commonweal* v144 no8 p36 My 5 2017

Halfpap, Brad
Storm in a Teacup: The Physics of Everyday Life *Physics Today* v70 no8 p59 Ag 2017

Haliburton Highlands (Ont.)
Chantal Kreviazuk A. Kylie color *Canadian Geographic* v135 no6 p86 D 2015

Halibut
FOOLPROOF HALIBUT M. HENNESSY color *Chicago* v66 no4 p58 Ap 2017

Halides
Improving efficiency and stability of perovskite solar cells with photocurable fluoropolymers F. Bella, G. Griffini et al bibl chart graph *Science* v354 no6309 p203 O 14 2016

Halifax (Bomber)
On the Nose bw *Military History* v34 no1 p80 My 2017

Halifax Explosion, Halifax, N.S., 1917
Retelling a tragedy M. CAMPBELL bw *Maclean's* v129 no51/52 p33 D 26 2016

HALL, ALEXANDRA
BLEND THE PAST WITH THE PRESENT *Yankee* v81 no1 p33 Ja/F 2017

Hall, Anthony Michael
PULVERIZER T. Friend cartoon *New Yorker* v93 no17 p21 Je 19 2017

Hall, April
EQUAL OPPORTUNITY CLASSROOMS color *Literacy Today (2411-7862)* v34 no5 p38 Mr/Ap 2017

Hall, Beth
Holding All the Cards color *AARP: The Magazine* v60 no5A p64 Ag/S 2017

Hall, Brandon
Breaking Big BRANDON MICHEAL HALL D. Franich, N. Abrams et al color *Entertainment Weekly* no1482/1483 p65 S 22 2017

Hall, Brenten
WORLD SERIES FINALE XI B. WELCH color *Spin to Win Rodeo* v20 no11 p56 Ja 2017

Hall, Carla
Apple cider is amazing color *Redbook* p28 N 2017
Cauliflower miracles color *Redbook* p38 F 2017
The easiest crowd-pleasing brunch color *Redbook* p28 Ap 2017
Here's the dessert that bakes itself! color *Redbook* p23 Mr 2017

Meet your new favorite vegetable color *Redbook* p22 Je 2017
A perfect (and easy!) pot pie color *Redbook* p30 O 2017
Quick-pickle anything color *Redbook* p22 S 2017
Stellar, surprising salsas color *Redbook* p30 My 2017
The ultimate easy chicken dinner color *Redbook* p22 Jl/Ag 2017
Your ultimate busy-night meal color *Redbook* p34 D 2016

HALL, CAROL M.
Expanding the Portfolio: Conserving Nature's Masterpieces in a Changing World *BioScience* v67 no6 p568 Je 2017

HALL, CAROLYN J.
Damming, Lost Connectivity, and the Historical Role of Anadromous Fish in Freshwater Ecosystem Dynamics *BioScience* v67 no8 p713 Ag 2017

Hall, Carrie
Study: Customers Really Do Trust Family Businesses More *Harvard Business Review Digital Articles* p2 Ap 27 2015

HALL, CHARLES A. S.
Our Renewable Future: Laying the Path for One Hundred Percent Clean Energy *BioScience* v66 no12 p1080 D 1 2016

Hall, Christopher
DAVIS, CA color map *Sunset* v238 no4 p36 Ap 2017
In Search of Serenity color *AARP: The Magazine* v60 no3A p40B Ap/My 2017
Wine, Dine and Wine Some More color *AARP: The Magazine* v59 no5A p59 Ag/S 2016

Hall, David
EYES ON THE ROAD A. OHNSMAN color *Forbes* v200 no2 p78 S 5 2017

Hall, Dick
Where Buffett Failed N. Buhayar color *Bloomberg Businessweek* no4527 p41 Je 19 2017

Hall, Emily Nabors
CUT TO THE CAKES color *Southern Living* v51 no12 p156 D 2016
THE SOUTHERN LIVING CAST-IRON COOKBOOK color *Southern Living* v52 no9 p106 S 2017

Hall, George
Der Rosenkavalier *Opera News* v81 no9 p44 Mr 2017
Norma *Opera News* v81 no6 p46 D 2016
The Nose *Opera News* v81 no7 p43 Ja 2017
The Snow Maiden *Opera News* v81 no10 p46 Ap 2017

Hall, Gerrad
3 ROUNDS WITH HANSON color *Entertainment Weekly* no1467 p40 My 26 2017
Family Matters color *Entertainment Weekly* no1485 p24 O 6 2017
THE GOLDEN AGE OF HAIM color *Entertainment Weekly* no1467 p32 My 26 2017
KENDRICK & GAGA HEAT UP THE DESERT color *Entertainment Weekly* no1463/1464 p106 Ap/My 2017
THE TRANSFORMATION OF KATY PERRY color *Entertainment Weekly* no1467 p28 My 26 2017

Hall, Harley
1987 Jeep Grand Wagoneer color *Popular Mechanics* p66 D 2016/Ja 2017

Hall, Harriet
5 THINGS WE KNOW TO BE TRUE cartoon *Scientific American* v315 no5 p46 N 2016
My Personal Odyssey in Skepticism *Skeptical Inquirer* v40 no6 p37 N/D 2016
Odysseys in Skepticism T. Randall, J. Cooper et al *Skeptical Inquirer* v41 no2 p65 Mr/Ap 2017
Statin Denialism *Skeptical Inquirer* v41 no3 p40 My/Je 2017
The Story of the Gene *Skeptical Inquirer* v41 no1 p59 Ja/F 2017

Hall, Jeffrey
How FLAGSTAFF is preserving DARK SKIES color graph *Astronomy* v45 no9 p54 S 2017

Hall, Jeffrey C., 1945-
Revelations about rhythm of life rewarded E. Stokstad and G. Vogel color *Science* v357 no6359 p18 O 6 2017

Hall, John
Byzantine Tale *History Today* v67 no3 p66 Mr 2017
Content Marketers Should Find Spokespeople Outside the C-Suite *Harvard Business Review Digital Articles* p2 Ja 7 2016

Hall, Julia
Changing climate shifts timing of European floods color graph *Science* v357 no6351 p588 Ag 11 2017

HALL, KATE
Laugh Lines color *Reader's Digest* v189 no1130 p107 My 2017

Hall, Kim
BARN DOORS D. Howland color *Cabin Living* p9 Je 2017

HALL, KIRSTEN
A Hundred Years of Summer color *Weekly Standard* v22 no48 p34 S 4 2017

Hall, Larry
NORTHERN EXPOSURE B. COOK color map *Sail* v48 no11 p40 N 2017

Hall, Lauren
The Class of 2017: Seven new faces at New York Fashion Week S. Franklin img *New York* v50 no18 p49 S 4 2017
Rehumanizing Birth and Death in America *Society* v54 no3 p226 Je 2017

Hall, Marcia B., 1939-
Naples J. Gardner color *Magazine Antiques* v184 no4 p54 Jl/Ag 2017

HALL, MICHAEL
the FACES of OBAMACARE *Texas Monthly* v45 no3 p116 Mr 2017
THE TROUBLE WITH INNOCENCE *Texas Monthly* v45 no4 p96 Ap 2017
TYLER TWO-STEP *Texas Monthly* v45 no6 p118 Je 2017

Hall, Mitch—Interviews
Six's technical adviser, Mitch Hall D. Holbrook *TV Guide* v65 no8 p15 F 27 2017

Hall, Monty, 1921-2017
1921-2017 REMEMBERING MONTY HALL L. Rice color *Entertainment Weekly* no1486 p50 O 13 2017

Hall, Patricia
Cover Up color *Publishers Weekly* v264 no14 p55 Ap 3. 2017

Hall, Peter, 1930-2017
Milestones *Time* v190 no12 p15 S 25 2017

Hall, Rachel Howzell
City of Saviors *Publishers Weekly* v264 no26 p157 Je 26 2017

Hall, Rebecca, 1982-
Rebecca Hall J. Johnson color *Current Biography* v78 no4 p33 Ap 2017
The Women Behind Wonder Woman S. Zacharek color *Time* v190 no16/17 p103 O 23 2017

Hall, Rebecca—Interviews
Rebecca Hall S. Lansky color *Time* v188 no16/17 p89 O 24 2016

Hall, Regina
GIRL TRIPPING R. R. Robertson color *Essence* v48 no3 p82 Jl 2017
Starcation: New Orleans O. I. Williams color *Ebony* v72 no9 p58 Jl/Ag 2017

Hall, Regina—Interviews
DEEP DISH WITH THE STARS OF GIRLS TRIP T. Stack color *Entertainment Weekly* no1474/1475 p100 Jl 21-28 2017

Hall, Shannon
Fast Radio Burst Has Surprising Source *Sky & Telescope* v133 no4 p10 Ap 2017
Fire and Ice color *Scientific American* v317 no2 p22 Ag 2017
Kepler Team Releases Final Catalog *Sky & Telescope* v134 no4 p10 O 2017
The Milky Way, Transformed color *Scientific American* v315 no6 p14 D 2016

Hall, Stephen S.
The Cancer Lottery bw *MIT Technology Review* v120 no1 p34 Ja/F 2017
THE RED LINE color diag *Scientific American* v315 no3 p54 S 2016

Hall, Steven—Interviews
ON KOMPROMAT A. Dejean, H. Levintova et al bw *Mother Jones* v42 no4 p24 Jl/Ag 2017

Hall, Stuart, 1932-2014
A STARTING POINT FOR POLITICS B. ROBBINS bw *Nation* v303 no20 p27 N 14 2016

Hall, Susan L.
SO MANY WORDS, SO LITTLE TIME: How morphological awareness can help young learners with their vocabulary comprehension *Literacy Today (2411-7862)* v35 no1 p26 Jl/Ag 2017

Hall, Taddy
Searching for New Ideas in the Curious Things Your Customers

Do *Harvard Business Review Digital Articles* p2 Ap 13 2017

HALL, TAMRON
42 new ALL-STAR PRODUCTS of the year [Cover story] color *Redbook* p27 Jl/Ag 2017

Hall, Taylor
China's Twitter Returns From the Dead color graph *Bloomberg Businessweek* no4526 p28 Je 12 2017
Why Machines Still Can't Learn So Good cartoon *Bloomberg Businessweek* no4499 p55 N 14 2016

Hall, Thomas
The new Barbados color map *Canadian Geographic* v135 no6 p9 D 2015
Ziya Tong color *Canadian Geographic* v137 no5 p82 S/O 2017

Hall, Wendy
Science of the World Wide Web bibl color *Science* v354 no6313 p703 N 11 2016

Hall China Co.
FUN SIZE F. VIGNA color *Martha Stewart Living* p124 Jl/Ag 2017

Hall effect
See also
Anomalous Hall effect
Quantum spin Hall effect
Hall-effect metamaterials and "anti-Hall bars" M. Wegener, M. Kadic et al *Physics Today* v70 no10 p14 O 2017
Semiconductor metamaterial fools the Hall effect J. Miller *Physics Today* v70 no2 p21 F 2017

Halla, Brian
Piecing Together the Tesla Strategy Puzzle *Harvard Business Review Digital Articles* p2 S 16 2015

Hallam, Toby
All-printed thin-film transistors from networks of liquid-exfoliated nanosheets diag *Science* v356 no6333 p69 Ap 7 2017

Hallas, Tony
PLANETARY WEIGHT LOSS color *Astronomy* v45 no4 p34 Ap 2017
Stellarvue's Optimus eyepieces tested color *Astronomy* v45 no5 p62 My 2017

Hallast, Pille
Chimpanzee genomic diversity reveals ancient admixture with bonobos bibl diag graph map *Science* v354 no6311 p477 O 28 2016

Hallberg, David
All the Way Back R. Milzoff and R. Afanador img *New York* v50 no10 p81 My 15 2017
David Hallberg *Dance Magazine* v91 no6 p6 Je 2017
THE REBIRTH OF DAVID HALLBERG C. THOMPSON *Dance Magazine* v91 no6 p26 Je 2017

HALLBERG, DEBORAH
FROM THE ARCHIVES bw color *Reason* v49 no3 p70 Jl 2017

HALLBERG, GARTH RISK
The Lion Tamer's Dance: In a collection of finely honed miniature essays, Karl Ove Knausgaard describes the world for his unborn child *New York Times Book Review* p13 O 1 2017

Hallberg-Rassy Varvs AB
Magnus Rassy A. Schell color *Sail* v48 no3 p14 Mr 2017

Halldór Laxness, 1902-1998
FLESH AND BLOOD J. Taylor *Harper's Magazine* v333 no1998 p87 N 2016

Halleluiah (Music)
How the Light Gets In C. Raab bw *Commonweal* v144 no8 p15 My 5 2017

Haller, David
Legion M. Roffman *TV Guide* v65 no6 p38 Ja 30 2017

Hallett, Christine E.
SAVING LIVES ON THE FRONT LINE *History Today* v67 no7 p24 Jl 2017

Hallett, Joe
THE PERFECT CHIP color *Golf Magazine* v59 no5 p49 My 2017

Hallett, Michael
Faith at Angola Prison bw *Commonweal* v144 no7 p10 Ap 14 2017

Halley, Lexi
Psychology Of Green color *Alternatives Journal (AJ) - Canada's Environmental Voice* v42 no3 p51 2016

Halliday, Jo E. B.

Driving improvements in emerging disease surveillance through locally relevant capacity strengthening color diag *Science* v357 no6347 p146 Jl 14 2017

Halliday, Karen J.

Light-sensing phytochromes feel the heat bibl color *Science* v354 no6314 p832 N 18 2016

HALLIGAN, ASHLEY M.

Easy Living map *Backpacker* p19 O 2017

Halligan, Brian

How Decision Making Evolves as a Startup Grows *Harvard Business Review Digital Articles* p2 Mr 23 2016

Halligan, Jessi—Interviews

Q&A S. POTTER color *Discover* v27 no10 p10 D 2016

Halliwell, Geri, 1972-

Ginger Spice J. Goodman color *Entertainment Weekly* no1460/1461 p71 Ap 7-17 2017

HALLMAN, TOM

CAN'T ANYONE HEAR ME? color *Reader's Digest* v190 no1133 p98 S 2017

She Was My Prosecutor *Reader's Digest* v188 no1124 p90 O 2016

They Did the Right Thing cartoon *Reader's Digest* v190 no1134 p88 O 2017

Hallmark Cards Inc.

THE QUEEN OF CHRISTMAS M. Callahan color *Bloomberg Businessweek* no4499 p79 N 14 2016

Hallmundarhraun Volcanic Field (Iceland)

THE BLACKENER'S CAVE S. S. PATEL color *Archaeology* v70 no3 p36 My/Je 2017

HALLOCK, BETTY

THE BEST NEW RESTAURANTS *Los Angeles Magazine* p86 Ja 2017

THE HOT LIST *Los Angeles Magazine* p132 D 2016

The New Art of Dessert *Los Angeles Magazine* v61 no11 p124 N 2016

Ramen Gone Wild *Los Angeles Magazine* p48 F 2017

Halloran, Bernie

Deal the seal C. SORENSEN color *Maclean's* v130 no2 p11 Mr 2017

Halloran, Tim

A Simple Way to Measure How Much Customers Love Your Brand *Harvard Business Review Digital Articles* p2 F 3 2015

Halloween

> *See also*
>
> Halloween decorations

Blessings in Disguise M. Bodgas color *Working Mother* v40 no4 p6 O/N 2017

Chapman's RV campers host riverside trick-or-treat adventure E. CASE color *Nebraska Life* v21 no5 p81 S/O 2017

Suckers and Cemeteries S. CARR *Idaho Magazine* v16 no2 p54 N 2016

TWISTED TERRIBLE TAKES! *Atlanta* v57 no6 p52 O 2017

What In The World? color *National Geographic Kids* no474 p29 O 2017

WICKED GOOD TIME: New Orleans is a decadent location to spend Halloween D. ARTAVIA *Advocate* no1093 p62 O/N 2017

Halloween cooking

Boo-scotti color *Good Housekeeping* v265 no4 p131 O 2017

Halloween costumes

Costume Chaos cartoon *National Geographic Kids* no474 p28 O 2017

Funny Fill-In S. YOUNGSON cartoon *National Geographic Kids* no474 p31 O 2017

Pop-tastic! bw cartoon color *Martha Stewart Living* p25 O 2017

SPOOK - Tacular! JOHNSON *Treasures* v6 no2 p45 O/N 2016

Wild Things E. N. GAGE color *Martha Stewart Living* p31 O 2017

Halloween decorations

All Keyed Up F. VIGNA color *Martha Stewart Living* p144 O 2017

BEAUTIFUL CREATURES J. TUNG *Martha Stewart Living* no268 p33 O 2016

better S. LIAO color *Better Homes & Gardens* v95 no10 p172 O 2017

A Little Night Magic E. N. GAGE color *Martha Stewart Living* p104 O 2017

SPOOK - Tacular! JOHNSON *Treasures* v6 no2 p45 O/N 2016

What In The World? color *National Geographic Kids* no474 p29 O 2017

Halloween in art

IN GOOD SPIRITS D. DICKINSON color *Better Homes & Gardens* v95 no10 p140 O 2017

Halloween parties

Amazing Animals A. SILEN color *National Geographic Kids* no474 p8 O 2017

Costume Chaos cartoon *National Geographic Kids* no474 p28 O 2017

Funny Fill-In S. YOUNGSON cartoon *National Geographic Kids* no474 p31 O 2017

Halloween Wars (TV program)

ALL OF YOUR RETURNING FAVORITES! *TV Guide* v65 no39 p56 S 18 2017

Halloween—Exhibitions

ABOVE & BEYOND cartoon *New Yorker* v92 no34 p16 O 24 2016

Halloween—History

The Architecture of Belief C. Valentino color *Archaeology* v69 no6 p4 N/D 2016

SAMHAIN REVIVAL E. MULLALLY color *Archaeology* v69 no6 p34 N/D 2016

Halloween—Humor

UNBURIED I. FRAZIER cartoon *New Yorker* v92 no35 p41 O 31 2016

Halls of fame

the 2016 HALL of FAME J. WOLCOTT bw cartoon color *Vanity Fair* v59 no1 p117 Holiday 2017

Celebrating Four Decades of Fame N. Jaffer *In Stride* v12 no2 p53 Mr 2017

MAURICE SMITH bw *Black Belt* v55 no5 p12 Ag/S 2017

Hallstatt period

Iron Age trade secrets revealed B. BOWER color *Science News* v191 no4 p17 Mr 4 2017

Hallström, Lasse

A Dog's Purpose L. Greenblatt color *Entertainment Weekly* no1451/1452 p88 F 3-10 2017

Humans Give Meaning to A Dog's Purpose S. Zacharek color *Time* v189 no4 p52 F 6 2017

Hallucinations & illusions

> *See also*
>
> Optical illusions

CIRCLING LHASA J. HERTOG bw *Tricycle: The Buddhist Review* v26 no3 p74 Spr 2017

clock-stoppers C. Maldarelli color *Popular Science* v289 no5 p88 S/O 2017

Misperceptions S. MARTINEZ-CONDE and S. L. MACKNIK bw color *Natural History* v125 no10 p16 O 2017

Pavlovian conditioning–induced hallucinations result from overweighting of perceptual priors A. R. Powers, C. Mathys et al diag *Science* v357 no6351 p596 Ag 11 2017

SEASONS FLEETING D. Copaken color *O, The Oprah Magazine* p35 S 2017

Hallucinogenic drugs

> *See also*
>
> LSD (Drug)

Can You Trip Your Way Out of Anxiety? M. SHAER cartoon *Men's Health* v32 no4 p88 My 2017

Hallucinogenic drugs—Law & legislation

The Psychedelic Miracle M. McCLELLAND cartoon color *Rolling Stone* no1283 p40 Mr 23 2017

Hallucinogenic drugs—Therapeutic use

A DOORWAY TO CHANGE J. Bleyer *Psychology Today* v50 no3 p60 My/Je 2017

OUT OF THE DUSTBIN *Psychology Today* v49 no6 p16 N/D 2016

The Psychedelic Miracle M. McCLELLAND cartoon color *Rolling Stone* no1283 p40 Mr 23 2017

Hallucinogenic plants

CONNECTING TWO REALMS R. ATWOOD color *Archaeology* v70 no4 p55 Je-Ag 2017

Hallux valgus—Prevention

the secret bunion society L. GOLDMAN color *Parents* v92 no7 p84 Jl 2017

Hallux valgus—Risk factors

the secret bunion society L. GOLDMAN color *Parents* v92 no7 p84 Jl 2017

Halo effect (Psychology)

Revolution: Removing its Halo E. Goodheart *Society* v54 no2 p100 Ap 2017

HALPER, DANIEL

The Anatomy of Defeat *Commentary* v143 no6 p50 Je 2017

ELECTION BOMBSHELL: 'I SLEPT WITH BILL' color *Weekly Standard* v22 no9 p40 N 7 2016

Halperin, Jimmy

Live At A-Trane: Berlin B. Zimmerman bw *Downbeat* v84 no5 p59 My 2017

HALPERIN, JULIA

ENGINEERED TO DECEIVE bw color diag *Wired* v25 no5 p92 My 2017

HALPERN, ASHLEA

The Dark Art of How (and When) to Buy an Airline Ticket img *New York* v50 no10 p70 My 15 2017

ICE CYCLE color *Wired* v25 no6 p26 Je 2017

"I READ CRIME FICTION ON THE PLANE—IT TAKES MY MIND OFF MY OWN LIFE" color *Conde Nast Traveler* v51 no10 p42 N 2016

Mail Models color *Bon Appetit* v61 no12 p69 D 2016 /Jan2017

SNORKEL WITH SHARKS color *Wired* v25 no10 p38 O 2017

THE URBANIST: Seoul: Soy-brined fried pickhs, abandoned amusement parks, sneaker bars img *New York* v50 no16 p90 Ag 7 2017

HALPERN, BENJAMIN S.

Synthesis Centers as Critical Research Infrastructure *BioScience* v67 no8 p750 Ag 2017

HALPERN, DANIEL

A Few Questions for Poetry *New York Times Book Review* p25 Ja 1 2017

HALPERN, JAKE

Edgeland *Publishers Weekly* v264 no12 p73 Mr 20 2017

A NEW UNDERGROUND RAILROAD cartoon color *New Yorker* v93 no4 p32 Mr 13 2017

Halpern, Michael

Ensuring scientific integrity in the Age of Trump bibl cartoon *Science* v355 no6326 p696 F 17 2017

High Time S. Mower bw *Vogue* v207 no11 p117 N 2017

Halpern, Sue

ALTERNATIVE FACTS color *Nation* v304 no7 p27 Mr 6 2017

How He Used Facebook to Win [Cover story] color *New York Review of Books* v64 no10 p59 Je 8 2017

INTO THE MULTIVERSE color *Nation* v305 no10 p32 O 23 2017

The Nihilism of Julian Assange color *New York Review of Books* v64 no12 p13 Jl 13 2017

Our Driverless Future bw color *New York Review of Books* v63 no18 p18 N 24 2016

Robert B. Silvers (1929–2017) [Cover story] bw color *New York Review of Books* v64 no8 p31 My 11 2017

They Have, Right Now, Another You color *New York Review of Books* v63 no20 p32 D 22 2016

We Need More Alternatives to Facebook B. Bergstein color diag *MIT Technology Review* v120 no3 p86 My/Je 2017

Halpert, Gabriella

My Deluxe Dream Barn Will Have... color *Horse & Rider* v56 no4 p80 Ap 2017

HALPIN, DENNIS P.

Another Abduction by North Korea? *Weekly Standard* v22 no6 p12 O 17 2016

The Brothers Kim color *Weekly Standard* v22 no27 p22 Mr 20 2017

Halpin, Mikki

Nevertheless, She Persisted color *Glamour* v115 no5 p162 My 2017

What We Believe color *Glamour* v114 no12 p195 D 2016

HALPIN, PATRICK N.

Google Haul Out: Earth Observation Imagery and Digital Aerial Surveys in Coastal Wildlife Management and Abundance Estimation *BioScience* v67 no8 p760 Ag 2017

Halsey (Performer)

Freedom Rock: Halsey lost a boyfriend, a producer, and, for a time, her sense of self. What she gained was a new sound and

her first No. 1 album P. Reilly img *New York* v50 no13 p69 Je 26 2017

Halsey Aims for Pop Dominance B. HIATT color *Rolling Stone* no1284 p21 Ap 6 2017

The New Rebel Queen of Pop's Badlands [Cover story] R. SHEFFIELD color *Rolling Stone* no1289 p55 Je 15 2017

Halsey (Performer)—Interviews

HALSEY M. Vain color *Entertainment Weekly* no1468/1469 p104 Je 2-9 2017

Halsey, Cheryl

SURPRISE, SURPRISE K. Hunhoff *South Dakota Magazine* v32 no4 p6 N/D 2016

Halstead, Ted

A Tax with a Twist: A novel idea to distribute carbon dividends that's both fair and workable *Hoover Digest: Research & Opinion on Public Policy* no3 p73 Summ 2017

Halt & Catch Fire (TV program)

Halt and Catch Fire J. Russell *TV Guide* v65 no35 p37 Ag 21 2017

Halter classes (Horse shows)

2016 Canadian Nationals G. Dearth *Arabian Horse World* v57 no2 p50 N 2016

2016 U. S. NATIONAL RESULTS *Arabian Horse World* v57 no4 p144 Ja 2017

2016 U.S. NATIONALS HALTER DIVISION C. Reich *Arabian Horse World* v57 no4 p130 Ja 2017

GUEST EDITORIAL: MAKE HALTER GREAT AGAIN? C. Reich *Arabian Horse World* v57 no4 p142 Ja 2017

Hariry Al Shaqab C. Reich color *Arabian Horse World* v57 no7 p113 Ap 2017

Up to the Challenge - Changes Coming for U.S. Nationals Halter Classes C. Reich *Arabian Horse World* v57 no5 p235 F 2017

Halter classes (Horse shows)—Charts, diagrams, etc.

LEADING DAMS OF 2015 U.S. NATIONAL WINNERS *Arabian Horse World* v56 no12 p158 S 2016

Halterman, Jim

ALL ABOUT FEUD *TV Guide* v65 no8 p8 F 27 2017

American Gods *TV Guide* v65 no13 p34 Mr 20 2017

American Gods *TV Guide* v65 no25 p34 Je 2017

Anatomy of a Hit *TV Guide* p9 D 5 2016

ANIMAL KINGDOM: The Cody clan at the center of the California-set crime drama often get into hot water. But on set, they know how to keep it cool *TV Guide* v65 no27 p20 Je 26 2017

Animal Kingdom *TV Guide* v65 no35 p35 Ag 21 2017

The Art of the Reboot *TV Guide* p8 D 19 2016

THE BEAT GOES ON *TV Guide* p34 D 5 2016

Berlin Station *TV Guide* v65 no43 p36 O 16 2017

Better Call Saul *TV Guide* v65 no13 p31 Mr 20 2017

Better Call Saul *TV Guide* v65 no25 p32 Je 2017

Beyond the LAW color *TV Guide* v65 no7 p32 F 13 2017

Big Exits on Hawaii Five-0: The drama says "aloha" to actors Daniel Dae Kim and Grace Park *TV Guide* v65 no31 p3 Jl 24 2017

A Bloody Good Time at Code Black *TV Guide* v64 no46 p9 N 7 2016

Can Pitch Be a Major League Success? color *TV Guide* v64 no42 p8 O 10 2016

Chelsea's Back for More *TV Guide* v65 no14 p10 Ap 3 2017

Claws *TV Guide* v65 no23 p32 My 29 2017

Colin Hanks's SLICE OF LIFE *TV Guide* p32 D 5 2016

Comedies Get Serious *TV Guide* v64 no48 p7 N 21 2016

Dr. Ken *TV Guide* v64 no40 p58 O 3 2016

Fall Sneak Peek: What to Expect *TV Guide* v65 no23 p6 My 29 2017

THE FANTASTIC FOUR RETURN: Will. Grace. Karen. Jack. Need we say more? Behind the scenes of NBC's must-see revival [Cover story] *TV Guide* v65 no41 p16 O 2 2017

From thirtysomething to This Is Us: My Pop Culture Milestones *TV Guide* v65 no43 p12 O 16 2017

FUNNY MONEY: Robert De Niro and Michelle Pfeiffer play Bernie and Ruth Madoff in HBO's film about how the scandal wrecked their infamous family *TV Guide* v65 no21 p28 My 15 2017

GAME ON! The classic Battle of the Network Stars is back, and your TV favorites are ready to wage war--on each other! *TV Guide* v65 no27 p24 Je 26 2017

THE GOOD WIFE: She has our vote! Sela Ward makes a power

play in the dramatic new season of Graves *TV Guide* v65 no43 p16 O 16 2017

Graves color *TV Guide* v64 no42 p37 O 10 2016

Hawaii Five-0 *TV Guide* v64 no40 p56 O 3 2016

HAWAII FIVE-0 *TV Guide* v65 no39 p53 S 18 2017

Hawaii Five-O/MacGyver Crossover *TV Guide* v65 no11 p37 Mr 6 2017

HOLLYWOOD DISPATCH *TV Guide* v65 no35 p5 Ag 21 2017

JOHN RIDLEY *TV Guide* v65 no19 p9 My 1 2017

JOSH BERMAN *TV Guide* v64 no40 p14 O 3 2016

KEVIN CAN WAIT SHAKE-UP! *TV Guide* v65 no27 p5 Je 26 2017

Kevin Can Wait *TV Guide* v64 no46 p31 N 7 2016

KEVIN CAN WAIT *TV Guide* v65 no11 p28 Mr 6 2017

Kevin Can Wait *TV Guide* v65 no19 p30 My 1 2017

Killing Richard Glossip *TV Guide* p35 Ap 17 2017

The Last Tycoon *TV Guide* v65 no25 p19 Je 2017

Lethal Showdown *TV Guide* v64 no48 p11 N 21 2016

Lethal Weapon *TV Guide* p41 D 5 2016

LETHAL WEAPON *TV Guide* v65 no39 p39 S 18 2017

Lethal Weapon *TV Guide* v65 no4 p40 Ja 16 2017

Life in Pieces' Game Day *TV Guide* p13 D 19 2016

Lily at Large *TV Guide* v65 no4 p6 Ja 16 2017

MacGyver color *TV Guide* v65 no7 p42 F 13 2017

The Man in the High Castle *TV Guide* v64 no40 p36 O 3 2016

MARK JOHNSON AND MELISSA BERNSTEIN *TV Guide* p11 D 5 2016

Moon Bloodgood Joins Code Black *TV Guide* v65 no37 p14 S 4 2017

New Fall TV: Winners and Losers *TV Guide* v65 no43 p4 O 16 2017

A New PBS, Just for Kids *TV Guide* v65 no4 p9 Ja 16 2017

PETER M. LENKOV *TV Guide* v64 no48 p9 N 21 2016

Shut Eye *TV Guide* v64 no40 p32 O 3 2016

Somewhere Between *TV Guide* v65 no31 p30 Jl 24 2017

STEVEN MOLARO color *TV Guide* v64 no42 p12 O 10 2016

The Strain *TV Guide* v65 no31 p36 Jl 24 2017

Streaming's New Stars *TV Guide* v65 no2 p14 Ja 2 2017

TOGETHER WE STAND *TV Guide* v65 no8 p22 F 27 2017

THE TONIGHT SHOW STARRING JIMMY FALLON *TV Guide* v65 no11 p47 Mr 6 2017

TV Trends to Watch for in 2017 *TV Guide* v65 no6 p6 Ja 30 2017

WILL & GRACE *TV Guide* v65 no37 p38 S 4 2017

YOUNG SHELDON *TV Guide* v65 no37 p25 S 4 2017

Haltiwanger, Robert S.

Notch-Jagged complex structure implicates a catch bond in tuning ligand sensitivity bibl diag graph *Science* v355 no6331 p1320 Mr 24 2017

Halton, Tom

How Coty Reinvigorated Its Supply Chain *Harvard Business Review Digital Articles* p2 My 19 2016

Halvah

OPEN SESAME *Martha Stewart Living* no268 p90 O 2016

Halverson, Jeffrey B.

A Cyclone for All Seasons *Weatherwise* v70 no5 p44 S/O 2017

A Retrospective on the Historical Derecho of June 29, 2012 *Weatherwise* v70 no5 p52 S/O 2017

Weatherwatch color map *Weatherwise* v70 no4 p38 Jl/Ag 2017

Weatherwatch map *Weatherwise* v69 no6 p46 N-D 2016

Weatherwatch *Weatherwise* v70 no2 p38 Mr/Ap 2017

Halvorsen, Anne-Lise

Teaching with evidence diag *Phi Delta Kappan* v98 no7 p67 Ap 2017

Halvorson, Bengt

Canyonero? No cartoon color *Car & Driver* v62 no10 p86 Ap 2017

Halo Bender color *Car & Driver* v63 no1 p108 Jl 2017

Halvorson, Heidi Grant

3 Ways Managers Start Off On the Wrong Foot *Harvard Business Review Digital Articles* p2 O 6 2015

How to Show Trustworthiness in a Job Interview *Harvard Business Review Digital Articles* p2 My 11 2015

The Mindset That Leads People to Be Dangerously Overconfident *Harvard Business Review Digital Articles* p2 Ap 19 2016

Signs You Might Be a Toxic Colleague *Harvard Business Review Digital Articles* p2 Mr 2 2016

Stop Making Gratitude All About You *Harvard Business Review Digital Articles* p2 Je 29 2016

We're All Terrible at Understanding Each Other *Harvard Business Review Digital Articles* p2 Ap 16 2015

Halvorson, Mary

Mary Halvorson D. OUELLETTE color *Downbeat* v84 no7 p90 Jl 2017

MARY HALVORSON: 'MORE THAN I WOULD'VE HOPED FOR' D. Ouellette color *Downbeat* v84 no8 p42 Ag 2017

Halzen, Francis

New angle on cosmic rays color *Science* v357 no6357 p1240 S 22 2017

Halzen, Francis L.

Martin Moses Block *Physics Today* v69 no10 p66 O 2016

Ham

    See also

    Prosciutto

Ham, Becky

AAAS seeks to uphold science's role in policy-making color *Science* v355 no6332 p1383 Mr 31 2017

Ham, Jonathan

Lee Rubin: Our mentor and role model *Science* v355 no6327 p806 F 24 2017

Ham, Mary Katharine

MARY KATHARINE HAM E. PLOTT color *Washingtonian Magazine* v52 no7 p86 Ap 2017

Hamada, Naomi

Cyclin A2 is an RNA binding protein that controls Mre11 mRNA translation bibl graph *Science* v353 no6307 p1549 S 30 2016

Hamadey, Gina

BURST THE HEALTH BUBBLE! color *Women's Health* v14 no8 p102 O 2017

WANT SPROUTS WITH THAT? [Cover story] color *Women's Health* v14 no5 p96 Je 2017

Hamahashi, Mari

Release of mineral-bound water prior to subduction tied to shallow seismogenic slip off Sumatra graph *Science* v356 no6340 p841 My 26 2017

Hamamori, James

TOP CHEFS A. M. Panoringan color *Los Angeles Magazine* v62 no10 p8 O 2017

Hamann, Wiebke

Fructose-driven glycolysis supports anoxia resistance in the naked mole-rat diag graph *Science* v356 no6335 p307 Ap 21 2017

Hamasyan, Tigran

Manuel Valera T. PANKEN color *Downbeat* v84 no10 p202 O 2017

Hamberger, Björn

Characterization of a dynamic metabolon producing the defense compound dhurrin in sorghum bibl graph *Science* v354 no6314 p890 N 18 2016

Hamblin, James

ABOVE & BEYOND cartoon *New Yorker* v92 no45 p18 Ja 16 2017

HOW TO SLEEP color *Atlantic* v319 no1 p84 Ja/F 2017

Hambsch, Franz-Josef

The First Pulsing White Dwarf *Sky & Telescope* v133 no1 p84 Ja 2017

Hamburg (Germany)

European XFEL to shine as brightest, fastest x-ray source E. Cartlidge chart color *Science* v354 no6308 p22 O 7 2016

Hamburg, G. M.

Russia's Path Toward Enlightenment: Faith, Politics, and Reason, 1500–1801 R. Legvold *Foreign Affairs* v95 no6 p188 N/D 2016

Hamburg, Steven P.

Unmask temporal trade-offs in climate policy debates color *Science* v356 no6337 p492 My 5 2017

Hamburger, Philip

Philip Hamburger, Is Administrative Law Unlawful? D. Brand *Society* v53 no6 p668 D 2016

Hamburgers

2016 WASHINGTONIAN BUD & BURGER BATTLE *Washingtonian Magazine* v52 no1 p42 O 2016

20-MINUTE MEALS color *Good Housekeeping* v264 no5 p121 My 2017

An American Classic Goes Low-Cal T. Mowry color *Entertain-*

ment Weekly no1456 p20 Mr 10 2017

Beef, Buns & Brews Perryville J. B. Patton color *Missouri Life* v44 no3 p78 My 2017

BETTER BURGERS, HOTTER DOGS B. P. KATZ and G. LOFTS color *Martha Stewart Living* no275 p67 Je 2017

BIDWLL WINNING BURGER *Washingtonian Magazine* v52 no1 p152 O 2016

Big Earl's Greasy Eats: Although its building is listed on the National Register of Historic Places, the food at Big Earl's is anything but dated. The burgers are made with Harris Ranch or Kobe beef, and the delicious home made buns are baked daily N. B. TRULSSON *Arizona Highways* v93 no11 p12 N 2017

Burger [Cover story] J. S. GOLUB color *Runner's World* v52 no6 p69 Jl 2017

The Burger, Perfectly Done cartoon chart color *Men's Health* v32 no6 p63 Ag 2017

The Dark Prince D. SEARCY *Texas Monthly* v45 no3 p86 Mr 2017

Deal With It! *Atlanta* v57 no3 p56 Jl 2017

My LIST B. Mazurek bw color *Harper's Bazaar* no3654 p66 Je/Jl 2017

Outside-In Burgers: Reviving a family recipe with a tip for anyone seeking perfection A. TRAVERSO color *Yankee* p54 Jl 2017

Restaurant GUIDE *Indianapolis Monthly* v40 no10 p144 Je 2017

RETURN OF THE KING S. Schneider color *Sunset* v239 no1 p102 Jl 2017

SINGULAR Sensation M. Kiesel cartoon color *O, The Oprah Magazine* p137 Mr 2017

STACK THAT PATTY! color *Women's Health* v14 no4 p36 My 2017

A THANKSGIVING TURKEY TWIST FROM BOB'S BURGERS color *Entertainment Weekly* no1441 p16 N 25 2016

THAT'S BEERLICIOUS! [Cover story] Y. LEE color *Runner's World* v52 no4 p31 My 2017

WANT SPROUTS WITH THAT? [Cover story] G. Hamadey color *Women's Health* v14 no5 p96 Je 2017

When Burgers Go Bad *Atlanta* v56 no10 p58 F 2017

Hamburgers—Evaluation

Plevention CLEANEST PACKAGED FOOD AWARDS 2017 [Cover story] S. Eckelkamp color *Prevention* p60 Mr 2017

Hamburgers—History

Putting the Fast In Fast Food E. Berman color *Time* v189 no3 p53 Ja 30 2017

Hamburgers—Sales & prices

BIG MAC ATTACK C. Suddath color *Bloomberg Businessweek* no4508 p62 Ja 23 2017

Jack Huey Field B. PHILLIPS *Texas Monthly* v44 no11 p38 N 2016

Hameed, Abbas

God's Word to an Iraqi Interpreter color *Christianity Today* v61 no6 p95 Jl/Ag 2017

HAMEED, ASLAM

A Few Movie Stars Don't Make Happy Muslim Indians *Islamic Horizons* v46 no2 p52 Mr/Ap 2017

Hamel, Gary

The 15 Diseases of Leadership, According to Pope Francis *Harvard Business Review Digital Articles* p2 Ap 14 2015

The 5 Requirements of a Truly Innovative Company *Harvard Business Review Digital Articles* p2 Ap 27 2015

Bureaucracy Must Die *Harvard Business Review Digital Articles* p2 N 4 2014

The Core Incompetencies of the Corporation *Harvard Business Review Digital Articles* p2 O 31 2014

Excess Management Is Costing the U.S. $3 Trillion Per Year *Harvard Business Review Digital Articles* p2 S 5 2016

A Few Unicorns Are No Substitute for a Competitive, Innovative Economy color graph *Harvard Business Review Digital Articles* p2 F 8 2017

Innovation Starts with the Heart, Not the Head *Harvard Business Review Digital Articles* p2 Je 12 2015

More of Us Are Working in Big Bureaucratic Organizations than Ever Before *Harvard Business Review Digital Articles* p2 Jl 5 2016

Top-Down Solutions Like Holacracy Won't Fix Bureaucracy *Harvard Business Review Digital Articles* p2 Mr 22 2016

What We Learned About Bureaucracy from 7,000 HBR Readers *Harvard Business Review Digital Articles* p2 Ag 10 2017

Hamel, Perrine

Promoting human rights through science color *Science* v357 no6359 p34 O 6 2017

Hameline, Paul

PAUL HAMELINE *Interview* v47 no1 p50 F 2017

Hamerla, Sara

ACADEMIC CONVERSATIONS color *Literacy Today (2411-7862)* v34 no3 p30 N/D 2016

HAMERLIK, LADISLAV

The Arctic in the Twenty-First Century: Changing Biogeochemical Linkages across a Paraglacial Landscape of Greenland *BioScience* v67 no2 p118 F 2017

Hamerly, Ryan

A fully programmable 100-spin coherent Ising machine with all-to-all connections bibl diag graph *Science* v354 no6312 p614 N 4 2016

Hamermesh, Richard G.

The Harvard Contest That's Trying to Improve Health Care Delivery *Harvard Business Review Digital Articles* p2 O 2 2015

A New Approach to Safely Sharing Cancer Patients' Data *Harvard Business Review Digital Articles* p1 Je 21 2017

One Obstacle to Curing Cancer: Patient Data Isn't Shared *Harvard Business Review Digital Articles* p2 N 28 2016

What Cancer Researchers Can Learn from Direct-to-Consumer Companies color *Harvard Business Review Digital Articles* p2 Ja 12 2017

HAMERS, LAUREL

Algae speed up melting of glacial snow color *Science News* v192 no6 p10 O 14 2017

Amoeba gives clues to animal origins *Science News* v190 no10 p7 N 12 2016

Ancient fossils feature tube feet color *Science News* v192 no6 p12 O 14 2017

Ancient sea worm had a head full of spines bw color *Science News* v192 no3 p4 S 2 2017

Beyond Today's Opioids color graph *Science News* v191 no11 p22 Je 10 2017

Biggest organelle gets image update color *Science News* v190 no11 p10 N 26 2016

Brains encode faces piece by piece bw *Science News* v191 no13 p9 Jl 8 2017

Budget proposal would slash science *Science News* v191 no7 p15 Ap 15 2017

Built for SPEED bw color diag graph *Science News* v191 no4 p20 Mr 4 2017

Canopies of many colors color map *Science News* v191 no5 p32 Mr 18 2017

Carbon can exceed four-bond limit diag *Science News* v191 no2 p9 F 4 2017

Chemists observe oxidation up close color *Science News* v191 no10 p9 My 27 2017

Citizen scientists help planet in peril color *Science News* v190 no9 p29 O 29 2016

Deep heat intensified mega-quake *Science News* v191 no12 p7 Je 24 2017

Designing a better glue from slug goo color *Science News* v192 no5 p14 S 30 2017

Dinosaur eggs were slow to hatch color *Science News* v191 no2 p4 F 4 2017

Enzyme links up carbon and silicon color *Science News* v190 no13 p11 D 24 2016

Enzymes aid rice's arsenic defenses color *Science News* v191 no5 p14 Mr 18 2017

Flight may have steered egg evolution color *Science News* v192 no1 p9 Ag 5 2017

Fossil whale hints at baleen makeover color *Science News* v191 no11 p12 Je 10 2017

The Future of Cars color *Science News* v190 no13 p34 D 24 2016

Gene offers clues to grasses' success color *Science News* v191 no7 p12 Ap 15 2017

Gut microbes may spark Parkinson's [Cover story] color *Science News* v190 no13 p10 D 24 2016

How an itch hitches a ride to the brain *Science News* v192 no4 p18 S 16 2017

Human noises invade wilderness color map *Science News* v191

no11 p14 Je 10 2017

Immune proteins aid viral enemy *Science News* v190 no11 p16 N 26 2016

In the lungs, mold cells self-destruct color *Science News* v192 no5 p16 S 30 2017

Malaria molecule lures mosquitoes color *Science News* v191 no5 p10 Mr 18 2017

Mapping Life's NETWORKS cartoon chart graph *Science News* v190 no9 p24 O 29 2016

Neonicotinoids found in honey globally [Cover story] *Science News* v192 no7 p16 O 28 2017

New views snag science Nobels bw *Science News* v192 no7 p6 O 28 2017

Nobels honor the small and exotic cartoon color *Science News* v190 no9 p6 O 29 2016

Photosynthesis reinvented color diag *Science News* v192 no6 p20 O 14 2017

POWER UP color diag graph *Science News* v192 no1 p22 Ag 5 2017

Rattlesnakes have lost venom genes color *Science News* v190 no8 p9 O 15 2016

Red squirrels harbor leprosy bacteria color *Science News* v190 no12 p9 D 10 2016

Scientists watch superbugs evolve bw *Science News* v190 no8 p11 O 15 2016

Seagrasses combat harmful bacteria *Science News* v191 no5 p14 Mr 18 2017

Stem cells help sterile mice grow eggs color *Science News* v191 no12 p13 Je 24 2017

Timing of Europe's river floods shifting map *Science News* v192 no3 p14 S 2 2017

To understand rivers, let physics be your guide color *Science News* v191 no6 p29 Ap 1 2017

Two brain circuits help mice hunt *Science News* v191 no3 p8 F 18 2017

Vital enzyme adapted to cooling Earth *Science News* v191 no2 p8 F 4 2017

A whole new (tiny) ball game for color color *Science News* v192 no6 p32 O 14 2017

Who you gonna call? color *Science News* v191 no12 p4 Je 24 2017

Zika hides out in hard-to-reach spots color *Science News* v191 no10 p10 My 27 2017

HAMES, ELIZABETH

When You're Away, The Cats And Dogs Will Play color *Reader's Digest* v189 no1130 p43 My 2017

Hamid, Mohsin, 1971-

Caught Between Worlds Y. E. Rashidi color *New York Review of Books* v64 no7 p35 Ap 20 2017

DOOR TO DOOR F. Prose *Harper's Magazine* p98 Ap 2017

Exit West L. Greenblatt color *Entertainment Weekly* no1457/1458 p103 Mr 17 2017

Land of the Free, Home of the Brave color *Time* v188 no16/17 p68 O 24 2016

Love In the Time of Refugees S. Begley color *Time* v189 no10 p56 Mr 20 2017

Mohsin Hamid's 'Exit West' A. Flournoy *New York Times Magazine* p43 O 8 2017

Of Windows and Doors bw cartoon *New Yorker* v92 no37 p70 N 14 2016

Points of No Return Viet Thanh Nguyen *New York Times Book Review* p1 Mr 12 2017

Hamid, Shadi

Islamists and Liberal Values in the Middle East E. STEIN *Current History* v115 no785 p363 D 2016

Political Islam After the Arab Spring O. Roy color *Foreign Affairs* v96 no6 p127 N/D 2017

Hamill, Mark

THE CARRIE I KNEW A. Breznican color *Entertainment Weekly* no1448 p22 Ja 13 2017

Hamill, Pete

Hello, Gorgeous N. GABLER *Saturday Evening Post* v288 no6 p44 N/D 2016

Hamilton (Play)

Hamilton Goes to High School W. D'Orio *Education Digest* v83 no2 p4 O 2017

Hamilton (Theatrical production)

Christian hope in Hamilton B. F. Jones color *Christian Century* v134 no7 p45 Mr 29 2017

Hamilton Nation E. Berman color *Time* v188 no14 p50 O 10 2016

Hamilton's $849 Tickets Are Priced Too Low R. Mohammed *Harvard Business Review Digital Articles* p2 Je 24 2016

THE HAMILTON SATISFACTION SCALE M. Snetiker color *Entertainment Weekly* no1444/1445 p119 D 16 2016

Lin-Manuel Miranda M. Snetiker color *Entertainment Weekly* no1444/1445 p18 D 16 2016

Masterpiece Theater J. BERNSTEIN *Commentary* v142 no3 p11 O 2016

Phillipa Soo Doesn't Leave It All Onstage D. Itzkoff *New York Times Magazine* p54 Ap 2 2017

What's Next for Hamilton's Breakout Stars? I. Biedenharn, J. Derschowitz et al color *Entertainment Weekly* no1454/1455 p104 F 24 2017

Word Power E. COX and H. RATHVON *Reader's Digest* v188 no1124 p139 O 2016

Hamilton, Alexander, 1757-1804

ALEXANDER HAMILTON, SOLDIER D. Silbey *MHQ: Quarterly Journal of Military History* v29 no3 p38 Spr 2017

THE BIG QUESTION H. Minhaj, A. S. Cooper et al cartoon *Atlantic* v318 no4 p112 N 2016

FIRST IN WAR B. Hogan *MHQ: Quarterly Journal of Military History* v29 no3 p26 Spr 2017

Legacy. What is a legacy? A. Gordon-Reed *History Today* v66 no11 p4 N 2016

Hamilton, Alexander, 1757-1804—Political & social views

Paterson: Alexander Hamilton's Trickle-Down City [Cover story] R. KREITNER bw color *Nation* v304 no8 p18 Mr 13 2017

Hamilton, Anne Hamilton, Duchess of, 1631-1716

The Good Duchess J. Dismore *History Today* v66 no10 p4 O 2016

Hamilton, Brian

16 UCLA BRUINS chart color *Sports Illustrated* v125 no15 p75 N 7 2016

1 DUKE BLUE DEVILS chart color *Sports Illustrated* v125 no15 p60 N 7 2016

6 NORTH CAROLINA TAR HEELS chart color *Sports Illustrated* v125 no15 p65 N 7 2016

Big SHOTS color *Sports Illustrated* v126 no8 p32 Mr 20 2017

CASE FOR ... CLEMSON color *Sports Illustrated* v125 no19 p40 D 12 2016

The Case for ... The High School Combine color *Sports Illustrated* v126 no14 p31 My 15-22 2017

HERE WE GO, 'ZO color *Sports Illustrated* v125 no13 p42 O 17 2016

LEARNING TO FLY [Cover story] color *Sports Illustrated* v126 no2 p24 Ja 16 2017

LINE OF FIRE color *Sports Illustrated* v126 no1 p36 Ja 9 2017

Hamilton, Bruce A.

Regeneration of fat cells from myofibroblasts during wound healing bibl color graph *Science* v355 no6326 p748 F 17 2017

HAMILTON, DAVID

Chords & Discords color *Downbeat* v83 no11 p10 N 2016

Hamilton, Denise

BUILDING BLACK FAMILY WEALTH color *Ebony* v72 no9 p88 Jl/Ag 2017

Hamilton, Diane Musho

Calming Your Brain During Conflict *Harvard Business Review Digital Articles* p2 D 22 2015

HAMILTON, DUNCAN

ERIC LIDDELL'S GREATEST RACE *Saturday Evening Post* v289 no1 p52 Ja/F 2017

Hamilton, Gabrielle

Cooking in My Own Voice: Chowder-soaked toast is a dish any chef would want to claim *New York Times Magazine* p36 My 21 2017

FEAST IN NYC color *New York Times Magazine* p54 N 27 2016

Health Food You Can Love *New York Times Magazine* p20 Ag 13 2017

A Meal for Reuniting *New York Times Magazine* p30 S 10 2017

Mother Knows Best *New York Times Magazine* p24 F 26 2017

One Fine Piece of Meat: Braised tongue with sauce gribiche can make you appreciate a cut you might otherwise avoid *New York Times Magazine* p20 Jl 16 2017

On Your Way to Your New Year's Self *New York Times Magazine*

p20 Ja 1 2017

The Way It Was *New York Times Magazine* p24 O 23 2016

What We Really Eat color *New York Times Magazine* p26 Ja 29 2017

The Wonder of Three Ingredients *New York Times Magazine* p32 Mr 26 2017

Hamilton, Ian

The Couturier of Milan *Publishers Weekly* v264 no35 p108 Ag 28 2017

HAMILTON, JACK

The Unknowable Joni Mitchell bw *Atlantic* v320 no4 p36 N 2017

Hamilton, James T.

BUT WHO WILL COVER THE SWILL MILK? A. SCHIFFRIN color *Nation* v304 no5 p35 F 20 2017

Hamilton, Janet

ASK THE EXPERTS color *Runner's World* v52 no1 p50 Ja/F 2017

Magic Bullets M. KITA and J. McCOY color *Runner's World* v52 no4 p56 My 2017

Hamilton, Jared

Selling to Customers Who Do Their Homework Online *Harvard Business Review Digital Articles* p2 Mr 16 2016

Hamilton, Kim

oops *Parents* v92 no7 p132 Jl 2017

Hamilton, L. S.

Intonational speech prosody encoding in the human auditory cortex diag *Science* v357 no6353 p797 Ag 25 2017

Hamilton, Laird

THE TAO OF LAIRD HAMILTON J. Roth color *Esquire* p54 O 2017

WILD MAN OF A CERTAIN AGE C. Ballard color *Sports Illustrated* v127 no10 p48 O 2 2017

Hamilton, Latonya Sadler

MOTORCYCLE ROAD: The making of a photo essay color *Virginia Living* v15 no5 p13 Ag 2017

Hamilton, Lewis, 1985-

The Fastest Man on Wheels S. Gregory color *Time* v188 no27-28 p74 D 26 2016

Hamilton, Lewis, 1985——Interviews

Lewis HAMILTON S. WILLIAMS *Interview* v47 no6 p68 Ag 2017

HAMILTON, LINDA

advice for dancers *Dance Magazine* v91 no4 p24 Ap 2017

advice for dancers *Dance Magazine* v91 no7 p24 Jl 2017

advice for dancers *Dance Magazine* v91 no8 p24 Ag 2017

The Curse of Career Happiness *Dance Magazine* v90 no12 p36 D 2016

Home Alone color *Dance Magazine* v91 no3 p24 Mr 2017

The MOST INFLUENTIAL PEOPLE IN DANCE TODAY: THE MOVERS, SHAKERS AND CHANGEMAKERS HAVING THE BIGGEST IMPACT ON DANCE RIGHT NOW *Dance Magazine* v91 no7 p27 Jl 2017

Stage Mom Trauma *Dance Magazine* v90 no11 p24 N 2016

Trouble in Paradise *Dance Magazine* v91 no1 p48 Ja 2017

Hamilton, Lisa

Seniors That Still Have It N. Chirico color *Horse & Rider* v56 no2 p60 F 2017

Hamilton, Meghan

Save Our Science, Save Our Planet *Humanist* v77 no2 p6 Mr/Ap 2017

Hamilton, Michael P.

Photon Menace chart color *Sound & Vision* v82 no8 p62 O 2017

Hamilton, Michelle

ALISON O'BRIEN color *Runner's World* v52 no2 p21 Mr 2017

CASE STUDY: YOU cartoon *Runner's World* v52 no1 p44 Ja/F 2017

RUN AWAY! [Cover story] color *Runner's World* v52 no7 p54 Ag 2017

Running While Female [Cover story] bw cartoon *Runner's World* v51 no11 p78 D 2016

Western States Master bw color *Runner's World* v52 no5 p58 Je 2017

Hamilton, Normani Kordei

NO LONGER SILENT R. R. Robertson color *Essence* v47 no7 p82 N 2016

HAMILTON, SHAWN

THE CANADIANS WHO COULD color *Dressage Today* v23 no8 p28 Ap 2017

Going to Extremes color *Trail Rider* v29 no3 p38 Ap 2017

Slide into Ski Joring color *Trail Rider* v29 no1 p26 Ja/F 2017

HAMILTON, STEPHEN K.

Cellulosic biofuel contributions to a sustainable energy future: Choices and outcomes color *Science* v356 no6345 p1349 Je 30 2017

A Global Assessment of Inland Wetland Conservation Status *BioScience* v67 no6 p523 Je 2017

Hamilton, Tish

Front Row at the Revolution [Cover story] bw color *Runner's World* v51 no10 p72 N 2016

NOT FADE AWAY [Cover story] bw color *Runner's World* v52 no5 p80 Je 2017

RW 2016 COVER SEARCH [Cover story] color *Runner's World* v51 no11 p62 D 2016

Hamilton, Wesley

STRENGTH SERVICE K. PANG, C. BUTLER et al cartoon color *Men's Health* v32 no4 p116 My 2017

Hamilton County (Ind.)

Hamilton COUNTY R. Annis, S. Bahr et al color map *Indianapolis Monthly* v41 no2 p63 S 2017

Hamilton County (Ohio)—Description & travel

HAMILTON A. KONERMANN *Cincinnati Magazine* p38 Je 2017

Hamilton Mixtape, The (Music)

THE HAMILTON MIXTAPE M. J. Rose color *U.S. Catholic* v82 no3 p40 Mr 2017

HAMILTON REINVENTED I. Biedenharn color *Entertainment Weekly* no1442 p20 D 2 2016 Rebellious Special Issue

Making 'Hamilton' Even Greater Again J. DOLAN color *Rolling Stone* no1276 p61 D 15 2016

Hamilton's America (Film)

Hamilton Comes to TV! M. Roffman *TV Guide* v64 no40 p15 O 3 2016

Hamitouche, Johnny

FIT TO PRINT bw color *Wired* v25 no5 p14 My 2017

Hamlet (Play : Shakespeare)

Anticipation Index *New York* v50 no10 p92 My 15 2017

New Sentences S. Anderson *New York Times Magazine* p13 O 8 2017

Summer Preview M. Schulman cartoon *New Yorker* v93 no14 p8 My 22 2017

THE THEATRE cartoon *New Yorker* v93 no17 p14 Je 19 2017

To See; To Hear M. Bissett *Stage Directions* v30 no10 p14 O 2017

We Are the Dane: Director Sam Gold and his star, Oscar Isaac, stage & Hamlet that's both theatrical and honest S. HOLDREN img *New York* v50 no15 p69 Jl 24 2017

Hamlet, Murray

Staying Warm *Yankee* v81 no1 p24 Ja/F 2017

Hamlin, Kevin

The 33¢ T-Shirt *Bloomberg Businessweek* no4536 p41 S 4 2017

The Asian Jobs Ladder Is Broken *Bloomberg Businessweek* no4528 p58 Je 26 2017

China Unleashes Its Farmers color *Bloomberg Businessweek* no4540 p36 O 2 2017

'We Must As a Nation Be More Unpredictable' *Bloomberg Businessweek* no4503 p12 D 12 2016

Hamling, Ian J.

Complex multifault rupture during the 2016 Mw 7.8 Kaikōura earthquake, New Zealand color map *Science* v356 no6334 p154 Ap 14 2017

Hamm, Bob

Re-enacting Rio Grande narrow gauge [Cover story] color diag *Model Railroader* v84 no9 p40 S 2017

Hamm, Jon, 1971-

I AM HAMM color *InStyle* v24 no7 p118 Jl 2017

Hamm, Jon, 1971——Interviews

Groomed! K. Branch bw color *Glamour* v115 no2 p116 F 2017

Hamm, Mia, 1972-

The Fifty Greatest Living Athletes D. MAGARY, Z. BARON et al bw color *GQ: Gentlemen's Quarterly* v97 no11 p96 N 2017

Hammarström, Per

De novo design of a biologically active amyloid bibl graph *Science* v354 no6313 paah4949-1 N 11 2016

Hammel, Anna G.
A pathogenic role for T cell–derived IL-22BP in inflammatory bowel disease bibl graph *Science* v354 no6310 p358 O 21 2016

Hammel, Jonathan
How to Scale Up B. KITE color *Popular Mechanics* p37 S 2017
How to Scale Up B. KITE color *Popular Mechanics* v193 no7 p37 S 2016

Hammer, Armie, 1986—Interviews
Armie Hammer Has Two Turkeys D. WALTERS color *Bon Appetit* no11 p24 N 2017

Hammer, Joshua
Egypt: The New Dictatorship color *New York Review of Books* v64 no10 p20 Je 8 2017
His City of Ruins *New York Times Book Review* p21 Ja 8 2017
The Improbable Life and Stunning Death of a Child Warrior color *GQ: Gentlemen's Quarterly* v87 no1 p34 Ja 2017
Iraq: The Terrible Battle for Mosul bw map *New York Review of Books* v63 no17 p24 N 10 2016
A MODERN ODYSSEY *Smithsonian* v48 no1 p70 Ap 2017
No Promised Land: After a Dickensian childhood, an orphan in Congo must contend with poverty, political instability and tribal rivalries *New York Times Book Review* p18 Jl 23 2017
THE ROAD TO REVOLUTION bw color map *Smithsonian* v47 no10 p66 Mr 2017
THE SALVATION OF MOSUL: An Iraqi archaeologist braved ISIS snipers and booby-trapped ruins to rescue cultural treasures in the city and nearby legendary Nineveh and Nimrud *Smithsonian* v48 no6 p30 O 2017

Hammer, Langdon
At Home in Baltimore *American Scholar* v86 no4 p51 Aut 2017
The Genius and Generosity of Jimmy Merrill E. Mendelson bw *New York Review of Books* v63 no20 p73 D 22 2016
In Her Waiting Room: A biography-memoir by a former student of Elizabeth Bishop's looks to the life behind the poems *New York Times Book Review* p12 Mr 5 2017
Inside & Underneath Words [Cover story] bw color *New York Review of Books* v64 no14 p31 S 28 2017
Shorter Means Sweeter *American Scholar* v86 no2 p58 Spr 2017
Sound and Sense *American Scholar* v86 no3 p54 Summ 2017

Hammer, Markus
The Dirty Little Secret About Digitally Transforming Operations *Harvard Business Review Digital Articles* p2 My 31 2016

Hammerhead (Company)
SEMA NEW PRODUCTS 2016 M. EMERY color *Dirt Sports + Off-Road* v51 no4 p52 Ap 2017

Hammerness, Karen
What does it take to sustain a productive partnership in education? color *Phi Delta Kappan* v99 no1 p15 S 2017

HAMMERSCHLAG, NEIL
Extinction Risk and Conservation of the Earth's National Animal Symbols *BioScience* v67 no8 p744 Ag 2017
FASTER, DEEPER, HIGHER, STRONGER: EVERY DAY IN THE WILD IS THE OLYMPICS *BioScience* v66 no11 p1000 N 1 2016

Hammers—Evaluation
DeWalt Demo Hammer color *Bloomberg Businessweek* no4529 p79 Jl 3 2017
Light Hammer Heavy Hitter D. GERSHGORN and H. MURPHY color *Popular Science* v288 no6 p68 N/D 2016

Hammes-Schiffer, Sharon
A conundrum for density functional theory bibl diag *Science* v355 no6320 p28 Ja 6 2017

Hammett, Dashiell
SHOWDOWN IN THE ALEUTIANS *MHQ: Quarterly Journal of Military History* v29 no3 p54 Spr 2017

Hammett, Luke
Share with us color *House Beautiful* p8 Ag 2017

HAMMILL, MIKE O.
Google Haul Out: Earth Observation Imagery and Digital Aerial Surveys in Coastal Wildlife Management and Abundance Estimation *BioScience* v67 no8 p760 Ag 2017

Hammill, Peter—Interviews
Van der Graaf Generator Disturbs the Sonic Wavelength (But in a Good Way) M. METTLER bw color *Sound & Vision* v82 no4 p26 My 2017

Hammocks

BEST OF THE WEST N. Farrell, J. Silver et al color *Sunset* v238 no3 p7 Mr 2017
HAVE SEX IN TREES! color *Men's Health* v32 no6 p103 Ag 2017

Hammocks—Evaluation
GEARHEAD: TRAIL MIX P. SARCONI color *Wired* v25 no7 p40 Jl 2017
GEAR UP FOR SUMMER A. Wisch color *Sail* v48 no7 p28 Jl 2017
Hang Time H. B. ROCHFORT bw color *Backpacker* p51 Ag 2017
The Swing of Things J. K. Robinson *Sierra* v102 no4 p16 Jl/Ag 2017

Hammond, Caleb
Time Flies H. Als cartoon *New Yorker* v92 no42 p20 D 19 2016

Hammond, Claudia
How Mindfulness Can Save You Money *Time* v188 no15 p15 O 17 2016

Hammond, Ed.
Rockwell Collins Inc *Bloomberg Businessweek* no4537 p29 S 11 2017

Hammond, Gretchen Rachel—Trials, litigation, etc.
SNAP leader resigns while group faces suit on legal practices D. Gibson color *Christian Century* v134 no5 p15 Mr 1 2017

Hammond, Jan
What Harvard Business School Has Learned About Online Collaboration From HBX *Harvard Business Review Digital Articles* p2 Ap 14 2015

Hammond, Kristian J.
Please Don't Hire a Chief Artificial Intelligence Officer *Harvard Business Review Digital Articles* p2 Mr 29 2017

Hammond, Noah
Pluto's Hidden Ocean K. HAYNES bw color *Discover* v38 no1 p46 Ja/F 2017

Hammond, Patricia
Money in the Bag J. SerVaas *Saturday Evening Post* v289 no4 p25 Jl/Ag 2017

Hammond, Philip
WHALE CULTURE color graph *Natural History* v125 no11 p30 N 2017

Hammond, Philip A., 1955-
That's quite a statement... *People Management* p6 D 2016/Ja 2017

Hammond, Richard
BRINGING IN THE BEANS: Harvest on an American family farm T. Genoways *Harper's Magazine* p53 S 2017

Hammond, Timothy
The SAILING SCENE color *Sail* v48 no11 p6 N 2017

Hammonds, Kaylee
THE 5-INGREDIENT Farmers' Market Cookbook color *Southern Living* v52 no7 p61 Jl 2017
Branching Out color *Southern Living* v52 no2 p17 F 2017
Flowers with Flavor color *Southern Living* v52 no3 p36 Mr 2017
The No-Fuss Fig Tree color *Southern Living* v51 no11 p53 N 2016
OYSTER CASSEROLE color *Southern Living* v51 no12 p188 D 2016
SL cooking school color *Southern Living* v51 no11 p168 N 2016
THE SOUTHERN LIVING COOKIE COOKBOOK color *Southern Living* v51 no12 p190 D 2016
the SWEET spot [Cover story] color *Southern Living* v52 no7 p86 Jl 2017
Top with Cilantro color *Southern Living* v52 no2 p34 F 2017
The Versatile Herb color *Southern Living* v52 no4 p31 Ap 2017

Hammons, David, 1943-
Snowballs and Flags D. Adams and C. Lebowitz color *Art in America* v105 no3 p54 Mr 2017

Hammour, Amer
DAN ABOUT TOWN *Washingtonian Magazine* v52 no1 p30 O 2016

Hamon, Vincent
WE HEAR YOU *Progressive* v81 no10 p9 N 2016

Hampel, M. R.
Observation of a large-scale anisotropy in the arrival directions of cosmic rays above 8×10^{18} eV *Science* v357 no6357 p1266 S 22 2017

Hampshire (England)
BEAULIEU *British Heritage Travel* v38 no2 p20 Mr/Ap 2017

Hampson, Daphne

Kierkegaard's Rebellion P. E. Gordon bw color *New York Review of Books* v63 no17 p21 N 10 2016

Hampson, Katie

Driving improvements in emerging disease surveillance through locally relevant capacity strengthening color diag *Science* v357 no6347 p146 Jl 14 2017

Hampson, Thomas

Jan/2017 M. MAZZARO *Opera News* v81 no7 p6 Ja 2017

A Still-Dangerous Don J. NORDLINGER color *National Review* v69 no11 p40 Je 12 2017

Hampstead (London, England)

Happy Hijinks in Hampstead S. Lawrence *British Heritage Travel* v38 no2 p22 Mr/Ap 2017

HAMPTON, HOWARD

BLANK GENERATION bw color *Film Comment* v53 no3 p52 My/Je 2017

Hampton, Kris

Understanding What You're Part Of A. Ashley color *Climbing* no353 p24 My/Je 2017

Hampton, Natalie—Interviews

"I Made Kindness Go Viral" cartoon color *Seventeen* v76 no12 p22 D 2016/Ja 2017

Hampton, Randolph Y.

New developments for protein quality control diag *Science* v357 no6350 p450 Ag 4 2017

Hampton, Stephanie E.

Skills and Knowledge for Data-Intensive Environmental Research *BioScience* v67 no6 p546 Je 2017

Synthesis Centers as Critical Research Infrastructure *BioScience* v67 no8 p750 Ag 2017

Toward a national, sustained U.S. ecosystem assessment bibl color *Science* v354 no6314 p838 N 18 2016

Hampton Creek Foods Inc.

The Mayo Mogul B. Bosker color *Atlantic* v320 no4 p76 N 2017

Hampton Sun (Company)

Sunscreen Saviors color *Essence* v48 no3 p38 Jl 2017

Hampton Yacht Group LLC

Hampton 650 Pilothouse Motoryacht *Sea Magazine* v108 no12 p51 D 2016

HAMPTON 650 PILOTHOUSE M. WERLING *Sea Magazine* v108 no10 p38 O 2016 Maritimo M54 *Sea Magazine* v108 no12 p52 D 2016

STRONG SILENT TYPE R. THIEL chart color diag *Power & Motoryacht* v33 no2 p94 F 2017

Hamptons (N.Y.)

PERFECT FIT color *Architectural Digest* v74 no10 pCover O 1 2017

Hamri, Ghislaine Charpin-El

β-cell–mimetic designer cells provide closed-loop glycemic control bibl graph *Science* v354 no6317 p1296 D 9 2016

Hamrick, Karen

Americans Spend an Average of 37 Minutes a Day Preparing and Serving Food and Cleaning Up *Amber Waves: The Economics of Food, Farming, Natural Resources, & Rural America* p26 N 2016

Hamsters

Guinness World Records K. HUNT color *National Geographic Kids* no465 p5 N 2016

Hamstring muscle

5 WAYS...To Hit the Clute-Ham Tie-In K. LOREN color *Muscle & Performance* v9 no7 p66 Jl 2017

The Flexibility Factor L. MCGLASHAN color *Muscle & Performance* v9 no11 p28 N 2017

HAMSTRING HELPERS B. SABIN color *Runner's World* v51 no11 p54 D 2016

Move Like an Old Pro cartoon chart color *Men's Health* v32 no8 p54 O 2017

Pilates to Improve Your Lifts S. MAIN color *Muscle & Performance* v9 no7 p22 Jl 2017

POSITION STATEMENT [Cover story] B. Sabin color *Runner's World* v51 no11 p52 D 2016

Turn & Burn L. McGLASHAN chart color *Muscle & Performance* v9 no7 p16 Jl 2017

Why Your Hammies Are Tight C. ROSSI chart color *Muscle & Performance* v9 no8 p28 Ag 2017

Hamstring muscle—Anatomy

Get to know... your hamstrings J. Gudmestad color *Yoga Journal* p90 2017 SpecialIssue

Get to know ... Your hamstrings J. Miller color *Yoga Journal* no294 p62 S 2017

Han, Hahrie

A Guide to Managing a Volunteer Workforce *Harvard Business Review Digital Articles* p2 Mr 2 2016

Han, Hua

China's proper role in the global nuclear order bibl *Bulletin of the Atomic Scientists* v73 no2 p128 Mr 2017

Han, Jian

Nanocrystalline copper films are never flat diag graph *Science* v357 no6349 p397 Jl 28 2017

Han, Kang, 1970-

Body Language S. Begley color *Time* v189 no4 p49 Ja 23 2017

Han Kang D. Kiper color *Current Biography* v77 no10 p49 O 2016

No. 6 THE VEGETARIAN L. Greenblatt color *Entertainment Weekly* no1444/1445 p104 D 16 2016

A novel for frightening times *Christian Century* v134 no8 p1 Ap 12 2017

What the Dead Know NAMI MUN *New York Times Book Review* p12 Ja 15 2017

WHEN TIME STOPPED FOREVER E. T. KIM color *Nation* v304 no8 p32 Mr 13 2017

Han, Ming-Fei

Deterministic entanglement generation from driving through quantum phase transitions bibl color graph *Science* v355 no6325 p620 F 10 2017

Han, Murui

Restored iron transport by a small molecule promotes absorption and hemoglobinization in animals color graph *Science* v356 no6338 p608 My 12 2017

Han, Seung Baek

Restoring auditory cortex plasticity in adult mice by restricting thalamic adenosine signaling graph *Science* v356 no6345 p1352 Je 30 2017

Han, Shi-Lei

"Perfect" designer chromosome V and behavior of a ring derivative diag *Science* v355 no6329 p1046 Mr 10 2017

Han, Shu-Jen

Carbon nanotube transistors scaled to a 40-nanometer footprint color graph *Science* v356 no6345 p1369 Je 30 2017

Han, Ting

Anticancer sulfonamides target splicing by inducing RBM39 degradation via recruitment to DCAF15 color diag *Science* v356 no6336 p397 Ap 28 2017

Han, Wenqi

Control of species-dependent cortico-motoneuronal connections underlying manual dexterity diag graph *Science* v357 no6349 p400 Jl 28 2017

Han Lin

Prejudgment call color *Science* v355 no6320 p22 Ja 6 2017

Han Seok Ko

Pathological α-synuclein transmission initiated by binding lymphocyte-activation gene 3 bibl graph *Science* v353 no6307 paah3374-1 S 30 2016

Hana Takemoto

veggie bits. Vegan Ben & Jerry's *Vegetarian Journal* v35 no4 p28 2016

Hanako Mochimaru

Methane production from coal by a single methanogen bibl graph *Science* v354 no6309 p222 O 14 2016

Hanauer, Annie

Against All Odds L. Cappelle color *Dance Magazine* v91 no3 p52 Mr 2017

Hanauer, Cathi

The Other Side of 40 L. GOTTLIEB *New York Times Book Review* p23 O 9 2016

Hanbury, Mary

The BEST BANK FOR YOU color diag map *Money* v45 no10 p86 N 2016

Hanc, John

heavenly rest cartoon *Yoga Journal* p82 2017 Special Issue

MIKEY BRANNIGAN color *Runner's World* v52 no1 p88 Ja/F 2017

Hancock, Brian
ASK SAIL color *Sail* v48 no3 p58 Mr 2017
LOFTY THOUGHTS ALL ABOUT MAINSAILS color *Sail* v48 no3 p48 Mr 2017
New-look VOR Boats color *Sail* v48 no8 p20 Ag 2017

Hancock, Graham
ALTERNATIVE ARCHAEOLOGY *Scientific American* v317 no4 p9 O 2017
Romance of the Vanished Past M. Shermer color *Scientific American* v316 no6 p75 Je 2017

Hancock, Herbie, 1940-
Herbie Hancock's Synthesizer Solo on 'Chameleon' J. DURSO color *Downbeat* v84 no9 p96 S 2017

Hancock, Herbie, 1940-—Interviews
The Science of Jazz N. DEGRASSE TYSON color *National Geographic* v231 no3 p26 Mr 2017

Hancock, John Lee, 1956-
The Founder L. Greenblatt color *Entertainment Weekly* no1450 p46 Ja 27 2017
The Founder V. LUCCA color *Film Comment* v53 no1 p83 Ja/F 2017
Potted Kroc J. PODHORETZ *Weekly Standard* v22 no21 p39 F 6 2017

HANCOCK, LYNNELL
How School Desegregation Unraveled bw color *Nation* v303 no19 p16 N 7 2016

Hancock, Maryanne
Put the "and" Back in "Sales and Marketing" *Harvard Business Review Digital Articles* p2 O 30 2014

Hancock, Sarah
Rewriting a Family History color *Women's Health* v13 no10 p100 D 2016

HANCOCK, STEVEN
Doses of Neighborhood Nature: The Benefits for Mental Health of Living with Nature *BioScience* v67 no2 p147 F 2017

Hancock, Terry
READER GALLERY bw color *Astronomy* v45 no11 p72 N 2017

Hancock County (Ind.)
FRESH HEIR T. BRAND color *Indianapolis Monthly* p34 Ap 2017

Hancox, Edward
BIG TIME VIRTUAL REALITY *Iceland Review* v55 no1 p6 Ja/F 2017

Hand
See also
Fingers
To help you stabilize your hand position... M. LaBarre color *Dressage Today* v23 no6 p72 F 2017

Hand, Cynthia
My Lady Jane color *Publishers Weekly* v263 no49 p109 D 7 2016

Hand, Eric
Cosmic ray catcher will probe supernovae from new perch color *Science* v357 no6350 p437 Ag 4 2017
CubeSat networks hasten shift to commercial weather data color *Science* v357 no6347 p118 Jl 14 2017
Fossil leaves bear witness to ancient carbon dioxide levels color graph *Science* v355 no6320 p14 Ja 6 2017
LORD OF THE RINGS color diag *Science* v356 no6335 p236 Ap 21 2017
MANIPULATING ULTRACOLD MATTER [Cover story] color *Science* v357 no6355 p984 S 8 2017

HAND, GREG
NIGHT CLUBBING *Cincinnati Magazine* v50 no8 p51 My 2017
NIGHT MOVES *Cincinnati Magazine* v50 no8 p40 My 2017
What Does the Fox Say? *Cincinnati Magazine* v50 no6 p56 Mr 2017

Hand, Keith
Q: What is the most interesting family in history? color *Atlantic* v318 no5 p96 D 2016

Hand, Maureen
Wind on the Upswing *MIT Technology Review* v119 no6 p11 N/D 2016

Hand anatomy
Talk to the hand(s) C. T. Burns color *Health* v31 no9 p33 N 2017

Hand diseases
How to Fix Trigger Finger M. Gunch cartoon *New Orleans Magazine* v51 no7 p46 My 2017

Hand exercises
TRY THIS! STRONG & LONG S. Munroe and D. Denunzio color *Golf Magazine* v59 no11 p50 N 2017

Hand games
See also
Rock-paper-scissors (Game)
WHO KNEW? Win at Rock, Paper, Scissors (And Other Sly Gimmicks) A. SIMMONS *Reader's Digest* v189 no1127 p124 F 2017

Hand in art
Talk to the Hand H. MARTIN color *Architectural Digest* no5 p26 My 2017

Hand-railing
Replace warped handrails on an HO scale diesel C. Grivno color diag *Model Railroader* v84 no5 p22 My 2017

Hand sanitizers
KEEP YOUR HANDS CLEAN C. Barakat and M. McCluskey color *Equus* no480 p18 S 2017

Hand sanitizers—Evaluation
Guido Palau color *InStyle* v24 no11 p148 N 2017
Winter Is Coming color *InStyle* v24 no11 p134 N 2017

Hand surgery
A Spare Hand D. Robitzski color *Scientific American* v316 no5 p17 My 2017

Hand washing
This Just In J. Zorthian *Time* v189 no23 p21 Je 19 2017

Hand washing—Equipment & supplies
LET'S GET HEALTHY-ISH A. RAPOPORT color *Bon Appetit* no1 p8 F 2017
MESSAGE ON A BOTTLE A. Finney bw color *Women's Health* v14 no3 p(Sp)22 Ap 2017
starters M. Perello, L. MENNIES et al color *Bon Appetit* no1 p13 F 2017

Handahu, Mo
The most versatile dress color *Redbook* p82 F 2017

Handbag design
Too Much Baggage M. TINDERA color *Forbes* v198 no6 p48 N 8 2016

Handbag industry
ECOCHIC DESIGN K. ABNEY *Atlanta* v57 no2 p40 Je 2017

Handbags
See also
Tote bags
Anything to DECLARE? color *Esquire* p112 S 2017
The BUY Fashion color *Harper's Bazaar* no3656 p172 S 2017
Candy Crush color *Vogue* v206 no12 p160 D 2016
FRINGE BENEFITS color *Harper's Bazaar* no3656 p210 S 2017
THE HERO K. PIERI color *Harper's Bazaar* no3656 p154 S 2017
HOW TO WEAR IT... K. SALADINO and L. BERGAMOTTO color *Good Housekeeping* v265 no2 p14 Ag 2017
The In/Out LIST color *Harper's Bazaar* no3656 p227 S 2017
RED ZONE color *Harper's Bazaar* no3656 p314 S 2017
SMALL WONDER color *Harper's Bazaar* no3656 p311 S 2017
SPORTING NEWS color *Harper's Bazaar* no3656 p256 S 2017
TAILOR-MADE color *Harper's Bazaar* no3656 p255 S 2017
Tassels & Pom-Poms color *Good Housekeeping* v265 no2 p13 Ag 2017
WHAT WE LOVE color *Harper's Bazaar* no3656 p97 S 2017
WINE COUNTRY color *Harper's Bazaar* no3656 p316 S 2017
Work the LOOK: FALL'S MUST-HAVES color *Harper's Bazaar* no3656 p293 S 2017
Work Those Resale Sites F. Kane color *Glamour* v115 no10 p80 O 2017

Handbags—Evaluation
90 YEARS OF STYLE bw color *Harper's Bazaar* no3654 p44 Je/Jl 2017
Arm Candy A. R. Williams color *Southern Living* v52 no2 p67 F 2017
ARTFUL ACCESSORIES color *Harper's Bazaar* no3650 p192 F 2017
Bergen On Bags color *InStyle* v24 no7 p68 Jl 2017
BLANK SLATE color *Harper's Bazaar* no3652 p142 Ap 2017
Boho Mermaid cartoon color *Seventeen* v76 no12 p37 D 2016/Ja 2017
Bright Ideas M. BOBO color *Ebony* v72 no5 p35 Mr 2017

The Bucket List E. Velluto color *Glamour* v115 no3 p72 Mr 2017

CHERRY BOMB color *Harper's Bazaar* no3649 p191 D 2016/Ja 2017

Christmas Clutches color *Good Housekeeping* v263 no6 p40 D 2016

Define Yourself F. Kane, S. P. Nadella et al color *Glamour* v115 no3 p60 Mr 2017

Different Strokes color *Los Angeles Magazine* v62 no7 p26 Jl 2017

DOPE STUFF ON MY DESK J. Wilson color *Essence* v47 no7 p20 N 2016

DOPE STUFF ON MY DESK J. Wilson color *Essence* v48 no3 p26 Jl 2017

DREAM WEAVER color *Conde Nast Traveler* v52 no6 p24 Je/Jl 2017

ECOCHIC DESIGN K. ABNEY *Atlanta* v57 no2 p40 Je 2017

Genius Jeans color *InStyle* v24 no4 p127 Ap 2017

Get Your Art to Go L. IMMEDIATO *Los Angeles Magazine* p29 Ja 2017

THE GIRL Zoey Deutch E. Wilson color *InStyle* v24 no4 p89 Ap 2017

Go West! color *Glamour* v115 no10 p68 O 2017

GREAT BUYS color *O, The Oprah Magazine* p60 F 2017

HEAVY METALS color *Harper's Bazaar* no3652 p147 Ap 2017

HIGH ART color *Harper's Bazaar* no3649 p172 D 2016/Ja 2017

HOW ROUGE! Scarlet, crimson, ruby, fire-engine—whatever you call it, this season's hottest hue will have you seeing red S. STEVENSON color *Indianapolis Monthly* v42 no2 p30 O 2017

I Can't Believe It's RUBBER! color *Women's Health* v14 no3 p50 Ap 2017

In a Stitch color *Seventeen* v76 no3 p36 My 2017

The In Out LIST color *Harper's Bazaar* no3651 p214 Mr 2017

IN THE DETAILS color *Harper's Bazaar* no3650 p101 F 2017

The LIST color *Harper's Bazaar* no3649 p129 D 2016/Ja 2017

The LIST color *Harper's Bazaar* no3652 p93 Ap 2017

Lug your stuff in style color *Redbook* p67 F 2017

Market color *Vanity Fair* v59 no4 p102 Mr 2017

Market color *Vanity Fair* v59 no8 p45 Ag 2017

MINI BAGS color *Good Housekeeping* v264 no2 p18 F 2017

on demand color *InStyle* v24 no3 p113 Mr 2017

on demand color *InStyle* v24 no6 p29 Je 2017

Primary Picks! color *Good Housekeeping* v264 no4 p27 Ap 2017

ROOM TO MOVE color *Esquire* p56 Ap 2017

Safe Bet L. Bailey *Indianapolis Monthly* v40 no10 p27 Je 2017

Shear Genius color *Glamour* v115 no11 p54 N 2017

Shop Like an Editor color *InStyle* v23 no12 p151 N 2016

A skirt that goes anywhere K. Smith color *Redbook* p76 My 2017

SMALL WONDERS color *Essence* v47 no7 p16 N 2016

Start With Your Bag color *Glamour* v115 no10 p56 O 2017

Strap Happy! E. Velluto color *Glamour* v114 no12 p98 D 2016

Think Small E. Velluto color *Glamour* no8 p70 Ag 2017

Wait LIST color *Harper's Bazaar* no3649 p132 D 2016/Ja 2017

a week of awesome outfits color *Good Housekeeping* v264 no2 p30 F 2017

WHAT'S COOL NOW color *Harper's Bazaar* no3652 p224 Ap 2017

WHAT WE LOVE color *Harper's Bazaar* no3650 p44 F 2017

WHAT WE LOVE color *Harper's Bazaar* no3652 p42 Ap 2017

Why I Love MY EDIE PARKER CLUTCH T. P. Henson color *InStyle* v24 no5 p262 My 2017

Handbags—Sales & prices

Fashion's Great Handbag Crash P. Wahba color *Fortune* v175 no4 p18 Mr 15 2017

Safe Bet L. Bailey *Indianapolis Monthly* v40 no10 p27 Je 2017

Hand—Care & hygiene

Age-proof your hands M. OLIVA color *Redbook* p36 Mr 2017

Handcarts

IDEA OF THE MONTH P. Barbour *Successful Farming* v115 no2 p80 F 2017

Handedness

THE POLITICS OF LEFT-HANDEDNESS *Sea Magazine* v109 no4 p30 Ap 2017

Handel, George Frideric, 1685-1759. Messiah

Hastings traditions inspire ageless symphonic voices E. Case color *Nebraska Life* v20 no6 p64 N/D 2016

Handel, Karen

All Politics Are National C. DEATON color *Weekly Standard* v22 no39 p15 Je 19 2017

The Body Politic: Rebecca Traister: Georgia's Silver Lining A new game plan for the Democratic Party emerges out of Jon Ossofrs loss img *New York* v50 no13 p17 Je 26 2017

HANDEL, MICHAEL F.

What are middle skills? bw *Issues in Science & Technology* v33 no2 p6 Wint 2017

Handel: Alcina (Music)

Handel: Alcina J. Malafroute *Opera News* v81 no6 p53 D 2016

Handelsman, Jo

Not just Salk color *Science* v357 no6356 p1105 S 15 2017

HANDEY, JACK

NEVER GIVE UP cartoon *New Yorker* v92 no33 p37 O 17 2016

Handheld video game consoles—Evaluation

Turn your iPhone 7 into a handheld console A. Hayward color *Macworld - Digital Edition* p97 Ap 2017

Handicraft

See also

Egg decoration

Jewelry making

Leatherwork

Mask making

Paper work

Tape craft

Textile arts

Wreaths

ADDITIONAL LISTINGS *Arts & Crafts Homes & the Revival* v12 no1 p30 2017 Resouce Guide

All trails lead to Ash Hollow S. W. KANSTEINER color *Nebraska Life* v21 no4 p90 Jl/Ag 2017

cozy creations *Parents* p34 2015

Crafted with a Purpose L. A. Addington color *Missouri Life* v44 no4 p16 Je 2017

crafts for a cause! *Parents* v91 no11 p52 N 2016

fun [Cover story] color *Parents* v92 no7 p51 Jl 2017

The Future Perfect D. DANIEL color *American Craft* v76 no6 p28 D 2016-Ja 2017

Good Fortune C. M. Cunningham color *Southern Living* v52 no2 p43 F 2017

make sparks fly M. POLLITT color *Better Homes & Gardens* v95 no7 p68 Jl 2017

Make Your Fridge Even Cooler *Parents* v92 no2 p86 F 2017

map it out *Parents* v91 no9 p139 S 2016

Pass the Crayons color *AARP: The Magazine* v60 no1A p60 D 2016/Ja 2017

pop-up shop *Parents* v91 no6 p64 Je 2016

resources *Parents* p140 2015

RIPPLE EFFECT H. Yanagihara bw color *Conde Nast Traveler* v52 no5 p98 My 2017

a season of smiles *Parents* v91 no12 p81 D 2016

(sm)art idea C. Harris *Parents* v91 no11 p109 N 2016

To The Editor A. Mason, M. Carney et al color *American Craft* v76 no6 p10 D 2016-Ja 2017

very useful valentines *Parents* v92 no2 p54 F 2017

Who is pushing the craft field forward? J. VANGOOL, D. HARROW et al color *American Craft* v76 no6 p26 D 2016-Ja 2017

Handicraft equipment

1968 CRAFTING SPACE K. K. CONDON color *Better Homes & Gardens* v95 no7 p172 Jl 2017

My Collection B. Welch color *Horse & Rider* v56 no7 p112 Jl 2017

Handicraft in the home

house of sunshine M. E. POLSON color *Old House Journal* v45 no6 p14 S 2017

Handicraft—21st century

Collecting, Evolving color *American Craft* v77 no2 p8 Ap/My 2017

What do you collect and why? G. HUBERMAN, H. H. TIDWELL et al color *American Craft* v77 no2 p20 Ap/My 2017

Handicraft—Congresses

UP FRONT: EVENTS + EXHIBITS color *Arts & Crafts Homes & the Revival* v11 no5 p20 Wint 2017

Handicraft—Evaluation

Hand and Machine color *American Craft* v76 no6 p24 D 2016-Ja 2017

Handicraft—Exhibitions

Shows to See color *American Craft* v76 no6 p20 D 2016-Ja 2017

Handicraft—History

Collecting, Evolving color *American Craft* v77 no2 p8 Ap/My 2017

Handke, Peter, 1942-

A Balkans of the Mind J. COHEN *New York Times Book Review* p7 Ja 1 2017

SOUND AND FURY P. Handke *Harper's Magazine* v333 no1999 p19 D 2016

The Stranger in Love A. Kirsch bw *New York Review of Books* v64 no2 p37 F 9 2017

Handkerchiefs

LOVE STORY F. VIGNA color *Martha Stewart Living* no271 p116 Ja/F 2017

Handler, Chelsea, 1975-

What, Me Worry? color *InStyle* v24 no6 p156 Jc 2017

Handler, Chelsea, 1975- —Interviews

Chelsea's Back for More J. HALTERMAN *TV Guide* v65 no14 p10 Ap 3 2017

Handler, Daniel, 1970-

ABOVE & BEYOND bw *New Yorker* v93 no28 p14 S 18 2017

ALL THE DIRTY PARTS color *Entertainment Weekly* no1446/1447 p83 D 2016/Ja 2017

Gretchen Rubin *New York Times Book Review* p11 O 23 2016

Händler, Kristian

Mapping the human DC lineage through the integration of high-dimensional techniques diag *Science* v356 no6342 p1044 Je 9 2017

Handles

CAN YOU HANDLE IT? Statement-making cabinet hardware F. Stephanie *Washingtonian Magazine* v53 no1 p160 O 2017

Handles—Evaluation

PUNCH LIST K. SELZER color *Better Homes & Gardens* v95 no8 p66 Ag 2017

Handley Page airplanes

See also

Halifax (Bomber)

On the Nose bw *Military History* v34 no1 p80 My 2017

Handloading of ammunition

CONCENTRICITY R. MANN and J. B. SNOW color *Outdoor Life* v224 no5 pR4 Je/Jl 2017

THE SLIDE STOP R. MANN color *Outdoor Life* v224 no8 pP5 O 2017

Handly, Jim

THE NEW JIM A. Beaujon *Washingtonian Magazine* v52 no3 p45 D 2016

Handmaiden, The (Film)

The Handmaiden K. P. Sullivan color *Entertainment Weekly* no1436/1437 p87 O 21 2016

No. 6 THE HANDMAIDEN L. Greenblatt color *Entertainment Weekly* no1444/1445 p54 D 16 2016

To Do img *New York* v49 no22 p116 O 31 2016

WOMEN's WORK A. LANE cartoon *New Yorker* v92 no34 p84 O 24 2016

Handmaid's Tale, The (TV program)

THE Anticipation Index *New York* p61 Ja 23 2017

Dystopia, Now Playing J. Zinoman color *Bloomberg Businessweek* no4528 p74 Je 26 2017

The Dystopian Style in American Politics C. ROSEN *Commentary* v143 no6 p9 Je 2017

ELISABETH MOSS'S MAD WORLD M. Tedder color *Esquire* p26 My 2017

Emmy Races to Watch M. ROUSH *TV Guide* v65 no37 p10 S 4 2017

The Handmaid and the Despot J. Stites *In These Times* v41 no5 p38 My 2017

The Handmaid's Tale M. ROUSH *TV Guide* p18 Ap 17 2017

The Handmaid's Tale, Retold E. Dockterman color *Time* v189 no15 p45 Ap 24 2017

The Handmaid's Tale S. Vilkomerson color *Entertainment Weekly* no1442 p13 D 2 2016 Rebellious Special Issue

INSIDE THE HANDMAID'S STUDIO C. Brody color *Entertainment Weekly* no1467 p50 My 26 2017

Newly Resonant Nonsense color *Weekly Standard* v22 no33 p2 My 8 2017

The Next Chapter: Television's best shows are taking their cues from literature M. Z. SEITZ img *New York* v50 no10 p98 My 15 2017

A NIGHT of FIRSTS L. Rice, D. Snierson et al color *Entertainment Weekly* no1484 p18 S 29 2017

Real Housewives S. JONES *New Republic* v248 no5 p58 My 2017

A Strait-Laced America S. ERICKSON *Los Angeles Magazine* p64 My 2017

Trumped up TV J. WEINMAN color *Maclean's* v129 no51/52 p70 D 26 2016

TV's Great New Heroine Is Born In The Handmaid's Tale D. D'Addario color *Time* v189 no18 p53 My 15 2017

What to Watch C. Collis, S. Li et al color *Entertainment Weekly* no1470 p52 Je 16 2017

Women's Work C. Wren color *Commonweal* v144 no12 p30 Jl 7 2017

Handpicked: A Tutorial on Simple, Seasonal Arrangements (Film)

armchair inspiration color *Better Homes & Gardens* v95 no7 p96 Jl 2017

Handsaws—Evaluation

Roundup for Fall color *Old House Journal* v45 no6 p50 S 2017

Handshaking

Good Tidings, Fellow Male: A Modern Guide to Man-to-Man Greetings C. SKIPPER bw color diag graph *GQ: Gentlemen's Quarterly* v97 no10 p154 O 2017

gringo syndrome m. ferrentino bw *Bike Magazine* v24 no5 p50 Jl 2017

Handsome (Film)

Jeff Garlin R. Bruner color *Time* v189 no19 p50 My 22 2017

Handt, Kai—Interviews

Kai Handt: 'Never Blame the Horse' T. Conahan color *Practical Horseman* v45 no10 p22 O 2017

Handwerker, Elizabeth Weber

Longitudinal data from the Occupational Employment Statistics survey bibl chart color graph *Monthly Labor Review* p1 O 2016

HANDY, BRUCE

Another Brief (ONE HOPES) Shining (PERHAPS) Moment? color *Vanity Fair* v59 no2 p40 F 2017

THE DEADLIEST KLATCH bw *Vanity Fair* p170 Hollywood 2017 Supplement

DEAD RECKONING bw *Vanity Fair* v59 no6 p72 My 2017

Kyle MACLACHLAN bw *Esquire* p124 My 2017

PLAZA SUITE color *Vanity Fair* v59 no8 p94 Ag 2017

Reading Rock *New York Times Book Review* p19 Je 4 2017

Handy, Charles

The Seductions of the Infosphere *Harvard Business Review Digital Articles* p2 Jl 15 2015

Han dynasty, China, 202 B.C.-220 A.D.

139 BC: China S. Qian *Lapham's Quarterly* v10 no2 p167 Spr 2017

Hanemann, Michael W.

Best cost estimate of greenhouse gases *Science* v357 no6352 p655 Ag 18 2017

Contingent valuation: Flawed logic? color *Science* v357 no6349 p363 Jl 28 2017

HANEY, JESSICA

r.s.v.p bw *Bon Appetit* no11 p12 N 2017

Haney, Lisa

LISTEN UP, Doc! chart color *O, The Oprah Magazine* p75 S 2017

MOTHER SUCKER! color *Women's Health* v14 no5 p72 Je 2017

THE ODDS AND ENDS OF ZEN color *Women's Health* v14 no4 p121 My 2017

THE SECRETS OF HEALTHY PEOPLE *Martha Stewart Living* no267 p58 S 2016

STREET SMARTS color *Runner's World* v51 no10 p40 N 2016

Veg Out for Your HEALTH! cartoon *O, The Oprah Magazine* p94 F 2017

Haney, Matthew M.

Volcanic tremor and plume height hysteresis from Pavlof Volcano, Alaska bibl graph *Science* v355 no6320 p1 Ja 6 2017

HANEY, THOMAS

Baptism by Fire color *Backpacker* p84 Ag 2017

Hanfling, Dan

The right planning now will save countless lives after a nuclear attack bibl *Bulletin of the Atomic Scientists* v73 no4 p220 Jl 2017

Hangar design & construction
HANGIN' TOUGH M. Jancer color *Car & Driver* v63 no1 p24 Jl 2017

Hangard, L.
iPTF16geu: A multiply imaged, gravitationally lensed type Ia supernova color diag graph *Science* v356 no6335 p291 Ap 21 2017

Hangartner, Dominik
How economic, humanitarian, and religious concerns shape European attitudes toward asylum seekers bibl graph map *Science* v354 no6309 p217 O 14 2016

Hanging baskets
Comfort & Curb Appeal L. Elliott color *Old House Journal* v45 no4 p48 Je 2017
Get the Hang of It color *Martha Stewart Living* p17 Ap 2017

Hanging of art
AND...FADE-OUT E. N. GAGE color *Martha Stewart Living* p19 My 2017

Hanging plants—Evaluation
PLANT KINGDOM J. Silver color *Sunset* v238 no2 p60 F 2017

Hanging of the Schoolmarm, The (Short story)
The Hanging of the Schoolmarm R. Coover cartoon *New Yorker* v92 no39 p80 N 28 2016

Hangovers
HANGOVER B. LUTZ color *New Orleans Magazine* v51 no2 p36 D 2016
THE HANGOVER IS ... OVER M. Robin color *InStyle* v23 no13 p186 D 2016
HOW DO I PREVENT & SURVIVE A HANG OVER L. Krieger color *Harper's Bazaar* no3649 p268 D 2016/Ja 2017
I'll Drink to That! B. HOWARD color *AARP: The Magazine* v59 no1A p20 D 2015/Ja 2016

Hangzhou Qiandaohu Xunlong Sci-tech Co. Ltd.
The Chinese Caviar Connection K. Krader color *Bloomberg Businessweek* no4539 p73 S 25 2017

Haniffa, Muzlifah
Mapping the human DC lineage through the integration of high-dimensional techniques diag *Science* v356 no6342 p1044 Je 9 2017
Single-cell RNA-seq reveals new types of human blood dendritic cells, monocytes, and progenitors color *Science* v356 no6335 p283 Ap 21 2017

HANIS, MARK
A KINDER TRUMAN DOCTRINE *Foreign Affairs* v96 no6 p175 N/D 2017

Hanke, John
The Steve Jobs OF WEST TEXAS M. AGRESTA *Texas Monthly* v45 no2 p43 F 2017

Hanke, Steve
THE MAN WHO WOULD KILL YOUR HOLIDAYS M. Hongoltz-Hetling color *Popular Science* v289 no5 p22 S/O 2017

Hanke, W.
Bismuthene on a SiC substrate: A candidate for a high-temperature quantum spin Hall material diag graph *Science* v357 no6348 p287 Jl 21 2017

Hankemeier, Thomas
Activity-based protein profiling reveals off-target proteins of the FAAH inhibitor BIA 10-2474 chart color graph *Science* v356 no6342 p1084 Je 9 2017

Hankerson, Amanda
WHAT'S IN A NAME? V. Mallory Kotz color *Popular Photography* v81 no2 p22 Mr/Ap 2017

Hankins, Kevin
ask the experts color *Dressage Today* v23 no8 p66 Ap 2017
Position Your Horse for Success This Year color *Dressage Today* v23 no6 p14 F 2017
Q&A: Your Horse's Vaccinations [Cover story] color *Horse & Rider* v56 no5 p26 My 2017

Hankinson, Andrew
TABLE TALK cartoon *New Yorker* v93 no25 p33 Ag 28 2017

Hankison, Amanda—Interviews
AV CLUB Davidaisy bw *Snowboarder* v29 no5 p29 Ja 2017

Hanks, Colin, 1977-—Interviews
Colin Hanks's SLICE OF LIFE J. HALTERMAN *TV Guide* p32 D 5 2014

Hanks, Tom, 1956-

THE WORLD ACCORDING TO Gayle G. King color *O, The Oprah Magazine* p36 N 2017

Hanks, Tom, 1956-—Interviews
Tom Hanks *New York Times Book Review* p8 O 15 2017

Hanley, Brian
One Man's Quest to Hack His Own Genes A. Regalado color il *MIT Technology Review* v120 no2 p13 Mr/Ap 2017

Hanley, Nick
Driving improvements in emerging disease surveillance through locally relevant capacity strengthening color diag *Science* v357 no6347 p146 Jl 14 2017

Hanna, Janan
Law Pushing Back on Public Dissent color *Bloomberg Businessweek* no4511 p26 F 13 2017
More Poll Monitors May Mean More Trouble *Bloomberg Businessweek* no4495 p21 O 17 2016

Hanna, Mark G.
A Lot of What Is Known about Pirates Is Not True, and a Lot of What Is True Is Not Known *Humanities* v38 no1 p1 Wint 2017

Hanna, Rema
Citywide effects of high-occupancy vehicle restrictions: Evidence from "three-in-one" in Jakarta chart graph map *Science* v357 no6346 p89 Jl 7 2017
Technology beats corruption bibl color *Science* v355 no6322 p244 Ja 20 2017

HANNAFORD, ALEX
Wave GOODBYE *Texas Monthly* v45 no6 p35 Je 2017

Hannaford, Jamie
Changing climate shifts timing of European floods color graph *Science* v357 no6351 p588 Ag 11 2017

Hannah, Aja
Hawaiian Natives Fight for Their Land color *Progressive* v81 no10 p32 N 2016

Hannah, Kristin, 1960-
Deals R. DEAHL bw color *Publishers Weekly* v264 no22 p12 My 29 2017

HANNAH, MARTIN
AMERICAN IDEAL color *Architectural Digest* v73 no11 p60 N 2016

Hannah-Jones, Nikole
Common Sense *New York Times Magazine* p13 F 26 2017
DIVIDING LINES *New York Times Magazine* p40 S 10 2017
EQUAL OPPORTUNITY CLASSROOMS A. Hall color *Literacy Today (2411-7862)* v34 no5 p38 Mr/Ap 2017
Iowa *New York Times Magazine* p43 N 20 2016

Hannah-Jones, Nikole, 1976-—Interviews
'Conversations Aren't Enough' M. LINDBERG *Education Digest* v82 no9 p9 My 2017

HANNAM, MICHAEL
Submersed Aquatic Vegetation in Chesapeake Bay: Sentinel Species in a Changing World *BioScience* v67 no8 p698 Ag 2017

Hannan, Caleb
He Objects bw *Bloomberg Businessweek* no4533 p25 Ag 7 2017

Hannant, Larry
The First of Many *History Today* v67 no1 p17 Ja 2017

Hanneman, Eli
BEST 14 AND UNDER color *Surfing Magazine* v53 no1 p56 Ja 2017

Hanner, Dan
INSIDE THE RANKINGS color *Sports Illustrated* v125 no15 p56 N 7 2016

Hannesdóttir, Ellen Inga
EYE ON PARADISE R. Mercer *Iceland Review* v54 no6 p52 N/D 2016

Hannibal, 247 B.C.-182 B.C.
Hannibal's Lost Road F. Lidz *Smithsonian* v48 no4 p108 Jl/Ag 2017
HOW TO SNEAK UP ON AN EMPIRE K. BURKE *Smithsonian* v48 no4 p114 Jl/Ag 2017

Hannibal, Mary Ellen
Citizen Scientist C. Moskowitz color *Scientific American* v315 no6 p82 D 2016
Citizen scientists help planet in peril L. Hamers color *Science News* v190 no9 p29 O 29 2016
Natural Data Detectives G. WINGENBACH color *Earth Island Journal* v32 no1 p54 Spr 2017

Hannigan, Robert E.
The Great War and American Foreign Policy, 1914–24 W. Russell Mead *Foreign Affairs* v96 no3 p162 My/Je 2017

Hannigan, T. J.
Local R&D Won't Help You Go Global *Harvard Business Review Digital Articles* p2 Je 25 2015
Sometimes Cutting R&D Spending Can Yield More Innovation *Harvard Business Review Digital Articles* p2 Ja 8 2015

Hannity, Sean, 1961-
And Then There Was Hannity F. Gillette and A. Sakoui bw color *Bloomberg Businessweek* no4520 p54 My 1 2017
The Pyne Tree K. Cook *Smithsonian* v48 no3 p18 Je 2017

Hannon, Dolly
Uncover the Mystery of "On the Bit" color diag *Dressage Today* v23 no11 p24 Ag 2017

Hannon, Eric
Technology Is Changing Transportation, and Cities Should Adapt *Harvard Business Review Digital Articles* p2 S 13 2017

Hanoverian horse
DRESSAGE SNAPSHOTS color *Dressage Today* v23 no7 p15 Mr 2017
The Kindergarten Years D. K. Skvarla color *Dressage Today* v23 no6 p50 F 2017

HANRAHAN, ROBERT M.
ICING ABOVE cartoon *Flying* v144 no2 p24 F 2017

Hanren Dai
CAR T-cell-based therapeutic modality in solid tumors. How to achieve precision bibl color *Science* v354 no6319 p27 D 23 2016

Hänsch, Theodor W.
The Rydberg constant and proton size from atomic hydrogen bw chart color diag graph *Science* v357 no6359 p79 O 6 2017

Hanse, Gil
Bet On Black J. Passov and J. Marksbury color *Golf Magazine* v59 no10 p27 O 2017
GIL HANSE J. Passov color *Golf Magazine* v59 no1 p92 Ja 2017
Mississippi Queen J. Passov and C. Barrett color *Golf Magazine* v59 no1 p36 Ja 2017

Hanse, Gil—Interviews
All Over the Map J. Passov color *Golf Magazine* v59 no10 p82 O 2017

Hansel, Armin
Global atmospheric particle formation from CERN CLOUD measurements bibl graph map *Science* v354 no6316 p1119 D 2 2016

Hansel, Patrick Cabello
Cutting away *Christian Century* v134 no22 p11 O 25 2017

HANSELL, SALLY
FOXFIRE AT 50 *Atlanta* v56 no8 p27 D 2016

Hansen, Andreas W.
Big Data Is Only Half the Data Marketers Need *Harvard Business Review Digital Articles* p2 N 16 2015

Hansen, C.
Jupiter's interior and deep atmosphere: The initial pole-to-pole passes with the Juno spacecraft [Cover story] color graph *Science* v356 no6340 p821 My 26 2017

Hansen, Chris
HELLEBORES K. C. FREDERICK color *Better Homes & Gardens* v95 no2 p64 F 2016
SMARTEN UP TO SHRINK YOUR GUT color *Men's Health* v32 no4 p52 My 2017
SMARTEN UP TO SHRINK YOUR GUT color *Men's Health* v32 no6 p69 Ag 2017
SMARTEN UP TO SHRINK YOUR GUT color *Men's Health* v32 no9 p73 N 2017

Hansen, Dinah Jane—Interviews
The Fab Four R. MOSELY color *Seventeen* v76 no5 p80 S 2017

Hansen, Dörte
THE OUTSIDERS R. MARLER *New York Times Book Review* p50 D 4 2016

Hansen, E. B.
Majorana bound state in a coupled quantum-dot hybrid-nanowire system bibl graph *Science* v354 no6319 p1557 D 23 2016

Hansen, Eric
Your Move S. CHAPIN color *Walrus* v14 no9 p75 N 2017

Hansen, James
Nuclear power: Deployment speed—Response bibl *Science* v354 no6316 p1113 D 2 2016

Hansen, James E. (James Edward), 1941-—Interviews
WILL WE MISS OUR LAST CHANCE? J. Goodell bw color *Rolling Stone* no1278/1279 p28 Ja 12 2017

Hansen, Jeff—Interviews
JEFF HANSEN: THE OWNER OF IOWA SELECT FARMS IS IN EXPANSION MODE B. Freese color *Successful Farming* v115 no7 p48 My 2017

Hansen, K. C.
Xenon isotopes in 67P/Churyumov-Gerasimenko show that comets contributed to Earth's atmosphere diag *Science* v356 no6342 p1069 Je 9 2017

Hansen, Kenneth
Dog Catcher A. JUNG *Reader's Digest* v189 no1127 p8 F 2017

Hansen, Kristine
Cheers! color *Cabin Living* p12 S 2017
Cheers! color *Cabin Living* p13 Ap 2017
A GOLDEN RAY color *Cabin Living* p16 Ja/F 2017

HANSEN, LUKE
BRINGING DOCTRINE TO LIFE *America* v215 p36 N 28 2016

HANSEN, MARK
ADD FUEL TO THE FIRE WITH MORE OXYGEN color *Bicycling* v58 no7 p19 Ag 2017
TAKE HOME A WIN color *Dressage Today* v23 no10 p15 Jl 2017

Hansen, Matt
The 2018 Buyer's Guide color *Powder* p80 S 2017
593" bw color *Powder* p64 S 2017
The Best Boots of 2018 color *Powder* p95 S 2017
Common Ailments of the Common Skier color *Powder* v46 no2 p40 O 2017
An Ecoregion-Based Approach to Protecting Half the Terrestrial Realm *BioScience* v67 no6 p534 Je 2017
Forward cartoon color *Powder* v45 no4 p68 D 2016
The Heartbeat color *Powder* v45 no6 p36 F 2017
THE HUSTLE bw color *Powder* p72 S 2017
LATITUDES FAT TIMES [Cover story] color *Powder* v45 no6 p54 F 2017
MASHED color *Powder* v45 no3 p140 N 2016
MY MUSTACHE AND ME color *Powder* v45 no6 p48 F 2017
WHAT REALLY MATTERS color *Powder* v45 no5 p34 Ja 2017

Hansen, Matthew E. B.
Going global by adapting local: A review of recent human adaptation bibl diag graph *Science* v354 no6308 p54 O 7 2016

Hansen, Nathaniel F.
Hydraulic control of tuna fins: A role for the lymphatic system in vertebrate locomotion color *Science* v357 no6348 p310 Jl 21 2017

Hansen, P.
Observation of a large-scale anisotropy in the arrival directions of cosmic rays above 8×10^{18} eV *Science* v357 no6357 p1266 S 22 2017

HANSEN, PETER J.
Winners and Losers bw *Weekly Standard* v22 no36 p32 My 29 2017

Hansen, Rasmus Bech
How Tesla, Under Armour, and Sonos Do Branding *Harvard Business Review Digital Articles* p2 O 8 2015

Hansen, Ron
Inner Outlaw A. HAGY *New York Times Book Review* p22 N 20 2016

Hansen, Rose
AGENT DEFEAT Efforts Strike Gold *Science & Technology Review* p12 Mr 2017
A Center of Excellence Prepares for SIERRA *Science & Technology Review* p4 Mr 2017
CHASING THE AMERICAN Dream color *Missouri Life* v44 no4 p38 Je 2017
Laying the Groundwork for EXTREME-SCALE COMPUTING *Science & Technology Review* p5 S 2017
THE LONG GOODBYE bw color *Missouri Life* v44 no5 p52 Ag 2017
A NEW COMPOSITE-MANUFACTURING Approach Takes Shape *Science & Technology Review* p16 Je 2017
TINY BUILDING BLOCKS OFFER OUTSIZED PROTECTION AND BREATHABILITY *Science & Technology Review* p20 D 2016

Hansen, Ryan

Ryan Hansen Solves Crimes on Television* A. Bacle, K. Connolly et al *Entertainment Weekly* no1482/1483 p109 S 22 2017

Hansen, Stephen

A Survey of How 1,000 CEOs Spend Their Day Reveals What Makes Leaders Successful *Harvard Business Review Digital Articles* p2 O 12 2017

Hansen, Suzy

Another Innocent Abroad K. Vick color *Time* v190 no8 p58 Ag 28 2017

The Empire in the Mirror [Cover story] H. Matar *New York Times Book Review* p1 S 3 2017

GOING LOCAL *New York Times Magazine* p16 S 24 2017

Postcard from the EDGE color *Vogue* v207 no1 p26 Ja 2017

A Very American Endeavor K. Genç color *New York Review of Books* v64 no17 p23 N 9 2017

The View from Abroad M. URBAN bw *Publishers Weekly* v264 no24 p52 Je 12 2017

HANSEN, TONY

ATV AND UTV TEST 2017 chart color *Outdoor Life* v224 no7 p14 S 2017

BOW TEST 2017 chart color *Outdoor Life* v224 no6 p17 Ag 2017

CHOKE JOB chart color *Outdoor Life* v224 no2 p20 F/Mr 2017

DIRT, CHEAP cartoon color *Outdoor Life* v224 no4 p39 My 2017

DIY 3-D color diag *Outdoor Life* v224 no5 p92 Je/Jl 2017

EATON COUNTY, MI color *Outdoor Life* v224 no7 p7 S 2017

GAME FINDERS chart color *Outdoor Life* v224 no2 p15 F/Mr 2017

LOAD THE BOAT color diag *Outdoor Life* v224 no4 p48 My 2017

MAKE IT LAST color *Outdoor Life* v224 no7 p28 S 2017

MAKE THIS YOUR FUNNEST DEER SEASON EVER cartoon color *Outdoor Life* v224 no8 p35 O 2017

MAKING THE CASE FOR PROTECTION color *Outdoor Life* v224 no8 pB4 O 2017

ONE BUCK, MANY LESSONS color *Outdoor Life* v224 no8 p22 O 2017

PINS APLENTY color *Outdoor Life* v224 no6 pB1 Ag 2017

THE PROCRASTINATOR'S PLAYBOOK color *Outdoor Life* v224 no6 p55 Ag 2017

RAISING A RACKET color *Outdoor Life* v224 no9 p31 N 2017

TRANSITION SEASON color *Outdoor Life* v224 no8 pB1 O 2017

THE UNKNOWNS color *Outdoor Life* v224 no2 p67 F/Mr 2017

HANSEN-BUNDY, BENJY

2,190 MILES, 1,102 HOURS, 348,000 CALORIES, AND 1 WORLD RECORD bw color *GQ: Gentlemen's Quarterly* v86 no12 p152 D 2016

THE BREAK-OUTS 2016 color *GQ: Gentlemen's Quarterly* v86 no12 p198 D 2016

GQ's 2017: GROOMING AWARDS bw color *GQ: Gentlemen's Quarterly* v97 no11 p56 N 2017

The Great Escape color *GQ: Gentlemen's Quarterly* v97 no5 p114 My 2017

How to Have a Grown-up Dinner Party (Without Feeling Too Grown-up) cartoon *GQ: Gentlemen's Quarterly* v97 no5 p44 My 2017

I GOT YOU, BABE bw color *GQ: Gentlemen's Quarterly* v97 no6 p96 Je 2017

Manual cartoon color *GQ: Gentlemen's Quarterly* v97 no7 p11 Jl 2017

The New Vows of Wedding Style color *GQ: Gentlemen's Quarterly* v97 no6 p23 Je 2017

OFF the BEATEN PATH color *GQ: Gentlemen's Quarterly* v97 no9 p154 S 2017

THE PERFECT FIT color *GQ: Gentlemen's Quarterly* v87 no1 p68 Ja 2017

Sometimes when I get incredibly horny color *Glamour* v114 no12 p172 D 2016

Steel Yourself: You're Gonna Love Pittsburgh color *GQ: Gentlemen's Quarterly* v97 no9 p82 S 2017

Hansen-Love, Mia

Things to Come N. PINKERTON color *Film Comment* v52 no6 p85 N/D 2016

Hansman, Heather

Cascadia color *Powder* v45 no3 p108 N 2016

Posthole M. Grabijas, M. Englert et al color *Powder* v45 no4 p146 D 2016

There's Something in the Snow at Mount Baker color *Powder* v46 no2 p33 O 2017

Hanson, B.

Fostering reproducibility in industry-academia research color *Science* v357 no6353 p759 Ag 25 2017

Hanson, Brock

DALLYING TECHNIQUES with Brock Hanson C. Toy color *Spin to Win Rodeo* v20 no11 p21 Ja 2017

Hanson, Brooks

Enhancing reproducibility for computational methods bibl color *Science* v354 no6317 p1240 D 9 2016

Hanson, Curtis, 1945-2016

CURTIS HANSON R. Crowe color *Entertainment Weekly* no1446/1447 p96 D 2016/Ja 2017

Hanson, Dave

Land of Lakes color *Sunset* v239 no1 p66 Jl 2017

SKIING, BRITISH COLUMBIA—STYLE chart color *Sunset* v237 no6 p38 D 2016

Hanson, David T., 1948-

Wilderness to Wasteland T. Brorby *Orion Magazine* v35 no3 p58 My/Je 2016

Hanson, Hart

The Driver *Publishers Weekly* v264 no22 p44 My 29 2017

HANSON, JASON

DUCT-TAPE DEFENSE color *Black Belt* v55 no6 p58 O/N 2017

Hanson, Marisa

Learning From the Past *Dance Magazine* v90 no11 p52 N 2016

Hanson, Mark

READER GALLERY bw color *Astronomy* v45 no11 p72 N 2017

Hanson, R.

Entanglement distillation between solid-state quantum network nodes diag *Science* v356 no6341 p928 Je 1 2017

Hanson, Ronald

Diamond defects cooperate via light bibl diag *Science* v354 no6314 p835 N 18 2016

Hanson, Taylor—Interviews

3 ROUNDS WITH HANSON I. Biedenharn, A. Bacle et al color *Entertainment Weekly* no1467 p40 My 26 2017

Hanson, Tom

To CATCH the ZODIAC Killer C. Collis color *Entertainment Weekly* no1468/1469 p72 Je 2-9 2017

Hanson, Victor Davis

The Case For Trump [Cover story] il *National Review* v68 no19 p24 O 24 2016

Dam Politics: The drought is over, but don't expect Sacramento to take any meaningful action to avert the next water crisis. That well is still bone dry *Hoover Digest: Research & Opinion on Public Policy* no3 p83 Summ 2017

License to Hate: The label of "hate crime" is used to score political points, not to end violence. It should be eliminated *Hoover Digest: Research & Opinion on Public Policy* no2 p143 Spr 2017

Quo vadis, GOP? color *National Review* v68 no22 p39 D 5 2016

Writing on the Walls *Hoover Digest: Research & Opinion on Public Policy* no4 p163 Fall 2016

Hanson, Zac—Interviews

3 ROUNDS WITH HANSON I. Biedenharn, A. Bacle et al color *Entertainment Weekly* no1467 p40 My 26 2017

Hansoo Choi

Samsung, Lee Jae-yong's Conviction, and How Business in South Korea Is Changing *Harvard Business Review Digital Articles* p2 S 29 2017

Hanssens, Dominique M.

Why Strong Customer Relationships Trump Powerful Brands *Harvard Business Review Digital Articles* p2 Ap 14 2015

Hansson, AnneMarie

Discussion *Smithsonian* v48 no1 p10 Ap 2017

Hansson, Úlfur

MANY BRANCHES MAKE THE TREE R. Mercer color *Iceland Review* v54 no5 p38 S-O 2016

Hansteen, V. H.

On the generation of solar spicules and Alfvénic waves diag *Science* v356 no6344 p1269 Je 23 2017

Hanton, Bobby Holland

WHEN LIFE GOES BOOM T. DASWICK and P. Kita cartoon

color *Men's Health* v32 no2 p20 Mr 2017

Hantson, S.

A human-driven decline in global burned area chart graph map *Science* v356 no6345 p1356 Je 30 2017

Hanulak, Ted

MARTIAL LAWS J. VRABEL *Indianapolis Monthly* p34 My 2017

Hanus, Julie K.

The Big Picture color il *American Craft* v76 no6 p22 D 2016-Ja 2017

The Handmade Life: A Companion to Modern Crafting color *American Craft* v76 no6 p18 D 2016-Ja 2017

The New Crew color *American Craft* v77 no2 p74 Ap/My 2017

Hao, Guolin

Three-dimensional holey-graphene/niobia composite architectures for ultrahigh-rate energy storage color diag graph *Science* v356 no6338 p599 My 12 2017

Hao, Yan

Molecular and neural basis of contagious itch behavior in mice bibl diag *Science* v355 no6329 p1072 Mr 10 2017

Hao Wang

What Chinese Companies Want from International Deals *Harvard Business Review Digital Articles* p2 F 12 2015

Hao Weng

Quality management for precision medicine clinical applications: A consensus from the China Precision Medicine Clinical Research and Application Association bibl *Science* v354 no6319 p11 D 23 2016

Haotian Wang

Direct and continuous strain control of catalysts with tunable battery electrode materials bibl graph *Science* v354 no6315 p1031 N 25 2016

Hap & Leonard (TV program)

Hap and Leonard: Mucho Mojo B. Oates *TV Guide* v65 no11 p42 Mr 6 2017

Hapkido

On Hapkido Functioning in All Four Ranges color *Black Belt* v55 no5 p17 Ag/S 2017

Happer, William

Roger Wolfe Cohen *Physics Today* v70 no8 p70 Ag 2017

Happiest in the World, The (Short story)

The Happiest in the World L. CHAVEZ *Commentary* v143 no1 p41 Ja 2017

Happiness

See also

> Joy
>
> Mental health

Andrea MARTIN color *Vanity Fair* v59 no6 p140 My 2017

Apps That Make You Happy color *Health* v31 no4 p10 My 2017

Being Happy at Work Matters A. McKee *Harvard Business Review Digital Articles* p2 N 14 2014

The Big Reveal M. BECK cartoon *O, The Oprah Magazine* p40 My 2017

B×(M+F+A)+Att2 A. STANLEY cartoon *Seventeen* v76 no2 p110 Mr 2017

BREAK THE MOLD IN 2017! S. Riley color *Essence* v47 no9 p76 Ja 2017

Can relationships boost longevity and well-being? *Harvard Health Letter* v42 no8 p5 Je 2017

Damian LEWIS cartoon *Vanity Fair* v59 no4 p219 Mr 2017

Does Work Make You Happy? Evidence from the World Happiness Report De Neve and G. Ward *Harvard Business Review Digital Articles* p2 Mr 20 2017

Every marriage needs... a meeting? A. S. GRANT and A. GRANT color *Redbook* p110 Ap 2017

Fun as a Key to Success T. Johnston color *Practical Horseman* v45 no3 p20 Mr 2017

GETTING TO KNOW YOU *Saturday Evening Post* v289 no2 p67 Mr/Ap 2017

Happiness hacks that really work color *Health* v31 no9 p16 N 2017

Happiness Isn't the Absence of Negative Feelings J. Moss *Harvard Business Review Digital Articles* p2 Ag 20 2015

Happiness on Your Bookshelf color *Health* v31 no8 p14 O 2017

HAPPINESS TRAPS: HOW WE SABOTAGE OURSELVES AT WORK A. MCKEE color *Harvard Business Review* v95 no5 p66 S/O 2017

Happy Snaps color *Health* v31 no1 p12 Ja 2017

HAPPY starts here A. Ferretti color *Yoga Journal* p80 2017 Special Issue

Hold Yourself Accountable-You'll Be Happier J. G. Miller *Time* v188 no22-23 p20 N/D 2016

A home practice for open, happy hips [Cover story] V. Marino color *Yoga Journal* no291 p61 My 2017

How to Become a Happy Retiree N. K. Schlossberg color *Money* v46 no4 p28 My 2017

HOW TO BE HAPPY A. SPENCER color *Good Housekeeping* v264 no1 p75 Ja 1 2017

I'LL TELL YOU SOMETHING NICOLAS ARNAUD & THIBAUT BARDON: Happiness in the workplace is no laughing matter *People Management* p19 My 2017

It's all ELEMENTAL [Cover story] T. EICHENSEHER color *Yoga Journal* no290 p64 Mr 2017

It's What You Do That Counts A. K. SMITH color *Kiplinger's Personal Finance* v70 no12 p42 D 2016

Looking Out for Small Joys C. McHugh color *Health* v31 no3 p8 Ap 2017

My Dirty Little Secret: I'm Happy A. Libers and S. G. Levy color *Glamour* v114 no12 p156 D 2016

New Ways to Become Happier—and Healthier M. Heid, A. MacMillan et al color *Time* v190 no13 p30 O 2 2017

Overtaken by Joy A. WHITMAN *Reader's Digest* v189 no1128 p94 Mr 2017

Q: What do you consistently do to boost happiness? J. Hanson Lasater, N. Rizopoulos et al color *Yoga Journal* no296 p12 N 2017

The Research We've Ignored About Happiness at Work A. Spicer and C. Cederström *Harvard Business Review Digital Articles* p2 Jl 21 2015

THE SCRIPT OF IGNORANCE K. D. Singh color *Tricycle: The Buddhist Review* v27 no1 p18 Fall 2017

Seth ROGEN cartoon *Vanity Fair* v59 no8 p132 Ag 2017

Spending to Save F. TORABI cartoon *O, The Oprah Magazine* p48 My 2017

Squeeze More Joy Out of Life J. Andriakos color *Health* v31 no3 p24 Ap 2017

When Economic Growth Doesn't Make Countries Happier S. Kesebir *Harvard Business Review Digital Articles* p2 Ap 25 2016

When It's Not Quite A Wonderful Life J. MARSH *Reader's Digest* v188 no1126 p43 D 2016/Ja 2017

When Multitasking Makes You Happy and When It Doesn't J. Etkin and C. Mogilner *Harvard Business Review Digital Articles* p2 F 26 2015

Why Rich People Aren't as Happy as They Could Be R. Raghunathan *Harvard Business Review Digital Articles* p2 Je 8 2016

Happiness—Research

How to Buy Happiness I. KWAI color *Atlantic* v319 no3 p24 Ap 2017

Happiness—Social aspects

THE WORLD'S HAPPIEST PLACES [Cover story] D. BUETTNER color diag graph *National Geographic* v232 no5 p30 N 2017

Happy! (TV program)

HAPPY! C. Collis color *Entertainment Weekly* no1474/1475 p70 Jl 21-28 2017

Happy Days (TV program)

When Fonzie Lost His Cool: He was the epitome of '50s chill on TV's family-friendly "Happy Days." And then he went over the top J. MacGregor *Smithsonian* v48 no5 p20 S 2017

Happy Death Day (Film)

11 THINGS THAT GOT US THROUGH THIS ISSUE: Movies, a bitchin' album, paper dolls, and some celebrity comings out helped our editors get through the making of this issue *Advocate* no1093 p50 O/N 2017

Happy Endings (TV program)

HAPPY ENDINGS D. Snierson, A. Writing et al color *Entertainment Weekly* no1439 p20 N 11 2016

Happy Valley (TV program)

LIKE THAT? TRY THIS! A. D'Arminio *TV Guide* v65 no25 p24 Je 2017

Haque, Umair

3 Terrible Strategies for Companies Seeking Growth *Harvard Business Review Digital Articles* p2 O 6 2014

Are You a Leader, or Just Pretending to Be One? *Harvard Business Review Digital Articles* p2 F 3 2016

Business Leaders Have Abandoned the Middle Class *Harvard Business Review Digital Articles* p2 Je 27 2016

Google Glass Failed Because It Just Wasn't Cool *Harvard Business Review Digital Articles* p2 Ja 30 2015

Hedi Slimane: The Steve Jobs of Fashion *Harvard Business Review Digital Articles* p2 Ap 1 2016

Our Economy Is Obsessed with Efficiency and Terrible at Everything Else *Harvard Business Review Digital Articles* p2 Mr 1 2016

The Reason Twitter's Losing Active Users *Harvard Business Review Digital Articles* p2 F 12 2016

To Manage a Platform, Think of It as a Micromarket *Harvard Business Review Digital Articles* p2 Ap 13 2016

Why No One Will Implement the Best Solution to Economic Stagnation *Harvard Business Review Digital Articles* p2 N 26 2015

Your Digital Strategy Shouldn't Be About Attention *Harvard Business Review Digital Articles* p2 Ja 15 2015

Haque, Usman
Managing Privacy in the Internet of Things *Harvard Business Review Digital Articles* p2 F 5 2015

Harabadian, Eric
Allan Holdsworth: Changing Guitar for the Better color *Downbeat* v84 no6 p24 Je 2017

Harakat al-Muqawamah al-Islamiyah
Hamas Takes a Step Away from Isolation J. Malsin color *Time* v190 no13 p15 O 2 2017

Haraldsdóttir, Dagný Rut
A NEW TOMORROW E. S. ARNARSDÓTTIR *Iceland Review* v54 no6 p80 N/D 2016

Haraldseth, Geir
Making Spaces color *Art in America* v105 no5 p37 My 2017
Norwegian Tags color *Art in America* v104 no10 p51 N 2016

Haramis, Nick
AL GORE *Interview* v47 no5 p72 Je/Jl 2017
Mackenzie DAVIS *Interview* v47 no5 p45 Je/Jl 2017

Harare (Zimbabwe)
Harare, Zimbabwe S. ALLISON color *Foreign Policy* no225 p18 Jl/Ag 2017

Harari, D.
Observation of a large-scale anisotropy in the arrival directions of cosmic rays above 8 × 1018 eV *Science* v357 no6357 p1266 S 22 2017

Harari, Yuval Noah
Inevitably Posthuman? L. KLEPP color *Weekly Standard* v22 no45 p29 Ag 7 2017
More Than Human M. SHERMER *American Scholar* v86 no2 p113 Spr 2017
New, Improved, Obsolete S. MUKHERJEE *New York Times Book Review* p12 Mr 19 2017
Received Ideas We know less than we think we do. Groupthink fills in the gaps color *New York Times Book Review* p15 Ap 23 2017

Harari, Yuval Noah—Interviews
Dataism Is Our New God Y. N. Harari *NPQ: New Perspectives Quarterly* v34 no2 p36 My 2017
THE GOD COMPLEX O. SOLON color *Wired* v25 no3 p18 Mr 2017
Yuval Noah Harari N. Hopper color *Time* v189 no7/8 p116 F 27 2017

Harashima, Hirofumi
RETINOBLASTOMA RELATED1 mediates germline entry in Arabidopsis color diag *Science* v356 no6336 p396 Ap 28 2017

Harassment
See also
Sexual harassment

Harassment in our community: An open letter *Physics Today* v69 no10 p12 O 2016
My Teenage Patient's Mom Is Slipping Her Prozac. What Should I Do? K. A. Appiah *New York Times Magazine* p16 Jl 16 2017
The Unaccountable IRS color *Weekly Standard* v23 no3 p8 S 25 2017

Harassment—Government policy
Academic Gabfest M. HEMINGWAY color *Weekly Standard* v23 no2 p20 S 18 2017

Harassment—Prevention
Society labels harassment as research misconduct M. Kuo color *Science* v356 no6335 p233 Ap 21 2017
WOULD YOU STAND UP TO HATE? K. TRANELL *Scholastic Choices* v32 no6 p6 Mr 2017

Harbaugh, Jim, 1963-
The Fix Was In G. NORMAN color *Weekly Standard* v22 no14 p14 D 12 2016
Icons color *Time* v189 no16/17 p122 My 1-8 2017

Harberts, Aaron
STAR TREK'S NEW FRONTIER J. Hibberd color *Entertainment Weekly* no1472 p20 Je 30 2017

Harbison, Martha
CAMP MACAW *Audubon* v119 no1 p26 Spr 2017

Harbor access
How Sharks Became So Scary O. B. Waxman *Time* v189 no22 p17 Je 12 2017

Harbor seal
Seal of Honor J. Johnson color *Yankee* p24 My/Je 2017

Harbors
See also
Marinas
Mooring of ships
Piers
Pilots & pilotage
Waterfronts

Great Escapes P. LOBO bw color *Power & Motoryacht* v33 no3 p96 Mr 2017
HÓLMAVÍK'S HUTS P. STEFÁNSSON *Iceland Review* v54 no6 p7 N/D 2016
PICTURESQUE PORT OF EDMONDS: EDMONDS HAS NOT LOST SIGHT OF WHAT MAKES IT UNIQUE D. HISLOP color map *Sea Magazine* v109 no6 pPNW-10 Je 2017

Harbors—California
ESCAPE TO AVALON S. SHIBATA and M. WERLING *Sea Magazine* v108 no10 pCA-1 O 2016

Harbors—Congresses
DONT MISS LIST OCTOBER 2016 *Sea Magazine* v108 no10 pCA-7 O 2016

Harbors—Illinois—Chicago
THE LAST HARBOR BOSS R. J. NELSON bw cartoon color *Chicago* v65 no11 p110 N 2016

Harbors—Mediterranean Region
The Quiz T. BALAZO color *Maclean's* v129 no47 p64 N 28 2016

Harbors—Texas—Corpus Christi
Oil and WATER R. G. RATCLIFFE *Texas Monthly* v45 no9 p27 S 2017

Harbors—Texas—Houston
How the Coast Guard Reopened the Port of Houston K. DUPZYK color *Popular Mechanics* p13 N 2017

Harbors—United States
CHAPTER 6 THE ECONOMIC BENEFITS OF INVESTING IN U. S. INFRASTRUCTURE *Economic Indicators* p251 O 2016

Harbors—Washington (State)
Coal port terminal may reach its last stop color *National Wildlife (World Edition)* v55 no4 p48 Je/Jl 2017

Harbour, Ron
Prepare Your Workforce for the Automation Age *Harvard Business Review Digital Articles* p2 N 23 2016

Harcourt, Robert G.
Envisioning the Future of Aquatic Animal Tracking: Technology, Science, and Application *BioScience* v67 no10 p884 O 2017
Now is the time to protect the Arctic bibl color *Science* v354 no6317 p1243 D 9 2016

Hard, Michael
Life After Combat color *Log Home Living* v33 no7 p53 S 2016

Hard disks (Computer science)
Configure a Time Capsule as an ethernet-only storage device G. Fleishman color diag *Macworld - Digital Edition* p122 Ap 2017
How to know when your SSD could die J. NOREM color diag *PCWorld* v35 no11 p159 N 2016
Intel Optane Memory has a mission: Make hard drives faster than SSDs G. MAH UNG color graph *PCWorld* v35 no5 p33 My 2017
Intel's speed-boosting Optane Memory won't work with Celeron and Pentium PCs I. PAUL color *PCWorld* v35 no5 p39 My 2017

Plenty of Room at the Bottom J. KEATS color *Discover* v38 no1 p45 Ja/F 2017

WD My Passport SSD: Worthy competition for Samsung's T3 J. L. JACOBI color graph *PCWorld* v35 no9 p66 S 2017

Hard disks (Computer science)—Evaluation

DISKASHUR PRO2: CROSS-PLATFORM, MAXIMUM SECURITY PORTABLE HARD DRIVE J. R. BOOKWALTER color *Macworld - Digital Edition* v34 no8 p44 Ag 2017

Seagate Barracuda Pro 10TB hard drive: Vast and amazingly fast (for a hard drive) J. L. JACOBI color graph *PCWorld* p99 O 2016

Hardberger, John

54 GREAT THINGS TO DO THIS MONTH color *Chicago* v66 no1 p117 Ja 2017

58 GREAT THINGS TO DO THIS MONTH color *Chicago* v66 no2 p101 F 2017

62 GREAT THINGS TO DO THIS MONTH color *Chicago* v66 no6 p97 Je 2017

63 GREAT THINGS TO DO THIS MONTH color *Chicago* v66 no7 p87 Jl 2017

63 GREAT THINGS TO DO THIS MONTH color *Chicago* v66 no8 p105 Ag 2017

65 GREAT THINGS TO DO THIS MONTH color *Chicago* v65 no11 p115 N 2016

66 GREAT THINGS TO DO THIS MONTH color *Chicago* v66 no9 p139 S 2017

68 GREAT THINGS TO DO THIS MONTH color *Chicago* v66 no5 p119 My 2017

CAKES, PASTRIES, PIES, COOKIES, HOT FUDGE, GALATO, BROWNIES & MORE! chart color *Chicago* v65 no11 p70 N 2016

COMEDY CALENDAR cartoon *Chicago* v66 no1 p46 Ja 2017

DIY ICE RINK color *Chicago* v65 no12 p30 D 2016

GO: 69 GREAT THINGS TO DO THIS MONTH color *Chicago* v66 no11 p103 N 2017

GO bw color *Chicago* v66 no10 p105 O 2017

GO color *Chicago* v65 no12 p119 D 2016

GO color *Chicago* v66 no4 p113 Ap 2017

The Grit & the Glory bw *Chicago* v66 no2 p90 F 2017

PLUNGE INTO COOL POOLS color *Chicago* v66 no7 p62 Jl 2017

TOP CANCER DOCTORS color *Chicago* v66 no1 p84 Ja 2017

THE WAR AT HOME bw *Chicago* v65 no11 p40 N 2016

Hardberger, Max, 1948-

Pirate of the Caribbean B. PIKE color *Power & Motoryacht* v33 no3 p68 Mr 2017

Hardcore Henry (Film)

HARDCORE HENRY C. Gunnestad color *Sound & Vision* v82 no4 p70 My 2017

THE INCREDIBLY SPECIAL EFFECTS AWARDS T. GRIERSON bw color *Popular Mechanics* p75 F 2017

Hardcore music

Bring It Back M. Trammell cartoon *New Yorker* v92 no35 p26 O 31 2016

Harden, Greg

High STAKES P. Thamel color *Sports Illustrated* v126 no9 p32 Mr 27 2017

Harden, James

HOT | NOT T. Keith color *Sports Illustrated* v127 no2 p22 Jl 17 2017

The Joy of Sharing S. Gregory color *Time* v189 no7/8 p62 F 27 2017

A SIMPLE PLAN [Cover story] L. Jenkins color *Sports Illustrated* v126 no7 p36 Mr 6 2017

STAR ROCKET IN FLIGHT C. O'CONNELL *Texas Monthly* v45 no4 p90 Ap 2017

WHOSE TROPHY IS IT? R. Nadkarni color *Sports Illustrated* v126 no5 p56 F 13 2017

Harden, Krysta

KRYSTA HARDEN A. McConnell *Successful Farming* v115 no3 p8 Mid-F 2017

Harder, Charles

THE GAWKER STALKER J. ZENGERLE color *GQ: Gentlemen's Quarterly* v86 no12 p164 D 2016

Harder, Jeffrey M.

Vitamin B3 modulates mitochondrial vulnerability and prevents

glaucoma in aged mice bibl graph *Science* v355 no6326 p756 F 17 2017

HARDERGER, JOHN

67 GREAT THINGS TO DO THIS MONTH color *Chicago* v66 no3 p129 Mr 2017

Hardesty, Darren

LOORRS 2017 SEASON DEBUT REDUX [Cover story] R. JOHNSTON color *Dirt Sports + Off-Road* v51 no10 p60 O 2017

Hardie, Mel

Publish openly but responsibly color *Science* v357 no6347 p141 Jl 14 2017

Hardin, Drew

THE (SOGGY) RACE OF GENTLEMEN bw color *Hot Rod* v70 no3 p48 Mr 2017

HARDIN, JOSHUA

Heritage Highway color map *Nebraska Life* v21 no5 p22 S/O 2017

HARDIN, MELORA

I Love My Dining Room color *House Beautiful* v159 no5 p104 Je 2017

Hardin, Tyler

Pint-sized Dynamos: Tyler Hardin and "Zipy" C. Reich *Arabian Horse World* v57 no4 p110 Ja 2017

Harding, Aldous

Aldous HARDING A. WEISS *Interview* v47 no6 p24 Ag 2017

Harding, Andrew

His City of Ruins J. HAMMER *New York Times Book Review* p21 Ja 8 2017

The Mayor of Mogadishu: A Story of Chaos and Redemption in the Ruins of Somalia N. van de Walle *Foreign Affairs* v96 no2 p189 Mr/Ap 2017

Saints and Sinners in Somalia K. MENKHAUS *Current History* v116 no790 p197 My 2017

Harding, Christopher

Meiji Modernist *History Today* v67 no1 p28 Ja 2017

Harding, Daniel Jr.

2017 A Look Ahead color map *Power & Motoryacht* v32 no12 p38 D 2016

ALEN 55 color *Power & Motoryacht* v33 no1 p46 Ja 2017

Attitude Adjustment *Power & Motoryacht* v33 no2 p26 F 2017

Aquila 36 color *Power & Motoryacht* v34 no7 p34 Jl 2017

Aussie Adventure *Power & Motoryacht* v34 no9 p18 S 2017

Aussie Rules chart color *Power & Motoryacht* v32 no11 p122 N 2016

Axopar 37 Sport Cabin color *Power & Motoryacht* v33 no4 p42 Ap 2017

Baikal 16 Cat color *Power & Motoryacht* v33 no1 p50 Ja 2017

Bertram 35 color *Power & Motoryacht* v32 no11 p64 N 2016

Bilge Pump 2.0 color *Power & Motoryacht* v33 no2 p125 F 2017

Boston Whaler 330 Outrage color *Power & Motoryacht* v33 no3 p52 Mr 2017

Bound by Boating *Power & Motoryacht* v33 no4 p18 Ap 2017

CAT BE NIMBLE, CAT BE QUICK chart color *Power & Motoryacht* v34 no10 p100 O 2017

Catching Memories color *Power & Motoryacht* v34 no7 p12 Jl 2017

Cruisers 50 Cantius color *Power & Motoryacht* v34 no6 p28 Je 2017

Cutting Corners bw chart color *Power & Motoryacht* v34 no11 p124 N 2017

Dealers Choice color *Power & Motoryacht* v34 no11 p132 N 2017

ENDURING LEGACY chart color *Power & Motoryacht* v33 no1 p72 Ja 2017

EXPOSURE color *Power & Motoryacht* v32 no11 p70 N 2016

Ferretti 920 color *Power & Motoryacht* v34 no7 p36 Jl 2017

The Future Faces of Boatbuilding color *Power & Motoryacht* v33 no1 p32 Ja 2017

Gulfstream 52 color *Power & Motoryacht* v32 no12 p34 D 2016

Hargrave 80 color *Power & Motoryacht* v34 no11 p80 N 2017

Jeanneau Leader 10.5 color *Power & Motoryacht* v34 no8 p30 Ag 2017

Lessons Learned color *Power & Motoryacht* v34 no7 p16 Jl 2017

LOGBOOK *Power & Motoryacht* v33 no3 p26 Mr 2017

The More Things Change... color *Power & Motoryacht* v34 no6 p12 Je 2017

New Adventures, Same Kid From the Boatyard *Power & Motory-*

acht v33 no1 p24 Ja 2017

Notebook color *Power & Motoryacht* v32 no11 p68 N 2016

ODYSSEY AT THE CROSSROADS [Cover story] chart color diag *Power & Motoryacht* v34 no6 p40 Je 2017

Outer Reef 610 MY color *Power & Motoryacht* v34 no9 p46 S 2017

PLAYING BY HIS OWN RULES color *Power & Motoryacht* v34 no11 p100 N 2017

Princess 40M color *Power & Motoryacht* v33 no4 p40 Ap 2017

Private Party color *Power & Motoryacht* v33 no2 p32 F 2017

Protect and Serve color *Power & Motoryacht* v32 no12 p28 D 2016

Purchasing the Proper PFD color *Power & Motoryacht* v32 no11 p62 N 2016

PURSUIT OF PASSION bw chart color *Power & Motoryacht* v34 no8 p52 Ag 2017

Rio Yachts 58 GTS color *Power & Motoryacht* v33 no2 p46 F 2017

Riviera 4800 Sport Yacht color *Power & Motoryacht* v33 no2 p40 F 2017

Riviera 68 Sports Motor Yacht color *Power & Motoryacht* v34 no10 p62 O 2017

Salty & Satisfying color *Power & Motoryacht* v34 no10 p32 O 2017

Seas the Day [Cover story] color *Power & Motoryacht* v33 no4 p50 Ap 2017

Silver Lining color *Power & Motoryacht* v34 no11 p38 N 2017

Smooth Operator color *Power & Motoryacht* v33 no1 p95 Ja 2017

THE STAR OF THE SHOW [Cover story] color *Power & Motoryacht* v32 no11 p76 N 2016

Sweet Summertime color *Power & Motoryacht* v33 no2 p88 F 2017

Ten ADVENTURES color *Power & Motoryacht* v34 no9 p64 S 2017

The Untold Truth color *Power & Motoryacht* v34 no8 p12 Ag 2017

WATERFRONT color *Power & Motoryacht* v32 no11 p40 N 2016

WATERFRONT color *Power & Motoryacht* v32 no12 p18 D 2016

HARDING, DAVID

STRATEGY IN THE AGE OF SUPERABUNDANT CAPITAL color graph img *Harvard Business Review* v95 no2 p66 Mr/Ap 2017

HARDING, DAVID-MICHAEL

CORRUPTION SET IN CONCRETE *USA Today Magazine* v145 no2860 p26 Ja 2017

HARDING, HARRY R.

Shipbuilding Docks as Experimental Systems for Realistic Assessments of Anthropogenic Stressors on Marine Organisms *BioScience* v67 no9 p853 S 2017

Harding, Ryan A.

Synthesis of resveratrol tetramers via a stereoconvergent radical equilibrium bibl diag graph *Science* v354 no6317 p1260 D 9 2016

Harding, Thomas

If These Walls Could Sprechen A. HAZLETT color *Reason* v48 no9 p64 F 2017

HARDING, XAVIER

THE PROFESSIONAL PASSENGER color *Popular Science* v288 no6 p11 N/D 2016

RIGHT OF WAY FOR ROBO-CARS color *Popular Science* p16 Ja/F 2017

The Sweet Sound of Virtual Reality color *Popular Science* v288 no6 p48 N/D 2016

The United Nations of Mobile Networks color *Popular Science* v288 no6 p74 N/D 2016

Harding Loevner LP

One Family, Two Foreign Fund Winners R. ERMEY chart *Kiplinger's Personal Finance* v71 no4 p62 Ap 2017

Hard Nut, The (Theatrical production)

10 MINUTES WITH . . . Mark Morris Z. WHITTENBURG *Dance Magazine* v90 no12 p30 D 2016

The Not Too Hard Nut J. Acocella cartoon *New Yorker* v92 no41 p19 D 12 2016

Hardship

On Hardship & Hope: Two teachings to instill inspiration when we feel paralyzed by despair DAISAKU IKEDA color *Tricycle:*

The Buddhist Review v27 no1 p36 Fall 2017

Hardt, Lena

HOOP DREAMS A. Syrett color *InStyle* v24 no8 p158 Ag 2017

Hardt, Wolf-Dietrich

Inflammation boosts bacteriophage transfer between Salmonella spp bibl diag *Science* v355 no6330 p1211 Mr 17 2017

Hardware

See also

Bolts & nuts

Door fittings

Knives

Screws

Tools

lighting & METALWORK M. E. Polson color *Arts & Crafts Homes & the Revival* v12 no1 p44 2017 Resouce Guide

TRANSOM HARDWARE color *Old House Journal* v45 no3 p78 My 2017

Hardware design & construction

hardware *Design Center Sourcebook* p92 2017

Hardware—Evaluation

Czech Mate E. FAZZARE color *Architectural Digest* v74 no10 p64 O 1 2017

HARDWARE color *Arts & Crafts Homes & the Revival* v12 no1 p48 2017 Resouce Guide

Hardwick, Bess

Higher predation risk for insect prey at low latitudes and elevations graph *Science* v356 no6339 p742 My 19 2017

Hardwick, Chris, 1971-

PARTY LINES img *New York* p128 Mr 6 2017

Red Nose Day A. D'Arminio *TV Guide* v65 no21 p36 My 15 2017

Hardwick, Chris, 1971-—Interviews

King of The Nerds M. WAKIM *Los Angeles Magazine* p72 Mr 2017

Hardwick, Elizabeth, 1916-2007

Master Class D. Pinckney bw *New York Review of Books* v64 no15 p19 O 12 2017

Hardwick, Omari

MORE POWER TO YOU L. Rice color *Entertainment Weekly* no1473 p38 Jl 7 2017

POWER GRAB: Starz's No. 1-rated original series--sorry, Outlander!--is back for its juiciest (and most intense) season yet I. RATLEDGE *TV Guide* v65 no25 p28 Je 2017

POWER L. Rice color *Entertainment Weekly* no1468/1469 p54 Je 2-9 2017

Hardwired...to Self-Destruct (Music)

What To Stream color *Entertainment Weekly* no1441 p53 N 25 2016

YOU PLAY YOU S. Hyden color *New York Times Magazine* p82 Mr 12 2017

HARDY, ALEXANDER

Audio Therapy: How Music Improved One Man's Mental Health color *Ebony* v72 no5 p64 Mr 2017

Keeping Your Mind Right While Fighting the Good Fight color *Ebony* v72 no3 p84 D 2016/Ja 2017

Hardy, Alison

BRING VINTAGE WINDOWS BACK TO LIFE S. HERTZ *Yankee* v81 no1 p40 Ja/F 2017

Hardy, Bruce W.

U.S. attitudes on human genome editing color graph *Science* v357 no6351 p553 Ag 11 2017

Hardy, Dale

My loved ones would describe me as… color map *Reader's Digest* v189 no1130 p34 My 2017

Hardy, Elora

BUILDING GREEN A. PEASLEY color *Architectural Digest* no5 p142 My 2017

Hardy, Emma

Ulcers in the Dressage Horse *Dressage Today* v23 no4 p14 D 2016

Hardy, Gus

SOCIAL STUDIES color *America* v216 no5 p30 Mr 6 2017

Hardy, Jim

FIND YOUR POWER RELEASE chart color *Golf Magazine* v59 no9 p56 S 2017

HARDY, MICHAEL

Blood and SUGAR *Texas Monthly* v45 no1 p47 Ja 2017

Country REVIVAL: HOW THE STRAIGHT-TALKING, COY-

OTE-SHOOTING, TOBACCO CHEWING JOHN SHARP HAS LED A BONANZA AT TEXAS A&M *Texas Monthly* v45 no8 p78 Ag 2017

The Redneck Tenor *Texas Monthly* v44 no11 p82 N 2016

She's the SHERIFF *Texas Monthly* v45 no1 p60 Ja 2017

Hardy, Quentin

3 Ways Companies Are Building a Business Around AI *Harvard Business Review Digital Articles* p2 2017

Hardy, Robert, 1925-2017

Milestones *Time* v190 no7 p13 Ag 21 2017

Hardy, Tom, 1977-

Taboo D. Franich color *Entertainment Weekly* no1448 p54 Ja 13 2017

Hardy, Tom, 1977—Interviews

No Rest for the Wicked M. Z. SEITZ img *New York* p76 F 9 2017

HARE, DAVID

The Year in Reading [Cover story] *New York Times Book Review* p8 D 25 2016

HARE, EMILY

Autumn HARVEST color *Cabin Living* p58 O 2017

Cabin Fever color *Cabin Living* p84 Ja/F 2017

Catch OF the Day color *Cabin Living* p60 Ap 2017

Cold, Creamy GOODNESS color *Cabin Living* p58 Ag 2017

cooking WITH CRAFT BEER color *Cabin Living* p60 S 2017

Kid-Friendly Fare cartoon color *Cabin Living* p62 Je 2017

open-air Deliciousness color *Cabin Living* p56 S 2017

Wake to Cake color *Cabin Living* p66 Mr 2017

HAREL, MONICA CORCORAN

JILLIAN MICHAELS [Cover story] color *Redbook* p88 F 2017

SHE'S A JOY [Cover story] color *Redbook* p86 Jl/Ag 2017

Harford, Tim

History's Best Overlooked Inventions S. Begley color *Time* v190 no10/11 p26 S 18 2017

Make a Mess of It M. KONNIKOVA *New York Times Book Review* p21 O 16 2016

A New Chaos Theory to Live Your Best Life S. Stein color *Time* v188 no14 p60 O 10 2016

Hargis, Van

Create a Confident Mindset [Cover story] color *Horse & Rider* v56 no3 p32 Mr 2017

Hargitay, Mariska, 1964-

Law & Order: Special Victims Unit N. Abrams, B. L. Heldman et al *Entertainment Weekly* no1482/1483 p75 S 22 2017

LAW & ORDER: SVU COVER PARTY, NEW YORK CITY *TV Guide* v65 no6 p4 Ja 30 2017

LAW & ORDER: SVU I. Rudolph *TV Guide* v65 no39 p46 S 18 2017

Hargrave Custom Yachts (Company)

Hargrave 80 D. J. Harding color *Power & Motoryacht* v34 no11 p80 N 2017

HOME AND ABROAD J. WOOLDRIDGE color *Power & Motoryacht* v32 no11 p134 N 2016

HARGREAVE, RICHARD

Why You Should Become a Wine Snob color *GQ: Gentlemen's Quarterly* v97 no10 p80 O 2017

Hargrove, Brantley

Close to Her Heart *D: The Magazine of Dallas* v43 no10 p116 O 2016

HOW to STOP the WIND color *Popular Mechanics* p86 S 2017

HARGROVE, CHANNING

The Question *O, The Oprah Magazine* p16 D 2016

Haring, Keith, 1958-1990

PAINT BY NUMBERS bw *Advocate* no1091 p93 Je/Jl 2017

Häring, Martin

miR-183 cluster scales mechanical pain sensitivity by regulating basal and neuropathic pain genes diag graph *Science* v356 no6343 p1168 Je 16 2017

Harington, Kit, 1986-

DRAGONS AND WOLVES AND RATINGS, OH MY! J. Hibberd color *Entertainment Weekly* no1477 p12 Ag 11 2017

Harjo, Joy

BY THE WAY *New Yorker* v92 no40 p52 D 5 2016

Harkany, Tibor

miR-183 cluster scales mechanical pain sensitivity by regulating basal and neuropathic pain genes diag graph *Science* v356 no6343 p1168 Je 16 2017

Harkavy, Juliana

ARROW N. Abrams color *Entertainment Weekly* no1474/1475 p73 Jl 21-28 2017

Harkema, Tessa

I Wish My Horse's Mentor Could Be... color *Horse & Rider* v56 no6 p88 Je 2017

Harker, David, 1906-1991

Creating Scientific Controversies: Uncertainty and Bias in Science and Society G. BRANCH *Skeptical Inquirer* v41 no3 p60 My/Je 2017

Harkins, Timothy T.

Single-cell methylomes identify neuronal subtypes and regulatory elements in mammalian cortex diag *Science* v357 no6351 p600 Ag 11 2017

HARKINSON, JOSH

MAKE AMERICA HATE AGAIN bw cartoon *Mother Jones* v42 no1 p24 Ja/F 2017

Harkness, Peter A.

Chief Concerns *Governing* v30 no2 p16 N 2016

Conjectures from the Swamp *Governing* v30 no4 p16 Ja 2017

Fractured Federalism: It's hard to tell who's in charge of what in American government these days *Governing* v30 no12 p16 S 2017

Let's Give the Stimulus Its Due: It saved the economy, but that isn't always acknowledged *Governing* v30 no10 p16 Jl 2017

Outposts of Rationality *Governing* v30 no6 p16 Mr 2017

Trump-Watching from City Hall: His policy choices will challenge places from Manhattan to Mobile, Ala *Governing* v30 no8 p16 My 2017

Hark-Weber, Amara

Amara Hark-Weber A. Ranallo color *American Craft* v77 no3 p40 Je/Jl 2017

Harland, Richard M.

Emergent cellular self-organization and mechanosensation initiate follicle pattern in the avian skin color *Science* v357 no6353 p811 Ag 25 2017

HARLANDER, THOMAS

the arts district color *Los Angeles Magazine* v62 no7 p63 Jl 2017

Harlap, Shmuel

Wheeler-Dealer cartoon *Forbes* v199 no4 p20 Ap 25 2017

Harlem on My Mind (Music)

Catherine Russell T. Panken color *Downbeat* v84 no4 p98 Ap 2017

Harlem On My Mind J. McDonough color *Downbeat* v83 no11 p49 N 2016

Harlem Renaissance—Exhibitions

SPRING SHOWS color *Popular Photography* v81 no2 p20 Mr/Ap 2017

Harlequin (UK) Ltd.

Rhapsody in BLUE color *House Beautiful* p20 Ag 2017

Harley-Davidson Inc.

2017 HARLEY-DAVIDSON STREET GLIDE SPECIAL J. Gustafson color *Cycle World* v55 no11 p8 D 2016

AMERICAN FLAT-TRACK M. HOYER *Cycle World* v55 no11 p5 D 2016

HARLEY VS. INDIAN M. Hoyer color *Cycle World* v56 no5 p8 Je 2017

INDIAN THROWS DOWN THE GLOVE K. Cameron color *Cycle World* v55 no11 p26 D 2016

Harley-Davidson motorcycle

10 Best Bikes 2017 color diag *Cycle World* v56 no10 p35 N 2017

CHASING A FEELING S. MacDonald chart color *Cycle World* v56 no6 p42 Jl 2017

HITTING A MARK B. Adams chart color *Cycle World* v56 no6 p56 Jl 2017

SOFTAILS P. Egan color *Cycle World* v56 no9 p38 O 2017

Harley-Davidson motorcycle—Design & construction

DYNAMIC CHANGES AT HARLEY-DAVIDSON: ADIOS, DYNA! K. Cameron color *Cycle World* v56 no9 p30 O 2017

RUBBER SOUL *Cycle World* v56 no9 p8 O 2017

Harley-Davidson motorcycle—Evaluation

HIGHWAY TO HELL B. Catterson chart color *Cycle World* v56 no1 p36 Ja/F 2017

Harloe, Kate

A BRIEF HISTORY OF WITCH HUNTS color *Mother Jones* v42 no6 p60 N/D 2017

Harlots (TV program)
Antiheroines Are Resplendent In Harlots D. D'Addario color *Time* v189 no12 p55 Ap 3 2017

Harm (Ethics)
The Thread T. C. Eberhardt, K. Lawrence et al *New York Times Magazine* p10 Ja 15 2017

Harman, Justine
10 Years of Kardashians; Khloé Looks Back color *Glamour* v115 no10 p42 O 2017
The 3-Minute Interview bw *Glamour* no8 p40 Ag 2017
The 3-Minute Interview color *Glamour* v114 no12 p82 D 2016
5 Loaded Questions for Adam Scott color *Glamour* v115 no11 p44 N 2017
6 loaded questions for Rami Malek bw *Glamour* v115 no9 p44 S 2017
The Academy Will See Us Now color *Glamour* v115 no3 p50 Mr 2017
Bathleisure: It's a Thing color *Glamour* v115 no1 p16 Ja 2017
Can Dirty TV & Movies Ruin You? color *Glamour* v115 no7 p72 Jl 2017
Dear Diana, You Still Rule. Love, Everyone color *Glamour* v115 no9 p42 S 2017
Everything Is 25 This Summer color *Glamour* no8 p38 Ag 2017
Gang's All Here color *Glamour* v115 no5 p178 My 2017
The Glamour Do: No-Polish Mani color *Glamour* no8 p40 Ag 2017
Haim Doesn't Want to Be "Cool" color *Glamour* no8 p38 Ag 2017
Hoodie, Yes. Pants, No color *Glamour* v114 no12 p78 D 2016
How to Primp Your Pooch color *Glamour* v114 no12 p88 D 2016
How We Communicate Now bw color *Glamour* v115 no3 p52 Mr 2017
The No-Frills NEGRONI color *Glamour* v115 no1 p96 Ja 2017
Nothing Scares Louisa Krause color *Glamour* v115 no11 p41 N 2017
Now meet 39 more beauty game changers—each defining themselves [Cover story] bw color *Glamour* v115 no4 p166 Ap 2017
Oh, and Tiaras Too?! color *Glamour* no8 p36 Ag 2017
Read These and Weep color *Glamour* v115 no9 p40 S 2017
Some Like It Aught color *Glamour* v114 no12 p84 D 2016
TALKIN' PARTIES with LIL BUCK color *Glamour* v115 no1 p97 Ja 2017
Wait, Platform Sneakers Are Back? [Cover story] color *Glamour* no8 p35 Ag 2017
What's Inside SABINA KARLSSON'S Party Purse? color *Glamour* v115 no1 p94 Ja 2017
Where the Red-Carpet Madness Begins [Cover story] color *Glamour* v115 no3 p47 Mr 2017
The Who's Who of Summer bw color *Glamour* v115 no6 p29 Je 2017
The Woman Behind the Blowout bw color *Glamour* v115 no4 p42 Ap 2017
The Year of the Detail color *Glamour* v114 no12 p77 D 2016
Yes, They Can color *Glamour* v115 no9 p39 S 2017

Harmant, Christine
Dispersals and genetic adaptation of Bantu-speaking populations in Africa and North America diag *Science* v356 no6337 p543 My 5 2017

Harmer, Martin P.
Segregation-induced ordered superstructures at general grain boundaries in a nickel-bismuth alloy color *Science* v357 no6359 p97 O 6 2017

Harmer, Peter
Can Insurance Companies Incentivize Their Customers to Be Healthier? *Harvard Business Review Digital Articles* p2 Je 23 2017

Harmon, Bruce
Arthur J. Freeman *Physics Today* v69 no11 p69 N 2016

Harmon, Claude
LASER SHOW color *Golf Magazine* v59 no6 p44 Je 2017

Harmon, Mark, 1951-
NCIS A. D'Arminio *TV Guide* v65 no21 p32 My 15 2017
NCIS A. D'Arminio *TV Guide* v65 no39 p38 S 18 2017

Harmon, Nicholas
A unified continental thickness from seismology and diamonds suggests a melt-defined plate graph map *Science* v357 no6351 p580 Ag 11 2017

Harmon, Pat—Interviews
IF YOU BUILD IT K. Krichko color *Powder* v45 no3 p56 N 2016

Harmon, Shani
How to Make Sure Your Emails Give the Right Impression color *Harvard Business Review Digital Articles* p2 F 6 2017
Meetings That Work for Both Managers and Makers *Harvard Business Review Digital Articles* p2 Jl 4 2016

Harmonics (Electric waves)
High-harmonic generation in graphene enhanced by elliptically polarized light excitation N. Yoshikawa, T. Tamaya et al color graph *Science* v356 no6339 p736 My 19 2017

Harmonium (Film)
Harmonium J. CRONK color *Film Comment* v53 no3 p67 My/Je 2017

Harms, Alexander
Mechanisms of bacterial persistence during stress and antibiotic exposure bibl diag graph *Science* v354 no6318 paaf4268-1 D 16 2016

HARMSEN, HANS
THE GHOSTS OF KANGEQ color *Archaeology* v70 no3 p55 My/Je 2017

Harnesses—Evaluation
The Outdoorsman's Essentials S. RINELLA color *Men's Health* v32 no6 p32 Ag 2017

HARNEY, TRICIA
Humor in Uniform color *Reader's Digest* v189 no1129 p135 Ap 2017

Harney, William
For Lack of a Handshake B. HUNHOFF *South Dakota Magazine* v32 no4 p30 N/D 2016

Harnish, Verne
5 BOOKS TO LEARN FROM color *Fortune* v174 no8 p70 D 15 2016
5 TRENDS TO RIDE IN 2017 color *Fortune* v175 no4 p32 Mr 15 2017

Harnoss, Johann
Don't Let Your Company Get Trapped by Success *Harvard Business Review Digital Articles* p2 N 19 2015
Using M&A to Increase Your Capacity for Growth *Harvard Business Review Digital Articles* p2 Jl 13 2016

Harold, King of England, 1022?-1066
Shot through the Eye and who's to Blame? M. Foys *History Today* v66 no10 p6 O 2016

Haron, Muhammed
Ahmad Kathrada 1929 - 2017 *Islamic Horizons* v46 no4 p60 Jl/Ag 2017

Haroun, Mahamat Saleh, 1961-
Hissein Habré, A Chadian Tragedy *New Yorker* v93 no29 p26 S 25 2017

HARP, SETH
THE ANARCHISTS VS. ISIS color *Rolling Stone* no1281/1282 p42 F 23 2017

Harp, Walter
Into the Fun House: An Unpredictable Story of a Relentless Leukemia *Publishers Weekly* v264 no28 p80 Jl 10 2017

Harper & Brothers
150 YEARS OF BAZAR S. Mooallem cartoon *Harper's Bazaar* no3649 p326 D 2016/Ja 2017

HARPER, ALAN
The Art of Refreshment cartoon chart color *Power & Motoryacht* v32 no12 p50 D 2016
ASCENDING THE THRONE cartoon chart color *Power & Motoryacht* v32 no12 p62 D 2016
Conquering Hero chart color diag *Power & Motoryacht* v34 no6 p50 Je 2017
MEDITERRANEAN PASSAGE chart color *Power & Motoryacht* v33 no4 p68 Ap 2017
ONE STEP IN THE RIGHT DIRECTION chart color diag *Power & Motoryacht* v33 no3 p62 Mr 2017
Out from the Crowd chart color *Power & Motoryacht* v34 no9 p58 S 2017
RIVA'S REINVENTION chart color diag *Power & Motoryacht* v33 no2 p82 F 2017
THE SHAPE OF THINGS TO COME chart color diag *Power & Motoryacht* v34 no10 p78 O 2017
Small Wonder chart color *Power & Motoryacht* v32 no11 p108

What arguments motivate citizens to demand nuclear disarmament? bibl *Bulletin of the Atomic Scientists* v73 no4 p255 Jl 2017

Harrington, Brette
FLASH color *Climbing* no356 p8 S/O 2017

Harrington, Brooke
Capital Without Borders: Wealth Managers and the One Percent R. N. Cooper *Foreign Affairs* v95 no6 p175 N/D 2016
Not Like Us S. Adler-Bell color *Commonweal* v144 no4 p22 F 24 2017

HARRINGTON, CAITLIN
BRICK HØUSE: DENMARK'S LEGO LANDMARK diag *Wired* v25 no9 p22 S 2017
GAME CHANGER: A NEW PANTHEON OF SUPERHEROES *Wired* v25 no9 p20 S 2017
TREKKIE TECH color *Wired* v25 no10 p32 O 2017

Harrington, Darlene
The SAILING SCENE color *Sail* v48 no10 p8 O 2017

Harrington, Janice N.
Love, a Prairie Discourse *Orion Magazine* v35 no6 p57 N/D 2016

Harrington, Mary Dell
5 Gifts Your Grad Will Actually Use color *Money* v46 no5 p21 Je 2017

Harrington, Matt
Inexperience on Lake Ontario color *Sail* v48 no5 p24 My 2017

Harrington, Pat
ASPEN WEAVER cartoon color *Snowboarder* v29 no5 p38 Ja 2017
BROCK CROUCH color *Snowboarder* v29 no2 p44 O 2016
SEB PICARD bw cartoon color *Snowboarder* v29 no4 p50 D 2016

HARRINGTON, PHIL
25 HOT ECLIPSE PRODUCTS color *Astronomy* v45 no6 p54 Je 2017
Deep-sky objects in Cancer color *Astronomy* v45 no5 p66 My 2017
Eclipse time! color *Astronomy* v45 no8 p78 Ag 2017
Exploring Capricornus bw color *Astronomy* v45 no10 p68 O 2017
FINDING PATTERNS IN THE SKY chart color *Astronomy* v45 no1 p60 Ja 2017
Going deep for Andromeda color *Astronomy* v44 no12 p68 D 2016
Great Ursa Major galaxies color *Astronomy* v45 no6 p64 Je 2017
How to care for your telescope color *Astronomy* v45 no3 p54 Mr 2017
How to observe colorful open clusters color *Astronomy* v44 no12 p32 D 2016
Observe with both eyes open color *Astronomy* v45 no11 p58 N 2017
Orion's Sword color *Astronomy* v45 no2 p70 F 2017
Putting iOptron's new mount to the test color *Astronomy* v44 no12 p62 D 2016
Rogue globular clusters color *Astronomy* v45 no9 p68 S 2017
Sky-Watcher USA's new COMPOUND SCOPE color *Astronomy* v45 no3 p62 Mr 2017
Sparkling star clusters color *Astronomy* v45 no11 p68 N 2017
The star clusters of Puppis color *Astronomy* v45 no3 p68 Mr 2017
Summertime clusters color *Astronomy* v45 no7 p68 Jl 2017
Target open clusters color *Astronomy* v45 no1 p69 Ja 2017

Harris, Alexandra—Awards
The Longman-History Today Awards *History Today* v66 no10 p45 O 2016

Harris, Alton B.
Are U.S. Millennial Men Just as Sexist as Their Dads? *Harvard Business Review Digital Articles* p2 Je 15 2016
Why Women Feel More Stress at Work *Harvard Business Review Digital Articles* p2 Ag 4 2016

Harris, Audray
Rapid development of a DNA vaccine for Zika virus bibl graph *Science* v354 no6309 p237 O 14 2016

Harris, Barry
Chords & Discords L. THOMAS, R. JONES et al color *Downbeat* v84 no3 p10 Mr 2017

Harris, Brad
Should You Chat Informally Before an Interview? *Harvard Business Review Digital Articles* p2 S 14 2016
Teamwork Works Best When Top Performers Are Rewarded *Har-*
vard Business Review Digital Articles p2 Mr 14 2016

Harris, Brandon
Rotterdam 46: Tremors from a Nervous World *Film Quarterly* v70 no4 p113 Summ 2017

Harris, Carla
Carla Harris's 'Pearls' of Power S. Hill and A. GUMBS color *Black Enterprise* v47 no3 p35 O 2016

Harris, Caylin
(sm)art idea *Parents* v91 no11 p109 N 2016

Harris, Charlaine, 1951-
FROM THE PAGE TO THE SCREEN: True Blood and Midnight, Texas author Charlaine Harris shares what it's like to see her beloved characters on TV I. Rudolph *TV Guide* v65 no31 p12 Jl 24 2017
Sleep like a Baby *Publishers Weekly* v264 no27 p53 Jl 3 2017

Harris, Charles E.
STATEMENT OF OWNERSHIP *Natural History* v124 no10 p44 N 2016

Harris, Daniel M.
How boundaries shape chemical delivery in microfluidics bibl diag graph *Science* v354 no6317 p1252 D 9 2016

Harris, Dave
FIT TO PRINT bw color *Wired* v25 no5 p14 My 2017

Harris, David
FATHER OF THE NAVY bw color *Military History* v34 no5 p22 Ja 2018

Harris, David L.
DAVID L. HARRIS P. Lutz color *Downbeat* v84 no7 p27 Jl 2017

Harris, Diane
A Few More Words—Before I Go color *Money* v46 no3 p9 Ap 2017
Job No. 1: Act in Your Best Interests color *Money* v46 no2 p15 Mr 2017
Old and New Holiday Traditions color *Money* v45 no11 p10 D 2016

Harris, Ed
PARTY LINES img *New York* v50 no7 p86 Ap 3 2017

Harris, Ed, 1950-
ED HARRIS J. Hibberd color *Entertainment Weekly* no1438 p52 N 4 2016

Harris, Gordon
FEATURED FELLOW: GORDON HARRIS M. Rosano color *Canadian Geographic* v137 no3 p78 My 2017

Harris, Hardette
Chef Hardette Harris C. JAY color *Louisiana Life* v37 no3 p54 Ja/F 2017

Harris, Holly
The Prisoner Dilemma color *Foreign Affairs* v96 no2 p118 Mr/ Ap 2017

Harris, Hunter
TRENDING NOW color *Wired* v25 no4 p12 Ap 2017

Harris, Ian
#Hønnolding color *Climbing* no350 p17 D 2016/Ja 2017

Harris, J. Berton C.
The pet trade's role in defaunation color *Science* v356 no6341 p916 Je 1 2017

HARRIS, J. SELDEN JR.
An Islamic Approach to Christianity: Do people realize that the Quran, the New Testament and the Hebrew Scriptures all teach us to become involved in interfaith dialogue? *Islamic Horizons* v46 no4 p48 Jl/Ag 2017
No Place for Islamophobia in America: Islamophobia has its roots in the history of Western Christianity *Islamic Horizons* v46 no3 p30 My/Je 2017

Harris, Jack
Faith and Science at a Crossroad *Sky & Telescope* v134 no3 p6 S 2017

Harris, Jack G. E.
Ambient quantum optomechanics diag *Science* v356 no6344 p1232 Je 23 2017

Harris, Jane Alvey—Interviews
Meet the Finalists for the booklife Prize in Fiction N. AUDREY SPECTOR color *Publishers Weekly* v263 no52 p78 D 19 2016

Harris, Jane Ursula
Invisible-Exports color *Art in America* v105 no1 p82 Ja 2017
Participant Inc color *Art in America* v105 no6 p136 Je/Jl 2017

HARRIS, JANELLE
'90S Till Infinity bw color *Ebony* v72 no4 p96 F 2017
Support Black Businesses color *Essence* v47 no8 p83 D 2016
TRIUMPH THROUGH TRAGEDY color *Essence* v47 no7 p96
  N 2016

HARRIS, JARRARD
Listen To Learn the Jazz Language color *Downbeat* v84 no8 p86
  Ag 2017

Harris, John
BRITAIN'S MIDSUMMER FEVER DREAM color *Nation* v305
  no4 p16 Ag 14 2017
Can the Left Find Its Voice in the 21st Century? color il *Nation*
  v303 no22 p16 N 28 2016
THAT DIDN'T GO TO PLAN color *Nation* v304 no12 p27 Ap
  10 2017

Harris, Judith
THE MODIGLIANI CODE bw color *Vanity Fair* v59 no6 p110
  My 2017

Harris, Kamala D., 1964-
keeping score *Ms.* v27 no3 p6 Fall 2017
Leaders color *Time* v189 no16/17 p64 My 1-8 2017
SAY HELLO TO THE NEW GIRL T. M. Ferguson *Ebony* v72
  no11 p12 S 2017
SENATOR-ELECT KAMALA HARRIS D. BARTLOW *Ms.* v26
  no3 p6 Fall 2016
A WOMAN ON THE RISE B. VIERA color *Ebony* v72 no11 p22
  S 2017

HARRIS, KAREN
STRATEGY IN THE AGE OF SUPERABUNDANT CAPITAL
  color graph img *Harvard Business Review* v95 no2 p66 Mr/Ap
  2017

Harris, Katelynn
The effect of state parity laws on how providers treat substance
  use disorder *Monthly Labor Review* p1 Je 2017

Harris, Kenneth D.
Synaptic scaling in sleep bibl color *Science* v355 no6324 p457
  F 3 2017

HARRIS, KEVIN
How to Install a Solar Panel color *Boating World* v38 no7 p26
  Jl 2017
Outboard Towing Magic: Installing TurboSwing to tow skiers be-
  hind an outboard-powered boat is one-person simple *Boating
  World* v38 no8 p22 S/O 2017

Harris, L. Kasimu
L. Kasimu Harris F. ESKER color *Louisiana Life* v37 no3 p60
  Ja/F 2017

Harris, Lawren, 1885-1970
Framed by fortune M. CAMPBELL bw color *Maclean's* v129
  no50 p16 D 19 2016

HARRIS, LINDA
ALL IN A Day's Work cartoon color *Reader's Digest* v190 no1134
  p54 O 2017

HARRIS, MALCOLM
HOT SEATS *New York Times Magazine* p64 N 13 2016

Harris, Mark
Ambitious web fundraising startup fails to meet big goals *Science*
  v354 no6312 p534 N 4 2016
How Much to Laugh at Trump: For late-night hosts, the president
  is a gift, and a quandary img *New York* p40 Mr 6 2017
Is There Really Such a Thing As "Oscar Bait"? img *New York* v49
  no22 p97 O 31 2016
Is There Really Such a Thing As "Oscar Bait"? M. HARRIS and
  K. BUCHANAN img *New York* v49 no22 p97 O 31 2016
OBAMA'S AMERICA img *New York* v49 no20 p12 O 3 2016
STILL LOOKING color *Film Comment* v52 no6 p66 N/D 2016

HARRIS, MARQUITA
GUCCI, do better color *Ebony* v72 no11 p27 S 2017
HERE'S WHY BRITISH VOGUE'S NEW EDITOR-IN-CHIEF
  MATTERS color *Ebony* v72 no11 p30 S 2017

Harris, Matthew
Show of Strength R. WALDMAN cartoon color *Vogue* v207 no11
  p226 N 2017

Harris, Michael
LET YOUR MIND WANDER color *Discover* v38 no5 p30 Je
  2017
A Recognized Man color *Walrus* v14 no8 p52 O 2017

SOLITUDE: A SINGULAR LIFE IN A CROWDED WORLD E.
  DONALDSON color *Maclean's* v130 no4 p70 My 2017

Harris, Michael D.
When to Sell with Facts and Figures, and When to Appeal to Emotions *Harvard Business Review Digital Articles* p2 Ja 26 2015

HARRIS, MICHELLE
Bet you didn't know color *National Geographic Kids* no470 p10
  My 2017
By the Numbers RAIN FOREST *National Geographic Kids*
  no468 p8 Mr 2017
By the Numbers The Sweetest Countries *National Geographic
  Kids* no466 p6 D 2016/Ja 2017
Weird But True! color *National Geographic Kids* no474 p4 O
  2017
Weird but true! *National Geographic Kids* no466 p4 D 2016/Ja
  2017
Weird but true! *National Geographic Kids* no468 p4 Mr 2017

Harris, Mike
GOOD AS NEW color *Sports Illustrated* v127 no10 p20 O 2 2017

Harris, Naomie, 1976-
Letitia WRIGHT *Interview* v47 no5 p66 Je/Jl 2017
NAOMIE HARRIS L. SATENSTEIN, M. HOLGATE et al color
  Vogue v207 no3 p322 Mr 2017
NAOMIE'S MOMENT C. Shanahan color *InStyle* v23 no13 p232
  D 2016
Pipe Up E. Wilson color *InStyle* v23 no12 p62 N 2016

Harris, Neil Patrick, 1973-
A SERIES OF UNFORTUNATE EVENTS M. J. Rose bw *U.S.
  Catholic* v82 no6 p40 Je 2017
A Series of Unfortunate Events M. Snetiker color *Entertainment
  Weekly* no1448 p38 Ja 13 2017

Harris, Neil Patrick, 1973---Interviews
Guess who's in the new LEMONY SNICKET? C. KOPACZE-
  WSKI color *Good Housekeeping* v264 no2 p140 F 2017
Neil Patrick Harris E. Dockterman color *Time* v189 no3 p50 Ja
  30 2017
WHY AMERICA LOVES NEIL PATRICK HARRIS: THIS FOR-
  MER CHILD ACTOR IS AMONG OUR MOST BELOVED
  GAY ACTORS, BUT TO HIS KIDS HE'S JUST DAD S.
  ABADSIDIS and D. ANDERSON-MINSHALL color *Advocate*
  no1091 p85 Je/Jl 2017

Harris, Nicola L.
Specific repair by discerning macrophages diag *Science* v356
  no6342 p1014 Je 9 2017

HARRIS, RALPH TONY
ROAR OF THE CROWD *Texas Monthly* v45 no7 p12 Jl 2017

Harris, Reginald
Suicide in the workplace *Monthly Labor Review* p1 D 2016

Harris, Rennie—Interviews
STREET TO STAGE D. S. GRIMES and A. O'NEAL *Dance
  Magazine* v91 no7 p42 Jl 2017

Harris, Richard
My Competitiveness Was Hurting My Sales Team. Here's How I
  Realized It *Harvard Business Review Digital Articles* p2 S 29
  2017
On rigor and replication L. P. Freedman color *Science* v356
  no6333 p34 Ap 7 2017
Publish and Perish *Issues in Science & Technology* v33 no4 p29
  Summ 2017
Through the Roof color map *Alternatives Journal (AJ) - Canada's
  Environmental Voice* v42 no2 p30 2016

Harris, Robert
CARDINAL SINS V. FRIEDMAN color *New York Times Book
  Review* p65 D 4 2016
A Complex Conclave L. PICKER *Publishers Weekly* v263 no39
  p66 S 26 2016

Harris, Robert J.
Spiral density waves in a young protoplanetary disk bibl graph
  Science v353 no6307 p1519 S 30 2016

Harris, Rosie
Only Love Can Heal *Publishers Weekly* v264 no15 p59 Ap 10
  2017

Harris, Simon R.
Emergence and spread of a human-transmissible multidrug-resistant nontuberculous mycobacterium bibl diag graph *Science*
  v354 no6313 p751 N 11 2016

Harris, Stefon
MSM Hires Harris for Jazz Program J. Hale color *Downbeat* v84 no3 p118 Mr 2017
HARRIS, TAMARA WINFREY
OBAMA'S AMERICA img *New York* v49 no20 p12 O 3 2016
Harris, Thomas
IS THAT WHAT THEY SHOULD LOOK LIKE? bw color *Reader's Digest* v190 no1134 p98 O 2017
Harris, Tristan
TRISTAN HARRIS BELIEVES SILICON VALLEY IS ADDICTING US TO OUR PHONES. HE'S DETERMINED TO MAKE IT STOP B. Bosker color *Atlantic* v318 no4 p56 N 2016
Harris, Will
NATIONAL BURDEN W. Williams *New York Times Magazine* p26 Ja 22 2017
Harris Corp.
Harris Cruiser 220 *Boating World* v38 no1 p60 Ja 2017
Harris Media Systems Ltd.
The German Far Right Gets American Aid V. Silver and S. Frier color *Bloomberg Businessweek* no4540 p42 O 2 2017
Harris tweed
Common Threads D. Coggins color map *Conde Nast Traveler* v52 no3 p64 Mr 2017
Dressing the Part P. Guzmán bw *Conde Nast Traveler* v52 no3 p16 Mr 2017
Harrison (Idaho)
HARRISON G. HILL *Idaho Magazine* v16 no3 p32 D 2016
Harrison, Alana
Bits That Go Ouch! [Cover story] color *Horse & Rider* v56 no1 p44 Ja 2017
HARRISON, ALEXA
City of Alchemy color *New Orleans Magazine* v51 no12 p30 O 2017
Her Louisiana Love bw *New Orleans Magazine* v52 no1 p28 S 2017
Harrison, Benjamin, 1833-1901
Speech! Speech! T. B. BROWNE *Indianapolis Monthly* v40 no3 p26 N 2016
Harrison, Christopher
Magnetic monopole search, past and present *Physics Today* v70 no6 p13 Je 2017
Harrison, Colin
Dreamers and Schemers: In Colin Harrison's thriller, noir has a complicated relationship with nostalgia M. ABBOTT *New York Times Book Review* p17 Je 18 2017
You Belong to Me *Publishers Weekly* v264 no14 p48 Ap 3. 2017
Harrison, D. J.
BONUS LEVEL: With Hazy Moods, DJ Harrison reveals his perfect pitch D. HARRISON *Virginia Living* v15 no6 p29 O 2017
HARRISON, DON
BONUS LEVEL: With Hazy Moods, DJ Harrison reveals his perfect pitch *Virginia Living* v15 no6 p29 O 2017
FAMILY TRADITION: Roanoke's Rutledge is a little bit country, a little bit rock 'n' roll *Virginia Living* v15 no4 p31 Je 2017
LAST MAN STANDING: With The Richmond Sessions, the surviving Holmes brother goes it alone bw color *Virginia Living* v15 no5 p31 Ag 2017
THE MEM PHIS BEAT *Virginia Living* v15 no1 p56 D 2016
WHERE I STOOD *Virginia Living* v15 no2 p25 F 2017
HARRISON, EMILY C.
Comfort Food Swaps *Dance Magazine* v90 no11 p48 N 2016
Harrison, Gordon
GORDON HARRISON B. Merrill and N. Müller color *Snowboarder* v29 no3 p42 N 2016
Harrison, Guy P.
Think Before You Like: Social Media's Effect on the Brain and the Tools You Need to Navigate Your Newsfeed color *Publishers Weekly* v264 no38 p63 S 18 2017
Harrison, Hunter
THE LAST RAILROAD TYCOON S. Tully color diag map *Fortune* v176 no3 p84 S 1 2017
HARRISON, IAN
Freshwater Megafauna: Flagships for Freshwater Biodiversity under Threat *BioScience* v67 no10 p919 O 2017
Harrison, Jim, 1937-2016
The Ancient Minstrel D. Bakopoulos *Orion Magazine* v35 no4/5

p109 Jl-O 2016
Dear Jim ... K. Vaughn *Arizona Highways* v93 no4 p32 Ap 2017
Larger Than Life S. Sifton *New York Times Magazine* p22 Ap 2 2017
Harrison, Joel
Joel Harrison D. OUELLETTE color *Downbeat* v84 no2 p106 F 2017
HARRISON, JOHN A.
Greenhouse Gas Emissions from Reservoir Water Surfaces: A New Global Synthesis *BioScience* v66 no11 p949 N 1 2016
Harrison, Joseph
BUCKLE UP color *Team Roping Journal* p16 O 2017
Cowboy Cred J. Mankin color *Spin to Win Rodeo* v21 no5 p56 Jl 2017
Harrison, Joseph S.
Research: Board Directors Are More Likely to Leave When a Firm Is Getting Criticized *Harvard Business Review Digital Articles* p2 Ag 9 2017
HARRISON, JUSTINE
To Play Or Not To Play? color *Horse & Rider* v56 no11 p90 N 2017
HARRISON, KATHRYN
Over Her Shoulder: A contemporary 'Rebecca,' Lily Tuck's new novel exposes a second wife's obsession with the woman who got to her husband first *New York Times Book Review* p20 O 8 2017
Harrison, Kayla, 1990-
How Kayla Harrison's Judo Dreams Came True — Twice! M. Jacobs color *Black Belt* v55 no1 p16 D 2016/Ja 2017
Harrison, Kristina
ask the experts color *Dressage Today* v23 no7 p64 Mr 2017
Harrison, Lou, 1917-2003
To Lou, with Love A. Ross color *New Yorker* v93 no10 p18 Ap 24 2017
Harrison, Nick
If Your Company Isn't Good at Analytics, It's Not Ready for AI color *Harvard Business Review Digital Articles* p2 Je 7 2017
Using Data to Strengthen Your Connections to Customers *Harvard Business Review Digital Articles* p2 Ag 25 2016
HARRISON, RICHARD A.
Not So Fast, Golden State *American Scholar* v86 no3 p3 Summ 2017
Harrison, Robert Pogue
Dante: He Went Mad in His Hell cartoon *New York Review of Books* v63 no16 p30 O 27 2016
Harrison, Roger
John Phillips J. Phillips color *Car & Driver* v62 no11 p28 My 2017
HARRISON, SAM
Help Keep Cincinnati Safe *Cincinnati Magazine* v50 no5 p118 F 2017
Harrison, Sarah Ellys
Assembly of embryonic and extraembryonic stem cells to mimic embryogenesis in vitro diag *Science* v356 no6334 p153 Ap 14 2017
Harrison, T. A.
Observation of a large-scale anisotropy in the arrival directions of cosmic rays above 8×10^{18} eV *Science* v357 no6357 p1266 S 22 2017
Harrison, Tanya
THE PAST AND PRESENT OF WATER ON MARS [Cover story] color *Astronomy* v45 no7 p22 Jl 2017
Where has all the water gone? D. J. EICHER color *Astronomy* v45 no7 p6 Jl 2017
Harrison, Ted
THE DEATH AND RESURRECTION OF ELVIS PRESLEY B. BETHUNE color *Maclean's* v129 no45 p56 N 14 2016
Harrison, Teva
IN-BETWEEN DAYS: A Memoir About Living With Cancer A. Ulinich *New York Times Book Review* p28 My 21 2017
HARRISON, VEE L.
Tiwa Savage Is Roc Steady color *Ebony* v72 no8 p30 Je 2017
Harrison, William Henry, 1773-1841
Retrospect S. Potter *Weatherwise* v70 no2 p10 Mr/Ap 2017
Harrison Warren, Tish
GIVE US THIS DAY OUR DAILY CHORES J. A. HUGHES

color *Christianity Today* v60 no10 p65 D 2016

Harris-Perry, Melissa

Beyoncé color *Time* v188 no25-26 p124 D 19 2016 Double Issue

World's Greatest Female Athlete [Cover story] bw color *Glamour* v114 no7 p114 Jl 2016

Harrold, A. F.

New Worlds and Old: Two books for middle-grade readers evoke both the past and the future of fantasy novels J. Auxier *New York Times Book Review* p17 Jl 16 2017

HARROW, DEL

Who is pushing the craft field forward? color *American Craft* v76 no6 p26 D 2016-Ja 2017

Harrows

POCKET PRICE GUIDE: Dealer Prices on Late-Model Field Cultivators *Successful Farming* v115 no5 p23 Mid-Mr 2017

Harry (TV program)

Happy Holidays, Harry! color *AARP: The Magazine* v60 no1A p7 D 2016/Ja 2017

Harry, Debbie, 1945-

Debbie Harry What's your backstage essential? D. WALTERS color *Bon Appetit* v62 no4 p118 Ap 2017

EDITOR'S LETTER G. Bailey color *Harper's Bazaar* no3652 p88 Ap 2017

GOING Blondie L. REGENSDORF color *Vogue* v206 no12 p200 D 2016

ICONS C. Mueller bw color *Glamour* v115 no5 p190 My 2017

My Blond color *InStyle* v24 no5 p216 My 2017

THERE'S SOMETHING ABOUT HARRY T. Janowitz bw color *Harper's Bazaar* no3652 p244 Ap 2017

Harry, Debbie, 1945-—Interviews

Two Rock Icons Hop on a Conference Call... N. Feeney color *Entertainment Weekly* no1473 p56 Jl 7 2017

Harry Benson: Shoot First (Film)

A Star-Studded Tribute to a Lovable Lensman I. Guzmán color *Time* v188 no24 p64 D 12 2016

Harry Potter & the Cursed Child (Play)

BESTSELLERS C. JURIS *Publishers Weekly* v263 no39 p17 S 26 2016

Books Suffer from Potter Curse, Sales Tumble 17% chart *Publishers Weekly* v264 no33 p6 Ag 14 2017

J.K. ROWLING M. Snetiker color *Entertainment Weekly* no1444/1445 p23 D 16 2016

News Briefs *Publishers Weekly* v263 no39 p5 S 26 2016

Potter Tops Print, 'Girl' Rides E-book Train J. Maher chart *Publishers Weekly* v264 no2 p5 Ja 9 2017

Sales Recover from Potter Curse, Hold Even in the Week chart *Publishers Weekly* v264 no34 p8 Ag 21 2017

Unit Sales Dip 2% Compared to 2016 chart *Publishers Weekly* v264 no36 p5 S 4 2017

Harry Potter films

ALAN RICKMAN K. Winslet and C. Nashawaty color *Entertainment Weekly* no1446/1447 p92 D 2016/Ja 2017

Harry Potter: By the Numbers D. Coggan color *Entertainment Weekly* no1435 p10 O 14 2016

Harry Styles (Music)

Harry Styles L. Greenblatt color *Entertainment Weekly* no1466 p57 My 19 2017

HARSANYI, DAVID

The Eternal Scandal *National Review* v69 no11 p44 Je 12 2017

In the Groove color *National Review* v69 no7 p48 Ap 17 2017

Jerk Logic *National Review* v68 no21 p48 N 21 2016

Modified Limited Hangouts *National Review* v69 no18 p44 O 2 2017

Sensitive Senate *National Review* v69 no4 p48 Mr 6 2017

When Driving Is Obsolete *National Review* v68 no23 p44 D 19 2016

Harss, Marina

Double Life *Dance Magazine* v90 no12 p112 D 2016

Fall Preview color *New Yorker* v93 no25 p20 Ag 28 2017

Gemma Bond *Dance Magazine* v91 no8 p18 Ag 2017

In Character *Dance Magazine* v91 no1 p128 Ja 2017

The MOST INFLUENTIAL PEOPLE IN DANCE TODAY: THE MOVERS, SHAKERS AND CHANGEMAKERS HAVING THE BIGGEST IMPACT ON DANCE RIGHT NOW *Dance Magazine* v91 no7 p27 Jl 2017

Paloma Herrera *Dance Magazine* v91 no6 p20 Je 2017

Spring Preview cartoon *New Yorker* v93 no4 p20 Mr 13 2017

Starting Over: Betsy McBride chose ABT's corps de ballet over stardom at Texas Ballet Theater *Dance Magazine* v91 no7 p58 Jl 2017

Summer Preview cartoon *New Yorker* v93 no14 p6 My 22 2017

TILER PECK *Dance Magazine* v90 no12 p47 D 2016

Troy Schumacher: The choreographer is premiering three ballets in a span of four weeks *Dance Magazine* v91 no10 p18 O 2017

Unflappable *Dance Magazine* v91 no10 p30 O 2017

Winter Preview cartoon *New Yorker* v92 no37 p22 N 14 2016

Hart, Amanda

CURATOR OF CUTE A. NOLAN color *Runner's World* v52 no3 p17 Ap 2017

Hart, Ashley

THE JOY OF YOGA [Cover story] M. Stacey cartoon color *Women's Health* v14 no1 p77 Ja/F 2017

Hart, Christopher—Interviews

Policing Driverless Cars A. Rosenblum il *MIT Technology Review* v119 no6 p15 N/D 2016

Hart, D. G.

The Soul of Mencken L. WEINER color *National Review* v69 no1 p35 Ja 23 2017

HART, DAVID

HUNTBNB color *Outdoor Life* v224 no6 pH15 Ag 2017

A STUDENT LOAN color map *Outdoor Life* v224 no6 pH9 Ag 2017

SUPER SCATTERS color *Outdoor Life* v224 no8 pH7 O 2017

TWO-TIMING WHITE TAILS color *Outdoor Life* v224 no8 pH8 O 2017

WHAT'S HE SCORE? bw color *Outdoor Life* v224 no9 pH1 N 2017

Hart, David Bentley

Suggestions or Commands? bw *Commonweal* v143 no20 p9 D 16 2016

HART, DAVID M.

Advancing clean energy *Issues in Science & Technology* v33 no3 p5 Spr 2017

Hart, Edward

OBAMA'S AMERICA img *New York* v49 no20 p12 O 3 2016

Hart, Ellen

Fever in the Dark: A Jane Lawless Mystery *Publishers Weekly* v263 no45 p40 N 7 2016

HART, GEOFF

Fiction and Our Changing Climate *American Scholar* v86 no1 p3 Wint 2017

Hart, Hannah

Buffering: Unshared Tales of a Life Fully Loaded *Publishers Weekly* v263 no42 p62 O 17 2016

Hart, James

"I WANT TO TRY CYCLOCROSS." color *Bicycling* v58 no3 p66 Ap 2017

THANKS FOR THE RIDE color *Bicycling* v58 no10 p15 N/D 2017

Hart, James—Interviews

READ color *Advocate* no1091 p36 Je/Jl 2017

THAT SONG IS NOT ABOUT HIM: Carly Simon's ex-husband talks coming out, Hillary's loss, and how truth sets us free D. ANDERSON-MINSHALL color *Advocate* no1091 p34 Je/Jl 2017

Hart, Jessica

Arms Up! E. Wilson color *InStyle* v24 no11 p74 N 2017

Hart, Josh

Flying Start T. Blackmar *Sports Illustrated* v126 no1 p52 Ja 9 2017

Hart, Kevin, 1979-

Hart of a Lion: Making an Entire City Laugh at Once S. Zacharek color *Time* v188 no16/17 p88 O 24 2016

THE INTERSECTION color *Runner's World* v52 no3 p27 Ap 2017

Kevin Hart L. Greenblatt color *Entertainment Weekly* no1444/1445 p22 D 16 2016

No Joke, Kevin Hart Couldn't Make This Up M. KIMBLE color *Ebony* v72 no8 p31 Je 2017

THE SELFLESS Love OF A FATHER K. Hart color *Essence* v48 no2 p92 Je 2017

UNSTOPPABLE [Cover story] M. M. Lewis color *Essence* v48

no2 p88 Je 2017

WHAT MEN THINK ABOUT WHAT WOMEN WEAR color *Harper's Bazaar* no3648 p194 N 2016

Hart, Kevin, 1979——Interviews

KEVIN HART D. Lawrence color *Entertainment Weekly* no1474/1475 p120 Jl 21-28 2017

MINING COMEDY GOLD E. Griffith, A. Vandermey et al color *Fortune* v176 no3 p70 S 1 2017

Hart, Kimberly

The Power of the Pink Ranger E. Mahaney color *Glamour* v115 no4 p50 Ap 2017

Hart, Lorenz, 1895-1943

Broadway's Tiny Giant *Commentary* v143 no4 p4 Ap 2017

Hart, Maureen

THE GATEWAY TO ACTIVE SENIORS *Parks & Recreation* v52 no1 p32 Ja 2017

Hart, Miranda M.

Plant-soil feedbacks and mycorrhizal type influence temperate forest population dynamics bibl graph map *Science* v355 no6321 p1 Ja 13 2017

Hart, Oliver

Contract theory nabs econ Nobel *Science* v354 no6309 p152 O 14 2016

Serving Shareholders Doesn't Mean Putting Profit Above All Else *Harvard Business Review Digital Articles* p2 O 12 2017

Hart, Paul

hart-shaped trails: MEET THE FUTURE OF FEDERAL LAND MANAGEMENT k. gensheimer bw color *Bike Magazine* v24 no8 p32 N 2017

Hart, Peter

VOICES FROM THE TREHCHES *MHQ: Quarterly Journal of Military History* v29 no2 p18 Wint 2017

Hart, Sara

In the Nature of a Natural Material *Architectural Record* v204 no10 p46 O 2016

Hart, Valorie

In Transition *New Orleans Homes & Lifestyles* v20 no1 p54 Wint 2016

Let Them Eat Cake! *New Orleans Homes & Lifestyles* v20 no1 p66 Wint 2016

Middle Ground *New Orleans Homes & Lifestyles* v20 no2 p52 Spr 2017

The Old Grocery [Cover story] *New Orleans Homes & Lifestyles* v20 no2 p42 Spr 2017

PICNIC CHIC: A vintage-inspired outdoor spread to kick your summer off in style *New Orleans Homes & Lifestyles* v20 no3 p66 Summ 2017

pretty IS AS PRETTY does: A FLOOD DAMAGED OLD METAIRIE HOUSE IS GIVEN A SECOND CHANCE *New Orleans Homes & Lifestyles* v20 no4 p56 Aut 2017

Urban Oasis: Stylish New Orleans outdoor living spaces large, small and everything between *New Orleans Homes & Lifestyles* v20 no3 p56 Summ 2017

Harte, Julia

THE IMMUNITY DOCTRINE: Can officials be held liable for the suffering they inflict? color *Harper's Magazine* v335 no2005 p59 Je 2017

Harter, J. W.

A parity-breaking electronic nematic phase transition in the spin-orbit coupled metal Cd2Re2O7 diag *Science* v356 no6335 p295 Ap 21 2017

Harter, James

Engage Your Long-Time Employees to Improve Performance *Harvard Business Review Digital Articles* p2 Mr 16 2015

What Great Managers Do to Engage Employees *Harvard Business Review Digital Articles* p2 Ap 2 2015

Hartfelder, William A.

ENEMY color *Christian Century* v134 no5 p20 Mr 1 2017

Hartford, Huntington, 1911-2008

Don't Spend Your Life Making Up Your Mind M. Chussil *Harvard Business Review Digital Articles* p2 My 15 2017

Hartjoy, Jeff

THE LONG WAY HOME color map *Sail* v48 no2 p52 F 2017

THE ROARING FORTIES color map *Sail* v48 no1 p36 Ja 2017

UNFINISHED BUSINESS color map *Sail* v47 no12 p40 D 2016

Hartlage, Alex S.

Mouse models of acute and chronic hepacivirus infection *Science* v357 no6347 p204 Jl 14 2017

HARTLEY, JONATHAN

Every Student a Bond Seller color *National Review* v68 no19 p37 O 24 2016

Hartley, Justin

FAMILY TIES I. RATLEDGE *TV Guide* v65 no11 p32 Mr 6 2017

This Is Us D. Snierson, N. Abrams et al color *Entertainment Weekly* no1482/1483 p56 S 22 2017

Hartley, Marsden, 1877-1943—Exhibitions

ART *New Yorker* v93 no8 p13 Ap 10 2017

"My native continent" D. M. Cassidy, E. Finch et al cartoon *Magazine Antiques* v184 no2 p100 Mr/Ap 2017

Hartley, Matthew

Distinct phases of Polycomb silencing to hold epigenetic memory of cold in Arabidopsis diag *Science* v357 no6356 p1142 S 15 2017

Hartman, David

PHANTASM: RAVAGER B. A. DuHamel color *Sound & Vision* v82 no4 p71 My 2017

Hartman, Gary

Reclaiming the Past N. E. BERRY color diag *Timber Home Living* v27 no6 p26 D 2017

Hartman, Karen

The Thread *New York Times Magazine* p12 O 30 2016

Hartman, Kim

CANDID CONVERSATION ABOUT MENOPAUSE AT THE CHRIST HOSPITAL *Cincinnati Magazine* v50 no3 p62 D 2016

Hartman, Liz

A Bonanza of Book Events for Toddlers to Teens bw color *Publishers Weekly* v263 no44 p(Sp)29 O 31 2016

BookCon 2017: More of the Same, but Better color *Publishers Weekly* v264 no20 p(Sp)32 My 15 2017

By the Community, for the Community bw *Publishers Weekly* v263 no44 p(Sp)6 O 31 2016

How to Reach Across the Aisle? Get a Dog bw *Publishers Weekly* v263 no44 p(Sp)12 O 31 2016

Lives: A Reading from Three Novels bw *Publishers Weekly* v263 no44 p(Sp)10 O 31 2016

New York's Finest... Coffee color *Publishers Weekly* v264 no20 p(Sp)90 My 15 2017

N.Y.C.: Tales of the City—A Reading from Three Novels bw *Publishers Weekly* v263 no44 p(Sp)24 O 31 2016

The Rising Stars of the Industry bw color *Publishers Weekly* v264 no36 p(Sp)3 S 4 2017

STRIKING THE RIGHT BALANCE bw color *Publishers Weekly* v263 no50 p26 D 5 2016

Thursday, Friday BookExpo Author Highlights color *Publishers Weekly* v264 no20 p(Sp)24 My 15 2017

Wednesday's Focus *Publishers Weekly* v264 no20 p(Sp)16 My 15 2017

Weekend Closeup November 19–20 cartoon *Publishers Weekly* v263 no44 p(Sp)4 O 31 2016

What's Cookin'? bw color *Publishers Weekly* v263 no44 p(Sp)14 O 31 2016

HARTMAN, RACHEL

how to teach time *Parents* v92 no8 p133 Ag 2017

HARTMAN, VIRGINIA

MY MOTHER, SEWING *Washingtonian Magazine* v52 no3 p192 D 2016

Hartmann, Bernhard

What Low Oil Prices Really Mean *Harvard Business Review Digital Articles* p2 Mr 28 2016

Hartmann, Betsy

The Apocalyptic Style in American Politics C. LEHMANN *In These Times* v41 no6 p37 Je 2017

HARTNETT, JUSTIN

Cheers & Jeers color *Field & Stream* v122 no6 p12 N 2017

Hartnoll, Sean A.

Anomalously low electronic thermal conductivity in metallic vanadium dioxide bibl graph *Science* v355 no6323 p371 Ja 27 2017

Harton, J. L.

Observation of a large-scale anisotropy in the arrival directions of cosmic rays above 8 × 1018 eV *Science* v357 no6357 p1266 S 22 2017

HARTSHORN, IAN M.
Labor's Role in the Arab Uprisings and Beyond *Current History* v115 no785 p349 D 2016

Hartshorn, Jessica
cleared for takeoff! *Parents* v91 no11 p123 N 2016
CONNECT WITH YOUR CHILD'S CLASSROOM color *Parents* v92 no9 p86 S 2017
From the Mouths of (Celebs') Babes color *Parents* v92 no8 p20 Ag 2017
Heartthrob Celeb Dads, and What We Fantasize They're Good At color *Parents* v92 no6 p16 Je 2017
playing with purpose color *Parents* v92 no5 p60 My 2017
Relatable Days With Rebecca Minkoff color *Parents* v92 no9 p15 S 2017
These Celebs Win at Family Comedy color *Parents* v92 no5 p9 My 2017
TOY JOY color *Parents* v92 no11 p56 N 2017
the toys of childhood color *Parents* v92 no6 p56 Je 2017
What's on Jillian Michaels's Phone? *Parents* v91 no11 p22 N 2016

Hartsock, Robert W.
Metalloprotein entatic control of ligand-metal bonds quantified by ultrafast x-ray spectroscopy diag *Science* v356 no6344 p1276 Je 23 2017

Hartt School (West Hartford, Conn.)
The Hartt School University of Hartford *Dance Magazine* v90 p68 2016/2017 Supplement College Guide

HARTUNG, WILLIAM D.
Trump's Twisted Budget color *Nation* v304 no9 p3 Mr 20 2017

HARTWICK, JEFFREY
Trump's Wall *Commentary* v142 no2 p8 S 2016

Hartwig, John F.
An artificial metalloenzyme with the kinetics of native enzymes bibl diag graph *Science* v354 no6308 p102 O 7 2016
Snap deconvolution: An informatics approach to high-throughput discovery of catalytic reactions color *Science* v357 no6347 p175 Jl 14 2017

Hartwig, Melissa
Paleo-Friendly BBQ color *Amazing Wellness* v9 no3 p82 Early-Summ 2017

HARTZ, KEVIN
How Did I Get Here? color *Bloomberg Businessweek* no4494 p76 O 10 2016

Hartzband, Pamela
Putting Profits Ahead of Patients bw color *New York Review of Books* v64 no12 p47 Jl 13 2017

Hartzel, Dustin N.
Distribution and clinical impact of functional variants in 50,726 whole-exome sequences from the DiscovEHR study chart graph *Science* v354 no6319 paaf6814-1 D 23 2016
Genetic identification of familial hypercholesterolemia within a single U.S. health care system chart graph *Science* v354 no6319 paaf7000-1 D 23 2016

Hartzell, Vincent
What To Ask About Antibiotics Before You Start A Course M. LAUBERTE *Reader's Digest* v188 no1124 p64 O 2016

Harvard Business Review
HBR's Best on Saying No to More Work A. Gallo color *Harvard Business Review Digital Articles* p2 Ja 30 2017
Remember to Sport Your Integrity M. Babick *In Stride* v12 no4 p34 Jl 2017

Harvard Business School
Alexis DePree color *Working Mother* v40 no3 p12 Ag/S 2017
A Partial Defense of Our Obsession with Short-Term Earnings S. Cliffe *Harvard Business Review Digital Articles* p2 My 7 2015
PATRICK J. MCGINNIS WEIGHS THE RISKS *Lapham's Quarterly* v10 no3 p78 Summ 2017

Harvard Law School
LATE BLOOMER J. Toobin cartoon *New Yorker* v93 no32 p23 O 16 2017

Harvard University
BEST BANG FOR THE BUCK NORTHEAST COLLEGES chart *Washington Monthly* v49 no9/10 p50 S/O 2017
A CLASSROOM IN THE AGE OF ENLIGHTENMENT E. W. Lasser bw color *Magazine Antiques* v184 no3 p90 My/Je 2017
COLOR CORRECTED K. SANNEH cartoon color *New Yorker* v93 no31 p71 O 9 2017

Cost of Running Harvard K. Stock color diag *Bloomberg Businessweek* no4535 p19 Ag 28 2017
Good News at Harvard! color *Weekly Standard* v23 no2 p2 S 18 2017
Harvard's Club Brawl J. SEDGWICK color *Vanity Fair* v59 no9 p224 S 2017
Harvard's Shame J. NICHOLS *Nation* v305 no8 p4 O 9 2017
HOUSEKEEPERS VS. HARVARD [Cover story] S. LEONARD color *Nation* v304 no12 p12 Ap 10 2017
JARED KUSHNER'S HARVARD ADMISSIONS ESSAY M. AMRAM cartoon *New Yorker* v93 no27 p33 S 11 2017
The Mouse Parent Trap A. Marks color *Scientific American* v317 no1 p16 Jl 2017
NATIONAL UNIVERSITIES chart *Washington Monthly* v49 no9/10 p82 S/O 2017
Pursuing big dreams, Halberstam started small J. Friedman bw color *Columbia Journalism Review* v56 no1 p48 Spr 2017
When Your Paycheck Is Bigger Than His J. Baird and M. Mertens color *Glamour* v114 no12 p165 D 2016

Harvard University—Faculty
Harvard Finds a Scapegoat N. S. RILEY color *Weekly Standard* v22 no44 p16 Jl 31 2017

Harvard University—Finance
Movers K. Stock color *Bloomberg Businessweek* no4526 p13 Je 12 2017

Harvard University—Soccer
Talking Back A. Fenwick and T. Keith color *Sports Illustrated* v125 no16 p22 N 14 2016

Harvard University—Students
Soup and Fishy color *Weekly Standard* v22 no44 p2 Jl 31 2017

Harvell, C. Drew
Seagrass ecosystems reduce exposure to bacterial pathogens of humans, fishes, and invertebrates bibl graph *Science* v355 no6326 p731 F 17 2017

Harvest festivals
See also
Oktoberfest
Sukkot
Thanksgiving Day
Yankees guide to top events this season... J. Bills color diag *Yankee* v80 no6 p100 N/D 2016

Harvesting
See also
Logging
Sunken Treasure J. KERR *Yankee* v81 no1 p54 Ja/F 2017

Harvesting equipment
HOPPER-BOTTOM BUYING: SOFTNESS IN LATE-MODEL HOPPER-BOTTOM TRAILER VALUES OFFERS BUYING OPPORTUNITY D. Mowitz *Successful Farming* v115 no11 p21 S 2017
KEY SUMMER MAINTENANCE CHORES R. Bohacz *Successful Farming* v115 no8 p52 Je/Jl 2017

Harvesting machinery
THE NEW FACE OF FAMILY FARMS L. SHUTE *Nation* v305 no11 p16 O 30 2017

Harvesting machinery—Evaluation
ONE MASSIVE MACHINE A. McConnell and L. Bedord *Successful Farming* v115 no2 p32 F 2017

Harvesting software
Forage with the Falling Fruit Map *Mother Earth News* no284 p7 O/N 2017

Harvesting—Equipment & supplies
HARVESTING THE SUN C. Huttes *Successful Farming* v115 no2 p32 F 2017

Harvey, Adam
DISH OF THE MONTH A. SPIEGEL *Washingtonian Magazine* v52 no2 p263 N 2016

Harvey, Andrew
All-printed thin-film transistors from networks of liquid-exfoliated nanosheets diag *Science* v356 no6333 p69 Ap 7 2017
Sensitive electromechanical sensors using viscoelastic graphene-polymer nanocomposites bibl graph *Science* v354 no6317 p1257 D 9 2016

Harvey, Benjamin
The Purge That's Paralyzed Turkey *Bloomberg Businessweek* no4506 p15 Ja 9 2017

Who'll Pay to Protect Trump's Towers? *Bloomberg Businessweek* no4503 p35 D 12 2016

Harvey, Brandon K.

Chemogenetics revealed: DREADD occupancy and activation via converted clozapine graph *Science* v357 no6350 p503 Ag 4 2017

Harvey, Chelsea

Cells that kill cancer [Cover story] color *Popular Science* v289 no6 p12 N/D 2017

Harvey, Donald, 1952-2017

Milestones color *Time* v189 no14 p15 Ap 17 2017

HARVEY, DOUG

Outsider Art's Inner Santum *Los Angeles Magazine* p30 Mr 2017

Sweet Smell of Success *Los Angeles Magazine* p24 Ap 2017

Harvey, Ed

Singing seldom-told Sandhills stories A. J. Bartels color *Nebraska Life* v21 no1 p63 Ja/F 2017

HARVEY, EUAN S.

Accelerating Tropicalization and the Transformation of Temperate Seagrass Meadows *BioScience* v66 no11 p938 N 1 2016

Harvey, Frank P.

Fighting for Credibility: U.S. Reputation and International Politics G. J. Ikenberry *Foreign Affairs* v96 no6 p152 N/D 2017

HARVEY, GILES

WORST-CASE SCENARIO cartoon *New Yorker* v92 no39 p46 N 28 2016

Harvey, Katherine

The Perils of PIETY *History Today* v67 no1 p11 Ja 2017

Harvey, Kirsten

Increased spatiotemporal resolution reveals highly dynamic dense tubular matrices in the peripheral ER bibl bw color graph *Science* v354 no6311 paaf3928-1 O 28 2016

HARVEY, MILES

BEHIND THE SCENES bw color *In These Times* v40 no11 p48 N 2016

Harvey, Nicolas—Interviews

Miami Bound J. WOOLDRIDGE color *Power & Motoryacht* v33 no2 p62 F 2017

Harvey, Paul

Christianity, Social Justice, and the Japanese American Incarceration during World War II color *Christian Century* v134 no10 p41 My 10 2017

Harvey, Rick

Oh, My Aching Back *USA Today Magazine* v146 no2868 p23 S 2017

HARVEY, SHARON

ALL IN A Day's Work *Reader's Digest* v190 no1135 p56 N 2017

Harvey, Simon

Smuggling C. Jowitt *History Today* v66 no10 p61 O 2016

Harvey, Stephanie

Gunning For eSports Equality P. GREEN *Los Angeles Magazine* p26 Mr 2017

Harvey, Steve, 1957-

America's top TV critic Matt Roush answers your burning questions M. ROUSH *TV Guide* v65 no27 p2 Je 26 2017

Entrepreneurs Wanted for Steve Harvey's New Competition Show On ABC color *Black Enterprise* v47 no3 p16 O 2016

Harvey Lands His Big Shot M. SCHNEIDER *TV Guide* v64 no15 p6 Ap 4 2016

Harvey, William S.

Being an Ethical Business in a Corrupt Environment *Harvard Business Review Digital Articles* p2 Mr 23 2017

Harvey Lake (Vt.)

strength in numbers G. CHIODI GRENSING color *Cabin Living* p26 D 2016

Harvey Mudd College

THE MANY FACES OF HARVEY MUDD C. HOWARD chart color *Forbes* v200 no2 p19 S 5 2017

HARVKEY, MIKE

THE DARK SIDE color *Publishers Weekly* v264 no3 p30 Ja 16 2017

A Muscle That Makes Us Feel color *Publishers Weekly* v263 no48 p41 N 28 2016

HARWOOD, MATTHEW

The Insatiable Utopia color *Reason* v49 no6 p74 N 2017

What Uncle Sam and Jim Crow Taught Hitler bw *Reason* v49 no1

p64 My 2017

Hasan, Mehdi

ST. LOUIS SHINES POWER OF FAITH *Islamic Horizons* v46 no4 p9 Jl/Ag 2017

Hasay, Jordan

SHE'S GOING THE DISTANCE N. WELDON bw color *Runner's World* v52 no4 p53 My 2017

Haselhuhn, Michael

When Trust Is Easily Broken, and When It's Not *Harvard Business Review Digital Articles* p2 F 17 2016

Hasenkamp, Wendy

The Monastery and the Microscope C. Ferland-Beckham color *Science* v357 no6355 p968 S 8 2017

Hāshimī Rafsanjānī, Alī Akbar, 1934-2017

The Death of Iran's Ultimate Political Insider Gives Hard-Liners an Edge K. Vick and K. A. Serjoie color *Time* v189 no4 p13 Ja 23 2017

Hashimoto, K.

Crystallization and vitrification of electrons in a glass-forming charge liquid bw *Science* v357 no6358 p1381 S 29 2017

Hasidim

Among the Hasidim J. ROSEN cartoon *Walrus* v14 no2 p32 Mr 2017

Hasilo, Craig

STEM CELLS TO THE RESCUE! *Maclean's* v130 no9 p33 O 2017

Hasinoff, Amy Adele

Sometimes when I get incredibly horny A. Gesselman, A. A. Hasinoff et al color *Glamour* v114 no12 p172 D 2016

Haskell, Molly

AGENTS PROVOCATEURS color *Film Comment* v52 no6 p38 N/D 2016

Different Lenses L. SCHWARZBAUM *New York Times Book Review* p10 Ja 8 2017

A MAN APART bw color *Film Comment* v53 no3 p26 My/Je 2017

NATURAL PROGRESSION color *Film Comment* v53 no1 p38 Ja/F 2017

Spielberg: The Inner Lives of a Genius G. O'Brien color *New York Review of Books* v64 no3 p17 F 23 2017

Steven Spielberg: A Life in Films M. Koresky color *Film Comment* v53 no2 p78 Mr/Ap 2017

Steven Spielberg: A Life in Films *Publishers Weekly* v263 no46 p44 N 14 2016

This Isn't Fun Anymore: When Molly Haskell offered to take porn seriously, the movies didn't perform on command C. Bonanos img *New York* v50 no12 p14 Je 12 2017

Haskell, Rob

In Control *Vogue* v207 no6 p144 Je 2017

The LONG GAME color *Vogue* v207 no10 p292 O 2017

On Her Own Terms [Cover story] color *Vogue* v207 no4 p194 Ap 2017

SERENA SERENE color *Vogue* v207 no9 p672 S 2017

UNDER Pressure cartoon *Vogue* v206 no11 p225 N 2016

HASKINS, HENRY STANLEY

Quotable Quotes bw color *Reader's Digest* v190 no1132 p140 Jl/Ag 2017

Haskoli Islands

TOWARDS A CLEANER CONSCIENCE Z. ROBERT *Iceland Review* v55 no4 p50 Jl/Ag 2017

VERÖLD, THE HOUSE OF VIGDÍS V. HAFSTAÐ *Iceland Review* v55 no4 p82 Jl/Ag 2017

HASLAM, CHRIS

GARDEN REMEDIES color *House Beautiful* p145 Ag 2017

GO GLAMPING color *House Beautiful* p146 Ag 2017

A SLICE OF ALFRESCO EATING bw color *House Beautiful* p144 Ag 2017

Haslehurst, Robert

How Consumer Brands Can Connect with Customers in a Changing Retail Landscape *Harvard Business Review Digital Articles* p2 Ag 4 2017

How to Know Which Digital Trends Are Worth Chasing *Harvard Business Review Digital Articles* p2 Jl 7 2016

The Potential of Geolocation for Revolutionizing Retail *Harvard Business Review Digital Articles* p2 N 13 2015

Virtual and Augmented Reality Will Reshape Retail *Harvard Business Review Digital Articles* p2 S 9 2016

We Don't Need a Whole New Regulatory Regime for Platforms Like Uber and Airbnb *Harvard Business Review Digital Articles* p2 Ap 4 2016

HASLETT, ADAM

Crashing the Party color *Vogue* v206 no12 p132 D 2016

lake Love bw color *Conde Nast Traveler* v52 no6 p90 Je/Jl 2017

VANDAL in CHIEF [Cover story] color il *Nation* v303 no17 p14 O 24 2016

HASLETT, TOBI

A WOMAN UNDER THE INFLUENCE bw cartoon *New Yorker* v93 no15 p63 My 29 2017

HASS, CHRISTOPHER

Muckraking and Troublemaking bw *In These Times* v40 no11 p41 N 2016

A Time to Take Risks *In These Times* v41 no3 p5 Mr 2017

Hass, Clayton

Hass Takes Aim in Two Events K. Santos color *Spin to Win Rodeo* v21 no5 p22 Jl 2017

Hass, Nancy

MARRAKECH Moderne color *Conde Nast Traveler* v52 no8 p102 S 2017

Hass, Robert, 1941-

A Little Book on Form: An Exploration into the Formal Imagination of Poetry *Publishers Weekly* v264 no6 p60 F 6 2017

Hassam, Childe, 1859-1935

The Artist's Wife in a Garden, Villiers-le-Bel color *Magazine Antiques* v184 no3 p17 My/Je 2017

Hassan, Fabien

How to Regain the Lost Art of Reflection *Harvard Business Review Digital Articles* p2 S 25 2017

Hassan, Maggie, 1958-

SENATOR-ELECT MAGGIE HASSAN D. DECKER *Ms.* v26 no3 p5 Fall 2016

Hassan, Mohamed

Migration—the choices we face color *Science* v356 no6339 p667 My 19 2017

U.S. immigration ban undermines scientists bibl color *Science* v355 no6326 p704 F 17 2017

Hassan, Mohammed Th.

Imaging rotational dynamics of nanoparticles in liquid by 4D electron microscopy bibl diag graph *Science* v355 no6324 p494 F 3 2017

Hassani, Mahmud

Zero-Casualty Mine Sweeping C. McDONALD cartoon color *Popular Science* p82 Ja/F 2017

Hassani, Sadri

Hassani replies *Physics Today* v69 no11 p12 N 2016

Hasselbring, Bobbie

Sanity and Grace color *AARP: The Magazine* v59 no1A p54 D 2015/Ja 2016

Hasselhoff, David, 1952-

David Hasselhot? C. Ianzito color *AARP: The Magazine* v60 no4A p12 Je/Jl 2017

Hassell, Brian

Paneth cells secrete lysozyme via secretory autophagy during bacterial infection of the intestine color diag *Science* v357 no6355 p1047 S 8 2017

Hasselmann, P.

Surface changes on comet 67P/Churyumov-Gerasimenko suggest a more active past bw graph *Science* v355 no6332 p1392 Mr 31 2017

Hasselmo, Michael

Howard Eichenbaum (1947–2017) color *Science* v357 no6354 p875 S 1 2017

Hassett, Brenna

The TrowelBlazing women of ARCHAEOLOGY *History Today* v67 no2 p32 F 2017

HASSETT, KEVIN A.

No Coattails for Hillary? *National Review* v68 no20 p8 N 7 2016

A Pro-Growth Tax Reform graph *National Review* v69 no2 p8 F 6 2017

Recovery through Tax Reform graph *National Review* v68 no23 p9 D 19 2016

Restoring Work and Wages graph *National Review* v69 no6 p6 Ap 3 2017

The Road Back from France? graph *National Review* v69 no4 p8

Mr 6 2017

Hässig, M.

Xenon isotopes in 67P/Churyumov-Gerasimenko show that comets contributed to Earth's atmosphere diag *Science* v356 no6342 p1069 Je 9 2017

Hassinger, Maren

Center Stage S. Nengudi and L. A. Miller bw *Art in America* v105 no5 p51 My 2017

Hassler, Scott

Collection with THROUGHNESS and FORWARD DESIRE color *Dressage Today* v24 no1 p28 O 2017

Hassol, Susan Joy

Climate Trumps Everything color *Scientific American* v316 no2 p8 F 2017

Hasterok, Derrick

High-resolution lithosphere viscosity and dynamics revealed by magnetotelluric imaging bibl graph *Science* v353 no6307 p1515 S 30 2016

Hastie, Amelie

The Ministry of Information: Parsing the Facts of Fiction *Film Quarterly* v71 no1 p65 Fall 2017

PASSING TIME WITH CERTAIN WOMEN *Film Quarterly* v70 no3 p74 Spr 2017

Hastie, Kathryn M.

Structural basis for antibody-mediated neutralization of Lassa virus [Cover story] color diag *Science* v356 no6341 p923 Je 1 2017

Hastie, Reid

Great Teams Need Social Intelligence, Equal Participation, and More Women *Harvard Business Review Digital Articles* p2 D 16 2014

Hastings, Justin V.

A Most Enterprising Country: North Korea in the Global Economy A. J. Nathan *Foreign Affairs* v96 no3 p174 My/Je 2017

HASTINGS, MARIANNE

Let's Shut Down the Economy on January 20 *In These Times* v41 no1 p19 Ja 2017

Hastings, Max

Splendid Isolation [Cover story] bw color *New York Review of Books* v64 no15 p14 O 12 2017

Hastings, Reed

13 REED HASTINGS M. Lev-Ram color *Fortune* v174 no7 p87 D 1 2016

HASTINGS, STACEY

ask the experts cartoon color *Dressage Today* v23 no5 p64 Ja 2017

Hastings, Stephen

Lyric Tradition *Opera News* v81 no7 p16 Ja 2017

Madama Butterfly *Opera News* v81 no9 p41 Mr 2017

Otello *Opera News* v81 no9 p43 Mr 2017

Werther *Opera News* v81 no9 p42 Mr 2017

Hastreiter, Sara

Sara Hastreiter A. Schell color *Sail* v48 no8 p16 Ag 2017

Hasuwa, Hidetoshi

Mobile elements control stem cell potency bibl diag *Science* v355 no6325 p581 F 10 2017

Hat design & hat making

Craft Your Own COONSKIN CAP: Turn a raccoon hide into a warm and hardy hat D. Biswell *Mother Earth News* no284 p24 O/N 2017

HAT-P 7b (Planet)

Exoplanet's magnetism stirs up wild winds A. Yeager color *Science News* v191 no11 p32 Je 10 2017

Hatami, Homayoun

Put the "and" Back in "Sales and Marketing" *Harvard Business Review Digital Articles* p2 O 30 2014

To Improve Sales, Pay More Attention to Presales *Harvard Business Review Digital Articles* p2 F 17 2015

Why Salespeople Need to Develop "Machine Intelligence" *Harvard Business Review Digital Articles* p2 Je 10 2016

Hatch, Nina

Galaxy formation through cosmic recycling color *Science* v354 no6316 p1102 D 2 2016

HATCH, RACHEL

CLASH OF THE TITANS cartoon *Vanity Fair* p84 Hollywood 2017 Supplement

Hatch, Richard, 1945-2017

Milestones *Time* v189 no6 p13 F 20 2017

Hatch, Steven

The Plague and the Judgment: When Ebola became something other than a contagious disease A. N. Schulman *Commentary* v143 no6 p31 Je 2017

A Plague Year: An American doctor's account of his work at an Ebola treatment unit in rural Liberia C. MacDOUGALL color *New York Times Book Review* p18 Ap 23 2017

Hatchability of eggs

Dinosaur eggs were slow to hatch L. Hamers color *Science News* v191 no2 p4 F 4 2017

Hatcher, Robin Lee

You're Gonna Love Me *Publishers Weekly* v264 no41 p50 O 9 2017

Hatchery fishes

THE CATCH AT McNENNY: Where South Dakota hatches trout, salmon and researchers P. HIGBEE *South Dakota Magazine* v33 no2 p48 Jl/Ag 2017

Hate

Peace Over Politics M. PATTERSON *America* v215 no19 p14 D 19 2016

What drives hate? P. W. Marty *Christian Century* v134 no1 p3 Ja 4 2017

Hate crimes

See also

Violence against gay men

Twilight of the Narratives M. CONTINETTI *Commentary* v143 no2 p56 F 2017

Hate crimes—Prevention

Hate Crimes B. BERKOWITZ *In These Times* v41 no1 p23 Ja 2017

Hate crimes—United States

Allies All Around Us U. ABDULLAH *Islamic Horizons* v46 no2 p38 Mr/Ap 2017

FBI report shows surge in anti-Muslim attacks, rise in hate crimes L. Markoe *Christian Century* v133 no26 p15 D 21 2016

HANDBOOK FOR THE RESISTANCE *In These Times* v41 no1 p20 Ja 2017

Hate Crimes B. BERKOWITZ *In These Times* v41 no1 p23 Ja 2017

What drives hate? P. W. Marty *Christian Century* v134 no1 p3 Ja 4 2017

When hatred rises *Christian Century* v134 no7 p7 Mr 29 2017

Hate crimes—United States—Law & legislation

License to Hate: The label of "hate crime" is used to score political points, not to end violence. It should be eliminated V. D. Hanson *Hoover Digest: Research & Opinion on Public Policy* no2 p143 Spr 2017

Hate crimes—United States—Psychological aspects

Hate Incidents Sow Fear Across U.S C. Alter and J. Sanburn color *Time* v189 no9 p13 Mr 13 2017

Hate groups

Hate Groups in America: Organizations that spread hate have grown in the past two decades *New York Times Upfront* p9 S 18 2017

HATE IN THE AGE OF TRUMP V. JONES color *New Republic* v248 no3 p38 Mr 2017

Hate speech

Battle Cry A. Hess *New York Times Magazine* p9 Ag 20 2017

Cruel Intentions P. J. Williams bw color *Nation* v304 no11 p10 Ap 3 2017

A New 'Hate Symbol' color *Time* v188 no14 p22 O 10 2016

Hateful Eight, The (Film)

NEWLY AVAILABLE MOVIES M. FELL *TV Guide* v64 no48 p46 N 21 2016

Hategekimana, Bahati Ernestine

I'm Not Broken, Just Bent *UN Chronicle* v53 no4 p1 2016

I'm Not Broken Just Bent *UN Chronicle* v54 no4 p32 2017

Hate—Religious aspects

God among the gangs P. Jenkins *Christian Century* v133 no24 p45 N 23 2016

Haters Back Off (TV program)

Haters Back Off Takes a Star from YouTube to TV D. D'Addario color *Time* v188 no16/17 p92 O 24 2016

QUICK TAKES *TV Guide* v64 no40 p35 O 3 2016

Hatfield, Karen

From Dawn Till Dusk A. WANG color *Los Angeles Magazine* v62 no10 p46 O 2017

Hatfield, Philip

THE SEARCH FOR THE NORTHWEST PASSAGE *History Today* v67 no2 p10 F 2017

Hatfield, Ricky

Steaking His Claim S. KROWIAK *Indianapolis Monthly* v40 no7 p42 Mr 2017

Hatha yoga

Surprising Benefits of Aerial Yoga V. Tweed color *Amazing Wellness* v8 no2 p19 Spr 2016

Hathaway, Anne, 1982-

The Parties B. Fowler, J. Ferrise et al color *InStyle* v23 no12 p84 N 2016

Party Girl, Godzilla Girl P. Travers color *Rolling Stone* no1285 p55 Ap 20 2017

Hathaway, Anne, 1982-—Interviews

Anne Hathaway E. Dockterman color *Time* v189 no10 p60 Mr 20 2017

Hathaway, Donny, 1945-1979

Lalah Hathaway R. R. Robertson color *Essence* v48 no2 p36 Je 2017

Hathaway, Ian

The Gig Economy Is Real If You Know Where to Look *Harvard Business Review Digital Articles* p2 Ag 13 2015

Is America Encouraging the Wrong Kind of Entrepreneurship? *Harvard Business Review Digital Articles* p2 Je 13 2017

Start-Up Capital Is Spreading Across the U.S *Harvard Business Review Digital Articles* p2 F 23 2015

What Startup Accelerators Really Do *Harvard Business Review Digital Articles* p2 Mr 1 2016

Hathaway, Kristl

Sexism in Silicon Valley color *Atlantic* v319 no5 p10 Je 2017

Hathaway, Lalah, 1968-

Lalah Hathaway B. Muteba color *Current Biography* v77 no10 p53 O 2016

Lalah Hathaway R. R. Robertson color *Essence* v48 no2 p36 Je 2017

Hathaway, Oona Anne

The Pipes of Peace: A history of the international pact that promised to bring an end to war M. BOOT *New York Times Book Review* p25 S 24 2017

Hathi, Sejal

The Right Way to Reform Health Care color *Foreign Affairs* v96 no4 p17 Jl/Ag 2017

Hatmaker, Jen—Interviews

Jen Hatmaker B. Luscombe color *Time* v190 no8 p60 Ag 28 2017

Hatmaker, Mark

3 Things to Avoid as You Seek to Become a Fitter Fighter color *Black Belt* v55 no4 p20 Je/Jl 2017

Battling Nelson and the Scissor Punch bw *Black Belt* v55 no3 p18 Ap/My 2017

Boxing vs. Boxe Francaise: A History Lesson cartoon *Black Belt* v55 no5 p20 Ag/S 2017

Martial Arts Archeology and the Way of the Autodidact color *Black Belt* v55 no2 p18 F/Mr 2017

Pros and Cons of Randomized Training for Martial Artists bw *Black Belt* v55 no6 p20 O/N 2017

Your Fighting Skills Are First-Rate, But Is Your Physical Training Sufficient? color *Black Belt* v55 no1 p24 D 2016/Ja 2017

Hats

The Fine Print M. OZAWA color *Martha Stewart Living* no275 p48 Je 2017

Summer Hair 101 A. Jordan color *Essence* v48 no2 p49 Je 2017

Thoroughly Modern Millinery B. L. Walls color *AARP: The Magazine* v59 no2A p72 F/Mr 2016

Hatsa (African people)

Seasonal change in the gut [Cover story] S. Peddada color *Science* v357 no6353 p754 Ag 25 2017

Seasonal cycling in the gut microbiome of the Hadza hunter-gatherers of Tanzania S. A. Smits, J. Leach et al diag *Science* v357 no6353 p802 Ag 25 2017

Hats—Evaluation

A CASE OF THE BLUES A. R. Williams color *Southern Living* v52 no1 p39 Ja 2017

DOPE STUFF ON MY DESK J. Wilson color *Essence* v48 no2

p24 Je 2017

FASHION UNDER $100 S. AFFELT color *Redbook* p60 N 2017

Handles With Flair color *Martha Stewart Living* p28 Jl/Ag 2017

Hat Hair N. Spradley color *Essence* v47 no10 p45 F 2017

LET'S DO FALL IN VIRGINIA J. B. Hager color *Southern Living* v51 no11 p62 N 2016

LIKE A BOY color *Essence* v47 no9 p16 Ja 2017

LOVE SWIMSUIT SEASON! [Cover story] color *Redbook* p52 Je 2017

Modern Fashion Meets Traditional Details [Cover story] color *Horse & Rider* v56 no8 p54 Ag 2017

O'S SUMMER STYLE HANDBOOK color *O, The Oprah Magazine* p49 Je 2017

POM SQUAD: Three cheers for summer's peppiest trend *Indianapolis Monthly* v40 no11 p26 Jl 2017

SLOPE STYLE J. MOAZAMI color *Chicago* v66 no1 p48 Ja 2017

Street Style: FITNESS EDITION K. Bacher color *Women's Health* v14 no3 p18 Ap 2017

HATTAM, JENNIFER

SCIENCE, INTERRUPTED bw color graph map *Discover* v38 no7 p42 S 2017

The Secrets Beneath a Suburb color graph map *Discover* v38 no9 p14 N 2017

Hattar, Nahed

Christian writer's murder in Jordan reveals conflict on free speech, religion T. Luck *Christian Century* v133 no22 p15 O 26 2016

HATTENBACH, JAN

Gaia Maps a 1,000,000,000+ Stars *Sky & Telescope* v133 no1 p10 Ja 2017

Hatteras Yachts Inc.

AMERICAN ICON J. WOOLDRIDGE chart color *Power & Motoryacht* v33 no1 p60 Ja 2017

LEADING LADY B. PIKE chart color *Power & Motoryacht* v34 no11 p86 N 2017

Hatton, Erin

Temp workers, permanent effects: how temps changed the nature of the U.S. workforce M. Miller *Monthly Labor Review* p1 D 2016

Hatum, Andres

What Makes FC Barcelona Such a Successful Business *Harvard Business Review Digital Articles* p2 Je 16 2015

Hatzakis, Nikos S.

Characterization of a dynamic metabolon producing the defense compound dhurrin in sorghum bibl graph *Science* v354 no6314 p890 N 18 2016

Hatzis, Michelle

How Google Optimized Healthy Office Snacks *Harvard Business Review Digital Articles* p2 Mr 3 2016

Haubegger, Christy

The Woman Changing the Face of Hollywood D. Coggan color *Entertainment Weekly* no1476 p46 Ag 4 2017

Hauber, Mark E.

The biology of color color *Science* v357 no6350 p470 Ag 4 2017

HAUBRUGE, ERIC

The Odor of Death: An Overview of Current Knowledge on Characterization and Applications *BioScience* v67 no7 p600 Jl 2017

Haucap, Justus

Research: Innovation Suffers When Drug Companies Merge *Harvard Business Review Digital Articles* p2 Ag 3 2016

Haucke, Volker

mTORC1 activity repression by late endosomal phosphatidylinositol 3,4-bisphosphate diag *Science* v356 no6341 p968 Je 1 2017

Haueis, Cathleen

A pathogenic role for T cell–derived IL-22BP in inflammatory bowel disease bibl graph *Science* v354 no6310 p358 O 21 2016

Haueisen, Kathy

Refugee work *Christian Century* v134 no2 p6 Ja 18 2017

Hauer, Jerome M.

US cities are not medically prepared for a nuclear detonation *Bulletin of the Atomic Scientists* v73 no4 p215 Jl 2017

Hauer, Tomas

Speed, Wealth and Power *Society* v54 no2 p150 Ap 2017

HAUFLER, CHRISTOPHER H.

Sex and the Single Gametophyte: Revising the Homosporous Vascular Plant Life Cycle in Light of Contemporary Research

BioScience v66 no11 p928 N 1 2016

HAUG, LORE I.

What Causes Hostile Behavior? *Horse & Rider* v55 no12 p12 D 2016

Haugen, Barbara

ROCKET MAN color *American Craft* v76 no6 p50 D 2016-Ja 2017

Haugen, Brett

Crafting a Big Business D. Bortz color *Money* v45 no10 p33 N 2016

Haungs, A.

Observation of a large-scale anisotropy in the arrival directions of cosmic rays above 8×1018 eV *Science* v357 no6357 p1266 S 22 2017

Haunted houses

Haunted White House K. B. RATTINI color *National Geographic Kids* no474 p24 O 2017

Laughter cartoon *Reader's Digest* v190 no1134 p96 O 2017

Haunted houses (Amusements)

PANIC ROOMS Z. MATTHEW color *Los Angeles Magazine* v62 no10 p90 O 2017

Haunted houses (Amusements)—Evaluation

True Blood J. KENT-DOOLAN bw color *Indianapolis Monthly* v42 no2 p13 O 2017

Haunted Hotel Inc.—Trials, litigation, etc.

The Case Of the Terrifying Trail V. GLEMBOCKI *Reader's Digest* v188 no1124 p27 O 2016

Hauri, Erik H.

Experimental constraints on the damp peridotite solidus and oceanic mantle potential temperature bibl diag *Science* v355 no6328 p942 Mr 3 2017

Haus Love (Company)

Bear Necessity L. BAILEY *Indianapolis Monthly* v40 no4 p33 D 2016

Hausberger, Andreas

Andreas Hausberger Brings Classical Dressage to America A. Heintzberger color *Dressage Today* v23 no9 p54 Je 2017

Hauschild, Robert

Biased partitioning of the multidrug efflux pump AcrAB-TolC underlies long-lived phenotypic heterogeneity diag *Science* v356 no6335 p311 Ap 21 2017

Hauser, Brooke

Can We Get Real About Having It All? color *Health* v31 no6 p91 Jl 2017

I Tried Dieting Like My Mom color *Health* v30 no10 p55 D 2016

Hauser, Emily

For the Most Beautiful: A Novel of the Trojan War *Publishers Weekly* v263 no45 p37 N 7 2016

Hauser, Oliver

Good Communication Requires Experimenting with Your Language *Harvard Business Review Digital Articles* p2 F 4 2016

How to Design (and Analyze) a Business Experiment *Harvard Business Review Digital Articles* p2 O 29 2015

Your Company Is Full of Good Experiments (You Just Have to Recognize Them) *Harvard Business Review Digital Articles* p2 N 23 2015

Hausfather, Zeke

Stay Out of Scientists' E-mails *Scientific American* v316 no4 p12 Ap 2017

Hausknecht, Ivy

Essential Framework for Adaptive Aquatics *Parks & Recreation* v52 no10 p54 O 2017

Hausmann, Annika

Inflammation boosts bacteriophage transfer between Salmonella spp bibl diag *Science* v355 no6330 p1211 Mr 17 2017

Hausmann, Robert

Leadership Development Should Focus on Experiments *Harvard Business Review Digital Articles* p2 Ap 12 2016

Haute couture

Best-Dressed LIST B. Mazurek color *Harper's Bazaar* no3653 p100 My 2017

BEST DRESS E. Wilson color *InStyle* v24 no11 p69 N 2017

Haute couture—Exhibitions

Daring to Be Different color *Vogue* v207 no11 p140 N 2017

Look Who's Crashing COUTURE E. Wilson color *InStyle* v24 no4 p63 Ap 2017

Haute House (Company)
Fig Purple K. RENDA and B. REYNAERT color *House Beautiful* v159 no7 p29 S 2017

Hauter, Wenonah—Interviews
Frack Attack F. Madeson color *Progressive* p48 D 2016/Ja 2017

Hauver, Jesse
RNA polymerase motions during promoter melting color diag graph *Science* v356 no6340 p863 My 26 2017

Havana (Cuba)
THE WEEKLY PACKAGE: How Cubans deliver culture without internet K. Wall *Harper's Magazine* v335 no2006 p59 Jl 2017

Havana (Cuba)—Description & travel
8 Travel Ideas for the Winter-Weary A. Fitzpatrick color *Time* v189 no7/8 p114 F 27 2017

Havana, Cuba S. Murray color *Power & Motoryacht* v33 no2 p60 F 2017

Havasu Canyon (Ariz.)
THE CALL OF THE CANYON K. VAUGHN *Arizona Highways* v93 no1 p28 Ja 2017

Havel, Václav, 1936-2011
VÁCLAV HAVEL ON GOING ALONG TO GET ALONG *Lapham's Quarterly* v10 no3 p133 Summ 2017

Haven, Cynthia L.
Brodsky and His Muses: A new collection shows where the great émigré poet Joseph Brodsky found friendship, love, and inspiration *Hoover Digest: Research & Opinion on Public Policy* no3 p188 Summ 2017

Haven Custom Furnishing (Company)
ADVERTISING RESOURCE DIRECTORY *New Orleans Homes & Lifestyles* v20 no2 p100 Spr 2017

Haven Custom Furnishing P. Marquis *New Orleans Homes & Lifestyles* v20 no2 p84 Spr 2017

Haves & the Have Nots, The (TV program)
ALSO COMING . . *TV Guide* v65 no2 p35 Ja 2 2017

HAVILAND, JOHN
.25/06 TIMES THREE color *Outdoor Life* v224 no9 p70 N 2017

LIGHT UPLAND LOADS color *Outdoor Life* v224 no7 p68 S 2017

Havill, Steven F.
Easy Errors: A Posadas County Mystery *Publishers Weekly* v264 no35 p102 Ag 28 2017

Havrilesky, Heather
For Better, for Worse: Three memoirs report from the country of marriage *New York Times Book Review* p22 My 21 2017

My boyfriend of four years doesn't want to move in together color *Glamour* v115 no3 p144 Mr 2017

OBAMA'S AMERICA img *New York* v49 no20 p12 O 3 2016

WHAT DOES SHE SEE IN THAT GUY? bw color *Esquire* p80 Ap 2017

Havurah movement
Mother Brooklyn *Commentary* v143 no4 p19 Ap 2017

Haw Par Corp. Ltd.
TIGER BALM ULTRA M. PICKETT color *Wired* v25 no3 p21 Mr 2017

Hawaii Opera Theatre (Performer)
Hawaii Opera Theatre F. COHN *Opera News* v81 no6 p14 D 2016

Hawaiian cooking
Poke Go, Go, Go K. Krader color *Bloomberg Businessweek* no4529 p77 Jl 3 2017

Hawaiians
Hawaiian Natives Fight for Their Land A. Hannah color *Progressive* v81 no10 p32 N 2016

POI POWER J. MILLER *Sierra* v102 no2 p42 Mr/Ap 2017

Hawaii—Description & travel
Hawai'i ISLAND ACTIVITIES FOR YOU AND YOUR 'OHANA *Los Angeles Magazine* p94 Mr 2017

KOMO MAI E AI L. ANTHONY color map *Canadian Geographic* v137 p24 2017 Travel

Two Tickets to Paradise A. EDWARDS color *AARP: The Magazine* v60 no2A p43 F/Mr 2017

Where-to-Ride Guide map *Trail Rider* v29 no1 p58 Ja/F 2017

Hawaii—Economic conditions—1959-
HALEIWA, HAWAII P. Theroux *Harper's Magazine* p35 O 2017

Hawaii Five-0 (TV program : 2010-)
Big Exits on Hawaii Five-0: The drama says "aloha" to actors Daniel Dae Kim and Grace Park J. Halterman *TV Guide* v65

no31 p3 Jl 24 2017

CHEERS & JEERS D. HOLBROOK color *TV Guide* v64 no42 p88 O 10 2016

Hawaii Five-0 J. Halterman *TV Guide* v64 no40 p56 O 3 2016

HAWAII FIVE-0 J. Halterman *TV Guide* v65 no39 p53 S 18 2017

Hawaii Five-O/MacGyver Crossover J. Halterman *TV Guide* v65 no11 p37 Mr 6 2017

Hawaii Five-O N. Abrams, S. Highfill et al *Entertainment Weekly* no1482/1483 p99 S 22 2017

PETER M. LENKOV J. HALTERMAN *TV Guide* v64 no48 p9 N 21 2016

Hawaii—Officials & employees
NOISY BY NATURE *Harper's Magazine* v335 no2006 p17 Jl 2017

Hawco, Allan
ALLAN HAWCO A. POPE color *Canadian Geographic* v136 no6 p21 D 2016

HAWDON, JOHN
Transformational Principles for NEON Sampling of Mammalian Parasites and Pathogens: A Response to Springer and Colleagues *BioScience* v66 no11 p917 N 1 2016

Hawes, James
TELLING TRABBIES FROM JUNKERS: Though fast-paced and refreshingly diff erent, this short study of Germany is more political manifesto than historical analysis S. Williams *History Today* v67 no10 p104 O 2017

Hawk, Steve
Evans Calftone Drum Heads color *Downbeat* v83 no11 p81 N 2016

Hawk Mountain Sanctuary (Pa.)
GET CRACKIN' A. WUNDERMAN color *Backpacker* p14 Je 2017

Hawke, Ethan, 1970-
PARTY LINES img *New York* v49 no25 p140 D 12 2016

Valley of Violence Is Hounded by Its True Star S. Zacharek color *Time* v188 no19 p57 N 7 2016

Hawken, Paul
Climate optimism gets a road map F. Duchin color *Science* v356 no6340 p811 My 26 2017

Hawken, Paul—Interviews
100 BEST Climate Solutions—And Why They're Going to Work S. Mowe color *Tricycle: The Buddhist Review* v26 no4 p44 Summ 2017

Paul Hawken: "Game on" for global warming D. Stover bibl color *Bulletin of the Atomic Scientists* v73 no3 p145 My 2017

Hawking, Quinn
Stayin' Hollywood M. McKnight and T. Keith color *Sports Illustrated* v126 no17 p20 Je 19 2017

Hawking, Stephen, 1942-
A COSMIC CONTROVERSY color *Scientific American* v317 no1 p5 Jl 2017

For the Record color *Time* v189 no19 p8 My 22 2017

Getting Out the Word bw *Discover* v38 no4 p51 My 2017

Points to Ponder *Reader's Digest* v189 no1128 p33 Mr 2017

Hawkins, Buddy
IVY AND HAWKINS GET A GRIPP K. Gustave chart color *Team Roping Journal* p18 O 2017

Hawkins, Coleman
Treasures Abound in 'Savory Collection' T. Panken bw *Downbeat* v84 no1 p19 Ja 2017

Hawkins, Connie, 1942-2017
CONNIE HAWKINS J. McCallum and S. Kwak color *Sports Illustrated* v127 no12 p18 O 16 2017

Milestones color *Time* v190 no16/17 p20 O 23 2017

Hawkins, Corey, 1988-
24: Legacy C. Agard color *Entertainment Weekly* no1448 p44 Ja 13 2017

24: Legacy J. Jensen color *Entertainment Weekly* no1451/1452 p99 F 3-10 2017

The Art of the Reboot J. HALTERMAN *TV Guide* p8 D 19 2016

Corey Hawkins M. Hagan color *Current Biography* v78 no9 p32 S 2017

Corey Hawkins Takes the Lead in 24: Legacy L. CROSS color *Ebony* v72 no4 p39 F 2017

Long RANGE A. GREEN and V. STEIKER bw *Vogue* v207 no1 p43 Ja 2017

Racing the Clock In the ISIS Era D. D'addario color *Time* v188 no27-28 p108 D 26 2016

Straight Outta Kong L. Rice color *Entertainment Weekly* no1457/1458 p26 Mr 17 2017

Hawkins, Edwin D.

Click chemistry enables preclinical evaluation of targeted epigenetic therapies diag *Science* v356 no6345 p1397 Je 30 2017

Hawkins, Johnica Reed

THE ORGANIZER color *Essence* v47 no7 p60 N 2016

Hawkins, Julia

FACES IN THE CROWD T. Keith color *Sports Illustrated* v127 no2 p26 Jl 17 2017

JOIN THE RIDE L. FLICKINGER color *Bicycling* v58 no9 p16 O 2017

Keep on Moving J. Fuchs and T. Keith color *Sports Illustrated* v127 no6 p20 Ag 28 2017

Still Rolling A. Fenwick and T. Keith color *Sports Illustrated* v125 no17 p28 N 21 2016 Double Issue

Hawkins, Larycia

ACTS OF FAITH R. Graham *New York Times Magazine* p48 O 16 2016

Hawkins, Nick

Cutting the Lines color *Canadian Wildlife* v23 no1 p18 Mr/Ap 2017

in memoriam Joe Howlett color *Canadian Wildlife* v23 no4 p34 S/O 2017

HAWKINS, NOTLEY

ALL ABOARD! bw color *Missouri Life* v44 no6 p30 S 2017

Hawkins, Paula

The Girls Off the Cliff S. Begley color *Time* v189 no18 p56 My 15 2017

INTO THE WATER I. Biedenharn color *Entertainment Weekly* no1446/1447 p80 D 2016/Ja 2017

Into the Water *Publishers Weekly* v264 no12 p53 Mr 20 2017

Hawkins, Peter S.

Conjuring God *Christian Century* v134 no12 p12 Je 7 2017

Hawkins, Taylor

Taylor Hawkins color *Rolling Stone* no1283 p8 Mr 23 2017

Hawks

Raptors on the Mountain G. NORMAN *Weekly Standard* v22 no5 p16 O 10 2016

Hawks, Howard, 1896-1977

HIS GIRL FRIDAY F. Kaplan bw *Sound & Vision* v82 no5 p69 Je 2017

Hawks, Jeremy

FUN & GAMES color *Backpacker* p71 Je 2017

Hawks—Behavior

When Birds Become Bird Food M. A. Barker color *National Wildlife (World Edition)* v54 no6 p12 O/N 2016

HAWLEY, ALIX

My Pleasure color *Walrus* v14 no4 p52 My 2017

Hawley, Josh

Missouri's Political Phenom F. BARNES cartoon color *Weekly Standard* v22 no42 p16 Jl 17 2017

Hawley, Noah

HOW TWIN PEAKS INFLUENCED MY WORK: Fargo and Legion creator Noah Hawley pays homage to Peaks' mastermind, David Lynch *TV Guide* v65 no35 p10 Ag 21 2017

KELLER INSTINCT J. Black color *Esquire* v167 no2 p54 Mr 2017

Rachel Getting Married *New York Times Book Review* p24 Je 4 2017

WELCOME TO HAWLEYWOOD D. RILEY color *GQ: Gentlemen's Quarterly* v86 no12 p140 D 2016

When Writers Rule, TV Gets Wonderfully Weird E. Dockterman color *Time* v189 no7/8 p102 F 27 2017

Hawlk, Kali

TRENDING NOW color *Wired* v25 no4 p12 Ap 2017

Hawn, Goldie, 1945-

As Good as Gold(ie) R. Kinane color *Entertainment Weekly* no1466 p14 My 19 2017

GOLDIE Hawn L. Bans color *GQ: Gentlemen's Quarterly* v97 no6 p124 Je 2017

Goldie & Kate color *InStyle* p96 Home & Design 2016

SOLID GOLDIE M. Heyman color *Harper's Bazaar* no3654 p160 Je/Jl 2017

Hawn, Goldie, 1945—Interviews

Goldie HAWN: AFTER A 15-YEAR HIATUS, THE GREAT GLASS-CEILING-SHATTERING GOLDIE HAWN IS BACK IN THE PICTURE, AND HAVING A LAUGH WITH THE LADIES FOR WHOM SHE PAVED THE WAY K. HUDSON *Interview* v47 no3 p88 My 2017

Who's A PRETTY Girl? [Cover story] S. Vilkomerson color *Entertainment Weekly* no1462 p20 Ap 21 2017

Haworth, Charles S.

Emergence and spread of a human-transmissible multidrug-resistant nontuberculous mycobacterium bibl diag graph *Science* v354 no6313 p751 N 11 2016

HAWORTH, HOLLY

DESERT HISTORIES *Orion Magazine* v35 no3 p64 My/Je 2016

Unseen Fruit color *Orion Magazine* v35 no6 p7 N/D 2016

Hawran, Paul

Because It's There [Cover story] S. MURRAY color *Power & Motoryacht* v34 no6 p54 Je 2017

Hawthorn (Poem)

Hawthorn A. MOTION *American Scholar* v86 no4 p53 Aut 2017

Hawthorne, Nathaniel, 1804-1864

Try Hawthorne for Halloween, . . . but Leave the Light on D. Heitman *Humanities* v37 no4 p1 Fall 2016

Hawthorns

HEART-HEALING HERBS K. P. S. Khalsa color *Amazing Wellness* p34 Fall 2017

Hay

Building a Hay Barn: The Old Way in New Idaho J. AKENSON and H. AKENSON *Idaho Magazine* v16 no9 p24 Je 2017

Hay, Ashley

Falling Through Time: Three men, separated by three centuries, witness an Australian miracle J. McNAMARA *New York Times Book Review* p14 S 10 2017

Hay, Donna

MIRACULOUS, MULTITASKING RECIPES color *Redbook* p130 S 2017

Hay, William Anthony

KEYS TO IMMORTALITY *Claremont Review of Books* v17 no2 p32 Spr 2017

Hay as feed

6 Signs of Good-Quality Horse Hay color *Trail Rider* v29 no1 p33 Ja/F 2017

The Hay Man J. Paulson *Horse & Rider* v56 no11 p14 N 2017

Trip Tips J. Goodnight and H. MELOCCO color *Trail Rider* v29 no3 p6 Ap 2017

TWO WAYS TO SOAK HAY C. Barakat and M. Freckleton *Equus* no476 p24 My 2017

Hay fever

NOTHING TO SNEEZE AT J. Szabo color *Amazing Wellness* v9 no2 p76 Spr 2017

Hay fever treatment

More Sex Can Provide Hay Fever Relief *USA Today Magazine* v146 no2869 p3 O 2017

The secret to an easier allergy season *Harvard Health Letter* v42 no4 p1 F 2017

Hay fever—Prevention

Problem Solved! [Cover story] R. LALIBERTE cartoon *Prevention* v69 no5 p18 My 2017

Hayabusa (Spacecraft)

Asteroids N. SCHARPING diag graph map *Discover* v38 no6 p50 Jl/Ag 2017

Hayabusa Fishing Hooks Co. Ltd.

THE GREATEST RIG EVER MADE J. BRANDT color *Outdoor Life* v224 no1 p97 D 2016/Ja 2017

Hayasaki, Erika

From Cuba, With Dreams bw *Glamour* v115 no5 p176 My 2017

PAIN color *Wired* v25 no5 p84 My 2017

WOMEN VS. THE MACHINE color *Foreign Policy* no222 p38 Ja/F 2017

Hayden, Carla Diane, 1952-

BIG ADVANCES D. Stone diag *National Geographic* v231 no6 p10 Je 2017

Carla Hayden J. Johnson color *Current Biography* v78 no3 p28 Mr 2017

Carla Hayden: U.S. Librarian of Congress A. Albanese *Publishers Weekly* v263 no52 p27 D 19 2016

Changes Coming To the Copyright Office? A. Albanese color *Publishers Weekly* v263 no44 p6 O 31 2016

GUEST LIST *Washingtonian Magazine* v52 no2 p24 N 2016

Remember the Card Catalogue? color *Publishers Weekly* v264 no18 p64 My 1 2017

THE TOP 10 LIBRARY STORIES OF 2016 A. RICHARD ALBANESE color *Publishers Weekly* v263 no52 p34 D 19 2016

Hayden, Carla Diane, 1952-—Interviews

Carla Hayden color *New York Times Book Review* p8 Ag 6 2017

CARLA HAYDEN G. Weber *Washingtonian Magazine* v52 no3 p39 D 2016

Carla Hayden Thinks Libraries Are a Key to Freedom A. M. Cox *New York Times Magazine* p66 Ja 22 2017

PW TALKS WITH LIBRARIAN OF CONGRESS CARLA HAYDEN S. MAUGHAN color *Publishers Weekly* v263 no52 p54 D 19 2016

Hayden, Nicky, 1981-2017

A GREAT ONE REMEMBERED L. Lawrence color *Cycle World* v56 no7 p62 Ag 2017

NICKY FROM BEHIND THE NOTEPAD L. Lawrence *Cycle World* v56 no7 p67 Ag 2017

HAYDEN, SALLY

Why Wallonia wobbled color *Maclean's* v129 no45 p43 N 14 2016

Hayden, Sterling, 1916-1986

TROUBLED WATERS P. X. Rutz bw color map *Military History* v34 no1 p40 My 2017

Hayden, Tom, 1939-2016

THE FORGOTTEN POWER OF THE VIETNAM PEACE MOVEMENT bw color *Nation* v304 no3 p18 Ja 30 2017

Our New Left Pillar E. Leanza *Nation* v303 no20 p5 N 14 2016

A Sui Generis Radical M. DAVIS *Nation* v303 no20 p8 N 14 2016

Tom Hayden E. Garcetti color *Time* v188 no19 p11 N 7 2016

Haydon, Daniel T.

Driving improvements in emerging disease surveillance through locally relevant capacity strengthening color diag *Science* v357 no6347 p146 Jl 14 2017

Haydu, Corey Ann

The Careful Undressing of Love *Publishers Weekly* v263 no44 p77 O 31 2016

HAYEK, F. A.

FROM THE ARCHIVES cartoon *Reason* v48 no10 p66 Mr 2017

Hayek, Salma, 1968-

getting ready with SALMA HAYEK D. GLUCK color *Better Homes & Gardens* v95 no4 p16 Ap 2017

Pierce BROSNAN *Interview* v47 no3 p34 My 2017

With the BAND color *Vogue* v207 no7 p48 Jl 2017

Hayenga, Cal

THE FARM *Successful Farming* v115 no11 p75 S 2017

Hayeri, Kiana

THE MOTHERS *Harper's Magazine* v334 no2004 p63 My 2017

HAYES, ANNIE

THE PM GUIDE *People Management* p39 N 2016

Hayes, Bill

The Story of O C. BRAM *New York Times Book Review* p13 Mr 12 2017

Hayes, Chris

Chris Hayes's Book for the Times K. CLINTON *Progressive* v81 no5 p67 Je/Jl 2017

A COLONY IN A NATION color *Vanity Fair* v59 no4 p128 Mr 2017

A 'liberal white guy' T. Curran *America* v217 no2 p46 Jl 24 2017

POLICING THE COLONY [Cover story] color *Nation* v304 no13 p12 Ap 17 2017

HAYES, CHRISTOPHER, 1979

A Colony in a Nation L. Daniel *Christian Century* v134 no16 p31 Ag 2 2017

The Institutionalist color *Nation* v304 no1 p1 Ja 2 2017 The Obama Years

Thinking Again About Crime M. Cooper bw *Washington Monthly* v49 no3-5 p56 Mr-My 2017

Hayes, Christopher, 1979-—Interviews

Chris Hayes *New York Times Book Review* p8 Mr 19 2017

"THE POLITICAL EQUIVALENT OF ENRICHED URANIUM" A. RICHARD ALBANESE color *Publishers Weekly* v263 no52 p50 D 19 2016

HAYES, COLE

JUST A LITTLE PRICK: TRANS PEOPLE NEED TO BE HERE FOR EACH OTHER WHEN IT COMES TO OUR OWN HEALTH, color *Advocate* no1091 p51 Je/Jl 2017

MY HEALTH CARE IS NOT COSMETIC: Trans folks are up against a tidal wave of ignorance in the insurance industry color *Advocate* no1091 p110 Je/Jl 2017

Hayes, David

An Alternative to Health Care M&A *Harvard Business Review Digital Articles* p2 D 22 2014

THE TANGLED WEB cartoon *Canadian Wildlife* v22 no5 p18 N/D 2016

Hayes, Elaine M.

The Divine One: A classic jazz singer turned husbands into managers and listeners into fans J. GAVIN *New York Times Book Review* p22 Jl 23 2017

Sassy's Story J. MCDONOUGH color *Downbeat* v84 no9 p72 S 2017

Hayes, Erinn

KEVIN CAN WAIT SHAKE-UP! J. Halterman *TV Guide* v65 no27 p5 Je 26 2017

Hayes, Hannah

Adventures in Acadiana color map *Southern Living* v52 no5 p77 My 2017

Follow Us to Jazz Fest color *Southern Living* v52 no3 p78 Mr 2017

Memphis Gets Its Groove Back color *Southern Living* v52 no11 p69 N 2017

MY GRANDMOTHER, THE BEAUTY ICON color *Southern Living* v51 no11 p68 N 2016

THE SOUTHERN LIVING FOOD AWARDS color *Southern Living* v52 no6 p109 Je 2017

SOUTH'S BEST BAR color *Southern Living* v52 no4 p68 Ap 2017

SOUTH'S BEST RESTAURANT color *Southern Living* v52 no4 p88 Ap 2017

SUNNY DELIGHTS [Cover story] color *Southern Living* v52 no2 p88 F 2017

Hayes, Kevin J.

Curious George D. BRADBURN color *Weekly Standard* v22 no41 p24 Jl 3 2017

Hayes, Kieran

FIT TO PRINT bw color *Wired* v25 no5 p14 My 2017

Hayes, Louis

Chords & Discords R. S. BROADHEAD, P. TULOWIECKI et al bw color *Downbeat* v84 no10 p10 O 2017

Louis Hayes T. PANKEN color *Downbeat* v84 no9 p106 S 2017

Hayes, Margo

Let's Get Ready to Rambla! [Cover story] Z. GATES color *Climbing* no353 p31 My/Je 2017

HAYES, MOLLY

Crops and Robbers cartoon *Walrus* v13 no10 p19 D 2016

HAYES, RANDY

An Ecoregion-Based Approach to Protecting Half the Terrestrial Realm *BioScience* v67 no6 p534 Je 2017

Hayes, Rhonda Fleming

SOUTH'S BEST INN color *Southern Living* v52 no4 p80 Ap 2017

Hayes, Robin

The Summer Job I'll Never Forget color *Time* v190 no2/3 p55 Jl 10-17 2017

Hayes, Scott

Producing The FINEST P. Schofler color *Dressage Today* v23 no8 p58 Ap 2017

Hayes, Sean, 1970-

WILL & GRACE J. Halterman *TV Guide* v65 no37 p38 S 4 2017

Hayes, Sharon

SHARON HAYES M. Tomic *Art in America* v104 no9 p162 O 2016

Hayes, Stephen F.

Barack Obama, Neo-Hawk *Weekly Standard* v22 no17 p6 Ja 2 2017

Comey, Trump, and the GOP color *Weekly Standard* v22 no35 p6 My 22 2017

Comey v. Trump color *Weekly Standard* v22 no39 p7 Je 19 2017

The Courage Deficit color *Weekly Standard* v22 no26 p7 Mr 13 2017

Do You Hear Me Now? color *Weekly Standard* v22 no11 p7 N

21 2016

A Fight Worth Having color *Weekly Standard* v22 no28 p6 Mr 27 2017

The Final Obama Scandal [Cover story] color *Weekly Standard* v22 no21 p22 F 6 2017

The Flynn Affair *Weekly Standard* v22 no24 p6 F 27 2017

Getting to No color *Weekly Standard* v23 no6 p24 O 16 2017

Playing Defense color *Weekly Standard* v22 no46 p6 Ag 14 2017

Speeches and Herb color *Weekly Standard* v22 no7 p5 O 24 2016

Who We Are and Who He Is color *Weekly Standard* v22 no16 p7 D 26 2016

Winning the 9/11 Wars [Cover story] color *Weekly Standard* v22 no37 p6 Je 5 2017

Hayes, Susan Seaforth

DAYS OF OUR LIVES M. LOGAN *TV Guide* v65 no6 p44 Ja 30 2017

Hayes, Terrance

Too Far North *New York Times Magazine* p17 Jl 9 2017

Hayes, Thomas C.

Learning the Art of Electronics: A Hands-On Lab Course P. J. H. Tjossem *Physics Today* v70 no5 p61 My 2017

Hayes, Tiffany

BREAKOUT PLAYERS *Atlanta* v57 no1 p34 My 2017

Hayes-Bautista, David

The Surprising Evolution of Cinco de Mayo O. B. Waxman *Time* v189 no18 p25 My 15 2017

Haygoods, The (Performer)

Silver Streak color *Missouri Life* v44 no4 p22 Je 2017

Hay—Handling

TWO WAYS TO SOAK HAY C. Barakat and M. Freckleton *Equus* no476 p24 My 2017

Hayhoe, Katharine

The Roots of Science Denial color *Scientific American* v317 no4 p66 O 2017

Yeah, THE WEATHER Has Been WEIRD color *Foreign Policy* no224 p40 My/Je 2017

Haying equipment—Evaluation

HAY MOISTURE TESTERS G. Gullickson *Successful Farming* v115 no4 p57 Mr 2017

Hayman, David T. S.

As the bat flies bibl color *Science* v354 no6316 p1099 D 2 2016

Haymarket Books (Company)

Haymarket Books: Publishing Books in the Current Moment C. Kirch color *Publishers Weekly* v263 no42 p11 O 17 2016

Haymond, John A.

THE BLOODY CODE *MHQ: Quarterly Journal of Military History* v29 no2 p14 Wint 2017

LAWS OF WAR: FOUNDING FATHERS color *MHQ: Quarterly Journal of Military History* v30 no1 p16 Aut 2017

THE TRIAL OF THOMAS KNOX color *MHQ: Quarterly Journal of Military History* v29 no4 p14 Summ 2017

Haynal, John S.—Awards

MEMBER SPOTLIGHT color *Literacy Today (2411-7862)* v34 no3 p40 N/D 2016

Hayne, Anita

Who I am M. CALNAN *People Management* p53 O 2016

Hayner, Judith A.

Lulu and the Shadow Catcher bw color *Magazine Antiques* v184 no3 p82 My/Je 2017

Haynes, Barton F.

Developing an HIV vaccine bibl diag *Science* v355 no6330 p1129 Mr 17 2017

Haynes, Bruce D.

Harlem Heritage: How a family rose and rose again in a house on Convent Avenue E. DOWLING TAYLOR *New York Times Book Review* p30 My 14 2017

Haynes, Grace

Budding Artist color *Southern Living* v52 no5 p22 My 2017

Haynes, John Earl

The Two Worlds of a Soviet Spy bw *Commentary* v143 no3 p27 Mr 2017

Haynes, Korey

Bad Moon Rising color *Discover* v38 no1 p48 Ja/F 2017

BLACK AND BLUE MOON color *Astronomy* v44 no12 p44 D 2016

BROWN DWARFS FORMING PLANETS color *Astronomy* v45

no1 p10 Ja 2017

Fighting FOR Visibility bw color *Astronomy* v45 no2 p44 F 2017

Looking for Planet Nine color *Discover* v38 no1 p19 Ja/F 2017

Mapping the galaxy one star at a time color diag *Astronomy* v45 no6 p31 Je 2017

Meet the Next-Generation Space Telescope color diag *Discover* v38 no6 p84 Jl/Ag 2017

Pluto's Hidden Ocean bw color *Discover* v38 no1 p46 Ja/F 2017

Stars Explode in Earthly Skies color *Discover* v38 no3 p12 Ap 2017

Surviving Space color *Discover* v38 no6 p70 Jl/Ag 2017

The unsolved mysteries of the ICE GIANTS bw color *Astronomy* v45 no10 p46 O 2017

Haynes, Richard, 1927-2017

"Racehorse" Haynes, 1927-2017 J. N. LOMAX *Texas Monthly* v45 no6 p54 Je 2017

Haynes, Todd, 1961-

Fairground bw color *Vanity Fair* v58 no12 p95 D 2016

WONDERSTRUCK J. McGovern color *Entertainment Weekly* no1478 / 1479 p48 Ag 18-25 2017

Haynes, Warren

Jam's Working-Class Heroes D. FRICKE color *Rolling Stone* no1293 p19 Ag 10 2017

Hays, Chance

By Chance L. Feldman bw color *American Cowboy* v23 no5 p54 F/Mr 2017

Hays, Charlotte

Mind Your Manners color *Southern Living* v52 no11 p26 N 2017

Hays, Gregory

Found in Translation color *New York Review of Books* v64 no11 p56 Je 22 2017

Hays, Tyler, 1968-

Tyler HAYS H. PHELAN *Interview* v47 no1 p24 F 2017

HAYSOM, JENNY

The New Colonialism *Walrus* v13 no10 p65 D 2016

Hayton, Bill

Shadow on the South China Sea *History Today* v66 no10 p3 O 2016

Hayward, Andrew

10 great, older games that you can still play on iOS 11 color *Macworld - Digital Edition* v34 no11 p59 N 2017

DISNEY MEETS FINAL FANTASY (AND TEDIUM) IN KINGDOM HEARTS UNION X[CROSS] color *Macworld - Digital Edition* v34 no10 p55 O 2017

How to use the Nintendo Switch's Joy-Cons with your Mac—and why you'd want to color *Macworld - Digital Edition* v34 no4 p13 My 2017

Latest Mac games bw color *Macworld - Digital Edition* p81 Ap 2017

LIGHTSEEKERS SMART FIGURES color *Macworld - Digital Edition* v34 no8 p47 Ag 2017

MINECRAFT APPLE TV EDITION: BLOCK BUILDING ON THE BIG SCREEN color *Macworld - Digital Edition* p59 F 2017

Pokémon Go on Apple Watch vs. Pokémon Go Plus: Which should you wear? color *Macworld - Digital Edition* p43 Mr 2017

Round-up: Latest Mac games color diag *Macworld - Digital Edition* p89 Ja 2017

SPHERO R2-D2 APP-ENABLED DROID color *Macworld - Digital Edition* v34 no11 p35 N 2017

Turn your iPhone 7 into a handheld console color *Macworld - Digital Edition* p97 Ap 2017

Hayward, James

Abstract #139 color *Art in America* v105 no6 p34 Je/Jl 2017

HAYWARD, MATT W.

Conserving the World's Megafauna and Biodiversity: The Fierce Urgency of Now *BioScience* v67 no3 p197 Mr 2017

Saving the World's Terrestrial Megafauna color *BioScience* v66 no10 p807 O 1 2016

Hayward, Steven F.

A Conservative Takes on Climate Change color *Weekly Standard* v22 no29 p22 Ap 3 2017

The Crisis at Berkeley bw color *Weekly Standard* v22 no34 p26 My 15 2017

Crisis of the Conservative House Divided *Weekly Standard* v22 no8 p20 O 31 2016

First Principles J. CARL diag *National Review* v69 no4 p36 Mr 6 2017

FRIENDS AND ENEMIES M. J. Franck *Claremont Review of Books* v17 no2 p28 Spr 2017

Over the Edge bw color *Weekly Standard* v22 no44 p27 Jl 31 2017

A Strauss Divided T. LINDBERG *Commentary* v143 no6 p42 Je 2017

THE THREAT TO LIBERTY *Claremont Review of Books* v17 no1 p53 Wint 2016/2017

Hayward, Susan

FEROCIOUS SUSAN HAYWARD *Saturday Evening Post* v289 no2 p93 Mr/Ap 2017

FROM THE ARCHIVE J. Nilsson *Saturday Evening Post* v289 no2 p94 Mr/Ap 2017

Haywood, R. R.

A Zombie Success Story J. MCCARTNEY bw color *Publishers Weekly* v264 no13 p41 Mr 27 2017

HAZAN, RITA

42 new ALL-STAR PRODUCTS of the year [Cover story] color *Redbook* p27 Jl/Ag 2017

Hazard mitigation

See also

Hurricane protection

Hazards

See also

Weather hazards

Apocalypse AI M. Shermer color *Scientific American* v316 no3 p77 Mr 2017

Arousing Performance A. Hadhazy bw *Natural History* v125 no11 p7 N 2017

Hot-Weather Trail Hazards H. S. Thomas color *Horse & Rider* v56 no6 p64 Je 2017

Hazards—Prevention

HEAVE-HO HAZARDS C. Barakat and M. Freckleton color *Equus* no473 p16 F 2017

HAZEL, CHRISTIAN

BLUE-COLLAR HAULER color *Dirt Sports + Off-Road* v51 no11 p42 N 2017

Hazelnuts

EAT MO NUTS! D. BRESHEARS *Missouri Life* v43 no7 p70 D 2016/Ja 2017

Hazelwood, Janell

5 SMART SAVING TIPS FOR SINGLE WOMEN color *Black Enterprise* v47 no7 p17 My/Je 2017

Hazelzet, Jan

A Blueprint for Measuring Health Care Outcomes *Harvard Business Review Digital Articles* p2 D 12 2016

Hazen, Helen

Antiquarian Dreams: Sometimes it's okay to judge history by its cover *American Scholar* v86 no4 p118 Aut 2017

The Cloistered Books of Peru *American Scholar* v86 no2 p64 Spr 2017

Hazing

Fatal Initiation B. WALLACE color *Vanity Fair* v59 no11 p134 N 2017

Hazing—Universities & colleges

A DEATH AT PENN STATE C. FLANAGAN color *Atlantic* v320 no4 p92 N 2017

HAZLETT, ANDREW

If These Walls Could Sprechen color *Reason* v48 no9 p64 F 2017

Hazlett, Thomas Winslow

FROM THE ARCHIVES bw *Reason* v49 no6 p78 N 2017

FROM THE ARCHIVES cartoon *Reason* v48 no10 p66 Mr 2017

Go Ahead, Throw Your Vote Away color *Reason* v48 no7 p62 D 2016

A Short History of Radio Explains the iPhone's Success *Harvard Business Review Digital Articles* p2 Je 29 2017

We Could Have Had Cellphones Four Decades Earlier color *Reason* v49 no3 p60 Jl 2017

Hazzard, Oli

EARLY MODERN LOVE POEM *Harper's Magazine* v335 no2006 p22 Jl 2017

He, B. B.

High dislocation density–induced large ductility in deformed and partitioned steels bw color diag *Science* v357 no6355 p1029 S 8 2017

He, Daniel

CRISPRi-based genome-scale identification of functional long noncoding RNA loci in human cells bibl graph *Science* v355 no6320 p1 Ja 6 2017

He, David

What China's 13th Five-Year Plan Means for Business *Harvard Business Review Digital Articles* p2 D 7 2015

He, Dong

Satellite-based entanglement distribution over 1200 kilometers diag graph *Science* v356 no6343 p1140 Je 16 2017

He, Fangliang

Plant diversity increases with the strength of negative density dependence at the global scale diag *Science* v356 no6345 p1389 Je 30 2017

He, Feng

Regional and global sea-surface temperatures during the last interglaciation bibl color graph *Science* v355 no6322 p276 Ja 20 2017

He, Huaibing

Systemic pan-AMPK activator MK-8722 improves glucose homeostasis but induces cardiac hypertrophy graph *Science* v357 no6350 p507 Ag 4 2017

He, Jian

Advances in thermoelectric materials research: Looking back and moving forward diag *Science* v357 no6358 p1369 S 29 2017

Formation of α-chiral centers by asymmetric β-C(sp3)–H arylation, alkenylation, and alkynylation bibl diag *Science* v355 no6324 p499 F 3 2017

He, Lin

Deficiency of microRNA miR-34a expands cell fate potential in pluripotent stem cells diag *Science* v355 no6325 p596 F 10 2017

He, Meg

MEG HE J. Chen color *Bloomberg Businessweek* no4518 p79 Ap 10 2017

He, Xi

Engineering the ribosomal DNA in a megabase synthetic chromosome diag *Science* v355 no6329 p1049 Mr 10 2017

He, Yang

Direction-specific van der Waals attraction between rutile TiO2 nanocrystals diag *Science* v356 no6336 p434 Ap 28 2017

He, Yupeng

Single-cell methylomes identify neuronal subtypes and regulatory elements in mammalian cortex diag *Science* v357 no6351 p600 Ag 11 2017

He, Zuhua

Epigenetic regulation of antagonistic receptors confers rice blast resistance with yield balance bibl diag *Science* v355 no6328 p962 Mr 3 2017

He Leng

RPA binds histone H3-H4 and functions in DNA replication–coupled nucleosome assembly bibl graph *Science* v355 no6323 p415 Ja 27 2017

He Yan

Highly stretchable polymer semiconductor films through the nanoconfinement effect bibl graph *Science* v355 no6320 p1 Ja 6 2017

He-Yin Zhen

REGIME CHANGE He-Yin Zhen *Lapham's Quarterly* v10 no3 p47 Summ 2017

REGIME CHANGE *Lapham's Quarterly* v10 no3 p47 Summ 2017

Heacock, Summer

Diary of a Working Mom's Date Night cartoon *Working Mother* v40 no3 p50 Ag/S 2017

Head, Bessie, 1937-1986

1966: Botswana B. Head *Lapham's Quarterly* v10 no2 p94 Spr 2017

Head, James Philip

An Affair with Beauty: The Mystique of Howard Chandler Christy *Publishers Weekly* v264 no3 p35 Ja 16 2017

Head, James W.

Formation of the Orientale lunar multiring basin bibl graph *Science* v354 no6311 p441 O 28 2016

Gravity field of the Orientale basin from the Gravity Recovery and Interior Laboratory Mission bibl graph *Science* v354 no6311 p438 O 28 2016

Head, Jason

Merging paleobiology with conservation biology to guide the future of terrestrial ecosystems color *Science* v355 no6325 p594 F 10 2017

Head halters

Best Show-Halter Fit A. Dunning and J. Paulson color *Horse & Rider* v56 no2 p32 F 2017

Head injuries

Not Sinking In G. MICHAL *Boating World* v38 no8 p47 S/O 2017

Head injuries—Prevention

Keep Your Little Soccer Star Safe S. SEA GOLD color *Parents* v92 no4 p26 Ap 2017

Head-mounted displays

See also

Helmet-mounted displays

First Windows Mixed Reality headsets color *PCWorld* v35 no10 p132 O 2017

THE UNAWARE OLYMPICS T. Taylor color *Sports Illustrated* v126 no7 p46 Mr 6 2017

VIRTUAL REALITY'S MONEY QUEST J. Vanian color *Fortune* v75 no1 p28 Ja 1 2017

VR'S CROSSOVER MOMENT? N. Abrams color *Entertainment Weekly* no1439 p12 N 11 2016

Head-mounted displays—Design & construction

Making VR Matter J. Brustein cartoon color *Bloomberg Businessweek* no4496 p32 O 24 2016

Head-mounted displays—Evaluation

SHOP ON SI's GIFT GUIDE color *Sports Illustrated* v125 no18 p48 D 5 2016

Head of the Class (TV program)

From TV to Lab, and Back N. D. TYSON color *National Geographic* v231 no6 p26 Je 2017

Head-on collisions

Dennis Byrd 1966-2016 P. King and T. Keith color *Sports Illustrated* v125 no14 p22 O 24-31 2016

Head-Smashed-In Buffalo Jump National Historic Site (Alta.)

A REMOVABLE FEAST E. A. POWELL color *Archaeology* v70 no1 p20 Ja/F 2017

Head-up displays

GARMIN UNVEILS BIZJET HUD color *Flying* v144 no7 p18 Jl 2017

HEAD-UP DISPLAY R. Mark color *Flying* v144 no4 p26 Ap 2017

Headache

Diagnosis L. Sanders *New York Times Magazine* p26 N 20 2016

"I get orgasm headaches" A. Massey and S. G. Levy color *Glamour* v115 no3 p132 Mr 2017

Our Doc Will See You Now R. Rajapaksa color *Health* v30 no10 p72 D 2016

THE PATH TO GOOD POSTURE K. ROCKWOOD bw cartoon *Martha Stewart Living* no275 p52 Je 2017

What a Headache S. WYKES *USA Today Magazine* v145 no2858 p33 N 2016

What's Your Headache IQ? K. Rockwood color *O, The Oprah Magazine* p102 N 2017

Headache treatment

Headaches as you age [Cover story] *Mayo Clinic Health Letter* v35 no6 p1 Je 2017

Head CASE O. Manno *Dance Spirit* v21 no4 p26 Ap 2017

Head & neck pain color *Yoga Journal* p21 2017 SpecialIssue

Our doc will see you now R. Rajapaka color *Health* v31 no9 p66 N 2017

Soothe a headache C. Lee color *Yoga Journal* p30 2017 SpecialIssue

Headache—Case studies

She had plenty of headaches in the past, but this pain felt different. Could it be something more dangerous than a migraine? L. Sanders *New York Times Magazine* p24 S 17 2017

Headache—Diagnosis

ERASE YOUR PAIN: A USER'S MANUAL II. Levine color *Health* v31 no2 p97 Mr 2017

Headache—Patients

She had plenty of headaches in the past, but this pain felt different. Could it be something more dangerous than a migraine? L. Sanders *New York Times Magazine* p24 S 17 2017

Headache—Prevention

Linking Diet and Headaches: Certain foods and drinks are more often headache triggers than others [Cover story] *Tufts University Health & Nutrition Letter* v35 no7 p1 S 2017

Head—Anatomy

Ancient sea worm had a head full of spines L. Hamers bw color *Science News* v192 no3 p4 S 2 2017

Headbands—Evaluation

BEAUTY BUYS UNDER $25 color *Good Housekeeping* v264 no2 p20 F 2017

Headcase: Opera Introspective (Music)

Dietz: Headcase: Opera Introspective J. Rosenblum *Opera News* v81 no7 p50 Ja 2017

Headdresses

Getting Out the Vote M. Allen bw *Yankee* v80 no6 p168 N/D 2016

Heade, Martin Johnson, 1819-1904—Exhibitions

On the road with Martin Johnson Heade color *Magazine Antiques* v184 no4 p38 Jl/Ag 2017

Headgear

See also

Caps (Headgear)

Helmets

CAPS LOCK *Cincinnati Magazine* v50 no8 p28 My 2017

SCARVES AS HAIR ACCESSORIES O. Watson cartoon *Women's Health* v14 no9 p34 N 2017

Headgear—Evaluation

THE GOODS *Atlanta* v57 no5 p37 S 2017

STYLE color *Horse & Rider* v56 no3 p20 Mr 2017

TRAIL & CAMPING GEAR L. Berger O'connor color *Trail Rider* v29 no2 p54 Mr 2017

Headlee, Celeste

Listen Up *American Scholar* v86 no4 p16 Aut 2017

NOISES OFF C. PENDLEY *Atlanta* v56 no11 p28 Mr 2017

HEADLEE, JACOB

LEAF SPRINGS 101 color *Dirt Sports + Off-Road* v51 no9 p34 S 2017

NON-JEEPS INVADE EASTER JEEP SAFARI color *Dirt Sports + Off-Road* v51 no9 p40 S 2017

SOUND MACHINE color *Dirt Sports + Off-Road* v51 no8 p48 Ag 2017

HEADLEE, JAKE

UTV PROTECTION color *Dirt Sports + Off-Road* v51 no6 p24 Je 2017

Headless Woman, The (Film)

WHEN ALL IS LOST J. TEODORO color *Film Comment* v53 no5 p44 S/O 2017

Headley, Brooks

Cleans Up Real Nice *Bon Appetit* v61 no12 p96 D 2016 /Jan2017

tools of the trade color *Bon Appetit* p82 S 2017

Headlight glare

AM I NORMAL? S. Yeager color *AARP: The Magazine* v60 no2A p18 F/Mr 2017

Headlines of American newspapers

Situation Normal, All Trumped Up F. BARNES color *Weekly Standard* v22 no45 p10 Ag 7 2017

Headly, Glenne, 1955-2017

Milestones *Time* v189 no24 p11 Je 26 2017

Headphones

BUILD YOUR OWN CREW J. MIGALA color *Runner's World* v52 no8 p20 S 2017

CUTE REBOOT L. BAILEY *Indianapolis Monthly* p26 F 2017

GIFT GUIDE 2016 M. Khemsurov color *Bloomberg Businessweek* no4500 p67 N 21 2016

MILLENNIAL PINK: THE LASTING COLOR OF NOW T. M. FERGUSON color *Ebony* v72 no11 p40 S 2017

On-the-road organization J. Jones color *Redbook* p24 S 2017

Resistance Is Futile D. Pogue color *Scientific American* v315 no6 p30 D 2016

TURNIN' THE INSIDE OUT R. SABIN *Sound & Vision* v82 no6 p8 Jl/Ag 2017

The Well-Edited Tote color *Esquire* p133 BigBlackBook

Headphones—Equipment & supplies—Evaluation

Like a Rock color *Sound & Vision* v82 no3 p63 Ap 2017

Headphones—Evaluation

AirPods: They sound great, but Siri holds them back S. OCHS color *PCWorld* v35 no2 p116 F 2017

AirPods wish list: 3 ways Apple can make its Bluetooth earphones even better C. McGARRY color *Macworld - Digital Edition* p39 Mr 2017

The Art of Sound S. Guttenberg and C. Crowley color *Sound & Vision* v81 no9 p20 N 2016

Astell&Kern AK XB10 Bluetooth DAC and amp: Wireless, hi-res audio for any headphones T. NICOLAKIS color *Macworld - Digital Edition* v34 no11 p129 N 2017

BeatsX review: Just as magical as the AirPods, but more comfortable and convenient S. Ochs bw color *Macworld - Digital Edition* v34 no4 p72 My 2017

Bedazzled! S. Guttenberg and C. Crowley color *Sound & Vision* v82 no6 p22 Jl/Ag 2017

Bedazzled S. Guttenberg color *Sound & Vision* v82 no4 p22 My 2017

The Best 25 Inventions of 2016 E. Berman, E. Dockterman et al color *Time* v188 no22-23 p43 N/D 2016

THE BEST BET img *New York* p53 Ja 9 2017

Best Buds color *Men's Health* v32 no1 p36 Ja/F 2017

The Best of Technology 2016 A. GEORGE color *Popular Mechanics* p17 D 2016/Ja 2017

BEYERDYNAMIC AMIRON HOME HEADPHONES T. NICOLAKIS color *Macworld - Digital Edition* p35 Mr 2017

Both Sides Now S. Guttenberg color *Sound & Vision* v82 no3 p24 Ap 2017

Bring the Noise J. NOSEK cartoon color *Men's Health* v32 no4 p32 My 2017

Come Fly With Me S. Guttenberg color *Sound & Vision* v82 no3 p22 Ap 2017

The Earbud Revolution G. EMMANUEL color *Rolling Stone* no1274 p16 N 17 2016

Finding Sonic Paradise B. Ankosko color *Sound & Vision* v82 no4 p74 My 2017

Focal Utopia Headphones M. Fleischmann color *Sound & Vision* v82 no6 p42 Jl/Ag 2017

For the Social Animal color *Consumer Reports* v81 no12 p38 D 2016

Gadgets for the Edge of the World A. George color *Popular Mechanics* p46 Mr 2017

Game Changer S. Guttenberg color *Sound & Vision* v82 no3 p26 Ap 2017

GEAR color *Downbeat* v83 no12 p96 D 2016

GEAR ESSENTIALS FOR NEW PILOTS P. BERGQVIST color *Flying* v144 no3 p62 Mr 2017

Headphone Hall of Fame S. Grobart color *Bloomberg Businessweek* no4511 p64 F 13 2017

Hearing Is Believing S. Guttenberg and C. Crowley color *Sound & Vision* v82 no6 p18 Jl/Ag 2017

iOS Accessories J. Mathis color *Macworld - Digital Edition* p58 Je 13 2017

JAYBIRD FREEDOM WIRELESS HEADPHONES O. RAYMUNDO color *Macworld - Digital Edition* v33 no11 p52 N 2016

JBL E55BT review: These modestly priced cans deliver strong features T. NICOLAKIS color *Macworld - Digital Edition* p102 Je 13 2017

Jewels for the Ear S. Guttenberg color *Sound & Vision* v82 no7 p20 S 2017

The Joy of Sound S. Guttenberg color *Sound & Vision* v82 no3 p18 Ap 2017

LIFE MADE EASIER R. WALKER color *AARP: The Magazine* v60 no1A p34 D 2016/Ja 2017

Looking Good S. Guttenberg color *Sound & Vision* v82 no7 p22 S 2017

MrSpeakers Aeon Headphones S. Guttenberg color *Sound & Vision* v82 no8 p20 O 2017

New Gear color *Sound & Vision* v82 no1 p30 Ja 2017

New Gear color *Sound & Vision* v82 no3 p32 Ap 2017

New Gear color *Sound & Vision* v82 no5 p28 Je 2017

Noise Cancellation Goes Blue L. Dragan and C. Crowley color *Sound & Vision* v82 no2 p18 F/Mr 2017

Now Here This M. Mettler and C. Crowley color *Sound & Vision* v81 no9 p18 N 2016

Out of the Blue S. Guttenberg and C. Crowley color *Sound & Vision* v82 no5 p22 Je 2017

PLANTRONICS BACKBEAT PRO 2 S. J. PUREWAL color *Macworld - Digital Edition* p41 F 2017

Rated XXX S. Guttenberg and C. Crowley color *Sound & Vision* v82 no6 p20 Jl/Ag 2017

Razer Kraken V2: Two headsets, one leap forward H. DINGMAN color *PCWorld* v35 no2 p109 F 2017

Sennheiser Wireless Headphones color *Bloomberg Businessweek* no4527 p91 Je 19 2017

The Shock of the New S. Guttenberg color *Sound & Vision* v82 no4 p18 My 2017

Sony MDR-Z1R Headphones S. Guttenberg color *Sound & Vision* v82 no3 p62 Ap 2017

STRATEGIST img *New York* p53 F 9 2017

Street Style: FITNESS EDITION M. Legrand color *Women's Health* v14 no6 p18 Jl 2017

The Sweet Sound of Virtual Reality X. HARDING and A. SMITH color *Popular Science* v288 no6 p48 N/D 2016

Take It Easy S. Guttenberg color *Sound & Vision* v82 no4 p24 My 2017

Tell It Like It Is S. Guttenberg and C. Crowley color *Sound & Vision* v81 no10 p18 D 2016

This One Goes to 99 S. Guttenberg and C. Crowley color *Sound & Vision* v81 no9 p28 N 2016

This Year's Model S. Guttenberg and C. Crowley color *Sound & Vision* v82 no5 p18 Je 2017

TUNE OUT TRAVEL STRESS color *Men's Health* v31 no10 p(Sp)22 D 2016

ULTIMATE "IT" Gifts color *Good Housekeeping* v263 no6 p71 D 2016

VI AI PERSONAL TRAINER: HEART RATE-TRACKING BLUETOOTH EARBUDS WITH SERIOUS POTENTIAL C. McGARRY color *Macworld - Digital Edition* v34 no6 p68 Je 2017

Vive la Différence! S. Guttenberg and C. Crowley color *Sound & Vision* v82 no1 p20 Ja 2017

Wireless for Less R. Broida color *Money* v45 no10 p23 N 2016

The WIRELESS RUNNER J. Dengate color *Runner's World* v52 no4 p1 My 2017

Heads of state
    See also
    Executive power
    Kings & rulers
    Prime ministers
Castle Gothic M. KNOX BERAN *National Review* v69 no11 p30 Je 12 2017

Headsails
CRUISING TIPS T. Cunliffe color *Sail* v47 no12 p16 D 2016
Rigging Adjustable Sheet Leads G. Snook color *Sail* v48 no5 p44 My 2017

Headsets (Audio)
LIGHTSPEED ZULU 3 color *Flying* v144 no8 p18 Ag 2017

Headsets (Audio)—Evaluation
The $60 A10 headset is Astro's first budget-priced audio gear H. DINGMAN color *PCWorld* v35 no7 p29 Jl 2017

AIRPODS REVIEW: They sound great, but Siri holds them back S. Ochs color *Macworld - Digital Edition* p72 F 2017

AirPods teardown reveals the magic and glue that make Apple's wireless earphones work I. PAUL color *Macworld - Digital Edition* p52 F 2017

Apple's AirPods survive tough workouts with no sweat C. McGARRY color *Macworld - Digital Edition* p49 F 2017

Best Buds color *Men's Health* v32 no1 p36 Ja/F 2017

Bring the Noise J. NOSEK cartoon color *Men's Health* v32 no4 p32 My 2017

The Earbud Revolution G. EMMANUEL color *Rolling Stone* no1274 p16 N 17 2016

GEAR BOX color *Downbeat* v84 no2 p100 F 2017

Headphone Hall of Fame S. Grobart color *Bloomberg Businessweek* no4511 p64 F 13 2017

Necessity--The Father of Innovation *Stage Directions* v30 no4 p9 Ap 2017

Razer Kraken V2: Two headsets, one leap forward H. DINGMAN color *PCWorld* v35 no2 p109 F 2017

The Sweet Spot S. Guttenberg and C. Crowley color *Sound & Vision* v82 no2 p20 F/Mr 2017

VIRTUAL REALITY, ONE YEAR OUT: What went right, what didn't B. CHACOS color *PCWorld* p141 Mr 2017

HEADY, KRISTEN K.

THE HEALTH CARE SCHMOZZLE C. R. Kesler *Claremont Review of Books* v17 no3 p5 Summ 2017

Health Coverage Is No Slam Dunk *Kiplinger's Personal Finance* v71 no12 p22 D 2017

How Long to Hang on to Tax Records K. LANKFORD *Kiplinger's Personal Finance* v71 no5 p42 My 2017

How to Survive a High-Deductible Health Plan D. Rosato color *Consumer Reports* v82 no1 p16 Ja 2017

Living Out Loud: On good food, great reads, and strong women G. DUNCAN, M. E. ZIEGLER et al color *O, The Oprah Magazine* p20 S 2017

THE MONTHLY INTERVIEW: TOM PERRIELLO color *Washington Monthly* v49 no6-8 p16 Je-Ag 2017

MY HEALTH CARE IS NOT COSMETIC: Trans folks are up against a tidal wave of ignorance in the insurance industry C. HAYES color *Advocate* no1091 p110 Je/Jl 2017

A Proven New Model for Reimbursing Physicians G. D. Steele Jr. *Harvard Business Review Digital Articles* p2 S 15 2015

Reinventing the Way Medicaid Delivers Care S. H. Jain and L. Lessin *Harvard Business Review Digital Articles* p2 Mr 31 2015

Remaking Public Schools D. Ruth Wilson color *New Orleans Magazine* v51 no6 p32 Ap 2017

Running a State Health Insurance Marketplace A. R. Wallack *Harvard Business Review Digital Articles* p2 D 15 2015

STAY WELL AND SAVE MONEY G. Roberts-grey color *Essence* v47 no12 p117 Ap 2017

Urgent Care T. Castañares *Harper's Magazine* v334 no2000 p3 Ja 2017

What's Your Plan? K. Cicero color graph *Prevention* v68 no12 p86 D 2016

Health insurance claims

Cover the Cost of Care K. LANKFORD color *Kiplinger's Personal Finance* v71 no6 p64 Je 2017

Health insurance companies

Diagnosis: Heartburn J. Cost color *Weekly Standard* v22 no47 p17 Ag 21 2017

Health insurance companies—Mergers

Big Merger Review graph *Bloomberg Businessweek* no4496 p46 O 24 2016

The Risks of Health Insurance Company Mergers L. Dafny *Harvard Business Review Digital Articles* p2 S 24 2015

Health insurance exchanges

Navigating Health Care's Transition to Private Exchanges R. Birhanzel, S. Brown et al *Harvard Business Review Digital Articles* p2 N 7 2014

Running a State Health Insurance Marketplace A. R. Wallack *Harvard Business Review Digital Articles* p2 D 15 2015

Where Both the ACA and AHCA Fall Short, and What the Health Insurance Market Really Needs D. Blumenthal and S. Collins *Harvard Business Review Digital Articles* p2 Mr 21 2017

Health insurance laws—United States

The effect of state parity laws on how providers treat substance use disorder K. Harris *Monthly Labor Review* p1 Je 2017

Health care after Obama *Christian Century* v134 no9 p7 Ap 26 2017

To Pass Health Care, The Senate Needs Him S. T. Dennis color *Bloomberg Businessweek* no4524 p28 My 29 2017

Health insurance policies

The Bridge to Single-Payer R. KIM *Nation* v304 no13 p3 Ap 17 2017

Health insurance premiums

Obamacare: In Need of Intensive Care, or Terminally Ill? H. S. Edwards color *Time* v188 no16/17 p56 O 24 2016

Obamacare Meltdown color *Weekly Standard* v22 no9 p2 N 7 2016

Obamacare's Thousand Cuts S. Mukherjee color *Fortune* v176 no3 p13 S 1 2017

Obamacare Sticker Shock M. Rhodan *Time* v188 no19 p10 N 7 2016

The Risks of Health Insurance Company Mergers L. Dafny *Harvard Business Review Digital Articles* p2 S 24 2015

Why So Expensive? F. BARNES color *Weekly Standard* v22 no46 p16 Ag 14 2017

Health insurance reimbursement

See also

Prospective payment systems

Value-based purchasing (Medical care)

The Mayo Clinic Model for Running a Value-Improvement Program D. A. Haas, R. A. Helmers et al *Harvard Business Review Digital Articles* p2 O 22 2015

Turning Value-Based Health Care into a Real Business Model L. S. Kaiser and T. H. Lee *Harvard Business Review Digital Articles* p2 O 8 2015

Health insurance—California

Single Payer Here We Come J. BLEIFUSS *In These Times* v41 no5 p5 My 2017

Health insurance—California—Law & legislation

CENTURY marks graph *Christian Century* v134 no6 p8 Mr 15 2017

Health insurance—Government policy

Pants on Fire *Weekly Standard* v22 no10 p3 N 14 2016

Health insurance—Government policy—United States

After Obamacare *Christian Century* v134 no3 p7 F 2017

THE BIG IDEA *In These Times* v41 no10 p39 O 2017

AN EXPENSIVE EXPERIMENT WITH SINGLE-PAYER HEALTH CARE E. Boehm color *Reason* v49 no5 p15 O 2017

Mythbusting Health Care: How health insurance should work S. W. Atlas *Hoover Digest: Research & Opinion on Public Policy* no3 p38 Summ 2017

Health insurance—Law & legislation—United States

After Obamacare *Christian Century* v134 no3 p7 F 2017

Health Care Needs the Individual Mandate cartoon *Bloomberg Businessweek* no4515 p10 Mr 20 2017

How the Health Care Debate Reveals the GOP's Divisions S. Frizell color diag *Time* v189 no11 p16 Mr 27 2017

Time to Rethink Early Retirement B. Steverman graph *Bloomberg Businessweek* no4516 p40 Mr 27 2017

Health insurance—Oregon

national: SHORT TAKES *Ms.* v27 no3 p13 Fall 2017

Health insurance—Texas

the FACES of OBAMACARE M. HALL *Texas Monthly* v45 no3 p116 Mr 2017

Health insurance—United States

See also

Medicare

THE CASE FOR BEING UNINSURED *USA Today Magazine* v145 no2861 p4 F 2017

Don't Bother Complaining About High-Deductible Health Plans L. Binder *Harvard Business Review Digital Articles* p2 N 13 2014

FARMING WITHOUT A NET: HEALTH INSURANCE CAN SAVE THE FARM, BUT BETWEEN THE COMPLICATED PROCESS AND THE EXPENSE, SOME FARMERS ARE GOING WITHOUT L. F. Prater *Successful Farming* v115 no11 p58 S 2017

FOR MOST WORKERS, HEALTH CARE IS BUSINESS AS USUAL K. LANKFORD color *Kiplinger's Personal Finance* v71 no10 p11 O 2017

Help Make America Compassionate Again E. J. Schneidewind *AARP: The Magazine* v60 no5A p67 Ag/S 2017

The Man Who Knew Too Little [Cover story] M. W. O'Reilly bw *Commonweal* v144 no17 p6 O 20 2017

PUBLISHER'S PAGE color *Black Enterprise* v47 no5 p6 Ja/F 2017

ROBBING THE MIDDLE CLASS A. ECK *USA Today Magazine* v145 no2864 p26 My 2017

Stanford's Big Health Care Idea H. Boerner color *Washington Monthly* v49 no3-5 p48 Mr-My 2017

What Young Adults Need to Know About Buying Health Insurance A. Adamczyk color *Money* v46 no7 p17 Ag 2017

Health insurance—United States—Costs

See also

Medicaid—Costs

The Best Cure for Obamacare Woes L. Zamosky color *Money* v45 no10 p36 N 2016

Health insurance—United States—Law & legislation

NOT BACKING DOWN: We at Ms. promise to never let up with our reporting, rebelling and truth-telling K. SPILLAR *Ms.* v27 no3 p39 Fall 2017

Health literacy

test your nutrition IQ S. KUZEMCHAK *Parents* v92 no2 p72 F 2017

Health maintenance organizations

An Alternative to Health Care M&A D. Hayes *Harvard Business Review Digital Articles* p2 D 22 2014

Health of African Americans

The Forgotten Y. Stines color *Ebony* v72 no9 p60 Jl/Ag 2017

Health of cancer patients

A Critical Gap in Cancer Care A. Papmehl bw color *Maclean's* v130 no9 p38 O 2017

Health of college teachers

Mom Left Me the House. What Do I Owe My Brothers? K. A. Appiah *New York Times Magazine* p20 Ag 20 2017

Health of dancers

advice for dancers L. HAMILTON *Dance Magazine* v91 no7 p24 Jl 2017

Gut Feeling: Can probiotics and prebiotics really make you healthier? R. ZAR *Dance Magazine* v91 no7 p48 Jl 2017

Healthy Through History J. STAHL *Dance Magazine* v91 no7 p46 Jl 2017

PLANT-Powered J. D. Hench color *Dance Spirit* v21 no8 p50 O 2017

Relax & Refresh L. KAY *Dance Magazine* v91 no8 p40 Ag 2017

STRIKE a Pose H. Rolfe, J. Brilliant et al *Dance Spirit* v21 no7 p56 S 2017

Health of dogs

BONE APPÉTIT: Revery's chef-designed dog menu caters to a ruff crowd B. POWERS *Indianapolis Monthly* v40 no11 p39 Jl 2017

Health of farmers

YOUR FARM C. Tevis *Successful Farming* v115 no11 p14 S 2017

Health of LGBT people

THE LGBTQ HEALTH CARE BILL OF RIGHTS: New York City made an important step toward equality D. GUERRERO *Advocate* no1093 p60 O/N 2017

Health of mothers

No Sweat J. BARBERIO color *Working Mother* v40 no2 p58 Je/Jl 2017

Health of older people

FINDING FITNESS: Incorporating exercise and wellness can increase years of happiness and health S. Walsh *Washingtonian Magazine* v52 no8 p146 My 2017

Senior Living J. YOUNG cartoon color *Indianapolis Monthly* v42 no2 p95 O 2017

TO YOUR HEALTH: Physicians and specialists recommend baseline health exams to prolong active lifestyle Rin-rin Yu *Washingtonian Magazine* v52 no8 p150 My 2017

Health of pets

BONE-A FIDE ADVICE L. ROBERTS color *Indianapolis Monthly* v42 no2 p99 O 2017

IS YOUR PET STRESSED OUT? J. Szabo color *Amazing Wellness* v9 no4 p76 Summ 2017

Health of physicians

40 THINGS CARDIOLOGISTS AND OTHER DOCTORS DO TO PROTECT THEIR HEARTS C. HILTON ANDERSEN color *Reader's Digest* v189 no1131 p98 Je 2017

How One California Medical Group Is Decreasing Physician Burnout S. Arabadjis and E. E. Sullivan color *Harvard Business Review Digital Articles* p2 Je 7 2017

Health of transgender people

JUST A LITTLE PRICK: TRANS PEOPLE NEED TO BE HERE FOR EACH OTHER WHEN IT COMES TO OUR OWN HEALTH, C. HAYES color *Advocate* no1091 p51 Je/Jl 2017

Health planning

Community Corps M. Quinn *Governing* v30 no6 p44 Mr 2017

THE FOUR-DAY REBOOT I. Edwards and K. Lovato color *Sunset* v238 no2 p15 F 2017

A MONDAY J. Migala color *Women's Health* v14 no3 p86 Ap 2017

Health products

See also

Hygiene products

Nonprescription drugs

Skin care products

Reducing Health Disparities and Promoting Health Equity J. M. Weinstein and R. García *Parks & Recreation* v52 no5 p40 My 2017

WELL BEINGS N. SPORTELLI color *Forbes* v200 no1 p18 Jl

27 2017

Health products—Evaluation

AND THE WINNERS ARE... [Cover story] color *Amazing Wellness* v9 no6 p50 EarlyWint 2017

Does It Work?: Tech Trackers S. KLEIN color *Prevention* v69 no8 p24 Ag 2017

JUST BEAUTIFUL! color *Amazing Wellness* v8 no6 p100 Early Winter2016

Must-Haves color *Amazing Wellness* v9 no1 p92 Wint 2017

Winter Wellness color *Amazing Wellness* v9 no6 p96 EarlyWint 2017

Health programs

See also

National school lunch program

MARK YOUR CALENDAR *Cincinnati Magazine* v50 no12 p96 S 2017

Member Spotlight: Commit to Health Youth Ambassadors C. Jones *Parks & Recreation* v52 no6 p43 Je 2017

Our Team D. McConnacie color *Alternatives Journal (AJ) - Canada's Environmental Voice* v42 no3 p56 2016

WIRED FOR SUCCESS C. Cunningham *Washingtonian Magazine* v52 no9 p119 Je 2017

Health programs—Evaluation

A New Take on Shipshape M. CROSS color *Kiplinger's Personal Finance* v71 no3 p71 Mr 2017

Health promotion

See also

Employee health promotion

5 secrets for health and happiness color *Redbook* p100 O 2017

Ayurvedic HERB GUIDE V. Tweed color *Better Nutrition* p34 My 2017

Ayurvedic TRANSFORMATION [Cover story] T. EICHENSEHER color *Yoga Journal* no287 p52 N 2016

EXERCISE C. DOW *Nutrition Action Health Letter* v44 no3 p9 Ap 2017

A Family Affair *Atlanta* v56 no9 p140 Ja 2017

Feel-Good Foods L. TURNER color *Better Nutrition* v79 no1 p58 Ja 2017

ghee WIZ M. RABBITT color *Yoga Journal* no287 p63 N 2016

GO NATURAL IN 90 days V. Tweed color *Better Nutrition* v79 no6 p32 Je 2017

healthy & hearty L. TURNER color *Better Nutrition* v78 no11 p68 N 2016

How do you fold seva, or self less service, into everyday life? color *Yoga Journal* no295 p14 O 2017

Jessamyn Stanley Y. MOROZ ALPERT color *Yoga Journal* no287 p78 N 2016

Meet the Wellness Programs That Save Companies Money J. Purcell *Harvard Business Review Digital Articles* p2 Ap 20 2016

Meet your next teacher: Aadil Palkhivala [Cover story] color *Yoga Journal* no293 p90 Ag 2017

NEWSBITES [Cover story] *Tufts University Health & Nutrition Letter* v35 no5 p1 Jl 2017

NOTE FROM THE COORDINATORS. VEGAN TAKES VOWS D. Wasserman and C. Stahler *Vegetarian Journal* v35 no4 p4 2016

On the A-List J. Bowden and V. TWEED color *Better Nutrition* p16 My 2017

Power up your diet with plant-based meals *Harvard Health Letter* v42 no6 p6 Ap 2017

SLIM DOWN IN 2017 L. TURNER color *Better Nutrition* v79 no1 p36 Ja 2017

Summer Slim Down L. TURNER color *Better Nutrition* p54 My 2017

There's No Place Like Home M. L. Tellado *Consumer Reports* v82 no3 p5 Mr 2017

Transform Yourself N. BRECHKA color *Better Nutrition* v79 no7 p62 Jl 2017

trend WATCH V. TWEED color *Better Nutrition* v78 no11 p14 N 2016

Health promotion—Evaluation

ADJUST YOUR ATTITUDE AND LOSE BIG color *Health* v31 no1 p14 Ja 2017

THE BEAN SCENE L. MOYER and B. LIEBMAN *Nutrition Action Health Letter* v43 no10 p13 D 2016

My Shape-Up Secret? The Buddy System! L. Murray color *Health*

v31 no1 p46 Ja 2017

Restaurant Frauds & Finds L. MOYER and B. LIEBMAN *Nutrition Action Health Letter* v44 no1 p13 Ja/F 2017

Health resorts

CHOOSE YOUR Cruise P. BRADY bw color *Conde Nast Traveler* v52 no1 p72 Ja 2017

A Facial Worth the Flight E. FLORIO color map *Conde Nast Traveler* v52 no8 p50 S 2017

Get Your Vita-Fix P. E. Christiani color *Essence* v47 no7 p36 N 2016

SANTA BARBARA R. MISNER color *Conde Nast Traveler* v52 no5 p32 My 2017

THE URBANIST: MY SUPER CLASSY SPA DAY R. O'CONNOR color *Chicago* v66 no9 p44 S 2017

Health resorts—California

GETTING THE GLAMOURPUSSES BACK M. Callahan bw color *Bloomberg Businessweek* no4521 p64 My 8 2017

Palm Springs color *Los Angeles Magazine* v62 no10 p147 O 2017

Health resorts—Evaluation

BEST BETS img *New York* p54 Ja 9 2017

BEST OF WASHINGTON HALL OF FAME *Washingtonian Magazine* v52 no2 p302 N 2016

An Expert Opinion on Where to Recharge This Season bw chart *Conde Nast Traveler* v52 no1 p112 Ja 2017

Green Hotels and Inns K. K. BECKIUS color *Yankee* p74 Mr 2017

JET — SET SPAE SCAPES S. GRINNELL color map *Vanity Fair* v58 no12 p81 D 2016

SPA *Indianapolis Monthly* v40 no7 p84 Mr 2017

Start with a Clean Slate A. SESSA color *Conde Nast Traveler* v52 no1 p22 Ja 2017

Tighten Up F. VALDESOLO color *Vogue* v207 no4 p172 Ap 2017

Zen Palace A. Jones img *New York* p46 Ja 9 2017

Health resorts—Spain

Start with a Clean Slate A. SESSA color *Conde Nast Traveler* v52 no1 p22 Ja 2017

Health risk assessment

See also

Medical screening

HOG HELL A. SKOLNICK and L. BARRETT *Sierra* v102 no2 p28 Mr/Ap 2017

Health service areas

THE FOUR-DAY REBOOT I. Edwards and K. Lovato color *Sunset* v238 no2 p15 F 2017

Health services accessibility—History

Access to quality health care has improved in most places A. Cunningham map *Science News* v191 no12 p5 Je 24 2017

Health services administration

See also

Hospital administration

Value-based purchasing (Medical care)

Giving Patients an Active Role in Their Health Care L. Schlesinger and J. Fox *Harvard Business Review Digital Articles* p2 N 21 2016

WAITING ON HEALTH REFORM M. Rozier il *America* v216 no13 p26 Je 12 2017

When a Health Department Fails: Is a growing focus on community factors coming at the expense of basic care? M. Quinn color *Governing* v30 no11 p18 Ag 2017

Health services administration—Study & teaching

Bridging Health Care's Innovation-Education Gap R. Herzlinger, V. K. Ramaswamy et al *Harvard Business Review Digital Articles* p2 N 11 2014

Health services administrators—Training of

The impact of training informal health care providers in India: A randomized controlled trial J. Das, A. Chowdhury et al chart diag *Science* v354 no6308 paaf7384-1 O 7 2016

Health surveys—United States

Vets Endure Higher Severity than Nonvets *USA Today Magazine* v145 no2861 p9 F 2017

Health systems agencies

The Critical Skills for Leading Major Change in America's Health System D. Blumenthal *Harvard Business Review Digital Articles* p2 O 3 2017

How U.S. Hospitals and Health Systems Can Reverse Their Sliding Financial Performance J. Goldsmith *Harvard Business Review Digital Articles* p2 O 5 2017

The Value of Teaching Patients to Administer Their Own Care A. H. Anderson, L. A. Martin et al color *Harvard Business Review Digital Articles* p1 Je 2 2017

What Health Systems, Hospitals, and Physicians Need to Know About Implementing Electronic Health Records R. M. Pearl *Harvard Business Review Digital Articles* p2 Je 15 2017

Health—Computer network resources

Running with Apps M. ANTONOFF color *Sound & Vision* v82 no1 p24 Ja 2017

Health—Congresses

Fortune Brainstorm HEALTH C. Leaf and D. B. Agus color *Fortune* v175 no7 p20 Je 1 2017

Health—Equipment & supplies

GOOD-FOR-YOU gifts cartoon color *Amazing Wellness* v8 no6 p68 Early Winter2016

Why Fitness Trackers Aren't Making Us Healthier M. Oaklander color *Time* v188 no18 p19 O 31 2016

Health—Evaluation

surviving dr. facebook J. MIGALA *Parents* v92 no2 p36 F 2017

Health facility-based child care

When Parents and Doctors Disagree on What Futile Means A. Park color *Time* v190 no4 p17 Jl 24 2017

Health—Management

5 secrets for a good, long life color *Redbook* p80 Jl/Ag 2017

Personal Best M. Singer color *Vogue* v207 no11 p160 N 2017

Research. Parks and Recreation: Meeting Community Fitness Needs at All Levels K. Roth *Parks & Recreation* v52 no6 p12 Je 2017

Taking Health Into Your Own Hands D. B. Agus *AARP: The Magazine* v59 no1A p24 D 2015/Ja 2016

Health—News briefs

AMAZING NEWS V. Tweed color *Amazing Wellness* v9 no6 p14 EarlyWint 2017

Listening to ELVIS CURES Foot Fungus [Cover story] color *Women's Health* v14 no3 p70 Ap 2017

World of Medicine S. RIDEOUT *Reader's Digest* v188 no1125 p81 N 2016

Health—Psychological aspects

Let joy in [Cover story] R. Miller *Yoga Journal* no289 p22 F 2017

Health—Research

8 SERVINGS OF FRUITS AND VEGETABLES *Better Homes & Gardens* v95 no1 p115 Ja 2017

Health self-care

See also

Medical self-examination

6 Ways to Weave Self-Care into Your Workday A. J. Su *Harvard Business Review Digital Articles* p2 Je 19 2017

DO EVERYONE A FAVOUR CALL IN SICK R. Druzin color *Maclean's* v129 no40 p67 O 10 2016

"I just don't have any qualms about looking different" M. Mire and Ying Chu cartoon color *Glamour* v115 no2 p60 F 2017

It's Time to Be Good to Yourself C. Mchugh color *Health* v30 no10 p6 D 2016

Pampering with Purpose H. Dowdle color *Yoga Journal* p100 2017 Special Issue

Relax & Refresh L. KAY *Dance Magazine* v91 no8 p40 Ag 2017

REVIVE YOUR Soul V. Burton color *Essence* v47 no9 p72 Ja 2017

SelfCare and the Disappearance of the Adult *Commentary* v142 no2 p1 S 2016

take OM HOME A. Tust color *Yoga Journal* no287 p88 N 2016

TAKE YOUR SEAT ON THE THRONE L. Thomas color *Essence* v48 no6 p126 O 2017

Health self-care—Equipment & supplies

"Fall" in Love color *Better Nutrition* v79 no9 p20 S 2017

GO NATURAL IN 90 days color *Better Nutrition* v79 no7 p35 Jl 2017

Stronger, Shinier, Silkier! S. BREAKEY color *Parents* v92 no11 p75 N 2017

When Your Kid Is Sick and You're Tired A. MENCEL color *Parents* v92 no8 p28 Ag 2017

HEALY, CHRISTOPHER

In the Face of Danger: An overheating planet, a toxic spill, anthropod aliens—kids in these graphic novels bravely handle a panoply of threats *New York Times Book Review* p24 My 14 2017

Healy, Colm

When Tough Performance Goals Lead to Cheating *Harvard Business Review Digital Articles* p2 S 8 2016

Healy, David

Listening to Patients color *Issues in Science & Technology* v33 no2 p92 Wint 2017

Healy, Gene

AMERICANS SHOULD IMPEACH PRESIDENTS MORE OFTEN bw *Reason* v49 no4 p28 Ag/S 2017

Are We Any Safer? color *Atlantic* v318 no4 p14 N 2016

Goodbye, Obama color *Reason* v48 no9 p18 F 2017

HEALY, PAUL

Case Study: How Much Should a New CEO Shake Things Up? color il *Harvard Business Review* v95 no1 p157 Ja/F 2017

Healy, Paul M.

Case Study: How Much Should a New CEO Shake Things Up? *Harvard Business Review Digital Articles* p2 O 26 2016

Healy, Sarah

The Sisters Chase *Publishers Weekly* v264 no13 p76 Mr 27 2017

HEALY, TIM

ENERGY STRATEGY FOR THE C-SUITE color graph img *Harvard Business Review* v95 no1 p138 Ja/F 2017

Healy-Rae, Michael

BUSHWHACKERS color *Harper's Magazine* v335 no2005 p18 Je 2017

HEANEY, PAUL

DRIVERLESS DELAY *Scientific American* v315 no3 p6 S 2016

HEANEY, PETER J.

Animal, Vegetable, or Mineral? *Natural History* v125 no2 p32 F 2017

Heaney, Seamus, 1939-2013

Report from the Afterlife C. McNamara color *Commonweal* v144 no1 p32 Ja 6 2017

Heap, Imogen

Blockchain Could Help Musicians Make Money Again color *Harvard Business Review Digital Articles* p2 Je 5 2017

HEAP, SUSANN

Cherri Pitts: A Rose Amongst San Antonio's STARs *Humanist* v77 no5 p28 S/O 2017

Heaphy, Emily

We Learn More When We Learn Together *Harvard Business Review Digital Articles* p2 Ja 12 2016

HEARD, DARRYL

Anesthesia and Euthanasia of Amphibians and Reptiles Used in Scientific Research: Should Hypothermia and Freezing Be Prohibited? *BioScience* v67 no1 p53 Ja 2017

Heard, John, 1946-2017

John Heard J. McGovern color *Entertainment Weekly* no1476 p49 Ag 4 2017

Milestones *Time* v190 no6 p17 Ag 7 2017

Heard, M. S.

Country-specific effects of neonicotinoid pesticides on honey bees and wild bees diag map *Science* v356 no6345 p1393 Je 30 2017

Hearing

Jumping spider hears distant sounds S. MILIUS color *Science News* v190 no10 p9 N 12 2016

making sense T. REECE *Parents* v91 no9 p165 S 2016

PARDON? D. OWEN cartoon color *New Yorker* v93 no7 p38 Ap 3 2017

Hearing aids

See also

Cochlear implants

Cochlear implants and electronic hearing M. Svirsky *Physics Today* v70 no8 p52 Ag 2017

Dr. Weil [Cover story] A. Weil cartoon color *Prevention* p24 Mr 2017

Now Hear This K. PITSKER cartoon *Kiplinger's Personal Finance* v71 no10 p70 O 2017

PSST...WANNA TRY A PSAP? [Cover story] *Nutrition Action Health Letter* v43 no10 p4 D 2016

Hearing aids—Evaluation

No More Suffering in Silence? J. Calderone color graph il *Consumer Reports* v82 no3 p15 Mr 2017

Hearing clinics

Free Hearing Test color *AARP: The Magazine* v59 no3A p90 Ap/My 2016

Hearing disorders

Free Hearing Test color *AARP: The Magazine* v59 no3A p90 Ap/My 2016

Hearing impaired

SAY WHAT? J. L. Stein cartoon *Cycle World* v55 no11 p16 D 2016

Hearing protection

Earplugs R. Berendsohn color *Popular Mechanics* v193 no7 p35 S 2016

Hearing Loss Prevalence Declining in U.S *USA Today Magazine* v145 no2861 p3 F 2017

Hearing protection—Charts, diagrams, etc.

Sounds Like Trouble M. Fischetti diag graph *Scientific American* v316 no6 p78 Je 2017

Hearlson, Adam

Comic book truth color *Christian Century* v134 no2 p43 Ja 18 2017

Facing the opioid crisis [Cover story] color *Christian Century* v133 no23 p22 N 9 2016

Minister as detective color *Christian Century* v134 no19 p20 S 13 2017

The next monster color *Christian Century* v133 no22 p43 O 26 2016

Vulgar prophecies *Christian Century* v134 no6 p44 Mr 15 2017

Hearlson, Christiane Lang

A tough age for girls color *Christian Century* v133 no22 p32 O 26 2016

Hearn, Alex

What role could nuclear power play in limiting climate change? bibl *Bulletin of the Atomic Scientists* v73 no1 p2 Ja 2017

Hearn, Hank

Peekaboo cartoon color *National Wildlife (World Edition)* v55 no3 p50 Ap/My 2017

HEARN, JOHN

OPIATE OF THE MASSES *Humanist* v77 no1 p22 Ja/F 2017

Hearst, Denise

2017 Egyptian Event *Arabian Horse World* v57 no11 p26 Ag 2017

Bahrain host of the 2017 WAHO CONFERENCE [Cover story] *Arabian Horse World* v56 no12 p1 S 2016

Beating the Odds color *Arabian Horse World* v57 no7 p111 Ap 2017

A Breeder's Thoughts on Fanaticaa—Raymond Mazzei Speaks *Arabian Horse World* v57 no8 p10 My 2017

Cheers to a New Year *Arabian Horse World* v57 no4 p10 Ja 2017

A CONVERSATION WITH BOB AND DIXIE NORTH *Arabian Horse World* v57 no9 p13 Je 2017

A CONVRSATION with Thomas Fourcy Al Shaqab Racing-Ecurie Haras Bouquetot Sas *Arabian Horse World* v57 no6 p56 Mr 2017

RACING YEARBOOK *Arabian Horse World* v57 no6 p6 Mr 2017

Sold! To the Lady in Front! color *Arabian Horse World* v57 no7 p10 Ap 2017

WADEE AL SHAQAB *Arabian Horse World* v57 no9 p1 Je 2017

WADEE AL SHAQAB: A VICTORY BY THE SEA [Cover story] *Arabian Horse World* v57 no11 p97 Ag 2017

Hearst, Michael

Curious Constructions: A Peculiar Portfolio of Fifty Fascinating Structures color *Publishers Weekly* v264 no12 p72 Mr 20 2017

Hearst Communications, Inc.

Less Is More K. RENDA color *House Beautiful* v159 no4 p28 My 2017

Heart

7 heart-pumping facts E. WHITMER *National Geographic Kids* no467 p10 F 2017

Hearts and MINDS M. OZ color *O, The Oprah Magazine* p78 Je 2017

Hearts & Minds B. Gifford cartoon color *Men's Health* v32 no3 p112 Ap 2017

Heart beat

5 Signs You're Working Out Too Much A. Schlinger color *Health* v30 no9 p65 N 2016

GET FIT WITH FIDO color *Good Housekeeping* v265 no1 p94 Jl 2017

Off-Key but In Sync A. Gurwitch cartoon *Prevention* v69 no1 p34 Ja 2017

POP QUIZ C. Barakat and M. Freckleton cartoon *Equus* no472

heart M. N. Groves *Mother Earth News* no284 p14 O/N 2017

Hearths

FOREST TO TABLE J. KRAMER bw color *Bon Appetit* v62 no6 p98 Je 2017

Hearths—Design & construction

Hearth of the Matter color *Cabin Living* p51 D 2016

Heartney, Eleanor

Multiple Originals cartoon color *Art in America* v104 no11 p63 D 2016

"PERPETUAL REVOLUTION: THE IMAGE AND SOCIAL CHANGE" color *Art in America* v105 no4 p114 Ap 2017

Varieties of Faith color *Art in America* v105 no4 p47 Ap 2017

Heart Part Four, The (Music)

The Playlist color *Rolling Stone* no1285 p8 Ap 20 2017

Hearts & Stars (Music)

HAND JIVE A. BURGER *Missouri Life* v43 no7 p25 D 2016/ Ja 2017

Heart Wants What It Wants, The (Music)

On Her Own Terms [Cover story] R. Haskell color *Vogue* v207 no4 p194 Ap 2017

Heartworms (Music)

Indie Rock May Be Dislocated, but It's Far from Dead M. Johnston color *Time* v189 no11 p63 Mr 27 2017

The Shins' New Adventures in Alt-Pop Romance J. DOLAN color *Rolling Stone* no1283 p50 Mr 23 2017

Heat

See also

Temperature

BEAT THE HEAT *Health* v31 no5 p14 Je 2017

Snacks for Your Summer Travels M. DIANE SMITH color *Better Nutrition* v79 no6 p58 Je 2017

TAKE OM HOME T. Eichenseher color *Yoga Journal* no294 p96 S 2017

Warming Waters color *Earth Island Journal* v32 no2 p6 Summ 2017

YOU SHOULD KNOW color *Bicycling* v58 no6 p96 Jl 2017

Heat (Film)

HEAT J. Krebs color *Sound & Vision* v82 no8 p71 O 2017

The Must List color *Entertainment Weekly* no1465 p1 My 12 2017

RE-PACKING HEAT D. Franich color *Entertainment Weekly* no1466 p42 My 19 2017

Heat adaptation

BEAT the HEAT A. SHAFFER color *Better Homes & Gardens* v95 no7 p161 Jl 2017

Heat exhaustion—Prevention

THE HEAT IS ON K. CASTEEL color *Missouri Life* v44 no5 p80 Ag 2017

Heat pipes

Wickless heat pipes in microgravity J. L. Plawsky and Thao Nguyen *Physics Today* v70 no9 p82 S 2017

Heat radiation & absorption

Microbes quick to occupy impact site T. SUMNER *Science News* v191 no1 p15 Ja 21 2017

our swiftly dimming planet K. Pierre-Louis color *Popular Science* v289 no4 p23 Jl/Ag 2017

RISING HEAT CONTENT OF EARTH'S OCEANS *Physics Today* v70 no5 p23 My 2017

Heat stroke—Diagnosis

Beat the Heat *Cincinnati Magazine* v50 no10 p73 Jl 2017

Heat stroke—Prevention

Beat the Heat *Cincinnati Magazine* v50 no10 p73 Jl 2017

Heat transfer

Probing the limits of heat flow D. Segal bibl diag *Science* v355 no6330 p1125 Mr 17 2017

Surprising states of order for linear diblock copolymers G. E. Stein diag *Science* v356 no6337 p487 My 5 2017

Through the Looking-Glass of the Ocean Surface A. Bogdanoff color *Oceanus* v51 no2 p106 Wint 2016

Heat waves (Meteorology)

HEAT W. LANGEWIESCHE color *Vanity Fair* v59 no8 p102 Ag 2017

Reporting on global warming: A study in headlines P. T. Brown *Physics Today* v69 no10 p10 O 2016

HEATH, ALOÏSE BUCKLEY

A Christmas Carol color *National Review* v68 no24 p30 D 31 2016

Heath, Becky

Worth the Wait M. Darrisaw color *Southern Living* v52 no10 p44 O 2017

Heath, Chris

THE EXTRAORDINARY ORDINARY LIFE OF THE ARTIST FORMERLY KNOWN AS PRINCE bw color *GQ: Gentlemen's Quarterly* v86 no12 p220 D 2016

THE GOOD SEED bw color *GQ: Gentlemen's Quarterly* v97 no5 p124 My 2017

LEADING MAN bw color *GQ: Gentlemen's Quarterly* v87 no1 p40 Ja 2017

Heath, Kathryn

4 Strategies for Women Navigating Office Politics *Harvard Business Review Digital Articles* p2 Ja 14 2015

How Women Can Show Passion at Work Without Seeming "Emotional" *Harvard Business Review Digital Articles* p2 S 30 2015

Heath, Lorraine

The Viscount and the Vixen *Publishers Weekly* v263 no41 p62 O 10 2016

Heath, M. R.

Observation of coherent elastic neutrino-nucleus scattering diag *Science* v357 no6356 p1123 S 15 2017

Heath, Michael

The Price of Australia's Complacency color *Bloomberg Businessweek* no4541 p33 O 9 2017

Heathcote, Bella, 1988-

STYLE CRUSH Bella Heathcote S. Simon color *InStyle* v24 no5 p96 My 2017

Heathcott, Steve

FOR THE HORSE In the stable C. REICH *Arabian Horse World* v56 no12 p82 S 2016

Heatherwick, Thomas

Design Unveiled for Heatherwick's Vessel at Hudson Yards M. SITZ *Architectural Record* v204 no10 p24 O 2016

GOINGS ON ABOUT TOWN color *New Yorker* v93 no22 p6 Jl 31 2017

A TICKET TO RISE P. GOLDBERGER color *Vanity Fair* v58 no12 p152 D 2016

Two Major Heatherwick Projects Nixed A. KLIMOSKI *Architectural Record* v205 no6 p26 Je 2017

The Willy Wonka of Hudson Yards C. Swanson and I. Klink img *New York* v49 no19 p79 S 19 2016

Heating

See also

Fireplaces

How to Sear a Steak C. PALMER color *Esquire* p141 BigBlackBook

Heating & ventilation industry equipment—Evaluation

Internal Affairs K. L. Beamon *Architectural Record* v205 no10 p61 O 2017

Heating equipment—Evaluation

BOIL BARONS S. Chodosh color *Popular Science* v289 no5 p28 S/O 2017

Heating—Control—Equipment & supplies

Air Supply J. Taraska *Architectural Record* v204 no10 p63 O 2016

Heating—Equipment & supplies

Hot-Water Bottles C. Tattoli *New York Times Magazine* p20 Ja 22 2017

Heating—Equipment & supplies—Evaluation

Air Supply J. Taraska *Architectural Record* v204 no10 p63 O 2016

Get Fired Up color *Log Home Living* v34 no3 p36 Ap 2017

Heat-Moon, William Least

INNER HIGHWAYS E. WOOD color *Missouri Life* v44 no2 p20 Ap 2017

Least Heat-Moon Makes His Fiction Debut with Three Rooms J. Maher color *Publishers Weekly* v264 no15 p12 Ap 10 2017

Heaton, Laura

The WATSON FILES bw color *Foreign Policy* no224 p46 My/ Je 2017

Heaton, T. H.

The hidden simplicity of subduction megathrust earthquakes graph *Science* v357 no6357 p1277 S 22 2017

Heat—Physiological effect

COMBAT HEAT STRESS WITH A QUICK RUN AROUND WITH THE PIVOT D. Mowitz *Successful Farming* v115 no1 p58 Ja 2017

HEATWOLE, HAROLD

Glenn Beck's Regrets color *Rolling Stone* no1273 p44 N 3 2016

THE LAST HAIR METAL BAND color *Rolling Stone* no1288 p44 Je 1 2017

The Peculiar Mr. Herzog color *Rolling Stone* no1284 p46 Ap 6 2017

Heder, Thyra

Alfie (The Turtle That Disappeared) *Publishers Weekly* v264 no32 p69 Ag 7 2017

Hederman, Rea

Robert B. Silvers (1929–2017) [Cover story] bw color *New York Review of Books* v64 no8 p31 My 11 2017

Hedge funds

Hedge Fund Resurrection N. VARDI color *Forbes* v198 no8 p58 D 20 2016

Tomorrow: David Wallace-Wells img *New York* v49 no19 p20 S 19 2016

Hedge funds—Corrupt practices

Red Flags Abounded On Platinum Partners Z. Faux *Bloomberg Businessweek* no4506 p31 Ja 9 2017

Hedge funds—Economic aspects

Greenwich Lean Time S. KISHAN cartoon graph *Bloomberg Businessweek* no4496 p48 O 24 2016

Hedge funds—Officials & employees

MARTIN SHKRELI IS STILL TALKING S. Kolhatkar cartoon *New Yorker* v93 no9 p23 Ap 17 2017

Hedgehogs

Weird but true! M. HARRIS and J. BEER color *National Geographic Kids* no465 p4 N 2016

Hedges, Chris

SEEN & HEARD *Humanist* v77 no5 p7 S/O 2017

Hedges, Hazelle

String Beings M. W. SCHWARTZ *Missouri Life* v43 no7 p58 D 2016/Ja 2017

Hedges, Kristi

5 Questions to Help Your Employees Find Their Inner Purpose *Harvard Business Review Digital Articles* p2 2017

How to Rediscover Your Inspiration at Work *Harvard Business Review Digital Articles* p1 S 5 2017

New Managers Shouldn't Be Afraid to Express Their Emotions *Harvard Business Review Digital Articles* p2 Je 1 2017

Hedges, Lucas

A Boy's LIFE N. HELLER color *Vogue* v206 no12 p204 D 2016

Lucas HEDGES M. MARTIN *Interview* v46 no10 p30 D 2016/ Ja 2017

PARTY LINES img *New York* v50 no8 p138 Ap 17 2017

Hedges, S.

Observation of coherent elastic neutrino-nucleus scattering diag *Science* v357 no6356 p1123 S 15 2017

HEDGES, SIMON

Conserving the World's Megafauna and Biodiversity: The Fierce Urgency of Now *BioScience* v67 no3 p197 Mr 2017

Saving the World's Terrestrial Megafauna color *BioScience* v66 no10 p807 O 1 2016

HÉDL, RADIM

Combining Biodiversity Resurveys across Regions to Advance Global Change Research *BioScience* v67 no1 p73 Ja 2017

Hedleigh, Boze—Interviews

HOLLYWOOD LESBIANS ARE SLOWLY COMING OUT: Boze Hedleigh opened the closet to some of Hollywood's most famous lesbians. 23 years later, he's doing it again D. ANDERSON-MINSHALL color *Advocate* no1091 p37 Je/Jl 2017

Hedman, Britt

Metalloprotein entatic control of ligand-metal bonds quantified by ultrafast x-ray spectroscopy diag *Science* v356 no6344 p1276 Je 23 2017

Hedren, Tippi, 1930-

A HITCHCOCK FANTASY P. MONAHAN color *Vanity Fair* v58 no12 p146 D 2016

Hedrick, Catherine C.

Hematopoietic stem cells gone rogue bibl color diag *Science* v355 no6327 p798 F 24 2017

HEDRICK, LAUREN

1939 PET GEAR color *Better Homes & Gardens* v95 no8 p184 Ag 2017

1968 ORANGE color *Better Homes & Gardens* v95 no3 p156 Mr 2017

1972 KITCHEN COLOR color *Better Homes & Gardens* v95 no4 p160 Ap 2017

1975 PLAID color *Better Homes & Gardens* v95 no11 p156 N 2017

3-D PILLOWS color *Better Homes & Gardens* v95 no10 p76 O 2017

BH&G throwback 1961 MIDCENTURY MODERN color *Better Homes & Gardens* v95 no10 p186 O 2017

BHG throwback 1976 VELVET *Better Homes & Gardens* v95 no1 p124 Ja 2017

christiane LEMIEUX *Better Homes & Gardens* v95 no1 p54 Ja 2017

GREAT HEIGHTS *Better Homes & Gardens* v94 no12 p141 D 2016

MAKING THE CUT color *Better Homes & Gardens* v95 no11 p56 N 2017

PAPER POSIES color *Better Homes & Gardens* v95 no5 p39 My 2017

POT LUCK color *Better Homes & Gardens* v95 no4 p46 Ap 2017

second nature color *Better Homes & Gardens* v95 no9 p54 S 2017

to dye for *Better Homes & Gardens* v94 no11 p16 N 2016

Hedricks, Cynthia A.

The 20 Most Common Things That Come Up During Reference Checks *Harvard Business Review Digital Articles* p2 Ag 4 2016

References Should Come from a Candidate's Coworkers, Not Just Their Boss *Harvard Business Review Digital Articles* p2 2017

HEDSTROM, MATTHEW

SCIENTIFIC SPIRITUALITY cartoon *Tricycle: The Buddhist Review* v26 no3 p56 Spr 2017

Hedychium coronarium

AROUND THE GARDEN S. Bender color *Southern Living* v52 no9 p34 S 2017

Hee-Sung Park

A chemical biology route to site-specific authentic protein modifications bibl diag graph *Science* v354 no6312 p623 N 4 2016

Hee-Yoon Lee

A chemical biology route to site-specific authentic protein modifications bibl diag graph *Science* v354 no6312 p623 N 4 2016

Heed, Dan

WHERE THE BUS IS THE NEW TRAIN *Washingtonian Magazine* v52 no1 p55 O 2016

Heeg, K. P.

Spectral narrowing of x-ray pulses for precision spectroscopy with nuclear resonances diag *Science* v357 no6349 p375 Jl 28 2017

Heemskerk, Eelke

How Corporate Boards Connect, in Charts *Harvard Business Review Digital Articles* p2 Ap 21 2016

Heen, Sheila

Responding to Feedback You Disagree With *Harvard Business Review Digital Articles* p2 Ap 14 2017

HEER, JEET

#Always Trump color *New Republic* v248 no10 p28 O 2017

Horrible Histories [Cover story] color *New Republic* v248 no4 p52 Ap 2017

Killer Reboot il *New Republic* v247 no12 p67 D 2016

THE PATH OF MOST RESISTANCE diag il *New Republic* v248 no6 p22 Je 2017

SIBLING RIVALRY bw color il *New Republic* v248 no11 p26 N 2017

Worst-Case Trump il *New Republic* v247 no11 p14 N 2016

Hees, Bernardo

The Hatchet Men And the Hot Dog B. Gruley, C. Giammona et al color diag *Bloomberg Businessweek* no4533 p50 Ag 7 2017

Heffernan, Andrew

6 Rules of Recovery color *Men's Health* v32 no5 p54 Je 2017

THE LAB OF LEAN bw *Men's Health* v32 no7 p100 S 2017

One Wild Workout color *Men's Health* v32 no7 p48 S 2017

STRONG FOR LIFE color diag *Men's Health* v31 no10 p98 D 2016

Heffernan, Lisa

5 Gifts Your Grad Will Actually Use color *Money* v46 no5 p21 Je 2017

Heffernan, Margaret—Interviews

THERE ARE LOTS OF MIKE ASHLEYS OUT THERE R. JEFFERY *People Management* p46 O 2016

Heffernan, Virginia

Art for App's Sake D. GREEN *Commentary* v142 no1 p61 Jl/Ag 2016

ESCAPE THE MATRIX: THE INTERNET IS THE UNCANNIEST VALLEY. DON'T GET TRAPPED THERE *Wired* v25 no9 p92 S 2017

FULL-FRONTAL ASSAULT cartoon color *Wired* v25 no4 p68 Ap 2017

The Power of Play *New York Times Book Review* p12 N 27 2016

What We Believe M. Halpin color *Glamour* v114 no12 p195 D 2016

Heffernan, William

The Scientology Murders: A Dead Detective Novel *Publishers Weekly* v264 no6 p48 F 6 2017

Heffington, Ryan

Be Fearless J. Stahl *Dance Magazine* v91 no10 p10 O 2017

THE HOLLYWOOD HEALER: Choreographer Ryan Heffington has emerged as the most unlikely in-demand dancemaker working in the commercial world today B. SCHAEFER *Dance Magazine* v91 no10 p26 O 2017

Heflebower, Tammy

Get it right the first time! chart color *Phi Delta Kappan* v98 no6 p58 Mr 2017

Hefling, Charles

WRITERS' FEAST color *Christian Century* v134 no10 p30 My 10 2017

Hefner, Christie, 1952-

CHRISTIE HEFNER B. Zehme cartoon *Chicago* v66 no2 p160 F 2017

Hefner, Hugh, 1926-2017

HEF AS CHANGE AGENT T. WALDEN color *Chicago* v66 no4 p44 Ap 2017

Hugh Hefner L. Rothman color *Time* v190 no15 p13 O 16 2017

The Male-Gazer in Chief K. Pollitt *Nation* v305 no10 p6 O 23 2017

Milestones *Time* v190 no15 p13 O 16 2017

Hefner, Philip

The Market as God *Christian Century* v134 no15 p41 Jl 19 2017

Heft, James

It is time to get past the snobbery against pastoral theologians *America* v217 no2 p10 Jl 24 2017

Hefzy, Hebah

Show Up. Be You color *Glamour* v115 no5 p18 My 2017

Hegar, Glenn

THE ACCOUNTANT *Texas Monthly* v45 no2 p90 F 2017

Hegarty, Antony, 1971-

Anohni *Art in America* v104 no9 p37 O 2016

Hegde, Ramanujan S.

Mechanistic basis for a molecular triage reaction bibl color graph *Science* v355 no6322 p298 Ja 20 2017

UBE2O is a quality control factor for orphans of multiprotein complexes diag *Science* v357 no6350 p472 Ag 4 2017

Hegemann, Peter

Active cortical dendrites modulate perception bibl graph *Science* v354 no6319 p1587 D 23 2016

The form and function of channelrhodopsin diag *Science* v357 no6356 p1111 S 15 2017

Hegemony

IT PAYS TO INCREASE YOUR Word Power E. COX and H. RATHVON *Reader's Digest* v190 no1133 p137 S 2017

Heger, Rachael—Interviews

Rachael Heger Do-gooder M. RUBINO *Indianapolis Monthly* v40 no4 p60 D 2016

HEGGE, FRED

Understanding the Victors *American Scholar* v86 no2 p3 Spr 2017

Heggestad, Susan

AGING GRACEFULLY on the Homestead *Mother Earth News* no280 p34 F/Mr 2017

Heguy, Adriana

Synthesis, debugging, and effects of synthetic chromosome consolidation: synVI and beyond color *Science* v355 no6329 p1045 Mr 10 2017

Heid, Markham

Find Your Best Burn color *Time* v190 no4 p45 Jl 24 2017

Inside the New Standards for Kids and Screen Time color *Time* v188 no19 p15 N 7 2016

New Ways to Become Happier—and Healthier color *Time* v190

no13 p30 O 2 2017

Should You Finally Get It Fixed? color *Men's Health* v31 no10 p114 D 2016

STRONGER EVERYTHING! cartoon color *Men's Health* v32 no4 p102 My 2017

THE TRIUMPHANT RETURN OF RED MEAT color *Men's Health* v32 no2 p88 Mr 2017

Heidari-Robinson, Stephen

A 5-Step Process for Reorganizing After a Merger *Harvard Business Review Digital Articles* p2 D 21 2016

Getting Reorgs Right diag *Harvard Business Review* v94 no11 p84 N 2016

Making Government Reorgs Work color *Harvard Business Review Digital Articles* p2 Mr 30 2017

Reorg: How to Get it Right *People Management* p51 D 2016/Ja 2017

Heide, David

Winning Windows P. POORE color *Old House Journal* v45 no4 p63 Je 2017

Heidegger, Martin, 1889-1976

1954: Freiburg M. Heidegger *Lapham's Quarterly* v10 no1 p28 Wint 2017

Designed to Unsettle R. L. Kehoe Iii *Commonweal* v143 no19 p36 D 2 2016

EDISONIAN DEMOCRACY A. Valiunas *Claremont Review of Books* v17 no1 p89 Wint 2016/2017

Heidelberger, Kathryn Bradford

Racism in Port William *Christian Century* v134 no18 p36 Ag 30 2017

Heidenhof, Friederike

The Stretch color *Dressage Today* v23 no4 p30 D 2016

HEIDINGER, LISA SCHNEBLY

A WOMAN BY THE NAME OF Sedona *Arizona Highways* v93 no11 p48 N 2017

Heidinger, Sandra

Who I am *People Management* p55 N 2016

Heidle, Eric

You Never Forget Your First Time diag il *Backpacker* v45 no2 p64 Mr 2017

Heidrich, Grant

SAND HILL ROAD: AN ORAL HISTORY color *Wired* v25 no9 p24 S 2017

Heidt, Jim

UPSTATE NEW YORK IN 1948 color map *Model Railroader* v84 no2 p46 F 2017

Heifer International (Organization)

UZO ADUBA PAYS IT FORWARD M. L. Lenker color *Entertainment Weekly* no1472 p15 Je 30 2017

Heifers

Jennifer MacNeill bw *National Geographic* v232 no4 p6 O 2017

Heifers—Reproduction

A Farmer's Best Friend B. Hewitt and M. FLEMING color *Yankee* p104 Mr 2017

Heifetz, Hank

Mexico in the Full Light of Day [Cover story] bw color *New York Review of Books* v64 no10 p48 Je 8 2017

Heifetz, Jane

How to Use Your LinkedIn Profile to Power a Career Transition *Harvard Business Review Digital Articles* p2 My 28 2015

Improve Your Résumé by Turning Bullet Points into Stories *Harvard Business Review Digital Articles* p2 My 4 2016

Writing Your Résumé When Your Job Title Doesn't Reflect Your Responsibilities *Harvard Business Review Digital Articles* p2 My 16 2017

Yes, Your Résumé Needs a Summary *Harvard Business Review Digital Articles* p2 Jl 28 2015

Height measurement

ALTiTUDE ADJUSTMENT LAST M. Steinberger *New York Times Magazine* p38 Ag 27 2017

HEIGHTON, STEVEN

An Occurrence on the Beach at Varosha cartoon *Walrus* p50 Ja\F 2017

Heigl, Katherine, 1978-

Beyond the LAW J. Halterman color *TV Guide* v65 no7 p32 F 13 2017

Heigl's Star Quality Comes Through In the Courtroom D.

D'Addario color *Time* v189 no7/8 p103 F 27 2017

KATHERINE HEIGL GUARDS DOGS (AND CATS) C. M. Smith color *Entertainment Weekly* no1462 p16 Ap 21 2017

Heijmans, Philip

Myanmar's Hotel Room Glut color *Bloomberg Businessweek* no4528 p29 Je 26 2017

Heikenwalder, Mathias

Immune receptor for pathogenic α-synuclein bibl diag *Science* v353 no6307 p1498 S 30 2016

HEIL, NICK

79 IS THE NEW 29 bw color *Men's Health* v32 no5 p126 Je 2017

DOOMED *Reader's Digest* v188 no1125 p128 N 2016

HEILBRON, J. L.

Universal Joint *New York Times Book Review* p22 Mr 12 2017

Heilbron, Johan

Johan Heilbron, French Sociology J. Conley *Society* v54 no1 p86 F 2017

Heilbrunn, Jacob

The Birth of the Imperial Presidency *Washington Monthly* p14 Ja/F 2017

Stalin, 1929-1941: Brutal and Brilliant *American Conservative* v16 no5 p54 S/O 2017

Heilbut, Anthony

THE NUMBER THAT NO MAN COULD NUMBER *Harper's Magazine* v334 no2001 p60 F 2017

Heil Honey, I'm Home! (TV program)

THE MOST CONTROVERSIAL TV SHOW EVER S. Li color *Entertainment Weekly* no1460/1461 p80 Ap 7-17 2017

Heilig, Julian Vasquez

The War over Education and Civil Rights *Progressive* v81 no10 p13 N 2016

Heilig, Julian Vasquez—Interviews

Charter schools don't serve black children well J. Richardson color *Phi Delta Kappan* v98 no5 p41 F 2017

Heiligman, Deborah

Vincent and Theo: The Van Gogh Brothers color *Publishers Weekly* v264 no5 p207 Ja 30 2017

Heilmann, Mary, 1940-

MARY HEILMANN G. Coxhead *Art in America* v104 no9 p161 O 2016

Heim, David

A cop's view from the street *Christian Century* v134 no6 p32 Mr 15 2017

Understanding rural resentment *Christian Century* v134 no16 p10 Ag 2 2017

When Muslims talk to Jews color *Christian Century* v134 no4 p41 F 15 2017

When pro-lifers were progressives color *Christian Century* v133 no23 p32 N 9 2016

HEIM, MORGAN

SANDBOX IN THE SKY *National Parks* v91 no2 p40 Spr 2017

Heimann, P.

Observation of a large-scale anisotropy in the arrival directions of cosmic rays above 8 × 1018 eV *Science* v357 no6357 p1266 S 22 2017

Heimans, Jeremy

TED's Shift from Old to New Power *Harvard Business Review Digital Articles* p2 D 1 2014

Heimbuch, Jaymi

Bane—or Blessing? color *National Wildlife (World Edition)* v55 no6 p36 O/N 2017

Heimburger, Don

Lucerne is 'Essence of Switzerland' color *Christianity Today* v61 no5 p7 Je 2017

SWITZERLAND color *Christianity Today* v61 no4 p24 My 2017

SWITZERLAND color *Christianity Today* v61 no7 p12 S 2017

Heimer, Andrea Joyce—Exhibitions

ANDREA JOYCE HEIMER A. Cohen cartoon *Art in America* v105 no4 p116 Ap 2017

Heimer, Matt

THE 2017 Fortune Crystal Ball color diag *Fortune* v174 no7 p11 D 1 2016

BASKETBALL SALARIES GET SOME AIR color diag *Fortune* v75 no1 p24 Ja 1 2017

CHANGE THE WORLD !!!! color diag map *Fortune* v176 no4 p74 S 15 2017

HOW TO TURN SECOND PLACE INTO A WIN *Fortune* v176 no2 p72 Ag 1 2017

KEEPING AN EYE ON THE ANIMALS color *Fortune* v75 no1 p40 Ja 1 2017

MAKING A MOTOWN MIRACLE [Cover story] color *Fortune* v176 no4 p94 S 15 2017

PLAY YOUR CARDS RIGHT color diag *Fortune* v174 no7 p30 D 1 2016

"RISK ON, RISK OFF" *Fortune* v175 no4 p19 Mr 15 2017

Stay Cool and Stay Invested [Cover story] color diag *Fortune* v174 no8 p84 D 15 2016

Where Should Investors Turn Now? color *Fortune* v174 no8 p96 D 15 2016

WORLD'S 50 GREATEST LEADERS [Cover story] color *Fortune* v175 no5 p46 Ap 1 2017

Hein, David

WELCOME TO CANADA J. KELLY color *Vanity Fair* v59 no2 p98 F 2017

Hein, Margaux Y.

Seagrass ecosystems reduce exposure to bacterial pathogens of humans, fishes, and invertebrates bibl graph *Science* v355 no6326 p731 F 17 2017

HEINDEL, PATRICIA

Student Success Built on a Positive School Climate *Education Digest* v82 no7 p10 Mr 2017

Heine, Thomas

Two-dimensional sp2 carbon–conjugated covalent organic frameworks diag graph *Science* v357 no6352 p673 Ag 18 2017

Heinecke, Stu

How Top Salespeople Land Hard-to-Get Meetings *Harvard Business Review Digital Articles* p2 My 5 2016

Heineman, Ben W., Jr.

The "Business in Society" Imperative for CEOs *Harvard Business Review Digital Articles* p2 D 20 2016

Corporations Need a Better Approach to Public Policy *Harvard Business Review Digital Articles* p2 Ap 1 2016

How the CFO and General Counsel Can Partner More Effectively *Harvard Business Review Digital Articles* p2 Jl 25 2016

Heineman, Matthew

City of Ghosts C. Nashawaty color *Entertainment Weekly* no1473 p47 Jl 7 2017

Heineman, Paul

WORK AT THE PERFECT HEIGHT P. Barbour *Successful Farming* v115 no4 p80 Mr 2017

Heinerth, Jill

THE EXPEDITIONS color map *Canadian Geographic* v137 no4 p49 Jl/Ag 2017

EXPLORER-IN-RESIDENCE SCHOOL VISITS S. Doyle color *Canadian Geographic* v136 no6 p77 D 2016

Heiney, P. A.

Eye patches: Protein assembly of index-gradient squid lenses bw color graph *Science* v357 no6351 p564 Ag 11 2017

HEING, BRIDEY

A Fiery Scotswoman: The youngest MP in 350 years, Mhairi Black is making a name for herself as a leader on the left *Ms.* v27 no2 p16 Summ 2017

HEINKEN, THILO

Combining Biodiversity Resurveys across Regions to Advance Global Change Research *BioScience* v67 no1 p73 Ja 2017

HEINRICH, BERND

Birds, Bees, and Beauty color *Natural History* v125 no4 p14 Ap 2017

Cohabitating with Elephants color *Natural History* v125 no5 p16 My 2017

Cooperative Undertaking color *Natural History* v125 no6 p14 Je 2017

The Crow's Song color *Natural History* v125 no11 p10 N 2017

A Diabolical Pair color *Natural History* v125 no7 p14 Jl/Ag 2017

The Hunt color *Natural History* v125 no3 p12 Mr 2017

Reading Tree Leaves *Natural History* v125 no1 p10 D 2016/Ja 2017

Rock-Solid Foundation *Natural History* v125 no2 p14 F 2017

Heinrich, Megan L.

Structural basis for antibody-mediated neutralization of Lassa virus [Cover story] color diag *Science* v356 no6341 p923 Je 1 2017

Heinrich, Sonja

WHALE CULTURE color graph *Natural History* v125 no11 p30 N 2017

HEINRICHS, STEFFI

Combining Biodiversity Resurveys across Regions to Advance Global Change Research *BioScience* v67 no1 p73 Ja 2017

Heinrichs, Waldo

WWII in the Pacific: Horrors and Heroism S. DONOGHUE *American Conservative* v16 no4 p64 Jl/Ag 2017

Heinritzi, Martin

Global atmospheric particle formation from CERN CLOUD measurements bibl graph map *Science* v354 no6316 p1119 D 2 2016

Heintzberger, Amber

Andreas Hausberger Brings Classical Dressage to America color *Dressage Today* v23 no9 p54 Je 2017

Lessons with Silva color *Dressage Today* v23 no5 p50 Ja 2017

URBAN HORSEKEEPING color *Dressage Today* v23 no10 p30 Jl 2017

WIN A DAY with Boyd Martin color *Practical Horseman* v45 no1 p58 Ja 2017

Heiny, Katherine

Class Act: A former '90s wild child satirizes suburban parenthood *New York Times Book Review* p23 S 10 2017

Standard Deviation *Publishers Weekly* v264 no12 p48 Mr 20 2017

Was She the One? A stuffy banker reconsiders his bubbly second wife L. KIESLING *New York Times Book Review* p14 Jl 9 2017

Heinz, Ted

The SAILING SCENE color *Sail* v48 no9 p6 S 2017

Heinze, Cailin

Keep Them Moving! J. McCAFFERY color *Prevention* v69 no4 p92 Ap 2017

Heinze, Svenia D.

Male sex in houseflies is determined by Mdmd, a paralog of the generic splice factor gene CWC22 bw color *Science* v356 no6338 p642 My 12 2017

Heinzmann, Ulrich

Angular momentum–induced delays in solid-state photoemission enhanced by intra-atomic interactions chart color graph *Science* v357 no6357 p1274 S 22 2017

Heirlooms

EDIBLE HEIRLOOMS *Successful Farming* v115 no5 p62 Mid-Mr 2017

Heise, Henrike

Fibril structure of amyloid-β(1–42) by cryo–electron microscopy color diag *Science* v357 no6359 p116 O 6 2017

Heisenberg (Theatrical production)

It Has Momentum and a New Location *New York* v49 no21 p112 O 17 2016

Heisenberg, Elisabeth

The Private Heisenberg and the Absent Bomb T. Powers bw *New York Review of Books* v63 no20 p65 D 22 2016

Heisey, Paul

U.S. Agricultural R&D in an Era of Falling Public Funding *Amber Waves: The Economics of Food, Farming, Natural Resources, & Rural America* p1 N 2016

Heiskell, Elizabeth

What Can I Bring? color *Southern Living* v52 no10 p124 O 2017

Heisler, Joel

Structural basis of the day-night transition in a bacterial circadian clock bibl diag *Science* v355 no6330 p1174 Mr 17 2017

Heisler, Marcus

The source of plants' spiral symmetry *Physics Today* v69 no12 p92 D 2016

Heisler Hospitality (Company)

Matt Eisler and Kevin Heisner C. SCHEDLER color *Chicago* v66 no6 p80 Je 2017

Heisman Trophy

JUST MY TYPE D. Patrick and T. Keith color *Sports Illustrated* v125 no21 p26 D 26 2016

SAQUON BARKLEY'S TOUGHEST COMPETITION IN THE HEISMAN RACE B. Feldman color *Sports Illustrated* v127 no3 p97 Jl 24 2017

STRIKING THE POSE C. Johnson color *Sports Illustrated* v125 no19 p48 D 12 2016

Heiss, Alanna—Interviews

THE ART NEWS ACCORD A. Heiss and M. Gioni bw color *ARTnews* v116 no1 p32 Spr 2017

HEITGER-EWING, CHRISTY

A 15-Year Passion Project color *Cabin Living* p26 S 2017

Cabin Fever? color *Cabin Living* p18 D 2016

cabin in training bw cartoon color *Cabin Living* p30 Je 2017

from SOMETHING OLD to SOMETHING new color diag *Cabin Living* p34 Mr 2017

Gimme a Break color *Cabin Living* p16 S 2017

Goldilocks, the Chipmunk color *Cabin Living* p20 Je 2017

Grin & Bear It color *Cabin Living* p16 O 2017

Marinating in the Moment color *Cabin Living* p18 Mr 2017

My Social Butterfly color *Cabin Living* p16 Ap 2017

"Not I," said the Cabin Guest color *Cabin Living* p18 Ag 2017

A Walk on the Wild Side color *Cabin Living* p22 Ja/F 2017

Yoga at the CABIN color *Cabin Living* p56 Je 2017

HEITING, STEVE

THE ABYSS color *Outdoor Life* v224 no3 pF1 Ap 2017

HEITMAN, DANNY

The Agony of Writing color *Weekly Standard* v23 no6 p41 O 16 2017

FINDING A CLASSROOM, WHEREVER YOU ARE *Phi Kappa Phi Forum* v97 no2 p36 Summ 2017

In My Solitude color *Weekly Standard* v22 no21 p34 F 6 2017

John Ruskin Taught Victorian Readers and Travelers the Art of Cultivation *Humanities* v38 no1 p1 Wint 2017

The Labrador Muse color *Weekly Standard* v22 no10 p34 N 14 2016

OUR LIVING SPHERE *Phi Kappa Phi Forum* v97 no1 p36 Spr 2017

PLANTING A NEW HOBBY, OUTLOOK ON LIFE *Phi Kappa Phi Forum* v96 no4 p36 Wint 2016

True Confessions color *Weekly Standard* v22 no18 p39 Ja 16 2017

Try Hawthorne for Halloween, . . . but Leave the Light on *Humanities* v37 no4 p1 Fall 2016

Words and Music bw *Weekly Standard* v22 no41 p42 Jl 3 2017

Heitman, Elizabeth

Precaution and governance of emerging technologies bibl color *Science* v354 no6313 p710 N 11 2016

Hekman, David R.

If There's Only One Woman in Your Candidate Pool, There's Statistically No Chance She'll Be Hired *Harvard Business Review Digital Articles* p2 Ap 26 2016

Women and Minorities Are Penalized for Promoting Diversity *Harvard Business Review Digital Articles* p2 Mr 23 2016

Hekstra, Doeke R.

Polymeric peptide pigments with sequence-encoded properties color graph *Science* v356 no6342 p1064 Je 9 2017

HeLa cells

SAVED BY THE CELLS color *O, The Oprah Magazine* p30 My 2017

HELBERG, JAMES

A Useful David *Commentary* v144 no3 p5 O 2017

Helberg, Simon, 1980-

Simon Helberg C. Mari color *Current Biography* v78 no5 p35 My 2017

Helbig, Louis

Ice invasion M. HEMMADI color *Maclean's* v130 no7 p18 Ag 2017

HELD, KRISTIN S.

Make Medicine Great Again *USA Today Magazine* v145 no2860 p65 Ja 2017

HELD, SHARI

CANCER'S INVISIBLE INJURY color *Indianapolis Monthly* v42 no2 p88 O 2017

COSMETIC PROCEDURES color *Indianapolis Monthly* p89 Ap 2017

Far Out *Indianapolis Monthly* p14 My 2017

The Heart of the Matter *Indianapolis Monthly* p108 F 2017

INDOORS VERSUS OUTDOORS *Indianapolis Monthly* v40 no7 p94 Mr 2017

LET'S START AT THE VERY BEGINNING color *Indianapolis Monthly* v41 no2 p138 S 2017

WONDERFUL WESTFIELD color *Indianapolis Monthly* v41 no2 p20 S 2017

HELD, SUZANNE

Grant-Writing Bootcamp: An Intervention to Enhance the Research Capacity of Academic Women in STEM *BioScience* v67 no7 p638 Jl 2017

Heldman, Breanne L.

American Housewife *Entertainment Weekly* no1482/1483 p79 S 22 2017

Arrow *Entertainment Weekly* no1482/1483 p84 S 22 2017

Better Things color *Entertainment Weekly* no1482/1483 p91 S 22 2017

The Blacklist color *Entertainment Weekly* no1482/1483 p74 S 22 2017

Broad City color *Entertainment Weekly* no1482/1483 p79 S 22 2017

The Challenge Hall of Fame color *Entertainment Weekly* no1474/1475 p107 Jl 21-28 2017

Chicago Fire *Entertainment Weekly* no1482/1483 p91 S 22 2017

Chicago P.D *Entertainment Weekly* no1482/1483 p79 S 22 2017

Criminal Minds color *Entertainment Weekly* no1482/1483 p79 S 22 2017

DEMI MOORE OF Empire color *Entertainment Weekly* no1482/1483 p78 S 22 2017

Designated Survivor color *Entertainment Weekly* no1482/1483 p74 S 22 2017

Dynasty color *Entertainment Weekly* no1482/1483 p76 S 22 2017

GOING OUT WITH A BANG color *Entertainment Weekly* no1463/1464 p10 Ap/My 2017

The Goldbergs color *Entertainment Weekly* no1482/1483 p74 S 22 2017

The Good Place color *Entertainment Weekly* no1482/1483 p86 S 22 2017

Gotham *Entertainment Weekly* no1482/1483 p84 S 22 2017

Great News color *Entertainment Weekly* no1482/1483 p88 S 22 2017

Grey's Anatomy color diag *Entertainment Weekly* no1482/1483 p89 S 22 2017

Hot Date *Entertainment Weekly* no1482/1483 p74 S 22 2017

How to Get Away With Murder *Entertainment Weekly* no1482/1483 p91 S 22 2017

Law & Order: Special Victims Unit *Entertainment Weekly* no1482/1483 p75 S 22 2017

Life in Pieces *Entertainment Weekly* no1482/1483 p88 S 22 2017

THE MASK color *Entertainment Weekly* no1460/1461 p43 Ap 7-17 2017

Modern Family *Entertainment Weekly* no1482/1483 p75 S 22 2017

Mom color *Entertainment Weekly* no1482/1483 p85 S 22 2017

Mr. Robot color *Entertainment Weekly* no1482/1483 p77 S 22 2017

The Orville *Entertainment Weekly* no1482/1483 p85 S 22 2017

Reality Bites color *Entertainment Weekly* no1460/1461 p82 Ap 7-17 2017

Riverdale color *Entertainment Weekly* no1482/1483 p68 S 22 2017

Scandal *Entertainment Weekly* no1482/1483 p88 S 22 2017

SEAL Team color *Entertainment Weekly* no1482/1483 p76 S 22 2017

The Shannara Chronicles *Entertainment Weekly* no1482/1483 p79 S 22 2017

Speechless color *Entertainment Weekly* no1482/1483 p75 S 22 2017

Star color *Entertainment Weekly* no1482/1483 p76 S 22 2017

Supernatural color *Entertainment Weekly* no1482/1483 p84 S 22 2017

Superstore color *Entertainment Weekly* no1482/1483 p84 S 22 2017

Survivor: Heroes vs. Healers vs. Hustlers *Entertainment Weekly* no1482/1483 p75 S 22 2017

S.W.A.T color *Entertainment Weekly* no1482/1483 p90 S 22 2017

What to Watch color *Entertainment Weekly* no1451/1452 p100 F 3-10 2017

What to Watch color *Entertainment Weekly* no1472 p54 Je 30 2017

What to Watch color *Entertainment Weekly* no1476 p54 Ag 4 2017

Will & Grace color *Entertainment Weekly* no1482/1483 p80 S 22 2017

Your LGBTQ Pop Preview color *Entertainment Weekly* no1471 p44 Je 23 2017

YOUR NEXT LIFETIME OBSESSION color *Entertainment Weekly* no1450 p18 Ja 27 2017

Helen, of Troy, Queen of Sparta (Legendary character)

Bad Houseguests *Lapham's Quarterly* v10 no1 p141 Wint 2017

Helen Ouyang

WHERE HEALTH CARE WON'T GO: A tuberculosis crisis in the Black Belt color *Harper's Magazine* v335 no2005 p27 Je 2017

Helena (Mont.)

ARE YOU A BELIEVER IN SUFFERING? BELIEVING YOU AREN'T ALLOWED TO HAVE FUN UNTIL YOU'VE PUT IN SOME SOLID WORK? G. AVERILL bw color *Bike Magazine* v24 no4 p76 Je 2017

Helena, Cleyde

Sunshine outside the ivory tower bw *Science* v357 no6357 p1322 S 22 2017

Heleski, Camie

Here's How color diag graph *Practical Horseman* v45 no9 p66 S 2017

Here's How color *Practical Horseman* v45 no6 p64 Je 2017

Helfand, David

Mass Misinformation Author David Helfand Warns of 'Google-Fed Zombies' *Skeptical Inquirer* v41 no2 p13 Mr/Ap 2017

A Survival Guide to the Misinformation Age K. B. Marvel *Physics Today* v69 no12 p56 D 2016

SURVIVING THE MIS INFORMATION AGE *Skeptical Inquirer* v41 no3 p34 My/Je 2017

Helfer, Erwin

Mercy, Mercy, Mercy! HADLEY color *Downbeat* v83 no12 p72 D 2016

Helfman, Tara

Frank Exchange color *Weekly Standard* v22 no9 p32 N 7 2016

The Future of the Gerrymander *Commentary* v143 no3 p9 Mr 2017

Is the Gerrymander on Its Way Out? New court action may threaten a 200-year-old practice *Commentary* v143 no1 p34 Ja 2017

The Meaning of Scalia *Commentary* v142 no1 p13 Jl/Ag 2016

Who's in Charge? *Weekly Standard* v22 no22 p33 F 13 2017

Helft, Miguel

END OF THE BIOLOGICAL CLOCK [Cover story] color graph *Forbes* v198 no6 p84 N 8 2016

HACKING THE VISA RACKET color *Forbes* v198 no5 p74 O 25 2016

LESSONS AND IDEAS BY THE 100 GREATEST LIVING BUSINESS MINDS bw color *Forbes* v200 no3 p115 S 28 2017

UBER'S BOLD MOVE [Cover story] color *Forbes* v198 no9 p58 D 30 2016

THE WORLD'S MOST INNOVATIVE COMPANIES chart color *Forbes* v200 no2 p72 S 5 2017

Helget, Nicole

Frack Attack: As a new industry arrives to lift a struggling town, a young forager weighs its heavy costs J. L. HOLM *New York Times Book Review* p26 My 14 2017

Helgoland (Germany)

BLOW THE BLOODY PLACE UP! J. Rüger *History Today* v67 no8 p24 Ag 2017

Helguera, Pablo

For a Few Months, A Spanish-Language Bookstore in Boston A. Green color *Publishers Weekly* v264 no10 p18 Mr 6 2017

Heli-skiing

SERENDIPITY IN ALASKA J. Brown color *Powder* v45 no6 p46 F 2017

THIS COULD BE YOU D. Wolman color *Bloomberg Businessweek* no4499 p83 N 14 2016

Helical gears

REAREND REDUX S. RICHARDS color *Dirt Sports + Off-Road* v51 no11 p26 N 2017

Helical springs

COIL SCIENCE J. KOPYCINSKI color *Dirt Sports + Off-Road* v51 no6 p64 Je 2017

Helicases

The cryo-EM structure of a ribosome–Ski2-Ski3-Ski8 helicase complex C. Schmidt, E. Kowalinski et al bibl color graph *Science* v354 no6318 p1431 D 16 2016

Helicity (Chemistry)

Complete measurement of helicity and its dynamics in vortex

tubes M. W. Scheeler, W. M. van Rees et al color diag graph *Science* v357 no6350 p487 Ag 4 2017

Helicity—invariant even in a viscous fluid H. Keith Moffatt color *Science* v357 no6350 p448 Ag 4 2017

Taking the measure of water's whirl A. G. Smart *Physics Today* v70 no10 p20 O 2017

Helicity of nuclear particles

Complete measurement of helicity and its dynamics in vortex tubes M. W. Scheeler, W. M. van Rees et al color diag graph *Science* v357 no6350 p487 Ag 4 2017

Helicopters

CHOP, CHOP! color *Iceland Review* v54 no5 p102 S-O 2016

PELICAN BRIEFS L. LeBlanc-Berry color *Louisiana Life* v37 no5 p10 My/Je 2017

SKYWITNESS NEWS C. R. JOYNT *Washingtonian Magazine* v52 no2 p26 N 2016

Helicopters—Design & construction

Innovation J. Bachman color *Bloomberg Businessweek* no4517 p37 Ap 3 2017

Helioseismology

HERE COMES THE SUN R. MARR cartoon *Missouri Life* v44 no5 p64 Ag 2017

Helium

Buffer-gas cooling of antiprotonic helium to 1.5 to 1.7 K, and antiproton-to-electron mass ratio Masaki Hori, H. Aghai-Khozani et al bibl chart diag graph *Science* v354 no6312 p610 N 4 2016

Compound defies helium's inertness E. CONOVER color *Science News* v191 no5 p8 Mr 18 2017

HELIUM COMPOUND MAY FORM UNDER PRESSURE *Physics Today* v70 no4 p23 Ap 2017

Helium atom

A testing time for antimatter W. Ubachs bibl color diag *Science* v354 no6312 p546 N 4 2016

Helium—Sales & prices

Erratic helium prices create research havoc D. Kramer *Physics Today* v70 no1 p26 Ja 2017

Hell

Does hell exist? K. P. Considine color *U.S. Catholic* v82 no3 p49 Mr 2017

Hell, Maximilian

The fading American dream: Trends in absolute income mobility since 1940 bw graph *Science* v356 no6336 p398 Ap 28 2017

Hell, Stefan W.

Nanometer resolution imaging and tracking of fluorescent molecules with minimal photon fluxes bibl graph *Science* v355 no6325 p606 F 10 2017

Hell or High Water (Film)

Hell or High Water *New Yorker* v92 no32 p28 O 10 2016

No. 5 HELL OR HIGH WATER C. Nashawaty color *Entertainment Weekly* no1444/1445 p53 D 16 2016

NOW PLAYING color *Entertainment Weekly* no1434 p45 O 7 2016

The Ten Best Movies of the Year D. Edelstein img *New York* v49 no25 p116 D 12 2016

Hellboy (Fictitious character)

NO. 32 HELLBOY C. Holub color *Entertainment Weekly* no1436/1437 p69 O 21 2016

Hellebores

HELLEBORES K. C. FREDERICK color *Better Homes & Gardens* v95 no2 p64 F 2016

Hellenistic Greek poetry

SAPPHO and her brothers D. Gribble *History Today* v66 no10 p46 O 2016

Heller, Arnie

Advanced Laser Promises EXCITING Applications: The extremely powerful High-Repetition-Rate Advanced Petawatt Laser System (HAPLS) is poised to be an important tool for scientific research *Science & Technology Review* p4 Jl/Ag 2017

HIGH-PERFORMANCE COMPUTING TAKES AIM AT CANCER color *Science & Technology Review* p4 O/N 2016

INVESTING IN THE NATION'S FUTURE: The Laboratory Directed Research and Development Program has been a significant engine of scientific discovery for 25 years *Science & Technology Review* p4 Ap/My 2017

Mighty ATLAS Supports Precise Alignment *Science & Technology Review* p16 Mr 2017

A National Security Code Is Reborn for Industry *Science & Technology Review* p20 Je 2017

Nuclear Data Moves into the 21st Century *Science & Technology Review* p12 S 2016

Heller, Barbara

Sustaining Leadership Greatness *Parks & Recreation* v52 no5 p54 My 2017

HELLER, BECCA

What a Just Immigration Policy Looks Like cartoon *Foreign Policy* no226 p80 S/O 2017

Heller, Caleb

PARODY *Weekly Standard* v22 no37 p40 Je 5 2017

Heller, Jason

How Marketers Can Personalize at Scale *Harvard Business Review Digital Articles* p2 N 23 2015

Heller, Jean

The Hunting Ground: Deuce Mora Series, Vol. 2 *Publishers Weekly* v264 no5 p182 Ja 30 2017

Heller, Joseph

CORPORATE WELFARE *Lapham's Quarterly* v10 no3 p66 Summ 2017

Heller, Michael R.

Kilogram-scale prexasertib monolactate monohydrate synthesis under continuous-flow CGMP conditions chart diag *Science* v356 no6343 p1144 Je 16 2017

HELLER, NATHAN

A Boy's LIFE color *Vogue* v206 no12 p204 D 2016

CASHING OUT cartoon *New Yorker* v92 no32 p48 O 10 2016

Free Radical color *Vogue* v207 no9 p714 S 2017

THE GIG IS UP cartoon *New Yorker* v93 no13 p52 My 15 2017

New Wave color *Vogue* v207 no9 p614 S 2017

NOT OUR KIND cartoon *New Yorker* v92 no39 p87 N 28 2016

OUT OF ACTION cartoon color *New Yorker* v93 no24 p70 Ag 21 2017

Rooney on the Move [Cover story] color *Vogue* v207 no10 p243 O 2017

Swept Away color *Vogue* v207 no6 p87 Je 2017

Heller, Rafael

On the goals and outcomes of arts education color *Phi Delta Kappan* v98 no7 p15 Ap 2017

On the science and teaching of emotional intelligence color *Phi Delta Kappan* v98 no6 p20 Mr 2017

Rafael Heller joins Kappan color *Phi Delta Kappan* v98 no5 p79 F 2017

Heller, Ted

BEST of TIMES WORST of TIMES cartoon *Esquire* v166 no5 p138 D 2016/Ja 2017

HELLER, ZOË

HAUNTED HOUSES cartoon *New Yorker* v92 no33 p90 O 17 2016

MOST LIKELY TO SUCCEED cartoon *New Yorker* v93 no8 p66 Ap 10 2017

What's the best book, new or old, you read this year? *New York Times Book Review* p27 D 25 2016

Hellerstein, Daniel

Declines in Pollinator Forage Suitability Were Concentrated in the Midwest, the Over-Summering Grounds for Many Honeybees *Amber Waves: The Economics of Food, Farming, Natural Resources, & Rural America* p1 Jl 2017

Gathering Experimental Evidence To Improve the Design of Agricultural Programs *Amber Waves: The Economics of Food, Farming, Natural Resources, & Rural America* p1 Ag 2017

Hellickson, Mickey

The Four-Day Deer Drive cartoon color *Field & Stream* v121 no7 p52 D 2016/Ja 2017

Hellier, David

A Would-Be Uber Rival's Ride to Nowhere cartoon *Bloomberg Businessweek* no4501 p28 N 28 2016

Helling, Steve

HOW SAFE ARE CONCERTS? color *Entertainment Weekly* no1468/1469 p16 Je 2-9 2017

Hellis, Clayton

The Difference Is in the Details *Stage Directions* v30 no3 p32 Mr 2017

Hellmann, Jessica

Merging paleobiology with conservation biology to guide the future of terrestrial ecosystems color *Science* v355 no6325 p594 F 10 2017

Society Is Ready for a New Kind of Science--Is Academia? *Bio-Science* v67 no7 p591 Jl 2017

Hellmann, Thomas

The Very First Mistake Most Startup Founders Make *Harvard Business Review Digital Articles* p2 F 23 2016

Hellmich, Thomas R.

How RFID Technology Improves Hospital Care *Harvard Business Review Digital Articles* p2 D 31 2015

Hello, Dolly! (Theatrical production)

David Hyde Pierce B. Newcott color *AARP: The Magazine* v60 no3A p13 Ap/My 2017

Hello, Tonys! Broadway's big bloom of openings before the awards-season cutoff brings greatness and... other things too img *New York* v50 no9 p92 My 1 2017

THE STAR H. ALS color *New Yorker* v93 no11 p60 My 1 2017

Hello, My Name Is Doris (Film)

NEWLY AVAILABLE MOVIES M. FELL *TV Guide* v65 no2 p46 Ja 2 2017

Springtime for SALLY T. Brodesser-Akner color *AARP: The Magazine* v59 no3A p48 Ap/My 2016

Hello, Y.

Seasonal exposure of carbon dioxide ice on the nucleus of comet 67P/Churyumov-Gerasimenko bibl bw graph *Science* v354 no6319 p1563 D 23 2016

HelloFresh GmbH

DOMINIK RICHTER D. RICHTER color *Harvard Business Review* v95 no2 p156 Mr/Ap 2017

Hells Canyon (Idaho & Or.)

America's Wildest Hikes T. VanderMolen color *Backpacker* p61 Ag 2017

Get Low I. KORIC map *Backpacker* p26 Ag 2017

TRAILING THE HERD P. WILSON *Idaho Magazine* v16 no2 p48 N 2016

Hell's Kitchen (TV program)

Hell's Kitchen N. Abrams, S. Highfill et al *Entertainment Weekly* no1482/1483 p99 S 22 2017

Hellwig, Thomas

An Early Warning System for Your Team's Stress Level [Cover story] *Harvard Business Review Digital Articles* p2 Ap 26 2017

Helly Hansen AS

The Best New Lightweight Rain Jackets M. GOULET color *Popular Mechanics* p40 My 2017

Shells E. KWAK-HEFFERAN color diag graph il *Backpacker* v45 no3 p83 Ap 2017

Helm, Dieter

The next energy economy A. S. Hopkins color *Science* v356 no6339 p709 My 19 2017

HELMAN, CHRISTOPHER

Biting the Hand That Feeds You color map *Forbes* v198 no7 p48 N 29 2016

Green Gas color *Forbes* v199 no2 p50 F 28 2017

LESSONS AND IDEAS BY THE 100 GREATEST LIVING BUSINESS MINDS bw color *Forbes* v200 no3 p115 S 28 2017

Oil's Changing Face color graph *Forbes* v200 no1 p38 Jl 27 2017

A VIEW FROM THE TOP color *Forbes* v198 no5 p112 O 25 2016

THE WORLD'S BILLIONAIRES bw color diag graph map *Forbes* v199 no3 p84 Mr 28 2017

Helman, Lori

WHY WE NEED TO TRACK PROGRESS color *Literacy Today (2411-7862)* v34 no4 p10 Ja/F 2017

Helman, Sarah R.

Landscape of immunogenic tumor antigens in successful immunotherapy of virally induced epithelial cancer graph *Science* v356 no6334 p200 Ap 14 2017

Helmers, Richard A.

The Mayo Clinic Model for Running a Value-Improvement Program *Harvard Business Review Digital Articles* p2 O 22 2015

Helmet-mounted displays

VISION OF THE FUTURE? S. Macdonald color *Cycle World* v56 no9 p22 O 2017

Helmets

METAL OF HONOR color *MHQ: Quarterly Journal of Military History* v30 no1 p58 Aut 2017

WHY HELMETS MATTER C. Owen color *Dressage Today* v23

no4 p18 D 2016

Helmets—Evaluation

ARAI QUANTUM-X AND SIGNET-X HELMETS S. MacDonald cartoon color *Cycle World* v55 no11 p14 D 2016

BELL PRO STAR HELMET B. Adams color *Cycle World* v56 no3 p22 Ap 2017

THE BEST BET img *New York* v50 no11 p93 My 29 2017

GEAR BOX color *Dirt Sports + Off-Road* v51 no7 p68 Jl 2017

GEAR BOX color *Dirt Sports + Off-Road* v51 no9 p70 S 2017

Head Masters color *Equus* no478 p26 Jl 2017

PLUG 'N' PLAY D. Canet color *Cycle World* v56 no1 p17 Ja/F 2017

A Shoe Sole That Won't Slip on Ice B. BROUDY and G. MILLIKEN color *Popular Science* v288 no6 p58 N/D 2016

STYLE color *Horse & Rider* v56 no5 p28 My 2017

Helmets—History

What's the Point? J. GUTTMAN color *MHQ: Quarterly Journal of Military History* v29 no4 p11 Summ 2017

Helmholtz, Hermann von, 1821-1894

1891: Berlin H. von Helmholtz *Lapham's Quarterly* v10 no2 p143 Spr 2017

The pulsing Moon S. J. O'MEARA color *Astronomy* v45 no1 p64 Ja 2017

Helmholz, R. H.

NATURE IN THE DOCK J. Dyer *Claremont Review of Books* v16 no4 p31 Fall 2016

Helminthiasis—Treatment

Worms remodel immune responsiveness *Science* v354 no6312 p594 N 4 2016

Helms, Lanie L.

From the Laboratory to the WORLD *Science & Technology Review* p12 Je 2017

PROLONGED POWER in Remote Places *Science & Technology Review* p21 Ap/My 2017

Rapid Recovery of Critical Infrastructure color *Science & Technology Review* p20 O/N 2016

Helou, Anissa

WHERE IN THE WORLD TO EAT cartoon color *Conde Nast Traveler* v52 no9 p53 O 2017

Help, The (Film)

Allison Janney color *O, The Oprah Magazine* p24 Ap 2017

Help! I'm Stuck (Theatrical production)

Wigstock M. Schulman cartoon *New Yorker* v93 no28 p10 S 18 2017

Help-seeking behavior

5 Ways to Get Better at Asking for Help W. Baker *Harvard Business Review Digital Articles* p2 D 18 2014

Helping behavior

See also

Bystander effect (Psychology)

Personal coaching

Volunteer service

Do Good, Feel Great cartoon *Good Housekeeping* v263 no5 p91 N 2016

Faith Matters M. C. Barnes color *Christian Century* v133 no22 p2 O 26 2016

How to Offer Support to a Grieving Colleague S. Nawaz bw *Harvard Business Review Digital Articles* p2 Ap 3 2017

Leaders Who Get How to Give C. Nickisch color *Harvard Business Review Digital Articles* p2 Ja 24 2017

An Open Letter To the Shoppers Who Consoled Me [Cover story] D. GREENE *Reader's Digest* v188 no1125 p94 N 2016

A Random Act Of Roadside Assistance [Cover story] J. HORNER *Reader's Digest* v188 no1125 p93 N 2016

Research: Yes, Being Helpful Is Tiring K. Lanaj *Harvard Business Review Digital Articles* p2 S 6 2016

What I Learned About Helpfulness When I Used a Cane Instead of Crutches A. Rimm *Harvard Business Review Digital Articles* p2 D 30 2016

What Not to Say to a Stressed-Out Colleague H. Weeks *Harvard Business Review Digital Articles* p2 Ag 23 2016

Helprin, Mark

An Article V Convention *Claremont Review of Books* v17 no1 p98 Wint 2016/2017

As Europe Devolves, America Centralizes *Claremont Review of Books* v16 no4 p90 Fall 2016

Innovations Improving Lives in Canada's Hemophilia Community D. F. McCourt *Maclean's* v130 no9 p33 O 2017

Hemp

Hemp Harvest in Virginia S. Richardson *American History* v52 no1 p8 Ap 2017

Hemp, James

On the origins of oxygenic photosynthesis and aerobic respiration in Cyanobacteria chart diag *Science* v355 no6332 p1436 Mr 31 2017

Hemp industry—Economic aspects

HEMP COMES HOME R. Kobell color *Reason* v49 no5 p38 O 2017

Hemp seed oil

FIBER FOODS color *Muscle & Performance* v9 no9 p61 S 2017

HEMPEL, JESSI

Why Your Cell Phone Sounds Female *Reader's Digest* v189 no1127 p54 F 2017

HEMPHILL, JIM

Hollywood Divided: The 1950 Screen Directors Guild Meeting and the Impact of the Blacklist *Film Quarterly* v71 no1 p117 Fall 2017

Hemphill, Julius

Good for Circulation P. MARGASAK color *Downbeat* v84 no2 p16 F 2017

HEMPHILL, NINA

Culinary Queens color *Ebony* v72 no5 p56 Mr 2017

Hems

THE TIP SHEET M. Marden, M. Hainey color *Esquire* p52 Je/Jl 2017

Hemsworth, Chris, 1983-

5 — KEVIN'S INTERVIEW D. Rovenstine *Entertainment Weekly* no1444/1445 p60 D 16 2016

HOW I GOT MY STYLE J. Roth color *Esquire* p44 O 2017

IF HE HAD A HAMMER... [Cover story] T. Stack color *Entertainment Weekly* no1457/1458 p28 Mr 17 2017

Hemsworth, Liam, 1990-

Cause & Effect C. Shanahan color *InStyle* v23 no12 p58 N 2016

Hen, René

Pcdhαc2 is required for axonal tiling and assembly of serotonergic circuitries in mice diag *Science* v356 no6336 p406 Ap 28 2017

Hen of the Woods (Company)

CHIP SHOT M. BRANDSTETTER *Cincinnati Magazine* v50 no7 p154 Ap 2017

HENAGER, ROBIN

HEAVY DEBT color *Phi Kappa Phi Forum* v97 no2 p15 Summ 2017

PACK A PLAN color *Phi Kappa Phi Forum* v96 no4 p17 Wint 2016

WORLDLY WEALTH il *Phi Kappa Phi Forum* v97 no1 p17 Spr 2017

Henao-Mejia, Jorge

The DNA-sensing AIM2 inflammasome controls radiation-induced cell death and tissue injury bibl color graph *Science* v354 no6313 p765 N 11 2016

Hench, Julie Diana

Livin' the DREAM color *Dance Spirit* v21 no8 p72 O 2017

PLANT-Powered color *Dance Spirit* v21 no8 p50 O 2017

HENDER, AMY

Bon Appétit, America *Weekly Standard* v22 no4 p30 O 3 2016

Hendershot, Heather

Firing Line At 50 N. B. FREEMAN bw color *National Review* v68 no19 p44 O 24 2016

Henderson, Amy

Bohemian Rhapsody bw *Weekly Standard* v22 no41 p40 Jl 3 2017

Floral History color *Weekly Standard* v22 no23 p32 F 20 2017

Frozen Folly color *Weekly Standard* v22 no43 p33 Jl 24 2017

A Guide to Discovery bw *Weekly Standard* v22 no33 p40 My 8 2017

The Rebels' Art cartoon *Weekly Standard* v22 no13 p26 D 5 2016

Henderson, Brad

CAN NEUROSCIENCE HELP US UNDERSTAND TRUST AT WORK?: INTERACTION color *Harvard Business Review* v95 no2 p18 Mr/Ap 2017

Henderson, Brooke, 1997-

Brooke Henderson M. Hagan color *Current Biography* v78 no4 p38 Ap 2017

Henderson, Bruce B., 1946-

Fighting their way home B. BETHUNE bw *Maclean's* v130 no7 p62 Ag 2017

Henderson, Charles

From Dissemination to Propagation: A New Paradigm for Education Developers *Change* v49 no4 p35 Jl/Ag 2017

HENDERSON, DANIELLE

2016: A LOOK BACK AT THE YEAR IN BLACK CULTURE color *Essence* v47 no8 p100 D 2016

These Are Your Sexual Rights color *Glamour* v114 no7 p94 Jl 2016

HENDERSON, DAVID R.

Bribe Bully Beg Borrow Steal color *Reason* v48 no10 p18 Mr 2017

Henderson, Don

we asked you answered color *Timber Home Living* v27 no5 p18 O 2017

HENDERSON, ELEANOR

All Ablaze: A tale of community mistrust in '90s suburban America *New York Times Book Review* p9 O 1 2017

Not Even Past: A racist murder and the legacy of Jim Crow haunt generations of a family in Eleanor Henderson's novel A. MATHIS *New York Times Book Review* p21 O 8 2017

The Twelve-Mile Straight *Publishers Weekly* v264 no29 p191 Jl 17 2017

Henderson, Florence, 1934-2016

Cover *Entertainment Weekly* no1443 pC1 D 9 2016

Florence Henderson 1934-2016 D. D'Addario color *Time* v188 no24 p70 D 12 2016

FLORENCE HENDERSON E. Plumb and L. Rice color *Entertainment Weekly* no1446/1447 p94 D 2016/Ja 2017

A Wellspring of Comfort M. Mccormick color *Time* v188 no24 p70 D 12 2016

Henderson, Gabriel

Weather in the Courtroom: Memoirs from a Career in Forensic Meteorology *Physics Today* v70 no10 p61 O 2017

HENDERSON, GARNET

Ashley Mayeux *Dance Magazine* v91 no6 p46 Je 2017

Both Sides of the Curtain *Dance Magazine* v91 no8 p50 Ag 2017

Dancing Through Language Barriers *Dance Magazine* v91 no6 p48 Je 2017

The Foodie Ballerina *Dance Magazine* v91 no8 p42 Ag 2017

Side Gig Woes *Dance Magazine* v91 no1 p114 Ja 2017

What Is Countertechnique? The method that wants to change how you think about dancing *Dance Magazine* v91 no9 p50 S 2017

Henderson, Isabel

ZEBRAS IN THE STREETS color *Atlantic* v319 no2 p26 Mr 2017

Henderson, Josh

The Arrangement K. Freeze *TV Guide* v65 no8 p34 F 27 2017

Henderson, Karen

A danger in the water color *Equus* no478 p80 Jl 2017

Henderson, Leslie—Interviews

Crafting Down-Home Brews P. M. ESSWEIN color *Kiplinger's Personal Finance* v71 no2 p25 F 2017

Henderson, M. Todd

Do Lawyers Make Better CEOs Than MBAs? *Harvard Business Review Digital Articles* p2 2017

Henderson, Mark—Interviews

Crafting Down-Home Brews P. M. ESSWEIN color *Kiplinger's Personal Finance* v71 no2 p25 F 2017

HENDERSON, PETER H.

Toward a More Diverse Research Community Models of Success: A forward-looking group of colleges and universities are demonstrating effective ways to educate underrepresented minorities for careers in science and engineering *Issues in Science & Technology* v33 no3 p33 Spr 2017

Henderson, Rebecca

A Partial Defense of Our Obsession with Short-Term Earnings S. Cliffe *Harvard Business Review Digital Articles* p2 My 7 2015

Why Inequality Is an Urgent Business Problem *Harvard Business Review Digital Articles* p2 Mr 29 2017

HENDERSON, RICK

FROM THE ARCHIVES cartoon *Reason* v49 no2 p70 Je 2017

Henderson, Ron

THE ART OF STAYING ALIVE S. Henderson color *Popular Me-*

chanics p66 F 2017

Pieces of Truth *New York Times Book Review* p20 Ja 8 2017

Henderson, Smith

THE ART OF STAYING ALIVE color *Popular Mechanics* p66 F 2017

Henderson, Tamara

Redcat J. Griffin color *Art in America* v105 no1 p88 Ja 2017

HENDERSON-PREECE, LINDSEY

Paying Our Respects color *O, The Oprah Magazine* p15 Je 2017

Hendifar, Gabriel

APPARATUS J. V. BOND *Interview* v46 no9 p30 N 2016

Hendler, James

It's the Partnership, Stupid *Issues in Science & Technology* v33 no4 p37 Summ 2017

Science of the World Wide Web bibl color *Science* v354 no6313 p703 N 11 2016

HENDLEY, DENNIS

Chords & Discords color *Downbeat* v84 no8 p10 Ag 2017

Hendra, Sue

Norman the Slug with the Silly Shell *Publishers Weekly* v264 no40 p136 O 2 2017

Hendren, Nathaniel

The fading American dream: Trends in absolute income mobility since 1940 bw graph *Science* v356 no6336 p398 Ap 28 2017

Hendricks, Drew

3D Printing Is Already Changing Health Care *Harvard Business Review Digital Articles* p2 Mr 4 2016

Hendricks, Kyle

The Chicago Cubs and Their Unlikely Ace Could Make History S. Gregory color *Time* v188 no18 p50 O 31 2016

Hendricks, Terri

Wranglered N. Chirico color *Horse & Rider* v56 no5 p19 My 2017

Hendricks, William W.

Stay on Your Smartphone! *Parks & Recreation* v51 no11 p14 N 2016

Hendrickson, Brandon—Interviews

RISING STAR J. KINDELA chart color *Muscle & Performance* v9 no1 p32 Ja 2017

HENDRICKSON, CHERYL

CONNECTIONS BETWEEN THE UNCONNECTED color *Alternatives Journal (A.J) - Canada's Environmental Voice* v42 no3 p75 2016

Hendrickson, D. Scott

The literary genius of Cervantes *America* v216 no9 p48 Ap 24 2017

Hendrickson, Ronald C.

PI3K pathway regulates ER-dependent transcription in breast cancer through the epigenetic regulator KMT2D bibl graph *Science* v355 no6331 p1324 Mr 24 2017

Hendriks, Carolyn M.

Twelve Key Findings in Deliberative Democracy Research *Daedalus* v146 no3 p28 Summ 2017

Hendriks, Giel

Activity-based protein profiling reveals off-target proteins of the FAAH inhibitor BIA 10-2474 chart color graph *Science* v356 no6342 p1084 Je 9 2017

HENDRIX, GRADY

Hello, Cruel World bw color *Film Comment* v53 no2 p74 Mr/Ap 2017

HENDRIX, JENNY

No Strings Attached *New York Times Book Review* p9 My 28 2017

Hendrix, Jimi, 1942-1970

QUOTE MARKS P. Lockwood cartoon *New Yorker* v92 no39 p42 N 28 2016

Heneghan, Liam

Preserving biodiversity, preventing climate disaster: Childish dreams or audacious strategies? bibl *Bulletin of the Atomic Scientists* v73 no4 p284 Jl 2017

Heneghan, Tom

Berlin debates restoring cross atop City Palace *Christian Century* v134 no14 p16 Jl 5 2017

German Protestant church renounces mission aiming to convert Jewish people color *Christian Century* v133 no26 p17 D 21 2016

Polls say most Europeans want to ban Muslims from immigrating color *Christian Century* v134 no6 p13 Mr 15 2017

Reformed churches affirm Catholic-Lutheran accord *Christian Century* v134 no16 p12 Ag 2 2017

A toy figure of Luther sparked accusations of anti-Semitism color *Christian Century* v134 no3 p14 F 2017

Heneghan Peng Architects Ltd.

Breaking New Ground E. HECHT color diag *Architectural Record* v205 no3 p66 Mr 2017

Heng, Joseph

Community network for deaf scientists color *Science* v356 no6336 p386 Ap 28 2017

Heng Zhu

A nuclease that mediates cell death induced by DNA damage and poly(ADP-ribose) polymerase-1 bw graph *Science* v354 no6308 paad6872-1 O 7 2016

Henge Docks LLC

HENGE DOCKS TETHERED DOCKING STATION R. LOYOLA color *Macworld - Digital Edition* p39 F 2017

Hengeveld, Geerten M.

Positive biodiversity-productivity relationship predominant in global forests bibl chart graph map *Science* v354 no6309 paaf8957-1 O 14 2016

HENIG, ROBIN MARANTZ

In Defense of Fat *New York Times Book Review* p23 Ja 8 2017

Rethinking Gender cartoon chart color map *National Geographic* v231 no1 p48 Ja 2017

HENION, LEIGH ANN

Paleo-Tech *Sierra* v102 no1 p104 Ja/F 2017

Henke, Jodi

10 SUCCESSFUL FARMERS: RANDY CONSTANT *Successful Farming* v115 no8 p28 Je/Jl 2017

MORTALITY COMPOSTING *Successful Farming* v115 no2 p32 F 2017

TRENCH COMPOSTING *Successful Farming* v114 no13 p40 D 2016

WATERING SYSTEMS FOR ROTATIONAL GRAZING: KEEP ANIMALS HYDRATED WHILE MOVING THEM AROUND *Successful Farming* v115 no12 p54 O 2017

Henke, Katharina

Choosing the hard road cartoon *Science* v355 no6321 p218 Ja 13 2017

Henke, Nicolaus

Most Industries Are Nowhere Close to Realizing the Potential of Analytics *Harvard Business Review Digital Articles* p2 D 16 2016

Henkel, T. W.

Persistent effects of pre-Columbian plant domestication on Amazonian forest composition bibl chart graph map *Science* v355 no6328 p925 Mr 3 2017

Henkes, Judd—Interviews

JUDD HENKES P. Strout color *Snowboarder* v29 no5 p40 Ja 2017

Henkes, Kevin, 1960-

Egg *Publishers Weekly* v263 no43 p74 O 24 2016

Henley, Blair

HOLDING COURT color *Tennis* v53 no5 p38 S/O 2017

The Sun Rises Again *Tennis* v52 no6 p12 N/D 2016

Henley, Hanna

Control of meiotic pairing and recombination by chromosomally tethered 26S proteasome bibl graph *Science* v355 no6323 p408 Ja 27 2017

Henley, Robert Y.

Enhanced water permeability and tunable ion selectivity in sub-nanometer carbon nanotube porins chart color *Science* v357 no6353 p792 Ag 25 2017

Henley, Tara

Freedom Thirty-Five color *Walrus* v14 no5 p16 Je 2017

Henna (Dye)

HENNA 101 L. Turner color *Amazing Wellness* v9 no2 p70 Spr 2017

Hennawi, Joseph F.

Measurement of the small-scale structure of the intergalactic medium using close quasar pairs diag graph *Science* v356 no6336 p418 Ap 28 2017

Henneberger, Melinda

Why Does Congress Do So Little? *Washington Monthly* p16 Ja/F 2017

Hennekam, Raoul C. M.
Mapping the human DC lineage through the integration of high-dimensional techniques diag *Science* v356 no6342 p1044 Je 9 2017

HENNEMUTH, BRITT
Mapping It Out: Downtown L.A cartoon *Vanity Fair* p98 Hollywood 2017 Supplement

Hennessey, Gail Skroback
Amazing Animals color map *National Geographic Kids* no473 p12 S 2017

Hennessey, Susan
Deterring Cyberattacks color *Foreign Affairs* v96 no6 p39 N/D 2017

Hennessy, Kate
Martyrs & Saints P. Steinfels bw *Commonweal* v144 no5 p28 Mr 10 2017
A Saint for Difficult People J. PARKER bw *Atlantic* v319 no2 p32 Mr 2017
UNDER THE GAZE OF DOROTHY bw *America* v216 no12 p36 My 29 2017

HENNESSY, MAGGIE
BERRY GOOD SANGRÍA color *Chicago* v66 no8 p56 Ag 2017
THE CAN-DO SAUCE color *Chicago* v66 no5 p68 My 2017
CHEFFED-UP CASSEROLE color *Chicago* v66 no11 p52 N 2017
CHICAGO'S COZIEST BARS color *Chicago* v66 no10 p47 O 2017
FOOLPROOF HALIBUT color *Chicago* v66 no4 p58 Ap 2017
FROM ROME WITH AMORE color *Chicago* v66 no3 p62 Mr 2017
HIP TO BE SQUARE color *Chicago* v66 no1 p56 Ja 2017
IN THE KITCHEN color *Chicago* v66 no6 p50 Je 2017
IN THE KITCHEN: VENETIAN BITES color *Chicago* v66 no9 p68 S 2017
MUSSELS, REBOOTED color *Chicago* v65 no11 p60 N 2016
NACHO NIRVANA color *Chicago* v66 no2 p52 F 2017
PERFECT SPROUTS color *Chicago* v65 no12 p64 D 2016
SALAD DAYS color *Chicago* v66 no10 p50 O 2017
SPICE UP YOUR BLT color *Chicago* v66 no7 p42 Jl 2017

Henney, Daniel
Criminal Minds *TV Guide* v65 no41 p31 O 2 2017

HENNIGAN, TOM
About Face *Architectural Record* v205 no10 p102 O 2017
Two of a Kind *Architectural Record* v205 no6 p98 Je 2017

Henning, C. Randall
Tangled Governance: International Regime Complexity, the Troika, and the Euro Crisis A. Moravcsik *Foreign Affairs* v96 no6 p160 N/D 2017

Henning, Hans-Martin
Terawatt-scale photovoltaics: Trajectories and challenges chart graph *Science* v356 no6334 p141 Ap 14 2017

Henning, Thomas
Spiral density waves in a young protoplanetary disk bibl graph *Science* v353 no6307 p1519 S 30 2016

Henningsgard, Jon
A CONVERSATION with Jon and Krista Henningsgard S. Andersen *Arabian Horse World* v57 no6 p70 Mr 2017

Henretta, Deb
5 Ways to Help Employees Keep Up with Digital Transformation *Harvard Business Review Digital Articles* p2 S 27 2017

Henrich, Joseph
High fidelity color *Science* v356 no6340 p810 My 26 2017

Henrick, Erin
A better research-practice partnership color *Phi Delta Kappan* v98 no3 p23 N 2016

Henrie, David
Wizards of Waverly Place? color *Seventeen* v76 no3 p16 My 2017

Henriksen, Danah
Teachers are designers color il *Phi Delta Kappan* v99 no2 p60 O 2017

Henrique Pereira, Jose
Principles for designing proteins with cavities formed by curved β sheets bibl color graph *Science* v355 no6321 p1 Ja 13 2017

Henriques, Diana B.
A First-Class Catastrophe *Publishers Weekly* v264 no29 p210 Jl 17 2017

Henriquez, Jessica Ciencin
THE HALFWAY HOUSE color *O, The Oprah Magazine* p25 Mr 2017

Henroid, Ron
Dream Buddy on a Trail Ride cartoon *Horse & Rider* v56 no3 p72 Mr 2017

Henry, Bob
Railway Post Office color *Model Railroader* v84 no8 p16 Ag 2017

Henry, Brian
Warm Up for Horsemanship color *Horse & Rider* v55 no11 p25 N 2016

Henry, Colu
Noodling Around color *O, The Oprah Magazine* p135 Ap 2017
PASTA NIGHT MAGIC color *Redbook* p120 Mr 2017

Henry, Dave
Choosing Equipment for Eclipse Photography color *Astronomy* v45 no7 p7 Jl 2017

Henry, F.
Seasonal exposure of carbon dioxide ice on the nucleus of comet 67P/Churyumov-Gerasimenko bibl bw graph *Science* v354 no6319 p1563 D 23 2016

HENRY, GRAY
Timeless Teachings for Young Readers *Islamic Horizons* v45 no6 p34 N/D 2016

Henry, Gregg
Orange Julius K. Pollitt *Nation* v305 no2 p6 Jl 17 2017

Henry, Jake
Beauty to Behold B. Fishel color diag *Log Home Living* v34 no4 p26 My 2017

HENRY, KRISTINA TATUSKO
THE QUESTION *Washingtonian Magazine* v52 no5 p192 F 2017

Henry, Mary Kay, 1958-——Interviews
Mary Kay Henry I. Boudway color *Bloomberg Businessweek* no4496 p24 O 24 2016

Henry, Matt
GQHQ bw color *GQ: Gentlemen's Quarterly* v97 no7 p8 Jl 2017

Henry, Peter Blair
A DEAN FOR ALL SEASONS T. J. Huddleston color *Fortune* v174 no7 p38 D 1 2016

Henry, Prince, grandson of Elizabeth II, Queen of Great Britain, 1984-
For the Record color *Time* v190 no2/3 p4 Jl 10-17 2017
HARRY'S NEXT GAMES P. TREBLE color *Maclean's* v129 no51/52 p47 D 26 2016
Wild About Harry! S. KASHNER bw color *Vanity Fair* v59 no10 p148 O 2017

HENRY, RAOUL
Copepods Against Aedes Mosquitoes: A Very Risky Strategy *BioScience* v67 no6 p489 Je 2017

HENRY, SARAH
GROWING LEADERS *Sierra* v101 no5 p44 S/O 2016

Henry, Scott
ATLANTA *Atlanta* v56 no10 p70 F 2017
BeltLine BREWERS *Atlanta* v56 no11 p114 Mr 2017
INTO THE SPOTLIGHT *Atlanta* v56 no8 p38 D 2016
INTO THIN AIR *Atlanta* v57 no1 p24 My 2017
LARGER THAN LIFE *Atlanta* v56 no7 p23 N 2016
MOVIE MAN *Atlanta* v56 no12 p24 Ap 2017
OFF TO THE RACES *Atlanta* v56 no10 p32 F 2017
One for All: The Woodruff Arts Center's new CEO aims to boost arts groups citywide *Atlanta* v57 no6 p75 O 2017
A PARK FOR VINE CITY *Atlanta* v56 no9 p24 Ja 2017
ROBOTS, TAKE THE WHEEL!: Driverless cars are coming to Atlanta. Are we ready? *Atlanta* v57 no4 p15 Ag 2017

Henry Francis du Pont Winterthur Museum
Flim-flam and chicanery exposed at Winterthur color *Magazine Antiques* v184 no3 p35 My/Je 2017

Henry: Portrait of a Serial Killer (Film)
HENRY: PORTRAIT OF A SERIAL KILLER C. Chiarella color *Sound & Vision* v82 no4 p69 My 2017

Henry Repeating Arms Co.
THE ENDURING .45/70 J. B. SNOW color *Outdoor Life* v224 no7 p62 S 2017
HENRY .410 LEVER ACTION chart color *Outdoor Life* v224 no8 p30 O 2017

Henry II, King of England, 1133-1189

OFFICIAL TRANSCRIPTS R. LONG *National Review* v69 no15 p36 Ag 14 2017

Henry III, King of England, 1207-1272

God Save the King! - Gloucester crowns a young prince R. Gardner *British Heritage Travel* v37 no6 p8 N/D 2016

Henry IV, Holy Roman Emperor, 1050-1106

Henry IV of Germany: a 'Bad King'? L. Roach *History Today* v67 no3 p4 Mr 2017

Henrys, P.

Country-specific effects of neonicotinoid pesticides on honey bees and wild bees diag map *Science* v356 no6345 p1393 Je 30 2017

Henry VIII, King of England, 1491-1547

Hallowed Ground Bosworth Field, England [Cover story] C. Allsop color *Military History* v34 no4 p76 N 2017

Hens

APROPOS OF NOTHING *Saturday Evening Post* v289 no4 p30 Jl/Ag 2017

Extreme Weirdness A. SANDLIN color *National Geographic Kids* no471 p10 Je/Jl 2017

Improve Your Flock with TRAPNESTS H. Ussery *Mother Earth News* no281 p58 Ap/My 2017

Hens, Gregor, 1965-

ASHES TO ASHES J. ACOCELLA color *New Yorker* v92 no44 p66 Ja 9 2017

Hensen, Matthias

Angular momentum–induced delays in solid-state photoemission enhanced by intra-atomic interactions chart color graph *Science* v357 no6357 p1274 S 22 2017

Henser-Brownhill, Tristan

The linker histone H1.0 generates epigenetic and functional intratumor heterogeneity bibl graph *Science* v353 no6307 paaf1644-1 S 30 2016

Hensley, Lucinda

MAVS-dependent host species range and pathogenicity of human hepatitis A virus bibl graph *Science* v353 no6307 p1541 S 30 2016

Henson, Taraji P., 1970-

Hidden Figures Calculates the Sum of a Story Untold E. Berman color *Time* v188 no22-23 p94 N/D 2016

Hidden Figures L. Greenblatt color *Entertainment Weekly* no1448 p48 Ja 13 2017

L. A. NOIR W. MORRIS and A. O. SCOTT bw *New York Times Magazine* p64 D 11 2016

Movie celebrates NASA 'computers' E. Conover bw color *Science News* v191 no1 p28 Ja 21 2017

TARAJI TELLS HER OWN STORY T. P. Henson color *Essence* v47 no7 p52 N 2016

Why I Love MY EDIE PARKER CLUTCH color *InStyle* v24 no5 p262 My 2017

Henson, Taraji P., 1970—Interviews

Empire M. Logan *TV Guide* v64 no46 p34 N 7 2016

Taraji P. Henson K. B. Brown color *InStyle* v24 no7 p91 Jl 2017

Henstock, Timothy J.

Release of mineral-bound water prior to subduction tied to shallow seismogenic slip off Sumatra graph *Science* v356 no6340 p841 My 26 2017

Hentges, Donna—Interviews

Small Breeders BIG RESULTS M. Moore *Arabian Horse World* v56 no12 p74 S 2016

Henthorne, Colin

The Queen of the North Disaster: The Captain's Story *Publishers Weekly* v264 no4 p75 Ja 23 2017

Hentoff, Nat, 1925-2017

Chords & Discords P. D'RIVERA, D. ELLIS et al color *Downbeat* v84 no5 p10 My 2017

Love and Rage L. SMITH color *Weekly Standard* v22 no19 p13 Ja 23 2017

Remembering Journalist Nat Hentoff color *Downbeat* v84 no3 p21 Mr 2017

Henwick, Jessica

Jessica HENWICK S. LACAVA *Interview* v47 no1 p12 F 2017

Heon Shin, Joo

Intersection of diverse neuronal genomes and neuropsychiatric disease: The Brain Somatic Mosaicism Network color *Science* v356 no6336 p395 Ap 28 2017

Heos, Bridget

It's Getting Hot in Here: The Past, Present and Future of Climate Change color *Publishers Weekly* v263 no49 p122 D 7 2016

Heparin

DRUG SHOWS PROMISE IN PREVENTING NEUROLOGICAL COMPLICATION C. Barakat and M. McCluskey *Equus* no476 p20 My 2017

RESEARCH color *Science* v356 no6335 p280 Ap 21 2017

Heparin—Therapeutic use

A Gutsy Call D. G. ADLER color *Discover* v38 no2 p20 Mr 2017

Hepatitis A virus

MAVS-dependent host species range and pathogenicity of human hepatitis A virus Asuka Hirai-Yuki, L. Hensley et al bibl graph *Science* v353 no6307 p1541 S 30 2016

Hepatitis B vaccine

Europe's top court alarms vaccine experts G. Vogel color *Science* v356 no6345 p1320 Je 30 2017

New and Improved Vaccine Schedule color *Parents* v92 no9 p28 S 2017

Hepatitis C treatment

Immunology taught by rats P. Klenerman and E. J. Barnes graph *Science* v357 no6347 p129 Jl 14 2017

Mouse models of acute and chronic hepacivirus infection E. Billerbeck, R. Wolfisberg et al *Science* v357 no6347 p204 Jl 14 2017

Hepatotoxicology

Are Supplements Toxic to Liver? *Tufts University Health & Nutrition Letter* v35 no5 p3 Jl 2017

HEPBURN, ANDREW

Double bubble, toil and trouble color graph *Maclean's* v129 no45 p44 N 14 2016

Hepburn, Audrey, 1929-1993

NINA'S BEAUTY HEROES color *Harper's Bazaar* no3656 p335e S 2017

Hepburn, Katharine, 1907-2003

KATE STORMS HOLLYWOOD *Saturday Evening Post* v289 no4 p93 Jl/Ag 2017

WE WERE RIGHT ALL ALONG bw *Yankee* p26 My/Je 2017

Hepfer, Anne—Interviews

LADY OF THE LAKE K. RENDA color *House Beautiful* v159 no4 p116 My 2017

Hepinstall, Kathy

A MOTHER'S LOVE A. Orr color *Louisiana Life* v37 no6 p12 Jl/Ag 2017

Hepola, Sarah

Rwanda Reborn color *Bloomberg Businessweek* no4540 p71 O 2 2017

Hepworth, Shelley

THE BUDGET bw *Columbia Journalism Review* v56 no1 p85 Spr 2017

The drone files color *Columbia Journalism Review* p12 Fall/Wint 2016

THE FERNDALE ENTERPRISE bw *Columbia Journalism Review* v56 no1 p111 Spr 2017

Hey, big funder color *Columbia Journalism Review* v56 no1 p60 Spr 2017

Where the digital dollars have gone graph *Columbia Journalism Review* p58 Fall/Wint 2016

Hepworth-Warren, Kate

The truth about Tail Blocks color *Equus* no476 p50 My 2017

Her (Film)

The Seven Best Romantic Comedies of the Past Decade img *New York* p70 F 20 2017

Her Birthday As Ashes in Seawater (Poem)

HER BIRTHDAY AS ASHES IN SEAWATER S. Olds *New Yorker* v92 no32 p86 O 10 2016

Heracleous, Loizos

As Hopelessness Sets In, Grexit May Be Inevitable *Harvard Business Review Digital Articles* p2 S 1 2015

Why Greece and Cyprus May Be Better Off Without the Euro *Harvard Business Review Digital Articles* p2 Mr 10 2015

Heras, Ricardo

Commentary How to teach me physics: Tradition is not always a virtue *Physics Today* v70 no3 p10 Mr 2017

Hérault, Bruno

Positive biodiversity-productivity relationship predominant in global forests bibl chart graph map *Science* v354 no6309 paaf8957-1 O 14 2016

Hérault, Yann

The DNA methyltransferase DNMT3C protects male germ cells from transposon activity bibl diag graph *Science* v354 no6314 p909 N 18 2016

Herb gardening

HERBS FOR THE WIN J. Silver color *Sunset* v238 no6 p52 Je 2017

Timing is Everything P. Marquis *New Orleans Homes & Lifestyles* v20 no2 p64 Spr 2017

Herbal medicine

Bark, Birds, and Berries S. KLEIN color *Prevention* v69 no6 p22 Je 2017

DOCTOR WHO? M. Velasquez-Manoff color *New York Times Magazine* p68 My 21 2017

EXPERT ADVICE A. Nix *Amazing Wellness* p8 Fall 2017

First Aid on the Go T. L. Dog color *Prevention* v69 no6 p26 Je 2017

Growing Natural Cures [Cover story] T. L. Dog color *Prevention* v69 no5 p26 My 2017

HEALTHY TRAVELS K. P. S. Khalsa color *Amazing Wellness* v8 no6 p36 Early Winter2016

MEDICINAL HERBS for Difficult Growing Conditions R. Cech *Mother Earth News* no281 p20 Ap/My 2017

ONE LOVE G. Megroz color *Bloomberg Businessweek* no4524 p66 My 29 2017

TOP THREE HERBS FOR MEN K. P. S. Khalsa color *Amazing Wellness* v8 no2 p22 Spr 2016

Herbal teas

HERBAL SUPPORT for Wintertime Blues M. Adelmann *Mother Earth News* no280 p56 F/Mr 2017

Herbal teas—Therapeutic use

What's the healthiest herbal tea? L. Dog color *Prevention* v68 no12 p28 D 2016

Herbalife International Inc.—Trials, litigation, etc.

HOW THE FTC GOT THE HERBALIFE SETTLEMENT DISASTROUSLY WRONG J. Wieczner color *Fortune* v175 no3 p12 Mr 1 2017

Herbalists

Online Courses for Homestead Herbalists S. Stonebrook *Mother Earth News* no281 p9 Ap/My 2017

Herbaria

Validating Herbarium-Based Phenology Models Using Citizen-Science Data K. V. SPELLMAN and C. P. H. MULDER chart graph *BioScience* v66 no10 p897 O 1 2016

Herberger, Brian

Miss E *Publishers Weekly* v264 no10 p62 Mr 6 2017

Herbert, Andrew S.

A "Trojan horse" bispecific-antibody strategy for broad protection against ebolaviruses bibl graph *Science* v354 no6310 p350 O 21 2016

Herbert, David Gauvey

COSTCO cartoon *Atlantic* v320 no4 p24 N 2017

A Digital Fact-Checker Fights Fake News color *Bloomberg Businessweek* no4507 p27 Ja 16 2017

How Couples (and Throuples!) Do Money color *Bloomberg Businessweek* no4502 p74 D 5 2016

HERBERT, GERALDINE

6 DRIVES TO TAKE YOUR BREATH AWAY color *House Beautiful* p158 Ag 2017

Herbert, Jack

Things That Go *Treasures* v6 no3 p12 D 2016/Ja 2017

Herbert, Joe

16 LIFE LESSONS *Psychology Today* v49 no5 p62 S/O 2016

Herbert, Wray

Goodnight, Sun color *Weekly Standard* v22 no36 p30 My 29 2017

Love Conquers All bw *Weekly Standard* v22 no9 p30 N 7 2016

Remains of the Day color *Weekly Standard* v22 no26 p34 Mr 13 2017

Herbicides

BE WARY OF INVERSIONS K. Birchmier *Successful Farming* v115 no5 p14 Mid-Mr 2017

MASS EXPOSURE R. EBERSOLE color *Nation* v305 no11 p34 O 30 2017

MEET METABOLIC RESISTANCE G. Gullickson *Successful Farming* v115 no5 p44 Mid-Mr 2017

ONLY ON OUR WEBSITE *South Dakota Magazine* v32 no6 p19 Mr/Ap 2017

WHERE DICAMBA STANDS FOR 2017 G. Gullickson *Successful Farming* v115 no1 p16 Ja 2017

Herbicides—Application—Environmental aspects

MANAGING FOR LEAN TIMES R. Nickel *Successful Farming* v114 no11 p20 N 2016

Herbicides—Evaluation

Products *Parks & Recreation* v52 no6 p50 Je 2017

Herbivores

How do gut microbes help herbivores? Counting the ways E. Pennisi color *Science* v355 no6322 p236 Ja 20 2017

Herbolzheimer, Claus

Can You Put a Dollar Amount on Your Company's Cyber Risk? *Harvard Business Review Digital Articles* p2 O 5 2016

Limit Cyberattacks with a System-Wide Safe Mode *Harvard Business Review Digital Articles* p2 My 17 2017

Preparing for a Black Swan Cyberattack *Harvard Business Review Digital Articles* p2 S 14 2016

Herbs

Ayurvedic HERB GUIDE V. Tweed color *Amazing Wellness* v9 no2 p38 Spr 2017

EASE ECZEMA WITH HERBS K. Purkh Singh Khalsa color *Amazing Wellness* v9 no3 p38 EarlySumm 2017

Faster, Easier Gnocchi color *Vegetarian Today* no2 p40 Ap 2017

GARDEN REMEDIES C. HASLAM color *House Beautiful* p145 Ag 2017

GH TEST KITCHEN S. WESTMORELAND color *Good Housekeeping* v265 no4 p105 O 2017

HEART-HEALING HERBS K. P. S. Khalsa color *Amazing Wellness* p34 Fall 2017

HERB APPEAL J. BALL *Indianapolis Monthly* v12 no40 p66 Ag 2017

Mineral-Rich Herbs K. P. SINGH KHALSA color *Better Nutrition* v78 no12 p20 D 2016

SO FRESH AND SO CLEAN A. MASON color *Bon Appetit* v62 no2 p99 Mr 2017

Spring Clean Your Life [Cover story] S. Sims color *Prevention* v69 no4 p40 Ap 2017

Herbs—Physiological aspects

HERBAL HEART TONICS: Incorporate these five delicious herbs into your daily routine to strengthen and gladden your heart M. N. Groves *Mother Earth News* no284 p14 O/N 2017

HERBST, JULIA

ALICIA RIVERA: THE COMMUNITY ORGANIZER DETAILS HER QUEST FOR ENVIRONMENTAL JUSTICE IN WILMINGTON, WHERE RESIDENTS LIVE IN THE SHADOW OF AN OIL FACILITY *Los Angeles Magazine* v62 no9 p97 S 2017

chinatown color *Los Angeles Magazine* v62 no7 p70 Jl 2017

THE DTLA LOOP *Los Angeles Magazine* v62 no6 p72 Je 2017

Friends, Foes, and Felines color *Los Angeles Magazine* v62 no10 p98 O 2017

Happy Mix color *Los Angeles Magazine* v62 no7 p41 Jl 2017

HELEN LEUNG + ELIZABETH TIMME: THE "WONKISH" URBAN PLANNER AND "ARCHITECTURE GEEK" ARE OUT TO SOLVE SOME OF L.A.'S TOUGHEST HOUSING AND SMALL-BUSINESS PROBLEMS *Los Angeles Magazine* v62 no9 p93 S 2017

Highland Park *Los Angeles Magazine* p84 D 2016

The High Sign *Los Angeles Magazine* v61 no11 p32 N 2016

The Little Comedy Fest That Could *Los Angeles Magazine* p57 Ja 2017

Looking Past the Color Lines *Los Angeles Magazine* p21 Ap 2017

Oakland *Los Angeles Magazine* v62 no9 p68 S 2017

The Plot To End Homelessness *Los Angeles Magazine* p22 My 2017

Recycling And Rehab *Los Angeles Magazine* v62 no6 p15 Je 2017

Studio City *Los Angeles Magazine* p76 Mr 2017

Susan Burton *Los Angeles Magazine* v62 no9 p92 S 2017

To Stand And Deliver *Los Angeles Magazine* p19 F 2017

A Wealth of Experience *Los Angeles Magazine* p32 D 2016

West Adams *Los Angeles Magazine* p62 My 2017

Herculano-Houzel, Suzana

Our 86 Billion Neurons: She Showed It S. Mithen color *New York Review of Books* v63 no18 p42 N 24 2016

Hercules (Constellation)

The Kneeler J. RAO color *Natural History* v125 no6 p45 Je 2017

Herd, Tim

'Good' Times in Pennsylvania *Parks & Recreation* v52 no2 p18 F 2017

Herders

See also

Cowboys

Herders helped shape Silk Road B. BOWER color *Science News* v191 no7 p9 Ap 15 2017

Road to Greener Pastures A. Hadhazy color *Natural History* v125 no5 p8 My 2017

Herding behavior in animals

Why Won't He Move? J. FIELD and J. VON GELDERN color *Horse & Rider* v56 no8 p64 Ag 2017

Herdling, Glenn

Piper Houdini: Apprentice of Coney Island *Publishers Weekly* v264 no17 p92 Ap 24 2017

Here (Music)

Alicia Keys B. HIATT color *Rolling Stone* no1274 p18 N 17 2016

Heredia-Genestar, José María

Chimpanzee genomic diversity reveals ancient admixture with bonobos bibl diag graph map *Science* v354 no6311 p477 O 28 2016

Hereditary nonpolyposis colorectal cancer

Hidden Agenda N. Casey color *Vogue* v207 no10 p224 O 2017

Hereford, Joe

Precipitation drives global variation in natural selection bibl chart diag map *Science* v355 no6328 p959 Mr 3 2017

HEREFORD, MASON

Thanksgiving LESSONS [Cover story] color *Bon Appetit* no11 p82 N 2017

Hergenrader, Jamie

Mindfulness Takes Flight color *Women's Health* v14 no9 p102 N 2017

SYNC UP YOUR SEX DRIVES [Cover story] *Women's Health* v14 no1 p150 Ja/F 2017

URGENT CARE OR ER? color *Women's Health* v14 no6 p82 Jl 2017

Hergert, Jeff

Railway Post Office color *Model Railroader* v84 no8 p16 Ag 2017

Hergott, J. -F.

Attosecond dynamics through a Fano resonance: Monitoring the birth of a photoelectron bibl graph *Science* v354 no6313 p734 N 11 2016

Hergt, Brian

Producer prices, 2016: goods inflation returns and price increases for services move higher bibl chart color graph *Monthly Labor Review* p1 Mr 2017

Heringa, Nic

GARAGE BRANDS C. Liska color *Snowboarder* v29 no4 p32 D 2016

Herink, G.

Real-time spectral interferometry probes the internal dynamics of femtosecond soliton molecules diag *Science* v356 no6333 p50 Ap 7 2017

Heritability (Genetics)

Transgenerational inheritance: Models and mechanisms of non–DNA sequence–based inheritance E. A. Miska and A. C. Ferguson-Smith bibl color diag *Science* v354 no6308 p59 O 7 2016

Heritage Expeditions (Company)

The Southern Wild M. Shipstead bw *Conde Nast Traveler* v52 no7 p46 Ag 2017

Heritage Guitar Inc.

Heritage KB Groove Master Archtop K. Baumann color *Downbeat* v83 no12 p106 D 2016

Heritage tourism

BELLWETHER E. J. WALLACE *Virginia Living* v15 no2 p27 F 2017

once upon a time in Wales: Life in the Valleys of Glamorganshire D. Huntley *British Heritage Travel* v38 no4 p56 Jl/Ag 2017

Heritage Foundation (Washington, D.C.)

Cracked Foundation J. MCCORMACK color *Weekly Standard* v22 no34 p8 My 15 2017

THE RIGHT-WING MACHINE BEHIND THE CURTAIN T. ANDERSON *In These Times* v41 no4 p14 Ap 2017

Trump's Think Tank A. SHEPHARD color *New Republic* v248

no3 p10 Mr 2017

Tweetstorms and Circuses J. BLEIFUSS *In These Times* v41 no4 p5 Ap 2017

Herjavec, Robert, 1962-

BEFORE HE WAS A SHARK D. Eng color *Fortune* v174 no7 p34 D 1 2016

LIFE (AND LOVE) LESSONS WE'VE LEARNED FROM REALITY TV R. HERJAVEC and K. JOHNSON HERJAVEC *TV Guide* v64 no40 p20 O 3 2016

Herjavec Group (Company)

BEFORE HE WAS A SHARK D. Eng color *Fortune* v174 no7 p34 D 1 2016

HERKEN, GREGG

He's the Bomb *New York Times Book Review* p23 N 20 2016

Herkenhoff, K. E.

Redox stratification of an ancient lake in Gale crater, Mars color *Science* v356 no6341 p922 Je 1 2017

HERLINGER, CHRIS

THE LONELY EVERYMAN color *America* v215 no16 p33 N 21 2016

Youngblood: A Novel/War Is Beautiful: The New York Times Pictorial Guide to the Glamour of Armed Conflict *Christian Century* v133 no26 p38 D 21 2016

Herlitz, John

The Dream Car D. Freiburger color *Hot Rod* v70 no3 p106 Mr 2017

Herman, Andrew—Interviews

ANDREW HERMAN J. Chen color *Bloomberg Businessweek* no4508 p63 Ja 23 2017

Herman, Arthur

Dangerous Gamble color *National Review* v68 no24 p35 D 31 2016

He Has Returned M. BOOT *Commentary* v142 no1 p48 Jl/Ag 2016

The Pentagon's 'Smart' Revolution *Commentary* v142 no1 p25 Jl/Ag 2016

Restoring U.S. Strength color *National Review* v69 no6 p42 Ap 3 2017

HERMAN, CHRISTINE

A LESSON IN LISTENING bw *Christianity Today* v61 no5 p40 Je 2017

Herman, Max

SHREDDING ON THE SANDS OF TIME S. Lachenauer and W. Allison color diag *Hot Rod* v70 no12 p38 D 2017

Herman, Roger M.

LIGO backstory delights and displeases *Physics Today* v70 no6 p14 Je 2017

HERMAN, SANFORD

Library Catalogs Deny Science Denial *Skeptical Inquirer* v41 no3 p8 My/Je 2017

Herman, Tom—Interviews

JUST MY TYPE D. Patrick and T. Keith color *Sports Illustrated* v125 no19 p27 D 12 2016

Herman Melville (Short story)

HERMAN MELVILLE, VOLUME I V. LODATO cartoon color *New Yorker* v93 no6 p56 Mr 27 2017

Hermanis, Alvis

Madama Butterfly S. Hastings *Opera News* v81 no9 p41 Mr 2017

HERMANN, KEN

Flower Men color map *National Geographic* v231 no5 p112 My 2017

Hermans, I.

Selective oxidative dehydrogenation of propane to propene using boron nitride catalysts bibl diag graph *Science* v354 no6319 p1570 D 23 2016

HERMANSON, MARISSA

The Autumnal Table Throw a dinner party Featuring the hearty bounty of the season *Virginia Living* v15 no6 p68 O 2017

NEW WORLD CHARM: A neoclassical waterfront home in Williamsburg is a stylish basis for the Fang family *Virginia Living* v15 no4 p60 Je 2017

Retail Therapy *Virginia Living* v15 no1 p45 D 2016

Hermé, Pierre

Homemade Chic D. Greenspan *New York Times Magazine* p22 Ag 13 2017

HERMES, WILL

THE 50 GREATEST CONCERTS OF THE LAST 50 YEARS bw color *Rolling Stone* no1286 p30 My 4 2017

Arcade Fire Go Dancing in the Dark color *Rolling Stone* no1293 p53 Ag 10 2017

Beck's Day-Glo Vision of Modern Pop color *Rolling Stone* no1298 p49 O 19 2017

Dirty Projectors' Brave New Breakup Pop cartoon color *Rolling Stone* no1281/1282 p51 F 23 2017

Essential Lou Reed color *Rolling Stone* no1273 p52 N 3 2016

The Gospel of Father John Misty cartoon *Rolling Stone* no1285 p51 Ap 20 2017

The Jam Kings Come Down to Earth color *Rolling Stone* no1272 p49 O 20 2016

Leonard Cohen's Late-Night Serenade color *Rolling Stone* no1273 p49 N 3 2016

Lorde Throws an Epic House Party color *Rolling Stone* no1290 p53 Je 29 2017

Lou Reed's Final Look Back bw *Rolling Stone* no1272 p19 O 20 2016

Miranda Lambert: Blonde on the Tracks color *Rolling Stone* no1275 p59 D 1 2016

The Mystery of Otis bw color *Rolling Stone* no1293 p18 Ag 10 2017

The New Protest Singers color *Rolling Stone* no1283 p49 Mr 23 2017

The Outlaw Soul of Chris Stapleton color *Rolling Stone* no1287 p53 My 18 2017

Paying Respect to Country Music's Original Rebel color *Rolling Stone* no1285 p54 Ap 20 2017

Rhinestone Superstar bw color *Rolling Stone* no1295 p16 S 7 2017

Hermès International SA

Back from the Dead S. HINE bw color *GQ: Gentlemen's Quarterly* v97 no3 p60 Mr 2017

Hermès bracelet cartoon *Vogue* v206 no11 p264 N 2016

Men's Ware color *Architectural Digest* v74 no7 p17 Jl 2017

VIENNA BOTH THE CLASSIC AND MODERN SIDES R. MISNER color *Conde Nast Traveler* v52 no8 p32 S 2017

Wait LIST color *Harper's Bazaar* no3649 p132 D 2016/Ja 2017

Hermes Parcelnet Ltd.

We're happy not to be in the gig economy: How a courier company's commitment to values is marking it out from the competition *People Management* p22 My 2017

Hermia & Helena (Film)

Hermia & Helena *New Yorker* v93 no16 p28 Je 5 2017

Hermit crab shells

Hermit crab takes shelter in corals M. QUINTANILLA color *Science News* v192 no7 p14 O 28 2017

Hermitages

The Friendly Recluse: Medieval hermits were the agony aunts of their day S. L. Deboick *History Today* v67 no7 p18 Jl 2017

Hermits—History

The Friendly Recluse: Medieval hermits were the agony aunts of their day S. L. Deboick *History Today* v67 no7 p18 Jl 2017

Hermon, Mount (Lebanon & Syria)

THE TOWER OF SUN J. CLARY DAVIES color map *Powder* v46 no2 p52 O 2017

HERMOSO, VIRGILIO

A Global Assessment of Inland Wetland Conservation Status *BioScience* v67 no6 p523 Je 2017

HERMY, MARTIN

Combining Biodiversity Resurveys across Regions to Advance Global Change Research *BioScience* v67 no1 p73 Ja 2017

Hernandez, Aaron, 1989-2017

FOR THE DEFENSE A. French color *Esquire* p130 S 2017

TURNING HEADS J. Vrentas and S. Kwak color *Sports Illustrated* v127 no10 p14 O 2 2017

Hernandez, Aaron, 1989-2017—Trials, litigation, etc.

BROTHER TO BROTHER M. Rosenberg color *Sports Illustrated* v126 no12 p50 My 1 2017

Hernandez, Aileen, 1926-2017

Milestones color *Time* v189 no9 p14 Mr 13 2017

Hernandez, Alvaro

Wild emmer genome architecture and diversity elucidate wheat evolution and domestication color *Science* v357 no6346 p93 Jl 7 2017

Hernández, Antonia, 1948-

A Wealth of Experience J. HERBST *Los Angeles Magazine* p32 D 2016

Hernandez, Danny

How Our Company Learned to Make Better Predictions About Everything *Harvard Business Review Digital Articles* p2 My 15 2017

Hernandez, Esteban—Interviews

ESTEBAN HERNÁNDEZ N. Loeffler-Gladstone *Dance Spirit* v21 no3 p40 Mr 2017

HERNANDEZ, JASON

OBAMA'S AMERICA img *New York* v49 no20 p12 O 3 2016

Hernandez, Johnny

Cinco de Mayo San Antonio Style color *Southern Living* v52 no5 p110 My 2017

Hernandez, Jonathan

BROTHER TO BROTHER M. Rosenberg color *Sports Illustrated* v126 no12 p50 My 1 2017

Hernandez, L.

Persistent effects of pre-Columbian plant domestication on Amazonian forest composition bibl chart graph map *Science* v355 no6328 p925 Mr 3 2017

Hernandez, Laurie, 2000-

Laurie Hernandez J. Crelin color *Current Biography* v78 no2 p31 F 2017

Meet the Class of 2016 A. Park, S. Gregory et al color *Time* v188 no18 p22 O 31 2016

Sound Bites color *Entertainment Weekly* no1441 p5 N 25 2016

Hernandez, Laurie, 2000-—Awards

American Voices Laurie Hernandez T. Keith color *Sports Illustrated* v125 no15 p24 N 7 2016

Hernandez, Michael

SOCIAL JUSTICE IN A DIGITAL AGE [Cover story] color *Literacy Today (2411-7862)* v34 no3 p18 N/D 2016

HERNANDEZ, REBECCA R.

Skills and Knowledge for Data-Intensive Environmental Research *BioScience* v67 no6 p546 Je 2017

Hernandez, Richard

Raising the minimum wage in three different ways: what are the effects? *Monthly Labor Review* p30 Jl 2017

HERNANDEZ, SUSAN

RECENT OUTINGS color *Advocate* no1090 p15 Ap 2017

Hernández-Benítez, Reyna

Integration of CpG-free DNA induces de novo methylation of CpG islands in pluripotent stem cells diag *Science* v356 no6337 p503 My 5 2017

Hernandez-Miranda, Luis R.

Loss of a mammalian circular RNA locus causes miRNA deregulation and affects brain function color *Science* v357 no6357 p1254 S 22 2017

Hernandez-Rodriguez, Jessica

Chimpanzee genomic diversity reveals ancient admixture with bonobos bibl diag graph map *Science* v354 no6311 p477 O 28 2016

Herndon, Bekah

NEW YORK, NEW YORK color *Runner's World* v51 no10 p10 N 2016

Herndon, James

Nuclear Power and Risk Psychology *Skeptical Inquirer* v41 no2 p64 Mr/Ap 2017

HERNDON, KRIS

I Survived! [Cover story] *Reader's Digest* v189 no1128 p62 Mr 2017

Hernia

My Late Term Abortion A. K. MILLER *Washingtonian Magazine* v52 no9 p64 Je 2017

Sick and Tired P. GULLEY *Indianapolis Monthly* v40 no4 p63 D 2016

HERNNDEZ, DAISY

LEARNING TO SPEAK THE TRUTH bw *Tricycle: The Buddhist Review* v27 no1 p55 Fall 2017

HERNROTH-ROTHSTEIN, ANNIKA

A Biography of Zion *Commentary* v142 no3 p44 O 2016

Hero (Greek mythology)

A William Henry Rinehart Leander comes to the surface S. P. Feld bw color *Magazine Antiques* v184 no5 p54 S/O 2017

Hero, The (Film)

A Cowboy Makes a Comeback In The Hero S. Zacharek color *Time* v189 no23 p51 Je 19 2017

Herod, Lindsey—Interviews

THE GREENHOUSE EFFECT J. LASKY color *House Beautiful* v159 no4 p98 My 2017

Heroes

See also

Explorers

Dog Catcher A. JUNG *Reader's Digest* v189 no1127 p8 F 2017

Sing the Hero: A Hole in the Boat, And Ice in the Water K. WIDNER *Idaho Magazine* v16 no7 p21 Ap 2017

Your True Stories G. PLOZAY, R. PITTMAN et al *Reader's Digest* v189 no1127 p28 F 2017

Héroguel, Florent

Formaldehyde stabilization facilitates lignin monomer production during biomass depolymerization bibl diag graph *Science* v354 no6310 p329 O 21 2016

Heroin

BORN USERS L. MURTHA *Cincinnati Magazine* v50 no4 p68 Ja 2017

Does Legalized Pot Fuel Opioid Epidemic? *USA Today Magazine* v146 no2867 p12 Ag 2017

Opioid Deaths Soar M. Fischetti graph *Scientific American* v317 no4 p96 O 2017

S&T Policy Forum examines evolving opioid epidemic K. O'Neil color *Science* v356 no6336 p390 Ap 28 2017

Heroin abuse

THE HEROIN CRISIS WE'VE IGNORED K. LYDERSEN *In These Times* v41 no5 p44 My 2017

Heroin took over our town S. M. FERNÁNDEZ *Scholastic Choices* v32 no3 p6 N/D 2016

hope riseS M. SZALAVITZ color *Women's Health* v14 no5 p154 Je 2017

I didn't know I was an addict J. Gellar *Scholastic Choices* v32 no3 p8 N/D 2016

Measuring the Impact: Rising opioid abuse puts pressure on schools E. McINTYRE *Education Digest* v82 no5 p4 Ja 2017

Heroin abuse—Social aspects

Seattle Breaks New Ground on Opioids A. Arnold color graph *Bloomberg Businessweek* no4494 p28 O 10 2016

Heroin industry

The Heroin Business Is Booming in America J. Smialek color *Bloomberg Businessweek* no4522 p32 My 15 2017

Heroin—Marketing

GETTING DARK A. FLANGO and J. WILLIAMS *Cincinnati Magazine* v50 no3 p29 D 2016

HEROLD, ANN

Beach Life *Los Angeles Magazine* p86 Ag 2017

The Cocktail Hour *Los Angeles Magazine* v61 no11 p52 N 2016

Draw Close *Los Angeles Magazine* p52 Mr 2017

Earth Tones *Los Angeles Magazine* p36 F 2017

Fine Prints *Los Angeles Magazine* v62 no6 p30 Je 2017

Fire Power: SOUTHERN CALIFORNIA GRILL MAKERS TURN UP THE HEAT ON ALFRESCO COOKING color *Los Angeles Magazine* v62 no7 p30 Jl 2017

Homes with A Pedigree bw color *Los Angeles Magazine* v62 no10 p124 O 2017

JE T'AIME FRENCHIES *Los Angeles Magazine* p118 Mr 2017

JOANNE HEYLER *Los Angeles Magazine* v62 no9 p98 S 2017

THE LINC *Los Angeles Magazine* v62 no6 p74 Je 2017

Luz Rivas *Los Angeles Magazine* v62 no9 p92 S 2017

The Midcentury As Muse *Los Angeles Magazine* p40 Ap 2017

Old Hollywood Haunt *Los Angeles Magazine* p38 Ja 2017

Herold, Benjamin

1-to-1 Computing Under Microscope in Maine Schools *Education Digest* v82 no5 p48 Ja 2017

Poor Students Face Digital Divide in How Teachers Learn to Use Tech *Education Digest* v83 no3 p16 N 2017

Heron, Pam

Work With What You've Got cartoon *Canadian Wildlife* v22 no5 p38 N/D 2016

Herons—Behavior

Bane—or Blessing? J. Heimbuch color *National Wildlife (World Edition)* v55 no6 p36 O/N 2017

Heroux, Michael A.

Enhancing reproducibility for computational methods bibl color

Science v354 no6317 p1240 D 9 2016

HERPER, MATTHEW

FEVER HIGH color *Forbes* v199 no7 p26 Je 29 2017

HOW TO CHEAT DEATH [Cover story] color map *Forbes* v199 no2 p74 F 28 2017

LESSONS AND IDEAS BY THE 100 GREATEST LIVING BUSINESS MINDS bw color *Forbes* v200 no3 p115 S 28 2017

Moderna's Mystery Medicines color *Forbes* v198 no9 p46 D 30 2016

PAIN AND GAIN color graph *Forbes* v198 no5 p92 O 25 2016

THE PRICE OF INSPIRATION chart color *Forbes* v200 no2 p84 S 5 2017

Refer Madness color *Forbes* v198 no9 p78 D 30 2016

The Right Chemistry chart color *Forbes* v200 no4 p35 O 24 2017

THE WORLD'S MOST INNOVATIVE COMPANIES chart color *Forbes* v200 no2 p72 S 5 2017

Herpes labialis—Treatment

NATURAL REMEDIES FOR COLD SORES M. Stengler color *Amazing Wellness* v9 no3 p32 EarlySumm 2017

Herpes simplex—Prevention

Natural Remedies for Cold Sores M. STENGLER color *Better Nutrition* v79 no1 p30 Ja 2017

YOUR SMILE: A USER'S MANUAL H. Levine color *Health* v30 no10 p97 D 2016

Herpesvirus diseases

See also

Shingles (Disease)

Shingles A Pain That Lasts I. Nath color *Maclean's* v129 no40 p64 O 10 2016

Herpesvirus diseases—Diagnosis

Why was the 3-year-old so irritable, and what was wrong with her eye? L. Sanders *New York Times Magazine* p20 F 19 2017

Herr, Christine Bibbo

Fit for a Fashion Pro K. NEITZ color *Runner's World* v52 no8 p41 S 2017

Herrada, Susannah

TAKE A DRIVE: THE OUTER BANKS *Washingtonian Magazine* v52 no9 p133 Je 2017

Herrera, Carmen, 1915-

WORLDLY ABSTRACTION C. Ratcliff cartoon color *Art in America* v104 no11 p72 D 2016

Herrera, Carmen, 1915—Exhibitions

Art on the Line J. GARDNER color *Weekly Standard* v22 no15 p37 D 19 2016

THE BRILLIANCE OF LINES B. SCHWABSKY *Nation* v303 no20 p33 N 14 2016

Herrera, Carolina, 1939-

CAROLINA HERRERA A. CODINHA color *Vogue* v207 no3 p409 Mr 2017

CAROLINA HERRERA K. MOLVAR bw color *Conde Nast Traveler* v52 no1 p42 Ja 2017

Hello! L. Brown color *InStyle* v24 no4 p24 Ap 2017

The Power of Carolina E. Wilson color *InStyle* v24 no4 p196 Ap 2017

Herrera, Paloma

Paloma Herrera M. HARSS *Dance Magazine* v91 no6 p20 Je 2017

Herrero-Ruiz, Andrés

ZATT (ZNF451)–mediated resolution of topoisomerase 2 DNA-protein cross-links diag *Science* v357 no6358 p1412 S 29 2017

Herrick, Ellen

The Forbidden Garden *Publishers Weekly* v264 no9 p71 F 27 2017

HERRIMAN, KAT

Jordan CASTEEL *Interview* v47 no6 p22 Ag 2017

Herring, Andrew

YOUR SCHEDULE COULD BE KILLING YOU L. KAUFMAN cartoon color *Popular Science* v289 no5 p58 S/O 2017

HERRING, HAL

THIS LAND WAS YOUR LAND cartoon color diag map *Field & Stream* v122 no1 p40 My 2017

HERRINGTON, GREGG

Evergreen State Blues: How George Bridges fostered his own humiliation [Cover story] *American Conservative* v16 no5 p13 S/O 2017

Herrington, Sarah

Love IN THE YOGA STUDIO color *Yoga Journal* no296 p40 N 2017

Herrman, John

Amazon's acquisition of Whole Foods is not only a clash between online and brick-and-mortar retail—it is also one between vastly different visions for the future of service work *New York Times Magazine* p16 Jl 23 2017

Counter Offensive: The American far right has become remarkably adept at commandeering ideas from its enemies. Now it's pulling off its trickiest switch yet: billing itself as the new 'alternative' culture *New York Times Magazine* p11 Jl 2 2017

Full Disclosure color *New York Times Magazine* p11 F 12 2017

Online platforms annexed much of our public sphere, playacting as little democracies—until extremists made them reveal their true nature *New York Times Magazine* p18 Ag 27 2017

On Technology *New York Times Magazine* p14 O 8 2017

Platforms might soon consume huge swaths of our economy—but what do they want to do with their power? *New York Times Magazine* p16 Mr 26 2017

HERRMANN, DUSTIN L.

Ecology for the Shrinking City *BioScience* v66 no11 p965 N 1 2016

Herrmann, Frank R.

An amoral enterprise color *America* v216 no13 p54 Je 12 2017

Herrmann, Richard

Living Color color *National Wildlife (World Edition)* v55 no6 p20 O/N 2017

Hersch, Charles

Jewish Jazz C. WOLFF bw *Downbeat* v84 no3 p66 Mr 2017

Hersch, Fred

FRED HERSCH TRUTH TELLER P. Lutz color *Downbeat* v84 no9 p34 S 2017

Jazz Epiphany color *Downbeat* v84 no9 p38 S 2017

Herschel, William

The amazing William Herschel D. J. Eicher color *Astronomy* v45 no6 p8 Je 2017

Herschel Space Observatory (Spacecraft)

Witnessing a Supernova P. Tyson *Sky & Telescope* v133 no2 p4 F 2017

Hersh, David

Stop Letting Quarterly Numbers Dictate Your Strategy *Harvard Business Review Digital Articles* p2 D 13 2016

Hersh, Glenda

WHEN REAL HOUSEWIVES OF ATLANTA DEBUTED IN FALL 2008 *Atlanta* v57 no1 p80 My 2017

Hershberger, Robin—Interviews

Q&A S. Goldberg *Cincinnati Magazine* v50 no4 p90 Ja 2017

Hershey, Terry

Terry Hershey: 'A Force of Nature for Nature' S. Myrick *Parks & Recreation* v52 no3 p50 Mr 2017

Hershey Co.

Melts in Your Mouth N. SCHMIDT cartoon *Walrus* p22 Ja\F 2017

Hershman, Lisa

PARTY DOWN C. SAFAVI *Better Homes & Gardens* v95 no1 p33 Ja 2017

Herskovitz, Marshall—Interviews

Inside Nashville's Revamp S. Highfill color *Entertainment Weekly* no1443 p54 D 9 2016

Herslow, Kimberly

The Value of Equine Education K. Beaudoin color *Dressage Today* v23 no4 p42 D 2016

Hertel, Sean

Evicted color *Alternatives Journal (A.J) - Canada's Environmental Voice* v42 no2 p16 2016

Welcome Home *Alternatives Journal (A.J) - Canada's Environmental Voice* v42 no2 p7 2016

HERTOG, JUDITH

CIRCLING LHASA bw *Tricycle: The Buddhist Review* v26 no3 p74 Spr 2017

Hertog, Roger

The Commentary Roast of Dan Senor *Commentary* v142 no4 p8 N 2016

HERTSGAARD, MARK

Climate Changed color il *Nation* v304 no1 p70 Ja 2 2017 The Obama Years

Climate Denialism Kills *Nation* v305 no7 p3 S 25 2017

Climate's Trump Card *Nation* v304 no13 p4 Ap 17 2017

Enemy of Humanity *Nation* v305 no1 p10 Jl 3 2017

HOW LIES SPREAD color *Nation* v304 no9 p19 Mr 20 2017

How to Fight Fox and Friends color *Nation* v304 no9 p14 Mr 20 2017

A Roar of Resistance color *Nation* v304 no5 p4 F 20 2017

HERTZ, DANIEL KAY

WHY We LOVE CHICAGO bw cartoon color *Chicago* v66 no3 p75 Mr 2017

HERTZ, SUE

BRING VINTAGE WINDOWS BACK TO LIFE *Yankee* v81 no1 p40 Ja/F 2017

Hertz, Thomas

Increased Demand for U.S. Agricultural Exports Would Likely Lead to More U.S. Jobs *Amber Waves: The Economics of Food, Farming, Natural Resources, & Rural America* p1 Je 2017

Hertz Corp.

The March of the Machines: Automation seems cold, but it's actually a sign that society is getting richer A. Marshall *Governing* v31 no1 p24 O 2017

HERTZBERG, HENDRIK

Wind From Down East *Nation* v303 no20 p4 N 14 2016

HERTZIG, ALYSSA

The customized plan for younger eyes color *Redbook* p45 S 2017

SUPERCHARGE YOUR SKINCARE color *Redbook* p38 O 2017

Herve, A. E.

Observation of a large-scale anisotropy in the arrival directions of cosmic rays above 8×10^{18} eV *Science* v357 no6357 p1266 S 22 2017

Hervert, Lyle

Reducing Noise in Decision Making: Interaction color *Harvard Business Review* v94 no12 p18 D 2016

Hervey, Jillian

VANESSA + JILLIAN [Cover story] D. L. D'Oyley color *Essence* v47 no9 p58 Ja 2017

Herz, Laura M.

Perovskite-perovskite tandem photovoltaics with optimized band gaps bibl chart graph *Science* v354 no6314 p861 N 18 2016

Herz, Steven

Making Paris Work bibl color map *Environment* v59 no2 p29 Mr/Ap 2017

Herzig, Dave

Kite Runner M. B. Cortez color *AARP: The Magazine* v59 no4A p66 Je/Jl 2016

Herzlinger, Regina

Bridging Health Care's Innovation-Education Gap *Harvard Business Review Digital Articles* p2 N 11 2014

Herzog & de Meuron Architekten AG

Stacking the Deck: A New York residential tower presents a new take on the city's classic skyscrapers J. GONCHAR color map *Architectural Record* v205 no5 p91 My 2017

HERZOG, DAGMAR

Hitler's Little Helper *New York Times Book Review* p19 Ap 2 2017

HERZOG, HAL

SURVIVAL OF THE CUTEST *Psychology Today* v49 no6 p19 N/D 2016

Herzog, Isaac, 1960-

Grave Matter *Commentary* v143 no4 p15 Ap 2017

Herzog, Jacques

All Seeing, If Not All Knowing P. PLAGENS *Architectural Record* v205 no7 p51 Jl 2017

Cochlear Implants - Life Beyond Hearing Aids J. Herzog *Saturday Evening Post* v289 no5 p101 S/O 2017

Cochlear Implants - Life Beyond Hearing Aids *Saturday Evening Post* v289 no5 p101 S/O 2017

A Surprising Critique of a Modernist Landmark F. A. Bernstein *Architectural Record* v204 no11 p53 N 2016

Herzog, Werner, 1942-

A Lens On the Psyche S. ERICKSON *Los Angeles Magazine* p94 Ap 2017

The Peculiar Mr. Herzog E. Hedegaard color *Rolling Stone* no1284 p46 Ap 6 2017

Herzon, Seth B.

A modular and enantioselective synthesis of the pleuromutilin antibiotics diag graph *Science* v356 no6341 p956 Je 1 2017

Hesheles, Zimmel

A WINDOW TO THE WORLD I. B. Singer *Harper's Magazine* v334 no2000 p85 Ja 2017

Hesitation

Without Hesitation J. DWYER *Reader's Digest* v188 no1126 p10 D 2016/Ja 2017

Heslin, Peter A.

Good Leaders Are Good Learners *Harvard Business Review Digital Articles* p2 Ag 10 2017

Hess, Amanda

Battle Cry *New York Times Magazine* p9 Ag 20 2017

Click Bait *New York Times Magazine* p11 Mr 5 2017

FORCES IN OPPOSITION color *New York Times Magazine* p36 F 12 2017

Identity Theft *New York Times Magazine* p11 Ap 2 2017

Old Money *New York Times Magazine* p13 S 17 2017

Open Secrets *New York Times Magazine* p11 My 14 2017

Show of Strength *New York Times Magazine* p19 O 16 2016

Straight to Video: YouTube's chief business officer presses play on the platform's greatest-hits reel *New York Times Book Review* p19 S 24 2017

Touching Base color *New York Times Magazine* p15 D 4 2016

Hess, Danny

SHAPIN' SAFARI M. CALORE color *Wired* v25 no7 p46 Jl 2017

Hess, Ed

In the AI Age, "Being Smart" Will Mean Something Completely Different *Harvard Business Review Digital Articles* p2 Je 19 2017

HESS, FREDERICK M.

Classes of Kindergarteners il *National Review* v69 no19 p36 O 16 2017

Ten Priorities for Education Policy [Cover story] color *National Review* v68 no19 p30 O 24 2016

Hess, Harald F.

Increased spatiotemporal resolution reveals highly dynamic dense tubular matrices in the peripheral ER bibl bw color graph *Science* v354 no6311 paaf3928-1 O 28 2016

HESS, JASON

RUN AWAY! [Cover story] color *Runner's World* v52 no7 p54 Ag 2017

Hess, Joan

Amelia Peabody's Last Hurrah E. Foxwell color *Publishers Weekly* v264 no20 p38 My 15 2017

HESS, MARC

BRING IT ON! color *Sail* v48 no7 p36 Jl 2017

Hess, Peter

I WISH SOMEONE WOULD INVENT... cartoon *Popular Science* p98 Ja/F 2017

look at this trove, treasures untold cartoon *Popular Science* v289 no2 p76 Mr/Ap 2017

Masako Tominaga cartoon *Popular Science* p52 Ja/F 2017

The Modern Explorer's Survival Kit color *Popular Science* p80 Ja/F 2017

moisture misers cartoon *Popular Science* v289 no2 p10 Mr/Ap 2017

WHERE TO LIVE IN AMERICA, 2100 A.D cartoon *Popular Science* p32 Ja/F 2017

HESS, TANJA M.

ask the experts cartoon color *Dressage Today* v23 no5 p64 Ja 2017

Hess, Zen

Where the Bible has clout bw *Christian Century* v134 no19 p36 S 13 2017

Hesse, Dan

WHAT PRESIDENT TRUMP'S ELECTION CAN TEACH US ABOUT MANAGING OUR HUMAN RESOURCES *Vital Speeches of the Day* v83 no5 p141 My 2017

Hesse, Monica

American Fire T. Jordan color *Entertainment Weekly* no1477 p62 Ag 11 2017

Smoldering Ruins K. Vick color *Time* v189 no22 p53 Je 12 2017

HESSION, MICHELE

The Question *O, The Oprah Magazine* p16 D 2016

Hessler, Alissa

Ditch the City and Go Country: How to Master the Art of Rural Life from a Former City Dweller color *Publishers Weekly* v264 no25 p107 Je 19 2017

Going Country color *Publishers Weekly* v264 no12 p43 Mr 20 2017

Hessler, Peter

AFTERMATH bw cartoon *New Yorker* v92 no38 p48 N 21 2016

Akhenaten bw color diag map *National Geographic* v231 no5 p120 My 2017

Akhenaten: EGYPT'S FIRST REVOLUTIONARY bw color diag map *National Geographic* v231 no5 p120 My 2017

THE SHADOW GENERAL cartoon *New Yorker* v92 no43 p44 Ja 2 2017

TALK LIKE AN EGYPTIAN cartoon color *New Yorker* v93 no9 p48 Ap 17 2017

Hester, Carl

14 TRAINING TIPS FROM OLYMPIAN CARL HESTER [Cover story] K. F. Miller color *Practical Horseman* v45 no7 p42 Jl 2017

Riding with "GOD" K. F. Miller color *Dressage Today* v23 no10 p46 Jl 2017

Hester, Devin

Taking on the Animal Kingdom K. Samuelson color *Time* v190 no1 p12 Jl 3 2017

HESTER, JEFF

Cassandra smiling color *Astronomy* v45 no9 p16 S 2017

A Dunning-Kruger universe color *Astronomy* v45 no6 p14 Je 2017

Entropy redux color *Astronomy* v45 no11 p66 N 2017

Entropy's rainbow color *Astronomy* v45 no10 p16 O 2017

The hermeneutics of bunk color *Astronomy* v45 no7 p14 Jl 2017

In a shark's eye color *Astronomy* v44 no12 p14 D 2016

King Tut's dagger color *Astronomy* v45 no8 p82 Ag 2017

Oklahoma skies color *Astronomy* v45 no3 p18 Mr 2017

A Saguaro's universe color *Astronomy* v45 no4 p20 Ap 2017

Hester, Jessica Leigh

Black Gotham bw color map *Atlantic* v320 no1 p30 Jl/Ag 2017

The Greenhouse Effect bw cartoon color *Atlantic* v318 no4 p38 N 2016

Total Immersion *Architectural Record* v204 no11 p57 N 2016

YOUR OWN BACK YARD cartoon *New Yorker* v93 no30 p19 O 2 2017

Hester, Larry

DADDY'S HOME W. KETCHUM color *Ebony* v72 no8 p64 Je 2017

Hesterberg, Armin

Around the Campfire color *Trail Rider* v29 no4 p8 My 2017

Heston, Charlton, 1923-2008

The Hero As Actor M. MATTIX color *Weekly Standard* v22 no32 p34 My 1 2017

Heterochromatin

Aggregation of the Whi3 protein, not loss of heterochromatin, causes sterility in old yeast cells G. Schlissel, M. K. Krzyzanowski et al bibl diag *Science* v355 no6330 p1184 Mr 17 2017

Heterogeneity

Extracting the contents of living cells S. G. Higgins and M. M. Stevens color *Science* v356 no6336 p379 Ap 28 2017

Neurodiversity as a Competitive Advantage R. D. AUSTIN and G. P. PISANO color *Harvard Business Review* v95 no3 p96 My/Je 2017

Heterojunctions

Double-heterojunction nanorod light-responsive LEDs for display applications N. Oh, B. Hoon Kim et al bibl color graph *Science* v355 no6325 p616 F 10 2017

Heteropoda

CELEBRITY STATUS C. Zuckerman color *National Geographic* v232 no4 p29 O 2017

Heterostructures

Robust epitaxial growth of two-dimensional heterostructures, multiheterostructures, and superlattices Z. Zhang, P. Chen et al color *Science* v357 no6353 p788 Ag 25 2017

HETI, SHEILA

Life Studies *New York Times Book Review* p11 F 26 2017

NULL AND VOID bw *New Yorker* v93 no29 p98 S 25 2017

HETLAND, DICK

Humor in Uniform *Reader's Digest* v190 no1134 p136 O 2017

HETLAND, GABRIEL

Venezuela's Agony *Nation* v305 no5 p4 Ag 28 2017

Hetland, Lois

On the goals and outcomes of arts education R. Heller color *Phi Delta Kappan* v98 no7 p15 Ap 2017

HETTINGER, ANNALIESE

Long-Term Studies Contribute Disproportionately to Ecology and

Policy *BioScience* v67 no3 p271 Mr 2017

Hetzel, Rachael

POWER OF THE PRESS A. BRANDT *Cincinnati Magazine* v50 no5 p38 F 2017

Heu, P.

Direct frequency comb measurement of OD + CO→DOCO kinetics bibl graph *Science* v354 no6311 p444 O 28 2016

Heuer, André

The cryo-EM structure of a ribosome–Ski2-Ski3-Ski8 helicase complex bibl color graph *Science* v354 no6318 p1431 D 16 2016

Heuer, Christopher P.

THE TASK OF ART cartoon color *Art in America* v105 no4 p82 Ap 2017

Heughan, Sam, 1980-

CLASH OF THE TARTANS [Cover story] L. Rice color *Entertainment Weekly* no1434 p20 O 7 2016

Cover *Entertainment Weekly* no1434 pC1 O 7 2016

From CLAIRE To ETERNITY [Cover story] L. Rice color *Entertainment Weekly* no1480 p22 S 1 2017

Outlander L. Rice, A. Bacle et al color *Entertainment Weekly* no1482/1483 p26 S 22 2017

OUTLANDER L. Rice color *Entertainment Weekly* no1446/1447 p60 D 2016/Ja 2017

Outlander's FRENCH KISS K. HAHN *TV Guide* v64 no15 p22 Ap 4 2016

PARTY LINES J. Vineyard img *New York* v49 no15 p90 Jl 25 2016

SOMEWHERE IN TIME K. HAHN *TV Guide* v65 no39 p28 S 18 2017

TOP 5 ESSENTIAL OUTLANDER EPISODES *TV Guide* v65 no39 p31 S 18 2017

Heughan, Sam, 1980—Interviews

And Then God Gave Us... Sam Heughan color *Glamour* v115 no10 p46 O 2017

Out of the Highlands: Outlander stars Sam Heughan and Caitriona Balfe and writer Matthew B. Roberts on season three, post-Culloden Scotland and the resilient, far-reaching Scots culture S. Gutierrez color *British Heritage Travel* v38 no5 p42 S/O 2017

HEUPEL, MICHELLE

Envisioning the Future of Aquatic Animal Tracking: Technology, Science, and Application *BioScience* v67 no10 p884 O 2017

Heutink, Peter

β2-Adrenoreceptor is a regulator of the a-synuclein gene driving risk of Parkinson's disease cartoon chart graph *Science* v357 no6354 p891 S 1 2017

Hevelius, Johannes, 1611-1687

THE MAP THE MOON, 1647 K. Wiles *History Today* v67 no7 p4 Jl 2017

HEWITT, BEN

A Farmer's Best Friend color *Yankee* p104 Mr 2017

Good Well Hunting color *Yankee* p16 My/Je 2017

The Hurry-Up Season: As the days get shorter, the list of chores grows longer *Yankee* v81 no5 p16 S/O 2017

Moving In color map *Yankee* p16 Mr 2017

THE POPULAR MECHANICS GUIDE TO SELF-SUFFICIEN-CY [Cover story] color *Popular Mechanics* p55 F 2017

Settling In color *Yankee* v80 no6 p16 N/D 2016

The Wheel Deal *Yankee* v81 no1 p16 Ja/F 2017

Hewitt, Don

THEIR FINEST HOURS J. FAGER bw color *Vanity Fair* v59 no10 p192 O 2017

Hewitt, Hugh

TGI (TPRM) R. L. FISCHER *USA Today Magazine* v145 no2864 p16 My 2017

Hewitt, Leslie

LESLIE HEWITT A. Schriber color *Art in America* v104 no10 p152 N 2016

HEWITT, PENNY

Good Well Hunting color *Yankee* p16 My/Je 2017

Moving In color map *Yankee* p16 Mr 2017

Settling In color *Yankee* v80 no6 p16 N/D 2016

Hewitt, Perry

The White House Selfie: The Visual Web's Latest Victory *Harvard Business Review Digital Articles* p2 Jl 2 2015

Hewitt, Sian

Music's Scary New Reality color *Rolling Stone* no1289 p13 Je 15 2017

Hewitt-White, Ken

Gemini City Sights *Sky & Telescope* v133 no2 p58 F 2017

A Whale of a Galaxy Cluster: Reel in the denizens of Abell 194 — if those autumn skies ever clear color *Sky & Telescope* v134 no5 p58 N 2017

Hewlett, Jamie

Confessions of a Mad Animator L. Greenblatt color *Entertainment Weekly* no1463/1464 p107 Ap/My 2017

Hewlett, Sylvia Ann

Creating a Culture Where Employees Speak Up *Harvard Business Review Digital Articles* p2 Ja 8 2016

The Financial Services Industry's Untapped Market *Harvard Business Review Digital Articles* p2 D 8 2014

Leading Across Cultures Is More Complicated for Women *Harvard Business Review Digital Articles* p2 D 2 2015

LGBT-Inclusive Companies Are Better at 3 Big Things *Harvard Business Review Digital Articles* p2 F 2 2016

People Suffer at Work When They Can't Discuss the Racial Bias They Face Outside of It *Harvard Business Review Digital Articles* p2 Jl 10 2017

Qualified Black Women Are Being Held Back from Management *Harvard Business Review Digital Articles* p2 Je 11 2015

Research: Millennials Can't Afford to Job Hop *Harvard Business Review Digital Articles* p2 Ag 31 2016

When Employees Think the Boss Is Unfair, They're More Likely to Disengage and Leave *Harvard Business Review Digital Articles* p2 Ag 1 2017

Women in Asia Are More Financially Savvy than Women in the U.S *Harvard Business Review Digital Articles* p2 Ag 25 2015

Hewlett-Packard Co.

HP Elite x3: This could be the last great Windows phone M. HACHMAN color graph *PCWorld* v35 no11 p68 N 2016

HP Omen 17: Great gaming performance at a great price G. MAHUNG color graph *PCWorld* v35 no11 p90 N 2016

HP Spectre x360: The best just keeps getting better A. YEE color graph *PCWorld* v35 no5 p95 My 2017

HP Spectre x360: Faster, smaller, and better than before G. MAHUNG color graph *PCWorld* v35 no1 p77 Ja 2017

HP's Spectre x360 puts Kaby Lake and Thunderbolt into a thinner, faster package G. MAHUNG color *PCWorld* v35 no11 p8 N 2016

Hewson, Marillyn A., ca. 1954-

Hardened Target D. FISHER chart color *Forbes* v199 no1 p36 Ja 24 2017

Hexel, Ole

Hiring Discrimination Against Black Americans Hasn't Declined in 25 Years *Harvard Business Review Digital Articles* p2 O 11 2017

Hey, Good Lookin' (Music)

The Darkness of Hank Williams T. TEACHOUT *Commentary* v143 no2 p49 F 2017

Hey, Spencer Phillips

Influence, integrity, and the FDA: An ethical framework color *Science* v357 no6354 p876 S 1 2017

Hey Jude (Music)

5 Great Songs Almost Ruined by Their Original Titles B. SPECK-TOR *Reader's Digest* v188 no1124 p134 O 2016

Heyao Wang

Quality management for precision medicine clinical applications: A consensus from the China Precision Medicine Clinical Research and Application Association bibl *Science* v354 no6319 p11 D 23 2016

Heyday Wake Boats (Company)

Wakesports For Working Sorts: Heyday's WT-2 allows boaters to have their wake and eat it too ... for a lot less money A. JONES *Boating World* v38 no8 p36 S/O 2017

Heyduk, Tomasz

RNA polymerase motions during promoter melting color diag graph *Science* v356 no6340 p863 My 26 2017

HEYER, ANDREW

Discerning Desire color *America* v216 no1 p30 Ja 2 2017

Heyer, Evelyne

Dispersals and genetic adaptation of Bantu-speaking populations in Africa and North America diag *Science* v356 no6337 p543 My 5 2017

Heyer, Heather D., 1985-2017

THESE MONUMENTS WERE TRANSFORMED INTO LIGHTNING RODS *Vital Speeches of the Day* v83 no10 p285 O 2017

Heyes, Anthony—Interviews

AIR POLLUTION BRINGS DOWN THE STOCK MARKET S. Berinato *Harvard Business Review* v95 no2 p38 Mr/Ap 2017

Heyler, Joanne

JOANNE HEYLER A. HEROLD *Los Angeles Magazine* v62 no9 p98 S 2017

Heyman, Andrew

CNN *New York Times Magazine* p10 Ap 23 2017

Heyman, Brett

Brett Heyman color *Architectural Digest* v74 no4 p60 Ap 2017

Heyman, Bruce

The Ambassador of Art C. MORGAN-FEIR color *Walrus* v14 no2 p17 Mr 2017

Heyman, David

Wonder World H. FREEMAN color *Vogue* v206 no12 p242 D 2016

Heyman, Jd

RED-CARPET INTELLIGENCE Emmys Edition color *Entertainment Weekly* no1484 p22 S 29 2017

Heyman, Marshall

CARLA UNCENSORED bw *Harper's Bazaar* no3656 p325 S 2017

CAT WALKING DEAD color *Harper's Bazaar* no3651 p442 Mr 2017

Freida & a Pinto color *InStyle* v24 no5 p234 My 2017

KATE'S NEW OBSESSION bw color *Harper's Bazaar* no3656 p442 S 2017

SOLID GOLDIE color *Harper's Bazaar* no3654 p160 Je/Jl 2017

Heymann, David L.

From Contamination to Containment [Cover story] color *Natural History* v125 no9 p40 S 2017

In Sickness and in Health color *Natural History* v125 no9 p43 S 2017

Who should direct WHO? color *Science* v354 no6313 p685 N 11 2016

Heyward, Carter

She Flies On: A White, Southern, Christian Debutante Wakes Up A. Frykholm *Christian Century* v134 no19 p41 S 13 2017

Heywood, Suzanne

A 5-Step Process for Reorganizing After a Merger *Harvard Business Review Digital Articles* p2 D 21 2016

Getting Reorgs Right diag *Harvard Business Review* v94 no11 p84 N 2016

Heywood Hill Ltd.

Little Shop of Hoarders F. WHEEN bw color *Vanity Fair* v59 no2 p100 F 2017

Hezroni, Nir—Interviews

Pushing the Envelopes L. PICKER *Publishers Weekly* v264 no9 p76 F 27 2017

hhgregg Inc.

This Just In... M. Fleischmann color *Sound & Vision* v82 no7 p19 S 2017

Hi-Tech Pharmaceuticals Inc.

GET TO KNOW: IFORCE NUTRITION J. SCHILDHOUSE color *Muscle & Performance* v8 no12 p34 D 2016

Hiaasen, Carl

The Heat Made Them Do It T. RAFFERTY color *New York Times Book Review* p12 S 25 2016

Hiatt, Anna

Great moments in local journalism bw color *Columbia Journalism Review* v56 no1 p112 Spr 2017

Hiatt, Brian

Alessia Cara color *Rolling Stone* no1283 p18 Mr 23 2017

Alicia Keys color *Rolling Stone* no1274 p18 N 17 2016

Back to the Blues [Cover story] bw color *Rolling Stone* no1275 p40 D 1 2016

Elvis Costello [Cover story] *Rolling Stone* no1289 p22 Je 15 2017

Essential Chuck color *Rolling Stone* no1285 p36 Ap 20 2017

FALL ALBUM PREVIEW *Rolling Stone* no1297 p12 O 5 2017

The Galaxy's Hottest Mixtape bw color *Rolling Stone* no1286 p14

My 4 2017

Halsey Aims for Pop Dominance color *Rolling Stone* no1284 p21 Ap 6 2017

Hot Comedian Brandon Wardell color *Rolling Stone* no1274 p43 N 17 2016

THE HUMBLE KING color *Rolling Stone* no1294 p38 Ag 24 2017

Jidenna's Redemption Songs color *Rolling Stone* no1284 p42 Ap 6 2017

John Legend color *Rolling Stone* no1278/1279 p23 Ja 12 2017

John Mellencamp bw *Rolling Stone* no1286 p18 My 4 2017

John Oliver bw color *Rolling Stone* no1281/1282 p32 F 23 2017

King of the Stone Age color *Rolling Stone* no1295 p20 S 7 2017

Lena Dunham color *Rolling Stone* no1281/1282 p21 F 23 2017

Liam Gallagher's Sweet Revenge color *Rolling Stone* no1298 p16 O 19 2017

The Liberation of Kesha [Cover story] bw color *Rolling Stone* no1298 p26 O 19 2017

Little Steven Is His Own Boss Again bw color *Rolling Stone* no1288 p16 Je 1 2017

Neil Young: Restless as Ever color *Rolling Stone* no1278/1279 p19 Ja 12 2017

Paris Jackson's Family Secrets color *Rolling Stone* no1280 p34 F 9 2017

Paul and Elvis: The Fab Two bw *Rolling Stone* no1283 p16 Mr 23 2017

Q&A Mac Miller color *Rolling Stone* no1273 p22 N 3 2016

The Road Heats Up bw color *Rolling Stone* no1288 p11 Je 1 2017

Sheryl Crow cartoon *Rolling Stone* no1286 p82 My 4 2017

True Bruce [Cover story] bw color *Rolling Stone* no1272 p32 O 20 2016

THE WOUNDED HEART OF MACHINE GUN KELLY color *Rolling Stone* no1290 p40 Je 29 2017

HIATT, CLAUDIA

TRIUMPH AND TURMOIL *USA Today Magazine* v145 no2864 p74 My 2017

Hiatt, Kim

FATAL MISTAKES S. KLIFF *Reader's Digest* v189 no1128 p100 Mr 2017

Hiatt, Sky Sinclair

Discussion color *Smithsonian* v47 no10 p8 Mr 2017

Hibberd, James

5 MORE SHOWS YOU NEED TO SEE color *Entertainment Weekly* no1435 p24 O 14 2016

THE AMERICANS color *Entertainment Weekly* no1446/1447 p61 D 2016/Ja 2017

Back to Black: Inside the Making of Mirror color *Entertainment Weekly* no1436/1437 p91 O 21 2016

BREAKING BILLIONS' BOYS' CLUB color *Entertainment Weekly* no1454/1455 p20 F 24 2017

A CLASH OF QUEENS color *Entertainment Weekly* no1474/1475 p62 Jl 21-28 2017

Does HBO's Future Include a Game of Thrones Spin-off? color *Entertainment Weekly* no1435 p9 O 14 2016

DOUBLE TROUBLE color *Entertainment Weekly* no1462 p42 Ap 21 2017

DRAGONS AND WOLVES AND RATINGS, OH MY! color *Entertainment Weekly* no1477 p12 Ag 11 2017

ED HARRIS color *Entertainment Weekly* no1438 p52 N 4 2016

Editor's Note H. Goldblatt color *Entertainment Weekly* no1468/1469 p10 Je 2-9 2017

FANTASTIC BEASTS and WHERE TO FIND THEM color *Entertainment Weekly* no1438 p40 N 4 2016

A FIELD GUIDE TO FANTASTIC BEASTS color *Entertainment Weekly* no1442 p8 D 2 2016 Rebellious Special Issue

FROZEN color *Entertainment Weekly* no1460/1461 p97 Ap 7-17 2017

HEARTLAND OF DARKNESS color *Entertainment Weekly* no1462 p38 Ap 21 2017

Hollywood Takes a Knee color *Entertainment Weekly* no1485 p14 O 6 2017

Homeland color *Entertainment Weekly* no1448 p39 Ja 13 2017

A Homeland Death in the Line of Duty color *Entertainment Weekly* no1462 p16 Ap 21 2017

A HOUSE UNDIVIDED [Cover story] color *Entertainment Weekly* no1468/1469 p28 Je 2-9 2017

IDOL'S RETURN: ARE WE READY? color *Entertainment Weekly* no1467 p16 My 26 2017

JOHN LITHGOW color *Entertainment Weekly* no1456 p60 Mr 10 2017

THE LEFTOVERS color *Entertainment Weekly* no1446/1447 p58 D 2016/Ja 2017

Legion color *Entertainment Weekly* no1448 p40 Ja 13 2017

Mariah Carey Sounds Off color *Entertainment Weekly* no1448 p10 Ja 13 2017

Meet the New Faces of Avatar 2 color *Entertainment Weekly* no1485 p40 O 6 2017

The Never-Ending Story? color *Entertainment Weekly* no1466 p14 My 19 2017

THE NEW TV SHOWS YOU CAN'T GET ENOUGH OF color *Entertainment Weekly* no1436/1437 p20 O 21 2016

NO. 11 Buffy color *Entertainment Weekly* no1436/1437 p52 O 21 2016

NO. 20 Robin color *Entertainment Weekly* no1436/1437 p60 O 21 2016

One for the Books color *Entertainment Weekly* no1457/1458 p18 Mr 17 2017

QUEER EYE RETURNS! color *Entertainment Weekly* no1451/1452 p20 F 3-10 2017

A REUNION OF GALACTICA PROPORTIONS color diag *Entertainment Weekly* no1471 p14 Je 23 2017

SE7EN color *Entertainment Weekly* no1460/1461 p62 Ap 7-17 2017

Sherlock Shocker: Her Last Bow color *Entertainment Weekly* no1448 p13 Ja 13 2017

THE SHINING color *Entertainment Weekly* no1460/1461 p44 Ap 7-17 2017

THE SHOWS WILL GO ON color *Entertainment Weekly* no1465 p8 My 12 2017

The Sopranos Kiss Adriana Goodbye color *Entertainment Weekly* no1470 p46 Je 16 2017

A STAR-FLEET IS BORN [Cover story] color *Entertainment Weekly* no1476 p22 Ag 4 2017

Star Trek Discovery color *Entertainment Weekly* no1482/1483 p104 S 22 2017

STAR TREK: DISCOVERY color *Entertainment Weekly* p24 Jl 24 2017

STAR TREK'S NEW FRONTIER color *Entertainment Weekly* no1472 p20 Je 30 2017

Striking Out color *Entertainment Weekly* no1465 p9 My 12 2017

SUN VALLEY FILM FEST color *Entertainment Weekly* no1459 p48 Mr 31 2017

A TALE OF TWO BATMANS color *Entertainment Weekly* no1454/1455 p18 F 24 2017

TV chart color *Entertainment Weekly* no1444/1445 p66 D 16 2016

Westworld: Fall TV's Biggest Mystery color *Entertainment Weekly* no1435 p8 O 14 2016

What's Left for The Leftovers? color *Entertainment Weekly* no1466 p47 My 19 2017

What's the Most Bingeworthy Show? color *Entertainment Weekly* no1443 p21 D 9 2016

What to Watch color *Entertainment Weekly* no1446/1447 p112 D 2016/Ja 2017

WHAT YOU'LL BE WATCHING IN 2017 (AND BEYOND) color *Entertainment Weekly* no1450 p18 Ja 27 2017

Your Ridiculously Early Fall TV Preview color *Entertainment Weekly* no1453 p10 F 17 2017

Your Sunshiny, Stupendous, Seriously Spectacular SUMMER BUCKET LIST color *Entertainment Weekly* no1470 p32 Je 16 2017

Hibbert, Alex

The 10 Best Performances S. Zacharek color *Time* v188 no25-26 p134 D 19 2016 Double Issue

HIBBS, THOMAS S.

The Christian Encounter *National Review* v69 no18 p41 O 2 2017

Hibernation

    See also

      Mammals—Hibernation

Discoveries From the Deepest Sleep J. Ingram color *Canadian Wildlife* v22 no5 p13 N/D 2016

Hibiscus

HARDY HIBISCUS M. ROSS color *Better Homes & Gardens*

v95 no8 p100 Ag 2017

the life C. Stern and A. Vorrasi color *InStyle* v24 no3 p363 Mr 2017

A Sip of Summer M. BURKLAND and H. GRAY color *Better Nutrition* v79 no7 p28 Jl 2017

Hibler, Harry

Harry "Hand Grenade" Hibler at the 1971 March Meet T. Taylor color *Hot Rod* v70 no1 p14 Ja 2017

Hiccups—Diagnosis

It started as a normal bout of hiccups—but then it wouldn't stop. What was causing these relentless spasms? L. Sanders *New York Times Magazine* p22 Jl 23 2017

Hiccups—Treatment

It started as a normal bout of hiccups—but then it wouldn't stop. What was causing these relentless spasms? L. Sanders *New York Times Magazine* p22 Jl 23 2017

Hickenlooper, John W. (John Wright), 1952-

POLITICAL CLIMBERS R. Manning *Harper's Magazine* no2007 p45 Ag 2017

Hickenlooper, John—Interviews

Hickenlooper's Fellows K. Barrett and R. Greene *Governing* v30 no2 p58 N 2016

Hickey, Andria

MAGALI REUS IN THE STUDIO color *Art in America* v104 no10 p136 N 2016

Hickey, Kelsey I.

CAT-tailing as a fail-safe mechanism for efficient degradation of stalled nascent polypeptides diag *Science* v357 no6349 p414 Jl 28 2017

Hickler, Thomas

Merging paleobiology with conservation biology to guide the future of terrestrial ecosystems color *Science* v355 no6325 p594 F 10 2017

HICKLIN, AARON

EXIT, LEFT color *Advocate* no1089 p30 F/Mr 2017

Hickman, Adam

A BETTER BARBECUE color *Health* v31 no5 p90 Je 2017

Full of Flavor color *Southern Living* v52 no6 p123 Je 2017

Pressure-Cooker Chili color *Southern Living* v52 no10 p126 O 2017

Spring PASTA PRIMER color *Health* v31 no3 p88 Ap 2017

Start with a Rotisserie Chicken color *Health* v31 no4 p103 My 2017

Hickman, Janell M.

"No, I won't color my hair" color *Glamour* no8 p82 Ag 2017

Hickok, Chase

HIGHLIGHTS OF THE 2016 U.S. DRESSAGE FINALS *Dressage Today* v23 no6 p12 F 2017

Hicks, Ashley

editor's letter color *Architectural Digest* v74 no4 p30 Ap 2017

THE SON ALSO RISES M. OWENS color *Architectural Digest* v74 no4 p128 Ap 2017

Hicks, Christina

Committing to socially responsible seafood color *Science* v356 no6341 p912 Je 1 2017

Hicks, Clifford W.

Strong peak in Tc of Sr2RuO4 under uniaxial pressure bibl color graph *Science* v355 no6321 p1 Ja 13 2017

HICKS, DANIEL J.

Scientific Controversies as Proxy Politics *Issues in Science & Technology* v33 no2 p67 Wint 2017

Hicks, Hope

The Inner Circle of Trump's Inner Circle Z. J. Miller color *Time* v189 no3 p34 Ja 30 2017

HICKS, JENNIFER BOWEN

Prison Ecology *Orion Magazine* v35 no4/5 p7 Jl-O 2016

Hicks, Jesse

MISTAKEN IDENTITIES *Harper's Magazine* v334 no2001 p48 F 2017

Hicks, Maureen Soyars

Flexible jobs give workers choices *Monthly Labor Review* p1 My 2017

Hickson, Paul

The Road Less Traveled T. Forte color *Sky & Telescope* v134 no5 p34 N 2017

Hicks Pries, Caitlin E.

The whole-soil carbon flux in response to warming [Cover story] chart graph *Science* v355 no6332 p1420 Mr 31 2017

Hicok, Bob, 1960-

ORIGIN STORY B. Hicok *New Yorker* v93 no24 p46 Ag 21 2017

Hidaka, Kumi

Holliday junction resolvases mediate chloroplast nucleoid segregation diag *Science* v356 no6338 p631 My 12 2017

Hidalgo, Anne

Pioneers [Cover story] color *Time* v189 no16/17 p14 My 1-8 2017

Placing People at the Centre of Our Sustainable Urban Future *UN Chronicle* v53 no3 p13 2016

Hidalgo, Anne, 1959----Interviews

THE MAYOR IS IN M. Mawad, E. Chrepa et al color *Bloomberg Businessweek* no4534 p66 Ag 14 2017

Hidalgo, César A.

Income Inequality and Export "Complexity" *USA Today Magazine* v145 no2863 p12 Ap 2017

Think Like an Author, Not an Owner *Harvard Business Review Digital Articles* p2 O 15 2015

Hidalgo-Carcedo, Cristina

Transgenerational transmission of environmental information in C. elegans diag *Science* v356 no6335 p320 Ap 21 2017

Hidden camera photography

AMERICAN SEX POLICE E. N. BROWN color *Reason* v48 no11 p16 Ap 2017

Hidden Figures (Film)

Black Girl Magic Works in Tech Too B. Lee color *Essence* v48 no5 p124 S 2017

The BRIGHT Stuff T. Stack color *Entertainment Weekly* no1446/1447 p34 D 2016/Ja 2017

The Bullseye M. Snetiker color *Entertainment Weekly* no1449 p64 Ja 20 2017

Hidden Figures Calculates the Sum of a Story Untold E. Berman color *Time* v188 no22-23 p94 N/D 2016

HIDDEN FIGURES C. Chiarella color *Sound & Vision* v82 no7 p69 S 2017

Hidden Figures L. Greenblatt color *Entertainment Weekly* no1448 p48 Ja 13 2017

Hidden Figures Proves There's Power In Numbers S. Zacharek color *Time* v189 no3 p56 Ja 16 2017

Liftoff Uplift J. PODHORETZ *Weekly Standard* v22 no22 p39 F 13 2017

Limits of a feel-good movie L. H. Moses *Christian Century* v134 no4 p10 F 15 2017

Movie celebrates NASA 'computers' E. Conover bw color *Science News* v191 no1 p28 Ja 21 2017

NEWLY AVAILABLE MOVIES J. HOGAN *TV Guide* v65 no37 p52 S 4 2017

No Longer 'Hidden Figures' M. CHARLES and L. CROSS color *Ebony* v72 no3 p30 D 2016/Ja 2017

NOW PLAYING color *Entertainment Weekly* no1453 p49 F 17 2017

On the Cover C. Lindsey *Hoover Digest: Research & Opinion on Public Policy* no3 p200 Summ 2017

STOP TRYING TO MAKE HIDDEN FENCES HAPPEN color *Entertainment Weekly* no1449 p16 Ja 20 2017

Hidden God

LIVING BY The Word *Christian Century* v133 no25 p20 D 7 2016

Hidden Side of WW2, The (TV program)

News B. Manley color *Military History* v34 no4 p9 N 2017

Hiddleston, Tom, 1981-

The Kong Show C. M. Smith color *Entertainment Weekly* no1440 p16 N 18 2016

WE ♥ T. H [Cover story] T. BRODESSER-AKNER color *GQ: Gentlemen's Quarterly* v97 no3 p108 Mr 2017

Hiddleston, Tom, 1981----Awards

SOLID GOLD K. Peiffer, B. Fowler et al color *InStyle* v24 no3 p153 Mr 2017

Hiddleston, Tom, 1981----Interviews

GQHQ cartoon color *GQ: Gentlemen's Quarterly* v97 no3 p54 Mr 2017

TOM HIDDLESTON B. CUMBERBATCH *Interview* v46 no8 p62 O 2016

Hideaki Morishita

The ATG conjugation systems are important for degradation of

the inner autophagosomal membrane bibl graph *Science* v354 no6315 p1036 N 25 2016

Hideo Mabuchi

A fully programmable 100-spin coherent Ising machine with all-to-all connections bibl diag graph *Science* v354 no6312 p614 N 4 2016

Hides & skins

Craft Your Own COONSKIN CAP: Turn a raccoon hide into a warm and hardy hat D. Biswell *Mother Earth News* no284 p24 O/N 2017

Ionia County, MI color *Outdoor Life* v223 no9 p7 N 2016

LAMB SPICES & SHEEP PELTS *South Dakota Magazine* v33 no3 p30 S/O 2017

Romal Reins A. Dunning and J. Paulson color *Horse & Rider* v56 no6 p46 Je 2017

Hides & skins----Design & construction

How lizards are like computer programs E. Conover color *Science News* v191 no9 p32 My 13 2017

Hidewaki Nakagawa

Mutational signatures associated with tobacco smoking in human cancer bibl graph *Science* v354 no6312 p618 N 4 2016

Hideyoshi Yoshioka

Methane production from coal by a single methanogen bibl graph *Science* v354 no6309 p222 O 14 2016

Hideyuki Tamaki

Methane production from coal by a single methanogen bibl graph *Science* v354 no6309 p222 O 14 2016

Hiebert, James

Making teaching visible through learning opportunities color *Phi Delta Kappan* v98 no8 p54 My 2017

Hiemstra, Henk

Unequivocal determination of complex molecular structures using anisotropic NMR measurements color *Science* v356 no6333 p43 Ap 7 2017

Hienzsch, Antje

Click chemistry enables preclinical evaluation of targeted epigenetic therapies diag *Science* v356 no6345 p1397 Je 30 2017

Hieshetter, Janet

TALK TO US bw *Chicago* v66 no3 p23 Mr 2017

HiFiMan Corp.

Both Sides Now S. Guttenberg color *Sound & Vision* v82 no3 p24 Ap 2017

HiFiMan SuperMini Music Player M. Fleischmann color *Sound & Vision* v82 no1 p54 Ja 2017

Higashida, Naoki

Naoki Higashida N. Hopper color *Time* v190 no6 p60 Ag 7 2017

Higashiyama, Tetsuya

RETINOBLASTOMA RELATED1 mediates germline entry in Arabidopsis color diag *Science* v356 no6336 p396 Ap 28 2017

Higbee, Paul

THE BRIEF CRUSADE OF THE RED HAWK *South Dakota Magazine* v33 no3 p62 S/O 2017

Brother Builders *South Dakota Magazine* v32 no4 p90 N/D 2016

THE CATCH AT McNENNY: Where South Dakota hatches trout, salmon and researchers *South Dakota Magazine* v33 no2 p48 Jl/Ag 2017

THE COWBOY AND THE RICE WRITER *South Dakota Magazine* v32 no6 p58 Mr/Ap 2017

HORSE NATION *South Dakota Magazine* v32 no6 p70 Mr/Ap 2017

OUR CASE FOR HISTORY: Historian Leland Case's spirit can be felt in certain South Dakota places *South Dakota Magazine* v33 no3 p42 S/O 2017

SMALL TOWN COFFEE *South Dakota Magazine* v33 no2 p64 Jl/Ag 2017

SPEARFISH: HIPPIE HAVEN? *South Dakota Magazine* v32 no4 p54 N/D 2016

Higdon, Hal

ZOOM, ZOOM! color *Runner's World* v52 no3 p38 Ap 2017

Higginbotham, Stacey

THE FUTURE IS HERE color diag *Sunset* v238 no4 p54 Ap 2017

Smart Homes Could Be Cheaper to Insure color *MIT Technology Review* v120 no1 p23 Ja/F 2017

Higgins, Ben, 1988----Interviews

Ben Higgins Reality Star M. RUBINO *Indianapolis Monthly* v40 no3 p62 N 2016

Higgins, Clay
The Pros and Cons of the President's Immigrant Travel Ban *Congressional Digest* v96 no3 p26 Mr 2017
HIGGINS, DREW
Direct atomic-level insight into the active sites of a high-performance PGM-free ORR catalyst diag graph *Science* v357 no6350 p479 Ag 4 2017
TRAIN LIKE A GIRL color *Climbing* no356 p60 S/O 2017
Higgins, E. Tory
Male and Female Entrepreneurs Get Asked Different Questions by VCs—and It Affects How Much Funding They Get *Harvard Business Review Digital Articles* p2 Je 27 2017
HIGGINS, HEATHER R.
Trump as Communicator *National Review* v69 no4 p18 Mr 6 2017
Higgins, Jack
The Midnight Bell *Publishers Weekly* v263 no41 p57 O 10 2016
Higgins, John
5 Questions to Ask Before You Call Out Someone Powerful *Harvard Business Review Digital Articles* p2 Ap 7 2017
The Problem with Saying "My Door Is Always Open" color *Harvard Business Review Digital Articles* p2 Mr 9 2017
Higgins, Lindsey M.
Stay on Your Smartphone! *Parks & Recreation* v51 no11 p14 N 2016
HIGGINS, MARGOT
Ghost Dancers and Shadow Keepers *Orion Magazine* v35 no4/5 p53 Jl-O 2016
Higgins, Michael W.
A Dry Time for Catholics color *Commonweal* v144 no15 p8 S 22 2017
Priest, Writer, Mentor, Misfit color *Commonweal* v143 no20 p13 D 16 2016
Higgins, Nathaniel
Gathering Experimental Evidence To Improve the Design of Agricultural Programs *Amber Waves: The Economics of Food, Farming, Natural Resources, & Rural America* p1 Ag 2017
Higgins, Scott
Matinee Melodrama: Playing with Formula in the Sound Serial T. GOLDMAN *Film Quarterly* v70 no2 p106 Wint 2016
Higgins, Shawn
THE VANISHING [Cover story] J. SULLIVAN color *Field & Stream* v122 no6 p64 N 2017
Higgins, Steve
THE TONIGHT SHOW STARRING JIMMY FALLON J. Halterman *TV Guide* v65 no11 p47 Mr 6 2017
Higgins, Stuart G.
Extracting the contents of living cells color *Science* v356 no6336 p379 Ap 28 2017
HIGGINS, WINTON
TREADING THE PATH WITH CARE [Cover story] color *Tricycle: The Buddhist Review* v26 no2 p38 Wint 2016
Higgott, Andrew
Raw Concrete The Beauty of Brutalism *History Today* v67 no1 p60 Ja 2017
HIGGS, ERIC S.
Expanding the Portfolio: Conserving Nature's Masterpieces in a Changing World *BioScience* v67 no6 p568 Je 2017
Higgs, Stephen
Rapid development of a DNA vaccine for Zika virus bibl graph *Science* v354 no6309 p237 O 14 2016
Higgs bosons
A BRIDGE TOO FAR The demise of the Superconducting Super Collider M. Riordan *Physics Today* v69 no10 p48 O 2016
High (Music)
LOVING LIFE C. Arnold color *Essence* v48 no6 p70 O 2017
High altitude pulmonary edema
The Ups (and Downs) of Mountain Travel A. WISLOWSKI chart diag *Climbing* no355 p48 Ag 2017
High Anxiety (Film)
HIGH ANXIETY'S OBSCENE PHONE CALL D. Franich color *Entertainment Weekly* no1460/1461 p28 Ap 7-17 2017
High Art (Music)
High Art R. Platt cartoon *New Yorker* v93 no27 p12 S 11 2017
High-calorie diet
Are You Hungry Yet? color *Prevention* p10 Mr 2017
DOUBLE DIGITS? SWEET! J. GALLOWAY color *Runner's*

World v52 no8 p14 S 2017
High definition DVD players
Sony UBP-X800 Ultra HD Blu-ray Player A. Griffin color *Sound & Vision* v82 no6 p38 Jl/Ag 2017
High definition DVD players—Evaluation
Panasonic DMP-UB900 Ultra HD Blu-ray Player A. Griffin color *Sound & Vision* v82 no2 p40 F/Mr 2017
Philips BDP7501/F7 Ultra HD Blu-ray Player T. J. Norton color *Sound & Vision* v81 no10 p50 D 2016
UHD Star-Lord? T. J. Norton color *Sound & Vision* v82 no4 p54 My 2017
High Definition Multimedia Interface
HDMI Anxiety A. GRIFFIN color *Sound & Vision* v82 no7 p24 S 2017
Taking HDMI to the Next Level B. Ankosko color *Sound & Vision* v82 no4 p16 My 2017
TV Troubles A. GRIFFIN color *Sound & Vision* v82 no4 p19 My 2017
High definition television
See also
Ultrahigh definition television
HOW TO BUY AN ULTRA HDTV A. Griffin color *Sound & Vision* v82 no1 p32 Ja 2017
LG Signature OLED65W7P OLED Ultra HDTV T. J. Norton color graph *Sound & Vision* v82 no5 p44 Je 2017
High definition television—Evaluation
Q and Me T. J. Norton bw color graph *Sound & Vision* v82 no8 p48 O 2017
Sharp Aquos LC-75N8000U LCD Ultra HDTV A. Griffin color graph *Sound & Vision* v82 no1 p52 Ja 2017
TVS THAT HANG LIKE PAINTINGS color *Popular Mechanics* p16 S 2017
High density lipoproteins
How Good Is Good Cholesterol? L. M. KASE color *Discover* v38 no10 p70 D 2017
Rethinking 'Good' Cholesterol *Saturday Evening Post* v289 no1 p76 Ja/F 2017
High dynamic range imaging
DEEP BLACK AND WHITE D. Grossman color *Popular Photography* v81 no2 p36 Mr/Ap 2017
Jerry Seinfeld's M. Fleischmann and C. Crowley color *Sound & Vision* v82 no5 p17 Je 2017
Welcome to 'Wow!' TV J. K. Willcox chart color graph *Consumer Reports* v82 no11 p44 N 2017
High-fidelity sound systems
See also
Surround-sound systems
High-frequency trading (Securities)
Maybe the Flash Boys Are the Good Guys C. Russo and J. Detrixhe graph *Bloomberg Businessweek* no4498 p49 N 7 2016
High-fructose corn syrup
STICKY ICKY color *Road & Track* v68 no8 p100 My 2017
High heel shoes
20 WAYS TO DO PLUM S. Walter color *Good Housekeeping* v263 no5 p56C N 2016
GWYNETH PALTROW'S SHOE SECRETS N. Silva-Jelly color *Harper's Bazaar* no3657 p242 O 2017
Hoodie, Yes. Pants, No N. Silverstein and J. Harman color *Glamour* v114 no12 p78 D 2016
Style Your Home T. A. Christian color *Essence* v48 no5 p114 S 2017
High heel shoes—Evaluation
Find Your Shoe Style color *Glamour* v115 no10 p62 O 2017
Lady LIKE *Interview* v46 no8 p54 O 2016
TOP PICKS [Cover story] color *Redbook* p60 Mr 2017
THE WOMAN Solange Knowles E. Wilson color *InStyle* v24 no4 p90 Ap 2017
High-intensity interval training
SPRING CLEAN YOUR FITNESS ROUTINE [Cover story] L. LEICHT cartoon color *Women's Health* v14 no3 p130 Ap 2017
High jump (Track & field)—Competitions
The Last Leap J. Fuchs and T. Keith color *Sports Illustrated* v126 no18 p20 Je 26 2017
High Life (Film)
COMPLETELY MENTAL N. Rapold color *Film Comment* v53 no4 p27 Jl/Ag 2017

High Maintenance (TV program)

High-Profile Guest Stars S. Li color *Entertainment Weekly* no1435 p47 O 14 2016

High Museum of Art

RURAL RETROSPECTIVE T. MALONE *Atlanta* v56 no10 p40 F 2017

High Noon (Film)

HIGH NOON C. Chiarella bw *Sound & Vision* v82 no5 p70 Je 2017

High performance computing

Breakthroughs Advance U.S. Competitiveness B. E. Warner *Science & Technology Review* p3 Ja/F 2017

COMPUTATIONAL Innovation Boosts MANUFACTURING A. Parker color *Science & Technology Review* p4 Ja/F 2017

Laboratory Investments Drive Computational Advances R. Al-Ayat *Science & Technology Review* p3 S 2016

A New Paradigm for Medical Research P. Falcone color *Science & Technology Review* p3 O/N 2016

High pressure (Science)

HELIUM COMPOUND MAY FORM UNDER PRESSURE *Physics Today* v70 no4 p23 Ap 2017

High pressure (Science)—Research

New claim staked for metallic hydrogen E. CONOVER color *Science News* v191 no3 p14 F 18 2017

High-protein diet

FEAST FIRST L. APPLEGATE color *Runner's World* v52 no1 p56 Ja/F 2017

High resolution imaging

A finer look at a fine cellular meshwork M. Terasaki bibl color *Science* v354 no6311 p415 O 28 2016

Increased spatiotemporal resolution reveals highly dynamic dense tubular matrices in the peripheral ER J. Nixon-Abell, C. J. Obara et al bibl bw color graph *Science* v354 no6311 paaf3928-1 O 28 2016

Nanometer resolution imaging and tracking of fluorescent molecules with minimal photon fluxes F. Balzarotti, Y. Eilers et al bibl graph *Science* v355 no6325 p606 F 10 2017

High-rise apartment buildings

Double Vision in South Park: RISING UP OUT OF NOWHERE NEAR STAPLES CENTER, THE TWIN CIRCA TOWERS HAVE ALREADY ALTERED HOW WE SEE DOWNTOWN C. NICHOLS *Los Angeles Magazine* v62 no9 p24 S 2017

PYRAMID POWER S. COCHRAN color *Architectural Digest* v73 no11 p208 N 2016

High-rise apartment buildings—Design & construction

About Face T. HENNIGAN *Architectural Record* v205 no10 p102 O 2017

Stacking the Deck: A New York residential tower presents a new take on the city's classic skyscrapers J. GONCHAR color map *Architectural Record* v205 no5 p91 My 2017

High-rise apartment buildings—Economic aspects

Misdirected Investment C. R. Morris color *Commonweal* v143 no18 p6 N 11 2016

High school athletes

See also

High school football players

et al *Phi Kappa Phi Forum* v96 no4 p4 Wint 2016

High school athletes—United States

The Case for ... The High School Combine B. Hamilton and T. Keith color *Sports Illustrated* v126 no14 p31 My 15-22 2017

FACES IN THE CROWD T. Keith and S. Kwak color *Sports Illustrated* v127 no5 p30 Ag 14 2017

FACES IN THE CROWD T. Keith color *Sports Illustrated* v125 no14 p26 O 24-31 2016

FACES IN THE CROWD T. Keith color *Sports Illustrated* v126 no11 p28 Ap 17-24 2017

FACES IN THE CROWD T. Keith color *Sports Illustrated* v126 no17 p28 Je 19 2017

High school athletes—United States—Awards

THE BEST AND BRIGHTEST [Cover story] D. Greene color *Sports Illustrated* v127 no2 p28 Jl 17 2017

MACKENZIE GORE S. Apstein color *Sports Illustrated* v127 no2 p32 Jl 17 2017

Teen Titans color *Sports Illustrated* v127 no2 p16 Jl 17 2017

High school baseball

HUNTER GREENE IS EXACTLY WHAT BASEBALL NEEDS [Cover story] L. Jenkins color *Sports Illustrated* v126 no12 p22 My 1 2017

High school curriculum

Educating students for an outdated world S. Wolk bw color *Phi Delta Kappan* v99 no2 p46 O 2017

High school football players

The No. 2 College-Football Recruit in the Country Is From Canarsie and Wears a SpongeBob Backpack R. WIEDEMAN img *New York* v49 no25 p76 D 12 2016

High school football players—History—20th century

A TOWN, A TEAM AND FOOTBALL T. Layden color *Sports Illustrated* v127 no11 p46 O 9 2017

High school football players—Wounds & injuries

Rallying For Grant L. Flynn and T. Keith color *Sports Illustrated* v125 no21 p25 D 26 2016

High school football—Social aspects

High-School-Football Games D. Hill color *New York Times Magazine* p30 N 27 2016

High school freshmen

Detracked — And going strong P. Bavis chart color graph *Phi Delta Kappan* v98 no4 p37 D 2016/Ja 2017

High school reunions

The Reluctant Reunioner: Amid Friends and Strangers S. CARR *Idaho Magazine* v16 no12 p54 S 2017

THE SECRET LIFE OF ANIMALS E. RYLAN, P. CHANDLEE et al cartoon *Reader's Digest* v190 no1134 p38 O 2017

High school sophomores

THE SOPHOMORE S. TIGNOR *Tennis* v53 no3 p52 My/Je 2017

High school student activities

Backtalk J. M. Torres *Phi Delta Kappan* v98 no7 p80 Ap 2017

High school students

See also

Black high school students

BEATING Senioritis N. Loeffler-Gladstone *Dance Spirit* v21 no1 p90 Ja 2017

Do Teens Need Recess? *Scholastic Choices* v33 no1 p2 S 2017

FIELD TRIP R. Mead cartoon *New Yorker* v93 no4 p30 Mr 13 2017

HANGING ONTO HOPE H. M. CAULEY *Atlanta* v56 no11 p124 Mr 2017

THE SOPHOMORE S. TIGNOR *Tennis* v53 no3 p52 My/Je 2017

Taking the Fast Track: Online links to higher education D. Wilson color *New Orleans Magazine* v51 no10 p44 Ag 2017

WE ARE HERE L. Chan color map *Glamour* v115 no9 p206 S 2017

High school students—California

CYBERKIDS C. Battan cartoon *New Yorker* v92 no44 p20 Ja 9 2017

High school students—Interviews

Q&A: High-Level Help color *Maclean's* v130 no9 p64 O 2017

High school students—Psychology

YOUR CHEAT SHEET TO... School! Money! Jobs! L. SAXTON color *Seventeen* v76 no2 p100 Mr 2017

High school students—United States

Congratulations to Regeneron Science Talent Search Top 40 Finalists color *Science News* v191 no4 p29 Mr 4 2017

For the Record color *Time* v188 no18 p8 O 31 2016

High school teachers

'How can I build upon a career in aerospace to become a high school teacher?' K. Palmer color *AARP: The Magazine* v59 no6A p28 O/N 2016

High school teaching

What real high performance looks like J. Nehring, M. Charner-Laird et al chart diag *Phi Delta Kappan* v98 no7 p38 Ap 2017

High schools

THE BRIDGE TO COLLEGE N. CROWE color *Indianapolis Monthly* v41 no2 p144 S 2017

My Advice L. Graham bw color *Seventeen* v75 no11 p108 N 2016

High schools—California

CAT GOES TO HIGH SCHOOL S. Jose and K. Jazynka color map *National Geographic Kids* no465 p13 N 2016

A Southern California District Resists Bad Education Policy J. Bryant color *Progressive* v81 no6 p40 Ag/S 2017

High schools—Social aspects

A Separate Place A. B. LLOYD color *Weekly Standard* v22 no39 p16 Je 19 2017

High schools—United States

CAN FOOTBALL BE SAVED? N. SCHMIDLE cartoon color *New Yorker* v92 no44 p38 Ja 9 2017

Detracked — And going strong P. Bavis chart color graph *Phi Delta Kappan* v98 no4 p37 D 2016/Ja 2017

Educating students for an outdated world S. Wolk bw color *Phi Delta Kappan* v99 no2 p46 O 2017

High School of the Future J. JACOBS *Education Digest* v82 no4 p33 D 2016

HIGH SCHOOL THEATRE HONORS PROGRAM L. Mulcahy *Stage Directions* v29 no11 p24 N 2016

Later start time for teens improves grades, mood, and safety K. L. Wahlstrom chart color diag *Phi Delta Kappan* v98 no4 p8 D 2016/Ja 2017

ROOM TO GROW: A private school with a noble mission gets a new lease on life--and a new building F. REDDY *Atlanta* v57 no3 p24 Jl 2017

A Separate Place A. B. LLOYD color *Weekly Standard* v22 no39 p16 Je 19 2017

A Study in Materials J. GONCHAR *Architectural Record* v205 no1 p100 Ja 2017

High schools—Virginia

Code RVA: HIGH SCHOOL OF THE FUTURE *Virginia Living* v15 no6 p91 O 2017

High-speed video recording

INSIDE NASCAR'S VIDEO REVIEW TRAILER E. HILDEBRANDT color *Popular Mechanics* p28 O 2017

High technology

See also
    High technology & education
    Nanotechnology

THE CONTENT OF NO CONTENT E. KOLBERT cartoon *New Yorker* v93 no25 p42 Ag 28 2017

Fast Forward D. B. CLARK color graph *Wired* v25 no10 p58 O 2017

High-Tech Tools Won't Automatically Improve Your Operations S. Thomke *Harvard Business Review Digital Articles* p2 Je 10 2015

How Israel Took a Toy and Made It a High-Tech Weapon [Cover story] Y. KATZ and A. BOHBOT *Commentary* v143 no1 p19 Ja 2017

Right Tech, Wrong Time R. Adner and R. Kapoor color img *Harvard Business Review* v94 no11 p60 N 2016

Yves Béhar E. HOLT color *Architectural Digest* v74 no10 p57 O 1 2017

High technology & education

Reading in a digital age N. S. Baron graph il *Phi Delta Kappan* v99 no2 p15 O 2017

High technology equipment

High Tech, Low Profile M. Khemsurov color *Bloomberg Businessweek* no4520 p72 My 1 2017

High technology industries

See also
    Information technology industry

3 Ways Tech Companies Are Offering Parental Leave J. C. Williams *Harvard Business Review Digital Articles* p2 N 19 2015

The Business Issue N. Byrnes color *MIT Technology Review* v120 no4 p2 Jl/Ag 2017

DATA CENTERS GO EXOTIC J. Vanian color *Fortune* v175 no5 p20 Ap 1 2017

In the Land of the Blind Hire E. Huet cartoon color *Bloomberg Businessweek* no4508 p27 Ja 23 2017

THE IPO STATUS REPORT color *Fortune* v175 no6 p8 My 1 2017

IT'S TIME TO TAKE AI SERIOUSLY E. Griffith color *Fortune* v175 no3 p51 Mr 1 2017

Local R&D Won't Help You Go Global T. J. Hannigan and R. Mudambi *Harvard Business Review Digital Articles* p2 Je 25 2015

The Problem with Tech Copycats D. Pogue cartoon *Scientific American* v315 no5 p23 N 2016

Research: Why Best Practices Don't Translate Across Cultures P. Hinds *Harvard Business Review Digital Articles* p2 Je 27 2016

Saving Face K. Mehrotra color *Bloomberg Businessweek* no4531 p42 Jl 24 2017

Start-Up Palestine Y. Kaufmann color *Foreign Affairs* v96 no4 p113 Jl/Ag 2017

Tech Stocks Are Back ... in a Bubble P. J. Lim color diag *Money* v46 no9 p48 O 2017

WORKHORSE STOCKS GET TO SHINE *Fortune* v174 no8 p111 D 15 2016

High technology industries—California—Santa Clara Valley

AFTER THE PROCESS C. Ballard chart color *Sports Illustrated* v125 no18 p54 D 5 2016

THE RAND PACK N. BILTON cartoon *Vanity Fair* v58 no11 p120 N 2016

The Reason Silicon Valley Beat Out Boston for VC Dominance A. Gupta and Haiyan Wang *Harvard Business Review Digital Articles* p2 N 15 2016

Silicon Valley's New Reality Show B. Stone color *Bloomberg Businessweek* no4505 p6 D 26 2016

TRISTAN HARRIS BELIEVES SILICON VALLEY IS ADDICTING US TO OUR PHONES. HE'S DETERMINED TO MAKE IT STOP B. Bosker color *Atlantic* v318 no4 p56 N 2016

THE UGLY UNETHICAL UNDERSIDE OF SILICON VALLEY E. Griffith color *Fortune* v75 no1 p72 Ja 1 2017

THE VIEW FROM THE VALLEY cartoon graph *Atlantic* v318 no4 p66 N 2016

High technology industries—California—Santa Clara Valley— Political activity

IF SILICON VALLEY WENT TO WASHINGTON R. Hackett color *Fortune* v175 no2 p26 F 1 2017

High technology industries—Canada

Canada Welcomes Tech Companies That Are Spooked by Trump P. Elliott color *Time* v189 no14 p27 Ap 17 2017

High technology industries—Congresses

Talking Tech Disruption M. Lev-ram color *Fortune* v176 no3 p24 S 1 2017

High technology industries—Corrupt practices

THE UGLY UNETHICAL UNDERSIDE OF SILICON VALLEY E. Griffith color *Fortune* v75 no1 p72 Ja 1 2017

High technology industries—Economic aspects

Goodbye, Unicorns. Hello, IPOs! E. Griffith color *Fortune* v175 no6 p7 My 1 2017

Tech Moves to Head of the Class chart diag *Money* v46 no3 p76 Ap 2017

High technology industries—Employees

We're Making the Wrong Case for Diversity in Silicon Valley T. L. Pittinsky *Harvard Business Review Digital Articles* p2 Ap 11 2016

High technology industries—European Union countries

How Europe Can Create Its Own Silicon Valley L. Downes *Harvard Business Review Digital Articles* p2 Je 11 2015

High technology industries—Finance

NEW-TECH'S PROFIT BLACK HOLE D. Lyons color *Fortune* v174 no8 p82 D 15 2016

Tech Shares on a Tear chart diag *Money* v46 no6 p76 Jl 2017

High technology industries—India

Laid-Off Indian IT Workers Blame Trump S. Rai graph *Bloomberg Businessweek* no4525 p14 Je 5 2017

High technology industries—Moral & ethical aspects

GLOBALIZATION BITES BACK J. J. Roberts color diag *Fortune* v176 no2 p82 Ag 1 2017

High technology industries—Personnel management

What African Start-Ups Need to Do to Hire and Keep Great Talent N. Ekekwe *Harvard Business Review Digital Articles* p2 Ap 13 2015

High technology industries—Philippines

How the Philippines Became Tech Startups' New Source for Talent O. Segovia *Harvard Business Review Digital Articles* p2 Ag 5 2015

High technology industries—Political activity

Are Uber and Facebook Turning Users into Lobbyists? M. Stempeck *Harvard Business Review Digital Articles* p2 Ag 11 2015

High technology industries—Soviet Union

JUNE 12, 1989. CYBER-SOVIETS A. BROWN bw color *Forbes* v199 no7 p36 Je 29 2017

High technology industries—United States

See also
    Silicon Valley (Santa Clara County, Calif.)

The AI Doctor Orders More Tests M. Bergen cartoon *Bloomberg Businessweek* no4526 p39 Je 12 2017

The Fast Tech 25 color *Forbes* v199 no6 p48 Je 13 2017

2017

The Sixteen Most Innovative People in Higher Education G. Edelman *Washington Monthly* p1 S/O 2016

Speak Up!: Colleges and universities honor free inquiry in theory, but not always in fact. How to keep higher education true to its values P. Berkowitz *Hoover Digest: Research & Opinion on Public Policy* no3 p125 Summ 2017

Taking Student Success to Scale R. R. Martin *Change* v49 no1 p38 Ja/F 2017

A Tale of Two Universities D. C. Paris *Change* v49 no3 p4 My/Je 2017

TOP OF THEIR CLASS *Sierra* v102 no5 p42 St/O 2017

Will Higher Education Reform Become Another Ideological War Zone? P. GLASTRIS *Washington Monthly* v49 no9/10 p14 S/O 2017

Higher education—United States—Costs

College Promise: Pathway to the 21 Century M. J. Kanter, A. Armstrong et al *Change* v48 no6 p6 N/D 2016

Higher education—United States—Finance

One Small Step to College J. B. Wogan *Governing* v30 no6 p38 Mr 2017

Higher nervous activity

Stellate cells drive maturation of the entorhinal-hippocampal circuit F. Donato, R. I. Jacobsen et al diag *Science* v355 no6330 p1172 Mr 17 2017

Highfill, Samantha

13 REASONS WHY: INSIDE THE MOST DARING SHOW ON TELEVISION [Cover story] color *Entertainment Weekly* no1466 p24 My 19 2017

THE 20-WORD REVIEW color *Entertainment Weekly* no1473 p50 Jl 7 2017

ANIMAL KINGDOM color *Entertainment Weekly* no1468/1469 p65 Je 2-9 2017

Arrow *Entertainment Weekly* no1482/1483 p84 S 22 2017

The Bachelorette Gets Woke color *Entertainment Weekly* no1454/1455 p18 F 24 2017

THE BACHELORETTE WE'VE BEEN WAITING FOR color *Entertainment Weekly* no1468/1469 p18 Je 2-9 2017

Better Things color *Entertainment Weekly* no1482/1483 p91 S 22 2017

Blindspot color *Entertainment Weekly* no1482/1483 p95 S 22 2017

Blue Bloods color *Entertainment Weekly* no1482/1483 p99 S 22 2017

The Bold Type's IRL Inspo color *Entertainment Weekly* no1478 / 1479 p89 Ag 18-25 2017

Chicago Fire *Entertainment Weekly* no1482/1483 p91 S 22 2017

CHRISTINE EVANGELISTA color *Entertainment Weekly* no1456 p59 Mr 10 2017

Crazy Ex-Girlfriend color *Entertainment Weekly* no1482/1483 p98 S 22 2017

Dynasty color *Entertainment Weekly* no1482/1483 p76 S 22 2017

The Exorcist color *Entertainment Weekly* no1482/1483 p92 S 22 2017

THE FINAL FOUR CHAPTERS color *Entertainment Weekly* no1441 p24 N 25 2016

FRIDAY NIGHT LIGHTS color *Entertainment Weekly* no1434 p48 O 7 2016

GILMORE GIRLS: ANOTHER YEAR IN THE LIFE?! color *Entertainment Weekly* no1457/1458 p18 Mr 17 2017

Gilmore Girls: A Year in the Life color *Entertainment Weekly* no1439 p18 N 11 2016

Gilmore Girls Revival Guide color *Entertainment Weekly* no1443 p14 D 9 2016

GOING OUT WITH A BANG color *Entertainment Weekly* no1463/1464 p10 Ap/My 2017

The Good Place color *Entertainment Weekly* no1482/1483 p86 S 22 2017

Gotham *Entertainment Weekly* no1482/1483 p84 S 22 2017

THE GREATEST DISNEY SONGS OF ALL TIME color *Entertainment Weekly* no1454/1455 p36 F 24 2017

Great News color *Entertainment Weekly* no1482/1483 p88 S 22 2017

Grey's Anatomy color diag *Entertainment Weekly* no1482/1483 p89 S 22 2017

Hawaii Five-O *Entertainment Weekly* no1482/1483 p99 S 22 2017

Hell's Kitchen *Entertainment Weekly* no1482/1483 p99 S 22 2017

How to Get Away With Murder *Entertainment Weekly* no1482/1483 p91 S 22 2017

Inside Nashville's Revamp color *Entertainment Weekly* no1443 p54 D 9 2016

Jane the Virgin color *Entertainment Weekly* no1482/1483 p95 S 22 2017

JASON RITTER OF Kevin (Probably) Saves the World color *Entertainment Weekly* no1482/1483 p61 S 22 2017

KINGDOM'S KNOCKOUT color *Entertainment Weekly* no1477 p48 Ag 11 2017

Life in Pieces *Entertainment Weekly* no1482/1483 p88 S 22 2017

MacGyver *Entertainment Weekly* no1482/1483 p99 S 22 2017

Marvel's Inhumans color *Entertainment Weekly* no1482/1483 p99 S 22 2017

Meet Nashville's Newbies color *Entertainment Weekly* no1468/1469 p91 Je 2-9 2017

Mom color *Entertainment Weekly* no1482/1483 p85 S 22 2017

Nashville's Life After Death color *Entertainment Weekly* no1456 p16 Mr 10 2017

THE NEVER-ENDING STORY color *Entertainment Weekly* no1450 p11 Ja 27 2017

Next on Bachelor in Paradise color *Entertainment Weekly* no1473 p14 Jl 7 2017

ONCE MORE, WITH FEELING! color *Entertainment Weekly* no1450 p12 Ja 27 2017

Once Upon a Time color *Entertainment Weekly* no1482/1483 p96 S 22 2017

ONE LAST HOWL color *Entertainment Weekly* no1480 p30 S 1 2017

The Orville *Entertainment Weekly* no1482/1483 p85 S 22 2017

PRETTY LITTLE LIARS color *Entertainment Weekly* no1468/1469 p56 Je 2-9 2017

Scandal *Entertainment Weekly* no1482/1483 p88 S 22 2017

STARS HOLLOW HOMECOMING [Cover story] color *Entertainment Weekly* no1441 p18 N 25 2016

Suddenly Sutton color *Entertainment Weekly* no1440 p28 N 18 2016

Suitors to Watch color *Entertainment Weekly* no1468/1469 p19 Je 2-9 2017

Supernatural color *Entertainment Weekly* no1482/1483 p84 S 22 2017

Supernatural's Sister Act color *Entertainment Weekly* no1472 p16 Je 30 2017

Superstore color *Entertainment Weekly* no1482/1483 p84 S 22 2017

S.W.A.T color *Entertainment Weekly* no1482/1483 p90 S 22 2017

THERE WILL BE TEARS color *Entertainment Weekly* no1454/1455 p54 F 24 2017

What's the Most Bingeworthy Show? color *Entertainment Weekly* no1443 p21 D 9 2016

What to Watch color *Entertainment Weekly* no1446/1447 p112 D 2016/Ja 2017

What to Watch color *Entertainment Weekly* no1457/1458 p88 Mr 17 2017

What to Watch color *Entertainment Weekly* no1468/1469 p94 Je 2-9 2017

What to Watch color *Entertainment Weekly* no1478 / 1479 p97 Ag 18-25 2017

WHY YOU'LL (PROBABLY) NEVER SEE A LOST REBOOT color *Entertainment Weekly* no1450 p15 Ja 27 2017

Will & Grace color *Entertainment Weekly* no1482/1483 p80 S 22 2017

Your Sunshiny, Stupendous, Seriously Spectacular SUMMER BUCKET LIST color *Entertainment Weekly* no1470 p32 Je 16 2017

Highland Capital Management LP

This Fund Banks on Bank Loans R. ERMEY chart *Kiplinger's Personal Finance* v71 no10 p63 O 2017

Highlander sport utility vehicle

Family-Friendly Road Warrior *Consumer Reports* v82 no7 p63 Jl 2017

Highlander sport utility vehicle—Evaluation

Toyota Highlander SE chart color *Motor Trend* v69 no1 p58 Ja 2017

Highly active antiretroviral therapy

Sustained virologic control in SIV+ macaques after antiretroviral and α4β7 antibody therapy S. N. Byrareddy, J. Arthos et al bibl graph *Science* v354 no6309 p197 O 14 2016

Highmore, Freddie

Bates Motel *TV Guide* v65 no8 p17 F 27 2017

Becoming Psycho *TV Guide* v65 no14 p16 Ap 3 2017

FREDDIE HIGHMORE OF The Good Doctor N. Abrams, C. Holub et al color *Entertainment Weekly* no1482/1483 p54 S 22 2017

THE GOOD DOCTOR I. Rudolph *TV Guide* v65 no37 p24 S 4 2017

High Noon: A 50-Year Retrospective (Music)

At Home Anywhere C. WOLFF color *Downbeat* v84 no1 p79 Ja 2017

Hight, Edward Ariel

Community network for deaf scientists color *Science* v356 no6336 p386 Ap 28 2017

HIGHTOWER, JIM

ALEC's War on Local Control color *Progressive* v81 no7 p70 O/N 2017

The Awfulest of the Awful color *Progressive* v81 no6 p70 Ag/S 2017

The Essence of Ed Garvey cartoon *Progressive* v81 no4 p70 Ap/My 2017

For the Love of Fighting Bob cartoon *Progressive* v81 no10 p46 N 2016

Governor Goodhair Goes to Washington cartoon *Progressive* v81 no3 p46 Mr 2017

Has Our Country Gone Nuts? cartoon *Progressive* p70 D 2016/Ja 2017

Putting the Constitution Up for Sale cartoon *Progressive* v81 no2 p46 F 2017

Save the Postal Service color *Progressive* v81 no5 p70 Je/Jl 2017

Hightower, Royalty

L. A. NOIR W. MORRIS and A. O. SCOTT bw *New York Times Magazine* p64 D 11 2016

Hightower Group LLC

Santa Cruz: HIGHTOWER LT X01/CARBON CC W/ RESERVE 30 WHEEL UPGRADE J. Weber color *Bike Magazine* v24 no8 p66 N 2017

Highway, Tomson

Kiss of the Fur Queen *Maclean's* v129 no42 p45 O 24 2016

Highway engineering

Electric Avenues Smart roads might serve as off-board EV range extenders F. Markus color *Motor Trend* v69 no9 p28 S 2017

Highwayman (Music)

The Highwaymen Return D. Browne color *AARP: The Magazine* v59 no3A p15 Ap/My 2016

Higinbotham, Gable

backstory color *New Republic* v247 no11 p64 N 2016

Higuchi2, Y.

Structural basis of the redox switches in the NAD+-reducing soluble [NiFe]-hydrogenase diag *Science* v357 no6354 p928 S 1 2017

Hijab (Islamic clothing)

Asking for a Friend L. Featherstone color *Nation* v304 no5 p5 F 20 2017

Calendar: Power T. Berenson and J. Shapiro color *Time* v188 no27-28 p62 D 26 2016

Canadian Mounties Can Wear Hijab *Islamic Horizons* v45 no6 p12 N/D 2016

HALIMA'S WORLD S. Kitchens color *Glamour* v115 no9 p200 S 2017

Hijabi Fits: A tween is creating a rainbow of hijabs for girls of all ages S. MEEHAN *Islamic Horizons* v46 no4 p36 Jl/Ag 2017

Nura Afia S. Pulia color *InStyle* v24 no3 p174 Mr 2017

Hijacking of ships

Where Pirates Still Roam the Seas color *Time* v189 no18 p12 My 15 2017

Hijacking of ships—Lawsuits & claims

THE HIJACKING OF THE BRILLANTE VIRTUOSO K. CHEL-LEL, M. CAMPBELL et al color map *Bloomberg Businessweek* no4532 p48 Jl 31 2017

Hik, David S.

Higher predation risk for insect prey at low latitudes and elevations graph *Science* v356 no6339 p742 My 19 2017

Hikers

2017 THRU-HIKER AWARDS color *Backpacker* v45 no1 p59 Ja 2017

Cabin Convert J. WATERMAN color *Backpacker* p51 O 2017

CAN'T STOP NOW B. Donahue color *Backpacker* v45 no1 p70 Ja 2017

COME ONE, COME ALL C. Gerard color *Backpacker* v45 no1 p64 Ja 2017

Get a fresh perspective color *Backpacker* p16 Je 2017

Get Fit Fast T. VANDERMOLEN il *Backpacker* p28 Je 2017

Go far, far away color *Backpacker* p15 My 2017

Go the Distance L. ". THOMAS color *Backpacker* v45 no1 p6 Ja 2017

The Hiker and the Sexologist M. NORDSTROM *Sierra* v101 no6 p18 N/D 2016

JOURNEY OF A LIFETIME E. J. Wallace color diag *Backpacker* v45 no1 p65 Ja 2017

The latest word from our testers color *Backpacker* p47 O 2017

out alive: lost & blind C. Webber color *Backpacker* p43 My 2017

Out of the ORDINARY M. JAFFE *Arizona Highways* v92 no7 p42 Jl 2016

Permanent Paths color *Backpacker* v45 no1 p10 Ja 2017

PHOTO FINISH color *Backpacker* v45 no1 p96 Ja 2017

Runyon Canyon 911 C. KAZDIN color *Los Angeles Magazine* v62 no10 p15 O 2017

Savor the last snow diag *Backpacker* p19 Je 2017

Treat Aches and Pains C. GERARD diag *Backpacker* v45 no1 p32 Ja 2017

VIEW WITH A ROOM W. M. ROCHFORT JR. color *Backpacker* p48 O 2017

Hikers—Safety measures

Under Attack il *Backpacker* p47 My 2017

Hiking

See also

Backpacking

Mountaineering

Trails

10 BEST WALKS IN AMERICA K. Benjamin cartoon *Prevention* p46 Mr 2017

2018 INTERNATIONAL TRIPS (PLUS WINTER DOMESTIC TRIPS) *Sierra* v102 no5 p48 St/O 2017

Along with Tom M. STUBBS *Idaho Magazine* v16 no2 p18 N 2016

Aluminum Foil T. BROWN JR. color *Backpacker* p40 O 2017

The Amateur's Guide to Africa's Highest Peak J. CRIDER color diag *Conde Nast Traveler* v52 no5 p64 My 2017

Backpacking With Benefits P. Rauber *Sierra* v102 no1 p16 Ja/F 2017

Backpack with a Stranger W. McGOUGH il *Backpacker* p28 O 2017

A Bandana C. LYONS color *Backpacker* p38 Je 2017

BASE CAMP *Sierra* v102 no1 p69 Ja/F 2017

Better in Winter O. DWYER color *Backpacker* p34 N 2017

BUZZ color *Bike Magazine* v24 no7 p28 S 2017

CABIN LOOP K. VAUGHN *Arizona Highways* v92 no7 p32 Jl 2016

CHARMING DALIR *Iceland Review* v54 no6 p106 N/D 2016

cheat sheet: Backcountry Hygiene C. BUHAY *Backpacker* p30 S 2017

Come in for a landing color *Backpacker* p20 S 2017

Come Out and Play T. ALVAREZ color *Backpacker* p84 Je 2017

Conquer Slot Canyons M. SALVATI il *Backpacker* p26 O 2017

The Dayhiker's Triple Crown J. MONTALVO color *Backpacker* v45 no1 p14 Ja 2017

DIARY OF A BELTWAY HIKE *Washingtonian Magazine* v52 no12 p61 S 2017

Double your fun: Trail Running C. BUHAY *Backpacker* p22 O 2017

Down you go C. BUHAY color *Backpacker* p29 S 2017

DRAWN OUT K. Krichko il *Backpacker* v45 no1 p87 Ja 2017

Eat for Endurance C. Gerard color *Backpacker* v45 no1 p36 Ja 2017

EXTREME ATTRACTION M. JENKINS color map *Backpacker* p58 Ag 2017

Find your Stride: Hiking in the Zone L. ". Thomas color *Backpacker* v45 no1 p16 Ja 2017

The First Steps J. P. Davis *Backpacker* p71 Je 2017

Follow Randy *Backpacker* p20 Ag 2017

For the Birds K. POPE color *Backpacker* p18 N 2017

Free Flow R. WICHELNS *Backpacker* p21 O 2017

FUN & GAMES J. Kofron, A. Ramsey et al color *Backpacker* p71 Je 2017

Get lost color *Backpacker* p14 O 2017

Go Big: Superhike A. DRUMMOND map *Backpacker* p28 Ag 2017

Golden Rules color *Backpacker* v45 no1 p51 Ja 2017

Gold Rush H. B. ROCHFORT color map *Backpacker* p18 O 2017

Go Stoveless A. JAMESON il *Backpacker* v45 no1 p34 Ja 2017

Go the Distance L. ". THOMAS color *Backpacker* v45 no1 p6 Ja 2017

A GROWING TREND A. STEWART *Missouri Life* v43 no6 p84 O/N 2016

Hell's Half Acre: Strolling the Lava Trails B. BASH *Idaho Magazine* v16 no11 p15 Ag 2017

The Highest Order M. JOHANSON color *Backpacker* p10 N 2017

HIKE MORE, DRIVE LESS P. CHISHOLM color *Backpacker* p56 My 2017

Hikes Gone Wrong: We all love the trail. Sometimes love hurts T. Ross, C. Buhay et al color il *Backpacker* p69 S 2017

Hike your own hike color *Backpacker* v45 no1 p12 Ja 2017

Hit the high country color *Backpacker* p10 S 2017

Holiday Hike: Stephens State Forest, Iowa K. PETERSON map *Backpacker* p15 N 2017

Home on the Range M. PALEY color map *National Geographic* v231 no4 p64 Ap 2017

HOME TOWN HERO B. Blais-Billie color *Glamour* v115 no9 p174 S 2017

Increase your vocabulary R. ZURER *Backpacker* p14 S 2017

Independence color *Backpacker* p74 Je 2017

INTO THE ROCKY MOUNTAIN WILD A. Shoalts color *Canadian Geographic* v136 no6 p34 D 2016

LAND: ATLANTA'S OUTDOOR RECREATION PLAYGROUND J. GREEN *Atlanta* v57 no4 p56 Ag 2017

let go: AND SURRENDER TO THE NOW m. ferrentino color *Bike Magazine* v24 no8 p42 N 2017

Light Up Your Life K. FERRARO color *Backpacker* v45 no1 p24 Ja 2017

Link 10 Peaks in a Day B. TARAZI il *Backpacker* p36 Ag 2017

Local Hikes Just Got Better D. LEWON *Backpacker* p10 Ag 2017

Lonely at the Top C. LYONS color *Backpacker* p16 O 2017

LONG DRIVE, SHORT HIKE J. Davis color *Backpacker* v45 no1 p79 Ja 2017

The Long Way Home: Returns C. C. CHOJNACKY *Backpacker* p13 S 2017

Lost and Found D. LEWON color *Backpacker* p4 O 2017

LOST IN BIG BEND C. FRYE color map *Reader's Digest* v190 no1132 p88 Jl/Ag 2017

Love at First Sight M. HORJUS and J. MONTALVO color *Backpacker* v45 no2 p54 Mr 2017

Make Hiking Great Again T. ALVAREZ and T. VANDERMOLEN color il *Backpacker* p18 Je 2017

Making a Splash N. BOUCHARD color *Backpacker* p43 O 2017

THE MAMMOTH MINE R. BROOKS *Idaho Magazine* v16 no5 p12 F 2017

Mountain Magic N. PIPENBERG map *Backpacker* p24 Je 2017

A MOUNTAIN OF TROUBLE K. MILLER *Reader's Digest* v188 no1124 p108 O 2016

The Never-Ending Journey C. LYONS color *Backpacker* v45 no1 p20 Ja 2017

Oasis of Rock: Joshua Tree National Park, California R. WICHELNS color map *Backpacker* p8 N 2017

Off-Grid on Rainy Lake [Cover story] F. SIGURDSSON color *Cabin Living* p24 Ag 2017

Oh, Crap! O. DWYER color *Backpacker* p21 Ag 2017

ON THE ROCKS L. VACCARIELLO *Indianapolis Monthly* v40 no5 p30 Ja 2017

Oregon's Trail of Tears B. Robinson *Sierra* v102 no5 p14 St/O 2017

out alive: mauled by a grizzly. twice C. Webber color diag *Backpacker* p35 Je 2017

Pack Ice Cream K. CLOOS il *Backpacker* p30 Je 2017

pass fail: Summit at Sunset A. GULSBY il *Backpacker* p32 S 2017

Passing It Down E. OSBORN *Sierra* v101 no5 p64 S/O 2016

Pillars of the Earth L. LANCASTER color *Backpacker* p14 Je 2017

Play color *Backpacker* p72 Je 2017

Play hide-and-seek A. WUNDERMAN diag *Backpacker* p10 N 2017

the play list color il map *Backpacker* p6 N 2017

PRESIDENTIAL TRAIL *South Dakota Magazine* v32 no4 p109 N/D 2016

Restoration and Renewal S. K. TRAUTMAN *Parks & Recreation* v51 no10 p8 O 2016

Room at the Top D. GUASPARI color *Weekly Standard* v22 no21 p36 F 6 2017

Rules, Shmoolz Leslie Hsu Oh *Backpacker* p73 Je 2017

Savor the last snow diag *Backpacker* p19 Je 2017

Secret Garden: Big Cypress National Preserve, Florida M. RADZICKI MCMANUS color *Backpacker* p16 N 2017

See the Forest for the Trees L. LANCASTER map *Backpacker* v45 no1 p25 Ja 2017

September 2017 color *O, The Oprah Magazine* p113 S 2017

Sleep Warmer K. Karlson color *Backpacker* p27 N 2017

Smoke Signals il *Backpacker* p41 O 2017

SOARING UNDER THE RADAR C. GRAHAM *American Forests* v123 no2 p42 Summ 2017

The Sound of 6 Million Acres B. COSGROVE *Orion Magazine* v36 no2 p13 Mr/Ap 2017

Southern Charm E. KWAK-HEFFERAN color map *Backpacker* p12 O 2017

Spa Days: Lake Mead National Recreation Area, Nevada/Arizona K. KYLE color map *Backpacker* p14 N 2017

Stay dry in a downpour color *Backpacker* p25 O 2017

SUPPORTED TREKKING *Sierra* v102 no1 p71 Ja/F 2017

Take the scenic route color *Backpacker* v45 no1 p22 Ja 2017

Tall Trees Grove: Redwood National Park, CA diag *Backpacker* p104 N 2017

Tell Your Story G. FULLERTON and B. ". BENVIE color diag *Backpacker* v45 no1 p38 Ja 2017

THIS COULD BE YOU *Sierra* v102 no3 p64 My/Je 2017

Thoughts on previous issues R. Reuck, S. Emmen-Outen et al color *American Cowboy* v24 no1 p24 Je/Jl 2017

TIMBERLINE I. VORSTER *American Forests* v123 no3 p32 Fall 2017

Toughen Up L. ". THOMAS color *Backpacker* v45 no1 p31 Ja 2017

#trailchat color diag *Backpacker* p6 O 2017

#trailchat J. Kay, D. O'Dell et al color *Backpacker* p8 My 2017

#trailchat R. Bovee, S. West et al color il map *Backpacker* p6 Je 2017

TRAIL DAZE B. Donahue color *Backpacker* p62 O 2017

Trail Fails D. LEWON color *Backpacker* p6 S 2017

THE TREE FUNERAL M. W. Spencer color *Louisiana Life* v38 no1 p10 S/O 2017

An Unlikely Embrace W. SMITH *Sierra* v102 no3 p72 My/Je 2017

A WALK AROUND THE BEAT BELTWAY: THE HIGHWAY RINGING WASHINGTON IS G4 MILES LONG. NO ONE EVER CONFUSED IT WITH A SCENIC NATURE TRAIL. BUT ON A SIX-DAY HIKE ALONG ITS PERIPHERY, A BDRN AND BRED WASHINGTONIAN FOUND MOMENTS OF SURPRISING BEAUTY,... J. HIMMELMAN *Washingtonian Magazine* v52 no12 p58 S 2017

Walking the Walk H. CHAHINIAN *O, The Oprah Magazine* p136 My 2017

Walk on Snow M. ATTEBERRY il *Backpacker* p28 N 2017

Walk This Way: FIVE OF SHENANDOAH NATIONAL PARK'S BEST DAY HIKES E. V. Clark *Washingtonian Magazine* v53 no1 p96 O 2017

Water Hazard D. Mother il *Backpacker* p39 Je 2017

We're Number One! D. L. Wheeler, T. Murarik et al color *Backpacker* v45 no1 p8 Ja 2017

WHAT I LEARNED color *Backpacker* v45 no1 p88 Ja 2017

WHERE ARE YOU GOING? color *O, The Oprah Magazine* p104 Ap 2017

WHERE NOBODY KNOWS YOUR TRAIL NAME T. Alvarez color *Backpacker* v45 no1 p80 Ja 2017

Where to Run K. DUPZYK color *Popular Mechanics* v193 no7

p43 S 2016

Wild Alaska S. Slon and L. Grier *Saturday Evening Post* v289 no2 p54 Mr/Ap 2017

WOODCHUTE TRAIL R. STIEVE *Arizona Highways* v93 no4 p54 Ap 2017

Your Adventure Fuel Formula color *Men's Health* v32 no6 p68 Ag 2017

Hiking equipment

Cabin Convert J. WATERMAN color *Backpacker* p51 O 2017

GEAR WARS D. LEWON color *Backpacker* v45 no3 p8 Ap 2017

The latest word from our testers color *Backpacker* p47 O 2017

Raingear T. J. BROWN color *Backpacker* p46 My 2017

#trailchat color *Backpacker* p4 N 2017

TREKKING POLES/SOCKS P. CHISHOLM color *Backpacker* v45 no3 p126 Ap 2017

What Has Your Gear Done for the World Lately? color *Backpacker* p78 S 2017

Hiking equipment—Evaluation

APPAREL E. KWAK-HEFFERAN, S. YORKO et al color *Backpacker* p55 N 2017

Editors' Choice Awards C. Lyons color *Backpacker* p45 N 2017

EQUIPMENT N. BOUCHARD, W. M. ROCHFORT et al color *Backpacker* p73 N 2017

EQUIP THE KIDS K. Bastone color *Backpacker* p71 Je 2017

Equip the Kids L. H. Oh *Sierra* v101 no4 p20 Jl/Ag 2016

ESSENTIALS M. HORJUS, A. ROY et al bw color *Backpacker* p93 N 2017

Feet First color *Backpacker* p54 Ag 2017

GEARHEAD: TRAIL MIX P. SARCONI color *Wired* v25 no7 p40 Jl 2017

Hang Time H. B. ROCHFORT bw color *Backpacker* p51 Ag 2017

The latest word from our testers color *Backpacker* p48 Je 2017

The latest word from our testers color *Backpacker* p50 S 2017

Hiking footwear

GEAR WARS D. LEWON color *Backpacker* v45 no3 p8 Ap 2017

Science Friction S. LEMONICK color *Climbing* no352 p12 Ap 2017

Hiking footwear—Evaluation

The Buy color *Harper's Bazaar* no3657 p100 O 2017

Hiking injuries

survival C. Webber bw color *Backpacker* v45 no2 p39 Mr 2017

Hiking techniques

Left Behind O. DWYER *Backpacker* p20 N 2017

Navigate at Night C. BUHAY diag graph il map *Backpacker* p34 Ag 2017

SECRETS OF THE GUIDES T. ALVAREZ color il *Backpacker* p75 Ag 2017

See the Light R. ZURER color *Backpacker* v45 no2 p21 Mr 2017

Hiking—Awards

2017 THRU-HIKER AWARDS color *Backpacker* v45 no1 p59 Ja 2017

Hiking—Charts, diagrams, etc.

Plan a Big Trip D. LEWON diag *Backpacker* v45 no2 p32 Mr 2017

Hiking—Colorado

Mountain Magic D. LEWON color *Backpacker* v45 no2 p70 Mr 2017

Hiking—Competitions

Take your mark: Competition Hikes C. BUHAY *Backpacker* p22 N 2017

Victory Lap C. BUHAY *Backpacker* v45 no2 p20 Mr 2017

Hiking—Psychological aspects

The Totally Trail-Ready Workout L. McGLASHAN chart color *Muscle & Performance* v9 no9 p20 S 2017

Hiking—Safety measures

Keep Your Cool in the Cold il *Backpacker* v45 no2 p43 Mr 2017

Hiking—Study & teaching

Raise a Kid Who Loves Hiking D. WORCESTER il *Backpacker* v45 no2 p34 Mr 2017

Hiking—Texas

BIRD CRAZY B. Andrews color *Prevention* v69 no6 p64 Je 2017

LODGE *Sierra* v102 no1 p78 Ja/F 2017

Hilborn, Anne

Scientists stand with Standing Rock bibl color *Science* v353 no6307 p1506 S 30 2016

Hilborn, Robert C.

Lyapunov Exponents A Tool to Explore Complex Dynamics *Physics Today* v70 no3 p62 Mr 2017

Hildebrandt, Becky

CANDID CONVERSATION ABOUT MENOPAUSE AT THE CHRIST HOSPITAL *Cincinnati Magazine* v50 no3 p62 D 2016

Hildebrandt, Eleanor

BREAK THROUGH AWARDS 2017 [Cover story] bw color *Popular Mechanics* p56 N 2017

INSIDE NASCAR'S VIDEO REVIEW TRAILER color *Popular Mechanics* p28 O 2017

WILL IT KILL YOU? bw color *Popular Mechanics* p88 Jl 2017

HILDENBRAND, BRUCE

Identify Bad Bolts color *Climbing* no354 p40 Jl 2017

UNSOLICITED BETA *Climbing* no355 p14 Ag 2017

Hilder, Starry

Fresh, Homemade SALAD DRESSINGS *Mother Earth News* no281 p36 Ap/My 2017

Hilderbrand, Elin—Interviews

Elin Hilderbrand: The author of 'The Identicals' says that for a literary dinner party, she would invite J. D. Salinger, John Cheever and Flannery O'Connor: 'I'm serving very cold Veuve Clicquot and a bowl of mixed nuts' E. Hilderbrand *New York Times Book Review* p6 Je 11 2017

Hilderbrand, Terry—Interviews

Terry Hilderbrand S. STALL *Indianapolis Monthly* v40 no4 p29 D 2016

Hildreth, Angus

Powerful People Underperform When They Work Together *Harvard Business Review Digital Articles* p2 F 24 2016

Hilferty, Susan

CREATING EMERALD CITY COUTURE *Cincinnati Magazine* v50 no8 p22 My 2017

Hilfiger, Tommy, 1951-

TOMMY'S GREAT ESCAPE H. Rubenstein color *InStyle* p70 Home & Design 2016

Hilfiker, Hans

WAIT A SECOND (AND A HALF) R. Verger color *Popular Science* v289 no5 p24 S/O 2017

Hilger, Joan

Welcome to the Monkey House L. D. ROBERTS *Indianapolis Monthly* p134 My 2017

Hilgert, Jeffrey

Rethinking the right to refuse hazardous work S. P. Kissinger diag *Monthly Labor Review* p1 Ja 2017

Hilico, Adèle

Quantum optical circulator controlled by a single chirally coupled atom bibl graph *Science* v354 no6319 p1577 D 23 2016

Hilker, Timon A.

Revealing hidden antiferromagnetic correlations in doped Hubbard chains via string correlators bw diag graph *Science* v357 no6350 p484 Ag 4 2017

Hill, Aaron D.

10 Years of Data on Baseball Teams Shows When Pay Transparency Backfires *Harvard Business Review Digital Articles* p2 My 9 2017

Hill, Abby Williams, 1861-1943

Purple mountains' majesty in Tacoma color *Magazine Antiques* v184 no4 p42 Jl/Ag 2017

Hill, Alex

How to Turn Around a Failing School *Harvard Business Review Digital Articles* p2 Ag 5 2016

The One Type of Leader Who Can Turn Around a Failing School bw color *Harvard Business Review Digital Articles* p2 O 20 2016

Research: How the Best School Leaders Create Enduring Change *Harvard Business Review Digital Articles* p2 S 14 2017

Hill, Alex J.

Blockchain Will Transform Customer Loyalty Programs *Harvard Business Review Digital Articles* p2 Mr 14 2017

HILL, BRETT

eating out *Parents* v92 no2 p102 F 2017

Hill, Charles

Islamism Implacable *Hoover Digest: Research & Opinion on Public Policy* no1 p98 Wint 2017

Ten Ways to Rescue Mideast Policy: In the Middle East the previous administration established neither democracy nor security-

-and now Russia is on the scene *Hoover Digest: Research & Opinion on Public Policy* no2 p62 Spr 2017

Hill, Chris

North Korea: How to Stop Kim Jong Un color *Time* v189 no12 p40 Ap 3 2017

HILL, CHRISTOPHER T.

Leaders color *Time* v189 no16/17 p64 My 1-8 2017

Measuring research benefits *Issues in Science & Technology* v33 no4 p14 Summ 2017

Hill, Clint

60 Minutes Turns 50 I. RUDOLPH *TV Guide* v65 no41 p4 O 2 2017

Hill, David

High-School-Football Games color *New York Times Magazine* p30 N 27 2016

Males Show Their True Colors [Cover story] color *Natural History* v125 no4 p10 Ap 2017

Hill, David B.

Celebrating ADIRONDACK PARK'S 125th ANNIVERSARY P. Constantakes and E. Stegemann *New York State Conservationist* v71 no6 p2 Je 2017

Hill, David L.

advice every new mom needs [Cover story] color *Parents* v92 no7 p32 Jl 2017

IS YOUR CHILD SICK OR JUST FAKING IT? color *Parents* v92 no9 p34 S 2017

Hill, Debbie

A Different Way of THINKING J. M. Keeler color *Dressage Today* v23 no10 p38 Jl 2017

Hill, Emily

Emergence and spread of a human-transmissible multidrug-resistant nontuberculous mycobacterium bibl diag graph *Science* v354 no6313 p751 N 11 2016

Hill, Erin

Never Done: A History of Women's Work in Media Production M. FULTON *Film Quarterly* v70 no3 p101 Spr 2017

Hill, Fiona

The Next Mr. Putin? The Question of Succession *Daedalus* v146 no2 p41 Spr 2017

Hill, G. C.

Observation of a large-scale anisotropy in the arrival directions of cosmic rays above 8×1018 eV *Science* v357 no6357 p1266 S 22 2017

Hill, Geoffrey E.

The biology of color color *Science* v357 no6350 p470 Ag 4 2017

HILL, GINA

HARRISON *Idaho Magazine* v16 no3 p32 D 2016

Hill, Grant

Artists color *Time* v189 no16/17 p40 My 1-8 2017

HILL, JAMES

Separate and Unequal bw *Weekly Standard* v22 no38 p38 Je 12 2017

Hill, Jason D.

An Open Letter to Ta-Nehisi Coates: The Dream is real *Commentary* v144 no3 p35 O 2017

Hill, Jemele

For the Record color *Time* v190 no16/17 p6 O 23 2017

Shifting Center R. Deitsch and T. Keith color *Sports Illustrated* v126 no5 p25 F 13 2017

HILL, JOE

Tape Worms *New York Times Book Review* p13 F 19 2017

Hill, Joseph A.

An adipo-biliary-uridine axis that regulates energy homeostasis diag *Science* v355 no6330 p1173 Mr 17 2017

Hill, Linda A.

3 Things Managers Should Be Doing Every Day *Harvard Business Review Digital Articles* p2 S 24 2015

The Capabilities Your Organization Needs to Sustain Innovation *Harvard Business Review Digital Articles* p2 Ja 14 2015

How to Work for a Workaholic R. Knight *Harvard Business Review Digital Articles* p2 Mr 24 2016

The Inescapable Paradox of Managing Creativity *Harvard Business Review Digital Articles* p2 D 12 2014

Hill, Logan

FEEL THE Dern color *InStyle* v24 no4 p200 Ap 2017

KILL THE BoY... ...LET THE MaN BE BORN! [Cover story]

bw color *Esquire* p78 Je/Jl 2017

WELCOME TO MARS color *Wired* v24 no11 p134 N 2016

Hill, Lynn

Sisterhood of the Rope K. LAMBERT *Climbing* no356 p26 S/O 2017

Hill, Marc Lamont

DONALD TRUMP IS FAILING BLACK PEOPLE... WHERE DO WE GO FROM HERE? B. VIERA *Ebony* v72/73 no12/1 p24 O/N 2017

Hill, Mark—Interviews

The New Crew J. K. Hanus color *American Craft* v77 no2 p74 Ap/My 2017

Hill, McKel—Interviews

Strip Down J. DRILLING *Cincinnati Magazine* v50 no4 p148 Ja 2017

Hill, Megan

OH, SHUCKS! color *Louisiana Life* v37 no2 p104 N/D 2016

PASSION IN ACTION color *Louisiana Life* v38 no1 p64 S/O 2017

SOLDIERING ON color *Louisiana Life* v37 no4 p112 Mr/Ap 2017

SYSTEMIC SUCCESS color *Louisiana Life* v37 no5 p64 My/Je 2017

TRIBAL LEGACY color *Louisiana Life* v37 no6 p64 Jl/Ag 2017

Hill, Nancy

THE BUTTERFLY EFFECT color *Earth Island Journal* v32 no2 p30 Summ 2017

HILL, NATALIE

CLASH OF THE TITANS cartoon *Vanity Fair* p84 Hollywood 2017 Supplement

Hill, Nathan

No. 1 THE NIX L. Greenblatt color *Entertainment Weekly* no1444/1445 p102 D 16 2016

Hill, Paul

How States Can Promote Local Innovation, Options, and Problem-Solving in Public Education bw *Education Digest* v83 no3 p30 N 2017

Hill, Ray

THIS WASN'T HIS FIRST RODEO: LONE STAR STATE ACTIVISTS LIKE RAY HILL HAD A GREATER IMPACT THAN MANY KNOW J. ANDERSON-MINSHALL color *Advocate* no1091 p97 Je/Jl 2017

HILL, REBECCA

Righting Words color *O, The Oprah Magazine* p17 Jl 2017

Hill, Rosemary

Ten policies for pollinators bibl color *Science* v354 no6315 p975 N 25 2016

Hill, Sarah

Role for migratory wild birds in the global spread of avian influenza H5N8 bibl graph map *Science* v354 no6309 p213 O 14 2016

Hill, Sarah J.

Higher predation risk for insect prey at low latitudes and elevations graph *Science* v356 no6339 p742 My 19 2017

Hill, Selena

CALLING ALL ENTREPRENEURS color *Black Enterprise* v47 no8 p42 Jl/Ag 2017

Carla Harris's 'Pearls' of Power color *Black Enterprise* v47 no3 p35 O 2016

EVOLUTION color diag graph *Black Enterprise* v47 no7 p46 My/Je 2017

STANDING UP FOR OUR STUDENTS color *Black Enterprise* v47 no7 p28 My/Je 2017

Hill, Sharon R.

A key malaria metabolite modulates vector blood seeking, feeding, and susceptibility to infection bibl chart diag *Science* v355 no6329 p1076 Mr 10 2017

Hill, Susanna Leonard

When Your Elephant Has the Sniffles color *Publishers Weekly* v264 no25 p110 Jc 19 2017

Hill, Taylor

OFF - BOAT & OFF BEAT color *Sea Magazine* v109 no6 p22 Je 2017

THE ROAD HOME color *Vogue* v207 no9 p650 S 2017

Hill, Taylor—Interviews

Taylor Hill K. B. Brown color *InStyle* v24 no4 p148 Ap 2017

Hill, Tony

Birdman D. Bishop color *American Craft* v77 no2 p22 Ap/My 2017

Hill, Tyreek, 1994——Trials, litigation, etc.
CHIEF CONCERN J. Jones color *Sports Illustrated* v126 no2 p44 Ja 16 2017

Hill, Walter, 1942-
The Assignment N. LEE color *Film Comment* v53 no2 p70 Mr/Ap 2017

HILL, ZAHARA
APP TO EXCELLENCE bw *Ebony* v72/73 no12/1 p92 O/N 2017
MELLOW OUT IN THE MILE HIGH CITY color *Ebony* v72/73 no12/1 p28 O/N 2017
THURGOOD MARSHALL bw *Ebony* v72/73 no12/1 p98 O/N 2017
VERY NECESSARY BROTHAS color *Ebony* v72/73 no12/1 p25 O/N 2017

HILL-AGNUS, EVE
A Bar Lamp Like No Other *D: The Magazine of Dallas* v43 no10 p52 O 2016
Pot Twist *D: The Magazine of Dallas* v43 no10 p76 O 2016
Raising the Bar *D: The Magazine of Dallas* v43 no10 p72 O 2016

HILLARD, GRAHAM
David Mamet's Prescience *National Review* v69 no18 p20 O 2 2017
It's Cold Outside *Weekly Standard* v22 no7 p34 O 24 2016

Hillberry, Marcia
Cheers & Jeers color *Field & Stream* v121 no7 p14 D 2016/Ja 2017

Hilleary, Richard
Adaptation *Science* v356 no6335 p243 Ap 21 2017

Hillen, Sean
Pretty Ugly *Publishers Weekly* v264 no13 p83 Mr 27 2017

Hillenbrand, Rainer
Tuning quantum nonlocal effects in graphene plasmonics bw diag *Science* v357 no6347 p187 Jl 14 2017

Hillert, Albin
Egyptian theologians look to early church history after recent attacks color *Christian Century* v134 no2 p16 Ja 18 2017

Hilliard, Joseph
Quite a Catch color diag *Log Home Living* v34 no5 p36 Jl 2017

Hilliker, Kalani
Correction *Dance Spirit* v21 no8 p32 O 2017
We're 20! *Dance Spirit* v21 no7 p32 S 2017

HILLMAN, JOANNA
7 KEY PIECES color *Harper's Bazaar* no3656 p187 S 2017

HILLMER, NORMAN
King among PMs bw chart color *Maclean's* v129 no41 p19 O 17 2016

Hillmyer, Marc A.
Thermal processing of diblock copolymer melts mimics metallurgy diag graph *Science* v356 no6337 p520 My 5 2017

Hills, Bedford
THIS IS YOUR LAST SLICE color *Golf Magazine* v59 no2 p45 F 2017

Hills, Corey
THE SECRETS TO Floor Plan Perfection diag *Log Home Living* v34 no1 p44 F 2017

Hills Have Eyes, The (Film)
THE HILLS HAVE EYES C. Chiarella color *Sound & Vision* v82 no2 p70 F/Mr 2017

Hillside landscape architecture
UPS AND DOWNS color *Iceland Review* v54 no5 p22 S-O 2016

HILMANTEL, ROBIN
Can You "UBERIZE" Wellness? color *Women's Health* v13 no10 p86 D 2016
What's for Dinner? *Scholastic Choices* v32 no3 p12 N/D 2016

Hilmarsson, Björgvin
CLIMBING TO A BETTER FUTURE B. Broudy color *Climbing* no351 p64 F/Mr 2017

Hilmes, Oliver
Liszt: The Reluctant Superstar L. Carey bw *New York Review of Books* v63 no17 p31 N 10 2016

Hilo (Hawaii)
Hilo, Hawaii color *National Geographic* v231 no3 p12 Mr 2017

HILT, SABINE
Translating Regime Shifts in Shallow Lakes into Changes in Eco-

system Functions and Services *BioScience* v67 no10 p928 O 2017

Hiltbrunner, Andreas
Phytochrome B integrates light and temperature signals in Arabidopsis bibl graph *Science* v354 no6314 p897 N 18 2016

Hilton, Matt
Raw Wounds: A Tess Grey Thriller *Publishers Weekly* v264 no20 p39 My 15 2017

Hilton, Paris, 1981-
DAVID LETTERMAN D. MARCHESE img *New York* p28 Mr 6 2017

HILTON ANDERSEN, CHARLOTTE
40 THINGS CARDIOLOGISTS AND OTHER DOCTORS DO TO PROTECT THEIR HEARTS color *Reader's Digest* v189 no1131 p98 Je 2017

Hilts, Cynthia
CYNTHIA HILTS K. Micallef color *Downbeat* v84 no5 p26 My 2017

Hilts, Peter
Are Three School Chiefs Better Than One? A. PASCOPELLA *Education Digest* v82 no5 p21 Ja 2017

Himalaya Mountains
How the Himalayas primed the Indonesian tsunami P. Voosen color *Science* v356 no6340 p794 My 26 2017

Himes, Geoffrey
BOBBY WATSON color *Downbeat* v84 no7 p34 Jl 2017
Gibbons Adds Soul to Jazz Standards color *Downbeat* v84 no8 p20 Ag 2017
Melodic Devotion color *Downbeat* v84 no10 p28 O 2017

Himes, Katherine E.
The Fear Factor *Science* v357 no6355 p964 S 8 2017

Himmel, Mirko
Can everyone help verify the bioweapons convention? Perhaps, via open source monitoring bibl *Bulletin of the Atomic Scientists* v72 no6 p412 N 2016

Himmelbach, Axel
Wild emmer genome architecture and diversity elucidate wheat evolution and domestication color *Science* v357 no6346 p93 Jl 7 2017

HIMMELFARB, GERTRUDE
In Search of Mrs. T bw *Weekly Standard* v22 no25 p34 Mr 6 2017

HIMMELMAN, JEFF
A WALK AROUND THE BEAT BELTWAY: THE HIGHWAY RINGING WASHINGTON IS G4 MILES LONG. NO ONE EVER CONFUSED IT WITH A SCENIC NATURE TRAIL. BUT ON A SIX-DAY HIKE ALONG ITS PERIPHERY, A BDRN AND BRED WASHINGTONIAN FOUND MOMENTS OF SURPRISING BEAUTY,... *Washingtonian Magazine* v52 no12 p58 S 2017

Himmelman, Peter
How Thinking Like a Kid Can Spur Creativity *Time* v188 no16/17 p15 O 24 2016

HIMMELSBACH-WEINSTEIN, ERIK
Budding Film Careers: A VALLEY MIDDLE SCHOOL'S CINEMATIC ARTS ACADEMY IS GIVING BIGGER, OLDER PROGRAMS A RUN FOR THEIR MONEY *Los Angeles Magazine* p15 Ag 2017
THE MUSIC FEST THAT TIME FORGOT color *Los Angeles Magazine* v62 no7 p80 Jl 2017
SUBURBAN GLORY *Los Angeles Magazine* p126 Ap 2017

Himschoot, Malcolm
HOW DO YOU HOLD TOGETHER YOUR TRANS IDENTITY AND YOUR LIFE OF FAITH? color *Christian Century* v134 no2 p22 Ja 18 2017

HINCH, SCOTT G.
Envisioning the Future of Aquatic Animal Tracking: Technology, Science, and Application *BioScience* v67 no10 p884 O 2017

Hinchliffe, Colter
A DESERT ISLAND J. Brown bw color *Powder* v45 no5 p28 Ja 2017

Hinckley, John Warnock, Jr., 1955-
John Hinckley Left the Mental Hospital Seven Months Ago L. MILLER img *New York* v50 no6 p42 Mr 20 2017

Hinckley, Story
Counterprotesters greet "free speech rally" *Christian Century* v134 no19 p13 S 13 2017

Hinckley Co.
  HINCKLEY TALARIA 34 RUNABOUT *Sea Magazine* v108 no8 p38 Ag 2016

Hincks, Joseph
  The Angels of Irma [Cover story] color map *Time* v190 no12 p34 S 25 2017
  A Deadly New Front for ISIS color map *Time* v190 no1 p36 Jl 3 2017
  The U.S. Territory In the Line of North Korea's 'Enveloping Fire' color *Time* v190 no8 p14 Ag 28 2017
  Why There's Still an Ashtray on Your Airplane *Time* v190 no14 p23 O 9 2017

Hindawi, Orion
  Security Software, Insecurity Culture L. Chapman and S. McBride color *Bloomberg Businessweek* no4519 p38 Ap 24 2017

Hindemith, Paul, 1895-1963
  The Good Germany R. Platt cartoon *New Yorker* v92 no33 p16 O 17 2016

Hinderaker, Eric
  Boston's Massacre *Publishers Weekly* v264 no5 p191 Ja 30 2017

Hindley, Meredith
  An interview about interviewing with Lynn Novick and Sarah Botstein of The Vietnam War *Humanities* v38 no4 p1 Fall 2017

Hinds, Aisha
  Underground M. Logan *TV Guide* p41 Ap 17 2017

Hinds, Pamela
  Global Teams Should Have Office Visits, Not Offsites *Harvard Business Review Digital Articles* p2 Mr 3 2016
  Research: Why Best Practices Don't Translate Across Cultures *Harvard Business Review Digital Articles* p2 Je 27 2016

Hindu art & symbolism
  The embattled swastika C. MCINTYRE color *Maclean's* v130 no10 p15 N 2017

Hindu sects
  c . 900: India *Lapham's Quarterly* v10 no1 p91 Wint 2017

Hinduism
    See also
    Gurus
    Hindu sects
    Yoga
  A Hatred for Hindus M. Bose *History Today* v66 no12 p3 D 2016

Hinduism—Rituals
  Lightbox color *Time* v189 no10 p16 Mr 20 2017

Hindus—Political activity
  HINDUS FOR TRUMP R. Ali cartoon *New Yorker* v92 no36 p16 N 7 2016

HINE, SAMUEL
  Back from the Dead bw color *GQ: Gentlemen's Quarterly* v97 no3 p60 Mr 2017

Hiner, Sarah
  THE HIGH PRICE OF MEDICAL ERRORS-DON'T LET IT COST YOU YOUR LIFE *Vital Speeches of the Day* v82 no12 p381 D 2016

HINER, TRACY G.
  growing joy color map *Cabin Living* p16 Ag 2017

Hines, Alice
  Beware Google Ads for 'Abortion Consultations' color *Bloomberg Businessweek* no4516 p30 Mr 27 2017

HINES, CHRISTA MELNYK
  eager learners *Parents* v91 no10 p142 O 2016

Hines, Ellen M.
  Poor fisheries struggle with U.S. import rule bibl color *Science* v355 no6329 p1031 Mr 10 2017

Hines, Pamela J.
  REPAIR AND REGENERATION [Cover story] color *Science* v356 no6342 p1020 Je 9 2017

HINES, TERENCE
  Houdini's Remarkable Female Detective *Skeptical Inquirer* v41 no5 p62 S/O 2017
  Why We Often Get Risks Wrong *Skeptical Inquirer* v41 no4 p58 Jl/Ag 2017

Hines-Shah, Katie
  Reflections on the lectionary *Christian Century* v133 no24 p23 N 23 2016

HING, JULIANNE
  How to Make AMERICA WHITE AGAIN bw color *Nation* v304

no3 p24 Ja 30 2017
  ICE Amps Up color *Nation* v304 no9 p4 Mr 20 2017
  New Ban, No Relief color *Nation* v304 no10 p4 Mr 27 2017
  "We Are Not Leaving" il *Nation* v303 no23/24 p21 D 5 2016

Hinges—Evaluation
  All About Cabinet Hinges B. D. Coleman color *Old House Journal* v45 no1 p52 F 2017

Hingley, Liz
  Daughter of an Irish Catholic and Bengali Muslim, by Liz Hingley L. Copan color *Christian Century* v134 no4 p63 F 15 2017

HINGSTON, MICHAEL
  What Makes a Funny Word Funny *Reader's Digest* v189 no1128 p124 Mr 2017

Hinkie, Sam
  AFTER THE PROCESS C. Ballard chart color *Sports Illustrated* v125 no18 p54 D 5 2016
  HOT | NOT T. Keith color *Sports Illustrated* v126 no18 p16 Je 26 2017

Hinkle, Kenyatta A. C.
  Kenyatta A.C. Hinkle L. CROSS color *Ebony* v72 no5 p31 Mr 2017

Hinkley, Dan
  Martha's Month chart color *Martha Stewart Living* p6 S 2017

Hinlicky, Paul R.
  Purgatory now! *Christian Century* v134 no14 p30 Jl 5 2017

Hinman, Darlene Kostelac
  A meal for many color *U.S. Catholic* v82 no6 p5 Je 2017

Hinrichs, Christian S.
  Landscape of immunogenic tumor antigens in successful immunotherapy of virally induced epithelial cancer graph *Science* v356 no6334 p200 Ap 14 2017

Hinsdale (Ill.)
  HINSDALE J. REESE color map *Chicago* v66 no7 p20 Jl 2017

Hinterland
  BACKCOUNTRY BAKING D. LEWON color *Backpacker* p27 Je 2017
  Highlines & Picket Lines M. ANDERSON color *Trail Rider* v29 no3 p34 Ap 2017
  Pack Ice Cream K. CLOOS il *Backpacker* p30 Je 2017
  Rules, Shmoolz Leslie Hsu Oh *Backpacker* p73 Je 2017

Hinterleitner, Reinhard
  Reovirus infection triggers inflammatory responses to dietary antigens and development of celiac disease color diag *Science* v356 no6333 p44 Ap 7 2017

Hinton, David—Interviews
  WHERE NATURE & MIND MEET L. Tonino color *Tricycle: The Buddhist Review* v26 no4 p76 Summ 2017

Hinton, Elizabeth
  Equal Protection: Three books discuss how to confront and reform racist policing *New York Times Book Review* p13 Jl 30 2017
  FORTRESS AMERICA J. FORMAN JR. bw *Nation* v303 no16 p35 O 17 2016

Hinton, S. E.—Interviews
  The Outsiders Turns 50 I. Biedenharn color *Entertainment Weekly* no1463/1464 p110 Ap/My 2017

Hinueber, Jesse
  Looking race in the face bw *Phi Delta Kappan* v98 no5 p24 F 2017

Hip exercises
  AROUND THE HOUSE color *AARP: The Magazine* v59 no3A p44 Ap/My 2016

Hip-hop culture
  CHICER THAN RAP: HIP-HOP'S MOST FORMIDABLE FASHION VENTURES N. SANTOS and B. GARWOOD color map *Ebony* v72 no11 p80 S 2017

Hip-hop culture—History
  '90s TILL INFINITY: LEADERS OF THE NEW SCHOOL M. A. GONZALES bw color *Ebony* v72 no8 p90 Je 2017

Hip-hop dance
  GOINGS ON ABOUT TOWN color *New Yorker* v93 no18 p6 Je 26 2017

Hip joint
  DO THE TWIST S. Snyder color *Yoga Journal* p68 2017 Special Issue
  go with the flow color *Yoga Journal* p58 2017 Special Issue
  Help Me Transform My Thighs! T. Anderson color *Health* v31

no3 p52 Ap 2017

hip to it J. Crandell color *Yoga Journal* p48 2017 Special Issue

A home practice for open, happy hips [Cover story] V. Marino color *Yoga Journal* no291 p61 My 2017

A home practice for open, happy hips V. Marino color *Yoga Journal* p73 2017 SpecialIssue

open voyage color *Yoga Journal* p52 2017 Special Issue

A Scary New Hip Trend D. SCHUYLER color diag *Men's Health* v32 no6 p89 Ag 2017

Hip joint injuries

A Scary New Hip Trend D. SCHUYLER color diag *Men's Health* v32 no6 p89 Ag 2017

Hip joint injury prevention

Hips, Hopped M. Gainsburg bw diag *Women's Health* v14 no3 p55 Ap 2017

Hip joint—Anatomy

Get to know... your hips R. Long color *Yoga Journal* p68 2017 SpecialIssue

Hip surgery

See also

Total hip replacement

A MARTIAL ARTIST'S GUIDE TO HIP HEALTH T. CALLOS color *Black Belt* v55 no1 p32 D 2016/Ja 2017

Hippalgaonkar, Kedar

Anomalously low electronic thermal conductivity in metallic vanadium dioxide bibl graph *Science* v355 no6323 p371 Ja 27 2017

Hippe, Malte

The Dirty Little Secret About Digitally Transforming Operations *Harvard Business Review Digital Articles* p2 My 31 2016

Hipple, Steven F.

Labor force participation: what has happened since the peak? bibl chart color graph *Monthly Labor Review* p1 S 2016

Hippler, Thomas

Governing from the Skies: A Global History of Aerial Bombing color *Publishers Weekly* v263 no46 p46 N 14 2016

Hippocampus (Brain)

Stellate cells drive maturation of the entorhinal-hippocampal circuit F. Donato, R. I. Jacobsen et al diag *Science* v355 no6330 p1172 Mr 17 2017

Superficial layers of the medial entorhinal cortex replay independently of the hippocampus J. O'Neill, C. N. Boccara et al bibl graph *Science* v355 no6321 p1 Ja 13 2017

Vectorial representation of spatial goals in the hippocampus of bats A. Finkelstein, L. Las et al bibl graph *Science* v355 no6321 p1 Ja 13 2017

your brain: time machine C. Maldarelli color *Popular Science* v289 no5 p6 S/O 2017

Hipsters (Subculture)

What Hipsters and Monks Share D. J. Michael color *America* v217 no2 p40 Jl 24 2017

Why So Many Millennials Aren't Into Protest Movements N. Gafni *Harvard Business Review Digital Articles* p2 O 22 2015

Hirabayashi, Toshiyuki

Conversion of object identity to object-general semantic value in the primate temporal cortex color graph *Science* v357 no6352 p687 Ag 18 2017

Hirabayashi, Yusuke

Multicluster Pcdh diversity is required for mouse olfactory neural circuit assembly diag *Science* v356 no6336 p411 Ap 28 2017

Hirahara, Art

ART HIRAHARA D. Ouellette color *Downbeat* v84 no3 p22 Mr 2017

Hirano, Shingo

Supersonic gas streams enhance the formation of massive black holes in the early universe diag graph *Science* v357 no6358 p1375 S 29 2017

Hirano, Tatsuya

Mitotic chromosome assembly despite nucleosome depletion in Xenopus egg extracts diag *Science* v356 no6344 p1284 Je 23 2017

Hirofumi Nakagami

Regulation of sugar transporter activity for antibacterial defense in Arabidopsis bibl diag graph *Science* v354 no6318 p1427 D 16 2016

Hirofumi Nishizono

Overlapping memory trace indispensable for linking, but not recalling, individual memories bibl graph *Science* v355 no6323 p398 Ja 27 2017

Hirokazu Takenouchi

A coherent Ising machine for 2000-node optimization problems bibl diag graph *Science* v354 no6312 p603 N 4 2016

Hiroki Ikeda

A chemical genetic roadmap to improved tomato flavor bibl graph *Science* v355 no6323 p391 Ja 27 2017

Hiroki Sato

Metal-catalyzed reductive coupling of olefin-derived nucleophiles: Reinventing carbonyl addition diag *Science* v354 no6310 paah5133-1 O 21 2016

Hiroki Takesue

A coherent Ising machine for 2000-node optimization problems bibl diag graph *Science* v354 no6312 p603 N 4 2016

A fully programmable 100-spin coherent Ising machine with all-to-all connections bibl diag graph *Science* v354 no6312 p614 N 4 2016

Hiromitsu Nakauchi

Depleting dietary valine permits nonmyeloablative mouse hematopoietic stem cell transplantation bibl graph *Science* v354 no6316 p1152 D 2 2016

Hirono, Masafumi

Holliday junction resolvases mediate chloroplast nucleoid segregation diag *Science* v356 no6338 p631 My 12 2017

Hiroshi Kida

Role for migratory wild birds in the global spread of avian influenza H5N8 bibl graph map *Science* v354 no6309 p213 O 14 2016

Hiroshi Watarai

Depleting dietary valine permits nonmyeloablative mouse hematopoietic stem cell transplantation bibl graph *Science* v354 no6316 p1152 D 2 2016

Hirota, S.

Structural basis of the redox switches in the NAD+-reducing soluble [NiFe]-hydrogenase diag *Science* v357 no6354 p928 S 1 2017

Hirota, Takayuki

Fertile offspring from sterile sex chromosome trisomic mice chart diag *Science* v357 no6354 p932 S 1 2017

Hiroyuki Yamada

Buffer-gas cooling of antiprotonic helium to 1.5 to 1.7 K, and antiproton-to-electron mass ratio bibl chart diag graph *Science* v354 no6312 p610 N 4 2016

Hirsch, Barton J.

Wanted: Soft skills for today's jobs il *Phi Delta Kappan* v98 no5 p12 F 2017

Hirsch, E. D. (Eric Donald), 1928-

Elaine Pagels A. M. Gillis *Humanities* v37 no4 p1 Fall 2016

One and the Many P. GIBBON *Education Digest* v82 no7 p36 Mr 2017

One and the Many P. Gibbon *Humanities* v37 no4 p1 Fall 2016

HIRSCH, EDWARD

Invincible Reason color *New Republic* v248 no7 p60 Jl 2017

HIRSCH, JESSE

GMOs color *Popular Mechanics* p108 S 2017

GMOs color *Popular Mechanics* v193 no7 p108 S 2016

STUPID or AMAZING? color *Popular Mechanics* v193 no7 p108 S 2016

HIRSCH, JORDAN CHANDLER

Harassment Strategy color *Weekly Standard* v22 no44 p32 Jl 31 2017

Humility, Credibility, Prudence color *National Review* v68 no21 p29 N 21 2016

Hirsch, Judd

Superior Donuts N. Abrams, C. Holub et al color *Entertainment Weekly* no1482/1483 p52 S 22 2017

Hirsch, Judd—Interviews

JOKERS WILD J. RUSSELL *TV Guide* v65 no6 p30 Ja 30 2017

Hirsch, Ranella

BEST FACE MASKS B. Le Poer Trench color *Harper's Bazaar* no3650 p180 F 2017

OUT OF THE SHADOWS K. Donahue Hodes color *Women's Health* v14 no4 p45 My 2017

Hirsch, Robert L.

Necessary and sufficient conditions for practical fusion power

Physics Today v70 no10 p11 O 2017

Hirsch, Tim

Publish openly but responsibly color *Science* v357 no6347 p141 Jl 14 2017

Hirscher, Marcel, 1989-

Marcel Hirscher M. Hagan color *Current Biography* v78 no2 p35 F 2017

Hirschfeld, Al, 1903-2003

AL HIRSCHFELD A. Curry color *Film Comment* v53 no2 p80 Mr/Ap 2017

Hirschfeld, Katherine

Rethinking 'Structural Violence' *Society* v54 no2 p156 Ap 2017

Hirschfeld, P. J.

Discovery of orbital-selective Cooper pairing in FeSe diag *Science* v357 no6346 p75 Jl 7 2017

Hirschhorn, Sara Yael

Getting Settled E. GORDON *Commentary* v144 no2 p44 S 2017

Hirschi, Karen K.

Clonal hematopoiesis associated with TET2 deficiency accelerates atherosclerosis development in mice bibl diag *Science* v355 no6327 p842 F 24 2017

Hirschorn, Michael

How to Take Back the Counterculture *New York* v49 no24 p34 N 28 2016

OBAMA'S AMERICA img *New York* v49 no20 p12 O 3 2016

Hirsh, Haym

Postmodern Prometheus bw color *Science* v357 no6350 p460 Ag 4 2017

Hirsh, Jacob B.

Why Being a Middle Manager Is So Exhausting *Harvard Business Review Digital Articles* p2 Mr 22 2017

HIRSH, MICHAEL

Here's the Good News *New York Times Book Review* p23 O 2 2016

Hirshberg, Jeremy

4 Steps to Dispel a Bad Mood *Harvard Business Review Digital Articles* p2 Ap 6 2015

How Your State of Mind Affects Your Performance *Harvard Business Review Digital Articles* p2 D 8 2014

Hirshhorn Museum & Sculpture Garden

THE NEW QUEUE: Washington's strange new affinity for waiting in line M. Schaffer *Washingtonian Magazine* v52 no9 p17 Je 2017

Hirst, Daisy

Alphonse, That Is Not OK to Do! color *Publishers Weekly* v263 no49 p35 D 7 2016

Hirst, Joel D.

AMID THE RUINS OF A REVOLUTION, THE CHURCH ENDURES [Cover story] color il *America* v216 no11 p26 My 15 2017

HIRST, KARIE J.

Estimation of Relative Potency from Bioassay Data that Include Values below the Limit of Quantitation *BioScience* v66 no11 p983 N 1 2016

Hirst, Michael

Vikings K. Hahn *TV Guide* v64 no48 p38 N 21 2016

Hirst, Peter

How a Flex-Time Program at MIT Improved Productivity, Resilience, and Trust *Harvard Business Review Digital Articles* p2 Je 30 2016

Hirst, Peter—Interviews

What MIT Is Learning About Online Courses and Working from Home S. G. Carmichael *Harvard Business Review Digital Articles* p2 Mr 30 2015

His Girl Friday (Film)

HIS GIRL FRIDAY F. Kaplan bw *Sound & Vision* v82 no5 p69 Je 2017

Hisatomo Taki

Ten policies for pollinators bibl color *Science* v354 no6315 p975 N 25 2016

Hiscock, Jane

4 Ways for B2B Businesses to Keep Their Customers *Harvard Business Review Digital Articles* p2 D 6 2016

Hise, Phaedra

24 HOURS AT LAMBSTOCK *Virginia Living* v15 no1 p66 D 2016

Chill Out Cool Summer soups *Virginia Living* v15 no4 p72 Je 2017

Food from the Heart color *Virginia Living* v15 no5 p43 Ag 2017

GONE TO POT *Virginia Living* v15 no3 p15 Ap 2017

MADE IN VIRGINIA 2016 AWARDS *Virginia Living* v15 no1 p82 D 2016

NEW OYSTER CULT *Virginia Living* v15 no2 p38 F 2017

Petal Pushers color *Virginia Living* v15 no5 p46 Ag 2017

The proof is in the Pudding *Virginia Living* v15 no3 p54 Ap 2017

Hisense USA Corp.

Hisense 50H8C LCD Ultra HDTV A. Griffin color graph *Sound & Vision* v81 no9 p40 N 2016

Hishamunda, Jean Bernard

Transition from turbulent to coherent flows in confined three-dimensional active fluids color *Science* v355 no6331 p1284 Mr 24 2017

Hishida, Tomoaki

Integration of CpG-free DNA induces de novo methylation of CpG islands in pluripotent stem cells diag *Science* v356 no6337 p503 My 5 2017

Hiskes, Jonathan

A ferocious attention *Christian Century* v134 no14 p10 Jl 5 2017

HISLOP, DEANE

ART AND CULTURE PIT STOPS IN PUGET SOUND: LEARN THE RICH HISTORY OF THE SAN JUAN ISLANDS AT ONE OF THESE MUSEUMS ON PUGET SOUND *Sea Magazine* v109 no9 pPNW-8 S 2017

ART, HISTORY AND FUN *Sea Magazine* v109 no1 pPNW-8 Ja 2017

BEACHCOMBING IN GIBSONS *Sea Magazine* v108 no8 pPNW-10 Ag 2016

BLOOD-SUCKING VISITORS: BUGS IN THE PNW CAN BE VORACIOUS, SO DON'T BECOME THEIR NEXT VICTIM *Sea Magazine* v109 no5 pCA-10 My 2017

BOUNTY OF THE SEA: THE OCEAN PROVIDES SUSTENANCE THAT IS FRESH, NUTRITIOUS AND FUN TO HARVEST color *Sea Magazine* v109 no7 pPNW-14 Jl 2017

BREMERTON IS BOOMING: AN INTERESTING AND LIKABLE PORT OF CALL FOR PUGET SOUND BOATERS IS NOT FAR FROM SEATTLE color map *Sea Magazine* v109 no8 pPNW-1 Ag 2017

BUTCHART GARDENS *Sea Magazine* v108 no10 pPNW-9 O 2016

A CENTURY OLD & NEW AGAIN: ROSARIO RESORT GOT A FACELIFT, A NEW MARINA CONFIGURATION AND MUCH MORE color map *Sea Magazine* v109 no7 pPNW-1 Jl 2017

COMMON SENSE AND THE GOLDEN RULE GO A LONG WAY *Sea Magazine* v109 no1 p46 Ja 2017

A COMMUNITY EFFORT *Sea Magazine* v109 no1 pPNW-14 Ja 2017

COMPACT CRUISING color map *Sea Magazine* v109 no7 p16 Jl 2017

CRUISING INTO TRANQUILITY *Sea Magazine* v109 no4 p20 Ap 2017

DON'T OVERLOOK THE OUTBOARD *Sea Magazine* v108 no10 p30 O 2016

ENJOY THE CRUISING LIFE: WHEN IT'S TIME, CUT THE LINES AND GO! bw color *Sea Magazine* v109 no6 pPNW-1 Je 2017

FIRE AND ICE *Sea Magazine* v108 no12 pPNW-1 D 2016

HOSE HEALTH: USING THE CORRECT CLAMP IS VITAL FOR HOSES' LONG-TERM VIABILITY color *Sea Magazine* v109 no6 p28 Je 2017

KEEP AN EYE ON OVERHEATING *Sea Magazine* v109 no1 p30 Ja 2017

MIDSEASON PREVENTIVE MAINTENANCE: PERFORM SOME QUICK AND SIMPLE CHECKS FOR A CAREFREE BALANCE OF THE BOATING SEASON bw color *Sea Magazine* v109 no8 p28 Ag 2017

THE MORE THINGS CHANGE... *Sea Magazine* v109 no2 pPNW-6 F 2017

MURAL TOWN *Sea Magazine* v108 no10 pPNW-1 O 2016

THE NUTS AND BOLTS *Sea Magazine* v109 no2 p30 F 2017

ONBOARD HERB GARDENS: NO ONE HAS TO GIVE UP THE TASTE OF FRESH HERBS WHILE CRUISING *Sea*

Historical errors
See also
Conspiracy theories
CLIMB ABOARD, YE WHO SEEK THE TRUTH! B. DICKEY color *Popular Mechanics* v193 no7 p84 S 2016

Historical fiction
FROM THE EDITOR FACTS AND FICTIONS *History Today* v67 no7 p3 Jl 2017
Madeline Hunter color *Publishers Weekly* v264 no15 p15 Ap 10 2017
Something More than an Art S. Lipscomb *History Today* v67 no8 p106 Ag 2017

Historical geography—Maps
THE MAP ROME, 1942 K. Wiles *History Today* v67 no9 p4 S 2017

Historical museum design & construction
The Battle for History D. LIND *Architectural Record* v205 no7 p77 Jl 2017

Historical museums
An Abundance Of Bones M. SEGAL color *Los Angeles Magazine* v62 no7 p18 Jl 2017
Bryn Eryr Iron Age Farmstead at St Fagans *British Heritage Travel* v37 no6 p7 N/D 2016
HINSDALE J. REESE color map *Chicago* v66 no7 p20 Jl 2017
Living History at Open Air Museums S. Reeves *British Heritage Travel* v38 no1 p48 Ja/F 2017

Historical museums—Design & construction
SNMAAHC in the Middle of the Mall G. TATE color *ARTnews* v115 no4 p30 Wint 2016/2017

Historical museums—Evaluation
The Day Our Ship Came In J. Johnson bw *Yankee* p184 My/Je 2017
SUBURBAN GLORY E. HIMMELSBACH-WEINSTEIN *Los Angeles Magazine* p126 Ap 2017

Historical reenactments
BREATHING LIFE BACK INTO THE PAST: The hobby of historical reenactment now has a deep history of its own. The Sealed Knot Society, the first reenactment society, was formed as long ago as 1968, the last year steam was used on British Railways J. Graham *British Heritage Travel* v38 no4 p64 Jl/Ag 2017
God Save the King! - Gloucester crowns a young prince R. Gardner *British Heritage Travel* v37 no6 p8 N/D 2016
Living the Tudor Life at Kentwell Hall S. Lawrence *British Heritage Travel* v38 no4 p68 Jl/Ag 2017
Revolutionary Roles D. FOX *National Parks* v91 no4 p10 Fall 2017

Historical revisionism
Censoring Indian History A. Truschke *History Today* v67 no8 p14 Ag 2017

Historically black colleges & universities
2017 HBCU QUEENS B. WILLIAMS bw color *Ebony* v72/73 no12/1 p78 O/N 2017

Historically black colleges & universities—Congresses
Securing Opportunities for Students with Our HBCU Summit color *Black Enterprise* v47 no4 p7 N/D 2016
STANDING UP FOR OUR STUDENTS R. W. GOODE and S. Hill color *Black Enterprise* v47 no7 p28 My/Je 2017

Historically black colleges & universities—Finance
The College Endowment Gap K. Smith *Bloomberg Businessweek* no4531 p25 Jl 24 2017

Historical television programs—Charts, diagrams, etc.
A Game of Throne E. Dockterman color diag *Time* v189 no3 p51 Ja 30 2017

Historic Royal Palaces (London, England)
History and Fun Haunt the Royal Palaces S. Lawrence *British Heritage Travel* v37 no6 p24 N/D 2016

Historiography
See also
Turkey—Historiography
On and Off Script S. Lipscomb *History Today* v66 no12 p31 D 2016

History
See also
Archaeology
Architectural history
Art history
Battles
Christianity & history
Coups d'état
Historic sites
Historical reenactments
Human migrations
Inquisition
Literature—History & criticism
Massacres
Migrations of nations
Military history
Revolutions
4,000 KILOMETRES 6,000 YEARS OF HISTORY 500 PETROGLYPHS 2 COLONIAL FORTS 17 STUDENTS 4 CULTURES ONE COOL TRIP J. PEARCE color map *Canadian Geographic* v137 p47 2017 Travel
THE BIG QUESTION B. Percy, T. French et al cartoon *Atlantic* v320 no3 p100 O 2017
THE BRITISH HERITAGE TRAVEL PUZZLER D. Kniffen, D. Kniffen et al *British Heritage Travel* v38 no3 p78 My/Je 2017
History is at odds with our desire for simple certainties. Can its cultivation of complexity create a better future? P. Lay *History Today* v67 no9 p3 S 2017
A Kinder, Gentler History: The past can seem like a timeline of horrors. But might it also remind us of our own failings - and help to put them right? S. Lipscomb *History Today* v67 no10 p106 O 2017
MIRACLE in the MARCHES I. Bass *History Today* v67 no3 p40 Mr 2017
Months Past MARCH *History Today* v67 no3 p8 Mr 2017
Out of the margins E. Parker *History Today* v67 no3 p25 Mr 2017
The Quiz T. BALAZO color *Maclean's* v129 no41 p60 O 17 2016
Q: What is the most interesting family in history? J. Moyes, H. Rothschild et al color *Atlantic* v318 no5 p96 D 2016
Something to Laugh About K. Davison *History Today* v67 no3 p72 Mr 2017
Time and Tides H. Aldersey-Williams *History Today* v67 no3 p37 Mr 2017

History & politics
Are We Any Safer? S. Weart, D. N. Blair et al color *Atlantic* v318 no4 p14 N 2016

History associations
BREATHING LIFE BACK INTO THE PAST: The hobby of historical reenactment now has a deep history of its own. The Sealed Knot Society, the first reenactment society, was formed as long ago as 1968, the last year steam was used on British Railways J. Graham *British Heritage Travel* v38 no4 p64 Jl/Ag 2017

History education
See also
History education in middle schools

History education in middle schools
THINKING LIKE A HISTORIAN: Developing disciplinary literacy in history among middle school struggling readers E. B. Claravall *Literacy Today (2411-7862)* v35 no1 p32 Jl/Ag 2017

History in literature
See also
Historical fiction
Something More than an Art S. Lipscomb *History Today* v67 no8 p106 Ag 2017

History in popular culture
FROM THE EDITOR P. Lay *History Today* v67 no1 p2 Ja 2017

History of aerial photography
Altered State: Taking to the sky to show how industry shapes the earth A. CRAWFORD *Smithsonian* v48 no2 p12 My 2017

History of African American military personnel
ARTIFACT J. A. LOBELL color *Archaeology* v70 no5 p68 S/O 2017

History of architectural design
THE SAINTS OF PITTSBURGH: A TINY NEIGHBORHOOD CHURCH IS HOME TO THE GREATEST COLLECTION OF RELICS OUTSIDE OF THE VATICAN R. WILKINSON *Smithsonian* v48 no4 p98 Jl/Ag 2017

History of cartography
History's Most Misleading Maps: Today's high-tech devices

aren't the only tools leading voyagers astray. And some "mistakes" were made deliberately C. Thompson *Smithsonian* v48 no4 p18 Jl/Ag 2017

The Whole World in Your Hands: Are high-tech maps ruining our sense of direction--or giving us a new awareness of where we are? C. Thompson *Smithsonian* v48 no4 p16 Jl/Ag 2017

History of economic development

The Boom Was a Blip R. Sharma color *Foreign Affairs* v96 no3 p104 My/Je 2017

History of emigration & immigration

The first Australians arrived early A. Gibbons color map *Science* v357 no6348 p238 Jl 21 2017

History of emigration & immigration law

Piece of Mind: At Ellis Island, a jigsaw challenge could seal an immigrant's fate A. Cohen *Smithsonian* v48 no2 p46 My 2017

History of espionage

YUGOSLAVIA'S VERY SECRET SERVICE C. Deliso *History Today* v67 no8 p68 Ag 2017

History of federal governments

America's First Nation C. K. Ballatore *History Today* v67 no4 p51 Ap 2017

History of India

Censoring Indian History A. Truschke *History Today* v67 no8 p14 Ag 2017

History of nuclear weapons

REVISITING THE LOS ALAMOS PRIMER: A concise packet of lecture notes offers a window into one of the turning points of 20th-century history B. C. Reed *Physics Today* v70 no9 p42 S 2017

History of railroads

NARROW PATH TO VICTORY S. T. Smith bw color *Military History* v34 no2 p54 Jl 2017

History of research

NUTRITION HOTLINE R. Mangels *Vegetarian Journal* v36 no3 p2 2017

History of science

See also

Forensic sciences—History

Gathering the human stories of science G. A. Good *Physics Today* v70 no5 p74 My 2017

History of serial publications

25 BIG IDEAS THAT BEGAN HERE N. CHARNEY *Psychology Today* v50 no4 p44 Ag 2017

History of technological innovations

WHAT'S YOUR BEST INNOVATION BET? BY MAPPING A TECHNOLOGY'S PAST, YOU CAN PREDICT WHAT FUTURE CUSTOMERS WILL WANT M. SCHILLING bw chart color graph img *Harvard Business Review* v95 no4 p86 Jl/Ag 2017

History of the plague

Tracking Ancient Plagues M. A. SPYROU and K. I. BOS bw color *Natural History* v125 no9 p18 S 2017

History of the Soviet Union

RUSSIA'S GRASSROOTS REVOLUTION: Underneath the sweeping history of the Russian Revolution is another story, one told through the lesser-known people, moments and objects of a world in transformation S. Reed and K. Rogatchevskaia *History Today* v67 no6 p42 Je 2016

Transnational Jihadism & Civil Wars M. CRENSHAW *Daedalus* v146 no4 p59 Fall 2017

History teachers

THE LOOK BOOK A. SWERDLOFF img *New York* v49 no23 p57 N 14 2016

TRAUMARAMA color *Seventeen* v76 no3 p108 My 2017

History—Awards

The Longman-History Today Awards *History Today* v66 no10 p45 O 2016

History—Errors, inventions, etc.

See also

Conspiracy theories

FROM THE EDITOR P. Lay *History Today* v66 no12 p2 D 2016

History—Exhibitions

8,000 Years of Human History in London *British Heritage Travel* v38 no3 p10 My/Je 2017

National Museum of African American History & Culture A. KONERMANN *Cincinnati Magazine* p56 Je 2017

History of the Decline & Fall of the Roman Empire, The (Book)

AMBITION, STYLE AND SACRIFICE: The challenges that Edward Gibbon faced remain much the same for historians today P. Lay *History Today* v67 no6 p3 Je 2016

History—Sources

See also

Charters

Time capsules

American Treasures K. Donohue *Prologue* v48 no3 p32 Fall 2016

DOCUMENTS ON Loan *Prologue* v48 no3 p35 Fall 2016

History—Sources—Conservation & restoration

NHPRC Awards $2.1 Million to Preserve Historic Records *Prologue* v48 no4 p62 Wint 2016

Hit the Road (TV program)

Hit the Road N. Abrams, A. Bacle et al *Entertainment Weekly* no1482/1483 p60 S 22 2017

Hitaj, Claudia

Declines in Pollinator Forage Suitability Were Concentrated in the Midwest, the Over-Summering Grounds for Many Honeybees *Amber Waves: The Economics of Food, Farming, Natural Resources, & Rural America* p1 Jl 2017

Energy Consumption and Production in Agriculture *Amber Waves: The Economics of Food, Farming, Natural Resources, & Rural America* p15 F 2017

Growing Organic Demand Provides High-Value Opportunities for Many Types of Producers *Amber Waves: The Economics of Food, Farming, Natural Resources, & Rural America* p51 F 2017

Share of Farm Businesses Receiving Lease and Royalty Income From Energy Production Varies Across Regions *Amber Waves: The Economics of Food, Farming, Natural Resources, & Rural America* p37 N 2016

Hitchcock, Alfred, 1899-1980

ALFRED HITCHCOCK RESENTS *Saturday Evening Post* v289 no1 p97 Ja/F 2017

A HITCHCOCK FANTASY P. MONAHAN color *Vanity Fair* v58 no12 p146 D 2016

Hitch onto TCM W. D. GEHRING *USA Today Magazine* v146 no2866 p76 Jl 2017

Suspenseful Silence C. Fleming *Weekly Standard* v22 no47 p41 Ag 21 2017

The Vault *Saturday Evening Post* v289 no1 p97 Ja/F 2017

Hitchhiker (Music)

Neil Young Pulls a Lost Treasure Out of the Vault D. BROWNE bw *Rolling Stone* no1294 p54 Ag 24 2017

Hitchhiking

America's Original Frontier E. BENICH color *Backpacker* v45 no2 p28 Mr 2017

Desert Dream A. JURRIES color *Backpacker* v45 no2 p26 Mr 2017

TICKED OFF K. CASTEEL color *Missouri Life* v44 no4 p64 Je 2017

Up the River E. ZAZO *Backpacker* v45 no2 p27 Mr 2017

Hitchhiking—Safety measures

Discomfort Zone D. LEWON color *Backpacker* v45 no2 p8 Mr 2017

Hitchman, Sam

Apple seismology *Physics Today* v70 no10 p94 O 2017

Hitler, Adolf, 1889-1945

Frank Rich: TRUMP'S APPEASERS img *New York* v49 no22 p36 O 31 2016

When Stalin Faced Hitler S. Kotkin cartoon *Foreign Affairs* v96 no6 p48 N/D 2017

Hitman's Bodyguard, The (Film)

The Hitman's Bodyguard L. Greenblatt color *Entertainment Weekly* no1478 / 1479 p86 Ag 18-25 2017

Hitt, Jack

HILLARYS FOR PRESIDENT! il *New Republic* v247 no11 p18 N 2016

To the Extreme color *New York Times Magazine* p17 D 11 2016

Hittle, Mike

You Never Forget Your First Time diag il *Backpacker* v45 no2 p64 Mr 2017

Hittman, Eliza

Beach Rats M. Koresky color *Film Comment* v53 no4 p68 Jl/Ag 2017

A Portrait of Male Beauty In Anguish S. Zacharek color *Time* v190 no9 p56 S 4 2017

Hittmeier, Leslie
7 Days of LOCURA color *Skiing* p58 Wint 2017
EATING CAKE color *Skiing* p64 D 2016
Z color *Skiing* p58 D 2016

HIV (Viruses)
Drugs now reach millions more with HIV color *Science* v357 no6349 p336 Jl 28 2017
HIV/AIDS—A History K. M. DE COCK color *Natural History* v125 no9 p36 S 2017
A microbiome variable in the HIV-prevention equation S. Tuddenham and K. G. Ghanem color *Science* v356 no6341 p907 Je 1 2017
People F. Nzwili color *Christian Century* v134 no1 p18 Ja 4 2017
Priming HIV-1 broadly neutralizing antibody precursors in human Ig loci transgenic mice D. Sok, B. Briney et al bibl graph *Science* v353 no6307 p1557 S 30 2016
Shock and kill with caution R. C. Gallo bibl color *Science* v354 no6309 p177 O 14 2016
The structure and flexibility of conical HIV-1 capsids determined within intact virions S. Mattei, B. Glass et al bibl color *Science* v354 no6318 p1434 D 16 2016

HIV (Viruses)—Genetic aspects
Cryo-EM structures and atomic model of the HIV-1 strand transfer complex intasome D. Oliveira Passos, Min Li et al bibl color *Science* v355 no6320 p1 Ja 6 2017
HIV's U.S. arrival gets pushed back T. HESMAN SAEY diag map *Science News* v190 no11 p7 N 26 2016

HIV (Viruses)—Research
HIV's ACHILLES' HEEL R. W. Sanders, I. A. Wilson et al color diag *Scientific American* v315 no6 p50 D 2016
HIV's U.S. arrival gets pushed back T. HESMAN SAEY diag map *Science News* v190 no11 p7 N 26 2016
Vaginal microbes hamper HIV drug A. CUNNINGHAM *Science News* v191 no13 p8 Jl 8 2017

HIV antibodies
Antibodies defeat HIV by ganging up A. CUNNINGHAM *Science News* v192 no6 p8 O 14 2017
Cows make powerful HIV antibodies A. CUNNINGHAM color graph *Science News* v192 no2 p7 Ag 19 2017
Trispecific broadly neutralizing HIV antibodies mediate potent SHIV protection in macaques L. Xu, A. Pegu et al color graph *Science* v357 no6359 p85 O 6 2017

HIV infection risk factors
MORE LEADING HEALTH EXPERTS AND ORGANIZATIONS ENDORSE UNDETECTABLE = UNTRANSMITTABLE: WHEN IS THERE ZERO RISK OF TRANSMITTING HIV? D. GUERRERO *Advocate* no1093 p33 O/N 2017

HIV infections
See also
AIDS (Disease)
AIDS in Africa: Progress and Obstacles S. A. MOJOLA *Current History* v116 no790 p170 My 2017
GQHQ bw color *GQ: Gentlemen's Quarterly* v86 no12 p60 D 2016
Shock and kill with caution R. C. Gallo bibl color *Science* v354 no6309 p177 O 14 2016

HIV infections—Prevention
HIV REMAINS A PREVALENT ISSUE IN CANADA R. Druzin *Maclean's* v129 no50 p52 D 19 2016
The Race to Zero A. Park and M. Fabry color diag map *Time* v188 no22-23 p38 N/D 2016

HIV infections—Risk factors
LET'S STOP SHAMING BLACK MEN J. ANDERSON-MINSHALL color *Advocate* no1090 p16 Ap 2017

HIV infections—Transmission
HIV infections are spiking among young gay Chinese K. McLaughlin color graph *Science* v355 no6332 p1359 Mr 31 2017
LET'S STOP SHAMING BLACK MEN J. ANDERSON-MINSHALL color *Advocate* no1090 p16 Ap 2017

HIV infections—Treatment
Where HIV and Housing Intersect M. Quinn *Governing* v30 no7 p18 Ap 2017

HIV-positive gay men

BECOMING MY OWN WARRIOR: HE WASN'T EVEN OUT TO HIS PARENTS YET, BUT JOSHUA THOMAS HAD TO TELL THEM HE WAS HIV-POSITIVE. HE SURVIVED AND TELLS OTHERS HOW YOU CAN, TOO D. GUERRERO *Advocate* no1093 p33 O/N 2017

HIV-positive persons
AMERICA'S HIDDEN H.I.V. EPIDEMIC L. VILLAROSA *New York Times Magazine* p38 Je 11 2017
Don't Look Away M. GATES color *Reader's Digest* v189 no1131 p26 Je 2017
How Running Toward HIV Can Save Your Life: Taking meds can be easy. Learning how to breathe is the tricky part T. CURRY color *Advocate* no1091 p41 Je/Jl 2017
Take a Deep Breath: Living with HIV is Like Learning to hold your breath under water T. CURRY *Advocate* no1093 p23 O/N 2017
UNITED BY YOGA [Cover story] bw color *Yoga Journal* no292 p40 Je 2017

HIV-positive persons—Attitudes
DEAR GAY MEN, AN OPEN LETTER T. CURRY color *Advocate* no1089 p27 F/Mr 2017

HIV-positive persons—Medical care
Venezuela's HIV drug crisis color *Science* v355 no6325 p552 F 10 2017

HIV-positive women
Vaginal bacteria modify HIV tenofovir microbicide efficacy in African women N. R. Klatt, R. Cheu et al chart graph *Science* v356 no6341 p938 Je 1 2017

Hively, Kimberly—Trials, litigation, etc.
Judges Rule Queers Have Civil Rights J. ANDERSON-MINSHALL color *Advocate* no1091 p21 Je/Jl 2017

HIV infections—Charts, diagrams, etc.
Tracking the Monster L. HUNTER and D. POINTDUJOUR color *Ebony* v72 no3 p86 D 2016/Ja 2017

Hjelmare, Martin
A subcellular map of the human proteome color *Science* v356 no6340 p820 My 26 2017

Hjerling-Leffler, Jens
miR-183 cluster scales mechanical pain sensitivity by regulating basal and neuropathic pain genes diag graph *Science* v356 no6343 p1168 Je 16 2017

H.L. Hunley (Submarine)
H.L. HUNLEY SUBMARINERS' DEATHS STILL A MYSTERY B. Manley color *Military History* v34 no5 p10 Ja 2018

HLA histocompatibility antigens
A large fraction of HLA class I ligands are proteasome-generated spliced peptides J. Liepe, F. Marino et al bibl graph *Science* v354 no6310 p354 O 21 2016

Hmong (Asian people)—United States
CHASING THE AMERICAN Dream R. HANSEN color *Missouri Life* v44 no4 p38 Je 2017

H.M.S. Pinafore (Theatrical production)
Sullivan: H.M.S. Pinafore R. Pines *Opera News* v81 no5 p57 N 2016

HNA Group Co. Ltd.
The Conglomerate That Troubles China M. Campbell, Dong Lyu et al *Bloomberg Businessweek* no4533 p12 Ag 7 2017
YOU'VE NEVER HEARD OF *HNA GROUP. HERE'S WHY YOU WILL V. Walt color diag *Fortune* v176 no2 p86 Ag 1 2017

Hnath, Lucas
72 minutes with ... Laurie Metcalf J. MCHENRY img *New York* v50 no11 p18 My 29 2017
THE IBSEN MYSTERY J. KELLY color *Vanity Fair* v59 no5 p94 Ap 2017
I Would Like to Thank... *Stage Directions* v30 no6 p34 Je 2017

Ho, David
Dynamics of cortical dendritic membrane potential and spikes in freely behaving rats diag *Science* v355 no6331 p1281 Mr 24 2017

Ho, Jane
The Great Mall of China chart color *Forbes* v198 no8 p48 D 20 2016
THE WORLD'S BILLIONAIRES bw color diag graph map *Forbes* v199 no3 p84 Mr 28 2017

Ho, Jannie
Bear and Chicken *Publishers Weekly* v264 no38 p68 S 18 2017

HO, JOHN S.
Ergonomically Correct *USA Today Magazine* v146 no2866 p25 Jl 2017

Ho, Lena
ELABELA deficiency promotes preeclampsia and cardiovascular malformations in mice color diag graph *Science* v357 no6352 p707 Ag 18 2017

Ho, Madelyn
Double Life M. HARSS *Dance Magazine* v90 no12 p112 D 2016

Ho, Mason
MASON HO Z. MORTON color *Surfer* v58 no3 p38 Je 2017

Ho, Prudence
A Case of Chicken vs. Machine cartoon color *Bloomberg Businessweek* no4507 p18 Ja 16 2017

Ho, Rodney
CHANNEL SURFING WITH RODNEY HO C. BETHEA *Atlanta* v57 no1 p90 My 2017

Ho Chul Kang
Pathological α-synuclein transmission initiated by binding lymphocyte-activation gene 3 bibl graph *Science* v353 no6307 paah3374-1 S 30 2016

Ho-Chunk Nation of Wisconsin
FACE OF A NATION S. Davis color *Sports Illustrated* v125 no19 p86 D 12 2016

Ho Ho Ho: An agent wraps up 2016 (Poem)
Ho Ho Ho R. CURTIS *Publishers Weekly* v263 no52 p128 D 19 2016

Ho Kwan Cheung
Two Types of Diversity Training That Really Work *Harvard Business Review Digital Articles* p1 Jl 28 2017

Hoagland, Edward, 1932-
Fade to Black R. HOFFMAN *New York Times Book Review* p17 D 18 2016
Groping and Not Finding F. Prose bw color *New York Review of Books* v64 no5 p60 Mr 23 2017

HOAK, AMY
McMANSIONS TO SPARE color *Chicago* v66 no11 p22 N 2017

Hoang, Don
A placental growth factor is silenced in mouse embryos by the zinc finger protein ZFP568 color graph *Science* v356 no6339 p757 My 19 2017

HOARD, CHRISTIAN
Bob Odenkirk bw *Rolling Stone* no1285 p58 Ap 20 2017

Hoaxes in mass media
Misreporting Iran K. J. Torrance color *Weekly Standard* v22 no37 p16 Je 5 2017

Hobart & William Smith Colleges (Geneva, N.Y.)
Hobart and William Smith Colleges *Dance Magazine* v90 p69 2016/2017 Supplement College Guide

Hobbes, Thomas, 1588-1679
MUTUAL AID T. Hobbes *Lapham's Quarterly* v10 no3 p37 Summ 2017
Not My Philosopher R. R. Reilly *Claremont Review of Books* v17 no3 p47 Summ 2017

Hobbies
DOT-DOT-DOT-DASH MEMORABILIA color *Indianapolis Monthly* v42 no2 p73 O 2017
FINAL CUT C. TRILLIN cartoon color *New Yorker* v93 no27 p28 S 11 2017
Making Room for Hobbies P. Reichard *New Orleans Homes & Lifestyles* v20 no1 p90 Wint 2016
MEET THE filter guy D. Goldman color *Astronomy* v45 no11 p52 N 2017
Q: What did you let go of that changed your life? P. JOHNSON, M. LANGE et al color *O, The Oprah Magazine* p16 Ag 2017
she sheds color *Parents* v92 no7 p97 Jl 2017
The Tyranny of Tennis Rackets A. WHITING *Washingtonian Magazine* v52 no6 p54 Mr 2017

HOBBS, ALLYSON
I'm Not the Nanny *New York Times Book Review* p18 N 6 2016

Hobbs, Boyd
TRENDING NOW color *Wired* v25 no4 p12 Ap 2017

Hobbs, Jesse
FROM OUR READERS color *Sky & Telescope* v134 no2 p6 Ag 2017

HOBBS, RICHARD J.

Expanding the Portfolio: Conserving Nature's Masterpieces in a Changing World *BioScience* v67 no6 p568 Je 2017

Hobbs-Crawford, Jackie
BUCKLE UP with Jackie Hobbs-Crawford C. Toy color *Spin to Win Rodeo* v20 no12 p19 F 2017

Hobby, Oveta Culp, 1905-1995
Women bw cartoon color *American Cowboy* p34 LEGENDS OF TEXAS Special Issue 2017

Hobby, William P.
THE HOBBY NAME IS ONE B. D. SWEANY *Texas Monthly* v44 no12 p24 D 2016

Hobby-Eberly Telescope
Hobby-Eberly Telescope eyes sky with new capabilities T. Feder *Physics Today* v70 no6 p36 Je 2017

Hobby farms
Coop It Up E. Millard color *Log Home Living* v34 no2 p36 Mr 2017

Hobby Lobby Stores Inc.
Hobby Lobby purchase shows ethical problems in the antiquities trade M. Chabin color *Christian Century* v134 no19 p15 S 13 2017

Hobday, Alistair J.
Biodiversity redistribution under climate change: Impacts on ecosystems and human well-being color *Science* v355 no6332 p1389 Mr 31 2017

Hobdy-olibricc, Dominique
SAADA AHMED color *Essence* v48 no3 p24 Jl 2017

Hobe, Ben
Around the Campfire color *Trail Rider* v29 no1 p6 Ja/F 2017

Hober, Sophia
A pathology atlas of the human cancer transcriptome diag *Science* v357 no6352 p660 Ag 18 2017
A subcellular map of the human proteome color *Science* v356 no6340 p820 My 26 2017

HOBERG, ERIC P.
Transformational Principles for NEON Sampling of Mammalian Parasites and Pathogens: A Response to Springer and Colleagues *BioScience* v66 no11 p917 N 1 2016

HOBERMAN, J.
The Devil and Miss Mansfield bw *Film Comment* v53 no5 p79 S/O 2017
EVERY PEBBLE CAN BLOW US SKY-HIGH *Lapham's Quarterly* v10 no3 p198 Summ 2017

Hobern, Donald
Publish openly but responsibly color *Science* v357 no6347 p141 Jl 14 2017

Hobsbawm, Julia
Fully Connected *People Management* p50 My 2017
Fully Connected: Surviving and Thriving in an Age of Overload *Publishers Weekly* v264 no17 p80 Ap 24 2017

HOBSON, JANELL
CELEBRATING FEMINISM *Ms.* v26 no3 p12 Fall 2016
Transformation of Consciousness: The National Women's Studies Association and the Combahee River Collective's "Black Feminist Statement" turn 40 *Ms.* v27 no3 p48 Fall 2017

Hobson, Katherine
THE CROWNING TOUCH bw color diag *O, The Oprah Magazine* p95 O 2017
Solving the Alzheimer's PUZZLE color *O, The Oprah Magazine* p70 Je 2017

Hobson, Keith
Staying Ahead of the Curve *Parks & Recreation* v52 no3 p18 Mr 2017

Hobson, Mellody
Everyone's Jumping on the Yield Bandwagon color *Black Enterprise* v47 no2 p20 S 2016
THE HOUSING MARKET & BLACK AMERICA color *Black Enterprise* v47 no8 p22 Jl/Ag 2017
The Retirement of Baby Boomers [Cover story] color *Black Enterprise* v47 no3 p26 O 2016

Hobson, Peter R.
A global map of roadless areas and their conservation status bibl color graph map *Science* v354 no6318 p1423 D 16 2016

Hobush, Christian—Interviews
CHRISTIAN HOBUSH B. Merrill color *Snowboarder* v29 no3 p50 N 2016

HOBY, HERMIONE

Absurd and Realistic bw *New York Times Book Review* p18 S 25 2016

Her Inner Eel *New York Times Book Review* p19 My 28 2017

The Youngs *New York Times Book Review* p36 Je 4 2017

Hoch, Francis

Obama Deal Sparks $65 Million Mystery *Publishers Weekly* v264 no10 p8 Mr 6 2017

Hoch, Maureen

Advice on Running a Government Agency Like a Startup, from Someone Who's Tried It *Harvard Business Review Digital Articles* p2 Ap 12 2017

HOCHART, CINDY

The Foregone Alternative *USA Today Magazine* v145 no2862 p61 Mr 2017

Hochbein, Craig

Making grades more meaningful chart color il *Phi Delta Kappan* v98 no3 p49 N 2016

Hochberg, Neal

What Companies Have Learned from Losing Billions in Emerging Markets *Harvard Business Review Digital Articles* p2 S 16 2015

Hochberg, Yael

The Top 20 Start-Up Accelerators in the U.S *Harvard Business Review Digital Articles* p2 Mr 31 2015

HOCHDORF, RACE

WHY WRITE ABOUT HISTORY? *Humanist* v77 no4 p40 Jl/Ag 2017

Hochkirch, Axel

De-extinction, nomenclature, and the law color *Science* v356 no6342 p1016 Je 9 2017

Fossil data lacking for insects and fungi bibl color *Science* v355 no6329 p1032 Mr 10 2017

Hochman, David

The 7 Rules of Smarter Shopping color *AARP: The Magazine* v60 no2A p28 F/Mr 2017

HOW TED DANSON FOUND HIS Balance color *AARP: The Magazine* v30 no6A p54 O/N 2017

John Leguizamo color *AARP: The Magazine* v59 no4A p15 Je/Jl 2016

MAKE A POWER PLAY *Los Angeles Magazine* p114 Ap 2017

The Melting Point *Los Angeles Magazine* p118 D 2016

Never Too Late To Renovate color *AARP: The Magazine* v60 no5A p32 Ag/S 2017

A Pictorial Toast TO The Celebrated Life AND Stellar Career OF THE ACTOR Morgan Freeman bw color *AARP: The Magazine* v60 no2A p46 F/Mr 2017

Secrets of Single Super color *AARP: The Magazine* v30 no6A p20 O/N 2017

To Life! [Cover story] color *AARP: The Magazine* v59 no2A p56 F/Mr 2016

Hochschild, Adam

Soviet Spain? *Commentary* v142 no3 p9 O 2016

Spain in Our Hearts K. Baker *MHQ: Quarterly Journal of Military History* v29 no2 p92 Wint 2017

Wave of Anguish: Could disobedience have saved a group of Japanese students? *American Scholar* v86 no4 p114 Aut 2017

When Dissent Became Treason bw *New York Review of Books* v64 no14 p82 S 28 2017

Hochschild, Ann

A bacterial global regulator forms a prion bibl color diag graph *Science* v355 no6321 p1 Ja 13 2017

Hochschild, Arlie Russell

DEEP STORIES J. B. JUDIS *Nation* v303 no16 p32 O 17 2016

Feeling Their Pain J. DEPARLE color *New York Times Book Review* p16 S 25 2016

Great White Hopes il *New Republic* v248 no1/2 p16 Ja/F 2017

Inside the Sacrifice Zone N. Rich color *New York Review of Books* v63 no17 p15 N 10 2016

Listening to Louisiana A. B. Robinson color *Christian Century* v133 no26 p36 D 21 2016

Hochschild, Joshua P.

The Catholic Vision color *Commonweal* v144 no9 p8 My 19 2017

Hochstetler Milling, Ltd.

Something Old, Something New [Cover story] Yu color diag *Log Home Living* v34 no4 p60 My 2017

Hockemeyer, Dirk

Mutations in the promoter of the telomerase gene TERT contribute to tumorigenesis by a two-step mechanism diag *Science* v357 no6358 p1416 S 29 2017

Hockenos, Paul

Berlin Stories J. ROCKWELL *New York Times Book Review* p49 Je 4 2017

ON PIRATE ISLAND IN THE NORTH ATLANTIC bw color *Nation* v303 no19 p22 N 7 2016

Hockett, Paul

Coherent imaging of an attosecond electron wave packet bw chart diag *Science* v356 no6343 p1150 Je 16 2017

Hockey

See also

Hockey for children

Hockey playoffs

Hockey, David

NEW WAYS OF SEEING: A painter and a critic discuss the visual past in a beguiling and provocative way, but do they engage the reader? D. Brady *History Today* v67 no6 p96 Je 2016

Hockey arenas—Design & construction

DIY ICE RINK J. HARDBERGER color *Chicago* v65 no12 p30 D 2016

Hockey equipment

See also

Face masks

Look Sharp L. VACCARIELLO *Cincinnati Magazine* v50 no4 p160 Ja 2017

Hockey equipment—Economic aspects

Finally, the end of hockey S. FESCHUK color *Maclean's* v130 no4 p73 My 2017

Hockey for children

Finally, the end of hockey S. FESCHUK color *Maclean's* v130 no4 p73 My 2017

Hockey goalkeepers

BEING NO. 2 A. Prewitt color *Sports Illustrated* v125 no17 p98 N 21 2016 Double Issue

Pipe Dream A. Prewitt and T. Keith color *Sports Illustrated* v126 no1 p14 Ja 9 2017

Hockey Night in Canada (TV program)

Rookie Sensation B. POPPLEWELL bw *Walrus* v13 no9 p16 N 2016

Hockey on television

The Case for ... Showing Off the Kids A. Prewitt and T. Keith color *Sports Illustrated* v125 no14 p31 O 24-31 2016

ON COURSE FOR DRAMA R. A. BERENZ *TV Guide* v65 no25 p43 Je 2017

Hockey on television—Reviews

NHL HOCKEY T. WORGO color *TV Guide* v64 no42 p48 O 10 2016

Hockey players

See also

Rookie hockey players

The Case for ... JAROMIR JAGR J. Fuchs and T. Keith color *Sports Illustrated* v127 no9 p19 S 25 2017

FRINGE BENEFICIARIES A. Prewitt color *Sports Illustrated* v126 no14 p54 My 15-22 2017

MY TOWN: Caps star Braden Holtby on why he calls Old Town Alexandria home *Washingtonian Magazine* v53 no1 p186 O 2017

Tanner Brent Kaufmann A. A. DAVIS color *Maclean's* v129 no42 p66 O 24 2016

Hockey players—Biography

Braden Holtby M. Rich color *Current Biography* v78 no1 p27 Ja 2017

Hockey players—Canada

THE INTERVIEW J. GATEHOUSE color *Maclean's* v129 no41 p12 O 17 2016

Hockey players—Substance use

Death of a Goon Aug. 24, 1992 T. Keith and S. Kwak color *Sports Illustrated* v127 no5 p32 Ag 14 2017

Hockey players—Trading of

THE BIG BANG A. Prewitt and J. Fuchs color *Sports Illustrated* v125 no12 p50 O 10 2016

Hockey players—United States

Recouping their losses N. MACDONALD *Maclean's* v130 no4 p15 My 2017

How Five Lost Minutes Altered Our Class Culture *Education Digest* v82 no4 p30 D 2016

Hodgson, Marshall
The Life of Marshall Hodgson L. Kiesling color *New York Times Magazine* p30 O 9 2016

Hodson, James
How to Make Your Company Machine Learning Ready *Harvard Business Review Digital Articles* p2 N 7 2016

Hodson, Zoe
Style insight FOLK ART color *House Beautiful* p30 Ag 2017

Hoechlin, Tyler
ONE LAST HOWL S. Highfill color *Entertainment Weekly* no1480 p30 S 1 2017

Hoecht, Dietrich
FIT TO PRINT bw color *Wired* v25 no5 p14 My 2017

Hoedemaker, Steve
Pitch Perfect K. RENDA color *House Beautiful* p60 Jl 2017

Hoefler, Kate
Real Cowboys color *Publishers Weekly* v263 no49 p16 D 7 2016

Hoeger, Marie
De novo assembly of the Aedes aegypti genome using Hi-C yields chromosome-length scaffolds chart color diag *Science* v356 no6333 p92 Ap 7 2017

Hoegh, Jan
Get it right the first time! chart color *Phi Delta Kappan* v98 no6 p58 Mr 2017

Hoekema, David A.
Faith and family in Nigeria *Christian Century* v133 no24 p32 N 23 2016
O Sing unto the Lord: A History of English Church Music *Christian Century* v134 no19 p37 S 13 2017

Hoeks, Sylvia
SYLVIA HOEKS K. SMITH color *Vanity Fair* v59 no9 p113 S 2017

HOEKSTRA, HOPI E.
Transformational Principles for NEON Sampling of Mammalian Parasites and Pathogens: A Response to Springer and Colleagues *BioScience* v66 no11 p917 N 1 2016

Hoelzel, A. Rus
The road to speciation runs both ways bibl color map *Science* v354 no6311 p414 O 28 2016

Hoelzle, Tracey
Did you receive support from your faith community while you were experiencing depression and/or anxiety? graph *America* v216 no12 p6 My 29 2017

Hoemberger, Marc
Evolutionary drivers of thermoadaptation in enzyme catalysis [Cover story] bibl color graph *Science* v355 no6322 p289 Ja 20 2017

HOERBURGER, ROB
NATALIE COLE *New York Times Magazine* p28 D 25 2016

HOFER, VERLYN
THE INDEPENDENT CUSS *South Dakota Magazine* v33 no2 p96 Jl/Ag 2017

Höferle, Christian
Will That Cross-Cultural Coach Really Help Your Team? *Harvard Business Review Digital Articles* p2 Ap 29 2015

Hoffa, James P.
Drivers Wanted *MIT Technology Review* v120 no2 p10 Mr/Ap 2017

Hoffeld, David
To Increase Sales, Get Customers to Commit a Little at a Time *Harvard Business Review Digital Articles* p2 Jl 20 2016

HOFFER, ERIC
THOUGHTS ON Conflict *Forbes* v199 no4 p112 Ap 25 2017

Hoffert, Emily
Buzz M For Murder J. ELLROY bw color *Vanity Fair* v59 no11 p152 N 2017

Hoffman, Alice, 1952-
The Road Back H. WECKER *New York Times Book Review* p22 N 20 2016
Surviving J. ROSEN color *Publishers Weekly* v263 no42 p42 O 17 2016

HOFFMAN, ALLYSON
APPLES AND SAND *Phi Kappa Phi Forum* v96 no4 p30 Wint 2016

Hoffman, Anat
Hoffman: U.S. Jews need to speak out on religious pluralism in Israel *Successful Farming* v115 no1 p11 Ja 2017

Hoffman, Andrew J.
A Call to Keep the Faith B. P. BEER color *Earth Island Journal* v32 no4 p55 Wint 2017

Hoffman, Andy
How Does Tax Avoidance Play in Peoria? color *Bloomberg Businessweek* no4525 p42 Je 5 2017
The Rise and Fall of a Trading Giant in Asia color graph map *Bloomberg Businessweek* no4525 p39 Je 5 2017

Hoffman, Ashley
Hashtags color *Time* v188 no25-26 p28 D 19 2016 Double Issue
Stand-Up Finds a Home on Netflix color *Time* v189 no10 p52 Mr 20 2017
Tig Notaro color *Time* v190 no10/11 p116 S 18 2017

Hoffman, B.
Persistent effects of pre-Columbian plant domestication on Amazonian forest composition bibl chart graph map *Science* v355 no6328 p925 Mr 3 2017

Hoffman, Cara
Hustle and Flow J. TORRES *New York Times Book Review* p10 Mr 19 2017

Hoffman, Charley
Watch + Learn M. Perpich and J. Marksbury color *Golf Magazine* v59 no11 p28 N 2017

HOFFMAN, CHRIS
Google's Fuchsia OS is out in the open and shrouded in mystery color *PCWorld* p22 O 2016
How to get started with Linux: A beginner's guide color *PCWorld* v35 no10 p122 O 2017

Hoffman, David E.
Farewell to a Citizen-Scientist *Hoover Digest: Research & Opinion on Public Policy* no2 p160 Spr 2017

HOFFMAN, DEAN A.
The Lion in Autumn bw *Weekly Standard* v22 no12 p34 N 28 2016

Hoffman, Dustin, 1937-
Dustin Hoffman on Playing Fathers E. Berman color *Time* v190 no16/17 p105 O 23 2017

Hoffman, Emilee
SWINGING LOW E. Laase and S. Kwak color *Sports Illustrated* v127 no11 p21 O 9 2017

HOFFMAN, GEORGE
Institutional Decay *Commentary* v143 no2 p7 F 2017

Hoffman, Jeremy S.
Regional and global sea-surface temperatures during the last interglaciation color graph *Science* v355 no6322 p276 Ja 20 2017

Hoffman, Jon
Rescuing The Police A. STAPLETON color *Reader's Digest* v189 no1129 p12 Ap 2017

Hoffman, Louis
Sam & Louis *Scholastic Choices* v33 no1 p24 S 2017

Hoffman, Monty
The Wharf M. M. KASHINO color *Washingtonian Magazine* v52 no7 p104 Ap 2017

Hoffman, Neal
Does the Mensch Have Staying Power? M. Townsend color graph *Bloomberg Businessweek* no4503 p37 D 12 2016

Hoffman, Reid
Marissa Mayer Was Right to Ask Executives to Commit to Staying at Yahoo *Harvard Business Review Digital Articles* p2 N 11 2015

Hoffman, Reid, 1967-
SAN FRANCISCO A. Wiener *Harper's Magazine* p31 O 2017

Hoffman, Reid, 1967—Interviews
THE WARP-SPEED ENTREPRENEUR R. KARLGAARD color *Forbes* v200 no5 p34 N 14 2017

HOFFMAN, ROY
Fade to Black *New York Times Book Review* p17 D 18 2016

Hoffman, S. L.
Honor vs. Betrayal bw color *Military History* v34 no1 p70 My 2017
Men of War: The American Soldier in Combat at Bunker Hill, Gettysburg and Iwo Jima *Military History* v33 no6 p70 Mr 2017

Hoffman, William C.
Is America great? graph *America* v216 no5 p6 Mr 6 2017

Hoffman, William S.
In the Company of DINOSAURS *New York State Conservationist* v71 no5 p28 Ap 2017

Hoffmann, Ary A.
The broad footprint of climate change from genes to biomes to people bibl chart color *Science* v354 no6313 paaf7671-1 N 11 2016

Hoffmann, D. L.
Permanent human occupation of the central Tibetan Plateau in the early Holocene bibl bw color diag *Science* v355 no6320 p1 Ja 6 2017

Hoffmann, E. T. A. (Ernst Theodor Amadeus), 1776-1822
NIGHT VISION E. T. A. Hoffmann *Lapham's Quarterly* v10 no3 p136 Summ 2017

Hoffmann, Federico G.
Predictable convergence in hemoglobin function has unpredictable molecular underpinnings bibl graph *Science* v354 no6310 p336 O 21 2016

Hoffmann, Gaby, 1982-
High-Profile Guest Stars S. Li color *Entertainment Weekly* no1435 p47 O 14 2016

Hoffmann, Josef Franz Maria, 1870-1956
"Pleasure in the beautiful 'thing as such'": Fashion and the Wiener Werkstätte J. Staggs bw color *Magazine Antiques* v184 no5 p96 S/O 2017

HOFFMANN, MICHAEL
Conserving the World's Megafauna and Biodiversity: The Fierce Urgency of Now *BioScience* v67 no3 p197 Mr 2017
Saving the World's Terrestrial Megafauna color *BioScience* v66 no10 p807 O 1 2016

Hoffmann, Monika T.
A global map of roadless areas and their conservation status bibl color graph map *Science* v354 no6318 p1423 D 16 2016

Hoffmann, Morgan—Interviews
Morgan Hoffmann J. Marksbury and C. Barrett color *Golf Magazine* v59 no1 p37 Ja 2017

Hoffs, Gill
Lost at Sea: The Dangers of Emigration *History Today* v67 no4 p3 Ap 2017

HOFF SOMMERS, CHRISTINA
Is free speech under threat IN THE UNITED STATES? WE RECEIVED TWENTY-SEVEN RESPONSES. WE PUBLISH THEM HERE, IN ALPHABETICAL ORDER *Commentary* v144 no1 p13 Jl/Ag 2017

Hofheins, Seth
Epitaxial lift-off of electrodeposited single-crystal gold foils for flexible electronics bibl bw diag *Science* v355 no6330 p1203 Mr 17 2017

Hofman, Jake M.
Prediction and explanation in social systems bibl diag graph *Science* v355 no6324 p486 F 3 2017

Hofman, Michiel
Ebola: A postmortem W. F. Pewen bibl color *Science* v355 no6324 p463 F 3 2017

Hofmann, Axel
Titanium isotopic evidence for felsic crust and plate tectonics 3.5 billion years ago bw color graph *Science* v357 no6357 p1271 S 22 2017

Hofmann, David A.
Get Your Employees to Make Better Suggestions *Harvard Business Review Digital Articles* p2 Mr 5 2015

Hofmann, M.
Rosetta's comet 67P/Churyumov-Gerasimenko sheds its dusty mantle to reveal its icy nature bibl graph *Science* v354 no6319 p1566 D 23 2016
Surface changes on comet 67P/Churyumov-Gerasimenko suggest a more active past bw graph *Science* v355 no6332 p1392 Mr 31 2017

Hofmann, Michael
The Lion in Winter bw *New York Review of Books* v64 no10 p39 Je 8 2017
LISBURN ROAD *New Yorker* v93 no3 p31 Mr 6 2017
Personality Is Everything: A new life of Goethe surveys his seemingly boundless abilities *New York Times Book Review* p16 Je 18 2017

Hofmann, Raphael

A radical approach to posttranslational mutagenesis bibl diag *Science* v354 no6312 p553 N 4 2016

Hofmans, Joeri
Too Much Charisma Can Make Leaders Look Less Effective *Harvard Business Review Digital Articles* p2 S 26 2017

Hofreiter, Michael
Ancient genomic changes associated with domestication of the horse color diag *Science* v356 no6336 p442 Ap 28 2017

Hofstadter, Richard, 1916-1970
DISORDER OF THE DAY R. Hofstadter *Lapham's Quarterly* v10 no3 p27 Summ 2017

Hofstra University
Hofstra University *Dance Magazine* v90 p70 2016/2017 Supplement College Guide

Hoft, Jim
ALT DANCE-OFF A. Marantz cartoon *New Yorker* v93 no13 p34 My 15 2017

HOFVE, JEAN
Cat Calm and Carry On color *Better Nutrition* v78 no11 p42 N 2016

Hog Island Oyster Co.
Naked Lunch: Oysters on the half shell are on the menu this fall M. W. Spencer *New Orleans Homes & Lifestyles* v20 no4 p112 Aut 2017

Hogan, Ben
SEEDING SUCCESS L. BEDORD *Successful Farming* v114 no12 p42 Mid-N 2016

Hogan, Bill
THE BATTLE OF ANACOSTIA FLATS *MHQ: Quarterly Journal of Military History* v29 no2 p66 Wint 2017
FIRST IN WAR *MHQ: Quarterly Journal of Military History* v29 no3 p26 Spr 2017
LAST GASPS *MHQ: Quarterly Journal of Military History* v29 no2 p20 Wint 2017
LETTER FROM MHQ: SAILOR AND SAVIOR color *MHQ: Quarterly Journal of Military History* v30 no1 p28 Aut 2017
THAT SINKING FEELING color *MHQ: Quarterly Journal of Military History* v29 no4 p28 Summ 2017
WAR STORIES *MHQ: Quarterly Journal of Military History* v29 no2 p25 Wint 2017

Hogan, Caelainn
The War Without And the War Within *New York Times Magazine* p36 Ag 13 2017

Hogan, Hulk, 1953-
DOWN AND DIRTY M. Potter color *Esquire* v167 no1 p82 F 2017
Gawkermania M. CONTINETTI *Commentary* v142 no1 p64 Jl/Ag 2016
WHEN TRUTH IS NOT ENOUGH J. TOOBIN cartoon *New Yorker* v92 no42 p96 D 19 2016

Hogan, John
Blade Runner *TV Guide* v65 no41 p39 O 2 2017
The Chilbury Ladies' Choir: A Novel *British Heritage Travel* v38 no1 p72 Ja/F 2017
Military Dramas on FXM *TV Guide* v65 no27 p38 Je 26 2017
NEWLY AVAILABLE MOVIES *TV Guide* v65 no43 p40 O 16 2017
Resident Evil: The Final Chapter *TV Guide* v65 no39 p61 S 18 2017

Hogan, Kathleen
How Microsoft Uses a Growth Mindset to Develop Leaders *Harvard Business Review Digital Articles* p2 O 7 2016

Hogan, Kevin
The Surprising Persuasiveness of a Sticky Note *Harvard Business Review Digital Articles* p2 My 26 2015

Hogan, Larry, 1956-
LARRY HOGAN IS HAVING A GRAND OLD TIME AS GOVERNOR L. MULLINS *Washingtonian Magazine* v52 no5 p52 F 2017

Hogan, Sharon—Interviews
SHARON HORGAN A. D'ARMINIO *TV Guide* v64 no46 p8 N 7 2016

Hogarth, Robin M.
POLARIZED *USA Today Magazine* v145 no2860 p44 Ja 2017
Stop Reading Lists of Things Successful People Do *Harvard Business Review Digital Articles* p2 Mr 13 2017

Hogeg, Moshe

Patience You Must Have, My Young Investors G. Coppola, S. Yoon et al color *Bloomberg Businessweek* no4503 p27 D 12 2016

Hogeland, William

George Washington's 'Founding War of Conquest' A. H. Sturgis color *Reason* v49 no5 p74 O 2017

Hogg, Ima

EDITOR'S LETTER G. Cerio *Magazine Antiques* v184 no1 p20 Ja/F 2017

Lone star D. B. Warren bw cartoon *Magazine Antiques* v184 no1 p160 Ja/F 2017

Hogg, Kirsten F.

A general catalytic β-C–H carbonylation of aliphatic amines to β-lactams bibl diag *Science* v354 no6314 p851 N 18 2016

HOGUET, NANCY

where the wild things are color *Architectural Digest* v74 no7 p67 Jl 2017

Hoh, Christina

SNOWBIRDS *New York State Conservationist* v71 no3 p2 D 2016

Hoh River (Wash.)

The Most Silent Night A. Castleman *Sierra* v101 no6 p14 N/D 2016

Hohl, Mathias

Precursor processing for plant peptide hormone maturation by subtilisin-like serine proteinases bibl color graph *Science* v354 no6319 p1594 D 23 2016

Hohl, Tobias M.

Sterilizing immunity in the lung relies on targeting fungal apoptosis-like programmed cell death color diag *Science* v357 no6355 p1037 S 8 2017

Hohlbaum, Christine

advice every new mom needs [Cover story] color *Parents* v92 no7 p32 Jl 2017

Hohman, Robert

ROBERT HOHMAN color *Bloomberg Businessweek* no4509 p64 Ja 30 2017

Hoile, Christopher

Dido and Aeneas *Opera News* v81 no7 p40 Ja 2017

HOINESS, BEN

Opening Season color *Climbing* no355 p32 Ag 2017

Hoisting machinery

See also

Elevators

eZ-Hoist Has a Clear Mission: Scenic Automation Domination *Stage Directions* v30 no3 p54 Mr 2017

Kinesys - Progress is Never Stationary *Stage Directions* v30 no3 p60 Mr 2017

Model a modern log-grasping lift A. Taylor color *Model Railroader* v84 no6 p53 Je 2017

Moving a Giant L. Nemo color *Scientific American* v317 no4 p26 O 2017

WORK AT THE PERFECT HEIGHT P. Barbour *Successful Farming* v115 no4 p80 Mr 2017

Hoisting machinery—Rigging

iWeiss - Offering More Than You Might Know *Stage Directions* v30 no3 p53 Mr 2017

Hojvat, C.

Observation of a large-scale anisotropy in the arrival directions of cosmic rays above 8×10^{18} eV *Science* v357 no6357 p1266 S 22 2017

Hoka One One (Company)

FALL SHOE GUIDE [Cover story] J. DENGATE and M. SHORTEN color graph *Runner's World* v52 no8 p59 S 2017

RUNNING. SERIOUSLY?! YES! C. GIDDINGS color *Bicycling* v58 no9 p56 O 2017

Hoke, Chris

A church for every prisoner color *Christian Century* v133 no22 p24 O 26 2016

Hoke, Jane Hawkins—Interviews

MOUNTAINS' MAJESTY C. BARBOUR color *House Beautiful* v158 no10 p64 D 2016/Ja 2017

Hökfelt, Tomas

miR-183 cluster scales mechanical pain sensitivity by regulating basal and neuropathic pain genes diag graph *Science* v356 no6343 p1168 Je 16 2017

Holahan, Marie A.

Systemic pan-AMPK activator MK-8722 improves glucose homeostasis but induces cardiac hypertrophy graph *Science* v357 no6350 p507 Ag 4 2017

Holbox Island (Mexico)—Description & travel

OuT of SighT color *Condé Nast Traveler* v52 no10 p132 N 2017

Holbrook, Damian

5 SMALLER NETWORKS YOU NEED TO KNOW ABOUT *TV Guide* v65 no31 p6 Jl 24 2017

5 THINGS TO KNOW ABOUT THE ORVILLE *TV Guide* v65 no37 p44 S 4 2017

Arrow *TV Guide* v64 no40 p57 O 3 2016

THE ART OF THE DEAL *TV Guide* v64 no46 p20 N 7 2016

At Home With Amy Sedaris *TV Guide* v65 no43 p37 O 16 2017

Blindspot color *TV Guide* v64 no42 p35 O 10 2016

BROOKLYN NINE-NINE *TV Guide* v30 p8 D 5 2016

Brooklyn Nine-Nine *TV Guide* v65 no19 p38 My 1 2017

CHEERS & JEERS color *TV Guide* v65 no7 p92 F 13 2017

CHEERS & JEERS *TV Guide* v64 no46 p88 N 7 2016

CHEERS & JEERS *TV Guide* v65 no19 p88 My 1 2017

CHEERS & JEERS *TV Guide* v65 no39 p107 S 18 2017

CHEERS & JEERS *TV Guide* v65 no8 p68 F 27 2017

DAVID E. KELLEY *TV Guide* v65 no35 p6 Ag 21 2017

DC's Legends of Tomorrow color *TV Guide* v64 no42 p36 O 10 2016

The Detour color *TV Guide* v65 no7 p41 F 13 2017

THE DEVIL AND MISS DAVIS *TV Guide* v64 no46 p18 N 7 2016

DYNASTY *TV Guide* v65 no37 p34 S 4 2017

FALL TV MATH *TV Guide* v65 no41 p6 O 2 2017

First Dates *TV Guide* v65 no14 p34 Ap 3 2017

THE FLASH *TV Guide* v65 no39 p39 S 18 2017

The Great Pumpkin Turns 50! cartoon *TV Guide* v64 no42 p10 O 10 2016

Holiday Gift Guide *TV Guide* v20 p8 D 5 2016

HOLLYWOOD DISPATCH *TV Guide* v65 no35 p5 Ag 21 2017

HOMECOMING SCREAM *TV Guide* v64 no40 p52 O 3 2016

HONORABLE MENTIONS *TV Guide* v27 p27 D 19 2016

I Love Dick *TV Guide* v65 no13 p38 Mr 20 2017

I Was a Child Star--and Lived to Tell About It *TV Guide* v65 no19 p13 My 1 2017

KIMMY SCHMIDT GOES TO COLLEGE: Females are smart as hell! Season 3 of Unbreakable Kimmy Schmidt finds its titular heroine heading off to get a higher education *TV Guide* v65 no21 p24 My 15 2017

Life's a BEACH *TV Guide* v65 no4 p30 Ja 16 2017

Lucifer *TV Guide* v65 no19 p32 My 1 2017

LUCIFER *TV Guide* v65 no39 p34 S 18 2017

LUKE PERRY MY LIFE ON TV *TV Guide* v65 no8 p26 F 27 2017

Making History *TV Guide* v65 no8 p34 F 27 2017

Meet the crew... *TV Guide* v65 no35 p7 Ag 21 2017

MEN OF HONOR *TV Guide* v65 no4 p28 Ja 16 2017

Nathan Fillion Heads to Brooklyn *TV Guide* v65 no11 p14 Mr 6 2017

Our Reporter Heads to Gotham *TV Guide* v8 p8 Ap 17 2017

Playing House *TV Guide* v65 no23 p35 My 29 2017

Riverdale *TV Guide* v65 no2 p26 Ja 2 2017

Season Finale Shockers! *TV Guide* v65 no25 p4 Je 2017

SHIP HAPPENS: 25,000 square feet covering two sound-stages, with tons of high-tech touches--the spaceship on Fox's out-of-this world hit The Orville is a stunner *TV Guide* v65 no41 p22 O 2 2017

Six's technical adviser, Mitch Hall *TV Guide* v65 no8 p15 F 27 2017

Specials, Movies & Marathons *TV Guide* v65 no43 p27 O 16 2017

Suits *TV Guide* v65 no4 p38 Ja 16 2017

Supergirl *TV Guide* v65 no6 p35 Ja 30 2017

Superheroes Break Into Song *TV Guide* v65 no13 p6 Mr 20 2017

That's One Hell of an Evil Keg Party! *TV Guide* v64 no15 p10 Ap 4 2016

Time After Time *TV Guide* v65 no8 p32 F 27 2017

Tina Fey Is a Bossypants *TV Guide* v65 no37 p14 S 4 2017

TV's HOTTEST COUPLES *TV Guide* v64 no15 p28 Ap 4 2016

TV Trends to Watch for in 2017 *TV Guide* v65 no6 p6 Ja 30 2017

TWIN PEAKS A to Z [Cover story] *TV Guide* v65 no21 p18 My

15 2017
URBAN Cowboy *TV Guide* v65 no25 p16 Je 2017
VALOR *TV Guide* v65 no37 p26 S 4 2017
What Would Diplo Do? *TV Guide* v65 no31 p35 Jl 24 2017
Who's the BOSS? *TV Guide* v65 no41 p20 O 2 2017
THE WILD BUNC color *TV Guide* v64 no42 p24 O 10 2016
THE YEAR IN CHEERS & JEERS *TV Guide* p34 D 19 2016

HOLBROOK, J. BRITT
The philosopher's view *Issues in Science & Technology* v33 no3 p16 Spr 2017

Holbrook, Sara
The Enemy: Detroit, 1954 *Publishers Weekly* v264 no3 p60 Ja 16 2017

Holbrow, Charles H.
Anthony Philip French *Physics Today* v70 no6 p74 Je 2017

Holby, Edward F.
Direct atomic-level insight into the active sites of a high-performance PGM-free ORR catalyst diag graph *Science* v357 no6350 p479 Ag 4 2017

Holcomb, Eric, 1968-
One State's School Duel *Governing* v30 no8 p12 My 2017
A Step Up: I first met Governor Holcomb on the Statehouse stairs. Both he and Indiana were ascending P. GULLEY *Indianapolis Monthly* v40 no11 p48 Jl 2017

Holcomb, Steven, 1980-2017
Milestones *Time* v189 no19 p13 My 22 2017
Steven Holcomb (1980-2017) J. Fuchs and T. Keith color *Sports Illustrated* v126 no15 p20 My 29 2017

Holcombe, Kate
simple everyday practice color *Yoga Journal* p12 2017 Special Issue
You worry constantly color *Yoga Journal* p46 2016 Special Issue

Hold Dear the Lamp Light (Short story)
HOLD DEAR THE LAMPLIGHT J. R. DAYRIT cartoon *Wired* v25 no1 p82 Ja 2017

Hold My Mule (Music)
'Hold My Mule' G. HOWARD bw *New York Times Magazine* p46 Mr 12 2017

Holden, Kristian L.
Why make it hard for teachers to cross state borders? color il *Phi Delta Kappan* v98 no5 p55 F 2017

Holden, Reed K.
Negotiating with Clients You Can't Afford to Lose *Harvard Business Review Digital Articles* p2 Je 10 2016

Holden, Richard J.
Nursing and the Great Recession bibl *Monthly Labor Review* p1 Jl 2017

Holden, Seamus
Treadmilling by FtsZ filaments drives peptidoglycan synthesis and bacterial cell division bibl graph *Science* v355 no6326 p739 F 17 2017

Holder, Burkhard
Terawatt-scale photovoltaics: Trajectories and challenges chart graph *Science* v356 no6334 p141 Ap 14 2017

Holder, Curtis D.
Coping with class in science color *Science* v355 no6325 p658 F 10 2017

HOLDER, ERIC
OBAMA'S AMERICA img *New York* v49 no20 p12 O 3 2016

Holder, Jamie
METEORITE ORIGINS color *Astronomy* v45 no11 p44 N 2017

Holdhoff, Matthias
Mismatch repair deficiency predicts response of solid tumors to PD-1 blockade chart graph *Science* v357 no6349 p409 Jl 28 2017

HOLDING, LAUREL
GUNS FOR WOMEN color *Outdoor Life* v224 no6 p67 Ag 2017

Holding companies
Alphabet Isn't a Typical Conglomerate N. V. Venkatraman *Harvard Business Review Digital Articles* p2 Ag 18 2015

Holdman, Scharlette, 1946-2017
The Lasting Legacy of a Life Devoted to Loving the Sinner D. V. Drehle color *Time* v190 no5 p31 Jl 31 2017

Holdren, John P.
Ralph J. Cicerone (1943–2016) color *Science* v354 no6316 p1107 D 2 2016

Holdren, John P.—Interviews
Is Fusion in Our Future? F. Guterl color *Scientific American* v316 no3 p17 Mr 2017

Holdren, Matthew
Character Building: Carpenter and designer Matthew Holdren creates custom wood pieces with reclaimed materials J. DeBold *New Orleans Homes & Lifestyles* v20 no3 p30 Summ 2017

HOLDREN, SARA
We Are the Dane: Director Sam Gold and his star, Oscar Isaac, stage & Hamlet that's both theatrical and honest img *New York* v50 no15 p69 Jl 24 2017

Holdsworth, Allan, 1946-2017
Allan Holdsworth's Guitar Solo on 'Land Of The Bag Snake' J. DURSO bw *Downbeat* v84 no3 p112 Mr 2017
Remembering Allan Holdsworth B. Milkowski bw *Downbeat* v84 no7 p22 Jl 2017

Holdsworth, Allan, 1946-2017—Interviews
Allan Holdsworth: Changing Guitar for the Better E. Harabadian color *Downbeat* v84 no6 p24 Je 2017

Hole, Jackson
CAM FITZPATRICK P. G. Strout cartoon color *Snowboarder* v29 no4 p48 D 2016

HOLECKO, CATHERINE
where does the time go? cartoon *Parents* v92 no7 p80 Jl 2017

Holes (Golf)
ALTERNATE ROUTES B. Riggs and D. DeNunzio color *Golf Magazine* v59 no6 p54 Je 2017
FINISH IN STYLE T. Cooke and D. DeNunzio color *Golf Magazine* v59 no4 p62 Ap 2017
Five, Oh! E. Rothman chart *Golf Magazine* v59 no6 p72 Je 2017
HAWAII'S 5-OH! J. King and D. DeNunzio color *Golf Magazine* v59 no1 p54 Ja 2017
TAKE A CHANT! B. McCabe and D. Denunzio color *Golf Magazine* v59 no10 p44 O 2017

Holes in one
GAMESET & MATCH J. King color *Golf Magazine* v59 no9 p72 S 2017
Master of None A. Shipnuck and J. Marksbury color *Golf Magazine* v59 no9 p28 S 2017

HOLGATE, MARK
Babe RUTH color *Vogue* v207 no3 p348 Mr 2017
Belle CURVE color *Vogue* v207 no3 p346 Mr 2017
Brigitte Macron color *Vogue* v207 no9 p358 S 2017
Bulgari/Nicholas Kirkwood Bags color *Vogue* v207 no9 p368 S 2017
Eastern Promises color *Vogue* v207 no9 p346 S 2017
Finding Her LEGS color *Vogue* v207 no7 p40 Jl 2017
FLORENCE in Abundance color *Vogue* v207 no4 p150 Ap 2017
FORCES TO RECKON WITH bw color *Vogue* v207 no3 p357 Mr 2017
GIVENCHY'S Giacomettis color *Vogue* v207 no3 p350 Mr 2017
GLOBAL Warmth color *Vogue* v207 no1 p34 Ja 2017
Heart and Sole color *Vogue* v207 no9 p388 S 2017
Kwaidan Editions color *Vogue* v207 no9 p354 S 2017
La Femme Natacha color *Vogue* v207 no7 p94 Jl 2017
LEG Work color *Vogue* v207 no3 p338 Mr 2017
The Magic Numbers color *Vogue* v207 no11 p134 N 2017
Mansur Gavriel Coats color *Vogue* v207 no9 p386 S 2017
Model BEHAVIOR color *Vogue* v207 no1 p30 Ja 2017
NAOMIE Harris color *Vogue* v207 no3 p322 Mr 2017
OBJECTS of their DESIRE color *Vogue* v207 no3 p326 Mr 2017
Off the Menu color *Vogue* v207 no9 p380 S 2017
Once Upon a Time in America bw color *Vogue* v207 no9 p706 S 2017
Queen of the Jungle color *Vogue* v207 no9 p396 S 2017
Riley Keough color *Vogue* v207 no9 p372 S 2017
Sies Marjan Shoes color *Vogue* v207 no9 p362 S 2017
Sparkles FLY color *Vogue* v207 no3 p314 Mr 2017
Spot ON color *Vogue* v207 no1 p34 Ja 2017
Statement Belts color *Vogue* v207 no9 p382 S 2017
Taste MAKERS color *Vogue* v207 no3 p334 Mr 2017
TNT cartoon color *Vogue* v207 no3 p342 Mr 2017
TNT color *Vogue* v207 no9 p392 S 2017

Holi (Hindu festival)
HOLI MOLEY *Atlanta* v57 no1 p20 My 2017

Holiday, Billie, 1915-1959

The Two Billie Holidays T. Teachout *Commentary* v140 no2 p63 S 2015

Holiday Affair (Film)

HOLIDAY MOVIES M. FELL *TV Guide* p46 D 19 2016

Holiday cooking

    See also

      Halloween cooking

      Thanksgiving cooking

A BETTER BABKA A. BROWNLEE *Cincinnati Magazine* v50 no3 p134 D 2016

DELICIOUS RECIPES POP THE HAPPIEST OF HOLIDAYS *Martha Stewart Living* no270 p14 D 2016

full house W. Williams color *Bon Appetit* v61 no11 p96 N 2016

HOLIDAY COOKIES S. PUCKETT *Atlanta* v56 no8 p78 D 2016

SHORTCUT BAKING M. GLISAN color *Better Homes & Gardens* v95 no11 p100 N 2017

Holiday decorations

    See also

      Christmas decorations

      Halloween decorations

      New Year's decorations

      Thanksgiving decorations

All Decked Out L. P. Bailey and E. Poston color *Southern Living* v51 no12 p34 D 2016

The GREENEST HOLIDAY G. TOMAINE color *Rodale's Organic Life* v2 no7 p52 D 2016/Ja 2017

Happy Holidays D. Howland color *Cabin Living* p7 D 2016

Holiday parties

    See also

      Christmas parties

Let Them Eat Cake! V. Hart *New Orleans Homes & Lifestyles* v20 no1 p66 Wint 2016

Holiday pay

Employers 'must prepare to add commission to holiday pay' after landmark ruling M. CALNAN *People Management* p8 N 2016

Holiday stress

MONEY MANNERS M. CROSS chart color *Kiplinger's Personal Finance* v70 no12 p41 D 2016

Holiday Inn, the Irving Berlin Musical (Theatrical production)

Reimagining a Classic S. GOLD *Dance Magazine* v90 no11 p20 N 2016

Holidays

    See also

      Father's Day

      Halloween

      Labor Day

      Memorial Day

      Patriot Day

      Saint Peter's Day

      Thanksgiving Day

4 gifts kids give you A. TRAISTER *Parents* v91 no12 p114 D 2016

5 Sneaky Ways the Holidays Harm Your Immunity K. KLOSS *Reader's Digest* v188 no1125 p70 N 2016

Against-the-Grain Holidays M. D. SMITH color *Better Nutrition* v78 no11 p88 N 2016

ALL IS CALM E. Jardina color *Sunset* v237 no6 p41 D 2016

ANNA THOMAS N. Gregory color *Vegetarian Times* v43 no2 p86 N/D 2016

CHILL-GIVING J. BAINBRIDGE color *Bon Appetit* v61 no11 p116 N 2016

creative cookies *Parents* v91 no12 p98 D 2016

cupcakes in costume E. CLARK *Parents* v91 no10 p82 O 2016

Easter together J. HOWARD color *Parents* v92 no4 p108 Ap 2017

Every Recipe Has a Story A. CHERNILA color *Parents* v92 no11 p99 N 2017

Finding more happiness in the holidays V. Chambers color *Redbook* p116 D 2016

Foodie Festivities E. JACKSON *Atlanta* v56 no8 p72 D 2016

gather ROUND S. Sexton and K. O'Donnell chart color *Yoga Journal* no287 p68 N 2016

HAPPY HOLIDAY SHOPPING C. W. DINEEN *Better Homes & Gardens* v94 no12 p154 D 2016

HAPPY(?) NEW YEAR *Sea Magazine* v109 no2 p32 F 2017

Harvest Feast Quick Fixes [Cover story] color *Vegetarian Times* v43 no2 p32 N/D 2016

HOLIDAY Roasts [Cover story] S. Middleton color *Vegetarian Times* v43 no2 p76 N/D 2016

HOME FOR THE HOLIDAY L. MYERS *Missouri Life* v43 no7 p67 D 2016/Ja 2017

Home for the Holidays S. James *Parents* p17 2015

Let There Be Light M. BECK color *O, The Oprah Magazine* p51 D 2016

MAKE-AHEAD holiday meal J. Silverman Hough color *Yoga Journal* no296 p25 N 2017

make thanksgiving in four hours E. CLARK *Parents* v91 no11 p112 N 2016

MONEY MANNERS M. CROSS chart color *Kiplinger's Personal Finance* v70 no12 p41 D 2016

no-carve fun *Parents* v91 no10 p67 O 2016

No More Party Pounds J. Andriakos color *Health* v30 no10 p37 D 2016

O come, Emmanuel R. McCarty *U.S. Catholic* v81 no12 p4 D 2016

one dough, six cookies K. TACK *Parents* p94 2015

PLEASE DON'T FEED THE ANIMAL D. Denunzio color *Golf Magazine* v58 no11 p58 N 2016

presents with purpose H. M. BAUER *Parents* v91 no12 p89 D 2016

Santa's Watching K. Cicero *Parents* v91 no12 p14 D 2016

a season of smiles *Parents* v91 no12 p81 D 2016

SPECIAL DELIVERY E. Graves *Martha Stewart Living* no270 p10 D 2016

spooky snacks F. LARGEMAN-ROTH *Parents* v91 no10 p74 O 2016

TOFURKEY IN THE OVEN M. GUNCH cartoon *New Orleans Magazine* v51 no1 p48 N 2016

Tough Act to Follow K. CHONG cartoon *Walrus* v14 no6 p64 Jl/Ag 2017

true colors K. SULLIVAN MORFORD *Parents* v92 no2 p48 F 2017

very useful valentines *Parents* v92 no2 p54 F 2017

When It's Not Quite A Wonderful Life J. MARSH *Reader's Digest* v188 no1126 p43 D 2016/Ja 2017

Winter-Break Entertainment C. Grise *Parents* p22 2015

your 2015 gift list M. LILES *Parents* p107 2015

YOUR LIFE *USA Today Magazine* v145 no2860 p6 Ja 2017

Holidays in art

NORTH J. FROIS color *Louisiana Life* v37 no2 p88 N/D 2016

Holidays—Religious aspects

Clock out J. Ryan color *U.S. Catholic* v82 no7 p25 Jl 2017

Holidays—Social aspects

YOUR YEAREND BONUS M. OZ cartoon *O, The Oprah Magazine* p134 D 2016

Holidays—United States

    See also

      Election Day

      Fourth of July

      Groundhog Day

      Martin Luther King, Jr., Day

      Veterans Day

The Long Holiday W. Kristol *Weekly Standard* v22 no19 p8 Ja 23 2017

Smart Cookies L. WINGENROTH *Dance Magazine* v90 no12 p100 D 2016

WRITE A BETTER WISH LIST A. Giorgianni color *Consumer Reports* v81 no12 p41 D 2016

Holiness

Verso l'alto M. J. Rose bw *U.S. Catholic* v82 no11 p45 N 2017

Holistic medicine

    See also

      Health self-care

HEALTH AND HEALING IN HVERAGERÐI Z. Robert *Iceland Review* v54 no6 p40 N/D 2016

How do you fold seva, or self less service, into everyday life? color *Yoga Journal* no295 p14 O 2017

Holistic medicine—Societies, etc.

take OM HOME T. Eichenseher color *Yoga Journal* no291 p86 My 2017

Holl, Adelbert

THE SURVIVOR *MHQ: Quarterly Journal of Military History* v29 no3 p14 Spr 2017

Holl, Karen D.

Restoring tropical forests from the bottom up bibl color *Science* v355 no6324 p455 F 3 2017

Holl, Steven, 1947-

1 An Experiment in the Woods W. GOODMAN img *New York* v49 no21 p80 O 17 2016

HOLLAND, AGNIESZKA

The Human Voice bw color *Film Comment* v53 no1 p94 Ja/F 2017

Holland, Ashley

The Artist Formally Known as Cherokee color *Art in America* v105 no8 p19 S 2017

Holland, David—Interviews

probiotics and prebiotics V. Tweed color *Amazing Wellness* v8 no6 p10 Early Winter2016

Holland, Edward

Q&A: A "See" Change S. Goldberg *Cincinnati Magazine* v51 no1 p144 O 2017

Holland, Eva

How Couples (and Throuples!) Do Money color *Bloomberg Businessweek* no4502 p74 D 5 2016

Saving an Arctic oasis color map *Canadian Geographic* v137 no1 p57 F 2017

Holland, James

Genomic estimation of complex traits reveals ancient maize adaptation to temperate North America diag *Science* v357 no6350 p512 Ag 4 2017

Holland, Jeff

Saving the saola from extinction color *Science* v357 no6357 p1248 S 22 2017

Holland, Jennifer S.

A Fight to Survive color map *National Geographic* v231 no3 p86 Mr 2017

Oh, What Tangled Webs They Weave color *National Wildlife (World Edition)* v55 no6 p18 O/N 2017

HOLLAND, JOSHUA

FIELD GUIDE TO THE RESISTANCE [Cover story] color *Nation* v304 no10 p12 Mr 27 2017

Holland, Kelley

The Early-Bird Dividend color diag *Money* v46 no1 p27 Ja/F 2017

HOLLAND, KIM N.

Envisioning the Future of Aquatic Animal Tracking: Technology, Science, and Application *BioScience* v67 no10 p884 O 2017

Holland, Kimberly

The best cold & flu fighting secrets of all time color *Health* v31 no9 p71 N 2017

HOLLAND, MAX

The 'White Rat' bw color *Weekly Standard* v23 no5 p34 O 9 2017

Holland, Noy

Hard Places S. BRADFIELD *New York Times Book Review* p18 Ja 29 2017

Holland, Tom, 1996-

Tom Holland A. Breznican color *Entertainment Weekly* no1444/1445 p59 D 16 2016

Holland, Tom, 1996-—Interviews

Tom HOLLAND Zendaya *Interview* v47 no5 p50 Je/Jl 2017

Holland-Dozier-Holland (Music)

HOLLAND-DOZIER-HOLLAND V. Cunningham *New Yorker* v92 no42 p76 D 19 2016

Hollandbeck, Andy

THE GRID: HERE COMES THE SUN *Saturday Evening Post* v289 no4 p26 Jl/Ag 2017

The Logophile *Saturday Evening Post* v289 no2 p24 Mr/Ap 2017

The Logophile *Saturday Evening Post* v289 no3 p24 My/Je 2017

Hollande, François, 1954-

Party at the End of the World C. CALDWELL color *Weekly Standard* v22 no10 p23 N 14 2016

Hollander, Paul

Dictators' Devotees R. RADOSH *Commentary* v143 no6 p45 Je 2017

Rafael Rojas: Fighting Over Fidel: the New York Intellectuals and the Cuban Revolution *Society* v54 no2 p210 Ap 2017

Treason of The Clerks D. PRYCE-JONES diag *National Review* v69 no4 p35 Mr 6 2017

Hollander, Stacy C.

A stitch in wartime: The American Folk Art Museum presents a fascinating collection of quilts made by men at arms bw color *Magazine Antiques* v184 no4 p92 Jl/Ag 2017

HOLLAND MURPHY, S.

The $55,000 Closet *D: The Magazine of Dallas* v43 no10 p66 O 2016

Break Out! *D: The Magazine of Dallas* v43 no10 p56 O 2016

A New Mission *D: The Magazine of Dallas* v43 no10 p54 O 2016

Plum Crazy *D: The Magazine of Dallas* v43 no10 p63 O 2016

Hollandsworth, Skip

CUBAN REVOLUTION *Texas Monthly* v45 no4 p110 Ap 2017

LITTLE TOWN ON THE PRAIRIE *Texas Monthly* v45 no5 p87 My 2017

LOVE AND LOSS ON THE PLAINS: The day the fire came to the Franklin Ranch *Texas Monthly* v45 no8 p60 Ag 2017

The PRISONER *Texas Monthly* v45 no1 p92 Ja 2017

The Wild BUNCH *Texas Monthly* v45 no4 p47 Ap 2017

Hollars, B. J., 1984-

Flock Together: A Love Affair with Extinct Birds L. A. MARSCHALL color *Natural History* v125 no4 p46 Ap 2017

HOLLERAN, MAX

Bright Lights, Small Government bw color *New Republic* v247 no12 p74 D 2016

Freestyle Marxism *New Republic* v248 no5 p69 My 2017

Hollerich, Michael J.

The Enemy Within [Cover story] color *Commonweal* v143 no19 p10 D 2 2016

Hollerith, Randolph Marshall

People C. Kennel-Shank color *Christian Century* v133 no21 p19 O 12 2016

Hollett, Jennifer

Taking on the Haters J. KAY *Walrus* v13 no10 p74 D 2016

Holley, Eric R.

Nuclear Weapons in a Changing Climate: Probability, Increasing Risks, and Perception bibl chart color graph *Environment* v59 no4 p22 Jl-Ag 2017

Holley, Eugene Jr.

Fathers and Sons color *Publishers Weekly* v263 no43 p35 O 24 2016

L.A.'s Black Renaissance color *Publishers Weekly* v264 no17 p36 Ap 24 2017

Matthew Shipp's Evolution color *Downbeat* v84 no5 p16 My 2017

Remembering Emmett Till color *Publishers Weekly* v264 no2 p52 Ja 9 2017

Transformers color *Downbeat* v84 no8 p83 Ag 2017

WORKING THROUGH IDEAS WITH FICTION bw *Publishers Weekly* v264 no24 p34 Je 12 2017

Wynton Marsalis *Humanities* v37 no4 p1 Fall 2016

Holley, Michael

THE PAPI PAPERS color *Sports Illustrated* v126 no14 p68 My 15-22 2017

Holley, Stephen—Interviews

A New Mission S. HOLLAND MURPHY *D: The Magazine of Dallas* v43 no10 p54 O 2016

Holley Performance Products Inc.

Bowling Green's Variable-Cam Brawler P. Thomas color graph *Hot Rod* v70 no7 p34 Jl 2017

Holliday, Ava

Unconscious Bias in Parks and Recreation *Parks & Recreation* v52 no2 p32 F 2017

HOLLIDAY, DARRYL

Charlene Carruthers color *Chicago* v66 no6 p93 Je 2017

Holliday junctions

Holliday junction resolvases mediate chloroplast nucleoid segregation Y. Kobayashi, O. Misumi et al diag *Science* v356 no6338 p631 My 12 2017

Holliday Park (Indianapolis, Ind.)

INQUIRING MINDS: CFI schools, open-air conventions, and Holliday Park ruins. Ask the Hoosierist S. STALL *Indianapolis Monthly* v12 no40 p18 Ag 2017

Hollier, Larry

Dr. Larry Hollier F. ESKER color *Louisiana Life* v37 no3 p64 Ja/F 2017

Hollingworth, Clare, 1911-2017

Milestones *Time* v189 no4 p13 Ja 23 2017

Hollins, Jon

Dragon Lords: False Idols *Publishers Weekly* v264 no31 p67 Jl

31 2017

Hollins University (Roanake, Va.)
Hollins University *Dance Magazine* v90 p70 2016/2017 Supplement College Guide

HOLLIS, LARRY
Chords & Discords bw *Downbeat* v83 no12 p10 D 2016

Hollister, Stacy
Don't Be a Redheaded Stranger! *Texas Monthly* v45 no3 p8 Mr 2017

Holloran, Tessa
10 TIPS FROM U.S. OLYMPIAN LISA WILCOX color *Dressage Today* p44 My 2017

Holloway, Carson
TEAM OF RIVALS P. McNamara *Claremont Review of Books* v16 no4 p28 Fall 2016

Holloway, Josh
Colony I. Rudolph *TV Guide* v65 no2 p27 Ja 2 2017
Colony Is Back in Action I. Rudolph *TV Guide* p12 D 5 2016

Holloway, Josh—Interviews
5 JUICY QUESTIONS J. Holloway color *Women's Health* v14 no1 p148 Ja/F 2017

Holloway, Julie
Paint It White K. Owen color *Southern Living* v52 no1 p31 Ja 2017

Holloway, Richard
Open to Belief T. LOZANO *Weekly Standard* v22 no8 p38 O 31 2016

Holloway, Tomekia
Q: If you had an extra hour in your day, what would you do with it? color *O, The Oprah Magazine* p18 O 2017

Hollow Crown: The Wars of the Roses, The (TV program)
The Hollow Crown: The Wars of the Roses J. Russell *TV Guide* p42 D 5 2016

Hollub, Christian
PLAYING THE TRUMP CARD color *Entertainment Weekly* no1470 p12 Je 16 2017

Hollub, Vicki A., 1960-
Oil's Changing Face C. HELMAN color graph *Forbes* v200 no1 p38 Jl 27 2017

Hollway, Don
BOHEMIAN CATASTROPHY color map *Military History* v34 no5 p40 Ja 2018

Hollyoaks (TV program)
A SENTIMENTAL EDUCATION D. PINCKNEY cartoon *New Yorker* v93 no26 p58 S 4 2017

Hollywood Foreign Press Association
THE HFPA AND INSTYLE KICK OFF THE 2017 GOLDEN GLOBE AWARDS SEASON B. Fowler color *InStyle* v24 no1 p42 Ja 2017

Hollywood Game Night (TV program)
PUT ON YOUR GAME FACE! M. Roffman *TV Guide* v65 no31 p8 Jl 24 2017

Hollywood Vibe (Company)
HOLLYWOOD VIBE *Dance Spirit* v20 no10 p18 D 2016

Hollywood (Los Angeles, Calif.)
The Girl Who Loved Hollywood: The story of my mother B. Bawer *Commentary* v144 no2 p32 S 2017
HOLLYWOOD GRABS BACK *Interview* v47 no5 p40 Je/Jl 2017
On the March E. MERCADO *Los Angeles Magazine* v61 no11 p180 N 2016
Set the Stage S. AMELAR *Architectural Record* v205 no4 p158 Ap 2017
Sober, Seething Hollywood K. D. WILLIAMSON il *National Review* v69 no5 p33 Mr 20 2017
TALK TO US R. DePesa and J. P. Dave' color *Chicago* v66 no2 p11 F 2017

Holm, Jennifer L.
Frack Attack: As a new industry arrives to lift a struggling town, a young forager weighs its heavy costs *New York Times Book Review* p26 My 14 2017
Hard Times in Paradise L. SNYDER *New York Times Book Review* p25 N 13 2016

Holm, Katrina Niidas
Spring 2017 Flying Starts color *Publishers Weekly* v264 no27 p36 Jl 3 2017

HOLM, KATRINA NIIDS

Holman, Audrey Coulthurst color *Publishers Weekly* v263 no52 p68 D 19 2016

Holman, Jonas W., fl. 1833
THE PULPIT AND THE PAINTBRUSH C. M. Riley bw color *Magazine Antiques* v183 no6 p84 N/D 2016

Holman, Jordyn
FINANCE graph *Bloomberg Businessweek* no4532 p25 Jl 31 2017

Holman Ranch (Company)
A TOAST TO OUR HOLIDAY HOST *USA Today Magazine* v145 no2858 p74 N 2016

Holman rule (U.S.)
IN DEFENSE OF EXPERTISE A. Whiting *Washingtonian Magazine* v52 no5 p15 F 2017
You're Fired! P. J. Williams diag *Nation* v304 no4 p10 F 6 2017

Holmberg, Charlie N.
The Fifth Doll *Publishers Weekly* v264 no23 p35 Je 5 2017

Holmberg, Ryan
JIRO TAKAMATSU color *Art in America* v105 no3 p131 Mr 2017
LEO TWIGGS cartoon *Art in America* v105 no3 p134 Mr 2017
MAKOTO AIDA *Art in America* v104 no9 p165 O 2016
NINA CHANEL ABNEY color *Art in America* v105 no5 p132 My 2017

Holmer, Anna Rose
BODIES THAT MATTER: BLACK GIRLHOOD IN THE FITS P. White *Film Quarterly* v70 no3 p23 Spr 2017

Holmes, Anna
Bookends *New York Times Book Review* p31 O 2 2016
Bookends: What distinguishes cultural exchange from cultural appropriation? *New York Times Book Review* p27 Je 11 2017
What's the best book, new or old, you read this year? *New York Times Book Review* p27 D 25 2016

Holmes, Bob
Flavor: The Science of Our Most Neglected Sense color *Publishers Weekly* v264 no9 p90 F 27 2017

Holmes, Bob—Interviews
On the Tip of My Tongue E. NORTON color *Publishers Weekly* v264 no11 p71 Mr 13 2017

HOLMES, CHRIS
BEST OF LOUISIANA OUTDOORS color *Louisiana Life* v38 no1 p30 S/O 2017

Holmes, Colin
High Treason D. PRYCE-JONES color *National Review* v68 no21 p41 N 21 2016

Holmes, Courtney
The Storybook Barber A. SIMMONS *Reader's Digest* v188 no1126 p8 D 2016/Ja 2017

Holmes, Fred
The Ugly Teapot, Book 1: Hannah *Publishers Weekly* v263 no51 p148 D 12 2016

Holmes, J. B., 1982-
PURE GENIUS D. Denunzio and J. Murphy color *Golf Magazine* v58 no11 p50 N 2016
YOUNG GUN, OLD SOUL D. M. Clarke color *Golf Magazine* v59 no2 p10 F 2017

Holmes, J. B., 1982-—Interviews
HE'S THE alpha dog C. Morfit color *Golf Magazine* v59 no2 p58 F 2017

HOLMES, JAMES
Clouds over The Pacific color *National Review* v69 no3 p45 F 20 2017

Holmes, Kathryn
ASSESS Your Specialty color *Dance Spirit* v21 no1 p56 Ja 2017
CAUTION: Toxic! *Dance Spirit* v20 no10 p58 D 2016
Dancing Through the Dog Days *Dance Magazine* v91 no1 p130 Ja 2017
HELP! I'm Too Short! color *Dance Spirit* v21 no4 p38 Ap 2017
Help! I'm Too Tall! color *Dance Spirit* v21 no4 p36 Ap 2017
KIDA color *Dance Spirit* v20 no10 p36 D 2016
Post-Performance Done Right *Dance Magazine* v91 no4 p48 Ap 2017
Reach New Heights *Dance Spirit* v21 no7 p84 S 2017
Summer Study Regrets: Five pros share what they wish they'd done differently as summer intensive students *Dance Magazine* v91 no7 p52 Jl 2017

Holmes, Katie, 1978-

The Kennedys: After Camelot A. D'ARMINIO *TV Guide* v65 no13 p20 Mr 20 2017

Holmes, Maori Karmael
INVISIBLE SCRATCH LINES: AN INTERVIEW WITH JULIE DASH *Film Quarterly* v70 no2 p49 Wint 2016

Holmes, Mowgli
THE Great POT MONOPOLY Mystery A. Chicago Lewis color *GQ: Gentlemen's Quarterly* v97 no9 p164 S 2017

Holmes, Oliver Wendell, 1841-1935
How a Veteran Sees Life J. MARK JACKSON color *Reader's Digest* v189 no1130 p102 My 2017

Holmes, Pete
Crashing J. Russell color *TV Guide* v65 no7 p38 F 13 2017
CRASH LANDING A. Marantz cartoon *New Yorker* v92 no47 p21 Ja 30 2017
A Young Comic's Hope-Filled Crash D. D'Addario color *Time* v189 no7/8 p103 F 27 2017

Holmes, Pete—Interviews
Bromantic Comedy *Los Angeles Magazine* p56 F 2017
Is This Guy Making the Next Girls? R. Rahman color *Entertainment Weekly* no1454/1455 p86 F 24 2017

Holmes, Richard, 1946-2011
De Quincey: So Original, So Truly Weird bw cartoon *New York Review of Books* v63 no18 p24 N 24 2016
Richard Holmes *New York Times Book Review* p6 Mr 5 2017
Their Faithful Servant R. Scurr color *New York Review of Books* v64 no14 p4 S 28 2017
The Trail of Talent S. SCHIFF *New York Times Book Review* p9 Mr 26 2017
Travels in Literary Time J. Parini *American Scholar* v86 no2 p124 Spr 2017

Holmes, Richard T.
THINKING LIKE A WATERSHED J. ODENBAUGH *BioScience* v67 no9 p861 S 2017

Holmes, Ryan
Hootsuite's CEO on What He Learned from Getting Hacked on Social Media *Harvard Business Review Digital Articles* p2 O 6 2016

Holmes, Sherlock (Fictitious character)
More things to read and watch and learn R. A. Schroth color *America* v216 no9 p6 Ap 24 2017

Holmes, Sherman
LAST MAN STANDING: With The Richmond Sessions, the surviving Holmes brother goes it alone D. Harrison bw color *Virginia Living* v15 no5 p31 Ag 2017

Holmes, Tamara E.
BATTLING THE BURDEN OF SUCCESS color *Essence* v47 no7 p92 N 2016
The New #BankBlack Movement color *Essence* v47 no11 p73 Mr 2017
Yes, You Can Travel on a Dime! color map *Essence* v48 no2 p71 Je 2017
Your Foolproof Holiday Budget color *Essence* v47 no7 p69 N 2016

HOLMES, THOMAS H.
Assessing National Biodiversity Trends for Rocky and Coral Reefs through the Integration of Citizen Science and Scientific Monitoring Programs *BioScience* v67 no2 p134 F 2017

Holmes Brothers (Performer)
LAST MAN STANDING: With The Richmond Sessions, the surviving Holmes brother goes it alone D. Harrison bw color *Virginia Living* v15 no5 p31 Ag 2017

Holmlund, Chris
John Waters: Multiple Maniacs Relaunch *Film Quarterly* v71 no1 p98 Fall 2017

Holmstrom, Bengt
Contract theory nabs econ Nobel *Science* v354 no6309 p152 O 14 2016

Holocaust denial
SPECIAL Letters D. IRVING and A. NEIER color *Nation* v303 no17 p8 O 24 2016

Holocaust survivors
FROM OUR READERS S. Lower, C. McGee et al *Archaeology* v70 no3 p8 My/Je 2017
THE HOLOCAUST'S GREAT ESCAPE M. SHAER bw color map *Smithsonian* v47 no10 p42 Mr 2017

LIVING MEMORY E. KANG color *Chicago* v66 no10 p37 O 2017
Valor The Selfless Survivor J. Guttman bw color *Military History* v34 no1 p16 My 2017
WITNESS TO DARKNESS S. FENNESSY *Atlanta* v57 no1 p22 My 2017

Holocaust survivors—Services for
Christian and Jewish groups form partnerships to care for Holocaust survivors M. Chabin color *Christian Century* v134 no6 p15 Mr 15 2017

Holocaust (1939-1945)
See also
  Holocaust survivors
Christian and Jewish groups form partnerships to care for Holocaust survivors M. Chabin color *Christian Century* v134 no6 p15 Mr 15 2017
Discussion E. Sponsler, G. J. Wood et al *Smithsonian* v48 no1 p10 Ap 2017
THE HOLOCAUST'S GREAT ESCAPE M. SHAER bw color map *Smithsonian* v47 no10 p42 Mr 2017
The Many Lives of Babi Yar N. M. Naimark *Hoover Digest: Research & Opinion on Public Policy* no2 p176 Spr 2017

Holocaust (1939-1945)—Personal narratives
THE LAST TIME WE CLOSED THE GATES L. RATNER bw color *Nation* v304 no5 p20 F 20 2017

Holocene Epoch
See also
  Holocene extinction
THE SIXTH EXTINCTION *Change* v82 no3 p15 Mr 2017

Holocene extinction
THE SIXTH EXTINCTION *Change* v82 no3 p15 Mr 2017

Holroyde, Andy
Predicting the Fall of Anne Boleyn *History Today* v67 no5 p11 My 2017

HOLSCHUH, NICK
that time i bombed antarctica cartoon *Popular Science* v289 no2 p75 Mr/Ap 2017

HOLSINGER, ROGER
Old West Balloon Fest fills Panhandle skies color *Nebraska Life* v21 no5 p80 S/O 2017

Holst, Lisa
Living Leviathans *New York State Conservationist* v72 no1 p22 Ag 2017

Holsters
BIRD-DOGGING BEARS R. BRUGGEMAN and N. KREBS cartoon color *Outdoor Life* v224 no5 p12 Je/Jl 2017
HOLSTER IT RIGHT R. MANN color *Outdoor Life* v224 no4 pP8 My 2017
Missouri K. Grannan *New York Times Magazine* p40 N 20 2016

Holt, Anne
Beyond the Truth T. Jordan color *Entertainment Weekly* no1442 p62 D 2 2016 Rebellious Special Issue

Holt, Chris
Hospital Coalitions Save Money and Improve Care *Harvard Business Review Digital Articles* p2 D 18 2014

Holt, E.
Observation of a large-scale anisotropy in the arrival directions of cosmic rays above 8×10^{18} eV *Science* v357 no6357 p1266 S 22 2017

HOLT, EMILY
Yves Béhar color *Architectural Digest* v74 no10 p57 O 1 2017

Holt, Frank L.
An Alexander for the social media age? P. Cartledge *History Today* v66 no10 p60 O 2016

Holt, Genevieve
THE QUINTESSENTIAL DIRECTOR FOR THE QUINTESSENTIAL PRODUCTION *Cincinnati Magazine* v50 no8 p18 My 2017
SCHOOL OF ROCK TEACHES US TO BREAK THE MOLD *Cincinnati Magazine* v50 no8 p14 My 2017
WELCOME *Cincinnati Magazine* v50 no8 p2 My 2017

Holt, Jim
The Man With the Red Pencil: Harold Evans, editor par excellence, explains why good writing is a moral issue *New York Times Book Review* p24 My 21 2017
Something Faster Than Light? What Is It? color *New York Review*

of Books v63 no17 p50 N 10 2016

HOLT, JOSEPH

Lockn' Roll *Weekly Standard* v22 no6 p37 O 17 2016

Holt, Lester, 1959-

NBC's Fake News Show color *Weekly Standard* v22 no40 p2 Je 26 2017

Holt, Marilyn E.

The [4Fe4S] cluster of human DNA primase functions as a redox switch using DNA charge transport color *Science* v355 no6327 p813 F 24 2017

Holt, Nathalia

Hidden Figures/Rise of the Rocket Girls J. Levasseur *Physics Today* v70 no1 p57 Ja 2017

Holt, Rachel

GUEST LIST: A monthly roundup of people we'd like to have over for drinks, food, and conversation *Washingtonian Magazine* v53 no1 p24 O 2017

Holt, Rush

Act for science color *Science* v355 no6325 p551 F 10 2017

Moving forward after the march *Science* v356 no6337 p467 My 5 2017

Northeast Asia trip bolsters ongoing scientific cooperation M. Jarvis color *Science* v354 no6315 p979 N 25 2016

What now for science? cartoon *Science* v354 no6315 p947 N 25 2016

HOLT, VICTORIA

Morning Glory *Reader's Digest* v188 no1125 p57 N 2016

Holtby, Braden, 1989-

Braden Holtby M. Rich color *Current Biography* v78 no1 p27 Ja 2017

MY TOWN: Caps star Braden Holtby on why he calls Old Town Alexandria home *Washingtonian Magazine* v53 no1 p186 O 2017

Holtby, Fred

The Experiment D. KUKOFF *Los Angeles Magazine* v61 no11 p144 N 2016

Holtmaat, Anthony

Rejuvenating brain plasticity diag *Science* v356 no6345 p1335 Je 30 2017

Holtman, Inge R.

An environment-dependent transcriptional network specifies human microglia identity color *Science* v356 no6344 p1248 Je 23 2017

Holton, Brandon—Interviews

THE LION KING B. COSSAVELLA *Arizona Highways* v93 no1 p48 Ja 2017

Holton, M. Jan

Longing for Home: Forced Displacement and Postures of Hospitality W. Brueggemann *Christian Century* v134 no1 p38 Ja 4 2017

Holton, Nicholas

The receptor kinase FER is a RALF-regulated scaffold controlling plant immune signaling bibl graph *Science* v355 no6322 p287 Ja 20 2017

Holton, Terry—Interviews

TERRY HOLTON B. Freese *Successful Farming* v115 no1 p10 Ja 2017

Holtsberg, Frederick W.

A "Trojan horse" bispecific-antibody strategy for broad protection against ebolaviruses bibl graph *Science* v354 no6310 p350 O 21 2016

Holtz, Lou, 1937-

CATHOLICS VS. CONVICTS K. ROSEN *TV Guide* p52 D 5 2016

Holtzman, David M.

Mechanisms linking circadian clocks, sleep, and neurodegeneration bibl diag *Science* v354 no6315 p1004 N 25 2016

Holtzman, Michael J.

The microbial metabolite desaminotyrosine protects from influenza through type I interferon graph *Science* v357 no6350 p498 Ag 4 2017

Holtzmann, Roger

DOOMSDAY IN IGLOO *South Dakota Magazine* v33 no3 p52 S/O 2017

LET US GIVE THANKS *South Dakota Magazine* v32 no4 p46 N/D 2016

PACKING FOR ETERNITY *South Dakota Magazine* v32 no6 p66 Mr/Ap 2017

WHY ROBOTS WON'T FARM *South Dakota Magazine* v33 no2 p44 Jl/Ag 2017

Holub, Christian

47 METERS DOWN color *Entertainment Weekly* no1463/1464 p57 Ap/My 2017

9JKL color *Entertainment Weekly* no1482/1483 p49 S 22 2017

ALL EYEZ ON ME color *Entertainment Weekly* no1463/1464 p50 Ap/My 2017

American Housewife *Entertainment Weekly* no1482/1483 p79 S 22 2017

Art's Latest Inspiration? TRUMP color *Entertainment Weekly* no1476 p16 Ag 4 2017

BEST COMIC BOOKS color *Entertainment Weekly* no1444/1445 p110 D 16 2016

The Blacklist color *Entertainment Weekly* no1482/1483 p74 S 22 2017

Blindspot color *Entertainment Weekly* no1482/1483 p95 S 22 2017

Blue Bloods color *Entertainment Weekly* no1482/1483 p99 S 22 2017

The Brave color *Entertainment Weekly* no1482/1483 p55 S 22 2017

Breaking Big EMMA DUMONT color *Entertainment Weekly* no1482/1483 p51 S 22 2017

Broad City color *Entertainment Weekly* no1482/1483 p79 S 22 2017

Chicago P.D *Entertainment Weekly* no1482/1483 p79 S 22 2017

Crazy Ex-Girlfriend color *Entertainment Weekly* no1482/1483 p98 S 22 2017

Criminal Minds color *Entertainment Weekly* no1482/1483 p79 S 22 2017

Dancing With the Stars *Entertainment Weekly* no1482/1483 p48 S 22 2017

DEMI MOORE OF Empire color *Entertainment Weekly* no1482/1483 p78 S 22 2017

Designated Survivor color *Entertainment Weekly* no1482/1483 p74 S 22 2017

Dynasty color *Entertainment Weekly* no1482/1483 p76 S 22 2017

The Exorcist color *Entertainment Weekly* no1482/1483 p92 S 22 2017

FREDDIE HIGHMORE OF The Good Doctor color *Entertainment Weekly* no1482/1483 p54 S 22 2017

The Gifted color *Entertainment Weekly* no1482/1483 p50 S 22 2017

The Goldbergs color *Entertainment Weekly* no1482/1483 p74 S 22 2017

Hawaii Five-O *Entertainment Weekly* no1482/1483 p99 S 22 2017

Hell's Kitchen *Entertainment Weekly* no1482/1483 p99 S 22 2017

Hot Date *Entertainment Weekly* no1482/1483 p74 S 22 2017

Jane the Virgin color *Entertainment Weekly* no1482/1483 p95 S 22 2017

Kevin Can Wait color *Entertainment Weekly* no1482/1483 p52 S 22 2017

Law & Order: Special Victims Unit *Entertainment Weekly* no1482/1483 p75 S 22 2017

The LEGO Ninjago Movie color *Entertainment Weekly* no1484 p43 S 29 2017

Lucifer *Entertainment Weekly* no1482/1483 p48 S 22 2017

MacGyver *Entertainment Weekly* no1482/1483 p99 S 22 2017

Marvel's Inhumans color *Entertainment Weekly* no1482/1483 p99 S 22 2017

Me, Myself & I color *Entertainment Weekly* no1482/1483 p48 S 22 2017

Modern Family *Entertainment Weekly* no1482/1483 p75 S 22 2017

Mr. Robot color *Entertainment Weekly* no1482/1483 p77 S 22 2017

NO. 13 Thor color *Entertainment Weekly* no1436/1437 p56 O 21 2016

NO. 17 Green Lantern color *Entertainment Weekly* no1436/1437 p59 O 21 2016

NO. 32 HELLBOY color *Entertainment Weekly* no1436/1437 p69 O 21 2016

NO. 43 Beast color *Entertainment Weekly* no1436/1437 p75 O 21

Vision v81 no9 p62 N 2016

Home Bank (Company)
ADVERTISING RESOURCE DIRECTORY *New Orleans Homes & Lifestyles* v20 no2 p100 Spr 2017

Home Box Office Inc.
20. Watch Beware the Slenderman *New York* p87 F 9 2017
Difficult Pontiff M. Z. SEITZ img *New York* p82 F 9 2017
Does HBO's Future Include a Game of Thrones Spin-off? J. Hibberd color *Entertainment Weekly* no1435 p9 O 14 2016
What Sesame Street's Move to HBO Says About the Media Business J. Balis *Harvard Business Review Digital Articles* p2 Ag 20 2015

Home Capital Group Inc.
BANKING ON THE BUBBLE J. CASTALDO color *Maclean's* p44 Je 2017
Buffett's Bet on Canadian Real Estate N. Buhayar and K. Dmitrieva bw *Bloomberg Businessweek* no4529 p27 Jl 3 2017
Canadian Finance Gets Less Boring. That's Bad K. Chipman graph *Bloomberg Businessweek* no4521 p41 My 8 2017

Home care services
Should you try a home genetic test kit? *Harvard Health Letter* v42 no10 p4 Ag 2017
Virtual doctor visits: A new kind of house call *Harvard Health Letter* v41 no12 p4 O 2016
A Vision for "Hospital at Home" Programs B. Leff *Harvard Business Review Digital Articles* p2 D 21 2015

Home care services—Management
Yes, I Make House Calls: The once-antiquated practice of doctors' home visits is making a comeback--and saving states money M. Quinn *Governing* v30 no12 p48 S 2017

Home care services—United States
Right at Home: Seniors want doctors to come to them. States are still working out how to pay for it M. Quinn *Governing* v30 no10 p18 Jl 2017

Home Depot Inc.
Congratulations on Your New Job! B. HOROVITZ color *AARP: The Magazine* v59 no2A p33 F/Mr 2016
Good times, beautifully organized J. Jones color *Redbook* p18 Je 2017
Shopping with Apps M. ANTONOFF color *Sound & Vision* v82 no2 p24 F/Mr 2017
Why Data Breaches Don't Hurt Stock Prices E. Kvochko and R. Pant *Harvard Business Review Digital Articles* p2 Mr 31 2015

Home economics
See also
　　Cost & standard of living
　　Food
　　Grocery shopping
　　Housekeeping
　　Interior decoration
　　Sewing
Martha's Month *Martha Stewart Living* no268 p2 O 2016
The O List: ENTERTAINING SPECIAL color *O, The Oprah Magazine* p54 N 2017

Home entertainment industry—News briefs
MQA Is Coming to NAD's M. Fleischmann and C. Crowley color *Sound & Vision* v81 no9 p17 N 2016

Home entertainment systems
See also
　　Video game consoles
March 15, 1967: Tuned In to the Future A. BROWN bw color *Forbes* v198 no9 p26 D 30 2016

Home entertainment systems—Evaluation
Live Out Loud L. D. JOHNSON color *Ebony* v72 no8 p52 Je 2017

Home environment
Animal House color *Parents* v92 no7 p98 Jl 2017
big ideas for small spaces L. FENTON color *Parents* v92 no3 p86 Mr 2017
get back on the mat H. Dowdle color *Yoga Journal* p8 2017 Special Issue
A home practice for Better balance D. Burkman color *Yoga Journal* p57 2017 Special Issue
A home practice for open, happy hips V. Marino color *Yoga Journal* p73 2017 SpecialIssue
A home practice to get grounded and stable D. Burkman color *Yoga Journal* p93 2017 SpecialIssue

Home environment—Psychological aspects
if you ask me... S. JAMES *Parents* v91 no9 p132 S 2016

Home equity conversion
The best of both worlds B. BORZYKOWSKI color *Maclean's* v130 no2 p50 Mr 2017

Home field advantage (Sports)
All-Star Struck M. Rosenberg color *Sports Illustrated* v125 no19 p122 D 12 2016

Home fire prevention
Fire alarm J. GEDDES color *Maclean's* v130 no4 p34 My 2017

Home furnishings
See also
　　Candlesticks
　　Carpets
　　Clocks & watches
　　Furniture
　　Glassware
　　Lamps
　　Mirrors
　　Screens (Furniture)
ASK OLD HOUSE JOURNAL P. Poore color *Old House Journal* v45 no1 p60 F 2017
An Aspirational Ensemble color *Old House Journal* v45 no1 p72 F 2017
BACK AT THE RANCH L. CUTRONE color *Louisiana Life* v37 no4 p28 Mr/Ap 2017
A Battle Royal K. RENDA and B. REYNAERT color *House Beautiful* v159 no7 p34 S 2017
bolds & brights color *House Beautiful* v159 no7 p77 S 2017
BUTTER color *Good Housekeeping* v265 no2 p56B Ag 2017
BY SIMPLICITY SAVED R. DeCotis bw color *Old House Journal* v45 no1 p32 F 2017
CABBAGETOWN CHARACTER L. MOWRY *Atlanta* v56 no9 p48 Ja 2017
CAMERA READY L. O'KEEFFE *Better Homes & Gardens* v94 no11 pN1 N 2016
COLOR OUTSIDE THE LINES L. M. Labong color *Sunset* v239 no4 p36 O 2017
creative haven A. PEASLEY bw color *Architectural Digest* v74 no2 p100 F 2017
design ideas that don't fade P. POORE color *Old House Journal* v44 p10 2016 Design Center source Book
design ideas that don't fade P. POORE *Design Center Sourcebook* p10 2016
DESIGNING WOMAN A. PANOS color *Better Homes & Gardens* v95 no7 p54 Jl 2017
DIY DRAMA J. GARLOCK color *Better Homes & Gardens* v95 no7 p31 Jl 2017
DOCTOR'S ORDER B. WARREN color *New Orleans Magazine* v51 no1 p60 N 2016
everyday adventure J. GARLOCK *Better Homes & Gardens* v94 no11 p36 N 2016
From Our Editor S. Donelson color *House Beautiful* v159 no3 p8 Ap 2017
From Our Editor S. Donelson color *House Beautiful* v159 no9 p6 N 2017
GAME ON K. K. CONDON color *Better Homes & Gardens* v95 no7 p134 Jl 2017
Get Organized in 10 minutes [Cover story] color *Good Housekeeping* v265 no2 p41 Ag 2017
GOLDEN YELLOW M. B. EYERS color *Better Homes & Gardens* v95 no7 p24 Jl 2017
Hanging Heavy Ceiling Fixtures R. Tschoepe cartoon *Old House Journal* v45 no1 p58 F 2017
HEADS UP A. MAZE color *Better Homes & Gardens* v95 no7 p41 Jl 2017
I DID IT! K. SELZER color *Better Homes & Gardens* v95 no7 p72 Jl 2017
june & DECEMBER M. POLLITT color *Better Homes & Gardens* v95 no7 p60 Jl 2017
Let it Glow color *Log Home Living* v34 no9 p54 D 2017
A LITTLE BIT COUNTRY A. CHANTIM color *Good Housekeeping* v265 no2 p46 Ag 2017
LIVING THE LOWE LIFE S. WUNDERLICH *Better Homes & Gardens* v94 no11 p128 N 2016
Make It New J. Silverstein *New York Times Magazine* p22 N 13

2016

MAKING THE CUT L. HEDRICK color *Better Homes & Gardens* v95 no11 p56 N 2017

NORTHERN LIGHT R. BARRENECHE color *Architectural Digest* v74 no2 p78 F 2017

PHOTO FINISH M. RUS color *Architectural Digest* v74 no2 p96 F 2017

A PLACE TO BE S. ORR *Better Homes & Gardens* v95 no8 p6 Ag 2017

Playing with Scale K. L. Beamon *Architectural Record* v205 no9 p153 S 2017

Presidential appointments chart color *Magazine Antiques* v184 no2 p74 Mr/Ap 2017

PROVING GROUND D. SCHWARTZ color *Better Homes & Gardens* v95 no6 p126 Je 2017

Q&A WITH JULIAN PASTRANA *Texas Monthly* v45 no4 p30 Ap 2017

A REFINED AFFAIR F. SCHULTZ color *House Beautiful* v159 no3 p112 Ap 2017

Resources *Old House Journal* v45 no1 p87 F 2017

Soothing Sleep Solutions color *Good Housekeeping* v265 no2 p90 Ag 2017

the storyteller P. P. FISCHER color *Better Homes & Gardens* v95 no8 p132 Ag 2017

Sumptuous 19th-century Revival Kitchen P. Poore color *Old House Journal* v45 no2 p74 Ap 2017

vintage couture S. WUNDERLICH color *Better Homes & Gardens* v95 no7 p64 Jl 2017

A WARM WELCOME J. LEWIS color *House Beautiful* v159 no3 p104 Ap 2017

Wash and Wow C. SWANSON color *House Beautiful* v159 no7 p69 S 2017

Where do ideas come from? P. POORE bw cartoon color *Old House Journal* v45 no1 p64 F 2017

zen spirit D. BLASBERG color *Architectural Digest* v74 no2 p86 F 2017

Home furnishings design & construction
    See also
    Lamp design & construction

Werk It P. BOWIE LARSON color *Architectural Digest* v74 no10 p42 O 1 2017

Home furnishings industry

4 pretty, mini updates for your home color *Redbook* p136 F 2017

Made to Measure J. J. CONDON color *House Beautiful* v159 no7 p51 S 2017

RESOURCES *New Orleans Homes & Lifestyles* v20 no2 p102 Spr 2017

Resources *Old House Journal* v45 no1 p87 F 2017

Home furnishings industry—Equipment & supplies

HOME UNDER $150 color *Redbook* p118 F 2017

The ultimate kid-room cleanup J. Jones color *Redbook* p40 F 2017

Home furnishings industry—History

Totally Radical H. MARTIN color *Architectural Digest* v74 no10 p52 O 1 2017

Home furnishings stores

BIG HELP FOR YOUR SMALL SPACE J. Sergent *Washingtonian Magazine* v52 no6 p161 Mr 2017

Home furnishings stores—Evaluation

Moving the Merchandise B. PAYNTER *Treasures* v6 no5 p12 Ap/My 2017

NAUTI-CAL BY NATURE *Sea Magazine* v109 no1 pCA-1 Ja 2017

Home furnishings—Equipment & supplies

CASUAL FRIDAYS P. P. FISCHER color *Better Homes & Gardens* v95 no6 p138 Je 2017

i did it! K. SELZER color *Better Homes & Gardens* v95 no6 p66 Je 2017

Island Girl T. Anderson and K. O'SHEA-EVANS color *House Beautiful* v159 no4 p43 My 2017

OBSESSED WITH NAUTICAL A. MAZE color *Better Homes & Gardens* v95 no7 p14 Jl 2017

PARTY ON... THE CHEAP A. MAZE and D. DICKINSON color *Better Homes & Gardens* v95 no6 p46 Je 2017

PARTY station A. PANOS color *Better Homes & Gardens* v95 no6 p94 Je 2017

RHAPSODY IN BLUE AND WHITE color *House Beautiful* v158

no9 p128 N 2016

STAIR RODS & DUST CORNERS color *Old House Journal* v45 no1 p78 F 2017

WITH an ARTIST'S EYE A. PANOS color *Better Homes & Gardens* v95 no4 p120 Ap 2017

Home furnishings—Evaluation

15 Reasons to Become a Morning Person J. J. CONDON color *House Beautiful* v159 no7 p48 S 2017

15 WAYS TO DO PEACOCK color *Good Housekeeping* v264 no3 p52D Mr 2017

17 WAYS TO ADD COLOR TO EVERY ROOM A. LONGOBUCCO color *Good Housekeeping* v264 no4 p50 Ap 2017

BAR CART color *Good Housekeeping* v264 no4 p47 Ap 2017

BAYOU BEAUTY color *House Beautiful* v159 no8 p122 O 2017

The Belle Is Back K. O'SHEA-EVANS color *House Beautiful* v159 no8 p53 O 2017

THE BIG MIX-UP [Cover story] H. BROWN color *House Beautiful* v159 no8 p57 O 2017

Côte d'Azur color *House Beautiful* v159 no3 p23 Ap 2017

ESCAPE FROM L.A K. P. Badal color *Sunset* v239 no3 p72 S 2017

Fig Purple K. RENDA and B. REYNAERT color *House Beautiful* v159 no7 p29 S 2017

Homecoming Season K. O'SHEA-EVANS and J. J. CONDON color *House Beautiful* v159 no7 p41 S 2017

HOMESPUN RUSTIC color *House Beautiful* v159 no8 p120 O 2017

HOME UNDER $150 color *Redbook* p118 F 2017

HOW TO BUILD CHARACTER E. Moody color *Martha Stewart Living* p76 My 2017

In This Luxe Kitchen, Purple Reigns K. RENDA and B. REYNAERT color *House Beautiful* v159 no7 p38 S 2017

AN INVITING POOL PAVILION M. Braff and K. O'SHEA-EVANS color *House Beautiful* v159 no4 p60 My 2017

MOVE THE PARTY OUTSIDE color *House Beautiful* v159 no4 p74 My 2017

The New Classics color *House Beautiful* v159 no3 p31 Ap 2017

Pink Grapefruit K. RENDA color *House Beautiful* v159 no2 p23 Mr 2017

PORCH PREP B. THORKELSON color *Better Homes & Gardens* v95 no5 p54 My 2017

a pretty SMART HOME C. Knobloch color *Good Housekeeping* v265 no4 p54 O 2017

Roped In H. BROWN color *House Beautiful* v159 no3 p38 Ap 2017

SERVING UP SIMPLICITY H. BROWN and K. O'SHEA-EVANS color *House Beautiful* v159 no7 p58 S 2017

Setting the Rustic Table color *Log Home Living* v33 no9 p40 D 2016

shopping secrets OF THE PROS K. O'SHEA-EVANS and H. BROWN color *House Beautiful* v159 no3 p46 Ap 2017

TROPICAL BRUNCH K. O'SHEA-EVANS color *House Beautiful* v159 no4 p54 My 2017

True Colorist K. O'SHEA-EVANS color *House Beautiful* v159 no7 p55 S 2017

The ultimate kid-room cleanup J. Jones color *Redbook* p40 F 2017

WHAT WILL YOU CREATE? color *House Beautiful* v159 no7 p1 S 2017

Home furnishings—Maintenance & repair

You Must Remember This B. HOWARD color *AARP: The Magazine* v59 no5A p24 Ag/S 2016

Home health aides

The Home Health Aide E. Craig *New York Times Magazine* p38 F 26 2017

How to Hire In-Home Help D. Rosato *Consumer Reports* v82 no12 p50 D 2017

Home improvement television programs

HOME IMPROVEMENT? J. GREEN *Atlanta* v57 no1 p91 My 2017

Home Is Where The Heart (of Cable) Is G. Smith color diag *Bloomberg Businessweek* no4506 p18 Ja 9 2017

NaILed IT J. Vrabel *Indianapolis Monthly* p70 F 2017

Home inspection services

Buy Today, Take a Close Look Tomorrow K. Chipman color *Bloomberg Businessweek* no4518 p39 Ap 10 2017

Home invasion

NIGHTMARE IN MCLEAN J. FAGONE *Washingtonian Magazine* v52 no1 p66 O 2016

Home labor
See also
Telecommuting

5 Ways to Work from Home More Effectively C. O'Hara *Harvard Business Review Digital Articles* p2 O 2 2014

Hire the Best People, and Let Them Work from Wherever They Are C. Frangos *Harvard Business Review Digital Articles* p2 F 8 2016

How to Work from Home When You Have Kids D. Wademan Dowling *Harvard Business Review Digital Articles* p2 S 14 2017

Why Remote Work Thrives in Some Companies and Fails in Others S. Graber *Harvard Business Review Digital Articles* p2 Mr 20 2015

A Working from Home Experiment Shows High Performers Like It Better N. Bloom and J. Roberts *Harvard Business Review Digital Articles* p2 Ja 23 2015

Home movies
Hoover Family Films Are Likely First White House Color Movies *Prologue* v49 no2 p68 Summ 2017

Home offices
THE CORPORATE BEDROOM P. Clark color *Bloomberg Businessweek* no4503 p74 D 12 2016

Home Sweet Home Office T. Bufete color graph il *Consumer Reports* v82 no9 p8 S 2017

WORK THE ROOM J. TUNG *Martha Stewart Living* no267 p29 S 2016

Home offices—Design & construction
LIGHT WORK L. HOWARD *Better Homes & Gardens* v95 no1 pN2 Ja 2017

Home ownership
Cost-effective OWNERSHIP S. FREED color *Cabin Living* p32 Ja/F 2017

In Our Cities K. H. TAYLOR and L. CROSS bw color *Ebony* v72 no6 p32 Ap/My 2017

OF MANY THINGS K. WEBER *America* v215 no16 p2 N 21 2016

Rental Breakdown J. LORINC color *Walrus* v14 no7 p16 S 2017

What You Don't Know About Home Insurance J. Blyskal chart il *Consumer Reports* v82 no8 p36 Ag 2017

Home ownership—United States
Moving First-Time Buyers Off the Fence: Solving the Millennial Homebuyer Puzzle with Proven Online Solutions and Partnerships D. Dylla and D. Caldwell-Tautges *Bridges (Federal Reserve Bank of St. Louis)* p6 Summ 2016

Home prices
200,000 ALCOHOLICS CAN'T BE WRONG P. BAGGE cartoon *Reason* v48 no10 p32 Mr 2017

2016: United States *Lapham's Quarterly* v10 no1 p23 Wint 2017

The Beckers Make Their Move P. M. ESSWEIN color *Kiplinger's Personal Finance* v70 no12 p72 D 2016

EDGEWATER'S LUXE BOOM M. LAWLER color *Chicago* v66 no7 p16 Jl 2017

Evicted M. Moos and S. Hertel color *Alternatives Journal (A.J) - Canada's Environmental Voice* v42 no2 p16 2016

GONE BABY GONE R. MONROE color *New Republic* v248 no10 p34 O 2017

Home Buying Across America D. Johnson color *Time* v189 no21 p11 Je 5 2017

Home In the Range M. SEGAL color *Los Angeles Magazine* v62 no10 p10 O 2017

HOME PRICES RETURN TO PRE-CRASH LEVELS K. Close color *Money* v46 no1 p21 Ja/F 2017

Homes Below $760K C. NICHOLS color *Los Angeles Magazine* v62 no10 p120 O 2017

Homes Under $950K M. GLUCK color *Los Angeles Magazine* v62 no10 p122 O 2017

On the Market G. MONTES color *Architectural Digest* v73 no11 p138 N 2016

POISED FOR PROFIT K. FINN color *New Orleans Magazine* v51 no3 p28 Ja 2017

Preparing to Pop a Bubble, Just in Case S. Kahl and A. Blackman color *Bloomberg Businessweek* no4535 p29 Ag 28 2017

SHELTERED M. MICHELSON bw color *Powder* v45 no4 p102

D 2016

Something New Under the Sun P. Hope color *Consumer Reports* v82 no9 p18 S 2017

An Uneven Market T. Tepper *Money* v46 no9 p45 O 2017

Want the Most for Your Home? Buyers Favor Bold Colors M. C. White color diag *Money* v46 no8 p12 S 2017

When Local Control Backfires S. Beyer *Governing* v30 no4 p24 Ja 2017

WHERE TO BUY NOW C. ZULKEY cartoon chart color graph *Chicago* v66 no4 p77 Ap 2017

Home range (Animal geography)
On the move A. POPE color *Canadian Geographic* v136 no6 p32 D 2016

Home remodeling
See also
Kitchen remodeling

10 Misunderstood Materials color *Old House Journal* v45 no3 p44 My 2017

9 Upgrades That Pay You Back J. F. WASIK color *AARP: The Magazine* v59 no3A p21 Ap/My 2016

THE Arts & Crafts ROOM B. D. Coleman and M. E. Polson color *Arts & Crafts Homes & the Revival* v12 no1 p10 2017 Resouce Guide

ASK ROY R. BERENDSOHN color *Popular Mechanics* p36 F 2017

BETTER WITH AGE K. RENDA color *House Beautiful* v159 no3 p76 Ap 2017

Bungalow More Modern P. Poore color *Old House Journal* v45 no3 p8 My 2017

CAPE CATASTROPHE bw color *Old House Journal* v45 no1 p88 F 2017

The CR Guide to Smarter Remodeling P. Hope chart color il *Consumer Reports* v82 no7 p44 Jl 2017

Design, BUILD & remodel P. Poore color *Arts & Crafts Homes & the Revival* v12 no1 p55 2017 Resouce Guide

DIAMONDS ARE FOREVER F. A. BERNSTEIN color *Architectural Digest* v73 no11 p90 N 2016

Editor's Letter A. ASTLEY color *Architectural Digest* v73 no11 p48 N 2016

EVERYTHING ZEN: A McLean homeowner gets a hidden spot for unwinding J. Sergent *Washingtonian Magazine* v52 no8 p174 My 2017

The Fix is In D. PEAK color *Log Home Living* v34 no7 p6 S 2017

FORM AND FUNCTION J. Sergent *Washingtonian Magazine* v52 no4 p185 Ja 2017

GOTHIC HORROR bw color *Old House Journal* v45 no4 p88 Je 2017

A HOME OF HER OWN M. INGRAM *Virginia Living* v15 no2 p42 F 2017

HOME: REAL ESTATE. DESIGN. NEIGHBORHOODS *Washingtonian Magazine* v52 no11 p141 Ag 2017

home renovation without the hassle K. CHENEY *Parents* v91 no6 p118 Je 2016

A House Full of Memories M. Read color *Southern Living* v52 no2 p98 F 2017

Hudson Valley Rebirth P. POORE color *Old House Journal* v45 no5 p22 Ag 2017

kitchens *Design Center Sourcebook* p16 2017

LAKEFRONT LEGACY L. Cutrone color *Louisiana Life* v37 no6 p20 Jl/Ag 2017

LIVING HISTORY L. Cutrone color *Louisiana Life* v37 no5 p24 My/Je 2017

LUSH LIFE: An English-inspired oasis takes root in Vienna J. Sergent *Washingtonian Magazine* v52 no8 p172 My 2017

Modern Compromise M. k. Quinlan color *Southern Living* v52 no1 p15 Ja 2017

More Than a Revival P. Poore *Arts & Crafts Homes & the Revival* v12 no1 p8 2017 Resouce Guide

NEW CENTURY FOR A WRIGHT ROOF S. Jordan color *Old House Journal* v45 no3 p31 My 2017

Outliers: Is opportunity knocking in the suburbs? P. Reichard *New Orleans Homes & Lifestyles* v20 no3 p94 Summ 2017

Proud To Be a Rancher K. Owen color *Southern Living* v52 no2 p26 F 2017

Remuddling color *Old House Journal* v45 no7 p88 O 2017

Renovations Done Right P. MERTZ ESSWEIN color *Kiplinger's*

Personal Finance v71 no11 p64 N 2017

Righting Wright S. STEPHENS color diag *Architectural Record* v205 no2 p63 F 2017

SHINING STAR P. F. Stahls Jr. color *Louisiana Life* v37 no5 p44 My/Je 2017

Silver Linings B. Fishel color *Log Home Living* v33 no9 p28 D 2016

SOCAL SO COOL C. Hong color *Martha Stewart Living* p88 Mr 2017

TUDOR 101 J. BALL color *Indianapolis Monthly* v42 no2 p32 O 2017

Under Fyne skies C. EDNIE color *House Beautiful* p66 Ag 2017

Well-Aged L. CUTRONE color *Louisiana Life* v37 no5 p41 My/Je 2017

A WRIGHT HOUSE IN ROCHESTER M. DeFRANCO color *Old House Journal* v45 no3 p24 My 2017

Home Run Media Group (Company)

Shutting Down Your Business Gracefully A. Blickstein and J. Mullins *Harvard Business Review Digital Articles* p2 Mr 20 2017

Home runs (Baseball)

38,000 CUTS (GIVE OR TAKE) M. McKnight color *Sports Illustrated* v126 no16 p50 Je 5 2017

The Case for ... GIANCARLO STANTON J. Dickey, T. Keith et al color *Sports Illustrated* v127 no7 p30 S 4 2017

HOT | NOT T. Keith color *Sports Illustrated* v126 no13 p19 My 8 2017

TREND SPOTTING J. Sheehan chart color *Sports Illustrated* v126 no16 p44 Je 5 2017

Home runs (Baseball)—History

Catching Trout J. Fuchs and T. Keith color *Sports Illustrated* v127 no1 p26 Jl 3 2017

HOT | NOT T. Keith color *Sports Illustrated* v127 no6 p17 Ag 28 2017

Home sales

Cracking L.A.'s Real Estate Market bw color *Los Angeles Magazine* v62 no10 p118 O 2017

CURVES AHEAD L. MURTHA *Cincinnati Magazine* v50 no2 p34 N 2016

Fix-Ups Buyers Will Love P. M. ESSWEIN chart color *Kiplinger's Personal Finance* v71 no3 p41 Mr 2017

GONE BABY GONE R. MONROE *New Republic* v248 no10 p34 O 2017

GOT CURB APPEAL? bw cartoon *AARP: The Magazine* v60 no3A p8 Ap/My 2017

Historic Bargains color *Old House Journal* v45 no2 p36 Ap 2017

Homes Below $760K C. NICHOLS color *Los Angeles Magazine* v62 no10 p120 O 2017

HOMES by the sea J. DOWLE color *House Beautiful* p62 Ag 2017

HOUSE HUNTERS TRANSNATIONAL J. Levin and S. Treleaven *Harper's Magazine* v334 no2000 p48 Ja 2017

The Housing Crunch Hits the Heartland P. Gopal cartoon *Bloomberg Businessweek* no4516 p36 Mr 27 2017

LIVE LIKE A ROCKEFELLER S. SHARF color *Forbes* v200 no4 p28 O 24 2017

The Most Famous House in New Hampshire color *Yankee* p44 My/Je 2017

OFF THE MARKET!: The nuts and bolts of some of Washington's most expensive residential transactions *Washingtonian Magazine* v52 no8 p195 My 2017

OFF THE MARKET! *Washingtonian Magazine* v52 no4 p195 Ja 2017

OFF THE MARKET! *Washingtonian Magazine* v52 no6 p173 Mr 2017

OFF THE MARKET! *Washingtonian Magazine* v52 no9 p183 Je 2017

The Pride of Shelburne Falls: This village in the Berkshire foothills has lots to be proud of—the famous Bridge of Flowers, for instance. But we recently discovered something else very special there M. Cohn color *Yankee* p40 Jl 2017

REAL ESTATE gallery color *Log Home Living* p118 2018 Annual Buyers Guide

Romantic Revivals color *Old House Journal* v45 no3 p36 My 2017

SHOW HOME T. BRAND *Indianapolis Monthly* v40 no3 p44 N 2016

Home schooling

The Floating Classroom K. Laird color *Sail* v48 no4 p12 Ap 2017

Home security measures

13 Home Security Secrets You Should Know M. CROUCH color *Reader's Digest* v189 no1130 p130 My 2017

Home staging

5 Tips to sell a Super-Pricey House K. OLSEN color *Washingtonian Magazine* v52 no7 p98 Ap 2017

Home theaters—Design & construction

DAILY DOUBLE [Cover story] R. Sabin bw color *Sound & Vision* v82 no3 p34 Ap 2017

Home theaters—Equipment & supplies

Vizio M65-D0 Ultra HD Display A. Griffin color graph *Sound & Vision* v81 no10 p56 D 2016

YOU CAN'T BURY IT IF IT 'S NOT DEAD R. SABIN *Sound & Vision* v81 no9 p8 N 2016

Home theaters—Equipment & supplies—Evaluation

Anthem MRX 1120 A/V Receiver D. Vaughn chart color graph *Sound & Vision* v81 no9 p36 N 2016

Arcam AVR850 A/V Receiver D. Kumin chart color graph *Sound & Vision* v81 no9 p50 N 2016

Denon AVR-X4200W A/V Receiver D. Kumin chart color graph *Sound & Vision* v81 no9 p58 N 2016

HOW TO BUY AN A/V RECEIVER R. Sabin color *Sound & Vision* v81 no9 p32 N 2016

New Gear color *Sound & Vision* v82 no3 p32 Ap 2017

Onkyo TX-RZ610 A/V Receiver M. Fleischmann chart color graph *Sound & Vision* v81 no9 p44 N 2016

Home theaters—Evaluation

The Big Short [Cover story] A. Griffin color graph *Sound & Vision* v82 no8 p36 O 2017

This Just In... M. Fleischmann color *Sound & Vision* v82 no8 p19 O 2017

Homeboy Industries (Company)

Recycling And Rehab J. HERBST *Los Angeles Magazine* v62 no6 p15 Je 2017

Homecoming celebrations

HOME AGAIN S. ONEY *Atlanta* v56 no8 p136 D 2016

Homecoming King (Poem)

c . 270 BC: Chen Song Yu *Lapham's Quarterly* v10 no1 p61 Wint 2017

Homecoming queens

Crowned Beauties P. Guglielmetti color *Southern Living* v52 no11 p61 N 2017

Homeland (TV program)

A Homeland Death in the Line of Duty J. Hibberd color *Entertainment Weekly* no1462 p16 Ap 21 2017

Homeland I. Rudolph *TV Guide* v65 no11 p42 Mr 6 2017

Homeland I. Rudolph *TV Guide* v65 no2 p24 Ja 2 2017

Homeland J. Jensen color *Entertainment Weekly* no1449 p48 Ja 20 2017

Homeless children

RACHEL BROSNAHAN S. Pulia color *InStyle* v23 no13 p128 D 2016

Homeless children—Education

Educating Homeless Kids in New York City R. Nathanson color *Progressive* v81 no4 p38 Ap/My 2017

Under the Law J. Underwood color *Phi Delta Kappan* v98 no3 p76 N 2016

Homeless families

How Stable is the Condition of Family Homelessness? A. Donley, D. Crisafi et al chart *Society* v54 no1 p46 F 2017

Homeless persons

See also

    Homeless families

    Homeless students

A City On the Move M. SEGAL *Los Angeles Magazine* v62 no7 p10 Jl 2017

The Gratitude Meter Z. Donaldson color *O, The Oprah Magazine* p24 My 2017

Hallelujah, I'm a Bum bw *Weekly Standard* v22 no21 p2 F 6 2017

Innovation Labs: Opportunities to Share Ideas and Solutions S. ECKELBERRY *Parks & Recreation* v52 no3 p8 Mr 2017

you may be right L. Miller, J. Morrill et al color *U.S. Catholic* v81 no11 p5 N 2016

Homeless persons—California
Last Look E. Daigneau *Governing* v30 no2 p64 N 2016

Homeless persons—Employment
BAKE TO THE FUTURE E. O'NEILL *Missouri Life* v43 no7 p46 D 2016/Ja 2017

Homeless persons—Housing
Students Develop Modular Homeless Shelters for L.A J. ZARA color *Architectural Record* v205 no2 p24 F 2017

Homeless persons—Services for
Impacting Homelessness in Missouri A. Murphy *Bridges (Federal Reserve Bank of St. Louis)* p12 Summ 2016
A Plot To Feed The Homeless M. MACVEAN *Los Angeles Magazine* p30 D 2016

Homeless persons—United States
Denver's Crackdown on Being Homeless R. Nathanson color *Progressive* v81 no7 p30 O/N 2017
How Stable is the Condition of Family Homelessness? A. Donley, D. Crisafi et al chart *Society* v54 no1 p46 F 2017

Homeless students
Street matriculation: Chicago student finds a way out of homelessness J. Valente color *America* v216 no5 p15 Mr 6 2017

Homeless youth
See also
LGBT homeless youth
THIS NEW HOUSE color *O, The Oprah Magazine* p114 N 2017

Homelessness
The Plot To End Homelessness J. HERBST *Los Angeles Magazine* p22 My 2017
Two Views of Homelessness C. Bonanos img *New York* v50 no6 p8 Mr 20 2017

Homelessness—New York (State)
Record Homelessness Hits a High Rent City K. CLARKE *America* v215 no19 p12 D 19 2016

Homelessness—Prevention
New York Spends $1.2 Billion a Year on Homelessness And yet the problem is only getting worse D. GIBSON and G. Cohn img *New York* v50 no6 p32 Mr 20 2017

Homelessness—United States
New York Spends $1.2 Billion a Year on Homelessness And yet the problem is only getting worse D. GIBSON and G. Cohn img *New York* v50 no6 p32 Mr 20 2017

Homemakers—Government policy
Let Us Now Praise Homemakers R. STEIN bw *National Review* v69 no2 p18 F 6 2017

Homeopathic pharmacy
HOMEOPATHIC STRESS RELIEF I. Eliaz *Better Nutrition* v79 no9 p42 S 2017
Post-Traumatic Stress A. CONSTANTINIDES color *Better Nutrition* v79 no3 p32 Mr 2017

Homeopathic pharmacy—Law & legislation
FTC Will Regulate Marketing of Homeopathic Drugs R. A. Lindsay *Skeptical Inquirer* v41 no2 p6 Mr/Ap 2017

Homeopathic pharmacy—Therapeutic use
Natural Remedies for Cold Sores M. STENGLER color *Better Nutrition* v79 no1 p30 Ja 2017
Prevent, Treat, & Recover: A FLU GUIDE L. TURNER color *Better Nutrition* v79 no1 p44 Ja 2017

Homeopathy
See also
Homeopathic pharmacy
5 Top Homeopathic Cold Remedies A. Constantinides color *Amazing Wellness* v9 no1 p72 Wint 2017
Are These Remedies Safe? [Cover story] J. COOK color *Prevention* v69 no6 p74 Je 2017
EASE ECZEMA A. Constantinides color *Amazing Wellness* v8 no6 p38 Early Winter2016
NATURAL REMEDIES FOR COLD SORES M. Stengler color *Amazing Wellness* v9 no3 p32 EarlySumm 2017

Homeostasis
An adipo-biliary-uridine axis that regulates energy homeostasis Y. Deng, Z. V. Wang et al diag *Science* v355 no6330 p1173 Mr 17 2017
Mechanistic basis for a molecular triage reaction S. Shao, M. C. Rodrigo-Brenni et al bibl color graph *Science* v355 no6322 p298 Ja 20 2017
Rest and renew color *Yoga Journal* no291 p80 My 2017

Homeowners
Feeling Trapped? How to Sell in This Tricky Market C. Fried and T. Tepper color diag *Money* v46 no9 p43 O 2017
SIMPLY PERFECT S. SMITH color *House Beautiful* p122 Ag 2017
TOUCH WOOD S. SMITH color *House Beautiful* p128 Ag 2017
Under the Influence P. Poore *Old House Journal* v45 no6 p8 S 2017

Homeowners' associations
Not In Their Backyard G. KAHN *Los Angeles Magazine* p74 F 2017

Homeowners insurance
Bundled Policies Can Save You a Lot ... Sometimes M. C. White color *Money* v45 no10 p20 N 2016

Homeowners insurance policies
What You Don't Know About Home Insurance J. Blyskal chart il *Consumer Reports* v82 no8 p36 Ag 2017

Homeowners insurance—Massachusetts
HOUSE RULES: M. Desmond *New York Times Magazine* p48 My 14 2017

Homeowners—Awards
BEST of HOME WINNERS *New Orleans Homes & Lifestyles* v20 no3 p76 Summ 2017

Homeowners—Services for
Divide Your Home S. SHARF color *Forbes* v199 no7 p136 Je 29 2017

Homeowners—Social aspects
HOUSE RULES: M. Desmond *New York Times Magazine* p48 My 14 2017

Home Place, The (Theatrical production)
THE THEATRE cartoon *New Yorker* v93 no30 p9 O 2 2017

Homer, fl. ca. 900 B.C.-ca. 801 B.C.
An Iliad Odyssey J. QUEENAN color *Weekly Standard* v22 no17 p35 Ja 2 2017

Homer, Winslow, 1836-1910
Autumn Trees color *Magazine Antiques* v183 no6 p27 N/D 2016
A Masterpiece by the Ocean S. Jermanok *Yankee* p96 Mr 2017

Home runs (Baseball)—Charts, diagrams, etc.
Smashing Debuts A. McKiernan and T. Keith chart color *Sports Illustrated* v127 no9 p14 S 25 2017

HOMES, A. M.
TAKE ME OUT TO THE BALLROOM color *Vanity Fair* v59 no4 p191 Mr 2017

Homesites
Get the Perfect Getaway! D. Peak color diag *Log Home Living* v34 no3 p62 Ap 2017

Homework
better S. LIAO color *Better Homes & Gardens* v95 no9 p142 S 2017
Is Home work Out of Control? *Scholastic Choices* v32 no4 p2 Ja 2017
THE REAL SUMMER EXPERIENCE: Going beyond the vacation essay to foster deeper school-community relationships M. P. Ghiso and G. Campano *Literacy Today (2411-7862)* v35 no1 p8 Jl/Ag 2017

Homicide
See also
Murder
Suicide
A FORCE FOR GOOD D. Kennedy *O, The Oprah Magazine* p142 My 2017
NOR PRAYERS FOR MERCY R. Selcer *Military History* v33 no5 p23 Ja 2017

Homicide investigation
See also
Murder investigation
Serial murder investigation

Homicide rates
Murder No. 605 A. HUTCHINS color graph *Maclean's* v129 no45 p34 N 14 2016

Homicide—British Columbia—Victoria
Forced Confessions B. TRAVERS color *Walrus* v14 no4 p42 My 2017

Homicide—Canada
Canada's unspoken crisis S. GILMORE color graph map *Maclean's* v129 no50 p12 D 19 2016

Homicide—Lawsuits & claims
The Girl from Plainville J. Barron bw color *Esquire* p100 O 2017
Wrong TURN L. Rice color *Entertainment Weekly* no1474/1475 p86 Jl 21-28 2017
Hominids
See also
    Gorilla (Genus)
    Human beings
    Orangutans
Apes know what others believe F. B. M. de Waal bibl color *Science* v354 no6308 p39 O 7 2016
Great apes anticipate that other individuals will act according to false beliefs C. Krupenye, Fumihiro Kano et al bibl chart diag graph *Science* v354 no6308 p110 O 7 2016
Lucy had taller kin, footprints suggest B. BOWER color *Science News* v191 no1 p8 Ja 21 2017
Monkey flakes resemble hominid tools B. BOWER color *Science News* v190 no11 p16 N 26 2016
More Hobbitses, Precious! G. TARLACH color *Discover* v38 no1 p25 Ja/F 2017
NOT OUR KIND N. HELLER cartoon *New Yorker* v92 no39 p87 N 28 2016
Very Distant Relative N. Wilson color *Natural History* v125 no7 p8 Jl/Ag 2017
THE WANDERERS A. Gibbons bw color map *Science* v354 no6315 p958 N 25 2016
Homma, Kaori
Fore Shadowing bw *Christian Century* v133 no24 p47 N 23 2016
Homme, Joshua
King of the Stone Age B. HIATT color *Rolling Stone* no1295 p20 S 7 2017
QUEENS OF THE STONE AGE'S JOSHUA HOMME E. R. Brown color *Entertainment Weekly* no1480 p48 S 1 2017
Homo naledi
Homo Naledi Likely Coexisted With Humans J. Kluger color *Time* v189 no19 p13 My 22 2017
Homo naledi's age surprises scientists B. BOWER color *Science News* v191 no11 p6 Je 10 2017
Our Cousin Neo K. Wong color *Scientific American* v317 no2 p46 Ag 2017
Homo naledi—Anatomy
Chipped teeth hint at Homo naledi diet B. BOWER color graph *Science News* v192 no4 p12 S 16 2017
Homola, P.
Observation of a large-scale anisotropy in the arrival directions of cosmic rays above 8×1018 eV *Science* v357 no6357 p1266 S 22 2017
Homophobia
THE BIGGEST HOMOPHOBES: THE LGBT RIGHTS MOVEMENT HAS HAD ITS SHARE OF VILLAINS L. GRINDLEY, T. RING et al color *Advocate* no1091 p102 Je/Jl 2017
FAMILY VALUES M. Gessen *Harper's Magazine* v334 no2002 p35 Mr 2017
Homosexuality & politics
The Tories need to go gay S. GILMORE color *Maclean's* v130 no7 p10 Ag 2017
Homosexuality—China
NUMBER CRUNCH: QUEER CHINA bw color *Advocate* no1089 p28 F/Mr 2017
Homosexuality—Religious aspects—Evangelical churches
Evangelically liberal J. Byassee color *Christian Century* v133 no23 p26 N 9 2016
Homosexuality—Religious aspects—Methodism
The Methodists after unity G. J. MacDonald color *Christian Century* v133 no24 p28 N 23 2016
HONACHEFSKY, NICK
THE ART OF THE EEL color *Outdoor Life* v224 no4 p66 My 2017
DRONE ATTACK color *Outdoor Life* v224 no7 p58 S 2017
THE RUN color *Outdoor Life* v224 no8 p65 O 2017
Honami Sato
The formation of peak rings in large impact craters bibl color graph *Science* v354 no6314 p878 N 18 2016
Honda Accord automobile
2018 Honda Accord A. Priddle color *Motor Trend* v69 no10 p20 O 2017

Honda Accord automobile—Evaluation
2017 BEST NEW CAR AWARDS cartoon color *Good Housekeeping* v264 no2 p83 F 2017
CAN THIS CAR SAVE THE SEDAN? [Cover story] T. Quiroga color diag *Car & Driver* v63 no5 p34 N 2017
Honda Accord chart color *Motor Trend* v69 no1 p125 Ja 2017
THE INCUMBENTS D. GRANGER color diag *Car & Driver* v62 no7 p62 Ja 2017
The Smart Appliance E. Alterman color graph *Car & Driver* v62 no7 p76 Ja 2017
What Do We Mean by Best? J. Sabatini color *Car & Driver* v62 no7 p104 Ja 2017
Honda Aircraft Co. Inc.
FLYING THE HONDAJET color *Flying* v144 no5 p82 My 2017
Honda automobile
See also
    Acura automobile
    Del Sol automobile
    Honda Civic automobile
ALTERNATIVE AVENUES K. Reynolds cartoon chart color graph *Motor Trend* v69 no7 p62 Jl 2017
COMBO PLATE C. Walton chart color *Motor Trend* v69 no9 p88 S 2017
FROM THE ROAD & TRACK ARCHIVES bw color *Road & Track* v69 no2 p94 S 2017
Old Faithful D. VanderWerp color *Car & Driver* v63 no2 p98 Ag 2017
Honda automobile—Evaluation
THE ALCHEMISTS D. ZENLEA color *Road & Track* v69 no3 p86 O 2017
Connected Comfort for the Long Haul color *Consumer Reports* v82 no10 p63 O 2017
FIRST LOOK: HONDA 2017 PIONEER 1000 [Cover story] S. MEAD color *Dirt Sports + Off-Road* v51 no12 p50 D 2017
Leading from the Front C. Walton chart color *Motor Trend* v69 no3 p52 Mr 2017
Honda Civic automobile
CLASH OF CLANS B. MCALEER chart color *Road & Track* v69 no2 p28 S 2017
EDITOR'S LETTER K. WOLFKILL *Road & Track* v69 no2 p20 S 2017
Revolutionary war [Cover story] J. Gall chart color diag *Car & Driver* v63 no2 p36 Ag 2017
Honda Civic automobile—Evaluation
INCREMENTAL BUSINESS OR NEXT BIG THING? C. Walton chart color *Motor Trend* v69 no3 p70 Mr 2017
ONE-CAR WONDERS A. Robinson chart color *Car & Driver* v62 no10 p62 Ap 2017
Wear Your Flare A. Robinson color *Car & Driver* v62 no8 p86 F 2017
Honda Motor Co. Ltd.
2017 HONDA CBR1000RR/SP D. Canet color *Cycle World* v56 no3 p10 Ap 2017
2017 HONDA CRF250L RALLY J. Allen bw color *Cycle World* v56 no6 p16 Jl 2017
2017 HONDA REBEL 300 AND 500 D. Canet color *Cycle World* v56 no5 p20 Je 2017
2018 Honda Accord A. Priddle color *Motor Trend* v69 no10 p20 O 2017
Borrowed Time S. SMITH bw color *Road & Track* v69 no2 p24 S 2017
CAN THIS CAR SAVE THE SEDAN? [Cover story] T. Quiroga color diag *Car & Driver* v63 no5 p34 N 2017
Centurion A. JONES *Boating World* v38 no1 p24 Ja 2017
COMBO PLATE C. Walton chart color *Motor Trend* v69 no9 p88 S 2017
FIRST LOOK: HONDA 2017 PIONEER 1000 [Cover story] S. MEAD color *Dirt Sports + Off-Road* v51 no12 p50 D 2017
Honda Accord chart color *Motor Trend* v69 no1 p125 Ja 2017
Honda Opens Its Doors A. OHNSMAN and J. D. MARKMAN color *Forbes* v199 no2 p46 F 28 2017
Honda Ridgeline chart color *Motor Trend* v69 no1 p85 Ja 2017
INCREMENTAL BUSINESS OR NEXT BIG THING? C. Walton chart color *Motor Trend* v69 no3 p70 Mr 2017
THE LITTLE ADVENTURE B. Adams color *Cycle World* v56 no3 p38 Ap 2017

THE NEW, IMPROVED HYDROGEN CAR! A. George and E. Dyer color diag map *Popular Mechanics* p38 Jl 2017

Old Faithful D. VanderWerp color *Car & Driver* v63 no2 p98 Ag 2017

ONE-CAR WONDERS A. Robinson chart color *Car & Driver* v62 no10 p62 Ap 2017

Wear Your Flare A. Robinson color *Car & Driver* v62 no8 p86 F 2017

Honda motorcycle

2017 HONDA CRF250L RALLY J. Allen bw color *Cycle World* v56 no6 p16 Jl 2017

2017 HONDA REBEL 300 AND 500 D. Canet color *Cycle World* v56 no5 p20 Je 2017

Service R. NIERLICH color *Cycle World* v56 no4 p62 My 2017

TORTURE TEST B. Lutes color *Cycle World* v56 no4 p58 My 2017

Honda motorcycle—Evaluation

2017 HONDA CRF450R B. Lutes color *Cycle World* v56 no1 p12 Ja/F 2017

THE LITTLE ADVENTURE B. Adams color *Cycle World* v56 no3 p38 Ap 2017

THE NORTH RIM Z. Bowman color *Cycle World* v56 no10 p24 N 2017

THINGS COME APART K. Dupzyk color *Popular Mechanics* p24 S 2017

Honda trucks—Evaluation

The Truck YOU Really WANT vs. the Truck You NEED color *Esquire* v166 no4 p80 N 2016

Honda vans—Evaluation

2018 Honda Odyssey E. DYER color *Popular Mechanics* p40 S 2017

Honda CR-V sport utility vehicle

The People's Choice M. Monticello color diag graph *Consumer Reports* v82 no4 p7 Ap 2017

Honda CR-V sport utility vehicle—Awards

HEAD VS. HEART [Cover story] S. Evans chart color *Motor Trend* v69 no8 p38 Ag 2017

Hondo, Med

First-World Problems M. Nelson bw *Film Comment* v53 no5 p11 S/O 2017

Honduras—Politics & government—21st century

Under the Gun J. Gibler *Sierra* v102 no4 p28 Jl/Ag 2017

Honduras—Social conditions

A Dangerous Place for Women: Honduras is an epicenter of violence against women V. MAZATAUD *Ms.* v27 no2 p14 Summ 2017

Honduras—Social conditions—21st century

Under the Gun J. Gibler *Sierra* v102 no4 p28 Jl/Ag 2017

Hone, James

Electron optics with p-n junctions in ballistic graphene bibl graph *Science* v353 no6307 p1522 S 30 2016

Tuning quantum nonlocal effects in graphene plasmonics bw diag *Science* v357 no6347 p187 Jl 14 2017

HONE, JIM

The Effort-Outcomes Relationship in Applied Ecology: Evaluation and Implications *BioScience* v67 no9 p845 S 2017

Honest Abe Log Homes Inc.

Sweet Dreams are Made of This C. Johnson color *Timber Home Living* v27 no5 p58 O 2017

Honest Co.

grime fighter [Cover story] color *Good Housekeeping* v265 no5 p(Sp)61 N 2017

Honest Woman, An (Short story)

An Honest Woman O. Moshfegh cartoon color *New Yorker* v92 no34 p62 O 24 2016

Honesty

The Dark Side of Creativity T. Chamorro-Premuzic *Harvard Business Review Digital Articles* p2 N 24 2015

THE FRAUD WHO ISN'T C. FLORA *Psychology Today* v49 no6 p70 N/D 2016

Is It O.K. to Give Cigarettes To a Homeless Person? K. A. Appiah *New York Times Magazine* p18 O 8 2017

ON FEELING FRAUDULENT *Psychology Today* v49 no6 p4 N/D 2016

The Truth About Lies color *Prevention* v69 no7 p15 Jl 2017

'TRUTH' AND Consequences E. GILBERT color *O, The Oprah*

Magazine p28 Ja 2017

Why Creative People Are More Likely to Be Dishonest L. C. Vincent and M. Kouchaki *Harvard Business Review Digital Articles* p2 N 23 2015

Honesty (Short story)

Zen Master Raven Stories R. A. ROSHI bw *Tricycle: The Buddhist Review* v27 no1 p120 Fall 2017

Honesty, Judith

How to React to Biased Comments at Work *Harvard Business Review Digital Articles* p2 My 3 2017

Honey

BUZZ WORTHY color *Martha Stewart Living* p112 Ap 2017

HOW DO I PREVENT & SURVIVE A HANG OVER L. Krieger color *Harper's Bazaar* no3649 p268 D 2016/Ja 2017

The Last Honey Hunter M. Synnott color map *National Geographic* v232 no1 p80 Jl 2017

MANUKA HONEY V. Tweed color *Amazing Wellness* v8 no6 p24 Early Winter2016

Mixing Bowl color *O, The Oprah Magazine* p120 Ag 2017

Neonicotinoids found in honey globally [Cover story] L. HAMERS *Science News* v192 no7 p16 O 28 2017

STING OPERATION C. Zuckerman color *National Geographic* v231 no6 p152 Je 2017

Honey Ear Trio (Performer)

Swivel P. Margasak color *Downbeat* v83 no11 p52 N 2016

Honeybee behavior

Bees Prefer Country Blossoms to City Blooms *USA Today Magazine* v145 no2865 p6 Je 2017

Honeybees

See also

Honey

BACKUP BEES? C. Zuckerman color *National Geographic* v232 no4 p24 O 2017

Country Lore J. Poindexter, A. Sezak-Blatt et al *Mother Earth News* no280 p85 F/Mr 2017

For the Record color *Time* v189 no20 p4 My 29 2017

Hey Mr. Green! Do alien bees threaten native species? B. Schildgen *Sierra* v101 no5 p14 S/O 2016

How Capitalism Saved the Bees [Cover story] S. REGAN color graph *Reason* v49 no4 p62 Ag/S 2017

Play hide-and-seek A. WUNDERMAN diag *Backpacker* p10 N 2017

The Pollinator BLAME GAME K. Birchmier *Successful Farming* v114 no10 p36 O 2016

Honeycomb Studio (Company)

Splendid Setting B. RILEY *Atlanta* v56 no9 p44 Ja 2017

Honeyman, Gail

Eleanor Oliphant Is Completely Fine color *Publishers Weekly* v264 no31 p82 Jl 31 2017

Honeymoons

Hillingdon Street Blues E. S. MACLEAN *Weekly Standard* v22 no5 p5 O 10 2016

home to roost A. NICHOLS color map *Cabin Living* p19 Je 2017

Honey—Sales & prices

Buzz Feud J. SMITH cartoon *Walrus* v13 no9 p19 N 2016

Honey—Therapeutic use

Buzzworthy: Honey color *Health* v31 no2 p16 Mr 2017

Fun Party Snacks B. Lipton color *Health* v31 no2 p132 Mr 2017

A Natural Remedy for Cuts and Scrapes L. Dog color *Prevention* v69 no4 p28 Ap 2017

Shiny, Healthy Hair for Less L. Desantis color *Health* v31 no2 p33 Mr 2017

Honeywell Process Solutions (Company)

THE FUTURE OF PROFITS, TODAY R. Geraci color *Bloomberg Businessweek* no4502 p2 D 5 2016

Hong, Carrie

Dollar So Ripped, It Might Actually Rip color *Bloomberg Businessweek* no4506 p12 Ja 9 2017

HONG, CATHERINE

COOKING INDIAN WITH A MASTER color *Martha Stewart Living* p96 Mr 2017

Dog Day Doodles: Innovative activity books take doodlers and puzzle lovers under the sea, around the world and into the past *New York Times Book Review* p40 Je 4 2017

EASTER FEAST color *Martha Stewart Living* p100 Ap 2017

Frankly Speaking bw color *Architectural Digest* v74 no1 p40 Ja

2017

IN LIVING COLOR cartoon color *Martha Stewart Living* no275 p104 Je 2017

THE JOY OF JUGGLING color *Martha Stewart Living* p98 S 2017

ORNAMENTAL *Martha Stewart Living* no270 p122 D 2016

A PLACE IN TIME *Martha Stewart Living* no268 p130 O 2016

SOCAL SO COOL color *Martha Stewart Living* p88 Mr 2017

Summer Y.A.: Escape Artists *New York Times Book Review* p18 Jl 16 2017

WEAVE IT IN color *Martha Stewart Living* p94 Jl/Ag 2017

WITH LOVE AND GRATITUDE *Martha Stewart Living* no269 p98 N 2016

Hong, Cynthia M.

A catalytic fluoride-rebound mechanism for C(sp3)-CF3 bond formation diag *Science* v356 no6344 p1272 Je 23 2017

Hong, Haizheng

The complex effects of ocean acidification on the prominent N2-fixing cyanobacterium Trichodesmium graph *Science* v356 no6337 p527 My 5 2017

Hong, John D.

Restored iron transport by a small molecule promotes absorption and hemoglobinization in animals color graph *Science* v356 no6338 p608 My 12 2017

Hong, Seok-Hyun

Trump Is The Right Leader To Achieve Peace With North Korea *NPQ: New Perspectives Quarterly* v34 no3 p13 Jl 2017

Hong-Bin Yao

Synthetic nacre by predesigned matrix-directed mineralization bibl bw diag graph *Science* v354 no6308 p107 O 7 2016

Hong Fan

Quality management for precision medicine clinical applications: A consensus from the China Precision Medicine Clinical Research and Application Association bibl *Science* v354 no6319 p11 D 23 2016

Hong Hua

Oral precision medicine: Identification of microbes from saliva by mass spectrometry bibl *Science* v354 no6319 p60 D 23 2016

Hong Kong (China)—Description & travel

THE CITY ON THE HARBOR A. Erace color *Fortune* v175 no7 p28 Je 1 2017

Hong Kong (China)—Politics & government—21st century

BAD NEWS color *Maclean's* v129 no46 p9 N 21 2016

HONG LIU

Opportunities and Anxieties for the Chinese Diaspora in Southeast Asia *Current History* v115 no784 p312 N 2016

Hong Young Yan

Research night owls color *Science* v354 no6315 p964 N 25 2016

Hongbo, Wu

A Conference to #SaveOurOcean *UN Chronicle* v54 no1/2 p1 2017

Hongjie Xu

Nuclear power: Deployment speed—Response bibl *Science* v354 no6316 p1113 D 2 2016

Hongjun Song

A nuclease that mediates cell death induced by DNA damage and poly(ADP-ribose) polymerase-1 bw graph *Science* v354 no6308 paad6872-1 O 7 2016

Hong Kong (China)—Politics & government—1997-

Can Xi Pacify a Restless Hong Kong? Ting Shi bw *Bloomberg Businessweek* no4529 p37 Jl 3 2017

Hongoltz-Hetling, Matt

THE MAN WHO WOULD KILL YOUR HOLIDAYS color *Popular Science* v289 no5 p22 S/O 2017

Mod squad cartoon *Popular Science* v289 no4 p42 Jl/Ag 2017

Hongyuan Yuan

Direct and continuous strain control of catalysts with tunable battery electrode materials bibl graph *Science* v354 no6315 p1031 N 25 2016

Honky Chateau (Music)

Essential Elton John R. Sheffield bw color *Rolling Stone* no1283 p52 Mr 23 2017

Honneth, Axel, 1949-

POSITIVE FREEDOM M. JAY color *Nation* v305 no2 p32 Jl 17 2017

Honnold, Alex, 1985-

The Freerider J. LUCAS color *Climbing* no355 p18 Ag 2017

HOT | NOT T. Keith color *Sports Illustrated* v126 no17 p20 Je 19 2017

Honolulu (Hawaii)—Social conditions

Aloha, Poke A. Mason color *Bon Appetit* p89 S 2017

Honor

MICHAEL D. ECHANIS HONORED POSTHUMOUSLY G. Walker color *Black Belt* v55 no5 p12 Ag/S 2017

HONSBERGER, SUE

Living Out Loud: On good food, great reads, and strong women color *O, The Oprah Magazine* p20 S 2017

Honscheid, Janni

Stopover of a Lifetime: Nemberala Beach Resort bw color *Surfer* v57 no11 p35 D 2016

Honsek, S. D.

Gliogenic LTP spreads widely in nociceptive pathways bibl graph *Science* v354 no6316 p1144 D 2 2016

Hoock, Holger

Red, White, Black and Blue: A study of the American Revolution takes violence as its overriding focus J. Kamensky *New York Times Book Review* p27 My 21 2017

Scars of Independence M. W. Robbins *MHQ: Quarterly Journal of Military History* v29 no3 p93 Spr 2017

Hood, Ann

Days of Our Lives *Yankee* v81 no1 p116 Ja/F 2017

Hood, Gavin

EYE IN THE SKY J. Krebs color *Sound & Vision* v81 no9 p71 N 2016

HOOD, JOHN

The Reddening States color *National Review* v68 no22 p37 D 5 2016

Hood, Leroy

'Scientific wellness' study divides researchers R. Cross color *Science* v357 no6349 p345 Jl 28 2017

Hood, Mount (Or.)

THANKS, VOLCANOES K. CORRIGAN color *Climbing* no349 p69 N 2016

Hood, Suzanne Findlen

GROWING INTERESTS cartoon *Magazine Antiques* v184 no1 p118 Ja/F 2017

Hoodies (Sweatshirts)

Hoodie, Yes. Pants, No N. Silverstein and J. Harman color *Glamour* v114 no12 p78 D 2016

Hoodies (Sweatshirts)—Evaluation

The Essential: Raincoat M. M. GOLDSTEIN color *Martha Stewart Living* p52 Ap 2017

GEAR TO TIE DYE FOR P. Bridges color *Snowboarder* v29 no3 p128 N 2016

Labels We Love J. ORTVED bw color *GQ: Gentlemen's Quarterly* v86 no12 p106 D 2016

No Sweat E. Wilson color *InStyle* v24 no3 p146 Mr 2017

PICK OF THE LAYERS [Cover story] L. Jhung color *Runner's World* v52 no1 p62 Ja/F 2017

Twice? Nice! color *Glamour* v115 no5 p52 My 2017

Hoodoo (Cult)

Do Do That Voodoo That You Do So Well color *Weekly Standard* v23 no1 p3 S 11 2017

Hoofs

HOW TO SUPPORT HEALTHY HOOF GROWTH C. Barakat and M. Freckleton color *Equus* no480 p20 S 2017

Hoofs—Care & hygiene

Hoof-Care Help color *Horse & Rider* v56 no10 p40 O 2017

Hoofs—Diseases

Coping with brittle hooves B. A. Connally color *Equus* no478 p73 Jl 2017

Hoofs—Wounds & injuries

A field guide to HOOF CRACKS H. S. Thomas color *Equus* no474 p26 Mr 2017

Hoogland, Keith

The Last Video Chain N. KIRSCH and D. DREMAN color *Forbes* v199 no2 p52 F 28 2017

Hoogland, Sjoerd

Efficient and stable solution-processed planar perovskite solar cells via contact passivation bibl graph *Science* v355 no6326 p722 F 17 2017

Hoogstraten, Charles G.

Fighting through the darkness color *Science* v357 no6350 p522 Ag 4 2017

Hook & Albert (Company)

PIN IT TO WIN IT color *Bloomberg Businessweek* no4508 p58 Ja 23 2017

Hook, Casey

10 UP & COMERS: CASEY HOOK G. Gullickson *Successful Farming* v115 no8 p46 Je/Jl 2017

Hook, Michael

UNSOLICITED BETA color *Climbing* no351 p18 F/Mr 2017

Hookahs

CLEARING THE AIR: Hookah-smoking, motorboating, and immigrants S. Stall *Indianapolis Monthly* v40 no10 p17 Je 2017

Hooker, Jacob, 1980-

Jacob Hooker J. Crelin color *Current Biography* v78 no8 p44 Ag 2017

Hooker, Sascha

WHALE CULTURE color graph *Natural History* v125 no11 p30 N 2017

Hooks

i did it! K. SELZER color *Better Homes & Gardens* v95 no2 p54 F 2016

THE MEAT ROOM M. Pendley color *Field & Stream* v122 no6 p32 N 2017

organize your DROP ZONE A. MAZE color *Better Homes & Gardens* v95 no11 p62 N 2017

HOOKS, CHRISTOPHER

Amphibious Assault *Texas Monthly* v45 no2 p52 F 2017

CHANGING The Conversation *Texas Monthly* v45 no8 p44 Ag 2017

Final CUT: WHEN TEXAS'S FILM INCENTIVES PROGRAM COMES UP FOR RENEWAL, POLITICIANS AND MOVIE BIZZERS GIVE PERFORMANCES THAT MATTHEW MC-CONAUGHEY WOULD ENVY *Texas Monthly* v45 no7 p39 Jl 2017

Is the Best Offense a Good Defense Lawyer? *Texas Monthly* v44 no11 p62 N 2016

Hooks—Evaluation

BH&G throwback 1957 CLOSETS K. K. CONDON color *Better Homes & Gardens* v95 no2 p136 F 2016

Hooley, Joseph

State Street's CEO on Creating Employment for At-Risk Youths color graph img *Harvard Business Review* v95 no3 p41 My/Je 2017

Hoon, Shawn

Preventing mussel adhesion using lubricant-infused materials color diag graph *Science* v357 no6352 p668 Ag 18 2017

Hoon Kim

Formaldehyde stabilization facilitates lignin monomer production during biomass depolymerization bibl diag graph *Science* v354 no6310 p329 O 21 2016

Hoon Sul, Jae

Negative selection in humans and fruit flies involves synergistic epistasis chart graph *Science* v356 no6337 p539 My 5 2017

Hoop Dreams (Film)

Hoop Dreams G. YUE color *Film Comment* v53 no1 p63 Ja/F 2017

Hoop exercises

FOWLER PARK RECREATION CENTER CUMMING 35 MILES NORTH OF ATLANTA J. GREEN *Atlanta* v56 no8 p200 D 2016

Hooper, Dan

POINT-SIZED UNIVERSE? color *Astronomy* v45 no2 p34 F 2017

Hooper, Kay

Wait for Dark *Publishers Weekly* v264 no4 p56 Ja 23 2017

Hooper, Lora V.

The intestinal microbiota regulates body composition through NFIL3 and the circadian clock diag *Science* v357 no6354 p912 S 1 2017

Paneth cells secrete lysozyme via secretory autophagy during bacterial infection of the intestine color diag *Science* v357 no6355 p1047 S 8 2017

Hoostal, Matthew

Neonatal acquisition of Clostridia species protects against colonization by bacterial pathogens diag *Science* v356 no6335 p315

Ap 21 2017

Hootsen, Jan-Albert

As Nafta II begins, Mexico shows cautious optimism color *America* v217 no6 p15 S 18 2017

Bad neighbor policy? Mexico's President Peña Nieto struggles to respond to Trump administration color *America* v216 no8 p16 Ap 17 2017

In Mexico, journalists become targets color *America* v216 no11 p15 My 15 2017

IN SOUTHERN MEXICO, TRACKING THE LEGACY OF BISHOP SAMUEL RUIZ color *America* v217 no4 p18 Ag 21 2017

Is the third time the charm for Mexico's 'eternal candidate'? color *America* v216 no10 p17 My 1 2017

Hoover, Amanda

Germany cracks down on groups accused of recruiting terrorists *Christian Century* v133 no26 p17 D 21 2016

Sanctuary churches, cities may face consequences from federal authorities color *Christian Century* v134 no9 p13 Ap 26 2017

Hoover, David

Fry Away S. Krowiak *Indianapolis Monthly* v40 no10 p39 Je 2017

Hoover, Elizabeth

SOX2 promotes lineage plasticity and antiandrogen resistance in TP53- and RB1-deficient prostate cancer bibl graph *Science* v355 no6320 p1 Ja 6 2017

Hoover, Herbert, 1874-1964

Before CAMP DAVID R. SKLAREW *Washingtonian Magazine* v53 no1 p101 O 2017

A Foretaste of 2018: Hoover fellow David Brady, surveying the political landscape, sees "knife-edge electoral instability" L. Simmons *Hoover Digest: Research & Opinion on Public Policy* no3 p28 Summ 2017

Hoover and the Great Outdoors J. M. Cannon *Hoover Digest: Research & Opinion on Public Policy* no2 p187 Spr 2017

Hoover, Jessica

Ammonia activation at a metal bibl diag *Science* v354 no6313 p707 N 11 2016

Hoover, Joe

CHRISTIAN POETRY VS 'CHRISTIAN POETRY' bw *America* v217 no4 p46 Ag 21 2017

'Music Is Life and Life Is Poetry' il *America* v216 no13 p48 Je 12 2017

Hoover, Lou Henry, 1874-1944

Hoover Family Films Are Likely First White House Color Movies *Prologue* v49 no2 p68 Summ 2017

Hoover, Martha, 1954-

First Things First M. Rubino *Indianapolis Monthly* v40 no7 p14 Mr 2017

Hoover Institution on War, Revolution, & Peace

"A Thousand Things Going Wrong" C. Yip *Hoover Digest: Research & Opinion on Public Policy* no1 p44 Wint 2017

"Growth Is the Problem": Lower tax rates, broaden the base. Such simple changes are all that we need, says Hoover fellow John H. Cochrane P. Robinson *Hoover Digest: Research & Opinion on Public Policy* no3 p143 Summ 2017

Historical Harvest M. Siekierski *Hoover Digest: Research & Opinion on Public Policy* no1 p209 Wint 2017

A Miracle or a Relic P. Robinson *Hoover Digest: Research & Opinion on Public Policy* no1 p165 Wint 2017

Hope

Hope for Moms Who Need it Most S. Maglente color *Parents* v92 no7 p31 Jl 2017

HOPE M. WERNER *Humanist* v76 no6 p42 N/D 2016

Wishing and hoping P. W. Marty *Christian Century* v134 no15 p3 Jl 19 2017

Hope, Anna

Running the Asylum S. FERGUSON *New York Times Book Review* p19 O 2 2016

Hope, Clover

10 THINGS WE'RE ALREADY OBSESSING OVER IN 2017 color *Essence* v47 no9 p41 Ja 2017

Hope, Don

The Thread color *New York Times Magazine* p14 O 9 2016

Hope, Paul

The CR Guide to Smarter Remodeling chart color il *Consumer Reports* v82 no7 p44 Jl 2017

Know the Drill color diag *Consumer Reports* v82 no12 p8 D 2017

Mowers That Make the Cut chart color graph *Consumer Reports* v82 no5 p9 My 2017

Something New Under the Sun color *Consumer Reports* v82 no9 p18 S 2017

Winning Kitchen Combos chart color *Consumer Reports* v82 no10 p20 O 2017

HOPE, TONI GERBER

BONE SMART cartoon *Better Homes & Gardens* v95 no5 p164 My 2017

the cold (and flu) truth *Better Homes & Gardens* v94 no11 p150 N 2016

HARVEST OF HEALTH cartoon color *Better Homes & Gardens* v95 no3 p136 Mr 2017

jump in! by the pool color *Better Homes & Gardens* v95 no8 p168 Ag 2017

JUST LIKE MEDICINE *Prevention* v69 no5 p54 My 2017

PLAYING DOCTOR color *Prevention* v69 no8 p48 Ag 2017

START OF DARKNESS color *Better Homes & Gardens* v95 no11 p154 N 2017

TESTING, TESTING color *Better Homes & Gardens* v95 no8 p177 Ag 2017

Hope Credit Union (Company)

Innovative Partnership Brings Hope to Small Towns C. Williams *Bridges (Federal Reserve Bank of St. Louis)* p8 Summ 2016

Hope College (Holland, Mich.)

Hope College *Dance Magazine* v90 p71 2016/2017 Supplement College Guide

Hopeless (Music)

The Must List color *Entertainment Weekly* no1443 p3 D 9 2016

Hopeless Fountain Kingdom (Music)

Freedom Rock: Halsey lost a boyfriend, a producer, and, for a time, her sense of self. What she gained was a new sound and her first No. 1 album P. Reilly img *New York* v50 no13 p69 Je 26 2017

Halsey Aims for Pop Dominance B. HIATT color *Rolling Stone* no1284 p21 Ap 6 2017

HALSEY M. Vain color *Entertainment Weekly* no1468/1469 p104 Je 2-9 2017

The New Rebel Queen of Pop's Badlands [Cover story] R. SHEFFIELD color *Rolling Stone* no1289 p55 Je 15 2017

Hopeless Romantic (Music)

Michelle Branch's Second Act J. HUDAK color *Rolling Stone* no1283 p14 Mr 23 2017

Hope—Religious aspects—Christianity

How to live in hope C. R. Pinches color *Christian Century* v134 no15 p22 Jl 19 2017

Not Settling for Less [Cover story] P. J. WADELL color *America* v215 no16 p20 N 21 2016

Hopfe, Charlotte

Neandertal and Denisovan DNA from Pleistocene sediments bw color *Science* v356 no6338 p605 My 12 2017

Hopgood, Jeromy

Stage Presence: A Collaboration That Resulted in a New Approach to Design Communication *Stage Directions* v30 no10 p32 O 2017

Hopkins & Porter (Company)

Custom Home Builders Directory *Washingtonian Magazine* v52 no6 p162 Mr 2017

Hopkins, Anthony, 1937-

Killer Reboot J. HEER il *New Republic* v247 no12 p67 D 2016

Hopkins, Anthony, 1937-—Interviews

Anthony Hopkins M. ZIMMERMAN *Men's Health* v32 no5 p148 Je 2017

Hopkins, Asa S.

The next energy economy color *Science* v356 no6339 p709 My 19 2017

Hopkins, Donald

THE RADICATOR B. YEOMAN *Atlanta* v57 no4 p66 Ag 2017

Hopkins, Edwin

December 1941 T. CLARK and E. INGRAHAM bw *Yankee* v80 no6 p20 N/D 2016

Hopkins, Hayden

CIRQUE Queen C. Bowers *Dance Spirit* v21 no7 p52 S 2017

Hopkins, Jared S.

A Miracle Drug Big Pharma Doesn't Want color graph *Bloomberg*

Businessweek no4517 p22 Ap 3 2017

Opening the Door For Future Drug Sales color *Bloomberg Businessweek* no4533 p15 Ag 7 2017

U.S. Dental Labs Are Gritting Their Teeth color *Bloomberg Businessweek* no4519 p24 Ap 24 2017

Where County Lines Mean Life and Death graph *Bloomberg Businessweek* no4538 p31 S 18 2017

HOPKINS, JEANINE

ROAR OF THE CROWD *Texas Monthly* v44 no11 p14 N 2016

Hopkins, Karen Leigh

A Gym Teacher Visited The Breakfast Club D. Coggan color *Entertainment Weekly* no1460/1461 p40 Ap 7-17 2017

Hopkins, Lee Bennett, 1938-

WHY POETRY?: Lee Bennett Hopkins on why we must share poetry with our students S. Knell color *Literacy Today (2411-7862)* v34 no6 p16 My/Je 2017

Hopkins, Matt

GM's Stock Buyback Is Bad for America and the Company *Harvard Business Review Digital Articles* p2 Mr 11 2015

If the SEC Measured CEO Pay Packages Properly, They Would Look Even More Outrageous *Harvard Business Review Digital Articles* p2 D 22 2016

McDonald's Has to Do More than Manipulate Its Stock Price *Harvard Business Review Digital Articles* p2 My 14 2015

Hopkins, Michael Starr

Philanthropy Paves Road to Riches color *Ebony* v72 no9 p76 Jl/Ag 2017

RISE OF THE NEW BLACK WALL STREET color *Ebony* v72 no9 p72 Jl/Ag 2017

Hopkins, Mike

slow down a. smith bw *Bike Magazine* v24 no6 p23 Ag 2017

Hopkins, Nancy

Not just Salk color *Science* v357 no6356 p1105 S 15 2017

HOPKINS, NANCY WALL

ART OF THE TART color *Better Homes & Gardens* v95 no3 p124 Mr 2017

Hopkins, Philip F.

Supernovae, supercomputers, and galactic evolution *Physics Today* v70 no4 p70 Ap 2017

Hopkins, Sophie

BREAKING BIG CLASS C. Collis color *Entertainment Weekly* no1446/1447 p64 D 2016/Ja 2017

Hopkins, Tapani

Higher predation risk for insect prey at low latitudes and elevations graph *Science* v356 no6339 p742 My 19 2017

Hopkins, Telma—Interviews

Family Matters G. Hall color *Entertainment Weekly* no1485 p24 O 6 2017

Hopkins, Tracy E.

GET SCULPTED LIKE YOUR GIRL CRUSH color *Essence* v48 no3 p115 Jl 2017

Hopkinson, Deborah

A Bandit's Tale: The Muddled Misadventures of a Pickpocket *Publishers Weekly* v263 no49 p81 D 7 2016

Independence Cake: A Revolutionary Confection Inspired by Amelia Simmons, Whose True History Is Unfortunately Unknown *Publishers Weekly* v264 no10 p59 Mr 6 2017

HOPKINSON, NATALIE

HOME OF THE BRAVE: THE NATION'S ONLY TOWN FOUNDED BY AFRICAN-AMERICAN CIVIL WAR SOLDIERS REMAINS A BASTION OF RESILIENCE 150 YEARS LATER *Smithsonian* v48 no5 p56 S 2017

Hoplamazian, Mark S., 1964-

MARK HOPLAMAZIAN bw color *Bloomberg Businessweek* no4524 p72 My 29 2017

Hopley, Claire

ENLIGHTENED PRINCESSES *British Heritage Travel* v38 no3 p48 My/Je 2017

It's Always Time for Tea *British Heritage Travel* v38 no1 p68 Ja/F 2017

Hopp, Christian

Research: Writing a Business Plan Makes Your Startup More Likely to Succeed *Harvard Business Review Digital Articles* p2 Jl 14 2017

Hopp, Kristi

The 10TH Annual Scottsdale Farm Tours *Arabian Horse World*

v57 no5 p202 F 2017

Arabian National BREEDER FINALS *Arabian Horse World* v57 no2 p78 N 2016

Divyn Inspiration and Betsy Kelley *Arabian Horse World* v57 no10 p105 Jl 2017

Prince Sultan bin Abdulaziz: International Arabian Horse Festival color *Arabian Horse World* v57 no7 p90 Ap 2017

Wayne Newton's Aramus Arabians Open House *Arabian Horse World* v57 no9 p30 Je 2017

Hoppe, Hans-Hermann

THEIR THOUGHT LEADERS ARE OBSESSED WITH THE PAST—BUT SAW A WAY TO WIN THE FUTURE img *New York* v50 no9 p31 My 1 2017

Hoppe, Magnus

The Right Way to Use Competitive Intelligence *Harvard Business Review Digital Articles* p2 Je 16 2016

Hoppe, Robert

Large Family Farms Continue To Dominate U.S. Agricultural Production *Amber Waves: The Economics of Food, Farming, Natural Resources, & Rural America* p1 Mr 2017

Hopper, Edward, 1882-1967

Seal color *Magazine Antiques* v183 no6 pC1 N/D 2016

Hopper, Jim

THE THINKING MAN DAVID HARBOUR M. Khidekel bw *Women's Health* v14 no9 p104 N 2017

Hopper, Nate

The 2017 Fear Index color diag *Time* v188 no27-28 p68 D 26 2016

5 Issues That Deserve More Love-or Hate *Time* v188 no16/17 p36 O 24 2016

Bruce Feiler color *Time* v189 no12 p64 Ap 3 2017

Celebrities! They're Just Like Writers! color *Time* v190 no12 p64 S 25 2017

The Earth Moving Under Us color *Time* v190 no8 p58 Ag 28 2017

Limbo of the Patriarch color *Time* v189 no7/8 p101 F 27 2017

Naoki Higashida color *Time* v190 no6 p60 Ag 7 2017

Purple Coffee, Rainbow Toast and the Politics of Unicorns color *Time* v189 no18 p27 My 15 2017

United's No Good, Very Bad Day-and What It Means for All of Us color *Time* v189 no15 p22 Ap 24 2017

The Walt Whitman Workout Plan color *Time* v189 no5 p53 F 13 2017

Yuval Noah Harari color *Time* v189 no7/8 p116 F 27 2017

Hopper, Peter

A 4-Step Process to Help Senior Teams Prioritize Decisions color *Harvard Business Review Digital Articles* p2 Mr 27 2017

You Can't Make Good Predictions Without Embracing Uncertainty *Harvard Business Review Digital Articles* p2 My 18 2016

Hopper, Sheila

YOU LIKE H&R! color *Horse & Rider* v56 no10 p22 O 2017

Hoppers (Storage)

How to model REPAIRED HOPPERS M. R. Snell color *Model Railroader* v84 no9 p32 S 2017

WalthersMainline HO covered hopper C. Grivno color *Model Railroader* v84 no7 p64 Jl 2017

Hopps, Walter, 1933-2005

NO SHOW A. Doran bw color *ARTnews* v116 no1 p84 Spr 2017

Rebel In the House W. HOPPS, D. TREISMAN et al *Los Angeles Magazine* v62 no6 p60 Je 2017

HOPTON, MATTHEW E.

Ecology for the Shrinking City *BioScience* v66 no11 p965 N 1 2016

Hoque, M. E.

Humanlike helpers teach social skills B. Bower color *Science News* v192 no6 p19 O 14 2017

Horace, 65 B.C.-8 B.C.

Montaigne: What Was Truly Courageous? T. Parks cartoon *New York Review of Books* v63 no18 p59 N 24 2016

The Resurrection Will Be a Remix C. McNamara color *Commonweal* v143 no18 p46 N 11 2016

Horaczek, Stan

Big-screen blowout color *Popular Science* v289 no6 p22 N/D 2017

free the mouse color *Popular Science* v289 no6 p84 N/D 2017

GONE IN 2.3 SECONDS color *Popular Science* v289 no5 p32 S/O 2017

I can put an IMAX in your house color *Popular Science* v289 no6

p86 N/D 2017

MEANS TO A LENS color *Popular Science* v289 no4 p36 Jl/Ag 2017

MEMBRAINIAC color *Popular Science* v289 no4 p38 Jl/Ag 2017

A real console, really mobile color *Popular Science* v289 no6 p18 N/D 2017

SLOW DOWN THE WORLD color *Popular Science* v289 no5 p30 S/O 2017

A TIRE FOR EVERY SEASON color *Popular Science* v289 no4 p37 Jl/Ag 2017

Toy story color *Popular Science* v289 no6 p44 N/D 2017

Horan, Bridget

Graham Finale T. KIRTS color *Indianapolis Monthly* p39 Ap 2017

HORAN, DANIEL P.

AFTER ELECTION DAY *America* v215 no16 p32 N 21 2016

Horan, Niall, 1993-

NIALL HORAN J. Goodman *Entertainment Weekly* no1446/1447 p75 D 2016/Ja 2017

Sound Bites color *Entertainment Weekly* no1443 p6 D 9 2016

Horandel, J. R.

Observation of a large-scale anisotropy in the arrival directions of cosmic rays above 8×1018 eV *Science* v357 no6357 p1266 S 22 2017

Horecka, Gene

Exploring genetic suppression interactions on a global scale diag *Science* v354 no6312 p599 N 4 2016

Horecka, Ira

Exploring genetic suppression interactions on a global scale diag *Science* v354 no6312 p599 N 4 2016

Horford, Al, 1986-

Al Horford J. Crelin color *Current Biography* v78 no9 p37 S 2017

Horgan, John

Spreading Skepticism W. GROSSMAN *Skeptical Inquirer* v40 no6 p41 N/D 2016

Horgan, Sharon

NASTY WOMEN S. Vilkomerson color *Entertainment Weekly* no1463/1464 p76 Ap/My 2017

Horgan, Sharon—Interviews

CATASTROPHE A. D'Arminio *TV Guide* v64 no15 p48 Ap 4 2016

Horie, Masatsugu

Japan's Furniture King Caters to the Plebes color *Bloomberg Businessweek* no4526 p19 Je 12 2017

Nissan Tries Turning Over a New Leaf *Bloomberg Businessweek* no4536 p18 S 4 2017

Horikoshi, Naoki

Crystal structure of the overlapping dinucleosome composed of hexasome and octasome graph *Science* v356 no6334 p205 Ap 14 2017

Horiuchi, Wakako

Branch-specific plasticity of a bifunctional dopamine circuit encodes protein hunger graph *Science* v356 no6337 p534 My 5 2017

Horizon (TV program)

Project Greenglow: How Horizon Lost the Message in the Medium J. EADES *Skeptical Inquirer* v41 no1 p52 Ja/F 2017

Horizon Hobby LLC

Athearn HO scale class Z-8 Challenger D. Kawala chart color *Model Railroader* v84 no8 p58 Ag 2017

Athearn HO scale GP39-2 diesel features accurate details and realistic sound D. Kawala chart color diag *Model Railroader* v84 no3 p64 Mr 2017

Athearn HO Southern Pacific EMD SD40 S. Otte color *Model Railroader* v84 no6 p64 Je 2017

Electro-Motive Division SD40-2 diesel locomotive C. Grivno color *Model Railroader* v84 no7 p10 Jl 2017

N scale freight cars C. Grivno color *Model Railroader* v84 no7 p15 Jl 2017

Showcase C. Grivno color *Model Railroader* v84 no7 p13 Jl 2017

Horizon Yachts (Company)

Horizon E88 *Sea Magazine* v108 no12 p49 D 2016

HORIZON E98 *Sea Magazine* v108 no10 p53 O 2016

HORIZON: FD87 SKYLINE color *Sea Magazine* v109 no8 p37 Ag 2017

Horizon V80 Motoryacht *Sea Magazine* v108 no12 p49 D 2016

Horizontal gas well drilling

Don't Frack on Me C. Traywick color *Bloomberg Businessweek* no4541 p24 O 9 2017

Horjus, Maren

18 PERFECT MILES color *Backpacker* v45 no1 p62 Ja 2017

Cold Comfort color *Backpacker* v45 no2 p24 Mr 2017

EQUIPMENT color *Backpacker* p73 N 2017

ESSENTIALS bw color *Backpacker* p93 N 2017

EYEWEAR color diag *Backpacker* v45 no3 p112 Ap 2017

Haunted Hikes color *Backpacker* p10 O 2017

Instant Awesome color map *Backpacker* p76 Je 2017

Love at First Sight color *Backpacker* v45 no2 p54 Mr 2017

ROOF OF AMERICA color *Backpacker* v45 no1 p68 Ja 2017

ROOM WITH A VIEW color *Backpacker* v45 no1 p78 Ja 2017

Sierra Solitude color graph map *Backpacker* p20 Je 2017

WE'VE GOT YOUR BACK color *Backpacker* p43 Je 2017

You Never Forget Your First Time diag il *Backpacker* v45 no2 p64 Mr 2017

HORJUS, RYAN

ELECTRONICS color diag *Backpacker* v45 no3 p98 Ap 2017

EQUIPMENT color *Backpacker* p73 N 2017

Power Play: Amplify your next adventure with these cutting-edge outdoor gadgets color *Backpacker* p45 S 2017

Horka, Tyler

SEAT FILLER color *Sports Illustrated* v127 no9 p14 S 25 2017

Horlbeck, Max A.

CRISPRi-based genome-scale identification of functional long noncoding RNA loci in human cells bibl graph *Science* v355 no6320 p1 Ja 6 2017

Hormesis

The Oxidative Cost of Reproduction: Theoretical Questions and Alternative Mechanisms C. ALONSO-ALVAREZ, T. CANELO et al *BioScience* v67 no3 p258 Mr 2017

Hormone therapy

See also

Estrogen replacement therapy

Hormones

See also

Gastrointestinal hormones

Love on the Mind D. HOWARD color *Prevention* v69 no6 p30 Je 2017

SLEEP MORE, EAT LESS color *Health* v31 no2 p16 Mr 2017

Horn, Brita

Is Coal No Longer King? A. STREEP *New Republic* v247 no12 p8 D 2016

Horn, Jazzmeia

Free Jazzmeia N. CHINEN *Texas Monthly* v45 no6 p88 Je 2017

JAZZMEIA HORN J. Murph color *Downbeat* v84 no7 p24 Jl 2017

HORN, JOHN

COMP TARGETS THAT WORK: HOW TO KEEP EXECU-TIVES FROM GAMING THE SYSTEM color graph img *Harvard Business Review* v95 no5 p102 S/O 2017

Horn, Lawrence

Patent pools for CRISPR technology bibl color *Science* v355 no6331 p1274 Mr 24 2017

Horn, Matthias

Giant viruses with an expanded complement of translation system components diag *Science* v356 no6333 p82 Ap 7 2017

In situ architecture, function, and evolution of a contractile injection system color diag *Science* v357 no6352 p713 Ag 18 2017

Horn, Michael

VW's Problem Is Bad Management, Not Rogue Engineers M. Schrage *Harvard Business Review Digital Articles* p2 O 15 2015

Horn, Robyn

To The Editor color *American Craft* v77 no3 p10 Je/Jl 2017

Horn, Shirley

Horn of Plenty K. Silsbee bw *Downbeat* v83 no12 p13 D 2016

Hornaday, Ann

Film Studies L. SCHWARZBAUM *New York Times Book Review* p47 Je 4 2017

Hornady Manufacturing Co.

MEET THE TECH THAT MAKES BALLISTIC COEFFI-CIENTS OBSOLETE J. B. SNOW color diag *Outdoor Life* v224 no2 p40 F/Mr 2017

Hornback, D.

Observation of coherent elastic neutrino-nucleus scattering diag *Science* v357 no6356 p1123 S 15 2017

Hornblow, Arthur

Rodgers and Hammerstein R. STIEVE *Arizona Highways* v93 no4 p2 Ap 2017

Hornby Hobbies Ltd.

Rivarossi adds upgraded ESU LokSound DCC decoder in impressive HO Big Boy S. Otte chart color *Model Railroader* v84 no3 p66 Mr 2017

Horne, Johnny

The ASI 1600MC Cooled Camera *Sky & Telescope* v133 no4 p58 Ap 2017

Horne, William W.

Portraits of Courage color *AARP: The Magazine* v60 no3A p56 Ap/My 2017

Horner, Charles

ASIA WHOLE AND FREE? *Claremont Review of Books* v17 no1 p61 Wint 2016/2017

Horner, Christine—Interviews

woman to woman A. Nix color *Amazing Wellness* v9 no3 p40 EarlySumm 2017

HORNER, JODI

Golden color *Idaho Magazine* v16 no1 p10 O 2016

HORNER, JUSTIN

A Random Act Of Roadside Assistance [Cover story] *Reader's Digest* v188 no1125 p93 N 2016

Hornet (Jet fighter plane)

Still-present dangers M. FRISCOLANTI color *Maclean's* v129 no42 p22 O 24 2016

Hornfischer, James D.

The Fleet at Flood Tide: America at Total War in the Pacific, 1944-45 R. Guttman *Military History* v33 no6 p74 Mr 2017

Hornik, Heidi J.

Adoration of the Magi *Christian Century* v133 no25 p47 D 7 2016

Christ and the Woman of Samaria at the Well by Guercino (Giovanni Francesco Barbieri) color *Christian Century* v134 no5 p47 Mr 1 2017

Crucifixion color *Christian Century* v134 no1 p47 Ja 4 2017

Gathering Manna in the Desert color *Christian Century* v134 no19 p47 S 13 2017

The Good Shepherd, early fourth century, Museo Pio Cristiano, Vatican color *Christian Century* v134 no9 p39 Ap 26 2017

ON Art *Christian Century* v134 no13 p47 Je 21 2017

St. Peter Walking on Water color *Christian Century* v134 no15 p47 Jl 19 2017

The Supper at Emmaus color *Christian Century* v134 no7 p47 Mr 29 2017

Transfiguration color *Christian Century* v134 no3 p39 F 2017

Trinity with Saint Jerome color *Christian Century* v134 no11 p47 My 24 2017

Horning, Kathryn C.

Performance with purpose color *U.S. Catholic* v81 no11 p12 N 2016

Horning, Sandra J.

A new cancer ecosystem color *Science* v355 no6330 p1103 Mr 17 2017

Horns (Anatomy)

See also

Antlers

TINES UP *South Dakota Magazine* v32 no6 p94 Mr/Ap 2017

Hornsby, Bruce

Events *Virginia Living* v15 no4 p39 Je 2017

Hornsby, Michael

Redox-based reagents for chemoselective methionine bioconjugation bibl diag graph *Science* v355 no6325 p597 F 10 2017

Hornsey, Liane

"Uber is going to be the best company in the world for women": HR chief Liane Hornsey explains how she'll banish the sexist culture that has made the taxi app the world's most beleaguered business R. JEFFERY *People Management* p40 S 2017

HORNSTEIN, GAIL A.

The Doctor Is In bw color *Weekly Standard* v22 no19 p30 Ja 23 2017

Hornung, Mary

The Road More Traveled color *Money* v46 no3 p80 Ap 2017

Horoscopes

MY HOMETOWN PAPER: Dexter Filkins D. Filkins color *Columbia Journalism Review* v56 no1 p41 Spr 2017

Horoszowski, Mark

How to Use Stretch Assignments to Support Social Good *Harvard Business Review Digital Articles* p2 N 13 2015

HOROVITZ, BRUCE

Congratulations on Your New Job! color *AARP: The Magazine* v59 no2A p33 F/Mr 2016

Secrets of Single Super color *AARP: The Magazine* v30 no6A p20 O/N 2017

Horowitz, Adam—Interviews

ADAM HOROWITZ AND EDWARD KITSIS M. LOGAN *TV Guide* v65 no8 p12 F 27 2017

Horowitz, Alexandra

WATCHING THE CLOCKS *Popular Science* v289 no5 p45 S/O 2017

Horowitz, Anthony

A 21st-Century Agatha Christie L. PICKER color *Publishers Weekly* v264 no25 p84 Je 19 2017

Horowitz, Ben

SAND HILL ROAD: AN ORAL HISTORY color *Wired* v25 no9 p24 S 2017

Horowitz, Diane

Brave Hearts color *O, The Oprah Magazine* p14 Mr 2017

HOROWITZ, JULIANA

An "Age" - Old Problem *USA Today Magazine* v145 no2860 p28 Ja 2017

Horowitz, Rachel

Trend Watching color *Publishers Weekly* v264 no12 p28 Mr 20 2017

Horowitz, Ruth

Are We Still Friends? *Publishers Weekly* v263 no48 p65 N 28 2016

Horrigan, Loretta

CONSULTANTS bw *Equus* no474 p67 Mr 2017

Horror

The admiration of horror B. BETHUNE color *Maclean's* v129 no42 p50 O 24 2016

DAMAGE HISTORY: PART II L. Abend color *Flying* v144 no8 p74 Ag 2017

Encounters with the Other Side *Reader's Digest* v188 no1124 p116 O 2016

Santa Clarita Diet M. ROUSH *TV Guide* v65 no6 p18 Ja 30 2017

SCARY THINGS S. M. BRADLEY color *Cabin Living* p80 O 2017

Horror films

See also

Twilight Saga film series

Dispelling Demons: Detective Work at The Conjuring House J. NICKELL *Skeptical Inquirer* v40 no6 p20 N/D 2016

FIELD OF SCREAMS S. STALL color *Indianapolis Monthly* v42 no2 p18 O 2017

Horror films—Reviews

Appetite for Creation R. DOUTHAT color *National Review* v69 no19 p58 O 16 2017

RESIDENT EVIL: THE FINAL CHAPTER C. Gunnestad color *Sound & Vision* v82 no8 p68 O 2017

Horror tales

A cocreator of horror podcasts finds inspiration in fiction M. SOLLINGER color *Publishers Weekly* v263 no46 p60 N 14 2016

Horror Authors Take a Stab at Self-Publishing N. A. SPECTOR bw color *Publishers Weekly* v263 no43 p38 O 24 2016

Horror television programs—Reviews

The next monster A. Hearlson color *Christian Century* v133 no22 p43 O 26 2016

Horschel, Billy

Tilt for Speed M. Perpich and D. DeNunzio color *Golf Magazine* v59 no8 p50 Ag 2017

Horse & Rider (Company)

TALK color graph *Horse & Rider* v56 no5 p20 My 2017

Horse & Rider (Periodical)

Blazing a New Trail R. E. Riley *Trail Rider* v29 no4 p6 My 2017

YOU LIKE H&R! K. Kennedy, K. Adams et al color *Horse & Rider* v56 no10 p22 O 2017

Horse agility trials

YOUNG GUNS with Travis Graves C. Toy color *Spin to Win Rodeo* v21 no1 p28 Mr 2017

Horse anatomy

Horses traded toes for speed, strength E. UNDERWOOD color *Science News* v192 no5 p12 S 30 2017

Horse auctions

AUCTION PURCHASER TERMS AND CONDITIONS *Arabian Horse World* v57 no4 p15 Ja 2017

EGYPTIAN BREEDERS' CHALLENGE *Arabian Horse World* v57 no3 p74 D 2016

MARQUISE INVITATIONAL AUCTION color *Arabian Horse World* v57 no7 p130 Ap 2017

Sold! To the Lady in Front! D. Hearst color *Arabian Horse World* v57 no7 p10 Ap 2017

Horse behavior

Basic Horse Behavior for Dressage Success K. Dupont and A. Morris color *Dressage Today* v24 no1 p24 O 2017

The gift of friendship T. Charney color *Equus* no477 p88 Je 2017

SO THAT'S WHY THE LONG FACE J. Berlin color *National Geographic* v232 no4 p26 O 2017

Stampede: How the symbol of the frontier became a nuisance M. Shaer *Smithsonian* v48 no2 p11 My 2017

Why Won't He Move? J. FIELD and J. VON GELDERN color *Horse & Rider* v56 no8 p64 Ag 2017

Horse blankets

COLD WEATHER FRIENDS color *Equus* no481 p24 O 2017

Organize Your Blankets color *Horse & Rider* v56 no10 p36 O 2017

Ready for Fall? J. Paulson *Horse & Rider* v56 no10 p14 O 2017

Solve Blanket Problems N. CHIRICO color *Horse & Rider* v56 no10 p63 O 2017

STRAP SAFETY C. Barakat and M. Freckleton color *Equus* no472 p14 Ja 2017

WINTER PREP TO-DO LIST C. Barakat color *Equus* no482 p22 N 2017

Horse boarding facilities

Margaret's Blog *Dressage Today* v23 no10 p16 Jl 2017

URBAN HORSEKEEPING A. Heintzberger color *Dressage Today* v23 no10 p30 Jl 2017

WHERE WERE THE STABLES? color *Archaeology* v70 no3 p31 My/Je 2017

Horse breeders

2016 brazilian breeders cup G. Labadie *Arabian Horse World* v57 no2 p118 N 2016

2017 Egyptian BREEDER PROFILES *Arabian Horse World* v57 no11 p68 Ag 2017

2017 Egyptian Event D. Hearst *Arabian Horse World* v57 no11 p26 Ag 2017

2017 Egyptian Event Preview *Arabian Horse World* v57 no8 p30 My 2017

ARAB YEAR *Arabian Horse World* v56 no12 p257 S 2016

A CONVERSATION WITH MOHAMMED AL MARZOUQ *Arabian Horse World* v57 no8 p10 My 2017

EGYPTIAN EVENT HIGHLIGHTS *Arabian Horse World* v57 no3 p18 D 2016

Esperanza ARABIANS, LLC: FOUR DECADES OF DEVOTION TO THE BREED N. Pierce *Arabian Horse World* v57 no12 p1 S 2017

EXXALT *Arabian Horse World* v57 no9 p1 Je 2017

GREENER PASTURES: MAGIC DREAM CAHR N. VALAITHAM *Arabian Horse World* v57 no12 p160 S 2017

The Lodwick Family *Arabian Horse World* v57 no12 p124 S 2017

Moments in Time: A Queen in Winter B. FINKE *Arabian Horse World* v57 no8 p28 My 2017

Moments in Time: A Royal Gift B. FINKE *Arabian Horse World* v57 no9 p132 Je 2017

PRESIDENT'S PERSPECTIVE R. Rogers *Arabian Horse World* v57 no3 p10 D 2016

REMEMBERING A LEGEND D. E. Barber color *Dressage Today* v23 no11 p54 Ag 2017

Small Breeders BIG RESULTS M. J. Parkinson *Arabian Horse World* v57 no9 p82 Je 2017

Wayne Newton's Aramus Arabians Open House K. Hopp *Arabian Horse World* v57 no9 p30 Je 2017

Wit and Wisdom: Alexander Keene Richards M. J. Parkinson color *Arabian Horse World* v57 no7 p136 Ap 2017

Wit and Wisdom From our Early Breeders: Edna and Jim Draper M. J. PAREINSON *Arabian Horse World* v57 no8 p152 My 2017

Wit and Wisdom from Our Early Breeders: Garth and Joe Buchanan M. J. PARKINSON *Arabian Horse World* v57 no9 p134 Je 2017

Wit and Wisdom From our Early Breeders M. J. PARKINSON *Arabian Horse World* v57 no2 p130 N 2016

Wit and Wisdom From Our Early Breeders: THE ED TWEED FAMILY M. J. PARKINSON *Arabian Horse World* v57 no11 p94 Ag 2017

Horse breeders—Competitions

2017 Las Vegas Arabian Breeders World Cup J. Winlersteen *Arabian Horse World* v57 no9 p20 Je 2017

Horse Properties: ACROSS THE NATION W. Tinker *Arabian Horse World* v57 no11 p160 Ag 2017

Wortex Kalliste J. Wintersteen color *Arabian Horse World* v57 no7 p116 Ap 2017

Horse breeders—Interviews

Small Breeders BIG RESULTS M. Moore *Arabian Horse World* v56 no12 p74 S 2016

Horse breeding

2016 european championships *Arabian Horse World* v57 no3 p266 D 2016

The Arabian Horse C. CULBERTSON *Arabian Horse World* v57 no3 p8 D 2016

Arabian MEADOWS J. WINTERSTEEN *Arabian Horse World* v57 no8 p1 My 2017

ARABIANS LTD J. WINTERSTEEN *Arabian Horse World* v57 no3 p1 D 2016

ARAB YEAR *Arabian Horse World* v57 no3 p289 D 2016

BACK TO HIS ROOTS MASTER DESIGN GA B. FINKE *Arabian Horse World* v57 no1 p122 O 2016

A Breeder's Thoughts on Fanaticaa—Raymond Mazzei Speaks D. P. Hearst *Arabian Horse World* v57 no8 p10 My 2017

December Duties C. Reich *Arabian Horse World* v57 no3 p212 D 2016

EGYPTIAN BREEDER PROFILES *Arabian Horse World* v57 no8 p60 My 2017

EGYPTIAN BREEDERS' CHALLENGE *Arabian Horse World* v57 no3 p74 D 2016

ELEANOR'S ARABIAN FARM G. Dearth *Arabian Horse World* v57 no10 p1 Jl 2017

February Madness C. Reich *Arabian Horse World* v57 no5 p232 F 2017

Getting Ready for the Coming Season C. Reich *Arabian Horse World* v57 no4 p186 Ja 2017

GLOSSARY *Equus* no474 p71 Mr 2017

Hail to the MARES P. Schofler color *Dressage Today* v23 no11 p28 Ag 2017

Heritage Breeder: Abbas Pasha I M. J. PARKINSON *Arabian Horse World* v57 no11 p84 Ag 2017

Horse DNA Trading A. Popescu color *Bloomberg Businessweek* no4534 p20 Ag 14 2017

Moments in Time B. FINKE *Arabian Horse World* v56 no12 p78 S 2016

Moments in Time Forgotten Hero B. FINKE *Arabian Horse World* v57 no1 p98 O 2016

NEW LIFESTYLE FOR PRZEWALSKI'S HORSES C. Barakat and M. McCluskey color *Equus* no481 p14 O 2017

PEREGRINE BLOODSTOCK M. Wharton and Q. Naylor *Arabian Horse World* v57 no5 p1 F 2017

Playing the Hay Odds B. CRABBE color *Horse & Rider* v56 no11 p102 N 2017

Salon Du Cheval d'El Jadida C. REID *Arabian Horse World* v57 no3 p276 D 2016

SIRE LINE: SAKLAWI I - PART 2: A GIFT TO THE WORLD B. FINKE *Arabian Horse World* v57 no11 p72 Ag 2017

Small Breeders BIG RESULTS M. Moore *Arabian Horse World* v57 no4 p150 Ja 2017

STALLION PROFILES *Arabian Horse World* v57 no3 p124 D 2016

TO BREED OR NOT TO BREED? B. Crabbe bw color *Horse & Rider* v56 no4 p56 Ap 2017

Varian Arabians Summer Jubilee & CELEBRATION OF LIFE K. Youngberg *Arabian Horse World* v56 no12 p108 S 2016

Wadee Al Shaqab B. Finke color *Arabian Horse World* v57 no7 p1 Ap 2017

the WAY WE WERE B. Fauls *Arabian Horse World* v57 no8 p61 My 2017

What it takes to breed horses S. Steuck color *Equus* no475 p15 Ap 2017

Wit and Wisdom From our Early Breeders: Edna and Jim Draper M. J. PAREINSON *Arabian Horse World* v57 no8 p152 My 2017

Wit and Wisdom from our Early Breeders M. J. PARKINSON *Arabian Horse World* v57 no5 p158 F 2017

Wit & Wisdom from Our Early Breeders: The Dr. Joseph L. Doyle Family M. J. Parkinson *Arabian Horse World* v57 no10 p54 Jl 2017

ZOBEYNI SIRE LINE - PART 1 B. FINKE *Arabian Horse World* v57 no6 p36 Mr 2017

Horse breeding—Congresses

Moments in Time: A Royal Gift B. FINKE *Arabian Horse World* v57 no9 p132 Je 2017

Horse breeding—History

Moments in Time: FROM SMALL Beginnings B. Finke *Arabian Horse World* v57 no10 p90 Jl 2017

Horse breeds

See also

Arabian horse

Thoroughbred horse

ALL THE RIGHT PARTS G. Dearth *Arabian Horse World* v57 no5 p2 F 2017

BAIRACTAR--A ROYAL HERITAGE B. FINKE *Arabian Horse World* v57 no5 p208 F 2017

CONFORMATION CLINIC J. Pipkin color *Horse & Rider* v56 no6 p43 Je 2017

CONFORMATION CLINIC S. Curl color *Horse & Rider* v56 no1 p31 Ja 2017

THE DOWAGER CLUB *Arabian Horse World* v57 no12 p88 S 2017

EGYPTIAN BREEDER PROFILES *Arabian Horse World* v57 no8 p60 My 2017

HORSES OF THE CIVIL WAR D. Bennett bw color *Equus* no477 p55 Je 2017

IMPERIAL MADHEEN B. FINKE *Arabian Horse World* v57 no3 p36 D 2016

Junior Arabian Mares A. Causey color *Horse & Rider* v56 no7 p57 Jl 2017

Moments in Time First Contact B. FINKE *Arabian Horse World* v57 no5 p156 F 2017

PEREGRINE BLOODSTOCK M. Wharton and Q. Naylor *Arabian Horse World* v57 no5 p1 F 2017

PRESIDENT's PERSPECTIVE R. Rogers *Arabian Horse World* v57 no3 p10 D 2016

A PRINCE OF EGYPT B. FINKE *Arabian Horse World* v57 no12 p148 S 2017

The Rise of EVEREST S. ANDREWS *Arabian Horse World* v57 no12 p140 S 2017

THIRTY-THIRD PUNTA DEL ESTE: ARABIAN HORSE SHOW G. Labadie color *Arabian Horse World* v57 no7 p94 Ap 2017

The Varian Way Weekend C. Maupin *Arabian Horse World* v57 no12 p60 S 2017

ZOBEYNI SIRE LINE - PART 2: MAHRUSS, RIJM, AND THE UNLIKELY BROTHERS B. Finke bw chart color *Arabian Horse World* v57 no7 p58 Ap 2017

Horse breeds—History

SIRE LINE: SAKLAWI I PART I: A TALE OF TWO BROTHERS B. Finke *Arabian Horse World* v57 no10 p78 Jl 2017

Horse breeds—United States

See also

American paint horse

Appaloosa horse

Morgan horse

Quarter horse

AMERICA'S MAJOR HORSE BREEDS EMERGE D. Bennett bw color *Equus* no473 p45 F 2017

NAHMS SNAPSHOT: WHERE THE BREEDS ARE C. Barakat and M. McCluskey chart color *Equus* no476 p22 My 2017

Horse care

10 BLANKETING TIPS FROM EMMA FORD L. Threlkeld color *Practical Horseman* v45 no10 p60 O 2017

911 ACTION PLAN E. Pascoe and M. Mudge color *Practical Horseman* v45 no11 p42 N 2017

BANISH IMBALANCES IN THE MOUTH S. Wilson color diag *Practical Horseman* v45 no1 p40 Ja 2017

Calm Your Horse color *Horse & Rider* v56 no11 p38 N 2017

CLIPPING & BLANKETING Insights from Top Grooms K. Brittle color *Dressage Today* v24 no1 p56 O 2017

CONSULTANTS B. A. Connally and S. D. White color *Equus* no472 p67 Ja 2017

Control What You Can S. Oliynyk color *Practical Horseman* v45 no1 p8 Ja 2017

Ease every breath color *Horse & Rider* v56 no11 p32 N 2017

Fancy Barns J. Paulson *Horse & Rider* v56 no4 p11 Ap 2017

From sickness to health B. Jo Lieberman bw cartoon color *Equus* no473 p34 F 2017

GENETICS Going gray D. P. Sponenberg color *Equus* no470 p68 N 2016

GLOSSARY *Equus* no470 p71 N 2016

Healing Hands J. SULLIVAN color *Trail Rider* v29 no4 p26 My 2017

HEALTH color *Horse & Rider* v56 no6 p26 Je 2017

Horse Owner's Spring Notebook J. Jahiel, H. Melocco et al color *Trail Rider* v29 no4 p38 My 2017

NUTRITION REPORT: AMINO ACIDS E. L. Prax color *Practical Horseman* v45 no3 p56 Mr 2017

ON-TRAIL FIRST-AID KIT R. E. Smith and H. Melocco color *Trail Rider* v29 no3 p64 Ap 2017

Pal for life A. Sandstrom color *Equus* no470 p66 N 2016

POP QUIZ C. Barakat and M. Freckleton color *Equus* no470 p22 N 2016

REMOVING GRASS STAINS C. Barakat and M. Freckleton *Equus* no475 p32 Ap 2017

Researching Reflux and Its Link to Inflammation S. D. Wenholz color *Practical Horseman* v45 no3 p69 Mr 2017

Snowball Solutions F. Jurga color *Trail Rider* v29 no1 p30 Ja/F 2017

STALL vs. PASTURE E. Pascoe color *Practical Horseman* v45 no10 p48 O 2017

STOCK & TRADE color *Equus* no476 p92 My 2017

STUD FARM DIARIES C. Reich *Arabian Horse World* v57 no2 p134 N 2016

Tack Room color *Practical Horseman* v45 no10 p69 O 2017

TALK color graph *Horse & Rider* v56 no4 p20 Ap 2017

Tune In S. Oliynyk *Practical Horseman* v45 no11 p8 N 2017

WATCH WINTER WATER INTAKE C. Barakat and M. Freckleton *Equus* no473 p18 F 2017

Welcome OLD MAN WINTER K. Brittle color *Dressage Today* v23 no12 p56 S 2017

What to expect as your horse grows old [Cover story] C. Barakat color *Equus* no473 p24 F 2017

Winter Hoof Care F. Jurga color *Trail Rider* v29 no1 p30 Ja/F 2017

Horse care—Equipment & supplies

Barn Life, Made Easy H. S. Thomas color *Horse & Rider* v56 no4 p43 Ap 2017

emporium bw color *Dressage Today* v23 no11 p64 Ag 2017

GLOSSARY *Equus* no475 p87 Ap 2017

STOCK & TRADE color *Equus* no473 p68 F 2017

STOCK & TRADE color *Equus* no475 p84 Ap 2017

Why I Use Beneficial Insects For My Fly Control S. R. H. de Frey *Horse & Rider* v56 no4 p49 Ap 2017

Horse collars

Breast-Collar Fit color *Horse & Rider* v56 no10 p38 O 2017

Horse diseases

See also

Equine influenza

Foal diseases

Laminitis in horses

7 Arthritis risk factors [Cover story] C. Barakat color *Equus* no478 p42 Jl 2017

BENEATH THE SURFACE OF RAIN ROT L. Threlkeld color *Practical Horseman* v45 no6 p54 Je 2017

Cellulitis in Your Dressage Partner K. L. Marcella color *Dressage Today* v23 no10 p20 Jl 2017

COMBATING JOINT DISEASE L. Threlkeld color *Practical Horseman* v45 no9 p56 S 2017

DEEP BREATH: EQUINE RESPIRATORY DISEASE L. Threlkeld color diag *Practical Horseman* v45 no8 p48 Ag 2017

DISAPPOINTING RESULTS FOR ULCER BLOOD TEST C. Barakat and M. McCluskey color *Equus* no477 p17 Je 2017

EPM L. Bonner color *Equus* no478 p29 Jl 2017

GASTRIC ULCERS: THE TRUE STORY B. Crabbe color *Horse & Rider* v56 no8 p78 Ag 2017

Genetic Test: Squamous Cell Carcinoma S. Dulai Wenholz color *Practical Horseman* v45 no10 p68 O 2017

GLOSSARY *Equus* no478 p79 Jl 2017

IDENTIFYING LEG "CRUD" C. Barakat and M. Freckleton *Equus* no477 p24 Je 2017

Keeping Worms at Bay color *Horse & Rider* v56 no9 p38 S 2017

Mysterious Foot Injuries C. Toy color *Spin to Win Rodeo* v21 no6 p52 Ag 2017

ORTHOPEDICS: A late-in-life change in gaits? B. A. Connally color *Equus* no480 p74 S 2017

Rabies C. Barakat color *Equus* no477 p29 Je 2017

Rhinopneumonitis L. Bonner color diag *Equus* no480 p35 S 2017

STUD FARM DIARIES: A Very Curious Case, Plus Answers to Common Foaling Questions C. Reich *Arabian Horse World* v57 no9 p161 Je 2017

STUDY: GAS IS IMPORTANT SIGN IN SAND COLIC CASES C. Barakat and M. McCluskey *Equus* no481 p12 O 2017

What Affects Heart Health in Event Horses? S. Dulai Wenholz color *Practical Horseman* v45 no9 p76 S 2017

Horse-drawn buggies

REASSURING STUDY OF CARRIAGE HORSES C. Barakat and M. McCluskey color *Equus* no475 p25 Ap 2017

Horse equipment

See also

Horse blankets

Horse collars

Battle the Bugs color *Horse & Rider* v56 no7 p34 Jl 2017

Head Masters color *Equus* no478 p26 Jl 2017

STOCK&TRADE color *Equus* no480 p76 S 2017

Tack Room color *Practical Horseman* v45 no6 p77 Je 2017

Wash-Stall Organizer color *Horse & Rider* v56 no8 p34 Ag 2017

Horse equipment—Evaluation

Custom Silverwork color *Horse & Rider* v56 no8 p36 Ag 2017

Horse exercises

6 EXERCISES TO NAIL YOUR HUNTER DERBY L. Towell Boyd and T. Conahan color diag *Practical Horseman* v45 no6 p44 Je 2017

Tight Turns, Big Benefits A. K. Querbach color *Horse & Rider* v56 no7 p103 Jl 2017

Horse farm management

Welcome OLD MAN WINTER K. Brittle color *Dressage Today* v23 no12 p56 S 2017

Horse farms

Al Rashediah Stud [Cover story] J. Wintersteen *Arabian Horse World* v57 no1 p105 O 2016

EXPRESSAMO G. Dearth color *Arabian Horse World* v57 no7 p1 Ap 2017

Horse Properties: ACROSS THE NATION *Arabian Horse World* v57 no10 p70 Jl 2017

LIPICA: The Original Home of the LIPIZZANER A. Morris color *Dressage Today* v23 no11 p44 Ag 2017

STUD FARM DIARIES C. Reich *Arabian Horse World* v56 no12 p246 S 2016

Horse farms—Germany

Journey Through Germany J. Mellace *Dressage Today* v23 no7 p12 Mr 2017

Horse feeding & feeds

EQUINE CUISINE around the world C. Barakat color *Equus* no482 p30 N 2017

GET YOUR HORSE'S SHINE ON C. Barakat and M. Freckleton color *Equus* no478 p24 Jl 2017

STOCK&TRADE color *Equus* no480 p76 S 2017

STOCK & TRADE color *Equus* no481 p76 O 2017

Horse grooming

Horse Properties ACROSS THE NATION W. Tinker *Arabian Horse World* v57 no8 p146 My 2017

Horse grooming—Equipment & supplies

STOCK & TRADE color *Equus* no478 p76 Jl 2017

Horse growth

The Rise of EVEREST S. ANDREWS *Arabian Horse World* v57 no12 p140 S 2017

Horse health

BUILT-IN BUG CONTROL C. Barakat and M. Freckleton *Equus* no478 p22 Jl 2017

Calm Your Horse color *Horse & Rider* v56 no11 p38 N 2017

DEEP BREATH: EQUINE RESPIRATORY DISEASE L. Threlkeld color diag *Practical Horseman* v45 no8 p48 Ag 2017

Greener Pastures S. Koneman *Arabian Horse World* v57 no11 p165 Ag 2017

Hoof-Care Help color *Horse & Rider* v56 no10 p40 O 2017

HOW TO SUPPORT HEALTHY HOOF GROWTH C. Barakat and M. Freckleton color *Equus* no480 p20 S 2017

Keep him well-watered bw color *Horse & Rider* v56 no7 p32 Jl 2017

Keep Your COOL at SUMMER SHOWS K. Brittle chart color *Dressage Today* v23 no10 p58 Jl 2017

MAINTAIN FITNESS THROUGH CANTERING C. Barakat and M. McCluskey color *Equus* no477 p16 Je 2017

My love triangle S. Bennett color *Equus* no480 p70 S 2017

NAHMS SNAPSHOT: HOW WE FIGHT FLIES C. Barakat and M. McCluskey chart color *Equus* no478 p20 Jl 2017

PASS THE SALT C. Barakat and M. Freckleton color *Equus* no478 p22 Jl 2017

POP QUIZ C. Barakat and M. Freckleton color *Equus* no482 p16 N 2017

SAFE RECOVERY FROM SEDATION C. Barakat and M. Freckleton *Equus* no482 p16 N 2017

Sticky Stifle Management J. Sobota *Dressage Today* v23 no12 p20 S 2017

STUD FARM DIARIES: Less is More: Methods of Restraint C. Reich *Arabian Horse World* v57 no11 p166 Ag 2017

Twisted TALES: How Not to Electrolyte Your Horse D. WHYTE *Arabian Horse World* v57 no11 p90 Ag 2017

WHEN YOUR HORSE IS COLICKY C. Barakat and M. Freckleton *Equus* no480 p20 S 2017

Your Horse's Lumps & Bumps B. CRABBE color *Horse & Rider* v56 no10 p86 O 2017

Horse health—Equipment & supplies

emporium color *Dressage Today* v24 no2 p62 N 2017

Organize Your Blankets color *Horse & Rider* v56 no10 p36 O 2017

Solve Blanket Problems N. CHIRICO color *Horse & Rider* v56 no10 p63 O 2017

Horse industry

See also

Horse farms

EDUCATING THE NEXT GENERATION T. Booker color *Practical Horseman* v45 no8 p40 Ag 2017

Horse industry—Economic aspects

Remember: The Word 'Horse' Comes First in the Horse Business A. Thornbury *In Stride* v12 no4 p6 Jl 2017

Horse milk

STUD FARM DIARIES: "On the Bottle"—Feeding the Orphan or Rejected Foal C. Reich *Arabian Horse World* v57 no10 p98 Jl 2017

Horse owners

See also

Women horse owners

CHALLENGES OF DETECTING EARLY LAMINITIS C. Barakat and M. McCluskey *Equus* no482 p14 N 2017

Finding Balance in Horse Ownership M. Lacy *In Stride* v12 no5 p31 S 2017

The Hay Man J. Paulson *Horse & Rider* v56 no11 p14 N 2017

A LOOK BACK—CHAMPIONS OF 2016 *Arabian Horse World* v57 no4 p30 Ja 2017

Prepare for the Worst B. CRABBE color *Horse & Rider* v56 no9 p80 S 2017

Taking Ownership: Finding the Right Professional for You M. Lacy *In Stride* v12 no3 p30 My 2017

Taking Ownership: Tips for the New or Longtime Horse Owner M. Lacy *In Stride* v12 no2 p45 Mr 2017

To Play Or Not To Play? J. HARRISON color *Horse & Rider* v56 no11 p90 N 2017

The Young'ns B. Welch color *Horse & Rider* v56 no10 p17 O 2017

Horse physiology

No More Saddle Sore A. BOATWRIGHT color *Horse & Rider* v56 no8 p86 Ag 2017

Step Control L. Place and J. Paulson color *Horse & Rider* v56 no7 p41 Jl 2017

Horse race betting

A day at the races K. McNamara bw color *Equus* no477 p77 Je 2017

March Racing in Abu Dhabi Featuring Five Stakes Races S. Andersen color *Arabian Horse World* v57 no7 p100 Ap 2017

Horse racing

6 Things to Do in OCTOBER *Practical Horseman* v45 no10 p64 O 2017

Abu Dhabi Racing S. Andersen *Arabian Horse World* v57 no6 p141 Mr 2017

ARAB YEAR *Arabian Horse World* v57 no1 p164 O 2016

ARAB YEAR *Arabian Horse World* v57 no9 p170 Je 2017

BIG RESULTS M. Moore *Arabian Horse World* v57 no6 p146 Mr 2017

A CONVERSATION with Jean-Pierre Deroubaix of The Royal Cavalry of Oman S. Andersen *Arabian Horse World* v57 no6 p66 Mr 2017

CUSTOM OF THE COUNTRY A. MILLER FISHER *Virginia Living* v15 no3 p94 Ap 2017

The Emir's Sword S. Anderson *Arabian Horse World* v57 no6 p138 Mr 2017

European Racing Report S. Andersen *Arabian Horse World* v57 no1 p150 O 2016

FOR THE HORSE C. REICH *Arabian Horse World* v57 no6 p150 Mr 2017

Get It Right, Keep It Right [Cover story] J. Gibbs and A. Boatwright color *Horse & Rider* v56 no6 p48 Je 2017

GRADE 1: U.S. races *Arabian Horse World* v57 no6 p35 Mr 2017

GRADE 2: U.S. races *Arabian Horse World* v57 no6 p42 Mr 2017

GRADE 3: U.S. races *Arabian Horse World* v57 no6 p51 Mr 2017

GROUP 1: IFAHR pattern races *Arabian Horse World* v57 no6 p20 Mr 2017

GROUP 2: IFAHR pattern races *Arabian Horse World* v57 no6 p38 Mr 2017

GROUP 3: IFAHR pattern races *Arabian Horse World* v57 no6 p44 Mr 2017

HUNTING FOR PERFECTION [Cover story] T. Conahan color diag *Practical Horseman* v45 no11 p22 N 2017

Longines FEI World Cup North American League News color *Practical Horseman* v45 no11 p65 N 2017

Major Stakes for Arabians in Qatar and the U.A.E. January Racing S. Andersen *Arabian Horse World* v57 no5 p226 F 2017

Major Summer Stakes Races in England S. Andersen *Arabian Horse World* v56 no12 p190 S 2016

The Mysterious Case of the Heavy Rain and the Television Show C. Reich *Arabian Horse World* v57 no6 p152 Mr 2017

News BITS color *Practical Horseman* v45 no11 p66 N 2017

Now's Your Chance J. Wofford color *Practical Horseman* v45 no11 p12 N 2017

October Arabian Stakes in Texas S. Andersen *Arabian Horse World* v57 no2 p102 N 2016

The President of the UAE Cup at Deauville S. Andersen *Arabian Horse World* v57 no9 p146 Je 2017

Qatar World Cup Weekend in Paris S. Andersen *Arabian Horse World* v57 no2 p96 N 2016

RACING YEARBOOK D. Hearst *Arabian Horse World* v57 no6 p6 Mr 2017

Stay Positive V. Green-Gott color *Practical Horseman* v45 no11 p72 N 2017

Summer Racing in England—Tayf Claims England's Richest Arabian Race S. Andersen *Arabian Horse World* v57 no12 p178 S 2017

U.S. Summer Racing S. Andersen *Arabian Horse World* v57 no11 p150 Ag 2017

Winner's CIRCLE color *Practical Horseman* v45 no11 p64 N 2017

A WORLDWIDE LEGACY B. Finke *Arabian Horse World* v57 no8 p8 My 2017

Horse racing awards

Darley Awards S. Andersen *Arabian Horse World* v57 no8 p106 My 2017

HH Sheikh Mansoor Festival Races at Sam Houston Race Park S. Andersen color *Arabian Horse World* v57 no7 p98 Ap 2017

Horse racing—Betting

RANKINGS Top International Racehorses S. Andersen *Arabian Horse World* v57 no6 p60 Mr 2017

Horse racing—Competitions

The $100,000 Darley Awards Stake S. Andersen *Arabian Horse World* v57 no8 p114 My 2017

Bahrain and the ARABIAN FARM TOURS hosted under the patronage of His Majesty King Hamad bin Isa Al Khalifa and the Royal Arabian Studs of Bahrain, February 15, 2017 C. Reid *Arabian Horse World* v57 no8 p128 My 2017

AN EGYPTIAN PRINCESS TAKES THE CROWN IN VEGAS J. Ferriss *Arabian Horse World* v57 no8 p62 My 2017

Moments in Time The Polish Pioneers B. Finke bw *Arabian Horse World* v57 no7 p26 Ap 2017

SPRING RACING IN THE GULF Kahayla Classic and Qatar Gold Sword S. Andersen *Arabian Horse World* v57 no8 p117 My 2017

TALK color graph *Horse & Rider* v56 no3 p16 Mr 2017

Horse racing—Congresses

ARAB YEAR *Arabian Horse World* v57 no8 p158 My 2017

Horse racing—United States

  See also

   Triple Crown (U.S. horse racing)

Paddys Day Tours America S. Andersen *Arabian Horse World* v57 no1 p147 O 2016

Horse showing

Cow Horses in Cowtown color map *Horse & Rider* v56 no10 p30 O 2017

Horse shows

2016 brazilian breeders cup G. Labadie *Arabian Horse World* v57 no2 p118 N 2016

2016 british nationals B. Finke *Arabian Horse World* v57 no1 p128 O 2016

2016 egyption event europe B. Finke *Arabian Horse World* v57 no1 p140 O 2016

2016 elran cup F. Aragno *Arabian Horse World* v56 no12 p214 S 2016

2017 ströhen european c-show and international b-show B. Finke *Arabian Horse World* v57 no11 p132 Ag 2017

26th Qatar International Arabian Horse Show C. Reid *Arabian Horse World* v57 no9 p86 Je 2017

50 Years of IHSA L. A. Pomeroy bw *Practical Horseman* v45 no4 p72 Ap 2017

6 Things to Do in OCTOBER *Practical Horseman* v45 no10 p64 O 2017

all nations cup festival B. Finke *Arabian Horse World* v57 no3 p244 D 2016

American Endurance Ride Conference G. STEWART-SPEARS *Arabian Horse World* v57 no3 p72 D 2016

The Arab Horse Society National Show 2017 B. Finke *Arabian Horse World* v57 no12 p166 S 2017

Arabian Horse World presents the AWPA Western Pleasure Futurity *Arabian Horse World* v57 no5 p31 F 2017

Arabian Stakes at Deauville, France S. Andersen *Arabian Horse World* v56 no12 p196 S 2016

ARAB YEAR *Arabian Horse World* v57 no12 p191 S 2017

ARAB YEAR *Arabian Horse World* v57 no3 p289 D 2016

ARAB YEAR *Arabian Horse World* v57 no4 p198 Ja 2017

ARAB YEAR *Arabian Horse World* v57 no8 p158 My 2017

Captive Style N. Chirico color *Horse & Rider* v55 no11 p17 N 2016

The Company You Keep N. Chirico color *Horse & Rider* v56 no4 p19 Ap 2017

CONGRATULATIONS TO OUR 2016 WINNERS *Arabian Horse World* v57 no5 p27 F 2017

Dr. Karlan Downing's Trail Stars M. Moore *Arabian Horse World* v57 no3 p68 D 2016

Help for a Nervous Pattern Horse J. Mellott color *Horse & Rider* v56 no4 p73 Ap 2017

HORSE EXPOS *Trail Rider* v29 no2 p31 Mr 2017

Horse Properties ACROSS THE NATION W. Tinker *Arabian Horse World* v57 no9 p156 Je 2017

The Immortal N. Chirico color *Horse & Rider* v55 no12 p15 D 2016

Missy Clark: "Riding is a Master Class in Life" T. Conahan color *Practical Horseman* v44 no12 p18 D 2016

Moments in Time On THE Road B. FINKE *Arabian Horse World* v57 no4 p154 Ja 2017

Moments in Time: THE Russian Year B. FINKE *Arabian Horse World* v57 no11 p92 Ag 2017

News BITS color *Practical Horseman* v45 no8 p62 Ag 2017

Paris C. Reid *Arabian Horse World* v57 no5 p216 F 2017

Prince Sultan bin Abdulaziz: International Arabian Horse Festival K. Hopp color *Arabian Horse World* v57 no7 p90 Ap 2017

Salon Du Cheval d'El Jadida C. REID *Arabian Horse World* v57 no3 p276 D 2016

School With Class B. Avila and J. Paulson color *Horse & Rider* v56 no1 p28 Ja 2017

SHOWRING STARS *Arabian Horse World* v57 no3 p66 D 2016

Show-Time COUNTDOWN B. Jewett and A. Boatwright color *Horse & Rider* v55 no11 p56 N 2016

Up to the Challenge - Changes Coming for U.S. Nationals Halter Classes C. Reich *Arabian Horse World* v57 no5 p235 F 2017

The View from Center Ring G. Dearth *Arabian Horse World* v57 no1 p74 O 2016

WADEE AL SHAQAB: A VICTORY BY THE SEA [Cover story] D. Hearst *Arabian Horse World* v57 no11 p97 Ag 2017

We love Scottsdale... *Arabian Horse World* v57 no4 p4 Ja 2017

WHAT IN THE WORLD G. Knowles *Arabian Horse World* v57 no5 p10 F 2017

The Young'ns B. Welch color *Horse & Rider* v56 no10 p17 O 2017

Horse sports

  See also

   Games on horseback

   Horse racing

   Rodeos

2016 bruges international arabian horse event *Arabian Horse World* v56 no12 p218 S 2016

2016 WRANGLER NATIONAL FINALS RODEO PREVIEW B. Welch color *Spin to Win Rodeo* v20 no10 p78 D 2016

The 2017 Show Jumping Hall of Fame Inductees N. Jaffer *In Stride* v12 no4 p43 Jl 2017

7 Things to Do in JULY *Practical Horseman* v45 no7 p64 Jl 2017

Are You Qualified Just Because You Qualified? G. Teall and J. Winkel *In Stride* v12 no1 p48 Ja 2017

AT A GLANCE color *Horse & Rider* v56 no11 p63 N 2017

The 'Beehive' K. LENSEIGNE and J. PAULSON color *Horse & Rider* v56 no10 p43 O 2017

Beware the Ides Of Woff J. Wofford cartoon *Practical Horseman* v45 no4 p18 Ap 2017

Class of 2016 color *Spin to Win Rodeo* v20 no10 p70 D 2016

The Clinic PHOTO CRITIQUES S. von Dietze color *Dressage Today* v23 no9 p22 Je 2017

FIVE FLAT with Jake Long B. Welch color *Spin to Win Rodeo* v20 no10 p41 D 2016

GOTTA HAVE MORE RODEO?!? color *Horse & Rider* v56 no11 p69 N 2017

Longines FEI World Cup North American League News color *Practical Horseman* v45 no10 p65 O 2017

My Ever-Growing Bucket List *Dressage Today* v23 no11 p10 Ag 2017

My Most Amazing 24 Hours N. Sheridan color *Horse & Rider* v55 no12 p10 D 2016

News BITS color *Practical Horseman* v45 no10 p66 O 2017

News BITS color *Practical Horseman* v45 no7 p64 Jl 2017

Ready for Fall? J. Paulson *Horse & Rider* v56 no10 p14 O 2017

SHARING THE WEALTH color *Spin to Win Rodeo* v21 no6 p68 Ag 2017

SLACK SOMETIMES GETS A BAD RAP K. Santos color *Spin to Win Rodeo* v20 no10 p46 D 2016

TALK color graph *Horse & Rider* v55 no12 p16 D 2016

TDF ANNOUNCES WINNERS OF 2016 TWO-TEMPI CHALLENGE color *Dressage Today* v23 no8 p12 Ap 2017

THE VIEW FROM CENTER RING G. Dearth *Arabian Horse World* v57 no3 p46 D 2016

Which Rider Is Not Jumping Ahead? G. H. Morris color *Practical Horseman* v45 no5 p14 My 2017

Games on horseback
Horse paces, gaits, etc.
Horse training
Horsemen & horsewomen
Hunter seat equitation
Lungeing (Horsemanship)
Riding clubs
Trail riding

10 TIPS FOR RANCH LOGS R. Kail and L. Stanley color *Horse & Rider* v56 no2 p54 F 2017

2017 Mediterranean Championships C. Reid *Arabian Horse World* v57 no11 p124 Ag 2017

5 Tips to Improve MENTAL FOCUS A. Brock and E. S. Romm color *Dressage Today* v24 no1 p36 O 2017

7 Things to Do in SEPTEMBER *Practical Horseman* v45 no9 p70 S 2017

Acceptable, Not Acceptable or Preferable G. H. Morris color *Practical Horseman* v45 no11 p10 N 2017

Ace Your Pivot J. GIBBS and A. BOATWRIGHT color *Horse & Rider* v56 no9 p86 S 2017

Aged Paint Mares color *Horse & Rider* v56 no11 p51 N 2017

ALLOW YOUR HORSE TO 'HEAR' YOU A. Carter color diag *Practical Horseman* v45 no10 p42 O 2017

Alone on the Trail J. GOODNIGHT and H. MELOCCO color *Horse & Rider* v56 no11 p46 N 2017

Another reason to ride H. Ellis-Ashburn color *Equus* no476 p96 My 2017

Around the Campfire J. Barsanti, D. M. Johnston et al color *Trail Rider* v29 no4 p8 My 2017

ask the experts A. GILMOUR, S. HASTINGS et al cartoon color *Dressage Today* v23 no5 p64 Ja 2017

Asymmetrical Riding B. GODDARD cartoon *Trail Rider* v29 no1 p72 Ja/F 2017

The Balance Between Humility and Confidence N. Pine color *Dressage Today* v23 no8 p20 Ap 2017

Be Trail-Tack Savvy J. GOODNIGHT and H. MELOCCO color *Horse & Rider* v56 no9 p51 S 2017

Body Control B. AVILA and J. PAULSON color *Horse & Rider* v56 no11 p44 N 2017

Broaden Your Horizons B. Avila and J. Paulson color *Horse & Rider* v56 no3 p26 Mr 2017

BROOKLYN CF C. Maupin *Arabian Horse World* v57 no9 p35 Je 2017

Catch Fall COLOR A. PAVIA color *Horse & Rider* v56 no9 p72 S 2017

CEI Endurance at Marbach, Germany, July 21, 2017 G. Waiditschka *Arabian Horse World* v57 no11 p164 Ag 2017

Celebrate Simple S. Oliynyk *Practical Horseman* v45 no10 p10 O 2017

Change It Up! C. CROW and J. F. MEYER color *Horse & Rider* v56 no9 p55 S 2017

Chrystine Tauber: An Incredible Journey With Horses N. Jaffer *In Stride* v12 no1 p38 Ja 2017

Clean is What Horse-Keeping is All About G. H. Morris color *Practical Horseman* v45 no9 p14 S 2017

The Clinic PHOTO CRITIQUES S. von Dietze chart color *Dressage Today* v24 no1 p22 O 2017

The Clinic S. von Dietze color *Dressage Today* v23 no5 p20 Ja 2017

Collection with THROUGHNESS and FORWARD DESIRE S. Hassler and B. Baumert color *Dressage Today* v24 no1 p28 O 2017

COMING (Back) TO AMERICA E. Iliff Prax color *Practical Horseman* v45 no9 p30 S 2017

CONSULTANTS L. Horrigan and B. A. Connally bw *Equus* no474 p67 Mr 2017

Coping with the Loss of an Equine Partner J. Susser color *Dressage Today* v23 no12 p16 S 2017

Corner Control Down the Fence J. Paulson color *Horse & Rider* v56 no3 p66 Mr 2017

Correct Lead-Change Anticipation [Cover story] L. Lange color *Horse & Rider* v56 no1 p65 Ja 2017

Create a Confident Mindset [Cover story] V. Hargis and J. F. Meyer color *Horse & Rider* v56 no3 p32 Mr 2017

CREATING HARMONY AND EXPRESSION A. Carter color *Practical Horseman* v45 no2 p36 F 2017

A day at the races K. McNamara bw color *Equus* no477 p77 Je 2017

DEVELOPING COLLECTION WITHOUT RESISTANCE K. Adams color *Practical Horseman* v45 no9 p46 S 2017

Develop Your Feel and Find Harmony S. Geikie and A. Morris color *Dressage Today* v23 no10 p26 Jl 2017

Dream Buddy on a Trail Ride S. Savage, E. Gilbreath et al cartoon *Horse & Rider* v56 no3 p72 Mr 2017

Driggers Doesn't Let Roping Define Him K. Santos *Spin to Win Rodeo* v21 no1 p26 Mr 2017

The EAP Regionals Open Eyes--and Doors--Throughout the Country K. Rover *In Stride* v12 no5 p27 S 2017

Effective Transitions L. LaPLANTE and J. PAULSON color *Horse & Rider* v56 no9 p43 S 2017

EF KINGSTON *Arabian Horse World* v57 no9 p40 Je 2017

Equestrian Idols S. Oliynyk color *Practical Horseman* v45 no6 p8 Je 2017

EQUINE CUISINE around the world C. Barakat color *Equus* no482 p30 N 2017

EXERCISES AND ADVICE FROM ROBERT DOVER A. Carter color diag *Practical Horseman* v45 no9 p38 S 2017

Fallon Taylor's Best Advice for Any Rider F. TAYLOR and N. CHIRICO color *Horse & Rider* v56 no11 p118 N 2017

Feel the Footfalls L. LaPlante color *Horse & Rider* v56 no3 p23 Mr 2017

Finding Balance in Horse Ownership M. Lacy *In Stride* v12 no5 p31 S 2017

Finding Carawich J. Wofford bw *Practical Horseman* v45 no2 p16 F 2017

Finding my way T. Anderson color *Equus* no473 p63 F 2017

The Finer Points of Fencing B. Avila and J. Paulson *Horse & Rider* v56 no6 p40 Je 2017

FITTING TACK, PART 1: HALTER AND WESTERN C. REICH and C. MANGAN *Arabian Horse World* v57 no1 p89 O 2016

For the Love of the Horse S. Allan and S. Taylor color *Practical Horseman* v45 no2 p72 F 2017

Free Yourself from Feelings Of Guilt Over Barn Time J. Susser *Dressage Today* v24 no2 p16 N 2017

Freeze Frame K. Gustave color *Team Roping Journal* p74 S 2017

Get Moving! T. SHIELDS and J. F. MEYER color *Horse & Rider* v56 no11 p48 N 2017

Get Ready to Win B. Avila and J. Paulson color *Horse & Rider* v55 no12 p28 D 2016

Get Snaffle-Bit Smart A. DUNNING and J. PAULSON color *Horse & Rider* v56 no8 p48 Ag 2017

Glorious Uncertainty J. Wofford color *Practical Horseman* v45 no10 p16 O 2017

Going to Extremes S. HAMILTON color *Trail Rider* v29 no3 p38 Ap 2017

Gotta Lota Good N. Chirico color *Horse & Rider* v56 no2 p15 F 2017

Greetings from JACKSON HOLE, WYOMING D. Newman *Practical Horseman* v45 no2 p62 F 2017

A GUIDE TO ACCURACY AND BALANCE N. Lavoie and A. Morris color diag *Dressage Today* v23 no5 p24 Ja 2017

Happy New Year! J. Mellace *Dressage Today* v23 no5 p1 Ja 2017

Here's How [Cover story] S. Coles and L. Thompson color *Practical Horseman* v45 no7 p62 Jl 2017

Here's How H. Hugo-Vidal and R. Sargent color *Practical Horseman* v45 no2 p58 F 2017

Here's How J. Jo Tate and C. Heleski color diag graph *Practical Horseman* v45 no9 p66 S 2017

Here's How S. LICO and C. HELESKI color *Practical Horseman* v45 no6 p64 Je 2017

Horsemanship, 60 & Over E. P. DeRousse color *Horse & Rider* v55 no11 p12 N 2016

Horsemanship, Front and Center W. Allen *In Stride* v12 no5 p36 S 2017

How Can I Move Past Training Ruts? J. Susser *Dressage Today* v23 no5 p18 Ja 2017

How I Solved My Horse's Problem R. Vaal, J. Morris et al cartoon *Horse & Rider* v56 no1 p72 Ja 2017

How to Influence Zoning Changes C. HUGHES color *Trail Rider* v29 no4 p30 My 2017

Improve Body Awareness for a Better Seat D. Thind and A. Morris color *Dressage Today* v23 no8 p24 Ap 2017

Practical Horseman v45 no2 p10 F 2017

Universal Appeal S. Oliynyk *Practical Horseman* v45 no8 p8 Ag 2017

WARRIOR HORSE C. REICH *Arabian Horse World* v57 no9 p38 Je 2017

WC CIAO PSYCHE *Arabian Horse World* v57 no9 p33 Je 2017

We Deserve Fair Play T. Brennan *In Stride* v12 no2 p25 Mr 2017

We Hear You P. RENNEBERG, B. OVED et al color *Horse & Rider* v56 no2 p10 F 2017

WHAT IN THE WORLD *Arabian Horse World* v57 no9 p10 Je 2017

What school horses taught me C. Graf color *Equus* no481 p80 O 2017

Why Kids Should Ride J. F. MEYER color *Horse & Rider* v56 no9 p62 S 2017

Winner's CIRCLE color *Practical Horseman* v45 no10 p64 O 2017

Winner's CIRCLE color *Practical Horseman* v45 no6 p72 Je 2017

The Wisdom (and Challenges) of Age S. Mastous color *Horse & Rider* v56 no3 p8 Mr 2017

Worth the Effort S. Oliynyk *Practical Horseman* v45 no2 p8 F 2017

Yes, Teamwork Does Make the Dream Work T. Johnston color *Practical Horseman* v45 no9 p24 S 2017

Your Summer Savior J. Paulson *Horse & Rider* v56 no6 p15 Je 2017

Youth Riders Should Know... B. AVILA and J. PAULSON color *Horse & Rider* v56 no9 p47 S 2017

Horsemanship coaching

Loping 'Out Loud' D. Dauphin and J. F. Meyer bw color *Horse & Rider* v56 no7 p54 Jl 2017

TALK color graph *Horse & Rider* v56 no4 p20 Ap 2017

Horsemanship competitions

See also

Horse shows

11th Annual twenty seventeen Las Vegas: ARABIAN BREEDERS WORLD CUP SHOW M. Moore color *Arabian Horse World* v57 no7 p70 Ap 2017

Back-to-Back Wins for Ireland color *Practical Horseman* v45 no5 p72 My 2017

Competition & Camaraderie in the Children's and Adult Amateur Jumper Championships L. Taylor *In Stride* v11 no6 p36 N 2016

FULL CIRCLE J. Autry color *Practical Horseman* v45 no5 p44 My 2017

Get Your Mojo Back B. Avila and J. Paulson color *Horse & Rider* v55 no11 p30 N 2016

Gracie Marlowe Is Golden at the USHJA Emerging Athletes Program National Training Session T. Booker *In Stride* v12 no1 p16 Ja 2017

The IDA School Horse: A Breed of its Own K. Beaudoin color *Dressage Today* v23 no4 p36 D 2016

The Immortal N. Chirico color *Horse & Rider* v55 no12 p15 D 2016

Longines FEI World Cup™ North American League News color *Practical Horseman* v45 no1 p65 Ja 2017

Longines FEI World Cup North American League News color *Practical Horseman* v45 no8 p66 Ag 2017

A Passion for Horses and Horsemanship Lead Alix Morrison to Gold L. Taylor *In Stride* v12 no1 p26 Ja 2017

Racing Arabians Khataab and Joudh Make Statements in France S. Andersen *Arabian Horse World* v57 no12 p176 S 2017

Sur Teddy's Magna A Great One Retires G. Dearth *Arabian Horse World* v57 no1 p94 O 2016

TALK color graph *Horse & Rider* v56 no5 p20 My 2017

WIN A TRIP TO THE 2017 WORLD CUP DRESSAGE FINAL color *Dressage Today* v23 no4 p12 D 2016

Winner's CIRCLE color *Practical Horseman* v45 no1 p66 Ja 2017

Wranglered N. Chirico color *Horse & Rider* v56 no5 p19 My 2017

Horsemanship equipment

See also

Bits (Bridles)

Riding whips

Romal Reins A. Dunning and J. Paulson color *Horse & Rider* v56 no6 p46 Je 2017

Tack Room color *Practical Horseman* v45 no8 p69 Ag 2017

Tack Room color *Practical Horseman* v45 no9 p77 S 2017

Horsemanship equipment—Evaluation

Bits for Heel Horses: Tips from Professional Heelers color *Team Roping Journal* p76 S 2017

emporium color *Dressage Today* v23 no12 p64 S 2017

Pack Your Bags color *Horse & Rider* v56 no11 p34 N 2017

Horsemanship for people with disabilities

Learning to Dance in the Rain L. Ostrander color *Horse & Rider* v56 no5 p14 My 2017

Horsemanship instruction

Cloverleaf Over Poles W. Knabenshue, E. Knabenshue et al color diag *Horse & Rider* v56 no4 p31 Ap 2017

Get Out of the Way B. AVILA and J. PAULSON color *Horse & Rider* v56 no10 p46 O 2017

Handy Checklist A. Pavia color *Trail Rider* v29 no2 p14 Mr 2017

Horsemanship, 60 & Over E. P. DeRousse color *Horse & Rider* v55 no11 p12 N 2016

Mecate Tie Rope A. DUNNING and J. PAULSON color *Horse & Rider* v56 no10 p50 O 2017

Miles to go J. Woehr color *Equus* no478 p68 Jl 2017

Precise Circles J. Newcomb, M. Griggs et al color *Horse & Rider* v56 no2 p23 F 2017

Sitting pretty P. Nolf color *Equus* no480 p80 S 2017

Horsemanship techniques

See also

Lungeing (Horsemanship)

50 Reasons to Love Being 50+ S. O'Brien color *AARP: The Magazine* v59 no5A p65 Ag/S 2016

ALL ABOUT THAT BASE! S. Cashman color *Practical Horseman* v44 no12 p32 D 2016

ask the experts C. Coley, I. Norris et al color *Dressage Today* p66 My 2017

Barrel Arc and Counter-Arc [Cover story] F. Taylor, J. Smeenk et al color *Horse & Rider* v55 no12 p25 D 2016

Body Control B. AVILA and J. PAULSON color *Horse & Rider* v56 no11 p44 N 2017

The Clinic PHOTO CRITIQUES S. von Dietze color *Dressage Today* p26 My 2017

Close the Legs to Go Forward G. H. Morris color *Practical Horseman* v44 no12 p10 D 2016

Cloverleaf Over Poles W. Knabenshue, E. Knabenshue et al color diag *Horse & Rider* v56 no4 p31 Ap 2017

Control Across the Line color *Team Roping Journal* p68 O 2017

Develop Your Feel and Find Harmony S. Geikie and A. Morris color *Dressage Today* v23 no10 p26 Jl 2017

Equestrian Idols S. Oliynyk color *Practical Horseman* v45 no6 p8 Je 2017

A FIRST LOOK AT COUNTER CANTER C. Foxley color diag *Dressage Today* v23 no4 p21 D 2016

Get Out of the Way B. AVILA and J. PAULSON color *Horse & Rider* v56 no10 p46 O 2017

Gone Away! J. Wofford color *Practical Horseman* v45 no1 p16 Ja 2017

Here's How J. J. TATE, S. LICO et al color *Practical Horseman* v45 no8 p56 Ag 2017

Judging Rider Angles G. H. Morris color *Practical Horseman* v45 no6 p14 Je 2017

Lead-Change Precision B. Avila and J. Paulson color *Horse & Rider* v56 no2 p26 F 2017

Lessons In Listening J. Mellace *Dressage Today* p12 My 2017

Mecate Tie Rope A. DUNNING and J. PAULSON color *Horse & Rider* v56 no10 p50 O 2017

Monte Velho: AN EQUESTRIAN PARADISE A. Morris color *Dressage Today* v23 no11 p36 Ag 2017

Mounting Blocks B. Goddard color *Trail Rider* v29 no2 p72 Mr 2017

'Now' Exercise Makes Safety a Habit [Cover story] B. Lyons and J. F. Meyer color *Horse & Rider* v56 no5 p42 My 2017

Organize, Plan and Structure Your Ride J. Congdon and A. Morris color *Dressage Today* p30 My 2017

Oskar the Invisible Horse B. GODDARD color *Trail Rider* v29 no4 p72 My 2017

Precise Circles J. Newcomb, M. Griggs et al color *Horse & Rider* v56 no2 p23 F 2017

Reflections on the Meaning of Horsemanship A. Myers *In Stride* v12 no1 p33 Ja 2017

Reiner to Ranch Rider B. LYON and J. PAULSON bw color

Horse & Rider v56 no10 p72 O 2017

Ride Off the Rail W. WETHERELL and N. CHIRICO color *Horse & Rider* v56 no8 p92 Ag 2017

Simplify the Turn S. PARKINSON and J. PAULSON color *Horse & Rider* v56 no8 p42 Ag 2017

STILL LEAPIN' LESLIE N. Jaffer bw color *Practical Horseman* v45 no6 p34 Je 2017

'Stop and Drop' for Ultimate Control S. Purdum and J. F. Meyer color *Horse & Rider* v55 no11 p36 N 2016

To prevent collapsing your body when riding corners and turns... M. Mestas color *Dressage Today* v23 no11 p72 Ag 2017

To prevent your horse's shoulders from falling in or out... color *Dressage Today* v23 no10 p72 Jl 2017

To ride the walk in balance by being grounded to the earth and in harmony with the movement of your horse's barrel... A. Morris color *Dressage Today* v23 no12 p72 S 2017

Tune Your Riding Position to Put Your Horse into "Drive" [Cover story] A. Gilmour and A. Morris color diag *Dressage Today* v24 no2 p26 N 2017

Uncover the Mystery of "On the Bit" D. Hannon and A. Morris color diag *Dressage Today* v23 no11 p24 Ag 2017

We've All Been There... J. Wofford color *Practical Horseman* v45 no6 p16 Je 2017

WIN A DAY with Boyd Martin A. Heintzberger color *Practical Horseman* v45 no1 p58 Ja 2017

Horsemanship—Awards

aerc National Awards: Endurance riders and horses honored at the 2016 AERC Convention G. Stewart-Spears *Arabian Horse World* v57 no10 p58 Jl 2017

Winner's CIRCLE color *Practical Horseman* v45 no8 p63 Ag 2017

Horsemanship—Colorado

The Charms of Chama K. Krone and C. Krone color *Trail Rider* v29 no2 p32 Mr 2017

Horsemanship—Congresses

5 Things to Do in DECEMBER *Practical Horseman* v44 no12 p62 D 2016

7 Things to Do in JANUARY *Practical Horseman* v45 no1 p64 Ja 2017

Words of WISDOM from the West Coast L. Paulsen color *Dressage Today* v23 no8 p44 Ap 2017

Horsemanship—Equipment & supplies

See also

    Stirrups

Cowboy Up: How a Curb Bit Works L. FELDMAN color *American Cowboy* v23 no5 p64 F/Mr 2017

emporium color *Dressage Today* p64 My 2017

Handy Checklist A. Pavia color *Trail Rider* v29 no2 p14 Mr 2017

How to make mecate reins L. Feldman color *American Cowboy* v23 no5 p56 F/Mr 2017

Mounting Blocks B. Goddard color *Trail Rider* v29 no2 p72 Mr 2017

READY TO ROLL color *Equus* no475 p34 Ap 2017

The Right Equipment I. Klimke *Dressage Today* p50 My 2017

TACK CHANGES K. M. Brittle color *Dressage Today* p48 My 2017

Horsemanship—Equipment & supplies—Evaluation

BOOTING UP color *Equus* no473 p22 F 2017

emporium color *Dressage Today* v23 no8 p64 Ap 2017

NEW PRODUCTS color *Spin to Win Rodeo* v20 no9 p26 N 2016

ON-THE-GO GEAR L. BACK color *Trail Rider* v29 no1 p52 Ja/F 2017

ON-THE-GO GEAR L. BACK color *Trail Rider* v29 no4 p50 My 2017

SOLUTIONS M. Vogt chart color *Horse & Rider* v56 no5 p24 My 2017

Spring Fling color *Equus* no474 p24 Mr 2017

STOCK & TRADE color *Equus* no470 p64 N 2016

STYLE color *Horse & Rider* v56 no5 p28 My 2017

Tack Room color *Practical Horseman* v45 no4 p68 Ap 2017

TRAIL & CAMPING GEAR L. BERGER O'CONNOR color *Trail Rider* v29 no4 p48 My 2017

TRAIL & CAMPING GEAR L. B. O'CONNOR color *Trail Rider* v29 no1 p50 Ja/F 2017

TRENDS for 2017 [Cover story] J. Paulson color *Horse & Rider* v56 no3 p46 Mr 2017

Horsemanship—History

A DIFFERENT WORLD D. Bennett bw color *Equus* no475 p60 Ap 2017

Horsemanship—News briefs

News BITS color *Practical Horseman* v45 no8 p62 Ag 2017

News BITS D. O'Connor *Practical Horseman* v45 no1 p64 Ja 2017

Remembering Great Moments in Show Jumping *In Stride* v12 no1 p10 Ja 2017

Winner's CIRCLE color *Practical Horseman* v45 no2 p66 F 2017

Horsemanship—Physiological aspects

Overcome 5 Cold-Weather Challenges E. M. Kellon color *Trail Rider* v29 no1 p28 Ja/F 2017

Step Control L. Place and J. Paulson color *Horse & Rider* v56 no7 p41 Jl 2017

Sweet Pea L. Thompson *Arabian Horse World* v57 no10 p10 Jl 2017

Horsemanship—Psychological aspects

Open Up J. Paulson *Horse & Rider* v56 no8 p15 Ag 2017

Horsemanship—Safety measures

A POSITIVE FOR PEER PRESSURE C. Barakat and M. McCluskey color *Equus* no471 p12 D 2016

Safe Trailer ~ Safe Ride I. LICHTENSTEIN color *Trail Rider* v29 no3 p28 Ap 2017

Safety in Numbers J. GOODNIGHT and H. MELOCCO color *Trail Rider* v29 no3 p24 Ap 2017

Trip Tips J. Goodnight color *Trail Rider* v29 no4 p17 My 2017

Turn Back for Safety J. GOODNIGHT and H. MELOCCO color *Horse & Rider* v56 no10 p48 O 2017

WHY HELMETS MATTER C. Owen color *Dressage Today* v23 no4 p18 D 2016

Horsemanship—Societies, etc.

COLLEGIATE EVENTING COMES OF AGE K. F. Miller color *Practical Horseman* v44 no12 p24 D 2016

From Pony Club Mom to Horsemaster S. Rodell color *Practical Horseman* v44 no12 p72 D 2016

Look, Ma--No Hands! M. Babick *In Stride* v12 no1 p8 Ja 2017

Remembering Great Moments in Show Jumping *In Stride* v12 no1 p10 Ja 2017

Horsemanship—Training of

21 TRAINING TIPS FROM 3 OLYMPIANS S. Weakley color *Practical Horseman* v45 no4 p34 Ap 2017

Finding Your Lane B. Welch bw *Horse & Rider* v56 no7 p17 Jl 2017

Fit for Your Ride [Cover story] K. Altschwager and A. Bennett color *Horse & Rider* v56 no5 p60 My 2017

From One Horse Parent To Another A. Costello color *Dressage Today* v24 no2 p60 N 2017

Is the Tough Trainer Worth It? J. Susser *Dressage Today* v23 no11 p16 Ag 2017

Where WORK is PLAY K. Sanchez color *Dressage Today* v24 no2 p46 N 2017

Horsemen & horsewomen

See also

    Cowboys

    Dressage riders

    Horse breeders

    Horse owners

    Horse trainers

10 TIPS FROM U.S. OLYMPIAN LISA WILCOX T. Holloran, L. Tenney et al color *Dressage Today* p44 My 2017

5 STEPS TO LET YOUR HORSE TRAIN YOU J. Karol color *Dressage Today* p38 My 2017

Abu Dhabi Racing S. Andersen *Arabian Horse World* v57 no6 p141 Mr 2017

Alice Tarjan's RISE TO THE TOP N. Jaffer color *Dressage Today* v23 no12 p44 S 2017

ALL ABOUT THAT BASE! S. Cashman color *Practical Horseman* v44 no12 p32 D 2016

Another reason to ride H. Ellis-Ashburn color *Equus* no476 p96 My 2017

Beware the Ides Of Woff J. Wofford cartoon *Practical Horseman* v45 no4 p18 Ap 2017

BUCKLE UP B. Welch color *Spin to Win Rodeo* v20 no9 p19 N 2016

BUCKLE UP C. Toy color *Spin to Win Rodeo* v21 no4 p17 Je

2017

Celebrate Simple S. Oliynyk *Practical Horseman* v45 no10 p10 O 2017

Choose the Best Eventer J. Winkel color *Practical Horseman* v45 no5 p11 My 2017

The Clinic PHOTO CRITIQUES S. von Dietze color *Dressage Today* p26 My 2017

The Clinic PHOTO CRITIQUES S. von Dietze color *Dressage Today* v23 no12 p26 S 2017

Close the Legs to Go Forward G. H. Morris color *Practical Horseman* v44 no12 p10 D 2016

Confessions of a Nitpicker B. Steinkraus color *Practical Horseman* v45 no2 p20 F 2017

Control What You Can S. Oliynyk color *Practical Horseman* v45 no1 p8 Ja 2017

A CONVERSATION with Jean-Pierre Deroubaix of The Royal Cavalry of Oman S. Andersen *Arabian Horse World* v57 no6 p66 Mr 2017

Correct Lead-Change Anticipation [Cover story] L. Lange color *Horse & Rider* v56 no1 p65 Ja 2017

A DIFFERENT Kind of Ride J. Keeler color *Dressage Today* v23 no8 p52 Ap 2017

Dressage in a Land Far, Far Away J. M. Keeler color *Dressage Today* v23 no9 p46 Je 2017

The Emir's Sword S. Anderson *Arabian Horse World* v57 no6 p138 Mr 2017

EXERCISES AND ADVICE FROM ROBERT DOVER A. Carter color diag *Practical Horseman* v45 no9 p38 S 2017

Find Your Fit N. Fyffe and J. Shepherd color *Dressage Today* v23 no5 p28 Ja 2017

FIVE FLAT B. Welch color *Spin to Win Rodeo* v20 no9 p29 N 2016

From Pony Club Mom to Horsemaster S. Rodell color *Practical Horseman* v44 no12 p72 D 2016

Fun as a Key to Success T. Johnston color *Practical Horseman* v45 no3 p20 Mr 2017

GRADE 1: U.S. races *Arabian Horse World* v57 no6 p35 Mr 2017

GRADE 2: U.S. races *Arabian Horse World* v57 no6 p42 Mr 2017

GRADE 3: U.S. races *Arabian Horse World* v57 no6 p51 Mr 2017

GROUP 1: IFAHR pattern races *Arabian Horse World* v57 no6 p20 Mr 2017

GROUP 2: IFAHR pattern races *Arabian Horse World* v57 no6 p38 Mr 2017

GROUP 3: IFAHR pattern races *Arabian Horse World* v57 no6 p44 Mr 2017

A GUIDE TO ACCURACY AND BALANCE N. Lavoie and A. Morris color diag *Dressage Today* v23 no5 p24 Ja 2017

HORSEPOWER: WHAT IT TAKES TO WIN A WORLD CUP N. Jaffer color *Practical Horseman* v45 no3 p48 Mr 2017

How Can I Move Past Training Ruts? J. Susser *Dressage Today* v23 no5 p18 Ja 2017

How to Break Your Goals Into Manageable Pieces J. Susser *Dressage Today* v23 no7 p16 Mr 2017

Invite Your Horse to Be Round G. H. Morris color *Practical Horseman* v45 no10 p12 O 2017

John French: 'Try to Always Find the Good' T. Conahan color *Practical Horseman* v45 no2 p22 F 2017

Judging Rider Angles G. H. Morris color *Practical Horseman* v45 no6 p14 Je 2017

KING OF QUEENS color *Spin to Win Rodeo* v21 no4 p11 Je 2017

A LEAP OF FAITH J. Autry color *Practical Horseman* v45 no5 p30 My 2017

Little Horse, Big Heart L. Threlkeld color *Practical Horseman* v45 no5 p80 My 2017

MENACE TO THE COMPETITION J. Mankin color diag *Spin to Win Rodeo* v20 no9 p48 N 2016

The Mysterious Case of the Heavy Rain and the Television Show C. Reich *Arabian Horse World* v57 no6 p152 Mr 2017

A New Meaning for "Never" S. Jacobsen color *Dressage Today* p62 My 2017

NO BIGGIE color *Spin to Win Rodeo* v21 no4 p12 Je 2017

Organize, Plan and Structure Your Ride J. Congdon and A. Morris color *Dressage Today* p30 My 2017

PANTYHOSE color *Spin to Win Rodeo* v21 no6 p16 Ag 2017

PRINCIPLES OF CROSS-COUNTRY RIDING L. Threlkeld color *Practical Horseman* v45 no3 p42 Mr 2017

Rachel Long Is Making a Splash L. Taylor *In Stride* v12 no2 p49 Mr 2017

RIDE YOUR HUNTER ROUND LIKE A PRO [Cover story] T. Brennan color *Practical Horseman* v45 no2 p28 F 2017

RIDE YOUR HUNTER ROUND LIKE A PRO T. Brennan color *Practical Horseman* v45 no3 p36 Mr 2017

THE RIGHT CANTER FOR EVERY SITUATION [Cover story] E. Gingras bw chart color *Practical Horseman* v45 no10 p28 O 2017

Sarah Esqueda G. DEARTH *Arabian Horse World* v57 no1 p65 O 2016

socially speaking color *Horse & Rider* v56 no10 p24 O 2017

A Sport of Leaders E. Daily color *Practical Horseman* v45 no5 p8 My 2017

Stanley G. White Sr. July 31, 1936-April 3, 2017 G. DEARTH *Arabian Horse World* v57 no8 p90 My 2017

Stanley White AND Harold Ray—ADVENTURES IN EGYPT ~1978~ G. Dearth *Arabian Horse World* v57 no8 p91 My 2017

Stay Free in the Stop [Cover story] C. Deary and J. Paulson color *Horse & Rider* v56 no1 p25 Ja 2017

Taking on the Big-Sister Role K. F. Miller color *Practical Horseman* v45 no6 p80 Je 2017

To help develop length, stability and elasticity throughout your whole body... cartoon *Dressage Today* v23 no5 p72 Ja 2017

To maximize the straightness and evenness of your connection as your young horse develops into an upper-level horse... L. Fore color *Dressage Today* p80 My 2017

TOUGH MUDDERS color *Spin to Win Rodeo* v21 no4 p14 Je 2017

Tyler Merrill: Weatherford, Texas A. Gentry color *Spin to Win Rodeo* v21 no6 p26 Ag 2017

the WAY WE WERE: THE YEAR WAS 1993 *Arabian Horse World* v57 no10 p53 Jl 2017

We Hear You S. STACKPOLE, K. CHRISTENSEN et al color *Horse & Rider* v56 no1 p12 Ja 2017

We've All Been There... J. Wofford color *Practical Horseman* v45 no6 p16 Je 2017

Which Rider Is Not Jumping Ahead? G. H. Morris color *Practical Horseman* v45 no5 p14 My 2017

Winner's CIRCLE color *Practical Horseman* v45 no1 p66 Ja 2017

Winner's CIRCLE color *Practical Horseman* v45 no7 p65 Jl 2017

Yes, Teamwork Does Make the Dream Work T. Johnston color *Practical Horseman* v45 no9 p24 S 2017

Yes—You Can Develop Feel [Cover story] L. Walker and J. F. Meyer color *Horse & Rider* v56 no1 p34 Ja 2017

Horsemen & horsewomen's injuries

MORE EVIDENCE THAT HELMETS PROTECT AGAINST BRAIN TRAUMA C. Barakat and M. McCluskey color *Equus* no478 p16 Jl 2017

Horsemen & horsewomen—Awards

USET Foundation Honors Three color *Practical Horseman* v45 no4 p62 Ap 2017

Horsemen & horsewomen—Competitions

11th Annual twenty seventeen Las Vegas: ARABIAN BREEDERS WORLD CUP SHOW M. Moore color *Arabian Horse World* v57 no7 p70 Ap 2017

Competition & Camaraderie in the Children's and Adult Amateur Jumper Championships L. Taylor *In Stride* v11 no6 p36 N 2016

DRESSAGE SNAPSHOT color *Dressage Today* v23 no10 p16 Jl 2017

Hunter Championships Conclude in the North K. Rover *In Stride* v11 no6 p47 N 2016

The Perfect Horse at the Perfect Time A. Spiler color *Practical Horseman* v45 no7 p72 Jl 2017

The Top Three Derby Contenders: A Conformation Analysis J. Winkel *In Stride* v11 no6 p44 N 2016

Horsemen & horsewomen—Congresses

6 Things to Do in March *Practical Horseman* v45 no3 p64 Mr 2017

7 Things to Do in JANUARY *Practical Horseman* v45 no1 p64 Ja 2017

Horsemen & horsewomen—Equipment & supplies

emporium color *Dressage Today* v23 no9 p62 Je 2017

READY FOR AUTUMN color *Equus* no480 p32 S 2017

Horsemen & horsewomen—Equipment & supplies—Evaluation

STYLE color *Horse & Rider* v56 no4 p28 Ap 2017

no3 p62 Ap 2017

Pleasure of a Good Ride L. Nelson color *Horse & Rider* v56 no6 p18 Je 2017

POP QUIZ: ALL EARS C. Barakat and M. Freckleton color *Equus* no480 p20 S 2017

POP QUIZ C. Barakat and M. Freckleton color *Equus* no475 p30 Ap 2017

Pressure-Testing Equine Leg Wraps S. Wenholz color *Practical Horseman* v45 no1 p69 Ja 2017

Q&A: Feed-Through Fly Control color *Horse & Rider* v56 no6 p30 Je 2017

The Question My Horse Would Ask Me color *Horse & Rider* v55 no11 p72 N 2016

Raising the Bar [Cover story] C. Shaffer color *Team Roping Journal* p82 S 2017

REASSURING STUDY OF CARRIAGE HORSES C. Barakat and M. McCluskey color *Equus* no475 p25 Ap 2017

Reflections on the Meaning of Horsemanship A. Myers *In Stride* v12 no1 p33 Ja 2017

Retirement Gig C. Toy color diag *Spin to Win Rodeo* v21 no6 p50 Ag 2017

Riding an Offensive Corner with Ryan Motes R. Motes color *Team Roping Journal* p73 S 2017

Riding Out of the Box C. Shaffer color *Team Roping Journal* p66 S 2017

SADDLE CHAT J. Day, J. Beam et al bw color graph *Horse & Rider* v56 no7 p21 Jl 2017

SADDLE CHAT J. Sheldon, J. Bagot et al bw color graph *Horse & Rider* v56 no9 p21 S 2017

The Secret to Free, Forward Collection B. Baumert and A. Morris color *Dressage Today* v23 no9 p24 Je 2017

Seniors That Still Have It N. Chirico color *Horse & Rider* v56 no2 p60 F 2017

Slag for dry lot rehab? E. Fabian-Wheeler *Equus* no473 p67 F 2017

TALK color graph *Horse & Rider* v56 no3 p16 Mr 2017

TALK color graph *Horse & Rider* v56 no6 p24 Je 2017

Test your knowledge of POISONOUS PLANTS [Cover story] L. Bonner color *Equus* no477 p34 Je 2017

THE TOLL TRAVEL TAKES C. Barakat and M. Freckleton color *Equus* no477 p22 Je 2017

Train for Your Horse's Pleasure [Cover story] I. Klimke and S. Rottermann color *Dressage Today* v23 no9 p30 Je 2017

A Truly Timeless Love S. White color *Practical Horseman* v45 no1 p72 Ja 2017

Trust in the Classical System S. Oliynyk color *Practical Horseman* v45 no9 p12 S 2017

What school horses taught me C. Graf color *Equus* no481 p80 O 2017

When I Was a Horse-Crazy Kid, I... L. Prentiss, C. Zundel et al color *Horse & Rider* v56 no2 p72 F 2017

THE X FACTOR C. Toy color *Spin to Win Rodeo* v21 no5 p48 Jl 2017

Young Horse Life J. Paulson *Horse & Rider* v56 no9 p14 S 2017

Zippos ATM N. Chirico color *Horse & Rider* v56 no6 p23 Je 2017

Horses as aids for people with disabilities

Where Are They Now? Haji Rabba's Second Career K. Youngberg *Arabian Horse World* v57 no2 p10 N 2016

Horses in art

FROM THE ARTISTS *Arabian Horse World* v57 no11 p22 Ag 2017

FROM THE ARTISTS *Arabian Horse World* v57 no5 p230 F 2017

FROM THE ARTISTS: EDWARD TROYE color *Arabian Horse World* v57 no7 p138 Ap 2017

Horses' injuries

BEWARE BIOFILM FORMATION C. Barakat and M. McCluskey color *Equus* no480 p14 S 2017

POP QUIZ C. Barakat and M. Freckleton color *Equus* no481 p20 O 2017

SIGNS OF A HOOF ABSCESS C. Barakat and M. Freckleton *Equus* no481 p22 O 2017

Stronger Than You Think J. Mellace *Dressage Today* v23 no12 p10 S 2017

WHAT INFECTION LOOKS LIKE C. Barakat and M. Freckleton color *Equus* no482 p16 N 2017

Horses' injuries—Treatment

emporium color *Dressage Today* v24 no2 p62 N 2017

Wound care basics color *Horse & Rider* v56 no8 p32 Ag 2017

Horses—Accidents

Horses Don't Want To Fall J. Wofford color *Practical Horseman* v45 no3 p16 Mr 2017

Horses—Age

Should This Senior Mare Be Bred? J. H. KOZIOL *Horse & Rider* v56 no2 p12 F 2017

Thinking About Johnny T. Joyce color *Horse & Rider* v56 no2 p8 F 2017

Horses—Age—Research

Oldsters and Aerobics color *Horse & Rider* v56 no2 p17 F 2017

Horses—Anatomy

    See also

    Horses—Hoofs

CONFORMATION CLINIC color *Horse & Rider* v55 no11 p33 N 2016

POP QUIZ: ANATOMY C. Barakat and M. Freckleton color *Equus* no473 p16 F 2017

Horses—Awards

2017 Egyptian Event LEADING SIRES *Arabian Horse World* v57 no11 p52 Ag 2017

Beating the Odds D. Hearst color *Arabian Horse World* v57 no7 p111 Ap 2017

WADEE AL SHAQAB: A VICTORY BY THE SEA [Cover story] D. Hearst *Arabian Horse World* v57 no11 p97 Ag 2017

Horses—Behavior

Beyond the forever home C. Collins color *Equus* no470 p11 N 2016

Can Your Horse Ask You For Help? S. D. Wenholz color *Practical Horseman* v45 no4 p67 Ap 2017

Catch Me Is Uncatchable T. Booker *In Stride* v12 no2 p18 Mr 2017

FOR THE HORSE C. REICH *Arabian Horse World* v57 no6 p150 Mr 2017

How to listen to your horse S. Wilsie and G. Vogel color *Equus* no470 p55 N 2016

Just Joe N. Chirico color *Horse & Rider* v56 no3 p15 Mr 2017

leading riders and handlers D. Tatelman *Arabian Horse World* v57 no6 p29 Mr 2017

NOTHING BORING ABOUT YAWNING C. Barakat and M. McCluskey color *Equus* no470 p21 N 2016

REFORMING A Jigger [Cover story] C. Anderson and J. F. Meyer color *Horse & Rider* v56 no1 p52 Ja 2017

Saving Kasyd B. FINKE *Arabian Horse World* v57 no6 p46 Mr 2017

Settle Your Cinchy Horse J. Goodnight and H. Melocco color *Trail Rider* v29 no2 p42 Mr 2017

What Causes Hostile Behavior? L. I. HAUG *Horse & Rider* v55 no12 p12 D 2016

ZOBEYNI SIRE LINE - PART 1 B. FINKE *Arabian Horse World* v57 no6 p36 Mr 2017

Horses—Behavior—Research

HOW YOUR HORSE LEARNS BY WATCHING YOU C. Barakat and M. McCluskey color *Equus* no473 p10 F 2017

Horses—Case studies

Letting it be C. Barakat bw color *Equus* no472 p20 Ja 2017

Horses—Charts, diagrams, etc.

2016 SPORT HORSE NATIONALS LEADING SIRES D. Tatelman *Arabian Horse World* v57 no4 p108 Ja 2017

Horses—Competitions

American Endurance Ride Conference G. STEWART-SPEARS *Arabian Horse World* v57 no3 p72 D 2016

ARAB YEAR *Arabian Horse World* v57 no4 p198 Ja 2017

Cow Horses in Cowtown color map *Horse & Rider* v56 no10 p30 O 2017

EGYPTIAN EVENT HIGHLIGHTS *Arabian Horse World* v57 no3 p18 D 2016

Greener Pastures N. Valaitham *Arabian Horse World* v57 no3 p285 D 2016

GUEST EDITORIAL B. Finke *Arabian Horse World* v57 no3 p36 D 2016

THE JOURNEY TO NAMPA M. Moore *Arabian Horse World* v57 no4 p84 Ja 2017

SCOTTSDALE 2017: The View from Center Ring G. Dearth

color *Arabian Horse World* v57 no7 p104 Ap 2017

Sheikh Zayed bin sultan Al Nahyan Jewel Crown S. Andersen *Arabian Horse World* v57 no4 p156 Ja 2017

SPORT HORSE NATIONALS AND THE RALVON ELIJAH INFLUENCE M. Moore *Arabian Horse World* v57 no4 p102 Ja 2017

Up to the Challenge *Arabian Horse World* v57 no3 p284 D 2016

U. S. Nationals AWPA Futurities G. Dearth *Arabian Horse World* v57 no3 p54 D 2016

THE VIEW FROM CENTER RING G. Dearth *Arabian Horse World* v57 no3 p46 D 2016

Horses—Conformation

CONFORMATION CLINIC M. Ball color *Horse & Rider* v55 no12 p33 D 2016

Horses—Congresses

6 Things to Do in March *Practical Horseman* v45 no3 p64 Mr 2017

Horses—Diseases

See also

Colic in horses

Equine herpesvirus diseases

Foals—Diseases

Lameness in horses

Laminitis in horses

6 Things you may not have known about Pigeon fever H. S. Thomas color *Equus* no470 p44 N 2016

BEYOND INSULIN RESISTANCE H. S. Thomas and C. Barakat color *Equus* no475 p42 Ap 2017

CONSULTANTS L. L. Couetil color *Equus* no475 p81 Ap 2017

Deciphering Shivers color *Practical Horseman* v44 no12 p69 D 2016

GLOSSARY *Equus* no473 p71 F 2017

GLOSSARY *Equus* no474 p71 Mr 2017

Heaves flare-up L. Bonner color *Equus* no472 p18 Ja 2017

HIGH-TECH BOOST FOR RAINROT DIAGNOSIS C. Barakat and M. McCluskey color *Equus* no471 p11 D 2016

How to Deal with Choke H. W. Werner color *Dressage Today* v23 no8 p18 Ap 2017

LAMINITIS PREVENTION BASICS L. Bonner bw color *Equus* no475 p52 Ap 2017

My Soft Spot J. Paulson *Horse & Rider* v56 no2 p6 F 2017

NEW WAY TO ASSESS PAIN C. Barakat and M. McCluskey color *Equus* no473 p12 F 2017

POP QUIZ C. Barakat and M. Freckleton color *Equus* no470 p22 N 2016

Q&A: Navicular Syndrome [Cover story] color *Horse & Rider* v56 no3 p19 Mr 2017

Q&A: Your Horse's Arthritis color *Horse & Rider* v56 no2 p19 F 2017

TAKING STOCK C. Barakat and M. Freckleton color *Equus* no473 p16 F 2017

The truth about Tail Blocks K. Hepworth-Warren color *Equus* no476 p50 My 2017

Horses—Diseases—Diagnosis

From sickness to health B. Jo Lieberman bw cartoon color *Equus* no473 p34 F 2017

Horses—Diseases—Prevention

ask the experts L. PIERSON and K. HANKINS color *Dressage Today* v23 no8 p66 Ap 2017

INVESTIGATING REPEAT HOOF ABSCESSES C. Barakat and M. Freckleton color *Equus* no470 p22 N 2016

STUD FARM DIARIES C. Reich *Arabian Horse World* v57 no1 p153 O 2016

Horses—Diseases—Treatment

5 First-Aid Kit Essentials E. M. Kellon color *Trail Rider* v29 no2 p22 Mr 2017

Albert's odd ailment C. Barakat color *Equus* no471 p18 D 2016

Colic L. Bonner bw color *Equus* no470 p26 N 2016

ULCERS PART ONE M. DEPAOLO *Arabian Horse World* v57 no2 p138 N 2016

Horses—Diseases—Treatment—Research

THE BEST WAY TO TREAT SAND COLIC C. Barakat and M. McCluskey color *Equus* no474 p11 Mr 2017

SOME SMALL SARCOIDS GO AWAY ON THEIR OWN C. Barakat and M. McCluskey color *Equus* no473 p11 F 2017

Horses—Diseases—Vaccination

West Nile encephalitis L. Bonner bw color *Equus* no475 p36 Ap 2017

Horses—Equipment & supplies

See also

Horses—Transportation—Equipment & supplies

Horseshoes

Saddle blankets

Around the Campfire J. Barsanti, D. M. Johnston et al color *Trail Rider* v29 no4 p8 My 2017

Best Show-Halter Fit A. Dunning and J. Paulson color *Horse & Rider* v56 no2 p32 F 2017

Chaps by Discipline K. Navarra color *Horse & Rider* v55 no12 p58 D 2016

emporium color *Dressage Today* v23 no7 p62 Mr 2017

HEALTH color *Horse & Rider* v56 no2 p17 F 2017

How to make mecate reins L. Feldman color *American Cowboy* v23 no5 p56 F/Mr 2017

Which Saddle is for You? [Cover story] J. Jahiel color *Trail Rider* v29 no2 p36 Mr 2017

Horses—Equipment & supplies—Evaluation

ON-THE-GO GEAR L. BACK color *Trail Rider* v29 no1 p52 Ja/F 2017

PRACTICAL PRODUCTS L. BACK color *Trail Rider* v29 no1 p53 Ja/F 2017

SOLUTIONS L. Armstrong color *Horse & Rider* v56 no2 p18 F 2017

STOCK & TRADE color *Equus* no474 p69 Mr 2017

STYLE color *Horse & Rider* v56 no2 p20 F 2017

Horses—Evaluation

CONFORMATION CLINIC C. Brown color *Horse & Rider* v56 no5 p39 My 2017

CONFORMATION CLINIC J. Pipkin color *Horse & Rider* v56 no6 p43 Je 2017

Four Riders with Good Legs G. H. Morris color *Practical Horseman* v45 no7 p8 Jl 2017

Horses—Exercise

3 STEPS TO STRONGER STIFLES K. L. Marcella color diag *Practical Horseman* v45 no4 p48 Ap 2017

The Gymnastic Tool J. Wofford color graph *Practical Horseman* v44 no12 p16 D 2016

LET THE LEG YIELD WORK FOR YOU S. Dapper and A. Morris color *Dressage Today* v23 no6 p22 F 2017

Horses—Feeding & feeds

6 Signs of Good-Quality Horse Hay color *Trail Rider* v29 no1 p33 Ja/F 2017

DOWNTIME FEEDING C. Barakat and M. Freckleton color *Equus* no475 p30 Ap 2017

EATING ON THE GO AIDS WEIGHT LOSS C. Barakat and M. McCluskey color *Equus* no472 p12 Ja 2017

EFFECTS OF DIET ON ULCER TREATMENT STUDIED C. Barakat and M. McCluskey color *Equus* no472 p11 Ja 2017

HEAD OFF HAY SHORTAGES C. Barakat and M. Freckleton *Equus* no474 p14 Mr 2017

HEALTH color *Horse & Rider* v56 no3 p17 Mr 2017

NUTRITION REPORT: AMINO ACIDS E. L. Prax color *Practical Horseman* v45 no3 p56 Mr 2017

Purina Donates Timely Feed color *Trail Rider* v29 no2 p10 Mr 2017

Trip Tips color *Trail Rider* v29 no2 p16 Mr 2017

USING THE GLYCEMIC INDEX TO INCREASE HEALTH & PERFORMANCE M. DEPAOLO *Arabian Horse World* v57 no1 p156 O 2016

WHAT'S YOUR SUPPLEMENT IQ? C. Barakat color *Equus* no472 p36 Ja 2017

Horses—Feeding & feeds—Evaluation

SOLUTIONS chart color *Horse & Rider* v56 no4 p24 Ap 2017

Horses—Genetic aspects

GENETIC BASIS FOR "TIGER EYE" IDENTIFIED C. Barakat and M. McCluskey color *Equus* no480 p15 S 2017

GLOSSARY *Equus* no480 p79 S 2017

you should know color *Horse & Rider* v56 no8 p21 Ag 2017

Horses—Grooming

See also

Horseshoeing

Finding my way T. Anderson color *Equus* no473 p63 F 2017

Good Impressions chart color *Horse & Rider* v55 no11 p20 N

2016

HOT-TOWEL TECHNIQUES C. Barakat and M. Freckleton color *Equus* no472 p16 Ja 2017

Martha's Month *Martha Stewart Living* no267 p2 S 2016

WHIRLS AND HAIR WHORLS C. Barakat and M. McCluskey color *Equus* no470 p18 N 2016

Winter-Management Checklist J. Jahiel color *Trail Rider* v29 no1 p31 Ja/F 2017

Horses—Grooming—Equipment & supplies

TRENDS for 2017 [Cover story] J. Paulson color *Horse & Rider* v56 no3 p46 Mr 2017

Horses—Health

5 STEPS TO LET YOUR HORSE TRAIN YOU J. Karol color *Dressage Today* p38 My 2017

ask the experts G. DeMone and L. Borzynski color *Dressage Today* v23 no4 p67 D 2016

BEYOND INSULIN RESISTANCE H. S. Thomas and C. Barakat color *Equus* no475 p42 Ap 2017

Bits That Go Ouch! [Cover story] R. Gollehon and A. Harrison color *Horse & Rider* v56 no1 p44 Ja 2017

Bodies in Motion J. Mellace *Dressage Today* v23 no6 p10 F 2017

Curing a Stumbler C. Anderson and J. F. Meyer color *Horse & Rider* v56 no4 p64 Ap 2017

DIET, MORE THAN WEIGHT, CRUCIAL IN INSULIN RESISTANCE C. Barakat and M. McCluskey color *Equus* no470 p19 N 2016

DRY RUN C. Barakat and M. Freckleton color *Equus* no476 p24 My 2017

Equine Fitness and Strength M. T. Donaldson color *Dressage Today* v23 no5 p14 Ja 2017

FECAL SAMPLE 101 C. Barakat and M. Freckleton color *Equus* no475 p30 Ap 2017

FEED-BASED ALLERGY TREATMENT SHOWS PROMISE C. Barakat and M. McCluskey color *Equus* no475 p28 Ap 2017

Feel-Good Work for your Senior Horse [Cover story] J. Forsberg Meyer color *Horse & Rider* v56 no2 p34 F 2017

FIRST-AID PURGE C. Barakat and M. Freckleton *Equus* no476 p26 My 2017

Fit for Your Ride [Cover story] K. Altschwager and A. Bennett color *Horse & Rider* v56 no5 p60 My 2017

GENETIC TEST NOW AVAILABLE FOR "NAKED FOAL" SYNDROME C. Barakat and M. McCluskey color *Equus* no476 p19 My 2017

GLOSSARY *Equus* no470 p71 N 2016

GOOD NEWS ABOUT LIFE AFTER COLIC SURGERY C. Barakat and M. McCluskey color *Equus* no476 p18 My 2017

HEALTH color *Horse & Rider* v56 no1 p19 Ja 2017

HEALTH color *Horse & Rider* v56 no5 p22 My 2017

Insulin-Resistance Q&A [Cover story] color *Horse & Rider* v56 no1 p21 Ja 2017

Keep a Fresh, Clean Barn color *Horse & Rider* v56 no4 p26 Ap 2017

Let's Fix It J. Paulson *Horse & Rider* v56 no1 p8 Ja 2017

Meds or Management? [Cover story] B. Crabbe cartoon *Horse & Rider* v56 no1 p36 Ja 2017

New DIY Tapeworm Test S. Wenholz color *Practical Horseman* v45 no5 p76 My 2017

Oldsters and Aerobics color *Horse & Rider* v56 no2 p17 F 2017

Parasite control L. Bonner color *Equus* no476 p37 My 2017

POP QUIZ C. Barakat and M. Freckleton cartoon *Equus* no472 p14 Ja 2017

PREVENT WINTER WEIGHT LOSS C. Barakat and M. Freckleton color *Equus* no471 p14 D 2016

READING RADIOGRAPHS B. Crabbe color *Horse & Rider* v56 no2 p46 F 2017

REASSURING FINDINGS ABOUT PREDNISOLONE C. Barakat and M. McCluskey color *Equus* no476 p18 My 2017

Rehab Done Right C. Metcalf color *Horse & Rider* v55 no11 p66 N 2016

The Ride Inside T. SCHEVE and N. KITTRELL SCHEVE color *Trail Rider* v29 no4 p54 My 2017

Show-Horse Care at Home B. Avila and J. Paulson color *Horse & Rider* v56 no5 p35 My 2017

Spring Veterinary Checklist C. Toy color *Spin to Win Rodeo* v21 no1 p52 Mr 2017

Thinking about Johnny T. Joyce color *Horse & Rider* v56 no2

p8 F 2017

TOP 10 BLOOD TESTS B. Crabbe color *Horse & Rider* v55 no11 p50 N 2016

The truth about Tail Blocks K. Hepworth-Warren color *Equus* no476 p50 My 2017

Ulcers in the Dressage Horse E. Hardy *Dressage Today* v23 no4 p14 D 2016

VET'S TOP MUD TIPS B. Crabbe color *Horse & Rider* v55 no12 p48 D 2016

What My Horse Wears on His Feet A. Dominy, C. A. Sperti et al cartoon *Horse & Rider* v56 no5 p80 My 2017

What Price for a Plain Pony? K. Pando color *Horse & Rider* v56 no1 p10 Ja 2017

Winter-Management Checklist J. Jahiel color *Trail Rider* v29 no1 p31 Ja/F 2017

Your Health Matters, Too J. Paulson *Horse & Rider* v56 no5 p10 My 2017

Horses—Health—Equipment & supplies

SOLUTIONS chart color *Horse & Rider* v56 no4 p24 Ap 2017

Horses—History

The Arabian Horse C. CULBERTSON *Arabian Horse World* v57 no3 p8 D 2016

Horseshoe pitching

DRINKING GAMES D. Garner bw color *Esquire* v166 no4 p82 N 2016

Horseshoeing

Best Shoeing Method for Low Heels? C. GREGORY *Horse & Rider* v56 no5 p16 My 2017

Quarter-Crack Q&A color *Horse & Rider* v55 no11 p21 N 2016

Horseshoes

THE NEWS ABOUT SHOES E. Pascoe color *Practical Horseman* v44 no12 p46 D 2016

What My Horse Wears on His Feet A. Dominy, C. A. Sperti et al cartoon *Horse & Rider* v56 no5 p80 My 2017

Horseshoes—Design & construction

Best Shoeing Method for Low Heels? C. GREGORY *Horse & Rider* v56 no5 p16 My 2017

Horseshoes—Evaluation

STOCK & TRADE color *Equus* no474 p69 Mr 2017

Horses—Hoofs

Winter Hoof Care F. Jurga color *Trail Rider* v29 no1 p30 Ja/F 2017

Horses—Housing

NEW LIVING ARRANGEMENTS B. Welch color *Spin to Win Rodeo* v20 no11 p88 Ja 2017

Horses—Infections—Prevention

AN EQUITARIAN MISSION S. L. Bettison color map *Equus* no471 p32 D 2016

Horses—Judging

GUEST EDITORIAL B. Finke *Arabian Horse World* v57 no3 p36 D 2016

Horses—Periodicals

Cheers to a New Year D. Hearst *Arabian Horse World* v57 no4 p10 Ja 2017

Page after page T. Belcher color *Equus* no482 p65 N 2017

UPCOMING ISSUES *Arabian Horse World* v57 no4 p203 Ja 2017

YOU LIKE H&R! K. Kennedy, K. Adams et al color *Horse & Rider* v56 no10 p22 O 2017

Horses—Physiology

BANISH IMBALANCES IN THE MOUTH S. Wilson color diag *Practical Horseman* v45 no1 p40 Ja 2017

Choose the Best Warmblood Hunter J. Winkel color *Practical Horseman* v45 no2 p13 F 2017

CONFORMATION CLINIC C. Brown color *Horse & Rider* v56 no5 p39 My 2017

Spring Veterinary Checklist C. Toy color *Spin to Win Rodeo* v21 no1 p52 Mr 2017

Horses—Psychology

My love triangle S. Bennett color *Equus* no480 p70 S 2017

Prevent Disappointment in the Saddle J. Susser color *Dressage Today* v23 no9 p18 Je 2017

Rethinking the BOX STALL N. Moffitt color *Equus* no478 p34 Jl 2017

Horses—Research

ORIGINS OF AMBLING HORSES TRACED C. Barakat and M.

McCluskey bw color *Equus* no471 p13 D 2016

Horses—Safety measures

CHOOSE THE RIGHT FENCE H. Smith Thomas color *Equus* no476 p70 My 2017

Horses Don't Want To Fall J. Wofford color *Practical Horseman* v45 no3 p16 Mr 2017

Horses—Sales & prices

SADDLE CHAT T. Lynn, K. Streeter et al bw color graph *Horse & Rider* v56 no11 p21 N 2017

Horses—Showing

CONGRATULATIONS TO OUR 2016 WINNERS *Arabian Horse World* v57 no5 p27 F 2017

HORSE EXPOS *Trail Rider* v29 no2 p31 Mr 2017

Horses—Societies, etc.

BREED-ASSOCIATION TRAIL-RIDING PROGRAMS color *Trail Rider* v29 no3 p67 Ap 2017

ORGANIZED TRAIL RIDES *Trail Rider* v29 no3 p76 Ap 2017

Horses—Training

See also

Cavalletti

Dressage

10 TIPS FROM U.S. OLYMPIAN LISA WILCOX T. Holloran, L. Tenney et al color *Dressage Today* p44 My 2017

3 Steps to Safe Winter Hauling R. Gimenez color *Trail Rider* v29 no1 p34 Ja/F 2017

Barn-Bored to Trail-Ready [Cover story] H. S. Thomas color *Horse & Rider* v56 no5 p44 My 2017

Barrel Arc and Counter-Arc [Cover story] F. Taylor, J. Smeenk et al color *Horse & Rider* v55 no12 p25 D 2016

Beyond the forever home C. Collins color *Equus* no470 p11 N 2016

Cavalletti Training for Every Horse and Discipline I. Klimke color diag *Practical Horseman* v45 no5 p58 My 2017

CORKILL'S SAN ANTONIO ROSE C. Toy color diag *Spin to Win Rodeo* v21 no2 p52 Ap 2017

Corner Control Down the Fence J. Paulson color *Horse & Rider* v56 no3 p66 Mr 2017

Education vs. Strength H. Hugo-Vidal color *Practical Horseman* v45 no4 p22 Ap 2017

Fix Showmanship Dullness color *Horse & Rider* v56 no5 p73 My 2017

FUNDAMENTALS OF CONDITIONING C. Barakat and M. Freckleton color *Equus* no476 p24 My 2017

Get Ready to Win B. Avila and J. Paulson color *Horse & Rider* v55 no12 p28 D 2016

GETTING THE MOST OUT OF EVERY HORSE C. O. COOPER color *Spin to Win Rodeo* v21 no2 p46 Ap 2017

Ground Work at Liberty J. GOODNIGHT and H. MELOCCO color *Trail Rider* v29 no1 p40 Ja/F 2017

The Gymnastic Tool J. Wofford color graph *Practical Horseman* v44 no12 p16 D 2016

HIP-SAVING STRATEGIES C. Barakat and M. McCluskey color *Equus* no471 p16 D 2016

Horses and People *Arabian Horse World* v56 no12 p234 S 2016

How I Solved My Horse's Problem R. Vaal, J. Morris et al cartoon *Horse & Rider* v56 no1 p72 Ja 2017

IN HARMONY WITH HORSES E. S. ARNARSDÓTTIR *Iceland Review* v55 no1 p48 Ja/F 2017

The Kindergarten Years D. K. Skvarla color *Dressage Today* v23 no5 p42 Ja 2017

LEG BEFORE REIN D. Bluman color *Practical Horseman* v45 no1 p50 Ja 2017

Let's Fix It J. Paulson *Horse & Rider* v56 no1 p8 Ja 2017

MAKING THEIR HORSES — AND THEIR MARK K. F. Miller color *Practical Horseman* v45 no3 p28 Mr 2017

'Now' Exercise Makes Safety a Habit [Cover story] B. Lyons and J. F. Meyer color *Horse & Rider* v56 no5 p42 My 2017

School With Class B. Avila and J. Paulson color *Horse & Rider* v56 no1 p28 Ja 2017

SHOWMANSHIP TUNE-UP [Cover story] L. Lange color *Horse & Rider* v56 no3 p58 Mr 2017

'Stop and Drop' for Ultimate Control S. Purdum and J. F. Meyer color *Horse & Rider* v55 no11 p36 N 2016

TALK color graph *Horse & Rider* v56 no1 p18 Ja 2017

TRAINING TECHNIQUE HELPS HORSES "TALK" C. Barakat and M. McCluskey color *Equus* no472 p10 Ja 2017

Transition Turmoil B. Barkemeyer color *Horse & Rider* v55 no12 p66 D 2016

Trend-Spotting J. Paulson *Horse & Rider* v56 no3 p6 Mr 2017

Without limits T. Rice color *Equus* no472 p63 Ja 2017

Horses—Transportation

3 Steps to Safe Winter Hauling R. Gimenez color *Trail Rider* v29 no1 p34 Ja/F 2017

Moments in Time On THE Road B. FINKE *Arabian Horse World* v57 no4 p154 Ja 2017

The Open Road T. SCHEVE and N. K. SCHEVE color *Trail Rider* v29 no1 p56 Ja/F 2017

Horses—Transportation—Equipment & supplies

See also

Horse trailers

12 Trailering Myths: Busted! R. Gimenez color *Trail Rider* v29 no2 p18 Mr 2017

Trip Tips color *Trail Rider* v29 no2 p16 Mr 2017

Horses—Transportation—Safety measures

12 Trailering Myths: Busted! R. Gimenez color *Trail Rider* v29 no2 p18 Mr 2017

Horses—Weights & measures

What to expect as your horse grows old [Cover story] C. Barakat color *Equus* no473 p24 F 2017

Horses—Wounds & injuries

ADVANCES MADE IN FOAL SURVIVAL RATES C. Barakat and M. McCluskey color *Equus* no475 p26 Ap 2017

Building Your First-Aid Kit B. Crabbe *Dressage Today* p18 My 2017

On guard against EYE INJURIES [Cover story] K. Elizabeth Baril color *Equus* no476 p42 My 2017

OUTCOMES FOR ESOPHAGEAL SURGERY REVIEWED C. Barakat and M. McCluskey *Equus* no475 p25 Ap 2017

POP QUIZ? C. Barakat and M. Freckleton color *Equus* no474 p14 Mr 2017

A tale of two mandibles T. Moates bw cartoon *Equus* no474 p20 Mr 2017

Horses—Wounds & injuries—Prevention

HIP-SAVING STRATEGIES C. Barakat and M. McCluskey color *Equus* no471 p16 D 2016

Horses—Wounds & injuries—Treatment

COMPLEMENTARY CARE M. DEPAULO *Arabian Horse World* v57 no5 p238 F 2017

A field guide to HOOF CRACKS H. S. Thomas color *Equus* no474 p26 Mr 2017

Large laceration L. Bonner color *Equus* no473 p20 F 2017

Rehabilitation Basics L. Simons color *Dressage Today* v23 no5 p36 Ja 2017

Horseware Ireland (Company)

UNDER WRAPS color *Equus* no476 p34 My 2017

HORSLEY, CHELSEA

BUZZWORTHY *Indianapolis Monthly* p14 N 2017

Horta, Paulo Lemos

One Thousand and One Appropriations C. Wren cartoon *Commonweal* v144 no9 p34 My 19 2017

Horticultural exhibitions

MARCH 2017 *Idaho Magazine* v16 no6 p58 Mr 2017

Horticulture

See also

Garden centers (Retail trade)

Greenhouses

Hydroponics

Planting (Plant culture)

Pruning

Vegetable gardening

2 PARENTS, 3 BOYS, 50,000 FLOWERS color *Parents* v92 no8 p114 Ag 2017

ADVENTURES IN DRONE HORTICULTURE C. COLIN color *Popular Mechanics* p7 My 2017

Backyard bliss M. HAIKEN color *Yoga Journal* p104 2016 Special Issue

garden variety J. KOPF color *Better Homes & Gardens* v95 no6 p16 Je 2017

GROW, EAT, LOVE [Cover story] T. Karras and S. Beaucamp cartoon chart color *Yoga Journal* no291 p36 My 2017

How Gardening Beats the Gym V. TWEED color *Better Nutrition* v79 no7 p10 Jl 2017 a lawn that loves you back V. SOLE-SMITH bw color *Parents* v92 no4 p114 Ap 2017

Horticulture—Great Britain

Gallivanting Gardens of the Cotswolds S. Ellis *British Heritage Travel* v38 no3 p30 My/Je 2017

Horton, Berry

BERRY HORTON R. Rubinstein color *Art in America* v104 no10 p156 N 2016

Horton, Jay D.

An adipo-biliary-uridine axis that regulates energy homeostasis diag *Science* v355 no6330 p1173 Mr 17 2017

Horton, Jerry

Act of Love J. NORDLINGER color *National Review* v69 no3 p27 F 20 2017

Horton, Jessica L.

DRONES AND SNAKES color *Art in America* p104 O 2017

Horton, Robert

CRITICS' CHOICE bw chart color *Film Comment* v53 no2 p12 Mr/Ap 2017

True Believer color *Film Comment* v53 no4 p66 Jl/Ag 2017

Horton, Russell

ANNIE HALL'S TICKET LINE TELL-OFF A. Breznican color *Entertainment Weekly* no1460/1461 p29 Ap 7-17 2017

Horvath, Brent

GEUMS M. ROSS color *Better Homes & Gardens* v95 no4 p74 Ap 2017

Horváth, Dezsö

Buffer-gas cooling of antiprotonic helium to 1.5 to 1.7 K, and antiproton-to-electron mass ratio bibl chart diag graph *Science* v354 no6312 p610 N 4 2016

HORVATH, NORA

Connect the Dots cartoon color *Prevention* p96 Mr 2017

Power Poses color *Prevention* v69 no4 p96 Ap 2017

So Happy Together [Cover story] bw color *Prevention* v69 no2 p96 F 2017

Horvath, P.

Observation of a large-scale anisotropy in the arrival directions of cosmic rays above 8 × 1018 eV *Science* v357 no6357 p1266 S 22 2017

Horvitz, Eric

AI, people, and society *Science* v357 no6346 p7 Jl 7 2017

Horvitz, Nir

Mass seasonal bioflows of high-flying insect migrants bibl graph *Science* v354 no6319 p1584 D 23 2016

Horwitz, Alex

Hamilton Comes to TV! M. Roffman *TV Guide* v64 no40 p15 O 3 2016

Horwitz, Paul

Both Sides Have Their Reasons color *Commonweal* v144 no17 p26 O 20 2017

Horwitz, Rick

Whole cell maps chart a course for 21st-century cell biology color *Science* v356 no6340 p806 My 26 2017

HORWITZ, STEVEN

Getting the State Out of Marriage color *Reason* v49 no6 p56 N 2017

HORWITZ, TONY

The Spy Who Loved Me color *New Republic* v248 no5 p6 My 2017

Horwitz-Bennett, Barbara

Sustainability and Structural Steel: A Closer Look *Architectural Record* v205 no7 p160 Jl 2017

HORYN, CATHY

American Fashion Confronts America img *New York* p43 F 20 2017

SEE NOW, BUY NOW img *New York* v49 no19 p55 S 19 2016

Hosanagar, Kartik

The First Wave of Corporate AI Is Doomed to Fail *Harvard Business Review Digital Articles* p2 Ap 18 2017

Why We Don't Trust Driverless Cars — Even When We Should *Harvard Business Review Digital Articles* p2 O 18 2016

Hosch, Melanie Goforth

Country Lore *Mother Earth News* no280 p85 F/Mr 2017

Hose

HOSE HEALTH: USING THE CORRECT CLAMP IS VITAL FOR HOSES' LONG-TERM VIABILITY D. HISLOP color

Sea Magazine v109 no6 p28 Je 2017

TOOLS THEY USE color *Popular Mechanics* p108 Mr 2017

Hose fittings

Don't Get Hosed P. FREDERIKSEN color *Power & Motoryacht* v34 no11 p56 N 2017

Hosemann, Delbert

Resisting Trump's Voter Fraud Inquiry M. WARREN color *Weekly Standard* v22 no42 p10 Jl 17 2017

Hose—Safety measures

WHAT'S THAT ODOR? D. HISLOP *Sea Magazine* v108 no9 p28 S 2016

HOSEY, LANCE

Architects' Original Sin *Architectural Record* v205 no4 p59 Ap 2017

Hoshi, Namiko

Anti-inflammatory effect of IL-10 mediated by metabolic reprogramming of macrophages diag *Science* v356 no6337 p513 My 5 2017

Hosiery

See also

Socks

Extraordinary Reuses For Ordinary Things J. LABIANCA color *Reader's Digest* v189 no1129 p35 Ap 2017

The Tights Stuff K. Kankiewicz color *O, The Oprah Magazine* p126 Mr 2017

Hoskins, Diane—Awards

TRADE SECRETS L. Milk *Washingtonian Magazine* v52 no2 p63 N 2016

Hoskinson, Sarah A.

Clues in the Forest--Archaeology at Florence Hill State Forest *New York State Conservationist* v72 no1 p18 Ag 2017

Hoskisson, Robert E.

Research: When CEOs Don't Win Awards, They Make More Acquisitions *Harvard Business Review Digital Articles* p2 Mr 27 2017

Hoskyns, Barney

Joni: The Anthology color *Publishers Weekly* v264 no21 p81 My 22 2017

Hosmer, Robert

Critic, curator, broadcaster, scoundrel bw *America* v216 no8 p42 Ap 17 2017

Hosmillo, Myra

Neurodevelopmental protein Musashi-1 interacts with the Zika genome and promotes viral replication diag *Science* v357 no6346 p83 Jl 7 2017

Hosokawa, Takashi

Supersonic gas streams enhance the formation of massive black holes in the early universe diag graph *Science* v357 no6358 p1375 S 29 2017

Hospice care

CAN WE TALK? A. BRANDT *Cincinnati Magazine* v50 no4 p72 Ja 2017

Hospice, Fact and Fiction *Saturday Evening Post* v289 no3 p72 My/Je 2017

Hospice care—Psychological aspects

WASHING MY BOY'S BODY F. Ostaseski color *Tricycle: The Buddhist Review* v26 no4 p74 Summ 2017

Hospice patients

Hospice, Fact and Fiction *Saturday Evening Post* v289 no3 p72 My/Je 2017

Hospices (Terminal care facilities)—Design & construction

Elegant Finish H. PEARMAN *Architectural Record* v205 no7 p99 Jl 2017

Hospital administration

See also

Medical appointments & schedules

Health Care Providers Can Use Design Thinking to Improve Patient Experiences S. H. Kim, C. G. Myers et al *Harvard Business Review Digital Articles* p2 Ag 31 2017

Hospitals Can't Improve Without Better Management Systems J. S. Toussaint *Harvard Business Review Digital Articles* p2 O 21 2015

How Every Hospital Should Start the Day R. Sikka, K. Kovich et al *Harvard Business Review Digital Articles* p2 D 5 2014

Why The Best Hospitals Are Managed by Doctors J. K. Stoller, A. Goodall et al *Harvard Business Review Digital Articles* p2

D 27 2016

Hospital building design & construction

HEALTH CARE *Architectural Record* v205 no7 p93 Jl 2017

Northwest Passage M. SITZ *Architectural Record* v205 no7 p104 Jl 2017

Secret Garden A. FIXSEN *Architectural Record* v205 no7 p120 Jl 2017

Hospital buildings—Design & construction

Better Healing from Better Hospital Design Y. Yamaguchi *Harvard Business Review Digital Articles* p2 O 5 2015

How Design Thinking Turned One Hospital into a Bright and Comforting Place D. Deichmann and R. van der Heijde *Harvard Business Review Digital Articles* p2 D 2 2016

How Our Community Designed a Better Hospital J. J. Warner *Harvard Business Review Digital Articles* p2 D 7 2015

The Thread D. Davis, S. Aguado et al *New York Times Magazine* p12 N 27 2016

Hospital care

Better Healing from Better Hospital Design Y. Yamaguchi *Harvard Business Review Digital Articles* p2 O 5 2015

How RFID Technology Improves Hospital Care K. S. Pasupathy and T. R. Hellmich *Harvard Business Review Digital Articles* p2 D 31 2015

Hospital care of children

When Parents and Doctors Disagree on What Futile Means A. Park color *Time* v190 no4 p17 Jl 24 2017

Hospital emergency services

See also

Ambulance service

CALL US EARLY--CALL US FIRST DECREASES EMERGENCY ROOM VISITS V. Prevish *Cincinnati Magazine* v50 no12 p76 S 2017

How We Transformed Emergency Care at Our Hospital R. Zane *Harvard Business Review Digital Articles* p2 D 17 2015

The man had suffered two strokes and was on medication to prevent more. Was this another stroke? Or something else? L. Sanders *New York Times Magazine* p20 My 14 2017

URGENT CARE OR ER? J. Hergenrader color *Women's Health* v14 no6 p82 Jl 2017

Hospital financing

GLEANINGS graph *Christianity Today* v61 no5 p16 Je 2017

Hospital for Special Surgery

Teaching Hospitals Are the Best Place to Test Health Innovation L. A. Shapiro and C. M. Angelo *Harvard Business Review Digital Articles* p2 N 21 2014

Hospital medical staff

Where Are They Now? Catching Up with the Past VRG Interns and Scholarships Winners C. Brown and H. Francis *Vegetarian Journal* v36 no3 p9 2017

Hospital personnel—Wounds & injuries

Hospital workers: an assessment of occupational injuries and illnesses M. A. Dressner bibl *Monthly Labor Review* p1 Je 2017

Hospital records

'GENERAL CONDITION: FAIRLY GOOD': RESEARCHING TUBERCULOSIS PATIENTS AT AN ARMY HOSPITAL IN NEW MEXICO C. White *Prologue* v49 no2 p56 Summ 2017

Hospitality

Bad Houseguests *Lapham's Quarterly* v10 no1 p141 Wint 2017

Celebrate Good Times K. A. BACKER and D. POINTDUJOUR color *Ebony* v72 no3 p74 D 2016/Ja 2017

Christian Slater: How do you navigate a dinner party? D. WALTERS bw color *Bon Appetit* v62 no10 p112 O 2017

Designing for Guests [Cover story] D. MULFINGER color *Cabin Living* p20 Ag 2017

easy as PIE color *Good Housekeeping* v263 no5 p85 N 2016

Greek hospitality is put to a religious test A. Markovich color *Christian Century* v133 no25 p15 D 7 2016

"I'm That Guy Who Kept Old Chinatown Old." W. TANG color *Bon Appetit* v62 no2 p60 Mr 2017

Mind Your Manners C. Hays and G. Metcalfe color *Southern Living* v52 no11 p26 N 2017

MY RECIPE FOR SUCCESS color *Bon Appetit* v62 no10 p12 O 2017

Hospitality industry

See also

Bars (Drinking establishments)

Food service

Hotels

Resorts

Restaurants

Spiritual retreat centers

AMERICA'S GUIDE TO RETREATS *America* v217 no6 p31 S 18 2017

BEST IN THE WORLD color *Conde Nast Traveler* v51 no10 p87 N 2016

BEST IN THE WORLD HOTELS [Cover story] color *Conde Nast Traveler* v52 no10 p51 N 2017

Case Study: Which Customers Should This Restaurant Listen To? S. Puri, K. Khanzode et al *Harvard Business Review Digital Articles* p2 Mr 29 2016

Chalet C7 Hotel Portillo A. GILDEMEISTER color *Conde Nast Traveler* v52 no9 p112 O 2017

LOCKED AND LOADED J. Sidman *Washingtonian Magazine* v52 no4 p180 Ja 2017

Missouri Tiger J. Passov and C. Barrett color *Golf Magazine* v59 no8 p36 Ag 2017

PEAK RESTAURANT? J. Sidman *Washingtonian Magazine* v52 no4 p15 Ja 2017

RESORTS color *Conde Nast Traveler* v52 no10 p80 N 2017

This Food Podcast Turns It Up to 11 H. EATON *Los Angeles Magazine* p66 D 2016

The TIPPING Point D. Garner color *Esquire* v167 no2 p82 Mr 2017

WIZARD OF OZ S. TODD color *Conde Nast Traveler* v52 no9 p22 O 2017

Hospitality industry—Corrupt practices

Share This J. Eidelson graph *Bloomberg Businessweek* no4530 p24 Jl 17 2017

Hospitals

All the Doctors Will See You Now S. Grobart color diag *Bloomberg Businessweek* no4508 p55 Ja 23 2017

Bouncing Baby Boomers *Saturday Evening Post* v289 no1 p108 Ja/F 2017

THE FIVE-STROKE NORTON P. EGAN *Cycle World* v55 no10 p26 N 2016

Getting Buy-In for Predictive Analytics in Health Care M. Kakad, R. Rozenblum et al *Harvard Business Review Digital Articles* p2 Je 20 2017

IDENTITY CRISIS L. COLLINS color diag *New Yorker* v93 no23 p24 Ag 7 2017

What a Visit to an AIEnabled Hospital Might Look Like R. "Wang *Harvard Business Review Digital Articles* p2 N 16 2016

What Health Systems, Hospitals, and Physicians Need to Know About Implementing Electronic Health Records R. M. Pearl *Harvard Business Review Digital Articles* p2 Je 15 2017

Zero Tolerance H. Levine bw color graph *Consumer Reports* v82 no1 p32 Ja 2017

Hospitals—Customer services

One Hospital's Experiments in Virtual Health Care A. Licurse *Harvard Business Review Digital Articles* p2 D 9 2016

Hospitals—Directories

TOP HOSPITALS color *New Orleans Magazine* v51 no4 p80 F 2017

Hospitals—Evaluation

What Does the Fox Say? G. HAND *Cincinnati Magazine* v50 no6 p56 Mr 2017

Hospitals—Louisiana

TOP HOSPITALS 2017 *Louisiana Life* v37 no6 p39 Jl/Ag 2017

Hospitals—Missouri

Remuddling bw color *Old House Journal* v45 no5 p80 Ag 2017

Hospitals—Ohio—Cincinnati

THE CHRIST HOSPITAL ATTRACTS CAPACITY CROWD FOR WOMEN'S HEALTH EVENT color *Cincinnati Magazine* v51 no1 p131 O 2017

Hospitals—Religious aspects

Rise of the Zombie Hospitals S. RUSSELL-KRAFT il *New Republic* v247 no12 p12 D 2016

Hospitals—Safety measures

How Every Hospital Should Start the Day R. Sikka, K. Kovich et al *Harvard Business Review Digital Articles* p2 D 5 2014

Hospitals—United States

30% V. Tweed color *Amazing Wellness* v9 no2 p18 Spr 2017

Hospital Coalitions Save Money and Improve Care C. Holt *Harvard Business Review Digital Articles* p2 D 18 2014

How Safe Does a Hospital Need to Be? M. Quinn *Governing* v30 no6 p18 Mr 2017

How U.S. Hospitals and Health Systems Can Reverse Their Sliding Financial Performance J. Goldsmith *Harvard Business Review Digital Articles* p2 O 5 2017

TOP HOSPITALS color *New Orleans Magazine* v51 no4 p80 F 2017

Why The Best Hospitals Are Managed by Doctors J. K. Stoller, A. Goodall et al *Harvard Business Review Digital Articles* p2 D 27 2016

Hospitals—United States—Security measures

Keep Hospitals Weapons-Free N. P. Morris color *Scientific American* v316 no1 p8 Ja 2017

Hospitals—Virginia

A Baby Dies in Virginia E. BOEHM cartoon *Reason* v48 no11 p46 Ap 2017

Hospodarsky, G.

Jupiter's magnetosphere and aurorae observed by the Juno spacecraft during its first polar orbits diag graph *Science* v356 no6340 p826 My 26 2017

Hossain, Mokarram

Visualizing the function and fate of neutrophils in sterile injury and repair color graph *Science* v357 no6359 p111 O 6 2017

Hossbach, T. W.

Observation of coherent elastic neutrino-nucleus scattering diag *Science* v357 no6356 p1123 S 15 2017

Hossenfelder, Sabine

Why Quark Rhymes with Pork And Other Scientific Diversions *Physics Today* v69 no11 p57 N 2016

Hosszú, Katinka, 1989-

Katinka Hosszú C. Cullen color *Current Biography* v77 no10 p58 O 2016

Host plants

Fatty acids in arbuscular mycorrhizal fungi are synthesized by the host plant L. H. Luginbuehl, G. N. Menard et al diag graph *Science* v356 no6343 p1175 Je 16 2017

Long-Term Trends in Midwestern Milkweed Abundances and Their Relevance to Monarch Butterfly Declines D. N. ZAYA, I. S. PEARSE et al *BioScience* v67 no4 p343 Ap 2017

Plants transfer lipids to sustain colonization by mutualistic mycorrhizal and parasitic fungi Y. Jiang, W. Wang et al diag graph *Science* v356 no6343 p1172 Je 16 2017

Hostages—Interviews

IRAN HOSTAGE SERGEANT ROCKY SICKMANN REMEMBERS *Military History* v33 no6 p28 Mr 2017

Hostages—Iraq

ESCAPE FROM THE CALIPHATE J. Percy *Harper's Magazine* v333 no1998 p62 N 2016

HOSTETTER, BECKY

SUMMER *Indianapolis Monthly* v12 no40 p64 Ag 2017

Hostetter, Kristin

Day DREAMING: The best dayhike in every state color *Backpacker* p52 S 2017

Hostility (Psychology)—Religious aspects

LIVING BY The Word *Christian Century* v134 no3 p18 F 2017

Hostin, Sunny

FINDING YOUR REAL VOICE color *Essence* v48 no2 p118 Je 2017

THE VIEW M. LOGAN *TV Guide* v65 no21 p44 My 15 2017

Hosung Kim

Extensive migration of young neurons into the infant human frontal lobe color diag graph *Science* v354 no6308 paaf7073-1 O 7 2016

Hot, David

Reversion of antibiotic resistance in Mycobacterium tuberculosis by spiroisoxazoline SMARt-420 bibl diag *Science* v355 no6330 p1206 Mr 17 2017

Hot air balloons

Old West Balloon Fest fills Panhandle skies R. HOLSINGER color *Nebraska Life* v21 no5 p80 S/O 2017

TRIAL BALLOONS A. Mann color diag *Science* v356 no6344 p1227 Je 23 2017

Hot air balloons—Competitions

JULY/AUGUST K. Massicot color *Louisiana Life* v37 no6 p62 Jl/Ag 2017

Hot baths

IN HOT WATER [Cover story] color *Prevention* v69 no2 p6 F 2017

Hot carriers

Long-range hot-carrier transport in hybrid perovskites visualized by ultrafast microscopy Z. Guo, Y. Wan et al diag graph *Science* v356 no6333 p59 Ap 7 2017

Hot chocolate (Beverage)

Gather color *Rodale's Organic Life* v2 no7 p15 D 2016/Ja 2017

HAUTE CHOCOLATE M. C. Cairns color *Southern Living* v52 no1 p110 Ja 2017

Hot Chocolate Bar A. Larson *Idaho Magazine* v17 no1 p56 Ja 2017

WARM UP YOUR COOLDOWN L. APPLEGATE color *Runner's World* v51 no11 p50 D 2016

Hot Date (TV program)

Hot Date N. Abrams, B. L. Heldman et al *Entertainment Weekly* no1482/1483 p74 S 22 2017

Hot flashes

FADING FLOW J. Pinkerton color *Women's Health* v14 no2 p34 Mr 2017

Hot pepper sauces

THE BEST UNSUNG SAUCES color *Men's Health* v32 no4 p114 My 2017

Hot peppers

AMAZING NEWS V. Tweed color *Amazing Wellness* v9 no6 p14 EarlyWint 2017

SOME LIKE IT HOT B. ESPARZA *Los Angeles Magazine* p64 Mr 2017

Hot Rod (Periodical)

The HOT ROD Archives D. Wallace color *Hot Rod* v70 no11 p12 N 2017

The HOT ROD Archives D. Wallace color *Hot Rod* v70 no2 p12 F 2017

The HOT ROD Archives D. Wallace color *Hot Rod* v70 no8 p14 Ag 2017

Hot Rod Drag Week

Salt-Flat Racing Happens at a Different Pace E. Perkins color *Hot Rod* v69 no12 p10 D 2016

Hot rod engines

Things to Come E. Perkins color *Hot Rod* v70 no10 p8 O 2017

Hot rod racing

Chasing the SUMMIT P. Thomas bw color *Hot Rod* v69 no12 p26 D 2016

Hot rod speed

Horsepower Shaming D. Freiburger color *Hot Rod* v70 no7 p122 Jl 2017

Hot rods

The 350 in Bill Hedekin's 1967 Corvette Backfires, Stalls, and Uses Oil. Time for HOT ROD to Fix It M. Davis chart color *Hot Rod* v70 no3 p88 Mr 2017

The HOT ROD Archives D. Wallace color *Hot Rod* v70 no10 p16 O 2017

The HOT ROD Archives D. Wallace color *Hot Rod* v70 no3 p12 Mr 2017

The HOT ROD Archives D. Wallace color *Hot Rod* v70 no6 p20 Je 2017

HOT ROD D. Wallace color *Hot Rod* v69 no12 p14 D 2016

MPG HEADS CHAMPION SMALL-BLOCK FORD B. Gillogly color *Hot Rod* v70 no3 p58 Mr 2017

Pat Ganahl T. Taylor bw color *Hot Rod* v70 no5 p58 My 2017

THE (SOGGY) RACE OF GENTLEMEN D. Hardin bw color *Hot Rod* v70 no3 p48 Mr 2017

Take 5 With ROY BRIZIO T. Taylor color *Hot Rod* v70 no6 p14 Je 2017

V8 Anything D. Freiburger color *Hot Rod* v70 no5 p114 My 2017

Where Did T-Buckets Come From? T. Taylor bw *Hot Rod* v70 no7 p10 Jl 2017

Hot rods—Design & construction

Take 5 With TROY LADD J. P. Huffman color *Hot Rod* v70 no2 p14 F 2017

Hot shops (Glass blowing & working)

GLASSBLOWER PATRICK CASANOVA'S color *Cabin Living* p11 Ap 2017

Playing with Fire: Glass blowing at YAYA Studios K. Massicot

color *New Orleans Magazine* v51 no10 p214 Ag 2017
Hot spots (Geology)
 Hot Spots G. Almy color *Field & Stream* v122 no3 pB1 Ag 2017
Hot springs
 First among equals H. Wilson map *Canadian Geographic* v137 no1 p24 F 2017
 HOT SPRINGS *South Dakota Magazine* v33 no3 p37 S/O 2017
Hot Springs Village (Ark.)
 Go Big & Go Home J. Passov color *Golf Magazine* v59 no3 p106 Mr 2017
Hot Stix Golf LLC
 THIS MONTH: DRIVERS M. Chwasky, M. Dee et al color *Golf Magazine* v59 no3 p72 Mr 2017
Hot Thoughts (Music)
 Spoon's Secret Influences K. GROW bw color *Rolling Stone* no1284 p18 Ap 6 2017
Hot tubs
 perspective house of the month: A FIRM REVISITS THE SITE OF ITS FIRST RESIDENCE TO CREATE A RELAXING BACKYARD RETREAT FOR A LONGTIME CLIENT AND FRIEND M. SITZ color map *Architectural Record* v205 no5 p37 My 2017
Hot weather clothing
 Suit yourself S. Kennedy color *Bloomberg Businessweek* no4522 p85 My 15 2017
 Summer Living C. Rose cartoon *New Orleans Magazine* v51 no8 p44 Je 2017
Hot weather clothing—Evaluation
 HOW TO SUMMER IN STYLE J. ROTH color *Esquire* p54 2017 BigBlackBook
 WEEKEND GETAWAY color *Essence* v48 no3 p20 Jl 2017
 YOUR TWO-STEP SUMMER UPGRADE color *Esquire* p34 Ag 2017
Hot weather conditions—Physiological effect
 TAKE THE PLUNGE K. DOLD color *Runner's World* v52 no7 p14 Ag 2017
Hotard, Michael
 Protecting unauthorized immigrant mothers improves their children's mental health diag *Science* v357 no6355 p1041 S 8 2017
HOTCHKISS, SEAN
 Can a Manly Man Wear Makeup? color *GQ: Gentlemen's Quarterly* v97 no10 p72 O 2017
 Drift Back color *Conde Nast Traveler* v52 no7 p88 Ag 2017
 I Surrendered My Wardrobe color *GQ: Gentlemen's Quarterly* v87 no1 p30 Ja 2017
 Living on the Edge color *Esquire* v166 no5 p60 D 2016/Ja 2017
 What, This Old Thing? [Cover story] color *Esquire* p98 BigBlackBook
Hotel design & construction
 Baja Soul S. KELSO color *Conde Nast Traveler* v52 no6 p36 Je/Jl 2017
 Ett Hem Stockholm color *Conde Nast Traveler* v52 no8 p48 S 2017
 The Haute Bungalow A. ABEL color *Forbes* v199 no5 p118 My 16 2017
 A Look at What's New in Retail and Hospitality Design P. J. Arsenault color graph *Architectural Record* v205 no8 p128 Ag 2017
 Myanmar's Hotel Room Glut P. Heijmans color *Bloomberg Businessweek* no4528 p29 Je 26 2017
 Public Display S. STEPHENS *Architectural Record* v205 no9 p84 S 2017
 Puro Hotel A. Martins *Architectural Record* v205 no9 p145 S 2017
 REDUX I. Parker cartoon *New Yorker* v93 no26 p20 S 4 2017
 Richardson Revival B. BROOME *Architectural Record* v205 no9 p78 S 2017
Hotel design & construction—Evaluation
 HAUTE HOTELS: Designed down to the last perfect detail *Virginia Living* p116 2017 Best 20of Virginia
Hotel Employees & Restaurant Employees International Union
 The Naked Man at the Door: City ordinances seek to protect hotel workers from sexual harassment and assault S. CLOKE *Ms.* v27 no3 p11 Fall 2017
Hotel employees—Crimes against
 The Naked Man at the Door: City ordinances seek to protect hotel workers from sexual harassment and assault S. CLOKE *Ms.* v27

no3 p11 Fall 2017
Hotel evaluation
 Alpine Inn Bed & Breakfast K. MONTGOMERY *Arizona Highways* v93 no8 p14 Ag 2017
 DOWN AND OUT AT THE BULLFROG HOTEL K. LYDERSEN *In These Times* v41 no8 p42 Ag 2017
 FRESH ON THE SCENE: The new and exciting in the food world-ranked! A. Spiegel *Washingtonian Magazine* v52 no8 p136 My 2017
 The Haute Bungalow A. ABEL color *Forbes* v199 no5 p118 My 16 2017
 Plan It: A Prairie Weekend *American Cowboy* v24 no1 p37 Je/Jl 2017
 Siam Revival J. ADAMS color *Conde Nast Traveler* v52 no6 p38 Je/Jl 2017
Hotel food service
 The Mercer Sevilla color *Conde Nast Traveler* v52 no6 p49 Je/Jl 2017
Hotel laundry service
 How Our Hotel Used Data to Make Our Laundry Service Glamorous A. Brant color *Harvard Business Review Digital Articles* p2 Mr 1 2017
Hotel remodeling
 Changes In the 'Bu M. BUSICO color *Los Angeles Magazine* v62 no10 p18 O 2017
 RISE & SHINE A. MARSHALL color *Architectural Digest* v74 no8 p88 Ag 2017
Hotel restaurants—Design & construction
 snapshot A. Klimoski *Architectural Record* v205 no7 p176 Jl 2017
Hotel restaurants—Evaluation
 Babylonstoren, South Africa S. KHAN color *Conde Nast Traveler* v51 no10 p60 N 2016
 News From the Kitchens: Public Service, Piece of Meat Butcher & Restaurant, Sprout and Press R. Peyton color *New Orleans Magazine* v51 no10 p174 Ag 2017
Hotel rooms
 THE 12-MINUTE HOTEL-ROOM WORKOUT cartoon color *Esquire* p68 S 2017
 ROOM WITH A VIEW A. TAMBURRINI color *Conde Nast Traveler* v52 no10 p142 N 2017
Hotel suites—Evaluation
 CAMP CHRISTMAS N. DAYTON *Better Homes & Gardens* v94 no12 p96 D 2016
Hotel de Crillon (Paris, France)
 Above AND Crillon C. Bagley color *Conde Nast Traveler* v52 no8 p96 S 2017
 Crillon Redux color *Conde Nast Traveler* v52 no8 p41 S 2017
Hotelkeepers
 Grand Floatels A. KIRKMAN color *Conde Nast Traveler* v52 no7 p42 Ag 2017
Hotels
    See also
    Bed & breakfast accommodations
    Boutique hotels
    Lodging-houses
    Park lodging facilities
    Tourist camps, hostels, etc.
 BACK TO BASICS ICELAND AS IT'S MEANT TO BE SEEN T. SKINNER color map *Conde Nast Traveler* v52 no10 p40 N 2017
 Back to Big Sur J. WOGAN color *Conde Nast Traveler* v52 no10 p32 N 2017
 THE BEACH RESET K. Sintumuang color *Esquire* p18 Ag 2017
 BEST IN THE WORLD color *Conde Nast Traveler* v51 no10 p87 N 2016
 BEST IN THE WORLD HOTELS [Cover story] color *Conde Nast Traveler* v52 no10 p51 N 2017
 THE BEST OF THE WEST color *Iceland Review* v54 no5 p106 S O 2016
 Chalet C7 Hotel Portillo A. GILDEMEISTER color *Conde Nast Traveler* v52 no9 p112 O 2017
 COCK TAIL OF THE MONTH D. ALAN *Texas Monthly* v45 no1 p36 Ja 2017
 DAKAR A. MERRILL and D. JEFFERYS color *Conde Nast Traveler* v52 no4 p30 Ap 2017
 ETHIOPIA A. POSTMAN color *Conde Nast Traveler* v52 no4

p36 Ap 2017

HIDDEN GOLD: A VERMONT INSIDERS GUIDE to finding UNDERTHERADAR, OVERTHETOP COLOR B. SCHELLER *Yankee* v81 no5 p96 S/O 2017

THE LAST WORD *Conde Nast Traveler* v52 no4 p46 Ap 2017

LITTLE MANOR ON THE PRAIRIE K. HUNHOFF *South Dakota Magazine* v32 no4 p58 N/D 2017

Missouri Tiger J. Passov and C. Barrett color *Golf Magazine* v59 no8 p36 Ag 2017

MODERN ROYALS E. Malter color *Sunset* v239 no1 p36 Jl 2017

New Orleans B. P. KATZ color *Martha Stewart Living* p136 Ap 2017

The Nongambler's Guide to Vegas M. CROSS color *Kiplinger's Personal Finance* v71 no8 p34 Ag 2017

OuT of SighT color *Conde Nast Traveler* v52 no10 p132 N 2017

THE PROMISED LAND D. Slater color *Sunset* v238 no4 p68 Ap 2017

RWANDA + UGANDA A. WHITTLE color *Conde Nast Traveler* v52 no4 p32 Ap 2017

SOMEWHERE NEW R. MISNER color *Conde Nast Traveler* v52 no5 p34 My 2017

SOUTHERN AFRICA S. KHAN color *Conde Nast Traveler* v52 no4 p38 Ap 2017

SPRINGTIME IN HORSE COUNTRY V. F. Luesse color *Southern Living* v52 no3 p100 Mr 2017

The Suite of Power [Cover story] A. Altman, T. Berenson et al color *Time* v189 no23 p22 Je 19 2017

TOTAL ECLIPSE OF HOTEL AVAILABILITY J. Alsever color *Fortune* v176 no1 p11 Jl 1 2017

Turning the Tables *Conde Nast Traveler* v52 no9 p12 O 2017

Hotels—Argentina

Free Range M. Hranek color map *Conde Nast Traveler* v51 no11 p108 D 2016

Hitting BA Just Right K. LAGRAVE color *Conde Nast Traveler* v52 no3 p18 Mr 2017

Hotels—Arizona

Hotel San Ramón K. MONTGOMERY *Arizona Highways* v93 no3 p14 Mr 2017

The Inn at Castle Rock: Like so many things in Bisbee, this old hotel has its quirks, including 14 funky guest rooms with names such as Crying Shame and Last Chance, a "Ghost Book" and a "moat." K. MONTGOMERY *Arizona Highways* v93 no11 p14 N 2017

Hotels—Brazil

Getting Warmer E. FLORIO color *Conde Nast Traveler* v52 no4 p14 Ap 2017

Oscar Winner F. A. BERNSTEIN color *Architectural Digest* no5 p158 My 2017

Hotels—California

52 GREAT WEEKENDS *Los Angeles Magazine* p98 My 2017

BACK TO THE LAND A. Scott color *Sunset* v239 no4 p60 O 2017

Changes In the 'Bu M. BUSICO color *Los Angeles Magazine* v62 no10 p18 O 2017

Going Back to Cali Wine Country P. BRADY color *Conde Nast Traveler* v52 no3 p50 Mr 2017

Hotels—California—Los Angeles

Sunset Tower Hotel, Los Angeles A. WHITTLE color *Conde Nast Traveler* v52 no1 p58 Ja 2017

Hotels—California—San Francisco

San Francisco A. WHITTLE color map *Conde Nast Traveler* v52 no6 p50 Je/Jl 2017

Hotels—Colorado

A VIEW FROM THE TOP C. HELMAN color *Forbes* v198 no5 p112 O 25 2016

Hotels—Costs

GREAT WINTER STAYCATIONS N. KOKOTAS HAHN color *Chicago* v65 no12 p34 D 2016

Hotels—Design & construction

DEFENDING PARADISE A. DOUGLAS bw color *Surfer* v57 no13 p40 Mr 2017

DONALD TRUMP'S WORST DEAL A. DAVIDSON cartoon color *New Yorker* v93 no4 p48 Mr 13 2017

A Hidden Treasure S. AMELAR *Architectural Record* v204 no10 p90 O 2016

In the Cloud S. STEPHENS color diag *Architectural Record* v205

no3 p84 Mr 2017

The Italian Job J. MINUTILLO *Architectural Record* v204 no10 p84 O 2016

Oscar Winner F. A. BERNSTEIN color *Architectural Digest* no5 p158 My 2017

Suite Life K. Logan color *Architectural Record* v204 no12 p105 D 2016

Hotels—England

HIe THee TO HULL! D. Huntley *British Heritage Travel* v38 no1 p40 Ja/F 2017

Lonely Places Jor Ajternoon Tea *British Heritage Travel* v38 no1 p71 Ja/F 2017

On the Road I. MANNERS and V. STEIKER color *Vogue* v207 no3 p390 Mr 2017

Hotels—England—London

Crowned Jewels N. Ekstein chart color *Bloomberg Businessweek* no4532 p65 Jl 31 2017

Hotels—Europe

Alpine Escapes [Cover story] B. K. Taylor color *Vegetarian Times* v43 no2 p70 N/D 2016

SERENITY AND COMFORT *Iceland Review* v54 no6 p105 N/D 2016

Hotels—Evaluation

See also

Boutique hotels—Evaluation

Luxury hotels—Evaluation

52 GREAT WEEKENDS *Los Angeles Magazine* p98 My 2017

All Roads Lead to Dubai C. AJUDUA color *Conde Nast Traveler* v51 no10 p52 N 2016

Baccarat Hotel New York R. KHONG color *Conde Nast Traveler* v52 no3 p44 Mr 2017

THE BOOZE SLEUTH S. FREEMAN color *Chicago* v66 no1 p60 Ja 2017

chandigarh, india N. BRARA and M. OWENS color *Architectural Digest* no5 p78 My 2017

CHRISTMAS AT THE GREENBRIER C. Kling color *Southern Living* v51 no12 p112 D 2016

The Comeback J. WOGAN color *Conde Nast Traveler* v52 no3 p48 Mr 2017

COZY COUNTRY HIDEAWAY *Iceland Review* v54 no6 p128 N/D 2016

THE DEWBERRY B. RILEY *Atlanta* v57 no1 p99 My 2017

THE DWELL HOTEL *Atlanta* v57 no1 p95 My 2017

ESCAPE TO KEY WEST J. ANDERSON-MINSHALL color *Advocate* no1090 p50 Ap 2017

Euro Star M. W. NICKLIN color *Conde Nast Traveler* v52 no3 p42 Mr 2017

FIT FOR A WHALE C. R. JOYNT *Washingtonian Magazine* v52 no5 p26 F 2017

Get Off The Loop E. GLUSAC color *Conde Nast Traveler* v52 no2 p36 F 2017

The GOLD List 2017 H. YANAGIHARA color *Conde Nast Traveler* v52 no1 p62 Ja 2017

Green Hotels and Inns K. K. BECKIUS color *Yankee* p74 Mr 2017

Haute News color *Vanity Fair* v58 no12 p76 D 2016

THE HENDERSON T. MALONE *Atlanta* v57 no1 p97 My 2017

Hotel Castel Dracula R. Griffiths *History Today* v67 no2 p70 F 2017

HOTELS and B&B's *Texas Monthly* v45 no3 p102 Mr 2017

Hotel San Ramón K. MONTGOMERY *Arizona Highways* v93 no3 p14 Mr 2017

HOT LIST! color map *Conde Nast Traveler* v52 no5 p67 My 2017

THE HOT LIST *Los Angeles Magazine* v61 no11 p152 N 2016

In the Zone *Conde Nast Traveler* v52 no4 p19 Ap 2017

THE KIMPTON CARDINAL HOTEL J. R. MARQUEZ *Atlanta* v57 no1 p98 My 2017

Land of OZ K. BUTCHER bw cartoon color *Bike Magazine* v24 no1 p74 Ja/F 2017

LIVING IN COLOR A. Postman color *Conde Nast Traveler* v51 no11 p102 D 2016

The Majestic Ahwahnee Hotel A. Andrews *Sierra* v101 no4 p17 Jl/Ag 2016

MANDARIN ORIENTAL, LAS VEGAS *Los Angeles Magazine* p82 Mr 2017

Meet and Greet E. FLORIO color *Conde Nast Traveler* v52 no3 p40 Mr 2017

MIAMI Rhapsody L. RAMZI color *Vogue* v206 no11 p180 N 2016

MORONGO CASINO, RESORT & SPA *Los Angeles Magazine* p82 F 2017

NORTHERN SOUL color *Iceland Review* v54 no5 p100 S-O 2016

On the Road I. MANNERS and V. STEIKER color *Vogue* v207 no3 p390 Mr 2017

Out & About color *Martha Stewart Living* p10 Mr 2017

THE PERFECT GIRLS' GETAWAY color *Good Housekeeping* v263 no5 p202 N 2016

PLAN IT: San Antonio, Texas *American Cowboy* v23 no6 p33 Ap/My 2017

Playing Huis P. GUZMÁN color *Conde Nast Traveler* v51 no11 p56 D 2016

puerto escondido, mexico H. MARTIN color *Architectural Digest* no5 p86 My 2017

SANTA BARBARA R. MISNER color *Conde Nast Traveler* v52 no5 p32 My 2017

SLEEP ON IT A. KONERMANN *Cincinnati Magazine* v50 no2 p36 N 2016

SOUTH'S BEST HOTEL V. F. Luesse color *Southern Living* v52 no4 p78 Ap 2017

SOUTH'S BEST INN R. F. Hayes color *Southern Living* v52 no4 p80 Ap 2017

The SOUTH'S COOLEST NEW HOTELS *Atlanta* v57 no1 p92 My 2017

Staying Power H. YANAGIHARA color *Conde Nast Traveler* v52 no2 p38 F 2017

Sunset Tower Hotel, Los Angeles A. WHITTLE color *Conde Nast Traveler* v52 no1 p58 Ja 2017

Tavern Hotel N. AUSTIN *Arizona Highways* v92 no11 p14 N 2016

THOMPSON NASHVILLE *Atlanta* v57 no1 p96 My 2017

WELL TRAVELED C. Coen cartoon *Louisiana Life* v37 no2 p80 N/D 2016

Where to Sleep It Off E. FLORIO color *Conde Nast Traveler* v51 no10 p50 N 2016

WHERE Winter is Grand B. SGHELLER *Yankee* v81 no1 p84 Ja/F 2017

WHY NOW IS THE PERFECT TIME TO VISIT HAWAII *Los Angeles Magazine* p64 F 2017

Hotels—Florida
THE HENDERSON T. MALONE *Atlanta* v57 no1 p97 My 2017

Hotels—Florida—Miami
MIAMI Rhapsody L. RAMZI color *Vogue* v206 no11 p180 N 2016

Secrets of South Florida S. Granada and V. F. Luesse color map *Southern Living* v52 no1 p45 Ja 2017

Hotels—Florida—Miami Beach
The Comeback J. WOGAN color *Conde Nast Traveler* v52 no3 p48 Mr 2017

Hotels—France
In the Zone *Conde Nast Traveler* v52 no4 p19 Ap 2017

ROARING LYON THE REVITALIZED CITY GETS A SAVVY NEW DESIGN HOTEL H. GARVEY *Conde Nast Traveler* v52 no10 p32 N 2017

What Becomes a Legend color *Conde Nast Traveler* v52 no5 p20 My 2017

Hotels—France—Paris
Euro Star M. W. NICKLIN color *Conde Nast Traveler* v52 no3 p42 Mr 2017

Le Bristol Paris A. WHITTLE color *Conde Nast Traveler* v51 no11 p62 D 2016

Hotels—Furniture, equipment, etc.
Where to Sleep It Off E. FLORIO color *Conde Nast Traveler* v51 no10 p50 N 2016

Hotels—Georgia
HYATT REGENCY 1967 T. WHEATLEY *Atlanta* v57 no3 p176 Jl 2017

Hotels—Great Britain
Fancy a Call at the Pub? *British Heritage Travel* v38 no4 p9 Jl/Ag 2017

Hotels—Greece
Solo Flight P. Guzmán color *Conde Nast Traveler* v51 no11 p20 D 2016

Hotels—Hawaii

NEW HAWAII P. Orenstein color *Sunset* v237 no6 p23 D 2016

OAHU, HAWAII J. WOGAN color *Conde Nast Traveler* v52 no6 p26 Je/Jl 2017

Hotels—Illinois
A New Angle B. KAMIN color diag *Architectural Record* v205 no2 p74 F 2017

SKOKIE J. REESE cartoon color *Chicago* v66 no3 p37 Mr 2017

Hotels—Illinois—Chicago
'Tear Down This Big, Beautiful Wall' J. LILEKS *National Review* v68 no20 p37 N 7 2016

Hotels—India
chandigarh, india N. BRARA and M. OWENS color *Architectural Digest* no5 p78 My 2017

Hotels—Indonesia
Meet and Greet E. FLORIO color *Conde Nast Traveler* v52 no3 p40 Mr 2017

Hotels—Interior decoration
Hotels in Full Bloom C. TATTOLI color *Conde Nast Traveler* v52 no2 p108 F 2017

Hotels—Italy
Golden Rules P. Guzmán bw *Conde Nast Traveler* v52 no1 p20 Ja 2017

The Innkeeper's Diaries O. Cohane color *Conde Nast Traveler* v52 no3 p60 Mr 2017

The Italian Job J. MINUTILLO *Architectural Record* v204 no10 p84 O 2016

Rome O. COHANE, M. ELLWOOD et al bw chart color map *Conde Nast Traveler* v52 no3 p52 Mr 2017

TORY BURCH color *Vanity Fair* v58 no12 p78 D 2016

What Becomes a Legend color *Conde Nast Traveler* v52 no5 p20 My 2017

Hotels—Italy—Evaluation
An ODE to HOTELS on the Amalfi Coast P. GUZMÁN color *Conde Nast Traveler* v52 no1 p74 Ja 2017

TIME AND SPACE J. WOGAN color *Conde Nast Traveler* v52 no5 p42 My 2017

Hotels—Massachusetts
ISLAND TIME S. COCHRAN bw color *Architectural Digest* v73 no11 p94 N 2016

Hotels—Mexico
TAKE OM HOME T. Eichenseher color *Yoga Journal* no295 p104 O 2017

Hotels—New York (State)
DOWN AND OUT AT THE BULLFROG HOTEL K. LYDERSEN *In These Times* v41 no8 p42 Ag 2017

Hotels—New York (State)—Evaluation
It's All in the Name E. FLORIO color *Conde Nast Traveler* v52 no8 p42 S 2017

Hotels—New York (State)—New York
Baccarat Hotel New York R. KHONG color *Conde Nast Traveler* v52 no3 p44 Mr 2017

A Hidden Treasure S. AMELAR *Architectural Record* v204 no10 p90 O 2016

It's All in the Name E. FLORIO color *Conde Nast Traveler* v52 no8 p42 S 2017

Playing Huis P. GUZMÁN color *Conde Nast Traveler* v51 no11 p56 D 2016

Public Display S. STEPHENS *Architectural Record* v205 no9 p84 S 2017

Hotels—North Carolina
THE KIMPTON CARDINAL HOTEL J. R. MARQUEZ *Atlanta* v57 no1 p98 My 2017

Hotels—Ohio
Nobody's Home L. VACCARIELLO *Cincinnati Magazine* v50 no8 p128 My 2017

Hotels—Portugal
Monte Velho: AN EQUESTRIAN PARADISE A. Morris color *Dressage Today* v23 no11 p36 Ag 2017

Hotels—Rates
How to Stay in Premium Hotels Without Blowing Your Expense Account R. Mohammed *Harvard Business Review Digital Articles* p2 Ag 2 2016

Hotels—Remodeling
AROUND TOWN *D: The Magazine of Dallas* v43 no10 p287 O 2016

Hotels—Repair & reconstruction

Above AND Crillon C. Bagley color *Conde Nast Traveler* v52 no8 p96 S 2017

Crillon Redux color *Conde Nast Traveler* v52 no8 p41 S 2017

Hotels—Reviews

Doubling Down on DTLA M. WILLIAMS color *Conde Nast Traveler* v52 no9 p24 O 2017

Gal-Pal Getaway M. Santos color *Working Mother* v40 no3 p48 Ag/S 2017

HOUSEKEEPERS VS. HARVARD [Cover story] S. LEONARD color *Nation* v304 no12 p12 Ap 10 2017

MGM RESORT EXPERIENCES B. Wright color *Los Angeles Magazine* v62 no10 p109 O 2017

A PLACE INN THE SUN K. MONTGOMERY *Arizona Highways* v93 no2 p34 F 2017

ROARING LYON THE REVITALIZED CITY GETS A SAVVY NEW DESIGN HOTEL H. GARVEY *Conde Nast Traveler* v52 no10 p32 N 2017

THE ROOM TO BOOK A. SESSA color *Conde Nast Traveler* v52 no10 p36 N 2017

WIZARD OF OZ S. TODD color *Conde Nast Traveler* v52 no9 p22 O 2017

Hotels—Singapore

SINGAPORE H. SILVA color *Conde Nast Traveler* v52 no3 p24 Mr 2017

Hotels—Social aspects

Early Check-In color *Conde Nast Traveler* v51 no10 p24 N 2016

Hotels—South Africa

THE SPIRIT OF '17 A. ABEL color *Forbes* v199 no2 p66 F 28 2017

Hotels—Sri Lanka

Sri Lanka A. Solomon color *Conde Nast Traveler* v51 no11 p92 D 2016

Hotels—Tennessee

THE DWELL HOTEL *Atlanta* v57 no1 p95 My 2017

THOMPSON NASHVILLE *Atlanta* v57 no1 p96 My 2017

Hotels—Thailand

Siam Revival J. ADAMS color *Conde Nast Traveler* v52 no6 p38 Je/Jl 2017

Hotels—United States

BEST OF THE WEST L. Ladoceour and A. Young color *Sunset* v239 no4 p13 O 2017

THE DEWBERRY B. RILEY *Atlanta* v57 no1 p99 My 2017

Field to Vase B. MCKIBBEN *Atlanta* v57 no1 p55 My 2017

New Orleans Picks *Opera News* v81 no6 p17 D 2016

NORTH J. FROIS color map *Louisiana Life* v37 no4 p94 Mr/Ap 2017

Southern Living CAST YOUR VOTE FOR THE SOUTH'S BEST! *Southern Living* v52 no9 p14 S 2017

The SOUTH'S COOLEST NEW HOTELS *Atlanta* v57 no1 p92 My 2017

Table for Two, No Waiting S. Sifton color *New York Times Magazine* p24 F 12 2017

weekend getaways: romance *Washingtonian Magazine* v52 no11 p94 Ag 2017

Hotels—Virginia

CHRISTMAS AT THE GREENBRIER C. Kling color *Southern Living* v51 no12 p112 D 2016

HAUTE HOTELS: Designed down to the last perfect detail *Virginia Living* p116 2017 Best 20of Virginia

Hotels—Washington (D.C.)

The Empire Knocks One Back I. ALEKSANDER cartoon color diag *GQ: Gentlemen's Quarterly* v97 no7 p40 Jl 2017

INN THE MONEY A. WHITING *Washingtonian Magazine* v52 no8 p20 My 2017

Selling Trump's D.C. Hotel Wouldn't Be Easy Yu and B. Brody *Bloomberg Businessweek* no4505 p40 D 26 2016

Hotels—West Virginia

LIVING IN COLOR A. Postman color *Conde Nast Traveler* v51 no11 p102 D 2016

Hotels—Wisconsin

CAMP CHRISTMAS N. DAYTON *Better Homes & Gardens* v94 no12 p96 D 2016

Hotline Bling (Music)

Kidz Bop Z. Jason *New York Times Magazine* p24 Mr 26 2017

Hot Tub After Skiing, December, 2016 (Poem)

HOT TUB AFTER SKIING, DECEMBER, 2016 J. Bialosky *New Yorker* v93 no7 p60 Ap 3 2017

Hotz, George

GET OUT OF HIS LANE A. Zaleski color *Fortune* v176 no3 p33 S 1 2017

Hou, Amy

All the Ruffles color *Glamour* no8 p50 Ag 2017

Do You Know These Labels? bw color *Glamour* v115 no3 p86 Mr 2017

A Fresh Coat color *Glamour* no8 p48 Ag 2017

If You Like to Rework the Classics color *Glamour* v115 no9 p54 S 2017

If You Love a Good Throwback color *Glamour* v115 no9 p58 S 2017

If You're Gearing Up for Date Night color *Glamour* v115 no9 p48 S 2017

If You're Getting Your Girlboss On color *Glamour* v115 no9 p50 S 2017

If You're Living for the Weekend color *Glamour* v115 no9 p56 S 2017

Outdoor Adventure color *Glamour* v115 no6 p36 Je 2017

Twice? Nice! color *Glamour* v115 no4 p70 Ap 2017

Wide-Leg Wonders color *Glamour* no8 p46 Ag 2017

Hou, Sha

Engineering the ribosomal DNA in a megabase synthetic chromosome diag *Science* v355 no6329 p1049 Mr 10 2017

Houck, Ty

Year-Round, Paved-Trail Surface Maintenance *Parks & Recreation* v51 no11 p22 N 2016

Houdek, Petr

Economics of Sex: Cost-Benefit Analysis *Society* v54 no1 p18 F 2017

Professional Identity and Dishonest Behavior *Society* v54 no3 p253 Je 2017

Houdini, Harry, 1874-1926

Houdini and the Cancer of Superstition M. POLIDORO *Skeptical Inquirer* v40 no6 p32 N/D 2016

Houellebecq, Michel, 1958-

SIDELINE L. Collins cartoon *New Yorker* v93 no17 p22 Je 19 2017

Hougaard, Rasmus

How to Practice Mindfulness Throughout Your Work Day *Harvard Business Review Digital Articles* p2 Mr 4 2016

Spending 10 Minutes a Day on Mindfulness Subtly Changes the Way You React to Everything color *Harvard Business Review Digital Articles* p2 Ja 18 2017

HOUGH, DEREK

The Dance of Being a Judge *TV Guide* v65 no25 p12 Je 2017

Hough, Derek, 1985—Interviews

Can't Stop the Beat C. Bowers *Dance Spirit* v20 no10 p19 D 2016

Hough, Jill Silverman

MAKE-AHEAD holiday meal color *Yoga Journal* no296 p25 N 2017

Hough, Julianne, 1988-

ALL the RIGHT MOVES L. O'KEEFFE *Better Homes & Gardens* v95 no1 p80 Ja 2017

My Obsessions... *TV Guide* v65 no21 p8 My 15 2017

Hough, Nicole Gaggini

One church? *U.S. Catholic* v82 no7 p5 Jl 2017

HOUGHTON, BILL

A GOOD CONVERSATION *Commonweal* v144 no12 p4 Jl 7 2017

Houghton Hall (England)

Rock Steady S. COCHRAN color *Architectural Digest* v74 no8 p110 Ag 2017

Houghton Mifflin Harcourt Publishing Co.

Archive Dive *Publishers Weekly* v263 no39 p4 S 26 2016

Deals R. DEAHL bw color *Publishers Weekly* v264 no14 p7 Ap 3 2017

HMH Looks for More in Culinary, Lifestyle C. Swanson color *Publishers Weekly* v264 no16 p6 Ap 17 2017

Publishers Post Good Start to 2017 J. Milliot chart *Publishers Weekly* v264 no22 p6 My 29 2017

Houlder, Dominic

4 Hard Questions to Ask About Your Company's Purpose *Harvard Business Review Digital Articles* p2 Mr 22 2016

All Hail Medium-Term Planning *Harvard Business Review Digi-*

tal Articles p2 Je 23 2016
Corporate Governance Should Combine the Best of Private Equity and Family Firms *Harvard Business Review Digital Articles* p2 D 22 2016

Houlihan, J. V., Jr.
Christopher Walken color *AARP: The Magazine* v60 no2A p20 F/Mr 2017

Houliston, Scott
Global analysis of protein folding using massively parallel design, synthesis, and testing color diag *Science* v357 no6347 p168 Jl 14 2017

Hoult, Nicholas, 1989-
Sand Castle *TV Guide* p43 Ap 17 2017

Houma (North American people)
BATON ROUGE AT 200 E. Laborde *Louisiana Life* v37 no3 p4 Ja/F 2017

Hounds
COLD CASE A. ROBINSON color *Outdoor Life* v224 no6 p47 Ag 2017
HOG, WILD C. KEARNS color *Field & Stream* v121 no7 p68 D 2016/Ja 2017

Hounsou, Djimon, 1964-
The Good Knight K. P. Sullivan color *Entertainment Weekly* no1466 p22 My 19 2017

HOUPT, KATHERINE
Coping with a "macho" gelding color *Equus* no476 p89 My 2017
EQ CONSULTANTS color *Equus* no471 p66 D 2016 How Does Twitching Affect Horses? Lip twitching has legitimate uses, but ear twitching is detrimental and should be avoided *Horse & Rider* v56 no6 p20 Je 2017

Hourihan, Matt
Trump administration outlines budget shake-up *Issues in Science & Technology* v33 no3 p19 Spr 2017
Trump budget proposal: gloomy, but just a proposal *Issues in Science & Technology* v33 no4 p21 Summ 2017

House, Billy
Planned Parenthood Is a GOP Land Mine *Bloomberg Businessweek* no4513 p32 Mr 6 2017

House, Brian M.
Release of mineral-bound water prior to subduction tied to shallow seismogenic slip off Sumatra graph *Science* v356 no6340 p841 My 26 2017

House, Colin
Click chemistry enables preclinical evaluation of targeted epigenetic therapies diag *Science* v356 no6345 p1397 Je 30 2017

House, The (Film)
THE HOUSE N. Sperling color *Entertainment Weekly* no1463/1464 p49 Ap/My 2017
Jason Mantzoukas Bets On The House C. Collis color *Entertainment Weekly* no1473 p48 Jl 7 2017
Will Ferrell and Amy Poehler Bet on The House N. Sperling color *Entertainment Weekly* no1453 p12 F 17 2017

House, Truman
Truman House A. Gentry color *Spin to Win Rodeo* v21 no3 p28 My 2017

House Beautiful (Periodical)
Cover Stars K. O'SHEA-EVANS color *House Beautiful* v158 no9 p170 N 2016

House buying
COURTING THE COUNTRYSIDE H. Lárusson *Iceland Review* v55 no1 p44 Ja/F 2017
Home Buying Across America D. Johnson color *Time* v189 no21 p11 Je 5 2017
Home Prices Keep Climbing P. M. ESSWEIN cartoon chart *Kiplinger's Personal Finance* v71 no4 p40 Ap 2017
How Many Avocado Toasts It Takes to Buy a Home J. Calfas color *Money* v46 no7 p14 Ag 2017
OF MANY THINGS K. WEBER *America* v215 no16 p2 N 21 2016
Our 70th Anniversary J. Bodnar *Kiplinger's Personal Finance* v71 no4 p4 Ap 2017
Realty Check cartoon *Men's Health* v32 no5 p42 Je 2017
THE SECRET GUIDE TO FINDING THE RIGHT HOUSE D. Owen and R. Berendsohn color *Popular Mechanics* p66 Je 2017
Staying True T. SHESS color *Old House Journal* v45 no7 p24 O 2017

WHY BUYING A FIXER-UPPER MIGHT NOT BE WORTH IT K. Close color *Money* v45 no10 p21 N 2016

House buying—Canada
TOUGH LOVE REQUIRED J. CASTALDO color *Maclean's* v130 no10 p46 N 2017

House buying—United States
13 Coveted Streets *Washingtonian Magazine* v52 no7 p96 Ap 2017
HOW WE DID IT T. Tepper color diag *Money* v46 no4 p56 My 2017
OFF THE MARKET!: The nuts and bolts of some of Washington's most expensive residential transactions *Washingtonian Magazine* v53 no1 p197 O 2017
When It Pays to Bend the Rules M. CROSS color *Kiplinger's Personal Finance* v71 no10 p44 O 2017

House cleaning
CLEANING TRICKS FOR PEOPLE WHO HATE TO CLEAN color *Redbook* p127 N 2017
FILM SCHOOL H. LEVINE color *Martha Stewart Living* p43 Ap 2017
Maintaining the Dream color *Log Home Living* v34 no7 p25 S 2017
SPRING CLEANING P. Gulley *Saturday Evening Post* v289 no3 p16 My/Je 2017
THE WORK YOU DO, THE PERSON YOU ARE T. MORRISON cartoon *New Yorker* v93 no16 p66 Je 5 2017

House cleaning—Equipment & supplies
MOVING made easy J. PHILLIP color *Good Housekeeping* v264 no5 p58 My 2017

House construction
See also
Custom-designed houses
Dwelling maintenance & repair
Home remodeling
House drainage
4 Key Questions to Ask as You Plan Your Timber Home *Timber Home Living* p20 2017 Annual Buyers
9 TIPS TO GET YOUR DESIGN JUST RIGHT *Timber Home Living* p28 2017 Annual Buyers
9 Topics to Discuss With Timber Companies *Timber Home Living* p22 2017 Annual Buyers
Back to Nature color *Timber Home Living* v27 no6 p12 D 2017
A Big Tent P. Poore *Arts & Crafts Homes & the Revival* v11 no5 p8 Wint 2017
BUILDER PROFILES *Washingtonian Magazine* v53 no1 p174 O 2017
CLEAN LIVING: A minimalist home for a design sophisticate has maximum impact in its downtown neighborhood J. PAYTON *Indianapolis Monthly* p92 N 2017
Custom Home Builders Directory *Washingtonian Magazine* v52 no11 p150 Ag 2017
ELEMENTS OF STYLES L. MURTHA *Cincinnati Magazine* p36 Je 2017
Enjoy the Ride S. BROWN color *Timber Home Living* p6 2017 Annual Buyers
Even More Ways to Get Your Log Home Education color *Log Home Living* p12 2018 Annual Buyers Guide
The everything-proof house H. Murphy color *Popular Science* v289 no4 p56 Jl/Ag 2017
Eye on Design S. BROWN *Timber Home Living* v27 no2 p6 Ap 2017
A Frink Lloyd Wright Home Built in the 1950s E. Gaukel *Treasures* v6 no3 p4 D 2016/Ja 2017
from SITE PLAN to FLOOR PLAN color diag *Timber Home Living* v27 no2 p46 Ap 2017
Get the Lay of the Land cartoon *Timber Home Living* p30 2017 Annual Buyers
Homebuilders Look to Trump for a Mood Lift P. Gopal and J. Light cartoon *Bloomberg Businessweek* no4508 p35 Ja 23 2017
HOME: REAL ESTATE. DESIGN. NEIGHBORHOODS *Washingtonian Magazine* v52 no11 p141 Ag 2017
Home Un-Wrecker: How adam Rayne restored a crumbling Walnut Hills Victorian to royal status A. KONERMANN *Cincinnati Magazine* v50 no11 p72 Ag 2017
In Great Demand color diag *Log Home Living* v34 no5 p46 Jl 2017
Keep a High Profile color diag *Log Home Living* p30 2018 Annual

Buyers Guide

Knock on Wood color *Log Home Living* p18 2018 Annual Buyers Guide

Land Ho! color *Log Home Living* p16 2018 Annual Buyers Guide

A Lesson in Addition D. Mitchell color *Log Home Living* v33 no7 p28 S 2016

The Log Home Basics color *Log Home Living* p14 2018 Annual Buyers Guide

Lost Lake *Los Angeles Magazine* p16 Ag 2017

Managing Chaos: How cities can handle the demands that density puts on services S. Beyer *Governing* v30 no8 p23 My 2017

Material Gain color *Timber Home Living* v27 no6 p8 D 2017

THE MISSING MIDDLE: We talk endlessly about affordable housing, but we don't produce much. Could that change? J. Buntin *Governing* v30 no8 p24 My 2017

Move Over D. Paul *Indianapolis Monthly* v40 no3 p160 N 2016

NAME GAME L. MURTHA *Cincinnati Magazine* v50 no6 p42 Mr 2017

Packaged to Perfection color *Log Home Living* p38 2018 Annual Buyers Guide

Picking a Log Home Producer color *Log Home Living* p46 2018 Annual Buyers Guide

plan color *Timber Home Living* p16 2017 Annual Buyers

the profound delight in PERSONAL EXPRESSION [Cover story] B. D. COLEMAN color *Arts & Crafts Homes & the Revival* v12 no4 p40 Fall 2017

The Quest for H2O D. Mitchell color *Log Home Living* v34 no5 p24 Jl 2017

Quite a Catch J. Hilliard color diag *Log Home Living* v34 no5 p36 Jl 2017

Readers' votes & editors' picks color *Old House Journal* v44 no8 p10 D 2016

Reid's Heritage Homes on Constructing Residential to the Net-Zero Standard C. Metler color *Maclean's* v129 no50 p43 D 19 2016

Stop Paying for the Gym! C. SKIPPER color *GQ: Gentlemen's Quarterly* v87 no1 p15 Ja 2017

Style Standouts color *Log Home Living* p58 2018 Annual Buyers Guide

timber framing 101 color *Timber Home Living* p10 2017 Annual Buyers

To Stretch a Shoestring color *Yankee* p26 My/Je 2017

House construction—Awards

Timber Block Wins at America's Biggest Building Show color *Log Home Living* v34 no4 p16 My 2017

House drainage

See also

Sewerage

House dust mites

4 WAYS TO STOP THE SNEEZING S. LIAO color *Better Homes & Gardens* v95 no6 p160 Je 2017

House framing

timber framing 101 color *Timber Home Living* p10 2017 Annual Buyers

House Hunters (TV program)

What to Watch R. Rahman, D. Snierson et al color *Entertainment Weekly* no1471 p58 Je 23 2017

House lighting

Resources *Old House Journal* v45 no5 p79 Ag 2017

See the Light [Cover story] color *Timber Home Living* v27 no6 p14 D 2017

House of Antique Hardware Inc.

All About Cabinet Hinges B. D. Coleman color *Old House Journal* v45 no1 p52 F 2017

House of Bamboo (Film)

No Peace of Mind R. Brody color *New Yorker* v93 no28 p12 S 18 2017

House of Breath (Theatrical production)

Profile M. S. Eddy *Stage Directions* v30 no3 p20 Mr 2017

House of Cardinals (TV program)

The Young Pope M. ROUSH *TV Guide* v65 no4 p16 Ja 16 2017

House of Cards (TV program)

HOUSE OF CARDS ROCKS THE VOTE T. Stack color *Entertainment Weekly* no1463/1464 p20 Ap/My 2017

The Must List color *Entertainment Weekly* no1468/1469 p3 Je 2-9 2017

STREAMING A. D'ARMINIO *TV Guide* v65 no23 p38 My 29 2017

House of Lies (TV program)

HOUSE OF LIES I. Rudolph *TV Guide* v64 no15 p50 Ap 4 2016

House painting

GOT CURB APPEAL? bw cartoon *AARP: The Magazine* v60 no3A p8 Ap/My 2017

MAKE OVER YOUR HOME WITH COLOR color *Redbook* p142 D 2016

painting a BLUE STREAK K. K. CONDON color *Better Homes & Gardens* v95 no4 p38 Ap 2017

Pretty in Paint K. Janeway chart color il *Consumer Reports* v82 no5 p38 My 2017

PUT IT in NEUTRAL K. SELZER color *Better Homes & Gardens* v95 no4 p26 Ap 2017

House painting—Equipment & supplies—Evaluation

GINKGO GREENS S. EGGE color *Better Homes & Gardens* v95 no3 p22 Mr 2017

House plants

HOME GROWN P. P. FISCHER color *Better Homes & Gardens* v95 no3 p112 Mr 2017

Pothos J. Hughes *New York Times Magazine* p26 Je 11 2017

the return of the HOUSEPLANT M. HUGHES *Better Homes & Gardens* v95 no1 p57 Ja 2017

House plants in interior decoration

Green Room J. K. DE VALLE color *Architectural Digest* no6 p39 Je 1 2017

House plants—Sales & prices

garden variety J. KOPF color *Better Homes & Gardens* v95 no6 p16 Je 2017

House-raising parties

BANGIN' BASH (On a Budget) N. M. Pittmon color *Ebony* v72 no9 p54 Jl/Ag 2017

House selling

5 Tips to sell a Super-Pricey House K. OLSEN color *Washingtonian Magazine* v52 no7 p98 Ap 2017

Feeling Trapped? How to Sell in This Tricky Market C. Fried and T. Tepper color diag *Money* v46 no9 p43 O 2017

House selling—Social aspects

A border runs through it A. ABEL color *Maclean's* v130 no7 p15 Ag 2017

Houseboats

LIFE ON LONDON'S WATERWAYS S. Gutierrez *British Heritage Travel* v37 no6 p36 N/D 2016

slow boat on a big lake M. Allen bw color map *Yankee* p70 My/Je 2017

A Traveler's Best Friend M. ALLEN color *Yankee* p12 My/Je 2017

Houseboats—Design & construction

2 Sleep With the Fishes W. Goodman img *New York* v49 no21 p86 O 17 2016

Noah's Ark-itecture K. Logan *Architectural Record* v205 no4 p217 Ap 2017

Housefly

Male sex in houseflies is determined by Mdmd, a paralog of the generic splice factor gene CWC22 A. Sharma, S. D. Heinze et al bw color *Science* v356 no6338 p642 My 12 2017

Household (Short story)

1928: Tokyo Yasunari Kawabata *Lapham's Quarterly* v10 no1 p135 Wint 2017

Household appliance stores—Evaluation

CATCHING FIRE color *Architectural Digest* v73 no11 p108 N 2016

Household appliances

THE ART OF THE OBJECT J. FOUMBERG color *Chicago* v66 no5 p50 My 2017

Head Off Disasters il *Consumer Reports* v82 no3 p28 Mr 2017

I'M NOT SURE D. OWEN color *Popular Mechanics* p79 My 2017

OK, HOUSE. GET SMART P. SARCONI, D. PIERCE et al chart color *Wired* v25 no6 p39 Je 2017

STRATEGIST img *New York* v50 no7 p55 Ap 3 2017

Household appliances—Evaluation

Bring on the Joy T. Bufete and J. Willcox chart il *Consumer Reports* v82 no3 p31 Mr 2017

GET SMART C. Lamers and N. Farrell color *Sunset* v239 no3 p46 S 2017

It's Spring - Say Yes to Yellow! color *Treasures* v5 no5 p6 Ap/My 2016

product spotlight color *Timber Home Living* p51 2017 Annual Buyers

Household appliances—Management

Supersensor M. Belfiore color *Bloomberg Businessweek* no4538 p25 S 18 2017

Household electronics industry

DODOCOOL DC30 7-IN-1 USB-C HUB: AFFORDABLE HUB WITH PASSTHROUGH POWER ALONGSIDE THREE USB TYPE-A PORTS G. FLEISHMAN color *Macworld - Digital Edition* p30 Je 13 2017

Household electronics industry—News briefs

Expanded Oscar Coverage M. Fleischmann and C. Crowley color *Sound & Vision* v82 no6 p17 Jl/Ag 2017

Jerry Seinfeld's M. Fleischmann and C. Crowley color *Sound & Vision* v82 no5 p17 Je 2017

This Just In... M. Fleischmann color *Sound & Vision* v82 no7 p19 S 2017

Household electronics—Congresses

Kicking the Self-Driving Tires K. Naughton and M. Bergen color *Bloomberg Businessweek* no4506 p26 Ja 9 2017

Household electronics—Sales & prices

Kicking the Self-Driving Tires K. Naughton and M. Bergen color *Bloomberg Businessweek* no4506 p26 Ja 9 2017

Household employees

The Diplomacy of Dog Walking in Russia A. FERRIS-ROTMAN color *Foreign Policy* no225 p20 Jl/Ag 2017

Household linens

See also

Draperies

Napkins

Place mats

SERVE CHILLED E. N. GAGE color *Martha Stewart Living* p25 Jl/Ag 2017

Household linens industry

HOME IS WHERE THE PERCALE IS S. Marikar color *Bloomberg Businessweek* no4525 p58 Je 5 2017

Household linens—Evaluation

Pillow Talk color *Architectural Digest* v74 no4 p50 Ap 2017

Household moving

Advice from a Serial Life Reinventor S. G. Carmichael *Harvard Business Review Digital Articles* p2 Ap 2 2015

Decision time B. Jo Lieberman color *Equus* no480 p60 S 2017

DOWNSIZING MY DAD A. Cochran *Washingtonian Magazine* v52 no2 p279 N 2016

The Long Haul M. MATTIX cartoon *Weekly Standard* v22 no12 p5 N 28 2016

Moving in Retirement? How to Time It Right E. O'Brien color diag *Money* v46 no5 p27 Je 2017

MOVING made easy J. PHILLIP color *Good Housekeeping* v264 no5 p58 My 2017

OBJECT PERMANENCE J. MOYER color *Orion Magazine* v36 no2 p64 Mr/Ap 2017

Rent Control D. Frolovskiy *New York Times Magazine* p38 O 30 2016

RETIREES FLOCK SOUTH AND WEST D. Kadlec color *Money* v46 no2 p20 Mr 2017

Household sounds

TRANSLATING THE NOISES MY RADIATOR MAKES C. STOKES cartoon *New Yorker* v92 no47 p29 Ja 30 2017

Household supplies

See also

Groceries

Household linens

Adam's Home STYLE SHEET Adam color *O, The Oprah Magazine* p56 Ag 2017

Household surveys

FoodAPS Data Now Available to the General Public E. Larimore, E. Page et al chart color graph *Amber Waves: The Economics of Food, Farming, Natural Resources, & Rural America* p27 D 2016

Popular money-saving strategies prove elusive for low-income households S. Carter *Monthly Labor Review* p1 S 2016

Households

See also

Intergenerational households

Farm Households Experience High Levels of Income Volatility N. Key, D. Prager et al *Amber Waves: The Economics of Food, Farming, Natural Resources, & Rural America* p16 Mr 2017

Households Purchase More Produce and Low-Fat Dairy at Supermarkets, Supercenters, and Warehouse Club Stores A. Kuhns *Amber Waves: The Economics of Food, Farming, Natural Resources, & Rural America* p1 My 2017

THE NEXT GREAT PLACE I. Edwards color *Sunset* v238 no2 p4 F 2017

Households—United States

Young adults and trends in household formation S. Berridge *Monthly Labor Review* p1 S 2016

Households—United States—Charts, diagrams, etc.

What Is Very Low Food Security and Who Experiences It A. Coleman-Jensen and M. Smith color *Amber Waves: The Economics of Food, Farming, Natural Resources, & Rural America* p38 D 2016

House I Live In, The (Film)

quick takes bw color *U.S. Catholic* v82 no5 p39 My 2017

Housekeepers

The Hotel Cleaner A. Fortini *New York Times Magazine* p46 F 26 2017

Housekeeping

9 Tidy Resolutions J. PHILLIP color *Good Housekeeping* v264 no1 p46 Ja 1 2017

ASK CAROLYN C. FORTÉ color *Good Housekeeping* v264 no4 p58 Ap 2017

c. 1300: Paris *Lapham's Quarterly* v10 no1 p46 Wint 2017

Cute Ways to Organize Toys E. Walker color *Parents* v92 no4 p106 Ap 2017

Declutter that cabinet! J. Jones color *Redbook* p26 N 2017

FIND MORE ROOM IN EVERY ROOM A. LONGOBUCCO color diag *Good Housekeeping* v264 no3 p60 Mr 2017

GH CLEANING LAB C. FORTÉ bw color *Good Housekeeping* v265 no4 p62 O 2017

home * solutions *Parents* v91 no6 p115 Je 2016

how to ORGANIZE EVERYTHING J. PHILLIP color *Good Housekeeping* v264 no3 p47 Mr 2017

messy no more! *Parents* v92 no1 p55 Ja 2017

SPEED-CLEANING *Good Housekeeping* v264 no3 p54 Mr 2017

your DECLUTTERING CALENDAR *Good Housekeeping* v264 no3 p82 Mr 2017

Housekeeping—Social aspects

The Invisible Workload That Drags Women Down L. Wade color diag *Money* v46 no4 p64 My 2017

Housel, Fred

FROM OUR READERS *Sky & Telescope* v133 no4 p6 Ap 2017

HOUSEL, MORGAN

Son, Here Is How You Save color *Reader's Digest* v189 no1129 p38 Ap 2017

Housemaid, The (Film)

Hello, Cruel World G. HENDRIX bw color *Film Comment* v53 no2 p74 Mr/Ap 2017

Houser, Trevor

Estimating economic damage from climate change in the United States color graph *Science* v356 no6345 p1362 Je 30 2017

Housewives

A Nurse's Daughter Barbara *Prevention* v68 no12 p3 D 2016

Housing

See also

Congregate housing

Home ownership

Involuntary relocation

Lodging-houses

Public housing

Rental housing

BACK splash PROGRESSION M. ELLEN POLSON color *Arts & Crafts Homes & the Revival* v12 no5 p28 Wint 2018

The Best of Both Worlds D. Peak color *Log Home Living* p10 2018 Annual Buyers Guide

Closing the door: And opening another one [Cover story] C. Rose color *New Orleans Magazine* v51 no10 p54 Ag 2017

Cracking L.A.'s Real Estate Market bw color *Los Angeles Magazine* v62 no10 p118 O 2017

GAME PLAN S. BLOCK cartoon *Kiplinger's Personal Finance*

v71 no7 p40 Jl 2017

Habitat III Is the Citizens' Conference of the United Nations J. Clos *UN Chronicle* v53 no3 p9 2016

HIGHCOUNTRY EXODUS M. Davis bw *Skiing* p21 D 2016

HOT PROPERTY T. BRAND *Indianapolis Monthly* v40 no4 p42 D 2016

"I HAD TO WALK THROUGH FIRE for my kids" J. SMALL color *Good Housekeeping* v265 no1 p69 Jl 2017

Keeping it in the Family C. KOLB bw *New Orleans Magazine* v52 no1 p46 S 2017

Lightbox color *Time* v189 no19 p14 My 22 2017

Midwestern Masterpiece [Cover story] J. Brewster color diag *Log Home Living* p76 2018 Annual Buyers Guide

The New Urban Agenda's Road Map for Planning Urban Spatial Development: Tangible, Manageable and Measurable E. L. Birch *UN Chronicle* v53 no3 p18 2016

Our Acquired Taste P. Poore *Arts & Crafts Homes & the Revival* v12 no5 p8 Wint 2018

Perfect Pitch D. Mitchell color *Log Home Living* v34 no6 p24 Ag 2017

The Pride of Union, Maine J. Ianello color *Yankee* v80 no6 p44 N/D 2016

Restoration drama C. MACDONALD color *House Beautiful* p40 Ag 2017

What is the biggest obstacle to forming stable families? graph *America* v216 no11 p6 My 15 2017

WIRING THE UNWIRED G. LEWIS-KRAUS color *Wired* v24 no11 p74 N 2016

The World's Housing Crisis Doesn't Need a Revolutionary Solution J. Woetzel, J. Mischke et al *Harvard Business Review Digital Articles* p2 D 25 2014

Housing & health

Boost Your Health & Happiness at Home D. DiClerico il *Consumer Reports* v82 no3 p22 Mr 2017

Get Healthier J. Calderone and B. Deitrick il *Consumer Reports* v82 no3 p25 Mr 2017

Head Off Disasters il *Consumer Reports* v82 no3 p28 Mr 2017

Stay Safer C. Roberts il *Consumer Reports* v82 no3 p27 Mr 2017

Housing design & construction

7 Hot Home Design Trends color *Timber Home Living* v27 no3 p22 Je 2017

9 TIPS TO GET YOUR DESIGN JUST RIGHT *Timber Home Living* p28 2017 Annual Buyers

THE APPROVAL MATRIX img *New York* v49 no19 p116 S 19 2016

BIG DEAL T. BRAND *Indianapolis Monthly* v40 no7 p32 Mr 2017

design color map *Timber Home Living* p26 2017 Annual Buyers

Dream Destination color diag *Timber Home Living* v27 no3 p48 Je 2017

Grand Finale L. CUTRONE color *New Orleans Magazine* v52 no1 p62 S 2017

Haven in a Hayfield S. LOGAN color diag *Timber Home Living* v27 no3 p34 Je 2017

house of the month J. MINUTILLO *Architectural Record* v205 no9 p39 S 2017

In a League of Its Own S. DURR ALBERT color map *Timber Home Living* v27 no3 p42 Je 2017

LAKESIDE LANDMARK color *Timber Home Living* v27 no3 p88 Je 2017

On the Rocks S. Logan color diag *Log Home Living* v34 no6 p26 Ag 2017

q&a color *Timber Home Living* v27 no3 p20 Je 2017

Resolve to Help Our Heroes color *Log Home Living* v34 no1 p14 F 2017

Second-Home Plans color diag *Timber Home Living* v27 no3 p28 Je 2017

Small-House Design Strategies color diag *Timber Home Living* v27 no3 p56 Je 2017

Small Sacrifices S. Murphy color *Log Home Living* v34 no6 p22 Ag 2017

The Space Issue S. BROWN *Timber Home Living* v27 no3 p10 Je 2017

tip Take Cover B. Cochran color *Timber Home Living* v27 no3 p18 Je 2017

your DREAM HOME STARTS HERE *Timber Home Living* p17

2017 Annual Buyers

Housing development

ALARGAN : Aim To Lead K. K. Al-Mashaan *Foreign Affairs* v95 no6 p120g N/D 2016

Breaking Ground and Glass Ceilings F. TAMER cartoon *Alternatives Journal (AJ) - Canada's Environmental Voice* v42 no2 p49 2016

Peripheral vision J. Bouchard color *U.S. Catholic* v82 no5 p12 My 2017

Housing management

Seeking Asylum: The up-and-coming co-living concept lands in Indy at a refurbished psychiatric hospital J. KENT-DOOLAN *Indianapolis Monthly* v40 no11 p16 Jl 2017

Housing market

2016: United States *Lapham's Quarterly* v10 no1 p23 Wint 2017

Double bubble, toil and trouble A. HEPBURN color graph *Maclean's* v129 no45 p44 N 14 2016

POISED FOR PROFIT K. FINN color *New Orleans Magazine* v51 no3 p28 Ja 2017

WE'RE IN THE DARK HERE ON HOUSING DATA J. KIRBY color *Maclean's* v129 no44 p38 N 7 2016

Young adults and trends in household formation S. Berridge *Monthly Labor Review* p1 S 2016

Housing market—Economic aspects

Canadian Finance Gets Less Boring. That's Bad K. Chipman graph *Bloomberg Businessweek* no4521 p41 My 8 2017

Wage and employment fluctuations during the housing market cycle R. Meharenna *Monthly Labor Review* p1 D 2016

Housing market—History

CASTLES IN AIR L. H. Lapham *Lapham's Quarterly* v10 no1 p12 Wint 2017

Housing policy—Canada

Housing Heals and Saves K. Broadbelt color *Alternatives Journal (AJ) - Canada's Environmental Voice* v42 no2 p34 2016

WE'RE IN THE DARK HERE ON HOUSING DATA J. KIRBY color *Maclean's* v129 no44 p38 N 7 2016

Housing policy—United States

Housing's Drag on the Economy I. BRANNON *Weekly Standard* v22 no22 p24 F 13 2017

Welcoming the Stranger Means Welcoming New Housing *America* v216 no10 p8 My 1 2017

Housing rehabilitation

Remaking History K. O'Shea-Evans bw color *House Beautiful* v158 no9 p112 N 2016

Housing subsidies—United States

I Crunched the Numbers on the U.S. Government. Here's What I Learned S. Ballmer color *Time* v190 no5 p30 Jl 31 2017

Housing—Awards

HAUTE HOUSES: The 2017 Washingtonian Residential Design Awards' 12 winning projects M. M. Kashino *Washingtonian Magazine* v52 no11 p70 Ag 2017

Housing—California—Los Angeles

In Our Cities B. DANIELLE bw color *Ebony* v72 no5 p32 Mr 2017

THE MISSING MIDDLE: We talk endlessly about affordable housing, but we don't produce much. Could that change? J. Buntin *Governing* v30 no8 p24 My 2017

Housing—Canada

Affordability Is the Hardest Shade of Green Y. Afshar color *Alternatives Journal (AJ) - Canada's Environmental Voice* v42 no2 p40 2016

Evicted M. Moos and S. Hertel color *Alternatives Journal (AJ) - Canada's Environmental Voice* v42 no2 p16 2016

Hands off my bubble [Cover story] C. SORENSEN color graph *Maclean's* v129 no41 p36 O 17 2016

Home in the North A. WONG color *Alternatives Journal (AJ) - Canada's Environmental Voice* v42 no2 p60 2016

Montebello monument N. Walker color map *Canadian Geographic* v137 no1 p26 F 2017

Rental Breakdown J. LORINC color *Walrus* v14 no7 p16 S 2017

Room for All J. DEAN cartoon diag graph *Alternatives Journal (AJ) - Canada's Environmental Voice* v42 no2 p54 2016

A Slow Revolution A. FRIEDMAN color graph *Alternatives Journal (AJ) - Canada's Environmental Voice* v42 no2 p36 2016

Through the Roof R. HARRIS color map *Alternatives Journal (AJ) - Canada's Environmental Voice* v42 no2 p30 2016

Welcome Home M. MOOS and S. HERTEL *Alternatives Journal (AJ) - Canada's Environmental Voice* v42 no2 p7 2016

WHAT IT TOOK TO TAME CMHC K. CARMICHAEL color *Maclean's* v130 no4 p53 My 2017

Housing—Canada—Economic aspects

The best of both worlds B. BORZYKOWSKI color *Maclean's* v130 no2 p50 Mr 2017

Double bubble, toil and trouble A. HEPBURN color graph *Maclean's* v129 no45 p44 N 14 2016

Housing—Colorado

Road Rage D. C. Vock *Governing* v30 no7 p44 Ap 2017

Housing—Connecticut

Moving In B. HEWITT and P. HEWITT color map *Yankee* p16 Mr 2017

Housing—Design & construction—Evaluation

MINIMALIST MULTIPURPOSE M. M. Kashino *Washingtonian Magazine* v52 no6 p155 Mr 2017

perspective house of the month A. WEDER *Architectural Record* v205 no4 p39 Ap 2017

SMALL WONDERS *Washingtonian Magazine* v52 no6 p153 Mr 2017

Housing—Evaluation

REBUILD THE NEIGHBORHOOD L. MURTHA *Cincinnati Magazine* v50 no5 p34 F 2017

SAND CASTLE: A new downtown home channels chic Florida beach style M. FERNANDEZ color *Indianapolis Monthly* v41 no2 p32 S 2017

Housing—Exhibitions

HOME AND AWAY P. SCHJELDAHL color *New Yorker* v93 no18 p72 Je 26 2017

It's Show Time! color *Log Home Living* v34 no6 p21 Ag 2017

Housing—Finance

Our Mortgaged Future A. WALKS color graph *Alternatives Journal (AJ) - Canada's Environmental Voice* v42 no2 p22 2016

STOCKS WITH A SHAKY FOUNDATION R. Derousseau color diag *Fortune* v174 no6 p39 N 1 2016

Housing—Florida

A Sarasota Scenario: One developer's battle to build affordable housing *Governing* v30 no8 p27 My 2017

Housing—History

The Ghost in Our Midst J. ROSEN *Psychology Today* v49 no5 p44 S/O 2016

Housing—Illinois—Chicago

GILDED PLATEAU M. LAWLER color *Chicago* v66 no3 p27 Mr 2017

Housing—Law & legislation—United States

Home Is Where the Market Is: What we should do--and stop doing--in the quest for "affordable housing" R. A. Epstein *Hoover Digest: Research & Opinion on Public Policy* no3 p137 Summ 2017

Housing—Louisiana

SHINING STAR P. F. Stahls Jr. color *Louisiana Life* v37 no5 p44 My/Je 2017

Well-Aged L. CUTRONE color *Louisiana Life* v37 no5 p41 My/Je 2017

Housing—Maintenance & repair

Bathroom Aesthetic P. Poore color *Old House Journal* v45 no7 p72 O 2017

DELETING A POOR ADDITION C. Neff color diag *Old House Journal* v45 no7 p32 O 2017

Where Gustav Dreamed Big color *Arts & Crafts Homes & the Revival* v11 no5 p16 Wint 2017

Housing—New York (State)—New York

ASPHALT GARDENS S. James *Harper's Magazine* p50 Ap 2017

Boston Road Supportive Housing A. Klimoski *Architectural Record* v205 no4 p193 Ap 2017

Loft Life: The Early Years C. Bonanos img *New York* v50 no8 p12 Ap 17 2017

Housing—Research

Hip, Cool & Unaffordable R. FLORIDA chart color *Alternatives Journal (AJ) - Canada's Environmental Voice* v42 no2 p42 2016

Housing—Resident satisfaction

GUIDE TO Restfulness C. BROPHY, B. A. KIPFER et al color *House Beautiful* v159 no2 p61 Mr 2017

Housing—United States

An Affordable-Housing Fix J. JEWELL *American Conservative*

v16 no3 p36 My/Je 2017

Birth rate craters as housing costs rise *America* v216 no3 p8 F 6 2017

HOME INSECURITY A. de Tocqueville *Lapham's Quarterly* v10 no3 p65 Summ 2017

The Housing Crunch Hits the Heartland P. Gopal cartoon *Bloomberg Businessweek* no4516 p36 Mr 27 2017

Managing Chaos: How cities can handle the demands that density puts on services S. Beyer *Governing* v30 no8 p23 My 2017

No Vacancy S. TRICK cartoon *Walrus* v13 no10 p22 D 2016

Seeking Asylum: The up-and-coming co-living concept lands in Indy at a refurbished psychiatric hospital J. KENT-DOOLAN *Indianapolis Monthly* v40 no11 p16 Jl 2017

The Unaffordable Urban Paradise R. Florida color il *MIT Technology Review* v120 no4 p88 Jl/Ag 2017

Welcoming the Stranger Means Welcoming New Housing *America* v216 no10 p8 My 1 2017

Housley, Adam

THE WHITE HOUSE READING IT CLOSELY *New York* v50 no9 p46 My 1 2017

Housman, A. E. (Alfred Edward), 1859-1936

THE LAND OF LOST CONTENT C. McGRATH cartoon *New Yorker* v93 no18 p63 Je 26 2017

HOUSMAN, JUSTIN

The American "Meh" color *Surfer* v58 no3 p30 Je 2017

CYRUS SUTTON color *Surfer* v58 no3 p36 Je 2017

DO SOMETHING bw color *Surfer* v58 no6 p32 O 2017

EMBRACING COLOSSUS bw color *Surfer* v58 no4 p96 Ag 2017

More (or Less) Core Division color *Surfer* v58 no4 p34 Ag 2017

SAFETY NOT GUARANTEED color *Surfer* v58 no1 p68 Ap 2017

Screen, I Wish I Knew How to Quit You cartoon color *Surfer* v57 no13 p30 Mr 2017

THE SHAPE OF THINGS TO COME color *Surfer* v58 no2 p64 My 2017

SHOCK WAVES color *Surfer* v57 no12 p42 Ja/F 2017

The Significance of the Frontier in Surfing History color *Surfer* v58 no2 p40 My 2017

Splitting the Political Peak cartoon *Surfer* v58 no1 p42 Ap 2017

Warts and All color *Surfer* v58 no6 p42 O 2017

Wet Hot American Mixtape cartoon *Surfer* v58 no5 p42 S 2017

What's So Great About the Great Outdoors? cartoon color *Surfer* v57 no11 p32 D 2016

Whither the Thruster? cartoon color *Surfer* v57 no12 p30 Ja/F 2017

Wings on His Feet color *Surfer* v58 no5 p30 S 2017

Housseau, Franck

Mismatch repair deficiency predicts response of solid tumors to PD-1 blockade chart graph *Science* v357 no6349 p409 Jl 28 2017

Houston (Tex.)

Dangerous Legacy: Cities get themselves into a fiscal squeeze paying bills they ran up decades ago M. Maciag *Governing* v30 no12 p58 S 2017

Pure Gold HOUSTON color *Sports Illustrated* v126 no6 p84 F 20 2017

Houston (Tex.)—Description & travel

HOUSTON: THE AMERICAN CITY OF THE FUTURE T. M. FERGUSON color *Ebony* v72 no11 p30 S 2017

The Next Global Food Mecca Is in...Texas?! color *GQ: Gentlemen's Quarterly* v86 no12 p114 D 2016

TRAVEL Houston color *Sports Illustrated* v126 no6 p90 F 20 2017

HOUSTON, ANGELA

Rich Rituals color *O, The Oprah Magazine* p14 Ja 2017

Houston, Drew—Interviews

Dropbox's Drew Houston M. Chafkin and D. Bass color *Bloomberg Businessweek* no4526 p40 Je 12 2017

Houston, Keith

From signs in clay tablets to digital data J. Camplin *History Today* v66 no10 p59 O 2016

Houston, Sam, 1793-1863

On Being Texan J. R. Erickson color *American Cowboy* p8 LEGENDS OF TEXAS Special Issue 2017

TEXAS TITANS bw color *American Cowboy* p40 LEGENDS OF

TEXAS Special Issue 2017

Houston, Shirley J.

WE LOVE HEARING FROM YOU! color diag *Essence* v47 no9 p13 Ja 2017

Houston, Whitney, 1963-2012

Whitney: Can I Be Me I. Ratledge *TV Guide* v65 no35 p32 Ag 21 2017

WHITNEY HOUSTON'S WHITNEY TURNS 30 K. O'donnell color *Entertainment Weekly* no1468/1469 p103 Je 2-9 2017

Houston Astros (Baseball team)

1 ASTROS color *Sports Illustrated* v126 no9 p88 Mr 27 2017

EDITOR'S LETTER B. D. SWEANY *Texas Monthly* v44 no11 p24 N 2016

LOVE SPRINGS ETERNAL T. Verducci color *Sports Illustrated* v127 no4 p38 Ag 7 2017

ORANGE CRUSH J. N. LOMAX *Texas Monthly* v44 no11 p112 N 2016

PER ASPERA AD ASTRO B. Reiter color *Sports Illustrated* v127 no9 p20 S 25 2017

Houston Ballet

HARPER WATTERS *Dance Spirit* v21 no3 p41 Mr 2017

Houston Rockets (Basketball team)

2 ROCKETS color *Sports Illustrated* v127 no12 p80 O 16 2017

8 Rockets R. Nadkarni, B. Golliver et al color *Sports Illustrated* v125 no14 p106 O 24-31 2016

To think, three thousand years from now people will still be asking, "Who?" B. Brown *Texas Monthly* v45 no1 p88 Ja 2017

Houston Texans (Football team)

2 Houston Texans color *Sports Illustrated* v127 no7 p76 S 4 2017

THE PATRIOTS PROBLEM [Cover story] A. Benoit color *Sports Illustrated* v127 no7 p32 S 4 2017

Hout, Thomas

Where Trump Does (and Doesn't) Have Leverage with China *Harvard Business Review Digital Articles* p2 D 16 2016

Houts, Julie

Literally Me *Publishers Weekly* v264 no36 p76 S 4 2017

Hou Yong, Ee

Avian egg shape: Form, function, and evolution color diag *Science* v356 no6344 p1249 Je 23 2017

Houzz Shop LLC

Organize the whole family! J. Jones color *Redbook* p32 D 2016

Hover, David

Suppressing relaxation in superconducting qubits by quasiparticle pumping bibl graph *Science* v354 no6319 p1573 D 23 2016

Hoverstad, Ron

One church? *U.S. Catholic* v82 no7 p5 Jl 2017

Hovestadt, Volker

Decoupling genetics, lineages, and microenvironment in IDH-mutant gliomas by single-cell RNA-seq diag *Science* v355 no6332 p1391 Mr 31 2017

Hovey, Pauline

NO PLACE LIKE NOME color *America* v217 no7 p34 O 2 2017

Singing for shelter color *U.S. Catholic* v81 no12 p19 D 2016

Hovis, Joanne

Digitally Unequal *MIT Technology Review* v120 no1 p11 Ja/F 2017

How?? (Music)

The Playlist color *Rolling Stone* no1276 p10 D 15 2016

How I Met Your Mother (TV program)

Forever and Ever, Amen img *New York* v50 no12 p96 Je 12 2017

How to Get Away With Murder (TV program)

America's top TV critic Matt Roush answers your burning questions Jodi *TV Guide* v65 no37 p9 S 4 2017

CHEERS & JEERS D. HOLBROOK *TV Guide* v65 no11 p92 Mr 6 2017

Goodbye, Wes: Inside Murder's Blazing Loss N. Abrams color *Entertainment Weekly* no1442 p48 D 2 2016 Rebellious Special Issue

How to Get Away With Murder N. Abrams, B. L. Heldman et al *Entertainment Weekly* no1482/1483 p91 S 22 2017

VIBRANT, RAW & IN LIVING COLOR: EBONY'S 2017 FALL TV PREVIEW A. TINUBU color *Ebony* v72 no11 p78 S 2017

Howard, Agnes R.

Women & Children Last bw *Commonweal* v144 no9 p13 My 19 2017

Howard, Andrew

ZINGING THE BLUES [Cover story] K. RENDA color *House Beautiful* v158 no9 p120 N 2016

Howard, Ayanna

Ayanna Howard *Atlanta* v57 no2 p104 Je 2017

HOWARD, BETH

20 Best Medical Breakthroughs of 2016 bw color *Prevention* v68 no12 p48 D 2016

20 Quirky Summer Health Tips (That Actually Work) color *AARP: The Magazine* v59 no4A p19 Je/Jl 2016

Carry-On Health color *AARP: The Magazine* v60 no5A p19 Ag/S 2017

Fit for Life color *AARP: The Magazine* v59 no3A p44 Ap/My 2016

Hard to Swallow [Cover story] color *Prevention* v69 no9 p42 O 2017

I'll Drink to That! color *AARP: The Magazine* v59 no1A p20 D 2015/Ja 2016

The LATEST WORD on WEIGHT LOSS color *Prevention* v69 no11 p36 N 2017

Simple Steps to Forge an Iron Will cartoon color *Men's Health* v32 no4 p85 My 2017

You Must Remember This color *AARP: The Magazine* v59 no5A p24 Ag/S 2016

Howard, Brenda

THE MOTHER OF PRIDE: THE FIRST PRIDE WAS ORGANIZED BY A BISEXUAL WOMAN E. CRUZ and D. GUERRERO bw *Advocate* no1091 p120 Je/Jl 2017

Howard, Bryce Dallas, 1981-

Back to Black: Inside the Making of Mirror J. Hibberd color *Entertainment Weekly* no1436/1437 p91 O 21 2016

Gold *New Yorker* v92 no49 p14 F 13 2017

A 'Twilight Zone' for the iPhone Era R. SHEFFIELD color *Rolling Stone* no1274 p19 N 17 2016

HOWARD, CAROLINE

THE MANY FACES OF HARVEY MUDD chart color *Forbes* v200 no2 p19 S 5 2017

Howard, Charles

CHARACTER *Christian Century* v134 no17 p22 Ag 16 2017

Out-of-control ministry *Christian Century* v134 no12 p10 Je 7 2017

HOWARD, DAVID

Forward Motion color *Prevention* v69 no7 p76 Jl 2017

In Hog Heaven color *Rodale's Organic Life* v2 no7 p26 D 2016/Ja 2017

Love on the Mind color *Prevention* v69 no6 p30 Je 2017

Howard, Dwight, 1985-

REBOUND C. BETHEA *Atlanta* v56 no7 p37 N 2016

WHAT HAPPENED TO SUPERMAN? [Cover story] L. Jenkins color *Sports Illustrated* v127 no9 p46 S 25 2017

HOWARD, GREG

A Failed War: A Harvard professor mourns her cousin's short life, much of it spent behind bars *New York Times Book Review* p10 O 15 2017

'Hold My Mule' bw *New York Times Magazine* p46 Mr 12 2017

MUHAMMAD ALI *New York Times Magazine* p54 D 25 2016

Virginia *New York Times Magazine* p40 N 20 2016

HOWARD, JACINTA

Mass Transit, Mass Art: MARTA finds new ways to use its vast spaces as a canvas for local artists *Atlanta* v57 no6 p80 O 2017

Howard, Jordan

WHO'S GOT NEXT? [Cover story] M. BAZER color *Chicago* v66 no6 p78 Je 2017

HOWARD, JOY

Easter together color *Parents* v92 no4 p108 Ap 2017

JOY HOWARD bw color *Bloomberg Businessweek* no4512 p84 F 20 2017

sweets worth saluting [Cover story] color *Parents* v92 no7 p60 Jl 2017

Howard, Keisha

Sugar Mama L. D. JOHNSON and S. T. BROWN color *Ebony* v72 no6 p75 Ap/My 2017

HOWARD, LACEY

HIGH GLOSS color *Better Homes & Gardens* v95 no4 p18 Ap 2017

home *Better Homes & Gardens* v95 no1 p27 Ja 2017

LIGHT WORK *Better Homes & Gardens* v95 no1 pN2 Ja 2017

MERRY AND MOD *Better Homes & Gardens* v94 no12 p56 D 2016

Howard, Leslie Burr
STILL LEAPIN' LESLIE N. Jaffer bw color *Practical Horseman* v45 no6 p34 Je 2017

Howard, Martin
Distinct phases of Polycomb silencing to hold epigenetic memory of cold in Arabidopsis diag *Science* v357 no6356 p1142 S 15 2017

Howard, Nathan
All the President's LLCs color *Bloomberg Businessweek* no4534 p24 Ag 14 2017

Howard, P.
Best cost estimate of greenhouse gases *Science* v357 no6352 p655 Ag 18 2017

HOWARD, PAUL
Available Drugs, Affordable Drugs color *National Review* v69 no6 p34 Ap 3 2017

Howard, Peter
What Counts as Climate Consensus? *National Review* v69 no11 p2 Je 12 2017

Howard, Phillip
Made from Concentrate L. Douglas *Washington Monthly* p1 S/O 2016

HOWARD, PHOEBE
Have It Both Ways color *House Beautiful* v159 no4 p30 My 2017

Howard, R. T.
BIAFRA 50 YEARS ON: The civil war that resulted from the division of Nigeria was a major human disaster that should not be forgotten *History Today* v67 no6 p36 Je 2016
Revolt in Madagascar, 70 Years On *History Today* v67 no4 p4 Ap 2017

Howard, Raymond
CASTING PLASTER WALLS for a scratchbuilt structure [Cover story] color diag *Model Railroader* v84 no10 p24 O 2017

Howard, Roger
THE BRITISH HERITAGE TRAVEL PUZZLER *British Heritage Travel* v38 no3 p78 My/Je 2017

Howard, Ron, 1954-
INFERNO D. Vaughn color *Sound & Vision* v82 no5 p68 Je 2017
Inferno S. Perry color *Entertainment Weekly* no1438 p46 N 4 2016
IN THE HEART OF THE SEA T. J. Norton color *Sound & Vision* v81 no9 p68 N 2016
Want to Go to Mars? Ron Howard's New Series Gives Red Planet Fever a Boost J. Kluger color *Time* v188 no21 p68 N 21 2016

Howard, Ron, 1954—Interviews
Ron Howard E. Spitznagel bw *Men's Health* v32 no1 p38 Ja/F 2017
Three Qs color *Science* v354 no6313 p687 N 11 2016

HOWARD, SALLY
The Coat-Hanger Rebellion *Ms.* v26 no4 p18 Wint 2016

Howard, Soloman
True Believer: Bass Soloman Howard's success is built on a foundation of faith that has seen him through some unusual challenges L. T. Guinther *Opera News* v81 no12 p65 Je 2017

Howard, Terrence
The Latest Empire Hitmaker M. Logan *TV Guide* v65 no41 p7 O 2 2017

Howard, Thomas Albert
If They Could Turn Back Time bw *Commonweal* v144 no13 p27 Ag 11 2017
The man who fought papal infallibility J. W. O'Malley color *America* v217 no2 p44 Jl 24 2017

Howard, Vivian (Vivian S.), 1978-
A CAROLINA CHRISTMAS color *Southern Living* v51 no12 p170 D 2016
HOME AGAIN J. BLACK color *Better Homes & Gardens* v95 no11 p106 N 2017
THE KITCHEN COOKBOOK color *Better Homes & Gardens* v95 no11 p130 N 2017
SPRINGTIME IN THE SOUTHLAND color *Bon Appetit* v62 no4 p96 Ap 2017
Vivian Howard J. Crelin color *Current Biography* v78 no8 p49 Ag 2017

Howard-Tilton Memorial Library
BEST OF DESIGN J. P. Klingman color *New Orleans Magazine*

v51 no5 p74 Mr 2017

Howard University
An Open Letter to Ta-Nehisi Coates: The Dream is real J. D. Hill *Commentary* v144 no3 p35 O 2017

Howarth, Ashlee J.
Bottom-up construction of a superstructure in a porous uranium-organic crystal color graph *Science* v356 no6338 p624 My 12 2017

Howarth, Barrett—Interviews
MEET BARRETT HOWARTH *Sea Magazine* v108 no9 pCA-5 S 2016

Howarth, Jamie
Complex multifault rupture during the 2016 Mw 7.8 Kaikōura earthquake, New Zealand color map *Science* v356 no6334 p154 Ap 14 2017

HOWARTH, WILLIAM
Reading Thoreau at 200: WHY IS THE SEMINAL WORK OF THE GREAT AMERICAN TRANSCENDENTALIST HELD IN SUCH SCORN TODAY? *American Scholar* v86 no3 p44 Summ 2017

Howdy Doody Show, The (TV program)
Houdini's Handcuffs Teller *AARP: The Magazine* v60 no4A p62 Je/Jl 2017

Howe, Andy
The SAILING SCENE color *Sail* v48 no7 p6 Jl 2017
Traveling Man [Cover story] color *Sail* v48 no8 p56 Ag 2017

Howe, Carole
To The Editor color *American Craft* v76 no6 p10 D 2016-Ja 2017

Howe, Craig
TOP 7 Things Craig Howe Loves About South Dakota *South Dakota Magazine* v33 no2 p17 Jl/Ag 2017

Howe, David Everitt
Pornography of Power *Art in America* v104 no9 p29 O 2016

Howe, Fanny, 1940-
Scattered Lives A. Domestico *Commonweal* v144 no7 p36 Ap 14 2017

Howe, Gay
The SAILING SCENE color *Sail* v48 no7 p6 Jl 2017

Howe, Gordie, 1928-2016
Farewell M. Bechtel color *Sports Illustrated* v125 no21 p52 D 26 2016

Howe, Marie
Magdalene: Poems A. Frykholm color *Christian Century* v134 no10 p57 My 10 2017

Howe, Michele
Preparing, Adjusting, and Loving the Empty Nest *Publishers Weekly* v264 no24 p60 Je 12 2017

Howe, Rob
What Does an Aspiring Founder Need to Know? *Harvard Business Review Digital Articles* p1 Je 21 2017

Howe, Robert W.
Plant diversity increases with the strength of negative density dependence at the global scale diag *Science* v356 no6345 p1389 Je 30 2017

HOWE, STEFFAN A.
Assessing National Biodiversity Trends for Rocky and Coral Reefs through the Integration of Citizen Science and Scientific Monitoring Programs *BioScience* v67 no2 p134 F 2017

Howe, Stephanie
Fuel Injector J. Fuchs and T. Keith color *Sports Illustrated* v127 no2 p24 Jl 17 2017

Howe, Susan, 1937-
Inside & Underneath Words [Cover story] L. Hammer bw color *New York Review of Books* v64 no14 p31 S 28 2017
PAPER TRAIL D. CHIASSON cartoon color *New Yorker* v93 no23 p77 Ag 7 2017

HOWELL, BETSY L.
The Fire's Edge *American Forests* v122 no3 p16 Fall 2016

Howell, Emily L.
U.S. attitudes on human genome editing color graph *Science* v357 no6351 p553 Ag 11 2017

Howell, Hannah
The Scotsman Who Saved Me: Seven Brides for Seven Scotsmen, Book 1 *Publishers Weekly* v264 no32 p57 Ag 7 2017

Howell, James C.
The Face of Water: A Translator on Beauty and Meaning in the

Estimating economic damage from climate change in the United States color graph *Science* v356 no6345 p1362 Je 30 2017

Hsiang-Jung Tsai

Role for migratory wild birds in the global spread of avian influenza H5N8 bibl graph map *Science* v354 no6309 p213 O 14 2016

Hsiao-Wei Tsao

The epigenetic landscape of T cell exhaustion bibl graph *Science* v354 no6316 p1165 D 2 2016

Hsieh, Chang-Fu

Plant diversity increases with the strength of negative density dependence at the global scale diag *Science* v356 no6345 p1389 Je 30 2017

Hsieh, Chyi-Song

Lactobacillus reuteri induces gut intraepithelial CD4+CD8αα+ T cells diag graph *Science* v357 no6353 p806 Ag 25 2017

Hsieh, D.

A parity-breaking electronic nematic phase transition in the spin-orbit coupled metal Cd2Re2O7 diag *Science* v356 no6335 p295 Ap 21 2017

Hsieh, Tehching, 1950-

Time Out T. Jeppesen bw color map *Art in America* v105 no4 p27 Ap 2017

Hsu, Emily

BUILDING A Fitness Empire K. McGuire color *Dance Spirit* v21 no2 p58 F 2017

Hsu, Jeremy

Can Medical Cannabis Break the Painkiller Epidemic? color *Scientific American* v315 no3 p10 S 2016

Mosquitoes to the Rescue color diag map *Scientific American* v315 no5 p17 N 2016

NASA Fights Flight Delays color *Scientific American* v316 no4 p26 Ap 2017

Polar Ice Squad color *Scientific American* v316 no6 p10 Je 2017

Sailing on Sunshine color *Scientific American* v317 no4 p24 O 2017

Telescopic Tag Team color *Scientific American* v316 no1 p16 Ja 2017

Winds of Change color *Scientific American* v315 no5 p21 N 2016

Hsu, Joanne I.

Evolution of protein phosphorylation across 18 fungal species bibl graph *Science* v354 no6309 p229 O 14 2016

Hsu, Michael

A Splash from the Past: Sutro Baths *Parks & Recreation* p8 Aquatics Guide 2017

Hsu, Ya-Ju

Imaging the distribution of transient viscosity after the 2016 Mw 7.1 Kumamoto earthquake map *Science* v356 no6334 p163 Ap 14 2017

Hsu, Yen-Pang

Treadmilling by FtsZ filaments drives peptidoglycan synthesis and bacterial cell division bibl graph *Science* v355 no6326 p739 F 17 2017

HTTP (Computer network protocol)

How to use HTTPS to improve web security G. FLEISHMAN color *Macworld - Digital Edition* v34 no8 p95 Ag 2017

Hu, B.

High dislocation density–induced large ductility in deformed and partitioned steels bw color diag *Science* v357 no6355 p1029 S 8 2017

Hu, Cheng

"Perfect" designer chromosome V and behavior of a ring derivative diag *Science* v355 no6329 p1046 Mr 10 2017

Hu, Chunhua

Polymeric peptide pigments with sequence-encoded properties color graph *Science* v356 no6342 p1064 Je 9 2017

Hu, Fengling

Reovirus infection triggers inflammatory responses to dietary antigens and development of celiac disease color diag *Science* v356 no6333 p44 Ap 7 2017

Hu, Fred

Why Globalization Stalled color *Foreign Affairs* v96 no4 p54 Jl/Ag 2017

Hu, Hailan

History of winning remodels thalamo-PFC circuit to reinforce social dominance color *Science* v357 no6347 p162 Jl 14 2017

Hu, J.

Grain boundary stability governs hardening and softening in extremely fine nanograined metals bibl color graph *Science* v355 no6331 p1292 Mr 24 2017

Hu, Jane C.

Baby's Rainbow color *Scientific American* v317 no3 p16 S 2017

Hu, Meng-Long

"Perfect" designer chromosome V and behavior of a ring derivative diag *Science* v355 no6329 p1046 Mr 10 2017

Hu, Peijun

Global roadless areas: Consider terrain color *Science* v355 no6332 p1381 Mr 31 2017

Hu, X.

Surface changes on comet 67P/Churyumov-Gerasimenko suggest a more active past bw graph *Science* v355 no6332 p1392 Mr 31 2017

Hua, Fangyuan

The pet trade's role in defaunation color *Science* v356 no6341 p916 Je 1 2017

Hua, Susanna

A key malaria metabolite modulates vector blood seeking, feeding, and susceptibility to infection bibl chart diag *Science* v355 no6329 p1076 Mr 10 2017

Hua-Bing Li

The DNA-sensing AIM2 inflammasome controls radiation-induced cell death and tissue injury bibl color graph *Science* v354 no6313 p765 N 11 2016

HUA HSU

IDENTITY AND INTENTION cartoon color *New Yorker* v93 no28 p69 S 18 2017

INDEPENDENCE DAY cartoon *New Yorker* v92 no46 p76 Ja 23 2017

LEGACY MEDIA color *New Yorker* v93 no11 p74 My 1 2017

MOOD MUSIC color *New Yorker* v93 no14 p92 My 22 2017

OVER IT cartoon *New Yorker* v93 no26 p90 S 4 2017

PRAISE SONGS bw *New Yorker* v93 no10 p98 Ap 24 2017

Hua Zhang

Precision medicine for nasopharyngeal carcinoma bibl diag *Science* v354 no6319 p24 D 23 2016

Huadong Zhu

Expert consensus on point-of-care testing *Science* v354 no6319 p15 D 23 2016

Recommendations on the management and use of POCT in medical institutions (nosocomial) *Science* v354 no6319 p13 D 23 2016

Huai-Ling Gao

Synthetic nacre by predesigned matrix-directed mineralization bibl bw diag graph *Science* v354 no6308 p107 O 7 2016

Huaizong Shen

Structural basis for the gating mechanism of the type 2 ryanodine receptor RyR2 bibl color graph *Science* v354 no6310 paah5324-1 O 21 2016

Huajian Cai

Charting China's Rising Individualism in Names, Songs, and Attitudes *Harvard Business Review Digital Articles* p2 Mr 11 2016

Hualan Chen

Role for migratory wild birds in the global spread of avian influenza H5N8 bibl graph map *Science* v354 no6309 p213 O 14 2016

Hualiang Wang

Quality management for precision medicine clinical applications: A consensus from the China Precision Medicine Clinical Research and Application Association bibl *Science* v354 no6319 p11 D 23 2016

Huamantupa-Chuquimaco, I.

Persistent effects of pre-Columbian plant domestication on Amazonian forest composition bibl chart graph map *Science* v355 no6328 p925 Mr 3 2017

Huaming Chen

A transcription factor hierarchy defines an environmental stress response network diag *Science* v354 no6312 p598 N 4 2016

Huan Xu

Generation of influenza A viruses as live but replication-incompetent virus vaccines bibl graph *Science* v354 no6316 p1170 D 2 2016

Huang, Alexander C.

Epigenetic stability of exhausted T cells limits durability of reinvigoration by PD-1 blockade bibl graph *Science* v354 no6316

S 24 2015

Huawei's Culture Is the Key to Its Success D. De Cremer and Tian Tao *Harvard Business Review Digital Articles* p2 Je 11 2015

Huawei Technologies Co. Ltd.—Management

IS THE WORLD BIG ENOUGH FOR HUAWEI? S. Cendrowski color diag *Fortune* v175 no2 p66 F 1 2017

Hubbard, A.

Massive blow-out craters formed by hydrate-controlled methane expulsion from the Arctic seafloor graph map *Science* v356 no6341 p948 Je 1 2017

Hubbard, Basil P.

A conserved NAD+ binding pocket that regulates protein-protein interactions during aging bibl graph *Science* v355 no6331 p1312 Mr 24 2017

Hubbard, Charlotte

Weddings at Promise Lodge *Publishers Weekly* v264 no21 p78 My 22 2017

Hubbard, Freddie, 1938-2008

Band Class Heroes B. ZIMMERMAN color *Downbeat* v84 no6 p8 Je 2017

Hubbard, Ladee

The Talented Ribkins *Publishers Weekly* v264 no26 p150 Je 26 2017

Hubbard, Ruth, 1924-2016

RUTH HUBBARD S. CORBETT *New York Times Magazine* p46 D 25 2016

HUBBARD, SHANITA

Missing Mama color *Ebony* v72 no6 p65 Ap/My 2017

Hubbard, Thomas N.

Research: Delegating More Can Increase Your Earnings *Harvard Business Review Digital Articles* p2 Ag 12 2016

HUBBARD, VALERIE

Bivalve Revival *Virginia Living* p19 2017 Smoke & Salt

CAITI & JACK *Virginia Living* v15 no2 p96 F 2017

COMFORT ZONE: Stately and elegant, Four Acres in Charlottesville is also a warm and welcoming family retreat *Virginia Living* v15 no4 p94 Je 2017

HOME STRETCH: luxe outdoor living spaces create opportunities for gracious year-round entertaining *Virginia Living* v15 no4 p81 Je 2017

HOUSE PROUD: Customized rooms that are just your style *Virginia Living* v15 no4 p85 Je 2017

New Point of View: The Richmond home of George and Louise Freeman is a study in transformation *Virginia Living* v15 no6 p58 O 2017

SHELL GAME *Virginia Living* p60 2017 Smoke & Salt

Hubbard, W. B.

Jupiter's interior and deep atmosphere: The initial pole-to-pole passes from the Juno spacecraft [Cover story] color graph *Science* v356 no6340 p821 My 26 2017

Hubbard model

Spin-imbalance in a 2D Fermi-Hubbard system P. T. Brown, D. Mitra et al diag graph *Science* v357 no6358 p1385 S 29 2017

Hubbard Street Dance Co.

Training Wheels L. Warnecke *Dance Magazine* v91 no8 p14 Ag 2017

Hubbardton Forge LLC

Radiant Materials R. C. Orrell color *Architectural Record* v205 no5 p135 My 2017

Hubbart, Christina

Resistance to malaria through structural variation of red blood cell invasion receptors diag *Science* v356 no6343 p1139 Je 16 2017

Hubbell, Stephen P.

Plant diversity increases with the strength of negative density dependence at the global scale diag *Science* v356 no6345 p1389 Je 30 2017

Hubble constant

A GRAVITATIONAL-LENSING MEASUREMENT OF THE HUBBLE CONSTANT *Physics Today* v70 no4 p24 Ap 2017

Is the universe expanding faster than expected? color *Astronomy* v45 no5 p14 My 2017

Hubble constant—Research

A COSMIC CONTROVERSY J. You, C. Bickel et al diag *Science* v355 no6329 p1013 Mr 10 2017

Hubble deep field

Our universe just got a whole lot bigger color *Astronomy* v45 no2

p16 F 2017

Hubble Space Telescope (Spacecraft)

Caught in a spider's web color *Astronomy* v45 no3 p74 Mr 2017

Europa Geysers Point to Subsurface Ocean J. K. BEATTY *Sky & Telescope* v133 no2 p14 F 2017

The final frontier bw *Astronomy* v45 no11 p74 N 2017

GALAXY CLUSTERS The universe's cosmic lenses L. Kruesi color diag graph *Astronomy* v45 no2 p28 F 2017

Hope Springs Eternal for Easy Access to Water on Europa L. Billings color *Scientific American* v315 no6 p20 D 2016

HUBBLE GONE WILD E. MASTROIANNI color *Discover* v38 no7 p20 S 2017

Peering through a galaxy cluster color *Science* v356 no6338 p564 My 12 2017

Hubble Space Telescope (Spacecraft)—History

Long Live Hubble K. Peek color *Scientific American* v316 no3 p80 Mr 2017

Hubbs, Heather—Interviews

HEATHER HUBBS J. Chen color *Bloomberg Businessweek* no4503 p75 D 12 2016

Huber, Anna Lee

This Side of Murder *Publishers Weekly* v264 no32 p53 Ag 7 2017

Huber, Bill

BILL HUBER WINS '02 NATIONAL TITLE WITH ARENA RECORD J. Mankin color *Spin to Win Rodeo* v21 no3 p88 My 2017

Huber, David

Highly efficient electrocaloric cooling with electrostatic actuation bw diag *Science* v357 no6356 p1130 S 15 2017

HUBER, DJURO

An Unparalleled Opportunity for an Important Ecological Study *BioScience* v67 no10 p875 O 2017

Huber, Mary Taylor

Academic Knowledge *Change* v48 no5 p64 S/O 2016

Is College for Everyone? *Change* v49 no1 p7 Ja/F 2017

QUALITY IN UNDERGRADUATE EDUCATION *Change* v49 no3 p45 My/Je 2017

Huber, Samuel

A pathogenic role for T cell–derived IL-22BP in inflammatory bowel disease bibl graph *Science* v354 no6310 p358 O 21 2016

Huberman, Andrew D.

Regenerating optic pathways from the eye to the brain diag *Science* v356 no6342 p1031 Je 9 2017

HUBERMAN, GIGI

What do you collect and why? color *American Craft* v77 no2 p20 Ap/My 2017

Hubert, Raymond

Hot Seat bw *Military History* v34 no5 p80 Ja 2018

Hubric, Tom—Interviews

TOM THE EGG MAN *Washingtonian Magazine* v52 no1 p99 O 2016

Huckabee, Mike, 1955-

TWITTER FAMOUS E. Plott *Washingtonian Magazine* v52 no9 p20 Je 2017

Huckman, Robert

The Harvard Contest That's Trying to Improve Health Care Delivery *Harvard Business Review Digital Articles* p2 O 2 2015

A Simple Way to Measure Health Care Outcomes *Harvard Business Review Digital Articles* p2 D 8 2016

The Untapped Potential of Health Care APIs *Harvard Business Review Digital Articles* p2 D 23 2015

Hudak, Joseph

Dan Auerbach's Nashville Love Letter color *Rolling Stone* no1278/1279 p22 Ja 12 2017

Michelle Branch's Second Act color *Rolling Stone* no1283 p14 Mr 23 2017

The Road Heats Up bw color *Rolling Stone* no1288 p11 Je 1 2017

HUDAK, TOM

Chords & Discords bw *Downbeat* v83 no12 p10 D 2016

Huddle, Molly

MOLLY HUDDLE S. DOUGLAS cartoon color *Runner's World* v51 no11 p21 D 2016

Huddleston, Tom Jr.

THE 2017 Fortune Crystal Ball color diag *Fortune* v174 no7 p11 D 1 2016

A DEAN FOR ALL SEASONS color *Fortune* v174 no7 p38 D

1 2016

DREAM WEAVER color *Fortune* v176 no3 p74 S 1 2017

Football Absorbs a Knockout Blow color diag *Fortune* v176 no4 p21 S 15 2017

FORTY UNDER FORTY 2017 color *Fortune* v176 no3 p62 S 1 2017

The Hidden Figures of the Oscars Ad Blitz color *Fortune* v175 no2 p14 F 1 2017

Hollywood's Search for a Blockbuster Algorithm color *Fortune* v175 no6 p12 My 1 2017

HOLLYWOOD WRAPS ONE OF ITS WORST SUMMERS EVER color *Fortune* v176 no4 p27 S 15 2017

MAKING IT ON BROAD-WAY color *Fortune* v174 no8 p75 D 15 2016

MINING COMEDY GOLD color *Fortune* v176 no3 p70 S 1 2017

"Peak TV" Is Further Away Than We Think color *Fortune* v176 no1 p10 Jl 1 2017

SPANISH-LANGUAGE TV IS EN FUEGO color *Fortune* v75 no1 p34 Ja 1 2017

Taylor Swift's Battle of the Brands color *Fortune* v176 no5 p18 O 1 2017

THIS STUDIO HAS A SPECIAL EFFECT ON MOVIES color *Fortune* v175 no3 p26 Mr 1 2017

VIEWERS TUNE IN FOR CUBS' EPIC WIN, TUNE OUT THE REST color *Fortune* v174 no8 p22 D 15 2016

WALT DISNEY BREAKS RECORDS color *Fortune* v174 no8 p21 D 15 2016

WORLD'S 50 GREATEST LEADERS [Cover story] color *Fortune* v175 no5 p46 Ap 1 2017

You're Already Good. Here's How to Step It Up color *Fortune* v174 no6 p18 N 1 2016

YOUTH REVOLT color *Fortune* v176 no3 p64 S 1 2017

HUDEPOHL, DANA

Secrets of the Super Healthy [Cover story] cartoon color *Prevention* v69 no1 p74 Ja 2017

Hudgens, Vanessa, 1988-

DON'T BELIEVE HER SPORTS BRA [Cover story] C. Connors color *Women's Health* v14 no4 p61 My 2017

HUDGINS, ANDREW

Goodbye to Westbrook Acres: AS A WRITER WALKS AND MUSES, THE WORLD'S SORROWS INTRUDE UPON THE PEACEFUL STREETS HE WILL BE LEAVING *American Scholar* v86 no3 p80 Summ 2017

Hudlin, Reginald

24 HOURS with REGINALD HUDLIN O. J. WILLIAMS color *Ebony* v72/73 no12/1 p94 O/N 2017

THE BIG QUESTION cartoon *Atlantic* v320 no3 p100 O 2017

MARSHALL C. Agard color *Entertainment Weekly* no1478 / 1479 p55 Ag 18-25 2017

Hudock, Barry

A Larger Solidarity bw *Commonweal* v144 no5 p11 Mr 10 2017

Hudson (N.Y.)

EDITOR'S LETTER G. Cerio color *Magazine Antiques* v184 no3 p16 My/Je 2017

Hudson (N.Y.)—Description & travel

GUIDE TO Hudson NEW YORK and nearby points of interest S. Dalati and N. Anderson color map *Magazine Antiques* v184 no3 p49 My/Je 2017

Hudson, Carter

Snowfall I. Rudolph *TV Guide* v65 no27 p33 Je 26 2017

Hudson, Dawn—Interviews

The Academy Will See Us Now E. Strauss and J. Harman color *Glamour* v115 no3 p50 Mr 2017

HUDSON, E. K.

Record's Innovation Conference in NYC Considers the Public Realm *Architectural Record* v205 no10 p26 O 2017

Hudson, Ed

PICKLE RECIPES for the Picking: Ferment or quick-pickle your harvest with this assortment of ideas from Mother Earth News bloggers *Mother Earth News* no282 p56 Je/Jl 2017

Hudson, Eric R.

Synthesis of mixed hypermetallic oxide BaOCa+ from laser-cooled reagents in an atom-ion hybrid trap diag graph *Science* v357 no6358 p1370 S 29 2017

HUDSON, HANNAH L.

Doses of Neighborhood Nature: The Benefits for Mental Health of

Living with Nature *BioScience* v67 no2 p147 F 2017

Hudson, Hugh

The Eclipse Megamovie Project bw color *Sky & Telescope* v134 no2 p20 Ag 2017

Hudson, Jennifer, 1981-

HAPPILY UNMARRIED S. E. JAMISON color *Ebony* v72 no11 p66 S 2017

TOASTING FALL TV H. Goldblatt color *Entertainment Weekly* no1467 p12 My 26 2017

The Voice N. Abrams, C. Holub et al color *Entertainment Weekly* no1482/1483 p49 S 22 2017

Why I Love HEART STONES color *InStyle* v24 no4 p228 Ap 2017

Hudson, Jennifer, 1981—Interviews

ONE NIGHT ONLY C. Murray color *Essence* v47 no8 p70 D 2016

Hudson, Kate, 1979-

The Bullseye M. Snetiker color *Entertainment Weekly* no1484 p64 S 29 2017

Goldie & Kate color *InStyle* p96 Home & Design 2016

Goldie HAWN: AFTER A 15-YEAR HIATUS, THE GREAT GLASS-CEILING-SHATTERING GOLDIE HAWN IS BACK IN THE PICTURE, AND HAVING A LAUGH WITH THE LADIES FOR WHOM SHE PAVED THE WAY *Interview* v47 no3 p88 My 2017

Kate Hudson HER BEST EVER E. Wilson color *InStyle* v24 no10 p94 O 2017

Hudson, Paul

Bad Mind M. Trammell color *New Yorker* v92 no43 p10 Ja 2 2017

Hudson, Sara

Selling a Beach Redesign Project *Parks & Recreation* v52 no4 p56 Ap 2017

Hudson, William Henry, 1862-1918

Dreams of Argentina: The naturalist W.H. Hudson wrote one of the 20th century's greatest memoirs after a fever rekindled visions of his childhood P. Symmes *Smithsonian* v48 no2 p58 My 2017

Hudson Bay

Building Archean cratons from Hadean mafic crust J. O'Neil and R. W. Carlson bibl graph *Science* v355 no6330 p1199 Mr 17 2017

Hudson River (N.Y. & N.J.)

Tunnel Out of Danger S. Gregory color *Time* v189 no13 p37 Ap 10 2017

Hudson River (N.Y. & N.J.)—Environmental conditions

A River Runs Through It S. MORFORD *USA Today Magazine* v146 no2866 p66 Jl 2017

Hudson's Bay Co.

What Hudson's Bay Likes About Macy's L. Rupp graph *Bloomberg Businessweek* no4511 p21 F 13 2017

Hudson Theatre (New York, N.Y.)

Another Opening... Finally!: Broadway's Oldest Theater, The Hudson, Returns as Broadway's Newest Space M. S. Eddy *Stage Directions* v30 no6 p30 Je 2017

Hue, V.

Jupiter's interior and deep atmosphere: The initial pole-to-pole passes with the Juno spacecraft [Cover story] color graph *Science* v356 no6340 p821 My 26 2017

Hueber, John

REBUILD THE NEIGHBORHOOD L. MURTHA *Cincinnati Magazine* v50 no5 p34 F 2017

HUEBERT, DAVID

COLLOQUIUM: J.T. HENRY AND LADY SIMCOE ON EARLY ONTARIO PETROCOLONIALISM *Walrus* p73 Ja\F 2017

Huebner, Timothy S.

Culture Clash R. STRINER *Weekly Standard* v22 no40 p36 Je 26 2017

Huebschmann, Dan

Chicken Fight! color *Men's Health* v32 no8 p88 O 2017

Huege, T.

Observation of a large-scale anisotropy in the arrival directions of cosmic rays above 8 × 1018 eV *Science* v357 no6357 p1266 S 22 2017

Huerta, Dolores

One Tough (Rebel, Activist, Feminist) Mother: The documentary Dolores shines a light on an overlooked hero of farmworkers' and women's rights L. BARCA *Ms.* v27 no3 p46 Fall 2017

Huerta, Marcos

Is anyone out there? color *Science* v354 no6311 p424 O 28 2016

The origins of intelligent life color *Science* v357 no6351 p556 Ag 11 2017

Hueso, Luis E.

A molecular spin-photovoltaic device color diag *Science* v357 no6352 p677 Ag 18 2017

Huet, Ellen

$400 Million Richer By Pinching Pennies *Bloomberg Businessweek* no4515 p29 Mr 20 2017

America's got NO Talent color graph *Bloomberg Businessweek* no4500 p32 N 21 2016

Artificial People cartoon color *Bloomberg Businessweek* no4496 p40 O 24 2016

Bulls On Parole cartoon *Bloomberg Businessweek* no4496 p33 O 24 2016

In the Land of the Blind Hire cartoon color *Bloomberg Businessweek* no4508 p27 Ja 23 2017

Slack Technologies chart color *Bloomberg Businessweek* no4503 p42 D 12 2016

A Spotlight on Harassment at Google *Bloomberg Businessweek* no4525 p33 Je 5 2017

Huey-You, Cannan

LEGO BOOST color *Popular Mechanics* p96 S 2017

Preteen Astronomer Shines at AAS Meeting N. T. REDD *Sky & Telescope* v133 no4 p12 Ap 2017

HUEY-YOU, CARSON

LEGO BOOST color *Popular Mechanics* p96 S 2017

Huffington, Arianna

Artists color *Time* v189 no16/17 p40 My 1-8 2017

How to Keep Email from Ruining Your Vacation *Harvard Business Review Digital Articles* p2 2017

The Rest of Your Life *New York Times Book Review* p10 D 18 2016

Huffman, Bobby

IDEA OF THE MONTH P. Barbour *Successful Farming* v114 no10 p78 O 2016

Huffman, James

Too Much Democracy? *Hoover Digest: Research & Opinion on Public Policy* no4 p62 Fall 2016

Huffman, Jibade-Khalil

Jibade-Khalil Huffman S. Korman *Art in America* v104 no9 p25 O 2016

Huffman, John Pearley

BOOT SCOOT BOOGIE chart color *Car & Driver* v63 no1 p64 Jl 2017

COMFORTABLY DUMB cartoon *Car & Driver* v62 no11 p22 My 2017

A MIGHTY WIND color *Car & Driver* v62 no6 p24 D 2016

M Means Something New. Again color *Car & Driver* v62 no11 p104 My 2017

OILED UP color *Car & Driver* v63 no4 p28 O 2017

Space Invader color *Car & Driver* v63 no5 p118 N 2017

TACO BELL FANTASIES color *Car & Driver* v62 no7 p30 Ja 2017

Take 5 With BILLY GODBOLD color diag *Hot Rod* v70 no7 p16 Jl 2017

Take 5 With TROY LADD color *Hot Rod* v70 no2 p14 F 2017

What I'd Do Differently A.J. Foyt, 82 cartoon *Car & Driver* v62 no8 p92 F 2017

What I'd Do Differently Bob Chandler, 75 color *Car & Driver* v63 no1 p112 Jl 2017

What I'd Do Differently Ed Welburn, 66 color *Car & Driver* v62 no11 p120 My 2017

What I'd Do Differently Fake Elon Musk, not 45 cartoon *Car & Driver* v62 no7 p120 Ja 2017

What I'd Do Differently Johan de Nysschen, 57 *Car & Driver* v63 no4 p108 O 2017

What I'd Do Differently Kyle Petty, 57 color *Car & Driver* v63 no5 p128 N 2017

Huffman, Lukas—Interviews

AV CLUB C. Liska color *Snowboarder* v29 no2 p33 O 2016

Hug of Thunder (Music)

What to Stream color *Entertainment Weekly* no1473 p55 Jl 7 2017

Huganir, Richard L.

Homer1a drives homeostatic scaling-down of excitatory synapses during sleep bibl graph *Science* v355 no6324 p511 F 3 2017

Hugenholtz, Philip

On the origins of oxygenic photosynthesis and aerobic respiration in Cyanobacteria chart diag *Science* v355 no6332 p1436 Mr 31 2017

Huges, Cathy—Interviews

POWER IN LONGEVITY S. FLOYD color *Black Enterprise* v47 no5 p16 Ja/F 2017

Hughes, Alice C.

Global roadless areas: Hidden roads color *Science* v355 no6332 p1381 Mr 31 2017

Hughes, Allen

THE DEFINING ONES M. LYNCH color *Vanity Fair* v59 no7 p108 Summ 2017

Hughes, Blake

BIG BUCKS color *Spin to Win Rodeo* v20 no10 p22 D 2016

HUGHES, BRENT B.

Long-Term Studies Contribute Disproportionately to Ecology and Policy *BioScience* v67 no3 p271 Mr 2017

Hughes, Bronwen—Interviews

Harriet the Spy: Behind the Blue Paint Scene C. Brody color *Entertainment Weekly* no1440 p44 N 18 2016

Hughes, Charles

Still Pilgrim: Poems *Christian Century* v134 no17 p41 Ag 16 2017

HUGHES, CHRISTINE

How to Influence Zoning Changes color *Trail Rider* v29 no4 p30 My 2017

Hughes, Danielle D.

5 BOOKS TO GET YOU ON THE ROAD TO FINANCIAL FREEDOM color *Black Enterprise* v47 no5 p20 Ja/F 2017

Hughes, George

LIMERICK LAUGHS *Saturday Evening Post* v289 no4 p97 Jl/Ag 2017

Hughes, Howard

Rich and Strange N. Rapold color *Film Comment* v52 no6 p10 N/D 2016

HUGHES, JAMIE A.

GIVE US THIS DAY OUR DAILY CHORES color *Christianity Today* v60 no10 p65 D 2016

Hughes, Jazmine

AFENI SHAKUR *New York Times Magazine* p50 D 25 2016

Charlamagne Tha God Loves Telling Middle America About Black Privilege color *New York Times Magazine* p82 My 21 2017

The Hair Braider *New York Times Magazine* p40 F 26 2017

Pothos *New York Times Magazine* p26 Je 11 2017

Refashionista *New York Times Magazine* p28 S 3 2017

Hughes, Justin—Interviews

Q&A *People Management* p13 D 2016/Ja 2017

Hughes, Kathryn, 1959-

STRIPPING DOWN THE BUTTONED UP: An examination of the 'fleeting, fine-grained intimacies' of letters, diaries and memoirs produces a witty and scholarly account of Victorian attitudes to the body A. Lycett *History Today* v67 no9 p96 S 2017

Hughes, Kelly T.

Nanoscale-length control of the flagellar driveshaft requires hitting the tethered outer membrane color diag graph *Science* v356 no6334 p197 Ap 14 2017

Hughes, Langston, 1902-1967

1933: Harlem L. Hughes *Lapham's Quarterly* v10 no1 p168 Wint 2017

Hughes, Lindsey D.

Macrophage function in tissue repair and remodeling requires IL-4 or IL-13 with apoptotic cells diag *Science* v356 no6342 p1072 Je 9 2017

Hughes, Mallory

KITCHEN HELP *Washingtonian Magazine* v52 no1 p162 O 2016

Hughes, Matt

NEWS BITES color *Black Belt* v55 no5 p14 Ag/S 2017

HUGHES, MEGAN

the dirt *Better Homes & Gardens* v94 no11 p68 N 2016

HOMEGROWN STRAWBERRIES color *Better Homes & Gardens* v95 no5 p94 My 2017

"I Knew She Was Out There" [Cover story] M. PEYSER *Reader's Digest* v188 no1126 p73 D 2016/Ja 2017

Hulick, Kathryn
Science News for Students color *Science News* v192 no4 p33 S 16 2017

Hulk (Fictitious character)
NO. 8 THE HULK J. McGovern color *Entertainment Weekly* no1436/1437 p50 O 21 2016

Hull, Courtney
To The Editor color *American Craft* v76 no6 p10 D 2016-Ja 2017

Hull, Dana
The Everyman Ride For the Upper Half bw *Bloomberg Businessweek* no4533 p14 Ag 7 2017
FURY ROAD color *Bloomberg Businessweek* no4515 p54 Mr 20 2017
How Grand Theft Auto Steers Driverless Cars color *Bloomberg Businessweek* no4519 p23 Ap 24 2017

HULL, EDMUND
BRINGING ANNIE HOME color map *Sail* v48 no4 p40 Ap 2017

Hull, Jeffrey W.
How to Make Your Workplace Safe for Transgender Employees *Harvard Business Review Digital Articles* p2 Ag 3 2015
How Your Leadership Has to Change as Your Startup Scales *Harvard Business Review Digital Articles* p2 My 20 2016
Learn to Become a Less Autocratic Manager *Harvard Business Review Digital Articles* p2 Mr 6 2015

Hull, Kami L.
Illuminating amination bibl diag *Science* v355 no6326 p690 F 17 2017

Hull, Michael D.
THE FOREST FOR THE TREES bw color *Military History* v34 no5 p30 Ja 2018

Hull, Mike
Slog Through the Hürtgen Forest bw color map *Military History* v34 no5 p36 Ja 2018

Hulliung, Mark
Mark Hulliung, Ed., Rousseau and the Dilemmas of Modernity J. Marks *Society* v54 no1 p83 F 2017

Hulls (Naval architecture)
See also
Planing hulls
THE HULL STORY: WHEN'S THE LAST TIME YOU THOUGHT ABOUT HULL INNOVATION? NOW'S THE TIME T. SERIO *Boating World* v38 no8 p54 S/O 2017

HULME, PHILIP E.
Scientific and Normative Foundations for the Valuation of Alien-Species Impacts: Thirteen Core Principles *BioScience* v67 no2 p166 F 2017

Hulmes, L.
Country-specific effects of neonicotinoid pesticides on honey bees and wild bees diag map *Science* v356 no6345 p1393 Je 30 2017

Hulmes, S.
Country-specific effects of neonicotinoid pesticides on honey bees and wild bees diag map *Science* v356 no6345 p1393 Je 30 2017

Hulot, Nicolas
Ditching Dirty Cars color *Earth Island Journal* v32 no3 p8 Aut 2017

Hulse, Carl
Supreme BATTLE *New York Times Upfront* v149 no10 p14 Mr 13 2017

Hulsman, David
Paradise Reimagined J. YOUNG *Indianapolis Monthly* p8 My 2017

Hulsman, J.
Observation of a large-scale anisotropy in the arrival directions of cosmic rays above 8 × 1018 eV *Science* v357 no6357 p1266 S 22 2017

Hultgren, Kelly
Teach the Children Well: Money lessons for the grandkids cartoon color *AARP: The Magazine* v60 no5A p27 Ag/S 2017

HULTINE, KEVIN R.
The Role of Botanical Gardens in the Conservation of Cactaceae *BioScience* v66 no12 p1057 D 1 2016

Hulu (Web resource)
THE UNFOLDIN DRAMA OF REAL-TIME TV M. Lev-Ram color diag *Fortune* v175 no6 p50 My 1 2017

Hulu LLC
Hulu Reboots for A Post-Cable Age L. Shaw graph *Bloomberg*

Businessweek no4502 p30 D 5 2016

Hum, Jay
Why My Company Serves Free Breakfast to All Employees *Harvard Business Review Digital Articles* p1 My 1 2017

Humagain, Sunita
Polymeric peptide pigments with sequence-encoded properties color graph *Science* v356 no6342 p1064 Je 9 2017

Humala, Ollanta, 1963-
Ollanta Humala B. Lightner *Current Biography* v78 no3 p34 Mr 2017

Human abnormalities—Prevention
Baby on Board L. TURNER color *Better Nutrition* v79 no1 p26 Ja 2017

Human activity recognition
Under the Microscope color *Earth Island Journal* v32 no3 p12 Aut 2017
WANING WILDFIRES *Earth Island Journal* v32 no3 p5 Aut 2017

Human-alien encounters
LAST PAGE color *Wired* v25 no9 p96 S 2017

Human anatomy
See also
Brain
Breast
Hair
Hand
Skin
Body Gunk, Explained K. KLOSS *Reader's Digest* v188 no1126 p122 D 2016/Ja 2017

Human-animal communication
BECKER STABLES and Kheanne G. DEARTH *Arabian Horse World* v57 no6 p1 Mr 2017
Can Your Horse Ask You For Help? S. D. Wenholz color *Practical Horseman* v45 no4 p67 Ap 2017
et al il *Phi Kappa Phi Forum* v97 no2 p4 Summ 2017
How to listen to your horse S. Wilsie and G. Vogel color *Equus* no470 p55 N 2016
leading riders and handlers D. Tatelman *Arabian Horse World* v57 no6 p29 Mr 2017
RACING YEARBOOK D. Hearst *Arabian Horse World* v57 no6 p6 Mr 2017
Saving Kasyd B. FINKE *Arabian Horse World* v57 no6 p46 Mr 2017
The Secret Language of Pets [Cover story] J. MCCAFFERY color *Prevention* v69 no2 p92 F 2017
the WAY WE ARE E. Verdieck *Arabian Horse World* v57 no6 p48 Mr 2017

Human-animal relationships
Animal House! color *Parents* v92 no11 p72 N 2017
Asymmetrical Riding B. GODDARD cartoon *Trail Rider* v29 no1 p72 Ja/F 2017
A BOY'S BEST FRIEND HAS A SECRET PAST G. PAULSEN color *Reader's Digest* v190 no1134 p112 O 2017
Dinner with Arnold: And Burying the Sail-Cats S. CARR *Idaho Magazine* v16 no7 p54 Ap 2017
Get Moving! T. SHIELDS and J. F. MEYER color *Horse & Rider* v56 no11 p48 N 2017
Greener Pastures L. Black *Arabian Horse World* v57 no2 p137 N 2016
Homebodies K. MORI *American Scholar* v86 no1 p70 Wint 2017
HOW HORSES THINK F. De Giorgio and J. De Giorgio-Schoorl bw cartoon color *Equus* no474 p59 Mr 2017
Mischief on High: Investigating the Mysterious Wolverine M. TERRA-BERNS *Idaho Magazine* v16 no7 p27 Ap 2017
A New Case for Our First Friendship B. Lang *Discover* v27 no10 p6 D 2016
pet perks A. MENCEL color *Parents* v92 no8 p25 Ag 2017
Settle Your Cinchy Horse J. Goodnight and H. Melocco color *Trail Rider* v29 no2 p42 Mr 2017
SURVIVAL OF THE CUTEST H. HERZOG *Psychology Today* v49 no6 p19 N/D 2016
Webs of Perception J. Ingram color *Canadian Wildlife* v23 no4 p12 S/O 2017

Human-animal relationships—History
Hannibal's Lost Road F. Lidz *Smithsonian* v48 no4 p108 Jl/Ag 2017

Human body—History

The Living Dead: BRUTALLY KILLED THOUSANDS OF YEARS AGO, EUROPE'S FAMED BOG BODIES ARE STARTING TO REVEAL THEIR SECRETS J. LEVINE *Smithsonian* v48 no2 p65 My 2017

Human body—Physiology

I AM PLURAL C. CARLSON cartoon *Christianity Today* v60 no9 p60 N 2016

Human body—Religious aspects

Bodies in the vernacular B. Bantum color *Christian Century* v134 no7 p26 Mr 29 2017

Human capital

Companies Are Now Making Innovation Everyone's Job M. Schrage *Harvard Business Review Digital Articles* p2 Ja 21 2016

The Crumbs of Capitalism D. MAYER-FOULKES *Commentary* v142 no2 p11 S 2016

Explaining changes in educational attainment over time L. H. Leith *Monthly Labor Review* p1 S 2016

HOW TO MAKE HUMAN CAPITAL COUNT C. Leaf color *Fortune* v175 no2 p6 F 1 2017

HR Must Make People Analytics More User-Friendly J. Boudreau *Harvard Business Review Digital Articles* p2 Je 16 2017

What If Companies Managed People as Carefully as They Manage Money? E. Garton *Harvard Business Review Digital Articles* p2 My 24 2017

When Investors Want to Know How You Treat People D. Creelman and J. Boudreau *Harvard Business Review Digital Articles* p2 F 10 2015

Why (and How) HR Needs to Act More Like Marketing M. W. Schaefer *Harvard Business Review Digital Articles* p2 N 24 2016

Human capital—United States

HOW TO GET ON THIS LIST M. C. Bush and S. Lewis-kulin color *Fortune* v175 no4 p89 Mr 15 2017

Human cell membranes

Whole cell maps chart a course for 21st-century cell biology R. Horwitz and G. T. Johnson color *Science* v356 no6340 p806 My 26 2017

Human chromosomes

See also

Human genome

Your entire genome in 3D color *Science* v354 no6312 p532 N 4 2016

Human comfort

the bye-bye blues L. ANASTASIA *Parents* p132 2015

get the HOME you want diag *Timber Home Living* p15 2017 SpecialIssue

Human-computer interaction

See also

Human-artificial intelligence interaction

Human-robot interaction

Humans Can Make the Internet of Things Smarter C. Montero-Luque *Harvard Business Review Digital Articles* p2 O 28 2014

Human cytomegalovirus diseases

Atomic structure of the human cytomegalovirus capsid with its securing tegument layer of pp150 X. Yu, J. Jih et al color *Science* v356 no6345 p1350 Je 30 2017

Human decomposition

A Columbia Lab Is Trying to Turn Corpses Into Glowing Installation Art Under the Manhattan Bridge B. WALLACE img *New York* v49 no25 p82 D 12 2016

Human DNA

DNA reveals Canaanites' fate M. TEMMING color *Science News* v192 no3 p8 S 2 2017

Oldest Human DNA Revises Our Family Tree B. ALEX color map *Discover* v38 no1 p14 Ja/F 2017

A single wave of migration from Africa peopled the globe E. Culotta color *Science* v354 no6319 p1522 D 23 2016

Human DNA—Research

Three Qs *Science* v354 no6311 p395 O 28 2016

Human ecology

See also

Community life

Environmental health

Population

Quality of life

Social psychology

Sustainability

THE INTERVIEW C. SORENSEN color *Maclean's* v129 no44 p12 N 7 2016

Nature offers inspiration, and occasionally courage E. Quill *Science News* v192 no5 p2 S 30 2017

Rewilders S. PIKE *Orion Magazine* v35 no4/5 p10 Jl-O 2016

TROUBLED WATERS D. Stone map *National Geographic* v231 no4 p20 Ap 2017

Human embryology

See also

Human embryos

Edited embryos reveal gene's function T. H. SAEY bw *Science News* v192 no6 p8 O 14 2017

Human embryo editing yields results T. HESMAN SAEY color *Science News* v191 no7 p16 Ap 15 2017

Human embryonic stem cells

Mutations in the promoter of the telomerase gene TERT contribute to tumorigenesis by a two-step mechanism K. Chiba, F. K. Lorber et al diag *Science* v357 no6358 p1416 S 29 2017

Human embryos

Heart mutation fixed in embryos T. H. SAEY bw *Science News* v192 no3 p6 S 2 2017

PUSHING THE LIMITS OF LIFE IN THE LAB L. SCHLEY color *Discover* v38 no1 p38 Ja/F 2017

Regulating the Brave New World of Human Gene Editing P. SMAGLIK color diag *Discover* v38 no1 p30 Ja/F 2017

Human evolution

Detection of human adaptation during the past 2000 years Y. Field, E. A. Boyle et al bibl graph *Science* v354 no6313 p760 N 11 2016

Launch your imagination with Science News stories *Science News* v191 no12 p2 Je 24 2017

MISSING LINKS P. L. Reno color diag *Scientific American* v316 no5 p42 My 2017

Oldest Human DNA Revises Our Family Tree B. ALEX color map *Discover* v38 no1 p14 Ja/F 2017

We Are All Africans B. ALEX color *Discover* v38 no1 p26 Ja/F 2017

Human experimentation

What do revised U.S. rules mean for human research? L. Nichols, L. Brako et al color *Science* v357 no6352 p650 Ag 18 2017

Human experimentation—Computer network resources

THE SURPRISING POWER OF ONLINE EXPERIMENTS: GETTING THE MOST OUT OF A/B AND OTHER CONTROLLED TESTS R. Kohavi and S. Thomke color diag graph img *Harvard Business Review* v95 no5 p74 S/O 2017

Human experimentation—Government policy

Regulators drop controversial biospecimen consent proposal J. Kaiser color *Science* v355 no6323 p335 Ja 27 2017

Human face recognition (Computer science)

Is iPhone set to get facial recognition? D. Moren color *Macworld - Digital Edition* p93 Ap 2017

Our Panopticon, Ourselves P. J. Williams color *Nation* v33 no21 p12 N 21 2016

Paying with YOUR FACE W. KNIGHT color *MIT Technology Review* v120 no2 p72 Mr/Ap 2017

say "cheese" for border security S. Chodosh color *Popular Science* v289 no6 p78 N/D 2017

Smile, you're in the database! *Maclean's* v130 no4 p4 My 2017

Twitter Votes diag graph *MIT Technology Review* v120 no3 p9 My/Je 2017

Human face recognition (Computer science)—Software

NO INTERACTION REQUIRED B. GARDINER color *Popular Science* v289 no6 p68 N/D 2017

Human fertility

Spark of Life K. KORNEI bw color *Discover* v38 no1 p53 Ja/F 2017

Human fertility—United States

BABY BOOM: Shady Grove Fertility is the largest fertility clinic in the country. How it got that way involved business innovation as well as science C. Cunningham *Washingtonian Magazine* v52 no8 p119 My 2017

FERTILE GROUND: Who to see when nature needs a little help *Washingtonian Magazine* v52 no8 p124 My 2017

Rejuvenating the Chance of Motherhood? K. Weintraub color il *MIT Technology Review* v120 no1 p44 Ja/F 2017

Human gene mapping

Genome writing project confronts technology hurdles K. Servick color *Science* v356 no6339 p673 My 19 2017

MISSING LINKS P. L. Reno color diag *Scientific American* v316 no5 p42 My 2017

Human genes

40 more genes linked to intelligence L. SANDERS *Science News* v191 no12 p14 Je 24 2017

Alzheimer's-linked gene is triple threat T. H. SAEY color *Science News* v192 no6 p13 O 14 2017

Jumping genes are part of all that makes us human E. Quill color *Science News* v191 no10 p2 My 27 2017

A Mightier Mouse N. SCHARPING color *Discover* v38 no5 p10 Je 2017

Human genes—Social aspects

YOUR SUCCESS IS SHAPED BY YOUR GENES A. Beard *Harvard Business Review* v95 no1 p34 Ja/F 2017

Human genetics

See also

Human genes

BEYOND XX AND XY A. Montañez diag *Scientific American* v317 no3 p50 S 2017

Distribution and clinical impact of functional variants in 50,726 whole-exome sequences from the DiscovEHR study F. E. Dewey, M. F. Murray et al chart graph *Science* v354 no6319 paaf6814-1 D 23 2016

DNA data point to unknown hominid T. H. SAEY *Science News* v190 no10 p13 N 12 2016

UNLOCKING THE MYSTERY OF ALS L. Petrucelli and A. D. Gitler color *Scientific American* v316 no6 p46 Je 2017

Human genetics variation

Degrees of Separation L. SCHLEY *Discover* v38 no10 p14 D 2017

"Pheno"menal value for human health D. J. Rader and S. M. Damrauer bibl diag *Science* v354 no6319 p1534 D 23 2016

Human genome

The Difference Makers [Cover story] T. Hesman Saey color diag *Science News* v191 no10 p22 My 27 2017

Eugenics warning A. M. STERN *Issues in Science & Technology* v33 no1 p15 Fall 2016

Gene–environment interplay J. Berg color *Science* v354 no6308 p15 O 7 2016

Genome writing project confronts technology hurdles K. Servick color *Science* v356 no6339 p673 My 19 2017

Genomic databases: A WHO affair S. E. Antonarakis, B. P. Koch et al *Science* v356 no6340 p812 My 26 2017

Notes from a Revolution: Lessons from the Human Genome Project D. J. GALAS, A. PATRINOS et al *Issues in Science & Technology* v33 no3 p57 Spr 2017

U.S. attitudes on human genome editing D. A. Scheufele, M. A. Xenos et al color graph *Science* v357 no6351 p553 Ag 11 2017

Your entire genome in 3D color *Science* v354 no6312 p532 N 4 2016

Human Genome Project

Making big science decisions N. LANE *Issues in Science & Technology* v33 no4 p13 Summ 2017

Notes from a Revolution: Lessons from the Human Genome Project D. J. GALAS, A. PATRINOS et al *Issues in Science & Technology* v33 no3 p57 Spr 2017

Human geography—United States

When the World Is an Arcade J. PARKER cartoon *Atlantic* v318 no4 p40 N 2016

Human growth

ages+stages color *Parents* v92 no4 p123 Ap 2017

Furniture Growth Spurt *Parents* v91 no10 p108 O 2016

See How They Grow *Parents* v91 no9 p140 S 2016

Human hair color

MY BEAUTY MARK... Karen Elson color *InStyle* v24 no3 p288 Mr 2017

RIDE OR DYE L. DUNHAM color *Vogue* v207 no9 p728 S 2017

Human in vitro fertilization

Why I Froze My Eggs color *InStyle* v23 no12 p193 N 2016

Human in vitro fertilization—Religious aspects

INCONCEIVABLE K. BUTLER color *Mother Jones* v42 no5 p34

S/O 2017

Human life cycle

See also

Childbirth

Children

Death

Fetus

Old age

Youth

A BESTIARY OF THE MIND H. Macdonald bw *New York Times Magazine* p40 My 21 2017

Human Longevity Inc.

What A $25,000 Medical Test Can't Tell You C. Chen bw *Bloomberg Businessweek* no4539 p21 S 25 2017

Human-machine relationship

Artificial Intelligence Can't Replace Hard-Earned Knowledge - Yet W. Swap and D. Leonard *Harvard Business Review Digital Articles* p2 N 17 2014

Human-machine systems

See also

Control rooms

Sociotechnical systems

Sociotechnical transitions for deep decarbonization F. W. Geels, B. K. Sovacool et al color diag *Science* v357 no6357 p1242 S 22 2017

Human mechanics—Software

SMART MOTION: The New Body Language J. MULLICH color diag *Forbes* v200 no4 p78 O 24 2017

Human microbiota

ASK THE DOCTOR A. L. KOMAROFF *Harvard Health Letter* v42 no7 p2 My 2017

CAN NUTRITION CHANGE YOUR PERSONALITY? K. James color *Better Nutrition* v79 no6 p46 Je 2017

Creature Comforts M. DeSanctis and C. ELLENBERG color *Vogue* v207 no3 p380 Mr 2017

feed your child's gut E. SONNENBURG *Parents* v91 no10 p42 O 2016

Gut Feeling: Can probiotics and prebiotics really make you healthier? R. ZAR *Dance Magazine* v91 no7 p48 Jl 2017

HARD TO STOMACH *Wired* v24 no11 p50 N 2016

new products: microbiome color *Science* v356 no6339 p764 My 19 2017

Nourishing Your Microbiota *Tufts University Health & Nutrition Letter* v35 no3 p4 My 2017

Palate and Possibility H. ESTROFF MARANO *Psychology Today* v50 no1 p34 Ja/F 2017

PLAY DIRTY R. Dunn bw color *Men's Health* v32 no2 p108 Mr 2017

A prominent glycyl radical enzyme in human gut microbiomes metabolizes trans-4-hydroxy-L-proline B. J. Levin, Y. Y. Huang et al diag *Science* v355 no6325 p595 F 10 2017

Human migrations

BUSTING MYTHS OF ORIGIN A. Gibbons bw color graph *Science* v356 no6339 p678 My 19 2017

Humans' arrival in Australia redated M. TEMMING color *Science News* v192 no2 p10 Ag 19 2017

Ice Age Tibetans J. Qiu color *Scientific American* v316 no3 p14 Mr 2017

Human multitasking

The Curious Science of When Multitasking Works W. Frick *Harvard Business Review Digital Articles* p2 Ja 6 2015

Get More Done During Your Commute P. Bregman *Harvard Business Review Digital Articles* p2 Ja 27 2015

How to Break Your Addiction to Work R. Knight *Harvard Business Review Digital Articles* p2 My 18 2016

How to nurture a high-performing brain J. Brockis *People Management* p50 F 2017

Just Hearing Your Phone Buzz Hurts Your Productivity N. Torres *Harvard Business Review Digital Articles* p2 Jl 10 2015

MEDITATION AND MARGARITAS K. ROEST *USA Today Magazine* v146 no2868 p64 S 2017

When Multitasking Makes You Happy and When It Doesn't J. Etkin and C. Mogilner *Harvard Business Review Digital Articles* p2 F 26 2015

When Work Satisfaction Comes from Having 4 Jobs B. Caza and S. Moss *Harvard Business Review Digital Articles* p2 My 4

2015

Women Need Mindfulness Even More than Men Do B. Cabrera *Harvard Business Review Digital Articles* p2 Je 21 2016

Human origins

The Oldest Homo sapiens? K. Wong color *Scientific American* v317 no3 p12 S 2017

Human Papillomavirus vaccination

FIVE QUESTIONS bw *Los Angeles Magazine* v62 no10 p159 O 2017

Human powered vehicles

See also

Bicycles

Velocipedes

Build Your Own $500 Drift Trike D. Glad chart color *Hot Rod* v70 no10 p14 O 2017

Human proteins

De novo design of a biologically active amyloid R. Gallardo, M. Ramakers et al bibl graph *Science* v354 no6313 paah4949-1 N 11 2016

Human Race (Music)

Rik Emmett on the Allied Forces Behind the Sound of RESolution9 M. METTLER bw color *Sound & Vision* v82 no2 p22 F/ Mr 2017

Human remains (Archaeology)

See also

Fossil hominids

Mummies

Ancient Skeleton Discovered *Oceanus* v52 no2 p5 Spr 2017

STATE OF PRESERVATION J. C. Weber and N. Spooner *Archaeology* v70 no5 p8 S/O 2017

This Means War! H. WATERMAN color *Discover* v38 no3 p68 Ap 2017

Human remains (Archaeology)—Egypt

ROYAL GAMS D. WEISS color *Archaeology* v70 no2 p18 Mr/ Ap 2017

Human remains (Archaeology)—England

Richard III—Resting in Peace D. Huntley *British Heritage Travel* v38 no1 p8 Ja/F 2017

Human remains (Archaeology)—France

A PRINCELY UPDATE J. URBANUS color *Archaeology* v70 no5 p16 S/O 2017

Human reproductive technology

See also

Human in vitro fertilization

OK on mitochondrial replacement color *Science* v354 no6319 p1508 D 23 2016

Relying on--or Recoiling from--Reproductive Enhancement P. LEVINE *USA Today Magazine* v145 no2864 p62 My 2017

Human rights

See also

Civil rights

Right to water

Women's rights

Bridges, not walls? M. Jarvis color *Science* v356 no6336 p388 Ap 28 2017

Cyberbullying and its Implications for Human Rights L. Hackett *UN Chronicle* v53 no4 p1 2016

The Evolving Role of the United Nations in Securing Human Rights Z. R. Al Hussein *UN Chronicle* v53 no4 p1 2016

The Evolving Role of the United Nations in Securing Human Rights Z. R. AL HUSSEIN *UN Chronicle* v54 no4 p6 2017

A Feminism of Everything K. Pollitt diag il *Nation* v304 no12 p6 Ap 10 2017

FOREWORD M. Nasser *UN Chronicle* v54 no4 p5 2017

From International Law to Local Communities: The Role of the United Nations in the Realization of Human Rights M. KJAE-RUM *UN Chronicle* v54 no4 p34 2017

Human Rights in Cuba *Congressional Digest* v95 no10 p9 D 2016

Human Rights, Mass Atrocity Prevention and the United Nations Security Council: The Long Road Ahead H. S. Puri *UN Chronicle* v53 no4 p1 2016

Is the American Idea Over? Y. APPELBAUM color *Atlantic* v320 no4 p17 N 2017

A Midlife Crisis for the Treaty-Based Human Rights System? A. KUMAR *UN Chronicle* v54 no4 p38 2017

Protection of Human Rights under Universal International Law C.

TOMUSCHAT *UN Chronicle* v54 no4 p23 2017

Remedies Beyond Reach F. QUIGLEY color *America* v215 no14 p14 N 7 2016

THE TERRE HAUTE EXPERIMENT A. WREN *Indianapolis Monthly* p76 My 2017

TINARIWEN C. MUSMECI *Interview* v47 no2 p76 Mr 2017

We've made giving a damn surprisingly affordable *Skeptical Inquirer* v40 no6 p10 N/D 2016

WHO WILL WE SPEAK FOR? M. MILLER *Humanist* v77 no1 p17 Ja/F 2017

Human rights advocacy

BLESSED ARE THE LAWYERS T. C. MORGAN color *Christianity Today* v61 no5 p54 Je 2017

THE INTERVIEW B. BETHUNE color *Maclean's* v130 no9 p22 O 2017

Human Rights Campaign Foundation

10 THINGS WE'RE TALKING ABOUT T. A. Christian color *Essence* v48 no3 p71 Jl 2017

We Have Ways to Make You Conform J. V. LAST color *Weekly Standard* v22 no31 p27 Ap 17 2017

Human rights workers

See also

Women human rights workers

Liu Xiaobo, Leader of China, R.I.P color *National Review* v69 no15 p13 Ag 14 2017

POWER HUNGRY N. SAVKA *Sierra* v102 no5 p44 St/O 2017

Human rights—China

A Hero's Daughter J. NORDLINGER color *National Review* v69 no12 p20 Je 26 2017

Human rights—International cooperation

Protection of Human Rights under Universal International Law C. Tomuschat *UN Chronicle* v53 no4 p1 2016

Human rights—Iran

Human Rights against Human Rights: Sexism in Human Rights Discourse for Sakineh Mohammadi E. Shahghasemi *Society* v53 no6 p614 D 2016

Human rights—United States

The Will to Resist R. CONNIFF cartoon *Progressive* v81 no3 p6 Mr 2017

WILL WE BE LEFT BEHIND, OR WILL WE CONTINUE TO LEAD THE WAY? *Vital Speeches of the Day* v83 no6 p176 Je 2017

Human-robot interaction

THE CASE FOR Robot Disobedience [Cover story] G. Briggs and M. Scheutz color *Scientific American* v316 no1 p44 Ja 2017

How We'll Stereotype Our Robot Coworkers T. Park *Harvard Business Review Digital Articles* p2 O 2 2014

The Shape of Our Robo-Doom S. FESCHUK color *Maclean's* v130 no9 p81 O 2017

Staying Human in the Robot Age S. Caulkin *Harvard Business Review Digital Articles* p2 O 6 2015

What a Hitchhiking Robot Can Teach Us About Automated Coworkers F. Zeller and D. H. Smith *Harvard Business Review Digital Articles* p2 D 18 2014

WOMEN VS. THE MACHINE E. HAYASAKI color *Foreign Policy* no222 p38 Ja/F 2017

Human-robot interaction—Moral & ethical aspects

Is It Ethical to Have Sex With a Robot? E. Dockterman *Time* v189 no7/8 p104 F 27 2017

Human sacrifice—History

Murder on the Mountain? J. URBANUS bw color *Archaeology* v69 no6 p14 N/D 2016

Human services

See also

Disaster relief

Public health

Public safety

Social services

Veterans—Services for

LYNN KELLY color *Tricycle: The Buddhist Review* v26 no2 p22 Wint 2016

Human settlements

See also

Cities & towns

Communities

Infrastructure (Economics)

Israeli settlements (Occupied territories)
Prehistoric settlements
Foragers first settled Tibetan Plateau B. BOWER color *Science News* v191 no2 p8 F 4 2017
Foreword M. Nasser *UN Chronicle* v53 no3 p5 2016
Looking Beyond the Hillforts [Cover story] J. URBANUS color *Archaeology* v70 no4 p38 Je-Ag 2017

Human sexuality
See also
Drugs & sex
Human sexuality & law
LGBT people's sexual behavior
Men's sexual behavior
Sexual aggression
Sexual intercourse
Women's sexual behavior
EDITOR'S NOTE J. BARDI *Humanist* v77 no4 p3 Jl/Ag 2017
EROTIC INTELLIGENCE color *Men's Health* v32 no7 p112 S 2017
THE FUTURE OF SEX: How technology, morality, and politics are reshaping human sexuality C. F. NAFF *Humanist* v77 no4 p12 Jl/Ag 2017
Getting Comfortable I. Kerner color *Prevention* v69 no9 p26 O 2017
THE GIRLS NEXT DOOR N. PIERCEY, LI JUN LI et al color diag *Men's Health* v32 no9 p82 N 2017
I Am Nine Years Old E. CONANT color *National Geographic* v231 no1 p30 Ja 2017
"I get orgasm headaches" A. Massey and S. G. Levy color *Glamour* v115 no3 p132 Mr 2017
The Long-View Lover M. HUSTON *Psychology Today* v50 no2 p16 Mr/Ap 2017
Rethinking Gender R. M. Henig cartoon chart color map *National Geographic* v231 no1 p48 Ja 2017
SEX: OUR WONDERFUL GIFT M. WERNER *Humanist* v77 no4 p41 Jl/Ag 2017
SEXPECTATIONS *Health* v31 no2 p16 Mr 2017
Sexual Stimulation R. D. Grimaldi *Humanist* v77 no5 p5 S/O 2017
Then There Were Three J. FOX *USA Today Magazine* v145 no2860 p57 Ja 2017
THE UNITED STATES OF SEX A. DAVIES color *Women's Health* v14 no2 p140 Mr 2017
WELCOME TO THE GOLDEN AGE OF SEX E. Sherman and J. Covert cartoon chart color *Men's Health* v32 no2 p102 Mr 2017
Your Feminist Dilemmas, Solved color *Glamour* v115 no2 p72 F 2017
Your New Libido Booster color *Health* v30 no10 p12 D 2016
YOUR SENSUAL SUMMER IS HERE C. K. Jackson color *Essence* v48 no3 p103 Jl 2017

Human sexuality & law
See also
Abortion laws
Illegitimacy
THIS IS NOT A WOMEN'S ISSUE *Scientific American* v317 no3 p30 S 2017

Human sexuality in art—Exhibitions
AROUND LOS ANGELES M. DURÓN bw cartoon color *ARTnews* v115 no3 p154 Fall 2016
Outside the frame K. Reklis color *Christian Century* v133 no21 p58 O 12 2016

Human sexuality in motion pictures
What's Up With the Orgasm Double Standard? S. M. Broom color *Glamour* v115 no7 p70 Jl 2017

Human sexuality in photography
"Your sexuality and your naked body are not shameful." color *Glamour* v115 no7 p92 Jl 2017

Human sexuality—Economic aspects
Economics of Sex: Cost-Benefit Analysis P. Houdek and P. Koblovský *Society* v54 no1 p18 F 2017

Human sexuality—Psychological aspects
See also
Sexual excitement
Crowdsource This color *Glamour* v115 no4 p140 Ap 2017
Forecast: More Snowflakes cartoon diag *Weekly Standard* v22 no29 p2 Ap 3 2017

Human sexuality—Research
Born This Way M. Shermer color *Scientific American* v315 no6 p84 D 2016
Getting older... and wilder color *Redbook* p87 Je 2017
No-Fly Zones: A New Model for Male Sexuality B. Fleming *Society* v54 no1 p34 F 2017
Sexes Differ in Evolved Mate Preferences *USA Today Magazine* v145 no2865 p12 Je 2017

Human sexuality—Social aspects
Economics of Sex: Cost-Benefit Analysis P. Houdek and P. Koblovský *Society* v54 no1 p18 F 2017
Is Tech Making Our Sex Lives Better or Worse? D. Friedman color *Glamour* v115 no7 p71 Jl 2017
Sexual Stimulation R. D. Grimaldi *Humanist* v77 no5 p5 S/O 2017

Human skeleton
See also
Human remains (Archaeology)
Ancient Skeleton Discovered *Oceanus* v52 no2 p5 Spr 2017
DEM BONES L. Widdicombe cartoon *New Yorker* v93 no8 p18 Ap 10 2017

Human skeleton in art
NIGHTMARES REVISITED J. FOUMBERG color *Chicago* v66 no7 p28 Jl 2017

Human skin color
See also
Melanism
Do this to disguise dark circles M. Roncal color *Redbook* p29 D 2016
Families Don't Have to "Match" L. L. Tharps *Parents* v91 no10 p24 O 2016
On being white P. W. Marty *Christian Century* v134 no17 p3 Ag 16 2017
Walking the Walk H. CHAHINIAN *O, The Oprah Magazine* p136 My 2017

Human smuggling
HIGHWAY THROUGH HELL T. MCCORMICK color *Foreign Policy* no226 p34 S/O 2017

Human trafficking
Between Two Worlds K. Vick color *Time* v188 no18 p36 O 31 2016
Monica Modi Khant *Atlanta* v57 no2 p101 Je 2017
No Safe Haven S. MCCLELLAND *Ms.* v26 no4 p14 Wint 2016
YE OLDE IKEA SEX TRAFFICKERS L. SKENAZY color *Reason* v49 no6 p15 N 2017

Human trafficking victims
People K. Chick and K. L. Gilbert color *Christian Century* v134 no22 p20 O 25 2017

Human trafficking—History
BIG GAME, BIG MYTH L. J. Wertheim color *Sports Illustrated* v126 no4 p46 Ja 30 2017

Human trafficking—Prevention
JAMMING UP SEX TRAFFIC E. BARTON *USA Today Magazine* v145 no2864 p68 My 2017
OUT OF THE SHADOWS L. FARMER *Governing* v30 no4 p40 Ja 2017

Human-artificial intelligence interaction—Charts, diagrams, etc.
A BRIEF CHRONICLE OF ROBOTIC HELPERS bw cartoon *Atlantic* v319 no2 p28 Mr 2017

Humane Society of the United States (Organization)—Trials, litigation, etc.
USDA faces suit on animal records pull color *Science* v355 no6325 p552 F 10 2017

Humangear Inc.
HYDRATION A. JURRIES color diag *Backpacker* v45 no3 p116 Ap 2017

Humanism
EDITOR'S NOTE J. BARDI *Humanist* v77 no5 p3 S/O 2017
Evolution's Error: HOW HUMAN NATURE WENT AWRY R. GRIGG *Humanist* v77 no3 p30 My/Je 2017
GIVEN the EVIDENCE *Humanist* v77 no3 p8 My/Je 2017
HUMANISM and the CHALLENGE of PRIVILEGE A. B. PINN *Humanist* v77 no3 p22 My/Je 2017
HUMANIST PROFILE *Humanist* v77 no4 p2 Jl/Ag 2017
The Only Way Forward Slaughter color *Foreign Policy* no221 p64

N/D 2016

REMAKING OURSELVES M. WERNER *Humanist* v77 no2 p38 Mr/Ap 2017

THE RISE OF ATOMIC HUMANISM R. Bailey color *Reason* v49 no5 p6 O 2017

Technology Is Not Threatening Our Humanity—We Are G. Petriglieri *Harvard Business Review Digital Articles* p2 O 30 2015

THE VIRTUE OF DOING LESS: BERTRAND RUSSELL'S IDLENESS S. M. SEAWARD *Humanist* v77 no1 p38 Ja/F 2017

WHO WILL WE SPEAK FOR? M. MILLER *Humanist* v77 no1 p17 Ja/F 2017

Humanism—History

What Are We Doing Here? M. Robinson bw color *New York Review of Books* v64 no17 p28 N 9 2017

Humanism—Law & legislation

CLASSIC HUMANIST *Humanist* v77 no5 p10 S/O 2017

Humanism—Moral & ethical aspects

Cherri Pitts: A Rose Amongst San Antonio's STARs S. HEAP *Humanist* v77 no5 p28 S/O 2017

Humanism—News briefs

GIVEN the EVIDENCE *Humanist* v76 no6 p8 N/D 2016

WORTH NOTING K. A. GAJEWSKi *Humanist* v76 no6 p46 N/D 2016

Humanistic education

Putting your liberal arts degree to work D. Angeles and B. Roberts *Career Outlook* p1 Ag 2017

Humanistic education—Study & teaching

Sarah Lawrence College *Dance Magazine* v90 p97 2016/2017 Supplement College Guide

Humanistic ethics

LET'S CELEBRATE! (AKA HOW WE CAN BE OF SERVICE TO THE SECULAR COMMUNITY) M. WERNER *Humanist* v77 no3 p38 My/Je 2017

Humanistic trait model

Split Personality B. PIKE bw *Power & Motoryacht* v34 no10 p200 O 2017

Humanists

AN ACTION LIST FOR THE (UN) GAITHFUL C. T. QUAM *Humanist* v77 no1 p20 Ja/F 2017

Art for Secularism's Sake J. Spofforth *Humanist* v77 no3 p5 My/Je 2017

THE Arts FOR HUMANISTS D. T. MORAN *Humanist* v77 no2 p24 Mr/Ap 2017

EDITOR'S NOTE J. BARDI *Humanist* v77 no1 p3 Ja/F 2017

GIVEN the EVIDENCE *Humanist* v77 no2 p8 Mr/Ap 2017

HUMANIST PROFILE *Humanist* v76 no6 p2 N/D 2016

HUMANIST PROFILE *Humanist* v77 no3 p49 My/Je 2017

LET'S CELEBRATE! (AKA HOW WE CAN BE OF SERVICE TO THE SECULAR COMMUNITY) M. WERNER *Humanist* v77 no3 p38 My/Je 2017

NIKI MASSEY, AND WHY SOME HUMANIST VOICES DON'T GET HEARD G. CHRISTINA *Humanist* v76 no6 p40 N/D 2016

Humanists—Attitudes

RESIST G. CHRISTINA *Humanist* v77 no1 p32 Ja/F 2017

Humanists—Awards

EDITOR'S NOTE J. BARDI *Humanist* v76 no6 p3 N/D 2016

Humanitarian assistance

Before THE FLOOD A. NELSEN *Texas Monthly* v45 no5 p43 My 2017

Recovery Will Take Long-term Effort K. CLARKE color *America* v215 no13 p10 O 31 2016

The War on Terror vs. the War on Poverty W. Easterly bw graph *New York Review of Books* v63 no18 p64 N 24 2016

What You Said About ... color *Time* v188 no16/17 p2 O 24 2016

Humanitarian assistance—Evaluation

Four ways to strengthen humanitarian aid C. Y. Woo *America* v216 no5 p10 Mr 6 2017

Humanitarian assistance—Haiti

Haiti's 'Republic of NGOs' M. SCHULLER *Current History* v116 no787 p68 F 2017

Humanitarian intervention

A Foreign Policy Held Hostage J. CARDEN color il *Nation* v303 no20 p16 N 14 2016

Humanitarian intervention—International cooperation

Why Humanitarian Intervention Still Isn't a Global Norm R. ME-

NON *Current History* v116 no786 p35 Ja 2017

Humanitarian intervention—Social aspects

Why Humanitarian Intervention Still Isn't a Global Norm R. MENON *Current History* v116 no786 p35 Ja 2017

Humanitarian law

Cyberbullying and Its Implications for Human Rights L. HACKETT *UN Chronicle* v54 no4 p41 2017

Limiting Civilian Casualties as Part of a Winning Strategy: The Case of Courageous Restraint J. H. Felter and J. N. Shapiro *Daedalus* v146 no1 p44 Wint 2017

Humanitarianism

Why Not an Auction? I. M. STELZER color *Weekly Standard* v22 no28 p20 Mr 27 2017

Humanities

See also

Arts

Humanistic education

Philosophy

Build STEM Skills, but Don't Neglect the Humanities J. Roos *Harvard Business Review Digital Articles* p2 Je 24 2015

Commonplace Book *American Scholar* v86 no3 p126 Summ 2017

Elaine Pagels A. M. Gillis *Humanities* v37 no4 p1 Fall 2016

Rewarding Rigor N. S. RILEY color *Weekly Standard* v23 no4 p18 O 2 2017

Save the Arts, Save America L. Lalami *Nation* v304 no13 p10 Ap 17 2017

Humanities education

See also

Art education

Dance education

Music education

What Are We Doing Here? M. Robinson bw color *New York Review of Books* v64 no17 p28 N 9 2017

Humanities—Periodicals

Winter 2017 available on ISSUU *Humanities* v38 no1 p1 Wint 2017

Humanities—Research

Executive Function with Shannon Smith T. Linse *Humanities* v37 no4 p1 Fall 2016

Humanity

See also

Caring

Black Lives Matter Because All Lives Matter [Cover story] J. E. JONES *Islamic Horizons* v46 no1 p20 Ja/F 2017

From the Knowledge Economy to the Human Economy D. Seidman *Harvard Business Review Digital Articles* p2 N 12 2014

Human health D. L. Clinciu, D. Scarf et al color *Science* v356 no6338 p590 My 12 2017

NORMAN LEAR & KENYA BARRIS N. Sperling color *Entertainment Weekly* no1460/1461 p22 Ap 7-17 2017

Only Human W. Yang *New York Times Magazine* p9 F 19 2017

Humanity in literature

1945: Los Angeles A. Döblin *Lapham's Quarterly* v10 no2 p177 Spr 2017

Humanity—Social aspects

Confronting the Heart of Darkness R. Patti Nakai bw *Tricycle: The Buddhist Review* v26 no4 p28 Summ 2017

Forge ahead! A. Camille color *U.S. Catholic* v82 no5 p47 My 2017

Humanoid robots

BOTS LIKE US C. LOCKE color graph *Wired* v25 no4 p24 Ap 2017

Humans (TV program)

What to Watch R. Rahman, C. Collis et al color *Entertainment Weekly* no1453 p54 F 17 2017

When the Most Human Human Isn't Actually Human D. D'Addario color *Time* v189 no7/8 p104 F 27 2017

Humans, The (Theatrical production)

No. 1 THE HUMANS M. Snetiker and M. R. Bernardo color *Entertainment Weekly* no1444/1445 p116 D 16 2016

Human Surge, The (Film)

The Human Surge M. NELSON color *Film Comment* v53 no1 p82 Ja/F 2017

Humanz (Music)

Gorillaz Rave to the Apocalypse D. FRICKE color *Rolling Stone* no1287 p14 My 18 2017

in U.S. landfills. Can reducing the amount we throw away help end hunger—and protect the environment? L. ANASTASIA *New York Times Upfront* v149 no12 p14 Ap 24 2017

MANAGING THE HUNGER MOOD M. GRAZIANO *Saturday Evening Post* v289 no2 p46 Mr/Ap 2017

Hunger, Johannes

A water window on surface chemistry diag *Science* v357 no6353 p755 Ag 25 2017

Hunger After You're Fed, The (Short story)

THE HUNGER AFTER YOU'RE FED J. S. A. COREY cartoon *Wired* v25 no1 p56 Ja 2017

Hungerford, Ashley

Applications for the Noninsured Crop Disaster Program Increased After the Agricultural Act of 2014 *Amber Waves: The Economics of Food, Farming, Natural Resources, & Rural America* p5 Jl 2017

Managing Agricultural Risk Under Different Scenarios: Selected 2014 Farm Act Programs *Amber Waves: The Economics of Food, Farming, Natural Resources, & Rural America* p22 F 2017

Hunger—Prevention

The Gift of Food J. BALL-TUFFORD *Reader's Digest* v188 no1126 p50 D 2016/Ja 2017

Moringa: How One Plant Is Changing Lives N. Zevnik color *Better Nutrition* v79 no6 p16 Je 2017

Hunger—Psychological aspects

Are You Hungry Yet? color *Prevention* p10 Mr 2017

Hung Lui, Chun

Large, valley-exclusive Bloch-Siegert shift in monolayer WS2 bibl diag *Science* v355 no6329 p1066 Mr 10 2017

Hunhoff, Bernie

13 DAYS ON OAHE: Three friends' odyssey on a 22-foot sailboat *South Dakota Magazine* v33 no2 p74 Jl/Ag 2017

BRIDGING THE JAMES *South Dakota Magazine* v32 no6 p20 Mr/Ap 2017

The Entertainers of MILBANK: The Grant County city's downtown has become a fun place to visit and shop *South Dakota Magazine* v33 no3 p20 S/O 2017

FARMERS MARKER DISCOVERIS: Plus other joyful life lessons learned at the farmers markets *South Dakota Magazine* v33 no3 p27 S/O 2017

The Fix-it Man *South Dakota Magazine* v32 no4 p48 N/D 2016

For Lack of a Handshake *South Dakota Magazine* v32 no4 p30 N/D 2016

THE HOUSE MOVERS *South Dakota Magazine* v32 no6 p69 Mr/Ap 2017

THE MOBRIDGE ART COLLECTION *South Dakota Magazine* v33 no3 p64 S/O 2017

THE RIVER AT SPRINGFIELD *South Dakota Magazine* v32 no4 p28 N/D 2016

A Town Every 10 Miles: Trains don't stop in most Corson County towns today, but that doesn't mean you shouldn't *South Dakota Magazine* v33 no2 p20 Jl/Ag 2017

Wrong From Right *South Dakota Magazine* v32 no4 p87 N/D 2016

Hunhoff, Katie

10 Plants WE SHOULD KNOW *South Dakota Magazine* v33 no2 p27 Jl/Ag 2017

BOAT-CRAZY DAKOTANS *South Dakota Magazine* v33 no2 p6 Jl/Ag 2017

FARMERS MARKER DISCOVERIS: Plus other joyful life lessons learned at the farmers markets *South Dakota Magazine* v33 no3 p27 S/O 2017

THE HAPPY MINER *South Dakota Magazine* v32 no6 p65 Mr/Ap 2017

LITTLE MANOR ON THE PRAIRIE *South Dakota Magazine* v32 no4 p58 N/D 2016

OUR 'COUSIN' MERLE *South Dakota Magazine* v32 no6 p8 Mr/Ap 2017

SEEDING JOY *South Dakota Magazine* v33 no3 p6 S/O 2017

SURPRISE, SURPRISE *South Dakota Magazine* v32 no4 p6 N/D 2016

Hunnam, Charlie, 1980-

Come In, Charlie R. Gay color *InStyle* v24 no4 p208 Ap 2017

Jungle Fever R. DOUTHAT color *National Review* v69 no9 p42 My 15 2017

THE LOST CITY OF Z K. P. Sullivan color *Entertainment Weekly* no1446/1447 p57 D 2016/Ja 2017

A NEW KING WILL RISE K. P. Sullivan color *Entertainment Weekly* no1450 p34 Ja 27 2017

Huns

Romans, Huns sometimes got along B. BOWER color *Science News* v191 no8 p18 Ap 29 2017

Hunsberger, Maren

Facility Drives Hydrogen Vehicle Innovations *Science & Technology Review* p20 S 2016

Hunsinger, George

Can the Churches Be Reunited? [Cover story] color *Commonweal* v144 no17 p14 O 20 2017

Hunt, Andrew A.

Understanding Anchorage Systems for Natural Stone Cladding color *Architectural Record* v204 no12 p198 D 2016

HUNT, HOLLY

How Can I Add Excitement to a Boxy, Bland Room? cartoon color *Chicago* v66 no4 p72 Ap 2017

Hunt, James M.

4 Reasons Managers Should Spend More Time on Coaching *Harvard Business Review Digital Articles* p2 My 29 2015

Hunt, Jennifer

Crossing borders along an endless frontier color *Science* v356 no6339 p694 My 19 2017

HUNT, KRISTIN

Guinness World Records color *National Geographic Kids* no465 p5 N 2016

Hunt, Laird

Black History C. FEHRMAN *Indianapolis Monthly* p23 F 2017

Invitation to a Killing K. GREENIDGE *New York Times Book Review* p19 F 12 2017

HUNT, MARY ELLEN

scratching the MFA itch: Considering an advanced degree in dance? Learn how to choose the program that's right for you *Dance Magazine* v90 p26 2016/2017 Supplement College Guide

scratching the MFA itch *Dance Magazine* p26 2016/2017

Hunt, Michael

CURVES AHEAD color *Golf Magazine* v59 no11 p57 N 2017

OH, SNAP! color *Golf Magazine* v59 no9 p52 S 2017

READY? DRAW! color *Golf Magazine* v59 no5 p54 My 2017

Hunt, Patricia A.

Control of meiotic pairing and recombination by chromosomally tethered 26S proteasome bibl graph *Science* v355 no6323 p408 Ja 27 2017

Hunt, Paul

NONBINARY CODE M. MOLTENI cartoon *Wired* v25 no6 p20 Je 2017

Hunt, Richard

The Corona Rising C. J. Martin color *Art in America* v105 no3 p45 Mr 2017

Hunt, Samantha

A LOVE STORY cartoon *New Yorker* v93 no14 p70 My 22 2017

QUEER THEOREM *Lapham's Quarterly* v10 no2 p210 Spr 2017

Seeking Eureka *New York Times Book Review* p16 Mr 12 2017

Wrinkles in Time: In small-town Australia, a Vietnam veteran disappears as his family struggles with intergenerational trauma *New York Times Book Review* p20 O 8 2017

Hunt, Stacey Wilson

HOW TO CRASH THE OSCARS img *New York* v49 no24 p134 N 28 2016

PARTY LINES img *New York* v50 no9 p98 My 1 2017

Hunt, Stephen

The Archers M. RUS color *Architectural Digest* v74 no10 p106 O 1 2017

Hunt, Timothy

The Timothy Hunt Witch Hunt: A joke told, a reputation destroyed J. Foreman *Commentary* v140 no2 p41 S 2015

The Timothy Hunt Witch Hunt J. Foreman *Commentary* v140 no2 p56 S 2015

HUNT, TIMOTHY ANN

A Rubric to Evaluate Citizen-Science Programs for Long-Term Ecological Monitoring *BioScience* v67 no9 p834 S 2017

Hunt, Tristram, 1974-

PEOPLE *Art in America* v105 no3 p152 Mr 2017

Hunt, W. Ben
Currency bw color *Forbes* v198 no7 p112 N 29 2016

Hunt riding
6 EXERCISES TO NAIL YOUR HUNTER DERBY: Part 2: Master rollbacks, the hand gallop and finish with flair [Cover story] L. T. Boyd and T. Conahan color *Practical Horseman* v45 no7 p34 Jl 2017
TRADERS POINT HUNT G. PALMIERI *Indianapolis Monthly* p20 F 2017

Hunt Yachts Inc.
Hunt 32CC *Sea Magazine* v108 no12 p48 D 2016

Hunted (TV program)
Hunted I. Ratledge *TV Guide* v65 no4 p36 Ja 16 2017

Hunter, Anne Kristen
The Health Benefits of a Bicycle-Pedestrian Trail *Parks & Recreation* v51 no12 p16 D 2016

HUNTER, ASHLEY
Give 'Em Shell *Virginia Living* p21 2017 Smoke & Salt
Tools OF THE Trade: Everything you need to shuck it, slice it and smoke it *Virginia Living* p46 2017 Smoke & Salt

Hunter, Frances Tipton
LIMERICK LAUGHS *Saturday Evening Post* v289 no3 p100 My/Je 2017

Hunter, Georgia
We Were the Lucky Ones *Publishers Weekly* v263 no50 p43 D 5 2016

Hunter, Georgia—Interviews
Picking Up the Pieces N. CIPRI color *Publishers Weekly* v264 no1 p34 Ja 2 2017

Hunter, Holly, 1958-
HOLLY HUNTER MY LIFE IN PICTURES J. McGovern color *Entertainment Weekly* no1473 p32 Jl 7 2017
THE MOM SLOT T. Friend cartoon *New Yorker* v93 no20 p25 Jl 10 2017

Hunter, Jen
"HOW I LOST 90 LBS AFTER 2 SETS OF TWINS!" K. ROCKWOOD color *Good Housekeeping* v265 no5 p77 N 2017

Hunter, John
Bentonville Gets the Country's First-Ever Bike Playground D. Wright *Parks & Recreation* v52 no5 p24 My 2017

HUNTER, LASHIEKA
Tracking the Monster color *Ebony* v72 no3 p86 D 2016/Ja 2017

HUNTER, LINDA
THE WILD OYSTERP ROJECT: Saving Oysters to Save Ourselves color *Earth Island Journal* v32 no2 p13 Summ 2017

HUNTER, LUKE
Conserving the World's Megafauna and Biodiversity: The Fierce Urgency of Now *BioScience* v67 no3 p197 Mr 2017
International Wildlife Law: Understanding and Enhancing Its Role in Conservation *BioScience* v67 no9 p784 S 2017
Saving the World's Terrestrial Megafauna color *BioScience* v66 no10 p807 O 1 2016

Hunter, Madeline
Madeline Hunter color *Publishers Weekly* v264 no15 p15 Ap 10 2017

HUNTER, MITCHELL C.
Agriculture in 2050: Recalibrating Targets for Sustainable Intensification *BioScience* v67 no4 p386 Ap 2017

Hunter, Neil
A SUMO-ubiquitin relay recruits proteasomes to chromosome axes to regulate meiotic recombination bibl graph *Science* v355 no6323 p403 Ja 27 2017

Hunter, Philip
Committing to socially responsible seafood color *Science* v356 no6341 p912 Je 1 2017

Hunter, Sylvia Izzo
Season of Spells *Publishers Weekly* v263 no45 p45 N 7 2016

Hunter, Victoria
PALE Fire K. Molvar color *Vogue* v206 no12 p198 D 2016

Hunter, Wendy
advice every new mom needs [Cover story] color *Parents* v92 no7 p32 Jl 2017

Hunter attitudes
Young Blood W. BRANTLEY and M. PENDLEY color *Field & Stream* v122 no4 p54 S 2017

Hunter classes (Horse shows)

6 EXERCISES TO NAIL YOUR HUNTER DERBY: Part 2: Master rollbacks, the hand gallop and finish with flair [Cover story] L. T. Boyd and T. Conahan color *Practical Horseman* v45 no7 p34 Jl 2017

Hunter College
Hunter College City University of New York *Dance Magazine* v90 p72 2016/2017 Supplement College Guide
The Mikado *New York* v49 no25 p144 D 12 2016

Hunter seat equitation
Expanding Opportunities for Derby and Green Hunters R. Danta *In Stride* v12 no5 p6 S 2017

Hunter seat equitation division
Cuba: Conquers the $268,550 USHJA International Hunter Derby Championship T. Booker *In Stride* v12 no5 p12 S 2017

Hunter trials (Horsemanship)
Choose the Best Thoroughbred Hunter J. Winkel color *Practical Horseman* v45 no4 p15 Ap 2017

Hunter-Cevera, Kristen
A Green Thumb for Synechococcus color *Oceanus* v51 no2 p64 Wint 2016
Physiological and ecological drivers of early spring blooms of a coastal phytoplankter bibl graph *Science* v354 no6310 p326 O 21 2016

Hunter-Doniger, Tracey
The eugenics movement and its impact on art education in the United States bibl *Arts Education Policy Review* v118 no2 p83 2017
The power of the arts: Evaluating a community artist-in-residence program through the lens of studio thinking bibl chart *Arts Education Policy Review* v118 no1 p19 2017

Hunters
See also
Bowhunters
Hunting guides
THE BIG GAMERS W. BRANTLEY, B. HEAVEY et al cartoon color *Field & Stream* v121 no7 p82 D 2016/Ja 2017
A BREAK IN THE BREAKS R. KIRK cartoon color *Outdoor Life* v224 no7 p13 S 2017
Cheers & Jeers J. Payne, B. Fort et al color *Field & Stream* v121 no7 p14 D 2016/Ja 2017
Dad's Happy Place L. Simpson color *New York State Conservationist* v71 no2 p32 O 2016
Down and Out (of Sight) T. E. Nickens color *Field & Stream* v122 no5 pF1 O 2017
FIVE REASONS YOU MISSED THAT DOVE P. Bourjaily color *Field & Stream* v122 no4 p34 S 2017
FOUR OF A KIND W. Brantley cartoon *Field & Stream* v121 no9 p30 Ap 2017
FREE-RANGE A. McKEAN color *Outdoor Life* v224 no3 p43 Ap 2017
The Locals T. E. Nickens color *Field & Stream* v122 no4 p60 S 2017
MAKE THIS YOUR FUNNEST DEER SEASON EVER T. HANSEN and D. McDOUGAL cartoon color *Outdoor Life* v224 no8 p35 O 2017
METHANE MOUNTAIN D. E. Petzal color *Field & Stream* v121 no7 p48 D 2016/Ja 2017
Pencil Pusher's Day Out N. Lussier *New York State Conservationist* v72 no1 p40 Ag 2017
RUFF AND TUMBLE T. DAVIS bw color *Field & Stream* v122 no6 p14 N 2017
START WITH A BANG A. ROBINSON color *Outdoor Life* v224 no7 pW1 S 2017
STUDY ABROAD W. Brantley color *Field & Stream* v122 no6 p30 N 2017
SUPER SCATTERS D. HART color *Outdoor Life* v224 no8 pH7 O 2017
TOP 5 SHOOTING MISTAKES R. SPOMER and J. B. SNOW color *Outdoor Life* v224 no4 p22 My 2017
TWILIGHT IN DINOSAUR LAND: In Western Massachusetts, a family business unlike any other is in the hands of its last heir—a man who dutifully digs for dinosaur tracks as he ponders the end of an era J. SHATWELL color map *Yankee* p100 Jl 2017
TWIN BRIDGES, MT color *Outdoor Life* v224 no8 p5 O 2017
WALK SOFTLY R. SPOMER color *Outdoor Life* v224 no3 p30 Ap 2017

no9 p70 N 2017

AUTUMN IN AUGUST W. BRANTLEY color *Field & Stream* v122 no3 p14 Ag 2017

COLD BAY ALASKA J. B. SNOW color *Outdoor Life* v224 no9 p46 N 2017

THE FINDERS A. MCKEAN color *Outdoor Life* v224 no9 p11 N 2017

NOTEWORTHY ADVENTURES color *Field & Stream* v122 no5 p8 O 2017

OL FAMILY RECIPES N. KREBS bw color *Outdoor Life* v224 no9 p13 N 2017

REMOTE SCOUTING T. FAULKNER color *Outdoor Life* v224 no6 pH6 Ag 2017

ROOSTERS ON THE RUN B. RUZZO color *Outdoor Life* v224 no9 p29 N 2017

SHOTGUN SHOOTOUT 2017 [Cover story] P. Bourjaily color *Field & Stream* v122 no6 p72 N 2017

Hunting equipment—Evaluation

FIELD TEST R. Mann, J. Johnston et al color *Field & Stream* v122 no2 p99 Je/Jl 2017

STRAPPED A. McKEAN color *Outdoor Life* v224 no9 p19 N 2017

Hunting ethics

GAME FACES color *Outdoor Life* v224 no8 p9 O 2017

Hunting guides

READ A BEAR'S MIND L. CASE color *Outdoor Life* v224 no8 pH11 O 2017

TWO-TIMING WHITE TAILS D. HART color *Outdoor Life* v224 no8 pH8 O 2017

WHEN YOU SPOOK A BUCK B. VAZNIS color *Outdoor Life* v224 no8 pH13 O 2017

Hunting guns

See also

Hunting rifles

Shotguns

BARREL LENGTH WISDOM B. FITZPATRICK color *Outdoor Life* v224 no1 p92 D 2016/Ja 2017

COYOTE NATION T. CARPENTER color *Outdoor Life* v224 no1 p74 D 2016/Ja 2017

FIELD & STREAM'S ULTIMATE GUIDE TO HUNTING RIFLES D. E. PETZAL color *Field & Stream* v122 no3 p34 Ag 2017

GUN TEST 2017 [Cover story] J. B. SNOW bw chart color *Outdoor Life* v224 no5 p42 Je/Jl 2017

Q & A D. E. Petzal cartoon *Field & Stream* v121 no7 p22 D 2016/Ja 2017

SHOOT FASTER, SHOOT BETTER B. FITZPATRICK color *Outdoor Life* v224 no9 p66 N 2017

THE SQUIRREL RUT W. Brantley color *Field & Stream* v121 no7 p24 D 2016/Ja 2017

Hunting guns—Evaluation

2016 BEST OF THE BEST T. McIntyre, T. Leeson et al bw color *Field & Stream* v121 no7 p96 D 2016/Ja 2017

BENELLI SBE 3 J. B. SNOW chart color *Outdoor Life* v224 no4 p24 My 2017

CHEAP SHOTS P. Bourjaily color *Field & Stream* v121 no7 p30 D 2016/Ja 2017

HOLIDAY GIFT GUIDE 2016 J. Cermele, D. Hurteau et al color *Field & Stream* v121 no7 p92 D 2016/Ja 2017

RUGER MK IV J. B. SNOW chart color *Outdoor Life* v224 no1 p84 D 2016/Ja 2017

Hunting guns—Maintenance & repair

BIRD SEASON COUNTDOWN J. WILSON and J. B. SNOW color *Outdoor Life* v224 no4 p26 My 2017

Hunting Hitler (TV program)

PRIME TIME PACIFIC *TV Guide* v64 no48 p90 N 21 2016

Hunting instruction

BUCKS' BEDROOMS A. Mckean color *Outdoor Life* v223 no9 p34 N 2016

The Imperfect Opener M. D. Johnson color *Field & Stream* v122 no4 pF1 S 2017

Hunting lodges

WELCOME TO HUNTING CAMP cartoon *Field & Stream* v121 no7 p16 D 2016/Ja 2017

where the wild things are N. HOGUET color *Architectural Digest* v74 no7 p67 Jl 2017

Hunting rifles

Cheers & Jeers J. Nichols, M. Matuszak et al *Field & Stream* v122 no5 p12 O 2017

FIELD & STREAM'S ULTIMATE GUIDE TO HUNTING RIFLES D. E. PETZAL color *Field & Stream* v122 no3 p34 Ag 2017

FIT AND SHIM P. Bourjaily color *Field & Stream* v122 no3 p28 Ag 2017

GUN TEST 2017 [Cover story] J. B. SNOW bw chart color *Outdoor Life* v224 no5 p42 Je/Jl 2017

PARADISE FOUND A. McKEAN and A. ROBINSON color *Outdoor Life* v224 no1 p60 D 2016/Ja 2017

Q&A D. E. Petzal color *Field & Stream* v122 no2 p23 Je/Jl 2017

Hunting safety

Young Blood W. BRANTLEY and M. PENDLEY color *Field & Stream* v122 no4 p54 S 2017

Hunting techniques

See also

Game calling (Hunting)

.25/06 TIMES THREE J. HAVILAND color *Outdoor Life* v224 no9 p70 N 2017

7 WAYS TO TAKE TOUGH ELK T. Carpenter color *Outdoor Life* v223 no9 pH1 N 2016

ALONE TOGETHER J. Babincsak color *Outdoor Life* v224 no5 p82 Je/Jl 2017

BLOOD SWEAT & DEER [Cover story] S. Bestul and D. Hurteau color *Field & Stream* v121 no7 p44 D 2016/Ja 2017

BOMBS AWAY BUCKS G. Bethge color *Outdoor Life* v223 no9 pH12 N 2016

The Call of the Wild D. Myers color *Field & Stream* v121 no7 p50 D 2016/Ja 2017

COLD BAY ALASKA J. B. SNOW color *Outdoor Life* v224 no9 p46 N 2017

CUTT AND RUN 2.0 B. LOVETT and G. BETHGE color *Outdoor Life* v224 no3 pT1 Ap 2017

DOUBLE-TEAM GOBBLER DRAG B. RUZZO cartoon *Outdoor Life* v224 no3 p26 Ap 2017

The Four-Day Deer Drive M. Hellickson cartoon color *Field & Stream* v121 no7 p52 D 2016/Ja 2017

The Hill Workout J. Schefler cartoon color *Field & Stream* v121 no7 p46 D 2016/Ja 2017

THE KNOCKDOWN MYTH R. SPOMER color *Outdoor Life* v224 no8 p26 O 2017

The Long (Cold!) Vigil G. Greenwalt bw color *Field & Stream* v121 no7 p54 D 2016/Ja 2017

Pencil Pusher's Day Out N. Lussier *New York State Conservationist* v72 no1 p40 Ag 2017

The Perfect-Plot Ambush J. Simpson bw cartoon *Field & Stream* v121 no7 p49 D 2016/Ja 2017

RAISING A RACKET T. HANSEN color *Outdoor Life* v224 no9 p31 N 2017

RAPID RECOVERY N. KREBS *Outdoor Life* v224 no9 p32 N 2017

ROOSTERS ON THE RUN B. RUZZO color *Outdoor Life* v224 no9 p29 N 2017

SET THE STAGE T. Faulkner color *Outdoor Life* v223 no9 pH9 N 2016

TURBO-CHEETAH A. E. HURT cartoon color map *National Geographic Kids* no470 p16 My 2017

TURKEY TACTICS THROUGH THE AGES N. KREBS color *Outdoor Life* v224 no3 p10 Ap 2017

WALK SOFTLY R. SPOMER color *Outdoor Life* v224 no3 p30 Ap 2017

Hunting training & conditioning

THE PATH LESS TRAVELED D. Decker, M. Quartuch et al color *New York State Conservationist* v71 no2 p24 O 2016

Hunting trophies

Should We Kill Animals to Save Them? M. Paterniti bw color graph *National Geographic* v232 no4 p70 O 2017

Hunting—Alaska

THE DISTANCE J. ARTERBURN cartoon *Outdoor Life* v224 no8 p78 O 2017

THE WAGER A. McKEAN color *Outdoor Life* v224 no8 p57 O 2017

Hunting—California

AIR STRIKE J. CHAPMAN color *Outdoor Life* v224 no1 p29 D

2016/Ja 2017

Hunting—Competitions
PITCH PERFECT J. BRANDT color *Outdoor Life* v224 no6 pH1 Ag 2017

Hunting—Corrupt practices
On Patrol L. Bobseine and S. Scherry color *New York State Conservationist* v71 no2 p17 O 2016

Hunting—Environmental aspects
Hunting driving many mammals to edge color *Science* v354 no6310 p266 O 21 2016
Loss of the Wild B. Butler color *National Wildlife (World Edition)* v54 no6 p36 O/N 2016

Hunting—Equipment & supplies
   See also
      Scouting cameras
      Treestands (Hunting)
AIR STRIKE J. CHAPMAN color *Outdoor Life* v224 no1 p29 D 2016/Ja 2017
GOING LONG S. Reese color *Outdoor Life* v223 no9 p40 N 2016
Q & A D. E. Petzal cartoon *Field & Stream* v121 no7 p22 D 2016/Ja 2017
TECH THROWBACK N. KREBS bw color *Outdoor Life* v224 no2 p12 F/Mr 2017

Hunting—Equipment & supplies—Evaluation
2016 BEST OF THE BEST T. McIntyre, T. Leeson et al bw color *Field & Stream* v121 no7 p96 D 2016/Ja 2017
22 NOSLER J. B. SNOW chart color *Outdoor Life* v224 no4 p28 My 2017
BENELLI SBE 3 J. B. SNOW chart color *Outdoor Life* v224 no4 p24 My 2017
CHEAP SHOTS P. Bourjaily color *Field & Stream* v121 no7 p30 D 2016/Ja 2017
DIRT, CHEAP T. HANSEN cartoon color *Outdoor Life* v224 no4 p39 My 2017
HOLIDAY GIFT GUIDE 2016 J. Cermele, D. Hurteau et al color *Field & Stream* v121 no7 p92 D 2016/Ja 2017

Hunting—Florida
SWAMP GOBBLERS A. McKEAN color map *Outdoor Life* v224 no2 p73 F/Mr 2017

Hunting—Lawsuits & claims
DEADLY TRADE B. CHRISTY bw color graph map *National Geographic* v230 no4 p56 O 2016

Hunting—New York (State)
THE PATH LESS TRAVELED D. Decker, M. Quartuch et al color *New York State Conservationist* v71 no2 p24 O 2016

Hunting—News briefs
BRIEFLY color *New York State Conservationist* v71 no2 p28 O 2016

Hunting—North America
YOUR Wildest DREAMS W. Brantley, B. Fenson et al color *Field & Stream* v122 no5 p38 O 2017

Hunting—Social aspects
THE BEAR AT LAST LIGHT C. KEARNS color *Field & Stream* v122 no4 p48 S 2017
A CANINE ASSIST P. Masotti color *New York State Conservationist* v71 no2 p10 O 2016

Hunting—Software
GAME FINDERS T. HANSEN chart color *Outdoor Life* v224 no2 p15 F/Mr 2017

Huntingto, Tom
Escape from Harpers Ferry *American History* v52 no1 p42 Ap 2017

Huntington, Henry P.
From Alaska, a Lesson on the Value of Conservation Partnerships With Indigenous Communities color *Environment* v59 no1 p34 2017
Treating Arctic Ecosystems as Systems color *Environment* v59 no4 p34 Jl-Ag 2017

Huntington Beach Co.
Fire Power: SOUTHERN CALIFORNIA GRILL MAKERS TURN UP THE HEAT ON ALFRESCO COOKING A. HEROLD color *Los Angeles Magazine* v62 no7 p30 Jl 2017

Huntington Botanical Gardens
Maxx Echt: Huntington Botanical Department Systems Manager M. Branom *Weatherwise* v70 no5 p40 S/O 2017

Huntington National Bank Inc.

Kevin Jones A. BRANDT *Cincinnati Magazine* v50 no2 p32 N 2016

Huntington-Whiteley, Rosie, 1987-
THE CHICEST LADY AT THE AIRPORT S. Trong color *InStyle* v24 no2 p132 F 2017
contributors color *InStyle* v24 no2 p22 F 2017
Gold Rush K. Peiffer color *InStyle* v24 no5 p84 My 2017

Hunting—United States
AUTUMN IN AUGUST W. BRANTLEY color *Field & Stream* v122 no3 p14 Ag 2017
A BREAK IN THE BREAKS R. KIRK cartoon color *Outdoor Life* v224 no7 p13 S 2017
CHEAP ADVENTURES J. BRANDT and P. J. DELHOMME cartoon color *Outdoor Life* v224 no4 p30 My 2017
THE COMEBACK KID N. Krebs color *Outdoor Life* v223 no9 p62 N 2016
PUBLIC DOMAINS A. McKEAN color map *Outdoor Life* v224 no5 p64 Je/Jl 2017
WOODS WORK AMONG THE PLAYFUL HUNTERS C. WHITE *Idaho Magazine* v16 no2 p10 N 2016

Hunting—West (U.S.)
MULEYS ON YOUR OWN T. Walrath color *Outdoor Life* v223 no9 pH5 N 2016

Huntley, Dana
DELIGHT ON THE NORTH YORKSHIRE COAST *British Heritage Travel* v38 no1 p60 Ja/T 2017
EDINBURGH: Take a stroll around Auld Reekie, Scotland's photogenic capital city color *British Heritage Travel* v38 no5 p62 S/O 2017
English Cheddar Cheese *British Heritage Travel* v38 no1 p77 Ja/F 2017
GWR ON DISPLAY color *British Heritage Travel* v38 no5 p38 S/O 2017
Hands Across the Sea *British Heritage Travel* v37 no6 p26 N/D 2016
HIe THee TO HULL! *British Heritage Travel* v38 no1 p40 Ja/F 2017
How Shakespeare Put Politics on the Stage: Power and Succession in the History Plays *British Heritage Travel* v38 no1 p72 Ja/F 2017
THE MAKING OF THE PILGRIMS *British Heritage Travel* v38 no3 p36 My/Je 2017
Notes from an Un-Reeling Island bw color *British Heritage Travel* v38 no5 p26 S/O 2017
once upon a time in Wales: Life in the Valleys of Glamorganshire *British Heritage Travel* v38 no4 p56 Jl/Ag 2017
Revealed: World's Best Travel Destination *British Heritage Travel* v38 no2 p24 Mr/Ap 2017
Revolution: The History of England From the Battle of the Boyne to the Battle of Waterloo color *British Heritage Travel* v38 no5 p72 S/O 2017
Richard III—Resting in Peace *British Heritage Travel* v38 no1 p8 Ja/F 2017
SIMPLY THE WORLD'S GREATEST RAILWAY MUSEUM *British Heritage Travel* v38 no2 p54 Mr/Ap 2017
To the Great Beyond and North Yorkshire *British Heritage Travel* v38 no1 p28 Ja/F 2017

Huntley, John Warren
Increase in predator-prey size ratios throughout the Phanerozoic history of marine ecosystems diag *Science* v356 no6343 p1178 Je 16 2017

Huntley, Pana
THE COAST OF KENT *British Heritage Travel* v38 no4 p50 Jl/Ag 2017

Huntley, Swan
The Goddesses *Publishers Weekly* v264 no21 p67 My 22 2017

Huntley, Tricia
LESS SPACE. MORE GLAM J. Sergent *Washingtonian Magazine* v52 no6 p158 Mr 2017

Huntsman, Jon M., 1960-
"There's No Optimism": Hoover fellow Michael A. McFaul, former ambassador to Moscow, reflects on fading democratic hopes for Russia T. Varadarajan *Hoover Digest: Research & Opinion on Public Policy* no3 p97 Summ 2017

Huntsman: Winter's War, The (Film)
THE HUNTSMAN: WINTER'S WAR D. Vaughn color *Sound &*

Vision v82 no1 p69 Ja 2017

Huntsville (Ala.)

OUT OF THIS WORLD K. SCHNEIDER *Indianapolis Monthly* v40 no7 p36 Mr 2017

Huntsville (Utah)

GLASS color *Powder* v45 no4 p22 D 2016

Hunwick, Robert Foyle

MURDER VILLAGES AND SCAM TOWNS color *Atlantic* v319 no3 p21 Ap 2017

Hunziker, Mirjam

Architecture of the yeast small subunit processome bibl color *Science* v355 no6321 p1 Ja 13 2017

Huot, Ludovic

Reversion of antibiotic resistance in Mycobacterium tuberculosis by spiroisoxazoline SMARt-420 bibl diag *Science* v355 no6330 p1206 Mr 17 2017

Hupé, Jean-Michel

Lee Rubin: Our mentor and role model *Science* v355 no6327 p806 F 24 2017

Hüpers, Andre

Release of mineral-bound water prior to subduction tied to shallow seismogenic slip off Sumatra graph *Science* v356 no6340 p841 My 26 2017

HUPP, STEPHEN

Science vs. Silliness for Parents: Debunking the Myths of Child Psychology *Skeptical Inquirer* v41 no1 p44 Ja/F 2017

HUPPERT, BOYD

The Call of the Trumpet color *Reader's Digest* v190 no1135 p8 N 2017

Huppert, Isabelle, 1953-

BEST ACTRESS CONTENDER ISABELLE HUPPERT N. Sperling color *Entertainment Weekly* no1440 p46 N 18 2016

Isabella Huppert A. LAROCCA *New York* p20 F 9 2017

LEG Work M. GUIDUCCI and M. HOLGATE color *Vogue* v207 no3 p338 Mr 2017

Huppert, Isabelle, 1953—Interviews

36 MINUTES WITH ... Isabelle Huppert A. LAROCCA img *New York* p20 Ja 9 2017

Huppert, Martin

Time-resolved x-ray absorption spectroscopy with a water window high-harmonic source graph *Science* v355 no6322 p264 Ja 20 2017

Huq, Saleemul

Climate adaptation funding: Getting the money to those who need it bibl *Bulletin of the Atomic Scientists* v72 no6 p396 N 2016

Hur, Gyum

Double-heterojunction nanorod light-responsive LEDs for display applications bibl color graph *Science* v355 no6325 p616 F 10 2017

Hur, Seyoon

Colloidally prepared La-doped BaSnO3 electrodes for efficient, photostable perovskite solar cells graph *Science* v356 no6334 p167 Ap 14 2017

Hur, Sunghoon

Quantized thermal transport in single-atom junctions bibl diag graph *Science* v355 no6330 p1192 Mr 17 2017

HURD, BARBARA

GLIMPSES bw color *Orion Magazine* v35 no6 p38 N/D 2016

Listening to the Savage N. Davis color *Orion Magazine* v35 no6 p59 N/D 2016

Hurd, Gale Anne

Gale Anne HURD Y. N. BROWN *Interview* v47 no3 p26 My 2017

Hurd, Mark W.

Potential role of intratumor bacteria in mediating tumor resistance to the chemotherapeutic drug gemcitabine diag *Science* v357 no6356 p1156 S 15 2017

Hurdle, Justin

Smoke-Free Parks: Why Park and Recreation Departments Should Lead the Effort *Parks & Recreation* v51 no10 p42 O 2016

HURFORD, MOLLY

The Accidental Bike Shop color *Bicycling* v58 no4 p50 My 2017

STRAIGHT TO THE BIG TIME color *Bicycling* v58 no6 p42 Jl 2017

HURLBURT, HEATHER

How Not to Fight Terrorism *New Republic* v248 no5 p8 My 2017

Hurley, Bob

School Ties D. Hurley color *Sports Illustrated* v126 no11 p116 Ap 17-24 2017

Hurley, Dan

Let There Be Dark cartoon *Discover* v27 no10 p70 D 2016

No Denying It color *Discover* v38 no8 p78 O 2017

School Ties color *Sports Illustrated* v126 no11 p116 Ap 17-24 2017

Hurley, Declan

Kilogram-scale prexasertib monolactate monohydrate synthesis under continuous-flow CGMP conditions chart diag *Science* v356 no6343 p1144 Je 16 2017

Hurley, Jayne

Healthy Foods *Nutrition Action Health Letter* v44 p1 Je 2017 Supplement

Hurling (Game)

GIVE IT A HURL D. Grove color *Virginia Living* v15 no5 p17 Ag 2017

Hurly, Adam

CAN WHITE WHISKEY GROW UP? color *Bloomberg Businessweek* no4495 p74 O 17 2016

GQ's 2017: GROOMING AWARDS bw color *GQ: Gentlemen's Quarterly* v97 no11 p56 N 2017

Hurowitz, J. A.

Redox stratification of an ancient lake in Gale crater, Mars color *Science* v356 no6341 p922 Je 1 2017

Hurowitz, Richard

How a Briton Created the Almighty Dollar *History Today* v67 no1 p6 Ja 2017

Hurricane Boats (Company)

Hurricane 187 IO *Boating World* v38 no1 p48 Ja 2017

Transformer A. Jones *Boating World* v37 no9 p34 N/D 2016

Hurricane damage

Home Alone R. ESPINOSA color *Nation* v305 no11 p13 O 30 2017

Hurricane damage—Economic aspects

Cleaning up in the wake of hurricanes, tornadoes, and other catastrophes has become a lucrative business for companies such as Cavalry P. Gopal color *Bloomberg Businessweek* no4538 p17 S 18 2017

Irma inundates Florida and Caribbean color *Science* v357 no6356 p1078 S 15 2017

Hurricane Deck Boats (Company)

Hybrid Happiness A. JONES *Boating World* v38 no4 p30 Ap 2017

Hurricane insurance

A Category 5 Business Problem C. Dillow color *Fortune* v176 no5 p13 O 1 2017

Hurricane protection

HARNESSING MOTHER NATURE: The Storied History of Hurricane Control and Cloud Seeding J. Williams *Weatherwise* v70 no5 p25 S/O 2017

What If D.C. Is Next? [Cover story] J. NOBEL color *Rolling Stone* no1297 p26 O 5 2017

Hurricane research

HURRICANE PERCEPTION C. EMERY *USA Today Magazine* v146 no2868 p70 S 2017

Hurricane Harvey, 2017

CENTURY marks bw graph *Christian Century* v134 no20 p8 S 27 2017

COMING STORMS E. Kolbert cartoon *New Yorker* v93 no27 p23 S 11 2017

Coverage Skirts Hurricane's Outsized Impact on Poor N. deMause *Extra!* v30 no8 p3 O 2017

A Cruel Blow B. Bauer *Sail* v48 no11 p4 N 2017

Disaster Relief M. CROSS and K. LANKFORD color *Kiplinger's Personal Finance* v71 no12 p24 D 2017

Flood warning K. Clarke color *U.S. Catholic* v82 no11 p42 N 2017

Hard Rain and Hard Lessons P. Coy and C. Flavelle bw map *Bloomberg Businessweek* no4536 p12 S 4 2017

Harvey brought new threats, and hope, to the undocumented in Houston K. Zipple-Shedd *America* v217 no6 p10 S 18 2017

Harvey Response: 'That's What We're All About' E. J. Schneidewind *AARP: The Magazine* v30 no6A p73 O/N 2017

Houston After Harvey J. Kluger, C. Alter et al color *Time* v190 no10/11 p38 S 18 2017

How an ocean climate cycle favored Harvey J. Rosen color graph

p52 O 2017

Hurricanes—Florida

Eye of the Hurricane B. PIKE cartoon *Power & Motoryacht* v32 no12 p128 D 2016

Shelter from the Storm B. PIKE color *Power & Motoryacht* v32 no12 p74 D 2016

Weatherwatch B. Rippey, J. B. Halverson et al *Weatherwise* v70 no1 p50 Ja/F 2017

Hurricanes—Haiti

Lightbox color *Time* v188 no16/17 p10 O 24 2016

Hurricanes—History

Retrospect S. Potter bw map *Weatherwise* v69 no6 p10 N-D 2016

Hurricanes—Names

The Fight to Change How Hurricanes Are Named O. B. Waxman *Time* v190 no12 p23 S 25 2017

Hurricanes—Puerto Rico

The Island and the Storm K. Vick color *Time* v190 no14 p26 O 9 2017

THE PLIGHT OF PUERTO RICO J. j. Barea and C. Ballard color *Sports Illustrated* v127 no11 p56 O 9 2017

Puerto Rico in Crisis E. MORALES *Nation* v305 no9 p4 O 16 2017

Hurricanes—Safety measures

Blowin' in the Wind T. NINTEMANN *USA Today Magazine* v146 no2868 p73 S 2017

Hurricanes—Social aspects

MATTHEW'S AFTERMATH P. Nielsen color *Sail* v47 no12 p13 D 2016

Storm documentary proves timely C. Gramling color *Science News* v192 no7 p29 O 28 2017

Hurricanes—Texas

12,000 MARKS FOR TEXAS R. C. GREINER *Prologue* v49 no1 p18 Spr 2017

Hurricanes—United States

Beat Back the Sea J. Worland color *Time* v189 no13 p41 Ap 10 2017

HURT, AVERY ELIZABETH

Check out these outrageous facts *National Geographic Kids* no469 p4 Ap 2017

OUT ON A LIMB color *National Geographic Kids* no465 p18 N 2016

TURBO-CHEETAH cartoon color map *National Geographic Kids* no470 p16 My 2017

Weird but true! color map *National Geographic Kids* no470 p4 My 2017

Weird But True! color *National Geographic Kids* no473 p4 S 2017

Hurt, John, 1940-2017

Also In MEMORIAM C. Nashawaty, J. Jensen et al color *Entertainment Weekly* no1453 p39 F 17 2017

Milestones *Time* v189 no5 p13 F 13 2017

Hurtado, Larry W.

Larry W. Hurtado R. Farmer bw color *Publishers Weekly* v263 no45 p22 N 7 2016

What made early Christians a peculiar people? color *Christian Century* v134 no8 p1 Ap 12 2017

Hurteau, Dave

ANGRY BIRDS bw cartoon color *Field & Stream* v121 no9 p47 Ap 2017

BLOOD SWEAT & DEER [Cover story] color *Field & Stream* v121 no7 p44 D 2016/Ja 2017

BOW SHOOTOUT 2017 bw color *Field & Stream* v122 no3 p69 Ag 2017

BULLS AT THE WIRE color *Field & Stream* v121 no6 p34 N 2016

DEKE ATTACK bw color *Field & Stream* v122 no5 p16 O 2017

FIELD TEST color *Field & Stream* v122 no2 p99 Je/Jl 2017

A Free Trip color *Field & Stream* v122 no4 p40 S 2017

GO-TO GLASS color *Field & Stream* v121 no6 p75 N 2016

HARD-EARNED BUCKS C. Kearns color *Field & Stream* v122 no4 p9 S 2017

HOLIDAY GIFT GUIDE 2016 color *Field & Stream* v121 no7 p92 D 2016/Ja 2017

NO PAIN, NO GAME color diag *Field & Stream* v122 no3 p57 Ag 2017

PEAK GLASS color *Field & Stream* v122 no4 p69 S 2017

Hurtley, Stella

The Cell color *Science* v354 no6317 p1229 D 9 2016

Hurvitz, Eli

The Difficulties Of Cloning A CEO D. Leonard and Y. Benmeleh color graph *Bloomberg Businessweek* no4535 p50 Ag 28 2017

HURWITZ, GREGG

What Next? *Publishers Weekly* v263 no47 p93 N 21 2016

Hurwitz, Justin, ca. 1985-

Justin Hurwitz D. Kiper color *Current Biography* v78 no8 p54 Ag 2017

Hurwitz, Laurie

THE MODIGLIANI CODE bw color *Vanity Fair* v59 no6 p110 My 2017

Husain, Altaf

ISNA ELECTS 2016-18 MAJLIS ASH-SHURA *Islamic Horizons* v45 no6 p8 N/D 2016

Husband & wife

See also

Support (Domestic relations)

Can Dad Bring His Second Wife to Mom's Funeral? K. A. Appiah *New York Times Magazine* p24 My 14 2017

CRAWFISH MIRAGE M. W. Spencer color *Louisiana Life* v37 no5 p8 My/Je 2017

EASY CHAIR: Shopping-Mall Time Machine W. Kirn *Harper's Magazine* v335 no2005 p5 Je 2017

For This Issue, We're All Going a Little Bare color *Glamour* v115 no6 p20 Je 2017

Further Notes of a Recycled Housewife J. Rogers img *New York* v50 no11 p12 My 29 2017

Happiness Isn't the Absence of Negative Feelings J. Moss *Harvard Business Review Digital Articles* p2 Ag 20 2015

The Innkeeper's Diaries O. Cohane color *Conde Nast Traveler* v52 no3 p60 Mr 2017

The Last Promise L. Penny color *AARP: The Magazine* v59 no6A p66 O/N 2016

MOTORCYCLE DIARY: Two empty-nesters, two wheels, and becoming the people we wanted to be A. JARRELL *Washingtonian Magazine* v53 no1 p232 O 2017

Movin' on Up D. Paul *Indianapolis Monthly* p136 F 2017

My husband has habits that annoy me… color *Glamour* v115 no5 p118 My 2017

Husband & wife—Canada

A RETURN TO TRADITION FOR MILLENNIALS A. KINGSTON chart color *Maclean's* v130 no6 p12 Jl 2017

Husbands

Back to Life S. SANDBERG cartoon color *O, The Oprah Magazine* p46 My 2017

Dump the Emotional Manure E. TAYLOR *USA Today Magazine* v145 no2860 p61 Ja 2017

A FAST LIFE J. J. Buck bw color *Harper's Bazaar* no3651 p288 Mr 2017

"Her Father Lives in HER EYES" bw color *Good Housekeeping* v263 no5 p113 N 2016

Home on the Ranch H. WILHELM *National Review* v69 no17 p44 S 11 2017

Life IN THESE UNITED STATES color *Reader's Digest* v189 no1131 p34 Je 2017

My little barn T. Mitman color *Equus* no475 p77 Ap 2017

A SON'S PRAYER T. Price color *America* v217 no6 p42 S 18 2017

Husbands—Psychology

Your Feminist Dilemmas, Solved color *Glamour* v115 no2 p72 F 2017

Huscroft, Richard

A Medieval Royal Rollercoaster N. Vincent *History Today* v67 no3 p58 Mr 2017

Huse, David A.

Spin-imbalance in a 2D Fermi-Hubbard system diag graph *Science* v357 no6358 p1385 S 29 2017

HUSEYNOV, SAID

Saffron *Natural History* v125 no2 p28 F 2017

Hush, Michael R.

Machine learning for quantum physics bibl diag *Science* v355 no6325 p580 F 10 2017

Huskey, Brian

CORONA DEL MAR, CA R. Jones color map *Sunset* v238 no2 p28 F 2017

Husock, Howard
Ben Carson Is Right *Commentary* v143 no3 p34 Mr 2017
Hussain, Amir
Here All Along J. L. Fredericks bw *Commonweal* v144 no6 p29
Mr 24 2017
Hussain, M. Shazam
Get Smart About Stroke G. deGROOT REDFORD cartoon *AARP:
The Magazine* v60 no1A p18 D 2016/Ja 2017
Hussain, Z.
Femtosecond electron-phonon lock-in by photoemission and x-
ray free-electron laser chart diag *Science* v357 no6346 p71 Jl
7 2017
Hussam, Reshmaan
The impact of training informal health care providers in India:
A randomized controlled trial chart diag *Science* v354 no6308
paaf7384-1 O 7 2016
Hussein, Asad
Waiting for Maryan *New York Times Magazine* p29 N 20 2016
HUSSEIN, HAISAM
On the Waterfront: Millions of people live, work and play along
New York's rivers and harbor. Here, a snapshot of the marine
traffic on one recent day—March 22—shows the amazing range
of activity *Smithsonian* v48 no2 p36 My 2017
Hussein, Linnéa
OFF THE RECORD: REENACTMENT AND INTIMACY IN
CASTING JONBENET *Film Quarterly* v71 no1 p32 Fall 2017
Hussein, Saddam, 1937-2006
The Burning Sands of Iraq K. Vick color *Time* v189 no24 p30
Je 26 2017
Hussein, Taz
Even Life-Saving Innovations Don't Sell Themselves *Harvard
Business Review Digital Articles* p2 F 16 2017
Why Big Health Systems Are Investing in Community Health
Harvard Business Review Digital Articles p2 D 6 2016
Hussen, Ahmed
THE RISE AND RISE OF AHMED HUSSEN S. PROUDFOOT
bw *Maclean's* v130 no3 p28 Ap 2017
Hussey, Nigel E.
Envisioning the Future of Aquatic Animal Tracking: Technology,
Science, and Application *BioScience* v67 no10 p884 O 2017
Now is the time to protect the Arctic bibl color *Science* v354
no6317 p1243 D 9 2016
Hussmann, Jeffrey A.
CAT-tailing as a fail-safe mechanism for efficient degradation of
stalled nascent polypeptides diag *Science* v357 no6349 p414 Jl
28 2017
Hustad, C.
Fostering reproducibility in industry-academia research color *Sci-
ence* v357 no6353 p759 Ag 25 2017
HUSTAD, MEGAN
Innocent and Confused *New York Times Book Review* p20 Ja 8
2017
UP FROM CHAOS *Psychology Today* v50 no2 p72 Mr/Ap 2017
Huston, Anjelica, 1951-
A KEY TO ANJELICA J. J. BUCK color *Vanity Fair* v59 no10
p180 O 2017
HUSTON, MATT
Dispatches From the End of Life *Psychology Today* v50 no1 p18
Ja/F 2017
Don't Look Now *Psychology Today* v50 no2 p18 Mr/Ap 2017
A Double-Edged Hormone *Psychology Today* v50 no1 p22 Ja/F
2017
A FOUR-LETTER FAN *Psychology Today* v49 no5 p14 S/O 2016
THE HOT SEAT *Psychology Today* v49 no5 p9 S/O 2016
I COULD BE WORSE: IN ADMITTING OUR FAULTS, WE
STILL FIND WAYS TO CAST OURSELVES IN A POSITIVE
LIGHT *Psychology Today* v50 no4 p19 Ag 2017
In Search of Answers *Psychology Today* v50 no3 p10 My/Je 2017
An Invisible Edge *Psychology Today* v49 no6 p22 N/D 2016
The Long-View Lover *Psychology Today* v50 no2 p16 Mr/Ap
2017
THE LURE OF CHARISMA: COLORFUL LEADERS IN-
SPIRE, BUT THEY MAY HAVE UNEXPECTED LIMITS
Psychology Today v50 no5 p9 S/O 2017
On Our Own *Psychology Today* v50 no2 p9 Mr/Ap 2017
STATES OF ALARM *Psychology Today* v50 no5 p14 S/O 2017

Tear Down This Wall *Psychology Today* v49 no6 p9 N/D 2016
Welcome to Beard City *Psychology Today* v50 no1 p20 Ja/F 2017
What Love Really Looks Like *Psychology Today* v50 no1 p9 Ja/F
2017
Huston, Nicholas C.
Restored iron transport by a small molecule promotes absorption
and hemoglobinization in animals color graph *Science* v356
no6338 p608 My 12 2017
Huston, Therese
Research: We Are Way Harder on Female Leaders Who Make Bad
Calls *Harvard Business Review Digital Articles* p2 Ap 21 2016
Hustvedt, Siri
Mind-Body Problems V. GORNICK *New York Times Book Review*
p16 D 18 2016
Hustvedt, Siri—Interviews
DOES SEX MATTER? L. Christensen color *Harper's Bazaar*
no3648 p190 N 2016
Hutcherson, Bobby
The 'Always Striving' Bobby Hutcherson: 1941-2016 Y. Kato bw
Downbeat v83 no11 p16 N 2016
Hutcherson, Josh, 1992-
FUTURE MAN D. Franich color *Entertainment Weekly*
no1474/1475 p68 Jl 21-28 2017
Streaming's New Stars J. Halterman *TV Guide* v65 no2 p14 Ja
2 2017
Hutcherson, Kimberly
MEMBER SPOTLIGHT color *Literacy Today (2411-7862)* v34
no5 p50 Mr/Ap 2017
Hutcheson, Matthew
A Brand New Start color *Log Home Living* v33 no9 p54 D 2016
Hutchings, Graham J.
Identification of single-site gold catalysis in acetylene hydrochlo-
rination bw diag graph *Science* v355 no6332 p1399 Mr 31 2017
Hutchings, Sasha
why i dance *Dance Magazine* v91 no1 p216 Ja 2017
HUTCHINS, AARON
Baby want a kale salad? [Cover story] color *Maclean's* no1 p52
F 17 2017
Barbara McClatchie Andrews color *Maclean's* v129 no43 p66 O
31 2016
BOXING SHADOWS bw *Maclean's* v130 no9 p72 O 2017
Bringing out the big guns color *Maclean's* v130 no4 p13 My 2017
Canada's champion color *Maclean's* v129 no48/49 p66 D 5 2016
Corey Michael Mijac color *Maclean's* v129 no47 p66 N 28 2016
The depth of despair chart color *Maclean's* v130 no2 p59 Mr 2017
Down on the border color *Maclean's* v130 no7 p24 Ag 2017
THE FIRST FLIGHT color *Maclean's* v129 no48/49 p14 D 5
2016
Little mosque on Lake Erie color *Maclean's* v130 no10 p14 N
2017
A moment of painful truth color *Maclean's* v130 no2 p18 Mr 2017
Murder No. 605 color graph *Maclean's* v129 no45 p34 N 14 2016
The Olympian on campus color *Maclean's* v130 no10 p58 N 2017
A shellfish display color *Maclean's* v130 no8 p12 S 2017
STUDENT ISSUE chart color graph *Maclean's* v130 no2 p57 Mr
2017
There for ewe color *Maclean's* v130 no9 p13 O 2017
The very worst-case scenario color graph *Maclean's* v130 no9 p43
O 2017
WARNING, STRANGE DAYS AHEAD [Cover story] color *Ma-
clean's* v129 no51/52 p65 D 26 2016
Welcome to America? color *Maclean's* v130 no4 p14 My 2017
Yaaka Markusie Yaaka color *Maclean's* v129 no45 p62 N 14 2016
Hutchins, Robert Maynard, 1899-1977
UNIVERSITY OF CHICAGO DAYS J. Epstein *Claremont Re-
view of Books* v17 no3 p64 Summ 2017
HUTCHINSON, ALEX
EXTRA REPS color *Runner's World* v52 no4 p26 My 2017
FORMULA FOR SUCCESS color diag *Runner's World* v52 no1
p46 Ja/F 2017
HOW HAVE MARATHONS CHANGED OVER TIME? graph
Runner's World v51 no10 p86 N 2016
HOW TO RUN MORE LIKE THIS GUY [Cover story] cartoon
color *Runner's World* v51 no11 p38 D 2016
MOONSHOT [Cover story] bw cartoon color map *Runner's
World* v52 no5 p62 Je 2017

Hydrogels—Analysis

DNA sequence–directed shape change of photopatterned hydrogels via high-degree swelling A. Cangialosi, C. Yoon et al color diag *Science* v357 no6356 p1126 S 15 2017

Hydrogen

See also

Hydrogen as fuel

Atoms on the move—finding the hydrogen J. Cairney bibl diag *Science* v355 no6330 p1128 Mr 17 2017

The Drama-Ridden Couple of R Aquarii A. MacRobert *Sky & Telescope* v134 no4 p48 O 2017

Elemental haiku *Science* v357 no6350 p461 Ag 4 2017

Food for microbes seen on Enceladus A. YEAGER color *Science News* v191 no9 p6 My 13 2017

Green Machine C. Sisson color *Power & Motoryacht* v34 no10 p38 O 2017

Synthesis of FeH5: A layered structure with atomic hydrogen slabs C. M. Pépin, G. Geneste et al diag graph *Science* v357 no6349 p382 Jl 28 2017

Two for the price of one color *Astronomy* v45 no5 p74 My 2017

Hydrogen as fuel

Hydrogen-powered vehicles: A chicken and egg problem: Although the cost of fuel cells has rapidly decreased, the lack of a fueling infrastructure limits their use in vehicles D. Kramer *Physics Today* v70 no9 p31 S 2017

Hydrogen atom

Electron diffraction and the hydrogen atom L. B. McCusker bibl diag *Science* v355 no6321 p136 Ja 13 2017

Electron diffraction sees hydrogen atoms J. Miller *Physics Today* v70 no3 p16 Mr 2017

Molecular imaging at 1-femtosecond resolution Chong-Yu Ruan bibl diag *Science* v354 no6310 p283 O 21 2016

Hydrogen bomb

The secret of the SOVIET HYDROGEN BOMB A. Wellerstein and E. Geist *Physics Today* v70 no4 p40 Ap 2017

Hydrogen bonding

Fast-freezing hot water spurs debate E. CONOVER *Science News* v191 no2 p14 F 4 2017

Hydrogen bonding interactions

Fast-freezing hot water spurs debate E. CONOVER *Science News* v191 no2 p14 F 4 2017

Hydrogen cars

Hydrogen-powered vehicles: A chicken and egg problem: Although the cost of fuel cells has rapidly decreased, the lack of a fueling infrastructure limits their use in vehicles D. Kramer *Physics Today* v70 no9 p31 S 2017

THE NEW, IMPROVED HYDROGEN CAR! A. George and E. Dyer color diag map *Popular Mechanics* p38 Jl 2017

Hydrogen plasmas

FUSION FRAMEWORK E. MASTROIANNI color *Discover* v38 no6 p9 Jl/Ag 2017

Hydrogen production

Cassini finds molecular hydrogen in the Enceladus plume: Evidence for hydrothermal processes J. H. Waite, C. R. Glein et al chart graph *Science* v356 no6334 p155 Ap 14 2017

Hydrogen storage

Facility Drives Hydrogen Vehicle Innovations M. Hunsberger *Science & Technology Review* p20 S 2016

Hydrogen—Analysis

Observation of the Wigner-Huntington transition to metallic hydrogen R. P. Dias and I. F. Silvera bibl chart color graph *Science* v355 no6326 p715 F 17 2017

Hydrogenase

Methanogenic heterodisulfide reductase (HdrABC-MvhAGD) uses two noncubane [4Fe-4S] clusters for reduction T. Wagner, J. Koch et al color *Science* v357 no6352 p699 Ag 18 2017

Structural basis of the redox switches in the NAD+-reducing soluble [NiFe]-hydrogenase Y. Shomura, M. Taketa et al diag *Science* v357 no6354 p928 S 1 2017

Hydrogenation

Hydrogenation of fluoroarenes: Direct access to all-cis-(multi)fluorinated cycloalkanes M. P. Wiesenfeldt, Z. Nairoukh et al diag *Science* v357 no6354 p908 S 1 2017

TECHNICAL COMMENT ABSTRACTS J. Nakamura, T. Fujitani et al *Science* v357 no6354 p881 S 1 2017

Hydrogen—Research

New claim staked for metallic hydrogen E. CONOVER color *Science News* v191 no3 p14 F 18 2017

Hydrogen—Thermal properties

Observation of the Wigner-Huntington transition to metallic hydrogen R. P. Dias and I. F. Silvera bibl chart color graph *Science* v355 no6326 p715 F 17 2017

Hydrology

How Did Earth Gets Its Ocean? A. Sarafian color *Oceanus* v51 no2 p100 Wint 2016

Hydronic heating systems

Roundup for Fall color *Old House Journal* v45 no6 p50 S 2017

Hydroponics

Dome sweet dome M. Rosano color *Canadian Geographic* v137 no2 p26 Mr/Ap 2017

HOME HYDROPONICS D. KLUKO color diag *Popular Mechanics* p85 F 2017

Hydroponic Farming: Organic or Not? L. Noyes *Mother Earth News* no282 p8 Je/Jl 2017

Hydrorider (Company)

PRODUCT PREVIEW *Parks & Recreation* v52 no9 p92 S 2017

Hydrotherapy

NOT JUST DOG-PADDLING: Pups are getting into the pool for help with arthritis, chronic pain, and other ailments J. Curry *Washingtonian Magazine* v52 no12 p163 S 2017

SPECIAL DELIVERY K. DINAN *Cincinnati Magazine* v50 no4 p74 Ja 2017

Hydrothermal vent microbiology

Food for microbes abundant on Enceladus P. Voosen bw *Science* v356 no6334 p121 Ap 14 2017

Hydrothermal vents

Chris German K. GRAY cartoon *Popular Science* p49 Ja/F 2017

The Hot Spot Beneath Yellowstone Park C. Linder *Oceanus* v52 no2 p54 Spr 2017

Hydroxycut (Company)

Get to Know: MuscleTech J. SCHILDHOUSE color *Muscle & Performance* v9 no10 p34 O 2017

Hydroxyl group

Direct frequency comb measurement of $OD + CO \rightarrow DOCO$ kinetics B. J. Bjork, T. Q. Bui et al bibl graph *Science* v354 no6311 p444 O 28 2016

Scientists flag new causes for surge in methane levels P. Voosen color *Science* v354 no6319 p1513 D 23 2016

Hye-young Pyun

CARING FOR PLANTS cartoon color *New Yorker* v93 no20 p64 Jl 10 2017

Hyejin Park

A nuclease that mediates cell death induced by DNA damage and poly(ADP-ribose) polymerase-1 bw graph *Science* v354 no6308 paad6872-1 O 7 2016

Pathological α-synuclein transmission initiated by binding lymphocyte-activation gene 3 bibl graph *Science* v353 no6307 paah3374-1 S 30 2016

Hyeong Kim, Shi

Harvesting electrical energy from carbon nanotube yarn twist diag graph *Science* v357 no6353 p773 Ag 25 2017

Hyeon Soo Lim—Trials, litigation, etc.

People L. Markoe, E. M. Miller et al color *Christian Century* v134 no19 p17 S 13 2017

Hyers, Martin

Coming Into Focus F. Winston bw color *Conde Nast Traveler* v52 no3 p90 Mr 2017

Hygiene

See also

Baths

Exercise

Eyebrows—Care & hygiene

Personal beauty

Relaxation (Health)

Rest

Sexual health

Shaving

The Art of the Arch M. MILRAD GOLDSTEIN *Martha Stewart Living* no268 p58 O 2016

Can Tidying Up Change Your Life? P. M. ESSWEIN cartoon *Kiplinger's Personal Finance* v71 no7 p39 Jl 2017

a chemical-free clean *Parents* v92 no4 p105 Ap 2017

Potty Relief for Tired Trainers color *Parents* v92 no7 p30 Jl 2017
Strong BONES, Flat BELLY K. ASP color *Prevention* v69 no8 p70 Ag 2017

Hygiene products
See also
    Feminine hygiene products
    Toilet preparations
Best. Bath. Ever! K. FOSTER cartoon color *Seventeen* v76 no12 p47 D 2016/Ja 2017
cheap THRILLS E. STOVALL color *Seventeen* v76 no12 p54 D 2016/Ja 2017
DOUBLE HEADER M. Goldberg color *O, The Oprah Magazine* p92 N 2017
How to Be Vain: A Modern Man's Primer M. ANTHONY GREEN, G. MUNCE et al color *GQ: Gentlemen's Quarterly* v97 no9 p96 S 2017
MASCARA made easy K. FOSTER color *Seventeen* v76 no12 p50 D 2016/Ja 2017

Hygiene products—Awards
Natural Beauty Awards 2017 [Cover story] A. PATZ color *Prevention* v69 no7 p58 Jl 2017

Hygiene products—Evaluation
Cloud Nine color *O, The Oprah Magazine* p111 D 2016
Get more from your shower! M. OLIVA color *Redbook* p30 My 2017
JUST ADD WATER T. BRAND *Indianapolis Monthly* v40 no5 p26 Ja 2017
Natural Beauty Awards 2017 [Cover story] A. PATZ color *Prevention* v69 no7 p58 Jl 2017
O's 2016 BEAUTY GIFT GUIDE color *O, The Oprah Magazine* p112 D 2016
Steal Her Stuff S. NYGAARD color *Men's Health* v32 no4 p62 My 2017
STOCK YOUR SPA cartoon color *Better Homes & Gardens* v95 no2 p20 F 2016
Val's Guide to GORGEOUS V. Monroe color *O, The Oprah Magazine* p116 D 2016

HYLAND, VÉRONIQUE
How Has One Designer Spent Decades Defining the Avant-Garde? Rei Kawakubo's Comme des Garçons gets a restrospective at the Met img *New York* v50 no8 p74 Ap 17 2017

Hyler, Maria E.
The power and potential of teacher residencies color graph *Phi Delta Kappan* v98 no8 p31 My 2017
The Teacher Residency *Education Digest* v83 no2 p38 O 2017

Hylidae
Surprise Party! S. ELDER cartoon color map *National Geographic Kids* no473 p16 S 2017

Hylton, Wil S.
IN THE MIDST OF A NATIONAL CRISIS OF POLICE VIOLENCE, SHE GAMBLED THAT PROSECUTING SIX OFFICERS WOULD HELP HEAL HER CITY. SHE LOST MUCH MORE THAN JUST THE CASE *New York Times Magazine* p42 O 2 2017
THE MEGAPHONE *New York Times Magazine* p30 Ag 20 2017

Hyman, Anthony A.
ATP as a biological hydrotrope color graph *Science* v356 no6339 p753 My 19 2017

HYMAN, DAN
FALL ALBUM PREVIEW *Rolling Stone* no1297 p12 O 5 2017
A FRINGE FANTASIA color *Chicago* v66 no10 p77 O 2017
The ORWELLS *Interview* v47 no1 p16 F 2017
SAD 13 *Interview* v46 no9 p24 N 2016
Salomon FAYE *Interview* v47 no3 p24 My 2017
SONGS FROM THE HEART cartoon color *Esquire* p45 S 2017
WHY We LOVE CHICAGO bw cartoon color *Chicago* v66 no3 p75 Mr 2017

Hyman, Jeffrey
School Districts in the Northeast Are Most Likely To Serve Local Foods on a Daily Basis *Amber Waves: The Economics of Food, Farming, Natural Resources, & Rural America* p1 My 2017

Hyman, Ray
My Personal Odyssey in Skepticism H. HALL *Skeptical Inquirer* v40 no6 p37 N/D 2016

Hymenoptera
See also

Bees
A Bee or Not a Bee, That is the Question G. Lemmo *New York State Conservationist* v71 no6 p14 Je 2017

HYMORE, KHALIL
6 Easy ONE-PAN SUPPERS [Cover story] color *Prevention* p84 Mr 2017
Delicious SUMMER FRUIT [Cover story] color *Prevention* v69 no7 p84 Jl 2017
Easy Backyard BBQ [Cover story] color *Prevention* v69 no6 p82 Je 2017
Easy, Fast, Healthy! [Cover story] color *Prevention* v69 no4 p84 Ap 2017
Easy No-Cook Dinners color *Prevention* v69 no8 p86 Ag 2017
Fresh & Easy FROM THE FARMERS' MARKET color *Prevention* v69 no9 p86 O 2017
HEALTHY HOLIDAY DESSERTS color *Prevention* v68 no12 p40 D 2016
Love Your Leftovers color *Prevention* v69 no11 p86 N 2017
Make the Most of Your Meals color *Prevention* v68 no11 p58 N 2016
THE MINI AND MERRY PARTY PLAN color *Redbook* p126 D 2016
Quick, healthy, filling pudding! color *Redbook* p125 Ap 2017
Smooth Blends [Cover story] color *Prevention* v69 no5 p76 My 2017
Super BOWLS [Cover story] color *Prevention* v69 no2 p82 F 2017

Hymowitz, Carol
IT'S NOT JUST BRANGELINA *Bloomberg Businessweek* no4493 p53 O 3 2016
Me, Retire? color *Bloomberg Businessweek* no4540 p47 O 2 2017
The Same Gold Watch, It Just Arrives Later chart color *Bloomberg Businessweek* no4504 p20 D 19 2016
Training Day color *Bloomberg Businessweek* no4515 p18 Mr 20 2017
Welcome Freshmen! color *Bloomberg Businessweek* no4516 p39 Mr 27 2017
White Men Can Change At Rockwell Automation cartoon *Bloomberg Businessweek* no4520 p24 My 1 2017

HYMOWITZ, KAY
Deplorables for Dummies *Commentary* v144 no1 p48 Jl/Ag 2017
Where America Begins *New York Times Book Review* p12 N 6 2016

Hymowitz, Kay S.
Beyond Black and White A. EHRENHALT *New York Times Book Review* p11 F 5 2017
From SoHo to Bushwick R. KOSTELANETZ color *Reason* v49 no2 p66 Je 2017
Time to Grow Up diag *National Review* v69 no12 p38 Je 26 2017

HYNDES, GLENN A.
Accelerating Tropicalization and the Transformation of Temperate Seagrass Meadows *BioScience* v66 no11 p938 N 1 2016

Hyne, C. J. Cutcliffe
On to Atlantis! M. DIRDA bw *Weekly Standard* v22 no38 p36 Je 12 2017

HYNE, JANICE
Life cartoon *Reader's Digest* v190 no1132 p30 Jl/Ag 2017

HYNES, ERIC
Acting Out color *Film Comment* v53 no5 p18 S/O 2017
CENTER OF GRAVITY color *Film Comment* v52 no6 p28 N/D 2016
Form and Void color *Film Comment* v53 no1 p14 Ja/F 2017
GETTING ON WITH IT color *Film Comment* v53 no3 p31 My/Je 2017
Give and Take color *Film Comment* v53 no4 p14 Jl/Ag 2017
Living Proof bw color *Film Comment* v53 no3 p16 My/Je 2017
See Through Me color *Film Comment* v53 no2 p14 Mr/Ap 2017
UNITED WE SIT color *Film Comment* v53 no1 p66 Ja/F 2017
URBAN LEGENDS bw color *Film Comment* v53 no4 p22 Jl/Ag 2017

HYNES, JENNIFER
HERE I AM: A NOVEL color *Phi Kappa Phi Forum* v97 no1 p31 Spr 2017

Hynes, Richard O.
Evolving policy with science color *Science* v355 no6328 p889 Mr 3 2017

Scholar v86 no4 p94 Aut 2017

Hysteria (Social psychology)

Mass Panics *Lapham's Quarterly* v10 no3 p87 Summ 2017

Hytner, Nicholas, 1956-

Balancing Acts: Behind the Scenes at London's National Theatre bw *Publishers Weekly* v264 no38 p62 S 18 2017

Hyun, Insoo—Interviews

PUSHING THE LIMITS OF LIFE IN THE LAB L. SCHLEY color *Discover* v38 no1 p38 Ja/F 2017

Hyun-Ja Nam

Cyclin A2 is an RNA binding protein that controls Mre11 mRNA translation bibl graph *Science* v353 no6307 p1549 S 30 2016

Hyun Seok Kim

Positive biodiversity-productivity relationship predominant in global forests bibl chart graph map *Science* v354 no6309 paaf8957-1 O 14 2016

Hyundai automobile—Evaluation

ALTERNATIVE AVENUES K. Reynolds cartoon chart color graph *Motor Trend* v69 no7 p62 Jl 2017

The End of an Era D. V. Werp color *Car & Driver* v62 no7 p92 Ja 2017

Hyundai Kona A Korea-spec taste A. Priddle color *Motor Trend* v69 no9 p24 S 2017

PENNY WISER A. Robinson and E. Tingwall color diag *Car & Driver* v62 no11 p84 My 2017

Hyundai Genesis automobile

Genesis Reveals: Product Plan Through 2021 M. Rechtin color *Motor Trend* v69 no11 p22 N 2017

Hyundai Genesis automobile—Evaluation

LUXURY START UP A. Priddle chart color *Motor Trend* v68 no12 p70 D 2016

Hyundai Motor America Inc.

Dave Zuchowski A. Priddle color *Motor Trend* v68 no12 p35 D 2016

Hyundai Motor Co.

Genesis G90 chart color *Motor Trend* v69 no1 p139 Ja 2017

Genesis Reveals: Product Plan Through 2021 M. Rechtin color *Motor Trend* v69 no11 p22 N 2017

Hyundai Elantra chart color *Motor Trend* v69 no1 p126 Ja 2017

Hyundai Kona A Korea-spec taste A. Priddle color *Motor Trend* v69 no9 p24 S 2017

LUXURY START UP A. Priddle chart color *Motor Trend* v68 no12 p70 D 2016

Manfred Fitzgerald: SENIOR VICE PRESIDENT, GENESIS M. Rechtin color *Motor Trend* v69 no11 p30 N 2017

PENNY WISER A. Robinson and E. Tingwall color diag *Car & Driver* v62 no11 p84 My 2017

Road Test chart color *Consumer Reports* v82 no5 p58 My 2017

HYUNG-OAK LEE, CHRISTINE

Big Little Lives *New York Times Book Review* p18 Mr 12 2017

I

I, Daniel Blake (Film)

ALSO PLAYING: JUNE J. Nolfi color *Entertainment Weekly* no1463/1464 p53 Ap/My 2017

HOW THE OTHER HALF LIVES A. LANE color *New Yorker* v93 no17 p74 Je 19 2017

I, Daniel Blake C. Nashawaty color *Entertainment Weekly* no1448 p50 Ja 13 2017

I, Snow Leopard (Short story)

I, SNOW LEOPARD J. MAJIA *Orion Magazine* v35 no4/5 p82 Jl-O 2016

I Am Bolt (Film)

THE INTERSECTION bw color *Runner's World* v52 no1 p26 Ja/F 2017

I Am Jane Doe (Film)

TRAFFIC T. Friend cartoon *New Yorker* v92 no45 p24 Ja 16 2017

I Am Michael (Film)

I Am Michael Maps Painful Betrayal S. Zacharek color *Time* v189 no4 p51 F 6 2017

I Am My Own Wife (Theatrical production)

DOUG WRIGHT M. Musto *Advocate* no1088 p30 D 2016/Ja 2017

I Am Not Your Negro (Film)

BALDWIN'S RENDEZVOUS WITH THE TWENTY-FIRST CENTURY: I AM NOT YOUR NEGRO W. Crichlow *Film Quarterly* v70 no4 p9 Summ 2017

Dear America, James Baldwin Is Still 'Not Your Negro' B. DANI-ELLE and L. CROSS bw color *Ebony* v72 no4 p22 F 2017

FADE TO BLACK H. ALS bw cartoon *New Yorker* v92 no49 p84 F 13 2017

THE GREAT DIVIDE A. CHAN bw *Film Comment* v53 no1 p54 Ja/F 2017

HISTORICALLY SPEAKING L. Kennedy color *Essence* v47 no10 p56 F 2017

I Am Not Your Negro C. Nashawaty color *Entertainment Weekly* no1451/1452 p92 F 3-10 2017

Language in black and white A. Frykholm bw *Christian Century* v134 no9 p10 Ap 26 2017

More Notes of a Native Son S. Zacharek color *Time* v189 no7/8 p109 F 27 2017

The Must List color *Entertainment Weekly* no1451/1452 p4 F 3-10 2017

NOW PLAYING color *Entertainment Weekly* no1457/1458 p79 Mr 17 2017

Timely Provocations R. Alleva color *Commonweal* v144 no7 p24 Ap 14 2017

Trapped in History D. EDELSTEIN img *New York* p69 Ja 23 2017

Under Duress B. R. Rich *Film Quarterly* v70 no4 p5 Summ 2017

Under the Spell of James Baldwin D. Pinckney bw *New York Review of Books* v64 no5 p24 Mr 23 2017

I Am Twenty (Film)

BREAKING THE ICE N. DUNNE bw *Film Comment* v53 no1 p72 Ja/F 2017

I Called Him Morgan (Film)

TRUE NOTE B. Ratliff bw cartoon *Esquire* p33 Ap 2017

I Can Barely Stand To (Poem)

I Can Barely Stand To R. ZUCKER *Nation* v304 no3 p35 Ja 30 2017

I Decided (Music)

BIG SEAN M. Vain color *Entertainment Weekly* no1453 p58 F 17 2017

BIG SEAN M. Vain *Entertainment Weekly* no1446/1447 p73 D 2016/Ja 2017

I Do...Until I Don't (Film)

Big Kill Hunting D. EDELSTEIN img *New York* v50 no18 p84 S 4 2017

Land O' Lake M. WAKIM *Los Angeles Magazine* v62 no9 p62 S 2017

I Don't Feel at Home in This World Anymore (Film)

I Don't Feel at Home Aims for the Heart S. Zacharek color *Time* v189 no7/8 p110 F 27 2017

I don't feel at home in this world anymore C. Collis color *Entertainment Weekly* no1454/1455 p83 F 24 2017

I Don't Wanna Live Forever (Music)

Fifty Shades' Top 40 Freakfest N. Feeney color *Entertainment Weekly* no1453 p56 F 17 2017

The Playlist color *Rolling Stone* no1278/1279 p10 Ja 12 2017

I Due Foscari (Theatrical production)

Verdi: I Due Foscari P. Dillon *Opera News* v81 no5 p56 N 2016

I Go Back Home (Film)

Film Chronicles Scott's Final Work B. Doerschuk color *Downbeat* v84 no3 p13 Mr 2017

I Hear You Say (Short story)

I Hear You Say M. DANN *Commentary* v142 no3 p25 O 2016

I Love Dick (TV program)

THE 10 BEST SHOWS OF THE YEAR SO FAR J. Jensen color *Entertainment Weekly* no1471 p54 Je 23 2017

COCKEYED OPTIMISTS E. NUSSBAUM color *New Yorker* v93 no18 p74 Je 26 2017

Dick Comes to Marfa J. McBride img *New York* v49 no15 p80 Jl 25 2016

Eyes on the Guys R. SYME color *New Republic* v248 no5 p60 My 2017

INSPIRATION T. Friend cartoon *New Yorker* v93 no15 p17 My 29 2017

Kathryn Hahn's Awkward Artistry A. Bacle color *Entertainment Weekly* no1465 p48 My 12 2017

KEVIN BACON IS NOT A DICK E. Lepucki bw color *Esquire* p21 My 2017

On Amazon, a Troubled Letter-Writing Campaign from the Heart D. D'Addario color *Time* v189 no19 p49 My 22 2017

Prime Opportunity R. MONROE *Texas Monthly* v45 no5 p56 My 2017

I Love Wine! (Poem)

8. I Love Wine! S. Simonds *New York Times Magazine* p17 Ap 2 2017

I Now Pronounce You (Poem)

I NOW PRONOUNCE YOU D. Malech *New Yorker* v93 no15 p52 My 29 2017

I Promise (Music)

The Playlist bw color *Rolling Stone* no1290 p10 Je 29 2017

I See You (Music)

Downcast Brits Brew Up a Quiet Storm M. Johnston color *Time* v189 no4 p52 Ja 23 2017

Hot Tracks L. Robinson color *Vanity Fair* v59 no2 p38 F 2017

Secrets of the xx's Joyful New Sound M. Vain color *Entertainment Weekly* no1449 p57 Ja 20 2017

The xx N. Feeney color *Entertainment Weekly* no1449 p56 Ja 20 2017

The xx's Dreamy Late-Night Rapture J. DOLAN color *Rolling Stone* no1278/1279 p49 Ja 12 2017

I Want to Hold Your Hand (Music)

IT WAS FIFTY YEARS AGO TODAY. . D. T. MORAN *Humanist* v77 no3 p28 My/Je 2017

I Will Survive (Music)

CHILLI PEPPER B. Zehme cartoon *Chicago* v66 no1 p170 Ja 2017

I Would Be Remiss If I Didn't Consider the Possibility of Gratitude (Poem)

I would be remiss if I didn't consider the possibility of gratitude W. O'Leary *America* v217 no3 p43 Ag 7 2017

Iaconangelo, David

By number, Christians overrepresented in Congress color *Christian Century* v134 no3 p12 F 2017

Iacovone, Leonardo

Teaching personal initiative beats traditional training in boosting small business in West Africa chart graph *Science* v357 no6357 p1287 S 22 2017

Iafrate, A. John

Decoupling genetics, lineages, and microenvironment in IDH-mutant gliomas by single-cell RNA-seq diag *Science* v355 no6332 p1391 Mr 31 2017

Ialenti, Vincent

Death and succession among Finland's nuclear waste experts *Physics Today* v70 no10 p48 O 2017

Iamsirithaworn, Sopon

Dengue diversity across spatial and temporal scales: Local structure and the effect of host population size bibl graph *Science* v355 no6331 p1302 Mr 24 2017

Iandoli, Kathy

COMMISSARY KITCHEN K. MANGU-WARD color *Reason* v48 no10 p65 Mr 2017

Ianello, James

The Pride of Union, Maine color *Yankee* v80 no6 p44 N/D 2016

IANNACCI, ELIO

Bubbles comes back to life color *Maclean's* v129 no41 p50 O 17 2016

IANNOTTI, LAUREN

love times two *Parents* v91 no9 p134 S 2016

Iansiti, Marco

THE BLOCKCHAIN REVOLUTION: INTERACTION color *Harvard Business Review* v95 no2 p20 Mr/Ap 2017

The History and Future of Operations *Harvard Business Review Digital Articles* p2 Je 30 2015

MANAGING OUR HUB ECONOMY: STRATEGY, ETHICS, AND NETWORK COMPETITION IN THE AGE OF DIGITAL SUPERPOWERS color diag graph img *Harvard Business Review* v95 no5 p84 S/O 2017

Taylor Swift and the Economics of Music as a Service *Harvard Business Review Digital Articles* p2 N 6 2014

THE TRUTH ABOUT BLOCKCHAIN bw color diag img *Harvard Business Review* v95 no1 p118 Ja/F 2017

What the Companies on the Right Side of the Digital Business Divide Have in Common color *Harvard Business Review Digital Articles* p2 Ja 31 2017

Ianzito, Christina

25 People Who Bust the Myths color *AARP: The Magazine* v59 no4A p42 Je/Jl 2016

Benicio Del Toro color *AARP: The Magazine* v60 no2A p82 F/ Mr 2017

Big5-Oh color *AARP: The Magazine* v30 no6A p76 O/N 2017

Big 5-Oh color *AARP: The Magazine* v60 no5A p72 Ag/S 2017

Cindy Crawford color *AARP: The Magazine* v59 no2A p84 F/Mr 2016

David Hasselhot? color *AARP: The Magazine* v60 no4A p12 Je/ Jl 2017

David Schwimmer color *AARP: The Magazine* v59 no6A p80 O/N 2016

Endless Recess color *AARP: The Magazine* v60 no5A p16 Ag/S 2017

Halle Berry color *AARP: The Magazine* v59 no5A p80 Ag/S 2016

Heartland GETAWAYS color *AARP: The Magazine* v30 no6A p44 O/N 2017

Janet Jackson color *AARP: The Magazine* v59 no3A p92 Ap/My 2016

Julianna Margulies color *AARP: The Magazine* v59 no4A p76 Je/ Jl 2016

Kiefer Sutherland color *AARP: The Magazine* v60 no1A p64 D 2016/Ja 2017

Making Memories color *AARP: The Magazine* v59 no3A p75 Ap/ My 2016

Nicole Kidman color *AARP: The Magazine* v60 no4A p68 Je/Jl 2017

A Parks Bucket List: We'll Visit All 59! color *AARP: The Magazine* v59 no3A p84 Ap/My 2016

Patrick Dempsey color *AARP: The Magazine* v59 no1A p64 D 2015/Ja 2016

Supremely Retro color *AARP: The Magazine* v59 no5A p69 Ag/S 2016

Surviving the '80s color *AARP: The Magazine* v59 no5A p47 Ag/S 2016

Tim McGraw color *AARP: The Magazine* v60 no3A p74 Ap/My 2017

IASEVOLI, BRENDA

Video Links Professors to Far-Flung Student Teachers *Education Digest* v82 no9 p14 My 2017

Iavarone, Anthony T.

Redox-based reagents for chemoselective methionine bioconjugation bibl diag graph *Science* v355 no6325 p597 F 10 2017

Ibarguen, Ed

GAME ON! color *Golf Magazine* v59 no2 p57 F 2017

TEE SHEET color *Golf Magazine* v59 no1 p47 Ja 2017

Ibarra, Herminia

5 Misconceptions About Networking *Harvard Business Review Digital Articles* p2 Ap 18 2016

By Being Authentic, You May Just Be Conforming *Harvard Business Review Digital Articles* p2 Ja 19 2015

How to Capture Value from Collaboration, Especially If You're Skeptical About It *Harvard Business Review Digital Articles* p2 My 2 2017

How to Revive a Tired Network *Harvard Business Review Digital Articles* p2 F 3 2015

The Most Productive Way to Develop as a Leader *Harvard Business Review Digital Articles* p2 Mr 27 2015

Why Companies Are So Bad at Treating Employees Like People *Harvard Business Review Digital Articles* p2 O 29 2015

You're Never Too Experienced to Fake It Till You Learn It *Harvard Business Review Digital Articles* p2 Ja 8 2015

IBARRA, SONIA

Incorporating Sociocultural Phenomena into Ecosystem-Service Valuation: The Importance of Critical Pluralism *BioScience* v67 no3 p233 Mr 2017

Ibbotson, Paul

LANGUAGE IN A NEW KEY cartoon *Scientific American* v315 no5 p70 N 2016

IBER, PATRICK

Cold War World bw color il *New Republic* v248 no11 p60 N 2017

Literary Agents color il *New Republic* v248 no1/2 p68 Ja/F 2017

SOCIALISM'S RETURN bw color *Nation* v304 no8 p27 Mr 13 2017

Ibeyi (Performer)

Soul Sisters C. NNADI color *Vogue* v207 no10 p226 O 2017

Ibis Bikes Inc.

IBIS RIPLEY LS J. Weber color *Bike Magazine* v23 no9 p92 D 2016

Ibisch, Pierre L.

A global map of roadless areas and their conservation status bibl color graph map *Science* v354 no6318 p1423 D 16 2016

Global roadless areas: Consider terrain color *Science* v355 no6332 p1381 Mr 31 2017

Ibiza Island (Spain)

TREASURE ISLAND color *Vanity Fair* v59 no7 p49 Summ 2017

IBM Research (Company)

Building a New Brain-Inspired Supercompu *Science & Technology Review* p2 S 2016

IBM ThinkPad (Computer)—Evaluation

Lenovo ThinkPad X1 Yoga: This 2-in-1's OLED screen will color your computing world J. L. JACOBI color graph *PCWorld* p58 O 2016

IBM Watson Group (Company)

WATSON: NOT SO ELEMENTARY C. Leaf color *Fortune* v174 no6 p30 N 1 2016

Ibn Sa'd, Abu Abdullah Muhammad

c. 700: Medina A. A. Muhammad ibn Sa'd *Lapham's Quarterly* v10 no1 p118 Wint 2017

Ibogaine

GET CLEAN or DIE TRYING J. Nestor color diag *Scientific American* v315 no5 p62 N 2016

iBook (Computer)

iBooks Bestsellers chart color *Publishers Weekly* v263 no43 p17 O 24 2016

iBook Bestsellers chart color *Publishers Weekly* v264 no23 p14 Je 5 2017

iBooks Bestsellers C. JURIS chart color *Publishers Weekly* v263 no50 p20 D 5 2016

Ibrahim, Mareya S.

Confronting the Opioid Outbreak in Our Parks *Parks & Recreation* v52 no6 p34 Je 2017

Ibsen, Henrik, 1828-1906

1881: Norway *Lapham's Quarterly* v10 no1 p142 Wint 2017

DIAL-A-FEMINIST M. Schulman cartoon *New Yorker* v93 no14 p32 My 22 2017

Icahn, Carl C., 1936-

Carl 'I can' Z. Mider and J. A. Dlouhy bw color graph *Bloomberg Businessweek* no4515 p23 Mr 20 2017

Could a Four-Year-Old Do What Carl Icahn Does? J. Fox *Harvard Business Review Digital Articles* p2 O 27 2014

TRUMP'S FAVORITE TYCOON P. R. KEEFE cartoon *New Yorker* v93 no25 p46 Ag 28 2017

Ice

See also

Glaciers

Icebergs

Sea ice

2.7-million-year-old ice opens window on past P. Voosen color map *Science* v357 no6352 p630 Ag 18 2017

Active sites in heterogeneous ice nucleation—the example of K-rich feldspars A. Kiselev, F. Bachmann et al bibl bw diag *Science* v355 no6323 p367 Ja 27 2017

Estonia color *National Geographic* v231 no3 p6 Mr 2017

Ice S. PERKOWITZ bw color diag *Discover* v38 no6 p66 Jl/Ag 2017

INTO THE GLACIER: Delving into the Ice *Iceland Review* v55 no3 p100 My/Je 2017

LOOK TWICE ... *Reader's Digest* v189 no1127 p128 F 2017

Making a statement about parameter ranges A. Caldwell *Physics Today* v70 no8 p12 Ag 2017

Next L. KRATOCHWILL color *Popular Science* v288 no6 p24 N/D 2016

Ice calving

Giant Antarctic iceberg splits off A. YEAGER map *Science News* v192 no1 p6 Ag 5 2017

Ice caps

Icy Retreat R. F. Mandelbaum diag *Scientific American* v316 no2 p17 F 2017

Ice caps—Greenland

Quick Hits A. Marks map *Scientific American* v316 no6 p18 Je

2017

Ice caves

FROZEN WORLD *National Geographic Kids* no466 p26 D 2016/ Ja 2017

Ice cores—Arctic regions

Canada ice cores suffer meltdown color *Science* v356 no6334 p116 Ap 14 2017

Ice cream industry

See also

Ice cream parlors

TASTE: EATING. DRINKING. DINING A. Limpert, A. Spiegel et al *Washingtonian Magazine* v52 no11 p123 Ag 2017

Ice cream parlors

Get the Scoop in Seattle P. M. ESSWEIN cartoon color *Kiplinger's Personal Finance* v71 no7 p22 Jl 2017

Get the Scoop M. LANGE color *Bon Appetit* no8 p30 Ag 2017

JULIA STREET WITH POYDRAS THE PARROT bw color *New Orleans Magazine* v52 no1 p22 S 2017

My Favorite Block E. Laborde *New Orleans Magazine* v51 no6 p14 Ap 2017

This Is My Job J. Militare color *Glamour* v115 no5 p122 My 2017

THE WHOLE HILL J. SIDMAN, M. D. G. KAPLAN et al *Washingtonian Magazine* v52 no9 p162 Je 2017

Ice cream parlors—Evaluation

Paletas, Not Pops *Atlanta* v57 no2 p56 Je 2017

PRIME CUT A. WHITTLE color *Conde Nast Traveler* v52 no2 p30 F 2017

SCREAM QUEENS R. J. SMITH *Cincinnati Magazine* v50 no8 p104 My 2017

Ice cream pies

Easy as Peach Pie D. Wise color *Southern Living* v52 no6 p138 Je 2017

A PIE FROM THE SKY C. MUHLKE color *Bon Appetit* p140 S 2017

Ice cream sandwiches

Play It Cool C. SAFFITZ color *Bon Appetit* v62 no7 p29 Jl 2017

SUMMER SPECIAL color *Bon Appetit* v62 no7 p30 Jl 2017

Ice crystals

Cracking the problem of ice nucleation B. J. Murray bibl color diag *Science* v355 no6323 p346 Ja 27 2017

i catch clouds for a living K. Atherton cartoon *Popular Science* v289 no4 p86 Jl/Ag 2017

Ice fishing

Marvellous Maine S. Doyle map *Canadian Geographic* v135 no6 p16 D 2015

Ice formation & growth

VISIONS color *National Geographic* v230 no6 pc15 D 2016

Ice Guardians (Film)

BEST OF FILM J. Fuchs color *Sports Illustrated* v125 no18 p46 D 5 2016

Ice hotels

WHERE WE'VE SLEPT M. KOZIOL diag *Popular Science* p15 Ja/F 2017

Ice jams (Geology)

PREVENT ICE DAMS G. C. Grensing color *Cabin Living* p66 O 2017

Ice pops

ACCIDENTS Happen C. BOYER and J. ROCCO color *National Geographic Kids* no465 p20 N 2016

Ice sheets

exit, pursued by bear K. Pierre-Louis cartoon *Popular Science* v289 no4 p83 Jl/Ag 2017

Is ice sheet collapse in West Antarctica unstoppable? C. Hulbe color map *Science* v356 no6341 p910 Je 1 2017

The smoking gun of the ice ages D. A. Hodell bibl diag *Science* v354 no6317 p1235 D 9 2016

Ice sheets—Research

A SONG OF ICE E. KOLBERT cartoon color map *New Yorker* v92 no34 p50 O 24 2016

Ice sheets—Thawing

Ice, Wind & Fury M. Oltmanns color *Oceanus* v51 no2 p24 Wint 2016

MELTDOWN E. Kintisch color diag graph *Science* v355 no6327 p788 F 24 2017

Scientists Find Trigger That Cracks lakes L. Stevens color *Oceanus* v51 no2 p20 Wint 2016

Ice shelves—Antarctica
See also
Larsen Ice Shelf (Antarctica)
ICEFALL E. MASTROIANNI color *Discover* v38 no10 p9 D 2017
MELTDOWN [Cover story] E. BETZ color diag map *Discover* v38 no5 p36 Je 2017
Studies in Solitude B. Lang *Discover* v38 no5 p6 Je 2017

Ice storms
Storm kings K. Gray color *Popular Science* v289 no4 p60 Jl/Ag 2017

Ice—Antarctic Ocean
THE CRISIS ON THE ICE D. FOX bw color map *National Geographic* v232 no1 p30 Jl 2017

Icebergs
Ice invasion M. HEMMADI color *Maclean's* v130 no7 p18 Ag 2017

Icebreakers (Ships)—Design & construction
Polar Ice Squad J. Hsu color *Scientific American* v316 no6 p10 Je 2017

Ice cream, ices, etc.
See also
Gelato
Ice cream pies
The Best Tech. EveryDay color *Popular Science* v288 no6 p8 N/D 2016
Bon Appetit Best New Restaurants 2017 [Cover story] A. KNOWLTON and J. KRAMER color *Bon Appetit* p99 S 2017
Cold, Creamy GOODNESS E. HARE color *Cabin Living* p58 Ag 2017
Dive In! color *Amazing Wellness* v9 no4 p80 Summ 2017
Don't Have a Cow K. O'Reilly *Sierra* v102 no5 p8 St/O 2017
Fire Cones *Idaho Magazine* v16 no9 p57 Je 2017
Get the Scoop M. LANGE color *Bon Appetit* no8 p30 Ag 2017
HOW TO MAKE ICE CREAM J. BRITTON BAUER, J. Lynch et al bw color diag *Popular Mechanics* p80 S 2017
ICE CREAM DREAM C. K. Jackson color *Essence* v48 no2 p105 Je 2017
ICE DREAMS [Cover story] J. R. FULLER color *Chicago* v66 no6 p45 Je 2017
Ice, Ice (Pops), Baby! R. Kinane color *Entertainment Weekly* no1472 p18 Je 30 2017
IT'S NATIONAL ICE CREAM DAY S. LIAO color *Better Homes & Gardens* v95 no7 p158 Jl 2017
NEWSY SCOOP color *Women's Health* v14 no4 p29 My 2017
Nice Cream St. Louis A. Burger color *Missouri Life* v44 no3 p16 My 2017
Peach Ice Cream C. BOND *Texas Monthly* v45 no6 p28 Je 2017
Play It Cool C. SAFFITZ color *Bon Appetit* v62 no7 p29 Jl 2017
POP ART C. BOYD and D. CENTONI color *Better Homes & Gardens* v95 no7 p108 Jl 2017
The Scoop on Ice Cream's Health-Food Origins O. B. Waxman *Time* v190 no8 p21 Ag 28 2017
SCREAM QUEENS R. J. SMITH *Cincinnati Magazine* v50 no8 p104 My 2017
SUMMER FAVORITES S. Dry color *Louisiana Life* v37 no6 p54 Jl/Ag 2017
TASTE: EATING. DRINKING. DINING A. Limpert, A. Spiegel et al *Washingtonian Magazine* v52 no11 p123 Ag 2017
there's NO CREAM like snow CREAM color *Cabin Living* p62 D 2016
Top This Ice Cream K. O'SHEA-EVANS and C. SWANSON color *House Beautiful* v159 no7 p74 S 2017

Ice cream, ices, etc.—Equipment & supplies
ICE CREAM MAKERS M. XERAKIA color *Better Homes & Gardens* v95 no7 p154 Jl 2017

Ice cream, ices, etc.—Evaluation
NO SCOOP NECESSARY C. Battan color *Bloomberg Businessweek* no4498 p90 N 7 2016
SCOOPED! M. GLISAN color *Better Homes & Gardens* v95 no5 p134 My 2017

Ice Cube, 1969-
THE FIFTH QUARTER D. Bry color *Esquire* p24 Je/Jl 2017
GOINGS ON ABOUT TOWN color *New Yorker* v93 no27 p7 S 11 2017

Iced coffee

Perk Up Your Iced Coffee K. O'SHEA-EVANS and LULU color *House Beautiful* v159 no5 p64 Je 2017

Iced tea
Ask Men's Health color *Men's Health* v32 no2 p14 Mr 2017
My Tea Does What?! J. GREEN *Reader's Digest* v188 no1125 p140 N 2016
SUMMER "TEA-TOX" J. Bowden color *Amazing Wellness* v9 no4 p47 Summ 2017
TEA TIME L. REGE color *Martha Stewart Living* p78 Jl/Ag 2017

Ice—Equipment & supplies—Evaluation
MIRACLE IN ICE J. Brown color *Popular Science* v289 no2 p28 Mr/Ap 2017

Iceland
THE BEST OF THE WEST color *Iceland Review* v54 no5 p106 S-O 2016
CELEBRATING SOCCER SUCCESS Z. Robert color *Iceland Review* v54 no5 p32 S-O 2016
GOING PLACES? Z. Robert color *Iceland Review* v54 no5 p76 S-O 2016
NORDIC NEIGHBORS UNITE color *Iceland Review* v54 no5 p98 S-O 2016
NORTHERN SOUL color *Iceland Review* v54 no5 p100 S-O 2016
OFF THE LAND E. S. ARNARSDÓTTIR color *Iceland Review* v54 no5 p92 S-O 2016
OUT OF THE WOMB AND INTO THE POOL R. Mercer color *Iceland Review* v54 no5 p68 S-O 2016
SCHOOL'S OUT P. STEFÁNSSON *Iceland Review* v55 no3 p76 My/Je 2017

Iceland. Althingi—Elections
Timeline of Events *Iceland Review* v55 no1 p74 Ja/F 2017

Icelandair ehf
10-HOUR LAYOVER? LUCKY YOU A. Vandermey color *Fortune* v174 no6 p70 N 1 2016

Iceland—Antiquities
THE BLACKENER'S CAVE S. S. PATEL color *Archaeology* v70 no3 p36 My/Je 2017

Iceland—Climate
From the Editor M. Benner Smidt *Weatherwise* v70 no1 p4 Ja/F 2017
The Vedur of Iceland W. Lyons *Weatherwise* v70 no1 p20 Ja/F 2017

Iceland—Description & travel
10-HOUR LAYOVER? LUCKY YOU A. Vandermey color *Fortune* v174 no6 p70 N 1 2016
ADVENTURES OF A LIFETIME color *Iceland Review* v54 no5 p109 S-O 2016
BACK TO BASICS ICELAND AS IT'S MEANT TO BE SEEN T. SKINNER color map *Conde Nast Traveler* v52 no10 p40 N 2017
BRINGING VIKING-ERA ICELAND TO LIFE *Iceland Review* v54 no6 p104 N/D 2016
CHARMING DALIR *Iceland Review* v54 no6 p106 N/D 2016
A DIFFERENT EXPERIENCE WELCOME TO AKRANES *Iceland Review* v54 no6 p102 N/D 2016
ENTER THE UNDERWORLD *Iceland Review* v54 no6 p106 N/D 2016
EXPERIENCE THE PEAK OF MAGNIFICENCE *Iceland Review* v55 no3 p105 My/Je 2017
From the Editor P. Stefánsson *Iceland Review* v54 no6 p4 N/D 2016
GREEN LAND P. STEFÁNSSON *Iceland Review* v55 no3 p24 My/Je 2017
HISTORIC GROUNDS *Iceland Review* v54 no6 p104 N/D 2016
ICELAND FROM OLD TO NEW: NEW THINGS ARE AFOOT AT THE CULTURE HOUSE *Iceland Review* v55 no3 p119 My/Je 2017
My Place color *Vanity Fair* v59 no7 p46 Summ 2017
OUT WEST *Iceland Review* v54 no6 p98 N/D 2016
SAGALAND *Iceland Review* v54 no6 p100 N/D 2016
SERENITY AND COMFORT *Iceland Review* v54 no6 p105 N/D 2016
TINT AND TONE P. STEFÁNSSON color *Iceland Review* v54 no5 p86 S-O 2016
TRAVEL BACK IN TIME *Iceland Review* v54 no6 p103 N/D 2016
VISIONS OF VIÐEY E. S. ARNARSDÓTTIR *Iceland Review*

v54 no6 p45 N/D 2016

YOUR GUIDE TO THE BEST OUTDOOR ADVENTURES IN ICELAND *Iceland Review* v55 no3 p103 My/Je 2017

Your Own Lunar Landing: ICELAND, BUGGY STYLE *Iceland Review* v55 no3 p105 My/Je 2017

Iceland—Economic conditions

THE NEXT GENERATION: Join us as we meet a handful of Iceland's most promising young people P. STEFÁNSSON *Iceland Review* v55 no4 p72 Jl/Ag 2017

Iceland—Environmental conditions

GO EAST: From Langanes peninsula in the north to Höfn in the south, East Iceland has some of the best Iceland has to offer P. STEFÁNSSON *Iceland Review* v55 no4 p100 Jl/Ag 2017

LAST PAGE P. STEFÁNSSON *Iceland Review* v55 no4 p111 Jl/Ag 2017

Icelanders

AUTHENTIC ICELANDIC KNITWEAR color *Iceland Review* v54 no5 p102 S-O 2016

Icelandic art

THE BIG CHEESE M. ALLAN *Iceland Review* v55 no4 p54 Jl/Ag 2017

Icelandic literature

OF LOVE AND MURDER E. S. ARNARSDÓTTIR *Iceland Review* v54 no5 p42 S-O 2016

Iceland—News briefs

News Roundup E. S. ARNARSDÓTTIR color *Iceland Review* v54 no5 p18 S-O 2016

News Roundup V. HAFSTAD *Iceland Review* v55 no4 p8 Jl/Ag 2017

Iceland—Politics & government

COALITION CRISIS J. GOTTLIEB *Iceland Review* v55 no1 p72 Ja/F 2017

From the Editor P. Stefánsson *Iceland Review* v55 no1 p4 Ja/F 2017

ON PIRATE ISLAND IN THE NORTH ATLANTIC P. HOCK-ENOS bw color *Nation* v303 no19 p22 N 7 2016

PUTTING A PRICE ON NATURE H. Lárusson *Iceland Review* v54 no6 p58 N/D 2016

Iceland—Politics & government—21st century

A STRANGE CALM - EXIT THE RABBLE-ROUSERS H. Lárusson color *Iceland Review* v54 no5 p58 S-O 2016

Ichiro Fukumori

Kamifusen, the self-inflating Japanese paper balloon *Physics Today* v70 no1 p78 Ja 2017

Ichiro Misumi

MAVS-dependent host species range and pathogenicity of human hepatitis A virus bibl graph *Science* v353 no6307 p1541 S 30 2016

Ichneumon

Circle of Life color *National Wildlife (World Edition)* v55 no4 p50 Je/Jl 2017

Icing (Company)

Oh, and Tiaras Too?! J. Harman color *Glamour* no8 p36 Ag 2017

Icings (Confectionery)

IT PAYS TO INCREASE YOUR Word Power E. COX and H. RATHVON *Reader's Digest* v190 no1135 p133 N 2017

Let Them Eat Cake S. LODGE color *Weekly Standard* v22 no39 p34 Je 19 2017

NO FLOUR, NO PROBLEM G. LOFTS color *Martha Stewart Living* p88 Ap 2017

THE WORKBOOK color *Martha Stewart Living* p104 My 2017

Icon Aircraft Inc.

Trailer Queen A. Robinson color *Car & Driver* v62 no6 p102 D 2016

Icon painting

Iconography classes draw non-Orthodox in search of spiritual images A. M. Banks color *Christian Century* v134 no4 p16 F 15 2017

ID Software Inc.

9 — DOOM A. Morales color *Entertainment Weekly* no1444/1445 p123 D 16 2016

Ida y Vuelta (Music)

MAUREEN CHOI J. Hale color *Downbeat* v84 no9 p25 S 2017

Idaho

THE BEST PLAYHOUSE K. Campbell Winters *Idaho Magazine* v17 no1 p49 Ja 2017

Christmas at Bear P. WILSON *Idaho Magazine* v16 no3 p40 D 2016

Don't Call Him Goofy D. AGUIRRE *Idaho Magazine* v16 no2 p43 N 2016

Gratitude S. CARR *Idaho Magazine* v16 no3 p54 D 2016

Hemingway's Fishing Rod J. BEYL *Idaho Magazine* v16 no3 p24 D 2016

HIDDEN SPRINGS J. KARAMALES *Idaho Magazine* v17 no1 p32 Ja 2017

Marvin's Ashes K. STEINBERG *Idaho Magazine* v16 no3 p28 D 2016

No Janitor, No Lunch K. WRIGHT *Idaho Magazine* v16 no3 p12 D 2016

The Perfect Tree J. A. ABEL *Idaho Magazine* v16 no3 p20 D 2016

STACE J. DAVIDSON color *Idaho Magazine* v16 no1 p18 O 2016

A TOWN RECYCLED AND ITS MASTERFUL MOVER K. CAMPBELL WIDNER *Idaho Magazine* v17 no1 p42 Ja 2017

Trial by Fire M. BLACKBIRD color *Idaho Magazine* v16 no1 p14 O 2016

Idaho National Laboratory

A Train for a Plane T. WAITE *Idaho Magazine* v16 no5 p42 F 2017

Idaho State University

ON THE CUSP OF CHANGE E. BARKER *Idaho Magazine* v16 no9 p32 Je 2017

Idaho—Description & travel

ELK RIVER K. WRIGHT color *Idaho Magazine* v16 no1 p32 O 2016

Get Low I. KORIC map *Backpacker* p26 Ag 2017

Giant Red D. PENCE color *Idaho Magazine* v16 no1 p6 O 2016

Memorial Hike B. MORGAN color *Idaho Magazine* v16 no1 p24 O 2016

NOT REALLY LOOKING TO GROW J. D. EDLEFSEN *Idaho Magazine* v16 no2 p33 N 2016

Idaho—History

Ghost on the Plain: The Rugged Serenity of Gilmore S. POWELL *Idaho Magazine* v16 no12 p44 S 2017

RIVERSIDE: WEST OF THE WILD SNAKE G. MATHIAS *Idaho Magazine* v16 no12 p32 S 2017

Ide, Joe

Righteous: An IQ Novel color *Publishers Weekly* v264 no33 p46 Ag 14 2017

IDE, ROGER

CHRISTMAS in Boston color *Yankee* v80 no6 p108 N/D 2016

Ide, Satoshi

Recurring and triggered slow-slip events near the trench at the Nankai Trough subduction megathrust diag graph *Science* v356 no6343 p1157 Je 16 2017

Idea (Philosophy)

See also

Memes

In defense of Crazy Ideas D. Stevenson *Physics Today* v70 no4 p10 Ap 2017

Idea in Everything, An (Music)

Unplugged B. MEYER color *Downbeat* v84 no6 p72 Je 2017

Idealism

THE MOMENT CYNICISM JUST BURNED AWAY E. SOLO-MON color *Maclean's* v129 no44 p10 N 7 2016

Idemitsu Kosan Co. Ltd.

Why Japan's Idemitsu Isn't Feeling Blue P. Alpeyev, T. Taniguchi et al color *Bloomberg Businessweek* no4520 p34 My 1 2017

Identification

See also

Biometric identification

Mistaken identity

Personal identification numbers

Identification (Religion)

See also

Jewish identity

Breaking Faith P. BEINART color *Atlantic* v319 no3 p15 Ap 2017

By number, Christians overrepresented in Congress D. Iaconangelo and F. Kiefer color *Christian Century* v134 no3 p12 F 2017

Identity as a calling C. Zaleski *Christian Century* v133 no24 p35 N 23 2016

LIVING BY The Word *Christian Century* v134 no2 p20 Ja 18

2017

Identification cards—Forgeries

Piecing Together A Credit Fraud J. Surane color *Bloomberg Businessweek* no4538 p26 S 18 2017

Identity (Philosophical concept)

Who gets to be Indigenous? J. Boyden bw color *Maclean's* v130 no8 p36 S 2017

Identity (Psychology)

See also

Coming out (Sexual orientation)

Gender identity

Chasing beauty, finding grace M. Fitzgerald color *Christian Century* v134 no3 p27 F 2017

Identity in ink E. Sanna bw il *U.S. Catholic* v81 no12 p26 D 2016

Identity search P. W. Marty *Christian Century* v134 no2 p3 Ja 18 2017

Make Peace with Your Unlived Life M. F. R. K. de Vries *Harvard Business Review Digital Articles* p2 D 21 2016

To Foster Innovation, Connect Coworkers Who Share Aspirations C. de Anca and S. Aragón *Harvard Business Review Digital Articles* p2 Jl 14 2016

Identity crises (Psychology)

The Democrats' Quandary: Can they find a winning formula and return to power? A. Ehrenhalt *Governing* v30 no12 p14 S 2017

Identity politics

Identity Politician J. V. LAST color *Weekly Standard* v22 no18 p11 Ja 16 2017

"Identity Politics" Takes a Hit S. MUWAKKIL *In These Times* v41 no1 p16 Ja 2017

It's the Culture, Stupid L. DRUTMAN il *New Republic* v248 no11 p14 N 2017

Killing Aida J. NORDLINGER color *National Review* v68 no21 p22 N 21 2016

Killing the Messenger: Mark Lilla's 'End of Identity Liberalism' and its Critics G. Brahm *Society* v54 no4 p326 Ag 2017

Mistaken Names T. John color *Time* v188 no20 p10 N 14 2016

The Most Astonishing Easter Miracle [Cover story] M. Galli bw *Christianity Today* p28 Ap 2017

This Woman's Place L. Meriwether img *New York* v49 no24 p32 N 28 2016

Identity theft

Are Your Bank Accounts at Risk? L. GERSTNER chart *Kiplinger's Personal Finance* v71 no12 p42 D 2017

Cartoons *New York Times Upfront* v149 no7 p24 Ja 9 2017

Identity Theft A. Hess *New York Times Magazine* p11 Ap 2 2017

'Tis the Season for ID Theft G. CARDONE *USA Today Magazine* v145 no2860 p37 Ja 2017

TRUST ME: A nurse posing as a qualified A&E doctor is putting patients at risk *People Management* p62 S 2017

Identity theft—Prevention

FIGHTING THE INTERNET'S DARK SIDE L. GERSTNER *Kiplinger's Personal Finance* v71 no11 p12 N 2017

IDEO LLC

How IDEO Designers Persuade Companies to Accept Change A. Powell *Harvard Business Review Digital Articles* p2 My 17 2016

IDEO's Employee Engagement Formula D. Bray *Harvard Business Review Digital Articles* p2 D 18 2015

Ideology

See also

Organizational ideology

Political correctness

All the Way With J.F.K M. Malone *America* v216 no12 p3 My 29 2017

The Essence of Ed Garvey J. HIGHTOWER cartoon *Progressive* v81 no4 p70 Ap/My 2017

A Lack of Ideas Has Consequences J. W. CEASER *Weekly Standard* v23 no3 p14 S 25 2017

Portrait of the Author as a Historian A. Lee *History Today* v66 no11 p54 N 2016

Preamble H. E. Blake color *Orion Magazine* v35 no6 p1 N/D 2016

The Walking Dead P. R. Gregory *Hoover Digest: Research & Opinion on Public Policy* no4 p66 Fall 2016

Ideology in literature

CRACKING UP J. Fielden color *Esquire* p13 Je/Jl 2017

Ideology—Religious aspects

Fragmentation Of the Soul R. MOORE color *National Review* v68 no22 p45 D 5 2016

Ideology—Social aspects

The Ideological Challenge at the Core of Donald Trump's Radical Presidency J. Klein color *Time* v189 no4 p23 F 6 2017

Idioms

Six Idiotic Idioms—and What's Wrong with Them B. SPECKTOR color *Reader's Digest* v189 no1130 p134 My 2017

Idiopathic pulmonary fibrosis

BREATHING NEW LIFE INTO IPF TREATMENTS I. Nath *Maclean's* v129 no47 p44 N 28 2016

Iditarod Trail Sled Dog Race, Alaska

THE LOOP ANNIE, D. CRAIG chart color *Runner's World* v52 no3 p12 Ap 2017

Idomeneo (Theatrical production)

Idomeneo *Opera News* v81 no9 p60 Mr 2017

Idov, Michael

Russia: Life After Trust img *New York* p22 Ja 23 2017

THE TRUMP BUMP cartoon *Esquire* v167 no1 p54 F 2017

Idris, Damson

Lost Souls at the Dawn of the Crack Crisis R. SHEFFIELD color *Rolling Stone* no1293 p25 Ag 10 2017

IDUMA, EMMANUEL

AROUND NEW YORK cartoon *ARTnews* v115 no3 p134 Fall 2016

"RECENT HISTORIES" bw color *ARTnews* v116 no1 p115 Spr 2017

Idyll (Poem)

Idyll J. M. Pitas color *U.S. Catholic* v82 no2 p11 F 2017

IEEE 802.11 (Standard)

Staying Connected E. Vohr color *Sail* v48 no10 p24 O 2017

Ienatsch, Nick

BODY POSITION, AN OVERVIEW cartoon *Cycle World* v56 no3 p24 Ap 2017

CRASHING AND LEARNING color *Cycle World* v56 no7 p24 Ag 2017

FLAT-LAND PROBLEM: FREEWAY ON- AND OFF-RAMPS color *Cycle World* v55 no10 p20 N 2016

LOOK NOW. DON'T LOOK NOW color *Cycle World* v56 no1 p20 Ja/F 2017

SAFE AND SLOW THEN DANGEROUS color *Cycle World* v56 no5 p26 Je 2017

SCHOOL SMOOTH color *Cycle World* v56 no10 p20 N 2017

Ienca, Marcello

The Right to Cognitive Liberty color *Scientific American* v317 no2 p10 Ag 2017

Iess, L.

Jupiter's interior and deep atmosphere: The initial pole-to-pole passes with the Juno spacecraft [Cover story] color graph *Science* v356 no6340 p821 My 26 2017

Iezzi, Alexandra M.

Volcanic tremor and plume height hysteresis from Pavlof Volcano, Alaska bibl graph *Science* v355 no6320 p1 Ja 6 2017

If I Forget (Theatrical production)

THE THEATRE *New Yorker* v92 no48 p7 F 6 2017

If I Had My Time Again (Music)

It's Like Broadway, But for Your Ears M. M. Kircher img *New York* v50 no11 p117 My 29 2017

If Only (Theatrical production)

THE THEATRE color *New Yorker* v93 no24 p11 Ag 21 2017

IFATEYO, AJOWA NZINGA

Greenbelt Earns Its Cooperative Stripes *In These Times* v41 no8 p8 Ag 2017

Ifill, Gwen, 1955-2016

The Bullseye M. Snetiker color *Entertainment Weekly* no1441 p64 N 25 2016

Gwen Ifill M. Duffy color *Time* v188 no22-23 p13 N/D 2016

GWEN THE GREAT color *Essence* v47 no9 p44 Ja 2017

Ifill, Gwen, 1955-2016—Interviews

10 THINGS WE'RE TALKING ABOUT T. Lewis and T. A. Christian color *Essence* v47 no7 p57 N 2016

iFly Holdings LLC

We Have Lift Off! C. Winter color diag *Bloomberg Businessweek* no4520 p67 My 1 2017

iFORCE Nutrition (Company)

GET TO KNOW: IFORCE NUTRITION J. SCHILDHOUSE

color *Muscle & Performance* v8 no12 p34 D 2016

Ig Nobel prizes

Ig Nobels honor goat man, mirror scratching color *Science* v353 no6307 p1475 S 30 2016

Igarashi, Y.

Structural basis of the redox switches in the NAD+-reducing soluble [NiFe]-hydrogenase diag *Science* v357 no6354 p928 S 1 2017

Iger, Bradley

RETURN OF THE T/A color *Hot Rod* v70 no8 p48 Ag 2017

Iglehart, Sasha

Dior and Me bw color *Glamour* no8 p66 Ag 2017

Igloolik (Nunavut)

ᐱᐱᕐᖓᑦ N. WALKER color map *Canadian Geographic* v137 no2 p52 Mr/Ap 2017

Ignatieff, Michael

Think Locally, Act Locally: Michael Ignatieff questions whether universalist values can survive the disruptive forces of globalization J. TRAUB *New York Times Book Review* p19 O 15 2017

Which Way Are We Going? color *New York Review of Books* v64 no6 p4 Ap 6 2017

Ignatius, Adi

"Above All, Acknowledge the Pain" color *Harvard Business Review* v95 no3 p142 My/Je 2017

Are We Giving Shareholders Too Much Power? *Harvard Business Review* v95 no3 p8 My/Je 2017

Dealing with Unexpected Bias color *Harvard Business Review* v94 no12 p12 D 2016

"DON'T TRY TO PROTECT THE PAST": A CONVERSATION WITH IBM CEO GINNI ROMETTY color graph img *Harvard Business Review* v95 no4 p126 Jl/Ag 2017

The Future Economy Project *Harvard Business Review Digital Articles* p2 2017

THE GREAT TRANSFORMER bw img *Harvard Business Review* v95 no5 p10 S/O 2017

THE INSULATED LEADER bw img *Harvard Business Review* v95 no2 p12 Mr/Ap 2017

Larry Summers: Business Leaders Should Stand Up to President Trump bw *Harvard Business Review Digital Articles* p2 F 1 2017

A NEW LOOK FOR A NEW ERA img *Harvard Business Review* v95 no1 p10 Ja/F 2017

THE TRUTH ABOUT GLOBALIZATION bw img *Harvard Business Review* v95 no4 p10 Jl/Ag 2017

AN UNEASY CODEPENDENCE color il *Harvard Business Review* v95 no2 p156 Mr/Ap 2017

"WE NEED PEOPLE TO LEAN INTO THE FUTURE" color img *Harvard Business Review* v95 no2 p94 Mr/Ap 2017

What CEOs Really Worry About [Cover story] bw color img *Harvard Business Review* v94 no11 p52 N 2016

Where Are the Women? *Harvard Business Review* v94 no11 p12 N 2016

Ignatius, David

Le Carré Goes Back Into the Cold color *Atlantic* v320 no2 p42 S 2017

Ignatius, of Loyola, Saint, 1491-1556

OF MANY THINGS M. MALONE *America* v215 no14 p2 N 7 2016

Ignell, Rickard

A key malaria metabolite modulates vector blood seeking, feeding, and susceptibility to infection bibl chart diag *Science* v355 no6329 p1076 Mr 10 2017

Igneous Skis (Company)

TOOLS THEY USE color *Popular Mechanics* p96 F 2017

Igneri, Ariana

ALL THE FEELS color *Bloomberg Businessweek* no4515 p64 Mr 20 2017

NO MEN ALLOWED color *Bloomberg Businessweek* no4506 p66 Ja 9 2017

Ignorance (Theory of knowledge)

How America Lost Faith in Expertise T. Nichols *Foreign Affairs* v96 no2 p60 Mr/Ap 2017

Ignotofsky, Rachel

Rachel Ignotofsky: Sharing Her Passion for Science and History E. Kantor color *Publishers Weekly* v264 no11 p24 Mr 13 2017

Iguchi, S.

Crystallization and vitrification of electrons in a glass-forming charge liquid bw *Science* v357 no6358 p1381 S 29 2017

Ihara, Saikaku, 1642-1693

DIRTY MONEY Ihara Saikaku *Lapham's Quarterly* v10 no3 p63 Summ 2017

Ihara, Yusuke

Predicting human olfactory perception from chemical features of odor molecules bibl diag graph *Science* v355 no6327 p820 F 24 2017

iHeartMedia Inc.

Rock of Aged J. Gilbert *Cincinnati Magazine* v50 no12 p40 S 2017

IHRIG, MARTIN

HOW TO GET ECOSYSTEM BUY-IN chart img *Harvard Business Review* v95 no2 p102 Mr/Ap 2017

Ihrig, Stefan

Measured Terror *History Today* v67 no2 p38 F 2017

Ijjas, Anna

POP goes the universe color graph *Scientific American* v316 no2 p32 F 2017

IKEA (Company)

CUTTING EDGE D. DICKINSON and J. A. BAGGETT color *Better Homes & Gardens* v95 no9 p84 S 2017

Ikeda, Y.

Structural basis of the redox switches in the NAD+-reducing soluble [NiFe]-hydrogenase diag *Science* v357 no6354 p928 S 1 2017

Ikegami, Masako

Seeking a path toward missile nonproliferation bibl *Bulletin of the Atomic Scientists* v72 no6 p365 N 2016

Ikemoto, Y.

Crystallization and vitrification of electrons in a glass-forming charge liquid bw *Science* v357 no6358 p1381 S 29 2017

Ikenberry, G. John

Cheap Threats: Why the United States Struggles to Coerce Weak States *Foreign Affairs* v96 no1 p156 Ja/F 2017

The Chessboard and the Web: Strategies of Connection in a Networked World *Foreign Affairs* v96 no3 p154 My/Je 2017

The Despot's Accomplice: How the West Is Aiding and Abetting the Decline of Democracy *Foreign Affairs* v96 no2 p168 Mr/Ap 2017

Fighting for Credibility: U.S. Reputation and International Politics *Foreign Affairs* v96 no6 p152 N/D 2017

Forged Through Fire: War, Peace, and the Democratic Bargain *Foreign Affairs* v96 no2 p167 Mr/Ap 2017

In the Hegemon's Shadow: Leading States and the Rise of Regional Powers *Foreign Affairs* v95 no6 p173 N/D 2016

Once Within Borders: Territories of Power, Wealth, and Belonging Since 1500 *Foreign Affairs* v96 no1 p157 Ja/F 2017

Peacemaking From Above, Peace From Below: Ending Conflict Between Regional Rivals *Foreign Affairs* v95 no6 p172 N/D 2016

The Plot Against American Foreign Policy color *Foreign Affairs* v96 no3 p2 My/Je 2017

Post-Western World: How Emerging Powers Are Remaking Global Order *Foreign Affairs* v96 no2 p168 Mr/Ap 2017

Power Shift: On the New Global Order *Foreign Affairs* v95 no6 p173 N/D 2016

Power Without Victory: Woodrow Wilson and the American Internationalist Experiment *Foreign Affairs* v96 no6 p151 N/D 2017

A Question of Order: India, Turkey, and the Return of Strongmen *Foreign Affairs* v96 no3 p155 My/Je 2017

Realpolitik: A History *Foreign Affairs* v96 no3 p155 My/Je 2017

Reflections on Progress: Essays on the Global Political Economy *Foreign Affairs* v96 no2 p167 Mr/Ap 2017

Reordering the World: Essays on Liberalism and Empire *Foreign Affairs* v95 no6 p172 N/D 2016

A World in Disarray: American Foreign Policy and the Crisis of the Old Order *Foreign Affairs* v96 no1 p156 Ja/F 2017

The World Reimagined: Americans and Human Rights in the Twentieth Century *Foreign Affairs* v96 no6 p151 N/D 2017

Ikhwan as-Safa'

c. 950: Basra *Lapham's Quarterly* v10 no1 p39 Wint 2017

Ikizler, Mine

Reovirus infection triggers inflammatory responses to dietary antigens and development of celiac disease color diag *Science* v356

no6333 p44 Ap 7 2017

Ikon.5 Architects (Company)

Training Recreation Education Center *Architectural Record* v205 no4 p184 Ap 2017

Ikuko Koyama-Honda

The ATG conjugation systems are important for degradation of the inner autophagosomal membrane bibl graph *Science* v354 no6315 p1036 N 25 2016

Il Barbiere di Siviglia (Theatrical production)

CLASSICAL MUSIC *New Yorker* v92 no48 p5 F 6 2017

Il Barbiere di Siviglia G. ROSSINI and C. STERBINI *Opera News* v81 no7 p57 Ja 2017

Iles, Greg

The Big Trial J. L. BREEN *Weekly Standard* v22 no41 p33 Jl 3 2017

Iliad of Homer

The Art of Wrath H. Pelliccia color *New York Review of Books* v64 no15 p42 O 12 2017

An Iliad Odyssey J. QUEENAN color *Weekly Standard* v22 no17 p35 Ja 2 2017

TOP 5 Books More Christian High Schoolers Should Be Encouraged to Read M. FARRELLY color *Christianity Today* v61 no4 p65 My 2017

Iliffe, Rob

The enlightened empiricist M. Stanley color *Science* v356 no6345 p1341 Je 30 2017

Ilitch, Mike, 1929-2017

Hail and Farewell color *Forbes* v199 no3 p36 Mr 28 2017

I'll Sing the Blues for You (Music)

Trouble Free Hadley color *Downbeat* v84 no4 p59 Ap 2017

Illanes, Rodolfo

A DEATH IN THE ANDES M. Reel color *Bloomberg Businessweek* no4513 p62 Mr 6 2017

Illegal imports

The General and the Refugee E. REIDY color *New Republic* v248 no4 p38 Ap 2017

Illegal logging

Profiles in Courage J. Mark, H. Jensen et al *Sierra* v102 no4 p4 Jl/Ag 2017

Illegitimacy

A New Deal for Europe Y. VAROUFAKIS and J. K. GALBRAITH color *Nation* v305 no10 p22 O 23 2017

Illes, Les

Conquering Cajon in HO scale color diag *Model Railroader* v84 no1 p46 Ja 2017

ILLICA, LUIGI

La Bohème *Opera News* v81 no7 p55 Ja 2017

Illinois

Healthy Food Fun V. TWEED color *Better Nutrition* v79 no6 p8 Je 2017

Illinois State University

POWER TOUR'S Sun-Powered Hot Rod P. Thomas color *Hot Rod* v70 no12 p66 D 2017

Illinois State University—Sports

HOT | NOT T. Keith color *Sports Illustrated* v126 no5 p18 F 13 2017

Illinois—Description & travel

WILMETTE J. REESE color map *Chicago* v65 no11 p29 N 2016

Illinois—Politics & government—21st century

Budget Fight Bruises the Needy J. VALENTE *America* v215 no10 p12 O 10 2016

Illinois Budget Woes Head From Bad to Junk E. Campbell and J. McCormick graph map *Bloomberg Businessweek* no4529 p36 Jl 3 2017

Illiterate persons

RESEARCH color *Science* v356 no6340 p816 My 26 2017

ills, Joe B

Out & About color *Yankee* p80 Mr 2017

Illuminations (Short story)

Illuminations A. McDermott *Commonweal* v144 no12 p26 Jl 7 2017

Illustrated children's books—Charts, diagrams, etc.

CHILDREN'S BESTSELLERS C. JURIS chart *Publishers Weekly* v264 no7 p14 F 13 2017

CHILDREN'S BESTSELLERS SEPT. 26-OCT. 2, 2016 *Publishers Weekly* v263 no41 p17 O 10 2016

Illustration (Art)—Exhibitions

PAINTER AND POET *Atlanta* v56 no12 p34 Ap 2017

Illustrators

See also

Women illustrators

Adventures in Illustrating *South Dakota Magazine* p8 S/O 2017 Supplement

If We Ran the World (Or at Least the Country): A children's author's love letter to her colleagues' character, knowledge, and empathy D. UNDERWOOD *Publishers Weekly* v264 no29 p224 Jl 17 2017

The McGinnis Look M. CALLAHAN cartoon color *Vanity Fair* v59 no5 p134 Ap 2017

The One *Texas Monthly* v44 no11 p12 N 2016

STRESS TEST color *Wired* v25 no9 p8 S 2017

Illustrators—Exhibitions

LIFE AFTER ELOISE L. JACOBS color *Vanity Fair* v59 no5 p152 Ap 2017

Illy, Andrea—Interviews

Q&A I. Boudway color *Bloomberg Businessweek* no4496 p72 O 24 2016

Illycaffè SpA

Q&A I. Boudway color *Bloomberg Businessweek* no4496 p72 O 24 2016

Ilo, Stan Chu

Coming of age color *U.S. Catholic* v82 no9 p21 S 2017

I am, through you: God is in the ties that bind all of creation together, says this African priest S. C. Ilo color *U.S. Catholic* v82 no9 p18 S 2017

I Love You, Americans (TV program)

SARAH SILVERMAN I Love You, America R. Rahman, A. Bacle et al color *Entertainment Weekly* no1482/1483 p108 S 22 2017

Il Seok, Sang

Iodide management in formamidinium-lead-halide–based perovskite layers for efficient solar cells bw diag *Science* v356 no6345 p1376 Je 30 2017

ILZHOEFER, DAVID

Chords & Discords color *Downbeat* v84 no3 p10 Mr 2017

Im, Jino

Colloidally prepared La-doped BaSnO3 electrodes for efficient, photostable perovskite solar cells graph *Science* v356 no6334 p167 Ap 14 2017

I'm Better (Music)

'I'm Better' J. E. SHEPHERD *New York Times Magazine* p21 Mr 12 2017

I'm Dying up Here (TV program)

ARI GRAYNOR IS NO JOKE... C. Collis color *Entertainment Weekly* no1470 p48 Je 16 2017

I'M DYING UP HERE C. Collis color *Entertainment Weekly* no1446/1447 p63 D 2016/Ja 2017

I'm Dying Up Here M. Logan *TV Guide* v65 no23 p22 My 29 2017

I'm the One (Music)

DJ KHALED N. Feeney color *Entertainment Weekly* no1471 p60 Je 23 2017

iMac (Computer)

iMAC KABY LAKE (2017): THE iMAC'S EXCELLENCE CONTINUES ON R. LOYOLA color graph *Macworld - Digital Edition* v34 no8 p27 Ag 2017

Why the new Mac Pro might never come D. MOREN color *Macworld - Digital Edition* v34 no4 p10 My 2017

Image

See also

Corporate image

Destination image (Tourism)

Megatelescope releases its first image R. Austin *Physics Today* v69 no12 p42 D 2016

Image compression—Equipment & supplies

THEN SPEED IT UP color *Popular Science* v289 no5 p31 S/O 2017

Image files

See also

Thumbnail images (Image processing)

If we show you how to back up your PC for free, will you finally do it? M. CHIAPPETTA and L. SPECTOR color *PCWorld* p155 Mr 2017

Image processing

See also

Deconvolution of digital images

Restoring Detail with Deconvolution R. Brecher *Sky & Telescope* v134 no1 p68 Jl 2017

Image processing equipment

TECH MIRROR, TECH MIRROR ON THE WALL M. Meltzer color *Women's Health* v14 no6 p50 Jl 2017

Image processing—Software

Innovation M. Belfiore color *Bloomberg Businessweek* no4511 p33 F 13 2017

Image processing—Software—Evaluation

NEW PRODUCTS color *Astronomy* v44 no12 p64 D 2016

Image transmission

See also

JPEG (Image coding standard)

You May Hug The Screen V. Law bw *Bloomberg Businessweek* no4541 p20 O 9 2017

Imagery (Psychology)

See also

Body image

MAXIMIZING THE BENEFITS of Minimal Practice C. O'Brien and K. Santos color *Team Roping Journal* p56 S 2017

Imaginary histories

The Discontents of Counterfactualism P. Dukes *History Today* v67 no1 p72 Ja 2017

ON THE SPOT HELEN CASTOR H. Castor *History Today* v67 no5 p112 My 2017

Imaginary Mary (TV program)

Imaginary Mary I. Ratledge *TV Guide* v65 no13 p26 Mr 20 2017

Imaginary space vehicles

FLIGHT OF THE U-WING A. Breznican color *Entertainment Weekly* no1442 p18 D 2 2016 Rebellious Special Issue

Imagination

See also

Fantasy

Imagery (Psychology)

hand over that thought color *Parents* v92 no6 p27 Je 2017

LET YOUR MIND WANDER M. HARRIS color *Discover* v38 no5 p30 Je 2017

MEDITATE in the moment M. RABBITT color *Yoga Journal* no291 p47 My 2017

tooth-fairy time R. RABKIN PEACHMAN *Parents* v91 no6 p144 Je 2016

WRITERS' FEAST K. Norris, W. Brueggemann et al color *Christian Century* v134 no10 p30 My 10 2017

Imaging systems

See also

Cameras

Infrared imaging

Electron microscopy gets a multicolor makeover Sung Chang *Physics Today* v70 no1 p14 Ja 2017

THE POWER OF IMAGING WITH PHASE, NOT POWER G. Popescu *Physics Today* v70 no5 p34 My 2017

TOP THREE: TRICK SHOTS B. ROSE color *Wired* v25 no7 p44 Jl 2017

Imaging systems in biology

See also

Cells—Imaging

Imaging method catches DNA 'blinking' on R. Ehrenberg color *Science News* v191 no5 p16 Mr 18 2017

Imaging systems—Evaluation

Focus on lasers and imaging A. Mandelis *Physics Today* v70 no4 p61 Ap 2017

NEW PRODUCTS color *Science* v354 no6311 p485 O 28 2016

NEW PRODUCTS: MICROSCOPY/IMAGING color *Science* v354 no6313 p775 N 11 2016

Imams (Mosque officers)

Muslim clerics disappearing near Kenya-Somalia border F. Nzwili *Christian Century* v134 no1 p13 Ja 4 2017

QUEERING ISLAM S. HABIB color *Advocate* no1089 p56 F/ Mr 2017

Imamura Kawasawa, Yuka

Control of species-dependent cortico-motoneuronal connections underlying manual dexterity diag graph *Science* v357 no6349 p400 Jl 28 2017

Iman, 1955-

I Am Iman I. Abdulmajid bw color *Vogue* v207 no9 p302 S 2017

Imatinib—Therapeutic use

LIVING WITH CANCER S. BLOCK color *Kiplinger's Personal Finance* v71 no6 p58 Je 2017

IMAX Corp. (Entertainment industry)

Can VR Find a Seat In the Parlor? A. Sakoui color *Bloomberg Businessweek* no4524 p22 My 29 2017

Imber, Amantha

Help Employees Innovate By Giving Them the Right Challenge *Harvard Business Review Digital Articles* p2 O 17 2016

Imber, Jonathan

The Discomfitures of Academic Life color *Society* v54 no4 p337 Ag 2017

Imhof, Anne—Exhibitions

Paint It Black M. GUIDUCCI color *Vogue* v207 no9 p366 S 2017

Imitation

Ghosting M. Binyam bw *New York Times Magazine* p24 Ag 6 2017

THE YOUNG TRUMP [Cover story] A. Rice img *New York* p22 Ja 9 2017

Imitation in business

Health Care Needs Less Innovation and More Imitation A. M. Roth and T. H. Lee *Harvard Business Review Digital Articles* p2 N 19 2014

Imm, Gary

Faith and Science at a Crossroad *Sky & Telescope* v134 no3 p6 S 2017

Immediate-early genes

Loss of a mammalian circular RNA locus causes miRNA deregulation and affects brain function M. Piwecka, P. Glažar et al color *Science* v357 no6357 p1254 S 22 2017

IMMEDIATO, LINDA

Art of Letting Loose color *Los Angeles Magazine* v62 no7 p28 Jl 2017

Bethany Yellowtail *Los Angeles Magazine* v62 no9 p95 S 2017

Bling It On color *Los Angeles Magazine* v62 no10 p25 O 2017

Blush Hour: AFICIONADOS OF PRECIOUS METALS ARE TICKLED PINK BY TODAY'S ROSE GOLD ACCESSORIES *Los Angeles Magazine* v62 no9 p46 S 2017

Face Time *Los Angeles Magazine* v62 no6 p25 Je 2017

Get Personal *Los Angeles Magazine* p29 F 2017

Get Your Art to Go *Los Angeles Magazine* p29 Ja 2017

A House Divided color *Los Angeles Magazine* v62 no10 p133 O 2017

IRON MAN *Los Angeles Magazine* p27 My 2017

It's a Small World *Los Angeles Magazine* p31 Ap 2017

JEWEL TONES *Los Angeles Magazine* v62 no9 p29 S 2017

A NEW GROOVE *Los Angeles Magazine* p34 Ja 2017

One Love color *Los Angeles Magazine* v62 no7 p25 Jl 2017

Out of The Box *Los Angeles Magazine* p43 D 2016

Play Hard at ROW DTLA color *Los Angeles Magazine* v62 no7 p66 Jl 2017

Raise The Bar *Los Angeles Magazine* p38 My 2017

REEL BEAUTY *Los Angeles Magazine* p36 Ap 2017

SHAPE SHIFTERS color *Los Angeles Magazine* v62 no10 p32 O 2017

Slab City color *Los Angeles Magazine* v62 no10 p34 O 2017

STATE OF MIND *Los Angeles Magazine* v62 no6 p28 Je 2017

SUNSET JUNCTION *Los Angeles Magazine* v62 no6 p68 Je 2017

Immelt, Jeffrey, 1956-

Business: Localization Can Help America Win Around the World color *Time* v188 no27-28 p32 D 26 2016

FIVE TRANSFORMATIONS S. PROKESCH *Harvard Business Review* v95 no5 p47 S/O 2017

GE'S GLOBAL GROWTH EXPERIMENT: THE COMPANY PUSHED CROSS-BUSINESS COLLABORATION R. GULATI *Harvard Business Review* v95 no5 p52 S/O 2017

THE GREAT TRANSFORMER A. IGNATIUS bw img *Harvard Business Review* v95 no5 p10 S/O 2017

HOW I REMADE GE: AND WHAT I LEARNED ALONG THE WAY color *Harvard Business Review* v95 no5 p42 S/O 2017

IN BRIEF K. Stock color graph *Bloomberg Businessweek* no4527 p14 Je 19 2017

Immelt, Jeffrey, 1956-—Interviews

GE's Jeff Immelt J. Micklethwait color *Bloomberg Businessweek* no4511 p22 F 13 2017

Immersion method (Language teaching)
See also
English language—Study & teaching—Immersion method
Schools ... with superpowers M. S. Winters color diag *U.S. Catholic* v82 no3 p12 Mr 2017

Immersion suits
Suit Yourself S. MURRAY bw *Power & Motoryacht* v34 no9 p54 S 2017

Immersive VR Education Ltd.
Rocketing off to (cyber)space T. Trusock color *Astronomy* v45 no2 p62 F 2017

Immigrant, The (Film : 1917)
A DOUBLE LIFE G. SHAMBU bw color *Film Comment* v53 no5 p56 S/O 2017

Immigrant students—Social conditions
Boston's School for Immigrants E. Kaplan bw *Progressive* v81 no6 p38 Ag/S 2017

Immigrants
See also
Undocumented immigrants
AMERICAN STUDIES J. BLITZER cartoon *New Yorker* v93 no14 p40 My 22 2017
CROTONE, ITALY *In These Times* v41 no7 p7 Jl 2017
ESCAPE FROM VIETNAM K. Luu *Saturday Evening Post* v289 no2 p16 Mr/Ap 2017
Froth on the daydream C. Day *Physics Today* v69 no10 p8 O 2016
How American Are You, Really? The Citizenship Test for Citizens S. SHERRILL color graph *GQ: Gentlemen's Quarterly* v97 no6 p62 Je 2017
Immigrants Make America Great S. BARRY color *Working Mother* v40 no2 p50 Je/Jl 2017
An Open Letter to Ta-Nehisi Coates: The Dream is real J. D. Hill *Commentary* v144 no3 p35 O 2017
The Price We've Paid chart graph *Chicago* v66 no7 p69 Jl 2017
Protecting unauthorized immigrant mothers improves their children's mental health J. Hainmueller, D. Lawrence et al diag *Science* v357 no6355 p1041 S 8 2017
shalom y'all L. Brook *Successful Farming* v115 no1 p3 Ja 2017
Where Decency Resides M. Funkhouser *Governing* v30 no9 p4 Je 2017

Immigrants' rights
CARAVAN AGAINST FEAR S. ABRAMSKY color *Nation* v305 no3 p14 Jl 31 2017

Immigrants—Canada
EMERGENCY CANADIAN RESIDENCE APPLICATION B. MCCALL cartoon *New Yorker* v92 no39 p45 N 28 2016

Immigrants—Canada—Attitudes
The impulse to assimilate A. DOMISE chart color *Maclean's* v130 no6 p13 Jl 2017

Immigrants—Economic aspects
ARE "DREAMERS" WORTH BILLIONS TO STATES? E. Fry map *Fortune* v175 no2 p11 F 1 2017

Immigrants—Europe
HOW TO SEE INVISIBLE PEOPLE J. G. BOCK color map *Phi Kappa Phi Forum* v96 no4 p18 Wint 2016

Immigrants—Greece
Greek hospitality is put to a religious test A. Markovich color *Christian Century* v133 no25 p15 D 7 2016

Immigrants—Italy
Italy Lashes Out As Flow of Migrants Surges T. John color *Time* v190 no4 p9 Jl 24 2017
Lightbox color *Time* v189 no22 p12 Je 12 2017

Immigrants—Japan
THE BOY WITHOUT A COUNTRY J. Weisberg *Harper's Magazine* p73 Ap 2017

Immigrants—Medical care
Immigrants and the Jinn E. RASCHKE color *America* v216 no1 p24 Ja 2 2017

Immigrants—Psychology
To the University, with Love P. J. Griffiths color *Commonweal* v144 no11 p39 Je 16 2017

Immigrants—Religious life
Daughter of an Irish Catholic and Bengali Muslim, by Liz Hingley L. Copan color *Christian Century* v134 no4 p63 F 15 2017

Immigrants—Social conditions

THE MIGRANT MISSIONARIES A. Olsen color *Christianity Today* v61 no6 p38 Jl/Ag 2017

Immigrants—Social conditions—History
Lost at Sea: The Dangers of Emigration G. Hoffs *History Today* v67 no4 p3 Ap 2017
Piece of Mind: At Ellis Island, a jigsaw challenge could seal an immigrant's fate A. Cohen *Smithsonian* v48 no2 p46 My 2017

Immigrants—Societies, etc.
Q. & A A. Marantz cartoon *New Yorker* v93 no3 p22 Mr 6 2017

Immigrants—Spain
Arrival M. CAMPBELL color *Maclean's* v130 no3 p20 Ap 2017

Immigrants—United States
ALL THE (POTENTIAL) PRESIDENT'S MEN R. BEHAR bw color *Forbes* v198 no5 p77 O 25 2016
America Is Still the Future A. Sullivan img *New York* p16 Ja 23 2017
CITY OF HOPE C. ANDERSON and A. TOENSING color *Yankee* p118 Mr 2017
Grand Island's FORGOTTEN BIRTHPLACE B. SASS bw color *Nebraska Life* v21 no4 p44 Jl/Ag 2017
HARPER'S INDEX *Harper's Magazine* v334 no2000 p15 Ja 2017
Immigrants Make America Great S. BARRY color *Working Mother* v40 no2 p50 Je/Jl 2017
Immigrants Play a Disproportionate Role in American Entrepreneurship S. P. Kerr and W. R. Kerr *Harvard Business Review Digital Articles* p2 O 3 2016
Learning To Take A Stand N. DEUEL *Los Angeles Magazine* p88 Mr 2017
THE MAZE E. Goldman *Harper's Magazine* v335 no2006 p31 Jl 2017
Michigan's Iraqi Christians fear deportation T. Bach color *Christian Century* v134 no15 p12 Jl 19 2017
Near and Far W. Voegeli *Claremont Review of Books* v17 no3 p11 Summ 2017
Should They Stay or Should They Go? The debate over President Trump's crackdown on undocumented immigrants B. ROSS, J. Medina et al *New York Times Upfront* v149 no13 p6 My 15 2017
The Staff Of Life R. BROOKHISER *National Review* v69 no9 p43 My 15 2017
State of Rebellion H. GUZIK *In These Times* v41 no2 p8 F 2017
Undocumented on Patrol K. SURANA color *Foreign Policy* no226 p11 S/O 2017
"We Are Not Leaving" J. HING il *Nation* v303 no23/24 p21 D 5 2016
What If? D. Mills color *Commonweal* v144 no7 p39 Ap 14 2017
Young Americans L. P. Jobs color *Wired* v24 no11 p86 N 2016

Immigrants—United States—Attitudes
Quiet Time P. Beinart *New Republic* v248 no4 p4 Ap 2017

Immigrants—United States—Economic conditions
Welcome to America! Here's How Your Investment Is Doing S. Berfield color *Bloomberg Businessweek* no4493 p74 O 3 2016

Immigrants—United States—Economic conditions—21st century
THE AMERICAN DREAM IS ALIVE AND WELL...ON THE FORBES 400 M. BURKE, S. Sharf et al color graph map *Forbes* v198 no5 p58 O 25 2016

Immigrants—United States—Government policy
Language Haven J. CHASE-LUBITZ color *Foreign Policy* no226 p10 S/O 2017

Immigrants—United States—History
IMMIGRANTS KEEP CAPITALISM FRESH R. KARLGAARD *Forbes* v198 no5 p56 O 25 2016
OBSERVATIONS ON A VERY SENSITIVE SUBJECT *Forbes* v198 no5 p29 O 25 2016

Immigrants—United States—History—20th century
WITH POYDRAS THE PARROT J. STREET color *New Orleans Magazine* v51 no7 p22 My 2017

Immigrants—United States—Social conditions
If You Don't Have Solid Borders, You Get Walls N. Gardels *NPQ: New Perspectives Quarterly* v34 no3 p2 Jl 2017

Immigrants—United States—Social conditions—21st century
CITIZENS IN TRAINING L. Widdicombe cartoon *New Yorker* v92 no49 p32 F 13 2017
Deportations S. HAFIZ *In These Times* v41 no1 p25 Ja 2017
Our American Union G. J. Mitchell color *America* v216 no6 p54

Mr 20 2017

Immigrants—United States—Legal status, laws, etc.

THE BIG UNEASY R. WESTWOOD color *Maclean's* v130 no4 p42 My 2017

MIAMI E. Danticat *Harper's Magazine* p34 O 2017

Immigration courts

FORTY QUESTIONS *Harper's Magazine* no2007 p11 Ag 2017

Immigration enforcement

At the Threshold K. A. Sital color *New York Times Magazine* p28 D 4 2016

Immigration opponents

Blame Automation, Not Immigration M. Champion and A. van der Schoot color *Bloomberg Businessweek* no4513 p30 Mr 6 2017

A continent divided C. Matlack and A. van der Schoot color *Bloomberg Businessweek* no4496 p20 O 24 2016

EUROPE'S NEW CLOSED-DOOR POLICY S. ABRAMSKY bw *Nation* v303 no16 p16 O 17 2016

THE TRUMP BUMP M. Idov and A. Weinstein cartoon *Esquire* v167 no1 p54 F 2017

Immigration status

ARE "DREAMERS" WORTH BILLIONS TO STATES? E. Fry map *Fortune* v175 no2 p11 F 1 2017

LESSONS FROM 20TH-CENTURY EUROPE: Saving democracy G. Dorrien *Christian Century* v134 no13 p20 Je 21 2017

Immigration status—History

Lost at Sea: The Dangers of Emigration G. Hoffs *History Today* v67 no4 p3 Ap 2017

Immorality

Crime Doesn't Pay color *Prevention* v69 no9 p12 O 2017

Immortality of the body

See also

Cryonics

ALL TOO HUMAN H. Rosner color *Scientific American* v315 no3 p70 S 2016

THE SEARCH FOR IMMORTALITY H. JAFFE color *Men's Health* v32 no5 p132 Je 2017

Immortal Life of Henrietta Lacks, The (TV program)

BEHIND THE LENS T. Stack color *Entertainment Weekly* no1462 p34 Ap 21 2017

For the Love of Henrietta Z. Donaldson bw color *O, The Oprah Magazine* p28 My 2017

THE IMMORTAL LIFE OF HENRIETTA LACKS T. Jordan color *Entertainment Weekly* no1446/1447 p66 D 2016/Ja 2017

INTO THE LIGHT T. Y. Jeffries color *Essence* v47 no12 p88 Ap 2017

LIFE LESSONS M. LOGAN *TV Guide* p24 Ap 17 2017

Immune response

See also

Immunology of inflammation

Adapting to Outer Space L. E. Ogden color *Natural History* v125 no5 p7 My 2017

Avoiding Overreaction N. Wilson color *Natural History* v125 no4 p7 Ap 2017

HIDDEN INVADERS P. WEINTRAUB cartoon color diag *Discover* v38 no3 p46 Ap 2017

MAVS-dependent host species range and pathogenicity of human hepatitis A virus Asuka Hirai-Yuki, L. Hensley et al bibl graph *Science* v353 no6307 p1541 S 30 2016

MICRONEEDLE PATCH FOR FLU VACCINATION [Cover story] *USA Today Magazine* v146 no2869 p1 O 2017

Worms remodel immune responsiveness *Science* v354 no6312 p594 N 4 2016

Immune response—Genetic aspects

Chromosomal chaos silences immune surveillance M. Zanetti bibl chart color *Science* v355 no6322 p249 Ja 20 2017

Immune system

AUTOIMMUNE DISEASE: NATURAL SOLUTIONS J. Bowden color *Amazing Wellness* p30 Fall 2017

DIRT IS GOOD FOR YOU J. Jetsohn *Saturday Evening Post* v289 no2 p26 Mr/Ap 2017

GOOD-GUT GULP color *Prevention* v69 no7 p12 Jl 2017

The Hidden Power of Funky Foods T. CORSON color *Men's Health* v32 no4 p65 My 2017

Immune proteins aid viral enemy L. HAMERS *Science News* v190 no11 p16 N 26 2016

Intracellular innate immune surveillance devices in plants and animals J. D. G. Jones, R. E. Vance et al chart color diag graph *Science* v354 no6316 paaf6395-1 D 2 2016

Killing old cells to stay young M. Leslie color *Science* v354 no6319 p1519 D 23 2016

Light Activated A. Hadhazy color *Natural History* v125 no3 p8 Mr 2017

The Lowdown on Mold M. E. Polson color *Old House Journal* v45 no3 p52 My 2017

Social status alters immune regulation and response to infection in macaques N. Snyder-Mackler, J. Sanz et al bibl graph *Science* v354 no6315 p1041 N 25 2016

Social status alters immune system R. EHRENBERG color *Science News* v190 no13 p7 D 24 2016

What you need to know about... Immuno therapy [Cover story] A. PATUREL color *Prevention* v68 no11 p68 N 2016

Writ large: Genomic dissection of the effect of cellular environment on immune response N. Yosef and A. Regev bibl diag *Science* v354 no6308 p64 O 7 2016

Immune system—Physiology

5 amazing mushrooms FOR WHOLE-BODY HEALTH T. ISO-KAUPPILA color *Better Nutrition* v79 no9 p53 S 2017

Fighting cancer from within *Mayo Clinic Health Letter* v35 no9 p4 S 2017

Immunity

5 REASONS TO GO PLAY T. ROSS color *Rodale's Organic Life* v2 no7 p95 D 2016/Ja 2017

5 Sneaky Ways the Holidays Harm Your Immunity K. KLOSS *Reader's Digest* v188 no1124 p70 N 2016

Boost Your Immunity K. ASP color *Martha Stewart Living* p68 O 2017

Enhancement of Zika virus pathogenesis by preexisting antiflavivirus immunity S. V. Bardina, P. Bunduc et al graph *Science* v356 no6334 p175 Ap 14 2017

Gut Check S. SCHENCK cartoon *Rodale's Organic Life* v3 no1 p34 Ja 2017

Immunity around the clock K. Man, A. Loudon et al bibl diag graph *Science* v354 no6315 p999 N 25 2016

A macrophage relay for long-distance signaling during postembryonic tissue remodeling D. Seok Eom and D. M. Parichy bibl color graph *Science* v355 no6331 p1317 Mr 24 2017

The Right Way to Sleep—Uncovered! color *Men's Health* v32 no8 p71 O 2017

Secrets of the Super Healthy [Cover story] D. HUDEPOHL cartoon color *Prevention* v69 no1 p74 Ja 2017

YOUR BODY ON... BAKING [Cover story] J. Migala color *Women's Health* v13 no10 p84 D 2016

Immunoglobulin A

Pleasurable Health Hacks That Actually Work T. DUMAIN *Reader's Digest* v188 no1124 p60 O 2016

Immunoglobulin G

IgG antibodies to dengue enhanced for FcγRIIIA binding determine disease severity T. T. Wang, J. Sewatanon et al bibl graph *Science* v355 no6323 p395 Ja 27 2017

Immunoglobulins

The best time for a flu shot color *Redbook* p75 N 2017

Broadly neutralizing antibodies to prevent HIV-1 M. S. Cohen and L. Corey diag *Science* v357 no6359 p46 O 6 2017

GLOSSARY *Equus* no475 p87 Ap 2017

Making a difference, differently M. Tuthill cartoon *Science* v354 no6316 p1194 D 2 2016

One antibody for all and all antibodies for one *Science* v356 no6334 p149 Ap 14 2017

Priming HIV-1 broadly neutralizing antibody precursors in human Ig loci transgenic mice D. Sok, B. Briney et al bibl graph *Science* v353 no6307 p1557 S 30 2016

Promising Alzheimer's drug will test amyloid hypothesis L. Sanders color *Science News* v190 no13 p27 D 24 2016

WE WISH SOMEONE WOULD INVENT... C. Maldarelli and S. K. Watson color *Popular Science* v289 no6 p98 N/D 2017

YEAST OF BURDEN M. ZARASKA cartoon *Mother Jones* v41 no6 p64 N/D 2016

Immunoglobulins—Evaluation

new products: proteomics *Science* v357 no6356 p1168 S 15 2017

Immunoglobulins—Research

Agreeable antibodies: Antibody validation challenges and solu-

SIRE LINE: KRZYZYK DB THE ROOTS OF POLISH BREED-
ING B. FINKE *Arabian Horse World* v57 no8 p94 My 2017

Imports—Charts, diagrams, etc.

CUBA TANTALIZES U.S. INDUSTRY diag *Fortune* v174 no8
p16 D 15 2016

Imports—United States

U.S. CHALLENGES CHINA OVER CORN, WHEAT, AND
RICE IMPORT RULES *Successful Farming* v115 no2 p14 F
2017

Imports—United States—Charts, diagrams, etc.

Trade Give and Take D. Gambrell diag *Bloomberg Businessweek*
no4500 p18 N 21 2016

Impossible (Film)

Tom HOLLAND Zendaya *Interview* v47 no5 p50 Je/Jl 2017

Impostor phenomenon

Everyone Suffers from Impostor Syndrome—Here's How to Handle It A. Molinsky *Harvard Business Review Digital Articles*
p2 Jl 7 2016

The Personality Traits That Make Us Feel Like Frauds S. Berinato
Harvard Business Review Digital Articles p2 O 22 2015

When an Editor Writes Fiction J. STRAWSER *Publishers Weekly*
v264 no13 p104 Mr 27 2017

Impotence

Understanding ED I. Kerner color *Prevention* v69 no2 p28 F 2017

Impotence—Diagnosis

Erectile dysfunction [Cover story] *Mayo Clinic Health Letter* v34
no11 p1 N 2016

Impresarios

ART WITHOUT WALLS C. TOMKINS cartoon *New Yorker* v92
no40 p34 D 5 2016

Impression formation (Psychology)

See also

First impression (Psychology)

Good Impressions chart color *Horse & Rider* v55 no11 p20 N
2016

Impression management

The Right Way to Brag About Yourself F. Gino *Harvard Business
Review Digital Articles* p2 My 20 2015

When Networking, Being Yourself Really Does Work F. Gino
Harvard Business Review Digital Articles p2 S 27 2016

Impressionism (Art movement)—Exhibitions

Temp Works R. Knudson *Texas Monthly* v44 no11 p104 N 2016

Impressionism (Art movement)—France—Exhibitions

Of an artist dying young J. Gardner color *Magazine Antiques* v184
no3 p96 My/Je 2017

Impreza automobile

ROAD TESTED E. DYER color *Popular Mechanics* p46 Jl 2017

Small but Mighty *Consumer Reports* v82 no7 p62 Jl 2017

Imprinting (Psychology)

Which One Is Mom Again? J. G. Goldman color *Scientific American* v316 no4 p18 Ap 2017

Imprints (Publications)

At 30, Amistad Press Looks Ahead D. Patrick *Publishers Weekly*
v263 no41 p11 O 10 2016

Readers Respond B. T. Greive and S. Kimmel bw *Publishers
Weekly* v264 no2 p3 Ja 9 2017

Imprints (Publishers' & printers' statements)

Weise Reimagines Charlesbridge's Imagine C. Swanson *Publishers Weekly* v263 no39 p14 S 26 2016

Imprisonment

GUILT BY OMISSION E. BAZELON color *New York Times
Magazine* p40 Ag 6 2017

Look at Him Now img *New York* v49 no20 p124 O 3 2016

No Jail Over Bail C. J. Ciaramella *Reason* v48 no7 p9 D 2016

The University-Bound Mother Who Killed Her Child Deserves
Forgiveness B. Luscombe color *Time* v190 no13 p21 O 2 2017

Imprisonment rates

The Prisoner Dilemma H. Harris color *Foreign Affairs* v96 no2
p118 Mr/Ap 2017

Imprisonment—Law & legislation

Obama's broken legacy A. ABEL color *Maclean's* no1 p36 F 17
2017

Imprisonment—United States

All Criminal Justice Reform Is Local G. Edelman *Washington
Monthly* p2 Ja/F 2017

LAW AND DISORDER *Smithsonian* v47 no9 p79 Ja/F 2017

The Prisoner Dilemma H. Harris color *Foreign Affairs* v96 no2
p118 Mr/Ap 2017

Improvisation in music

See also

Rap music

Bach to Basics II: Using Melodies To Suggest Harmony [Cover
story] C. DAVIS bw color *Downbeat* v84 no5 p76 My 2017

Embracing Your Current Improv Vocabulary M. SHEVITZ bw
color *Downbeat* v84 no5 p80 My 2017

Improvisation in the arts

See also

Improvisation in music

Studio Improv P. MARGASAK bw *Downbeat* v84 no3 p19 Mr
2017

Impulse (Psychology)

Dear Readers B. Kelley *Reader's Digest* v189 no1127 p4 F 2017

In & Of Itself (Theatrical production)

DESIGNING the undefinable M. S. Eddy *Stage Directions* v30
no8 p18 Ag 2017

Elusive Illusions H. Sherman *Stage Directions* v30 no8 p16 Ag
2017

In a Valley of Violence (Film)

Valley of Violence Is Hounded by Its True Star S. Zacharek color
Time v188 no19 p57 N 7 2016

In Cloud Country (Poem)

In Cloud Country M. PRIOR *Walrus* v14 no6 p53 Jl/Ag 2017

In Dubious Battle (Film)

In Dubious Battle L. Greenblatt color *Entertainment Weekly*
no1454/1455 p82 F 24 2017

In-line skating

Rollerblading the Little Miami A. COHEN *Cincinnati Magazine*
p62 Je 2017

In loco parentis

The Evolution of in loco parentis Plus B. A. Carlisle *Change* v49
no1 p48 Ja/F 2017

In-N-Out Burgers Inc.

Burger Queen C. SORVINO color *Forbes* v199 no6 p22 Je 13
2017

In Pursuit of Silence (Film)

Code of Silence K. O'Reilly *Sierra* v102 no3 p10 My/Je 2017

In the Heart of the Sea (Film)

IN THE HEART OF THE SEA T. J. Norton color *Sound & Vision*
v81 no9 p68 N 2016

In the Palace of Cats (Short story)

In the Palace of Cats C. P. BOYKO color *Walrus* v14 no6 p54 Jl/
Ag 2017

In the Park (Theatrical Production)

Odd Man In H. Als color *New Yorker* v93 no32 p8 O 16 2017

In These Times (Periodical)

40 Years J. BLEIFUSS bw *In These Times* v40 no11 p9 N 2016

In This One (Short story)

IN THIS ONE S. Dixon *Harper's Magazine* v333 no1998 p75 N
2016

In to America (Theatrical production)

COMING TO AMERICA N. PARSI bw color *Chicago* v66 no3
p47 Mr 2017

In-vehicle entertainment equipment

Outfitting Robo Car M. ANTONOFF color graph *Sound & Vision*
v82 no7 p21 S 2017

In vitro meat

TRENDING L. SCHLEY color diag graph *Discover* v38 no6 p12
Jl/Ag 2017

Where's the Beef? M. STONE color *Discover* v38 no4 p17 My
2017

In War & Peace (Theatrical production)

In War and Peace D. Shengold *Opera News* v81 no9 p34 Mr 2017

Inaba, Carrie Ann

Let's Dance! bw color *AARP: The Magazine* v59 no6A p52 O/N
2016

**In a Rented Cabin in the Haliburton Highlands, Oriented to-
ward Algonquin Park (Poem)**

In a Rented Cabin in the Haliburton Highlands, Oriented toward
Algonquin Park J. ARTHUR *Walrus* v14 no9 p38 N 2017

Inbal, Asaf

Localized seismic deformation in the upper mantle revealed by
dense seismic arrays bibl graph *Science* v354 no6308 p88 O 7

7 2016

Income distribution—Canada

THE EDITORIAL *Maclean's* v129 no40 p5 O 10 2016

Income distribution—China

China's Numbers Man D. Roberts and X. Pi color *Bloomberg Businessweek* no4516 p12 Mr 27 2017

Income distribution—Great Britain

Money's too tight to mention P. Cheese *People Management* p5 F 2017

Income distribution—United States

FINDINGS *Harper's Magazine* v334 no2000 p104 Ja 2017

Paid In Semi Full C. Suddath color diag *Bloomberg Businessweek* no4528 p42 Je 26 2017

Q: IS SLOW WAGE GROWTH BOOMERS' FAULT? J. Porter *Fortune* v176 no4 p28 S 15 2017

The Redistribution Fallacy J. Piereson *Commentary* v140 no2 p51 S 2015

Your Neighbor's Fancy Car Should Make You Feel Better About Income Inequality J. V. C. NYE color graph *Reason* v49 no3 p42 Jl 2017

Income gap

WAGE GROWTH LOOKS GREAT—AT THE TOP diag *Fortune* v176 no4 p23 S 15 2017

Income gap—History—21st century

Shrinking the Gap Is Key for Democracy B. Obama color *Time* v188 no16/17 p36 O 24 2016

Income maintenance programs

No Strings Attached Z. Patton color *Governing* v30 no11 p32 Ag 2017

Income tax

See also

Capital gains tax

Withholding tax

Breakdown of Federal Spending *USA Today Magazine* v146 no2867 p7 Ag 2017

Reversal of Fortunes: Local income taxes were once blamed for causing businesses to flee to the suburbs J. Marlowe *Governing* v31 no1 p62 O 2017

Income tax—United States

Blue State Blues A. EBELING map *Forbes* v199 no2 p102 F 28 2017

Last-Minute Tax Savers S. BLOCK cartoon *Kiplinger's Personal Finance* v71 no4 p46 Ap 2017

Income tax—United States—History

DON'T MESS WITH TAXES W. BALDWIN color *Forbes* v200 no3 p74 S 28 2017

Income—Canada

GOOD NEWS color *Maclean's* v129 no50 p8 D 19 2016

Through the Roof R. HARRIS color map *Alternatives Journal (AJ) - Canada's Environmental Voice* v42 no2 p30 2016

Income—Charts, diagrams, etc.

Survey Says R. Klemko and T. Keith diag *Sports Illustrated* v126 no18 p14 Je 26 2017

Income—Law & legislation

CENTURY marks *Christian Century* v134 no16 p8 Ag 2 2017

Income tax—Charts, diagrams, etc.

FEDERAL FINANCE *Economic Indicators* p32 Ag 2017

Income—United States

APPENDIX B STATISTICAL TABLES RELATING TO IN-COME, EMPLOYMENT, AND PRODUCTION *Economic Indicators* p395 O 2016

HOW MUCH YOUNG PEOPLE ARE MAKING map *Fortune* v175 no5 p11 Ap 1 2017

If the SEC Measured CEO Pay Packages Properly, They Would Look Even More Outrageous W. Lazonick and M. Hopkins *Harvard Business Review Digital Articles* p2 D 22 2016

The Indestructible IDEA of the Basic INCOME J. WALKER color *Reason* v49 no3 p32 Jl 2017

It's Okay to Reach for Yield J. R. KOSNETT *Kiplinger's Personal Finance* v71 no10 p60 O 2017

REFERENCES *Economic Indicators* p331 O 2016

We Tracked Every Dollar 235 U.S. Households Spent for a Year, and Found Widespread Financial Vulnerability J. Morduch and R. Schneider *Harvard Business Review Digital Articles* p2 Ap 12 2017

Where the Living Is Easy Wei Lu map *Bloomberg Businessweek*

no4514 p41 Mr 13 2017

Income—United States—Charts, diagrams, etc.

WAGE GROWTH LOOKS GREAT—AT THE TOP diag *Fortune* v176 no4 p23 S 15 2017

WHERE A $100K SALARY WILL TAKE YOU THE FAR-THEST map *Fortune* v176 no2 p15 Ag 1 2017

Inconvenient Sequel: Truth to Power, An (Film)

Al Gore J. Worland color *Time* v190 no5 p66 Jl 31 2017

Al Gore's inconvenient update V. Thompson color *Science* v357 no6349 p361 Jl 28 2017

An Inconvenient Sequel: Truth to Power C. Nashawaty color *Entertainment Weekly* no1476 p47 Ag 4 2017

An Inconvenient Truth sequel: Hope for a clean energy future color *National Wildlife (World Edition)* v55 no5 p46 Ag/S 2017

Planet Earth As Spectacle-and Cautionary Tale J. Worland color *Time* v189 no7/8 p111 F 27 2017

Q&A: AL GORE J. McGovern color *Entertainment Weekly* no1463/1464 p64 Ap/My 2017

Save the Earth, Save Our Health B. O'DAIR color *Prevention* v69 no8 p18 Ag 2017

Inconvenient Truth, An (Film)

AL GORE N. Haramis *Interview* v47 no5 p72 Je/Jl 2017

Truth Be Told: Former vice president Al Gore returns to theaters to discuss our continuing climate crisis K. O'Reilly *Sierra* v102 no4 p10 Jl/Ag 2017

Incord (Company)

Playing It Safe: Orchestra Pit Safety Net Systems from InCord. Ltd *Stage Directions* v30 no3 p38 Mr 2017

Incredible Jessica James, The (Film)

Jessica Williams Gives You Permission to Chill img *New York* v50 no16 p105 Ag 7 2017

The Must List color *Entertainment Weekly* no1476 p1 Ag 4 2017

Incredibles, The (Film)

The Bullseye M. Snetiker color *Entertainment Weekly* no1436/1437 p108 O 21 2016

Incubators

Build Your Own INCUBATOR J. Gauthier *Mother Earth News* no280 p46 F/Mr 2017

Incubators—Evaluation

new products color *Science* v356 no6334 p209 Ap 14 2017

Incumbency (Public officers)

Don't Sweat the Primaries A. Greenblatt *Governing* v30 no2 p17 N 2016

Incyte Corp.

The Right Chemistry M. HERPER and K. KAM chart color *Forbes* v200 no4 p35 O 24 2017

Indecent (Theatrical production)

David Dorfman K. SCHWAB *Dance Magazine* v91 no4 p18 Ap 2017

The Moral Indecency of Indecent: A play revisited, a struggle imagined R. R. Wisse *Commentary* v144 no1 p43 Jl/Ag 2017

STAGE OF ENLIGHTENMENT S. CROSLEY color *Vanity Fair* v59 no6 p74 My 2017

Independence Day (Texas)

Happy Texas Week, Y'all! D. COURTNEY *Texas Monthly* v45 no3 p212 Mr 2017

Independence Day: Resurgence (Film)

INDEPENDENCE DAY: RESURGENCE B. A. DuHamel color *Sound & Vision* v82 no3 p68 Ap 2017

THE WORST FILMS OF THE YEAR C. Nashawaty, D. Coggan et al color *Entertainment Weekly* no1444/1445 p62 D 16 2016

Independence Hall (Philadelphia, Pa.)

My Kind of Landscape K. Roosevelt III color *AARP: The Magazine* v59 no3A p76 Ap/My 2016

Independent bookstores

Dangerous Books Ahead color *Publishers Weekly* v264 no2 p10 Ja 9 2017

Happy Holidays for Indies in 2016 J. Rosen, C. Kirch et al color *Publishers Weekly* v264 no2 p6 Ja 9 2017

Why Backlist Matters J. Rosen color *Publishers Weekly* v264 no7 p4 F 13 2017

Independent bookstores—Evaluation

A New Concept for Indie Bookstores P. GOODMAN *Publishers Weekly* v264 no20 p60 My 15 2017

Independent churches

WORSHIP WITH A DROP J. Neely color *Christianity Today* v61

p51 N 2016

High on the Hog J. SPALDING *Indianapolis Monthly* v40 no5 p38 Ja 2017

New Wave J. SPALDING *Indianapolis Monthly* v40 no4 p56 D 2016

PINEWOOD DERBY L. SAXE color *Indianapolis Monthly* p17 Ap 2017

RAW-RAH! S. KROWIAK *Indianapolis Monthly* v40 no3 p52 N 2016

Restaurant GUIDE *Indianapolis Monthly* p149 N 2017

Restaurant GUIDE *Indianapolis Monthly* v40 no3 p144 N 2016

A Short Ride C. ZEIGLER *Indianapolis Monthly* p20 My 2017

SHOW HOME T. BRAND *Indianapolis Monthly* v40 no3 p44 N 2016

Small But Meaty J. SPALDING *Indianapolis Monthly* v40 no3 p58 N 2016

SQUARE MEALS T. Kirts *Indianapolis Monthly* v40 no10 p40 Je 2017

TIBBS DRIVE-IN THEATRE N. MONDAY *Indianapolis Monthly* v12 no40 p20 Ag 2017

TOP DENTISTS *Indianapolis Monthly* v40 no4 p105 D 2016

Indianapolis (Ind.)—Description & travel

TRAVEL J. YOUNG bw color *Indianapolis Monthly* p79 Ap 2017

Indianapolis (Ind.)—Social conditions

CHANGE the CITY L. BAILEY, D. S. COMISKEY et al *Indianapolis Monthly* p55 Ap 2017

Indianapolis (Ship)

PAUL ALLEN PINPOINTS WRECK OF USS INDIANAPOLIS B. Manley bw *Military History* v34 no5 p8 Ja 2018

Indianapolis 500 (Automobile race)

Road to Joy J. Feldman and T. Keith color *Sports Illustrated* v126 no17 p26 Je 19 2017

Indianapolis Colts (Football team)

3 Indianapolis Colts color *Sports Illustrated* v127 no7 p78 S 4 2017

AFC + SOUTH color *Sports Illustrated* v126 no5 p46 F 13 2017

Indianapolis Monthly (Periodical)

The Best Medicine M. Rubino *Indianapolis Monthly* p12 N 2017

Indianapolis Museum of Art

Encounter L. BAILEY *Indianapolis Monthly* v40 no3 p24 N 2016

Indianapolis Recorder (Newspaper)

Extra! Extra! Pie-eating contests, swimming, junk food. For years, the annual Indianapolis Recorder picnics were a summertime highlight C. ZEIGLER *Indianapolis Monthly* v12 no40 p22 Ag 2017

Indianapolis Symphony Orchestra

DECEMBER'S COOLEST EVENTS *Indianapolis Monthly* v40 no4 p28 D 2016

JUNE'S HOTTEST EVENTS *Indianapolis Monthly* v40 no10 p22 Je 2017

WHAT TO DO color *Indianapolis Monthly* p78 Ap 2017

Indiana—Social life & customs

BEST OF THE FESTS L. Roberts color *Indianapolis Monthly* v41 no2 p92 S 2017

Indian Creek (San Juan County, Utah)

Scarface J. ELLISON color *Climbing* no354 p33 Jl 2017

India—Officials & employees

India at 70 *Vital Speeches of the Day* v83 no10 p281 O 2017

India-Pakistan Conflict, 1947-1949

Seasons of Discontent and Revolt in Kashmir C. ZUTSHI *Current History* v116 no789 p123 Ap 2017

Indic authors

INDIAN AUTHORS AT SIBF R. DeeCee bw color *Publishers Weekly* v263 no43 p(Sp)18 O 24 2016

Indictments

LEGAL BRIEF M. McCann *Sports Illustrated* v127 no11 p24 O 9 2017

Prosecuting Politics D. FRENCH color *National Review* v69 no16 p16 Ag 28 2017

Indigenous children—Medical care

Jordan's Principle L. CHAMBERS and K. BURNETT *American Indian Quarterly* v41 no2 p101 Spr 2017

Indigenous languages of the Americas

Preamble *Orion Magazine* v36 no2 p1 Mr/Ap 2017

Indigenous peoples

THE END OF ICE B. MCKIBBEN color *New Republic* v247

no12 p32 D 2016

NATIONAL GALLERY FINLAND R. Griffiths *History Today* v67 no9 p78 S 2017

Indigenous peoples of the Americas

See also

Indigenous peoples—Canada

Native Americans

GENEALOGY BUG BITE: Alt-facts, fake news, obsession and wasted days in the land of the dead R. NELSON *Virginia Living* v15 no4 p112 Je 2017

Indigenous peoples—Attitudes

Indigenous peoples: Conservation paradox P. O'B. Lyver and J. M. Tylianakis color *Science* v357 no6347 p142 Jl 14 2017

Indigenous peoples—Brazil

Modern Amazonia Y. Gross color map *National Geographic* v231 no2 p120 F 2017

Indigenous peoples—Canada

CANADIAN INJUSTICE K. EDWARDS color *Maclean's* v130 no10 p36 N 2017

FEATURED FELLOW: BRANDON PARDY M. Rosano color *Canadian Geographic* v137 no2 p70 Mr/Ap 2017

NOT ON THEIR WATCH M. PATRIQUIN and J. MARKUSOFF color *Maclean's* v129 no40 p16 O 10 2016

A pilgrimage for indigenous rights mobilizes faith communities in Canada D. Dettloff bw *America* v216 no10 p15 My 1 2017

RCGS AND PARTNERS ANNOUNCE THE INDIGENOUS PEOPLES ATLAS OF CANADA N. Walker color *Canadian Geographic* v137 no4 p75 Jl/Ag 2017

Take Back the Parks R. JAGO bw *Walrus* v14 no8 p14 O 2017

Indigenous peoples—Canada—Attitudes

THE EDITORIAL *Maclean's* v129 no44 p5 N 7 2016

Indigenous peoples—Canada—Crimes against

Canada's unspoken crisis S. GILMORE color graph map *Maclean's* v129 no50 p12 D 19 2016

Indigenous peoples—Canada—Political activity

THE EDITORIAL *Maclean's* v129 no44 p5 N 7 2016

Indigenous peoples—Canada—Social conditions

Celebrate Canada? Not yet S. WHITECLOUD-BRASS chart color *Maclean's* v130 no6 p21 Jl 2017

Indigenous peoples—Canada—Social conditions—21st century

MISPLACED PRIDE S. GILMORE color *Maclean's* v130 no6 p22 Jl 2017

Indigenous peoples—Government relations

FROM HOPE TO FURY IN 12 MONTHS N. MACDONALD color *Maclean's* v129 no42 p24 O 24 2016

Indigenous peoples—Panama

See also

Cuna (Central American people)

HIGHER GROUND Z. SLOBIG *Orion Magazine* v35 no4/5 p20 Jl-O 2016

Indigenous rights

A pilgrimage for indigenous rights mobilizes faith communities in Canada D. Dettloff bw *America* v216 no10 p15 My 1 2017

Indigenous women—America

Broken before it begins B. HUTCHINSON color *Maclean's* p34 Je 2017

Indigenous women—America—Crimes against

Lost and broken [Cover story] N. Macdonald and M. Campbell color *Maclean's* v130 no9 p24 O 2017

Indigenous women—Crimes against

A SEARCH FOR ANSWERS N. MACDONALD color *Maclean's* v129 no51/52 p31 D 26 2016

Indignation (Film)

Dead Man on Campus D. EDELSTEIN img *New York* v49 no15 p86 Jl 25 2016

Indigo

Oldest indigo-dyed fabric found B. BOWER color *Science News* v190 no8 p8 O 15 2016

Indigo (Poem)

INDIGO E. Bass *New Yorker* v93 no32 p60 O 16 2017

Indigo Books & Music Inc.

A Book Lover's Cultural Department Store E. NAWOTKA *Publishers Weekly* v263 no39 p10 S 26 2016

Is This Indigo's Moment? J. Milliot chart *Publishers Weekly* v264 no30 p4 Jl 24 2017

Indio (Calif.)

COACHELLA IS HELLA QUEER THIS YEAR D. GUERRERO color *Advocate* no1090 p51 Ap 2017

Individual differences

THE BEGINNER'S GUIDE TO Making a Difference B. ROBINSON, K. SILVER et al cartoon color diag *O, The Oprah Magazine* p114 S 2017

What I Know for Sure Oprah color *O, The Oprah Magazine* p144 Mr 2017

Individual retirement accounts

GAME PLAN S. BLOCK cartoon *Kiplinger's Personal Finance* v71 no3 p31 Mr 2017

Last-Minute Tax Savers S. BLOCK cartoon *Kiplinger's Personal Finance* v71 no4 p46 Ap 2017

Roll Your Money Into an IRA? S. BLOCK color *Kiplinger's Personal Finance* v71 no5 p38 My 2017

Tax Reform and IRA Conversions K. LANKFORD *Kiplinger's Personal Finance* v71 no11 p44 N 2017

When Your Broker Goes Rogue K. LANKFORD *Kiplinger's Personal Finance* v71 no3 p36 Mr 2017

Individual retirement accounts—Investments

IRAs Gone Wild A. EBELING color *Forbes* v198 no6 p62 N 8 2016

Individual retirement accounts—Law & legislation

California's Big IRA Push P. Wang color *Money* v45 no10 p21 N 2016

Individual retirement accounts—Taxation

ASK THE EXPERT E. O'Brien and A. Mondalek chart *Money* v46 no4 p20 My 2017

This Tax Do-Over Could Be Handy P. Wang color diag *Money* v46 no4 p26 My 2017

Individual retirement accounts—United States

BROKERS CHANGE THEIR GAME PLAN S. BLOCK cartoon *Kiplinger's Personal Finance* v71 no4 p9 Ap 2017

You're Retiring Should Your Savings Move On Too? E. O'Brien color diag *Money* v46 no4 p23 My 2017

Your IRA Withdrawal May Be Reversible K. Damato color *Money* v46 no6 p30 Jl 2017

Individualism

Charting China's Rising Individualism in Names, Songs, and Attitudes Xi Zou and Huajian Cai *Harvard Business Review Digital Articles* p2 Mr 11 2016

Research: How You Feel About Individualism Is Influenced by Your Social Class N. Stephens and S. Townsend *Harvard Business Review Digital Articles* p2 My 22 2017

Individualism—Social aspects

Rugged Individualism: Two of the gravest threats to this distinctively American value: nanny states and helicopter parents D. Davenport and G. Lloyd *Hoover Digest: Research & Opinion on Public Policy* no2 p42 Spr 2017

Individualized medicine

Breast cancer research in the era of precision medicine Yi-Zhou Jiang and Zhi-Ming Shao bibl color *Science* v354 no6319 p30 D 23 2016

Cancer precision medicine in China Yuankai Shi bibl *Science* v354 no6319 p20 D 23 2016

Cardiovascular precision medicine in China Lei Song and Rutai Hui bibl *Science* v354 no6319 p66 D 23 2016

The challenges and prospects of precision oncology Lun-Xiu Qin bibl *Science* v354 no6319 p22 D 23 2016

Gene expression profiling–guided clinical precision treatment for patients with endometrial carcinoma Xiaoping Li, Jingyi Zhou et al bibl color diag *Science* v354 no6319 p33 D 23 2016

Glycomics and its application potential in precision medicine Youxin Wang, E. Adua et al bibl diag *Science* v354 no6319 p36 D 23 2016

How economics can shape precision medicines A. D. Stern, B. M. Alexander et al bibl color *Science* v355 no6330 p1131 Mr 17 2017

Opportunities and advantages for the development of precision medicine in China Qimin Zhan and Haili Qian *Science* v354 no6319 p6 D 23 2016

Opportunities and challenges for precision medicine in pancreatic cancer prevention and treatment Chengfeng Wang bibl *Science* v354 no6319 p42 D 23 2016

Personalized tumor vaccines keep cancer in check J. Kaiser color *Science* v356 no6334 p122 Ap 14 2017

Precision Medicine *Congressional Digest* v96 no2 p3 F 1 2017

Precision medicine development in Beijing Qian Li, Ke Huang et al *Science* v354 no6319 p61 D 23 2016

Precision medicine for Chinese women with familial breast cancer: Opportunities and challenges Xinyi Chen, Cong Fan et al bibl *Science* v354 no6319 p43 D 23 2016

Precision medicine for nasopharyngeal carcinoma Lin-Quan Tang, Hua Zhang et al bibl diag *Science* v354 no6319 p24 D 23 2016

Precision medicine in the 21st century S. Sanders *Science* v354 no6319 p3 D 23 2016

Quality management for precision medicine clinical applications: A consensus from the China Precision Medicine Clinical Research and Application Association Chen Wang, Shukun Yao et al bibl *Science* v354 no6319 p11 D 23 2016

Urgent need for implementation of precision medicine in gastric cancer in China Shuqin Jia, Lianhai Zhang et al bibl chart *Science* v354 no6319 p39 D 23 2016

Indochino Apparel Inc.

MADE TO MEASURE S. Marikar color *Fortune* v176 no4 p55 S 15 2017

Indole-3-carbinol

I-3-C and DIM V. Tweed color *Amazing Wellness* p12 Fall 2017

Indonesia—Description & travel

DO AS I SAY, NOT AS I DO B. CALVERT *Sea Magazine* v109 no1 p23 Ja 2017

Drift Back S. HOTCHKISS color *Conde Nast Traveler* v52 no7 p88 Ag 2017

Indonesian authors

PORTRAIT OF THE AUTHOR AS A HISTORIAN NO. 11: PRAMOEDYA ANANTA TOER A. Lee *History Today* v67 no5 p86 My 2017

Indonesian cooking

AN INDONESIAN FEAST J. R. FULLER color *Chicago* v66 no7 p44 Jl 2017

Indoor air pollution

Clearing the Air M. H. J. Farrell bw color graph *Consumer Reports* v82 no11 p8 N 2017

clear THE AIR M. RABBITT color *Yoga Journal* no290 p17 Mr 2017

Indoor air pollution—Prevention

MAKE YOUR HOME HEALTHIER K. Rockwood color *Health* v31 no4 p59 My 2017

See How They Grow *Parents* v91 no9 p140 S 2016

Indoor air quality

Research: Stale Office Air Is Making You Less Productive J. G. Allen *Harvard Business Review Digital Articles* p2 Mr 21 2017

Indoor gardening

GONE TO POT P. HISE *Virginia Living* v15 no3 p15 Ap 2017

Indoor rock climbing

Lift Off M. Brown cartoon *Vogue* v206 no11 p170 N 2016

Rotating-Wall Workouts H. MOORE bw *Climbing* no353 p47 My/Je 2017

Induced pluripotent stem cells

iPS cell therapy reported safe D. Normile color *Science* v355 no6330 p1109 Mr 17 2017

Induced pluripotent stem cells—Therapeutic use

A NEW WAY TO REPRODUCE A. Regalado color *MIT Technology Review* v120 no5 p32 S/O 2017

Induced seismicity

See also

Reservoir-triggered seismicity

Fault activation by hydraulic fracturing in western Canada Xuewei Bao and D. W. Eaton bibl graph map *Science* v354 no6318 p1406 D 16 2016

Human Activity Shakes Up Geological Hazard Map M. BARNA color map *Discover* v38 no1 p64 Ja/F 2017

Localized seismic deformation in the upper mantle revealed by dense seismic arrays A. Inbal, J. P. Ampuero et al bibl graph *Science* v354 no6308 p88 O 7 2016

Understanding induced seismicity D. Elsworth, C. J. Spiers et al bibl color graph *Science* v354 no6318 p1380 D 16 2016

Industria de Diseño Textil SA

SECRET FORMULA S. Baker cartoon color graph *Bloomberg Businessweek* no4501 p18 N 28 2016

Industrial applications

See also

L. S. PAINE chart img *Harvard Business Review* v95 no3 p50 My/Je 2017

Evaluate Your Leadership Development Program H. Monarth *Harvard Business Review Digital Articles* p2 Ja 22 2015

EXECUTIVE SUMMARIES color *Harvard Business Review* v95 no5 p150 S/O 2017

Finally, Proof That Managing for the Long Term Pays Off D. Barton, J. Manyika et al color graph *Harvard Business Review Digital Articles* p2 F 7 2017

The Former Head of the CIA on Managing the Hunt for Bin Laden L. E. Panetta and J. Bash *Harvard Business Review Digital Articles* p2 My 2 2016

The Four Phases of Project Management *Harvard Business Review Digital Articles* p2 N 3 2016

Getting an Intricate Operation Back in Sync E. Mady *Harvard Business Review Digital Articles* p2 My 20 2016

Good Leaders Are Good Learners L. A. Keating, P. A. Heslin et al *Harvard Business Review Digital Articles* p2 Ag 10 2017

Go West, Young Man map *Weekly Standard* v22 no47 p3 Ag 21 2017

Having a Difficult Conversation with Someone from a Different Culture M. Hahn and A. Molinsky *Harvard Business Review Digital Articles* p2 Mr 25 2016

Here's How Managers Can Be Replaced by Software D. Fidler *Harvard Business Review Digital Articles* p2 Ap 21 2015

How Senior Executives Stay Passionate About Their Work J. Morgan *Harvard Business Review Digital Articles* p2 2017

How to Bounce Back After a Failed Negotiation C. O'Hara *Harvard Business Review Digital Articles* p2 Ap 21 2016

How to Get Your Salespeople to Execute Your Strategy S. Edinger *Harvard Business Review Digital Articles* p2 Mr 1 2016

How to Manage Someone Who Thinks Everything Is Urgent L. Kislik *Harvard Business Review Digital Articles* p2 Ag 2 2017

How to Stop People Who Bog Things Down with Bureaucracy J. Allen *Harvard Business Review Digital Articles* p2 Jl 12 2016

How to Work Confidently with Numbers People R. Knight *Harvard Business Review Digital Articles* p2 S 2 2015

Innovation Is as Much About Finding Partners as Building Products C. Gnanasambandam and M. Uhl *Harvard Business Review Digital Articles* p2 Jl 20 2017

Innovation Isn't the Answer to All Your Problems S. Anthony, D. S. Duncan et al *Harvard Business Review Digital Articles* p2 Je 2 2015

The Internet Is Finally Forcing Management to Care About People S. Denning *Harvard Business Review Digital Articles* p2 My 5 2015

A Little Competition Could Improve Your HR, IT, and Legal Departments R. L. Martin *Harvard Business Review Digital Articles* p2 F 21 2017

The Management Thinker We Should Never Have Forgotten J. Macht *Harvard Business Review Digital Articles* p2 Je 24 2016

Managing in an Age of Winner-Take-All R. Straub *Harvard Business Review Digital Articles* p2 Ap 7 2015

Movers K. Stock color *Bloomberg Businessweek* no4525 p11 Je 5 2017

Optimizing Each Part of a Firm Doesn't Optimize the Whole Firm G. Satell *Harvard Business Review Digital Articles* p2 Ja 27 2016

Reflecting on David Garvin's Imprint on Management S. Cliffe *Harvard Business Review Digital Articles* p2 My 18 2017

RESTRUCTURE OR RECONFIGURE? S. J. G. GIROD and S. KARIM *Harvard Business Review* v95 no2 p128 Mr/Ap 2017

Signs That You're a Micromanager M. M. Wilkins *Harvard Business Review Digital Articles* p2 N 11 2014

The Social Cost of Bad Online Marketing A. Samuel *Harvard Business Review Digital Articles* p2 Ap 20 2016

Study: More Frequent Sales Quotas Help Volume but Hurt Profits D. J. Chung and D. Narayandas *Harvard Business Review Digital Articles* p2 2017

Tackle Bias in Your Company Without Making People Defensive A. Wittenberg-Cox *Harvard Business Review Digital Articles* p2 Mr 10 2015

Technology Changes, Good Management Doesn't Z. First *Harvard Business Review Digital Articles* p2 Ap 7 2016

Think Like an Author, Not an Owner C. A. Hidalgo *Harvard Business Review Digital Articles* p2 O 15 2015

To Lead Change, Explain the Context R. Ashkenas *Harvard Business Review Digital Articles* p2 N 24 2015

To Reduce Complexity in Your Company, Start with Pen and Paper R. McGrath *Harvard Business Review Digital Articles* p2 Ag 22 2016

To Win People Over, Speak to Their Wants and Needs N. Duarte *Harvard Business Review Digital Articles* p2 My 12 2015

'We Are as Gods and Might as Well Get Good at It' K. D. WILLIAMSON color *National Review* v69 no19 p29 O 16 2017

We Need to Expand Our Definition of Entrepreneurship J. Hagel III *Harvard Business Review Digital Articles* p2 S 28 2016

What Does an Aspiring Founder Need to Know? T. R. Eisenmann and R. Howe *Harvard Business Review Digital Articles* p1 Je 21 2017

What Economists Know That Managers Don't (and Vice Versa) P. Ghemawat *Harvard Business Review Digital Articles* p2 N 6 2014

What Hospitals Can Learn from Airlines About Buying Equipment P. Pronovost, S. Palmer et al *Harvard Business Review Digital Articles* p2 Je 13 2017

What to Do When a Colleague Can't Stick to a Decision A. Jen Su *Harvard Business Review Digital Articles* p2 Mr 25 2016

What You Can and Should Be Doing with Your Customer Journeys A. Richardson *Harvard Business Review Digital Articles* p2 Mr 25 2016

Why CEOs Should Commit to Many Small Battles Instead of a Single Big One J. Allen *Harvard Business Review Digital Articles* p2 D 14 2016

Why Leadership Training Fails—and What to Do About It: Interaction B. Palmer, C. Sharma et al *Harvard Business Review* v94 no12 p19 D 2016

You Don't Need to Adopt Holacracy to Get Some of Its Benefits G. Satell *Harvard Business Review Digital Articles* p2 Ag 28 2015

Your Customers Still Want to Talk to a Human Being G. Johnson *Harvard Business Review Digital Articles* p2 Jl 26 2017

Zombie Projects: How to Find Them and Kill Them S. Anthony, D. S. Duncan et al *Harvard Business Review Digital Articles* p2 Mr 4 2015

Industrial management education (Higher)
Shenandoah University *Dance Magazine* v90 p98 2016/2017 Supplement College Guide

Industrial management—European Union countries
SECRET FORMULA S. Baker cartoon color graph *Bloomberg Businessweek* no4501 p18 N 28 2016

Industrial management—International cooperation
But all I said was 'nice buns, ladies' J. SIMMS *People Management* p40 O 2016

Industrial management—Law & legislation
DIGITAL DOINGS IN DELAWARE J. J. Roberts *Fortune* v176 no3 p50 S 1 2017

Industrial management—Methodology
MANAGEMENT IS MUCH MORE THAN A SCIENCE: THE LIMITS OF DATA-DRIVEN DECISION MAKING R. L. MARTIN and T. GOLSBY-SMITH il *Harvard Business Review* v95 no5 p128 S/O 2017

Proof That Good Managers Really Do Make a Difference W. Frick *Harvard Business Review Digital Articles* p2 Ap 11 2016

WHY DO WE UNDERVALUE COMPETENT MANAGEMENT? NEITHER GREAT LEADERSHIP NOR BRILLIANT STRATEGY MATTERS WITHOUT OPERATIONAL EXCELLENCE R. SADUN, N. BLOOM et al graph il img *Harvard Business Review* v95 no5 p120 S/O 2017

Industrial management—Social aspects
From the Knowledge Economy to the Human Economy D. Seidman *Harvard Business Review Digital Articles* p2 N 12 2014

Industrial marketing
Avoid These Common B2B Content Marketing Mistakes B. Adamson and P. Spenner *Harvard Business Review Digital Articles* p2 F 10 2016

Why Self Image Matters in B2B Sales B. Adamson, K. Schmidt et al *Harvard Business Review Digital Articles* p2 Ap 2 2015

Industrial organization (Management)
See also
Facilitation (Business)
Teams in the workplace

ployee morale and her firm's reputation *People Management* p62 Ap 2017

editor's note. ON BECOMING A LEADER K. Perina *Psychology Today* v50 no1 p3 Ja/F 2017

Followers Don't See Their Leaders as Real People N. T. Washburn and B. Galvin color *Harvard Business Review Digital Articles* p2 Ja 23 2017

Get What You Need from Your Hands-Off Boss S. Stibitz *Harvard Business Review Digital Articles* p2 Je 12 2015

Half of Employees Don't Feel Respected by Their Bosses C. Porath *Harvard Business Review Digital Articles* p2 N 19 2014

Helping a Coworker Who's Stressed Out L. Davey *Harvard Business Review Digital Articles* p2 S 10 2015

How to Break Through Deadlock on Your Team R. Schwarz *Harvard Business Review Digital Articles* p2 Jl 7 2015

How to Deliver Bad News to Your Employees A. Gallo *Harvard Business Review Digital Articles* p2 Mr 30 2015

How to Get Out from Under Your Boss's Shadow P. Claman *Harvard Business Review Digital Articles* p2 D 2 2014

How to Navigate a Turf War at Work A. Gallo *Harvard Business Review Digital Articles* p2 S 27 2017

How to Negotiate Nicely Without Being a Pushover C. O'Hara *Harvard Business Review Digital Articles* p2 Ap 9 2015

How to Work for a Gossipy Boss R. Knight color *Harvard Business Review Digital Articles* p2 Ja 23 2017

How to Work with Someone Who Isn't a Team Player C. O'Hara *Harvard Business Review Digital Articles* p2 Ap 21 2017

How to Work with Someone Who's Always Stressed Out R. Knight *Harvard Business Review Digital Articles* p2 Ag 7 2017

ISAAC GETZ: Hierarchies are unnatural - it's time for a liberating revolution I. GETZ *People Management* p16 Mr 2017

Love Your Ex-Employees and They'll Love You Back M. Schrage *Harvard Business Review Digital Articles* p2 N 18 2015

Millennials Want to Be Coached at Work K. Willyerd *Harvard Business Review Digital Articles* p2 F 27 2015

New Managers Should Focus on Helping Their Teams, Not Pleasing Their Bosses K. Dillon *Harvard Business Review Digital Articles* p2 Jl 7 2017

Overcoming the Toughest Common Coaching Challenges A. Gallo *Harvard Business Review Digital Articles* p2 Ap 15 2015

Research: Insecure Managers Don't Want Your Suggestions N. J. Fast, E. R. Burris et al *Harvard Business Review Digital Articles* p2 N 24 2014

Research: Yes, Being Helpful Is Tiring K. Lanaj *Harvard Business Review Digital Articles* p2 S 6 2016

Small Talk Is an Overrated Way to Build Relationships with Your Employees K. Scott *Harvard Business Review Digital Articles* p1 Jl 25 2017

To Get Better at Your Job, Work Practice into Your Routine R. H. Schaffer *Harvard Business Review Digital Articles* p2 Ja 29 2016

View from the Top C. FLORA *Psychology Today* v50 no1 p62 Ja/F 2017

Want to Be More Productive? Sit Next to Someone Who Is J. Corsello and D. Minor *Harvard Business Review Digital Articles* p2 F 14 2017

Want Your Employees to Trust You? Show You Trust Them H. H. Brower, S. W. Lester et al *Harvard Business Review Digital Articles* p2 Jl 5 2017

What Amazing Bosses Do Differently S. Finkelstein *Harvard Business Review Digital Articles* p2 N 27 2015

What Bosses Gain by Being Vulnerable E. Seppala *Harvard Business Review Digital Articles* p2 D 11 2014

What Really Happens When Companies Nix Performance Ratings D. Rock and B. Jones *Harvard Business Review Digital Articles* p2 N 6 2015

What to Do When a Coworker Goes Over Your Head A. Gallo *Harvard Business Review Digital Articles* p2 D 22 2016

What to Do When You and Your Boss Aren't Getting Along R. Knight *Harvard Business Review Digital Articles* p2 Ag 18 2016

What to Do When Your Boss Says No S. Sonenshein color *Harvard Business Review Digital Articles* p2 F 6 2017

What to Do When You're the Target of a Hurtful Office Rumor E. Seppala *Harvard Business Review Digital Articles* p2 D 2 2016

What to Do When Your Peer Becomes Your Boss A. Gallo *Harvard Business Review Digital Articles* p2 O 24 2016

What You Can Do If You Have a Gossiping Boss J. Grenny *Harvard Business Review Digital Articles* p2 N 21 2016

Industrial relations—Great Britain

Strong unions are fighting against technology A. Cook *People Management* p15 F 2017

Industrial relations—Management

Great Strategy Begins with a CEO on the Frontlines B. Saunders and K. Banta *Harvard Business Review Digital Articles* p2 O 7 2014

Put Yourself in Your Colleague's Shoes J. Cohen *Harvard Business Review Digital Articles* p2 O 6 2014

Industrial relations—Methodology

2 Ways to Regain Your Boss's Trust D. DeSteno *Harvard Business Review Digital Articles* p2 N 26 2014

How to Disagree with Your Boss J. Grenny *Harvard Business Review Digital Articles* p2 N 25 2014

When Your Boss Gives You Conflicting Messages L. Schlesinger and C. Kiefer *Harvard Business Review Digital Articles* p2 N 27 2014

Industrial relations—Psychological aspects

THE SCIENCE OF PEP TALKS: TO FIRE UP YOUR TEAM, DRAW ON A RESEARCH-PROVEN, THREE-PART FORMULA D. MCGINN il *Harvard Business Review* v95 no4 p133 Jl/Ag 2017

Industrial relations—United States

Navigating Political Talk at Work D. W. Ballard color graph *Harvard Business Review Digital Articles* p2 Mr 2 2017

Industrial research laboratories

Celebrating Targeted Investments in Innovative Research P. Falcone *Science & Technology Review* p3 Ap/My 2017

INVESTING IN THE NATION'S FUTURE: The Laboratory Directed Research and Development Program has been a significant engine of scientific discovery for 25 years A. Heller *Science & Technology Review* p4 Ap/My 2017

Industrial revolution

Industrial Evolution A. SCHUKAR *American Scholar* v86 no3 p10 Summ 2017

A (Working) Woman's Place: As the Industrial Revolution wrought widespread social changes, female cotton industry workers' lives changed dramatically S. Wilkes *History Today* v67 no6 p16 Je 2016

Industrial revolution—Economic aspects

Is Canadian Philanthropy Ready for the Future? A. Chunilall color *Walrus* v14 no5 p36 Je 2017

Industrial robot design & construction

DARK FACTORY S. KOLHATKAR bw color *New Yorker* v93 no33 p70 O 23 2017

Industrial robots

See also

Automated guided vehicle systems

The Age of Smart, Safe, Cheap Robots Is Already Here M. Miremadi, S. Narayanan et al *Harvard Business Review Digital Articles* p2 Je 15 2015

ARMLESS DROID CALLS COPS AFTER BEING ASSAULTED BY DRUNKEN MAN K. MANGU-WARD color *Reason* v49 no3 p4 Jl 2017

Breaking the Death Grip of Legacy Technologies W. C. Shih *Harvard Business Review Digital Articles* p2 My 28 2015

How to Give a Robot a Job Review M. Schrage *Harvard Business Review Digital Articles* p2 Mr 30 2016

How We'll Really Feel if Robots Take Our Jobs G. Gavett *Harvard Business Review Digital Articles* p2 Ja 16 2015

The impact of technology on labor markets R. Works *Monthly Labor Review* p1 Je 2017

A Pizza-Making Robot J. Zorthian color *Time* v189 no7/8 p27 F 27 2017

Prepare Your Workforce for the Automation Age C. Knoess, R. Harbour et al *Harvard Business Review Digital Articles* p2 N 23 2016

ROBOPOCALYPSE NOT: EVERYONE THINKS THAT AUTOMATION WILL TAKE AWAY OUR JOBS. THE EVIDENCE DISAGREES J. SUROWIECKI cartoon color graph *Wired* v25 no9 p40 S 2017

THE ROBOTS ARE COMING (But You'll Still Need to Work) P. Coy *Bloomberg Businessweek* no4528 p8 Je 26 2017

ROLE REVERSAL color *Wired* v25 no10 p14 O 2017

teach AI when to say hi C. Mayeda diag *Popular Science* v289 no5 p8 S/O 2017

What Happens to Society When Robots Replace Workers? W. H. Davidow and M. S. Malone *Harvard Business Review Digital Articles* p2 D 10 2014

Industrial robots—Design & construction

Beware the Blue-Collar Bots E. BETZ color *Discover* v38 no2 p12 Mr 2017

Industrial robots—Economic aspects

The 33¢ T-Shirt K. Hamlin and Yinan Zhao *Bloomberg Businessweek* no4536 p41 S 4 2017

Robots Seem to Be Improving Productivity, Not Costing Jobs M. Muro and S. Andes *Harvard Business Review Digital Articles* p2 Je 16 2015

Industrial robots—Programming

Beware the Blue-Collar Bots E. BETZ color *Discover* v38 no2 p12 Mr 2017

Industrial safety

See also

Occupational hazards

Chemical safety K. REST *Issues in Science & Technology* v33 no1 p17 Fall 2016

Counting injuries and illnesses in the workplace: an international review [Cover story] bibl *Monthly Labor Review* p1 S 2017

Ergonomically Correct J. S. HO *USA Today Magazine* v146 no2866 p25 Jl 2017

How to Make Your Workplace Safe for Transgender Employees J. W. Hull *Harvard Business Review Digital Articles* p2 Ag 3 2015

Why Workplace Accidents Tend to Happen Late in a Project N. Swidey *Harvard Business Review Digital Articles* p2 F 20 2015

Industrial safety—United States

U.S. WORKERS ARE SAFER, BUT NOT IN ALL JOBS diag *Fortune* v175 no2 p11 F 1 2017

Industrial surveys

Workers Are Bad at Filling Out Timesheets, and It Costs Billions a Day G. Gavett *Harvard Business Review Digital Articles* p2 Ja 12 2015

Industrial technicians

Theater Needs Tomorrow's Technicians Today W. Djerf *Stage Directions* v30 no10 p34 O 2017

Industrial tours

THE Chef of the Future MAKES ONLY ONE DISH CRAB BISQUE à la robot D. MARCHESE img *New York* p40 Ja 9 2017

Industrial workers

Making Waves *Reader's Digest* v188 no1125 p40 N 2016

Industrial capacity—Charts, diagrams, etc.

PRODUCTION AND BUSINESS ACTIVITY *Economic Indicators* p17 F 2017

PRODUCTION AND BUSINESS ACTIVITY *Economic Indicators* p17 S 2016

Industrialization

BORDERLINE WILDERNESS C. Mihell *Sierra* v101 no6 p28 N/D 2016

The Shaman Masters of Hohhot Have Returned color *Foreign Policy* no225 p5 Jl/Ag 2017

Industrialization—Environmental aspects

THE LONG VIEW R. KHATCHADOURIAN cartoon color *New Yorker* v92 no42 p80 D 19 2016

Industrial production index—Charts, diagrams, etc.

INTERNATIONAL STATISTICS *Economic Indicators* p35 F 2017

INTERNATIONAL STATISTICS *Economic Indicators* p35 Je 2017

PRODUCTION AND BUSINESS ACTIVITY *Economic Indicators* p17 F 2017

PRODUCTION AND BUSINESS ACTIVITY *Economic Indicators* p17 Je 2017

Industrial productivity—Charts, diagrams, etc.

INTERNATIONAL STATISTICS *Economic Indicators* p35 Ag 2017

INTERNATIONAL STATISTICS *Economic Indicators* p35 Ja 2017

PRODUCTION AND BUSINESS ACTIVITY *Economic Indicators* p17 Ag 2017

PRODUCTION AND BUSINESS ACTIVITY *Economic Indica-*

tors p17 Ja 2017

PRODUCTION AND BUSINESS ACTIVITY *Economic Indicators* p17 O 2016

Industrial productivity—United States—Charts, diagrams, etc.

PRODUCTION AND BUSINESS ACTIVITY *Economic Indicators* p17 Ap 2017

PRODUCTION AND BUSINESS ACTIVITY *Economic Indicators* p17 D 2016

Industries

See also

Boating industry

Cigarette industry

Do-it-yourself products industry

Energy industries

Fisheries

Health care industry

High technology industries

Home furnishings industry

Hospitality industry

Industries—Social aspects

Luxury goods industry

Manufacturing industries

Mineral industries

Pharmaceutical industry

Prison industries

Real estate business

Regulated industries

Service industries

Transportation industry

The Gig Economy Is Real If You Know Where to Look I. Hathaway *Harvard Business Review Digital Articles* p2 Ag 13 2015

How Industrial Systems Are Turning into Digital Services J. Sinfield, N. Calder et al *Harvard Business Review Digital Articles* p2 Je 23 2015

Industries & society

CHANGE THE WORLD !!!! C. Leaf, E. Fry et al color diag map *Fortune* v176 no4 p74 S 15 2017

E=MC× EARTH FRIENDLY = MANUFACTURING × CONSCIENTIOUSNESS× E. Fry color *Fortune* v176 no4 p120 S 15 2017

RISING STARS S. Agus and J. Vanian color *Fortune* v176 no4 p89 S 15 2017

Industries & society—United States

FROM BOOM TO DOOM E. Griffith color *Fortune* v176 no4 p68 S 15 2017

Industries—Classification

Why Are We Still Classifying Companies by Industry? B. Libert, M. Beck et al *Harvard Business Review Digital Articles* p2 Ag 18 2016

Industries—Computer network resources

Most Industries Are Nowhere Close to Realizing the Potential of Analytics N. Henke, J. Bughin et al *Harvard Business Review Digital Articles* p2 D 16 2016

Industries—India

Doing Business in India Requires a Mobile-First Strategy V. Govindarajan and G. Bagla *Harvard Business Review Digital Articles* p2 D 23 2016

Industries—Social aspects

See also

Factories—Environmental aspects

Petroleum industry—Environmental aspects

Restaurants—Social aspects

Social entrepreneurship

Business Can Help End Child Labor V. Govindarajan *Harvard Business Review Digital Articles* p2 Ap 9 2015

Industries—United States

50, 100 & 150 YEARS AGO color *Scientific American* v317 no2 p83 Ag 2017

Industrywide conditions

BEEF IS BOUNCING BACK A. McConnell *Successful Farming* v114 no10 p31 O 2016

Clean, Well-Lighted Places A. RUSSETH bw *ARTnews* v115 no3 p46 Fall 2016

ONE BIG FIELD M. McGinnis *Successful Farming* v114 no10 p22 O 2016

Indvik, Lauren

Cashmere color *InStyle* v23 no12 p217 N 2016
Puffer Coats color *InStyle* v23 no13 p205 D 2016

Indy Racing League LLC
Auto Pilots A. Lawrence, T. Keith et al color *Sports Illustrated* v126 no7 p26 Mr 6 2017
GOOD AS NEW M. Harris and S. Kwak color *Sports Illustrated* v127 no10 p20 O 2 2017
RETRO FIRE S. Kwak color *Sports Illustrated* v127 no10 p20 O 2 2017

Inertia (Mechanics)
See also
    Momentum (Mechanics)
Angular momentum–induced delays in solid-state photoemission enhanced by intra-atomic interactions F. Siek, S. Neb et al chart color graph *Science* v357 no6357 p1274 S 22 2017

Infant care
See also
    Swaddling
why poop changes N. PRENTIS *Parents* v92 no8 p130 Ag 2017

Infant carriers—Evaluation
A Natural Start A. Andrews *Sierra* v102 no1 p9 Ja/F 2017

Infant development
See also
    Infant psychology
bizarre behavior A. BROWN *Parents* v92 no1 p72 Ja 2017
control freaks J. BURT COTE *Parents* v91 no9 p166 S 2016
sign up for fun I. COHEN *Parents* v92 no6 p134 Je 2017

Infant diseases
SHOULD BABIES BE SEQUENCED? [Cover story] B. Rochman color *Scientific American* v316 no3 p72 Mr 2017

Infant formulas
Formula for Feeding *Parents* v91 no11 p34 N 2016

Infant mortality
Welfare Pasts and Futures S. King *History Today* v67 no3 p6 Mr 2017

Infant mortality—Economic aspects
BLACK BIRTHS MATTER Z. CARPENTER color il *Nation* v304 no7 p12 Mr 6 2017

Infant nutrition
See also
    Baby foods
    Breastfeeding (Humans)
eating issues E. KLEIN *Parents* v91 no6 p138 Je 2016
Meals for Munchkins J. Laird color *Working Mother* v40 no3 p18 Ag/S 2017

Infant nutrition—Equipment & supplies
parents to parents *Parents* v91 no6 p14 Je 2016

Infant psychology
See also
    Parent & infant
bizarre behavior A. BROWN *Parents* v92 no1 p72 Ja 2017
coming attractions J. DETZ *Parents* v91 no9 p52 S 2016
control freaks J. BURT COTE *Parents* v91 no9 p166 S 2016
reasons your baby isn't sleeping (abridged) J. VICK color *Parents* v92 no4 p136 Ap 2017
show how to share J. RAINEY MARQUEZ *Parents* v92 no6 p136 Je 2017
The Smarter Way to Play *Parents* v91 no11 p30 N 2016

Infantile amnesia
The Great Forgetting K. OHLSON *Reader's Digest* v189 no1127 p41 F 2017

Infantile colic—Treatment
Acupuncture for Colicky Babies?! Yes, It's a Thing! K. Rockwood color *Parents* v92 no7 p26 Jl 2017

Infant mortality—Charts, diagrams, etc.
Yes, There Is Good News! *New York Times Upfront* v149 no11 p12 Ap 3 2017

Infantry—History
THE FOREST FOR THE TREES M. D. Hull bw color *Military History* v34 no5 p30 Ja 2018

Infants
See also
    Newborn infants
    Premature infants
Baby's Rainbow J. C. Hu color *Scientific American* v317 no3 p16 S 2017

Boardwalk Empire *Reader's Digest* v188 no1124 p136 O 2016
Bouncing Baby Boomers *Saturday Evening Post* v289 no1 p108 Ja/F 2017
Cooper's HEART R. GUMMERE cartoon color *O, The Oprah Magazine* p110 Ap 2017
GREAT EXPECTATIONS C. Agard color *Entertainment Weekly* no1463/1464 p18 Ap/My 2017
I Ain't Got No Body: Need a dead body for a show? Get an intern and Saran Wrap J. Duckworth *Stage Directions* v30 no9 p28 S 2017
Infants make more attempts to achieve a goal when they see adults persist J. A. Leonard, Y. Lee et al chart color *Science* v357 no6357 p1290 S 22 2017
Myanmar color *National Geographic* v230 no5 p5 N 2016
THE SEVEN AGES OF ME AND TV R. CHAST cartoon *New Yorker* v93 no26 p31 S 4 2017
The social origins of persistence L. P. Butler color *Science* v357 no6357 p1236 S 22 2017

Infants' supplies
See also
    Breast pumps
Baby, Monitored A. LAFRANCE bw color *Atlantic* v318 no5 p24 D 2016
Bringing Up Bébé E. A. ACHARA color *Vogue* v206 no11 p164 N 2016
wear with care J. KELLY GEDDES *Parents* v92 no5 p116 My 2017

Infants' supplies—Evaluation
TEST DRIVE: DOONA INFANT CAR SEAT/STROLLER bw *Conde Nast Traveler* v51 no10 p175 N 2016
WHOA, BABY H. Kelly *Washingtonian Magazine* v52 no5 p148 F 2017

Infants' supplies—History
Vintage Views bw *Parents* v92 no9 p18 S 2017

Infants—Care
baby no. 2 C. W. DINEEN *Parents* v91 no11 p90 N 2016
BABY ON BOARD I. CORTES *USA Today Magazine* v145 no2858 p68 N 2016
crying out loud H. KARP *Parents* v92 no1 p71 Ja 2017
FIGHTING FOR A HEALTHY BLACK PREGNANCY D. McCLAIN bw color *Nation* v304 no7 p17 Mr 6 2017
getting physical T. REECE *Parents* v91 no11 p140 N 2016
have a nicer trip R. RABKIN PEACHMAN *Parents* v91 no11 p142 N 2016
the sleep fix H. GOWEN WALSH *Parents* v91 no11 p58 N 2016
spending time apart J. MIGALA *Parents* v92 no3 p106 Mr 2017
wear with care J. KELLY GEDDES *Parents* v92 no5 p116 My 2017

Infants—Care—Equipment & supplies—Evaluation
Baby's First Virtual Assistant F. Gillette color *Bloomberg Businessweek* no4506 p27 Ja 9 2017

Infants—United States
America's Buzziest Baby Names C. Wilson color *Time* v189 no20 p9 My 29 2017

Infection
See also
    Communicable diseases
    Respiratory infections
WHAT INFECTION LOOKS LIKE C. Barakat and M. Freckleton color *Equus* no482 p16 N 2017

Infection prevention
ASK THE DOCTOR A. L. KOMAROFF color *Harvard Health Letter* v42 no2 p2 D 2016
Buzzworthy: Honey color *Health* v31 no2 p16 Mr 2017
KEEPING IT CLEAN K. Donohue *Maclean's* v129 no40 p71 O 10 2016
Your Travel Beauty Problems, Solved C. T. Burns color *Health* v31 no6 p27 Jl 2017

Infection—Diagnosis
Microbial Mystery C. P. DUNAVAN bw color diag *Discover* v27 no10 p22 D 2016

Infection—Treatment
icky infections D. KOENIG *Parents* v91 no12 p34 D 2016

Inferno (Film)
INFERNO D. Vaughn color *Sound & Vision* v82 no5 p68 Je 2017
Inferno S. Perry color *Entertainment Weekly* no1438 p46 N 4 2016

Possibly E. Curran, J. Black et al color *Bloomberg Businessweek* no4507 p14 Ja 16 2017

Inflation (Finance)—News briefs

Asia K. Stock color *Bloomberg Businessweek* no4538 p11 S 18 2017

Inflation (Finance)—United States

Hedging Inflation Without Gold J. Waggoner color diag *Money* v46 no4 p34 My 2017

Job Switchers Solve An Inflation Mystery S. Matthews diag *Bloomberg Businessweek* no4513 p22 Mr 6 2017

Inflation (Finance)—United States—Economic aspects

INFLATION PLAY W. BALDWIN chart color graph *Forbes* v198 no9 p88 D 30 2016

Inflation (Finance)—Venezuela

Hyperinflation B. Bartenstein and M. Glassman graph *Bloomberg Businessweek* no4505 p19 D 26 2016

Inflation-indexed bonds

GREAT IDEAS for $1,000, $10,000 or even $100,000 color *Kiplinger's Personal Finance* v71 no2 p26 F 2017

Inflation (Finance)—Charts, diagrams, etc.

Hyperinflation B. Bartenstein and M. Glassman graph *Bloomberg Businessweek* no4505 p19 D 26 2016

Influence (Psychology)

See also

Influence (Literary, artistic, etc.)

Social influence

3 Rules for Experts Who Want More Influence D. Clark *Harvard Business Review Digital Articles* p2 My 22 2015

5 FOR FIGHTING: LEADERS AND ADVOCATE STAFF TELL US THE FIVE LGBT PEOPLE WHO INFLUENCED THEM THE MOST bw color *Advocate* no1091 p42 Je/Jl 2017

Are You Following the Herd? H. CORBETT *Scholastic Choices* v32 no8 p16 My 2017

Focus on Winning Either Hearts or Minds L. Lai *Harvard Business Review Digital Articles* p2 My 20 2015

Influence People by Leveraging the Brain's Laziness A. Markman *Harvard Business Review Digital Articles* p2 My 29 2015

Measuring Your Employees' Invisible Forms of Influence C. Nielsen, D. Niu et al *Harvard Business Review Digital Articles* p2 N 7 2016

Understand the 4 Components of Influence N. Morgan *Harvard Business Review Digital Articles* p2 My 19 2015

Influence (Literary, artistic, etc.)

A cocreator of horror podcasts finds inspiration in fiction M. SOLLINGER color *Publishers Weekly* v263 no46 p60 N 14 2016

WHAT DO YOU DO WITH THE MAD THAT YOU FEEL? [Cover story] D. Dark color *America* v216 no10 p26 My 1 2017

Influencer marketing

Snapchat vs. the 'Influencers' S. Frier color *Bloomberg Businessweek* no4537 p24 S 11 2017

Influenza

See also

Equine influenza

Ask Men's Health® bw color *Men's Health* v32 no3 p8 Ap 2017

BOOSTER CLUB L. Krieger color *O, The Oprah Magazine* p78 Ag 2017

Flu Season J. RAO color *Natural History* v125 no9 p46 S 2017

HOW TO OUTSMART COLD+FLU SEASON [Cover story] J. MIGALA cartoon chart color *Good Housekeeping* v263 no5 p163 N 2016

SAVED BY THE CELLS color *O, The Oprah Magazine* p30 My 2017

SICK SEASON SURVIVAL GUIDE J. R. MARQUEZ *Scholastic Choices* v32 no4 p16 Ja 2017

Influenza A H5N1

First flu is forever C. Viboud and S. L. Epstein bibl diag *Science* v354 no6313 p706 N 11 2016

Potent protection against H5N1 and H7N9 influenza via childhood hemagglutinin imprinting K. M. Gostic, M. Ambrose et al bibl chart graph *Science* v354 no6313 p722 N 11 2016

Influenza A H7N9

Potent protection against H5N1 and H7N9 influenza via childhood hemagglutinin imprinting K. M. Gostic, M. Ambrose et al bibl chart graph *Science* v354 no6313 p722 N 11 2016

Warning: The Next Global Security Threat Isn't What You Think

[Cover story] B. Walsh color diag *Time* v189 no18 p32 My 15 2017

Influenza A virus

See also

Avian influenza A virus

Generation of influenza A viruses as live but replication-incompetent virus vaccines Longlong Si, Huan Xu et al bibl graph *Science* v354 no6316 p1170 D 2 2016

Influenza epidemiology

Can we beat influenza? W. Zhang and R. G. Webster color *Science* v357 no6347 p111 Jl 14 2017

Influenza prevention

See also

Influenza vaccination

ASK THE DOCTOR A. L. KOMAROFF color *Harvard Health Letter* v42 no2 p2 D 2016

fall immunity guide V. TWEED color *Better Nutrition* v79 no10 p42 O 2017

Got a Cold? Do This M. Santos color *Working Mother* p57 F/Mr 2017

immunity now! S. SEA GOLD *Parents* v91 no11 p38 N 2016

Keeping Winter Bugs at Bay V. TWEED color *Better Nutrition* v78 no12 p60 D 2016

The microbial metabolite desaminotyrosine protects from influenza through type I interferon A. L. Steed, G. P. Christophi et al graph *Science* v357 no6350 p498 Ag 4 2017

Prevent, Treat, & Recover: A FLU GUIDE L. TURNER color *Better Nutrition* v79 no1 p44 Ja 2017

PROTECTING OUR COMMUNITIES B. Keyes-Bevan *Maclean's* v129 no40 p68 O 10 2016

STAGES OF COLDS & FLU J. Rice color *Amazing Wellness* v8 no6 p52 Early Winter2016

Vaccination roundup *Harvard Health Letter* v41 no12 p7 O 2016

Influenza vaccination

See also

Flu vaccine efficacy

The best time for a flu shot color *Redbook* p75 N 2017

THE BEST & WORST OF 2016 bw color *Men's Health* v31 no10 p90 D 2016

Fall vaccination roundup *Harvard Health Letter* v42 no11 p6 S 2017

HEALTHFESSIONS K. Peterson color *Women's Health* v14 no2 p86 Mr 2017

MICRONEEDLE PATCH FOR FLU VACCINATION [Cover story] *USA Today Magazine* v146 no2869 p1 O 2017

New and Improved Vaccine Schedule color *Parents* v92 no9 p28 S 2017

One and Done [Cover story] L. Beil color graph *Science News* v192 no7 p18 O 28 2017

Patch could someday replace flu shot A. CUNNINGHAM color *Science News* v192 no1 p8 Ag 5 2017

PROTECTING OUR COMMUNITIES B. Keyes-Bevan *Maclean's* v129 no40 p68 O 10 2016

Influenza viruses

Autopsy of a Deadly Virus J. K. TAUBENBERGER bw color *Natural History* v125 no9 p14 S 2017

Why is the flu vaccine so mediocre? J. Cohen color graph *Science* v357 no6357 p1222 S 22 2017

Influenza—Complications

Avoiding winter heart attacks *Harvard Health Letter* v41 no12 p3 O 2016

Influenza Epidemic, 1918-1919

Death March of 1918 G. CHOWELL, L. SIMONSEN et al bw color *Natural History* v125 no9 p11 S 2017

In Flew Enza N. J. COX color *Natural History* v125 no9 p16 S 2017

Profiling a Pandemic MAMELUND bw color *Natural History* v125 no9 p6 S 2017

Influenza—History

Profiling a Pandemic MAMELUND bw color *Natural History* v125 no9 p6 S 2017

Influenza—Patients

Forecasting the Flu B. LUTZ color *New Orleans Magazine* v52 no1 p40 S 2017

Influenza—Risk factors

The best cold & flu fighting secrets of all time E. Crain, K. Hol-

land et al color *Health* v31 no9 p71 N 2017
Influenza—Transmission
EVIDENCE SUGGESTS EQUINE INFLUENZA VIRUS IS ZOONOTIC C. Barakat and M. McCluskey color *Equus* no470 p18 N 2016
Influenzavirus A
 See also
 Influenza A virus
Generation of influenza A viruses as live but replication-incompetent virus vaccines Longlong Si, Huan Xu et al bibl graph *Science* v354 no6316 p1170 D 2 2016
Infocomm Academy (Company)
Hey... What Are You Doing Next January? T. Lowe *Stage Directions* v30 no8 p2 Ag 2017
Infor Inc.
SEEKING NEW HIRES, INFOR GOES STRAIGHT TO THE SOURCE P. Marinova color *Fortune* v175 no4 p16 Mr 15 2017
Information & communication technologies
 See also
 Electronic services
To Really Help the Global Poor, Create Technology They'll Pay For A. Deng *Harvard Business Review Digital Articles* p2 Ag 5 2015
The Two Essential Entrepreneurial Types P. Formica *Harvard Business Review Digital Articles* p2 Ag 5 2015
Information design
A note from the editor K. Pope *Columbia Journalism Review* p10 Fall/Wint 2016
Information display systems
 See also
 Head-mounted displays
 Radar indicators
Computation BOOSTS Materials Discovery A. Chen *Science & Technology Review* p16 Jl/Ag 2017
Information display systems—Evaluation
JOHN DEERE 4640 UNIVERSAL DISPLAY UNVEILED: PORTABLE DISPLAY FEATURES THE LATEST TECHNOLOGY IN A USER-FRIENDLY GEN 4 EXPERIENCE L. Bedord *Successful Farming* v115 no11 p24 S 2017
Information economy
Is the Era of Mass Manufacturing Coming to an End? P. Acton *Harvard Business Review Digital Articles* p2 D 5 2014
Information filtering systems
 See also
 Recommender systems (Information filtering)
Great Digital Companies Build Great Recommendation Engines M. Schrage *Harvard Business Review Digital Articles* p2 Ag 1 2017
Information overload
Turn Digital Overload to Your Advantage A. Samuel *Harvard Business Review Digital Articles* p2 My 12 2015
Information policy
 See also
 Data protection
The Business Implications of the EU-U.S. "Privacy Shield" L. Downes *Harvard Business Review Digital Articles* p2 F 10 2016
Information resources
 See also
 Electronic information resources
 Reference sources
Special Dolls for Special Kids S. Watts color *Parents* v92 no3 p18 Mr 2017
Information resources management
 See also
 Data modeling
 Information sharing
Dispel Your Team's Fear of Data T. C. Redman *Harvard Business Review Digital Articles* p2 Jl 16 2015
Firms Need a Blueprint for Building Their IT Systems D. A. Marchand and J. Peppard *Harvard Business Review Digital Articles* p2 Je 18 2015
Good Presentations Need to Make People Uncomfortable J. Bersin *Harvard Business Review Digital Articles* p2 S 9 2016
IGNORANCE WAS BLISS S. Manguso bw *O, The Oprah Magazine* p32 D 2016
Information resources management—Software

Defend The Bottom Line L. Bedord *Successful Farming* v114 no12 p14 Mid-N 2016
Information resources—Evaluation
surviving dr. facebook J. MIGALA *Parents* v92 no2 p36 F 2017
Information retrieval
 See also
 Internet searching
Information scientists
 See also
 Librarians
Retaining Your Data Scientists M. Li *Harvard Business Review Digital Articles* p2 N 20 2014
The Two Questions You Need to Ask Your Data Analysts M. Li *Harvard Business Review Digital Articles* p2 O 27 2015
What Kind of Data Scientist Do You Need? Michael Li *Harvard Business Review Digital Articles* p2 F 1 2016
Information scientists—Employment
The Best Data Scientists Know How to Tell Stories M. Li *Harvard Business Review Digital Articles* p2 O 13 2015
Information services
 See also
 Information storage & retrieval systems
 Location-based services
 Medicine information services
 Preprints
Seven Ways to Leverage Mobile Technology in Aquatics M. Pierce *Parks & Recreation* v52 no5 p50 My 2017
You Don't Have to Be an Expert: As cities become inundated with data, they're turning to citizens for help T. Newcombe color *Governing* v30 no11 p60 Ag 2017
Information sharing
8 Ground Rules for Great Meetings R. Schwarz *Harvard Business Review Digital Articles* p2 Je 15 2016
The Benefits of Giving Away What Your Company Knows C. V. Harquail *Harvard Business Review Digital Articles* p2 O 14 2014
Fostering reproducibility in industry-academia research B. R. Jasny, N. Wigginton et al color *Science* v357 no6353 p759 Ag 25 2017
Good Presentations Need to Make People Uncomfortable J. Bersin *Harvard Business Review Digital Articles* p2 S 9 2016
Hey! You! Get Off of My Cloud! And Other Tales from the Family-Data-Sharing Economy K. V. Ogtrop color *Time* v190 no14 p55 O 9 2017
HOW YOU'LL SHARE DATA SAFELY *Governing* v30 no1 p28 O 2016
Is Your Company Encouraging Employees to Share What They Know? C. G. Myers *Harvard Business Review Digital Articles* p2 N 6 2015
A New Approach to Safely Sharing Cancer Patients' Data K. Giusti and R. G. Hamermesh *Harvard Business Review Digital Articles* p1 Je 21 2017
Preprint ecosystems J. Berg color *Science* v357 no6358 p1331 S 29 2017
A VAST WING CON-SPIRACY? C. Leonard color *Bloomberg Businessweek* no4512 p62 F 20 2017
Information storage & retrieval systems
 See also
 Information filtering systems
6 quick ways to clear space on an overstuffed Android device B. PATTERSON color *PCWorld* v35 no9 p101 S 2017
IBM stores one bit of data on a single atom, showing how small storage could become S. LAWSON color *PCWorld* v35 no4 p21 Ap 2017
Reinventing Intel T. Simonite color *MIT Technology Review* v119 no6 p20 N/D 2016
Information storage & retrieval systems—Medical care
Making Predictive Analytics a Routine Part of Patient Care R. B. Parikh, Z. Obermeyer et al *Harvard Business Review Digital Articles* p2 Ap 21 2016
Information storage & retrieval systems—Security measures
HOW MUCH IS SECURITY WORTH? J. J. Roberts *Fortune* v175 no2 p14 F 1 2017
HOW YOU'LL SHARE DATA SAFELY *Governing* v30 no1 p28 O 2016
Information technology

Business Review Digital Articles p2 F 27 2015

Leadership May Not Be the Problem with Your Innovation Team D. Dworkin and M. Spiegel *Harvard Business Review Digital Articles* p2 Ag 25 2016

Leading Digital Transformation Is Like Urban Planning P. Beswick *Harvard Business Review Digital Articles* p2 Ag 2 2017

To Encourage Innovation, Make It a Competition A. Rathi *Harvard Business Review Digital Articles* p2 N 19 2014

Unlock Employee Innovation That Fits with Your Strategy B. Fischer *Harvard Business Review Digital Articles* p2 O 27 2014

What Big Companies Get Wrong About Innovation Metrics S. Kirsner *Harvard Business Review Digital Articles* p2 My 6 2015

Innovations in business

The 4 Main Ways to Innovate in a Digital Economy T. J. Marion and S. K. Fixson *Harvard Business Review Digital Articles* p2 Je 2 2016

The 5 Requirements of a Truly Innovative Company G. Hamel and N. Tennant *Harvard Business Review Digital Articles* p2 Ap 27 2015

The 6 Most Common Innovation Mistakes Companies Make S. Anthony, D. S. Duncan et al *Harvard Business Review Digital Articles* p2 Je 23 2015

ACTIVE STYLE AWARDS B. BOYÉ, B. COURT et al bw color *Men's Health* v32 no7 p(Sp)17 S 2017

AI Can Be a Troublesome Teammate K. Gray *Harvard Business Review Digital Articles* p2 Jl 20 2017

Are Most CEOs Too Old to Innovate? W. Frick *Harvard Business Review Digital Articles* p2 N 20 2014

The Best Digital Companies Are Set Up to Never Stop Innovating B. Power *Harvard Business Review Digital Articles* p2 My 17 2016

The Best Entrepreneurs Think Globally, Not Just Digitally M. Schrage *Harvard Business Review Digital Articles* p2 Mr 10 2016

The Best Way to Improve Health Care Delivery Is with a Small, Dedicated Team C. Trimble *Harvard Business Review Digital Articles* p2 Mr 9 2016

The Biases That Keep Good R&D Projects from Getting Funded P. Criscuolo, L. Dahlander et al *Harvard Business Review Digital Articles* p2 Mr 17 2017

Blockchain Can Grow More Than Just Money M. Leising color diag *Bloomberg Businessweek* no4516 p33 Mr 27 2017

Blockchain Could Make the Insurance Industry Much More Transparent D. Disparte *Harvard Business Review Digital Articles* p2 Jl 12 2017

BUILD YOUR BRAND B. COURT color *Men's Health* v32 no7 p(Sp)6 S 2017

THE BUSINESS OF ARTIFICIAL INTELLIGENCE: WHAT IT CAN—AND CANNOT—DO FOR YOUR ORGANIZATION E. BRYNJOLFSSON and A. MCAFEE *Harvard Business Review Digital Articles* p3 Jl 1 2017

Choose the Right Innovation Method at the Right Time N. Furr and J. Dyer *Harvard Business Review Digital Articles* p2 D 31 2014

Companies Are Now Making Innovation Everyone's Job M. Schrage *Harvard Business Review Digital Articles* p2 Ja 21 2016

Countries with High English Proficiency Are More Innovative M. Tran *Harvard Business Review Digital Articles* p2 N 17 2015

The Dirty Little Secret About Digitally Transforming Operations M. Hammer, M. Hippe et al *Harvard Business Review Digital Articles* p2 My 31 2016

Employees Will Use Tools They Helped Build T. Erwin *Harvard Business Review Digital Articles* p3 Ap 22 2015

EXECUTIVE SUMMARIES *Harvard Business Review* v94 no11 p113 N 2016

Franchise Innovators M. RONEY *Forbes* v200 no3 p176 S 28 2017

Get More Innovative by Rethinking the Way You Think M. Schrage *Harvard Business Review Digital Articles* p2 N 5 2015

A Hands-Off Approach to Open Innovation Doesn't Work R. Narsalay, J. Kavathekar et al *Harvard Business Review Digital Articles* p2 My 3 2016

Help Employees Innovate By Giving Them the Right Challenge A. Imber *Harvard Business Review Digital Articles* p2 O 17 2016

How Corporate HQ Can Get More from Innovation Outposts A. Di Fiore *Harvard Business Review Digital Articles* p2 My 2 2017

HOW HIGH-TECH KITCHENS ARE LEVERAGING THE INTERNET OF THINGS D. F. McCourt color *Maclean's* v129 no40 p21 O 10 2016

How the Meaning of Digital Transformation Has Evolved T. Puthiyamadam *Harvard Business Review Digital Articles* p2 My 29 2017

How to Break Up with an Innovation Project S. Anthony *Harvard Business Review Digital Articles* p2 Ag 7 2015

How to Invent the Future N. Merchant *Harvard Business Review Digital Articles* p2 O 17 2014

How Understanding Disruption Helps Strategists S. Anthony *Harvard Business Review Digital Articles* p2 N 18 2015

Improving Innovation in Africa N. Ekekwe *Harvard Business Review Digital Articles* p2 F 18 2015

Innovate Without Diluting Your Core Idea J. Campbell *Harvard Business Review Digital Articles* p2 Mr 25 2015

Innovation Is as Much About Finding Partners as Building Products C. Gnanasambandam and M. Uhl *Harvard Business Review Digital Articles* p2 Jl 20 2017

Innovation Springs from the Unexpected Meeting of Minds B. Comstock *Harvard Business Review Digital Articles* p2 Mr 9 2016

The Innovative Coworking Spaces of 15th-Century Italy P. Formica *Harvard Business Review Digital Articles* p2 Ap 27 2016

The Innovative Mindset Your Company Can't Afford to Lose S. Ahuja *Harvard Business Review Digital Articles* p2 O 13 2015

Inside Adobe's Innovation Kit D. Burkus *Harvard Business Review Digital Articles* p2 F 23 2015

Is R&D Getting Harder, or Are Companies Just Getting Worse At It? A. M. Knott *Harvard Business Review Digital Articles* p2 Mr 21 2017

It's Time to Bury the Idea of the Lone Genius Innovator G. Satell *Harvard Business Review Digital Articles* p2 Ap 6 2016

Just Using Big Data Isn't Enough Anymore R. Bean *Harvard Business Review Digital Articles* p2 F 9 2016

Leadership May Not Be the Problem with Your Innovation Team D. Dworkin and M. Spiegel *Harvard Business Review Digital Articles* p2 Ag 25 2016

Maybe Your Team Doesn't Need to Be More Creative T. Chamorro-Premuzic *Harvard Business Review Digital Articles* p2 N 27 2015

The Most Innovative Companies Have Long-Term Leadership M. Wessel *Harvard Business Review Digital Articles* p2 D 30 2014

The Power of Designing Products for Customers You Don't Have Yet K. Dillon *Harvard Business Review Digital Articles* p2 Ag 31 2016

The President's Policy Changes Are Already Hurting U.S. Innovation M. Wessel color *Harvard Business Review Digital Articles* p2 F 1 2017

The Problem with Product Proliferation M. MOCKER and J. W. ROSS color *Harvard Business Review* v95 no3 p104 My/Je 2017

Renaissance Florence Was a Better Model for Innovation than Silicon Valley Is E. Weiner *Harvard Business Review Digital Articles* p2 Ja 25 2016

Research: 10 Traits of Innovative Leaders J. Zenger and J. Folkman *Harvard Business Review Digital Articles* p2 D 15 2014

The Right Way to Plan an Innovation Tour D. Isenberg *Harvard Business Review Digital Articles* p2 Jl 7 2015

Sometimes "Small Data" Is Enough to Create Smart Products P. Saklani *Harvard Business Review Digital Articles* p2 Jl 19 2017

Stop Saying Big Companies Can't Innovate V. Govindarajan *Harvard Business Review Digital Articles* p2 Je 6 2016

There's No Such Thing As an Average Business, Just Average Ways to Do Business B. Taylor *Harvard Business Review Digital Articles* p2 Ag 11 2016

What Big Companies Get Wrong About Innovation Metrics S. Kirsner *Harvard Business Review Digital Articles* p2 My 6 2015

What Business Can Learn from Government L. Greenspun and R. Wartzman *Harvard Business Review Digital Articles* p2 Ja 12 2015

What Do You Really Mean by Business "Transformation"? S. Anthony *Harvard Business Review Digital Articles* p2 F 29 2016

What Frugal Innovators Do N. Radjou and J. Prabhu *Harvard Business Review Digital Articles* p2 D 10 2014

What Makes Some Silicon Valley Companies So Successful H. Martins, Y. B. Dias et al *Harvard Business Review Digital Articles* p2 Ap 26 2016

What Ruthless Innovators Can Learn from the New England Patriots V. Govindarajan *Harvard Business Review Digital Articles* p2 Mr 9 2016

When It Comes to Digital Innovation, Less Action, More Thought S. Anthony *Harvard Business Review Digital Articles* p2 Ja 21 2015

When Treating Workers Well Leads to More Innovation W. Frick *Harvard Business Review Digital Articles* p2 N 3 2015

Why You Can't Just Tell a Company "Be More Like a Startup" S. Blank *Harvard Business Review Digital Articles* p2 Je 19 2017

Why Your Employees' Suggestions Aren't Going Anywhere J. Aurik *Harvard Business Review Digital Articles* p2 Ag 31 2015

THE WORLD'S MOST INNOVATIVE COMPANIES N. Karmali, M. Helft et al chart color *Forbes* v200 no2 p72 S 5 2017

You Can Talk About Innovation Without Resorting to Cliches K. Gordon *Harvard Business Review Digital Articles* p2 F 4 2016

Your Leadership Development Program Needs an Overhaul M. Samani and R. J. Thomas *Harvard Business Review Digital Articles* p2 D 5 2016

Zipcar Doesn't Just Ask Employees to Innovate — It Shows Them How S. Kaplan color *Harvard Business Review Digital Articles* p2 F 1 2017

Innovations in business—Economic aspects

THE PROBLEM WITH PRODUCT PROLIFERATION: INTERACTION M. MOCKER and J. W. ROSS color graph *Harvard Business Review* v95 no5 p16 S/O 2017

Innovations in business—History—20th century

How the Rise of the Post Office Explains American Innovation W. Frick *Harvard Business Review Digital Articles* p2 F 3 2016

Innovations in business—Management

Don't Treat Innovation as a Cure-All W. McKinley, S. Latham et al *Harvard Business Review Digital Articles* p2 D 8 2014

When Not to Celebrate Failure R. Ashkenas *Harvard Business Review Digital Articles* p2 D 11 2014

Innovations in business—Charts, diagrams, etc.

HOW COMPANIES REALLY USE BIG DATA graph il img *Harvard Business Review* v95 no5 p26 S/O 2017

Innovia (Company)

A License to Print Plastic A. Satariano color *Bloomberg Businessweek* no4498 p41 N 7 2016

Innovus Pharmaceuticals Inc.

New Male Potency Formula Makes "The Little Blue Pill" Obsolete H. S. Waxman *Saturday Evening Post* v289 no2 p103 Mr/Ap 2017

Inohara, Naohiro

Neonatal acquisition of Clostridia species protects against colonization by bacterial pathogens diag *Science* v356 no6335 p315 Ap 21 2017

Inorganic Chemistry (Periodical)

Fortune favors the well read J. G. West color *Science* v355 no6329 p1090 Mr 10 2017

Inosanto, Dan—Interviews

STILL KICKING! (and Punching and Grappling) [Cover story] M. CHENG bw color *Black Belt* v55 no1 p26 D 2016/Ja 2017

Inoue, Fukashi

Mitotic chromosome assembly despite nucleosome depletion in Xenopus egg extracts diag *Science* v356 no6344 p1284 Je 23 2017

Inoue, Kae

Globalism Is Alive and Well: Just Ask Carlos Ghosn color *Bloomberg Businessweek* no4531 p50 Jl 24 2017

Inoue, Rintaro

Crystal structure of the overlapping dinucleosome composed of hexasome and octasome graph *Science* v356 no6334 p205 Ap 14 2017

Inoue, Yoshihiro

Evolution of the wheat blast fungus through functional losses in a host specificity determinant diag map *Science* v357 no6346 p80 Jl 7 2017

Inouye, David

Words alone will not protect pollinators bibl color *Science* v355 no6323 p357 Ja 27 2017

Inquisition

No One Expects the Inquisition [Cover story] E. Brende color *Commonweal* v144 no10 p17 Je 2 2017

SYMBOLIC GESTURES R. SULLIVAN *Commonweal* v144 no13 p2 Ag 11 2017

Insco, Mathew

Nursing and the Great Recession bibl *Monthly Labor Review* p1 Jl 2017

Insdorf, Annette

Intimations: The Cinema of Wojciech Has V. Lucca color *Film Comment* v53 no4 p78 Jl/Ag 2017

Insect anatomy

   See also
      Insect wings

Insect baits & repellents

BUG OFF! V. Tweed color *Amazing Wellness* v9 no4 p26 Summ 2017

BUGS, BEGONE! *Health* v31 no5 p13 Je 2017

Day-Ride Essentials J. JAHIEL color *Trail Rider* v29 no3 p63 Ap 2017

How to Keep the Bugs Away: Discover which repellents work well—and those that don't—against mosquitoes and ticks J. Interlandi *Consumer Reports* v82 no9 p16 S 2017

NATURAL INSECT REPELLENTS: Don't get bugged out—follow these simple DIY recipes to keep pests at bay J. Cox *Mother Earth News* no282 p53 Je/Jl 2017

Tomorrow: Carl Swanson: Where's Our Laser-Shooting Mosquito Death Machine? Nathan Myhrvold said he was making just that in 2010. We re still waiting img *New York* v50 no15 p8 Jl 24 2017

Insect baits & repellents—Evaluation

5 high-tech gadgets for an outdoor cookout color *PCWorld* p168 O 2016

Why I Use Beneficial Insects For My Fly Control S. R. H. de Frey *Equus* no475 p17 Ap 2017

Insect behavior

Home Itch Remedies B. RADFORD *Skeptical Inquirer* v41 no1 p66 Ja/F 2017

One of Earth's most massive aerial migrations color *National Wildlife (World Edition)* v55 no6 p9 O/N 2017

Insect bites & stings

SUSCEPTIBILITY TO SWEET ITCH INVESTIGATED C. Barakat and M. McCluskey color *Equus* no478 p18 Jl 2017

Insect bites & stings—Prevention

BLOOD-SUCKING VISITORS: BUGS IN THE PNW CAN BE VORACIOUS, SO DON'T BECOME THEIR NEXT VICTIM D. HISLOP *Sea Magazine* v109 no5 pCA-10 My 2017

Insect bites & stings—Treatment

Home Itch Remedies B. RADFORD *Skeptical Inquirer* v41 no1 p66 Ja/F 2017

Insect migration

   See also
      Butterfly migration

One of Earth's most massive aerial migrations color *National Wildlife (World Edition)* v55 no6 p9 O/N 2017

Insect pest control

   See also
      Insect baits & repellents
      Mosquito control

BUILT-IN BUG CONTROL C. Barakat and M. Freckleton *Equus* no478 p22 Jl 2017

THE GRUMPY GARDENER S. Bender color *Southern Living* v52 no10 p46 O 2017

Insect pests

Buffalo Gnats J. R. Erickson cartoon *American Cowboy* v23 no5 p22 F/Mr 2017

Insect-plant relationships

Using Plant-Animal Interactions to Inform Tree Selection in Tree-Based Agroecosystems for Enhanced Biodiversity V. E. PETERS, T. A. CARLO et al *BioScience* v66 no12 p1046 D 1 2016

Insect pollinators

FLIGHT OF FANCY M. REAGIN color *Louisiana Life* v37 no5 p28 My/Je 2017

Insect population density

Bees once again making headlines color map *National Wildlife*

(World Edition) v55 no5 p8 Ag/S 2017

Insect population estimates

A cocktail of toxins J. T. Kerr color diag map *Science* v356 no6345 p1331 Je 30 2017

Insect populations

Invest in insects D. Schar color *Science* v356 no6343 p1131 Je 16 2017

Insect spermatozoa

Blocking promiscuous activation at cryptic promoters directs cell type–specific gene expression J. Kim, C. Lu et al diag *Science* v356 no6339 p717 My 19 2017

Insect wings

The strangest insect wings S. Milius bw color *Science News* v191 no13 p4 Jl 8 2017

Insecticide resistance

Revenge of the Super Lice K. Weintraub color *Scientific American* v316 no6 p24 Je 2017

Insecticides—Application

PICK YOUR POISON K. Kupferschmidt bw color map *Science* v354 no6309 p171 O 14 2016

Insecticides—Government policy

Better Living Through Chemistry? A. Lappé *Earth Island Journal* v32 no2 p12 Summ 2017

Insects

See also
Ants
Beetles
Butterflies
Flies
Introduced insects
Photography of insects
Wasps

Bet you didn't know M. HARRIS color *National Geographic Kids* no470 p10 My 2017

Bringing Back the Light L. Tangley color *National Wildlife (World Edition)* v55 no4 p12 Je/Jl 2017

Creating a Haven for Beneficial Bugs J. Marinelli color *National Wildlife (World Edition)* v55 no2 p12 F/Mr 2017

Funny Fill-In E. WHITMER cartoon *National Geographic Kids* no471 p31 Je/Jl 2017

INSECT'S-EYE VIEW *Sierra* v102 no5 p4 St/O 2017

A Little Birdie *Arizona Highways* v93 no6 p5 Je 2017

NATURAL INSECT REPELLENTS: Don't get bugged out—follow these simple DIY recipes to keep pests at bay J. Cox *Mother Earth News* no282 p53 Je/Jl 2017

Nature's Jewels A. Bolen color *National Wildlife (World Edition)* v55 no4 p22 Je/Jl 2017

WHERE HAVE ALL THE INSECTS GONE? G. Vogel color graph *Science* v356 no6338 p576 My 12 2017

Insects as carriers of disease

How to Keep the Bugs Away: Discover which repellents work well—and those that don't—against mosquitoes and ticks J. Interlandi *Consumer Reports* v82 no9 p16 S 2017

Insects as feed

BURGER WITH FLIES T. PHILPOTT cartoon *Mother Jones* v42 no2 p64 Mr/Ap 2017

Insects—Exhibitions

A big, bug science party C. M. Gibson color *Science* v355 no6321 p141 Ja 13 2017

Insects—Migration

See also
Seasonal distribution of insects

Like birds, insects may travel in sync with the seasons E. Pennisi color *Science* v354 no6319 p1515 D 23 2016

Mass seasonal bioflows of high-flying insect migrants Gao Hu, K. S. Lim et al bibl graph *Science* v354 no6319 p1584 D 23 2016

Trillions of Insects Migrate M. Fischetti color graph *Scientific American* v316 no4 p84 Ap 2017

Insects—Population biology

'We know that insect species are being lost across the planet … but no one is really looking.' L. ANTHONY color *Canadian Geographic* v135 no6 p50 D 2015

Insecure (TV program)

Insecure J. Jensen color *Entertainment Weekly* no1474/1475 p106 Jl 21-28 2017

Issa Rae B. SPANOS bw *Rolling Stone* no1295 p47 S 7 2017

Issa Rae's Insecure Is the Sharpest Comedy of the Year D. D'addario color *Time* v190 no4 p50 Jl 24 2017

Meet the Awkward Black Supergirl R. SHEFFIELD color *Rolling Stone* no1275 p28 D 1 2016

The Must List color *Entertainment Weekly* no1474/1475 p6 Jl 21-28 2017

Rap Sesh M. WAKIM color *Los Angeles Magazine* v62 no7 p44 Jl 2017

Insel, Joan

What I Wear to Work: JOAN INSEL J. Chen color *Bloomberg Businessweek* no4516 p71 Mr 27 2017

Insel, Tom

THE SMARTPHONE PSYCHIATRIST D. DOBBS color *Atlantic* v320 no1 p78 Jl/Ag 2017

Inside Out (Film)

INSIDE OUT *People Management* p62 F 2017

Inside Passage—Description & travel

READY, SET, GO D. HISLOP *Sea Magazine* v108 no10 pPNW-8 O 2016

Inside the NBA (TV program)

Care Taker B. Golliver and T. Keith color *Sports Illustrated* v126 no10 p26 Ap 10 2017

Insider Software Inc.

FONTAGENT 7 AND FONTAGENT SYNC: ALL-NEW INTERFACE AND FONT SYNCING ACROSS USERS AND MACS J. J. NELSON color *Macworld - Digital Edition* p31 D 2016

Insider trading in securities—Lawsuits & claims

We Have Better Things to Do Than Prosecute Insider Trading J. Fox *Harvard Business Review Digital Articles* p2 D 11 2014

Insider trading in securities—United States—Lawsuits & claims

INSIDER-TRADING LAW: A SUPREME COURT RULING GIVES PROSECUTORS A BOOST J. J. Roberts *Fortune* v75 no1 p94 Ja 1 2017

Insight

3 Questions to Get the Most Out of Your Company's Data J. Allworth, M. Wessel et al *Harvard Business Review Digital Articles* p2 Ja 29 2015

Insight Editions (Company)

Insight Editions Launches Comics Imprint C. Reid color *Publishers Weekly* v263 no43 p10 O 24 2016

Insolia, A.

Observation of a large-scale anisotropy in the arrival directions of cosmic rays above 8 × 1018 eV *Science* v357 no6357 p1266 S 22 2017

Insomnia

6 COMPENSATIONS FOR SLEEPLESSNESS D. URBANSKI *Orion Magazine* v35 no3 p4 My/Je 2016

DO I HAVE THIS? color *Men's Health* v32 no8 p72 O 2017

Don't Sleep on MELATONIN J. WUEBBEN color *Muscle & Performance* v9 no6 p11 Je 2017

Great Sleep Starts Here A. Patz color *Health* v30 no9 p92 N 2016

INSOMNIA SOLUTIONS E. Kane color *Amazing Wellness* v9 no2 p28 Spr 2017

Insomnia treatment

Does It Work? Melatonin [Cover story] S. KLEIN color *Prevention* v69 no9 p22 O 2017

Experts say Americans get an hour or two less shut-eye every night than we once did. What's keeping us up, and is there a way to make a restless nation go to bed? D. Dudley color *AARP: The Magazine* v59 no5A p54 Ag/S 2016

Insomnia—Prevention

7 supplements for better sleep L. TURNER color *Better Nutrition* v79 no10 p52 O 2017

Enjoy deep sleep color *Yoga Journal* p88 2016 Special Issue

Great Sleep Starts Here A. Patz color *Health* v30 no9 p92 N 2016

Insourcing

Why and How to Build an In-House Consulting Team M. Bernholz and A. Teng *Harvard Business Review Digital Articles* p2 S 11 2015

Inspection & review

Flipping the Safety Switch K. Barrett and R. Greene *Governing* v30 no5 p60 F 2017

Inspector Morse (TV program)

Murder in Paradise A. JACOBS *American Conservative* v15 no6 p42 N/D 2016

Inspiration

THE CHANGE MAKER M. Goldstein color *Sunset* v238 no1 p17 Ja 2017

GREAT INSPIRATIONS D. KASTOR color *Runner's World* v51 no10 p28 N 2016

How to Rediscover Your Inspiration at Work K. Hedges *Harvard Business Review Digital Articles* p1 S 5 2017

Live Your Best Life bw *O, The Oprah Magazine* p19 Mr 2017

Live Your Best Life color *O, The Oprah Magazine* p25 S 2017

One-on-Wonderful: What makes a good competition coach and how do you find one? K. BRADY *Dance Magazine* v91 no10 p42 O 2017

THE ORGANIZER J. R. Hawkins color *Essence* v47 no7 p60 N 2016

Pop Radio Rocks Again D. BROWNE color *Rolling Stone* no1290 p18 Je 29 2017

The POWER of the Aha! MOMENT I. MARSHALL color *Prevention* v68 no12 p60 D 2016

Power Tools: Pioneers C. Alter color *Time* v189 no16/17 p36 My 1-8 2017

Raise a Fitter Family P. CARLOTTI cartoon color *Men's Health* v32 no5 p92 Je 2017

Secrets of Single Super B. HOROVITZ, D. HOCHMAN et al color *AARP: The Magazine* v30 no6A p20 O/N 2017

the stylemaker event BIG IDEAS *Better Homes & Gardens* v95 no1 p9 Ja 2017

Inspired by Nature (Music)

Ozella's Northern Stars J. EPHLAND color *Downbeat* v84 no10 p60 O 2017

Instagram (Web resource)

DAVIDE GRASSO IS THE CEO OF CONVERSE D. GRASSO *Harvard Business Review* v95 no3 p160 My/Je 2017

Fitness feeds on Instagram can perpetuate harmful ideas about the perfect body—but they can also inspire us with bodies that are more like ours J. Wortham *New York Times Magazine* p14 Jl 9 2017

How Much Is an Instagram Story Worth? N. Ekstein color *Bloomberg Businessweek* no4513 p38 Mr 6 2017

An Inquiry Into the Nature and Causes of the Wealth of Rich People C. ROSEN *Commentary* v144 no3 p7 O 2017

Insta-fluencer M. Chafkin color *Bloomberg Businessweek* no4502 p66 D 5 2016

INSTAGRAM EVERYWHERE E. STEIN color *Wired* v24 no12 p91 D 2016

Instagram Explore M. Young *New York Times Magazine* p18 Ja 8 2017

Instagram Feeding Frenzies J. SCHERER *Los Angeles Magazine* p42 My 2017

Instagram Tries to Ease Users Into Shopping S. Frier cartoon *Bloomberg Businessweek* no4499 p49 N 14 2016

LASER-SHARP FAT REDUCTION E. MUSIWA color *Ebony* v72 no11 p56 S 2017

Love, Cleo L. Goodman img *New York* v49 no25 p89 D 12 2016

THE NEW WAY TO TRAVEL color *Wired* v24 no12 p81 D 2016

POPULAR MACHINE EVERYWHERE color diag *Popular Mechanics* p14 D 2016/Ja 2017

Sarah Dewald A. BROWNLEE *Cincinnati Magazine* v50 no11 p34 Ag 2017

Selena On Fire [Cover story] L. Brown color *InStyle* v24 no9 p366 S 2017

#SHOPNOW M. MELTZER cartoon *Wired* v24 no12 p28 D 2016

Social Climbers T. Keith color *Sports Illustrated* v125 no19 p24 D 12 2016

SOCIAL SET S. ORR *Better Homes & Gardens* v95 no9 p10 S 2017

Tap Twice to Like color *National Geographic* v230 no4 p16 O 2016

This Just In J. Zorthian *Time* v189 no23 p21 Je 19 2017

WE LOVE HEARING FROM YOU! color diag *Essence* v47 no9 p13 Ja 2017

Would You Rather... cartoon chart color *Seventeen* v76 no12 p112 D 2016/Ja 2017

Installation art

Arc of Joan A. K. Scott color *New Yorker* v93 no15 p7 My 29 2017

ART *New Yorker* v93 no15 p8 My 29 2017

Breaking Through C. MORGAN-FEIR color *Walrus* v14 no7 p58

S 2017

DAWN DEDEAUX J. R. Kemp bw color *Louisiana Life* v38 no1 p22 S/O 2017

The Fire Within; Sky Steps L. Copan color *Christian Century* v134 no22 p47 O 25 2017

FOREST GATE *Atlanta* v56 no8 p42 D 2016

Glow, Baby, Glow D. ROTHBART color *Los Angeles Magazine* v62 no7 p45 Jl 2017

Going the Distance D. White and L. A. Miller bw *Art in America* v104 no11 p59 D 2016

THE LURE OF LACMA B. COLACELLO color *Vanity Fair* v58 no12 p138 D 2016

RADICAL DESTABILIZATION D. Ebony bw color *Art in America* v105 no3 p106 Mr 2017

TAKE ME OUT TO THE BALLROOM A. M. HOMES color *Vanity Fair* v59 no4 p191 Mr 2017

WHAT GOES UP S. STALL *Indianapolis Monthly* v12 no40 p26 Ag 2017

Installation art exhibitions

Dancing in the Streets M. SLENSKE bw color *Architectural Digest* v74 no3 p62 Mr 2017

EMERGE A Festival of Futures *Issues in Science & Technology* v33 no3 p96 Spr 2017

ERIC WESLEY G. Kroeber color *Art in America* v105 no3 p135 Mr 2017

A Gateway In DTLA *Los Angeles Magazine* p85 Ap 2017

HEAVEN SENT G. Adamson cartoon color *Art in America* v105 no4 p90 Ap 2017

KOCHI-MUZIRIS BIENNALE B. Augustine color *Art in America* v105 no3 p140 Mr 2017

LUBAINA HIMID E. Fullerton cartoon *Art in America* v105 no4 p122 Ap 2017

ROBERT RAUSCHENBERG E. Fullerton color *Art in America* v105 no3 p123 Mr 2017

SAM DURANT J. S. Li color *Art in America* v105 no3 p136 Mr 2017

Watch the Throne img *New York* v49 no23 p80 N 14 2016

YUKI KIMURA L. M. Green color *Art in America* v105 no3 p137 Mr 2017

Installation of electric lighting

LIGHTER FARE color *Timber Home Living* v27 no5 p30 O 2017

Installation of equipment

Art of the SOUND INSTALL B. Reesman *Stage Directions* v29 no11 p14 N 2016

Hiding in Plain Sight J. SCIACCA color *Sound & Vision* v82 no5 p23 Je 2017

ONE-HOUR WONDERS M. EMERY color *Dirt Sports + Off-Road* v51 no3 p44 Mr 2017

ONE-HOUR WONDER S. RICHARDS color *Dirt Sports + Off-Road* v51 no7 p58 Jl 2017

Top Four System Install Mistakes J. SCIACCA color *Sound & Vision* v82 no7 p28 S 2017

Installation of industrial equipment

Outboard Towing Magic: Installing TurboSwing to tow skiers behind an outboard-powered boat is one-person simple K. HARRIS *Boating World* v38 no8 p22 S/O 2017

Instant messaging

The Next Frontier of Collaborative Communications D. Gould color *Bloomberg Businessweek* no4500 pC1 N 21 2016

The Rise of WhatsApp in Brazil Is About More than Just Messaging F. Saboia *Harvard Business Review Digital Articles* p2 Ap 15 2016

Why Facebook Messenger Is a Big Deal for Customer Service J. Gans *Harvard Business Review Digital Articles* p2 My 6 2016

Instant messaging software

Messaging Apps Are Changing How Companies Talk with Customers G. BenMark and D. Venkatachari *Harvard Business Review Digital Articles* p2 S 23 2016

What Happens When Work Becomes a Nonstop Chat Room M. FISCHER *New York* v50 no10 p40 My 15 2017

Instant replay systems in sports

ALL WORK AND REPLAY A. Prewitt color *Sports Illustrated* v126 no11 p87 Ap 17-24 2017

Upon Further Review T. Taylor and T. Keith color *Sports Illustrated* v127 no2 p18 Jl 17 2017

Instinct (Behavior)

Bumble bees prove their smarts color *Science* v354 no6309 p154 O 14 2016

Epigenetics and the evolution of instincts G. E. Robinson and A. B. Barron color diag *Science* v356 no6333 p26 Ap 7 2017

Gut Instinct E. C. Peyton cartoon *New Orleans Magazine* v51 no7 p48 My 2017

We aren't so great at assessing risk G. Miller color *Science* v354 no6310 p278 O 21 2016

Institute, The (Film)

FUTURE FRANCO FILMS D. Coggan color *Entertainment Weekly* no1454/1455 p82 F 24 2017

Institute for Social Policy & Understanding

Healthy Mosques Hold the Future: ISNA teams up with ISPU to help make mosques welcoming, inclusive and dynamic I. BAG-BY *Islamic Horizons* v46 no3 p36 My/Je 2017

Institute of Medicine (U.S.)

NAS: Pot does help chronic pain color *Science* v355 no6322 p228 Ja 20 2017

Institute of Museum & Library Services (U.S.)

Follow the (Grant) Money B. Kenney *Publishers Weekly* v263 no42 p21 O 17 2016

Institutional advertising

DC, WHERE POLITICAL ADS NEVER END A. BEAUJON and C. CUNNINGHAM *Washingtonian Magazine* v52 no5 p24 F 2017

Institutional autonomy

It's Wrong to Bully Central Banks cartoon *Bloomberg Businessweek* no4501 p8 N 28 2016

Institutional Critique (Art movement)

INSIDE JOB A. RUSSETH color *ARTnews* v115 no4 p102 Wint 2016/2017

Institutional environment

DOWN TO THE ATP K. Pandolfi *Cincinnati Magazine* p64 Je 2017

Institutional ownership (Stocks)

One Big Reason There's So Little Competition Among U.S. Banks M. Schmalz *Harvard Business Review Digital Articles* p2 Je 13 2016

Institutional racism

Diversity at the Oscars Is More than a Numbers Game K. H. Banks *Harvard Business Review Digital Articles* p2 F 24 2016

Institutionalized persons

See also

Prisoners

Injuries Differ for Outdoors and Indoors *USA Today Magazine* v145 no2861 p1 F 2017

Jail Break C. Menzel color *Powder* p42 S 2017

TALK TO US P. Bella, B. Antcliff et al color graph *Chicago* v66 no11 p16 N 2017

Instructional systems

See also

Curricula (Courses of study)

Get it right the first time! T. Heflebower, J. Hoegh et al chart color *Phi Delta Kappan* v98 no6 p58 Mr 2017

Instrument landing systems

See also

Runway localizing beacons

CONSIDER THE OPERATING ENVIRONMENT AROUND AN ILS APPROACH R. MARK and J. BLAIR color *Flying* v144 no10 p27 O 2017

EVEN AN ILS APPROACH DEMANDS ATTENTION R. MARK and J. BLAIR bw *Flying* v144 no7 p25 Jl 2017

Instrumental music

See also

Dance music

Orchestral music

The Beat Goes On color *Prevention* v68 no11 p12 N 2016

InStyle (Periodical)

Welcome L. Brown color *InStyle* v23 no12 p20 N 2016

Insulating materials

See also

Electric insulators & insulation

Magnetic insulators

Robust spin-polarized midgap states at step edges of topological crystalline insulators P. Sessi, D. Di Sante et al bibl graph *Science* v354 no6317 p1269 D 9 2016

Sleep Warmer K. Karlson color *Backpacker* p27 N 2017

Insulin

THE BIG DIABETES IS AMERICA'S STEALTHY KILLER L. SCHULER cartoon color *Men's Health* v32 no2 p96 Mr 2017

A Cure for Diabetes? M. Munson color *O, The Oprah Magazine* p104 N 2017

Drosophila insulin release is triggered by adipose Stunted ligand to brain Methuselah receptor R. Delanoue, E. Meschi et al bibl graph *Science* v353 no6307 p1553 S 30 2016

Insulin-dependent diabetes

The Artificial Pancreas Gets Real E. Sheng bw *Scientific American* v315 no5 p14 N 2016

Insulin-dependent diabetes—Diagnosis

The Most Significant Advance in Diabetes Care Since Insulin B. Keyes-Bevan color *Maclean's* v129 no48/49 p46 D 5 2016

Insulin-dependent diabetes—Treatment

Insulin Pump Technology Gives Greater Freedom and Flexibility M. Sponagle cartoon *Maclean's* v129 no48/49 p42 D 5 2016

MAX DOMI'S Success Depends on Accuracy R. Druzin bw *Maclean's* v129 no48/49 p40 D 5 2016

pet projects *Parents* v91 no12 p23 D 2016

Insulin pumps

Insulin Pump Technology Gives Greater Freedom and Flexibility M. Sponagle cartoon *Maclean's* v129 no48/49 p42 D 5 2016

Insulin resistance

ALOE AGAIN, NATURALLY color *Prevention* v69 no1 p8 Ja 2017

DIET, MORE THAN WEIGHT, CRUCIAL IN INSULIN RESISTANCE C. Barakat and M. McCluskey color *Equus* no470 p19 N 2016

Insulin-Resistance Q&A [Cover story] color *Horse & Rider* v56 no1 p21 Ja 2017

Insulin—Sales & prices

The Crazy Math Behind Drug Prices P. M. Barrett, R. Langreth et al graph *Bloomberg Businessweek* no4529 p14 Jl 3 2017

Insurance

See also

Climate change insurance

Health insurance

Insurance companies

Insurance policies

Life insurance

BOAT INSURANCE INS AND OUTS B. M. KENYON *Sea Magazine* v109 no2 p44 F 2017

How the Insurance Industry Can Push Us to Prepare for Climate Change M. E. Kahn, B. Casey et al *Harvard Business Review Digital Articles* p2 Ag 28 2017

HOW TO SELL YOUR HOUSE—FAST *Los Angeles Magazine* pFS1 Mr 2017

Need That Insurance? J. GARSKOF color *AARP: The Magazine* v60 no1A p24 D 2016/Ja 2017

PARODY color *Weekly Standard* v22 no24 p44 F 27 2017

THE RIGHT WAY TO PAY A CAREGIVER T. Stanger *Consumer Reports* v82 no12 p51 D 2017

Save with NRPA-Sponsored Insurance Plans *Parks & Recreation* v52 no1 p48 Ja 2017

What the Insurance Industry Can Do to Fix Health Care S. Soderland *Harvard Business Review Digital Articles* p2 D 23 2014

Insurance advertising

SCARE TACTICS *Saturday Evening Post* v289 no4 p95 Jl/Ag 2017

Insurance agents

CAN THEIR PROBLEM BE SOLVED? M. Friesen *Successful Farming* v115 no5 p66 Mid-Mr 2017

Insurance claims

When a Tree Falls, Who Pays? K. LANKFORD *Kiplinger's Personal Finance* v71 no8 p38 Ag 2017

Insurance companies

See also

Health insurance companies

Cover the Cost of Care K. LANKFORD color *Kiplinger's Personal Finance* v71 no6 p64 Je 2017

Fresh-Squeezed Insurance L. BRODY color *Forbes* v198 no7 p92 N 29 2016

How One Insurance Firm Learned to Create an Innovation Culture S. Kaplan *Harvard Business Review Digital Articles* p2 2017

Insurance companies—China

It's Insurance. It's an Investment. It's Trouble *Bloomberg Businessweek* no4528 p25 Je 26 2017

Insurance consultants

Get Your Insurer to Pay Up K. LANKFORD color *Kiplinger's Personal Finance* v71 no8 p30 Ag 2017

Insurance eligibility

When Small Changes Can Earn You Big Bucks L. RICHARDS color *Reader's Digest* v190 no1134 p52 O 2017

Insurance policies

See also

Disability insurance policies

Health insurance policies

Life insurance policies

Bundled Policies Can Save You a Lot ... Sometimes M. C. White color *Money* v45 no10 p20 N 2016

When to Get a Second Opinion N. S. HUANG *Kiplinger's Personal Finance* v70 no12 p68 D 2016

Insurance premiums

Exposing Unfair Pricing in Auto Insurance Rates R. Root, R. Fischer et al color *Consumer Reports* v82 no5 p6 My 2017

Obamacare Unravels, Cont'd R. PONNURU il *National Review* v68 no21 p16 N 21 2016

Insurance premiums—Economic aspects

THE FARM INSURANCE GAMBIT: DO YOU HAVE ENOUGH OR TOO MUCH INSURANCE? IT'S WORTH ASKING S. Williamson color *Successful Farming* v115 no7 p12 My 2017

Insurance—Economic aspects

Smart Homes Could Be Cheaper to Insure S. Higginbotham color *MIT Technology Review* v120 no1 p23 Ja/F 2017

Insurance—Government policy

Federal Agencies Play 'Not It' With Flood Insurance C. Flavelle, H. Perlberg et al *Bloomberg Businessweek* no4538 p28 S 18 2017

Insurance—History

Why the U.S. Needs Wage Insurance L. G. Kletzer *Harvard Business Review Digital Articles* p2 Ja 25 2016

Insurgency

See also

Terrorism

In the Horrorscape of Aleppo C. Glass color *New York Review of Books* v64 no9 p18 My 25 2017

Lightbox I. Grillo and J. Benezra color *Time* v190 no7 p14 Ag 21 2017

Still waiting D. D. Collum color *U.S. Catholic* v82 no11 p38 N 2017

With Aleppo's Fall, Syria's Civil War Reaches a Grim Turning Point J. Malsin color diag *Time* v188 no27-28 p11 D 26 2016

Insurgent, The (Poem)

The Insurgent E. KHALIL WILSON *Progressive* v81 no6 p69 Ag/S 2017

INSYS Therapeutics Inc.—Officials & employees

PAIN AND GAIN M. HERPER and M. TINDERA color graph *Forbes* v198 no5 p92 O 25 2016

Intangible property

See also

Intellectual property

Licenses

Patents

Entrepreneurs, Economic Growth, and the Enlightenment T. Sullivan *Harvard Business Review Digital Articles* p2 Ag 10 2015

What the U.S. Should Be Doing to Protect Intellectual Property D. Breznitz and M. Murphree *Harvard Business Review Digital Articles* p2 Ja 27 2016

Intasomes

Cryo-EM structures and atomic model of the HIV-1 strand transfer complex intasome D. Oliveira Passos, Min Li et al bibl color *Science* v355 no6320 p1 Ja 6 2017

Integers (Short story)

INTEGERS D. W. MILLIKEN *Humanist* v77 no3 p41 My/Je 2017

Integrase genetics

Structures of the CRISPR genome integration complex A. V. Wright, Liu et al color *Science* v357 no6356 p1113 S 15 2017

Integrases—Genetics

A supramolecular assembly mediates lentiviral DNA integration

A. Ballandras-Colas, D. P. Maskell et al bibl color *Science* v355 no6320 p1 Ja 6 2017

Integrated circuit design

Google's Quantum Leap T. Simonite color *MIT Technology Review* v120 no4 p22 Jl/Ag 2017

Integrated circuits

Chip Implants Make It Impossible to Forget Your Keys C. Britschgi bw *Reason* v48 no7 p64 D 2016

Ryzen CPUs explained: Everything you need to know about AMD's disruptive multicore chips B. CHACOS color *PCWorld* v35 no5 p13 My 2017

Integrated circuits industry—Mergers

China Is Missing the Chips Rush I. King *Bloomberg Businessweek* no4529 p22 Jl 3 2017

Integrated circuits—Evaluation

Intel Core i9: The fastest consumer CPU prepares for Ryzen war G. MAH UNG chart color graph *PCWorld* v35 no8 p42 Ag 2017

Integrated delivery of health care

Health Care Providers Must Stop Wasting Patients' Time N. R. Shah, L. M. Garofalo-Wright et al *Harvard Business Review Digital Articles* p2 My 24 2017

Why Health Care Mergers Can Be Good for Patients J. D. Birkmeyer *Harvard Business Review Digital Articles* p2 S 30 2015

Integrated reporting (Corporation reports)

When Investors Want to Know How You Treat People D. Creelman and J. Boudreau *Harvard Business Review Digital Articles* p2 F 10 2015

Integrative medicine

Nature's Medicine B. ANDREWS color *Prevention* v69 no8 p54 Ag 2017

Integrity

Green works of mercy K. Clarke color *U.S. Catholic* v81 no11 p42 N 2016

Mission before Identity D. O'Brien color *Commonweal* v144 no6 p8 Mr 24 2017

Research integrity revisited M. McNutt and R. M. Nerem color *Science* v356 no6334 p115 Ap 14 2017

Intel Corp.

Deal Snapshot Intel + Mobileye I. King and G. Coppola diag graph *Bloomberg Businessweek* no4515 p21 Mr 20 2017

Intel buys Mobileye for $15 billion to challenge Nvidia for the future of self-driving cars I. PAUL color *PCWorld* v35 no4 p27 Ap 2017

Intel Core i9: The fastest consumer CPU prepares for Ryzen war G. MAH UNG chart color graph *PCWorld* v35 no8 p42 Ag 2017

Intel revealed the Core i9 ship dates, but you won't like them GORDON MAH UNG chart color *PCWorld* v35 no7 p9 Jl 2017

Intel SSD 545s: The next great budget SSD has arrived J. L. JACOBI color graph *PCWorld* v35 no8 p82 Ag 2017

Intel's speed-boosting Optane Memory won't work with Celeron and Pentium PCs I. PAUL color *PCWorld* v35 no5 p39 My 2017

Is Intel's Buying Binge a Good Thing? K. KRISTOF *Kiplinger's Personal Finance* v71 no6 p54 Je 2017

Optane Memory: Why you may want Intel's futuristic cache in your PC GORDON MAH UNG color diag graph *PCWorld* v35 no7 p101 Jl 2017

Reinventing Intel T. Simonite color *MIT Technology Review* v119 no6 p20 N/D 2016

Intel Corp.—Officials & employees

How Did I Get Here? DANIELLE BROWN bw color *Bloomberg Businessweek* no4514 p76 Mr 13 2017

Intel microprocessors

Intel revealed the Core i9 ship dates, but you won't like them GORDON MAH UNG chart color *PCWorld* v35 no7 p9 Jl 2017

Intellect

See also

Genius

Intelligence levels

Memory

Perception

Reason

Stupidity

CAN YOU MAKE YOURSELF SMARTER? J. RAINEY MARQUEZ *Atlanta* v56 no9 p115 Ja 2017

Direction Finder P. J. RYAN color *America* v215 no13 p28 O 31 2016

For Leaders, Looking Healthy Matters More than Looking Smart D. Burkus *Harvard Business Review Digital Articles* p2 Ja 2 2015

Gender stereotypes about intellectual ability emerge early and influence children's interests L. Bian, Leslie et al bibl graph *Science* v355 no6323 p389 Ja 27 2017

Good leaders aren't all that smart *People Management* p59 Je 2017

In Praise of $%!#?! J. Murph cartoon chart *AARP: The Magazine* v60 no1A p12 D 2016/Ja 2017

JOE NAVARRO AGENT PROVOCATEUR H. ESTROFF MARANO *Psychology Today* v50 no2 p56 Mr/Ap 2017

Massively Intelligent G. DREVITCH *Psychology Today* v50 no2 p44 Mr/Ap 2017

SMART PEOPLE DO THE Dumbest THINGS! [Cover story] A. MARIE, S. CONNOR et al *Reader's Digest* v190 no1134 p62 O 2017

Why Ladies Pick Guitar Players E. Spitznagel bw *Men's Health* v31 no10 p42 D 2016

Intellect & genetics

40 more genes linked to intelligence L. SANDERS *Science News* v191 no12 p14 Je 24 2017

Intellectual development

The Case of the Missing Stylist L. Smith color *Weekly Standard* v22 no37 p5 Je 5 2017

Intellectual life

See also
Learning & scholarship
Popular culture
Prisoners—Intellectual life

The Intellectual Species: Evolution or Extinction? J. Rodden *Society* v54 no4 p352 Ag 2017

Intellectual property

See also
Patents

Everyday Business Travelers Are Easy Targets for Espionage L. Bencie *Harvard Business Review Digital Articles* p2 N 10 2015

How an Airplane Laptop Ban Would Expose Company Data to Espionage L. Bencie *Harvard Business Review Digital Articles* p2 My 25 2017

How to Protect Your Company's Inventions *Harvard Business Review Digital Articles* p2 N 24 2014

IP: The Roots of Innovation T. J. Donohue *Weekly Standard* v22 no23 p11 F 20 2017

Market Rules J. PODHORETZ color *Weekly Standard* v22 no38 p39 Je 12 2017

Patent Trolling Isn't Dead—It's Just Moving to Delaware L. H. Cohen, U. G. Gurun et al *Harvard Business Review Digital Articles* p2 Je 28 2017

What the Rise of Russian Hackers Means for Your Business M. Sulmeyer *Harvard Business Review Digital Articles* p2 My 12 2017

Intellectual property theft

It Doesn't Matter If Competitors Know Your Strategy F. V. Cespedes *Harvard Business Review Digital Articles* p2 N 25 2014

Intellectual property theft—Lawsuits & claims

Chinese scientist jailed over theft of hybrid corn M. Hvistendahl color *Science* v354 no6309 p160 O 14 2016

Intellectual property—United States

What the U.S. Should Be Doing to Protect Intellectual Property D. Breznitz and M. Murphree *Harvard Business Review Digital Articles* p2 Ja 27 2016

Intellectuals

America's Dimming Stars: Our nation has always depended on public intellectuals to guide us. How come we no longer see the light? E. Mitchell *Smithsonian* v48 no4 p31 Jl/Ag 2017

I WANT YOU TO MAKE HISTORY, NOT BE HISTORY I. X. KENDI *Vital Speeches of the Day* v83 no8 p232 Ag 2017

Intellectuals—Political activity

SECRET ADMIRERS K. SANNEH cartoon *New Yorker* v92 no44 p24 Ja 9 2017

Intellectuals—United States

Discussion C. H. Schwefel, P. Ensley et al *Smithsonian* v48 no5 p4 S 2017

Intelligence (Theatrical production)

POWER PLAYWRIGHT P. O'Donnell *Washingtonian Magazine*

v52 no6 p41 Mr 2017

Intelligence levels

See also
Genius

THE BRILLIANCE TRAP A. CIMPIAN and LESLIE color graph *Scientific American* v317 no3 p60 S 2017

Nearly Half of Companies Say They Don't Have the Digital Skills They Need J. Goldman *Harvard Business Review Digital Articles* p1 Jl 28 2017

Testing R. J. Sternberg chart color *Phi Delta Kappan* v98 no4 p66 D 2016/Ja 2017

TEST YOUR ECO IQ *National Geographic Kids* no469 p30 Ap 2017

Intelligence officers—Attitudes

GENERAL CHAOS N. SCHMIDLE cartoon *New Yorker* v93 no2 p40 F 27 2017

Intelligence service

See also
Espionage

Both Sides Now M. HEMINGWAY color *Weekly Standard* v22 no46 p22 Ag 14 2017

Spies Like Us *American Scholar* v86 no1 p14 Wint 2017

Susan Rice: Talking Trump and tennis with the former national-security adviser M. TOMASKY *New York* v50 no13 p16 Je 26 2017

Intelligence service—United States

Exposing Shabby Intelligence P. GIRALDI bw *American Conservative* v16 no2 p6 Mr/Ap 2017

Hacking Democracy Inside Russia's Social Media War on America M. Calabresi and P. Rebala color *Time* v189 no20 p30 My 29 2017

Helicopter President J. BAMFORD color *Foreign Policy* no223 p66 Mr/Ap 2017

How Intelligence Works (When It Does) H. E. MEYER *USA Today Magazine* v145 no2864 p10 My 2017

IARPA Director Jason Matheny advances tech tools for US espionage E. Eaves color *Bulletin of the Atomic Scientists* v73 no2 p67 Mr 2017

Intelligence and the Presidency J. Miscik color *Foreign Affairs* v96 no3 p57 My/Je 2017

The Ministry of Preemption J. BAMFORD color *Foreign Policy* no224 p78 My/Je 2017

SLEUTHING FOR CLICHÉS bw color *Reader's Digest* v190 no1133 p124 S 2017

Trump Versus the Spies: All presidents clash with their intelligence experts, but the hostility the new administration has displayed is unusual--and risky A. B. Zegart *Hoover Digest: Research & Opinion on Public Policy* no2 p117 Spr 2017

WAR GAMES D. Smith cartoon *New Yorker* v92 no40 p22 D 5 2016

Intelligence service—United States—History—21st century

Russia, a Dossier of Rumors and a President-Elect M. Calabresi color diag *Time* v189 no4 p9 Ja 23 2017

Intelligence tests

Taking the IQ Test: ONE OF THE HARDEST TRICKS IS COMING UP WITH A WAY TO MEASURE DOG INTELLIGENCE R. ARDEN *Psychology Today* v50 no5 p74 S/O 2017

Intelligent personal assistants (Computer software)

AI TEST DRIVE: IS ALEXA ON YOUR PHONE AS GOOD AS IT IS IN YOUR HOME? M. SIMON color *PCWorld* v35 no5 p149 My 2017

"Alexa, Understand Me" G. Anders *MIT Technology Review* v120 no5 p26 S/O 2017

Google Searches for Its Voice L. Eadicicco color diag *Time* v190 no16/17 p68 O 23 2017

How People Will Use AI to Do Their Jobs Better H. J. Wilson and C. Bataller *Harvard Business Review Digital Articles* p2 My 27 2015

How to use Siri in macOS Sierra to find pictures in Photos on the fly L. SNIDER color *Macworld - Digital Edition* p125 F 2017

How We Built a Virtual Scheduling Assistant at Microsoft A. Monroy-Hernández and J. Cranshaw *Harvard Business Review Digital Articles* p1 Jl 28 2017

MY VOICE — ACTIVATED HOUSE G. DELL'ABATE color *Popular Mechanics* p70 My 2017

PRODUCTIVITY Bots Won't Just Help Us Buy Stuff. They'll

Help Us Become Better Versions of Ourselves M. Schrage *Harvard Business Review Digital Articles* p2 Je 1 2017

Siri vs. Google Assistant: Which is better for iPhone users? O. RAYMUNDO and M. SIMON color *Macworld - Digital Edition* p37 Je 13 2017

TAKEAWAY M. A. WOJNO cartoon *Kiplinger's Personal Finance* v71 no12 p72 D 2017

This AI flushes out trolls R. Verger and J. Will color *Popular Science* v289 no6 p65 N/D 2017

Intelligent personal assistants (Computer software)—Evaluation

Alexa, please define knowledge E. Sundrup color *America* v216 no4 p51 F 20 2017

Hello? Alexa? K. C. POHLMANN *Sound & Vision* v82 no2 p28 F/Mr 2017

Intelligent personal assistants (Computer software)—Social aspects

Growing Up with Alexa R. Metz color graph il *MIT Technology Review* v120 no5 p70 S/O 2017

The Octogenarians Who Love Amazon's Alexa E. Woyke il *MIT Technology Review* v120 no5 p17 S/O 2017

Our Bots, Ourselves M. HUTSON color *Atlantic* v319 no2 p28 Mr 2017

Intelligent sensors

Do Your Customers Actually Want a "Smart" Version of Your Product? C. Smith *Harvard Business Review Digital Articles* p2 Ag 8 2017

Supersensor M. Belfiore color *Bloomberg Businessweek* no4538 p25 S 18 2017

Intensive care units

AFTER THE ICU K. MILLER color *Prevention* v69 no1 p84 Ja 2017

How Systems Engineering Can Help Fix Health Care P. Pronovost, A. Ravitz et al *Harvard Business Review Digital Articles* p2 F 9 2017

Intention

intention INSPIRATION [Cover story] M. RABBITT color *Yoga Journal* no290 p45 Mr 2017

Intentionality (Philosophy)

THE BUDDHA'S BAGGAGE T. BHIKKHU bw *Tricycle: The Buddhist Review* v26 no2 p78 Wint 2016

Interactive motion pictures

ALTERNATE ENDINGS R. KHATCHADOURIAN cartoon *New Yorker* v92 no47 p46 Ja 30 2017

Interactive multimedia

A Case for Multimedia Storytelling M. GREER *Publishers Weekly* v264 no26 p184 Je 26 2017

Interactive television

When Television Was a Medical Device J. A. Greene *Humanities* v38 no2 p6 Spr 2017

Interactive videos

See also

Video on demand

Watch, Play, Learn cartoon *AARP: The Magazine* v60 no2A p78 F/Mr 2017

Interamerica Stage Inc.

Defining Space: Staging Products that let you re-shape a space *Stage Directions* v30 no6 p26 Je 2017

Intercontinental ballistic missile bases

backstory color *New Republic* v248 no10 p68 O 2017

Intercontinental ballistic missiles

No Good Options on North Korea P. Elliott, M. Scherer et al color *Time* v190 no4 p10 Jl 24 2017

NORTH KOREA: HOW BIG A THREAT? J. PAPPALARDO color *Popular Mechanics* p16 Jl 2017

Nuclear Wake-Up Call M. T. KLARE *Nation* v305 no3 p4 Jl 31 2017

Interdisciplinary approach in education

Doubling up J. LEWINGTON color *Maclean's* v130 no10 p77 N 2017

Updating the Two Cultures: How Structures Can Promote Interdisciplinary Cultures S. A. Valles, D. B. Luckie et al *Change* v48 no6 p28 N/D 2016

Uptown Squirrels C. Kimmett color *Walrus* v14 no5 p26 Je 2017

Interdisciplinary research

Choosing the hard road K. Henke cartoon *Science* v355 no6321 p218 Ja 13 2017

Incorporating Sociocultural Phenomena into Ecosystem-Service Valuation: The Importance of Critical Pluralism C. J. VAN RIPER, A. C. LANDON et al *BioScience* v67 no3 p233 Mr 2017

Science of the World Wide Web J. Hendler and W. Hall bibl color *Science* v354 no6313 p703 N 11 2016

Interest (Psychology)

See also

Curiosity

When to Stay Inside Your Comfort Zone A. Molinsky *Harvard Business Review Digital Articles* p2 S 7 2016

Interest rate forecasting

Investors: Don't Fear Higher Rates J. J. SIEGEL *Kiplinger's Personal Finance* v70 no12 p52 D 2016

Interest rate risk

How to Buy Bonds Now J. BODNAR *Kiplinger's Personal Finance* v71 no6 p8 Je 2017

Interest rates

See also

Discount

3 Ways to Budget for a Windfall color *Black Enterprise* v47 no4 p15 N/D 2016

Replot Your Income Plan C. Fried color diag *Money* v45 no10 p39 N 2016

STORE CARDS POSE CREDIT HAZARDS K. Close color *Money* v45 no11 p14 D 2016

Interest rates—United States

Dodge & Cox Stock Comes Roaring Back N. S. HUANG chart *Kiplinger's Personal Finance* v71 no2 p60 F 2017

THE FALLOUT FROM RISING RATES A. K. SMITH cartoon *Kiplinger's Personal Finance* v71 no3 p11 Mr 2017

Leaving Money on the Table A. Greenblatt *Governing* v30 no7 p9 Ap 2017

Milestones *Time* v188 no27-28 p17 D 26 2016

UNLOCKING THE VAULT FOR SHAREHOLDERS diag *Fortune* v174 no8 p112 D 15 2016

Why Interest Rates Matter D. FONDA cartoon graph *Kiplinger's Personal Finance* v71 no2 p57 F 2017

Interest rates—United States—Economic aspects

How to Invest When Rates Rise J. Waggoner diag *Money* v46 no5 p38 Je 2017

Interest rates—United States—Government policy

The Fed Is Driving Blind P. Coy color graph *Bloomberg Businessweek* no4527 p43 Je 19 2017

Janet Yellen Can't Help Retirees C. Condon color *Bloomberg Businessweek* no4540 p50 O 2 2017

Why a Rate Hike Is an Indicator of a Healthy Economy B. Saporito color *Time* v189 no11 p30 Mr 27 2017

Interfacial bonding

Combining polyethylene and polypropylene: Enhanced performance with PE/iPP multiblock polymers J. M. Eagan, J. Xu et al bibl chart graph *Science* v355 no6327 p814 F 24 2017

Interfaith dialogue

Interfaith women's group marches for peace in Israel N. Darom *Christian Century* v133 no25 p16 D 7 2016

Interfaith marriage

Interfaith Marriages: Do Muslims realize that interfaith unions could be an existential threat to their community? M. MIRZA *Islamic Horizons* v46 no3 p34 My/Je 2017

Interfaith worship

A church where Black lives matter B. Massingale color *U.S. Catholic* v81 no12 p8 D 2016

An Islamic Approach to Christianity: Do people realize that the Quran, the New Testament and the Hebrew Scriptures all teach us to become involved in interfaith dialogue? J. S. HARRIS JR. *Islamic Horizons* v46 no4 p48 Jl/Ag 2017

Interference (Telecommunication)

Your self-driving car could kill radio astronomy D. Clery color *Science* v355 no6322 p232 Ja 20 2017

Interferometry

Ambient quantum optomechanics J. G. E. Harris diag *Science* v356 no6344 p1232 Je 23 2017

Real-time spectral interferometry probes the internal dynamics of femtosecond soliton molecules G. Herink, F. Kurtz et al diag *Science* v356 no6333 p50 Ap 7 2017

Interferons

Immune proteins aid viral enemy L. HAMERS *Science News*

v190 no11 p16 N 26 2016

Intergenerational households

CAN THEIR PROBLEM BE SOLVED? D. J. Jonovic *Successful Farming* v115 no3 p62 Mid-F 2017

Intergenerational relations

See also

Generation gap

if you ask me... S. JAMES *Parents* v91 no9 p132 S 2016

Indigenous Intergenerational Teachings J. BURNS ROSS bw chart il map *American Indian Quarterly* v40 no3 p216 Summ 2016

Living With Grandma? Don't Knock It Till You Try It *Parents* v91 no10 p18 O 2016

Intergenerational relations in the workplace

What Younger Workers Can Learn from Older Workers, and Vice Versa L. Gratton and A. Scott *Harvard Business Review Digital Articles* p2 N 18 2016

Interglacials

Regional and global sea-surface temperatures during the last interglaciation J. S. Hoffman, P. U. Clark et al bibl color graph *Science* v355 no6322 p276 Ja 20 2017

Intergroup relations

See also

Interorganizational relations

There's a Difference Between Cooperation and Collaboration R. Ashkenas *Harvard Business Review Digital Articles* p2 Ap 20 2015

Interior architecture

See also

Bathrooms—Design & construction

Office layout

HOUSE PROUD: Customized rooms that are just your style V. Hubbard *Virginia Living* v15 no4 p85 Je 2017

The Most 25 Electrifying Minutes of My Life M. S. PAZHOOR *Islamic Horizons* v46 no1 p60 Ja/F 2017

Southern Comforts color *House Beautiful* v158 no10 p31 D 2016/ Ja 2017

Interior architecture—Evaluation

Creating a Getaway to Share J. Brewster color diag *Log Home Living* v34 no3 p38 Ap 2017

interiors C. A. PEARSON color diag *Architectural Record* v205 no2 p33 F 2017

On the SPLIT LEVEL G. TOON color *House Beautiful* p137 Ag 2017

Interior decoration

See also

Bathroom design & construction

Color in interior decoration

Dining room design & construction

Interior decoration of cottage

Interior decoration of dwellings

Interior decoration of entrance halls

Interior decoration of farmhouses

Interior decoration of restaurants

Interior decoration of yachts

Interior painting

Living room design & construction

Mural painting & decoration

Restroom design & construction

Screens (Furniture)

Staircases

Wall coverings

1840: Philadelphia E. A. Poe *Lapham's Quarterly* v10 no1 p102 Wint 2017

#2: In California, decorator Chloe Warner transforms a modernist glass box into a family house that is both beautiful and kid-proof. All it takes is pattern-andcolor confidence—and 200 yards of sheer pink fabric D. A. KEEPS color *House Beautiful* v159 no2 p90 Mr 2017

#5: In a classic Southern home, Melissa Rufty keeps the best of the past while injecting chic colors and patterns—from cantaloupe walls to animal prints—that say, "This isn't your grandmother's house" M. READ color *House Beautiful* v159 no2 p116 Mr 2017

ALL the RIGHT MOVES L. O'KEEFFE *Better Homes & Gardens* v95 no1 p80 Ja 2017

AND...FADE-OUT E. N. GAGE color *Martha Stewart Living* p19 My 2017

Animal House color *Parents* v92 no7 p98 Jl 2017

ASK OLD HOUSE JOURNAL P. Poore color *Old House Journal* v45 no1 p60 F 2017

An Aspirational Ensemble color *Old House Journal* v45 no1 p72 F 2017

As you are: logan killen interiors renews northshore house lo reflect couples personalities and lifestyle L. CUTRONE *New Orleans Homes & Lifestyles* v20 no3 p46 Summ 2017

At Play: Antique toys add history and whimsy to any room L. Claverie *New Orleans Homes & Lifestyles* v20 no3 p28 Summ 2017

back at the ranch color *Better Homes & Gardens* v95 no2 p29 F 2016

BACK TO CALI M. RUS color *Architectural Digest* v74 no10 p140 O 1 2017

backyard hideaway B. MOLLENKAMP color *Better Homes & Gardens* v95 no8 p84 Ag 2017

BACKYARD RETREAT L. MOWRY *Atlanta* v57 no4 p32 Ag 2017

THE BEACH color *InStyle* p68 Home & Design 2016

BEAMS & in between P. Poore color *Arts & Crafts Homes & the Revival* v11 no5 p28 Wint 2017

BEARDED IRIS M. ROSS color *Better Homes & Gardens* v95 no6 p72 Je 2017

BELGIAN BEAUTY L. MOWRY *Atlanta* v57 no1 p44 My 2017

BEST OF THE WEST color *Sunset* v239 no1 p11 Jl 2017

big ideas for small spaces L. FENTON color *Parents* v92 no3 p86 Mr 2017

the big picture bw color *Parents* v92 no3 p83 Mr 2017

BLUES CLUES B. RILEY *Atlanta* v57 no6 p50 O 2017

Branching Out K. Hammonds color *Southern Living* v52 no2 p17 F 2017

Bright Ideas T. MARTIN *Indianapolis Monthly* p38 My 2017

Bungalow More Modern P. Poore color *Old House Journal* v45 no3 p8 My 2017

BY SIMPLICITY SAVED R. DeCotis bw color *Old House Journal* v45 no1 p32 F 2017

CABBAGETOWN CHARACTER L. MOWRY *Atlanta* v56 no9 p48 Ja 2017

CAMERA READY L. O'KEEFFE *Better Homes & Gardens* v94 no11 pN1 N 2016

CASUAL FRIDAYS P. P. FISCHER color *Better Homes & Gardens* v95 no6 p138 Je 2017

CAT HOUSE D. Keeps color *InStyle* p22 Home & Design 2016

CHAINS OF LOVE E. Wilson color *InStyle* p52 Home & Design 2016

The cheap, joyful HOME MAKEOVER [Cover story] color *Redbook* p108 Jl/Ag 2017

Chicken-wire Glass B. D. Coleman bw color *Old House Journal* v45 no1 p56 F 2017

CLEAR INTENTIONS J. GIOVANNINI bw color *Architectural Digest* v74 no1 p202 Ja 2017

CLUB ROOM L. MOWRY *Atlanta* v56 no8 p64 D 2016

color of the month: NAVY color *Good Housekeeping* v265 no4 p64a O 2017

COLOR OUTSIDE THE LINES L. M. Labong color *Sunset* v239 no4 p36 O 2017

COLOR THEORY S. ORR *Better Homes & Gardens* v95 no4 p2 Ap 2017

Cover *Southern Living* v52 no2 pC1 F 2017

A CRAFTSMAN HOME in Perfect Pitch [Cover story] D. PIZZI color *Arts & Crafts Homes & the Revival* v12 no5 p40 Wint 2018

creative haven A. PEASLEY bw color *Architectural Digest* v74 no2 p100 F 2017

CURTAINS TO CARPETS *Design Center Sourcebook* p83 2016

DARRYL CARTER ON MIXING MODERN WITH TRADITIONAL K. O'SHEA-EVANS color *House Beautiful* v159 no2 p56 Mr 2017

Décor Fresh for Spring K. Wilburn *New Orleans Homes & Lifestyles* v20 no2 p88 Spr 2017

DESIGNED for COMPANY K. Owen color *Southern Living* v51 no12 p120 D 2016

design ideas FROM THE PAST FOR TODAY'S STYLE P.

MIAMI HEAT H. SILVA color *Architectural Digest* v74 no9 p149 S 2017

Midwestern Masterpiece [Cover story] J. Brewster color diag *Log Home Living* p76 2018 Annual Buyers Guide

minding the manor K. BETTS color *Architectural Digest* v74 no3 p86 Mr 2017

Mix and Match color *House Beautiful* v159 no1 p21 F 2017

Mix and Match: Inccrporating art and antiques with style and panache K. Wilburn *New Orleans Homes & Lifestyles* v20 no4 p102 Aut 2017

Modern Compromise M. k. Quinlan color *Southern Living* v52 no1 p15 Ja 2017

Modernity H. MARTIN color *Architectural Digest* no6 p34 Je 1 2017

Modern Mix S. LOGAN color *Timber Home Living* v27 no4 p44 Ag 2017

The More the Merrier Z. Gowen color *Southern Living* v52 no5 p50 My 2017

MOUNTAINS' MAJESTY C. BARBOUR color *House Beautiful* v158 no10 p64 D 2016/Ja 2017

my write space L. Vaccariello *Parents* v92 no7 p10 Jl 2017

A New Americana D. BRENNER color *House Beautiful* v159 no9 p94 N 2017

New House, Old Soul C. BARBOUR color *House Beautiful* v159 no9 p100 N 2017

New Point of View: The Richmond home of George and Louise Freeman is a study in transformation V. HUBBARD *Virginia Living* v15 no6 p58 O 2017

NIGHT AND DEY H. MITCHELL color *Chicago* v66 no4 p63 Ap 2017

NORTHERN LIGHT R. BARRENECHE color *Architectural Digest* v74 no2 p78 F 2017

not your granny's slipcover color *Parents* v92 no6 p109 Je 2017

OBSESSED WITH NAUTICAL A. MAZE color *Better Homes & Gardens* v95 no7 p14 Jl 2017

ON CUE L. MOWRY *Atlanta* v56 no11 p50 Mr 2017

OPEN invitation K. BARNES color *Better Homes & Gardens* v95 no6 p57 Je 2017

Our Acquired Taste P. Poore *Arts & Crafts Homes & the Revival* v12 no5 p8 Wint 2018

Outside the Box T. MARTIN *Indianapolis Monthly* p42 My 2017

painting a BLUE STREAK K. K. CONDON color *Better Homes & Gardens* v95 no4 p38 Ap 2017

PARTY DOWN C. SAFAVI *Better Homes & Gardens* v95 no1 p33 Ja 2017

PARTY ON... THE CHEAP A. MAZE and D. DICKINSON color *Better Homes & Gardens* v95 no6 p46 Je 2017

PERSIMMON + SAND color *Martha Stewart Living* p27 My 2017

PHOTO FINISH M. RUS color *Architectural Digest* v74 no2 p96 F 2017

A Place To DREAM H. Rubenstein color *InStyle* p28 Home & Design 2016

PLAN TO PERFECTION C. RODRIGUES color *House Beautiful* p92 Ag 2017

professional services *Design Center Sourcebook* p140 2016

PROVING GROUND D. SCHWARTZ color *Better Homes & Gardens* v95 no6 p126 Je 2017

(PUMPKIN) SPICE UP YOUR DECOR R. Kinane color *Entertainment Weekly* no1486 p52 O 13 2017

PURPOSE-BUILT M. M. Kashino color *Washingtonian Magazine* v52 no7 p46 Ap 2017

PUT IT in NEUTRAL K. SELZER color *Better Homes & Gardens* v95 no4 p26 Ap 2017

q&a color *Timber Home Living* v27 no4 p26 Ag 2017

QUIET UPGRADES: A MODERN BUNGALOW MAKE R. COLE color *Arts & Crafts Homes & the Revival* v12 no5 p50 Wint 2018

RAISE THE ROOF C. Lamers color *Sunset* v238 no1 p33 Ja 2017

Renovating a Victorian? P. Poore cartoon color *Old House Journal* v45 no2 p64 Ap 2017

resource guide color *Timber Home Living* p59 2017 SpecialIssue

Resources *Old House Journal* v45 no4 p87 Je 2017

Restoration drama C. MACDONALD color *House Beautiful* p40 Ag 2017

Retail Therapy M. HERMANSON *Virginia Living* v15 no1 p45

D 2016

RETOOLED JEWEL L. MURTHA *Cincinnati Magazine* v50 no4 p38 Ja 2017

Return TO GLORY B. BROWN color *House Beautiful* p48 Ag 2017

RISE & SHINE A. MARSHALL color *Architectural Digest* v74 no8 p88 Ag 2017

ROBERT COUTURIER ON FIRE! K. O'SHEA-EVANS color *House Beautiful* v158 no10 p34 D 2016/Ja 2017

Rolling the Dice K. RENDA color *House Beautiful* v159 no9 p84 N 2017

Room to Improve M. RICAPITO color *Women's Health* v14 no9 p98 N 2017

Room with a View color *Timber Home Living* v27 no4 p38 Ag 2017

RUSTIC REVISITED K. HACKETT color *Better Homes & Gardens* v95 no10 p132 O 2017

SAVE THE PLANET AT HOME T. A. Christian color *Essence* v47 no12 p126 Ap 2017

score more storage *Parents* p93 2015

second nature L. HEDRICK color *Better Homes & Gardens* v95 no9 p54 S 2017

Second Time's the Charm S. LOGAN color *Timber Home Living* p54 2017 Annual Buyers

SERENE QUEEN [Cover story] J. Bober color *InStyle* p4 Home & Design 2016

Share with us L. Hammett, A. Marie O'Leary et al color *House Beautiful* p8 Ag 2017

shelf expression *Better Homes & Gardens* v94 no11 pN8 N 2016

shelf help L. FENTON color *Parents* v92 no8 p121 Ag 2017

SIMPLE LIVING in Santa Barbara B. D. COLEMAN chart color *Arts & Crafts Homes & the Revival* v11 no5 p38 Wint 2017

SPACE SAVERS color *Martha Stewart Living* p41 O 2017

SPRING DESIGN: ART W. GOODMAN img *New York* v50 no8 p81 Ap 17 2017

Spring Forward T. BROOKS and D. POINTDUJOUR color *Ebony* v72 no5 p53 Mr 2017

A Storybook ODYSSEY D. Pizzi color *Old House Journal* v44 no8 p28 D 2016

Stroke of Genius K. O'SHEA-EVANS color *House Beautiful* p31 Jl 2017

STUNING MADE SIMPLE P. GUGLIELMETTI *Martha Stewart Living* no270 p114 D 2016

STYLE *New Orleans Homes & Lifestyles* v20 no3 p18 Summ 2017

The Suite Life color *Log Home Living* v34 no1 p10 F 2017

Summer Lovin' M. W. Spencer *New Orleans Homes & Lifestyles* v20 no3 p14 Summ 2017

Sweet Dreams are Made of This C. Johnson color diag *Cabin Living* p72 Je 2017

Sweet Dreams L. D. ROBERTS *Indianapolis Monthly* p24 My 2017

SWEET ON CARNATIONS A. PANOS color *Better Homes & Gardens* v95 no2 p96 F 2017

That's the Ticket Z. KUMOK *Indianapolis Monthly* p46 My 2017

This Old Boardinghouse: A once-abandoned Boerum Hill building got stripped down to its bones and built back up again W. GOODMAN img *New York* v50 no13 p63 Je 26 2017

TINY HOME BIG DREAMS J. Chamberlain color *Sunset* v238 no1 p70 Ja 2017

top design QUESTIONS ANSWERED! A. LONGOBUCCO chart color *Good Housekeeping* v264 no2 p41 F 2017

TORY'S GLORY H. Rubenstein color *InStyle* p46 Home & Design 2016

Totally Rockin' Idea color *Good Housekeeping* v265 no1 p121 Jl 2017

Tricks of the Trim Trade color *House Beautiful* v159 no1 p26 F 2017

TURN AN UNUSED GARAGE INTO A Guest Retreat A. CHANTIM color diag *Good Housekeeping* v265 no1 p44 Jl 2017

Turning the Tide D. A. KEEPS color *House Beautiful* v159 no9 p68 N 2017

up to the CHALLENGE B. MOLLENKAMP color diag *Better Homes & Gardens* v95 no11 p40 N 2017

Vintage Holiday Homemaking JOHNSON *Treasures* v6 no3 p28

D 2016/Ja 2017
WALL & FLOOR TILES *Design Center Sourcebook* p33 2016
WALLS & CEILINGS *Design Center Sourcebook* p47 2016
WE ASKED THE PROS *Washingtonian Magazine* v52 no6 p160 Mr 2017
Welcome to the Monkey House L. D. ROBERTS *Indianapolis Monthly* p134 My 2017
Well Schooled L. CUTRONE color *New Orleans Magazine* v51 no12 p64 O 2017
What Lies Beneath [Cover story] S. Durr Albert color *Log Home Living* v33 no7 p56 S 2016
WHAT SHE DID *Better Homes & Gardens* v94 no11 p60 N 2016
Where do ideas come from? P. POORE bw cartoon color *Old House Journal* v45 no1 p64 F 2017
Wonder Brothers: The Goethe-, Tolstoy-, and Melnikov-inspired Carroll Gardens apartment of two young siblings and business partners W. GOODMAN img *New York* v50 no12 p78 Je 12 2017
Work Hard, Play Hard J. YOUNG *Indianapolis Monthly* p34 My 2017
WORK OF ART: A happy, light-filled space in Brookland proves that multifunctional doesn't have to mean cluttered and confused J. Sergent *Washingtonian Magazine* v52 no12 p137 S 2017
zen spirit D. BLASBERG color *Architectural Digest* v74 no2 p86 F 2017
ZINGING THE BLUES [Cover story] K. RENDA color *House Beautiful* v158 no9 p120 N 2016

Interior decoration accessories
HOME, sweet HOME A. MAZE and J. O'BRIEN color *Better Homes & Gardens* v95 no10 p70 O 2017

Interior decoration accessories—Evaluation
Finishing Touch J. J. CONDON color *House Beautiful* v159 no4 p38 My 2017
Get in Line J. J. CONDON color *House Beautiful* v159 no4 p40 My 2017

Interior decoration accessories—Sales & prices
$1 million Day V. Kagan and J. Dubuffet *Treasures* v6 no2 p8 O/N 2016

Interior decoration equipment
Rhymes with Smiles K. O'Shea-Evans color *House Beautiful* p26 Jl 2017
SEA SHADES M. B. EYERS color *Better Homes & Gardens* v95 no6 p26 Je 2017
STRIPE RIGHT K. O'SHEA-EVANS color *House Beautiful* p21 Jl 2017

Interior decoration equipment—Evaluation
Designers' Favorites UNDER $150 color *Redbook* p140 O 2017
In the Western HOME color *Sunset* v239 no3 p58 S 2017
Lime Light color *Timber Home Living* v27 no5 p16 O 2017

Interior decoration exhibitions
Frankly Speaking C. HONG bw color *Architectural Digest* v74 no1 p40 Ja 2017
Girl Just Wants to Have Fun S. COCHRAN color *Architectural Digest* v74 no9 p94 S 2017

Interior decoration firms
DECOR & FURNISHINGS color *Timber Home Living* p60 2017 SpecialIssue

Interior decoration of apartments
TRUE BLUE J. LEVINE bw color *Architectural Digest* v74 no8 p48 Ag 2017

Interior decoration of bathrooms
MAKE A SPLASH: Bathrooms done up in unexpected colors, patterns, and accessories will make you forget basic, boring white M. M. Kashino *Washingtonian Magazine* v52 no12 p130 S 2017
REVIVAL BATHS *Design Center Sourcebook* p41 2016

Interior decoration of bungalows
California dreamy K. P. Badal color *Sunset* v238 no6 p46 Je 2017
Pleasures of TAKING IT BACK D. Pizzi color *Arts & Crafts Homes & the Revival* v12 no3 p25 Summ 2017

Interior decoration of chapels
Pray Tell M. OWENS color *Architectural Digest* no11 p162 N 1 2017

Interior decoration of cottage
A Makeover on LAKE CHARLEVOIX P. POORE color *Arts & Crafts Homes & the Revival* v12 no3 p50 Summ 2017

PERFECT FIT K. BARNES color *Better Homes & Gardens* v95 no6 p35 Je 2017
a real charmer G. C. GRENSING color diag *Cabin Living* p36 Je 2017

Interior decoration of cottages
A FAIRY TALE L. MURTHA color *Cincinnati Magazine* v51 no1 p30 O 2017
make a WOODSY statement D. Howland color *Cabin Living* p7 S 2017

Interior decoration of country homes
SLEEPING BEAUTY M. RUS color *Architectural Digest* v74 no10 p160 O 1 2017

Interior decoration of dwellings
2017'S HOTTEST COLOR COMBOS color *Good Housekeeping* v264 no6 p48A Je 2017
ANGLO FILE D. F. WOOD bw color *Architectural Digest* no6 p110 Je 1 2017
ARTISTIC TRIUMPH S. THORNTON color *Architectural Digest* v74 no8 p62 Ag 2017
DOMINICAN DREAM C. Malle color *Architectural Digest* no6 p124 Je 1 2017
A Fine Vintage D. THOMAS color *Architectural Digest* v74 no8 p94 Ag 2017
From Our Editor S. Donelson *House Beautiful* v159 no5 p8 Je 2017
Garden District E. MacSweeney color *Vogue* v207 no11 p202 N 2017
House Beautiful GUIDE TO Small Spaces [Cover story] color *House Beautiful* v159 no5 p21 Je 2017
AN IDEAL SETTING: JEWELRY ARTIST CAROLYN MORRIS BACH TRANSFORMS AN OVERGROWN 18TH-CENTURY CAPE INTO A POLISHED WORK-AND-LIVING SPACE A. GRAVES *Yankee* v81 no5 p32 S/O 2017
Industrial Lite: Designer Shauna Leftwich softens industrial edges of warehouse district condo L. Cutrone *New Orleans Homes & Lifestyles* v20 no4 p65 Aut 2017
THE LIFE AQUATIC R. BECKER color *Architectural Digest* no6 p142 Je 1 2017
MY LATEST DIY PROJECT, COMPLETED M. Bristol bw color *Old House Journal* v45 no4 p32 Je 2017
One Room, Two Ways J. Blaise Kramer color *Good Housekeeping* v264 no6 p43 Je 2017
Playing (High-Design) House J. MURPHY color *Conde Nast Traveler* v52 no8 p44 S 2017
pretty IS AS PRETTY does: A FLOOD DAMAGED OLD METAIRIE HOUSE IS GIVEN A SECOND CHANCE V. HART *New Orleans Homes & Lifestyles* v20 no4 p56 Aut 2017
Prime of Their Lives: Retiring in style on St. Charles Avenue L. Cutrone color *New Orleans Magazine* v51 no10 p66 Ag 2017
RENOVATION DIARY: Behind the scenes of my $140,000, six-month remodel in Arlington J. Sergent *Washingtonian Magazine* v52 no11 p142 Ag 2017
sea for days D. BLASBERG color *Architectural Digest* no6 p98 Je 1 2017
TOWN COUNTRY K. FRANZMAN color *Indianapolis Monthly* v42 no2 p78 O 2017
VERN YIP ON PERFECT MEASUREMENTS K. O'SHEA-EVANS color *House Beautiful* v159 no5 p57 Je 2017
WINNING COMBINATION [Cover story] color diag *Timber Home Living* v27 no6 p72 D 2017
Worth the Wait color *Timber Home Living* v27 no4 p30 Ag 2017

Interior decoration of entrance halls
Keys to a tidy, pretty entryway S. JEAN SHELTON color *Redbook* p132 N 2017

Interior decoration of farmhouses
COMING CLEAN K. P. Badal color *Sunset* v239 no1 p43 Jl 2017
living HISTORY P. P. FISCHER color *Better Homes & Gardens* v95 no11 p122 N 2017

Interior decoration of log cabins
Built On a Dream E. O'Brien color diag *Log Home Living* v34 no6 p64 Ag 2017

Interior decoration of restaurants
KENGO KUMA INFUSES A MODEST RESTAURANT IN PORTLAND, OREGON, WITH THE CRAFT AND AURA OF JAPAN N. R. POLLOCK *Architectural Record* v205 no7 p43 Jl 2017

snapshot A. Klimoski *Architectural Record* v205 no9 p188 S 2017

Interior decoration of yachts

How It's Done L. BECKETT chart color diag *Power & Motoryacht* v34 no10 p88 O 2017

REGENCY: P65 MOTOR YACHT R. McAFEE color *Sea Magazine* v109 no8 p34 Ag 2017

TECHNOLOGY IS CHANGING HOW YACHTS ARE BUILT AND, IN TURN, HOW DECKS AND INTERIORS ARE BEING DESIGNED Z. PROCHAZKA color *Sea Magazine* v109 no6 p46 Je 2017

Interior decoration—California

ALL IS CALM E. Jardina color *Sunset* v237 no6 p41 D 2016

BEAUTY & THE BEACH D. Keeps color *InStyle* p78 Home & Design 2016

A Cottage All Grown Up B. D. Coleman color *Old House Journal* v44 no8 p16 D 2016

The many shades of AMBER L. Sandell color *InStyle* p88 Home & Design 2016

PURSUIT OF BEAUTY S. DONELSON color *House Beautiful* v159 no3 p94 Ap 2017

Interior decoration—England

how sweet it is A. BROOKS color *Architectural Digest* v74 no9 p166 S 2017

IN FULL FLOWER J. K. DE VALLE color *Architectural Digest* v74 no9 p146 S 2017

MODERN ENGLISH D. BLASBERG color *Architectural Digest* no11 p152 N 1 2017

Interior decoration—Equipment & supplies

BERRY REDS S. EGGE *Better Homes & Gardens* v94 no12 p33 D 2016

Christmas in the country S. S. SORIA *Better Homes & Gardens* v94 no12 p39 D 2016

COLOR REGAL PURPLES N. DAYTON *Better Homes & Gardens* v94 no11 p33 N 2016

GREAT HEIGHTS L. HEDRICK *Better Homes & Gardens* v94 no12 p141 D 2016

Magnate School R. L. BOFFERDING color *Architectural Digest* v74 no4 p69 Ap 2017

Make It Your Own S. ORR *Better Homes & Gardens* v94 no12 p4 D 2016

Max Volume color *House Beautiful* v159 no3 p43 Ap 2017

Mobile Home H. MARTIN color *Architectural Digest* no5 p118 My 2017

No Limits cartoon color *Architectural Digest* v74 no1 p51 Ja 2017

PERSONAL EFFECTS S. Morrow color *Martha Stewart Living* no271 p96 Ja/F 2017

A REFINED AFFAIR F. SCHULTZ color *House Beautiful* v159 no3 p112 Ap 2017

A WARM WELCOME J. LEWIS color *House Beautiful* v159 no3 p104 Ap 2017

Interior decoration—Equipment & supplies

BERRY REDS S. EGGE *Better Homes & Gardens* v94 no12 p33 D 2016

Christmas in the country S. S. SORIA *Better Homes & Gardens* v94 no12 p39 D 2016

COLOR REGAL PURPLES N. DAYTON *Better Homes & Gardens* v94 no11 p33 N 2016

GREAT HEIGHTS L. HEDRICK *Better Homes & Gardens* v94 no12 p141 D 2016

Magnate School R. L. BOFFERDING color *Architectural Digest* v74 no4 p69 Ap 2017

Make It Your Own S. ORR *Better Homes & Gardens* v94 no12 p4 D 2016

Max Volume color *House Beautiful* v159 no3 p43 Ap 2017

Mobile Home H. MARTIN color *Architectural Digest* no5 p118 My 2017

No Limits cartoon color *Architectural Digest* v74 no1 p51 Ja 2017

PERSONAL EFFECTS S. Morrow color *Martha Stewart Living* no271 p96 Ja/F 2017

A REFINED AFFAIR F. SCHULTZ color *House Beautiful* v159 no3 p112 Ap 2017

A WARM WELCOME J. LEWIS color *House Beautiful* v159 no3 p104 Ap 2017

Interior decoration—Equipment & supplies—Evaluation

1968 ORANGE L. HEDRICK color *Better Homes & Gardens* v95 no3 p156 Mr 2017

AMERICAN IDEAL M. HANNAH color *Architectural Digest* v73 no11 p60 N 2016

art + craft color *Arts & Crafts Homes & the Revival* v11 no5 p10 Wint 2017

ART OBJECTS color *Arts & Crafts Homes & the Revival* v12 no1 p28 2017 Resouce Guide

be so bold bw color *Architectural Digest* v74 no4 p100 Ap 2017

BHG throwback 1976 VELVET L. HEDRICK *Better Homes & Gardens* v95 no1 p124 Ja 2017

Bright Ideas J. Taraska *Architectural Record* v204 no11 p159 N 2016

Burning, Man! E. Reimel cartoon color *Glamour* v114 no12 p124 D 2016

coat check color *Better Homes & Gardens* v95 no3 p44 Mr 2017

DESIGN NOTES color *Architectural Digest* no5 p116 My 2017

Family Reading Time color *Old House Journal* v45 no3 p72 My 2017

Faux Arts H. BROWN color *House Beautiful* v159 no1 p30 F 2017

FLORA & FAUNA color *Architectural Digest* v73 no11 p55 N 2016

FORAGED FINDS *Better Homes & Gardens* v94 no11 p12 N 2016

GINKGO GREENS S. EGGE color *Better Homes & Gardens* v95 no3 p22 Mr 2017

guiding lights W. T. Georgis color *Architectural Digest* v74 no4 p102 Ap 2017

Have It Both Ways K. RENDA, P. GORRIVAN et al color *House Beautiful* v159 no4 p30 My 2017

HOME UNDER $150 color *Redbook* p114 Mr 2017

Inside Job J. Taraska color *Architectural Record* v205 no2 p48 F 2017

In the House J. Minutillo *Architectural Record* v204 no10 p53 O 2016

into the light A. MAZE color *Better Homes & Gardens* v95 no3 p30 Mr 2017

Let's get Cozy N. DAYTON *Better Homes & Gardens* v95 no1 p88 Ja 2017

Modern and Sporty color *Old House Journal* v45 no3 p50 My 2017

OBSESSED WITH RUSHES, REEDS & GRASSES E. S. SOTO color *Better Homes & Gardens* v95 no3 p10 Mr 2017

OBSESSED WITH WOODSY DECOR E. S. SOTO *Better Homes & Gardens* v94 no11 p11 N 2016

PUNCH LIST K. SELZER color *Better Homes & Gardens* v95 no3 p56 Mr 2017

RHAPSODY IN BLUE AND WHITE color *House Beautiful* v158 no9 p128 N 2016

small wonders K. Ridder color *Architectural Digest* v74 no4 p93 Ap 2017

soak it up bw color *Architectural Digest* v74 no4 p104 Ap 2017

Interior decoration—Evaluation

bragging rights color *Better Homes & Gardens* v95 no5 p78 My 2017

THE BUILD & THE BLOG K. R. KEGANS color *Better Homes & Gardens* v95 no5 p128 My 2017

A COZY SITTING ROOM color *House Beautiful* v158 no10 p35 D 2016/Ja 2017

DESIGN NOTES color *Architectural Digest* no5 p150 My 2017

Domestic Harmony J. LEVINE color *Architectural Digest* no5 p66 My 2017

Game Changer K. Sutton color *House Beautiful* v159 no2 p45 Mr 2017

A group effort—led by AD100 designer Dan Fink—transforms the dancers' lounge for American Ballet Theatre into a triumphant tour de force S. COCHRAN bw color *Architectural Digest* v74 no7 p76 Jl 2017

a happy medium J. GARLOCK color diag *Better Homes & Gardens* v95 no5 p30 My 2017

Modern Marriage color *House Beautiful* v159 no2 p43 Mr 2017

MUSEUM–WORTHY K. GIVEN color *Architectural Digest* v73 no12 p41 D 2016

Pattern Play color *Architectural Digest* v74 no3 p33 Mr 2017

SARAH STORMS M. B. EYERS color *Better Homes & Gardens* v95 no9 p18 S 2017

SEASIDE BOHEMIA J. A. RUDICK color *Architectural Digest*

v74 no7 p36 Jl 2017

Tuscan Olive K. RENDA and B. REYNAERT color *House Beautiful* v159 no8 p21 O 2017

Young at Heart S. HARRELSON color *Architectural Digest* v74 no1 p160 Ja 2017

Interior decoration—France

Domestic Harmony J. LEVINE color *Architectural Digest* no5 p66 My 2017

Interior decoration—History—20th century

Totally Radical H. MARTIN color *Architectural Digest* v74 no10 p52 O 1 2017

Interior decoration—History—21st century

ALL THE RAJ D. THOMAS color *Architectural Digest* v74 no4 p146 Ap 2017

FAMILY STYLE D. BRENNER bw color *Architectural Digest* v74 no4 p168 Ap 2017

GREEK REVIVAL M. ROZZO color *Architectural Digest* v74 no4 p118 Ap 2017

perch perfect A. FLEETWOOD color *Architectural Digest* v74 no4 p140 Ap 2017

THE SON ALSO RISES M. OWENS color *Architectural Digest* v74 no4 p128 Ap 2017

Southern Comfort H. MARTIN color *Architectural Digest* v74 no4 p43 Ap 2017

Interior decoration—Illinois

ROYALE MESS A. AMBROSIUS color *Chicago* v65 no11 p22 N 2016

Interior decoration—Latin America

PORT OF CALL M. OWENS bw color *Architectural Digest* v73 no11 p192 N 2016

Interior decoration—New York (State)—New York

Artistic License color *Architectural Digest* v73 no11 pCover N 2016

editor's letter color *Architectural Digest* v74 no7 p10 Jl 2017

Flip the Script M. RUS color *Architectural Digest* no11 p104 N 1 2017

In Mr. Fulk's Neighborhood H. MARTIN bw color *Architectural Digest* v73 no11 p186 N 2016

In the Bag M. OWENS color *Architectural Digest* v74 no9 p52 S 2017

keep it classic M. RUS color *Architectural Digest* v74 no10 p134 O 1 2017

Sitting Pretty J. K. DE VALLE color *Architectural Digest* v74 no9 p41 S 2017

Interior decoration—United States

Artistic License [Cover story] M. HAINEY color *Architectural Digest* v73 no11 p142 N 2016

GET PLASTERED T. MCKEOUGH color *Architectural Digest* v73 no11 p68 N 2016

polishing a gem [Cover story] J. BREWSTER color diag *Cabin Living* p26 O 2017

Resources color *House Beautiful* v159 no1 p102 F 2017

Royal Barry Wills COLONIAL REVIVAL P. POORE color *Old House Journal* v45 no1 p14 F 2017

Interior decorators

See also

Women interior decorators

2017 KITCHEN OF THE YEAR K. Renda color *House Beautiful* v159 no8 p76 O 2017

Aging Gracefully K. Owen color *Southern Living* v52 no7 p15 Jl 2017

ALL DRESSED UP D. A. Keeps color *House Beautiful* v159 no8 p104 O 2017

all in the family K. HACKETT color *House Beautiful* v159 no7 p112 S 2017

All you need is Paint! color *Redbook* p126 O 2017

AT YOUR SERVICE B. THORKLESON color *Better Homes & Gardens* v95 no9 p48 S 2017

The Avant-Garde color *Architectural Digest* v74 no1 p94 Ja 2017

BACK TO THE LAND D. Brenner color *House Beautiful* v159 no8 p96 O 2017

Bohemian Rhapsody M. OWENS color *Architectural Digest* no6 p42 Je 1 2017

Bridle Party K. RENDA color *House Beautiful* v159 no5 p78 Je 2017

BRITISH ACCENT [Cover story] K. RENDA color *House Beau-*

tiful v158 no10 p82 D 2016/Ja 2017

British Invasion color *Architectural Digest* v74 no1 p120 Ja 2017

BUILDER PROFILES *Washingtonian Magazine* v52 no1 p170 O 2016

Chrestia Staub Pierce P. Marquis *New Orleans Homes & Lifestyles* v20 no1 p92 Wint 2016

Color Geniuses color *Architectural Digest* v74 no1 p144 Ja 2017

The Connoisseurs color *Architectural Digest* v74 no1 p116 Ja 2017

Crowned Beauties P. Guglielmetti color *Southern Living* v52 no11 p61 N 2017

The Daredevils color *Architectural Digest* v74 no1 p136 Ja 2017

Design, BUILD & remodel P. Poore color *Arts & Crafts Homes & the Revival* v12 no1 p55 2017 Resouce Guide

DESIGNER PROFILES *Atlanta* v56 no7 p38 N 2016

Eclectic Home P. Marquis *New Orleans Homes & Lifestyles* v20 no1 p94 Wint 2016

EVENT CHAIRS *Atlanta* v56 no7 p12 N 2016

fantasy island M. K. QUINLAN color *House Beautiful* v159 no7 p78 S 2017

Flight of Fancy C. BARBOUR color *House Beautiful* v159 no5 p68 Je 2017

French Connection color *Architectural Digest* v74 no1 p124 Ja 2017

Hall of Fame color *Architectural Digest* v74 no1 p92 Ja 2017

Hitmakers bw color *Architectural Digest* v74 no1 p140 Ja 2017

in the pink C. BARBOUR color *House Beautiful* v159 no7 p104 S 2017

A LABOR OF LOVE K. RENDA color *House Beautiful* v159 no1 p66 F 2017

Living the Lush Life D. A. KEEPS color *House Beautiful* v159 no5 p84 Je 2017

loving Fall D. Howland color *Cabin Living* p7 O 2017

luxe be a lady K. RENDA color *House Beautiful* v159 no7 p88 S 2017

MAKE IT HUM C. BARBOUR color *House Beautiful* v159 no1 p76 F 2017

MAN OF THE WORLD J. LEVINE color *Architectural Digest* v74 no3 p132 Mr 2017

The Modernists color *Architectural Digest* v74 no1 p107 Ja 2017

NEW OPULENCE H. MARTIN color *Architectural Digest* v74 no1 p186 Ja 2017

The New Traditionalists color *Architectural Digest* v74 no1 p128 Ja 2017

PALETTE CLEANSER M. READ color *House Beautiful* v158 no10 p76 D 2016/Ja 2017

POLISHING A JEWEL K. HACKETT color *House Beautiful* v159 no1 p92 F 2017

READY, FETE, GO ! L. CREGAN color *House Beautiful* v158 no10 p92 D 2016/Ja 2017

RESOURCES *Architectural Digest* no6 p152 Je 1 2017

Roll the Tape K. O'SHEA-EVANS color *House Beautiful* v159 no1 p25 F 2017

Room to Improve M. RICAPITO color *Women's Health* v14 no9 p98 N 2017

Style insight FOLK ART color *House Beautiful* p30 Ag 2017

Three's Company K. HACKETT color *House Beautiful* v159 no5 p92 Je 2017

TURNING BACK TIME M. READ color *House Beautiful* v159 no1 p58 F 2017

untamed chic A. PREISER color *House Beautiful* v159 no7 p96 S 2017

WHAT TO DO WITH A WHITE BOX L. CREGAN color *House Beautiful* v159 no1 p84 F 2017

Young Guns color *Architectural Digest* v74 no1 p138 Ja 2017

Interior decorators—Interviews

what's your HANG-UP? P. GUGLIELMETTI color *Better Homes & Gardens* v95 no9 p50 S 2017

Interior landscaping

BEARDED IRIS M. ROSS color *Better Homes & Gardens* v95 no6 p72 Je 2017

Interior lighting

BRIGHT IDEAS: The perfect pendant lights are like jewelry for your kitchen. Here are a few of our favorites F. Stephanie *Washingtonian Magazine* v53 no1 p157 O 2017

LIGHTING *Design Center Sourcebook* p91 2016

See the Light [Cover story] color *Timber Home Living* v27 no6 p14 D 2017

up to the CHALLENGE B. MOLLENKAMP color diag *Better Homes & Gardens* v95 no11 p40 N 2017

Interior painting

INTERIOR PAINTING color *Cabin Living* p64 D 2016

Want the Most for Your Home? Buyers Favor Bold Colors M. C. White color diag *Money* v46 no8 p12 S 2017

Interior space acoustics

Stop Noise from Ruining Your Open Office C. Calisi and J. Stout *Harvard Business Review Digital Articles* p2 Mr 16 2015

Interlandi, Jeneen

An Essential Heart-Surgery Device Has a Rare But Deadly Side Effect color *Consumer Reports* v82 no1 p41 Ja 2017

How to Keep the Bugs Away: Discover which repellents work well—and those that don't—against mosquitoes and ticks *Consumer Reports* v82 no9 p16 S 2017

Interleukin-10

Anti-inflammatory effect of IL-10 mediated by metabolic reprogramming of macrophages W. K. Eddie Ip, N. Hoshi et al diag *Science* v356 no6337 p513 My 5 2017

Interleukin-4

Local amplifiers of IL-4Rα-mediated macrophage activation promote repair in lung and liver C. M. Minutti, L. H. Jackson-Jones et al diag *Science* v356 no6342 p1076 Je 9 2017

Interlochen Center for the Arts

Interlochen Center for the Arts focuses on performance and design and production *Stage Directions* v30 no3 p74 Mr 2017

Interlocking directorates

How Corporate Boards Connect, in Charts E. Heemskerk *Harvard Business Review Digital Articles* p2 Ap 21 2016

Intermediate-Range Nuclear Forces Treaty (1987)

Seeking a path toward missile nonproliferation W. P. S. (. Sidhu bibl *Bulletin of the Atomic Scientists* v72 no6 p360 N 2016

Intermediate state (Religion)—Buddhism

IF SUPER MARIO WENT TO THE BARDO M. SCARLES color *Tricycle: The Buddhist Review* v26 no2 p19 Wint 2016

Intermittent fasting

Feast. Fast. Repeat C. SAGON color *AARP: The Magazine* v60 no1A p14 D 2016/Ja 2017

Intermolecular forces

See also

Van der Waals forces

Direction-specific van der Waals attraction between rutile TiO2 nanocrystals X. Zhang, Y. He et al diag *Science* v356 no6336 p434 Ap 28 2017

InterMountain Railway Co.

Electro-Motive Division SD40-2 diesel locomotive C. Grivno color *Model Railroader* v84 no7 p12 Jl 2017

InterMountain HO scale GP10 diesel C. Grivno color *Model Railroader* v84 no10 p60 O 2017

Internal colonialism

'Civilization' and 'Mission' A. Babo *Society* v54 no2 p124 Ap 2017

'Civilization' and the Self-Critical Tradition D. Gordon *Society* v54 no2 p106 Ap 2017

Internal combustion engines—Evaluation

Old Engine, New Tricks E. DYER cartoon color *Popular Mechanics* p38 Je 2017

Internal migration

See also

Geographic mobility

Labor mobility

Seasonal residents

Internal migration—Economic aspects

STAYING PUT IN A MOBILE ERA R. D. Sullivan chart color graph map *America* v217 no2 p12 Jl 24 2017

Internal migration—United States

See also

Great Migration, 1910-1970

ON THE MOVE M. TODD *Phi Kappa Phi Forum* v96 no4 p1 Wint 2016

Internal revenue

See also

Lottery proceeds

Internal revenue law—United States

For Rich Families, A Change in Tax Plans S. Foxman *Bloomberg Businessweek* no4502 p45 D 5 2016

A Recipe for 3% Growth: The ingredients: boost productivity, rationalize the tax code, and put more Americans to work (and keep them there). All that, and add a dash of luck E. P. Lazear *Hoover Digest: Research & Opinion on Public Policy* no3 p9 Summ 2017

Internal revenue law—United States—History—21st century

A Tax Showdown At the Border L. Browning and S. Kapur cartoon *Bloomberg Businessweek* no4514 p25 Mr 13 2017

Internal migration—Charts, diagrams, etc.

TEXAS IN-MIGRATION AND OUT-MIGRATION K. TASKER *Texas Monthly* v45 no2 p50 F 2017

Internal migration—United States—Charts, diagrams, etc.

Migration The Sun Belt Rises Again S. Matthews graph map *Bloomberg Businessweek* no4521 p15 My 8 2017

International advertising

The Most Common Mistakes Companies Make with Global Marketing N. Kelly *Harvard Business Review Digital Articles* p2 S 7 2015

International agencies—Officials & employees

We wanted to prove learning can be fun M. CALNAN *People Management* p25 O 2016

International AIDS Society

We still need to beat HIV F. Dabis and Bekker color *Science* v357 no6349 p335 Jl 28 2017

International airports—Awards

EUROPE'S BEST AIRPORT color *Iceland Review* v54 no5 p36 S-O 2016

EUROPE'S BEST AIRPORT *Iceland Review* v54 no6 p62 N/D 2016

International Alliance of Theatrical Stage Employees & Moving Picture Machine Operators of the United States & Canada

Paying My Dues J. Coakley *Stage Directions* v30 no1 p2 Ja 2017

International arbitration

How To Address Strategic Insecurity In A Turbulent Age Z. Brzezinski *NPQ: New Perspectives Quarterly* v34 no2 p29 My 2017

Justice at Sea color *Earth Island Journal* v32 no3 p9 Aut 2017

What Donald Trump Doesn't Understand About Negotiation D. Malhotra and J. Powell *Harvard Business Review Digital Articles* p2 Ap 8 2016

International armistice cooperation

CLEANING UP OBAMA'S SYRIA MESS M. BOOT *Commentary* v142 no4 p20 N 2016

International Astronomical Union

NAME THAT STAR C. Zuckerman color *National Geographic* v232 no2 p16 Ag 2017

International Bank Note Society

And the Nominees For Best New Bill Are... J. Tarmy color *Bloomberg Businessweek* no4502 p60 D 5 2016

International banking industry

See also

World Bank

Can Bankers Fight Terrorism? M. Levitt, K. Bauer et al *Foreign Affairs* v96 no6 p144 N/D 2017

Florida S. Burnell color *Forbes* v198 no9 p27 D 30 2016

International broadcasting

The Urbanist: The Globalization of Local Radio B. ELLMAN img *New York* v49 no25 p32 D 12 2016

International business enterprises

80% of Companies Don't Know If Their Products Contain Conflict Minerals Y. H. Kim and G. F. Davis color *Harvard Business Review Digital Articles* p2 Ja 4 2017

Africa's Maker Movement Offers Opportunity for Growth N. Ekekwe *Harvard Business Review Digital Articles* p2 My 29 2015

DATA IS EVERYTHING I. Paz, R. Gruia et al color *Maclean's* v129 no51/52 p17 D 26 2016

How Multinationals Can Adapt to a Political Mood That Doesn't Care for Them at All D. Taliente and C. Windorfer *Harvard Business Review Digital Articles* p2 My 23 2017

HOW TO RESTORE THE U.S.'s ECONOMIC MOBILITY F. BUCKLEY *USA Today Magazine* v145 no2860 p18 Ja 2017

Multinationals Have a Bright Future, If You Know Where to Look A. Gupta and Haiyan Wang *Harvard Business Review Digital Articles* p2 Je 14 2017

The Rise of the Not-So- Experienced CEO R. Torres *Harvard*

v198 no7 p44 N 29 2016

International English Language Testing System

Are English tests for nurses fair? Experts make the case for and against new language quizzes said to be deterring applicants *People Management* p13 Ag 2017

International Equestrian Federation

BRINGING THE BEST TO OMAHA N. Jaffer color *Practical Horseman* v45 no3 p53 Mr 2017

Longines FEI World Cup™ North American League News color *Practical Horseman* v45 no1 p65 Ja 2017

International finance

How Blockchain Is Changing Finance A. Tapscott and D. Tapscott color *Harvard Business Review Digital Articles* p2 Mr 1 2017

International Ice Patrol

At Work With U.S. Coast Guard Ice Patrol C. Suddath color *Bloomberg Businessweek* no4528 p37 Je 26 2017

International Justice Mission

BRINGING LIGHT TO THE TRAFFICKING FIGHT [Cover story] K. SHELLNUTT color graph *Christianity Today* v61 no5 p26 Je 2017

International law

See also

Civil war

Sanctions (International law)

Sovereignty (Political science)

Protection of Human Rights under Universal International Law C. Tomuschat *UN Chronicle* v53 no4 p1 2016

Protection of Human Rights under Universal International Law C. TOMUSCHAT *UN Chronicle* v54 no4 p23 2017

International Maritime Organization

The Role of the International Maritime Organization in Preventing the Pollution of the World's Oceans from Ships and Shipping K. Lim *UN Chronicle* v54 no1/2 p1 2017

International markets

ALL ABOUT THE Benjamins D. Welch chart color *Bloomberg Businessweek* no4523 p20 My 22 2017

International mediation

How long, O Lord? K. Clarke color *U.S. Catholic* v81 no12 p42 D 2016

International Meteor Organization

The Taurids Are Back color *Sky & Telescope* v134 no5 p50 N 2017

International Monetary Fund

Christine LAGARDE A. Robb color *Glamour* v114 no12 p220 D 2016

International Monetary Fund—Officials & employees

New world disorder K. CARMICHAEL color *Maclean's* v129 no48/49 p60 D 5 2016

International obligations

World Order 2.0 R. Haass color *Foreign Affairs* v96 no1 p2 Ja/F 2017

International Olympic Committee (IOC)

THE OLYMPIC MOVEMENT THE UNITED NATIONS AND THE PURSUIT OF COMMON IDEALS T. BACH *UN Chronicle* v53 no2 p14 2016

International organization

See also

Reconstruction (1914-1939)

Is the Liberal Order in Peril? A. APPLEBAUM and M. MATTHIJS color graph *Foreign Affairs* v96 no3 p178 My/Je 2017

International Polar Foundation (Company)

Science suffers in cold war over polar base M. Enserink color *Science* v355 no6322 p231 Ja 20 2017

International relations

See also

Economic sanctions

Globalization

International arbitration

International conflict

International security

Jihad

Nationalism

Nuclear crisis control

Peace

Political realism

War

Break Up the Bromance: Just getting along with Russia isn't going

to be good enough. If the new administration wants a "reset" of its own, it will need to demonstrate clarity and strength M. A. McFaul *Hoover Digest: Research & Opinion on Public Policy* no2 p86 Spr 2017

Chicken Soup for the Russian Soul: A strongman with a messianic streak, Vladimir Putin might almost have stepped from the pages of Russian history R. Peters *Hoover Digest: Research & Opinion on Public Policy* no2 p101 Spr 2017

The China Challenge Z. KHALILZAD *American Conservative* v16 no3 p32 My/Je 2017

Civil Wars as Challenges to the Modern International System H. Spruyt *Daedalus* v146 no4 p112 Fall 2017

Civil War & the Current International System J. D. Fearon chart graph *Daedalus* v146 no4 p18 Fall 2017

Credibility Counts [Cover story] J. KIRCHICK bw color *Weekly Standard* v22 no16 p18 D 26 2016

The Dirtbag Left's Man in Syria R. Wiedeman img *New York* v50 no7 p40 Ap 3 2017

"It's Best Not to Mess with Us": The nuclear poker game with Moscow has already begun--or, rather, resumed P. R. Gregory *Hoover Digest: Research & Opinion on Public Policy* no2 p97 Spr 2017

Kim Jong Un Isn't the Only Wild Card In the North Korea Crisis P. Elliott, C. Campbell et al color *Time* v190 no10/11 p11 S 18 2017

Legislative Background on the Cuba Embargo *Congressional Digest* v95 no10 p11 D 2016

MEXICO IMAGE vs. REALITY S. McCOLLUM and P. SMITH *New York Times Upfront* v149 no4 p8 O 31 2016

Moscow's Wounded Pride S. Kotkin *Hoover Digest: Research & Opinion on Public Policy* no4 p99 Fall 2016

Obama's Gift to Iran R. D. WILKINS *Commentary* v142 no5 p8 D 2016

OLIGARCHY 2.0 J. YAFFA cartoon color *New Yorker* v93 no15 p46 My 29 2017

The Only Way Forward Slaughter color *Foreign Policy* no221 p64 N/D 2016

Organized Crime, Illicit Economies, Civil Violence & International Order: More Complex Than You Think V. Felbab-Brown *Daedalus* v146 no4 p98 Fall 2017

The Plucky Little Emirate Vs. Old Foes P. Waldman, M. Sergie et al color *Bloomberg Businessweek* no4535 p36 Ag 28 2017

President Obama's Cuba Policy *Congressional Digest* v95 no10 p6 D 2016

The QUIZ J. R. KEMP bw color diag *New Orleans Magazine* v51 no12 p68 O 2017

Red Dawn E. Cawthorne *Hoover Digest: Research & Opinion on Public Policy* no2 p108 Spr 2017

The Revolutionary Roots of Russian Foreign Policy J. FRIEDMAN *Current History* v116 no792 p258 O 2017

Rough Road Ahead? *Change* v82 no3 p26 Mr 2017

The Russia Question: American relations with Moscow have become a geopolitical mess--a mess, very largely, of our own making N. Ferguson *Hoover Digest: Research & Opinion on Public Policy* no2 p76 Spr 2017

Stop Listening to the Obamas and Merkels *USA Today Magazine* v145 no2863 p5 Ap 2017

Strength in a Tougher World M. SINGH color *National Review* v68 no22 p43 D 5 2016

TRUMPING OBAMA ON CUBA J. A. NATHAN *USA Today Magazine* v145 no2862 p30 Mr 2017

Trump's Penchant for Chaos Brings Less World Order K. Vick color *Time* v190 no8 p9 Ag 28 2017

U.S.-Cuba Relations Timeline *Congressional Digest* v95 no10 p2 D 2016

What Trade Deals Are Good For G. Grossman *Harvard Business Review Digital Articles* p2 My 24 2016

YOU SAY SLOVAKIA L. Mirani cartoon *New Yorker* v93 no15 p16 My 29 2017

International relations—Government policy

Diplomacy Over War P. BENNIS color *Nation* v304 no2 p18 Ja 16 2017

International relations—History—21st century

Britain's Bridge to Nowhere G. Younge il *Nation* v304 no6 p10 F 27 2017

Donald Trump's New World Disorder bw *Bloomberg Business-*

week no4505 p8 D 26 2016

International relations—Study & teaching
    See also
    Diplomacy—Study & teaching
Obama's Gift to Iran R. D. Wilkins *Commentary* v141 no10 p1 D 2016
Obama's Gift to Iran R. D. Wilkins *Commentary* v142 no5 p1 D 2016

International relief
Somalia on the Verge of Famine As U.N. Pleads for Help T. John color *Time* v189 no7/8 p17 F 27 2017

International Science & Engineering Fair
Society seeks new sponsor for International Science and Engineering Fair color *Science News* v191 no5 p29 Mr 18 2017

International security
Building Security Forces & Stabilizing Nations: The Problem of Agency S. Biddle *Daedalus* v146 no4 p126 Fall 2017
Changing Climates for Arctic Security S. Goodman bw color *Wilson Quarterly* p1 Summ 2017
The Harm in Trying E. ABRAMS color *Weekly Standard* v22 no41 p8 Jl 3 2017
Introduction: International security in the age of renewables J. Mecklin *Bulletin of the Atomic Scientists* v72 no6 p377 N 2016

International Security Assistance Force (Afghanistan)
Pakistan's Deadly Grip on Afghanistan C. C. FAIR *Current History* v116 no789 p136 Ap 2017

International Space Station
Cosmic ray catcher will probe supernovae from new perch E. Hand color *Science* v357 no6350 p437 Ag 4 2017
Lessons of Mir B. BERMAN color *Astronomy* v45 no4 p10 Ap 2017
A New Cosmopolitanism P. Tyson color *Sky & Telescope* v134 no5 p4 N 2017
on a space walk, flying blind S. Fecht cartoon *Popular Science* v289 no5 p78 S/O 2017
Stormy skies and starry nights R. Shubinski color graph *Astronomy* v45 no4 p52 Ap 2017
TRAPPED IN ORBIT A. Cho color diag graph *Science* v357 no6355 p986 S 8 2017

International Standard Book Numbers
The Bar Code Revolution L. Dawson *Publishers Weekly* v264 no21 p34 My 22 2017

International Tennis Federation
Angelique Kerber M. Hagan color *Current Biography* v78 no4 p42 Ap 2017
Golden Opportunity T. Perrotta *Tennis* v52 no6 p10 N/D 2016

International Thermonuclear Experimental Reactor (Project)
Private fusion machines aim to beat massive global effort D. Clery chart color *Science* v356 no6336 p360 Ap 28 2017
Re-creating The Sun On Earth Jing Cao color *Bloomberg Businessweek* no4529 p20 Jl 3 2017

International trade
CHAPTER 3 THE GLOBAL MACROECONOMIC SITUATION *Economic Indicators* p119 O 2016
Globalism and Its Discontents M. Spence *Hoover Digest: Research & Opinion on Public Policy* no1 p40 Wint 2017
GLOBALIZATION IN THE AGE OF TRUMP: PROTECTIONISM WILL CHANGE HOW COMPANIES DO BUSINESS—BUT NOT IN THE WAYS YOU THINK [Cover story] P. GHEMAWAT color graph img *Harvard Business Review* v95 no4 p112 Jl/Ag 2017
Globalization Is Becoming More About Data and Less About Stuff S. Lund, J. Manyika et al *Harvard Business Review Digital Articles* p2 Mr 14 2016
If Trump Abandons the TPP, China Will Be the Biggest Winner P. Ghemawat *Harvard Business Review Digital Articles* p2 D 12 2016
Rough seas ahead for trade C. SORENSEN color *Maclean's* v129 no45 p40 N 14 2016
Rounding Error cartoon color *Weekly Standard* v22 no42 p3 Jl 17 2017
Russia, Japan, and China Fill the Trade Gap B. Einhorn and I. Arkhipov *Bloomberg Businessweek* no4502 p22 D 5 2016
The U.S. Can Win a Trade War With China. That Doesn't Mean It Should Try I. Bremmer color *Time* v190 no8 p19 Ag 28 2017
The World Is Still Not Flat J. Fox *Harvard Business Review Digital Articles* p2 N 3 2014

International trade disputes
Here's How Donald Trump Can Win a Trade War With China C. Matthews color diag *Fortune* v75 no1 p22 Ja 1 2017
Retaliation Nation I. M. STELZER color *Weekly Standard* v22 no36 p26 My 29 2017

International trade—Computer network resources
We Don't Need Political Solutions for Global Trade — We Need Practical Ones R. Knight color *Harvard Business Review Digital Articles* p2 Mr 9 2017

International trade—History—21st century
Global Trade Is Slowing B. Einhorn, N. Brautlecht et al color *Bloomberg Businessweek* no4500 p16 N 21 2016
Has the World Reached Peak Trade? R. Foroohar color *Time* v188 no16/17 p44 O 24 2016

International trade—International cooperation
An Important Trade Agreement You Haven't Heard Of T. J. DONOHUE *Weekly Standard* v22 no22 p19 F 13 2017

International travel
    See also
    Border crossing
2018 WINTER AND SPRING INTERNATIONAL TRIPS *Sierra* v102 no2 p50 Mr/Ap 2017
7 Amazing Adventures That Won't Cost a Fortune M. Leonhardt and K. A. Renzulli color *Money* v46 no6 p12 Jl 2017
Florence's Mud Angels R. I. Jobs *History Today* v67 no8 p8 Ag 2017

International Union for Conservation of Nature & Natural Resources—Congresses
FIVE QUESTIONS ON THE IUCN WORLD CONGRESS WITH Rick Bates color *Canadian Wildlife* v22 no5 p42 N/D 2016
A Seat at the Conservation Table color *Earth Island Journal* v32 no4 p10 Wint 2017

International Union of Geological Sciences
DUST IN THE WIND M. O. SIMINGTON color *Phi Kappa Phi Forum* v97 no1 p11 Spr 2017
WELCOME TO THE ANTHROPOCENE N. SCHARPING color *Discover* v38 no1 p89 Ja/F 2017

International Union of Pure & Applied Physics
International Union of Pure and Applied Physics and you B. H. J. McKellar *Physics Today* v70 no10 p9 O 2017

International Women's Day
Female Privilege M. A. MIRANDA ALCAZAR and K. D. GRIFFITHS *Nation* v304 no10 p4 Mr 27 2017
March for Every Woman: Far too many feminists in the West prove reluctant to condemn practices that harm their sisters in the developing world A. H. Ali *Hoover Digest: Research & Opinion on Public Policy* no3 p128 Summ 2017
THE WOMEN AT BESSASTAÐIR: A look at how the role of the first lady of Iceland has evolved over the years Z. ROBERT *Iceland Review* v55 no3 p21 My/Je 2017

International Covenant on Economic, Social & Cultural Rights (1966)
From International Law to Local Communities: The Role of the United Nations in the Realization of Human Rights M. Kjaerum *UN Chronicle* v53 no4 p1 2016
Half a Century of a Right to Health? J. Bhabha *UN Chronicle* v53 no4 p1 2016
A Midlife Crisis for the Treaty-Based Human Rights System? A. Kumar *UN Chronicle* v53 no4 p1 2016

International Dark-Sky Association
LOOK UP T. WHEATLEY *Atlanta* v56 no11 p22 Mr 2017

International trade—Charts, diagrams, etc.
INTERNATIONAL STATISTICS *Economic Indicators* p35 D 2016
INTERNATIONAL STATISTICS *Economic Indicators* p35 O 2016

Internet
    See also
    Internet & youth
    Internet celebrities
    Internet in higher education
    Wireless Internet
9 parent click-bait headlines you never see online M. DUBIN cartoon *Parents* v92 no7 p94 Jl 2017

After 20 Years, It's Harder to Ignore the Digital Economy's Dark Side D. Tapscott *Harvard Business Review Digital Articles* p2 Mr 11 2016

apps we wish existed S. GIVEN color *Parents* v92 no4 p102 Ap 2017

The Blockchain Will Do to the Financial System What the Internet Did to Media Joichi Ito, N. Narula et al color *Harvard Business Review Digital Articles* p2 Mr 8 2017

Business Competition Has Not Gotten Fiercer J. T. Landry *Harvard Business Review Digital Articles* p2 Jl 22 2015

Cognitive Offloading L. SCHLEY cartoon *Discover* v27 no10 p14 D 2016

Governing the Smart, Connected City S. Crawford *Harvard Business Review Digital Articles* p2 O 31 2014

How the Internet Wrecked College Admissions A. Kim *Washington Monthly* p1 S/O 2016

The Internet As You Know It Does Not Exist B. FELDMAN *New York* v49 no21 p54 O 17 2016

The Internet Is Finally Forcing Management to Care About People S. Denning *Harvard Business Review Digital Articles* p2 My 5 2015

The internet should have made zines obsolete. Their resilience shows the limitations of the web as a place to nurture young creativity J. Wortham *New York Times Magazine* p14 Mr 5 2017

The Internet Shouldn't Run on Dirty Energy N. Springer and K. Gallo *Harvard Business Review Digital Articles* p2 D 17 2015

Jessamyn Stanley, Internet Yogi M. Oaklander color *Time* v188 no20 p22 N 14 2016

On Technology J. Wortham *New York Times Magazine* p16 Je 11 2017

We Don't Need Political Solutions for Global Trade — We Need Practical Ones R. Knight color *Harvard Business Review Digital Articles* p2 Mr 9 2017

What Kids Expect of Parents *USA Today Magazine* v145 no2859 p6 D 2016

Why You Should Never Date Anyone You Meet IRL D. Schwartz color *Glamour* v115 no9 p126 S 2017

Your Best Cyberself G. D. MELTON cartoon *O, The Oprah Magazine* p35 Ap 2017

Internet & activism

The Geography of Mercy V. J. MILLER color *America* v215 no11 p14 O 17 2016

Internet & children

Tackling Technology Tactfully H. QUADRI *Islamic Horizons* v45 no6 p36 N/D 2016

Internet & privacy

4 ways to bolster your online privacy J. NOREM color *PCWorld* v35 no5 p205 My 2017

Being Professionally Personable on Facebook A. Samuel *Harvard Business Review Digital Articles* p2 Ag 14 2015

Broadband Privacy: Protecting Personal Information in the Digital Age *Congressional Digest* v96 no5 p2 My 2017

The Downside of the FCC's New Internet Privacy Rules L. Downes *Harvard Business Review Digital Articles* p2 My 27 2016

How to browse privately and avoid persistent tracking on a Mac, iPhone, and iPad G. FLEISHMAN color *Macworld - Digital Edition* p93 Mr 2017

Internet Privacy *Congressional Digest* v96 no4 p31 Ap 2017

Managing Privacy in the Internet of Things U. Haque *Harvard Business Review Digital Articles* p2 F 5 2015

Privacy legislation reintroduced for mail older than 180 days J. RIBEIRO color *PCWorld* v35 no2 p43 F 2017

Three privacy tools that block your Internet provider from tracking you I. PAUL color *PCWorld* v35 no5 p51 My 2017

'Tis the Season for Stress-Free Shopping M. L. Tellado *Consumer Reports* v82 no12 p4 D 2017

When a Private Message Ends Up in the Wrong Place K. Dillon *Harvard Business Review Digital Articles* p2 D 22 2014

WHEN YOUR STUFF SPIES ON YOU J. J. Roberts color *Fortune* v175 no7 p26 Je 1 2017

Why We're So Hypocritical About Online Privacy T. Chamorro-Premuzic and N. Nahai *Harvard Business Review Digital Articles* p1 My 1 2017

Internet & privacy—Government policy

How Not to Regulate The Internet bw *Bloomberg Businessweek*

no4498 p16 N 7 2016

Internet Regulation Is About the Common Good, Not Just Competition *America* v216 no8 p8 Ap 17 2017

The Pros and Cons of the FCC's Broadband Consumer Privacy Rules *Congressional Digest* v96 no5 p10 My 2017

Would You Pay for Your Online Privacy? bw *Bloomberg Businessweek* no4519 p12 Ap 24 2017

Internet & society

Art for App's Sake *Commentary* v142 no1 p1 Jl/Ag 2016

BEFORE THE INTERNET E. RATHBONE cartoon *New Yorker* v93 no18 p29 Je 26 2017

ESCAPE THE MATRIX: THE INTERNET IS THE UNCANNIEST VALLEY. DON'T GET TRAPPED THERE V. HEFFERNAN, L. PANDELL et al *Wired* v25 no9 p92 S 2017

LIFE, ACCORDING TO MARTHA color *Fortune* v175 no8 p44 Je 15 2017

Internet & women

Why Do So Few Women Edit Wikipedia? N. Torres *Harvard Business Review Digital Articles* p2 Je 2 2016

Internet & youth

HAS THE SMARTPHONE DESTROYED A GENERATION? J. M. Twenge color graph *Atlantic* v320 no2 p58 S 2017

Internet access

See also

Wireless Internet

No Internet connection? Be prepared for iTunes to drive you crazy K. MCELHEARN color *Macworld - Digital Edition* p113 Mr 2017

Internet access—Social aspects

The Hole in the Digital Economy D. Talbot color graph map *MIT Technology Review* v120 no1 p88 Ja/F 2017

Internet advertising

Ad Blockers and the Next Chapter of the Internet D. Searls *Harvard Business Review Digital Articles* p2 N 6 2015

Beware Google Ads for 'Abortion Consultations' A. Hines color *Bloomberg Businessweek* no4516 p30 Mr 27 2017

EXTREME REACH M. RONEY color *Forbes* v198 no9 p30 D 30 2016

Has Google Finally Proven That Online Ads Cause Offline Purchases? N. Dawar *Harvard Business Review Digital Articles* p1 Je 1 2017

Here we go again: Microsoft's popping up ads from the Windows 10 taskbar M. HACHMAN color *PCWorld* p52 D 2016

Is Programmatic Advertising the Future of Marketing? J. F. Rayport *Harvard Business Review Digital Articles* p2 Je 22 2015

Microsoft ads invade Windows 10's File Explorer I. PAUL color *PCWorld* v35 no5 p61 My 2017

The New Advertising, As Seen on TV V. Vara color *Bloomberg Businessweek* no4502 p41 D 5 2016

Why Fraudulent Ad Networks Continue to Thrive K. Fung *Harvard Business Review Digital Articles* p2 O 28 2015

Internet advertising—Corrupt practices

The Online Ad Scams Every Marketer Should Watch Out For B. Edelman *Harvard Business Review Digital Articles* p2 O 13 2015

Internet advertising—Social aspects

In Ads We Trust A. Vance color *Bloomberg Businessweek* no4521 p6 My 8 2017

Internet art

THE TROLL OF INTERNET ART A. CHEN cartoon color *New Yorker* v92 no47 p30 Ja 30 2017

Internet auctions

HOLY GRAILS S. Perman color *Fortune* v176 no4 p59 S 15 2017

Internet auctions—Government policy

Why You Need the Internet to Drill M. Frazier *Bloomberg Businessweek* no4512 p33 F 20 2017

Internet banking

BANK ON IT J. YOUNG color *Indianapolis Monthly* v41 no2 p30 S 2017

Best Bets: Online Banks T. Cettina cartoon color *Working Mother* p56 F/Mr 2017

Who's Afraid of Online Banking? E. J. MARTIN chart color *AARP: The Magazine* v59 no3A p22 Ap/My 2016

Internet celebrities

8 MILLION FOLLOWERS CANT BE WRONG: Why Tyler Oakley has an army of YouTube fans D. ARTAVIA *Advocate*

THE FINANCIAL PAGE: CLEANING UP A. Davidson color *New Yorker* v93 no33 p40 O 23 2017

THE FUTURE OF PROFITS, TODAY R. Geraci color *Bloomberg Businessweek* no4502 p2 D 5 2016

Gestures Will Be the Interface for the Internet of Things P. Daugherty, O. Schybergson et al *Harvard Business Review Digital Articles* p2 Jl 8 2015

The House That Actually Makes the Internet of Things Easy S. G. Carmichael *Harvard Business Review Digital Articles* p2 N 12 2014

HOW HIGH-TECH KITCHENS ARE LEVERAGING THE INTERNET OF THINGS D. F. McCourt color *Maclean's* v129 no40 p21 O 10 2016

How Industrial Systems Are Turning into Digital Services J. Sinfield, N. Calder et al *Harvard Business Review Digital Articles* p2 Je 23 2015

How People Are Actually Using the Internet of Things H. J. Wilson, B. Shah et al *Harvard Business Review Digital Articles* p2 O 28 2015

How to quickly check that your home IoT devices are secure I. PAUL color *PCWorld* v35 no2 p198 F 2017

How We Think About Innovation at Cisco S. Monterde *Harvard Business Review Digital Arttcles* p2 Je 8 2016

Humans Can Make the Internet of Things Smarter C. Montero-Luque *Harvard Business Review Digital Articles* p2 O 28 2014

I'M NOT SURE D. OWEN color *Popular Mechanics* p79 My 2017

The Internet of Things Changes the Company-Customer Relationship P. Weichselbaum *Harvard Business Review Digital Articles* p2 Je 29 2015

The Internet of Things Needs Design, Not Just Technology S. A. Nelson and P. Metaxatos *Harvard Business Review Digital Articles* p2 Ap 29 2016

The Internet of Things Will Change Your Company, Not Just Your Products J. Fitts *Harvard Business Review Digital Articles* p2 O 24 2014

IoT IS NOT A TREND: IT IS TRANSFORMATIVE AND HERE TO STAY color *Maclean's* v129 no40 p23 O 10 2016

Make the Internet of Things More Human-Friendly H. J. Wilson *Harvard Business Review Digital Articles* p2 O 16 2014

Managing Privacy in the Internet of Things U. Haque *Harvard Business Review Digital Articles* p2 F 5 2015

Manufacturing Companies Need to Sell Outcomes, Not Products M. Connerty, E. Navales et al *Harvard Business Review Digital Articles* p2 Je 2 2016

Put the Hammer Down J. Y. WOOD color *Power & Motoryacht* v33 no1 p40 Ja 2017

The Sectors Where the Internet of Things Really Matters S. Jankowski *Harvard Business Review Digital Articles* p2 O 22 2014

Setting Standards for the Internet of Things T. H. Davenport and S. E. Sarma *Harvard Business Review Digital Articles* p2 N 21 2014

Success with the Internet of Things Requires More Than Chasing the Cool Factor M. Kranz *Harvard Business Review Digital Articles* p2 Ag 7 2017

To Predict the Trajectory of the Internet of Things, Look to the Software Industry B. Iyer *Harvard Business Review Digital Articles* p2 F 25 2016

The U.S. Can't Count on Technology to Revive the Job Market U. Karmarkar *Harvard Business Review Digital Articles* p2 Je 4 2015

Using IoT Data to Understand How Your Products Perform S. Ramaswamy *Harvard Business Review Digital Articles* p2 Je 16 2016

Who Provides Tech Support for the Internet of Things? P. Weichselbaum *Harvard Business Review Digital Articles* p2 D 31 2014

Internet of things—Case studies

The Boundaries Around Your Industry Are About to Change D. Chivers *Harvard Business Review Digital Articles* p2 N 3 2014

Internet of things—Economic aspects

DATA IS EVERYTHING I. Paz, R. Gruia et al color *Maclean's* v129 no51/52 p17 D 26 2016

Finding the Money in the Internet of Things J. Hagel III *Harvard Business Review Digital Articles* p2 N 11 2014

Internet of things—Security measures

Why Do IoT Companies Keep Building Devices with Huge Security Flaws? [Cover story] A. Tannenbaum *Harvard Business Review Digital Articles* p2 Ap 27 2017

Internet pornography

See also

Revenge porn

PORNHUB IS THE KINSEY REPORT OF OUR TIME M. O'CONNOR *New York* v50 no12 p30 Je 12 2017

Internet publishing

Ad Blocking's Unintended Consequences F. Bhat *Harvard Business Review Digital Articles* p2 Ag 12 2015

Internet Relay Chat

Skype like a boss with these hidden chat commands I. PAUL color *PCWorld* v35 no4 p149 Ap 2017

Internet research

THE SURPRISING POWER OF ONLINE EXPERIMENTS: GETTING THE MOST OUT OF A/B AND OTHER CONTROLLED TESTS R. Kohavi and S. Thomke color diag graph img *Harvard Business Review* v95 no5 p74 S/O 2017

Internet searching

Google, Yelp, and the Future of Search J. Gans *Harvard Business Review Digital Articles* p2 Jl 10 2015

Inspired by Athena and Aided by Facebook R. SCHABAUER and K. INCHINGALO *USA Today Magazine* v145 no2862 p74 Mr 2017

Internet security

11 Things the Health Care Sector Must Do to Improve Cybersecurity R. Weintraub and J. Borenstein *Harvard Business Review Digital Articles* p2 Je 1 2017

AI Is the Future of Cybersecurity, for Better and for Worse R. V. Yampolskiy *Harvard Business Review Digital Articles* p2 My 8 2017

The Best Cybersecurity Investment You Can Make Is Better Training D. Disparte and C. Furlow *Harvard Business Review Digital Articles* p2 My 16 2017

Cybersecurity Has a Serious Talent Shortage. Here's How to Fix It M. van Zadelhoff *Harvard Business Review Digital Articles* p2 My 4 2017

Cyber security is too important to be left to the IT department: As hackers increasingly exploit human vulnerability, HR has a vital role to play - not least in ensuring businesses have the technical talent to fight back H. KIRTON *People Management* p42 Jl 2017

The Flaws in Obama's Cybersecurity Initiative D. M. Upton *Harvard Business Review Digital Articles* p2 Ja 20 2015

Good Cybersecurity Can Be Good Marketing J. Lucas, L. Minsky et al *Harvard Business Review Digital Articles* p2 S 23 2016

Good Cybersecurity Doesn't Try to Prevent Every Attack G. Bell *Harvard Business Review Digital Articles* p2 O 25 2016

A Heightened State Of Security L. Chapman graph *Bloomberg Businessweek* no4514 p45 Mr 13 2017

How—and why—you should use a VPN any time you hop on the Internet I. PAUL color diag *PCWorld* v35 no2 p173 F 2017

How Facebook Uses Empathy to Keep User Data Safe M. Luu-Van *Harvard Business Review Digital Articles* p2 Ap 28 2016

How to use HTTPS to improve web security G. FLEISHMAN color *Macworld - Digital Edition* v34 no8 p95 Ag 2017

Lurking in the Shadows T. Newcombe *Governing* v30 no7 p60 Ap 2017

Managing nuclear risk in South Asia J. Sarkar bibl *Bulletin of the Atomic Scientists* v73 no1 p59 Ja 2017

"Netwar": The unwelcome militarization of the Internet has arrived J. Zittrain bibl *Bulletin of the Atomic Scientists* v73 no5 p300 2017

Not All Russian Hackers Are Bad V. Walt color *Fortune* v175 no2 p12 F 1 2017

Now Is the Greatest Time to Be Alive color *Wired* v24 no11 p30 N 2016

Security Breaches: No End in Sight *USA Today Magazine* v145 no2863 p10 Ap 2017

Soft law: New tools for governing emerging technologies G. E. Marchant and B. Allenby bibl *Bulletin of the Atomic Scientists* v73 no2 p108 Mr 2017

THINK LIKE A HACKER S. ORNES bw color graph *Discover* v38 no8 p48 O 2017

To Fix Your Terrible Passwords, Kill Them N. Lanxon color *Bloomberg Businessweek* no4524 p36 My 29 2017

Training Companies To Handle a Hack M. Riley *Bloomberg Businessweek* no4501 p29 N 28 2016

Trump and Tech Companies Make Nice N. Syeed color *Bloomberg Businessweek* no4514 p43 Mr 13 2017

What the Rise of Russian Hackers Means for Your Business M. Sulmeyer *Harvard Business Review Digital Articles* p2 My 12 2017

Why Cybersecurity Is So Difficult to Get Right J. M. Olejarz *Harvard Business Review Digital Articles* p2 Jl 27 2015

Why Is Cybersecurity So Hard? M. Daniel *Harvard Business Review Digital Articles* p2 My 22 2017

Why You Really Need to Stop Using Public Wi-Fi L. Bencie *Harvard Business Review Digital Articles* p2 My 3 2017

Your Biggest Cybersecurity Weakness Is Your Phone L. Dignan *Harvard Business Review Digital Articles* p2 S 22 2016

Internet security—Economic aspects

A BIG PAYOFF FOR CYBERCOP STOCKS R. Derousseau color diag *Fortune* v176 no3 p28 S 1 2017

Internet security—Government policy

8 Ways Governments Can Improve Their Cybersecurity [Cover story] M. Chertoff and J. Grant *Harvard Business Review Digital Articles* p2 Ap 25 2017

EXECUTIVE ORDER: How Virginia Governs Cybersecurity *Governing* v30 no1 p1 O 2016

Germany Builds An Election Firewall S. Nicola, C. Matlack et al *Bloomberg Businessweek* no4527 p48 Je 19 2017

Our Failed Cybersecurity Policy L. THOMPSON color *National Review* v69 no1 p30 Ja 23 2017

Internet security—Software

That Seventies Startup S. McBride color *Bloomberg Businessweek* no4532 p21 Jl 31 2017

Internet service providers

BAD RATINGS S. Kolhatkar color *New Yorker* v93 no23 p23 Ag 7 2017

How to Win at Wi-Fi J. SCIACCA color *Sound & Vision* v82 no4 p23 My 2017

Internet service providers—Evaluation

Comcast is the fastest ISP, and T-Mobile is the fastest wireless carrier, Ookla says M. HACHMAN color graph *PCWorld* v35 no10 p18 O 2017

Internet service providers—Law & legislation

The Downside of the FCC's New Internet Privacy Rules L. Downes *Harvard Business Review Digital Articles* p2 My 27 2016

HOW TO HIDE YOUR ONLINE FOOTPRINT S. BLOCK cartoon *Kiplinger's Personal Finance* v71 no7 p13 Jl 2017

Internet stores

Amazon's Brick-and-Mortar Store Shouldn't Come as a Surprise A. Bernstein *Harvard Business Review Digital Articles* p2 O 10 2014

Little Bit Country L. BAILEY *Indianapolis Monthly* p27 F 2017

NEVER PAY FULL PRICE AGAIN K. Dold color *Men's Health* v31 no10 p73 D 2016

Online Retailers Should Care More About the Post-Purchase Experience A. Sharma *Harvard Business Review Digital Articles* p2 My 24 2016

SPORTS CANVAS ART GETS A BIG RA-RAH-RAH! *USA Today Magazine* v146 no2866 p78 Jl 2017

Internet stores—Evaluation

Living & Recreation *Virginia Living* p143 2017 Best 20of Virginia

Nothing to Wear To Work R. Greenfield color *Bloomberg Businessweek* no4535 p68 Ag 28 2017

Internet strategy

Why Costco Is Lagging Online J. E. Ellis graph *Bloomberg Businessweek* no4535 p14 Ag 28 2017

You Don't Need to Be a Silicon Valley Startup to Have a Network-Based Strategy M. Bonchek and B. Libert *Harvard Business Review Digital Articles* p2 Jl 14 2017

Internet surveys

and the survey says *U.S. Catholic* v82 no10 p29 O 2017

How to Click Your Way to Cash M. C. White color *Money* v46 no5 p24 Je 2017

Is It Safe for CEOs to Voice Strong Political Opinions? L. Gaines-Ross *Harvard Business Review Digital Articles* p2 Je 23 2016

Internet television

The Best Ways to Stream Live TV A. D'Arminio *TV Guide* v65 no19 p12 My 1 2017

Coming Soon To A Device Near You L. BRODY color *Forbes* v200 no2 p64 S 5 2017

The Entertainment Weekly Must List R. Kinane color *Entertainment Weekly* no1478 / 1479 p10 Ag 18-25 2017

How to cut the cord without resorting to a pricey streaming-TV bundle J. NEWMAN color *PCWorld* v35 no6 p47 Je 2017

HOW TO WATCH IT ALL D. PIERCE cartoon color *Wired* v25 no4 p42 Ap 2017

THE MILLENNIAL CORD CUTTING SINGULARITY IS NIGH F. Gillette and L. Shaw color *Bloomberg Businessweek* no4513 p56 Mr 6 2017

Internet television programmers & programming

THE UNFOLDIN DRAMA OF REAL-TIME TV M. Lev-Ram color diag *Fortune* v175 no6 p50 My 1 2017

Internet traffic

Why Fraudulent Ad Networks Continue to Thrive K. Fung *Harvard Business Review Digital Articles* p2 O 28 2015

Internet usage monitoring

Three privacy tools that block your Internet provider from tracking you I. PAUL color *PCWorld* v35 no5 p51 My 2017

Internet users

MR. KNOW-IT-ALL J. MOOALLEM cartoon *Wired* v25 no7 p28 Jl 2017

The Myth of 'Going Viral' on the Internet D. Thompson *Time* v189 no6 p21 F 20 2017

Internet videos

Apple's updated Android 'Switch' campaign explains why people move to iPhone M. SIMON color *Macworld - Digital Edition* p44 Je 13 2017

CNN Has Had Enough S. Frier and G. Smith color graph *Bloomberg Businessweek* no4528 p20 Je 26 2017

DIGITAL MR D. Kawala color il *Model Railroader* v84 no3 p6 Mr 2017

ESCAPE THE MATRIX: THE INTERNET IS THE UNCANNIEST VALLEY. DON'T GET TRAPPED THERE V. HEFFERNAN, L. PANDELL et al *Wired* v25 no9 p92 S 2017

Gone Viral Z. WHITTENBURG and S. SKYBETTER *Dance Magazine* v90 no12 p59 D 2016

Google Chrome will start blocking noisy autoplay videos in January B. CHACOS color *PCWorld* v35 no10 p14 O 2017

HOT | NOT T. Keith color *Sports Illustrated* v126 no14 p22 My 15-22 2017

How to be a Video Star S. Bockmaster and J. Lewczuk color *Sail* v48 no9 p10 S 2017

Just for Clicks S. STALL *Indianapolis Monthly* v40 no7 p20 Mr 2017

Skin DEEP J. Francisco color *Good Housekeeping* v264 no5 p9 My 2017

Video Metrics Every Marketer Should Be Watching K. Craft *Harvard Business Review Digital Articles* p2 Ap 24 2015

What an OTT Future Means for Brands J. Balis *Harvard Business Review Digital Articles* p2 My 13 2015

Internet videos—Social aspects

PAID FOR BY THE SAME PEOPLE WHO PAID FOR THE VIDEO YOU'RE ABOUT TO WATCH S. Issenberg color *Bloomberg Businessweek* no4497 p26 O 31 2016

Internet—China

Cartoons *New York Times Upfront* v149 no5 p24 N 21 2016

Streaming Away From The Censors C. Larson color *Bloomberg Businessweek* no4537 p50 S 11 2017

Internet—Economic aspects

The Internet Has Been a Colossal Economic Disappointment W. H. Davidow *Harvard Business Review Digital Articles* p2 Mr 30 2015

What We Know, Now, About the Internet's Disruptive Power A. Ovans *Harvard Business Review Digital Articles* p2 Ja 28 2015

Where Buying Data Is as Easy as Buying Cabbage C. Larson color *Bloomberg Businessweek* no4493 p41 O 3 2016

Where the Digital Economy Is Moving the Fastest B. Chakravorti, C. Tunnard et al *Harvard Business Review Digital Articles* p2 F 19 2015

Internet—Government policy

How to Understand the EU-U.S. Digital Divide L. Downes *Har-*

vard Business Review Digital Articles p2 O 19 2015

No One Actually Knows How to Regulate the Internet J. Fox *Harvard Business Review Digital Articles* p2 N 18 2014

Why the Public Utility Model Is the Wrong Approach for Internet Regulation L. Downes *Harvard Business Review Digital Articles* p2 N 11 2014

Internet—History

Our new website C. Day *Physics Today* v70 no1 p8 Ja 2017

Where Buying Data Is as Easy as Buying Cabbage C. Larson color *Bloomberg Businessweek* no4493 p41 O 3 2016

Internet—Performance

Consumers Don't Understand the Relationship Between Time and Speed S. Puntoni and B. de Langhe *Harvard Business Review Digital Articles* p2 N 3 2015

Islands Stranded Offline T. John color *Time* v189 no4 p12 Ja 23 2017

Maximizing Your Network Performance J. SCIACCA color *Sound & Vision* v82 no3 p21 Ap 2017

Internet pop-up advertising

Here we go again: Microsoft's popping up ads from the Windows 10 taskbar M. HACHMAN color *PCWorld* p52 D 2016

Internet—Psychological aspects

Why We're So Hypocritical About Online Privacy T. Chamorro-Premuzic and N. Nahai *Harvard Business Review Digital Articles* p1 My 1 2017

Internet—Safety measures

8 Ways Governments Can Improve Their Cybersecurity [Cover story] M. Chertoff and J. Grant *Harvard Business Review Digital Articles* p2 Ap 25 2017

Parents Need to Be Clued in on Teens *USA Today Magazine* v145 no2863 p11 Ap 2017

Internet—Social aspects

See also

Internet videos—Social aspects

How New Technologies Push Us Toward the Past W. H. Davidow and M. S. Malone *Harvard Business Review Digital Articles* p2 My 8 2015

An Internet of Our Own N. SCHNEIDER *Nation* v303 no18 p4 O 31 2016

A Smarter Web H. Derakhshan *MIT Technology Review* v120 no1 p12 Ja/F 2017

Tokens of Our Affection M. KAUFMAN, E. SPINNER et al cartoon *O, The Oprah Magazine* p17 F 2017

Internet—United States

FAKE NEWS FREAKOUT J. E. USCINSKI bw *Reason* v48 no10 p54 Mr 2017

Internists

Your body's got something to tell you L. KRIEGER *Redbook* p92 S 2017

Interns

6 Ways to Make the Most of Your Internship J. Coleman *Harvard Business Review Digital Articles* p2 Jl 11 2016

CASE STUDY: FOLLOW DUBIOUS ORDERS OR SPEAK UP? AN INTERN CONTEMPLATES WHETHER SHE SHOULD COMPROMISE HER VALUES FOR A JOB S. SUCHER and M. PREBLE il *Harvard Business Review* v95 no4 p139 Jl/Ag 2017

KATNISS EVERDEEN, WHITE HOUSE INTERN APPLICATION C. FRAZIER cartoon *New Yorker* v92 no42 p65 D 19 2016

Internship programs

6 Ways to Make the Most of Your Internship J. Coleman *Harvard Business Review Digital Articles* p2 Jl 11 2016

Code RVA: HIGH SCHOOL OF THE FUTURE *Virginia Living* v15 no6 p91 O 2017

Empowering Youth to Care for Local Parks and Their Neighborhoods M. Talbert *Parks & Recreation* v52 no8 p30 Ag 2017

If You Offer Mid-Career Internships, Flaunt It C. F. Cohen *Harvard Business Review Digital Articles* p2 Jl 4 2016

Inside Out A. TOWER color *Climbing* no354 p30 Jl 2017

Score a Great Summer Internship K. Mulhere chart color *Money* v46 no1 p34 Ja/F 2017

Internship programs—Economic aspects

Does work experience have to be paid? Sandwich chains woes demonstrate nuances of engaging students *People Management* p16 My 2017

Interorganizational relations

See also

Bureaucracy

What I Learned from Trying to Innovate at the New York Times J. Geraci *Harvard Business Review Digital Articles* p2 Ap 7 2016

Interpersonal attraction

WHAT DOES SHE SEE IN THAT GUY? H. HAVRILESKY bw color *Esquire* p80 Ap 2017

Interpersonal communication

See also

Body language

Email

Letter writing

Supportive communication

Teacher-student communication

Donald Trump, James Comey, and the Ambiguity of "Hope" R. T. Lakoff *Harvard Business Review Digital Articles* p2 Je 13 2017

A Gateway In DTLA *Los Angeles Magazine* p85 Ap 2017

How to Get Feedback When No One Is Volunteering It K. Willyerd and B. Mistick *Harvard Business Review Digital Articles* p2 Ag 14 2015

How to Handle Interrupting Colleagues F. Gino *Harvard Business Review Digital Articles* p2 F 22 2017

How to Tell If Someone Wants to Stop Talking to You D. Clark *Harvard Business Review Digital Articles* p2 O 19 2015

Making a S.P.E.C.I.A.L. first impression A. Dovico *Phi Delta Kappan* v98 no3 p55 N 2016

The real truth about gossip *Redbook* p132 Je 2017

Standing up to fear A. Khaledi-Nasab color *Science* v356 no6336 p458 Ap 28 2017

YARD CARE T. Hale color *Sail* v48 no10 p72 O 2017

You Just Had a Difficult Conversation at Work. Here's What to Do Next D. Bernardo *Harvard Business Review Digital Articles* p2 My 29 2017

Your Elevator Pitch Needs an Elevator Pitch T. David *Harvard Business Review Digital Articles* p2 D 30 2014

Interpersonal conflict

Defusing an Emotionally Charged Conversation with a Colleague R. Friedman *Harvard Business Review Digital Articles* p2 Ja 12 2016

Feuds M. Gajanan color *Time* v188 no25-26 p34 D 19 2016 Double Issue

The Good FIGHT A. Atkins cartoon *O, The Oprah Magazine* p92 F 2017

HOW TO FIGHT FAIR K. TRANELL and C. RIDSDALE *Scholastic Choices* v32 no4 p12 Ja 2017

The Real Big Lie E. Alterman il *Nation* v305 no7 p6 S 25 2017

The Summer of Bad Blood A. GREENE bw color *Rolling Stone* no1295 p22 S 7 2017

Interpersonal conflict—History

Celebrity Squabbles for the Ages C. Lang color *Time* v189 no9 p53 Mr 13 2017

Interpersonal confrontation

Learning to Appreciate Disagreement at Work W. Johnson *Harvard Business Review Digital Articles* p2 Jl 6 2016

Interpersonal relations

See also

Competition (Psychology)

Compliments

Couples

Dating (Social customs)

Discrimination

Emotional competence

Family relations

Friendship

Grandparent & child

Interpersonal communication

Interpersonal conflict

Intimacy (Psychology)

Love-hate relationships

Man-woman relationships

Non-monogamous relationships

Parent & child

Personal criticism

Physician & patient

Professional relationships

raise happy siblings R. SAGIV RIEBLING *Parents* v91 no6 p56 Je 2016

Regarding People Who Don't Have Period Sex A. L. Grecoq color *Glamour* no8 p110 Ag 2017

#RelationshipGoals Z. HUGHES and S. TIABROWN color *Ebony* v72 no4 p78 F 2017

RELATIONSHIP MATH H. ESTROFF MARANO *Psychology Today* v50 no1 p25 Ja/F 2017

The Right (and Wrong) Way to Network D. Clark *Harvard Business Review Digital Articles* p2 Mr 10 2015

RISK MANAGEMENT A. BONEVELLE and E. BALDINI *Psychology Today* v50 no4 p6 Ag 2017

Saving a Family Business from Emotional Dysfunction M. F. R. Kets de Vries color *Harvard Business Review Digital Articles* p2 F 1 2017

Sex matters: Report experimenter gender C. D. Chapman, C. Benedict et al *Science* v356 no6341 p916 Je 1 2017

Sleeping with the Enemy M. BECK color *O, The Oprah Magazine* p40 Ag 2017

SLEEP WITH ANY WOMAN D. Roe cartoon color *Men's Health* v32 no1 p94 Ja/F 2017

Stop Making Gratitude All About You H. G. Halvorson *Harvard Business Review Digital Articles* p2 Je 29 2016

Stranger Danger? W. Patrick *Psychology Today* v50 no4 p12 Ag 2017

Stressproof Your Work Life G. Saltz color *Health* v31 no4 p68 My 2017

SWING TIME L. MCCAFFREY *Psychology Today* v50 no4 p20 Ag 2017

Tightening Your Bond With Boo S. TIABROWN color *Ebony* v72 no4 p76 F 2017

TIME FOR A MAN-CATION! D. Sax, J. GORDINIER et al color *Esquire* p114 O 2017

TIME FOR TRUST H. ESTROFF MARANO *Psychology Today* v50 no3 p22 My/Je 2017

We are one J. Bleem color *U.S. Catholic* v82 no5 p50 My 2017

What comes after I. Kerner cartoon *Prevention* v69 no7 p26 Jl 2017

Why Do We Lash Out? IT MIGHT BE MORE THAN A BAD MOOD S. POLAN *Psychology Today* v50 no5 p16 S/O 2017

Why I Stopped Sleeping with the Love of My Life J. VRABEL color *GQ: Gentlemen's Quarterly* v97 no9 p84 S 2017

Work Friends Make Us More Productive (Except When They Stress Us Out) D. Burkus *Harvard Business Review Digital Articles* p2 My 26 2017

You Are Not Alone M. JONES color *Reader's Digest* v189 no1131 p54 Je 2017

You are struggling to feel sympathy S. Kempton color *Yoga Journal* p41 2016 Special Issue

YOUR FROZEN EGG HAS A QUESTION S. FOGEL cartoon *New Yorker* v93 no14 p39 My 22 2017

Interpersonal relations in children

first teacher C. WIRA DINEEN *Parents* v91 no9 p168 S 2016

New Orleans High School Turbocharges Restorative Justice J. SHAW cartoon *Education Digest* v82 no7 p4 Mr 2017

Interpersonal relations—Research

The secret to a relationship that lasts color *Redbook* p99 F 2017

Interpersonal relations—Software

Am I Going to Post This, or Are You? B. GREGORY cartoon graph *Men's Health* v32 no9 p80 N 2017

Interracial dating

Are We Biased When We Date? Yes, but things are improving. Here's a look at our semi-enlightened hearts *Glamour* v115 no6 p94 Je 2017

LOVE IN BLACK & WHITE L. L. Joiner color *Essence* v47 no8 p129 D 2016

Interracial friendship

Are We Biased When We Date? Yes, but things are improving. Here's a look at our semi-enlightened hearts *Glamour* v115 no6 p94 Je 2017

Interracial marriage

Interstates E. BERNARD *American Scholar* v86 no2 p43 Spr 2017

The Loving Legacy A. Haglage and E. Mahaney bw color *Glamour* v114 no11 p141 N 2016

Telling the Lovings' Story In 1966 L. Rothman color *Time* v188

no20 p50 N 14 2016

Interracial marriage—Social aspects

A Silk Road Marriage R. STANDISH color *Foreign Policy* no226 p8 S/O 2017

Interruption (Psychology)

How to Handle Interrupting Colleagues F. Gino *Harvard Business Review Digital Articles* p2 F 22 2017

Intersectionality (Social sciences)

Is "Intersectionality" a Religion? img *New York* v50 no6 p11 Mr 20 2017

Intersexuality

See also

Gynandromorphism

Interstate 80

BORDER to BORDER I-80 Adventure A. J. BARTELS bw color *Nebraska Life* v21 no1 p18 Ja/F 2017

Interstate 95

SWEET SMELL OF SUCCESS A. Davidson color *New Yorker* v93 no10 p39 Ap 24 2017

Interstate agreements

Collective Edge K. Barrett and R. Greene *Governing* v30 no3 p58 D 2016

Interstellar matter

See also

Cosmic dust

Dark matter (Astronomy)

Planetary nebulae

A fast radio boom V. M. Kaspi bibl color *Science* v354 no6317 p1230 D 9 2016

GALLERY color *Sky & Telescope* v134 no2 p74 Ag 2017

Measurement of the small-scale structure of the intergalactic medium using close quasar pairs A. Rorai, J. F. Hennawi et al diag graph *Science* v356 no6336 p418 Ap 28 2017

Preteen Astronomer Shines at AAS Meeting N. T. REDD *Sky & Telescope* v133 no4 p12 Ap 2017

Interstellar travel

NEAR-LIGHT-SPEED MISSION TO ALPHA CENTAURI [Cover story] A. Finkbeiner color *Scientific American* v316 no3 p30 Mr 2017

Interstitial helium generation—Research

Helium Fields Forever? J. KEATS color map *Discover* v38 no1 p87 Ja/F 2017

Interstitial hydrogen generation

Atomic-layered Au clusters on α-MoC as catalysts for the low-temperature water-gas shift reaction S. Yao, X. Zhang et al chart diag graph *Science* v357 no6349 p389 Jl 28 2017

Intertidal ecology

THE ROCKWEED RUSH R. Jacobsen cartoon color *Mother Jones* v41 no6 p8 N/D 2016

Wonderful Wetlands B. Friedlander *USA Today Magazine* v146 no2866 p68 Jl 2017

Interval training

18-MINUTE MIRACLE WORKOUT E. SAMUEL bw color *Men's Health* v32 no7 p96 S 2017

A BODY IN MOTION & A BODY AT REST [Cover story] M. GAINSBURG color *Women's Health* v14 no4 p156 My 2017

A New Way to Attack Your Six-Pack L. SCHULER cartoon color *Men's Health* v32 no5 p47 Je 2017

Powerhouse Renovation G. Reynolds *New York Times Magazine* p22 Mr 26 2017

Intervention (International law)

All Quiet on the Balkan Front? N. M. Naimark and A. Matovski *Hoover Digest: Research & Opinion on Public Policy* no1 p120 Wint 2017

America's Longest War: U.S. troops have been fighting in Afghanistan for the past 16 years. And there's no end in sight P. Smith *New York Times Upfront* v150 no1 p16 S 4 2017

No More Anti-War Liberals? T. G. CARPENTER *USA Today Magazine* v145 no2862 p15 Mr 2017

Should the United States intervene when other countries are in crisis? chart graph *America* v217 no5 p6 S 4 2017

Trump's Broken Promises: Foreign-policy realists need a new congressional caucus W. S. LIND *American Conservative* v16 no4 p9 Jl/Ag 2017

TRUMP'S INTERVENTION S. Coll cartoon *New Yorker* v93 no9 p19 Ap 17 2017

Intervention (Social services)
Proactive Intervention T. Barton diag graph *Alternatives Journal (AJ) - Canada's Environmental Voice* v42 no3 p40 2016
Interviewing
See also
Artists—Interviews
Cooks interviews
Employment interviewing
Hunters and Scavengers J. POCOCK color *Orion Magazine* v36 no2 p11 Mr/Ap 2017
IN QUOTES *People Management* p10 Je 2017
'No.' Is that all you're telling unsuccessful applicants? Most employers have given up on offering interview feedback - but if you handle it carefully, there s no reason to stay silent A. MAKOFF-CLARK *People Management* p14 Jl 2017
Tactics for Asking Good Follow-Up Questions R. Davis *Harvard Business Review Digital Articles* p2 N 7 2014
Why You Should Interview People Who Turn Down a Job with Your Company B. Dattner *Harvard Business Review Digital Articles* p2 Ag 1 2016
Interviews with librarians
Carla Hayden color *New York Times Book Review* p8 Ag 6 2017
Reflections on a "Busy and Wonderful Year" S. MAUGHAN *Publishers Weekly* v264 no25 p75 Je 19 2017
Interwar Period (1918-1939)
The Limits of Nationhood: In the interwar period, France and Germany worked towards an integrated Europe C. Fischer *History Today* v67 no6 p12 Je 2016
Intestinal absorption
The intestinal microbiota regulates body composition through NFIL3 and the circadian clock Y. Wang, Z. Kuang et al diag *Science* v357 no6354 p912 S 1 2017
Intestines—Anatomy
The intestinal microbiota regulates body composition through NFIL3 and the circadian clock Y. Wang, Z. Kuang et al diag *Science* v357 no6354 p912 S 1 2017
Intimacy (Psychology)
See also
Separation (Psychology)
Are You in The Wrong Relationship? J. KIM *Psychology Today* v50 no3 p38 My/Je 2017
The Great Divide M. Caine-Barrett and Shonin color *Tricycle: The Buddhist Review* v26 no4 p80 Summ 2017
My Funny Valentine: ONE QUESTION FOR KUMAIL NANJIANI AND EMILY V. GORDON J. BLEYER *Psychology Today* v50 no4 p96 Ag 2017
Sex WHILE PARENTING J. Press color *Parents* v92 no9 p106 S 2017
A Star is Reborn [Cover story] L. Brown color *InStyle* v24 no7 p104 Jl 2017
WHAT YOU NEED IS LOVE C. Lee color *O, The Oprah Magazine* p24 Je 2017
Intimacy (Psychology)—Social aspects
NOT JUST US: Is an open marriage a happier marriage? S. Dominus *New York Times Magazine* p34 My 14 2017
Into the Badlands (TV program)
Into the Badlands J. Russell *TV Guide* v65 no11 p43 Mr 6 2017
Into the Breach (Poem)
You're so quiet you're almost tomorrow S. Anderson *New York Times Magazine* p13 Ap 2 2017
Intonation (Phonetics)
Intonational speech prosody encoding in the human auditory cortex C. Tang, L. S. Hamilton et al diag *Science* v357 no6353 p797 Ag 25 2017
Intracranial aneurysms
BROUGHT TO LIGHT color *Women's Health* v14 no3 p32 Ap 2017
Her Healing Garden G. GRAVES color *Prevention* v69 no4 p30 Ap 2017
Intravenous drug abusers
Harm reduction underused *Science* v354 no6315 p948 N 25 2016
Shooting Up in Public Bathrooms Common *USA Today Magazine* v145 no2859 p12 D 2016
Intravenous drug abusers—Services for
A SHOT IN THE DARK J. Lurie color graph *Mother Jones* v42 no2 p6 Mr/Ap 2017

Intravenous therapy—Psychological aspects
STICK IT TO ME K. Massicot color *New Orleans Magazine* v51 no2 p38 D 2016
Introduced insects
Farewell to the World's Smallest Tarantula? J. Schneider color *National Wildlife (World Edition)* v55 no6 p10 O/N 2017
Introduced organism prevention
Black Tiger Shrimp C. BOND *Texas Monthly* v45 no5 p34 My 2017
Introduced organisms
See also
Introduced insects
Goldfish Gone Wild *New York Times Upfront* v149 no10 p2 Mr 13 2017
Listing Foreign Species under the Endangered Species Act: A Primer for Conservation Biologists C. M. FOLEY, M. A. LYNCH et al *BioScience* v67 no7 p627 Jl 2017
Mexico's invasive species plan in context J. Golubov, A. Aguirre-Muñoz et al bw *Science* v356 no6336 p386 Ap 28 2017
Scientific and Normative Foundations for the Valuation of Alien-Species Impacts: Thirteen Core Principles F. ESSL, P. E. HULME et al *BioScience* v67 no2 p166 F 2017
A welcome invasion *Maclean's* v130 no8 p4 S 2017
Introduced organisms & the environment
Invasive Species, Indigenous Stewards, and Vulnerability Discourse N. J. REO, K. WHYTE et al chart diag map *American Indian Quarterly* v41 no3 p201 Summ 2017
Introducing Karl Blau (Music)
Trailblazers and Hybrids HADLEY color *Downbeat* v83 no12 p76 D 2016
Introns
Crystal structures of a group II intron lariat primed for reverse splicing M. Costa, H. Walbott et al color diag *Science* v354 no6316 paaf9258-1 D 2 2016
Introspection
EMBRACING YOUR "Type" A. Smith color *Dance Spirit* v21 no2 p52 F 2017
John Lithgow A. Nash color *AARP: The Magazine* v60 no5A p17 Ag/S 2017
Manage Stress by Knowing What You Value D. Brendel *Harvard Business Review Digital Articles* p2 S 8 2015
On Our Own M. Huston *Psychology Today* v50 no2 p9 Mr/Ap 2017
Why You Should Make Time for Self-Reflection (Even If You Hate Doing It) J. Porter *Harvard Business Review Digital Articles* p2 Mr 21 2017
Introverts
How to Talk in Meetings When You Hate Talking in Meetings D. Rousmaniere *Harvard Business Review Digital Articles* p2 Ap 21 2016
Introverts, Extroverts, and the Complexities of Team Dynamics F. Gino *Harvard Business Review Digital Articles* p2 Mr 16 2015
People like me don't normally speak up V. SMART *People Management* p32 F 2017
Intuit Inc.
6 BRAD SMITH G. Colvin color *Fortune* v174 no7 p84 D 1 2016
A CONVERSATION WITH INTUIT CHAIRMAN AND CO-FOUNDER SCOTT COOK [Cover story] D. CHAMPION color *Harvard Business Review* v95 no1 p62 Ja/F 2017
Intuit Inc.—Officials & employees
Tech's Resilient Force color *Forbes* v199 no5 p30 My 16 2017
Intuition (Psychology)
3 Questions to Get the Most Out of Your Company's Data J. Allworth, M. Wessel et al *Harvard Business Review Digital Articles* p2 Ja 29 2015
HOW TO TRUST YOUR GUT color *Health* v31 no5 p10 Je 2017
It's gut-check time M. Malone *America* v216 no5 p3 Mr 6 2017
Mastering Your Mental Game... TANIA SACHDEV J. bleyer *Psychology Today* v50 no2 p96 Mr/Ap 2017
When It's Safe to Rely on Intuition (and When It's Not) Connson Chou Locke *Harvard Business Review Digital Articles* p2 Ap 30 2015
IntuView (Company)
Good Deals Make Good Neighbors J. Ferziger and P. Waldman color map *Bloomberg Businessweek* no4510 p36 F 6 2017
Inuit

OUR SCHOOL: An Arctic community prepares its young people for the future L. MARKHAM color *Orion Magazine* v35 no6 p20 N/D 2016

Inuit hunters

WAZED AND CONFUSED D. DOBBS cartoon *Mother Jones* v41 no6 p53 N/D 2016

Yaaka Markusie Yaaka A. HUTCHINS color *Maclean's* v129 no45 p62 N 14 2016

Invasion

BATTLE OF BAGHDAD color *AARP: The Magazine* v59 no3A p69 Ap/My 2016

Invasive plant prevention

NATIVE or INVASIVE: What it means to adapt in a postcolonial world A. VAIDYA color *Orion Magazine* v36 no2 p52 Mr/Ap 2017

Weeds Be Gone! color *Cabin Living* p21 S 2017

Invasive plants

FLOATING IN PLAIN SIGHT: Invasive Aquatic Garden Plants C. McGlynn *New York State Conservationist* v71 no5 p32 Ap 2017

NATIVE or INVASIVE: What it means to adapt in a postcolonial world A. VAIDYA color *Orion Magazine* v36 no2 p52 Mr/Ap 2017

Invective

ALFRED HITCHCOCK RESENTS *Saturday Evening Post* v289 no1 p97 Ja/F 2017

SLING STATE C. FEHRMAN *Cincinnati Magazine* v50 no2 p20 N 2016

The Vault *Saturday Evening Post* v289 no1 p97 Ja/F 2017

Invective—Psychological aspects

Abuse at work linked to shopping binges *People Management* p57 S 2017

Inventions

See also

Inventors

Technological innovations

ACCIDENTS Happen C. BOYER and J. ROCCO color *National Geographic Kids* no465 p20 N 2016

COOL inventions C. M. TOMLIN cartoon color *National Geographic Kids* no470 p11 My 2017

COOL inventions C. M. TOMLIN *National Geographic Kids* no467 p11 F 2017

FLUX CAPACITOR A. FLANGO *Cincinnati Magazine* p39 Je 2017

Frankenstein's Nightmares *Lapham's Quarterly* v10 no2 p170 Spr 2017

How to Protect Your Company's Inventions *Harvard Business Review Digital Articles* p2 N 24 2014

THOUGHTS ON Inventions bw color *Forbes* v200 no2 p112 S 5 2017

WHO REALLY INVENTED MONOPOLY? M. Pilon *Saturday Evening Post* v289 no5 p80 S/O 2017

Inventions—History

THE BIG QUESTION cartoon *Atlantic* v320 no1 p104 Jl/Ag 2017

Inventories

PICKIN' OFF THE CHERRY PRE-TIER 4 SEMIS *Successful Farming* v114 no10 p26 O 2016

Inventories—Charts, diagrams, etc.

PRODUCTION AND BUSINESS ACTIVITY *Economic Indicators* p17 Ja 2017

Inventors

Frankenstein's Nightmares *Lapham's Quarterly* v10 no2 p170 Spr 2017

Jacques Isaac Pankove T. D. Moustakas and B. Monemar *Physics Today* v70 no4 p64 Ap 2017

John Michael Julius Madey Pui Lam, V. Shiltsev et al *Physics Today* v70 no1 p70 Ja 2017

This Year's 35 Innovators Under the Age of 35 *MIT Technology Review* v120 no5 p2 S/O 2017

Inventors—History

THE RELIC HUNTER B. Underwood color *MHQ: Quarterly Journal of Military History* v29 no4 p24 Summ 2017

Inventors—United States

Research: Arab Inventors Make the U.S. More Innovative S. Mahroum, G. Zahradnik et al *Harvard Business Review Digital Articles* p2 F 23 2017

Inventory control—Management

Inventory Management in the Age of Big Data M. A. Cohen *Harvard Business Review Digital Articles* p2 Je 24 2015

Invertebrates

See also

Tardigrada

HOW VERTEBRATES GOT THEIR COATS M. GresÜo color *National Geographic* v232 no4 p14 O 2017

Investigation reports

Paul Manafort Wasn't the Problem *Commentary* v142 no1 p1 Jl/Ag 2016

Investigations

See also

Criminal investigation

Missing persons investigation

The Monster of Florence: Case Closed? The Terrifying Story of the Most Infamous Ritual Murders in Italian History, Part 2 M. POLIDORO *Skeptical Inquirer* v41 no5 p20 S/O 2017

Skeptical Activism from the Bottom Up M. MARSHALL *Skeptical Inquirer* v40 no6 p49 N/D 2016

An Unparalleled Opportunity for an Important Ecological Study L. D. MECH, S. BARBER-MEYER et al *BioScience* v67 no10 p875 O 2017

Investigative reporting

Dr. Cristin Kearns A. Sifferlin color *Time* v188 no27-28 p97 D 26 2016

The drone files S. Hepworth color *Columbia Journalism Review* p12 Fall/Wint 2016

The Early Scoops A. GREENE bw color *Rolling Stone* no1283 p20 Mr 23 2017

Finding new ways to follow the story S. Coll *Columbia Journalism Review* p21 Fall/Wint 2016

Journalism's Last Hurrah? M. BAUERLEIN and C. JEFFERY *Mother Jones* v42 no5 p5 S/O 2017

Muckraking and Troublemaking C. HASS bw *In These Times* v40 no11 p41 N 2016

Where Did All the Investigative Journalism Go? J. SHAFER bw cartoon *Reason* v48 no11 p64 Ap 2017

Investment advisors

See also

Wealth management services

Women investment advisors

3 Reality Checks You Must Face To Fix Your Finances A. Edmond Jr. color *Black Enterprise* v47 no4 p14 N/D 2016

Are You Betting Too Big on Trump? W. BALDWIN chart color graph *Forbes* v199 no2 p90 F 28 2017

Financial Life A. McKINNEY color *Missouri Life* v44 no5 p82 Ag 2017

FINDING THAT Special Someone F. TORABI color *O, The Oprah Magazine* p41 Je 2017

LONG ON TRUMP J. Pressler img *New York* p26 Ja 23 2017

THE RIGHT PRICE FOR ADVICE N. S. HUANG cartoon diag *Kiplinger's Personal Finance* v71 no12 p44 D 2017

Untangling Dividend Stocks C. Taylor color diag *Fortune* v174 no8 p132 D 15 2016

Investment advisors—Employment

Coming for Your Trading Desk S. Kishan color *Bloomberg Businessweek* no4528 p22 Je 26 2017

Trying to Make Active Funds Cool Again R. Evans and A. Massa cartoon diag *Bloomberg Businessweek* no4518 p40 Ap 10 2017

Investment advisors—Government policy

A Case for Caution I. M. STELZER *Weekly Standard* v22 no25 p20 Mr 6 2017

Investment advisors—Ratings & rankings

America's Top 100 Wealth Advisors H. Touryalai chart *Forbes* v200 no4 p105 O 24 2017

Investment advisors—Software

Robot Advisers Can Be Conflicted, Too H. Son cartoon *Bloomberg Businessweek* no4532 p28 Jl 31 2017

Investment advisors—United States

America's Top 100 Wealth Advisors H. Touryalai chart *Forbes* v200 no4 p105 O 24 2017

Best Places to Get Investment Advice N. S. HUANG cartoon *Kiplinger's Personal Finance* v71 no1 p52 Ja 2017

BROKERS CHANGE THEIR GAME PLAN S. BLOCK cartoon *Kiplinger's Personal Finance* v71 no4 p9 Ap 2017

Harvard Business Review Digital Articles p2 Mr 28 2016

Why Your Portfolio Should Be Stocked With Global Shares P. J. Lim color *Time* v189 no20 p12 My 29 2017

WORKHORSE STOCKS GET TO SHINE *Fortune* v174 no8 p111 D 15 2016

The World Is Still Not Flat J. Fox *Harvard Business Review Digital Articles* p2 N 3 2014

The Worry-Free Life J. KITA color *AARP: The Magazine* v59 no2A p28 F/Mr 2016

Worrying About the Bear? Don't J. K. GLASSMAN chart *Kiplinger's Personal Finance* v71 no4 p16 Ap 2017

YOUR ETF, YOUR LIBERATOR W. BALDWIN *Forbes* v198 no8 p65 D 20 2016

Investments & the environment

The Challenge of Socially Responsible Investing T. Tepper color diag *Money* v46 no7 p31 Ag 2017

Investments—Australia

Active Funds Still Rule Down Under. For Now E. Cadman and R. Liew color *Bloomberg Businessweek* no4526 p33 Je 12 2017

Investments—Charts, diagrams, etc.

ANNUAL ARTIFICIAL INTELLIGENCE DEALS diag *Fortune* v175 no2 p11 F 1 2017

Tech Stocks Join Market Rally chart diag *Money* v46 no2 p84 Mr 2017

Investments—Computer network resources

Why Machines Still Can't Learn So Good N. Kumar and T. Hall cartoon *Bloomberg Businessweek* no4499 p55 N 14 2016

The XX Factor S. SHARF color *Forbes* v199 no4 p58 Ap 25 2017

Investments—Economic aspects

Don't Let Current Events Spook You K. KRISTOF *Kiplinger's Personal Finance* v71 no11 p57 N 2017

EARNINGS SURPRISES IN THE HEARTLAND J. OBERWEIS *Forbes* v198 no6 p70 N 8 2016

Investments—European Union countries

Boring Funds Get Weird S. Jones color *Bloomberg Businessweek* no4499 p52 N 14 2016

Progressive Developments in Greek Trade and Industry color *Foreign Affairs* v96 no3 p86f My/Je 2017

Investments—History—21st century

2017 INVESTMENT GUIDE [Cover story] color *Forbes* v198 no9 p87 D 30 2016

Investments—Management

Inflation-Proof Your Assets A. K. SMITH cartoon chart *Kiplinger's Personal Finance* v71 no4 p59 Ap 2017

One Family, Two Foreign Fund Winners R. ERMEY chart *Kiplinger's Personal Finance* v71 no4 p62 Ap 2017

A truly happy way to spend your money N. Lapin color *Redbook* p36 D 2016

Investments—Moral & ethical aspects

Doing Good While Doing Well J. Marlowe *Governing* v30 no7 p62 Ap 2017

Impact Investing Needs Millennials V. Dhar and J. Fetherston *Harvard Business Review Digital Articles* p2 O 3 2014

Making Sense of the Many Kinds of Impact Investing B. Trelstad *Harvard Business Review Digital Articles* p2 Ja 28 2016

Passive Investing for The Social Activist S. Foxman color *Bloomberg Businessweek* no4511 p40 F 13 2017

Investments—Psychological aspects

Investing Can Be About Feelings Too M. Statman color *Money* v46 no5 p30 Je 2017

Investments—United States

ASK THE EXPERT E. O'Brien and A. Mondalek chart *Money* v46 no4 p20 My 2017

Beware the Gender Investing Gap S. Krawcheck color *Glamour* v115 no2 p74 F 2017

EARNINGS SURPRISES IN THE HEARTLAND J. OBERWEIS *Forbes* v198 no6 p70 N 8 2016

How to Brace Yourself C. Bigda color diag *Money* v45 no11 p45 D 2016

HOW TO BUY CLASSIC CARS D. Bentley and K. Korosec color *Fortune* v175 no4 p53 Mr 15 2017

Infrastructure Investment *Congressional Digest* v96 no4 p30 Ap 2017

Investors Try to Predict Trump H. S. Edwards color diag *Time* v188 no22-23 p30 N/D 2016

Time to Fix Fannie and Freddie I. BRANNON color *Weekly Stan-*

dard v22 no30 p18 Ap 10 2017

We Pick the Best Online Brokers D. FONDA chart color *Kiplinger's Personal Finance* v71 no10 p48 O 2017

WORLDLY WEALTH R. HENAGER il *Phi Kappa Phi Forum* v97 no1 p17 Spr 2017

YOUR 20 BEST MONEY MOVES FOR 2017 P. J. Lim, K. Bahler et al color diag *Money* v45 no11 p60 D 2016

Investments—United States—Government policy

Job No. 1: Act in Your Best Interests D. Harris color *Money* v46 no2 p15 Mr 2017

Investments—United States—Charts, diagrams, etc.

CEO SOOTHSAYERS A. Murray diag *Fortune* v175 no8 p340 Je 15 2017

IF YOU BET ON THE FORTUNE 500, YOU BEAT THE MARKET diag *Fortune* v175 no8 p36 Je 15 2017

Invictus Yacht (Company)

Conquering Hero A. HARPER chart color diag *Power & Motoryacht* v34 no6 p50 Je 2017

Invisibility

Vanishing Act E. UNDERWOOD *Smithsonian* v47 no9 p16 Ja/F 2017

Invisible Children (Organization)

THE ACTIVIST SOUL J. Medefind color *Christianity Today* v61 no6 p70 Jl/Ag 2017

Invisible Web

See also

Darknets (File sharing)

The Darknet: A Quick Introduction for Business Leaders A. Delamarter *Harvard Business Review Digital Articles* p2 D 9 2016

Invocation

COMMUNITY MATTERS *Islamic Horizons* v46 no3 p13 My/Je 2017

Invoices

See also

Health care industry—Billing

What Should I Do With My Father's Nazi Keepsake? K. A. Appiah *New York Times Magazine* p28 Mr 26 2017

Involuntary relocation

Can We Leave Now? V. FAIRBANK cartoon *Walrus* p18 Ja\F 2017

HOT ZONES J. Benko *New York Times Magazine* p54 Ap 23 2017

How to Move a Town J. Dean color *Bloomberg Businessweek* no4537 p68 S 11 2017

JULIA STREET color *New Orleans Magazine* v51 no12 p24 O 2017

Invoxia (Company)

INVOXIA NVX 200: TURN YOUR iPHONE INTO A DESK PHONE J. R. BOOKWALTER color *Macworld - Digital Edition* v34 no9 p48 S 2017

Inxile Entertainment (Company)

TORMENT: TIDES OF NUMENERA: ONE OF THE BEST BOOKS YOU'LL EVER PLAY S. BELLAMY color *Macworld - Digital Edition* p26 Je 13 2017

'Torment: Tides of Numenera': The 'Planescape' successor you've been waiting for H. DINGMAN color *PCWorld* v35 no4 p103 Ap 2017

Inzpire (Company)

"Unlimited holiday works because of our culture": Why a defence SME did away with leave limits *People Management* p23 Ag 2017

Io (Satellite)—Research

IO'S ATMOSPHERE PERIODICALLY COLLAPSES J. Rice color *Astronomy* v44 no12 p8 D 2016

Ioannidis, John P. A.

Enhancing reproducibility for computational methods bibl color *Science* v354 no6317 p1240 D 9 2016

Iodides

Iodide management in formamidinium-lead-halide–based perovskite layers for efficient solar cells W. S. Yang, Park et al bw diag *Science* v356 no6345 p1376 Je 30 2017

Iodine—Physiological aspects

shake it off A. OGLETHORPE, J. Brill et al color *Better Homes & Gardens* v95 no7 p168 Jl 2017

Ioffe, Julia

THE PUTIN GENERATION bw color graph map *National Geo-*

graphic v230 no6 p76 D 2016

ION, FLORENCE
Galaxy S8 battery life tips: How to control battery drain color *PC-World* v35 no10 p116 O 2017
How to stop Google Home or Amazon Echo from making unwanted online purchases color *PCWorld* v35 no9 p107 S 2017

Ion channels
The form and function of channelrhodopsin K. Deisseroth and P. Hegemann diag *Science* v357 no6356 p1111 S 15 2017

Ionescu, Mihai
CUSTOMER LOYALTY IS OVERRATED: INTERACTION color *Harvard Business Review* v95 no3 p18 My/Je 2017

Ionization (Atomic physics)
See also
Auger effect
Scintillators
Cause of cosmic makeover reassessed A. YEAGER *Science News* v191 no4 p10 Mr 4 2017

Ionization energy
Long-standing gold mystery solved E. CONOVER *Science News* v191 no3 p11 F 18 2017

Ions—Therapeutic use
On the value of carbon-ion therapy M. Story, A. Pompos et al *Physics Today* v69 no11 p14 N 2016

Ioptron Corp.
Get Up and Go with AZ Mount Pro: Follow this observers guide to find one of the best H II regions in the night sky R. T. Fienberg *Sky & Telescope* v134 no3 p60 S 2017
Putting iOptron's new mount to the test P. Harrington color *Astronomy* v44 no12 p62 D 2016

Iordansky, Sergey
Lev Petrovich Gor'kov *Physics Today* v70 no5 p68 My 2017

iOS (Operating system)
10 great, older games that you can still play on iOS 11 A. HAYWARD color *Macworld - Digital Edition* v34 no11 p59 N 2017
Ask the iTunes Guy: Your questions about the iOS 10 Music app K. McELHEARN cartoon color *Macworld - Digital Edition* v33 no11 p151 N 2016
Dual-processor Fusion Mac makes sense D. Moren color *Macworld - Digital Edition* p125 Ap 2017
Hackintosh: Build a DIY Mac mini K. McELHEARN color *Macworld - Digital Edition* v34 no8 p16 Ag 2017
Hackintosh: Should you build one? R. GRIFFITHS color *Macworld - Digital Edition* v34 no8 p7 Ag 2017
How Control Center works J. SNELL color *Macworld - Digital Edition* v34 no11 p51 N 2017
How to downgrade to iOS 9 if you don't like iOS 10 R. LOYOLA *PCWorld* p157 O 2016
The iOS 11 To-Do List D. Pogue color *Scientific American* v316 no6 p26 Je 2017
iOS Accessories J. Mathis color *Macworld - Digital Edition* v34 no8 p80 Ag 2017
Mac 911 G. FLEISHMAN color *Macworld - Digital Edition* p111 Je 13 2017
Mac 911 G. FLEISHMAN color *Macworld - Digital Edition* v34 no11 p135 N 2017
RAW TO GO T. Nikitas color *Popular Photography* v80 no11 p40 D 2016
The Rule of Cool K. C. POHLMANN color *Sound & Vision* v82 no7 p26 S 2017
Sitters in a Snap J. Laird color *Working Mother* v40 no4 p18 O/N 2017

iOS (Operating system)—Equipment & supplies
iMazing 2.2: Use your Mac to manage your iPhone and iPad J. R. BOOKWALTER color *Macworld - Digital Edition* p93 Je 13 2017
iOS Accessories J. Mathis color *Macworld - Digital Edition* p58 Je 13 2017
iOS Accessories J. Mathis color *Macworld - Digital Edition* p62 Mr 2017
iOS Accessories J. Mathis color *Macworld - Digital Edition* v34 no9 p56 S 2017

iOS (Operating system)—Evaluation
Apple will allow developers to respond to App Store user reviews R. LOYOLA color *Macworld - Digital Edition* p19 Mr 2017
Hey, Apple Fixed This! K. MCELHEARN color *Macworld - Digi-*

tal Edition v34 no8 p24 Ag 2017
iOS 11 FAQ: EVERYTHING WE KNOW ABOUT NEW SIRI, PHOTOS, APPLE PAY, & MESSAGES [Cover story] O. Raymundo color *Macworld - Digital Edition* p65 Je 13 2017
iOS 11 J. Snell color *Macworld - Digital Edition* v34 no9 p62 S 2017
iOS 11 REVIEW [Cover story] J. Snell color *Macworld - Digital Edition* v34 no11 p87 N 2017
Update to iOS 10.3.3 now: Apple patches serious Wi-Fi exploit G. FLEISHMAN color *Macworld - Digital Edition* v34 no9 p39 S 2017

IOSSEL, MIKHAIL
Santa Barbara Forevah! color *Foreign Policy* no225 p54 Jl/Ag 2017

IOU, The (Short story)
The I.O.U F. S. FITZGERALD cartoon *New Yorker* v93 no5 p80 Mr 20 2017

IOVENKO, CHRIS
The Voice of Trump *New Republic* v248 no5 p12 My 2017

Iovine, Jimmy, 1953-
THE DEFINING ONES M. LYNCH color *Vanity Fair* v59 no7 p108 Summ 2017
Dre and Jimmy's Excellent Adventure D. BROWNE bw *Rolling Stone* no1291/1292 p16 Jl 13 2017
A Star Is Born L. Shaw and A. Webb color graph *Bloomberg Businessweek* no4520 p22 My 1 2017

Iovine, Jimmy, 1953——Interviews
JIMMY IOVINE Wants to Learn A. Grant color *Esquire* p72 Je/Jl 2017

Iovino, Nicola
Germ line–inherited H3K27me3 restricts enhancer function during maternal-to-zygotic transition diag *Science* v357 no6347 p212 Jl 14 2017

Iowa Select Farms (Company)
JEFF HANSEN: THE OWNER OF IOWA SELECT FARMS IS IN EXPANSION MODE B. Freese color *Successful Farming* v115 no7 p48 My 2017

Iowa Soybean Association (Company)
10 UP & COMERS: GRANT BERLEY K. Birchmier *Successful Farming* v115 no8 p48 Je/Jl 2017

Iowa State University
10 UP & COMERS: MEAGHAN ANDERSON G. Gullickson *Successful Farming* v115 no8 p36 Je/Jl 2017

Iowa State University—Sports
Week 5 color *Sports Illustrated* v127 no5 p62 Ag 14 2017

Iowa—Economic conditions
IOWA CITY, IOWA M. Robinson *Harper's Magazine* p37 O 2017

Iozzio, Corinne
THE CAMERA MAN color *Popular Photography* v81 no1 p76 Ja/F 2017
CARRY WATER color *Popular Science* v289 no2 p26 Mr/Ap 2017
THIRTY YEARS LATER... color *Popular Science* v289 no6 p8 N/D 2017
UNDER PRESSURE color *Popular Science* v289 no2 p32 Mr/Ap 2017

Ip, Hon S.
Role for migratory wild birds in the global spread of avian influenza H5N8 bibl graph map *Science* v354 no6309 p213 O 14 2016

Ip, W. K. Eddie
Anti-inflammatory effect of IL-10 mediated by metabolic reprogramming of macrophages diag *Science* v356 no6337 p513 My 5 2017

Ip, W.-H.
Rosetta's comet 67P/Churyumov-Gerasimenko sheds its dusty mantle to reveal its icy nature bibl graph *Science* v354 no6319 p1566 D 23 2016
Seasonal exposure of carbon dioxide ice on the nucleus of comet 67P/Churyumov-Gerasimenko bibl bw graph *Science* v354 no6319 p1563 D 23 2016
Surface changes on comet 67P/Churyumov-Gerasimenko suggest a more active past bw graph *Science* v355 no6332 p1392 Mr 31 2017

iPad (Computer)
10.5- and 12.9in iPad Pros on the way L. Yamshon color *Macworld - Digital Edition* p17 Ap 2017

10.5-INCH iPAD PRO: IF ANY iPAD REPLACES THE MAC-BOOK, IT'S THIS ONE O. RAYMUNDO color *Macworld - Digital Edition* v34 no8 p69 Ag 2017

DITCH THE LAPTOP? K. Sintumuang cartoon color *Esquire* p52 S 2017

IPAD (2017) REVIEW: WITH A STRIPPED-DOWN iPAD FOR $329, YOU MAY NOT NEED TO GO PRO S. Ochs color *Macworld - Digital Edition* v34 no4 p67 My 2017

The iPad Pro: Now a true photographer's tool J. CARLSON color *Macworld - Digital Edition* v34 no8 p57 Ag 2017

iPAD PRO SMART KEYBOARD VS. LOGITECH SLIM COMBO: WHICH iPAD PRO KEYBOARD SHOULD YOU BUY? J. NEWMAN color *Macworld - Digital Edition* v34 no8 p75 Ag 2017

The iPad's popularity is on the rise, and it's all thanks to cheaper prices D. MOREN color *Macworld - Digital Edition* v34 no10 p42 O 2017

IRRESISTIBLE: The business of technology is the business of addiction A. Alter *Saturday Evening Post* v289 no4 p12 Jl/Ag 2017

TAXI AT LARGE AIRPORTS LIKE A PRO B. Koebbe color *Flying* v144 no8 p30 Ag 2017

iPad (Computer)—Equipment & supplies

WATERFIELD iPAD PRO SLEEVECASE S. J. PUREWAL *Macworld - Digital Edition* v34 no9 p37 S 2017

iPad (Computer)—Equipment & supplies—Evaluation

iPhone and iPad Cases J. MATHIS color *Macworld - Digital Edition* v33 no11 p96 N 2016

iPad (Computer)—Evaluation

SHOULD I REPLACE MY LAPTOP WITH A TABLET? C. MUELLER color *Popular Science* v288 no6 p18 N/D 2016

iPad (Computer)—Sales & prices

Why the future is bright for Apple's iPad J. Snell color diag *Macworld - Digital Edition* p103 Ap 2017

iPad (Computer)—Software—Evaluation

WHAT'S NEW AT THE APP STORE J. MATHIS cartoon *Macworld - Digital Edition* p61 Mr 2017

Iphigénie en Tauride (Theatrical production)

Gluck: Iphigénie en Tauride D. J. Baker *Opera News* v81 no7 p49 Ja 2017

iPhone (Smartphone)

AFTER 10 YEARS, WHERE DOES THE iPHONE GO NEXT? D. Moren color *Macworld - Digital Edition* v34 no8 p91 Ag 2017

Apple investigates iPhone 7 Plus that 'blew up' O. Raymundo color *Macworld - Digital Edition* p15 Ap 2017

GEARHEAD: ROCK GROUP D. PIERCE color *Wired* v25 no8 p42 Ag 2017

How Control Center works J. SNELL color *Macworld - Digital Edition* v34 no11 p51 N 2017

How to unlock your iPhone on Verizon, AT&T, Sprint, T-Mobile, and Virgin Mobile J. CARLSON color *Macworld - Digital Edition* v34 no8 p61 Ag 2017

How to use your iPhone or iPad as a wireless hotspot N. MEDIATI color *Macworld - Digital Edition* v34 no6 p105 Je 2017

The iPhone's Home button is gone: What's next to go? D. MOREN color *Macworld - Digital Edition* v34 no11 p56 N 2017

Letter Head C. BONANOS color *Conde Nast Traveler* v52 no3 p102 Mr 2017

The Reader Page R. G. Elmendorf and B. Porter color *Popular Mechanics* p8 D 2016/Ja 2017

SHOOT PHOTOS LIKE THIS with an iPhone P. K. Søeborg color diag *Model Railroader* v84 no11 p42 N 2017

A Short History of Radio Explains the iPhone's Success T. W. Hazlett *Harvard Business Review Digital Articles* p2 Je 29 2017

Sleep, Thy Name Is Gadget L. Eadicicco color *Time* v189 no13 p20 Ap 10 2017

A wish list for the iPhone in 2017 J. SNELL color *Macworld - Digital Edition* p43 F 2017

iPhone (Smartphone)—Design & construction

Face ID on the iPhone X: Apple releases Face ID white paper and support document G. FLEISHMAN color *Macworld - Digital Edition* v34 no11 p39 N 2017

News: Apple to replace faulty iPhone 6s batteries J. Ribeiro color *Macworld - Digital Edition* p4 Ja 2017

Resistance Is Futile D. Pogue color *Scientific American* v315 no6

p30 D 2016

iPhone (Smartphone)—Equipment & supplies

6 ACCESSORIES that make the iPhone an even BETTER VIDEO CAMERA [Cover story] T. Larson and D. Masaoka color *Macworld - Digital Edition* v34 no6 p83 Je 2017

BEZALEL OMNIA: STYLISH WIRELESS AUTOMOBILE CHARGER FOR IPHONE 6/7 J. R. BOOKWALTER color *Macworld - Digital Edition* v34 no6 p45 Je 2017

ELAGO M4 STAND FOR iPHONE 7 J. MATHIS color *Macworld - Digital Edition* v34 no6 p45 Je 2017

iMazing 2.2: Use your Mac to manage your iPhone and iPad J. R. BOOKWALTER color *Macworld - Digital Edition* p93 Je 13 2017

iOS Accessories J. Mathis color *Macworld - Digital Edition* v34 no6 p76 Je 2017

K'ABLEKEY REVIEW: VERSATILE IPHONE FLASH DRIVE DOUBLES AS LIGHTNING CHARGE CABLE J. R. BOOKWALTER color *Macworld - Digital Edition* p51 Je 13 2017

MY MIGGO PICTAR FOR iPHONE 7 J. MATHIS color *Macworld - Digital Edition* p34 Je 13 2017

O6 PORTABLE SMART BLUETOOTH REMOTE J. R. BOOKWALTER color *Macworld - Digital Edition* v34 no10 p36 O 2017

PERI DUO: BULKY iPHONE BATTERY CASE WITH SPEAKERS DOESN'T QUITE GO TO 11 J. R. BOOKWALTER color *Macworld - Digital Edition* v34 no6 p65 Je 2017

WORKS FOR US! M. Santos color *Working Mother* p19 F/Mr 2017

iPhone (Smartphone)—Equipment & supplies—Evaluation

iPhone and iPad Cases J. MATHIS color *Macworld - Digital Edition* v33 no11 p96 N 2016

Turn your smartphone into an astro-camera T. Trusock color *Astronomy* v45 no3 p58 Mr 2017

iPhone (Smartphone)—Evaluation

8 times Google savagely burned Apple during the Pixel announcement L. YAMSHON cartoon color diag *PCWorld* v35 no11 p127 N 2016

8 WAYS THE iPHONE 8 CAN BEAT THE GALAXY S8 [Cover story] M. Simon color graph *Macworld - Digital Edition* v34 no6 p91 Je 2017

Have More Fun With Your Phone M. Gikas chart color il *Consumer Reports* v82 no3 p48 Mr 2017

How the iPhone 8 can live up to all the crazy hype O. RAYMUNDO color *Macworld - Digital Edition* v34 no9 p42 S 2017

How to use Messages in iOS 10, from special effects to iMessage apps O. RAYMUNDO cartoon color *Macworld - Digital Edition* v33 no11 p67 N 2016

iPhone 7 and 7 Plus FAQ: Everything you need to know about Apple's new phones C. McGARRY bw color *PCWorld* p8 O 2016

iPhone 7: ITS SPEED AND CAMERA ARE CRAZY-GOOD, BUT IT STILL DRIVES ME CRAZY S. OCHS color graph *Macworld - Digital Edition* v33 no11 p101 N 2016

iPHONE 7 PLUS REVIEW: THE DUAL-LENS CAMERA MAKES IT A WINNER S. OCHS color graph *Macworld - Digital Edition* p85 D 2016

iPhone 8 has the best smartphone camera, DxOMark says, but iPhone X will probably beat it M. SIMON color *Macworld - Digital Edition* v34 no11 p54 N 2017

iPHONE AT 10 J. Snell color *Macworld - Digital Edition* v34 no8 p86 Ag 2017

Photo shootout: We tested Portrait mode with an iPhone 7 Plus fashion shoot S. OCHS and A. P. MURRAY color *Macworld - Digital Edition* p47 D 2016

TESTED: GALAXY NOTE 8 LIVE FOCUS VS. iPHONE 7 PLUS PORTRAIT MODE A. P. Murray color *Macworld - Digital Edition* v34 no10 p75 O 2017

iPhone (Smartphone)—Marketing

Apple's risky balancing act with the next iPhone J. SNELL color *Macworld - Digital Edition* v34 no9 p43 S 2017

iPhone (Smartphone)—Mobile apps—Evaluation

Blow up: iPhone 7 Plus uses digital zoom instead of optical more often than you'd expect G. FLEISHMAN color *Macworld - Digital Edition* v33 no11 p57 N 2016

Evernote overhauls its iOS app with focus on speed and simplicity C. McGARRY color *Macworld - Digital Edition* p49 Mr 2017

iPhone (Smartphone)—Sales & prices

The Battle Over iPhones in India B. Chakravorti *Harvard Business Review Digital Articles* p2 Ap 19 2016

Finally, a Cheap(ish) iPhone S. Rai color *Bloomberg Businessweek* no4527 p30 Je 19 2017

THE IPHONE DECADE A. Pressman color diag *Fortune* v175 no7 p23 Je 1 2017

iPhones outsell Samsung smartphones P. Sayer color *Macworld - Digital Edition* p12 Ap 2017

The Psychology Behind the New iPhone's Four-Digit Price R. Mohammed *Harvard Business Review Digital Articles* p2 S 21 2017

iPhone (Smartphone)—Security measures

INVADING APPLE B. BURROUGH color *Vanity Fair* v59 no1 p144 Holiday 2017

Is iPhone set to get facial recognition? D. Moren color *Macworld - Digital Edition* p93 Ap 2017

iPhone (Smartphone)—Software—Evaluation

Apple Music in iTunes just got more enjoyable and easier to use K. McELHEARN color *Macworld - Digital Edition* v33 no11 p147 N 2016

iPhone software

Face ID on the iPhone X: Apple releases Face ID white paper and support document G. FLEISHMAN color *Macworld - Digital Edition* v34 no11 p39 N 2017

iPod (Digital music player)

Apple discontinues iPod nano and iPod shuffle R. LOYOLA color *Macworld - Digital Edition* v34 no9 p87 S 2017

Ippati, Stefania

Site-specific phosphorylation of tau inhibits amyloid-β toxicity in Alzheimer's mice bibl graph *Science* v354 no6314 p904 N 18 2016

Ippoliti, Amy

REACH FOR MORE color *Yoga Journal* p38 2017 Special Issue

Supta Padangusthasana to Ardha Chandra Chapasana [Cover story] color *Yoga Journal* no295 p55 O 2017

Ippolito, Jacy

SIDE-BY-SIDE LEARNING: A summer program focused on science disciplinary literacy *Literacy Today (2411-7862)* v35 no1 p30 Jl/Ag 2017

Ipsa Dixit (Theatrical production)

SINGING PHILOSOPHY A. ROSS cartoon *New Yorker* v93 no2 p74 F 27 2017

Iqbal, Muhammad, Sir, 1877-1938

Mysteries of the Self: The poet-philosopher Mohammad Iqbal stressed discovering and valuing the self for ever-lasting success S. ATTAR *Islamic Horizons* v46 no4 p58 Jl/Ag 2017

Iqbal, Sonny

Why Family Firms in East Asia Struggle with Succession *Harvard Business Review Digital Articles* p2 Mr 24 2015

Irabu, Hideki

THE SEEKER B. Reiter color *Sports Illustrated* v127 no4 p60 Ag 7 2017

Irac, Sergio Erdal

Mapping the human DC lineage through the integration of high-dimensional techniques diag *Science* v356 no6342 p1044 Je 9 2017

Iran. Army of the Guardians of the Islamic Revolution

How Deep Is Iran's State? A. Vatanka *Foreign Affairs* v96 no4 p155 Jl/Ag 2017

Iran—Description & travel

IRAN *New York Times Magazine* p70 S 24 2017

VACATION IN IRAN N. Tavakolian color map *New Yorker* v93 no10 p74 Ap 24 2017

Iran—Economic conditions—1997-

Iran Has a 1 Percent Too, and It's Pro-West M. Champion and G. Motevalli cartoon *Bloomberg Businessweek* no4495 p14 O 17 2016

Iran—Foreign relations—United States

THE BREAKING POINT D. FILKINS cartoon *New Yorker* v93 no32 p42 O 16 2017

Doomed Deal L. Smith color *Weekly Standard* v22 no12 p7 N 28 2016

Iran Sanctions *Congressional Digest* v95 no10 p13 D 2016

The Leveling of Tehran *USA Today Magazine* v145 no2860 p16 Ja 2017

Pipe Dreams of a Normal Iran T. Donnelly *Hoover Digest: Re-*

search & Opinion on Public Policy no1 p131 Wint 2017

Saudi Arms Deal Stories Omitted Who the Weapons Would Be Killing A. Johnson *Extra!* v30 no6 p4 Jl/Ag 2017

The Tehran Two-Step J. Lifhits color *Weekly Standard* v22 no33 p11 My 8 2017

Iran—Foreign relations—United States—History—21st century

The Iran Paradox A. J. Stavridis color *Time* v188 no16/17 p33 O 24 2016

The U.S. and Iran's New Relationship Status: Enemies, With Benefits K. Vick color *Time* v189 no6 p9 F 20 2017

Iran—Foreign relations—1997-

Taking On Iran [Cover story] R. TAKEYH *National Review* v68 no24 p28 D 31 2016

Iranian Americans—Social conditions

They Can't Go Home Again A. P. Q. Wittmeyer and J. Chase-Lubitz color *Foreign Policy* no226 p16 S/O 2017

Iranian Revolution, 1979

Winning Iran's Election Is Just The Beginning Of Rouhani's Political Struggles S. H. Mousavian *NPQ: New Perspectives Quarterly* v34 no3 p22 Jl 2017

Iran—Military history

The Pentagon's 'Smart' Revolution A. Herman *Commentary* v142 no1 p25 Jl/Ag 2016

Iran—Politics & government

Iran: Still Waiting for Democracy C. de Bellaigue color *New York Review of Books* v64 no12 p25 Jl 13 2017

Iran—Politics & government—21st century

How Deep Is Iran's State? A. Vatanka *Foreign Affairs* v96 no4 p155 Jl/Ag 2017

Iran—Politics & government—History

Iran's Next Supreme Leader S. Vakil and H. Rassam color *Foreign Affairs* v96 no3 p76 My/Je 2017

Iran—Politics & government—1979-1997

Iran's Islamic Evolution M. Champion and L. Nasseri color *Bloomberg Businessweek* no4524 p14 My 29 2017

Iran—Politics & government—1997-

Iran Has a 1 Percent Too, and It's Pro-West M. Champion and G. Motevalli cartoon *Bloomberg Businessweek* no4495 p14 O 17 2016

Iran's Islamic Evolution M. Champion and L. Nasseri color *Bloomberg Businessweek* no4524 p14 My 29 2017

Iran—Social conditions

Tortured by 'Moderates' K. Jane Torrance color *Weekly Standard* v22 no47 p34 Ag 21 2017

Iraq antiquities

See also

Calah (Extinct city)

THE SALVATION OF MOSUL: An Iraqi archaeologist braved ISIS snipers and booby-trapped ruins to rescue cultural treasures in the city and nearby legendary Nineveh and Nimrud J. HAMMER *Smithsonian* v48 no6 p30 O 2017

Iraq—Armed Forces

THE LIVING AND THE DEAD J. Verini *New York Times Magazine* p36 Jl 23 2017

Iraq—Foreign relations—United States

A Second Chance in Iraq D. FRENCH color *National Review* v68 no21 p26 N 21 2016

Iraq—Foreign relations—United States—History—21st century

New Travel Ban Helps U.S.-Iraq Relations but Still Stings Elsewhere J. Malsin and R. Collard color *Time* v189 no10 p7 Mr 20 2017

Iraq—History—2003-

See also

Iraq—History—Anti-ISIL intervention, 2014-

Iraq War, 2003-2011

Iraq—History—Anti-ISIL intervention, 2014-

Iraq: The Terrible Battle for Mosul J. Hammer bw map *New York Review of Books* v63 no17 p24 N 10 2016

Quagmire A. R. KHAN color *Maclean's* v129 no45 p30 N 14 2016

Iraqi painting

ART OF WAR V. LOWRY color *Architectural Digest* v73 no11 p92 N 2016

Iraqi refugees

Fight for Mosul Drags On While Displaced Numbers Grow K. CLARKE *America* v216 no1 p8 Ja 2 2017

The Iraqis Who Fled Mosul C. YAR color *Foreign Policy* no226

p5 S/O 2017

Iraqis
Fleeing Iraq *Smithsonian* v48 no1 p82 Ap 2017

Iraq—Military relations—United States—History—21st century
Beating ISIS-and Saving Iraq M. Thompson color *Time* v188 no16/17 p32 O 24 2016
Mission Still Not Accomplished in Iraq E. Sky color *Foreign Affairs* v96 no6 p9 N/D 2017

Iraq—Politics & government
Why 'Artificiality' Fails to Explain Iraq's Woes F. HADDAD *Current History* v115 no785 p343 D 2016

Iraq—Politics & government—2003-
Mission Still Not Accomplished in Iraq E. Sky color *Foreign Affairs* v96 no6 p9 N/D 2017

Iraq War, 2003-2011
BATTLE OF BAGHDAD color *AARP: The Magazine* v59 no3A p69 Ap/My 2016
God's Word to an Iraqi Interpreter A. Hameed color *Christianity Today* v61 no6 p95 Jl/Ag 2017
Humility, Credibility, Prudence J. C. HIRSCH color *National Review* v68 no21 p29 N 21 2016
THE LONG ROAD BACK B. CARPENTER *USA Today Magazine* v145 no2864 p42 My 2017
Mission Critical G. REPPENHAGEN *Sierra* v101 no4 p42 Jl/Ag 2016

Iraq War, 2003-2011—Refugees
Fleeing Iraq *Smithsonian* v48 no1 p82 Ap 2017
A MODERN ODYSSEY J. HAMMER *Smithsonian* v48 no1 p70 Ap 2017

Irasburg (Vt.)
Irasburg J. Johnson bw color *Old House Journal* v45 no4 p34 Je 2017

Irby, Charlotte M.
Disabled veterans and veterans with service-connected disabilities: are they the same? *Monthly Labor Review* p1 D 2016
Words pack a punch in online job recruiting bibl *Monthly Labor Review* p1 Ap 2017

Irby, Samantha
TALK TO US chart color *Chicago* v66 no7 p11 Jl 2017
Voted Most Inappropriate: Samantha Irby took up her confessional writing to "impress a dude"--and wound up marrying a woman. She also picked up a lot of famous fans K. Bolonik img *New York* v50 no11 p120 My 29 2017
THE WORLD'S LOUDES INNER MONOLOGUE C. CHEDLER color *Chicago* v66 no5 p94 My 2017

Ireland
Armagh Archbishop Martin contemplates changing times in Ireland R. Tarrant color *America* v216 no4 p15 F 20 2017
Four-Leaf Dining and Drinking J. Passov color *Golf Magazine* v59 no7 p94 Jl 2017
Letter from... IRELAND K. Cairns *Advocate* no1088 p28 D 2016/Ja 2017
Two Kinds of Wilderness: On foot through an ecological experiment J. MILLER bw *Orion Magazine* v36 no2 p34 Mr/Ap 2017

Ireland, Dave
Birthday Bioblitzes color *Canadian Wildlife* v23 no2 p30 My/Je 2017

Irenaeus, Saint, Bishop of Lyon
Egyptian theologians look to early church history after recent attacks A. Hillert color *Christian Century* v134 no2 p16 Ja 18 2017

IRESON, BRYHN
ASK RW color *Runner's World* v52 no4 p35 My 2017

Irfan, M.
Demonstration of an ac Josephson junction laser bibl diag *Science* v355 no6328 p939 Mr 3 2017

Iris (Eye)
BLINK OF AN EYE J. J. Roberts color *Fortune* v175 no4 p36 Mr 15 2017

I.R.I.S. SA
READIRIS PRO 16: OCR SOFTWARE MORE FOCUSED ON SPEED THAN ACCURACY J. R. BOOKWALTER color *Macworld - Digital Edition* v34 no6 p29 Je 2017

Irish authors
Luck and Book Sales J. FOSTER *Publishers Weekly* v264 no3

p41 Ja 16 2017

Irish history—To 1172
The Other Invasion: The Anglo-Norman invasion of Ireland in 1167 sowed the seeds for centuries of tension between England and the Irish C. Ellis *History Today* v67 no9 p12 S 2017

Irish whiskey
THE TIPSY TEXAN'S COOK TAIL OF THE MONTH D. ALAN *Texas Monthly* v45 no2 p40 F 2017

Irish whiskey—Evaluation
Multi-Flasking J. Passov color *Golf Magazine* v59 no7 p95 Jl 2017

Irishman, The (Film)
"Every Man Has to Go Through Hell to Reach Paradise" A. STERNBERGH img *New York* p114 Mr 6 2017

Irman (Short story)
IRMAN S. Schweblin *Harper's Magazine* p18 O 2017

Irmen, Andreas
What a Study of 33 Countries Found About Aging Populations and Innovation bw *Harvard Business Review Digital Articles* p2 Ja 18 2017

Irmer, Henriette
Sterilizing immunity in the lung relies on targeting fungal apoptosis-like programmed cell death color diag *Science* v357 no6355 p1037 S 8 2017

Irmis, Randall
Dinosaur family tree gets a makeover R. EHRENBERG diag *Science News* v191 no7 p7 Ap 15 2017

IRMSCHER, CHRISTOPH
Ambiguous Eye color *Weekly Standard* v22 no30 p34 Ap 10 2017
Birdman of America bw color *Weekly Standard* v22 no13 p30 D 5 2016
Selective Memory *American Scholar* v86 no1 p113 Wint 2017

Iron
Diamonds from the deep *Physics Today* v70 no2 p80 F 2017
Synthesis of FeH5: A layered structure with atomic hydrogen slabs C. M. Pépin, G. Geneste et al diag graph *Science* v357 no6349 p382 Jl 28 2017

Iron age
See also
Hallstatt period
Iron Age trade secrets revealed B. BOWER color *Science News* v191 no4 p17 Mr 4 2017

Iron catalysts
A bioinspired iron catalyst for nitrate and perchlorate reduction C. L. Ford, Yun Ji Park et al bibl diag *Science* v354 no6313 p741 N 11 2016

Iron deficiency anemia
A vigorous 81-year-old had struggled with high blood pressure for years—but suddenly it was dangerously low. Why? L. Sanders *New York Times Magazine* p22 Ja 15 2017

Iron Fist (TV program)
How Iron Fist Packs a Punch K. P. Sullivan color *Entertainment Weekly* no1457/1458 p84 Mr 17 2017
Iron Fist A. D'ARMINIO *TV Guide* v65 no11 p45 Mr 6 2017

Iron Man (Fictitious character)
NO. 6 IRON MAN K. P. Sullivan color *Entertainment Weekly* no1436/1437 p49 O 21 2016
WHO WOULD WIN? WOLVERINE VS. IRON MAN K. P. Sullivan and T. Stack *Entertainment Weekly* no1436/1437 p49 O 21 2016

Iron meteorites
Huge "Gancedo" Found in Argentina D. DICKINSON *Sky & Telescope* v133 no1 p18 Ja 2017

Iron oxidation
Chemists observe oxidation up close L. HAMERS color *Science News* v191 no10 p9 My 27 2017

Iron oxide nanoparticles
Quantitative 3D evolution of colloidal nanoparticle oxidation in solution Y. Sun, X. Zuo et al diag graph *Science* v356 no6335 p303 Ap 21 2017

Iron selenides
Discovery of orbital-selective Cooper pairing in FeSe P. O. Sprau, A. Kostin et al diag *Science* v357 no6346 p75 Jl 7 2017
Hunting down unconventional superconductors Lee diag *Science* v357 no6346 p32 Jl 7 2017

Ironbridge Gorge Museum Trust

How the Pieces all Came Together in Ironbridge Gorge *British Heritage Travel* v37 no6 p49 N/D 2016

Iron Eyes, Tokata

"I Led a Movement to Protect My Land" J. ABIDOR color *Seventeen* v76 no2 p24 Mr 2017

Ironing boards—Evaluation

SPRING CLEANING LAUNDRY SPECIAL C. FORTÉ and S. BOGDAN color *Good Housekeeping* v264 no5 p81 My 2017

Irons (Pressing)—Evaluation

IRONS color *Good Housekeeping* v264 no5 p86 My 2017

Irons, Jan

13 Ways To Ensure BBQ Success color *Sail* v48 no7 p10 Jl 2017

The SAILING SCENE color *Sail* v48 no11 p6 N 2017

Irons, Jeremy, 1948-

Jeremy Irons M. Rochlin color *AARP: The Magazine* v59 no2A p14 F/Mr 2016

Kingdom by the Sea D. KAMP color *Vanity Fair* v59 no10 p198 O 2017

PARTY LINES img *New York* p85 F 9 2017

Ironwood Forest National Monument (Ariz.)

IRONWOOD FOREST N. AUSTIN *Arizona Highways* v93 no1 p52 Ja 2017

Irony

When Kanye Met Donald R. THEDE cartoon color *Wired* v25 no4 p66 Ap 2017

Iroquois (North American people)—History

America's First Nation C. K. Ballatore *History Today* v67 no4 p51 Ap 2017

Irregular warfare

Hybrid war: Russian contemporary political warfare C. S. Chivvis bibl *Bulletin of the Atomic Scientists* v73 no5 p316 2017

Introduction: The evolving threat of hybrid war J. Mecklin bibl *Bulletin of the Atomic Scientists* v73 no5 p298 2017

Thinking clearly about China's layered Indo-Pacific strategy Z. Cooper and A. Shearer bibl *Bulletin of the Atomic Scientists* v73 no5 p305 2017

Irrigation

See also

Water requirements of plants

IDEA OF THE MONTH: SHOP-BUILT SIDEDRESSER CONVERTED FROM SPRAYER ALLOWS SPLIT APPLICATIONS P. Barbour *Successful Farming* v115 no6 p78 Ap 2017

IRRIGATION + INNOVATION = SAVING WATER IN KANSAS L. Bedord *Successful Farming* v115 no6 p47 Ap 2017

MOBILE PIVOT PAYOFF: TOWABLE SPRINKLERS ARE A LOWER INVESTMENT PER ACRE WHILE STILL OFFERING THE YIELD POTENTIAL FROM IRRIGATION T. Gaines *Successful Farming* v115 no12 p56 O 2017

Irrigation farming—United States

Understanding Irrigated Agriculture G. Schaible *Amber Waves: The Economics of Food, Farming, Natural Resources, & Rural America* p9 Je 2017

Irrigation management

GIVE-AND-TAKE IRRIGATION: TEXAS FARMER USES MULTIPLE PRACTICES TO EARN STRONG YIELDS ON MINIMAL ACRE-INCHES OF WATER T. Gaines *Successful Farming* v115 no11 p46 S 2017

Irrigation—Equipment & supplies—Evaluation

INNOVATION IN IRRIGATION T. Gaines *Successful Farming* v115 no2 p58 F 2017

Irrigation—India

HUMANITARIANS E. Gent, N. Byrnes et al color il *MIT Technology Review* v120 no5 p62 S/O 2017

Irritable colon

ASK JACKIE J. LONDON color *Good Housekeeping* v264 no5 p104 My 2017

The Gut Diaries K. Dold color *Women's Health* v13 no10 p78 D 2016

Irritable colon—Risk factors

Natural Solutions for IBS E. A. Kane cartoon *Better Nutrition* v79 no4 p28 Ap 2017

Irritable colon—Treatment

Are Your Bowels Irritable or Just Angry? D. Keating cartoon color *Maclean's* v129 no48/49 p78 D 5 2016

Foods to Soothe Digestive Woes [Cover story] *Tufts University Health & Nutrition Letter* v35 no1 p1 Mr 2017

Natural Solutions for IBS E. A. Kane cartoon *Better Nutrition* v79 no4 p28 Ap 2017

Problem Solved! [Cover story] R. LALIBERTE cartoon *Prevention* v68 no11 p18 N 2016

Irschick, Duncan

DIGITIZED MENAGERIE R. H. Shea color *National Geographic* v231 no5 p8 My 2017

FASTER, DEEPER, HIGHER, STRONGER: EVERY DAY IN THE WILD IS THE OLYMPICS N. HAMMERSCHLAG *Bio-Science* v66 no11 p1000 N 1 2016

Irvin, Doyle

Blisters, Beetles and British Columbia: Global ReLeaf in Canada *American Forests* v123 no1 p6 Wint/Spr 2017

Conservation Begins With Your Boots On The Ground *American Forests* v123 no2 p46 Summ 2017

Doubling Down on Urban Forests *American Forests* v123 no2 p7 Summ 2017

ONE TREE, MANY FUTURES *American Forests* v123 no3 p24 Fall 2017

Protecting One of America's Premier Wildernesses: American ReLeaf in Tahoe National Forest *American Forests* v123 no1 p7 Wint/Spr 2017

Irvin, Nick

LIFE: ***½ color *Art in America* v104 no10 p100 N 2016

IRVINE, HEATHER MAYER

AGONY—AND ECSTASY [Cover story] color *Runner's World* v52 no5 p17 Je 2017

Irvine, Mike

BEYOND THE KALE color *Sunset* v239 no4 p46 O 2017

THE NEW WINERY GARDEN color *Sunset* v239 no4 p42 O 2017

Your CHECKLIST color *Sunset* v239 no1 p58 Jl 2017

Your CHECKLIST color *Sunset* v239 no4 p50 O 2017

Irvine, William T. M.

Complete measurement of helicity and its dynamics in vortex tubes color diag graph *Science* v357 no6350 p487 Ag 4 2017

Irving, Blake

6 CEOs on How Business Can Do Better color *Time* v190 no13 p34 O 2 2017

How Did I Get Here? BLAKE IRVING bw color *Bloomberg Businessweek* no4497 p72 O 31 2016

Irving, Carolina

Bohemian Rhapsody M. OWENS color *Architectural Digest* no6 p42 Je 1 2017

IRVING, DAVID

SPECIAL Letters color *Nation* v303 no17 p8 O 24 2016

IRVING, JOHN

It Takes a Commune *New York Times Book Review* p9 F 5 2017

Irving, Kyrie, 1992-

BLOWN COVER T. Keith and S. Kwak color *Sports Illustrated* v127 no7 p22 S 4 2017

Rounding Error T. Keith color *Sports Illustrated* v126 no9 p23 Mr 27 2017

Irving, Washington, 1783-1859

Cleaning Up Christmas G. BOWLER cartoon *Walrus* v13 no10 p71 D 2016

The Cross Timbers J. GIFFORD *American Forests* v123 no1 p32 Wint/Spr 2017

What's in a Name? A. Morrow bw color *American History* v52 no3 p48 Ag 2017

Irwin, Douglas A.

The False Promise of Protectionism color *Foreign Affairs* v96 no3 p45 My/Je 2017

In a Trade War, No One Wins *Hoover Digest: Research & Opinion on Public Policy* no4 p22 Fall 2016

Irwin, Jaimey

THE CANADIANS WHO COULD S. Hamilton color *Dressage Today* v23 no8 p28 Ap 2017

Trust the Journey J. Mellace *Dressage Today* v23 no8 p10 Ap 2017

Irwin, Janice

Benefits of a Local Lumber Mill *Mother Earth News* no282 p83 Je/Jl 2017

Irwin, Jim

JIM IRWIN D. Pimentel bw color *Flying* v144 no2 p67 F 2017

Irwin, John T.

Back From Oblivion: A writer who refused to live in a world robbed of meaning *American Scholar* v86 no3 p119 Summ 2017

Darkness at Noon C. J. SCALIA bw *Weekly Standard* v22 no38 p33 Je 12 2017

Irwin, Julie

Ethical Consumerism Isn't Dead, It Just Needs Better Marketing *Harvard Business Review Digital Articles* p2 Ja 12 2015

Loyalty to a Leader Is Overrated, Even Dangerous *Harvard Business Review Digital Articles* p2 D 16 2014

Why Companies Are Blind to Child Labor *Harvard Business Review Digital Articles* p2 Ja 28 2016

Irwin, L. Gail

Blurring the lines color *Christian Century* v134 no3 p20 F 2017

Love that can't be shamed *Christian Century* v133 no24 p12 N 23 2016

Irwin, Levi

Turbines can use CO2 to cut CO2 diag *Science* v356 no6340 p805 My 26 2017

Irwin, P.

Seasonal exposure of carbon dioxide ice on the nucleus of comet 67P/Churyumov-Gerasimenko bibl bw graph *Science* v354 no6319 p1563 D 23 2016

Irwin, Robert, 1928-

THE LURE OF LACMA B. COLACELLO color *Vanity Fair* v58 no12 p138 D 2016

Irwin, Tina

THE CANADIANS WHO COULD S. Hamilton color *Dressage Today* v23 no8 p28 Ap 2017

Irwin Naturals (Company)

WEIGHT-LOSS SUPPORTERS color *Amazing Wellness* v9 no1 p42 Wint 2017

Is It Me...? (Music)

Gibbons Adds Soul to Jazz Standards G. Himes color *Downbeat* v84 no8 p20 Ag 2017

Is There Nowhere Else Where We Can Meet? (Short story)

IT CAME N. Gordimer *Lapham's Quarterly* v10 no3 p34 Summ 2017

Is This the Life We Really Want? (Music)

Roger Waters Returns to Rock K. GROW color *Rolling Stone* no1283 p11 Mr 23 2017

What to Stream color *Entertainment Weekly* no1468/1469 p102 Je 2-9 2017

Isaac, Bobby

The ghost of Bobby Isaac G. Stunkard color *Hot Rod* v70 no9 p62 S 2017

Isaac, Oscar, 1979-

HOUSE OF SHADOWS A. GREEN color *Vogue* v207 no7 p96 Jl 2017

Isaacman-Beck, Jesse

Glia put visual map in sync color *Science* v357 no6354 p867 S 1 2017

Isaacs, Jason, 1963-

Chills, Pills and Spills on Verbinski's Magic Mountain S. Zacharek color *Time* v189 no7/8 p109 F 27 2017

A STAR-FLEET IS BORN [Cover story] J. Hibberd color *Entertainment Weekly* no1476 p22 Ag 4 2017

Isaacs, Kate

4 Ways CEOs Can Conquer Short-Termism *Harvard Business Review Digital Articles* p2 F 24 2017

Isaacs, Nora

Have the time of your life color *Yoga Journal* p69 2017 Special Issue

peace of mind cartoon *Yoga Journal* p96 2017 Special Issue

SAGE MOVES FOR MEDITATION color *Yoga Journal* p54 2017 Special Issue

YOUR BRAIN ON MEDITATION color *Yoga Journal* p36 2017 Special Issue

Isaacson, Richard

I sometimes call my children by other family members' names S. Yeager cartoon *AARP: The Magazine* v60 no3A p18 Ap/My 2017

Isaacson, Walter

How Leonardo Made Mona Lisa Smile bw color *Atlantic* v320 no4 p50 N 2017

THE NEW ESTABLISHMENT 2017 bw color *Vanity Fair* v59 no11 p87 N 2017

Resistance Is Futile *New York Times Book Review* p1 Je 25 2017

THE SOUL IN THE MACHINE color *Vanity Fair* v59 no11 p110 N 2017

The Year in Reading [Cover story] *New York Times Book Review* p8 D 25 2016

Isaacson, Walter—Awards

ADL presents Torch awards to Isaacson, Suggs *Successful Farming* v115 no1 p14 Ja 2017

Isaakievskiĭ sobor (Saint Petersburg, Russia)

State museum or church? Russians debate future of iconic cathedral F. Weir color *Christian Century* v134 no7 p14 Mr 29 2017

Isabel Marant SA

Give Em the Boot bw color *Glamour* v115 no7 p100 Jl 2017

Isabelle, Jay

we asked you answered color *Cabin Living* p8 D 2016

Isackson, Noah

CHICAGOANS OF THE YEAR [Cover story] color *Chicago* v65 no12 p74 D 2016

Isacoff, Stuart

When the World Stopped to Listen: Van Cliburn's Cold War Triumph and Its Aftermath *Publishers Weekly* v263 no48 p58 N 28 2016

Isaiah (Biblical prophet)

Be the peace A. Camille il *U.S. Catholic* v81 no12 p47 D 2016

Isalska, Barbara

Emergence and spread of a human-transmissible multidrug-resistant nontuberculous mycobacterium bibl diag graph *Science* v354 no6313 p751 N 11 2016

Isamu Matsuyama

Gravity field of the Orientale basin from the Gravity Recovery and Interior Laboratory Mission bibl graph *Science* v354 no6311 p438 O 28 2016

Isar, P. G.

Observation of a large-scale anisotropy in the arrival directions of cosmic rays above 8 × 1018 eV *Science* v357 no6357 p1266 S 22 2017

Isbell, Jason, 1979-—Interviews

Hot Tracks: JASON ISBELL L. ROBINSON color *Vanity Fair* v59 no11 p76 N 2017

Q&A: Jason Isbell P. DOYLE color *Rolling Stone* no1293 p26 Ag 10 2017

ISBERG, ART

MAPPING MULEYS color *Outdoor Life* v224 no8 p18 O 2017

Ischinger, Wolfgang

Europe: The E.U. Can Emerge from 2017 Stronger, If It Survives color *Time* v188 no27-28 p24 D 26 2016

Isele, Klaus

Next-Gen Visualization J. FLASHMAN color *Climbing* no357 p16 N 2017

Isella, Andrea

Spiral density waves in a young protoplanetary disk bibl graph *Science* v353 no6307 p1519 S 30 2016

Isenberg, Daniel

Do Startups Really Create Lots of Good Jobs? *Harvard Business Review Digital Articles* p2 Je 6 2016

How Involved Should CEOs Be in Social Causes? *Harvard Business Review Digital Articles* p2 My 15 2015

Midsize Cities Are Entrepreneurship's Real Test color *Harvard Business Review Digital Articles* p2 Ja 24 2017

The Right Way to Plan an Innovation Tour *Harvard Business Review Digital Articles* p2 Jl 7 2015

Using Supply Chains to Grow Your Businesss *Harvard Business Review Digital Articles* p2 N 20 2015

Isenberg, Nancy

The Great White Nope J. Cowie color *Foreign Affairs* v95 no6 p147 N/D 2016

WHITE TRASH T. DEIGNAN color *America* v215 no12 p33 O 24 2016

Isenberg, Noah

We'll Always Have Casablanca: The Life, Legend, and Afterlife of Hollywood's Most Beloved Movie *Publishers Weekly* v263 no51 p139 D 12 2016

Isenberg, Noah—Interviews

Of World Wars and Cold Wars and Hollywood Classics: Noah Isenberg on We'll Always Have Casablanca: The Life, Legend, and Afterlife of Hollywood's Most Beloved Movie and Glenn

Frankel on High Noon: The Hollywood Blacklist and the Making of an American... R. Longo *Film Quarterly* v70 no3 p84 Spr 2017

Iserloh, Jennifer

All wrapped up color *Yoga Journal* no289 p68 F 2017

Chili fest color *Yoga Journal* no287 p64 N 2016

consider this *Yoga Journal* no293 p12 Ag 2017

Mindful meals color *Yoga Journal* no294 p38 S 2017

Roast onions color *Yoga Journal* no291 p34 My 2017

Summer-fresh pastas color *Yoga Journal* no293 p40 Ag 2017

Ishag, Daniel

A Would-Be Uber Rival's Ride to Nowhere A. Satariano and D. Hellier cartoon *Bloomberg Businessweek* no4501 p28 N 28 2016

Ishchenko, Andrii

Mechanism of transmembrane signaling by sensor histidine kinases color *Science* v356 no6342 p1043 Je 9 2017

Ishibashi, Kota

Holliday junction resolvases mediate chloroplast nucleoid segregation diag *Science* v356 no6338 p631 My 12 2017

Ishiguro, Kazuo, 1954-

For the Record color *Time* v190 no16/17 p6 O 23 2017

Knopf to Print 200,000 Copies of Nobel Winner Ishiguro's Works J. Maher and J. Milliot color *Publishers Weekly* v264 no41 p10 O 9 2017

Ishii, M.

Structural basis of the redox switches in the NAD+-reducing soluble [NiFe]-hydrogenase diag *Science* v357 no6354 p928 S 1 2017

ISHIYAMA, NORIKO

Unofficial Paths: Memories of Poston *Orion Magazine* v35 no4/5 p51 Jl-O 2016

Ishiyama, S.

Neural correlates of ticklishness in the rat somatosensory cortex bibl graph *Science* v354 no6313 p757 N 11 2016

Ishmael (Biblical figure)

CRY HAVOC Pseudo-Methodius *Lapham's Quarterly* v10 no3 p147 Summ 2017

ISHMAEL, GIGI

HOW TO MAKE THE SHARJAH INTERNATIONAL BOOK FAIR PROFESSIONAL PROGRAM & TRANSLATION GRANT REWARDING color *Publishers Weekly* v263 no43 p(Sp)14 O 24 2016

Ising model

A coherent Ising machine for 2000-node optimization problems Takahiro Inagaki, Yoshitaka Haribara et al bibl diag graph *Science* v354 no6312 p603 N 4 2016

A fully programmable 100-spin coherent Ising machine with all-to-all connections P. L. McMahon, A. Marandi et al bibl diag graph *Science* v354 no6312 p614 N 4 2016

Odd computer zips through knotty tasks A. Cho color *Science* v354 no6310 p269 O 21 2016

Iskarpatyoti, Jason A.

Reovirus infection triggers inflammatory responses to dietary antigens and development of celiac disease color diag *Science* v356 no6333 p44 Ap 7 2017

Islam

See also

Christian-Islam relations

Islamic law

Ummah (Islam)

Europe in Transition *American Conservative* v16 no2 p58 Mr/Ap 2017

NATIONAL GALLERY SAUDI ARABIA R. Griffiths *History Today* v67 no10 p78 O 2017

No hate, no fear W. Massey color *U.S. Catholic* v82 no4 p12 Ap 2017

Reformation 2.0 [Cover story] E. Simon color *Commonweal* v144 no17 p31 O 20 2017

Stop Listening to the Obamas and Merkels *USA Today Magazine* v145 no2863 p5 Ap 2017

Was the FIRST CRUSADE really a war against ISLAM? N. Merton *History Today* v67 no3 p11 Mr 2017

Wellsprings of Violence R. M. Gerecht *Hoover Digest: Research & Opinion on Public Policy* no4 p94 Fall 2016

WHO AWAITS THE MESSIAH MOST? MUSLIMS J. CASPER

cartoon *Christianity Today* v61 no1 p17 Ja/F 2017

Islam & politics

COMIX NATION J. Sorensen *Nation* v305 no1 p8 Jl 3 2017

The Nationalist Origins of Political Islam J. CESARI *Current History* v116 no786 p31 Ja 2017

Islam—Congresses

Engaging with Our Trials and Tribulations A. KARIM *Islamic Horizons* v46 no1 p19 Ja/F 2017

Islam—History

ARAB CONQUESTS and SASANIAN IRAN K. Rezakhani *History Today* v67 no4 p28 Ap 2017

Islamic art & symbolism

SPANISH & ART DECO tile FANTASY P. POORE color *Arts & Crafts Homes & the Revival* v12 no4 p28 Fall 2017

Islamic art & symbolism—Exhibitions

Exhibit at Smithsonian captures art of the Qur'an L. Markoe color *Christian Century* v133 no24 p18 N 23 2016

Salaam to the Keir Collection in Dallas color *Magazine Antiques* v184 no3 p32 My/Je 2017

Islamic civilization

The Life of Marshall Hodgson L. Kiesling color *New York Times Magazine* p30 O 9 2016

Islamic clothing & dress

See also

Hijab (Islamic clothing)

There's More to Haya Than the Hijab: To understand hijab as an act of worship, it is first crucial to consider other common acts of worship and see the correlation between them S. MEHDI *Islamic Horizons* v46 no4 p38 Jl/Ag 2017

Islamic clothing & dress—Government policy

Chancellor Angela Merkel of Germany calls for a ban of burqas as election nears D. Iaconangelo and J. Bhatti *Christian Century* v134 no1 p15 Ja 4 2017

Islamic countries—Congresses

WE ARE NOT HERE TO LECTURE D. TRUMP *Vital Speeches of the Day* v83 no7 p190 Jl 2017

Islamic education

Adding Value to Learning [Cover story] K. JAMIL *Islamic Horizons* v46 no2 p28 Mr/Ap 2017

Deepening Students' Understanding of the Qur'anic Text [Cover story] P. SALAHUDDIN *Islamic Horizons* v46 no2 p34 Mr/Ap 2017

Preparing the Brave *Islamic Horizons* v46 no2 p6 Mr/Ap 2017

Teaching Social Justice at Islamic Schools [Cover story] A. YILDIZ-ODEH and S. AZMAT *Islamic Horizons* v46 no2 p30 Mr/Ap 2017

Why Can't They All be Doctors? [Cover story] K. KEYWORTH and F. SHAMMA *Islamic Horizons* v46 no2 p22 Mr/Ap 2017

Islamic education—Congresses

A Focus on the Literary and Creative Arts Curricula [Cover story] S. KHAN *Islamic Horizons* v46 no2 p29 Mr/Ap 2017

Rejuvenation through Nature [Cover story] FAWZIA MAI TUNG *Islamic Horizons* v46 no2 p36 Mr/Ap 2017

Islamic Empire—History

Islam's forgotten scholars A. Azad *History Today* v66 no10 p24 O 2016

Islamic fundamentalism

The Growing Lone Wolf Threat from ISIS and Other Players M. E. NATHANSON *USA Today Magazine* v145 no2860 p48 Ja 2017

Terror's Afterlife: Do suicide bombers think their victims are headed to paradise as well? B. Challman *Humanist* v77 no4 p6 Jl/Ag 2017

Islamic fundamentalists

See also

Taliban

Islamic law

Tired of Halal Chicken? Try the Eyeshadow L. Colby color *Bloomberg Businessweek* no4505 p24 D 26 2016

THE TRUMP CONSPIRACY, EXPLAINED *In These Times* v41 no8 p32 Ag 2017

The Unbreakable Relationship M. H. BAWANY, A. MILHAN et al *Islamic Horizons* v45 no6 p48 N/D 2016

What the Burqini Ban Reveals N. GARDELS *NPQ: New Perspectives Quarterly* v33 no4 p28 O 2016

Islamic law—Indonesia

On Mecca's Front Porch D. Pinault color *Commonweal* v144 no7 p8 Ap 14 2017

Islamic leadership

IN MEMORIAM *Islamic Horizons* v46 no1 p41 Ja/F 2017

Islamic learning & scholarship

Young Achievers *Islamic Horizons* v46 no4 p14 Jl/Ag 2017

Islamic Society of North America

Healthy Mosques Hold the Future: ISNA teams up with ISPU to help make mosques welcoming, inclusive and dynamic I. BAG-BY *Islamic Horizons* v46 no3 p36 My/Je 2017

MUSLIM-CHRISTIAN DIALOGUE *Islamic Horizons* v46 no3 p10 My/Je 2017

The Power of Faith: Muslim Houstonians welcome ISNA with flair S. ESSA *Islamic Horizons* v46 no3 p20 My/Je 2017

The Stage Sets for Convention 2017: In selecting the theme, the ISNA leadership considered the situation as challenges facing Muslims intensify B. Saleem *Islamic Horizons* v46 no3 p18 My/Je 2017

Islamic Society of North America—Congresses

Convention 2017 *Islamic Horizons* v46 no2 p16 Mr/Ap 2017

Harnessing the Power of Faith F. M. KHATRI *Islamic Horizons* v46 no2 p19 Mr/Ap 2017

Hope & Guidance through the Quran: The ISNA convention will show attendees how to apply the Quran's lessons today O. ABDUL-SALAAM *Islamic Horizons* v46 no4 p26 Jl/Ag 2017

Interfaith Understanding *Islamic Horizons* v45 no6 p21 N/D 2016

Islamic Schools for a Changing World: Are Islamic schools preparing their students to function effectively in a rapidly changing world? F. M. KHATRI *Islamic Horizons* v46 no4 p24 Jl/Ag 2017

Navigating Challenges and Seizing Opportunities S. NAGEEB and M. D. A. NIEMI *Islamic Horizons* v45 no6 p16 N/D 2016

On the Sidelines & More *Islamic Horizons* v45 no6 p18 N/D 2016

Preventing Radicalization A. KANJI *Islamic Horizons* v46 no2 p18 Mr/Ap 2017

ST. LOUIS SHINES POWER OF FAITH *Islamic Horizons* v46 no4 p9 Jl/Ag 2017

Striving for Justice: The Prophetic Way of Life *Islamic Horizons* v46 no2 p20 Mr/Ap 2017

Striving for Quality Mosques *Islamic Horizons* v46 no1 p18 Ja/F 2017

Islamic Society of North America—Officials & employees

Shifting Gears J. WILLOUGHBY *Islamic Horizons* v46 no2 p14 Mr/Ap 2017

Islamic State (Organization)

After the Bombs Have Fallen R. Ratnesar, C. Simpson et al color *Bloomberg Businessweek* no4531 p34 Jl 24 2017

AFTER THE ISLAMIC STATE R. WRIGHT cartoon *New Yorker* v92 no41 p30 D 12 2016

AMERICAN JIHADI G. Wood cartoon color *Atlantic* v319 no2 p74 Mr 2017

Are We Winning the Battle Against Terrorism? T. MOCKAITIS and J. ALTERMAN *New York Times Upfront* v149 no7 p22 Ja 9 2017

THE AVENGERS OF MOSUL L. MOGELSON bw cartoon map *New Yorker* v92 no48 p34 F 6 2017

BAD NEWS color *Maclean's* v129 no40 p9 O 10 2016

The Battle for Mosul: A Humanitarian Disaster B. SMITH color *Progressive* v81 no7 p12 O/N 2017

Beating ISIS-and Saving Iraq M. Thompson color *Time* v188 no16/17 p32 O 24 2016

Black death A. R. KHAN color *Maclean's* v129 no48/49 p28 D 5 2016

Brave Hearts J. DI GIOVANNI color *Vogue* v206 no11 p94 N 2016

Cover *Time* v190 no4 pC1 Jl 24 2017

Cyber-Extremism: Isis and the Power of Social Media I. Awan chart color *Society* v54 no2 p138 Ap 2017

A Deadly New Front for ISIS J. Hincks and M. Manos color map *Time* v190 no1 p36 Jl 3 2017

ESCAPE FROM THE CALIPHATE J. Percy *Harper's Magazine* v333 no1998 p62 N 2016

The Fighters In the Battle for Mosul J. Malsin color *Time* v188 no18 p10 O 31 2016

Fight for Mosul Drags On While Displaced Numbers Grow K. CLARKE *America* v216 no1 p8 Ja 2 2017

General Mattis Advances on Washington J. Mattis *Hoover Digest: Research & Opinion on Public Policy* no1 p84 Wint 2017

GOOD NEWS color *Maclean's* v129 no42 p8 O 24 2016

Greetings from ISIS M. D. Silber *Commentary* v140 no2 p13 S 2015

How to Beat ISIS J. COLE *Nation* v304 no7 p5 Mr 6 2017

How to Defeat ISIS L. Smith *Weekly Standard* v22 no29 p8 Ap 3 2017

'I came to fight for all Iraqis' C. MACDIARMID color *Maclean's* v129 no44 p32 N 7 2016

In Hock to Bad History J. Wakeley *History Today* v66 no11 p3 N 2016

Iraq Takes on ISIS J. Malsin and M. Thompson color map *Time* v188 no19 p32 N 7 2016

Iraq: The Terrible Battle for Mosul J. Hammer bw map *New York Review of Books* v63 no17 p24 N 10 2016

LIFE AFTER ISIS J. Verini color map *National Geographic* v231 no4 p96 Ap 2017

Life under ISIS [Cover story] A. R. KHAN color *Maclean's* v129 no51/52 p22 D 26 2016

Life With ISIS & After ISIS E. Trieb color *Glamour* no8 p117 Ag 2017

Lightbox color *Time* v188 no18 p16 O 31 2016

Lightbox I. Bremmer color *Time* v190 no4 p14 Jl 24 2017

Lightbox J. Malsin color *Time* v189 no15 p14 Ap 24 2017

THE LIVING AND THE DEAD J. Verini *New York Times Magazine* p36 Jl 23 2017

LOADED QUESTIONS *Harper's Magazine* v334 no2000 p25 Ja 2017

Medics on a mission A. R. KHAN color *Maclean's* v130 no3 p39 Ap 2017

The Middle East *New York Times Upfront* p2 S 18 2017 Supplement

A Military in Need M. Eaglen and G. Schmitt color *Weekly Standard* v22 no32 p9 My 1 2017

Mission aims to salvage what's left of Nimrud J. Couzin-Frankel color map *Science* v357 no6358 p1340 S 29 2017

THE MOST DANGEROUS ARMY IN IRAQ A. R. KHAN color *Maclean's* no1 p44 F 17 2017

Nadia MURAD E. Griswold color *Glamour* v114 no12 p206 D 2016

Nineveh Christians Await Outcome Of Mosul Offensive Against ISIS color *America* v215 no14 p8 N 7 2016

Obama's JV Jibe Still Stings E. PEPPERS *USA Today Magazine* v145 no2864 p47 My 2017

The Other Forever War J. Goldsmith and M. C. Waxman *Hoover Digest: Research & Opinion on Public Policy* no1 p92 Wint 2017

THE PEACE PRIZE WINNER WHO WAGED WAR E. KRAYEWSKI cartoon *Reason* v48 no9 p14 F 2017

Postcard from the EDGE S. HANSEN color *Vogue* v207 no1 p26 Ja 2017

The Qatar Rift Is the Middle East's 'Trump Effect' In Action I. Bremmer color *Time* v189 no23 p14 Je 19 2017

A Second Chance in Iraq D. FRENCH color *National Review* v68 no21 p26 N 21 2016

Syria, slums, and health security S. Berkley color *Science* v356 no6336 p353 Ap 28 2017

Tiny Ruins J. Berlin color *National Geographic* v231 no4 p124 Ap 2017

Uneasy on the Mosul front A. R. KHAN color *Maclean's* v129 no47 p40 N 28 2016

We Got Lucky...This Time T. JOSCELYN *Weekly Standard* v22 no4 p8 O 3 2016

Islamic State (Organization)—History

A Legacy in Ruins: What now for Iraq's Mosul Museum, recently liberated from ISIS? C. OTTEN *American Scholar* v86 no3 p99 Summ 2017

Islamic State (Organization)—History—21st century

The Beginning of the End J. Malsin color map *Time* v189 no15 p30 Ap 24 2017

Islamic Cultural Centre of Quebec City Shooting, Quebec, Quebec (Province), 2017

A moment of painful truth M. CAMPBELL, A. HUTCHINS et al color *Maclean's* v130 no2 p18 Mr 2017

More than just America's foil *Maclean's* v130 no2 p4 Mr 2017

Islamists

Germany cracks down on groups accused of recruiting terrorists A. Hoover *Christian Century* v133 no26 p17 D 21 2016

In Hock to Bad History J. Wakeley *History Today* v66 no11 p3 N 2016

RADICAL AMBITION T. C. Williams *New York Times Magazine* p24 Ap 2 2017

Islamization

French Catholics' political awakening color *Christian Century* v134 no8 p1 Ap 12 2017

Islamophobia

Advice for Young Muslims O. S. Ghobash color *Foreign Affairs* v96 no1 p96 Ja/F 2017

Expelling Islamophobia S. McCOLLUM *Education Digest* v82 no8 p14 Ap 2017

Guiding the Youth Amidst Islamophobia N. ALI *Islamic Horizons* v45 no6 p40 N/D 2016

Islamophobia in Focus E. ABDELKADER *Islamic Horizons* v46 no1 p32 Ja/F 2017

Muslim cleric to lead national association of chaplains in higher ed C. Kennel-Shank *Christian Century* v134 no8 p1 Ap 12 2017

Muslims on the Front Lines: Countering violent Islamophobia with knowledge and organizing I. QAIYIM *Islamic Horizons* v46 no4 p44 Jl/Ag 2017

No Place for Islamophobia in America: Islamophobia has its roots in the history of Western Christianity J. S. HARRIS *Islamic Horizons* v46 no3 p30 My/Je 2017

Standing against Islamophobia in California School Curricula M. THANGE *Islamic Horizons* v45 no6 p32 N/D 2016

The terrorists on the right S. GILMORE color *Maclean's* v130 no9 p12 O 2017

"The Only Good Muslim Is a Dead Muslim" T. GENOWAYS color *New Republic* v248 no6 p30 Je 2017

What Catholics owe their Muslim brothers and sisters J. Denari Duffner *America* v216 no3 p10 F 6 2017

Islamophobia—Social aspects

Denial of a nation M. WILLIAMS chart color *Maclean's* v130 no6 p18 Jl 2017

Islam—Relations—Judaism

Jews and Muslims partner in efforts to defend religious minorities J. Mendoza *Christian Century* v134 no2 p17 Ja 18 2017

Islam—Societies, etc.

Mosque wins $3.25 million in legal settlement from New Jersey township L. Markoe *Christian Century* v134 no14 p16 Jl 5 2017

Islam—Study & teaching

Filling the Void in Spanish-language Islamic Material W. DÍAZ *Islamic Horizons* v46 no1 p40 Ja/F 2017

Islam—United States

White Women and the Specter of Islam R. ZAKARIA color il *Nation* v305 no5 p20 Ag 28 2017

Island gray fox

Tree-Climbing Foxes and Other Success Stories K. R. FAULKNER and C. Graham *Natural History* v125 no2 p18 F 2017

Island life

in harmony L. WATERMAN color *Architectural Digest* v74 no7 p52 Jl 2017

Island Moving Co.

The 2017 Jobs Guide *Dance Magazine* v91 no3 p54 Mr 2017

Islands

See also

Coral reefs & islands

The Garden of the Great Spirit: A Photo Essay of the Thousand Islands C. Murray *New York State Conservationist* v72 no1 p2 Ag 2017

ISLANDS color *Conde Nast Traveler* v52 no10 p96 N 2017

The Magic of Maui: Turn your summer vacation into a wellness retreat on this laid-back Hawaiian isle R. WALLWORK color *Tennis* v53 no5 p22 S/O 2017

Manitoulin Island F. Bagley color *Sail* v48 no6 p43 Je 2017

Tourism: Committed to Preserving Life below Water T. Rifai *UN Chronicle* v54 no1/2 p1 2017

Islands of the Pacific—Environmental conditions

Cleanup on Isle Nine J. Greenspan color *Scientific American* v315 no3 p20 S 2016

Islands of the South China Sea

See also

Spratly Islands

Islands of the South China Sea—History

Shadow on the South China Sea B. Hayton *History Today* v66 no10 p3 O 2016

Islands—California

See also

Santa Catalina Island (Calif.)

Santa Catalina Island Z. Prochazka color *Sail* v48 no6 p42 Je 2017

Islands—Florida

See also

Florida Keys (Fla.)

The Dry Tortugas M. Doyle and D. Doyle color *Sail* v48 no6 p40 Je 2017

Islands—Indonesia

CURSED LAND color *Surfer* v57 no11 p72 D 2016

Islands—Louisiana

Swimming with Bacteria D. Lutz color *New Orleans Magazine* v51 no8 p34 Je 2017

Islands—Maine

Mount Desert Island T. Egan color *Sail* v48 no6 p38 Je 2017

Islands—Maldives

the Best Beaches for Black Women B. Atufunwa color *Essence* v48 no3 p94 Jl 2017

Islands—Mauritius

Forgotten Island Of Santosha M. WARSHAW bw color *Surfer* v58 no2 p30 My 2017

Islands—Scotland

A DANGEROUS ISLAND [Cover story] J. URBANUS color *Archaeology* v70 no4 p14 Je-Ag 2017

Islands—Washington (State)

See also

Bainbridge Island (Wash.)

WILDLIFE ADVENTURES AT EAGLE HARBOR:FIND AN UNTOUCHED ISLAND THAT IS A HIKER'S PARADISE D. HISLOP *Sea Magazine* v109 no5 pPNW-1 My 2017

Islas, Indira

'The Only Way We Can Fight Back Is to Excel' D. Russakoff color *New York Times Magazine* p36 Ja 29 2017

Isle of Man

Out of Place S. BLACK *Natural History* v125 no2 p48 F 2017

Ism Racing (Company)

ISM PL 1.0 S. Yeager color *Bicycling* v58 no6 p68 Jl 2017

Ismailites—India

IT HAPPENS HERE T. Raja color *Mother Jones* v42 no4 p13 Jl/Ag 2017

Isner, John

Pet Project *Tennis* v52 no6 p66 N/D 2016

ISOKAUPPILA, TERO

5 amazing mushrooms FOR WHOLE-BODY HEALTH color *Better Nutrition* v79 no9 p53 S 2017

Isolation (Philosophy)

LIVING BY The Word A. H. K. Apple *Christian Century* v134 no10 p25 My 10 2017

What it means to belong A. Chunilall color *Walrus* v14 no9 p12 N 2017

Isometric exercise

Brace Yourself for Big Gains N. PLISKE cartoon *Men's Health* v32 no4 p52 My 2017

Isopoda

Deep Dive L. SCHLEY color *Discover* v38 no4 p14 My 2017

Isotopes

Moon formation idea takes a violent turn color *Astronomy* v45 no1 p12 Ja 2017

Quantum and isotope effects in lithium metal G. J. Ackland, M. Dunuwille et al color diag graph *Science* v356 no6344 p1254 Je 23 2017

Isoya, Junichi

Nanoscale nuclear magnetic resonance with chemical resolution diag *Science* v357 no6346 p67 Jl 7 2017

ISP (Computer program language)

How to Win at Wi-Fi J. SCIACCA color *Sound & Vision* v82 no4 p23 My 2017

Ispahani, Farahnaz

Purifying the Land of the Pure: A History of Pakistan's Religious Minorities A. J. Nathan *Foreign Affairs* v96 no6 p171 N/D 2017

iSpy (Music)

JUKEBOX JURY SONG OF THE SUMMER EDITION N. Feeney color *Entertainment Weekly* no1467 p38 My 26 2017

KYLE N. Feeney color *Entertainment Weekly* no1462 p61 Ap 21 2017

Israel

Defending the State M. Wolfish and J. Blankfort *Commentary* v140 no2 p11 S 2015

HOT NOT T. Keith color *Sports Illustrated* v126 no8 p24 Mr 20 2017

Israel, Abay

Radial Revolution L. D. JOHNSON color *Ebony* v72 no8 p73 Je 2017

Israel, Gian Luca

An accreting pulsar with extreme properties drives an ultraluminous x-ray source in NGC 5907 bibl chart graph *Science* v355 no6327 p817 F 24 2017

THE BRIGHTEST, MOST DISTANT PULSAR A. Klesman color *Astronomy* v45 no6 p12 Je 2017

Israel, Harold

SALVATION K. ARMSTRONG *Smithsonian* v47 no9 p70 Ja/F 2017

Israel, Jonathan

The Expanding Blaze: How the American Revolution Ignited the World, 1775-1848 *Publishers Weekly* v264 no30 p53 Jl 24 2017

Israel. Keneset

People M. Jaffe-Hoffman *Christian Century* v133 no24 p21 N 23 2016

Israel—Antiquities

ARTIFACT J. A. LOBELL color *Archaeology* v70 no2 p68 Mr/Ap 2017

Israel-Arab War, 1967

THE IRON CURTAIN TORN BY ISRAEL G. Laron *History Today* v67 no5 p36 My 2017

The Six-Day War at 50 D. PRYCE-JONES *National Review* v69 no11 p17 Je 12 2017

Israel-Arab War, 1967—Occupied territories

See also

Israeli settlements (Occupied territories)

Israel—Description & travel

FRESH START IN THE OLD CITY L. J. Wertheim color *Sports Illustrated* v126 no2 p46 Ja 16 2017

Israel—Foreign relations

Bibi the Strategist: A close look at Benjamin Netanyahu's foreign policy reveals an underappreciated and misunderstood record of accomplishment L. Berman *Commentary* v142 no2 p33 S 2016

Israel—Foreign relations—Palestine

The Department of Pay-for-Slay *Commentary* v143 no4 p29 Ap 2017

Israel—Foreign relations—Palestine—History

Shimon Peres Could Change. Can the Israelis and the Palestinians? K. Vick color *Time* v188 no14 p7 O 10 2016

Israel—Foreign relations—United States

An Ally Betrayed color *National Review* v69 no1 p14 Ja 23 2017

The Maligning Of Israel D. PRYCE-JONES *National Review* v69 no1 p20 Ja 23 2017

Israel—Foreign relations—United States—History—21st century

The U.S. Should Form a Closer Military Alliance With Israel A. J. Stavridis color *Time* v189 no3 p20 Ja 16 2017

Israeli art—Exhibitions

ART *New Yorker* v92 no44 p8 Ja 9 2017

Israeli authors

By the Book A. Oz *New York Times Book Review* p8 N 27 2016

Israeli settlements (Occupied territories)

CLEANING UP OBAMA'S FOREIGN POLICY MESS A. GREENWALD *Commentary* v142 no4 p15 N 2016

Israeli Settlements Are Illegal. Equipping Their Guards Is Tax-Deductible A. KANE *In These Times* v41 no3 p28 Mr 2017

Israeli West Bank Barrier

Room With a View (of a Wall and Barbed Wire) J. Ferziger and F. Hodali color *Bloomberg Businessweek* no4516 p14 Mr 27 2017

Israelis

Assessing Bibi S. CHESTER *Commentary* v142 no4 p14 N 2016

Protecting Palestine R. M. GERECHT color *Weekly Standard* v22 no18 p30 Ja 16 2017

Israelis—Social conditions

HOUSE HUNTERS TRANSNATIONAL J. Levin and S. Treleaven *Harper's Magazine* v334 no2000 p48 Ja 2017

Israel—Politics & government

How Israel Took a Toy and Made It a High-Tech Weapon [Cover story] Y. KATZ and A. BOHBOT *Commentary* v143 no1 p19 Ja 2017

Is Israeli Democracy in Danger? D. WAXMAN *Current History* v115 no785 p360 D 2016

A New Strategy for Israeli Victory D. PIPES *Commentary* v143 no1 p13 Ja 2017

Israel—Politics & government—1993-

Netanyahu, the Almost-American: Bibi's unique feel for the United States hasn't always paid off S. Mandel *Commentary* v142 no2 p40 S 2016

Israel—Social conditions—21st century

Occupational Hazards F. G. MOHAMED *American Scholar* v86 no4 p6 Aut 2017

Israel—Social life & customs

Team Israel 2017-17 J. Fuchs and T. Keith color *Sports Illustrated* v126 no9 p26 Mr 27 2017

ISSA, ALI

THIS MONTH: The U.S. Is Bombing at Least Six Countries. How Can the Anti-War Movement Step Up? *In These Times* v41 no10 p14 O 2017

Issa, Darrell, 1953-

The Fight of His Life M. FLEMING color *Weekly Standard* v22 no7 p15 O 24 2016

Issenberg, Sasha

PAID FOR BY THE SAME PEOPLE WHO PAID FOR THE VIDEO YOU'RE ABOUT TO WATCH color *Bloomberg Businessweek* no4497 p26 O 31 2016

THE TRUMP MACHINE IS BUILT TO LAST. BIGLY color map *Bloomberg Businessweek* no4497 p44 O 31 2016

Trump's Path To Victory color *Bloomberg Businessweek* no4499 p20 N 14 2016

Isserman, Maurice

HIGHER GROUND G. Long color *American History* v52 no4 p71 O 2017

Issler, Lutz

Posthole color *Powder* v45 no3 p148 N 2016

Issler, Orna

Early life stress confers lifelong stress susceptibility in mice via ventral tegmental area OTX2 diag *Science* v356 no6343 p1185 Je 16 2017

Issues management (Public relations)

When Public Opinion Shifts, How Should Your Company Respond? P. G. Audia *Harvard Business Review Digital Articles* p2 S 29 2015

Istanbul Nightclub Shooting, Istanbul, Turkey, 2017

Lightbox J. Malsin color *Time* v189 no3 p12 Ja 16 2017

Istanbul (Turkey)—Buildings, structures, etc.

High Times: Skyscrapers continue to capture the imagination of architects, who are finding more freedom to innovate and enliven the skylines of our cities bw color *Architectural Record* v205 no5 p20 My 2017

The Ripple Effect: Concealing a straightforward office tower within, a curvilinear exterior commands attention, S. MORENO color map *Architectural Record* v205 no5 p98 My 2017

Istomin, Kirill

A DARLING SITTING ROOM color *House Beautiful* v159 no1 p38 F 2017

Istomina, Tatiana

Clearing color *Art in America* v105 no1 p81 Ja 2017

DAVID DIAO color *Art in America* v105 no5 p128 My 2017

KAARI UPSON color *Art in America* p123 O 2017

KERRY JAMES MARSHALL cartoon *Art in America* v105 no4 p109 Ap 2017

SADIE BENNING *Art in America* v104 no9 p153 O 2016

iStorage Ltd.

DISKASHUR PRO2: CROSS-PLATFORM, MAXIMUM SECURITY PORTABLE HARD DRIVE J. R. BOOKWALTER color *Macworld - Digital Edition* v34 no8 p44 Ag 2017

Istvan, Zoltan

THE BIONIC CANDIDATE A. Marantz cartoon *New Yorker* v92 no37 p34 N 14 2016

S 2017
Staying On Message With the First Lady *Los Angeles Magazine* p19 Ja 2017
WHEN SEEING IS FEELING *Los Angeles Magazine* p98 F 2017

Ito, Toyo, 1941-
Grand Opera N. R. POLLOCK color diag *Architectural Record* v204 no12 p60 D 2016

ITOCHU Corp.
Traditional Values Bring Tectonic Shift to Trading Sector M. Foster and D. W. Russell color *Forbes* v199 no1 p(Sp)3 Ja 24 2017

Itoh, K.
Crystallization and vitrification of electrons in a glass-forming charge liquid bw *Science* v357 no6358 p1381 S 29 2017

Itokawa (Asteroid)
Interplanetary sand traps T. Shinbrot *Physics Today* v70 no8 p78 Ag 2017

It's a Summer Day (Short story)
It's a Summer Day A. S. Greer color *New Yorker* v93 no17 p54 Je 19 2017

It's a Wonderful Life (Theatrical production)
It's a Wonderful Life G. Barnett *Opera News* v81 no9 p38 Mr 2017

It's Complicated (Film)
CLAUDIA O'DOHERTY: LOVES OF MY LIFE A. Bacle color *Entertainment Weekly* no1457/1458 p81 Mr 17 2017

It's Hard (Music)
NIGHT LIFE *New Yorker* v92 no43 p11 Ja 2 2017

It's the World Committing Suicide Said One Mom (Poem)
It's the World Committing Suicide Said One Mom R. ZUCKER *Nation* v304 no3 p30 Ja 30 2017

It's a Mad, Mad, Mad, Mad World (Film)
NEWLY AVAILABLE MOVIES M. FELL *TV Guide* v65 no13 p46 Mr 20 2017

It's the Great Pumpkin, Charlie Brown (TV program)
The Great Pumpkin Turns 50! D. Holbrook cartoon *TV Guide* v64 no42 p10 O 10 2016

Ittner, Arne
Site-specific phosphorylation of tau inhibits amyloid-β toxicity in Alzheimer's mice bibl graph *Science* v354 no6314 p904 N 18 2016

Ittner, Lars M.
Site-specific phosphorylation of tau inhibits amyloid-β toxicity in Alzheimer's mice bibl graph *Science* v354 no6314 p904 N 18 2016

Ittoop, Elisheba
Balancing Audio and Life V. Olivieri *Stage Directions* v30 no3 p10 Mr 2017

iTunes (Digital music program)
Apple's confusing method of device authorization and association K. McELHEARN bw color *Macworld - Digital Edition* v34 no6 p14 Je 2017
Ask the iTunes Guy: A look at new features in iTunes 12.6 K. McELHEARN cartoon color *Macworld - Digital Edition* v34 no4 p101 My 2017
Ask the iTunes Guy: iTunes libraries on the new MacBook Pro K. MCELHEARN cartoon color *Macworld - Digital Edition* p116 Mr 2017
Ask the iTunes Guy K. McElhearn cartoon diag *Macworld - Digital Edition* p108 Ap 2017
The difference between backing up an iPhone to iCloud and iTunes J. BATTERSBY cartoon color *Macworld - Digital Edition* v33 no11 p123 N 2016
Feature: Ask the iTunes Guy K. McElhearn cartoon color *Macworld - Digital Edition* p102 Ja 2017
iTunes needs to go (well, the name, anyway) D. MOREN color *Macworld - Digital Edition* v34 no6 p123 Je 2017
No Internet connection? Be prepared for iTunes to drive you crazy K. MCELHEARN color *Macworld - Digital Edition* p113 Mr 2017

Itzkoff, Dave
Abbi Jacobson Didn't Expect Hillary to Come On Her Show *New York Times Magazine* p54 O 23 2016
Gene Luen Yang Thinks Superheroes Are For Everyone *New York Times Magazine* p66 N 20 2016
Iggy Pop Traded In His Sports Car color *New York Times Magazine* p70 D 4 2016

Phillipa Soo Doesn't Leave It All Onstage *New York Times Magazine* p54 Ap 2 2017

Itzkovitz, Shalev
Global mRNA polarization regulates translation efficiency in the intestinal epithelium diag *Science* v357 no6357 p1299 S 22 2017

IUPUI (Campus)
IUPUI T. KIRTS *Indianapolis Monthly* v40 no4 p40 D 2016

Ivanchev, Yavor
Does bankruptcy hurt an individual's ability to be hired or borrow money? *Monthly Labor Review* p1 My 2017
The future of oil prices: a break with the past? *Monthly Labor Review* p1 Jl 2017
Reducing barriers of occupational licensing: insights from nursing *Monthly Labor Review* p1 D 2016

Ivanko, John
Fresh, Homemade SALAD DRESSINGS *Mother Earth News* no281 p36 Ap/My 2017

Ivanov, Vladimir V.
Greater role for Atlantic inflows on sea-ice loss in the Eurasian Basin of the Arctic Ocean chart diag graph *Science* v356 no6335 p285 Ap 21 2017

Ivanova, Natalia N.
Giant viruses with an expanded complement of translation system components diag *Science* v356 no6333 p82 Ap 7 2017

Ivany, Christopher G.
How the U.S. Army Personalized Its Mental Health Care *Harvard Business Review Digital Articles* p2 D 7 2016

Ivascyn, Dan
Dan Ivascyn J. Gittelsohn *Bloomberg Businessweek* no4531 p72 Jl 24 2017

Ive, Jonathan, 1967-
One More Thing S. Levy bw color *Wired* v25 no6 p52 Je 2017

Iverson, Allen, 1975-
Allen IVERSON [Cover story] L. Jenkins color *Sports Illustrated* v127 no1 p32 Jl 3 2017

Iverson, E. B.
Observation of coherent elastic neutrino-nucleus scattering diag *Science* v357 no6356 p1123 S 15 2017

Iverson, Ellen
DRY by DESIGN K. BARNES *Better Homes & Gardens* v95 no1 pZ1 Ja 2017

IVERSON, SARA J.
Envisioning the Future of Aquatic Animal Tracking: Technology, Science, and Application *BioScience* v67 no10 p884 O 2017

Ives, Lucy
Impossible Views of the World *Publishers Weekly* v264 no24 p36 Je 12 2017
Mystery at the Museum: A smart debut about a disappearance in the art world S. COLL *New York Times Book Review* p18 Ag 20 2017
THE REPATRIATION OF F$ color *Art in America* v105 no8 p94 S 2017

IVES, MIKE
A MATTER OF FAITH *Sierra* v101 no6 p40 N/D 2016

Ives, Susanna
How to Impress a Marquess *Publishers Weekly* v263 no39 p72 S 26 2016

Ivester, Roger
FROM OUR READERS *Sky & Telescope* v133 no1 p6 Ja 2017

Ivey, Kimberly Smith
GROWING INTERESTS cartoon *Magazine Antiques* v184 no1 p118 Ja/F 2017

Ivinskaya, Olga
A Grand Passion A. Pasternak bw color *Vogue* v206 no12 p120 D 2016

Ivory
Hope for Elephants *Earth Island Journal* v32 no1 p9 Spr 2017
Illegal wildlife trade: Look to the elephants G. Wittemyer bibl *Science* v353 no6307 p1507 S 30 2016
WE ARE ALLIES IN EARTH'S CARE G. E. Knell *National Geographic* v230 no6 pc7 D 2016

Ivory, James
MERCHANT'S IVORY: James Ivory sails on without his partner Ismail Merchant, lovingly restoring the films that were their lives's work, like the newly re-released Maurice T. RING color

Advocate no1091 p28 Je/Jl 2017

Ivory, James—Interviews

JAMES IVORY C. BOLLEN *Interview* v47 no3 p94 My 2017

Ivory, Tom

READER COMMENTS *America* v216 no3 p7 F 6 2017

Ivory industry

The Ivory Trade Loses Its Biggest Player K. Samuelson color *Time* v189 no3 p6 Ja 16 2017

Ivory—Research

The Elephant Detective E. KOLBERT *Smithsonian* v47 no9 p29 Ja/F 2017

IWANIEC, DAVID

Incorporating Sociocultural Phenomena into Ecosystem-Service Valuation: The Importance of Critical Pluralism *BioScience* v67 no3 p233 Mr 2017

Iwasaki, Akiko

Stay warm to beat a cold color *Redbook* p85 F 2017

Iwasaki, Augusta

St. Jacques and Iwasaki Claim Hunterdon Cup Titles T. Booker *In Stride* v12 no5 p42 S 2017

Iwasaki, Hiroshi

Holliday junction resolvases mediate chloroplast nucleoid segregation diag *Science* v356 no6338 p631 My 12 2017

iWeiss (Company)

iWeiss - Offering More Than You Might Know *Stage Directions* v30 no3 p53 Mr 2017

Iyaituk, Mattiusi

Shape Shifters S. Madwar color *Walrus* v14 no6 p75 Jl/Ag 2017

Iyamah, Dumebi—Interviews

CULTURAL WAVES J. Amay color *Ebony* v72 no9 p40 Jl/Ag 2017

Iyengar, Rishi

The Killing Season Inside Philippine President Rodrigo Duterte's War on Drugs color *Time* v188 no14 p46 O 10 2016

Iyer, Bala

Are You Using APIs to Gain Competitive Advantage? *Harvard Business Review Digital Articles* p2 Ap 13 2015

The Benefits of Virtual Mentors *Harvard Business Review Digital Articles* p2 Ap 26 2014

Corporate Alliances Matter Less Thanks to APIs *Harvard Business Review Digital Articles* p2 Je 8 2015

Google vs. the EU Explains the Digital Economy *Harvard Business Review Digital Articles* p2 D 12 2016

A New Way for Entrepreneurs to Think About IT *Harvard Business Review Digital Articles* p2 Je 28 2016

The Next Battle in Antitrust Will Be About Whether One Company Knows Everything About You *Harvard Business Review Digital Articles* p2 Jl 6 2017

The Strategic Value of APIs *Harvard Business Review Digital Articles* p2 Ja 7 2015

To Predict the Trajectory of the Internet of Things, Look to the Software Industry *Harvard Business Review Digital Articles* p2 F 25 2016

What Comes After Smart Products *Harvard Business Review Digital Articles* p2 Jl 1 2015

Iyer, Dhruv

Young science officers lead by example color *Science* v355 no6322 p256 Ja 20 2017

Iyer, Pico

Last Rites cartoon *Walrus* p67 Ja\F 2017

Nymphets in the New Japan [Cover story] bw *New York Review of Books* v64 no10 p16 Je 8 2017

Izatt, Gregory

A cargo-sorting DNA robot color *Science* v357 no6356 p1112 S 15 2017

Izaurralde, R. Cesar

Cellulosic biofuel contributions to a sustainable energy future: Choices and outcomes color *Science* v356 no6345 p1349 Je 30 2017

Izbicki, Jakob R.

A pathogenic role for T cell–derived IL-22BP in inflammatory bowel disease bibl graph *Science* v354 no6310 p358 O 21 2016

iZombie (TV program)

iZombie M. Roffman *TV Guide* v65 no14 p33 Ap 3 2017

Rob Thomas Belts It Out on iZombie M. Roffman *TV Guide* v64 no15 p15 Ap 4 2016

Izpisúa Belmonte, Juan Carlos

HUMAN ORGANS FROM ANIMAL BODIES cartoon color diag *Scientific American* v315 no5 p32 N 2016

Integration of CpG-free DNA induces de novo methylation of CpG islands in pluripotent stem cells diag *Science* v356 no6337 p503 My 5 2017

Izzard, Eddie, 1962-

Believe Me: A Memoir of Love, Death, and Jazz Chickens *Publishers Weekly* v264 no17 p79 Ap 24 2017

Izzard, Eddie, 1962-—Interviews

Beyond High Heels and Lipstick W. WERRIS color *Publishers Weekly* v264 no19 p48 My 8 2017

J

J. Craig Venter Institute Inc.

Biologists Create Organism With Smallest Genome J. KEATS chart color graph *Discover* v38 no1 p15 Ja/F 2017

J. Crew Group Inc.

4 dress-up & date-night solutions color *Redbook* p62 Je 2017

Flats? For Evening? Why, Yes color *Women's Health* v13 no10 p62 D 2016

J. Jill Group Inc.

5 amazing gifts that give back color *Redbook* p78 D 2016

J. Paul Getty Museum

Treasures beyond gold: A new exhibition examines the luxury arts of the ancient Americas J. Pillsbury color *Magazine Antiques* v184 no5 p108 S/O 2017

J. Walter Thompson Co. Inc.—Management

They said we'd never get creatives to learn G. GYTON *People Management* p20 O 2016

Jabbour, Nassib

Emergence and spread of a human-transmissible multidrug-resistant nontuberculous mycobacterium bibl diag graph *Science* v354 no6313 p751 N 11 2016

Jaber, David

Design, Place and Indigenous Ways: Working with Local Communities *Parks & Recreation* v51 no12 p30 D 2016

Jablonski, Nina G.

The biology of color color *Science* v357 no6350 p470 Ag 4 2017

Jabr, Ferris

Blue Light Blues cartoon *Scientific American* v315 no5 p24 N 2016

CAN WE TALK? AN ARIZONA BIOLOGIST BELIEVES THAT THE SOUNDS MADE BY MANY ANIMAL SPECIES, INCLUDING THE HUMBLE PRAIRIE DOG, SHOULD BE CONSIDERED LANGUAGE—AND THAT SOMEDAY WE'LL UNDERSTAND WHAT THEY HAVE TO SAY *New York Times Magazine* p28 My 14 2017

Probiotics Are No Panacea color *Scientific American* v317 no1 p26 Jl 2017

Jabri, Bana

Reovirus infection triggers inflammatory responses to dietary antigens and development of celiac disease color diag *Science* v356 no6333 p44 Ap 7 2017

Jacanidae—Behavior

SHE MATES, HE INCUBATES P. Edmonds color *National Geographic* v231 no5 p29 My 2017

Jacco, Charlie

Passwords Are Terrible, but Will Biometrics Be Any Better? *Harvard Business Review Digital Articles* p1 My 11 2017

JACHIMOWICZ, JON

A 5-Step Process to Get More Out of Your Organization's Data *Harvard Business Review Digital Articles* p2 Mr 16 2017

Reclaim Your Commute color *Harvard Business Review* v95 no3 p149 My/Je 2017

What to Do When Someone Angrily Challenges Your Data color *Harvard Business Review Digital Articles* p2 Ap 5 2017

Jack, William

The long-run poverty and gender impacts of mobile money bibl chart graph *Science* v354 no6317 p1288 D 9 2016

Jack Reacher: Never Go Back (Film)

Cobie Smulders' Guide to Getting Action D. Franich color *Entertainment Weekly* no1436/1437 p84 O 21 2016

JACK REACHER: NEVER GO BACK C. Gunnestad color *Sound & Vision* v82 no5 p65 Je 2017

Pump Up the volume! color *Essence* v48 no6 p100 O 2017

Queen of Cool L. SINGER *Chicago* v66 no10 p74 O 2017

QUICKSILVER cartoon color *Snowboarder* v29 no4 p120 D 2016

READY FOR AUTUMN color *Equus* no480 p32 S 2017

RIDE HARD, LOUNGE HARDER M. YOZELL color *Bicycling* v58 no10 p78 N/D 2017

RISE & SHINE bw color *Vogue* v207 no1 p45 Ja 2017

THE RULES OF CASUAL COOL S. NYGAARD color *Men's Health* v32 no7 p(Sp)10 S 2017

Shear Genius color *Glamour* v115 no11 p54 N 2017

Shells E. KWAK-HEFFERAN color diag graph il *Backpacker* v45 no3 p83 Ap 2017

SHE SHREDS, SHE SCORES! color *Women's Health* v13 no10 p118 D 2016

SHORT STORY color *Esquire* p47 N 2017

SLATIN MOTOGEAR EZ-1 SUPERFABRIC MESH JACKET P. Dean color *Cycle World* v55 no10 p18 N 2016

SMOOTH MOVE color *Esquire* v167 no2 p70 Mr 2017

SNOW BALLERS P. Bridges color *Snowboarder* v29 no4 p128 D 2016

SO BAZAAR bw *Harper's Bazaar* no3649 p342 D 2016/Ja 2017

SQUALL PARKA color *Good Housekeeping* v264 no1 p136 Ja 1 2017

The Start color *InStyle* v24 no1 p11 Ja 2017

STORM STOPPERS J. Dengate color *Runner's World* v52 no3 p51 Ap 2017

Street Style: FITNESS EDITION M. Legrand color *Women's Health* v14 no6 p18 Jl 2017

STRIKING GOLD color *Essence* v47 no10 p52 F 2017

STYLE color *Horse & Rider* v56 no2 p20 F 2017

STYLE color *Horse & Rider* v56 no6 p32 Je 2017

STYLISH SOIRÉE bw color *Vanity Fair* v58 no12 p74 D 2016

Summer Weekend Checklist color *Glamour* v115 no6 p35 Je 2017

THIS OUTFIT USED TO BE 44 WATER BOTTLES color diag *Good Housekeeping* v264 no5 p94 My 2017

This vest does it all color *Redbook* p67 D 2016

THREE WISE MEN N. Sullivan, J. Roth et al bw color *Esquire* p88 2017 BigBlackBook

TOUGH ENOUGH *Los Angeles Magazine* p32 My 2017

TOUGH LOVE color *O, The Oprah Magazine* p61 O 2017

Ultralight Baggage K. Boelte *Sierra* v102 no1 p19 Ja/F 2017

VELVET CRUSH color *Ebony* v72 no3 p64 D 2016/Ja 2017

Velvet Crush color *Vogue* v207 no10 p294 O 2017

A WEEK OF AWESOME OUTFITS color *Good Housekeeping* v264 no3 p36 Mr 2017

WELCOME TO PEAK STYLE SEASON N. SULLIVAN color *Esquire* p61 S 2017

THE WELL-SPENT $ DOLLAR color *Harper's Bazaar* no3653 p114 My 2017

THE WELL-SPENT $ DOLLAR color *Harper's Bazaar* no3655 p72 Ag 2017

WHERE FASHION GETS PERSONAL color *Harper's Bazaar* no3652 p129 Ap 2017

WHERE TO BUY color *Essence* v48 no2 p114 Je 2017

Work the LOOK color *Harper's Bazaar* no3652 p134 Ap 2017

WOWZA! color *Bicycling* v58 no8 p68 S 2017

Jackfruit

A FEW WORDS WITH JACKFRUIT ANNIE R. Jacobsen color *Rodale's Organic Life* v3 no1 p57 Ja 2017

SERVING UP JACKFRUIT S. Stukin color *National Geographic* v230 no6 p14 D 2016

Jackie (Film)

19 THINGS YOU REALLY OUGHT TO 00 THIS MONTH M. J. Gaynor, A. Beaujon et al *Washingtonian Magazine* v52 no3 p31 D 2016

AMERICAN Women color *Vogue* v206 no12 p212 D 2016

Being Jackie Kennedy color *Entertainment Weekly* no1442 p42 D 2 2016 Rebellious Special Issue

CRITICS' CHOICE chart color *Film Comment* v53 no1 p12 Ja/F 2017

Jackie *New Yorker* v92 no46 p10 Ja 23 2017

Jackie Places the First Lady Under a Microscope S. Zacharek color *Time* v188 no24 p63 D 12 2016

OUR FIRST LADY OF SORROWS B. KACHKA img *New York* v49 no24 p46 N 28 2016

THE STATE THAT I AM IN J. TEODORO bw color *Film Com-*

ment v52 no6 p42 N/D 2016

Telling Her Story C. Benson-Allott *Film Quarterly* v70 no4 p88 Summ 2017

The Umbrellas of Silver Lake D. EDELSTEIN img *New York* v49 no24 p148 N 28 2016

With Camelot Behind Her S. ERICKSON *Los Angeles Magazine* p72 Ja 2017

WIVES AND HUSBANDS A. LANE cartoon *New Yorker* v92 no40 p86 D 5 2016

Jackman, Hugh, 1968-

Hugh Jackman in The Greatest Showman T. Stack color *Entertainment Weekly* no1467 p46 My 26 2017

Shane, With Claws and Bloodlust to Spare S. Zacharek color *Time* v189 no9 p56 Mr 13 2017

WHAT'S NEXT FOR WOLVERINE? K. P. Sullivan color *Entertainment Weekly* no1457/1458 p16 Mr 17 2017

WOLVERINE NO MORE [Cover story] K. P. Sullivan color *Entertainment Weekly* no1456 p22 Mr 10 2017

Jackrel, Meredith E.

Ratchet-like polypeptide translocation mechanism of the AAA+ disaggregase Hsp104 diag *Science* v357 no6348 p273 Jl 21 2017

JACKS, DWAYNE N.

PUT FAT AT A LOSS color *Muscle & Performance* v9 no5 p12 My 2017

Jackson (Miss.)—Politics & government

The Battle for the Soul of Black Politics M. CUNNINGHAM-COOK *In These Times* v41 no5 p15 My 2017

Jackson (Wyo.)

20 HOT SPOTS to view the eclipse M. E. Bakich color map *Astronomy* v45 no8 p38 Ag 2017

Jackson, Andrew, 1767-1845

THE ANDREW BROTHERS R. BROOKHISER bw color *American History* v52 no3 p18 Ag 2017

Fit for a King S. Jenkins bw *Smithsonian* v47 no10 p40 Mr 2017

A PECULIAR VIRTUE G. W. Johnson *Harper's Magazine* v334 no2000 p9 Ja 2017

Trump and the "New Nationalism": It's not new at all. Andrew Jackson, almost two centuries ago, also championed a populist style--and, in the end, strengthened American democracy K. N. Schake *Hoover Digest: Research & Opinion on Public Policy* no3 p23 Summ 2017

TRUMP TAKES UP THE MANTLE OF OLD HICKORY T. CHAMBERS *USA Today Magazine* v145 no2864 p14 My 2017

THE TWO ANDREW JACKSONS M. KAZIN il *Nation* v305 no5 p35 Ag 28 2017

Jackson, Angela

Our Ms. Brooks P. H. Bass color *Essence* v48 no2 p63 Je 2017

JACKSON, BETHANNA M.

When, Where, and How Nature Matters for Ecosystem Services: Challenges for the Next Generation of Ecosystem Service Models *BioScience* v67 no9 p820 S 2017

Jackson, Charreah K.

APPRECIATE color *Essence* v47 no7 p124 N 2016

BEST SUPPORTING DISH color *Essence* v47 no7 p113 N 2016

BLACK LOVE THROUGH THE AGES color *Essence* v47 no10 p97 F 2017

CELEBRATE color *Essence* v47 no8 p152 D 2016

A DATE WITH Niecy color *Essence* v48 no5 p84 S 2017

EAT YOUR WAY TO PROSPERITY color *Essence* v47 no9 p83 Ja 2017

GRILLED GOODNESS color *Essence* v48 no3 p109 Jl 2017

ICE CREAM DREAM color *Essence* v48 no2 p105 Je 2017

MERRY TRANSIT color *Essence* v47 no8 p92 D 2016

OUR FATHERS IN THEIR OWN WORDS color *Essence* v48 no2 p94 Je 2017

RAISE A GLASS color *Essence* v47 no10 p105 F 2017

SANTA'S LITTLE CHEFS color *Essence* v47 no8 p133 D 2016

STAR IN YOUR OWN LOVE STORY color *Essence* v48 no5 p105 S 2017

TABLE FOR ONE color *Essence* v47 no11 p111 Mr 2017

#THXBIRTHCONTROL color *Essence* v47 no7 p104 N 2016

YOUR SENSUAL SUMMER IS HERE color *Essence* v48 no3 p103 Jl 2017

JACKSON, CHERISSA

OBAMA'S AMERICA img *New York* v49 no20 p12 O 3 2016

Jackson, Chris, ca. 1971-
Chris Jackson M. Rich *Current Biography* v77 no10 p63 O 2016
Jackson, Christal
GIVING BACK WITH IMPACT CHRISTAL JACKSON'S J. McKINNEY color *Black Enterprise* v47 no5 p22 Ja/F 2017
JACKSON, CHRISTINE
NEITHER GUYS NOR DOLLS: A theater's experiment in gender-blind casting *Washingtonian Magazine* v52 no12 p23 S 2017
WHERE & WHEN: 17 THINGS YOU REALLY OUGHT TO DO THIS MONTH *Washingtonian Magazine* v53 no1 p31 O 2017
WHERE & WHEN: 18 THINGS YOU REALLY OUGHT TO DO THIS MONTH *Washingtonian Magazine* v52 no12 p29 S 2017
Jackson, Constanza
Xist recruits the X chromosome to the nuclear lamina to enable chromosome-wide silencing bibl graph *Science* v354 no6311 p468 O 28 2016
Jackson, Danielle
8 — 2 DOPE QUEENS color *Entertainment Weekly* no1444/1445 p114 D 16 2016
Jackson, David
CHASING THE DREAM WAVE color *Canoe & Kayak Magazine* v45 no1 p25 Wint 2017
Jackson, Don
Why We Ride: Great bikes and the people who love them W. Sheppard bw color *Virginia Living* v15 no5 p90 Ag 2017
Jackson, Doug
Nuclear Power and Risk Psychology *Skeptical Inquirer* v41 no2 p64 Mr/Ap 2017
JACKSON, DWAYNE N.
AMINOS: ATHLETIC ASSETS color diag *Muscle & Performance* v9 no11 p58 N 2017
THE A-Z ON VITAMIN B color *Muscle & Performance* v9 no4 p26 Ap 2017
BEET THE COMPETITION color *Muscle & Performance* v9 no9 p16 S 2017
Free Radicals & Antioxidants chart color *Muscle & Performance* v9 no5 p58 My 2017
GET ENERGIZED color *Muscle & Performance* v9 no10 p18 O 2017
I HEART TAURINE color *Muscle & Performance* v9 no10 p18 O 2017
Max Out With Capsaicin color *Muscle & Performance* v9 no11 p33 N 2017
MICROMINERALS FOR MAXIMUM PERFORMANCE color *Muscle & Performance* v9 no4 p58 Ap 2017
Milk Your Inflammation! color *Muscle & Performance* v9 no11 p32 N 2017
PICKING THE PERFECT PROTEIN color *Muscle & Performance* v9 no6 p51 Je 2017
POWER-PACKED VITAMINS color *Muscle & Performance* v9 no10 p56 O 2017
SAVVY SUPPLEMENTATION FOR ATHLETES cartoon *Muscle & Performance* v8 no12 p58 D 2016
Supplement Strategy color diag *Muscle & Performance* v9 no6 p57 Je 2017
Supplement Support For Your New Year's Resolutions color *Muscle & Performance* v9 no1 p58 Ja 2017
TEST YOUR KNOWLEDGE color *Muscle & Performance* v9 no9 p16 S 2017
Jackson, Eddie
AMERICA'S FITTEST CHEFS J. DEAN cartoon color *Men's Health* v32 no3 p104 Ap 2017
Jackson, Eliot—Interviews
GO AHEAD, OVERTHINK IT B. BROUDY color *Bicycling* v58 no8 p32 S 2017
JACKSON, EMILY
Foodie Festivities *Atlanta* v56 no8 p72 D 2016
FOODSTUFFS *Atlanta* v56 no9 p54 Ja 2017
POP REVIVAL *Atlanta* v56 no7 p83 N 2016
Sugar Rush *Atlanta* v56 no7 p59 N 2016
Jackson, Evan
Caring for Aging Loved Ones color *Consumer Reports* v82 no12 p6 D 2017
Jackson, Georgina
#Dynos color *Climbing* no351 p19 F/Mr 2017

JACKSON, J. MARK
How a Veteran Sees Life color *Reader's Digest* v189 no1130 p102 My 2017
Life Lessons From Boot Camp color *Reader's Digest* v190 no1135 p26 N 2017
Jackson, Janet, 1966-
Janet Jackson C. Ianzito color *AARP: The Magazine* v59 no3A p92 Ap/My 2016
Jackson, Janet, 1966—Interviews
SWEET & STRONG [Cover story] J. D. Tatum color *Redbook* p104 My 2017
Jackson, Janine
'Elites Not Only Benefit From Racism, but Use Racism to Their Advantage" *Extra!* v30 no8 p4 O 2017
Freedom of Speech Doesn't Guarantee the Right to a Megaphone *Extra!* v30 no7 p4 S 2017
In Trump's America, Protest Is Criminalized While Reporters Are Literally Assaulted *Extra!* v30 no6 p1 Jl/Ag 2017
Rebranding Trump's White Supremacist Strategist *Extra!* v30 no1 p1 Ja/F 2017
Syrian Airstrikes Rekindle Media's Love Affair With US Violence [Cover story] *Extra!* v30 no4 p1 My 2017
Jackson, Jeff
DEMOCRACY ON THE LINE B. YEOMAN color map *Nation* v305 no9 p16 O 16 2017
Jackson, Jesse, 1941-
Cozying Up to the Dictator F. BARNES bw *Weekly Standard* v22 no14 p11 D 12 2016
Jackson, John David
John David Jackson C. Quigg *Physics Today* v69 no10 p68 O 2016
Jackson, Josh
Leading Off color *Sports Illustrated* v127 no2 p8 Jl 17 2017
Jackson, Justine—Awards
news & notes color *Literacy Today (2411-7862)* v34 no4 p42 Ja/F 2017
Jackson, K. M.
Insert Groom Here *Publishers Weekly* v263 no48 p53 N 28 2016
Jackson, Lamar
HOT | NOT T. Keith color *Sports Illustrated* v127 no8 p20 S 18 2017
Players Of the Year C. Johnson, S. Kwak et al color *Sports Illustrated* v125 no20 p92 D 19 2016
STRIKING THE POSE C. Johnson color *Sports Illustrated* v125 no19 p48 D 12 2016
Jackson, Lamar—Interviews
JUST MY TYPE D. Patrick and T. Keith color *Sports Illustrated* v125 no21 p26 D 26 2016
Jackson, Lawrence Patrick, 1968-
HYMN TO HARM CITY *Harper's Magazine* v334 no2001 p31 F 2017
LIBERATION STRUGGLE T. Chatterton Williams *Harper's Magazine* no2007 p88 Ag 2017
MYSTERY MAN A. Belth color *Esquire* p20 Ag 2017
The Rage in Harlem, and Beyond M. P. JEFFRIES *New York Times Book Review* p18 Ag 27 2017
JACKSON, LINK
The Crown Jewel: A Rare Float on the Best Wilderness River in America *Idaho Magazine* v16 no12 p6 S 2017
Jackson, Lisa
Lisa Jackson color *Publishers Weekly* v264 no13 p13 Mr 27 2017
Jackson, Mahalia, 1911-1972
Shared Vision, Common Spirit Hadley bw *Downbeat* v84 no4 p61 Ap 2017
JACKSON, MAJOR
'Making Is the Mirror': A career retrospective shows how Frank Bidart shed the masks of his early poems to create a kind of self-mythology *New York Times Book Review* p14 O 8 2017
Jackson, Matthew G.
Tungsten-182 heterogeneity in modern ocean island basalts chart diag *Science* v356 no6333 p66 Ap 7 2017
Jackson, Michael
'I feel like I'm 20' CANDIDO [Cover story] color *Downbeat* v84 no5 p44 My 2017
JAMES MORRISON THE ADVENTURER color *Downbeat* v84 no10 p176 O 2017
Jackson, Michael, 1958-2009

Paris Jackson's Family Secrets B. Hiatt color *Rolling Stone* no1280 p34 F 9 2017

Jackson, Michael, 1958-2009—Finance

Top-Earning Dead Celebrities color *Forbes* v198 no6 p28 N 8 2016

Jackson, Mick

Denial L. Greenblatt color *Entertainment Weekly* no1434 p41 O 7 2016

Sighs, Tears, and Jogging R. R. Cooper color *Commonweal* v143 no19 p24 D 2 2016

Jackson, Niyah—Interviews

Niyah Jackson A. BRANDT *Cincinnati Magazine* v50 no7 p32 Ap 2017

Jackson, Paris, 1998-

PARIS IN APRIL D. BLASBERG color *Vanity Fair* v59 no6 p90 My 2017

Paris Jackson Is a Star *TV Guide* v65 no8 p10 F 27 2017

Paris Jackson's Family Secrets B. Hiatt color *Rolling Stone* no1280 p34 F 9 2017

Jackson, Phil, 1945-

No Exit C. P. Pierce, T. Keith et al color *Sports Illustrated* v126 no7 p30 Mr 6 2017

Jackson, Phil, 1945-—Interviews

PHIL JACKSON E. SPITZNAGEL color *Men's Health* v32 no2 p120 Mr 2017

Jackson, Rachel W.

Human-in-the-loop optimization of exoskeleton assistance during walking diag *Science* v356 no6344 p1280 Je 23 2017

Jackson, Randall D.

Cellulosic biofuel contributions to a sustainable energy future: Choices and outcomes color *Science* v356 no6345 p1349 Je 30 2017

Jackson, Rasheedah

Memorial Community Development Corporation: Putting Faith to Work *Bridges (Federal Reserve Bank of St. Louis)* p11 Wint 2016/2017

Jackson, Rebecca

A Mooring in Iceberg Alley color *Oceanus* v51 no2 p16 Wint 2016

Jackson, Richard

In Plain Sight color *Publishers Weekly* v263 no49 p32 D 7 2016

This Beautiful Day *Publishers Weekly* v264 no24 p63 Je 12 2017

Jackson, Ricky

EXONERATION M. SHAER *Smithsonian* v47 no9 p80 Ja/F 2017

Jackson, Ryan B.

STEAM-POWERED READERS color *Literacy Today (2411-7862)* v34 no4 p14 Ja/F 2017

Jackson, Simon A.

CRISPR-Cas: Adapting to change color *Science* v356 no6333 p40 Ap 7 2017

Jackson, Stephen T.

Merging paleobiology with conservation biology to guide the future of terrestrial ecosystems color *Science* v355 no6325 p594 F 10 2017

Toward a national, sustained U.S. ecosystem assessment bibl color *Science* v354 no6314 p838 N 18 2016

Jackson, Stephen—Interviews

MEET STEPHEN JACKSON *Sea Magazine* v109 no2 pCA-5 F 2017

Jackson, Stonewall, 1824-1863

FROM OUR READERS F. Housel, D. Kreuer et al *Sky & Telescope* v133 no4 p6 Ap 2017

Jackson, Stuart

Boards Must Be More Combative color *Harvard Business Review Digital Articles* p2 Ja 27 2017

Jackson, Susan

Click chemistry enables preclinical evaluation of targeted epigenetic therapies diag *Science* v356 no6345 p1397 Je 30 2017

Jackson, Timothy F.

Selected Poems of Edna St. Vincent Millay: An Annotated Edition J. W. Barbeau *Christian Century* v133 no24 p41 N 23 2016

Jackson, Tom

Uber's Africa Push Hits Roadblocks color *Fortune* v175 no6 p14 My 1 2017

Jackson, Vivien

Perfect Gravity *Publishers Weekly* v264 no38 p60 S 18 2017

Jackson, Will

Empire's Other Whites *History Today* v66 no12 p43 D 2016

Jackson, William—Interviews

A GOOD MAN EMERGES D. Snierson color *Entertainment Weekly* no1471 p56 Je 23 2017

Jackson 5 (Performer)

THE MUSIC MAN N. Santos bw *Ebony* v72 no9 p98 Jl/Ag 2017

Jackson Hole (Wyo.)

Greetings from JACKSON HOLE, WYOMING D. Newman *Practical Horseman* v45 no2 p62 F 2017

Jackson Hole Mountain Resorts (Company)

TURNED SCREWS GONE LOOSE D. Bertsch color *Powder* v45 no6 p90 F 2017

Jacksonian democracy

The Jacksonian Revolt W. R. Mead color *Foreign Affairs* v96 no2 p2 Mr/Ap 2017

Jackson-Jones, Lucy H.

Local amplifiers of IL-4Rα-mediated macrophage activation promote repair in lung and liver diag *Science* v356 no6342 p1076 Je 9 2017

Jackson Lee, Sheila, 1950-

Honorable Sheila Jackson Lee *Congressional Digest* v95 no9 p22 N 2016

Jackson Park (Chicago, Ill.)

The Obamas Unveil Preliminary Design for Presidential Center J. GAUER *Architectural Record* v205 no6 p23 Je 2017

Jackson State University (Jackson, Miss.)

THINGS THAT GO BOOM R. GRANT *Smithsonian* v47 no9 p54 Ja/F 2017

Jacksonville Jaguars (Football team)

4 Jacksonville Jaguars color *Sports Illustrated* v127 no7 p79 S 4 2017

Jacksonville University

Jacksonville University *Dance Magazine* v90 p77 2016/2017 Supplement College Guide

Jacksonville University—Curricula

JU Creates 'Holistic' Musicians J. Hale color *Downbeat* v84 no10 p198 O 2017

JACOB, BRIAN A.

The Wisdom of Mandatory Grade Retention *Education Digest* v82 no7 p29 Mr 2017

Jacob, Daniel J.

Unmask temporal trade-offs in climate policy debates color *Science* v356 no6337 p492 My 5 2017

Jacob, George

FEATURED FELLOW: GEORGE JACOB M. Rosano color *Canadian Geographic* v136 no6 p78 D 2016

Jacob, Mira

"Don't Be Afraid of Who You Are" color *Glamour* v115 no6 p116 Je 2017

Navigating a world of bullies color *Redbook* p108 O 2017

What the Church Ladies Know *New York Times Book Review* p10 N 6 2016

Jacob, Sophia

Clonal hematopoiesis associated with TET2 deficiency accelerates atherosclerosis development in mice bibl diag *Science* v355 no6327 p842 F 24 2017

JACOBI, JON L.

Apricorn Aegis Secure Key 3z: This USB thumbdrive is small, secure, and device-agnostic color graph *PCWorld* p79 Mr 2017

Back up all your data—and we mean all of it—to your NAS box without installing any software color *Macworld - Digital Edition* v34 no4 p86 My 2017

External drive died? Your data may still be easy to recover color *PCWorld* v35 no7 p196 Jl 2017

How Babelsoft Media Preview reveals less-common file types in Explorer color *PCWorld* v35 no4 p152 Ap 2017

Intel SSD 545s: The next great budget SSD has arrived color graph *PCWorld* v35 no8 p82 Ag 2017

Lenovo ThinkPad X1 Yoga: This 2-in-1's OLED screen will color your computing world color graph *PCWorld* p58 O 2016

OCZ VX500: A featherlight SATA SSD that's ideal for laptop upgrades color graph *PCWorld* v35 no11 p100 N 2016

Samsung KS9800 4K UHD, 65-inch smart TV: Quantum dots + HDR = Wow! color graph *PCWorld* p141 D 2016

Samsung 960 Pro NVMe SSD: Ludicrously fast PC storage color graph *PCWorld* v35 no2 p104 F 2017

Seagate Barracuda Pro 10TB hard drive: Vast and amazingly fast (for a hard drive) color graph *PCWorld* p99 O 2016

Toshiba OCZ's TL100: A budget SSD that's not a bargain color graph *PCWorld* p95 D 2016

WD MY CLOUD HOME DUO: SUPER EASY TO USE, BUT ALSO SUPER SLOW AND SHORT ON FEATURES color *Macworld - Digital Edition* v34 no11 p28 N 2017

WD My Passport SSD: Worthy competition for Samsung's T3 color graph *PCWorld* v35 no9 p66 S 2017

Jacobides, Michael G.

Greece and Its Misguided Champions *Harvard Business Review Digital Articles* p2 Ag 24 2015

Greece's Problem Is More Complicated than Austerity *Harvard Business Review Digital Articles* p2 Jl 27 2015

Grexit Would Be Even More Dangerous than Economists Realize *Harvard Business Review Digital Articles* p2 Je 29 2015

What Greece Has to Do Now: Fix Its Economy *Harvard Business Review Digital Articles* p2 F 27 2015

What Managers Really Need from Academics *Harvard Business Review Digital Articles* p2 N 26 2014

Jacobite Rebellion, 1745-1746—Campaigns

See also

Battle of Culloden, Scotland, 1746

Blades not bullets M. Pittock *History Today* v67 no1 p45 Ja 2017

Jacobites

PRELUDE TO REVOLUTION J. Bertrand *Military History* v33 no5 p61 Ja 2017

Jacobovici, Sara

CAN NEUROSCIENCE HELP US UNDERSTAND TRUST AT WORK?: INTERACTION color *Harvard Business Review* v95 no2 p18 Mr/Ap 2017

JACOBS, A. J.

Book Learning *New York Times Book Review* p17 D 25 2016

Fairy Tales, Gently Fractured: Audiobooks for kids play around in the Grimm brothers' universe *New York Times Book Review* p21 My 21 2017

Jacobs, Alan

How to Think: A Survival Guide for a World at Odds *Publishers Weekly* v264 no30 p51 Jl 24 2017

Murder in Paradise *American Conservative* v15 no6 p42 N/D 2016

JACOBS, ALEXANDRA

Funny Women *New York Times Book Review* p16 N 20 2016

Jacobs, Ben

In Trump's America, Protest Is Criminalized While Reporters Are Literally Assaulted J. Jackson *Extra!* v30 no6 p1 Jl/Ag 2017

Jacobs, Bonnie F.

Global climatic drivers of leaf size [Cover story] graph *Science* v357 no6354 p917 S 1 2017

Jacobs, Dean

the SWEETNESS of AN AGE M. Teague color *Southern Living* v52 no9 p100 S 2017

Jacobs, Douglas

Employers Should Offer Free Screenings for Depression *Harvard Business Review Digital Articles* p2 D 11 2015

Jacobs, Gillian

GILLIAN JACOBS L. M. M. BLUME bw *Vanity Fair* v59 no4 p124 Mr 2017

The Tech Visionary You've Never Heard Of color *Glamour* v115 no5 p186 My 2017

Jacobs, Jane, 1916-2006

Bright Lights, Small Government M. HOLLERAN bw color *New Republic* v247 no12 p74 D 2016

Jacobs, Jennifer

'Chairman Cohn' Has a Nice Ring to It color graph *Bloomberg Businessweek* no4533 p32 Ag 7 2017

Do You Love It Now? color *Bloomberg Businessweek* no4530 p36 Jl 17 2017

Thanks to Ivanka, We May Always Have Paris color *Bloomberg Businessweek* no4519 p50 Ap 24 2017

The Unmaking Of American Dreams chart *Bloomberg Businessweek* no4537 p36 S 11 2017

JACOBS, JOANNE

High School of the Future *Education Digest* v82 no4 p33 D 2016

Jacobs, Katharine L.

Toward a national, sustained U.S. ecosystem assessment bibl color

Science v354 no6314 p838 N 18 2016

JACOBS, LAURA

LIFE AFTER ELOISE color *Vanity Fair* v59 no5 p152 Ap 2017

ONCE IN LOVE WITH GIGI cartoon *Vanity Fair* v59 no4 p212 Mr 2017

POINTE OF PERFECTION color *Vanity Fair* v59 no10 p172 O 2017

Pride and Prejudice bw color *Vanity Fair* p146 Hollywood 2017 Supplement

WHY SHOULD KIDS HAVE ALL THE FUN? cartoon *Vanity Fair* v59 no8 p108 Ag 2017

Jacobs, Marc, 1963-

Can fashion be FEMINIST? E. Wilson color *InStyle* v24 no2 p49 F 2017

Jacobs, Mark

For the Good of the People color *Black Belt* v55 no6 p74 O/N 2017

How Kayla Harrison's Judo Dreams Came True — Twice! color *Black Belt* v55 no1 p16 D 2016/Ja 2017

Jita Kyoei: Mutual Welfare and Benefit in Judo color *Black Belt* v55 no4 p24 Je/Jl 2017

Martial Arts the Old-Fashioned Way bw color *Black Belt* v55 no5 p24 Ag/S 2017

RICHARD BUSTILLO (1942-2017) bw color *Black Belt* v55 no5 p42 Ag/S 2017

That's "Combatives" Spelled With Four C's color *Black Belt* v55 no2 p22 F/Mr 2017

WHEN EASTERN MOVIES MEET WESTERN MUSIC color *Black Belt* v55 no1 p12 D 2016/Ja 2017

Jacobs, Marshall

Fairways to Heaven M. Bamberger color *Golf Magazine* v59 no9 p112 S 2017

Jacobs, Michael

Diversification Drives Gains at Abrams J. Milliot color *Publishers Weekly* v264 no35 p8 Ag 28 2017

GO LOW, GET FAST color *Golf Magazine* v59 no3 p52 Mr 2017

SURVIVAL TACTICS color *Golf Magazine* v59 no9 p60 S 2017

TRY THIS! Feast On the Green color *Golf Magazine* v59 no8 p59 Ag 2017

YOUR EXIT PLAN color *Golf Magazine* v59 no6 p50 Je 2017

Jacobs, René

René Jacobs: The Countertenor, The Accent Recordings, 1978-1982 D. Minter *Opera News* v81 no10 p56 Ap 2017

Jacobs, Samuel P.

Channel Your Inner Bill Gates With These Beach Reads color *Money* v46 no7 p19 Ag 2017

Class Dismissed color *Time* v189 no15 p49 Ap 24 2017

Why I Love Books-and Which Ones You'll Enjoy color *Time* v189 no21 p25 Je 5 2017

JACOBS, STEPHI

kitchen refresh color *Cabin Living* p52 Je 2017

Neandertal and Denisovan DNA from Pleistocene sediments bw color *Science* v356 no6338 p605 My 12 2017

Jacobsen, Annie

Weird Vibrations: The federal government spent a bundle looking into spoon bending, ESP in cats and things that go bump in the night D. TERESI *New York Times Book Review* p18 Ap 30 2017

Jacobsen, Eric N.

Macrocyclic bis-thioureas catalyze stereospecific glycosylation reactions bibl diag *Science* v355 no6321 p1 Ja 13 2017

Jacobsen, Karsten W.

Making the most of materials computations bibl diag *Science* v354 no6309 p180 O 14 2016

JACOBSEN, KIM

International Wildlife Law: Understanding and Enhancing Its Role in Conservation *BioScience* v67 no9 p784 S 2017

JACOBSEN, PATRICIA

r.s.v.p color *Bon Appetit* no8 p14 Ag 2017

Jacobsen, R. Irene

Stellate cells drive maturation of the entorhinal-hippocampal circuit diag *Science* v355 no6330 p1172 Mr 17 2017

Jacobsen, Rebecca

Building a better measure of school quality color il *Phi Delta Kappan* v98 no7 p43 Ap 2017

Teaching with evidence diag *Phi Delta Kappan* v98 no7 p67 Ap

Jacobsen, Rowan

Designer Genes color *Mother Jones* v42 no5 p44 S/O 2017

A FEW WORDS WITH JACKFRUIT ANNIE color *Rodale's Organic Life* v3 no1 p57 Ja 2017

ON THE RISE: A CADRE OF NEW ENGLAND WHEAT GROWERS AND ARTISAN BAKERS WHO PROUDLY CALL THEMSELVES "GRAINIACS" ARE CREATING SOME OF THE BEST BREADS IN THE COUNTRY *Yankee* v81 no5 p118 S/O 2017

THE ROCKWEED RUSH cartoon color *Mother Jones* v41 no6 p8 N/D 2016

Seaweed Dreaming *Yankee* v81 no1 p120 Ja/F 2017

Jacobsen, Sandy

A New Meaning for "Never" color *Dressage Today* p62 My 2017

Jacobsen, Thomas W.

Modern Guide, Historic City D. KUNIAN color *Downbeat* v84 no1 p81 Ja 2017

Jacobs-Jenkins, Branden

GOD ONLY KNOWS H. ALS cartoon *New Yorker* v93 no3 p80 Mr 6 2017

Jacobs-Lorena, Marcelo

Driving mosquito refractoriness to Plasmodium falciparum with engineered symbiotic bacteria color graph *Science* v357 no6358 p1399 S 29 2017

Jacobson, Abbi, 1984-

Abbi Jacobson D. Kiper color *Current Biography* v77 no10 p68 O 2016

Broad City N. Abrams, B. L. Heldman et al color *Entertainment Weekly* no1482/1483 p79 S 22 2017

BROAD CITY R. Rahman color *Entertainment Weekly* no1468/1469 p50 Je 2-9 2017

Jacobson, Abbi, 1984—Interviews

ABBI GETS ARTSY I. Biedenharn color *Entertainment Weekly* no1473 p58 Jl 7 2017

Abbi Jacobson Didn't Expect Hillary to Come On Her Show D. Itzkoff *New York Times Magazine* p54 O 23 2016

JACOBSON, ALISON

MAKING EVERY HOME A SAFER PLACE *Parents* v91 no6 p30 Je 2016

Jacobson, Barry D.

Community network for deaf scientists color *Science* v356 no6336 p386 Ap 28 2017

Jacobson, Chris

Garden in motion E. Jardina color *Sunset* v238 no3 p36 Mr 2017

JACOBSON, ELLIOTT

Anesthesia and Euthanasia of Amphibians and Reptiles Used in Scientific Research: Should Hypothermia and Freezing Be Prohibited? *BioScience* v67 no1 p53 Ja 2017

Jacobson, Howard

A Touch of Woody Allen A. Sargeant bw *Commonweal* v143 no20 p26 D 16 2016

Jacobson, Ken

McDonald's Has to Do More than Manipulate Its Stock Price *Harvard Business Review Digital Articles* p2 My 14 2015

Jacobson, Kurt

PICKLE RECIPES for the Picking: Ferment or quick-pickle your harvest with this assortment of ideas from Mother Earth News bloggers *Mother Earth News* no282 p56 Je/Jl 2017

Jacobson, Linda

Building a Culture of Literacy: Ideas for making literacy the foundation in your school [Cover story] *Literacy Today (2411-7862)* v35 no1 p20 Jl/Ag 2017

Jacobson, Lisa

TAMING Migraines G. Graves color *O, The Oprah Magazine* p83 Ap 2017

JACOBSON, MARK

OBAMA'S AMERICA img *New York* v49 no20 p12 O 3 2016

Riding With Chuck color *Rolling Stone* no1285 p35 Ap 20 2017

The Trump Voters Who'd Become My Friends *New York* v49 no23 p23 N 14 2016

JACOBSON, MATT

HOW I DISCOVERED MY STYLE cartoon color *Esquire* p48 My 2017

Jacobson, Michael F.

2017: the Year of Plant-Based Meat? *Nutrition Action Health Letter* v44 no5 p2 Je 2017

Conflict Resolution *Nutrition Action Health Letter* v44 no2 p2 Mr 2017

Evidence Matters *Nutrition Action Health Letter* v44 no3 p2 Ap 2017

Fixin' for a Fight *Nutrition Action Health Letter* v44 no1 p2 Ja/F 2017

Industry Giveaway *Nutrition Action Health Letter* v44 no4 p2 My 2017

Turning Over the Reins *Nutrition Action Health Letter* v44 no7 p2 S 2017

We Deserve Better *Nutrition Action Health Letter* v44 no6 p2 Jl/Ag 2017

What a Year! *Nutrition Action Health Letter* v43 no10 p2 D 2016

Jacobson, Mireille

Research: When a Retail Store Closes, Crime Increases Around It *Harvard Business Review Digital Articles* p2 Je 29 2017

Jacobson, Peter

Discussion *Smithsonian* v48 no4 p6 Jl/Ag 2017

Jacobson, Roni

We All Speed-Read color *Scientific American* v315 no3 p23 S 2016

Your Pun-Divided Attention color *Scientific American* v315 no6 p17 D 2016

Jacobson, Shavonne

BOOK BREAK color *Literacy Today (2411-7862)* v34 no5 p46 Mr/Ap 2017

Jacob's Pillow (Becket, Mass.)

Farm to Theater J. Peters *Dance Magazine* v91 no1 p42 Ja 2017

Jacoby-Garrett, Paula M.

Arts Unleashed: Creating Successful, Lasting Arts Programs *Parks & Recreation* v52 no8 p38 Ag 2017

Creating a Vibrant Public Space on the Lafitte Greenway: Parks Build Community project to add several amenities to the southeast portion of the greenway *Parks & Recreation* v52 no8 p44 Ag 2017

Meet Me in ST. LOUIS *Parks & Recreation* v51 no10 p60 O 2016

Monumental Achievements... and Controversy *Parks & Recreation* v52 no4 p32 Ap 2017

St. Louis Parks and Green Spaces *Parks & Recreation* v51 no10 p66 O 2016

Trojan Park: Welcome to the Parks Build Community Family [Cover story] *Parks & Recreation* v51 no12 p36 D 2016

We're Headed to the Big Eassy *Parks & Recreation* v52 no9 p78 S 2017

Jacofsky, David J.

A Payment Model That Prevents Unnecessary Medical Treatment *Harvard Business Review Digital Articles* p2 D 19 2016

JACOT, PATRICIA

circle j lodge color *Cabin Living* p16 D 2016

JACQUES, MOLLY

THE WORLD'S Greatest STAG PARTY [Cover story] color *Field & Stream* v122 no6 p52 N 2017

Jacques, Phil

ENDER/ENDER color *Snowboarder* v29 no4 p136 D 2016

Jacquier, Alain

The cryo-EM structure of a ribosome–Ski2-Ski3-Ski8 helicase complex bibl color graph *Science* v354 no6318 p1431 D 16 2016

Jacquinod, S.

Seasonal exposure of carbon dioxide ice on the nucleus of comet 67P/Churyumov-Gerasimenko bibl bw graph *Science* v354 no6319 p1563 D 23 2016

Jacquot, Josh

2016 CHEVROLET CAMARO SS color graph *Car & Driver* v63 no2 p72 Ag 2017

2017 FORD F-150 RAPTOR SUPERCREW color *Car & Driver* v63 no2 p78 Ag 2017

Appetite for Destruction color *Car & Driver* v62 no10 p90 Ap 2017

Ballistic Leaf Blower [Cover story] color diag *Car & Driver* v62 no6 p42 D 2016

BRINGING THE 'SHINE BACK cartoon *Car & Driver* v62 no10 p16 Ap 2017

DODGE VIPER color graph *Car & Driver* v63 no5 p26 N 2017

ENGINES color *Car & Driver* v62 no7 p26 Ja 2017

Feel Lucky, Punk? [Cover story] color *Car & Driver* v63 no1 p36 Jl 2017

Four Play color diag *Car & Driver* v62 no11 p102 My 2017

Ghost of the White Dame color diag *Car & Driver* v62 no8 p60 F 2017

LIGHTNING LAP [Cover story] color graph map *Car & Driver* v63 no4 p45 O 2017

Little Feat color graph *Car & Driver* v62 no7 p98 Ja 2017

NAMING RITES bw chart color *Car & Driver* v63 no5 p48 N 2017

RAISING ARIZONA chart color graph map *Car & Driver* v63 no1 p56 Jl 2017

SPARE CHANGE chart color *Car & Driver* v62 no8 p22 F 2017

With Porsche's transcendent new 911 GT3, you won't need any damn luck color *Car & Driver* v63 no1 p42 Jl 2017

Jade

Battling for Blood Jade H. Beech and S. Nang color map *Time* v189 no10 p40 Mr 20 2017

Jadue, Pam

A life with loss color *U.S. Catholic* v82 no1 p5 Ja 2017

Jae-Hoon Jung

Phytochromes function as thermosensors in Arabidopsis bibl graph *Science* v354 no6314 p886 N 18 2016

Jae-Hwang Lee

Dynamic creation and evolution of gradient nanostructure in single-crystal metallic microcubes bibl bw *Science* v354 no6310 p312 O 21 2016

Jaeger, Baptiste N.

An environment-dependent transcriptional network specifies human microglia identity color *Science* v356 no6344 p1248 Je 23 2017

Jaeger, Katja E.

Phytochromes function as thermosensors in Arabidopsis bibl graph *Science* v354 no6314 p886 N 18 2016

Jaeggy, Fleur

AN ENCOUNTER IN THE BRONX color *Harper's Magazine* v335 no2005 p21 Je 2017

NULL AND VOID S. HETI bw *New Yorker* v93 no29 p98 S 25 2017

Jaegher (Company)

JAEGHER TS-38 INTERCEPTOR S-STIFF J. Southerland color *Bicycling* v58 no10 p52 N/D 2017

Jaehoon Kim

A chemical biology route to site-specific authentic protein modifications bibl diag graph *Science* v354 no6312 p623 N 4 2016

Jaekel, Astrid

Why Women Aren't Making It to the Top of Financial Services Firms *Harvard Business Review Digital Articles* p2 O 25 2016

Jafa, Arthur

The Ten Best Art Shows of the Year J. Saltz img *New York* v49 no25 p128 D 12 2016

Jafa, Arthur—Exhibitions

On Message A. K. Scott color *New Yorker* v92 no46 p13 Ja 23 2017

Jaffe, Andrew E.

Intersection of diverse neuronal genomes and neuropsychiatric disease: The Brain Somatic Mosaicism Network color *Science* v356 no6336 p395 Ap 28 2017

JAFFE, HARRY

A Beautiful Trump? *Washingtonian Magazine* v52 no4 p103 Ja 2017

THE SEARCH FOR IMMORTALITY color *Men's Health* v32 no5 p132 Je 2017

The TRAGEDY of CHRISTOPHER BARRY *Washingtonian Magazine* v52 no4 p62 Ja 2017

JAFFE, MATT

Cambria *Los Angeles Magazine* p90 Ap 2017

editor's LETTER R. STIEVE *Arizona Highways* v93 no10 p2 O 2017

FRINGE BENEFITS *Arizona Highways* v93 no1 p32 Ja 2017

HE KNOWS WHAT HE'S TALKING ABOUT *Arizona Highways* v93 no10 p46 O 2017

IDENTIFYING FLYING OBJECTS *Arizona Highways* v93 no6 p32 Je 2017

THE LAST TRADING POSTS *Arizona Highways* v92 no11 p16 N 2016

A LITTLE CAT GOES A LONG WAY *Arizona Highways* v93 no9 p48 S 2017

Out of the ORDINARY *Arizona Highways* v92 no7 p42 Jl 2016

JAFFE, SARAH

HER REVOLUTION Zephyr Teachout bw color *Nation* v303 no20 p12 N 14 2016

Molar Mobility *New York Times Book Review* p21 Mr 26 2017

THE WORKERS TRUMP FORGOT color *Nation* v304 no15 p18 My 8 2017

Jaffe, Sarah—Interviews

BEYOND HOPE [Cover story] E. BATES color il *New Republic* v248 no1/2 p20 Ja/F 2017

Q&A S. JAFFE il *Nation* v303 no19 p5 N 7 2016

Jaffe-Hoffman, Maayan

People *Christian Century* v133 no24 p21 N 23 2016

Jaffer, Ali

A Better Metric for the Value of a Worker Training Program *Harvard Business Review Digital Articles* p2 F 14 2017

To Better Train Workers, Figure Out Where They Struggle *Harvard Business Review Digital Articles* p2 Je 30 2017

Jaffer, Nancy

The 2017 Show Jumping Hall of Fame Inductees *In Stride* v12 no4 p43 Jl 2017

Alice Tarjan's RISE TO THE TOP color *Dressage Today* v23 no12 p44 S 2017

Bill Moroney Sets Sail for New Challenges *In Stride* v11 no6 p50 N 2016

Bound For Omaha! color *Dressage Today* v23 no7 p48 Mr 2017

BRINGING THE BEST TO OMAHA color *Practical Horseman* v45 no3 p53 Mr 2017

Celebrating Four Decades of Fame *In Stride* v12 no2 p53 Mr 2017

Chrystine Tauber: An Incredible Journey With Horses *In Stride* v12 no1 p38 Ja 2017

COMING HOME color *Dressage Today* v23 no6 p58 F 2017

The Future of Midwestern Dressage color *Dressage Today* v23 no10 p52 Jl 2017

HORSEPOWER: WHAT IT TAKES TO WIN A WORLD CUP color *Practical Horseman* v45 no3 p48 Mr 2017

Old Dominion and Strapless Find Fame *In Stride* v12 no5 p45 S 2017

Omaha: A World Cup Legacy *In Stride* v12 no3 p20 My 2017

OMAHA RAISES THE BAR [Cover story] color *Practical Horseman* v45 no6 p22 Je 2017

Ray Francis: A True Friend and Horseman *In Stride* v12 no1 p55 Ja 2017

A Rising STAR color *Dressage Today* v24 no1 p42 O 2017

Safety a Key Issue at USEA Annual Meeting color *Practical Horseman* v45 no3 p65 Mr 2017

STILL LEAPIN' LESLIE bw color *Practical Horseman* v45 no6 p34 Je 2017

THOROUGHBREDS ARE MADE FOR EVENTING color *Practical Horseman* v45 no2 p40 F 2017

JAFFREY, MADHUR

COOKING INDIAN WITH A MASTER color *Martha Stewart Living* p96 Mr 2017

Jag, Michael

Ultrafast many-body interferometry of impurities coupled to a Fermi sea bibl diag graph *Science* v354 no6308 p96 O 7 2016

Jagadeesh, Karthik A.

Deriving genomic diagnoses without revealing patient genomes chart *Science* v357 no6352 p692 Ag 18 2017

Jagannathan, P.

Molecular gas in the halo fuels the growth of a massive cluster galaxy at high redshift bibl graph *Science* v354 no6316 p1128 D 2 2016

Jagannathan, Vidhya

Ancient genomic changes associated with domestication of the horse color diag *Science* v356 no6336 p442 Ap 28 2017

Jagde, Brian

Nov/2016 M. MAZZARO *Opera News* v81 no5 p8 N 2016

Jager, Wander

Social norms as solutions bibl color *Science* v354 no6308 p42 O 7 2016

Jagers, Gerard A. J. M.

HIERARCHY AND COMPLEXITY PONGE *BioScience* v67 no7 p672 Jl 2017

Jagger, Bianca

My Stuff: BIANCA JAGGER color *Vanity Fair* v59 no9 p124 S 2017

Jagger, Mick, 1943-

MICK TALKS S. Mooallem bw color *Harper's Bazaar* no3649 p336 D 2016/Ja 2017

The Playlist bw color *Rolling Stone* no1294 p10 Ag 24 2017

Jag-Lauber, Katharina

Bloch oscillations in the absence of a lattice graph *Science* v356 no6341 p945 Je 1 2017

JAGO, ROBERT

Take Back the Parks bw *Walrus* v14 no8 p14 O 2017

Jagoda, Evelyn

We Are All Africans B. ALEX color *Discover* v38 no1 p26 Ja/F 2017

Jagodzinski, Andrzej M.

Positive biodiversity-productivity relationship predominant in global forests bibl chart graph map *Science* v354 no6309 paaf8957-1 O 14 2016

Jagr, Jaromir

The Case for ... JAROMIR JAGR J. Fuchs and T. Keith color *Sports Illustrated* v127 no9 p19 S 25 2017

Jaguar

MIGRANTS J. Mark *Sierra* v102 no5 p30 St/O 2017

Jaguar automobile—Evaluation

2017 JAGUAR XE 35T AWD R-SPORT J. Sabatini color *Car & Driver* v62 no10 p/8 Ap 2017

2018 Jaguar: E-Pace K. Pleskot color *Motor Trend* v69 no11 p18 N 2017

THE CHALLENGERS T. QUIROGA color *Car & Driver* v62 no7 p54 Ja 2017

CONVERGENCE THEORY A. MacKenzie color *Motor Trend* v69 no7 p118 Jl 2017

EVERYDAY HEROES [Cover story] C. Seabaugh, A. MacKenzie et al chart color *Motor Trend* v69 no5 p34 My 2017

The Finalists... color *Motor Trend* v69 no1 p134 Ja 2017

Fleet Files D. VanderWerp, J. Sabatini et al color diag *Car & Driver* v63 no1 p88 Jl 2017

Jaguar F-Pace chart color *Motor Trend* v69 no1 p66 Ja 2017

Jaguar XE chart color *Motor Trend* v69 no1 p140 Ja 2017

The New Luxury Trucks E. DYER color *Popular Mechanics* v193 no7 p50 S 2016

VS cartoon *Car & Driver* v62 no7 p44 Ja 2017

Jaguar Cars Ltd.

Wayne Burgess A. Priddle color *Motor Trend* v69 no10 p26 O 2017

Jaguar Land Rover Automotive PLC

2017 Land Rover Discovery color *Motor Trend* v69 no3 p28 Mr 2017

CONVERGENCE THEORY A. MacKenzie color *Motor Trend* v69 no7 p118 Jl 2017

DISCO IS BACK A. Priddle chart color *Motor Trend* v69 no6 p98 Je 2017

Exclusive Land Rover Discovery S. Evans color *Motor Trend* v69 no12 p18 D 2016

FJORD EXPLORER E. Loh chart color *Motor Trend* v69 no11 p100 N 2017

HIGH RANGE A. MacKenzie color *Motor Trend* v69 no5 p102 My 2017

Jaguar F-Pace chart color *Motor Trend* v69 no1 p66 Ja 2017

Jaguar XE chart color *Motor Trend* v69 no1 p140 Ja 2017

Jaguar XF chart color *Motor Trend* v69 no1 p127 Ja 2017

Suburban Safari D. Pund color *Car & Driver* v62 no11 p98 My 2017

Velar–Oh! D. G. Johnson color *Car & Driver* v63 no5 p112 N 2017

WHICH Luxury SUV Are YOU? color *Esquire* v166 no4 p78 N 2016

Jaguar XF automobile—Evaluation

CLIMB EVERY MOUNTAIN T. Quiroga chart color *Car & Driver* v62 no11 p54 My 2017

Proceed With Caution color *Consumer Reports* v82 no4 p20 Ap 2017

Jaguar E-type automobile

2018 Jaguar: E-Pace K. Pleskot color *Motor Trend* v69 no11 p18 N 2017

Jaguarundi

A LITTLE CAT GOES A LONG WAY M. JAFFE *Arizona Highways* v93 no9 p48 S 2017

Wild Cat Academy A. KLEPEIS color map *National Geographic Kids* no473 p30 S 2017

Jahiel, Jessica

Day-Ride Essentials color *Trail Rider* v29 no3 p63 Ap 2017

Horse Owner's Spring Notebook color *Trail Rider* v29 no4 p38 My 2017

Which Saddle is for You? [Cover story] color *Trail Rider* v29 no2 p36 Mr 2017

Winter-Management Checklist color *Trail Rider* v29 no1 p31 Ja/F 2017

JÄHNIG, SONJA C.

Freshwater Megafauna: Flagships for Freshwater Biodiversity under Threat *BioScience* v67 no10 p919 O 2017

Jahren, Hope

Engineered Food Holds Our Future color *Time* v188 no16/17 p78 O 24 2016

Lab Girl E. T. Cloyd color *Issues in Science & Technology* v33 no1 p92 Fall 2016

No. 9 LAB GIRL L. Greenblatt color *Entertainment Weekly* no1444/1445 p108 D 16 2016

Jails—United States

Jailhouse Experiments *Governing* v30 no10 p11 Jl 2017

Jaimes, Truen

DYE HARD J. KENT-DOOLAN color *Indianapolis Monthly* p30 Ap 2017

Jain, Amy—Interviews

AMY JAIN J. Chen *Bloomberg Businessweek* no4521 p67 My 8 2017

JAIN, ANDREA

THE CASE OF BIKRAM YOGA color *Tricycle: The Buddhist Review* v26 no3 p53 Spr 2017

Jain, Ankit

Efficient and stable solution-processed planar perovskite solar cells via contact passivation bibl graph *Science* v355 no6326 p722 F 17 2017

Jain, Piyanka

Improving Customer Satisfaction with Simple Analytics *Harvard Business Review Digital Articles* p2 N 17 2015

Jain, Rakesh K.

Origins of lymphatic and distant metastases in human colorectal cancer diag graph *Science* v357 no6346 p55 Jl 7 2017

Jain, Sachin H.

How Pharma Can Offer More than Pills *Harvard Business Review Digital Articles* p2 Jl 23 2015

Redesigning Care for High-Cost, High-Risk Patients color *Harvard Business Review Digital Articles* p2 F 7 2017

Reinventing the Way Medicaid Delivers Care *Harvard Business Review Digital Articles* p2 Mr 31 2015

The Skills Doctors and Nurses Need to Be Effective Executives *Harvard Business Review Digital Articles* p2 Ap 7 2015

Start-Ups Are Helping Consumers Make Better Health Care Purchases *Harvard Business Review Digital Articles* p2 Ja 13 2015

Two Ways to Better Care for Patients with Dementia *Harvard Business Review Digital Articles* p2 Ag 11 2015

Jain, Umang

The microbial metabolite desaminotyrosine protects from influenza through type I interferon graph *Science* v357 no6350 p498 Ag 4 2017

Jaipur (India)—Description & travel

India Full-On S. McAlpine bw color *Conde Nast Traveler* v52 no10 p100 N 2017

More Is More H. YANAGIHARA color *Conde Nast Traveler* v52 no5 p50 My 2017

Jais, Nina

Can Insurance Companies Incentivize Their Customers to Be Healthier? *Harvard Business Review Digital Articles* p2 Je 23 2017

Jakes, T. D.

Making Room at the Table color *Ebony* v72 no4 p73 F 2017

Jakiel, Richard

Napoleon's Comets *Sky & Telescope* v133 no5 p52 My 2017

The obsessive comet hunter bw color *Astronomy* v45 no2 p54 F 2017

Phantoms of the Deep Sky *Sky & Telescope* v133 no6 p70 Je 2017

JAKIN, STEVE

THE SECRET LIFE OF ANIMALS cartoon *Reader's Digest* v190 no1134 p38 O 2017

Jaklenec, Ana

Fabrication of fillable microparticles and other complex 3D microstructures color diag *Science* v357 no6356 p1138 S 15 2017

Jakobsen, Amalie

AMALIE JAKOBSEN L. DeLand color *Art in America* v104 no10 p154 N 2016

Jakosky, B. M.

Mars' atmospheric history derived from upper-atmosphere measurements of 38 Ar/36Ar diag *Science* v355 no6332 p1408 Mr 31 2017

Jakowenko, Laura

TAKING THE Radio City STAGE color *Dance Spirit* v20 no10 p30 D 2016

Jalali, B.

Real-time spectral interferometry probes the internal dynamics of femtosecond soliton molecules diag *Science* v356 no6333 p50 Ap 7 2017

Jalebi, Mojtaba Abdi

High-performance light-emitting diodes based on carbene-metal-amides chart graph *Science* v356 no6334 p159 Ap 14 2017

Jallow, Muminatou

Resistance to malaria through structural variation of red blood cell invasion receptors diag *Science* v356 no6343 p1139 Je 16 2017

JAM

CLUCK OFF bw *Advocate* no1091 p26 Je/Jl 2017

A Controversial Orientation? color *Advocate* no1091 p111 Je/Jl 2017

KUNG-FU APPALACHIAN PUNK color *Advocate* no1091 p34 Je/Jl 2017

OUT OF THE MOUTHS OF BABES cartoon *Advocate* no1091 p34 Je/Jl 2017

Jam (Preserves)

A Fair to Remember K. WISE *D: The Magazine of Dallas* v43 no10 p7 O 2016

MAKE JAMS WITH LESS SUGAR: These recipes and tips offer a variety of options for preserving low-sugar jams without commercial pectin A. Chesman *Mother Earth News* no283 p16 Ag/S 2017

Jamaica

I Tried a Runcation N. Blades color *Health* v31 no6 p57 Jl 2017

Jamal, Ahmad

Marseille M. Mercer color *Downbeat* v84 no9 p59 S 2017

James, Aaron

Being and Gnarliness: A philosopher explains why surfers are right and Sartre is wrong J. RYERSON *New York Times Book Review* p16 Ag 20 2017

James, Bill

Close *Publishers Weekly* v264 no12 p56 Mr 20 2017

James, Bill, 1949——Interviews

Murder Analytics L. PICKER *Publishers Weekly* v264 no35 p116 Ag 28 2017

James, C. Renee

CONFESSIONS OF A master sketcher bw color *Astronomy* v45 no2 p58 F 2017

Pulsars at 50 still going strong [Cover story] bw color diag graph *Astronomy* v45 no5 p22 My 2017

JAMES, CARYN

The Talented Mr. Gilmour: Elizabeth Day's psychological thriller, about an aristocrat's birthday party gone awry, updates Waugh, Highsmith and Fitzgerald *New York Times Book Review* p14 S 10 2017

James, Chenault

Worth the Wait K. Owen color *Southern Living* v52 no5 p28 My 2017

James, Clive, 1939-

The Joys of Binge-Watching J. PARKER *New York Times Book Review* p10 O 9 2016

James, Dan

Coaching With Purpose *Tennis* v52 no6 p75 N/D 2016

James, David

Extensive migration of young neurons into the infant human frontal lobe color diag graph *Science* v354 no6308 paaf7073-1 O

7 2016

James, Eric

The Spooky Express Texas *Publishers Weekly* v264 no26 p179 Je 26 2017

JAMES, FRANK A. III

Wrestling with Eternity *Christianity Today* v60 no10 p58 D 2016

James, Garrett

MATT "ARCHY" ARCHBOLD 47, SAN CLEMENTE, CALIFORNIA bw *Surfer* v57 no12 p34 Ja/F 2017

James, Henry, 1843-1916

The Portrait of a Man D. Green color *Weekly Standard* v22 no47 p42 Ag 21 2017

James, José, 1978-

JOSÉ JAMES 'TORNADO OF CREATIVITY' [Cover story] P. Lutz color *Downbeat* v84 no5 p28 My 2017

James, Joshua Isaac

Promoting human rights through science color *Science* v357 no6359 p34 O 6 2017

James, Kat

CAN NUTRITION CHANGE YOUR PERSONALITY? chart color *Amazing Wellness* v9 no1 p48 Wint 2017

CAN NUTRITION CHANGE YOUR PERSONALITY? color *Better Nutrition* v79 no6 p46 Je 2017

recent study correlates multi-strain probiotics with blood sugar benefit color *Better Nutrition* v79 no10 p18 O 2017

James, Kevin, 1965-

KEVIN CAN WAIT I. Ratledge *TV Guide* v65 no39 p32 S 18 2017

Kevin Can Wait J. Halterman *TV Guide* v64 no46 p31 N 7 2016

KEVIN CAN WAIT J. HALTERMAN *TV Guide* v65 no11 p28 Mr 6 2017

James, King of England

THE MAKING OF THE PILGRIMS D. Huntley *British Heritage Travel* v38 no3 p36 My/Je 2017

James, LeBron, 1984-

COMFORT EATS & TREATS FROM SOME OF OUR FAVORITE CELEBS S. E. JAMISON color *Ebony* v72/73 no12/1 p62 O/N 2017

For the Record color *Time* v189 no22 p6 Je 12 2017

HOT | NOT T. Keith color *Sports Illustrated* v126 no12 p17 My 1 2017

In It to Win It R. Sullivan color *Vogue* v207 no9 p330 S 2017

KEEPING IT 100 S. MEHTA color *Vanity Fair* v58 no11 p42 N 2016

Leading Off color *Sports Illustrated* v125 no20 p10 D 19 2016

Power Players T. Keith color *Sports Illustrated* v125 no20 p22 D 19 2016

SAVE US, LEBRON! G. Wahl and J. Feldman color *Sports Illustrated* v126 no11 p68 Ap 17-24 2017

SI's Top 100 B. Golliver, R. Mahoney et al color *Sports Illustrated* v125 no14 p94 O 24-31 2016

Social Climbers T. Keith color *Sports Illustrated* v125 no19 p24 D 12 2016

Starring The King [Cover story] M. Anthony Green color *GQ: Gentlemen's Quarterly* v97 no11 p86 N 2017

We Knew Them When Z. O'MALLEY GREENBURG, M. BERG et al color *Forbes* v199 no1 p22 Ja 24 2017

James, LeBron, 1984-——Awards

Cover *Sports Illustrated* v125 no20 pC1 D 19 2016

Greatest of the Great color *Sports Illustrated* v125 no20 p18 D 19 2016

Sportsperson of the Year LEBRON JAMES [Cover story] L. Jenkins color *Sports Illustrated* v125 no20 p32 D 19 2016

James, M. R. (Montague Rhodes), 1862-1936

BAD MOON RISING M. R. James *Lapham's Quarterly* v10 no3 p95 Summ 2017

The Greatest of Ghost Stories N. CLARK bw *American Conservative* v15 no6 p55 N/D 2016

James, Marlon

DOUBLE THE DENIM color *Esquire* p54 My 2017

Screaming Karaoke *New York Times Magazine* p42 O 8 2017

James, Max

'THE HARDER I FALL, THE HIGHER THE BOUNCE' D. Eng color *Fortune* v175 no8 p72 Je 15 2017

James, Nathan R.

Translational termination without a stop codon bibl color *Science*

v354 no6318 p1437 D 16 2016

James, Peter
You need nature, stat color *Redbook* p81 My 2017

James, Richard
BENCHMARK: SPRING FLING J. KEATS color *Wired* v25 no9 p50 S 2017

James, Sabrina
3 Ways to Show "Mumpathy" *Parents* v91 no6 p13 Je 2016
4 "Mom" Things People Insult That Are Actually Pretty Darn Awesome *Parents* v92 no1 p7 Ja 2017
Bikers Who Deliver Breast Milk color *Parents* v92 no5 p14 My 2017
Dads Are So Hot Right Now *Parents* v91 no12 p11 D 2016
Home for the Holidays *Parents* p17 2015
if you ask me... color *Parents* v92 no4 p100 Ap 2017
if you ask me... color *Parents* v92 no6 p100 Je 2017
if you ask me... or me *Parents* v91 no6 p108 Je 2016
if you ask me ... *Parents* v91 no10 p96 O 2016
if you ask me... *Parents* v91 no9 p132 S 2016
The Kids Are All Right *Parents* v92 no2 p13 F 2017
Let's Hear It for the Dads color *Parents* v92 no6 p15 Je 2017
PARENT CRUSH *Parents* v91 no9 p15 S 2016
parents 2 parents cartoon color graph *Parents* v92 no3 p9 Mr 2017
Try These Five Fun Ideas! color *Parents* v92 no8 p30 Ag 2017
We Swear It's Okay! color *Parents* v92 no8 p16 Ag 2017

James, Samuel
ASPHALT GARDENS *Harper's Magazine* p50 Ap 2017

JAMES, SAMUEL D.
WELCOMING THE STRANGER ... AND UPHOLDING THE LAW color *Christianity Today* v61 no4 p59 My 2017

James, Stephan
Shots Fired M. ROUSH *TV Guide* v65 no13 p18 Mr 20 2017

James, Steve
Hoop Dreams G. YUE color *Film Comment* v53 no1 p63 Ja/F 2017

James, Warren
ELEMENTAL VISION color *Old House Journal* v45 no3 p32 My 2017

James, William, 1842-1910
Walking Backward Toward the Future J. BRICKLIN cartoon *Tricycle: The Buddhist Review* v26 no3 p26 Spr 2017

James Bay Region
OUT OF SIGHT J. GAMBLE color map *Canadian Geographic* v137 no2 p38 Mr/Ap 2017

James Bond films
What keeps me feeling cozy M. Rollins *Redbook* p14 N 2017

James Chance & the Contortions (Performer)
NIGHT LIFE *New Yorker* v92 no37 p12 N 14 2016

James L. Taylor Manufacturing Co.
Make Poughkeepsie Great Again W. BALDWIN color *Forbes* v199 no5 p40 My 16 2017

James River Batteau Festival Trail (Va.)
JOURNEY DOWN THE JAMES: James River Batteau Festival gears up for its 32nd trip downriver E. J. Wallace *Virginia Living* v15 no4 p25 Je 2017

James Webb Space Telescope (Spacecraft)
Eyes In the Sky J. Kluger color *Time* v190 no1 p42 Jl 3 2017
Meet the Next-Generation Space Telescope K. HAYNES color diag *Discover* v38 no6 p84 Jl/Ag 2017
POPULAR MECHANICS EVERYWHERE color *Popular Mechanics* p10 N 2017

James Bender, A.
How the EMR Is Increasing Innovation and Creativity in Health Care *Harvard Business Review Digital Articles* p1 O 10 2017

Jameson, A.
The magnetic field and turbulence of the cosmic web measured using a brilliant fast radio burst bibl chart graph *Science* v354 no6317 p1249 D 9 2016

JAMESON, AMANDA
Go Stoveless il *Backpacker* v45 no1 p34 Ja 2017
WHAT I LEARNED color *Backpacker* v45 no1 p88 Ja 2017

Jameson, David
perspective interiors B. AGNESE *Architectural Record* v205 no4 p45 Ap 2017

Jameson, Fredric, 1934-
Philip Marlowe's Revolution J. Banville bw *New York Review of*

Books v63 no16 p38 O 27 2016

James Shen, Che-Kun
A placental growth factor is silenced in mouse embryos by the zinc finger protein ZFP568 color graph *Science* v356 no6339 p757 My 19 2017

Jami, Ata
Praising Customers for Ethical Purchases Can Backfire *Harvard Business Review Digital Articles* p2 O 6 2016

Jamieson, A.
An ecosystem-based deep-ocean strategy bibl color map *Science* v355 no6324 p452 F 3 2017

Jamieson, Victoria
... When You Can't Help Standing Out M. INGALL *New York Times Book Review* p25 Ag 27 2017

JAMIESON, WENDELL
Birth of the Blue: Bumbling constables led to the rise of New York's police force *New York Times Book Review* p16 Jl 2 2017

JAMIL, KATHY
Adding Value to Learning [Cover story] *Islamic Horizons* v46 no2 p28 Mr/Ap 2017

JAMIN, MENEDITH BEN
NETWORKING 101 color *Dance Spirit* v21 no8 p68 O 2017

Jamison, Darly
Strawberry Wine color *Publishers Weekly* v263 no51 p130 D 12 2016

Jamison, Judith, 1943-
ICONS C. Mueller bw color *Glamour* v115 no5 p190 My 2017
There's No One Right Age to Be Awesome C. Leive color *Glamour* v115 no5 p16 My 2017

Jamison, Kay Redfield
His Skunk Hours: A psychological biography of Robert Lowell explores the overlap of poetry and pathology P. BOSWORTH *New York Times Book Review* p13 Mr 5 2017
THE MANIA AND THE MUSE D. CHIASSON cartoon *New Yorker* v93 no5 p94 Mr 20 2017
Robert Lowell, Setting the River on Fire: A Study of Genius, Mania, and Character *Publishers Weekly* v263 no48 p60 N 28 2016

Jamison, Leslie
Chris KRAUS *Interview* v47 no6 p18 Ag 2017
Leslie Jamison *New York Times Book Review* p31 Ja 8 2017
THE MARCH ON EVERYWHERE *Harper's Magazine* p25 Ap 2017
Motherhood Lost *New York Times Book Review* p10 Ap 9 2017
What's the best book, new or old, you read this year? *New York Times Book Review* p27 D 25 2016

Jamison, Shantell E.
7 GREAT READS TO FALL INTO color *Ebony* v72 no11 p84 S 2017
AYESHA CURRY SCORES WITH HER TV SHOW & FOOD DELIVERY SERVICE color *Ebony* v72 no11 p60 S 2017
Be Innclusive color *Ebony* v72 no9 p77 Jl/Ag 2017
BOOK IT: FAVORITE READS FROM CHARLAMAGNE THA GOD color *Ebony* v72/73 no12/1 p85 O/N 2017
COMFORT EATS & TREATS FROM SOME OF OUR FAVORITE CELEBS color *Ebony* v72/73 no12/1 p62 O/N 2017
DON'T SETTLE, BOO: HOLD OUT FOR MR. RIGHT INSTEAD OF MR. RIGHT NOW color *Ebony* v72/73 no12/1 p67 O/N 2017
Getting Real with Detroit's Myya D. Jones color *Ebony* v72 no8 p24 Je 2017
HAPPILY UNMARRIED color *Ebony* v72 no11 p66 S 2017
How Alternative Medicine Saved My Life color *Ebony* v72 no9 p62 Jl/Ag 2017
THE MARIJUANA REVIVAL: A LOOK AT WEED'S CHANGING DEMOGRAPHIC color *Ebony* v72/73 no12/1 p66 O/N 2017
Meet Eritha Akilè Cainion, Millennial of Change color *Ebony* v72 no9 p25 Jl/Ag 2017
The Road to Freedom: How One Woman Became Debt-Free color *Ebony* v72 no9 p71 Jl/Ag 2017
STARCATION: TOKYO color *Ebony* v72/73 no12/1 p68 O/N 2017
The Truth About 'Black Love' color *Ebony* v72 no9 p66 Jl/Ag 2017

Jamiyat al-Ikhwan al-Muslimin (Egypt)
O Brotherhood, Where Art Thou? A. A. Zeid and Cook *Foreign*

Japan—Military policy

Is Japan Ready To Abandon Pacifism? A. Sharp, Yuki Hagiwara et al color *Bloomberg Businessweek* no4536 p37 S 4 2017

Japanese military entices academics to break taboo D. Normile color *Science* v355 no6323 p338 Ja 27 2017

Japan—Politics & government

Abe Tries To Polish His Tarnished Image I. Reynolds color *Bloomberg Businessweek* no4534 p30 Ag 14 2017

Recovering from Disaster, Reinventing Japan? S. KLIEN *Current History* v116 no791 p241 S 2017

Japan—Religion

Japan's Priests Turn to Property Development J. Clenfield, K. Kuwako et al color *Bloomberg Businessweek* no4521 p38 My 8 2017

JAPHARIDZE, IRINA

GEORGIAN RUGBY UNiTES TO END VIOLENCE AGAINST WOMEN AND GIRLS *UN Chronicle* v53 no2 p33 2016

Jaquess, James F.

A HALF A DOZEN BATTLES J. Goldberg bw *Atlantic* v320 no4 p10 N 2017

Jaramillo, Thomas F.

Combining theory and experiment in electrocatalysis: Insights into materials design bibl color graph *Science* v355 no6321 p1 Ja 13 2017

Jarche, Harold

The Best Leaders Are Constant Learners *Harvard Business Review Digital Articles* p2 O 16 2015

Jardina, Elizabeth

ALL IS CALM color *Sunset* v237 no6 p41 D 2016

Garden in motion color *Sunset* v238 no3 p36 Mr 2017

WILD AT HEART color *Sunset* v238 no3 p66 Mr 2017

Your CHECKLIST color *Sunset* v238 no1 p46 Ja 2017

Your CHECKLIST color *Sunset* v238 no5 p56 My 2017

Your CHECKLIST color *Sunset* v239 no1 p58 Jl 2017

Your CHECKLIST color *Sunset* v239 no4 p50 O 2017

Jardine, Joseph G.

Priming HIV-1 broadly neutralizing antibody precursors in human Ig loci transgenic mice bibl graph *Science* v353 no6307 p1557 S 30 2016

Jardine, Laura

Single-cell RNA-seq reveals new types of human blood dendritic cells, monocytes, and progenitors color *Science* v356 no6335 p283 Ap 21 2017

Jardine-Wright, Lisa

Rethinking the arrow of time color *Science* v353 no6307 p1504 S 30 2016

Jarman, Richard G.

Dengue diversity across spatial and temporal scales: Local structure and the effect of host population size bibl graph *Science* v355 no6331 p1302 Mr 24 2017

Rapid development of a DNA vaccine for Zika virus bibl graph *Science* v354 no6309 p237 O 14 2016

Jarmusch, Jim, 1953-

A Heart Full of Napalm J. JARMUSCH *Los Angeles Magazine* v61 no11 p92 N 2016

Paterson Sings the Poetry of Everyday Life In the City S. Zacharek color *Time* v189 no4 p50 Ja 23 2017

Jarmusch, Jim, 1953-—Interviews

COMMON SENSE A. TAUBIN bw color *Film Comment* v52 no6 p32 N/D 2016

Jarnow, Jesse

The Road Heats Up bw color *Rolling Stone* no1288 p11 Je 1 2017

Jarosh, Willow

the health nut A. Brightfield cartoon color *Better Homes & Gardens* v95 no3 p146 Mr 2017

Jarosz, Daniel F.

Old moms say, no Sir bibl diag *Science* v355 no6330 p1126 Mr 17 2017

JAROSZEWICZ, BOGDAN

Combining Biodiversity Resurveys across Regions to Advance Global Change Research *BioScience* v67 no1 p73 Ja 2017

Positive biodiversity-productivity relationship predominant in global forests bibl chart graph map *Science* v354 no6309 paaf8957-1 O 14 2016

Jaroussky, Philippe, 1978-

Philippe Jaroussky: Sacred Cantatas W. R. Braun *Opera News* v81 no9 p55 Mr 2017

Jarreau, Al, 1940-2017

Al Jarreau M. Vain color *Entertainment Weekly* no1454/1455 p22 F 24 2017

THE ESSENTIALS M. Vain *Entertainment Weekly* no1454/1455 p22 F 24 2017

Milestones *Time* v189 no7/8 p19 F 27 2017

Remembering Al Jarreau bw *Downbeat* v84 no5 p20 My 2017

VIRTUOSO VOCALIST G. BLACK color *Ebony* v72 no8 p98 Je 2017

JARRELL, ANDREA

MOTORCYCLE DIARY: Two empty-nesters, two wheels, and becoming the people we wanted to be *Washingtonian Magazine* v53 no1 p232 O 2017

Jarrell, Debbie

Around the Campfire color *Trail Rider* v29 no1 p6 Ja/F 2017

Jarrell, Randall, 1914-1965

The Gogol Notebook A. DAVIS-GARDNER *American Scholar* v86 no1 p106 Wint 2017

Jarrett, Keith, 1945-

Jarrett's Pivotal Moment D. OULLETTE color *Downbeat* v84 no2 p80 F 2017

JARRETT, KEVIN

Makerspaces and Design Thinking: Perfect Together! *Education Digest* v82 no4 p50 D 2016

Jarrett, Michael

THE INSIDE STORIES OF CLASSIC JAZZ RECORDINGS K. Micallef color *Downbeat* v84 no2 p95 F 2017

Jarrett, Ryan

RYAN JARRETT IS TOP '05 ALL-AROUND COWBOY J. Mankin color *Spin to Win Rodeo* v20 no10 p120 D 2016

JARRETT, VALERIE

OBAMA'S AMERICA img *New York* v49 no20 p12 O 3 2016

Jarrett, Valerie B., 1956-—Interviews

EXIT, LEFT A. HICKLIN color *Advocate* no1089 p30 F/Mr 2017

Jars (Containers)

A SINGULAR LANDSCAPE K. COATES color *Archaeology* v70 no1 p55 Ja/F 2017

Jarvis, Brooke

THE DISENROLLED *New York Times Magazine* p52 Ja 22 2017

UNDER WATER *New York Times Magazine* p64 Ap 23 2017

JARVIS, CLAIRE

Let Me Go: Women and girls eke out an existence in a patriarchal dystopia *New York Times Book Review* p18 O 15 2017

JARVIS, DEBRA

Down Off The Cross *Reader's Digest* v188 no1124 p18 O 2016

Jarvis, Erich

New technologies boost genome quality E. Pennisi chart color *Science* v357 no6346 p10 Jl 7 2017

Jarvis, Michaela

AAAS Leshner fellow aligns science with public service color *Science* v356 no6345 p1344 Je 30 2017

AAAS Leshner Fellows help confront climate impacts color *Science* v353 no6307 p1508 S 30 2016

AAAS Members Stand Up for Science color *Science* v357 no6349 p365 Jl 28 2017

AAAS reaches out to theology students color *Science* v354 no6319 p1544 D 23 2016

AAAS urges Trump team to value science and its benefits color *Science* v355 no6323 p359 Ja 27 2017

Bridges, not walls? color *Science* v356 no6336 p388 Ap 28 2017

Conference navigates gap between science and government color *Science* v354 no6311 p427 O 28 2016

New AAAS president emphasizes making the case for science color *Science* v355 no6327 p807 F 24 2017

Northeast Asia trip bolsters ongoing scientific cooperation color *Science* v354 no6315 p979 N 25 2016

Results of the 2016 election of AAAS officers *Science* v355 no6323 p360 Ja 27 2017

U.S.-Cuba scientific collaboration advances color *Science* v357 no6358 p1364 S 29 2017

Video games: The bad, the ugly, and the (potentially) good color *Science* v355 no6332 p1385 Mr 31 2017

Jarvis, Stephen

Q: What was the most important letter in history? color *Atlantic* v320 no2 p104 S 2017

Jarzyna, Marta A.
Biodiversity redistribution under climate change: Impacts on ecosystems and human well-being color *Science* v355 no6332 p1389 Mr 31 2017

JARZYNIECKI, TOM
Letters color *Nation* v303 no25/26 p2 D 19 2016

JASANOFF, SHEILA
Back from the Brink: Truth and Trust in the Public Sphere *Issues in Science & Technology* v33 no4 p25 Summ 2017

Jasinski, Adam
Confessions of a Reality TV FELON L. Rice color *Entertainment Weekly* no1463/1464 p80 Ap/My 2017

Jasinski, Laurie E.
A Rainbow in the Velvet of the Night *Sky & Telescope* v133 no2 p84 F 2017

JASKUNAS, PAUL
A Shrine That Endures color *America* v215 no16 p25 N 21 2016

Jasmine
AROUND THE GARDEN S. Bender color map *Southern Living* v52 no2 p46 F 2017
GARDEN-HOPPING WITH CHRISTIAN LOUBOUTIN color *Harper's Bazaar* no3653 p137 My 2017

Jasny, B. R.
Fostering reproducibility in industry-academia research color *Science* v357 no6353 p759 Ag 25 2017

Jasny, Barbara R.
PREDICTION AND ITS LIMITS [Cover story] color *Science* v355 no6324 p468 F 3 2017

Jason, Zachary
Kidz Bop *New York Times Magazine* p24 Mr 26 2017

Jason Bourne (Film)
JASON BOURNE C. Gunnestad color *Sound & Vision* v82 no4 p69 My 2017

Jasper, Christopher
Big Jets Get Squeezed color *Bloomberg Businessweek* no4539 p16 S 25 2017
A German, a Swede, and A Brit Walk Into a Hotel... cartoon chart *Bloomberg Businessweek* no4518 p18 Ap 10 2017
Long Reach, Big Problems bw *Bloomberg Businessweek* no4523 p22 My 22 2017

Jasper, Geremy
PATTI CAKE$ C. Agard color *Entertainment Weekly* no1463/1464 p70 Ap/My 2017

Jasper National Park (Alta.)
all access A. FINDLAY bw color *Bike Magazine* v24 no5 p70 Jl 2017

JASRA, ABDUL WAHID
Bridging the Gaps between Science and Policy for the Sustainable Management of Rangeland Resources in the Developing World *BioScience* v67 no7 p656 Jl 2017

Jastroch, Martin
Fat controls U bibl diag *Science* v355 no6330 p1124 Mr 17 2017

Jastrzembski, Frank
Valor The Fighting Parson color *Military History* v34 no4 p16 N 2017

Jaszberenyi, Sandor
The Cat Named Morphine *New York Times Magazine* p23 F 19 2017

Jaumann, R.
Seasonal exposure of carbon dioxide ice on the nucleus of comet 67P/Churyumov-Gerasimenko bibl bw graph *Science* v354 no6319 p1563 D 23 2016

Jauregui, Lauren—Interviews
The Fab Four R. MOSELY color *Seventeen* v76 no5 p80 S 2017

Javey, Ali
MoS2 transistors with 1-nanometer gate lengths bibl color graph *Science* v354 no6308 p99 O 7 2016

Javier, Christian
British Columbia Ry.'s FORT ST. JOHN SUB color diag *Model Railroader* v84 no11 p55 N 2017

Javornik, Ana
What Marketers Need to Understand About Augmented Reality *Harvard Business Review Digital Articles* p2 Ap 18 2016

Jawaid, Ali
Promoting human rights through science color *Science* v357 no6359 p34 O 6 2017

Jawlensky, Alexej von, 1864-1941—Exhibitions
NEW LIVES P. SCHJELDAHL cartoon *New Yorker* v93 no2 p72 F 27 2017

Jaws
CHINS UP: More Washington men are getting cosmetic injections to create stronger jawlines. What's behind the trend? C. Cunningham *Washingtonian Magazine* v53 no1 p113 O 2017

Jaws—Evolution
The first jaws J. A. Long bibl color *Science* v354 no6310 p280 O 21 2016
Fossil find revises history of jaws M. ROSEN color *Science News* v190 no11 p12 N 26 2016
A Silurian maxillate placoderm illuminates jaw evolution Min Zhu, P. E. Ahlberg et al bibl color *Science* v354 no6310 p334 O 21 2016

JAY, CHRIS
Chef Hardette Harris color *Louisiana Life* v37 no3 p54 Ja/F 2017
SECOND ACT color *Louisiana Life* v37 no3 p18 Ja/F 2017
SPRING FESTIVALS *Louisiana Life* v37 no4 p62 Mr/Ap 2017
SUGAR BUZZ color *Louisiana Life* v37 no2 p102 N/D 2016

JAY, MARTIN
POSITIVE FREEDOM color *Nation* v305 no2 p32 Jl 17 2017

Jay, Mike
'A Safe Place to Go Mad' P. MCGRATH *New York Times Book Review* p12 O 30 2016

Jayachandran, Seema
Cash for carbon: A randomized trial of payments for ecosystem services to reduce deforestation bw chart *Science* v357 no6348 p267 Jl 21 2017
A Friend's Support Can Make Women Better Entrepreneurs *Harvard Business Review Digital Articles* p2 Je 19 2015

Jayapal, Pramila
BANNED TOGETHER T. MURPHY color *Mother Jones* v42 no4 p39 Jl/Ag 2017

Jayapal, Pramila—Interviews
Resistance Is Not Enough [Cover story] J. WALSH color *Nation* v304 no17 p16 Je 5 2017

Jayaraman, Saru
THE OTHER NRA *Nation* v305 no11 p15 O 30 2017
Saru Jayaraman J. Eidelson color *Bloomberg Businessweek* no4528 p76 Je 26 2017

Jayaraman, Vivek
Ring attractor dynamics in the Drosophila central brain diag graph *Science* v356 no6340 p849 My 26 2017

Jay-Z, 1969-
BEY AND JAY'S DOUBLE DEBUT M. Vain chart color *Entertainment Weekly* no1472 p12 Je 30 2017
A TO Z W. Mason color *Esquire* p112 Je/Jl 2017
THE WORLD ACCORDING TO Gayle Gayle color *O, The Oprah Magazine* p25 Je 2017

Jazynka, Kitson
Amazing Animals color map *National Geographic Kids* no470 p12 My 2017
CAT GOES TO HIGH SCHOOL color map *National Geographic Kids* no465 p13 N 2016
DOG EATS SOCKS *National Geographic Kids* no466 p13 D 2016/Ja 2017
DONKEY LIVES IN HOUSE *National Geographic Kids* no469 p12 Ap 2017
Guinness World Records color *National Geographic Kids* no473 p5 S 2017
INTeRNATiONAL PHOTOgrAPHY CONTeST 2016 FOR KiDS Winners! color *National Geographic Kids* no470 p14 My 2017
RED FOX color *National Geographic Kids* no465 p30 N 2016
SECRETS OF THE GOLDEN GATE BRIDGE *National Geographic Kids* no467 p20 F 2017

Jazz
1917 [Cover story] J. McDonough bw color *Downbeat* v84 no1 p27 Ja 2017
81st READERS POLL COMPLETE RESULTS bw chart color *Downbeat* v83 no12 p56 D 2016
ARCHIVES PROVIDE WINDOW TO JAZZ HISTORY color *Downbeat* v84 no10 p115 O 2017
BECCA STEVENS: Regal Strength A. Morrison color *Downbeat* v84 no8 p52 Ag 2017
Boppin' Savoy Sessions T. PANKEN bw *Downbeat* v84 no3 p64

Mr 2017

Chords & Discords H. STEVEN MOFFIC, J. GARMAN et al color *Downbeat* v84 no9 p10 S 2017

Closing the Book, Opening the Ears J. SIMS bw *Downbeat* v84 no8 p84 Ag 2017

DRAWN TO JAZZ Y. Kato color *Downbeat* v84 no6 p114 Je 2017

EAST color *Downbeat* v84 no3 p73 Mr 2017

EVENT CALENDAR *Washingtonian Magazine* v52 no4 p206 Ja 2017

FOSTERING A WINNING TEAM T. Perkins color *Downbeat* v84 no6 p118 Je 2017

GEORGE GERSHWIN: HERE TO STAY J. McDonough bw *Downbeat* v84 no8 p38 Ag 2017

HOW TO BUY RECORDS R. D'AGOSTINO color *Popular Mechanics* p38 My 2017

Hungarian Jazz Showcase: 10 Years in the Spotlight H. Mandel color *Downbeat* v84 no5 p14 My 2017

Integrating Afro Caribbean Rhythms into Straightahead Jazz L. PERDOMO bw *Downbeat* v84 no10 p190 O 2017

INTERNATIONAL color *Downbeat* v83 no11 p96 N 2016

INTERNATIONAL color *Downbeat* v84 no3 p106 Mr 2017

JEN SHYU: Perpetually Compelling K. Micallef color *Downbeat* v84 no8 p53 Ag 2017

Listen To Learn the Jazz Language J. HARRIS color *Downbeat* v84 no8 p86 Ag 2017

The Main Harmonic Movement Principles Used in Jazz Composition F. CARUSO bw color *Downbeat* v84 no3 p108 Mr 2017

Matsuda Embraces Challenge K. Micallef color *Downbeat* v84 no8 p15 Ag 2017

Matthew Shipp's Evolution E. J. Holley color *Downbeat* v84 no5 p16 My 2017

Movers, Groovers & Shakers Prevail at New Orleans Jazz Fest D. Kunian color *Downbeat* v84 no8 p21 Ag 2017

Sound & Vision B. ZIMMERMAN color *Downbeat* v83 no11 p8 N 2016

SOUTH color *Downbeat* v84 no3 p84 Mr 2017

Still Chasin' the Trane cartoon *Weekly Standard* v22 no43 p34 Jl 24 2017

STRENGTH IN DIVERSITY Y. Kato color *Downbeat* v84 no6 p106 Je 2017

UNITED STATES color *Downbeat* v83 no11 p90 N 2016

Widner Big Band Camp Turns 30, Remains True to Kenton's Format T. Perkins color *Downbeat* v84 no6 p134 Je 2017

Jazz at Lincoln Center Orchestra (Performer)

JAZZ AT LINCOLN CENTER ORCHESTRA P. LUTZ color *Downbeat* v83 no12 p50 D 2016

JLCO Launches '100 Years of Jazz' Series with Jazz Age Suite B. Zimmerman color *Downbeat* v84 no1 p14 Ja 2017

Jazz concerts

Birthday Milestone: Corea Relives Davis Years at Blue Note T. Panken color *Downbeat* v84 no1 p13 Ja 2017

Brainfeeder Showcase Fuses Enlightened Funk, Innovative Jazz S. J. O'Connell color *Downbeat* v83 no12 p19 D 2016

'Ella 100' Celebrates First Lady of Song R. Musto color *Downbeat* v84 no1 p18 Ja 2017

Horn of Plenty K. Silsbee bw *Downbeat* v83 no12 p13 D 2016

JAZZ AT LINCOLN CENTER ORCHESTRA P. LUTZ color *Downbeat* v83 no12 p50 D 2016

JLCO Launches '100 Years of Jazz' Series with Jazz Age Suite B. Zimmerman color *Downbeat* v84 no1 p14 Ja 2017

MEHMET ALI SANLIKOL F. Bouchard color *Downbeat* v84 no1 p22 Ja 2017

A Note on the Big Picture D. WILENSKY color *Downbeat* v84 no3 p110 Mr 2017

Russell 'Dazzles' in Denver N. Provizer color *Downbeat* v84 no8 p17 Ag 2017

UNPLUGGING AT JAZZ CAMP WEST Y. Kato color *Downbeat* v84 no3 p97 Mr 2017

Jazz dance

I DON'T COMPETE. Madison Warnick color *Dance Spirit* v21 no8 p67 O 2017

Jazz ensembles

LITCHFIELD FOSTERS 'LIFETIME CONNECTIONS' J. Hale color *Downbeat* v84 no3 p72 Mr 2017

TOM TEASLEY j. poet color *Downbeat* v83 no11 p24 N 2016

Jazz exercise

REVAMPING RESOLUTIONS K. Massicot color *New Orleans Magazine* v51 no3 p32 Ja 2017

Jazz festivals

50 Years of Greatness E. Enright bw color *Downbeat* v83 no11 p86 N 2016

Almost Too Much Music M. Griffith color *New Orleans Magazine* v51 no7 p50 My 2017

The Art of Mosaic-Making at Vossa Jazz J. Woodard color *Downbeat* v84 no7 p20 Jl 2017

Atlanta Jazz Fest Mixes Global Icons, Local Talent J. Ross color *Downbeat* v84 no5 p105 My 2017

Bold in the Cold: Finland's Tampere Jazz Happening Makes an Impact J. Woodard color *Downbeat* v84 no2 p17 F 2017

CANADA color *Downbeat* v84 no5 p128 My 2017

EAST color *Downbeat* v84 no5 p96 My 2017

Edgefest Now Bigger Than Ever A. Drouot color *Downbeat* v83 no11 p95 N 2016

Elkhart Hosts Massive Jazz Party T. Perkins color *Downbeat* v84 no5 p111 My 2017

Festive Activism T. Panken color *Downbeat* v83 no11 p99 N 2016

Frisell, Lloyd Assert Mastery in Funchal T. Panken color *Downbeat* v84 no10 p25 O 2017

Generations Unite at Litchfield Jazz Fest B. Zimmerman color *Downbeat* v84 no10 p18 O 2017

Hampton Fest Spotlights Stars, Students J. Ross color *Downbeat* v84 no5 p15 My 2017

Hot Jazz Festival Sizzles in New York B. Milkowski color *Downbeat* v83 no12 p17 D 2016

Java Jazz Provides Sonic Travelogue J. Ephland color *Downbeat* v84 no6 p14 Je 2017

Jazz at the Limits: Avant Artists Convene at Edgefest A. Drouot color *Downbeat* v84 no2 p18 F 2017

Jazz on the French Riviera A. Drouot color *Downbeat* v84 no5 p132 My 2017

MAY/JUNE K. Massicot color *Louisiana Life* v37 no5 p62 My/Je 2017

Mellow Moods, Deep Grooves in Montreal E. Enright color *Downbeat* v84 no10 p17 O 2017

Memorable Tributes Enliven Newport Sets B. Milkowski color *Downbeat* v84 no10 p14 O 2017

MIDWEST color *Downbeat* v84 no5 p112 My 2017

MOKSHA J. Ephland color *Downbeat* v84 no1 p25 Ja 2017

Monterey Nurtured by Music D. Ouellette bw color *Downbeat* v84 no5 p92 My 2017

Motor City Magic T. Panken color *Downbeat* v83 no11 p14 N 2016

Mutually Beneficial Exchange B. REED color *Downbeat* v84 no9 p8 S 2017

Rare Gems Stand Out at North Sea Fest D. Ouellette color *Downbeat* v84 no9 p21 S 2017

Reaching Youngsters B. REED color *Downbeat* v84 no7 p8 Jl 2017

Rhythm Rules at PDX Jazz Fest P. de Barros color *Downbeat* v84 no5 p13 My 2017

Rocking Grooves, Roaring Oceans at DR Jazz Fest T. Panken color *Downbeat* v84 no2 p14 F 2017

Shorter, Metheny Play it Cool at Monterey Jazz Fest D. Ouellette color *Downbeat* v83 no12 p14 D 2016

SOUTH color *Downbeat* v84 no5 p106 My 2017

Toronto Highlights Diversity J. Hale color *Downbeat* v84 no5 p127 My 2017

Vocal Dynamos Add Spark to Umbria Jazz Fest D. Ouellette color *Downbeat* v84 no10 p22 O 2017

Vocal Identity T. Panken color *Downbeat* v83 no11 p26 N 2016

WEST color *Downbeat* v84 no5 p118 My 2017

Winter Jazzfest Artists Address Social Justice M. J. West color *Downbeat* v84 no3 p14 Mr 2017

Yankee's favorite events this season color *Yankee* p70 Jl 2017

Jazz festivals—Idaho

Thriving in Idaho J. Ross color *Downbeat* v84 no1 p92 Ja 2017

Jazz instruction

EAST color *Downbeat* v84 no10 p86 O 2017

INTERNATIONAL color *Downbeat* v84 no10 p180 O 2017

MIDWEST color *Downbeat* v84 no10 p130 O 2017

SOUTH color *Downbeat* v84 no10 p116 O 2017

WEST bw color *Downbeat* v84 no10 p156 O 2017

Jazz musicians
See also
Women jazz musicians
AFTER PETE J. BERRY color *New Orleans Magazine* v51 no1 p56 N 2016
Atlanta Jazz Fest Mixes Global Icons, Local Talent J. Ross color *Downbeat* v84 no5 p105 My 2017
Cécile McLorin Salvant: True Character [Cover story] P. Lutz color *Downbeat* v84 no10 p34 O 2017
Center of the Storm B. Bambarger bw *Downbeat* v84 no10 p32 O 2017
Chords & Discords S. COMINGS, G. MILLIKEN et al bw color *Downbeat* v84 no2 p10 F 2017
DRIVEN & DETERMINED B. Bambarger color *Downbeat* v84 no9 p54 S 2017
EAST color *Downbeat* v84 no5 p96 My 2017
Elkhart Hosts Massive Jazz Party T. Perkins color *Downbeat* v84 no5 p111 My 2017
Embracing Your Current Improv Vocabulary M. SHEVITZ bw color *Downbeat* v84 no5 p80 My 2017
FRED HERSCH TRUTH TELLER P. Lutz color *Downbeat* v84 no9 p34 S 2017
Giordano's Future in the Past K. Micallef color *Downbeat* v83 no11 p20 N 2016
Good for Circulation P. MARGASAK color *Downbeat* v84 no2 p16 F 2017
Improvising over Contemporary Harmonies Using Common Tones A. J. GARCÍA bw color *Downbeat* v84 no1 p98 Ja 2017
MARIA SCHNEIDER ATTACKING THE 'DATA LORDS' [Cover story] A. MORRISON color *Downbeat* v83 no12 p26 D 2016
MATT WILSON: LIFE'S CALLING D. Ouellette color *Downbeat* v84 no9 p44 S 2017
Monterey Nurtured by Music D. Ouellette bw color *Downbeat* v84 no5 p92 My 2017
A Note on the Big Picture D. WILENSKY color *Downbeat* v84 no3 p110 Mr 2017
ONE FAN AT A TIME J. Garelick color *Downbeat* v84 no9 p50 S 2017
ROSCOE MITCHELL: 'PEOPLE DON'T WANT TO BE CATEGORIZED' T. Panken color *Downbeat* v84 no9 p40 S 2017
SOUTH color *Downbeat* v84 no5 p106 My 2017
Thielemans Remembered as Pioneer bw *Downbeat* v83 no11 p21 N 2016
Tom Sancton J. Berry color *New Orleans Magazine* v51 no9 p28 Jl 2017
Trost Records Fuses Punk Ethos with Jazz Artistry P. MARGASAK bw *Downbeat* v83 no11 p18 N 2016
VIRTUOSO VOCALIST G. BLACK color *Ebony* v72 no8 p98 Je 2017
Jazz musicians—United States
Living the Dream J. B. Dyas color *Downbeat* v84 no1 p84 Ja 2017
Jazz singers
Al Jarreau M. Vain color *Entertainment Weekly* no1454/1455 p22 F 24 2017
And All That Jazz *Los Angeles Magazine* p67 Mr 2017
Ella by Starlight T. Gioia bw *Weekly Standard* v22 no29 p30 Ap 3 2017
Ella Fitzgerald J. McDonough bw *Downbeat* v84 no1 p38 Ja 2017
Remembering Al Jarreau bw *Downbeat* v84 no5 p20 My 2017
Jazz—2011-2020—Reviews
Chrome/Vertical P. Margasak color *Downbeat* v84 no10 p61 O 2017
Classical Confluence Y. KATO color *Downbeat* v84 no10 p68 O 2017
The Hot Box chart *Downbeat* v84 no10 p57 O 2017
Ozella's Northern Stars J. EPHLAND color *Downbeat* v84 no10 p60 O 2017
Jazz—Awards
See also
Down Beat Student Music Awards
OUTREACH YIELDS REWARDS IN VAIL P. de Barros color *Downbeat* v84 no6 p132 Je 2017
Jazz—Competitions
JAZZMEIA HORN J. Murph color *Downbeat* v84 no7 p24 Jl 2017

Jazz—Congresses
Bimhuis Eschews Trends P. Margasak color *Downbeat* v84 no2 p63 F 2017
Jazzie B (Performer)—Interviews
Jazzie B L. BRADLEY *Interview* v47 no1 p74 F 2017
Jazz—Instruction & study
Improvising over Contemporary Harmonies Using Common Tones A. J. GARCÍA bw color *Downbeat* v84 no1 p98 Ja 2017
Jazz Essential at Oberlin P. Lutz color *Downbeat* v84 no1 p110 Ja 2017
Jazz Studies Thrives at New Jersey's MSU P. Lutz color *Downbeat* v83 no12 p110 D 2016
Living the Dream J. B. Dyas color *Downbeat* v84 no1 p84 Ja 2017
University of the Pacific Fosters Collaborations Y. Kato color *Downbeat* v83 no11 p102 N 2016
Jazz—Instruction & study—Congresses
JEN Grows Up F. Alkyer color *Downbeat* v84 no4 p19 Ap 2017
Jazz—Reviews
JD Allen D. OUELLETTE color *Downbeat* v84 no5 p146 My 2017
Lloyd Marks Milestone at Oslo Fest J. Ephland color *Downbeat* v83 no11 p22 N 2016
Jazz—Social aspects
Bach to Basics II: Using Melodies To Suggest Harmony [Cover story] C. DAVIS bw color *Downbeat* v84 no5 p76 My 2017
Rocking Grooves, Roaring Oceans at DR Jazz Fest T. Panken color *Downbeat* v84 no2 p14 F 2017
Jazz—To 1921
All That Jass *Smithsonian* v47 no9 p13 Ja/F 2017
JB & FD (Short story)
JB & FD J. E. Wideman *Harper's Magazine* v334 no2001 p73 F 2017
JBL Inc.
JBL E55BT review: These modestly priced cans deliver strong features T. NICOLAKIS color *Macworld - Digital Edition* p102 Je 13 2017
J/Boats Inc.
J/112e A. Cort cartoon color diag *Sail* v48 no4 p26 Ap 2017
JBS SA
Will Bad Beef Taint Brazil's Meat Master? G. Freitas Jr., J. Brice et al cartoon chart *Bloomberg Businessweek* no4516 p20 Mr 27 2017
J.C. Penney Co. Inc.
CHAPTER UPDATE K. WHITE color *Phi Kappa Phi Forum* v96 no4 p8 Wint 2016
PENNEY WISE A. Gumbs color *Black Enterprise* v47 no2 p34 S 2016
A Thought for Your Penneys J. LILEKS *National Review* v69 no12 p33 Je 26 2017
JD Allen Trio (Performer)
JD Allen D. OUELLETTE color *Downbeat* v84 no5 p146 My 2017
JD.com Inc.
The Great Mall of China M. SCHUMAN and J. Ho chart color *Forbes* v198 no8 p48 D 20 2016
Jealousy
13 Resolutions Other People Really Need to Make This Year K. Bonnell and P. R. Satran color *Glamour* v115 no1 p99 Ja 2017
Listening to Jealousy [Cover story] S. ECKEL *Psychology Today* v49 no6 p50 N/D 2016
You're jealous of a colleague or friend S. Kempton color *Yoga Journal* p45 2016 Special Issue
Jean Lafitte National Historical Park & Preserve (La.)
BATTLE OF NEW ORLEANS ANNIVERSARY color *New Orleans Magazine* v51 no3 p25 Ja 2017
Jean Paul Gaultier SA
SNATCH That STYLE T. Ebony color *Ebony* v72 no9 p35 Jl/Ag 2017
Jeanneau (Company)
JEANNEAU NC 895: A NEW CONCEPT GETS AN OUTBOARD REDESIGN BUT KEEPS ITS PERFORMANCE CHOPS AND WEEKEND CRUISING ABILITY M. WERLING *Sea Magazine* v109 no9 p38 S 2017
LEADER OF THE PACK J. WOOLDRIDGE chart color *Power & Motoryacht* v32 no11 p114 N 2016
Sweet Summertime D. HARDING color *Power & Motoryacht*

v33 no2 p88 F 2017

Jeanneau America Inc.

Jeanneau 51 A. Cort color *Sail* v48 no7 p24 Jl 2017

JEANNEAU LEADER 30 M. WERLING *Sea Magazine* v109 no2 p38 F 2017

Jeanneret, Neryl

Research, practice, and policy connections: The ArtPlay case study bibl chart diag *Arts Education Policy Review* v118 no1 p37 2017

Jeanneret, Pierre

Hot Seat H. MARTIN bw color *Architectural Digest* v74 no2 p12 F 2017

Jean-Pierre, Azede, 1988-

Azéde Jean-Pierre J. Crelin color *Current Biography* v78 no6 p50 Je 2017

Jeans (Clothing)

Adam's DENIM GUIDE A. Glassman bw color *O, The Oprah Magazine* p51 Ag 2017

Ashley Graham DOES DENIM color *InStyle* v24 no2 p90 F 2017

ATTENTION, PLEASE! color *Essence* v47 no9 p14 Ja 2017

Being an Original color *InStyle* v24 no3 p180 Mr 2017

In Bloom S. ZLOTNICK and H. G. PHILLIPS color *Washingtonian Magazine* v52 no7 p80 Ap 2017

Jean Queens E. Wilson color *InStyle* v24 no7 p44 Jl 2017

THE MODERN GIRL A. Syrett color *InStyle* v24 no7 p110 Jl 2017

my style color *InStyle* v24 no4 p120 Ap 2017

Three Writers. Three Sizes. Three Perfect Pairs of Jeans L. Chan color *Glamour* v115 no2 p38 F 2017

Jeans (Clothing)—Evaluation

...And Now Just Jeans color *Glamour* no8 p52 Ag 2017

apparel color *Climbing* no352 p49 Ap 2017

Beach Bum cartoon color *Seventeen* v76 no12 p44 D 2016/Ja 2017

BEST BETS img *New York* v50 no15 p42 Jl 24 2017

CORNER OFFICE MATERIAL color *Esquire* p53 Je/Jl 2017

Denim, Your Way color *Glamour* no8 p45 Ag 2017

AN EYE FOR STYLE color *Martha Stewart Living* p50 Ap 2017

FEST FORWARD L. TUDOR color *New Orleans Magazine* v51 no6 p76 Ap 2017

Genius Jeans color *InStyle* v24 no4 p127 Ap 2017

If You're Living for the Weekend S. P. Nadella and A. Hou color *Glamour* v115 no9 p56 S 2017

MATTIE JAMES L. CROSS color *Ebony* v72 no6 p27 Ap/My 2017

MOM ON A MISSION color *Martha Stewart Living* p40 My 2017

my style color *InStyle* v24 no8 p96 Ag 2017

NEW PRODUCTS color *Spin to Win Rodeo* v20 no12 p30 F 2017

ONES TO WATCH color *Harper's Bazaar* no3651 p284 Mr 2017

Outfits for Days R. Wang color *Glamour* v115 no9 p74 S 2017

Return of the Kicking Jeans R. W. Young color *Black Belt* v55 no4 p76 Je/Jl 2017

THE RULES OF CASUAL COOL S. NYGAARD color *Men's Health* v32 no7 p(Sp)10 S 2017

Spring Fling color *Equus* no474 p24 Mr 2017

the start color *InStyle* v24 no3 p99 Mr 2017

STYLE color *Horse & Rider* v56 no1 p22 Ja 2017

Tapped Off B. Welch color *American Cowboy* v24 no1 p42 Je/Jl 2017

That Robe Life F. Kane, S. P. Nadella et al color *Glamour* v115 no3 p64 Mr 2017

The Thousand-Dollar Pair of Jeans J. MOORE color *GQ: Gentlemen's Quarterly* v87 no1 p9 Ja 2017

Turn and Burn color *American Cowboy* v24 no1 p44 Je/Jl 2017

We Made Plus-Size Jeans! L. Chan color *Glamour* no8 p54 Ag 2017

Wish LIST N. Fritton color *Harper's Bazaar* no3649 p130 D 2016/Ja 2017

JEAN SHELTON, SARAH

GET OUTSIDE! color *Good Housekeeping* v265 no1 p35 Jl 2017

Jeansonne, Glen, 1946-

Humanitarian Relief G. H. NASH bw *Weekly Standard* v22 no20 p34 Ja 30 2017

Unpopular Vote G. KABASERVICE *New York Times Book Review* p15 N 27 2016

Jebelli, Joseph

In Pursuit of Memory: The Fight Against Alzheimer's *Publishers*

Weekly v264 no36 p84 S 4 2017

Jecks, Michael

A Murder Too Soon *Publishers Weekly* v264 no30 p43 Jl 24 2017

Jeep automobile

See also

Cherokee automobile

Wagoneer automobile

5 THINGS TO KNOW ABOUT THE 2017 JEEP GRAND CHEROKEE SUMMIT C. Seabaugh color *Motor Trend* v69 no2 p57 F 2017

GARAGE C. Walton, J. Bishop et al chart color diag *Motor Trend* v69 no9 p104 S 2017

Jeep Grand Cherokee Trackhawk F. Markus and J. Udy color *Motor Trend* v69 no7 p20 Jl 2017

Jeep Yuntu concept E. Tahaney color *Motor Trend* v69 no8 p20 Ag 2017

Lost in Last Place color *Consumer Reports* v82 no8 p59 Ag 2017

Jeep automobile—Evaluation

GET USED TO THIS MUG C. Seabaugh and E. Ayapana chart color *Motor Trend* v69 no6 p82 Je 2017

A New Heading G. Fink cartoon color *Car & Driver* v62 no10 p88 Ap 2017

OVER LANDER'S DREAM C. Seabaugh chart color *Motor Trend* v69 no2 p54 F 2017

Jeet Kune Do

5 JEET KUNE DO FIGHTING PRINCIPLES L. M. I. DAVIS color *Black Belt* v55 no4 p40 Je/Jl 2017

KICKING TOOLS OF JKD T. TACKETT color *Black Belt* v55 no4 p46 Je/Jl 2017

Jeff, Kevin Iega

KEVIN IEGA JEFF J. BERG color *Chicago* v66 no2 p32 F 2017

Jefferies, Harold B. J.

A switch from canonical to noncanonical autophagy shapes B cell responses bibl graph *Science* v355 no6325 p641 F 10 2017

Jefferies, Sam

The D.C. Working Man's True Power Suit color *Washington Monthly* v49 no3-5 p6 Mr-My 2017

JEFFERS, GLENN

Father's Day: The Real Stories of Black Single Dads color *Ebony* v72 no8 p58 Je 2017

Moving to the Middle color *Ebony* v72 no6 p70 Ap/My 2017

THE WAY FORWARD bw color *Ebony* v72 no4 p84 F 2017

WOMEN UP color *Ebony* v72 no5 p70 Mr 2017

Your Guide to Recycling Black Dollars cartoon color *Ebony* v72 no3 p100 D 2016/Ja 2017

JEFFERS, THOMAS L.

So Long, Mary Ann *Commentary* v144 no3 p60 O 2017

Jefferson, Margo

Buddy System color *O, The Oprah Magazine* p150 My 2017

Buddy System M. Jefferson and E. Kendall color *O, The Oprah Magazine* p150 My 2017

'THE TROLLEY SONG' color *New York Times Magazine* p53 Mr 12 2017

Jefferson, Robin Seaton

Marceline bw color *Missouri Life* v44 no6 p44 S 2017

Jefferson, Sherri

Motor City *Publishers Weekly* v263 no44 p51 O 31 2016

Jefferson, Thomas, 1743-1826

Before the Scandal Broke M. SILK *Smithsonian* v47 no7 p25 N 2016

CENTRHL REGIOFL *Virginia Living* p22 2017 Best 20of Virginia

Thomas Jefferson's Letter Rack: David Esterly carves our past E. Pochoda color *Magazine Antiques* v184 no5 p92 S/O 2017

Weird But True! M. TERRELL color map *National Geographic Kids* no471 p4 Je/Jl 2017

Jefferson, Tony—Finance

TONY JEFFERSON'S Wild Ride A. Benoit color *Sports Illustrated* v126 no8 p68 Mr 20 2017

JEFFERY, CLARA

Don't Mourn. Fight cartoon *Mother Jones* v42 no1 p6 Ja/F 2017

HOW TO DEFLATE A DEMAGOGUE *Mother Jones* v42 no6 p4 N/D 2017

Journalism's Last Hurrah? *Mother Jones* v42 no5 p5 S/O 2017

Moscow on the Potomac color *Mother Jones* v42 no4 p5 Jl/Ag 2017

Readers of the Year *Mother Jones* v42 no3 p3 My/Je 2017

JEFFERY, ROBERT

HR should stand for humane rigour *People Management* p42 N 2016

"I'M A RECOVERING HR DIRECTOR": Lucy Adams has recast herself as a tough-talking consultant asking difficult questions about the future of HR. We posed a few of our own - on the BBC, the tabloids and the death of the HR manual *People Management* p42 Mr 2017

THERE ARE LOTS OF MIKE ASHLEYS OUT THERE *People Management* p46 O 2016

These are the experts deciding the future of HR... ...shouldn't you know who they are? [Cover story] *People Management* p24 Ag 2017

"Uber is going to be the best company in the world for women": HR chief Liane Hornsey explains how she'll banish the sexist culture that has made the taxi app the world's most beleaguered business *People Management* p40 S 2017

"We trained the whole organisation - and it didn't cost us anything": Britain's biggest nature charity shows how everyone can benefit from leadership training - not just leaders *People Management* p18 Mr 2017

"Without migrants, we don't have a business" *People Management* p34 Je 2017

JEFFERYS, DAVID

DAKAR color *Conde Nast Traveler* v52 no4 p30 Ap 2017

Jeffreys, Anna E.

Resistance to malaria through structural variation of red blood cell invasion receptors diag *Science* v356 no6343 p1139 Je 16 2017

Jeffreys-Jones, Rhodri

Public and Private Eyes J. Daskal cartoon *Foreign Affairs* v96 no6 p139 N/D 2017

We Know All About You: The Story of Surveillance in Britain and America *Publishers Weekly* v264 no12 p63 Mr 20 2017

JEFFRIES, MICHAEL P.

The Rage in Harlem, and Beyond *New York Times Book Review* p18 Ag 27 2017

JEFFRIES, STUART

Pop Goes German Philosophy color *Foreign Policy* no225 p70 Jl/Ag 2017

Jeffries, Tamara Y.

INTO THE LIGHT color *Essence* v47 no12 p88 Ap 2017

Jeganathan, Karthik B.

Cyclin A2 is an RNA binding protein that controls Mre11 mRNA translation bibl graph *Science* v353 no6307 p1549 S 30 2016

Jehovah's Witnesses

Defending the Faith (of Others) K. SHELLNUTT *Christianity Today* v61 no5 p17 Je 2017

Jeko, Anita

A large fraction of HLA class I ligands are proteasome-generated spliced peptides bibl graph *Science* v354 no6310 p354 O 21 2016

Jelassi, Tawfik

What I Learned from Leading a Tunisian Ministry During the Arab Spring *Harvard Business Review Digital Articles* p2 My 16 2016

Jelezko, Fedor

An integrated diamond nanophotonics platform for quantum-optical networks bibl graph *Science* v354 no6314 p847 N 18 2016

Submillihertz magnetic spectroscopy performed with a nanoscale quantum sensor diag *Science* v356 no6340 p832 My 26 2017

Jelicic, Katija

Sustained virologic control in SIV+ macaques after antiretroviral and α4β7 antibody therapy bibl graph *Science* v354 no6309 p197 O 14 2016

Jelinek, Kelly

To The Editor color *American Craft* v76 no6 p10 D 2016-Ja 2017

Jellicoe, Nicholas

Victory (?) at Sea J. F. CALLO bw *Weekly Standard* v22 no40 p37 Je 26 2017

Jellyfishes

BREATHE color *Prevention* v69 no8 p36 Ag 2017

The Immortal Jellyfish J. BERWALD color diag *Discover* v38 no10 p58 D 2017

Mozambique color *National Geographic* v231 no3 p8 Mr 2017

Persistence Counts B. Lang *Discover* v38 no10 p6 D 2017

Sleeping with the jellyfish color *Science* v357 no6358 p1333 S 29 2017

VISIONS color *National Geographic* v231 no3 p6 Mr 2017

Jellyfishes—Behavior

Lion's Mane Jelly (Cyanea capillata) S. MIDDLETON color *Issues in Science & Technology* v33 no2 p96 Wint 2017

Upside-down jellyfish pass sleep test M. QUINTANILLA color *Science News* v192 no7 p10 O 28 2017

Jelly's Last Jam (Theatrical production)

CALENDAR F. Esker *New Orleans Magazine* v51 no4 p26 F 2017

Jelly-Schapiro, Joshua

ISLANDS IN THE SUN T. GJELTEN *New York Times Book Review* p45 D 4 2016

MONARCHS cartoon *New Yorker* v93 no31 p20 O 9 2017

Where Globalization Began? C. Thubron color *New York Review of Books* v64 no10 p28 Je 8 2017

Jemisin, N. K.

COMMENTS color *Wired* v25 no3 p16 Mr 2017

THE EVALUATORS bw cartoon *Wired* v25 no1 p64 Ja 2017

Otherworldly *New York Times Book Review* p27 Mr 26 2017

Otherworldly *New York Times Book Review* p83 D 4 2016

Otherworldly: Science Fiction and Fantasy *New York Times Book Review* p35 My 21 2017

Science Fiction and Fantasy color *New York Times Book Review* p27 Ja 29 2017

Science Fiction and Fantasy *New York Times Book Review* p35 O 9 2016

Jemison, G. Peter

HISTORY & CULTURE COME TO LIFE—The Seneca Art & Culture Center at Ganondagan color *New York State Conservationist* v71 no2 p14 O 2016

Jemison, Mae, 1956-—Interviews

10 THINGS WE'RE TALKING ABOUT T. A. Christian color *Essence* v47 no8 p75 D 2016

Jena, Anupam B.

Do Doctors Get Worse as They Get Older? *Harvard Business Review Digital Articles* p2 My 23 2017

Immigrant Doctors Provide Better Care, According to a Study of 1.2 Million Hospitalizations color *Harvard Business Review Digital Articles* p2 F 3 2017

Research: Higher U.S. Physician Spending Doesn't Lead to Better Patient Outcomes *Harvard Business Review Digital Articles* p2 Mr 13 2017

To Increase Vaccination Rates, Share Information on Disease Outbreaks *Harvard Business Review Digital Articles* p2 F 22 2017

When Roads Are Closed for Marathons, More Elderly People Die of Heart Attacks *Harvard Business Review Digital Articles* p2 Ap 12 2017

Jenkin, Tim

Scary (and true) tales from a crag near you *Climbing* no352 p11 Ap 2017

JENKINS, ADAM

BE MORE METICULOUS *Sea Magazine* v109 no1 p24 Ja 2017

Sophia Hears the Siren's Song *Sea Magazine* v108 no8 p16 Ag 2016

Jenkins, Barry, 1979-

Barry Jenkins M. Rich bw *Current Biography* v78 no5 p39 My 2017

Black and blue J. SEMLEY color *Maclean's* v129 no43 p56 O 31 2016

BLACK POWER H. ALS color *New Yorker* v92 no34 p70 O 24 2016

THE MAKING OF BARRY JENKINS C. SWANSON img *New York* v49 no24 p122 N 28 2016

Mark BRADFORD: THE AMERICAN ARTIST HEADS TO VENICE WITH THE HOPE OF TURNING ACTIVISM INTO AN ART FORM *Interview* v47 no5 p106 Je/Jl 2017

THE MAVERICKS OF HOLLYWOOD J. Black, K. Sintumuang et al bw color *Esquire* v167 no2 p89 Mr 2017

Moonlight B. A. DuHamel chart color *Sound & Vision* v82 no6 p68 Jl/Ag 2017

Moonlight color *New Yorker* v93 no5 p14 Mr 20 2017

Moonlight Enchants by Revealing Itself In a Thousand Facets S. Zacharek color *Time* v188 no18 p43 O 31 2016

Moonlight *New Yorker* v92 no40 p17 D 5 2016

Moon Over Miami D. Pinckney color *New York Review of Books* v64 no7 p24 Ap 20 2017

The MORNING AFTER N. Sperling color *Entertainment Weekly* no1456 p52 Mr 10 2017

No. 2 MOONLIGHT L. Greenblatt color *Entertainment Weekly* no1444/1445 p50 D 16 2016

No Refuge R. Alleva color *Commonweal* v143 no20 p18 D 16 2016

One Part, Three Breakouts J. Yuan img *New York* v49 no21 p104 O 17 2016

Pioneers [Cover story] color *Time* v189 no16/17 p14 My 1-8 2017

Portrait of a Hustler T. CHATTERTON WILLIAMS color *Esquire* v166 no4 p40 N 2016

When History Makes the Cut B. R. Rich *Film Quarterly* v70 no3 p6 Spr 2017

Jenkins, Barry, 1979——Interviews

Barry Jenkins E. Berman color *Time* v189 no5 p56 F 13 2017

ONE STEP AHEAD: A CONVERSATION WITH BARRY JENKINS M. Boyce Gillespie *Film Quarterly* v70 no3 p52 Spr 2017

Jenkins, Barry, 1979——Political & social views

For the Record color *Time* v189 no9 p6 Mr 13 2017

Jenkins, Beverly

Chasing Down a Dream *Publishers Weekly* v264 no22 p40 My 29 2017

JENKINS, CLINTON N.

Mapping Conservation Strategies under a Changing Climate *BioScience* v67 no6 p494 Je 2017

Jenkins, Craig

6. See Gucci Mane and Zaytoven *New York* v50 no9 p100 My 1 2017

Is Culture Borrowing Always Theft? img *New York* v49 no15 p75 Jl 25 2016

OBAMA'S AMERICA img *New York* v49 no20 p12 O 3 2016

Run the Jewels Enter Their Blue Period img *New York* p79 F 9 2017

The Ten Best Pop Albums of the Year img *New York* v49 no25 p118 D 12 2016

To Do img *New York* p72 Ja 23 2017

To Do img *New York* v49 no20 p136 O 3 2016

To Do: Twenty-five things to see, hear, watch, and read img *New York* v50 no10 p106 My 15 2017

Tyler, the Obfuscator: The Odd Future leader sends mixed messages on his best album so far img *New York* v50 no16 p106 Ag 7 2017

Jenkins, Daniell Nielsen

Step Up to a Breakthrough color *Women's Health* v14 no9 p88 N 2017

JENKINS, EMILY

In Her Storied Land *New York Times Book Review* p22 N 13 2016

Jenkins, Florence Foster, 1868-1944

Accidental Diva *Opera News* v81 no5 p6 N 2016

Jenkins, Jack

Acts of Faith *Harper's Magazine* v333 no1998 p2 N 2016

Jenkins, Jo Ann

ARE WE READY FOR AN AGING WORLD? *Vital Speeches of the Day* v83 no10 p301 O 2017

"I wasn't over the hill, I was on top of the mountain, and I liked being there." color *AARP: The Magazine* v59 no2A p26 F/Mr 2016

PREPARING FOR THE 100-YEAR LIFE *Vital Speeches of the Day* v83 no4 p120 Ap 2017

Jenkins, John I.

LAND O' LAKES 50 YEARS ON bw color *America* v217 no2 p28 Jl 24 2017

Jenkins, Kris

The Power Of Three color *Sports Illustrated* v125 no15 p76 N 7 2016

Jenkins, Lee

Allen IVERSON [Cover story] color *Sports Illustrated* v127 no1 p32 Jl 3 2017

BIG LITTLE MAN color *Sports Illustrated* v127 no12 p42 O 16 2017

BRICKTOWN Bricolage color *Sports Illustrated* v126 no11 p76 Ap 17-24 2017

Embiid, Indiid color *Sports Illustrated* v125 no16 p42 N 14 2016

FO' BETTER OR FO' WORSE? [Cover story] color *Sports Illustrated* v126 no16 p34 Je 5 2017

FREAK UNLEASHED chart color *Sports Illustrated* v126 no1 p40 Ja 9 2017

Fun & Gun color *Sports Illustrated* v126 no3 p44 Ja 23 2017

HE'S THE ONE DURANT [Cover story] color *Sports Illustrated* v126 no17 p32 Je 19 2017

HOW OKC GOT ITS MAN color *Sports Illustrated* v127 no3 p50 Jl 24 2017

HUNTER GREENE IS EXACTLY WHAT BASEBALL NEEDS [Cover story] color *Sports Illustrated* v126 no12 p22 My 1 2017

THE HUSTLE color *Sports Illustrated* v126 no14 p32 My 15-22 2017

JIMMY BUTLER [Cover story] color *Sports Illustrated* v127 no12 p34 O 16 2017

PEYTON'S (OTHER) PLACE color *Sports Illustrated* v126 no11 p48 Ap 17-24 2017

A SIMPLE PLAN [Cover story] color *Sports Illustrated* v126 no7 p36 Mr 6 2017

Sportsperson of the Year LEBRON JAMES [Cover story] color *Sports Illustrated* v125 no20 p32 D 19 2016

Staying Power [Cover story] color *Sports Illustrated* v125 no14 p56 O 24-31 2016

The Stopper color *Sports Illustrated* v125 no14 p64 O 24-31 2016

That's Shoe Business color *Sports Illustrated* v125 no21 p68 D 26 2016

TROJAN FORCE color *Sports Illustrated* v127 no5 p78 Ag 14 2017

WHAT HAPPENED TO SUPERMAN? [Cover story] color *Sports Illustrated* v127 no9 p46 S 25 2017

WONDER WALL color *Sports Illustrated* v126 no12 p30 My 1 2017

JENKINS, MARK

Chess with Death color *Climbing* no355 p13 Ag 2017

EXTREME ATTRACTION color map *Backpacker* p58 Ag 2017

Forlorn Pinnacle bw color *Climbing* no355 p72 Ag 2017

Jenkins, McKay

Food Fight: GMOs and the Future of the American Diet *Publishers Weekly* v263 no43 p69 O 24 2016

Jenkins, Melissa

It Starts With a Fever A. WISNIEWSKI *American Forests* v123 no3 p46 Fall 2017

Jenkins, Michael

You Never Forget Your First Time diag il *Backpacker* v45 no2 p64 Mr 2017

Jenkins, Nash

After the Massacre [Cover story] color diag *Time* v190 no15 p22 O 16 2017

Congress Confronts a Daunting to-Do List color *Time* v190 no10/11 p16 S 18 2017

Death Reigns on the Streets of Duterte's Philippines color *Time* v189 no3 p28 Ja 16 2017

Do Androids Dream of Electric Sequels? color *Time* v190 no15 p53 O 16 2017

Duterte's Fiercest Critic Finds Herself In Jail color *Time* v189 no9 p11 Mr 13 2017

Next Generation Leaders color *Time* v188 no15 p41 O 17 2016

Otto Warmbier color *Time* v190 no1 p13 Jl 3 2017

Republicans Launch a Last-Ditch Effort to Repeal Obamacare *Time* v190 no13 p16 O 2 2017

Jenkins, Patty

Comic Critics J. PODHORETZ *Weekly Standard* v22 no39 p43 Je 19 2017

FINALLY [Cover story] N. Sperling color *Entertainment Weekly* no1467 p20 My 26 2017

The Superhero We've Been Waiting For L. Cornish and E. Mahaney color *Glamour* v115 no6 p110 Je 2017

WONDER WOMAN N. Sperling color *Entertainment Weekly* no1446/1447 p56 D 2016/Ja 2017

WONDER WOMAN N. Sperling color *Entertainment Weekly* no1463/1464 p50 Ap/My 2017

WONDER WOMAN WINS N. Sperling color *Entertainment Weekly* no1470 p8 Je 16 2017

Jenkins, Patty—Interviews

Patty Jenkins B. Luscombe color *Time* v189 no24 p56 Je 26 2017

Jenkins, Philip

The Baptist exception *Christian Century* v134 no10 p61 My 10

2017

The Catholic surge in Africa *Christian Century* v134 no6 p45 Mr 15 2017

Charismatic in Chile *Christian Century* v134 no12 p44 Je 7 2017

China's many revivals *Christian Century* v134 no13 p34 Je 21 2017

Crucible of Faith: The Ancient Revolution That Made Our Modern Religious World T. Jones *Christian Century* v134 no22 p39 O 25 2017

Ethiopia's martyred monks *Christian Century* v134 no2 p45 Ja 18 2017

Films against the church color *Christian Century* v134 no22 p44 O 25 2017

Goa, Rome of the East color *Christian Century* v134 no18 p44 Ag 30 2017

God among the gangs *Christian Century* v133 no24 p45 N 23 2016

Jakarta's Christian governor *Christian Century* v133 no26 p45 D 21 2016

The Maori: separate and equal? *Christian Century* v133 no22 p45 O 26 2016

Mission in the vernacular *Christian Century* v134 no4 p61 F 15 2017

The other Eastern churches *Christian Century* v134 no14 p44 Jl 5 2017

Pearl River Delta Christians *Christian Century* v134 no16 p36 Ag 2 2017

Speak of the devil *Christian Century* v134 no20 p44 S 27 2017

When God is silent color *Christian Century* v134 no5 p44 Mr 1 2017

Jenkins, Sally

Fit for a King bw *Smithsonian* v47 no10 p40 Mr 2017

JENKINS, STEVE

The Pig That Changed My Life color *Reader's Digest* v189 no1129 p74 Ap 2017

JENKINS,, MICHAEL A.

Combining Biodiversity Resurveys across Regions to Advance Global Change Research *BioScience* v67 no1 p73 Ja 2017

JENKS, TOM

Come, Labor On *American Scholar* v86 no1 p92 Wint 2017

Jennen, Birgit

An Establishment Firebrand in Germany color *Bloomberg Businessweek* no4514 p28 Mr 13 2017

Germany Builds An Election Firewall *Bloomberg Businessweek* no4527 p48 Je 19 2017

How Facebook Could Stop bw color *Bloomberg Businessweek* no4524 p56 My 29 2017

It's Merkel 3, Schulz 0 In German Campaign color *Bloomberg Businessweek* no4523 p16 My 22 2017

Jenner, Brian

BECAUSE WE THINK RHETORIC IS IMPORTANT *Vital Speeches of the Day* v83 no9 p275 S 2017

Jenner, Caitlyn, 1949-

CAITLYN JENNER I. Biedenharn color *Entertainment Weekly* no1463/1464 p108 Ap/My 2017

Jenner, Kendall, 1995-

The A-LIST K. Jenner color *Harper's Bazaar* no3653 p86 My 2017

Best-Dressed LIST color *Harper's Bazaar* no3655 p64 Ag 2017

Better to Gather color *Vogue* v207 no11 p138 N 2017

The Bullseye M. Snetiker color *Entertainment Weekly* no1462 p70 Ap 21 2017

KENDALL COMES OF AGE D. Peres bw color *Harper's Bazaar* no3653 p246 My 2017

Kendall Jenner color *InStyle* v24 no2 p109 F 2017

Kendall's Rules for Low-Key Beauty S. Kitchens color *Glamour* v114 no12 p130 D 2016

The Legs Have It color *Vogue* v207 no7 p116 Jl 2017

Oh Hey, Thongs: Welcome Back! A. Edwards Walker color *Glamour* v114 no7 p40 Jl 2016

Spot ON M. HOLGATE and M. GUIDUCCI color *Vogue* v207 no1 p34 Ja 2017

Jenner, Kylie, 1998-

E!'s Teen Queen of Screens D. D'addario color *Time* v190 no6 p52 Ag 7 2017

Jean on Jean? Genius! color *Glamour* no8 p162 Ag 2017

Kendall's Rules for Low-Key Beauty S. Kitchens color *Glamour* v114 no12 p130 D 2016

Jennett, Maggie

FARMER UP! AT THE 2017 COMMODITY CLASSIC *Successful Farming* v115 no3 p48 Mid-F 2017

Jenney, Andrea

Caesar's Last Breath color *Science* v356 no6342 p1009 Je 9 2017

Jennings, Austin

Still-Hunt Rule Breaker color *Field & Stream* v121 no6 pW7 N 2016

Jennings, Brian

Exposing Unfair Pricing in Auto Insurance Rates color *Consumer Reports* v82 no5 p6 My 2017

Jennings, Chris

Paradise Lost: The Mysterious Case of the Missing Utopian Novels S. Begley color *Time* v190 no14 p52 O 9 2017

JENNINGS, DAVID JOSHUA

THE QUEEN PASSED ON, BUT THE QUEEN LIVES ON bw color *Louisiana Life* v37 no2 p40 N/D 2016

Jennings, Edward David

HACKER CRACK-UP color *Wired* v25 no6 p10 Je 2017

Jennings, Erin M.

SAP TO SYRUP *New York State Conservationist* v71 no4 p14 F 2017

Jennings, Garth

Sing D. Coggan color *Entertainment Weekly* no1446/1447 p103 D 2016/Ja 2017

SING T. J. Norton color *Sound & Vision* v82 no7 p70 S 2017

Jennings, Jay

Ozark Magic color *Southern Living* v52 no9 p63 S 2017

JENNINGS, JUNE

O's 2017 HEALTH HEROES color *O, The Oprah Magazine* p57 Ja 2017

Jennings, Oshin Liam—Interviews

Oshin Liam Jennings M. Gesicki color *Tricycle: The Buddhist Review* v26 no2 p24 Wint 2016

JENNINGS, PETER

The Shark in the Shallows *Reader's Digest* v189 no1127 p110 F 2017

JENNINGS, RALPH

Asia's Rising Stars color *Forbes* v199 no5 p20 My 16 2017

Jennings, Sarah

Biodiversity redistribution under climate change: Impacts on ecosystems and human well-being color *Science* v355 no6332 p1389 Mr 31 2017

Jennings, Stephen

DROPPING INTO WORK E. MASTROIANNI color *Discover* v27 no10 p7 D 2016

Jennings, Waylon, 1937-2002

The Highwaymen Return D. Browne color *AARP: The Magazine* v59 no3A p15 Ap/My 2016

Jennings, Willie James

Reflections on the lectionary *Christian Century* v134 no14 p21 Jl 5 2017

Jennis, Stephanie

HANDING OVER THE PEN: Empowering students by encouraging them to write their own stories *Literacy Today (2411-7862)* v35 no1 p36 Jl/Ag 2017

Jenny Sabin Studio LLC

Jenny Sabin to Design PS1 Pavilion A. Klimoski color *Architectural Record* v205 no3 p23 Mr 2017

JENSEN, BRENNEN

25 People Who Bust the Myths color *AARP: The Magazine* v59 no4A p42 Je/Jl 2016

Find an Empty Beach: There's no need to go far to find a deserted island--they're all along the Delmarva coast *Washingtonian Magazine* v52 no11 p84 Ag 2017

NEXT EXIT: AMERICANA: FROM FIBERGLASS DINOSAURS TO STONEWALL JACKSON'S STUFFED HORSE TO PATSY CLINE'S ICE-CREAM SCOOP, SHENANDOAH IS HOME TO SOME PARTICULARLY AMERICAN ATTRACTIONS *Washingtonian Magazine* v53 no1 p104 O 2017

Surviving the '80s color *AARP: The Magazine* v59 no5A p47 Ag/S 2016

Jensen, Christine

INGRID & CHRISTINE JENSEN: 'Our Gift Is What We Do' P.

Jeong, Wonho

Quantized thermal transport in single-atom junctions bibl diag graph *Science* v355 no6330 p1192 Mr 17 2017

Jeong-Il Kim

Photoactivation and inactivation of Arabidopsis cryptochrome 2 bibl graph *Science* v354 no6310 p343 O 21 2016

Jeong Kwan

Michelin Monastic M. Scarles color *Tricycle: The Buddhist Review* v26 no4 p17 Summ 2017

Jeopardy! (TV program)

Game Show Philosophy J. S. J. Conley *America* v216 no10 p54 My 1 2017

Jeplan Inc.—Officials & employees

A Real Mr. Fusion Feeds on Used Clothing P. Alpeyev *Bloomberg Businessweek* no4509 p29 Ja 30 2017

JEPPESEN, ERIK

Translating Regime Shifts in Shallow Lakes into Changes in Ecosystem Functions and Services *BioScience* v67 no10 p928 O 2017

Jeppesen, Travis

AUGUSTAS SERAPINAS IN THE STUDIO color *Art in America* v105 no3 p114 Mr 2017

Film Brut bw color *Art in America* v104 no10 p41 N 2016

KURT SCHWITTERS *Art in America* v104 no9 p163 O 2016

Time Out bw color map *Art in America* v105 no4 p27 Ap 2017

Jeppson, Tamara N.

Release of mineral-bound water prior to subduction tied to shallow seismogenic slip off Sumatra graph *Science* v356 no6340 p841 My 26 2017

Jepsen, Carly Rae, 1985—Interviews

HOW CARLY RAE JEPSEN AND LEAP! GAVE US SUMMER'S BEST POP ANTHEM M. Snetiker color *Entertainment Weekly* no1480 p50 S 1 2017

Jepson, Paul D.

Europe's insufficient pollutant remediation color *Science* v356 no6334 p148 Ap 14 2017

Jerabek, John

Lifetime experience #25 color *Canadian Geographic* v137 no1 p27 F 2017

Jeremiah Tower: The Last Magnificent (Film)

The Fundamentals R. R. Cooper color *Commonweal* v144 no12 p28 Jl 7 2017

Jeremias, Gunnar

Can everyone help verify the bioweapons convention? Perhaps, via open source monitoring bibl *Bulletin of the Atomic Scientists* v72 no6 p412 N 2016

Jeremy, Rob

The Morning After color *Field & Stream* v122 no4 pF12 S 2017

Jericho

The Architecture of Belief C. Valentino color *Archaeology* v69 no6 p4 N/D 2016

Jerkins, Morgan

Do Writers Deserve to Make a Living? M. LAPOINTE cartoon *Walrus* p64 Ja\F 2017

Out of the Shadow *New York Times Book Review* p24 D 11 2016

Jermalavičius, Tomas

A plausible scenario of nuclear war in Europe, and how to deter it: A perspective from Estonia bibl *Bulletin of the Atomic Scientists* v73 no4 p233 Jl 2017

Jermanok, Steve

A Masterpiece by the Ocean *Yankee* p96 Mr 2017

Jermyn, Alexander

Alexander Jermyn Architecture A. Klimoski bw color *Architectural Record* v204 no12 p50 D 2016

Jerome, Saint, d. 419 or 20

Trinity with Saint Jerome H. J. Hornik and M. C. Parsons color *Christian Century* v134 no11 p47 My 24 2017

Jerry Maguire (Film)

Hello Again T. Keith color *Sports Illustrated* v125 no21 p24 D 26 2016

JERRY MAGUIRE F. Kaplan color *Sound & Vision* v82 no5 p70 Je 2017

Jersey (Music)

The Hot Box chart *Downbeat* v84 no10 p57 O 2017

Jersey J. Murph color *Downbeat* v84 no10 p55 O 2017

Jersey City (N.J.)

an after noon in JERSEY CITY color *Good Housekeeping* v263 no5 p44 N 2016

Jerusalem Post (Newspaper)

Dispatches from the World's Most Parochial Newspaper *Weekly Standard* v22 no18 p2 Ja 16 2017

Jerusalem—Antiquities—Exhibitions

Jerusalem 1000 - 1400: Every People Under Heaven M. MIRZA *Islamic Horizons* v45 no6 p52 N/D 2016

Museum exhibit reveals many sides of Jerusalem in Middle Ages and today D. Van Biema color *Christian Century* v133 no22 p17 O 26 2016

Jerusalem—Description & travel

Center of The World R. BROOKHISER bw *National Review* v69 no7 p47 Ap 17 2017

Jerzembeck, Fabian

Strong peak in Tc of Sr2RuO4 under uniaxial pressure bibl color graph *Science* v355 no6321 p1 Ja 13 2017

JESCHKE, JONATHAN M.

Scientific and Normative Foundations for the Valuation of Alien-Species Impacts: Thirteen Core Principles *BioScience* v67 no2 p166 F 2017

Jeske, Sandra

pontoon mania color *Cabin Living* p60 Je 2017

Jesse trees

Waiting by the Jesse Tree M. Wilson O'Reilly color *Commonweal* v143 no20 p7 D 16 2016

Jesser, Mallory

You + your Body color diag graph *Seventeen* v76 no5 p86 S 2017

Jessica Jones (TV program)

JONESING ON JONES J. Jensen color *Entertainment Weekly* no1436/1437 p73 O 21 2016

Jeste, Dilip

MIDLIFE CRISIS APPARENTLY IS A MYTH *USA Today Magazine* v145 no2859 p1 D 2016

JESTER, SUSAN

ALL IN A Day's Work *Reader's Digest* v190 no1135 p56 N 2017

Jesuit missions—History

Mission in the vernacular P. Jenkins *Christian Century* v134 no4 p61 F 15 2017

Jesuit Refugee Service

How the church can prevent climate displacement T. Pulaski *America* v216 no6 p10 Mr 20 2017

Learning on the Margins W. Massey color *America* v216 no3 p17 F 6 2017

Jesuit universities & colleges

A Pledge to Protect 'Dreamers' color *America* v215 no19 p10 D 19 2016

Jesuit Volunteer Corps (Organization)

Out of service H. G. Gary color *U.S. Catholic* v82 no4 p26 Ap 2017

Jesuits

Here are the "America Jeopardy!" questions, er, answers M. Malone *America* v217 no2 p3 Jl 24 2017

Jesuits Admirable and Execrable G. Wills bw cartoon *New York Review of Books* v64 no2 p39 F 9 2017

Jesuits: Models of Reconciliation For a World in Need of Mercy color *America* v215 no19 p9 D 19 2016

New Leader of Jesuits Worldwide Is Latin American 'Historic Choice' G. O'CONNELL color *America* v215 no13 p9 O 31 2016

No-Collateral Damage N. S. RILEY color *Weekly Standard* v22 no36 p15 My 29 2017

OF MANY THINGS M. MALONE *America* v215 no19 p2 D 19 2016

OF MANY THINGS M. MALONE *America* v216 no1 p2 Ja 2 2017

Jesuits—Attitudes

A Brush of the Butterfly's Wing W. C. Birdsall color *Commonweal* v143 no19 p39 D 2 2016

Jesuits—History

OF MANY THINGS M. MALONE *America* v215 no14 p2 N 7 2016

Jesus Christ

See also

Incarnation

April 30, Third Sunday of Easter J. M. Gallagher *Christian Cen-*

IT'S ALL IN THE WRIST color *Conde Nast Traveler* v52 no3 p26 Mr 2017

JEWEL TONES L. IMMEDIATO *Los Angeles Magazine* v62 no9 p29 S 2017

MAKING WAVES: From dainty frills to major flounces, fashion is currently rife with ruffles S. STEVENSON bw color *Indianapolis Monthly* v41 no2 p30 S 2017

Market bw color *Vanity Fair* p90 Hollywood 2017 Supplement

Necklace Party E. Velluto color *Glamour* v115 no6 p50 Je 2017

Shoot for Some Hoops color *Glamour* v115 no10 p66 O 2017

SHOW YOUR METAL color *Esquire* p41 Ag 2017

Stone AGE color *InStyle* v23 no13 p150 D 2016

SWING LOW SEXY PENDANT NECKLACES YOU CAN WEAR ANYWHERE, WITH ANYTHING (OR NOTHING AT ALL) color *Conde Nast Traveler* v52 no10 p42 N 2017

Wearable Sculpture M. L. BIKOFF *Atlanta* v56 no10 p43 F 2017

WHAT WE LOVE color *Harper's Bazaar* no3649 p44 D 2016/Ja 2017

Jewelry—Exhibitions

Daring to Be Different color *Vogue* v207 no11 p140 N 2017

INSPIRED BY NATURE *Virginia Living* v15 no2 p69 F 2017

Kyoto Crush J. K. DE VALLE color *Architectural Digest* v74 no8 p21 Ag 2017

Jewels (Theatrical production)

SHINE ON: George Balanchine's Jewels celeb rates its 50th anniversary this year. But what is it that makes this plotless full-length so timeless? P. BOAL *Dance Magazine* v91 no7 p35 Jl 2017

Jewett, Brad

Show-Time COUNTDOWN color *Horse & Rider* v55 no11 p56 N 2016

Jewish actors

Mystery Woman H. Als cartoon *New Yorker* v92 no33 p10 O 17 2016

Jewish artists

People C. Kennel-Shank color *Christian Century* v133 no24 p20 N 23 2016

Jewish calendar

The Quiz T. BALAZO color *Maclean's* v130 no3 p71 Ap 2017

Jewish communists

BETWEEN HEAVEN AND EARTH: HIGH IN THE MOUNTAINS OF WESTERN ETHIOPIA, AN ISOLATED CHRISTIAN COMMUNITY CLINGS TO AN ANCIENT WAY OF LIFE T. A. FRAIL *Smithsonian* v48 no4 p88 Jl/Ag 2017

Jewish day schools

Kindergarten on our minds S. Pollin *Successful Farming* v115 no1 p4 Ja 2017

Jewish identity

shalom y'all L. Brook *Successful Farming* v115 no1 p3 Ja 2017

Jewish laity

Saving Conservative Judaism *Commentary* v143 no4 p24 Ap 2017

Jewish law

    See also

    Jewish identity

God's Perfect Instructions M. R. Simone *America* v216 no3 p50 F 6 2017

Jewish museums—Exhibitions

Chicken Soup and Other Remedies P. Wasley *Humanities* v37 no4 p1 Fall 2016

Jewish refugees

No Safe Haven A. L. CORREA *Publishers Weekly* v263 no40 p128 O 3 2016

Jewish refugees—History—20th century

THE LAST TIME WE CLOSED THE GATES L. RATNER bw color *Nation* v304 no5 p20 F 20 2017

Jewish refugees—United States

An Illegal Immigrant J. Tytell *Commonweal* v144 no10 p8 Je 2 2017

Jewish students

Tulane, Emory, Vandy make best-of list for Jewish students *Successful Farming* v115 no1 p36 Ja 2017

Jewish studies

Millsaps starts Jewish studies minor, Professor James Bowley honored L. J. Green *Successful Farming* v115 no1 p37 Ja 2017

Jewish way of life

29TH DELTA JEWISH OPEN *Successful Farming* v115 no1 p19 Ja 2017

Jewish women

LET THEM EAT MEAT R. Serkin *History Today* v67 no8 p50 Ag 2017

Jewish Museum (New York, N.Y.)

exhibition J. MINUTILLO color *Architectural Record* v204 no12 p31 D 2016

Jews

    See also

    American Jews

agenda *Successful Farming* v115 no1 p5 Ja 2017

Commentary on Commentary *Commentary* v143 no4 p14 Ap 2017

Defining Jewish Conservatism G. EPSTEIN and J. STERN *Commentary* v144 no1 p4 Jl/Ag 2017

IT HAPPENED HERE D. Goodyear diag *New Yorker* v93 no29 p40 S 25 2017

The Park Bench Joke *Commentary* v140 no2 p10 S 2015

WHEN A JEW & A CATHOLIC MARRY M. Oppenheimer color *America* v217 no5 p18 S 4 2017

Jews in motion pictures

Fix the Fixer J. Podhoretz color *Weekly Standard* v22 no33 p47 My 8 2017

Jews—Antiquities

Archaeologists discover ancient Jewish artifacts, part of Jerusalem walls M. Chabin color *Christian Century* v133 no24 p16 N 23 2016

Jews—Conversion to Christianity

German Protestant church renounces mission aiming to convert Jewish people T. Heneghan color *Christian Century* v133 no26 p17 D 21 2016

Jews—Egypt—Alexandria

To promote diversity, Egypt plans to restore Alexandria synagogue J. Wirtschafter color *Christian Century* v134 no18 p13 Ag 30 2017

Jews—Europe—History

Synagogues, Cemeteries, and Frontiers: Anti-Semitism in Switzerland L. Tartakoff *Society* v54 no1 p56 F 2017

Jews—Italy—Venice

Chief rabbi of Venice works for return of Jewish community J. McKenna *Christian Century* v134 no7 p15 Mr 29 2017

Jews—Social conditions

Grave Matter *Commentary* v143 no4 p15 Ap 2017

Jews—Societies, etc.

Nonprofit offers Talmud in English online for free M. Chabin *Christian Century* v134 no8 p1 Ap 12 2017

Jeyasingh, Shobana

A Gender-Bent Bayadére *Dance Magazine* v91 no10 p13 O 2017

Jha, Ashish K.

Health Care Providers Should Publish Physician Ratings *Harvard Business Review Digital Articles* p2 O 23 2015

Immigrant Doctors Provide Better Care, According to a Study of 1.2 Million Hospitalizations color *Harvard Business Review Digital Articles* p2 F 3 2017

JHS Pedals (Company)

Vintage Sounds J. Weir *Missouri Life* v43 no6 p17 O/N 2016

Jhung, Lisa

COOL RUNNERS color *Runner's World* v52 no7 p26 Ag 2017

PICK OF THE LAYERS [Cover story] color *Runner's World* v52 no1 p62 Ja/F 2017

Rock the Gym color *Men's Health* v31 no10 p32 D 2016

Skishoe il *Backpacker* p30 N 2017

Ultra days color *Runner's World* v52 no6 p50 Jl 2017

Ji, Yining

A multifunctional catalyst that stereoselectively assembles prodrugs diag *Science* v356 no6336 p426 Ap 28 2017

Ji-Youn Seo

Incorporation of rubidium cations into perovskite solar cells improves photovoltaic performance bibl graph *Science* v354 no6309 p206 O 14 2016

Ji-Young Youn

Exploring genetic suppression interactions on a global scale diag *Science* v354 no6312 p599 N 4 2016

Jia, Bin

Bug mapping and fitness testing of chemically synthesized chromosome X diag *Science* v355 no6329 p1048 Mr 10 2017

"Perfect" designer chromosome V and behavior of a ring derivative diag *Science* v355 no6329 p1046 Mr 10 2017

Jia, C.

Femtosecond electron-phonon lock-in by photoemission and x-ray free-electron laser chart diag *Science* v357 no6346 p71 Jl 7 2017

Jia, Jian-Jun

Satellite-based entanglement distribution over 1200 kilometers diag graph *Science* v356 no6343 p1140 Je 16 2017

Jia, Jimmy

Companies That Don't Manage Utilities Strategically Are Throwing Money Away *Harvard Business Review Digital Articles* p2 Mr 22 2016

Jia, Nan

"Perfect" designer chromosome V and behavior of a ring derivative diag *Science* v355 no6329 p1046 Mr 10 2017

Jia, Shang

Redox-based reagents for chemoselective methionine bioconjugation bibl diag graph *Science* v355 no6325 p597 F 10 2017

Jia, T.

Femtosecond electron-phonon lock-in by photoemission and x-ray free-electron laser chart diag *Science* v357 no6346 p71 Jl 7 2017

Jia Fu Ji

Quality management for precision medicine clinical applications: A consensus from the China Precision Medicine Clinical Research and Application Association bibl *Science* v354 no6319 p11 D 23 2016

Urgent need for implementation of precision medicine in gastric cancer in China bibl chart *Science* v354 no6319 p39 D 23 2016

Jian-Wei Pan

Realization of two-dimensional spin-orbit coupling for Bose-Einstein condensates bibl graph *Science* v354 no6308 p83 O 7 2016

Jian Zhang

Quality management for precision medicine clinical applications: A consensus from the China Precision Medicine Clinical Research and Application Association bibl *Science* v354 no6319 p11 D 23 2016

Jian-Zhou Zhao

A selective insecticidal protein from Pseudomonas for controlling corn rootworms bibl chart graph *Science* v354 no6312 p634 N 4 2016

Jian Chye, Sam Tan

ELABELA deficiency promotes preeclampsia and cardiovascular malformations in mice color diag graph *Science* v357 no6352 p707 Ag 18 2017

Jiang, Danhua

DNA replication–coupled histone modification maintains Polycomb gene silencing in plants diag *Science* v357 no6356 p1146 S 15 2017

Jiang, Donglin

Two-dimensional sp2 carbon–conjugated covalent organic frameworks diag graph *Science* v357 no6352 p673 Ag 18 2017

Jiang, Guo-Zhen

Bug mapping and fitness testing of chemically synthesized chromosome X diag *Science* v355 no6329 p1048 Mr 10 2017

"Perfect" designer chromosome V and behavior of a ring derivative diag *Science* v355 no6329 p1046 Mr 10 2017

Jiang, Hui

Deep functional analysis of synII, a 770-kilobase synthetic yeast chromosome diag *Science* v355 no6329 p1047 Mr 10 2017

Jiang, Jiansen

Atomic structure of the human cytomegalovirus capsid with its securing tegument layer of pp150 color diag *Science* v356 no6345 p1350 Je 30 2017

Jiang, Nan

Harvesting electrical energy from carbon nanotube yarn twist diag graph *Science* v357 no6353 p773 Ag 25 2017

Jiang, Qingwen

Engineering the ribosomal DNA in a megabase synthetic chromosome diag *Science* v355 no6329 p1049 Mr 10 2017

Jiang, Shuangying

Engineering the ribosomal DNA in a megabase synthetic chromosome diag *Science* v355 no6329 p1049 Mr 10 2017

Jiang, Xuntian

Lysosomal cholesterol activates mTORC1 via an SLC38A9–Nie-

mann-Pick C1 signaling complex bibl diag graph *Science* v355 no6331 p1306 Mr 24 2017

Jiang, Yina

Plants transfer lipids to sustain colonization by mutualistic mycorrhizal and parasitic fungi diag graph *Science* v356 no6343 p1172 Je 16 2017

Jiang, Yiran

Double-heterojunction nanorod light-responsive LEDs for display applications bibl color graph *Science* v355 no6325 p616 F 10 2017

Jiang, Zi-Qing

Satellite-based entanglement distribution over 1200 kilometers diag graph *Science* v356 no6343 p1140 Je 16 2017

Jiang Qian

A nuclease that mediates cell death induced by DNA damage and poly(ADP-ribose) polymerase-1 bw graph *Science* v354 no6308 paad6872-1 O 7 2016

Jianhua Wang

Large gem diamonds from metallic liquid in Earth's deep mantle bibl color *Science* v354 no6318 p1403 D 16 2016

Quality management for precision medicine clinical applications: A consensus from the China Precision Medicine Clinical Research and Application Association bibl *Science* v354 no6319 p11 D 23 2016

Jianlin Yao

Biaxially strained PtPb/Pt core/shell nanoplate boosts oxygen reduction catalysis bibl color graph *Science* v354 no6318 p1410 D 16 2016

Jianliu Wang

Gene expression profiling–guided clinical precision treatment for patients with endometrial carcinoma bibl color diag *Science* v354 no6319 p33 D 23 2016

Jianlong Yang

Expert consensus on point-of-care testing *Science* v354 no6319 p15 D 23 2016

Recommendations on the management and use of POCT in medical institutions (nosocomial) *Science* v354 no6319 p13 D 23 2016

Jianmin Wang

Rb1 and Trp53 cooperate to suppress prostate cancer lineage plasticity, metastasis, and antiandrogen resistance bibl graph *Science* v355 no6320 p1 Ja 6 2017

Jianmin Wu

Urgent need for implementation of precision medicine in gastric cancer in China bibl chart *Science* v354 no6319 p39 D 23 2016

Jianmin Zhang

Pathological α-synuclein transmission initiated by binding lymphocyte-activation gene 3 bibl graph *Science* v353 no6307 paah3374-1 S 30 2016

Jianping Wu

Structural basis for the gating mechanism of the type 2 ryanodine receptor RyR2 bibl color graph *Science* v354 no6310 paah5324-1 O 21 2016

Jianshi Yu

Sustained virologic control in SIV+ macaques after antiretroviral and α4β7 antibody therapy bibl graph *Science* v354 no6309 p197 O 14 2016

Jianwei Sun

Density functional theory is straying from the path toward the exact functional bibl chart graph *Science* v355 no6320 p1 Ja 6 2017

Jianxun Feng

RPA binds histone H3-H4 and functions in DNA replication–coupled nucleosome assembly bibl graph *Science* v355 no6323 p415 Ja 27 2017

Jiao, Deling

Inactivation of porcine endogenous retrovirus in pigs using CRISPR-Cas9 diag *Science* v357 no6357 p1303 S 22 2017

Jiawang Hong

Anomalously low electronic thermal conductivity in metallic vanadium dioxide bibl graph *Science* v355 no6323 p371 Ja 27 2017

Jiaxin Du

LAST BATTLE ON THE GREAT WALL *Military History* v33 no5 p30 Ja 2017

Jiayang Fan

Jindra, Michael

Poverty and the Controversial Work of Nonprofits *Society* v53 no6 p634 D 2016

Jing Cai

Quality management for precision medicine clinical applications: A consensus from the China Precision Medicine Clinical Research and Application Association bibl *Science* v354 no6319 p11 D 23 2016

Jing Cao

Boxed In color graph *Bloomberg Businessweek* no4535 p23 Ag 28 2017

Re-creating The Sun On Earth color *Bloomberg Businessweek* no4529 p20 Jl 3 2017

Jing jing Liang

Forest value: More than commercial *Science* v354 no6319 p1541 D 23 2016

Positive biodiversity-productivity relationship predominant in global forests bibl chart graph map *Science* v354 no6309 paaf8957-1 O 14 2016

Jing Li

Biaxially strained PtPb/Pt core/shell nanoplate boosts oxygen reduction catalysis bibl color graph *Science* v354 no6318 p1410 D 16 2016

Jing Lu

A Silurian maxillate placoderm illuminates jaw evolution bibl color *Science* v354 no6310 p334 O 21 2016

Jing-Yuan Ma

Biaxially strained PtPb/Pt core/shell nanoplate boosts oxygen reduction catalysis bibl color graph *Science* v354 no6318 p1410 D 16 2016

Jinghua Guo

Ultrafine jagged platinum nanowires enable ultrahigh mass activity for the oxygen reduction reaction bibl chart graph *Science* v354 no6318 p1414 D 16 2016

Jingping Zhang

Apple, Spotify, and the Battle over Freemium *Harvard Business Review Digital Articles* p2 My 13 2015

Jingyi Zhou

Gene expression profiling–guided clinical precision treatment for patients with endometrial carcinoma bibl color diag *Science* v354 no6319 p33 D 23 2016

Jinhua Cui

Self-renewal of a purified Tie2+ hematopoietic stem cell population relies on mitochondrial clearance bibl graph *Science* v354 no6316 p1156 D 2 2016

Jin Kim, Young

Liquefied gas electrolytes for electrochemical energy storage devices graph *Science* v356 no6345 p1351 Je 30 2017

Jinming Li

China's policies regarding next-generation sequencing diagnostic tests *Science* v354 no6319 p9 D 23 2016

Jin Mun, Tae

Harvesting electrical energy from carbon nanotube yarn twist diag graph *Science* v357 no6353 p773 Ag 25 2017

Jinnan Wang

Protecting China's soil by law bibl *Science* v354 no6312 p562 N 4 2016

Jiřičná, Eva

interiors L. C. LENTZ *Architectural Record* v205 no10 p35 O 2017

JISI, WANG

As Distrust Mounts, US and China Battle Over New Rules of Global Order *NPQ: New Perspectives Quarterly* v33 no4 p44 O 2016

Ji-Sun Kim, Grace

Beyond black and white: To make conversations about race more productive, try using different metaphors for God color *U.S. Catholic* v82 no10 p25 O 2017

Jitney (Theatrical production)

August Wilson will not go quietly: revisiting "Fences" and "Jitney" R. Weinert-Kendt color *America* v216 no5 p44 Mr 6 2017

It's All in the Details B. Reesman *Stage Directions* v30 no3 p42 Mr 2017

THE THEATRE *New Yorker* v92 no44 p9 Ja 9 2017

Jitterbug Waltz (Music)

Lewis Nash's Drum Solo on 'Jitterbug Waltz' J. LIEN color

Downbeat v83 no11 p78 N 2016

Jiu-jitsu

From the Archives color *Black Belt* v55 no3 p66 Ap/My 2017

GEORGE KIRBY JUJITSU PIONEER FOR 50 YEARS bw color *Black Belt* v55 no3 p10 Ap/My 2017

HUMILITY & EMPOWERMENT S. RAVITS color *New Orleans Magazine* v51 no3 p167 Ja 2017

Jiyu Tong

The DNA-sensing AIM2 inflammasome controls radiation-induced cell death and tissue injury bibl color graph *Science* v354 no6313 p765 N 11 2016

JL Audio Inc.

JL Audio Dominion d110 Subwoofer D. Vaughn color graph *Sound & Vision* v82 no3 p64 Ap 2017

JL Audio Fathom IWS-SYS-1 In-Wall Subwoofer System D. Wilkinson color *Sound & Vision* v82 no6 p50 Jl/Ag 2017

Jno-Charles, Alisa

Why Startups Shouldn't Chase Media Buzz color *Harvard Business Review Digital Articles* p2 Je 5 2017

Joachim, David

AMERICA'S TRENDIEST COMFORT FOOD chart color *AARP: The Magazine* v59 no6A p10 O/N 2016

SOUPING IS THE NEW JUICING color *AARP: The Magazine* v60 no2A p12 F/Mr 2017

Joachim, Mitchell

Gym with a View S. MURRAY color *Power & Motoryacht* v33 no3 p32 Mr 2017

Joan, of Arc, Saint, 1412-1431

History's Greatest Hits K. BOATNER cartoon *National Geographic Kids* no473 p10 S 2017

JOAN OF ARC'S 'VOICES': INSPIRED OR EPILEPTIC? *Military History* v33 no5 p12 Ja 2017

MONTHS PAST MAY *History Today* v67 no5 p22 My 2017

Joan Biddlecombe, Wendy

Anchorage Zen Community color *Tricycle: The Buddhist Review* v26 no4 p24 Summ 2017

Tsewang Rinzing color *Tricycle: The Buddhist Review* v26 no4 p22 Summ 2017

Joanne (Music)

Gaga's Totally Nineties Cowgirl Blues R. SHEFFIELD color *Rolling Stone* no1274 p57 N 17 2016

Lady Gaga COMES DOWN to EARTH N. Feeney color *Entertainment Weekly* no1434 p26 O 7 2016

PORTRAIT OF A LADY bw color *Harper's Bazaar* no3649 p292 D 2016/Ja 2017

WELCOME TO THE ISSUE color *Harper's Bazaar* no3649 p40 D 2016/Ja 2017

Joans, Ted

Ted Joans: Poet Painter/Former Villager Now/World Traveller *Publishers Weekly* v263 no47 p85 N 21 2016

Joaquin, Nick

Uncanny Powers: Feminist fiction by one of the Philippines' greatest (male) writers M. CHADBURN *New York Times Book Review* p8 S 3 2017

Job analysis

See also

Job descriptions

When You Realize You'll Never Get Your Dream Job S. Friedman *Harvard Business Review Digital Articles* p2 Ap 1 2015

Job applications

See also

Employment references

Job vacancies

Have I Got a Job for You J. A. CHALLENGER *USA Today Magazine* v145 no2864 p25 My 2017

How to Choose the Right References R. Knight *Harvard Business Review Digital Articles* p2 O 21 2014

How to Get the Most Out of an Informational Interview R. Knight *Harvard Business Review Digital Articles* p2 F 26 2016

How to Handle Stress During a Job Interview A. Ranieri *Harvard Business Review Digital Articles* p2 Jl 17 2017

How to Interview and Assess a Serial Job Hopper P. Claman *Harvard Business Review Digital Articles* p2 Ja 27 2016

Improve Your Résumé by Turning Bullet Points into Stories J. Heifetz *Harvard Business Review Digital Articles* p2 My 4 2016

'No.' Is that all you're telling unsuccessful applicants? Most employers have given up on offering interview feedback - but if you handle it carefully, there s no reason to stay silent A. MA-KOFF-CLARK *People Management* p14 Jl 2017

The Right Time to Mention Your Vacation Plans in a Job Interview J. Lees *Harvard Business Review Digital Articles* p2 Je 1 2015

Setting the Record Straight on Job Interviews A. Gallo *Harvard Business Review Digital Articles* p2 N 11 2014

Should employers be barred from asking job applicants what they earn? K. KIPLINGER *Kiplinger's Personal Finance* v71 no8 p14 Ag 2017

Wearing Luxury Brands Makes You Seem More Qualified for the Job J. M. Olejarz *Harvard Business Review Digital Articles* p2 Ap 9 2015

What a Year of Job Rejections Taught Me About Pitching Myself N. Mufleh *Harvard Business Review Digital Articles* p2 S 9 2015

When Someone Asks You for a Reference R. Knight *Harvard Business Review Digital Articles* p2 O 30 2015

Writing Your Résumé When Your Job Title Doesn't Reflect Your Responsibilities J. Heifetz *Harvard Business Review Digital Articles* p2 My 16 2017

Yes, Your Résumé Needs a Summary J. Heifetz *Harvard Business Review Digital Articles* p2 Jl 28 2015

Job creation

Do Startups Really Create Lots of Good Jobs? D. Isenberg *Harvard Business Review Digital Articles* p2 Je 6 2016

The Internet Has Been a Colossal Economic Disappointment W. H. Davidow *Harvard Business Review Digital Articles* p2 Mr 30 2015

Midsize Cities Are Entrepreneurship's Real Test D. Isenberg and V. Onyemah color *Harvard Business Review Digital Articles* p2 Ja 24 2017

The U.S. Economy Is Doing Only Half Its Job J. W. Rivkin *Harvard Business Review Digital Articles* p2 D 17 2015

Job creation—United States

AT THIS MOMENT WE ALL FACE A CHOICE B. OBAMA *Vital Speeches of the Day* v82 no11 p322 N 2016

Back to Work B. COVERT color *New Republic* v248 no8/9 p16 Ag/S 2017

Can Sneaker Makers Come Home Again? M. Townsend cartoon *Bloomberg Businessweek* no4510 p17 F 6 2017

CHAPTER 1 INCLUSIVE GROWTH IN THE UNITED STATES *Economic Indicators* p21 O 2016

Deconstricting the Administrative State A. Kim color *Washington Monthly* v49 no6-8 p36 Je-Ag 2017

Economic Growth Isn't Over, but It Doesn't Create Jobs Like It Used To M. Ford *Harvard Business Review Digital Articles* p2 Mr 14 2016

ECONOMIC REPORT OF THE PRESIDENT *Economic Indicators* p3 O 2016

Fix the Global Economy, Don't Flee It L. FINK *In These Times* v41 no1 p15 Ja 2017

Make America Make Again K. S. Newman and H. Winston color *Foreign Affairs* v96 no1 p114 Ja/F 2017

The Republican Future W. Kristol *Weekly Standard* v22 no39 p8 Je 19 2017

Smoke, Mirrors and Job Creation M. Maciag *Governing* v30 no6 p56 Mr 2017

Job descriptions

ALL IN A Day's Work *Reader's Digest* v189 no1127 p60 F 2017

Stake Your Claim H. VILLA *Publishers Weekly* v264 no12 p76 Mr 20 2017

When Should You Fire a "Good Enough" Employee? J. Glickman and A. Bassuk *Harvard Business Review Digital Articles* p2 My 25 2015

Words pack a punch in online job recruiting C. M. Irby bibl *Monthly Labor Review* p1 Ap 2017

Job evaluation

Creating an Effective Peer Review System E. Mosley *Harvard Business Review Digital Articles* p2 Ag 19 2015

How Adobe Structures Feedback Conversations D. Burkus *Harvard Business Review Digital Articles* p2 Jl 20 2017

How to Get Feedback as a Freelancer S. King *Harvard Business Review Digital Articles* p2 Ag 19 2015

If Your Boss Thinks You're Awesome, You Will Become More Awesome J. Zenger and J. Folkman *Harvard Business Review*

Digital Articles p2 Ja 27 2015

Job hunting

See also

Résumés (Employment)

30 DAYS TO YOUR DREAM JOB [Cover story] S. Floyd color *Black Enterprise* v47 no4 p34 N/D 2016

How Can I ... Wow an Adult? *Scholastic Choices* v32 no6 p24 Mr 2017

How to Get Back in the Game K. Bahler *Money* v46 no1 p31 Ja/F 2017

How to Get the Most Out of an Informational Interview R. Knight *Harvard Business Review Digital Articles* p2 F 26 2016

New year, new career: 5 tips for changing occupations E. Torpey *Career Outlook* p4 F 2017

Nurturing Success J. Caplin color *Money* v46 no2 p26 Mr 2017

Optimists Are Better at Finding New Jobs M. Gielan *Harvard Business Review Digital Articles* p2 Ap 15 2016

Robots and Automation May Not Take Your Desk Job After All D. Finnigan *Harvard Business Review Digital Articles* p2 N 22 2016

SKIRTING THE SALARY QUESTION K. PITSKER color *Kiplinger's Personal Finance* v71 no7 p14 Jl 2017

SOLUTIONS TO END YOUR JOB DROUGHT K. Bahler *Money* v46 no6 p75 Jl 2017

Strategies for Crowdsourcing Your Job Search L. Zoref *Harvard Business Review Digital Articles* p2 My 8 2015

To Ace Your Job Interview, Get into Character and Rehearse C. Salit *Harvard Business Review Digital Articles* p2 Ap 21 2017

What a Year of Job Rejections Taught Me About Pitching Myself N. Mufleh *Harvard Business Review Digital Articles* p2 S 9 2015

Why You Should Always Go Off-Script in a Job Interview T. Menon and L. Thompson *Harvard Business Review Digital Articles* p2 Jl 14 2016

Job hunting—Computer network resources

LinkedIn Makes It Easier to Sneak In a Job Hunt K. Bahler color *Money* v45 no11 p14 D 2016

Job hunting—United States

Have I Got a Job for You J. A. CHALLENGER *USA Today Magazine* v145 no2864 p25 My 2017

How to Be a Stealthy Job Seeker When You Know It's Time to Go K. Bahler color *Money* v46 no4 p17 My 2017

Job involvement

4 Steps to Sustaining Improvement in Health Care K. S. Mate and J. Rakover *Harvard Business Review Digital Articles* p2 N 9 2016

4 Ways to Make Conference Calls Less Terrible R. Bellmar *Harvard Business Review Digital Articles* p2 Ja 28 2015

Being Engaged at Work Is Not the Same as Being Productive R. Fuller and N. Shikaloff *Harvard Business Review Digital Articles* p2 F 16 2017

Being Happy at Work Matters A. McKee *Harvard Business Review Digital Articles* p2 N 14 2014

CEOs Can't Give Feedback Only to Their Direct Reports D. R. Conant *Harvard Business Review Digital Articles* p2 Ag 24 2015

Companies Have Always Struggled to Engage Young People A. Ovans *Harvard Business Review Digital Articles* p2 N 18 2014

The Dark Side of High Employee Engagement L. Garrad and T. Chamorro-Premuzic *Harvard Business Review Digital Articles* p2 Ag 16 2016

Don't Let Your Company Culture Just Happen A. Osterwalder, Y. Pigneur et al *Harvard Business Review Digital Articles* p2 Jl 7 2016

Employee Engagement Depends on What Happens Outside of the Office S. LaMotte *Harvard Business Review Digital Articles* p2 Ja 13 2015

Engagement Is a Means, Not an End M. Schrage *Harvard Business Review Digital Articles* p2 F 22 2016

Engage Your Long-Time Employees to Improve Performance J. Harter *Harvard Business Review Digital Articles* p2 Mr 16 2015

Engaging Your Employees Is Good, but Don't Stop There E. Garton and M. C. Mankins *Harvard Business Review Digital Articles* p2 D 9 2015

Engaging Your Older Workers P. Cappelli *Harvard Business Review Digital Articles* p2 N 5 2014

Burnout (Psychology)

The 10 Best Workplaces for Millennials C. Austin color *Fortune* v176 no2 p20 Ag 1 2017

28 Years of Stock Market Data Shows a Link Between Employee Satisfaction and Long-Term Value A. Edmans *Harvard Business Review Digital Articles* p2 Mr 24 2016

Before You Agree to Take on New Work, Ask 3 Questions R. Walsh *Harvard Business Review Digital Articles* p2 My 23 2017

Do You Hate Your Boss? M. F. R. Kets de Vries color il *Harvard Business Review* v94 no12 p98 D 2016

An Easy Way to Make Your Employees Happier L. Wiseman *Harvard Business Review Digital Articles* p2 N 13 2014

Fall Back in Love With Your Job G. Roberts-Grey color *Essence* v47 no10 p71 F 2017

Get Your Employees to Make Better Suggestions D. A. Hofmann and J. J. Sumanth *Harvard Business Review Digital Articles* p2 Mr 5 2015

THE HAPPINESS FACTOR: A look at career satisfaction *Cincinnati Magazine* v50 no11 pCG10 Ag 2017

HAPPINESS TRAPS: HOW WE SABOTAGE OURSELVES AT WORK A. MCKEE color *Harvard Business Review* v95 no5 p66 S/O 2017

How to Fall Back in Love with Your Job C. O'Hara *Harvard Business Review Digital Articles* p2 Jl 23 2015

How to Make Employees Feel Like They Own Their Work F. Gino *Harvard Business Review Digital Articles* p2 D 7 2015

How to Prioritize Your Work When Your Manager Doesn't A. J. Su color *Harvard Business Review Digital Articles* p2 Ja 24 2017

If You Can't Take a Vacation, Get the Most Out of Minibreaks E. Seppala *Harvard Business Review Digital Articles* p2 Jl 14 2015

If Your Boss Could Do Your Job, You're More Likely to Be Happy at Work B. Artz, A. Goodall et al *Harvard Business Review Digital Articles* p2 D 29 2016

Let Employees Choose When, Where, and How to Work N. Koloc *Harvard Business Review Digital Articles* p2 N 10 2014

Meaningful Work Should Be Every CEO's Top Priority J. Keane *Harvard Business Review Digital Articles* p2 N 5 2015

A No-Layoffs Policy Can Work, Even in an Unpredictable Economy C. Van Gorder *Harvard Business Review Digital Articles* p2 Ja 26 2015

Research Shows Unionized Workers Are Less Happy, but Why? P. Laroche *Harvard Business Review Digital Articles* p1 Ag 30 2017

A SMART INVESTMENT IN AMERICA A. Murray color *Fortune* v175 no4 p8 Mr 15 2017

What High Performers Want at Work K. Willyerd *Harvard Business Review Digital Articles* p2 N 18 2014

What to Do When Your Heart Isn't in Your Work Anymore A. Molinsky *Harvard Business Review Digital Articles* p2 Jl 10 2017

WHAT WORKERS WANT cartoon diag map *Forbes* v199 no4 p76 Ap 25 2017

where does the time go? C. HOLECKO cartoon *Parents* v92 no7 p80 Jl 2017

Why So Many of Us Experience a Midlife Crisis Why So Many of Us Experience a Midlife Crisis H. Schwandt *Harvard Business Review Digital Articles* p2 Ap 20 2015

Why You Should Watch Out for Your 5-Year Job Anniversary J. Zenger and J. Folkman *Harvard Business Review Digital Articles* p2 Ap 10 2015

You find your job uninspiring S. Kempton color *Yoga Journal* p47 2016 Special Issue

Job satisfaction—Great Britain

Job satisfaction hits new peak *People Management* p14 D 2016/ Ja 2017

Job security

Job insecurity K. Clarke color *U.S. Catholic* v82 no8 p42 Ag 2017

The new tissue culture R. L. Ruben color *Science* v356 no6335 p342 Ap 21 2017

We Need to Move Beyond the Employee vs. Contractor Debate J. Boudreau *Harvard Business Review Digital Articles* p2 Jl 8 2015

What Happens at Home When People Can't Depend on Stable Work A. J. Pugh *Harvard Business Review Digital Articles* p2 Ap 4 2017

What If Socially Useful Jobs Were Taxed Less Than Other Jobs?

B. B. Lockwood, C. G. Nathanson et al *Harvard Business Review Digital Articles* p2 O 11 2017

Job skills

A 2×2 Matrix to Help You Prioritize the Skills to Learn Right Now M. Zao-Sanders *Harvard Business Review Digital Articles* p2 S 27 2017

Augmented Reality Is Already Improving Worker Performance M. Abraham and M. Annunziata *Harvard Business Review Digital Articles* p2 Mr 13 2017

A Great Deal J. Epstein *Claremont Review of Books* v17 no3 p67 Summ 2017

How to Decide What Skill to Work On Next E. Andersen *Harvard Business Review Digital Articles* p2 Ja 25 2016

HOW TO GET A JOB AT GOOGLE V. STEVENSON color *Maclean's* v129 no47 p48 N 28 2016

Providing Students with Pathways to High-Value Careers R. Craig *Change* v48 no5 p58 S/O 2016

Putting your liberal arts degree to work D. Angeles and B. Roberts *Career Outlook* p1 Ag 2017

Time Management Training Doesn't Work M. Thomas *Harvard Business Review Digital Articles* p2 Ap 22 2015

To Build Your Resilience, Ask Yourself Two Simple Questions S. Rao *Harvard Business Review Digital Articles* p2 Je 13 2017

TRAINING FOR YOUR NEXT JOB, THE ONE THAT MIGHT NOT EXIST YET diag *Fortune* v175 no6 p9 My 1 2017

Wage and job-skill distributions in the National Compensation Survey C. M. Cunningham and R. D. Mohr bibl chart color graph *Monthly Labor Review* p1 F 2017

We need to talk about skills *People Management* p5 My 2017

What Kind of Data Scientist Do You Need? Michael Li *Harvard Business Review Digital Articles* p2 F 1 2016

What Younger Managers Should Know About How They're Perceived J. Zenger and J. Folkman *Harvard Business Review Digital Articles* p2 S 29 2015

You Can Learn and Get Work Done at the Same Time L. Davey *Harvard Business Review Digital Articles* p2 Ja 11 2016

Job skills—Government policy

UK sleepwalking into a low-skills economy': Skills policy overhaul needed to avert disaster, warns CIPD *People Management* p10 My 2017

Job skills—Research

WHAT SKILLS WILL KEEP YOU AHEAD OF AI? graph img *Harvard Business Review* v95 no2 p36 Mr/Ap 2017

Job stress

See also

Burnout (Psychology)

3 Small Things Every Person Can Do to Reduce Stress in Their Office D. Clark *Harvard Business Review Digital Articles* p2 Mr 31 2017

A 3-Step Process to Break a Cycle of Frustration, Stress, and Fighting at Work A. McKee *Harvard Business Review Digital Articles* p2 Jl 12 2017

5 Signs Your Job is Completely Stressing You Out S. Floyd and A. GUMBS color *Black Enterprise* v47 no4 p29 N/D 2016

5 Work Stresses You Can Alleviate with Tech A. Samuel *Harvard Business Review Digital Articles* p2 Ag 25 2015

7 Tricky Work Situations, and How to Respond to Them A. Bassuk *Harvard Business Review Digital Articles* p2 O 11 2017

Are You Too Stressed to Be Productive? Or Not Stressed Enough? F. Gino *Harvard Business Review Digital Articles* p2 Ap 14 2016

Don't Let Your Stressed-Out Boss Stress You Out A. McKee *Harvard Business Review Digital Articles* p2 S 11 2015

Don't Take Work Stress Home with You J. Coleman and J. Coleman *Harvard Business Review Digital Articles* p2 Jl 28 2016

An Early Warning System for Your Team's Stress Level [Cover story] T. Hellwig, C. Rook et al *Harvard Business Review Digital Articles* p2 Ap 26 2017

Handle Your Stress Better by Knowing What Causes It A. Grady *Harvard Business Review Digital Articles* p1 Je 21 2017

How to Deal with a Boss Who Stresses You Out T. Chamorro-Premuzic *Harvard Business Review Digital Articles* p2 Jl 19 2017

How to Evaluate, Manage, and Strengthen Your Resilience D. Kopans *Harvard Business Review Digital Articles* p2 Je 14 2016

How to Put the Right Amount of Pressure on Your Team L. Davey *Harvard Business Review Digital Articles* p2 Jl 1 2016

How to Work with Someone Who's Always Stressed Out R. Knight *Harvard Business Review Digital Articles* p2 Ag 7 2017

Manage Your Stress by Monitoring Your Body's Reactions to It E. A. Fox *Harvard Business Review Digital Articles* p2 O 2 2017

Millions struggling with mental ill-health *People Management* p13 N 2016

My Energy Makeover B. O'Dair *Prevention* v69 no2 p3 F 2017

New Hires Create More Anxiety at a Midsized Company K. Firestone *Harvard Business Review Digital Articles* p2 Ap 23 2015

Office De-stress Ideas D. L. GORDON and D. L. KATZ color *Reader's Digest* v189 no1130 p49 My 2017

The Right Kind of Stress Can Bond Your Team Together S. Achor *Harvard Business Review Digital Articles* p2 D 14 2015

Steps to Take When You're Starting to Feel Burned Out M. Valcour *Harvard Business Review Digital Articles* p2 Je 20 2016

Stressing mental health M. Notaras color *Science* v356 no6340 p878 My 26 2017

Stress Leads to Bad Decisions. Here's How to Avoid Them R. Carucci *Harvard Business Review Digital Articles* p2 Ag 29 2017

The Two Main Sources of Stress for High-Status Workers S. Damaske, M. J. Zawadzki et al *Harvard Business Review Digital Articles* p2 Ap 25 2016

Why People Cry at Work A. Ranieri *Harvard Business Review Digital Articles* p2 My 1 2015

Work stress could be good for your health *People Management* p57 D 2016/Ja 2017

Job stress—Management

4 Ways to Own Your Personal Power During Extremely Stressful Work Periods S. Franklin and A. GUMBS *Black Enterprise* v47 no4 p29 N/D 2016

How Making Time for Books Made Me Feel Less Busy H. McGuire *Harvard Business Review Digital Articles* p2 S 1 2015

A One-Page Exercise to Get Stress Under Control A. Rimm *Harvard Business Review Digital Articles* p2 S 15 2015

A Simple Yet Powerful Way to Handle a Stress Episode M. Valcour *Harvard Business Review Digital Articles* p2 Ag 27 2015

Work Grind Killing You? E. Lowe and A. GUMBS color *Black Enterprise* v47 no4 p28 N/D 2016

Job stress—Prevention

4 Ways to Own Your Personal Power During Extremely Stressful Work Periods S. Franklin and A. GUMBS *Black Enterprise* v47 no4 p29 N/D 2016

5 Ways to Boost Your Resilience at Work R. Fernandez *Harvard Business Review Digital Articles* p2 Je 27 2016

5 Ways to Focus Your Energy During a Work Crunch A. Jen Su *Harvard Business Review Digital Articles* p2 S 22 2017

5 Ways to Minimize Office Distractions J. Grenny *Harvard Business Review Digital Articles* p2 D 17 2015

Don't Get Surprised by Burnout S. D'Souza *Harvard Business Review Digital Articles* p2 Je 17 2016

Help Your Team Manage Stress, Anxiety, and Burnout R. Fernandez *Harvard Business Review Digital Articles* p2 Ja 21 2016

How to Handle Stress in the Moment R. Knight *Harvard Business Review Digital Articles* p2 N 5 2014

How to Overcome Burnout and Stay Motivated R. Knight *Harvard Business Review Digital Articles* p2 Ap 2 2015

SECRETS of People with HIGHLY STRESSFUL JOBS M. CROUCH cartoon *Prevention* v69 no2 p64 F 2017

A Simple Way to Stay Grounded in Stressful Moments L. Weiss *Harvard Business Review Digital Articles* p2 N 18 2016

Stressproof Your Work Life G. Saltz color *Health* v31 no4 p68 My 2017

Job titles

How to Ask for the Job Title You Deserve R. Knight *Harvard Business Review Digital Articles* p2 Jl 17 2017

The More Senior Your Job Title, the More You Need to Keep a Journal D. Ciampa *Harvard Business Review Digital Articles* p2 Jl 7 2017

Job vacancies

93 AT&T A. Pressman color *Fortune* v175 no4 p124 Mr 15 2017

Hellllp! S. Mohsin and R. Schmidt color *Bloomberg Businessweek* no4526 p22 Je 12 2017

Job openings, hires, and separations return to prerecession levels in 2015 A. MacLeod bibl chart color graph *Monthly Labor Review* p1 S 2016

Job openings, hires, and separations rise, but at a slower pace, in 2016 B. M. Thibaud bibl *Monthly Labor Review* p1 Ag 2017

MANY AMERICANS ARE OUT OF WORK, OR NEED BETTER JOBS. MANY EMPLOYERS HAVE GOOD JOBS THEY CAN'T FILL. CAN TRAINING PROGRAMS MORE INTELLIGENTLY MATCH THEM UP? R. Graham *New York Times Magazine* p48 F 26 2017

Top industries for job openings, July 2016 graph *Career Outlook* p1 S 2016

Why Social Networks Still Haven't Cracked the Job Search Puzzle J. P. V. Sampere *Harvard Business Review Digital Articles* p2 Ja 13 2015

Jobbágy, Esteban

Forest conservation: Remember Gran Chaco bibl color *Science* v355 no6324 p465 F 3 2017

Jobs, Laurene Powell, 1963-

Classroom: Lisa Miller img *New York* v49 no21 p22 O 17 2016

Young Americans color *Wired* v24 no11 p86 N 2016

Jobs, Richard Ivan

Florence's Mud Angels *History Today* v67 no8 p8 Ag 2017

Jobs, Steven, 1955-2011

IRRESISTIBLE: The business of technology is the business of addiction A. Alter *Saturday Evening Post* v289 no4 p12 Jl/Ag 2017

One More Thing S. Levy bw color *Wired* v25 no6 p52 Je 2017

Turtleneck 2.0 T. Patterson color *Bloomberg Businessweek* no4529 p76 Jl 3 2017

WHEN YOU ACHIEVE ALL OF YOUR GOALS, YOU STILL WAKE UP AS YOU L. DUCA *Vital Speeches of the Day* v83 no8 p226 Ag 2017

Job security—Charts, diagrams, etc.

How Screwed Is Your Job? M. Whitehouse and D. Gambrell diag *Bloomberg Businessweek* no4528 p50 Je 26 2017

Jobson, Gary—Interviews

Gary Jobson A. Schell color *Sail* v48 no1 p14 Ja 2017

Jockel, Luci

Luci Jockel B. MARTIN color *American Craft* v77 no2 p10 Ap/My 2017

Jockeys

See also

Women jockeys

The $100,000 Darley Awards Stake S. Andersen *Arabian Horse World* v57 no8 p114 My 2017

REIN MEN *Los Angeles Magazine* v62 no6 p100 Je 2017

Very Light Jockeys color *MIT Technology Review* v120 no2 p18 Mr/Ap 2017

Jockeys—United States

Stella Bella Arabians C. Reich color *Arabian Horse World* v57 no7 p118 Ap 2017

Jocko, Willink

Quotable Quotes *Reader's Digest* v188 no1124 p144 O 2016

Jodi

America's top TV critic Matt Roush answers your burning questions *TV Guide* v65 no37 p9 S 4 2017

Jodyjazz Inc.

JodyJazz Super Jet Alto Saxophone Mouthpiece B. Gibson color *Downbeat* v84 no5 p86 My 2017

Joe, Andrew

Mismatch repair deficiency predicts response of solid tumors to PD-1 blockade chart graph *Science* v357 no6349 p409 Jl 28 2017

Joel, Billy, 1949—Interviews

Billy Joel [Cover story] P. DOYLE bw *Rolling Stone* no1289 p62 Je 15 2017

Joel, Daphna

IS THERE A "FEMALE" BRAIN? L. DENWORTH color diag graph *Scientific American* v317 no3 p38 S 2017

Joel, Emmy

Wild for the Warrior *Publishers Weekly* v264 no29 p204 Jl 17 2017

Joergens, Ben

12 Steps to Financial Success: Empowering At-Risk Adults *Bridges (Federal Reserve Bank of St. Louis)* p9 Wint 2016/2017

Joffrey Ballet

HANSOL JEONC *Dance Spirit* v21 no3 p41 Mr 2017

Joffroy, Thierry

Learning from Local Building Cultures to Improve Housing Project Sustainability *UN Chronicle* v53 no3 p11 2016

Jogging
On the run S. FESCHUK color *Maclean's* v130 no8 p65 S 2017
PEAK 26.2 PLAN [Cover story] chart *Runner's World* v52 no6 p66 Jl 2017
SAFETY FIRST color *Women's Health* v13 no10 p32 D 2016

Johannsen, Jamie
Critical consciousness A key to student achievement bw il *Phi Delta Kappan* v98 no5 p18 F 2017

Johannsen, Niels N.
A composite window into human history color map *Science* v356 no6343 p1118 Je 16 2017

Johansen, Erika
The Fate of the Tearling N. Serrao color *Entertainment Weekly* no1442 p62 D 2 2016 Rebellious Special Issue

Johansen, Iris, 1938-
Look Behind You *Publishers Weekly* v264 no21 p73 My 22 2017
No Easy Target *Publishers Weekly* v264 no7 p49 F 13 2017

JOHANSON, MARK
The Highest Order color *Backpacker* p10 N 2017

Johanson, Michael
DeepStack: Expert-level artificial intelligence in heads-up no-limit poker [Cover story] chart diag *Science* v356 no6337 p508 My 5 2017

Johansson, Fredric
A subcellular map of the human proteome color *Science* v356 no6340 p820 My 26 2017

Johansson, J.
iPTF16geu: A multiply imaged, gravitationally lensed type Ia supernova color diag graph *Science* v356 no6335 p291 Ap 21 2017

Johansson, Jeaneth
We Recorded VCs' Conversations and Analyzed How Differently They Talk About Female Entrepreneurs *Harvard Business Review Digital Articles* p2 My 17 2017

Johansson, Mathias
Ridding the World of Bad Sound bw color *Sound & Vision* v82 no3 p16 Ap 2017

Johansson, Scarlett, 1984-
THE CULTURAL SATURATION CHART C. WEAVER and J. WILLIS bw cartoon color *GQ: Gentlemen's Quarterly* v97 no4 p59 Ap 2017
Scarlett Johansson: What's your go-to movie snack? D. WALTERS color *Bon Appetit* v62 no7 p108 Jl 2017
Sound Bites color *Entertainment Weekly* no1472 p8 Je 30 2017

Johar, Gita V.
Research: Being in a Group Makes Us Less Likely to Fact-Check *Harvard Business Review Digital Articles* p2 Ag 1 2017

Johka, Sharifa
Illuminations Debuts Online J. Coakley *Stage Directions* v29 no10 p2 O 2016

John, Arit
Planned Parenthood Is a GOP Land Mine *Bloomberg Businessweek* no4513 p32 Mr 6 2017

John, Elton
Artists color *Time* v189 no16/17 p40 My 1-8 2017

John, Jasper
Triple Bull's-Eye R. SULLIVAN and C. SCHAMA color *Vogue* v207 no9 p624 S 2017

JOHN, JORY
Should I Stop Bringing Up My Cat? *Reader's Digest* v189 no1127 p14 F 2017

John, King of England, 1167-1216
King John dies in Newark R. Cavendish *History Today* v66 no10 p8 O 2016

John, Leslie K.
We Say We Want Privacy Online, But Our Actions Say Otherwise *Harvard Business Review Digital Articles* p2 O 16 2015
WHAT'S THE VALUE OF A LIKE? color *Harvard Business Review* v95 no2 p108 Mr/Ap 2017

John, Leslie—Interviews
Blindsided by Trump's Victory? Behavioral Science Explains E. Harrell *Harvard Business Review Digital Articles* p2 N 9 2016

John, Rebecca
The Good Bohemian: The Letters of Ida John color *Publishers Weekly* v264 no23 p40 Je 5 2017

John, Roland
Put the "and" Back in "Sales and Marketing" *Harvard Business Review Digital Articles* p2 O 30 2014

John, Simon W. M.
Vitamin B3 modulates mitochondrial vulnerability and prevents glaucoma in aged mice bibl graph *Science* v355 no6326 p756 F 17 2017

John, Sir
the Glow Up A. Jordan color *Essence* v48 no2 p31 Je 2017
Sir John K. B. Brown color *InStyle* v24 no6 p86 Je 2017

John, Tara
Acid Attacks Have Become a Brutal New Trend In the U.K *Time* v190 no5 p16 Jl 31 2017
Adama Barrow color *Time* v189 no4 p12 F 6 2017
America's New Cardinals color *Time* v188 no16/17 p6 O 24 2016
The Angels of Irma [Cover story] color map *Time* v190 no12 p34 S 25 2017
Australia Has Its Say on Same-Sex Marriage color *Time* v190 no15 p11 O 16 2017
Best Excuses for Sleeping on the Job color *Time* v189 no20 p11 My 29 2017
Big Data Breaches color *Time* v188 no14 p10 O 10 2016
Britain Keeps Calm and Carries on After Parliament Attack color *Time* v189 no13 p12 Ap 10 2017
Changing the Laws That Let Rapists Wed Victims color *Time* v189 no18 p13 My 15 2017
The Developing Space Race color *Time* v188 no14 p8 O 10 2016
Female-Only Transport color *Time* v189 no3 p10 Ja 30 2017
France's Battle Royale color *Time* v189 no5 p9 F 13 2017
France's Golden Boy Loses His Luster color *Time* v190 no9 p10 S 4 2017
France's Man to Take on the Far Right color *Time* v188 no24 p14 D 12 2016
Google's $2.7 Billion Antitrust Fine color *Time* v190 no2/3 p9 Jl 10-17 2017
How Antarctica Is Being Invaded color *Time* v190 no1 p10 Jl 3 2017
How China Could Weaponize Water color *Time* v190 no13 p14 O 2 2017
How 'Golden Visas' Work color *Time* v189 no19 p10 My 22 2017
How to Treat Phobias color *Time* v189 no6 p12 F 20 2017
Islands Stranded Offline color *Time* v189 no4 p12 Ja 23 2017
Italy Lashes Out As Flow of Migrants Surges color *Time* v190 no4 p9 Jl 24 2017
Japan's Deadly Culture of Overwork color *Time* v190 no16/17 p14 O 23 2017
The Legal Rights of Nature color *Time* v189 no14 p14 Ap 17 2017
Lightbox color *Time* v189 no6 p16 F 20 2017
The Longest Meals color *Time* v189 no24 p10 Je 26 2017
The Lost Colony color *Time* v190 no15 p32 O 16 2017
Martin Schulz, Germany's Bernie Sanders color diag *Time* v189 no12 p14 Ap 3 2017
Meet the World's 'Newest' Plants color *Time* v189 no21 p12 Je 5 2017
Mistaken Names color *Time* v188 no20 p10 N 14 2016
Nepal Criminalizes Period Huts *Time* v190 no8 p10 Ag 28 2017
A New Face for the Republic of Ireland color *Time* v189 no23 p13 Je 19 2017
The New Gold Rush for Our e-Waste color *Time* v190 no15 p10 O 16 2017
New Zealand's Rising Star Puts Election In Play color *Time* v190 no10/11 p13 S 18 2017
Next Generation Leaders color *Time* v188 no15 p41 O 17 2016
Next Generation Leaders color *Time* v189 no9 p38 Mr 13 2017
The Pirate Party Sets Sail for Election Victory In Iceland color *Time* v188 no19 p9 N 7 2016
Saudi Women In the Driver's Seat color *Time* v190 no14 p10 O 9 2017
Savagery In the U.K. Britain Comes Under Attack at a Turning Point color *Time* v189 no21 p34 Je 5 2017
The Science of Making Food Taste Better color *Time* v189 no5 p12 F 13 2017
Six Months In, Is Britain's Theresa May Bungling Brexit? color *Time* v189 no4 p10 Ja 23 2017
The Sky Is Falling color *Time* v188 no22-23 p12 N/D 2016
Somalia on the Verge of Famine As U.N. Pleads for Help color

Time v189 no7/8 p17 F 27 2017

Stolen Art That Made a Return color *Time* v188 no15 p8 O 17 2016

The 'Super-Malaria' on the Rise In Southeast Asia color *Time* v190 no14 p11 O 9 2017

Under the Influence color *Time* v188 no16/17 p8 O 24 2016

Unpresidential Palaces color *Time* v189 no11 p14 Mr 27 2017

Wave of Unrest Crashes on Ethiopia color *Time* v188 no15 p6 O 17 2016

Ways to Rid the World's Oceans of Plastic Trash color *Time* v189 no24 p9 Je 26 2017

What Not to Wear Flying color *Time* v189 no13 p10 Ap 10 2017

What's Next After the Peace Deal In Colombia color *Time* v188 no14 p9 O 10 2016

Where Artists Fall Afoul of Blasphemy Laws color *Time* v189 no19 p13 My 22 2017

Where Catcalling Is Criminalized color *Time* v188 no27-28 p12 D 26 2016

Where National Breakups Are In the Cards color *Time* v189 no7/8 p18 F 27 2017

Why Brazil's Prisoners Are Rioting color *Time* v189 no4 p11 Ja 23 2017

World Elections: Races to Watch color *Time* v188 no27-28 p63 D 26 2016

The World's Costliest Typos *Time* v189 no10 p10 Mr 20 2017

The World's New Diplomat In Chief color *Time* v188 no27-28 p13 D 26 2016

The World's Unlikeliest Star Athletes color *Time* v189 no9 p12 Mr 13 2017

The World Won't Ignore Chechnya's Purge of Gay Men color *Time* v189 no22 p9 Je 12 2017

John, the Apostle, Saint, 6-100

Reflections on the lectionary C. J. LaRue *Christian Century* v133 no25 p19 D 7 2016

John, the Baptist, Saint

LIVING BY The Word *Christian Century* v133 no24 p22 N 23 2016

John Deere tractors

DEERE DEALERS' DEALS ON 4WDs D. Mowitz *Successful Farming* v115 no3 p20 Mid-F 2017

NEW LIFE FOR WORN CABS: REPLACE DILAPIDATED IN-TERIORS IN HOURS WITH PREFORMED KITS T. Gaines *Successful Farming* v115 no9 p34 Ag 2017

John Deere tractors—Evaluation

GOING ELECTRIC J. Scott *Successful Farming* v115 no4 p46 Mr 2017

John F. Kennedy Presidential Library & Museum

And the Oscar Goes to... color *Weekly Standard* v22 no35 p2 My 22 2017

Beyond Camelot J. BILLS color *Yankee* p76 Mr 2017

EDITOR'S NOTE J. WORSHAM *Prologue* v49 no1 p1 Spr 2017

JFK 100 Centennial Events *Prologue* v49 no1 p34 Spr 2017

JFK 100 Milestones & Mementos S. Bredhoff *Prologue* v49 no1 p48 Spr 2017

John Frieda Professional Hair Care Inc.

Little ways to boost your color M. OLIVA color *Redbook* p54 O 2017

John Muir Wilderness (Calif.)

Find a higher calling color *Backpacker* v45 no1 p18 Ja 2017

John Pizzarelli Quartet (Performer)

Yankee's favorite events this season color *Yankee* p70 Jl 2017

John Rigby & Co.

THE RETURN OF RIGBY W. van Zwoll bw *Outdoor Life* v224 no2 p63 F/Mr 2017

John Wick (Film)

JOHN WICK – CHAPTER 2 D. Vaughn color *Sound & Vision* v82 no8 p67 O 2017

John Wick: Chapter 2 (Film)

The Hit Parade J. QUEENAN *Weekly Standard* v22 no36 p39 My 29 2017

JOHN WICK: CHAPTER 2 C. Collis color *Entertainment Weekly* no1446/1447 p51 D 2016/Ja 2017

John Wick: Chapter 2 C. Nashawaty color *Entertainment Weekly* no1453 p45 F 17 2017

Keanu Reeves' Contract Killer With Feelings Returns S. Lansky color *Time* v189 no5 p49 F 13 2017

Surprise Ending J. Podhoretz color *Weekly Standard* v22 no24 p43 F 27 2017

Vengeance, the Slow Way S. Zacharek color *Time* v189 no6 p50 F 20 2017

John Deere tractors—Charts, diagrams, etc.

POCKET PRICE GUIDE: Dealer Prices on Deere 500-hp. 4WDs *Successful Farming* v115 no3 p23 Mid-F 2017

John F. Kennedy Center Plaza (Washington, D.C.)

Quick Hits A. Marks map *Scientific American* v316 no5 p20 My 2017

John McDonogh Senior High School (New Orleans, La.)

JULIA STREET / WITH POYDRAS THE PARROT J. STREET bw *New Orleans Magazine* v51 no3 p20 Ja 2017

John Paul II, Pope, 1920-2005

you follow? LOLs and hashtags from Twitter *U.S. Catholic* v82 no7 p8 Jl 2017

JOHNS, DAVID

POLITICAL SCIENCE color *Scientific American* v317 no3 p7 S 2017

We Need a Biologically Sound North American Conservation Plan *BioScience* v67 no8 p685 Ag 2017

Johns, Jasper, 1930-

Surface Depth L. D. ALSPAUGH cartoon *Weekly Standard* v22 no17 p37 Ja 2 2017

Johns, Jerry L.—Awards

news & notes color *Literacy Today (2411-7862)* v34 no4 p42 Ja/F 2017

Johns, Mallory

ONE NIGHTSTAND color *Popular Science* v289 no5 p34 S/O 2017

RUGGEDLY HANDSOME color *Popular Science* v289 no4 p28 Jl/Ag 2017

Johns, Zach

FUN & GAMES color *Backpacker* p71 Je 2017

Johnsen, Dawn

The Lawyers' War *Foreign Affairs* v96 no1 p148 Ja/F 2017

Johnsen, Erik

The Costumer Is Thriving At 100 Years Young L. Mulcahy *Stage Directions* v30 no8 p23 Ag 2017

Johnsen, J. A.

Observation of a large-scale anisotropy in the arrival directions of cosmic rays above 8×1018 eV *Science* v357 no6357 p1266 S 22 2017

Johnsen Schmaling Architects (Company)

house of the month M. SITZ color diag *Architectural Record* v205 no3 p33 Mr 2017

Johnsgard, Paul

Nebraskans of a feather let new crane book fly N. Buck cartoon color *Nebraska Life* v21 no2 p77 Mr/Ap 2017

Johnson, A. J.

GET SCULPTED LIKE YOUR GIRL CRUSH T. E. Hopkins color *Essence* v48 no3 p115 Jl 2017

Johnson, A. Ross

The Cold War's Pivot *Hoover Digest: Research & Opinion on Public Policy* no4 p199 Fall 2016

Johnson, Abigail P., 1961-

Massachusetts M. TINDERA color *Forbes* v199 no1 p29 Ja 24 2017

Johnson, Adam

Centrist Pundits Prepared Way for Trump Smear of 'Alt-Left' *Extra!* v30 no8 p1 O 2017

Declining to Label Lies, NPR Picks Diplomacy Over Reality *Extra!* v30 no2 p4 Mr 2017

NPR Sees 'Restraint' in Thump's Threat-Filled Foreign Policy *Extra!* v30 no3 p3 Ap 2017

NYT Exposes a Favorite Source as War Industry Flack *Extra!* v29 no8 p4 O 2016

NYT, Reviewing Trump's '100 Days,' Shows Folly of 'Both Sides' Journalism *Extra!* v30 no5 p1 Je 2017

'Perseverance Porn' Bolsters System by Celebrating Survivors of Its Cruelties *Extra!* v30 no7 p3 S 2017

Pundits Told Dems to Spurn Sanders for 'Electable' Clinton *Extra!* v29 no10 p3 D 2016

Saudi Arms Deal Stories Omitted Who the Weapons Would Be Killing *Extra!* v30 no6 p4 Jl/Ag 2017

Trump's 'Presidential' Moment: Turning a Massacre Into Political

2017

From Retreat to Forever color *Log Home Living* v34 no5 p(Sp)6 Jl 2017

High Forest Hideout color *Cabin Living* p46 S 2017

High Forest Hideout color *Log Home Living* v34 no1 p60 F 2017

Sweet Dreams are Made of This color diag *Cabin Living* p72 Je 2017

Sweet Dreams are Made of This color *Timber Home Living* v27 no5 p58 O 2017

Johnson, Cookie—Interviews

The Good Wife P. H. Bass color *Essence* v47 no7 p90 N 2016

JOHNSON, CRAIG

Yep, There Are Books color *Publishers Weekly* v264 no32 p76 Ag 7 2017

Johnson, Craig Hella

Johnson: Considering Matthew Shepard J. Rosenblum *Opera News* v81 no6 p51 D 2016

Johnson, Craig, 1961-

Lovably Unlikable D. EDELSTEIN img *New York* v50 no6 p85 Mr 20 2017

Wilson C. Nashawaty color *Entertainment Weekly* no1459 p47 Mr 31 2017

Johnson, Daisy

Fen *Publishers Weekly* v264 no11 p53 Mr 13 2017

Her Inner Eel H. HOBY *New York Times Book Review* p19 My 28 2017

Johnson, Dakota, 1989-

"I'm complicated, but my beauty routine is simple" F. Valdesolo color *Glamour* v115 no9 p94 S 2017

The Quiz T. BALAZO color *Maclean's* v130 no3 p71 Ap 2017

Johnson, Dana

In the Not Quite Dark: Stories M. Earley *Christian Century* v134 no4 p55 F 15 2017

Johnson, Daniel J.

Plant diversity increases with the strength of negative density dependence at the global scale diag *Science* v356 no6345 p1389 Je 30 2017

Johnson, Dashon

The Guru of Abs J. SCHILDHOUSE color *Muscle & Performance* v9 no11 p40 N 2017

Johnson, Davey G.

Velar–Oh! color *Car & Driver* v63 no5 p112 N 2017

Johnson, David

America's Happiest Incomes color *Time* v189 no19 p11 My 22 2017

birds of a feather color *Cabin Living* p19 Ap 2017

Home Buying Across America color *Time* v189 no21 p11 Je 5 2017

THE X-MAN FACTOR G. Bishop color *Sports Illustrated* v127 no7 p46 S 4 2017

Johnson, David V.

LET'S MAKE FOOTBALL A COLLEGE MAJOR *Saturday Evening Post* v288 no6 p12 N/D 2016

Johnson, Demetrious

Demetrious Johnson L. J. Wertheim color *Sports Illustrated* v126 no15 p44 My 29 2017

Johnson, Denis, 1949-2017

ABOVE & BEYOND cartoon *New Yorker* v93 no30 p14 O 2 2017

Denis Johnson: A Lot Like Prayer W. Blythe *New York Times Book Review* p14 Jl 30 2017

Denis Johnson: An Editor's Love Story J. Maher color *Publishers Weekly* v264 no41 p5 O 9 2017

Strangler Bob bw color *New Yorker* v93 no33 p82 O 23 2017

Johnson, Dennis

Woodworker's Refuge: Cedar and Oak *South Dakota Magazine* v33 no2 p70 Jl/Ag 2017

Johnson, Diane

Frail, Funny, and Prescient About Our Mess bw *New York Review of Books* v64 no3 p41 F 23 2017

Postmodern Mom bw *New York Review of Books* v64 no15 p37 O 12 2017

JOHNSON, DONALD-BRIAN

CERAMICS TRIAD *Treasures* v6 no4 p28 F/Mr 2017

Dream Homes color *Treasures* v5 no5 p44 Ap/My 2016

Gene Marshall, Hollywood Fashion Icon *Treasures* v6 no3 p38 D 2016/Ja 2017

THE GOLDEN AGE OF BRONZE *Treasures* v6 no6 p24 Je/Jl 2017

HEADS UP *Treasures* v6 no5 p38 Ap/My 2017

Hello? *Treasures* v6 no2 p36 O/N 2016

HERE COME THE BRIDE'S BASKETS! *Treasures* v6 no6 p30 Je/Jl 2017

It's a Small World After All color *Treasures* v5 no5 p53 Ap/My 2016

OVER THERE, OVER HERE *Treasures* v6 no5 p30 Ap/My 2017

SPOOK - Tacular! *Treasures* v6 no2 p45 O/N 2016

VAUDEVILLE TONITE! *Treasures* v6 no4 p38 F/Mr 2017

Vintage Holiday Homemaking *Treasures* v6 no3 p28 D 2016/Ja 2017

Johnson, Doug

Granf Island Painter A. J. Bartels color *Nebraska Life* v21 no1 p60 Ja/F 2017

Johnson, Dustin

The DJ Universe M. Chwasky color *Golf Magazine* v59 no1 p68 Ja 2017

DUSTIN'S YEAR TO REMEMBER D. M. Clarke color *Golf Magazine* v59 no1 p12 Ja 2017

Dustin' the Competition M. Broadie chart color *Golf Magazine* v59 no1 p72 Ja 2017

Game of Thrones A. Shipnuck and C. Barrett color *Golf Magazine* v59 no5 p30 My 2017

His Brother's Looper S. Zak color *Golf Magazine* v59 no1 p76 Ja 2017

"I Want to Make Them Proud" A. Shipnuck color *Golf Magazine* v59 no1 p58 Ja 2017

PLAYER OF THE YEAR color *Golf Magazine* v59 no1 p56 Ja 2017

TEEING OFF J. Sens color *Golf Magazine* v59 no5 p18 My 2017

THE ULTIMATE DRIVING MACHINE [Cover story] D. De-Nunzio color *Golf Magazine* v59 no1 p78 Ja 2017

What He's Really Like S. Zak color *Golf Magazine* v59 no1 p67 Ja 2017

You're Up! color *Golf Magazine* v59 no3 p13 Mr 2017

Johnson, Dustin, 1984-

DJ's Secret Sauce M. Broadie and C. Barrett color *Golf Magazine* v59 no6 p28 Je 2017

Johnson and Johnson A. Shipnuck color *Sports Illustrated* v126 no17 p48 Je 19 2017

LASER SHOW C. Harmon and D. DeNunzio color *Golf Magazine* v59 no6 p44 Je 2017

Johnson, Dustin, 1984—Interviews

Public Defender J. Marksbury and C. Barrett color *Golf Magazine* v59 no6 p19 Je 2017

Johnson, Dwayne, 1972-

6 — "YOU'RE WELCOME" D. Coggan *Entertainment Weekly* no1444/1445 p60 D 16 2016

BATTLE OF THE BALD, ETHNICALLY AMBIGUOUS AC-TION HEROES chart color *Esquire* p25 Ap 2017

The Celebrity We Need [Cover story] D. FRENCH color *National Review* v69 no9 p21 My 15 2017

Cover *Sports Illustrated* v125 no18 pC1 D 5 2016

David Hasselhot? C. Ianzito color *AARP: The Magazine* v60 no4A p12 Je/Jl 2017

DWAYNE JOHNSON ROCKS D. Coggan color *Entertainment Weekly* no1441 p11 N 25 2016

JUMANJI: WELCOME TO THE JUNGLE D. Coggan color *Entertainment Weekly* no1478 / 1479 p73 Ag 18-25 2017

Sexy as the Rock S. FESCHUK color *Maclean's* v129 no50 p65 D 19 2016

VOTE tHE ROCK [Cover story] C. WEAVER bw color *GQ: Gentlemen's Quarterly* v97 no6 p84 Je 2017

Johnson, Dwayne, 1972—Finance

Dwayne Johnson ALMIGHTY BALLER [Cover story] A. Shipnuck color *Sports Illustrated* v125 no18 p28 D 5 2016

Johnson, E. Pauline, 1861-1913

Flint, Feather, and Other Material Selves M. Jones and N. Ferris *American Indian Quarterly* v41 no2 p125 Spr 2017

Johnson, Edward Hibberd

Bright Idea J. Malanowski *Smithsonian* v47 no8 p11 D 2016

Johnson, Elaine

BEST OF THE WEST color *Sunset* v238 no6 p9 Je 2017

BEYOND THE KALE color *Sunset* v239 no4 p46 O 2017

BIG-BATCH GIFTS color *Sunset* v237 no6 p81 D 2016

CHOCOLATE PARTY! color *Sunset* v238 no2 p77 F 2017

FILIPINO FOOD'S MOMENT color *Sunset* v238 no3 p73 Mr 2017

A FOOLPROOF FEAST color *Sunset* v237 no5 p81 N 2016

In the SUNSET KITCHEN color *Sunset* v237 no6 p98 D 2016

In the SUNSET KITCHEN color *Sunset* v238 no5 p94 My 2017

In the SUNSET KITCHEN color *Sunset* v239 no4 p92 O 2017

PEAR POWER color *Sunset* v238 no1 p77 Ja 2017

spring awakening color *Sunset* v238 no4 p76 Ap 2017

SWEET ON PEPPERS color *Sunset* v239 no3 p91 S 2017

TRAILBLAZERS color *Sunset* v238 no5 p74 My 2017

WORLD OF FLAVOR color *Sunset* v239 no1 p74 Jl 2017

JOHNSON, ELIANA

Maine Divided il *National Review* v68 no20 p16 N 7 2016

Johnson, Elsbeth

How Leaders Can Focus on the Big Picture *Harvard Business Review Digital Articles* p2 N 9 2016

How to Communicate Clearly During Organizational Change *Harvard Business Review Digital Articles* p2 Je 13 2017

Johnson, Emily

THE FIX cartoon *Old House Journal* v45 no6 p56 S 2017

Johnson, Emma

OPRAH'S Favorite Things, Unwrapped color *O, The Oprah Magazine* p94 D 2016

Johnson, Eric

Brought to You by the Letter K color *Golf Magazine* v58 no11 p52 N 2016

SEE IT AND SPIETH IT! color *Golf Magazine* v59 no1 p50 Ja 2017

Johnson, Erik

Braking Bad color *Car & Driver* v62 no11 p116 My 2017

SECOND CHANCES color *Car & Driver* v62 no7 p52 Ja 2017

The Stoic Beast color *Car & Driver* v63 no4 p100 O 2017

Johnson, Ernie

Care Taker B. Golliver and T. Keith color *Sports Illustrated* v126 no10 p26 Ap 10 2017

Take Me Out to the Blackberry Patch E. JOHNSON JR. color *Reader's Digest* v190 no1132 p36 Jl/Ag 2017

Johnson, Gene

10 SUCCESSFUL FARMERS: JOE BREKER *Successful Farming* v115 no8 p14 Je/Jl 2017

JOHNSON, GEORGE

Awakenings *New York Times Book Review* p13 Ag 27 2017

Johnson, Gerald W.

A PECULIAR VIRTUE *Harper's Magazine* v334 no2000 p9 Ja 2017

Johnson, Graham

VARIETY AMONG CLONES E. MASTROIANNI color *Discover* v38 no7 p9 S 2017

Johnson, Graham R.

Emergence and spread of a human-transmissible multidrug-resistant nontuberculous mycobacterium bibl diag graph *Science* v354 no6313 p751 N 11 2016

Johnson, Graham T.

Whole cell maps chart a course for 21st-century cell biology color *Science* v356 no6340 p806 My 26 2017

Johnson, Gregg

Your Customers Still Want to Talk to a Human Being *Harvard Business Review Digital Articles* p2 Jl 26 2017

Johnson, Harold

Evil Spirits J. Kay color *Walrus* v14 no5 p64 Je 2017

Johnson, Henry

Valor Heroic Hellfighter C. Lyons *Military History* v33 no6 p12 Mr 2017

Johnson, Hillary C.

Teaching personal initiative beats traditional training in boosting small business in West Africa chart graph *Science* v357 no6357 p1287 S 22 2017

Johnson, Ian

CATHOLICS AT A CROSSROADS color map *America* v217 no7 p18 O 2 2017

China's Astounding Religious Revival [Cover story] R. MacFarquhar color *New York Review of Books* v64 no10 p36 Je 8 2017

China's Great Awakening color *Foreign Affairs* v96 no2 p83 Mr/Ap 2017

China's many revivals P. Jenkins *Christian Century* v134 no13 p34 Je 21 2017

China: The Virtues of the Awful Convulsion bw cartoon *New York Review of Books* v63 no16 p70 O 27 2016

Chronicles of China's Spiritual Revival R. P. WELLER *Current History* v116 no791 p244 S 2017

Novels from China's Moral Abyss color *New York Review of Books* v64 no11 p53 Je 22 2017

Recreating China's Imagined Empire color map *New York Review of Books* v64 no7 p33 Ap 20 2017

Sexual Life in Modern China color *New York Review of Books* v64 no16 p63 O 26 2017

The Souls of China: The Return of Religion After Mao A. J. Nathan *Foreign Affairs* v96 no3 p172 My/Je 2017

When the Chinese Were Unspeakable color map *New York Review of Books* v64 no1 p22 Ja 19 2017

Johnson, Ian—Interviews

A Thousand Religions Bloom Again R. MOLL bw color *Christianity Today* p70 Ap 2017

Johnson, Jack

Seeing the Light R. KOBELL *National Parks* v91 no1 p24 Wint 2017

Johnson, Jack, 1975-

Jack Johnson's New Wave K. GROW bw color *Rolling Stone* no1291/1292 p20 Jl 13 2017

JOHNSON, JARED

Coam Over *Boating World* v38 no6 p24 Je 2017

Install Yacht-like Non-Skid *Boating World* v38 no2 p22 F 2017

Rebuild a Rotten Transom *Boating World* v38 no3 p22 Mr 2017

Johnson, Jeff

Genius at Work color *Downbeat* v83 no12 p91 D 2016

Guitar Hero, Chicago Born color *Downbeat* v83 no12 p80 D 2016

Knottspeed: A Love Story *Publishers Weekly* v264 no1 p35 Ja 2 2017

Living Waters M. Malone *America* v217 no6 p3 S 18 2017

Motown Treasures color *Downbeat* v83 no12 p94 D 2016

Next Stop: Otis in 1966 color *Downbeat* v83 no12 p90 D 2016

Otis Taylor: 'TRIUMPH IS THE KEY' color *Downbeat* v84 no4 p40 Ap 2017

Remembering James Cotton bw *Downbeat* v84 no6 p25 Je 2017

Johnson, Jeffrey

Forever Words: The Unknown Poems *Christian Century* v134 no6 p42 Mr 15 2017

The Whole Harmonium: The Life of Wallace Stevens *Christian Century* v134 no9 p36 Ap 26 2017

Johnson, Jeffrey O.

MYSTERY SPOT *Sky & Telescope* v133 no6 p76 Je 2017

Johnson, Jenn

The Day Our Ship Came In bw *Yankee* p184 My/Je 2017

How to Give a Great Speech color *Yankee* p28 My/Je 2017

Markdown Memories: When the original Filene's Basement closed 10 years ago this fall, Boston lost a quirky shopping experience-and a kind of common ground *Yankee* v81 no5 p156 S/O 2017

Seal of Honor color *Yankee* p24 My/Je 2017

The Write Stuff color *Yankee* p26 Jl 2017

Johnson, Jenny

In Full Velvet N. Davis color *Orion Magazine* v36 no2 p60 Mr/Ap 2017

Life IN THESE UNITED STATES *Reader's Digest* v189 no1128 p38 Mr 2017

Johnson, Jerry

Irasburg bw color *Old House Journal* v45 no4 p34 Je 2017

JOHNSON, JESSICA

The Age of Canlandia cartoon *Walrus* v13 no10 p26 D 2016

Johnson, Jimmie, 1975——Awards

Magnificent Sevens T. Keith chart color *Sports Illustrated* v125 no18 p19 D 5 2016

The Standout M. Bechtel color *Sports Illustrated* v125 no20 p102 D 19 2016

Johnson, John Asher

How Do You Find an Exoplanet? S. J. Thompson *Physics Today* v69 no11 p59 N 2016

Johnson, John R.

Reintroducing the Game of Golf *Parks & Recreation* v52 no1 p50 Ja 2017

Johnson, John—Interviews

IQ P. O'Donnell *Washingtonian Magazine* v52 no4 p39 Ja 2017

Johnson, Joseph

To Survive, Health Care Data Providers Need to Stop Selling Data *Harvard Business Review Digital Articles* p2 Je 14 2017

Johnson, Joshua

MEET JOSHUA JOHNSON A. BEAUJON *Washingtonian Magazine* v52 no4 p22 Ja 2017

Johnson, Josiah—Interviews

Stayin' Hollywood M. McKnight and T. Keith color *Sports Illustrated* v126 no17 p20 Je 19 2017

Johnson, Judy

Carla Hayden color *Current Biography* v78 no3 p28 Mr 2017

Daveed Diggs color *Current Biography* v78 no2 p26 F 2017

Emily Nussbaum color *Current Biography* v77 no10 p82 O 2016

The Great Day-Care Sexual-Abuse Panic P. TERZIAN bw *Weekly Standard* v22 no42 p12 Jl 17 2017

Janicza Bravo color *Current Biography* v78 no8 p8 Ag 2017

Katia Beauchamp color *Current Biography* v77 no11 p21 N 2016

Kellie Jones color *Current Biography* v78 no5 p44 My 2017

Kelly Fremon Craig color *Current Biography* v78 no9 p13 S 2017

Kelsea Ballerini color *Current Biography* v78 no5 p8 My 2017

Kwame Alexander color *Current Biography* v78 no1 p8 Ja 2017

Lily Collins color *Current Biography* v78 no8 p22 Ag 2017

Melissa Benoist color *Current Biography* v78 no6 p15 Je 2017

Olivia Bee color *Current Biography* v78 no6 p10 Je 2017

Ottessa Moshfegh color *Current Biography* v78 no2 p53 F 2017

Rebecca Hall color *Current Biography* v78 no4 p33 Ap 2017

Sara Mearns color *Current Biography* v78 no9 p57 S 2017

Vanita Gupta color *Current Biography* v78 no1 p22 Ja 2017

JOHNSON, K. C.

Assault on Justice A. B. Lloyd color *Weekly Standard* v22 no26 p30 Mr 13 2017

Campus Chaos *Commentary* v142 no1 p15 Jl/Ag 2016

The Campus Sex-Crime Tribunals Are Losing: How the courts are intervening to block some of the most unjust punishments of our time *Commentary* v144 no3 p20 O 2017

Is free speech under threat IN THE UNITED STATES? WE RECEIVED TWENTY-SEVEN RESPONSES. WE PUBLISH THEM HERE, IN ALPHABETICAL ORDER *Commentary* v144 no1 p13 Jl/Ag 2017

Kafka U *Commentary* v143 no6 p46 Je 2017

Overruled color *Weekly Standard* v23 no5 p15 O 9 2017

The Persistently Misleading Media color graph *Weekly Standard* v22 no46 p17 Ag 14 2017

RAGE OF THE SNOWFLAKES *Claremont Review of Books* v17 no3 p62 Summ 2017

Salem, Montana *Commentary* v140 no2 p63 S 2015

Johnson, Kandia

6 WAYS TO GET MEDIA COVERAGE FOR YOUR STARTUP color *Black Enterprise* v47 no8 p14 Jl/Ag 2017

7 SECRETS OF A SIDE HUSTLER color *Black Enterprise* v47 no7 p14 My/Je 2017

Bouncing Back After Breast Cancer color *Black Enterprise* v47 no3 p69 O 2016

BRINGING SILICON VALLEY TO DETROIT color *Black Enterprise* v47 no7 p21 My/Je 2017

WANT TO SPREAD THE WORD ABOUT YOUR WORK? FIND YOUR TRIBE *Black Enterprise* v47 no8 p32 Jl/Ag 2017

Johnson, Katherine

SHOOT FOR THE STARS V. K. De Luca color *Essence* v47 no10 p14 F 2017

Johnson, Katherine Coleman Goble, 1918-

Fighting FOR Visibility K. Haynes bw color *Astronomy* v45 no2 p44 F 2017

Johnson, Kij

The River Bank *Publishers Weekly* v264 no31 p59 Jl 31 2017

Johnson, Kirsten

INDESTRUCTIBLE *Film Comment* v53 no2 p6 Mr/Ap 2017

Johnson, Kristen A.

Decarboxylative borylation color *Science* v356 no6342 p1045 Je 9 2017

JOHNSON, KRISTEN DEEDE

SPIRITUAL DISCIPLINES ARE NOT ABOUT YOU color *Christianity Today* v61 no7 p77 S 2017

JOHNSON, KYLE

FIREWORKS, FLASHLIGHTS AND FIREFLIES color *Flying* v144 no11 p26 N 2017

Johnson, Kym, 1976-

LIFE (AND LOVE) LESSONS WE'VE LEARNED FROM REALITY TV R. HERJAVEC and K. JOHNSON HERJAVEC *TV Guide* v64 no40 p20 O 3 2016

Johnson, Laura

AGING GRACEFULLY on the Homestead *Mother Earth News* no280 p34 F/Mr 2017

r.s.v.p cartoon *Bon Appetit* v62 no2 p14 Mr 2017

JOHNSON, LEROY

READERS' THOUGHTS ON PAST ISSUES color *Motor Trend* v69 no2 p26 F 2017

Johnson, Lily

Don't Let A Drought Hit The Progressive! color *Progressive* v81 no5 p37 Je/Jl 2017

Johnson, Lise

Five reasons to leave your science bubble C. Tachibana color *Science* v357 no6353 p823 Ag 25 2017

Johnson, Liz

HOLIDAY FOOD G. DUFFY img *New York* v49 no22 p71 O 31 2016

SALT-BAKED VENISON FOR 18 L. JOHNSON img *New York* v49 no22 p76 O 31 2016

Johnson, Lora

ASK THE EXPERTS color *Runner's World* v51 no11 p42 D 2016

Johnson, Luke Timothy

The Church & Transgender Identity cartoon *Commonweal* v144 no5 p15 Mr 10 2017

Flourishing bw *Commonweal* v144 no3 p37 F 10 2017

The Letters of Robert Giroux and Thomas Merton bw *Commonweal* v144 no3 p35 F 10 2017

An Ordinary Sunday [Cover story] color *Commonweal* v144 no15 p11 S 22 2017

RELIGION BOOKNOTES color *Commonweal* v144 no10 p34 Je 2 2017

The Triumph of Faith color *Commonweal* v144 no3 p35 F 10 2017

We Have Been Friends Together & Adventures in Grace bw *Commonweal* v144 no3 p36 F 10 2017

Johnson, Lyndon B. (Lyndon Baines), 1908-1973

SAVING THE CABINET OAK W. FERGUSON *Texas Monthly* v45 no7 p46 Jl 2017

JOHNSON, LYNNE d.

3 BUSINESS BOOKS TO DRIVE YOUR SUCCESS IN 2017 color *Black Enterprise* v47 no5 p30 Ja/F 2017

Live Out Loud color *Ebony* v72 no8 p52 Je 2017

Minding Our Business color *Ebony* v72 no3 p108 D 2016/Ja 2017

Mixing Dollars and Sense color *Ebony* v72 no5 p74 Mr 2017

Radial Revolution color *Ebony* v72 no8 p73 Je 2017

Sugar Mama color *Ebony* v72 no6 p75 Ap/My 2017

Johnson, M. D.

The Coot Surprise color *Field & Stream* v122 no5 pF8 O 2017

The Imperfect Opener color *Field & Stream* v122 no4 pF1 S 2017

Operation Black Duck color *Field & Stream* v122 no5 p80 O 2017

TARGET: Bluebills color *Field & Stream* v122 no4 pF6 S 2017

Johnson, Marcus

The Vogue R. ANNIS *Indianapolis Monthly* v40 no7 p18 Mr 2017

Johnson, Mari-Vaughn V.

Dinner with Darwin color *Science* v357 no6355 p968 S 8 2017

Johnson, Mark A.

Spectroscopic snapshots of the proton-transfer mechanism in water bibl diag graph *Science* v354 no6316 p1131 D 2 2016

JOHNSON, MARK R.

THE affordable LOG CABIN color diag *Cabin Living* p28 Ap 2017

ARE YOU FIREWISE? color *Cabin Living* p72 Ap 2017

creating Joy color *Cabin Living* p5 Ja/F 2017

Feeling Grateful *Cabin Living* p5 D 2016

Grandpa Ernie's Wool Jacket color *Cabin Living* p5 Ag 2017

IT'S A SMALL World *Cabin Living* p5 Je 2017

LET'S COZY UP TO small CABINS! bw color *Cabin Living* p5 Mr 2017

Oh! The Stories They Tell *Cabin Living* p5 S 2017

Rustic Lighting color *Cabin Living* p38 Ja/F 2017

What is a cabin? color *Cabin Living* p5 Ap 2017

Johnson, Mark W.

toon color *Military History* v34 no1 p76 My 2017

Johnson, Steve
DIARY OF A SEASON *Tennis* v53 no1 p36 Ja/F 2017
THE MONSTER MAN C. Collis color *Entertainment Weekly* no1453 p62 F 17 2017

Johnson, Steven
Lighten Up! N. BEACH color *O, The Oprah Magazine* p70 Ja 2017
NATURAL MAGIC *New York Times Magazine* p48 N 6 2016
TO WHOM IT MAY CONCERN *New York Times Magazine* p32 Jl 2 2017
Triviality Is the Mother of Invention S. Begley color *Time* v188 no20 p18 N 14 2016
When Play Drives Progress V. POSTREL color *Reason* v48 no10 p60 Mr 2017

Johnson, Steven L.
How to Get Experts to Work Together Effectively *Harvard Business Review Digital Articles* p2 My 10 2017

Johnson, Steven, 1968-
The Power of Play V. HEFFERNAN *New York Times Book Review* p12 N 27 2016

Johnson, Steven, 1968—Interviews
Steven Johnson *New York Times Book Review* p8 D 18 2016

Johnson, Sylvester A., 1972-
God and Man at the FBI A. THEOHARIS bw color *Reason* v49 no3 p66 Jl 2017

Johnson, Tara
Kid Sports Inc [Cover story] color diag *Time* v190 no9 p42 S 4 2017

JOHNSON, TODD
UNDER DISCUSSION *Christianity Today* p17 Ap 2017

Johnson, Tom M.
MAN OF STEEL A. Ryder color *Popular Photography* v81 no2 p90 Mr/Ap 2017

Johnson, Trent
My Collection color *Horse & Rider* v56 no11 p136 N 2017

Johnson, Vicki
STRANGE & WONDERFUL TOPIARY GARDENS color *Old House Journal* v45 no4 p20 Je 2017

Johnson, W. Brad
How to Mentor a Narcissist *Harvard Business Review Digital Articles* p2 S 19 2017
How to Mentor a Perfectionist *Harvard Business Review Digital Articles* p2 F 21 2017
Male Mentors Shouldn't Hesitate to Challenge Their Female Mentees *Harvard Business Review Digital Articles* p2 My 29 2017
Men Can Improve How They Mentor Women. Here's How *Harvard Business Review Digital Articles* p2 D 5 2016
Men Shouldn't Refuse to Be Alone with Female Colleagues *Harvard Business Review Digital Articles* p2 My 5 2017
Too Many Men Are Silent Bystanders to Sexual Harassment *Harvard Business Review Digital Articles* p2 Mr 13 2017

Johnson, Warren
KICK-ASS CUSTOMER SERVICE: INTERACTION color *Harvard Business Review* v95 no3 p16 My/Je 2017

Johnson, Wayne E.
The Militarized Zone: What Did You Do in the Army, Grandpa? *Publishers Weekly* v264 no31 p58b Jl 31 2017

Johnson, Wendy
Ecology of the Heart color *Tricycle: The Buddhist Review* v26 no2 p32 Wint 2016
The Whole Earth Is Medicine color *Tricycle: The Buddhist Review* v27 no1 p29 Fall 2017
Wild Mustard and the Way of Zen color *Tricycle: The Buddhist Review* v26 no4 p27 Summ 2017

Johnson, Whitney
Building Rapport Across Cultures *Harvard Business Review Digital Articles* p2 My 25 2016
Can You Really Not Afford to Change Jobs? *Harvard Business Review Digital Articles* p2 Ap 9 2015
I'm a Female Author, So Why Did I Want a Man to Narrate My Audiobook? *Harvard Business Review Digital Articles* p2 N 25 2015
Is Your Company Experiencing Good Times? Time for a Plan B *Harvard Business Review Digital Articles* p2 N 18 2016
Keeping Anxious Thoughts at Bay *Harvard Business Review*
Digital Articles p2 F 22 2016
Learning to Appreciate Disagreement at Work *Harvard Business Review Digital Articles* p2 Jl 6 2016
Managing Up Without Sucking Up *Harvard Business Review Digital Articles* p2 D 15 2014
Rejecting Ideas Doesn't Have to Cause Resentment *Harvard Business Review Digital Articles* p2 Je 22 2015
Should You Give Up on Your New Dream? *Harvard Business Review Digital Articles* p2 Ja 28 2016
What Do You Do Well That Others Don't? *Harvard Business Review Digital Articles* p2 O 6 2015
What It's Like When a Stay-at-Home Dad Goes Back to Work *Harvard Business Review Digital Articles* p2 Ap 19 2016
What to Do When Your Personal Growth Stalls *Harvard Business Review Digital Articles* p2 S 28 2015
Why Today's Teens Are More Entrepreneurial than Their Parents *Harvard Business Review Digital Articles* p2 My 25 2015

Johnson, William H.
The 2018 revision of the Consumer Price Index geographic sample bibl chart color diag map *Monthly Labor Review* p1 O 2016

Johnson, Winifred
A Mighty & Mysterious Molecule color *Oceanus* v51 no2 p76 Wint 2016

Johnson, Zachary P.
Social status alters immune regulation and response to infection in macaques bibl graph *Science* v354 no6315 p1041 N 25 2016

Johnson Outdoors Inc.
KITCHEN A. JURRIES color diag *Backpacker* v45 no3 p102 Ap 2017

JOHNSON-FREESE, JOAN
Future of space color *Issues in Science & Technology* v33 no1 p15 Fall 2016

JOHNSON-GROH, MARA
Show Time color diag *Backpacker* p30 Ag 2017

JOHNSON HERJAVEC, KYM
LIFE (AND LOVE) LESSONS WE'VE LEARNED FROM REALITY TV *TV Guide* v64 no40 p20 O 3 2016

Johnson & Johnson (Company)—Trials, litigation, etc.
The Lawsuits Keep Coming for J&J M. C. Fisk, J. Feeley et al bw *Bloomberg Businessweek* no4514 p21 Mr 13 2017

JOHNSON JR., ERNIE
Take Me Out to the Blackberry Patch color *Reader's Digest* v190 no1132 p36 Jl/Ag 2017

JOHNSON-ROEHR, S. N.
Evening Entertainment: Go out early and stay out late to catch the best meteor shower of the year *Sky & Telescope* v134 no6 p48 D 2017
Other Worlds: THE PLANET FACTORY: Exoplanets and the Search for a Second Earth *Sky & Telescope* v134 no6 p39 D 2017
Pure & Simple *Sky & Telescope* v133 no4 p57 Ap 2017
Totality Changes Everything *Sky & Telescope* v133 no2 p57 F 2017
X-Ray Revelations color *Sky & Telescope* v134 no2 p57 Ag 2017

Johnsson, Julie
Big Jets Get Squeezed color *Bloomberg Businessweek* no4539 p16 S 25 2017
A Fast-Track Promotion—With a Catch diag *Bloomberg Businessweek* no4536 p19 S 4 2017
Rockwell Collins Inc *Bloomberg Businessweek* no4537 p29 S 11 2017
Will Boeing Become Collateral Damage? color graph *Bloomberg Businessweek* no4500 p23 N 21 2016

Johnston, Abby
AUSTIN, TEXAS *Atlanta* v56 no9 p50 Ja 2017
KNIVES OUT *Texas Monthly* v44 no12 p90 D 2016

Johnston, Alison
From Convergence to Crisis: Labor Markets and the Instability of the Euro A. Moravcsik *Foreign Affairs* v96 no1 p165 Ja/F 2017

Johnston, Carolyn Ross
Voices of Cherokee Women V. LaPoe *American Indian Quarterly* v40 no3 p277 Summ 2016

Johnston, Daniel
NIGHT LIFE *New Yorker* v93 no31 p5 O 9 2017

Johnston, David
THE CONVERSATION color *Atlantic* v319 no1 p10 Ja/F 2017

JOHNSTON, DAVID CAY
Simplify, Simplify, Simplify *New York Times Book Review* p10 Je 25 2017

JOHNSTON, DAVID W.
Google Haul Out: Earth Observation Imagery and Digital Aerial Surveys in Coastal Wildlife Management and Abundance Estimation *BioScience* v67 no8 p760 Ag 2017

Johnston, Dennis M.
Around the Campfire color *Trail Rider* v29 no4 p8 My 2017

Johnston, Gene
10 UP & COMERS: ROB LECLERC *Successful Farming* v115 no8 p38 Je/Jl 2017
4 TIPS TO TELLING YOUR FARM'S STORY: NEBRASKA DIETITIAN AMBER PANKONIN SAYS WE CAN DO BETTER AT ENGAGING PASSIONATE CONSUMERS AND FOOD ACTIVISTS *Successful Farming* v115 no11 p16 S 2017
BEEF INDUSTRY PAST, PRESENT, AND FUTURE: NCBA PRESIDENT CRAIG UDEN HAS A FAMILY HISTORY OF INDUSTRY ACTIVISM AND HOPES TO UNITE PRODUCERS AROUND COMMON GOALS *Successful Farming* v115 no9 p63 Ag 2017
BEFORE THEY'RE BORN *Successful Farming* v115 no3 p54 Mid-F 2017
BY-PRODUCTS NO MORE *Successful Farming* v115 no1 p64 Ja 2017
ECONOMICAL PRODUCTS *Successful Farming* v115 no5 p53 Mid-Mr 2017
ERADICATE? CATTLE INDUSTRY CONTEMPLATES THE POTENTIAL TO ELIMINATE BVD AS A SIGNIFICANT DISEASE *Successful Farming* v115 no6 p58 Ap 2017
Farm Moneyball *Successful Farming* v114 no12 p24 Mid-N 2016
FEEDING CROPS IN TOUGH TIMES: FRUGAL AND FERTILIZER ARE TWO WORDS THAT GO TOGETHER IN TODAY'S FARM ECONOMY *Successful Farming* v115 no12 p50 O 2017
FIVE TRENDS THAT COULD CHANGE YOUR FARM *Successful Farming* v114 no11 p54 N 2016
FOOD TRENDS *Successful Farming* v114 no10 p60 O 2016
GROWING PAINS FOR ILLINOIS CANNABIS FARM *Successful Farming* v115 no1 p56 Ja 2017
HERD REPLACEMENTS: RAISE OR BUY? THAT QUESTION IS BACK ON THE RADAR WITH MUCH LOWER PRICES *Successful Farming* v115 no6 p59 Ap 2017
LOOKING UNDER THE HOOD *Successful Farming* v115 no3 p50 Mid-F 2017
MORE PREVENTION, LESS TREATMENT *Successful Farming* v115 no5 p52 Mid-Mr 2017
THE NEW RULES OF FEED ANTIBIOTICS *Successful Farming* v115 no1 p60 Ja 2017
OLD-SCHOOL PIG FARMING: NIMAN RANCH PORK IS LOOKING FOR GROWERS TO PRODUCE PIGS IN BEDDED PENS AND PASTURES FOR HEALTH-CONSCIOUS CONSUMERS OF NATURAL PORK *Successful Farming* v115 no6 p40 Ap 2017
$100 MORE PER COW! *Successful Farming* v115 no5 p60 Mid-Mr 2017
SCOUT FOR SUDDEN DEATH SYNDROME: IOWA STATE UNIVERSITY EXTENSION PLANT PATHOLOGIST DAREN MUELLER ANSWERS FIVE QUESTIONS WITH THE LATEST RESEARCH RESULTS ON SDS color *Successful Farming* v115 no7 p34 My 2017
SMART APP TELLS WHEN TO IRRIGATE: INTERNET PROGRAM TAPS INTO NATIONAL WEATHER SERVICE AND OTHER DATA TO GUIDE IRRIGATION SCHEDULING FOR MISSOURI FARMERS *Successful Farming* v115 no9 p56 Ag 2017

Johnston, Jake Wyatt
Artificial intelligence in research color *Science* v357 no6346 p28 Jl 7 2017

Johnston, Jeff
2016 BEST OF THE BEST bw color *Field & Stream* v121 no7 p96 D 2016/Ja 2017
FIELD TEST color *Field & Stream* v122 no2 p99 Je/Jl 2017
FIRE DRILLS bw color *Field & Stream* v121 no8 p64 F/Mr 2017
GET YOUR GOBBLER color *Outdoor Life* v224 no4 p43 My 2017

SILENCE, PLEASE color *Field & Stream* v122 no2 p34 Je/Jl 2017
SQUEEZE PLAY color *Field & Stream* v121 no8 p33 F/Mr 2017
WAYNE'S WORLD color *Outdoor Life* v224 no8 p69 O 2017
YOUR Wildest DREAMS color *Field & Stream* v122 no5 p38 O 2017

JOHNSTON, KATHERINE
DEHORNING dilemma *Earth Island Journal* v32 no4 p33 Wint 2017

Johnston, Kyle
Tailored semiconductors for high-harmonic optoelectronics graph *Science* v357 no6348 p303 Jl 21 2017

Johnston, Maura
Country That Melds Tried-and-True With Utterly New color *Time* v189 no7/8 p107 F 27 2017
Downcast Brits Brew Up a Quiet Storm color *Time* v189 no4 p52 Ja 23 2017
FALL ALBUM PREVIEW *Rolling Stone* no1297 p12 O 5 2017
George Michael color *Time* v189 no3 p11 Ja 16 2017
Indie Rock May Be Dislocated, but It's Far from Dead color *Time* v189 no11 p63 Mr 27 2017
Lightbox color *Time* v190 no15 p14 O 16 2017

Johnston, Michael B.
Perovskite-perovskite tandem photovoltaics with optimized band gaps bibl chart graph *Science* v354 no6314 p861 N 18 2016

Johnston, Peter
Identification of single-site gold catalysis in acetylene hydrochlorination bw diag graph *Science* v355 no6332 p1399 Mr 31 2017

Johnston, Randy
STEPPIN' OUT E. J. Wallace *Virginia Living* v15 no3 p25 Ap 2017

JOHNSTON, RUSSELL
LOORRS 2017 SEASON DEBUT REDUX [Cover story] color *Dirt Sports + Off-Road* v51 no10 p60 O 2017

Johnston, S.
The magnetic field and turbulence of the cosmic web measured using a brilliant fast radio burst bibl chart graph *Science* v354 no6317 p1249 D 9 2016

Johnston, Stephen E.
Potential role of intratumor bacteria in mediating tumor resistance to the chemotherapeutic drug gemcitabine diag *Science* v357 no6356 p1156 S 15 2017

Johnston, Tony
A Small Thing... but Big color *Publishers Weekly* v263 no49 p25 D 7 2016

Johnston, Tonya
Airplane Mode color *Practical Horseman* v45 no11 p16 N 2017
Fun as a Key to Success color *Practical Horseman* v45 no3 p20 Mr 2017
Harnessing the Power Of Observation [Cover story] color *Practical Horseman* v45 no7 p20 Jl 2017
Mistakes: The Big Picture color *Practical Horseman* v45 no1 p22 Ja 2017
Yes, Teamwork Does Make the Dream Work color *Practical Horseman* v45 no9 p24 S 2017

Johnstone, Philip
Nuclear power: Serious risks *Science* v354 no6316 p1112 D 2 2016

Joichi Ito
The Blockchain Will Do to the Financial System What the Internet Did to Media color *Harvard Business Review Digital Articles* p2 Mr 8 2017

Joiner, Lottie L.
LOVE IN BLACK & WHITE color *Essence* v47 no8 p129 D 2016
THE LUST LOCKDOWN color *Essence* v47 no11 p107 Mr 2017

Joining processes
See also
Solder & soldering
Seven tips for better solder connections L. Puckett color diag *Model Railroader* v84 no8 p56 Ag 2017

JOINSON, SUZANNE
Long Haul *New York Times Book Review* p14 Je 4 2017

Joint, Ian
How microbes survive in the open ocean color diag *Science* v357 no6352 p646 Ag 18 2017

Joint Comprehensive Plan of Action (2015)

The Art of Undoing the Iran Deal L. SMITH color *Weekly Standard* v22 no11 p25 N 21 2016

Borrowed Time color *Weekly Standard* v22 no44 p6 Jl 31 2017

Doomed Deal L. Smith color *Weekly Standard* v22 no12 p7 N 28 2016

The Face-Off [Cover story] R. Marc Gerecht color *Weekly Standard* v22 no24 p22 F 27 2017

Getting to No S. F. HAYES and M. WARREN color *Weekly Standard* v23 no6 p24 O 16 2017

He Still Hasn't Torn It Up M. WARREN and J. LIFHITS color *Weekly Standard* v22 no43 p9 Jl 24 2017

How Restraint Leads to War H. R. Nau *Commentary* v140 no2 p17 S 2015

Iran on Notice L. Smith color *Weekly Standard* v22 no32 p8 My 1 2017

Keeping the Deal and Cracking Down on Iran color *Bloomberg Businessweek* no4504 p8 D 19 2016

Mad, Democrats? Blame the Iran Deal *Commentary* p1 Ja 2017

Mad, Democrats? Blame the Iran Deal *Commentary* v143 no1 p1 Ja 2017

No Easy Way Out R. MARC GERECHT color *Weekly Standard* v23 no6 p11 O 16 2017

Notes on a Disaster J. Podhoretz *Commentary* v140 no2 p27 S 2015

The Nuclear Deal Is Only Half of It L. SMITH *Weekly Standard* v23 no3 p16 S 25 2017

Nuclear Summer C. H. KAHL color *New Republic* v248 no8/9 p6 Ag/S 2017

The Park Bench Joke *Commentary* v140 no2 p50 S 2015

Trump's Desire for a Better Deal With Iran Could Isolate the U.S I. Bremmer *Time* v190 no15 p12 O 16 2017

Trump's Right About Iran color *Weekly Standard* v23 no6 p8 O 16 2017

Joint custody of children—Psychological aspects

The Growing Case for Shared Parenting After Divorce B. Luscombe color *Time* v188 no14 p21 O 10 2016

Joint diseases

See also

Arthritis

COMBATING JOINT DISEASE L. Threlkeld color *Practical Horseman* v45 no9 p56 S 2017

Joint infections

BLOOD TEST HELPS MONITOR JOINT INFECTIONS C. Barakat and M. McCluskey color *Equus* no480 p16 S 2017

Joint ownership of personal property

THE INTRINSIC VALUE OF BUSINESS AVIATION T. VELOCCI color *Forbes* v198 no5 p121 O 25 2016

Joint pain

Aching In The Rain K. Massicot color *New Orleans Magazine* v51 no8 p36 Je 2017

Joint pain—Treatment

Cold Comfort D. F. Maron color *Scientific American* v316 no1 p22 Ja 2017

Joint ventures

Need to Change? Keep a Diary C. Vlachoutsicos *Harvard Business Review Digital Articles* p2 N 27 2014

Joints (Anatomy)—Abnormalities

A MARTIAL ARTIST'S GUIDE TO HIP HEALTH [Cover story] T. CALLOS bw color *Black Belt* v55 no2 p54 F/Mr 2017

Joints (Anatomy)—Diseases

See also

Arthritis

LOOKING FOR HELP B. LUT color *New Orleans Magazine* v51 no3 p30 Ja 2017

Q&A: Your Horse's Arthritis color *Horse & Rider* v56 no2 p19 F 2017

Joints (Engineering)

See also

Brackets

Fasteners

FLEX JOINTS J. KOPYCINSKI color *Dirt Sports + Off-Road* v51 no2 p64 F 2017

U-JOINT SURVIVAL J. KOPYCINSKI color *Dirt Sports + Off-Road* v51 no11 p66 N 2017

Jojo (Performer)

The LIBERATION of JOJO I. Biedenharn and N. Feeney color

Entertainment Weekly no1436/1437 p30 O 21 2016

MUSIC MADE THE PEOPLE COME TOGETHER R. Kinane, A. Writing et al color *Entertainment Weekly* no1439 p22 N 11 2016

JOKINEN, TOM

The Line King cartoon *Walrus* v14 no6 p12 Jl/Ag 2017

What Is the CBC Good For? [Cover story] bw color *Walrus* v14 no7 p20 S 2017

Jokinen, Tuija

Global atmospheric particle formation from CERN CLOUD measurements bibl graph map *Science* v354 no6316 p1119 D 2 2016

Jolene (Music)

'Jolene' A. PHILLIPS color *New York Times Magazine* p24 Mr 12 2017

Jolie, Angelina, 1975-

A Child Survives the Khmer Rouge S. Zacharek color *Time* v190 no13 p65 O 2 2017

A HOT TIME IN THE OLD TOWN K. SMITH color *Vanity Fair* v59 no9 p78 S 2017

A Life in Bold [Cover story] E. PERETZ bw color *Vanity Fair* v59 no9 p182 S 2017

"Style," bw color *Vanity Fair* v59 no9 p1c S 2017

WHAT'S IN THE CARDS FOR '17? color *Esquire* v167 no1 p5 F 2017

Jo Lieberman, Bobbie

Digging Deeper color diag *Equus* no478 p60 Jl 2017

Falling in love with New Mexico color *Equus* no477 p46 Je 2017

Jolla, Wayne

Contributors color *InStyle* v23 no12 p24 N 2016

Jolly, David, 1972-

Honorable David Jolly *Congressional Digest* v95 no9 p25 N 2016

Jolma, Arttu

Impact of cytosine methylation on DNA binding specificities of human transcription factors diag *Science* v356 no6337 p502 My 5 2017

JOLNA, KARON

Transformation of Consciousness: The National Women's Studies Association and the Combahee River Collective's "Black Feminist Statement" turn 40 *Ms.* v27 no3 p48 Fall 2017

Jolt Athletics (Company)

A JOLT TO THE SENSES R. MATHESON *USA Today Magazine* v145 no2860 p66 Ja 2017

Joly, Nicolas

Guanine glycation repair by DJ-1/Park7 and its bacterial homologs chart color diag graph *Science* v357 no6347 p208 Jl 14 2017

Jompa, Jamaluddin

Seagrass ecosystems reduce exposure to bacterial pathogens of humans, fishes, and invertebrates bibl graph *Science* v355 no6326 p731 F 17 2017

Jonas, Elizabeth

The MIFstep in parthanatos bibl diag *Science* v354 no6308 p36 O 7 2016

Jonas, Joe, 1989-

3 ROUNDS WITH DNCE M. Snetiker color *Entertainment Weekly* no1441 p26 N 25 2016

Joe Jonas' Low-Key Chic S. EXPOSITO color *Rolling Stone* no1275 p24 D 1 2016

Jonas, Nick, 1992-

Entertainment WEEKLY POPFEST TM color *Entertainment Weekly* no1436/1437 p8 O 21 2016

KINGDOM'S KNOCKOUT S. Highfill color *Entertainment Weekly* no1477 p48 Ag 11 2017

Jonas, Oliver H.

Potential role of intratumor bacteria in mediating tumor resistance to the chemotherapeutic drug gemcitabine diag *Science* v357 no6356 p1156 S 15 2017

Jonas, Victoria

MEET A WARRIOR color *Essence* v48 no6 p118 O 2017

Jonathan Adler Enterprises LLC

Blush Hour: AFICIONADOS OF PRECIOUS METALS ARE TICKLED PINK BY TODAY'S ROSE GOLD ACCESSORIES L. IMMEDIATO *Los Angeles Magazine* v62 no9 p46 S 2017

JONES, ADAM

The Crimson Tide's "CAST" Is Cresting *USA Today Magazine* v146 no2868 p46 S 2017

Jones, Alan
  Advanced Retreat *Boating World* v38 no2 p36 F 2017
  Alt Boating *Boating World* v38 no3 p4 Mr 2017
  Best Boating Week *Boating World* v38 no4 p4 Ap 2017
  Budget Cuts Bad for Boaters *Boating World* v38 no5 p4 My 2017
  Centurion *Boating World* v38 no1 p24 Ja 2017
  Chasing the Sun for Less *Boating World* v38 no2 p40 F 2017
  Crown Jewel *Boating World* v38 no5 p32 My 2017
  Diamond Setting: The first-class cabin at G3 pontoons just got a
    lot more plush and stylish *Boating World* v38 no8 p44 S/O 2017
  En Vogue *Boating World* v37 no9 p38 N/D 2016
  Extreme Boating *Boating World* v38 no1 p4 Ja 2017
  Find your Center *Boating World* v38 no3 p40 Mr 2017
  Fish It Up *Boating World* v37 no9 p30 N/D 2016
  Flexible Formula: The 310 BR is a bowrider that can cruise to the
    sandbar ... or the Bahamas ... in style *Boating World* v38 no8
    p40 S/O 2017
  Frankenboat *Boating World* v38 no4 p6 Ap 2017
  Going Big *Boating World* v38 no8 p4 S/O 2017
  The Good Life In the Fast Lane: You don't have to give up go-fast
    performance to embrace the pontoon lifestyle *Boating World*
    v38 no5 p42 My 2017
  Grand Opening *Boating World* v38 no3 p32 Mr 2017
  Hitting the Spot *Boating World* v38 no6 p42 Je 2017
  Hybrid Happiness *Boating World* v38 no4 p30 Ap 2017
  The Industry Bottom Line *Boating World* v38 no2 p4 F 2017
  Keep It Legal: Think that fish you caught is a keeper? Not so fast
    Boating World v38 no5 p18 My 2017
  Kid Power *Boating World* v38 no6 p4 Je 2017
  Let's Go Racing color *Boating World* v38 no7 p24 Jl 2017
  Let the Sun Shine In color *Boating World* v38 no7 p38 Jl 2017
  Locked and Loaded *Boating World* v38 no6 p38 Je 2017
  Make It a Double *Boating World* v38 no4 p38 Ap 2017
  Malibu Did What? Malibu's new 21 VLX is the boat many people
    wanted to own but didn't think they could afford *Boating World*
    v38 no6 p34 Je 2017
  Monsters of the Midrange *Boating World* v38 no3 p20 Mr 2017
  New Wave *Boating World* v38 no2 p44 F 2017
  On The Road Again *Boating World* v37 no9 p4 N/D 2016
  Platinum Upgrade: The Catalina series gets elevated styling and
    remains multitalented color *Boating World* v38 no7 p42 Jl 2017
  Pontoon For the Populous *Boating World* v38 no3 p44 Mr 2017
  Positive Spin: Suzuki raises the bar on high-horsepower outboards
    with a testosterone-laced engine that has a pair ... of propellers
    Boating World v38 no8 p20 S/O 2017
  Power Trip *Boating World* v38 no2 p20 F 2017
  Propless Surfing *Boating World* v38 no6 p46 Je 2017
  Protect Your Rig From Theft: Every year, about 5,000 boats are
    stolen. Here's how to keep it from happening *Boating World*
    v38 no8 p14 S/O 2017
  Protect Yourself *Boating World* v38 no5 p24 My 2017
  Qwest For the Best color *Boating World* v38 no7 p34 Jl 2017
  Ranger Rover *Boating World* v38 no4 p42 Ap 2017
  Return of the Beast: Light weight converges with extreme power
    and channels a bit of checkered (flag) history *Boating World* v38
    no5 p38 My 2017
  Shade Is Good color *Boating World* v38 no7 p4 Jl 2017
  Ski Boats Take Control *Boating World* v38 no5 p22 My 2017
  Skiff's Notes: A skiff provides an inexpensive alternative to the
    big boat and delivers a different sort of boating experience *Boat-
    ing World* v38 no8 p48 S/O 2017
  Ski, Fish, Cruise, Save: The flagship of Chaparral's H2O line has
    something never seen before: outboard power *Boating World*
    v38 no8 p32 S/O 2017
  Stayin' Alive *Boating World* v38 no3 p18 Mr 2017
  Transformer *Boating World* v37 no9 p34 N/D 2016
  Triple Threat *Boating World* v38 no3 p36 Mr 2017
  TRIXX Aren't Just For Kids: The Spark TRIXX makes everyone
    a PWC trick artist hero in a matter of minutes *Boating World*
    v38 no5 p36 My 2017
  TUBE TEST 2017 *Boating World* v38 no6 p50 Je 2017
  Wakesports For Working Sorts: Heyday's WT-2 allows boaters to
    have their wake and eat it too ... for a lot less money *Boating
    World* v38 no8 p36 S/O 2017
  Wake Up *Boating World* v38 no4 p34 Ap 2017
  What Am I Looking At? *Boating World* v38 no6 p20 Je 2017
  You Can Have a V-8 *Boating World* v37 no9 p20 N/D 2016
Jones, Alex, 1974-
  NEWS BLUES A. Marantz cartoon *New Yorker* v92 no42 p44 D
    19 2016
Jones, Alexander
  THE ANCIENTS HAD STARS IN THEIR EYES: Since its sur-
    prising discovery on the Aegean seabed over a century ago, the
    Antikythera Mechanism has intrigued astrologers, classicists
    and historians of science A. Robinson *History Today* v67 no9
    p97 S 2017
Jones, Alexis—Interviews
  The Jock Whisperer color *O, The Oprah Magazine* p25 Ap 2017
Jones, Allie
  Lele Pons Is the Most Popular Girl in Hollywood: A day in the
    life of YouTube's reigning queen of teens img *New York* v50
    no9 p53 My 1 2017
  Zen Palace img *New York* p46 F 9 2017
Jones, Amelia
  Editors Tell All! bw color *Women's Health* v14 no2 p60 Mr 2017
Jones, Andrew
  Emergence and spread of a human-transmissible multidrug-re-
    sistant nontuberculous mycobacterium bibl diag graph *Science*
    v354 no6313 p751 N 11 2016
  New Heart, New Mission color *Men's Health* v32 no1 p8 Ja/F
    2017
Jones, Andrew M.
  Emergence and spread of a human-transmissible multidrug-re-
    sistant nontuberculous mycobacterium bibl diag graph *Science*
    v354 no6313 p751 N 11 2016
Jones, Anna
  it's not all gravy color *Bon Appetit* v61 no11 p58 N 2016
Jones, Bart
  On the trail of Jorge Bergoglio *America* v216 no4 p48 F 20 2017
JONES, BENJAMIN
  An Ecoregion-Based Approach to Protecting Half the Terrestrial
    Realm *BioScience* v67 no6 p534 Je 2017
Jones, Benjamin F.
  The dual frontier: Patented inventions and prior scientific advance
    graph *Science* v357 no6351 p583 Ag 11 2017
Jones, Beth
  What Really Happens When Companies Nix Performance Ratings
    Harvard Business Review Digital Articles p2 N 6 2015
  Why More and More Companies Are Ditching Performance Rat-
    ings *Harvard Business Review Digital Articles* p2 S 8 2015
Jones, Beth Felker
  Christian hope in Hamilton color *Christian Century* v134 no7 p45
    Mr 29 2017
  Episodes in hell color *Christian Century* v133 no23 p43 N 9 2016
  Wizards in New York color *Christian Century* v133 no26 p44 D
    21 2016
Jones, Bill
  How to Take the Plunge J. BILLS *Yankee* v81 no1 p26 Ja/F 2017
Jones, Bill T., 1954-
  35 Years Ago This Month *Dance Magazine* v90 no11 p67 N 2016
Jones, Bill T., 1954-—Interviews
  MR. JONES: THERE ARE FEW THINGS MORE INTEREST-
    ING THAN WATCHING THIS DANCER/CHOREOGRA-
    PHER MOVE HIS BODY S. ABADSIDIS color *Advocate*
    no1091 p89 Je/Jl 2017
Jones, Blair
  How Incentives for Long-Term Management Backfire *Harvard
    Business Review Digital Articles* p2 My 6 2016
Jones, Bruce D.
  Civil Wars & the Post–Cold War International Order *Daedalus*
    v146 no4 p33 Fall 2017
Jones, Carey
  PAINT IT BLACK color *Bloomberg Businessweek* no4497 p67
    O 31 2017
Jones, Charles Aron
  STORIES WITH VALUE: Inspiring positive student conduct with
    children's picture books *Literacy Today (2411-7862)* v35 no1
    p28 Jl/Ag 2017
Jones, Chris
  BASEBALL BLOOD *New York Times Magazine* p38 S 17 2017
  BODIES IN TRANSIT bw color *New York Times Magazine* p90
    D 11 2016

FLIGHT color *Popular Mechanics* p90 Je 2017

Why were electric cars of the early 1900s advertised as "ladies' cars"? *Smithsonian* v47 no9 p140 Ja/F 2017

WILL IT KILL YOU? bw color *Popular Mechanics* p88 Jl 2017

JONES, CHRISTOPHER

Infrastructure and Democracy *Issues in Science & Technology* v33 no2 p24 Wint 2017

Jones, Chuck—Interviews

The Local Labor Leader Who Defied Trump M. UETRICHT *In These Times* v41 no2 p32 F 2017

Jones, Cleve

When We Rise: My Life in the Movement *Publishers Weekly* v263 no40 p112 O 3 2016

Jones, Colin

Did Emotions Cause the Terror? bw *New York Review of Books* v64 no11 p38 Je 22 2017

Jones, Cort

Confronting the Opioid Outbreak in Our Parks *Parks & Recreation* v52 no6 p34 Je 2017

Member Spotlight: Commit to Health Youth Ambassadors *Parks & Recreation* v52 no6 p43 Je 2017

Member Spotlight: Diane Drake *Parks & Recreation* v52 no10 p47 O 2017

Member Spotlight: Maria Nardi *Parks & Recreation* v52 no9 p97 S 2017

Park Bench: Nomadic Nourishment in NorCal *Parks & Recreation* v52 no6 p56 Je 2017

Jones, Cynan

The Edge of the Shoal cartoon *New Yorker* v92 no33 p72 O 17 2016

JONES, DAFYDD

A LIFE IN FOCUS bw *Vanity Fair* v59 no6 p100 My 2017

Jones, Dan

The Templars: The Rise and Spectacular Fall of God's Holy Warriors W. J. Shepherd color *Military History* v34 no5 p74 Ja 2018

Jones, Daniel Lawson

Kinetics of dCas9 target search in Escherichia coli diag *Science* v357 no6358 p1420 S 29 2017

Jones, David R.

Riding Toward Equality *Nation* v304 no3 p4 Ja 30 2017

STRONG AS OAK D. T. Dingle color *Black Enterprise* v47 no7 p72 My/Je 2017

JONES, DIANE

Shipbuilding Docks as Experimental Systems for Realistic Assessments of Anthropogenic Stressors on Marine Organisms *BioScience* v67 no9 p853 S 2017

Jones, Digby, 1955-

Fixing Business *People Management* p53 Je 2017

Jones, Doug—Interviews

AN ALIEN ENCOUNTER WITH DOUG JONES S. Li color *Entertainment Weekly* no1476 p27 Ag 4 2017

Jones, Duncan, 1971-

WARCRAFT C. Gunnestad color *Sound & Vision* v82 no2 p69 F/Mr 2017

JONES, EILEEN

Guerrilla Chic *In These Times* v41 no6 p38 Je 2017

Marx in Westworld *In These Times* v41 no1 p34 Ja 2017

Jones, Everett

Essays & Literary Criticism bw color *Publishers Weekly* v263 no51 p46 D 12 2016

Essays & Literary Criticism bw color *Publishers Weekly* v264 no26 p48 Je 26 2017

Lifestyle color *Publishers Weekly* v263 no51 p56 D 12 2016

Lifestyle color *Publishers Weekly* v264 no26 p64 Je 26 2017

Jones, Felicity, 1984-

Cover *Entertainment Weekly* no1442 pC1 D 2 2016 Rebellious Special Issue

Feminist Force S. Whitlock, A. Taylor et al color *Glamour* v115 no3 p38 Mr 2017

Going Rogue R. DOUTHAT color *National Review* v69 no1 p42 Ja 23 2017

Your Hair Lookbook J. Mulrow color *Glamour* v115 no7 p50 Jl 2017

Jones, Felicity, 1984-—Interviews

Felicity Goes Rogue K. Valby color *Glamour* v115 no1 p88 Ja 2017

Jones, Finn

How Iron Fist Packs a Punch K. P. Sullivan color *Entertainment Weekly* no1457/1458 p84 Mr 17 2017

Iron Fist A. D'ARMINIO *TV Guide* v65 no11 p45 Mr 6 2017

PARTY LINES T. Rami and K. Van Syckle img *New York* v50 no16 p110 Ag 7 2017

Jones, Gareth

Authentic Workplaces Don't Try to Make Everyone the Same *Harvard Business Review Digital Articles* p2 N 12 2015

Volkswagen and the End of Corporate Spin *Harvard Business Review Digital Articles* p2 O 28 2015

Jones, Gareth Stedman

Call Him Karl P. E. GORDON *New York Times Book Review* p24 O 23 2016

MARX'S REVENGE B. KUNKEL color *Nation* v304 no6 p27 F 27 2017

Jones, Glenn

Unplugged B. MEYER color *Downbeat* v84 no6 p72 Je 2017

Jones, Grace

GRACE JONES color *Ebony* v72 no11 p98 S 2017

Jones, Heather

The formation of peak rings in large impact craters bibl color graph *Science* v354 no6314 p878 N 18 2016

Jones, Howard

My Lai Murders D. T. Zabecki bw color *Military History* v34 no2 p70 Jl 2017

Jones, Jace W.

Sustained virologic control in SIV+ macaques after antiretroviral and α4β7 antibody therapy bibl graph *Science* v354 no6309 p197 O 14 2016

Jones, Jacqueline

Goddess of Anarchy: The Life and Times of Lucy Parsons, American Radical color *Publishers Weekly* v264 no40 p127 O 2 2017

Jones, James Earl, 1931-—Awards

The Tonys You Didn't See J. Derschowitz color *Entertainment Weekly* no1471 p16 Je 23 2017

Jones, Janet L.

Cory's second wind color diag *Equus* no470 p32 N 2016

The limits of Negative Reinforcement [Cover story] bw color *Equus* no480 p40 S 2017

The power of INDIRECT TRAINING color diag *Equus* no478 p52 Jl 2017

Training BY Reward bw color *Equus* no481 p46 O 2017

JONES, JANNA

WHAT CHRISTIAN COLLEGE PROFESSORS WANT YOU TO KNOW bw chart color *Christianity Today* v60 no9 p75 N 2016

Jones, Jason

The Detour J. Russell *TV Guide* v65 no8 p35 F 27 2017

JONES, JEFF

RUN AWAY! [Cover story] color *Runner's World* v52 no7 p54 Ag 2017

Jones, Jen

Declutter that cabinet! color *Redbook* p26 N 2017

Get a do-it-all organizer! color *Redbook* p28 O 2017

Good times, beautifully organized color *Redbook* p18 Je 2017

The great plastic basket makeover color *Redbook* p20 Mr 2017

On-the-road organization color *Redbook* p24 S 2017

Organize the whole family! color *Redbook* p32 D 2016

A pantry that stays organized color *Redbook* p30 Ap 2017

Tame that junk drawer for good [Cover story] color *Redbook* p32 My 2017

The ultimate kid-room cleanup color *Redbook* p40 F 2017

Jones, Jeremy

KING OF THE MOUNTAIN J. Dean color *Sunset* v238 no2 p25 F 2017

JONES, JERROD

DIFFERENTIAL DIFFERENCES chart color *Dirt Sports + Off-Road* v51 no11 p32 N 2017

MOUNTAIN HAVOC 2017 color *Dirt Sports + Off-Road* v51 no11 p48 N 2017

JONES, JIMMY E.

Black Lives Matter Because All Lives Matter [Cover story] *Islamic Horizons* v46 no1 p20 Ja/F 2017

Jones, John

Safely Home color *Sail* v48 no3 p28 Mr 2017

Jones, Jonathan
  AT ARM'S LENGTH color *Sports Illustrated* v127 no10 p38 O 2 2017
  CHIEF CONCERN color *Sports Illustrated* v126 no2 p44 Ja 16 2017
  Foul Language color *Sports Illustrated* v125 no14 p19 O 24-31 2016
  GAME of THROWS color *Sports Illustrated* v127 no5 p34 Ag 14 2017
  RUN THIS TOWN [Cover story] color *Sports Illustrated* v126 no4 p24 Ja 30 2017
  SUSPENDED DISBELIEF [Cover story] color *Sports Illustrated* v126 no5 p26 F 13 2017
  Value Judgments chart color *Sports Illustrated* v125 no19 p28 D 12 2016

Jones, Jonathan D. G.
  Intracellular innate immune surveillance devices in plants and animals chart color diag graph *Science* v354 no6316 paaf6395-1 D 2 2016

Jones, Julio, 1989-
  Leading Off color *Sports Illustrated* v126 no5 p6 F 13 2017

Jones, Katherine
  Gender discrimination lawsuit at Salk ignites controversy M. Wadman color *Science* v357 no6348 p237 Jl 21 2017

Jones, Kellie, 1959-
  Kellie Jones J. Johnson color *Current Biography* v78 no5 p44 My 2017
  L.A.'s Black Renaissance E. J. HOLLEY color *Publishers Weekly* v264 no17 p36 Ap 24 2017
  Looking Past the Color Lines J. HERBST *Los Angeles Magazine* p21 Ap 2017

Jones, Kent
  Frederick WISEMAN *Interview* v47 no2 p88 Mr 2017
  THE MARGINALIZATION OF CINEMA color *Film Comment* v52 no6 p54 N/D 2016
  A Six-Letter Word bw color *Film Comment* v53 no4 p58 Jl/Ag 2017

Jones, Kerry
  Gender Can Be a Bigger Factor than Race in Raise Negotiations *Harvard Business Review Digital Articles* p2 S 1 2016
  The Most Desirable Employee Benefits *Harvard Business Review Digital Articles* p2 F 15 2017
  The Work Conversations We Dread the Most, According to Research *Harvard Business Review Digital Articles* p2 Ap 11 2016

Jones, Kevin—Interviews
  Kevin Jones A. BRANDT *Cincinnati Magazine* v50 no2 p32 N 2016

Jones, Kristen
  The Right and Wrong Ways to Help Pregnant Workers *Harvard Business Review Digital Articles* p2 S 27 2016
  Stop "Protecting" Women from Challenging Work *Harvard Business Review Digital Articles* p2 S 9 2016
  Why Subtle Bias Is So Often Worse than Blatant Discrimination *Harvard Business Review Digital Articles* p2 Jl 13 2016

JONES, KRISTIN M.
  HARD TIMES color *Film Comment* v53 no3 p36 My/Je 2017
  Heal the Living color *Film Comment* v53 no2 p66 Mr/Ap 2017

JONES, LANDON
  REMEMBERING DIANA color *AARP: The Magazine* v60 no5A p50 Ag/S 2017

Jones, Laney K.
  Genetic identification of familial hypercholesterolemia within a single U.S. health care system chart graph *Science* v354 no6319 paaf7000-1 D 23 2016

Jones, Leslie, 1967-
  Big 5-Oh C. Ianzito color *AARP: The Magazine* v60 no5A p72 Ag/S 2017
  Icons color *Time* v189 no16/17 p122 My 1-8 2017
  Sound Bites color *Entertainment Weekly* no1438 p14 N 4 2016

Jones, Lisa Renee
  Damage Control color *Publishers Weekly* v263 no52 p104 D 19 2016

Jones, Lynai
  what's your HANG-UP? P. GUGLIELMETTI color *Better Homes & Gardens* v95 no9 p50 S 2017

JONES, MAGGIE

DANA RAPHAEL *New York Times Magazine* p53 D 25 2016

Jones, Manina
  Flint, Feather, and Other Material Selves *American Indian Quarterly* v41 no2 p125 Spr 2017

Jones, Margaret
  Drawing on the Past *Natural History* v124 no10 p16 N 2016

Jones, Martha F.
  What do revised U.S. rules mean for human research? color *Science* v357 no6352 p650 Ag 18 2017

Jones, Marty
  BUSINESS RULEMAKING IN THE U.S.: A BRIEF HISTORY color *Fortune* v174 no6 p80 N 1 2016

Jones, Martyn Wendell
  Chesterton's Throne bw *Commonweal* v144 no13 p39 Ag 11 2017

JONES, MATTHEW B.
  Skills and Knowledge for Data-Intensive Environmental Research *BioScience* v67 no6 p546 Je 2017

Jones, Matthew R.
  Single-particle mapping of nonequilibrium nanocrystal transformations bibl bw graph *Science* v354 no6314 p874 N 18 2016

Jones, Meaghan
  Priming HIV-1 broadly neutralizing antibody precursors in human Ig loci transgenic mice bibl graph *Science* v353 no6307 p1557 S 30 2016

JONES, MEGAN
  You Are Not Alone color *Reader's Digest* v189 no1131 p54 Je 2017

Jones, Michelle
  The University-Bound Mother Who Killed Her Child Deserves Forgiveness B. Luscombe color *Time* v190 no13 p21 O 2 2017

Jones, Mikala
  Perfect Day, Somewhere color *Surfer* v58 no2 p134 My 2017

JONES, MIMI
  Establishing the Perfect Groove color diag *Downbeat* v84 no7 p74 Jl 2017

Jones, Myya D.
  Getting Real with Detroit's Myya D. Jones S. E. Jamison color *Ebony* v72 no8 p24 Je 2017

Jones, Nolan
  How the Insurance Industry Can Push Us to Prepare for Climate Change *Harvard Business Review Digital Articles* p2 Ag 28 2017

Jones, Norah, 1979-
  The New Norah J. WEINER bw color *Rolling Stone* no1273 p18 N 3 2016
  Welcome to the 40th Annual DownBeat Student Music Awards B. Reed color *Downbeat* v84 no6 p94 Je 2017

Jones, Norah, 1979-—Interviews
  NORAH JONES N. Feeney color *Entertainment Weekly* no1434 p55 O 7 2016

Jones, Parneshia
  Parneshia Jones C. Kirch color *Publishers Weekly* v264 no19 p6 My 8 2017

Jones, Paul
  THE BIG QUESTION cartoon *Atlantic* v320 no3 p100 O 2017

Jones, Peter
  2018 BMW K1600B color *Cycle World* v56 no10 p12 N 2017
  HURRICANES, POOP, AND FLAT-TRACKS color *Cycle World* v56 no2 p24 Mr 2017
  A MAD, MONSTROUS MOTUS color *Cycle World* v56 no6 p38 Jl 2017
  NO PARTICULAR NIGHT OR MORNING color *Cycle World* v56 no6 p24 Jl 2017
  NOT BY THE HAIR ON MY CHINNY, CHIN, CHIN bw color *Cycle World* v56 no10 p21 N 2017
  A QUESTION OF BALANCE color *Cycle World* v56 no8 p18 S 2017
  THE RISE AND FALL OF SPORTBIKES color *Cycle World* v56 no4 p32 My 2017
  VIRTUAL COMBUSTION *Cycle World* v55 no11 p20 D 2016

Jones, Preston
  Polished Performances: Classic and contemporary silver in dialogue at the Museum of the City of New York M. Bartolucci color *Magazine Antiques* v184 no5 p78 S/O 2017

Jones, Quincy, 1933-
  GQ HQ bw color *GQ: Gentlemen's Quarterly* v97 no4 p38 Ap

2017

Jones, Radhika

Death and the Maiden *New York Times Book Review* p14 Jl 16 2017

In Zadie Smith's New Novel, Performance Is the Tie That Binds, and Divides color *Time* v188 no21 p70 N 21 2016

JONES, RAMAKUMAR

Chords & Discords color *Downbeat* v84 no3 p10 Mr 2017

Jones, Rashida, 1976-

Angie Tribeca J. Russell *TV Guide* v65 no14 p37 Ap 3 2017

Jones, Rashida, 1976—Interviews

Rashida Jones Changed Her Mind About Porn A. M. Cox *New York Times Magazine* p54 Jl 30 2017

Jones, Reece

Visions of a Borderless World N. SIGONA *Current History* v116 no786 p38 Ja 2017

Jones, Richard

Primal Edge H. Als cartoon *New Yorker* v93 no6 p6 Mr 27 2017

Jones, Richard S.

Committing to socially responsible seafood color *Science* v356 no6341 p912 Je 1 2017

Jones, Rob

CATCH HIM IF YOU CAN M. Rosenberg and S. Kwak color *Sports Illustrated* v127 no12 p18 O 16 2017

Jones, Robert P.

Negotiating Surrender M. Peppard bw *Commonweal* v144 no10 p30 Je 2 2017

Jones, Robin

CORONA DEL MAR, CA color map *Sunset* v238 no2 p28 F 2017

Jones, Roger

The Family Dynamics We Grew Up with Shape How We Work *Harvard Business Review Digital Articles* p2 Jl 19 2016

What CEOs Are Afraid Of *Harvard Business Review Digital Articles* p2 F 2015

Jones, Ron Cephas

This Is Us Can't Quit Ron Cephas Jones D. Snierson color *Entertainment Weekly* no1484 p52 S 29 2017

Jones, Samantha H.

Choose a program, have a life color *Science* v357 no6355 p1058 S 8 2017

Jones, Sarah

All of ME color *InStyle* v24 no8 p156 Ag 2017

Boring Funds Get Weird color *Bloomberg Businessweek* no4499 p52 N 14 2016

CLASS-CONFLICT CUISINE bw *Nation* v305 no11 p28 O 30 2017

IN LA FOLLETTE TERRITORY color *Nation* v305 no4 p27 Ag 14 2017

The New Blue *New Republic* v248 no10 p27 O 2017

Ramp Hollow: The Ordeal of Appalachia color *Publishers Weekly* v264 no36 p79 S 4 2017

Real Housewives *New Republic* v248 no5 p58 My 2017

THE WAR ON HILLBILLIES color *New Republic* v248 no6 p42 Je 2017

Jones, Saul

High-performance light-emitting diodes based on carbene-metal-amides chart graph *Science* v356 no6334 p159 Ap 14 2017

Jones, Serene, 1959-

marks bw graph *Christian Century* v133 no21 p8 O 12 2016

Jones, Sharon, 1956-2016

SHARON JONES B. Kopple and E. R. Brown color *Entertainment Weekly* no1446/1447 p96 D 2016/Ja 2017

Jones, Sheep

IN THE GROOVE: Sheep Jones' striking textured surfaces imbue simple subjects with soulful wonder S. SARGENT *Virginia Living* v15 no4 p33 Je 2017

Jones, Sidney

WAIT FOR IT ... G. Bishop color *Sports Illustrated* v126 no13 p36 My 8 2017

JONES, SOPHIA

MERCY DENIED *Ms.* v27 no3 p26 Fall 2017

TURKISH WOMEN RISING *Ms.* v27 no1 p34 Spr 2017

Jones, Stella J.

The Perfect Present *Publishers Weekly* v263 no39 p88 S 26 2016

Jones, Stephen

BREATH OF FRESH HEIR A. Murphy color *Sports Illustrated*

v126 no2 p34 Ja 16 2017

Jones, Stephen Graham

Mapping the Interior *Publishers Weekly* v264 no15 p56 Ap 10 2017

Jones, Stephen Mack

August Snow *Publishers Weekly* v263 no47 p89 N 21 2016

Jones, Tim

In Ohio, the Ground War Goes Door-to-Door color *Bloomberg Businessweek* no4494 p26 O 10 2016

Jones, Tom

On a Burning Deck: The Road to Akron; An Oral History of the Great Migration, Vol. 1, 1900-1920 *Publishers Weekly* v264 no39 p80c S 25 2017

Jones, Tommy Lee, 1946-

Actors bw cartoon color *American Cowboy* p24 LEGENDS OF TEXAS Special Issue 2017

Jones, Tony

Crucible of Faith: The Ancient Revolution That Made Our Modern Religious World *Christian Century* v134 no22 p39 O 25 2017

Pax Romana: War, Peace and Conquest in the Roman World *Christian Century* v134 no11 p41 My 24 2017

Jones, Van

HATE IN THE AGE OF TRUMP color *New Republic* v248 no3 p38 Mr 2017

Serenity Prayer *GQ: Gentlemen's Quarterly* v87 no1 p24 Ja 2017

Jones, Van, 1968—Interviews

Is Bigotry a Parking Ticket or a Capital Offense? R. Carroll *New York* v49 no23 p27 N 14 2016

Jones, Wayne

Autumn Spectacle *New York State Conservationist* v72 no2 p2 O 2017

Recollections of Wayne Trimm *New York State Conservationist* v72 no1 p14 Ag 2017

Jones, Whitney

design masters l. cutrone *New Orleans Homes & Lifestyles* v20 no4 p70 Aut 2017

Jones, Williams B.

Discussion color *Smithsonian* v47 no10 p8 Mr 2017

Jones, Wilm

Identification of single-site gold catalysis in acetylene hydrochlorination bw diag graph *Science* v355 no6332 p1399 Mr 31 2017

Jones Day (Company)

Donald Trump's Favorite Law Firm P. M. Barrett color *Bloomberg Businessweek* no4515 p25 Mr 20 2017

Jones Soda Co.

Fizzy Math color *Weekly Standard* v22 no26 p2 Mr 13 2017

JONES CONDON, JENNIFER

Beach, Please! color *House Beautiful* p28 Jl 2017

The Life Aquatic color *House Beautiful* p24 Jl 2017

Jong, Erica

THE BOOK THAT CHANGED MY LIFE color *AARP: The Magazine* v59 no1A p12 D 2015/Ja 2016

Quotable Quotes bw color *Reader's Digest* v190 no1132 p140 Jl/Ag 2017

Jong Won Chung

Highly stretchable polymer semiconductor films through the nanoconfinement effect bibl graph *Science* v355 no6320 p1 Ja 6 2017

Jonlin, Erica C.

Our best shot bw *Science* v355 no6324 p464 F 3 2017

Jonnes, Jill

Jill Jonnes *American Forests* v123 no2 p4 Summ 2017

Jonovic, Donald J.

CAN THEIR PROBLEM BE SOLVED? *Successful Farming* v115 no3 p62 Mid-F 2017

CAN THEIR PROBLEM SOLVED? *Successful Farming* v114 no11 p67 N 2016

THE PROBLEM: HOW CAN PAY BE USED TO LEAD AND KEEP VALUED EMPLOYEES? color *Successful Farming* v115 no7 p56 My 2017

Jonson, Ben, 1573?-1637

BUBBLING UNDER D. STEWART color *America* v215 no15 p30 N 14 2016

Jönsson, Bodil

Emergence and spread of a human-transmissible multidrug-resistant nontuberculous mycobacterium bibl diag graph *Science*

v354 no6313 p751 N 11 2016

Jonsson, Patrik

In black Charleston, a struggle to find both justice and mercy color *Christian Century* v134 no4 p13 F 15 2017

Jónsson, Stefán R.

A supramolecular assembly mediates lentiviral DNA integration bibl color *Science* v355 no6320 p1 Ja 6 2017

Jonze, Spike, 1969-

JR'S BREAKOUT ARTISTS color *Harper's Bazaar* no3654 p136 Je/Jl 2017

Joo-Ho Shin

Pathological α-synuclein transmission initiated by binding lymphocyte-activation gene 3 bibl graph *Science* v353 no6307 paah3374-1 S 30 2016

Joonki Suh

Anomalously low electronic thermal conductivity in metallic vanadium dioxide bibl graph *Science* v355 no6323 p371 Ja 27 2017

Joppa, Lucas N.

Toward a national, sustained U.S. ecosystem assessment bibl color *Science* v354 no6314 p838 N 18 2016

Jorda, L.

Rosetta's comet 67P/Churyumov-Gerasimenko sheds its dusty mantle to reveal its icy nature bibl graph *Science* v354 no6319 p1566 D 23 2016

Surface changes on comet 67P/Churyumov-Gerasimenko suggest a more active past bw graph *Science* v355 no6332 p1392 Mr 31 2017

JORDAAN, ADRIAN

Damming, Lost Connectivity, and the Historical Role of Anadromous Fish in Freshwater Ecosystem Dynamics *BioScience* v67 no8 p713 Ag 2017

JORDAN, ALAN

Assessing National Biodiversity Trends for Rocky and Coral Reefs through the Integration of Citizen Science and Scientific Monitoring Programs *BioScience* v67 no2 p134 F 2017

Jordan, Alex

Research: Narcissists Don't Like Flat Organizations *Harvard Business Review Digital Articles* p2 Jl 27 2016

Jordan, Andrea

DOES IT REALLY WORK? color *Essence* v48 no2 p43 Je 2017

GET CHEEKY color *Essence* v48 no3 p36 Jl 2017

the Glow Up color *Essence* v48 no2 p31 Je 2017

KELSEY & KENDRA color *Essence* v48 no2 p38 Je 2017

Makeup Marvels color *Essence* v48 no5 p37 S 2017

MALAIKA CHANEY color *Essence* v48 no6 p46 O 2017

NOT-SO-BASIC BRUSHES color *Essence* v47 no9 p34 Ja 2017

Scalp Care 101 color *Essence* v48 no5 p50 S 2017

Summer Hair 101 color *Essence* v48 no2 p49 Je 2017

Trending Tresses color *Essence* v48 no5 p53 S 2017

Jordan, Andrew N.

Classical-quantum sensors keep better time graph *Science* v356 no6340 p802 My 26 2017

Jordan, Betty Ann

Art at the edge color map *Canadian Geographic* v137 no2 p24 Mr/Ap 2017

JORDAN, EDOUARDO

r.s.v.p bw *Bon Appetit* v62 no4 p10 Ap 2017

Jordan, Jason

Companies with a Formal Sales Process Generate More Revenue *Harvard Business Review Digital Articles* p2 Ja 21 2015

Jordan, Jennifer Szweda

Belonging color *U.S. Catholic* v82 no5 p28 My 2017

Finding refuge color *U.S. Catholic* v82 no8 p12 Ag 2017

JORDAN, KAREN

When The Past Is Present *Los Angeles Magazine* v62 no7 p15 Jl 2017

Jordan, Katherine W.

Wild emmer genome architecture and diversity elucidate wheat evolution and domestication color *Science* v357 no6346 p93 Jl 7 2017

Jordan, Keagan

KSU FOOTBALL *Atlanta* v56 no7 p26 N 2016

Jordan, Kelly

BEST OF ATLANTA *Atlanta* v56 no8 p106 D 2016

RADICAL REMEDIES *Atlanta* v56 no9 p43 Ja 2017

Jordan, Kenneth D.

Spectroscopic snapshots of the proton-transfer mechanism in water bibl diag graph *Science* v354 no6316 p1131 D 2 2016

Jordan, Kim

Growing Pains S. ADAMS color *Forbes* v200 no1 p35 Jl 27 2017

Jordan, Mark D.

Teaching Bodies: Moral Formation in the Summa of Thomas Aquinas P. Christman color *Christian Century* v134 no10 p36 My 10 2017

WRITERS' FEAST color *Christian Century* v134 no10 p30 My 10 2017

JORDAN, MICHAEL

CALIFORNIA CALLING color *Road & Track* v68 no7 p92 Mr/Ap 2017

RETURN TO FORM color *Road & Track* v68 no9 p88 Je 2017

Jordan, Michael B. (Michael Bakari), 1987-

How I Got My Style MICHAEL B. JORDAN J. CHEN color *Esquire* v166 no4 p49 N 2016

Jordan, Michael, 1963-

WHAT IF? ... MICHAEL JORDAN HAD NEVER BAGGED IT? T. Keith and J. Feldman color *Sports Illustrated* v126 no11 p60 Ap 17-24 2017

Jordan, Niema

EAT YOUR WAY TO PROSPERITY color *Essence* v47 no9 p83 Ja 2017

MARRIED TO MY BUSINESS PARTNER color *Essence* v47 no12 p113 Ap 2017

JORDAN, PAT

Welcome to Paradise color *Power & Motoryacht* v32 no11 p92 N 2016

Jordán, Patricia Arriaga

Letter from Mexico City: Juana Inés, the Miniseries P. J. Smith *Film Quarterly* v70 no4 p83 Summ 2017

Jordan, Patrick

Dorothy Day's 'Second Conversion'? bw *Commonweal* v144 no11 p31 Je 16 2017

Jordan, Sheldon

THE TANGLED WEB D. Hayes cartoon *Canadian Wildlife* v22 no5 p18 N/D 2016

Jordan, Sophie

While the Duke Was Sleeping *Publishers Weekly* v263 no40 p105 O 3 2016

Jordan, Steve

NEW CENTURY FOR A WRIGHT ROOF color *Old House Journal* v45 no3 p31 My 2017

Jordan, Tina

THE 24-WORD REVIEW color *Entertainment Weekly* no1474/1475 p118 Jl 21-28 2017

American Fire color *Entertainment Weekly* no1477 p62 Ag 11 2017

Beyond the Truth color *Entertainment Weekly* no1442 p62 D 2 2016 Rebellious Special Issue

BOLD TALES FOR COLD NIGHTS color *Entertainment Weekly* no1454/1455 p100 F 24 2017

Burning Bright color *Entertainment Weekly* no1449 p63 Ja 20 2017

DAISY GOODWIN color *Entertainment Weekly* no1451/1452 p110 F 3-10 2017

Eat, Think & Be Merry color *Entertainment Weekly* no1443 p62 D 9 2016

Hungry Heart color *Entertainment Weekly* no1436/1437 p106 O 21 2016

THE IMMORTAL LIFE OF HENRIETTA LACKS color *Entertainment Weekly* no1446/1447 p66 D 2016/Ja 2017

Last Girl Before Freeway color *Entertainment Weekly* no1440 p62 N 18 2016

The Lost Boy color *Entertainment Weekly* no1438 p63 N 4 2016

No. 10 EVICTED color *Entertainment Weekly* no1444/1445 p108 D 16 2016

PAT CONROY color *Entertainment Weekly* no1446/1447 p86 D 2016/Ja 2017

The Pie-Chart Review color diag *Entertainment Weekly* no1468/1469 p109 Je 2-9 2017

Settle for More color *Entertainment Weekly* no1441 p57 N 25 2016

Summer's 20 MUST-READ BOOKS color *Entertainment Weekly*

no1467 p58 My 26 2017

Sweet Stuff color *Entertainment Weekly* no1441 p60 N 25 2016

We: A Manifesto for Women Everywhere color *Entertainment Weekly* no1459 p63 Mr 31 2017

WHAT THE H IS HYGGE? color *Entertainment Weekly* no1459 p62 Mr 31 2017

What to Watch color *Entertainment Weekly* no1436/1437 p94 O 21 2016

Jordan, Vernon E. (Vernon Eulion), 1935—Interviews

THE POWER BROKER D. T. Dingle *Black Enterprise* v47 no8 p50 Jl/Ag 2017

Jordan—Description & travel

Arabian Nights K. Corrigan and J. Lucas color *Climbing* no357 p48 N 2017

Jorgensen, Bryan

10 SUCCESSFUL FARMERS: BRYAN JORGENSEN G. Gullickson *Successful Farming* v115 no8 p22 Je/Jl 2017

Jorgensen, Gwen

DOMESTIQUE BLISS N. WELDON color *Runner's World* v51 no11 p22 D 2016

Jorgensen, J. L.

Jupiter's interior and deep atmosphere: The initial pole-to-pole passes with the Juno spacecraft [Cover story] color graph *Science* v356 no6340 p821 My 26 2017

Jupiter's magnetosphere and aurorae observed by the Juno spacecraft during its first polar orbits diag graph *Science* v356 no6340 p826 My 26 2017

Jorgensen, Timothy J.

Strange Glow M. Lavine *Physics Today* v70 no1 p58 Ja 2017

Jorio, Ado

Mildred S. Dresselhaus *Physics Today* v70 no6 p73 Je 2017

Jorn, Asger, 1914-1973

ASGER JORN D. Ebony *Art in America* v104 no9 p150 O 2016

Joscelyn, Thomas

A Fateful Decision color *Weekly Standard* v22 no47 p7 Ag 21 2017

The Final Obama Scandal [Cover story] color *Weekly Standard* v22 no21 p22 F 6 2017

The Flynn Affair *Weekly Standard* v22 no24 p6 F 27 2017

Take Two at the NSC cartoon *Weekly Standard* v22 no25 p11 Mr 6 2017

Trump Got This One Right color *Weekly Standard* v22 no45 p14 Ag 7 2017

Unfinished Business [Cover story] color map *Weekly Standard* v22 no37 p22 Je 5 2017

We Got Lucky...This Time *Weekly Standard* v22 no4 p8 O 3 2016

When Loretta Met Bill color *Weekly Standard* v22 no47 p6 Ag 21 2017

Jose, San

CAT GOES TO HIGH SCHOOL color map *National Geographic Kids* no465 p13 N 2016

José Alava, Juan

Illegal fishing on the Galápagos high seas color *Science* v357 no6358 p1362 S 29 2017

Josebachuili, M.

Observation of a large-scale anisotropy in the arrival directions of cosmic rays above 8×1018 eV *Science* v357 no6357 p1266 S 22 2017

Joselow, Maxine

FOTOWEEKDC *Washingtonian Magazine* v52 no2 p35 N 2016

Joseph, Annette

CREATIVE CLASS A. MAZE color *Better Homes & Gardens* v95 no2 p40 F 2016

Joseph, Caleb

Nobody Home S. Apstein and T. Keith chart color *Sports Illustrated* v125 no12 p18 O 10 2016

Joseph, John

When First Movers Are Rewarded, and When They're Not *Harvard Business Review Digital Articles* p2 Ag 11 2015

Joseph, Lawanda

Posthole color *Powder* v45 no5 p108 Ja 2017

Joseph, Lawrence, 1948-

Portrait of Our Time A. Domestico color *Commonweal* v144 no15 p34 S 22 2017

THAT SEPTEMBER AND OCTOBER *Commonweal* v143 no17 p26 O 21 2016

Joseph, Nimesh

Neurodevelopmental protein Musashi-1 interacts with the Zika genome and promotes viral replication diag *Science* v357 no6346 p83 Jl 7 2017

Joseph, Peniel E.

THE BLACK PANTHERS' RADICAL HUMANISM *In These Times* v41 no1 p38 Ja 2017

WHY BLACK LIVES MATTER STILL MATTERS [Cover story] bw *New Republic* v248 no5 p16 My 2017

Joseph, Phillip

Understanding Acoustics: An Experimentalist's View of Acoustics and Vibration *Physics Today* v70 no10 p61 O 2017

JOSEPH, ROBERT

Bring Back Containment color *Weekly Standard* v22 no47 p18 Ag 21 2017

Cheney Was Right color *Weekly Standard* v23 no5 p27 O 9 2017

Trump's Nuclear Tweets color *Weekly Standard* v22 no18 p24 Ja 16 2017

Joseph, Rosara

Sports Funnies K. MILLER color *National Geographic Kids* no475 p6 N 2017

Joseph, Saint

Encounters With Angels M. R. SIMONE *America* v215 no18 p42 D 5 2016

JOSEPH, SAM

Dominate Fake Football color diag *Men's Health* v32 no7 p38 S 2017

Joseph, Shahadi Wright

Shahadi WRIGHT JOSEPH N. Loeffier-Giadstore *Dance Spirit* v21 no3 p71 Mr 2017

Josephs, Margaret

The Real Housewives of New Jersey I. Ratledge *TV Guide* v65 no41 p32 O 2 2017

Josephson effect

See also

Josephson junctions

Demonstration of an ac Josephson junction laser M. C. Cassidy, A. Bruno et al bibl diag *Science* v355 no6328 p939 Mr 3 2017

Josephson junctions

Demonstration of an ac Josephson junction laser M. C. Cassidy, A. Bruno et al bibl diag *Science* v355 no6328 p939 Mr 3 2017

RESEARCH bw color *Science* v355 no6328 p920 Mr 3 2017

Josey, Darren

UNSOLICITED BETA color *Climbing* no350 p16 D 2016/Ja 2017

Joshi, Aditya

Technology Questions Every CMO Must Ask *Harvard Business Review Digital Articles* p2 O 2 2014

JOSHI, ANUP

An Ecoregion-Based Approach to Protecting Half the Terrestrial Realm *BioScience* v67 no6 p534 Je 2017

Joshi, Aparna

Do Conservative Managers Give Smaller Bonuses to Women? *Harvard Business Review Digital Articles* p2 D 2 2016

Joshi, Rajiv

WE ARE THE LAW: We took employment lawyers from top firms and asked them about what really matters to HR - from Brexit and the Taylor review to staying out of court *People Management* p34 S 2017

Joshua tree

STRESSED OUT K. MOORE *Natural History* v125 no1 p2 D 2016/Ja 2017

Joshua Tree National Park (Calif.)

Hang In There L. Addison color *AARP: The Magazine* v59 no3A p83 Ap/My 2016

Oasis of Rock: Joshua Tree National Park, California R. WICHELNS color map *Backpacker* p8 N 2017

Joshua Tree, The (Music)

How U2 Got Back to 'The Joshua Tree' A. GREENE bw *Rolling Stone* no1280 p11 F 9 2017

THE JOSHUA TREE – SUPER DELUXE EDITION M. Mettler color *Sound & Vision* v82 no7 p72 S 2017

JOSPE, CHRISTOPHE

Climate Change is a Waste Management Problem *Issues in Science & Technology* v33 no3 p83 Spr 2017

JOSS, LIZ

A New Level: When Gen Con lands on planet Indianapolis August

17 and turns 50, the annual gathering of gamers will look quite different than it did during the beta phase *Indianapolis Monthly* v12 no40 p16 Ag 2017

Josse, Sebastien

Vraiment Incroyable! color *Sail* v48 no7 p18 Jl 2017

Jossinet, Fabrice

Transient compartmentalization of RNA replicators prevents extinction due to parasites bibl chart graph *Science* v354 no6317 p1293 D 9 2016

Jost, Colin—Interviews

"When life gets bad, make it funny" [Cover story] W. Paskin color *Glamour* v115 no3 p190 Mr 2017

Jost, Timothy Stoltzfus

Health Care & the Gospel color *Commonweal* v144 no8 p10 My 5 2017

Jothen, Peder

The Matter of Voice: Sensual Soundings *Christian Century* v134 no2 p38 Ja 18 2017

Jouet, Mugambi

Code Switch cartoon color graph *Mother Jones* v42 no1 p17 Ja/F 2017

THE UNEXCEPTIONAL DONALD TRUMP *In These Times* v41 no6 p38 Je 2017

Joules Ltd.

THE WORLD ACCORDING TO Gayle G. King bw color *O, The Oprah Magazine* p36 S 2017

Joung, Julia

High-resolution interrogation of functional elements in the noncoding genome bibl graph *Science* v353 no6307 p1545 S 30 2016

Nucleic acid detection with CRISPR-Cas13a/C2c2 color diag *Science* v356 no6336 p438 Ap 28 2017

Journal of Experimental Biology (Periodical)

Mixed-up mammal mixes soil Down Under S. Milius color *Science News* v190 no11 p4 N 26 2016

Journal of Geophysical Research (Periodical)

Extreme-Weather Winters More Common *USA Today Magazine* v145 no2859 p8 D 2016

Journal of Interpersonal Violence (Periodical)

Men Who Buy Sex Prove Sexually Coercive *USA Today Magazine* v145 no2859 p10 D 2016

Journal of Physical Chemistry (Periodical)

Fortune favors the well read J. G. West color *Science* v355 no6329 p1090 Mr 10 2017

Journal writing

Mom's Dinner Party Diaries A. SEAN GREER *Reader's Digest* v188 no1125 p62 N 2016

Want to Be an Outstanding Leader? Keep a Journal N. J. Adler *Harvard Business Review Digital Articles* p2 Ja 13 2016

What Thoreau Saw A. WULF color *Atlantic* v320 no4 p106 N 2017

Journalism

    See also

    Citizen journalism

    Newsletters

    Newspaper reading

    Periodical publishing

    Photojournalism

    Press conferences

    Reporters & reporting

    Science journalism

COLLAPSE OF THE FOURTH ESTATE *Change* v82 no3 p22 Mr 2017

Consumed by the news P. W. Marty *Christian Century* v133 no24 p3 N 23 2016

The Facebook rescue that wasn't E. Bell color graph *Columbia Journalism Review* v56 no1 p19 Spr 2017

Finding common ground over barbecue S. Blanchard color *Columbia Journalism Review* v56 no1 p42 Spr 2017

FIT TO PRINT T. McWilliam, S. Arnswald et al bw color *Wired* v25 no5 p14 My 2017

Gannett and the last great local hope D. Uberti color map *Columbia Journalism Review* v56 no1 p64 Spr 2017

Great moments in local journalism A. Hiatt bw color *Columbia Journalism Review* v56 no1 p112 Spr 2017

The new meaning of new media V. Vara color *Columbia Journal-*

ism Review v56 no1 p104 Spr 2017

OF MANY THINGS A. McKINLESS *America* v215 no15 p2 N 14 2016

Readers of the Year C. JEFFERY *Mother Jones* v42 no3 p3 My/ Je 2017

Save the Postal Service J. HIGHTOWER color *Progressive* v81 no5 p70 Je/Jl 2017

THE SPIRITUAL ACT OF SUBSCRIPTION M. GALLI color *Christianity Today* v60 no8 p29 O 2016

Welcome to Macedonia, Fake News Factory to the World S. Subramanian color graph *Wired* v25 no3 p68 Mr 2017

What if the right-wing media wins? M. Coppins and P. Vernon bw color *Columbia Journalism Review* v56 no2 p52 Fall 2017

Journalism & politics

Wow If True M. Hemingway color *Weekly Standard* v22 no33 p17 My 8 2017

Journalism—Editing

"Are you Tony?" T. Koester *Model Railroader* v84 no6 p82 Je 2017

Journalism—Finance

Hey, big funder S. Hepworth, C. Spike et al color *Columbia Journalism Review* v56 no1 p60 Spr 2017

Journalism—History—19th century

Fire and Faith: The coverage of a disaster in Chile revealed religious divisions among the world's press S. J. Martland *History Today* v67 no7 p14 Jl 2017

Journalism—Objectivity

The Harm of Smarm *Commentary* v142 no1 p1 Jl/Ag 2016

Journalism—Political aspects—United States

How the Press Should Cover TRUMP N. DAWES color il *Nation* v304 no9 p22 Mr 20 2017

Journalism—Social aspects

Journalism under Attack K. KLOOR *Issues in Science & Technology* v33 no2 p60 Wint 2017

Journalism—Standards

Television Fail E. Alterman il *Nation* v303 no22 p6 N 28 2016

Journalism—Style manuals

Sniffing Out Dog Whistles K. Steinmetz *Time* v188 no16/17 p65 O 24 2016

Journalism—Technological innovations

The age of the cyborg J. Stray color *Columbia Journalism Review* p70 Fall/Wint 2016

Can journalism be virtual? T. Owen cartoon *Columbia Journalism Review* p102 Fall/Wint 2016

Finding new ways to follow the story S. Coll *Columbia Journalism Review* p21 Fall/Wint 2016

Innovation gone bad E. Wemple *Columbia Journalism Review* p30 Fall/Wint 2016

A note from the editor K. Pope *Columbia Journalism Review* p10 Fall/Wint 2016

Journalism—United States

The Collapse of Fair-Minded Journalism M. GOODWIN *USA Today Magazine* v146 no2868 p12 S 2017

Democracy's Eulogists *Weekly Standard* v22 no25 p3 Mr 6 2017

The limits of story cartoon *Christian Century* v133 no22 p7 O 26 2016

When local stopped being cool M. Oreskes color *Columbia Journalism Review* v56 no1 p15 Spr 2017

Journalism—United States—Social aspects

Journalism in Trump's America M. MASSING color diag *Nation* v304 no4 p24 F 6 2017

Journalistic errors

CORRECTION *House Beautiful* v158 no9 p168 N 2016

Just the Facts D. COURTNEY *Texas Monthly* v45 no6 p288 Je 2017

The Straight Story N. Gibbs color *Time* v189 no4 p4 F 6 2017

Journalistic ethics

The COASTER CORRESPONDENCE E. J. COASTER cartoon color *Vanity Fair* v59 no5 p56 Ap 2017

FIGHTING FAKE NEWS: Made-up stories are taking over the internet. Are tech companies doing enough to stop the spread? S. GROSSBART *New York Times Upfront* v150 no1 p12 S 4 2017

Gawkermania *Commentary* v142 no1 p1 Jl/Ag 2016

How We Honor The First Amendment L. D'VORKIN *Forbes* v199 no2 p14 F 28 2017

Journalists

Joyce, Barnaby, 1967-
The Dual-Citizenship Crisis Rocking Politics Down Under R. Lewis color *Time* v190 no8 p11 Ag 28 2017

Joyce, James, 1882-1941
Joyce and His Jesuits R. Cavanaugh color *America* v216 no9 p18 Ap 24 2017

Joyce, John-Pierre
The Road to Equality: The Sexual Offences Act of 1967 was not the great step forward it is sometimes purported to be *History Today* v67 no7 p11 Jl 2017

JOYCE, KATHRYN
the silence of the lambs color *New Republic* v248 no7 p38 Jl 2017

Joyce, Richard
DRONES ON MARS color *Astronomy* v45 no7 p34 Jl 2017

Joyce, Sara
What Few Have Seen S. PETTICORD *Idaho Magazine* v17 no1 p12 Ja 2017

Joyce, Tim
The Forecasting Sweet Spot Between Micro and Macro *Harvard Business Review Digital Articles* p2 Ag 26 2016

Joyce, Tina
Thinking About Johnny color *Horse & Rider* v56 no2 p8 F 2017

Joyeux, Jean-Christophe
Fringe on the brink: Intertidal reefs at risk color *Science* v357 no6348 p261 Jl 21 2017

JOYNT, CAROL ROSS
FIT FOR A WHALE *Washingtonian Magazine* v52 no5 p26 F 2017
OLDIES AND GOODIES *Washingtonian Magazine* v52 no3 p26 D 2016
OLD MONEY *Washingtonian Magazine* v52 no4 p26 Ja 2017
SKYWITNESS NEWS *Washingtonian Magazine* v52 no2 p26 N 2016

Joysticks
ADVANCEMENT FOR ALL C. CASWELL color *Sea Magazine* v109 no7 p46 Jl 2017

Joysticks—Evaluation
Ski Boats Take Control A. JONES *Boating World* v38 no5 p22 My 2017
Stick the Landing P. FREDERIKSEN color *Power & Motoryacht* v34 no9 p30 S 2017

J.P. Morgan Chase & Co.
BANKING L. Shen *Fortune* v175 no7 p64 Je 1 2017
How Jamie Dimon's Minimum Wage Hike Could Backfire W. Frick *Harvard Business Review Digital Articles* p2 Jl 13 2016
Jamie Dimon and Other People's Money [Cover story] D. DAYEN color *Nation* v305 no10 p12 O 23 2017
JPMorgan Traders Get Into Property Deals S. Mulholland and H. Son *Bloomberg Businessweek* no4504 p35 D 19 2016
MAKING A MOTOWN MIRACLE [Cover story] M. Heimer color *Fortune* v176 no4 p94 S 15 2017

J.P. Morgan Chase & Co.—Management
How Fancy Private Bankers Cross-Sell N. Weinberg graph *Bloomberg Businessweek* no4510 p35 F 6 2017

J.P. Morgan Chase & Co.—Officials & employees
'If you can duplicate what they've done in Detroit around the country, you're going to have a huge renaissance' M. Murphy color *Bloomberg Businessweek* no4505 p46 D 26 2016

J.P. Sauer & Sohn (Company)
SAUER 100 CLASSIC XT J. B. Snow chart color *Outdoor Life* v223 no9 p74 N 2016

JPEG (Image coding standard)
How to split a raw+JPEG photo file into its separate parts G. FLEISHMAN bw color *Macworld - Digital Edition* v34 no10 p107 O 2017

Jørgensen, P. Møller
Persistent effects of pre-Columbian plant domestication on Amazonian forest composition bibl chart graph map *Science* v355 no6328 p925 Mr 3 2017

Ju, Sungtaek Yongho
Highly efficient electrocaloric cooling with electrostatic actuation bw diag *Science* v357 no6356 p1130 S 15 2017

Juana Inés (TV program)
A brilliant nun with no time for short-sighted men N. Ripatrazone color *America* v216 no7 p49 Ap 3 2017
Letter from Mexico City: Juana Inés, the Miniseries P. J. Smith

Film Quarterly v70 no4 p83 Summ 2017

Juarez, Aimee
The Sitting Room *Publishers Weekly* v264 no9 p66f F 27 2017

Jucker, Mathias
Immune receptor for pathogenic α-synuclein bibl diag *Science* v353 no6307 p1498 S 30 2016

Jucker, Tommaso
Positive biodiversity-productivity relationship predominant in global forests bibl chart graph map *Science* v354 no6309 paaf8957-1 O 14 2016

Judah, Tim
Hey, Judah J. Kirchick *Commentary* v143 no1 p53 Ja 2017
In Wartime: Stories From Ukraine R. Legvold *Foreign Affairs* v95 no6 p186 N/D 2016
Mad, Democrats? Blame the Iran Deal *Commentary* p1 Ja 2017
Mad, Democrats? Blame the Iran Deal *Commentary* v143 no1 p1 Ja 2017
Will Ukraine Ever Change? color *New York Review of Books* v64 no9 p47 My 25 2017

Judaism
See also
Conservative Judaism
Havurah movement
Assessing Spinoza R. K. MASON *Commentary* v142 no2 p13 S 2016
Commentary on Commentary J. PODHORETZ *Commentary* v143 no4 p1 Ap 2017
Deep State of Affairs T. Troy *Commentary* v143 no4 p4 Ap 2017

Judaism & culture
Holla for Challah! J. Miller color *Bloomberg Businessweek* no4517 p67 Ap 3 2017

Judaism—United States
Saving Conservative Judaism: The case for ballasting the tent rather than widening it until it collapses R. Rosenthal Kwall *Commentary* v143 no4 p31 Ap 2017

JUDAR, NINA
healthy summer HAIR HABITS cartoon color *Better Homes & Gardens* v95 no8 p22 Ag 2017
the secret to BOLD BROWS color *Better Homes & Gardens* v95 no5 p18 My 2017

Judd, Alan, 1946-
A Throne in the Rearview Mirror T. KENEALLY *New York Times Book Review* p15 Ja 15 2017

Judd, Ashley, 1968-
Berlin Station J. Halterman *TV Guide* v65 no43 p36 O 16 2017

Judd, Dan
Flavin JUDD S. LACAVA *Interview* v46 no10 p38 D 2016/Ja 2017

Judd, Donald, 1928-1994
SPECIFIC OBJECTIVES Z. LESCAZE bw color *ARTnews* v115 no3 p110 Fall 2016

JUDD, ELIZABETH
The Joy and Terror of Shirley Jackson *American Conservative* v15 no6 p53 N/D 2016

Judd, Flavin, 1968-
Flavin JUDD S. LACAVA *Interview* v46 no10 p38 D 2016/Ja 2017
A Visionary of the Real J. Perl bw color *New York Review of Books* v64 no16 p30 O 26 2017

Jude, Radu
Scarred Hearts color *New Yorker* v92 no46 p11 Ja 23 2017

Judge, Aaron
Aaron Judge Sizes Up As Baseball's Best New Hope S. Gregory color *Time* v190 no8 p22 Ag 28 2017
ALL RISE [Cover story] S. Apstein chart color *Sports Illustrated* v126 no14 p76 My 15-22 2017
NEW YORK GIANT A. Belth color *Esquire* p30 O 2017
Smashing Debuts A. McKiernan and T. Keith chart color *Sports Illustrated* v127 no9 p14 S 25 2017
Why are some stats—like baseball's 'exit velocity' this year—embraced more than others? J. Caspian Kang *New York Times Magazine* p14 S 3 2017

JUDGE, CLARK S.
Reagan In the Wilderness bw color *National Review* v69 no7 p40 Ap 17 2017

Judge, Lauren

Power of Art cartoon *Alternatives Journal (AJ) - Canada's Environmental Voice* v42 no3 p68 2016

Judge, Marie

When I Was a Horse-Crazy Kid, I... color *Horse & Rider* v56 no2 p72 F 2017

Judge, Mike

Mike Judge R. MCCAMMON color *GQ: Gentlemen's Quarterly* v97 no6 p128 Je 2017

Judge, Paul

THIS MAN WANTS TO DISRUPT YOUR DOWNLOAD S. LYNN color *Black Enterprise* v47 no5 p25 Ja/F 2017

Judge Ventures (Company)

THIS MAN WANTS TO DISRUPT YOUR DOWNLOAD S. LYNN color *Black Enterprise* v47 no5 p25 Ja/F 2017

Judges

See also

Judgments (Law)

Here's How H. Hugo-Vidal and R. Sargent color *Practical Horseman* v45 no2 p58 F 2017

My Obsessions... *TV Guide* v65 no21 p8 My 15 2017

Judges—Biography

Neil Gorsuch M. Rich color *Current Biography* v78 no9 p23 S 2017

Judges—Italy

The Pros and Cons of Doing One Thing at a Time A. O'Connell *Harvard Business Review Digital Articles* p2 Ja 20 2015

Judges—Selection & appointment

Patriotic Gorsuch *Commentary* v143 no3 p23 Mr 2017

Judges—Selection & appointment—United States

The Judiciary: Realigning the Courts P. M. Barrett graph *Bloomberg Businessweek* no4530 p41 Jl 17 2017

Supreme BATTLE P. SMITH, D. Victor et al *New York Times Upfront* v149 no10 p14 Mr 13 2017

Judges—United States

See also

Supreme Court justices (U.S.)

ANTONIN SCALIA E. BAZELON *New York Times Magazine* p34 D 25 2016

Bad Faith? *Commonweal* v144 no16 p5 O 6 2017

Fighting Words E. SHOWALTER bw color il *New Republic* v247 no11 p42 N 2016

Lone Star Legal Show A. Greenblatt color *Governing* v30 no11 p38 Ag 2017

ORDER IN THE COURTS: Some judges are severely overworked while others don't have enough to do. But fixing that can be politically impossible J. B. Wogan *Governing* v30 no9 p30 Je 2017

What He Could Do [Cover story] M. Danner color *New York Review of Books* v64 no5 p4 Mr 23 2017

When Is a Judge Too Old? A. Greenblatt *Governing* v30 no1 p10 O 2016

Judging

2016 british nationals B. Finke *Arabian Horse World* v57 no1 p128 O 2016

Health Care HERO K. CICERO color *Prevention* v69 no6 p34 Je 2017

Judgment (Ethics)

When We Don't Blame People for Their Bad Deeds J. Martin and F. Cushman *Harvard Business Review Digital Articles* p2 F 16 2016

Why It's Dangerous to Love Your Boss A. McKee *Harvard Business Review Digital Articles* p2 D 4 2014

Judgment (Psychology)

See also

Attitude change (Psychology)

Public opinion

The Big Picture: The snap judgments we make based on people's online photographs may predict how we act toward them in person S. M. BUCKLIN *Psychology Today* v50 no5 p43 S/O 2017

Coping with Judgment J. Susser *Dressage Today* v23 no8 p16 Ap 2017

Judgments (Law)

A FREE MARKET FRIEND AT THE FTC D. ROOT *Reason* v48 no8 p16 Ja 2017

What Young vs. UPS Means for Pregnant Workers and Their Bosses L. Morris, C. T. Calvert et al *Harvard Business Review*

Digital Articles p2 Mr 26 2015

Judgments (Law)—Great Britain

Court rules small groups can bring whistleblowing claims: Landmark case could influence future decisions defining what is in the public interest *People Management* p14 Ag 2017

Judgments (Law)—Michigan

CAN YOU GO TO JAIL FOR HANDING OUT PAMPHLETS? J. SULLUM bw *Reason* v49 no6 p8 N 2017

Judicial corruption

Judge on Trial L. YOUNG *Ms.* v26 no4 p8 Wint 2016

Judicial impartiality

ORDER IN THE COURTS: Some judges are severely overworked while others don't have enough to do. But fixing that can be politically impossible J. B. Wogan *Governing* v30 no9 p30 Je 2017

Judicial process—United States

Courtroom forensic evidence often lacks scientific validity, report finds T. Feder *Physics Today* v69 no11 p32 N 2016

Judicial review—United States

WHY MARBURY MATTERS D. B. MOSKOWITZ color *American History* v52 no4 p24 O 2017

JUDIS, JOHN B.

DEEP STORIES *Nation* v303 no16 p32 O 17 2016

Just Say No to Just Say No color *New Republic* v248 no5 p14 My 2017

The Loyalty Freak color *New Republic* v248 no7 p14 Jl 2017

POWER TO THE PEOPLE J. W. Ceaser *Claremont Review of Books* v17 no3 p38 Summ 2017

Redoing the Electoral Math color *New Republic* v248 no10 p16 O 2017

Trans-Atlantic Populism J. ALTER *New York Times Book Review* p24 O 9 2016

THE TWO POPULISMS J. PURDY color *Nation* v303 no18 p27 O 31 2016

Judo—History

Judo Back in the Day H. NISHIOKA bw *Black Belt* v55 no4 p54 Je/Jl 2017

Judson, Olivia

The Power of Eight chart color *National Geographic* v230 no5 p62 N 2016

What the Octopus Knows color *Atlantic* v319 no1 p34 Ja/F 2017

Judson, Phoebe

1853: Nooksack, WA P. Judson *Lapham's Quarterly* v10 no1 p55 Wint 2017

JUDUA, CHRISTINEA

London color *Conde Nast Traveler* v52 no2 p64 F 2017

Judy & Arthur Zankel Hall (New York, N.Y.)

Less Is More R. Platt cartoon *New Yorker* v93 no7 p20 Ap 3 2017

Jugular vein

TECH RX S. STANKORB *Cincinnati Magazine* v50 no4 p69 Ja 2017

JUHASZ, ANTONIA

The United States of Exxon *In These Times* v41 no2 p18 F 2017

Juicers—Evaluation

YOUR MAIN SUMMER TEST KITCHEN SQUEEZE color *Better Homes & Gardens* v95 no5 p118 My 2017

Juilliard Orchestra

CLASSICAL MUSIC cartoon *New Yorker* v93 no26 p14 S 4 2017

Juilliard School

no average day: The busy lives of dancers at Juilliard, Indiana University and Harvard K. BRADY *Dance Magazine* v90 p18 2016/2017 Supplement College Guide

Jukebox musicals

March Events F. Esker color *New Orleans Magazine* v51 no5 p26 Mr 2017

Jukes, Calum

Treadmilling by FtsZ filaments drives peptidoglycan synthesis and bacterial cell division bibl graph *Science* v355 no6326 p739 F 17 2017

Julavits, Heidi

THE ART AT THE END OF THE WORLD *New York Times Magazine* p44 Jl 9 2017

KIKI SMITH *Interview* v47 no6 p86 Ag 2017

Juliana Bicycles (Company)

HOT DAMN! color *Bicycling* v58 no6 p71 Jl 2017

Julie's Greenroom (TV program)

Julie Andrews S. Begley color *Time* v189 no12 p54 Ap 3 2017

LUCKY M. Schulman cartoon *New Yorker* v93 no2 p25 F 27 2017

Julieta (Film)

Julieta A. Lane *New Yorker* v92 no44 p12 Ja 9 2017

Letter from Madrid: Spanish Screenings and Julieta P. J. Smith *Film Quarterly* v70 no2 p63 Wint 2016

MOTHER LODE A. LANE cartoon *New Yorker* v92 no42 p130 D 19 2016

Pedro Almodóvar Grows Up J. THOMAS *Advocate* no1088 p60 D 2016/Ja 2017

Julietta (Music)

Martinů: Ariane/Martinů Julietta *Opera News* v81 no7 p47 Ja 2017

JULIOUS, BRITT

54 GREAT THINGS TO DO THIS MONTH color *Chicago* v66 no1 p117 Ja 2017

58 GREAT THINGS TO DO THIS MONTH color *Chicago* v66 no2 p101 F 2017

62 GREAT THINGS TO DO THIS MONTH color *Chicago* v66 no6 p97 Je 2017

63 GREAT THINGS TO DO THIS MONTH color *Chicago* v66 no7 p87 Jl 2017

63 GREAT THINGS TO DO THIS MONTH color *Chicago* v66 no8 p105 Ag 2017

65 GREAT THINGS TO DO THIS MONTH color *Chicago* v65 no11 p115 N 2016

66 GREAT THINGS TO DO THIS MONTH color *Chicago* v66 no9 p139 S 2017

67 GREAT THINGS TO DO THIS MONTH color *Chicago* v66 no3 p129 Mr 2017

68 GREAT THINGS TO DO THIS MONTH color *Chicago* v66 no5 p119 My 2017

GO: 69 GREAT THINGS TO DO THIS MONTH color *Chicago* v66 no11 p103 N 2017

GO bw color *Chicago* v66 no10 p105 O 2017

GO color *Chicago* v65 no12 p119 D 2016

GO color *Chicago* v66 no4 p113 Ap 2017

WHY We LOVE CHICAGO bw cartoon color *Chicago* v66 no3 p75 Mr 2017

Juliska Inc.

Melamine Scene color *House Beautiful* v159 no3 p40 Ap 2017

Julius Caesar (Play : Shakespeare)

Never Mind Trump. We Need Shakespeare More Than Ever D. V. Drehle color *Time* v189 no24 p17 Je 26 2017

The Quiz T. BALAZO color *Maclean's* v129 no48/49 p37 D 5 2016

Julius Caesar (Theatrical production)

Orange Julius K. Pollitt *Nation* v305 no2 p6 Jl 17 2017

Jullapat, Roxana

The New Wonder Bread P. KUH *Los Angeles Magazine* p60 Mr 2017

July

Summer Madness T. Verducci and T. Keith color *Sports Illustrated* v126 no8 p20 Mr 20 2017

July, Miranda

Icons color *Time* v189 no16/17 p122 My 1-8 2017

The Metal Bowl cartoon color *New Yorker* v93 no26 p72 S 4 2017

Juma, Calestous

Change's Challengers A. Trembath color *Issues in Science & Technology* v33 no2 p94 Wint 2017

Jumanji: Welcome to the Jungle (Film)

JUMANJI: WELCOME TO THE JUNGLE D. Coggan color *Entertainment Weekly* no1478 / 1479 p73 Ag 18-25 2017

Jumbo, Cush, 1985——Interviews

Q&A WITH CUSH JUMBO M. M. Toby color *Essence* v47 no11 p60 Mr 2017

Jump (Music)

1984 L. Greenblatt color *Entertainment Weekly* no1456 p66 Mr 10 2017

Jump Trading LLC

The Battle of the Microwave Antennas B. Louis and M. Leising color *Bloomberg Businessweek* no4523 p40 My 22 2017

JUMPERTZ, CAROLINE

Battling Depression with LSD color *Publishers Weekly* v263 no52 p110 D 19 2016

Jumping

Jumping Seat Medal Finals Debut *In Stride* v12 no3 p10 My 2017

SPRING TRAINING C. KUZMA color *Runner's World* v52 no5 p22 Je 2017

Why Not...Jump into Shape! color *Health* v31 no3 p11 Ap 2017

Jumping (Horsemanship)

See also

Cavalletti

The 2017 Show Jumping Hall of Fame Inductees N. Jaffer *In Stride* v12 no4 p43 Jl 2017

Four Good Legs, Two Faulty Releases G. H. Morris color *Practical Horseman* v45 no8 p10 Ag 2017

HORSEPOWER: WHAT IT TAKES TO WIN A WORLD CUP N. Jaffer color *Practical Horseman* v45 no3 p48 Mr 2017

Let Your Horse Figure It Out S. Oliynyk *Practical Horseman* v45 no3 p8 Mr 2017

SHARPEN YOUR COURSE-RIDING SKILLS T. Brooks and C. Brooks color diag *Practical Horseman* v45 no8 p30 Ag 2017

Three Solid Leg Positions G. H. Morris color *Practical Horseman* v45 no3 p10 Mr 2017

'What the Horse Takes, the Rider Gives' G. H. Morris color *Practical Horseman* v45 no4 p12 Ap 2017

Jumping spiders

Males Show Their True Colors [Cover story] J. OTTO, D. KNOWLES et al color *Natural History* v125 no4 p10 Ap 2017

Jumping techniques

Reach New Heights K. Holmes *Dance Spirit* v21 no7 p84 S 2017

Jumpsuits—Evaluation

Anything GOES! color *Seventeen* p41 Ja 1 2017

The GIFT GUIDE 2016 img *New York* v49 no24 p79 N 28 2016

Jump Around S. Kennedy color *Bloomberg Businessweek* no4514 p70 Mr 13 2017

LOUNGE HAPPY! color *Women's Health* v14 no1 p178 Ja/F 2017

Nail Your Holiday Style! color *Glamour* v114 no12 p91 D 2016

the start color *InStyle* v24 no4 p41 Ap 2017

Jun, Shelma

FLASH bw color *Climbing* no353 p8 My/Je 2017

Jun, Sora

The Unintended Consequences of Diversity Statements *Harvard Business Review Digital Articles* p2 Mr 29 2016

Jun-Hyuk Bang

High Score G. CHUNG color *Forbes* v198 no6 p30 N 8 2016

Jun Kobayashi

A three-dimensional movie of structural changes in bacteriorhodopsin bibl diag graph *Science* v354 no6319 p1552 D 23 2016

Jun Li

A Better Way to Fight Discrimination in the Sharing Economy color *Harvard Business Review Digital Articles* p2 F 27 2017

Jun Seop Jeong

A nuclease that mediates cell death induced by DNA damage and poly(ADP-ribose) polymerase-1 bw graph *Science* v354 no6308 paad6872-1 O 7 2016

Jun Yan

Application of MALDI-TOF mass spectrometry for identifying clinical microorganisms bibl *Science* v354 no6319 p58 D 23 2016

Jun Yan Wu

Quality management for precision medicine clinical applications: A consensus from the China Precision Medicine Clinical Research and Application Association bibl *Science* v354 no6319 p11 D 23 2016

Jun Yang

Application of MALDI-TOF mass spectrometry for identifying clinical microorganisms bibl *Science* v354 no6319 p58 D 23 2016

Jun Ye

Deborah S. Jin (1968–2016) color *Science* v354 no6313 p709 N 11 2016

Jun Zhao

Quality management for precision medicine clinical applications: A consensus from the China Precision Medicine Clinical Research and Application Association bibl *Science* v354 no6319 p11 D 23 2016

Jun-Zhi Wei

A selective insecticidal protein from Pseudomonas for controlling corn rootworms bibl chart graph *Science* v354 no6312 p634 N

4 2016

Jun Zhu

Positive biodiversity-productivity relationship predominant in global forests bibl chart graph map *Science* v354 no6309 paaf8957-1 O 14 2016

Junchompoo, Chalatip

Poor fisheries struggle with U.S. import rule bibl color *Science* v355 no6329 p1031 Mr 10 2017

Juncker, Jean-Claude, 1954-

How Europe Can Create Its Own Silicon Valley L. Downes *Harvard Business Review Digital Articles* p2 Je 11 2015

STATE OF THE EUROPEAN UNION: AN "EXISTENTIAL CRISIS" JUNCKER *Vital Speeches of the Day* v82 no11 p328 N 2016

We Will Move On Because Brexit Isn't Everything *Vital Speeches of the Day* v83 no10 p270 O 2017

Juncker, Jean-Claude, 1954—Interviews

The E.U.'s Chief Executive on Trump, Populism and Russia C. McDonald-Gibson color *Time* v189 no7/8 p19 F 27 2017

Juncos

Bird's-Eye View R. BROOKHISER il *National Review* v69 no1 p43 Ja 23 2017

June (Month)

JUNE NIGHTS OUT *Natural History* v125 no6 p45 Je 2017

June, Carl H.

CANCER KILLERS color *Scientific American* v316 no3 p38 Mr 2017

June, Carl—Interviews

Our Bodies Can Kill Cancer color *Popular Science* v288 no6 p40 N/D 2016

June, Valerie

"My dreads gave me time" S. Kitchens and Ying Chu color *Glamour* v115 no3 p118 Mr 2017

Why Valerie June Sings the Blues D. BROWNE bw *Rolling Stone* no1287 p18 My 18 2017

June Life Inc.

A CHEF'S TEST: THE AUTOMATIC OVEN W. DUFRESNE color *Popular Mechanics* p77 My 2017

JUNG, ALYSSA

8 Silent Signs Stress Is Making You Sick *Reader's Digest* v189 no1127 p56 F 2017

Bridge Builder color *Reader's Digest* v190 no1133 p8 S 2017

Dog Catcher *Reader's Digest* v189 no1127 p8 F 2017

HEALING With Light color *Prevention* v69 no11 p72 N 2017

Simple Ways To Cut the Top Blood Pressure Number color *Reader's Digest* v190 no1134 p56 O 2017

Stopping A Kidnapper color *Reader's Digest* v189 no1131 p8 Je 2017

Sweet Pickings *Reader's Digest* v188 no1125 p14 N 2016

JUNG, E. ALEX

52 MINUTES WITH ... Andrew Rannells img *New York* v50 no8 p18 Ap 17 2017

Can You Love This Super-Pig? It's one thing to dream up a nonexistent creature. But just try bringing it adorably to life img *New York* v50 no13 p72 Je 26 2017

HOW TO: Play 11 Different Characters (And Counting) on One TV Show img *New York* v50 no11 p118 My 29 2017

Jung, Eui Hyuk

Iodide management in formamidinium-lead-halide–based perovskite layers for efficient solar cells bw diag *Science* v356 no6345 p1376 Je 30 2017

Jung, Gowoon

Evangelical Christian Discourse in South Korea on the LGBT: the Politics of Cross-Border Learning *Society* v54 no1 p29 F 2017

Jung, Jiwook

Research: Hiring Chief Risk Officers Led Banks to Take on Even More Risk *Harvard Business Review Digital Articles* p2 Jl 13 2017

Jung-Hoon Kwon

Role for migratory wild birds in the global spread of avian influenza H5N8 bibl graph map *Science* v354 no6309 p213 O 14 2016

Jünger, Ernst, 1895-1998

1957: Germany E. Jünger *Lapham's Quarterly* v10 no2 p171 Spr 2017

Valor The Last Blue Max D. T. Zabecki bw *Military History* v34 no5 p16 Ja 2018

Junger, Sebastian, 1962-

Now Shut Up and Shop A. J. Bacevich color *Commonweal* v143 no17 p33 O 21 2016

Tribe: On Home coming and Belonging W. Kinghorn color *Christian Century* v133 no21 p39 O 12 2016

Junger, Sebastian, 1962——Interviews

HOW WE SHOW ALL SIDES OF WAR color *National Geographic* v231 no2 p6 F 2017

Jungle animals

Personality Quiz color diag *National Geographic Kids* no473 p14 S 2017

Jungle Book, The (Film)

THE JUNGLE BOOK C. Chiarella color *Sound & Vision* v81 no10 p71 D 2016

Junior high schools

Northern Hills Middle School *American Forests* v123 no3 p10 Fall 2017

Junior riders (Horsemanship)

Carol Kozlowski: 'Don't Ever Close Your Mind' T. Conahan color *Practical Horseman* v45 no5 p24 My 2017

Juniper Ridge (Company)

Beauty J. Chamberlain color *Sunset* v237 no5 p60 N 2016

Junipers

Made in the Shade E. Millard color map *Log Home Living* v34 no3 p34 Ap 2017

Junji Cao

Nuclear power: Deployment speed—Response bibl *Science* v354 no6316 p1113 D 2 2016

Junk bonds

Get a 6.5% Yield With a Stew of Junk Bonds R. ERMEY chart *Kiplinger's Personal Finance* v71 no1 p61 Ja 2017

Junk food

Laugh Out Loud *National Geographic Kids* no469 p33 Ap 2017

THE SINISTER SCIENCE OF IRRESISTIBLE JUNK FOOD M. CROUCH and A. ACHILLEOS *Scholastic Choices* v32 no4 p6 Ja 2017

Junk loans

A Sun-Dappled Tuscan Banking Mess L. Casiraghi and C. Albanese color *Bloomberg Businessweek* no4511 p36 F 13 2017

Junk sculpture—Exhibitions

One man's trash J. Bleem color *U.S. Catholic* v82 no7 p50 Jl 2017

Junkers airplanes

FIRST CLASS L. STRAUSS bw color *Vanity Fair* v58 no12 p84 D 2016

Junkin Media Inc.

click doctors J. L. Keiles *New York Times Magazine* p24 Ja 1 2017

Junkluggers (Company)

OUT WITH THE OLD P. Marx cartoon *New Yorker* v92 no44 p22 Ja 9 2017

Juno (Company)

THE ANTI-UBER S. KOLHATKAR cartoon *New Yorker* v92 no32 p40 O 10 2016

Juno Got Sold, and Its Drivers Got Stiffed J. Brustein *Bloomberg Businessweek* no4521 p33 My 8 2017

NO MORE MR. NICE GUY S. Kolhatkar cartoon *New Yorker* v93 no16 p44 Je 5 2017

Juno (Space probe)

How Juno Met Jupiter B. ANDREWS color *Discover* v38 no1 p73 Ja/F 2017

Juno reveals more complex Jupiter A. YEAGER color *Science News* v191 no12 p14 Je 24 2017

Juno's early results reveal a mysterious Jupiter color *Astronomy* v45 no10 p17 O 2017

Juno Will Stay in Current Orbit Around Jupiter D. DICKINSON *Sky & Telescope* v133 no6 p8 Je 2017

Juno will stay put for the rest of its mission color *Astronomy* v45 no6 p17 Je 2017

Jupiter's interior and deep atmosphere: The initial pole-to-pole passes with the Juno spacecraft [Cover story] S. J. Bolton, A. Adriani et al color graph *Science* v356 no6340 p821 My 26 2017

NASA's Juno Makes First Science Pass D. DICKINSON *Sky & Telescope* v133 no1 p16 Ja 2017

A recurring rendezvous E. DeMarco color *Science News* v191 no12 p32 Je 24 2017

Junqiao Wu

Anomalously low electronic thermal conductivity in metallic

vanadium dioxide bibl graph *Science* v355 no6323 p371 Ja 27 2017

Junqing Li

Premature downgrade of panda's status color *Science* v354 no6310 p295 O 21 2016

Junqueira, A. B.

Persistent effects of pre-Columbian plant domestication on Amazonian forest composition bibl chart graph map *Science* v355 no6328 p925 Mr 3 2017

Junqueira, Bruna

Emission of volatile organic compounds from petunia flowers is facilitated by an ABC transporter diag *Science* v356 no6345 p1386 Je 30 2017

Junwon Choi

A general, modular method for the catalytic asymmetric synthesis of alkylboronate esters bibl color *Science* v354 no6317 p1265 D 9 2016

Jupiter (Planet)

Aim High F. Schaaf *Sky & Telescope* v133 no6 p46 Je 2017

April 2017: Jupiter rules the night M. RATCLIFFE and A. LING color *Astronomy* v45 no4 p36 Ap 2017

Hail to the King M. Wedel *Sky & Telescope* v133 no5 p41 My 2017

January 2017: Venus climbs high at dusk M. RATCLIFFE and A. LING color *Astronomy* v45 no1 p36 Ja 2017

Juno will stay put for the rest of its mission color *Astronomy* v45 no6 p17 Je 2017

Jupiter at Dawn *Sky & Telescope* v132 no6 p50 D 2016

Jupiter High at Dawn *Sky & Telescope* v133 no2 p50 F 2017

Shadow transit double header G. CHAPLE color *Astronomy* v45 no5 p18 My 2017

Solar system birthed Jupiter early on L. GROSSMAN color *Science News* v191 no13 p18 Jl 8 2017

Spacecraft eyes Great Red Spot color *Science* v357 no6348 p232 Jl 21 2017

Weird But True! J. SWAIN and A. E. HURT color *National Geographic Kids* no473 p4 S 2017

Jupiter (Planet)—Observations

Jupiter Enters the Evening Sky A. MacRobert *Sky & Telescope* v133 no4 p48 Ap 2017

Jupiter High at Dawn *Sky & Telescope* v133 no1 p50 Ja 2017

NASA's Juno Makes First Science Pass D. DICKINSON *Sky & Telescope* v133 no1 p16 Ja 2017

Jupiter (Planet)—Ring system

Jupiter – From Earth to Juno J. H. Rogers color *Sky & Telescope* v134 no5 p52 N 2017

Jupiter (Planet)—Satellites

See also

Europa (Satellite)

Jupiter High at Dawn *Sky & Telescope* v133 no1 p50 Ja 2017

The planets in December 2016 M. RATCLIFFE and A. LING chart diag graph map *Astronomy* v44 no12 p40 D 2016

Jupiter's Great Red Spot

A JunoCam close-up *Physics Today* v70 no8 p80 Ag 2017

Jupiter's orbit

Juno Will Stay in Current Orbit Around Jupiter D. DICKINSON *Sky & Telescope* v133 no6 p8 Je 2017

Juraschek, Dominik M.

Sounding out optical phonons diag *Science* v357 no6354 p873 S 1 2017

Jurczak, Jonathan

Discussion *Smithsonian* v48 no2 p8 My 2017

Jurek, Scott

HOW TO GO GREEN [Cover story] cartoon color *Runner's World* v52 no2 p38 Mr 2017

Jurga, Fran

Snowball Solutions color *Trail Rider* v29 no1 p30 Ja/F 2017

Winter Hoof Care color *Trail Rider* v29 no1 p30 Ja/F 2017

JURIS, CAROLYN

AUDIO BESTSELLERS chart color *Publishers Weekly* v264 no41 p16 O 9 2017

AUDIO BESTSELLERS chart *Publishers Weekly* v264 no28 p16 Jl 10 2017

AUDIO BESTSELLERS chart *Publishers Weekly* v264 no7 p15 F 13 2017

BESTSELLERS chart color graph *Publishers Weekly* v264 no20 p12 My 15 2017

BESTSELLERS chart *Publishers Weekly* v263 no50 p17 D 5 2016

BESTSELLERS chart *Publishers Weekly* v264 no30 p12 Jl 24 2017

BESTSELLERS chart *Publishers Weekly* v264 no31 p13 Jl 31 2017

BESTSELLERS chart *Publishers Weekly* v264 no7 p12 F 13 2017

BESTSELLERS OCTOBER 17–23 2016 chart color *Publishers Weekly* v263 no44 p13 O 31 2016

BESTSELLERS SEPTEMBER 26-OCTOBER 2, 2016 *Publishers Weekly* v263 no41 p15 O 10 2016

CATEGORY BESTSELLERS chart *Publishers Weekly* v263 no42 p17 O 17 2016

CATEGORY BESTSELLERS chart *Publishers Weekly* v264 no16 p17 Ap 17 2017

CATEGORY BESTSELLERS chart *Publishers Weekly* v264 no41 p15 O 9 2017

CATEGORY BESTSELLERS chart *Publishers Weekly* v264 no7 p16 F 13 2017

CHILDREN'S BESTSELLERS chart *Publishers Weekly* v263 no42 p16 O 17 2016

CHILDREN'S BESTSELLERS chart *Publishers Weekly* v264 no10 p16 Mr 6 2017

CHILDREN'S BESTSELLERS chart *Publishers Weekly* v264 no24 p15 Je 12 2017

CHILDREN'S BESTSELLERS chart *Publishers Weekly* v264 no30 p14 Jl 24 2017

CHILDREN'S BESTSELLERS chart *Publishers Weekly* v264 no39 p19 S 25 2017

Ferrante Hot in Summer chart *Publishers Weekly* v264 no35 p26 Ag 28 2017

France Loves Calendar Girl chart map *Publishers Weekly* v264 no12 p22 Mr 20 2017

Game Face chart color graph *Publishers Weekly* v264 no32 p10 Ag 7 2017

'History of Bees' Still Buzzing chart *Publishers Weekly* v264 no30 p16 Jl 24 2017

iBook Bestsellers chart color *Publishers Weekly* v264 no12 p21 Mr 20 2017

iBook Bestsellers chart color *Publishers Weekly* v264 no21 p18 My 22 2017

iBook Bestsellers chart color *Publishers Weekly* v264 no30 p15 Jl 24 2017

iBook Bestsellers chart color *Publishers Weekly* v264 no31 p16 Jl 31 2017

iBOOKS AUDIO TOP 10 chart color *Publishers Weekly* v264 no19 p17 My 8 2017

iBooks Bestsellers chart color *Publishers Weekly* v263 no50 p20 D 5 2016

iBooks Bestsellers chart color *Publishers Weekly* v264 no38 p21 S 18 2017

iBooks Bestsellers chart color *Publishers Weekly* v264 no7 p17 F 13 2017

Royal Family chart color graph *Publishers Weekly* v264 no8 p11 F 20 2017

SMASHWORDS SELF-PUBLISHED BESTSELLERS LIST, AUGUST 2017 bw chart color *Publishers Weekly* v264 no41 p18 O 9 2017

SMASHWORDS SELF-PUBLISHED BESTSELLERS LIST, MAY 2017 chart color *Publishers Weekly* v264 no28 p19 Jl 10 2017

SMASHWORDS SELF-PUBLISHED BESTSELLERS LIST, NOVEMBER 2016 chart color *Publishers Weekly* v264 no3 p20 Ja 16 2017

Spring Fever chart color graph *Publishers Weekly* v264 no15 p17 Ap 10 2017

Springsteen Plays Well Abroad chart map *Publishers Weekly* v263 no42 p18 O 17 2016

'Trees' Takes Root in France, Germany chart color *Publishers Weekly* v264 no39 p21 S 25 2017

Trump Bump bw color *Publishers Weekly* v264 no6 p37 F 6 2017

Jurisdiction

U.S. Court Jurisdiction and Foreign States *Congressional Digest* v95 no9 p5 N 2016

The Zone of Death K. PETERSON *Idaho Magazine* v16 no5 p45 F 2017

KADISH, SETH
C-SUITE GIGS: A WEB OF MAD SKILLS diag *Wired* v25 no9 p18 S 2017
DATA IN THE HOUSE: WHERE TO MOVE NOW color graph *Wired* v25 no8 p18 Ag 2017

Kadivar, Mohsen
People K. L. Gilbert color *Christian Century* v134 no6 p17 Mr 15 2017

Kadlec, Dan
The Military's Got a New Spin on Retirement color diag *Money* v46 no6 p28 Jl 2017
RETIREES FLOCK SOUTH AND WEST color *Money* v46 no2 p20 Mr 2017

Kae Nemoto
Optical circulators reach the quantum level bibl diag *Science* v354 no6319 p1532 D 23 2016

Kaebnick, Gregory E.
Precaution and governance of emerging technologies bibl color *Science* v354 no6313 p710 N 11 2016

Kael, Pauline
The Critic AND THE STAR L. ANOLIK bw cartoon *Vanity Fair* p180 Hollywood 2017 Supplement

Kaepernick, Colin, 1987-
Boycotts and Brain Damage Cast a Dark Shadow Over Football Season S. Gregory color *Time* v190 no10/11 p25 S 18 2017
Citizenship on Its Knees P. J. Williams *Nation* v305 no10 p10 O 23 2017
Everything All the Time D. FOSTER color *National Review* v69 no19 p60 O 16 2017
Getting Riled Up Over the Knee Jerk J. COST color *Weekly Standard* v23 no5 p18 O 9 2017
HOT | NOT T. Keith color *Sports Illustrated* v125 no17 p24 N 21 2016 Double Issue
HOT | NOT T. Keith color *Sports Illustrated* v126 no9 p24 Mr 27 2017
Kaepernick's Legacy Lives On D. ZIRIN color *Progressive* v81 no7 p68 O/N 2017
Knee High M. Rosenberg and T. Keith color *Sports Illustrated* v126 no10 p21 Ap 10 2017
The Season for Dissent D. ZIRIN *Progressive* v81 no10 p44 N 2016
Star-Spangled PROTEST [Cover story] C. STOFFERS and S. Borden *New York Times Upfront* v149 no3 p8 O 10 2016
Taking a Knee Deserves a Knee—in the Gut *USA Today Magazine* v145 no2860 p15 Ja 2017
What Kaepernick Started E. Thomas bw *Progressive* v81 no10 p29 N 2016

Kaepernick, Colin, 1987——Political & social views
Beyond Words L. J. Wertheim and T. Keith color *Sports Illustrated* v125 no12 p16 O 10 2016
On Sports J. C. Kang *New York Times Magazine* p22 O 16 2016
Taking on the Bully Empire cartoon *Progressive* v81 no10 p6 N 2016

Kaeser, Joe
Looking for Answers to the World's Biggest Challenges In the Eternal City color *Time* v188 no24 p31 D 12 2016

Kaesŏng-si (Korea)
A Last Glance at North Korea D. STONE color map *National Geographic* v232 no5 p136 N 2017

Kafina, Martin D.
Restored iron transport by a small molecule promotes absorption and hemoglobinization in animals color graph *Science* v356 no6338 p608 My 12 2017

Kafka, Franz, 1883-1924
BREATHE F. KAFKA color *Prevention* v69 no6 p38 Je 2017
THE ESCAPE ARTIST: Nicole Krauss and her precursors R. Franklin *Harper's Magazine* p90 S 2017

Kagan, Elena, 1960-
Supreme Court may lean toward Lutheran school in public funds dispute R. Wolf color *Christian Century* v134 no11 p15 My 24 2017

Kagan, Vladimir
$1 million Day *Treasures* v6 no2 p8 O/N 2016

Kageleiyr, Jamie
swim your way stronger [Cover story] chart color *Redbook* p77 Je 2017

Kahan, Tamar
Host cell attachment elicits posttranscriptional regulation in infecting enteropathogenic bacteria bibl graph *Science* v355 no6326 p735 F 17 2017

Kaha:wi (Performer)
THE WIDE WORLD OF CONTEMPORARY DANCE N. LOEFFLER-GLADSTONE color *Dance Spirit* v20 no10 p42 D 2016

KAHL, COLIN H.
Nuclear Summer color *New Republic* v248 no8/9 p6 Ag/S 2017

Kahl, P.
Revealing the subfemtosecond dynamics of orbital angular momentum in nanoplasmonic vortices bibl diag *Science* v355 no6330 p1187 Mr 17 2017

Kahl, Stephan
Preparing to Pop a Bubble, Just in Case color *Bloomberg Businessweek* no4535 p29 Ag 28 2017

Kahlenberg, Richard D.
Why Segregated Neighborhoods Persist color *Washington Monthly* v49 no6-8 p72 Je-Ag 2017

Kahler, David M.
Clockwork Futures color *Science* v357 no6355 p967 S 8 2017

Kahler, Kalyn
Leading Off color *Sports Illustrated* v126 no17 p8 Je 19 2017
WHAT IF? ... GEORGE HALAS—AND THE NFL—HAD SUNK IN LAKE MICHIGAN? color *Sports Illustrated* v126 no11 p51 Ap 17-24 2017

Kahlstatt, Josefine
Activity-dependent spatially localized miRNA maturation in neuronal dendrites bibl graph *Science* v355 no6325 p634 F 10 2017

Kahn, Anna
Data Can Do for Change Management What It Did for Marketing *Harvard Business Review Digital Articles* p2 Jl 31 2017
Email and Calendar Data Are Helping Firms Understand How Employees Work *Harvard Business Review Digital Articles* p2 Ag 28 2017

Kahn, Claire
Change & Continuity M. McCowan color *American Craft* v77 no3 p72 Je/Jl 2017

Kahn, David
Flashback color *Sports Illustrated* v126 no18 p12 Je 26 2017

Kahn, Eve M.
Setting the stage bw color *Magazine Antiques* v184 no3 p74 My/Je 2017

KAHN, GABRIEL
Civil Rights And Trump *Los Angeles Magazine* p98 Ap 2017
A Local Pol with A Global Profile color *Los Angeles Magazine* v62 no7 p58 Jl 2017
Not In Their Backyard *Los Angeles Magazine* p74 F 2017
Of Scorched Earth and Skyscrapers *Los Angeles Magazine* v61 no11 p26 N 2016

Kahn, Jennifer
'Primitive Technology' color *New York Times Magazine* p24 D 4 2016

Kahn, Jeremy
Digital Banks Take On The High Street Giants *Bloomberg Businessweek* no4493 p50 O 3 2016
Europe's Startup Factory Sputters color *Bloomberg Businessweek* no4495 p31 O 17 2016
From Angry Birds to Particle Physics color *Bloomberg Businessweek* no4508 p30 Ja 23 2017
How Facebook Could Stop bw color *Bloomberg Businessweek* no4524 p56 My 29 2017
The Smartest Machines Are Playing Games color *Bloomberg Businessweek* no4517 p34 Ap 3 2017

Kahn, Matthew E.
Can America's Blue States Tackle Climate Change on Their Own? color *Harvard Business Review Digital Articles* p2 Je 6 2017
How the Insurance Industry Can Push Us to Prepare for Climate Change *Harvard Business Review Digital Articles* p2 Ag 28 2017
The More Climate Skeptics There Are, the Fewer Climate Entrepreneurs *Harvard Business Review Digital Articles* p2 Mr 16 2017
Requiring Companies to Disclose Climate Risks Helps Everyone *Harvard Business Review Digital Articles* p2 F 16 2017
Rising Sea Levels Won't Doom U.S. Coastal Cities *Harvard Busi-*

ness Review Digital Articles p2 Ja 20 2016

Kahn, Mattie

Every Woman Is an Activist color *Glamour* v115 no3 p162 Mr 2017

Kahn, Misha

CHAOS THEORY H. MARTIN color *Architectural Digest* no11 p142 N 1 2017

Kahraman, Abdullah

Cell-wide analysis of protein thermal unfolding reveals determinants of thermostability color *Science* v355 no6327 p812 F 24 2017

Kahraman, Hayv

ART OF WAR V. LOWRY color *Architectural Digest* v73 no11 p92 N 2016

Kahuno, Elizabeth

Deconstructing behavioral neuropharmacology with cellular specificity color *Science* v356 no6333 p42 Ap 7 2017

Kai Chen

Directed evolution of cytochrome c for carbon–silicon bond formation: Bringing silicon to life bibl diag graph *Science* v354 no6315 p1048 N 25 2016

Kai Chi (Sam) Yam

Leadership Takes Self-Control. Here's What We Know About It color *Harvard Business Review Digital Articles* p2 Je 5 2017

Kai Liu

Anomalously low electronic thermal conductivity in metallic vanadium dioxide bibl graph *Science* v355 no6323 p371 Ja 27 2017

Kaibab National Forest (Ariz.)

Jacob Lake Ranger Station N. AUSTIN *Arizona Highways* v96 no7 p6 Jl 2017

Kaidi, Austin

Fixing the Recruiting and Retention Problems in Britain's NHS *Harvard Business Review Digital Articles* p2 2017

Kaifala, Joseph

The Man Who Would Be King or Vicar: Was the new king of Sierra Leone poisoned on his return voyage from England? *History Today* v67 no10 p14 O 2017

Kaifu Chen

RPA binds histone H3-H4 and functions in DNA replication–coupled nucleosome assembly bibl graph *Science* v355 no6323 p415 Ja 27 2017

Kaihoi, David

"YOU CAN GET AWAY WITH MORE IN A SMALL SPACE," D. SCHWARTZ color *Better Homes & Gardens* v95 no9 p36 S 2017

Kaijie Zheng

High-resolution interrogation of functional elements in the noncoding genome bibl graph *Science* v353 no6307 p1545 S 30 2016

Kaiko, Gerard E.

The microbial metabolite desaminotyrosine protects from influenza through type I interferon graph *Science* v357 no6350 p498 Ag 4 2017

Kail, Ryan

10 TIPS FOR RANCH LOGS color *Horse & Rider* v56 no2 p54 F 2017

Kail, Thomas

YOURS Truly A. GREEN color *Vogue* v206 no11 p182 N 2016

Kailus, Katie

MUSICIANS' GEAR GUIDE BEST OF THE 2017 NAMM SHOW color *Downbeat* v84 no4 p70 Ap 2017

Kain, Karen

30 Years Ago This Month color *Dance Magazine* v91 no3 p67 Mr 2017

Kaine, Timothy M. (Timothy Michael), 1958-

KAINE COUNTRY E. OSNOS bw cartoon *New Yorker* v92 no34 p40 O 24 2016

A KINDER TRUMAN DOCTRINE M. HANIS *Foreign Affairs* v96 no6 p175 N/D 2017

Leaders color *Time* v189 no16/17 p64 My 1-8 2017

A New Truman Doctrine color *Foreign Affairs* v96 no4 p36 Jl/Ag 2017

Tim Kaine's Top Five A. GREENE color *Rolling Stone* no1273 p15 N 3 2016

Why Pence Matters W. Kristol *Weekly Standard* v22 no6 p6 O

17 2016

Kaine, Timothy M. (Timothy Michael), 1958—Political & social views

For the Record color *Time* v188 no15 p4 O 17 2016

Kaino, Glenn—Interviews

DESIGNING the undefinable M. S. Eddy *Stage Directions* v30 no8 p18 Ag 2017

Kains, Noé

Relativistic deflection of background starlight measures the mass of a nearby white dwarf star chart color graph *Science* v356 no6342 p1046 Je 9 2017

Kaiser, Cheryl R.

Diversity Policies Rarely Make Companies Fairer, and They Feel Threatening to White Men *Harvard Business Review Digital Articles* p2 Ja 4 2016

Kaiser, David

The Rockefeller Family Fund Takes on ExxonMobil color *New York Review of Books* v63 no20 p60 D 22 2016

The Rockefeller Family Fund vs. Exxon color *New York Review of Books* v63 no19 p31 D 8 2016

The Rockefeller Family Fund vs. Exxon D. Kaiser and L. Wasserman color *New York Review of Books* v63 no19 p31 D 8 2016

KAISER, DAVID I.

A COSMIC CONTROVERSY color *Scientific American* v317 no1 p5 Jl 2017

Kaiser, Henry

Kaiser Dives into Intriguing Waters J. Ephland color *Downbeat* v84 no3 p17 Mr 2017

Kaiser, Jocelyn

Baby genome screening needs more time to gestate color *Science* v354 no6311 p398 O 28 2016

Congress votes on sweeping biomedical bill color *Science* v354 no6316 p1085 D 2 2016

Critics challenge NIH finding that bigger labs aren't necessarily better color *Science* v356 no6342 p997 Je 9 2017

How biologists pioneered preprints—with paper and postage bw *Science* v357 no6358 p1348 S 29 2017

Mixed results from cancer replications unsettle field graph *Science* v355 no6322 p234 Ja 20 2017

NIH abandons grant cap, offers new help to younger scientists *Science* v356 no6343 p1108 Je 16 2017

NIH overhead plan draws fire color *Science* v356 no6341 p893 Je 1 2017

NIH redefines clinical trials, attracting critics color *Science* v357 no6348 p236 Jl 21 2017

NIH's massive health study is off to a slow start color *Science* v357 no6355 p955 S 8 2017

NIH to cap grants for well-funded investigators graph *Science* v356 no6338 p574 My 12 2017

Personalized tumor vaccines keep cancer in check color *Science* v356 no6334 p122 Ap 14 2017

THE PREPRINT DILEMMA chart color graph *Science* v357 no6358 p1344 S 29 2017

Qatar's genome effort slowly gears up color *Science* v354 no6317 p1220 D 9 2016

Regulators drop controversial biospecimen consent proposal color *Science* v355 no6323 p335 Ja 27 2017

WHEN DNA AND CULTURE CLASH color map *Science* v354 no6317 p1217 D 9 2016

WHEN LESS IS MORE color graph *Science* v355 no6330 p1144 Mr 17 2017

Kaiser, Laura S.

Turning Value-Based Health Care into a Real Business Model *Harvard Business Review Digital Articles* p2 O 8 2015

Kaiser, M.

Inhibitors of PEX14 disrupt protein import into glycosomes and kill Trypanosoma parasites chart color diag graph *Science* v355 no6332 p1416 Mr 31 2017

Kaiser, Robert B.

Too Much Charisma Can Make Leaders Look Less Effective *Harvard Business Review Digital Articles* p2 S 26 2017

What Science Says About Identifying High-Potential Employees *Harvard Business Review Digital Articles* p2 O 3 2017

Kaiser, Robert G.

The Closed Mind of Mitch color *New York Review of Books* v63 no17 p38 N 10 2016

Kaiser Fung
An Important Data Lesson from an Inconsequential Football Scandal *Harvard Business Review Digital Articles* p2 Ja 30 2015

Kaivalya, Alanna
A home practice to re-energize and find greater joy color *Yoga Journal* no288 p55 D 2016

Kaiyuan Zheng
The biosynthetic pathway of coenzyme F430 in methanogenic and methanotrophic archaea bibl diag graph *Science* v354 no6310 p339 O 21 2016

Kaizuka, Izumi
Terawatt-scale photovoltaics: Trajectories and challenges chart graph *Science* v356 no6334 p141 Ap 14 2017

Kajastila, Raine—Interviews
Augmented Climbing Games B. BLANCHARD color *Climbing* no351 p20 F/Mr 2017

Kakad, Meetali
Getting Buy-In for Predictive Analytics in Health Care *Harvard Business Review Digital Articles* p2 Je 20 2017

Kakaes, Konstantin
Bad Math Props Up Border Wall diag graph il *MIT Technology Review* v119 no6 p18 N/D 2016

Kakkar, Rita
Atomic and Molecular Spectroscopy K. Lehmann *Physics Today* v69 no10 p57 O 2016

Kakuda, Shinako
Notch-Jagged complex structure implicates a catch bond in tuning ligand sensitivity bibl diag graph *Science* v355 no6331 p1320 Mr 24 2017

Kakui, Yasutaka
Building chromosomes without bricks [Cover story] diag *Science* v356 no6344 p1233 Je 23 2017

Kakutani, Michiko
The End of the Lone-Wolf Critic The Times after "Voice of God" Michiko Kakutani B. Kachka img *New York* v50 no17 p36 Ag 21 2017
Who Critiques The Critic? I. TUTTLE color *National Review* v69 no16 p21 Ag 28 2017

Kala, Namrata
An Experiment in India Shows How Much Companies Have to Gain by Investing in Their Employees *Harvard Business Review Digital Articles* p1 Jl 25 2017

Kalahari Development LLC
THE ULTIMATE FAMILY GETAWAY color *Good Housekeeping* v264 no4 p142 Ap 2017

Kalamazoo (Mich.)—Economic conditions
Another Way to Tap the 1 Percent S. Friess and A. Albright color *Bloomberg Businessweek* no4493 p39 O 3 2016

Kalamboglas, John
Control of species-dependent cortico-motoneuronal connections underlying manual dexterity diag graph *Science* v357 no6349 p400 Jl 28 2017

Kalan, Elliott
SOUL CHECK *Harper's Magazine* v334 no2001 p19 F 2017

Kalanick, Travis, 1976-
15 TRAVIS KALANICK A. Lashinsky color *Fortune* v174 no7 p88 D 1 2016
ASK A FLOWCHART R. CAPPS diag *Wired* v25 no7 p96 Jl 2017
CORPORATE CONTRITION: WHO GROVELED BEST? color *Fortune* v175 no6 p15 My 1 2017
RIDING SHOTGUN WITH TRAVIS KALANICK [Cover story] A. Lashinsky color diag *Fortune* v175 no7 p36 Je 1 2017
Uber's CEO Has a Little Bit of Vanderbilt in Him J. Fox *Harvard Business Review Digital Articles* p2 N 25 2014
Uber's Taxicab Confessions E. Newcomer color *Bloomberg Businessweek* no4513 p26 Mr 6 2017
THE VALUE OF NOTHING A. MacKenzie color *Motor Trend* v68 no12 p118 D 2016
What Silicon Valley Can Learn from Travis Kalanick's Uber Fail M. Vella color *Time* v190 no1 p23 Jl 3 2017
What Uber Means for the Valley E. Griffith color *Fortune* v176 no1 p12 Jl 1 2017

Kalanick, Travis, 1976—Interviews
UBER'S RECKLESS DRIVER C. Leaf color *Fortune* v175 no7 p6 Je 1 2017

Kalanithi, Paul, 1977-2015

Cancer Does Discriminate M. Garb *In These Times* v40 no12 p40 D 2016
No. 2 WHEN BREATH BECOMES AIR L. Greenblatt color *Entertainment Weekly* no1444/1445 p104 D 16 2016

Kalanty, Michael
How to Bake More Bread: Modern Breads, Wild Yeast color *Publishers Weekly* v263 no43 p50e O 24 2016

Kalayanarooj, Siripen
Dengue diversity across spatial and temporal scales: Local structure and the effect of host population size bibl graph *Science* v355 no6331 p1302 Mr 24 2017

KALB, CLAUDIA
GENIUS bw color diag *National Geographic* v231 no5 p30 My 2017
Icons, Analyzed color *National Geographic* v231 no5 p144 My 2017

Kalb, Claudia—Interviews
Is There a Connection Between Entrepreneurship and Mental Health Conditions? D. McGinn *Harvard Business Review Digital Articles* p2 F 22 2016

Kalb, N.
Entanglement distillation between solid-state quantum network nodes diag *Science* v356 no6341 p928 Je 1 2017

Kalbermatten, Fredi
ELEMENTS bw color *Snowboarder* v29 no4 p84 D 2016

Kaldun, A.
Observing the ultrafast buildup of a Fano resonance in the time domain bibl diag graph *Science* v354 no6313 p738 N 11 2016
Spectral narrowing of x-ray pulses for precision spectroscopy with nuclear resonances diag *Science* v357 no6349 p375 Jl 28 2017

Kale
Buy 5, Drop 5 K. Glassman color *Women's Health* v13 no10 p98 D 2016
Can I video-chat with my kids even though I have an iPhone and they all have Androids? il *Consumer Reports* v82 no5 p23 My 2017
Go Green for Speed color *Health* v31 no1 p11 Ja 2017

Kalec, Will
Rob Gaudet color *Louisiana Life* v37 no3 p52 Ja/F 2017
Waterscapes bw color *Louisiana Life* v37 no4 p40 Mr/Ap 2017

Kaleidescape Inc.
THE ADVENTURES OF K'SCAPE R. SABIN *Sound & Vision* v81 no10 p8 D 2016
Did Streaming Finally Kill Serving? J. SCIACCA color *Sound & Vision* v81 no10 p26 D 2016

Kalel, V. C.
Inhibitors of PEX14 disrupt protein import into glycosomes and kill Trypanosoma parasites chart color diag graph *Science* v355 no6332 p1416 Mr 31 2017

Kalesse, Markus
RNA polymerase motions during promoter melting color diag graph *Science* v356 no6340 p863 My 26 2017

Kalev, Alexandra
How "Neutral" Layoffs Disproportionately Affect Women and Minorities *Harvard Business Review Digital Articles* p2 Jl 26 2016

Kalfar, Jaroslav
Space Oddities H. KUNZRU *New York Times Book Review* p11 Mr 26 2017

Kaliardos, James
Visionaire M. MULLEN *Interview* v46 no9 p42 N 2016

Kalimat Publishing (Company)
OUR STORIES TRAVEL THE WORLD T. SAID color *Publishers Weekly* v263 no43 p(Sp)9 O 24 2016
U.A.E.'s Kalimat Celebrates 10th Anniversary E. Nawotka color *Publishers Weekly* v264 no29 p4 Jl 17 2017

Kalina, Richard
THE HERE AND THEN bw cartoon color *Art in America* v105 no4 p72 Ap 2017

Kaling, Mindy
THE MINDY PROJECT A. Bacle color *Entertainment Weekly* no1477 p32 Ag 11 2017
THE MINDY PROJECT R. Moynihan *TV Guide* v64 no15 p53 Ap 4 2016
WHY I LOVE MY CUSTOM PEARL NECKLACE color *InStyle* v24 no10 p254 O 2017

KALISH, ABRAHAM H.
FROM THE ARCHIVES bw cartoon *Reason* v48 no11 p70 Ap 2017

Kalish, Susan
A Globally Rare eco system *Parks & Recreation* v52 no4 p38 Ap 2017

Kalisky, Tomer
Stromal Gli2 activity coordinates a niche signaling program for mammary epithelial stem cells color *Science* v356 no6335 p284 Ap 21 2017

Kalitta, Connie—Interviews
Take 5 With CONNIE KALITTA T. Taylor bw color *Hot Rod* v70 no1 p20 Ja 2017

KALLET, BRAD
James Blake's Next Challenge *Tennis* v52 no6 p22 N/D 2016

Kallman, Neil J.
Kilogram-scale prexasertib monolactate monohydrate synthesis under continuous-flow CGMP conditions chart diag *Science* v356 no6343 p1144 Je 16 2017

Kalloch, Sarah
How 4 Retailers Became "Best Places to Work" color *Harvard Business Review Digital Articles* p2 Ja 2 2017
Transforming Today's Bad Jobs into Tomorrow's Good Jobs *Harvard Business Review Digital Articles* p2 Je 12 2017

Kallor, Amber
But First, SKIN CARE color *Women's Health* v14 no1 p54 Ja/F 2017
GLITTER FOR GROWN-UPS cartoon *Harper's Bazaar* no3651 p418 Mr 2017

KALLOSH, RENATA
A COSMIC CONTROVERSY color *Scientific American* v317 no1 p5 Jl 2017

Kallquist & Associates Architects LLP
ARCHITECTS, DESIGNERS & ENGINEERS color *Log Home Living* p127 2018 Annual Buyers Guide

KALMAN, CHRIS
A League of Her Own color *Climbing* no351 p26 F/Mr 2017
Slow Children color *Climbing* no350 p26 D 2016/Ja 2017

KALMAN, MAIRA
SKETCHBOOK cartoon *New Yorker* v92 no38 p73 N 21 2016

Kalmansohn, David
Black COHOSH color *Vegetarian Times* v43 no2 p30 N/D 2016

Kalmbach, Al
Was Al Kalmbach a railroader? J. Dziedzic color *Model Railroader* v84 no4 p100 Ap 2017

Kalodimos, Charalampos G.
Enzymes at work are enzymes in motion diag *Science* v355 no6322 p247 Ja 20 2017

Kalogera, Vicky
3 Cosmic Chirps & Counting *Sky & Telescope* v134 no3 p24 S 2017

Kalotay, Daphne
The Shortlist: Essays *New York Times Book Review* p26 D 18 2016

Kalsi, Priti
How One Law Measurably Lifted the Status of Women in India *Harvard Business Review Digital Articles* p2 Mr 16 2017

Kaltenheuser, Steve
FIGHTING BACK K. Birchmier *Successful Farming* v114 no10 p42 O 2016

Kaluuya, Daniel
Fear of a White Village R. DOUTHAT color *National Review* v69 no8 p43 My 2017

Kalyuzhniy, Oleksandr
Priming HIV-1 broadly neutralizing antibody precursors in human Ig loci transgenic mice bibl graph *Science* v353 no6307 p1557 S 30 2016

Kam, Kaiwen
Breathing control center neurons that promote arousal in mice diag graph *Science* v355 no6332 p1411 Mr 31 2017

KAM, KEN
Driven color *Forbes* v199 no5 p46 My 16 2017
The Right Chemistry chart color *Forbes* v200 no4 p35 O 24 2017

Kamal, Archana
Suppressing relaxation in superconducting qubits by quasiparticle pumping bibl graph *Science* v354 no6319 p1573 D 23 2016

Kamal, Maha
Finding Trump's Refugee Policy *Humanist* v77 no2 p9 Mr/Ap 2017

Kamali, Norma, 1945-
Norma Kamali E. Wilson color *InStyle* v23 no12 p87 N 2016

KAMATA, JUN
Unofficial Paths: Memories of Poston *Orion Magazine* v35 no4/5 p51 Jl-O 2016

Kamath, Ganesh
Quantitative 3D evolution of colloidal nanoparticle oxidation in solution diag graph *Science* v356 no6335 p303 Ap 21 2017

Kamau, Khalid
RED DAWN T. Murphy *Mother Jones* v42 no3 p10 My/Je 2017

KAMBACH, STEPHAN
Harmonizing Biodiversity Conservation and Productivity in the Context of Increasing Demands on Landscapes graph *BioScience* v66 no10 p890 O 1 2016

Kambeitz, O.
Observation of a large-scale anisotropy in the arrival directions of cosmic rays above 8×1018 eV *Science* v357 no6357 p1266 S 22 2017

Kamcev, Jovan
Maximizing the right stuff: The trade-off between membrane permeability and selectivity color *Science* v356 no6343 p1137 Je 16 2017

Kamel, Deena
THE WORLD IS NOT ENOUGH [Cover story] color *Bloomberg Businessweek* no4506 p34 Ja 9 2017

Kamenev, Dmitry
Multipotent peripheral glial cells generate neuroendocrine cells of the adrenal medulla color *Science* v357 no6346 p46 Jl 7 2017

Kamensky, Jane
DEPICTING REVOLUTION AND INDEPENDENCE G. Goodwin *History Today* v67 no8 p102 Ag 2017
Red, White, Black and Blue: A study of the American Revolution takes violence as its overriding focus *New York Times Book Review* p27 My 21 2017

KAMEON, JUDY
everyday getaway color *Better Homes & Gardens* v95 no6 p77 Je 2017

Kamer, Foster
Craps *New York Times Magazine* p28 O 16 2016

Kameradschaft (Film)
Between Two Fires M. Nelson bw *Film Comment* v53 no1 p11 Ja/F 2017

Kamerling, S. J.
Entanglement distillation between solid-state quantum network nodes diag *Science* v356 no6341 p928 Je 1 2017

Kamil, Alan
Cognition-mediated evolution of low-quality floral nectars bibl graph *Science* v355 no6320 p1 Ja 6 2017

KAMIN, BLAIR
A New Angle color diag *Architectural Record* v205 no2 p74 F 2017
Packing a Punch: A new corporate headquarters makes a big impact both inside and out color map *Architectural Record* v205 no5 p104 My 2017

Kamin, Jennie
America's growing news deserts map *Columbia Journalism Review* v56 no1 p34 Spr 2017

Kaminski, Clemens F.
De novo design of a biologically active amyloid bibl graph *Science* v354 no6313 paah4949-1 N 11 2016

Kaminski, James
The epigenetic landscape of T cell exhaustion bibl graph *Science* v354 no6316 p1165 D 2 2016

Kamiński, Lukasz
WWI'S WONDER DRUG *MHQ: Quarterly Journal of Military History* v29 no2 p44 Wint 2017

Kaminsky, Adolfo
THE FORGER J. BERGER *New York Times Upfront* v149 no8 p16 Ja 30 2017

KAMINSKY, ILYA
Red Ripening *New York Times Book Review* p20 F 12 2017

Kamisetty, Hetunandan
Protein structure determination using metagenome sequence data color graph *Science* v355 no6322 p294 Ja 20 2017

KAMIYA, GARY

THE WILDERNESS OUT YOUR FRONT DOOR *Sierra* v102 no3 p42 My/Je 2017

KAMMEN, DANIEL M.

Advancing clean energy *Issues in Science & Technology* v33 no3 p5 Spr 2017

Kammerlander, Nadine

Research: Family Firms Are More Innovative Than Other Companies color *Harvard Business Review Digital Articles* p2 Ja 25 2017

Kammhuber, J.

Demonstration of an ac Josephson junction laser bibl diag *Science* v355 no6328 p939 Mr 3 2017

Kamo, Chomei, 1153?-1216?

1212: Hino Kamo no Chomei *Lapham's Quarterly* v10 no1 p187 Wint 2017

Kamookak, Louie

THE EXPEDITIONS color map *Canadian Geographic* v137 no4 p49 Jl/Ag 2017

KAMP, DAVID

THE ACCIDENTAL BOOKSHOP color *Vanity Fair* v58 no12 p112 D 2016

THE FORCE WAS WITH HER color *Vanity Fair* v59 no7 p36 Summ 2017

GOOD EVENING, VIETNAM bw *Vanity Fair* v59 no8 p58 Ag 2017

GRAND MOTEL color *Vanity Fair* v59 no1 p166 Holiday 2017

HANK AZARIA bw *Vanity Fair* v59 no5 p58 Ap 2017

ISABELLA ROSSELLINI bw *Vanity Fair* v59 no1 p106 Holiday 2017

IT'S A WONKA WORLD color *Vanity Fair* p187 Hollywood 2017 Supplement

Kingdom by the Sea color *Vanity Fair* v59 no10 p198 O 2017

MEGAN MULLALLY color *Vanity Fair* v59 no6 p60 My 2017

Nighty Night: Two books about the necessity and virtue of slumber *New York Times Book Review* p16 O 15 2017

PHILIPPE STARCK bw *Vanity Fair* v58 no12 p100 D 2016

What You Should Know About ADAM SCOTT bw *Vanity Fair* p108 Hollywood 2017 Supplement

WHAT YOU SHOULD KNOW ABOUT BECK bw *Vanity Fair* v59 no11 p78 N 2017

KAMP, MARIANNE

Broken Ties in the Ferghana Valley *Current History* v116 no792 p285 O 2017

The Soviet Legacy and Women's Rights in Central Asia *Current History* v115 no783 p270 O 2016

Kampert, K. H.

Observation of a large-scale anisotropy in the arrival directions of cosmic rays above 8×1018 eV *Science* v357 no6357 p1266 S 22 2017

Kampeska, Lake (S.D.)

TOP 7 Things Christine Erickson Loves About South Dakota *South Dakota Magazine* v32 no4 p17 N/D 2016

Kamphorst, Alice O.

Rescue of exhausted CD8 T cells by PD-1-targeted therapies is CD28-dependent bw diag graph *Science* v355 no6332 p1423 Mr 31 2017

KAMPION, DREW

Lessons From John bw color *Surfer* v58 no6 p56 O 2017

Kamps, Louisa

INDEPENDENT SPIRIT color *O, The Oprah Magazine* p113 My 2017

THE SUMMER EFFECT color *Martha Stewart Living* p50 Jl/Ag 2017

The Surprising Power of Self-Compassion color *Martha Stewart Living* no271 p42 Ja/F 2017

Kamran, Tahir

PAKISTAN: A FAILED STATE? Seventy years on from its creation, crisis-ridden Pakistan is a very different country from the one envisioned by its founder, Muhammad Ali Jinnah *History Today* v67 no9 p24 S 2017

KAN, MICHAEL

Old Windows PCs can stop WannaCry ransomware with new Microsoft patch color map *PCWorld* v35 no6 p22 Je 2017

WikiLeaks dump brings CIA spying powers into the spotlight color *PCWorld* v35 no4 p33 Ap 2017

Yahoo data breach affects at least 500 million users, company says color *PCWorld* p48 O 2016

Kan, S. B. Jennifer

Directed evolution of cytochrome c for carbon–silicon bond formation: Bringing silicon to life bibl diag graph *Science* v354 no6315 p1048 N 25 2016

Kan, Yinan

Inactivation of porcine endogenous retrovirus in pigs using CRISPR-Cas9 diag *Science* v357 no6357 p1303 S 22 2017

Kana Nishizawa

Is Japan Ready To Abandon Pacifism? color *Bloomberg Businessweek* no4536 p37 S 4 2017

Kanagaraj, Manoj

Distribution and clinical impact of functional variants in 50,726 whole-exome sequences from the DiscovEHR study chart graph *Science* v354 no6319 paaf6814-1 D 23 2016

Kanai, Aya

We're Heading Back to Project Runway Junior! color *Seventeen* v76 no12 p10 D 2016/Ja 2017

Kanakkanthara, Arun

Cyclin A2 is an RNA binding protein that controls Mre11 mRNA translation bibl graph *Science* v353 no6307 p1549 S 30 2016

Kanakri, Terry

The Transformation of the Puente Hills Landfill *Parks & Recreation* v52 no3 p20 Mr 2017

Kanan, Matthew W.

Bragg coherent diffractive imaging of single-grain defect dynamics in polycrystalline films color graph *Science* v356 no6339 p739 My 19 2017

Kanatzidis, M. G.

Extremely efficient internal exciton dissociation through edge states in layered 2D perovskites bibl graph *Science* v355 no6331 p1288 Mr 24 2017

Kanbach, Dominik

What BMW's Corporate VC Offers That Regular Investors Can't *Harvard Business Review Digital Articles* p2 Jl 27 2017

Kandemir, Asli

In Turkey It's Purge, Then Splurge *Bloomberg Businessweek* no4529 p31 Jl 3 2017

Kander, Diana

Help Your Team Stop Overcommitting by Empowering Them to Say No color *Harvard Business Review Digital Articles* p2 Je 6 2017

Kander, John, 1927-

THE REAL WOMEN OF "MURDERESS ROW" AND THE WOMAN WHO TOLD THEIR STORY R. Price *Cincinnati Magazine* v50 no8 p16 My 2017

KANDIAH, KRISH

WHEN GOD DOES THE UNEXPECTED color *Christianity Today* p52 Mr 2017

KANE, ALEX

Israeli Settlements Are Illegal. Equipping Their Guards Is Tax-Deductible *In These Times* v41 no3 p28 Mr 2017

Kane, Carol

GENE WILDER color *Entertainment Weekly* no1446/1447 p90 D 2016/Ja 2017

Kane, Colleen

THE INTERNET OF THINGS ... IN BED color *Fortune* v174 no6 p72 N 1 2016

KANE, EMILY A.

Antihistamine Alternatives color *Better Nutrition* p24 My 2017

Bounce Back color *Better Nutrition* v79 no7 p26 Jl 2017

Building a Better Gut color *Better Nutrition* v78 no12 p32 D 2016

CAN ALZHEIMER'S DISEASE BE PREVENTED? color *Amazing Wellness* v9 no3 p30 EarlySumm 2017

Feet First color *Better Nutrition* v79 no9 p26 S 2017

INSOMNIA SOLUTIONS color *Amazing Wellness* v9 no2 p28 Spr 2017

Natural Solutions for IBS cartoon *Better Nutrition* v79 no4 p28 Ap 2017

Potent Pigments color *Better Nutrition* v79 no10 p30 O 2017

Reduce Cancer Risk color *Amazing Wellness* v9 no1 p28 Wint 2017

Remember When? color *Better Nutrition* v79 no1 p32 Ja 2017

Sinus Solutions color *Better Nutrition* v78 no11 p28 N 2016

Sugar Swings [Cover story] color *Better Nutrition* v79 no11 p30

N 2017

Top 10 Natural Pain Relievers color *Better Nutrition* v79 no3 p28 Mr 2017

What is Hemochromatosis? color *Better Nutrition* v79 no6 p24 Je 2017

Kane, Florence

All Hail Annie Hall color *Glamour* v115 no4 p210 Ap 2017

AMERICA IS A STATE OF MIND color map *Glamour* v115 no9 p182 S 2017

Define Yourself color *Glamour* v115 no3 p60 Mr 2017

Do You Know These Labels? bw color *Glamour* v115 no3 p86 Mr 2017

Find Your Passion bw color *Glamour* v115 no3 p194 Mr 2017

For the Win color *Glamour* v115 no4 p62 Ap 2017

Hey, Jenna! color *Glamour* v115 no3 p92 Mr 2017

Hey, Stores: Where's My Size? cartoon color *Glamour* v115 no4 p76 Ap 2017

How to Look Less Tired bw color *Glamour* v115 no3 p120 Mr 2017

"I feel my best in this dress" color *Glamour* v115 no4 p55 Ap 2017

Katy's Got Sole color *Glamour* v115 no2 p25 F 2017

The Man Who Loves Women color *Glamour* v115 no3 p94 Mr 2017

Mix and Remix color *Glamour* v115 no4 p60 Ap 2017

Our Fall Favorites color *Glamour* no8 p62 Ag 2017

Outfits for Days color *Glamour* v115 no4 p74 Ap 2017

Pack Your Bags color *Glamour* v115 no3 p206 Mr 2017

Pretty, Please! color *Glamour* v115 no4 p58 Ap 2017

Purple's Reign color *Glamour* v115 no3 p212 Mr 2017

Recycled Style color *Glamour* v115 no4 p72 Ap 2017

Red-Carpet Revolution color *Glamour* v115 no3 p82 Mr 2017

Rihanna's Midnight Magic color *Glamour* v114 no11 p40 N 2016

Sleeve Game Strong color *Glamour* v115 no3 p62 Mr 2017

That Robe Life color *Glamour* v115 no3 p64 Mr 2017

Twice? Nice! color *Glamour* v115 no3 p74 Mr 2017

What to Know NOW color *Glamour* v114 no11 p72 N 2016

Work Those Resale Sites color *Glamour* v115 no10 p80 O 2017

Work Your Look color *Glamour* v115 no3 p166 Mr 2017

Your Spring Look Is Here color *Glamour* v115 no3 p59 Mr 2017

Kane, Jim

ELK THE KANE WAY T. CHRISTIE color *Outdoor Life* v224 no6 p37 Ag 2017

Kane, John F.

A CONCRETE FAITH B. McLAUGHLIN color *America* v215 no13 p35 O 31 2016

Without Walls S. Schloesser bw *Commonweal* v144 no11 p35 Je 16 2017

Kane, Julie Braman

Are We Any Safer? color *Atlantic* v318 no4 p14 N 2016

Kane, Maureen A.

Sustained virologic control in SIV+ macaques after antiretroviral and α4β7 antibody therapy bibl graph *Science* v354 no6309 p197 O 14 2016

Kane, Michael

Systematic mapping of functional enhancer–promoter connections with CRISPR interference bibl graph *Science* v354 no6313 p769 N 11 2016

KANE, MORGAN

HOW TO MAKE ANYTHING [Cover story] color diag *Popular Mechanics* p56 S 2017

Kane, Tim

The Crumbs of Capitalism *Commentary* v142 no2 p11 S 2016

Sanctuary and Sanctimony: Defying the law is defying the law—even if it's immigration law *Hoover Digest: Research & Opinion on Public Policy* no3 p69 Summ 2017

Kanefield, Teri, 1960-

Free to Be: Ruth Bader Ginsburg; The Story of Women and Law *Publishers Weekly* v263 no41 p72 O 10 2016

Kanekar, Nissim

[C II] 158-μm emission from the host galaxies of damped Lyman-alpha systems bibl color graph *Science* v355 no6331 p1285 Mr 24 2017

Kaneko, Yuki

Into the Snow color *Publishers Weekly* v263 no49 p13 D 7 2016

Kanellos, Nicolás, 1945-

Nicolás Kanellos Wins Tejano Association for Historical Preservation Award L. Ahuile color *Publishers Weekly* v264 no23 p16 Je 5 2017

KANG, DAVID C.

A New President Aims to Change South Korea's Course *Current History* v116 no791 p217 S 2017

KANG, ESTHER

Anna Valencia color *Chicago* v66 no6 p89 Je 2017

THE BOW TRUSS BEEF color *Chicago* v66 no5 p28 My 2017

Carlos Ramirez-Rosa color *Chicago* v66 no6 p95 Je 2017

LIVING MEMORY color *Chicago* v66 no10 p37 O 2017

Kang, Jay Caspian

Baseball is flirting with new rules. But if it really wants to embrace change - and speed things up - it should look to its ancient, woolier past *New York Times Magazine* p14 Ap 2 2017

A father's dilemma: Which baseball team will my baby daughter root for? *New York Times Magazine* p14 Jl 2 2017

The future of basketball as both sport and marketing enterprise can be glimpsed in the moves of seven-foot wonder athletes who handle the ball like point guards *New York Times Magazine* p17 Ja 22 2017

If sports betting is legalized, could its hunger for analytics restore an older, purer version of fandom? *New York Times Magazine* p16 Ap 30 2017

Not Without My Brothers [Cover story] *New York Times Magazine* p30 Ag 13 2017

On Sports *New York Times Magazine* p18 N 20 2016

Should professional athletes be allowed to use their status to talk about things more important than the games they play? *New York Times Magazine* p12 F 19 2017

Why are some stats—like baseball's 'exit velocity' this year—embraced more than others? *New York Times Magazine* p14 S 3 2017

Would major professional sports be better if the star athletes made more money and ran the leagues? *New York Times Magazine* p14 Jl 30 2017

Kang, S. Peter

Mismatch repair deficiency predicts response of solid tumors to PD-1 blockade chart graph *Science* v357 no6349 p409 Jl 28 2017

Kang, Shichang

Melting glaciers: Hidden hazards color *Science* v356 no6337 p495 My 5 2017

Kang, Sonia

The Unintended Consequences of Diversity Statements *Harvard Business Review Digital Articles* p2 Mr 29 2016

Kangaroo rats—Behavior

moisture misers P. Hess cartoon *Popular Science* v289 no2 p10 Mr/Ap 2017

Kangaroos

Laughter THE BEST MEDICINE *Reader's Digest* v189 no1127 p74 F 2017

Look! Kangaroos? B. PIKE cartoon *Power & Motoryacht* v34 no8 p160 Ag 2017

Kangasluoma, Juha

Global atmospheric particle formation from CERN CLOUD measurements bibl graph map *Science* v354 no6316 p1119 D 2 2016

Kangeq (Greenland)

THE GHOSTS OF KANGEQ H. HARMSEN color *Archaeology* v70 no3 p55 My/Je 2017

Kanigel, Robert

THE LIVING CITY B. C. Anderson *Claremont Review of Books* v17 no3 p80 Summ 2017

AN URBAN DEFENDER J. R. KELLY color *America* v215 no14 p32 N 7 2016

KANJI, AZEEZAH

Preventing Radicalization *Islamic Horizons* v46 no2 p18 Mr/Ap 2017

Kankiewicz, Kim

The Tights Stuff color *O, The Oprah Magazine* p126 Mr 2017

Kann, Victoria

Peterrific *Publishers Weekly* v264 no14 p75 Ap 3, 2017

Kannan, Harini

Cognitive science in the field: A preschool intervention durably enhances intuitive but not formal mathematics chart color diag graph *Science* v357 no6346 p47 Jl 7 2017

Kannan, Krishna

Yeast genome, by design bibl color *Science* v355 no6329 p1024 Mr 10 2017

Kanninen, Barbara

Contingent valuation: Flawed logic? color *Science* v357 no6349 p363 Jl 28 2017

Putting a value on injuries to natural assets: The BP oil spill chart *Science* v356 no6335 p253 Ap 21 2017

Kanoda, K.

Electronic crystal growth bw diag graph *Science* v357 no6358 p1378 S 29 2017

Kanon, Joseph

Collaborations P. KERR *New York Times Book Review* p26 Je 4 2017

Kanon, Joseph—Interviews

By the Book *New York Times Book Review* p10 Je 18 2017

Kansas

Grassroots Movements Invigorate Communities *Mother Earth News* no280 p5 F/Mr 2017

We're All in Kansas Now K. Wright il *Nation* v304 no12 p10 Ap 10 2017

Kansas City Chiefs (Football team)

2 Kansas City Chiefs color *Sports Illustrated* v127 no7 p81 S 4 2017

CHIEF CONCERN J. Jones color *Sports Illustrated* v126 no2 p44 Ja 16 2017

Kansas City Royals (Baseball team)

3 ROYALS color *Sports Illustrated* v126 no9 p85 Mr 27 2017

For the Record color *Time* v190 no13 p10 O 2 2017

Kansas State University—Sports

19 Kansas State color *Sports Illustrated* v127 no5 p108 Ag 14 2017

Kansas—Economic conditions

Burying Bad News A. Greenblatt *Governing* v30 no4 p11 Ja 2017

Kansteiner, Sarah

Pioneering painter leaves glowing mark on Ashland cartoon *Nebraska Life* v20 no6 p58 N/D 2016

Shaking up the BURGER SCENE in Kearney cartoon color *Nebraska Life* v20 no6 p30 N/D 2016

Kansteiner, Sarah Woodman

All trails lead to Ash Hollow color *Nebraska Life* v21 no4 p90 Jl/Ag 2017

Chester's Pencil Lady color *Nebraska Life* v21 no1 p62 Ja/F 2017

Delightful fusion of worldly food in Omaha color *Nebraska Life* v21 no4 p50 Jl/Ag 2017

Hunting for Nebraska spring treasure color *Nebraska Life* v21 no2 p16 Mr/Ap 2017

Into the Wild Blue Yonder with the Air National Guard color *Nebraska Life* v21 no4 p20 Jl/Ag 2017

THE SKINNY ON BLACK COW FAT PIG color *Nebraska Life* v21 no2 p28 Mr/Ap 2017

Volunteers launch Cold War icon back to life color *Nebraska Life* v21 no5 p18 S/O 2017

Winter fun heats up in Bellevue color *Nebraska Life* v21 no1 p66 Ja/F 2017

Kanstul Musical Instruments Inc.

Kanstul 1603 Committee Trumpet B. Zimmerman color *Downbeat* v84 no4 p92 Ap 2017

Kantae, Vasudev

Activity-based protein profiling reveals off-target proteins of the FAAH inhibitor BIA 10-2474 chart color graph *Science* v356 no6342 p1084 Je 9 2017

Kanter, Martha J.

College Promise: Pathway to the 21 Century *Change* v48 no6 p6 N/D 2016

Kanter, Michael

Health Care Providers Must Stop Wasting Patients' Time *Harvard Business Review Digital Articles* p2 My 24 2017

Kanter, Nancy

How Did I Get Here? N. KANTER bw color *Bloomberg Businessweek* no4504 p68 D 19 2016

Kanter, Rosabeth Moss

America's Leaders Need to Tell a New Story About Infrastructure *Harvard Business Review Digital Articles* p2 My 15 2015

America's Transportation Infrastructure Needs Entrepreneurs *Harvard Business Review Digital Articles* p2 My 13 2015

Small Wins Go a Long Way in Improving U.S. Rail Transportation *Harvard Business Review Digital Articles* p2 My 12 2015

Too Many Infrastructure Projects Go It Alone *Harvard Business Review Digital Articles* p2 My 14 2015

What It Will Take to Fix America's Crumbling Infrastructure *Harvard Business Review Digital Articles* p2 My 11 2015

Kanton (Kiribati)

ECLIPSED BY WAR N. Strochlic bw *National Geographic* v232 no2 p26 Ag 2017

Kantor, Emma

Rachel Ignotofsky: Sharing Her Passion for Science and History color *Publishers Weekly* v264 no11 p24 Mr 13 2017

Kantor, Jessica

The 3-Minute Interview bw *Glamour* no8 p40 Ag 2017

The 3-Minute Interview [Cover story] color *Glamour* v114 no11 p46 N 2016

Dear Diana, You Still Rule. Love, Everyone color *Glamour* v115 no9 p42 S 2017

The Scenes That Changed Everything color *Glamour* v115 no10 p50 O 2017

The Ultimate Beauty How-tos... color *Glamour* v115 no4 p204 Ap 2017

Kantor, Linda

Americans' Seafood Consumption Below Recommendations *Amber Waves: The Economics of Food, Farming, Natural Resources, & Rural America* p1 O 2016

Kantrowitz, David S.

Equifax and Why It's So Hard to Sue a Company for Losing Your Personal Information *Harvard Business Review Digital Articles* p2 S 22 2017

Kantrowitz, Tiby

50 Reasons to Love Being 50+ color *AARP: The Magazine* v60 no2A p67 F/Mr 2017

Kanze, Dana

Male and Female Entrepreneurs Get Asked Different Questions by VCs—and It Affects How Much Funding They Get *Harvard Business Review Digital Articles* p2 Je 27 2017

KANZE, EDWARD

In the Presence of Greatness color *Natural History* v125 no5 p48 My 2017

Kanzow, Torsten

Greater role for Atlantic inflows on sea-ice loss in the Eurasian Basin of the Arctic Ocean chart diag graph *Science* v356 no6335 p285 Ap 21 2017

Kao, Kaity C.

LITERATURE AS AN AGENT OF SOCIAL CHANGE: Promoting awareness of critical social issues in schools color *Literacy Today (2411-7862)* v34 no6 p40 My/Je 2017

Kao, Shuh-Ji

The complex effects of ocean acidification on the prominent N2-fixing cyanobacterium Trichodesmium graph *Science* v356 no6337 p527 My 5 2017

KAO USA Inc.

4 beauty tricks I just learned V. Kirby color *Redbook* p56 Ap 2017

Kaoru Inokuchi

Overlapping memory trace indispensable for linking, but not recalling, individual memories bibl graph *Science* v355 no6323 p398 Ja 27 2017

Kaos (Film)

Mother Tongue R. Brody color *New Yorker* v92 no45 p14 Ja 16 2017

Kapic, Kelly M.

Do We Need a New Word for 'Faith'? color *Christianity Today* v61 no6 p90 Jl/Ag 2017

Kaplan, Alice

Algeria's New Imprint bw color *Nation* v304 no11 p20 Ap 3 2017

Enigma Machine W. H. PRITCHARD color *Weekly Standard* v22 no17 p33 Ja 2 2017

LOOKING FOR 'THE STRANGER' E. DONALDSON bw color *Maclean's* v129 no43 p62 O 31 2016

Kaplan, David

CLASSICAL MUSIC *New Yorker* v93 no20 p10 Jl 10 2017

Lee Rubin: Our mentor and role model *Science* v355 no6327 p806 F 24 2017

Kaplan, Emily

Boston's School for Immigrants bw *Progressive* v81 no6 p38

KAPUR, DEVESH
Diasporas' Impacts on Economic Development *Current History* v115 no784 p298 N 2016

Kapur, Ratika
Underground Affair A. SRIRAM *New York Times Book Review* p9 D 18 2016

Kapur, Sahil
Chillary Clinton color *Bloomberg Businessweek* no4493 p35 O 3 2016

In Congress, It's Do-or-Die Time for the GOP cartoon *Bloomberg Businessweek* no4530 p39 Jl 17 2017

Planned Parenthood Is a GOP Land Mine *Bloomberg Businessweek* no4513 p32 Mr 6 2017

The Republican't Party *Bloomberg Businessweek* no4517 p27 Ap 3 2017

Show Us Your Tax Reforms color *Bloomberg Businessweek* no4517 p8 Ap 3 2017

A Tax Showdown At the Border cartoon *Bloomberg Businessweek* no4514 p25 Mr 13 2017

Trump vows to cut the corporate tax rate from 35% to 15%. Suppose Republicans could raise $2 trillion to pay for cuts (not an easy task). That would require hiking other taxes or ending popular deductions. And it can't all go to corporate giants, so... *Bloomberg Businessweek* no4538 p34 S 18 2017

UHMM...CARE *Bloomberg Businessweek* no4506 p20 Ja 9 2017

The Unmaking Of American Dreams chart *Bloomberg Businessweek* no4537 p36 S 11 2017

Kapur, Shekhar
Will Has a Famous Name, but It Lacks Light-Footed Grace D. D'addario color *Time* v190 no4 p51 Jl 24 2017

KAPUSHION, MARVIN
Senior Quarter Horse Geldings color *Horse & Rider* v56 no10 p53 O 2017

Kapustin, Eugene A.
Water harvesting from air with metal-organic frameworks powered by natural sunlight diag *Science* v356 no6336 p430 Ap 28 2017

Karabell, Zachary
Presidential Biographies A. Coe *New York Times Magazine* p18 F 19 2017

Karageorge, Eleni
My coworkers are making me sick *Monthly Labor Review* p1 N 2016

"Superstar" companies to blame for workers' falling share of income *Monthly Labor Review* p1 Ap 2017

Karako, Thomas
Homeland missile defense: How the United States got here bibl chart diag *Bulletin of the Atomic Scientists* v73 no3 p159 My 2017

A Missile Defense Agenda *National Review* v69 no18 p29 O 2 2017

Karalidi, T.
Zones, spots, and planetary-scale waves beating in brown dwarf atmospheres color graph *Science* v357 no6352 p683 Ag 18 2017

KARAMALES, JAY
HIDDEN SPRINGS *Idaho Magazine* v17 no1 p32 Ja 2017

Kara-Murza, Vladimir
A Defender Of His Country J. NORDLINGER color *National Review* v69 no7 p22 Ap 17 2017

Karamustafa, Gülsün, 1946-
GÜLSÜN KARAMUSTAFA A. Bier cartoon *Art in America* v104 no11 p130 D 2016

Karaoke
ABOVE & BEYOND bw *New Yorker* v93 no20 p20 Jl 10 2017

Karaoke at Home J. Zhang *New York Times Magazine* p24 Jl 9 2017

TESTING? TESTING? B. CROWDER *Virginia Living* v15 no1 p27 D 2016

Trap Karaoke Lets Fans Take Center Stage B. Danielle color *Ebony* v72 no9 p22 Jl/Ag 2017

Karaoke—Software
WHAT'S NEW AT THE APP STORE color *Macworld - Digital Edition* p65 F 2017

Karasawa, Takatoshi
Community network for deaf scientists color *Science* v356 no6336 p386 Ap 28 2017

Karate
AAU'S ROLE IN OLYMPIC KARATE TO BE DETERMINED color *Black Belt* v55 no1 p50 D 2016/Ja 2017

KARATE WINS ITS OLYMPIC BID F. BURK color *Black Belt* v55 no1 p44 D 2016/Ja 2017

REFLECTIONS ON A LIFETIME OF MARTIAL ARTS bw *Black Belt* v55 no2 p44 F/Mr 2017

Karate training
FINE-TUNE YOUR KARATE! D. LOWRY color *Black Belt* v55 no6 p40 O/N 2017

The Intricacies of Power D. Lowry color *Black Belt* v55 no4 p26 Je/Jl 2017

KARATE STRONG S. LENZI color *Black Belt* v55 no3 p34 Ap/My 2017

Karate—Competitions
KARATEPRO AWARDS BIG BUCKS IN LAS VEGAS color *Black Belt* v55 no1 p10 D 2016/Ja 2017

Karáth, Kata
'Safe spaces' may save the European mink color *Science* v357 no6352 p636 Ag 18 2017

Karaveli, Halil
Erdogan's Journey color *Foreign Affairs* v95 no6 p121 N/D 2016

KARBHARI, NADEEM
I'LL TELL YOU SOMETHING NADEEM KARBHARI *People Management* p18 F 2017

Karch, Fritz
LOVE STORY F. VIGNA color *Martha Stewart Living* no271 p116 Ja/F 2017

Karcher, Carolyn L., 1945-
Albion's Seeds E. M. YODER JR. bw *Weekly Standard* v22 no7 p37 O 24 2016

Karchmer-Klein, Rachel
TECHNOLOGY-SUPPORTED LEARNING color *Literacy Today (2411-7862)* v34 no3 p8 N/D 2016

Karchner, Sibel I.
The genomic landscape of rapid repeated evolutionary adaptation to toxic pollution in wild fish bibl graph *Science* v354 no6317 p1305 D 9 2016

KARCZYNSKI, DAVID
BRING ON THE NIGHT color *Outdoor Life* v224 no5 p36 Je/Jl 2017

BROWN UNIVERSITY color *Outdoor Life* v224 no2 p28 F/Mr 2017

PAIN, SUFFERING & MUSKIES color *Outdoor Life* v224 no8 p63 O 2017

Kardashian, Khloe, 1984-
10 Years of Kardashians: Khloé Looks Back J. Harman color *Glamour* v115 no10 p42 O 2017

KEEPING UP WITH THE KARDASHIANS: TEN YEARS AND COUNTING... D. Bianculli *TV Guide* v65 no39 p20 S 18 2017

Kardashian, Khloe, 1984-—Interviews
"It's OK to be whatever size you are" L. Chan color *Glamour* v114 no12 p116 D 2016

Kardashian, Kim, 1980-
GQHQ bw color *GQ: Gentlemen's Quarterly* v86 no12 p60 D 2016

L'Affaire Kardashian M. SEAL color *Vanity Fair* v59 no1 p150 Holiday 2017

Things M. McCluskey color *Time* v188 no25-26 p20 D 19 2016 Double Issue

KARDIAN, STEVE
BEWARE THE RED ZONE *USA Today Magazine* v146 no2868 p42 S 2017

Kardol, Paul
Plant-soil feedback and the maintenance of diversity in Mediterranean-climate shrublands bibl graph *Science* v355 no6321 p1 Ja 13 2017

Kardon, Gabrielle
Step out of the lab and engage color *Science* v355 no6330 p1234 Mr 17 2017

KAREIVA, PETER
Society Is Ready for a New Kind of Science--Is Academia? *BioScience* v67 no7 p591 Jl 2017

KAREN, JULIE
42 new ALL-STAR PRODUCTS of the year [Cover story] color *Redbook* p27 Jl/Ag 2017

Karenina, Anna (Fictitious character)
Throwing Anna Under the Train T. GITLIN *New York Times Book Review* p49 N 13 2016

KARETZKY, STEPHEN
Free Speech and Its Enemies *Commentary* v144 no3 p4 O 2017

Kargil War, 1999
TURNING POINT IN KARGIL P. Shukla color map *Military History* v34 no2 p38 Jl 2017

Karhoo (Company)
A Would-Be Uber Rival's Ride to Nowhere A. Satariano and D. Hellier cartoon *Bloomberg Businessweek* no4501 p28 N 28 2016

KARIM, ALIYA
Engaging with Our Trials and Tribulations *Islamic Horizons* v46 no1 p19 Ja/F 2017

KARIM, PERSIS
Driving While Female *Ms.* v27 no2 p43 Summ 2017

KARIM, SAMINA
RESTRUCTURE OR RECONFIGURE? *Harvard Business Review* v95 no2 p128 Mr/Ap 2017

Karimova, Gulnara, 1972-
Succession in the Silk Roads P. Frankopan *History Today* v67 no1 p4 Ja 2017

Karl, Andy
Time After Time A. Green color *Vogue* v207 no4 p240 Ap 2017

Karl, Dick
AN ADDICT SEEKS TO CHANGE color *Flying* v144 no1 p62 Ja 2017
AN AIRPLANE HANGER-ON color *Flying* v144 no7 p68 Jl 2017
AVIATION SIGHTS color *Flying* v144 no6 p70 Je 2017
CONSIDERING A CAREER IN THE CHARTER WORLD color *Flying* v144 no9 p70 S 2017
THE END OF A LOVE AFFAIR color *Flying* v143 no12 p70 D 2016
FLYING THE BOSS color *Flying* v144 no5 p70 My 2017
FLYING THE CANINE HIGHWAY color *Flying* v144 no4 p78 Ap 2017
LOOKING FOR A NEW AIRPLANE color *Flying* v144 no11 p68 N 2017
ON TENTERHOOKS bw *Flying* v144 no8 p70 Ag 2017
SHE'S GONE: A 17-YEAR LOVE AFFAIR COMES TO AN ABRUPT END color *Flying* v144 no10 p70 O 2017
THE SPLENDID END color *Flying* v144 no2 p70 F 2017
THERE, I SAID IT bw color *Flying* v144 no3 p78 Mr 2017
WE FLY: CESSNA CITATION CJ3+ chart color *Flying* v144 no11 p40 N 2017

Karl Lagerfeld SAS
WELCOME TO THE ISSUE *Harper's Bazaar* no3657 p50 O 2017

Karl Marx City (Film)
I HEARD A FLY BUZZ S. KLAWANS color *Nation* v304 no13 p36 Ap 17 2017

Karlan, Dean
Making Microfinance More Effective *Harvard Business Review Digital Articles* p2 O 5 2016

Karlesky, Matthew J.
Why Companies Are Becoming B Corporations *Harvard Business Review Digital Articles* p2 Je 17 2016

KARLGAARD, RICH
BEST SPORTS BOOKS FOR BUSINESS *Forbes* v198 no9 p34 D 30 2016
CITIES ARE THE FUTURE *Forbes* v198 no7 p38 N 29 2016
COMBAT CONSULTANT color *Forbes* v200 no4 p26 O 24 2017
DELL'S NEW DESTINY color *Forbes* v200 no2 p24 S 5 2017
DIGITAL DEATH STAR color *Forbes* v198 no6 p44 N 8 2016
FLIGHT'S NEXT ACE color *Forbes* v200 no1 p22 Jl 27 2017
How to Survive a Stampeding Elephant color *Forbes* v199 no6 p28 Je 13 2017
IMMIGRANTS KEEP CAPITALISM FRESH *Forbes* v198 no5 p56 O 25 2016
INVESTMENT THEMES 2017-20 *Forbes* v199 no4 p34 Ap 25 2017
TRUMP INFRASTRUCTURE SMART? *Forbes* v198 no8 p39 D 20 2016
TRUMP'S ECONOMIC ROAD MAP *Forbes* v199 no2 p41 F 28

2017
THE WARP-SPEED ENTREPRENEUR color *Forbes* v200 no5 p34 N 14 2017
WHAT TRUMP CAN DO—AND CAN'T *Forbes* v199 no1 p33 Ja 24 2017

Karlin, Mara
Why Military Assistance Programs Disappoint color *Foreign Affairs* v96 no6 p111 N/D 2017

Karlseder, Jan
TZAP: A telomere-associated protein involved in telomere length control bibl diag graph *Science* v355 no6325 p638 F 10 2017

Karlson, Krista
Basecamp Thanksgiving color *Backpacker* p32 N 2017
Sleep Warmer color *Backpacker* p27 N 2017

Karlsruher Institut für Technologie
THE UNBEARABLE LIGHTNESS OF NEUTRINOS A. Cho color diag map *Science* v356 no6345 p1322 Je 30 2017

Karlsson, Erik
"GOD BLESS ERIK KARLSSON" M. Farber chart color *Sports Illustrated* v126 no13 p46 My 8 2017

Karlsson, Mia
After 15,000 Miles: LESSONS LEARNED FROM HARDCORE OCEAN SAILING [Cover story] A. Schell color *Sail* v48 no8 p46 Ag 2017

Karlsson, Per-Ola
CEOs Are Getting Fired for Ethical Lapses More Than They Used To *Harvard Business Review Digital Articles* p2 Je 6 2017
Why CEOs Don't Get Fired as Often as They Used To *Harvard Business Review Digital Articles* p2 Je 15 2015

Karlsson, Sabina
BAND OF SISTERS color *Glamour* v115 no9 p164 S 2017
What's Inside SABINA KARLSSON'S Party Purse? J. Harman color *Glamour* v115 no1 p94 Ja 2017

Karlstrom, Leif
Mega-earthquakes rupture flat megathrusts bibl graph *Science* v354 no6315 p1027 N 25 2016

Karma
10,000 Dharma Doors J. Shaheen *Tricycle: The Buddhist Review* v26 no2 p12 Wint 2016
THE BUDDHA'S BAGGAGE T. BHIKKHU bw *Tricycle: The Buddhist Review* v26 no2 p78 Wint 2016
DAVID NICHTERN color *Tricycle: The Buddhist Review* v26 no2 p20 Wint 2016

Karma Automotive LLC
Karma Revero Back to the future C. Walton color *Motor Trend* v69 no9 p18 S 2017

Karmali, Naazneen
The Bitterest Pill cartoon color *Forbes* v199 no4 p38 Ap 25 2017
SALESMEN OF THE SUBCONTINENT color *Forbes* v199 no3 p80 Mr 28 2017
THE WORLD'S BILLIONAIRES bw color diag graph map *Forbes* v199 no3 p84 Mr 28 2017
THE WORLD'S MOST INNOVATIVE COMPANIES chart color *Forbes* v200 no2 p72 S 5 2017

KARMAN, PETE
DEAR ITT IDEOLOGIST *In These Times* v40 no12 p7 D 2016
DEAR ITT IDEOLOGIST *In These Times* v41 no8 p7 Ag 2017
snapshot *In These Times* v41 no1 p7 Ja 2017
snapshot *In These Times* v41 no3 p7 Mr 2017

Karman, Tawakkol
Women and the Arab Spring *UN Chronicle* v53 no4 p1 2016
WOMEN AND THE ARAB SPRING *UN Chronicle* v54 no4 p21 2017

Karmarkar, Uday
The U.S. Can't Count on Technology to Revive the Job Market *Harvard Business Review Digital Articles* p2 Je 4 2015

Karmarkar, Uma R.
Marketers Should Pay Attention to fMRI *Harvard Business Review Digital Articles* p2 N 3 2015

KARNAZES, DEAN
YOU DON'T KNOW PHEIDIPPIDES! [Cover story] bw cartoon color map *Runner's World* v51 no11 p72 D 2016

KARNES, ANDREA
SELF-PORTRAIT *Texas Monthly* v44 no11 p101 N 2016

Karnicar, Davo
Downhill dynamo R. VERGER color *Popular Science* v289 no6

p34 N/D 2017

KARNS, GABRIEL R.

Modernization, Risk, and Conservation of the World's Largest Carnivores *BioScience* v67 no7 p646 Jl 2017

KARO, PEGGY BAKER

Holt County's Christmas Lesson cartoon *Nebraska Life* v20 no6 p48 N/D 2016

Karol, Jane

5 STEPS TO LET YOUR HORSE TRAIN YOU color *Dressage Today* p38 My 2017

Karolina Fund ehf

PEOPLE POWER FOR POSITIVE CHANGE S. DANIELS *Iceland Review* v55 no2 p46 Mr/Ap 2017

Karoll, Albert

BESPOKEN FOR R. O'CONNOR cartoon *Chicago* v66 no2 p22 F 2017

KARP, HARVEY

crying out loud *Parents* v92 no1 p71 Ja 2017

Karp, Jeff

Play On color *Sports Illustrated* v127 no6 p10 Ag 28 2017

Karp, Marshall

Terminal: A Lomax and Biggs Mystery *Publishers Weekly* v263 no41 p60 O 10 2016

KARP, MATT

THE ENDURING STRUGGLE color *Nation* v304 no11 p27 Ap 3 2017

Karp, Matthew

Q: Who Is the Worst Leader of All Time? color *Atlantic* v319 no1 p100 Ja/F 2017

The Slave Owners' Foreign Policy D. S. Reynolds bw *New York Review of Books* v64 no11 p51 Je 22 2017

This Vast Southern Empire: Slaveholders at the Helm of American Foreign Policy W. R. Mead *Foreign Affairs* v96 no1 p163 Ja/F 2017

Karpay, Kenneth

3 Health Care Trends That Don't Hinge on the ACA *Harvard Business Review Digital Articles* p2 My 25 2017

Karpowicz, Nicholas

Angular momentum can slow down photoemission color *Science* v357 no6357 p1239 S 22 2017

Soft x-ray excitonics bw diag *Science* v357 no6356 p1134 S 15 2017

Karr, Doug

we asked you answered color *Cabin Living* p8 D 2016

KARR, KENDRA A.

Long-Term Studies Contribute Disproportionately to Ecology and Policy *BioScience* v67 no3 p271 Mr 2017

Karr, Kevin

Cultivating a school-university partnership for teacher learning color *Phi Delta Kappan* v98 no8 p48 My 2017

Karr, Mary

AFTERMATH bw cartoon *New Yorker* v92 no38 p48 N 21 2016

MESSENGER *Commonweal* v144 no5 p23 Mr 10 2017

KARRAS, TULA

GROW, EAT, LOVE [Cover story] cartoon chart color *Yoga Journal* no291 p36 My 2017

"I was only 9 WHEN MY MOM GOT SICK" color *Good Housekeeping* v264 no4 p107 Ap 2017

KARST, MORRIE

KEEPING SHOP IN MILLER *South Dakota Magazine* v32 no4 p112 N/D 2016

Kartaloff, Plamen

Mussorgsky: Boris Godunov D. J. Baker *Opera News* v81 no7 p46 Ja 2017

Karthaus, Wouter R.

SOX2 promotes lineage plasticity and antiandrogen resistance in TP53- and RB1-deficient prostate cancer bibl graph *Science* v355 no6320 p1 Ja 6 2017

Karting

THE MAGIC OF KARTS S. SMITH color *Road & Track* v68 no5 p111 D 2016/Ja 2017

Purple Kart S. SMITH color *Road & Track* v68 no5 p38 D 2016/Ja 2017

There's No Match for Nintendo Gameplay *USA Today Magazine* v146 no2866 p79 Jl 2017

WITH KIDS *Indianapolis Monthly* p61 F 2017

Karts (Automobiles)

The Diesel Weasel Mow-Kart! P. Thomas chart color *Hot Rod* v70 no6 p12 Je 2017

THE MAGIC OF KARTS S. SMITH color *Road & Track* v68 no5 p111 D 2016/Ja 2017

Purple Kart S. SMITH color *Road & Track* v68 no5 p38 D 2016/Ja 2017

Karts (Automobiles)—Evaluation

The Kid-Proof Go-Kart color *Popular Mechanics* p52 D 2016/Ja 2017

Karty, Mary

CIRCLE CITY AERODROME A. SHULER *Indianapolis Monthly* p21 My 2017

Karunakaran, Bipin

How an Early Adopter of Electronic Health Records Uses Big Data *Harvard Business Review Digital Articles* p2 D 15 2016

Karuppagounder, Senthilkumar S.

Pathological α-synuclein transmission initiated by binding lymphocyte-activation gene 3 bibl graph *Science* v353 no6307 paah3374-1 S 30 2016

Karwah, Salome

Salome Karwah A. Baker color *Time* v189 no9 p14 Mr 13 2017

Kaschock, Kirsten

Confessional Sci-Fi: A Primer *Publishers Weekly* v264 no16 p40 Ap 17 2017

KASE, LORI MILLER

How Good Is Good Cholesterol? color *Discover* v38 no10 p70 D 2017

Kaser, Arthur

The road to Crohn's disease diag *Science* v357 no6355 p976 S 8 2017

Kashdan, Todd

16 LIFE LESSONS *Psychology Today* v49 no5 p62 S/O 2016

Kashdan, Todd B.

Companies Value Curiosity but Stifle It Anyway *Harvard Business Review Digital Articles* p2 O 21 2015

Kashino, Marisa M.

2017'S COOLEST DEVELOPMENTS *Washingtonian Magazine* v52 no4 p188 Ja 2017

Around here, developers don't just build buildings—they build entire neighborhoods color *Washingtonian Magazine* v52 no7 p102 Ap 2017

THE BARN BY THE BEACH *Washingtonian Magazine* v52 no9 p151 Je 2017

Capitol Crossing color *Washingtonian Magazine* v52 no7 p103 Ap 2017

DAVID COLE *Washingtonian Magazine* v52 no5 p39 F 2017

Downtown Columbia color *Washingtonian Magazine* v52 no7 p102 Ap 2017

FAB FIRST IMPRESSIONS *Washingtonian Magazine* v52 no9 p156 Je 2017

GALLERY IN THE GARDEN *Washingtonian Magazine* v52 no3 p164 D 2016

HAUTE HOUSES: The 2017 Washingtonian Residential Design Awards' 12 winning projects *Washingtonian Magazine* v52 no11 p70 Ag 2017

MAKE A SPLASH: Bathrooms done up in unexpected colors, patterns, and accessories will make you forget basic, boring white *Washingtonian Magazine* v52 no12 p130 S 2017

MINIMALIST MULTIPURPOSE *Washingtonian Magazine* v52 no6 p155 Mr 2017

NOT THE PRESIDENT'S MEN: Top lawyers are passing up a career-making opportunity. Why? *Washingtonian Magazine* v52 no11 p16 Ag 2017

PARENTAL GUIDANCE *Washingtonian Magazine* v52 no3 p122 D 2016

THE POTOMAC PROBLEM *Washingtonian Magazine* v52 no1 p183 O 2016

PURPOSE-BUILT color *Washingtonian Magazine* v52 no7 p46 Ap 2017

SEEKING SANCTUARY *Washingtonian Magazine* v52 no2 p274 N 2016

THERE'S A SECRET STASH OF HOUSES FOR SALE color *Washingtonian Magazine* v52 no7 p107 Ap 2017

The Wharf color *Washingtonian Magazine* v52 no7 p104 Ap 2017

WHERE & WHEN color *Washingtonian Magazine* v52 no7 p31

Ap 2017

THE WHOLE HILL *Washingtonian Magazine* v52 no9 p162 Je 2017

YOUNG GLOVE *Washingtonian Magazine* v53 no1 p26 O 2017

Kashkari, Neel T. (Neel Tushar), 1973-

Neel Kashkari M. Boesler and J. Smialek color *Bloomberg Businessweek* no4527 p92 Je 19 2017

Kashkush, Khalil

Wild emmer genome architecture and diversity elucidate wheat evolution and domestication color *Science* v357 no6346 p93 Jl 7 2017

Kashmir conflict (India & Pakistan)

A Merciless Occupation A. R. MIR *Islamic Horizons* v45 no6 p60 N/D 2016

A Road to Peace or Disaster? Isn't it time for the world powers to ask the Kashmiris what they really want? G. N. FAI *Islamic Horizons* v46 no4 p54 Jl/Ag 2017

KASHNER, SAM

Chanel's Costume Drama bw color *Vanity Fair* p158 Hollywood 2017 Supplement

THE HIT MAN bw color *Vanity Fair* p172 Hollywood 2017 Supplement

Hollywood Can Wait bw color *Vanity Fair* v58 no11 p186 N 2016

Santa Gets His Claws bw cartoon color *Vanity Fair* v59 no1 p168 Holiday 2017

Wild About Harry! bw color *Vanity Fair* v59 no10 p148 O 2017

Kashuk, Sonia

BEST CASE Scenario color *O, The Oprah Magazine* p48 Ja 2017

Kasibhatla, P. S.

A human-driven decline in global burned area chart graph map *Science* v356 no6345 p1356 Je 30 2017

Kasich, John, 1952-

The Tea Party Centrists: A lot of the governors elected as hardliners in 2010 have surprised their states A. Ehrenhalt *Governing* v30 no9 p14 Je 2017

KASIM, ABUBAKAR N.

The Never-Ending Mosque Parking Syndrome *Islamic Horizons* v46 no1 p50 Ja/F 2017

Kasischke, Laura

March *New York Times Magazine* p20 Mr 26 2017

Kask SpA

THE BEST BET img *New York* v50 no11 p93 My 29 2017

Kaske, Michelle

Cries In the Dark color graph *Bloomberg Businessweek* no4540 p16 O 2 2017

Kaskey, Jack

Ethylene color *Bloomberg Businessweek* no4537 p21 S 11 2017

Kasler, Suzanne

Kitchens color *Architectural Digest* no11 p73 N 1 2017

Star-Spangled Style K. O'SHEA-EVANS color *House Beautiful* p50 Jl 2017

Kasliwal, M.

iPTF16geu: A multiply imaged, gravitationally lensed type Ia supernova color diag graph *Science* v356 no6335 p291 Ap 21 2017

Kasowitz, Marc

NOT THE PRESIDENT'S MEN: Top lawyers are passing up a career-making opportunity. Why? M. M. Kashina *Washingtonian Magazine* v52 no11 p16 Ag 2017

Trump Taps His Personal Lawyer for Russia Probe A. Altman color *Time* v189 no24 p13 Je 26 2017

Kasparian, Ana—Interviews

Are The Young Turks Progressive Media's Rising Stars? L. FLANDERS color *Nation* v304 no9 p38 Mr 20 2017

Kasparov, G. K. (Garri Kimovich), 1963-

Garry KASPAROV J. Dickey color *Sports Illustrated* v127 no1 p78 Jl 3 2017

KASPAROV, GARRY

Vladimir Putin's PR Victory color *Weekly Standard* v22 no43 p13 Jl 24 2017

Kasparov, Garry—Interviews

Garry KASPAROV M. Potter color *Esquire* p124 Je/Jl 2017

Kasper, Karen

MEMBERS IN MOTION *Arabian Horse World* v57 no3 p50 D 2016

Kaspersky Labs Ltd.

Stand By...Scanning for Viruses and Secrets J. Robertson, M. Riley et al cartoon *Bloomberg Businessweek* no4530 p21 Jl 17 2017

Kaspi, Victoria M.

A fast radio boom bibl color *Science* v354 no6317 p1230 D 9 2016

Kaspi, Y.

Jupiter's interior and deep atmosphere: The initial pole-to-pole passes with the Juno spacecraft [Cover story] color graph *Science* v356 no6340 p821 My 26 2017

Kassabova, Kapka

Border: A Journey to the Edge of Europe A. Greenwald *Christian Century* v134 no18 p39 Ag 30 2017

Kassam, Karim-Aly S.

Toward a national, sustained U.S. ecosystem assessment bibl color *Science* v354 no6314 p838 N 18 2016

Kassar, Chris

COMMITTED color *Climbing* no355 p62 Ag 2017

Kassem, Amirah

Our Relationship, in Pictures bw color *Glamour* v115 no3 p142 Mr 2017

Kassengaliyeva, Madina

Better Questions to Ask Your Data Scientists *Harvard Business Review Digital Articles* p2 N 15 2016

Kassianidou, Elena

Emergent cellular self-organization and mechanosensation initiate follicle pattern in the avian skin color *Science* v357 no6353 p811 Ag 25 2017

Kassis, Judith A.

Passing epigenetic silence to the next generation diag *Science* v356 no6333 p28 Ap 7 2017

Kaste, Martin

Evergreen Evasion color *Weekly Standard* v22 no39 p4 Je 19 2017

Kastelein, Richard

What Initial Coin Offerings Are, and Why VC Firms Care *Harvard Business Review Digital Articles* p2 Mr 24 2017

KASTOR, DEENA

GREAT INSPIRATIONS color *Runner's World* v51 no10 p28 N 2016

Kastriti, Maria Eleni

Multipotent peripheral glial cells generate neuroendocrine cells of the adrenal medulla color *Science* v357 no6346 p46 Jl 7 2017

Kasumba, Florence

Emerald City M. Logan *TV Guide* v65 no2 p30 Ja 2 2017

Katagiri, Tomoe

ONENESS WITH EVERY STITCH B. CONNELLY color *Tricycle: The Buddhist Review* v26 no2 p74 Wint 2016

Katahdin, Mount (Me.)

Terra Incognita R. WICHELNS color *Backpacker* p14 My 2017

Katahdin Cedar Log Homes (Company)

LET THE SUNSHINE IN color *Log Home Living* v34 no9 p21 D 2017

Katan, C.

Extremely efficient internal exciton dissociation through edge states in layered 2D perovskites bibl graph *Science* v355 no6331 p1288 Mr 24 2017

Kataria, Tiffany

HAT-P-26b: A Neptune-mass exoplanet with a well-constrained heavy element abundance chart diag graph *Science* v356 no6338 p628 My 12 2017

Kate Spade LLC

Flats? For Evening? Why, Yes color *Women's Health* v13 no10 p62 D 2016

KATES, MARGARET TRACEY

The Question *O, The Oprah Magazine* p12 Mr 2017

Kathakali

Déjeuner sur l'Herbe J. Acocella cartoon *New Yorker* v92 no34 p14 O 24 2016

Kathrada, Ahmed, 1929-2017

Ahmed Kathrada 1929 - 2017 M. Haron *Islamic Horizons* v46 no4 p60 Jl/Ag 2017

Milestones color *Time* v189 no13 p12 Ap 10 2017

Kati, Vassiliki

A global map of roadless areas and their conservation status bibl color graph map *Science* v354 no6318 p1423 D 16 2016

Katkov, I.

Observation of a large-scale anisotropy in the arrival directions

of cosmic rays above 8 × 1018 eV *Science* v357 no6357 p1266 S 22 2017

Kato, Daiki

Crystal structure of the overlapping dinucleosome composed of hexasome and octasome graph *Science* v356 no6334 p205 Ap 14 2017

Kato, Kenji

Evolution of the wheat blast fungus through functional losses in a host specificity determinant diag map *Science* v357 no6346 p80 Jl 7 2017

Kato, Yoshi

The 'Always Striving' Bobby Hutcherson: 1941-2016 bw *Downbeat* v83 no11 p16 N 2016

AMBROSE AKINMUSIRE: THE THINKER [Cover story] color *Downbeat* v84 no9 p28 S 2017

Blue Note Takes Root in Napa color *Downbeat* v84 no2 p57 F 2017

Bunnett Continues Cuban Journey color *Downbeat* v83 no11 p13 N 2016

Classical Confluence color *Downbeat* v84 no10 p68 O 2017

DRAWN TO JAZZ color *Downbeat* v84 no6 p114 Je 2017

Kamasi Turns Bay Residency into Party color *Downbeat* v84 no3 p20 Mr 2017

Music Of Miles Davis & Original Compositions color *Downbeat* v84 no7 p58 Jl 2017

Round Trip/Ternion Quartet color *Downbeat* v84 no9 p65 S 2017

STRENGTH IN DIVERSITY color *Downbeat* v84 no6 p106 Je 2017

University of the Pacific Fosters Collaborations color *Downbeat* v83 no11 p102 N 2016

UNPLUGGING AT JAZZ CAMP WEST color *Downbeat* v84 no3 p97 Mr 2017

WITNESSING HIS OWN LEGACY color *Downbeat* v84 no6 p130 Je 2017

Kato USA Inc.

Kato HO scale Dash 9 features upgraded mechanism and road-name-specific detail D. Kawala chart color diag *Model Railroader* v84 no2 p68 F 2017

Kato N scale SDP40F diesel locomotive C. Grivno color *Model Railroader* v84 no5 p65 My 2017

Kato N scale SDP40F with ESU LokSound D. Kawala *Model Railroader* v84 no10 p63 O 2017

Katrib, Ruba

MOLECULAR SCULPTURE color *Art in America* v105 no8 p68 S 2017

Katsowich, Naama

Host cell attachment elicits posttranscriptional regulation in infecting enteropathogenic bacteria bibl graph *Science* v355 no6326 p735 F 17 2017

Kattan, Huda

The World According to Huda F. Valdesolo color *Glamour* v115 no11 p82 N 2017

Kattan, Michael W.

Why Cleveland Clinic Shares Its Outcomes Data with the World *Harvard Business Review Digital Articles* p2 S 22 2015

Kattel, Shyam

Active sites for CO2 hydrogenation to methanol on Cu/ZnO catalysts bibl graph *Science* v355 no6331 p1296 Mr 24 2017

TECHNICAL COMMENT ABSTRACTS *Science* v357 no6354 p881 S 1 2017

Kattoor, James

Speak up color *U.S. Catholic* v82 no4 p5 Ap 2017

Katz, Andrew

Moments color *Time* v188 no25-26 p18 D 19 2016 Double Issue

Katz, Benjamin

Big Jets Get Squeezed color *Bloomberg Businessweek* no4539 p16 S 25 2017

Surviving a Classic Car Slump color *Bloomberg Businessweek* no4530 p64 Jl 17 2017

Katz, Brooke Porter

BETTER BURGERS, HOTTER DOGS color *Martha Stewart Living* no275 p67 Je 2017

BUTTERMILK PANCAKES color *Martha Stewart Living* p55 My 2017

CAKES FOR any OCCASION [Cover story] color *Martha Stewart Living* p70 My 2017

CHICKEN ON THE GRILL color *Martha Stewart Living* p71 Jl/Ag 2017

Do the Charleston color *Martha Stewart Living* p110 My 2017

LEFTOVER RICE color *Martha Stewart Living* p69 S 2017

Meatball Makeovers color *Martha Stewart Living* p83 O 2017

New Orleans color *Martha Stewart Living* p136 Ap 2017

TRIPS THAT TRANSPORT AND TRANSFORM color *Martha Stewart Living* p102 Mr 2017

TRUE-BLUE WINNERS color *Martha Stewart Living* no271 p76 Ja/F 2017

WE SAY TOMATOES color *Martha Stewart Living* p102 Jl/Ag 2017

a whole lot of wholesome color *Martha Stewart Living* p82 Mr 2017

Katz, Bruce J.

Priorities for Jumpstarting the U.S. Industrial Economy *Harvard Business Review Digital Articles* p2 F 2 2015

The Rise of Urban Innovation Districts *Harvard Business Review Digital Articles* p2 N 12 2014

Why Today's Corporate Research Centers Need to Be in Cities *Harvard Business Review Digital Articles* p2 Mr 1 2016

Katz, Daniel Martin

Harnessing legal complexity diag graph *Science* v355 no6332 p1377 Mr 31 2017

Katz, David

7 FOODS DOCTORS PRESCRIBE B. Risher cartoon color *Men's Health* v32 no1 p55 Ja/F 2017

KATZ, DAVID L.

Office De-stress Ideas color *Reader's Digest* v189 no1130 p49 My 2017

KATZ, DEBRA S.

Not OK *Ms.* v26 no4 p38 Wint 2016

Katz, Farley

YOUR GUIDE TO WINNING MOVEMBER cartoon *Esquire* p30 N 2017

Katz, Gwen C.

Among the Red Stars *Publishers Weekly* v264 no35 p130 Ag 28 2017

KATZ, HOWARD

I'M DOING MY PART, ARE YOU? *Humanist* v77 no3 p39 My/Je 2017

Katz, Jon

Talking to Animals: A New Approach to Living Alongside Animals color *Publishers Weekly* v263 no52 p108 D 19 2016

KATZ, JONATHAN M.

SEEING IS BELIEVING *Smithsonian* v48 no4 p77 Jl/Ag 2017

Katz, Joseph

The Two Worlds of a Soviet Spy H. Klehr, J. E. Haynes et al bw *Commentary* v143 no3 p27 Mr 2017

Katz, Josh

Style and Substance: Can genius be graphed? The word choices that explain why Jane Austen's work survives and thrives *New York Times Book Review* p13 Jl 16 2017

You Say Tomato ... map *Reader's Digest* v190 no1132 p124 Jl/Ag 2017

Katz, Lawrence F.

Documenting decline in U.S. economic mobility graph *Science* v356 no6336 p382 Ap 28 2017

Katz, Lily

The Mystery of the 4,555 Percent Return graph *Bloomberg Businessweek* no4517 p40 Ap 3 2017

Katz, Matthew

Potential role of intratumor bacteria in mediating tumor resistance to the chemotherapeutic drug gemcitabine diag *Science* v357 no6356 p1156 S 15 2017

The Thread *New York Times Magazine* p7 Jl 2 2017

Katz, Miriam E.

Impact ejecta at the Paleocene-Eocene boundary bibl bw graph *Science* v354 no6309 p225 O 14 2016

Katz, Robert

Peak Performance D. FISHER color graph *Forbes* v198 no8 p44 D 20 2016

Katz, Ross

Feather in His Cap S. KROWIAK *Indianapolis Monthly* v40 no5 p37 Ja 2017

Katz, Steve

A NOTE FROM OUR PUBLISHER *Mother Jones* v42 no3 p44 My/Je 2017

A NOTE FROM OUR PUBLISHER *Mother Jones* v42 no5 p19 S/O 2017

Katz, Yaakov

How David Became Goliath R. BROOKS *New York Times Book Review* p21 F 5 2017

How Israel Took a Toy and Made It a High-Tech Weapon [Cover story] *Commentary* v143 no1 p19 Ja 2017

Katzenberger, Jeremy

FOR THOSE LEFT BEHIND M. GRIMM *USA Today Magazine* v145 no2858 p38 N 2016

Katzenstein, Terese L.

Emergence and spread of a human-transmissible multidrug-resistant nontuberculous mycobacterium bibl diag graph *Science* v354 no6313 p751 N 11 2016

Katzer, Nathan

10 UP & COMERS: NATHAN KATZER J. Scott *Successful Farming* v115 no8 p42 Je/Jl 2017

Katzman, Susan

CULINARY SURPRISES color *Missouri Life* v44 no2 p92 Ap 2017

DELI DELIGHTS color *Missouri Life* v44 no3 p72 My 2017

Katzman, David J.

Cyclin A2 is an RNA binding protein that controls Mre11 mRNA translation bibl graph *Science* v353 no6307 p1549 S 30 2016

Katznelson, Ira

The Borrowers bw *Foreign Affairs* v95 no6 p159 N/D 2016

What America Taught the Nazis color *Atlantic* v320 no4 p42 N 2017

Kauai (Hawaii)—Description & travel

My Place bw color *Vanity Fair* v59 no5 p48 Ap 2017

Kauffman, Anne

American Carnage M. Schulman color *New Yorker* v93 no20 p12 Jl 10 2017

KAUFFMAN, BILL

Buffalo's Fall and Rise: An inspiring case history of an urban turnaround *American Conservative* v16 no5 p20 S/O 2017

California Split *American Conservative* v16 no2 p39 Mr/Ap 2017

Censorship Tale *American Conservative* v16 no3 p43 My/Je 2017

Election-Night Giddiness *American Conservative* v16 no1 p45 Ja/F 2017

He Was a Lifelong Buddy *American Conservative* v16 no5 p45 S/O 2017

The Liberty Boys *American Conservative* v16 no4 p52 Jl/Ag 2017

Populism Needs Place-ism *American Conservative* v15 no6 p45 N/D 2016

Kauffman, Gary

Mysterious Foot Injuries C. Toy color *Spin to Win Rodeo* v21 no6 p52 Ag 2017

Kauffman, Gretel

A Muslim police officer sues the NYPD, citing religious harassment *Christian Century* v134 no6 p15 Mr 15 2017

Kauffman, James M.

It's instruction over place — not the other way around! color diag il *Phi Delta Kappan* v98 no4 p55 D 2016/Ja 2017

Kauffman, Marta—Interviews

FRIENDS: PHOEBE'S SEDUCTION A. Wilkinson color *Entertainment Weekly* no1460/1461 p63 Ap 7-17 2017

KAUFLIN, JEFF

AMERICA'S TOP 50 COMPANIES 1917-2017 chart graph *Forbes* v200 no3 p38 S 28 2017

Lightbulb Moment color *Forbes* v199 no6 p58 Je 13 2017

Shark Tank's Toothless Deals color graph *Forbes* v198 no7 p24 N 29 2016

THE WORLD'S MOST INNOVATIVE COMPANIES chart color *Forbes* v200 no2 p72 S 5 2017

Kaufman, Andy, 1949-1984

It Is Not About Race cartoon *New Orleans Magazine* v51 no12 p22 O 2017

Kaufman, Anne

The Thread *New York Times Magazine* p9 F 12 2017

KAUFMAN, BEN

How to Make a... ROOT BEER color *Popular Mechanics* p76 S 2017

Kaufman, Bruce

RACE A RIDING MOWER bw cartoon chart color *Men's Health* v32 no6 p102 Ag 2017

Kaufman, Don

The Fix-it Man B. HUNHOFF *South Dakota Magazine* v32 no4 p48 N/D 2016

Kaufman, Heather

The Story People *Publishers Weekly* v263 no39 p73 S 26 2016

Kaufman, Kenn

Grail Bird *Audubon* v118 no6 p46 Wint 2016

MOST BIRDS LIVE THREE-DIMENSIONAL LIVES color *Audubon* v119 no3 p46 Fall 2017

Kaufman, L. J.

Observation of coherent elastic neutrino-nucleus scattering diag *Science* v357 no6356 p1123 S 15 2017

Kaufman, Leslie

The Fertility Problem No One Talks About color *Health* v31 no1 p72 Ja 2017

HIGH AND DRY color *Popular Science* v289 no2 p36 Mr/Ap 2017

YOUR SCHEDULE COULD BE KILLING YOU cartoon color *Popular Science* v289 no5 p58 S/O 2017

Kaufman, Mark

Space Age Firefighters color *Scientific American* v316 no6 p14 Je 2017

Kaufman, Mark D.

the elusive green flash color *Popular Science* v289 no4 p93 Jl/Ag 2017

I WISH SOMEONE WOULD INVENT... cartoon *Popular Science* v289 no4 p102 Jl/Ag 2017

weather gets weird diag *Popular Science* v289 no4 p10 Jl/Ag 2017

KAUFMAN, MELISSA

Tokens of Our Affection cartoon *O, The Oprah Magazine* p17 F 2017

Kaufman, Mervyn

A Dish of Tea *British Heritage Travel* v38 no4 p76 Jl/Ag 2017

Tea's Noble Afternoon Ritual color *British Heritage Travel* v38 no5 p76 S/O 2017

Kaufman, Scott Barry

The Emotions That Make Us More Creative *Harvard Business Review Digital Articles* p2 Ag 12 2015

Executives, Protect Your Alone Time *Harvard Business Review Digital Articles* p2 D 16 2015

People Favor Naturals Over Strivers—Even Though They Say Otherwise *Harvard Business Review Digital Articles* p2 My 19 2016

Kaufman, Smylie—Interviews

Grin to Win C. Barrett and S. Zak color *Golf Magazine* v58 no11 p23 N 2016

Kaufman, Tanner Brent

Tanner Brent Kaufmann A. A. DAVIS color *Maclean's* v129 no42 p66 O 24 2016

Kaufmann, Miranda

Black Tudors: The Untold Story *Publishers Weekly* v264 no35 p115 Ag 28 2017

Kaufmann, Yadin

Start-Up Palestine color *Foreign Affairs* v96 no4 p113 Jl/Ag 2017

Kauk, Lonnie

BOARDER SECURITY P. BRIDGES color *Snowboarder* v29 no2 p26 O 2016

Kaur, Rupi

Canadian Voices, Global Bestsellers E. NAWOTKA color *Publishers Weekly* v264 no41 p20 O 9 2017

Rupi Kaur: Bestselling Poet C. Kirch *Publishers Weekly* v263 no52 p28 D 19 2016

Kaur, Sirinder

Flying scares you color *Yoga Journal* p43 2016 Special Issue

Kaus, Boris J. P.

Constraining lithospheric flow bibl color graph *Science* v353 no6307 p1495 S 30 2016

KAUSCH, MEGAN

5TH ANNUAL RAPTOR WINTER WONDERLAND color *Dirt Sports + Off-Road* v51 no6 p58 Je 2017

DEEP IN THE HEART OF TEXAS color *Dirt Sports + Off-Road* v51 no3 p38 Mr 2017

HANDY ADJUSTABILITY color *Dirt Sports + Off-Road* v51 no9 p62 S 2017

HUCKING IT AT HAVOC 4 color *Dirt Sports + Off-Road* v51 no2 p54 F 2017

TEARING IT UP IN TEXAS [Cover story] color *Dirt Sports + Off-Road* v51 no12 p10 D 2017

THE X FACTOR color *Dirt Sports + Off-Road* v51 no7 p46 Jl 2017

Kausikan, Bilahari

Asia in the Trump Era color *Foreign Affairs* v96 no3 p146 My/ Je 2017

Kautonen, Teemu

Starting a Business Can Increase Older Workers' Quality of Life (Even When It Doesn't Pay Well) *Harvard Business Review Digital Articles* p2 S 19 2017

Kautsky, Nils

Social norms as solutions bibl color *Science* v354 no6308 p42 O 7 2016

Kautzsch, Thomas

German Manufacturing Is Leading a Digital Industrial Revolution *Harvard Business Review Digital Articles* p2 Je 1 2016

Kavanagh, Tasha

Things We Have in Common *Publishers Weekly* v263 no44 p48 O 31 2016

Kavathekar, Jitendra

A Hands-Off Approach to Open Innovation Doesn't Work *Harvard Business Review Digital Articles* p2 My 3 2016

Kaveny, Cathleen

Prophecy without Contempt: Religious Discourse in the Public Square D. O'Brien color *Christian Century* v133 no21 p45 O 12 2016

Seventh-Circuit Shakedown color *Commonweal* v144 no16 p8 O 6 2017

KAVULLA, TRAVIS

Indian Country bw color *National Review* v69 no1 p38 Ja 23 2017

Kawa, Luke

Markets Reactions graph *Bloomberg Businessweek* no4536 p31 S 4 2017

Kawabata, Yasunari, 1899-1972

1928: Tokyo Yasunari Kawabata *Lapham's Quarterly* v10 no1 p135 Wint 2017

Dandelions *Publishers Weekly* v264 no40 p113 O 2 2017

Kawae, Yukinori

The Anti-Indiana Jones Measures the Pyramids N. Strochlic color *National Geographic* v230 no5 p27 N 2016

Kawai (Company)

Kawai ES110 Digital Piano J. Ann Daugherty color *Downbeat* v84 no9 p99 S 2017

Kawajiri, Mei

How We Communicate Now C. de León, A. L. Greco et al bw color *Glamour* v115 no3 p52 Mr 2017

Kawakubo, Rei

Rei KAWAKUBO *Interview* v47 no3 p104 My 2017

REI L. SHAPTON *New York Times Magazine* p50 Ap 30 2017

Kawakubo, Rei—Exhibitions

ART bw *New Yorker* v93 no26 p8 S 4 2017

Clothes That Don't Need You [Cover story] D. Salle bw color *New York Review of Books* v64 no14 p10 S 28 2017

How Has One Designer Spent Decades Defining the Avant-Garde? Rei Kawakubo's Comme des Garçons gets a restrospective at the Met V. HYLAND img *New York* v50 no8 p74 Ap 17 2017

SHOWCASE P. DUKOVIC color *New Yorker* v93 no11 p52 My 1 2017

Kawala, Dana

Accurail HO scale 36-foot double-sheathed boxcar kit color *Model Railroader* v84 no8 p62 Ag 2017

Athearn HO scale class Z-8 Challenger chart color *Model Railroader* v84 no8 p58 Ag 2017

Athearn HO scale GP39-2 diesel features accurate details and realistic sound chart color diag *Model Railroader* v84 no3 p64 Mr 2017

Atlas HO scale NJ Transit commuter train [Cover story] color *Model Railroader* v84 no7 p60 Jl 2017

Bachmann HO SoundValue USRA light 4-6-2 chart color *Model Railroader* v84 no4 p92 Ap 2017

Bachmann SoundValue HO scale EMD E7A chart color diag *Model Railroader* v84 no5 p60 My 2017

Bachmann Sound Value HO scale GS-4 [Cover story] color *Model Railroader* v84 no10 p58 O 2017

BlueRail Trains App upgrade *Model Railroader* v84 no9 p63 S 2017

Broadway Limited Imports HO scale P70 color *Model Railroader* v84 no11 p66 N 2017

Detailed SD45 from Walthers rumbles to life in HO scale with SoundTraxx DCC chart color diag *Model Railroader* v83 no12 p66 D 2016

DIGITAL MR color map *Model Railroader* v84 no2 p6 F 2017

DIGITALMR color *Model Railroader* v83 no12 p6 D 2016

A hybrid DCC system *Model Railroader* v84 no4 p47 Ap 2017

InterMountain N scale SD40-2 with sound color *Model Railroader* v84 no9 p66 S 2017

Kato HO scale Dash 9 features upgraded mechanism and road-name-specific detail chart color diag *Model Railroader* v84 no2 p68 F 2017

Kato N scale SDP40F with ESU LokSound *Model Railroader* v84 no10 p63 O 2017

Kitbashing an early B&O wagontop boxcar color *Model Railroader* v84 no9 p22 S 2017

Making a multimedia HIGHWAY OVERPASS color diag *Model Railroader* v84 no5 p50 My 2017

Model Power N scale 2-6-0 Mogul chart color *Model Railroader* v84 no11 p64 N 2017

On the Web color *Model Railroader* v84 no7 p6 Jl 2017

ScaleTrains.com HO Union Pacific GTEL lives up to Museum Quality expectations color *Model Railroader* v84 no1 p68 Ja 2017

WalthersMainline HO scale Plymouth ML-8 color *Model Railroader* v84 no6 p62 Je 2017

Woodland Scenics Built & Ready Work Shed *Model Railroader* v84 no6 p67 Je 2017

Kawan, Mona

UBE2O remodels the proteome during terminal erythroid differentiation diag *Science* v357 no6350 p471 Ag 4 2017

Kawasaki (Company)

The Requiem J. L. Stein color *Cycle World* v55 no11 p40 D 2016

Service R. NIERLICH color *Cycle World* v55 no11 p56 D 2016

Kawasaki, Guy

The Art of Aggressive Social Sharing *Harvard Business Review Digital Articles* p2 D 5 2014

Kawasaki motorcycle—Evaluation

2017 KAWASAKI NINJA 650 T. Montano color *Cycle World* v56 no3 p14 Ap 2017

2017 KAWASAKI Z900 D. Canet color *Cycle World* v56 no4 p22 My 2017

THREE OF A KIND B. Adams chart color *Cycle World* v56 no4 p42 My 2017

Kawasaki Motors Corp. USA

2017 KAWASAKI NINJA 1000 ABS J. Gustafson color *Cycle World* v56 no7 p14 Ag 2017

2017 KAWASAKI NINJA 650 T. Montano color *Cycle World* v56 no3 p14 Ap 2017

2017 KAWASAKI Z900 D. Canet color *Cycle World* v56 no4 p22 My 2017

ATV AND UTV TEST 2017 T. HANSEN chart color *Outdoor Life* v224 no7 p14 S 2017

Kawasaki's Hellcat for the Water P. Thomas color *Hot Rod* v70 no11 p10 N 2017

SUPER MIDDLEWEIGHT MATCHUP D. Canet chart color *Cycle World* v56 no6 p50 Jl 2017

Kawka, A.

An unusual white dwarf star may be a surviving remnant of a sub-luminous Type Ia supernova chart diag *Science* v357 no6352 p680 Ag 18 2017

Kaxiras, E.

Magnetic resonance spectroscopy of an atomically thin material using a single-spin qubit bibl color diag graph *Science* v355 no6324 p503 F 3 2017

Kay, Annie B.

Herbs and spices with benefits cartoon *Redbook* p87 Mr 2017

Kay, Chris

Brands Pump Up the Volume in Pakistan color graph *Bloomberg Businessweek* no4530 p34 Jl 17 2017

Kay, John

#trailchat color *Backpacker* p8 My 2017

Kay, Jonathan

Case Study cartoon *Walrus* v14 no2 p63 Mr 2017
Evil Spirits color *Walrus* v14 no5 p64 Je 2017
The Helsinki Formula *Walrus* v13 no9 p74 N 2016
Je M'Excuse cartoon *Walrus* p71 Ja\F 2017
Pop-Tarts for Dinner *Walrus* v14 no4 p66 My 2017
Taking on the Haters *Walrus* v13 no10 p74 D 2016
The Wingman *Walrus* v14 no3 p66 Ap 2017

Kay, Kelly O.

3 Mistakes Executives Make When Telling People That They're Leaving *Harvard Business Review Digital Articles* p2 Jl 27 2017

KAY, LAUREN

Elena d'Amario *Dance Magazine* v91 no1 p118 Ja 2017
Jonalyn Saxer *Dance Magazine* v90 no12 p34 D 2016
Relax & Refresh *Dance Magazine* v91 no8 p40 Ag 2017
What's a Jellicle Cat? *Dance Magazine* v90 no12 p70 D 2016

Kayaking

2016 PHOTO ANNUAL color *Canoe & Kayak Magazine* v45 no1 p14 Wint 2017
ALASKA CROSSING M. HAGE color *Canoe & Kayak Magazine* v45 no1 p56 Wint 2017
CANOE & KAYAK *Sierra* v102 no1 p73 Ja/F 2017
CHASING THE DREAM WAVE D. Jackson color *Canoe & Kayak Magazine* v45 no1 p25 Wint 2017
CLOSE TO HOME N. WARREN color *Canoe & Kayak Magazine* v45 no1 p36 Wint 2017
EXPANDING THE REALM C. Mihell color *Canoe & Kayak Magazine* v45 no1 p28 Wint 2017
FLORIDA'S NATURAL WONDERS B. BROUDY *Sierra* v102 no3 p28 My/Je 2017
from AROUND the WORLD A. SHAW *National Geographic Kids* no467 p5 F 2017
A JOURNEYMAN'S TALE T. WILLIAMS color *Canoe & Kayak Magazine* v45 no1 p44 Wint 2017
A PLACE IN THE SUN M. SIMMS color *O, The Oprah Magazine* p130 S 2017
The Ultimate Winter Adventure Guide color *Conde Nast Traveler* v51 no11 p41 D 2016

Kayaking equipment

See also
Spray skirts (Kayaks)
EVOKE color *Canoe & Kayak Magazine* v45 no1 p81 Wint 2017
ORU KAYAK color *Canoe & Kayak Magazine* v45 no1 p97 Wint 2017
PAKBOATS/SCANSPORT color *Canoe & Kayak Magazine* v45 no1 p98 Wint 2017
PELICAN/ELIE color *Canoe & Kayak Magazine* v45 no1 p99 Wint 2017
PERCEPTION color *Canoe & Kayak Magazine* v45 no1 p102 Wint 2017
SUN DOLPHIN color *Canoe & Kayak Magazine* v45 no1 p101 Wint 2017

Kayaking—Accidents

LCAC ATTACK M. GOFF cartoon *Canoe & Kayak Magazine* v45 no1 p40 Wint 2017

Kayaking—Equipment & supplies

ADVANCED ELEMENTS color *Canoe & Kayak Magazine* v45 no1 p65 Wint 2017
AIRE color *Canoe & Kayak Magazine* v45 no1 p68 Wint 2017
CASCADE CREEK color *Canoe & Kayak Magazine* v45 no1 p67 Wint 2017

Kayaks

Life Magazine P. Theroux *New York Times Magazine* p20 Ap 2 2017

Kayaks—Evaluation

ADVANCED ELEMENTS color *Canoe & Kayak Magazine* v45 no1 p65 Wint 2017
CURRENT DESIGNS color *Canoe & Kayak Magazine* v45 no1 p72 Wint 2017
DAGGER color *Canoe & Kayak Magazine* v45 no1 p80 Wint 2017
DELTA KAYAKS color *Canoe & Kayak Magazine* v45 no1 p82 Wint 2017
EDDYLINE color *Canoe & Kayak Magazine* v45 no1 p84 Wint 2017
EPIC KAYAKS color *Canoe & Kayak Magazine* v45 no1 p88

Wint 2017
EVOKE color *Canoe & Kayak Magazine* v45 no1 p81 Wint 2017
OLD TOWN color *Canoe & Kayak Magazine* v45 no1 p95 Wint 2017
ORU KAYAK color *Canoe & Kayak Magazine* v45 no1 p97 Wint 2017
PAKBOATS/SCANSPORT color *Canoe & Kayak Magazine* v45 no1 p98 Wint 2017
PELICAN/ELIE color *Canoe & Kayak Magazine* v45 no1 p99 Wint 2017
PERCEPTION color *Canoe & Kayak Magazine* v45 no1 p102 Wint 2017
PLACID BOATWORKS color *Canoe & Kayak Magazine* v45 no1 p100 Wint 2017
THE POWER 'YAK REVIEW R. BURNLEY chart color *Outdoor Life* v224 no4 p14 My 2017
SEA EAGLE BOATS color *Canoe & Kayak Magazine* v45 no1 p104 Wint 2017
STELLAR KAYAKS color *Canoe & Kayak Magazine* v45 no1 p106 Wint 2017
SUN DOLPHIN color *Canoe & Kayak Magazine* v45 no1 p101 Wint 2017
WILDERNESS SYSTEMS color *Canoe & Kayak Magazine* v45 no1 p108 Wint 2017

KAYANO, CECILIA

High-Desert Adventure color *Trail Rider* v29 no4 p58 My 2017

Kaye, Ariel

HOME IS WHERE THE PERCALE IS S. Marikar color *Bloomberg Businessweek* no4525 p58 Je 5 2017

Kaye, Cheryl Kramer

ZEN AND THE ART OF HAIR [Cover story] color *Women's Health* v14 no3 p(Sp)24 Ap 2017

Kaye, Laura

Ride Rough: Raven Riders color *Publishers Weekly* v264 no7 p55 F 13 2017

Ka Yi, Ling

ELABELA deficiency promotes preeclampsia and cardiovascular malformations in mice color diag graph *Science* v357 no6352 p707 Ag 18 2017

Kayle, Hilary S.

Best. Interview. Ever bw *Publishers Weekly* v263 no44 p(Sp)8 O 31 2016

KAYLIN, LUCY

Let it go! [Cover story] color *O, The Oprah Magazine* p92 Ag 2017

Kaynor, Grace

LABOR OF LOVE M. Z. Roux color *Southern Living* v52 no3 p92 Mr 2017

Kaytis, Clay

THE ANGRY BIRDS MOVIE T. J. Norton cartoon *Sound & Vision* v82 no1 p69 Ja 2017

Kaytranada (Performer)

KAY-TRANADA D. Valdez color *Surfing Magazine* v53 no1 p30 Ja 2017

Kazakhs

A Silk Road Marriage R. STANDISH color *Foreign Policy* no226 p8 S/O 2017

Kazakhstan—Description & travel

Astana, Kazakhstan J. LILLIS color *Foreign Policy* no223 p70 Mr/Ap 2017

Kazakina, Katya

Globalism Is Alive and Well: Just Ask Carlos Ghosn color *Bloomberg Businessweek* no4531 p50 Jl 24 2017
How Do You Sell A Priceless Watch? color *Bloomberg Businessweek* no4535 p66 Ag 28 2017
Managing the Boss's Art Collection color *Bloomberg Businessweek* no4520 p38 My 1 2017

Kazan, Zoe

I Am Not Interchangeable A. Sternbergh img *New York* v50 no11 p109 My 29 2017
Love and Its Complications R. DOUTHAT color *National Review* v69 no17 p42 S 11 2017

KAZANJIAN, DODIE

BEAUTIFUL DREAMERS color *Vogue* v207 no7 p100 Jl 2017
Object Lesson bw cartoon *Vogue* v207 no3 p388 Mr 2017
VISIBLE DIFFERENCE color *Vogue* v207 no4 p208 Ap 2017

The X Factor color *Vogue* v206 no12 p126 D 2016

Kazansky, Andrey K.

Angular momentum–induced delays in solid-state photoemission enhanced by intra-atomic interactions chart color graph *Science* v357 no6357 p1274 S 22 2017

Kazantsev, Kira—Interviews

Kira Kazantsev J. Marksbury and C. Barrett color *Golf Magazine* v59 no2 p41 F 2017

KAZDIN, COLE

Runyon Canyon 911 color *Los Angeles Magazine* v62 no10 p15 O 2017

Kazez, Jean

The Philosophical Parent: Asking the Hard Questions About Having and Raising Children color *Publishers Weekly* v264 no23 p49 Je 5 2017

KAZI, JASON

1-to-1 Computing Under Microscope in Maine Schools *Education Digest* v82 no5 p48 Ja 2017

Kazin, Michael, 1948-

The Century That Could Have Been T. Anderson *In These Times* v41 no2 p40 F 2017

The Odds Against Antiwar Warriors A. J. BACEVICH *American Conservative* v16 no2 p46 Mr/Ap 2017

Trump and American Populism color *Foreign Affairs* v95 no6 p17 N/D 2016

THE TWO ANDREW JACKSONS il *Nation* v305 no5 p35 Ag 28 2017

THE WAR TO END ALL WARS G. WHEATCROFT color *Nation* v305 no10 p35 O 23 2017

Kazlauskiene, Migle

A cyclic oligonucleotide signaling pathway in type III CRISPR-Cas systems *Science* v357 no6351 p605 Ag 11 2017

Kazuhisa Goto

The formation of peak rings in large impact craters bibl color graph *Science* v354 no6314 p878 N 18 2016

Kazumasa Oda

A three-dimensional movie of structural changes in bacteriorhodopsin bibl diag graph *Science* v354 no6319 p1552 D 23 2016

Kazumura Cave (Hawaii)

CARVED BY LAVA J. Foer color diag map *National Geographic* v231 no6 p112 Je 2017

Kazuyuki Aihara

A coherent Ising machine for 2000-node optimization problems bibl diag graph *Science* v354 no6312 p603 N 4 2016

A fully programmable 100-spin coherent Ising machine with all-to-all connections bibl diag graph *Science* v354 no6312 p614 N 4 2016

K. E., Anna, 1986—Exhibitions

ART cartoon *New Yorker* v93 no12 p6 My 8 2017

Ke, Yazi D.

Site-specific phosphorylation of tau inhibits amyloid-β toxicity in Alzheimer's mice bibl graph *Science* v354 no6314 p904 N 18 2016

Ke, Yonggang

Reconfiguration of DNA molecular arrays driven by information relay diag *Science* v357 no6349 p371 Jl 28 2017

Ke Huang

Precision medicine development in Beijing *Science* v354 no6319 p61 D 23 2016

Ke Xu

Aerobic glycolysis promotes T helper 1 cell differentiation through an epigenetic mechanism bibl graph *Science* v354 no6311 p481 O 28 2016

Kean, Hilda

The War on Pets: The fate of London's companion animals before the Blitz E. PASSARELLO bw *New York Times Book Review* p22 Ap 23 2017

Kean, Sam

1895: Würzburg S. Kean *Lapham's Quarterly* v10 no2 p154 Spr 2017

Caesar's Last Breath A. Jenney color *Science* v356 no6342 p1009 Je 9 2017

Every breath contains a molecule of history E. Engelhaupt color *Science News* v191 no13 p38 Jl 8 2017

MAKERS cartoon *New Yorker* v92 no30 p25 S 26 2016

ON THE TRAIL OF YELLOW FEVER [Cover story] color diag map *Science* v357 no6352 p637 Ag 18 2017

Quotable Quotes color *Reader's Digest* v190 no1135 p136 N 2017

THE SCIENTIFIC NIGHT SHIFT color *Science* v354 no6315 p988 N 25 2016

The Shortlist *New York Times Book Review* p30 N 27 2016

Sisters of the Night Sky *American Scholar* v86 no1 p121 Wint 2017

Keane, Claire—Interviews

A FAMILY AFFAIR I. Biedenharn color *Entertainment Weekly* no1440 p61 N 18 2016

Keane, E. F.

The magnetic field and turbulence of the cosmic web measured using a brilliant fast radio burst bibl chart graph *Science* v354 no6317 p1249 D 9 2016

Keane, James T.

Formation of the Orientale lunar multiring basin bibl graph *Science* v354 no6311 p441 O 28 2016

Gravity field of the Orientale basin from the Gravity Recovery and Interior Laboratory Mission bibl graph *Science* v354 no6311 p438 O 28 2016

A guide to holy places and people T. Wadkins color *America* v217 no2 p46 Jl 24 2017

A LEGACY CORRUPTED color *America* v215 no10 p38 O 10 2016

Northern Warning *America* v215 no16 p12 N 21 2016

Keane, Jim

Meaningful Work Should Be Every CEO's Top Priority *Harvard Business Review Digital Articles* p2 N 5 2015

Keane, Margaret

What Spinning Off a GE Business Taught Me About Managing Ultra-Fast Change *Harvard Business Review Digital Articles* p2 Jl 24 2017

Keane, Tim

MAKE NO LITTLE PLANS T. WHEATLEY *Atlanta* v57 no1 p17 My 2017

Keanu (Film)

KEANU C. Gunnestad color *Sound & Vision* v81 no10 p70 D 2016

Kearney (Neb.)

3 Days in... Kearney, Neb color *American Cowboy* v23 no4 p40 D 2016/Ja 2017

Kearney, Cynthia

A meal for many color *U.S. Catholic* v82 no6 p5 Je 2017

Kearney, Melissa S.

How Should Governments Address Inequality? color *Foreign Affairs* v96 no6 p133 N/D 2017

The "marriage premium" and the economic impact it can have on children J. C. Roach *Monthly Labor Review* p1 My 2017

Kearns, Chris—Interviews

Dr. Cristin Kearns A. Sifferlin color *Time* v188 no27-28 p97 D 26 2016

Kearns, Colin

THE BEAR AT LAST LIGHT color *Field & Stream* v122 no4 p48 S 2017

BREAK EVEN *Field & Stream* v121 no9 p10 Ap 2017

THE COLD OPEN cartoon color *Field & Stream* v121 no7 p18 D 2016/Ja 2017

¿CÓMO SE DICE CAST & BLAST? cartoon color *Field & Stream* v121 no8 p83 F/Mr 2017

FIELD TEST color *Field & Stream* v122 no2 p99 Je/Jl 2017

GIFT OF A LIFETIME color *Field & Stream* v121 no7 p10 D 2016/Ja 2017

HARD-EARNED BUCKS color *Field & Stream* v122 no4 p9 S 2017

HOG, WILD color *Field & Stream* v121 no7 p68 D 2016/Ja 2017

HOLIDAY GIFT GUIDE 2016 color *Field & Stream* v121 no7 p92 D 2016/Ja 2017

OLD FLAMES color *Field & Stream* v121 no8 p8 F/Mr 2017

THE Perfect SHOOTER color *Field & Stream* v121 no6 p67 N 2016

A PLACE IN THE SUN color *Field & Stream* v122 no2 p10 Je/Jl 2017

RIGHT ON TARGET *Field & Stream* v122 no3 p6 Ag 2017

THE TIME HAS COME color *Field & Stream* v122 no6 p8 N 2017

Kearns, Cristin

Sugar industry shifted health focus L. BEIL *Science News* v190 no8 p7 O 15 2016

Kearns, Michael

Building Trust Between Your Employees and Freelancers *Harvard Business Review Digital Articles* p2 Mr 15 2017

Kearns, Natalie

Present to Past L. Mulcahy *Stage Directions* v30 no10 p60 O 2017

Kearns, Shannon T. L.

HOW DO YOU HOLD TOGETHER YOUR TRANS IDENTITY AND YOUR LIFE OF FAITH? color *Christian Century* v134 no2 p22 Ja 18 2017

Keating, Brian

The Big Picture *Physics Today* v69 no12 p55 D 2016

Keating, Brian—Interviews

FEATURED FELLOW: BRIAN KEATING M. Wang color *Canadian Geographic* v137 no5 p78 S/O 2017

Keating, Daryl

Are Your Bowels Irritable or Just Angry? cartoon color *Maclean's* v129 no48/49 p78 D 5 2016

CURBING THE HABIT Your Own Way color *Maclean's* v129 no47 p47 N 28 2016

SAVE YOUR VACATION color *Maclean's* v129 no50 p54 D 19 2016

Keating, Lauren A.

Good Leaders Are Good Learners *Harvard Business Review Digital Articles* p2 Ag 10 2017

Keaton, Diane, 1946-

All Hail Annie Hall F. Kane color *Glamour* v115 no4 p210 Ap 2017

Diane Keaton CAN'T STOP M. GRANT *AARP: The Magazine* v59 no1A p30 D 2015/Ja 2016

A Long-Form Miracle M. Bayles *Claremont Review of Books* v17 no2 p93 Spr 2017

Keaton, Michael, 1951-

Empire Builder R. DOUTHAT color *National Review* v69 no4 p47 Mr 6 2017

Fast-Food Godfather P. Travers color *Rolling Stone* no1280 p56 F 9 2017

The Founder Finds Drama Under the Golden Arches S. Zacharek color *Time* v189 no3 p53 Ja 30 2017

Missions Accomplished R. Alleva color *Commonweal* v144 no4 p20 F 24 2017

Twilight Cowboy or (Why Michael Keaton Would Rather Be a Dog) B. Luscombe color *Time* v188 no24 p56 D 12 2016

KEATS, JONATHON

The Animal Mummy Business color *Discover* v38 no10 p64 D 2017

The Atomic Movie Machine color *Discover* v38 no7 p10 S 2017

Babylonian Tablets Tracked Jupiter color diag *Discover* v38 no1 p54 Ja/F 2017

Bacteria Beef Up New Tree of Life diag *Discover* v38 no1 p90 Ja/F 2017

BENCHMARK PARALLAX VIEW color diag *Wired* v25 no5 p48 My 2017

BENCHMARK: SAFE PASSAGE color *Wired* v25 no10 p52 O 2017

BENCHMARK: SPRING FLING color *Wired* v25 no9 p50 S 2017

Biologists Create Organism With Smallest Genome chart color graph *Discover* v38 no1 p15 Ja/F 2017

Bypassing Paralysis Altogether color *Discover* v38 no1 p81 Ja/F 2017

Caring Computers [Cover story] color *Discover* v38 no4 p10 My 2017

Catching a Criminal color diag *Discover* v38 no6 p40 Jl/Ag 2017

The Electric Touch color *Discover* v38 no9 p10 N 2017

Helium Fields Forever? color map *Discover* v38 no1 p87 Ja/F 2017

Plenty of Room at the Bottom color *Discover* v38 no1 p45 Ja/F 2017

A Quantum Machine for All... color *Discover* v38 no1 p57 Ja/F 2017

Return of the Aurochs color *Discover* v38 no2 p24 Mr 2017

Story Time color *Discover* v38 no4 p16 My 2017

To Floss or Not to Floss color *Discover* v38 no1 p88 Ja/F 2017

Urban Biodiversity color *Discover* v38 no10 p12 D 2017

Walking With Venus' Wind color diag *Discover* v38 no3 p10 Ap 2017

Kebabs

Spring Chicken! L. Cericola color *Southern Living* v52 no3 p119 Mr 2017

YOUR PANTRY color *Good Housekeeping* v264 no6 p120 Je 2017

Kechiche, Abdellatif, 1960-

THE APPROVAL MATRIX img *New York* v50 no12 p128 Je 12 2017

Kedia, Hridesh

Complete measurement of helicity and its dynamics in vortex tubes color diag graph *Science* v357 no6350 p487 Ag 4 2017

Kedia, Simi

Research: Firms Give More Stock Options When They're Committing Fraud color *Harvard Business Review Digital Articles* p2 Ja 26 2017

KEDIGIAN, GARROW

Have It Both Ways color *House Beautiful* v159 no4 p30 My 2017

Keeble, John

At Home with Moose color *Natural History* v125 no7 p48 Jl/Ag 2017

SYNCHRONICITY *Harper's Magazine* p75 S 2017

Keech, Pamela

TIME TRAVEL J. Blitzer cartoon *New Yorker* v92 no42 p46 D 19 2016

KEECH, ROGER

VANISHING EARTH color *Flying* v144 no8 p24 Ag 2017

KEEFE, PATRICK RADDEN

JOURNEYMAN cartoon color *New Yorker* v92 no49 p52 F 13 2017

LIMITED LIABILITY cartoon color *New Yorker* v93 no22 p28 Jl 31 2017

TRUMP'S FAVORITE TYCOON cartoon *New Yorker* v93 no25 p46 Ag 28 2017

Keegan, Jessica

GO FORTH AND READ: How one Long Island school district started a literacy movement in its community color *Literacy Today (2411-7862)* v34 no6 p36 My/Je 2017

KEEGAN, REBECCA

AND THE OSCAR COMES FROM... color *Vanity Fair* v59 no11 p79 N 2017

GEEK IDOLS color *Vanity Fair* v59 no9 p147a S 2017

PRIME-TIME HUNGER GAMES color *Vanity Fair* v59 no7 p61 Summ 2017

Keehan, Carol

Catholic hospitals' C.E.O. ready to fix health care after G.O.P. 'skinny repeal' fails K. Clarke color *America* v217 no4 p17 Ag 21 2017

Healing With God color *America* v216 no13 p62 Je 12 2017

KEELER, BONNIE L.

Society Is Ready for a New Kind of Science--Is Academia? *BioScience* v67 no7 p591 Jl 2017

Keeler, Jennifer M.

A DIFFERENT Kind of Ride color *Dressage Today* v23 no8 p52 Ap 2017

A Different Way of THINKING color *Dressage Today* v23 no10 p38 Jl 2017

Dressage in a Land Far, Far Away color *Dressage Today* v23 no9 p46 Je 2017

From FEEDLOT to FINALS color *Dressage Today* p56 My 2017

Keeping It LEGAL color *Dressage Today* v23 no8 p60 Ap 2017

Keeling, Jonathan

The new era of POLARITON CONDENSATES *Physics Today* v70 no10 p54 O 2017

Keely, Louise

4 Strategies for Reaching the Chinese Consumer *Harvard Business Review Digital Articles* p2 Jl 22 2015

Your Business Is Going to Depend on Connected Spenders, So You'd Better Understand Who They Are color *Harvard Business Review Digital Articles* p2 F 8 2017

Keen, Helen

COULD THAT REALLY HAPPEN ON GAME OF THRONES? N. Serrao color *Entertainment Weekly* no1441 p62 N 25 2016

Keen, Judy

Insider Trading *Science* v357 no6355 p966 S 8 2017

Keenan, Fran
Get Creative with Turkey Plates color *Southern Living* v52 no11 p15 N 2017

Keenan, James F.
All the Pope's Men cartoon *Commonweal* v143 no18 p36 N 11 2016
Called to Conscience color *America* v216 no1 p14 Ja 2 2017

Keenan, Perry
A Way to Assess and Prioritize Your Change Efforts *Harvard Business Review Digital Articles* p2 Jl 9 2015

Keenan, Sasha
A GUIDE TO VEGAN CHEESE *Vegetarian Journal* v36 no2 p12 2017

Keene, Marcus
KEENESANITY D. Greene color *Sports Illustrated* v126 no4 p52 Ja 30 2017

KEENER, CRAIG
WHO COMES TO STEAL KILL AND DESTROY? *Christianity Today* p48 Ap 2017

Keeney, George
You're a what? Insectary manager A. Chen color *Career Outlook* p1 Ap 2017

Keeney, Scott
A global view of meiotic double-strand break end resection bibl graph *Science* v355 no6320 p1 Ja 6 2017

KEEP, ELMO
LIFE WITHOUT END *Smithsonian* v48 no3 p43 Je 2017

Keep It Moving (Music)
THE ULTIMATE FALL SINGLES SWAP color *Entertainment Weekly* no1440 p56 N 18 2016

Keepers, The (Film)
quick takes *U.S. Catholic* v82 no10 p39 O 2017

Keepers, The (TV program)
In 'The Keepers,' the Hopes of Vatican II Crumble Amid Sexual Abuse and Murder N. Ripatrazone bw color *America* v216 no13 p42 Je 12 2017
The Keepers Avoids True Crime's Ghastliest Pitfalls D. D'Addario color *Time* v189 no21 p63 Je 5 2017
YOUR NEXT TRUE-CRIME OBSESSION IS HERE C. Agard color *Entertainment Weekly* no1466 p48 My 19 2017

Keeping up With the Joneses (Film)
The Joneses Tries to Shake Up the 'Hood S. Zacharek color *Time* v188 no18 p44 O 31 2016

Keeping up With the Kardashians (TV program)
10 Years of Kardashians: Khloé Looks Back J. Harman color *Glamour* v115 no10 p42 O 2017
KEEPING UP WITH THE KARDASHIANS: TEN YEARS AND COUNTING... D. Bianculli *TV Guide* v65 no39 p20 S 18 2017
KENDALL COMES OF AGE D. Peres bw color *Harper's Bazaar* no3653 p246 My 2017

KEEPNEWS, PETER
JEWISH HUMOR *New York Times Book Review* p49 D 4 2016
Music *New York Times Book Review* p44 Je 4 2017

KEEPS, DAVID A.
#2: In California, decorator Chloe Warner transforms a modernist glass box into a family house that is both beautiful and kid-proof. All it takes is pattern-and-color confidence—and 200 yards of sheer pink fabric color *House Beautiful* v159 no2 p90 Mr 2017
BEAUTY & THE BEACH color *InStyle* p78 Home & Design 2016
CAT HOUSE color *InStyle* p22 Home & Design 2016
ALL DRESSED UP color *House Beautiful* v159 no8 p104 O 2017
LEAVING NO STONE UNTURNED color *House Beautiful* v159 no4 p90 My 2017
Living the Lush Life color *House Beautiful* v159 no5 p84 Je 2017
Turning the Tide color *House Beautiful* v159 no9 p68 N 2017

KEER, TOM
8 Safety Hacks *Boating World* v38 no1 p20 Ja 2017
FOR THE BIRDS chart color *Outdoor Life* v224 no6 pH5 Ag 2017
ONE, TWO PUNCH chart color *Outdoor Life* v224 no6 p40 Ag 2017

Kees, Ashley L.
Dynamics of cortical dendritic membrane potential and spikes in freely behaving rats diag *Science* v355 no6331 p1281 Mr 24 2017

Keesling, Alexander
Atom-by-atom assembly of defect-free one-dimensional cold atom arrays bibl diag graph *Science* v354 no6315 p1024 N 25 2016

Keeves, Gareth
Research: Executives Who Flatter Their CEOs Are More Likely to Criticize Them to the Press bw *Harvard Business Review Digital Articles* p2 Ap 5 2017

Keflezighi, Meb, 1975-
THE INTERSECTION bw color *Runner's World* v51 no11 p25 D 2016
THE LOVELY LONELINESS J. BEVERLY cartoon *Runner's World* v51 no11 p26 D 2016

KEGANS, KELLY RYAN
THE BUILD & THE BLOG color *Better Homes & Gardens* v95 no5 p128 My 2017
FUN HOUSE color *Better Homes & Gardens* v95 no4 p112 Ap 2017

Kegel exercises
LEAK PROOF YOUR LIFE C. PIKUL color *Parents* v92 no11 p86 N 2017
Sound Bites color *Entertainment Weekly* no1482/1483 p8 S 22 2017

KEGLEY, CHARLES W.
THE GRAVE IS A GATEWAY *USA Today Magazine* v145 no2862 p48 Mr 2017

KEGLEY, DEBRA J.
THE GRAVE IS A GATEWAY *USA Today Magazine* v145 no2862 p48 Mr 2017

Kehayas, Vassilis
Rejuvenating brain plasticity diag *Science* v356 no6345 p1335 Je 30 2017

Kehe, Emily—Interviews
One Couple, Two Pregnancies, One Year Later A. Tsoulis-Reay img *New York* v49 no26 p10 D 26 2016

KEHE, JASON
MR. ROBOT color *Wired* v24 no12 p30 D 2016
WISH LIST 2016 color *Wired* v24 no12 p45 D 2016

Kehlani, 1995-
Kehlani Turns Candor Into Virtue J. Cox color *Time* v189 no6 p51 F 20 2017

Kehoe, Ashley
DRONES ON MARS color *Astronomy* v45 no7 p34 Jl 2017

KEHOE, JACQUELINE
Summer Solitude color *Backpacker* p19 S 2017

Kehoe, Jeff
What's at Stake in an Economy with Low Oil Prices *Harvard Business Review Digital Articles* p2 F 15 2016
Why Europe Tops 2015's List of Global Risks *Harvard Business Review Digital Articles* p2 Ja 9 2015

Kehoe, Robert L. III
Designed to Unsettle *Commonweal* v143 no19 p36 D 2 2016

Keiler, James A.
Pathological α-synuclein transmission initiated by binding lymphocyte-activation gene 3 bibl graph *Science* v353 no6307 paah3374-1 S 30 2016

Keiles, Jamie Lauren
click doctors *New York Times Magazine* p24 Ja 1 2017
'One Night' color *New York Times Magazine* p28 Mr 12 2017
VOYAGES *New York Times Magazine* p37 Mr 26 2017

Keilhauer, B.
Observation of a large-scale anisotropy in the arrival directions of cosmic rays above 8×10^{18} eV *Science* v357 no6357 p1266 S 22 2017

Keillor, Garrison, 1942-
THE BEAUTY OF IT IS THAT A. Streep *New York Times Magazine* p31 O 2 2016
MARCH BADNESS P. Gulley *Saturday Evening Post* v289 no2 p14 Mr/Ap 2017

Keim, Paul S.
TIME TO WORRY ABOUT ANTHRAX AGAIN color diag *Scientific American* v316 no4 p70 Ap 2017

Keinan, Anat
Research: Why Americans Are So Impressed by Busyness *Harvard Business Review Digital Articles* p2 D 15 2016

Keiper, Adam

Shut Up, They Explained color *Weekly Standard* v22 no47 p15 Ag 21 2017

KEISER, DAKOTA

Rocket Redux *Idaho Magazine* v16 no2 p40 N 2016

Keisling, Jason

WHAT DO CRIME VICTIMS WANT FROM CRIMINAL JUSTICE REFORM? cartoon graph *Reason* v48 no7 p8 D 2016

Keisling, Phil

How to Bring Home Democratic Voters *Washington Monthly* p7 Ja/F 2017

KEISMAN, JENNIFER

Submerged Aquatic Vegetation in Chesapeake Bay: Sentinel Species in a Changing World *BioScience* v67 no8 p698 Ag 2017

KEISTER, KIM

Surviving the '80s color *AARP: The Magazine* v59 no5A p47 Ag/S 2016

Keisuke Ito

Self-renewal of a purified Tie2+ hematopoietic stem cell population relies on mitochondrial clearance bibl graph *Science* v354 no6316 p1156 D 2 2016

Keita Tamura

Causal neural network of metamemory for retrospection in primates bibl diag graph *Science* v355 no6321 p1 Ja 13 2017

Keitany, Mary Jepkosgei, 1982-

Mary Jepkosgei Keitany M. Hagan color *Current Biography* v78 no9 p48 S 2017

Keitel, C. H.

Spectral narrowing of x-ray pulses for precision spectroscopy with nuclear resonances diag *Science* v357 no6349 p375 Jl 28 2017

Keith, Bill

A GAY Old Timeline color diag *Entertainment Weekly* no1471 p32 Je 23 2017

HAPPY HOUR! color *Entertainment Weekly* no1465 p28 My 12 2017

THIRTYSOMETHING UNDER COVERS color *Entertainment Weekly* no1460/1461 p40 Ap 7-17 2017

Keith, David W.

Toward a Responsible Solar Geoengineering Research Program *Issues in Science & Technology* v33 no3 p71 Spr 2017

Unmask temporal trade-offs in climate policy debates color *Science* v356 no6337 p492 My 5 2017

Keith, Jourdan Imani

Nature's Pied Piper color *AARP: The Magazine* v59 no3A p82 Ap/My 2016

Keith, Kool

ABOVE & BEYOND bw *New Yorker* v93 no22 p14 Jl 31 2017

Keith, Sam

REFLECTIONS ON A MAN IN HIS WILDERNESS *National Parks* v91 no2 p52 Spr 2017

Keith, Ted

Actionable Offenses color diag *Sports Illustrated* v126 no7 p20 Mr 6 2017

American Dreamer color *Sports Illustrated* v126 no5 p16 F 13 2017

American Voices Ernesto Escobedo color *Sports Illustrated* v126 no12 p18 My 1 2017

American Voices J.J. Barea color *Sports Illustrated* v126 no10 p34 Ap 10 2017

American Voices Laurie Hernandez color *Sports Illustrated* v125 no15 p24 N 7 2016

American Voices Meghan Klingenberg color *Sports Illustrated* v126 no11 p24 Ap 17-24 2017

American Voices Michael Mmoh color *Sports Illustrated* v125 no18 p22 D 5 2016

American Voices Nneka Ogwumike color *Sports Illustrated* v125 no12 p20 O 10 2016

American Voices Pierre Garçon color *Sports Illustrated* v125 no17 p26 N 21 2016 Double Issue

American Voices Sean Doolittle color *Sports Illustrated* v126 no8 p30 Mr 20 2017

And the Award Goes to ... color *Sports Illustrated* v126 no5 p18 F 13 2017

Anything You Can Do ... color *Sports Illustrated* v126 no2 p23 Ja 16 2017

Arrival Instincts color *Sports Illustrated* v125 no14 p24 O 24-31 2016

Ask the Host color *Sports Illustrated* v126 no4 p19 Ja 30 2017

Austin Power color *Sports Illustrated* v125 no19 p22 D 12 2016

Auto Pilots color *Sports Illustrated* v126 no7 p26 Mr 6 2017

Awesome Foursomes color *Sports Illustrated* v126 no10 p28 Ap 10 2017

Back at the Starting Line color *Sports Illustrated* v126 no1 p18 Ja 9 2017

Back to the Basket color *Sports Illustrated* v126 no14 p28 My 15-22 2017

Bader Up color *Sports Illustrated* v127 no5 p30 Ag 14 2017

Bambi Wulf 1954-2017 color *Sports Illustrated* v126 no17 p18 Je 19 2017

Beyond Words color *Sports Illustrated* v125 no12 p16 O 10 2016

Bickell Brave color *Sports Illustrated* v126 no11 p21 Ap 17-24 2017

Big Man on Campus color *Sports Illustrated* v125 no13 p16 O 17 2016

Biter Beware color *Sports Illustrated* v127 no1 p22 Jl 3 2017

BLOWN COVER color *Sports Illustrated* v127 no7 p22 S 4 2017

Body of Work color *Sports Illustrated* v125 no21 p22 D 26 2016

Book of Joe color *Sports Illustrated* v125 no16 p20 N 14 2016

The 'Boys Are Back color *Sports Illustrated* v126 no1 p12 Ja 9 2017

Bracket of Brackets color diag *Sports Illustrated* v125 no16 p18 N 14 2016

Brats Amore color *Sports Illustrated* v126 no17 p24 Je 19 2017

Broadcast Muse color *Sports Illustrated* v126 no12 p17 My 1 2017

Broga? color *Sports Illustrated* v126 no14 p24 My 15-22 2017

Care Taker color *Sports Illustrated* v126 no10 p26 Ap 10 2017

The Case for ... A Stadium-Funding Stiff-Arm color *Sports Illustrated* v126 no2 p20 Ja 16 2017

The Case for ... Athletes In Office color *Sports Illustrated* v125 no15 p28 N 7 2016

The Case for ... Banishing Beanballs color *Sports Illustrated* v126 no15 p26 My 29 2017

The Case for ... Boxing's Big Summer color *Sports Illustrated* v126 no17 p30 Je 19 2017

The Case for ... CHANGING THE TRANSFER RULE color *Sports Illustrated* v127 no8 p26 S 18 2017

The Case for ... Christian in The Middle color *Sports Illustrated* v126 no9 p28 Mr 27 2017

The Case for ... Clarity color *Sports Illustrated* v126 no1 p19 Ja 9 2017

The Case for ... Exercising Caution color *Sports Illustrated* v126 no8 p29 Mr 20 2017

The Case for ... Fewer Cowboys color *Sports Illustrated* v126 no11 p29 Ap 17-24 2017

The Case for ... GIANCARLO STANTON color *Sports Illustrated* v127 no7 p30 S 4 2017

The Case for ... JAROMIR JAGR color *Sports Illustrated* v127 no9 p19 S 25 2017

The Case for ... Killing TNF color *Sports Illustrated* v125 no18 p26 D 5 2016

The Case for ... Monica Abbott color *Sports Illustrated* v126 no18 p22 Je 26 2017

The Case for ... Peak NBA color *Sports Illustrated* v127 no2 p27 Jl 17 2017

The Case for ... Showing Off the Kids color *Sports Illustrated* v125 no14 p31 O 24-31 2016

The Case for ... Starting College Early color *Sports Illustrated* v126 no3 p19 Ja 23 2017

The Case for ... The Career Slam color *Sports Illustrated* v127 no4 p24 Ag 7 2017

The Case for ... The High School Combine color *Sports Illustrated* v126 no14 p31 My 15-22 2017

The Case for ... The White Sox color *Sports Illustrated* v126 no12 p21 My 1 2017

The Case for ... Time Off color *Sports Illustrated* v127 no1 p28 Jl 3 2017

Catching Trout color *Sports Illustrated* v127 no1 p26 Jl 3 2017

Checkmate color *Sports Illustrated* v125 no19 p26 D 12 2016

Cheer to Eternity color *Sports Illustrated* v126 no9 p23 Mr 27 2017

Chuck Redux color *Sports Illustrated* v126 no13 p22 My 8 2017

Strike of 1913 *Harper's Magazine* v335 no2006 p53 Jl 2017

KEIZER, GREGG

Another 40 million people bolt from Microsoft's browsers as mass exodus continues color graph *PCWorld* p58 D 2016

Microsoft tells some Mac Office users to pass on Apple's High Sierra color *Macworld - Digital Edition* v34 no10 p86 O 2017

Kelanic, Rosemary A.

Getting Out of the Gulf color *Foreign Affairs* v96 no1 p122 Ja/F 2017

Kelber, Almut

The biology of color color *Science* v357 no6350 p470 Ag 4 2017

Kelce, Travis

TRAVIS KELCE DOES A VERY TRAVIS KELCE THING D. Greene color *Sports Illustrated* v127 no12 p26 O 16 2017

Kelchen, Robert

America's Best Bang for the Buck Colleges 2016 *Washington Monthly* p1 S/O 2016

AMERICA'S BEST BANG FOR THE BUCK COLLEGES 2017 *Washington Monthly* v49 no9/10 p46 S/O 2017

Keldysh, Leonid

Leonid Keldysh F. Capasso, P. Corkum et al *Physics Today* v70 no6 p75 Je 2017

Kelela (Performer)

'REWIND' J. WORTHAM color *New York Times Magazine* p29 Mr 12 2017

Kelin, Daniel A. II

Purposefully poetic bibl chart diag *Arts Education Policy Review* v118 no4 p202 2017

Kelkar, Supriya

Ahimsa *Publishers Weekly* v264 no32 p73 Ag 7 2017

Kell, John

THE 2017 Fortune Crystal Ball color diag *Fortune* v174 no7 p11 D 1 2016

Big Food Is Going to Get Even Bigger color diag *Fortune* v175 no4 p11 Mr 15 2017

Celebs Dabble in Weird Food color *Fortune* v176 no1 p14 Jl 1 2017

DIGITAL DIET color *Fortune* v175 no4 p38 Mr 15 2017

Drink Local, Buy Global color map *Fortune* v176 no1 p13 Jl 1 2017

FORGET STEMWARE. BEHOLD THE RISE OF WINE IN A CAN color *Fortune* v174 no6 p10 N 1 2016

FROM THE GYM TO THE RUNWAY color diag *Fortune* v174 no6 p67 N 1 2016

GENERAL MILLS LOSES THE CULTURE WARS color diag *Fortune* v175 no7 p66 Je 1 2017

A HOUSE UNITED BY ROSÉ color *Fortune* v176 no2 p44 Ag 1 2017

Is Craft Beer All Froth? color diag *Fortune* v175 no6 p15 My 1 2017

Lunch Is Dead color *Fortune* v175 no5 p12 Ap 1 2017

MEET THE WORKPLACE CULTURE WARRIORS color *Fortune* v175 no4 p117 Mr 15 2017

NEXT GIN color *Fortune* v175 no2 p28 F 1 2017

RESTAURANTS' DIGITAL DILEMMA color *Fortune* v175 no8 p57 Je 15 2017

WATCH OUT, NIKE, THE GERMANS ARE COMING color *Fortune* v175 no8 p46 Je 15 2017

Kellam, Ed

All in the Family K. Andrews *Virginia Living* v15 no3 p72 Ap 2017

Kelleher, Katy

Practical Magic color map *American Craft* v77 no3 p86 Je/Jl 2017

Keller, Andreas

Predicting human olfactory perception from chemical features of odor molecules bibl diag graph *Science* v355 no6327 p820 F 24 2017

KELLER, BILL

Cop to It *New York Times Book Review* p12 F 26 2017

Keller, Cathryne

5 JUICY CONFESSIONS with... Keanu Reeves color *Women's Health* v14 no2 p126 Mr 2017

5 JUICY QUESTIONS with... Riz Ahmed color *Women's Health* v13 no10 p108 D 2016

5 JUICY QUESTIONS with... SCOTT SPEEDMAN color *Women's Health* v14 no4 p128 My 2017

5 JUICY QUESTIONS with... The Chainsmokers color *Women's Health* v14 no3 p128 Ap 2017

The Fine Tint color *O, The Oprah Magazine* p30 O 2017

Keller, Christoph

We're On: A June Jordan Reader A. MONET color *Publishers Weekly* v264 no34 p86 Ag 21 2017

Keller, Des

MICROLOANS *Successful Farming* v114 no10 p61 O 2016

Keller, Father Paul

When politics trumps faith color *U.S. Catholic* v81 no11 p23 N 2016

Keller, H. U.

Rosetta's comet 67P/Churyumov-Gerasimenko sheds its dusty mantle to reveal its icy nature bibl graph *Science* v354 no6319 p1566 D 23 2016

Surface changes on comet 67P/Churyumov-Gerasimenko suggest a more active past bw graph *Science* v355 no6332 p1392 Mr 31 2017

Keller, J. R.

The Best Way to Hire from Inside Your Company *Harvard Business Review Digital Articles* p2 Je 1 2015

Keller, Joyce

REMEMBERING PEARL HARBOR *Saturday Evening Post* v288 no6 p6 N/D 2016

KELLER, KELLER

GRILLING 101 with Andy Husbands color *Yankee* p54 My/Je 2017

Keller, Kevin Lane

The Branding Logic Behind Google's Creation of Alphabet *Harvard Business Review Digital Articles* p2 Ag 14 2015

Keller, Laura J.

Hot Tickets and Wall Street Marks *Bloomberg Businessweek* no4540 p33 O 2 2017

Traders' New Favorite Way to Swap Secrets color *Bloomberg Businessweek* no4518 p41 Ap 10 2017

Keller, M. Jean

Older Adults *Parks & Recreation* v52 no1 p36 Ja 2017

Keller, M. Jean—Interviews

Member Spotlight: M. Jean Keller V. Paynich *Parks & Recreation* v52 no3 p51 Mr 2017

Keller, Rachel

Head Trip img *New York* p72 F 20 2017

Rachel KELLER S. LACAVA *Interview* v46 no8 p28 O 2016

KELLER, REUBEN

Ecology for All *BioScience* v67 no8 p769 Ag 2017

Scientific and Normative Foundations for the Valuation of Alien-Species Impacts: Thirteen Core Principles *BioScience* v67 no2 p166 F 2017

Keller, Scott

ABNEY AND KELLER BANK color *Team Roping Journal* p26 O 2017

Keller, Thomas, 1955-

GOLDEN TICKET S. Lyon cartoon *New Yorker* v93 no3 p24 Mr 6 2017

Keller, Timothy

Leaning Toward God A. B. LLOYD *Weekly Standard* v22 no6 p32 O 17 2016

Lessons from the Keller controversy M. C. Barnes *Christian Century* v134 no17 p35 Ag 16 2017

PTS cancels award to Keller but not lecture C. Kennel-Shank color *Christian Century* v134 no9 p12 Ap 26 2017

Keller, U.

Dual-comb spectroscopy of water vapor with a free-running semiconductor disk laser diag *Science* v356 no6343 p1164 Je 16 2017

Keller, Valerie

Find Purpose in Even Your Most Mundane Tasks at Work color graph *Harvard Business Review Digital Articles* p2 Mr 8 2017

Keller, Warren

GALLERY *Sky & Telescope* v133 no4 p74 Ap 2017

Narrowband Color in PixInsight *Sky & Telescope* v133 no4 p36 Ap 2017

READER GALLERY color *Astronomy* v45 no1 p72 Ja 2017

Keller Williams Realty Inc.

The Neighborhood Naming Game: What people call a community can have a big impact on its self-image A. Ehrenhalt *Governing*

v31 no1 p14 O 2017

KELLER LAIRD, AMY

(A HAPPY) LIFE'S A BEACH color *Women's Health* v14 no5 p8 Je 2017

Editors Tell All! bw color *Women's Health* v14 no2 p60 Mr 2017

INCONCEIVABLE? PERHAPS. IMPOSSIBLE? NEVER! color *Women's Health* v14 no8 p8 O 2017

I'VE GOT SOMETHING TO CONFESS... color *Women's Health* v14 no2 p8 Mr 2017

LIKE MOTHER, LIKE DAUGHTER *Women's Health* v14 no4 p8 My 2017

THE POWER OF "WHY" color *Women's Health* v14 no6 p10 Jl 2017

WELLNESS IS BEAUTIFUL color *Women's Health* v14 no3 p8 Ap 2017

Kelley, Bruce

Dear Readers *Reader's Digest* v189 no1127 p4 F 2017

Kelley, Cody

old dog's tricks r. cleek bw color *Bike Magazine* v24 no4 p42 Je 2017

Kelley, David E.

Systemic pan-AMPK activator MK-8722 improves glucose homeostasis but induces cardiac hypertrophy graph *Science* v357 no6350 p507 Ag 4 2017

Kelley, David E., 1956-

DAVID E. KELLEY D. HOLBROOK *TV Guide* v65 no35 p6 Ag 21 2017

A TV Legend's Unremarkable Return D. D'addario color *Time* v188 no15 p54 O 17 2016

Kelley, Linda Molner

Learning from schools that close opportunity gaps *Phi Delta Kappan* v99 no1 p8 S 2017

Kelley, Moe

Deciding to Fix or Kill a Problem Product *Harvard Business Review Digital Articles* p2 Je 19 2015

Kelley, Norman

The Revolution Will Be Analyzed *Washington Monthly* p9 N/D 2016

Kelley, Owen

John Phillips J. Phillips color *Car & Driver* v62 no8 p24 F 2017

Kelley, Reid

Can competitive product markets reduce workplace discrimination? *Monthly Labor Review* p1 Ag 2017

Kelley, Tom

3 Things the Most Creative Leaders Do *Harvard Business Review Digital Articles* p2 D 10 2015

Kellner, Mark A.

State Department to keep anti-Semitism envoy but scrap many others *Christian Century* v134 no20 p15 S 27 2017

Kellner, Peter

To fight climate change, we need to improve capitalism, not get rid of it *America* v216 no11 p10 My 15 2017

KELLOGG, CRAIG

COOL & COLLECTED color *House Beautiful* v158 no9 p150 N 2016

Kellogg, Kristin

BEST OF ATLANTA *Atlanta* v56 no8 p106 D 2016

Kellogg, Richard

Mossberg Memories *New York State Conservationist* v72 no2 p32 O 2017

Kellogg, W. K. (Will Keith), 1860-1951

Wit and Wisdom from Our Early Breeders M. J. PARKINSON *Arabian Horse World* v57 no1 p100 O 2016

Kellogg-Briand Pact (1928)

DROP YOUR WEAPONS L. MENAND cartoon color *New Yorker* v93 no28 p61 S 18 2017

Kellogg Co.

How General Mills and Kellogg Are Tackling Greenhouse Gas Emissions A. Winston *Harvard Business Review Digital Articles* p2 Je 1 2016

Kellon, Eleanor M.

5 First-Aid Kit Essentials color *Trail Rider* v29 no2 p22 Mr 2017

Overcome 5 Cold-Weather Challenges color *Trail Rider* v29 no1 p28 Ja/F 2017

Your Horse's Coggins Test color *Trail Rider* v29 no3 p14 Ap 2017

KELLOW, BRIAN

PATRICE MUNSEL. SPOKANE, WA, MAY 14, 1925-SCHROON LAKE, NY, AUGUST 4, 2016 *Opera News* v81 no5 p62 N 2016

Sarah Mesko *Opera News* v81 no5 p12 N 2016

Kelly & Stone Architects Inc.

Mountain Modern color *Timber Home Living* p46 2017 SpecialIssue

Kelly, Adam G.

All-printed thin-film transistors from networks of liquid-exfoliated nanosheets diag *Science* v356 no6333 p69 Ap 7 2017

Kelly, Aileen M.

Controlled Experiments *American Scholar* v86 no1 p116 Wint 2017

The Discovery of Chance: The Life and Thought of Alexander Herzen R. Legvold *Foreign Affairs* v96 no1 p169 Ja/F 2017

Herzen: The Hero of Skeptical Idealism G. S. Morson bw *New York Review of Books* v63 no18 p45 N 24 2016

Kelly, Ben

Q: What is the most interesting family in history? color *Atlantic* v318 no5 p96 D 2016

Kelly, Betsy

Divyn Inspiration and Betsy Kelley K. Hopp *Arabian Horse World* v57 no10 p105 Jl 2017

Kelly, Brett

BROUGHT UP BAD C. Collis color *Entertainment Weekly* no1441 p35 N 25 2016

Kelly, Bruce

Dear Readers *Reader's Digest* v188 no1124 p4 O 2016

KELLY, CAITLIN

The Best Boots of 2018 color *Powder* p95 S 2017

Sea Change color *House Beautiful* p86 Jl 2017

THE TITUS MIRACLE color *Powder* v46 no2 p30 O 2017

Kelly, Catherine E.

Republic of Taste: Art, Politics, and Everyday Life in Early America E. Pochoda color *Magazine Antiques* v183 no6 p52 N/D 2016

Kelly, Chris

an unpredicted journey n. formosa color *Bike Magazine* v24 no3 p46 My 2017

KELLY, CHRISTOPHER

REVENGE OF THE FILM NERDS *Texas Monthly* v45 no7 p70 Jl 2017

Kelly, Clinton—Interviews

CLINTON KELLY M. LOGAN *TV Guide* v65 no19 p14 My 1 2017

Kelly, David

Killer Crossover T. S. YOUNG and S. T. BROWN color *Ebony* v72 no6 p74 Ap/My 2017

KELLY, DEIRDRE

Natasha Sheehan *Dance Magazine* v91 no4 p22 Ap 2017

Kelly, Devin

This, a Gospel *America* v217 no7 p43 O 2 2017

Kelly, Donika

Bestiary S. Kleinman color *Orion Magazine* v35 no6 p59 N/D 2016

Kelly, Eileen

"I feel sexually powerful always." color *Glamour* v115 no7 p91 Jl 2017

KELLY, EMILY

look at this trove, treasures untold cartoon *Popular Science* v289 no2 p76 Mr/Ap 2017

Kelly, Gail

What Kind of Leader Do You Want to Be? R. Newton *Harvard Business Review Digital Articles* p2 Ja 26 2015

Kelly, Gene, 1912-1996

Dancer with Alvin Ailey American Dance Theater R. McLaren *Dance Magazine* v91 no9 p72 S 2017

A Man in Motion bw *Weekly Standard* v22 no46 p30 Ag 14 2017

Working It M. KORESKY color *Film Comment* v53 no3 p42 My/Je 2017

Kelly, Grace, 1992-

JAZZ ALBUM OF THE YEAR bw color *Downbeat* v83 no12 p38 D 2016

Kelly, Helena

The Austenista E. SHOWALTER *New Republic* v248 no8/9 p72 Ag/S 2017

Jane Austen, the Secret Radical *Publishers Weekly* v264 no7 p60 F 13 2017

You Don't Know Jane: A new reading of Jane Austen's novels depicts her as a critic of her society J. Sutherland *New York Times Book Review* p11 Jl 16 2017

Kelly, Hillary

COOK, EAT, LAUGH, REPEAT *Washingtonian Magazine* v52 no1 p155 O 2016

DECK THE TABLE *Washingtonian Magazine* v52 no2 p271 N 2016

GIFT GUIDE 2016 *Washingtonian Magazine* v52 no3 p84 D 2016

How Do Young Women Feel About Hillary Clinton? [Cover story] *Glamour* v114 no11 p174 N 2016

"I made this decision for her" color *Glamour* v115 no4 p126 Ap 2017

PACK A PRETTY PICNIC: No yard? No problem. Turn one of Washington's beautiful parks into your own outdoor dining room *Washingtonian Magazine* v52 no8 p169 My 2017

A TALE OF TWO BAR CARTS *Washingtonian Magazine* v52 no3 p170 D 2016

WHOA, BABY *Washingtonian Magazine* v52 no5 p148 F 2017

Why I'm Running color *Glamour* v115 no10 p146 O 2017

KELLY, IVAN W.

Tests of Astrology: A Critical Review of Hundreds of Studies *Skeptical Inquirer* v41 no3 p58 My/Je 2017

KELLY, JAMES R.

AN URBAN DEFENDER color *America* v215 no14 p32 N 7 2016

Kelly, Jason

A One-Stop Hit Shop bw *Bloomberg Businessweek* no4538 p61 S 18 2017

There's No 'I' in Tone House color *Bloomberg Businessweek* no4528 p72 Je 26 2017

Kelly, Jean P.

One bread? color *U.S. Catholic* v82 no6 p28 Je 2017

KELLY, JEFFREY F.

From Agricultural Benefits to Aviation Safety: Realizing the Potential of Continent-Wide Radar Networks *BioScience* v67 no10 p912 O 2017

Kelly, Jerrie

Around the Campfire color *Trail Rider* v29 no4 p8 My 2017

Kelly, Jim

Body-mounted couplers on auto racks color *Model Railroader* v84 no11 p24 N 2017

Bringing engines back from the dead color *Model Railroader* v84 no1 p26 Ja 2017

Derailments of the curious kind color *Model Railroader* v84 no7 p22 Jl 2017

Easier access to an N scale sneak track color *Model Railroader* v84 no3 p24 Mr 2017

Horseshoe curves work better in N scale color *Model Railroader* v84 no5 p20 My 2017

THE IBSEN MYSTERY color *Vanity Fair* v59 no5 p94 Ap 2017

A little paint can improve N scale ready-to-run freight cars color *Model Railroader* v84 no9 p20 S 2017

PARTNERS IN RHYME bw *Vanity Fair* v58 no11 p113 N 2016

That Other Clinton *New York Times Book Review* p7 Ja 22 2017

WELCOME TO CANADA color *Vanity Fair* v59 no2 p98 F 2017

Kelly, Jim, 1960-

Death Ship *Publishers Weekly* v263 no42 p53 O 17 2016

KELLY, JOHN

Laugh Lines color *Reader's Digest* v190 no1132 p86 Jl/Ag 2017

Kelly, John F. (John Francis), 1950-

Country First [Cover story] M. Duffy, A. Altman et al color *Time* v190 no7 p26 Ag 21 2017

The Pros and Cons of a Mexico Border Wall *Congressional Digest* v96 no8 p8 O 2017

KELLY, JON

A DIFFERENT REALITY bw color *Vanity Fair* v59 no4 p140 Mr 2017

KELLY, JOSEPH

COSMIC CAN-DO *Scientific American* v316 no6 p6 Je 2017

Kelly, Justin

A God worthy of belief color *America* v217 no4 p51 Ag 21 2017

I Am Michael Maps Painful Betrayal S. Zacharek color *Time* v189 no4 p51 F 6 2017

Kelly, Karen

diet for a green planet color *Yoga Journal* p117 2017 Special Issue

Kelly, Kathleen

Reprogramming to resist bibl diag *Science* v355 no6320 p29 Ja 6 2017

Kelly, L. T.

Using fire to promote biodiversity bibl color *Science* v355 no6331 p1264 Mr 24 2017

Kelly, Lesley

A Fine House in Trinity *Publishers Weekly* v263 no40 p101 O 3 2016

Kelly, Lois

5 Mistakes Employees Make When Challenging the Status Quo *Harvard Business Review Digital Articles* p2 N 24 2016

Kelly, Lynn

LYNN KELLY color *Tricycle: The Buddhist Review* v26 no2 p22 Wint 2016

Kelly, Matthew

TV guide M. J. Rose color *U.S. Catholic* v82 no4 p22 Ap 2017

Kelly, Megyn, 1970-

Can MEGYN KELLY ESCAPE Her Past? C. FLANAGAN cartoon color *Atlantic* v319 no2 p88 Mr 2017

FOX EATS CROW E. NUSSBAUM cartoon *New Yorker* v92 no36 p64 N 7 2016

Freedom of Speech Doesn't Guarantee the Right to a Megaphone J. Jackson *Extra!* v30 no7 p4 S 2017

Megyn KELLY color *Vanity Fair* v59 no1 p125 Holiday 2017

Megyn Kelly, Queen of TV Sparring, Meets Her Match D. D'Addario color *Time* v189 no23 p53 Je 19 2017

Movers K. Stock color graph *Bloomberg Businessweek* no4506 p11 Ja 9 2017

ONLY CONNECT M. Daum bw *Vogue* v207 no9 p680 S 2017

Quotable Quotes *Reader's Digest* v189 no1130 p140 My 2017

Settle for More T. Jordan color *Entertainment Weekly* no1441 p57 N 25 2016

Kelly, Megyn, 1970——Interviews

By the Book *New York Times Book Review* p7 N 13 2016

"I Have Zero Doubt I Can Do This Job": Former Fox News anchor Megyn Kelly faces off against 60 Minutes and Kelly Ripa in her quest to take over both primetime and daytime with two new NBC shows I. RUDOLPH *TV Guide* v65 no27 p14 Je 26 2017

Megyn in the Morning: The former Fox News golden girl turned NBC multitasker hopes to rise--and shine--as her new a.m. talk show debuts I. RUDOLPH *TV Guide* v65 no39 p10 S 18 2017

Kelly, Michelle

What Lilly Pulitzer Learned About Marketing to Millennials *Harvard Business Review Digital Articles* p2 Mr 31 2016

KELLY, MILIARY

THE Loving STORY *Washingtonian Magazine* v52 no2 p92 N 2016

Kelly, Nataly

7 Traits of Companies on the Fast Track to International Growth *Harvard Business Review Digital Articles* p2 Mr 6 2015

How Marketing Is Evolving in Latin America *Harvard Business Review Digital Articles* p2 Je 1 2015

The Most Common Mistakes Companies Make with Global Marketing *Harvard Business Review Digital Articles* p2 S 7 2015

Kelly, Patrick

Improving Alignment between Educational Supply and Labor Market Needs *Change* v49 no1 p34 Ja/F 2017

The Production and Migration of Educational Capital *Change* v49 no3 p71 My/Je 2017

Should Catholics be feeling March Madness? color *America* v216 no6 p36 Mr 20 2017

Kelly, Robert

Companies with a Formal Sales Process Generate More Revenue *Harvard Business Review Digital Articles* p2 Ja 21 2015

Kelly, Robert E.

Pop Chart R. Bruner, C. Lang et al color *Time* v189 no12 p62 Ap 3 2017

Kelly, Robert L.

How America Lost Its Mind color *Atlantic* v320 no4 p12 N 2017

KELLY, SANDRA

A Family Reunion with a Twist [Cover story] bw color *Cabin Living* p46 Ag 2017

Kelly, Sarah

The Secret Life of the Mind *Science* v356 no6342 p1006 Je 9 2017

Kelly, Scott, 1964-

The Man Who Fell to Earth: America's longest-orbiting astronaut describes his rocky return home in this adaptation from his book Endurance *Smithsonian* v48 no5 p29 S 2017

ROCKET MAN E. NAWOTKA color *Publishers Weekly* v264 no32 p44 Ag 7 2017

Scott Kelly T. WOLFE color *Vanity Fair* v59 no9 p222 S 2017

Space Odyssey S. Kelly color *National Geographic* v232 no2 p66 Ag 2017

WHAT I LEARNED IN SPACE color *AARP: The Magazine* v30 no6A p41 O/N 2017

Kelly, Scott, 1964-—Interviews

OUT OF THIS WORLD: SCOTT KELLY'S YEAR IN SPACE N. STOCKTON bw color *Wired* v25 no9 p15 S 2017

Kelly, Simon

Life at the top cartoon *Magazine Antiques* v184 no1 p124 Ja/F 2017

Kelly, Sofie

A Tale of Two Kitties: A Magical Cats Mystery *Publishers Weekly* v264 no28 p66 Jl 10 2017

Kelly-Irving, Michelle

Promoting human rights through science color *Science* v357 no6359 p34 O 6 2017

Kelman, Glenn

How Did I Get Here? GLENN KELMAN bw color *Bloomberg Businessweek* no4515 p68 Mr 20 2017

Kelman, James

11. Read Dirt Road *New York* v50 no15 p75 Jl 24 2017

Living the Blues: After a family tragedy, two Scots seek solace in the American South B. MARKOVITS *New York Times Book Review* p21 S 10 2017

Kelp bed ecology

Scientists snoop to check on kelp R. EHRENBERG *Science News* v192 no1 p10 Ag 5 2017

Kelp bed ecology—California

Invasion of the Kelp Snatchers A. DOUGLAS color *Surfer* v58 no1 p38 Ap 2017

Underwater Barrens D. SIMPSON *Natural History* v125 no2 p24 F 2017

Kelps

KELP IS ON THE WAY C. Zuckerman color *National Geographic* v232 no5 p14 N 2017

Seaweed Dreaming R. Jacobsen *Yankee* v81 no1 p120 Ja/F 2017

Kelsey, Blythe

Hawaii Opera Theatre F. COHN *Opera News* v81 no6 p14 D 2016

KELSEY, COLLEEN

Dua LIPA: THE BRITISH SINGER SONGWRITER FUSES SOUL AND POP BY MAKING IT PERSONAL *Interview* v47 no3 p22 Ap 2017

Gus BIRNEY *Interview* v46 no10 p28 D 2016/Ja 2017

Jacqueline RABUN: THE LONDON-BASED JEWELRY DESIGNER CREATES MODERN, COVETABLE WORKS OF ART MEANT TO BE WORN AND CHERISHED *Interview* v47 no3 p38 Ap 2017

Jonathan SAUNDERS *Interview* v47 no2 p112 Mr 2017

Junichi ABE *Interview* v47 no1 p32 F 2017

RISE UP *Interview* v47 no3 p36 Ap 2017

KELSEY, ELIZABETH

Show Me The Money *Psychology Today* v49 no6 p35 N/D 2016

Kelsey, Frances Oldham, 1914-2015—Awards

The Heroine of the FDA N. KRIPLEN bw *Discover* v38 no2 p68 Mr 2017

Kelsey, Gavin

Single-cell epigenomics: Recording the past and predicting the future diag *Science* v357 no6359 p69 O 6 2017

Kelsey, Quinn

Patience Rewarded: Quinn Kelsey waited to sing the great Verdi baritone roles until the time was right. This month, he's San Francisco Opera's Rigoletto F. P. Driscoll *Opera News* v81 no12 p45 Je 2017

KELSEY, RICK G.

Physiological Stress and Ethanol Accumulation in Tree Stems and Woody Tissues at Sublethal Temperatures from Fire *BioScience* v67 no5 p443 My 2017

Kelso, Janet

Neandertal and Denisovan DNA from Pleistocene sediments bw color *Science* v356 no6338 p605 My 12 2017

Kelso, Johnathon

Black churches in North Carolina have responded to cutbacks in early voting by the Republican legislature by organizing "Souls to the Polls" marches after services color *Bloomberg Businessweek* no4498 p37 N 7 2016

Kelso, Scott

Big Daddy Medicine Man J. Kirkpatrick color *American Cowboy* v24 no1 p19 Je/Jl 2017

Kelso, Stirling

Baja Soul color *Conde Nast Traveler* v52 no6 p36 Je/Jl 2017

BEST IN TRAVEL 2017 color *Money* v46 no3 p58 Ap 2017

Just Wait Till Next Year color *Money* v45 no11 p17 D 2016

Save While You Serve color *Money* v46 no2 p24 Mr 2017

TOP 10 EUROPE TRIPS FOR YOUR MONEY color *Money* v46 no5 p48 Je 2017

TRIPS THAT TRANSPORT AND TRANSFORM color *Martha Stewart Living* p102 Mr 2017

Where to go in 2017 color *Money* v46 no1 p124 Ja/F 2017

Kelton, Elmer

Writers bw cartoon color *American Cowboy* p28 LEGENDS OF TEXAS Special Issue 2017

Kelton, Ketch

Raising a Phenom J. Mankin color *Spin to Win Rodeo* v20 no10 p34 D 2016

KELTY, CATRINE

GRILLING 101 with Andy Husbands color *Yankee* p54 My/Je 2017

Strawberry-Rhubarb Coffee Cake color *Yankee* p68 My/Je 2017

"WEEKENDS" WARRIOR color *Yankee* p50 Mr 2017

Kelty, Edward J.

CIRCUS DAYS R. Smith bw *American History* v52 no3 p56 Ag 2017

Kem, Erin

Deviled Egg Taco color *Indianapolis Monthly* p47 Ap 2017

Kemalism

From Abdulhamid II to Ataturk: Change or Continuity in Turkey's History M. GÖKÇEK *Islamic Horizons* v46 no3 p54 My/Je 2017

Kemberling, Holly

Mismatch repair deficiency predicts response of solid tumors to PD-1 blockade chart graph *Science* v357 no6349 p409 Jl 28 2017

Kemble, Celerie—Interviews

THE GREENHOUSE EFFECT J. LASKY color *House Beautiful* v159 no4 p98 My 2017

Kemeny, John G., 1926-1992

How to Fix Democracy color *MIT Technology Review* v120 no1 p112 Ja/F 2017

Kemmer, Christian

Reversion of antibiotic resistance in Mycobacterium tuberculosis by spiroisoxazoline SMARt-420 bibl diag *Science* v355 no6330 p1206 Mr 17 2017

Kemmerich, N.

Observation of a large-scale anisotropy in the arrival directions of cosmic rays above 8 × 1018 eV *Science* v357 no6357 p1266 S 22 2017

Kemp, Christopher

Collections Matter color *Natural History* v125 no10 p38 O 2017

Darwin, the crowdsourcer color *Science* v357 no6356 p1104 S 15 2017

The First Art: The Earliest Hominin Engraving bw color diag *Natural History* v125 no10 p34 O 2017

Travels through time bw color *Science* v355 no6321 p138 Ja 13 2017

Kemp, Daniel M.

Systemic pan-AMPK activator MK-8722 improves glucose homeostasis but induces cardiac hypertrophy graph *Science* v357 no6350 p507 Ag 4 2017

Kemp, E.

Observation of a large-scale anisotropy in the arrival directions of cosmic rays above 8 × 1018 eV *Science* v357 no6357 p1266 S 22 2017

Kemp, J.

Observation of a large-scale anisotropy in the arrival directions of cosmic rays above 8 × 1018 eV *Science* v357 no6357 p1266

S 22 2017

Kemp, John R.
BATON ROUGE AND THE VISUAL ARTS cartoon color *Louisiana Life* v37 no4 p32 Mr/Ap 2017
CAROLINE YOUNGBLOOD color *Louisiana Life* v37 no5 p20 My/Je 2017
DAWN DEDEAUX bw color *Louisiana Life* v38 no1 p22 S/O 2017
MICHEL VARISCO bw color *Louisiana Life* v37 no6 p16 Jl/Ag 2017
PARALLEL WORLDS bw color *Louisiana Life* v37 no3 p30 Ja/F 2017
The QUIZ bw color diag *New Orleans Magazine* v51 no12 p68 O 2017
XAVIER GONZALEZ cartoon *Louisiana Life* v37 no2 p32 N/D 2016

Kemp, Kristen
playing favorites *Parents* v91 no12 p128 D 2016
YA Stories You Should Snatch Up color *Parents* v92 no7 p16 Jl 2017

kemp, lacy
curators of self bw color *Bike Magazine* v24 no6 p102 Ag 2017
FORWARD MOMENTUM color *Bike Magazine* v24 no1 p116 Ja/F 2017
GET IN GEAR bw color *Bike Magazine* v24 no1 p122 Ja/F 2017
Liv Pique color *Bike Magazine* v24 no5 p92 Jl 2017
made rad color *Bike Magazine* v24 no2 p38 Mr 2017

Kemp, Melissa
Merging paleobiology with conservation biology to guide the future of terrestrial ecosystems color *Science* v355 no6325 p594 F 10 2017

Kemp, Mike
WAYPOINT N. KREBS color *Outdoor Life* v224 no1 p9 D 2016/Ja 2017

Kempa, Stefan
Fructose-driven glycolysis supports anoxia resistance in the naked mole-rat diag graph *Science* v356 no6335 p307 Ap 21 2017

Kempainen, Bob
A SICK FINISH K. A. FETTERS color *Runner's World* v51 no10 p33 N 2016

Kemper, Ellie, 1980-
KIMMY SCHMIDT GOES TO COLLEGE: Females are smart as hell! Season 3 of Unbreakable Kimmy Schmidt finds its titular heroine heading off to get a higher education D. HOLBROOK *TV Guide* v65 no21 p24 My 15 2017
Unbreakable Kimmy Schmidt J. Jensen color *Entertainment Weekly* no1466 p46 My 19 2017
With Kimmy Schmidt in the land of the happy fools J. McDermott color *America* v217 no2 p48 Jl 24 2017

Kempkes, Taylor
Hot Rod Anything! Motorized Picnic Table Because—Why Not? color *Hot Rod* v70 no1 p16 Ja 2017

Kempner, Randall
Startup Accelerators Have Become More Popular in Emerging Markets—and They're Working *Harvard Business Review Digital Articles* p2 O 2 2017

Kempski, Jan
A pathogenic role for T cell–derived IL-22BP in inflammatory bowel disease bibl graph *Science* v354 no6310 p358 O 21 2016

Kempton, Sally
The yoga of give & take color *Yoga Journal* no288 p28 D 2016
You are struggling to feel sympathy color *Yoga Journal* p41 2016 Special Issue
You can't help being overly critical of others bw *Yoga Journal* p40 2016 Special Issue
You find your job uninspiring color *Yoga Journal* p47 2016 Special Issue
You're in a funk color *Yoga Journal* p39 2016 Special Issue
You're jealous of a colleague or friend color *Yoga Journal* p45 2016 Special Issue
Your energy is flagging color *Yoga Journal* p48 2016 Special Issue
Your family is driving you crazy color *Yoga Journal* p44 2016 Special Issue

Kemsley, William "BackpackerBill", Jr.
MIND THE GAPS *Backpacker* v45 no1 p75 Ja 2017

Ken-ichi Kawarabayashi

A coherent Ising machine for 2000-node optimization problems bibl diag graph *Science* v354 no6312 p603 N 4 2016

KEN YASUKAWA
Bird Brains or Avian Einsteins? *BioScience* v67 no7 p672 Jl 2017

Kendall, Elizabeth
Buddy System color *O, The Oprah Magazine* p150 My 2017

Kendall, Greg
OLD FLAMES color *Field & Stream* v122 no1 p10 My 2017

Kendall, Jake
Fintech Companies Could Give Billions of People More Banking Options color *Harvard Business Review Digital Articles* p2 Ja 20 2017
Making Microfinance More Effective *Harvard Business Review Digital Articles* p2 O 5 2016

Kendall, Kelly
Best New Restaurants *Indianapolis Monthly* p58 My 2017
best of Indy *Indianapolis Monthly* v40 no4 p73 D 2016
BLAST from the PAST *Indianapolis Monthly* v40 no10 p86 Je 2017
CHANGE the CITY *Indianapolis Monthly* p55 Ap 2017
DOCTORING THE TRUTH: The worst lies you tell your physician *Indianapolis Monthly* p74 N 2017
IT'S a MaB, MaB, MaB, MaB WORLD *Indianapolis Monthly* v12 no40 p81 Ag 2017
Let's Get Stitched: A Bloomington seamstress does wedding wear that's more off-the-wall than off-the-rack *Indianapolis Monthly* v40 no11 p28 Jl 2017
Looking Fly color *Indianapolis Monthly* v42 no2 p29 O 2017
Pieces de Résistance: Outgoing Planned Parenthood CEO Betty Cockrum packs up a collection of quirky office tchotchkes *Indianapolis Monthly* v40 no10 p18 Je 2017
Speed Read *Indianapolis Monthly* v40 no3 p18 N 2016

Kendall, Mark—Interviews
"THE MAGIC NEGRO" G. GODFREY *Atlanta* v56 no11 p40 Mr 2017

KENDI, IBRAM X.
I WANT YOU TO MAKE HISTORY, NOT BE HISTORY *Vital Speeches of the Day* v83 no8 p232 Ag 2017
Rights, Wrongs and Roots *New York Times Book Review* p16 F 26 2017

Kendra Scott LLC
GEM DANDY color *O, The Oprah Magazine* p53 S 2017
Rock Solid color *Forbes* v199 no6 p77 Je 13 2017

Kendrick, Anna, 1985-
ACCORDING TO: Anna Kendrick J. DUBOFF bw *Vanity Fair* v59 no1 p100 Holiday 2017
"He just wasn't that into me" A. Kendrick color *Glamour* v114 no11 p121 N 2016

Kendrick, Anna, 1985—Interviews
Anna Kendrick color *New York Times Book Review* p10 D 4 2016
Boss Lady M. WAKIM *Los Angeles Magazine* p74 D 2016
Somebody to Love B. VOSS *Advocate* no1088 p64 D 2016/Ja 2017

Kendrick, Denise
A FAMILY BUILT BY FOSTER CARE color *Good Housekeeping* v263 no5 p110 N 2016

KENDRICK, GARY A.
Accelerating Tropicalization and the Transformation of Temperate Seagrass Meadows *BioScience* v66 no11 p938 N 1 2016

Kendsersky, Nathan M.
Ratchet-like polypeptide translocation mechanism of the AAA+ disaggregase Hsp104 diag *Science* v357 no6348 p273 Jl 21 2017

Keneally, Thomas, 1935-
Crimes of the Father *Publishers Weekly* v264 no33 p45 Ag 14 2017
A Throne in the Rearview Mirror *New York Times Book Review* p15 Ja 15 2017

Kenfack, David
Plant diversity increases with the strength of negative density dependence at the global scale diag *Science* v356 no6345 p1389 Je 30 2017

Kengo Kuma & Associates (Company)
Man and Nature bw color *Architectural Record* v205 no8 p12 Ag 2017

Kenigsberg, Abby R.

Release of mineral-bound water prior to subduction tied to shallow seismogenic slip off Sumatra graph *Science* v356 no6340 p841 My 26 2017

Keniston-Pond, Kymberly

SCENTS THAT SLIM color *Amazing Wellness* v8 no2 p70 Spr 2016

Kenji Watanabe

Ballistic miniband conduction in a graphene superlattice bibl graph *Science* v353 no6307 p1526 S 30 2016

Electron optics with p-n junctions in ballistic graphene bibl graph *Science* v353 no6307 p1522 S 30 2016

Kenji Yoshino

LGBT-Inclusive Companies Are Better at 3 Big Things *Harvard Business Review Digital Articles* p2 F 2 2016

Kenley, Casey

AHEAD OF THE CURRENT color *Indianapolis Monthly* v41 no2 p68 S 2017

Broad RIPPLE color map *Indianapolis Monthly* v41 no2 p66 S 2017

CAN YOU DIG IT? diag *Indianapolis Monthly* v41 no2 p72 S 2017

CONFESSIONS OF A FREE-RANGE PARENT *Indianapolis Monthly* v40 no4 p100 D 2016

A DAM SHAME *Indianapolis Monthly* v41 no2 p64 S 2017

Downtown color map *Indianapolis Monthly* v41 no2 p73 S 2017

Farther Downstream color map *Indianapolis Monthly* v41 no2 p77 S 2017

GM STAMPING PLANT color map *Indianapolis Monthly* v41 no2 p75 S 2017

Hamilton COUNTY color map *Indianapolis Monthly* v41 no2 p63 S 2017

Hot on the TRAILS: A ROAD-FREE GUIDE TO EXPLORING CENTRAL INDIANA *Indianapolis Monthly* v40 no10 p59 Je 2017

Last Rites: Leaders at St. Joseph's College allowed its finances to get so bad for so long, the situation became impossible to fix. If the historic Catholic school ever returns now, it will be a miracle *Indianapolis Monthly* v12 no40 p54 Ag 2017

MAKING A SPLASH color *Indianapolis Monthly* v41 no2 p76 S 2017

Mounds STATE PARK color map *Indianapolis Monthly* v41 no2 p60 S 2017

On the Brand Wagon *Indianapolis Monthly* v40 no3 p20 N 2016

Riverside PARK color map *Indianapolis Monthly* v41 no2 p68 S 2017

TOUR OF DOODY diag *Indianapolis Monthly* v41 no2 p65 S 2017

WHERE THE WILD THINGS ARE color *Indianapolis Monthly* v41 no2 p62 S 2017

THE White RIVER diag *Indianapolis Monthly* v41 no2 p59 S 2017

Kenmark Inc.

Kenmark - Exceptional scenic images, on time shipping, and outstanding customer service *Stage Directions* v30 no3 p30 Mr 2017

KENNARD, MATT

HOW ISRAEL PRIVATIZED ITS OCCUPATION OF PALESTINE color il *Nation* v303 no20 p20 N 14 2016

Kenneally, Miranda

Coming Up for Air *Publishers Weekly* v264 no20 p58 My 15 2017

Kennedy, A. L.

Neurotics Need Love Too J. THOMPSON *New York Times Book Review* p19 N 6 2016

KENNEDY, ADRIENNE

Watching Michelle color *Nation* v304 no1 p62 Ja 2 2017 The Obama Years

Kennedy, Anthony M., 1936-

A FREE MARKET FRIEND AT THE FTC D. ROOT *Reason* v48 no8 p16 Ja 2017

Kennedy, Blake

Who Said a Collared Shirt Needs a Collar? color *GQ: Gentlemen's Quarterly* v97 no4 p46 Ap 2017

Kennedy, Chris

CLASH OF THE TITANS J. DUGDALE color *Chicago* v66 no4 p26 Ap 2017

Kennedy, Dara

"Every time I've had a really good idea, it was because I thought, I would so buy that." color *Glamour* v115 no4 p114 Ap 2017

Kennedy, David

A FORCE FOR GOOD *O, The Oprah Magazine* p142 My 2017

Kennedy, Deborah E.

Our Town: Deborah E. Kennedy's first novel delves into a community's secrets and silences E. Fridlund *New York Times Book Review* p18 Ag 13 2017

Kennedy, Edward Moore, 1932-2009

A Bridge Too Far bw cartoon *Weekly Standard* v23 no3 p2 S 25 2017

Permanent Crisis P. TERZIAN bw *Weekly Standard* v22 no32 p20 My 1 2017

Kennedy, Elizabeth

The Hour of Land *Orion Magazine* v35 no4/5 p106 Jl-O 2016

KENNEDY, GERARD J.

Justice for Some color *Walrus* v14 no9 p47 N 2017

Kennedy, Hugh

THE RETURN OF THE CALIPH P. A. Rahe *Claremont Review of Books* v17 no1 p22 Wint 2016/2017

Kennedy, Janelle

THINGS I LEARNED THIS PAST WEEK *Sail* v48 no1 p16 Ja 2017

Kennedy, Jeffe

The Edge of the Blade *Publishers Weekly* v263 no48 p55 N 28 2016

Kennedy, Jessica A.

When Trust Is Easily Broken, and When It's Not *Harvard Business Review Digital Articles* p2 F 17 2016

Kennedy, Joe

Should Antitrust Regulators Stop Companies from Collecting So Much Data? *Harvard Business Review Digital Articles* p2 Ap 17 2017

Kennedy, John F. (John Fitzgerald), 1917-1963

All the Way With J.F.K M. Malone *America* v216 no12 p3 My 29 2017

Another Brief (ONE HOPES) Shining (PERHAPS) Moment? B. HANDY color *Vanity Fair* v59 no2 p40 F 2017

THE CLASS OF 1917 M. SOLOMON color *Forbes* v200 no3 p32 S 28 2017

A GIFT for the PRESIDENT... GARDEN GNOMES *Prologue* v49 no1 p72 Spr 2017

An inaugural accolade *America* v216 no12 p40 My 29 2017

JFK 100 Centennial Events *Prologue* v49 no1 p34 Spr 2017

JFK IN CONGRESS D. McMillen *Prologue* v49 no1 p36 Spr 2017

John F. Kennedy's America Answered a Call to Leadership No Longer Given Voice D. Von Drehle color *Time* v189 no21 p32 Je 5 2017

KENNEDY KILLING STILL A MYSTERY J. DUFFY *USA Today Magazine* v145 no2858 p44 N 2016

Kennedy, John F. (John Fitzgerald), 1917-1963—Assassination

25th JFK Assassination Secrets Scheduled for 2017 Release J. Sanburn color *Time* v188 no27-28 p119 D 26 2016

53 Years of Evading the Truth color *Weekly Standard* v22 no13 p2 D 5 2016

The '60s C. R. Kesler *Claremont Review of Books* v17 no3 p31 Summ 2017

WHO REALLY KILLED JFK? A. ABEL bw color *Maclean's* v129 no51/52 p42 D 26 2016

Kennedy, John F. (John Fitzgerald), 1917-1963—Exhibitions

EDITOR'S NOTE J. WORSHAM *Prologue* v49 no1 p1 Spr 2017

JFK 100 Milestones & Mementos S. Bredhoff *Prologue* v49 no1 p48 Spr 2017

Kennedy, Julia Taylor

The Health Care Industry Needs to Start Taking Women Seriously *Harvard Business Review Digital Articles* p2 My 28 2015

Kennedy, Katie

Learning to Swear in America color *Publishers Weekly* v263 no49 p98 D 7 2016

Kennedy, Kitty

YOU LIKE H&R! color *Horse & Rider* v56 no10 p22 O 2017

Kennedy, Lisa

HISTORICALLY SPEAKING color *Essence* v47 no10 p56 F 2017

Kennedy, Mary Lee

How Employees Shaped Strategy at the New York Public Library *Harvard Business Review Digital Articles* p2 D 5 2016

KENNEDY, MICHAEL

The Meaning of Scalia *Commentary* v142 no1 p12 Jl/Ag 2016

KENNEDY, NOAH

The Story of Reason in Islam *Humanist* v77 no1 p44 Ja/F 2017

Kennedy, Oliver

Getting to Know Your Zone Committee Chairs K. Rover *In Stride* v12 no2 p39 Mr 2017

Kennedy, Pamela

No, No, Bunny *Publishers Weekly* v264 no5 p203 Ja 30 2017

Kennedy, Robert F., 1925-1968

50 Years in 15 Photos H. BENSON bw color *AARP: The Magazine* v30 no6A p58 O/N 2017

Is It 1968? *Commentary* v142 no2 p1 S 2016

Kennedy, Robert Francis, 1954-

Kill This Idea E. Epstein color *Weekly Standard* v22 no19 p6 Ja 23 2017

Kennedy, Ryan

Growing pains for global monitoring of societal events bibl graph *Science* v353 no6307 p1502 S 30 2016

Improving election prediction internationally bibl graph *Science* v355 no6324 p515 F 3 2017

Kennedy, Shibon

CHECK THIS OUT color *Bloomberg Businessweek* no4504 p64 D 19 2016

Give Up Your Boring Gray Suit color *Bloomberg Businessweek* no4513 p69 Mr 6 2017

Jump Around color *Bloomberg Businessweek* no4514 p70 Mr 13 2017

SLIP ON A PAIR OF WHITE SOCKS color *Bloomberg Businessweek* no4518 p74 Ap 10 2017

Suit yourself color *Bloomberg Businessweek* no4522 p85 My 15 2017

These Jackets Are the Bomb color *Bloomberg Businessweek* no4498 p88 N 7 2016

Kennedy, Simon

Alpine Disconnect cartoon *Bloomberg Businessweek* no4507 p35 Ja 16 2017

Kennedy, Thomas D.

What makes a family? color *Christian Century* v134 no7 p36 Mr 29 2017

Kennedy, Tom

Out of Tune E. FELTEN color *Weekly Standard* v22 no35 p5 My 22 2017

Kennedy Center Honors, The (TV program)

Kennedy Center Honors M. Roffman *TV Guide* p39 D 19 2016

Kennedy-Moore, Eileen, 1964-

2017 BACK-TO-SCHOOL GUIDE K. ROCKWOOD color *Good Housekeeping* v265 no3 p139 S 2017

advice every new mom needs [Cover story] color *Parents* v92 no7 p32 Jl 2017

"Bad Mommy" Guilt Busters J. K. Geddes cartoon color *Working Mother* p54 F/Mr 2017

fickle friendships *Parents* v92 no1 p76 Ja 2017

Kennedys: After Camelot, The (TV program)

The Kennedys: After Camelot A. D'ARMINIO *TV Guide* v65 no13 p20 Mr 20 2017

Kennel, Charles F.

Making climate science more relevant bibl color *Science* v354 no6311 p421 O 28 2016

Kennels—Design & construction

TOUGH TIMES LEAD TO TOUGH KENNELS *South Dakota Magazine* v32 no6 p14 Mr/Ap 2017

Kennel-Shank, Celeste

Clergy on the front lines in Charlottesville color *Christian Century* v134 no19 p12 S 13 2017

Congo's churches face rising violence *Christian Century* v134 no13 p12 Je 21 2017

Duke Divinity professor disciplined amid complaint over antiracism event *Christian Century* v134 no12 p16 Je 7 2017

Episcopal Divinity School to affiliate with Union Theological in New York *Christian Century* v134 no7 p13 Mr 29 2017

Episcopal Divinity School to join Union Seminary, Brown Douglas named dean *Christian Century* v134 no13 p15 Je 21 2017

Faith-based groups, others put pressure on UN for its role in Haiti

cholera deaths *Christian Century* v133 no24 p15 N 23 2016

Forming priests among the people color *Christian Century* v134 no4 p30 F 15 2017

Fund supports historic congregations color *Christian Century* v134 no4 p12 F 15 2017

Indonesian Christian leader jailed under blasphemy law *Christian Century* v134 no12 p16 Je 7 2017

Muslim cleric to lead national association of chaplains in higher ed *Christian Century* v134 no8 p1 Ap 12 2017

Pastor resists extremism in Nigeria *Christian Century* v134 no14 p14 Jl 5 2017

People *Christian Century* v134 no13 p17 Je 21 2017

People color *Christian Century* v133 no24 p20 N 23 2016

People color *Christian Century* v134 no5 p17 Mr 1 2017

PTS cancels award to Keller but not lecture color *Christian Century* v134 no9 p12 Ap 26 2017

Seminary returns rare manuscript to Greek Orthodox color *Christian Century* v133 no26 p14 D 21 2016

KENNER, DAVID

Farewell, Lebanon's First Brewery color *Foreign Policy* no225 p21 Jl/Ag 2017

How to Fund a Refugee Camp School color *Foreign Policy* no224 p28 My/Je 2017

Kenneth, O.

Deterministic generation of a cluster state of entangled photons bibl diag graph *Science* v354 no6311 p434 O 28 2016

Kenneth Cole Productions Inc.

STAR PLAYERS color *O, The Oprah Magazine* p59 F 2017

Kenney, Brian

ALA, Chicago Style *Publishers Weekly* v264 no25 p40 Je 19 2017

Follow the (Grant) Money *Publishers Weekly* v263 no42 p21 O 17 2016

A Time to Lead *Publishers Weekly* v264 no3 p21 Ja 16 2017

Kenney, Chris

Manufacturing Companies Need to Sell Outcomes, Not Products *Harvard Business Review Digital Articles* p2 Je 2 2016

Kenney, Jason—Interviews

THE INTERVIEW S. PROUDFOOT color *Maclean's* v129 no40 p14 O 10 2016

Kenney, John

2017 MaVeRicks OF Style bw color *Esquire* p81 S 2017

THE MAVERICKS OF HOLLYWOOD 2017 bw color *Esquire* v167 no2 p89 Mr 2017

Kenney, Linny

LOVE and MUSIC and LEATHER and RACE CARS color *Popular Mechanics* p48 S 2017

KENNICOTT, PHILIP

Senta's CHOICE *Opera News* v81 no10 p32 Ap 2017

Kennicott, Robert

The Preservation of a Naturalist S. Bartram *Parks & Recreation* v52 no5 p20 My 2017

KENNINGTON, TONI

The Way Forward color *O, The Oprah Magazine* p18 My 2017

Kenny, Charles

Seven Habits of Successful Nations *Washington Monthly* p7 N/D 2016

Kenny, David—Interviews

WATSON: NOT SO ELEMENTARY C. Leaf color *Fortune* v174 no6 p30 N 1 2016

Kenny, Graham

Build an Organization That's Less Busy and More Strategic *Harvard Business Review Digital Articles* p2 Ap 7 2015

The False Promise of the Single Metric *Harvard Business Review Digital Articles* p2 Ag 26 2015

Fixing Performance Appraisal Is About More than Ditching Annual Reviews *Harvard Business Review Digital Articles* p2 F 2 2016

How Boards Can Rein in CEO Pay *Harvard Business Review Digital Articles* p2 D 1 2014

A List of Goals Is Not a Strategy *Harvard Business Review Digital Articles* p2 N 19 2014

Making (a Little) Progress on CEO Pay *Harvard Business Review Digital Articles* p2 F 16 2015

Repositioning Is Not a New Business Model *Harvard Business Review Digital Articles* p2 Ap 12 2016

Should a CEO's Bonus Be Based on Financial Performance

p44 F 2017

KEEP PONTOON TUBES SHIPSHAPE: They keep the family afloat, so make sure the pontoon's logs are ready for action color *Boating World* v38 no7 p52 Jl 2017

METAL BOAT Q & A *Sea Magazine* v108 no9 p54 S 2016

Kenyon, Mark

CRAZY FOR THE RUT color *Outdoor Life* v223 no9 p44 N 2016

REAL-WORLD RUT [Cover story] color *Outdoor Life* v224 no9 p39 N 2017

Kenyon, Sherrilyn, 1965-

Deadmen Walking *Publishers Weekly* v264 no13 p85 Mr 27 2017

KENZY, CHLOE

An Original River Town *South Dakota Magazine* v32 no4 p20 N/D 2016

Keogh, Caitlin

CAITLIN KEOGH S. Korman color *Art in America* v104 no10 p153 N 2016

Keoghan, Phil

THE BIG QUESTION cartoon *Atlantic* v319 no5 p96 Je 2017

Quotable Quotes color *Reader's Digest* v190 no1134 p140 O 2017

Keohane, Joe

Robots Wrote This Story cartoon *Wired* v25 no3 p62 Mr 2017

Keohane, Nathaniel O.

Unmask temporal trade-offs in climate policy debates color *Science* v356 no6337 p492 My 5 2017

Keohane, Robert O.

The Liberal Order Is Rigged *Foreign Affairs* v96 no3 p36 My/Je 2017

KEOHANE, WEWER

GIFTS that UPLIFT! cartoon *O, The Oprah Magazine* p148 D 2016

Keough, Joe

One church? *U.S. Catholic* v82 no7 p5 Jl 2017

Keough, Riley

Riley Keough R. SULLIVAN, M. HOLGATE et al color *Vogue* v207 no9 p372 S 2017

Keown, Christopher L.

Single-cell methylomes identify neuronal subtypes and regulatory elements in mammalian cortex diag *Science* v357 no6351 p600 Ag 11 2017

Kepel, Gilles, 1955-

Generation Jihad J. KIRCHICK *Commentary* v144 no3 p50 O 2017

Lost amid Anxiety C. Stangler color *Commonweal* v144 no13 p33 Ag 11 2017

Kepenekian, M.

Extremely efficient internal exciton dissociation through edge states in layered 2D perovskites bibl graph *Science* v355 no6331 p1288 Mr 24 2017

Kepko, L.

Structure, force balance, and topology of Earth's magnetopause diag graph *Science* v356 no6341 p960 Je 1 2017

Kepler (Spacecraft)

Get ready for the next generation planet hunter J. Wenz color *Astronomy* v45 no7 p44 Jl 2017

The hunt for Earth's BIGGER COUSINS [Cover story] M. Carroll color diag *Astronomy* v45 no4 p22 Ap 2017

The Most Mysterious Star in the Galaxy B. Montet and T. Boyajian *Sky & Telescope* v133 no6 p16 Je 2017

STRANGE NEWS FROM Another Star K. Cartier and J. T. Wright color diag graph *Scientific American* v316 no5 p36 My 2017

Tabby's Star Dims on Cue M. YOUNG *Sky & Telescope* v134 no3 p13 S 2017

Kepner, Christopher

Deals R. DEAHL color *Publishers Weekly* v264 no27 p9 Jl 3 2017

Kepnes, Caroline

YOUR NEXT LIFETIME OBSESSION B. L. Heldman color *Entertainment Weekly* no1450 p18 Ja 27 2017

Keppler, Selina Jessica

A switch from canonical to noncanonical autophagy shapes B cell responses bibl graph *Science* v355 no6325 p641 F 10 2017

Keqiang, Li

"Economic Openness Serves Everyone Better" bw *Bloomberg Businessweek* no4509 p8 Ja 30 2017

Keratin

Body Gunk, Explained K. KLOSS *Reader's Digest* v188 no1126 p122 D 2016/Ja 2017

KERATIN V. Tweed color *Amazing Wellness* v9 no4 p24 Summ 2017

Kerber, Angelique, 1988-

Angelique Kerber M. Hagan color *Current Biography* v78 no4 p42 Ap 2017

Angelique Kerber *Tennis* v53 no1 p44 Ja/F 2017

Finishing Strong C. Evert *Tennis* v52 no6 p4 N/D 2016

Kéré, Diébédo Francis

Francis Kéré Envisions House of Parliament for Burkina Faso J. M. MCKNIGHT *Architectural Record* v204 no11 p25 N 2016

Kéré, Diébédo Francis, 1965-—Interviews

Diébédo Francis Kéré A. FIXSEN and M. SITZ *Architectural Record* v205 no6 p28 Je 2017

Kere Architecture (Company)

Raising the Grade J. M. MCKNIGHT *Architectural Record* v205 no1 p96 Ja 2017

Kerekes, Ryan A.

Restoring auditory cortex plasticity in adult mice by restricting thalamic adenosine signaling graph *Science* v356 no6345 p1352 Je 30 2017

Kerensky, Aleksandr Fyodorovich, 1881-1970

KERENSKY IN HINDSIGHT: Alexander Kerensky, the last Russian premier before the Bolsheviks took power, decided to continue the war with Germany. He and his country would pay the price G. Darby *History Today* v67 no7 p48 Jl 2017

KERET, EDGAR

A cartoon *Wired* v25 no1 p38 Ja 2017

A E. KERET cartoon *Wired* v25 no1 p38 Ja 2017

SKETCHBOOK cartoon *New Yorker* v92 no38 p73 N 21 2016

Keret, Etgar

FLY ALREADY color *New Yorker* v93 no13 p76 My 15 2017

Kerfeld, Cheryl A.

Assembly principles and structure of a 6.5-MDa bacterial microcompartment shell color diag *Science* v356 no6344 p1293 Je 23 2017

Kering SA—Officials & employees

WHERE DID YOU GET THAT LOVELY SUPPLY CHAIN? K. Bhasin color *Bloomberg Businessweek* no4505 p62 D 26 2016

KERLEY, GRAHAM I. H.

Conserving the World's Megafauna and Biodiversity: The Fierce Urgency of Now *BioScience* v67 no3 p197 Mr 2017

Saving the World's Terrestrial Megafauna color *BioScience* v66 no10 p807 O 1 2016

Kerman, Andrew J.

Suppressing relaxation in superconducting qubits by quasiparticle pumping bibl graph *Science* v354 no6319 p1573 D 23 2016

Kerman, Piper

WRITERS BLOC color *Mother Jones* v42 no3 p61 My/Je 2017

Kern, Ashley—Awards

DanceSPIRIT FutureSTAR 2016 N. Loeffler-Gladstone *Dance Spirit* v20 no10 p63 D 2016

Kern, Christian

Hall-effect metamaterials and "anti-Hall bars" *Physics Today* v70 no10 p14 O 2017

KERN, DEANNA

petal POWER color *Yoga Journal* no293 p17 Ag 2017

Kern, Dorothee

Evolutionary drivers of thermoadaptation in enzyme catalysis [Cover story] bibl color graph *Science* v355 no6322 p289 Ja 20 2017

KERN, LAURA

Back on the Slab color *Film Comment* v53 no1 p20 Ja/F 2017

CAUGHT color *Film Comment* v53 no3 p24 My/Je 2017

Death-Defying Acts color *Film Comment* v53 no2 p64 Mr/Ap 2017

Hell Houses color *Film Comment* v53 no3 p22 My/Je 2017

Kern, Matt

Crescent by Sabian Stanton Moore Collection color *Downbeat* v83 no12 p108 D 2016

Finale Notation Software color *Downbeat* v83 no12 p107 D 2016

Mojave Audio MA-50 color *Downbeat* v84 no2 p99 F 2017

PreSonus Studio 192 Mobile color *Downbeat* v84 no2 p98 F 2017

Sabian Artisan Elites color *Downbeat* v84 no6 p86 Je 2017

Steinberg Dorico color *Downbeat* v84 no3 p114 Mr 2017

Yamaha Recording Custom Series color *Downbeat* v83 no11 p81 N 2016

KERN, MERILEE

SHATTERING THE STATUS QUO *USA Today Magazine* v146 no2866 p72 Jl 2017

Kern, R. J.

The Unchosen color *National Geographic* v232 no5 p104 N 2017

Kern, Roger

ASTRO LETTERS color *Astronomy* v45 no4 p9 Ap 2017

KERN, STUART

MEN BEHAVING BADLY color *Vanity Fair* v59 no11 p54 N 2017

Kernan, Christopher

GIFTS OF A FOREST *New York State Conservationist* v71 no5 p24 Ap 2017

Kernan, Patricia

GIFTS OF A FOREST *New York State Conservationist* v71 no5 p24 Ap 2017

Kerner, Ian

Getting Comfortable color *Prevention* v69 no9 p26 O 2017

Is It "Manopause"? color *Prevention* v69 no11 p26 N 2017

Moving Beyond Betrayal color *Prevention* v69 no5 p28 My 2017

Say What You Want [Cover story] color *Prevention* v69 no1 p32 Ja 2017

SYNC UP YOUR SEX DRIVES [Cover story] J. Hergenrader *Women's Health* v14 no1 p150 Ja/F 2017

Understanding ED color *Prevention* v69 no2 p28 F 2017

What comes after cartoon *Prevention* v69 no7 p26 Jl 2017

Kerns, Joanna

ALAN THICKE color *Entertainment Weekly* no1446/1447 p84 D 2016/Ja 2017

Kerouac, Jack, 1922-1969

America in the Time of Kerouac's Travels J. ZOBENICA il *American Conservative* v16 no2 p40 Mr/Ap 2017

On le Road D. E. BÉCHARD cartoon *Walrus* v13 no10 p67 D 2016

Kerpelman, Larry C.

Race to Remember bw color *American History* v52 no2 p48 Je 2017

Kerr, Eve A.

How to Stop the Overconsumption of Health Care *Harvard Business Review Digital Articles* p2 D 11 2014

KERR, JEAN

Sunken Treasure *Yankee* v81 no1 p54 Ja/F 2017

Kerr, Jeremy T.

A cocktail of toxins color diag map *Science* v356 no6345 p1331 Je 30 2017

KERR, JOHN

CAN'T AFFORD A LAWYER? NO FREE SPEECH FOR YOU *Reason* v48 no8 p44 Ja 2017

Kerr, Lindsey

Acts of Faith *Harper's Magazine* v333 no1998 p2 N 2016

Kerr, Lucy

Time of Death: A Stillwater General Mystery *Publishers Weekly* v263 no40 p99 O 3 2016

Kerr, M.

The magnetic field and turbulence of the cosmic web measured using a brilliant fast radio burst bibl chart graph *Science* v354 no6317 p1249 D 9 2016

Kerr, Maddie

"My View of the Country" A. STANLEY color *Seventeen* v76 no5 p14 S 2017

Kerr, Miranda, 1983-

Best-Dressed LIST color *Harper's Bazaar* no3652 p104 Ap 2017

Everybody Is a Star color *Glamour* v115 no11 p158 N 2017

Everybody Loves Stripes color *Glamour* v115 no6 p148 Je 2017

Miranda Kerr A. Syrett color *InStyle* v24 no10 p113 O 2017

Kerr, Philip, 1956-

THE PLOT THICKENS J. KRAMER cartoon color *New Yorker* v93 no20 p78 Jl 10 2017

Kerr, Sari Pekkala

The Average Mid-Forties Male College Graduate Earns 55% More Than His Female Counterparts *Harvard Business Review Digital Articles* p2 Je 12 2017

Immigrants Play a Disproportionate Role in American Entrepreneurship *Harvard Business Review Digital Articles* p2 O 3 2016

Kerr, Steve

BRING US TOGETHER color *Sports Illustrated* v127 no10 p28 O 2 2017

Kerr, Steve—Health

NO COACH, NO PROBLEM C. Ballard color *Sports Illustrated* v126 no15 p28 My 29 2017

Kerr, Tom

Cities for People and by People *UN Chronicle* v53 no3 p1 2016

Kerr, William

Crossing borders along an endless frontier color *Science* v356 no6339 p694 My 19 2017

Kerr, William R.

How Local Context Shapes Digital Business Abroad *Harvard Business Review Digital Articles* p2 Je 24 2015

Immigrants Play a Disproportionate Role in American Entrepreneurship *Harvard Business Review Digital Articles* p2 O 3 2016

Kerr electro-optical effect

Quantized Faraday and Kerr rotation and axion electrodynamics of a 3D topological insulator Liang Wu, M. Salehi et al bibl graph *Science* v354 no6316 p1124 D 2 2016

Kerrick Sullivan, Sean

RIGA, LATVIA color *Snowboarder* v29 no2 p104 O 2016

Kerry, John, 1943-

The Case for Optimism In These Strange Times color *Time* v189 no22 p20 Je 12 2017

CLEANING UP OBAMA'S SYRIA MESS M. BOOT *Commentary* v142 no4 p20 N 2016

CLIMATE CHANGE SHOULDN'T BE A PARTISAN ISSUE IN THE FIRST PLACE J. KERRY *Vital Speeches of the Day* v83 no1 p8 Ja 2017

Leaders color *Time* v189 no16/17 p64 My 1-8 2017

OBAMA'S AMERICA img *New York* v49 no20 p12 O 3 2016

SETTLEMENTS ARE NOT THE CAUSE OF THE CONFLICT, BUT NO ONE CAN IGNORE THE THREAT THEY POSE TO PEACE *Vital Speeches of the Day* v83 no2 p30 F 2017

WITHOUT CORRUPTION *Vital Speeches of the Day* v82 no10 p303 O 2016

Kerry, John, 1943-—Interviews

The Envoy color *Foreign Affairs* v95 no6 p56 N/D 2016

Kerry J. Vahala

Microresonator soliton dual-comb spectroscopy bibl diag graph *Science* v354 no6312 p600 N 4 2016

Kerry Smith, V.

Contingent valuation: Flawed logic? color *Science* v357 no6349 p363 Jl 28 2017

Deciphering dueling analyses of clean water regulations color *Science* v357 no6359 p49 O 6 2017

Putting a value on injuries to natural assets: The BP oil spill chart *Science* v356 no6335 p253 Ap 21 2017

Kershner, Vicki

oops *Parents* v92 no7 p132 Jl 2017

Kersten, Jason

THE NINETEENTH HOLE cartoon *New Yorker* v92 no34 p25 O 24 2016

TOTALLY cartoon *New Yorker* v93 no25 p28 Ag 28 2017

KERSTEN, KATHERINE

Experimenting on the Young color *Weekly Standard* v22 no43 p19 Jl 24 2017

Kertes, Darlene

5 ways to simply feel better color *Redbook* p94 S 2017

Kertes, Joseph

On the Way to a New World J. ORRINGER *New York Times Book Review* p8 Ja 22 2017

Kertész, Imre, 1929-2016

Portrait of the Author as a Historian A. Lee *History Today* v67 no3 p54 Mr 2017

Kesebir, Selin

When Economic Growth Doesn't Make Countries Happier *Harvard Business Review Digital Articles* p2 Ap 25 2016

Kesey, Ken

IS THAT WHAT THEY SHOULD LOOK LIKE? bw color *Reader's Digest* v190 no1134 p98 O 2017

Kesha, 1987-

Kesha E. R. Brown color *Entertainment Weekly* no1478 / 1479 p103 Ag 18-25 2017

Kesha's Battle Cry of Many Colors B. SPANOS color *Rolling*

Kevin (Probably) Saves the World (TV program)
JASON RITTER OF Kevin (Probably) Saves the World S. Highfill, N. Abrams et al color *Entertainment Weekly* no1482/1483 p61 S 22 2017
KEVIN (PROBABLY) SAVES THE WORLD M. Roffman *TV Guide* v65 no37 p30 S 4 2017

KEVIN, BRIAN
WILD ABANDON *Audubon* v118 no6 p38 Wint 2016

Kevin Can Wait (TV program)
Anatomy of a Hit J. HALTERMAN *TV Guide* p9 D 5 2016
KEVIN CAN WAIT I. Ratledge *TV Guide* v65 no39 p32 S 18 2017
Kevin Can Wait J. Halterman *TV Guide* v64 no46 p31 N 7 2016
KEVIN CAN WAIT J. HALTERMAN *TV Guide* v65 no11 p28 Mr 6 2017
Kevin Can Wait J. Halterman *TV Guide* v65 no19 p30 My 1 2017
KEVIN CAN WAIT SHAKE-UP! J. Halterman *TV Guide* v65 no27 p5 Je 26 2017
PRIME TIME EASTERN *TV Guide* v64 no48 p50 N 21 2016
PRIMETIME: EASTERN *TV Guide* v65 no27 p42E Je 26 2017

Kevin Hart: What Now? (Film)
Hart of a Lion: Making an Entire City Laugh at Once S. Zacharek color *Time* v188 no16/17 p88 O 24 2016

Kevyn Aucoin Beauty & the Beast in Me (Film)
Boy on Film L. M. M. BLUME and C. ELLENBERG bw color *Vogue* v207 no9 p458 S 2017

Kew, Janice
Mobile Carriers Start Hanging Up on Africa cartoon *Bloomberg Businessweek* no4530 p18 Jl 17 2017

Key, David
Key and Woodard Win Sandhills Invitational Jackpot color *Spin to Win Rodeo* v21 no1 p24 Mr 2017

Key, H. M.
An artificial metalloenzyme with the kinetics of native enzymes bibl diag graph *Science* v354 no6308 p102 O 7 2016

Key, Keegan-Michael, 1971-
FIVE THINGS: OBAMA WHISTLES CONSTANTLY C. FELSENTHAL color *Chicago* v66 no9 p38 S 2017
KEEGAN-MICHAEL KEY'S NEW COURSE S. Li color *Entertainment Weekly* no1474/1475 p104 Jl 21-28 2017

Key, Nigel
Examining Farm Sector and Farm Household Income *Amber Waves: The Economics of Food, Farming, Natural Resources, & Rural America* p23 Ag 2017
Farm Households Experience High Levels of Income Volatility *Amber Waves: The Economics of Food, Farming, Natural Resources, & Rural America* p43 F 2017
For Beginning Farmers, Business Survival Rates Increase With Scale and With Direct Sales to Consumers *Amber Waves: The Economics of Food, Farming, Natural Resources, & Rural America* p14 S 2016

Key employees
How to Prepare for Your Star's Exit L. Braham *Bloomberg Businessweek* no4517 p46 Ap 3 2017

Key Largo (Company)
Key Largo 216 LX *Boating World* v38 no1 p67 Ja 2017

Key performance indicators (Management)
Appraising the performance of performance appraisals P. C. Fisk *Monthly Labor Review* p1 D 2016
Deliver Feedback That Sticks L. Davey *Harvard Business Review Digital Articles* p2 Ag 20 2015
Identify the Marketing Metrics That Actually Matter L. J. Popky *Harvard Business Review Digital Articles* p2 Jl 14 2015
To Get Better at Your Job, Work Practice into Your Routine R. H. Schaffer *Harvard Business Review Digital Articles* p2 Ja 29 2016
A Way to Know If Your Corporate Goals Are Too Aggressive M. E. Raynor and D. Pankratz *Harvard Business Review Digital Articles* p2 Jl 13 2015

Key West (Fla.)
ESCAPE TO KEY WEST J. ANDERSON-MINSHALL color *Advocate* no1090 p50 Ap 2017

Key West (Fla.)—Description & travel
A Key West Road Trip A. FLANGO *Cincinnati Magazine* p57 Je 2017

Keyboard instruments—Evaluation

Korg monologue C. Neville color *Downbeat* v84 no3 p114 Mr 2017

Keyboard players
See also
Pianists
Enter Sampha B. RATLIFF color *Esquire* v167 no1 p18 F 2017

Keyboards (Electronics)
6 Keyboard Shortcuts For Faster Web Browsing color *Reader's Digest* v190 no1133 p49 S 2017
HANDS-ON: THE MACBOOK PRO'S INNOVATIVE TOUCH BAR GRAB YOU S. OCHS color *Macworld - Digital Edition* p79 D 2016
How to incorporate keyboard shortcuts into your workflow I. PAUL color *PCWorld* v35 no2 p180 F 2017

Keyboards (Electronics)—Equipment & supplies—Evaluation
ZAGG RUGGED BOOK KEYBOARD CASE FOR THE iPAD PRO S. BELLAMY color *Macworld - Digital Edition* v33 no11 p54 N 2016

Keyboards (Electronics)—Evaluation
THE BEST BET img *New York* v50 no18 p55 S 4 2017
The Best Tech Gifts for $50 or Less R. Broida color *Money* v45 no11 p18 D 2016
HEAD-TO-HEAD D. PIERCE color *Wired* v25 no3 p36 Mr 2017
iPAD PRO SMART KEYBOARD VS. LOGITECH SLIM COMBO: WHICH iPAD PRO KEYBOARD SHOULD YOU BUY? J. NEWMAN color *Macworld - Digital Edition* v34 no8 p75 Ag 2017
LOFREE KEYBOARD: THE FEELING OF A TYPEWRITER ON YOUR MAC OR iOS DEVICE R. LOYOLA color *Macworld - Digital Edition* v34 no4 p23 My 2017
Logitech Craft hands-on: This keyboard's mini-Surface Dial is truly innovative M. HACHMAN color *PCWorld* v35 no10 p67 O 2017

Keyboards (Musical instruments)—Evaluation
ROLI Seaboard Rise C. Neville color *Downbeat* v83 no12 p107 D 2016

Keyes, Brice E.
Spatiotemporal antagonism in mesenchymal-epithelial signaling in sweat versus hair fate decision graph *Science* v354 no6319 paah6102-1 D 23 2016

Keyes, Scott—Interviews
THE BEST ROUTE TO BARGAIN AIRFARES R. ERMEY color *Kiplinger's Personal Finance* v71 no4 p10 Ap 2017

Keyes-Bevan, Bronwen
AGING GRACEFULLY WITH HOWIE MANDEL color *Maclean's* v129 no40 p58 O 10 2016
The Most Significant Advance in Diabetes Care Since Insulin color *Maclean's* v129 no48/49 p46 D 5 2016
PROTECTING OUR COMMUNITIES *Maclean's* v129 no40 p68 O 10 2016

Keylor, Mitchell H.
Synthesis of resveratrol tetramers via a stereoconvergent radical equilibrium bibl diag graph *Science* v354 no6317 p1260 D 9 2016

Keys, Alicia, 1981-
Alicia Keys color *InStyle* v24 no4 p156 Ap 2017
ALICIA KEYS & STELLA McCARTNEY TEAM UP FOR BREAST CANCER AWARENESS color *Harper's Bazaar* no3657 p202 O 2017
Show Up. Be You Z. Malin, H. Hefzy et al color *Glamour* v115 no5 p18 My 2017

Keys, Alicia, 1981—Interviews
Alicia Keys B. HIATT color *Rolling Stone* no1274 p18 N 17 2016
Use Your Gift [Cover story] K. Drew bw color *Glamour* v115 no3 p174 Mr 2017

Keys, Henson
Elīna Garanča: Revive *Opera News* v81 no10 p56 Ap 2017

Keys, Madison, 1995-
Madison Keys *Tennis* v53 no1 p58 Ja/F 2017

Keyser, Christine
Ancient genomic changes associated with domestication of the horse color diag *Science* v356 no6336 p442 Ap 28 2017

Keyser, Samuel Jay
The Best Health Care Money Can't Buy bw color *Washington Monthly* v49 no6-8 p55 Je-Ag 2017

Keystone (Colo.)

Just Wait Till Next Year S. Kelso color *Money* v45 no11 p17 D 2016

Keystone pipeline project

THE FIGHT OF OUR LIFETIME K. ARONOFF *In These Times* v41 no3 p20 Mr 2017

A Final Fight for the Keystone Pipeline S. ELBEIN color *Rolling Stone* no1298 p24 O 19 2017

The Man Who Fell for Earth N. STOCKTON bw color graph *Wired* v25 no4 p46 Ap 2017

Reviving Keystone XL Is No Sure Thing P. Coy and R. Tuttle *Bloomberg Businessweek* no4510 p23 F 6 2017

STARVING THE BLACK SNAKE T. BOSNIC *In These Times* v41 no5 p11 My 2017

A Tale of Two Pipelines J. Worland color map *Time* v189 no5 p13 F 13 2017

Why the Keystone Pipeline Is the Wrong U.S. Energy Debate A. Winston *Harvard Business Review Digital Articles* p2 Ja 30 2015

Keywords

I Always Hated Keywords L. Dawson *Publishers Weekly* v264 no16 p23 Ap 17 2017

Keyworth, Karen

Karen Keyworth *Islamic Horizons* v46 no2 p37 Mr/Ap 2017

Why Can't They All be Doctors? [Cover story] *Islamic Horizons* v46 no2 p22 Mr/Ap 2017

Keyzer, Carl de, 1958-

Land of the Hermit King J. H. LEE color *New Republic* v248 no10 p38 O 2017

Kezar, Adrianna

Consortial Leadership Toward Large-Scale Change *Change* v48 no6 p50 N/D 2016

Increasing Student Success in STEM: Summary of A Guide to Systemic Institutional Change *Change* v49 no4 p26 Jl/Ag 2017

Khabarova, Ksenia

The Rydberg constant and proton size from atomic hydrogen bw chart color diag graph *Science* v357 no6359 p79 O 6 2017

Khademhosseini, Ali

Advances in engineering hydrogels diag *Science* v356 no6337 p500 My 5 2017

Khadivi, Laleh

Death of a Dream D. NAYERI *New York Times Book Review* p12 Je 25 2017

Khadr, Omar, 1986-

A Jihadist Hits the Jackpot C. MALCOLM color *Weekly Standard* v22 no43 p16 Jl 24 2017

Khaki

Radical Chinos J. MOORE color *GQ: Gentlemen's Quarterly* v97 no5 p29 My 2017

Khaki, El-Farouk

QUEERING ISLAM S. HABIB color *Advocate* no1089 p56 F/Mr 2017

Khalack, V.

An unusual white dwarf star may be a surviving remnant of a sub-luminous Type Ia supernova chart diag *Science* v357 no6352 p680 Ag 18 2017

Khaled, DJ

Titans color *Time* v189 no16/17 p94 My 1-8 2017

Khaledi-Nasab, Ali

Standing up to fear color *Science* v356 no6336 p458 Ap 28 2017

Khalfani-Cox, Lynnette

THE THOUSAND DOLLAR PAGE bw color *Men's Health* v32 no7 p42 S 2017

Khalid (Performer)

2017 MaVeRicks OF Style J. Roth, N. Zarinsky et al bw color *Esquire* p81 S 2017

Khalid's Teenage Dream N. Feeney color *Entertainment Weekly* no1456 p65 Mr 10 2017

A Pop Prodigy Breaks Out J. LEVY color *Rolling Stone* no1283 p15 Mr 23 2017

Khalid (Performer)—Interviews

How Khalid Makes Music R. Bruner color *Time* v189 no14 p51 Ap 17 2017

Khalid, Adeeb

Making Uzbekistan: Nation, Empire, and Revolution in the Early USSR R. Legvold *Foreign Affairs* v96 no1 p172 Ja/F 2017

KHALID, ZAIN

MYSTERY NOVELS INSPIRED BY A CO-WORKING SPACE cartoon *New Yorker* v93 no3 p33 Mr 6 2017

Khalil, Amina

When the Call Comes color map *Time* v189 no6 p32 F 20 2017

Khalil, Osamah F.

America's Dream Palace: Middle East Expertise and the Rise of the National Security State J. Waterbury *Foreign Affairs* v96 no2 p183 Mr/Ap 2017

Behold, the Jihad of Freedom A. J. Bacevich bw *Commonweal* v144 no9 p36 My 19 2017

KHALILZAD, ZALMAY

The China Challenge *American Conservative* v16 no3 p32 My/Je 2017

Khalsa, Karta Purkh Singh

BLADDER CONTROL color *Amazing Wellness* v9 no4 p36 Summ 2017

EASE GAS WITH HERBS color *Amazing Wellness* v9 no6 p40 EarlyWint 2017

HEALTHY TRAVELS color *Amazing Wellness* v8 no6 p36 Early Winter2016

HEART-HEALING HERBS color *Amazing Wellness* p34 Fall 2017

KIDNEY CARE color *Amazing Wellness* v9 no2 p32 Spr 2017

TOP THREE HERBS FOR MEN color *Amazing Wellness* v8 no2 p22 Spr 2016

Khamsi, Roxanne

POOCHED OUT color *New York Times Magazine* p44 My 21 2017

KHAN, ADNAN R.

Black death color *Maclean's* v129 no48/49 p28 D 5 2016

Enemies of the state color *Maclean's* p42 Je 2017

Escape to Canada color *Maclean's* v130 no8 p42 S 2017

Hell on Earth color *Maclean's* v129 no46 p16 N 21 2016

INSIDE MOSUL color *Maclean's* v129 no50 p14 D 19 2016

Life under ISIS [Cover story] color *Maclean's* v129 no51/52 p22 D 26 2016

Medics on a mission color *Maclean's* v130 no3 p39 Ap 2017

THE MOST DANGEROUS ARMY IN IRAQ color *Maclean's* no1 p44 F 17 2017

Quagmire color *Maclean's* v129 no45 p30 N 14 2016

Uneasy on the Mosul front color *Maclean's* v129 no47 p40 N 28 2016

KHAN, AROOBA

THE WORLD'S BILLIONAIRES bw color diag graph map *Forbes* v199 no3 p84 Mr 28 2017

Khan, Ausma Zehanat

Among the Ruins *Publishers Weekly* v263 no48 p45 N 28 2016

KHAN, COCO

The Urbanist: What Does London Think of Brexit Now? img *New York* v49 no22 p22 O 31 2016

Khan, LeeAndra

The Challenge of Being a Black Principal in Today's Racial and Political Climate *Education Digest* v82 no4 p4 D 2016

Khan, Maola

Posttranslational mutagenesis: A chemical strategy for exploring protein side-chain diversity diag *Science* v354 no6312 p597 N 4 2016

Khan, Natasha

Are Drugs Samsung's Next Big Thing? color graph *Bloomberg Businessweek* no4523 p23 My 22 2017

China Needs Help Having Babies bw *Bloomberg Businessweek* no4530 p15 Jl 17 2017

Hong Kong and Shenzhen Band Together to Lure Startups color *Bloomberg Businessweek* no4527 p44 Je 19 2017

Park in Limbo color *Bloomberg Businessweek* no4498 p22 N 7 2016

Khan, Naveed

Ancient genomic changes associated with domestication of the horse color diag *Science* v356 no6336 p442 Ap 28 2017

Khan, Omar

Epigenetic stability of exhausted T cells limits durability of rein-vigoration by PD-1 blockade bibl graph *Science* v354 no6316 p1160 D 2 2016

Khan, Romana

Even a 14-Cent Food Tax Could Lead to Healthier Choices *Harvard Business Review Digital Articles* p2 S 29 2016

Khan, Sadiq, 1970-
Sadiq Khan J. Crelin color *Current Biography* v77 no10 p72 O 2016
Sadiq Khan T. Penny color *Bloomberg Businessweek* no4540 p80 O 2 2017
WEATHERING THE STORM S. KNIGHT bw cartoon *New Yorker* v93 no22 p34 Jl 31 2017

KHAN, SARAH
Babylonstoren, South Africa color *Conde Nast Traveler* v51 no10 p60 N 2016
SOUTHERN AFRICA color *Conde Nast Traveler* v52 no4 p38 Ap 2017

Khan, Shaji
Security Breaches: No End in Sight *USA Today Magazine* v145 no2863 p10 Ap 2017

KHAN, SHAZA
A Focus on the Literary and Creative Arts Curricula [Cover story] *Islamic Horizons* v46 no2 p29 Mr/Ap 2017

Khan, Umar
Sensitive electromechanical sensors using viscoelastic graphene-polymer nanocomposites bibl graph *Science* v354 no6317 p1257 D 9 2016

Khan, Uzma
Having More Options Can Make Us Evaluate Risk Differently color *Harvard Business Review Digital Articles* p2 F 9 2017

KHANDAKER, TAMARA
When Hate Goes Mainstream color *Walrus* v14 no9 p14 N 2017

Khanna, Gaurav
Crossing borders along an endless frontier color *Science* v356 no6339 p694 My 19 2017

Khanna, Kanika
Assembly of a nucleus-like structure during viral replication in bacteria bibl color graph *Science* v355 no6321 p1 Ja 13 2017

Khanna, Parag—Interviews
Swiss Direct Democracy + Singapore's Smart Rulers = Direct Technocracy P. Khanna *NPQ: New Perspectives Quarterly* v34 no3 p40 Jl 2017

Khanna, Somesh
What Makes Some Silicon Valley Companies So Successful *Harvard Business Review Digital Articles* p2 Ap 26 2016
Which Industries Are the Most Digital (and Why)? *Harvard Business Review Digital Articles* p2 Ap 1 2016

Khanna, Vik
Corporate Wellness Programs Lose Money *Harvard Business Review Digital Articles* p2 O 15 2015

Khant, Monica Modi
Monica Modi Khant *Atlanta* v57 no2 p101 Je 2017

Khanzode, Kirti
Case Study: Which Customers Should This Restaurant Listen To? *Harvard Business Review Digital Articles* p2 Mr 29 2016

Kharchenko, Peter V.
Multipotent peripheral glial cells generate neuroendocrine cells of the adrenal medulla color *Science* v357 no6346 p46 Jl 7 2017

Kharif, Olga
Blockchain May Help Walmart Stop Bad Food cartoon *Bloomberg Businessweek* no4501 p20 N 28 2016
The Greatest Generation Is Around the Corner chart color *Bloomberg Businessweek* no4512 p41 F 20 2017
Holding Down the Costs of the Cloud *Bloomberg Businessweek* no4508 p29 Ja 23 2017
Innovation bw color *Bloomberg Businessweek* no4506 p28 Ja 9 2017
Innovation color *Bloomberg Businessweek* no4513 p39 Mr 6 2017
Is AT&T Buying a Big Dog to Get a Fancy Tail? *Bloomberg Businessweek* no4498 p30 N 7 2016
Portable Hydropower cartoon color *Bloomberg Businessweek* no4493 p45 O 3 2016
Rare Jewelry That Isn't So Rare Anymore color *Bloomberg Businessweek* no4514 p36 Mr 13 2017

Khartabil, Bassel
THE #FREEBASSEL EFFECT E. STEUER color *Wired* v25 no10 p17 O 2017

Khasnabis, Debi
Cultivating a school-university partnership for teacher learning color *Phi Delta Kappan* v98 no8 p48 My 2017

Khatami, Ehsan
Spin-imbalance in a 2D Fermi-Hubbard system diag graph *Science* v357 no6358 p1385 S 29 2017

KHATCHADOURIAN, RAFFI
ALTERNATE ENDINGS cartoon *New Yorker* v92 no47 p46 Ja 30 2017
THE LONG VIEW cartoon color *New Yorker* v92 no42 p80 D 19 2016
MAN WITHOUT A COUNTRY cartoon color *New Yorker* v93 no24 p36 Ag 21 2017

KHATIB, JOUMANA
Paperback Row *New York Times Book Review* p24 Ap 2 2017

KHATRI, FARYAL M.
Harnessing the Power of Faith *Islamic Horizons* v46 no2 p19 Mr/Ap 2017
Islamic Schools for a Changing World: Are Islamic schools preparing their students to function effectively in a rapidly changing world? *Islamic Horizons* v46 no4 p24 Jl/Ag 2017

Khatri, Raina
From Dissemination to Propagation: A New Paradigm for Education Developers *Change* v49 no4 p35 Jl/Ag 2017

Khattak, Asif Khan
Phytochromes function as thermosensors in Arabidopsis bibl graph *Science* v354 no6314 p886 N 18 2016

Khattala, Ahmed Abu, ca. 1971-
Benghazi at the Bar J. LIFHITS color *Weekly Standard* v23 no6 p14 O 16 2017

KHAWAJA, JEMAYEL
A Trance to Remember *Los Angeles Magazine* p22 Ja 2017

Khazan, Olga
The QUEEN BEE in the CORNER OFFICE color *Atlantic* v320 no2 p50 S 2017

Khedoori, Toba
Los Angeles County Museum of Art J. S. Li color *Art in America* v105 no1 p89 Ja 2017

Khemiri, Jonas Hassen
As You Would Have Told It to Me (Sort Of) If We Had Know Each Other Before You Died cartoon color *New Yorker* v93 no29 p86 S 25 2017

Khemsurov, Monica
GIFT GUIDE 2016 color *Bloomberg Businessweek* no4500 p67 N 21 2016
High Tech, Low Profile color *Bloomberg Businessweek* no4520 p72 My 1 2017
Morning Glory color *Bloomberg Businessweek* no4494 p72 O 10 2016
PACK IT UP, PACK IT IN color *Bloomberg Businessweek* no4493 p84 O 3 2016
Sit Back, Relax color *Bloomberg Businessweek* no4512 p80 F 20 2017
Top Brass color *Bloomberg Businessweek* no4509 p58 Ja 30 2017
WHEELS UP color *Bloomberg Businessweek* no4507 p65 Ja 16 2017

Khepra, Nza-Ari
Home of the Brave R. Sullivan bw color *Vogue* v207 no1 p60 Ja 2017
"I'm Doing This for Hadiya" L. Brody color *Glamour* v114 no7 p102 Jl 2016

Khestanova, E.
High-temperature quantum oscillations caused by recurring Bloch states in graphene superlattices color *Science* v357 no6347 p181 Jl 14 2017

Khidekel, Marina
THE THINKING MAN: ANSEL ELGORT color *Women's Health* v14 no6 p118 Jl 2017
THE THINKING MAN DAVID HARBOUR bw *Women's Health* v14 no9 p104 N 2017
THE THINKING MAN: MIKE COLTER color *Women's Health* v14 no8 p118 O 2017
THE THINKING MAN RYAN PHILLIPPE color *Women's Health* v14 no7 p128 S 2017
THE THINKING MAN SAM CLAFLIN color *Women's Health* v14 no5 p106 Je 2017

Khilnani, Sunil
India Personified V. BAJAJ *New York Times Book Review* p24 N 20 2016

Khim, David Ly

HIRED! T. SPIKER cartoon color graph *Men's Health* v32 no3 p96 Ap 2017

Khmer language

RELATED LINKS T. OLSEN *Christianity Today* v61 no5 p9 Je 2017

Khodaparast, Ladan

De novo design of a biologically active amyloid bibl graph *Science* v354 no6313 paah4949-1 N 11 2016

Khodaparast, Laleh

De novo design of a biologically active amyloid bibl graph *Science* v354 no6313 paah4949-1 N 11 2016

Khomandiak, Solomiia

Reovirus infection triggers inflammatory responses to dietary antigens and development of celiac disease color diag *Science* v356 no6333 p44 Ap 7 2017

Khong, Rachel

Baccarat Hotel New York color *Conde Nast Traveler* v52 no3 p44 Mr 2017

Goodbye, Vitamin *Publishers Weekly* v264 no22 p42 My 29 2017

Just Out of Reach: This novel's heroine has turned 30, but she still doesn't have her life figured out D. SHAFRIR *New York Times Book Review* p18 Jl 30 2017

Khong Yuen Foong—Interviews

MEANING OF New American Leadership FOR Asia color *Foreign Affairs* v95 no6 p64a N/D 2016

Khorana, Aditi

The Library of Fates *Publishers Weekly* v264 no21 p93 My 22 2017

Khosla, Chaitan

Reovirus infection triggers inflammatory responses to dietary antigens and development of celiac disease color diag *Science* v356 no6333 p44 Ap 7 2017

Khosrowshahi, Dara

The Bull Case for Uber's New Chief Executive A. Lashinsky color *Fortune* v176 no4 p26 S 15 2017

Dara Khosrowshahi color *Bloomberg Businessweek* no4522 p92 My 15 2017

Uber's New CEO Will Have to Win on Two Fronts Simultaneously C. Zook *Harvard Business Review Digital Articles* p1 Ag 30 2017

Khouri, Hala

Stronger together color *Yoga Journal* no295 p19 O 2017

Khrennikov, Ilya

A Billionaire Emerges On the Silicon Steppe bw *Bloomberg Businessweek* no4527 p28 Je 19 2017

Buying Syrian Shoes To Bolster Putin's Pride color *Bloomberg Businessweek* no4524 p24 My 29 2017

For Manufacturers, Russia Is Now a Bargain graph *Bloomberg Businessweek* no4501 p15 N 28 2016

Microsoft Isn't Feeling Any Russian Thaw *Bloomberg Businessweek* no4500 p35 N 21 2016

Now on EBay: Russian Micro-Multinationals *Bloomberg Businessweek* no4515 p19 Mr 20 2017

Toys 'R' Russia? Retailer Detsky Mir Says, 'Da' color *Bloomberg Businessweek* no4512 p23 F 20 2017

Khromov, A.

Observation of coherent elastic neutrino-nucleus scattering diag *Science* v357 no6356 p1123 S 15 2017

Khrushcheva, Nina

The Historian of the Soul bw *Atlantic* v320 no2 p36 S 2017

Khullar, Dhruv

To Increase Vaccination Rates, Share Information on Disease Outbreaks *Harvard Business Review Digital Articles* p2 F 22 2017

Khund-Sayeed, Syed

Impact of cytosine methylation on DNA binding specificities of human transcription factors diag *Science* v356 no6337 p502 My 5 2017

Khurana, Ishant

Dynamic multinuclear sites formed by mobilized copper ions in NOx selective catalytic reduction bw color diag graph *Science* v357 no6354 p898 S 1 2017

Khurana, Vikram

β2-Adrenoreceptor is a regulator of the a-synuclein gene driving risk of Parkinson's disease cartoon chart graph *Science* v357 no6354 p891 S 1 2017

Khutzeymateen Grizzly Bear Sanctuary (B.C.)

big picture bw color *Canadian Geographic* v137 no1 p12 F 2017

Ki, S.

Observation of coherent elastic neutrino-nucleus scattering diag *Science* v357 no6356 p1123 S 15 2017

Ki Youl Yang

Microresonator soliton dual-comb spectroscopy bibl diag graph *Science* v354 no6312 p600 N 4 2016

Kia automobiles—Evaluation

A Boost for the Soul J. Capparella color *Car & Driver* v62 no8 p82 F 2017

Canyonero? No B. Halvorson cartoon color *Car & Driver* v62 no10 p86 Ap 2017

Comfort With Class *Consumer Reports* v82 no7 p62 Jl 2017

Kia Cadenza chart color *Motor Trend* v69 no1 p128 Ja 2017

Kia Forte chart color *Motor Trend* v69 no1 p129 Ja 2017

Kia Sportage chart color *Motor Trend* v69 no1 p50 Ja 2017

KIA Stinger GT color *Motor Trend* v69 no3 p18 Mr 2017

Kia Stinger GT Track Drive S. Evans color *Motor Trend* v69 no9 p22 S 2017

REVIEWS E. DYER color *Popular Mechanics* p42 F 2017

SPLITTING THE HAIRS OF LUXURY A. Bassett chart color *Motor Trend* v68 no12 p74 D 2016

STINGS SO GOOD C. CHILTON color *Road & Track* v69 no3 p94 O 2017

Kia Motors Corp.

A Boost for the Soul J. Capparella color *Car & Driver* v62 no8 p82 F 2017

Comfort With Class *Consumer Reports* v82 no7 p62 Jl 2017

Kia Stinger GT Track Drive S. Evans color *Motor Trend* v69 no9 p22 S 2017

SPLITTING THE HAIRS OF LUXURY A. Bassett chart color *Motor Trend* v68 no12 p74 D 2016

STINGS SO GOOD C. CHILTON color *Road & Track* v69 no3 p94 O 2017

Kiarostami, Abbas, 1940-2016

JACQUES RIVETTE & ABBAS KIAROSTAM A. O. SCOTT *New York Times Magazine* p57 D 25 2016

Kiass, Mehdi

Reversion of antibiotic resistance in Mycobacterium tuberculosis by spiroisoxazoline SMARt-420 bibl diag *Science* v355 no6330 p1206 Mr 17 2017

Kibaroglu, Mustafa

Ban the bomb by... banning the bomb? bibl *Bulletin of the Atomic Scientists* v73 no3 p199 My 2017

Kibbe, Michael

OUR FUTURE IN THE FACE OF JESUS color *Christianity Today* v61 no6 p66 Jl/Ag 2017

Kibble, Tom, 1932-2016

Thomas Walter Bannerman Kibble E. Copeland, N. Turok et al *Physics Today* v69 no12 p68 D 2016

Kiberstis, Paula A.

FRONTIERS IN CANCER THERAPY *Science* v355 no6330 p1143 Mr 17 2017

Kibler, Ewald

Starting a Business Can Increase Older Workers' Quality of Life (Even When It Doesn't Pay Well) *Harvard Business Review Digital Articles* p2 S 19 2017

Kibler, Michael E.

Prevent Your Star Performers from Losing Passion for Their Work *Harvard Business Review Digital Articles* p2 Ja 14 2015

Treat Promises to Yourself as Seriously as Promises to Others *Harvard Business Review Digital Articles* p2 S 9 2015

Kibsgaard, Jakob

Combining theory and experiment in electrocatalysis: Insights into materials design bibl color graph *Science* v355 no6321 p1 Ja 13 2017

Kicheva, Anna

Decoding of position in the developing neural tube from antiparallel morphogen gradients diag *Science* v356 no6345 p1379 Je 30 2017

Kickboxing

See also

Muay Thai

Beauty and the Beast Mode M. SAGER cartoon color *Men's Health* v32 no3 p19 Ap 2017

FIGHT CLUB L. SCHOLZ *Atlanta* v57 no6 p46 O 2017

Kicking Butt D. Love color *AARP: The Magazine* v59 no6A p70 O/N 2016

Kickboxing—Thailand

See also

Muay Thai

PRADAL SEREY M. ANDERSON, L. ELLIOTT et al bw color *Black Belt* v55 no5 p48 Ag/S 2017

Kickstarter PBC

Kickstarter Publishing in 2016 C. Reid *Publishers Weekly* v264 no6 p7 F 6 2017

To Innovate, Think Like a 19th-Century Barn Raiser J. Geraci and C. Chavez *Harvard Business Review Digital Articles* p2 Ag 4 2016

Kid Mero (Performer)

Desus and Mero L. SCHWARTZBERG img *New York* v50 no6 p14 Mr 20 2017

KIDA, JEFF

The Big Pictures: LAKE POWELL color *Arizona Highways* v93 no5 p16 My 2017

The Big Pictures: SANTA CATALINA MOUNTAINS *Arizona Highways* v93 no6 p16 Je 2017

Q&A: Karen Shell *Arizona Highways* v93 no8 p9 Ag 2017

Visualization—or "Pre-Visualization" *Arizona Highways* v93 no2 p9 F 2017

Kidal (Music)

International Studies HADLEY color *Downbeat* v84 no9 p68 S 2017

KIDD, CHARLENE

SMART PEOPLE DO THE Dumbest THINGS! [Cover story] *Reader's Digest* v190 no1134 p62 O 2017

Kidd, Chip

Chip Kidd: Book Two color *Publishers Weekly* v264 no30 p49 Jl 24 2017

Kidd, David

Last Look *Governing* v30 no10 p64 Jl 2017

Last Look *Governing* v30 no4 p64 Ja 2017

Last Look *Governing* v30 no7 p64 Ap 2017

Last Look *Governing* v31 no1 p64 O 2017

Kidd, Jeffrey M.

Intersection of diverse neuronal genomes and neuropsychiatric disease: The Brain Somatic Mosaicism Network color *Science* v356 no6336 p395 Ap 28 2017

KIDD, SARAH

Incorporating Sociocultural Phenomena into Ecosystem-Service Valuation: The Importance of Critical Pluralism *BioScience* v67 no3 p233 Mr 2017

KIDD, THOMAS S.

The Ghosts of Wars on Christmas Past color *Christianity Today* v60 no10 p70 D 2016

Kidd, Timothy J.

Emergence and spread of a human-transmissible multidrug-resistant nontuberculous mycobacterium bibl diag graph *Science* v354 no6313 p751 N 11 2016

Kidder, Tracy

From Techie to Titan J. GERTNER *New York Times Book Review* p20 O 16 2016

Kidder, Tracy—Interviews

Pulitzer-winning author Tracy Kidder: Looking for the soul of the machine makers D. Drollette color *Bulletin of the Atomic Scientists* v73 no2 p74 Mr 2017

Kiddrane, Jonathan

The Thread *New York Times Magazine* p20 N 13 2016

Kidman, Nicole, 1967-

The Beguiled L. Greenblatt color *Entertainment Weekly* no1472 p44 Je 30 2017

BEST DRESS E. Wilson color *InStyle* v24 no8 p71 Ag 2017

BRANDON MAXWELL Simply Irresistible E. Wilson color *InStyle* v24 no6 p136 Je 2017

the cover color *InStyle* v24 no7 p18 Jl 2017

Feeling Social color *InStyle* v23 no12 p18 N 2016

THE GUIDE TO LIES L. Acken *TV Guide* v65 no7 p26 F 13 2017

Hello! L. Brown color *InStyle* v24 no7 p16 Jl 2017

THE INSTYLE AWARDS Fashion Goes to Hollywood K. Peiffer color *InStyle* v24 no1 p39 Ja 2017

Nicole Kidman C. Ianzito color *AARP: The Magazine* v60 no4A p68 Je/Jl 2017

NICOLE KIDMAN'S BAD WOMEN K. BUCHANAN img *New York* v49 no24 p130 N 28 2016

Ooh La La! N. Sperling color *Entertainment Weekly* no1468/1469 p22 Je 2-9 2017

PASSION PLAYER J. Powers color *Vogue* v207 no9 p676 S 2017

TV Trends to Watch for in 2017 J. HALTERMAN and D. HOLBROOK *TV Guide* v65 no6 p6 Ja 30 2017

Who Won Fashion? J. Ferrise color *InStyle* v24 no5 p82 My 2017

Kidman, Nicole, 1967—Interviews

A Star is Reborn [Cover story] L. Brown color *InStyle* v24 no7 p104 Jl 2017

Kidnapping

Hollywood's ORIGINAL GONE GIRL J. McGovern color *Entertainment Weekly* no1485 p30 O 6 2017

Kidnapping—Lawsuits & claims

WHY DID THIS INNOCENT MAN PLEAD GUILTY? A. GOLDET color *Reader's Digest* v189 no1131 p118 Je 2017

Kidney diseases

How Alternative Medicine Saved My Life S. E. Jamison color *Ebony* v72 no9 p62 Jl/Ag 2017

Kidney function tests

HYDRATION VITAL FOR SHIPPING FEVER RECOVERY C. Barakat and M. McCluskey color *Equus* no477 p18 Je 2017

Kidney stones—Alternative treatment—Research

Roller coaster knocks out stones in kidney model L. Beil color *Science News* v190 no10 p4 N 12 2016

Kidney stones—Treatment

FINDINGS *Harper's Magazine* v333 no1999 p96 D 2016

Kidney transplants

The Gift That Keeps on Giving T. ANDERSON and D. POINTDUJOUR color *Ebony* v72 no6 p62 Ap/My 2017

Xenotransplant advances may prompt human trials K. Servick *Science* v357 no6358 p1338 S 29 2017

Kidneys

See also

Urine

KIDNEY CARE K. P. S. Khalsa color *Amazing Wellness* v9 no2 p32 Spr 2017

Kid Rock, 1971-

MEET Rock 'n' Roll Hair Stylists B. CALLOWAY and R. SHELABARGER *Indianapolis Monthly* v40 no4 p24 D 2016

The Road to Statism... J. COST color *Weekly Standard* v22 no45 p11 Ag 7 2017

Kids & Co. Ltd.

DAYCARE MADE SIMPLE C. MCINTYRE color *Maclean's* v130 no7 p50 Ag 2017

Kiechel, Walter

The Case Against Competing *Harvard Business Review Digital Articles* p2 Ap 30 2015

Kieckhafer, R. M.

Observation of a large-scale anisotropy in the arrival directions of cosmic rays above 8×10^{18} eV *Science* v357 no6357 p1266 S 22 2017

Kiefer, Anselm, 1945-

BEAUTIFUL RUINS I. Parker cartoon *New Yorker* v93 no19 p21 Jl 3 2017

Kiefer, Charlie

When Your Boss Gives You Conflicting Messages *Harvard Business Review Digital Articles* p2 N 27 2014

Kiefer, Francine

By number, Christians overrepresented in Congress color *Christian Century* v134 no3 p12 F 2017

Kiefer, Kara

SPLASH PAD L. MOWRY *Atlanta* v56 no12 p50 Ap 2017

Kiefer, Walter S.

Gravity field of the Orientale basin from the Gravity Recovery and Interior Laboratory Mission bibl graph *Science* v354 no6311 p438 O 28 2016

Kiefert, Nicole

DETAILS ARRIVE ON TRAPPIST-1'S OUTERMOST PLANET color *Astronomy* v45 no9 p12 S 2017

Kieft, Jeffrey S.

Zika virus produces noncoding RNAs using a multi-pseudoknot structure that confounds a cellular exonuclease bibl color graph *Science* v354 no6316 p1148 D 2 2016

Kiehl's Since 1851 LLC

BEAUTY WITH BENEFITS color *Good Housekeeping* v263 no5 p26 N 2016

BODY SUNSCREEN color *Good Housekeeping* v264 no6 p28 Je 2017

Smooth Operators: From New York's East Village to The Fashion Mall: brand-new digs for Kiehl's J. Kent-Doolan *Indianapolis Monthly* v40 no10 p29 Je 2017

Kielb, Karolina

The Urbanist: What Does London Think of Brexit Now? C. KHAN img *New York* v49 no22 p22 O 31 2016

Kielsmeier-Cook, Stina

The Song Poet: A Memoir of My Father *Christian Century* v134 no12 p37 Je 7 2017

Kiely, Christopher J.

Atomic-layered Au clusters on α-MoC as catalysts for the low-temperature water-gas shift reaction chart diag graph *Science* v357 no6349 p389 Jl 28 2017

Identification of single-site gold catalysis in acetylene hydrochlorination bw diag graph *Science* v355 no6332 p1399 Mr 31 2017

KIENER, ROBERT

50 SECONDS FROM DEATH color *Reader's Digest* v189 no1131 p88 Je 2017

Kieper, Sebastian N.

CRISPR-Cas: Adapting to change color *Science* v356 no6333 p40 Ap 7 2017

Kiermer, V.

Fostering reproducibility in industry-academia research color *Science* v357 no6353 p759 Ag 25 2017

Kiernan, Caitlín R.

A BEAUTIFUL LIFE color *Women's Health* v14 no8 p52 O 2017

Dear Sweet Filthy World *Publishers Weekly* v264 no4 p60 Ja 23 2017

Kiernan, Denise

The Money Pit: America's largest private home and the history of its inhabitants V. WARD *New York Times Book Review* p21 O 15 2017

Kies, Thomas

Random Road: Introducing Geneva Chase *Publishers Weekly* v264 no10 p41 Mr 6 2017

Kiesel, Marcia

The Power of 3 color *O, The Oprah Magazine* p173 D 2016

SINGULAR Sensation cartoon color *O, The Oprah Magazine* p131 Ap 2017

SINGULAR Sensation color *O, The Oprah Magazine* p118 Ag 2017

SINGULAR Sensation color *O, The Oprah Magazine* p143 N 2017

Kiesling, Lydia

The Life of Marshall Hodgson color *New York Times Magazine* p30 O 9 2016

'This Girl' *New York Times Magazine* p34 Mr 12 2017

Was She the One? A stuffy banker reconsiders his bubbly second wife *New York Times Book Review* p14 Jl 9 2017

KIFFEL-ALCHEH, JAMIE

Epic Animal Fake Outs *National Geographic Kids* no469 p14 Ap 2017

Ghost Cat [Cover story] color map *National Geographic Kids* no475 p12 N 2017

Guinness World Records *National Geographic Kids* no468 p9 Mr 2017

Guinness World Records color *National Geographic Kids* no470 p8 My 2017

Panda Patrol color map *National Geographic Kids* no472 p12 Ag 2017

Rebel Penguins color map *National Geographic Kids* no473 p26 S 2017

Rise of the Tiger *National Geographic Kids* no466 p14 D 2016/Ja 2017

Secrets of Fake Photos Revealed *National Geographic Kids* no469 p22 Ap 2017

The Richest PETS OF ALL TIME! *National Geographic Kids* no467 p22 F 2017

Wild Vacation color *National Geographic Kids* no471 p6 Je/Jl 2017

Kiffin, Lane

Back at the Starting Line J. Fuchs and T. Keith color *Sports Il-*

lustrated v126 no1 p18 Ja 9 2017

KIGER, PATRICK

Surviving the '80s color *AARP: The Magazine* v59 no5A p47 Ag/S 2016

Kiger, Patrick J.

MASTERMIND OF DUNKIRK [Cover story] bw color map *MHQ: Quarterly Journal of Military History* v30 no1 p30 Aut 2017

Kikkoman Corp.

Healthy, Sustainable Growth on the Menu M. Foster and D. W. Russell color *Forbes* v199 no1 p(Sp)5 Ja 24 2017

KILACHAND, SEAN

THE WORLD'S BILLIONAIRES bw color diag graph map *Forbes* v199 no3 p84 Mr 28 2017

Kilauea Volcano (Hawaii)

GO WITH THE FLOW M. Roacti *Smithsonian* v48 no1 p48 Ap 2017

Hawaii's Lava Waterfall *New York Times Upfront* v149 no12 p2 Ap 24 2017

HEAVEN AND EARTH E. MASTROIANNI color *Discover* v38 no4 p9 My 2017

Twice-setting stars S. J. O'MEARA color *Astronomy* v45 no3 p20 Mr 2017

Kilbane, D.

Revealing the subfemtosecond dynamics of orbital angular momentum in nanoplasmonic vortices bibl diag *Science* v355 no6330 p1187 Mr 17 2017

Kilby, Karen

Life amid Loss *Commonweal* v144 no4 p13 F 24 2017

Kilday, Alyson

People TO WATCH [Cover story] K. SINGLETARY color *New Orleans Magazine* v52 no1 p76 S 2017

Kilday, Anne-Marie

A FORENSIC TAKE ON DEVIANCE: Microhistories, examining a range of notorious and mundane crimes, can help recover marginalised figures and forge links to wider cultural histories C. Wildman *History Today* v67 no9 p94 S 2017

Kilgannon, David

Whose idea was it? *History Today* v66 no11 p7 N 2016

Kilgariff, Karen

2 — MY FAVORITE MURDER J. Goodman color *Entertainment Weekly* no1444/1445 p114 D 16 2016

DEATH BECOMES THEM A. Wilkinson color *Entertainment Weekly* no1457/1458 p98 Mr 17 2017

Kilgore, Caroline C.

BEST OF ATLANTA *Atlanta* v56 no8 p106 D 2016

Kilgore, Ed

1968 Versus 2016 *Washington Monthly* p1 S/O 2016

DO MAYORS DO IT BETTER? img *New York* v50 no18 p30 S 4 2017

Will This Midterm Be Different From All Other Midterms? *New York* v50 no7 p26 Ap 3 2017

Kilgore, Marcia

Heir TRANSPARENT K. Molvar color *Vogue* v207 no4 p174 Ap 2017

Kilgore, Marcia—Interviews

"Every time I've had a really good idea, it was because I thought, I would so buy that." D. Kennedy and Ying Chu color *Glamour* v115 no4 p114 Ap 2017

Kilimanjaro, Mount (Tanzania)

The Amateur's Guide to Africa's Highest Peak J. CRIDER color diag *Conde Nast Traveler* v52 no5 p64 My 2017

Kilkenny, Joe

Patents and Awards *Science & Technology Review* p24 Je 2017

Killam, Taran, 1982-—Interviews

3 Rounds WITH TARAN Killam & COUBIE Smulders S. Vilkomerson color *Entertainment Weekly* no1457/1458 p50 Mr 17 2017

Killeen, T. J.

Persistent effects of pre-Columbian plant domestication on Amazonian forest composition bibl chart graph map *Science* v355 no6328 p925 Mr 3 2017

Killer Hurricanes (TV program)

Storm documentary proves timely C. Gramling color *Science News* v192 no7 p29 O 28 2017

Killer Instinct (TV program)

Your Ridiculously Early Fall TV Preview J. Hibberd color *Entertainment Weekly* no1453 p10 F 17 2017

Killer Mike (Performer)

Run the Jewels Enter Their Blue Period C. JENKINS img *New York* p79 F 9 2017

Killer whale

Milestones *Time* v189 no4 p13 Ja 23 2017

Killer whale—Behavior

Species IN THE Making R. Riesch color diag *Scientific American* v315 no5 p54 N 2016

Killers, The (Performer)

IN TUNE color *New Orleans Magazine* v51 no12 p51 O 2017

THE KILLERS' WONDERFUL RETURN N. Feeney color *Entertainment Weekly* no1472 p56 Je 30 2017

The Playlist color *Rolling Stone* no1273 p10 N 3 2016

Killian, Mary Lea

Role for migratory wild birds in the global spread of avian influenza H5N8 bibl graph map *Science* v354 no6309 p213 O 14 2016

Killifishes—Behavior

Swimming in polluted waters M. Tobler and Z. W. Culumber bibl diag *Science* v354 no6317 p1232 D 9 2016

Killing Reagan (Film)

REAGAN REVISITED I. RUDOLPH color *TV Guide* v64 no42 p26 O 10 2016

Killing Richard Glossip (TV program)

Killing Richard Glossip J. Halterman *TV Guide* p35 Ap 17 2017

Killing of a Sacred Deer, The (Film)

ALSO PLAYING D. Heching color *Entertainment Weekly* no1478 / 1479 p56 Ag 18-25 2017

MOVIES A. Lane *New Yorker* v93 no33 p18 O 23 2017

Killjoys (TV program)

ALSO COMING... A. D'Arminio *TV Guide* v65 no23 p31 My 29 2017

Killoren, Robert

READER COMMENTS *America* v216 no7 p7 Ap 3 2017

Kilmer, Joyce, 1886-1918

A Tree Grows on the Marne M. S. J. Malone *America* v216 no10 p3 My 1 2017

Kilmurray, Erin

THE HONEY HIVE B. GOLDEN color *Chicago* v66 no8 p44 Ag 2017

Kilogram

The Kilogram Makeover K. Sheikh color graph *Scientific American* v315 no3 p18 S 2016

Plot to redefine the kilogram nears climax A. Cho color *Science* v356 no6339 p670 My 19 2017

Kilpert, Fabian

Germ line–inherited H3K27me3 restricts enhancer function during maternal-to-zygotic transition diag *Science* v357 no6347 p212 Jl 14 2017

Kilroy, Jessica

Scaling New Heights K. Wong *Sierra* v102 no3 p26 My/Je 2017

KIM, ANN

r.s.v.p color *Bon Appetit* no8 p14 Ag 2017

Kim, Anne

Deconstructing the Administrative State color *Washington Monthly* v49 no6-8 p36 Je-Ag 2017

How the Internet Wrecked College Admissions *Washington Monthly* p1 S/O 2016

IVY LEAGUE ENDOWMENTS UNDER FIRE color *Washington Monthly* v49 no9/10 p67 S/O 2017

Minority Retort *Washington Monthly* p9 Ja/F 2017

Time to Abolish Cash Bail *Washington Monthly* p15 Ja/F 2017

Kim, Bong Hoon

Double-heterojunction nanorod light-responsive LEDs for display applications bibl color graph *Science* v355 no6325 p616 F 10 2017

Kim, Byron

COLOR IS A BOUNDARY W. S. Smith color *Art in America* v105 no3 p74 Mr 2017

Kim, Charles

Deconstructing behavioral neuropharmacology with cellular specificity color *Science* v356 no6333 p42 Ap 7 2017

Kim, Chloe, 2000-

Chloe Kim J. Crelin color *Current Biography* v78 no1 p32 Ja 2017

HOT IN THE COLD color *Sports Illustrated* v126 no5 p88 F 13 2017

Kim, Chŏng-nam, 1971-2017

Murder at Terminal 2 C. Campbell color *Time* v189 no9 p34 Mr 13 2017

The UNTOLD STORY of the ACCIDENTAL ASSASSINS of NORTH KOREA D. Bock Clark color *GQ: Gentlemen's Quarterly* v97 no10 p168 O 2017

Kim, Chŏng-ŭn, 1984-

About 200 Americans Have Been Living In North Korea E. Dias color *Time* v190 no9 p36 S 4 2017

THE APPROVAL MATRIX img *New York* v50 no18 p124 S 4 2017

A Blockade by Any Other Name color *Weekly Standard* v23 no5 p6 O 9 2017

Cigarette Fiend color *Weekly Standard* v22 no21 p2 F 6 2017

Esquipedia D. Dernavich cartoon color graph *Esquire* p30 S 2017

Feeding the Crocodile P. TERZIAN color *Weekly Standard* v23 no1 p17 S 11 2017

From the Twitter feed of Kim Jong Un, @youthcaptain R. LONG il *National Review* v69 no1 p34 Ja 23 2017

How the Kims Came to Love The Bomb M. J. Schuman color *Bloomberg Businessweek* no4537 p12 S 11 2017

KIM JONG-UN NO PATSY B. McCALL cartoon *New Yorker* v93 no6 p29 Mr 27 2017

KINGS OF COMMUNISM J. H. LEE bw color diag *Esquire* p94 S 2017

Land of the Hermit King J. H. LEE color *New Republic* v248 no10 p38 O 2017

North Korea: How to Stop Kim Jong Un W. Sherman, E. Revere et al color *Time* v189 no12 p40 Ap 3 2017

NORTH KOREA VS. THE WORLD R. ZISSOU *New York Times Upfront* v149 no9 p14 F 20 2017

People L. Markoe, E. M. Miller et al color *Christian Century* v134 no19 p17 S 13 2017

The U.S. Territory In the Line of North Korea's 'Enveloping Fire' J. Hincks and Guam color *Time* v190 no8 p14 Ag 28 2017

Kim, Connie

Why NYU's B-School Teaches Mindfulness *Harvard Business Review Digital Articles* p2 D 31 2015

Kim, Daniel

Science in litigation, the third branch of U.S. climate policy graph *Science* v357 no6355 p979 S 8 2017

Kim, Daniel Dae

Hawaii Five-O/MacGyver Crossover J. Halterman *TV Guide* v65 no11 p37 Mr 6 2017

HOLLYWOOD DISPATCH J. Halterman, D. Holbrook et al *TV Guide* v65 no35 p5 Ag 21 2017

Kim, David E.

Protein structure determination using metagenome sequence data bibl color graph *Science* v355 no6322 p294 Ja 20 2017

Kim, E. Tammy

FAMILY BUSINESS cartoon *New Yorker* v92 no49 p33 F 13 2017

WHEN TIME STOPPED FOREVER color *Nation* v304 no8 p32 Mr 13 2017

Kim, Eric

I would like to try dating women bw *Glamour* v115 no6 p98 Je 2017

Kim, Eun Kyu

Iodide management in formamidinium-lead-halide–based perovskite layers for efficient solar cells bw diag *Science* v356 no6345 p1376 Je 30 2017

Kim, Heejin

A Scandal at Korea's Retirement Giant color *Bloomberg Businessweek* no4507 p31 Ja 16 2017

Kim, Helen Kiyong

When East Meets East *Commentary* v141 no9 p1 N 2016

When East Meets East N. S. RILEY *Commentary* v142 no4 p40 N 2016

KIM, HYUNG-EUN

DOLL STORY bw *Archaeology* v70 no5 p12 S/O 2017

GUIDE TO THE AFTERLIFE color *Archaeology* v70 no1 p16 Ja/F 2017

Korea's Half Moon Palace color *Archaeology* v69 no6 p44 N/D 2016

Kim, Hyunho

Water harvesting from air with metal-organic frameworks powered by natural sunlight diag *Science* v356 no6336 p430 Ap 28 2017

Kim, Jae-Hwan
Double-heterojunction nanorod light-responsive LEDs for display applications bibl color graph *Science* v355 no6325 p616 F 10 2017

Kim, Jeong M.
T cell costimulatory receptor CD28 is a primary target for PD-1–mediated inhibition color diag graph *Science* v355 no6332 p1428 Mr 31 2017

Kim, Jiwoong
Anticancer sulfonamides target splicing by inducing RBM39 degradation via recruitment to DCAF15 color diag *Science* v356 no6336 p397 Ap 28 2017

KIM, JOHN
Are You in The Wrong Relationship? *Psychology Today* v50 no3 p38 My/Je 2017

Kim, Jonghan
Restored iron transport by a small molecule promotes absorption and hemoglobinization in animals color graph *Science* v356 no6338 p608 My 12 2017

Kim, Jongmin
Blocking promiscuous activation at cryptic promoters directs cell type–specific gene expression diag *Science* v356 no6339 p717 My 19 2017

Kim, Joseph
ESCAPE FROM NORTH KOREA P. Smith *New York Times Upfront* v149 no9 p17 F 20 2017

Kim, K. W.
Femtosecond electron-phonon lock-in by photoemission and x-ray free-electron laser chart diag *Science* v357 no6346 p71 Jl 7 2017

Kim, Keon Jung
Harvesting electrical energy from carbon nanotube yarn twist diag graph *Science* v357 no6353 p773 Ag 25 2017

Kim, Kirk
Bringing Better Hip-Hop To Asia N. SCARVELIS *Los Angeles Magazine* p22 F 2017

Kim, Kyungtae
Thermal processing of diblock copolymer melts mimics metallurgy diag graph *Science* v356 no6337 p520 My 5 2017

Kim, Michael
Potential role of intratumor bacteria in mediating tumor resistance to the chemotherapeutic drug gemcitabine diag *Science* v357 no6356 p1156 S 15 2017

Kim, Min Gyu
Colloidally prepared La-doped BaSnO3 electrodes for efficient, photostable perovskite solar cells graph *Science* v356 no6334 p167 Ap 14 2017

Kim, Minkyu
Low-temperature activation of methane on the IrO2(110) surface bw diag graph *Science* v356 no6335 p299 Ap 21 2017

KIM, MONICA
Legend Status color *Vogue* v207 no9 p442 S 2017

Kim, Moon
Harvesting electrical energy from carbon nanotube yarn twist diag graph *Science* v357 no6353 p773 Ag 25 2017
MoS2 transistors with 1-nanometer gate lengths bibl color graph *Science* v354 no6308 p99 O 7 2016

Kim, P.
Magnetic resonance spectroscopy of an atomically thin material using a single-spin qubit bibl color diag graph *Science* v355 no6324 p503 F 3 2017

KIM, RICHARD
The Bridge to Single-Payer *Nation* v304 no13 p3 Ap 17 2017

Kim, Rira
A chemical biology route to site-specific authentic protein modifications bibl diag graph *Science* v354 no6312 p623 N 4 2016

Kim, Sam
Are Drugs Samsung's Next Big Thing? color graph *Bloomberg Businessweek* no4523 p23 My 22 2017
THE BILLION-DOLLAR WAR Over an $18 Part color graph *Bloomberg Businessweek* no4541 p52 O 9 2017
Playing Dumb Didn't Help Samsung's Heir Apparent color *Bloomberg Businessweek* no4536 p22 S 4 2017
Samsung Would Love to Talk About This Phone color *Bloomberg*

Businessweek no4517 p36 Ap 3 2017
Summer of Samsung bw color diag graph *Bloomberg Businessweek* no4532 p42 Jl 31 2017

Kim, Sangman M.
Reovirus infection triggers inflammatory responses to dietary antigens and development of celiac disease color diag *Science* v356 no6333 p44 Ap 7 2017

Kim, Sarah A.
Madam Secretary, help us improve social-emotional learning color *Phi Delta Kappan* v98 no8 p64 My 2017

Kim, Seon Jeong
Harvesting electrical energy from carbon nanotube yarn twist diag graph *Science* v357 no6353 p773 Ag 25 2017

Kim, Sharon H.
Health Care Providers Can Use Design Thinking to Improve Patient Experiences *Harvard Business Review Digital Articles* p2 Ag 31 2017

Kim, Sheila
Wine Country Farmhouse *Architectural Record* v205 no9 p142 S 2017

Kim, Simon C.—Interviews
Who is us? color *U.S. Catholic* v82 no5 p18 My 2017

Kim, Sohee
K-Pop Eyes Its 'Michael Jackson Moment' bw color *Bloomberg Businessweek* no4535 p31 Ag 28 2017
Samsung's New Board Gets Back to Business color *Bloomberg Businessweek* no4513 p21 Mr 6 2017

Kim, Stephen
The Negotiator color *Time* v189 no18 p40 My 15 2017

Kim, Sung Soo
Ring attractor dynamics in the Drosophila central brain diag graph *Science* v356 no6340 p849 My 26 2017

Kim, Suntae
Why Companies Are Becoming B Corporations *Harvard Business Review Digital Articles* p2 Je 17 2016

Kim, Susan C.
Character study color *Sunset* v238 no2 p38 F 2017

Kim, Tae Hun
The role of dimer asymmetry and protomer dynamics in enzyme catalysis diag *Science* v355 no6322 p262 Ja 20 2017

Kim, Thomas Aquinas
Deficiency of microRNA miR-34a expands cell fate potential in pluripotent stem cells diag *Science* v355 no6325 p596 F 10 2017

KIM, VIVEKAE
Why I'm For Hillary Clinton [Cover story] *New York Times Upfront* v149 no4 p12 O 31 2016

Kim, W. Chan
Closing the Gap Between Blue Ocean Strategy and Execution *Harvard Business Review Digital Articles* p2 F 5 2015
Identify Blue Oceans by Mapping Your Product Portfolio *Harvard Business Review Digital Articles* p2 F 12 2015

Kim, Yong H.
80% of Companies Don't Know If Their Products Contain Conflict Minerals color *Harvard Business Review Digital Articles* p2 Ja 4 2017

Kim, Yoochul
StarCraft Pros Are Ready to Battle AI color *MIT Technology Review* v120 no5 p18 S/O 2017

Kim, Young Chan
Iodide management in formamidinium-lead-halide–based perovskite layers for efficient solar cells bw diag *Science* v356 no6345 p1376 Je 30 2017

Kim, Young-ha, 1968-
I Hear Your Voice *Publishers Weekly* v264 no23 p28 Je 5 2017

Kim Yuna, 1990-
Sport Can Transform Children's Lives and the World Y. KIM *UN Chronicle* v53 no2 p42 2016

Kim, Yun-Gi
Neonatal acquisition of Clostridia species protects against colonization by bacterial pathogens diag *Science* v356 no6335 p315 Ap 21 2017

KIM, YUNHEE
MORNING GLORIES *Martha Stewart Living* no270 p91 D 2016

Kimani, Peter
Dance of the Jakaranda color *Publishers Weekly* v263 no51 p119 D 12 2016

Laying the Lunatic Express F. ROCCO *New York Times Book Review* p10 F 19 2017

Kimball, Christopher, 1951-
Christopher Kimball M. Rich color *Current Biography* v78 no6 p59 Je 2017
Kimball Returns to Cookbook Publishing J. Rosen color *Publishers Weekly* v264 no5 p3 Ja 30 2017

KIMBALL, ROGER
Shooting Blanks *Weekly Standard* v22 no31 p37 Ap 17 2017

Kimber America (Company)
KIMBER M84 HUNTER J. B. SNOW chart color *Outdoor Life* v224 no2 p88 F/Mr 2017
KIMBER SUPER JAGARE J. B. SNOW chart color *Outdoor Life* v224 no9 p68 N 2017

Kimberley, Grant
10 UP & COMERS: GRANT BERLEY K. Birchmier *Successful Farming* v115 no8 p48 Je/Jl 2017

Kimble, David
1966 CHAPARRAL 2E bw color *Hot Rod* v70 no1 p60 Ja 2017

Kimble, Judith
Not just Salk color *Science* v357 no6356 p1105 S 15 2017

KIMBLE, MELISSA
EBONY POWER 100 Celebrated Black Excellence, Community and Creativity color *Ebony* v72 no4 p26 F 2017
No Joke, Kevin Hart Couldn't Make This Up color *Ebony* v72 no8 p31 Je 2017
Ooh, Ladies First! color *Ebony* v72 no5 p30 Mr 2017

Kimbler, Tammy
PICKLE RECIPES for the Picking: Ferment or quick-pickle your harvest with this assortment of ideas from Mother Earth News bloggers *Mother Earth News* no282 p56 Je/Jl 2017

Kimbrel, Craig
SPECIAL K T. Verducci color *Sports Illustrated* v126 no18 p40 Je 26 2017
STRIKE FORCE color *Sports Illustrated* v126 no18 p43 Je 26 2017

Kimbrell, Tristan
Biology and the Law J. SALZMAN *BioScience* v66 no11 p999 N 1 2016

Kimchi
YOU WON'T FIND THIS IN LAOS. AND THAT'S THE POINT J. SYHABOUT color *Bon Appetit* v62 no2 p72 Mr 2017

Kimetto, Dennis, 1984-
Great Barrier Reach C. Chavez and T. Keith color *Sports Illustrated* v126 no8 p22 Mr 20 2017

Kimmel, Barbara Brooks
CAN NEUROSCIENCE HELP US UNDERSTAND TRUST AT WORK?: INTERACTION color *Harvard Business Review* v95 no2 p18 Mr/Ap 2017

Kimmel, Jimmy, 1967-
CHEERS & JEERS D. HOLBROOK *TV Guide* v65 no21 p84 My 15 2017
Jimmy Kimmel D. BROWNE bw *Rolling Stone* no1281/1282 p58 F 23 2017
A Modest Proposal J. Kimmel color *GQ: Gentlemen's Quarterly* v97 no3 p78 Mr 2017
Sound Bites color *Entertainment Weekly* no1462 p7 Ap 21 2017

Kimmel, Joyce
SWEEPSTAKES *Nebraska Life* v20 no6 p13 N/D 2016

Kimmel, Sarah
Readers Respond bw *Publishers Weekly* v264 no2 p3 Ja 9 2017

KIMMERER, ROBIN WALL
SPEAKING OF NATURE: Finding language that affirms our kinship with the natural world color *Orion Magazine* v36 no2 p14 Mr/Ap 2017
Teaching Biology in the Field: Importance, Challenges, and Solutions *BioScience* v67 no6 p558 Je 2017
Weaving Science with Tradition *South Dakota Magazine* p13 S/O 2017 Supplement

Kimmett, Colleen
Uptown Squirrels color *Walrus* v14 no5 p26 Je 2017

Kimoto, Benny—Interviews
THE DIRT C. Bowers *Dance Spirit* v21 no1 p24 Ja 2017

Kim's Convenience (TV program)
Convenience truth A. LEE color *Maclean's* v129 no42 p59 O 24 2016

Kimura, Tim
The 'Man of Trail' SHARES HIS TIPS color *Horse & Rider* v55 no12 p52 D 2016

Kimura, Toshinori
Recurring and triggered slow-slip events near the trench at the Nankai Trough subduction megathrust diag graph *Science* v356 no6343 p1157 Je 16 2017

Kimura, Yuki—Exhibitions
YUKI KIMURA L. M. Green color *Art in America* v105 no3 p137 Mr 2017

Kin selection (Evolution)
Beyond Hamilton's rule H. P. de Vladar and E. Szathmáry color *Science* v356 no6337 p485 My 5 2017

Kinane, Ruth
39 Perfect Pop Culture Presents color *Entertainment Weekly* no1442 p31 D 2 2016 Rebellious Special Issue
9JKL color *Entertainment Weekly* no1482/1483 p49 S 22 2017
All Men Must Dine color *Entertainment Weekly* no1480 p44 S 1 2017
Arrow *Entertainment Weekly* no1482/1483 p84 S 22 2017
As Good as Gold(ie) color *Entertainment Weekly* no1466 p14 My 19 2017
The Beautiful Dead color *Entertainment Weekly* no1449 p63 Ja 20 2017
Better Things color *Entertainment Weekly* no1482/1483 p91 S 22 2017
THE BLAIR WITCH PROJECT color *Entertainment Weekly* no1460/1461 p75 Ap 7-17 2017
Blindspot color *Entertainment Weekly* no1482/1483 p95 S 22 2017
Blue Bloods color *Entertainment Weekly* no1482/1483 p99 S 22 2017
THE BOOK OF HENRY color *Entertainment Weekly* no1463/1464 p57 Ap/My 2017
The Brave color *Entertainment Weekly* no1482/1483 p55 S 22 2017
Breaking Big EMMA DUMONT color *Entertainment Weekly* no1482/1483 p51 S 22 2017
Cake Fit for a Queen color diag *Entertainment Weekly* no1474/1475 p24 Jl 21-28 2017
Can Fans Save The Sackett Sisters? color *Entertainment Weekly* no1468/1469 p92 Je 2-9 2017
Chicago Fire *Entertainment Weekly* no1482/1483 p91 S 22 2017
Cinnamon Crumb Cake color *Entertainment Weekly* no1465 p18 My 12 2017
Crazy Ex-Girlfriend color *Entertainment Weekly* no1482/1483 p98 S 22 2017
Dancing With the Stars *Entertainment Weekly* no1482/1483 p48 S 22 2017
The Entertainment Weekly Must List color *Entertainment Weekly* no1441 p4 N 25 2016
The Entertainment Weekly Must List color *Entertainment Weekly* no1457/1458 p9 Mr 17 2017
The Entertainment Weekly Must List color *Entertainment Weekly* no1478 / 1479 p10 Ag 18-25 2017
ESSENCE'S GLAM GRAMMY WARM-UP color *Entertainment Weekly* no1454/1455 p14 F 24 2017
EW PULLS DOUBLE PARTY DUTY AT NY COMIC CON color *Entertainment Weekly* no1436/1437 p18 O 21 2016
The Exorcist color *Entertainment Weekly* no1482/1483 p92 S 22 2017
"Express Yourself" color *Entertainment Weekly* no1460/1461 p47 Ap 7-17 2017
Fancy a Nightcap With These Folks? color *Entertainment Weekly* no1470 p49 Je 16 2017
FREDDIE HIGHMORE OF The Good Doctor color *Entertainment Weekly* no1482/1483 p54 S 22 2017
A GAY Old Timeline color diag *Entertainment Weekly* no1471 p32 Je 23 2017
The Gifted color *Entertainment Weekly* no1482/1483 p50 S 22 2017
The Good Place color *Entertainment Weekly* no1482/1483 p86 S 22 2017
Gotham *Entertainment Weekly* no1482/1483 p84 S 22 2017
THE GREATEST DISNEY SONGS OF ALL TIME color *Entertainment Weekly* no1454/1455 p36 F 24 2017

Great News color *Entertainment Weekly* no1482/1483 p88 S 22 2017

Grey's Anatomy color diag *Entertainment Weekly* no1482/1483 p89 S 22 2017

Hawaii Five-O *Entertainment Weekly* no1482/1483 p99 S 22 2017

Hell's Kitchen *Entertainment Weekly* no1482/1483 p99 S 22 2017

HOLLYWOOD HONORS LGBTQ YOUTH ADVOCATES color *Entertainment Weekly* no1438 p20 N 4 2016

HOME AGAIN color *Entertainment Weekly* no1478 / 1479 p44 Ag 18-25 2017

How to Get Away With Murder *Entertainment Weekly* no1482/1483 p91 S 22 2017

Hungry for S'more? color *Entertainment Weekly* no1486 p52 O 13 2017

Ice, Ice (Pops), Baby! color *Entertainment Weekly* no1472 p18 Je 30 2017

Jane the Virgin color *Entertainment Weekly* no1482/1483 p95 S 22 2017

Kevin Can Wait color *Entertainment Weekly* no1482/1483 p52 S 22 2017

LADY MACBETH color *Entertainment Weekly* no1463/1464 p71 Ap/My 2017

LAFAYETTE'S BON TEMPS color *Entertainment Weekly* no1474/1475 p20 Jl 21-28 2017

Life in Pieces *Entertainment Weekly* no1482/1483 p88 S 22 2017

Lobster-and-Celery Rolls color *Entertainment Weekly* no1470 p16 Je 16 2017

Lucifer *Entertainment Weekly* no1482/1483 p48 S 22 2017

MacGyver *Entertainment Weekly* no1482/1483 p99 S 22 2017

MALIN AKERMAN FIGHTS GLOBAL POVERTY color *Entertainment Weekly* no1465 p16 My 12 2017

Marvel's Inhumans color *Entertainment Weekly* no1482/1483 p99 S 22 2017

Meanwhile, 3 Doors Down... color *Entertainment Weekly* no1451/1452 p19 F 3-10 2017

Me, Myself & I color *Entertainment Weekly* no1482/1483 p48 S 22 2017

Mermaid Marshmallow Pie color *Entertainment Weekly* no1466 p20 My 19 2017

MET GALA MADNESS color *Entertainment Weekly* no1465 p12 My 12 2017

Mom color *Entertainment Weekly* no1482/1483 p85 S 22 2017

MUSIC color *Entertainment Weekly* no1444/1445 p88 D 16 2016

MUSIC MADE THE PEOPLE COME TOGETHER color *Entertainment Weekly* no1439 p22 N 11 2016

MY BEST FRIEND'S WEDDING color *Entertainment Weekly* no1460/1461 p67 Ap 7-17 2017

Once Upon a Time color *Entertainment Weekly* no1482/1483 p96 S 22 2017

The Opposition With Jordan Klepper *Entertainment Weekly* no1482/1483 p55 S 22 2017

The Orville *Entertainment Weekly* no1482/1483 p85 S 22 2017

PITCH PERFECT 3 color *Entertainment Weekly* no1478 / 1479 p78 Ag 18-25 2017

PRAISE (JUST) JACK—WILL & GRACE IS BACK! color *Entertainment Weekly* no1484 p50 S 29 2017

(PUMPKIN) SPICE UP YOUR DECOR color *Entertainment Weekly* no1486 p52 O 13 2017

Quidditch for Muggles color *Entertainment Weekly* no1476 p20 Ag 4 2017

Scandal *Entertainment Weekly* no1482/1483 p88 S 22 2017

Scorpion color *Entertainment Weekly* no1482/1483 p55 S 22 2017

A Starry Night color *Entertainment Weekly* no1446/1447 p25 D 2016/Ja 2017

Supergirl *Entertainment Weekly* no1482/1483 p49 S 22 2017

Superior Donuts color *Entertainment Weekly* no1482/1483 p52 S 22 2017

Supernatural color *Entertainment Weekly* no1482/1483 p84 S 22 2017

Superstore color *Entertainment Weekly* no1482/1483 p84 S 22 2017

SURREAL SUPPERS color *Entertainment Weekly* no1439 p62 N 11 2016

S.W.A.T color *Entertainment Weekly* no1482/1483 p90 S 22 2017

A Tale of Two Sheldons color *Entertainment Weekly* no1482/1483 p44 S 22 2017

Toss Like a Boss color *Entertainment Weekly* no1484 p50 S 29 2017

Valor color *Entertainment Weekly* no1482/1483 p52 S 22 2017

The Voice color *Entertainment Weekly* no1482/1483 p49 S 22 2017

A WESTEROS TEST(EROS) color *Entertainment Weekly* no1480 p44 S 1 2017

What to Watch color *Entertainment Weekly* no1446/1447 p112 D 2016/Ja 2017

What to Watch color *Entertainment Weekly* no1457/1458 p88 Mr 17 2017

WHAT TO WATCH color *Entertainment Weekly* no1468/1469 p68 Je 2-9 2017

Will & Grace color *Entertainment Weekly* no1482/1483 p80 S 22 2017

KINARD, KYLE

ANALYZE THIS color *Road & Track* v69 no3 p102 O 2017

CHEMISTRY LESSON color *Road & Track* v68 no6 p80 F 2017

THE FULL KIT color *Road & Track* v69 no2 p86 S 2017

SLEEPER STREAKER color *Road & Track* v68 no5 p102 D 2016/Ja 2017

SLOW LEARNERS cartoon *Road & Track* v68 no7 p96 Mr/Ap 2017

Kinases

See also

Adenylate kinase

Optical control of cell signaling by single-chain photoswitchable kinases X. X. Zhou, L. Z. Fan et al bibl diag *Science* v355 no6327 p836 F 24 2017

Kincade, Trudy

Around the Campfire color *Trail Rider* v29 no2 p6 Mr 2017

Kincaid, Hannah

Just Choose Hope *Mother Earth News* no279 p3 D/Ja 2017

Kincaid, Kimberly

Crossing Hearts: Cross Creek, Book 1 *Publishers Weekly* v264 no1 p44 Ja 2 2017

KINCAID, STEPHEN

What Sets Successful CEOs Apart [Cover story] color *Harvard Business Review* v95 no3 p70 My/Je 2017

Kinch, Michael

Arrested development G. Painter color *Science* v354 no6316 p1111 D 2 2016

Food and microbiota in the FDA regulatory framework color *Science* v357 no6346 p39 Jl 7 2017

Kind LLC

How Did I Get Here? DANIEL LUBETZKY color *Bloomberg Businessweek* no4501 p64 N 28 2016

KINDELA, JERRY

AFTER THE BARRE chart color *Muscle & Performance* v8 no12 p32 D 2016

A Born Natural chart color *Muscle & Performance* v9 no8 p30 Ag 2017

Hybrid Powerlifter color *Muscle & Performance* v9 no7 p28 Jl 2017

LITTLE DYNAMITE chart color *Muscle & Performance* v9 no4 p28 Ap 2017

NEVER LOOK BACK color *Muscle & Performance* v9 no4 p30 Ap 2017

THE NEW MR. OLYMPIA? chart color *Muscle & Performance* v9 no5 p30 My 2017

RISING STAR chart color *Muscle & Performance* v9 no1 p32 Ja 2017

Kindem, Jonathan M.

Nanophotonic rare-earth quantum memory with optically controlled retrieval diag graph *Science* v357 no6358 p1392 S 29 2017

Kinder, Donald R.

Tribalists and Ideologues L. Drutman color *Washington Monthly* v49 no6-8 p74 Je-Ag 2017

Kinder, Joe

Sending Southern Smoke H. MOORE chart color *Climbing* no351 p32 F/Mr 2017

Kindergarten

Back to School S. Myrick *Parks & Recreation* v52 no9 p120 S 2017

College, Careers, and Kindergarten D. YAFFE *Education Digest*

King, Gayle, 1954-
GAYLE KING and FRANK EDWARDS color *AARP: The Magazine* v59 no2A p50 F/Mr 2016
My Days in Morning TV *TV Guide* v65 no2 p16 Ja 2 2017
Princess Diana: Her Life, Her Death, the Truth B. Oates *TV Guide* v65 no21 p37 My 15 2017
THE WORLD ACCORDING TO Gayle Gayle color *O, The Oprah Magazine* p28 Jl 2017
THE WORLD ACCORDING TO Gayle color *O, The Oprah Magazine* p32 Ap 2017
THE WORLD ACCORDING TO Gayle color *O, The Oprah Magazine* p32 Ag 2017
THE WORLD ACCORDING TO Gayle bw color *O, The Oprah Magazine* p36 S 2017
THE WORLD ACCORDING TO Gayle color *O, The Oprah Magazine* p38 O 2017

King, Homay
VIRTUAL REALITY IN REAL TIME: A CONVERSATION *Film Quarterly* v71 no1 p51 Fall 2017

King, I. Marlene—Interviews
PRETTY LITTLE LIARS S. Highfill color *Entertainment Weekly* no1468/1469 p56 Je 2-9 2017

King, Ian
Apple Tries the Full-Court Press color graph *Bloomberg Businessweek* no4509 p28 Ja 30 2017
THE BILLION-DOLLAR WAR Over an $18 Part color graph *Bloomberg Businessweek* no4541 p52 O 9 2017
China Is Missing the Chips Rush *Bloomberg Businessweek* no4529 p22 Jl 3 2017
Deal Snapshot Intel + Mobileye diag graph *Bloomberg Businessweek* no4515 p21 Mr 20 2017
The End of Terrible Wi-Fi May Be Near color diag *Bloomberg Businessweek* no4510 p27 F 6 2017
Summer of Samsung bw color diag graph *Bloomberg Businessweek* no4532 p42 Jl 31 2017

King, J. C. H.
The Cultural Resilience of a Continent's Dispossessed J. Porter *History Today* v67 no4 p59 Ap 2017

KING, JEFF
UNDER DISCUSSION *Christianity Today* p17 Ap 2017

King, Jerry
GAMESET & MATCH color *Golf Magazine* v59 no9 p72 S 2017
HAWAII'S 5-OH! color *Golf Magazine* v59 no1 p54 Ja 2017
PARADISE LOST color *Golf Magazine* v59 no10 p51 O 2017

King, John
FLYING JETS: WHAT'S THE BIG DEAL? color *Flying* v144 no1 p28 Ja 2017
OBSERVING A LOT JUST BY WATCHING color *Flying* v144 no5 p30 My 2017
POLISHING OFF THE RUST color *Flying* v144 no9 p30 S 2017

KING, JOHN B., JR.
Giving Every Student a Fair Shot *Education Digest* v82 no7 p16 Mr 2017

King, Kimberley
Who I am Kimberley King *People Management* p49 Jl 2017

King, Larry, 1933—Interviews
FIVE QUESTIONS FOR LARRY KING color *Fortune* v175 no6 p14 My 1 2017

King, Laurie R.
Lockdown *Publishers Weekly* v264 no17 p68 Ap 24 2017

King, Lisa
Survivance, Sovereignty, and Story: Teaching American Indian Rhetorics M. N. Boyer-Kelly *American Indian Quarterly* v41 no2 p190 Spr 2017

KING, MARA
love your BELLY color *Yoga Journal* p102 2017 SpecialIssue

King, Marissa
Burnout at Work Isn't Just About Exhaustion. It's Also About Loneliness *Harvard Business Review Digital Articles* p2 Je 29 2017
Having Work Friends Can Be Tricky, but It's Worth It *Harvard Business Review Digital Articles* p2 Ag 8 2017

King, Martha
THE GREATEST AIRPORT PARTY EVER color *Flying* v144 no11 p32 N 2017
IT TAKES AN AVIATION VILLAGE color *Flying* v144 no7 p32

Jl 2017
SAFETY CAUSE DU JOUR color *Flying* v144 no3 p32 Mr 2017

King, Martin Luther, Jr., 1929-1968
BIRTHDAY WISHES J. Cobb bw cartoon *New Yorker* v92 no45 p21 Ja 16 2017
In Search of MLK's Atlanta N. SHAVIN *Smithsonian* v47 no9 p18 Ja/F 2017
King & His Mentors G. Dorrien bw *Commonweal* v144 no16 p17 O 6 2017
A MESSAGE OF PEACE J. RAINEY MARQUEZ *Atlanta* v56 no9 p31 Ja 2017
ON MARTIN LUTHER KING D. Halberstam *Harper's Magazine* v334 no2001 p39 F 2017
THE POLITICS OF ANGER S. Coll cartoon *New Yorker* v93 no18 p17 Je 26 2017
The Quiz *History Today* v67 no1 p71 Ja 2017
Q: What was the most important letter in history? C. Carson, N. Sparks et al color *Atlantic* v320 no2 p104 S 2017
Successful Movements All Have 3 Acts N. Duarte *Harvard Business Review Digital Articles* p2 Mr 24 2016

King, Mary-Claire
Home of the Brave cartoon *Reader's Digest* v190 no1132 p99 Jl/Ag 2017
Not just Salk color *Science* v357 no6356 p1105 S 15 2017

King, Mervyn A., 1948-
Hello, Central J. SHELTON color *Weekly Standard* v22 no9 p34 N 7 2016

King, Michael D.
Why Higher Ed and Business Need to Work Together *Harvard Business Review Digital Articles* p2 Jl 17 2015

King, Michelle
To Address Gender Bias at Your Company, Start with Teams color *Harvard Business Review Digital Articles* p2 Ja 27 2017

King, Nicholas
Spirituality that makes sense *America* v216 no11 p54 My 15 2017

King, Peter
Dennis Byrd 1966-2016 color *Sports Illustrated* v125 no14 p22 O 24-31 2016
FIVE WILL GET YOU ZEN color *Sports Illustrated* v126 no7 p74 Mr 6 2017
GOLD MINED color *Sports Illustrated* v126 no13 p42 My 8 2017
HATERS GONNA FLUCTUATE color *Sports Illustrated* v127 no1 p40 S 4 2017
LIVE AND LEARN color *Sports Illustrated* v127 no10 p34 O 2 2017

King, R. Daniel
HEALTH CARE NEEDS REAL COMPETITION: INTERACTION img *Harvard Business Review* v95 no2 p19 Mr/Ap 2017

King, Rachel
MEANWHILE, ELSEWHERE IN CANADA ... *Fortune* v176 no2 p31 Ag 1 2017

King, Regina, 1971-
American Crime J. Jensen and A. Wilkinson color *Entertainment Weekly* no1456 p58 Mr 10 2017
AMERICAN CRIME T. Stack color *Entertainment Weekly* no1446/1447 p61 D 2016/Ja 2017
FIELD NOTES E. NUSSBAUM color *New Yorker* v93 no11 p76 My 1 2017
My Obsessions... *TV Guide* v65 no13 p8 Mr 20 2017

King, Richard H.
Richard H. King, Arendt and America T. Wheatland *Society* v54 no2 p199 Ap 2017

King, Richard, 1824-1885
Building a Legacy: The King Ranch R. Soodalter bw *American Cowboy* p64 LEGENDS OF TEXAS Special Issue 2017

King, Ross
CLAUDE MONET D. SOLOMON *New York Times Book Review* p68 D 4 2016
Mad Enchantment Claude Monet and the Painting of the Water Lilies T. Fowle *History Today* v67 no1 p57 Ja 2017

King, Stephen, 1947-
A Hunger of the Soul *New York Times Book Review* p14 O 2 2016
IS THAT WHAT THEY SHOULD LOOK LIKE? bw color *Reader's Digest* v190 no1134 p98 O 2017
Maternal Claws: It isn't Mother's Day in Paul Theroux's portrait of dysfunction running in the family *New York Times Book Re-*

view p13 My 14 2017

Sound Bites color *Entertainment Weekly* no1439 p8 N 11 2016

STEPHEN KING & SON A. Breznican color *Entertainment Weekly* no1484 p60 S 29 2017

Stephen King's September L. Feldman *Time* v190 no12 p61 S 25 2017

King, Steve

How PwC and The Washington Post Are Finding and Hiring External Talent *Harvard Business Review Digital Articles* p2 Mr 29 2016

How to Get Feedback as a Freelancer *Harvard Business Review Digital Articles* p2 Ag 19 2015

The Pros and Cons of the President's Immigrant Travel Ban *Congressional Digest* v96 no3 p16 Mr 2017

Your Company Needs Independent Workers *Harvard Business Review Digital Articles* p2 N 23 2015

King, Steve, 1949——Interviews

The Freelance Economy Still Runs on Word of Mouth J. Fox *Harvard Business Review Digital Articles* p2 O 9 2014

King, Steven

Welfare Pasts and Futures *History Today* v67 no3 p6 Mr 2017

King, Sue

Borg's Jesus *Christian Century* v134 no17 p6 Ag 16 2017

KING, TIMOTHY

JUST SAY NO TO SHAME [Cover story] cartoon color *Christianity Today* v60 no10 p34 D 2016

OUR SUSTAINING FORCE R. CLARK *Christianity Today* v60 no10 p9 D 2016

King Arthur (Theatrical production)

King Arthur A. J. Goldmann *Opera News* v81 no10 p42 Ap 2017

King Arthur (TV program)

A NEW KING WILL RISE K. P. Sullivan color *Entertainment Weekly* no1450 p34 Ja 27 2017

King Arthur: Legend of the Sword (Film)

The Good Knight K. P. Sullivan color *Entertainment Weekly* no1466 p22 My 19 2017

King Arthur as a Knockabout Guy S. Zacharek color *Time* v189 no19 p54 My 22 2017

KING ARTHUR: LEGEND OF THE SWORD K. P. Sullivan color *Entertainment Weekly* no1463/1464 p40 Ap/My 2017

King cakes

tops OF THE TOWN bw color *New Orleans Magazine* v51 no3 p68 Ja 2017

King Kong (Fictitious character)

SIZE KINGS D. Coggan color diag *Entertainment Weekly* no1456 p54 Mr 10 2017

King Lear (Play : Shakespeare)

Commonplace Book *American Scholar* v86 no1 p126 Wint 2017

Glenda Jackson's Great Lear F. O'Toole color *New York Review of Books* v63 no20 p16 D 22 2016

Professor Shakespeare *Lapham's Quarterly* v10 no2 p114 Spr 2017

King of Hearts (Film)

Stir Crazy M. Nelson color *Film Comment* v53 no4 p11 Jl/Ag 2017

King Ranch (Tex.)

Building a Legacy: The King Ranch R. Soodalter bw *American Cowboy* p64 LEGENDS OF TEXAS Special Issue 2017

Kingdom (TV program)

KINGDOM'S KNOCKOUT S. Highfill color *Entertainment Weekly* no1477 p48 Ag 11 2017

What to Watch D. Heching, R. Rahman et al color *Entertainment Weekly* no1476 p54 Ag 4 2017

Kingdom of God

Faith Matters S. Wells *Christian Century* v134 no9 p30 Ap 26 2017

Kinge, Sachin

All-printed thin-film transistors from networks of liquid-exfoliated nanosheets diag *Science* v356 no6333 p69 Ap 7 2017

Kinghorn, Warren

Tribe: On Home coming and Belonging color *Christian Century* v133 no21 p39 O 12 2016

King & I, The (Theatrical production)

THE QUINTESSENTIAL DIRECTOR FOR THE QUINTESSENTIAL PRODUCTION G. Holt *Cincinnati Magazine* v50 no8 p18 My 2017

KINGLOFF, AMANDA

ENJOY A NATURAL CRAFTERNOON color *Parents* v92 no11 p108 N 2017

King-Miller, Lindsay

21 Ways to Please Your SELF C. Leive color *Glamour* v115 no7 p12 Jl 2017

Why Didn't Anyone Teach Us the Good Stuff? color *Glamour* v115 no7 p64 Jl 2017

Kingo, Audrey Goodson

Making the Grade? color *Working Mother* v40 no3 p44 Ag/S 2017

WHEN WE RUN, WE WIN [Cover story] color *Working Mother* v40 no2 p46 Je/Jl 2017

King of Dauphin Island, The (Short story)

THE KING OF DAUPHIN ISLAND M. KNIGHT *Saturday Evening Post* v289 no5 p62 S/O 2017

Kings & rulers

See also

Governors

Royal houses

Bhumibol Adulyadej C. Campbell color *Time* v188 no18 p13 O 31 2016

An Empowering Rule Z. PARVEZ *Islamic Horizons* v46 no1 p54 Ja/F 2017

A General State of Mourning R. Wilson *History Today* v67 no3 p7 Mr 2017

Thailand's Royal Mess D. DEVOSS *Weekly Standard* v22 no8 p14 O 31 2016

The Universe M. McCluskey color *Time* v190 no2/3 p76 Jl 10-17 2017

Kings & rulers of China—History

c. 400 BC: China *Lapham's Quarterly* v10 no2 p107 Spr 2017

Kings & rulers—Children

Prince and princess charming color *Maclean's* v129 no41 p44 O 17 2016

Kings of Leon (Performer)

Kings of Leon K. O'Donnell color *Entertainment Weekly* no1436/1437 p99 O 21 2016

KINGS OF LEON'S CALEB FOLLOWILL M. Vain color *Entertainment Weekly* no1436/1437 p98 O 21 2016

Kingsland, Dave

PAYING IT FORWARD *New York State Conservationist* v71 no5 p11 Ap 2017

Kingsley, Laura

Friendship *Science* v354 no6308 p46 O 7 2016

Kingsley, Patrick

TRUMP'S TRAVEL BAN *New York Times Upfront* v149 no10 p6 Mr 13 2017

Kingsman: The Golden Circle (Film)

Kingsman: The Golden Circle C. Nashawaty color *Entertainment Weekly* no1484 p42 S 29 2017

KINGSMAN: THE GOLDEN CIRCLE J. McGovern color *Entertainment Weekly* no1462 p46 Ap 21 2017

Return of the Kingsman S. Zacharek color *Time* v190 no13 p65 O 2 2017

Kingsnorth, Bob

FREELANCED PAINT SCHEMES from factory-painted models color *Model Railroader* v84 no2 p42 F 2017

Model a LARGE STATION using 3-D PRINTING color *Model Railroader* v84 no8 p24 Ag 2017

Kingsnorth, Paul

THE AXIS AND THE SYCAMORE color *Orion Magazine* v36 no1 p34 Ja/F 2017

The Beast *Publishers Weekly* v264 no24 p37 Je 12 2017

Confessions of a Recovering Environmentalist and Other Essays *Publishers Weekly* v264 no19 p46 My 8 2017

Fantastic Beast: An itinerant hero hunts for a creature and a purpose T. KOELB *New York Times Book Review* p18 S 17 2017

Kingsolver, Barbara, 1955-

THOUGHTS ON Treating Others Well bw color *Forbes* v198 no8 p112 D 20 2016

Kingsolver, Joel G.

Precipitation drives global variation in natural selection bibl chart diag map *Science* v355 no6328 p959 Mr 3 2017

KINGSTON, ANNE

The algebra of sexual violence *Maclean's* v130 no9 p10 O 2017

Behind the Big Red Machine color *Maclean's* v130 no10 p24 N

2017

Blood money color *Maclean's* no1 p18 F 17 2017

Contraception mans up color *Maclean's* v130 no4 p8 My 2017

False equivalencies color *Maclean's* v129 no45 p35 N 14 2016

Feminism's wrong turn color *Maclean's* v130 no3 p10 Ap 2017

THE GRIEF OF SUSAN B. ANTHONY color *Maclean's* v129 no46 p39 N 21 2016

A HARROWING LINGUISTIC MOMENT *Maclean's* v129 no48/49 p10 D 5 2016

JUSTIN TRUDEAU IS JUST NOT THAT INTO YOU color *Maclean's* v129 no51/52 p12 D 26 2016

KEEPING SEX ASSAULT UNDERGROUND color *Maclean's* v129 no45 p10 N 14 2016

More than just safety pins color *Maclean's* v129 no47 p31 N 28 2016

NEW PILL, OLD HEADACHES color *Maclean's* v130 no2 p26 Mr 2017

PREDICTABLE PATTERNS AND SEXUAL ASSAULT *Maclean's* v129 no41 p10 O 17 2016

The problem with men color *Maclean's* v130 no3 p66 Ap 2017

The real taboo in 13 Reasons Why color *Maclean's* p8 Je 2017

A RETURN TO TRADITION FOR MILLENNIALS chart color *Maclean's* v130 no6 p12 Jl 2017

Shackled and abandoned *Maclean's* v130 no8 p10 S 2017

THE SMILE THAT TRUMPED THE DONALD color *Maclean's* v129 no40 p10 O 10 2016

A symptom of a deeper problem color *Maclean's* v130 no7 p8 Ag 2017

Trump's way with women color *Maclean's* v129 no42 p37 O 24 2016

WHO PAYS FOR THE RCMP'S EPIC FAILURE? *Maclean's* v129 no43 p10 O 31 2016

WHY WE ALL NEED TO HYGGE [Cover story] color *Maclean's* v129 no51/52 p50 D 26 2016

The year of the 'nasty woman' color *Maclean's* v129 no48/49 p73 D 5 2016

KINGSTON, MAXINE HONG

The Year in Reading [Cover story] *New York Times Book Review* p8 D 25 2016

Kingston, Robert E.

Mutation of a nucleosome compaction region disrupts Polycomb-mediated axial patterning bibl chart diag *Science* v355 no6329 p1081 Mr 10 2017

Kingston, Tigga

Can we protect island flying foxes? color *Science* v355 no6332 p1368 Mr 31 2017

KINGWELL, MARK

Philosopher Up to Bat cartoon *Walrus* v14 no2 p59 Mr 2017

Kingzette, Jonathon

The need for a translational science of democracy bibl color *Science* v355 no6328 p914 Mr 3 2017

Kini, Tara

Sticky schools color graph *Phi Delta Kappan* v98 no8 p19 My 2017

Kinias, Zoe

A Simple Exercise Can Help Women Overcome Self-Doubt to Succeed *Harvard Business Review Digital Articles* p2 Ag 11 2016

KININMONTH, STUART

Assessing National Biodiversity Trends for Rocky and Coral Reefs through the Integration of Citizen Science and Scientific Monitoring Programs *BioScience* v67 no2 p134 F 2017

Kinks (Performer)

Ray Davies A. GREENE bw *Rolling Stone* no1284 p58 Ap 6 2017

Kinlaw, Joshua

Contentious Christians color *Commonweal* v144 no16 p14 O 6 2017

Kinloch, Nicolas

HULEGU THE MONGOL: Unlike his grandfather Chinggis Khan, the Mongol ruler Hulegu Khan is little known in the West. But his destruction of two Islamic empires, as well as a failed attempt to forge an alliance with Christendom, gave him a notoriety... *History Today* v67 no6 p52 Je 2016

Kinnamon, Michael

The Witness of Religion in an Age of Fear W. Willimon *Christian Century* v134 no12 p39 Je 7 2017

Kinney, Courtney

What Do YOU Think Should Be Hot? color *Literacy Today (2411-7862)* v34 no4 p43 Ja/F 2017

Kinney, Jeff, 1971-

A New Chapter J. BILLS *Yankee* v81 no1 p76 Ja/F 2017

Kinney, Julie

A New Chapter J. BILLS *Yankee* v81 no1 p76 Ja/F 2017

Kinney, Marcey A.

Changing the Praxis of Retention in Higher Education: A Plan to TEACH All Learners *Change* v48 no6 p58 N/D 2016

Kinney, Morgan

...AND NINE THEY NEED TO PROTECT *New York* v50 no7 p31 Ap 3 2017

Kinney, Taylor, 1981-

Chicago Fire N. Abrams, B. L. Heldman et al *Entertainment Weekly* no1482/1483 p91 S 22 2017

Chicago Fire's Severide in Custody! I. Rudolph *TV Guide* p13 D 19 2016

Out & About *TV Guide* v65 no19 p4 My 1 2017

Kinokuniya Co. Ltd.

Kinokuniya Seeing Steady Growth In the U.S E. Nawotka color *Publishers Weekly* v264 no35 p15 Ag 28 2017

Kinsey, Erin

GREEN GODDESS A. WALL color *Rodale's Organic Life* v3 no1 p43 Ja 2017

Kinship

NAME DROPPING D. Garner cartoon color *Esquire* v166 no5 p92 D 2016/Ja 2017

Kinski, Nastassja, 1960-

STYLE CRUSH Kenya Kinski-Jones S. Simon color *InStyle* v24 no3 p170 Mr 2017

KINSLEY, MICHAEL

AMERICA NEEDS TALENT color *Vanity Fair* v59 no11 p82 N 2017

CAPITALISM, BY GEORGE! color *Vanity Fair* v59 no10 p142 O 2017

ENVY IS THE NEW GREED color *Vanity Fair* v58 no12 p102 D 2016

Naked Justice *New York Times Book Review* p21 Ap 2 2017

Kinstler, Linda

THE 2017 Fortune Crystal Ball color diag *Fortune* v174 no7 p11 D 1 2016

First the Cold War, Now the Flame War color *Fortune* v176 no2 p19 Ag 1 2017

HAVE LAPTOP WILL TRAVEL cartoon *Bloomberg Businessweek* no4515 p63 Mr 20 2017

Kintisch, Eli

THE LOST NORSE color graph map *Science* v354 no6313 p696 N 11 2016

MELTDOWN color diag graph *Science* v355 no6327 p788 F 24 2017

Kinzer, Stephen

The Birth of the Imperial Presidency J. Heilbrunn *Washington Monthly* p14 Ja/F 2017

The dawning of America's imperial ambitions M. J. Davis color *America* v216 no6 p45 Mr 20 2017

From Isolation to Intervention M. LIND *New York Times Book Review* p19 Ja 29 2017

How the US Began Its Empire J. Lears cartoon color *New York Review of Books* v64 no3 p37 F 23 2017

The True Flag: Theodore Roosevelt, Mark Twain, and the Birth of American Empire color *Publishers Weekly* v263 no45 p50 N 7 2016

WHEN TITANS TANGLED bw cartoon color *American History* v52 no4 p40 O 2017

Kinzie, Jillian

REFRAMING STUDENT SUCCESS IN COLLEGE: Advancing Know-What and Know-How *Change* v49 no3 p19 My/Je 2017

Kinzler, Kenneth W.

Mismatch repair deficiency predicts response of solid tumors to PD-1 blockade chart graph *Science* v357 no6349 p409 Jl 28 2017

Kiowa (North American people)

Color Country K. BASTONE color *Backpacker* v45 no2 p16 Mr 2017

Kipchoge, Eliud, 1984-

1:59:59 E. CAESAR color *Wired* v25 no7 p84 Jl 2017

MOONSHOT [Cover story] A. Hutchinson bw cartoon color map *Runner's World* v52 no5 p62 Je 2017

KIPEN, DAVID

Going From Door to Door *Los Angeles Magazine* p18 F 2017

Kiper, Dmitry

Abbi Jacobson color *Current Biography* v77 no10 p68 O 2016

Alex Sharp color *Current Biography* v78 no2 p74 F 2017

Damien Chazelle color *Current Biography* v78 no6 p25 Je 2017

Han Kang color *Current Biography* v77 no10 p49 O 2016

Jessie Mueller color *Current Biography* v78 no1 p41 Ja 2017

Justin Hurwitz color *Current Biography* v78 no8 p54 Ag 2017

Kate McKinnon color *Current Biography* v77 no11 p54 N 2016

Kathryn Schulz *Current Biography* v78 no6 p92 Je 2017

Keith Stanfield color *Current Biography* v78 no8 p73 Ag 2017

Mac DeMarco color *Current Biography* v77 no11 p35 N 2016

Madeleine Thien color *Current Biography* v78 no3 p73 Mr 2017

Maggie Nelson color *Current Biography* v78 no5 p68 My 2017

Nicky Jam color *Current Biography* v78 no3 p36 Mr 2017

Rukmini Callimachi color *Current Biography* v78 no2 p17 F 2017

Shawn Mendes color *Current Biography* v78 no4 p59 Ap 2017

Sturgill Simpson color *Current Biography* v78 no4 p77 Ap 2017

Viet Thanh Nguyen color *Current Biography* v78 no6 p73 Je 2017

KIPFER, BARBARA ANN

GUIDE TO Restfulness color *House Beautiful* v159 no2 p61 Mr 2017

KIPLINGER, KNIGHT

How can we discourage bogus news stories? *Kiplinger's Personal Finance* v71 no2 p18 F 2017

How should I handle a tax windfall that I don't want? *Kiplinger's Personal Finance* v71 no3 p15 Mr 2017

Should bank customers be allowed to file class-action suits? *Kiplinger's Personal Finance* v70 no12 p16 D 2016

Should colleges use collection agencies for overdue student bills? *Kiplinger's Personal Finance* v71 no11 p12 N 2017

Should employers be barred from asking job applicants what they earn? *Kiplinger's Personal Finance* v71 no8 p14 Ag 2017

Should ethics determine who you do business with? *Kiplinger's Personal Finance* v71 no12 p12 D 2017

Should soft-drink makers be held liable for the health risks of sugar? *Kiplinger's Personal Finance* v71 no10 p14 O 2017

What should doctors and drugmakers do to stop painkiller addiction? color *Kiplinger's Personal Finance* v71 no5 p14 My 2017

Kiplinger Business Forecasts (Company)

From Pain to Gain for This Fidelity Fund N. S. HUANG chart *Kiplinger's Personal Finance* v70 no12 p60 D 2016

Kipnis, Laura

Forecast: More Snowflakes cartoon diag *Weekly Standard* v22 no29 p2 Ap 3 2017

Is free speech under threat IN THE UNITED STATES? WE RECEIVED TWENTY-SEVEN RESPONSES. WE PUBLISH THEM HERE, IN ALPHABETICAL ORDER *Commentary* v144 no1 p13 Jl/Ag 2017

Kafka U K. C. JOHNSON *Commentary* v143 no6 p46 Je 2017

The politics of sexual assault [Cover story] J. Dailey color *Christian Century* v134 no22 p28 O 25 2017

Screw Wisdom cartoon color *Atlantic* v319 no5 p31 Je 2017

Sexual Panic J. Filipovic *New York Times Book Review* p11 Ap 9 2017

Kipping, David

Seeking unexpected worlds L. Grossman color *Science News* v192 no6 p22 O 14 2017

KIRABO, SINCERE

STANDING WITH STANDING ROCK *Humanist* v77 no1 p25 Ja/F 2017

When Colorblindness Isn't the Answer: Humanism and the Challenge of Race *Humanist* v77 no4 p44 Jl/Ag 2017

Kiraly, Drew D.

Early life stress confers lifelong stress susceptibility in mice via ventral tegmental area OTX2 diag *Science* v356 no6343 p1185 Je 16 2017

Kiranti (Asian people)

The Last Honey Hunter M. Synnott color map *National Geographic* v232 no1 p80 Jl 2017

Kirby, Alisha

Workshop Builds Students' Writing Skills *Education Digest* v83 no2 p55 O 2017

KIRBY, DAVID

Evermore *New York Times Book Review* p14 Ag 27 2017

Kirby, George

GEORGE KIRBY JUJITSU PIONEER FOR 50 YEARS bw color *Black Belt* v55 no3 p10 Ap/My 2017

KIRBY, JASON

Avoid the crowds map *Maclean's* v130 no4 p17 My 2017

COUNTRIES CLOSEST IN SIZE TO EACH PROVINCE map *Maclean's* v130 no2 p15 Mr 2017

GRANDPA, WHAT'S A RATE HIKE? color *Maclean's* v129 no51/52 p48 D 26 2016

THE INTERVIEW color *Maclean's* v130 no4 p20 My 2017

The space between us map *Maclean's* v130 no3 p19 Ap 2017

WE'RE IN THE DARK HERE ON HOUSING DATA color *Maclean's* v129 no44 p38 N 7 2016

Kirby, Julia

4 Reasons to Kill the Office Holiday Party—and One Reason to Save It *Harvard Business Review Digital Articles* p2 D 17 2014

Automation Won't Replace People as Your Competitive Advantage *Harvard Business Review Digital Articles* p2 Ag 10 2015

Clay Christensen on Peter Drucker *Harvard Business Review Digital Articles* p2 N 10 2014

An Inside Look at Facebook's Approach to Automation and Human Work *Harvard Business Review Digital Articles* p2 Je 12 2015

The Knowledge Jobs Most Likely to Be Automated *Harvard Business Review Digital Articles* p2 Je 23 2016

Meaningful Work Should Not Be a Privilege of the Elite color *Harvard Business Review Digital Articles* p2 Ap 3 2017

KIRBY, KEITH J.

Combining Biodiversity Resurveys across Regions to Advance Global Change Research *BioScience* v67 no1 p73 Ja 2017

Kirby, Matthew J.

A Taste for Monsters color *Publishers Weekly* v263 no49 p117 D 7 2016

Kirby, Victoria

4 beauty tricks I just learned color *Redbook* p54 N 2017

4 beauty tricks I just learned color *Redbook* p56 Ap 2017

5 beauty tricks I just learned bw color *Redbook* p43 Jl/Ag 2017

5 beauty tricks I just learned color *Redbook* p48 Mr 2017

5 beauty tricks I just learned color *Redbook* p58 O 2017

5 beauty tricks I just learned color *Redbook* p64 F 2017

Hot-weather-proof your skin color *Redbook* p39 Je 2017

Jo Malone's secrets to picking a fragrance bw color *Redbook* p59 D 2016

Q&A:Gabrielle Union's inspiring advice color *Redbook* p48 N 2017

Secrets of a 52-year-old beauty color *Redbook* p48 S 2017

Kirby, William C.

China Still Isn't Ready to Be a True Global Leader *Harvard Business Review Digital Articles* p2 Ja 5 2015

The Real Reason Uber Is Giving Up in China *Harvard Business Review Digital Articles* p2 Ag 2 2016

Kirch, Claire

The Allure of Decay color *Publishers Weekly* v264 no15 p44 Ap 10 2017

Bookselling As a Second Career color *Publishers Weekly* v264 no34 p11 Ag 21 2017

BOOKSELLING IN THE TWIN CITIES color *Publishers Weekly* v264 no3 p10 Ja 16 2017

Bookstores Engage in Diverse Forms of Protest color *Publishers Weekly* v264 no11 p6 Mr 13 2017

CONVERSATIONS WITH KEYNOTERS color *Publishers Weekly* v264 no3 p4 Ja 16 2017

Everything Happens to King David bw *Publishers Weekly* v263 no44 p(Sp)16 O 31 2016

Fast-Growing Independent Publishers, 2017 chart color *Publishers Weekly* v264 no15 p36 Ap 10 2017

Greystone Builds on Last Year's Bestseller color *Publishers Weekly* v264 no41 p8 O 9 2017

Happy Holidays for Indies in 2016 color *Publishers Weekly* v264 no2 p6 Ja 9 2017

Haymarket Books: Publishing Books in the Current Moment color *Publishers Weekly* v263 no42 p11 O 17 2016

Independent Bookstore Day 2017: A Perfect Storm for Sales color map *Publishers Weekly* v264 no17 p6 Ap 24 2017

Indie Booksellers See Early Holiday Boost color *Publishers Weekly* v263 no50 p4 D 5 2016

KIDS' SUBSCRIPTION SERVICES TAKE OFF color *Publishers Weekly* v264 no11 p26 Mr 13 2017

Parneshia Jones color *Publishers Weekly* v264 no19 p6 My 8 2017

Politics Was Front and Center At This Year's AWP Conference color *Publishers Weekly* v264 no8 p4 F 20 2017

Post Election—Dowd Dishes color *Publishers Weekly* v263 no44 p(Sp)23 O 31 2016

Rupi Kaur: Bestselling Poet *Publishers Weekly* v263 no52 p28 D 19 2016

Shining a Light on YA, MG Fiction *Publishers Weekly* v264 no3 p11 Ja 16 2017

Summer in the Bookstore color *Publishers Weekly* v264 no27 p5 Jl 3 2017

TIME FOR A GOOD BOOK color *Publishers Weekly* v263 no46 p12 N 14 2016

Wayne State Benefits From Move into Trade color *Publishers Weekly* v263 no48 p10 N 28 2016

Weinstein Preps New Children's Series By Indie Favorite color *Publishers Weekly* v264 no31 p9 Jl 31 2017

Wild Rumpus: PW's Bookstore of the Year color *Publishers Weekly* v264 no20 p(Sp)8 My 15 2017

Kirchenschlager, Dakota

FIVE FLAT with Dakota Kirchenschlager C. Toy color *Spin to Win Rodeo* v20 no12 p33 F 2017

Kirchenschlager, Dakota—Interviews

Thumbs Up on Dakota K's Recovery K. Santos *Spin to Win Rodeo* v20 no10 p32 D 2016

Kircher, Madison Malone

It's Like Broadway, But for Your Ears img *New York* v50 no11 p117 My 29 2017

THE YEAR IN MEMES img *New York* v49 no26 p38 D 26 2016

Kirchfeld, Aaron

The New Barbarian at The Cate color graph *Bloomberg Businessweek* no4497 p39 O 31 2016

Kirchheimer, Manfred, 1931-

Sanctuary City R. Brody bw *New Yorker* v92 no49 p12 F 13 2017

Kirchick, James

Coming Apart M. M. ROSEN color *Weekly Standard* v22 no35 p34 My 22 2017

Credibility Counts [Cover story] bw color *Weekly Standard* v22 no16 p18 D 26 2016

The Dark Continent C. BERLINSKI diag *National Review* v69 no5 p40 Mr 20 2017

Generation Jihad *Commentary* v144 no3 p50 O 2017

Hey, Judah *Commentary* v143 no1 p53 Ja 2017

How Putin Plays Trump Like a Piano: The Republican nominee and his team of paid Moscow apologists *Commentary* v142 no2 p25 S 2016

Trump's Anti-Semites *Commentary* v142 no2 p7 S 2016

Kirchmann, P. S.

Femtosecond electron-phonon lock-in by photoemission and x-ray free-electron laser chart diag *Science* v357 no6346 p71 Jl 7 2017

KIRCHNER, BEN

EURO STARS *Opera News* v81 no7 p20 Ja 2017

Kirchner, Bharti

Season of Sacrifice: A Maya Mallick Mystery *Publishers Weekly* v264 no27 p55 Jl 3 2017

Kirchner, H. Lester

Distribution and clinical impact of functional variants in 50,726 whole-exome sequences from the DiscovEHR study chart graph *Science* v354 no6319 paaf6814-1 D 23 2016

Genetic identification of familial hypercholesterolemia within a single U.S. health care system chart graph *Science* v354 no6319 paaf7000-1 D 23 2016

Kirchner, Lauren

A World Apart color *Consumer Reports* v82 no7 p52 Jl 2017

Kirchofner, Dustin

ONE MONTH TO A BIGGER 1RM M. BERG bw *Muscle & Performance* v9 no6 p18 Je 2017

Kireeva, Maria

Changing climate shifts timing of European floods color graph *Science* v357 no6351 p588 Ag 11 2017

Kirillova, Mariia S.

Synthesis of resveratrol tetramers via a stereoconvergent radical equilibrium bibl diag graph *Science* v354 no6317 p1260 D 9 2016

Kirilov, Emil

Bloch oscillations in the absence of a lattice graph *Science* v356 no6341 p945 Je 1 2017

Kirk, Barry—Interviews

PROTECT POINTS AND MILES FROM THEFT L. GERSTNER color *Kiplinger's Personal Finance* v71 no3 p12 Mr 2017

Kirk, James T. (Fictitious character)

Sky Gods for Skeptics M. Shermer color *Scientific American* v317 no4 p88 O 2017

Kirk, Justin, 1969-

APB K. Freeze *TV Guide* v65 no6 p39 Ja 30 2017

The Best Police Money Can Buy K. Williams *In These Times* v41 no4 p54 Ap 2017

Kirk, Katherine

Human health color *Science* v356 no6338 p590 My 12 2017

Kirk, Kevin

How to Build a Swing You Can Believe in color *Golf Magazine* v59 no9 p71 S 2017

PATRICK READS color *Golf Magazine* v59 no1 p44 Ja 2017

ROUGH CUTS color *Golf Magazine* v59 no4 p65 Ap 2017

Kirk, Marjorie

60 Years of Campus Changemakers J. Militare color *Glamour* v115 no5 p138 My 2017

Kirk, Randy

COURT of APPEALS WITH REBEL GOOD *Tennis* v52 no6 p6 N/D 2016

KIRK, RONALD

A BREAK IN THE BREAKS cartoon color *Outdoor Life* v224 no7 p13 S 2017

KIRK, SAM

CAN I TOUCH YOUR HAIR? WHY DO YOU DRESS LIKE A BOY IF YOU LIKE GIRLS? *In These Times* v41 no10 p24 O 2017

Kirkbride, Jasmin

Publishers Keep Calm And Carry On color *Publishers Weekly* v264 no12 p5 Mr 20 2017

Kirkby, Jasper

Global atmospheric particle formation from CERN CLOUD measurements bibl graph map *Science* v354 no6316 p1119 D 2 2016

Kirke, Jemima, 1985-—Interviews

Girls I. Ratledge *TV Guide* v65 no14 p36 Ap 3 2017

In Girls We Trust L. Dunham and J. Konner color *Glamour* v115 no2 p98 F 2017

Kirke, Lola, 1990-

LOLA color *InStyle* v24 no1 p92 Ja 2017

Mozart in the Jungle J. Russell *TV Guide* v64 no40 p37 O 3 2016

Kirkland, Gelsey

Coached by Gelsey A. BRANDT *Dance Magazine* v91 no1 p134 Ja 2017

KIRKLAND, GLORIA

Life *Reader's Digest* v188 no1124 p40 O 2016

Kirkland, Irene

BREAK THE FAST color *Essence* v48 no6 p123 O 2017

Kirkland, Isaiah—Interviews

THE LOOK BOOK A. SWERDLOFF and B. Doherty img *New York* v49 no15 p65 Jl 25 2016

Kirkland, Justin

How to Stalk Your Pet color *AARP: The Magazine* v60 no4A p10 Je/Jl 2017

Kirkland, Sally

Exile on Main Street N. DAVIS color *Film Comment* v52 no6 p18 N/D 2016

KIRKMAN, ALEXANDRA

Grand Floatels color *Conde Nast Traveler* v52 no7 p42 Ag 2017

Kirkman, Bradley

Research: The Biggest Culture Gaps Are Within Countries, Not Between Them *Harvard Business Review Digital Articles* p2 My 18 2016

Team Leaders Should Play Favorites (but Only in Moderation) *Harvard Business Review Digital Articles* p2 Ja 13 2016

Teamwork Works Best When Top Performers Are Rewarded *Harvard Business Review Digital Articles* p2 Mr 14 2016

Railway Post Office color *Model Railroader* v84 no8 p16 Ag 2017

Kischkewitz, Marvin

Radical-polar crossover reactions of vinylboron ate complexes bibl diag *Science* v355 no6328 p936 Mr 3 2017

Kiselev, Alexei

Active sites in heterogeneous ice nucleation—the example of K-rich feldspars bibl bw diag *Science* v355 no6323 p367 Ja 27 2017

Kish, Kara

To Ph.D. or Not to Ph.D.? *Parks & Recreation* v52 no9 p38 S 2017

Kish, Kilo

GOINGS ON ABOUT TOWN color *New Yorker* v93 no7 p7 Ap 3 2017

Kish, Kristen

WHERE ARE YOU GOING? color *O, The Oprah Magazine* p166 D 2016

Kishan, Saijel

Coming for Your Trading Desk color *Bloomberg Businessweek* no4528 p22 Je 26 2017

Greenwich Lean Time cartoon graph *Bloomberg Businessweek* no4496 p48 O 24 2016

Lies, Damn Lies, and Financial Statistics cartoon *Bloomberg Businessweek* no4518 p8 Ap 10 2017

Kisida, Brian

The art of partnerships color graph il *Phi Delta Kappan* v98 no7 p8 Ap 2017

Kisin, Evgeniĭ, 1971-

A Salzburg Trio J. NORDLINGER color *National Review* v69 no17 p40 S 11 2017

Kiskinis, Evangelos

Dopamine oxidation mediates mitochondrial and lysosomal dysfunction in Parkinson's disease graph *Science* v357 no6357 p1255 S 22 2017

Kislik, Liz

Being the Boss's Favorite Is Great, Until It's Not *Harvard Business Review Digital Articles* p2 My 19 2017

How to Manage Someone Who Thinks Everything Is Urgent *Harvard Business Review Digital Articles* p2 Ag 2 2017

Kislyak, Sergey I., 1950-

THE INCONVENIENT COMRADE G. M. Graff color *Esquire* p90 Je/Jl 2017

Kismet, Drake

Dr. Kismet's Cure J. Queenan *Weekly Standard* v22 no23 p38 F 20 2017

Kisner, Jordan

The Natural: Frances McDormand has built a career, and a passionate fan base, playing supporting roles; now, at 60, she has become an unconventional star *New York Times Magazine* p44 O 8 2017

Kiss, Andrea

Changing climate shifts timing of European floods color graph *Science* v357 no6351 p588 Ag 11 2017

Kiss My Face Corp.

LOVE YOUR LIPS J. Martin color *Amazing Wellness* v8 no6 p78 Early Winter2016

Kisseih, Nene

Nene Kisseih *Atlanta* v56 no9 p46 Ja 2017

Kissileff, Beth

Reading Genesis: Beginnings A. L. Rosen color *Christian Century* v134 no10 p47 My 10 2017

Kissing Walls (TV program)

BROWN GIRL AUTEUR B. GOLDEN color *Chicago* v66 no2 p25 F 2017

Kissinger, Henry

Pioneers [Cover story] color *Time* v189 no16/17 p14 My 1-8 2017

Kissinger, Henry, 1923-—Interviews

THE LESSONS OF HENRY KISSINGER J. Goldberg bw color *Atlantic* v318 no5 p50 D 2016

KISSINGER, JESSIE

OFF the BEATEN PATH color *GQ: Gentlemen's Quarterly* v97 no9 p154 S 2017

Kissinger, Samuel P.

Rethinking the right to refuse hazardous work diag *Monthly Labor Review* p1 Ja 2017

Kistemaker, Jos C. M.

Locked synchronous rotor motion in a molecular motor diag *Sci-*

ence v356 no6341 p964 Je 1 2017

Kit, Lee, 1978-

LEE KIT G. Leung color *Art in America* v104 no10 p155 N 2016

KITA, JOE

THE BEAST OF WALL STREET [Cover story] bw cartoon color *Men's Health* v32 no2 p80 Mr 2017

BUILD COVER GUY MUSCLE [Cover story] bw cartoon chart color *Men's Health* v32 no1 p98 Ja/F 2017

ME VS. THE BOY bw color graph map *Men's Health* v32 no8 p108 O 2017

Plan the Perfect Vacation cartoon color *AARP: The Magazine* v59 no6A p46 O/N 2016

Undo the Damage (of Your ROCK 'N' ROLL Years) bw cartoon color *AARP: The Magazine* v60 no1A p48 D 2016/Ja 2017

The Worry-Free Life color *AARP: The Magazine* v59 no2A p28 F/Mr 2016

KITA, MEGHAN

GET READY, GET SET... chart color *Runner's World* v52 no7 p71 Ag 2017

Magic Bullets color *Runner's World* v52 no4 p56 My 2017

My Immune System Attacked My Hair color *Health* v31 no2 p91 Mr 2017

Kita, Paul

24 TOP MUSCLE FOODS color *Men's Health* v32 no7 p108 S 2017

THE BEST FOOD FOR MEN 2017 [Cover story] cartoon color *Men's Health* v32 no1 p106 Ja/F 2017

Carly Chaikin cartoon color *Men's Health* v32 no9 p38 N 2017

The Cheesecake Factory color *Men's Health* v32 no3 p70 Ap 2017

Cooler Gear, Hotter Deals color *Men's Health* v32 no2 p24 Mr 2017

Craft a New Coffee Rig color *Men's Health* v32 no2 p34 Mr 2017

Drink the Beer, Skip the Gut color *Men's Health* v32 no5 p67 Je 2017

Eggplant and Zucchini Lasagna color *Men's Health* v32 no7 p30 S 2017

Egg & Tomato Breakfast Sandwich color *Men's Health* v32 no8 p38 O 2017

Emily Skye bw color *Men's Health* v32 no6 p40 Ag 2017

Gabrielle Union color *Men's Health* v32 no2 p28 Mr 2017

The Guys Next Door color *Women's Health* v14 no1 p26 Ja/F 2017

The Guys Next Door *Women's Health* v14 no2 p20 Mr 2017

How This Dad Lost 100 Pounds color *Men's Health* v32 no2 p26 Mr 2017

How to Sell a Crazy Idea cartoon color *Men's Health* v32 no2 p32 Mr 2017

Jenna Dewan Tatum bw color *Men's Health* v32 no5 p36 Je 2017

Jessie Graff cartoon color *Men's Health* v32 no8 p35 O 2017

ME VS. THE BOY bw color graph map *Men's Health* v32 no8 p108 O 2017

Screw the Turkey! cartoon color *Men's Health* v32 no9 p57 N 2017

Sizzlin' Campfire Nachos bw color *Men's Health* v32 no6 p36 Ag 2017

Skillet Wings cartoon color *Men's Health* v32 no2 p31 Mr 2017

The Sports Bar cartoon *Men's Health* v32 no2 p30 Mr 2017

WHEN LIFE GOES BOOM cartoon color *Men's Health* v32 no2 p20 Mr 2017

The Wright Way to Keep Your Cool color *Men's Health* v32 no2 p25 Mr 2017

Kitamura, Katie

COLD HEART A. SCHWARTZ color *New Yorker* v92 no48 p73 F 6 2017

Gone Guy F. EBERSTADT *New York Times Book Review* p14 F 19 2017

SCENES FROM A MARRIAGE A. WHITWHAM cartoon *O, The Oprah Magazine* p102 Mr 2017

The Stranger on the Shore *New York Times Book Review* p1 Jl 9 2017

Kitamura, Takashi

Engrams and circuits crucial for systems consolidation of a memory diag *Science* v356 no6333 p73 Ap 7 2017

Kitaoka, Akiyoshi

snakes on a plane M. Shieh color *Popular Science* v289 no5 p84 S/O 2017

Kitaru Yachts (Company)

MODERN THROWBACK S. SHIBATA *Sea Magazine* v108 no12 p8 D 2016

Kitazawa, Taro

Gene bivalency at Polycomb domains regulates cranial neural crest positional identity diag *Science* v355 no6332 p1390 Mr 31 2017

Kitchen appliances

See also

Blenders (Cooking)

Dishwashing machines

DISHWASHERS K. SELZER bw color *Better Homes & Gardens* v95 no11 p52 N 2017

thanks, bro N. Berkus and K. SELZER color diag *Better Homes & Gardens* v95 no10 p54 O 2017

Kitchen appliances industry

1972 KITCHEN COLOR L. HEDRICK color *Better Homes & Gardens* v95 no4 p160 Ap 2017

Kitchen appliances—Evaluation

1972 KITCHEN COLOR L. HEDRICK color *Better Homes & Gardens* v95 no4 p160 Ap 2017

Blenders color *Good Housekeeping* v265 no1 p60 Jl 2017

Countertop Intelligence K. Janeway chart color graph *Consumer Reports* v82 no11 p34 N 2017

Country Chic color *Architectural Digest* v73 no11 p116 N 2016

family matters P. P. FISCHER color *Better Homes & Gardens* v95 no5 p46 My 2017

GH'S KITCHEN of the FUTURE color *Good Housekeeping* v264 no6 p48K Je 2017

GOOD HOUSEKEEPING REGISTRY WISH LIST N. SAPORITA color *Good Housekeeping* v264 no6 p49 Je 2017

It's Getting Bot In the Kitchen L. Eadicicco color *Time* v189 no22 p18 Je 12 2017

KITCHEN WIZARDS color *Good Housekeeping* v264 no3 p94 Mr 2017

Meet in the Middle K. Renda color *House Beautiful* v158 no10 p39 D 2016/Ja 2017

the (mostly) clean eater color *House Beautiful* v159 no8 p74 O 2017

point, CLICK, DECORATE B. THORKLESON color *Better Homes & Gardens* v95 no9 p40 S 2017

The Slice Is Right A. BARAGHANI color *Bon Appetit* p78 S 2017

STIR CRAZY color *Runner's World* v52 no7 p24 Ag 2017

TOP TOOLS color *Good Housekeeping* v265 no4 p64e O 2017

Kitchen cabinets

BEHIND THE SCENES I. Edwards color *Sunset* v239 no3 p8 S 2017

THE BUILD & THE BLOG K. R. KEGANS color *Better Homes & Gardens* v95 no5 p128 My 2017

Kitchen Creativity S. Murphy color *Log Home Living* v34 no4 p22 My 2017

Kitchen cabinets—Evaluation

Meet in the Middle K. Renda color *House Beautiful* v158 no10 p39 D 2016/Ja 2017

Kitchen design & construction

American Beauty S. BROWN color *Timber Home Living* v27 no5 p10 O 2017

Better Built-Ins C. MARTIN color *Timber Home Living* v27 no5 p21 O 2017

DESIGN MOTIFS FOR A KITCHEN T. Guarino color *Old House Journal* v45 no6 p32 S 2017

English Sensibility B. D. Coleman color *Old House Journal* v45 no6 p74 S 2017

Grow Together R. Newhouse color *Log Home Living* p90 2018 Annual Buyers Guide

Into the Woods E. O'Brien color diag *Log Home Living* p84 2018 Annual Buyers Guide

KITCHEN HELP: Resources for creating your own dream kitchen *Washingtonian Magazine* v53 no1 p166 O 2017

KITCHENS *Design Center Sourcebook* p17 2016

Kitchens S. KASLER, D. NETTO et al color *Architectural Digest* no11 p73 N 1 2017

LIGHTER FARE color *Timber Home Living* v27 no5 p30 O 2017

LOFTY AMBITIONS L. M. Labong color *Sunset* v239 no4 p33 O 2017

Mudroom, Pantry, and Kitchen All in a Row P. Poore color *Old House Journal* v45 no4 p74 Je 2017

PROFESSIONAL GRADE: Curious how the experts live? Take a look inside four kitchens belonging to people who design or work in them for a living J. Barger *Washingtonian Magazine* v53 no1 p161 O 2017

The Secret to Layered Lighting K. O'SHEA-EVANS color *House Beautiful* p46 Jl 2017

thanks, bro N. Berkus and K. SELZER color diag *Better Homes & Gardens* v95 no10 p54 O 2017

Kitchen design & construction—Awards

BEST KITCHEN color *Timber Home Living* p20 2017 SpecialIssue

Kitchen equipment

The 8 Best Kitchen Essentials color *Men's Health* v32 no8 p81 O 2017

the crowd-pleaser color *House Beautiful* v159 no8 p66 O 2017

The Great Outdoors: Creating backyard living spaces fit for your indoor style K. Wilburn *New Orleans Homes & Lifestyles* v20 no3 p100 Summ 2017

A Housewife's Kitchen, 1931 color *Old House Journal* v45 no7 p70 O 2017

Kitchens S. KASLER, D. NETTO et al color *Architectural Digest* no11 p73 N 1 2017

KITCHEN WHISPERER B. Gold color *Good Housekeeping* v265 no1 p8 Jl 2017

A Nigerian President's Disappointing Return E. OBADARE *Current History* v116 no790 p194 My 2017

Kitchen gardens

Your CHECKLIST E. Jardina and J. Mccausland color *Sunset* v238 no1 p46 Ja 2017

Kitchen-middens

WORD EXCHANGE A. Ward, E. Cummings et al *Natural History* v125 no2 p9 F 2017

Kitchen remodeling

kitchen refresh S. JACOBS color *Cabin Living* p52 Je 2017

KITCHEN REMODELING J. Kneiszel color *Cabin Living* p68 Je 2017

MY DIY KITCHEN RENO: How I built my dream kitchen on a budget-no pricey professional designer needed K. Bennell *Washingtonian Magazine* v52 no11 p148 Ag 2017

New Point of View: The Richmond home of George and Louise Freeman is a study in transformation V. HUBBARD *Virginia Living* v15 no6 p58 O 2017

Play the Blues K. Owen chart color *Southern Living* v52 no10 p24 O 2017

Under Fyne skies C. EDNIE color *House Beautiful* p66 Ag 2017

Kitchen utensils

See also

Cookware

Cutlery

Graters

Peelers (Utensils)

A CUT ABOVE F. VIGNA *Martha Stewart Living* no268 p148 O 2016

KNIVES OUT *Los Angeles Magazine* p46 F 2017

Make your kitchen wall work color *Redbook* p113 Mr 2017

SPACE SAVERS color *Martha Stewart Living* p41 O 2017

Kitchen utensils in art

Modern Metals E. GAUKEL *Treasures* v6 no2 p10 O/N 2016

Where new meets Old E. Gaukel *Treasures* v5 no5 p4 Ap/My 2016

Kitchen utensils—Evaluation

See also

Baking pans—Evaluation

Cookware—Evaluation

the aspiring pastry chef color *House Beautiful* v159 no8 p72 O 2017

the crowd-pleaser color *House Beautiful* v159 no8 p66 O 2017

Editors' Picks color *Prevention* v68 no11 p5 N 2016

FIERCE FEMME color *House Beautiful* v159 no8 p124 O 2017

the global gourmand color *House Beautiful* v159 no8 p68 O 2017

the on-the-fly entertainer color *House Beautiful* v159 no8 p70 O 2017

SERVING UP SIMPLICITY H. BROWN and K. O'SHEA-EVANS color *House Beautiful* v159 no7 p58 S 2017

Splendid Setting B. RILEY *Atlanta* v56 no9 p44 Ja 2017

TO HAVE AND TO HOLD color *Martha Stewart Living* p38 S 2017

TOP BRASS color *Bon Appetit* v62 no4 p92 Ap 2017

VEGGIE TOOLS M. XERAKIA color *Better Homes & Gardens* v95 no8 p164 Ag 2017

WHAT'S NEW? *USA Today Magazine* v145 no2862 p78 Mr 2017

Kitchener, Caroline

Learning CURVE color *Vogue* v207 no4 p116 Ap 2017

Kitchenettes

AN OPEN INVITATION A. Preiser color *Southern Living* v52 no6 p84 Je 2017

Kitchens

See also

Kitchen cabinets

Restaurant kitchens

70 WAYS TO BE FASTER, HAPPIER, AND MORE CONFIDENT IN THE KITCHEN color *Redbook* p117 S 2017

backstory color *New Republic* v248 no1/2 p72 Ja/F 2017

BEST KITCHENS color *Log Home Living* p34 2017 SpecialIssue

THE BEST-LAID (KITCHEN) PLANS J. TUNG *Martha Stewart Living* no268 p98 O 2016

Built On a Dream E. O'Brien color diag *Log Home Living* v34 no6 p64 Ag 2017

Gordon–Van Tine Homes: Davenport, Iowa: "The Kitchen," 1926 B. Sullivan color *Arts & Crafts Homes & the Revival* v12 no5 p72 Wint 2018

I Love My Kitchen L. BERGER color *House Beautiful* v159 no1 p104 F 2017

KITCHEN OF THE MONTH: In With the Old World color *House Beautiful* v159 no9 p57 N 2017

kitchens *Design Center Sourcebook* p16 2017

Never Too Late To Renovate D. Hochman color *AARP: The Magazine* v60 no5A p32 Ag/S 2017

On the Rocks S. Logan color diag *Log Home Living* v34 no6 p26 Ag 2017

pretty ENOUGH TO EAT P. P. FISCHER color *Better Homes & Gardens* v95 no9 p114 S 2017

The Right Flooring for Every Room J. Garskof chart color diag *Consumer Reports* v82 no8 p44 Ag 2017

SHARPEN YOUR KNIFE SKILLS color *Redbook* p122 S 2017

SINK SMARTS color *Good Housekeeping* v265 no4 p64d O 2017

Kitchens, Simone

All Night Long color *Glamour* v115 no7 p84 Jl 2017

Beauty for the Future color *Glamour* v115 no5 p80 My 2017

Best. Beauty Gifts. Ever cartoon color *Glamour* v114 no12 p128 D 2016

Ciara Demystifies Her Whole Beauty Approach color *Glamour* v115 no3 p114 Mr 2017

Curly Bangs, the Modern Way color *Glamour* v115 no2 p49 F 2017

HALIMA'S WORLD color *Glamour* v115 no9 p200 S 2017

"I felt pride, and that changed everything." color *Glamour* v115 no6 p72 Je 2017

Is Beauty Self-Care? color *Glamour* v115 no7 p55 Jl 2017

Kendall's Rules for Low-Key Beauty color *Glamour* v114 no12 p130 D 2016

Let's Talk Curly Hair bw color *Glamour* v115 no5 p86 My 2017

"My body was telling me to go back to basics—and stop straightening my hair" color *Glamour* v115 no6 p74 Je 2017

"My dreads gave me time" color *Glamour* v115 no3 p118 Mr 2017

Now meet 39 more beauty game changers—each defining themselves [Cover story] bw color *Glamour* v115 no4 p166 Ap 2017

She Air-Dried Her Hair This Morning color *Glamour* v115 no11 p69 N 2017

Supermodel Makeup School color *Glamour* v114 no12 p119 D 2016

"They Said I Didn't Have the Face for Short Hair" color *Glamour* v114 no7 p76 Jl 2016

The Ultimate Beauty How-tos... color *Glamour* v115 no4 p204 Ap 2017

Kitchens—Cleaning

Clean It Like You Mean It A. ANDREWS color *Martha Stewart Living* no271 p30 Ja/F 2017

Fast Fixes for a Sparkling Kitchen color *Good Housekeeping* v263 no5 p58 N 2016

Kitchen Cleanups L. Elliott cartoon *Old House Journal* v45 no2 p48 Ap 2017

Save Time IN THE KITCHEN B. GOLD color *Good Housekeep-*

ing v264 no3 p87 Mr 2017

Kitchens—Design & construction

The 7 Kitchen Essentials D. Peak color diag *Log Home Living* v34 no4 p54 My 2017

Cabin Patterns D. MULFINGER color *Cabin Living* p20 Mr 2017

Cause a Stir color *Log Home Living* v34 no4 p10 My 2017

COOK, EAT, LAUGH, REPEAT H. Kelly *Washingtonian Magazine* v52 no1 p155 O 2016

From Our Editor S. Donelson color *House Beautiful* v158 no9 p18 N 2016

i did it! K. SELZER *Better Homes & Gardens* v94 no11 p58 N 2016

I Love My Kitchen C. ROCHA color *House Beautiful* v159 no4 p128 My 2017

In the Western HOME color *Sunset* v237 no6 p44 D 2016

Inviting and Efficient T. Tanner color *Old House Journal* v44 no8 p70 D 2016

Kitchen Creativity S. Murphy color *Log Home Living* v34 no4 p22 My 2017

KITCHEN HELP M. Hughes *Washingtonian Magazine* v52 no1 p162 O 2016

Kitchens *New Orleans Homes & Lifestyles* v20 no2 p58 Spr 2017

make a SPLASH J. BREWSTER color *Cabin Living* p52 Ap 2017

Make your kitchen wall work color *Redbook* p113 Mr 2017

PEACEFUL GRANDEUR B. WARREN color *New Orleans Magazine* v51 no3 p52 Ja 2017

Playing Favorites D. PEAK *Log Home Living* v34 no4 p8 My 2017

SHOW US YOUR kitchens color *Log Home Living* v34 no4 p80 My 2017

SPLENDID CRAFTSMAN on the East Coast P. Poore color diag *Arts & Crafts Homes & the Revival* v12 no2 p24 Spr 2017

STEPS IN TIME C. SWANSON bw color *House Beautiful* v158 no9 p95 N 2016

Sumptuous 19th-century Revival Kitchen P. Poore color *Old House Journal* v45 no2 p74 Ap 2017

TRUE VINTAGE STYLE R. Wampler and M. Gill color *Old House Journal* v45 no2 p32 Ap 2017

A TRULY Special PLACE M. PAULSEN bw color diag *Cabin Living* p46 Mr 2017

WHAT SHE DID *Better Homes & Gardens* v94 no11 p60 N 2016

Your DREAM KITCHEN is right here N. Voulgaris color *Redbook* p134 My 2017

Kitchens—Equipment & supplies

The 7 Kitchen Essentials D. Peak color diag *Log Home Living* v34 no4 p54 My 2017

Chef-spector Gadget M. Kronsberg color *Bloomberg Businessweek* no4516 p63 Mr 27 2017

Off-Grid in Alaska F. SIGURDSSON color *Cabin Living* p22 D 2016

Playing Favorites D. PEAK *Log Home Living* v34 no4 p8 My 2017

Kitchens—Equipment & supplies—Evaluation

ALL SET *Martha Stewart Living* no267 p50 S 2016

Cleaning House color *Bon Appetit* v62 no4 p27 Ap 2017

In the SUNSET KITCHEN E. Johnson and S. Spencer color *Sunset* v238 no5 p94 My 2017

KITCHEN A. JURRIES color diag *Backpacker* v45 no3 p102 Ap 2017

KITCHEN WIZARDS color *Good Housekeeping* v264 no3 p94 Mr 2017

Top Chef color *Log Home Living* v34 no4 p38 My 2017

Kitchens—History

KITCHENS color *Old House Journal* v44 p17 2016 Design Center source Book

STEPS IN TIME C. SWANSON bw color *House Beautiful* v158 no9 p95 N 2016

Kitchens—Maintenance & repair

DECO delight D. Pizzi color *Old House Journal* v45 no2 p14 Ap 2017

from SOMETHING OLD to SOMETHING new C. HEITGER-EWING color diag *Cabin Living* p34 Mr 2017

kitchen & bath renovations WITH A BUDGET IN MIND P. Poore color *Old House Journal* v44 no8 p62 D 2016

Kitchens—Remodeling

Full of Grace K. Renda color *House Beautiful* v159 no3 p65 Ap

2017

good bones *Indianapolis Monthly* p99 F 2017

Kitchen + BATH + TILE P. Poore color *Arts & Crafts Homes & the Revival* v12 no1 p32 2017 Resouce Guide

KITCHEN HELP M. Hughes *Washingtonian Magazine* v52 no1 p162 O 2016

Kitchen in the Craftsman Spirit P. Poore color diag *Arts & Crafts Homes & the Revival* v11 no5 p23 Wint 2017

kitchens & baths *New Orleans Homes & Lifestyles* v20 no1 p60 Wint 2016

KITCHENS color *Old House Journal* v44 p17 2016 Design Center source Book

RECIPE FOR SUCCESS H. MARTIN color *Architectural Digest* v73 no11 p104 N 2016

SHOW US YOUR kitchens color *Log Home Living* v34 no4 p80 My 2017

Tricks of the Trade C. Swanson color *House Beautiful* v159 no2 p69 Mr 2017

Kit Cheung, Man

Adaptation *Science* v356 no6335 p243 Ap 21 2017

KITE, BUDDY

How to Scale Up color *Popular Mechanics* p37 S 2017

How to Scale Up color *Popular Mechanics* v193 no7 p37 S 2016

Kite Pharma Inc.

Americas K. Stock color *Bloomberg Businessweek* no4536 p10 S 4 2017

Kites

Fishing for the Moon R. Bragg color *Southern Living* v52 no3 p140 Mr 2017

Off script A. Kylie color *Canadian Geographic* v137 p6 2017 Travel

Kites—Design & construction

Kite Runner M. B. Cortez color *AARP: The Magazine* v59 no4A p66 Je/Jl 2016

Kitt Peak (Ariz.)

Arizona A to Z H. Wilson color *Canadian Geographic* v135 no6 p14 D 2015

Kittens

Amazing Animals K. JAZYNKA color map *National Geographic Kids* no470 p12 My 2017

Wild Cat Academy A. KLEPEIS color map *National Geographic Kids* no473 p30 S 2017

Kittinger, John N.

Committing to socially responsible seafood color *Science* v356 no6341 p912 Je 1 2017

Kitty Hawk (Company)

Where's my flying car? C. Day *Physics Today* v70 no6 p8 Je 2017

Kitzhaber, John A. (John Albert), 1947-

Operating Room K. Barrett and R. Greene *Governing* v30 no6 p58 Mr 2017

Kivi, Lea Karen

The church must build 'spiritual ramps' for abuse survivors *America* v216 no12 p10 My 29 2017

Kiviet, Daniel J.

Biased partitioning of the multidrug efflux pump AcrAB-TolC underlies long-lived phenotypic heterogeneity diag *Science* v356 no6335 p311 Ap 21 2017

Kivinen, Katja

Resistance to malaria through structural variation of red blood cell invasion receptors diag *Science* v356 no6343 p1139 Je 16 2017

Kivioja, Teemu

Impact of cytosine methylation on DNA binding specificities of human transcription factors diag *Science* v356 no6337 p502 My 5 2017

Kivipelto, Miia

A RARE SUCCESS AGAINST ALZHEIMER'S [Cover story] color graph *Scientific American* v316 no4 p32 Ap 2017

Kivirist, Lisa

Country Lore *Mother Earth News* no281 p84 Ap/My 2017

Fresh, Homemade SALAD DRESSINGS *Mother Earth News* no281 p36 Ap/My 2017

Kivlen, Maryann H.

Mechanistic basis for a molecular triage reaction color graph *Science* v355 no6322 p298 Ja 20 2017

Kivshar, Yuri S.

Optically resonant dielectric nanostructures bibl graph *Science*

v354 no6314 paag2472-1 N 18 2016

Kiwifruit

Better, slimmer smoothies L. Lillien color *Redbook* p74 Jl/Ag 2017

Kiwis (Birds)

The Kiwi Connection J. CAREY *Audubon* v118 no6 p16 Wint 2016

KIX, PAUL

THE ACCIDENTAL GETAWAY DRIVER cartoon color *GQ: Gentlemen's Quarterly* v97 no5 p110 My 2017

KIZER, BILLIE

Rich Rituals color *O, The Oprah Magazine* p14 Ja 2017

Kizer, DeShone

UPSIDE-DOWNSIDE A. Benoit color *Sports Illustrated* v126 no11 p40 Ap 17-24 2017

Kizilcec, René F.

Closing global achievement gaps in MOOCs bibl graph *Science* v355 no6322 p251 Ja 20 2017

Kjaerum, Morten

From International Law to Local Communities: The Role of the United Nations in the Realization of Human Rights *UN Chronicle* v53 no4 p1 2016

From International Law to Local Communities: The Role of the United Nations in the Realization of Human Rights *UN Chronicle* v54 no4 p34 2017

Kjartansson, Ragnar

19 THINGS YOU REALLY OUGHT TO DO THIS MONTH M. J. Gaynor, B. Freed et al *Washingtonian Magazine* v52 no1 p33 O 2016

Kjeldsen, Thomas R.

Changing climate shifts timing of European floods color graph *Science* v357 no6351 p588 Ag 11 2017

KKR & Co. LP—Finance

Letting Workers Have a Share A. Melin and M. Mittelman bw color *Bloomberg Businessweek* no4527 p37 Je 19 2017

Klaas, Brian

The Despot's Accomplice: How the West Is Aiding and Abetting the Decline of Democracy color *Publishers Weekly* v264 no6 p55 F 6 2017

Klages, Ellen

Wicked Wonders color *Publishers Weekly* v264 no16 p50 Ap 17 2017

Klages, H. O.

Observation of a large-scale anisotropy in the arrival directions of cosmic rays above 8 × 1018 eV *Science* v357 no6357 p1266 S 22 2017

Klajn, Rafal

Clathrates grow up bibl color *Science* v355 no6328 p912 Mr 3 2017

Klam, Matthew

MONEY HONEY color *Esquire* p86 Je/Jl 2017

Rich Is Rabbit: Matthew Klam's debut novel tells the tale of a conflicted adulterer M. SCHAUB *New York Times Book Review* p11 Jl 30 2017

Klamkin, Chris

PLAYING FAVORITES R. Sauerhaft color *Golf Magazine* v59 no7 p86 Jl 2017

Klapars, Artis

A multifunctional catalyst that stereoselectively assembles prodrugs diag *Science* v356 no6336 p426 Ap 28 2017

Klapmeier, Dale

FLIGHT'S NEXT ACE R. KARLGAARD color *Forbes* v200 no1 p22 Jl 27 2017

Klapper, Robert

A modern diagnosis of an ancient cat L. E. Ogden color *Science News* v192 no7 p5 O 28 2017

Klare, Hendrik F. T.

Teaching nature the unnatural bibl diag *Science* v354 no6315 p970 N 25 2016

KLARE, MICHAEL T.

Billionaires vs. Bombardiers diag *Nation* v304 no8 p3 Mr 13 2017

From Scarcity to Abundance: The New Geopolitics of Energy *Current History* v116 no786 p3 Ja 2017

Learning to Bargain bw *Nation* v304 no2 p15 Ja 16 2017

Nuclear Wake-Up Call *Nation* v305 no3 p4 Jl 31 2017

OFF-TARGET *Foreign Affairs* v95 no6 p196 N/D 2016

Toward a New Foreign Policy [Cover story] bw *Nation* v304 no2 p12 Ja 16 2017

War Crimes in Yemen *Nation* v33 no21 p4 N 21 2016

Klarna AB—Officials & employees

Buy Now, Pay Later P. OLSON color *Forbes* v198 no7 p88 N 29 2016

Klatt, Nichole R.

Vaginal bacteria modify HIV tenofovir microbicide efficacy in African women chart graph *Science* v356 no6341 p938 Je 1 2017

Klausner, Julie

Difficult People A. D'Arminio *TV Guide* v65 no35 p36 Ag 21 2017

A POP CULTURE LEXICON C. Agard color *Entertainment Weekly* no1468/1469 p41 Je 2-9 2017

Sadness: A Love Story color *InStyle* v24 no9 p218 S 2017

Klaver, Becca

Empire Wasted *Publishers Weekly* v263 no47 p87 N 21 2016

Klaw, Irving

Why I Love MY BETTIE PAGE PUMPS D. Von Teese color *InStyle* v24 no6 p172 Je 2017

KLAWANS, STUART

BIG NAMES EVERYWHERE *Nation* v304 no16 p44 My 22 2017

BOOK RATS color *Nation* v305 no8 p36 O 9 2017

FREEDOM OF MOVEMENT bw color *Nation* v303 no19 p33 N 7 2016

HUMAN PRESENCE *Nation* v303 no17 p36 O 24 2016

I HEARD A FLY BUZZ color *Nation* v304 no13 p36 Ap 17 2017

ORNAMENTS TO THE SEASON color *Nation* v304 no2 p35 Ja 16 2017

SPOTTING BIGFOOT AT LINCOLN CENTER color *Nation* v303 no22 p35 N 28 2016

THOSE WONDROUS POWERS *Nation* v303 no23/24 p35 D 5 2016

UNSEEN AND UNHEARD color *Nation* v304 no7 p36 Mr 6 2017

The Woman Who Left bw *Film Comment* v53 no3 p72 My/Je 2017

WONDER WOMEN color *Nation* v305 no1 p44 Jl 3 2017

Klawe, Maria

THE MANY FACES OF HARVEY MUDD C. HOWARD chart color *Forbes* v200 no2 p19 S 5 2017

KLAY, PHIL

INTO THE VOID bw cartoon color *Mother Jones* v42 no5 p56 S/O 2017

Klaymoon, Nicole

STREET TO STAGE D. S. GRIMES and A. O'NEAL *Dance Magazine* v91 no7 p42 Jl 2017

Klebanoff, Christopher A.

Landscape of immunogenic tumor antigens in successful immunotherapy of virally induced epithelial cancer graph *Science* v356 no6334 p200 Ap 14 2017

Klebnikov, Sergei

THE BEST PLACES TO LIVE IN AMERICA [Cover story] chart color map *Money* v46 no9 p54 O 2017

Kleckner, Dustin

Complete measurement of helicity and its dynamics in vortex tubes color diag graph *Science* v357 no6350 p487 Ag 4 2017

Klee, Harry

A chemical genetic roadmap to improved tomato flavor bibl graph *Science* v355 no6323 p391 Ja 27 2017

Kleeb, Jane

Bolder Is Better A. Scher color *Progressive* v81 no3 p30 Mr 2017

Building the Resistance R. CONNIFF *Progressive* v81 no3 p5 Mr 2017

Kleeb, Jane—Interviews

Lighting a Fire on the Prairie J. BLEIFUSS *In These Times* v41 no7 p30 Jl 2017

KLEEMAN, ALEXANDRA

Passing: A novel grapples with the impossibility of transcending race *New York Times Book Review* p10 O 8 2017

The Slowness of 'Twin Peaks' *New York Times Magazine* p38 O 8 2017

Kleeman, Alexandra, 1986-

Absurd and Realistic H. HOBY bw *New York Times Book Review* p18 S 25 2016

COOKED DATA cartoon *New Yorker* v92 no39 p76 N 28 2016

Things Fall Apart C. LORENTZEN img *New York* v49 no20 p131 O 3 2016

Kleese, Karl

FROM OUR READERS *Sky & Telescope* v133 no4 p6 Ap 2017

Klehr, Harvey

The Old Terrorists *Commentary* v140 no2 p48 S 2015

Spy vs. Spy *Commentary* v142 no5 p38 D 2016

The Spy Who Loved Animals bw *Weekly Standard* v23 no3 p30 S 25 2017

Stalin's Second String *Weekly Standard* v22 no4 p31 O 3 2016

The Two Worlds of a Soviet Spy bw *Commentary* v143 no3 p27 Mr 2017

Kleifges, M.

Observation of a large-scale anisotropy in the arrival directions of cosmic rays above 8×1018 eV *Science* v357 no6357 p1266 S 22 2017

Kleiman, Evan

LIMA BEAN LEGACY color *Los Angeles Magazine* v62 no10 p18 O 2017

Kleiman, Mark A. R.

High Stakes color *Foreign Affairs* v96 no2 p130 Mr/Ap 2017

KLEIN, ADAM I.

The Hacking Bear il *National Review* v68 no21 p33 N 21 2016

Klein, Alex

THE IMPROBABLE ENCORE E. FISHMAN bw color *Chicago* v66 no2 p72 F 2017

TALK TO US J. Hieshetter, N. Malitz et al bw *Chicago* v66 no3 p23 Mr 2017

Klein, Allen

Sam Cooke Had a Hammer F. Goodman bw color *American History* v52 no2 p56 Je 2017

KLEIN, AMY

HOW TO Wean When Your Toddler Resists *Parents* v92 no11 p119 N 2017

Klein, Bruce S.

The balance between immunity and inflammation diag *Science* v357 no6355 p973 S 8 2017

Klein, Calvin, 1942-

Once Upon a Time in America M. HOLGATE bw color *Vogue* v207 no9 p706 S 2017

Klein, Carol Swartout

PROMOTING PEACE: How libraries, schools, and art help in a time of crisis color *Literacy Today (2411-7862)* v34 no6 p18 My/Je 2017

Klein, Debby

REUNITED S. Koslow color *AARP: The Magazine* v59 no2A p46 F/Mr 2016

Klein, Emily

eating issues *Parents* v91 no6 p138 Je 2016

Without inclusion, diversity initiatives may not be enough color *Science* v357 no6356 p1101 S 15 2017

KLEIN, GARY

ALL IN A Day's Work *Reader's Digest* v189 no1128 p60 Mr 2017

Klein, Ionia

Finders Keepers, Losers Weepers J. SerVaas *Saturday Evening Post* v289 no2 p23 Mr/Ap 2017

Klein, Jessi, 1975-

You'll Grow Out of It *Publishers Weekly* v263 no40 p119 O 3 2016

Klein, Joe

Alienating Friends and Comforting Enemies color *Bloomberg Businessweek* no4527 p16 Je 19 2017

All the Right Moves [Cover story] *New York Times Book Review* p1 My 14 2017

Amazing Grace color *Time* v188 no25-26 p160 D 19 2016 Double Issue

Beware the Toxic Sequel to Donald Trump's Flailing Presidential Campaign color *Time* v188 no18 p25 O 31 2016

Beware the Tricks and Traps of Donald Trump, News Manipulator In Chief color *Time* v188 no27-28 p34 D 26 2016

Closing Argument: Why Hillary Clinton Is the Only Choice to Keep America Great color *Time* v188 no20 p24 N 14 2016

The Debate Stage Reveals Character, Preparation and the Candidate Who Is Still a Child color *Time* v188 no14 p28 O 10 2016

The Ideological Challenge at the Core of Donald Trump's Radical

Presidency color *Time* v189 no4 p23 F 6 2017

Running Mates from the Past Prove the Need for a New Politics of the Future color *Time* v188 no15 p18 O 17 2016

Style Over Substance: Why Fidel Castro's Revolutionary Chic Was a Fraud color *Time* v188 no24 p38 D 12 2016

The Teddy Awards, Even In a Year That Set New Lows for Politicians color *Time* v188 no25-26 p39 D 19 2016 Double Issue

The Ultimate Insider Who Could Still Change the Game In the Oval Office color *Time* v188 no19 p24 N 7 2016

What Comes Next With President Trump color *Time* v188 no21 p26 N 21 2016

Why the Russian Hacks of Hillary Clinton's Campaign Should Reassure Us All color *Time* v188 no16/17 p18 O 24 2016

Why We Must Focus Now on Maintaining Democracy, Civility and Perspective color *Time* v188 no22-23 p22 N/D 2016

Yes He Did *Foreign Affairs* v96 no4 p134 Jl/Ag 2017

Klein, Marty

His Porn, Her Pain: Confronting Americas PornPanic With Honest Talk About Sex H. SILVERMAN *Humanist* v77 no1 p42 Ja/F 2017

Klein, Melissa

Go Ahead... Ask Us Anything color *Popular Science* v288 no6 p102 N/D 2016

Klein, Naomi

DARING TO DREAM IN THE AGE OF TRUMP [Cover story] color *Nation* v305 no1 p14 Jl 3 2017

No Is Not Enough: Resisting Trump's Shock Politics and Winning the World We Need color *Publishers Weekly* v264 no36 p88 S 4 2017

W.W.E. THE PEOPLE *Harper's Magazine* p11 S 2017

Klein, Naomi—Interviews

'Every Day, There Is Some New Shock': An Interview with Naomi Klein, on Her New Book and Donald Trump N. Stockwell color *Progressive* v81 no6 p60 Ag/S 2017

We Need a Plan, Not a Brand K. ARONOFF *In These Times* v41 no8 p28 Ag 2017

Klein, Roland

De-extinction, nomenclature, and the law color *Science* v356 no6342 p1016 Je 9 2017

Klein, S. R.

Observation of coherent elastic neutrino-nucleus scattering diag *Science* v357 no6356 p1123 S 15 2017

Klein, Samuel

An adipo-biliary-uridine axis that regulates energy homeostasis diag *Science* v355 no6330 p1173 Mr 17 2017

KLEIN, SARAH

5 Myths About STRESS [Cover story] cartoon *Prevention* v69 no5 p38 My 2017

America's Opioid Crisis (Might Be Different Than You Think) color *Prevention* p32 Mr 2017

Aspirin to Prevent Heart Attacks *Prevention* v69 no4 p22 Ap 2017

Bark, Birds, and Berries color *Prevention* v69 no6 p22 Je 2017

Before You Take It color *Prevention* p22 Mr 2017

Before You Take It color *Prevention* v69 no1 p22 Ja 2017

BOOST YOUR BRAIN POWER [Cover story] color *Prevention* v69 no9 p68 O 2017

Does It Work? Melatonin [Cover story] color *Prevention* v69 no9 p22 O 2017

Does It Work?: Tech Trackers color *Prevention* v69 no8 p24 Ag 2017

Food Coloring bw color *Prevention* v68 no12 p96 D 2016

High-tech Hydration [Cover story] color *Prevention* v69 no7 p28 Jl 2017

Mind Games cartoon *Prevention* v68 no11 p30 N 2016

NOT YOUR AVERAGE NOODLE color *Runner's World* v52 no9 p39 O 2017

Snow Days bw color *Prevention* v69 no1 p96 Ja 2017

This Is Not Your Mother's Mammogram. It's a... 3-D Medical Breakthrough bw *Prevention* v69 no2 p32 F 2017

Your Perfect Day cartoon color *Prevention* v68 no11 p50 N 2016

Klein, Spencer

ULTRAPERIPHERAL NUCLEAR COLLISIONS *Physics Today* v70 no10 p40 O 2017

Klein, Stephanie

Quotable Quotes color *Reader's Digest* v190 no1133 p140 S 2017

KLEIN, STEPHEN

Trump Theory *Commentary* v142 no1 p8 Jl/Ag 2016

Klein, Tal M.

The Punch Escrow *Publishers Weekly* v264 no25 p96 Je 19 2017

Klein, Todd

Why Are Startup Founders So Bad at Changing Their Own Companies? *Harvard Business Review Digital Articles* p2 O 13 2017

Kleinberg, Jon

A Guide to Solving Social Problems with Machine Learning *Harvard Business Review Digital Articles* p2 D 8 2016

Kleinberg, Neil

Ask anything bw color *Women's Health* v14 no4 p18 My 2017

KLEINBERGER, HERB

CURING THE ADDICTION TO GROWTH color graph il img *Harvard Business Review* v95 no1 p66 Ja/F 2017

Kleindienst, Josef

2 Sleep With the Fishes W. Goodman img *New York* v49 no21 p86 O 17 2016

KLEINE, DENNIS

Cheers & Jeers color *Field & Stream* v122 no6 p12 N 2017

Kleiner, Art

5 Ways to Close the Strategy-to-Execution Gap *Harvard Business Review Digital Articles* p2 D 22 2015

Develop Your Company's Cross-Functional Capabilities *Harvard Business Review Digital Articles* p2 F 2 2016

Only 8% of Leaders Are Good at Both Strategy and Execution *Harvard Business Review Digital Articles* p2 D 30 2015

KLEINER, GREGG

SHOVELING BLOSSOMS color *Orion Magazine* v36 no1 p64 Ja/F 2017

Kleiner Perkins Caufield & Byers (Company)—Officials & employees

VENTURE BALL A. POWELL cartoon *Wired* v25 no10 p42 O 2017

Kleinfeller, J.

Observation of a large-scale anisotropy in the arrival directions of cosmic rays above 8×10^{18} eV *Science* v357 no6357 p1266 S 22 2017

Kleinfelter, Lara M.

Structural basis for antibody-mediated neutralization of Lassa virus [Cover story] color diag *Science* v356 no6341 p923 Je 1 2017

Kleinjung, Jens

Lineage-dependent spatial and functional organization of the mammalian enteric nervous system color graph *Science* v356 no6339 p722 My 19 2017

Kleinman, Steven

Bestiary color *Orion Magazine* v35 no6 p59 N/D 2016

Kleinschmidt, Dörte

A pathogenic role for T cell–derived IL-22BP in inflammatory bowel disease bibl graph *Science* v354 no6310 p358 O 21 2016

Klementieff, Pom, 1986-

Pom KLEMENTIEFF A. LEDGERWOOD *Interview* v47 no3 p18 My 2017

Klementová, M.

Hydrogen positions in single nanocrystals revealed by electron diffraction bibl color *Science* v355 no6321 p1 Ja 13 2017

Klemko, Robert

BE COOL, MAN chart color *Sports Illustrated* v127 no11 p34 O 9 2017

THE GREAT SUPER BOWL JERSEY CAPER color *Sports Illustrated* v126 no11 p98 Ap 17-24 2017

INTERNAL DEBATE color *Sports Illustrated* v127 no10 p33 O 2 2017

Survey Says diag *Sports Illustrated* v126 no18 p14 Je 26 2017

Klemme, Bob

Making his Mark E. Putfark bw *American Cowboy* v23 no6 p19 Ap/My 2017

Klempa, William

A Unique Time of God: Karl Barth's WWI Sermons W. Brueggemann *Christian Century* v134 no13 p37 Je 21 2017

Klenerman, Paul

Immunology taught by rats graph *Science* v357 no6347 p129 Jl 14 2017

Kleopatra (Asteroid)

Interplanetary sand traps T. Shinbrot *Physics Today* v70 no8 p78 Ag 2017

KLEPEIS, ALICIA
PADEMELON *National Geographic Kids* no466 p20 D 2016/Ja 2017
Wild Cat Academy color map *National Geographic Kids* no473 p30 S 2017
KLEPP, LAWRENCE
Fear Is the Spur *Weekly Standard* v22 no41 p26 Jl 3 2017
Inevitably Posthuman? color *Weekly Standard* v22 no45 p29 Ag 7 2017
Lovers of Wisdom cartoon *Weekly Standard* v22 no7 p33 O 24 2016
The Simpler Life *Weekly Standard* v22 no22 p35 F 13 2017
Klepper, E. Dan
High Sierras, Low Stress color map *American Cowboy* p78 LEGENDS OF TEXAS Special Issue 2017
Klepper, Jordan
Fake News Tonight: Comedy Central's latest news satire show pokes fun at the right and left *TV Guide* v65 no39 p12 S 18 2017
The Opposition With Jordan Klepper N. Abrams, C. Holub et al *Entertainment Weekly* no1482/1483 p55 S 22 2017
Klesman, Alison
An astronomical workhorse D. J. EICHER *Astronomy* v45 no5 p6 My 2017
THE BRIGHTEST, MOST DISTANT PULSAR color *Astronomy* v45 no6 p12 Je 2017
Coming soon: Our first picture of a black hole color *Astronomy* v45 no8 p13 Ag 2017
Could life lurk within Pluto's ocean? color *Astronomy* v45 no4 p13 Ap 2017
HUBBLE WEIGHS A WHITE DWARF color *Astronomy* v45 no10 p12 O 2017
METEORITE ORIGINS color *Astronomy* v45 no11 p44 N 2017
OUR MOON'S MANTLE IS WETTER THAN WE THOUGHT bw *Astronomy* v45 no11 p12 N 2017
Our trillion-galaxy universe [Cover story] color *Astronomy* v45 no6 p18 Je 2017
Kletzer, Lori G.
Why the U.S. Needs Wage Insurance *Harvard Business Review Digital Articles* p2 Ja 25 2016
KLIBANOFF, HANK
THE PATTERSON PAPERS *Atlanta* v56 no10 p90 F 2017
Klick, John
What Companies Have Learned from Losing Billions in Emerging Markets *Harvard Business Review Digital Articles* p2 S 16 2015
KLIEN, SUSANNE
Recovering from Disaster, Reinventing Japan? *Current History* v116 no791 p241 S 2017
KLIFF, SARAH
FATAL MISTAKES *Reader's Digest* v189 no1128 p100 Mr 2017
Kligerman, Tom
TOM KLIGERMAN ON CRUCIAL DETAILS K. O'SHEA-EVANS bw color *House Beautiful* v159 no1 p41 F 2017
Klim (Company)
KLIM KRIOS KARBON ADVENTURE HELMET M. Hoyer color *Cycle World* v56 no5 p24 Je 2017
Klimas, Michael
Systemic pan-AMPK activator MK-8722 improves glucose homeostasis but induces cardiac hypertrophy graph *Science* v357 no6350 p507 Ag 4 2017
Klimburg, Alexander
The Darkening Web: The War for Cyberspace *Publishers Weekly* v264 no21 p86 My 22 2017
Klimczak, Karen
Hope for all R. Miska color *U.S. Catholic* v82 no2 p45 F 2017
Klimke, Ingrid
Cavalletti Training for Every Horse and Discipline color diag *Practical Horseman* v45 no5 p58 My 2017
The Right Equipment *Dressage Today* p50 My 2017
Train for Your Horse's Pleasure [Cover story] color *Dressage Today* v23 no9 p30 Je 2017
Klimke, Ingrid, 1968-
16 Questions with INGRID KLIMKE C. Wyllie color *Dressage Today* v23 no12 p52 S 2017
Klimoski, Alex
Alexander Jermyn Architecture bw color *Architectural Record* v204 no12 p50 D 2016

Boston Road Supportive Housing *Architectural Record* v205 no4 p193 Ap 2017
A CALIFORNIA FIRM WORKS WITH AN INDUSTRIAL-DESIGNER CLIENT TO CREATE A CONTEMPORARY HOME IN THE SANTA BARBARA HILLS *Architectural Record* v205 no7 p41 Jl 2017
Diplomacy in Design color *Architectural Record* v205 no3 p44 Mr 2017
Gehry Archive Goes to Getty color *Architectural Record* v205 no5 p28 My 2017
Gilles & Boissier Bardula Studio color *Architectural Record* v205 no2 p109 F 2017
Guggenheim Helsinki Scrapped *Architectural Record* v205 no1 p20 Ja 2017
interiors color *Architectural Record* v204 no12 p29 D 2016
Jenny Sabin to Design PS1 Pavilion color *Architectural Record* v205 no3 p23 Mr 2017
Newport Street Art Gallery Wins 2016 RIBA Stirling Prize *Architectural Record* v204 no11 p29 N 2016
perspective: house of the month color map *Architectural Record* v205 no8 p27 Ag 2017
Rules of Engagement *Architectural Record* v204 no11 p47 N 2016
Set in Stone *Architectural Record* v205 no10 p74 O 2017
snapshot *Architectural Record* v204 no10 p184 O 2016
snapshot *Architectural Record* v205 no10 p172 O 2017
snapshot color *Architectural Record* v205 no3 p144 Mr 2017
Step Right Up *Architectural Record* v205 no9 p122 S 2017
Summer Follies color *Architectural Record* v205 no8 p46 Ag 2017
Two Major Heatherwick Projects Nixed *Architectural Record* v205 no6 p26 Je 2017
Women in Architecture Forum & Awards 2016 color *Architectural Record* v204 no12 p17 D 2016
Klimoski, Thomas
Modeling a COMPACT DIESEL SERVICE TERMINAL color *Model Railroader* v84 no1 p40 Ja 2017
Klimowski, Andrzej
ANDRZEJ KLIMOWSKI A. Curry color *Film Comment* v53 no4 p80 Jl/Ag 2017
Kline, Josh
Editor's Letter L. POLLOCK color *Art in America* v104 no10 p16 N 2016
TERMINAL VELOCITY B. Droitcour color *Art in America* v104 no10 p92 N 2016
Kline, Ronald R.
A Coming of (Information) Age Story: The Cybernetics Moment: Or Why We Call Our Age the Information Age D. Auerbach *Issues in Science & Technology* v33 no4 p89 Summ 2017
Klinenberg, Eric
Social Infrastructure *Foreign Policy* no222 p76 Ja/F 2017
STRENGTH IN NUMBERS color *Wired* v24 no11 p106 N 2016
Kling, Cynthia
CHRISTMAS AT THE GREENBRIER color *Southern Living* v51 no12 p112 D 2016
Klinge, Sebastian
Architecture of the yeast small subunit processome bibl color *Science* v355 no6321 p1 Ja 13 2017
Klingebiel, Ronald
3 Things Driving Entrepreneurial Growth in Africa color *Harvard Business Review Digital Articles* p2 F 1 2017
What Western Investors Want from African Entrepreneurs *Harvard Business Review Digital Articles* p2 N 11 2014
When First Movers Are Rewarded, and When They're Not *Harvard Business Review Digital Articles* p2 Ag 11 2015
Klingenberg, Meghan, 1988-
American Voices Meghan Klingenberg G. Wahl and T. Keith color *Sports Illustrated* v126 no11 p24 Ap 17-24 2017
Klingman, John P.
BEST OF DESIGN color *New Orleans Magazine* v51 no5 p74 Mr 2017
Klingner, Bruce
Getting Tough on North Korea color *Foreign Affairs* v96 no3 p65 My/Je 2017
Klink, Immo
The Willy Wonka of Hudson Yards img *New York* v49 no19 p79 S 19 2016
KLINKENBERG, ABBY LYNN

THE ART OF DISOBEDIENCE *In These Times* v41 no10 p40 O 2017

Klinkenborg, Verlyn

Running With the Pack: Running With the Pack *American Scholar* v86 no4 p120 Aut 2017

What's Happening to the Bees and Butterflies? color *New York Review of Books* v63 no20 p68 D 22 2016

Klinsmann, Jürgen, 1964-

HOT | NOT T. Keith color *Sports Illustrated* v125 no18 p20 D 5 2016

Klipsch Group Inc.

Klipsch Reference Premiere RP-140SA Atmos Elevation Module M. Fleischmann color graph *Sound & Vision* v81 no9 p54 N 2016

New Gear color *Sound & Vision* v81 no9 p30 N 2016

Retro Elegance B. Ankosko and C. Crowley color *Sound & Vision* v82 no5 p20 Je 2017

Klironomos, Filippos

Loss of a mammalian circular RNA locus causes miRNA deregulation and affects brain function color *Science* v357 no6357 p1254 S 22 2017

Klironomos, John

Plant-soil feedbacks and mycorrhizal type influence temperate forest population dynamics bibl graph map *Science* v355 no6321 p1 Ja 13 2017

Kloberdanz, Chad

PUT YOUR POWER USE UNDER THE MICROSCOPE L. BEDORD *Successful Farming* v114 no10 p50 O 2016

Klock, Alice—Interviews

GET Her Look H. Rolfe color *Dance Spirit* v21 no1 p54 Ja 2017

Klöckner, Jan C.

Quantized thermal transport in single-atom junctions bibl diag graph *Science* v355 no6330 p1192 Mr 17 2017

Kloetzel, Peter M.

A large fraction of HLA class I ligands are proteasome-generated spliced peptides bibl graph *Science* v354 no6310 p354 O 21 2016

Klomhaus, Sam

It Happened Here: Ranger, Texas bw *American Cowboy* p54 LEGENDS OF TEXAS Special Issue 2017

Klompmaker, Adiël A.

Increase in predator-prey size ratios throughout the Phanerozoic history of marine ecosystems diag *Science* v356 no6343 p1178 Je 16 2017

Klonsky, Karen

The California Leafy Greens Industry Provides an Example of an Established Food Safety System *Amber Waves: The Economics of Food, Farming, Natural Resources, & Rural America* p43 Je 2017

KLOOR, KEITH

Journalism under Attack *Issues in Science & Technology* v33 no2 p60 Wint 2017

The Science Police: On highly charged issues, such as climate change and endangered species, peer review literature and public discourse are aggressively patrolled by self-appointed sheriffs in the scientific community *Issues in Science & Technology* v33 no4 p78 Summ 2017

Kloos, Julia

Making SDGs Work for Climate Change Hotspots bibl *Environment* v58 no6 p24 N/D 2016

Kloppenberg, James T.

A Fitful Union color *Commonweal* v144 no1 p22 Ja 6 2017

HERE THE PEOPLE RULE D. J. Mahoney *Claremont Review of Books* v17 no1 p49 Wint 2016/2017

Klose, Cornelia

Phytochrome B integrates light and temperature signals in Arabidopsis bibl graph *Science* v354 no6314 p897 N 18 2016

Phytochromes function as thermosensors in Arabidopsis bibl graph *Science* v354 no6314 p886 N 18 2016

KLÖSER, HEINZ

An Ecoregion-Based Approach to Protecting Half the Terrestrial Realm *BioScience* v67 no6 p534 Je 2017

Klosin, Adam

Transgenerational transmission of environmental information in C. elegans diag *Science* v356 no6335 p320 Ap 21 2017

Kloss, Karlie, 1992-

Hello! L. Brown color *InStyle* v24 no6 p20 Je 2017

Kloss, Karlie, 1992-—Interviews

KARLIE KLOSS SUPER MODEL [Cover story] L. Brown color *InStyle* v24 no6 p118 Je 2017

KLOSS, KELSEY

30 Superfoods for a Healthier Life color *Prevention* v69 no11 p44 N 2017

5 Sneaky Ways the Holidays Harm Your Immunity *Reader's Digest* v188 no1125 p70 N 2016

Body Gunk, Explained *Reader's Digest* v188 no1126 p122 D 2016/Ja 2017

Is It Germier To...? *Reader's Digest* v188 no1124 p48 O 2016

Neat Eats: 6 Great Food-Container Tricks *Reader's Digest* v189 no1127 p46 F 2017

Undo a Sugar Binge *Reader's Digest* v188 no1124 p58 O 2016

Kloster, S.

A human-driven decline in global burned area chart graph map *Science* v356 no6345 p1356 Je 30 2017

Klosterman, Chuck

Fire in the Sky color *AARP: The Magazine* v59 no1A p26 D 2015/Ja 2016

Klosterman, Chuck, 1972-—Interviews

FOR THE CULTURE J. WILLIAMS *Cincinnati Magazine* v50 no11 p22 Ag 2017

Klostermann, T.

Soft x-ray excitonics bw diag *Science* v357 no6356 p1134 S 15 2017

Klotz, Anthony C.

7 Ways People Quit Their Jobs *Harvard Business Review Digital Articles* p2 S 15 2016

How to Motivate Employees to Go Beyond Their Jobs *Harvard Business Review Digital Articles* p2 S 15 2017

Will Refusing an International Assignment Derail Your Career? *Harvard Business Review Digital Articles* p2 Ap 18 2017

KLOTZ, STEFAN

Harmonizing Biodiversity Conservation and Productivity in the Context of Increasing Demands on Landscapes graph *BioScience* v66 no10 p890 O 1 2016

National Ecosystem Assessments in Europe: A Review chart *BioScience* v66 no10 p813 O 1 2016

Kluber, Corey

The Case for ... KLUBOT AS MVP G. Baumgaertner and S. Kwak color *Sports Illustrated* v127 no10 p24 O 2 2017

Kluge, Alexander, 1932-

SINKING SHIPS AND SEA DRAMAS A. Kluge *Harper's Magazine* v334 no2002 p22 Mr 2017

Kluger, Jeffrey

The Angels of Irma [Cover story] color map *Time* v190 no12 p34 S 25 2017

Apollo 8: The Thrilling Story of the First Mission to the Moon L. Billings color *Scientific American* v316 no5 p74 My 2017

The Best 25 Inventions of 2016 color *Time* v188 no22-23 p43 N/D 2016

Birdbrain Is a Misnomer: New Studies Show Birds' Remarkable Cognitive Skills color *Time* v190 no7 p24 Ag 21 2017

Burning Questions color *Time* v189 no7/8 p88 F 27 2017

The Deeper Meaning of the Great American Eclipse color map *Time* v190 no7 p19 Ag 21 2017

Eugene Cernan color *Time* v189 no3 p11 Ja 30 2017

Eyes In the Sky color *Time* v190 no1 p42 Jl 3 2017

Glen Campbell color *Time* v190 no7 p13 Ag 21 2017

Homo Naledi Likely Coexisted With Humans color *Time* v189 no19 p13 My 22 2017

Houston After Harvey color *Time* v190 no10/11 p38 S 18 2017

How a War on Science Could Hurt the U.S.-and Its Citizens color *Time* v189 no5 p17 F 13 2017

John Glenn color *Time* v188 no27-28 p17 D 26 2016

Lightbox color *Time* v190 no9 p18 S 4 2017

Moon Missions, Imperfect and Magnificent color *Time* v189 no13 p19 Ap 10 2017

NASA Has a New Way to Fly color *Time* v188 no27-28 p90 D 26 2016

NASA Hopes to Make History With Its Latest Mission—to the Sun color *Time* v189 no22 p7 Je 12 2017

Obama Says NASA Will Put a Human on Mars 'by the 2030s.' Can It? color *Time* v188 no16/17 p9 O 24 2016

Searching for Life on the Newly Discovered Earthlike Planets color diag *Time* v189 no9 p24 Mr 13 2017

Secrets of the Canine Mind color *Time* v189 no19 p42 My 22 2017

A 'Teleportation' to Outer Space color *Time* v190 no4 p13 Jl 24 2017

Want to Go to Mars? Ron Howard's New Series Gives Red Planet Fever a Boost color *Time* v188 no21 p68 N 21 2016

Kluger, Lotta C.

Panama's impotent mangrove laws bibl *Science* v355 no6328 p918 Mr 3 2017

Kluis, Al

BASIS MANAGEMENT M. McGinnis *Successful Farming* v115 no4 p25 Mr 2017

CORN REVENUE MOVES LOWER: A LONG-TERM LOW IS DUE IN 2017 *Successful Farming* v115 no12 p22 O 2017

FINE-TUNE YOUR 2017 MARKETING PLAN *Successful Farming* v115 no4 p22 Mr 2017

GET READY TO MAKE MORE SALES: HERE ARE THE KEY WEEKS YOU'LL WANT TO WATCH IN 2017 graph *Successful Farming* v115 no7 p14 My 2017

GLOBAL GRAIN FUNDAMENTALS BEGIN TO IMPROVE: IS THE FIVE-YEAR BEAR MARKET FINALLY OVER? *Successful Farming* v115 no9 p22 Ag 2017

GRAIN DROPS TO BARGAIN-BASEMENT PRICES: EXPECT GLOBAL DEMAND TO SOAR *Successful Farming* v115 no11 p18 S 2017

LONG-TERM FARM PROFIT ANALYSIS *Successful Farming* v115 no2 p20 F 2017

PUT TOGETHER YOUR SEASONAL PLAN: WATCH WHAT TO DO EACH MONTH THIS SPRING AND SUMMER *Successful Farming* v115 no6 p18 Ap 2017

RISK MANAGEMENT SAVES THE FARM *Successful Farming* v114 no10 p18 O 2016

SEASONAL PRICE PATTERNS WORK AGAIN *Successful Farming* v115 no1 p18 Ja 2017

SOYBEAN-TO-CORN PRICE RATIO FAVORS BEANS *Successful Farming* v115 no3 p17 Mid-F 2017

THINK OF YOUR CROPS LIKE MONEY. BECAUSE THEY ARE D. KURNS *Successful Farming* v114 no10 p4 O 2016

WEATHERING THE STORM *Successful Farming* v114 no11 p21 N 2016

WHAT IS YOUR CMV? *Successful Farming* v114 no13 p22 D 2016

WHEN WILL TRENDS CHANGE? *Successful Farming* v115 no5 p18 Mid-Mr 2017

KLUKO, DANIEL

HOME HYDROPONICS color diag *Popular Mechanics* p85 F 2017

Klum, Heidi, 1973-

Heidi Klum A. Syrett color *InStyle* v24 no4 p96 Ap 2017

Klungthong, Chonticha

Dengue diversity across spatial and temporal scales: Local structure and the effect of host population size bibl graph *Science* v355 no6331 p1302 Mr 24 2017

Klymkowsky, Michael

Lee Rubin: Our mentor and role model *Science* v355 no6327 p806 F 24 2017

Kmart Corp.

'Plus Size' Goes Out of Fashion K. Samuelson color *Time* v190 no12 p14 S 25 2017

Knaak, Richard A.

Black City Demon *Publishers Weekly* v264 no3 p45 Ja 16 2017

Knäbe, S.

Country-specific effects of neonicotinoid pesticides on honey bees and wild bees diag map *Science* v356 no6345 p1393 Je 30 2017

Knabenshue, Elizabeth

Cloverleaf Over Poles color diag *Horse & Rider* v56 no4 p31 Ap 2017

Knabenshue, Will

Cloverleaf Over Poles color diag *Horse & Rider* v56 no4 p31 Ap 2017

Knap, Michael

Bloch oscillations in the absence of a lattice graph *Science* v356 no6341 p945 Je 1 2017

Ultrafast many-body interferometry of impurities coupled to a Fermi sea bibl diag graph *Science* v354 no6308 p96 O 7 2016

KNAPP, ALEX

Old World, Young Promise color *Forbes* v199 no1 p20 Ja 24 2017

Knapp, Christian

THE BEST DEAL IN SKIING S. Davis color *Powder* v45 no3 p54 N 2016

Knapp, D. E.

Airborne laser-guided imaging spectroscopy to map forest trait diversity and guide conservation bibl chart graph *Science* v355 no6323 p385 Ja 27 2017

Knapp, Eli

CHOMPING AT NATURE'S BIT *New York State Conservationist* v71 no6 p7 Je 2017

Knapp, Jackson

THE MAKING OF WASHINGTON color *Washingtonian Magazine* v52 no7 p10 Ap 2017

THE PURSGLOVES' TOP ONE PERCENT *Washingtonian Magazine* v52 no5 p12 F 2017

THE SPY WHO CAME TO DINNER *Washingtonian Magazine* v52 no6 p10 Mr 2017

STRANGE BANDFELLOWS *Washingtonian Magazine* v52 no5 p19 F 2017

WHERE & WHEN *Washingtonian Magazine* v52 no8 p35 My 2017

XBOX WIZARD: We challenged NBA star Bradley Beal to a game of basketball--on his couch *Washingtonian Magazine* v53 no1 p19 O 2017

Knapp, Robert

The Dawn of Christianity: People and Gods in a Time of Magic and Miracles *Publishers Weekly* v264 no24 p59 Je 12 2017

KNAPP, RYAN

ASK RW color *Runner's World* v52 no4 p35 My 2017

Knausgaard, Karl Ove—Interviews

Karl Ove Knausgaard *New York Times Book Review* p7 Ag 20 2017

Knausgård, Karl Ove, 1968-

THE BRIEF bw color *Art in America* v105 no5 p27 My 2017

Gum *New York Times Magazine* p18 Ag 13 2017

Home and Away: Writing the Beautiful Game S. SATTERLEE color *Publishers Weekly* v263 no50 p60 D 5 2016

The Lion Tamer's Dance: In a collection of finely honed miniature essays, Karl Ove Knausgaard describes the world for his unborn child G. R. HALLBERG *New York Times Book Review* p13 O 1 2017

New Sentences S. Anderson *New York Times Magazine* p13 S 3 2017

ONLY A GAME K. O. Knausgaard *Harper's Magazine* v333 no1999 p17 D 2016

Knee

Better Kneebars J. LUCAS color *Climbing* no350 p48 D 2016/Ja 2017

KNEE, JONATHAN A.

Why For-Profit Education Fails color *Atlantic* v318 no4 p30 N 2016

Knee anatomy

Get to know... your knee R. Long color *Yoga Journal* p96 2017 SpecialIssue

Knee pain—Prevention

Age-proof your knees *Harvard Health Letter* v42 no7 p1 My 2017

Get to know... your knee R. Long color *Yoga Journal* p96 2017 SpecialIssue

Knee physiology

ARTHRITIS: What works. What doesn't [Cover story] D. Felson *Nutrition Action Health Letter* v44 no8 p3 O 2017

Knee surgery

See also

Total knee replacement

Boomers Go Bionic P. MERTZ ESSWEIN color *Kiplinger's Personal Finance* v71 no5 p64 My 2017

Kneeboarding

10 Tips for Kneeboarding Success: Minimize wipeouts by following a few simple suggestions T. KOHL *Boating World* v38 no8 p16 S/O 2017

Knee—Diseases—Treatment

Knee Pain from Arthritis? Try Tai Chi *Tufts University Health & Nutrition Letter* v34 no9 p3 N 2016

Kneen, Simon

HORSE POWER bw color *Esquire* p104 2017 BigBlackBook

Kneer, Luisa M.

Molecular force spectroscopy with a DNA origami–based nanoscopic force clamp bibl diag graph *Science* v354 no6310 p305 O 21 2016

Knefel, Molly

Media Embrace of Ed 'Reform' Paved Way for Betsy DeVos *Extra!* v30 no2 p3 Mr 2017

Kneiszel, Jim

KITCHEN REMODELING color *Cabin Living* p68 Je 2017

Knell, Gary E.

ROLEX PARTNERS WITH NATIONAL GEOGRAPHIC ON A VITAL MISSION color *National Geographic* v232 no1 p9 Jl 2017

WE ARE ALLIES IN EARTH'S CARE *National Geographic* v230 no6 pc7 D 2016

Knell, Susan

WHY POETRY?: Lee Bennett Hopkins on why we must share poetry with our students color *Literacy Today (2411-7862)* v34 no6 p16 My/Je 2017

Knibbs, Luke D.

Emergence and spread of a human-transmissible multidrug-resistant nontuberculous mycobacterium bibl diag graph *Science* v354 no6313 p751 N 11 2016

Knick, Shelby

CAPTURING THE LIFE AT SPEED OLD CARS, CHANGING TIMES color *Road & Track* v68 no8 p8 My 2017

Knife cases—Evaluation

ASK JEFFREY J. PHILLIP color *Good Housekeeping* v264 no4 p49 Ap 2017

Knife fighting

THE EVERYTHING GUIDE TO: Sucking at Stuff D. MARCHESE img *New York* v49 no23 p64 N 14 2016

Knife Lake (Minn. & Ont.)

BORDERLINE WILDERNESS C. Mihell *Sierra* v101 no6 p28 N/D 2016

Knife manufacturing

BLADE CITY P. J. DELHOMME color *Outdoor Life* v224 no6 p58 Ag 2017

Trusty Bargains A. McKEAN and N. KREBS color *Outdoor Life* v224 no4 p8 My 2017

Knife Merchant Inc.

LEAVE IT TO CLEAVER color *Bon Appetit* v61 no12 p168 D 2016 /Jan2017

Knifesmithing

BLADE CITY P. J. DELHOMME color *Outdoor Life* v224 no6 p58 Ag 2017

SKINNING KNIVES 101 B. FITZPATRICK color *Outdoor Life* v224 no8 pH15 O 2017

Kniffen, Donna

THE BRITISH HERITAGE TRAVEL PUZZLER *British Heritage Travel* v38 no3 p78 My/Je 2017

Kniffin, Kevin

Being a Good Leader Makes You More Attractive *Harvard Business Review Digital Articles* p2 D 4 2014

Upbeat Music Can Make Employees More Cooperative *Harvard Business Review Digital Articles* p2 Ag 30 2016

Knight, Amy P.

Lost, Almost *Publishers Weekly* v264 no38 p46 S 18 2017

Knight, Anthony P.

CONSULTANTS *Equus* no482 p68 N 2017

Knight, Bob, 1940-

Chatter M. Thomas and C. B. Cooper *Indianapolis Monthly* v40 no10 p13 Je 2017

Knight, Joe

The Most Common Mistake People Make In Calculating ROI *Harvard Business Review Digital Articles* p2 Ap 9 2015

A Refresher on Cost of Capital A. Gallo *Harvard Business Review Digital Articles* p2 Ap 30 2015

A Refresher on Net Present Value A. Gallo *Harvard Business Review Digital Articles* p2 N 19 2014

A Refresher on Payback Method A. Gallo *Harvard Business Review Digital Articles* p2 Ap 18 2016

When It Pays to Think Like a Finance Manager *Harvard Business Review Digital Articles* p2 Mr 23 2015

Knight, Kelly

"Any HR person working here will be out of their comfort zone": An industry-leading ad agency needed bold thinking to address a drastic gender imbalance *People Management* p20 Ag 2017

Knight, Kip

Get Buy-in for Your Global Strategy with Local Partners *Harvard Business Review Digital Articles* p2 O 21 2014

Knight, Lloyd

face off N. Loeffler-Gladstone color *Dance Spirit* v20 no9 p44 N 2016

whyidance L. Knight color *Dance Magazine* v91 no3 p72 Mr 2017

KNIGHT, MICHAEL

THE KING OF DAUPHIN ISLAND *Saturday Evening Post* v289 no5 p62 S/O 2017

Knight, Michael, 1969-

They Do Declare R. BASS *New York Times Book Review* p16 Ap 2 2017

KNIGHT, MIKE

Plant Yourself Here cartoon *Indianapolis Monthly* p23 Ap 2017

Knight, Rebecca

7 Practical Ways to Reduce Bias in Your Hiring Process *Harvard Business Review Digital Articles* p2 Je 12 2017

Convincing Skeptical Employees to Adopt New Technology *Harvard Business Review Digital Articles* p2 Mr 19 2015

Get Your Passion Project Moving Without Quitting Your Day Job *Harvard Business Review Digital Articles* p2 F 19 2015

A Guide to Winning Support for Your New Idea or Project *Harvard Business Review Digital Articles* p2 Je 19 2015

How Freelancers Can Make Sure They Get Paid on Time *Harvard Business Review Digital Articles* p2 2017

How Managers Can Avoid Playing Favorites *Harvard Business Review Digital Articles* p2 Mr 15 2017

How to Ask for the Job Title You Deserve *Harvard Business Review Digital Articles* p2 Jl 17 2017

How to Be Good at Managing Both Introverts and Extroverts *Harvard Business Review Digital Articles* p2 N 16 2015

How to Boost Your Team's Productivity *Harvard Business Review Digital Articles* p2 Ja 29 2016

How to Bounce Back After Getting Laid Off *Harvard Business Review Digital Articles* p2 Jl 31 2015

How to Break Your Addiction to Work *Harvard Business Review Digital Articles* p2 My 18 2016

How to Choose the Right References *Harvard Business Review Digital Articles* p2 O 21 2014

How to Conduct an Effective Job Interview *Harvard Business Review Digital Articles* p2 Ja 23 2015

How to Convince Your Boss to Let You Work from Home *Harvard Business Review Digital Articles* p2 My 5 2017

How to Earn Your Manager's Respect *Harvard Business Review Digital Articles* p2 D 2 2016

How to Fake It When You're Not Feeling Confident *Harvard Business Review Digital Articles* p2 Je 7 2016

How to Get the Most Out of a Conference *Harvard Business Review Digital Articles* p2 Jl 8 2015

How to Get the Most Out of an Informational Interview *Harvard Business Review Digital Articles* p2 F 26 2016

How to Get Your Employees to Speak Up *Harvard Business Review Digital Articles* p2 O 10 2014

How to Give a Stellar Presentation *Harvard Business Review Digital Articles* p2 N 25 2014

How to Handle Difficult Conversations at Work *Harvard Business Review Digital Articles* p2 Ja 9 2015

How to Handle Stress in the Moment *Harvard Business Review Digital Articles* p2 N 5 2014

How to Help an Employee Who Rubs People the Wrong Way *Harvard Business Review Digital Articles* p2 S 21 2017

How to Improve Your Finance Skills (Even If You Hate Numbers) *Harvard Business Review Digital Articles* p2 Mr 31 2017

How to Improve Your Sales Skills, Even If You're Not a Salesperson *Harvard Business Review Digital Articles* p2 My 22 2017

How to Know If Joining a Startup Is Right for You *Harvard Business Review Digital Articles* p2 My 16 2016

How to Make a Great First Impression *Harvard Business Review Digital Articles* p2 S 12 2016

How to Make Your One-on-Ones with Employees More Productive *Harvard Business Review Digital Articles* p2 Ag 8 2016

How to Manage a Needy Employee color *Harvard Business Re-*

view *Digital Articles* p2 Je 5 2017

How to Manage People Who Are Smarter than You *Harvard Business Review Digital Articles* p2 Ag 6 2015

How to Manage Remote Direct Reports *Harvard Business Review Digital Articles* p2 F 10 2015

How to Manage Your Star Employee *Harvard Business Review Digital Articles* p2 Je 30 2017

How to Overcome Burnout and Stay Motivated *Harvard Business Review Digital Articles* p2 Ap 2 2015

How to Quit Your Job Without Burning Bridges *Harvard Business Review Digital Articles* p2 D 4 2014

How to Refocus a Meeting After Someone Interrupts *Harvard Business Review Digital Articles* p2 Ap 16 2015

How to Run a Meeting of People from Different Cultures *Harvard Business Review Digital Articles* p2 D 4 2015

How to Say No to Taking on More Work *Harvard Business Review Digital Articles* p2 D 29 2015

How to Stop Micromanaging Your Team *Harvard Business Review Digital Articles* p2 Ag 21 2015

How to Tell Someone They're Being Laid Off *Harvard Business Review Digital Articles* p2 Je 26 2015

How to Tell Your Boss You Have Too Much Work color *Harvard Business Review Digital Articles* p2 Ja 13 2017

How to Work Confidently with Numbers People *Harvard Business Review Digital Articles* p2 S 2 2015

How to Work for a Gossipy Boss color *Harvard Business Review Digital Articles* p2 Ja 23 2017

How to Work for a Narcissistic Boss *Harvard Business Review Digital Articles* p2 Ap 1 2016

How to Work for a Workaholic *Harvard Business Review Digital Articles* p2 Mr 24 2016

How to Work with a Bad Listener *Harvard Business Review Digital Articles* p2 2017

How to Work with Someone Who's Always Stressed Out *Harvard Business Review Digital Articles* p2 Ag 7 2017

Make Sure Your Team's Workload Is Divided Fairly *Harvard Business Review Digital Articles* p2 N 14 2016

Make Your Work Resolutions Stick *Harvard Business Review Digital Articles* p2 D 29 2014

Planning Maternity or Paternity Leave: A Professional's Guide *Harvard Business Review Digital Articles* p2 My 29 2015

The Right Way to Check Someone's References *Harvard Business Review Digital Articles* p2 Jl 29 2016

The Right Way to Fire Someone *Harvard Business Review Digital Articles* p2 F 5 2016

The Right Way to Off-Board a Departing Employee *Harvard Business Review Digital Articles* p2 Ja 15 2016

Should You Talk About Politics at Work? *Harvard Business Review Digital Articles* p2 S 26 2016

To Boost Your Career, Get to Know Your Boss's Boss *Harvard Business Review Digital Articles* p2 S 2 2016

What to Do and Say After a Tough Reorganization *Harvard Business Review Digital Articles* p2 O 23 2015

What to Do When You and Your Boss Aren't Getting Along *Harvard Business Review Digital Articles* p2 Ag 18 2016

What to Do When You Get a New Boss Every Few Months *Harvard Business Review Digital Articles* p2 Jl 1 2016

What to Do When Your Boss Has a Favorite (and It's Not You) *Harvard Business Review Digital Articles* p2 Je 16 2016

What to Do When Your Boss Is Socially Awkward *Harvard Business Review Digital Articles* p2 D 7 2016

What to Do When Your Employee Asks for a Raise Too Soon *Harvard Business Review Digital Articles* p2 Jl 15 2016

What to Do When You're Returning to a Company You Used to Work For *Harvard Business Review Digital Articles* p2 Ag 4 2017

When an Employee Quits and You Didn't See It Coming *Harvard Business Review Digital Articles* p2 Mr 12 2015

When Someone Asks You for a Reference *Harvard Business Review Digital Articles* p2 O 30 2015

When the Competition Is Trying to Poach Your Top Employee *Harvard Business Review Digital Articles* p2 S 29 2015

When You Find Out a Coworker Makes More Money than You Do *Harvard Business Review Digital Articles* p2 Mr 7 2016

When Your Boss Is Younger than You *Harvard Business Review Digital Articles* p2 O 9 2015

You Can't Move Up If You're Stuck in Your Boss's Shadow *Harvard Business Review Digital Articles* p2 My 8 2015

Knight, Rob

How Blockchain Could Help Emerging Markets Leap Ahead *Harvard Business Review Digital Articles* p2 My 17 2017

Seasonal cycling in the gut microbiome of the Hadza hunter-gatherers of Tanzania diag *Science* v357 no6353 p802 Ag 25 2017

We Don't Need Political Solutions for Global Trade — We Need Practical Ones color *Harvard Business Review Digital Articles* p2 Mr 9 2017

KNIGHT, SAM

BACK TO THE GARDEN cartoon color *New Yorker* v93 no26 p24 S 4 2017

WEATHERING THE STORM bw cartoon *New Yorker* v93 no22 p34 Jl 31 2017

Knight, Shahira

Hidden Hand L. Browning bw *Bloomberg Businessweek* no4522 p35 My 15 2017

Knight, T. R., 1973-

A KNIGHT'S Tale N. Abrams color *Entertainment Weekly* no1454/1455 p64 F 24 2017

T.R. Knight Is J. Edgar Hoover M. Roffman *TV Guide* v65 no14 p8 Ap 3 2017

Knight, Travis

The Unfolding Story T. J. Norton color *Sound & Vision* v82 no3 p66 Ap 2017

Knight, Will

AI's Future Is Not So Scary il *MIT Technology Review* v119 no6 p17 N/D 2016

China's Central Bank Has Begun Cautiously Testing a Digital Currency color *MIT Technology Review* v120 no5 p22 S/O 2017

The Dark Secret at the Heart of AI [Cover story] bw color *MIT Technology Review* v120 no3 p54 My/Je 2017

ENTREPRENEURS color il *MIT Technology Review* v120 no5 p48 S/O 2017

INVENTORS color il *MIT Technology Review* v120 no5 p56 S/O 2017

Making AI Smarter, Faster *MIT Technology Review* v120 no1 p22 Ja/F 2017

Paying with YOUR FACE color *MIT Technology Review* v120 no2 p72 Mr/Ap 2017

Real or Fake? AI Is Making It Very Hard to Know il *MIT Technology Review* v120 no4 p26 Jl/Ag 2017

Reinforcement LEARNING color il *MIT Technology Review* v120 no2 p32 Mr/Ap 2017

Why Poker Is a Big Deal for Artificial Intelligence *MIT Technology Review* v120 no2 p16 Mr/Ap 2017

Your Driverless Ride Is Arriving color il *MIT Technology Review* v119 no6 p34 N/D 2016

Knight Inlet (B.C.)

Where the Wild Things Are P. Rauber *Sierra* v101 no5 p18 S/O 2016

Knightley, Keira, 1985-

Keira Knightley color *InStyle* v23 no13 p188 D 2016

Pirates of the Caribbean: The Curse of the Black Pearl M. FELL *TV Guide* v65 no21 p42 My 15 2017

Knights & knighthood

THE PASSION OF DANIEL J. GORDINIER bw color *Esquire* v167 no2 p136 Mr 2017

Knights of Columbus (Poem)

KNIGHTS OF COLUMBUS T. Burns *America* v216 no9 p37 Ap 24 2017

Knightscope Inc.

ARMLESS DROID CALLS COPS AFTER BEING ASSAULTED BY DRUNKEN MAN K. MANGU-WARD color *Reason* v49 no3 p4 Jl 2017

KNIPPENBERG, CANDY

The Question *O, The Oprah Magazine* p18 S 2017

Knipper, Johanna A.

Local amplifiers of IL-4Rα-mediated macrophage activation promote repair in lung and liver diag *Science* v356 no6342 p1076 Je 9 2017

Knit goods industry

the life C. Stern color *InStyle* v24 no5 p249 My 2017

Knitter, Matt

IT'S HY TIME M. Chwasky and D. Denunzio color *Golf Maga-*

zine v58 no11 p56 N 2016

Knitting
Knitting Classes N. NOEL *Los Angeles Magazine* p60 F 2017
THE LOOK BOOK L. RUIZ img *New York* v49 no25 p97 D 12 2016

Knitting—Societies, etc.
AUTHENTIC ICELANDIC KNITWEAR color *Iceland Review* v54 no5 p102 S-O 2016

Knitwear
Out & About *Martha Stewart Living* no270 p18 D 2016

Knives
ANTHONY BOURDAIN A. BOURDAIN color *Esquire* v166 no4 p141 N 2016
CODE'S KNIFE J. ARTERBURN cartoon *Outdoor Life* v224 no6 p82 Ag 2017
THE KNIFE R. CHAST cartoon *New Yorker* v93 no30 p30 O 2 2017
MEN OF STEEL B. HEAVEY *Field & Stream* v121 no8 p110 F/Mr 2017
RAZOR'S EDGE B. CAMPBELL color *Black Belt* v55 no5 p60 Ag/S 2017
THE SCRODE-HOLE MYSTERY J. ARTERBURN *Outdoor Life* v224 no2 p98 F/Mr 2017
SHARPEN YOUR KNIFE SKILLS color *Redbook* p122 S 2017
SL cooking school K. Hammonds color *Southern Living* v51 no11 p168 N 2016
SO FRESH AND SO CLEAN A. MASON color *Bon Appetit* v62 no2 p99 Mr 2017

Knives—Evaluation
Chef's Knives [Cover story] color *Good Housekeeping* v265 no3 p99 S 2017
Cut 'Em Loose S. MURRAY color *Power & Motoryacht* v34 no11 p84 N 2017
gear *Boating World* v38 no6 p30 Je 2017
Gear P. Nielsen color *Sail* v48 no9 p28 S 2017
Invest in American Steel color *Men's Health* v32 no9 p33 N 2017
KNIVES/ACCESSORIES J. NYQUIST color *Backpacker* v45 no3 p122 Ap 2017
KNIVES OUT *Los Angeles Magazine* p46 F 2017
Looking Sharp A. GARDNER *Indianapolis Monthly* p33 N 2017
Miyabi Knife color *Bloomberg Businessweek* no4532 p67 Jl 31 2017
MOTHER'S Product Picks *Mother Earth News* no283 p14 Ag/S 2017
MY FIRST TOOL KIT color *Popular Mechanics* p102 Jl 2017
The Next Generation of Multitools bw *Popular Mechanics* p42 Mr 2017
the on-the-fly entertainer color *House Beautiful* v159 no8 p70 O 2017
OUR HOLIDAY GIFT GUIDE E. N. GAGE *Martha Stewart Living* no270 p31 D 2016
Tools OF THE Trade: Everything you need to shuck it, slice it and smoke it S. GEROUX and A. HUNTER *Virginia Living* p46 2017 Smoke & Salt
VEGGIE TOOLS M. XERAKIA color *Better Homes & Gardens* v95 no8 p164 Ag 2017

Knives—Maintenance & repair
SKINNING KNIVES 101 B. FITZPATRICK color *Outdoor Life* v224 no8 pH15 O 2017

Knoblich, Juergen A.
Human tissues in a dish: The research and ethical implications of organoid technology diag *Science* v355 no6322 p260 Ja 20 2017
LAB-BUILT BRAINS [Cover story] color *Scientific American* v316 no1 p26 Ja 2017

Knobloch, Carley
a pretty SMART HOME color *Good Housekeeping* v265 no4 p54 O 2017

Knock, Thomas J.
THE LAST POPULIST R. COOPER bw *Nation* v305 no5 p27 Ag 28 2017

Knocked Up (Film)
The Seven Best Romantic Comedies of the Past Decade img *New York* p70 F 20 2017

Knoepfler, Paul
THE STEM CELL SKEPTIC K. Servick color graph *Science* v357 no6350 p441 Ag 4 2017

Knoess, Christoph
Prepare Your Workforce for the Automation Age *Harvard Business Review Digital Articles* p2 N 23 2016

Knoke, Thomas
Forest value: More than commercial bibl color *Science* v354 no6319 p1541 D 23 2016

Knoll, Jeremy
My President Was Black *Atlantic* v319 no2 p8 Mr 2017
Pathways to Adulthood *Education Digest* v82 no4 p13 D 2016

Knoll, John
Knoll R. Capps color *Wired* v24 no12 p124 D 2016

Knolle, Johannes
Neutron scattering in the proximate quantum spin liquid a-RuCl3 bw diag *Science* v356 no6342 p1055 Je 9 2017

Knollenberg, J.
Rosetta's comet 67P/Churyumov-Gerasimenko sheds its dusty mantle to reveal its icy nature bibl graph *Science* v354 no6319 p1566 D 23 2016
Surface changes on comet 67P/Churyumov-Gerasimenko suggest a more active past bw graph *Science* v355 no6332 p1392 Mr 31 2017

Knols, Bart
THE ELIMINATOR K. Kupferschmidt and M. Enserink color diag *Science* v354 no6309 p168 O 14 2016

Knopf, Joan Didion
Time Travel With Joan Didion img *New York* p116 Mr 6 2017

Knopf Doubleday Publishing Group (Company)—Officials & employees
Erroll McDonald D. Patrick color *Publishers Weekly* v264 no30 p8 Jl 24 2017

KNOPPER, STEVE
THE 50 GREATEST CONCERTS OF THE LAST 50 YEARS bw color *Rolling Stone* no1286 p30 My 4 2017
The Biggest Tours of 2017, From GNR to Bieber color *Rolling Stone* no1278/1279 p14 Ja 12 2017
Concert Security's New Frontier color *Rolling Stone* no1293 p16 Ag 10 2017
How Spotify Creates Hits color *Rolling Stone* no1294 p17 Ag 24 2017
Inside the War Over Album Exclusives color *Rolling Stone* no1272 p13 O 20 2016
Music's Scary New Reality color *Rolling Stone* no1289 p13 Je 15 2017
Predicting Pop's Big Night color *Rolling Stone* no1280 p18 F 9 2017
The Puberty Problem img *New York* v49 no20 p118 O 3 2016
Rock's New Protest Era color *Rolling Stone* no1281/1282 p13 F 23 2017
Summer Forecast color *Rolling Stone* no1291/1292 p28 Jl 13 2017

Knorke, Harald
Spectroscopic snapshots of the proton-transfer mechanism in water bibl diag graph *Science* v354 no6316 p1131 D 2 2016

Knorr, M. A.
Long-term pattern and magnitude of soil carbon feedback to the climate system in a warming world chart graph *Science* v357 no6359 p101 O 6 2017

Knost, Alex
ALL TO YOURSELF bw color *Surfer* v58 no6 p62 O 2017

Knots & splices
READY or KNOT *Better Homes & Gardens* v95 no1 p14 Ja 2017

Knots & splices—Methodology
How to Knot a Cherry Stem With Your Tongue M. Wollan *New York Times Magazine* p28 Je 25 2017

Knott, Anne Marie
Is R&D Getting Harder, or Are Companies Just Getting Worse At It? *Harvard Business Review Digital Articles* p2 Mr 21 2017
What the Two Most Innovation-Friendly States Have in Common *Harvard Business Review Digital Articles* p2 D 4 2014

Knott, Bill, 1940-
THE FUGITIVE D. CHIASSON cartoon *New Yorker* v93 no7 p98 Ap 3 2017
I Am Flying Into Myself: Selected Poems, 1960-2014 J. STUCKY color *Publishers Weekly* v264 no3 p38 Ja 16 2017
One Hand Slapping K. Rooney *New York Times Book Review* p18 Ap 9 2017

Knott, Cheryl

Out on a Limb M. White color map *National Geographic* v230 no6 p56 D 2016

Knott, Gavin J.

Structures of the CRISPR genome integration complex color *Science* v357 no6356 p1113 S 15 2017

KNOTT, NATHAN A.

Assessing National Biodiversity Trends for Rocky and Coral Reefs through the Integration of Citizen Science and Scientific Monitoring Programs *BioScience* v67 no2 p134 F 2017

Knottenbelt, Derek

WHEN WOUNDS DON'T HEAL [Cover story] color *Equus* no471 p24 D 2016

Know Your Enemy (Short story)

KNOW YOUR ENEMY M. GALLAGHER cartoon *Wired* v25 no1 p22 Ja 2017

Knowledge gap theory (Communication)

You Know What . . . D. T. PUTERBAUGH *USA Today Magazine* v145 no2864 p80 My 2017

Knowledge management

Develop Deep Knowledge in Your Organization—and Keep It D. Leonard *Harvard Business Review Digital Articles* p2 S 29 2016

Do Doctors Get Worse as They Get Older? Yusuke Tsugawa, D. M. Blumenthal et al *Harvard Business Review Digital Articles* p2 My 23 2017

How to Prevent Experts from Hoarding Knowledge D. Leonard *Harvard Business Review Digital Articles* p2 D 18 2014

Sometimes the Best Ideas Come from Outside Your Industry M. Poetz, N. Franke et al *Harvard Business Review Digital Articles* p2 N 21 2014

Knowledge management—Equipment & supplies

The Benefits of Virtual Mentors B. Iyer and W. Murphy *Harvard Business Review Digital Articles* p2 Ap 26 2016

Knowledge process outsourcing

Why Some Crowdsourcing Efforts Work and Others Don't L. Dahlander and H. Piezunka *Harvard Business Review Digital Articles* p2 F 21 2017

Knowledge workers

4 Organizational Mistakes That Plague Modern Knowledge Workers M. Thomas *Harvard Business Review Digital Articles* p2 My 10 2016

Knowles, Barbara B.

ELABELA deficiency promotes preeclampsia and cardiovascular malformations in mice color diag graph *Science* v357 no6352 p707 Ag 18 2017

KNOWLES, DAVID

Males Show Their True Colors [Cover story] color *Natural History* v125 no4 p10 Ap 2017

KNOWLES, DREW

Get Your Kicks... *USA Today Magazine* v146 no2866 p74 Jl 2017

Knowles, Greg

WHAT IN THE WORLD *Arabian Horse World* v57 no5 p10 F 2017

Knowles, Jonathan

CUSTOMER LOYALTY IS OVERRATED: INTERACTION color *Harvard Business Review* v95 no3 p18 My/Je 2017

Knowles, Michael J.

Shooting Blanks R. KIMBALL *Weekly Standard* v22 no31 p37 Ap 17 2017

Knowles, Robert R.

Catalytic intermolecular hydroaminations of unactivated olefins with secondary alkyl amines bibl diag *Science* v355 no6326 p727 F 17 2017

KNOWLTON, ANDREW

THE ART of SIMPLICITY color *Bon Appetit* no8 p56 Ag 2017

BON APPETIT BEST NEW RESTAURANTS 2017 [Cover story] color *Bon Appetit* p99 S 2017

Cook Like a Pro: Summer Edition [Cover story] bw color diag *Bon Appetit* v62 no7 p56 Jl 2017

The French Are Coming! bw color *Bon Appetit* v62 no4 p15 Ap 2017

RESTAURANT OF THE YEAR color *Bon Appetit* p103 S 2017

starters color *Bon Appetit* no1 p13 F 2017

Thanksgiving LESSONS [Cover story] color *Bon Appetit* no11 p82 N 2017

A Very Organized Thanksgiving color *Bon Appetit* no11 p19 N 2017

Knowlton, Christopher

Cattle Kingdom: The Hidden History of the Cowboy West color *Publishers Weekly* v264 no16 p58 Ap 17 2017

Range Rovers E. DOLNICK *New York Times Book Review* p37 Je 4 2017

Knowlton, Nancy

Why Earth Optimism? color *Science* v356 no6335 p225 Ap 21 2017

Knox, Henry, 1750-1806

BEHIND THE LINES: TRAIN MAN M. G. DeSantis color map *MHQ: Quarterly Journal of Military History* v30 no1 p24 Aut 2017

Knox, John

Applied Thermodynamics for Meteorologists *Physics Today* v69 no12 p58 D 2016

Knox, Rachel

Memphis & Beyond: Assessing the Market for CRA Investment *Bridges (Federal Reserve Bank of St. Louis)* p1 Spr 2017

Knox, Taylor

TAYLOR KNOX, NORTHERN BAJA color *Surfer* v57 no13 p12 Mr 2017

Knox, Thomas W.

THE TRIAL OF THOMAS KNOX J. A. Haymond color *MHQ: Quarterly Journal of Military History* v29 no4 p14 Summ 2017

Knox, Wyatt

LOVE and MUSIC and LEATHER and RACE CARS color *Popular Mechanics* p48 S 2017

Knox County (Neb.)

Creighton creates magic in holiday SantaLand B. SCHWINDT color *Nebraska Life* v21 no6 p69 N/D 2017

Knox-Johnston, Robin—Interviews

Sir Robin Knox-Johnston color *Sail* v48 no9 p12 S 2017

Knudsen, Camilla

Characterization of a dynamic metabolon producing the defense compound dhurrin in sorghum bibl graph *Science* v354 no6314 p890 N 18 2016

Knudson, Rainey

Temp Works *Texas Monthly* v44 no11 p104 N 2016

Knudstorp, Jørgen Vig, 1968—Interviews

A CONVERSATION WITH JØRGEN VIG KNUDSTORP, CO-CHAIRMAN OF THE LEGO BRAND GROUP [Cover story] D. CHAMPION color *Harvard Business Review* v95 no1 p58 Ja/F 2017

Knul, Monika V.

Neandertal and Denisovan DNA from Pleistocene sediments bw color *Science* v356 no6338 p605 My 12 2017

Knupfer, Stefan M.

Technology Is Changing Transportation, and Cities Should Adapt *Harvard Business Review Digital Articles* p2 S 13 2017

Knuth, Rachel

STRIKE a Pose *Dance Spirit* v21 no7 p56 S 2017

Knuth, Randy

A schoolwide investment in problem-based learning chart il *Phi Delta Kappan* v99 no2 p65 O 2017

Knutson, Brian

Brains, environments, and policy responses to addiction color *Science* v356 no6344 p1237 Je 23 2017

Knutson, Heather

HAT-P-26b: A Neptune-mass exoplanet with a well-constrained heavy element abundance chart diag graph *Science* v356 no6338 p628 My 12 2017

Knútsson, Tómas J.—Interviews

SOLDIER FOR SUSTAINABILITY Z. Robert *Iceland Review* v55 no1 p62 Ja/F 2017

KO, GENEVIEVE

LIGHTEN UP THE GRILL color *Parents* v92 no8 p58 Ag 2017

meal mash -ups *Parents* v91 no10 p126 O 2016

Ko, Kwang

A Brief History of Imperial Examination and Its Influences *Society* v54 no3 p272 Je 2017

Ko, Lisa

The ICE-Men Cometh R. BACON *Ms.* v27 no1 p43 Spr 2017

Scene, Not Heard *O, The Oprah Magazine* p149 My 2017

Unmoored: A Chinese-American boy struggles with his mother's disappearance Gish Jen *New York Times Book Review* p25 My 21 2017

Ko, Lydia, 1997——Interviews
Under Pressure M. Washchyshyn and C. Barrett color *Golf Magazine* v59 no7 p25 Jl 2017

Kołakowski, Leszek, 1927-2009
6684 AGC: Earth *Lapham's Quarterly* v10 no2 p159 Spr 2017

Koala
KOALAS SNAP "SELFIES" S. Schwartz *National Geographic Kids* no468 p12 Mr 2017

Koane, Bonny
Higher predation risk for insect prey at low latitudes and elevations graph *Science* v356 no6339 p742 My 19 2017

Koasati (North American people)
Asserting Tribal Sovereignty through Compact Negotiations J. PRECHT *American Indian Quarterly* v41 no1 p67 Wint 2017

Kobayashi, K.
Crystallization and vitrification of electrons in a glass-forming charge liquid bw *Science* v357 no6358 p1381 S 29 2017

Kobayashi, R.
Crystallization and vitrification of electrons in a glass-forming charge liquid bw *Science* v357 no6358 p1381 S 29 2017

Kobayashi, Yusuke
Holliday junction resolvases mediate chloroplast nucleoid segregation diag *Science* v356 no6338 p631 My 12 2017

KOBELL, RONA
HEMP COMES HOME color *Reason* v49 no5 p38 O 2017
Remember Aunt Harriet [Cover story] *National Parks* v91 no4 p26 Fall 2017
Seeing the Light *National Parks* v91 no1 p24 Wint 2017

Kobernick, Hillary
Flood, followed by a rainbow *Christian Century* v134 no3 p22 F 2017

Koberstein, Paul
EDITING EVOLUTION diag *Earth Island Journal* v32 no1 p36 Spr 2017

Kobi, Simi
Host cell attachment elicits posttranscriptional regulation in infecting enteropathogenic bacteria bibl graph *Science* v355 no6326 p735 F 17 2017

Kobi Co.
Innovation Yardbot M. Belfiore color *Bloomberg Businessweek* no4504 p33 D 19 2016

Kobiela, Dorota
Loving Vincent J. McGovern color *Entertainment Weekly* no1485 p41 O 6 2017

Kobilka, Brian K.
Corrigendum: Biology and Light Sources *BioScience* v67 no8 p774 Ag 2017

KOBLIN, JOHN
WHEN FAKE NEWS WAS FUNNY color *New York Times Book Review* p41 D 4 2016

Kobliner, Beth
MAKE YOUR KID AN INVESTING GENIUS color diag *Money* v46 no1 p102 Ja/F 2017

Koblovský, Petr
Economics of Sex: Cost-Benefit Analysis *Society* v54 no1 p18 F 2017

Kobuk Valley National Park (Alaska)
A Parks Bucket List: We'll Visit All 59! C. Ianzito color *AARP: The Magazine* v59 no3A p84 Ap/My 2016

Kobylianskii, Ilia J.
A catalytic fluoride-rebound mechanism for C(sp3)-CF3 bond formation diag *Science* v356 no6344 p1272 Je 23 2017

Koçer, Suncem
Invented Myths in Contemporary Turkish Political Advertising *Society* v53 no6 p603 D 2016

Koch, Alexander
Get to the Heart of Fitness color *Men's Health* v32 no2 p12 Mr 2017

Koch, Boris P.
Dissolved organic sulfur in the ocean: Biogeochemistry of a petagram inventory bibl chart diag graph *Science* v354 no6311 p456 O 28 2016
Genomic databases: A WHO affair *Science* v356 no6340 p812 My 26 2017

Koch, Ed, 1924-2013
I SAY KOCH N. Paumgarten cartoon *New Yorker* v93 no8 p19

Ap 10 2017

Koch, Jim
Thirst Cruncher M. M. WOOSTER color *Weekly Standard* v22 no12 p32 N 28 2016

Koch, Johannes
J&J Plays the Spurned Suitor cartoon *Bloomberg Businessweek* no4503 p20 D 12 2016
A Miracle Drug Big Pharma Doesn't Want color graph *Bloomberg Businessweek* no4517 p22 Ap 3 2017

Koch, Jonathan
ANATOMY OF A PERFECT HAND TRANSPLANT A. WALLACE color *Reader's Digest* v190 no1134 p102 O 2017
HEART OF A CHAMPION A. WALLACE *Los Angeles Magazine* p120 Ap 2017
A Winning Hand *Los Angeles Magazine* v62 no6 p8 Je 2017

Koch, Jürgen
Methanogenic heterodisulfide reductase (HdrABC-MvhAGD) uses two noncubane [4Fe-4S] clusters for reduction color *Science* v357 no6352 p699 Ag 18 2017

Koch, Leah
Bricks and Amour-tar color *Publishers Weekly* v264 no23 p20 Je 5 2017

Koch, Paul L.
Merging paleobiology with conservation biology to guide the future of terrestrial ecosystems color *Science* v355 no6325 p594 F 10 2017

Koch, Ron
#BIKECRUSH color *Bicycling* v58 no8 p53 S 2017
CAMELBAK K.U.D.U. PROTECTOR 10 color *Bicycling* v58 no9 p70 O 2017
DIAMONDBACK RELEASE 5C color *Bicycling* v58 no10 p64 N/D 2017
EASY ON, EASY OFF! color *Bicycling* v58 no7 p82 Ag 2017
GIANT ANTHEM ADVANCED PRO 29 0 color *Bicycling* v58 no9 p68 O 2017
"I'M GOING THROUGH A MIDLIFE CRISIS AND WANT SOMETHING BETTER THAN A CORVETTE." color *Bicycling* v58 no3 p96 Ap 2017
"I WANT TO GO BIKE CAMPING." color *Bicycling* v58 no3 p24 Ap 2017
Oooh... Cozy! color *Bicycling* v58 no1 p64 Ja/F 2017
"SHOULD I GET AN ENDURO BIKE?" color *Bicycling* v58 no3 p94 Ap 2017
TERN CARGO NODE color *Bicycling* v58 no1 p70 Ja/F 2017
THANKS FOR THE RIDE color *Bicycling* v58 no10 p15 N/D 2017
THAT FRESH TIRE FEEL color *Bicycling* v58 no7 p84 Ag 2017
Totally Worth It! color *Bicycling* v58 no4 p22 My 2017
TURBO LEVO FSR COMP CARBON 6FATTIE color *Bicycling* v58 no8 p(Sp)20 S 2017
"WHY SHOULD I SPEND $5,000 ON A BIKE?" color *Bicycling* v58 no3 p46 Ap 2017
WHY WHEELS MATTER color *Bicycling* v58 no3 p57 Ap 2017
YOUR VISION QUEST PACKING LIST color *Bicycling* v58 no1 p78 Ja/F 2017

KOCH, TOM
COMMON GROUND bw color *Black Belt* v55 no5 p54 Ag/S 2017

Koch Industries Inc.
Designing the Next Generation of Business Leaders D. T. Dingle color *Black Enterprise* v47 no4 p24 N/D 2016
Yard Spiel color *Weekly Standard* v22 no34 p3 My 15 2017

Kochan, Thomas A.
Why Isn't Jamie Dimon Telling Clients to Raise Wages Too? *Harvard Business Review Digital Articles* p2 Jl 20 2016

Kocharovskaya, Olga
Leonid Keldysh *Physics Today* v70 no6 p75 Je 2017

Kochen, Lisa
Activity-dependent spatially localized miRNA maturation in neuronal dendrites bibl graph *Science* v355 no6325 p634 F 10 2017

Kocher, Bob
How the U.S. Can Reduce Waste in Health Care Spending by $1 Trillion *Harvard Business Review Digital Articles* p2 O 13 2015
The Right Way to Reform Health Care color *Foreign Affairs* v96 no4 p17 Jl/Ag 2017
Why So Many New Tech Companies Are Getting into Health Care

FUN & GAMES color *Backpacker* p71 Je 2017

KOGAN, LISA

Best Laid Plans, Straight Talk, Helicopter Daughter cartoon *O, The Oprah Magazine* p39 Ap 2017

bold & beautiful color *Better Homes & Gardens* v95 no9 p106 S 2017

The Drinking Game, Ladies Who Lunch, Mother's Day color *O, The Oprah Magazine* p35 Jl 2017

Permission to Speak Freely L. Kogan color *O, The Oprah Magazine* p44 O 2017

Road Trip, Bad Romance, Future Fashionista cartoon *O, The Oprah Magazine* p44 F 2017

Sex and the Single Girl, Puppy Love, Oy Vey color *O, The Oprah Magazine* p38 Ag 2017

A Slacker, a Sticky Situation, a Sensitive Subject color *O, The Oprah Magazine* p30 Ja 2017

Sometimes Life Doesn't Go According to Plan color *O, The Oprah Magazine* p45 N 2017

KOGAN, SVETLANA

HOW TO GET OVER IT *USA Today Magazine* v146 no2866 p28 Jl 2017

Koger, Susan

Beyond the roots of human inaction: Fostering collective effort toward ecosystem conservation color diag *Science* v356 no6335 p275 Ap 21 2017

Koh, Gou Young

Organotypic vasculature: From descriptive heterogeneity to functional pathophysiology color *Science* v357 no6353 p771 Ag 25 2017

Kohan, Jenji

RIOT GIRL E. NUSSBAUM cartoon color *New Yorker* v93 no26 p38 S 4 2017

Kohavi, Ron

THE SURPRISING POWER OF ONLINE EXPERIMENTS: GETTING THE MOST OUT OF A/B AND OTHER CONTROLLED TESTS color diag graph img *Harvard Business Review* v95 no5 p74 S/O 2017

Kohl, Gary

THE BIG QUESTION cartoon *Atlantic* v319 no5 p96 Je 2017

THE CONVERSATION color *Atlantic* v319 no1 p10 Ja/F 2017

Kohl, Helmut, 1930-2017

CRACKDOWN ON NORTH KOREA UNAVOIDABLE NOW S. FORBES color *Forbes* v200 no1 p11 Jl 27 2017

Helmut Kohl S. Shuster color *Time* v190 no1 p13 Jl 3 2017

One Europe Under Kohl L. J. O'Donovan *America* v217 no3 p54 Ag 7 2017

Kohl, Michel T.

Without inclusion, diversity initiatives may not be enough color *Science* v357 no6356 p1101 S 15 2017

KOHL, TOM

10 Tips for Kneeboarding Success: Minimize wipeouts by following a few simple suggestions *Boating World* v38 no8 p16 S/O 2017

Kohlbrenner, Tea

Male sex in houseflies is determined by Mdmd, a paralog of the generic splice factor gene CWC22 bw color *Science* v356 no6338 p642 My 12 2017

Kohler, Hubertus

Gene bivalency at Polycomb domains regulates cranial neural crest positional identity diag *Science* v355 no6332 p1390 Mr 31 2017

Kohler, Judith

Home at Last [Cover story] color *National Wildlife (World Edition)* v55 no5 p22 Ag/S 2017

KÖHLER, NICHOLAS

THE NEW ORANGE CRUSH color *Maclean's* v130 no8 p26 S 2017

STORAGE WARS color *Maclean's* v130 no7 p52 Ag 2017

Kohler, R.

Architecture of a transcribing-translating expressome diag graph map *Science* v356 no6334 p194 Ap 14 2017

Kohler, Sheila

The Purest Bond J. VAN DER LEUN *New York Times Book Review* p9 Ja 29 2017

Kohlhaas, Jacob

Can Catholics celebrate the Reformation? color *U.S. Catholic* v82 no2 p49 F 2017

Kohlrabi

COLONY KOHLRABI *South Dakota Magazine* v33 no3 p38 S/O 2017

Kohl's Corp.

FASHION UNDER $100 [Cover story] color *Redbook* p51 Jl/Ag 2017

get the looks for less color *Good Housekeeping* v265 no5 p41 N 2017

MATCH POINT color *O, The Oprah Magazine* p41 Ja 2017

So pretty, so useful color *Redbook* p45 Jl/Ag 2017

Kohn, Chase

A Caring Place for every step of your journey color *Cincinnati Magazine* v51 no1 p144 O 2017

Q & A: Long-term Care S. Goldberg *Cincinnati Magazine* v50 no10 p74 Jl 2017

Kohn, Jordan N.

Social status alters immune regulation and response to infection in macaques bibl graph *Science* v354 no6315 p1041 N 25 2016

Köhn, Michael D.

INTERESTING AND UPSETTING color *American History* v52 no2 p12 Je 2017

Kohn Pedersen Fox Associates PC

River Dance: A chiseled skyscraper anchors Manhattan's new west-side neighborhood color diag map *Architectural Record* v205 no5 p116 My 2017

Kohnhorst, Amber

survival C. Webber bw color *Backpacker* v45 no2 p39 Mr 2017

Kohnová, Silvia

Changing climate shifts timing of European floods color graph *Science* v357 no6351 p588 Ag 11 2017

KOHUT, MERIDITH

Desperate for a Cure color *National Geographic* v232 no1 p74 Jl 2017

Koichi Todoroki

Buffer-gas cooling of antiprotonic helium to 1.5 to 1.7 K, and antiproton-to-electron mass ratio bibl chart diag graph *Science* v354 no6312 p610 N 4 2016

KOINOVA, MARIA

How Refugee Diasporas Respond to Trauma *Current History* v115 no784 p322 N 2016

Koirala, N.

Quantized Faraday and Kerr rotation and axion electrodynamics of a 3D topological insulator bibl graph *Science* v354 no6316 p1124 D 2 2016

Kojevnikov, Alexei

Kojevnikov replies *Physics Today* v70 no2 p14 F 2017

Koji

Breaking the Mold A. STANEK bw color *Bon Appetit* v61 no11 p34 N 2016

KOJI WHIZ T. KIRTS *Indianapolis Monthly* v40 no7 p40 Mr 2017

Koji Enbutsu

A coherent Ising machine for 2000-node optimization problems bibl diag graph *Science* v354 no6312 p603 N 4 2016

Koji Igarashi

A coherent Ising machine for 2000-node optimization problems bibl diag graph *Science* v354 no6312 p603 N 4 2016

Kokai, Mitch

The Future of the Gerrymander *Commentary* v143 no3 p8 Mr 2017

Kokalitcheva, Kia

BREAKTHROUGH BRANDS 2017 color diag *Fortune* v75 no1 p64 Ja 1 2017

PERSON OF INTEREST color *Fortune* v174 no8 p40 D 15 2016

Koki, George

A Neolithic expansion, but strong genetic structure, in the independent history of New Guinea diag *Science* v357 no6356 p1160 S 15 2017

Kokomo (Ind.)

Buckeye Street: Get to know the darling of Kokomo's historic district L. FISHER *Indianapolis Monthly* v12 no40 p38 Ag 2017

DESTINATION KOKOMO ANTIQUES color *Indianapolis Monthly* v42 no2 p65 O 2017

Kokomo Opalescent Glass Co.

BULL'S-EYE GLASS color *Old House Journal* v45 no4 p78 Je

2017

Kolachevsky, Nikolai

The Rydberg constant and proton size from atomic hydrogen bw chart color diag graph *Science* v357 no6359 p79 O 6 2017

Kolata, Gina

Fatal Genes A. Solomon color *New York Review of Books* v64 no17 p25 N 9 2017

Kolb, Carolyn

Cross Current bw *New Orleans Magazine* v51 no12 p48 O 2017

DOLLS THROUGH THE AGES bw *New Orleans Magazine* v51 no2 p42 D 2016

Glass Act color *New Orleans Magazine* v51 no5 p40 Mr 2017

Keeping it in the Family bw *New Orleans Magazine* v52 no1 p46 S 2017

Legacy of Nature color *New Orleans Magazine* v51 no9 p38 Jl 2017

LIGHT 'EM UP! color *New Orleans Magazine* v51 no1 p42 N 2016

PENTHOUSE PEOPLE color *New Orleans Magazine* v51 no3 p36 Ja 2017

Picturing Mardi Gras bw *New Orleans Magazine* v51 no4 p38 F 2017

A Rose is A Rose: Bayou Road Renaissance color *New Orleans Magazine* v51 no10 p50 Ag 2017

Spinning Platters color *New Orleans Magazine* v51 no6 p38 Ap 2017

Stitches in Time color *New Orleans Magazine* v51 no8 p40 Je 2017

Vive la Différence color *New Orleans Magazine* v51 no7 p40 My 2017

Kolb, Deborah M.

How to Negotiate for Vacation Time *Harvard Business Review Digital Articles* p2 Je 19 2015

How to Negotiate for Yourself When People Don't Expect You To *Harvard Business Review Digital Articles* p2 Je 17 2016

"Office Housework" Gets in Women's Way *Harvard Business Review Digital Articles* p2 Ap 16 2015

Would the World Be Different with Merkel, May, and Clinton in Charge? *Harvard Business Review Digital Articles* p2 S 12 2016

Kolbert, Elizabeth

COMING STORMS cartoon *New Yorker* v93 no27 p23 S 11 2017

THE CONTENT OF NO CONTENT cartoon *New Yorker* v93 no25 p42 Ag 28 2017

The Elephant Detective *Smithsonian* v47 no9 p29 Ja/F 2017

INCIDENTS bw cartoon *New Yorker* v93 no17 p23 Je 19 2017

MINORITY REPORT cartoon *New Yorker* v93 no6 p20 Mr 27 2017

RAGE AGAINST THE MACHINE cartoon *New Yorker* v92 no42 p114 D 19 2016

A SONG OF ICE cartoon color map *New Yorker* v92 no34 p50 O 24 2016

THAT'S WHAT YOU THINK cartoon *New Yorker* v93 no2 p66 F 27 2017

Kolbjørnsrud, Vegard

How Artificial Intelligence Will Redefine Management *Harvard Business Review Digital Articles* p2 N 2 2016

Kolhatkar, Sheelah

ALGORITHM BLUES cartoon *New Yorker* v92 no32 p38 O 10 2016

THE ANTI-UBER cartoon *New Yorker* v92 no32 p40 O 10 2016

BAD RATINGS color *New Yorker* v93 no23 p23 Ag 7 2017

THE COMEBACK KID K. Burton color *Bloomberg Businessweek* no4509 p62 Ja 30 2017

DARK FACTORY bw color *New Yorker* v93 no33 p70 O 23 2017

Inside Additions A. R. SORKIN *New York Times Book Review* p12 F 19 2017

MAR-A-LAGO RULES cartoon *New Yorker* v93 no5 p34 Mr 20 2017

MARTIN SHKRELI IS STILL TALKING cartoon *New Yorker* v93 no9 p23 Ap 17 2017

NATIONAL DISASTER color *New Yorker* v93 no28 p21 S 18 2017

NO MORE MR. NICE GUY cartoon *New Yorker* v93 no16 p44 Je 5 2017

PLAYED OUT color *New Yorker* v93 no31 p23 O 9 2017

SHORTING A RAINBOW cartoon color *New Yorker* v93 no3 p56

Mr 6 2017

STICKLER STATUS cartoon *New Yorker* v93 no13 p37 My 15 2017

TOTAL RETURN cartoon *New Yorker* v92 no45 p34 Ja 16 2017

UBER AND OUT cartoon *New Yorker* v93 no20 p27 Jl 10 2017

Kolin, Philip C.

Benedict's Daughter: Poems P. Mariani *Christian Century* v134 no14 p42 Jl 5 2017

Smell like Sheep bw *U.S. Catholic* v82 no7 p11 Jl 2017

Kolker, Robert

COMING TO TERMS WITH CRISPR color *Bloomberg Businessweek* no4525 p62 Je 5 2017

EVEN IN THE AGE OF ZIKA, THE PEOPLE OF KEY WEST WANT NOTHING TO DO WITH OXITEC'S GENETICALLY MODIFIED MOSQUITOES [Cover story] color *Bloomberg Businessweek* no4494 p48 O 10 2016

MURDER, HE CALCULATED color diag graph *Bloomberg Businessweek* no4511 p48 F 13 2017

THE OLIGARCH WAITS bw color *Bloomberg Businessweek* no4512 p56 F 20 2017

PAUL MANAFORT IS BACK (BECAUSE HE NEVER WENT AWAY) color *Bloomberg Businessweek* no4501 p50 N 28 2016

Project Spade bw *Walrus* v14 no7 p44 S 2017

RICH KIDS ANONYMOUS color *Bloomberg Businessweek* no4500 p48 N 21 2016

THIS CAWSUIT GOES TO 11 bw color *Bloomberg Businessweek* no4519 p72 Ap 24 2017

Kolko, Jon

Dysfunctional Products Come from Dysfunctional Organizations *Harvard Business Review Digital Articles* p2 Ja 21 2015

For Any Product to be Successful, Empathy Is Key *Harvard Business Review Digital Articles* p2 N 20 2014

Lean Doesn't Always Create the Best Products *Harvard Business Review Digital Articles* p2 My 14 2015

Make Enterprise Software People Actually Love *Harvard Business Review Digital Articles* p2 F 12 2015

The Problem of Bolt-On Acquisitions in a Digital World *Harvard Business Review Digital Articles* p2 Jl 5 2016

A Process for Empathetic Product Design *Harvard Business Review Digital Articles* p2 Ap 23 2015

Kolle, Stefan

Preventing mussel adhesion using lubricant-infused materials color diag graph *Science* v357 no6352 p668 Ag 18 2017

Koller, Daphne

Who's Benefiting from MOOCs, and Why *Harvard Business Review Digital Articles* p2 S 22 2015

Koller, Dennis

The Custer Conspiracy *Publishers Weekly* v264 no3 p44 Ja 16 2017

Kollsman Inc.

ALL ABOUT ALTITUDE R. Lengel bw *Flying* v144 no2 p28 F 2017

Koloc, Nathaniel

Let Employees Choose When, Where, and How to Work *Harvard Business Review Digital Articles* p2 N 10 2014

Kolodziejczyk, Aleksandra A.

Aging increases cell-to-cell transcriptional variability upon immune stimulation color diag graph *Science* v355 no6332 p1433 Mr 31 2017

Kolonia, Peter

ADD SNAP color *Popular Photography* v81 no1 p50 Ja/F 2017

CLOUDSCAPES color *Popular Photography* v81 no1 p36 Ja/F 2017

FREEZE FRAME color *Popular Photography* v80 no11 p44 D 2016

High Concepts bw color *Popular Photography* v81 no2 p68 Mr/Ap 2017

LIGHT REPAST color *Popular Photography* v81 no2 p40 Mr/Ap 2017

SCREEN GEMS color *Popular Photography* v81 no2 p28 Mr/Ap 2017

Kolonko, M.

Inhibitors of PEX14 disrupt protein import into glycosomes and kill Trypanosoma parasites chart color diag graph *Science* v355 no6332 p1416 Mr 31 2017

Kolp, Alan

Corporate Ethics Can't Be Reduced to Compliance *Harvard Business Review Digital Articles* p2 Ap 29 2016

KOLSON HURLEY, AMANDA

Time-Travel Therapy bw color *Atlantic* v319 no1 p28 Ja/F 2017

Kolstad, Charles

Reforming the U.S. coal leasing program color graph *Science* v354 no6316 p1096 D 2 2016

Koltai, Steven R.

Entrepreneurship Needs to Be a Bigger Part of U.S. Foreign Aid *Harvard Business Review Digital Articles* p2 Ag 15 2016

Refugees Need Jobs. Entrepreneurship Can Help *Harvard Business Review Digital Articles* p2 D 29 2016

Kolton, Adam

Beyond Politics color *National Wildlife (World Edition)* v54 no6 p40 O/N 2016

Kolvenbach, Peter-Hans, 1928-2016

OF MANY THINGS M. MALONE *America* v215 no19 p2 D 19 2016

Komaki, Shinichiro

RETINOBLASTOMA RELATED1 mediates germline entry in Arabidopsis color diag *Science* v356 no6336 p396 Ap 28 2017

KOMAROFF, ANTHONY L.

ASK THE DOCTOR color *Harvard Health Letter* v42 no2 p2 D 2016

ASK THE DOCTOR *Harvard Health Letter* v42 no7 p2 My 2017

The benefits of vitamin pills and chocolate color *Harvard Health Letter* v41 no12 p2 O 2016

Should you increase HDL, and how? *Harvard Health Letter* v42 no9 p2 Jl 2017

KOMATSU, EIICHIRO

A COSMIC CONTROVERSY color *Scientific American* v317 no1 p5 Jl 2017

Komatsuda, Takao

Wild emmer genome architecture and diversity elucidate wheat evolution and domestication color *Science* v357 no6346 p93 Jl 7 2017

Kombucha tea

FASHIONING FOOD WASTE C. Zuckerman color *National Geographic* v231 no5 p14 My 2017

STRANGE BREW M. P. Lowry color *O, The Oprah Magazine* p32 My 2017

Kombucha tea—Evaluation

Sour Power S. KROWIAK color *Indianapolis Monthly* p41 Ap 2017

Kominers, Scott Duke

Patent Trolling Isn't Dead—It's Just Moving to Delaware *Harvard Business Review Digital Articles* p2 Je 28 2017

Komnene, Anna

Succession in the Silk Roads P. Frankopan *History Today* v67 no1 p4 Ja 2017

Komnenic, Ana

In Canada, case spurs concern over misconduct secrecy color *Science* v354 no6318 p1361 D 16 2016

Komodo dragon

A ONE-PARENT FAMILY, LITERALLY P. Edmonds color *National Geographic* v232 no5 p29 N 2017

A TRIO OF WEAPONS TO FIGHT BACTERIA... color *Prevention* v69 no8 p11 Ag 2017

Komunyakaa, Yusef, 1947-

The Mushroom Gatherers *Progressive* p69 D 2016/Ja 2017

THE SOUL'S SOUNDTRACK *New Yorker* v93 no13 p70 My 15 2017

Kon Leong

Is Your Company Using Employee Data Ethically? *Harvard Business Review Digital Articles* p2 Mr 13 2017

Kona (Company)

"I QUIT MY JOB, AND I WANT TO RIDE ACROSS THE COUNTRY." C. Giddings and B. STRICKLAND color *Bicycling* v58 no3 p62 Ap 2017

Kona Honzo J. Weber and I. Schmitt color *Bike Magazine* v24 no6 p118 Ag 2017

Konadu, Kwasi

The Ghana Reader: History, Culture, Politics N. van de Walle *Foreign Affairs* v95 no6 p195 N/D 2016

Konar, Affinity

Mischling: A Novel E. L. Brown color *Christian Century* v133 no21 p37 O 12 2016

Konczal, Mike

Accidental Advocates *Nation* v305 no8 p9 O 9 2017

Art of the Trade Deal il *Nation* v303 no18 p5 O 31 2016

A Battle for Fair Rates *Nation* v305 no4 p5 Ag 14 2017

Beyond Affirmative Action *Nation* v305 no6 p5 S 11 2017

Funemployment il *Nation* v304 no2 p5 Ja 16 2017

The Great Pretender *Nation* v304 no17 p5 Je 5 2017

Imaginary Inner Cities il *Nation* v303 no22 p5 N 28 2016

Liberalism's Half-Life color graph *Nation* v304 no1 p14 Ja 2 2017

The Obama Years

Man Without a Plan diag il *Nation* v304 no10 p5 Mr 27 2017

Naming Names diag graph *Nation* v304 no15 p5 My 8 2017

Kondo, Marie

2011: Tokyo *Lapham's Quarterly* v10 no1 p72 Wint 2017

Kondov, Stanimir S.

Spin-imbalance in a 2D Fermi-Hubbard system diag graph *Science* v357 no6358 p1385 S 29 2017

Kondrashov, Alexey S.

Negative selection in humans and fruit flies involves synergistic epistasis chart graph *Science* v356 no6337 p539 My 5 2017

Kondrat, Simon A.

Identification of single-site gold catalysis in acetylene hydrochlorination bw diag graph *Science* v355 no6332 p1399 Mr 31 2017

Koneman, Sandi

Greener Pastures *Arabian Horse World* v57 no11 p165 Ag 2017

Konermann, Alyssa

AU NATUREL: Eighty miles east of downtown, Edge of Appalachia Nature Preserve is expanding, and late summer is peak time to visit its prairie lands *Cincinnati Magazine* v50 no11 p26 Ag 2017

Can't Go Home *Cincinnati Magazine* v50 no5 p64 F 2017

DOG DAZE *Cincinnati Magazine* v50 no10 p52 Jl 2017

ENCYCLOPEDIA CINCINNATI bw cartoon color *Cincinnati Magazine* v51 no1 p42 O 2017

GOOD CHEMISTRY *Cincinnati Magazine* v50 no6 p28 Mr 2017

HAMILTON *Cincinnati Magazine* p38 Je 2017

Home Un-Wrecker: How adam Rayne restored a crumbling Walnut Hills Victorian to royal status *Cincinnati Magazine* v50 no11 p72 Ag 2017

Leaving On That Late- Night Train *Cincinnati Magazine* p59 Je 2017

LETTERS OF NOTE: The Cincinnati Type & Print Museum is looking to make the past present *Cincinnati Magazine* v50 no10 p30 Jl 2017

National Museum of African American History & Culture *Cincinnati Magazine* p56 Je 2017

NIGHT MOVES *Cincinnati Magazine* v50 no8 p40 My 2017

OUR FATHER *Cincinnati Magazine* v50 no12 p24 S 2017

PARTY LINES color *Cincinnati Magazine* v51 no1 p24 O 2017

POOL PARTY *Cincinnati Magazine* v50 no4 p21 Ja 2017

RAP SESSION *Cincinnati Magazine* v50 no7 p19 Ap 2017

SLEEP ON IT *Cincinnati Magazine* v50 no2 p36 N 2016

Spice World color *Cincinnati Magazine* v51 no1 p156 O 2017

STORY TIME *Cincinnati Magazine* v50 no7 p22 Ap 2017

STREET ART *Cincinnati Magazine* v50 no7 p62 Ap 2017

You Are Now Entering the Money Pit *Cincinnati Magazine* v50 no11 p77 Ag 2017

Kong, Benson

BACK TO WORK color map *Motor Trend* v69 no1 p80 Ja 2017

GARAGE chart color diag *Motor Trend* v69 no11 p106 N 2017

A NEW HOPE chart color *Motor Trend* v69 no3 p64 Mr 2017

TOW MASTERS chart color *Motor Trend* v68 no12 p64 D 2016

VELOCITY RAPTOR chart color *Motor Trend* v69 no3 p56 Mr 2017

Kong, Jing

Large, valley-exclusive Bloch-Siegert shift in monolayer WS2 bibl diag *Science* v355 no6329 p1066 Mr 10 2017

Kong, Kanga

Park in Limbo color *Bloomberg Businessweek* no4498 p22 N 7 2016

South Korea's High-Value Targets *Bloomberg Businessweek* no4520 p17 My 1 2017

South Korea Tries to Curb the Chaebol color *Bloomberg Businessweek* no4504 p15 D 19 2016

Kong, Liang

A paralogous decoy protects Phytophthora sojae apoplastic effector PsXEG1 from a host inhibitor bibl graph *Science* v355 no6326 p710 F 17 2017

Kong, Yong
Macrophage function in tissue repair and remodeling requires IL-4 or IL-13 with apoptotic cells diag *Science* v356 no6342 p1072 Je 9 2017

Kong: Skull Island (Film)
ANIMAL KINGDOMS A. LANE color *New Yorker* v93 no4 p84 Mr 13 2017
Gorilla Theater J. Podhoretz color *Weekly Standard* v22 no29 p39 Ap 3 2017
A Grand, Nutty and Visually Splendid Kong: Skull Island S. Zacharek color *Time* v189 no10 p49 Mr 20 2017
The Kong Show C. M. Smith color *Entertainment Weekly* no1440 p16 N 18 2016
Kong: Skull Island *New Yorker* v93 no7 p23 Ap 3 2017
Straight Outta Kong L. Rice color *Entertainment Weekly* no1457/1458 p26 Mr 17 2017

Konieczny, Bogumila T.
Rescue of exhausted CD8 T cells by PD-1-targeted therapies is CD28-dependent bw diag graph *Science* v355 no6332 p1423 Mr 31 2017

König, Alexandra
A pathogenic role for T cell–derived IL-22BP in inflammatory bowel disease bibl graph *Science* v354 no6310 p358 O 21 2016

König, Andreas
What BMW's Corporate VC Offers That Regular Investors Can't *Harvard Business Review Digital Articles* p2 Jl 27 2017

KONIGSBERG, Eric
The Real Ex-Husband of Beverly Hills color diag *Vanity Fair* p164 Hollywood 2017 Supplement
SOCK IT TO HIM color *Esquire* p74 Ag 2017
What Have They Done to The Four Seasons? img *New York* p46 Mr 6 2017

KONIK, MICHAEL
FROM THE ARCHIVES bw cartoon *Reason* v48 no11 p70 Ap 2017

Koning Eizenberg Architecture (Company)
Sanctuary for the Stars S. AMELAR color diag *Architectural Record* v205 no2 p90 F 2017

Koninklijke DSM NV
E=MC× EARTH FRIENDLY = MANUFACTURING × CONSCIENTIOUSNESS× E. Fry color *Fortune* v176 no4 p120 S 15 2017

Koninklijke Gazelle NV
GAZELLE GAZELLENL C7 HMB R. Missel color *Bicycling* v58 no9 p82 O 2017

Konner, Jenni
5 Minutes With a TV Pioneer *Glamour* v115 no10 p32 O 2017
In Girls We Trust color *Glamour* v115 no2 p98 F 2017
The New Girls color *Glamour* v115 no2 p108 F 2017

Konner, Jenni—Interviews
Hannah and Her Sisters S. Vilkomerson color *Entertainment Weekly* no1463/1464 p95 Ap/My 2017

KONNIKOVA, MARIA
THE ART OF THE CON *Saturday Evening Post* v289 no1 p34 Ja/F 2017
Make a Mess of It *New York Times Book Review* p21 O 16 2016
Maria Konnikova on Stories as a Force for Evil *Skeptical Inquirer* v41 no2 p11 Mr/Ap 2017
Maria Konnikova Wins CSI's Balles Prize in Critical Thinking for The Confidence Game P. FIDALGO *Skeptical Inquirer* v41 no4 p37 Jl/Ag 2017

Kono, Hidetoshi
Crystal structure of the overlapping dinucleosome composed of hexasome and octasome graph *Science* v356 no6334 p205 Ap 14 2017

Konopelski, Sara E.
Regeneration of fat cells from myofibroblasts during wound healing bibl color graph *Science* v355 no6326 p748 F 17 2017

Konopka, Matthew
Contingent valuation: Flawed logic? color *Science* v357 no6349 p363 Jl 28 2017
Putting a value on injuries to natural assets: The BP oil spill chart *Science* v356 no6335 p253 Ap 21 2017

Konopliv, Alexander S.
Gravity field of the Orientale basin from the Gravity Recovery and Interior Laboratory Mission bibl graph *Science* v354 no6311 p438 O 28 2016

Konovalov, A.
Observation of coherent elastic neutrino-nucleus scattering diag *Science* v357 no6356 p1123 S 15 2017

KONRAD, ALEX
Big Pharma's Friend color *Forbes* v199 no6 p46 Je 13 2017
CLOUD'S NEW CAPITAL chart color graph map *Forbes* v200 no1 p74 Jl 27 2017
FEVER HIGH color *Forbes* v199 no7 p26 Je 29 2017
LESSONS AND IDEAS BY THE 100 GREATEST LIVING BUSINESS MINDS bw color *Forbes* v200 no3 p115 S 28 2017
Power Player color diag *Forbes* v199 no4 p84 Ap 25 2017
SIEBEL'S SECOND ACT color *Forbes* v200 no1 p90 Jl 27 2017
Trash Tech color *Forbes* v199 no1 p46 Ja 24 2017
THE WORLD'S BILLIONAIRES bw color diag graph map *Forbes* v199 no3 p84 Mr 28 2017

Konrad, Walecia
Tidy Up Your Files color *AARP: The Magazine* v59 no3A p26 Ap/My 2016

Konshuh, Courtnay
CHRONICLES OF THE CONQUERED *History Today* v66 no10 p15 O 2016

Konta, Johanna
Johanna Konta *Tennis* v53 no1 p62 Ja/F 2017

KONTOROVICH, EUGENE
Is free speech under threat IN THE UNITED STATES? WE RECEIVED TWENTY-SEVEN RESPONSES. WE PUBLISH THEM HERE, IN ALPHABETICAL ORDER *Commentary* v144 no1 p13 Jl/Ag 2017

Konzum (Company)
Friendship Is a Bountiful Thing Z. Simon bw *Bloomberg Businessweek* no4532 p27 Jl 31 2017

Koob, Frank
Still worried *U.S. Catholic* v82 no10 p5 O 2017

Koolhaas, Rem, 1944-
Buildings Seeking Art V. Camblin bw color *Art in America* v104 no11 p48 D 2016
SIGHTLINES color *Art in America* v105 no5 p45 My 2017

Koomey, Jonathan
Arthur Hinton Rosenfeld *Physics Today* v70 no9 p72 S 2017

Koonin, Eugene V.
Giant viruses with an expanded complement of translation system components diag *Science* v356 no6333 p82 Ap 7 2017
Nucleic acid detection with CRISPR-Cas13a/C2c2 color diag *Science* v356 no6336 p438 Ap 28 2017

Koons, Cynthia
Guarding Big Pharma's Crown Jewel *Bloomberg Businessweek* no4537 p17 S 11 2017

Koons, Jeff, 1955-
The Society PAGE *Interview* v46 no10 p72 D 2016/Ja 2017

Koonse, Emma
LEADING BY EXAMPLE color *Publishers Weekly* v264 no2 p34 Ja 9 2017
Publishers Plan for Future Without Family Christian *Publishers Weekly* v264 no9 p5 F 27 2017

Koontz, Kory
whatever IT Takes B. Welch color *Spin to Win Rodeo* v21 no1 p62 Mr 2017

Koop, Meredith
THE STYLIST & THE FIRST LADY L. Christensen color *Harper's Bazaar* no3648 p268 N 2016

Koop, Meredith—Interviews
WELCOME TO THE ISSUE color *Harper's Bazaar* no3648 p42 N 2016

Koopmans, Marion P.
Role for migratory wild birds in the global spread of avian influenza H5N8 bibl graph map *Science* v354 no6309 p213 O 14 2016

Kooyman, Robert
Global climatic drivers of leaf size [Cover story] graph *Science* v357 no6354 p917 S 1 2017

Kopaczewski, Christine
awesome women Awards 2017 [Cover story] bw color *Good Housekeeping* v265 no3 p67 S 2017

Character Builders cartoon color *Good Housekeeping* v263 no6 p75 D 2016

EVERYDAY HERO LIP SERVICE cartoon color *Good Housekeeping* v263 no5 p96 N 2016

Front-Yard Friends color *Good Housekeeping* v264 no6 p59 Je 2017

Give-Back Getaways color *Good Housekeeping* v264 no5 p69 My 2017

Guess who's in the new LEMONY SNICKET? color *Good Housekeeping* v264 no2 p140 F 2017

NOT-SO-SILENT NIGHTS color *Good Housekeeping* v263 no6 p170 D 2016

STRONGER than EVER color *Good Housekeeping* v263 no6 p85 D 2016

Kopans, David

How to Evaluate, Manage, and Strengthen Your Resilience *Harvard Business Review Digital Articles* p2 Je 14 2016

Kopecky, Elyse

THE WEEK AHEAD [Cover story] color *Runner's World* v52 no1 p52 Ja/F 2017

KOPECKÝ, MARTIN

Combining Biodiversity Resurveys across Regions to Advance Global Change Research *BioScience* v67 no1 p73 Ja 2017

Kopel, Dana

POOH KAYE color *Art in America* v105 no8 p119 S 2017

Kopelson, Gene

He Liked Ike F. BARNES *Weekly Standard* v22 no5 p30 O 10 2016

Kopf, Achim J.

Recurring and triggered slow-slip events near the trench at the Nankai Trough subduction megathrust diag graph *Science* v356 no6343 p1157 Je 16 2017

KOPF, JENNIFER

garden variety color *Better Homes & Gardens* v95 no6 p16 Je 2017

Koplewicz, Harold S.

advice every new mom needs [Cover story] color *Parents* v92 no7 p32 Jl 2017

Kopp, E.

Xenon isotopes in 67P/Churyumov-Gerasimenko show that comets contributed to Earth's atmosphere diag *Science* v356 no6342 p1069 Je 9 2017

Kopp, Raymond J.

Contingent valuation: Flawed logic? color *Science* v357 no6349 p363 Jl 28 2017

Putting a value on injuries to natural assets: The BP oil spill chart *Science* v356 no6335 p253 Ap 21 2017

Kopp, Robert

Estimating economic damage from climate change in the United States color graph *Science* v356 no6345 p1362 Je 30 2017

Kopp, Shannon

"How Shelter Dogs Rescued Me" S. Bower color *Good Housekeeping* v263 no6 p166 D 2016

Koppel, Alan

Exquisite Copse color *Architectural Digest* v73 no12 p90 D 2016

Koppel, Nitzan

Chemical transformation of xenobiotics by the human gut microbiota diag *Science* v356 no6344 p1246 Je 23 2017

Koppens, Frank H. L.

Tuning quantum nonlocal effects in graphene plasmonics bw diag *Science* v357 no6347 p187 Jl 14 2017

KOPPISCH, JOHN

THE WORLD'S BILLIONAIRES bw color diag graph map *Forbes* v199 no3 p84 Mr 28 2017

Kopple, Barbara

SHARON JONES color *Entertainment Weekly* no1446/1447 p96 D 2016/Ja 2017

Kopta, Emry

MASTER OF THE ARTS K. VAUGHN *Arizona Highways* v92 no11 p22 N 2016

KOPYCINSKI, JAY

BEARING TIPS & TRICKS color *Dirt Sports + Off-Road* v51 no5 p64 My 2017

CLEVER STORAGE color *Dirt Sports + Off-Road* v51 no7 p64 Jl 2017

COIL SCIENCE color *Dirt Sports + Off-Road* v51 no6 p64 Je 2017

DIY POWER MANAGEMENT [Cover story] color *Dirt Sports + Off-Road* v51 no12 p66 D 2017

DIY STEEL SHEET FAB color *Dirt Sports + Off-Road* v51 no3 p64 Mr 2017

EXPLORERS, GUNFIGHTERS & SMUGGLERS [Cover story] color *Dirt Sports + Off-Road* v51 no10 p30 O 2017

FIXING TRAIL FAILURESL color *Dirt Sports + Off-Road* v51 no9 p66 S 2017

FLEX JOINTS color *Dirt Sports + Off-Road* v51 no2 p64 F 2017

GRAND CANYON EXPEDITION color *Dirt Sports + Off-Road* v51 no5 p46 My 2017

IFS ARM UPGRADES color *Dirt Sports + Off-Road* v51 no8 p66 Ag 2017

SHEETMETAL WITH A FLARE [Cover story] color *Dirt Sports + Off-Road* v51 no1 p64 Ja 2017

SHOP TIPS color *Dirt Sports + Off-Road* v51 no10 p66 O 2017

U-JOINT SURVIVAL color *Dirt Sports + Off-Road* v51 no11 p66 N 2017

VALVE STEM VITALS color *Dirt Sports + Off-Road* v51 no4 p64 Ap 2017

Kora Organics (Company)

Miranda Kerr A. Syrett color *InStyle* v24 no10 p113 O 2017

Korb, Lawrence J.

Rising tensions, nuclear modernizations: How Washington can turn down the heat bibl *Bulletin of the Atomic Scientists* v73 no3 p173 My 2017

The third offset strategy: A misleading slogan bibl *Bulletin of the Atomic Scientists* v73 no2 p92 Mr 2017

Korban, Ryan

cool customer A. BEVAN color *Architectural Digest* v74 no9 p130 S 2017

Körbes, Carla—Interviews

Carla Körbes G. BERARDI *Dance Magazine* v91 no1 p44 Ja 2017

Kord, Victor

Tense color *Art in America* v104 no10 p36 N 2016

KORDA, JOSH

A SAFE CONTAINER FOR FEAR: WHEN YOU EMBRACE YOUR EMOTIONAL EXPERIENCE, ANXIETY FADES AWAY bw *Tricycle: The Buddhist Review* v27 no1 p64 Fall 2017

Kordei, Normani

FIFTH HARMONY'S NORMANI KORDEI HELPS FIGHT CANCER M. L. Lenker color *Entertainment Weekly* no1484 p59 S 29 2017

Kordic, John

Death of a Goon Aug. 24, 1992 T. Keith and S. Kwak color *Sports Illustrated* v127 no5 p32 Ag 14 2017

Kordick, Rusty

LAUNCHING A START-UP *Successful Farming* v115 no3 p32 Mid-F 2017

Kordus, Bryan

Hot Rod Anything! Motorized Picnic Table Because—Why Not? T. Kempkes color *Hot Rod* v70 no1 p16 Ja 2017

Korea (North)

Korean War Drums B. CUMINGS *Nation* v304 no12 p5 Ap 10 2017

Land of the Hermit King J. H. LEE color *New Republic* v248 no10 p38 O 2017

Korea (North)—Economic conditions

North Korea, Then and Now E. Epstein *Weekly Standard* v22 no33 p7 My 8 2017

Korea (North)—Foreign economic relations

A FRAGILE BORDER P. Martin and S. Chen color *Bloomberg Businessweek* no4539 p33 S 25 2017

Korea (North)—Foreign relations

NORTH KOREA VS. THE WORLD R. ZISSOU *New York Times Upfront* v149 no9 p14 F 20 2017

The South Korean Mirage M. Schuman cartoon *Bloomberg Businessweek* no4515 p8 Mr 20 2017

With North Korea, No Alternative to Patience *Bloomberg Businessweek* no4530 p12 Jl 17 2017

Korea (North)—Foreign relations—Korea (South)

South Korea's High-Value Targets B. Einhorn, K. Kong et al *Bloomberg Businessweek* no4520 p17 My 1 2017

Korea (North)—Foreign relations—United States

KORMOS, CYRIL
An Ecoregion-Based Approach to Protecting Half the Terrestrial Realm *BioScience* v67 no6 p534 Je 2017

Korn, Kim C.
The 7 Laws of Regenerative Enterprises *Harvard Business Review Digital Articles* p2 N 17 2014

KORN, MARJORIE
Compassion in action bw *Yoga Journal* p18 2016 Special Issue

Kornacki, Steve
POLITICAL RACE N. WELDON color *Runner's World* v51 no10 p26 N 2016

KORNBLUH, PETER
After Fidel bw color *Nation* v303 no25/26 p4 D 19 2016

Kornbluh, Roy
Highly efficient electrocaloric cooling with electrostatic actuation bw diag *Science* v357 no6356 p1130 S 15 2017

KORNEI, KATHERINE
Spark of Life bw color *Discover* v38 no1 p53 Ja/F 2017

Kornelis, Chris
What My Music Teacher Taught Me About Money color *Money* v46 no6 p80 Jl 2017

Körner, Christian
A matter of tree longevity bibl color *Science* v355 no6321 p130 Ja 13 2017

Kornfeld, Ari
Mobile MUTE specifies subsidiary cells to build physiologically improved grass stomata bibl diag *Science* v355 no6330 p1215 Mr 17 2017

KORNHABER, SPENCER
RuPaul Gets Political bw *Atlantic* v319 no5 p20 Je 2017
Toby Keith's Happy Hour cartoon *Atlantic* v320 no4 p20 N 2017
TV Gets Metaphysical color *Atlantic* v320 no1 p44 Jl/Ag 2017

Kornilovich, Pavel
African Arrow sees hints of structure in the fabric of space *Physics Today* v69 no12 p49 D 2016

Korol, Abraham
Wild emmer genome architecture and diversity elucidate wheat evolution and domestication color *Science* v357 no6346 p93 Jl 7 2017

KOROM, FRANK J.
A Mixed-Up World *Current History* v115 no784 p325 N 2016

Korosec, Kirsten
BREAKTHROUGH BRANDS 2017 color diag *Fortune* v75 no1 p64 Ja 1 2017
DREAM WEAVER color *Fortune* v176 no3 p74 S 1 2017
FORTY UNDER FORTY 2017 color *Fortune* v176 no3 p62 S 1 2017
HOW TO BUY CLASSIC CARS color *Fortune* v175 no4 p53 Mr 15 2017
MINING COMEDY GOLD color *Fortune* v176 no3 p70 S 1 2017
TESLA'S GOOD DEED SPARKS A (MISPLACED) BACKLASH color *Fortune* v176 no5 p14 O 1 2017
WORLD'S 50 GREATEST LEADERS [Cover story] color *Fortune* v175 no5 p46 Ap 1 2017
YOUTH REVOLT color *Fortune* v176 no3 p64 S 1 2017

Korosec, Marko
VISIONS color *National Geographic* v230 no6 pc15 D 2016

Korovilas, Maria—Interviews
Maria Korovilas *Los Angeles Magazine* p36 Ja 2017

KORS, ALAN CHARLES
FROM THE ARCHIVES bw cartoon *Reason* v48 no11 p70 Ap 2017

Kors, Michael, 1959-
MICHAEL KORS'S Icons A. Serrano color *InStyle* v24 no8 p108 Ag 2017
Why I Love color *InStyle* v24 no3 p378 Mr 2017

Korsgaard, M. Audrey
Want Your Employees to Trust You? Show You Trust Them *Harvard Business Review Digital Articles* p2 Jl 5 2017

Kortava, David
Cheeseboat color *New Yorker* v93 no28 p15 S 18 2017

Korte, Lisa
Plant diversity increases with the strength of negative density dependence at the global scale diag *Science* v356 no6345 p1389 Je 30 2017

KORTEN, TRISTRAM

INTO THE STORM color map *GQ: Gentlemen's Quarterly* v86 no11 p140 N 2016
STORM TROOPERS color map *Reader's Digest* v190 no1135 p116 N 2017

Korteti, Tristram
State of Denial *Sierra* v101 no5 p22 S/O 2016

Korth, A.
Xenon isotopes in 67P/Churyumov-Gerasimenko show that comets contributed to Earth's atmosphere diag *Science* v356 no6342 p1069 Je 9 2017

Kosa, Lauren
Unchosen Hardships color *Commonweal* v144 no6 p47 Mr 24 2017

KOSABA, MAY
Made-to-Please Religious Reforms: Egyptian strongman El-Sisi seeks ways to please Western supporters *Islamic Horizons* v46 no4 p50 Jl/Ag 2017

Kosann, Laura
PARTY HEARTY A. Vorrasi color *InStyle* v24 no1 p98 Ja 2017

Kosar, Kevin R.
Still Life with Corn W. GROOM *Weekly Standard* v22 no41 p29 Jl 3 2017
The Strongest Branch of Liberty *Washington Monthly* p10 N/D 2016

Kosbie, David
How to Prepare the Next Generation for Jobs in the AI Economy color *Harvard Business Review Digital Articles* p2 Je 5 2017

Koschny, D.
Rosetta's comet 67P/Churyumov-Gerasimenko sheds its dusty mantle to reveal its icy nature bibl graph *Science* v354 no6319 p1566 D 23 2016
Surface changes on comet 67P/Churyumov-Gerasimenko suggest a more active past bw graph *Science* v355 no6332 p1392 Mr 31 2017

Koschwanez, John
Exploring genetic suppression interactions on a global scale diag *Science* v354 no6312 p599 N 4 2016

Koseki, Haruhiko
PCGF3/5–PRC1 initiates Polycomb recruitment in X chromosome inactivation color *Science* v356 no6342 p1081 Je 9 2017

Koseki, Yoko
PCGF3/5–PRC1 initiates Polycomb recruitment in X chromosome inactivation color *Science* v356 no6342 p1081 Je 9 2017

koselak, Jeremy
The revitalized tutoring center chart color graph *Phi Delta Kappan* v98 no5 p61 F 2017

Kosher restaurants—Evaluation
Kosher Cool P. KUH color *Los Angeles Magazine* v62 no7 p36 Jl 2017

Kosher salt
ALL RISE M. SHIH and G. LOFTS color *Martha Stewart Living* p110 O 2017
BRAISED AND SMOKED BOAR RIBS J. Miles color *Field & Stream* v122 no6 p24 N 2017
GOLDENRODS G. LOFTS color *Martha Stewart Living* p82 Ap 2017
tools of the trade B. HEADLEY color *Bon Appetit* p82 S 2017

Kosinski, Michal
Promoting human rights through science color *Science* v357 no6359 p34 O 6 2017

Koskela, Jarkko J.
Changing climate shifts timing of European floods color graph *Science* v357 no6351 p588 Ag 11 2017

Koski, Olivia
Vacation Guide to the Solar System: Science for the Savvy Space Traveler *Publishers Weekly* v264 no14 p66 Ap 3 2017

Kosky, Barrie
The Nose G. Hall *Opera News* v81 no7 p43 Ja 2017

Kosloff, Janet
What's Your Most Awkward Team-Building Experience? K. Morell cartoon *Bloomberg Businessweek* no4518 p78 Ap 10 2017

KOSLOFF, MARSHALL
The Uses and Abuses of Cultural Identity *National Review* v69 no17 p17 S 11 2017

Koslow, Jessica
Crunch TIME color *O, The Oprah Magazine* p112 Ja 2017

Koslow, Sally

REUNITED color *AARP: The Magazine* v59 no2A p46 F/Mr 2016

Sorry, Kids: We Made You This Way color *AARP: The Magazine* v59 no3A p55 Ap/My 2016

KOSNETT, JEFFREY R.

Better Rates for Savers, Finally color *Kiplinger's Personal Finance* v71 no6 p53 Je 2017

Don't Dump Your Dividend Stocks *Kiplinger's Personal Finance* v71 no3 p60 Mr 2017

Get a Boost From a Floating-Rate Fund color *Kiplinger's Personal Finance* v70 no12 p58 D 2016

It's Okay to Reach for Yield *Kiplinger's Personal Finance* v71 no10 p60 O 2017

These Supersavers Spend a Little color *Kiplinger's Personal Finance* v71 no11 p72 N 2017

What I'm Telling Worried Readers *Kiplinger's Personal Finance* v71 no5 p62 My 2017

When Everything Is Working, Sit Tight color *Kiplinger's Personal Finance* v71 no7 p53 Jl 2017

Why Income Investors Shouldn't Panic *Kiplinger's Personal Finance* v71 no11 p62 N 2017

You'll Still Make Money in Bonds *Kiplinger's Personal Finance* v71 no1 p49 Ja 2017

Kosoff, Maya

THE NEW ESTABLISHMENT 2017 bw color *Vanity Fair* v59 no11 p87 N 2017

NEW ESTABLISHMENT bw cartoon color *Vanity Fair* v58 no11 p124 N 2016

Kost, Korey A.

Distribution and clinical impact of functional variants in 50,726 whole-exome sequences from the DiscovEHR study chart graph *Science* v354 no6319 paaf6814-1 D 23 2016

Kostel, Ken

Our Ship Comes In *Oceanus* v52 no1 p36 Summ 2016

Shipshape and Well-Equipped *Oceanus* v52 no1 p38 Summ 2016

To Track a Sea Turtle: UNDERWATER VEHICLES FOLLOW TAGGED TURTLES IN THE WILD *Oceanus* v52 no2 p18 Spr 2017

KOSTELANETZ, RICHARD

From SoHo to Bushwick color *Reason* v49 no2 p66 Je 2017

Kostelnick, Peter

BREAK THE TRANSCONTINENTAL RECORD! K. FOX color *Runner's World* v52 no2 p22 Mr 2017

KOSTEN, SARIAN

Translating Regime Shifts in Shallow Lakes into Changes in Ecosystem Functions and Services *BioScience* v67 no10 p928 O 2017

Kosten, Tetiana

Fructose-driven glycolysis supports anoxia resistance in the naked mole-rat diag graph *Science* v356 no6335 p307 Ap 21 2017

Koster, John

Fair and Balanced *American History* v52 no2 p12 Je 2017

WHEN FRANCE DEFIED HITLER'S PANZERS [Cover story] bw color map *Military History* v34 no4 p30 N 2017

Kostin, A.

Discovery of orbital-selective Cooper pairing in FeSe diag *Science* v357 no6346 p75 Jl 7 2017

Kostis, Peter

It's Tome for a Change color *Golf Magazine* v58 no11 p34 N 2016

Peter's Parting Shot color *Golf Magazine* v59 no1 p32 Ja 2017

You're Up! color *Golf Magazine* v59 no3 p13 Mr 2017

Kostiuk, Georgij

A cyclic oligonucleotide signaling pathway in type III CRISPR-Cas systems *Science* v357 no6351 p605 Ag 11 2017

Kostova, Kamena K.

CAT-tailing as a fail-safe mechanism for efficient degradation of stalled nascent polypeptides diag *Science* v357 no6349 p414 Jl 28 2017

Kostyal, K. M.

The Ghost Ship of Brooklyn: An Untold Story of the American Revolution bw *MHQ: Quarterly Journal of Military History* v30 no1 p92 Aut 2017

The Locomotive of War: Money, Empire, Power, and Guilt bw *MHQ: Quarterly Journal of Military History* v29 no4 p92 Summ 2017

Koszul, Romain

3D organization of synthetic and scrambled chromosomes diag *Science* v355 no6329 p1050 Mr 10 2017

Deep functional analysis of synII, a 770-kilobase synthetic yeast chromosome diag *Science* v355 no6329 p1047 Mr 10 2017

Koszycki, Nate

A Day in the Life of a Teen Birder color *Audubon* v119 no3 p45 Fall 2017

Kota, Subu

Trump Plays Six Degrees of the KGB D. Kocieniewski and P. Robison color *Bloomberg Businessweek* no4506 p22 Ja 9 2017

Kotack, Madison

Get-Around Work-Arounds *Sierra* v101 no6 p19 N/D 2016

WISH LIST 2016 color *Wired* v24 no12 p45 D 2016

Kotaro Tsuboyama

The ATG conjugation systems are important for degradation of the inner autophagosomal membrane bibl graph *Science* v354 no6315 p1036 N 25 2016

Kotcheff, Ted

Canadian Hustle N. PINKERTON color *Film Comment* v53 no2 p79 Mr/Ap 2017

Kotchen, Matthew J.

Deciphering dueling analyses of clean water regulations color *Science* v357 no6359 p49 O 6 2017

Kotecha, Abhay

A supramolecular assembly mediates lentiviral DNA integration bibl color *Science* v355 no6320 p1 Ja 6 2017

Koter, Dominika

Beyond Ethnic Politics in Africa N. van de Walle *Foreign Affairs* v96 no2 p189 Mr/Ap 2017

KOTESKEY, TYLER

A BETTER CHANCE FOR NATIVE EDUCATION cartoon *Reason* v49 no1 p18 My 2017

UBER, BUT FOR SCHOOL BUSES color *Reason* v49 no3 p10 Jl 2017

WHY ARE COPS PUTTING KIDS IN CUFFS? color *Reason* v48 no10 p46 Mr 2017

KOTHARI, S.P.

DECODING CEO PAY: *THE TRUTH IS BURIED IN THE FINE PRINT—AND THAT'S A PROBLEM color graph img *Harvard Business Review* v95 no4 p78 Jl/Ag 2017

Kothari, Yogin

Ensuring scientific integrity in the Age of Trump bibl cartoon *Science* v355 no6326 p696 F 17 2017

KOTITE, ROB

ANOTHER LAP color map *Sail* v48 no10 p50 O 2017

KOTIKALAPUDI, CHAITANYA

Advancing clean energy *Issues in Science & Technology* v33 no3 p5 Spr 2017

Kotkin, Stephen

Moscow's Wounded Pride *Hoover Digest: Research & Opinion on Public Policy* no4 p99 Fall 2016

Stalin, 1929-1941: Brutal and Brilliant J. HEILBRUNN *American Conservative* v16 no5 p54 S/O 2017

Stalin at the Movies bw *New York Review of Books* v64 no16 p39 O 26 2017

When Stalin Faced Hitler cartoon *Foreign Affairs* v96 no6 p48 N/D 2017

Kotkow, Karen

Lee Rubin: Our mentor and role model *Science* v355 no6327 p806 F 24 2017

Kotsantonis, Sakis

ExxonMobil's Shareholder Vote Is a Tipping Point for Climate Issues color *Harvard Business Review Digital Articles* p2 Je 7 2017

If CEOs Care About the Long Term, Why Don't They Talk About It? *Harvard Business Review Digital Articles* p2 N 13 2015

Kottick, Gloria

THE BIG QUESTION cartoon *Atlantic* v320 no3 p100 O 2017

Kotz, Vanessa Mallory

GHOSTS IN WINTER color *Popular Photography* v80 no11 p20 D 2016

WHAT'S IN A NAME? color *Popular Photography* v81 no2 p22 Mr/Ap 2017

Kou, Xufeng

Chiral Majorana fermion modes in a quantum anomalous Hall insulator–superconductor structure diag *Science* v357 no6348

Kouchaki, Maryam

Praising Customers for Ethical Purchases Can Backfire *Harvard Business Review Digital Articles* p2 O 6 2016

We're Unethical at Work Because We Forget Our Misdeeds *Harvard Business Review Digital Articles* p2 My 18 2016

Why Creative People Are More Likely to Be Dishonest *Harvard Business Review Digital Articles* p2 N 23 2015

Koudstaal, Maarten

A Blueprint for Measuring Health Care Outcomes *Harvard Business Review Digital Articles* p2 D 12 2016

KOUL, SCAACHI

Get the Scissors cartoon *Walrus* v14 no3 p52 Ap 2017

Kounios, John, 1956-

Step Up to a Breakthrough K. ASP, D. N. Jenkins et al color *Women's Health* v14 no9 p88 N 2017

Koup, Richard A.

Trispecific broadly neutralizing HIV antibodies mediate potent SHIV protection in macaques color graph *Science* v357 no6359 p85 O 6 2017

KOURLAS, GIA

Isabella LaFreniere *Dance Magazine* v91 no6 p22 Je 2017

Rachel Richardson *Dance Magazine* v90 no11 p22 N 2016

KOURY, DAN

Trump's Wall *Commentary* v142 no2 p8 S 2016

Kouvalis, Nick

How to make a candidate M. PATRIQUIN and C. GILLIS color *Maclean's* no1 p26 F 17 2017

Kouwenhoven, L. P.

Demonstration of an ac Josephson junction laser bibl diag *Science* v355 no6328 p939 Mr 3 2017

KOVAC, JOE, JR.

OUR TIME? NOT THIS TIME *Atlanta* v56 no11 p19 Mr 2017

Kovac, Mark

Social Media Works for B2B Sales, Too *Harvard Business Review Digital Articles* p2 Ja 4 2016

Using Digital Exhaust to Improve Sales *Harvard Business Review Digital Articles* p2 Jl 8 2016

When You Need Sales Specialists, Not Sales Generalists *Harvard Business Review Digital Articles* p2 F 18 2016

Kovac, Mirko

Beyond Schrödinger's cat color *Science* v355 no6322 p253 Ja 20 2017

Mechanized creatures color *Science* v355 no6332 p1379 Mr 31 2017

Kovach, Robert

How Tribalism Hurts Companies, and What to Do About It *Harvard Business Review Digital Articles* p2 Jl 26 2017

Kovačić, Damir

Community network for deaf scientists color *Science* v356 no6336 p386 Ap 28 2017

Kovacs, G.

Rosetta's comet 67P/Churyumov-Gerasimenko sheds its dusty mantle to reveal its icy nature bibl graph *Science* v354 no6319 p1566 D 23 2016

Surface changes on comet 67P/Churyumov-Gerasimenko suggest a more active past bw graph *Science* v355 no6332 p1392 Mr 31 2017

Kovacs, Kit M.

The broad footprint of climate change from genes to biomes to people bibl chart color *Science* v354 no6313 paaf7671-1 N 11 2016

KOVEL, ANNA

fast & fresh color *Better Homes & Gardens* v95 no10 p114 O 2017

FAST & FRESH color *Better Homes & Gardens* v95 no2 p76 F 2016

FAST & FRESH color *Better Homes & Gardens* v95 no4 p98 Ap 2017

FAST & FRESH color *Better Homes & Gardens* v95 no7 p114 Jl 2017

Kovich, Kate

How Every Hospital Should Start the Day *Harvard Business Review Digital Articles* p2 D 5 2014

Kovind, Ram Nath, 1945-

The Low-Caste Farmer's Son Taking High Office In India N. Kumar color *Time* v190 no5 p15 Jl 31 2017

Kowal, Joseph

Producer prices, 2016: goods inflation returns and price increases for services move higher bibl chart color graph *Monthly Labor Review* p1 Mr 2017

Kowalewski, Dan

Blockchain Will Transform Customer Loyalty Programs *Harvard Business Review Digital Articles* p2 Mr 14 2017

Kowalewski, Michaż

Increase in predator-prey size ratios throughout the Phanerozoic history of marine ecosystems diag *Science* v356 no6343 p1178 Je 16 2017

Kowalinski, Eva

The cryo-EM structure of a ribosome–Ski2-Ski3-Ski8 helicase complex bibl color graph *Science* v354 no6318 p1431 D 16 2016

Kowalski, David

David Kowalski *Atlanta* v57 no2 p42 Je 2017

Kowalski, Joel

CHASING THE DREAM WAVE D. Jackson color *Canoe & Kayak Magazine* v45 no1 p25 Wint 2017

Kowitt, Beth

100 FASTEST-GROWING COMPANIES chart color diag map *Fortune* v176 no4 p157 S 15 2017

THE 2017 Fortune Crystal Ball color diag *Fortune* v174 no7 p11 D 1 2016

APPLE REBOOTS IN CHINA color *Fortune* v176 no5 p106 O 1 2017

As Oceans Rise, Insurers Flee color *Fortune* v176 no2 p18 Ag 1 2017

BIG FOOD'S MASS CEO EXODUS color *Fortune* v176 no4 p138 S 15 2017

THE BLACK CEILING color *Fortune* v176 no5 p94 O 1 2017

BOXED IN color diag *Fortune* v176 no5 p86 O 1 2017

CHANGE THE WORLD !!!! color diag map *Fortune* v176 no4 p74 S 15 2017

The Deal That Made an Industry Shudder color diag *Fortune* v176 no1 p7 Jl 1 2017

DREAM WEAVER color *Fortune* v176 no3 p74 S 1 2017

The Food Industry's Urgent Question: What Is Milk? color *Fortune* v176 no3 p17 S 1 2017

FOOD TECH'S NEW BUZZWORD: "FERMENTATION" color *Fortune* v175 no5 p15 Ap 1 2017

FORTY UNDER FORTY 2017 color *Fortune* v176 no3 p62 S 1 2017

HOWARD SCHULTZ HAS SOMETHING LEFT TO PROVE chart color *Fortune* v175 no8 p114 Je 15 2017

IT ISN'T EASY BEING GREEN color *Fortune* v174 no7 p100 D 1 2016

LOW ALCOHOL COULD MEAN HIGH PERCENTAGE GROWTH color *Fortune* v176 no5 p33 O 1 2017

MINING COMEDY GOLD color *Fortune* v176 no3 p70 S 1 2017

MOST POWERFUL WOMEN color *Fortune* v176 no5 p54 O 1 2017

MOST POWERFUL WOMEN INTERNATIONAL color *Fortune* v176 no5 p111 O 1 2017

THE QUEEN OF POP [Cover story] color diag *Fortune* v176 no5 p70 O 1 2017

The Rise of the Ailment Shopper diag *Fortune* v174 no6 p14 N 1 2016

SUGAR RUSH color diag *Fortune* v175 no3 p102 Mr 1 2017

TECH TAKEOVER IN TOYLAND color diag *Fortune* v176 no5 p76 O 1 2017

WANTED: FRESH SOLUTIONS FOR AGE-OLD PROBLEMS color diag *Fortune* v175 no6 p68 My 1 2017

WORLD'S 50 GREATEST LEADERS [Cover story] color *Fortune* v175 no5 p46 Ap 1 2017

YOUTH REVOLT color *Fortune* v176 no3 p64 S 1 2017

Koyama, Motomichi

Bone-like crack resistance in hierarchical metastable nanolaminate steels bibl color diag *Science* v355 no6329 p1055 Mr 10 2017

Koz, Rich

RICH KOZ B. Zehme color *Chicago* v66 no10 p152 O 2017

KOZAK, JANET

Muslims in the Halls of Justice *Islamic Horizons* v45 no6 p46 N/D 2016

no16 p22 O 6 2017

Krakowski, Jane, 1968-

Sound Bites color *Entertainment Weekly* no1474/1475 p4 Jl 21-28 2017

Král, Kamil

Plant diversity increases with the strength of negative density dependence at the global scale diag *Science* v356 no6345 p1389 Je 30 2017

Kramer, Andrea S.

Are U.S. Millennial Men Just as Sexist as Their Dads? *Harvard Business Review Digital Articles* p2 Je 15 2016

Why Women Feel More Stress at Work *Harvard Business Review Digital Articles* p2 Ag 4 2016

Kramer, David

Atmospheric research in the Rocky Mountain foothills: As an NSF-funded center approaches its 60th birthday, scientific and fiscal challenges lie ahead *Physics Today* v70 no8 p32 Ag 2017

Biology leads the race to turn sunlight into fuels *Physics Today* v70 no4 p30 Ap 2017

Breakthrough battery hinged on funding from program in Trump's crosshairs *Physics Today* v70 no6 p34 Je 2017

Can a trusting relationship between DOE and its labs be restored? *Physics Today* v70 no3 p27 Mr 2017

Cleanup of Cold War nuclear waste drags on: Despite billions of dollars spent preparing to treat and stabilize liquid radioactive wastes, cleaning out leaking tanks at the former nuclear production site in Hanford, Washington, will take decades more *Physics Today* v70 no7 p28 Jl 2017

Climate change in the Arctic accelerates: Improved models, new icebreakers, and more observations are needed to gauge global effects of the polar region's diminishing ice cover *Physics Today* v70 no9 p24 S 2017

Clinton and Trump: Where do they stand on science? *Physics Today* v69 no10 p24 O 2016

Effort in asteroid defense under way despite funding constraints *Physics Today* v70 no2 p31 F 2017

Erratic helium prices create research havoc *Physics Today* v70 no1 p26 Ja 2017

First physicist in Congress dies *Physics Today* v70 no10 p38 O 2017

The Gathering Storms till looms *Physics Today* v69 no11 p29 N 2016

High-energy-density science blooms at NIF *Physics Today* v70 no2 p33 F 2017

Hydrogen-powered vehicles: A chicken and egg problem: Although the cost of fuel cells has rapidly decreased, the lack of a fueling infrastructure limits their use in vehicles *Physics Today* v70 no9 p31 S 2017

Illinois budget impasse damaging state universities *Physics Today* v70 no6 p32 Je 2017

MINIATURIZED GPS COLLARS, SOPHISTICATED DNA MAPPING, AND CROWDSOURCED DATA ARE CHANGING THE WAY WE MANAGE OUR WILDLIFE cartoon color *Outdoor Life* v224 no2 p50 F/Mr 2017

Nevada and Trump administration face off over Yucca Mountain *Physics Today* v70 no10 p32 O 2017

President Obama's science legacy is big on climate change and clean energy *Physics Today* v69 no12 p26 D 2016

Steady, strong growth is expected for open-access journals *Physics Today* v70 no5 p24 My 2017

White House science adviser talks space, climate change, and budgets *Physics Today* v69 no10 p27 O 2016

With Trump in charge, uncharted waters lie ahead for science *Physics Today* v70 no1 p29 Ja 2017

KRAMER, GARY M.

"Only Tell the Best Stories" color *Publishers Weekly* v264 no31 p72 Jl 31 2017

KRAMER, JANE

THE PLOT THICKENS cartoon color *New Yorker* v93 no20 p78 Jl 10 2017

Kramer, Jennifer Blaise

One Room, Two Ways color *Good Housekeeping* v264 no6 p43 Je 2017

Kramer, Julia

Bon Appetit Best New Restaurants 2017 [Cover story] color *Bon Appetit* p99 S 2017

fish out of water color *Bon Appetit* v62 no2 p50 Mr 2017

FOREST TO TABLE bw color *Bon Appetit* v62 no6 p98 Je 2017

OLD CHiNESE IS THE NEIII CHiNESə [Cover story] color *Bon Appetit* p114 S 2017

r.s.v.p.: BEST NEW RESTAURANTS EDITION bw color *Bon Appetit* p16 S 2017

r.s.v.p cartoon *Bon Appetit* v62 no2 p14 Mr 2017

The Second Coming of the Schnecken *Bon Appetit* v61 no12 p82 D 2016 /Jan2017

SECOND to NONE [Cover story] bw color *Bon Appetit* p134 S 2017

starters bw color diag *Bon Appetit* v62 no2 p19 Mr 2017

starters color *Bon Appetit* p25 S 2017

Kramer, Karen

SHARED AUTHORITY bw *Art in America* p76 O 2017

Kramer, Kirk

Nonprofits Can't Keep Ignoring Talent Development *Harvard Business Review Digital Articles* p2 D 17 2015

Kramer, Laura Shapiro

Scouting Report color *Publishers Weekly* v264 no17 p44 Ap 24 2017

Kramer, Mark R.

How Big Business Created the Politics of Anger *Harvard Business Review Digital Articles* p2 Mr 8 2016

Kramer, Peter

16 LIFE LESSONS *Psychology Today* v49 no5 p62 S/O 2016

Kramer, Peter D.

Listening to Patients D. Healy color *Issues in Science & Technology* v33 no2 p92 Wint 2017

Kramer, Sara

CHANGING COURSE T. Adler color *Vogue* v207 no9 p724 S 2017

Kramm, J.-R.

Surface changes on comet 67P/Churyumov-Gerasimenko suggest a more active past bw graph *Science* v355 no6332 p1392 Mr 31 2017

Kramm, R.

Rosetta's comet 67P/Churyumov-Gerasimenko sheds its dusty mantle to reveal its icy nature bibl graph *Science* v354 no6319 p1566 D 23 2016

Krammer, Florian

Enhancement of Zika virus pathogenesis by preexisting antiflavivirus immunity graph *Science* v356 no6334 p175 Ap 14 2017

Kranish, Michael

The Real Trump M. Danner color *New York Review of Books* v63 no20 p8 D 22 2016

Kranz, Holly

The Clinic PHOTO CRITIQUES S. von Dietze color *Dressage Today* v23 no8 p22 Ap 2017

Kranz, Maciej

Success with the Internet of Things Requires More Than Chasing the Cool Factor *Harvard Business Review Digital Articles* p2 Ag 7 2017

Kranz, Sven A.

The complex effects of ocean acidification on the prominent N2-fixing cyanobacterium Trichodesmium graph *Science* v356 no6337 p527 My 5 2017

Krapcha, Elisa

This Is Our Time color *Glamour* v115 no7 p14 Jl 2017

Krar, Rob

SO FAR. SO GOOD K. VAUGHN *Arizona Highways* v93 no1 p40 Ja 2017

Krasemann, Susanne

A pathogenic role for T cell–derived IL-22BP in inflammatory bowel disease bibl graph *Science* v354 no6310 p358 O 21 2016

Krasikov, Sana

Back to the U.S.S.R T. Donnellan color *America* v216 no8 p46 Ap 17 2017

The Future Wasn't There WYNN WHELDON *Commentary* v143 no1 p61 Ja 2017

Mad, Democrats? Blame the Iran Deal *Commentary* v143 no1 p1 Ja 2017

Moscow Believes in Tears N. RICH color *New York Times Book Review* p11 Ja 29 2017

Krasner, Stephen D.

Introduction *Daedalus* v146 no4 p6 Fall 2017

Krasnow, Mark A.
Breathing control center neurons that promote arousal in mice
diag graph *Science* v355 no6332 p1411 Mr 31 2017

Krasny, Michael
JEWISH HUMOR P. KEEPNEWS *New York Times Book Review*
p49 D 4 2016

Krasovskii, Eugene E.
Angular momentum–induced delays in solid-state photoemission
enhanced by intra-atomic interactions chart color graph *Science*
v357 no6357 p1274 S 22 2017

Krastev, Ivan
After Europe A. Moravcsik *Foreign Affairs* v96 no6 p161 N/D
2017

KRATOCHWILL, LINDSEY
The End of the Language Barrier color *Popular Science* v288 no6
p84 N/D 2016
Next color *Popular Science* v288 no6 p24 N/D 2016

Kratom
IS KRATOM A DEADLY DRUG Or A Life-Saving Medicine? B.
GRULEY cartoon color *Bloomberg Businessweek* no4503 p54
D 12 2016
IS KRATOM THE NEW MARIJUANA? J. SULLUM color *Reason* v48 no8 p8 Ja 2017

KRATTENMAKER, TOM
THE NEW SECULAR MOMENT *Humanist* v77 no2 p16 Mr/
Ap 2017

Kratz, Jessie
The Bill of Right *Prologue* v48 no4 p34 Wint 2016
Electrious and the ELECTORAL COLLEGE *Prologue* v48 no3
p34 Fall 2016
The FIRST RECORDS *Prologue* v49 no2 p40 Summ 2017
The National Archives' ROLE IN Amending the Constitution *Prologue* v49 no1 p32 Spr 2017

Krauland, Konrad
ADVANCES IN FISHING LINE THAT WILL CHANGE THE
WAY WE FISH T. KUHN color *Outdoor Life* v224 no2 p47 F/
Mr 2017

Kraus, Chris
A FEMALE ANTIHERO E. BLAIR cartoon color *New Yorker*
v92 no38 p42 N 21 2016

Kraus, Chris—Interviews
Chris KRAUS L. JAMISON *Interview* v47 no6 p18 Ag 2017

Kraus, Karl, 1874-1936
Kraus Revisited A. Valiunas bw color *Weekly Standard* v22 no24
p41 F 27 2017

Kraus, Laurie
Post-traumatic ministry [Cover story] color *Christian Century*
v134 no7 p22 Mr 29 2017

Krause, Bernie
Call of the Wild color *O, The Oprah Magazine* p26 F 2017

Krause, Johannes
Genomic estimation of complex traits reveals ancient maize adaptation to temperate North America diag *Science* v357 no6350
p512 Ag 4 2017

Krause, Kea
SPECIAL EXPERIENCE *Lapham's Quarterly* v10 no2 p192 Spr
2017

Krause, Kenneth W.
The Delectable Myths of Healthy and Healthier Obesity *Skeptical
Inquirer* v41 no2 p33 Mr/Ap 2017
On Obesity S. Vyse *Skeptical Inquirer* v40 no6 p64 N/D 2016

Krause, Louisa
Nothing Scares Louisa Krause J. Harman color *Glamour* v115
no11 p41 N 2017

Krause, Peter, 1965-
A Lighter Touch L. Rice color *Entertainment Weekly* no1456 p30
Mr 10 2017

Krause, R.
Observation of a large-scale anisotropy in the arrival directions
of cosmic rays above 8 × 1018 eV *Science* v357 no6357 p1266
S 22 2017

Krauss, Alison, 1971-
ALISON KRAUSS M. Vain *Entertainment Weekly* no1446/1447
p72 D 2016/Ja 2017

Krauss, Lawrence
The Amazing Cosmos of Gravitational Waves K. Frazier *Skeptical*

Inquirer v41 no2 p14 Mr/Ap 2017
A COSMIC CONTROVERSY color *Scientific American* v317
no1 p5 Jl 2017
The Greatest Story Ever Told—So Far: Why Are We Here? *Publishers Weekly* v264 no2 p53 Ja 9 2017
Stranger than fiction M. Livio color *Science* v355 no6331 p1273
Mr 24 2017

KRAUSS, MARGARET J.
Funny FiLL-IN *National Geographic Kids* no468 p30 Mr 2017

Krauss, Nicole
Home Away from Home J. BUNTIN color *Publishers Weekly*
v264 no34 p78 Ag 21 2017
INTO THE MULTIVERSE S. HALPERN color *Nation* v305
no10 p32 O 23 2017
THE SEEKERS R. Makkai color *O, The Oprah Magazine* p96
O 2017
Two Places at Once P. Orner *New York Times Book Review* p1 S
17 2017

Krauss, Nicole—Interviews
By the Book *New York Times Book Review* p8 S 10 2017

Kräusslich, Hans-Georg
The structure and flexibility of conical HIV-1 capsids determined
within intact virions bibl color *Science* v354 no6318 p1434 D
16 2016

Krauthammer, Daniel
What Makes America Great? [Cover story] color *Weekly Standard*
v22 no33 p26 My 8 2017

Krauze, Enrique
Mexico in the Full Light of Day [Cover story] bw color *New York
Review of Books* v64 no10 p48 Je 8 2017

Krav maga
GO ON STRIKE C. RUSHTON bw *Runner's World* v52 no7 p36
Ag 2017

Kravchenko, Stepan
Microsoft Isn't Feeling Any Russian Thaw *Bloomberg Businessweek* no4500 p35 N 21 2016
Putin's Rival Targets Provincial Russians color *Bloomberg Businessweek* no4517 p28 Ap 3 2017

Kravetz, Lee Daniel—Interviews
Stopping Suicdes M. GEFFNER color *Publishers Weekly* v264
no25 p104 Je 19 2017

Kravetz, Pam
Pam Kravetz A. BRANDT *Cincinnati Magazine* v50 no10 p38 Jl
2017

Kravitz, Zoë
Zoë Kravitz and Karl Glusman L. RAMZI color *Vogue* v207 no6
p58 Je 2017
Zoë Kravitz color *InStyle* v24 no9 p356 S 2017

Kravitz, Zoë—Interviews
Zoë Kravitz S. Zuckerman color *InStyle* v23 no13 p197 D 2016

Kraviz, Nina
As Is K. Sanneh cartoon *New Yorker* v93 no5 p24 Mr 20 2017

Krawcheck, Sallie
Beware the Gender Investing Gap color *Glamour* v115 no2 p74
F 2017
How Technology Can Help Close the Gender Gap color *Harvard
Business Review Digital Articles* p2 Ja 25 2017
THE IMPOSSIBLE CLIMB R. Greenfield cartoon *Bloomberg
Businessweek* no4508 p59 Ja 23 2017

Kray, Laura
When Trust Is Easily Broken, and When It's Not *Harvard Business Review Digital Articles* p2 F 17 2016

KRAYEWSKI, ED
DIAL * FOR TRUMP cartoon *Reason* v49 no1 p6 My 2017
THE PEACE PRIZE WINNER WHO WAGED WAR cartoon
Reason v48 no9 p14 F 2017

Kreamer, Anne
Not Taking Risks Is the Riskiest Career Move of All *Harvard
Business Review Digital Articles* p2 Ap 16 2015
The Rise of the Rude Hiring Manager *Harvard Business Review
Digital Articles* p2 N 3 2014

KREBS, CHARLES J.
Ecology for All R. P. KELLER *BioScience* v67 no8 p769 Ag 2017
The Effort-Outcomes Relationship in Applied Ecology: Evaluation and Implications *BioScience* v67 no9 p845 S 2017

Krebs, Josef

CAFÉ SOCIETY color *Sound & Vision* v82 no5 p67 Je 2017

CRIMINAL color *Sound & Vision* v81 no10 p70 D 2016

EYE IN THE SKY color *Sound & Vision* v81 no9 p71 N 2016

HEAT color *Sound & Vision* v82 no8 p71 O 2017

LEONARD COHEN: I'M YOUR MAN color *Sound & Vision* v82 no5 p69 Je 2017

MANCHESTER BY THE SEA color *Sound & Vision* v82 no6 p71 Jl/Ag 2017

The Night Manager chart color *Sound & Vision* v82 no1 p68 Ja 2017

NOCTURNAL ANIMALS color *Sound & Vision* v82 no6 p71 Jl/Ag 2017

OUR KIND OF TRAITOR color *Sound & Vision* v82 no3 p70 Ap 2017

WOMAN IN THE DUNES bw *Sound & Vision* v82 no4 p70 My 2017

KREBS, MITCH

Case Study: How Much Should a New CEO Shake Things Up? color il *Harvard Business Review* v95 no1 p157 Ja/F 2017

Krebs, Natalie

BIRD-DOGGING BEARS cartoon color *Outdoor Life* v224 no5 p12 Je/Jl 2017

THE COMEBACK KID color *Outdoor Life* v223 no9 p62 N 2016

Cutting Edges *Outdoor Life* v224 no2 p11 F/Mr 2017

DOUBLE JEOPARDY cartoon color *Outdoor Life* v224 no3 p12 Ap 2017

DROP SHOT cartoon color *Outdoor Life* v224 no4 p12 My 2017

Full Circles *Outdoor Life* v224 no5 p10 Je/Jl 2017

LAND CLAIMS color *Outdoor Life* v224 no4 p10 My 2017

THE MOST UNUSUAL GAME bw color *Outdoor Life* v223 no9 p14 N 2016

New electronic lure may catch too many fish; one state bans it color *Outdoor Life* v224 no3 p6 Ap 2017

OL FAMILY RECIPES bw color *Outdoor Life* v224 no9 p13 N 2017

RAPID RECOVERY *Outdoor Life* v224 no9 p32 N 2017

The Redneck Stradivari color *Outdoor Life* v224 no3 p8 Ap 2017

SECRETS OF A SCOUTMASTER color *Outdoor Life* v224 no7 pW6 S 2017

SUPER WOMAN color *Outdoor Life* v223 no9 p13 N 2016

TECH THROWBACK bw color *Outdoor Life* v224 no2 p12 F/Mr 2017

Trusty Bargains color *Outdoor Life* v224 no4 p8 My 2017

TURKEY TACTICS THROUGH THE AGES color *Outdoor Life* v224 no3 p10 Ap 2017

AN UNEXPECTED ALL-NIGHTER cartoon color *Outdoor Life* v224 no2 p13 F/Mr 2017

WAYPOINT color *Outdoor Life* v224 no2 p7 F/Mr 2017

WAYPOINT color *Outdoor Life* v224 no4 p5 My 2017

WAYPOINT color *Outdoor Life* v224 no5 p7 Je/Jl 2017

KREBSBACH, FRED

Still Resonating a Half-Century Later *USA Today Magazine* v145 no2864 p40 My 2017

Kreeft, Peter J.

A God by any other name *Christian Century* v134 no19 p24 S 13 2017

Kreeger, Keith

Q&A WITH KEITH KREEGER *Texas Monthly* v45 no1 p26 Ja 2017

Kreft, Stefan

A global map of roadless areas and their conservation status bibl color graph map *Science* v354 no6318 p1423 D 16 2016

KREICK, DIANNE

Your True Stories IN 100 WORDS color *Reader's Digest* v189 no1130 p32 My 2017

Kreimer, Julian

BENNY ANDREWS color *Art in America* v105 no3 p128 Mr 2017

DRASTIC TIMES bw color *Art in America* v105 no8 p76 S 2017

EMILY MULLIN color *Art in America* v105 no3 p124 Mr 2017

GLADYS NILSSON cartoon *Art in America* v105 no4 p112 Ap 2017

GUY GOODWIN color *Art in America* p122 O 2017

PAM GLICK *Art in America* v104 no9 p154 O 2016

SUELLEN ROCCA cartoon *Art in America* v104 no11 p121 D 2016

Kreindler, Gabriel

Citywide effects of high-occupancy vehicle restrictions: Evidence from "three-in-one" in Jakarta chart graph map *Science* v357 no6346 p89 Jl 7 2017

Kreinheder, Deanna

Ask the Biologist *New York State Conservationist* v72 no2 p31 O 2017

Kreisberg, Andrew

Superheroes Break Into Song D. HOLBROOK *TV Guide* v65 no13 p6 Mr 20 2017

Kreisel, A.

Discovery of orbital-selective Cooper pairing in FeSe diag *Science* v357 no6346 p75 Jl 7 2017

Kreiss-Tomkins, Jonathan

PIPE DREAM T. Alvarez color *Backpacker* v45 no1 p77 Ja 2017

KREITNER, RICHARD

Paterson: Alexander Hamilton's Trickle-Down City [Cover story] bw color *Nation* v304 no8 p18 Mr 13 2017

A Usable Past A conversation on Politics & History with Eric Foner color *Nation* v304 no15 p16 My 8 2017

Kreizman, Maris

This Vacation Could Save Your Life! color *Bloomberg Businessweek* no4522 p81 My 15 2017

Kremen, Claire

Merging paleobiology with conservation biology to guide the future of terrestrial ecosystems color *Science* v355 no6325 p594 F 10 2017

Kremer, M.

Observation of coherent elastic neutrino-nucleus scattering diag *Science* v357 no6356 p1123 S 15 2017

Kreml, Nancy

South Carolina Dharma Group W. J. Biddlecombe color *Tricycle: The Buddhist Review* v27 no1 p24 Fall 2017

Krentcil, Faran

Lens Crafter bw *Glamour* v115 no3 p36 Mr 2017

A Quick Lesson in Rock Herstory color *Glamour* no8 p33 Ag 2017

Wait, Platform Sneakers Are Back? [Cover story] color *Glamour* no8 p35 Ag 2017

KRESE, META

Toiling for King Cotton *In These Times* v41 no4 p22 Ap 2017

Kresge, Naomi

A Few Tweaks to Keep Pharma Profits Rolling *Bloomberg Businessweek* no4535 p15 Ag 28 2017

Germany's Maternity Wards Are Booked color graph *Bloomberg Businessweek* no4504 p16 D 19 2016

J&J Plays the Spurned Suitor cartoon *Bloomberg Businessweek* no4503 p20 D 12 2016

Kresge Foundation

THE GIFT OF LENI SINCLAIR: INTERTWINED ART, ACTIVISIM AND LOVE FOR COMMUNITY R. RAPSON *Vital Speeches of the Day* v83 no1 p21 Ja 2017

Kress, Steve

Birds of a (Faux) Feather L. FOPPICK color *Audubon* v119 no3 p14 Fall 2017

Kressel, Henry

Why the Fail-Fast Approach Isn't Right for Breakthrough Ventures *Harvard Business Review Digital Articles* p2 N 6 2015

Kretinin, A. V.

High-temperature quantum oscillations caused by recurring Bloch states in graphene superlattices color *Science* v357 no6347 p181 Jl 14 2017

Kretschmer, John—Interviews

John Kretschmer A. Schell *Sail* v48 no2 p14 F 2017

Kreuer, Dieter

FROM OUR READERS *Sky & Telescope* v133 no4 p6 Ap 2017

Kreviazuk, Chantal

Chantal Kreviazuk A. Kylie color *Canadian Geographic* v135 no6 p86 D 2015

Krichels, Jennifer

Page *Architectural Record* v205 no4 p104 Ap 2017

Studio Akkerhuis bw color *Architectural Record* v204 no12 p42 D 2016

Krichko, Kade

THE ART OF FUN bw color *Powder* v45 no5 p92 Ja 2017

AWAKENING bw color *Powder* v45 no4 p80 D 2016

COMMANDER IN CHAIN color *Powder* v45 no5 p38 Ja 2017

DRAWN OUT il *Backpacker* v45 no1 p87 Ja 2017

IF YOU BUILD IT color *Powder* v45 no3 p56 N 2016

MAGIC CARPET RIDE color *Powder* v45 no4 p52 D 2016

The Skis of the Year color *Powder* p82 S 2017

A Taste of the Far East in the Northeast color *Powder* v46 no2 p32 O 2017

TURN THIS MOTHER OUT color *Powder* v45 no4 p140 D 2016

Krieger, Dylan

Primal Wounds: A poetry collection rooted in the grotesque weaves the religious with the obscene T. SIMMONS bw *New York Times Book Review* p10 Ag 6 2017

KRIEGER, EMILY

REAL OR FAKE? *National Geographic Kids* no469 p18 Ap 2017

Krieger, Liz

BETTER SLEEP A to Z color *Good Housekeeping* v264 no3 p107 Mr 2017

BOOSTER CLUB color *O, The Oprah Magazine* p78 Ag 2017

Eat smart, waste less chart color *Yoga Journal* no295 p29 O 2017

Gold-Medal Moms *Parents* v91 no9 p22 S 2016

HEAL YOUR GUT TO LOSE WEIGHT color *Harper's Bazaar* no3654 p114 Je/Jl 2017

HOW DO I PREVENT & SURVIVE A HANG OVER color *Harper's Bazaar* no3649 p268 D 2016/Ja 2017

HOW TO PREVENT & TREAT LYME DISEASE color *Harper's Bazaar* no3653 p242 My 2017

I GOT A FACE LIFT AT 35 color *Harper's Bazaar* no3648 p220 N 2016

The Real Reason I Work Out color *Health* v31 no2 p120 Mr 2017

Under Pressure color *O, The Oprah Magazine* p100 N 2017

Your body's got something to tell you *Redbook* p92 S 2017

Kriegman, Josh

Flies on the wall D. D. Collum color *U.S. Catholic* v81 no11 p38 N 2016

No. 8 WEINER C. Nashawaty color *Entertainment Weekly* no1444/1445 p55 D 16 2016

Krigbaum, Megan

Notes from Underground color *Conde Nast Traveler* v51 no11 p118 D 2016

Krikalev, Sergei

THE LAST SOVIET CITIZEN E. BETZ bw cartoon color *Discover* v27 no10 p40 D 2016

KRIKORIAN, MARK

The Facts on Immigration color *National Review* v68 no20 p39 N 7 2016

Two Immigration Priorities color *National Review* v68 no23 p18 D 19 2016

The War over Enforcement [Cover story] diag *National Review* v69 no5 p30 Mr 20 2017

Krikorian, Raffi—Interviews

THE PROFESSIONAL PASSENGER X. HARDING color *Popular Science* v288 no6 p11 N/D 2016

Kril, Jillian J.

Site-specific phosphorylation of tau inhibits amyloid-β toxicity in Alzheimer's mice bibl graph *Science* v354 no6314 p904 N 18 2016

Krill, John

Against Big-Government Conservatism *National Review* v69 no2 p2 F 6 2017

Krimmel, Katherine

Research: Opposition to Federal Spending Is Driven by Racial Resentment *Harvard Business Review Digital Articles* p2 S 1 2017

Kring, David A.

The formation of peak rings in large impact craters bibl color graph *Science* v354 no6314 p878 N 18 2016

Kringle, Alaina

TALK color graph *Horse & Rider* v56 no2 p16 F 2017

KrioRus (Company)

Decapitate And Chill J. Dean bw *Bloomberg Businessweek* no4498 p64 N 7 2016

Kripke, Eric—Interviews

ERIC KRIPKE AND SHAWN RYAN I. RUDOLPH *TV Guide* v65 no6 p10 Ja 30 2017

KRIPLEN, NANCY

The Heroine of the FDA bw *Discover* v38 no2 p68 Mr 2017

KRISAI, LAUREN

FLORIDA CHANGES HARSH SENTENCING LAW, TOO LATE FOR MANY INMATES color *Reason* v49 no3 p48 Jl 2017

Krische, Michael J.

Metal-catalyzed reductive coupling of olefin-derived nucleophiles: Reinventing carbonyl addition diag *Science* v354 no6310 paah5133-1 O 21 2016

Ruthenium-catalyzed insertion of adjacent diol carbon atoms into C-C bonds: Entry to type II polyketides diag *Science* v357 no6353 p779 Ag 25 2017

KRISCHER, HAYLEY

Here, Kitty Kitty! *Reader's Digest* v190 no1134 p41 O 2017

Krishfield, Richard

Greater role for Atlantic inflows on sea-ice loss in the Eurasian Basin of the Arctic Ocean chart diag graph *Science* v356 no6335 p285 Ap 21 2017

KRISHNA, ANIRUDH

Demonetization in India: One More Rock in the River *Current History* v116 no789 p154 Ap 2017

Krishna, Ben A.

Neurodevelopmental protein Musashi-1 interacts with the Zika genome and promotes viral replication diag *Science* v357 no6346 p83 Jl 7 2017

Krishna, Mrinalini

THE AMERICAN DREAM IS ALIVE AND WELL...ON THE FORBES 400 color graph map *Forbes* v198 no5 p58 O 25 2016

Krishna, Priya

home & help img *New York* p96 Mr 6 2017

Krishna Kumar, R.

High-temperature quantum oscillations caused by recurring Bloch states in graphene superlattices color *Science* v357 no6347 p181 Jl 14 2017

Krishnamoorthy, Raghu

The Corporate HQ Is an Anachronism *Harvard Business Review Digital Articles* p2 Mr 13 2015

Corporate Universities Should Reflect a Company's Ideals *Harvard Business Review Digital Articles* p2 O 16 2014

GE's Culture Challenge After Welch and Immelt *Harvard Business Review Digital Articles* p2 Ja 26 2015

Krishnan, Priyanka

Divergent Realities color *Publishers Weekly* v264 no41 p26 O 9 2017

Krishnan, Unni

The ABCs of India's GST color graph *Bloomberg Businessweek* no4496 p19 O 24 2016

Krishnan, Yamuna

ATP as a biological hydrotrope color graph *Science* v356 no6339 p753 My 19 2017

Kriss, Sam

The Nakagin Capsule Tower *New York Times Magazine* p26 O 2 2016

Kristal, Marc

On the Home Front W. Moonan color *Architectural Record* v205 no5 p61 My 2017

Kristensen, Hans M.

Indian nuclear forces, 2017 bibl chart *Bulletin of the Atomic Scientists* v73 no4 p205 Jl 2017

Pakistani nuclear forces, 2016 bibl chart *Bulletin of the Atomic Scientists* v72 no6 p368 N 2016

Russian nuclear forces, 2017 bibl chart *Bulletin of the Atomic Scientists* v73 no2 p115 Mr 2017

United States nuclear forces, 2017 bibl *Bulletin of the Atomic Scientists* v73 no1 p48 Ja 2017

Worldwide deployments of nuclear weapons, 2017 bibl *Bulletin of the Atomic Scientists* v73 no5 p289 2017

Kristeva, Julia, 1941-

Tied in Knots V. GORNICK color il *New Republic* v248 no1/2 p56 Ja/F 2017

Kristinsdóttir, Ólafía Þórunn

News Roundup V. HAFSTAÐ *Iceland Review* v55 no1 p18 Ja/F 2017

ON PAR WITH NONE A. M. I. GRÍMSSON *Iceland Review* v55 no2 p14 Mr/Ap 2017

KRISTOF, KATHY

Can This Fallen Biotech Be Revived? *Kiplinger's Personal Finance* v71 no5 p61 My 2017

Don't Let Current Events Spook You *Kiplinger's Personal Finance* v71 no11 p57 N 2017

How One Bad Year Can Wreck Results color *Kiplinger's Personal Finance* v71 no7 p57 Jl 2017

I'm Still Cheering for GM and Gilead color *Kiplinger's Personal Finance* v71 no2 p61 F 2017

Is Intel's Buying Binge a Good Thing? *Kiplinger's Personal Finance* v71 no6 p54 Je 2017

A Kickstarter Business Takes Off color *Kiplinger's Personal Finance* v71 no1 p72 Ja 2017

My Portfolio's Uninvited Guests *Kiplinger's Personal Finance* v71 no1 p56 Ja 2017

A Takeover Boosts My Portfolio *Kiplinger's Personal Finance* v71 no4 p58 Ap 2017

Why Am I Lagging? Blame It on 2015 chart *Kiplinger's Personal Finance* v70 no12 p56 D 2016

Why I'm Hanging On to a Loser *Kiplinger's Personal Finance* v71 no10 p62 O 2017

Kristol, Bill

The Commentary Roast of Dan Senor *Commentary* v142 no4 p8 N 2016

Must Listening *Weekly Standard* v22 no20 p4 Ja 30 2017

Kristol, Irving, 1920-2009

The Populist Ploy W. McCORMACK il *New Republic* v248 no3 p8 Mr 2017

KRISTOL, SUSAN

Lost and Founder color *Weekly Standard* v23 no2 p38 S 18 2017

Kristol, William

After Obama *Weekly Standard* v22 no20 p8 Ja 30 2017

After Trump color *Weekly Standard* v22 no34 p6 My 15 2017

'A Sense of Responsibility' *Weekly Standard* v22 no35 p8 My 22 2017

As Time Goes By bw *Weekly Standard* v22 no43 p7 Jl 24 2017

The 'Car 54' Model bw *Weekly Standard* v22 no27 p10 Mr 20 2017

Country First bw *Weekly Standard* v22 no21 p6 F 6 2017

Critical but Not Serious *Weekly Standard* v22 no26 p8 Mr 13 2017

Dunkirk and Us bw *Weekly Standard* v22 no45 p7 Ag 7 2017

An Empire for Liberty *Weekly Standard* v23 no4 p7 O 2 2017

Generation Trump? *Weekly Standard* v22 no37 p8 Je 5 2017

Governing Matters Most color *Weekly Standard* v22 no14 p7 D 12 2016

Keep Your Panic Dry cartoon *Weekly Standard* v22 no13 p7 D 5 2016

The Long Holiday *Weekly Standard* v22 no19 p8 Ja 23 2017

The Loser *Weekly Standard* v22 no8 p6 O 31 2016

Make 50 the New 60 color *Weekly Standard* v22 no22 p6 F 13 2017

Meanwhile... *Weekly Standard* v22 no46 p9 Ag 14 2017

No Way Out But Up *Weekly Standard* v22 no5 p6 O 10 2016

Obama's Legacy color *Weekly Standard* v22 no32 p7 My 1 2017

Onward *Weekly Standard* v22 no11 p8 N 21 2016

'Our Progress in Degeneracy' bw *Weekly Standard* v22 no29 p7 Ap 3 2017

The Party of Liberty bw *Weekly Standard* v22 no16 p6 D 26 2016

A Populist-Nationalist Right? No Thanks! color *Weekly Standard* v22 no9 p7 N 7 2016

Question Time cartoon *Weekly Standard* v22 no38 p6 Je 12 2017

Remember Henry Clay bw *Weekly Standard* v22 no25 p7 Mr 6 2017

The Republican Challenge *Weekly Standard* v22 no23 p6 F 20 2017

A Republican Crackup? *Weekly Standard* v23 no6 p10 O 16 2017

The Republican Future *Weekly Standard* v22 no39 p8 Je 19 2017

The Road to Liberty *Weekly Standard* v22 no17 p7 Ja 2 2017

Speak for America *Weekly Standard* v22 no7 p10 O 24 2016

Steal the March *Weekly Standard* v22 no28 p8 Mr 27 2017

True American Greatness color *Weekly Standard* v22 no44 p8 Jl 31 2017

The Trump Administration bw color *Weekly Standard* v22 no12 p6 N 28 2016

Why Pence Matters *Weekly Standard* v22 no6 p6 O 17 2016

Wouldn't It Be Nice? *Weekly Standard* v22 no48 p8 S 4 2017

The Year's at the Spring *Weekly Standard* v22 no30 p8 Ap 10 2017

Krivak, Andrew

Bound by War R. ROBINSON color *New York Times Book Review*

p17 Ja 29 2017

Krivit, Danny

NIGHT LIFE *New Yorker* v93 no19 p6 Jl 3 2017

Krivkovich, Alexis

How CMOs and CROs Can Be Allies *Harvard Business Review Digital Articles* p2 Mr 26 2015

Krizan, Paul

OUT OF THE WILD L. Feldman color *American Cowboy* v23 no5 p50 F/Mr 2017

Kroc, Joan B., 1928-2003

BEHIND THE BUNS S. WATTS bw *Chicago* v65 no11 p26 N 2016

Kroeber, Gavin

"ENCODED" color *Art in America* v105 no4 p117 Ap 2017

ERIC WESLEY color *Art in America* v105 no3 p135 Mr 2017

Krannert Art Museum color *Art in America* v105 no6 p141 Je/Jl 2017

SUBURBAN FUTURISM bw color *Art in America* v104 no11 p106 D 2016

Kroeger, Brad

You Never Forget Your First Time diag il *Backpacker* v45 no2 p64 Mr 2017

Kroeger, Brooke

Metropolis Rising: How the Big Apple took its place among the world's great cities *American Scholar* v86 no4 p116 Aut 2017

Kroenert, Tim

Arcade Fire looks for God in a material world color *America* v217 no5 p50 S 4 2017

Kroenig, Matthew

The Case for Trump's Foreign Policy color *Foreign Affairs* v96 no3 p30 My/Je 2017

Nuclear Trash Talk cartoon *Weekly Standard* v22 no7 p18 O 24 2016

Kroes, Rob

Signs of Fascism Rising *Society* v54 no3 p218 Je 2017

KROFEL, MIHA

International Wildlife Law: Understanding and Enhancing Its Role in Conservation *BioScience* v67 no9 p784 S 2017

Krog, Karin

The Art of Mosaic-Making at Vossa Jazz J. Woodard color *Downbeat* v84 no7 p20 Jl 2017

Kroger Co.

Money in the Bag J. SerVaas *Saturday Evening Post* v289 no4 p25 Jl/Ag 2017

Krogstrup, P.

Majorana bound state in a coupled quantum-dot hybrid-nanowire system bibl graph *Science* v354 no6319 p1557 D 23 2016

Krogue, Ken

The End-of-Quarter Sales Rush Costs Companies Money *Harvard Business Review Digital Articles* p2 2017

Krohm, N.

Observation of a large-scale anisotropy in the arrival directions of cosmic rays above 8×10^{18} eV *Science* v357 no6357 p1266 S 22 2017

Krohn, Jason

OAK HAVEN FARMS G. Dearth *Arabian Horse World* v57 no12 p97 S 2017

Krolewski, Richard

Lee Rubin: Our mentor and role model *Science* v355 no6327 p806 F 24 2017

Kroll, Andy

BETTER CALL DON [Cover story] color *Mother Jones* v42 no3 p24 My/Je 2017

CHECKS AND BALANCES color *Mother Jones* v42 no4 p36 Jl/Ag 2017

GOSPEL OF THE CLIMATE DENIERS cartoon color *Rolling Stone* no1274 p24 N 17 2016

HERE COMES THE BRIBE chart color *Mother Jones* v42 no4 p8 Jl/Ag 2017

MIGHTY MORPHIN POWER PLAYER cartoon *Mother Jones* v41 no6 p46 N/D 2016

THE QUIET CRUSADER color *Rolling Stone* no1291/1292 p38 Jl 13 2017

REMOTE CONTROLLED color graph *Mother Jones* v42 no6 p48 N/D 2017

Swamp Creature cartoon *Mother Jones* v42 no1 p16 Ja/F 2017

Kroll, Luisa
The Class of 2016 cartoon chart *Forbes* v198 no5 p36 O 25 2016
LESSONS AND IDEAS BY THE 100 GREATEST LIVING BUSINESS MINDS bw color *Forbes* v200 no3 p115 S 28 2017
THE WORLD'S BILLIONAIRES bw color diag graph map *Forbes* v199 no3 p84 Mr 28 2017

Kroll, Nick
NICK KROLL D. BLASBERG color *Vanity Fair* v58 no12 p92 D 2016

Kroll, Thomas
Metalloprotein entatic control of ligand-metal bonds quantified by ultrafast x-ray spectroscopy diag *Science* v356 no6344 p1276 Je 23 2017

Kromdijk, Johannes
Improving photosynthesis and crop productivity by accelerating recovery from photoprotection bibl chart color graph *Science* v354 no6314 p857 N 18 2016

Krone, Charlene
The Charms of Chama color *Trail Rider* v29 no2 p32 Mr 2017
Great Basin Getaway [Cover story] color *Trail Rider* v29 no4 p32 My 2017
Southwest Solitude color *Horse & Rider* v56 no9 p94 S 2017
Working Vacation color *Trail Rider* v29 no3 p46 Ap 2017

KRONE, KENT
The Charms of Chama color *Trail Rider* v29 no2 p32 Mr 2017
Great Basin Getaway [Cover story] color *Trail Rider* v29 no4 p32 My 2017
PLAN. WORK. ACHIEVE K. NAVARRA color *Horse & Rider* v56 no8 p71 Ag 2017
Southwest Solitude color *Horse & Rider* v56 no9 p94 S 2017
Working Vacation color *Trail Rider* v29 no3 p46 Ap 2017

Kronman, Hope G.
Early life stress confers lifelong stress susceptibility in mice via ventral tegmental area OTX2 diag *Science* v356 no6343 p1185 Je 16 2017

Kronsberg, Matthew
Chef-spector Gadget color *Bloomberg Businessweek* no4516 p63 Mr 27 2017

Kronschläger, M. T.
Gliogenic LTP spreads widely in nociceptive pathways bibl graph *Science* v354 no6316 p1144 D 2 2016

Kropff, M. J.
Improving global integration of crop research color *Science* v357 no6349 p359 Jl 28 2017

Kroposki, Benjamin
Terawatt-scale photovoltaics: Trajectories and challenges chart graph *Science* v356 no6334 p141 Ap 14 2017

Kropp, Delia—Interviews
A STAR IS REBORN N. PARSI color *Chicago* v65 no11 p37 N 2016

Krosner, Yudit C.
Delivering Higher Value Care Means Spending More Time with Patients *Harvard Business Review Digital Articles* p2 D 26 2014

Krosnick, Jon
Contingent valuation: Flawed logic? color *Science* v357 no6349 p363 Jl 28 2017
Putting a value on injuries to natural assets: The BP oil spill chart *Science* v356 no6335 p253 Ap 21 2017

Kross, Ethan
How "you" makes meaning bibl diag graph *Science* v355 no6331 p1299 Mr 24 2017
Pronouns Matter when Psyching Yourself Up *Harvard Business Review Digital Articles* p2 F 6 2015

KROWIAK, SUZANNE
Against the Grain *Indianapolis Monthly* v40 no7 p39 Mr 2017
ALL THE THINGS *Indianapolis Monthly* v40 no4 p54 D 2016
BEARING FRUIT: In Bill Weghorst's world, one great Honeysmith always beats a bag full of garden-variety produce color *Indianapolis Monthly* v41 no2 p42 S 2017
Best New Restaurants *Indianapolis Monthly* p58 My 2017
best of Indy *Indianapolis Monthly* v40 no4 p73 D 2016
Branching Out *Indianapolis Monthly* v40 no3 p54 N 2016
Business Perks *Indianapolis Monthly* v40 no4 p52 D 2016
CITIZEN CANE: Chris Coy gets a little tiki behind the bar at The Inferno Room, opening this fall *Indianapolis Monthly* v12 no40 p46 Ag 2017

Crust Belt *Indianapolis Monthly* p37 F 2017
CSA CONFIDENTIAL: If you've splurged on a COMMUNITY SUPPORTED AGRICULTURE membership, take these simple steps to protect your investment. Because thyme is money *Indianapolis Monthly* v12 no40 p65 Ag 2017
Feather in His Cap *Indianapolis Monthly* v40 no5 p37 Ja 2017
FLOUR GIRL: Head baker Jessica Flores is a rising star at Open Society Public House *Indianapolis Monthly* v40 no11 p40 Jl 2017
Fry Away *Indianapolis Monthly* v40 no10 p39 Je 2017
HAIL TO THE CHEESE *Indianapolis Monthly* p47 N 2017
The HOOSIER KITCHEN *Indianapolis Monthly* v12 no40 p60 Ag 2017
HOW TO HUNT AND GUT YOUR OWN DINNER ... AND OTHER LIFE LESSONS FROM A HOOSIER KITCHEN RENAISSANCE WOMAN *Indianapolis Monthly* v12 no40 p72 Ag 2017
LOCAL FLAVOR: Kimbal Musk considers Indy fertile ground for continuing his food fight *Indianapolis Monthly* v40 no10 p42 Je 2017
NEW COURSE: A fresh start awaits pastry chef Pete Schmutte after five years spent preparing finales at Cerulean *Indianapolis Monthly* p48 N 2017
NEW JAM *Indianapolis Monthly* p42 My 2017
RAW-RAH! *Indianapolis Monthly* v40 no3 p52 N 2016
Rebel Yell color *Indianapolis Monthly* p42 Ap 2017
RISING STARS: The humble biscuit goes big-time color *Indianapolis Monthly* v41 no2 p41 S 2017
Sour Power color *Indianapolis Monthly* p41 Ap 2017
Spice Girl *Indianapolis Monthly* p43 F 2017
Steaking His Claim *Indianapolis Monthly* v40 no7 p42 Mr 2017
TAKING FLIGHT color *Indianapolis Monthly* v42 no2 p44 O 2017
Toast of the Town color *Indianapolis Monthly* v42 no2 p41 O 2017
TOP PICKS *Indianapolis Monthly* v12 no40 p62 Ag 2017
What a Catch! *Indianapolis Monthly* v40 no11 p37 Jl 2017

Krucoff, Carol
Lovely BONES color *Yoga Journal* p60 2017 Special Issue
TAKE A SEAT color *Yoga Journal* p62 2017 Special Issue

Krueger, Alan B.
Documenting decline in U.S. economic mobility graph *Science* v356 no6336 p382 Ap 28 2017

Krueger, Joachim I.
16 LIFE LESSONS *Psychology Today* v49 no5 p62 S/O 2016

Krueger, Roland
Roland Krueger A. Priddle color *Motor Trend* v69 no8 p32 Ag 2017

Krueger, Shawn
Artist Shawn Krueger B. D. Coleman color *Arts & Crafts Homes & the Revival* v12 no5 p48 Wint 2018

Kruesi, Liz
Close encounters with the RINGED PLANET bw color diag *Astronomy* v45 no10 p28 O 2017
The cosmic bullies next door color *Astronomy* v45 no7 p28 Jl 2017
A Dark Milky Way color *Discover* v38 no1 p78 Ja/F 2017
GALAXY CLUSTERS The universe's cosmic lenses color diag graph *Astronomy* v45 no2 p28 F 2017
I'll have a Cosmo cartoon color *Astronomy* v44 no12 p58 D 2016
Missing Matter Found color *Discover* v38 no7 p70 S 2017
SUPERNOVA 1987A 30 years later color *Astronomy* v45 no3 p28 Mr 2017
Top 10 space stories of 2016 [Cover story] color *Astronomy* v45 no1 p18 Ja 2017

Krüger, Anneke
Braiding a molecular knot with eight crossings bibl diag graph *Science* v355 no6321 p1 Ja 13 2017

Kruger, Diane, 1976-
Hello! L. Brown color *InStyle* v24 no11 p30 N 2017
jason × diane E. Wilson color *InStyle* v24 no11 p166 N 2017
Short Stories E. Wilson color *InStyle* v24 no5 p70 My 2017

Krüger, Rejko
Dopamine oxidation mediates mitochondrial and lysosomal dysfunction in Parkinson's disease graph *Science* v357 no6357 p1255 S 22 2017

Kruglyak, Leonid
A genetic signature of the evolution of loss of flight in the Galapa-

gos cormorant color diag *Science* v356 no6341 p921 Je 1 2017

A maternal-effect selfish genetic element in Caenorhabditis elegans diag *Science* v356 no6342 p1051 Je 9 2017

KRUGMAN, PAUL

All That's Left *New York Times Book Review* p12 My 7 2017

Kruip, Jochen

Trispecific broadly neutralizing HIV antibodies mediate potent SHIV protection in macaques color graph *Science* v357 no6359 p85 O 6 2017

Krulak, Charles

Chanukah around the South *Successful Farming* v115 no1 p20 Ja 2017

KRULWICH, DAVID

Alternatives to Workshops *Education Digest* v82 no6 p38 F 2017

Krummel, Matthew F.

Visualizing dynamic microvillar search and stabilization during ligand detection by T cells color *Science* v356 no6338 p598 My 12 2017

Krupat, Arnold

Companion to James Welch's "The Heartsong of Charging Elk." L. R. Cooper *American Indian Quarterly* v41 no2 p182 Spr 2017

Krupenye, Christopher

Great apes anticipate that other individuals will act according to false beliefs bibl chart diag graph *Science* v354 no6308 p110 O 7 2016

Krupic, Julija

Wire together, fire apart diag *Science* v357 no6355 p974 S 8 2017

Krupnick, Alan

Reforming the U.S. coal leasing program color graph *Science* v354 no6316 p1096 D 2 2016

Krupp, Fred

Trump and the Environment color *Foreign Affairs* v96 no4 p73 Jl/Ag 2017

Kruse, Carl

HACKER CRACK-UP color *Wired* v25 no6 p10 Je 2017

Kruse-Peeples, Melissa

Genomic estimation of complex traits reveals ancient maize adaptation to temperate North America diag *Science* v357 no6350 p512 Ag 4 2017

Kruss GmbH

ECO-FRIENDLY AND HEALTHY color *Iceland Review* v54 no5 p93 S-O 2016

Kruuk, Loeske E. B.

Precipitation drives global variation in natural selection bibl chart diag map *Science* v355 no6328 p959 Mr 3 2017

Krylon Inc.

KRYLON CAMO T. FREEL and A. McKEAN bw color *Outdoor Life* v224 no5 p94 Je/Jl 2017

Krynicki, Ryszard, 1943-

Magnetic Point: Selected Poems C. SIMIC bw *Publishers Weekly* v264 no38 p51 S 18 2017

Krypton (TV program)

KRYPTON D. Franich color *Entertainment Weekly* p24 Jl 24 2017

Krysl, Terri

Mother Nature's Quilt color *Nebraska Life* v21 no5 p45 S/O 2017

Krysztof, David

Enhancement of Zika virus pathogenesis by preexisting antiflavivirus immunity graph *Science* v356 no6334 p175 Ap 14 2017

Krzentowski, Clémence—Interviews

Galerie Kreo H. MARTIN bw color *Architectural Digest* no5 p30 My 2017

Krzentowski, Didier—Interviews

Galerie Kreo H. MARTIN bw color *Architectural Digest* no5 p30 My 2017

Krzykowski, Matylda

MATYLDA KRZYKOWSKI *Interview* v46 no9 p28 N 2016

Krzywonos, Henryka

The Rise of the Dwarf P. CYWIŃSKI *American Conservative* v16 no2 p36 Mr/Ap 2017

Krzyzanowski, Marek K.

Aggregation of the Whi3 protein, not loss of heterochromatin, causes sterility in old yeast cells bibl diag *Science* v355 no6330 p1184 Mr 17 2017

Krzyzewski, Mike, 1947——Interviews

Life's Work: An Interview with Mike Krzyzewski A. Beard bw

Harvard Business Review v95 no2 p164 Mr/Ap 2017

KS USA (Company)

KS LEV CI R. Palmer color *Bike Magazine* v24 no2 p84 Mr 2017

Ksionzek, Kerstin B.

Dissolved organic sulfur in the ocean: Biogeochemistry of a petagram inventory bibl chart diag graph *Science* v354 no6311 p456 O 28 2016

Genomic databases: A WHO affair *Science* v356 no6340 p812 My 26 2017

Kteily, Nour

Why CEOs Can't Stay Silent in the Wake of Events Like Charlottesville *Harvard Business Review Digital Articles* p2 2017

KTM motorcycle—Evaluation

THE BEAST 2.0 B. Adams color *Cycle World* v56 no2 p52 Mr 2017

ENDURO ESCAPE J. Bradshaw color *Cycle World* v55 no10 p52 N 2016

MAKING IT S. MacDonald chart color *Cycle World* v55 no10 p38 N 2016

KTM-Sportmotorcycle AG

2017 KTM 1090 ADVENTURE R B. Adams color *Cycle World* v56 no5 p44 Je 2017

HIGH ADVENTURE D. Canet color *Cycle World* v55 no10 p16 N 2016

Kuan, Debora

Lunch Portraits *Publishers Weekly* v263 no47 p86 N 21 2016

Kuang, Zheng

Bug mapping and fitness testing of chemically synthesized chromosome X diag *Science* v355 no6329 p1048 Mr 10 2017

Engineering the ribosomal DNA in a megabase synthetic chromosome diag *Science* v355 no6329 p1049 Mr 10 2017

The intestinal microbiota regulates body composition through NFIL3 and the circadian clock diag *Science* v357 no6354 p912 S 1 2017

"Perfect" designer chromosome V and behavior of a ring derivative diag *Science* v355 no6329 p1046 Mr 10 2017

Synthesis, debugging, and effects of synthetic chromosome consolidation: synVI and beyond color *Science* v355 no6329 p1045 Mr 10 2017

Kubacki, Kevin

The Pros and Cons of Federally Funded School Choice Programs *Congressional Digest* v96 no7 p12 S 2017

KUBE, KATHI

Frogs cartoon color *Discover* v27 no10 p74 D 2016

Kubes, Paul

Visualizing the function and fate of neutrophils in sterile injury and repair color graph *Science* v357 no6359 p111 O 6 2017

Kubitz, Michael

Priming HIV-1 broadly neutralizing antibody precursors in human Ig loci transgenic mice bibl graph *Science* v353 no6307 p1557 S 30 2016

Kubo, Masato

The intestinal microbiota regulates body composition through NFIL3 and the circadian clock diag *Science* v357 no6354 p912 S 1 2017

Kubo and the Two Strings (Film)

The Unfolding Story T. J. Norton color *Sound & Vision* v82 no3 p66 Ap 2017

KUBOTA, TYSON

Choose Wisely color *Film Comment* v52 no6 p20 N/D 2016

Kubrick, Stanley, 1928-1999

DR. STRANGELOVE F. Kaplan bw color *Sound & Vision* v81 no9 p71 N 2016

THE SHINING J. Hibberd color *Entertainment Weekly* no1460/1461 p44 Ap 7-17 2017

Kućan, Željko

Neandertal and Denisovan DNA from Pleistocene sediments bw color *Science* v356 no6338 p605 My 12 2017

Kuchar, Matt

Watch + Learn C. O'connell and C. Barrett color *Golf Magazine* v58 no11 p30 N 2016

Kucharski, Joe

Curating the Character's Closet *Stage Directions* v30 no8 p20 Ag 2017

Digital Weaving *Stage Directions* v30 no5 p18 My 2017

Kucharski, Timothy J.

Experimentally realized mechanochemistry distinct from force-accelerated scission of loaded bonds diag graph *Science* v357 no6348 p299 Jl 21 2017

Kuchibhotla, Srinivas

MURDER IN THE HEARTLAND L. SMILEY bw color map *Wired* v25 no7 p72 Jl 2017

Kuchler, Fred

Increased Consumer Sensitivity to Food Safety Raised Financial Costs of Ground Beef Recalls *Amber Waves: The Economics of Food, Farming, Natural Resources, & Rural America* p1 O 2016

Kuchler, Sebastian

In the Best Sales Teams, About Half of the People Are in Support Roles *Harvard Business Review Digital Articles* p2 My 25 2016

Kuchler, William

Nuclear Power and Risk Psychology *Skeptical Inquirer* v41 no2 p64 Mr/Ap 2017

Kuchment, Anna

Man-Made Solutions for Man-Made Quakes color *Scientific American* v316 no2 p10 F 2017

Kuczynski, Alex

CAN A DNA TEST GIVE YOU A BETTER BODY? color *Harper's Bazaar* no3656 p468 S 2017

Copycats and Confidantes: Friendship or identity theft? In a French best seller, it's hard to tell *New York Times Book Review* p11 Jl 2 2017

School's Over *New York Times Book Review* p20 N 6 2016

Kuczynski, Doug

ILLUMINATED PRIVACY SCREEN color *Cabin Living* p58 Mr 2017

RUSTIC CEDAR PICKET SIGN color *Cabin Living* p62 Ag 2017

Kuczynski Godard, Pedro-Pablo, 1938-

Peru Is a Bright Spot on the Global Stage I. Bremmer color *Time* v188 no24 p19 D 12 2016

Kudacki, Andres

The Ethics of Watching Gymnastics img *New York* v49 no15 p54 Jl 25 2016

Kudaravalli, Sri

How to Get Experts to Work Together Effectively *Harvard Business Review Digital Articles* p2 My 10 2017

Kuder, Pat

Dear Readers B. Kelly *Reader's Digest* v188 no1124 p4 O 2016

Kuderna, Lukas F. K.

Ancient genomic changes associated with domestication of the horse color diag *Science* v356 no6336 p442 Ap 28 2017

Chimpanzee genomic diversity reveals ancient admixture with bonobos bibl diag graph map *Science* v354 no6311 p477 O 28 2016

Kudinha, Timothy

A brief overview of matrix-assisted laser desorption/ionization time-of-flight mass spectrometry (MALDI-TOF MS) applications in clinical microbiology in China *Science* v354 no6319 p55 D 23 2016

Kudisch, Erica

Don't Feed the Trolls *Publishers Weekly* v264 no9 p84 F 27 2017

Kudlow, Lawrence

The Ture-Kennedy Blueprint I. BRANNON *National Review* v69 no9 p37 My 15 2017

Kudrow, Lisa, 1963——Interviews

Lisa Kudrow E. Berman color *Time* v189 no10 p51 Mr 20 2017

KUEFFER, CHRISTOPH

Scientific and Normative Foundations for the Valuation of Alien-Species Impacts: Thirteen Core Principles *BioScience* v67 no2 p166 F 2017

Kuehl, Sheila James, 1941-

L.A. Women LEAD THE WAY N. L. COHEN and J. M. PIS-COPO *Ms.* v27 no1 p32 Spr 2017

Kuehler, Darin

Code and Coops *Stage Directions* v30 no2 p28 F 2017

KUEHN, STEFFEN

Latin Lead Trumpet vs. Jazz Soloist: Developing Different Concepts color *Downbeat* v84 no6 p82 Je 2017

Kuehne, Ana I.

A "Trojan horse" bispecific-antibody strategy for broad protection against ebolaviruses bibl graph *Science* v354 no6310 p350 O 21 2016

Kuehnle, Nathalie

UBE2O remodels the proteome during terminal erythroid differentiation diag *Science* v357 no6350 p471 Ag 4 2017

Kuehrt, E.

Seasonal exposure of carbon dioxide ice on the nucleus of comet 67P/Churyumov-Gerasimenko bibl bw graph *Science* v354 no6319 p1563 D 23 2016

Kuemmerle, Tobias

Forest conservation: Remember Gran Chaco bibl color *Science* v355 no6324 p465 F 3 2017

Kuempel, D.

Observation of a large-scale anisotropy in the arrival directions of cosmic rays above 8×1018 eV *Science* v357 no6357 p1266 S 22 2017

Kueppers, Mark

Promoting Student Academic Achievement Through Faculty Development about Inclusive Teaching *Change* v48 no5 p16 S/O 2016

Kuerten, Gustavo

WORLD ON A STRING S. TIGNOR color *Tennis* v53 no2 p42 Mr/Ap 2017

Kuh, George

REFRAMING STUDENT SUCCESS IN COLLEGE: Advancing Know-What and Know-How *Change* v49 no3 p19 My/Je 2017

KUH, PATRIC

THE BEST NEW RESTAURANTS *Los Angeles Magazine* p86 Ja 2017

Culinary Power Plants *Los Angeles Magazine* p62 D 2016

Green Giant *Los Angeles Magazine* p44 My 2017

Hot Biscuits *Los Angeles Magazine* p50 Ja 2017

How We Love To Look *Los Angeles Magazine* v61 no11 p64 N 2016

Kosher Cool color *Los Angeles Magazine* v62 no7 p36 Jl 2017

The Last Bento-Ya In Boyle Heights *Los Angeles Magazine* v62 no9 p116 S 2017

A Maestro Returns: AT FELIX IN VENICE, EVAN FUNKE ROLLS OUT SUBLIMELY REGIONAL ITALIAN FOOD color *Los Angeles Magazine* v62 no7 p38 Jl 2017

Majestic Baja *Los Angeles Magazine* v62 no6 p36 Je 2017

Man On Fire color *Los Angeles Magazine* v62 no10 p44 O 2017

Minimalist Appeal *Los Angeles Magazine* p42 Ja 2017

The New Wonder Bread *Los Angeles Magazine* p60 Mr 2017

The Nobu Effect: HOW AMERICA'S MOST INFLUENTIAL SUSHI CHEF REDEFINED JAPANESE FOOD IN L.A *Los Angeles Magazine* v62 no9 p106 S 2017

On Top of the World *Los Angeles Magazine* p58 D 2016

Pass the Mike *Los Angeles Magazine* p58 Mr 2017

The Pita Rising *Los Angeles Magazine* v62 no6 p42 Je 2017

Secret Sauce: WHAT MAKES THE BOLOGNESE AT STEVE SAMSON'S ROSSOBLU SO GOOD? *Los Angeles Magazine* v62 no9 p53 S 2017

A Side of Drama *Los Angeles Magazine* p42 F 2017

A Sugar High *Los Angeles Magazine* p50 Ap 2017

Kühl, Hjalmar

Chimpanzee genomic diversity reveals ancient admixture with bonobos bibl diag graph map *Science* v354 no6311 p477 O 28 2016

Kuhl, Joan Snyder

Research: Millennials Can't Afford to Job Hop *Harvard Business Review Digital Articles* p2 Ag 31 2016

Kuhl, Nadine

Macrocyclic bis-thioureas catalyze stereospecific glycosylation reactions bibl diag *Science* v355 no6321 p1 Ja 13 2017

Kuhl, Stephen

HOT SEATS M. HARRIS *New York Times Magazine* p64 N 13 2016

Kuhlenbeck, Mike

CHRISTIAN HEGEMONY IN THE AGE OF TRUMP *Humanist* v77 no3 p12 My/Je 2017

Kuhlman, Evan

Hank's Big Day: The Story of a Bug *Publishers Weekly* v263 no49 p12 D 7 2016

Kuhlmeier, Theodore

COMMENTS KICKIN' BACK *MHQ: Quarterly Journal of Military History* v29 no2 p10 Wint 2017

Kuhlwilm, Martin

Chimpanzee genomic diversity reveals ancient admixture with bonobos bibl diag graph map *Science* v354 no6311 p477 O 28 2016

KUHN, JENS H.
Bats and human health *Issues in Science & Technology* v33 no4 p15 Summ 2017

Kuhn, Larry
READER GALLERY color *Astronomy* v45 no1 p72 Ja 2017

Kuhn, Laura
John Cage's Gift to Us T. Page bw *New York Review of Books* v63 no16 p42 O 27 2016

Kühn, Ralf
Loss of a mammalian circular RNA locus causes miRNA deregulation and affects brain function color *Science* v357 no6357 p1254 S 22 2017

KUHN, TODD
ADVANCES IN FISHING LINE THAT WILL CHANGE THE WAY WE FISH color *Outdoor Life* v224 no2 p47 F/Mr 2017
TACKLE TEST 2017 chart color *Outdoor Life* v224 no3 p14 Ap 2017

Kühn, Ulrich
Europe's nuclear woes: Mitigating the challenges of the next years bibl *Bulletin of the Atomic Scientists* v73 no4 p245 Jl 2017
Introduction: Nuclear disarmament and arms control for the next decade *Bulletin of the Atomic Scientists* v73 no4 p244 Jl 2017
Keine Atombombe, Bitte color *Foreign Affairs* v96 no4 p103 Jl/Ag 2017

Kuhns, Annemarie
Consumers Paid Less for Grocery Store Foods in 2016 Than in 2015 *Amber Waves: The Economics of Food, Farming, Natural Resources, & Rural America* p8 Mr 2017
Households Purchase More Produce and Low-Fat Dairy at Supermarkets, Supercenters, and Warehouse Club Stores *Amber Waves: The Economics of Food, Farming, Natural Resources, & Rural America* p1 My 2017
Percent of Income Spent on Food Falls as Income Rises *Amber Waves: The Economics of Food, Farming, Natural Resources, & Rural America* p31 S 2016
Since 2009, Restaurant Prices Have Generally Risen Faster Than Grocery Store Prices *Amber Waves: The Economics of Food, Farming, Natural Resources, & Rural America* p53 Ag 2017

Kührt, E.
Rosetta's comet 67P/Churyumov-Gerasimenko sheds its dusty mantle to reveal its icy nature bibl graph *Science* v354 no6319 p1566 D 23 2016
Surface changes on comet 67P/Churyumov-Gerasimenko suggest a more active past bw graph *Science* v355 no6332 p1392 Mr 31 2017

Kuich, P. Henning J. L.
Fructose-driven glycolysis supports anoxia resistance in the naked mole-rat diag graph *Science* v356 no6335 p307 Ap 21 2017

Kuiken, Thijs
Role for migratory wild birds in the global spread of avian influenza H5N8 bibl graph map *Science* v354 no6309 p213 O 14 2016

Kuiper, Rolf
Supersonic gas streams enhance the formation of massive black holes in the early universe diag graph *Science* v357 no6358 p1375 S 29 2017

Kuiper belt
Chasing the Elusive 2014 MU69 D. Grinspoon color *Sky & Telescope* v134 no5 p12 N 2017
A double target for a distant probe? color *Science* v357 no6351 p532 Ag 11 2017
Is New Horizons' Next Target a Binary Body? J. K. BEATTY color *Sky & Telescope* v134 no5 p9 N 2017
Observers Track New Horizons' Next Target J. K. BEATTY *Sky & Telescope* v134 no4 p11 O 2017

Kuipers, Dean
The Lady In the Camper color *Los Angeles Magazine* v62 no7 p50 Jl 2017
THE PANTHER YOU WANT color *Orion Magazine* v35 no6 p49 N/D 2016
Witness to Spirit *Orion Magazine* v35 no4/5 p108 Jl-O 2016

KUITENBROUWER, PETER
"O Canada, Beloved Country, Thou!" cartoon *Walrus* v14 no6 p23 Jl/Ag 2017

Kukec Mezek, G.
Observation of a large-scale anisotropy in the arrival directions of cosmic rays above 8×1018 eV *Science* v357 no6357 p1266 S 22 2017

Kukk, Christopher L.
The Compassionate Achiever: How Helping Others Fuels Success *Publishers Weekly* v264 no2 p55 Ja 9 2017

Kukla, Jon
Patrick Henry: Champion of Liberty *Publishers Weekly* v264 no22 p58 My 29 2017

Ku Klux Klan (1915-)
Radical Reconciliation B. McGarvey *America* v216 no11 p62 My 15 2017
Trump's Troubling Attorney General Pick J. SULLUM color *Reason* v48 no10 p6 Mr 2017

KUKOFF, DAVID
The Experiment *Los Angeles Magazine* v61 no11 p144 N 2016

Kulacki, Gregory
China's proper role in the global nuclear order bibl *Bulletin of the Atomic Scientists* v73 no2 p131 Mr 2017

Kuld, Sebastian
TECHNICAL COMMENT ABSTRACTS *Science* v357 no6354 p881 S 1 2017

KULISH, NICHOLAS
Escape From East Berlin *New York Times Book Review* p10 N 20 2016

Kulkarni, Aditya
All-printed thin-film transistors from networks of liquid-exfoliated nanosheets diag *Science* v356 no6333 p69 Ap 7 2017

Kulkarni, Girish
Measurement of the small-scale structure of the intergalactic medium using close quasar pairs diag graph *Science* v356 no6336 p418 Ap 28 2017

Kulkarni, Prajwal
The Penultimate Curiosity: How Science Swims in the Slipstream of Ultimate Questions color *Issues in Science & Technology* v33 no1 p94 Fall 2016

Kulkarni, S. R.
iPTF16geu: A multiply imaged, gravitationally lensed type Ia supernova color diag graph *Science* v356 no6335 p291 Ap 21 2017

Kullgren, Jeffrey T.
How to Teach People About Health Care Pricing *Harvard Business Review Digital Articles* p2 S 29 2015

Kulmala, Markku
Global atmospheric particle formation from CERN CLOUD measurements bibl graph map *Science* v354 no6316 p1119 D 2 2016

KULP, ADRIAN
breaking binky *Parents* v91 no10 p60 O 2016

Kulp, Daniel W.
Priming HIV-1 broadly neutralizing antibody precursors in human Ig loci transgenic mice bibl graph *Science* v353 no6307 p1557 S 30 2016

Kuma, Kengo, 1954-
Common Ground N. R. POLLOCK color *Architectural Record* v205 no8 p71 Ag 2017
MAKING HIS MARK B. LIBBY color *Architectural Digest* v74 no7 p80 Jl 2017

Kumai, R.
Crystallization and vitrification of electrons in a glass-forming charge liquid bw *Science* v357 no6358 p1381 S 29 2017

Kumanogoh, Atsushi
Control of species-dependent cortico-motoneuronal connections underlying manual dexterity diag graph *Science* v357 no6349 p400 Jl 28 2017

Kumar, Akshaya
A Midlife Crisis for the Treaty-Based Human Rights System? *UN Chronicle* v53 no4 p1 2016
A Midlife Crisis for the Treaty-Based Human Rights System? *UN Chronicle* v54 no4 p38 2017

Kumar, Amit
TRADING VS. TRUMP S. Marikar cartoon *New Yorker* v92 no33 p24 O 17 2016

KUMAR, AMITAVA
CONFESSIONS OF A BEEF EATER color *Nation* v305 no11 p32 O 30 2017

Kumar, Anil
 Evidence for bulk superconductivity in pure bismuth single crystals at ambient pressure bibl color graph *Science* v355 no6320 p1 Ja 6 2017
Kumar, B. Mohan
 Forestry for a Low-Carbon Future: Integrating Forests and Wood Products Into Climate Change Strategies bibl color *Environment* v59 no2 p16 Mr/Ap 2017
Kumar, Brijesh
 Promoting human rights through science color *Science* v357 no6359 p34 O 6 2017
Kumar, Manish
 The Mauritania Exploit J. ROBERTSON, M. RILEY et al bw *Bloomberg Businessweek* no4508 p48 Ja 23 2017
Kumar, Manoj
 Decarboxylative borylation color *Science* v356 no6342 p1045 Je 9 2017
 De novo design of a biologically active amyloid bibl graph *Science* v354 no6313 paah4949-1 N 11 2016
 Phytochromes function as thermosensors in Arabidopsis bibl graph *Science* v354 no6314 p886 N 18 2016
Kumar, Nikhil
 'Afghanistan Is the Front Line' color *Time* v189 no22 p38 Je 12 2017
 How Bad Air Came Back color *Time* v188 no27-28 p94 D 26 2016
 India Pays Steep Price for Cash Withdrawal color *Time* v188 no22-23 p11 N/D 2016
 The Low-Caste Farmer's Son Taking High Office In India color *Time* v190 no5 p15 Jl 31 2017
 Message Delivered [Cover story] color *Time* v188 no21 p28 N 21 2016
 Modi's Turbulent Priest Signals Change In Approach color *Time* v189 no13 p9 Ap 10 2017
 Next Generation Leaders color *Time* v188 no15 p41 O 17 2016
 Next Generation Leaders color *Time* v190 no16/17 p74 O 23 2017
 A State Election In India Reinforces Narendra Modi's Grip on Power color map *Time* v189 no11 p12 Mr 27 2017
Kumar, Nishant
 Why Machines Still Can't Learn So Good cartoon *Bloomberg Businessweek* no4499 p55 N 14 2016
Kumar, Prashant
 Harvesting electrical energy from carbon nanotube yarn twist diag graph *Science* v357 no6353 p773 Ag 25 2017
Kumar, Sanjay
 Critics assail India's attempt to 'validate' folk remedy color *Science* v355 no6328 p898 Mr 3 2017
 Emergent cellular self-organization and mechanosensation initiate follicle pattern in the avian skin color *Science* v357 no6353 p811 Ag 25 2017
 India resurrects forgotten leprosy vaccine color *Science* v356 no6342 p999 Je 9 2017
Kumar, Sanjit
 CANCER SCANNERS L. BELLOWS *Atlanta* v56 no10 p22 F 2017
Kumar, Srijan
 Predicting human behavior: The next frontiers bibl color *Science* v355 no6324 p489 F 3 2017
Kumarasamy, Akil
 NEW WORLD *Harper's Magazine* no2007 p77 Ag 2017
Kumari, Veena
 Beyond Diagnostic Categories: Comprehensive Assessment of Psychopathology in Addiction and Mental Health Disorders *Psychology Today* v50 no3 p14 My/Je 2017
 Improving Cognitive Function in Behavioral Health Treatment: Sovereign Health asks Veena Kumari, Ph.D., about Cognitive Remediation Therapy *Psychology Today* v50 no5 p12 S/O 2017
 Increasing Cognitive Function May Improve Addiction Treatment Outcomes *Psychology Today* v49 no6 p12 N/D 2016
Kumin, Daniel
 Anthem AVM 60 A/V Processor color graph *Sound & Vision* v82 no1 p56 Ja 2017
 Arcam AVR850 A/V Receiver chart color graph *Sound & Vision* v81 no9 p50 N 2016
 Bluesound Pulse Soundbar and Pulse Sub color graph *Sound & Vision* v82 no5 p52 Je 2017
 Denon AVR-X4200W A/V Receiver chart color graph *Sound &*

 Vision v81 no9 p58 N 2016
 Elac Element EA101EQ-G Integrated Amplifier/DAC chart color graph *Sound & Vision* v82 no3 p58 Ap 2017
 Emotiva Airmotiv 5CH Speaker System color graph *Sound & Vision* v82 no1 p42 Ja 2017
 Legacy Audio Powerbloc2 and Powerbloc4 Amplifiers chart color graph *Sound & Vision* v82 no6 p58 Jl/Ag 2017
 Line 'Em Up color graph *Sound & Vision* v82 no7 p36 S 2017
 Old Faithful color graph *Sound & Vision* v82 no8 p42 O 2017
 Onkyo TX-RZ1100 A/V Receiver chart color graph *Sound & Vision* v82 no2 p44 F/Mr 2017
 Polk Signature S60 Speaker System color graph *Sound & Vision* v82 no6 p34 Jl/Ag 2017
 RSL Speakers CG3 5.1 Speaker System color graph *Sound & Vision* v82 no3 p44 Ap 2017
 Solidly Serious chart color graph *Sound & Vision* v82 no7 p58 S 2017
KUMMER, CORBY
 50 Best, Refreshed *Atlanta* v56 no11 p2 Mr 2017
 Dishing It Out *New York Times Book Review* p19 Ja 8 2017
 HAIKAN *Washingtonian Magazine* v52 no3 p148 D 2016
 JEWEL IN THE ROUGH *Washingtonian Magazine* v52 no4 p175 Ja 2017
 Look Inward, ATL *Atlanta* v56 no8 p82 D 2016
 LOVING SPOONFUL *Atlanta* v56 no9 p73 Ja 2017
 Noble Fin *Atlanta* v56 no7 p68 N 2016
 PIE IN THE SKY *New York Times Magazine* p67 O 9 2016
KUMOK, ZINA
 CLASS IS IN SESSION *Indianapolis Monthly* p142 My 2017
 That's the Ticket *Indianapolis Monthly* p46 My 2017
Kumpan, A.
 Observation of coherent elastic neutrino-nucleus scattering diag *Science* v357 no6356 p1123 S 15 2017
Kun, Ádám
 Transient compartmentalization of RNA replicators prevents extinction due to parasites bibl chart graph *Science* v354 no6317 p1293 D 9 2016
Kun-tao
 Dropping Bombs, Kuntaw Style A. Graceffo color *Black Belt* v55 no4 p22 Je/Jl 2017
Kun Xia
 Recent progress in autism spectrum disorder research in China bibl chart diag *Science* v354 no6319 p48 D 23 2016
Kun Zhang
 Recent progress in autism spectrum disorder research in China bibl chart diag *Science* v354 no6319 p48 D 23 2016
Kundig, Tom
 Steeling the Show J. GAUER *Architectural Record* v205 no6 p112 Je 2017
Kundla, John, 1916-2017
 Milestones *Time* v190 no6 p17 Ag 7 2017
Kundu, Sharmistha
 Mutation of a nucleosome compaction region disrupts Polycomb-mediated axial patterning bibl chart diag *Science* v355 no6329 p1081 Mr 10 2017
Kungliga Baletten (Stockholm, Sweden)
 Johannes Öhman M. Hagan color *Current Biography* v78 no1 p55 Ja 2017
Kunian, David
 Modern Guide, Historic City color *Downbeat* v84 no1 p81 Ja 2017
 Movers, Groovers & Shakers Prevail at New Orleans Jazz Fest color *Downbeat* v84 no8 p21 Ag 2017
KUNICHOFF, YANA
 THE NEW SANCTUARY MOVEMENT [Cover story] *In These Times* v41 no6 p16 Je 2017
 Outrage Is Not Optional *In These Times* v41 no5 p30 My 2017
 A Rust Belt Town Goes Green--And Non-Union *In These Times* v41 no10 p9 O 2017
Kunis, Mila, 1983-
 Mila Kunis: What's on your Thanksgiving table? D. WALTERS color *Bon Appetit* no11 p136 N 2017
KUNITZ, DANIEL
 MUSCLE IN THE AGE OF INSTAGRAM color *Men's Health* v32 no9 p90 N 2017
Kunka, N.
 Observation of a large-scale anisotropy in the arrival directions

of cosmic rays above 8 × 1018 eV *Science* v357 no6357 p1266 S 22 2017

KUNKEL, BENJAMIN

MARX'S REVENGE color *Nation* v304 no6 p27 F 27 2017

VOYAGE TO THE INTERIOR color *New Yorker* v92 no46 p72 Ja 23 2017

Kunnus, Kristjan

Metalloprotein entatic control of ligand-metal bonds quantified by ultrafast x-ray spectroscopy diag *Science* v356 no6344 p1276 Je 23 2017

Kúnos, Ignácz

FEAR NOT *Lapham's Quarterly* v10 no3 p38 Summ 2017

Kunst, Wendy

How My Horse De-Stresses Me color *Horse & Rider* v55 no12 p72 D 2016

Künstler, Mort—Interviews

Painting the American Adventure S. Slon *Saturday Evening Post* v289 no1 p40 Ja/F 2017

Kuntz, Martin

Martin Kuntz Sculptor S. BAHR color *Indianapolis Monthly* v42 no2 p49 O 2017

Kuntz, Taryn L

Building Better Cause-Marketing Relationships *Parks & Recreation* v52 no5 p60 My 2017

Kunzig, Robert

Dubai's Audacious Goal color map *National Geographic* v232 no4 p52 O 2017

THE NEW EUROPEANS color graph map *National Geographic* v230 no4 p82 O 2016

Kunzru, Hari

Blues Dabblers S. ERICKSON *New York Times Book Review* p15 Ap 2 2017

SINGING THE BLUES J. W. MCCORMACK bw color *Publishers Weekly* v263 no51 p117 D 12 2016

The Thrill Is Here C. Howorth color *Time* v189 no11 p61 Mr 27 2017

Kunzru, Hari—Interviews

Hari Kunzru *New York Times Book Review* p8 Mr 12 2017

Kuo, Maggie

Society labels harassment as research misconduct color *Science* v356 no6335 p233 Ap 21 2017

Kuotb Awad, A.

Observation of a large-scale anisotropy in the arrival directions of cosmic rays above 8 × 1018 eV *Science* v357 no6357 p1266 S 22 2017

Kupc, Agnieszka

Global atmospheric particle formation from CERN CLOUD measurements bibl graph map *Science* v354 no6316 p1119 D 2 2016

Kuper, Simon

Soccer's Culture of Corruption [Cover story] color *New York Review of Books* v64 no14 p55 S 28 2017

KUPERBERG, ETHAN

NUCLEAR MINDFULNESS cartoon *New Yorker* v93 no31 p31 O 9 2017

WHAT I HAVE IN COMMON WITH TRUMP cartoon *New Yorker* v93 no7 p45 Ap 3 2017

Kupernik, Tammy

Hang some curtains! color *Redbook* p140 My 2017

Kupfer, David

Doctor on Call color *Progressive* p24 D 2016/Ja 2017

Kupfer, Harry

Lady Macbeth of Mtsensk J. A. Leipsic *Opera News* v81 no9 p46 Mr 2017

Kupfer, Sonia S.

Reovirus infection triggers inflammatory responses to dietary antigens and development of celiac disease color diag *Science* v356 no6333 p44 Ap 7 2017

Kupfer, T.

iPTF16geu: A multiply imaged, gravitationally lensed type Ia supernova color diag graph *Science* v356 no6335 p291 Ap 21 2017

Kupferschmidt, Kai

Anthrax cousin wreaks havoc in the rainforest color *Science* v357 no6350 p438 Ag 4 2017

At 10, Europe's 'excellence' fund ponders changes color graph *Science* v355 no6329 p1002 Mr 10 2017

BAT PATROL color *Science* v356 no6341 p901 Je 1 2017

Bot-hunters eye mischief in German election color *Science* v357 no6356 p1081 S 15 2017

Cholera vaccine faces major test in Yemen color *Science* v356 no6345 p1316 Je 30 2017

THE ELIMINATOR color diag *Science* v354 no6309 p168 O 14 2016

Fears of Ebola resurgence quickly dispelled in Liberia color *Science* v356 no6338 p575 My 12 2017

Germany seeks 'big flip' in publishing model color graph *Science* v357 no6353 p744 Ag 25 2017

Labmade smallpox is possible, study shows color *Science* v357 no6347 p115 Jl 14 2017

Life-saving diphtheria drug is running out bw *Science* v355 no6321 p118 Ja 13 2017

New bird flu strain brings death and questions color diag *Science* v354 no6318 p1363 D 16 2016

PICK YOUR POISON bw color map *Science* v354 no6309 p171 O 14 2016

THE SCIENCE OF PERSUASION color *Science* v356 no6336 p366 Ap 28 2017

Study suggests hidden epidemic in CF patients color *Science* v354 no6313 p695 N 11 2016

Kupor, Daniella

Having More Options Can Make Us Evaluate Risk Differently color *Harvard Business Review Digital Articles* p2 F 9 2017

Research: Consumers Prefer Products Created by Mistake *Harvard Business Review Digital Articles* p2 S 20 2017

Küppers, M.

Rosetta's comet 67P/Churyumov-Gerasimenko sheds its dusty mantle to reveal its icy nature bibl graph *Science* v354 no6319 p1566 D 23 2016

Surface changes on comet 67P/Churyumov-Gerasimenko suggest a more active past bw graph *Science* v355 no6332 p1392 Mr 31 2017

Küppers, Michael

Dwarf planet Ceres and the ingredients of life bibl color *Science* v355 no6326 p692 F 17 2017

Kuranaga, Mebae

Release of mineral-bound water prior to subduction tied to shallow seismogenic slip off Sumatra graph *Science* v356 no6340 p841 My 26 2017

Kuranaga, Misa

The Talent Question J. Stahl *Dance Magazine* v90 no11 p10 N 2016

Unstoppable A. RIVERS *Dance Magazine* v90 no11 p26 N 2016

Kurbjuweit, Dirk

Fear *Publishers Weekly* v264 no33 p48 Ag 14 2017

Kurdish refugees

Trump Cracks Down on Refugees in Nashville's Little Kurdistan [Cover story] M. Petti color *Reason* v49 no5 p20 O 2017

Kurdistan—Politics & government—21st century

The Kurds Get Under Way D. DEVOSS color *Weekly Standard* v23 no5 p19 O 9 2017

Kurds—Iraq

Lightbox color *Time* v190 no14 p18 O 9 2017

Kurihara, Laurie

Single-cell methylomes identify neuronal subtypes and regulatory elements in mammalian cortex diag *Science* v357 no6351 p600 Ag 11 2017

Kuriloff, Aaron

HOW TO GET FORGOTTEN G. ALLEN bw color *ARTnews* v116 no1 p90 Spr 2017

KURIN, RICHARD

Innovation Nation *New York Times Book Review* p11 Ja 1 2017

Kurlander, Eric

Gods and Monsters A. STUTTAFORD *National Review* v69 no18 p36 O 2 2017

KURLANSKY, MARK

Points to Ponder color *Reader's Digest* v190 no1134 p35 O 2017

Kurlansky, Mark, 1948-—Interviews

Mark Kurlansky S. Begley color *Time* v190 no1 p56 Jl 3 2017

Kurlantzick, Joshua

The Arc of Trump *Bloomberg Businessweek* no4501 p6 N 28 2016

Donald Trump's Long Tail color *Bloomberg Businessweek* no4495 p6 O 17 2016

From Spying to Killing B. Dakin *Washington Monthly* p6 Ja/F 2017

A Great Place to Have a War: America in Laos and the Birth of a Military CIA *Publishers Weekly* v263 no46 p43 N 14 2016

The Not-So-Secret War S. SHANE *New York Times Book Review* p12 F 5 2017

Return Of the Strongman color *Bloomberg Businessweek* no4522 p8 My 15 2017

A Survival Guide for Democracies color *Bloomberg Businessweek* no4535 p10 Ag 28 2017

Trade's Coming Rough Turn *Bloomberg Businessweek* no4507 p8 Ja 16 2017

Kurns, Dave

DOWN TO BUSINESS: WE COVER THE BUSINESS, PRODUCTION, AND FUN ASPECTS OF FARMING color *Successful Farming* v115 no7 p4 My 2017

FARMING IN SPACE: CAN WE GROW CROPS ON MARS? RESEARCHERS ARE TRYING TO FEED ASTRONAUTS *Successful Farming* v115 no12 p6 O 2017

IT ALL STARTS NOW *Successful Farming* v115 no4 p4 Mr 2017

IT'LL BE A CLASSIC! *Successful Farming* v115 no2 p4 F 2017

A LIFE IN FARMING: THE NEXT CHAPTER *Successful Farming* v115 no3 p4 Mid-F 2017

A NEW DAY DAWNS IN AGRICULTURE *Successful Farming* v115 no1 p6 Ja 2017

NO-TILL OR NEVER-TILL? STORY ON THE EFFECT OF TILLAGE GETS READER REACTIONS *Successful Farming* v115 no11 p4 S 2017

A SIDE BUSINESS COMES FULL CIRCLE *Successful Farming* v114 no13 p4 D 2016

A STAR-STUDDED CAST: THE STAFF AT SUCCESSFUL FARMING MAGAZINE IS A STELLAR TEAM *Successful Farming* v115 no9 p6 Ag 2017

THINK OF YOUR CROPS LIKE MONEY. BECAUSE THEY ARE *Successful Farming* v114 no10 p4 O 2016

WE CAN FEED 9 BILLION: HOW DOES AMERICAN AGRICULTURE HELP FEED THE POPULATION? LET'S DO THE MATH *Successful Farming* v115 no6 p2 Ap 2017

WE OWE A LOT TO OUR VETERANS *Successful Farming* v114 no11 p6 N 2016

WHAT MAKES A FARMER SUCCESSFUL? *Successful Farming* v115 no8 p3 Je/Jl 2017

WORDS MATTER *Successful Farming* v115 no5 p4 Mid-Mr 2017

Kuroiwa, Tsuneyoshi

Holliday junction resolvases mediate chloroplast nucleoid segregation diag *Science* v356 no6338 p631 My 12 2017

Kurokawa, Kishō, 1934-2007

The Nakagin Capsule Tower S. Kriss *New York Times Magazine* p26 O 2 2016

Kurpanek, Detlef

Build a signal system with Arduino microcontrollers color diag *Model Railroader* v83 no12 p42 D 2016

Kursinski, Anne

21 TRAINING TIPS FROM 3 OLYMPIANS S. Weakley color *Practical Horseman* v45 no4 p34 Ap 2017

Winner's CIRCLE color *Practical Horseman* v45 no7 p65 Jl 2017

Kürten, Andreas

Global atmospheric particle formation from CERN CLOUD measurements bibl graph map *Science* v354 no6316 p1119 D 2 2016

Kurth, W. S.

Jupiter's magnetosphere and aurorae observed by the Juno spacecraft during its first polar orbits diag graph *Science* v356 no6340 p826 My 26 2017

Kurth, Wally

DAYS OF OUR LIVES M. LOGAN *TV Guide* v65 no25 p42 Je 2017

Kurtis, Bill

WHY We LOVE CHICAGO bw cartoon color *Chicago* v66 no3 p75 Mr 2017

Kurtz, Annalyn

STATE STREET'S GENDER SHOWDOWN color diag *Fortune* v175 no7 p58 Je 1 2017

Kurtz, F.

Real-time spectral interferometry probes the internal dynamics of femtosecond soliton molecules diag *Science* v356 no6333 p50

Ap 7 2017

Kurtz, Marc M.

Systemic pan-AMPK activator MK-8722 improves glucose homeostasis but induces cardiac hypertrophy graph *Science* v357 no6350 p507 Ag 4 2017

Kurtz, Sarah

Terawatt-scale photovoltaics: Trajectories and challenges chart graph *Science* v356 no6334 p141 Ap 14 2017

Kurtzman, Alex

THE MUMMY D. Franich color *Entertainment Weekly* no1446/1447 p52 D 2016/Ja 2017

THE MUMMY D. Franich color *Entertainment Weekly* no1463/1464 p48 Ap/My 2017

The Other Tom J. PODHORETZ *Weekly Standard* v22 no40 p39 Je 26 2017

Kurtzman, Harvey

The Fleeting Glory of Trump Magazine P. BAGGE color *Reason* v49 no3 p64 Jl 2017

Kurtz-Phelan, Daniel

The Clash of Victimizations color *Washington Monthly* v49 no6-8 p63 Je-Ag 2017

Kuru, Erkin

Treadmilling by FtsZ filaments drives peptidoglycan synthesis and bacterial cell division bibl graph *Science* v355 no6326 p739 F 17 2017

Kurumizaka, Hitoshi

Crystal structure of the overlapping dinucleosome composed of hexasome and octasome graph *Science* v356 no6334 p205 Ap 14 2017

Kurup, Seema

Understanding Louise Erdrich D. Miller *American Indian Quarterly* v41 no3 p287 Summ 2017

Kurup, Smita

Fatty acids in arbuscular mycorrhizal fungi are synthesized by the host plant diag graph *Science* v356 no6343 p1175 Je 16 2017

Kurz, Gretchen

THE COMFORTS OF PASTA color *Los Angeles Magazine* v62 no10 p14 O 2017

FIFTY Favorites *Los Angeles Magazine* p8 Ap 2017

Kurz, Mark D.

Tungsten-182 heterogeneity in modern ocean island basalts chart diag *Science* v356 no6333 p66 Ap 7 2017

Kurzel, Justin

ASSASSIN'S CREED C. Gunnestad color *Sound & Vision* v82 no7 p68 S 2017

Kurzmann, Christof

Trost Records Fuses Punk Ethos with Jazz Artistry P. MARGASAK bw *Downbeat* v83 no11 p18 N 2016

Kurzweil, Ray

Integrated Circuits *New York Times Book Review* p13 Mr 19 2017

Pioneers [Cover story] color *Time* v189 no16/17 p14 My 1-8 2017

Kurzweil, Ray, 1948——Interviews

TECH'S MAGIC 8 BALL SAYS EMBRACE THE FUTURE M. Lev-ram color *Fortune* v176 no5 p28 O 1 2017

Kusama, Yayoi, 1929-

The Art of Repetition M. WAKIM color *Los Angeles Magazine* v62 no10 p86 O 2017

Kusama, Yayoi, 1929——Exhibitions

Yayoi Kusama's Existential Circus S. BOXER color *Atlantic* v320 no1 p94 Jl/Ag 2017

Kushner, Charles

The Kushner Kingdom C. SORVINO color *Forbes* v199 no2 p32 F 28 2017

KUSHNER, DAVID

WHERE THE @#$% AM I? color map *Reader's Digest* v189 no1130 p88 My 2017

Kushner, Ellen

Tremontaine *Publishers Weekly* v264 no15 p57 Ap 10 2017

Kushner, Howard I.

Sleight of hand D. Casasanto color *Science* v357 no6357 p1246 S 22 2017

KUSHNER, JACOB

LETTER FROM KAKUMA color *Nation* v304 no6 p12 F 27 2017

Kushner, Jared C., 1981-

AGENTS AND ASSETS A. Davidson color *New Yorker* v93 no22

p21 Jl 31 2017

BLAND AMBITION S. ELLISON color *Vanity Fair* v59 no10 p174 O 2017

Family First [Cover story] Z. J. Miller, M. Scherer et al color *Time* v189 no22 p24 Je 12 2017

JARED KUSHNER'S HARVARD ADMISSIONS ESSAY M. AMRAM cartoon *New Yorker* v93 no27 p33 S 11 2017

The Kushner Kingdom C. SORVINO color *Forbes* v199 no2 p32 F 28 2017

The Most Expensive Building in NYC D. Kocieniewski and C. Melby color *Bloomberg Businessweek* no4515 p27 Mr 20 2017

The Potem kin Prince R. COHEN color *Vanity Fair* v59 no11 p124 N 2017

The Son-in-Law Also Rises [Cover story] S. BERTONI color *Forbes* v198 no8 p70 D 20 2016

TRUMP'S KEY ADVISERS BY THE NUMBERS T. Newmyer *Fortune* v174 no8 p17 D 15 2016

The Voice in His Ear M. WARREN color *Weekly Standard* v22 no34 p20 My 15 2017

What You Said About ... color *Time* v189 no23 p6 Je 19 2017

THE YOUNG TRUMP A. Rice img *New York* p21 F 9 2017

Kushner, Josh

The Other Brother [Cover story] S. BERTONI color *Forbes* v199 no4 p70 Ap 25 2017

KUSHNER, RACHEL

Castro's Cuba Is the Only Way of Life Many Have Known *Time* v188 no24 p45 D 12 2016

'WE ARE ORPHANS HERE' LIFE AND DEATH IN EAST JE-RUSALEM'S PALESTINIAN REFUGEE CAMP color *New York Times Magazine* p44 D 4 2016

Kushner, Steven A.

Activity-based protein profiling reveals off-target proteins of the FAAH inhibitor BIA 10-2474 chart color graph *Science* v356 no6342 p1084 Je 9 2017

Kushner Cos.

Cost of 666 Fifth Avenue D. Kocieniewski and C. Melby color diag graph *Bloomberg Businessweek* no4537 p39 S 11 2017

Kusmin, Lorin

Using the ERS County Economic Types To Explore Demographic and Economic Trends in Rural Areas color graph *Amber Waves: The Economics of Food, Farming, Natural Resources, & Rural America* p1 D 2016

Kustra-Olszewska, Magdalena

What Makes Someone an Engaging Leader *Harvard Business Review Digital Articles* p2 N 7 2014

Kutcher, Ashton, 1978—Interviews

URBAN Cowboy D. HOLBROOK *TV Guide* v65 no25 p16 Je 2017

Kutkiewicz, Anna

Climber Art color *Climbing* no349 p9 N 2016

Kutska, Kenneth S.

Playground Safety: A Shared Responsibility *Parks & Recreation* p12 2017 Supplement Field Guide - Supplier and Resource Directory

Kutter, Steffen

Evolutionary drivers of thermoadaptation in enzyme catalysis [Cover story] bibl color graph *Science* v355 no6322 p289 Ja 20 2017

Kutterolf, Steffen

Release of mineral-bound water prior to subduction tied to shallow seismogenic slip off Sumatra graph *Science* v356 no6340 p841 My 26 2017

KUTZ, SUSAN J.

Transformational Principles for NEON Sampling of Mammalian Parasites and Pathogens: A Response to Springer and Colleagues *BioScience* v66 no11 p917 N 1 2016

Kuwait. Communication & Information Technology Regulatory Authority

CITRA: The ICT sector role on boosting Kuwait's economy S. Alozainah color *Foreign Affairs* v95 no6 p120e N/D 2016

Kuwait—Economic policy

Kuwait: The Race For Economic Diversification color *Foreign Affairs* v95 no6 p120a N/D 2016

Kuwako, Katsuyo

Japan's Priests Turn to Property Development color *Bloomberg Businessweek* no4521 p38 My 8 2017

Kuyda, Eugenia—Interviews

Artificial People E. Huet cartoon color *Bloomberg Businessweek* no4496 p40 O 24 2016

Kuylenstierna, J. C. I.

A climate policy pathway for near- and long-term benefits color *Science* v356 no6337 p493 My 5 2017

KUZEMCHAK, SALLY

Is This the Perfect POWER SNACK! *Scholastic Choices* v33 no1 p16 S 2017

Let's get granular about SUGAR color *Redbook* p96 Ap 2017

not picky [Cover story] color *Parents* v92 no7 p44 Jl 2017

test your nutrition IQ *Parents* v92 no2 p72 F 2017

Kuzma, Cindy

ALIA GRAY color *Runner's World* v52 no1 p21 Ja/F 2017

American Dreamer color *Runner's World* v52 no5 p47 Je 2017

Beer Money color *Runner's World* v52 no7 p43 Ag 2017

BE SELFIE-AWARE cartoon *Runner's World* v52 no3 p32 Ap 2017

Chicago Style color *Runner's World* v52 no9 p50 O 2017

COOL (DUDE) RUNNING color *Runner's World* v52 no1 p48 Ja/F 2017

CRUSH IT. THEN COOL IT [Cover story] color *Runner's World* v52 no2 p28 Mr 2017

Down But Not Out cartoon chart *Prevention* v68 no11 p76 N 2016

Embrace the Tough Stuff color *Runner's World* v52 no8 p56 S 2017

FOOD FOR THOUGHT [Cover story] color *Runner's World* v52 no6 p30 Jl 2017

HOME RUN color *Runner's World* v52 no3 p20 Ap 2017

MAKE OVER YOUR Metabolism [Cover story] cartoon color graph *Prevention* v69 no5 p66 My 2017

POSE PRIORITIES color *Runner's World* v52 no2 p46 Mr 2017

SPRING TRAINING color *Runner's World* v52 no5 p22 Je 2017

STRETCH YOUR LIMITS [Cover story] color *Runner's World* v52 no2 p44 Mr 2017

STRIDE WITH PRIDE color *Runner's World* v52 no9 p26 O 2017

Style for Miles cartoon color *Runner's World* v52 no4 p46 My 2017

YOU CAN FLY! chart color *Runner's World* v52 no5 p18 Je 2017

YOUR BEST BODY [Cover story] color *Prevention* v69 no6 p40 Je 2017

KUZMA, JENNIFER

Rethinking biosecurity diag *Issues in Science & Technology* v33 no2 p12 Wint 2017

Kuzmanovic, Jasmina

From Russia, With Debt color *Bloomberg Businessweek* no4517 p42 Ap 3 2017

Kuzmin, Elena

Exploring genetic suppression interactions on a global scale diag *Science* v354 no6312 p599 N 4 2016

Kuznetsov, Arseniy I.

Optically resonant dielectric nanostructures bibl graph *Science* v354 no6314 paag2472-1 N 18 2016

Kuznetsova, Svetlana

Svetlana Kuznetsova *Tennis* v53 no1 p60 Ja/F 2017

Kuzyk, Jake

JAKE KUZYK T. Monterosso cartoon color *Snowboarder* v29 no4 p42 D 2016

Kvaran, Gunnar

THE SHIPPING EXPERT *Iceland Review* v54 no6 p122 N/D 2016

Kvaratskhelia, Mamuka

Cryo-EM structures and atomic model of the HIV-1 strand transfer complex intasome bibl color *Science* v355 no6320 p1 Ja 6 2017

Kvedar, Joseph C.

Simple Digital Technologies Can Reduce Health Care Costs *Harvard Business Review Digital Articles* p2 N 14 2016

Telemedicine Is Vital to Reforming Health Care Delivery *Harvard Business Review Digital Articles* p2 O 7 2015

Kvitová, Petra, 1990-

Best of the Rest E. D. McGROGAN *Tennis* v53 no1 p64 Ja/F 2017

Kvochko, Elena

Why Data Breaches Don't Hurt Stock Prices *Harvard Business Review Digital Articles* p2 Mr 31 2015

KWAI, ISABELLA

How to Buy Happiness color *Atlantic* v319 no3 p24 Ap 2017

KWAK, CHANEY

I Got the Powder color *Bon Appetit* v62 no4 p22 Ap 2017

Kwak, James

Getting Away With It: Why America's top prosecutors no longer go after corporations or their executives *New York Times Book Review* p10 Jl 9 2017

What Econ 101 gets wrong C. R. Morris color *America* v216 no7 p47 Ap 3 2017

Kwak, Sarah

ALLOWANCE TO PLAY color map *Sports Illustrated* v127 no10 p18 O 2 2017

Bader Up color *Sports Illustrated* v127 no5 p30 Ag 14 2017

BLOWN COVER color *Sports Illustrated* v127 no7 p22 S 4 2017

The Case for ... GIANCARLO STANTON color *Sports Illustrated* v127 no7 p30 S 4 2017

The Case for ... KLUBOT AS MVP color *Sports Illustrated* v127 no10 p24 O 2 2017

The Case for ... LOWERING THE NBA AGE MINIMUM color *Sports Illustrated* v127 no12 p24 O 16 2017

CATCH HIM IF YOU CAN color *Sports Illustrated* v127 no12 p18 O 16 2017

CONNIE HAWKINS color *Sports Illustrated* v127 no12 p18 O 16 2017

DAWG DAYS color *Sports Illustrated* v127 no5 p28 Ag 14 2017

Death of a Goon Aug. 24, 1992 color *Sports Illustrated* v127 no5 p32 Ag 14 2017

Disaster Relief color *Sports Illustrated* v127 no7 p20 S 4 2017

DOWNWARD-FACING BULL color *Sports Illustrated* v127 no7 p24 S 4 2017

DUELING ROLES color *Sports Illustrated* v127 no10 p17 O 2 2017

EXECUTIVE ORDERS color *Sports Illustrated* v127 no11 p18 O 9 2017

FACE OF THE FRANCHISE color *Sports Illustrated* v127 no11 p20 O 9 2017

FACES IN THE CROWD color *Sports Illustrated* v127 no11 p21 O 9 2017

Finishing Rush color *Sports Illustrated* v127 no5 p26 Ag 14 2017

GOOD AS NEW color *Sports Illustrated* v127 no10 p20 O 2 2017

HAIR TO BE DIFFERENT color *Sports Illustrated* v127 no12 p20 O 16 2017

Handsome Is ... color *Sports Illustrated* v127 no5 p28 Ag 14 2017

HOCKEY AND HEALING color *Sports Illustrated* v127 no12 p15 O 16 2017

HOT | NOT color *Sports Illustrated* v127 no11 p20 O 9 2017

JAKE LAMOTTA (1922-2017) color *Sports Illustrated* v127 no10 p22 O 2 2017

LONDON CALLING color *Sports Illustrated* v127 no11 p14 O 9 2017

MIKED VICK color *Sports Illustrated* v127 no7 p20 S 4 2017

Players Of the Year color *Sports Illustrated* v125 no20 p92 D 19 2016

Reign Over color *Sports Illustrated* v127 no5 p22 Ag 14 2017

RETRO FIRE color *Sports Illustrated* v127 no10 p20 O 2 2017

SHELL GAME color *Sports Illustrated* v127 no7 p26 S 4 2017

Slam Bunk color *Sports Illustrated* v127 no5 p19 Ag 14 2017

SWINGING LOW color *Sports Illustrated* v127 no11 p21 O 9 2017

Total Eclipse of the Park color map *Sports Illustrated* v127 no5 p24 Ag 14 2017

TRIBUTES color *Sports Illustrated* v127 no5 p22 Ag 14 2017

TURNING HEADS color *Sports Illustrated* v127 no10 p14 O 2 2017

VENUS VENERATED color *Sports Illustrated* v127 no7 p17 S 4 2017

VIEW SOME TWOSOME color *Sports Illustrated* v127 no11 p18 O 9 2017

WHY DO I FEEL SO EMPTY INSIDE? color *Sports Illustrated* v127 no10 p16 O 2 2017

Y.A. TITTLE (1926-2017) color *Sports Illustrated* v127 no12 p22 O 16 2017

YOUTH BE KNOWN color *Sports Illustrated* v127 no10 p20 O 2 2017

Kwak-Hefferan, Elisabeth

APPAREL color *Backpacker* p55 N 2017

Day DREAMING: The best dayhike in every state color *Back-*

packer p52 S 2017

EQUIPMENT color *Backpacker* p73 N 2017

FROM BACKYARD TO BACKCOUNTRY [Cover story] color *Sunset* v238 no5 p60 My 2017

The Great Wide Open color map *Backpacker* p12 Je 2017

Hall of Fame color *Backpacker* v45 no2 p45 Mr 2017

THE LONG WAY 'ROUND il *Backpacker* p83 My 2017

Mercy Rule color *Backpacker* p22 My 2017

Shells color diag graph il *Backpacker* v45 no3 p83 Ap 2017

Southern Charm color map *Backpacker* p12 O 2017

Water's Edge: Pictured Rocks National Lakeshore, Michigan color *Backpacker* p12 S 2017

Kwall, Roberta Rosenthal

Conservative Judaism and Its Discontents A. COOPER and S. GLICK *Commentary* v143 no6 p4 Je 2017

Saving Conservative Judaism: The case for ballasting the tent rather than widening it until it collapses *Commentary* v143 no4 p31 Ap 2017

Thou Shalt Not Reprint *Commentary* v142 no2 p58 S 2016

Kwan, Eugene E.

Macrocyclic bis-thioureas catalyze stereospecific glycosylation reactions bibl diag *Science* v355 no6321 p1 Ja 13 2017

Kwan, Harry

Caring for Aging Loved Ones color *Consumer Reports* v82 no12 p6 D 2017

Kwan, Kenneth Y.

Intersection of diverse neuronal genomes and neuropsychiatric disease: The Brain Somatic Mosaicism Network color *Science* v356 no6336 p395 Ap 28 2017

Kwang-Je Kim

Moo-Young Han *Physics Today* v69 no11 p70 N 2016

Kwanzaa

December! T. PAYNE and L. CROSS color *Ebony* v72 no3 p34 D 2016/Ja 2017

Kwate, Naa Oyo

Fast Food's Urban Invasion *American Scholar* v86 no2 p16 Spr 2017

Kwiatkowski, Dominic P.

Resistance to malaria through structural variation of red blood cell invasion receptors diag *Science* v356 no6343 p1139 Je 16 2017

Kwikset Corp.

Pick Your Lock color *Log Home Living* v34 no3 p16 Ap 2017

Kwoh, Stewart

To Stand And Deliver J. HERBST *Los Angeles Magazine* p19 F 2017

KWOK, ROBERTA

The Secret Lives of Birds *Audubon* v119 no2 p18 Summ 2017

Kwok, Ronald

Greater role for Atlantic inflows on sea-ice loss in the Eurasian Basin of the Arctic Ocean chart diag graph *Science* v356 no6335 p285 Ap 21 2017

Kwokyung Lo

Kwok-Yung Lo P. A. Vanden Bout and A. I. Sargent *Physics Today* v70 no8 p71 Ag 2017

Kwon, Minseok

Intersection of diverse neuronal genomes and neuropsychiatric disease: The Brain Somatic Mosaicism Network color *Science* v356 no6336 p395 Ap 28 2017

Kwon, Tae-woo

Highly elastic binders integrating polyrotaxanes for silicon microparticle anodes in lithium ion batteries diag *Science* v357 no6348 p279 Jl 21 2017

Kwong, Lily

Lily Kwong H. MARTIN color *Architectural Digest* v74 no9 p50 S 2017

Kwong, Peter D.

Trispecific broadly neutralizing HIV antibodies mediate potent SHIV protection in macaques color graph *Science* v357 no6359 p85 O 6 2017

Kwon Lee, Tae

Giant viruses with an expanded complement of translation system components diag *Science* v356 no6333 p82 Ap 7 2017

Kwun, Aileen

Look Out, Below! *Architectural Record* v205 no4 p99 Ap 2017

Water, Water Everywhere color *Architectural Record* v205 no3 p59 Mr 2017

Welcome Effects *Architectural Record* v205 no4 p93 Ap 2017

Kyanon Kamera KK
GLASS APPEAL A. Ryder color *Popular Photography* v81 no2 p18 Mr/Ap 2017

Kyle (Performer)
KYLE N. Feeney color *Entertainment Weekly* no1462 p61 Ap 21 2017

Kyle, Benjamin
The Last Unknown Man M. WOLFE color *New Republic* v247 no12 p40 D 2016

KYLE, KATHY
Spa Days: Lake Mead National Recreation Area, Nevada/Arizona color map *Backpacker* p14 N 2017

Kyles, Kyra
Bigotry is the Monster in Jordan Peele's New Film color *Ebony* v72 no5 p20 Mr 2017
Black History, Black Future *Ebony* v72 no4 p16 F 2017
In Our Cities bw color *Ebony* v72 no4 p42 F 2017
Musically Inclined color *Ebony* v72 no8 p16 Je 2017
My Sister's Keeper *Ebony* v72 no5 p14 Mr 2017
Powered Up color *Ebony* v72 no3 p20 D 2016/Ja 2017
The World Is Yours color *Ebony* v72 no6 p14 Ap/My 2017

Kylie, Aaron
Black-capped chickadee color *Canadian Geographic* v135 no6 p71 D 2015
Chantal Kreviazuk color *Canadian Geographic* v135 no6 p86 D 2015
From polo to paddleboarding color map *Canadian Geographic* v137 p11 2017 Travel
NEVADA color *Canadian Geographic* v135 no6 p30 D 2015
Off script color *Canadian Geographic* v137 p6 2017 Travel
Where we go color *Canadian Geographic* v135 no6 p4 D 2015

Kylstra, Carolyn—Interviews
Celebrating 16 Years of THE GIRL NEXT DOOR cartoon color *Men's Health* v32 no8 p94 O 2017

Kymata Ltd.
Kyma Sandals color *Bloomberg Businessweek* no4531 p71 Jl 24 2017

Kyncl, Robert
Straight to Video: YouTube's chief business officer presses play on the platform's greatest-hits reel A. HESS *New York Times Book Review* p19 S 24 2017

Kyo Inoue
A coherent Ising machine for 2000-node optimization problems bibl diag graph *Science* v354 no6312 p603 N 4 2016

Kyoko Ito
Self-renewal of a purified Tie2+ hematopoietic stem cell population relies on mitochondrial clearance bibl graph *Science* v354 no6316 p1156 D 2 2016

Kyosuke Yamamoto
Methane production from coal by a single methanogen bibl graph *Science* v354 no6309 p222 O 14 2016

Kyoto (Japan)—Description & travel
On our radar color *Canadian Geographic* v137 p18 2017 Travel
Ready, Set, Kyoto! C. POLIS color *Bon Appetit* v62 no4 p58 Ap 2017

Kyoung Kim, Tae
Liquefied gas electrolytes for electrochemical energy storage devices graph *Science* v356 no6345 p1351 Je 30 2017

Kyprianou, Christos
Assembly of embryonic and extraembryonic stem cells to mimic embryogenesis in vitro diag *Science* v356 no6334 p153 Ap 14 2017

Kyrgios, Nick, 1995-
THE KYRGIOS ENIGMA L. THOMAS cartoon color *New Yorker* v93 no20 p28 Jl 10 2017
OPEN SEASON *Atlanta* v57 no3 p23 Jl 2017

Kyrpides, Nikos C.
Giant viruses with an expanded complement of translation system components diag *Science* v356 no6333 p82 Ap 7 2017
Protein structure determination using metagenome sequence data color graph *Science* v355 no6322 p294 Ja 20 2017

Kyunghee Park
Beijing Is Mad About Thaad color *Bloomberg Businessweek* no4514 p16 Mr 13 2017

KYZER, LARISSA

FINE PRINT *Iceland Review* v55 no2 p62 Mr/Ap 2017

L

L. & J.G. Stickley Inc.
L. & J.G. STICKLEY: Fayetteville, N.Y. "A Living Room," 1912 B. Sullivan color *Arts & Crafts Homes & the Revival* v12 no4 p72 Fall 2017

LA 92 (Film)
Past Tense R. Brody color *New Yorker* v93 no10 p22 Ap 24 2017

La Bamba (Film)
Crossing Artistic Borders M. WAKIM *Los Angeles Magazine* v62 no9 p59 S 2017

La Bohème (Theatrical production)
A HOT TIME IN THE OLD TOWN K. SMITH color *Vanity Fair* v59 no9 p78 S 2017
La Bohème G. PUCCINI, G. GIACOSA et al *Opera News* v81 no7 p55 Ja 2017

La Cienaga (Film)
WHEN ALL IS LOST J. TEODORO color *Film Comment* v53 no5 p44 S/O 2017

La Fanciulla del West (Music)
CLASSICAL MUSIC *New Yorker* v93 no27 p13 S 11 2017

La Favorite (Theatrical production)
La Favorite J. A. Leipsic *Opera News* v81 no7 p41 Ja 2017

La Havana Madrid (Theatrical production)
HAVANA RESURRECTED B. GOLDEN color *Chicago* v66 no4 p42 Ap 2017

La La Land (Film)
5 ways to ditch the winter blahs color *Redbook* p121 D 2016
BEST PICTURE CONTENDER LA LA LAND N. Sperling color *Entertainment Weekly* no1442 p44 D 2 2016 Rebellious Special Issue
CAN ANYTHING STOP LA LA LAND? N. Sperling color *Entertainment Weekly* no1449 p12 Ja 20 2017
DANCING WITH THE STARS A. LANE cartoon *New Yorker* v92 no41 p88 D 12 2016
EMMA STONE J. McGovern color *Entertainment Weekly* no1444/1445 p21 D 16 2016
The Entertainer S. MARCHE cartoon color *Esquire* v166 no5 p45 D 2016/Ja 2017
Fairground color *Vanity Fair* p105 Hollywood 2017 Supplement
FINDING LA LA LAND J. McGovern color *Entertainment Weekly* no1443 p44 D 9 2016
Glittering Prizes R. DOUTHAT color *National Review* v69 no6 p47 Ap 3 2017
Hollywood On Hollywood R. DOUTHAT color *National Review* v69 no2 p47 F 6 2017
La La Land, a Truly Modern Hollywood Musical, Strikes All the Best Chords R. Bruner color *Time* v188 no24 p61 D 12 2016
La La Land C. Chiarella color *Sound & Vision* v82 no7 p66 S 2017
La La Land: Haters Shall Be Lovers S. Zacharek color *Time* v188 no24 p62 D 12 2016
LA LA LAND IS A MUSICAL LOVE LETTER TO THE CITY M. WAKIM *Los Angeles Magazine* p124 D 2016
LA LA LAND J. Mcgovern color *Entertainment Weekly* no1438 p36 N 4 2016
Let's Face the Music and Dance G. O'Brien color *New York Review of Books* v64 no6 p16 Ap 6 2017
The Missing Piece M. KORESKY color *Film Comment* v53 no1 p50 Ja/F 2017
'Moonlight' Sonata J. Podhoretz color *Weekly Standard* v22 no26 p39 Mr 13 2017
MOVIES OF THE YEAR P. TRAVERS color *Rolling Stone* no1276 p24 D 15 2016
A Musical Triumph P. Travers color *Rolling Stone* no1276 p64 D 15 2016
NEWLY AVAILABLE MOVIES J. HOGAN *TV Guide* v65 no37 p52 S 4 2017
No. 1 LA LA LAND C. Nashawaty and L. Greenblatt color *Entertainment Weekly* no1444/1445 p48 D 16 2016
NOW PLAYING color *Entertainment Weekly* no1448 p50 Ja 13 2017
NOW PLAYING color *Entertainment Weekly* no1451/1452 p92 F 3-10 2017

On with the Show J. Gay color *Vogue* v206 no11 p212 N 2016

ORNAMENTS TO THE SEASON S. KLAWANS color *Nation* v304 no2 p35 Ja 16 2017

The Oscar Race Is On! N. Sperling color *Entertainment Weekly* no1436/1437 p24 O 21 2016

Out of Step with Movie History S. ERICKSON *Los Angeles Magazine* p66 F 2017

PICTURE J. McGovern, D. Franich et al color diag *Entertainment Weekly* no1451/1452 p70 F 3-10 2017

Song and Solitude R. R. Cooper *Commonweal* v144 no2 p22 Ja 27 2017

A Star Is Born J. PODHORETZ color *Weekly Standard* v22 no16 p39 D 26 2016

The Ten Best Movies of the Year D. Edelstein img *New York* v49 no25 p116 D 12 2016

THIS STUDIO HAS A SPECIAL EFFECT ON MOVIES T. J. Huddleston color *Fortune* v175 no3 p26 Mr 1 2017

A tonic for the times B. D. JOHNSON color *Maclean's* v129 no50 p56 D 19 2016

Two visions of creativity K. Reklis color *Christian Century* v134 no4 p59 F 15 2017

The Umbrellas of Silver Lake D. EDELSTEIN img *New York* v49 no24 p148 N 28 2016

UNDER THE INFLUENCE D. MARCHESE img *New York* v49 no24 p120 N 28 2016

Who Should Really Win *Los Angeles Magazine* p68 F 2017

WONDER WOMEN A. LEIBOVITZ and J. WOLCOTT bw color *Vanity Fair* p126 Hollywood 2017 Supplement

Your Golden Globes Workout Plan E. Berman color diag *Time* v189 no3 p55 Ja 16 2017

La La Land (Music)

WHERE & WHEN: 18 THINGS YOU REALLY OUGHT TO DO THIS MONTH M. J. Gaynor, R. Cartagena et al *Washingtonian Magazine* v52 no11 p31 Ag 2017

La La Land (Theatrical production)

L.A. Law (TV program)

DAVID E. KELLEY D. HOLBROOK *TV Guide* v65 no35 p6 Ag 21 2017

La Mere Coupable (Theatrical production)

Family Dynamics R. Platt color *New Yorker* v93 no18 p8 Je 26 2017

La Notte (Film)

La Notte *New Yorker* v93 no14 p21 My 22 2017

La nueva Cuba (Short story)

La nueva Cuba [Cover story] P. BLAIR color *Canadian Geographic* v135 no6 p42 D 2015

La Paz (Bolivia)—Social conditions—21st century

ZEBRAS IN THE STREETS I. Henderson color *Atlantic* v319 no2 p26 Mr 2017

La Sal Mountains (Utah)

SALT OF THE EARTH E. Catino bw color *Skiing* p30 D 2016

La Traviata (Theatrical production)

La Traviata *Opera News* v81 no9 p58 Mr 2017

THE MUSIC OF TIME NO 3: THE SOUND OF SILENCE: How and why did concert-going change from a raucous, noisy affair to one of hushed appreciation? A. Lee *History Today* v67 no9 p86 S 2017

Orange S. J. Mudge *Opera News* v81 no5 p52 N 2016

La Tuile a Loup (Company)

La Tuile à Loup M. OWENS color *Architectural Digest* no5 p46 My 2017

La zingara (Music)

CLASSICAL MUSIC cartoon *New Yorker* v93 no16 p10 Je 5 2017

LAAKMANN, PETER

The Price Is Right *National Review* v69 no19 p18 O 16 2017

Laase, Eden

Goal Oriented color *Sports Illustrated* v127 no4 p20 Ag 7 2017

NEW FOOTING color *Sports Illustrated* v127 no9 p18 S 25 2017

SWINGING LOW color *Sports Illustrated* v127 no11 p21 O 9 2017

This Old House color *Sports Illustrated* v127 no6 p16 Ag 28 2017

Winning Ways color *Sports Illustrated* v127 no2 p26 Jl 17 2017

Labadie, Gastón

2016 brazilian breeders cup *Arabian Horse World* v57 no2 p118 N 2016

THIRTY-THIRD PUNTA DEL ESTE: ARABIAN HORSE

SHOW color *Arabian Horse World* v57 no7 p94 Ap 2017

LABADIE, THOMAS

Easy Rider color *Road & Track* v68 no8 p108 My 2017

Labahn, Jörg

Fibril structure of amyloid-β(1–42) by cryo–electron microscopy color diag *Science* v357 no6359 p116 O 6 2017

LABAN, TERRY

COMICS *In These Times* v41 no10 p46 O 2017

La Barbara, Joan

Classical Music & Dance img *New York* v50 no17 p140 Ag 21 2017

LaBarre, Michelle

To help you stabilize your hand position… color *Dressage Today* v23 no6 p72 F 2017

Labash, Matt

A Beating in Berkeley [Cover story] color *Weekly Standard* v23 no1 p18 S 11 2017

Release Me color *Weekly Standard* v22 no25 p5 Mr 6 2017

Sweet Dreams Are Made of This color *Weekly Standard* v22 no33 p5 My 8 2017

Unhappy Meal color *Weekly Standard* v22 no11 p5 N 21 2016

LaBastille, Anne

An Enduring & Inspiring Vision *New York State Conservationist* v71 no3 p13 D 2016

ORIGINAL WOODSWOMAN: Preserving the legacy of Anne LaBastille L. Surprenant *New York State Conservationist* v71 no3 p10 D 2016

Labbé, David P.

Rb1 and Trp53 cooperate to suppress prostate cancer lineage plasticity, metastasis, and antiandrogen resistance bibl graph *Science* v355 no6320 p1 Ja 6 2017

Labbé, Romain

Row bots *Physics Today* v70 no6 p82 Je 2017

Labberton, Mark

More than a Plain Reading cartoon *Christianity Today* v61 no1 p64 Ja/F 2017

The plain, difficult sense of scripture *Christian Century* v134 no8 p1 Ap 12 2017

Labeling laws

How to Avoid Glyphosate M. DIANE SMITH color *Better Nutrition* v79 no7 p54 Jl 2017

Labels

See also

Food labeling

BEHIND THE LABEL color *Prevention* v69 no4 p6 Ap 2017

The Long Haul M. MATTIX cartoon *Weekly Standard* v22 no12 p5 N 28 2016

Labels—Evaluation

ASK SUSAN S. WESTMORELAND color *Good Housekeeping* v264 no2 p108 F 2017

HOW TO READ A Multivitamin Label [Cover story] *Nutrition Action Health Letter* v43 no9 p6 N 2016

LaBeouf, Shia, 1986-

CAPTURE THE FLAG A. Marantz cartoon *New Yorker* v93 no7 p34 Ap 3 2017

LABIANCA, JULIANA

7 Times The Airline Likely Owes You Money color *Reader's Digest* v190 no1134 p46 O 2017

8 Things You Should Never Do on an Airplane color *Reader's Digest* v189 no1129 p52 Ap 2017

Dinner in a Dumpster *Reader's Digest* v188 no1125 p12 N 2016

Extraordinary Reuses For Ordinary Things color *Reader's Digest* v189 no1129 p35 Ap 2017

He Paints Their Final Portraits *Reader's Digest* v188 no1124 p8 O 2016

High-Wire Act color *Reader's Digest* v189 no1129 p8 Ap 2017

How to (Shamelessly) Regift This Holiday Season *Reader's Digest* v188 no1126 p54 D 2016/Ja 2017

I Survived! [Cover story] *Reader's Digest* v189 no1128 p62 Mr 2017

Meet the Celebrity Judge color *Reader's Digest* v190 no1135 p80 N 2017

Mr. Clean Is on the Scene color *Reader's Digest* v190 no1135 p12 N 2017

Snap Dynamite Fireworks Photos color *Reader's Digest* v190 no1132 p33 Jl/Ag 2017

They Did the Right Thing cartoon *Reader's Digest* v190 no1134 p88 O 2017

Vacation Items You'll Almost Always Regret Packing *Reader's Digest* v188 no1126 p52 D 2016/Ja 2017

Labienus, d. 45 B.C.

The Quiz *History Today* v67 no1 p71 Ja 2017

Labille-Guiard, Adélaïde, 1749-1803

The Gratitude Meter Z. Donaldson color *O, The Oprah Magazine* p20 Mr 2017

Labong, Leilani Marie

COLOR OUTSIDE THE LINES color *Sunset* v239 no4 p36 O 2017

THE FAB LIFE color *Sunset* v238 no4 p50 Ap 2017

LOFTY AMBITIONS color *Sunset* v239 no4 p33 O 2017

Labor

See also

Contract labor

Home labor

Skilled labor

A Guide to Finding and Hiring the Best Contractors A. Merwin *Harvard Business Review Digital Articles* p2 Jl 17 2017

Labor (Obstetrics)

View from the Top C. FLORA *Psychology Today* v50 no1 p62 Ja/F 2017

Labor arbitration

Ellen Pao E. Dockterman color *Time* v190 no14 p56 O 9 2017

Labor complications (Obstetrics)

See also

Premature labor

What to Extopect K. BUTLER cartoon diag graph *Mother Jones* v42 no1 p38 Ja/F 2017

Labor contracts

5 ROADBLOCKS TO REFORM IN CHICAGO'S POLICE UNION CONTRACT *In These Times* v41 no6 p22 Je 2017

Trump Theory A. NAGANO *Commentary* v142 no1 p11 Jl/Ag 2016

We Need to Move Beyond the Employee vs. Contractor Debate J. Boudreau *Harvard Business Review Digital Articles* p2 Jl 8 2015

Labor contracts—Mexico

Why Mexico's Autoworkers Aren't Prospering D. Welch, N. Cattan et al color graph *Bloomberg Businessweek* no4521 p12 My 8 2017

Labor costs

See also

Wages

Labor courts—Great Britain

TRIBUNAL FEES ARE FINISHED - and here's what happens next: Should employers brace themselves for a tsunami of claims? And will the government reintroduce fees in a different form? H. KIRTON *People Management* p8 S 2017

Labor Day

DON'T MISS THIS *Atlanta* v57 no5 p34 S 2017

DROWNING ON MY CUSHION K. LARRABEE bw *Tricycle: The Buddhist Review* v27 no1 p58 Fall 2017

Here We Go! Oprah color *O, The Oprah Magazine* p19 Jl 2017

Thank You, American Workers T. J. DONOHUE *Weekly Standard* v23 no1 p8 S 11 2017

Washington View M. Ferguson diag *Phi Delta Kappan* v98 no4 p74 D 2016/Ja 2017

WEST RIVER EVENTS *South Dakota Magazine* v33 no3 p87 S/O 2017

Why Argue About a Day Off? P. TERZIAN color *Weekly Standard* v23 no2 p19 S 18 2017

Wine, Dine and Wine Some More C. HALL color *AARP: The Magazine* v59 no5A p59 Ag/S 2016

Labor discipline

Could HR solve...? *People Management* p62 D 2016/Ja 2017

Labor discipline—Lawsuits & claims

Mechanic wins unfair dismissal appeal after attack: Case highlights importance of policies and proper investigations, say legal experts *People Management* p15 Mr 2017

Labor economics

See also

Human capital

Labor law reform

History of child labor in the United States--part 2: the reform movement M. Schuman bibl bw color *Monthly Labor Review* p1 Ja 2017

Macron vs. The Unions C. Matlack and G. Viscusi graph *Bloomberg Businessweek* no4529 p30 Jl 3 2017

Severance à la Française C. Matlack color *Bloomberg Businessweek* no4540 p34 O 2 2017

Labor laws & legislation

See also

Equal pay for equal work laws

Parental leave laws

Retirement—Law & legislation

Working hours—Law & legislation

THE FRENCH DEFECTION J. ANGELOS bw color *New York Times Magazine* p44 Ja 29 2017

THE GIG ECONOMY IN COURT *People Management* p13 F 2017

Sense and License S. E. RHOADS color *Weekly Standard* v23 no6 p23 O 16 2017

Labor laws & legislation—France

French 'right to disconnect' law comes into force *People Management* p17 F 2017

Severance à la Française C. Matlack color *Bloomberg Businessweek* no4540 p34 O 2 2017

Labor laws & legislation—Great Britain

Change is in the air for employers *People Management* p6 My 2017

EXTRA EXTRA *People Management* p65 N 2016

Get ready for #HRmegamonth: From gender pay reporting to the minimum wage, People Management rounds up key legal and practical changes coming to the UK in April M. CALNAN *People Management* p8 Ap 2017

Most employment rights 'indispensable', say businesses: Survey finds majority want to avoid post-Brexit 'bonfire' *People Management* p13 Je 2017

Most gig economy workers 'want employment rights': But survey says few rely on platforms for their main income, and most are happy with pay *People Management* p15 Ap 2017

Who's the best choice for the future of work? As Britain goes to the polls, the CIPD asks for legislation on zero hours and action on diversity H. KIRTON *People Management* p8 Je 2017

Labor laws & legislation—United States

Bright Sides to a Trump Presidency W. DURST cartoon *Progressive* p67 D 2016/Ja 2017

Changes in federal and state unemployment insurance legislation in 2016 L. Lancaster *Monthly Labor Review* p1 Ag 2017

The New Fight for Labor Rights R. M. COHEN *New Republic* v248 no10 p6 O 2017

'Unjust Discrimination' *America* v215 no14 p5 N 7 2016

Labor leaders—United States

The Local Labor Leader Who Defied Trump M. UETRICHT *In These Times* v41 no2 p32 F 2017

Labor market

See also

Gig economy

Labor supply

Supply & demand of teachers

Building a 21st Century Workforce T. J. DONOHUE *Weekly Standard* v22 no48 p9 S 4 2017

Research: The Rise of Superstar Firms Has Been Better for Investors than for Employees J. Van Reenen and C. Patterson *Harvard Business Review Digital Articles* p1 My 11 2017

Saudi Arabia's Labor Market Challenge L. El-Katiri *Harvard Business Review Digital Articles* p2 Jl 6 2016

Starting a Business Can Increase Older Workers' Quality of Life (Even When It Doesn't Pay Well) M. Minniti, T. Kautonen et al *Harvard Business Review Digital Articles* p2 S 19 2017

Unemployment holds steady for much of 2016 but edges down in the fourth quarter V. Brundage Jr. and E. Cunningham bibl chart color graph *Monthly Labor Review* p1 Mr 2017

Young people are just smarter *People Management* p26 D 2016/Ja 2017

Labor market research

The 'Wisdom of the Crowd' Has a Pretty Bad Track Record at Predicting Jobs Reports D. Cassino *Harvard Business Review Digital Articles* p2 Jl 8 2016

South Africa's Divided Working-Class Movements M. PARET *Current History* v116 no790 p176 My 2017

Labor unions—United States

The Conservative Case for Unions J. RAUCH color graph *Atlantic* v320 no1 p15 Jl/Ag 2017

The decline of unions is part of a bad 50 years for American workers K. Clarke *America* v217 no5 p10 S 4 2017

IN THE AGE OF TRUMP, CAN LABOR UNITE? [Cover story] A. BRADBURY *In These Times* v41 no5 p18 My 2017

Labor pains graph *America* v217 no5 p14 S 4 2017

More Perfect Unions L. J. Wertheim and T. Keith color *Sports Illustrated* v125 no19 p19 D 12 2016

The New Fight for Labor Rights R. M. COHEN color *New Republic* v248 no10 p6 O 2017

Unions Want Hotels to Give ICE The Cold Shoulder J. Eidelson bw *Bloomberg Businessweek* no4539 p44 S 25 2017

Laboratories

THE CYBERSCIENTIST J. Bohannon color diag *Science* v357 no6346 p18 Jl 7 2017

MAKERS S. Kean cartoon *New Yorker* v92 no30 p25 S 26 2016

Storm kings K. Gray color *Popular Science* v289 no4 p60 Jl/Ag 2017

Laboratories—Furniture, equipment, etc.

new products color *Science* v355 no6328 p973 Mr 3 2017

Laboratories—Government policy

When Medical Tests Mislead C. Schmidt color *Scientific American* v315 no6 p28 D 2016

Laboratories—Universities & colleges

Undergraduate labs lag in science and technology T. Feder *Physics Today* v70 no4 p26 Ap 2017

Laboratory equipment & supplies

new products color *Science* v355 no6328 p973 Mr 3 2017

new products: general lab equipment color *Science* v357 no6352 p721 Ag 18 2017

Laboratory equipment & supplies—Evaluation

new products color *Science* v355 no6331 p1335 Mr 24 2017

new products: general lab equipment color *Science* v356 no6335 p334 Ap 21 2017

Laboratory for Visionary Architecture (Company)

LAVA C. Foges color *Architectural Record* v205 no2 p120 F 2017

Laborde, Errol

BACCHUS STORIES bw *New Orleans Magazine* v51 no3 p168 Ja 2017

BATON ROUGE AT 200 *Louisiana Life* v37 no3 p4 Ja/F 2017

BEST POOR BOY *New Orleans Magazine* v51 no2 p16 D 2016

Bud and Friends *New Orleans Magazine* v51 no5 p14 Mr 2017

Carnival SOME OF OUR FAVORITE THINGS color *New Orleans Magazine* v51 no4 p68 F 2017

CHRISTMAS OF '89 bw *New Orleans Magazine* v51 no2 p152 D 2016

Custer at Mardi Gras bw *New Orleans Magazine* v51 no4 p144 F 2017

EDWIN EDWARDS AT 90 *Louisiana Life* v37 no5 p4 My/Je 2017

Election Day in Liverpool: Victory for The Fab Four Party bw *New Orleans Magazine* v51 no10 p216 Ag 2017

Fish on the Half Shell *New Orleans Magazine* v51 no9 p14 Jl 2017

French vs. Italian *New Orleans Magazine* v51 no7 p14 My 2017

THE GREAT FLOOD: AN ANNIVERSARY *Louisiana Life* v37 no4 p4 Mr/Ap 2017

How Dixie Got Its 45 color *New Orleans Magazine* v52 no1 p168 S 2017

ICED *New Orleans Magazine* v51 no3 p12 Ja 2017

Jacques Chirac in New Orleans cartoon *New Orleans Magazine* v51 no8 p152 Je 2017

James Rivers and the 'Pipes *New Orleans Magazine* v51 no8 p16 Je 2017

JOLE BLON'S ANNIVERSARY *Louisiana Life* v38 no1 p6 S/O 2017

Krauss bw *New Orleans Magazine* v51 no9 p136 Jl 2017

Lessons From a Streetcar bw *New Orleans Magazine* v51 no6 p160 Ap 2017

Lundi Gras *New Orleans Magazine* v51 no4 p14 F 2017

My Favorite Block *New Orleans Magazine* v51 no6 p14 Ap 2017

A NIGHT AT THE OLD MANSION *Louisiana Life* v37 no6 p4 Jl/Ag 2017

THE QUIZ OF KINGS color *Louisiana Life* v37 no3 p110 Ja/F 2017

Roffignac cartoon *New Orleans Magazine* v51 no12 p168 O 2017

Sounds In the Night bw *New Orleans Magazine* v51 no5 p152 Mr 2017

Tennessee Williams Stories bw cartoon *New Orleans Magazine* v51 no7 p152 My 2017

Tricentennial: The Montreal Influence *New Orleans Magazine* v51 no12 p16 O 2017

The Truth About Ticks *New Orleans Magazine* v51 no10 p22 Ag 2017

TWO WOMEN IN BURKAS cartoon *New Orleans Magazine* v51 no1 p184 N 2016

WHEN IT SNOWS *Louisiana Life* v37 no2 p6 N/D 2016

LaBorde, Lauren

Ink in Her Blood *New Orleans Homes & Lifestyles* v20 no1 p30 Wint 2016

Labor market—Charts, diagrams, etc.

HOW DATA SCIENCE IS DISRUPTING THE JOB MARKET diag img *Harvard Business Review* v95 no5 p24 S/O 2017

Labor supply—Charts, diagrams, etc.

EMPLOYMENT, UNEMPLOYMENT, AND WAGES *Economic Indicators* p11 Ag 2017

Labor supply statistics—Charts, diagrams, etc.

EMPLOYMENT, UNEMPLOYMENT, AND WAGES *Economic Indicators* p11 Je 2017

Labor—United States

Computers Don't Kill Jobs but Do Increase Inequality J. Bessen *Harvard Business Review Digital Articles* p2 Mr 24 2016

Labor pains graph *America* v217 no5 p14 S 4 2017

Muckraking and Troublemaking C. HASS bw *In These Times* v40 no11 p41 N 2016

Labor—United States—History—20th century

LEARNING TO WORK THE NIGHT SHIFT: With the war effort, suddenly many more factories were working around the clock to fulfill their defense contracts G. Bijur and P. Martin *Saturday Evening Post* v289 no4 p96 Jl/Ag 2017

LABOU, STEPHANIE G.

Skills and Knowledge for Data-Intensive Environmental Research *BioScience* v67 no6 p546 Je 2017

Labour Party (Great Britain)

Labour's Corbyn Faced Media Attacks From Right and Center-on Both Sides of Atlantic B. Norton *Extra!* v30 no6 p3 Jl/Ag 2017

The Party of Left-Wing Anti-Semitism *Commentary* v141 no9 p1 N 2016

The Party of Left-Wing Anti-Semitism *Commentary* v142 no4 p1 N 2016

The Party of Left-Wing Anti-Semitism: The shocking decline and fall of Labour D. Murray *Commentary* v142 no4 p29 N 2016

Winning Isn't Everything G. Younge *Nation* v305 no8 p10 O 9 2017

Labour Party (Great Britain)—Officials & employees

Jeremy Corbyn M. Leftly color *Time* v188 no16/17 p96 O 24 2016

Labrador retriever

MAN'S FAVORITE BEST FRIEND color *Outdoor Life* v224 no6 p13 Ag 2017

THE UNDERDOG T. DOKKEN and T. PETERSON color *Outdoor Life* v224 no6 p46 Ag 2017

Labrador retriever—Behavior

A LABRADOR OF LOVE J. M. TURNER cartoon *Outdoor Life* v224 no1 p16 D 2016/Ja 2017

Labrecque, Jeff

THE 25 MOST PATRIOTIC MOVIES OF ALL TIME color *Entertainment Weekly* no1472 p30 Je 30 2017

MUHAMMAD ALI color *Entertainment Weekly* no1446/1447 p90 D 2016/Ja 2017

WarReN BEAtty An ORAL HISTORY color *Entertainment Weekly* no1440 p30 N 18 2016

What to Watch color *Entertainment Weekly* no1477 p50 Ag 11 2017

Labrijn, Aran F.

Hitting Ebola, to the power of two bibl diag *Science* v354 no6310 p284 O 21 2016

Labriola, Anthony

The Lonely Barber *Publishers Weekly* v264 no9 p83 F 27 2017

Labuz, D.
A nontoxic pain killer designed by modeling of pathological receptor conformations bibl diag graph *Science* v355 no6328 p966 Mr 3 2017

Labyrinths
Trying to Lose My Religion S. DIMITROPOULOS bw *Discover* v38 no7 p26 S 2017

La Caille, Nicolas Louis de, 1713-1762
The Father of Southern Astronomy B. Ventrudo *Sky & Telescope* v134 no4 p34 O 2017

LaCapra, Véronique
As Bay Warms, Harmful Algae Bloom *Oceanus* v52 no1 p9 Summ 2016

Crabs Swarm on the Seafloor *Oceanus* v52 no1 p6 Summ 2016

Endangered Whales Get a High-Tech Checkup: DRONES GIVE RESEARCHERS AN UNPARALLELED VIEW OF MARINE MAMMAL HEALTH *Oceanus* v52 no2 p10 Spr 2017

Keeping Whales Free from Fishing Gear: NEW "ON-CALL" BUOY FOR LOBSTER TRAPS COULD HELP PREVENT ENTANGLEMENTS *Oceanus* v52 no2 p16 Spr 2017

A Scientist-Fisherman Partnership: COLLABORATION SPURS MUTUAL BENEFITS FOR RESEARCH AND INDUSTRY *Oceanus* v52 no2 p4 Spr 2017

See Those Black Dots? They're Penguins. Now Count Them *Oceanus* v52 no1 p13 Summ 2016

Warming Ocean Drove Catastrophic Australian Floods *Oceanus* v52 no1 p11 Summ 2016

When the Hunter Became the Hunted *Oceanus* v52 no1 p21 Summ 2016

La Cava, Gregory
Mad, Democrats? Blame the Iran Deal *Commentary* p1 Ja 2017

Mad, Democrats? Blame the Iran Deal *Commentary* v143 no1 p1 Ja 2017

LaCAVA, STEPHANIE
Asia Kate DILION *Interview* v47 no6 p8 Ag 2017

Flavin JUDD *Interview* v46 no10 p38 D 2016/Ja 2017

Herizen GUARDIOLA *Interview* v46 no9 p20 N 2016

Jessica HENWICK *Interview* v47 no1 p12 F 2017

Rachel KELLER *Interview* v46 no8 p28 O 2016

Lacey, Catherine
BECAUSE YOU HAVE TO *Harper's Magazine* v335 no2006 p18 Jl 2017

CONNECT THE DOTS (AND THE ARTISTS) color *Entertainment Weekly* no1449 p62 Ja 20 2017

Help Wanted: In Catherine Lacey's novel, a famous actor tries to design the perfect partner piece by piece M. YOUNG *New York Times Book Review* p16 Jl 30 2017

LACEY, EILEEN A.
Teaching Biology in the Field: Importance, Challenges, and Solutions *BioScience* v67 no6 p558 Je 2017

Lacey, James
THE DAY WASHINGTON WOKE UP *MHQ: Quarterly Journal of Military History* v29 no3 p46 Spr 2017

Pax Romana *MHQ: Quarterly Journal of Military History* v29 no3 p92 Spr 2017

Lacey, John, 1755-1814
CLOSE CALL AT CROOKED BILLET A. A. Zellers-Frederick cartoon color map *Military History* v34 no1 p48 My 2017

LACEY, ROBERT
REMEMBERING DIANA color *AARP: The Magazine* v60 no5A p50 Ag/S 2017

Lachanze (Performer)
MAY'S HOTTEST EVENTS *Indianapolis Monthly* p22 My 2017

Lachel, Christian
The Brand Benefits of Places Like the Guinness Storehouse *Harvard Business Review Digital Articles* p2 O 20 2015

Lachenauer, Rob
The 5 Models of Family Business Ownership *Harvard Business Review Digital Articles* p2 S 20 2016

Dealing with the Unique Work-Life Challenges of Family Businesses *Harvard Business Review Digital Articles* p2 Mr 19 2015

Family Businesses Need One Person to Conquer and Another to Rule *Harvard Business Review Digital Articles* p2 D 3 2014

Making Better Decisions in Your Family Business *Harvard Business Review Digital Articles* p2 S 8 2015

Signs You're Losing Control of Your Family Business *Harvard Business Review Digital Articles* p2 Ap 7 2017

Surviving in a Family Business When You're Not Part of the Family *Harvard Business Review Digital Articles* p2 Ja 15 2015

Warren Buffett's Risky Final Bet *Harvard Business Review Digital Articles* p2 Ap 21 2016

What to Do If a Feud Threatens Your Family Business *Harvard Business Review Digital Articles* p2 Ap 15 2015

When You've Made Enough Money to Cause Family Tension *Harvard Business Review Digital Articles* p2 Ja 8 2016

Lachenauer, Scotty
BLACK BULLION color *Hot Rod* v70 no2 p60 F 2017

PURPLE MAJESTY color *Hot Rod* v70 no5 p38 My 2017

PUT AWAY WET bw color *Hot Rod* v70 no3 p40 Mr 2017

SHREDDING ON THE SANDS OF TIME color diag *Hot Rod* v70 no12 p38 D 2017

Lachow, Irving
The upside and downside of swarming drones bibl *Bulletin of the Atomic Scientists* v73 no2 p96 Mr 2017

Lacillade, Bruce
Still worried *U.S. Catholic* v82 no10 p5 O 2017

Lacity, Mary C.
What Knowledge Workers Stand to Gain from Automation *Harvard Business Review Digital Articles* p2 Je 19 2015

Lackberg, Camilla, 1974-
The Lost Boy T. Jordan color *Entertainment Weekly* no1438 p63 N 4 2016

LACKNER, KLAUS S,
Climate Change is a Waste Management Problem *Issues in Science & Technology* v33 no3 p83 Spr 2017

The promise of negative emissions bibl color *Science* v354 no6313 p714 N 11 2016

Laclette, Juan P.
Mexico's basic science funding falls short *Science* v357 no6348 p260 Jl 21 2017

Lacob, Joe
VENTURE BALL A. POWELL cartoon *Wired* v25 no10 p42 O 2017

Iaconangelo, David
Chancellor Angela Merkel of Germany calls for a ban of burqas as election nears *Christian Century* v134 no1 p15 Ja 4 2017

Lacoste SA
Primary Picks! color *Good Housekeeping* v264 no4 p27 Ap 2017

Lacour, Julie—Interviews
CELEBRATION IN THE OAKS color *New Orleans Magazine* v51 no1 p29 N 2016

LaCour, Sarah E.
Learning from schools that close opportunity gaps *Phi Delta Kappan* v99 no1 p8 S 2017

LACOVARA, KENNETH
In Defense of Dinosaurs color *Natural History* v125 no11 p36 N 2017

Lacquer & lacquering
COLOR THEORY S. ORR *Better Homes & Gardens* v95 no4 p2 Ap 2017

Lacreek National Wildlife Refuge (S.D.)
ON THE RISE *South Dakota Magazine* v32 no4 p110 N/D 2016

Lacrimal apparatus—Physiology
Second opinion *Mayo Clinic Health Letter* v35 no2 p8 F 2017

Lactic acid
TURN UP THE HEAT M. BERG color *Muscle & Performance* v9 no6 p20 Je 2017

Lactose intolerance
The Gut Diaries K. Dold color *Women's Health* v13 no10 p78 D 2016

Lacy, Megan
Finding Balance in Horse Ownership *In Stride* v12 no5 p31 S 2017

Navigating the Purchase Process *In Stride* v12 no4 p24 Jl 2017

Taking Ownership: Finding the Right Professional for You *In Stride* v12 no3 p30 My 2017

Taking Ownership: Tips for the New or Longtime Horse Owner *In Stride* v12 no2 p45 Mr 2017

Lacy, Sarah
A Uterus Is a Feature, Not a Bug: The Working Woman's Guide to Overthrowing the Patriarchy *Publishers Weekly* v264 no31

p71 Jl 31 2017

Ladas, Alice K.
Diamond's Space *Humanist* v77 no1 p5 Ja/F 2017

Ladd, Cheryl
SPREADING HER WINGS C. Mann color *Amazing Wellness* v9 no2 p20 Spr 2017

Ladd, Diane
The Stars Are Out R. Love color *AARP: The Magazine* v59 no3A p4 Ap/My 2016

LADD, GARY
HUGE UNDERTAKING bw *Arizona Highways* v93 no5 p32 My 2017

Ladd, Helen F.
Self-governing schools, parental choice, and the need to protect the public interest *Phi Delta Kappan* v99 no1 p31 S 2017

Ladd, Ted
The Limits of the Lean Startup Method *Harvard Business Review Digital Articles* p2 Mr 7 2016

Ladd, Troy—Interviews
Take 5 With TROY LADD J. P. Huffman color *Hot Rod* v70 no2 p14 F 2017

Ladder, The (Music)
The Purple One color *Ebony* v72 no8 p82 Je 2017

Ladders—Equipment & supplies
Modern and Sporty color *Old House Journal* v45 no3 p50 My 2017

Ladders—Evaluation
Ladders color *Popular Mechanics* p34 S 2017
Ladders color *Popular Mechanics* v193 no7 p34 S 2016
The Right Ladder M. E. Polson color *Old House Journal* v45 no2 p52 Ap 2017

Ladders—Safety measures
The Right Ladder M. E. Polson color *Old House Journal* v45 no2 p52 Ap 2017

Laden, Charles
Fall to Winter *South Dakota Magazine* v32 no4 p106 N/D 2016

LADENDORF, ROBERT
A Brilliant Climate Collaboration *Skeptical Inquirer* v41 no5 p60 S/O 2017

LADER, ELLIS
Understanding the Victors *American Scholar* v86 no2 p3 Spr 2017

Ladge, Jamie J.
Coping with the Effects of Emotionally Difficult Work *Harvard Business Review Digital Articles* p2 Ag 16 2016

Ladies' Lunch (Short story)
Ladies' Lunch L. SEGAL cartoon *New Yorker* v93 no2 p62 F 27 2017

Ladies Professional Golf Association
Cheyenne Woods J. Marksbury and C. Barrett color *Golf Magazine* v59 no6 p34 Je 2017
Hitting the Sweet Spot N. Lopez color *AARP: The Magazine* v30 no6A p64 O/N 2017

Ladinsky, Mark S.
Nanoscale-length control of the flagellar driveshaft requires hitting the tethered outer membrane color diag graph *Science* v356 no6334 p197 Ap 14 2017

Ladoceour, Lauren
BEST OF THE WEST color *Sunset* v239 no4 p13 O 2017
COEUR D'ALENE, ID color *Sunset* v238 no4 p34 Ap 2017
soul FOOD color *Yoga Journal* no288 p75 D 2016
sound bites color *Yoga Journal* p111 2017 Special Issue

Lady Humps (Music)
BEN FERGUSON T. Monterosso cartoon color *Snowboarder* v29 no4 p40 D 2016

Lady in the Water (Film)
M. NIGHT SHYAMALAN'S SCORECARD color *Entertainment Weekly* no1450 p43 Ja 27 2017

Lady Macbeth (Film)
Lady Macbeth C. Nashawaty color *Entertainment Weekly* no1474/1475 p98 Jl 21-28 2017
LADY MACBETH R. Kinane color *Entertainment Weekly* no1463/1464 p71 Ap/My 2017

Lady Macbeth (Theatrical production)
Hey, Lady! M. GUIDUCCI color *Vogue* v207 no7 p58 Jl 2017

Lady Macbeth of Mtsensk (Theatrical production)
Lady Macbeth of Mtsensk J. A. Leipsic *Opera News* v81 no9 p46

Mr 2017

Lady Wood (Music)
COOL GIRL INTERRUPTED N. Feeney color *Entertainment Weekly* no1438 p28 N 4 2016
LADY WOOD M. Vain color *Entertainment Weekly* no1438 p31 N 4 2016
Tove Lo's High Life B. SPANOS color *Rolling Stone* no1275 p18 D 1 2016

Lady Gaga, 1986-
THE 25-WORD REVIEW N. Feeney color *Entertainment Weekly* no1463/1464 p104 Ap/My 2017
Gaga Hitches a Ride on Drag Race J. Nolfi color *Entertainment Weekly* no1457/1458 p17 Mr 17 2017
Gaga's Totally Nineties Cowgirl Blues R. SHEFFIELD color *Rolling Stone* no1274 p57 N 17 2016
GOING GAGA AT HALFTIME! K. ROSEN *TV Guide* v65 no6 p48 Ja 30 2017
'Grigio Girls' B. FINGER *New York Times Magazine* p57 Mr 12 2017
INSIDE LADY GAGA'S SUPER-SECRET SUPER BOWL SET N. Feeney color *Entertainment Weekly* no1451/1452 p14 F 3-10 2017
Lady Gaga color *InStyle* v24 no3 p274 Mr 2017
Lady Gaga COMES DOWN to EARTH N. Feeney color *Entertainment Weekly* no1434 p26 O 7 2016
Marina Abramovic at 70 C. Swanson img *New York* v49 no21 p99 O 17 2016
Pop Chart R. Bruner, C. Lang et al color *Time* v188 no16/17 p94 O 24 2016
PORTRAIT OF A LADY bw color *Harper's Bazaar* no3649 p292 D 2016/Ja 2017
Random Notes color *Rolling Stone* no1287 p22 My 18 2017
Sound Bites color *Entertainment Weekly* no1485 p2 O 6 2017
WHAT'S NEXT FOR LADY GAGA M. Vain color *Entertainment Weekly* no1453 p17 F 17 2017

Ladzinski, Keith
THE PARKS OF TOMORROW color diag graph map *National Geographic* v230 no6 p102 D 2016

Laennec, R. T. H. (René Théophile Hyacinthe), 1781-1826
THOU SIMPLE TUBE M. Dickson *History Today* v67 no5 p66 My 2017

Laestadius, Lars
The extent of forest in dryland biomes [Cover story] chart map *Science* v356 no6338 p635 My 12 2017

La Farge, Paul
For the Love of Lovecraft D. T. MAX *New York Times Book Review* p14 Mr 12 2017
The Night Ocean P. CANNON bw *Publishers Weekly* v263 no51 p120 D 12 2016

LaFave Jr., Tim
Pseudoscience versus science *Physics Today* v69 no11 p10 N 2016

LAFAVORE, MIKE
WAR! WOMEN! WEASELS! bw color *Men's Health* v32 no5 p120 Je 2017

LaFayette (N.Y.)
Atla S. Lyon color *New Yorker* v93 no16 p32 Je 5 2017

Lafayette, Marie Joseph Paul Yves Roch Gilbert Du Motier, marquis de, 1757-1834
The Surprisingly Peaceful Origins of Bastille Day M. Fabry *Time* v190 no4 p19 Jl 24 2017

Lafee, Scott
CODING: The New 21st-Century Literacy? *Education Digest* v83 no2 p25 O 2017

Lafer, Gordon
Work Hard, Die Poor: The Corporate Attack on Employee Pensions color *Progressive* v81 no6 p30 Ag/S 2017

Laff, Becky
Joseph the Dreamer *Publishers Weekly* v263 no41 p82 O 10 2016

Lafferty, Kelsey
Sister Act color *Glamour* v115 no5 p188 My 2017

Laffont, Jean-Pierre, 1935-
This Magic Moment: For more than 50 years, photographer Jean-Pierre Laffont has proved that in New York, you never know what you might see A. STERNBERGH img *New York* v50 no15 p64 Jl 24 2017

LAFFOON, POLK IV

Crystal Visions *Cincinnati Magazine* v50 no6 p50 Mr 2017

Growing Up color *Cincinnati Magazine* v51 no1 p38 O 2017

LaFleur, Martin W.

The epigenetic landscape of T cell exhaustion bibl graph *Science* v354 no6316 p1165 D 2 2016

Lafleur-Vetter, Sara

NATIONS RISING color *Earth Island Journal* v32 no4 p18 Wint 2017

LAFLEY, A.G.

CUSTOMER LOYALTY IS OVERRATED [Cover story] color *Harvard Business Review* v95 no1 p45 Ja/F 2017

Lafont, Cristina

Can Democracy be Deliberative & Participatory? The Democratic Case for Political Uses of Mini-Publics *Daedalus* v146 no3 p85 Summ 2017

LaFountain, Michael

The Requiem J. L. Stein color *Cycle World* v55 no11 p40 D 2016

LAFRANCE, ADRIENNE

Baby, Monitored bw color *Atlantic* v318 no5 p24 D 2016

Lafranchi, Howard

Refugee plan divides religious leaders color *Christian Century* v134 no5 p12 Mr 1 2017

LaFranco Scheuch, Lisa

Systemic pan-AMPK activator MK-8722 improves glucose homeostasis but induces cardiac hypertrophy graph *Science* v357 no6350 p507 Ag 4 2017

LaFreniere, Isabelle

Isabella LaFreniere G. KOURLAS *Dance Magazine* v91 no6 p22 Je 2017

Lagacé, Patrick

BAD NEWS color *Maclean's* v129 no45 p9 N 14 2016

Lagarde, Christine, 1956-

The Best Leaders Allow Themselves to Be Persuaded A. Pittampalli *Harvard Business Review Digital Articles* p2 Mr 3 2016

"I've always loved stories about women" bw color *Glamour* v114 no12 p68 D 2016

New world disorder K. CARMICHAEL color *Maclean's* v129 no48/49 p60 D 5 2016

Lagarde, Christine, 1956—Interviews

Christine LAGARDE A. Robb color *Glamour* v114 no12 p220 D 2016

Lagasse, Emeril, 1959-

Emeril Lagasse J. Forman color *New Orleans Magazine* v51 no2 p68 D 2016

Lage, Julian

Jazzahead! Draws Record Number of Attendees B. Zimmerman color *Downbeat* v84 no7 p16 Jl 2017

Lagerfeld, Karl, 1933-

THE BRIDE WORE BLUSH color *Harper's Bazaar* no3653 p147 My 2017

FENDI'S FAIRY TALE J. J. Martin color *Harper's Bazaar* no3648 p272 N 2016

French Twist E. Wilson color *InStyle* v23 no12 p260 N 2016

My Desk color *Vanity Fair* p93 Hollywood 2017 Supplement

Lagerfeld, Nathalie

Feeling No Pain img *American Scholar* v86 no1 p124 Wint 2017

Lagerstroemia

ask THE GRUMPY GARDENER S. Bender color *Southern Living* v51 no11 p48 N 2016

THE GRUMPY GARDENER S. Bender color *Southern Living* v52 no4 p48 Ap 2017

THE GRUMPY GARDENER S. Bender color *Southern Living* v52 no7 p31 Jl 2017

Summer's Confetti K. Owen color *Southern Living* v52 no6 p32 Je 2017

Lageschaar, Lisa

A GRAND ENTRY! color *Horse & Rider* v56 no11 p56 N 2017

Lagomarsino, Marco Cosentino

Quantitative Viral Ecology *Physics Today* v70 no6 p65 Je 2017

Lagrange, Pierre

Savile Row Arrives Stateside T. Patterson bw color *Bloomberg Businessweek* no4530 p59 Jl 17 2017

LAGRAVE, KATHERINE

Do Como Right color *Conde Nast Traveler* v52 no2 p14 F 2017

Hitting BA Just Right color *Conde Nast Traveler* v52 no3 p18 Mr 2017

One Step Beyond color *Conde Nast Traveler* v52 no7 p41 Ag 2017

La Guardia, Fiorello H. (Fiorello Henry), 1882-1947

New Yorkers I. M. STELZER bw *Weekly Standard* v22 no46 p5 Ag 14 2017

LaGuardia, Pete

SIMPLE route selection color *Model Railroader* v84 no7 p39 Jl 2017

La Guardia Airport (New York, N.Y.)

I LOVE LAGUARDIA C. Suddath color *Bloomberg Businessweek* no4514 p72 Mr 13 2017

Makeover in Queens *Governing* v30 no3 p53 D 2016

The Universally Acknowledged Dump That Is La Guardia Airport Is Finally Getting an Upgrade C. BONANOS img *New York* v49 no25 p72 D 12 2016

Lagudah, Evans S.

Starving the enemy bibl diag *Science* v354 no6318 p1377 D 16 2016

Lagum, Aamito

cuff love A. Syrett color *InStyle* v24 no2 p128 F 2017

Laguna Beach (Calif.)

Laguna Beach Festival of Arts *Saturday Evening Post* v288 no6 p32 N/D 2016

Laguna Beach (TV program)

CHEERS & JEERS D. HOLBROOK *TV Guide* v65 no35 p76 Ag 21 2017

Laha, Bireswar

Regenerating optic pathways from the eye to the brain diag *Science* v356 no6342 p1031 Je 9 2017

Lahav, Alexandra

How Lawsuits Help Democracy S. Begley color *Time* v189 no4 p18 F 6 2017

Lahav, Ofer

Survey finds galaxy clumps stirred up by dark energy D. Clery color *Science* v357 no6351 p537 Ag 11 2017

Lahaye, Thierry

An atom-by-atom assembler of defect-free arbitrary two-dimensional atomic arrays bibl bw diag graph *Science* v354 no6315 p1021 N 25 2016

Laheru, Dan

Mismatch repair deficiency predicts response of solid tumors to PD-1 blockade chart graph *Science* v357 no6349 p409 Jl 28 2017

LAHEY, ANITA

Feed the Birds color *Walrus* v14 no8 p21 O 2017

In the Palm of Her Hand *Walrus* v14 no9 p72 N 2017

LAHEY, EMILY

Shop 'til Your Eyes Pop *USA Today Magazine* v146 no2868 p79 S 2017

Lahm, Brandon

#trailchat color il map *Backpacker* p6 Je 2017

LAHR, JOHN

ACT OF GRACE cartoon color *New Yorker* v92 no42 p52 D 19 2016

WALKING TALL bw cartoon *New Yorker* v92 no34 p34 O 24 2016

Lahsen, Myanna

Civil Society and Environmental Change in Brazil's Cerrado bibl *Environment* v58 no6 p16 N/D 2016

Precaution Needs to Abound, Not Wither *Environment* v59 no5 p2 S/O 2017

Undervaluing and Overexploiting the Brazilian Cerrado at Our Peril bibl *Environment* v58 no6 p4 N/D 2016

LaHurd, D.

Observation of a large-scale anisotropy in the arrival directions of cosmic rays above 8×10^{18} eV *Science* v357 no6357 p1266 S 22 2017

Lai, Jonathan R.

A "Trojan horse" bispecific-antibody strategy for broad protection against ebolaviruses bibl graph *Science* v354 no6310 p350 O 21 2016

Lai, Lisa

Being a Strategic Leader Is About Asking the Right Questions color *Harvard Business Review Digital Articles* p2 Ja 18 2017

Focus on Winning Either Hearts or Minds *Harvard Business Review Digital Articles* p2 My 20 2015

Motivating Employees Is Not About Carrots or Sticks *Harvard*

Business Review Digital Articles p2 Je 27 2017

Lai, Peter
A Tiny Village By Little Tokyo J. CARREIRO *Los Angeles Magazine* v61 no11 p24 N 2016

Lai, Prerna
We're Not Going Back in the Shadows *In These Times* v40 no12 p19 D 2016

Lai, Trevor
Piggy *Publishers Weekly* v263 no41 p77 O 10 2016

Laiacona, Michael
Whirlwind's 42 Years of Rock-Solid Reliability and Diversity *Stage Directions* v30 no3 p13 Mr 2017

Laidlaw, Eli
SECOND COURSE T. KIRTS *Indianapolis Monthly* v40 no4 p50 D 2016

LAIDLAW, KATHERINE
Central Parc color *Walrus* v13 no9 p68 N 2016
Period Drama color *Walrus* v14 no3 p18 Ap 2017

Laif, Paul
FROM THE EDITOR *History Today* v67 no3 p2 Mr 2017

Laine, Romain F.
De novo design of a biologically active amyloid bibl graph *Science* v354 no6313 paah4949-1 N 11 2016

LAING, JOANN M.
AI Apparently Is for Real *USA Today Magazine* v145 no2862 p35 Mr 2017

Lainhart, Brendan C.
Catalytic intermolecular hydroaminations of unactivated olefins with secondary alkyl amines bibl diag *Science* v355 no6326 p727 F 17 2017

LAIRD, AMY KELLER
GREAT BEFORE, GREATER AFTER! *Women's Health* v14 no1 p12 Ja/F 2017

LAIRD, FRANK N.
Advancing clean energy *Issues in Science & Technology* v33 no3 p5 Spr 2017

Laird, Jessica
Meals for Munchkins color *Working Mother* v40 no3 p18 Ag/S 2017
Sitters in a Snap color *Working Mother* v40 no4 p18 O/N 2017

Laird, Kate
The Floating Classroom color *Sail* v48 no4 p12 Ap 2017
Northern Lights color *Sail* v48 no1 p12 Ja 2017

Laird, Nick, 1975-
Myths, Tribes & Troubles J. Walton bw *New York Review of Books* v64 no12 p34 Jl 13 2017
Nick LAIRD M. Chabon *Interview* v47 no5 p16 Je/Jl 2017
Two Islands: Northern Ireland and Papua New Guinea don't seem so different in Nick Laird's new novel J. EGAN *New York Times Book Review* p8 Jl 2 2017

Laird-Hopkins, Benita
Higher predation risk for insect prey at low latitudes and elevations graph *Science* v356 no6339 p742 My 19 2017

LAISKONIS, MICHAEL
EXPENSIVE TASTE color *Women's Health* v14 no8 p30 O 2017

Laitin, David D.
Protecting unauthorized immigrant mothers improves their children's mental health diag *Science* v357 no6355 p1041 S 8 2017

La Jolla (San Diego, Calif.)—Description & travel
GRACE AND FRANKIES SAN DIEGO: The artsy burg of La Jolla, California, deserves all the attention it gets D. ANDERSON-MINSHALL *Advocate* no1093 p52 O/N 2017

Lak, Sander
OBJECTS of their DESIRE R. SULLIVAN, M. HOLGATE et al color *Vogue* v207 no3 p326 Mr 2017

Lakdawalla, Darius
It's Easier to Measure the Cost of Health Care than Its Value *Harvard Business Review Digital Articles* p2 N 18 2014

Lakdawalla, Emily
Curiosity's Discoveries on Mars *Sky & Telescope* v133 no4 p14 Ap 2017

Lake, Greg, 1947-2016—Interviews
Greg Lake and ELP Welcome Us Back to the Hi-Fi Show That Never Ends M. METTLER and C. Crowley bw color *Sound & Vision* v81 no10 p24 D 2016

Lake, Oliver—Interviews

Trio 3: SURVIVAL SYNDROME T. Panken color *Downbeat* v84 no4 p34 Ap 2017

Lake, Peter
How Shakespeare Put Politics on the Stage: Power and Succession in the History Plays D. Huntley *British Heritage Travel* v38 no1 p72 Ja/F 2017

Lake, Robin
How States Can Promote Local Innovation, Options, and Problem-Solving in Public Education bw *Education Digest* v83 no3 p30 N 2017

Lake, Thomas
Stop Hitting Yourself C. Lehmann *In These Times* v41 no1 p38 Ja 2017

Lake acidification
POLLUTION IN PARADISE V. HAFSTAÐ *Iceland Review* v55 no3 p70 My/Je 2017

Lake District National Park (England)
Touring in the Lake District *British Heritage Travel* v38 no3 p20 My/Je 2017

Lake Havasu City (Ariz.)
BURNING MEN S. Hely color *Esquire* p28 Je/Jl 2017

Lake management
Is Your Property Lake-Friendly? E. Bye color *Cabin Living* p54 S 2017

Lake Mead National Recreation Area (Ariz. & Nev.)
Spa Days: Lake Mead National Recreation Area, Nevada/Arizona K. KYLE color map *Backpacker* p14 N 2017

Lake sediment analysis
Paleoecology--Looking to the Past to Inform the Future: Researchers uncover the buried history of lakes and estuaries S. LEVY *BioScience* v67 no9 p791 S 2017

Lake sturgeon
Living Leviathans L. Holst *New York State Conservationist* v72 no1 p22 Ag 2017

Lake trout fishing
FALL IN LINE W. RYAN color *Field & Stream* v122 no4 p16 S 2017

Lakefield College School (Peterborough, Ont.)
An elite school's dark past M. FRISCOLANTI bw color *Maclean's* v130 no10 p32 N 2017

Lake|Flato Architects Inc.
Confluence Park M. Sitz *Architectural Record* v205 no4 p208 Ap 2017

Lakeland, Paul
When Art & Spirit Meet E. T. Wheeler color *Commonweal* v144 no16 p35 O 6 2017

Laker, Ben
How to Turn Around a Failing School *Harvard Business Review Digital Articles* p2 Ag 5 2016
The One Type of Leader Who Can Turn Around a Failing School bw color *Harvard Business Review Digital Articles* p2 O 20 2016
Research: How the Best School Leaders Create Enduring Change *Harvard Business Review Digital Articles* p2 S 14 2017

Lakes
10! P. ROBBINS, L. VICK et al cartoon color *Field & Stream* v122 no1 p30 My 2017
Imagining Imogene N. OWENS BARNES *Idaho Magazine* v17 no1 p6 Ja 2017
LAKE ASSOCIATION SPOTLIGHT color *Cabin Living* p10 Ag 2017
THE LAKE HOUSE T. George cartoon *Cabin Living* p88 Mr 2017
LET'S COZY UP TO small CABINS! M. R. JOHNSON bw color *Cabin Living* p5 Mr 2017
Marinating in the Moment C. HEITGER-EWING color *Cabin Living* p18 Mr 2017
Think big color *Backpacker* p20 O 2017
Translating Regime Shifts in Shallow Lakes into Changes in Ecosystem Functions and Services S. HILT, S. BROTHERS et al *BioScience* v67 no10 p928 O 2017
Weatherscapes. The Snowy Range – Hidden Alpine Gem E. Darack *Weatherwise* v69 no6 p8 N-D 2016

Lakes in art
On the Lake — Central Park cartoon *Magazine Antiques* v184 no1 p29 Ja/F 2017

Lakes—Arizona
   See also
      Powell, Lake (Utah & Ariz.)
   EXPLORE THE WHITE MOUNTAINS *Arizona Highways* v96 no7 p16 Jl 2017
Lakes—British Columbia
   Seeing Red A. CRAWFORD *Smithsonian* v47 no7 p14 N 2016
Lakes—California
   Lost Lake *Los Angeles Magazine* p16 Ag 2017
Lakes—Canada
   Coast over Corridor Z. ZORICH color *Archaeology* v69 no6 p17 N/D 2016
Lakes—Germany
   A JOURNEY Through Germany L. Paulsen color *Dressage Today* v23 no7 p32 Mr 2017
Lakes—Iceland
   HIGHS & LOWS *Iceland Review* v55 no1 p28 Ja/F 2017
Lakes—Indiana
   EASY ESCAPES [Cover story] N. K. HAHN color *Chicago* v66 no6 p54 Je 2017
Lakes—Michigan
   LAKE ASSOCIATION SPOTLIGHT color *Cabin Living* p11 S 2017
Lakes—Russia—Siberia
   Cold Comfort S. Roberts color *Conde Nast Traveler* v51 no11 p74 D 2016
   Solo Flight P. Guzmán color *Conde Nast Traveler* v51 no11 p20 D 2016
Lakes—Texas
   5 East Texas Hideaways color *American Cowboy* p55 LEGENDS OF TEXAS Special Issue 2017
   CREATURE FROM THE GREEN LAGOON L. BEIL *Texas Monthly* v45 no9 p72 S 2017
Lakes—United States
   See also
      Great Lakes (North America)
      Michigan, Lake
   lake Love A. HASLETT bw color *Conde Nast Traveler* v52 no6 p90 Je/Jl 2017
Lakes—Wisconsin
   EASY ESCAPES [Cover story] N. K. HAHN color *Chicago* v66 no6 p54 Je 2017
Lakhani, Karim R.
   The Antidote to HiPPOs: Crowd Voting *Harvard Business Review Digital Articles* p2 F 2 2016
   THE BLOCKCHAIN REVOLUTION: INTERACTION color *Harvard Business Review* v95 no2 p20 Mr/Ap 2017
   MANAGING OUR HUB ECONOMY: STRATEGY, ETHICS, AND NETWORK COMPETITION IN THE AGE OF DIGITAL SUPERPOWERS color diag graph img *Harvard Business Review* v95 no5 p84 S/O 2017
   Taylor Swift and the Economics of Music as a Service *Harvard Business Review Digital Articles* p2 N 6 2014
   THE TRUTH ABOUT BLOCKCHAIN bw color diag img *Harvard Business Review* v95 no1 p118 Ja/F 2017
   What the Companies on the Right Side of the Digital Business Divide Have in Common color *Harvard Business Review Digital Articles* p2 Ja 31 2017
Lakin, Joshua
   Changing How Patients and Doctors Talk About Death *Harvard Business Review Digital Articles* p2 D 1 2016
Lakoff, Robin Tolmach
   Donald Trump, James Comey, and the Ambiguity of "Hope" *Harvard Business Review Digital Articles* p2 Je 13 2017
Lakota (Company)
   Trailer Innovations K. Navarra bw color *Horse & Rider* v56 no7 p78 Jl 2017
Lakota (North American people)
   At Home With... D. BRISBY color *American Cowboy* v23 no6 p16 Ap/My 2017
   CRUDE AWAKENING W. ENZINNA color *Mother Jones* v42 no1 p32 Ja/F 2017
Lakota (North American people)—History—19th century
   Grant's Uncivil War P. COZZENS *Smithsonian* v47 no7 p46 N 2016
Lakshmi, Padma, 1970-

   Kitchen Wisdom color *AARP: The Magazine* v59 no3A p9 Ap/My 2016
   Pioneers [Cover story] color *Time* v189 no16/17 p14 My 1-8 2017
   the stylemaker event BIG IDEAS *Better Homes & Gardens* v95 no1 p9 Ja 2017
Lakshmi, Radha
   Kitchen Ritual A. BRANDT *Cincinnati Magazine* v50 no5 p162 F 2017
Lal, Deepak
   RISING TIDES AND MEGA-YACHTS *Claremont Review of Books* v16 no4 p55 Fall 2016
Lalami, Laila
   Blending In color *New York Times Magazine* p11 Ag 6 2017
   The Change We Believed In il *Nation* v304 no1 p8 Ja 2 2017 The Obama Years
   The Color of Terrorism *Nation* v305 no11 p12 O 30 2017
   Divided We Stand il *Nation* v303 no22 p10 N 28 2016
   Free Press Under Assault diag *Nation* v304 no18 p10 Je 19 2017
   The GOP Empathy Gap il *Nation* v303 no18 p12 O 31 2016
   Group Think *New York Times Magazine* p15 N 27 2016
   How to Win the Culture War il *Nation* v305 no5 p10 Ag 28 2017
   No Time for Silence bw color *Nation* v304 no5 p12 F 20 2017
   Over the Edge *New York Times Magazine* p13 Ap 30 2017
   Save the Arts, Save America *Nation* v304 no13 p10 Ap 17 2017
   Unprepared for Disaster il *Nation* v305 no7 p10 S 25 2017
   Who Belongs in America? il *Nation* v304 no9 p12 Mr 20 2017
Laland, Kevin N.
   High fidelity J. Henrich color *Science* v356 no6340 p810 My 26 2017
Lalanne, François-Xavier
   Herd Mentality H. MARTIN bw color *Architectural Digest* v74 no3 p26 Mr 2017
Laliberté, Etienne
   Plant-soil feedback and the maintenance of diversity in Mediterranean-climate shrublands bibl graph *Science* v355 no6321 p1 Ja 13 2017
LALIBERTE, MARISSA
   Homegrown Medical Mystery color map *Reader's Digest* v190 no1132 p42 Jl/Ag 2017
   The Priceless Car Loan color *Reader's Digest* v189 no1131 p86 Je 2017
   Silent Signs Your Body Craves a Diet Tweak *Reader's Digest* v188 no1126 p46 D 2016/Ja 2017
   Water—To Your Health! color *Reader's Digest* v190 no1133 p33 S 2017
LALIBERTE, RICHARD
   5 Surprising Reasons You're Not Losing Weight cartoon *AARP: The Magazine* v60 no2A p24 F/Mr 2017
   Can the World Be Your doctor? cartoon *Men's Health* v32 no9 p119 N 2017
   Dry Eyes *Prevention* v69 no7 p18 Jl 2017
   MISERABLE? HERE'S WHY cartoon chart color *Men's Health* v32 no3 p73 Ap 2017
   Plantar Fasciitis [Cover story] cartoon *Prevention* v69 no4 p18 Ap 2017
   Problem Solved! color *Prevention* v68 no12 p22 D 2016
   Problem Solved Constipation *Prevention* v69 no9 p24 O 2017
   Problem Solved! [Cover story] cartoon *Prevention* v69 no5 p18 My 2017
   Problem Solved: Gum Disease *Prevention* v69 no6 p18 Je 2017
   Problem Solved: Heartburn *Prevention* v69 no8 p22 Ag 2017
   Problem Solved: Warts *Prevention* v69 no11 p20 N 2017
Lallemend, Francois
   miR-183 cluster scales mechanical pain sensitivity by regulating basal and neuropathic pain genes diag graph *Science* v356 no6343 p1168 Je 16 2017
   Multipotent peripheral glial cells generate neuroendocrine cells of the adrenal medulla color *Science* v357 no6346 p46 Jl 7 2017
Lalueza-Fox, Carles
   The growth pattern of Neandertals, reconstructed from a juvenile skeleton from El Sidrón (Spain) color graph *Science* v357 no6357 p1282 S 22 2017
   Neandertal and Denisovan DNA from Pleistocene sediments bw color *Science* v356 no6338 p605 My 12 2017
Lalvani, Kartar
   The troubled history of the 'jewel in the Crown' M. Bose *History*

Today v67 no1 p59 Ja 2017

Lam, Bao H.

Mismatch repair deficiency predicts response of solid tumors to PD-1 blockade chart graph *Science* v357 no6349 p409 Jl 28 2017

Lam, Enid Y. N.

Click chemistry enables preclinical evaluation of targeted epigenetic therapies diag *Science* v356 no6345 p1397 Je 30 2017

Lam, Francis

A Middle Eastern Layer Cake for Dinner *New York Times Magazine* p22 Ja 8 2017

Shamelessly French color *New York Times Magazine* p26 D 4 2016

A Shorter Road to Singapore *New York Times Magazine* p34 O 30 2016

What My Chinese Mother Made *New York Times Magazine* p22 F 5 2017

Lam, Fred C.

The DNA-sensing AIM2 inflammasome controls radiation-induced cell death and tissue injury bibl color graph *Science* v354 no6313 p765 N 11 2016

Lam, Richard

How to Eat a Regular-Size Soup Dumpling H. GOLDFIELD img *New York* v49 no25 p106 D 12 2016

Lam, Sharon

Pathological α-synuclein transmission initiated by binding lymphocyte-activation gene 3 bibl graph *Science* v353 no6307 paah3374-1 S 30 2016

Lam, Wifredo, 1902-1982

Hermes Trismegiste color *Art in America* v104 no10 p61 N 2016

Lamach, Michael W.

3 Ways to Incorporate Sustainability into Everyday Work *Harvard Business Review Digital Articles* p2 O 1 2015

LAMAN, ALLEN

best of Indy *Indianapolis Monthly* v40 no4 p73 D 2016

Pitter Patter *Indianapolis Monthly* v40 no4 p38 D 2016

LaManna, Joseph A.

Plant diversity increases with the strength of negative density dependence at the global scale diag *Science* v356 no6345 p1389 Je 30 2017

Lamar, Kendrick, 1987-

63 GREAT THINGS TO DO THIS MONTH J. FOUMBERG, J. HARDBERGER et al color *Chicago* v66 no7 p87 Jl 2017

KENDRICK & GAGA HEAT UP THE DESERT G. Hall color *Entertainment Weekly* no1463/1464 p106 Ap/My 2017

LEGACY MEDIA HUA HSU color *New Yorker* v93 no11 p74 My 1 2017

Lamar, Kendrick, 1987—Interviews

THE HUMBLE KING B. HIATT color *Rolling Stone* no1294 p38 Ag 24 2017

Kendrick LAMAR D. CHAPPELLE *Interview* v47 no6 p34 Ag 2017

LAMARCHE, GARA

IN FREE-SPEECH TERRITORY color *Nation* v305 no8 p34 O 9 2017

LA MARR, DIANE

Your True Stories *Reader's Digest* v188 no1126 p30 D 2016/Ja 2017

LaMattina, John L.

Approving new drugs color *Science* v355 no6327 p777 F 24 2017

Lamb, Christopher

Pope visits Egypt to join imams, Coptic church in rejecting violence *Christian Century* v134 no12 p14 Je 7 2017

Lamb, Joleah B.

Seagrass ecosystems reduce exposure to bacterial pathogens of humans, fishes, and invertebrates bibl graph *Science* v355 no6326 p731 F 17 2017

Lamb, Jonathan

The Disease of Discovery *Publishers Weekly* v263 no40 p111 O 3 2016

Scurvy C. Jowitt *History Today* v67 no4 p60 Ap 2017

Lamb, Matthew L.

A Church That Can & Did Change R. R. Gaillardetz color *Commonweal* v144 no16 p29 O 6 2017

Lamb, Wally

HARPER LEE color *Entertainment Weekly* no1446/1447 p92 D

2016/Ja 2017

Lambert, Adam, 1982—Interviews

Adam Lambert S. Lansky color *Time* v189 no4 p49 F 6 2017

Lambert, Craig

Louis Menand *Humanities* v37 no4 p1 Fall 2016

Lambert, John

Cal Poly Pomona Auction Grosses $126,950 C. Reich *Arabian Horse World* v57 no11 p162 Ag 2017

FOR THE HORSE In the training barn: LONG LINING, PART 2 WITH JOHN LAMBERT C. REICH *Arabian Horse World* v57 no12 p64 S 2017

LAMBERT, JOSH

I Swear *New York Times Book Review* p17 O 2 2016

LAMBERT, KATIE

The Curated Image color *Climbing* no350 p38 D 2016/Ja 2017

Head, Fingers, Knees, and Toes *Climbing* no355 p30 Ag 2017

Sisterhood of the Rope *Climbing* no356 p26 S/O 2017

Lambert, Lance

MBA Programs Tout Entrepreneurship diag *Bloomberg Businessweek* no4522 p50 My 15 2017

The Real Cost Of an MBA graph *Bloomberg Businessweek* no4500 p41 N 21 2016

Lambert, Liz

Baja Soul S. KELSO color *Conde Nast Traveler* v52 no6 p36 Je/Jl 2017

The QUEEN of COOL L. S. FORD *Texas Monthly* v45 no8 p66 Ag 2017

LAMBERT, MICHAEL

PEOPLE OF THE YEAR: THE HEROES OF PULSE *Advocate* no1088 p34 D 2016/Ja 2017

Lambert, Miranda, 1983-

Miranda Lambert: Blonde on the Tracks W. HERMES color *Rolling Stone* no1275 p59 D 1 2016

Miranda Lambert L. Greenblatt color *Entertainment Weekly* no1441 p52 N 25 2016

PINK LEMONADE K. SANNEH cartoon *New Yorker* v92 no37 p89 N 14 2016

What keeps me feeling cozy M. Rollins *Redbook* p14 N 2017

Lambert, Miranda, 1983—Interviews

Miranda's RULES of friendship [Cover story] D. EVANS PRICE color *Redbook* p96 N 2017

Lambert, Richard S.

SKEPTICAL ANNIVERSARIES B. RADFORD and T. Farley *Skeptical Inquirer* v40 no6 p66 N/D 2016

Lambert, Samuel A.

Transcription factors read epigenetics diag *Science* v356 no6337 p489 My 5 2017

Lambert, Valère

Imaging the distribution of transient viscosity after the 2016 Mw 7.1 Kumamoto earthquake map *Science* v356 no6334 p163 Ap 14 2017

LAMBERT, VALERIE

The Big Black Box of Indian Country *American Indian Quarterly* v40 no4 p333 Fall 2016

Lamberton, Cait

Men Choose Differently When They Choose with Other Men *Harvard Business Review Digital Articles* p2 S 14 2016

Lambin, Eric F.

Cash for carbon: A randomized trial of payments for ecosystem services to reduce deforestation bw chart *Science* v357 no6348 p267 Jl 21 2017

Lamborghini automobile

See also

Lamborghini Murcielago automobile

Aaron Robinson A. Robinson color *Car & Driver* v62 no6 p32 D 2016

Arresting Development bw *Car & Driver* v62 no6 p41 D 2016

Bullet with Butterfly Wings C. Csere color *Car & Driver* v63 no2 p90 Ag 2017

Ezra Dyer E. Dyer color *Car & Driver* v62 no10 p26 Ap 2017

Go color *Road & Track* v69 no1 p10 Ag 2017

IN THE BELLY OF THE BRAZEN BULL D. Bentley color *Fortune* v176 no3 p37 S 1 2017

Lamborghini automobile—Evaluation

A NEW FORCE J. Lieberman chart color *Motor Trend* v69 no4 p76 Ap 2017

RENAISSANCE J. H. HARPER bw color *Road & Track* v69 no4 p46 N 2017

Ringing the Bull A. Robinson color diag *Car & Driver* v62 no6 p52 D 2016

SHOW STEALER C. CHILTON color *Road & Track* v68 no8 p86 My 2017

Viva La RIVOLUZIONE S. Evans chart color *Motor Trend* v69 no5 p46 My 2017

Lamborghini Murcielago automobile

Aging Bull M. Duff color *Car & Driver* v63 no5 p120 N 2017

Lambrecht, Anja

The 4 Mistakes Most Managers Make with Analytics *Harvard Business Review Digital Articles* p2 Jl 12 2016

Lambright, Kelly J.

Emergence of hierarchical structural complexities in nanoparticles and their assembly bibl color *Science* v354 no6319 p1580 D 23 2016

Lambs

Christmas DELUXE A. Baraghani color *Bon Appetit* v61 no12 p126 D 2016 /Jan2017

GIANT ZIPLOCK BAGGIES FULL OF LAMBS ARE GOING TO CHANGE EVERYTHING K. MANGU-WARD color *Reason* v49 no4 p4 Ag/S 2017

HOMESTEAD HACKS J. Desjardins and S. Walker *Mother Earth News* no280 p66 F/Mr 2017

Learning Lessons from Lambing Season *Mother Earth News* no281 p5 Ap/My 2017

RACK OF LAMB WITH SMOKED HERBED POTATOES AND POMEGRANATE SAUCE: WANT A BEAUTIFUL MAIN COURSE FOR EASTER DINNER? TRY THIS DISH *Successful Farming* v115 no6 p64 Ap 2017

Lamb's Ear (Poem)

LAMB'S EAR S. Burt *New Yorker* v93 no14 p72 My 22 2017

Lame duck sessions (Political science)

"LAME DUCK" /LĀM DŬK/ B. PETERSON *Washingtonian Magazine* v52 no2 p20 N 2016

Lameness in horses

CONSULTANTS B. A. Connally and S. D. White color *Equus* no472 p67 Ja 2017

One horse's journey T. Boros color *Equus* no476 p85 My 2017

A WAY TO GET MORE FROM HOCK INJECTIONS C. Barakat and M. McCluskey color *Equus* no472 p12 Ja 2017

Laments

How to Lament M. Wollan diag *New York Times Magazine* p25 Ag 6 2017

Lamers, Chantal

A+ REVIVAL [Cover story] color *Sunset* v238 no4 p60 Ap 2017

BEST OF THE WEST color *Sunset* v238 no1 p11 Ja 2017

BEST OF THE WEST color *Sunset* v238 no4 p17 Ap 2017

BEST OF THE WEST color *Sunset* v238 no6 p9 Je 2017

BEST OF THE WEST color *Sunset* v239 no3 p11 S 2017

THE FUTURE IS HERE color diag *Sunset* v238 no4 p54 Ap 2017

GET SMART color *Sunset* v239 no3 p46 S 2017

NEXT-LEVEL DESIGN color diag *Sunset* v237 no5 p31 N 2016

O CHRISTMAS TREE [Cover story] color *Sunset* v237 no6 p62 D 2016

RAISE THE ROOF color *Sunset* v238 no1 p33 Ja 2017

Laminated plastics

WALL PANELS IN THE AGE OF PLASTICS M. E. Polson color *Old House Journal* v45 no2 p20 Ap 2017

Laminitis

See also

Laminitis in horses

GLOSSARY *Equus* no472 p71 Ja 2017

Laminitis in horses

CHALLENGES OF DETECTING EARLY LAMINITIS C. Barakat and M. McCluskey *Equus* no482 p14 N 2017

GLOSSARY *Equus* no476 p95 My 2017

LAMINITIS PREVENTION BASICS L. Bonner bw color *Equus* no475 p52 Ap 2017

NEW WAY TO ASSESS PAIN C. Barakat and M. McCluskey color *Equus* no473 p12 F 2017

Laminitis in horses—Treatment

GENE THERAPY FOR LAMINITIS? C. Barakat and M. McCluskey color diag *Equus* no474 p10 Mr 2017

LAMM, CATE

6 Dutch-Oven Recipes color *Trail Rider* v29 no3 p32 Ap 2017

Lamm, Ross

Sky Net D. STARR cartoon map *Wired* v25 no3 p38 Mr 2017

Lamond, Joe—Interviews

The Parnelli Awards and NAMM: Industry Convergence K. M. Mitchell *Stage Directions* v30 no6 p16 Je 2017

Lamont, Corliss

HUMANIST PROFILE *Humanist* v77 no1 p2 Ja/F 2017

LAMONT, JAN

The Question *O, The Oprah Magazine* p18 S 2017

Lamott, Anne

5 ways to feel inspired and empowered color *Redbook* p115 Ap 2017

LaMotta, Jake, 1922-2017

JAKE LAMOTTA (1922-2017) J. Fuchs and S. Kwak color *Sports Illustrated* v127 no10 p22 O 2 2017

LaMotte, Susan

Employee Engagement Depends on What Happens Outside of the Office *Harvard Business Review Digital Articles* p2 Ja 13 2015

Lamour, Tobias

The Rydberg constant and proton size from atomic hydrogen bw chart color diag graph *Science* v357 no6359 p79 O 6 2017

L'amour de Loin (Theatrical production)

L'Amour de Loin *New York* v49 no24 p158 N 28 2016

L'Amour de Loin W. R. Braun *Opera News* v81 no9 p32 Mr 2017

Lamoureux, Kevin

MOST KNOWLEDGEABLE S. PROUDFOOT color *Maclean's* v129 no47 p22 N 28 2016

Lamoureux, Scott

A scenic showcase color diag *Model Railroader* v84 no5 p32 My 2017

Lamouri, Aazdine

Guanine glycation repair by DJ-1/Park7 and its bacterial homologs chart color diag graph *Science* v357 no6347 p208 Jl 14 2017

Lamp design & construction

IT'S LIT H. MARTIN color *Architectural Digest* v74 no10 p156 O 1 2017

Lamp Plus Inc.

HOME UNDER $150 color *Redbook* p130 Ap 2017

Lampe, Jordan

The Ways Americans Pay for Things Are Woefully Out of Date *Harvard Business Review Digital Articles* p2 O 14 2015

Lampel, Ayala

Polymeric peptide pigments with sequence-encoded properties color graph *Science* v356 no6342 p1064 Je 9 2017

Lampert, Jo

GIRL ON FIRE A. Green color *Vogue* v207 no3 p464 Mr 2017

Lamphere, Dale

Dignity of Earth and Sky *South Dakota Magazine* v32 no4 p13 N/D 2016

Lampoon

QUIET ON THE SET R. STIEVE *Arizona Highways* v93 no11 p42 N 2017

LAMPRINAKOS, PATTY

The Question *O, The Oprah Magazine* p16 D 2016

Lampropeltis

King snake's strength is in its squeeze E. S. EATON color *Science News* v191 no7 p13 Ap 15 2017

Lamps

See also

Candelabra

Chandeliers

Electric lamps

Flashlights

Daffodil Table Lamp color *Magazine Antiques* v183 no6 p4 N/D 2016

Earthy Delights color *Architectural Digest* v74 no9 p44 S 2017

A LITTLE BIT COUNTRY A. CHANTIM color *Good Housekeeping* v265 no2 p46 Ag 2017

ON CUE L. MOWRY *Atlanta* v56 no11 p50 Mr 2017

QUIET UPGRADES: A MODERN BUNGALOW MAKE R. COLE color *Arts & Crafts Homes & the Revival* v12 no5 p50 Wint 2018

SADNESS LAMP F.A.Q S. HUTTO cartoon *New Yorker* v93 no4 p41 Mr 13 2017

STYLE *New Orleans Homes & Lifestyles* v20 no3 p18 Summ 2017

Lamps—Evaluation

Adam's Home STYLE SHEET: HAUTE PINK Adam color *O, The Oprah Magazine* p66 O 2017

BAR CART color *Good Housekeeping* v264 no4 p47 Ap 2017

Euroluce: The biennial lighting trade show, which took place alongside the Salone del Mobile last month, spanned four large pavilions at Milan's sprawling fairgrounds. Additional exhibitors showcased their introductions at off-site venues throughout... J. Minutillo color *Architectural Record* v205 no5 p137 My 2017

Family Reading Time color *Old House Journal* v45 no3 p72 My 2017

FIND YOUR INNER PREPPER R. Verger color *Popular Science* v289 no4 p32 Jl/Ag 2017

go to your ROOM K. K. CONDON color *Better Homes & Gardens* v95 no8 p34 Ag 2017

HOME UNDER $150 color *Redbook* p108 Je 2017

HOME UNDER $150 color *Redbook* p130 Ap 2017

A Luxury Bath of 1924 G. Louise cartoon color *Old House Journal* v45 no2 p72 Ap 2017

Make your bathroom beautiful color *Redbook* p142 S 2017

Natural Beauty color *Timber Home Living* v27 no3 p16 Je 2017

The Natural K. O'SHEA-EVANS bw color *House Beautiful* v159 no5 p51 Je 2017

NEBRASKA MADE D. VAN BUREN color *Nebraska Life* v20 no6 p54 N/D 2016

PERIOD LANTERNS color *Old House Journal* v45 no5 p30 Ag 2017

PUNCH LIST K. SELZER color *Better Homes & Gardens* v95 no2 p58 F 2016

The Secret to Layered Lighting K. O'SHEA-EVANS color *House Beautiful* p46 Jl 2017

Slab City L. IMMEDIATO color *Los Angeles Magazine* v62 no10 p34 O 2017

STYLE *New Orleans Homes & Lifestyles* v20 no1 p16 Wint 2016

THROWING SHADE color *Esquire* v167 no2 p42 Mr 2017

WEAVE IT IN C. Hong color *Martha Stewart Living* p94 Jl/Ag 2017

Lampshades—Evaluation

MOODBOARD MASTERCLASS color *House Beautiful* p81 Ag 2017

LAMSTER, MARK

Building Confidence *Architectural Record* v205 no7 p114 Jl 2017

Lamy, Nicole

Match Book *New York Times Book Review* p53 Je 4 2017

Match Book *New York Times Book Review* p9 O 8 2017

Lamy, P. L.

Rosetta's comet 67P/Churyumov-Gerasimenko sheds its dusty mantle to reveal its icy nature bibl graph *Science* v354 no6319 p1566 D 23 2016

Surface changes on comet 67P/Churyumov-Gerasimenko suggest a more active past bw graph *Science* v355 no6332 p1392 Mr 31 2017

Lan, Da

All-oxide–based synthetic antiferromagnets exhibiting layer-resolved magnetization reversal diag *Science* v357 no6347 p191 Jl 14 2017

Lan, Xinzheng

Efficient and stable solution-processed planar perovskite solar cells via contact passivation bibl graph *Science* v355 no6326 p722 F 17 2017

Lanaj, Klodiana

Feeling Powerful at Work Makes Us Feel Worse When We Get Home *Harvard Business Review Digital Articles* p2 Je 13 2017

Research: Yes, Being Helpful Is Tiring *Harvard Business Review Digital Articles* p2 S 6 2016

Lancaster (Ohio)—Economic conditions

PIRATES OF THE RUST BELT J. Fox color *Bloomberg Businessweek* no4511 p63 F 13 2017

THE POSTWAR DREAM: NOV. 15, 1947 A. BROWN bw color *Forbes* v200 no4 p30 O 24 2017

Lancaster, Andy

How to take learning to the next level: L&D hacks from smartphones to shared practice *People Management* p12 Ag 2017

LANCASTER, LAURA

ESSENTIALS bw color *Backpacker* p93 N 2017

Life Finds a Way: Gifford Pinchot National Forest, Washington color map *Backpacker* p22 S 2017

Pillars of the Earth color *Backpacker* p14 Je 2017

See the Forest for the Trees map *Backpacker* v45 no1 p25 Ja 2017

Lancaster, Loryn

Changes in federal and state unemployment insurance legislation in 2016 *Monthly Labor Review* p1 Ag 2017

Lancaster Sound (Nunavut)

Saving an Arctic oasis E. HOLLAND color map *Canadian Geographic* v137 no1 p57 F 2017

Lance, Jennifer

Cat Ladies, Unite! [Cover story] color *Glamour* v114 no11 p45 N 2016

Monopoly's Feminist History bw color *Glamour* v115 no5 p20 My 2017

Yves, Please! cartoon *Glamour* v114 no12 p56 D 2016

Lancefield, David

Reimagining the Boardroom for an Age of Virtual Reality and AI *Harvard Business Review Digital Articles* p2 Ap 3 2015

What to Know Before You Sign a Payment-by-Results Contract *Harvard Business Review Digital Articles* p2 S 5 2016

Lanchester, John

Can We Escape from Time? bw color *New York Review of Books* v63 no18 p30 N 24 2016

Economics is still struggling with its self-conception after the financial crisis—a disaster that economists were supposed to foresee but didn't *New York Times Magazine* p14 F 12 2017

HOW CIVILIZATION STARTED cartoon *New Yorker* v93 no28 p22 S 18 2017

Many economists would like to abolish cash, which enables tax avoidance and crime. But would a cashless world be a fairer one? *New York Times Magazine* p18 Ja 15 2017

MONEY TRAP cartoon *New Yorker* v92 no34 p73 O 24 2016

On Money *New York Times Magazine* p18 N 6 2016

SIGNAL cartoon *New Yorker* v93 no7 p78 Ap 3 2017

THINK TWICE cartoon *New Yorker* v92 no37 p85 N 14 2016

LANCY, DAVID F.

20 Dad Hacks for Enjoying Dadhood cartoon chart color *GQ: Gentlemen's Quarterly* v97 no7 p32 Jl 2017

Land, Ali

Good Me Bad Me color *Publishers Weekly* v264 no29 p196 Jl 17 2017

Land capability for agriculture

Grow a Community GIVING GARDEN P. Stone *Mother Earth News* no279 p46 D/Ja 2017

Land Cruiser sport utility vehicle—Evaluation

Toyota Land Cruiser chart color *Motor Trend* v69 no1 p60 Ja 2017

Land economics

The Bad Modern History of Farming W. Berry bw *Progressive* v81 no5 p46 Je/Jl 2017

Land grants

See also

Ranches

BARRY DUNN: SOUTH DAKOTA STATE UNIVERSITY'S NEW PRESIDENT TACKLES RESTRUCTURING WITH WEB-BASED TOOL AND AIMS TO EXTEND THE LAND-GRANT MISSION G. Gullickson *Successful Farming* v115 no6 p10 Ap 2017

Garden Rule: Taking advantage of extension programs like the Master Gardeners of New Orleans P. Marquis *New Orleans Homes & Lifestyles* v20 no3 p26 Summ 2017

Land management

Sweet Deal P. SAHA *Audubon* v119 no1 p17 Spr 2017

Land management—Law & legislation

Legislative Background on Public Land Use: Recent Action by Congress on Federal Land Management *Congressional Digest* v96 no6 p9 Je 2017

Land of Mine (Film)

INTERNATIONAL RELATIONS A. LANE cartoon *New Yorker* v92 no49 p100 F 13 2017

Land of Mine M. J. ROWIN color *Film Comment* v53 no1 p86 Ja/F 2017

Land of Mine *New Yorker* v93 no3 p10 Mr 6 2017

Land reform—China

Landing of airplanes
TRAINING & TECHNIQUE cartoon *Flying* v144 no3 p25 Mr 2017

Landis, Abbie Gascho
The Complex Lives of Freshwater Mussels color *Natural History* v125 no3 p30 Mr 2017
LIFE at River Bottom color *Earth Island Journal* v32 no1 p49 Spr 2017
What lies beneath J. S. Weis color *Science* v356 no6336 p384 Ap 28 2017

Landis, Dana—Interviews
Hiring C-Suite Executives by Algorithm S. G. Carmichael *Harvard Business Review Digital Articles* p2 Ap 6 2015

Landis, Douglas A.
Cellulosic biofuel contributions to a sustainable energy future: Choices and outcomes color *Science* v356 no6345 p1349 Je 30 2017

Landis, Wayne G.
Precaution and governance of emerging technologies bibl color *Science* v354 no6313 p710 N 11 2016

Landler, Mark
ALTER EGOS: Hillary Clinton, Barack Obama, and the Twilight Struggle Over American Power R. L. FISCHER *USA Today Magazine* v145 no2860 p80 Ja 2017
To NYT, Trump's 'Populism' Still an 'Open Question' J. Naureckas *Extra!* v30 no2 p1 Mr 2017

Landles-Cobb, Libbie
Nonprofits Can't Keep Ignoring Talent Development *Harvard Business Review Digital Articles* p2 D 17 2015

Landline (Film)
Jenny Slate Hates Being Oversimplified A. M. Cox *New York Times Magazine* p54 Jl 16 2017
Landline Is a Message from a Lost World: the 1990s S. Zacharek color *Time* v190 no5 p58 Jl 31 2017
Landline L. Greenblatt color *Entertainment Weekly* no1474/1475 p99 Jl 21-28 2017
MIX MASTER J. BLACK color *Esquire* v167 no1 p88 F 2017
Stupid QUESTIONS WITH... Jenny Slate D. Snierson color *Entertainment Weekly* no1474/1475 p22 Jl 21-28 2017
Summer Movie Preview: July S. Begley, E. Berman et al color *Time* v189 no20 p56 My 29 2017

Landlord & tenant—California
SAN FRANCISCO BURNING J. Ronson color *GQ: Gentlemen's Quarterly* v97 no7 p92 Jl 2017

Landlords—Corrupt practices
GET OUT S. VAN ZUYLEN-WOOD color *Bloomberg Businessweek* no4495 p50 O 17 2016

Landman, Tanya
Hell and High Water *Publishers Weekly* v264 no16 p67 Ap 17 2017

LANDON, ADAM C.
Incorporating Sociocultural Phenomena into Ecosystem-Service Valuation: The Importance of Critical Pluralism *BioScience* v67 no3 p233 Mr 2017

Landon, Isla
Timber Treehouse Makes One Girl's Dreams Come True color *Timber Home Living* v27 no2 p7 Ap 2017

Landon, Sydney
Keeping It Hot *Publishers Weekly* v264 no22 p50 My 29 2017

Landowners
See also
Forest landowners
Financial Life J. Dobbs color *Missouri Life* v44 no6 p78 S 2017
A Grouse About Government D. YARNOLD color *Audubon* v119 no3 p8 Fall 2017
Working Lands as Wild Lands M. Cimitile color *National Wildlife (World Edition)* v55 no5 p40 Ag/S 2017

LANDRETTI, JOHN
A FISH IN THE TREE color *Orion Magazine* v36 no2 p45 Mr/Ap 2017

Landrieu, Mitch J., 1960-
THE CONFEDERACY WAS ON THE WRONG SIDE OF HUMANITY *Vital Speeches of the Day* v83 no7 p214 Jl 2017
The Longest Yard A. J. Johnson color *New Orleans Magazine* v51 no4 p36 F 2017
Mitch's Fault M. GUNCH cartoon *New Orleans Magazine* v51

no12 p54 O 2017
The Monuments cartoon *New Orleans Magazine* v51 no9 p20 Jl 2017
The Monuments: Demythifying the "Cult" bw *New Orleans Magazine* v51 no10 p32 Ag 2017

Landrigan, Marissa
Coming of Age at the End of Nature *Orion Magazine* v36 no2 p59 Mr/Ap 2017
Trace *Orion Magazine* v35 no3 p55 My/Je 2016
The Vegetarian's Guide to Eating Meat K. Babine color *Orion Magazine* v36 no2 p59 Mr/Ap 2017

Landry, Christian R.
Gene duplication can impart fragility, not robustness, in the yeast protein interaction network bibl color graph *Science* v355 no6325 p630 F 10 2017

LANDRY, J. BROOKE
Submersed Aquatic Vegetation in Chesapeake Bay: Sentinel Species in a Changing World *BioScience* v67 no8 p698 Ag 2017

Landry, John T.
Business Competition Has Not Gotten Fiercer *Harvard Business Review Digital Articles* p2 Jl 22 2015

Lands Besieged & in Flames (Poem)
Reality check B. J. Lieberman color *Equus* no481 p54 O 2017

Lands' End Inc.
The BUY Fashion color *Harper's Bazaar* no3654 p52 Je/Jl 2017
find your BEST BATHING SUIT color *Good Housekeeping* v264 no6 p16 Je 2017
Must-Buys M. Santos color *Working Mother* v40 no4 p16 O/N 2017
This vest does it all color *Redbook* p67 D 2016

Landsbaum, Claire
TO UNDERSTAND THIS NEW RIGHT, IT HELPS TO SEE IT NOT AS A FRINGE MOVEMENT, BUT A POWERFUL COUNTERCULTURE img *New York* v50 no9 p24 My 1 2017

Landscape architects
See also
Golf course architects

Landscape architecture
See also
Front yards & backyards
Garden design
Landscape design
Park design
Blurring the Boundaries J. SANDERS *Architectural Record* v205 no1 p34 Ja 2017
Designing for Landscape Architecture E. M. Pascarella color *Architectural Record* v204 no12 p166 D 2016
Groundbreakers color *Architectural Digest* v74 no1 p146 Ja 2017
THE NEW WINERY GARDEN M. Irvine color *Sunset* v239 no4 p42 O 2017
THE NINETEENTH HOLE J. Kersten cartoon *New Yorker* v92 no34 p25 O 24 2016

Landscape architecture—Evaluation
MLH-024 color diag *Log Home Living* v34 no3 p50 Ap 2017
SHENANDOAH VALLEY *Virginia Living* p138 2017 Best 20of Virginia
UNDER A CANOPY OF FLOWERS... H. BROWN color *House Beautiful* p154 Ag 2017

Landscape design
See also
Garden design
Artistic Retreat A. LUBOW color *Architectural Digest* v73 no12 p134 D 2016
dream scape M. Silva color *Martha Stewart Living* p116 O 2017
Exquisite Copse color *Architectural Digest* v73 no12 p90 D 2016
fertile imagination S. MEDFORD color *Architectural Digest* v74 no9 p138 S 2017
A Growing Concern color *Canadian Wildlife* v22 no5 p44 N/D 2016
HOME BETWEEN THE HEDGES: MARY BETH AND KIRBY SMART COMBINE FAMILY AND UGA LIFE IN ONE CHARMING ATHENS HOUSE L. MOWRY *Atlanta* v57 no6 p84 O 2017
INSIDE TRACK K. SELZER color *Better Homes & Gardens* v95 no9 p76 S 2017
italian idyll M. OWENS bw color *Architectural Digest* v74 no2

p46 F 2017

Lily Kwong H. MARTIN color *Architectural Digest* v74 no9 p50 S 2017

LIVING THE DREAM R. MURPHY color *Architectural Digest* v74 no2 p60 F 2017

NATIVE ROSES ARE FOR THE BIRDS J. L. Baker color *Cabin Living* p9 Ag 2017

A NEW EDEN color *Architectural Digest* v73 no11 p172 N 2016

ROCKY MOUNTAIN HIGH J. Silver color *Sunset* v239 no1 p50 Jl 2017

rooms IN BLOOM C. Rogers color *Southern Living* v52 no3 p88 Mr 2017

UNCOMMON GROUND N. SAVAL *New York Times Magazine* p72 N 13 2016

UNDER A CANOPY OF FLOWERS... H. BROWN color *House Beautiful* p154 Ag 2017

A WALK IN THE GARDEN C. Rogers color *Southern Living* v52 no7 p78 Jl 2017

WARM WELCOME D. NETTO color *Architectural Digest* v73 no11 p182 N 2016

WILD AT HEART E. Jardina color *Sunset* v238 no3 p66 Mr 2017

Landscape gardening

    See also
        Bedding plants
        Topiary work

THE SHAPE OF THINGS T. MARTIN bw color *Better Homes & Gardens* v95 no11 p118 N 2017

STRANGE & WONDERFUL TOPIARY GARDENS V. Johnson color *Old House Journal* v45 no4 p20 Je 2017

Landscape gardening—California

Living laboratory J. Silver color *Sunset* v238 no5 p52 My 2017

Landscape painting

Lewellen artist takes 'most unlikely' journey home E. SCHWARTZ color *Nebraska Life* v21 no4 p72 Jl/Ag 2017

Pioneering painter leaves glowing mark on Ashland S. Kansteiner cartoon *Nebraska Life* v20 no6 p58 N/D 2016

Landscape painting—19th century

Autumn Trees color *Magazine Antiques* v183 no6 p27 N/D 2016

Landscape painting—Exhibitions

A hallucinatory Old Master at the Met color *Magazine Antiques* v184 no2 p34 Mr/Ap 2017

Landscape photographers

CAPTURED BY CURIOSITY G. V. Andrésson *Iceland Review* v55 no1 p52 Ja/F 2017

FOG MACHINE J. Roedel bw color *Louisiana Life* v37 no5 p16 My/Je 2017

Super Soaker color *O, The Oprah Magazine* p28 F 2017

Landscape photography

FROZEN P. STEFÁNSSON *Iceland Review* v55 no2 p32 Mr/Ap 2017

HIGHS & LOWS *Iceland Review* v55 no1 p28 Ja/F 2017

HOT SPOT J. Wignall color *Popular Photography* v81 no2 p34 Mr/Ap 2017

In the Frame *Arizona Highways* v93 no1 p5 Ja 2017

Lost in Space color *Popular Photography* v81 no1 p12 Ja/F 2017

Love at First Sight M. HORJUS and J. MONTALVO color *Backpacker* v45 no2 p54 Mr 2017

NEW YORK'S TIMELESS BEAUTY *New York State Conservationist* v71 no4 p6 F 2017

Picturesque and Memorable Villages *British Heritage Travel* v38 no1 p14 Ja/F 2017

SHOWCASE SHOTS color *Nebraska Life* v21 no5 p96 S/O 2017

THAT'S A STRETCH T. WHEATLEY *Atlanta* v57 no2 p26 Je 2017

That Was Then *National Parks* v91 no4 p60 Fall 2017

VISIONS color *National Geographic* v230 no4 p6 O 2016

WINNING LIGHT C. Murray color *Popular Photography* v81 no1 p42 Ja/F 2017

A WINNING YEAR [Cover story] S. Cravatts bw color *Popular Photography* v81 no2 p50 Mr/Ap 2017

Landscape photography—Competitions

Your Top Shots color *Backpacker* v45 no2 p78 Mr 2017

Landscape photography—Exhibitions

Neglected viewpoints at the National Gallery of Art color *Magazine Antiques* v184 no3 p30 My/Je 2017

Landscape protection

Bold Push to Save Wildlife—and Inspire Kids L. Moore color *National Wildlife (World Edition)* v55 no3 p18 Ap/My 2017

Landscapes

1925 VERTICAL GARDENS M. MANNARINO color *Better Homes & Gardens* v95 no6 p168 Je 2017

Bogs H. Wismayer *New York Times Magazine* p24 N 20 2016

Escape to Alaska *American Forests* v122 no3 p40 Fall 2016

From the Editor P. Stefánsson *Iceland Review* v54 no6 p4 N/D 2016

FROM THE EDITOR P. Stefánsson *Iceland Review* v55 no3 p4 My/Je 2017

Ha-has & other cool beans P. Poore cartoon *Arts & Crafts Homes & the Revival* v12 no3 p8 Summ 2017

last look *American Forests* v123 no1 p48 Wint/Spr 2017

A Night at the Crossroads of America G. WOOD color *Missouri Life* v44 no4 p98 Je 2017

OFF THE LAND E. S. ARNARSDÓTTIR color *Iceland Review* v54 no5 p92 S-O 2016

THE ONE DESN'T EVEN NEED A HEADLINE M. DO-BROWNER *Arizona Highways* v92 no11 p32 N 2016

PICTURE POWER *Iceland Review* v55 no3 p64 My/Je 2017

Summer Quests bw color *Yankee* p10 Jl 2017

What In The World? color *National Geographic Kids* no472 p31 Ag 2017

Whose Moors Are They? C. Newman color map *National Geographic* v231 no5 p84 My 2017

Landseer, John

CAPTURING THE CAT: The arrival of big cats to 19th-century London forced a change in the image left by mythology and the Old Masters C. Good *History Today* v67 no10 p36 O 2017

Landslide prediction

Soil in the Forecast L. Laursen color *Scientific American* v316 no5 p18 My 2017

Landslides

LIFE ON THE EDGE R. Rivera *Sierra* v102 no4 p42 Jl/Ag 2017

Mitigating coastal landslide damage B. Leshchinsky, M. J. Olsen et al color *Science* v357 no6355 p981 S 8 2017

LANDUYT, DRIES

Combining Biodiversity Resurveys across Regions to Advance Global Change Research *BioScience* v67 no1 p73 Ja 2017

Landuyt, Eric H.

Why manufacturing matters diag *Monthly Labor Review* p1 O 2016

Landy, Dick

The HOT ROD Magazine Championship Drag Races T. Taylor bw *Hot Rod* v70 no2 p10 F 2017

Lane, Andrew A.

Single-cell RNA-seq reveals new types of human blood dendritic cells, monocytes, and progenitors color *Science* v356 no6335 p283 Ap 21 2017

LANE, ANTHONY

ACROSS THE AGES color *New Yorker* v93 no33 p98 O 23 2017

ACROSS THE DIVIDE color *New Yorker* v93 no18 p76 Je 26 2017

ANIMAL KINGDOMS color *New Yorker* v93 no4 p84 Mr 13 2017

BOOKISH color *New Yorker* v93 no28 p72 S 18 2017

COME BACK color *New Yorker* v93 no20 p92 Jl 10 2017

COME TOGETHER cartoon *New Yorker* v92 no30 p78 S 26 2016

DANCING WITH THE STARS cartoon *New Yorker* v92 no41 p88 D 12 2016

Deepwater Horizon *New Yorker* v92 no34 p15 O 24 2016

DEPTHS OF FEAR cartoon *New Yorker* v92 no47 p76 Ja 30 2017

DESPERADOES color *New Yorker* v93 no24 p82 Ag 21 2017

FAMILY PACKS cartoon *New Yorker* v92 no45 p86 Ja 16 2017

FIGHTING DEMONS cartoon *New Yorker* v92 no39 p96 N 28 2016

The Founder *New Yorker* v92 no47 p8 Ja 30 2017

GOOD FIGHTS cartoon *New Yorker* v92 no36 p82 N 7 2016

HAPPY RETURNS cartoon *New Yorker* v93 no25 p86 Ag 28 2017

HOW THE OTHER HALF LIVES color *New Yorker* v93 no17 p74 Je 19 2017

IN DEEP cartoon *New Yorker* v92 no32 p108 O 10 2016

INQUIRING MINDS cartoon *New Yorker* v93 no27 p82 S 11 2017

LANGBERG, JASON
Busting the School-to-Prison Pipeline *Education Digest* v82 no5 p42 Ja 2017

Langbord, Joan
The Case of the Double Eagle Gold Coins V. GLEMBOCKI color *Reader's Digest* v190 no1135 p23 N 2017

Lange, Bob
THE EDISON OF MEDICINE S. PROKESCH color img *Harvard Business Review* v95 no2 p134 Mr/Ap 2017

Lange, Christian
Trispecific broadly neutralizing HIV antibodies mediate potent SHIV protection in macaques color graph *Science* v357 no6359 p85 O 6 2017

Lange, Jessica, 1949-
Jessica Lange Can Finally Relax K. Miller color *AARP: The Magazine* v60 no5A p40 Ag/S 2017
On FX, a Bonfire of the Vain Biddies D. D'Addario color *Time* v189 no9 p52 Mr 13 2017

Lange, Leslie
Correct Lead-Change Anticipation [Cover story] color *Horse & Rider* v56 no1 p65 Ja 2017
Get Through the Line color *Horse & Rider* v56 no7 p86 Jl 2017
SHOWMANSHIP TUNE-UP [Cover story] color *Horse & Rider* v56 no3 p58 Mr 2017

LANGE, MAGGIE
Get the Scoop color *Bon Appetit* no8 p30 Ag 2017
starters color *Bon Appetit* v62 no6 p17 Je 2017

Lange, Matthew
The problem of violence in the modern world J. J. Carney *America* v216 no12 p51 My 29 2017

LANGE, MAUREEN
Q: What did you let go of that changed your life? color *O, The Oprah Magazine* p16 Ag 2017

Lange, Richard
The Smack *Publishers Weekly* v264 no21 p71 My 22 2017

Langeberg, Lorene K.
Local protein kinase A action proceeds through intact holoenzymes color diag graph *Science* v356 no6344 p1288 Je 23 2017

Langehanenberg, Helen
At HOME with Three of Germany's Elite Riders L. Paulsen color *Dressage Today* v23 no7 p40 Mr 2017
DRESSAGE SNAPSHOTS color *Dressage Today* v23 no7 p15 Mr 2017
The Swinging Back color *Dressage Today* v23 no7 p26 Mr 2017

LANGELAN, MARTY
Stop a Bigot: A five-step tool kit for dealing with white supremacists in the era of Trump *Ms.* v27 no3 p56 Fall 2017

Langenberg, Tobias
De novo design of a biologically active amyloid bibl graph *Science* v354 no6313 paah4949-1 N 11 2016

LANGER, ANDY
THE ELI YOUNG BAND PLAYS THE GAME *Texas Monthly* v45 no6 p48 Je 2017
LEMME HEAR YOU Say, "Ha!" *Texas Monthly* v45 no6 p66 Je 2017
Meet the Texas Gentlemen *Texas Monthly* v45 no9 p36 S 2017
The No-GPS Road Trip color *Popular Mechanics* p32 S 2017
The Sons Also Rise *Texas Monthly* v45 no2 p70 F 2017

Langer, Ellen
Mindfulness Isn't Much Harder than Mindlessness *Harvard Business Review Digital Articles* p2 Ja 13 2016

Langer, Richard
The gospel in a violent culture *Christian Century* v134 no12 p30 Je 7 2017

Langer, Robert
Fabrication of fillable microparticles and other complex 3D microstructures color diag *Science* v357 no6356 p1138 S 15 2017

Langergraber, Kevin
Chimpanzee genomic diversity reveals ancient admixture with bonobos bibl diag graph map *Science* v354 no6311 p477 O 28 2016

Langevin, Y.
Seasonal exposure of carbon dioxide ice on the nucleus of comet 67P/Churyumov-Gerasimenko bibl bw graph *Science* v354 no6319 p1563 D 23 2016

LANGEWIESCHE, WILLIAM

HEAT color *Vanity Fair* v59 no8 p102 Ag 2017

LANGFORD, DANIELLE
Brave Hearts color *O, The Oprah Magazine* p14 Mr 2017
The Question *O, The Oprah Magazine* p16 My 2017

Langford, Katherine, 1996-
13 Reasons Why E. Aslanian *TV Guide* v65 no19 p38 My 1 2017

LANGHANS, SIMONE D.
Freshwater Megafauna: Flagships for Freshwater Biodiversity under Threat *BioScience* v67 no10 p919 O 2017

LANGILLE, ERINN BETH
THE LESSER BOHEMIANS color *Maclean's* v129 no42 p61 O 24 2016

Langjökull Glacier (Iceland)
JOURNEY TO THE CENTER OF THE GLACIER *Iceland Review* v54 no6 p108 N/D 2016

Langley, Bruce
American Gods M. ROUSH *TV Guide* v65 no19 p18 My 1 2017

Langley, Bryan
PITCH PERFECT J. BRANDT color *Outdoor Life* v224 no6 pH1 Ag 2017

Langmann, Brady
CONSCIOUS COUPLING bw color *Esquire* p116 N 2017
THE NEW NBA LEXICON bw color *Esquire* p20 N 2017

Langness, Felix
WHY FACEBOOK IS KEEPING PERFORMANCE REVIEWS: INTERACTION color *Harvard Business Review* v95 no1 p18 Ja/F 2017

Langreth, Robert
The Crazy Math Behind Drug Prices graph *Bloomberg Businessweek* no4529 p14 Jl 3 2017
Drug Costs Too High? Fire the Middleman *Bloomberg Businessweek* no4513 p28 Mr 6 2017
Your Prescription Gets A Rebate—for Insurers *Bloomberg Businessweek* no4494 p23 O 10 2016

Langridge, Robert
Complex multifault rupture during the 2016 Mw 7.8 Kaikōura earthquake, New Zealand color map *Science* v356 no6334 p154 Ap 14 2017

Langrock, Carsten
A fully programmable 100-spin coherent Ising machine with all-to-all connections bibl diag graph *Science* v354 no6312 p614 N 4 2016

Langstaff, David
4 Ways CEOs Can Conquer Short-Termism *Harvard Business Review Digital Articles* p2 F 24 2017

LANGSTON, ERICA
DIM-WITTED cartoon *Mother Jones* v41 no6 p61 N/D 2016

LANGSTON, JENNIFER
I Need (an App) Consult *USA Today Magazine* v145 no2862 p51 Mr 2017

Language & color
Colorful Language L. E. Ogden color *Natural History* v125 no4 p7 Ap 2017

Language & languages
See also
Judgment (Psychology)
Language policy
Multilingualism
Native language
Translating & interpreting
Translations
Writing
Written communication
An AI stereotype catcher A. G. Greenwald color *Science* v356 no6334 p133 Ap 14 2017
A Few Questions for Poetry D. HALPERN *New York Times Book Review* p25 Ja 1 2017
A FOUR-LETTER FAN M. HUSTON *Psychology Today* v49 no5 p14 S/O 2016
Learning from monkey "talk" C. T. Snowdon bibl chart color *Science* v355 no6330 p1120 Mr 17 2017
The Long Road to "Politically Correct" J. MCWHORTER *Psychology Today* v49 no6 p48 N/D 2016
LOVE, HATE, AND CULTURE WARS O. B. AREWA color il *Phi Kappa Phi Forum* v97 no1 p26 Spr 2017
The Power of Language G. Bastidas *Parents* v91 no10 p16 O 2016

snapshots 2017 img *New York Times Upfront* v149 no6 p38 D 12 2016

Talking of Taste: Umami? Kokumi? The search for new tastes goes way beyond gastronomy K. GOLDYNIA *Psychology Today* v50 no5 p36 S/O 2017

Toward Essentials M. ROBINSON *New York Times Book Review* p13 S 24 2017

What is a Jewish state? M. Beck *Christian Century* v134 no13 p30 Je 21 2017

Woeful Words S. POLAN *Psychology Today* v50 no2 p21 Mr/Ap 2017

Language & languages—Ability
See also
Verbal ability

The English Lesson E. K. HUMMEL bw color *Reader's Digest* v190 no1133 p94 S 2017

Rating the English Proficiency of Countries and Industries Around the World M. Tran and P. Burman *Harvard Business Review Digital Articles* p2 N 21 2016

Language & languages—Grammars
See also
English grammar

Grammar School E. C. Peyton color *New Orleans Magazine* v51 no5 p48 Mr 2017

Language & languages—Political aspects
A HARROWING LINGUISTIC MOMENT A. KINGSTON *Maclean's* v129 no48/49 p10 D 5 2016

How Political Language Got So Coded K. Steinmetz *Time* v188 no16/17 p65 O 24 2016

Use Vivid Language A. NABAUM color *New Republic* v248 no3 p34 Mr 2017

Language & languages—Study & teaching
See also
Immersion method (Language teaching)

Teaching Arabic to Non-Native Speakers [Cover story] N. ZAKI *Islamic Horizons* v46 no2 p32 Mr/Ap 2017

Language acquisition
Family Is What You Make It A. Davies *Parents* v91 no10 p24 O 2016

Serve and return: Communication foundations for early childhood music policy stakeholders A. M. Reynolds and S. L. Burton bibl *Arts Education Policy Review* v118 no3 p140 2017

Language arts (Middle school)
How Five Lost Minutes Altered Our Class Culture K. HODGSON *Education Digest* v82 no4 p30 D 2016

Language arts (Secondary)
LIT BITS color *Literacy Today (2411-7862)* v34 no4 p4 Ja/F 2017

Language policy
Language policy, language ideology, and visual art education for emergent bilingual students B. A. Thomas bibl *Arts Education Policy Review* v118 no4 p228 2017

Language revival
TRIBAL LEGACY M. Hill color *Louisiana Life* v37 no6 p64 Jl/Ag 2017

Language schools
LOST IN TRANSLATION H. MACGREGOR *Los Angeles Magazine* v61 no11 p140 N 2016

Languedoc (France)
Of Land and Sea K. Wheelock color map *Conde Nast Traveler* v52 no6 p60 Je/Jl 2017

Langworth, Richard M.
Win-Winston A. ROBERTS *Commentary* v144 no3 p52 O 2017

Lanham, Richard A.
RHETORICAL QUESTIONS *Claremont Review of Books* v17 no2 p44 Spr 2017

LANIER, FRANK
11 COMMONSENSE TIPS FOR SAFE BOATING *Sea Magazine* v108 no12 p36 D 2016

ANCHORING 201: SOMETIMES, SIMPLY FIGURING OUT SCOPE AND DROPPING THE HOOK ISN'T ENOUGH color *Sea Magazine* v109 no6 p52 Je 2017

CLEAN FUEL, HAPPY BOAT *Sea Magazine* v108 no9 p48 S 2016

Intro to Electronic Charts *Sea Magazine* v108 no8 p40 Ag 2016

KNOW YOUR NAV LIGHTS *Sea Magazine* v108 no8 p26 Ag 2016

MAKE THE SWITCH *Sea Magazine* v109 no4 p28 Ap 2017

MOUNTING OPTIONS *Sea Magazine* v109 no9 p28 S 2017

Q+A *Boating World* v37 no9 p24 N/D 2016

Q+A *Boating World* v38 no5 p26 My 2017

Q+A *Boating World* v38 no8 p24 S/O 2017

Stay Put *Boating World* v38 no4 p54 Ap 2017

Lanier, Heather Kirn
MY DAUGHTER HAS A DISABILITY. I DON'T WANT JESUS TO 'FIX' HER [Cover story] il *America* v216 no11 p36 My 15 2017

Lanier, Randy—Trials, litigation, etc.
INDYCAP VICE L. J. Wertheim color *Sports Illustrated* v126 no2 p54 Ja 16 2017

LANKFORD, KIMBERLY
50 WAYS TO SAVE ON HEALTH CARE color *Kiplinger's Personal Finance* v71 no11 p26 N 2017

Brokerage Account Fraud Protection *Kiplinger's Personal Finance* v71 no1 p40 Ja 2017

Cash In on Your Good Health color *Kiplinger's Personal Finance* v70 no12 p62 D 2016

Charitable Giving Is a Family Affair *Kiplinger's Personal Finance* v71 no12 p41 D 2017

Cover the Cost of Care color *Kiplinger's Personal Finance* v71 no6 p64 Je 2017

Disaster Relief color *Kiplinger's Personal Finance* v71 no12 p24 D 2017

Estate Planning for Snowbirds *Kiplinger's Personal Finance* v71 no4 p49 Ap 2017

Estimate Your Social Security Benefit *Kiplinger's Personal Finance* v71 no2 p50 F 2017

A Fighter Pilot's New Career Takes Off color *Kiplinger's Personal Finance* v71 no4 p72 Ap 2017

Financial Gifts for New Graduates *Kiplinger's Personal Finance* v71 no6 p38 Je 2017

A Flexible Way to Give to Charity color *Kiplinger's Personal Finance* v70 no12 p44 D 2016

FOR MOST WORKERS, HEALTH CARE IS BUSINESS AS USUAL color *Kiplinger's Personal Finance* v71 no10 p11 O 2017

Get Your Insurer to Pay Up color *Kiplinger's Personal Finance* v71 no8 p30 Ag 2017

How Long to Hang on to Tax Records *Kiplinger's Personal Finance* v71 no5 p42 My 2017

How to Find a Home's Claims History color *Kiplinger's Personal Finance* v71 no10 p42 O 2017

How to Help Hurricane Victims Rebuild color *Kiplinger's Personal Finance* v71 no11 p18 N 2017

Managing a Family (and Cash Flow) color *Kiplinger's Personal Finance* v71 no10 p72 O 2017

A Single Mom Plans Her Next Act color *Kiplinger's Personal Finance* v71 no8 p72 Ag 2017

Tax Reform and IRA Conversions *Kiplinger's Personal Finance* v71 no11 p44 N 2017

A Tech Entrepreneur Goes Global color *Kiplinger's Personal Finance* v71 no6 p72 Je 2017

These Super Savers Reap Big Rewards color *Kiplinger's Personal Finance* v71 no3 p72 Mr 2017

Thriving After an Early Retirement color *Kiplinger's Personal Finance* v71 no7 p72 Jl 2017

When a Tree Falls, Who Pays? *Kiplinger's Personal Finance* v71 no8 p38 Ag 2017

When You Crash a Rental Car *Kiplinger's Personal Finance* v71 no7 p43 Jl 2017

When Your Broker Goes Rogue *Kiplinger's Personal Finance* v71 no3 p36 Mr 2017

Why You Need Disability Coverage color *Kiplinger's Personal Finance* v71 no3 p38 Mr 2017

Your Medicare FAQs color *Kiplinger's Personal Finance* v71 no5 p34 My 2017

Lanman, Scott
It's Hard to Label China A Currency Manipulator *Bloomberg Businessweek* no4500 p17 N 21 2016

Lannamann, Taylor
10 TITLES TO PICK UP NOW color *O, The Oprah Magazine* p110 N 2017

10 TITLES TO PICK UP NOW color *O, The Oprah Magazine*

p86 Ag 2017

10 TITLES TO PICK UP NOW color *O, The Oprah Magazine* p99 O 2017

WHAT A BOOK CAN DO [Cover story] color *O, The Oprah Magazine* p76 Jl 2017

Lanney, Jessica

How Large NGOs Are Using Data to Transform Themselves *Harvard Business Review Digital Articles* p2 My 18 2016

Lanning, Carly

THE VLOGGING CURE *Psychology Today* v50 no3 p68 My/Je 2017

Lanouette, William

The Little Match's Momentous Legacy: The Pope of Physics: Enrico Fermi and the Birth of the Atomic Age *Issues in Science & Technology* v33 no3 p93 Spr 2017

Timely counsel from America's first commander in chief color *America* v216 no7 p44 Ap 3 2017

Lansdale, Joe R., 1951-

Coco Butternut *Publishers Weekly* v263 no45 p41 N 7 2016

Lansing, Robert, 1864-1928

Big Lie [Cover story] J. Connor bw *American History* v52 no2 p30 Je 2017

Lansing, Sherry

Sherry Lansing color *Vanity Fair* p153 Hollywood 2017 Supplement

Lansky, Sam

Adam Lambert color *Time* v189 no4 p49 F 6 2017

Andrew Garfield color *Time* v188 no19 p57 N 7 2016

Becky G, Actor color *Time* v189 no12 p58 Ap 3 2017

A Global Hit Machine Scores Again color *Time* v189 no10 p53 Mr 20 2017

Gregg Allman color *Time* v189 no22 p11 Je 12 2017

Harry Styles' Solo Album Is an Unexpected Tour of Rock History color *Time* v189 no19 p52 My 22 2017

How Andrew Garfield Learned to Suffer Like the Saints color *Time* v189 no4 p51 Ja 23 2017

If There's Pain In Fifty Shades, There's Pleasure In Its Soundtrack color *Time* v189 no6 p52 F 20 2017

In Arrival, Amy Adams Takes a Listening Tour of the Universe color *Time* v188 no21 p65 N 21 2016

In a Tragedy, Casey Affleck Finds Triumph color *Time* v188 no22-23 p98 N/D 2016

Jack Antonoff Shines a Light In the Dark color *Time* v189 no22 p56 Je 12 2017

John Legend's Light Shines Even Brighter color *Time* v188 no24 p65 D 12 2016

Keanu Reeves' Contract Killer With Feelings Returns color *Time* v189 no5 p49 F 13 2017

Life of the Party color *Time* v189 no23 p44 Je 19 2017

Mark Wahlberg color *Time* v188 no14 p57 O 10 2016

Meet the Class of 2016 color *Time* v188 no18 p22 O 31 2016

Pop's Young a-Listers Look to the Past color *Time* v189 no21 p64 Je 5 2017

Rebecca Hall color *Time* v188 no16/17 p89 O 24 2016

Ryan Tedder color *Time* v188 no15 p55 O 17 2016

Solange Takes a Seat but Stands on Her Own color *Time* v188 no15 p55 O 17 2016

Lanterns (Lamps)—Evaluation

ALL ATWITTER L. MOWRY *Atlanta* v57 no2 p44 Je 2017

Cooler Gear, Hotter Deals C. Carter and P. Kita color *Men's Health* v32 no2 p24 Mr 2017

CREATE A HAPPY SUMMER SPACE [Cover story] color *Redbook* p110 Je 2017

GO GLAMPING C. HASLAM color *House Beautiful* p146 Ag 2017

PERIOD LANTERNS color *Old House Journal* v45 no5 p30 Ag 2017

Lanthimos, Yorgos

No. 4 THE LOBSTER C. Nashawaty color *Entertainment Weekly* no1444/1445 p51 D 16 2016

Lantz, Erin—Interviews

MORTGAGE OUTLOOK: MOSTLY GOOD NEWS P. M. ESSWEIN color *Kiplinger's Personal Finance* v71 no1 p14 Ja 2017

Lanvin (Company)

Shake A Leg *Los Angeles Magazine* p34 Ap 2017

Lanxon, Nate

To Fix Your Terrible Passwords, Kill Them color *Bloomberg Businessweek* no4524 p36 My 29 2017

Lanza, Katherine

EVENTS color *Magazine Antiques* v184 no4 p122 Jl/Ag 2017

Lao, Oscar

Chimpanzee genomic diversity reveals ancient admixture with bonobos bibl diag graph map *Science* v354 no6311 p477 O 28 2016

Lao Brewery Co.

Getting a Taste of Laos *Foreign Affairs* v95 no6 p(Sp)16 N/D 2016

Laos

Powering Ahead: Turning Laos into ASEAN's 'Battery' *Foreign Affairs* v95 no6 p(Sp)6 N/D 2016

Telecommunications Taking Off *Foreign Affairs* v95 no6 p(Sp)12 N/D 2016

Laos—Description & travel

LUANG PRABANG, LAOS color *Runner's World* v52 no2 p8 Mr 2017

Towards a World-Class Destination *Foreign Affairs* v95 no6 p(Sp)19 N/D 2016

Laos—Economic conditions—21st century

Getting a Taste of Laos *Foreign Affairs* v95 no6 p(Sp)16 N/D 2016

The Intelligent Way to Market *Foreign Affairs* v95 no6 p(Sp)18 N/D 2016

LAOS color *Foreign Affairs* v95 no6 p(Sp)1 N/D 2016

Laos' New Breed of Entrepreneurs *Foreign Affairs* v95 no6 p(Sp)17 N/D 2016

Local Leaders in the Power Industry *Foreign Affairs* v95 no6 p(Sp)7 N/D 2016

The Reward of Taking the Initiative *Foreign Affairs* v95 no6 p(Sp)14 N/D 2016

Laos—Foreign economic relations

ASEAN – Turning Vision into Reality *Foreign Affairs* v95 no6 p(Sp)2 N/D 2016

The U.S. Dimension *Foreign Affairs* v95 no6 p(Sp)2 N/D 2016

Lapeña, Shari

For Shari Lapena, Entering Crowded Category Proved An Asset R. Deahl color *Publishers Weekly* v264 no33 p6 Ag 14 2017

Lapham, Lewis H.

CASTLES IN AIR *Lapham's Quarterly* v10 no1 p12 Wint 2017

HOMO FABER *Lapham's Quarterly* v10 no2 p13 Spr 2017

PETRIFIED FOREST *Lapham's Quarterly* v10 no3 p12 Summ 2017

Lapierre, Isabelle

Longines FEI World Cup North American League News color *Practical Horseman* v45 no10 p65 O 2017

Lapierre, Pascal

Intercellular communication and conjugation are mediated by ESX secretion systems in mycobacteria bibl diag graph *Science* v354 no6310 p347 O 21 2016

LAPIN, LISA

Money Talks *USA Today Magazine* v145 no2862 p77 Mr 2017

Lapin, Nicole

Get more cash for what you care about color *Redbook* p33 Ap 2017

Get the money you deserve color *Redbook* p26 S 2017

Grow your hard-earned cash color *Redbook* p24 Je 2017

MAKE YOUR VOICE HEARD [Cover story] cartoon color *Redbook* p98 Mr 2017

Need more money? Read this [Cover story] color *Redbook* p34 My 2017

Organize your way richer color *Redbook* p25 Jl/Ag 2017

Secrets to being smart with money color *Redbook* p30 N 2017

Smart ways to pay down debt color *Redbook* p43 F 2017

A truly happy way to spend your money color *Redbook* p36 D 2016

Your secret weapon for saving more color *Redbook* p32 O 2017

LaPlante, Lindsay

Effective Transitions color *Horse & Rider* v56 no9 p43 S 2017

Feel the Footfalls color *Horse & Rider* v56 no3 p23 Mr 2017

LaPoe, Victoria

Voices of Cherokee Women *American Indian Quarterly* v40 no3 p277 Summ 2016

LaPointe, Anne M.

Combining polyethylene and polypropylene: Enhanced performance with PE/iPP multiblock polymers bibl chart graph *Science* v355 no6327 p814 F 24 2017

LAPOINTE, MICHAEL
Do Writers Deserve to Make a Living? cartoon *Walrus* p64 Ja\F 2017
A Portrait of the Artist as a Young Convict color *Atlantic* v320 no3 p40 O 2017

Lapowsky, Issie
THE JUSTICE MACHINE color *Wired* v24 no11 p68 N 2016
NEXT LIST 2017 bw graph *Wired* v25 no5 p63 My 2017
A STARTUP ON THE INSIDE color *Wired* v24 no11 p42 N 2016

Lappé, Anna
Better Living Through Chemistry? *Earth Island Journal* v32 no2 p12 Summ 2017
De-Junking Paradise *Earth Island Journal* v32 no3 p13 Aut 2017
Good Food Rising color *Earth Island Journal* v32 no4 p13 Wint 2017
Hope's Edge color *Earth Island Journal* v32 no1 p13 Spr 2017
Q&A: DANNY MEYER *Nation* v305 no11 p5 O 30 2017

Lappe, Meg
Dance It Out color *Glamour* v115 no4 p132 Ap 2017

Laprell, Friederike
Propagation of Polycomb-repressed chromatin requires sequence-specific recruitment to DNA diag *Science* v356 no6333 p85 Ap 7 2017

Lapsley, Jacqueline E.
Old Testament color *Christian Century* v134 no10 p28 My 10 2017

Laptop computer equipment
ANKER POWERCORE 26800 PD: QUICKLY RECHARGE YOUR USB-C MACBOOK OR MACBOOK PRO G. FLEISHMAN color *Macworld - Digital Edition* v34 no10 p27 O 2017
Finsix Dart-C charger: Tiny, powerful, and worth the expense G. MAH UNG chart color *PCWorld* v35 no7 p145 Jl 2017
NONDA USB-C TO HDMI ADAPTER G. FLEISHMAN color *Macworld - Digital Edition* v34 no10 p35 O 2017
URBAN ARMOR GEAR RUGGED CASE: AN EXCELLENT TOUGH CASE FOR YOUR DELICATE FLOWER OF A LAPTOP S. BELLAMY color *Macworld - Digital Edition* v34 no9 p33 S 2017
URBAN ARMOR GEAR RUGGED CASE S. BELLAMY color *Macworld - Digital Edition* v34 no8 p49 Ag 2017

Laptop computers
See also
    Chromebook (Computer)
    iBook (Computer)
    MacBook (Computer)
How To: Get a Touch Bar without buying a MacBook R. Loyola color *Macworld - Digital Edition* p106 Ja 2017
How To: Migrate an old Mac's system to a new Mac G. Fleishman color *Macworld - Digital Edition* p108 Ja 2017
I want to buy my husband a laptop that comes with great tech support because he always has a million questions. Who has the best? il *Consumer Reports* v81 no12 p16 D 2016
Microsoft Surface Laptops Are No Longer Recommended *Consumer Reports* v82 no11 p16 N 2017
Mom Wins & Fails color *Working Mother* v40 no4 p7 O/N 2017
What You Miss When You Take Notes on Your Laptop M. McGloin *Harvard Business Review Digital Articles* p2 Jl 31 2015
Why Google plans to stop supporting your Chromebook after five years J. NEWMAN color *PCWorld* p43 O 2016
Why you should cover up your laptop's webcam J. NOREM color *PCWorld* p172 Mr 2017

Laptop computers—Evaluation
Acer Predator 21 X: The most insane laptop ever built [Cover story] G. MAH UNG color graph *PCWorld* v35 no10 p48 O 2017
Acer's Switch 7 could overpower the Surface Pro and MacBook Pro G. MAH UNG color *PCWorld* v35 no10 p12 O 2017
Acer Swift 7: The world's thinnest laptop is starving for power A. YEE color graph *PCWorld* v35 no1 p90 Ja 2017
Alienware 13 (2016): The first OLED gaming laptop has landed J. NOREM color graph *PCWorld* p102 D 2016
Alienware 17 R4: Worth its weight in gold H. DINGMAN color graph *PCWorld* v35 no9 p49 S 2017
Asus ZenBook Flip: A sleek, affordable 2-in-1 for everyday tasks

J. NOREM color graph *PCWorld* p84 Mr 2017
Best cheap laptops: We rate the best-sellers on Amazon and Best Buy G. M. UNG color *PCWorld* v35 no9 p56 S 2017
Consumer Reports' Surface Laptop flap is based on data from past Surface models M. HACHMAN color *PCWorld* v35 no9 p7 S 2017
Consumer Reports updates its MacBook Pro review R. LOYOLA color *PCWorld* v35 no2 p41 F 2017
Dell Inspiron 15 7000: A gaming laptop at a decidedly non-gaming price H. DINGMAN color graph *PCWorld* v35 no6 p84 Je 2017
Dell XPS 13 Kaby Lake: Yes, this is the best one so far G. UNG color graph *PCWorld* v35 no1 p67 Ja 2017
GEARHEAD: OK, COMMUTER A. MARSHALL color *Wired* v25 no10 p50 O 2017
Gigabyte Aero 15: A near-perfect power user's laptop G. MAH UNG color graph *PCWorld* v35 no8 p87 Ag 2017
Go PC! 5 killer MacBook Pro alternatives for disappointed Apple fans [Cover story] B. CHACOS color *PCWorld* p41 D 2016
HP Omen 17. Great gaming performance at a great price G. MAH UNG color graph *PCWorld* v35 no11 p90 N 2016
HP's 15-inch Spectre x360 features upgraded hardware and a new look A. YEE color *PCWorld* p30 Mr 2017
HP Spectre x360: Faster, smaller, and better than before G. MAH UNG color graph *PCWorld* v35 no1 p77 Ja 2017
HP's Spectre x360 puts Kaby Lake and Thunderbolt into a thinner, faster package G. MAH UNG color *PCWorld* v35 no11 p8 N 2016
Lenovo ThinkPad X1 Yoga: This 2-in-1's OLED screen will color your computing world J. L. JACOBI color graph *PCWorld* p58 O 2016
Lenovo Yoga 910: A host of excellent upgrades make it a winner J. NOREM color graph *PCWorld* v35 no2 p82 F 2017
MACBOOK 2017: THE BANG FOR YOUR BUCK GETS BETTER R. LOYOLA color graph *Macworld - Digital Edition* v34 no8 p32 Ag 2017
MACBOOK PRO (2017): THE FUTURE STARTS WITH KABY LAKE R. LOYOLA color graph *Macworld - Digital Edition* v34 no8 p37 Ag 2017
Microsoft Surface Pro (2017): More power for more money M. HACHMAN color graph *PCWorld* v35 no7 p57 Jl 2017
MSI's GT75VR Titan brings high-end HDR display tech to a gaming laptop H. DINGMAN color *PCWorld* v35 no8 p102 Ag 2017
The new Dell XPS 13 Developer Edition is the little Linux laptop that can A. CAMPBELL chart color graph *PCWorld* p94 Mr 2017
Razer Blade Pro (2016) review: Now this is how you do a 'Pro' laptop H. DINGMAN color graph *PCWorld* v35 no4 p80 Ap 2017
Samsung Galaxy Book: An excellent 2-in-1 for a good price M. HACHMAN color graph *PCWorld* v35 no7 p71 Jl 2017
SURFACE BOOK i7 vs. MACBOOK PRO: FIGHT! G. MAH UNG color graph *PCWorld* v35 no1 p155 Ja 2017
Surface Laptop: Microsoft's MacBook Air killer nails what students need M. HACHMAN color graph *PCWorld* v35 no8 p62 Ag 2017
TOP 3: BOOK SMARTS D. PIERCE color *Wired* v25 no9 p44 S 2017

Laptop computers—Performance
Razer Blade Pro (2016) review: Now this is how you do a 'Pro' laptop H. DINGMAN color graph *PCWorld* v35 no4 p80 Ap 2017

Laptop computers—Universities & colleges
1-to-1 Computing Under Microscope in Maine Schools B. HEROLD and J. KAZI *Education Digest* v82 no5 p48 Ja 2017

Laqueur, Thomas W.
The Weight of Bodies T. Lynch color *Commonweal* v143 no20 p28 D 16 2016

Lara, M. L.
Rosetta's comet 67P/Churyumov-Gerasimenko sheds its dusty mantle to reveal its icy nature bibl graph *Science* v354 no6319 p1566 D 23 2016
Surface changes on comet 67P/Churyumov-Gerasimenko suggest a more active past bw graph *Science* v355 no6332 p1392 Mr 31 2017

Larbi, Anis

Mapping the human DC lineage through the integration of high-dimensional techniques diag *Science* v356 no6342 p1044 Je 9 2017

Larche, Raoul, 1860-1912

Chicago's most famous Dancer color *Magazine Antiques* v184 no3 p22 My/Je 2017

Larcker, David

We Studied 38 Incidents of CEO Bad Behavior and Measured Their Consequences *Harvard Business Review Digital Articles* p2 Je 9 2016

What It's Like to Be Owned by Berkshire Hathaway *Harvard Business Review Digital Articles* p2 D 14 2015

Why Is CEO Pay Rising? Maybe There Aren't Enough Good CEOs *Harvard Business Review Digital Articles* p2 O 5 2017

Large art works

Place Markers G. Moreno bw color *Art in America* v105 no3 p33 Mr 2017

Large art works—Exhibitions

"THE STAND" D. Markus color *Art in America* v105 no4 p115 Ap 2017

Large astronomical telescopes

HOUSE OF THE SUN I. Loomis color map *Science* v357 no6350 p444 Ag 4 2017

Large astronomical telescopes—Design & construction

As Hawaii deliberates, giant telescope considers new home D. Clery color *Science* v354 no6309 p156 O 14 2016

Large-breasted women

Sports Bras That Don't Suck color *Glamour* v115 no6 p85 Je 2017

Large capitalization stocks

Foreign Stocks Emerge I. Salisbury chart *Money* v46 no8 p77 S 2017

Large Hadron Collider (France & Switzerland)

2016 Nobels: Science News fans read it here first *Science News* v190 no9 p2 O 29 2016

Aloof light particles nudged to interact E. CONOVER color *Science News* v192 no4 p7 S 16 2017

An electron- proton collider could bridge the gap between the LHC and its successor T. Feder *Physics Today* v70 no5 p29 My 2017

THE LARGE HADRON COLLIDER: AN ORAL HISTORY E. G. ELLIS bw color *Wired* v25 no7 p20 Jl 2017

Large Hadron Collider (France & Switzerland)—Congresses

Collider data hint at new particle E. CONOVER color *Science News* v191 no9 p16 My 13 2017

Large magellanic cloud

Our fastest stars could be runaways color *Astronomy* v45 no11 p13 N 2017

LARGEMAN-ROTH, FRANCES

Capital Grilled Cheese color *Parents* v92 no9 p46 S 2017

Happy Apple Discs color *Parents* v92 no11 p70 N 2017

spooky snacks *Parents* v91 no10 p74 O 2016

L'Argent (Film)

L'Argent R. Brody *New Yorker* v92 no33 p13 O 17 2016

Larimore, Elizabeth

FoodAPS Data Now Available to the General Public chart color graph *Amber Waves: The Economics of Food, Farming, Natural Resources, & Rural America* p27 D 2016

LaRiviere, Jacob

Where Predictive Analytics Is Having the Biggest Impact *Harvard Business Review Digital Articles* p2 My 25 2016

LARK, EDIEC

Turkey Trot color *Yankee* v80 no6 p14 N/D 2016

Larkin, Chris

Black Sails' New Adversary *TV Guide* v65 no2 p13 Ja 2 2017

LARKIN, EMMA

Trust and Trauma *New York Times Book Review* p18 My 28 2017

LARKIN, JOAN

Flamingo *Progressive* v81 no5 p69 Je/Jl 2017

Larkin, Joseph

Coupling between distant biofilms and emergence of nutrient time-sharing bw color graph *Science* v356 no6338 p638 My 12 2017

Larkin, Philip, 1922-1985

1955: Hull *Lapham's Quarterly* v10 no1 p145 Wint 2017

Larkum, Matthew E.

Active cortical dendrites modulate perception bibl graph *Science*

v354 no6319 p1587 D 23 2016

Larkworthy, Jane

My Obsessions color *InStyle* v24 no10 p226 O 2017

LARMER, BROOK

Chinese projects all over the world can create debt traps for the countries they're in—and perhaps also trap China on the road to empire *New York Times Magazine* p18 S 17 2017

THE NEW KIDS *New York Times Magazine* p40 F 5 2017

Without a Home, and Without Hope bw color map *National Geographic* v232 no4 p100 O 2017

LAROCCA, AMY

36 MINUTES WITH ... Isabelle Huppert img *New York* p20 Ja 9 2017

FALL FASHION img *New York* v50 no16 p29 Ag 7 2017

Isabella Huppert *New York* p20 F 9 2017

POLITICAL PEROXIDE: Blonde privilege img *New York* v50 no16 p44 Ag 7 2017

QUEEN OF THE WOOD NYMPHS: Who else but KIRSTEN DUNST could star in the Rodarte sisters' trippy first film? img *New York* v50 no16 p52 Ag 7 2017

This + That img *New York* v49 no23 p49 N 14 2016

TOM FORD OVER SEX, SEEKING EMOTION img *New York* v50 no16 p48 Ag 7 2017

The Wellness Epidemic img *New York* v50 no13 p38 Je 26 2017

LaRocco, Leah

You Never Forget Your First Time diag il *Backpacker* v45 no2 p64 Mr 2017

Laroche, Loretta

Genella Macintyre color *Publishers Weekly* v263 no43 p51 O 24 2016

Laroche, Patrice

Research Shows Unionized Workers Are Less Happy, but Why? *Harvard Business Review Digital Articles* p1 Ag 30 2017

La Roche-Posay LLC

Don't Get Burned! T. Calvo chart color *Consumer Reports* v82 no7 p8 Jl 2017

LaRocque, Joshua J.

Reactivation of latent working memories with transcranial magnetic stimulation. bibl graph *Science* v354 no6316 p1136 D 2 2016

Laroia, Rajiv

Pocket DSLR M. Belfiore bw color *Bloomberg Businessweek* no4508 p31 Ja 23 2017

Laron, Guy

THE IRON CURTAIN TORN BY ISRAEL *History Today* v67 no5 p36 My 2017

LaRossa, Ralph, 1965-

The Forgotten Origins of Father's Day O. B. Waxman *Time* v189 no24 p19 Je 26 2017

LARRABEE, KIM

DROWNING ON MY CUSHION bw *Tricycle: The Buddhist Review* v27 no1 p58 Fall 2017

Larraín, Pablo

Jackie L. Greenblatt color *Entertainment Weekly* no1443 p47 D 9 2016

Jackie Places the First Lady Under a Microscope S. Zacharek color *Time* v188 no24 p63 D 12 2016

A Love Poem to Neruda M. ATKINSON *In These Times* v41 no1 p37 Ja 2017

OUR FIRST LADY OF SORROWS B. KACHKA img *New York* v49 no24 p46 N 28 2016

Telling Her Story C. Benson-Allott *Film Quarterly* v70 no4 p88 Summ 2017

Larremore, Daniel B.

Data-driven predictions in the science of science bibl color diag *Science* v355 no6324 p477 F 3 2017

LARRICK, RICHARD

Linear Thinking in a Nonlinear World bw chart diag graph img *Harvard Business Review* v95 no3 p130 My/Je 2017

Larroquette, John

Me, Myself & I R. Rahman, N. Abrams et al color *Entertainment Weekly* no1482/1483 p48 S 22 2017

Larroquette, John—Interviews

ME, MYSELF & I A. D'Arminio *TV Guide* v65 no37 p22 S 4 2017

Larsen, Don, 1929-

MAGIC ON THE MOUND A. BARRA *American History* v51 no6 p22 F 2017

Larsen, Eric
The Art and Science of LAYERING color diag *Backpacker* p71 My 2017

Larsen, Erika
Both Clinton and Trump are trying to win over Latinos in Florida, about 16 percent of all registered voters. Democrats have an advantage of 284,000 among them color *Bloomberg Businessweek* no4498 p36 N 7 2016

Larsen, Gavin
JACK OF ALL TRADES, OR MASTER OF ONE? color *Dance Spirit* v21 no2 p40 F 2017

LARSEN, JENNIFER
decorating: TRICKS OF THE TRADE [Cover story] color *Timber Home Living* v27 no6 p46 D 2017

Larsen, Jon
WHERE STARDUST HIDES ON EARTH A. R. Williams color *National Geographic* v232 no2 p14 Ag 2017

Larsen, Josh
HOLLYWOOD AT PRAYER E. Davidson color *Christianity Today* v61 no6 p85 Jl/Ag 2017

Larsen, Kate
Estimating economic damage from climate change in the United States color graph *Science* v356 no6345 p1362 Je 30 2017

Larsen, Orin
Thoughts on previous issues D. Bruce and J. Freeman color *American Cowboy* v23 no5 p24 F/Mr 2017

Larsen, Timothy
The fasts we choose *Christian Century* v134 no5 p10 Mr 1 2017

Larsen Ice Shelf (Antarctica)
Giant Antarctic iceberg splits off A. YEAGER map *Science News* v192 no1 p6 Ag 5 2017

Larson, Amy
Bacon Bomb Potato Salad *Idaho Magazine* v16 no10 p56 Jl 2017
Bonfire Pizza Chips *Idaho Magazine* v16 no9 p56 Je 2017
Dill Pickle Dip *Idaho Magazine* v16 no3 p57 D 2016
Holiday S'mores Rolls *Idaho Magazine* v16 no3 p56 D 2016
Hot Chocolate Bar *Idaho Magazine* v17 no1 p56 Ja 2017
Lyman Lemon Zucchini Bread *Idaho Magazine* v16 no12 p57 S 2017
RECIPES *Idaho Magazine* v16 no11 p56 Ag 2017
RECIPES *Idaho Magazine* v16 no7 p56 Ap 2017
Rex's Potato and Ham Soup *Idaho Magazine* v16 no1 p56 O 2016
Zippy Grilled Cheese *Idaho Magazine* v16 no5 p56 F 2017

Larson, Andrew J.
Plant diversity increases with the strength of negative density dependence at the global scale diag *Science* v356 no6345 p1389 Je 30 2017

Larson, Brie, 1989-
Artists color *Time* v189 no16/17 p40 My 1-8 2017
Brie Spirit [Cover story] K. SMITH color *Vanity Fair* v59 no6 p76 My 2017
A Grand, Nutty and Visually Splendid Kong: Skull Island S. Zacharek color *Time* v189 no10 p49 Mr 20 2017

Larson, Christina
China Gets Physical color *Bloomberg Businessweek* no4499 p47 N 14 2016
How Long Can DJI Rule the Sky? color *Bloomberg Businessweek* no4518 p36 Ap 10 2017
OVER THE HANDLEBARS color *Bloomberg Businessweek* no4534 p50 Ag 14 2017
Streaming Away From The Censors color *Bloomberg Businessweek* no4537 p50 S 11 2017
Where Buying Data Is as Easy as Buying Cabbage color *Bloomberg Businessweek* no4493 p41 O 3 2016

Larson, Daniel R.
The genome—seeing it clearly now diag *Science* v357 no6349 p354 Jl 28 2017

Larson, Erik
Blue State AGs: The Dems' New Resistance bw *Bloomberg Businessweek* no4516 p25 Mr 27 2017
A Checklist for Making Faster, Better Decisions *Harvard Business Review Digital Articles* p2 Mr 7 2016

Larson, Frank
Forecasting Weather the Old-Fashioned Way bw color diag il *Weatherwise* v70 no4 p28 Jl/Ag 2017

Larson, Gary O.
Chords & Discords color *Downbeat* v84 no4 p10 Ap 2017

Larson, Greger
A composite window into human history color map *Science* v356 no6343 p1118 Je 16 2017

Larson, Jeff
A World Apart color *Consumer Reports* v82 no7 p52 Jl 2017

Larson, John
Fructose-driven glycolysis supports anoxia resistance in the naked mole-rat diag graph *Science* v356 no6335 p307 Ap 21 2017

Larson, Jordan
200 YEARS OF ABORTION img *New York* p32 F 9 2017
...AND NINE THEY NEED TO PROTECT *New York* v50 no7 p31 Ap 3 2017
BEYOND LE PEN: The world's nationalists img *New York* v50 no9 p32 My 1 2017
IN THE ROOM img *New York* p69 F 20 2017
OBAMA'S AMERICA img *New York* v49 no20 p12 O 3 2016
THE RISE OF THE FAKE FAMOUS JACKASS NOVELIST img *New York* v50 no6 p80 Mr 20 2017
TO UNDERSTAND THIS NEW RIGHT, IT HELPS TO SEE IT NOT AS A FRINGE MOVEMENT, BUT A POWERFUL COUNTERCULTURE img *New York* v50 no9 p24 My 1 2017

Larson, Kyle
NASCAR SHOWDOWN R. A. BERENZ *TV Guide* v65 no21 p46 My 15 2017

Larson, Lauren
THE BREAK-OUTS 2016 color *GQ: Gentlemen's Quarterly* v86 no12 p198 D 2016
Drink color *GQ: Gentlemen's Quarterly* v86 no11 p50 N 2016
How to Be Vain: A Modern Man's Primer color *GQ: Gentlemen's Quarterly* v97 no9 p96 S 2017
Mating bw color *GQ: Gentlemen's Quarterly* v86 no11 p58 N 2016
One NaTiON UNDER PencE color *GQ: Gentlemen's Quarterly* v97 no6 p112 Je 2017
Rethink Your Ink color *GQ: Gentlemen's Quarterly* v97 no11 p48 N 2017
What Ever Happened to the Romantic Gesture? color *GQ: Gentlemen's Quarterly* v97 no10 p78 O 2017

LARSON, PARKER BOWIE
Werk It color *Architectural Digest* v74 no10 p42 O 1 2017

Larson, Paul
cozy MOUNTAIN CABIN [Cover story] M. MYLCHREEST color *Cabin Living* p42 D 2016

Larson, Richard
WATCHING THE CLOCKS *Popular Science* v289 no5 p45 S/O 2017

Larson, Sara B.
Dark Breaks the Dawn *Publishers Weekly* v264 no13 p99 Mr 27 2017

Larson, Sarah
THE ELEMENTS cartoon *New Yorker* v93 no12 p19 My 8 2017
FLOWER POWER cartoon *New Yorker* v92 no40 p25 D 5 2016
TELEVISION'S COMEDY AUTEURS bw *New Yorker* v93 no26 p62 S 4 2017

Larson, Tyler
6 ACCESSORIES that make the iPhone an even BETTER VIDEO CAMERA [Cover story] color *Macworld - Digital Edition* v34 no6 p83 Je 2017

Larson-Green, Julie
You Just Got Promoted. Now What? W. Naugle bw *Glamour* v115 no6 p104 Je 2017

Larsson, Zara, 1997-
Zara Larsson C. Mari color *Current Biography* v78 no2 p39 F 2017
Zara Larsson Is Wide A-Woke N. Feeney color *Entertainment Weekly* no1457/1458 p94 Mr 17 2017

Larsson, Zara, 1997——Interviews
ZARA LARSSON color *Seventeen* v76 no2 p37 Mr 2017

LaRue, Bailey
EDITORS' 100 bw color *Skiing* p36 Wint 2017

LaRue, Cleophus J.
Reflections on the lectionary *Christian Century* v133 no25 p19 D 7 2016

WRITERS' FEAST color *Christian Century* v134 no10 p30 My 10 2017

Larue, James

THE TOP 10: MOST CHALLENGED BOOKS OF 2016 S. MAUGHAN color *Publishers Weekly* v264 no25 p60 Je 19 2017

LARUE, KRISHNA

FLAT BELLY INDULGENCE *USA Today Magazine* v145 no2858 p70 N 2016

Laruelle, Elise

The preprophase band of microtubules controls the robustness of division orientation in plants graph *Science* v356 no6334 p186 Ap 14 2017

Laruelle, Marlene

Is Nationalism a Force for Change in Russia? *Daedalus* v146 no2 p89 Spr 2017

Larusmiani SpA

Guglielmo Miani J. Roth color *Esquire* p134 2017 BigBlackBook

Lárusson, Halldór

COURTING THE COUNTRYSIDE *Iceland Review* v55 no1 p44 Ja/F 2017

PUTTING A PRICE ON NATURE *Iceland Review* v54 no6 p58 N/D 2016

A STRANGE CALM - EXIT THE RABBLE-ROUSERS color *Iceland Review* v54 no5 p58 S-O 2016

Larvae

HENS, PISTOLS, AND SHEDDERS: A BASIC LOBSTER LEXICON *Yankee* p97 Jl 2017

SUPER FLY: YOU'RE GONNA LARVA IT M. CHIU cartoon *Wired* v25 no8 p32 Ag 2017

Larvae—Food

FISHY BUSINESS M. Enserink color *Science* v355 no6331 p1254 Mr 24 2017

Laryngeal diseases

Cory's second wind J. L. Jones color diag *Equus* no470 p32 N 2016

Las, Liora

Vectorial representation of spatial goals in the hippocampus of bats bibl graph *Science* v355 no6321 p1 Ja 13 2017

Las Vegas (Nev.)

ALL IN A. Prewitt color *Sports Illustrated* v125 no19 p92 D 12 2016

At a Glance color *American Cowboy* v23 no4 p52 D 2016/Ja 2017

THE FORUM SHOPS AT CAESARS PALACE MARKS ITS 25TH ANNIVERSARY *Los Angeles Magazine* p80 Mr 2017

HOT ICE A. Prewitt color *Sports Illustrated* v126 no10 p64 Ap 10 2017

MANDARIN ORIENTAL, LAS VEGAS *Los Angeles Magazine* p82 Mr 2017

Las Vegas (Nev.)—Description & travel

The Nongambler's Guide to Vegas M. CROSS color *Kiplinger's Personal Finance* v71 no8 p34 Ag 2017

SHOW OFF SIN CITY bw color *Runner's World* v52 no3 p24 Ap 2017

Top 5 Dog-Friendly Cities map *Good Housekeeping* v265 no3 p144 S 2017

Lasagna

Lasagna With Meat, 3 Cheeses, Eggplant, Asparagus and Peas T. SCALICI color *AARP: The Magazine* v59 no1A p50 D 2015/Ja 2016

Tiers of JOY A. Guarnaschelli color *O, The Oprah Magazine* p140 O 2017

LaSala, John

Emergent consciousness decoded *Physics Today* v69 no12 p52 D 2016

La Salle, John

Publish openly but responsibly color *Science* v357 no6347 p141 Jl 14 2017

LaSalle, Ryan

If Data Is Money, Why Don't Businesses Keep It Secure? *Harvard Business Review Digital Articles* p2 F 10 2015

Lasater, Judith Hanson

Chasing contentment color *Yoga Journal* no296 p14 N 2017

Get to know... your SI joint color *Yoga Journal* p60 2017 SpecialIssue

Q: What do you consistently do to boost happiness? color *Yoga Journal* no296 p12 N 2017

LaScala, Marisa

At Jimmy Fallon's House color *Parents* v92 no11 p11 N 2017

Dad to Dad Gift Guide color *Parents* v92 no6 p22 Je 2017

Goop vs. Slime color *Parents* v92 no11 p16 N 2017

Helping Dads Boost Their Styling Mojo *Parents* v92 no2 p20 F 2017

How SHE-roes Raise Girls color *Parents* v92 no5 p17 My 2017

Rewind: Back-to-School Movies chart color *Parents* v92 no9 p16 S 2017

Royalty Gets a Rethink color *Parents* v92 no8 p15 Ag 2017

Savannah Guthrie Looks Back at 2016 *Parents* v91 no12 p12 D 2016

What I Learned at My Parent's Job color *Parents* v92 no4 p13 Ap 2017

When the weather gets hotter, so do your choices at the multiplex color *Parents* v92 no7 p14 Jl 2017

You've Come a Long Way, Baby ... Bump! *Parents* v91 no11 p15 N 2016

Lascaux Cave (France)

Cave Dweller J. MINUTILLO *Architectural Record* v205 no4 p142 Ap 2017

Quick Hits map *Scientific American* v316 no3 p22 Mr 2017

Lasch, Pat—Exhibitions

Shows to See color *American Craft* v77 no2 p18 Ap/My 2017

Lasdun, James

APPOINTMENT WITH DEATH cartoon color *New Yorker* v93 no19 p30 Jl 3 2017

The Fall Guy *Publishers Weekly* v263 no50 p67 D 5 2016

Odd Coupling: Why does a young writer fall in love with a misognyist bully? *New York Times Book Review* p11 My 21 2017

Laser communication systems

The Atomic Movie Machine J. KEATS color *Discover* v38 no7 p10 S 2017

Laser cooling

Molecules face the biggest chill E. CONOVER color *Science News* v192 no4 p18 S 16 2017

Laser design & construction

LORD OF THE RINGS E. Hand color diag *Science* v356 no6335 p236 Ap 21 2017

Laser fusion

High-energy-density science blooms at NIF D. Kramer *Physics Today* v70 no2 p33 F 2017

Laser-induced fluorescence

Fleshing Out Dinosaurs A. Braun color *Natural History* v125 no6 p6 Je 2017

Laser interferometers

LIGO backstory delights and displeases R. M. Herman *Physics Today* v70 no6 p14 Je 2017

Laser research

Advanced Laser Promises EXCITING Applications: The extremely powerful High-Repetition-Rate Advanced Petawatt Laser System (HAPLS) is poised to be an important tool for scientific research A. Heller *Science & Technology Review* p4 Jl/Ag 2017

Cutting through the Fog P. Patel *Scientific American* v317 no3 p216 S 2017

Laser spectroscopy

Let There Be Laser Light G. Schanker *Oceanus* v52 no1 p26 Summ 2016

Laser ultrasonics

A Powerful Petawatt Laser for Experimental Science W. H. Goldstein *Science & Technology Review* p3 Jl/Ag 2017

Laser Interferometer Gravitational-Wave Observatory

The cosmos aquiver A. Cho color *Science* v354 no6319 p1516 D 23 2016

European gravitational wave detector falters D. Clery color *Science* v355 no6326 p673 F 17 2017

GRAVITATIONAL WAVES: From novelty to science [Cover story] R. Naeye color diag *Astronomy* v45 no11 p18 N 2017

LIGO backstory delights and displeases R. M. Herman *Physics Today* v70 no6 p14 Je 2017

LIGO Detects Third Black Hole Merger C. M. CARLISLE *Sky & Telescope* v134 no3 p10 S 2017

Lasers

Eastern Europe's laser centers will debut without a star E. Car-

trated v125 no20 p29 D 19 2016

Last Supper

A meal for many D. K. Hinman, G. Byerly et al color *U.S. Catholic* v82 no6 p5 Je 2017

Were women at the Last Supper? A. Camilleis color *U.S. Catholic* v82 no4 p49 Ap 2017

Last Week Tonight With John Oliver (TV program)

Election 2016: Winners & Losers I. RUDOLPH *TV Guide* v64 no46 p6 N 7 2016

John Oliver B. Hiatt bw color *Rolling Stone* no1281/1282 p32 F 23 2017

John Oliver is good for the Republic. Or not J. Martin and Z. Davis color *America* v216 no6 p47 Mr 20 2017

My Obsessions... *TV Guide* v65 no19 p8 My 1 2017

Last Words (Poem)

Last Words M. J. Salter *American Scholar* v86 no3 p57 Summ 2017

Last Days of Mankind, The (Theatrical production)

Kraus Revisited A. Valiunas bw color *Weekly Standard* v22 no24 p41 F 27 2017

Last of England, The (Poem)

The Last of England A. MOTION *American Scholar* v86 no4 p52 Aut 2017

Lastpass (Company)

LastPass password manager fixes serious password leak vulnerabilities L. CONSTANTIN color *PCWorld* v35 no5 p59 My 2017

Last Picture Show, The (Film)

THE LAST PICTURE SHOW C. Nashawaty color *Entertainment Weekly* no1460/1461 p14 Ap 7-17 2017

Last Ship, The (TV program)

The Last Ship's Captain Takes a Break I. Rudolph *TV Guide* v65 no21 p11 My 15 2017

Last Tycoon, The (TV program)

AMAZON BETS ON THE LAST TYCOON T. Stack color *Entertainment Weekly* no1476 p53 Ag 4 2017

Amazon Tries to Complete F. Scott Fitzgerald's Unfinished Novel D. D'addario color *Time* v190 no5 p60 Jl 31 2017

From the Great Beyond: HOLLYWOOD HELPED DRIVE F. SCOTT FITZGERALD TO THE GRAVE, BUT THE AUTHOR'S GHOST HAUNTS AMAZON'S COMPELLING NEW SERIES THE LAST TYCOON S. ERICKSON *Los Angeles Magazine* p60 Ag 2017

The Last Tycoon J. Halterman *TV Guide* v65 no25 p19 Je 2017

The Last Tycoon M. ROUSH *TV Guide* v65 no31 p15 Jl 24 2017

Last Waltz, The (Music)

THE BAND M. Mettler bw color *Sound & Vision* v82 no3 p72 Ap 2017

Las Vegas Strip (Las Vegas, Nev.)

STRIP TEASE N. Padova chart color *Sunset* v238 no2 p20 F 2017

Las Vegas Strip shooting, Las Vegas, Nev., 2017

After the Massacre [Cover story] P. Elliott, H. S. Edwards et al color diag *Time* v190 no15 p22 O 16 2017

Can Anyone Keep Fans Safe? M. Vain color *Entertainment Weekly* no1486 p22 O 13 2017

The Case for Suppressor Technology R. J. Duncan *Time* v190 no15 p30 O 16 2017

The Color of Terrorism L. Lalami *Nation* v305 no11 p12 O 30 2017

HOCKEY AND HEALING A. Prewitt and S. Kwak color *Sports Illustrated* v127 no12 p15 O 16 2017

To Vegas, With Love from Orlando R. J. Negron-almodovar *Time* v190 no15 p26 O 16 2017

The Tragedies of 2017 Will Test the Bonds That Connect Us, Now and for Years to Come S. Schrobsdorff color *Time* v190 no15 p59 O 16 2017

Unthinkable. Unspeakable. The Language of Tragedy K. Steinmetz *Time* v190 no15 p25 O 16 2017

WMDs in Las Vegas [Cover story] G. ZORNICK *Nation* v305 no10 p3 O 23 2017

Laszlo, Anna—Interviews

Training Police Departments to Be Less Biased S. G. Carmichael *Harvard Business Review Digital Articles* p2 Mr 6 2015

Laszlo, Victor (Fictitious character)

VICTOR LASZLO'S BLOG I. FRAZIER bw *New Yorker* v93 no28 p27 S 18 2017

Late blight of potato

"What a Painfully Interesting Subject": Charles Darwin's Studies of Potato Late Blight J. B. RISTAINO and D. H. PFISTER *BioScience* v66 no12 p1035 D 1 2016

Late Late Show With James Corden, The (TV program)

THE LATE LATE SHOW WITH JAMES CORDEN M. ROFFMAN *TV Guide* p45 Ap 17 2017

THE WORLD ACCORDING TO Gayle cartoon color *O, The Oprah Magazine* p34 My 2017

Late Night (Talk programs)

How Much to Laugh at Trump: For late-night hosts, the president is a gift, and a quandary M. HARRIS img *New York* p40 Mr 6 2017

LATE-NIGHT POLIT-O-METER R. Rahman color diag *Entertainment Weekly* no1457/1458 p15 Mr 17 2017

The Politics of Late-Night Comedy M. Gerson, T. Noah et al color *Atlantic* v320 no1 p10 Jl/Ag 2017

Poll Watchers: A Late-Night Guide R. Rahman color *Entertainment Weekly* no1438 p18 N 4 2016

Late Night (TV program)

LADIES' NIGHT WITH SETH MEYERS F. Penn color *InStyle* v24 no6 p150 Je 2017

LATE NIGHT E. ASLANIAN *TV Guide* v65 no23 p43 My 29 2017

A Mother in Arms J. Ferrise color *InStyle* v24 no6 p148 Je 2017

Late Night With David Letterman (TV program)

Thirty Years Ago, at 12:30 img *New York* p14 Mr 6 2017

Late Show With Stephen Colbert, The (TV program)

AUTHORITY ALWAYS WINS E. NUSSBAUM cartoon *New Yorker* v93 no9 p64 Ap 17 2017

BETTER LATE THAN NEVER R. Rahman color *Entertainment Weekly* no1457/1458 p14 Mr 17 2017

The Most Trusted Name in News L. Brown color *InStyle* v24 no9 p386 S 2017

Lateral dominance

See also

Handedness

THE POLITICS OF LEFT-HANDEDNESS *Sea Magazine* v109 no4 p30 Ap 2017

Latex paint

INTERIOR PAINTING color *Cabin Living* p64 D 2016

Latham, Andrew

Is the 'Common Good' Obsolete? [Cover story] bw color *Commonweal* v143 no19 p12 D 2 2016

Latham, Jennifer

Dreamland Burning *Publishers Weekly* v263 no46 p57 N 14 2016

Latham, Richard

A global brain state underlies C. elegans sleep behavior diag *Science* v356 no6344 p1247 Je 23 2017

Latham, Scott

Don't Treat Innovation as a Cure-All *Harvard Business Review Digital Articles* p2 D 8 2014

LATHAM, WARREN

DROP SHOT cartoon color *Outdoor Life* v224 no4 p12 My 2017

Lathan, Sanaa

Bad Boys (and Girls) Return to Fox In Shots Fired D. D'Addario color *Time* v189 no12 p53 Ap 3 2017

Mother. Daughter. Repeat K. Brown color *Glamour* v115 no5 p189 My 2017

LATIF, ADREES

Top Dog color *Nation* v305 no7 p11 S 25 2017

Latifah, Queen, 1970-

Girls Trip *New Yorker* v93 no25 p17 Ag 28 2017

Star N. Abrams, B. L. Heldman et al color *Entertainment Weekly* no1482/1483 p76 S 22 2017

Latifah, Queen, 1970—Interviews

IT'S GOOD TO BE QUEEN M. LOGAN *TV Guide* v65 no4 p24 Ja 16 2017

Q&A: QUEEN LATIFAH & JADA PINKETT SMITH T. Stack color *Entertainment Weekly* no1463/1464 p68 Ap/My 2017

LATIMER, JOANNE

THE FRENCH CHEF IN AMERICA color *Maclean's* v129 no45 p57 N 14 2016

Latimer, Matt

Upstart D.C. Agents Making Waves in N.Y.C R. Deahl color *Publishers Weekly* v264 no36 p5 S 4 2017

Latimer, Matthew

OFF THE MARKET! *Washingtonian Magazine* v52 no9 p183 Je 2017

Latimer, Michelle
Sacred Water: Standing Rock K. Servick *Science* v356 no6337 p480 My 5 2017

Latimore, Jacob
HOLDING HIS OWN T. A. Christian color *Essence* v47 no8 p67 D 2016

Latin America
Super Salsas B. Lipton color *Health* v31 no6 p132 Jl 2017

Latin America—Economic conditions
The Challenges of Formalizing Labor in Latin America M. E. CARNES *Current History* v116 no787 p43 F 2017

Latin America—Foreign economic relations—United States
Soundbites *Extra!* v30 no8 p2 O 2017

Latin American authors
New Publishers Give Readers More Choices L. Ahuile *Publishers Weekly* v264 no6 p18 F 6 2017

Latin American films
Film Criticism in the Era of Algorithms R. Rich *Film Quarterly* v70 no2 p5 Wint 2016
WHOSE LATIN AMERICAN CINEMA? M. Betancourt *Film Quarterly* v70 no2 p9 Wint 2016

Latin American women
I'M A CONSERVATIVE LATINA [Cover story] A. Menchaca-Bagnulo color *America* v217 no6 p28 S 18 2017

Latin America—News briefs
South America img *New York Times Upfront* v149 no6 p35 D 12 2016

Latin Americans—United States—Government policy
White Out color *Weekly Standard* v22 no25 p2 Mr 6 2017

Latin America—Politics & government—History
Latin America's Populist Hangover S. K. O'Neil color *Foreign Affairs* v95 no6 p31 N/D 2016

Latin History for Morons (Theatrical production)
John Leguizamo, Actor E. Berman color *Time* v189 no15 p50 Ap 24 2017

Latin language
NAKED [Cover story] color *Women's Health* v14 no7 p31 S 2017

Latin language—Terms & phrases
The Resurrection Will Be a Remix C. McNamara color *Commonweal* v143 no18 p46 N 11 2016

Latin Percussion Inc.
LP Peruvian Cajons R. Bennett color *Downbeat* v83 no11 p80 N 2016

Latin teachers
Houdini's Handcuffs Teller *AARP: The Magazine* v60 no4A p62 Je/Jl 2017

Latin School of Chicago (Chicago, Ill.)
BEST PRIVATE SCHOOLS [Cover story] R. BERTSCHE chart color *Chicago* v66 no9 p104 S 2017

Latitude
How latitude affects biotic interactions L. S. Comita color *Science* v356 no6345 p1328 Je 30 2017
A latitudinal gradient for genetic diversity H. M. Pereira bibl color *Science* v353 no6307 p1494 S 30 2016

LATONA, VALERIE
Be kind to body and mind color *Yoga Journal* p14 2016 Special Issue

Latonero, Mark
Tech Companies Should Speak Up for Refugees, Not Only High-Skilled Immigrants *Harvard Business Review Digital Articles* p2 My 16 2017

Latour, Bruno
THE NEW CLIMATE *Harper's Magazine* v334 no2004 p13 My 2017

LATOURRETTE, DEAN
Carving Giants bw color *Surfer* v58 no2 p46 My 2017

Latson, Jennifer
All His Loving R. PADAWER *New York Times Book Review* p17 Je 25 2017

Lattice dynamics
See also
Phonons
Spin-imbalance in a 2D Fermi-Hubbard system P. T. Brown, D. Mitra et al diag graph *Science* v357 no6358 p1385 S 29 2017

Latza, Greg
THE BIG PICTURE *South Dakota Magazine* v33 no3 p50 S/O 2017

Lau, Amy
Perfect Harmony D. SHAW color *Architectural Digest* v73 no12 p112 D 2016

Lau, Amy—Interviews
COOL & COLLECTED C. KELLOGG color *House Beautiful* v158 no9 p150 N 2016

Lau, Brian
She Makes More (Way More) M. Mertens color *Glamour* v114 no12 p168 D 2016

Lau, Jason
PRINCIPLES FOR ELEMENTARY PRINCIPALS: Keys to remember when it comes to being a literacy leader *Literacy Today (2411-7862)* v35 no2 p24 S/O 2017

Lau, Jonathan
Three-dimensional holey-graphene/niobia composite architectures for ultrahigh-rate energy storage color diag graph *Science* v356 no6338 p599 My 12 2017

Lau, Martin
TENCENT GOES GLOBAL MAYBE B. Stone and Lulu Chen color diag *Bloomberg Businessweek* no4529 p50 Jl 3 2017

Lau, Megan
She Makes More (Way More) M. Mertens color *Glamour* v114 no12 p168 D 2016

Laub, Michael T.
Bacillus subtilis SMC complexes juxtapose chromosome arms as they travel from origin to terminus bibl graph *Science* v355 no6324 p524 F 3 2017

LAUBERTE, MARISSA
What To Ask About Antibiotics Before You Start A Course *Reader's Digest* v188 no1124 p64 O 2016

LAUCHT, LUCY
Room 8 Albergo Barbara color *Conde Nast Traveler* v52 no8 p122 S 2017

Lauckner, Bruce
AJ CREATORS *Alternatives Journal (AJ) - Canada's Environmental Voice* v42 no3 p8 2016
Community Medicine cartoon diag *Alternatives Journal (AJ) - Canada's Environmental Voice* v42 no3 p36 2016

Laudato si' (Papal encyclical)
Whose Land? [Cover story] J. D. WILSEY color *America* v215 p20 N 28 2016

Lauder, Aerin, 1970-
DESIGN NOTES color *Architectural Digest* no5 p116 My 2017

Lauder, Robert E.
Present in Every Page *Commonweal* v144 no16 p39 O 6 2017

Lauds (Poem)
Lauds C. V. Paintner *U.S. Catholic* v82 no10 p51 O 2017

Lauer, David Walter
ENEMY color *Christian Century* v134 no5 p20 Mr 1 2017

Lauer, Georg M.
The epigenetic landscape of T cell exhaustion bibl graph *Science* v354 no6316 p1165 D 2 2016

Lauer, Matt, 1957-
THE PEACOCK THRONE S. ELLISON color *Vanity Fair* v59 no4 p184 Mr 2017

Lauerman, John
This Hospital Operator Needs A Prescription graph *Bloomberg Businessweek* no4539 p18 S 25 2017

Laufer, Alex
The Great Whiskey Mash-Up F. MAROUKIAN color *Popular Mechanics* p22 Mr 2017

Laughlin, Robert B., 1950-
EXPANDING THE REAL P. E. DINTER *Commonweal* v144 no11 p2 Je 16 2017

Laughlin, Tim
AFTER PETE J. BERRY color *New Orleans Magazine* v51 no1 p56 N 2016

Laughlin, Trella
Discussion *Smithsonian* v48 no1 p10 Ap 2017

Laughter
See also
Smiling
ages+stages color *Parents* v92 no3 p105 Mr 2017

A Laughing Matter color *Earth Island Journal* v32 no2 p5 Summ 2017

Laughter & health

Letters J. ROSS, G. CHIARA et al color *Reader's Digest* v189 no1130 p6 My 2017

Laughter—Health aspects

Voyages J. Lowe *New York Times Magazine* p24 N 6 2016

Laughter—Religious aspects

May You Be Inscribed for a Good Laugh M. Y. SOLOVEICHIK *Commentary* v144 no2 p11 S 2017

Laukkanen, Liisa

Higher predation risk for insect prey at low latitudes and elevations graph *Science* v356 no6339 p742 My 19 2017

Laun, Jack

Will There Be Peace in Colombia? color *Progressive* p45 D 2016/Ja 2017

Laundry

See also

Hotel laundry service

Adulting 101 L. SAXTON color *Seventeen* v76 no12 p100 D 2016/Ja 2017

LOONEY FUMES M. Zeitler color *Women's Health* v14 no4 p40 My 2017

Laundry Co.

a week of AWESOME OUTFITS [Cover story] color *Good Housekeeping* v263 no5 p32 N 2016

Laundry equipment

See also

Laundry machinery

LAUNDRY QUANDARIES E. MOODY color *Martha Stewart Living* p34 S 2017

Laundry machinery

Can Your Washing Machine Work Harder? K. Janeway chart color il *Consumer Reports* v82 no10 p14 O 2017

Clothes Quarters K. Janeway color *Consumer Reports* v82 no1 p12 Ja 2017

Laundry rooms

7 Hot Home Design Trends color *Timber Home Living* v27 no3 p22 Je 2017

LAUNDRY QUANDARIES E. MOODY color *Martha Stewart Living* p34 S 2017

Rolling on the River J. Brewster bw color diag *Log Home Living* v34 no6 p40 Ag 2017

Wash and Wow C. SWANSON color *House Beautiful* v159 no7 p69 S 2017

Laundry—Equipment & supplies

Laundroid Y. Nakamura and H. Nakagawa color *Bloomberg Businessweek* no4510 p28 F 6 2017

Laundry—Equipment & supplies—Evaluation

IRONS color *Good Housekeeping* v264 no5 p86 My 2017

Launi, Stephen

FROM OUR READERS *Sky & Telescope* v134 no6 p6 D 2017

Lauper, Cyndi, 1953-

Guide to Life, Career & Kids color *AARP: The Magazine* v59 no5A p44 Ag/S 2016

Random Notes color *Rolling Stone* no1278/1279 p26 Ja 12 2017

Lauper, Cyndi, 1953—Awards

Still Having FUN! J. NEWMAN color *AARP: The Magazine* v59 no5A p42 Ag/S 2016

Laur, Katie

He's Funny That Way: THE LIFE, TIMES, AND PICKLED GARLIC OF ALAN KIGER *Cincinnati Magazine* v50 no11 p40 Ag 2017

In the Garden *Cincinnati Magazine* v50 no5 p44 F 2017

Radio Days *Cincinnati Magazine* p44 Je 2017

A Song for J.D K. LAUR *Cincinnati Magazine* v50 no3 p50 D 2016

Sparkle and Dance *Cincinnati Magazine* v50 no7 p38 Ap 2017

Laurance, S. G. W.

Persistent effects of pre-Columbian plant domestication on Amazonian forest composition bibl chart graph map *Science* v355 no6328 p925 Mr 3 2017

Laurance, William F.

Persistent effects of pre-Columbian plant domestication on Amazonian forest composition bibl chart graph map *Science* v355 no6328 p925 Mr 3 2017

Wildlife-snaring crisis in Asian forests color *Science* v355 no6322 p255 Ja 20 2017

Laurel & Wolf (Company)

AT YOUR SERVICE B. THORKLESON color *Better Homes & Gardens* v95 no9 p48 S 2017

Lauren, Greg

Living on the Edge S. HOTCHKISS color *Esquire* v166 no5 p60 D 2016/Ja 2017

LAUREN, LAUREN BUSH

THE DO-GOOD DESIGNER color *Martha Stewart Living* p42 Mr 2017

Lauren, Ralph

THE WINNING LOOK color *Golf Magazine* v59 no9 p40 S 2017

Laurence, Hannah M.

Zika virus produces noncoding RNAs using a multi-pseudoknot structure that confounds a cellular exonuclease bibl color graph *Science* v354 no6316 p1148 D 2 2016

Laurence Scherer, Barrymore

The ancien régime's master of precious metals color *Magazine Antiques* v183 no6 p90 N/D 2016

Laurens, Camille

Who You Think I Am *Publishers Weekly* v264 no5 p173 Ja 30 2017

Laurens, Stephanie

Lord of the Privateers color *Publishers Weekly* v263 no50 p56 D 5 2016

Laurenson, Ian

Emergence and spread of a human-transmissible multidrug-resistant nontuberculous mycobacterium bibl diag graph *Science* v354 no6313 p751 N 11 2016

Laurenson, Lydia

Don't Try to Be a Publisher and a Platform at the Same Time *Harvard Business Review Digital Articles* p2 Ja 19 2015

Secret's Problem Wasn't Trolls *Harvard Business Review Digital Articles* p2 My 20 2015

Laurentian Suite (Poem)

Laurentian Suite S. GLICKMAN *Walrus* v14 no8 p58 O 2017

Laurie, Hugh, 1959-

Chance A. D'ARMINIO color *TV Guide* v64 no42 p43 O 10 2016

Laurie's New Healing Sleuth Takes a Dubious Chance D. D'Addario color *Time* v188 no18 p45 O 31 2016

Laurie, Victoria

A Panicked Premonition: A Psychic Eye Mystery *Publishers Weekly* v264 no18 p39 My 1 2017

Lauritzen, Paul

A necessary evil? color *America* v217 no4 p50 Ag 21 2017

Oh the Places We'll Go color *Commonweal* v144 no6 p30 Mr 24 2017

Laursen, Lucas

Emission Permission color *Scientific American* v317 no2 p17 Ag 2017

Soil in the Forecast color *Scientific American* v316 no5 p18 My 2017

Laursen, Tomas

Characterization of a dynamic metabolon producing the defense compound dhurrin in sorghum bibl graph *Science* v354 no6314 p890 N 18 2016

Lausanne (Switzerland)

ON THE GRAND LAKE A. Erace color *Fortune* v175 no8 p90 Je 15 2017

Lauscher, M.

Observation of a large-scale anisotropy in the arrival directions of cosmic rays above 8×10^{18} eV *Science* v357 no6357 p1266 S 22 2017

LAUSSADE, ALICE

THE GREASE-STAINED SUGAR-DUSTED INSANELY TEXAN TRUE BUT IMPROBABLE INSIDE STORY ABOUT THE INVENTION OF FRIED JELL~O *D: The Magazine of Dallas* v43 no10 p138 O 2016

Lautenberg, Frank R., 1924-2013

Not'Til the Fat Lady Sings TSCA's Next Act D. GOLDSTON *Issues in Science & Technology* v33 no1 p73 Fall 2016

Lauterbach, Christiane

50 Best, Refreshed *Atlanta* v56 no11 p2 Mr 2017

BEST NEW RESTAURANTS *Atlanta* v57 no5 p78 S 2017

BEST OF ATLANTA *Atlanta* v56 no8 p106 D 2016

2017

Law, Elizabeth A.

Global climatic drivers of leaf size [Cover story] graph *Science* v357 no6354 p917 S 1 2017

Law, Jude, 1972-

On HBO, a Tyrannical New Pope Lusts for Power D. D'Addario color *Time* v189 no3 p53 Ja 16 2017

The Young Pope A. D'Arminio *TV Guide* v65 no2 p32 Ja 2 2017

The Young Pope J. Jensen color *Entertainment Weekly* no1448 p52 Ja 13 2017

The Young Pope M. ROUSH *TV Guide* v65 no4 p16 Ja 16 2017

Law, Keith

Smart Baseball: The Story Behind the Old Stats That Are Ruining the Game, the New Ones That Are Running It, and the Right Way to Think About Baseball *Publishers Weekly* v264 no9 p93 F 27 2017

Law, Oliver

UNKNOWN: LOST LEADER P. Brecher bw *MHQ: Quarterly Journal of Military History* v30 no1 p87 Aut 2017

Law, Robin J.

Europe's insufficient pollutant remediation color *Science* v356 no6334 p148 Ap 14 2017

Law, Victoria

You May Hug The Screen bw *Bloomberg Businessweek* no4541 p20 O 9 2017

LAW, YAO-HUA

Rock-a-Bye Baby's Rocky Roots color *Discover* v38 no5 p66 Je 2017

Law enforcement

See also

Arrest (Police methods)

Criminal investigation

Peace officers

Racial profiling in law enforcement

HATE SPEECH W. Wilson *Lapham's Quarterly* v10 no3 p60 Summ 2017

THE JUSTICE MACHINE I. Lapowsky color *Wired* v24 no11 p68 N 2016

To the Extreme J. Hitt color *New York Times Magazine* p17 D 11 2016

Law enforcement agencies

THE OPAQUE BLUE LINE C. J. CIARAMELLA color *Reason* v49 no1 p16 My 2017

Law enforcement officials

A Vocation to Protect And Serve *America* v217 no4 p8 Ag 21 2017

Law enforcement—Equipment & supplies

Real-Life Robocops J. Zorthian color *Time* v189 no21 p10 Je 5 2017

Law enforcement—United States

A Vocation to Protect And Serve *America* v217 no4 p8 Ag 21 2017

Why Our Policing Is So Ineffective: Racism results in misdirected resources. Technology could help M. Funkhouser *Governing* v31 no1 p59 O 2017

Law firms

See also

Law partnership

Flex Equity L. NARGI diag *Working Mother* v40 no3 p26 Ag/S 2017

LAWYER PROFILES *Washingtonian Magazine* v52 no3 p125 D 2016

Law firms—United States

Why Your Diversity Program May Be Helping Women but Not Minorities (or Vice Versa) E. Apfelbaum *Harvard Business Review Digital Articles* p2 Ag 8 2016

Law offices—Automation

Rise of the Robolawyers J. KOEBLER bw color *Atlantic* v319 no3 p26 Ap 2017

Law partnership

HELL IS OTHER LAWYERS P. M. Barrett color *Bloomberg Businessweek* no4499 p72 N 14 2016

Law reform

See also

Labor law reform

FLORIDA CHANGES HARSH SENTENCING LAW, TOO LATE FOR MANY INMATES L. KRISAI and C. J. CIARAMELLA color *Reason* v49 no3 p48 Jl 2017

Law schools

Massimo Bottura M. Rich color *Current Biography* v78 no4 p12 Ap 2017

A More Practical Model for Law Schools A. Armitage and R. Feldman *Harvard Business Review Digital Articles* p2 D 24 2015

Lawal, Olawale

Dynamic creation and evolution of gradient nanostructure in single-crystal metallic microcubes bibl bw *Science* v354 no6310 p312 O 21 2016

Law—China

China Retailers' Latest Woe: Food Vigilantes color *Bloomberg Businessweek* no4535 p18 Ag 28 2017

Law—France

Jump-starting French startups *Science* v355 no6327 p778 F 24 2017

Lawhon, Cynthia

from you, the reader color graph *Horse & Rider* v56 no8 p22 Ag 2017

Lawler, Debbie

Fear Factor *Lapham's Quarterly* v10 no3 p146 Summ 2017

Lawler, Janet

Leaves: An Autumn Pop-up Book color *Publishers Weekly* v264 no35 p126 Ag 28 2017

LAWLER, KATE

Check You Out! cartoon *AARP: The Magazine* v60 no5A p20 Ag/S 2017

Mysteries of the Human Body EXPLAINED! cartoon color *AARP: The Magazine* v60 no3A p26 Ap/My 2017

Lawler, Louise

LOOKING AND SEEING P. SCHJELDAHL color *New Yorker* v93 no12 p72 My 8 2017

Lawler, Louise—Exhibitions

ART color *New Yorker* v93 no20 p16 Jl 10 2017

Lawler, Michael J.

Global atmospheric particle formation from CERN CLOUD measurements bibl graph map *Science* v354 no6316 p1119 D 2 2016

LAWLER, MOIRA

EDGEWATER'S LUXE BOOM color *Chicago* v66 no7 p16 Jl 2017

GILDED PLATEAU color *Chicago* v66 no3 p27 Mr 2017

HOT MOD color *Chicago* v66 no5 p32 My 2017

OSCAR MUNOZ'S NEW DIGS color *Chicago* v66 no8 p28 Ag 2017

QUIRK APPEAL color *Chicago* v66 no2 p16 F 2017

SQUARE FEET: THE WAITING GAME color *Chicago* v66 no9 p36 S 2017

TAKE THEM TO THE RIVER color map *Chicago* v66 no6 p26 Je 2017

Lawler, Peter Augustine, 1951-2017

PETER AUGUSTINE LAWLER, 1951-2017 D. J. Mahoney *Claremont Review of Books* v17 no3 p83 Summ 2017

Lawless, Jack—Interviews

3 ROUNDS WITH DNCE M. Snetiker color *Entertainment Weekly* no1441 p26 N 25 2016

Lawless, Jennifer

GUEST LIST: A monthly roundup of people we'd like to have over for drinks, food, and conversation *Washingtonian Magazine* v52 no11 p22 Ag 2017

LAWLESS, KRISTIN WARTMAN

Salt. a love/hate story color *Women's Health* v13 no10 p132 D 2016

Lawn aeration—Equipment & supplies

Products *Parks & Recreation* v52 no1 p52 Ja 2017

Lawn chairs

See also

Adirondack chairs

THE Adirondack CHAIR [Cover story] D. Howland color *Cabin Living* p8 Ag 2017

Lawn mowers—Equipment & supplies

Mowers That Make the Cut P. Hope chart color graph *Consumer Reports* v82 no5 p9 My 2017

Lawn mowers—Evaluation

CORDLESS YARD GEAR S. Vaglica color *Men's Health* v32 no3 p26 Ap 2017

ELECTRIC MOWERS J. SCHADEWALD color *Popular Me-*

chanics p22 Je 2017

Mowers That Make the Cut P. Hope chart color graph *Consumer Reports* v82 no5 p9 My 2017

WHAT'S NEW? *USA Today Magazine* v146 no2866 p77 Jl 2017

Lawner, Damon Emanuel

THE LONELY HEDONIST M. SAGER bw color *Esquire* v166 no4 p116 N 2016

Lawns

A Real Grass Act J. SerVaas *Saturday Evening Post* v289 no5 p25 S/O 2017

Lawns—Design & construction

FARMING the Neighborhood K. Quillen and K. C. Compton *Mother Earth News* no279 p24 D/Ja 2017

Lawns—Equipment & supplies—Evaluation

The New Yardwork Essentials R. BERENDSOHN color *Popular Mechanics* p14 Ap 2017

Lawns—Management

THIRSTY GRASS E. LITVAK and D. PATAKI *USA Today Magazine* v146 no2866 p70 Jl 2017

Law—Political aspects

For the Record color *Time* v189 no12 p9 Ap 3 2017

Lawrence, Andrew

Auto Pilots color *Sports Illustrated* v126 no7 p26 Mr 6 2017

Leading Off color *Sports Illustrated* v126 no7 p6 Mr 6 2017

PATRIOT GAMES color *Sports Illustrated* v126 no3 p52 Ja 23 2017

Players Of the Year color *Sports Illustrated* v125 no20 p92 D 19 2016

Seven for The Road color *Sports Illustrated* v125 no20 p122 D 19 2016

WALL? WHAT WALL? color *Sports Illustrated* v126 no5 p74 F 13 2017

Lawrence, Cameron Alexander

To the Ghost *America* v216 no11 p49 My 15 2017

To the Ghost C. A. Lawrence *America* v216 no11 p49 My 15 2017

Lawrence, D. J.

Extensive water ice within Ceres' aqueously altered regolith: Evidence from nuclear spectroscopy bibl graph *Science* v355 no6320 p1 Ja 6 2017

Lawrence, Dave

The Fathers of Our Wisdom M. Bean bw color *Men's Health* v32 no5 p8 Je 2017

Lawrence, Derek

After the Verdict color *Entertainment Weekly* no1482/1483 p62 S 22 2017

American Housewife *Entertainment Weekly* no1482/1483 p79 S 22 2017

Baby Daddy Marks 100 Episodes color *Entertainment Weekly* no1454/1455 p21 F 24 2017

BEYOND BLACK AND WHITE *Entertainment Weekly* no1451/1452 p43 F 3-10 2017

black-ish *Entertainment Weekly* no1482/1483 p63 S 22 2017

The Blacklist color *Entertainment Weekly* no1482/1483 p74 S 22 2017

Breaking Big BRANDON MICHEAL HALL color *Entertainment Weekly* no1482/1483 p65 S 22 2017

Broad City color *Entertainment Weekly* no1482/1483 p79 S 22 2017

Bull color *Entertainment Weekly* no1482/1483 p66 S 22 2017

The Cast of Grey's Anatomy color *Entertainment Weekly* no1439 p23 N 11 2016

Chicago P.D *Entertainment Weekly* no1482/1483 p79 S 22 2017

Criminal Minds color *Entertainment Weekly* no1482/1483 p79 S 22 2017

DC's Legends of Tomorrow color *Entertainment Weekly* no1482/1483 p66 S 22 2017

DEMI MOORE OF Empire color *Entertainment Weekly* no1482/1483 p78 S 22 2017

Designated Survivor color *Entertainment Weekly* no1482/1483 p74 S 22 2017

DIVE INTO Brooklyn Nine-Nine color *Entertainment Weekly* no1482/1483 p67 S 22 2017

Dynasty color *Entertainment Weekly* no1482/1483 p76 S 22 2017

Editor's Note color *Entertainment Weekly* no1439 p23 N 11 2016

Fantastic Beasts and Where to Find Them color *Entertainment Weekly* no1439 p18 N 11 2016

The Flash color *Entertainment Weekly* no1482/1483 p66 S 22 2017

Fresh Off the Boat color *Entertainment Weekly* no1482/1483 p63 S 22 2017

Gilmore Girls: A Year in the Life color *Entertainment Weekly* no1439 p18 N 11 2016

The Goldbergs color *Entertainment Weekly* no1482/1483 p74 S 22 2017

HAPPY ENDINGS color *Entertainment Weekly* no1439 p20 N 11 2016

Hit the Road *Entertainment Weekly* no1482/1483 p60 S 22 2017

Hot Date *Entertainment Weekly* no1482/1483 p74 S 22 2017

JASON RITTER OF Kevin (Probably) Saves the World color *Entertainment Weekly* no1482/1483 p61 S 22 2017

KEVIN HART color *Entertainment Weekly* no1474/1475 p120 Jl 21-28 2017

Law & Order: Special Victims Unit *Entertainment Weekly* no1482/1483 p75 S 22 2017

Law & Order True Crime: The Menendez Murders color *Entertainment Weekly* no1482/1483 p62 S 22 2017

Lethal Weapon color *Entertainment Weekly* no1482/1483 p60 S 22 2017

Major Crimes *Entertainment Weekly* no1482/1483 p66 S 22 2017

The Mick *Entertainment Weekly* no1482/1483 p67 S 22 2017

The Middle color *Entertainment Weekly* no1482/1483 p60 S 22 2017

Modern Family *Entertainment Weekly* no1482/1483 p75 S 22 2017

Mr. Robot color *Entertainment Weekly* no1482/1483 p77 S 22 2017

MUSIC MADE THE PEOPLE COME TOGETHER color *Entertainment Weekly* no1439 p22 N 11 2016

NCIS *Entertainment Weekly* no1482/1483 p60 S 22 2017

NCIS: New Orleans *Entertainment Weekly* no1482/1483 p67 S 22 2017

ORPHAN BLACK A TO Z color *Entertainment Weekly* no1470 p24 Je 16 2017

Riverdale color *Entertainment Weekly* no1482/1483 p68 S 22 2017

THE SCOOP, STARS & SONGS color *Entertainment Weekly* no1439 p16 N 11 2016

SEAL Team color *Entertainment Weekly* no1482/1483 p76 S 22 2017

The Shannara Chronicles *Entertainment Weekly* no1482/1483 p79 S 22 2017

Speechless color *Entertainment Weekly* no1482/1483 p75 S 22 2017

Star color *Entertainment Weekly* no1482/1483 p76 S 22 2017

Survivor: Heroes vs. Healers vs. Hustlers *Entertainment Weekly* no1482/1483 p75 S 22 2017

This Is Us color *Entertainment Weekly* no1482/1483 p56 S 22 2017

What to Watch color *Entertainment Weekly* no1453 p54 F 17 2017

What to Watch color *Entertainment Weekly* no1468/1469 p94 Je 2-9 2017

What to Watch color *Entertainment Weekly* no1480 p46 S 1 2017

Lawrence, Destiney

CROWNED jewels S. T. Brown color *Ebony* v72 no6 p90 Ap/My 2017

Lawrence, Dorothy

DOROTHY LAWRENCE 4 OCTOBER 1896 - 4 OCTOBER 1964 J. Pollard and S. Pollard *History Today* v67 no10 p22 O 2017

Lawrence, Duncan

Protecting unauthorized immigrant mothers improves their children's mental health diag *Science* v357 no6355 p1041 S 8 2017

Lawrence, Dune

Can Jigsaw's Designers Make the Internet Safer? cartoon *Bloomberg Businessweek* no4539 p49 S 25 2017

A China Moonshot for Chicago's Exchange *Bloomberg Businessweek* no4514 p40 Mr 13 2017

Cloud Armor That's Not Quite So Fluffy *Bloomberg Businessweek* no4504 p32 D 19 2016

ICO Is the New IPO *Bloomberg Businessweek* no4527 p35 Je 19 2017

It's the U.S. Army Vs. the Drone Army *Bloomberg Businessweek*

no4536 p26 S 4 2017

Neighborhood Watch cartoon *Bloomberg Businessweek* no4514 p42 Mr 13 2017

The Right To Run Sex Ads *Bloomberg Businessweek* no4493 p14 O 3 2016

SAVING THE SOUTH CHINA SEA color map *Bloomberg Businessweek* no4505 p78 D 26 2016

Seriously, Beware the 'Shadow Brokers' color *Bloomberg Businessweek* no4521 p34 My 8 2017

Will Bosch Choke on VW's Exhaust? bw color *Bloomberg Businessweek* no4534 p12 Ag 14 2017

Your Money Or Your Data! color *Bloomberg Businessweek* no4523 p15 My 22 2017

Lawrence, Ian

Reovirus infection triggers inflammatory responses to dietary antigens and development of celiac disease color diag *Science* v356 no6333 p44 Ap 7 2017

Lawrence, Jacob, 1917-2000

Missing pieces E. H. Turner bw cartoon *Magazine Antiques* v184 no1 p146 Ja/F 2017

Lawrence, Jennifer, 1990-

Best-Dressed LIST color *Harper's Bazaar* no3651 p218 Mr 2017

CELEBRATING FEMINISM J. HOBSON *Ms.* v26 no3 p12 Fall 2016

Covering the Past A. WINTOUR bw color *Vogue* v207 no9 p232 S 2017

Joy M. FELL color *TV Guide* v64 no42 p45 O 10 2016

Star Without a Script J. MILLER bw color *Vanity Fair* v59 no1 p136 Holiday 2017

We Knew Them When Z. O'MALLEY GREENBURG, M. BERG et al color *Forbes* v199 no1 p22 Ja 24 2017

WITHOUT A NET J. Gay color *Vogue* v207 no9 p630 S 2017

Lawrence, Josh

High Brass Fantasy B. ZIMMERMAN color *Downbeat* v84 no5 p54 My 2017

LAWRENCE, KERRI

PHOTOGRAPHS OF ALASKA *Prologue* v49 no2 p28 Summ 2017

Lawrence, Larry

A GREAT ONE REMEMBERED color *Cycle World* v56 no7 p62 Ag 2017

NICKY FROM BEHIND THE NOTEPAD *Cycle World* v56 no7 p67 Ag 2017

Lawrence, Mark

MINIMALIST MULTIPURPOSE M. M. Kashino *Washingtonian Magazine* v52 no6 p155 Mr 2017

Lawrence, Mark Atwood

Studying the Vietnam War: How the scholarship has changed *Humanities* v38 no4 p1 Fall 2017

Lawrence, Patrick

From Destiny to Purpose color *Nation* v304 no2 p14 Ja 16 2017

Toward a New Foreign Policy [Cover story] bw *Nation* v304 no2 p12 Ja 16 2017

LAWRENCE, RANDOLPH S.

In Spite of Education ... *American Scholar* v86 no1 p3 Wint 2017

Lawrence, Regina G.

The Trump Conundrum color graph *Columbia Journalism Review* v56 no2 p42 Fall 2017

Lawrence, Sandra

Celebrating Jane Austen 2017 color *British Heritage Travel* v38 no5 p28 S/O 2017

GOD'S WONDERFUL RAILWAY *British Heritage Travel* v38 no2 p38 Mr/Ap 2017

Happy Hijinks in Hampstead *British Heritage Travel* v38 no2 p22 Mr/Ap 2017

HEARTS OF OAK *British Heritage Travel* v38 no3 p54 My/Je 2017

History and Fun Haunt the Royal Palaces *British Heritage Travel* v37 no6 p24 N/D 2016

It's Eccentric Glamor in Regents Park color *British Heritage Travel* v38 no5 p24 S/O 2017

Living the Tudor Life at Kentwell Hall *British Heritage Travel* v38 no4 p68 Jl/Ag 2017

Regal Echoes in Royal Greenwich *British Heritage Travel* v38 no1 p26 Ja/F 2017

Take a Walk on the South Side *British Heritage Travel* v38 no3

p26 My/Je 2017

Teatime at Christmas *British Heritage Travel* v37 no6 p83 N/D 2016

Lawrence, Savannah

reviews. EAT AND RUN: MY UNLIKELY JOURNEY TO ULTRAMARATHON GREATNESS *Vegetarian Journal* v36 no3 p31 2017

Vegan Snacks for Runners *Vegetarian Journal* v36 no2 p24 2017

Vegetarian Action. Scott Jurek: An Example for Vegan Athletes *Vegetarian Journal* v36 no3 p35 2017

Lawrence, Ty

Why, That Son of a Steak! L. STEFFY *Texas Monthly* v45 no1 p56 Ja 2017

Lawrence, Wendy

SPACESHIP EARTH color map *Phi Kappa Phi Forum* v97 no1 p18 Spr 2017

WHAT ON EARTH IS IT? J. BERNHARD chart *Phi Kappa Phi Forum* v97 no1 p32 Spr 2017

Lawrence Berkeley National Laboratory

Swirls possible in infant cosmos E. CONOVER *Science News* v190 no12 p9 D 10 2016

Lawrence Livermore National Laboratory

AGENT DEFEAT Efforts Strike Gold R. Hansen *Science & Technology Review* p12 Mr 2017

Facility Drives Hydrogen Vehicle Innovations M. Hunsberger *Science & Technology Review* p20 S 2016

Forcing Failure in Granular Materials H. Auten *Science & Technology Review* p20 Mr 2017

From the Laboratory to the WORLD L. L. Helms *Science & Technology Review* p12 Je 2017

HUMAN-FREE HUMAN TRIALS S. PALUS color *Popular Science* v288 no6 p32 N/D 2016

Laboratory Investments Drive Computational Advances R. Al-Ayat *Science & Technology Review* p3 S 2016

Looking Forward to New Generations of Supercomputers color *Science & Technology Review* p8 O/N 2016

A National Security Code Is Reborn for Industry A. Heller *Science & Technology Review* p20 Je 2017

A New Paradigm for Medical Research P. Falcone color *Science & Technology Review* p3 O/N 2016

Nuclear Data Moves into the 21st Century A. Heller *Science & Technology Review* p12 S 2016

Program Supports BLAZING NEW TRAILS A. Chen *Science & Technology Review* p13 Ap/My 2017

Ready, Set, Innovate! ENTREPRENEURSHIP FLOURISHES AT THE LABORATORY H. Auten *Science & Technology Review* p4 Je 2017

Law reports, digests, etc.

A Maze Called Workers' Comp A. Greenblatt *Governing* v30 no3 p11 D 2016

UMC court rules against consecrating gay bishops K. L. Gilbert, L. Bloom et al color *Christian Century* v134 no11 p13 My 24 2017

Laws, Kevin

Successful Startups Don't Make Money Their Primary Mission *Harvard Business Review Digital Articles* p2 Jl 10 2015

Laws, Malcolm

Teachers Who Teach J. J. CONLEY *America* v215 no19 p28 D 19 2016

Lawson, Chip

Drilling Stainless Steel color *Sail* v48 no5 p49 My 2017

Refit Tips color *Sail* v48 no1 p46 Ja 2017

Lawson, Crystal

Control of meiotic pairing and recombination by chromosomally tethered 26S proteasome bibl graph *Science* v355 no6323 p408 Ja 27 2017

Lawson, Dave

NO COMMENT cartoon *Progressive* v81 no5 p8 Je/Jl 2017

Lawson, Deana

ART *New Yorker* v92 no48 p9 F 6 2017

Lawson, Ian Robert

Ian Robert Lawson A. A. DAVIS bw *Maclean's* v129 no40 p82 O 10 2016

Lawson, Ivy

MAKING A BEELINE TO SELF-EMPLOYMENT C. M. BROWN color *Black Enterprise* v47 no5 p13 Ja/F 2017

Lawson, Jonathan N.
Faculty Expressions of (No) Confidence in Institutional Leadership *Change* v49 no1 p62 Ja/F 2017

Lawson, Michael J.
Kinetics of dCas9 target search in Escherichia coli diag *Science* v357 no6358 p1420 S 29 2017

Lawson, Richard—Interviews
ART WALK AT HOME WITH THE LAWSONS T. M. FERGUSON color *Ebony* v72/73 no12/1 p58 O/N 2017

LAWSON, STEPHEN
IBM stores one bit of data on a single atom, showing how small storage could become color *PCWorld* v35 no4 p21 Ap 2017

Lawson, Tina
ART WALK AT HOME WITH THE LAWSONS T. M. FERGUSON color *Ebony* v72/73 no12/1 p58 O/N 2017
I, TINA P. H. Bass color *Essence* v47 no8 p104 D 2016

Lawson, Wesley
THE SECRETS TO Floor Plan Perfection diag *Log Home Living* v34 no1 p44 F 2017

Lawton, Colin
Red squirrels in the British Isles are infected with leprosy bacilli bibl color diag map *Science* v354 no6313 p744 N 11 2016

Lawton, Jacqueline
POWER PLAYWRIGHT P. O'Donnell *Washingtonian Magazine* v52 no6 p41 Mr 2017

Law—United States
THE Wackiest Law IN EVERY STATE B. SPECKTOR color *Reader's Digest* v190 no1132 p68 Jl/Ag 2017

Lawyer, Natasha
TINY HOME BIG DREAMS J. Chamberlain color *Sunset* v238 no1 p70 Ja 2017

Lawyers
> *See also*
> Civil rights lawyers
> Defense attorneys
> Patent lawyers
> Prosecutors
> Women lawyers

2016 TOP LAWYERS color *New Orleans Magazine* v51 no1 p80 N 2016
ALL THE PRESIDENT'S LAWYERS: DONALD TRUMP'S LIFE AND CAREER HAVE BEEN DEFINED BY HIS LEGAL BATTLES. BUT DO THE ATTORNEYS WHO GUIDED HIM THROUGH THE COURTROOMS OF NEW YORK AND NEW JERSEY KNOW HOW TO NAVIGATE WASHINGTON? J. MAHLER *New York Times Magazine* p28 Jl 9 2017
Do Lawyers Make Better CEOs Than MBAs? M. T. Henderson *Harvard Business Review Digital Articles* p2 2017
IN DEFENSE OF LAWYERS: The widely held belief that lawyers are untrustworthy and unprincipled is dead wrong L. Tesser *Saturday Evening Post* v289 no5 p12 S/O 2017
Justice for Some G. J. KENNEDY color *Walrus* v14 no9 p47 N 2017
KEEPING YOUR CABIN IN THE FAMILY [Cover story] C. R. Barden *Cabin Living* p12 Ag 2017
Law Firms' Grueling Hours Are Turning Defectors into Competitors J. C. Williams *Harvard Business Review Digital Articles* p2 Ag 25 2015
Nancy Rafuse *Atlanta* v57 no2 p102 Je 2017
SECURITY BREACH: Trump's tussle with the bureaucratic state M. J. Glennon color *Harper's Magazine* v335 no2005 p40 Je 2017
TV SKILLS: Ever dream of being on television? Here's where you go to learn how to sound like an expert C. Neuhaus *Saturday Evening Post* v289 no4 p16 Jl/Ag 2017
Vanita Gupta J. Johnson color *Current Biography* v78 no1 p22 Ja 2017
A Wealth of Experience J. HERBST *Los Angeles Magazine* p32 D 2016

Lawyers—China
The Last Line of Defense A. W. PALMER *New York Times Magazine* p24 Jl 30 2017

Lawyers—Employment
Bad at Doing Good L. Featherstone color *Nation* v304 no16 p5 My 22 2017

Lawyers—Great Britain
'For £750,000 Per Dear, I'll Call Anyone Sir' S. AKAM color *Bloomberg Businessweek* no4524 p48 My 29 2017

Lawyers—Humor
That's Outrageous! SO SUE ME *Reader's Digest* v188 no1125 p137 N 2016

Lawyers—Interviews
JOHN MANGIN J. Chen color *Bloomberg Businessweek* no4512 p83 F 20 2017
What I Wear to Work: MAURICIO URIBE J. Chen color *Bloomberg Businessweek* no4507 p67 Ja 16 2017

Lawyers—Louisiana
Mourning a Friend, Losing a Hero E. C. Peyton color *New Orleans Magazine* v51 no8 p48 Je 2017

Lawyers—Malpractice
FLUNKING THE BAR *Governing* v30 no6 p10 Mr 2017

Lawyers—Salaries, wages, etc.
LAWYERS LEAD, PASTORAL WORKERS LAG ON PAY SCALE IN CATHOLIC CHURCH M. O'Loughlin il *America* v217 no5 p12 S 4 2017

Lawyers—United States
> *See also*
> African American lawyers

FLUNKING THE BAR *Governing* v30 no6 p10 Mr 2017
GAMM ON: The Humanist Interview with Philanthropist Gordon Gamm J. BARDI *Humanist* v77 no5 p20 S/O 2017
"Racehorse" Haynes, 1927-2017 J. N. LOMAX *Texas Monthly* v45 no6 p54 Je 2017
THURGOOD MARSHALL Z. HILL bw *Ebony* v72/73 no12/1 p98 O/N 2017
Why You Won't Get Your Day in Court J. S. Rakoff bw cartoon *New York Review of Books* v63 no18 p4 N 24 2016

Lawyers—United States—Attitudes
THE GAWKER STALKER J. ZENGERLE color *GQ: Gentlemen's Quarterly* v86 no12 p164 D 2016

Lawyers—United States—Employment
Mueller's Dream Team Gears Up T. Schoenberg and D. Voreacos bw *Bloomberg Businessweek* no4527 p46 Je 19 2017

Lawyers—United States—Political activity
The Trump-Loving Lawyer Who Won't Stop Suing Fox News F. Gillette color *Bloomberg Businessweek* no4540 p60 O 2 2017

Laxminarayan, Ramanan
Reducing antimicrobial use in food animals color graph *Science* v357 no6358 p1350 S 29 2017

Lay, Benjamin
THE CAVE-DWELLING VEGAN WHO TOOK ON QUAKER SLAVERY AND WON: THE NATION'S FIRST RADICAL ABOLITIONIST WAS ONE OF THE MOST DRAMATIC OUTSPOKEN FIGURES OF THE 18TH CENTURY. YET FEW HISTORIANS HAVE EVEN HEARD OF THE AMAZING BENJAMIN LAY M. REDIKER *Smithsonian* v48 no5 p34 S 2017

Lay, Paul
AMBITION, STYLE AND SACRIFICE: The challenges that Edward Gibbon faced remain much the same for historians today *History Today* v67 no6 p3 Je 2016
FROM THE EDITOR 1917: THE FRAGILITY OF POWER: The First World War ensured the success of the Russian Revolution. Peace would have strangled it at birth *History Today* v67 no10 p3 O 2017
FROM THE EDITOR *History Today* v66 no12 p2 D 2016
FROM THE EDITOR *History Today* v67 no2 p2 F 2017
FROM THE EDITOR *History Today* v67 no4 p2 Ap 2017
History is at odds with our desire for simple certainties. Can its cultivation of complexity create a better future? *History Today* v67 no9 p3 S 2017
THE TRUE NORTH *History Today* v67 no8 p3 Ag 2017

Lay readers
Raise your voice: To be a lector is to live out the Catholic commitment to prayer, community, and storytelling J. Bazan color *U.S. Catholic* v82 no10 p45 O 2017

Laya, Patricia
Can Puerto Rico Corral Its Tax Dodgers? color graph *Bloomberg Businessweek* no4524 p17 My 29 2017
How Much Room to Grow? color *Bloomberg Businessweek* no4511 p8 F 13 2017

Layback Co.
BEST OF THE WEST N. Farrell, J. Silver et al color *Sunset* v238 no3 p7 Mr 2017

Laycock, Douglas
Free speech in the pulpit *Christian Century* v134 no6 p10 Mr 15 2017

Layden, Tim
ALL ABOUT CONNECTIONS [Cover story] color *Sports Illustrated* v126 no3 p22 Ja 23 2017
ALL-TIME DRAFT chart color *Sports Illustrated* v127 no3 p64 Jl 24 2017
ATHLETE GETS CANCER. ATHLETE FIGHTS CANCER. REPEAT, AGAIN & AGAIN ... color *Sports Illustrated* v127 no2 p54 Jl 17 2017
CARDINALS' SINS color *Sports Illustrated* v127 no11 p26 O 9 2017
Continental Divide color *Sports Illustrated* v125 no17 p20 N 21 2016 Double Issue
DREAM Team color *Sports Illustrated* v126 no14 p50 My 15-22 2017
THE GOLD STANDARD [Cover story] chart color *Sports Illustrated* v125 no21 p30 D 26 2016
Horse Nonsense color *Sports Illustrated* v126 no13 p18 My 8 2017
LITTLE MAN, BIG SHOTS color *Sports Illustrated* v126 no5 p52 F 13 2017
Players Of the Year color *Sports Illustrated* v125 no20 p92 D 19 2016
PUMP IT UP color *Sports Illustrated* v126 no11 p58 Ap 17-24 2017
Reign Over color *Sports Illustrated* v127 no5 p22 Ag 14 2017
Seven for The Road color *Sports Illustrated* v125 no20 p122 D 19 2016
A TOWN, A TEAM AND FOOTBALL color *Sports Illustrated* v127 no11 p46 O 9 2017
Victor CONTE color *Sports Illustrated* v127 no1 p66 Jl 3 2017
WIN ONE MORE? ROGER color *Sports Illustrated* v126 no4 p31 Ja 30 2017

Laying-out (Woodwork)
Home with a View J. Brewster color diag *Log Home Living* v34 no5 p52 Jl 2017

Layla Mehdi, B.
Bottom-up construction of a superstructure in a porous uranium-organic crystal color graph *Science* v356 no6338 p624 My 12 2017

LAYNE, CHRISTOPHER
The Big Forces of History il *American Conservative* v16 no1 p10 Ja/F 2017
Contemplating Decline: China's challenge to America percolates on many fronts *American Conservative* v16 no4 p29 Jl/Ag 2017
FROM THE ARCHIVES cartoon *Reason* v49 no2 p70 Je 2017

Layoffs
THE APPROVAL MATRIX img *New York* v49 no22 p136 O 31 2016
The disappearance of SoundCloud has become a real possibility. What would that mean for the music culture that thrives on the site? J. Wortham color *New York Times Magazine* p14 Ag 6 2017
A Guide to Being Compassionate During Layoffs K. W. Freeman *Harvard Business Review Digital Articles* p2 F 25 2016
I Got Fired: Rebuild your career after you've been shown the door K. BRADY *Dance Magazine* v91 no7 p56 Jl 2017
Job openings, hires, and separations return to prerecession levels in 2015 A. MacLeod bibl chart color graph *Monthly Labor Review* p1 S 2016
The Jobs That Weren't Saved S. Gregory color *Time* v189 no20 p36 My 29 2017
News Roundup V. HAFSTAÐ *Iceland Review* v55 no2 p18 Mr/Ap 2017

Layous, Kristin
Ask anything [Cover story] color *Women's Health* v14 no1 p24 Ja/F 2017

Laytham, D. Brent
Reflections on the lectionary *Christian Century* v134 no11 p21 My 24 2017

LAZAN, MARK
Your Say... color *Motor Trend* v69 no7 p32 Jl 2017

Lazar, Mitchell A.
Circadian time signatures of fitness and disease bibl diag map *Science* v354 no6315 p994 N 25 2016
Regeneration of fat cells from myofibroblasts during wound healing bibl color graph *Science* v355 no6326 p748 F 17 2017

Lazar, Sara W.
Mindfulness Can Literally Change Your Brain *Harvard Business Review Digital Articles* p2 Ja 8 2015

Lazar, Seth
Evaluating the Revisionist Critique of Just War Theory *Daedalus* v146 no1 p113 Wint 2017

Lazar, Wendi—Interviews
SPEAK OUT J. OWENS bw *Working Mother* p16 F/Mr 2017

Lazar, Zachary
Evicted: The Israeli immigrants in Joshua Cohen's novel spend their days displacing delinquent tenants *New York Times Book Review* p11 Ag 13 2017

Lazar, Zohar
STRESS TEST color *Wired* v25 no9 p8 S 2017

Lazare, Gerald
A Walrus Tribute color *Walrus* v14 no2 p56 Mr 2017

LAZARONY, LUCY
Hidden Bank Fees cartoon *AARP: The Magazine* v60 no5A p25 Ag/S 2017

Lazarus (Music)
David Bowie's Parting Gift A. GREENE color *Rolling Stone* no1273 p16 N 3 2016

Lazarus, Emma, 1849-1887
Wretched Refuse, Indeed K. D. WILLIAMSON bw *National Review* v69 no16 p14 Ag 28 2017

Lazarus, of Bethany, Saint, d. 1st century
LIVING BY The Word *Christian Century* v134 no6 p18 Mr 15 2017

Lazcano, Antonio
Mexican and U.S. scientists: Partners bibl color *Science* v355 no6330 p1139 Mr 17 2017

Lazear, Edward Paul
The Latest German Model *Hoover Digest: Research & Opinion on Public Policy* no1 p61 Wint 2017
A Recipe for 3% Growth: The ingredients: boost productivity, rationalize the tax code, and put more Americans to work (and keep them there). All that, and add a dash of luck *Hoover Digest: Research & Opinion on Public Policy* no3 p9 Summ 2017
Steady and Rising: The American economy, going from strength to strength *Hoover Digest: Research & Opinion on Public Policy* no2 p9 Spr 2017

Lazer, David M. J.
Fostering reproducibility in industry-academia research color *Science* v357 no6353 p759 Ag 25 2017
Growing pains for global monitoring of societal events bibl graph *Science* v353 no6307 p1502 S 30 2016
Improving election prediction internationally bibl graph *Science* v355 no6324 p515 F 3 2017
The need for a translational science of democracy bibl color *Science* v355 no6328 p914 Mr 3 2017

Laziness
See also
Procrastination
5 Research-Based Strategies for Overcoming Procrastination C. Bailey *Harvard Business Review Digital Articles* p2 O 4 2017
Make Time for Boredom J. STEWART cartoon *Atlantic* v319 no5 p23 Je 2017

Lazio, Joseph
Spiral density waves in a young protoplanetary disk bibl graph *Science* v353 no6307 p1519 S 30 2016

Lazo, Suzan
Single-cell RNA-seq reveals new types of human blood dendritic cells, monocytes, and progenitors color *Science* v356 no6335 p283 Ap 21 2017

Lazonick, William
Clinton's Proposals on Stock Buybacks Don't Go Far Enough *Harvard Business Review Digital Articles* p2 Ag 11 2015
GM's Stock Buyback Is Bad for America and the Company *Harvard Business Review Digital Articles* p2 Mr 11 2015
If the SEC Measured CEO Pay Packages Properly, They Would Look Even More Outrageous *Harvard Business Review Digital*

Articles p2 D 22 2016

McDonald's Has to Do More than Manipulate Its Stock Price *Harvard Business Review Digital Articles* p2 My 14 2015

Numbers Show Apple Shareholders Have Already Gotten Plenty *Harvard Business Review Digital Articles* p2 O 16 2014

U.S. Corporations Don't Need Tax Breaks on Foreign Profits *Harvard Business Review Digital Articles* p2 D 21 2015

What Apple Should Do with Its Massive Piles of Money *Harvard Business Review Digital Articles* p2 O 20 2014

Lazowska, Ed

Academia's failure to retain data scientists bibl *Science* v355 no6323 p357 Ja 27 2017

Lazzarin, M.

Rosetta's comet 67P/Churyumov-Gerasimenko sheds its dusty mantle to reveal its icy nature bibl graph *Science* v354 no6319 p1566 D 23 2016

Surface changes on comet 67P/Churyumov-Gerasimenko suggest a more active past bw graph *Science* v355 no6332 p1392 Mr 31 2017

LCD Soundsystem (Performer)

A Disco-Punk Epic for the Age of Trump R. SHEFFIELD color *Rolling Stone* no1295 p53 S 7 2017

LCD Soundsystem L. Greenblatt color *Entertainment Weekly* no1480 p53 S 1 2017

OVER IT HUA HSU cartoon *New Yorker* v93 no26 p90 S 4 2017

The Playlist color *Rolling Stone* no1288 p8 Je 1 2017

Someone Great Is Back D. MARCHESE img *New York* v50 no17 p112 Ag 21 2017

Lceffler-Gladstone, Nicoie

THE TRUTH ABOUT Sugar *Dance Spirit* v21 no3 p30 Mr 2017

Le, A.-T.

Ultrafast electron diffraction imaging of bond breaking in di-ionized acetylene bibl graph *Science* v354 no6310 p308 O 21 2016

Le, Chip

Photosensitized, energy transfer-mediated organometallic catalysis through electronically excited nickel(II) bibl diag graph *Science* v355 no6323 p380 Ja 27 2017

Le, Dung T.

Mismatch repair deficiency predicts response of solid tumors to PD-1 blockade chart graph *Science* v357 no6349 p409 Jl 28 2017

Le, G.

COMPRESSION LOCKS A. Zerling color *Black Belt* v55 no6 p52 O/N 2017

Flamingos' bones favor one-leg stance S. MILIUS color *Science News* v191 no12 p15 Je 24 2017

A home practice for powerful legs N. Costello color *Yoga Journal* p98 2017 SpecialIssue

IN THIS SECTION color *Yoga Journal* p52 2017 Special Issue

Leg pain color *Yoga Journal* p89 2017 SpecialIssue

LIVE JOY N. Doane and E. Modestini color *Yoga Journal* p66 2017 Special Issue

My Legs A. Sedaris and S. Cristobal color *InStyle* v24 no10 p224 O 2017

Structure, force balance, and topology of Earth's magnetopause diag graph *Science* v356 no6341 p960 Je 1 2017

TAKE A SEAT C. Krucoff color *Yoga Journal* p62 2017 Special Issue

Le, Khoa M.

Priming HIV-1 broadly neutralizing antibody precursors in human Ig loci transgenic mice bibl graph *Science* v353 no6307 p1557 S 30 2016

Le, Tung B. K.

Bacillus subtilis SMC complexes juxtapose chromosome arms as they travel from origin to terminus bibl graph *Science* v355 no6324 p524 F 3 2017

Le Boeuf Brothers (Performer)

GOINGS ON ABOUT TOWN bw *New Yorker* v92 no38 p9 N 21 2016

Le Bon Marché SA

Le Click! E. ELWICK-BATES color *Vogue* v207 no6 p62 Je 2017

Le Brad (Theatrical production)

Tutino: Le Braci J. Rosenblum *Opera News* v81 no5 p56 N 2016

Le Canard Enchaine (Periodical)

The Duck That Clipped Fillon's Wings A. Boksenbaum-Granier and G. Amiel color *Bloomberg Businessweek* no4518 p17 Ap

10 2017

Le Chatelier's principle

Super-dry reforming of methane intensifies CO_2 utilization via Le Chatelier's principle L. C. Buelens, V. V. Galvita et al bibl diag graph *Science* v354 no6311 p449 O 28 2016

Le Clemenza di Tito (Theatrical production)

La Clemenza di Tito J. Malafronte *Opera News* v81 no9 p36 Mr 2017

Le Mans: Racing is Everything (Film)

STREAMING A. D'ARMINIO *TV Guide* v65 no23 p38 My 29 2017

Leach, Jeff

Seasonal cycling in the gut microbiome of the Hadza hunter-gatherers of Tanzania diag *Science* v357 no6353 p802 Ag 25 2017

Leach, Mark Richard

Where Making Matters color *American Craft* v76 no6 p66 D 2016-Ja 2017

Leach, Mike

WHAT IF THE PIRATE NEVER LEFT THE ISLAND? A. Staples color *Sports Illustrated* v127 no9 p36 S 25 2017

Leach, Patrick

Containing Trump *Atlantic* v319 no5 p10 Je 2017

Leach, Samantha

Bald & Beautiful: A Timeline bw color *Glamour* v115 no11 p46 N 2017

Pink Power color *Glamour* v115 no10 p36 O 2017

The Scenes That Changed Everything color *Glamour* v115 no10 p50 O 2017

Leach, Steve

Runnerhood of the Traveling Singlet K. FOX color *Runner's World* v52 no7 p50 Ag 2017

Leacock, Matt

EVERY DAY I'M SIDE-HUSTLIN' cartoon color *GQ: Gentlemen's Quarterly* v97 no4 p60 Ap 2017

Leacock, Patrick

Do You Know the Mushroom Man? R. O'CONNOR color *Chicago* v66 no4 p100 Ap 2017

Lead

charging up a battery conference M. B. Griggs color *Popular Science* v289 no6 p80 N/D 2017

HEAVY METAL J. Yuskavitch color *Earth Island Journal* v32 no3 p41 Aut 2017

Toxicologists look to epigenetics T. H. SAEY color graph *Science News* v190 no13 p12 D 24 2016

Lead based paint—Health aspects

Backtalk J. M. Torres *Phi Delta Kappan* v98 no7 p80 Ap 2017

Lead in water

See also

Drinking water—Lead content

CAN AMERICA AVOID ANOTHER FLINT? N. SCHARPING color *Discover* v38 no1 p18 Ja/F 2017

WHAT'S IN A GLASS OF WATER? R. FELTMAN color *Popular Science* v289 no2 p56 Mr/Ap 2017

Lead poisoning

Early Emissions H. Leifert color *Natural History* v125 no10 p7 O 2017

Leadbetter, C.

Observation of coherent elastic neutrino-nucleus scattering diag *Science* v357 no6356 p1123 S 15 2017

Leader, Joseph B.

Distribution and clinical impact of functional variants in 50,726 whole-exome sequences from the DiscovEHR study chart graph *Science* v354 no6319 paaf6814-1 D 23 2016

Genetic identification of familial hypercholesterolemia within a single U.S. health care system chart graph *Science* v354 no6319 paaf7000-1 D 23 2016

Leaders

See also

Religious leaders

Women leaders

4 Ways to Overcome a Bad First Impression D. Clark *Harvard Business Review Digital Articles* p2 My 13 2016

5 Questions to Ask About Corporate Culture to Get Beyond the Usual Meaningless Blather B. Taylor *Harvard Business Review Digital Articles* p2 Je 1 2017

The 5 Skills That Innovative Leaders Have in Common K. Gra-

J. Folkman *Harvard Business Review Digital Articles* p2 F 26 2015

Your Company's Networks Might Matter More than Its Strategy G. Satell *Harvard Business Review Digital Articles* p2 Je 10 2015

You're Never Too Experienced to Fake It Till You Learn It H. Ibarra *Harvard Business Review Digital Articles* p2 Ja 8 2015

Your Team's Time Management Problem Might Be a Focus Problem M. Thomas color *Harvard Business Review Digital Articles* p2 F 27 2017

Leadership in children
A JACK-OF-ALL-TRADES N. Cremen color *Literacy Today (2411-7862)* v34 no4 p12 Ja/F 2017
WHY WE NEED TO TRACK PROGRESS L. Helman color *Literacy Today (2411-7862)* v34 no4 p10 Ja/F 2017

Leadership in Energy & Environmental Design Green Building Rating System
GREEN HOUSES B. RILEY *Atlanta* v56 no10 p28 F 2017
A Slow Revolution A. FRIEDMAN color graph *Alternatives Journal (AJ) - Canada's Environmental Voice* v42 no2 p36 2016

Leadership—Awards
Patents and Awards *Science & Technology Review* p24 Je 2017

Leadership—Congresses
Build Your Own Company J. BODNAR cartoon *Kiplinger's Personal Finance* v71 no3 p37 Mr 2017
Los Angeles *Los Angeles Magazine* p147 D 2016

Leadership—Methodology
The Hard Data on Being a Nice Boss E. Seppala *Harvard Business Review Digital Articles* p2 N 24 2014
How to Pull Your Company Out of a Tailspin C. Zook *Harvard Business Review Digital Articles* p2 S 8 2016
Leaders Win Trust When They Show a Bit of Humanity T. Leberecht *Harvard Business Review Digital Articles* p2 Ap 1 2015
Learning New Things Means Getting Up From Your Desk B. Power *Harvard Business Review Digital Articles* p2 N 27 2014
The Most Productive Way to Develop as a Leader H. Ibarra *Harvard Business Review Digital Articles* p2 Mr 27 2015
People Remember What You Say When You Paint a Picture A. M. Carton *Harvard Business Review Digital Articles* p2 Je 12 2015
You Don't Need Charisma to Be an Inspiring Leader N. Tasler *Harvard Business Review Digital Articles* p2 O 27 2015

Leadership—Moral & ethical aspects
THE FOUR PILLARS OF MORAL LEADERSHIP D. Seidman and C. Leaf color *Fortune* v176 no4 p90 S 15 2017

Leadership—Psychological aspects
3 Ways to Better Understand Your Emotions S. David *Harvard Business Review Digital Articles* p2 N 10 2016
When Was the Last Time You Took On a New Challenge? K. Firestone *Harvard Business Review Digital Articles* p2 F 17 2017

Leadership—Study & teaching
Fixing the Leadership Gap in Southeast Asia V. Ratanjee and A. Pyrka *Harvard Business Review Digital Articles* p2 My 27 2015
How One Hospital Turns Doctors into Leaders J. Dudley *Harvard Business Review Digital Articles* p2 D 12 2014
Research: How Leadership Experience Affects Students M. L. Anderson and Fangwen Lu *Harvard Business Review Digital Articles* p2 F 21 2017
We're serious about putting patients at the heart of learning M. CALNAN *People Management* p22 F 2017
Why Leadership Training Fails—and What to Do About It: Interaction B. Palmer, C. Sharma et al *Harvard Business Review* v94 no12 p19 D 2016
Your Leadership Development Program Needs an Overhaul M. Samani and R. J. Thomas *Harvard Business Review Digital Articles* p2 D 5 2016

Leadership—United States
America's Leaders Need to Tell a New Story About Infrastructure R. M. Kanter *Harvard Business Review Digital Articles* p2 My 15 2015
How Learning and Development Are Becoming More Agile J. Younger *Harvard Business Review Digital Articles* p2 O 11 2016
How the Navy SEALs Train for Leadership Excellence M. Schrage *Harvard Business Review Digital Articles* p2 My 28 2015

Leaders—Moral & ethical aspects

Time for purposeful leadership P. Cheese *People Management* p5 Jl 2017

Leaders—Moral & religious aspects
We're Unethical at Work Because We Forget Our Misdeeds F. Gino and M. Kouchaki *Harvard Business Review Digital Articles* p2 My 18 2016

Leaf, Clifton
14 DELOS "TOBY" COSGROVE color *Fortune* v174 no7 p88 D 1 2016
THE BUSINESS OF HUMANITY color *Fortune* v75 no1 p9 Ja 1 2017
CHANGE THE WORLD !!!! color diag map *Fortune* v176 no4 p74 S 15 2017
FORGING A NEW SOCIAL COMPACT color *Fortune* v174 no7 p8 D 1 2016
Fortune Brainstorm HEALTH color *Fortune* v175 no7 p20 Je 1 2017
FORTUNE'S MPW VIPs color *Fortune* v176 no5 p10 O 1 2017
THE FOUR PILLARS OF MORAL LEADERSHIP color *Fortune* v176 no4 p90 S 15 2017
THE GREATEST ASSIGNMENT color *Fortune* v175 no5 p6 Ap 1 2017
HOW TO MAKE HUMAN CAPITAL COUNT color *Fortune* v175 no2 p6 F 1 2017
IDEAS KNOW NO BORDERS color *Fortune* v176 no2 p10 Ag 1 2017
KEYS TO THE KINGDOM color *Fortune* v176 no1 p4 Jl 1 2017
NEW KIDS ON THE BLOCKCHAIN color *Fortune* v176 no3 p9 S 1 2017
NO MARGIN, NO MISSION color *Fortune* v176 no4 p12 S 15 2017
NO TIME TO WAIT color *Fortune* v174 no8 p11 D 15 2016
REBEL TERRITORY color *Fortune* v175 no8 p24 Je 15 2017
SEEING TOMORROW color *Fortune* v175 no6 p4 My 1 2017
UBER'S RECKLESS DRIVER color *Fortune* v175 no7 p6 Je 1 2017
WATSON: NOT SO ELEMENTARY color *Fortune* v174 no6 p30 N 1 2016

Leaf, Jonathan
Acts of Undermining I. TUTTLE *National Review* v69 no9 p38 My 15 2017
Parsimonious Eye color *Weekly Standard* v22 no19 p38 Ja 23 2017
Reconsidering August Wilson *National Review* v69 no5 p44 Mr 20 2017

Leaf, June
Precision Drawing and Useless Categories D. Nadel color *Art in America* v104 no10 p29 N 2016

Leaf area index
Satellites reveal contrasting responses of regional climate to the widespread greening of Earth G. Forzieri, R. Alkama et al diag *Science* v356 no6343 p1180 Je 16 2017

Leaf blowers—Evaluation
CORDLESS YARD GEAR S. Vaglica color *Men's Health* v32 no3 p26 Ap 2017

League, Tim
REVENGE OF THE FILM NERDS D. SOLOMON, C. KELLY et al *Texas Monthly* v45 no7 p70 Jl 2017

Leah Remini: Scientology & the Aftermath (TV program)
Leah Remini's Divine Intervention J. Nolfi color *Entertainment Weekly* no1472 p52 Je 30 2017

LEAHY, IAN
Vibrant Cities Lab: A State-of-the-Art Platform to Connect Urban Forest Leaders *American Forests* v123 no3 p40 Fall 2017

LEAK, ALLYSON
Killing the Competition color *Ebony* v72 no5 p66 Mr 2017

Leak detection
Pressure Test M. FAWCETT diag *Walrus* v14 no2 p14 Mr 2017

Leak detection—Equipment & supplies
The Internet of "Meh" D. GERSHGORN color *Popular Science* v288 no6 p72 N/D 2016

Leakey, Richard E., 1944-—Interviews
WILDLIFE WARRIOR R. Schiffman color *Scientific American* v316 no1 p64 Ja 2017

Leaks (Disclosure of information)—Law & legislation
Cleaning Up Leaks Is a Messy Business P. M. Barrett *Bloomberg Businessweek* no4533 p35 Ag 7 2017

Leaks (Disclosure of information)—Prevention

Leading in a World Without Secrets R. D. Austin and R. Nolan *Harvard Business Review Digital Articles* p2 D 2 2016

Leal, Tess

Paneth cells secrete lysozyme via secretory autophagy during bacterial infection of the intestine color diag *Science* v357 no6355 p1047 S 8 2017

Leamer, Laurence

Q: Who Is the Worst Leader of All Time? color *Atlantic* v319 no1 p100 Ja/F 2017

Lean management

The Barriers Big Companies Face When They Try to Act Like Lean Startups S. Kirsner *Harvard Business Review Digital Articles* p2 Ag 16 2016

Can Lean Manufacturing Put an End to Sweatshops? G. Distelhorst *Harvard Business Review Digital Articles* p2 My 26 2016

Lean Doesn't Always Create the Best Products J. Kolko *Harvard Business Review Digital Articles* p2 My 14 2015

A Lean Startup Approach to International Development S. Netessine and I. Popescu *Harvard Business Review Digital Articles* p2 D 11 2014

The Limits of the Lean Startup Method T. Ladd *Harvard Business Review Digital Articles* p2 Mr 7 2016

Lean-tos (Dwellings)

RESTORING LEAN-TOS, VOLUNTEERS WORK TO SAVE THESE HISTORIC STRUCTURES D. Nelson and P. Constantakes *New York State Conservationist* v72 no1 p34 Ag 2017

Leandros Moschovakis, G.

Repulsive behavior in germinal centers diag *Science* v356 no6339 p703 My 19 2017

LEANE, ELIZABETH

Where is the South Pole? *Natural History* v124 no10 p48 N 2016

Leane, Shaun

Sculpted Jewels color *Vogue* v207 no11 p142 N 2017

Leanza, Emilio

Nation Voices 2016 *Nation* v304 no2 p8 Ja 16 2017

Our New Left Pillar *Nation* v303 no20 p5 N 14 2016

Lear, Kristen

A looming tragedy of the sand commons color *Science* v357 no6355 p970 S 8 2017

Lear, Norman, 1922-

Los Angeles ICON P. BROWNFIELD *Los Angeles Magazine* p110 F 2017

NORMAN LEAR M. Paterniti color *GQ: Gentlemen's Quarterly* v97 no6 p120 Je 2017

One (More) Day at a Time img *New York* v49 no26 p78 D 26 2016

Lear, Norman, 1922-—Interviews

NORMAN LEAR & KENYA BARRIS N. Sperling color *Entertainment Weekly* no1460/1461 p22 Ap 7-17 2017

Learned institutions & societies

See also

Research institutes

TREE ENTERPRISE *Arizona Highways* v92 no7 p48 Jl 2016

Why Today's Corporate Research Centers Need to Be in Cities B. J. Katz and S. Andes *Harvard Business Review Digital Articles* p2 Mr 1 2016

Learning

See also

Experiential learning

Memorization

Organizational learning

A 2×2 Matrix to Help You Prioritize the Skills to Learn Right Now M. Zao-Sanders *Harvard Business Review Digital Articles* p2 S 27 2017

4 Ways to Become a Better Learner M. Valcour *Harvard Business Review Digital Articles* p2 D 31 2015

The Antidote to Our Anxious Times Is a Learning Mindset C. Dweck *Harvard Business Review Digital Articles* p2 Jl 28 2016

Commentary How to teach me physics: Tradition is not always a virtue R. Heras *Physics Today* v70 no3 p10 Mr 2017

Don't Be a Hypocrite About Failure J. Brady *Harvard Business Review Digital Articles* p2 Ag 4 2016

eager learners C. MELNYK HINES *Parents* v91 no10 p142 O 2016

Getting better together K. MacConnell and S. Caillier color il *Phi Delta Kappan* v98 no3 p16 N 2016

Gliogenic LTP spreads widely in nociceptive pathways M. T. Kronschläger, R. Drdla-Schutting et al bibl graph *Science* v354 no6316 p1144 D 2 2016

How to Teach Employees Skills They Don't Know They Lack U. J. Christensen *Harvard Business Review Digital Articles* p2 S 29 2017

It's the Company's Job to Help Employees Learn T. Chamorro-Premuzic and M. Swan *Harvard Business Review Digital Articles* p2 Jl 18 2016

Learning, Professionalism, and Change D. C. Paris *Change* v49 no1 p4 Ja/F 2017

Learn to Layer R. S. Frazier color *Health* v31 no2 p54 Mr 2017

Make Learning a Lifelong Habit J. Coleman bw *Harvard Business Review Digital Articles* p2 Ja 24 2017

More time for learning A. Magaña, M. Saab et al color *Phi Delta Kappan* v98 no4 p26 D 2016/Ja 2017

parents to parents color graph *Parents* v92 no4 p14 Ap 2017

The social origins of persistence L. P. Butler color *Science* v357 no6357 p1236 S 22 2017

Teaching the arts as a second language: A school-wide policy approach to arts integration B. H. Martin bibl *Arts Education Policy Review* v118 no2 p116 2017

They said we'd never get creatives to learn G. GYTON *People Management* p20 O 2016

What I Learned at My Parent's Job M. LaScala color *Parents* v92 no4 p13 Ap 2017

What I Learned AT MY Summer Job T. CHIARELLA, H. ROLLINS et al cartoon *Popular Mechanics* p64 Je 2017

Learning & scholarship

See also

Humanities

Islamic learning & scholarship

2016 SCHOLARSHIP winners *Vegetarian Journal* v35 no4 p20 2016

2017 Dance Magazine Scholarship Guide *Dance Magazine* v91 no8 p52 Ag 2017

Learning ability

GENIUS SPICE color *Prevention* v68 no11 p8 N 2016

How to Make Learning More Automatic G. Rubin *Harvard Business Review Digital Articles* p2 Ja 6 2016

Learning ability—Research

HOW YOUR HORSE LEARNS BY WATCHING YOU C. Barakat and M. McCluskey color *Equus* no473 p10 F 2017

Learning by teaching

EDUCATIONAL options JULIE YOUNG *Indianapolis Monthly* v40 no3 p107 N 2016

Learning curve (Education)

Averages can conceal how people and science learn E. Emerson *Science News* v190 no11 p2 N 26 2016

Learning disabled persons—Employment

We're accessing a whole new pool of talent *People Management* p18 N 2016

Learning in animals

WHALE CULTURE P. Hammond, S. Heinrich et al color graph *Natural History* v125 no11 p30 N 2017

Learning management

Strategies for Implementing Personalized Learning in Rural Schools *Education Digest* v83 no3 p40 N 2017

Learning Management System (Computer software)

Reaching Full Digitization in the Classroom S. Wilson *Education Digest* v83 no3 p61 N 2017

Learning models (Stochastic processes)

Tele-Mentoring Is Creating Global Communities of Practice in Health Care D. Barash *Harvard Business Review Digital Articles* p2 N 22 2016

Learning strategies

Make it stick S. Gaidos color *Science News* v192 no4 p30 S 16 2017

Learning—Equipment & supplies

How to take learning to the next level: L&D hacks from smartphones to shared practice *People Management* p12 Ag 2017

Learning—Physiological aspects

Flex Time [Cover story] L. Sanders color diag graph *Science News* v192 no4 p22 S 16 2017

Learning is a ubiquitous, mysterious phenomenon E. Quill *Science News* v192 no4 p2 S 16 2017

Lears, Jackson

How the US Began Its Empire cartoon color *New York Review of Books* v64 no3 p37 F 23 2017

LEARY, ANN

Dating Game *New York Times Book Review* p23 Je 4 2017

LEARY, ELIZABETH

INVESTING AT EVERY AGE [Cover story] color *Kiplinger's Personal Finance* v71 no11 p48 N 2017

Lend Online and Earn Up to 11% cartoon *Kiplinger's Personal Finance* v71 no1 p58 Ja 2017

Lease & rental services

See also

Bicycle sharing programs

Sailboats—Chartering

At Work With Rent-a-Dad P. Alpeyev color *Bloomberg Businessweek* no4535 p41 Ag 28 2017

Q: I'd like to invest in a rental property. Can I use my IRA to buy real estate? S. BLOCK color *Kiplinger's Personal Finance* v70 no12 p43 D 2016

ROAD WARRIORS E. Malter color *Sunset* v239 no1 p24 Jl 2017

Lease & rental services—China

Airbnb Finds China Is A Crowded House D. Ramli and O. Zaleski color *Bloomberg Businessweek* no4527 p23 Je 19 2017

Lease & rental services—Economic aspects

How to Get a Great Deal on a Lease D. MUHLBAUM *Kiplinger's Personal Finance* v71 no1 p38 Ja 2017

Lease & rental services—Evaluation

Renting Just Got Better N. Silverstein color *Glamour* v114 no12 p112 D 2016

Lease & rental services—United States

Reforming the U.S. coal leasing program K. Gillingham, J. Bushnell et al color graph *Science* v354 no6316 p1096 D 2 2016

Leather

Handcrafted Creations color *Horse & Rider* v56 no7 p36 Jl 2017

How to Make Your Own MOCCASINS D. Biswell *Mother Earth News* no280 p26 F/Mr 2017

THE ILLUSTRATED HISTORY OF WORKER J. VRABEL bw color *Men's Health* v32 no2 p(Sp)8 Mr 2017

Leather garments—Design & construction

Meet Our Challenge Winner! color *Seventeen* v76 no2 p49 Mr 2017

Leather garments—Evaluation

Craft Culture color *Vogue* v207 no4 p242 Ap 2017

Leather goods

Breast-Collar Fit color *Horse & Rider* v56 no10 p38 O 2017

The Essential: Workbag J. TUNG *Martha Stewart Living* no267 p36 S 2016

My Studio L. BAILEY *Indianapolis Monthly* v40 no3 p46 N 2016

Leather goods stores

Hatton Henry *Texas Monthly* v44 no12 p35 D 2016

Leather goods—Evaluation

Fabulous Finds S. M. MULLINS *Cincinnati Magazine* v50 no2 pH4 N 2016

New Apple Watch buyers face limited band selection C. McGARRY color *Macworld - Digital Edition* v34 no4 p49 My 2017

Leather handbags

Add to Cart: Five bright accessories, served five ways img *New York* v50 no12 p57 Je 12 2017

Leather handbags—Evaluation

27 Great Gifts *Atlanta* v56 no8 p55 D 2016

her style color *InStyle* v24 no4 p34 Ap 2017

The SCORE color *InStyle* v24 no1 p50 Ja 2017

Leather jackets—Evaluation

BABY'S IN BLACK *Cincinnati Magazine* v50 no7 p29 Ap 2017

LEATHERMAN, DALE

Be Starstruck: Remote Primland Resort is off the grid yet finely attuned to creature comforts, outdoor fun, and the human fascination with stars in the night sky *Washingtonian Magazine* v52 no11 p92 Ag 2017

TAKE A DRIVE: SNOWSHOE *Washingtonian Magazine* v52 no4 p116 Ja 2017

What Lies Beneath: THE VALLEY'S BEAUTY ISN'T ALL ABOVE GROUND *Washingtonian Magazine* v53 no1 p102 O 2017

LEATHERMAN, TIM

What I Learned AT MY Summer Job cartoon *Popular Mechanics*

p64 Je 2017

Leatherwork

See also

Saddlery

Cowboy DIY Leather key fob L. Feldman color *American Cowboy* v23 no6 p46 Ap/My 2017

Léaud, Jean-Pierre—Interviews

THE LONG GOODBYE Y. TALU color *Film Comment* v53 no2 p27 Mr/Ap 2017

Leaumont, Lori

Slush Fun T. KIRTS *Indianapolis Monthly* p41 My 2017

Leave of absence

How to Manage Your Team's Vacation Requests K. Dillon *Harvard Business Review Digital Articles* p2 Je 10 2015

Make It Easier for Your Boss to Say Yes to a Vacation Request H. Weeks *Harvard Business Review Digital Articles* p2 Je 3 2015

Sick employee wants no contact *People Management* p49 Ag 2017

VACATION MODE V. K. De Luca color *Essence* v48 no3 p10 Jl 2017

Vacation Policy in Corporate America Is Broken M. Thomas *Harvard Business Review Digital Articles* p2 Je 26 2015

Why Won't My Employees Admit They're Going on Vacation? K. Firestone *Harvard Business Review Digital Articles* p2 Ag 28 2015

Leave of absence—Law & legislation

GUEST LIST *Washingtonian Magazine* v52 no5 p20 F 2017

Why Paid Leave Matters for the Future of Business S. Friedman *Harvard Business Review Digital Articles* p2 S 16 2015

Leavell, Chuck

THE AGE OF WOOD *Vital Speeches of the Day* v83 no6 p170 Je 2017

Leavens, Dan

TWIN BRIDGES, MT color *Outdoor Life* v224 no8 p5 O 2017

Leaves

Reading Tree Leaves B. HEINRICH *Natural History* v125 no1 p10 D 2016/Ja 2017

Leavitt, Caroline

Are You My Father? *New York Times Book Review* p18 Je 25 2017

School's Over A. KUCZYNSKI *New York Times Book Review* p20 N 6 2016

Leavitt, David

Love and Revolution *New York Times Book Review* p20 N 20 2016

Where the Willed Things Are: When a renowned children's book author dies, his longtime assistant must unravel his knotty legacy *New York Times Book Review* p19 Ag 13 2017

LEAVITT, PETER R.

Synthesis Centers as Critical Research Infrastructure *BioScience* v67 no8 p750 Ag 2017

LEAVY, THOM

Build a Record Player Powered by Wind color *Popular Science* v288 no6 p88 N/D 2016

The Sun Stove color *Popular Science* p88 Ja/F 2017

Lebanon (Kan.)

SIGNS and WONDERS J. D. DANIELS color *Esquire* p107 My 2017

Lebanon, Mount (Lebanon)

Joe Manganiello C. Mari color *Current Biography* v78 no3 p50 Mr 2017

Lebanon. Majlis al-Nuwab

Lebanon's New Leader Aims to Keep 'Regional Fires' at Bay J. Malsin color *Time* v188 no20 p9 N 14 2016

LeBaron, Anna

Out of the Cult and into the Church color *Christianity Today* p79 Ap 2017

Lebda, Doug

AT LENDINGTREE, IT'S ALL FIST BUMPS—AND HYPERGROWTH S. Tully color diag *Fortune* v176 no4 p166 S 15 2017

LeBell, Gene

Gene LeBell [Cover story] T. L. WILSON color *Black Belt* v55 no2 p46 F/Mr 2017

Le Ber, Erwan

The formation of peak rings in large impact craters bibl color graph *Science* v354 no6314 p878 N 18 2016

Leberecht, Tim

In the Age of Loneliness, Connections at Work Matter *Harvard Business Review Digital Articles* p2 S 18 2015

Leaders Win Trust When They Show a Bit of Humanity *Harvard Business Review Digital Articles* p2 Ap 1 2015

Make IT Delightful, and Other Ways to Enchant Your Employees *Harvard Business Review Digital Articles* p2 F 1 2016

LEBLANC, SIMONE

TALENTED & GIFTED color *Martha Stewart Living* no275 p46 Je 2017

LeBlanc-Berry, Lisa

COMMON GROUND color *Louisiana Life* v37 no3 p12 Ja/F 2017

HOLLYWOOD SOUTH'S RIPPLE EFFECT color *Louisiana Life* v37 no4 p12 Mr/Ap 2017

PELICAN BRIEFS bw color *Louisiana Life* v38 no1 p12 S/O 2017

PELICAN BRIEFS color *Louisiana Life* v37 no6 p10 Jl/Ag 2017

THAT'S A WRAP *Louisiana Life* v37 no2 p14 N/D 2016

Lebo, Matthew S.

Distribution and clinical impact of functional variants in 50,726 whole-exome sequences from the DiscovEHR study chart graph *Science* v354 no6319 paaf6814-1 D 23 2016

Le Bon, Joël

Why the Best Salespeople Get So Lucky *Harvard Business Review Digital Articles* p2 Ap 13 2015

Lebowitz, Cathy

Snowballs and Flags color *Art in America* v105 no3 p54 Mr 2017

Lebowitz, Fran—Interviews

Fran Lebowitz *New York Times Book Review* p7 Mr 26 2017

Le Bras, Isabela

Oceanic Highway color *Oceanus* v51 no2 p40 Wint 2016

Lebrilla, Carlito B.

Microbiota-activated PPAR-γ signaling inhibits dysbiotic Enterobacteriaceae expansion graph *Science* v357 no6351 p570 Ag 11 2017

Le Carré, John, 1931-

1931: Poole J. le Carré *Lapham's Quarterly* v10 no1 p164 Wint 2017

Inside the Circus M. F. BISHOP color *National Review* v68 no19 p49 O 24 2016

John le CARRÉ C. MURPHY color *Vanity Fair* v59 no10 p156 O 2017

Le Carré Goes Back Into the Cold D. Ignatius color *Atlantic* v320 no2 p42 S 2017

Le Carré's People M. Bayles *Claremont Review of Books* v17 no1 p95 Wint 2016/2017

THE PIGEON TUNNEL C. GILLIS color *Maclean's* v129 no41 p58 O 17 2016

Le Carré, John, 1931—Interviews

Spies Like Us [Cover story] S. Lyall *New York Times Book Review* p1 Ag 27 2017

LECHOWICZ, MARTIN J.

Plant Functional Diversity: Organism Traits, Community Structure, and Ecosystem Properties *BioScience* v66 no12 p1082 D 1 2016

Lechtenfeld, Oliver J.

Dissolved organic sulfur in the ocean: Biogeochemistry of a petagram inventory bibl chart diag graph *Science* v354 no6311 p456 O 28 2016

Genomic databases: A WHO affair *Science* v356 no6340 p812 My 26 2017

LECKART, STEVEN

That '80s Show bw color *Esquire* v166 no5 p144 D 2016/Ja 2017

Leckey, Mark

MARK LECKEY A. Considine color *Art in America* v105 no5 p123 My 2017

MARK LECKEY S. Sandhu color *Art in America* v104 no11 p88 D 2016

Leckey, Mark—Exhibitions

AROUND NEW YORK A. GREENBERGER color *ARTnews* v116 no1 p110 Spr 2017

LeCLAIR, TOM

Psychic Friend Network: A novel about mind reading, repressed memories and the self-styled superhero Brainstorm *New York Times Book Review* p11 Je 18 2017

Le Cleac'h, Armel

A Separate Reality C. J. Doane color *Sail* v48 no3 p96 Mr 2017

Leclerc, Marc-Andre

Being There D. Copeland bw color *Climbing* no355 p22 Ag 2017

LeClerc, Rob

10 UP & COMERS: ROB LECLERC G. Johnston *Successful Farming* v115 no8 p38 Je/Jl 2017

Le Clercq, Tanaquil, 1929-2000

60 Years Ago This Month *Dance Magazine* v91 no10 p75 O 2017

Le Corbusier, 1887-1965

1923: Paris L. Corbusier *Lapham's Quarterly* v10 no1 p40 Wint 2017

interiors M. PEPCHINSKI *Architectural Record* v205 no6 p33 Je 2017

Le Cornu, Elodie

Committing to socially responsible seafood color *Science* v356 no6341 p912 Je 1 2017

Lectrosonics Inc.

Lectrosonics is Dedicated to Pushing the Envelope on Wireless Technology *Stage Directions* v30 no3 p40 Mr 2017

Lecture method in teaching

get more yj color *Yoga Journal* no291 p8 My 2017

Lecturers

Defending Milo T. J. FLANNERY *Publishers Weekly* v264 no8 p88 F 20 2017

Love and Justice for Each: Martha C. Nussbaum Through the Eyes of a Friend and Colleague H. Richardson *Humanities* v38 no2 p3 Spr 2017

NEW VICE PRESIDENT AND BOARD MEMBERS NAMED *Literacy Today (2411-7862)* v35 no1 p40 Jl/Ag 2017

Lecturers—Interviews

Martha C. Nussbaum Talks About the Humanities, Mythmaking, and International Development *Humanities* v38 no2 p4 Spr 2017

Lectures & lecturing

His Bleak Materials J. Meyers bw *Commonweal* v144 no12 p18 Jl 7 2017

"THE ACTIVE MANY CAN OVERCOME THE RUTHLESS FEW" B. McKIBBEN bw color il *Nation* v303 no25/26 p10 D 19 2016

LED displays

Double-heterojunction nanorod light-responsive LEDs for display applications N. Oh, B. Hoon Kim et al bibl color graph *Science* v355 no6325 p616 F 10 2017

LED lamps

WHELEN LEDS color *Flying* v144 no7 p16 Jl 2017

LED lamps—Evaluation

FETISH B. BARRETT color *Wired* v25 no3 p33 Mr 2017

Haute News color *Vanity Fair* v58 no12 p76 D 2016

LED lighting

DOCK BOX color *Sea Magazine* v109 no6 p32 Je 2017

LED ERS-Style Fixtures J. Coakley *Stage Directions* v30 no2 p8 F 2017

Lightbulb Moment J. KAUFLIN and J. D. MARKMAN color *Forbes* v199 no6 p58 Je 13 2017

Light Refreshment P. Nielsen color *Sail* v48 no3 p56 Mr 2017

NAVE-GAZING K. OLSEN color *Washingtonian Magazine* v52 no7 p24 Ap 2017

Tools: New To Take Note Of... *Stage Directions* v30 no9 p6 S 2017

LED lighting—Congresses

The Show's the Thing J. Coakley *Stage Directions* v29 no11 p2 N 2016

LED lighting—Equipment & supplies

All the Right Moves J. Taraska color *Architectural Record* v205 no2 p124 F 2017

Antari - A New Generation of UV LED Lights *Stage Directions* v30 no3 p47 Mr 2017

BEST OF THE WEST J. Chamberlain, J. Ritz et al color *Sunset* v238 no4 p17 Ap 2017

A Bright Idea *Stage Directions* v30 no3 p3 Mr 2017

Light Show B. PIKE color *Power & Motoryacht* v34 no6 p71 Je 2017

Mega-Lite Offers Feature-Packed Drama *Stage Directions* v30 no3 p14 Mr 2017

ONE NIGHTSTAND M. Johns color *Popular Science* v289 no5 p34 S/O 2017

THE SETUP UNREAL ESTATE P. SARCONI cartoon *Wired* v25 no4 p40 Ap 2017

Leda Burning, Immendorf Palace, 1945 (Poem)
'Leda' Burning, Immendorf Palace, 1945 T. J. Welch *New York Times Magazine* p21 Ja 15 2017

Ledbetter, David H.
Distribution and clinical impact of functional variants in 50,726 whole-exome sequences from the DiscovEHR study chart graph *Science* v354 no6319 paaf6814-1 D 23 2016
Genetic identification of familial hypercholesterolemia within a single U.S. health care system chart graph *Science* v354 no6319 paaf7000-1 D 23 2016

Ledbetter, James
NUGGETS, AND BULLION, AND BILLS, OH MY! color *Fortune* v175 no8 p42 Je 15 2017

Ledeen, Michael
MEN IN BLACK *Claremont Review of Books* v17 no2 p39 Spr 2017

Ledeen, Michael Arthur, 1941-
The Uses and Misuses of 'Fascism' P. Gottfried *Society* v54 no4 p315 Ag 2017

Leder, Jonathan
This Year's GIRL [Cover story] C. Bagley color *InStyle* v24 no3 p300 Mr 2017

LEDERER, ADAM
Rio Tinto and the Mines bw color *Natural History* v125 no5 p36 My 2017

Lederer, Richard
WORD PLAY *Saturday Evening Post* v289 no3 p28 My/Je 2017

Lederman, Jason
The enforcer color *Popular Science* v289 no6 p28 N/D 2017
nap your way to Mars cartoon *Popular Science* v289 no5 p18 S/O 2017

Lederman, Larry
Eastern Exposure M. OWENS color *Architectural Digest* no5 p59 My 2017

Lederman, Meg
mom wins... ...and fails color *Working Mother* v40 no2 p8 Je/Jl 2017

Ledesma, John
GET GOOD! DO IT FAST! [Cover story] color *Golf Magazine* v59 no11 p58 N 2017
POWER: PURE & SIMPLE [Cover story] color *Golf Magazine* v59 no10 p55 O 2017

LEDGER, KATE
more than skin deep *Parents* v91 no6 p80 Je 2016
when a parent is about to snap [Cover story] cartoon *Parents* v92 no3 p76 Mr 2017

LEDGERWOOD, ANGELA
Pom KLEMENTIEFF *Interview* v47 no3 p18 My 2017

Ledisi, 1972-—Interviews
LOVING LIFE C. Arnold color *Essence* v48 no6 p70 O 2017

LEDOUX, JEANÉE
Always Use a Condiment *Atlanta* v56 no7 p84 N 2016

LeDray, Charles—Exhibitions
The Genius of Making It Small S. Schwartz color *New York Review of Books* v63 no17 p12 N 10 2016

Ledvinka, Ondrej
Changing climate shifts timing of European floods color graph *Science* v357 no6351 p588 Ag 11 2017

Ledyard, John, 1751-1789
RESTLESS ROAMER S. RICHARDSON color *American History* v52 no4 p26 O 2017

LEE, ADRIAN
Convenience truth color *Maclean's* v129 no42 p59 O 24 2016
INSIDE THE KEN PAGAN WITCHHUNT color *Maclean's* v129 no42 p11 O 24 2016
THE INTERVIEW color *Maclean's* v129 no45 p14 N 14 2016

Lee, Alec
Doing Business in a Post-Fidel Cuba *Harvard Business Review Digital Articles* p2 D 19 2016
The Potential and Pitfalls of Doing Business in Cuba *Harvard Business Review Digital Articles* p2 Mr 16 2016

Lee, Alexander
THE MUSIC OF TIME NO 1: FOR WHOM THE BELLS TOLL: In Renaissance Florence, church and civic bells frequently rang out across the city's crowded soundscape. Their calls were far from impartial *History Today* v67 no7 p86 Jl 2017
THE MUSIC OF TIME NO 2: ANGELIC CHOIRS AND DEVILISH VOICES *History Today* v67 no8 p86 Ag 2017
THE MUSIC OF TIME NO 3: THE SOUND OF SILENCE: How and why did concert-going change from a raucous, noisy affair to one of hushed appreciation? *History Today* v67 no9 p86 S 2017
THE MUSIC OF TIME NO 4: LISTENING FOR THE CHANGES: Understanding the period and context in which a piece of music was created can offer great rewards for the listener *History Today* v67 no10 p86 O 2017
Portrait of the Author as a Historian *History Today* v66 no12 p54 D 2016
Portrait of the Author as a Historian *History Today* v67 no2 p54 F 2017
Portrait of the Author as a Historian *History Today* v67 no4 p54 Ap 2017
PORTRAIT OF THE AUTHOR AS A HISTORIAN NO. 11: PRAMOEDYA ANANTA TOER *History Today* v67 no5 p86 My 2017
PORTRAIT OF THE AUTHOR AS A HISTORIAN NO. 12: SVETLANA ALEXIEVICH: Attempting to recover the human experience of Communism in the post-Soviet era, a Belarusian investigative journalist found pessimistic nostalgia in place of hope for the future *History Today* v67 no6 p86 Je 2016

Lee, Alison
What A Girl Wants A. Shipnuck and C. Barrett color *Golf Magazine* v59 no4 p32 Ap 2017

Lee, Amy
EVANESCENCE'S AMY LEE J. Goodman color *Entertainment Weekly* no1443 p60 D 9 2016

Lee, Ang, 1954-
BILLY LYNN'S LONG HALFTIME WALK D. Vaughn color *Sound & Vision* v82 no6 p69 Jl/Ag 2017
Billy Lynn's Long Halftime Walk N. RAPOLD color *Film Comment* v52 no6 p84 N/D 2016

Lee, Barbara
Black Girl Magic Works in Tech Too color *Essence* v48 no5 p124 S 2017

Lee, Bruce Y.
Drones to the Rescue *MIT Technology Review* v120 no4 p12 Jl/Ag 2017

Lee, Bruce, 1940-1973
5 JEET KUNE DO FIGHTING PRINCIPLES L. M. I. DAVIS color *Black Belt* v55 no4 p40 Je/Jl 2017
From the Archives J. Chong color *Black Belt* v55 no6 p82 O/N 2017
KICKING TOOLS OF JKD T. TACKETT color *Black Belt* v55 no4 p46 Je/Jl 2017

Lee, Carole J.
Promote scientific integrity via journal peer review data color *Science* v357 no6348 p256 Jl 21 2017

Lee, Chain
Three-dimensional holey-graphene/niobia composite architectures for ultrahigh-rate energy storage color diag graph *Science* v356 no6338 p599 My 12 2017

Lee, Chien-Hsiu
Artificial intelligence in research color *Science* v357 no6346 p28 Jl 7 2017

Lee, Choli
Comprehensive single-cell transcriptional profiling of a multicellular organism diag *Science* v357 no6352 p661 Ag 18 2017

Lee, Chris
Billy on How to Lighten Up cartoon color *Men's Health* v32 no9 p26 N 2017
STARK BEAUTY color *InStyle* v24 no6 p142 Je 2017

Lee, Chrishaunda
WHAT YOU NEED IS LOVE color *O, The Oprah Magazine* p24 Je 2017

Lee, Christina
TRAP TO RICHES *Atlanta* v57 no5 p32 S 2017

Lee, Christine Hyung-Oak
Unstuck in Time M. MARKOWITZ *New York Times Book Review* p18 F 26 2017

Lee, Cris

One Bao to Rule All *Los Angeles Magazine* v61 no11 p68 N 2016

Lee, Cyndi

Serenity Now! color *Yoga Journal* p90 2017 Special Issue

Soothe a headache color *Yoga Journal* p30 2017 SpecialIssue

Lee, Daniel J.

Rise of the thought leader color *Science* v356 no6333 p35 Ap 7 2017

Lee, Deborah

Five Years of Vigils and Protests at the West County Detention Center D. BACON color *Progressive* v81 no2 p12 F 2017

Lee, Deron

The pleasure and pain of going nonprofit color *Columbia Journalism Review* v56 no1 p54 Spr 2017

LEE, DONALD

Correction Course *America* v215 no15 p27 N 14 2016

Lee, Dong Uk

Iodide management in formamidinium-lead-halide–based perovskite layers for efficient solar cells bw diag *Science* v356 no6345 p1376 Je 30 2017

Lee, Dong Youn

Harvesting electrical energy from carbon nanotube yarn twist diag graph *Science* v357 no6353 p773 Ag 25 2017

Lee, Dongwon

Design of a synthetic yeast genome bibl chart color graph *Science* v355 no6329 p1040 Mr 10 2017

Lee, Dong-yeon D.

Coupling between distant biofilms and emergence of nutrient time-sharing bw color graph *Science* v356 no6338 p638 My 12 2017

Lee, Dung-Hai

Hunting down unconventional superconductors diag *Science* v357 no6346 p32 Jl 7 2017

LEE, ED

LONG NIGHT IN FOSSIL BAY *Sea Magazine* v109 no9 p22 S 2017

Lee, Eddie

In Perfect Harmony C. Swanson color *House Beautiful* v158 no10 p49 D 2016/Ja 2017

LEE, ELIZABETH

The Absence of Assorted Things: Where Nothing Is Everything *Idaho Magazine* v16 no12 p12 S 2017

LEE, ELLEN

HOW TO GET A Work-from-Home Job AT THE BEST COMPANIES *Working Mother* v40 no4 p74 O/N 2017

Paying It Forward color *Working Mother* v40 no2 p44 Je/Jl 2017

Lee, Eugene L. Q.

Research night owls color *Science* v354 no6315 p964 N 25 2016

Lee, Frances E.

Why Does Congress Do So Little? M. Henneberger *Washington Monthly* p16 Ja/F 2017

Lee, Gabi

Gabi Lee G. CHAPMAN *Atlanta* v57 no6 p48 O 2017

Lee, Greta—Interviews

The New Girls L. Dunham and J. Konner color *Glamour* v115 no2 p108 F 2017

Lee, Harper, 1926-2016

HARPER LEE W. Lamb and I. Biedenharn color *Entertainment Weekly* no1446/1447 p92 D 2016/Ja 2017

Lee, Heesu

THE PRICE OF A DIGITAL WORLD color *Bloomberg Businessweek* no4527 p58 Je 19 2017

Lee, Hye-Lim

Regeneration of fat cells from myofibroblasts during wound healing bibl color graph *Science* v355 no6326 p748 F 17 2017

Lee, I-Hsiu

Inactivation of porcine endogenous retrovirus in pigs using CRISPR-Cas9 diag *Science* v357 no6357 p1303 S 22 2017

Lee, J.

J Lee C. Collis color *Entertainment Weekly* no1485 p45 O 6 2017

Lee, J. J.

Femtosecond electron-phonon lock-in by photoemission and x-ray free-electron laser chart diag *Science* v357 no6346 p71 Jl 7 2017

Lee, J. M.

The Boy Who Escaped Paradise *Publishers Weekly* v263 no39 p63 S 26 2016

Lee, J.-S.

Femtosecond electron-phonon lock-in by photoemission and x-ray free-electron laser chart diag *Science* v357 no6346 p71 Jl 7 2017

Lee, James J.

Mismatch repair deficiency predicts response of solid tumors to PD-1 blockade chart graph *Science* v357 no6349 p409 Jl 28 2017

Lee, Janet

Not Your Average Joe chart color *Consumer Reports* v82 no10 p8 O 2017

Lee, Jason, 1970-—Interviews

CANDID Cameraman: JASON LEE EXPLAINS WHY HE LEFT LOS ANGELES FOR DENTON AND WHY, RIGHT NOW, HE PREFERS TAKING PHOTOGRAPHS TO ACTING M. J. MOONEY *Texas Monthly* v45 no7 p52 Jl 2017

Lee, Jay Y., 1968-

Samsung, Lee Jae-yong's Conviction, and How Business in South Korea Is Changing Hansoo Choi *Harvard Business Review Digital Articles* p2 S 29 2017

Lee, Jay Y., 1968-—Trials, litigation, etc.

Playing Dumb Didn't Help Samsung's Heir Apparent S. Kim color *Bloomberg Businessweek* no4536 p22 S 4 2017

Samsung, Shame, and Corporate Atonement R. Chun *Harvard Business Review Digital Articles* p2 My 17 2017

Samsung's New Board Gets Back to Business B. Einhorn, S. Kim et al color *Bloomberg Businessweek* no4513 p21 Mr 6 2017

Lee, Jean H.

For North Koreans, the War Never Ended *Wilson Quarterly* p1 Spr 2017

KINGS OF COMMUNISM bw color diag *Esquire* p94 S 2017

Land of the Hermit King *New Republic* v248 no10 p38 O 2017

Lee, Jeffrey

God's Wolf: The Life of the Most Notorious of All Crusaders, Scourge of Saladin D. Saunders *Military History* v34 no1 p71 My 2017

Lee, Jim III

THE BIG QUESTION cartoon *Atlantic* v320 no3 p100 O 2017

Lee, Jiyeun

Park in Limbo color *Bloomberg Businessweek* no4498 p22 N 7 2016

Lee, Joann H.

Reflections on the lectionary *Christian Century* v134 no13 p19 Je 21 2017

Lee, Joyce

OH, HOW I HAVE ENJOYED *Arizona Highways* v93 no10 p4 O 2017

Lee, Julia

The Benefits of Saying Nice Things About Your Colleagues *Harvard Business Review Digital Articles* p2 Ag 1 2017

Reclaim Your Commute color *Harvard Business Review* v95 no3 p149 My/Je 2017

Lee, Jungah

LG Sees an Opening In the Smart Home *Bloomberg Businessweek* no4498 p44 N 7 2016

Samsung's New Board Gets Back to Business color *Bloomberg Businessweek* no4513 p21 Mr 6 2017

South Korea Tries to Curb the Chaebol color *Bloomberg Businessweek* no4504 p15 D 19 2016

Lee, Jungyup

Double-heterojunction nanorod light-responsive LEDs for display applications bibl color graph *Science* v355 no6325 p616 F 10 2017

Lee, Jussara

Jussara Lee R. Gollin bw *Rodale's Organic Life* v3 no1 p54 Ja 2017

Lee, Justina

Show Us Your Tax Reforms color *Bloomberg Businessweek* no4517 p8 Ap 3 2017

Lee, Kate

Kate Lee S. Zuckerman color *InStyle* v24 no5 p146 My 2017

LEE, KATIE

ALL MY RIVERS ARE GONE: The Prologue color *Arizona Highways* v93 no5 p48 My 2017

AT MY HOUSE with Katie Lee L. Benoit and A. Chantim color *Good Housekeeping* v264 no6 p30 Je 2017

I Love My Bar L. BENOIT color *House Beautiful* p96 Jl 2017

A Song FOR Katie K. VAUGHN bw *Arizona Highways* v93 no5 p50 My 2017

Lee, Keli

INCLUSION S. Marikar cartoon *New Yorker* v93 no31 p22 O 9 2017

Lee, Khee-Gan

Measurement of the small-scale structure of the intergalactic medium using close quasar pairs diag graph *Science* v356 no6336 p418 Ap 28 2017

LEE, KRYS

Home but Not Home *New York Times Book Review* p18 F 5 2017

Lee, Kyung Mi

FRESHMAN YEAR VS. SENIOR YEAR J. BARTOLOMEO and A. STANLEY color *Seventeen* v76 no3 p102 My 2017

Lee, Leon

THE BLEEDING EDGE E. BOEHM color *Reason* v49 no1 p68 My 2017

Lee, Lydia

Boeddeker Park *Architectural Record* v205 no4 p182 Ap 2017

house of the month *Architectural Record* v204 no10 p31 O 2016

Mark Cavagnero Associates *Architectural Record* v205 no4 p130 Ap 2017

Spruce Street Residence San Francisco *Architectural Record* v204 no10 p132 O 2016

Lee, Malcolm D.

Buoyant, Breezy and Brassy, Girls Trip Never Trips Up S. Zacharek color *Time* v190 no5 p57 Jl 31 2017

Girls Trip *New Yorker* v93 no27 p9 S 11 2017

Lee, Mark R.

Around the Campfire color *Trail Rider* v29 no1 p6 Ja/F 2017

Lee, Mary

TNT color *Vogue* v206 no12 p172 D 2016

LEE, MICHAEL H.

The Raw Deal *Los Angeles Magazine* v62 no9 p111 S 2017

Lee, Mike

Obamacare Lives J. McCORMACK cartoon *Weekly Standard* v22 no44 p9 Jl 31 2017

Principled Populism *National Review* v68 no22 p32 D 5 2016

Lee, Min Jin

Home but Not Home K. LEE *New York Times Book Review* p18 F 5 2017

Lee, Morgan

GONE FOR A RIDE S. Granada color *Sunset* v238 no3 p24 Mr 2017

The Indigenous Worship War *Christianity Today* v61 no7 p20 S 2017

My Home Has 'Murder' in Its Name bw color *Christianity Today* v60 no10 p68 D 2016

Why Africa Needed Its Own Study Bible map *Christianity Today* v60 no9 p22 N 2016

Lee, Nancy Wolske

THE BIG QUESTION cartoon *Atlantic* v319 no2 p100 Mr 2017

LEE, NATHAN

The Assignment color *Film Comment* v53 no2 p70 Mr/Ap 2017

Lee, Nelson

The SAILING SCENE color *Sail* v48 no7 p6 Jl 2017

Lee, Peter S.

Redox-based reagents for chemoselective methionine bioconjugation bibl diag graph *Science* v355 no6325 p597 F 10 2017

Lee, Precious—Interviews

PRECIOUS LEE J. Wilson color *Essence* v47 no8 p38 D 2016

Lee, R. Alton

RELIEF IF WE MUST *South Dakota Magazine* v32 no6 p45 Mr/Ap 2017

LEE, REBECCA

La-La Land color *O, The Oprah Magazine* p89 S 2017

Southern Echoes color *New York Times Book Review* p18 Ja 29 2017

Lee, Rhonda Mawhood

THE WORK OF LOVE color *America* v216 no3 p32 F 6 2017

Lee, Robert E. (Robert Edward), 1807-1870

Clergy on the front lines in Charlottesville C. Kennel-Shank color *Christian Century* v134 no19 p12 S 13 2017

THE CONFEDERACY WAS ON THE WRONG SIDE OF HUMANITY M. LANDRIEU *Vital Speeches of the Day* v83 no7

p214 Jl 2017

FACING HISTORY R. Sullivan cartoon *New Yorker* v93 no17 p20 Je 19 2017

Monumental BATTLE: Why a movement to topple Confederate monuments has sparked debate, protests, and even violence [Cover story] *New York Times Upfront* p6 S 18 2017

Lee, Roger

New Life for Old Windmill *South Dakota Magazine* v32 no6 p18 Mr/Ap 2017

Lee, Sandra, 1966-

My Obsessions... *TV Guide* p10 D 19 2016

Sandra Lee Favorites *TV Guide* v65 no6 p14 Ja 30 2017

UNICHEF: Uniting Through Food K. Hahn *TV Guide* v64 no46 p35 N 7 2017

Lee, Sangmin

Clathrate colloidal crystals bibl color *Science* v355 no6328 p931 Mr 3 2017

Lee, Shannon—Interviews

BRUCE LEE ENTER THE COMIC BOOK - AND THEN ENTER THE TV! [Cover story] R. W. YOUNG bw color *Black Belt* v55 no4 p32 Je/Jl 2017

Lee, Sheryl

Twin Peaks *TV Guide* v65 no13 p39 Mr 20 2017

Lee, Spike, 1957-

THE SHADOW BEHIND THE REAL: SPIKE LEE DOES CHICAGO J. D. Petermon *Film Quarterly* v70 no2 p30 Wint 2016

Lee, Sung-Yoon

Getting Tough on North Korea color *Foreign Affairs* v96 no3 p65 My/Je 2017

Lee, Sunjae

A pathology atlas of the human cancer transcriptome diag *Science* v357 no6352 p660 Ag 18 2017

A subcellular map of the human proteome color *Science* v356 no6340 p820 My 26 2017

Lee, Thomas

THE Adirondack CHAIR D. Howland color *Cabin Living* p7 Ag 2017

Structure of histone-based chromatin in Archaea diag *Science* v357 no6351 p609 Ag 11 2017

Lee, Thomas H.

5 Examples of Great Health Care Management *Harvard Business Review Digital Articles* p2 N 6 2014

Health Care Needs Less Innovation and More Imitation *Harvard Business Review Digital Articles* p2 N 19 2014

Health Care Needs Real Competition color diag graph img *Harvard Business Review* v94 no12 p76 D 2016

Health Care Transparency Should Be About Strategy, Not Marketing *Harvard Business Review Digital Articles* p2 My 21 2015

How U.S. Health Care Got Safer by Focusing on the Patient Experience *Harvard Business Review Digital Articles* p2 My 31 2017

Turning Value-Based Health Care into a Real Business Model *Harvard Business Review Digital Articles* p2 O 8 2015

What Makes Doctors Value Patient Feedback *Harvard Business Review Digital Articles* p2 N 30 2015

What the Trump Administration Needs to Do About Health Care *Harvard Business Review Digital Articles* p2 N 10 2016

Lee, Vivian S.

Why Doctors Shouldn't Be Afraid of Online Reviews *Harvard Business Review Digital Articles* p2 Mr 29 2016

Lee, W.-S.

Femtosecond electron-phonon lock-in by photoemission and x-ray free-electron laser chart diag *Science* v357 no6346 p71 Jl 7 2017

Lee, Wayne E.

Waging War: Conflict, Culture, and Innovation in World History M. W. ROBBINS *MHQ: Quarterly Journal of Military History* v29 no4 p94 Summ 2017

Lee, Yi-Hsien

Large, valley-exclusive Bloch-Siegert shift in monolayer WS2 bibl diag *Science* v355 no6329 p1066 Mr 10 2017

LEE, YISHANE

HEADS ABOVE color *Runner's World* v52 no9 p42 O 2017

TANGLED UP IN BLUE[BERRIES] color *Runner's World* v52 no7 p18 Ag 2017

THAT'S BEERLICIOUS! [Cover story] color *Runner's World* v52 no4 p31 My 2017

THIS IS BANANAS! color *Runner's World* v52 no3 p44 Ap 2017

Lee, Yuna

Infants make more attempts to achieve a goal when they see adults persist chart color *Science* v357 no6357 p1290 S 22 2017

Leeb, Tosso

Ancient genomic changes associated with domestication of the horse color diag *Science* v356 no6336 p442 Ap 28 2017

Lee Byrd, Tommy

One Man's Junk color *Hot Rod* v70 no4 p26 Ap 2017

UNEARTHING A LEGEND color *Hot Rod* v70 no4 p20 Ap 2017

Leeches—Therapeutic use

OUT OF THE DUSTBIN *Psychology Today* v49 no6 p16 N/D 2016

Leeds (England)—Description & travel

LEEDS R. Gardner color *British Heritage Travel* v38 no5 p58 S/O 2017

Leeds, Phillip

Phillip LEEDS: A NEW BOOK REVIVES THE INTIMATE ART OF THE POLAROID WITH IMAGES OF ICONS AND IN-SURGENTS IN MUSIC AND FASHION *Interview* v47 no3 p26 Ap 2017

Leemon, Daniel

An Emotional Connection Matters More than Customer Satisfaction *Harvard Business Review Digital Articles* p2 Ag 29 2016

What Separates the Best Customers from the Merely Satisfied *Harvard Business Review Digital Articles* p2 D 3 2015

Leendertz, Lia

FIFTY SHADES OF GREEN D. DILWORTH color *Publishers Weekly* v264 no12 p39 Mr 20 2017

LEEPER, MARGARET SUE

Your True Stories *Reader's Digest* v188 no1126 p30 D 2016/Ja 2017

Leepson, Marc

The Birth of America's Flag Obsession O. B. Waxman *Time* v189 no23 p21 Je 19 2017

Lees, John

The Right Time to Mention Your Vacation Plans in a Job Interview *Harvard Business Review Digital Articles* p2 Je 1 2015

Stop Fantasizing About the Perfect Job *Harvard Business Review Digital Articles* p2 Ap 22 2015

What You Should (and Shouldn't) Focus on Before a Job Interview K. Dillon *Harvard Business Review Digital Articles* p2 Ag 28 2015

Lees, Joshua A.

Lipid transport by TMEM24 at ER-plasma membrane contacts regulates pulsatile insulin secretion diag *Science* v355 no6326 p709 F 17 2017

Lee Shetterly, Margot

Hidden Figures: The American Dream and the Untold Story of the Black Women Mathematicians Who Helped Win the Space Race A. DOVE-VIEBAHN *Ms.* v26 no4 p41 Wint 2016

Leeson, Lynn Hershman

A New Future from the Passed A. Greenberger color *ARTnews* v116 no1 p66 Spr 2017

Leeson, Ted

2016 BEST OF THE BEST bw color *Field & Stream* v121 no7 p96 D 2016/Ja 2017

Leess, Ingrid Bjelland

12 DAYS of DECORATING A. LONGOBUCCO color *Good Housekeeping* v263 no6 p124 D 2016

Lee-Talbot, Deb

THE SPEARS OF PEACE: The arrival of a Christian mission on the island of Dobu in Papua New Guinea was met with ambivalence, but it resulted in a mixing of cultures and the development of new traditions *History Today* v67 no10 p50 O 2017

Lefavour, Cree

The Tolerable Stranger: A memoir explores the relationship between a woman and her therapist as she struggles with, and eventually overcomes, self-abuse D. MERKIN *New York Times Book Review* p12 Jl 30 2017

LEFCHECK, JONATHAN S.

Assessing National Biodiversity Trends for Rocky and Coral Reefs through the Integration of Citizen Science and Scientific Monitoring Programs *BioScience* v67 no2 p134 F 2017

Submersed Aquatic Vegetation in Chesapeake Bay: Sentinel Species in a Changing World *BioScience* v67 no8 p698 Ag 2017

Lefebure, Pum

The Art of Fashion color *Working Mother* v40 no3 p14 Ag/S 2017

Lefebvre, Liz

BUILDING A BRIDGE *U.S. Catholic* v82 no10 p41 O 2017

Lefebvre, Ludo

"I Love Being on an Airplane. It's Like Going to the Spa for Six Hours." H. GARVEY color *Conde Nast Traveler* v52 no9 p20 O 2017

SNOWED IN C. SAFFITZ bw color *Bon Appetit* v61 no12 p108 D 2016 /Jan2017

LEFEVERS, DELANA

On the trail of Peru's enigmatic cliff artist color *Nebraska Life* v21 no5 p82 S/O 2017

Snowmen, ice skates and lights make Nebraska's holiday bucket list color *Nebraska Life* v21 no6 p68 N/D 2017

LeFevre, Camille

Shyamali: Sprouting Words *Dance Magazine* v91 no9 p12 S 2017

Lefèvre, François

Emission of volatile organic compounds from petunia flowers is facilitated by an ABC transporter diag *Science* v356 no6345 p1386 Je 30 2017

Lefevre, Joe

NEW YORK'S TIMELESS BEAUTY *New York State Conservationist* v71 no4 p6 F 2017

Leff, Bruce

A Vision for "Hospital at Home" Programs *Harvard Business Review Digital Articles* p2 D 21 2015

LEFFERTS, DANIEL

Deals color *Publishers Weekly* v263 no50 p14 D 5 2016

Deals color *Publishers Weekly* v264 no6 p8 F 6 2017

Flour Power bw color *Publishers Weekly* v264 no33 p22 Ag 14 2017

Mind-Body Connection color *Publishers Weekly* v264 no17 p28 Ap 24 2017

A WINNING COMBINATION bw color *Publishers Weekly* v263 no45 p19 N 7 2016

WRITERS TO WATCH bw color *Publishers Weekly* v264 no27 p41 Jl 3 2017

WRITERS TO WATCH bw color *Publishers Weekly* v264 no7 p20 F 13 2017

Leffler, Ellen M.

Resistance to malaria through structural variation of red blood cell invasion receptors diag *Science* v356 no6343 p1139 Je 16 2017

Left, Andrew, 1970-

THE VIGILANTE OF WALL STREET-ANDREW LEFT HUNTS FOR CORPORATE FRAUD--AND GETS RICH DO-ING IT J. BARRON *New York Times Magazine* p30 Je 11 2017

Left-wing extremism

WHEN VIOLENCE COMES S. ABRAMSKY color *Nation* v305 no10 p16 O 23 2017

Lefthand, Nathan

I JUST STARTED READING THE *Arizona Highways* v92 no11 p4 N 2016

Leftly, Mark

Jeremy Corbyn color *Time* v188 no16/17 p96 O 24 2016

Savagery In the U.K. Britain Comes Under Attack at a Turning Point color *Time* v189 no21 p34 Je 5 2017

Leftovers, The (TV program)

THE 10 BEST SHOWS OF THE YEAR SO FAR J. Jensen color *Entertainment Weekly* no1471 p54 Je 23 2017

Five Rejected Ideas for How to End The Leftovers img *New York* v50 no12 p98 Je 12 2017

Goodbyes Are Hard B. Kachka img *New York* v50 no12 p84 Je 12 2017

KEVIN'S GATE E. NUSSBAUM cartoon *New Yorker* v93 no16 p108 Je 5 2017

THE LEFTOVERS J. Hibberd color *Entertainment Weekly* no1446/1447 p58 D 2016/Ja 2017

The Leftovers J. Russell *TV Guide* v65 no13 p30 Mr 20 2017

The Left overs J. Russell *TV Guide* v65 no14 p38 Ap 3 2017

The Leftovers *TV Guide* v65 no21 p34 My 15 2017

THE MUST LIST color *Entertainment Weekly* p2 Jl 24 2017

The Postmortem *New York* v50 no12 p104 Je 12 2017

Previously, on The Leftovers...: An introduction to (or reminder of) the show's sprawling cast of characters img *New York* v50 no12 p86 Je 12 2017

TV Gets Metaphysical S. KORNHABER color *Atlantic* v320 no1 p44 Jl/Ag 2017

What's Left for The Leftovers? J. Hibberd color *Entertainment Weekly* no1466 p47 My 19 2017

A wild ride with The Leftovers K. Reklis color *Christian Century* v134 no15 p44 Jl 19 2017

Wrath of the Showrunners M. ZOLLER SEITZ img *New York* v50 no8 p130 Ap 17 2017

Leg exercises

> *See also*
> Squat (Weight lifting)
> Thigh exercises

The Beach-Towel WORKOUT *Seventeen* v76 no4 p54 Jl/Ag 2017

Leg Drop With Abduction color *Prevention* v69 no6 p16 Je 2017

THE LEG PRESS, PERFECTED L. McGLASHAN chart color *Muscle & Performance* v8 no12 p18 D 2016

NEVER SKIP LEG DAY [Cover story] M. Gainsburg color *Women's Health* v14 no6 p(Sp)20 Jl 2017

One minute to a better butt A. Swan cartoon color *Redbook* p99 My 2017

One Wild Workout A. HEFFERNAN color *Men's Health* v32 no7 p48 S 2017

Prep Your Legs for Winter L. BEDOSKY color *Men's Health* v32 no9 p54 N 2017

SQUAT TO GET LEAN? YEP L. MCGLASHAN cartoon chart *Muscle & Performance* v8 no12 p22 D 2016

STRONG MUSCLES, HEALTHY JOINTS A. C. SHILTON color *Runner's World* v51 no10 p58 N 2016

THE ULTIMATE SPLIT-STANCE TRAINING GUIDE L. BOYCE color *Muscle & Performance* v9 no6 p44 Je 2017

Leg injuries

Gimme a Break C. HEITGER-EWING color *Cabin Living* p16 S 2017

Leg muscles

> *See also*
> Hamstring muscle
> Thigh muscles

POSITION STATEMENT [Cover story] B. Sabin color *Runner's World* v51 no11 p52 D 2016

QUAD GOALS A. HUTCHINSON color *Runner's World* v52 no8 p16 S 2017

Leg warmers—Evaluation

All in the Details S. FRISCIA *Dance Magazine* v91 no1 p110 Ja 2017

Legacies

Obama's Legacy W. Kristol color *Weekly Standard* v22 no32 p7 My 1 2017

THE UNDISCOVERED FRANK LLOYD WRIGHT P. Goldberger bw color *Bloomberg Businessweek* no4528 p67 Je 26 2017

Legacy (TV program)

FRESH FACE: ANNA DIOP color *Essence* v47 no12 p38 Ap 2017

STAY TUNED L. Rice color *Entertainment Weekly* no1440 p13 N 18 2016

Legacy Yachts (Company)

ENDURING LEGACY D. HARDING chart color *Power & Motoryacht* v33 no1 p72 Ja 2017

Legal aid

In India, a legal group defends Muslims accused in terrorism cases B. Dore color *Christian Century* v134 no7 p16 Mr 29 2017

Legal bibliography

Politics, Biography Hot Categories So Far in 2017: With the adult coloring book phenomenon on the decline, other categories step up J. Milliot chart *Publishers Weekly* v264 no29 p1 Jl 17 2017

Legal consultants

Bring on the lawyers M. Campbell and S. Baker color *Bloomberg Businessweek* no4496 p16 O 24 2016

Legal documents

Equine Traveling Papers R. GIMENEZ color *Trail Rider* v29 no3 p10 Ap 2017

Organize your way richer N. Lapin color *Redbook* p25 Jl/Ag 2017

Legal instruments

> *See also*
> Contracts
> Financial instruments

Recording & registration

Legal professions

> *See also*
> Lawyers

The Last Line of Defense A. W. PALMER *New York Times Magazine* p24 Jl 30 2017

Virginia's Best Women Lawyers *Virginia Living* v15 no5 p67 Ag 2017

Legal rights

Deals R. DEAHL bw color *Publishers Weekly* v264 no36 p10 S 4 2017

SHUT UP! K. A. STRASSEL *USA Today Magazine* v146 no2866 p10 Jl 2017

Legal status of businessmen

The Big Case: 'Pharma Bro' on Trial P. M. Barrett color *Bloomberg Businessweek* no4527 p29 Je 19 2017

Legal status of cancer patients

Harassed cancer patient wins £47,000 compensation *People Management* p14 Ag 2017

Legal status of farmers

Who martyred the Tolpuddle Labourers? R. Quinault *History Today* v67 no4 p10 Ap 2017

Legal status of financial planners

The New Financial Rule You Need to Know About M. Leonhardt color map *Money* v46 no7 p23 Ag 2017

Legal status of gay men

RUSSIAN ROULETTE: Alarming reports indicate that Chechnya is detaining hundreds of gay men and some aren't making it out alive color *Advocate* no1091 p16 Je/Jl 2017

Legal status of homeless people

Denver's Crackdown on Being Homeless R. Nathanson color *Progressive* v81 no7 p30 O/N 2017

Legal status of Jehovah's Witnesses

Russia's top court bans Jehovah's Witnesses D. Stanglin *Christian Century* v134 no11 p14 My 24 2017

Legal status of Jews

What is a Jewish state? M. Beck *Christian Century* v134 no13 p30 Je 21 2017

Legal status of journalists

The Grave Hunter, Hunted J. NORDLINGER color *National Review* v69 no19 p24 O 16 2017

Legal status of LGBT people

Hidden but not lost C. Burns *History Today* v67 no5 p8 My 2017

The Non-Virtue of Intolerance D. ZIRIN color *Progressive* v81 no6 p68 Ag/S 2017

The Road to Equality: The Sexual Offences Act of 1967 was not the great step forward it is sometimes purported to be Joyce *History Today* v67 no7 p11 Jl 2017

Legal status of Native Americans

> *See also*
> Indian country (United States law)

Freedom for Indian Country: The federal government has long been proven unworthy of Indians' trust. How the new administration can do better T. L. Anderson *Hoover Digest: Research & Opinion on Public Policy* no2 p136 Spr 2017

Legal status of noncitizens

> *See also*
> Immigration status

The Scary New Normal for Immigrants A. Gupta color *Progressive* v81 no5 p55 Je/Jl 2017

Legal status of older people

THE TAKEOVER R. AVIV cartoon color *New Yorker* v93 no31 p48 O 9 2017

Legal status of political refugees

> *See also*
> Political asylum

Nations That Take Refugees *Smithsonian* v48 no1 p78 Ap 2017

Legal status of rape victims

Changing the Laws That Let Rapists Wed Victims T. John color *Time* v189 no18 p13 My 15 2017

Legal status of rapists

Changing the Laws That Let Rapists Wed Victims T. John color *Time* v189 no18 p13 My 15 2017

Legal status of slaves

Stolen Birthright L. Douglas color map *Nation* v305 no2 p18 Jl 17 2017

Legal status of voters
Real Representation: What if every voter in every election had the chance to cast a meaningful vote? L. YOUNG *Ms.* v27 no3 p8 Fall 2017

Legal status of whistleblowers
Why the U.K.'s Whistles Remain Mostly Unblown L. Vaughan color *Bloomberg Businessweek* no4525 p38 Je 5 2017

Legal status of women
See also
Husband & wife
Women's suffrage
global: SHORT TAKES *Ms.* v27 no3 p19 Fall 2017

Legal tender
See also
Polymer currency
Many economists would like to abolish cash, which enables tax avoidance and crime. But would a cashless world be a fairer one? J. Lanchester *New York Times Magazine* p18 Ja 15 2017

Legalization
Public Health and Safety Issues Remain *USA Today Magazine* v146 no2867 p12 Ag 2017

Legant, Wesley R.
Increased spatiotemporal resolution reveals highly dynamic dense tubular matrices in the peripheral ER bibl bw color graph *Science* v354 no6311 paaf3928-1 O 28 2016

Legend, John, 1978-
Artists H. Belafonte, Z. Efron et al color *Time* v189 no16/17 p40 My 1-8 2017
A *Atlanta* v57 no1 p30 My 2017
Do You See Me? color *Time* v188 no16/17 p60 O 24 2016
THE EBONY POWER 100 bw color *Ebony* v72 no3 p110 D 2016/Ja 2017
John Legend J. ZAMBRANO color *O, The Oprah Magazine* p23 Ja 2017
John Legend's Light Shines Even Brighter S. Lansky color *Time* v188 no24 p65 D 12 2016
One Legend Plays Another C. Holub and A. Wilkinson color *Entertainment Weekly* no1456 p61 Mr 10 2017

Legend, John, 1978-—Interviews
John Legend B. HIATT color *Rolling Stone* no1278/1279 p23 Ja 12 2017
John Legend Can't Pretend Times Are Normal A. M. Cox *New York Times Magazine* p66 F 26 2017
John Legend Shows His Soul N. Feeney color *Entertainment Weekly* no1443 p58 D 9 2016
John's Legendary Role M. LOGAN *TV Guide* v65 no11 p8 Mr 6 2017

Legend of Zelda (Game)
An Ancient Power Awakens, and Evolves, In New Zelda M. Peckham color *Time* v189 no9 p54 Mr 13 2017

Legend of Tarzan, The (Film)
The Legend of Tarzan M. Fell color *TV Guide* v65 no7 p49 F 13 2017

Legends
See also
Mythology
THE WYOMING COWBOY B. Welch color *Spin to Win Rodeo* v21 no1 p96 Mr 2017

Legends of Tomorrow (TV program)
DC's Legends of Tomorrow D. Holbrook color *TV Guide* v64 no42 p36 O 10 2016
DC's Legends of Tomorrow N. Abrams, A. Bacle et al color *Entertainment Weekly* no1482/1483 p66 S 22 2017
DC'S LEGENDS OF TOMORROW *TV Guide* v65 no35 p22 Ag 21 2017

Legends—History
6684 AGC: Earth L. Kolakowski *Lapham's Quarterly* v10 no2 p159 Spr 2017

Leger, Thibaut
Guanine glycation repair by DJ-1/Park7 and its bacterial homologs chart color diag graph *Science* v357 no6347 p208 Jl 14 2017

Legere, John
T-MOBILE'S CEO ON WINNING MARKET SHARE BY TRASH-TALKING RIVALS color graph img *Harvard Business Review* v95 no1 p37 Ja/F 2017

Légeret, Bertrand
An algal photoenzyme converts fatty acids to hydrocarbons color graph *Science* v357 no6354 p903 S 1 2017

Leggings
BACK TO BLACK (AND WHITE) H. Rolfe bw *Dance Spirit* v21 no8 p76 O 2017
#STYLESQUARED H. ROLFE *Dance Spirit* v21 no4 p45 Ap 2017

Leggings—Evaluation
ASHLEY GRAHAM'S GYM PICKS color *InStyle* v24 no1 p52 Ja 2017
DOPE STUFF ON MY DESK J. Wilson color *Essence* v47 no9 p20 Ja 2017
Dressed for the Season A. R. Williams color *Southern Living* v51 no12 p65 D 2016
GIFTS WE Love color *Rodale's Organic Life* v2 no7 p20 D 2016/Ja 2017
Leggings for Days G. Porcaro color *Women's Health* v14 no2 p72 Mr 2017
Meet The FITNESS Suit color *Women's Health* v14 no3 p152 Ap 2017
THIS OUTFIT USED TO BE 44 WATER BOTTLES color diag *Good Housekeeping* v264 no5 p94 My 2017
WORKOUT LEGGINGS chart color *Good Housekeeping* v264 no1 p106 Ja 1 2017
Work Your Look F. Kane, S. P. Nadella et al color *Glamour* v115 no3 p166 Mr 2017

Leggings—Sales & prices
FOOD FOR THOUGHT J. CAPITAIN color *O, The Oprah Magazine* p14 Ag 2017

Legion (TV program)
THE ANTICIPATION INDEX img *New York* p80 F 9 2017
Head Trip img *New York* p72 F 20 2017
KELLER INSTINCT J. Black color *Esquire* v167 no2 p54 Mr 2017
LEGION C. Collis color *Entertainment Weekly* no1474/1475 p69 Jl 21-28 2017
Legion J. Hibberd color *Entertainment Weekly* no1448 p40 Ja 13 2017
Legion J. Jensen color *Entertainment Weekly* no1451/1452 p96 F 3-10 2017
A New Class of Hard-Ass Heroes D. D'addario color *Time* v188 no27-28 p109 D 26 2016
Show Me a Superhero E. Dockterman color *Time* v189 no11 p60 Mr 27 2017
Which Legion Hairstyle Is Right for You? A. WEATHERFORD img *New York* v50 no8 p121 Ap 17 2017
X MARKS THE SPOT E. NUSSBAUM cartoon *New Yorker* v92 no49 p98 F 13 2017

Legionnaires' disease
FINDINGS *Harper's Magazine* p96 S 2017

Legislation
See also
Delegated legislation
Legislative bills
Legislative resolutions
Repeal of legislation
Industry Giveaway M. F. Jacobson *Nutrition Action Health Letter* v44 no4 p2 My 2017
The Social Safety Net Doesn't Exist in America M. POTTS bw il *Nation* v303 no18 p22 O 31 2016
WHAT WOULD IT MEAN FOR 24 MILLION AMERICANS TO LOSE HEALTH INSURANCE? A. BONAVOGLIA color *Nation* v304 no12 p20 Ap 10 2017

Legislative amendments
WHY DID A CONSERVATIVE JUDGE UPHOLD AN ASSAULT WEAPONS BAN? D. ROOT color *Reason* v49 no3 p6 Jl 2017

Legislative auditing
Flipping the Safety Switch K. Barrett and R. Greene *Governing* v30 no5 p60 F 2017

Legislative bills
Celebrating ADIRONDACK PARK'S 125th ANNIVERSARY P. Constantakes and E. Stegemann *New York State Conservationist* v71 no6 p2 Je 2017
Closing Options for Adoptions N. SCHAEFER RILEY color

Weekly Standard v22 no40 p12 Je 26 2017

Nepal Criminalizes Period Huts T. John *Time* v190 no8 p10 Ag 28 2017

Republicans Launch a Last-Ditch Effort to Repeal Obamacare N. Jenkins *Time* v190 no13 p16 O 2 2017

That'll Be the Day bw *Weekly Standard* v22 no39 p2 Je 19 2017

U.S. Congress wants to know the weather weeks ahead P. Voosen color *Science* v354 no6317 p1212 D 9 2016

The Wisdom of Mandatory Grade Retention B. A. JACOB *Education Digest* v82 no7 p29 Mr 2017

Legislative bills—United States

Bernie's Brilliant Bill *Nation* v305 no8 p3 O 9 2017

BRICKBATS cartoon *Reason* v48 no11 p72 Ap 2017

The Case for Skills-Based Immigration [Cover story] R. SALAM color *National Review* v69 no16 p24 Ag 28 2017

Green Climate Fund *Congressional Digest* v96 no6 p31 Je 2017

Legislative Background on School Choice: Recent Action by Congress on Funding for Private Education *Congressional Digest* v96 no7 p11 S 2017

Playing Defense S. F. Hayes color *Weekly Standard* v22 no46 p6 Ag 14 2017

Shortcut for stem cell therapies color *Science* v354 no6318 p1356 D 16 2016

State of Rebellion H. GUZIK *In These Times* v41 no2 p8 F 2017

YOUR FLIGHT IS DELAYED R. W. J. POOLE color *Reason* v49 no6 p16 N 2017

Legislative bills—United States—History—21st century

A Bipartisan Wall C. DEATON *Weekly Standard* v22 no19 p15 Ja 23 2017

Legislative bodies

See also

Lame duck sessions (Political science)

Legislative reform

Pan de Campo C. BOND *Texas Monthly* v44 no11 p42 N 2016

Legislative bodies—United States

The Legislative Time Machine A. Ehrenhalt *Governing* v30 no4 p14 Ja 2017

Legislative committees

Open Wide: Why can't legislative websites be less opaque? K. Barrett and R. Greene color *Governing* v30 no11 p58 Ag 2017

Legislative hearings—Humor

PARODY *Weekly Standard* v22 no29 p40 Ap 3 2017

Legislative hearings—United States—History—21st century

Who, Me? Nah... *Weekly Standard* v22 no19 p3 Ja 23 2017

Legislative power

See also

Repeal of legislation

War & emergency powers

The Three Branches of Government *New York Times Upfront* v149 no7 p27 Ja 9 2017

Legislative reform

Apathy in the Executive G. ALEXANDER and Y. LEVIN color *Weekly Standard* v22 no14 p24 D 12 2016

Legislative resolutions

Stream Protection *Congressional Digest* v96 no3 p30 Mr 2017

Legislators

See also

United States legislators

The 702 Problem J. LIFHITS color *Weekly Standard* v23 no4 p14 O 2 2017

A NIGHT AT THE OLD MANSION E. Laborde *Louisiana Life* v37 no6 p4 Jl/Ag 2017

The Year New York Almost Lost the Right to Choose C. Bonanos img *New York* p10 F 9 2017

Legislators—Attitudes

A Culture War Casualty M. Hemingway *Weekly Standard* v22 no12 p7 N 28 2016

Legislators—Canada

THE INTERVIEW S. PROUDFOOT color *Maclean's* v129 no40 p14 O 10 2016

The puck stops here S. PROUDFOOT color *Maclean's* v130 no3 p16 Ap 2017

Legislators—Georgia

TROLLEY TROUBLE J. GREEN *Atlanta* v56 no7 p28 N 2016

Legislators—United States

See also

Senators (U.S.)

BRICKBATS cartoon *Reason* v48 no11 p72 Ap 2017

CORRUPTION SET IN CONCRETE HARDING *USA Today Magazine* v145 no2860 p26 Ja 2017

Cory Booker's Challenge K. B. VLAHOS *American Conservative* v16 no3 p28 My/Je 2017

Home from the Capitol A. Greenblatt *Governing* v30 no5 p12 F 2017

IN HINDSIGHT E. Plott color *Washingtonian Magazine* v52 no7 p22 Ap 2017

Introducing Jim Banks J. J. MILLER color *National Review* v68 no23 p24 D 19 2016

JAMIE RASKIN P. O'Donnell *Washingtonian Magazine* v52 no7 p41 Ap 2017

Play Hardball in Congress T. E. Mann *New Republic* v248 no3 p32 Mr 2017

The Pros and Cons of the President's Deregulation Agenda *Congressional Digest* v96 no4 p12 Ap 2017

THE PROTEST CANDIDATE V. CUNNINGHAM cartoon color *New Yorker* v93 no2 p34 F 27 2017

Legislators—United States—Interviews

UP AGAINST the Wall E. BENSON *Texas Monthly* v44 no11 p66 N 2016

Legitimacy of governments

Can Democracy be Deliberative & Participatory? The Democratic Case for Political Uses of Mini-Publics C. Lafont *Daedalus* v146 no3 p85 Summ 2017

Decisions and Revisions That a Moment Will Reverse N. Rothman color *Commentary* v143 no2 p1 F 2017

Is It 1968? *Commentary* v142 no2 p1 S 2016

A New Deal for Europe Y. VAROUFAKIS and J. K. GALBRAITH color *Nation* v305 no10 p22 O 23 2017

Our Legitimacy Crisis R. FEINGOLD *Nation* v304 no11 p4 Ap 3 2017

Legland, David

The preprophase band of microtubules controls the robustness of division orientation in plants graph *Science* v356 no6334 p186 Ap 14 2017

LEGLER, GRETCHEN

TRACKS: How many lives intersect our own, just out of view? color *Orion Magazine* v36 no1 p54 Ja/F 2017

Lego Gruppe (Denmark)

A CONVERSATION WITH JØRGEN VIG KNUDSTORP, CO-CHAIRMAN OF THE LEGO BRAND GROUP [Cover story] D. CHAMPION color *Harvard Business Review* v95 no1 p58 Ja/F 2017

Lego Is the Perfect Toy G. Smith img *New York* v49 no24 p54 N 28 2016

Lego Offensive cartoon color *Weekly Standard* v22 no12 p2 N 28 2016

LEGO toys

LEGO BOOST C. HUEY-YOU and C. HUEY-YOU color *Popular Mechanics* p96 S 2017

LEGO BOOST CREATIVE TOOLBOX: YUP, TABLET-CONNECTED LEGO ROBOTS ARE AS COOL AS THEY SOUND S. OCHS color *Macworld - Digital Edition* v34 no11 p67 N 2017

The Lego House J. Zorthian color *Time* v190 no9 p25 S 4 2017

Lego Is the Perfect Toy G. Smith img *New York* v49 no24 p54 N 28 2016

Pop Chart R. Bruner, C. Lang et al color *Time* v188 no18 p54 O 31 2016

Lego Batman Movie, The (Film)

ALL ABOUT LEGO BATMAN'S ROGUES' GALLERY M. Snetiker color *Entertainment Weekly* no1454/1455 p19 F 24 2017

Lego Batman Finds the Funny In Existential Angst S. Zacharek color *Time* v189 no6 p50 F 20 2017

THE LEGO BATMAN MOVIE C. Chiarella color *Sound & Vision* v82 no8 p68 O 2017

The LEGO Batman Movie C. Nashawaty color *Entertainment Weekly* no1453 p44 F 17 2017

THE LEGO BATMAN MOVIE M. Snetiker color *Entertainment Weekly* no1446/1447 p55 D 2016/Ja 2017

Not So Super R. DOUTHAT color *National Review* v69 no5 p46 Mr 20 2017

Lego Ninjago Movie, The (Film)

THE LEGO NINJAGO MOVIE D. Coggan color *Entertainment Weekly* no1478 / 1479 p47 Ag 18-25 2017

Legrain, Milli

Churches in El Salvador help youths find life beyond gangs color *Christian Century* v134 no22 p16 O 25 2017

Legrand, Claire

Some Kind of Happiness *Publishers Weekly* v263 no49 p76 D 7 2016

Legrand, Marnie

Street Style: FITNESS EDITION color *Women's Health* v14 no6 p18 Jl 2017

Legris, Martina

Phytochrome B integrates light and temperature signals in Arabidopsis bibl graph *Science* v354 no6314 p897 N 18 2016

Legro, Nicole

Exploring genetic suppression interactions on a global scale diag *Science* v354 no6312 p599 N 4 2016

Leguillon, Pierre—Exhibitions

"THE ARTIST'S MUSEUM" C. Barliant color *Art in America* v105 no3 p133 Mr 2017

Le Guin, Ursula K., 1929-

The Journeys of Ursula K. Le Guin Z. CARPENTER bw color *Nation* v303 no17 p22 O 24 2016

OUT OF BOUNDS J. PHILLIPS cartoon *New Yorker* v92 no33 p38 O 17 2016

World Apart E. MUNDAHL bw *Weekly Standard* v22 no16 p36 D 26 2016

Leguizamo, John

John Leguizamo, Actor E. Berman color *Time* v189 no15 p50 Ap 24 2017

John Leguizamo D. Hochman color *AARP: The Magazine* v59 no4A p15 Je/Jl 2016

John LEGUIZAMO MIRANDA color *Vanity Fair* p144 Hollywood 2017 Supplement

Legumes

Aquafabulous L. McGuiness *Vegetarian Journal* v36 no2 p19 2017

THE BEAN SCENE L. MOYER and B. LIEBMAN *Nutrition Action Health Letter* v43 no10 p13 D 2016

Beans & Rice! K. SHERWOOD *Nutrition Action Health Letter* v43 no10 p12 D 2016

diet for a green planet K. Kelly color *Yoga Journal* p117 2017 Special Issue

Enjoy Hunger-Busting Beans and Peas *Tufts University Health & Nutrition Letter* v35 no3 p3 My 2017

NUTRITION HOTLINE R. MANGELS *Vegetarian Journal* v36 no1 p2 2017

A Passion for Peas D. DANIELS-ZELLER *Vegetarian Journal* v35 no2 p22 2016

Peanut Butter Power Snack Dip J. BOWDEN and J. BESSINGER color *Better Nutrition* v79 no7 p56 Jl 2017

VEGGIE BURGERS ROCK! From B.C.E to OMG! Z. Allen *Vegetarian Journal* v35 no2 p10 2016

Weeknight Warriors color *Vegetarian Today* no2 p42 Ap 2017

What Is Aquafaba? L. TURNER color *Better Nutrition* p60 My 2017

Legumes—Harvesting

Winter HARVEST A. J. BARTELS color *Nebraska Life* v20 no6 p72 N/D 2016

Legumina, R.

Observation of a large-scale anisotropy in the arrival directions of cosmic rays above 8×10^{18} eV *Science* v357 no6357 p1266 S 22 2017

Legutko, Ryszard

You Can't Say That! M. B. Crawford color *Weekly Standard* v22 no47 p38 Ag 21 2017

Legvold, Dave

10 SUCCESSFUL FARMERS: DAVE LEGVOLD K. Birchmier *Successful Farming* v115 no8 p26 Je/Jl 2017

Legvold, Robert

Bosnia's Paralyzed Peace *Foreign Affairs* v96 no2 p182 Mr/Ap 2017

Communism's Shadow: Historical Legacies and Contemporary Political Attitudes *Foreign Affairs* v96 no6 p164 N/D 2017

Dictators Without Borders: Power and Money in Central Asia *Foreign Affairs* v96 no3 p169 My/Je 2017

The Discovery of Chance: The Life and Thought of Alexander Herzen *Foreign Affairs* v96 no1 p169 Ja/F 2017

Everyone Loses: The Ukraine Crisis and the Ruinous Contest for Post-Soviet Eurasia *Foreign Affairs* v96 no3 p167 My/Je 2017

Fragile Conviction: Changing Ideological Landscapes in Urban Kyrgyzstan *Foreign Affairs* v96 no6 p165 N/D 2017

The House of Government: A Saga of the Russian Revolution *Foreign Affairs* v96 no6 p166 N/D 2017

In Wartime: Stories From Ukraine *Foreign Affairs* v95 no6 p186 N/D 2016

The Last Days of Stalin *Foreign Affairs* v96 no1 p170 Ja/F 2017

Making Uzbekistan: Nation, Empire, and Revolution in the Early USSR *Foreign Affairs* v96 no1 p172 Ja/F 2017

Milosz: A Biography *Foreign Affairs* v96 no3 p169 My/Je 2017

Near Abroad: Putin, the West, and the Contest Over Ukraine and the Caucasus *Foreign Affairs* v96 no2 p183 Mr/Ap 2017

The New Russia *Foreign Affairs* v95 no6 p186 N/D 2016

The NGO Game: Postconflict Peacebuilding in the Balkans and Beyond *Foreign Affairs* v96 no6 p164 N/D 2017

Opposing Forces: Plotting the New Russia *Foreign Affairs* v96 no1 p170 Ja/F 2017

Property Rights in Post-Soviet Russia: Violence, Corruption, and the Demand for Law *Foreign Affairs* v96 no6 p165 N/D 2017

Rasputin: Faith, Power, and the Twilight of the Romanovs *Foreign Affairs* v95 no6 p187 N/D 2016

Russia's Path Toward Enlightenment: Faith, Politics, and Reason, 1500–1801 *Foreign Affairs* v95 no6 p188 N/D 2016

Russia: What Everyone Needs to Know *Foreign Affairs* v96 no2 p182 Mr/Ap 2017

Should We Fear Russia? *Foreign Affairs* v96 no2 p181 Mr/Ap 2017

Violence as a Generative Force: Identity, Nationalism, and Memory in a Balkan Community *Foreign Affairs* v96 no3 p168 My/Je 2017

The War Within: Diaries From the Siege of Leningrad *Foreign Affairs* v96 no2 p181 Mr/Ap 2017

Lehane, Dennis

The Bostonian: Novelist Dennis Lehane is drawn to restless characters who aren't quite sure where they fit in. It's a feeling he can relate to D. L. Ulin *New York* v50 no9 p88 My 1 2017

Rachel Getting Married N. HAWLEY *New York Times Book Review* p24 Je 4 2017

Since We Fell *Publishers Weekly* v264 no13 p77 Mr 27 2017

Summer Reading color *Time* v189 no22 p49 Je 12 2017

Lehane, Dennis—Interviews

DENNIS LEHANE'S PLACE IN THE SUN A. Breznican color *Entertainment Weekly* no1465 p58 My 12 2017

Lehleitner, John

You Never Forget Your First Time diag il *Backpacker* v45 no2 p64 Mr 2017

Lehman, Nathan

ALL AROUND THE FARM *Successful Farming* v115 no2 p79 F 2017

Lehmann, Chris

The Apocalyptic Style in American Politics *In These Times* v41 no6 p37 Je 2017

Doubting Thomas Friedman *In These Times* v40 no12 p39 D 2016

Koched-Up Economics *In These Times* v41 no8 p37 Ag 2017

Lincoln's Grief, and Ours *In These Times* v41 no3 p40 Mr 2017

MASTERS OF SCHISM color *Nation* v304 no17 p38 Je 5 2017

MR. BRIGHT SIDE color *Nation* v303 no17 p32 O 24 2016

Neoliberalism, Cranked Up to 11 *In These Times* v41 no2 p39 F 2017

Our Philanthropic Overlords *In These Times* v41 no5 p37 My 2017

Stop Hitting Yourself *In These Times* v41 no1 p38 Ja 2017

To Form a Mo re Corporate Union *In These Times* v41 no4 p53 Ap 2017

When Money Talks Too Much *In These Times* v41 no7 p38 Jl 2017

LEHMANN, CLAIRE

THE XX FACTOR: WHEN GENDER DIFFERENCES ARE IGNORED IN HEALTH STUDIES, IT'S WOMEN WHO PAY THE PRICE [Cover story] *Commentary* v143 no4 p13 Ap 2017

Lehmann, Herman, 1859-1932

Double Life L. Feldman bw cartoon *American Cowboy* v23 no4 p20 D 2016/Ja 2017

Lehmann, Kevin

Atomic and Molecular Spectroscopy *Physics Today* v69 no10 p57 O 2016

Lehmann, Philipp

A key malaria metabolite modulates vector blood seeking, feeding, and susceptibility to infection bibl chart diag *Science* v355 no6329 p1076 Mr 10 2017

LEHMANN, RICHARD

TRUMP ON, RISK OFF *Forbes* v198 no9 p102 D 30 2016

Lehmann, Ruth

Not just Salk color *Science* v357 no6356 p1105 S 15 2017

LEHMER-CHANG, AARON

CALIFORNIA TRADE JUSTICE COALITION: Hope for a New Trade Agenda color *Earth Island Journal* v32 no2 p15 Summ 2017

Lehn, Arianne Braithwaite

Casting Lots: Creating a Family in a Beautiful, Broken World *Christian Century* v134 no3 p34 F 2017

Lehn, Dirk

Four-to-the-Floor: The Techno Discourse and Aesthetic Work in Berlin color *Society* v53 no6 p608 D 2016

Lehner, Anita

The receptor kinase FER is a RALF-regulated scaffold controlling plant immune signaling bibl graph *Science* v355 no6322 p287 Ja 20 2017

Lehner, Ben

Transgenerational transmission of environmental information in C. elegans diag *Science* v356 no6335 p320 Ap 21 2017

LEHNER, BERNHARD

A Global Assessment of Inland Wetland Conservation Status *BioScience* v67 no6 p523 Je 2017

Lehnert, M. D.

Molecular gas in the halo fuels the growth of a massive cluster galaxy at high redshift bibl graph *Science* v354 no6316 p1128 D 2 2016

LeHoullier, Craig

TERRIFIC TOMATOES for Spectacular Sauces and Creative Canning *Mother Earth News* no280 p20 F/Mr 2017

Lehr, Jennifer

Parentspeak: What's Wrong with How We Talk to Our Children—and What to Say Instead *Publishers Weekly* v263 no40 p115 O 3 2016

LEHRER, ELI

Do Less Harm *Weekly Standard* v22 no5 p18 O 10 2016

LEHRER, JONAH

MORE ENERGY NOW! color *Men's Health* v32 no6 p108 Ag 2017

Lehrer, Michael B.

Central Recreation Center Pool *Architectural Record* v205 no4 p182 Ap 2017

Lehrer, Ruth

Being Fishkill *Publishers Weekly* v264 no38 p72 S 18 2017

Lehrman, Celia Kuperszmid

Pillow Talk color *Consumer Reports* v82 no2 p22 F 2017

Lehrman, Lewis E.

Grand Alliance M. KNOX BERAN bw diag *National Review* v69 no5 p41 Mr 20 2017

Lehtipalo, Katrianne

Global atmospheric particle formation from CERN CLOUD measurements bibl graph map *Science* v354 no6316 p1119 D 2 2016

Lehto, Steve

A Man, A Plan W. VATTER bw color *Weekly Standard* v22 no27 p41 Mr 20 2017

Lei, Danni

Transformation of bulk alloys to oxide nanowires bibl color graph *Science* v355 no6322 p267 Ja 20 2017

Lei Bao

A nuclease that mediates cell death induced by DNA damage and poly(ADP-ribose) polymerase-1 bw graph *Science* v354 no6308 paad6872-1 O 7 2016

Lei Feng

Universal space-time scaling symmetry in the dynamics of bosons across a quantum phase transition bibl graph *Science* v354 no6312 p606 N 4 2016

Lei Liu

Synthetic nacre by predesigned matrix-directed mineralization bibl bw diag graph *Science* v354 no6308 p107 O 7 2016

Lei Song

Cardiovascular precision medicine in China bibl *Science* v354 no6319 p66 D 23 2016

Lei Wang

Electron optics with p-n junctions in ballistic graphene bibl graph *Science* v353 no6307 p1522 S 30 2016

Leibach, Julie

AMERICAN FLAMINGO BY DAN WINTERS *Audubon* v119 no2 p60 Summ 2017

Leiber, Nick

Baby, You Can Rent My Car *Bloomberg Businessweek* no4494 p36 O 10 2016

Folding Bike Helmet color *Bloomberg Businessweek* no4539 p48 S 25 2017

Hey Guys, Watch This color *Bloomberg Businessweek* no4498 p45 N 7 2016

Innovation color diag *Bloomberg Businessweek* no4509 p31 Ja 30 2017

Innovation Walker-Chair color *Bloomberg Businessweek* no4501 p31 N 28 2016

Innovation WindTree bw color *Bloomberg Businessweek* no4515 p32 Mr 20 2017

Pollinator Drones bw color *Bloomberg Businessweek* no4516 p31 Mr 27 2017

A Recovery That's Not Micro Enough graph *Bloomberg Businessweek* no4517 p46 Ap 3 2017

U.S. B-Schools Grapple With the 'Trump Effect' color *Bloomberg Businessweek* no4522 p49 My 15 2017

Leibler, Ludwik

High-performance vitrimers from commodity thermoplastics through dioxaborolane metathesis color diag *Science* v356 no6333 p62 Ap 7 2017

Leibovich, Mark

HER WAY *New York Times Magazine* p40 O 16 2016

NORMALIZE THIS color *New York Times Magazine* p40 N 27 2016

This Town Melts Down: At large in Trump's Washington *New York Times Magazine* p30 Jl 16 2017

Leibovitz, Annie, 1949-

A DIFFERENT REALITY bw color *Vanity Fair* v59 no4 p140 Mr 2017

FANTASY LEAGUE K. SMITH color *Vanity Fair* p77 Hollywood 2017 Supplement

THE FORCE WAS WITH HER D. KAMP color *Vanity Fair* v59 no7 p36 Summ 2017

Gathering FORCE [Cover story] bw color *Vanity Fair* v59 no7 p80 Summ 2017

REFLECTIONS IN A CAMERA color *Vanity Fair* v59 no11 p128 N 2017

WONDER WOMEN bw color *Vanity Fair* p126 Hollywood 2017 Supplement

Leibovitz, Annie, 1949-—Exhibitions

WOMEN: NEW PORTRAITS A. LEIBOVITZ bw color *Vogue* v206 no11 p147 N 2016

Leibovitz, Annie, 1949-—Interviews

Annie Leibovitz bw *Rolling Stone* no1299 p82 N 2 2017

LEIBOWITZ, ED

Hard Times At The L.A. Times *Los Angeles Magazine* p104 Ja 2017

Nashville color *Los Angeles Magazine* v62 no7 p48 Jl 2017

Leica Camera AG

GRAY LEICA Q TITANIUM'S REFINED STYLE *USA Today Magazine* v145 no2862 p78 Mr 2017

Leica camera—Evaluation

BEST STUFF OF THE YEAR 2016 color *GQ: Gentlemen's Quarterly* v86 no12 p63 D 2016

Leica digital cameras—Evaluation

GRAY LEICA Q TITANIUM'S REFINED STYLE *USA Today Magazine* v145 no2862 p78 Mr 2017

Leicester City Football Club PLC

Leicester City FC and the Benefits of an Underdog Brand R. Angell, P. Bottomley et al *Harvard Business Review Digital Articles* p2 Ag 12 2016

Leicht, Laurel

12 Ways to Blast Calories in a Hurry color *Health* v30 no10 p62 D 2016

How to Be Unbreakable cartoon color *Women's Health* v14 no9 p68 N 2017

SPRING CLEAN YOUR FITNESS ROUTINE [Cover story] cartoon color *Women's Health* v14 no3 p130 Ap 2017

Work That Body color *Glamour* v114 no7 p138 Jl 2016

Leidner, Alan

TUNNEL VISION G. Milner color *Bloomberg Businessweek* no4534 p52 Ag 14 2017

Leifert, Harvey

Air Waves Over Antarctica *Natural History* v125 no2 p8 F 2017

A Bit Tipsy map *Natural History* v125 no3 p7 Mr 2017

Charged Atmosphere color *Natural History* v125 no7 p7 Jl/Ag 2017

Cooling Effect of an Eclipse *Natural History* v125 no1 p7 D 2016/Ja 2017

Cooling Element color *Natural History* v125 no5 p8 My 2017

Early Emissions color *Natural History* v125 no10 p7 O 2017

How Dry the Moon bw color *Natural History* v125 no11 p7 N 2017

Lunar Birth bw *Natural History* v125 no4 p6 Ap 2017

Space Weather Forecast color *Natural History* v125 no6 p7 Je 2017

Tiny Food color *Atlantic* v319 no1 p19 Ja/F 2017

Leigh, David

Addicted to alcohol and sex and haunted by God bw *America* v216 no3 p42 F 6 2017

Leigh, David A.

Braiding a molecular knot with eight crossings bibl diag graph *Science* v355 no6321 p1 Ja 13 2017

Leigh, Gene

STUFF THERMALS SCREWED UP cartoon *Old House Journal* v45 no1 p54 F 2017

Leigh, Makenzie

MAKENZIE LEIGH K. SMITH color *Vanity Fair* v58 no11 p77 N 2016

Leigh, Matthew

War & Peace alla Romana *History Today* v67 no2 p56 F 2017

Leigh, Melinda

Say You're Sorry *Publishers Weekly* v264 no13 p87 Mr 27 2017

Leighton, Clare, 1898-1989—Exhibitions

Depression-era prints from the Woodcut Society cartoon *Magazine Antiques* v184 no1 p44 Ja/F 2017

LEIJNSE, HIDDE

From Agricultural Benefits to Aviation Safety: Realizing the Potential of Continent-Wide Radar Networks *BioScience* v67 no10 p912 O 2017

Leijnse, M.

Majorana bound state in a coupled quantum-dot hybrid-nanowire system bibl graph *Science* v354 no6319 p1557 D 23 2016

Leijtens, Tomas

Perovskite-perovskite tandem photovoltaics with optimized band gaps bibl chart graph *Science* v354 no6314 p861 N 18 2016

Lein, Ed

The promise of spatial transcriptomics for neuroscience in the era of molecular cell typing color diag *Science* v357 no6359 p64 O 6 2017

LEINBERGER, CHRISTOPHER B.

The Politics of Infrastructure *American Conservative* v16 no2 p30 Mr/Ap 2017

The Thinking Person's Guide to Infrastructure color *Washington Monthly* v49 no3-5 p22 Mr-My 2017

Leininger, Rob

Gumshoe for Two: A Mortimer Angel Novel *Publishers Weekly* v264 no6 p49 F 6 2017

Leinwand, Paul

The 3 Elements of a Strong Corporate Identity *Harvard Business Review Digital Articles* p2 D 9 2014

5 Ways to Close the Strategy-to-Execution Gap *Harvard Business Review Digital Articles* p2 D 22 2015

Connect Your Firm's Strategy to Its Identity *Harvard Business Review Digital Articles* p2 S 28 2016

Develop Your Company's Cross-Functional Capabilities *Harvard Business Review Digital Articles* p2 F 2 2016

Growth Needs to Come from the Entire Company *Harvard Business Review Digital Articles* p2 Je 17 2016

How Starbucks's Culture Brings Its Strategy to Life *Harvard Business Review Digital Articles* p2 D 30 2016

How to Cut Costs More Strategically color *Harvard Business Review Digital Articles* p2 Mr 10 2017

Only 8% of Leaders Are Good at Both Strategy and Execution *Harvard Business Review Digital Articles* p2 D 30 2015

Why Top Management Should Listen to Activist Investors *Harvard Business Review Digital Articles* p2 N 30 2016

Your Whole Company Needs to Be Distinctive, Not Just Your Product *Harvard Business Review Digital Articles* p2 My 19 2016

Leipsic, Jeffrey

Bayreuth *Opera News* v81 no5 p46 N 2016

La Favorite *Opera News* v81 no7 p41 Ja 2017

Lady Macbeth of Mtsensk *Opera News* v81 no9 p46 Mr 2017

Leiris, Antoine

Hatred for Thee S. BECK color *Weekly Standard* v22 no15 p30 D 19 2016

Leisheng Shi

Recent progress in autism spectrum disorder research in China bibl chart diag *Science* v354 no6319 p48 D 23 2016

Leishman, Jeff

ATTACK MODE color *Golf Magazine* v59 no10 p42 O 2017

COURT ORDERS! color *Golf Magazine* v59 no9 p63 S 2017

Leishman, Michelle R.

Global climatic drivers of leaf size [Cover story] graph *Science* v357 no6354 p917 S 1 2017

Leising, Matthew

Amber Baldet color *Bloomberg Businessweek* no4536 p72 S 4 2017

The Battle of the Microwave Antennas color *Bloomberg Businessweek* no4523 p40 My 22 2017

Blockchain Can Grow More Than Just Money color diag *Bloomberg Businessweek* no4516 p33 Mr 27 2017

Dirty Deeds Hidden In a Mess of Data *Bloomberg Businessweek* no4512 p38 F 20 2017

Maybe a Good Manager Can't Run Everything *Bloomberg Businessweek* no4510 p32 F 6 2017

Leisner, Thomas

Active sites in heterogeneous ice nucleation—the example of K-rich feldspars bibl bw diag *Science* v355 no6323 p367 Ja 27 2017

Leiss, Jonathan—Interviews

SLOW FLOWERS and a Solar Home K. C. Compton *Mother Earth News* no279 p16 D/Ja 2017

Leiss, Megan—Interviews

SLOW FLOWERS and a Solar Home K. C. Compton *Mother Earth News* no279 p16 D/Ja 2017

Leisure

    See also

    Hobbies

    Work & leisure

25 best vacation spots for big kids [Cover story] K. CICERO color *Parents* v92 no6 p66 Je 2017

and the survey says... *U.S. Catholic* v81 no11 p27 N 2016

Are You Wasting Food? V. TWEED color *Better Nutrition* v78 no11 p92 N 2016

awesome ideas for your little one's summer K. ROCKWOOD color *Parents* v92 no8 p68 Ag 2017

BEFORE THE INTERNET E. RATHBONE cartoon *New Yorker* v93 no18 p29 Je 26 2017

Free up your "me time" color *Redbook* p93 Mr 2017

get ready to relax E. Seidman color *Health* v31 no6 p116 Jl 2017

It's the Weekend! Why Are You Working? F. Gino and B. Staats *Harvard Business Review Digital Articles* p2 Ap 10 2015

Lyme Disease Facts V. TWEED color *Better Nutrition* v79 no6 p64 Je 2017

MAKE YOUR BACKYARD more FUN! color *Parents* v92 no6 p114 Je 2017

PADMA LAKSHMI What I love color *Health* v31 no8 p18 O 2017

parent-pleasing media picks color *Parents* v92 no4 p76 Ap 2017

photographic memories color *Parents* v92 no6 p55 Je 2017

Planning Events Make Them Seem Like Work *USA Today Magazine* v145 no2863 p7 Ap 2017

Reclaim Your Weekends! M. C. White color *Money* v46 no9 p28 O 2017

Skinny Dips B. Lipton color *Health* v31 no1 p120 Ja 2017

THINKING OUTSIDE S. ORR *Better Homes & Gardens* v95 no6 p6 Je 2017

When the weather gets hotter, so do your choices at the multiplex M. LaScala color *Parents* v92 no7 p14 Jl 2017

Leisure—Charts, diagrams, etc.

A BRIEF HISTORY OF LEISURE L. Smith bw color *Mother Jones* v42 no4 p59 Jl/Ag 2017

Leitch, David

Atomic Blonde Kicks You Where It Hurts S. Zacharek color *Time* v190 no6 p54 Ag 7 2017

ATOMIC BLONDE N. Sperling color *Entertainment Weekly* no1463/1464 p60 Ap/My 2017

Charlize Theron in Atomic Blonde N. Sperling color *Entertainment Weekly* no1457/1458 p76 Mr 17 2017

GENTLEMEN BEWARE BLONDES S. Vilkomerson color *Entertainment Weekly* no1474/1475 p50 Jl 21-28 2017

Leitch, Luke

Fingers On the Prints color *Vogue* v207 no6 p134 Je 2017

Leitch, Will

City of Angles color *Sports Illustrated* v126 no3 p14 Ja 23 2017

Dreams Redeemed color *Sports Illustrated* v127 no1 p24 Jl 3 2017

Entitled Behavior color *Sports Illustrated* v125 no20 p20 D 19 2016

Hidden Cam color *Sports Illustrated* v125 no15 p18 N 7 2016

Run It Back color *Sports Illustrated* v126 no11 p17 Ap 17-24 2017

Leiter, Saul

COOL MOM R. Mead cartoon *New Yorker* v93 no7 p36 Ap 3 2017

Leith, Lawrence H.

Explaining changes in educational attainment over time *Monthly Labor Review* p1 S 2016

Leitus, Gregory

Biological fabrication of cellulose fibers with tailored properties color *Science* v357 no6356 p1118 S 15 2017

Leive, Cindi

21 Ways to Please Your SELF color *Glamour* v115 no7 p12 Jl 2017

Emily Doe color *Glamour* v114 no12 p214 D 2016

In Praise of Women Who Speak Their Minds color *Glamour* v115 no3 p28 Mr 2017

It's Election Time Are You Ready? color *Glamour* v114 no11 p30 N 2016

Miuccia PRADA color *Glamour* v114 no12 p208 D 2016

Should You Talk About Race at Work? color *Glamour* v114 no7 p98 Jl 2016

Strong Is Stylish. End of Story color *Glamour* v114 no7 p26 Jl 2016

There's No One Right Age to Be Awesome color *Glamour* v115 no5 p16 My 2017

This Issue Was Brought to You by... Women color *Glamour* v115 no2 p18 F 2017

TV Will Save Us All color *Glamour* v115 no10 p28 O 2017

What Makes a Woman of the Year in 2016? color *Glamour* v114 no12 p48 D 2016

Why Beauty Matters color *Glamour* v115 no4 p28 Ap 2017

Women and Power: What Happens Next? bw color *Glamour* v115 no1 p10 Ja 2017

LeJeune, Geneviève

NETWORKING AT NIGHT M. Koester color *Bloomberg Businessweek* no4501 p60 N 28 2016

Lekberg, Ylva

Plant-soil feedbacks and mycorrhizal type influence temperate forest population dynamics bibl graph map *Science* v355 no6321 p1 Ja 13 2017

Lekic, Vedran

Tungsten-182 heterogeneity in modern ocean island basalts chart diag *Science* v356 no6333 p66 Ap 7 2017

Lekman, Jens

JENS LEKMAN N. Feeney *Entertainment Weekly* no1446/1447 p72 D 2016/Ja 2017

Lelyveld, Joseph

Last Days L. OLSON bw *New York Times Book Review* p11 S 25 2016

LeMahieu, Paul G.

The right network for the right problem color diag *Phi Delta Kappan* v98 no3 p8 N 2016

Lemak, Alexander

Global analysis of protein folding using massively parallel design, synthesis, and testing color diag *Science* v357 no6347 p168 Jl 14 2017

Lemann, Jorge Paulo

Run! It's 3G Capital! C. Giammona and N. Buhayar cartoon *Bloomberg Businessweek* no4510 p31 F 6 2017

Lemann, Nicholas

AFTERMATH bw cartoon *New Yorker* v92 no38 p48 N 21 2016

Hero, Traitor Or Spy? [Cover story] *New York Times Book Review* p1 Ja 15 2017

Is free speech under threat IN THE UNITED STATES? WE RECEIVED TWENTY-SEVEN RESPONSES. WE PUBLISH THEM HERE, IN ALPHABETICAL ORDER *Commentary* v144 no1 p13 Jl/Ag 2017

MANAGER-IN-CHIEF color *New Yorker* v93 no33 p93 O 23 2017

What Happened to Clintonism? [Cover story] color *New York Review of Books* v64 no10 p4 Je 8 2017

LeMay, Nancy

To The Editor color *American Craft* v76 no6 p10 D 2016-Ja 2017

Lemay, Violet

Babies Around the World color *Publishers Weekly* v264 no13 p100 Mr 27 2017

Lembeck, Michael, 1948-

FRIENDS: PHOEBE'S SEDUCTION A. Wilkinson color *Entertainment Weekly* no1460/1461 p63 Ap 7-17 2017

LEMBO, DANIEL

Understanding the Victors *American Scholar* v86 no2 p3 Spr 2017

Lembo, Tiziana

Driving improvements in emerging disease surveillance through locally relevant capacity strengthening color diag *Science* v357 no6347 p146 Jl 14 2017

Lemerond, Terry

I promise you a pain-free life or your money back color *Better Nutrition* v78 no11 p76 N 2016

Lemeshko, Andrey

For Manufacturers, Russia Is Now a Bargain graph *Bloomberg Businessweek* no4501 p15 N 28 2016

Lemieux, Christiane

christiane LEMIEUX L. HEDRICK *Better Homes & Gardens* v95 no1 p54 Ja 2017

LEMIEUX, KATY

Better Call Tina Parker *Texas Monthly* v45 no6 p52 Je 2017

Lemieux, Patrick

DOMESTIQUE BLISS N. WELDON color *Runner's World* v51 no11 p22 D 2016

Lemke, Hilmar

Maternal antibodies' role in immunity bibl color *Science* v355 no6326 p704 F 17 2017

LEMKE, WILFRIED

The Role of Sport in Achieving the Sustainable Development Goals *UN Chronicle* v53 no2 p6 2016

Lemmich, Bjarne

Compliance Alone Won't Make Your Company Safe *Harvard Business Review Digital Articles* p2 My 18 2015

Lemmo, Gerry

A Bee or Not a Bee, That is the Question *New York State Conservationist* v71 no6 p14 Je 2017

Lemmon (S.D.)

VACATION ON THE ROAD LESS TRAVELED: Big things happen in small towns ... Welcome to Lemmon, SD! *South Dakota Magazine* v33 no3 p9 S/O 2017

Lemmon, Gayle Tzemach

The Female Soldiers Who've Already Joined Special Ops Teams *Harvard Business Review Digital Articles* p2 Ag 21 2015

Girls in White Dresses *Ms.* v27 no2 p31 Summ 2017

Lemmon, Jessica

Shut Up and Kiss Me *Publishers Weekly* v263 no45 p48 N 7 2016

Lemmon, Mount (Ariz.)

MOUNT LEMMON C. ABBOTT *Arizona Highways* v93 no6 p42 Je 2017

LEMOINE, DENISE

Q: What adventure would you love to share with your best friend? color *O, The Oprah Magazine* p12 Ja 2017

Lemoine, Frank G.
Gravity field of the Orientale basin from the Gravity Recovery and Interior Laboratory Mission bibl graph *Science* v354 no6311 p438 O 28 2016

Lemon
ask THE GRUMPY GARDENER S. Bender color *Southern Living* v51 no12 p60 D 2016
Ciao Time! [Cover story] J. Waldbieser color *Women's Health* v13 no10 p89 D 2016
STEM SKILLS E. N. GAGE cartoon color *Martha Stewart Living* p19 Mr 2017

Lemon (Film)
Lemon *New Yorker* v93 no26 p12 S 4 2017
Rotterdam 46: Tremors from a Nervous World B. Harris *Film Quarterly* v70 no4 p113 Summ 2017

Lemon, Don, 1966-
CHEERS & JEERS *TV Guide* v65 no4 p88 Ja 16 2017

Lemon, Stanley M.
MAVS-dependent host species range and pathogenicity of human hepatitis A virus bibl graph *Science* v353 no6307 p1541 S 30 2016

Lemon balm—Therapeutic use
Growing Natural Cures [Cover story] T. L. Dog color *Prevention* v69 no5 p26 My 2017

Lemon juice
FOOLPROOF HALIBUT M. HENNESSY color *Chicago* v66 no4 p58 Ap 2017
Kick back with a cocktail color *Redbook* p107 Je 2017
SL COOKING SCHOOL color *Southern Living* v52 no7 p126 Jl 2017
Spring Goes Fancy T. McNally color *New Orleans Magazine* v51 no6 p90 Ap 2017

Lemonade
Female Chefs Teach You to Cook S. Dreisbach and S. G. Levy color *Glamour* v115 no2 p66 F 2017

Lemonade (Music)
ALBUMS OF THE YEAR bw color *Rolling Stone* no1276 p13 D 15 2016
The Ten Best Pop Albums of the Year C. Jenkins img *New York* v49 no25 p118 D 12 2016
WAIT FOR THE DROP: THE YEAR THE SURPRISE ALBUM TOOK OVER MUSIC V. Staples color *GQ: Gentlemen's Quarterly* v86 no12 p147 D 2016
What can Beyoncé and Pope Francis teach us about love? O. Segura color *America* v216 no11 p56 My 15 2017

Lemonade Inc.
Can Lemonade Lure Insurance Skeptics? R. Walker *Bloomberg Businessweek* no4503 p40 D 12 2016

Lemonade Inc.—Officials & employees
Fresh-Squeezed Insurance L. BRODY color *Forbes* v198 no7 p92 N 29 2016

LEMOND, GREG
THANKS FOR THE RIDE color *Bicycling* v58 no10 p15 N/D 2017

Lemonick, Michael
Artist's amnesia could unlock brain mysteries D. Steele color *Science News* v191 no3 p28 F 18 2017

Lemonick, Michael D.
The Perpetual Now: A Story of Amnesia, Memory, and Love *Publishers Weekly* v263 no52 p116 D 19 2016

LEMONICK, SAM
Science Friction color *Climbing* no352 p12 Ap 2017

Lemonis, Marcus
THE BOW TRUSS BEEF E. KANG color *Chicago* v66 no5 p28 My 2017

Lemonnier, Jean-François
Braiding a molecular knot with eight crossings bibl diag graph *Science* v355 no6321 p1 Ja 13 2017

Lemons, Don S.
A History of Physics Worth Fifty-One Thousand Words C. WARD *Skeptical Inquirer* v41 no5 p58 S/O 2017

Lemon Twigs, The (Performer)
The LEMON TWIGS T. Rundgren *Interview* v47 no5 p12 Je/Jl 2017
Random Notes color *Rolling Stone* no1287 p22 My 18 2017

Le Moullec, Yann

Turbines can use CO2 to cut CO2 diag *Science* v356 no6340 p805 My 26 2017

Lemze, Doron
Global mRNA polarization regulates translation efficiency in the intestinal epithelium diag *Science* v357 no6357 p1299 S 22 2017

Le Nain Brothers, 17th century—Exhibitions
Plain Can Be Powerful L. J. O'Donovan cartoon *Commonweal* v143 no18 p30 N 11 2016

LENDE, HEATHER
What Matters in the End *New York Times Book Review* p19 N 27 2016

Lender, Stacey
City Mouse *Publishers Weekly* v264 no15 p50 Ap 10 2017

LendingTree LLC
AT LENDINGTREE, IT'S ALL FIST BUMPS—AND HYPER-GROWTH S. Tully color diag *Fortune* v176 no4 p166 S 15 2017

LENDON, J. E.
Devise and Conquer *Weekly Standard* v22 no36 p36 My 29 2017
Hannibal's Heel cartoon *Weekly Standard* v22 no7 p35 O 24 2016

Lenehan, Michael
HOW TO GET 3,000 POUNDS OF BEEF JERKY from Reno to Seattle cartoon *Chicago* v66 no5 p98 My 2017

Lengel, Edward G.
THE DAY THE EARTH BLEW OPEH *MHQ: Quarterly Journal of Military History* v29 no2 p51 Wint 2017

Lengel, Richie
ALL ABOUT ALTITUDE bw *Flying* v144 no2 p28 F 2017
ALTIMETRY AROUND THE WORLD color *Flying* v144 no10 p32 O 2017
CLASS D AIRSPACE map *Flying* v144 no11 p30 N 2017
EVERYTHING ABOUT V SPEEDS EXPLAINED: PART ONE color *Flying* v144 no8 p28 Ag 2017
EVERYTHING ABOUT V SPEEDS EXPLAINED: PART TWO color *Flying* v144 no9 p28 S 2017
RUNWAY STATUS LIGHTS color *Flying* v144 no4 p34 Ap 2017
THE SPEED OF SOUND chart color *Flying* v144 no1 p24 Ja 2017
STANDARD CLASS B AIRPORT color *Flying* v144 no7 p30 Jl 2017
THUNDERSTORM AVOIDANCE, PENETRATION AND SURVIVAL color *Flying* v144 no6 p28 Je 2017
VASI LIGHT SYSTEMS color *Flying* v144 no5 p28 My 2017
THE VISUAL APPROACH color *Flying* v143 no12 p24 D 2016
WEIGHT & BALANCE diag *Flying* v144 no3 p30 Mr 2017

Leniency (Law)
How to Design a Return Policy N. Janakiraman, H. Syrdal et al *Harvard Business Review Digital Articles* p2 Ag 2 2016

Lenihan, Michael D.
Why People Quit Their Jobs: Interaction *Harvard Business Review* v94 no11 p18 N 2016

Lenin, Vladimir Ilich, 1870-1924
How to Pull Down a Statue M. Wollan *New York Times Magazine* p32 S 17 2017
THE ROAD TO REVOLUTION J. HAMMER bw color map *Smithsonian* v47 no10 p66 Mr 2017

Lenk, Katrina
Dancing in a Chair and in the Air: in the Air Katrina Lenk's Broadway gigs are wildly diverse. Her latest is The Bands visit S. GOLD *Dance Magazine* v91 no10 p20 O 2017

Lenker, Maureen Lee
THE 25 MOST PATRIOTIC MOVIES OF ALL TIME color *Entertainment Weekly* no1472 p30 Je 30 2017
ALLISON WILLIAMS' HOPE ON THE HORIZON color *Entertainment Weekly* no1474/1475 p18 Jl 21-28 2017
AMERICAN IDOL IS BACK! color *Entertainment Weekly* no1466 p16 My 19 2017
ANTHONY ANDERSON'S MISSION color *Entertainment Weekly* no1471 p18 Je 23 2017
Casting Call: The Jetsons color *Entertainment Weekly* no1480 p43 S 1 2017
CHRISTINA APPLEGATE FIGHTS FOR WOMEN'S HEALTH CARE color *Entertainment Weekly* no1486 p45 O 13 2017
FIFTH HARMONY'S NORMANI KORDEI HELPS FIGHT CANCER color *Entertainment Weekly* no1484 p59 S 29 2017

HOT STUFF color *Entertainment Weekly* no1486 p60 O 13 2017

LEIGHTON MEESTER FIGHTS HUNGER color *Entertainment Weekly* no1477 p17 Ag 11 2017

UZO ADUBA PAYS IT FORWARD color *Entertainment Weekly* no1472 p15 Je 30 2017

Lenkov, Peter M.—Interviews

PETER M. LENKOV J. HALTERMAN *TV Guide* v64 no48 p9 N 21 2016

Lenkowsky, Leslie

A Party of One D. DISALVO *Commentary* v143 no2 p46 F 2017

LENNERS, JACKI

Pato Thai Cuisine *Arizona Highways* v92 no7 p12 Jl 2016

Lennerz, Jochen K.

Origins of lymphatic and distant metastases in human colorectal cancer diag graph *Science* v357 no6346 p55 Jl 7 2017

LENNIHAN, BURKE

Quiet Your Cough color *Better Nutrition* v78 no12 p26 D 2016

Lennon, J. Robert

Don't Look Now; A small town in upstate New York turns out to be anything but a refuge for a Brooklyn family T. Rafferty *New York Times Book Review* p14 Ag 13 2017

Lennon, John, 1940-1980

THE BALLAD OF SEAN & YOKO S. Mooallem bw color *Harper's Bazaar* no3655 p162 Ag 2017

Between the Covers J. HAGAN bw color *Vanity Fair* v59 no11 p144 N 2017

Lennon Revealed A. GREENE bw color *Rolling Stone* no1291/1292 p32 Jl 13 2017

The Photo Issue [Cover story] D. Browne, P. Doyle et al bw *Rolling Stone* no1299 p24 N 2 2017

Lennon, Thomas

Common faith: Documentary film Sacred explores ritual and prayer as primary human experiences D. Duncan Collum color *U.S. Catholic* v82 no8 p38 Ag 2017

LENNOX, ANNIE

Marina ABRAMOVIĆ color *Vanity Fair* v58 no11 p154 N 2016

LENNOX, ROBERT J.

Envisioning the Future of Aquatic Animal Tracking: Technology, Science, and Application *BioScience* v67 no10 p884 O 2017

Lenny, Kai

8 Beach-Body Secrets from the Life of Kai M. ANDERS color *Men's Health* v32 no6 p47 Ag 2017

KAI LENNY Z. MORTON color *Surfer* v58 no3 p40 Je 2017

Leno, Jay, 1950-

THOUGHTS ON Inflation bw color *Forbes* v198 no9 p114 D 30 2016

Lenoir, Jonathan

Biodiversity redistribution under climate change: Impacts on ecosystems and human well-being color *Science* v355 no6332 p1389 Mr 31 2017

Combining Biodiversity Resurveys across Regions to Advance Global Change Research *BioScience* v67 no1 p73 Ja 2017

Lenovo Group Ltd.

Lenovo's ThinkPad X1 Tablet modules add features but limit functionality M. HACHMAN color *PCWorld* p128 D 2016

Lenovo Yoga 910: A host of excellent upgrades make it a winner J. NOREM color graph *PCWorld* v35 no2 p82 F 2017

Lenovo Yoga Book: Unique touch features let you be hands-on creative M. RIOFRIO color *PCWorld* v35 no11 p82 N 2016

TOP 3: BOOK SMARTS D. PIERCE color *Wired* v25 no9 p44 S 2017

Lenox, Jason

House of Style color *Log Home Living* p74 2018 Annual Buyers Guide

Lens (Music)

The Playlist bw color *Rolling Stone* no1287 p8 My 18 2017

Lenschow, Deborah J.

The microbial metabolite desaminotyrosine protects from influenza through type I interferon graph *Science* v357 no6350 p498 Ag 4 2017

LENSEIGNE, KENDA

The 'Beehive' color *Horse & Rider* v56 no10 p43 O 2017

Lenses

See also

Concave lenses

Gravitational lenses

Ophthalmic lenses

Metalenses, megapromise R. F. Service color *Science* v354 no6319 p1523 D 23 2016

OFF LINE color *Bike Magazine* v24 no6 p136 Ag 2017

Lenses—Evaluation

Stellarvue's Optimus eyepieces tested T. Hallas color *Astronomy* v45 no5 p62 My 2017

YEAR'S END color *Popular Photography* v80 no11 p10 D 2016

Lenski, Richard E.

Ecological speciation of bacteriophage lambda in allopatry and sympatry bibl graph *Science* v354 no6317 p1301 D 9 2016

Lent

Disrupting the Cradle to Prison Pipeline, by Ndume Olatushani L. Copan color *Christian Century* v134 no8 p1 Ap 12 2017

Winter together A. Scobey color *U.S. Catholic* v82 no3 p36 Mr 2017

Lentils

12 Superfoods You Should Be Eating [Cover story] P. O. BLUMBERG color *Prevention* v69 no4 p60 Ap 2017

Q I'm craving comfort food. Recipes, please?! [Cover story] color *Good Housekeeping* v264 no2 p110 F 2017

Lentrodt, D.

Spectral narrowing of x-ray pulses for precision spectroscopy with nuclear resonances diag *Science* v357 no6349 p375 Jl 28 2017

Lents, Thomas

Chicken Fight! color *Men's Health* v32 no8 p88 O 2017

Lentz & Co.

SPACE ODDITIES *Cincinnati Magazine* p32 Je 2017

Lentz, Linda

Record Products 2016 color *Architectural Record* v204 no12 p113 D 2016

Lentz, Linda C.

Command Performance color *Architectural Record* v205 no8 p109 Ag 2017

Downtown Style *Architectural Record* v204 no11 p37 N 2016

ESI Design with HOK and Available Light color *Architectural Record* v205 no2 p118 F 2017

Fashion Statement *Architectural Record* v204 no10 p72 O 2016

interiors *Architectural Record* v205 no10 p35 O 2017

Leny Cuellar, Rosa

Forest conservation: Remember Gran Chaco bibl color *Science* v355 no6324 p465 F 3 2017

LENZER, SUZANNE

count your chickens! color *Parents* v92 no3 p94 Mr 2017

LENZI, SCOTT

KARATE STRONG color *Black Belt* v55 no3 p34 Ap/My 2017

Lenzner, Steven J.

Philosopher's Guide *Weekly Standard* v22 no8 p39 O 31 2016

Stop, Look, Listen color *Weekly Standard* v22 no23 p36 F 20 2017

Leo (Constellation)

Amateurs Track a DISINTEGRATING Planet M. Motta *Sky & Telescope* v133 no4 p66 Ap 2017

The Lion-Guarded Gate S. French *Sky & Telescope* v133 no4 p54 Ap 2017

Occulting the Little King J. RAO color *Natural History* v125 no10 p45 O 2017

Leo, Julie

The Last Four Digits *Publishers Weekly* v264 no26 p146a Je 26 2017

Leo, Leonard

FULL-COURT PRESS J. TOOBIN cartoon color *New Yorker* v93 no9 p24 Ap 17 2017

Leo, Melissa, 1960-

American atheist is hated, murdered, revived in new film J. Martin color *America* v216 no11 p57 My 15 2017

I'M DYING UP HERE C. Collis color *Entertainment Weekly* no1446/1447 p63 D 2016/Ja 2017

I'm Dying Up Here M. Logan *TV Guide* v65 no23 p22 My 29 2017

Melissa LEO color *O, The Oprah Magazine* p32 N 2017

Leocha, Charles—Interviews

United's No Good, Very Bad Day-and What It Means for All of Us N. Hopper color *Time* v189 no15 p22 Ap 24 2017

Leon, Adam

Girl on the RUN J. POWERS and V. STEIKER color *Vogue* v207 no1 p42 Ja 2017

Book Review p17 S 17 2017

THE UNDOING PROJECT [Cover story] *New York Times Book Review* p1 D 18 2016

Leonhardt, Megan

10 TRIPS TO ASIA THAT WON'T COST A FORTUNE color map *Money* v46 no7 p71 Ag 2017

THE 2017 WASHINGTON WISH LIST color diag *Money* v46 no1 p96 Ja/F 2017

36 APPS THAT WILL SAVE YOU MONEY color *Money* v46 no4 p46 My 2017

7 Amazing Adventures That Won't Cost a Fortune color *Money* v46 no6 p12 Jl 2017

Ace the Money Question color *Money* v46 no8 p20 S 2017

The BEST BANK FOR YOU color diag map *Money* v45 no10 p86 N 2016

The Best Cell Phone Plan for You color diag *Money* v46 no6 p64 Jl 2017

BEST IN TRAVEL 2017 color *Money* v46 no3 p58 Ap 2017

The Best Way to Beat the Lines diag *Money* v46 no3 p26 Ap 2017

DINNER IN A BOX chart color *Money* v46 no8 p67 S 2017

Insurers Ding Innocent Drivers After Accidents color *Money* v46 no3 p18 Ap 2017

It's Not Just You: Robocalls and Scams Are on the Rise color diag *Money* v46 no9 p25 O 2017

THE MONEY CHAMPIONS [Cover story] color *Money* v45 no11 p52 D 2016

The New Financial Rule You Need to Know About color map *Money* v46 no7 p23 Ag 2017

THE RIGHT ROBOT FOR YOUR MONEY chart color *Money* v46 no1 p86 Ja/F 2017

Self-Defense Can Ward Off Senior Financial Abuse color *Money* v46 no1 p20 Ja/F 2017

THE TERRIFYING TRUE STORY OF A $1 MILLION SCAM color *Money* v46 no5 p68 Je 2017

TOP 10 EUROPE TRIPS FOR YOUR MONEY color *Money* v46 no5 p48 Je 2017

Watchdog Lacks Bite? color *Money* v45 no11 p15 D 2016

What to Do if You Get Bumped color *Money* v46 no6 p19 Jl 2017

Who's Using Meal Kits? chart *Money* v46 no8 p72 S 2017

YOUR 20 BEST MONEY MOVES FOR 2017 color diag *Money* v45 no11 p60 D 2016

Leoni, Téa, 1966-

DOMESTIC AFFAIRS: Madam Secretary's Elizabeth McCord handles global crises on a daily basis. So challenges at home must be a cakewalk. Right? M. LOGAN *TV Guide* v65 no41 p26 O 2 2017

Madam Secretary A. Bacle, D. Coggan et al color *Entertainment Weekly* no1482/1483 p39 S 22 2017

Who runs the world? P. H. Nettleton color *U.S. Catholic* v82 no6 p38 Je 2017

Leonids (Meteors)

75, 50 & 25 YEARS AGO R. W. Sinnott *Sky & Telescope* v133 no1 p7 Ja 2017

Leontine Linens (Company)

A Stitch in Time M. OZAWA *Martha Stewart Living* no269 p44 N 2016

Leopard

Keep Earth Wild A. SHAW *National Geographic Kids* no468 p14 Mr 2017

Rare Encounter color *National Wildlife (World Edition)* v55 no4 p20 Je/Jl 2017

Leopard frogs

Chiricahua Leopard Frogs E. Balli color *Arizona Highways* v93 no5 p13 My 2017

Leopard lizards

Attractive Advantage *Natural History* v125 no4 p5 Ap 2017

SEX APPEAL K. MOORE color *Natural History* v125 no4 p2 Ap 2017

Leopard seal

The Seal who Loved Me MY UNDERWATER ADVENTURE ANTARCTICA P. NICKLEN *National Geographic Kids* no466 p28 D 2016/Ja 2017

Leopard tortoise

Guinness World Records J. KIFFEL-ALCHEH *National Geographic Kids* no468 p9 Mr 2017

Léopold, Pierre

Drosophila insulin release is triggered by adipose Stunted ligand to brain Methuselah receptor bibl graph *Science* v353 no6307 p1553 S 30 2016

Leotards (Clothing)

#STYLESQUARED H. ROLFE *Dance Spirit* v21 no4 p45 Ap 2017

Leotards (Clothing)—Evaluation

Dare to Stand Out S. FRISCIA *Dance Magazine* v91 no4 p45 Ap 2017

Leovy, Jill

Robocops and Robbers *American Scholar* v86 no2 p115 Spr 2017

Leo XIII, Pope, 1810-1903

Sanctifying the Acela K. J. Lopez color *America* v216 no8 p54 Ap 17 2017

LePage, Paul, 1948-

The COASTER CORRESPONDENCE E. J. COASTER cartoon color *Vanity Fair* v59 no5 p56 Ap 2017

Lepage, Robert, 1957-

L'Amour de Loin W. R. Braun *Opera News* v81 no9 p32 Mr 2017

Lepak, Nicholas

Genomic estimation of complex traits reveals ancient maize adaptation to temperate North America diag *Science* v357 no6350 p512 Ag 4 2017

Le Parc, Julio

RADICAL DESTABILIZATION D. Ebony bw color *Art in America* v105 no3 p106 Mr 2017

Le Parc, Julio—Exhibitions

Estrellita Brodsky R. Simonini color *Art in America* v104 no10 p37 N 2016

LEPCZYK, CHRISTOPHER A.

Biodiversity in the City: Fundamental Questions for Understanding the Ecology of Urban Green Spaces for Biodiversity Conservation *BioScience* v67 no9 p799 S 2017

Le Pen, Marine, 1968-

CAN THE CENTER HOLD? L. COLLINS bw cartoon *New Yorker* v93 no12 p20 My 8 2017

France Picks a Novice C. CALDWELL color *Weekly Standard* v22 no35 p23 My 22 2017

French Muslims and a Changed Scenario: What does the future hold for France's Muslims after Marine Le Pen's defeat? A. ALOUSH *Islamic Horizons* v46 no4 p56 Jl/Ag 2017

La Nostalgie et l'Oubli M. O. Steinfels bw *Commonweal* v144 no9 p7 My 19 2017

THE POWER OF POPULISM G. Rose *Foreign Affairs* v95 no6 p1g N/D 2016

Thatcherism Redux in France C. Matlack, M. Deen et al bw color *Bloomberg Businessweek* no4502 p21 D 5 2016

Le Pen, Marine, 1968—Interviews

France's Next Revolution? color *Foreign Affairs* v95 no6 p2 N/D 2016

Le Pen, Marine, 1968—Political & social views

The Power of Le Pen V. Walt color *Time* v189 no11 p34 Mr 27 2017

Lepetit, F.

Attosecond dynamics through a Fano resonance: Monitoring the birth of a photoelectron bibl graph *Science* v354 no6313 p734 N 11 2016

Lepetz, Sébastien

Ancient genomic changes associated with domestication of the horse color diag *Science* v356 no6336 p442 Ap 28 2017

Lepido, Daniele

Hello, Ericsson. 'The Butcher' Is on the Line color *Bloomberg Businessweek* no4526 p35 Je 12 2017

When Coders Become Stickup Artists color *Bloomberg Businessweek* no4517 p35 Ap 3 2017

Lepidochelys kempii

Arrested Recovery L. Tangley color *National Wildlife (World Edition)* v55 no5 p34 Ag/S 2017

Lepidoptera

See also

Butterflies

Caterpillars

Discovering the Perilous Life of Monarchs E. BLAKER *Natural History* v125 no1 p12 D 2016/Ja 2017

Lepine, Nate

Leadership Premieres M. LONGLEY color *Downbeat* v84 no1

p69 Ja 2017

Lepler, Lori Moskowitz
How We Closed the Gap Between Men's and Women's Retention Rates *Harvard Business Review Digital Articles* p2 My 19 2017

Le Poer Trench, Brooke
BEST FACE MASKS color *Harper's Bazaar* no3650 p180 F 2017

Lepore, Chiara
More tornadoes in the most extreme U.S. tornado outbreaks bibl chart graph *Science* v354 no6318 p1419 D 16 2016

Lepore, Jill
AFTERMATH bw cartoon *New Yorker* v92 no38 p48 N 21 2016
AUTUMN OF THE ATOM cartoon color *New Yorker* v92 no47 p22 Ja 30 2017
DEAD WEIGHT cartoon *New Yorker* v93 no32 p83 O 16 2017
ESMÉ IN NEVERLAND cartoon *New Yorker* v92 no38 p34 N 21 2016
THE HISTORY TEST cartoon *New Yorker* v93 no6 p66 Mr 27 2017
INQUIETUDE cartoon *New Yorker* v93 no31 p17 O 9 2017
NO, WE CANNOT bw cartoon *New Yorker* v93 no16 p102 Je 5 2017
THE STRATEGY OF TRUTH cartoon *New Yorker* v93 no16 p37 Je 5 2017

Lepore, Kirsten
A New Era In Toon Town R. ITO *Los Angeles Magazine* v62 no9 p82 S 2017

Lepore, Tim
THE ISLAND DOCTOR I. ALDRICH and M. FLEMING bw color *Yankee* p98 My/Je 2017

Leporidae—Research
A VANISHING LEGACY R. Dewitt chart color *Outdoor Life* v224 no1 p48 D 2016/Ja 2017

LEPPI, JASON C.
Mapping Conservation Strategies under a Changing Climate *BioScience* v67 no6 p494 Je 2017

Leprino, James
THE BIG CHEESE C. SORVINO color *Forbes* v199 no6 p100 Je 13 2017

Leprino Foods Co.
THE BIG CHEESE C. SORVINO color *Forbes* v199 no6 p100 Je 13 2017

Lepró, Xavier
Harvesting electrical energy from carbon nanotube yarn twist diag graph *Science* v357 no6353 p773 Ag 25 2017

Leprosy
Red squirrels harbor leprosy bacteria L. HAMERS color *Science News* v190 no12 p9 D 10 2016

Leprosy treatment
India resurrects forgotten leprosy vaccine S. Kumar color *Science* v356 no6342 p999 Je 9 2017

Leprosy vaccination
India resurrects forgotten leprosy vaccine S. Kumar color *Science* v356 no6342 p999 Je 9 2017

Leptospirosis
Athlete, Interrupted C. P. DUNAVAN color *Discover* v38 no4 p20 My 2017

Leptospirosis in animals—Vaccination
ADDITIONAL APPROVAL FOR LEPTOSPIROSIS VACCINE C. Barakat and M. McCluskey *Equus* no471 p12 D 2016

Lepucki, Edan
KEVIN BACON IS NOT A DICK bw color *Esquire* p21 My 2017
Mother's Little Helper: A novel plays on genre, but is less interested in noir than in richer questions of identity, art and the ties that bind E. UMANSKY *New York Times Book Review* p18 Je 11 2017

Lequn Su
Quality management for precision medicine clinical applications: A consensus from the China Precision Medicine Clinical Research and Application Association bibl *Science* v354 no6319 p11 D 23 2016

Lerchenmueller, Marc J.
Research: Junior Female Scientists Aren't Getting the Credit They Deserve *Harvard Business Review Digital Articles* p2 Mr 22 2017

Lercher, Lukas
Posttranslational mutagenesis: A chemical strategy for exploring

protein side-chain diversity diag *Science* v354 no6312 p597 N 4 2016

Lerman, Eleanor
The Stargazer's Embassy *Publishers Weekly* v264 no20 p42 My 15 2017

Lerman, Katrina
The Brands That Make Customers Feel Respected *Harvard Business Review Digital Articles* p2 N 1 2016

LERMAN, SUSANNAH B.
Biodiversity in the City: Fundamental Questions for Understanding the Ecology of Urban Green Spaces for Biodiversity Conservation *BioScience* v67 no9 p799 S 2017

Lerner, Ben, 1979-
Must Lerner Connect? C. Simic bw *New York Review of Books* v64 no6 p31 Ap 6 2017

LERNER, JEFF
WILDLAMDS FOR WILDLIFE: Working to protect and restore forest habitat for at-risk wildlife across the United States *American Forests* v123 no2 p20 Summ 2017

LERNER, JON
The View From Pennsylvania color *National Review* v68 no22 p27 D 5 2016

Lerner, Josh—Interviews
The Economics of Knowledge Sharing J. Fox *Harvard Business Review Digital Articles* p2 O 16 2014

Lerner, Lois—Trials, litigation, etc.
The Unaccountable IRS color *Weekly Standard* v23 no3 p8 S 25 2017

LERNER, PRESTON
Abuzz In the Drone Age *Los Angeles Magazine* p76 Ja 2017
FERRARI INVADES DAYTONA color *Road & Track* v68 no7 p8 Mr/Ap 2017
HIDDEN FIGURES color *Road & Track* v68 no8 p56 My 2017
IMPERFECT PIPES color *Road & Track* v69 no3 p98 O 2017
IN THE DRAFT color *Road & Track* v69 no4 p62 N 2017
"M" IS FOR MOST color *Road & Track* v68 no8 p92 My 2017
SPORTS-CAR RACING 101 color *Road & Track* v68 no8 p50 My 2017
STAR POWER color *Road & Track* v68 no9 p66 Je 2017
A Tennis Tourney Moves Forward *Los Angeles Magazine* p24 Mr 2017
THROWBACK color diag graph *Road & Track* v68 no8 p68 My 2017
TURNING POINTS color *Road & Track* v68 no10 p98 Jl 2017

Lerner, Ralph
REREADING THE ENLIGHTENMENT *Claremont Review of Books* v17 no2 p58 Spr 2017
Stop, Look, Listen S. J. Lenzner color *Weekly Standard* v22 no23 p36 F 20 2017

Lerner, Robert E.
He Remade Kings G. PROCHNIK *New York Times Book Review* p17 Ja 8 2017

LERNER, SALLY
75 YEARS OF FIGHTING color *Alternatives Journal (AJ) - Canada's Environmental Voice* v42 no3 p78 2016

LERNERYD, FREDRIK
Ballet Without Borders *Dance Magazine* v90 no12 p80 D 2016

Leroi, Arnaud
3 Ways M&A Is Different When You're Acquiring a Digital Company *Harvard Business Review Digital Articles* p2 Jl 11 2017

Leroux, Scott David
Scott David Leroux A. A. DAVIS color *Maclean's* v129 no50 p66 D 19 2016

Le Roy, L.
Xenon isotopes in 67P/Churyumov-Gerasimenko show that comets contributed to Earth's atmosphere diag *Science* v356 no6342 p1069 Je 9 2017

Leroy, Prune
Kinetics of dCas9 target search in Escherichia coli diag *Science* v357 no6358 p1420 S 29 2017

Les Contes d'Hoffmann (Theatrical production)
CLASSICAL MUSIC *New Yorker* v93 no32 p6 O 16 2017

Les Liaisons Dangereuses (Theatrical production)
Eternal Quadrangle C. YOUNG color *Weekly Standard* v22 no16 p37 D 26 2016
THEATER OF THE MOMENT R. WEINERT-KENDT color

America v215 no18 p30 D 5 2016

Les Liaisons Dangereuses 1960 (Music)

Record Store Day's Spring Awakening P. MARGASAK color *Downbeat* v84 no6 p22 Je 2017

Lesbian comedians—Interviews

In Search Of Girls town? Keep on Looking M. WAKIM *Los Angeles Magazine* v62 no6 p83 Je 2017

Lesbian dating

I would like to try dating women L. Morelli, R. Bernard et al bw *Glamour* v115 no6 p98 Je 2017

Lesbian employees

What a Study of French Auditors Shows About Homophobia at Work T. Roulet and S. Stenger *Harvard Business Review Digital Articles* p2 Mr 29 2017

Lesbian marriage

Love that can't be shamed L. G. Irwin *Christian Century* v133 no24 p12 N 23 2016

Lesbian relationships

DID HOLLYWOOD SABOTAGE MY MARRIAGE? Perhaps a lack of examples doomed me to fail in love T. E. GILCHRIST *Advocate* no1093 p16 O/N 2017

I would like to try dating women L. Morelli, R. Bernard et al bw *Glamour* v115 no6 p98 Je 2017

Lesbians

The Fellowship A. BECHDEL cartoon *New Yorker* v92 no32 p82 O 10 2016

A Tale of Two Sisters L. Carrera color *Glamour* v115 no2 p69 F 2017

Lesbians—Identity

Finding Herself at 36 K. BOLONIK color *Prevention* v69 no1 p38 Ja 2017

Lesbians—Legal status, laws, etc.

Can I Pretend to Be A Lesbian to Get a Couples Discount? K. A. Appiah *New York Times Magazine* p26 O 16 2016

Lesbians—Travel

Letter from... ZIMBABWE M. Goba color *Advocate* no1089 p20 F/Mr 2017

Lesbos (Greece : Municipality)—Social conditions—21st century

Island Escape A. WARDAK *Ms.* v27 no2 p24 Summ 2017

LESCAZE, ZOË

SPECIFIC OBJECTIVES bw color *ARTnews* v115 no3 p110 Fall 2016

Leschin-Hoar, Clare

OCEAn TO TABLE color *Sunset* v238 no2 p68 F 2017

Lescroart, John

Fatal *Publishers Weekly* v263 no43 p56 O 24 2016

Lescure, Roland

On the Stump for Macron—in Florida E. Schine and S. Rastello color *Bloomberg Businessweek* no4525 p12 Je 5 2017

Lesha, Emal

Inactivation of porcine endogenous retrovirus in pigs using CRISPR-Cas9 diag *Science* v357 no6357 p1303 S 22 2017

LESHAW, LISA

Your True Stories IN 100 WORDS color *Reader's Digest* v189 no1129 p25 Ap 2017

Leshchinsky, Ben

Mitigating coastal landslide damage color *Science* v357 no6355 p981 S 8 2017

Leshko, Drew

In the Clouds, Down to Earth color *American Craft* v77 no3 p8 Je/Jl 2017

Ode to the Corner Store B. Martin color *American Craft* v77 no3 p30 Je/Jl 2017

Lesica, Ivan

Ivan Lesica color *National Geographic* v230 no4 p15 O 2016

Lesko, Frank

Still worried *U.S. Catholic* v82 no10 p5 O 2017

Leslie, Christina S.

Aerobic glycolysis promotes T helper 1 cell differentiation through an epigenetic mechanism bibl graph *Science* v354 no6311 p481 O 28 2016

PI3K pathway regulates ER-dependent transcription in breast cancer through the epigenetic regulator KMT2D bibl graph *Science* v355 no6331 p1324 Mr 24 2017

Leslie, Jacques

AN ENERGY-GENERATING BEAVER DAM *Harper's Magazine* v333 no1998 p72 N 2016

Leslie, Lisa—Interviews

The Factors That Lead to a Pay Premium for Women G. Gavett *Harvard Business Review Digital Articles* p2 My 9 2016

Leslie, Mitch

Can flu shots help women get pregnant? color *Science* v355 no6331 p1247 Mr 24 2017

THE CASE OF THE MACHO CROCS color map *Science* v357 no6354 p859 S 1 2017

Cell-like giant viruses found color *Science* v356 no6333 p15 Ap 7 2017

A division of labor in cells' protein factories color *Science* v356 no6344 p1218 Je 23 2017

Is the cell's garbage disposal sending messages? color *Science* v355 no6332 p1361 Mr 31 2017

Killing old cells to stay young color *Science* v354 no6319 p1519 D 23 2016

THE POST-OP BRAIN color *Science* v356 no6341 p898 Je 1 2017

Zebrafish larvae could help to personalize cancer treatments color *Science* v357 no6353 p745 Ag 25 2017

Leslie, Rose

My Obsessions... *TV Guide* p10 Ap 17 2017

Leslie, Ryan

TECH TRENDS CHANGING OUR WORLD color *Black Enterprise* v47 no2 p46 S 2016

Leslie, Sarah-Jane

THE BRILLIANCE TRAP color graph *Scientific American* v317 no3 p60 S 2017

Gender stereotypes about intellectual ability emerge early and influence children's interests bibl graph *Science* v355 no6323 p389 Ja 27 2017

Leslie, Victoria

Fallen Women *History Today* v67 no1 p35 Ja 2017

Lesniak, Wojciech

Chemogenetics revealed: DREADD occupancy and activation via converted clozapine graph *Science* v357 no6350 p503 Ag 4 2017

LESSER, ELIZABETH

Let it go! [Cover story] color *O, The Oprah Magazine* p92 Ag 2017

Lesser, Wendy

The Battles Over Julia Ward Howe bw cartoon *New York Review of Books* v63 no18 p54 N 24 2016

Eternal Flames *New York Times Book Review* p16 F 12 2017

A Long Look Back K. Frampton *Architectural Record* v205 no9 p59 S 2017

THE MYSTIC P. GOLDBERGER color *Nation* v304 no17 p33 Je 5 2017

What the Brick Says: The tangled life and transcendent work of the architect Louis Kahn I. SAFFRON bw *New York Times Book Review* p12 Ap 23 2017

"You Say to Brick": Louis Kahn Begins to Articulate the Ideas that Define His Architecture *Humanities* v38 no2 p1 Spr 2017

LESSIG, LAWRENCE

ALL TOGETHER NOW *Sierra* v101 no5 p30 S/O 2016

Lessin, Jessica

Inside (The) Information M. Marr color *Columbia Journalism Review* p62 Fall/Wint 2016

Lessin, Leeba

Reinventing the Way Medicaid Delivers Care *Harvard Business Review Digital Articles* p2 Mr 31 2015

Lessler, Justin

Dengue diversity across spatial and temporal scales: Local structure and the effect of host population size bibl graph *Science* v355 no6331 p1302 Mr 24 2017

Opportunities and challenges in modeling emerging infectious diseases diag graph *Science* v357 no6347 p149 Jl 14 2017

Lessner, Joanne Sydney

Anna Netrebko: Verismo *Opera News* v81 no9 p54 Mr 2017

The Ouroboros Trilogy *Opera News* v81 no6 p44 D 2016

Lessons (Poem)

Lessons J. RUNGE *America* v215 no13 p36 O 31 2016

Lester, Harry

DAN ABOUT TOWN color *Washingtonian Magazine* v52 no7

p26 Ap 2017

Lester, Jeff

WAPITI WISDOM B. FITZPATRICK color *Outdoor Life* v224 no7 p26 S 2017

Lester, Karl

Vietnam Shrugs Off the Loss of a Trade Pact *Bloomberg Businessweek* no4512 p15 F 20 2017

Lester, Kent

The Seventh Sun *Publishers Weekly* v264 no6 p47 F 6 2017

Lester, Richard

Nuclear power: Deployment speed—Response bibl *Science* v354 no6316 p1113 D 2 2016

Lester, Scott Wayne

Want Your Employees to Trust You? Show You Trust Them *Harvard Business Review Digital Articles* p2 Jl 5 2017

Let Freedom Ring (Music)

Marian Anderson: Let Freedom Ring I. Siff *Opera News* v81 no9 p55 Mr 2017

Let Me Be Your Girl (Music)

The Must List color *Entertainment Weekly* no1434 p3 O 7 2016

Let the Right One In (Film)

They Came to Slay E. Dockterman color *Time* v189 no9 p56 Mr 13 2017

Let the Sunshine In (Film)

Parting the Clouds N. Rapold bw *Film Comment* v53 no4 p10 Jl/Ag 2017

Let Us Now Praise Famous Men (Book : Agee)

Run SILENT, Run DEEP D. Garner bw *Esquire* p58 O 2017

Letessier-Selvon, A.

Observation of a large-scale anisotropy in the arrival directions of cosmic rays above 8×1018 eV *Science* v357 no6357 p1266 S 22 2017

Lethal Weapon (TV program)

Anatomy of a Hit J. HALTERMAN *TV Guide* p9 D 5 2016

Everything New Is Old Again E. Dockterman color *Time* v189 no4 p49 F 6 2017

Lethal Showdown J. Halterman *TV Guide* v64 no48 p11 N 21 2016

Lethal Weapon J. Halterman *TV Guide* p41 D 5 2016

Lethal Weapon J. Halterman *TV Guide* v65 no4 p40 Ja 16 2017

Lethal Weapon N. Abrams, A. Bacle et al color *Entertainment Weekly* no1482/1483 p60 S 22 2017

Lethem, Jonathan

IT ALL CONNECTS *New York Times Magazine* p60 O 30 2016

Reading Rock B. HANDY *New York Times Book Review* p19 Je 4 2017

Rolls Of the Dice [Cover story] K. Andersen *New York Times Book Review* p1 O 16 2016

Shake Those Dice Again J. Walton bw *New York Review of Books* v63 no19 p38 D 8 2016

LETNIC, MIKE

Conserving the World's Megafauna and Biodiversity: The Fierce Urgency of Now *BioScience* v67 no3 p197 Mr 2017

Saving the World's Terrestrial Megafauna color *BioScience* v66 no10 p807 O 1 2016

Leto, Jared, 1971-

Artists color *Time* v189 no16/17 p40 My 1-8 2017

LET'S PLAY JOKER'S WILD! K. P. Sullivan color *Entertainment Weekly* no1444/1445 p64 D 16 2016

Leto, Jared, 1971—Interviews

JARED LETO TELLS ALL R. Oltuski color *Harper's Bazaar* no3648 p192 N 2016

L'Etoile, James

At What Cost: A Detective Penley Mystery *Publishers Weekly* v263 no40 p98 O 3 2016

Letonja, Marko

Manon S. J. Mudge *Opera News* v81 no6 p49 D 2016

LeTourneau, Nancy

Obama's Top 50 Accomplishments, Revisited *Washington Monthly* p12 Ja/F 2017

Let's Make a Deal (TV program)

THE ART OF THE DEAL D. HOLBROOK *TV Guide* v64 no46 p20 N 7 2016

Lett, Kathryn

IGNITING THE FLAME K. Lett *Literacy Today (2411-7862)* v35 no2 p12 S/O 2017

IGNITING THE FLAME *Literacy Today (2411-7862)* v35 no2 p12 S/O 2017

Letter openers

A Letter Opener M. Schnaidt bw *Men's Health* v32 no5 p140 Je 2017

Letter to My Son (Poem)

Letter to My Son M. Alexander *America* v216 no3 p41 F 6 2017

Letter writing

Dear Younger Me *Scholastic Choices* pT10 S 2017 Supplement

Letter Head C. BONANOS color *Conde Nast Traveler* v52 no3 p102 Mr 2017

The "Write" Way to Show Gratitude L. M. Smith *USA Today Magazine* v145 no2862 p64 Mr 2017

Letter writing—Competitions

Posthole M. Viola, A. Forsyth et al color *Powder* v45 no3 p148 N 2016

Letterman, David, 1947-

Q+A D. S. COMISKEY *Indianapolis Monthly* p73 Ap 2017

Thirty Years Ago, at 12:30 img *New York* p14 Mr 6 2017

Letterman, David, 1947—Interviews

Dave Is Back! S. Vilkomerson color *Entertainment Weekly* no1478 / 1479 p18 Ag 18-25 2017

David Letterman B. MARTIN color *GQ: Gentlemen's Quarterly* v97 no6 p130 Je 2017

DAVID LETTERMAN D. MARCHESE img *New York* p28 Mr 6 2017

Why I Started Acting on Climate Change color *National Geographic* v230 no4 p4 O 2016

Letters

See also

Celebrities' correspondence

Open letters

Postcards

Prisoners' correspondence

BOOK NOOK KOOKS *Reader's Digest* v189 no1130 p69 My 2017

NO SHOW A. Doran bw color *ARTnews* v116 no1 p84 Spr 2017

Notes, Asides, And Memories J. NORDLINGER color *National Review* v69 no18 p31 O 2 2017

ONLY A GAME K. O. Knausgaard *Harper's Magazine* v333 no1999 p17 D 2016

THE PURLOINED LETTER B. Freed *Washingtonian Magazine* v52 no6 p18 Mr 2017

Special Delivery R. Marech *National Parks* v91 no1 p4 Wint 2017

THE TIP SHEET M. Marden, M. Hainey color *Esquire* p52 Je/Jl 2017

VÁCLAV HAVEL ON GOING ALONG TO GET ALONG *Lapham's Quarterly* v10 no3 p133 Summ 2017

Letters from Baghdad (Film)

LINES IN THE SAND A. LANE cartoon *New Yorker* v93 no16 p110 Je 5 2017

Letters in motion pictures

READING INTO IT M. NELSON bw color *Film Comment* v53 no2 p48 Mr/Ap 2017

Letters—History

Q: What was the most important letter in history? C. Carson, N. Sparks et al color *Atlantic* v320 no2 p104 S 2017

Letting My Hair Down (Poem)

Letting My Hair Down S. OLDS *Nation* v304 no4 p37 F 6 2017

Letting of contracts

See also

Contracting out

LETTOW, PAUL

Preserving American Power *National Review* v69 no7 p42 Ap 17 2017

Letts, Elizabeth

THE PERFECT HORSE: A Conversation with Author Elizabeth Letts G. DEARTH *Arabian Horse World* v57 no11 p154 Ag 2017

Lettuce

Fried Fish Lettuce Wraps img *New York* p59 F 20 2017

Lighter Manicotti color *Vegetarian Today* no1 p28 F 2017

Summa Cum Lettuce G. SINGER color *Walrus* v14 no9 p82 N 2017

WEEKNIGHT MEALS [Cover story] color *Good Housekeeping* v265 no3 p121 S 2017

Lettuce growing
 Love Story, With Lettuce K. Washington and Nancy Matsumoto
  color *AARP: The Magazine* v60 no4A p59 Je/Jl 2017
 Raising Lettuce, Buddhist Style J. D. OLIVER color *Tricycle: The
  Buddhist Review* v27 no1 p28 Fall 2017
 Your CHECKLIST E. Jardina and J. Silver color *Sunset* v239 no3
  p60 S 2017
LEU, CHELSEA
 THE CLIQUE THAT'S CHANGING HOW SCHOOLKIDS EAT
  Sierra v101 no5 p46 S/O 2016
 Get Cultured *Sierra* v101 no5 p8 S/O 2016
 IT'S NOT JUST ROCKET SCIENCE color *Wired* v24 no11 p138
  N 2016
 K2R SPOT-LIFTER: NO PAIN, NO STAIN color *Wired* v25 no9
  p36 S 2017
 LITHIUM-ION BATTERIES color *Wired* v25 no4 p20 Ap 2017
 OK, HOUSE. GET SMART chart color *Wired* v25 no6 p39 Je
  2017
 Raw Appeal *Sierra* v101 no4 p8 Jl/Ag 2016
 Salt for the Earth *Sierra* v101 no6 p11 N/D 2016
 SCOTCH MAGIC TAPE color *Wired* v24 no12 p36 D 2016
 TRIPLE-ACTION MACE: CRY, FRY, AND DYE color *Wired*
  v25 no7 p26 Jl 2017
 WHAT LIES BENEATH bw *Wired* v24 no12 p26 D 2016
Leube, Kurt R.
 Warning: Semantic Traps Ahead: Environmental politics are lit-
  tered with language that obscures meaning and hinders good
  policy *Hoover Digest: Research & Opinion on Public Policy*
  no3 p77 Summ 2017
Leuchtenburg, William E.
 Commanders-in-chief R. Cook *History Today* v67 no1 p62 Ja
  2017
Leuchter, Miriam
 Do You Still Need a 'Real' Camera? color *Popular Photography*
  v81 no2 p60 Mr/Ap 2017
 HAIRSTORY color *Popular Photography* v81 no1 p106 Ja/F
  2017
 In Praise of Craft *Popular Photography* v81 no2 p8 Mr/Ap 2017
 Making It New *Popular Photography* v81 no1 p10 Ja/F 2017
 POETRY IN MOTION color *Popular Photography* v81 no1 p28
  Ja/F 2017
 Speaking Volumes color *Popular Photography* v80 no11 p6 D
  2016
 A STAR'S TURN color *Popular Photography* v81 no1 p64 Ja/F
  2017
Leucine
 Epigenetic regulation of antagonistic receptors confers rice blast
  resistance with yield balance Y. Deng, K. Zhai et al bibl diag
  Science v355 no6328 p962 Mr 3 2017
 IT'S WHEY BETTER WITH LEUCINE J. WUEBBEN bw *Mus-
  cle & Performance* v9 no10 p17 O 2017
Leuenberger, D.
 Femtosecond electron-phonon lock-in by photoemission and x-
  ray free-electron laser chart diag *Science* v357 no6346 p71 Jl
  7 2017
Leuenberger, Pascal
 Cell-wide analysis of protein thermal unfolding reveals determi-
  nants of thermostability color *Science* v355 no6327 p812 F 24
  2017
Leuinson, Megan
 face off N. Loeffler-Gladstone color *Dance Spirit* v20 no9 p44
  N 2016
Leukemia
 FATHER FIGURE: Franciscan Health's cancer center has a se-
  cret weapon: a medical director who knows what it's like to be
  the parent of a leukemia patient A. GARCEAU *Indianapolis
  Monthly* p76 N 2017
Leukemia—Treatment
 The Healing Hoagie J. SHAHIN *Reader's Digest* v189 no1128
  p48 Mr 2017
Leung, Diamond
 Mind Over Mascot color *Sports Illustrated* v125 no13 p23 O 17
  2016
Leung, Godfre
 LEE KIT color *Art in America* v104 no10 p155 N 2016
Leung, Helen

 HELEN LEUNG + ELIZABETH TIMME: THE "WONKISH"
  URBAN PLANNER AND "ARCHITECTURE GEEK" ARE
  OUT TO SOLVE SOME OF L.A.'S TOUGHEST HOUSING
  AND SMALL-BUSINESS PROBLEMS J. HERBST *Los An-
  geles Magazine* v62 no9 p93 S 2017
LEUNG, IRIS
 Asia's Rising Stars color *Forbes* v199 no5 p20 My 16 2017
Leung, Ken
 Inhumans Come to Life—Finally N. Abrams color *Entertainment
  Weekly* no1465 p15 My 12 2017
 MARVEL'S INHUMANS J. Russell *TV Guide* v65 no37 p40 S
  4 2017
Leuschner, Rudolf
 The Rise of FinTech in Supply Chains *Harvard Business Review
  Digital Articles* p2 Je 22 2016
Leuschner, Wulf Dirk
 Trispecific broadly neutralizing HIV antibodies mediate potent
  SHIV protection in macaques color graph *Science* v357 no6359
  p85 O 6 2017
Leutwyler, Henry
 HORSE POWER bw color *Esquire* p104 2017 BigBlackBook
Levad, Amy
 Locked In: The True Causes of Mass Incarceration and How to
  Achieve Real Reform *Christian Century* v134 no17 p37 Ag 16
  2017
Levant, Ezra
 CANADA'S ANTI-MEDIA MOGUL J. MARKUSOFF color *Ma-
  clean's* v130 no2 p28 Mr 2017
 Conservatives in Cruise Wear P. NORMAN cartoon *Walrus* v14
  no3 p26 Ap 2017
 The Wingman J. KAY *Walrus* v14 no3 p66 Ap 2017
LEVASSEUR, JENNIFER
 THE CRIMINAL'S MASK color *America* v215 no13 p37 O 31
  2016
 Hidden Figures/Rise of the Rocket Girls *Physics Today* v70 no1
  p57 Ja 2017
Levay, Zoltan G.
 Relativistic deflection of background starlight measures the mass
  of a nearby white dwarf star chart color graph *Science* v356
  no6342 p1046 Je 9 2017
LEVE, ARIEL
 His Dark Material *New York Times Book Review* p43 N 13 2016
Leveaux, David
 Gradations of Badness: The Exception pays little fealty to the his-
  tory of Kaiser Wilhelm, but, oh, that glorious acting D. EDEL-
  STEIN img *New York* v50 no11 p122 My 29 2017
Levees
 Vital wetlands saved from proposed levee color *National Wildlife
  (World Edition)* v55 no4 p44 Je/Jl 2017
Level of difficulty
 An Easy Way to Make Your Employees Happier L. Wiseman *Har-
  vard Business Review Digital Articles* p2 N 13 2014
Leven, Brody
 Have Skis, Will Travel S. Davis color *Powder* v45 no3 p44 N 2016
LevenBetts (Company)
 perspective house of the month: A FIRM REVISITS THE SITE
  OF ITS FIRST RESIDENCE TO CREATE A RELAXING
  BACKYARD RETREAT FOR A LONGTIME CLIENT AND
  FRIEND M. SITZ color map *Architectural Record* v205 no5
  p37 My 2017
Levendusky, Matthew
 Research: Political Polarization Is Changing How Americans
  Work and Shop *Harvard Business Review Digital Articles* p2
  My 19 2017
Levens Hall (England)
 SHEAR GENIUS M. OWENS color *Architectural Digest* no11
  p146 N 1 2017
Levensaler, Leighanne
 Build a Great Company Culture with Help from Technology *Har-
  vard Business Review Digital Articles* p2 F 24 2016
LEVENSON, JON D.
 Rome and Jerusalem *Commentary* v142 no5 p47 D 2016
Levenstein, Daniel
 Layer-specific modulation of neocortical dendritic inhibition dur-
  ing active wakefulness bibl diag *Science* v355 no6328 p954 Mr
  3 2017

Leveraged buyouts
Private Equity Can Make Firms More Innovative N. Torres *Harvard Business Review Digital Articles* p2 Je 29 2015

LEVERETT, HILLARY MANN
How Progressives Can Change Middle East Policy color *Nation* v304 no2 p17 Ja 16 2017
Toward a New Foreign Policy [Cover story] bw *Nation* v304 no2 p12 Ja 16 2017

Levering, Donald
UNRAPTURED *Commonweal* v144 no15 p38 S 22 2017

Leverington, David
Observatories and Telescopes of Modern Times: Ground-Based Optical and Radio Astronomy Facilities Since 1945 Eun-Joo Ahn *Physics Today* v70 no10 p64 O 2017

Levesque, Joanna
The LIBERATION of JOJO I. Biedenharn and N. Feeney color *Entertainment Weekly* no1436/1437 p30 O 21 2016

LEVEY, JON
CROWD PLEASERS color *Tennis* v53 no2 p20 Mr/Ap 2017
Dual Threats *Tennis* v53 no4 p18 Jl/Ag 2017
GUT CHECK color *Tennis* v53 no2 p32 Mr/Ap 2017
Multiple Personalities color *Tennis* v53 no2 p12 Mr/Ap 2017
The PRO SHOP *Tennis* v53 no4 p16 Jl/Ag 2017
The PRO SHOP *Tennis* v53 no5 p12 S/O 2017

Levez, Olivia
The Island color *Publishers Weekly* v263 no49 p114 D 7 2016

Levi, Anthea
Beat the Heat color *Health* v31 no5 p72 Je 2017
DETOX MOVES YOU SHOULD NEVER TRY *Health* v31 no7 p86 S 2017
From Obese to Ironman color *Health* v31 no5 p51 Je 2017
Getting slim with my sister color *Health* v31 no8 p46 O 2017
How Clean Is Your Pet? color *Health* v31 no7 p104 S 2017
How I Found My Feel-Great Weight color *Health* v31 no6 p48 Jl 2017
I'm Almost Half My Size! color *Health* v31 no4 p56 My 2017
I'm hooked on taking care of my body color *Health* v31 no9 p47 N 2017
Me, Minus 108 Pounds color *Health* v31 no3 p44 Ap 2017
Social Media Changed My Body color *Health* v31 no7 p66 S 2017
This Is You on Sex color *Health* v31 no6 p86 Jl 2017
This Is You on Sugar color *Health* v31 no3 p68 Ap 2017
What's in that kibble? color *Health* v31 no8 p86 O 2017
Which Teas Are Healthiest? color *Health* v31 no7 p151 S 2017

Levi, Helen
This Is My Job L. Liebman color *Glamour* v115 no1 p56 Ja 2017

Levi, Primo, 1919-1987
1985: Turin *Lapham's Quarterly* v10 no1 p93 Wint 2017

Levi, Renalto
The Father of Modern Powerboat Design M. PETERS color *Power & Motoryacht* v34 no6 p20 Je 2017

LEVI, TAAL
Conserving the World's Megafauna and Biodiversity: The Fierce Urgency of Now *BioScience* v67 no3 p197 Mr 2017
Saving the World's Terrestrial Megafauna color *BioScience* v66 no10 p807 O 1 2016

Levi Strauss & Co.
Google's next wearable is a $350 Levi's jacket that controls music by brushing your sleeve M. SIMON color *PCWorld* v35 no4 p29 Ap 2017
THE TIES THAT BIND AT LEVI'S E. Fry color map *Fortune* v176 no4 p104 S 15 2017

Levie, Aaron
3 Questions to Get the Most Out of Your Company's Data *Harvard Business Review Digital Articles* p2 Ja 29 2015
Old Management Systems Stifle New Business Models *Harvard Business Review Digital Articles* p2 Ap 28 2015
The Problem with Legacy Ecosystems il *Harvard Business Review* v94 no11 p68 N 2016
Why Some Digital Companies Should Delay Profitability for as Long as They Can *Harvard Business Review Digital Articles* p2 My 4 2017

Levin, Alan
2.5m color *Bloomberg Businessweek* no4514 p29 Mr 13 2017
Apple Is Bringing Drones to a Map Fight *Bloomberg Businessweek* no4503 p29 D 12 2016

The Debate Over Drone IDs bw *Bloomberg Businessweek* no4534 p36 Ag 14 2017

Levin, B. J.
A prominent glycyl radical enzyme in human gut microbiomes metabolizes trans-4-hydroxy-L-proline diag *Science* v355 no6325 p595 F 10 2017

Levin, Bess
THE NEW ESTABLISHMENT 2017 bw color *Vanity Fair* v59 no11 p87 N 2017
Work Mistakes to Avoid in 2017 color *Glamour* v115 no1 p59 Ja 2017

Levin, David
Blue Hotes Hurricanes: GEOLOGICAL MARVELS ARE GOLD MINES FOR CLIMATE HISTORY *Oceanus* v52 no2 p44 Spr 2017
Consumers Paid Less for Grocery Store Foods in 2016 Than in 2015 *Amber Waves: The Economics of Food, Farming, Natural Resources, & Rural America* p8 Mr 2017

Levin, E.
Hawkmoths use nectar sugar to reduce oxidative damage from flight bibl graph *Science* v355 no6326 p733 F 17 2017

Levin, Frances
SPECIALISTS *New York* v50 no11 p60 My 29 2017

Levin, Jamie
Home Wrecker cartoon *Walrus* v14 no6 p28 Jl/Ag 2017
HOUSE HUNTERS TRANSNATIONAL *Harper's Magazine* v334 no2000 p48 Ja 2017

LEVIN, JANNA
Ladies Who Launch *New York Times Book Review* p10 Ja 1 2017

Levin, Jonathan
Can Puerto Rico Corral Its Tax Dodgers? color graph *Bloomberg Businessweek* no4524 p17 My 29 2017
Cries In the Dark color graph *Bloomberg Businessweek* no4540 p16 O 2 2017
Google's Opioid Ad Addiction color *Bloomberg Businessweek* no4540 p21 O 2 2017
Miami's Mayor Climbs Aboard the Trump Train color *Bloomberg Businessweek* no4512 p28 F 20 2017
A Political Scion Tries To Right Puerto Rico color *Bloomberg Businessweek* no4519 p18 Ap 24 2017
Trading Wall Street For Jacksonville color *Bloomberg Businessweek* no4509 p34 Ja 30 2017
Trump's Tax Bill For Global Warming color *Bloomberg Businessweek* no4504 p26 D 19 2016

Levin, Mark D.
A catalytic fluoride-rebound mechanism for C(sp3)-CF3 bond formation diag *Science* v356 no6344 p1272 Je 23 2017

Levin, Rachel
STRANDED... AND LOVING IT color *Sunset* v238 no3 p13 Mr 2017

Levin, S. M.
Jupiter's interior and deep atmosphere: The initial pole-to-pole passes with the Juno spacecraft [Cover story] color graph *Science* v356 no6340 p821 My 26 2017
Jupiter's magnetosphere and aurorae observed by the Juno spacecraft during its first polar orbits diag graph *Science* v356 no6340 p826 My 26 2017

Levin, Simon A.
Reducing antimicrobial use in food animals color graph *Science* v357 no6358 p1350 S 29 2017
Social norms as solutions bibl color *Science* v354 no6308 p42 O 7 2016

Levin, Steve
AERO-SPACE K. D. ATHERTON and S. BUSHWICK color *Popular Science* v288 no6 p52 N/D 2016

Levin, Yuval
Apathy in the Executive color *Weekly Standard* v22 no14 p24 D 12 2016
Can the Right Reform? P. Steinfels cartoon *Commonweal* v143 no17 p29 O 21 2016
A Changed GOP il *National Review* v68 no22 p16 D 5 2016
CONSTITUTIONALISM FOR REALISTS *Claremont Review of Books* v17 no2 p14 Spr 2017
The Cronyist Threat *National Review* v68 no20 p32 N 7 2016
DAVID FRUM D. FRUM *Commentary* v142 no1 p36 Jl/Ag 2016
David Frum on Yuval Levin's 'The Fractured Republic' M. Conti-

netti, M. Soloveichik et al *Commentary* v142 no1 p1 Jl/Ag 2016

The Fractured Republic: Renewing America's Social Contract in the Age of Individualism W. Russell Mead *Foreign Affairs* v95 no6 p178 N/D 2016

Getting past the past A. B. Robinson color *Christian Century* v133 no22 p36 O 26 2016

Infrastructure Dangers Ahead map *Weekly Standard* v22 no18 p18 Ja 16 2017

Kevin D. Williamson on Yuval Levin's 'The Fractured Republic' M. Continetti, D. Frum et al *Commentary* v142 no1 p1 Jl/Ag 2016

MATTHEW CONTINETTI M. CONTINETTI *Commentary* v142 no1 p35 Jl/Ag 2016

Matthew Continetti on Yuval Levin's 'The Fractured Republic' D. Frum, M. Soloveichik et al *Commentary* v142 no1 p1 Jl/Ag 2016

MEIR SOLOVEICHIK M. SOLOVEICHIK *Commentary* v142 no1 p37 Jl/Ag 2016

Meir Soloveichik on Yuval Levin's 'The Fractured Republic' M. Continetti, D. Frum et al *Commentary* v142 no1 p1 Jl/Ag 2016

Scoring the GOP Health-Care Plan color *National Review* v69 no6 p14 Ap 3 2017

TIES THAT BIND D. Azerrad *Claremont Review of Books* v16 no4 p18 Fall 2016

TRUMP FILLS THE VACUUM: HE EXEMPLIFIES AND AC-CELERATES THE DECLINE OF AMERICA'S INSTITU-TIONS [Cover story] *Commentary* v142 no5 p16 D 2016

Levine, Aaron

KILL THE CHILL S. Nygaard cartoon color *Men's Health* v32 no1 p77 Ja/F 2017

Levine, Adam, 1979-

Sound Bites color *Entertainment Weekly* no1439 p8 N 11 2016

Levine, Alaina G.

From selfies to selfless: Managing multigenerational teams color *Science* v357 no6356 p1170 S 15 2017

Navigating technology transfer issues color *Science* v355 no6328 p975 Mr 3 2017

LEVINE, ALLAN

TRUDEAUMANIA color *Maclean's* v129 no40 p76 O 10 2016

Levine, Beth

Closing the loop bibl bw *Science* v354 no6315 p968 N 25 2016

Open to Possibilities bw *Publishers Weekly* v263 no44 p(Sp)18 O 31 2016

Tavis Smiley Smiles on the KING of POP bw *Publishers Weekly* v263 no44 p(Sp)28 O 31 2016

The Thread *New York Times Magazine* p8 Ja 8 2017

Levine, Bruce L.

CANCER KILLERS color *Scientific American* v316 no3 p38 Mr 2017

Levine, Hallie

6 Things Every Woman Should Know About Her Heart color *Health* v31 no1 p83 Ja 2017

ALL ABOUT MUSCLES: A USER'S MANUAL color *Health* v31 no5 p77 Je 2017

BIRTH CONTROL UPDATE: A USER'S MANUAL color *Health* v31 no6 p95 Jl 2017

Breast Cancer Breaking News color *Health* v31 no8 p74 O 2017

EAT GREAT & LOSE WEIGHT *Better Homes & Gardens* v95 no1 p116 Ja 2017

ERASE YOUR PAIN: A USER'S MANUAL color *Health* v31 no2 p97 Mr 2017

FILM SCHOOL color *Martha Stewart Living* p43 Ap 2017

it takes two *Better Homes & Gardens* v94 no11 p156 N 2016

KNOW YOUR FLOW: A USER'S MANUAL color *Health* v31 no3 p75 Ap 2017

LIVE YOUR DREAM color *Yoga Journal* p28 2016 Special Issue

Teddy's Wisdom Made Me Weep color *Parents* v92 no5 p10 My 2017

THE TRUTH ABOUT WOMEN AND CONCUSSIONS color *Health* v30 no9 p132 N 2016

UNSTOPPABLE ENERGY: A USER'S MANUAL color *Health* v31 no4 p75 My 2017

UTI Myths, Cleared Up color *Glamour* v114 no12 p160 D 2016

What your mom's body says about you color *Health* v31 no9 p59 N 2017

WORK YOUR BODY CLOCK: A USER'S MANUAL color

Health v31 no7 p109 S 2017

YOUR METABOLISM: A USER'S MANUAL color *Health* v30 no9 p109 N 2016

YOUR SMILE: A USER'S MANUAL color *Health* v30 no10 p97 D 2016

Zero Tolerance bw color graph *Consumer Reports* v82 no1 p32 Ja 2017

Levine, Harry

Atom-by-atom assembly of defect-free one-dimensional cold atom arrays bibl diag graph *Science* v354 no6315 p1024 N 25 2016

Levine, James, 1943-

CLASSICAL MUSIC *New Yorker* v93 no30 p13 O 2 2017

Levine, Jessica

Just breathe color *Yoga Journal* p42 2017 Special Issue

Levine, Jonathan, 1976-

Snatched L. Greenblatt color *Entertainment Weekly* no1466 p42 My 19 2017

LEVINE, JOSHUA

Domestic Harmony color *Architectural Digest* no5 p66 My 2017

The Living Dead: BRUTALLY KILLED THOUSANDS OF YEARS AGO, EUROPE'S FAMED BOG BODIES ARE STARTING TO REVEAL THEIR SECRETS *Smithsonian* v48 no2 p65 My 2017

MAN OF THE WORLD color *Architectural Digest* v74 no3 p132 Mr 2017

Statement Piece color *Architectural Digest* v74 no9 p85p S 2017

TRUE BLUE bw color *Architectural Digest* v74 no8 p48 Ag 2017

Levine, Matt

Trump Vs. The Rule Of Law color *Bloomberg Businessweek* no4510 p6 F 6 2017

Levine, Max

Committing to socially responsible seafood color *Science* v356 no6341 p912 Je 1 2017

Levine, Naomi M.

Putting the spotlight on organic sulfur bibl color diag *Science* v354 no6311 p418 O 28 2016

LEVINE, PHILIPPA

Relying on--or Recoiling from--Reproductive Enhancement *USA Today Magazine* v145 no2864 p62 My 2017

Levine, Shira

Biking the Legends of Wales *British Heritage Travel* v38 no1 p10 Ja/F 2017

Levings, Megan

Harnessing Cellular Tools from Immune Systems to Help Prevent Graft Rejection color *Maclean's* v130 no9 p34 O 2017

Levingston, Steven

Kennedy, King and a Call to Coretta color *Time* v190 no1 p54 Jl 3 2017

Kennedy, King and a Call to Coretta S. Levingston color *Time* v190 no1 p54 Jl 3 2017

Profiles in Caution: In the heart of the civil rights struggle, a politician and an activist found common ground J. GOODMAN *New York Times Book Review* p9 Jl 2 2017

Levin-Reisman, Irit

Antibiotic tolerance facilitates the evolution of resistance bibl bw chart diag graph *Science* v355 no6327 p826 F 24 2017

Levinsen, Jesper

Ultrafast many-body interferometry of impurities coupled to a Fermi sea bibl diag graph *Science* v354 no6308 p96 O 7 2016

Levinsky, Addie

38 REASONS TO GO GA-GA FOR THE TOUR DE FRANCE color *Bicycling* v58 no7 p24 Ag 2017

Levinson, Barry, 1942-

THE SINS OF THE FATHER K. Burton color *Bloomberg Businessweek* no4524 p70 My 29 2017

Levinson, Marc

The Problem with the U.S. Economy Isn't Something Politicians Can Fix *Harvard Business Review Digital Articles* p2 N 29 2016

Prospects For Growth J. PETHOKOUKIS color *National Review* v69 no2 p37 F 6 2017

WHEN THE GOING WAS GOOD M. Barone *Claremont Review of Books* v17 no1 p85 Wint 2016/2017

Levintova, Hannah

HACKER, BANKER, SOLDIER, SPY bw color *Mother Jones* v42 no4 p19 Jl/Ag 2017

HACKS, LEAKS, AND TWEETS color *Mother Jones* v42 no4 p22 Jl/Ag 2017

IF YOU DEFUND IT, THEY WON'T COME color *Mother Jones* v42 no5 p15 S/O 2017

THE KREMLIN'S GREMLINS color *Mother Jones* v42 no4 p20 Jl/Ag 2017

ON KOMPROMAT bw *Mother Jones* v42 no4 p24 Jl/Ag 2017

PUTIN'S LONG GAME color *Mother Jones* v42 no4 p26 Jl/Ag 2017

THE RUSSIAN CONNECTION color *Mother Jones* v42 no4 p16 Jl/Ag 2017

WIKILEAKS' ROLE *Mother Jones* v42 no4 p30 Jl/Ag 2017

Levirne, Jake
The Most Overlooked Way of Stimulating Team Creativity *Harvard Business Review Digital Articles* p2 My 15 2015

Levis, Carolina
Forest conservation: Humans' handprints bibl color *Science* v355 no6324 p466 F 3 2017

Persistent effects of pre-Columbian plant domestication on Amazonian forest composition bibl chart graph map *Science* v355 no6328 p925 Mr 3 2017

Levi-Strauss, Claude, 1908-2009
1955: Paris *Lapham's Quarterly* v10 no2 p145 Spr 2017

Levitov, Leonid S.
An on/off Berry phase switch in circular graphene resonators diag graph *Science* v356 no6340 p845 My 26 2017

Levitsky, Steven
Is America Still Safe for Democracy? color *Foreign Affairs* v96 no3 p20 My/Je 2017

LEVITT, ANDREA AU
Simple Ways To Cut the Top Blood Pressure Number color *Reader's Digest* v190 no1134 p56 O 2017

Levitt, Emma
Woodville versus the Bastard *History Today* v66 no11 p6 N 2016

Levitt, Matthew
Can Bankers Fight Terrorism? *Foreign Affairs* v96 no6 p144 N/D 2017

LEVITT, MOLLY
Educators Share 10 Best Teaching, Technology Practices *Education Digest* v82 no8 p56 Ap 2017

Levitt, Rob
Level Up Your Grilling Game C. BOERS color *Chicago* v66 no7 p54 Jl 2017

LEVITZ, ERIC
A NATIVIST IS IN CHARGE OF THE POLICE STATE img *New York* v50 no9 p48 My 1 2017

TRUMP'S CAMPAIGN HAS BEEN SO INSANE *New York* v49 no22 p46 O 31 2016

Levorse, John
Coupling organelle inheritance with mitosis to balance growth and differentiation diag *Science* v355 no6324 p493 F 3 2017

Lev-ram, Michal
100 FASTEST-GROWING COMPANIES chart color diag map *Fortune* v176 no4 p157 S 15 2017

13 REED HASTINGS color *Fortune* v174 no7 p87 D 1 2016

THE 2017 Fortune Crystal Ball color diag *Fortune* v174 no7 p11 D 1 2016

APPLE REBOOTS IN CHINA color *Fortune* v176 no5 p106 O 1 2017

THE BLACK CEILING color *Fortune* v176 no5 p94 O 1 2017

BOXED IN color diag *Fortune* v176 no5 p86 O 1 2017

BREAKTHROUGH BRANDS 2017 color diag *Fortune* v75 no1 p64 Ja 1 2017

Can China Save Hollywood? color *Fortune* v175 no7 p9 Je 1 2017

CHANGE THE WORLD !!!! color diag map *Fortune* v176 no4 p74 S 15 2017

#DEFEATUBER [Cover story] color *Fortune* v176 no2 p66 Ag 1 2017

DEREK JETER'S NEXT SWING color *Fortune* v175 no3 p30 Mr 1 2017

DREAM WEAVER color *Fortune* v176 no3 p74 S 1 2017

FORTY UNDER FORTY 2017 color *Fortune* v176 no3 p62 S 1 2017

THE GAMBLERS BEHIND TECH'S BIGGEST DEAL EVER color *Fortune* v75 no1 p82 Ja 1 2017

A GIANT ENTERS A NEW ARENA chart color *Fortune* v175

no8 p192 Je 15 2017

IF I RAN THE CIRCUS color *Fortune* v175 no3 p132 Mr 1 2017

MINING COMEDY GOLD color *Fortune* v176 no3 p70 S 1 2017

MOST POWERFUL WOMEN color *Fortune* v176 no5 p54 O 1 2017

MOST POWERFUL WOMEN INTERNATIONAL color *Fortune* v176 no5 p111 O 1 2017

PROBLEM SOLVING WITH TECH'S HOTTEST SELF-HELP GURU color *Fortune* v174 no7 p40 D 1 2016

THE QUEEN OF POP [Cover story] color diag *Fortune* v176 no5 p70 O 1 2017

SECURING MCAFEE color *Fortune* v175 no6 p24 My 1 2017

SLACK'S QUEST TO MAKE WORK EASIER color *Fortune* v176 no1 p21 Jl 1 2017

Talking Tech Disruption color *Fortune* v176 no3 p24 S 1 2017

TECH'S MAGIC 8 BALL SAYS EMBRACE THE FUTURE color *Fortune* v176 no5 p28 O 1 2017

TECH TAKEOVER IN TOYLAND color diag *Fortune* v176 no5 p76 O 1 2017

THE UNFOLDIN DRAMA OF REAL-TIME TV color diag *Fortune* v175 no6 p50 My 1 2017

What Disney's Netflix Snub Means color *Fortune* v176 no3 p18 S 1 2017

YOUTH REVOLT color *Fortune* v176 no3 p64 S 1 2017

Levs, Josh
... And There's an Invisible Workload That Drags Men Down Too color *Money* v46 no4 p66 My 2017

Stop Punishing the Family Man *Harvard Business Review Digital Articles* p2 My 14 2015

Levy, Albert
PRIMARY-CARE PHYSICIANS *New York* v50 no11 p58 My 29 2017

Levy, Allegra
Memorable Melodies A. Morrison color *Downbeat* v84 no6 p30 Je 2017

Levy, Allen
Article So Long Love Songs *Commentary* v140 no2 p5 S 2015

Levy, Ariel
FINDING STRENGTH IN GREAT LOSS [Cover story] cartoon color *Redbook* p122 My 2017

A LONG HOMECOMING bw color *New Yorker* v93 no11 p22 My 1 2017

Motherhood Lost L. Jamison *New York Times Book Review* p10 Ap 9 2017

Rewriting the Rules of Womanhood E. Dockterman color *Time* v189 no11 p61 Mr 27 2017

The Rules Do Not Apply L. Greenblatt color *Entertainment Weekly* no1457/1458 p105 Mr 17 2017

SECRET SELVES cartoon color *New Yorker* v93 no4 p58 Mr 13 2017

THE WOMEN cartoon *New Yorker* v92 no39 p34 N 28 2016

Levy, Avraham A.
Wild emmer genome architecture and diversity elucidate wheat evolution and domestication color *Science* v357 no6346 p93 Jl 7 2017

Lévy, Bernard-Henri
The Jewish Thread D. MERKIN *New York Times Book Review* p17 F 12 2017

Judaism Doesn't Need This 'Genius' *Commentary* v143 no3 p40 Mr 2017

The Year in Reading [Cover story] *New York Times Book Review* p8 D 25 2016

Lévy, Bernard-Henri—Interviews
Bernard-Henri Lévy *New York Times Book Review* p6 Ja 1 2017

Levy, Daniel
What I Learned From My Dad color *TV Guide* v65 no7 p17 F 13 2017

Levy, David H.
FROM OUR READERS color *Sky & Telescope* v134 no2 p6 Ag 2017

Levy, DeAndre
Getting Serious About Locker-Room Talk D. ZIRIN color *Progressive* p68 D 2016/Ja 2017

Levy, Deborah, 1959-
Deborah Levy M. Rich color *Current Biography* v78 no5 p49 My 2017

view of Books v64 no7 p62 Ap 20 2017

Mind Games Y. Foong Khong color *Foreign Affairs* v96 no3 p139 My/Je 2017

THE NOT-SO-DISMAL SCIENCE J. K. Glassman *Washingtonian Magazine* v52 no6 p45 Mr 2017

THE UNDOING PROJECT [Cover story] D. Leonhardt *New York Times Book Review* p1 D 18 2016

LEWIS, MICHAEL J.

The Art of War: A history of how a bitter controversy over the Vietnam Veterans Memorial ended in national reconciliation *New York Times Book Review* p21 S 17 2017

Is free speech under threat IN THE UNITED STATES? WE RECEIVED TWENTY-SEVEN RESPONSES. WE PUBLISH THEM HERE, IN ALPHABETICAL ORDER *Commentary* v144 no1 p13 Jl/Ag 2017

A Museum That Overcomes Its Correctness: In Philadelphia, the American Revolution comes alive despite contemporary curatorial ideology *Commentary* v144 no1 p39 Jl/Ag 2017

Lewis, Miles Marshall

LET FREEDOM RING color *Essence* v47 no7 p50 N 2016

ON A ROLE color *Essence* v47 no10 p55 F 2017

UNSTOPPABLE [Cover story] color *Essence* v48 no2 p88 Je 2017

Lewis, Nathan

WHY IS THE KEY TO PROSPERITY IGNORED? color *Forbes* v200 no4 p11 O 24 2017

Lewis, Nicole

THE SECESSION MOVEMENT IN EDUCATION bw color graph map *Nation* v305 no7 p12 S 25 2017

Lewis, Nikole K.

HAT-P-26b: A Neptune-mass exoplanet with a well-constrained heavy element abundance chart diag graph *Science* v356 no6338 p628 My 12 2017

Lewis, Owen T.

Higher predation risk for insect prey at low latitudes and elevations graph *Science* v356 no6339 p742 My 19 2017

Lewis, Phillip

Spectral Baggage J. SILBER *New York Times Book Review* p18 Mr 26 2017

Lewis, Rachel

The Dual-Citizenship Crisis Rocking Politics Down Under color *Time* v190 no8 p11 Ag 28 2017

Lewis, Ronald M. III

Thermal processing of diblock copolymer melts mimics metallurgy diag graph *Science* v356 no6337 p520 My 5 2017

Lewis, Russell D.

Directed evolution of cytochrome c for carbon–silicon bond formation: Bringing silicon to life bibl diag graph *Science* v354 no6315 p1048 N 25 2016

Lewis, Shantrelle P.

Black Dandies img *New York* p60 Mr 6 2017

Lewis, Simon L.

Positive biodiversity-productivity relationship predominant in global forests bibl chart graph map *Science* v354 no6309 paaf8957-1 O 14 2016

Lewis, Sinclair, 1885-1951

1922: Zenith S. Lewis *Lapham's Quarterly* v10 no1 p42 Wint 2017

... How It Ends B. GAGE *New York Times Book Review* p15 Ja 22 2017

LEWIS, SUSANNAH B.

The Things I Wish My Dad Knew About Me Before He Died color *Reader's Digest* v189 no1131 p50 Je 2017

Lewis, Tanya

The Stuff of Dreams color *Scientific American* v317 no1 p16 Jl 2017

Lewis, Taylor

10 THINGS WE'RE TALKING ABOUT color *Essence* v47 no7 p57 N 2016

LEADERS of the NEW SCHOOL color *Essence* v47 no11 p100 Mr 2017

LEWIS, WALTER

I Survived! [Cover story] *Reader's Digest* v189 no1128 p62 Mr 2017

Lewis, Willette

Brave Hearts color *O, The Oprah Magazine* p14 Mr 2017

Lewis acids

The broadening reach of frustrated Lewis pair chemistry D. W. Stephan bibl diag *Science* v354 no6317 paaf7229-1 D 9 2016

Lewis pairs (Chemistry)

The broadening reach of frustrated Lewis pair chemistry D. W. Stephan bibl diag *Science* v354 no6317 paaf7229-1 D 9 2016

Lewis-Jones, Huw

Explorers' Sketchbooks: The Art of Discovery & Adventure A. Gawrylewski color *Scientific American* v316 no4 p76 Ap 2017

LEWIS-KRAUS, GIDEON

THE KNIGHT'S MOVE il *Nation* v304 no15 p27 My 8 2017

WIRING THE UNWIRED color *Wired* v24 no11 p74 N 2016

Lewis-kulin, Sarah

100 BEST COMPANIES TO WORK FOR 2017 [Cover story] color diag map *Fortune* v175 no4 p79 Mr 15 2017

HOW TO GET ON THIS LIST color *Fortune* v175 no4 p89 Mr 15 2017

Lewison, Rebecca L.

Poor fisheries struggle with U.S. import rule bibl color *Science* v355 no6329 p1031 Mr 10 2017

A Rubric to Evaluate Citizen-Science Programs for Long-Term Ecological Monitoring *BioScience* v67 no9 p834 S 2017

LEWIT, IDO

The Curious Humanist: Siegfried Kracauer in America *Film Quarterly* v70 no4 p131 Summ 2017

Lewon, Dennis

BACKCOUNTRY BAKING color *Backpacker* p27 Je 2017

Discomfort Zone color *Backpacker* v45 no2 p8 Mr 2017

GEAR WARS color *Backpacker* v45 no3 p8 Ap 2017

Local Hikes Just Got Better *Backpacker* p10 Ag 2017

Lost and Found color *Backpacker* p4 O 2017

Mountain Magic color *Backpacker* v45 no2 p70 Mr 2017

Plan a Big Trip diag *Backpacker* v45 no2 p32 Mr 2017

There's an App for That color *Backpacker* p38 My 2017

Trail Fails color *Backpacker* p6 S 2017

LEWSEN, SIMON

The Politics of Rotting Blubber color *Walrus* v14 no3 p59 Ap 2017

Ready for Our Close-Up color *Walrus* v14 no6 p79 Jl/Ag 2017

Lexicon (Linguistics)

THE NEW NBA LEXICON B. Langmann bw color *Esquire* p20 N 2017

Lexus (Company)

2018 Lexus LC 500 E. DYER color *Popular Mechanics* p36 Je 2017

The Big Show M. Sutton color *Car & Driver* v63 no1 p102 Jl 2017

Lexus LX 570 chart color *Motor Trend* v69 no1 p51 Ja 2017

Lexus RX chart color *Motor Trend* v69 no1 p52 Ja 2017

Lexus Sport Yacht 42 S. Murray color *Power & Motoryacht* v33 no4 p44 Ap 2017

RELEASE THE BEAST K. Sintumuang color *Esquire* p24 My 2017

WHEN CONCEPT MEETS REALITY J. Lieberman chart color *Motor Trend* v69 no4 p68 Ap 2017

Lexus automobile

2018 Lexus LC 500 E. DYER color *Popular Mechanics* p36 Je 2017

The Big Show M. Sutton color *Car & Driver* v63 no1 p102 Jl 2017

RELEASE THE BEAST K. Sintumuang color *Esquire* p24 My 2017

Lexus automobile—Evaluation

Lexus LX 570 chart color *Motor Trend* v69 no1 p51 Ja 2017

WHEN CONCEPT MEETS REALITY J. Lieberman chart color *Motor Trend* v69 no4 p68 Ap 2017

Lexus RX sport utility vehicle—Evaluation

Lexus RX chart color *Motor Trend* v69 no1 p52 Ja 2017

Leynaud, Gerardo

Forest conservation: Remember Gran Chaco bibl color *Science* v355 no6324 p465 F 3 2017

Leyrat, C.

Seasonal exposure of carbon dioxide ice on the nucleus of comet 67P/Churyumov-Gerasimenko bibl bw graph *Science* v354 no6319 p1563 D 23 2016

LG Display Co. Ltd.

South Korea's High-Value Targets B. Einhorn, K. Kong et al *Bloomberg Businessweek* no4520 p17 My 1 2017

LG Electronics

3D TV Is Dead K. C. POHLMANN *Sound & Vision* v82 no5 p21 Je 2017

BINGE BIGGER K. Sintumuang color *Esquire* v167 no2 p60 Mr 2017

LG OLED65E6P OLED Ultra HDTV T. J. Norton color graph *Sound & Vision* v82 no2 p54 F/Mr 2017

LG Sees an Opening In the Smart Home B. Einhorn and J. Lee *Bloomberg Businessweek* no4498 p44 N 7 2016

LG Signature OLED65W7P OLED Ultra HDTV T. J. Norton color graph *Sound & Vision* v82 no5 p44 Je 2017

LG V20 hands-on: A 5.7-inch phablet for smartphone content creators J. PHILLIPS color *PCWorld* p104 O 2016

LG V20 Smartphone M. Fleischmann color *Sound & Vision* v82 no3 p52 Ap 2017

LG V30 hands-on: A 6-inch beast with more power and fewer gimmicks M. SIMON color *PCWorld* v35 no10 p74 O 2017

Not Your Father's HDTV T. J. Norton color *Sound & Vision* v82 no7 p42 S 2017

LGA Architectural Partners Ltd.

Fresh Start J. MINUTILLO color diag *Architectural Record* v205 no2 p86 F 2017

LGBT accommodations

ALONE ON A ROMANTIC COUPLES GETAWAY D. DURAN color *Advocate* no1090 p48 Ap 2017

LGBT activists

See also

Transgender activists

50 FOR 50: EVERY STATE HAS ITS OWN LGBT LEADERS AND HEROES. 50 CURRENT LGBT LEADERS SHARE THEIR STATE'S HEROES D. ARTAVIA, D. GUERRERO et al map *Advocate* no1091 p98 Je/Jl 2017

ASIAN AWAKENING D. ANDERSON-MINSHALL color *Advocate* no1090 p11 Ap 2017

EDITOR'S LETTER D. ANDERSON-MINSHALL bw color *Advocate* no1091 p8 Je/Jl 2017

FORBIDDEN LIVES M. GESSEN cartoon color *New Yorker* v93 no19 p22 Jl 3 2017

HALL OF FAME: THESE HEROES MADE THE LGBT RIGHTS MOVEMENT-- AND THE ADVOCATE ITSELF— WHAT IT IS TODAY bw color *Advocate* no1091 p52 Je/Jl 2017

LGBTQ ICON-O-METER color *Entertainment Weekly* no1473 p14 Jl 7 2017

THIS WASN'T HIS FIRST RODEO: LONE STAR STATE ACTIVISTS LIKE RAY HILL HAD A GREATER IMPACT THAN MANY KNOW J. ANDERSON-MINSHALL color *Advocate* no1091 p97 Je/Jl 2017

LGBT activists—Awards

HOLLYWOOD HONORS LGBTQ YOUTH ADVOCATES R. Kinane color *Entertainment Weekly* no1438 p20 N 4 2016

LGBT artists—Exhibitions

SAFE SPACE P. SCHJELDAHL color *New Yorker* v93 no31 p78 O 9 2017

LGBT athletes

THE BOYS' CLUB A. Barronian cartoon *Powder* v45 no4 p50 D 2016

LGBT bars

See also

Gay bars

LGBT bookstores

"The Library Saved My Life" J. BOOG color *Publishers Weekly* v264 no22 p29 My 29 2017

Welcoming Spaces A. GREEN color *Publishers Weekly* v264 no22 p23 My 29 2017

LGBT characters

GAY (SUPER) POWER J. PEEPLES *Advocate* no1088 p22 D 2016/Ja 2017

LGBT clergy

A church for the kids I. S. Villegas *Christian Century* v133 no22 p10 O 26 2016

LGBT communities

See also

Gay community

2016 YEAR IN REVIEW M. BREEN *Advocate* no1088 p32 D

2016/Ja 2017

EDITOR'S LETTER N. Rapold color *Film Comment* v52 no6 p4 N/D 2016

EVENTS OF THE YEAR *Advocate* no1088 p38 D 2016/Ja 2017

The Gratitude Meter Z. Donaldson bw color *O, The Oprah Magazine* p26 D 2016

NO CONGRESS? NO PROBLEM M. J. STERN *Advocate* no1088 p12 D 2016/Ja 2017

PRIDE OF PLACE D. PENER *Los Angeles Magazine* v62 no6 p80 Je 2017

STILL LOOKING M. HARRIS color *Film Comment* v52 no6 p66 N/D 2016

THERE GOES THE GAYBORHOOD: As DC's LGBTQ community has evolved, traditional gay areas have grown less vital. It's a welcome sign of progress--and also a bit sad D. Reed *Washingtonian Magazine* v53 no1 p47 O 2017

LGBT community centers

HATE IN THE AGE OF TRUMP: Are America's LGBT centers under attack? D. REYNOLDS color *Advocate* no1091 p19 Je/Jl 2017

LGBT couples

See also

Gay couples

LGBT-friendly businesses

LGBT-Inclusive Companies Are Better at 3 Big Things Sylvia Ann Hewlett and Kenji Yoshino *Harvard Business Review Digital Articles* p2 F 2 2016

Welcoming Spaces A. GREEN color *Publishers Weekly* v264 no22 p23 My 29 2017

LGBT homeless youth

TEEN, TRANS AND HOMELESS: ON THE STREETS OF NEW YORK WITH AMERICA'S MOST VULNERABLE POPULATION L. R. MURRAY color *Rolling Stone* no1297 p44 O 5 2017

LGBT identity

See also

Coming out (Sexual orientation)

Outing (Sexual orientation)

LGBT judges

COURT'S IN SESSION: THE COUNTRY'S FIRST TRANS-GENDER JUDGE WAS ALWAYS A RABBLE ROUSER J. ANDERSON-MINSHALL bw *Advocate* no1091 p96 Je/Jl 2017

LGBT literature

"The Library Saved My Life" J. BOOG color *Publishers Weekly* v264 no22 p29 My 29 2017

LGBT musicians

AN ICON REMEMBERED J. Goodman and K. O'Donnell color *Entertainment Weekly* no1448 p33 Ja 13 2017

LGBT organizations

ON A QUEST I. R. Björnsdottir *Iceland Review* v54 no6 p76 N/D 2016

LGBT people

See also

LGBT people in popular culture

LGBT people on television

Transgender people

10 THINGS WE'RE TALKING ABOUT T. A. Christian color *Essence* v48 no6 p79 O 2017

50 MOST INFLUENTIAL LGBT PEOPLE IN MEDIA *Advocate* no1093 p44 O/N 2017

ABOVE & BEYOND cartoon *New Yorker* v93 no18 p14 Je 26 2017

CAN I TOUCH YOUR HAIR? WHY DO YOU DRESS LIKE A BOY IF YOU LIKE GIRLS? S. KIRK *In These Times* v41 no10 p24 O 2017

COLORING OUTSIDE THE LINES J. Berlin cartoon *National Geographic* v231 no6 pC19 Je 2017

Know Thyself (And Try to Understand Everyone Else): Our 101 guide to gender identities and sexual orientations R. NEIRENE and J. ANDERSON-MINSHALL *Advocate* no1093 p17 O/N 2017

MAKING SMALL TALK: THE CASE FOR LGBT DIVERSITY AND INCLUSION *Vital Speeches of the Day* v82 no12 p384 D 2016

Your LGBTQ Pop Preview C. Agard, A. Bacle et al color *Entertainment Weekly* no1471 p44 Je 23 2017

LGBT people in mass media
50 MOST INFLUENTIAL LGBT PEOPLE IN MEDIA *Advocate* no1093 p44 O/N 2017

LGBT people in popular culture
DID HOLLYWOOD SABOTAGE MY MARRIAGE? Perhaps a lack of examples doomed me to fail in love T. E. GILCHRIST *Advocate* no1093 p16 O/N 2017
A GAY Old Timeline C. Brody, H. Goldblatt et al color diag *Entertainment Weekly* no1471 p32 Je 23 2017

LGBT people in the military
See also
Transgender military personnel

LGBT people on television
IT'S GO TIME [Cover story] L. Rice color *Entertainment Weekly* no1477 p20 Ag 11 2017
WHY AMERICA LOVES NEIL PATRICK HARRIS: THIS FORMER CHILD ACTOR IS AMONG OUR MOST BELOVED GAY ACTORS, BUT TO HIS KIDS HE'S JUST DAD S. ABADSIDIS and D. ANDERSON-MINSHALL color *Advocate* no1091 p85 Je/Jl 2017

LGBT people's sexual behavior
BLURRED LINES: CHEMSEX & CONSENT: It's time to talk about the elephant in the room Z. ZANE *Advocate* no1093 p58 O/N 2017

LGBT people—Crimes against
BEST of TIMES WORST of TIMES T. Heller and D. Schofield cartoon *Esquire* v166 no5 p138 D 2016/Ja 2017

LGBT people—History
See also
Transgender people—History
Hidden but not lost C. Burns *History Today* v67 no5 p8 My 2017

LGBT people—Social conditions—21st century
LETTER FROM KAKUMA J. KUSHNER color *Nation* v304 no6 p12 F 27 2017

LGBT people—Travel
ALONE ON A ROMANTIC COUPLES GETAWAY D. DURAN color *Advocate* no1090 p48 Ap 2017

LGBT people—United States
See also
Transgender people—United States
5 FOR FIGHTING: LEADERS AND ADVOCATE STAFF TELL US THE FIVE LGBT PEOPLE WHO INFLUENCED THEM THE MOST bw color *Advocate* no1091 p42 Je/Jl 2017
Nearly Half of LGBTs Over 50 Are Disabled And Other Alarming Facts color *Advocate* no1091 p26 Je/Jl 2017

LGBT people—United States—Social conditions
TIME TO PANIC M. GESSEN color *Advocate* no1089 p38 F/Mr 2017

LGBT politicians
50 FOR 50: EVERY STATE HAS ITS OWN LGBT LEADERS AND HEROES. 50 CURRENT LGBT LEADERS SHARE THEIR STATE'S HEROES D. ARTAVIA, D. GUERRERO et al map *Advocate* no1091 p98 Je/Jl 2017

LGBT pride celebrations
See also
Gay Pride Day
Jasper Pride's Tory supporter J. MARKUSOFF color *Maclean's* v130 no8 p15 S 2017
Pride & Moonlight DA color *Advocate* no1091 p117 Je/Jl 2017
VIVA PRIDE! Celebrate LGBT Life at World Pride in Gay Madrid J. ANDERSON-MINSHALL color *Advocate* no1091 p116 Je/Jl 2017

LGBT rights
See also
Gay rights
Transgender rights
HALL OF FAME: THESE HEROES MADE THE LGBT RIGHTS MOVEMENT-- AND THE ADVOCATE ITSELF--- WHAT IT IS TODAY bw color *Advocate* no1091 p52 Je/Jl 2017
Left, Right, Reverse I. Cost *Weekly Standard* v22 no33 p20 My 8 2017
Mennonite Pride J. NEUFELD cartoon *Walrus* v13 no9 p48 N 2016
THE QUIET CRUSADER A. Kroll color *Rolling Stone* no1291/1292 p38 Jl 13 2017
Survey: Americans accept contraception, divide over LGBT rights

L. Markoe *Christian Century* v133 no23 p18 N 9 2016

LGBT rights—Lawsuits & claims
Edith Windsor D. D'addario color *Time* v190 no12 p15 S 25 2017

LGBT students
10 THINGS WE'RE TALKING ABOUT T. A. Christian color *Essence* v48 no3 p71 Jl 2017

LGBT theater
ACTING OUT W. BROCK *Atlanta* v56 no12 p38 Ap 2017

LGBT travelers
GRACE AND FRANKIES SAN DIEGO: The artsy burg of La Jolla, California, deserves all the attention it gets D. ANDERSON-MINSHALL *Advocate* no1093 p52 O/N 2017

Lhenry-Yvon, I.
Observation of a large-scale anisotropy in the arrival directions of cosmic rays above 8×10^{18} eV *Science* v357 no6357 p1266 S 22 2017

L'HEUREUX, CATIE
Self-less Portrait img *New York* v49 no22 p65 O 31 2016

Li, Alexander H.
Distribution and clinical impact of functional variants in 50,726 whole-exome sequences from the DiscovEHR study chart graph *Science* v354 no6319 paaf6814-1 D 23 2016

Li, Bai, 701-762
THE LONG WAR L. Bai *MHQ: Quarterly Journal of Military History* v29 no4 p89 Summ 2017
OF SOLDIERS AND GENERALS color *MHQ: Quarterly Journal of Military History* v29 no4 p89 Summ 2017

Li, Bingzhi
Bug mapping and fitness testing of chemically synthesized chromosome X diag *Science* v355 no6329 p1048 Mr 10 2017
Deep functional analysis of synII, a 770-kilobase synthetic yeast chromosome diag *Science* v355 no6329 p1047 Mr 10 2017
Engineering the ribosomal DNA in a megabase synthetic chromosome diag *Science* v355 no6329 p1049 Mr 10 2017
"Perfect" designer chromosome V and behavior of a ring derivative diag *Science* v355 no6329 p1046 Mr 10 2017

Li, Bo
Neandertal and Denisovan DNA from Pleistocene sediments bw color *Science* v356 no6338 p605 My 12 2017
Satellite-based entanglement distribution over 1200 kilometers diag graph *Science* v356 no6343 p1140 Je 16 2017

Li, C.
Jupiter's interior and deep atmosphere: The initial pole-to-pole passes with the Juno spacecraft [Cover story] color graph *Science* v356 no6340 p821 My 26 2017

Li, Cai
Systemic pan-AMPK activator MK-8722 improves glucose homeostasis but induces cardiac hypertrophy graph *Science* v357 no6350 p507 Ag 4 2017

Li, Chao
Decarboxylative borylation color *Science* v356 no6342 p1045 Je 9 2017

Li, Charlene
Why No One Uses the Corporate Social Network *Harvard Business Review Digital Articles* p2 Ap 7 2015

LI, DAIJIANG
Combining Biodiversity Resurveys across Regions to Advance Global Change Research *BioScience* v67 no1 p73 Ja 2017

Li, Danielle
The applied value of public investments in biomedical research diag graph *Science* v356 no6333 p78 Ap 7 2017

Li, Da-Shuai
"Perfect" designer chromosome V and behavior of a ring derivative diag *Science* v355 no6329 p1046 Mr 10 2017

LI, DUOLAN
BAO WOW color *Bon Appetit* v61 no11 p118 N 2016

Li, Enbang
Methods for teaching traditional physics K. K. Shah *Physics Today* v69 no12 p12 D 2016

Li, F.
A human-driven decline in global burned area chart graph map *Science* v356 no6345 p1356 Je 30 2017

Li, Fei-Fei
Bug mapping and fitness testing of chemically synthesized chromosome X diag *Science* v355 no6329 p1048 Mr 10 2017
"Perfect" designer chromosome V and behavior of a ring deriva-

tive diag *Science* v355 no6329 p1046 Mr 10 2017

Li, Feng
Charge delivery goes the distance color *Science* v356 no6338 p582 My 12 2017

Li, Feng-Zhi
Satellite-based entanglement distribution over 1200 kilometers diag graph *Science* v356 no6343 p1140 Je 16 2017

Li, G.
Bismuthene on a SiC substrate: A candidate for a high-temperature quantum spin Hall material diag graph *Science* v357 no6348 p287 Jl 21 2017

Li, Guang-Bing
Satellite-based entanglement distribution over 1200 kilometers diag graph *Science* v356 no6343 p1140 Je 16 2017

Li, Haiyang
A paralogous decoy protects Phytophthora sojae apoplastic effector PsXEG1 from a host inhibitor bibl graph *Science* v355 no6326 p710 F 17 2017

Li, Heng
Single-cell whole-genome analyses by Linear Amplification via Transposon Insertion (LIANTI) graph *Science* v356 no6334 p189 Ap 14 2017

Li, Hui
BRINGING LEGENDS TO LIFE K. McLaughlin color *Science* v354 no6316 p1094 D 2 2016
A central neural circuit for itch sensation color graph *Science* v357 no6352 p695 Ag 18 2017
China Needs Help Having Babies bw *Bloomberg Businessweek* no4530 p15 Jl 17 2017
Control of muscle formation by the fusogenic micropeptide myomixer diag *Science* v356 no6335 p323 Ap 21 2017
Dynamic multinuclear sites formed by mobilized copper ions in NOx selective catalytic reduction bw color diag graph *Science* v357 no6354 p898 S 1 2017
Pharma's Worst Nightmare cartoon *Bloomberg Businessweek* no4508 p18 Ja 23 2017

Li, J.
Tough adhesives for diverse wet surfaces diag *Science* v357 no6349 p378 Jl 28 2017

Li, Jennifer S.
KATHLEEN RYAN color *Art in America* v105 no4 p118 Ap 2017
KISHIO SUGA color *Art in America* v105 no5 p135 My 2017
Los Angeles County Museum of Art color *Art in America* v105 no1 p89 Ja 2017
MADE IN LA *Art in America* v104 no9 p158 O 2016
NEIL RAITT color *Art in America* v104 no10 p159 N 2016
SAM DURANT color *Art in America* v105 no3 p136 Mr 2017

Li, Jiangyu
An organic-inorganic perovskite ferroelectric with large piezoelectric response graph *Science* v357 no6348 p306 Jl 21 2017

Li, Jin Billy
Deficiency of microRNA miR-34a expands cell fate potential in pluripotent stem cells diag *Science* v355 no6325 p596 F 10 2017

Li, Jun
A conserved NAD+ binding pocket that regulates protein-protein interactions during aging bibl graph *Science* v355 no6331 p1312 Mr 24 2017

LI, JUN LI
THE GIRLS NEXT DOOR color diag *Men's Health* v32 no9 p82 N 2017

Li, Junhao
Single-cell methylomes identify neuronal subtypes and regulatory elements in mammalian cortex diag *Science* v357 no6351 p600 Ag 11 2017

Li, L.
Observation of coherent elastic neutrino-nucleus scattering diag *Science* v357 no6356 p1123 S 15 2017

Li, Lili
miR-183 cluster scales mechanical pain sensitivity by regulating basal and neuropathic pain genes diag graph *Science* v356 no6343 p1168 Je 16 2017

Li, Ling
Controlled growth and form of precipitating microsculptures bw color diag graph *Science* v355 no6332 p1395 Mr 31 2017

Li, Lu
Stem cell divisions, somatic mutations, cancer etiology, and cancer prevention bibl chart diag graph *Science* v355 no6331 p1330 Mr 24 2017

Li, Mei
Structure and assembly mechanism of plant C2S2M2-type PSII-LHCII supercomplex color *Science* v357 no6353 p815 Ag 25 2017

Li, Michael
The 3 Things That Make Technical Training Worthwhile *Harvard Business Review Digital Articles* p2 Mr 18 2016
The Best Data Scientists Know How to Tell Stories *Harvard Business Review Digital Articles* p2 O 13 2015
Better Questions to Ask Your Data Scientists *Harvard Business Review Digital Articles* p2 N 15 2016
The Promise and Challenge of Big Data for Pharma *Harvard Business Review Digital Articles* p2 N 29 2016
Retaining Your Data Scientists *Harvard Business Review Digital Articles* p2 N 20 2014
The Two Questions You Need to Ask Your Data Analysts *Harvard Business Review Digital Articles* p2 O 27 2015
What Kind of Data Scientist Do You Need? *Harvard Business Review Digital Articles* p2 F 1 2016

Li, Ming
Satellite-based entanglement distribution over 1200 kilometers diag graph *Science* v356 no6343 p1140 Je 16 2017

Li, Ming O.
Aerobic glycolysis promotes T helper 1 cell differentiation through an epigenetic mechanism bibl graph *Science* v354 no6311 p481 O 28 2016

Li, Mo
Integration of CpG-free DNA induces de novo methylation of CpG islands in pluripotent stem cells diag *Science* v356 no6337 p503 My 5 2017

Li, Mufan
Three-dimensional holey-graphene/niobia composite architectures for ultrahigh-rate energy storage color diag graph *Science* v356 no6338 p599 My 12 2017

Li, Na
Coseismic rupturing stopped by Aso volcano during the 2016 Mw 7.1 Kumamoto earthquake, Japan bibl color graph *Science* v354 no6314 p869 N 18 2016
Harvesting electrical energy from carbon nanotube yarn twist diag graph *Science* v357 no6353 p773 Ag 25 2017

Li, Peicheng
Efficient and stable solution-processed planar perovskite solar cells via contact passivation bibl graph *Science* v355 no6326 p722 F 17 2017

Li, Peng
Bottom-up construction of a superstructure in a porous uranium-organic crystal color graph *Science* v356 no6338 p624 My 12 2017

Li, Peng-Fei
An organic-inorganic perovskite ferroelectric with large piezoelectric response graph *Science* v357 no6348 p306 Jl 21 2017

Li, Pengpeng
Optical control of cell signaling by single-chain photoswitchable kinases bibl diag *Science* v355 no6327 p836 F 24 2017

Li, Qun
Epigenetic regulation of antagonistic receptors confers rice blast resistance with yield balance bibl diag *Science* v355 no6328 p962 Mr 3 2017

Li, Rosa
Behavior management color *Science* v356 no6335 p244 Ap 21 2017
Time Warp *Natural History* v124 no10 p7 N 2016

Li, Sheng
Structural basis of the day-night transition in a bacterial circadian clock bibl diag *Science* v355 no6330 p1174 Mr 17 2017

Li, Shirley
The 100 color *Entertainment Weekly* no1448 p41 Ja 13 2017
THE 25 BEST MOVIES AND TV SHOWS TO STREAM RIGHT NOW color *Entertainment Weekly* no1443 p34 D 9 2016
THE 25 MOST PATRIOTIC MOVIES OF ALL TIME color *Entertainment Weekly* no1472 p30 Je 30 2017
5 MORE SHOWS YOU NEED TO SEE color *Entertainment Weekly* no1435 p24 O 14 2016
616 PUBLiC ENEMiES DEFENDERS [Cover story] color *Enter-*

tainment Weekly no1449 p26 Ja 20 2017

ALEXANDRA THE GREAT color *Entertainment Weekly* no1474/1475 p78 Jl 21-28 2017

AN ALIEN ENCOUNTER WITH DOUG JONES color *Entertainment Weekly* no1476 p27 Ag 4 2017

ALL THE MONEY IN THE WORLD color *Entertainment Weekly* no1478 / 1479 p75 Ag 18-25 2017

American Housewife *Entertainment Weekly* no1482/1483 p79 S 22 2017

Arrow *Entertainment Weekly* no1482/1483 p84 S 22 2017

BAYWATCH color *Entertainment Weekly* no1463/1464 p30 Ap/ My 2017

BEST SUPPORTING ACTOR color diag *Entertainment Weekly* no1451/1452 p50 F 3-10 2017

Better Things color *Entertainment Weekly* no1482/1483 p91 S 22 2017

The Blacklist color *Entertainment Weekly* no1482/1483 p74 S 22 2017

BOYZ N THE HOOD color *Entertainment Weekly* no1460/1461 p76 Ap 7-17 2017

Breaking Big EMMA DUMONT color *Entertainment Weekly* no1482/1483 p51 S 22 2017

Breaking the Other Color Line color *Entertainment Weekly* no1439 p10 N 11 2016

Broad City color *Entertainment Weekly* no1482/1483 p79 S 22 2017

Chicago Fire *Entertainment Weekly* no1482/1483 p91 S 22 2017

Chicago P.D *Entertainment Weekly* no1482/1483 p79 S 22 2017

COLD WAR CONFIDENTIAL color *Entertainment Weekly* no1457/1458 p36 Mr 17 2017

Criminal Minds color *Entertainment Weekly* no1482/1483 p79 S 22 2017

CRITICS' CHOICE AWARDS NOMINATIONS color *Entertainment Weekly* no1441 p13 N 25 2016

DEMI MOORE OF Empire color *Entertainment Weekly* no1482/1483 p78 S 22 2017

Designated Survivor color *Entertainment Weekly* no1482/1483 p74 S 22 2017

The Dirty Dancing Drinking Game color *Entertainment Weekly* no1467 p51 My 26 2017

Dynasty color *Entertainment Weekly* no1482/1483 p76 S 22 2017

The Exorcist color *Entertainment Weekly* no1482/1483 p92 S 22 2017

THE FOREIGNER color *Entertainment Weekly* no1478 / 1479 p53 Ag 18-25 2017

FRIENDS FROM COLLEGE color *Entertainment Weekly* no1468/1469 p40 Je 2-9 2017

The Gifted color *Entertainment Weekly* no1482/1483 p50 S 22 2017

The Goldbergs color *Entertainment Weekly* no1482/1483 p74 S 22 2017

The Good Place color *Entertainment Weekly* no1482/1483 p86 S 22 2017

Gotham *Entertainment Weekly* no1482/1483 p84 S 22 2017

THE GREATEST DISNEY SONGS OF ALL TIME color *Entertainment Weekly* no1454/1455 p36 F 24 2017

Great News color *Entertainment Weekly* no1482/1483 p88 S 22 2017

Grey's Anatomy color diag *Entertainment Weekly* no1482/1483 p89 S 22 2017

GRIFFIN NEWMAN color *Entertainment Weekly* no1468/1469 p39 Je 2-9 2017

High-Profile Guest Stars color *Entertainment Weekly* no1435 p47 O 14 2016

Hot Date *Entertainment Weekly* no1482/1483 p74 S 22 2017

How to Get Away With Murder *Entertainment Weekly* no1482/1483 p91 S 22 2017

The Invisible Minority *Entertainment Weekly* no1439 p11 N 11 2016

JACOB TREMBLAY 2.0? color *Entertainment Weekly* no1442 p10 D 2 2016 Rebellious Special Issue

KEEGAN-MICHAEL KEY'S NEW COURSE color *Entertainment Weekly* no1474/1475 p104 Jl 21-28 2017

Law & Order: Special Victims Unit *Entertainment Weekly* no1482/1483 p75 S 22 2017

Life in Pieces *Entertainment Weekly* no1482/1483 p88 S 22 2017

MARVELOUS MAHERSHALA color *Entertainment Weekly* no1434 p30 O 7 2016

Marvel's The Punisher color *Entertainment Weekly* no1482/1483 p106 S 22 2017

Modern Family *Entertainment Weekly* no1482/1483 p75 S 22 2017

Mom color *Entertainment Weekly* no1482/1483 p85 S 22 2017

THE MOST CONTROVERSIAL TV SHOW EVER color *Entertainment Weekly* no1460/1461 p80 Ap 7-17 2017

THE MOUNTAIN BETWEEN US color *Entertainment Weekly* no1478 / 1479 p56 Ag 18-25 2017

Mr. Robot color *Entertainment Weekly* no1482/1483 p77 S 22 2017

NEW YORK COMIC CON'S GREATEST HITS color *Entertainment Weekly* no1436/1437 p18 O 21 2016

NO. 21 RAPHAEL OF TEENAGE MUTANT NINJA TURTLES color *Entertainment Weekly* no1436/1437 p60 O 21 2016

NO. 40 KITTY PRYDE color *Entertainment Weekly* no1436/1437 p74 O 21 2016

THE ORIGINAL color *Entertainment Weekly* no1474/1475 p76 Jl 21-28 2017

The Orville *Entertainment Weekly* no1482/1483 p85 S 22 2017

POWER RANGERS VILLAIN GETS MELTY MAKEOVER color *Entertainment Weekly* no1457/1458 p74 Mr 17 2017

THE PROS OF CON color *Entertainment Weekly* no1476 p32 Ag 4 2017

Riverdale color *Entertainment Weekly* no1482/1483 p68 S 22 2017

RIZ AHMED: THE NEW BOY ON GIRLS color *Entertainment Weekly* no1453 p52 F 17 2017

Scandal *Entertainment Weekly* no1482/1483 p88 S 22 2017

SEAL Team color *Entertainment Weekly* no1482/1483 p76 S 22 2017

The Shannara Chronicles *Entertainment Weekly* no1482/1483 p79 S 22 2017

Smooth Criminal color *Entertainment Weekly* no1440 p50 N 18 2016

Speechless color *Entertainment Weekly* no1482/1483 p75 S 22 2017

Star color *Entertainment Weekly* no1482/1483 p76 S 22 2017

Streaming color *Entertainment Weekly* no1442 p46 D 2 2016 Rebellious Special Issue

Streaming color *Entertainment Weekly* no1451/1452 p94 F 3-10 2017

Streaming color *Entertainment Weekly* no1470 p44 Je 16 2017

Streaming color *Entertainment Weekly* no1477 p44 Ag 11 2017

Streaming Jr color *Entertainment Weekly* no1436/1437 p88 O 21 2016

Supernatural color *Entertainment Weekly* no1482/1483 p84 S 22 2017

Superstore color *Entertainment Weekly* no1482/1483 p84 S 22 2017

Survivor: Heroes vs. Healers vs. Hustlers *Entertainment Weekly* no1482/1483 p75 S 22 2017

S.W.A.T color *Entertainment Weekly* no1482/1483 p90 S 22 2017

THINGS ARE LOOKING UP... SIDE DOWN [Cover story] color *Entertainment Weekly* no1485 p16 O 6 2017

THE TICK color *Entertainment Weekly* no1468/1469 p38 Je 2-9 2017

TORI THE DOG color *Entertainment Weekly* no1454/1455 p88 F 24 2017

TV chart color *Entertainment Weekly* no1444/1445 p66 D 16 2016

A Very Timeless Script color *Entertainment Weekly* no1436/1437 p92 O 21 2016

What's the Most Bingeworthy Show? color *Entertainment Weekly* no1443 p21 D 9 2016

What to Watch color *Entertainment Weekly* no1443 p56 D 9 2016

What to Watch color *Entertainment Weekly* no1459 p56 Mr 31 2017

What to Watch color *Entertainment Weekly* no1463/1464 p99 Ap/ My 2017

What to Watch color *Entertainment Weekly* no1478 / 1479 p97 Ag 18-25 2017

Will & Grace color *Entertainment Weekly* no1482/1483 p80 S 22 2017

WONDER WHEEL color *Entertainment Weekly* no1478 / 1479

p76 Ag 18-25 2017

YOU'RE NOT FROM AROUND HERE, ARE YOU? color *Entertainment Weekly* no1440 p49 N 18 2016

Your Sunshiny, Stupendous, Seriously Spectacular SUMMER BUCKET LIST color *Entertainment Weekly* no1470 p32 Je 16 2017

Li, Shuang-Lin

Satellite-based entanglement distribution over 1200 kilometers diag graph *Science* v356 no6343 p1140 Je 16 2017

Li, Shuzhao

mTOR regulates metabolic adaptation of APCs in the lung and controls the outcome of allergic inflammation graph *Science* v357 no6355 p1014 S 8 2017

Li, Sichi

Dynamic multinuclear sites formed by mobilized copper ions in NOx selective catalytic reduction bw color diag graph *Science* v357 no6354 p898 S 1 2017

Li, Tai-De

Polymeric peptide pigments with sequence-encoded properties color graph *Science* v356 no6342 p1064 Je 9 2017

Li, Tao

Low-temperature activation of methane on the IrO2(110) surface bw diag graph *Science* v356 no6335 p299 Ap 21 2017

Li, Tianyi

Engineering the ribosomal DNA in a megabase synthetic chromosome diag *Science* v355 no6329 p1049 Mr 10 2017

Li, Ting

"Perfect" designer chromosome V and behavior of a ring derivative diag *Science* v355 no6329 p1046 Mr 10 2017

Li, W.

Femtosecond electron-phonon lock-in by photoemission and x-ray free-electron laser chart diag *Science* v357 no6346 p71 Jl 7 2017

Li, Wei

A cargo-sorting DNA robot color *Science* v357 no6356 p1112 S 15 2017

Hydrogenation of fluoroarenes: Direct access to all-cis-(multi)fluorinated cycloalkanes diag *Science* v357 no6354 p908 S 1 2017

Li, Weibo

Single-cell RNA-seq reveals new types of human blood dendritic cells, monocytes, and progenitors color *Science* v356 no6335 p283 Ap 21 2017

Li, Weizhen

Atomic-layered Au clusters on α-MoC as catalysts for the low-temperature water-gas shift reaction chart diag graph *Science* v357 no6349 p389 Jl 28 2017

LI, WINNIE M.

A Life-Changing Trauma color *Publishers Weekly* v264 no28 p64 Jl 10 2017

Li, Xia

Bug mapping and fitness testing of chemically synthesized chromosome X diag *Science* v355 no6329 p1048 Mr 10 2017

"Perfect" designer chromosome V and behavior of a ring derivative diag *Science* v355 no6329 p1046 Mr 10 2017

Li, Xue

Neonatal acquisition of Clostridia species protects against colonization by bacterial pathogens diag *Science* v356 no6335 p315 Ap 21 2017

Li, Xue-Nan

"Perfect" designer chromosome V and behavior of a ring derivative diag *Science* v355 no6329 p1046 Mr 10 2017

Li, Y.

Femtosecond electron-phonon lock-in by photoemission and x-ray free-electron laser chart diag *Science* v357 no6346 p71 Jl 7 2017

Li, Ying

Systemic pan-AMPK activator MK-8722 improves glucose homeostasis but induces cardiac hypertrophy graph *Science* v357 no6350 p507 Ag 4 2017

Li, Yue

Photonic doping of epsilon-near-zero media bibl diag *Science* v355 no6329 p1058 Mr 10 2017

Li, Yu-Huai

Satellite-based entanglement distribution over 1200 kilometers diag graph *Science* v356 no6343 p1140 Je 16 2017

Li, Yun

Paneth cells secrete lysozyme via secretory autophagy during bacterial infection of the intestine color diag *Science* v357 no6355 p1047 S 8 2017

Why Trump Is Making Bond Markets Nervous *Bloomberg Businessweek* no4500 p39 N 21 2016

Li, Yun Rose

Regeneration of fat cells from myofibroblasts during wound healing bibl color graph *Science* v355 no6326 p748 F 17 2017

Li, Zhangqiang

Structure of a eukaryotic voltage-gated sodium channel at near-atomic resolution diag graph *Science* v355 no6328 p924 Mr 3 2017

Li, Zhan-Yang

Late Pleistocene archaic human crania from Xuchang, China bibl color diag graph *Science* v355 no6328 p969 Mr 3 2017

Li, Zhe

Reconfiguration of DNA molecular arrays driven by information relay diag *Science* v357 no6349 p371 Jl 28 2017

Li, Zhen

Control of species-dependent cortico-motoneuronal connections underlying manual dexterity diag graph *Science* v357 no6349 p400 Jl 28 2017

Li, Zhuo

Control of species-dependent cortico-motoneuronal connections underlying manual dexterity diag graph *Science* v357 no6349 p400 Jl 28 2017

Li-Bo Mao

Synthetic nacre by predesigned matrix-directed mineralization bibl bw diag graph *Science* v354 no6308 p107 O 7 2016

Li Di

Radio telescope gets no-fly zone color *Science* v357 no6353 p736 Ag 25 2017

Li Ma

What Chinese Companies Want from International Deals *Harvard Business Review Digital Articles* p2 F 12 2015

Li Shuai

Formaldehyde stabilization facilitates lignin monomer production during biomass depolymerization bibl diag graph *Science* v354 no6310 p329 O 21 2016

LI ZHANG

Conserving the World's Megafauna and Biodiversity: The Fierce Urgency of Now *BioScience* v67 no3 p197 Mr 2017

Saving the World's Terrestrial Megafauna color *BioScience* v66 no10 p807 O 1 2016

Liabilities (Accounting)

Rising Pension Liabilities K. Roth *Parks & Recreation* v52 no2 p12 F 2017

Towering Debts M. SWARTZ *Texas Monthly* v45 no2 p20 F 2017

Liability for mountaineering accidents

Goodbye to Unbelayvable K. CORRIGAN *Climbing* no354 p17 Jl 2017

Liachko, Ivan

Evolution of protein phosphorylation across 18 fungal species bibl graph *Science* v354 no6309 p229 O 14 2016

Lian, Biao

Chiral Majorana fermion modes in a quantum anomalous Hall insulator–superconductor structure diag *Science* v357 no6348 p294 Jl 21 2017

Lian, Zhong

Palladium-catalyzed carbon-sulfur or carbon-phosphorus bond metathesis by reversible arylation diag *Science* v356 no6342 p1059 Je 9 2017

Lianfeng Gu

Photoactivation and inactivation of Arabidopsis cryptochrome 2 bibl graph *Science* v354 no6310 p343 O 21 2016

Liang, Cunren

Complex multifault rupture during the 2016 Mw 7.8 Kaikōura earthquake, New Zealand color map *Science* v356 no6334 p154 Ap 14 2017

Liang, Hexing

History of winning remodels thalamo-PFC circuit to reinforce social dominance color *Science* v357 no6347 p162 Jl 14 2017

Liang, Jingjing

Forest value: More than commercial C. B. Barrett, Mo Zhou et al *Science* v354 no6319 p1541 D 23 2016

Liang, Junfei

Three-dimensional holey-graphene/niobia composite architectures for ultrahigh-rate energy storage color diag graph *Science* v356 no6338 p599 My 12 2017

Liang, Qiren

An adipo-biliary-uridine axis that regulates energy homeostasis diag *Science* v355 no6330 p1173 Mr 17 2017

Liang, Sicheng, 1901-1972

The Lovers of Shanxi T. PERROTTET *Smithsonian* v47 no9 p110 Ja/F 2017

Liang, Wendy

Exploring genetic suppression interactions on a global scale diag *Science* v354 no6312 p599 N 4 2016

Liang, Zhu

Low-temperature activation of methane on the IrO2(110) surface bw diag graph *Science* v356 no6335 p299 Ap 21 2017

Liang Song

A transcription factor hierarchy defines an environmental stress response network diag *Science* v354 no6312 p598 N 4 2016

Liang Wu

Quantized Faraday and Kerr rotation and axion electrodynamics of a 3D topological insulator bibl graph *Science* v354 no6316 p1124 D 2 2016

Liang Yang

Photoactivation and inactivation of Arabidopsis cryptochrome 2 bibl graph *Science* v354 no6310 p343 O 21 2016

Liang Zhang

Ultrafine jagged platinum nanowires enable ultrahigh mass activity for the oxygen reduction reaction bibl chart graph *Science* v354 no6318 p1414 D 16 2016

Liang Zong

Urgent need for implementation of precision medicine in gastric cancer in China bibl chart *Science* v354 no6319 p39 D 23 2016

Lianhai Zhang

Urgent need for implementation of precision medicine in gastric cancer in China bibl chart *Science* v354 no6319 p39 D 23 2016

Liantao Jia

A Silurian maxillate placoderm illuminates jaw evolution bibl color *Science* v354 no6310 p334 O 21 2016

Liao, Hsin-Kai

Integration of CpG-free DNA induces de novo methylation of CpG islands in pluripotent stem cells diag *Science* v356 no6337 p503 My 5 2017

Liao, Nick

THE RANDY NEWMAN SONGBOOK bw *U.S. Catholic* v82 no6 p40 Je 2017

Liao, Pei-Qin

Controlling guest conformation for efficient purification of butadiene bw diag *Science* v356 no6343 p1193 Je 16 2017

LIAO, SHARON

2 weeks is all it takes to feel an energy boost after upping your intake of FRUITS & VEGGIES color *Better Homes & Gardens* v95 no6 p150 Je 2017

4 WAYS TO STOP THE SNEEZING color *Better Homes & Gardens* v95 no6 p160 Je 2017

better color *Better Homes & Gardens* v95 no2 p123 F 2016

better color *Better Homes & Gardens* v95 no3 p134 Mr 2017

better color *Better Homes & Gardens* v95 no9 p142 S 2017

IT'S NATIONAL ICE CREAM DAY color *Better Homes & Gardens* v95 no7 p158 Jl 2017

NATIONAL WATERMELON DAY color *Better Homes & Gardens* v95 no8 p167 Ag 2017

TUMMY TROUBLE TOOLBOX *Better Homes & Gardens* v94 no12 p144 D 2016

WHAT'S IN YOUR BASKET? color *Better Homes & Gardens* v95 no4 p146 Ap 2017

Liao, Sheng-Kai

Satellite-based entanglement distribution over 1200 kilometers diag graph *Science* v356 no6343 p1140 Je 16 2017

Liao, Wei-Qiang

An organic-inorganic perovskite ferroelectric with large piezoelectric response graph *Science* v357 no6348 p306 Jl 21 2017

Liau, Y-Sing

Philippine Leader Scares Off Investors color *Bloomberg Businessweek* no4493 p23 O 3 2016

Liaudet, Nicolas

Three-dimensional Ca2+ imaging advances understanding of as-

trocyte biology diag *Science* v356 no6339 p715 My 19 2017

Libaire, Jardine

12. Read White Fur *New York* v50 no12 p114 Je 12 2017

LIBBY, BRIAN

Eileen Gray: For many years a forgotten name, today Eileen Gray's designs are more popular than ever *Treasures* v6 no6 p16 Je/Jl 2017

Eva Zeisel color *Treasures* v5 no5 p19 Ap/My 2016

Gio Ponti *Treasures* v6 no5 p16 Ap/My 2017

Jean Prouvé *Treasures* v6 no2 p18 O/N 2016

MAKING HIS MARK color *Architectural Digest* v74 no7 p80 Jl 2017

Modern Traditions *Treasures* v6 no4 p22 F/Mr 2017

Peter Bristol color *Architectural Digest* v74 no10 p112 O 1 2017

Underrated Icon: Jens Quistgaard *Treasures* v6 no3 p22 D 2016/Ja 2017

Libby, Stephen B.

Abraham Szöke *Physics Today* v70 no10 p76 O 2017

Libecap, Gary D.

Time to Count the Costs--And Adapt: Environmental activists must quit playing politics and begin to practice one of the fundamental disciplines of good governance: weighing benefits against costs *Hoover Digest: Research & Opinion on Public Policy* no2 p127 Spr 2017

Li-Beisson, Yonghua

An algal photoenzyme converts fatty acids to hydrocarbons color graph *Science* v357 no6354 p903 S 1 2017

Libel & slander

See also

Hate speech

Right of privacy

Libel & slander—United States

"ADORE ME, MEDIA SCUM, OR ELSE!" G. TRUDEAU *Nation* v304 no9 p30 Mr 20 2017

Libenson, Terri

Invisible Emmie *Publishers Weekly* v264 no10 p61 Mr 6 2017

Liberal, Iñigo

Photonic doping of epsilon-near-zero media bibl diag *Science* v355 no6329 p1058 Mr 10 2017

Liberal Party in British Columbia

A Speaker on mute B. HUTCHINSON color *Maclean's* v130 no10 p12 N 2017

Liberal Party of Canada

Behind the Big Red Machine A. KINGSTON color *Maclean's* v130 no10 p24 N 2017

CHILLY TIMES AHEAD FOR THE LIBERALS E. SOLOMON color *Maclean's* v129 no40 p12 O 10 2016

MOST KNOWLEDGEABLE S. PROUDFOOT color *Maclean's* v129 no47 p22 N 28 2016

Reforming the reformers J. GEDDES color *Maclean's* v129 no42 p18 O 24 2016

Still-present dangers M. FRISCOLANTI color *Maclean's* v129 no42 p22 O 24 2016

Liberalism

See also

New left (Politics)

Is Publishing's Liberal Bias a Liability? R. Deahl color *Publishers Weekly* v264 no15 p8 Ap 10 2017

Is the Liberal Order in Peril? A. APPLEBAUM and M. MATTHIJS color graph *Foreign Affairs* v96 no3 p178 My/Je 2017

Liberalism in Retreat R. Niblett color *Foreign Affairs* v96 no1 p17 Ja/F 2017

Liberalism is founded on the belief that we should tolerate one another's error A. Kirsch *New York Times Book Review* p27 O 1 2017

The Old New Left C. R. Kesler *Claremont Review of Books* v17 no3 p32 Summ 2017

Liberalism—Canada

CONFESSIONS OF A SELF-LOATHING TORY S. GILMORE color *Maclean's* v130 no4 p32 My 2017

Liberalism—Europe

Liberal Democracy Is Eroding Right In Europe's Backyard I. Bremmer *Time* v190 no6 p16 Ag 7 2017

Shape-Shifting Illiberalism in East-Central Europe H. CASE *Current History* v116 no788 p112 Mr 2017

Liberalism—European Union countries

Liberty—Philosophy
Becoming America P. Gorski *Christian Century* v134 no5 p28 Mr 1 2017

Liberty—Religious aspects—Christianity
From the publisher P. W. Marty *Christian Century* v134 no5 p3 Mr 1 2017

Liberty—Social aspects
France's Next Revolution? color *Foreign Affairs* v95 no6 p2 N/D 2016
PROTEST IS A PATRIOTIC DUTY *Saturday Evening Post* v289 no3 p96 My/Je 2017

Liberty State Park (Jersey City, N.J.)
Let It Grow P. Saha *Audubon* v119 no3 p13 Fall 2017

Libido
SYNC UP YOUR SEX DRIVES [Cover story] J. Hergenrader *Women's Health* v14 no1 p150 Ja/F 2017

Libido—Research
This Just In J. Zorthian *Time* v189 no9 p23 Mr 13 2017

Libman, Leslie
Britney Ever After A. D'arminio color *TV Guide* v65 no7 p38 F 13 2017

Librado, Pablo
Ancient genomic changes associated with domestication of the horse color diag *Science* v356 no6336 p442 Ap 28 2017

Librarians
See also
Women librarians
CARLA HAYDEN G. Weber *Washingtonian Magazine* v52 no3 p39 D 2016
HIVE MIND B. COLEMAN *Cincinnati Magazine* p20 Je 2017
THE LIBRARY IS NOT DEAD I. Collins *Saturday Evening Post* v289 no1 p10 Ja/F 2017

Librarians, The (TV program)
The Librarians E. Aslanian *TV Guide* v64 no46 p37 N 7 2016

Librarians—Congresses
Librarians, Check This Out A. R. ALBANESE color *Publishers Weekly* v264 no20 p(Sp)28 My 15 2017

Librarians—Political activity
Librarians Take Capitol Hill A. Albanese color *Publishers Weekly* v264 no19 p4 My 8 2017

Librarians—Services for
Carla Hayden Thinks Libraries Are a Key to Freedom A. M. Cox *New York Times Magazine* p66 Ja 22 2017

Librarians—United States
How to Maximize ALA Midwinter S. MAUGHAN color *Publishers Weekly* v263 no52 p62 D 19 2016
A Time to Lead B. Kenney *Publishers Weekly* v264 no3 p21 Ja 16 2017

Libraries
See also
Data libraries
THE BUNGALOW BOOK LADY D. RUTH WILSON color *New Orleans Magazine* v51 no2 p34 D 2016
How Do You CHOOSE? color *Literacy Today (2411-7862)* v34 no6 p51 My/Je 2017
Overdue Notice R. J. Smith *Cincinnati Magazine* v50 no5 p68 F 2017
Story Stroll S. Myrick *Parks & Recreation* v52 no10 p64 O 2017

Libraries & state—United States
For Librarians, 2017 Is Off To a Rough Start A. Albanese color *Publishers Weekly* v264 no5 p2 Ja 30 2017

Libraries—Congresses
STORY TIME M. Meltzer cartoon *New Yorker* v92 no38 p33 N 21 2016

Libraries—France
Look Up B. BERGDOLL color *Architectural Digest* v74 no4 p178 Ap 2017

Libraries—United States
ALA Annual 2017: Picks for Advocacy Panels *Publishers Weekly* v264 no25 p72 Je 19 2017
THE TOP 10 LIBRARY STORIES OF 2016 A. RICHARD ALBANESE color *Publishers Weekly* v263 no52 p34 D 19 2016

Libraries—Washington (D.C.)
Churchill in Washington T. BROMUND color *Weekly Standard* v22 no10 p12 N 14 2016

Library buildings—Design & construction

Boston Public Library D. S. Glenn *Architectural Record* v205 no4 p180 Ap 2017
Look Up B. BERGDOLL color *Architectural Digest* v74 no4 p178 Ap 2017
Open Book S. STEPHENS *Architectural Record* v204 no10 p102 O 2016
Ramped Up J. MINUTILLO color diag *Architectural Record* v205 no3 p100 Mr 2017
The X Factor J. MINUTILLO color diag *Architectural Record* v205 no3 p112 Mr 2017

Library directors
New Director Named For Eisenhower Library *Prologue* v49 no2 p68 Summ 2017

Library exhibits
LEAVE USA STORY: We are in challenging times! We need your help S. DeBoer *South Dakota Magazine* p6 S/O 2017 Supplement
WELCOME... Festival of Books Visitors C. Turbiville *South Dakota Magazine* p4 S/O 2017 Supplement

Library legislation
Library Demand for Graphic Novels Keeps Growing H. MACDONALD color *Publishers Weekly* v264 no20 p19 My 15 2017

Library materials
See also
Books
Periodicals
Serial publications
Bookends A. Kirsch and A. Holmes *New York Times Book Review* p31 O 2 2016

Library of Congress
A Century Later, The Great War Lives On *USA Today Magazine* v145 no2863 p16 Ap 2017
Information Bias in Library Catalogs T. BINGA *Skeptical Inquirer* v41 no3 p9 My/Je 2017
Lie on Sigmund Freud's Couch ... Online *USA Today Magazine* v146 no2867 p11 Ag 2017
Remember the Card Catalogue? C. HAYDEN color *Publishers Weekly* v264 no18 p64 My 1 2017

Library of Congress. Copyright Office
Copyright Reform Is Never Happening A. R. Albanese *Publishers Weekly* v264 no16 p21 Ap 17 2017

Library of Congress—Exhibitions
Rediscovering Our Past *USA Today Magazine* v146 no2868 p76 S 2017

Library planning
How Employees Shaped Strategy at the New York Public Library B. A. Strong and M. L. Kennedy *Harvard Business Review Digital Articles* p2 D 5 2016

Library science
Remember the Card Catalogue? C. HAYDEN color *Publishers Weekly* v264 no18 p64 My 1 2017

Library special collections
A gem of a discovery B. Carver Wees color *Magazine Antiques* v183 no6 p48 N/D 2016

Library users—Attitudes
You Found What? C. FULLER *Publishers Weekly* v264 no11 p88 Mr 13 2017

Library users—Research
You Found What? C. FULLER *Publishers Weekly* v264 no11 p88 Mr 13 2017

Libresco, Leah
INSIDE THE CHANGING U.S. CATHOLIC CHURCH color diag *America* v216 no5 p12 Mr 6 2017
THE LARGEST PARISH IN AMERICA [Cover story] color *America* v216 no10 p18 My 1 2017

Libya—Economic conditions
LIBYA VS GOLDMAN M. CAMPBELL and K. CHELLEL cartoon *Bloomberg Businessweek* no4493 p66 O 3 2016

Libya—Foreign relations—2011-
LIBYA VS GOLDMAN M. CAMPBELL and K. CHELLEL cartoon *Bloomberg Businessweek* no4493 p66 O 3 2016

LICATA, ANNIE
Daveed Diggs' Dad-Chic color *Rolling Stone* no1273 p20 N 3 2016

Licata, Anthony
84 Great Days color *Field & Stream* v121 no6 p8 N 2016

WHERE MONSTERS ROAR color *Field & Stream* v121 no7 p62 D 2016/Ja 2017

Lice control

How to Get Rid of Lice M. Wollan *New York Times Magazine* p19 My 14 2017

License agreements

Patent pools for CRISPR technology L. Horn, J. L. Contreras et al bibl color *Science* v355 no6331 p1274 Mr 24 2017

Licensed products

Tracking Tie-in Trends K. Raugust color *Publishers Weekly* v264 no16 p19 Ap 17 2017

Licenses

See also
    License agreements
    Professional licenses
8 STEPS TO A SMOOTH BUILD *Timber Home Living* p37 2017 Annual Buyers
A Baby Dies in Virginia E. BOEHM cartoon *Reason* v48 no11 p46 Ap 2017
License for three-parent babies *Science* v355 no6331 p1244 Mr 24 2017

Licenses—Congresses

Licensing Expo 2017 Highlights Synergies Between Books and Tie-in Products K. Raugust color *Publishers Weekly* v264 no24 p20 Je 12 2017

Licenses—Lawsuits & claims

Liberty and License color *Weekly Standard* v22 no23 p3 F 20 2017

Lice—Physiology

Revenge of the Super Lice K. Weintraub color *Scientific American* v316 no6 p24 Je 2017

Lice—Treatment

NIT-PICKING IN ANCIENT CHILE A. R. Williams color *National Geographic* v231 no3 p20 Mr 2017

Lichen conservation

A Lift for Lichens R. Drouin color *Scientific American* v316 no4 p22 Ap 2017

Lichens

The Meaning of Lichen E. Gies color *Scientific American* v316 no6 p52 Je 2017
SENTINELS OF FOREST HEALTH [Cover story] A. McDermott color graph map *Science News* v190 no11 p20 N 26 2016
Triple Symbiosis N. Wilson *Natural History* v124 no10 p7 N 2016

LICHTBLAU, JULIA

Smart Girls *American Scholar* v86 no1 p6 Wint 2017

LICHTENHELD, TOM

Gone Guppy: In four imaginative new picture books, cherished pets are nowhere to be found *New York Times Book Review* p14 Je 18 2017

Lichtenstein, Alice H.

ASK TUFTS EXPERTS *Tufts University Health & Nutrition Letter* v34 no10 p8 D 2016
ASK TUFTS EXPERTS *Tufts University Health & Nutrition Letter* v35 no1 p8 Mr 2017
Breaking up exercise ... Canola oil ... Probiotics ... Roasting vegetables *Tufts University Health & Nutrition Letter* v34 no11 p8 Ja 2017

Lichtenstein, Andrew

MISSISSIPPI MARTYR: Recalling a lynching that shocked America and galvanized the civil rights movement A. Crawford *Smithsonian* v48 no6 p16 O 2017

Lichtenstein, Donald R.

High Online User Ratings Don't Actually Mean You're Getting a Quality Product *Harvard Business Review Digital Articles* p2 Jl 4 2017

LICHTENSTEIN, IRVIN

Safe Trailer ~ Safe Ride color *Trail Rider* v29 no3 p28 Ap 2017

Lichtenstein, Roy, 1923-1997

Study of Hands color *ARTnews* v115 no4 p2 Wint 2016/2017

Lichtenstein, Roy, 1923-1997—Exhibitions

Regarding Henri Matisse G. Stavitsky cartoon *Magazine Antiques* v184 no1 p180 Ja/F 2017

Lichtman, Joshua S.

Seasonal cycling in the gut microbiome of the Hadza hunter-gatherers of Tanzania diag *Science* v357 no6353 p802 Ag 25 2017

Lick, James

They Don't Know When They're Licked color *Weekly Standard*

v23 no6 p3 O 16 2017

Lickteig, Paul S.J.

The case for (and problem with) Christian movies color *America* v216 no10 p50 My 1 2017

LICO, SCOTT

Here's How color *Practical Horseman* v45 no8 p56 Ag 2017

Licona, Michael

Why Don't the Gospel Writers Tell the Same Story? New Testament scholar and apologist Michael Licona's new book argues that ancient literary devices are the answer—and that's a good thing for Christians C. LINDGREN color *Christianity Today* v61 no4 p42 My 2017

Licona-Limon, Paula

Macrophage function in tissue repair and remodeling requires IL-4 or IL-13 with apoptotic cells diag *Science* v356 no6342 p1072 Je 9 2017

Licorice (Plant)

10 Plants WE SHOULD KNOW K. HUNHOFF *South Dakota Magazine* v33 no2 p27 Jl/Ag 2017

Licorice-root

How to Make a... ROOT BEER B. KAUFMAN color *Popular Mechanics* v193 no7 p76 S 2016

Licurse, Adam

One Hospital's Experiments in Virtual Health Care *Harvard Business Review Digital Articles* p2 D 9 2016

LIDA, GRETCHEN

The Benefits of Biophilia color *Earth Island Journal* v32 no2 p55 Summ 2017

LIDAR (Optics)

Laser Vision J. Condliffe color *MIT Technology Review* v120 no5 p88 S/O 2017
Self-Driving Cars' Spinning-Laser Problem T. Simonite color *MIT Technology Review* v120 no4 p27 Jl/Ag 2017

Liddell, Eric

ERIC LIDDELL'S GREATEST RACE D. HAMILTON *Saturday Evening Post* v289 no1 p52 Ja/F 2017

Liddiard, Izzy

Who I am M. CALNAN *People Management* p51 F 2017

LIDDICOAT, CRAIG

Environmental Change and Human Health: Can Environmental Proxies Inform the Biodiversity Hypothesis for Protective Microbial-Human Contact? *BioScience* v66 no12 p1023 D 1 2016

Liddle, Ann

To The Editor color *American Craft* v77 no3 p10 Je/Jl 2017

Lidocaine—Therapeutic use

LIDOCAINE NERVE BLOCKS CAN BE TRICKY C. Barakat and M. McCluskey *Equus* no482 p12 N 2017
A Salve for the Shot S. SEA GOLD color *Parents* v92 no4 p24 Ap 2017

Lidow, Derek

A Better Way to Set Strategic Priorities *Harvard Business Review Digital Articles* p2 F 13 2017

Lidz, Franz

Game Changers: The spectacular play you see today owes a mighty debt to the revolutionary, slam-dunking ABA *Smithsonian* v48 no6 p26 O 2017
Hannibal's Lost Road *Smithsonian* v48 no4 p108 Jl/Ag 2017
THE MAGIC MOUNTAIN *Smithsonian* v48 no2 p48 My 2017
Special Delivery *Smithsonian* v47 no7 p46 N 2016

Lie, Sonia Destri—Interviews

Sonia Destri Lie S. E. Scherpf color *Dance Magazine* v91 no3 p18 Mr 2017

LIEB, JOSH

TRUMP'S CADDY color *New Yorker* v93 no10 p47 Ap 24 2017

Liebart, Jean-Claude

Guanine glycation repair by DJ-1/Park7 and its bacterial homologs chart color diag graph *Science* v357 no6347 p208 Jl 14 2017

Liebenson-Morse, Kelsey

EDITORS' CHOICE FOOD AWARDS 2016 color *Yankee* v80 no6 p73 N/D 2016
The Mapparium *Yankee* v81 no1 p28 Ja/F 2017

Lieberher, Jaeden, 2003-

THE BERET BUNCH M. LOSGAR color *Vanity Fair* v59 no6 p66 My 2017

Lieberman, Bari

About Those HPV Rumors... color *Glamour* v115 no7 p57 Jl 2017

What Before-and-After Pictures Don't Tell You bw color *Glamour* no8 p99 Ag 2017

Lieberman, Bobbie Jo

Decision time color *Equus* no480 p60 S 2017

From sickness to health bw cartoon color *Equus* no473 p34 F 2017

Keep calm and carry on color *Equus* no470 p72 N 2016

Reality check color *Equus* no481 p54 O 2017

Lieberman, Charlotte

Is Something Lost When We Use Mindfulness as a Productivity Tool? *Harvard Business Review Digital Articles* p2 Ag 25 2015

What You're Hiding from When You Constantly Check Your Phone *Harvard Business Review Digital Articles* p2 Ja 19 2016

Lieberman, Jonny

2018 Mercedes-AMG GT Roadster and GT C Roadster color *Motor Trend* v69 no3 p26 Mr 2017

A BIGGER HAMMER chart color *Motor Trend* v69 no5 p62 My 2017

BRUTE SQUAD GOALS chart color *Motor Trend* v69 no4 p62 Ap 2017

DUNEKHANA color *Motor Trend* v69 no5 p78 My 2017

THE FOREVER WAR [Cover story] chart color diag graph *Motor Trend* v69 no8 p48 Ag 2017

GARAGE chart color diag *Motor Trend* v69 no11 p106 N 2017

the leftovers... [Cover story] chart color *Motor Trend* v69 no4 p36 Ap 2017

A NEW FORCE chart color *Motor Trend* v69 no4 p76 Ap 2017

SECOND TIME'S A CHARMER [Cover story] chart color *Motor Trend* v69 no1 p70 Ja 2017

WHEELS OF DESIRE chart color *Motor Trend* v69 no7 p80 Jl 2017

WHEN CONCEPT MEETS REALITY chart color *Motor Trend* v69 no4 p68 Ap 2017

Lieberman, Trudy

"DON'T TOUCH MY MEDICARE!" *Harper's Magazine* v333 no1998 p45 N 2016

Liebesman, Jonathan

TEENAGE MUTANT NINJA TURTLES: OUT OF THE SHAD-OWS C. Gunnestad color *Sound & Vision* v82 no2 p71 F/Mr 2017

LIEBMAN, BONNIE

An Anti-Aging Diet? [Cover story] *Nutrition Action Health Letter* v44 no4 p3 My 2017

APRIL FOOLS *Nutrition Action Health Letter* v44 no3 p8 Ap 2017

THE BEAN SCENE *Nutrition Action Health Letter* v43 no10 p13 D 2016

Bone Smarts... Bess Dawson-Hughes [Cover story] *Nutrition Action Health Letter* v44 no6 p3 Jl/Ag 2017

BREAD WINNERS *Nutrition Action Health Letter* v44 no2 p13 Mr 2017

Cereal Smarts *Nutrition Action Health Letter* v43 no9 p12 N 2016

DIABETES DEFENSE *Nutrition Action Health Letter* v44 no1 p3 Ja/F 2017

DODGE DISEASE WITH DIET [Cover story] *Nutrition Action Health Letter* v44 no5 p3 Je 2017

The Fruit Case *Nutrition Action Health Letter* v44 no4 p13 My 2017

Headline Headaches: Are you getting the full story? [Cover story] *Nutrition Action Health Letter* v44 no7 p3 S 2017

Healthy Foods *Nutrition Action Health Letter* v44 p1 Je 2017 Supplement

NEWtrition Facts|Labels *Nutrition Action Health Letter* v44 no7 p10 S 2017

NOTHING BUT THE TRUTH? *Nutrition Action Health Letter* v44 no8 p8 O 2017

Raising the Bar *Nutrition Action Health Letter* v44 no5 p13 Je 2017

Restaurant Frauds & Finds *Nutrition Action Health Letter* v44 no1 p13 Ja/F 2017

Savvy Swaps: How to cut calories in half *Nutrition Action Health Letter* v44 no8 p13 O 2017

Say Cheese: Pitfalls on the path to a better cheddar *Nutrition Action Health Letter* v44 no7 p14 S 2017

Short on Sleep? *Nutrition Action Health Letter* v44 no5 p8 Je 2017

what makes us EAT too much [Cover story] *Nutrition Action Health Letter* v44 no3 p3 Ap 2017

XTREME EATING 2017 *Nutrition Action Health Letter* v44 no6 p13 Jl/Ag 2017

Liebman, Lisa

At Work I'm the Only... color *Glamour* v115 no4 p148 Ap 2017

This Is My Job color *Glamour* v115 no1 p56 Ja 2017

Liedl, Tim

Molecular force spectroscopy with a DNA origami–based nano-scopic force clamp bibl diag graph *Science* v354 no6310 p305 O 21 2016

Liedtke, Eric

BUILD YOUR BRAND B. COURT color *Men's Health* v32 no7 p(Sp)6 S 2017

Liefert, Olga

Agricultural Recovery in Russia and the Rise of Its South *Amber Waves: The Economics of Food, Farming, Natural Resources, & Rural America* p10 Ap 2017

Liefert, William

Agricultural Recovery in Russia and the Rise of Its South *Amber Waves: The Economics of Food, Farming, Natural Resources, & Rural America* p10 Ap 2017

Liem, Tess

My Body in Three Movements T. LIEM *Walrus* v14 no7 p53 S 2017

LIEN, JEFFREY

Lewis Nash's Drum Solo on 'Jitterbug Waltz' color *Downbeat* v83 no11 p78 N 2016

Lien, Terry

Slow Children C. KALMAN color *Climbing* no350 p26 D 2016/Ja 2017

LIENHARD, JUDD

MY LONGEST DAY *Humanist* v77 no1 p34 Ja/F 2017

Lienhard, Vincent

An atom-by-atom assembler of defect-free arbitrary two-dimen-sional atomic arrays bibl bw diag graph *Science* v354 no6315 p1021 N 25 2016

Liepe, Juliane

A large fraction of HLA class I ligands are proteasome-generated spliced peptides bibl graph *Science* v354 no6310 p354 O 21 2016

LIERLE, EMILY

NATIONAL PARKS TIMELINE *Arizona Highways* v92 no8 p10 Ag 2016

A RIM COUNTRY ALMANAC *Arizona Highways* v92 no7 p28 Jl 2016

Lieshout, Robert H.

BEYOND BALFOUR AND SYKES-PICOT: Steering clear of Orientalist fantasy and patriotic British myth, this innovative analysis brings clarity to the complexities of the Middle East in the early 20th century C. Beckerman *History Today* v67 no9 p100 S 2017

Lieu, Ted

Inaction Isn't an Option *Earth Island Journal* v32 no3 p56 Aut 2017

Lieutenant governors

LESSONS OF UTAH BEACH ARE MORE IMPORTANT THAN EVER *Vital Speeches of the Day* v82 no12 p377 D 2016

Lieutenant governors—United States

Behaving Badly *Governing* v30 no10 p12 Jl 2017

A Step Up: I first met Governor Holcomb on the Statehouse stairs. Both he and Indiana were ascending P. GULLEY *Indianapolis Monthly* v40 no11 p48 Jl 2017

Liew, Ruth

Active Funds Still Rule Down Under. For Now color *Bloomberg Businessweek* no4526 p33 Je 12 2017

Liew, Sonny

LAST CHANCE TO SEE *New York Times Book Review* p27 O 15 2017

Life

See also

Everyday life

Quality of life

Faith Matters C. Zaleski *Christian Century* v134 no11 p38 My 24 2017

Finding a fresh start M. Rollins *Redbook* p21 F 2017

A Greater Whole LARRY YANG *Orion Magazine* v35 no4/5 p50 Jl-O 2016

I'M WITH STUPID J. Gordinier color *Esquire* p15 Je/Jl 2017

James PATTERSON J. Black color *Esquire* p76 S 2017

Let it go! [Cover story] R. ROMM, K. ARNOLD-RATLIFF et al color *O, The Oprah Magazine* p92 Ag 2017

Live Well, Die Well: Does Neil Gorsuch Understand Epicurus? H. Crespo *Humanist* v77 no3 p6 My/Je 2017

Live Your Best Life bw *O, The Oprah Magazine* p21 Ap 2017

My Life, Before and After National Parks A. PETERMAN *Orion Magazine* v35 no4/5 p54 Jl-O 2016

Points to Ponder color *Reader's Digest* v189 no1129 p31 Ap 2017

PRAYING ATTENTION G. DOYLE color *O, The Oprah Magazine* p34 Ag 2017

The Question F. G. BASS, J. LAMONT et al *O, The Oprah Magazine* p18 S 2017

Saving Your First Life T. RODOCKER color *Reader's Digest* v189 no1129 p98 Ap 2017

Sometimes Life Doesn't Go According to Plan L. KOGAN color *O, The Oprah Magazine* p45 N 2017

Sound and Sense L. HAMMER *American Scholar* v86 no3 p54 Summ 2017

TIME DIFFERENCES J. Brown *Popular Science* v289 no5 p5 S/O 2017

WE WERE RIGHT ALL ALONG bw *Yankee* p26 My/Je 2017

WHAT YOU REALLY NEED FOR A HAPPY LIFE A. Traister color *Redbook* p100 F 2017

When the sky falls A. Camille color *U.S. Catholic* v81 no11 p47 N 2016

Life (Biology)
See also
Biosphere
Longevity
Transgenic organisms

The laws of life C. S. Cockell *Physics Today* v70 no3 p42 Mr 2017

The Nature of Humans *Natural History* v125 no1 p5 D 2016/Ja 2017

Life (Film)
In Life, the Blob from Mars Is Small and Very Scary S. Zacharek color *Time* v189 no12 p56 Ap 3 2017

The / MUST LIST color *Entertainment Weekly* no1460/1461 p3 Ap 7-17 2017

Life (Periodical)
c. 1880: Río Santiago M. Sabina *Lapham's Quarterly* v10 no2 p161 Spr 2017

Life Magazine P. Theroux *New York Times Magazine* p20 Ap 2 2017

Life (Theatrical production)
Bunny Masks and a Ballet Barre *Dance Magazine* v91 no1 p39 Ja 2017

Life, A (Theatrical production)
SHOWOFFS H. ALS cartoon *New Yorker* v92 no36 p80 N 7 2016

Life care communities
A Caring Place for every step of your journey color *Cincinnati Magazine* v51 no1 p144 O 2017

SENIOR LIVING COMMUNITY DIRECTORY *Cincinnati Magazine* v50 no4 p92 Ja 2017

Life care communities—Finance
A Home for Now and Later C. Fried chart color *Money* v45 no11 p37 D 2016

Life change events
BE THE CHANGE [Cover story] K. Fowler color *Yoga Journal* no296 p74 N 2017

Fate G. Bakker *Skeptical Inquirer* v41 no1 p62 Ja/F 2017

Life unexpected: When plans go awry, consider the possibilities A. Scobey color *U.S. Catholic* v82 no8 p43 Ag 2017

The middle ages J. M. Griffith color *U.S. Catholic* v82 no7 p38 Jl 2017

TRAUMARAMA color *Seventeen* v76 no4 p92 Jl/Ag 2017

Life Changes (Music)
On the Road With Thomas Rhett M. Vain color *Entertainment Weekly* no1484 p58 S 29 2017

Life cycle funds
CRISIS AMONG The Palms J. Conant color *Earth Island Journal* v32 no2 p33 Summ 2017

Life cycles (Biology)

See also
Human life cycle

A BESTIARY OF THE MIND H. Macdonald bw *New York Times Magazine* p40 My 21 2017

Life expectancy
LIVING TO 120 B. Gifford color *Scientific American* v315 no3 p62 S 2016

Retirement's Scariest Question: How Long? B. Steverman bw *Bloomberg Businessweek* no4498 p51 N 7 2016

This Just In J. Zorthian color *Time* v189 no20 p19 My 29 2017

Violence, boys, and the labor market S. Hyde *Monthly Labor Review* p1 O 2016

Life expectancy—Abstracts
PREPARING FOR THE 100-YEAR LIFE J. A. JENKINS *Vital Speeches of the Day* v83 no4 p120 Ap 2017

Life in Pieces (TV program)
Colin Hanks's SLICE OF LIFE J. HALTERMAN *TV Guide* p32 D 5 2016

Life in Pieces' Game Day J. Halterman *TV Guide* p13 D 19 2016

Life in Pieces N. Abrams, B. L. Heldman et al *Entertainment Weekly* no1482/1483 p88 S 22 2017

Life insurance
CAN THEIR PROBLEM BE SOLVED? M. Friesen *Successful Farming* v115 no5 p66 Mid-Mr 2017

HOW LIFE INSURANCE CAN BUILD WEALTH FOR BLACKS J. McKinney color *Black Enterprise* v47 no8 p19 Jl/Ag 2017

Life insurance companies
How Life Insurers Can Bring Their Business into the 21st Century P. Lyons and B. Demaster *Harvard Business Review Digital Articles* p2 Mr 25 2015

Life insurance policies
Charitable Giving Is a Family Affair K. LANKFORD *Kiplinger's Personal Finance* v71 no12 p41 D 2017

Why Women Need Life Insurance *USA Today Magazine* v145 no2861 p2 F 2017

Life insurance—Evaluation
DO YOU NEED LIFE INSURANCE? *Health* v31 no1 p16 Ja 2017

Life insurance—United States—History
YOUR MONEY OR YOUR LIFE V. POSTREL color *Reason* v49 no3 p8 Jl 2017

Life jackets (Garments)
float & live J. NEPORADNY JR. color *Cabin Living* p80 Ja/F 2017

Lessons Learned D. J. Harding color *Power & Motoryacht* v34 no7 p16 Jl 2017

Purchasing the Proper PFD D. J. HARDING color *Power & Motoryacht* v32 no11 p62 N 2016

Shade Is Good A. JONES color *Boating World* v38 no7 p4 Jl 2017

Surf's SUP! D. Wolman color *Bloomberg Businessweek* no4518 p76 Ap 10 2017

Trapped! W. Bailey cartoon *Sail* v47 no12 p20 D 2016

Life jackets (Garments)—Evaluation
ONYX color *Canoe & Kayak Magazine* v45 no1 p96 Wint 2017

Life of Kylie (TV program)
E!'s Teen Queen of Screens D. D'addario color *Time* v190 no6 p52 Ag 7 2017

Life partners
Who's Your Leading Man? *Dance Spirit* v21 no3 p20 Mr 2017

Life preservers (Safety equipment)
See also
Life jackets (Garments)

Purchasing the Proper PFD D. J. HARDING color *Power & Motoryacht* v32 no11 p62 N 2016

Life preservers (Safety equipment)—Evaluation
STUFF YOU WANT *Boating World* v38 no8 p28 S/O 2017

Life science education
See also
Agricultural education
Biology education

Addressing the Gender Gap in Distinguished Speakers at Professional Ecology Conferences C. M. FARR, S. P. BOMBACI et al *BioScience* v67 no5 p464 My 2017

Life sciences
See also

Agriculture

Biology

Medicine

An Exercise to Get Your Team Thinking Differently About the Future L. M. Fuld *Harvard Business Review Digital Articles* p2 Ja 23 2015

He Knows Where the Bodies Are Buried G. DREVITCH *Psychology Today* v50 no2 p27 Mr/Ap 2017

Research: Junior Female Scientists Aren't Getting the Credit They Deserve M. J. Lerchenmueller and O. Sorenson *Harvard Business Review Digital Articles* p2 Mr 22 2017

Life sciences research

Calendar of meetings *BioScience* v67 no3 p313 Mr 2017

Life sciences—Congresses

Calendar of meetings *BioScience* v66 no10 p910 O 1 2016

Life sciences—Equipment & supplies

NEW PRODUCTS color *Science* v354 no6316 p1174 D 2 2016

new products color *Science* v355 no6327 p871 F 24 2017

new products color *Science* v356 no6340 p867 My 26 2017

new products color *Science* v357 no6353 p822 Ag 25 2017

new products: sample prep-handling color *Science* v356 no6343 p1197 Je 16 2017

Life sciences—Equipment & supplies—Evaluation

NEW PRODUCTS color *Science* v354 no6309 p241 O 14 2016

new products color *Science* v355 no6332 p1441 Mr 31 2017

Life sciences—Government policy

From Politics to Science: The Way Forward R. E. GROPP *BioScience* v66 no12 p1007 D 1 2016

Life sentences

WOMEN WITHOUT PAROLE D. WOLFFE color *Nation* v305 no1 p21 Jl 3 2017

Life skills

See also

Conduct of life

A 3-Step Plan for Turning Weaknesses into Strengths J. Grenny color *Harvard Business Review Digital Articles* p2 Ja 26 2017

CHARACTER A. R. Caldwell, K. Logan et al *Christian Century* v134 no17 p22 Ag 16 2017

Life skills—Study & teaching (Secondary)

What real high performance looks like J. Nehring, M. Charner-Laird et al chart diag *Phi Delta Kappan* v98 no7 p38 Ap 2017

Life spans (Biology)

See also

Animal life spans

Life expectancy

Longevity

Life Time Fitness Inc.

Liquid Crunch B. Marston and T. Keith color *Sports Illustrated* v127 no1 p20 Jl 3 2017

Living & Recreation *Virginia Living* p92 2017 Best 20of Virginia

Life Will See You Now (Music)

JENS LEKMAN N. Feeney *Entertainment Weekly* no1446/1447 p72 D 2016/Ja 2017

Life Without a Spine (Poem)

LIFE WITHOUT A SPINE S. R. NORDGREN *Humanist* v77 no3 p33 My/Je 2017

Life Without Sound (Music)

NIGHT LIFE *New Yorker* v92 no48 p8 F 6 2017

Life zones

Microbial mass movements Zhu, M. Gillings et al color *Science* v357 no6356 p1099 S 15 2017

Life & Adventures of Jack Engle: An Auto-Biography (Short story)

A Common Language: Two newly discovered works enrich and complicate our view of Walt Whitman T. GENOWAYS *New York Times Book Review* p21 S 3 2017

LifeBEAM Technologies Ltd.

VI AI PERSONAL TRAINER: HEART RATE-TRACKING BLUETOOTH EARBUDS WITH SERIOUS POTENTIAL C. McGARRY color *Macworld - Digital Edition* v34 no6 p68 Je 2017

Life-Changing Magic of Tidying Up: The Japanese Art of Decluttering & Organizing, The (Book : Kondo)

Correction *Publishers Weekly* v264 no36 p13 S 4 2017

Lifeguard stations—Design & construction

Standing Guard *Los Angeles Magazine* p20 Ag 2017

Life—Moral & ethical aspects

Guide to Life, Career & Kids color *AARP: The Magazine* v59 no5A p44 Ag/S 2016

What I Know for Sure Oprah *O, The Oprah Magazine* p142 O 2017

Life of Pablo, The (Music)

Chaos Reigns B. RATLIFF cartoon *Esquire* v166 no5 p40 D 2016/Ja 2017

GETTING TO YES C. BATTAN cartoon *New Yorker* v93 no15 p72 My 29 2017

Life's About to Get Good (Music)

THE 28-WORD REVIEW K. O'donnell color *Entertainment Weekly* no1472 p56 Je 30 2017

Lifesaving

See also

Drowning—Prevention

Syria's First Responders N. Gibbs color *Time* v188 no15 p3 O 17 2016

The White Helmets of Syria [Cover story] J. Malsin, Turkey et al color *Time* v188 no15 p20 O 17 2016

Lifesaving—Equipment & supplies

See also

Immersion suits

Suit Yourself S. MURRAY bw *Power & Motoryacht* v34 no9 p54 S 2017

Lifestyles

50 SMART WAYS TO Feel Great Now! color *AARP: The Magazine* v59 no3A p31 Ap/My 2016

78 fun ways to spend less color *Redbook* p8 Je 2017

BETTER WITH BEAVERS R. Rich color *Earth Island Journal* v32 no1 p30 Spr 2017

BO Brummell color *Weekly Standard* v22 no39 p3 Je 19 2017

Contributors color *InStyle* v23 no13 p40 D 2016

EDITOR'S LETTER E. PARKHURST *Virginia Living* p17 2017 Best 20of Virginia

GENES UNDER PRESSURE L. M. Zahn and B. A. Purnell color *Science* v354 no6308 p52 O 7 2016

The Good, the Dad, and the Ugly S. NYGAARD bw cartoon color *Men's Health* v32 no5 p59 Je 2017

I Need (an App) Consult J. LANGSTON *USA Today Magazine* v145 no2862 p51 Mr 2017

The Innovation Issue M. Bean color *Men's Health* v32 no7 p4 S 2017

IN THIS CORNER... J. FIELDEN bw *Esquire* v166 no5 p28 D 2016/Ja 2017

Jimmy Buffett A. MCLELLAN color *New Orleans Magazine* v51 no12 p32 O 2017

JUST DO IT C. KETTLEWELL *Virginia Living* v15 no3 p13 Ap 2017

Just Us girls [Cover story] E. Wilson color *InStyle* v24 no4 p180 Ap 2017

Life IN THESE UNITED STATES color graph *Reader's Digest* v189 no1129 p32 Ap 2017

My favorite star M. Rollins color *Redbook* p12 S 2017

NEW VISIONS OF THE VIKINGS H. Pringle color *National Geographic* v231 no3 p30 Mr 2017

NORTHERN VIRGINIA *Virginia Living* p86 2017 Best 20of Virginia

Sober, Seething Hollywood K. D. WILLIAMSON il *National Review* v69 no5 p33 Mr 20 2017

Trips for Weight Loss Success in 2017 J. Fortenberry *Successful Farming* v115 no1 p39 Ja 2017

The #VanLife Checklist H. VANDERSMITH color *Surfer* v58 no2 p132 My 2017

Walking on Air chart color *AARP: The Magazine* v60 no2A p76 F/Mr 2017

WHY WE ALL NEED TO HYGGE [Cover story] A. KINGSTON color *Maclean's* v129 no51/52 p50 D 26 2016

Wonder Beyond Words R. GRIJALVA *Sierra* v101 no4 p68 Jl/Ag 2016

Would You Rather... chart color *Seventeen* v76 no3 p112 My 2017

Wow. Just Wow color *Glamour* v114 no12 p201 D 2016

YOUR SCHEDULE COULD BE KILLING YOU L. KAUFMAN cartoon color *Popular Science* v289 no5 p58 S/O 2017

Lifestyles & health

HAPPIER, HEALTHIER, WELLTHIER K. Dold color *Women's*

Health v14 no4 p89 My 2017

Simple Ways To Cut the Top Blood Pressure Number A. A. LEVITT and A. JUNG color *Reader's Digest* v190 no1134 p56 O 2017

Working Together for a Healthier Wichita B. Tuttle *Parks & Recreation* v52 no1 p28 Ja 2017

Lifestyles—Periodicals

Scared Straight A. FERGUSON cartoon *Weekly Standard* v22 no17 p5 Ja 2 2017

Lifestyles—Social aspects

DRESSING DOWN D. Clemente *Saturday Evening Post* v289 no3 p80 My/Je 2017

Imperfect Home E. C. PEYTON cartoon *New Orleans Magazine* v51 no12 p56 O 2017

LifeWay Christian Resources

How Small Churches Make Disciples chart *Christianity Today* v61 no7 p17 S 2017

Lifford, Tina

Queen Sugar M. Logan color *TV Guide* v64 no42 p40 O 10 2016

LIFHITS, JENNA

The 702 Problem color *Weekly Standard* v23 no4 p14 O 2 2017

Benghazi at the Bar color *Weekly Standard* v23 no6 p14 O 16 2017

He Still Hasn't Torn It Up color *Weekly Standard* v22 no43 p9 Jl 24 2017

It's Mueller Time [Cover story] color *Weekly Standard* v22 no36 p18 My 29 2017

Overseeing What's Overheard color *Weekly Standard* v22 no28 p16 Mr 27 2017

The Tehran Two-Step color *Weekly Standard* v22 no33 p11 My 8 2017

Trump's Democracy Man color *Weekly Standard* v23 no3 p19 S 25 2017

Lifson, Amy

Terry Gross *Humanities* v37 no4 p1 Fall 2016

Lifting & carrying (Human mechanics)

WE'VE GOT YOURBACK A. SHAFFER color *Better Homes & Gardens* v95 no10 p174 O 2017

Lifting & carrying (Human mechanics)—Competitions

How to Carry Your Wife: Giving new meaning to "spousal support" Elliot and Giana Storey share their secrets for winning a sports competition like no other J. BILLS *Yankee* v81 no5 p28 S/O 2017

Lifting-jacks

CHANGE A TIRE color *Good Housekeeping* v265 no3 p96 S 2017

ROADSIDE ASSISTANCE D. Canet color *Cycle World* v56 no6 p20 Jl 2017

Ligament injuries

SIGNS OF A HOOF ABSCESS C. Barakat and M. Freckleton *Equus* no481 p22 O 2017

Ligament surgery

See also
　　Ulnar collateral ligament reconstruction

advice for dancers L. HAMILTON *Dance Magazine* v91 no10 p24 O 2017

Ligands

Metalloprotein entatic control of ligand-metal bonds quantified by ultrafast x-ray spectroscopy M. W. Mara, R. G. Hadt et al diag *Science* v356 no6344 p1276 Je 23 2017

Visualizing dynamic microvillar search and stabilization during ligand detection by T cells E. Cai, K. Marchuk et al color *Science* v356 no6338 p598 My 12 2017

Ligands (Biochemistry)

ELABELA deficiency promotes preeclampsia and cardiovascular malformations in mice L. Ho, M. van Dijk et al color diag graph *Science* v357 no6352 p707 Ag 18 2017

Light

See also
　　Color
　　Photons

1665: Cambridge I. Newton *Lapham's Quarterly* v10 no2 p88 Spr 2017

20 Things You Didn't Know About ... Color S. MORROW color *Discover* v38 no9 p74 N 2017

Bear Necessity L. BAILEY *Indianapolis Monthly* v40 no4 p33 D 2016

Look-back Time Peter *Sky & Telescope* v132 no6 p4 D 2016

Mystery of the Paulding Light B. RADFORD *Skeptical Inquirer* v41 no2 p36 Mr/Ap 2017

WORK THE ROOM J. TUNG *Martha Stewart Living* no267 p29 S 2016

Light & darkness (Aesthetics)

LAND OF DARKNESS Suki Kim *Lapham's Quarterly* v10 no3 p205 Summ 2017

LIGHT, ALAN

The Big O *New York Times Book Review* p28 Je 4 2017

ROCK LIVES *New York Times Book Review* p54 D 4 2016

Light, Caroline E.

AMERICA'S STAND ON SELF-DEFENSE N. TAPPAN bw *American History* v52 no4 p16 O 2017

Light, David

A Hands-Off Approach to Open Innovation Doesn't Work *Harvard Business Review Digital Articles* p2 My 3 2016

How Manufacturers Can Get Faster, More Flexible, and Cheaper bw *Harvard Business Review Digital Articles* p2 F 27 2017

Light, Duncan

ROMANIA'S PROBLEM WITH DRACULA *History Today* v67 no5 p62 My 2017

LIGHT, JESSICA E.

Transformational Principles for NEON Sampling of Mammalian Parasites and Pathogens: A Response to Springer and Colleagues *BioScience* v66 no11 p917 N 1 2016

Light, Joe

Fannie and Freddie's Many Happy Returns graph *Bloomberg Businessweek* no4520 p30 My 1 2017

Federal Agencies Play 'Not It' With Flood Insurance *Bloomberg Businessweek* no4538 p28 S 18 2017

Homebuilders Look to Trump for a Mood Lift cartoon *Bloomberg Businessweek* no4508 p35 Ja 23 2017

John Paulson's Long Bet on Trump Pays Off color graph *Bloomberg Businessweek* no4501 p33 N 28 2016

Mamas, Don't Let Your Babies Grow Up to Be Appraisers color *Bloomberg Businessweek* no4530 p29 Jl 17 2017

Light, Judith, 1949-—Interviews

WHO'S THE BOSS? 1984-1992 S. Vilkomerson color *Entertainment Weekly* no1434 p34 O 7 2016

LIGHT, LISA

FULL HOUSE color *Architectural Digest* v74 no1 p212 Ja 2017

Light, Steve

School Days M. RUSSO *New York Times Book Review* p27 Ag 27 2017

Light aircraft

FIREWORKS, FLASHLIGHTS AND FIREFLIES K. JOHNSON color *Flying* v144 no11 p26 N 2017

AN ODE TO AUGUST color *Flying* v144 no8 p8 Ag 2017

SPORTING FUN color *Flying* v144 no4 p90 Ap 2017

VANISHING EARTH R. KEECH color *Flying* v144 no8 p24 Ag 2017

Light aircraft—Evaluation

WE FLY: REMOS GXiS [Cover story] R. MARK chart color *Flying* v144 no4 p50 Ap 2017

Light art

A Bar Lamp Like No Other E. HILL-AGNUS *D: The Magazine of Dallas* v43 no10 p52 O 2016

MASTER OF ILLUSION V. HAFSTAÐ color *Iceland Review* v54 no5 p12 S-O 2016

Light boxes—Evaluation

LET THERE BE LIGHT BOXES! [Cover story] cartoon *Prevention* p9 Mr 2017

Light bulbs—Evaluation

4 Could This Be in Your Living Rooms Future? T. Rami img *New York* v49 no21 p92 O 17 2016

Light curves

Amateur astronomer sheds light on pulsar companion's odd behavior color *Astronomy* v45 no4 p18 Ap 2017

Light emitting diodes

The Danger of Chromotherapy: Despite the lack of scientific evidence for its effectiveness and its use of esoteric theories to describe its mechanisms of action, chromotherapy has become popular. But is It safe? S. POINT *Skeptical Inquirer* v41 no4 p50 Jl/Ag 2017

Glow Sticks S. STEVENSON color *Indianapolis Monthly* v41

Profile of a Profile C. Rutherford *Stage Directions* v30 no3 p76 Mr 2017

Show Offs J. Coakley and N. Schoenfeld *Stage Directions* v29 no12 p6 D 2016

Lighting—Evaluation

2017 Renovation SHOWCASE J. BREWSTER color *Cabin Living* p47 Je 2017

DOCK BOX: GEAR, TOOLS AND TOYS *Sea Magazine* v109 no4 p32 Ap 2017

Lighting & Electrical color *Architectural Record* v204 no12 p128 D 2016

Light Work K. L. Beamon color *Architectural Record* v205 no8 p123 Ag 2017

Products *Parks & Recreation* v52 no1 p52 Ja 2017

The Wellness Factor R. C. Orrell *Architectural Record* v205 no7 p69 Jl 2017

Lighting—Mergers

In the Greenroom *Stage Directions* v29 no11 p4 N 2016

Lighting—Special effects

See also

Christmas lights

NOT-SO-SILENT NIGHTS C. Kopaczewski color *Good Housekeeping* v263 no6 p170 D 2016

Lighting—Special effects—Exhibitions

DON'T MISS LIST *Sea Magazine* v108 no12 p102 D 2016

EVENTS *Sea Magazine* v108 no12 pPNW-14 D 2016

Lightneer Inc.

From Angry Birds to Particle Physics J. Kahn color *Bloomberg Businessweek* no4508 p30 Ja 23 2017

Lightner, Barb

Ameenah Gurib *Current Biography* v78 no4 p30 Ap 2017

Dennis Daugaard color *Current Biography* v78 no3 p12 Mr 2017

Manuel Valls *Current Biography* v77 no11 p90 N 2016

Ollanta Humala *Current Biography* v78 no3 p34 Mr 2017

Shannon Walker *Current Biography* v77 no11 p93 N 2016

Lightner, Lindsay

Putting paraeducators on the path to teacher certification color *Phi Delta Kappan* v98 no8 p43 My 2017

Lightning

The 2017 PHOTO CONTEST *Weatherwise* v70 no5 p12 S/O 2017

ADDITIONAL LISTINGS *Arts & Crafts Homes & the Revival* v12 no1 p52 2017 Resouce Guide

FLASH POINTS C. Zuckerman graph map *National Geographic* v230 no6 p8 D 2016

Lightbox color *Time* v189 no5 p14 F 13 2017

Storm WARNING [Cover story] J. Pitts color *Sail* v48 no8 p26 Ag 2017

Surge Protector K. J. P. Smith color *Scientific American* v315 no6 p21 D 2016

Tallying the tropical toll on trees from lightning M. Price color *Science* v356 no6344 p1222 Je 23 2017

upside-down lightning C. Maldarelli color *Popular Science* v289 no4 p90 Jl/Ag 2017

Venezuelan lake is a lightning hot spot color *Science* v355 no6320 p10 Ja 6 2017

Weird But True! M. TERRELL color map *National Geographic Kids* no472 p4 Ag 2017

When Thunder Roars, Go Indoors color *Parents* v92 no7 p24 Jl 2017

Lightning strike injuries—Diagnosis

On the Job M. Branom color map *Weatherwise* v70 no4 p32 Jl/Ag 2017

Lightning strike injuries—Prevention

When Thunder Roars, Go Indoors color *Parents* v92 no7 p24 Jl 2017

Lightning—Equipment & supplies

Hanging Heavy Ceiling Fixtures R. Tschoepe cartoon *Old House Journal* v45 no1 p58 F 2017

Lightning—Equipment & supplies—Evaluation

LIGHTING & ART GLASS color *Arts & Crafts Homes & the Revival* v12 no1 p46 2017 Resouce Guide

Lightspeed Aviation Inc.

LIGHTSPEED ZULU 3 color *Flying* v144 no8 p18 Ag 2017

Light—Wave-length

Innovation N. Leiber color diag *Bloomberg Businessweek* no4509 p31 Ja 30 2017

Lightweight materials

A NEW COMPOSITE-MANUFACTURING Approach Takes Shape R. Hansen *Science & Technology Review* p16 Je 2017

Sailing on Sunshine J. Hsu color *Scientific American* v317 no4 p24 O 2017

Lignins

Formaldehyde stabilization facilitates lignin monomer production during biomass depolymerization Li Shuai, M. T. Amiri et al bibl diag graph *Science* v354 no6310 p329 O 21 2016

Ligorio, Matteo

Potential role of intratumor bacteria in mediating tumor resistance to the chemotherapeutic drug gemcitabine diag *Science* v357 no6356 p1156 S 15 2017

Lihe Zhang

Generation of influenza A viruses as live but replication-incompetent virus vaccines bibl graph *Science* v354 no6316 p1170 D 2 2016

Lihua Jin

Highly stretchable polymer semiconductor films through the nanoconfinement effect bibl graph *Science* v355 no6320 p1 Ja 6 2017

Lihui Wei

Gene expression profiling–guided clinical precision treatment for patients with endometrial carcinoma bibl color diag *Science* v354 no6319 p33 D 23 2016

Lijuan Wang

Bifurcating electron-transfer pathways in DNA photolyases determine the repair quantum yield bibl graph *Science* v354 no6309 p209 O 14 2016

Lijun Liu

High-resolution lithosphere viscosity and dynamics revealed by magnetotelluric imaging bibl graph *Science* v353 no6307 p1515 S 30 2016

Lijun Zhao

Gene expression profiling–guided clinical precision treatment for patients with endometrial carcinoma bibl color diag *Science* v354 no6319 p33 D 23 2016

Like a Mountain (Poem)

Emily Dickinson wrote poems R. STIEVE *Arizona Highways* v96 no7 p2 Jl 2017

Like kind exchange

ORCHESTRATING 1031 AND REVERSE 1031 EXCHANGES S. Williamson *Successful Farming* v115 no2 p16 F 2017

Liker, Jeffrey

Assessing the Sins of Volkswagen, Toyota, and General Motors *Harvard Business Review Digital Articles* p2 S 24 2015

Likes & dislikes

My Obsessions... *TV Guide* v65 no25 p7 Je 2017

WHY WE HATE TO CHANGE OUR MINDS il *Harvard Business Review* v95 no5 p28 S/O 2017

Likes (Short story)

Likes S. Shun-lien Bynum cartoon color *New Yorker* v93 no31 p58 O 9 2017

Likitalo, Leena

The Sisters of the Crescent Empress *Publishers Weekly* v264 no40 p121 O 2 2017

Lil Buck (Performer)

TALKIN' PARTIES with LIL BUCK J. Harman color *Glamour* v115 no1 p97 Ja 2017

Lil Yachty (Performer)

Hot Rebel MC Lil Yachty J. WEINER bw color *Rolling Stone* no1274 p38 N 17 2016

'One Night' J. L. KEILES color *New York Times Magazine* p28 Mr 12 2017

Q&A: Lil Yachty A. GREENE color *Rolling Stone* no1290 p24 Je 29 2017

LILEKS, JAMES

Apocalypse Hound *National Review* v69 no16 p37 Ag 28 2017

Athwart *National Review* v68 no19 p41 O 24 2016

Athwart *National Review* v69 no6 p39 Ap 3 2017

Dads in Ads *National Review* v69 no15 p37 Ag 14 2017

Executive Disorder *National Review* v69 no3 p41 F 20 2017

Foodie Feud *National Review* v69 no11 p33 Je 12 2017

New-Year Trump Fears *National Review* v69 no1 p33 Ja 23 2017

Rated PC *National Review* v69 no17 p33 S 11 2017

The Razor's Edge *National Review* v69 no7 p39 Ap 17 2017

Real News, Fake Panic *National Review* v69 no5 p39 Mr 20 2017

'She Said What?' *National Review* v69 no8 p33 My 2017

Standing athwart Hillary *National Review* v68 no22 p51 D 5 2016

Sufficient unto the Day *National Review* v69 no4 p33 Mr 6 2017

Take a Small Knee *National Review* v69 no19 p51 O 16 2017

'Tear Down This Big, Beautiful Wall' *National Review* v68 no20 p37 N 7 2016

That's a Lot of Broken Eggs *National Review* v68 no23 p33 D 19 2016

A Thought for Your Penneys *National Review* v69 no12 p33 Je 26 2017

Thoughts from an Ocean Crossing *National Review* v69 no18 p33 O 2 2017

The Way Forward *National Review* v68 no21 p37 N 21 2016

'We Have Science!' *National Review* v69 no9 p33 My 15 2017

LILES, MARYN

stop fighting about money! *Parents* v91 no9 p156 S 2016

your 2015 gift list *Parents* p107 2015

LILIENFELD, SCOTT O.

Superstition Masquerading as Science *Skeptical Inquirer* v40 no6 p14 N/D 2016

Teaching Skepticism: How Early Can We Begin? *Skeptical Inquirer* v41 no5 p30 S/O 2017

Lilies—Varieties

LILIES FOR DAYS M. OZAWA color *Martha Stewart Living* p90 My 2017

Lilium Polska (Company)

Flying Jet Taxis J. Zorthian color *Time* v189 no18 p25 My 15 2017

Liliuokalani, Queen of Hawaii, 1838-1917

QUEEN'S RANSOM [Cover story] P. X. Rutz bw color map *Military History* v34 no4 p62 N 2017

Lilla, Mark

Identity Bites: An intellectual historian urges liberals to overcome their differences B. GAGE *New York Times Book Review* p12 Ag 20 2017

Identity Crisis D. Oppenheimer bw *Washington Monthly* v49 no9/10 p129 S/O 2017

If They Could Turn Back Time T. A. Howard bw *Commonweal* v144 no13 p27 Ag 11 2017

The New Manichaeans M. KNOX BERAN *National Review* v69 no16 p39 Ag 28 2017

OBAMA'S AMERICA img *New York* v49 no20 p12 O 3 2016

THE RIGHT IDEA S. TANENHAUS bw cartoon *New Yorker* v92 no34 p77 O 24 2016

Robert B. Silvers (1929–2017) [Cover story] bw color *New York Review of Books* v64 no8 p31 My 11 2017

Speaking as a... J. Rauch bw color *New York Review of Books* v64 no17 p10 N 9 2017

Lillard, Damian, 1990-

Damian Lillard C. Cullen color *Current Biography* v77 no11 p49 N 2016

Lillebaek, Troels

Emergence and spread of a human-transmissible multidrug-resistant nontuberculous mycobacterium bibl diag graph *Science* v354 no6313 p751 N 11 2016

LILLESØ, JENS-PETER BARNEKOW

An Ecoregion-Based Approach to Protecting Half the Terrestrial Realm *BioScience* v67 no6 p534 Je 2017

Lilley, Kathryn S.

A subcellular map of the human proteome color *Science* v356 no6340 p820 My 26 2017

Lillien, Lisa

Better, slimmer smoothies color *Redbook* p74 Jl/Ag 2017

Build the perfect snack color *Redbook* p86 D 2016

Fresh & slimming snacks [Cover story] color *Redbook* p74 Je 2017

The frozen-meal makeover color *Redbook* p86 My 2017

Happy, healthy pizza night color *Redbook* p87 N 2017

More treats, fewer calories color *Redbook* p85 Mr 2017

Reasons to have more chocolate color *Redbook* p85 S 2017

Simple, slimming sides color *Redbook* p98 O 2017

Slim and satisfying soups color *Redbook* p94 F 2017

LILLIS, JOANNA

Astana, Kazakhstan color *Foreign Policy* no223 p70 Mr/Ap 2017

LILLO, VICKIE

The Dragon's Lair color map *Backpacker* p16 Ag 2017

Lilly Pulitzer (Company)

Lilly Pulitzer's Target Disaster Was Actually a Success D. Lee Yohn *Harvard Business Review Digital Articles* p2 My 22 2015

What Lilly Pulitzer Learned About Marketing to Millennials O. Artun and M. Kelly *Harvard Business Review Digital Articles* p2 Mr 31 2016

LILLYWHITE, HARVEY B.

Anesthesia and Euthanasia of Amphibians and Reptiles Used in Scientific Research: Should Hypothermia and Freezing Be Prohibited? *BioScience* v67 no1 p53 Ja 2017

Lil Wayne, 1982-

Look at Him Now img *New York* v49 no20 p124 O 3 2016

Lim, Agnes

Stromal Gli2 activity coordinates a niche signaling program for mammary epithelial stem cells color *Science* v356 no6335 p284 Ap 21 2017

Lim, Carol

WILD THINGS L. McCarthy color *Harper's Bazaar* no3648 p187 N 2016

Lim, Chae Ho

Regeneration of fat cells from myofibroblasts during wound healing bibl color graph *Science* v355 no6326 p748 F 17 2017

Lim, Chin Yan

ELABELA deficiency promotes preeclampsia and cardiovascular malformations in mice color diag graph *Science* v357 no6352 p707 Ag 18 2017

Lim, Daniel A.

CRISPRi-based genome-scale identification of functional long noncoding RNA loci in human cells bibl graph *Science* v355 no6320 p1 Ja 6 2017

Lim, Dennis

Cemetery of Splendor *Film Comment* v53 no1 p46 Ja/F 2017

Keeping at It bw color *Film Comment* v53 no4 p62 Jl/Ag 2017

Lim, Eugene

We Can Be Heroes: A new novel engages the post-Occupy moment C. LORENTZEN img *New York* v50 no13 p81 Je 26 2017

Lim, Hyeongtaek

Metalloprotein entatic control of ligand-metal bonds quantified by ultrafast x-ray spectroscopy diag *Science* v356 no6344 p1276 Je 23 2017

LIM, JASON

Asia's Rising Stars color *Forbes* v199 no5 p20 My 16 2017

Lim, Jean K.

Enhancement of Zika virus pathogenesis by preexisting antiflavivirus immunity graph *Science* v356 no6334 p175 Ap 14 2017

Lim, Ka S.

Mass seasonal bioflows of high-flying insect migrants bibl graph *Science* v354 no6319 p1584 D 23 2016

Lim, Kitack

The Role of the International Maritime Organization in Preventing the Pollution of the World's Oceans from Ships and Shipping *UN Chronicle* v54 no1/2 p1 2017

Lim, Paul J.

10 THINGS THE FINANCIAL CRISIS TAUGHT US color diag *Money* v46 no1 p46 Ja/F 2017

THE CASE FOR INVESTING ABROAD chart *Money* v46 no6 p36 Jl 2017

Everything You Need to Know About P/E Ratios chart diag *Money* v46 no8 p36 S 2017

FAST-GROWING ECONOMIES, FOR CHEAP *Fortune* v174 no8 p115 D 15 2016

OTHER LESSONS FROM THE RICH *Money* v46 no9 p37 O 2017

Stock X-Ray: Priceline color diag *Money* v46 no9 p52 O 2017

A Strange Trumphoria Rules the U.S. Stock Market. For Now diag *Time* v188 no24 p16 D 12 2016

Tech Stocks Are Back ... in a Bubble color diag *Money* v46 no9 p48 O 2017

That ETF May Not Be as Cheap as You Think diag *Money* v46 no5 p36 Je 2017

When Is a Bubble Not a Bubble? Why This Tech-Stock Boom Is Different color *Time* v189 no24 p20 Je 26 2017

Why Your Portfolio Should Be Stocked With Global Shares color *Time* v189 no20 p12 My 29 2017

YOUR 20 BEST MONEY MOVES FOR 2017 color diag *Money* v45 no11 p60 D 2016

Lim, Stacey R.

Community network for deaf scientists color *Science* v356 no6336 p386 Ap 28 2017

Lim, Tony

Mapping the human DC lineage through the integration of high-dimensional techniques diag *Science* v356 no6342 p1044 Je 9 2017

Lima, Adriana

ICONS UNPLUGGED BRIGITTE LACOMBE [Cover story] C. ROITFELD bw color *Harper's Bazaar* no3656 p397 S 2017

Lima, Jamie Kern

The Beauty Queen of QVC L. Wells img *New York* v49 no26 p44 D 26 2016

The IT Girl C. SORVINO color *Forbes* v199 no6 p80 Je 13 2017

Lima, Jamie Kern—Interviews

"I take my makeup off on QVC 100 times a year." B. Selene, K. Lima et al color *Glamour* v115 no4 p112 Ap 2017

The New Beauty Pioneers B. Meyer and Ying Chu color *Glamour* v115 no4 p110 Ap 2017

Lima, Kern

"I take my makeup off on QVC 100 times a year." color *Glamour* v115 no4 p112 Ap 2017

Lima, Manuel

Making the rounds K. Cooperrider color *Science* v356 no6341 p914 Je 1 2017

Lima, Mario Sergio

How do you maximize the profits of a drug that treats a very rare disease? [Cover story] color *Bloomberg Businessweek* no4524 p42 My 29 2017

Liman, Doug, 1965-

American Made C. Nashawaty color *Entertainment Weekly* no1485 p38 O 6 2017

Cruise, the Smuggest of Drug Smugglers S. Zacharek color *Time* v190 no14 p50 O 9 2017

JOHN CENA: UNDER FIRE K. P. Sullivan color *Entertainment Weekly* no1466 p41 My 19 2017

Limanto, John

A multifunctional catalyst that stereoselectively assembles pro-drugs diag *Science* v356 no6336 p426 Ap 28 2017

Limburg, Joanne

God Help the Queen K. GRANT *New York Times Book Review* p17 D 18 2016

Limehouse Golem, The (Film)

INQUIRING MINDS A. LANE cartoon *New Yorker* v93 no27 p82 S 11 2017

Limerick, Patricia Nelson, 1951-

HINDSIGHT I. Frazier cartoon *New Yorker* v93 no12 p17 My 8 2017

Limericks

LIMERICK LAUGHS *Saturday Evening Post* v288 no6 p112 N/D 2016

LIMERICK LAUGHS *Saturday Evening Post* v289 no2 p100 Mr/Ap 2017

Limericks—Competitions

LIMERICK LAUGHS *Saturday Evening Post* v289 no4 p97 Jl/Ag 2017

Limestone

See also
Coquina

LITTLE DEVILS TOWER TRAIL *South Dakota Magazine* v32 no6 p93 Mr/Ap 2017

Rain G. TARLACH color *Discover* v38 no3 p74 Ap 2017

Limestone figurines

FIGURE OF DISTINCTION J. A. LOBELL color *Archaeology* v70 no1 p22 Ja/F 2017

Limey, The (Film)

Search History L. Poitras color *Film Comment* v53 no3 p6 My/Je 2017

Limited Stores LLC

Movers K. Stock color graph *Bloomberg Businessweek* no4505 p11 D 26 2016

Limited English-proficient students

Language Haven J. CHASE-LUBITZ color *Foreign Policy* no226 p10 S/O 2017

Mariachi and Spanish speaking English learners: District initiatives, models, and education policy M. M. Neel bibl graph *Arts Education Policy Review* v118 no4 p208 2017

Lim Lee, Yae

A cargo-sorting DNA robot color *Science* v357 no6356 p1112 S 15 2017

Limnodromus griseus

SHORT-BILLED DOWITCHERS color *Canadian Wildlife* v23 no4 p6 S/O 2017

Limoli, Charles L.

DEEP-SPACE DEAL BREAKER color diag *Scientific American* v316 no2 p54 F 2017

Limonene

TRIPLE-ACTION MACE: CRY, FRY, AND DYE C. LEU color *Wired* v25 no7 p26 Jl 2017

Limpert, Ann

BINDAAS *Washingtonian Magazine* v52 no2 p255 N 2016

CASOLARE *Washingtonian Magazine* v52 no1 p145 O 2016

CHAIN REACTION: At the Smith, the menu aims to please all tastes *Washingtonian Magazine* v52 no8 p125 My 2017

DISH OF THE MONTH color *Washingtonian Magazine* v52 no7 p144 Ap 2017

DISH OF THE MONTH *Washingtonian Magazine* v52 no9 p142 Je 2017

FAVORITE FLAVORS *Washingtonian Magazine* v52 no3 p154 D 2016

THE GENEALOGY OF WASHINGTON RESTAURANTS *Washingtonian Magazine* v52 no1 p64 O 2016

MEATY MATTERS: Red Apron Burger Bar is doing wonders with Virginia beef *Washingtonian Magazine* v52 no8 p132 My 2017

MIRABELLE *Washingtonian Magazine* v52 no9 p139 Je 2017

MR. MOMO: A former Blue Duck Tavern server brings a taste of Nepal to Del Ray *Washingtonian Magazine* v53 no1 p146 O 2017

PICK-ME-UP ARTISTS color *Washingtonian Magazine* v52 no7 p141 Ap 2017

Q BY PETER CHANG: The famed Chinese chef puts down roots in Bethesda *Washingtonian Magazine* v53 no1 p143 O 2017

QUICK TAKES color *Washingtonian Magazine* v52 no7 p140 Ap 2017

QUICK TAKES: First impressions of three new seafood-focused restaurants *Washingtonian Magazine* v53 no1 p148 O 2017

QUICK TAKES: First impressions of three restaurants *Washingtonian Magazine* v52 no11 p132 Ag 2017

QUICK TAKES *Washingtonian Magazine* v52 no2 p258 N 2016

THE SALT LINE: Chef Kyle Bailey makes a splash right next door to Nats Park *Washingtonian Magazine* v52 no11 p130 Ag 2017

SEASON OF THE 'WICH color *Washingtonian Magazine* v52 no7 p137 Ap 2017

TAPABAR *Washingtonian Magazine* v52 no2 p259 N 2016

TASTE: EATING. DRINKING. DINING *Washingtonian Magazine* v52 no11 p123 Ag 2017

THE WHOLE HILL *Washingtonian Magazine* v52 no9 p162 Je 2017

'WICH CRAFT: Italian-sub lovers have reason to rejoice at Capo Delicatessen *Washingtonian Magazine* v52 no11 p136 Ag 2017

L'important c'est d'aimer (Film)

L'Important c'est d'aimer E. Bittencourt color *Film Comment* v53 no4 p71 Jl/Ag 2017

Limulidae

EVERYWHERE color *Popular Mechanics* p6 Ap 2017

Limzerwala, Jazeel F.

Cyclin A2 is an RNA binding protein that controls Mre11 mRNA translation bibl graph *Science* v353 no6307 p1549 S 30 2016

Lin, C. D.

Observing the ultrafast buildup of a Fano resonance in the time domain bibl graph *Science* v354 no6313 p738 N 11 2016

Ultrafast electron diffraction imaging of bond breaking in di-ionized acetylene bibl graph *Science* v354 no6310 p308 O 21 2016

Lin, Chao-Po

Deficiency of microRNA miR-34a expands cell fate potential in pluripotent stem cells diag *Science* v355 no6325 p596 F 10 2017

Lin, Charles P.

Self-renewal of a purified Tie2+ hematopoietic stem cell population relies on mitochondrial clearance bibl graph *Science* v354 no6316 p1156 D 2 2016

Lin, Chenxiang
Directing reconfigurable DNA nanoarrays color *Science* v357 no6349 p352 Jl 28 2017

Lin, Eddie
How One Chef Created THE WORLD'S BEST BOWL OF RAMEN color *Los Angeles Magazine* v62 no10 p4 O 2017

Lin, Eric
How to Survive a Company Scandal You Had Nothing to Do With *Harvard Business Review Digital Articles* p2 Ag 31 2016

Lin, Grace, 1974-
In Her Storied Land E. JENKINS *New York Times Book Review* p22 N 13 2016

Lin, Haixin
Clathrate colloidal crystals bibl color *Science* v355 no6328 p931 Mr 3 2017

Lin, Jeremy, 1988-
HAIR TO BE DIFFERENT S. Kwak color *Sports Illustrated* v127 no12 p20 O 16 2017
Jeremy Lin R. WIEDEMANN img *New York* v49 no22 p18 O 31 2016

Lin, JiaBei
Ratchet-like polypeptide translocation mechanism of the AAA+ disaggregase Hsp104 diag *Science* v357 no6348 p273 Jl 21 2017

Lin, Jiwei
Engineering the ribosomal DNA in a megabase synthetic chromosome diag *Science* v355 no6329 p1049 Mr 10 2017

Lin, Justin Yifu, 1952-
Beating the Odds: Jump-Starting Developing Countries R. N. Cooper *Foreign Affairs* v96 no6 p153 N/D 2017

Lin, Justin, 1971-
STAR TREK BEYOND D. Vaughn color *Sound & Vision* v82 no3 p69 Ap 2017

Lin, Lili
Atomic-layered Au clusters on α-MoC as catalysts for the low-temperature water-gas shift reaction chart diag graph *Science* v357 no6349 p389 Jl 28 2017

Lin, Lin
Inactivation of porcine endogenous retrovirus in pigs using CRISPR-Cas9 diag *Science* v357 no6357 p1303 S 22 2017

Lin, Longnian
History of winning remodels thalamo-PFC circuit to reinforce social dominance color *Science* v357 no6347 p162 Jl 14 2017

Lin, Maya
The Summer Job I'll Never Forget color *Time* v190 no2/3 p55 Jl 10-17 2017

Lin, Michael Z.
Optical control of cell signaling by single-chain photoswitchable kinases bibl diag *Science* v355 no6327 p836 F 24 2017

Lin, Qiu-Hui
Bug mapping and fitness testing of chemically synthesized chromosome X diag *Science* v355 no6329 p1048 Mr 10 2017
"Perfect" designer chromosome V and behavior of a ring derivative diag *Science* v355 no6329 p1046 Mr 10 2017

Lin, Shixian
Redox-based reagents for chemoselective methionine bioconjugation bibl diag graph *Science* v355 no6325 p597 F 10 2017

Lin, Song
Metal-catalyzed electrochemical diazidation of alkenes diag *Science* v357 no6351 p575 Ag 11 2017

Lin, Szu-Yen
Rain of Terror L. PICKER color *Publishers Weekly* v264 no39 p86 S 25 2017

Lin, Wenfang
The complex effects of ocean acidification on the prominent N2-fixing cyanobacterium Trichodesmium graph *Science* v356 no6337 p527 My 5 2017

Lin, Yachun
A paralogous decoy protects Phytophthora sojae apoplastic effector PsXEG1 from a host inhibitor bibl graph *Science* v355 no6326 p710 F 17 2017

Lin, Yicong
Bug mapping and fitness testing of chemically synthesized chromosome X diag *Science* v355 no6329 p1048 Mr 10 2017
Engineering the ribosomal DNA in a megabase synthetic chromosome diag *Science* v355 no6329 p1049 Mr 10 2017

Lin, Z.-Yi
Surface changes on comet 67P/Churyumov-Gerasimenko suggest a more active past bw graph *Science* v355 no6332 p1392 Mr 31 2017

Lin, Zhanmin
Activity-based protein profiling reveals off-target proteins of the FAAH inhibitor BIA 10-2474 chart color graph *Science* v356 no6342 p1084 Je 9 2017

Lin Gu
Ultrafine jagged platinum nanowires enable ultrahigh mass activity for the oxygen reduction reaction bibl chart graph *Science* v354 no6318 p1414 D 16 2016

Lin-Quan Tang
Precision medicine for nasopharyngeal carcinoma bibl diag *Science* v354 no6319 p24 D 23 2016

Lin Wang
Recent progress in autism spectrum disorder research in China bibl chart diag *Science* v354 no6319 p48 D 23 2016

Liñán-Cembrano, Gustavo
Effects of network modularity on the spread of perturbation impact in experimental metapopulations diag graph *Science* v357 no6347 p199 Jl 14 2017

Linares-Palomino, Reynaldo
Forest conservation: Humans' handprints bibl color *Science* v355 no6324 p466 F 3 2017
Forest conservation: Remember Gran Chaco bibl color *Science* v355 no6324 p465 F 3 2017

Linberg, Joanna
NATURAL WONDERS color *Better Homes & Gardens* v95 no10 p150 O 2017
URBANE FARM color *Sunset* v239 no1 p60 Jl 2017

LINC Housing Corp.
BBVA COMPASS & LINC HOUSING CHARITY EVENT *TV Guide* v64 no42 p4 O 10 2016

Lincoln (Neb.)
Best Places to Retire [Cover story] S. BLOCK, P. MERTZ ESSWEIN et al color *Kiplinger's Personal Finance* v71 no8 p56 Ag 2017

Lincoln, Abraham
THIS LAND WAS MADE FOR YOU AND ME [Cover story] T. TEMPEST WILLIAMS color *O, The Oprah Magazine* p78 Ja 2017

Lincoln, Abraham, 1809-1865
America's Evolving Idea T. T. Williams *Sierra* v101 no4 p31 Jl/Ag 2016
Athwart J. LILEKS *National Review* v68 no19 p41 O 24 2016
The changing face of the GOP T. Stanley *History Today* v66 no11 p11 N 2016
THE COLD CIVIL WAR *Claremont Review of Books* v17 no2 p24 Spr 2017
How to Fix Congress chart color *Popular Mechanics* p11 F 2017
Lightbox color *Time* v188 no19 p12 N 7 2016
Lincoln's Killer Is Killed J. W. EMORD *USA Today Magazine* v145 no2862 p19 Mr 2017
Lying Low C. Chocano color *New York Times Magazine* p13 Ja 29 2017
OFFICIAL TRANSCRIPTS R. LONG *National Review* v69 no15 p36 Ag 14 2017
'Our Progress in Degeneracy' W. Kristol bw *Weekly Standard* v22 no29 p7 Ap 3 2017
The Requisite Darkness B. Doyle color *U.S. Catholic* v82 no4 p11 Ap 2017
Self-Restraint in the Executive C. NADON bw *Weekly Standard* v22 no28 p28 Mr 27 2017
UNCOMMON COURTESIES bw color *O, The Oprah Magazine* p102 Ap 2017

Lincoln, Abraham, 1809-1865. Gettysburg address
Why the Gettysburg Address Is Still a Great Case Study in Persuasion T. David *Harvard Business Review Digital Articles* p2 Ap 9 2015

Lincoln, Abraham, 1809-1865—Military leadership
To Win the Civil War, Lincoln Had to Change His Leadership V. Govindarajan and H. Faber *Harvard Business Review Digital Articles* p2 My 30 2016

Lincoln, Abraham, 1809-1865—Political & social views
Allen C. Guelzo, Redeeming the Great Emancipator D. Schaub

"WHERE DO I WANT TO RIDE? DUH, EVERYWHERE."
color *Bicycling* v58 no3 p48 Ap 2017

YAY WINTER! bw cartoon color *Bicycling* v58 no1 p30 Ja/F
2017

Lindsey, Lawrence B.

The Right Cure color *Weekly Standard* v22 no23 p10 F 20 2017

Lindsey, Payne

INTO THIN AIR S. HENRY *Atlanta* v57 no1 p24 My 2017

LINDSEY, PETER A.

Conserving the World's Megafauna and Biodiversity: The Fierce
Urgency of Now *BioScience* v67 no3 p197 Mr 2017

Saving the World's Terrestrial Megafauna color *BioScience* v66
no10 p807 O 1 2016

LINDSEY, URSULA

Moroccan Rules color *Nation* v303 no22 p20 N 28 2016

Lindskog, Cecilia

A pathology atlas of the human cancer transcriptome diag *Science*
v357 no6352 p660 Ag 18 2017

A subcellular map of the human proteome color *Science* v356
no6340 p820 My 26 2017

Lindt, Suzanne F.

Movement and learning in elementary school color *Phi Delta
Kappan* v98 no7 p34 Ap 2017

Line-of-sight radio links

Danger Zone? J. Y. WOOD color *Power & Motoryacht* v34 no11
p62 N 2017

Lineage

Moments in Time Forgotten Hero B. FINKE *Arabian Horse World*
v57 no1 p98 O 2016

Retracing embryological fate S. Behjati bibl diag *Science* v354
no6316 p1109-B D 2 2016

Linear models (Statistics)

Linear Thinking in a Nonlinear World B. DE LANGHE, S. PUN-
TONI et al bw chart diag graph img *Harvard Business Review*
v95 no3 p130 My/Je 2017

Lineback, Kent

3 Things Managers Should Be Doing Every Day *Harvard Business Review Digital Articles* p2 S 24 2015

The Capabilities Your Organization Needs to Sustain Innovation
Harvard Business Review Digital Articles p2 Ja 14 2015

The Inescapable Paradox of Managing Creativity *Harvard Business Review Digital Articles* p2 D 12 2014

Lineberry, Cate

CATE LINEBERRY: Be Free or Die K. DONOHUE *Prologue*
v49 no2 p26 Summ 2017

Linehan, Allison R.

Fabrication of fillable microparticles and other complex 3D microstructures color diag *Science* v357 no6356 p1138 S 15 2017

Linehan, Dennis M.

OF MANY THINGS M. MALONE *America* v215 no10 p2 O 10
2016

Linen

MAKING A PROPER BED M. B. EYERS color diag *Better
Homes & Gardens* v95 no10 p38 O 2017

Linen—Evaluation

In Stitches color *House Beautiful* v159 no8 p48 O 2017

A SERENE DRAWING ROOM H. BROWN and K. O'SHEA-
EVANS color *House Beautiful* v159 no7 p65 S 2017

LING, ALISTER

April 2017: Jupiter rules the night color *Astronomy* v45 no4 p36
Ap 2017

August 2017: Totality comes to America color *Astronomy* v45 no8
p44 Ag 2017

Comet viewing the whole night through color *Astronomy* v45 no5
p42 My 2017

December 2016: Inner planet convention chart color *Astronomy*
v44 no12 p36 D 2016

February 2017: Venus blazes after sunset color *Astronomy* v45
no2 p36 F 2017

January 2017: Venus climbs high at dusk color *Astronomy* v45
no1 p36 Ja 2017

July 2017: A warm-weather showcase color *Astronomy* v45 no7
p36 Jl 2017

June 2017: Peak for the ringed planet color *Astronomy* v45 no6
p36 Je 2017

March 2017: The Moon hides Aldebaran bw chart color *Astrono-*

my v45 no3 p36 Mr 2017

May 2017: Venus dazzles before dawn color *Astronomy* v45 no5
p36 My 2017

November 2017: Venus meets Jupiter color *Astronomy* v45 no11
p36 N 2017

October 2017: Uranus glows brightly bw chart color *Astronomy*
v45 no10 p36 O 2017

On the shoals of a rainy sea color *Astronomy* v45 no4 p37 Ap 2017

Pickin' up good librations bw *Astronomy* v45 no5 p37 My 2017

The planets in December 2016 chart diag graph map *Astronomy*
v44 no12 p40 D 2016

September 2017: An ice giant pinnacle chart color *Astronomy* v45
no9 p36 S 2017

STAR DOME chart color *Astronomy* v44 no12 p38 D 2016

Ling, Alvin J. Y.

A conserved NAD+ binding pocket that regulates protein-protein
interactions during aging bibl graph *Science* v355 no6331
p1312 Mr 24 2017

Ling, Princess Der

1903: Forbidden City *Lapham's Quarterly* v10 no1 p162 Wint
2017

LING, SCOTT D.

Assessing National Biodiversity Trends for Rocky and Coral
Reefs through the Integration of Citizen Science and Scientific
Monitoring Programs *BioScience* v67 no2 p134 F 2017

Ling-Lie Chau

Stanley Mandelstam *Physics Today* v70 no5 p69 My 2017

Ling Zhang

RABBIT IN AND OUT OF THE MOON: A RETROSPECTIVE
OF EMIKO OMORI *Film Quarterly* v71 no1 p42 Fall 2017

L'inganno Felice (Theatrical production)

Rossini: L'Inganno Felice P. Dillon *Opera News* v81 no9 p53 Mr
2017

Lingerie

ERICA M J. Wilson color *Essence* v47 no10 p26 F 2017

The Guys Next Door D. Stattmann, P. Kita et al color *Women's
Health* v14 no4 p20 My 2017

Ta-da! The Bra R. Beach bw color *Glamour* v115 no6 p24 Je 2017

Lingerie industry

WHAT'S NEW IN LINGERIE L. McCarthy color *Harper's Bazaar* no3650 p196 F 2017

Lingerie stores—Evaluation

PANTY RAID A. BROWNLEE *Cincinnati Magazine* v50 no4
p44 Ja 2017

Shop *Los Angeles Magazine* p27 Ag 2017

Lingerie—Evaluation

Delicate Subject: Bust a move to Carmel's new lingerie boutique
S. BAHR *Indianapolis Monthly* p36 N 2017

MORE UNDER STATEMENTS! color *Women's Health* v14 no7
p54 S 2017

PRETTY INTIMATE color *Essence* v47 no10 p21 F 2017

Lingner, Joachim

TZAP or not to zap telomeres bibl diag *Science* v355 no6325 p578
F 10 2017

Lingner, Linda

FREE FOR ALL color *O, The Oprah Magazine* p20 O 2017

Lingzheng Bu

Biaxially strained PtPb/Pt core/shell nanoplate boosts oxygen reduction catalysis bibl color graph *Science* v354 no6318 p1410
D 16 2016

Lin He, Qing

Chiral Majorana fermion modes in a quantum anomalous Hall
insulator–superconductor structure diag *Science* v357 no6348
p294 Jl 21 2017

Linherr Hollingsworth (Company)

Faux Arts H. BROWN color *House Beautiful* v159 no1 p30 F
2017

Liniers

Sketchbook *New York Times Book Review* p30 Ag 27 2017

LINK, ALBERT N.

Putting technology to work *Issues in Science & Technology* v33
no3 p14 Spr 2017

Link, Jonathan M.

Scattering neutrinos caught in the act [Cover story] color *Science*
v357 no6356 p1098 S 15 2017

Link, K.

Lion's Pride, The (Poem)

The Lion's Bride *American Scholar* v86 no1 p58 Wint 2017

LIOTTA, ELIZABETH A.

THE SURPRISING WAYS AGING AFFECTS YOUR SKIN color *Redbook* p26 Mr 2017

Lioumi, Irene

Children of No Nation [Cover story] color map *Time* v188 no27-28 p38 D 26 2016

When the Call Comes color map *Time* v189 no6 p32 F 20 2017

Lip care preparations

beauty NEWSFEED K. FOSTER color *Seventeen* v76 no2 p72 Mr 2017

Cold Weather FIXES K. FOSTER color *Seventeen* v76 no12 p62 D 2016/Ja 2017

Dr. Low Dog [Cover story] cartoon color *Prevention* v68 no11 p24 N 2016

EVERYDAY HERO LIP SERVICE C. Kopaczewski cartoon color *Good Housekeeping* v263 no5 p96 N 2016

LIP SERVICE color *Vogue* v207 no9 p432 S 2017

saved by: Lip Balm T. BROWN JR. color *Backpacker* p42 S 2017

Sleepover color *Seventeen* v76 no3 p42 My 2017

Val's Guide to GORGEOUS O's beauty director, Valerie Monroe, finds a new way to appreciate April showers, and more... V. Monroe color *O, The Oprah Magazine* p64 Ap 2017

Lip care preparations—Evaluation

6 incredible lip protectors color *Redbook* p51 D 2016

Blooming BRILLIANT! cartoon *O, The Oprah Magazine* p75 Mr 2017

cheap THRILLS E. STOVALL color *Seventeen* v76 no2 p84 Mr 2017

CITRUS SPLASH J. MOAZAMI color *Chicago* v66 no7 p32 Jl 2017

DARE TO WEAR COLOR Guarnieri color *Harper's Bazaar* no3653 p286 My 2017

DOPE STUFF ON MY DESK J. Wilson color *Essence* v48 no3 p26 Jl 2017

Gym color *Seventeen* v76 no3 p48 My 2017

her style color *InStyle* v24 no7 p20 Jl 2017

LOVE YOUR LIPS J. Martin color *Amazing Wellness* v8 no6 p78 Early Winter2016

MESSAGE ON A BOTTLE A. Finney bw color *Women's Health* v14 no3 p(Sp)22 Ap 2017

the pick color *InStyle* v24 no6 p96 Je 2017

the pick color *InStyle* v24 no9 p344 S 2017

Pretty in pink lips color *Redbook* p25 Mr 2017

SIX WAYS TO WAKE UP BETTER-LOOKING color *Esquire* p42 Ag 2017

Val's Guide to GORGEOUS V. Monroe color *O, The Oprah Magazine* p78 F 2017

White Now! color *Essence* v47 no7 p34 N 2016

Lip diseases—Prevention

kiss chapped lips goodbye *Parents* p79 2015

Lip-syncing

LIP SYNC BATTLE J. MATHIS color *Macworld - Digital Edition* p73 D 2016

Lipa, Dua

DUA LIPA C. Stern color *InStyle* v24 no6 p33 Je 2017

Dua Lipa's Tough Love A. GOLD color *Rolling Stone* no1291/1292 p18 Jl 13 2017

Lipginski, Mary

Dream Buddy on a Trail Ride cartoon *Horse & Rider* v56 no3 p72 Mr 2017

Lipid rafts

Lipid transport by TMEM24 at ER-plasma membrane contacts regulates pulsatile insulin secretion J. A. Lees, M. Messa et al diag *Science* v355 no6326 p709 F 17 2017

Why Antidepressants Are So Slow M. LOCKLEAR color *Discover* v38 no1 p62 Ja/F 2017

Lipids

See also

Fat

Fats & oils

STRAWBERRIES PRESERVED D. Stone color *National Geographic* v232 no5 p20 N 2017

Liping Yang

Quality management for precision medicine clinical applications: A consensus from the China Precision Medicine Clinical Research and Application Association bibl *Science* v354 no6319 p11 D 23 2016

Lipinski, Edward

THE LOOK BOOK A. SWERDLOFF img *New York* v50 no15 p43 Jl 24 2017

Lipinski, Paul

How to Integrate Data and Analytics into Every Part of Your Organization *Harvard Business Review Digital Articles* p2 Je 23 2017

Lipkin, W. Ian

Mouse models of acute and chronic hepacivirus infection *Science* v357 no6347 p204 Jl 14 2017

Lipkind, Dina

Encoding vocal culture bibl color *Science* v354 no6317 p1234 D 9 2016

Lipman, Elinor

IT'S ALWAYS SUNNY in Everton, Massachusetts L. HABER cartoon color *O, The Oprah Magazine* p104 Mr 2017

This Old House M. WILDGEN *New York Times Book Review* p9 F 12 2017

Tick-Tock *New York Times Book Review* p25 Je 4 2017

Lipman, Victor

How to Steer Clear of Office Gossip *Harvard Business Review Digital Articles* p2 O 19 2016

To Reduce Stress, Embrace Your Inner Type-B *Harvard Business Review Digital Articles* p2 S 22 2015

Why Do We Spend So Much Developing Senior Leaders and So Little Training New Managers? *Harvard Business Review Digital Articles* p2 Je 28 2016

Liposuction

LASER-SHARP FAT REDUCTION E. MUSIWA color *Ebony* v72 no11 p56 S 2017

Lipp, Susan

Full Compass - Contributing to Customers and Community via the Arts *Stage Directions* v30 no3 p16 Mr 2017

Lippa, Jacob

What Health Care Leaders Need to Do to Improve Value for Patients *Harvard Business Review Digital Articles* p2 D 3 2015

Lippard, Stephen J.

Roger Y. Tsien (1952–2016) color *Science* v354 no6308 p41 O 7 2016

Lippert, John

Globalism Is Alive and Well: Just Ask Carlos Ghosn color *Bloomberg Businessweek* no4531 p50 Jl 24 2017

Remodeling a Sedan Plant for the SUV Era bw *Bloomberg Businessweek* no4529 p18 Jl 3 2017

Rental Cars to The Rescue cartoon graph *Bloomberg Businessweek* no4526 p18 Je 12 2017

STILL UGLY, AFTER ALL THESE YEARS color graph *Bloomberg Businessweek* no4494 p22 O 10 2016

LIPPERT, MARISSA

Your HEALTHY, FRESH, DELICIOUS meal plan [Cover story] color *Redbook* p120 F 2017

Lippincott-Schwartz, Jennifer

Increased spatiotemporal resolution reveals highly dynamic dense tubular matrices in the peripheral ER bibl bw color graph *Science* v354 no6311 paaf3928-1 O 28 2016

Lippit, Akira Mizuta

Cinema without Reflection: Jacques Derrida's Echopoiesis and Narcissism Adrift S. CHAKRAVORTY *Film Quarterly* v70 no3 p98 Spr 2017

Lippman, Andrew

The Potential for Blockchain to Transform Electronic Health Records bw *Harvard Business Review Digital Articles* p2 Mr 3 2017

LIPPMAN, LAURA

Friends Without Benefits: In Claire Messud's new novel, a teenage girl takes a dangerous path to adulthood *New York Times Book Review* p12 S 10 2017

Lippsett, Lonny

Attracted to Magnetics *Oceanus* v52 no1 p52 Summ 2016

Coral Coring *Oceanus* v52 no1 p7 Summ 2016

Expanding the Scientific Arsenal *Oceanus* v52 no2 p60 Spr 2017

Girls Just Wanna Be Engineers *Oceanus* v52 no2 p29 Spr 2017

How Do Larvae Find a Place to Settle Down?: NOT WITH

SOUND CUES, SURPRISED SCIENTISTS SAY *Oceanus* v52 no2 p30 Spr 2017

More Floods and Faster-Rising Sea Levels: GEOLOGICAL RECORDS HELP FORECAST ESCALATING COASTAL HAZARDS *Oceanus* v52 no2 p8 Spr 2017

Mummified Microbes *Oceanus* v52 no1 p18 Summ 2016

A New Eye on Deep-Sea Fisheries *Oceanus* v52 no1 p23 Summ 2016

The Quest for the Moho *Oceanus* v52 no1 p44 Summ 2016

Scientists and the Navy Join Forces: NATO SEEKS ADVICE TO AVOID COLLATERAL ENVIRONMENTAL DAMAGE *Oceanus* v52 no2 p6 Spr 2017

Signs of Big Changes in the Arctic *Oceanus* v52 no1 p14 Summ 2016

To Forecast Rain, Look to the Ocean: SCIENTISTS EXPLORE COMPELLING NEW WAY TO PREDICT SEASONAL RAINFALL *Oceanus* v52 no2 p6 Spr 2017

Lips

Does It Really Work? color *InStyle* v24 no3 p281 Mr 2017

Find Your Power color *Glamour* v114 no11 p147 N 2016

MODEL MOMENTS BEST LIP LOOKS color *Harper's Bazaar* no3656 p385 S 2017

Lips, Karen R.

Amphibians on the brink color map *Science* v357 no6350 p454 Ag 4 2017

Lips—Anatomy

I Want Her...Coral Lips L. Desantis color *Health* v31 no6 p32 Jl 2017

LIP-READING C. Zuckerman color *National Geographic* v232 no3 p22 S 2017

Lips—Care & hygiene

6 incredible lip protectors color *Redbook* p51 D 2016

LIP SERVICE color *Vogue* v207 no9 p432 S 2017

MERRY AND BRIGHT M. M. GOLDSTEIN *Martha Stewart Living* no270 p72 D 2016

THE NEW CONTOUR N. Spradley color *Essence* v47 no7 p30 N 2016

SEXY, EASY SHORTCUTS M. OLIVA color *Redbook* p52 D 2016

Lipschitz, Vanessa

Research: How Female CEOs Actually Get to the Top *Harvard Business Review Digital Articles* p2 N 6 2014

Lipscomb, Suzannah

A Case of Double Standards *History Today* v66 no10 p53 O 2016

The Hardest Word? Is it ahistorical for public figures to say sorry for events that took place before they were born? The issue cuts to the heart of the relationship between the living and the dead *History Today* v67 no6 p106 Je 2016

A Kinder, Gentler History: The past can seem like a timeline of horrors. But might it also remind us of our own failings - and help to put them right? *History Today* v67 no10 p106 O 2017

No Island is an Island *History Today* v67 no2 p31 F 2017

On and Off Script *History Today* v66 no12 p31 D 2016

Remembrance of Things Past *History Today* v67 no4 p40 Ap 2017

Something More than an Art *History Today* v67 no8 p106 Ag 2017

Lipsitch, Marc

Improving vaccine trials in infectious disease emergencies graph *Science* v357 no6347 p153 Jl 14 2017

LIPSKY, SETH

Tracing the WSJ's Editorial Page Journey *American Conservative* v16 no5 p58 S/O 2017

Lipson, Adrienne—Interviews

Hubbard Street Dance Chicago's Season of Premieres color *Dance Spirit* v20 no9 p23 N 2016

Lipson, Hod

Our Driverless Future S. Halpern bw color *New York Review of Books* v63 no18 p18 N 24 2016

Lipson, Michael

To Fix a Chronic Problem, Try Winging It *Harvard Business Review Digital Articles* p2 Ja 20 2016

To Improve Your Focus, Notice How You Lose It *Harvard Business Review Digital Articles* p2 N 4 2015

Lipstick

About Face E. Graves *Martha Stewart Living* p8 O 2017

ASK APRIL A. FRANZINO color *Good Housekeeping* v264 no3 p25 Mr 2017

HEAVY METAL T. M. FERGUSON color *Ebony* v72 no11 p48 S 2017

The In/Out LIST color *Harper's Bazaar* no3656 p227 S 2017

In the Nude color *InStyle* v24 no3 p292 Mr 2017

The key to lipstick that lasts M. Roncal color *Redbook* p24 O 2017

LIP SERVICE color *Ebony* v72 no4 p54 F 2017

Look gorgeous with just one product M. Roncal color *Redbook* p17 Jl/Ag 2017

LOUD MOUTH L. Dunham color *Vogue* v207 no6 p145 Je 2017

Nail Every Photo Op M. ABERMAN bw color *Seventeen* p106 Ja 1 2017

Plum Crazy S. HOLLAND-MURPHY *D: The Magazine of Dallas* v43 no10 p63 O 2016

Power Tools: Leaders C. Alter color *Time* v189 no16/17 p90 My 1-8 2017

Read My Lips Y. Chu color *Glamour* v114 no11 p166 N 2016

Shopping List color *InStyle* v24 no5 p205 My 2017

SUPER NATURAL SUMMER color *O, The Oprah Magazine* p106 Ag 2017

VELVET REVOLUTION color *O, The Oprah Magazine* p83 N 2017

WELLNESS IS BEAUTIFUL A. K. LAIRD color *Women's Health* v14 no3 p8 Ap 2017

Lipstick—Evaluation

10 New Rules of Southern Style A. R. Williams color *Southern Living* v52 no3 p45 Mr 2017

15 ways to do CARAMEL color diag *Good Housekeeping* v264 no5 p68C My 2017

4 beauty tricks I just learned V. Kirby color *Redbook* p54 N 2017

5 beauty tricks I just learned V. Kirby bw color *Redbook* p43 Jl/Ag 2017

BEAUTY BUYS from $6 color *Good Housekeeping* v265 no1 p16 Jl 2017

BEAUTY NEWS A. Parnass color *Harper's Bazaar* no3654 p112 Je/Jl 2017

BEAUTY NEWS A. Parnass color *Harper's Bazaar* no3657 p194 O 2017

BEAUTY UNDER $25 color *Redbook* p46 F 2017

Berry Lips color *InStyle* v24 no9 p336 S 2017

Best Beauty Gifts. Ever S. Kitchens cartoon color *Glamour* v114 no12 p128 D 2016

BETH'S PICKS color *Harper's Bazaar* no3649 p248 D 2016/Ja 2017

Black Is Beautiful color *Essence* v47 no10 p40 F 2017

Bring some wine to your lips color *Redbook* p29 S 2017

the buzz color *InStyle* v24 no2 p114 F 2017

the buzz color *InStyle* v24 no3 p295 Mr 2017

CHANDRA POINTER K. NEITZ color *Runner's World* v51 no10 p23 N 2016

CHARLOTTE TILBURY'S Magic Touch A. Serrano color *InStyle* v24 no10 p171 O 2017

CHERRY PICKED A. B. RAYA color *Chicago* v65 no11 p48 N 2016

CHIC WAVES color *Harper's Bazaar* no3649 p254 D 2016/Ja 2017

the COMPACT N. Spradley color *Essence* v47 no12 p46 Ap 2017

COUNTER INTELLIGENCE M. MILRAD GOLDSTEIN color *Martha Stewart Living* p48 S 2017

DOPE STUFF ON MY DESK J. Wilson color *Essence* v47 no7 p20 N 2016

DOPE STUFF ON MY DESK J. Wilson color *Essence* v48 no6 p32 O 2017

Dune K. RENDA color *House Beautiful* v159 no4 p25 My 2017

Fabulous Gifts [Cover story] color *Good Housekeeping* v263 no6 p59 D 2016

Fiery Ombré Lips E. Reimel and Y. Chu color *Glamour* v115 no1 p39 Ja 2017

FIND YOUR WINNING STYLE! [Cover story] color *Redbook* p56 S 2017

Glow Up E. Reimel color *Glamour* v115 no10 p94 O 2017

THE HEALING POWER OF LIPSTICK F. Valdesolo color *Women's Health* v14 no3 p(Sp)6 Ap 2017

"I love looking a little disheveled" M. Deem color *Glamour* v115 no5 p74 My 2017

JANET JACKSON J. AMAY color *Ebony* v72/73 no12/1 p56 O/N 2017

CAN WHITE WHISKEY GROW UP? A. Hurly color *Bloomberg Businessweek* no4495 p74 O 17 2016

Liquor industry—China

A Little Sugar Helps The Baijiu Go Down color *Bloomberg Businessweek* no4495 p18 O 17 2016

Liquor industry—Export & import trade

A Little Sugar Helps The Baijiu Go Down color *Bloomberg Businessweek* no4495 p18 O 17 2016

Liquor laws

See also

Prohibition

FREE RANGE? An "old hen" found in Harrisonburg was caught before she could work her prohibited ways B. CROWDER *Virginia Living* v15 no2 p23 F 2017

ICED E. Laborde *New Orleans Magazine* v51 no3 p12 Ja 2017

A Sobering Race E. Conant bw *National Geographic* v230 no4 p148 O 2016

Liquor stores—Evaluation

SUGAR BUZZ C. JAY color *Louisiana Life* v37 no2 p102 N/D 2016

Liquors

See also

Gin

Vodka

Whiskey

6 Things to Eat, Drink, & Buy This Month color *Bon Appetit* v62 no10 p19 O 2017

Amaro for Everyone R. Schaap color *New York Times Magazine* p37 N 27 2016

Bourbon. In Ohio F. MAROUKIAN color *Popular Mechanics* p16 S 2017

Drink Like a Scandinavian F. MAROUKIAN color map *Popular Mechanics* p16 F 2017

Drink the World color *Conde Nast Traveler* v52 no7 p82 Ag 2017

Halloween Spirits T. MCNALLY color *New Orleans Magazine* v51 no12 p116 O 2017

OUT THE BOX T. MCNALLY color *New Orleans Magazine* v51 no1 p118 N 2016

RAISING THE BAR J. TUNG *Martha Stewart Living* no269 p38 N 2016

The Secret to Drinking More Is... Drinking Less M. BYRNE color *GQ: Gentlemen's Quarterly* v97 no6 p42 Je 2017

A Short History of My Long Drinking Life color *Bon Appetit* v62 no10 p96 O 2017

Liquors—Evaluation

Drink Bitter Than You're Used To R. McCAMMON color *GQ: Gentlemen's Quarterly* v97 no9 p88 S 2017

Not Throwin' Away My Shot J. Passov color *Golf Magazine* v59 no9 p96 S 2017

Why You Should Become a Wine Snob R. HARGREAVE, J. SALCITO et al color *GQ: Gentlemen's Quarterly* v97 no10 p80 O 2017

Liquors—Marketing

NOT NEW (MEXICAN!) DRINK ALERT! MEZCAL J. Kaplan, T. Buckley et al color *Bloomberg Businessweek* no4496 p66 O 24 2016

Liquors—Packaging

See also

Liquor bottles

Amaro for Everyone R. Schaap color *New York Times Magazine* p37 N 27 2016

Lis, Steve

Shaper Hall of Fame A. GOGGANS color *Surfer* v58 no2 p40 My 2017

Lisanti, Jamie

American Voices Ernesto Escobedo color *Sports Illustrated* v126 no12 p18 My 1 2017

American Voices Michael Mmoh color *Sports Illustrated* v125 no18 p22 D 5 2016

Arrival Instincts color *Sports Illustrated* v125 no14 p24 O 24-31 2016

BODY COUNT chart color diag *Sports Illustrated* v127 no9 p40 S 25 2017

FASHIONABLE 50 [Cover story] color *Sports Illustrated* v127 no3 p26 Jl 24 2017

Old School Food color *Sports Illustrated* v126 no2 p18 Ja 16 2017

When Pain Surpasses Gain color *Sports Illustrated* v126 no4 p20 Ja 30 2017

Lisbon (Portugal)

Brunch, Lunch, Lanche, and Dinner: Four Lisboan chefs on where to eat four Lisboan meals img *New York* v50 no9 p65 My 1 2017

THE URBANIST: Lisbon: Why the European expats are coming by the EasyJet-ful Z. NIEMTUS img *New York* v50 no9 p62 My 1 2017

Lisbon (Portugal)—Description & travel

High Heat S. COCHRAN color *Architectural Digest* v74 no3 p51 Mr 2017

Lisburn Road (Poem)

LISBURN ROAD M. Hofmann *New Yorker* v93 no3 p31 Mr 6 2017

Lischer, Richard

George Herbert: 100 Poems color *Christian Century* v133 no21 p55 O 12 2016

A Pursued Justice: Black Preaching from the Great Migration to Civil Rights *Christian Century* v134 no10 p42 My 10 2017

Lischer, Sarah Kenyon

The Global Refugee Crisis: Regional Destabilization & Humanitarian Protection *Daedalus* v146 no4 p85 Fall 2017

Lisée, Jean-François

Behind the curve M. PATRIQUIN color *Maclean's* v129 no42 p28 O 24 2016

Lish, Atticus

SOCIAL CONTRACT *Lapham's Quarterly* v10 no3 p181 Summ 2017

Lish, Gordon

Still Vibrant After All These Years L. THOMSON bw color *Publishers Weekly* v264 no27 p47 Jl 3 2017

Lishan Zhao

Strong peak in Tc of Sr2RuO4 under uniaxial pressure bibl color graph *Science* v355 no6321 p1 Ja 13 2017

LISICKY, PAUL

Obscure Objects of Desire *New York Times Book Review* p20 Ja 22 2017

Liska, Adam J.

Nuclear Weapons in a Changing Climate: Probability, Increasing Risks, and Perception bibl chart color graph *Environment* v59 no4 p22 Jl-Ag 2017

Liska, Cody

AV CLUB color *Snowboarder* v29 no2 p33 O 2016

THE EIGHTH PHASE bw cartoon color *Snowboarder* v29 no4 p54 D 2016

GARAGE BRANDS color *Snowboarder* v29 no4 p32 D 2016

LISKA, RACHEL

9 Easy Eco-Friendly Backyard Tips color *Reader's Digest* v189 no1131 p45 Je 2017

Liskey, Eric

SUMMER BUMMERS: PESTS, WEEDS, STRESSED PLANTS. EVERY YEAR, THEY SHOW UP OUT OF NOWHERE. SEND THEM PACKING WITH THESE EASY TIPS color *Successful Farming* v115 no7 p54 My 2017

LISOTTA, CHRISTOPHER

Greenland: Singular, Spectacular, Surprising color *Advocate* no1089 p50 F/Mr 2017

LISS, SARAH

HOW TO: Assemble a Sketch-Comedy Troupe From Scratch img *New York* v50 no15 p63 Jl 24 2017

LISSACK, MICHAEL

Consensual Sex Under Title IX *USA Today Magazine* v145 no2864 p67 My 2017

Lissner, Elaine

The Elusive Male Pill *MIT Technology Review* v120 no3 p10 My/Je 2017

LISS-SCHULTZ, NINA

THE CLOSET IN THE CLOUD cartoon *Mother Jones* v42 no1 p61 Ja/F 2017

"SOME FORM OF PUNISHMENT" color *Mother Jones* v42 no3 p48 My/Je 2017

List, John

Contingent valuation: Flawed logic? color *Science* v357 no6349 p363 Jl 28 2017

Putting a value on injuries to natural assets: The BP oil spill chart *Science* v356 no6335 p253 Ap 21 2017

recognizes both rising stars and lifetime contributions [Cover story] A. O'Donnell *Literacy Today (2411-7862)* v35 no2 p26 S/O 2017

A JACK-OF-ALL-TRADES N. Cremen color *Literacy Today (2411-7862)* v34 no4 p12 Ja/F 2017

POWERFUL PARTNERSHIPS: Literacy, your librarian, and you J. K. Valenza and M. A. Scheuer *Literacy Today (2411-7862)* v35 no1 p14 Jl/Ag 2017

PRINCIPLES FOR ELEMENTARY PRINCIPALS: Keys to remember when it comes to being a literacy leader T. Meidl and J. Lau *Literacy Today (2411-7862)* v35 no2 p24 S/O 2017

TRANSFORMING THE NARRATIVE: The director and producer of Teach Us All on literacy's role in the fight for educational equity S. Lowman *Literacy Today (2411-7862)* v35 no1 p10 Jl/Ag 2017

What Does It TAKE? *Literacy Today (2411-7862)* v35 no2 p43 S/O 2017

WHY WE NEED TO TRACK PROGRESS L. Helman color *Literacy Today (2411-7862)* v34 no4 p10 Ja/F 2017

Literacy programs

Choices Are Here! color *Literacy Today (2411-7862)* v34 no6 p4 My/Je 2017

DIFFERENTIATED AND MEANINGFUL INSTRUCTION: Turning around districtwide performance by immersing students in an engaging, literacy-rich environment L. Moody and J. Morrow *Literacy Today (2411-7862)* v35 no1 p18 Jl/Ag 2017

Literacy—Congresses

EVENTS *Literacy Today (2411-7862)* v34 no3 p38 N/D 2016

EVENTS *Literacy Today (2411-7862)* v35 no2 p40 S/O 2017

LIT BITS *Literacy Today (2411-7862)* v35 no2 p4 S/O 2017

OUR ORLANDO FIVE: Favorite highlights from ILA 2017--or, some of the best of what you may have missed! *Literacy Today (2411-7862)* v35 no2 p8 S/O 2017

PUTTING BOOKS TO WORK: Create lessons based on children's and YA books, side by side with the authors themselves, at ILA 2017 M. Cotillo and E. O'Leary color *Literacy Today (2411-7862)* v34 no6 p30 My/Je 2017

Literacy—Government policy

WHAT'S HOT 2017 C. P. Clark *Literacy Today (2411-7862)* v34 no4 p3 Ja/F 2017

Literacy—Social aspects

PROVIDING DIRECTION J. Williams *Literacy Today (2411-7862)* v34 no4 p16 Ja/F 2017

Literacy—Societies, etc.

BEYOND NATIONAL borders O. Aina color *Literacy Today (2411-7862)* v34 no5 p52 Mr/Ap 2017

Elevating the Profession D. Fisher *Literacy Today (2411-7862)* v35 no2 p6 S/O 2017

FROM TEACHER to leader S. Kaplan color *Literacy Today (2411-7862)* v34 no3 p44 N/D 2016

Get Involved With ILA D. Fisher *Literacy Today (2411-7862)* v34 no4 p6 Ja/F 2017

ILA—an Evolving Organization and Conference Experience M. Craig Post *Literacy Today (2411-7862)* v34 no5 p6 Mr/Ap 2017

LIT BITS *Literacy Today (2411-7862)* v35 no2 p4 S/O 2017

Using Technology to Enhance Our Community D. Barone *Literacy Today (2411-7862)* v34 no3 p6 N/D 2016

Literacy—Standards

WHAT'S HOT 2017 C. P. Clark *Literacy Today (2411-7862)* v34 no4 p3 Ja/F 2017

WHAT'S HOT IN LITERACY [Cover story] R. Edward chart color graph *Literacy Today (2411-7862)* v34 no4 p18 Ja/F 2017

Literacy—Study & teaching

CRACKING THE CONTENT AREAS S. Zaidi color *Literacy Today (2411-7862)* v34 no3 p32 N/D 2016

SKIRTING QUESTIONS D. L. Wolter color *Literacy Today (2411-7862)* v34 no3 p10 N/D 2016

WHAT'S HOT IN LITERACY [Cover story] R. Edward chart color graph *Literacy Today (2411-7862)* v34 no4 p18 Ja/F 2017

Literacy—Study & teaching (Middle school)

LEADERSHIP BY COMMITTEE: Our middle school's journey to create a culture of literacy A. Osborn *Literacy Today (2411-7862)* v35 no2 p20 S/O 2017

Literacy—United States

THE KEY IS DIFFERENTIATION: Recognizing the literacy and linguistic needs of indigenous Hispanic students L. J. Pentón

Herrera color *Literacy Today (2411-7862)* v34 no6 p8 My/Je 2017

WE'RE IN THIS TOGETHER L. Elion color *Literacy Today (2411-7862)* v34 no4 p36 Ja/F 2017

Literary errors & blunders

FROM THE EDITOR P. Lay *History Today* v66 no12 p2 D 2016

Literary explication

FEEDING TWO BIRDS WITH ONE WORM B. I. Bailey color *Literacy Today (2411-7862)* v34 no4 p26 Ja/F 2017

Literary festivals

ALL AROUND Missouri color *Missouri Life* v44 no2 p103 Ap 2017

BULLISH ON BOOKS L. Martin *Virginia Living* v15 no3 p27 Ap 2017

CALENDAR *New Orleans Magazine* v51 no5 p26 Mr 2017

Diversity on Display L. Ahuile color *Publishers Weekly* v263 no50 p24 D 5 2016

HOW TO MAKE THE SHARJAH INTERNATIONAL BOOK FAIR PROFESSIONAL PROGRAM & TRANSLATION GRANT REWARDING G. ISHMAEL color *Publishers Weekly* v263 no43 p(Sp)14 O 24 2016

INDIAN AUTHORS AT SIBF R. DeeCee bw color *Publishers Weekly* v263 no43 p(Sp)18 O 24 2016

INTRODUCTION R. TAGHOLM *Publishers Weekly* v263 no43 p(Sp)4 O 24 2016

LEAVE USA STORY: We are in challenging times! We need your help S. DeBoer *South Dakota Magazine* p6 S/O 2017 Supplement

Lionel Shriver Is Out of Line: And thank God J. Foreman *Commentary* v142 no5 p31 D 2016

Rick Bragg L. Monk Carter color *New Orleans Magazine* v51 no6 p28 Ap 2017

SELECT BOOK CONFERENCES, FESTIVALS, AND FAIRS IN 2017 J. MAHER *Publishers Weekly* v264 no1 p23 Ja 2 2017

SIBF BOOK FAIR AWARDS 2016 R. Tagholm *Publishers Weekly* v263 no43 p(Sp)8 O 24 2016

Thirty Years of Telling Great Stories L. AHUILE *Publishers Weekly* v263 no46 p4 N 14 2016

WELCOME A. A. AMERI *Publishers Weekly* v263 no43 p(Sp)2 O 24 2016

WELCOME... Festival of Books Visitors C. Turbiville *South Dakota Magazine* p4 S/O 2017 Supplement

WORLDVIEWS A. R. ALBANESE *Publishers Weekly* v263 no39 p32 S 26 2016

Literary form

See also

Allegory

Essay (Literary form)

Fiction genres

Short story (Literary form)

NEW VOICES ON TIMELESS SUBJECTS L. GARRETT color *Publishers Weekly* v264 no32 p24 Ag 7 2017

Literary interpretation

Book on Sakharov raises issues S. D. Drell and G. P. Shultz *Physics Today* v70 no2 p14 F 2017

Kojevnikov replies A. Kojevnikov *Physics Today* v70 no2 p14 F 2017

Literary prizes

See also

National Book Awards

THE 2017 BOOK AWARDS M. Reynolds *Christianity Today* v61 no1 p52 Ja/F 2017

Award Kremlinology B. BETHUNE color *Maclean's* v129 no44 p108 N 7 2016

The Carnegie Medals Turn Six A. RICHARD ALBANESE color *Publishers Weekly* v264 no25 p38 Je 19 2017

NEWS ROUNDUP bw *Publishers Weekly* v264 no18 p18 My 1 2017

SIBF BOOK FAIR AWARDS 2016 R. Tagholm *Publishers Weekly* v263 no43 p(Sp)8 O 24 2016

WHALES AND DINOSAURS D. T. Max cartoon *New Yorker* v93 no13 p32 My 15 2017

Literary prizes—United States

See also

Newbery Medal

A Night for Winners J. Maher color *Publishers Weekly* v263 no47

p4 N 21 2016

Literary research

READING THAT UNITES US: Discovering the science of literature through our favorite books N. Smetannikova color *Literacy Today (2411-7862)* v34 no6 p46 My/Je 2017

Literary style

Style and Substance: Can genius be graphed? The word choices that explain why Jane Austen's work survives and thrives K. A. Flynn and J. Katz *New York Times Book Review* p13 Jl 16 2017

Literature

See also

Characters & characteristics in literature

Children's literature

Drama

Fiction

First person narrative

Journalism

Letters

Quotations

Satire

Wit & humor

Young adult literature

The Brutal Dreams That Came True M. Filler color *New York Review of Books* v63 no20 p22 D 22 2016

Mission Impossible W. Teale *Literacy Today (2411-7862)* v34 no6 p6 My/Je 2017

On le Road D. E. BÉCHARD cartoon *Walrus* v13 no10 p67 D 2016

On Optimism and Despair Z. Smith color *New York Review of Books* v63 no20 p36 D 22 2016

parents to parents *Parents* v91 no6 p14 Je 2016

popular authors' favorite children's books J. PACTON color *Parents* v92 no5 p48 My 2017

Literature & history

Portrait of the Author as a Historian A. Lee *History Today* v66 no10 p54 O 2016

Literature & society

CURATING A DIVERSE AND ANTI-BIASED COLLECTION: Building capacity to identify and use diverse youth literature in the classroom R. E. Quiroa color *Literacy Today (2411-7862)* v34 no6 p22 My/Je 2017

International Literature: Writers have found freedom and restriction working in other languages. For Leonora Carrington, alternatives to English offered her access to secret selves P. Sehgal *New York Times Book Review* p59 Je 4 2017

Literature publishing

Literary Publishing in SINGAPORE T. TAN *Publishers Weekly* v263 no41 p23 O 10 2016

Literature—Adaptations

Avenue of the Idealists J. Davidson img *New York* v50 no7 p76 Ap 3 2017

Skybound's Walking Dead Graphic Novel Sales Won't Die C. Reid chart color *Publishers Weekly* v263 no45 p5 N 7 2016

Literature—Congresses

Roving Eye T. Parks *New York Times Book Review* p27 F 12 2017

Literature—History & criticism

FEEDING TWO BIRDS WITH ONE WORM B. I. Bailey color *Literacy Today (2411-7862)* v34 no4 p26 Ja/F 2017

Master Class D. Pinckney bw *New York Review of Books* v64 no15 p19 O 12 2017

Literature—Religious aspects

Stand & Wait K. S. Franklin cartoon *Commonweal* v144 no3 p39 F 10 2017

Literature—Research

Novel Math M. Fischetti graph *Scientific American* v316 no2 p76 F 2017

Literature—Study & teaching (Secondary)

LIT BITS color *Literacy Today (2411-7862)* v34 no4 p4 Ja/F 2017

Literature—Study & teaching—Congresses

A Focus on the Literary and Creative Arts Curricula [Cover story] S. KHAN *Islamic Horizons* v46 no2 p29 Mr/Ap 2017

Literes, Antonio

For the People R. Platt cartoon *New Yorker* v93 no12 p8 My 8 2017

Litespeed Bicycles (Company)

LITESPEED GRAVEL J. Lindsey color *Bicycling* v58 no9 p86

O 2017

Lithgow, John, 1945-

JOHN LITHGOW J. Hibberd and A. Wilkinson color *Entertainment Weekly* no1456 p60 Mr 10 2017

Lithgow, John, 1945—Interviews

BEING JOHN LITHGOW J. RUSSELL *TV Guide* v65 no11 p26 Mr 6 2017

John Lithgow A. Nash color *AARP: The Magazine* v60 no5A p17 Ag/S 2017

Lithium

Quantum and isotope effects in lithium metal G. J. Ackland, M. Dunuwille et al color diag graph *Science* v356 no6344 p1254 Je 23 2017

Lithium cobalt oxide

LITHIUM-ION BATTERIES C. LEU color *Wired* v25 no4 p20 Ap 2017

Lithium hydride

NEW INSIGHT INTO AN INTRIGUING MATERIAL A. Parker color graph *Science & Technology Review* p12 O/N 2016

Lithium-ion batteries

GREAT EXPECTATIONS K. Cameron *Cycle World* v56 no9 p28 O 2017

Help Desk G. Fleishman color *Macworld - Digital Edition* p57 Ap 2017

Highly elastic binders integrating polyrotaxanes for silicon microparticle anodes in lithium ion batteries S. Choi, Kwon et al diag *Science* v357 no6348 p279 Jl 21 2017

LITHIUM-ION BATTERIES C. LEU color *Wired* v25 no4 p20 Ap 2017

Lithium-ion batteries—Evaluation

Find Your Power *Log Home Living* v33 no9 p18 D 2016

Lithium-ion batteries—Research

A BETTER BATTERY E. Tingwall cartoon *Car & Driver* v62 no8 p18 F 2017

Lithium-ion battery manufacturing

Charged Up: Batteries Are the Next Target In China's Clean-Energy Conquest J. Worland color *Time* v190 no15 p20 O 16 2017

Lithium mines & mining

An Account of Clayton Valley and the Great Nevada LITHIUM RUSH P. Tullis color graph *Bloomberg Businessweek* no4517 p60 Ap 3 2017

We're Going To Need More Lithium D. Merrill, J. Shankleman et al diag graph map *Bloomberg Businessweek* no4537 p60 S 11 2017

Lithosphere

High-resolution lithosphere viscosity and dynamics revealed by magnetotelluric imaging Lijun Liu and D. Hasterok bibl graph *Science* v353 no6307 p1515 S 30 2016

Mega-earthquakes rupture flat megathrusts Q. Bletery, A. M. Thomas et al bibl graph *Science* v354 no6315 p1027 N 25 2016

Lithosphere—Research

Constraining lithospheric flow B. J. P. Kaus bibl color graph *Science* v353 no6307 p1495 S 30 2016

Lithuania—Foreign relations

backstory color *New Republic* v248 no4 p64 Ap 2017

Litina, Anastasia

What a Study of 33 Countries Found About Aging Populations and Innovation bw *Harvard Business Review Digital Articles* p2 Ja 18 2017

Litke, Justin

Bradley J. Birzer, Russell Kirk: American Conservative *Society* v54 no3 p299 Je 2017

Litt, David

More Than Words: A speechwriter for Barack Obama recalls coming of age at the White House R. E. THOMAS *New York Times Book Review* p19 S 24 2017

Litterateurs

See also

Authors

I HAVE FALLEN IN LOVE WITH AMERICAN NAMES P. ROTH bw *New Yorker* v93 no16 p46 Je 5 2017

LITTLE, AIESHA D.

THE MAN BEHIND THE MASKS *Cincinnati Magazine* v50 no10 p28 Jl 2017

Little, Ann M.

The Many Captivities of Esther Wheelwright M. Bendroth *Chris-*

tian Century v134 no7 p40 Mr 29 2017

Little, Benilde
   The Meaning of Michelle bw color *Glamour* v114 no12 p198 D 2016

Little, Dawn
   Sustained virologic control in SIV+ macaques after antiretroviral and α4β7 antibody therapy bibl graph *Science* v354 no6309 p197 O 14 2016

LITTLE, JANE BRAXTON
   Waiting for Water *Audubon* v118 no6 p17 Wint 2016

Little, Joel
   Life of the Party S. Lansky color *Time* v189 no23 p44 Je 19 2017

LITTLE, MELANIE
   Body of Work bw *Walrus* v14 no3 p63 Ap 2017

Little, Tias
   Poses of the month [Cover story] color *Yoga Journal* no291 p49 My 2017

Little, Tim
   Complex multifault rupture during the 2016 Mw 7.8 Kaikōura earthquake, New Zealand color map *Science* v356 no6334 p154 Ap 14 2017

Little Big Shots (TV program)
   Harvey Lands His Big Shot M. SCHNEIDER *TV Guide* v64 no15 p6 Ap 4 2016

Little Big Town (Performer)
   Country That Melds Tried-and-True With Utterly New M. Johnston color *Time* v189 no7/8 p107 F 27 2017
   LITTLE BIG TOWN K. O'Donnell color *Entertainment Weekly* no1446/1447 p77 D 2016/Ja 2017

Little Giant Ladder Systems (Company)
   Ladders color *Popular Mechanics* v193 no7 p34 S 2016

Little Golden Books (Company)
   Commemorating 75 Years Of Little Golden Books S. Lodge color *Publishers Weekly* v264 no8 p18 F 20 2017

Little Guy Trailers (Company)
   Happy Campers R. DeBruhl color *AARP: The Magazine* v60 no4A p11 Je/Jl 2017

Little Men (Film)
   7 — THE ACTING CLASS J. McGovern *Entertainment Weekly* no1444/1445 p60 D 16 2016
   Dead Man on Campus D. EDELSTEIN img *New York* v49 no15 p86 Jl 25 2016

Little Mix (Performer)
   THE SECRET INGREDIENTS OF LITTLE MIX N. Feeney color *Entertainment Weekly* no1441 p55 N 25 2016

Little Passports Inc.—Finance
   Oh, the Places You'll Go! S. ADAMS color *Forbes* v198 no7 p52 N 29 2016

Little Sister (Film)
   From Marilyn Manson to Marian prayer T. Donnellan color *America* v216 no5 p45 Mr 6 2017

Little Women: Atlanta (TV program)
   BEHIND THE SCENES C. BETHEA *Atlanta* v57 no1 p86 My 2017

Little Bighorn, Battle of the, Mont., 1876
   The Face of Battle without the Rules of War: Lessons from Red Horse & the Battle of the Little Bighorn S. D. Sagan *Daedalus* v146 no1 p25 Wint 2017

Little Foxes, The (Theatrical production)
   THE THEATRE *New Yorker* v93 no8 p5 Ap 10 2017

Little Hours, The (Film)
   The Little Hours D. Coggan color *Entertainment Weekly* no1473 p48 Jl 7 2017
   Medieval Laughs for the Modern Day S. Zacharek color *Time* v190 no2/3 p90 Jl 10-17 2017
   Our bad habit: The recent film that fixates on nuns having fun isn't all that funny J. M. Griffith color *U.S. Catholic* v82 no10 p38 O 2017
   The Return of Nunsploitation M. ATKINSON *In These Times* v41 no6 p36 Je 2017

Little Mermaid, The (Theatrical production)
   Sounds From Under the Sea G. Petersen *Stage Directions* v30 no5 p16 My 2017
   Tituss Burgess J. Crelin color *Current Biography* v78 no3 p3 Mr 2017

Little Night Music, A (Music)

Eliogabalo S. J. Mudge *Opera News* v81 no6 p48 D 2016
Manon S. J. Mudge *Opera News* v81 no6 p49 D 2016
Norma G. Hall *Opera News* v81 no6 p46 D 2016
The Ouroboros Trilogy J. S. Lessner *Opera News* v81 no6 p44 D 2016

Little Night Music, A (Theatrical production)
   Judi Dench My Life in Pictures J. McGovern color *Entertainment Weekly* no1484 p32 S 29 2017

Little Prince, The (Film)
   Finding the Little Prince R. MILZOFF img *New York* v49 no15 p84 Jl 25 2016

Little Rascals, The (Film)
   SAVE THE PAST LIFE FOR ME R. O'CONNOR cartoon *Chicago* v66 no1 p34 Ja 2017

Liturgics
         See also
      Church music
      Fasts & feasts
   From the ground up M. Francis *U.S. Catholic* v81 no12 p22 D 2016
   A liturgy for families suffering a miscarriage E. Sanna *U.S. Catholic* v81 no11 p35 N 2016

Liturgies
         See also
      Catholic liturgy
      Funeral service
      Mass (Liturgy)
   How do you rate the quality of liturgy in your parish? Mary, Thomas et al graph *America* v217 no7 p6 O 2 2017

LITVAK, ELIZAVETA
   THIRSTY GRASS *USA Today Magazine* v146 no2866 p70 Jl 2017

Litvak, Yael
   Microbiota-activated PPAR-γ signaling inhibits dysbiotic Enterobacteriaceae expansion graph *Science* v357 no6351 p570 Ag 11 2017

Litvan, Laura
   Repeal and _____ *Bloomberg Businessweek* no4509 p22 Ja 30 2017
   The Unmaking Of American Dreams chart *Bloomberg Businessweek* no4537 p36 S 11 2017

LITVIN, STEVEN Y.
   The Resilience of Marine Ecosystems to Climatic Disturbances *BioScience* v67 no3 p208 Mr 2017

Liu, Albert Tianxiang
   A general, modular method for the catalytic asymmetric synthesis of alkylboronate esters bibl color *Science* v354 no6317 p1265 D 9 2016

Liu, Alfred
   A New Caribbean Bank For Chinese Money color *Bloomberg Businessweek* no4523 p38 My 22 2017

Liu, Amy
   A Blueprint for More Inclusive Economic Growth *Harvard Business Review Digital Articles* p2 Mr 3 2016

Liu, Bao-Li
   Bug mapping and fitness testing of chemically synthesized chromosome X diag *Science* v355 no6329 p1048 Mr 10 2017

Liu, Cailing
   Guanine glycation repair by DJ-1/Park7 and its bacterial homologs chart color diag graph *Science* v357 no6347 p208 Jl 14 2017

Liu, Cindy D.
   Thirst-associated preoptic neurons encode an aversive motivational drive diag *Science* v357 no6356 p1149 S 15 2017

Liu, Duo
   Bug mapping and fitness testing of chemically synthesized chromosome X diag *Science* v355 no6329 p1048 Mr 10 2017

Liu, Franklin
   Systemic pan-AMPK activator MK-8722 improves glucose homeostasis but induces cardiac hypertrophy graph *Science* v357 no6350 p507 Ag 4 2017

Liu, Fuchen
   Control of species-dependent cortico-motoneuronal connections underlying manual dexterity diag graph *Science* v357 no6349 p400 Jl 28 2017

Liu, Gloria

18 FOR 18 color *Bicycling* v58 no9 p63 O 2017

#BIKECRUSH color *Bicycling* v58 no8 p53 S 2017

CANYON ULTIMATE WMN CF SLX DISC 9.0 TEAM CSR color *Bicycling* v58 no9 p90 O 2017

CORYN RIVERA IS NOT LIKE THE REST OF US color *Bicycling* v58 no10 p32 N/D 2017

EASY ON, EASY OFF! color *Bicycling* v58 no7 p82 Ag 2017

"I WANT TO GO FAST." color *Bicycling* v58 no3 p68 Ap 2017

MAVIC ECHAPPÉE W SHOE color *Bicycling* v58 no4 p89 My 2017

ON THE MOUNTAIN color *Bicycling* v58 no3 p84 Ap 2017

Oooh... Cozy! color *Bicycling* v58 no1 p64 Ja/F 2017

SEND-IT SHOES color *Bicycling* v58 no7 p80 Ag 2017

THOSE LEGS! bw *Bicycling* v58 no8 p39 S 2017

WAHOO ELEMNT color *Bicycling* v58 no1 p61 Ja/F 2017

"WHAT'S A GOOD BIKE FOR RIDING HOME FROM THE BAR?" color *Bicycling* v58 no3 p54 Ap 2017

YETI SB5+ TURQ X01 EAGLE color *Bicycling* v58 no4 p84 My 2017

Liu, Hong

Bug mapping and fitness testing of chemically synthesized chromosome X diag *Science* v355 no6329 p1048 Mr 10 2017

Mitotic transcription and waves of gene reactivation during mitotic exit color graph *Science* v357 no6359 p119 O 6 2017

Liu, Hui-Min

"Perfect" designer chromosome V and behavior of a ring derivative diag *Science* v355 no6329 p1046 Mr 10 2017

Liu, Jia

Direction-specific van der Waals attraction between rutile TiO2 nanocrystals diag *Science* v356 no6336 p434 Ap 28 2017

Liu, Jianguo

A looming tragedy of the sand commons color *Science* v357 no6355 p970 S 8 2017

Liu, Jiayu

DNA sequence–directed shape change of photopatterned hydrogels via high-degree swelling color diag *Science* v357 no6356 p1126 S 15 2017

Liu, Jin-Gui

"Perfect" designer chromosome V and behavior of a ring derivative diag *Science* v355 no6329 p1046 Mr 10 2017

Liu, Jinqi

Systemic pan-AMPK activator MK-8722 improves glucose homeostasis but induces cardiac hypertrophy graph *Science* v357 no6350 p507 Ag 4 2017

Liu, Jintao

Coupling between distant biofilms and emergence of nutrient time-sharing bw color graph *Science* v356 no6338 p638 My 12 2017

Liu, Jun-Jie

Structures of the CRISPR genome integration complex color *Science* v357 no6356 p1113 S 15 2017

Liu, Jun-Ming

An organic-inorganic perovskite ferroelectric with large piezoelectric response graph *Science* v357 no6348 p306 Jl 21 2017

Liu, Junzhong

Epigenetic regulation of antagonistic receptors confers rice blast resistance with yield balance bibl diag *Science* v355 no6328 p962 Mr 3 2017

Liu, Kai

Chiral Majorana fermion modes in a quantum anomalous Hall insulator–superconductor structure diag *Science* v357 no6348 p294 Jl 21 2017

Liu, Ke-Fei

A central neural circuit for itch sensation color graph *Science* v357 no6352 p695 Ag 18 2017

Liu, Kun Connie

Driving mosquito refractoriness to Plasmodium falciparum with engineered symbiotic bacteria color graph *Science* v357 no6358 p1399 S 29 2017

Liu, Lixia

Plants transfer lipids to sustain colonization by mutualistic mycorrhizal and parasitic fungi diag graph *Science* v356 no6343 p1172 Je 16 2017

Liu, Na

Plants transfer lipids to sustain colonization by mutualistic mycorrhizal and parasitic fungi diag graph *Science* v356 no6343 p1172 Je 16 2017

Liu, Nai-Le

Satellite-based entanglement distribution over 1200 kilometers diag graph *Science* v356 no6343 p1140 Je 16 2017

Liu, Ning-Zhi

"Perfect" designer chromosome V and behavior of a ring derivative diag *Science* v355 no6329 p1046 Mr 10 2017

Liu, Ping

Active sites for CO2 hydrogenation to methanol on Cu/ZnO catalysts bibl graph *Science* v355 no6331 p1296 Mr 24 2017

Atomic-layered Au clusters on α-MoC as catalysts for the low-temperature water-gas shift reaction chart diag graph *Science* v357 no6349 p389 Jl 28 2017

TECHNICAL COMMENT ABSTRACTS *Science* v357 no6354 p881 S 1 2017

Liu, Pingfang

DNA damage is a pervasive cause of sequencing errors, directly confounding variant identification bibl graph *Science* v355 no6326 p752 F 17 2017

Liu, Qi

Deterministic entanglement generation from driving through quantum phase transitions bibl color graph *Science* v355 no6325 p620 F 10 2017

Liu, Qili

Branch-specific plasticity of a bifunctional dopamine circuit encodes protein hunger graph *Science* v356 no6337 p534 My 5 2017

Liu, Richard Y.

Macrocyclic bis-thioureas catalyze stereospecific glycosylation reactions bibl diag *Science* v355 no6321 p1 Ja 13 2017

Liu, S. John

CRISPRi-based genome-scale identification of functional long noncoding RNA loci in human cells bibl graph *Science* v355 no6320 p1 Ja 6 2017

Liu, Sha

Branch-specific plasticity of a bifunctional dopamine circuit encodes protein hunger graph *Science* v356 no6337 p534 My 5 2017

Liu, Shi-Yang

"Perfect" designer chromosome V and behavior of a ring derivative diag *Science* v355 no6329 p1046 Mr 10 2017

Liu, Ting

"Perfect" designer chromosome V and behavior of a ring derivative diag *Science* v355 no6329 p1046 Mr 10 2017

Liu, Tsung-Li

Visualizing dynamic microvillar search and stabilization during ligand detection by T cells color *Science* v356 no6338 p598 My 12 2017

Liu, Wei

Deep functional analysis of synII, a 770-kilobase synthetic yeast chromosome diag *Science* v355 no6329 p1047 Mr 10 2017

"Perfect" designer chromosome V and behavior of a ring derivative diag *Science* v355 no6329 p1046 Mr 10 2017

Liu, Wei-Yue

Satellite-based entanglement distribution over 1200 kilometers diag graph *Science* v356 no6343 p1140 Je 16 2017

Liu, Wu

Late Pleistocene archaic human crania from Xuchang, China bibl color diag graph *Science* v355 no6328 p969 Mr 3 2017

Liu, Xiaobo, 1955-2017

Liu Xiaobo C. Campbell color *Time* v190 no5 p17 Jl 31 2017

Liu Xiaobo, Leader of China, R.I.P color *National Review* v69 no15 p13 Ag 14 2017

Liu Xiaobo's Last Text L. Xiaobo bw *New York Review of Books* v64 no14 p8 S 28 2017

Liu, Xing-Jun

A central neural circuit for itch sensation color graph *Science* v357 no6352 p695 Ag 18 2017

Liu, Xue-Ting

Molecular and neural basis of contagious itch behavior in mice bibl diag *Science* v355 no6329 p1072 Mr 10 2017

Liu, Yi-Lin

"Perfect" designer chromosome V and behavior of a ring derivative diag *Science* v355 no6329 p1046 Mr 10 2017

Liu, Ying-Chau

Epitaxial lift-off of electrodeposited single-crystal gold foils for flexible electronics bibl bw diag *Science* v355 no6330 p1203 Mr 17 2017

Liu, Yizhou
Unequivocal determination of complex molecular structures using anisotropic NMR measurements color *Science* v356 no6333 p43 Ap 7 2017

Liu, Yue
Bug mapping and fitness testing of chemically synthesized chromosome X diag *Science* v355 no6329 p1048 Mr 10 2017
"Perfect" designer chromosome V and behavior of a ring derivative diag *Science* v355 no6329 p1046 Mr 10 2017

Liu, Zhenfeng
Structure and assembly mechanism of plant C2S2M2-type PSII-LHCII supercomplex color *Science* v357 no6353 p815 Ag 25 2017

Liu, Zhengtao
A pathology atlas of the human cancer transcriptome diag *Science* v357 no6352 p660 Ag 18 2017

Liu, Zhen-Ning
"Perfect" designer chromosome V and behavior of a ring derivative diag *Science* v355 no6329 p1046 Mr 10 2017

Liu, Zunfeng
Harvesting electrical energy from carbon nanotube yarn twist diag graph *Science* v357 no6353 p773 Ag 25 2017

LIU YONGMOU
The Benefits of Technocracy in China *Issues in Science & Technology* v33 no1 p25 Fall 2016

Liu Cixin, 1963-
THE HIDDEN MIND P. SUDERMAN color *Reason* v48 no8 p50 Ja 2017

LIUHTO, MAIJA
The Afghan Field Medic color *Foreign Policy* no225 p14 Jl/Ag 2017

Liv & Maddie (TV program)
Disney's Next Teen Queen M. Snetiker color *Entertainment Weekly* no1474/1475 p106 Jl 21-28 2017

Liv Cycling (Company)
"I WISH MY RIDES COULD GO ON FOREVER." C. Giddings and B. STRICKLAND color *Bicycling* v58 no3 p110 Ap 2017
Liv Pique L. Kemp color *Bike Magazine* v24 no5 p92 Jl 2017

Live action/animation films
Disney Brings Good Things to Life D. Coggan color *Entertainment Weekly* no1459 p11 Mr 31 2017
MULAN RIDES BACK INTO BATTLE—FOR REAL D. Coggan color *Entertainment Weekly* no1435 p10 O 14 2016
NOW (RE)PLAYING M. YARM cartoon graph *Wired* v25 no3 p20 Mr 2017
TALE AS OLD AS TIME [Cover story] C. Collis color *Entertainment Weekly* no1439 p28 N 11 2016

Live at the New Penelope Cafe (Music)
Nettwerk, Justin Time Records Resurrect Rising Sun K. MICALLEF bw *Downbeat* v83 no12 p16 D 2016

Live at the Whisky a Go Go: The Complete Recordings (Music)
Good to Us C. FLEMING bw *Weekly Standard* v22 no21 p33 F 6 2017

Live by Night (Film)
BEN AFFLECK'S LIVE BY NIGHT N. Sperling color *Entertainment Weekly* no1439 p42 N 11 2016
Ben Affleck S. Vilkomerson color *Entertainment Weekly* no1444/1445 p20 D 16 2016
Live by Night L. Greenblatt color *Entertainment Weekly* no1446/1447 p101 D 2016/Ja 2017

Live From Jazz at the Bistro (Music)
The Hot Box J. Murph, J. Macnie et al *Downbeat* v84 no8 p69 Ag 2017

Live in London (Music)
Magic on the Bandstand K. Silsbee bw *Downbeat* v84 no4 p65 Ap 2017

Live in Los Angeles (Music)
The Hot Box chart *Downbeat* v84 no3 p55 Mr 2017

Live In New York 2010 (Music)
William Parker: A Sonic Trisection B. MEYER bw *Downbeat* v84 no9 p64 S 2017

Live television programs
The Best Ways to Stream Live TV A. D'Arminio *TV Guide* v65 no19 p12 My 1 2017

Hulu Reboots for A Post-Cable Age L. Shaw graph *Bloomberg Businessweek* no4502 p30 D 5 2016

Live With Kelly & Ryan (TV program)
Seacrest IN! D. Coggan and E. Strohm color *Entertainment Weekly* no1465 p17 My 12 2017

Live at A-Trane: Berlin (Music)
Live At A-Trane: Berlin B. Zimmerman bw *Downbeat* v84 no5 p59 My 2017

Lively, Blake, 1987-
Velvet for Day color *Glamour* v114 no11 p184 N 2016

Lively, Blake, 1987—Interviews
THIS PICTURE IS PERFECT. BLAKE LIVELY IS NOT A. Morris color *Glamour* v115 no9 p188 S 2017

Lively, Penelope, 1933-
When Past Is Present C. McGrath *New York Times Book Review* p1 My 7 2017

Liver disease prevention
NEWSBITES [Cover story] *Tufts University Health & Nutrition Letter* v35 no7 p1 S 2017

Liver diseases—Prevention
Is Your Liver Cooked? A. Swartz color *Men's Health* v32 no1 p90 Ja/F 2017

Liver diseases—Risk factors
The downside of taking pills to treat chronic pain *Harvard Health Letter* v42 no5 p6 Mr 2017

Liver tumors
protect your watershed S. Moen color *Cabin Living* p13 Ag 2017

Liveris, Andrew
Looking for Answers to the World's Biggest Challenges In the Eternal City color *Time* v188 no24 p31 D 12 2016

Livermore, David
Leading a Brainstorming Session with a Cross-Cultural Team *Harvard Business Review Digital Articles* p2 My 27 2016

Livermore, M.
Best cost estimate of greenhouse gases *Science* v357 no6352 p655 Ag 18 2017

Liver—Physiology
ASK THE DOCTOR A. L. KOMAROFF *Harvard Health Letter* v42 no4 p2 F 2017

Liverpool (England)
Election Day in Liverpool: Victory for The Fab Four Party E. Laborde bw *New Orleans Magazine* v51 no10 p216 Ag 2017

Liverpool (England)—Description & travel
Love me Do, in Liverpool *British Heritage Travel* v37 no6 p59 N/D 2016

Liversidge, Helen
The growth pattern of Neandertals, reconstructed from a juvenile skeleton from El Sidrón (Spain) color graph *Science* v357 no6357 p1282 S 22 2017

Lives of Performers (Film)
MOVING BEYOND V. Lucca bw *Film Comment* v53 no4 p42 Jl/Ag 2017

LIVESEY, BRUCE
Science for Sale color *Walrus* v14 no4 p24 My 2017

Livesey, Margot
The Stallion in the Room C. SCHAMA *New York Times Book Review* p22 O 9 2016

Lives of Many Others, The (Music)
Convergence Factor P. MARGASAK color *Downbeat* v84 no7 p19 Jl 2017

Livestock
    See also
    Cattle
    Donkeys
    Horses
    Poultry
    Sheep
CARBON FARMING WILL (HELP) SAVE THE PLANET J. MCDOUGALL color *Rodale's Organic Life* v3 no1 p68 Ja 2017
ERADICATE? CATTLE INDUSTRY CONTEMPLATES THE POTENTIAL TO ELIMINATE BVD AS A SIGNIFICANT DISEASE G. Johnston *Successful Farming* v115 no6 p58 Ap 2017
Wagonhound Land and Livestock B. Welch color *American Cowboy* v23 no4 p96 D 2016/Ja 2017

Livestock exhibitions

TO LIFE *Physics Today* v70 no6 p25 Je 2017
Skin-Deep Evolutionary Link B. ALEX color *Discover* v38 no1 p58 Ja/F 2017

Lizards—Behavior

The Thermal Edge S. K. WILSON color *Natural History* v125 no3 p48 Mr 2017

Liz-Marzán, Luis M.

Growing anisotropic crystals at the nanoscale color diag *Science* v356 no6343 p1120 Je 16 2017

Lizotte, Heather

The Clinic PHOTO CRITIQUES S. von Dietze color *Dressage Today* v23 no6 p19 F 2017

LIZZA, JENNIFER

Laugh Lines color *Reader's Digest* v189 no1130 p107 My 2017

Lizza, Ryan

Bet the Ranch *New Republic* v248 no8/9 p5 Ag/S 2017
FIRING BACK bw cartoon color *New Yorker* v93 no15 p20 My 29 2017
TAMING TRUMP cartoon *New Yorker* v92 no33 p30 O 17 2016

Lizzie Fortunato Jewels (Company)

Lizzie Fortunato Earrings color *Bloomberg Businessweek* no4535 p71 Ag 28 2017

Lizzo (Performer)

Lizzo's Feel-Good Revolution N. Feeney color *Entertainment Weekly* no1435 p56 O 14 2016

Ljubuncic, Igor

The Amazing Adventures of Dashing Prince Dietrich. Woes & Hose, Book 1 *Publishers Weekly* v263 no47 p96 N 21 2016

Ljunggren, Tim

Koan Kreativity *Publishers Weekly* v264 no17 p58d Ap 24 2017

Llactayo, W.

Airborne laser-guided imaging spectroscopy to map forest trait diversity and guide conservation bibl chart graph *Science* v355 no6323 p385 Ja 27 2017

Llana, Sara Miller

British strive to build interfaith bridges amid terrorist attacks color *Christian Century* v134 no15 p14 Jl 19 2017

Llano, Matt

MATT LLANO S. DOUGLAS color *Runner's World* v51 no10 p32 N 2016

LLEWELLYN, OTHMAN A.

An Ecoregion-Based Approach to Protecting Half the Terrestrial Realm *BioScience* v67 no6 p534 Je 2017

Llinas, Juan Pablo

MoS2 transistors with 1-nanometer gate lengths bibl color graph *Science* v354 no6308 p99 O 7 2016

Llona, Ramiro

TABLE GAMES color *ARTnews* v115 no4 p23 Wint 2016/2017

Llopis, Roger

A molecular spin-photovoltaic device color diag *Science* v357 no6352 p677 Ag 18 2017

Lloyd, Alice B.

The Appalachian Work College color *Weekly Standard* v22 no10 p26 N 14 2016
Assault on Justice color *Weekly Standard* v22 no26 p30 Mr 13 2017
Can This State Be Saved? color *Weekly Standard* v23 no6 p27 O 16 2017
The Cassandra of Vanderbilt color *Weekly Standard* v22 no34 p32 My 15 2017
The Family Leave Dilemma color graph *Weekly Standard* v22 no48 p21 S 4 2017
Leaning Toward God *Weekly Standard* v22 no6 p32 O 17 2016
The Little College That Couldn't color *Weekly Standard* v22 no45 p17 Ag 7 2017
A Separate Place color *Weekly Standard* v22 no39 p16 Je 19 2017

Lloyd, Carli

At Any Cost color *Sports Illustrated* v125 no12 p44 O 10 2016

Lloyd, Carli, 1982-

Carli Lloyd J. Crelin color *Current Biography* v78 no2 p44 F 2017

Lloyd, Gordon

Rugged Individualism: Two of the gravest threats to this distinctively American value: nanny states and helicopter parents *Hoover Digest: Research & Opinion on Public Policy* no2 p42 Spr 2017

Lloyd, Harold, 1893-1971

Talk of the Town: In a city temporarily teeming with Shriners, silent-film star Harold Lloyd was the most famous man in a fez C. Zeigler *Indianapolis Monthly* v40 no10 p21 Je 2017

Lloyd, Howard R.

A RAIL-MARINE SHOWCASE [Cover story] color *Model Railroader* v84 no7 p42 Jl 2017

LLOYD, JARED

Losing Ground *American Forests* v123 no2 p12 Summ 2017
Woodpeckers THE ENGINEERS OF ECOSYSTEMS *American Forests* v123 no3 p16 Fall 2017

LLOYD, JENNY

BETTER THAN BESPOKE color *House Beautiful* p139 Ag 2017

Lloyd, K. C. Kent

Deficiency of microRNA miR-34a expands cell fate potential in pluripotent stem cells diag *Science* v355 no6325 p596 F 10 2017

Lloyd, M. Cooper

Attacking the Roots of Violence cartoon *Scientific American* v315 no5 p9 N 2016

Lloyd, Nick

Passchendaele: The Lost Victory of World War I *Publishers Weekly* v264 no13 p95 Mr 27 2017

Lloyd, Robin

Dissent with Modification diag *Scientific American* v316 no5 p14 My 2017
Gasping for Air color *Scientific American* v316 no3 p26 Mr 2017

LLOYD, WILLIAM FORSTER

OLD and RIGHT *American Conservative* v16 no1 p25 Ja/F 2017

Lloyd-Smith, James O.

Maternal antibodies' role in immunity bibl color *Science* v355 no6326 p704 F 17 2017
Potent protection against H5N1 and H7N9 influenza via childhood hemagglutinin imprinting bibl chart graph *Science* v354 no6313 p722 N 11 2016

Lloyd Webber, Andrew, 1948-

SCHOOL OF ROCK TEACHES US TO BREAK THE MOLD G. Holt *Cincinnati Magazine* v50 no8 p14 My 2017

LMC Truck (Company)

TAILGATE PARTY B. W. SMITH color *Dirt Sports + Off-Road* v51 no3 p52 Mr 2017

LMK (Music)

The Playlist bw color *Rolling Stone* no1295 p10 S 7 2017

Lmt, Bleu Andersen

Still worried *U.S. Catholic* v82 no10 p5 O 2017

Lo, Cody

Research night owls color *Science* v354 no6315 p964 N 25 2016

Lo, Wen-Ting

mTORC1 activity repression by late endosomal phosphatidylinositol 3,4-bisphosphate diag *Science* v356 no6341 p968 Je 1 2017

Loa, Ingo

Quantum and isotope effects in lithium metal color diag graph *Science* v356 no6344 p1254 Je 23 2017

Loach, Ken, 1936-

HOW THE OTHER HALF LIVES A. LANE color *New Yorker* v93 no17 p74 Je 19 2017
I, Daniel Blake C. Nashawaty color *Entertainment Weekly* no1448 p50 Ja 13 2017

Loaded Precision Inc.

flat out A. Smith and J. Weber color *Bike Magazine* v24 no3 p112 My 2017

Loaders (Machines)

Trackside Photos color *Model Railroader* v84 no7 p68 Jl 2017

Loaders (Machines)—Sales & prices

POCKET PRICE GUIDE: 2013 Midsize Skid Steer Loaders *Successful Farming* v115 no2 p29 F 2017

Loaders (Machines)—Charts, diagrams, etc.

POCKET PRICE GUIDE: 2013 Midsize Skid Steer Loaders *Successful Farming* v115 no2 p29 F 2017

Loads (Mechanics)

See also

Compression loads

Make a pipe load from plastic and stripwood D. Popp bw color *Model Railroader* v84 no4 p36 Ap 2017

Loafers (Shoes)

500,000 Miles Logged in the Past Year *Conde Nast Traveler* v51 no11 p128 D 2016

Loafers (Shoes)—Evaluation

The Essential: Loafer M. MILRAD GOLDSTEIN color *Martha Stewart Living* p50 S 2017

The Loafer Steps Out T. Patterson color *Bloomberg Businessweek* no4532 p64 Jl 31 2017

NOT Business as USUAL color *Esquire* p92 Ap 2017

ROCK STEADY J. MOAZAMI color *Chicago* v66 no4 p48 Ap 2017

Slide right into these color *Redbook* p59 Ap 2017

SMOOTH MOVE color *Esquire* v167 no2 p70 Mr 2017

this Way In: HIT THE LINKS FLASH SOME GREEN N. Sullivan color *Esquire* p27 S 2017

Loans

See also
Automobile loans

Does bankruptcy hurt an individual's ability to be hired or borrow money? Y. Ivanchev *Monthly Labor Review* p1 My 2017

Gettin' Better M. Werling *Sea Magazine* v109 no5 p54 My 2017

LAKE COMPOUNCE *Yankee* p25 Jl 2017

SEPTEMBER QUESTIONS *Sea Magazine* v109 no9 p61 S 2017

Loans for use

Lend Online and Earn Up to 11% E. LEARY cartoon *Kiplinger's Personal Finance* v71 no1 p58 Ja 2017

Loans—Great Britain

Diamonds Aren't A Bank's Best Friend F. Wild, T. Biesheuvel et al color *Bloomberg Businessweek* no4537 p26 S 11 2017

Loarie, Scott R.

Publish openly but responsibly color *Science* v357 no6347 p141 Jl 14 2017

LoBaido, Scott

MR. "T" I. Frazier cartoon *New Yorker* v92 no39 p32 N 28 2016

Lobbies (Rooms)—Design & construction

ESI Design with HOK and Available Light L. C. Lentz color *Architectural Record* v205 no2 p118 F 2017

Lobbying

Geopolitical Shell Game: Washington and the fraudulent freedom fighters T. G. CARPENTER *American Conservative* v16 no5 p31 S/O 2017

Lobbyists Are Behind the Rise in Corporate Profits J. Bessen *Harvard Business Review Digital Articles* p2 My 26 2016

Lobbying—United States

ACCESS 2 PREZ WHILE U WAIT: THE BUCKS START HERE N. Confessore *New York Times Magazine* p32 S 3 2017

Lobbying Is Not Enough to Build Influence Among U.S. Lawmakers M. D. Gottlieb and E. Gurney *Harvard Business Review Digital Articles* p2 D 28 2016

A Monument to Trump Hatred color *Weekly Standard* v22 no31 p2 Ap 17 2017

The NRA's New Scare Tactics L. RESTON il *New Republic* v248 no11 p6 N 2017

Work Hard, Die Poor: The Corporate Attack on Employee Pensions G. Lafer color *Progressive* v81 no6 p30 Ag/S 2017

Lobbying—United States—Government policy

How to Lobby But Not Be a Lobbyist B. Allison and B. Brody *Bloomberg Businessweek* no4511 p25 F 13 2017

Lobbying—United States—Charts, diagrams, etc.

THE REAL DC POWER PLAY graph img *Harvard Business Review* v95 no1 p24 Ja/F 2017

Lobbyists

THE TAX REFORM HUNGER GAMES ARE AFOOT IN WASHINGTON A. Vandermey diag *Fortune* v176 no5 p16 O 1 2017

Will Women Ever Break the Bronze Ceiling? M. Rhodan color *Time* v190 no9 p28 S 4 2017

Lobbyists—United States

THE LOBBYIST *Texas Monthly* v45 no2 p91 F 2017

Trump's K Street Office J. Green color *Bloomberg Businessweek* no4508 p22 Ja 23 2017

Lobel, Orly

Stop Trying to Control How Ex-Employees Use Their Knowledge *Harvard Business Review Digital Articles* p2 O 9 2014

Why California Is Such a Talent Magnet *Harvard Business Review Digital Articles* p2 Ja 19 2016

LOBELL, JARRETT A.

And They're Off! color *Archaeology* v69 no6 p20 N/D 2016

ARTIFACT color *Archaeology* v70 no1 p68 Ja/F 2017

ARTIFACT color *Archaeology* v70 no2 p68 Mr/Ap 2017

ARTIFACT color *Archaeology* v70 no4 p68 Je-Ag 2017

ARTIFACT color *Archaeology* v70 no5 p68 S/O 2017

BATHING, ANCIENT ROMAN STYLE color *Archaeology* v70 no2 p20 Mr/Ap 2017

FIGURE OF DISTINCTION color *Archaeology* v70 no1 p22 Ja/F 2017

MEMENTO MORI color *Archaeology* v70 no2 p38 Mr/Ap 2017

ONE + ONE = FORTY-NINE color *Archaeology* v70 no3 p42 My/Je 2017

Painted Worlds [Cover story] color *Archaeology* v70 no5 p26 S/O 2017

SECRET SPACES bw color *Archaeology* v70 no2 p12 Mr/Ap 2017

Shifting Sands color *Archaeology* v69 no6 p22 N/D 2016

TOP 10 DISCOVERIES OF 2016 bw cartoon color *Archaeology* v70 no1 p26 Ja/F 2017

THE WALL AT THE END OF THE EMPIRE [Cover story] color *Archaeology* v70 no3 p26 My/Je 2017

LOBO, PAUL

Great Escapes bw color *Power & Motoryacht* v33 no3 p96 Mr 2017

Lobo, Rebecca

AT HOME IN THE HALL S. Rushin color *Sports Illustrated* v127 no8 p68 S 18 2017

LOBRANO, ALEC

Riviera Revival color *Conde Nast Traveler* v52 no7 p34 Ag 2017

Lobster, The (Film)

No. 4 THE LOBSTER C. Nashawaty color *Entertainment Weekly* no1444/1445 p51 D 16 2016

Lobster fishers

Is There a Doctor on the Boat? B. MORGAN *USA Today Magazine* v146 no2866 p69 Jl 2017

The Lobsterman's Commute *Saturday Evening Post* v289 no3 p104 My/Je 2017

TENANTS HARBOR, MAINE S. Mumford *Harper's Magazine* p30 O 2017

Lobsters

FEEDING FRENZY: WHEN COMPETITIVE EATERS TACKLE LOBSTER ROLLS, YOU MIGHT WANT TO AVERT YOUR EYES. WE COULDN'T J. BILLS color *Yankee* p94 Jl 2017

FOOD FOR THOUGHT: Five tasty trivia tidbits color *Yankee* p98 Jl 2017

HENS, PISTOLS, AND SHEDDERS: A BASIC LOBSTER LEXICON *Yankee* p97 Jl 2017

LOBSTER 411: Answers to frequently asked questions color *Yankee* p97 Jl 2017

The Lobsterman's Commute *Saturday Evening Post* v289 no3 p104 My/Je 2017

SHE'S YOUR LOBSTER': MEMORABLE MOMENTS IN POP CULTURE bw color *Yankee* p99 Jl 2017

TALES & TRIVIA: WHEREIN WE CONSIDER THE LOBSTER, A CREATURE AS FASCINATING AS IT IS DELICIOUS S. SHOCKERS color *Yankee* p96 Jl 2017

TIPPING THE SCALES: A SALUTE TO SOME COLOSSAL CRUSTACEANS *Yankee* p98 Jl 2017

Lobsters—Reproduction

CRUSTACEAN ASSIGNATION P. Edmonds color *National Geographic* v232 no1 p29 Jl 2017

Local building materials

Learning from Local Building Cultures to Improve Housing Project Sustainability T. Joffroy *UN Chronicle* v53 no3 p11 2016

Local elections—Canada

Running from office K. EDWARDS *Maclean's* v130 no10 p16 N 2017

Local elections—United States

Resistance Is Rising in the Heartland J. NICHOLS color il *Nation* v305 no1 p30 Jl 3 2017

Local foods

Dig In: The Food Freedom Act L. Noyes *Mother Earth News* no282 p10 Je/Jl 2017

A great campus food makeover A. HECK color *Maclean's* v129 no44 p74 N 7 2017

Local foods—Sales & prices

School Districts in the Northeast Are Most Likely To Serve Local Foods on a Daily Basis J. Hyman and K. Ralston *Amber Waves:*

The Economics of Food, Farming, Natural Resources, & Rural America p1 My 2017

Local government

See also

Mayors

How Local Governments Are Using Technology to Serve Citizens Better S. Ressler *Harvard Business Review Digital Articles* p2 Ja 12 2016

The Most Important Work M. Funkhouser *Governing* v31 no1 p4 O 2017

Your tax dollars at work L. Zagare and B. Smith color *Columbia Journalism Review* v56 no1 p30 Spr 2017

Local government—California

The Road Ahead: BIKE LANES, CROSSWALKS, RAMPED-UP POLICE ENFORCEMENT— THERE'S LOTS OF CHANGE AFOOT AS LOS ANGELES MOVES TO REDUCE TRAFFIC-RELATED DEATHS S. CARPENTER *Los Angeles Magazine* v62 no9 p76 S 2017

Local government—United States

The Innovation Equation M. Funkhouser *Governing* v30 no1 p4 O 2016

No Urge to Merge A. Greenblatt *Governing* v31 no1 p12 O 2017

When Local Control Backfires S. Beyer *Governing* v30 no4 p24 Ja 2017

Local Group (Astronomy)

Void "Repels" Milky Way's Galaxy Group C. M. CARLISLE *Sky & Telescope* v133 no5 p8 My 2017

Local taxation—United States

Who Pays the Tax Bill? A progressive local tax is hard to find J. Marlowe *Governing* v30 no9 p63 Je 2017

Locane, Amy

Wrong TURN L. Rice color *Entertainment Weekly* no1474/1475 p86 Jl 21-28 2017

Locascio, Joseph J.

β2-Adrenoreceptor is a regulator of the a-synuclein gene driving risk of Parkinson's disease cartoon chart graph *Science* v357 no6354 p891 S 1 2017

LoCash (Performer)

After Dark on The Strip color *American Cowboy* v23 no4 p82 D 2016/Ja 2017

Locatelli, Massimiliano

ode to beauty J. J. MARTIN bw color *Architectural Digest* v74 no3 p120 Mr 2017

Location (Music)

A Pop Prodigy Breaks Out J. LEVY color *Rolling Stone* no1283 p15 Mr 23 2017

Location-based services

How to stop websites from asking for your location in Chrome, Edge, Firefox, Opera, Safari I. PAUL color *PCWorld* v35 no6 p35 Je 2017

You Are Here (So Buy Something) J. Wise *Bloomberg Businessweek* no4536 p24 S 4 2017

Location marketing

The Secret to Smartphone Marketing Is Still Email N. Mele *Harvard Business Review Digital Articles* p2 N 2 2015

L'Occitane International SA

What Sunrise Smells Like K. Erickson color *Glamour* v115 no5 p82 My 2017

Lochery, Neill

The 'Iron Wall' of Israel G. BECKERMAN *New York Times Book Review* p28 D 11 2016

Lochsa River (Idaho)

Hooked on Rafting: A Lochsa River Adventure A. SCHENK *Idaho Magazine* v16 no12 p40 S 2017

Locht, Camille

Reversion of antibiotic resistance in Mycobacterium tuberculosis by spiroisoxazoline SMARt-420 bibl diag *Science* v355 no6330 p1206 Mr 17 2017

Lochte, Ryan, 1984-

Ryan Lochte J. PRESSLER img *New York* v49 no21 p18 O 17 2016

Lock, Michael

AMERICAN FLAT-TRACK REVIVAL A. Wilson color *Cycle World* v56 no2 p68 Mr 2017

Lock picking

Secrets of a Weekend Lock Picker [Cover story] D. DUBNO color

Popular Mechanics v193 no7 p29 S 2016

Locke, Attica

DOWN ON HIGHWAY 59 *Texas Monthly* v45 no9 p34 S 2017

MURDER AND RACE IN EAST TEXAS W. WERRIS color *Publishers Weekly* v264 no28 p58 Jl 10 2017

LOCKE, CHARLEY

BOTS LIKE US color graph *Wired* v25 no4 p24 Ap 2017

Locke, Connson Chou

When It's Safe to Rely on Intuition (and When It's Not) *Harvard Business Review Digital Articles* p2 Ap 30 2015

Locke, Harvey

An Ecoregion-Based Approach to Protecting Half the Terrestrial Realm *BioScience* v67 no6 p534 Je 2017

Harvey wants half N. WALKER color map *Canadian Geographic* v137 no1 p42 F 2017

Locke, James C, W.

Phytochromes function as thermosensors in Arabidopsis bibl graph *Science* v354 no6314 p886 N 18 2016

Locke, Julia

A supramolecular assembly mediates lentiviral DNA integration bibl color *Science* v355 no6320 p1 Ja 6 2017

Locke, Margaret

A Man of Character *Publishers Weekly* v264 no10 p47 Mr 6 2017

Locked-in syndrome—Patients

A Mind-Reading Device Gives Words to "Locked In" Patients E. Mullin color *MIT Technology Review* v120 no3 p18 My/Je 2017

Locker rooms

Getting Serious About Locker-Room Talk D. ZIRIN color *Progressive* p68 D 2016/Ja 2017

Lifestyles of the Top 100 J. Passov color *Golf Magazine* v59 no10 p88 O 2017

Locker rooms—Social aspects

"We're standing up for respect" J. PRESS *Scholastic Choices* v32 no7 p6 Ap 2017

Lockers

Is Your Locker MAKING YOU SICK? A. STANLEY color *Seventeen* v76 no2 p92 Mr 2017

Lockers D. Everitt color *Sail* v48 no9 p64 S 2017

Lockets

One Suit, Two Ways S. P. Nadella color *Glamour* v115 no9 p62 S 2017

Wait LIST color *Harper's Bazaar* no3657 p120 O 2017

Lockett, Kyle

YOUNG GUNS with Kyle Lockett C. Toy color *Spin to Win Rodeo* v21 no6 p24 Ag 2017

Lockett, Ronald

RONALD LOCKETT D. Ebony color *Art in America* v104 no10 p150 N 2016

Lockhart, James Macdonald

Raptor: A Journey Through Birds L. A. MARSCHALL color *Natural History* v125 no7 p46 Jl/Ag 2017

Lockhart, Rob

Creating a Better Playground Experience for Children *Parks & Recreation* p28 2017 Supplement Field Guide - Supplier and Resource Directory

Lockhart, Ross

Seminary at the megachurch color *Christian Century* v134 no4 p24 F 15 2017

Lockheed Martin aircraft—Evaluation

GIANTS OF THE SKY K. ATHERTON color *Popular Science* p54 Ja/F 2017

Lockheed Martin Space Systems Co.

A Look Inside Lockheed Martin's Space-Age Operations B. Watson *Harvard Business Review Digital Articles* p2 Je 25 2015

Lockheed Martin—Finance

Hardened Target D. FISHER chart color *Forbes* v199 no1 p36 Ja 24 2017

Locklear, Gina

Saving the Family Business A. Reliford color *Good Housekeeping* v265 no1 p63 Jl 2017

LOCKLEAR, MALLORY

Disrupting Dopamine Dogma diag *Discover* v38 no1 p39 Ja/F 2017

Why Antidepressants Are So Slow color *Discover* v38 no1 p62 Ja/F 2017

LOCKLEAR, SUZANNE

The Snow People *Idaho Magazine* v17 no1 p27 Ja 2017

Lockmiller-Stretch, Jeanette
i did it! K. SELZER *Better Homes & Gardens* v95 no1 p50 Ja 2017

Locks & keys
> *See also*
> Automobile keys
> Cabinet hardware

All Keyed Up F. VIGNA color *Martha Stewart Living* p144 O 2017

KEYS TO THE ALAMO B. SHACKELFORD *Texas Monthly* v44 no11 p98 N 2016

Secrets of a Weekend Lock Picker [Cover story] D. DUBNO color *Popular Mechanics* p29 S 2017

Secrets of a Weekend Lock Picker [Cover story] D. DUBNO color *Popular Mechanics* v193 no7 p29 S 2016

Locks & keys—Design & construction
Cowboy DIY Leather key fob L. Feldman color *American Cowboy* v23 no6 p46 Ap/My 2017

Locks & keys—Equipment & supplies
The Key to Your Next Fashion Move color *GQ: Gentlemen's Quarterly* v97 no5 p32 My 2017

Locks, Mia
GOINGS ON ABOUT TOWN color *New Yorker* v93 no5 p9 Mr 20 2017

TNT M. HOLGATE and M. GUIDUCCI cartoon color *Vogue* v207 no3 p342 Mr 2017

Lockwood, Benjamin B.
What If Socially Useful Jobs Were Taxed Less Than Other Jobs? *Harvard Business Review Digital Articles* p2 O 11 2017

Lockwood, C. C.
C.C. Lockwood F. ESKER color *Louisiana Life* v37 no3 p62 Ja/F 2017

Lockwood, Jeffrey A.
A state of denial G. Wong-Parodi color *Science* v356 no6336 p385 Ap 28 2017

Lockwood, John
FROM OUR READERS *Sky & Telescope* v134 no4 p6 O 2017

Lockwood, Lewis
'There Is Only One Beethoven' bw cartoon *New York Review of Books* v64 no1 p48 Ja 19 2017

Lockwood, Meghan
Using data wisely at the system level chart color *Phi Delta Kappan* v99 no1 p25 S 2017

Lockwood, Patricia, 1982-
Going Bare... color *Glamour* v115 no6 p138 Je 2017

The Most Catholic of Families K. Daniels color *Commonweal* v144 no13 p29 Ag 11 2017

OUR FATHER A. Konermann *Cincinnati Magazine* v50 no12 p24 S 2017

QUOTE MARKS cartoon *New Yorker* v92 no39 p42 N 28 2016

Locomotive engineers
Stepping in for Gls J. Nilsson *Saturday Evening Post* v289 no4 p98 Jl/Ag 2017

Locomotive models
Atlas HO scale FMC 5347 boxcar C. Grivno color *Model Railroader* v84 no9 p62 S 2017

Atlas HO scale NJ Transit commuter train [Cover story] D. Kawala color *Model Railroader* v84 no7 p60 Jl 2017

Bachmann Sound Value HO scale GS-4 [Cover story] D. Kawala color *Model Railroader* v84 no10 p58 O 2017

Dual engines with a WOWSound decoder [Cover story] L. Puckett color *Model Railroader* v84 no7 p58 Jl 2017

Electro-Motive Division SD40-2 diesel locomotive C. Grivno color *Model Railroader* v84 no7 p12 Jl 2017

HO scale details and accessories C. Grivno color *Model Railroader* v84 no7 p14 Jl 2017

HO scale locomotives C. Grivno color *Model Railroader* v84 no7 p10 Jl 2017

InterMountain N scale SD40-2 with sound D. Kawala color *Model Railroader* v84 no9 p60 S 2017

On the Web color *Model Railroader* v84 no9 p6 S 2017

Tangent HO 40-foot Mini Hy-Cube boxcar C. Grivno *Model Railroader* v84 no9 p63 S 2017

WalthersProto HO scale EMD GP35 diesel E. White color *Model Railroader* v84 no9 p58 S 2017

Where is Canadian spelled with an "e"? S. Otte color *Model Railroader* v84 no7 p18 Jl 2017

Z scale locomotives C. Grivno color *Model Railroader* v84 no7 p16 Jl 2017

Locomotives
> *See also*
> Steam locomotives

Hot Rod Anything! Clearing Snow With 4,000 HP P. Thomas bw color *Hot Rod* v70 no3 p10 Mr 2017

Into the Woods: The Patten Lumbermen's Museum takes visitors into the rugged and essential lives of those who felled the trees that helped build a nation I. ALDRICH *Yankee* v81 no5 p80 S/O 2017

Locomotives—Evaluation
Bachmann SoundValue HO scale EMD E7A D. Kawala chart color diag *Model Railroader* v84 no5 p60 My 2017

Locomotives—Maintenance & repair
Modeling a COMPACT DIESEL SERVICE TERMINAL T. Klimoski color *Model Railroader* v84 no1 p40 Ja 2017

Locomotives—Models
THE FUTURE OF MODEL RAILROADING L. Mindheim color diag *Model Railroader* v84 no4 p52 Ap 2017

Replace warped handrails on an HO scale diesel C. Grivno color diag *Model Railroader* v84 no5 p22 My 2017

Locomotives—Models—Evaluation
News & Products color *Model Railroader* v84 no4 p10 Ap 2017

LOCONTE, JOSEPH
A Marxist Manifesto *Weekly Standard* v22 no5 p20 O 10 2016

Locrian Chamber Players (Performer)
CLASSICAL MUSIC *New Yorker* v93 no25 p8 Ag 28 2017

Loda, Massimo
Rb1 and Trp53 cooperate to suppress prostate cancer lineage plasticity, metastasis, and antiandrogen resistance bibl graph *Science* v355 no6320 p1 Ja 6 2017

Lodato, Giuseppe
Modern Fluid Dynamics for Physics and Astrophysics *Physics Today* v70 no5 p60 My 2017

Lodato, Michael A.
Intersection of diverse neuronal genomes and neuropsychiatric disease: The Brain Somatic Mosaicism Network color *Science* v356 no6336 p395 Ap 28 2017

Lodato, Victor
HERMAN MELVILLE, VOLUME I V. LODATO cartoon color *New Yorker* v93 no6 p56 Mr 27 2017

Loden, Barbara
HER WAY D. Thomson bw color *Film Comment* v53 no4 p50 Jl/Ag 2017

Wanda *New Yorker* v93 no9 p12 Ap 17 2017

Lodge, Gabriel
YOU SHOULD KNOW cartoon *Bicycling* v58 no9 p100 O 2017

Lodge, Henry S.
Younger Next Year cartoon color *AARP: The Magazine* v59 no6A p32 O/N 2016

Lodge, Michael
The International Seabed Authority and Deep Seabed Mining *UN Chronicle* v54 no1/2 p1 2017

Lodge, Sally
Commemorating 75 Years Of Little Golden Books color *Publishers Weekly* v264 no8 p18 F 20 2017

LODGE, SARA
Let Them Eat Cake color *Weekly Standard* v22 no39 p34 Je 19 2017

Lyrical Isles color *Weekly Standard* v22 no46 p32 Ag 14 2017

Secret Gardens bw cartoon color *Weekly Standard* v22 no7 p30 O 24 2016

Lodge Looks (Company)
Make it Yours D. PEAK *Log Home Living* v34 no1 p8 F 2017

Lodge Manufactoring Co.
RESOURCES *New Orleans Homes & Lifestyles* v20 no1 p102 Wint 2016

Lodges (Architecture)
BEST OF THE WEST J. Chamberlain, C. Dash et al color *Sunset* v238 no6 p9 Je 2017

CENTRAL KENYA S. ROBERTS bw color *Conde Nast Traveler* v52 no4 p88 Ap 2017

In Colombia, You'll Get Beach and Then Some L. MORRIS color

Conde Nast Traveler v52 no1 p51 Ja 2017

QUIET THE MIND C. Menzel bw color *Powder* v45 no3 p64 N 2016

Lodges (Architecture)—Design & construction

Living Lodge color *Timber Home Living* p60 2017 Annual Buyers

Lodges (Architecture)—Evaluation

CAJUN COUNTRY J. FROIS color map *Louisiana Life* v37 no4 p97 Mr/Ap 2017

Into the WILD color *Vogue* v207 no6 p84 Je 2017

Lodging-houses

See also

Tourist camps, hostels, etc.

Nobody's Home L. VACCARIELLO *Cincinnati Magazine* v50 no8 p128 My 2017

POSTHOLE C. CAPELLI, S. CUNHA et al color *Powder* v46 no2 p94 O 2017

Lodriguss, Jerry

The Astro-Physics 1100GTO: This powerful German equatorial mount offers many features for astrophotographers *Sky & Telescope* v134 no1 p60 Jl 2017

Ethics in Astrophotography: Seeing isn't always believing in the digital age *Sky & Telescope* v134 no3 p66 S 2017

Portable Star Trackers *Sky & Telescope* v133 no5 p66 My 2017

Loeb, Abraham

POP goes the universe color graph *Scientific American* v316 no2 p32 F 2017

Loebbermann, Jens

mTOR regulates metabolic adaptation of APCs in the lung and controls the outcome of allergic inflammation graph *Science* v357 no6355 p1014 S 8 2017

Loechner, Erin

NO FILTER E. LOECHNER *Indianapolis Monthly* v40 no5 p54 Ja 2017

NO FILTER *Indianapolis Monthly* v40 no5 p54 Ja 2017

Loeffler-Gladstone, Nicole

Annabelle LOPEZ OCHOA color *Dance Spirit* v20 no10 p28 D 2016

BEATING Senioritis *Dance Spirit* v21 no1 p90 Ja 2017

Dancehall 101 color *Dance Spirit* v21 no4 p54 Ap 2017

DanceSPIRIT FutureSTAR 2016 *Dance Spirit* v20 no10 p63 D 2016

Eden GALLOWAY color *Dance Spirit* v20 no9 p80 N 2016

Emma THE ENIGMA color *Dance Spirit* v20 no9 p38 N 2016

Emma WYLIE *Dance Spirit* v21 no1 p95 Ja 2017

ESTEBAN HERNÁNDEZ *Dance Spirit* v21 no3 p40 Mr 2017

face off color *Dance Spirit* v20 no9 p44 N 2016

FIGHTING Fatigue *Dance Spirit* v20 no10 p34 D 2016

GET YOUR Head IN THE Game color *Dance Spirit* v20 no9 p68 N 2016

Lior MELNIKOV *Dance Spirit* v20 no10 p71 D 2016

Madison PENNEY color *Dance Spirit* v21 no2 p71 F 2017

MONEY MATTERS: Ways you can pay for school *Dance Magazine* v90 p20 2016/2017 Supplement College Guide

Moving THE Needle *Dance Spirit* v21 no7 p58 S 2017

POST-ACCEPTANCE LETTER Hurdles *Dance Spirit* v21 no4 p56 Ap 2017

Samantha BULSTRODE *Dance Spirit* v21 no4 p71 Ap 2017

Shahadi WRIGHT JOSEPH *Dance Spirit* v21 no3 p71 Mr 2017

TRICIA MIRANDA'S TOP 10 WAYS TO OWN YOUR CAREER color *Dance Spirit* v21 no2 p46 F 2017

THE WIDE WORLD OF CONTEMPORARY DANCE color *Dance Spirit* v20 no10 p42 D 2016

Loehfelm, Bill

The Devil's Muse *Publishers Weekly* v264 no18 p37 My 1 2017

LOERZEL, ROBERT

WHY We LOVE CHICAGO bw cartoon color *Chicago* v66 no3 p75 Mr 2017

LOESCHKE, CAROL

enjoying lake life color *Cabin Living* p16 Mr 2017

Loeser, Eva

Germ line–inherited H3K27me3 restricts enhancer function during maternal-to-zygotic transition diag *Science* v357 no6347 p212 Jl 14 2017

Loesser, Frank

I Hear Music: Songs of Frank Loesser img *New York* v49 no24 p156 N 28 2016

Loewe SA

THE HERO K. PIERI color *Harper's Bazaar* no3656 p154 S 2017

The Loewe* Way E. Wilson color *InStyle* v24 no2 p142 F 2017

LOEWEN, JAMES

LEARNING CODE color *Scientific American* v317 no4 p8 O 2017

LOEWENSTEIN, ANTONY

HOW ISRAEL PRIVATIZED ITS OCCUPATION OF PALESTINE color il *Nation* v303 no20 p20 N 14 2016

Loewy, Raymond

SERVICE CHECK J. Gordinier bw color *Esquire* p34 O 2017

Loewy, Raymond, 1893-1986

WHAT MAKES THINGS COOL D. THOMPSON color *Atlantic* v319 no1 p68 Ja/F 2017

Lofgren, Edward Joseph

Edward Joseph Lofgren W. Barletta and J. Alonso *Physics Today* v70 no2 p69 F 2017

Lofi, Johanna

The formation of peak rings in large impact craters bibl color graph *Science* v354 no6314 p878 N 18 2016

Lofrisco, Anthony F.

LoFrisco Family Cookbook: How Josie Brought Sicily to Brooklyn *Publishers Weekly* v264 no3 p54 Ja 16 2017

Lofts

Loft Life: The Early Years C. Bonanos img *New York* v50 no8 p12 Ap 17 2017

PORTERDALE MILL LOFTS/PORTERDALE 35 MILES SOUTHEAST OF ATLANTA J. GREEN *Atlanta* v56 no11 p232 Mr 2017

LOFTS, GREG

ALL RISE color *Martha Stewart Living* p110 O 2017

BETTER BURGERS, HOTTER DOGS color *Martha Stewart Living* no275 p67 Je 2017

Buttermilk Biscuit color *Martha Stewart Living* p79 Ap 2017

CAKES FOR any OCCASION [Cover story] color *Martha Stewart Living* p70 My 2017

GOLDENRODS color *Martha Stewart Living* p82 Ap 2017

LEFTOVER RICE color *Martha Stewart Living* p69 S 2017

MAGIC IN A JAR color *Martha Stewart Living* p74 Jl/Ag 2017

MASHED POTATOES *Martha Stewart Living* no269 p77 N 2016

NO FLOUR, NO PROBLEM color *Martha Stewart Living* p88 Ap 2017

SWEETS FOR YOUR SWEETIE color *Martha Stewart Living* no271 p90 Ja/F 2017

WITH LOVE AND GRATITUDE *Martha Stewart Living* no269 p98 N 2016

Loftus, Elizabeth F., 1944-

The John Maddox Prize Nomination for Elizabeth Loftus C. FRENCH *Skeptical Inquirer* v41 no2 p20 Mr/Ap 2017

TO ENHANCE JUSTICE: The Risk and Reward of Studying Memory *Humanist* v76 no6 p29 N/D 2016

Loftus, Elizabeth F., 1944——Awards

Elizabeth Loftus Wins 2016 John Maddox Prize for Standing Up for Science *Skeptical Inquirer* v41 no2 p7 Mr/Ap 2017

Loftus, Matthew

Awareness Is Good. Attention Is Better *Christianity Today* v60 no8 p31 O 2016

FOUR ASPECTS of RECOVERY [Cover story] cartoon *Christianity Today* v60 no10 p40 D 2016

Frail of Mind, Human in Full color *Christianity Today* v61 no7 p82 S 2017

Loftus-Farren, Zoe

AMERICA'S TOXIC PRISONS color map *Earth Island Journal* v32 no2 p17 Summ 2017

Cheap Food is a Myth color *Earth Island Journal* v32 no4 p45 Wint 2017

LOSING HOME color *Earth Island Journal* v32 no1 p19 Spr 2017

UP IN SMOKE *Earth Island Journal* v32 no4 p44 Wint 2017

"We're All in the Same Boat" color *Earth Island Journal* v32 no3 p46 Aut 2017

Youth Voices Are Powerful color *Earth Island Journal* v32 no1 p47 Spr 2017

Log buildings

See also

Log cabins

p44 Ja 2 2017

NEW WORLD ORDER *TV Guide* v64 no48 p20 N 21 2016

NO MORE MR. NICE GUY: On HBO's Ballers, good egg Steve Guttenberg breaks bad--and puts Dwayne Johnson between a rock and a hard place *TV Guide* v65 no31 p22 Jl 24 2017

Once Upon a Time *TV Guide* v65 no19 p36 My 1 2017

ONCE UPON A TIME *TV Guide* v65 no39 p51 S 18 2017

One Day at a Time *TV Guide* v65 no2 p28 Ja 2 2017

PEG + CAT cartoon color *TV Guide* v64 no42 p46 O 10 2016

PETE NOWALK *TV Guide* v65 no4 p12 Ja 16 2017

Queen Sugar color *TV Guide* v64 no42 p40 O 10 2016

Queen Sugar *TV Guide* v65 no25 p39 Je 2017

Queen Sugar *TV Guide* v65 no31 p37 Jl 24 2017

Ray Donovan *TV Guide* v65 no41 p36 O 2 2017

Scandal *TV Guide* v65 no14 p39 Ap 3 2017

SEACREST IN! *TV Guide* v65 no21 p13 My 15 2017

Season Finale Shockers! *TV Guide* v65 no25 p4 Je 2017

Shades of Blue *TV Guide* v65 no14 p34 Ap 3 2017

SHAUN CASSIDY color *TV Guide* v65 no7 p11 F 13 2017

THE SIMPSONS *TV Guide* v65 no43 p26 O 16 2017

So You Think You Can Dance *TV Guide* v65 no25 p34 Je 2017

STARFLEET RISING: The new prequel goes where no Star Trek series has gone before: gay romance, major crew conflicts and a Spock sister *TV Guide* v65 no35 p18 Ag 21 2017

Star *TV Guide* p44 D 5 2016

Still Star-Crossed *TV Guide* v65 no23 p20 My 29 2017

Still Star-Crossed *TV Guide* v65 no31 p32 Jl 24 2017

THE TALK *TV Guide* v65 no27 p40 Je 26 2017

Tangled Before Ever After *TV Guide* v65 no11 p39 Mr 6 2017

TV's HOTTEST COUPLES *TV Guide* v64 no15 p28 Ap 4 2016

Underground *TV Guide* p41 Ap 17 2017

THE VIEW *TV Guide* v64 no46 p40 N 7 2016

THE VIEW *TV Guide* v65 no11 p46 Mr 6 2017

THE VIEW *TV Guide* v65 no21 p44 My 15 2017

THE WALKING DEAD *TV Guide* v65 no39 p55 S 18 2017

THE YOUNG AND THE RESTLESS *TV Guide* v65 no14 p44 Ap 3 2017

Younger *TV Guide* v65 no23 p34 My 29 2017

Logan, Nicola

Local amplifiers of IL-4Rα-mediated macrophage activation promote repair in lung and liver diag *Science* v356 no6342 p1076 Je 9 2017

Logan, Peter B.

The Labrador Muse D. HEITMAN color *Weekly Standard* v22 no10 p34 N 14 2016

Logan, Suzanna

Haven in a Hayfield color diag *Timber Home Living* v27 no3 p34 Je 2017

Lake Minded color diag *Log Home Living* v34 no2 p24 Mr 2017

Modern Mix color *Timber Home Living* v27 no4 p44 Ag 2017

On the Rocks color diag *Log Home Living* v34 no6 p26 Ag 2017

Renovation Re-imagined [Cover story] color *Log Home Living* v34 no7 p28 S 2017

Second Time's the Charm color *Timber Home Living* p54 2017 Annual Buyers

LOGAN, WILLIAM

Lately Blooming *New York Times Book Review* p22 O 23 2016

Subdued Exuberance *New York Times Book Review* p18 N 27 2016

Logan County (W. Va.)

TRUMPTOWN L. MACFARQUHAR cartoon color *New Yorker* v92 no32 p56 O 10 2016

Logan Lucky (Film)

GAMBLING MAN K. P. Sullivan color *Entertainment Weekly* no1477 p34 Ag 11 2017

HAPPY RETURNS A. LANE cartoon *New Yorker* v93 no25 p86 Ag 28 2017

A Hillbilly Heist R. R. Cooper color *Commonweal* v144 no16 p27 O 6 2017

A Hillbilly 'Ocean's 11' P. Travers color *Rolling Stone* no1295 p56 S 7 2017

How to Steal a Million-and Then Some E. Dockterman color diag *Time* v190 no8 p49 Ag 28 2017

Logan Lucky C. Nashawaty color *Entertainment Weekly* no1478 / 1479 p82 Ag 18-25 2017

The Must List color *Entertainment Weekly* no1478 / 1479 p1 Ag 18-25 2017

Striking It Logan Lucky S. Zacharek color *Time* v190 no8 p48 Ag 28 2017

Logano, Joey, 1990-

Ezra Dyer E. Dyer color *Car & Driver* v63 no5 p32 N 2017

Logan-Robinson, Nidia

Memphis & Beyond: Assessing the Market for CRA Investment *Bridges (Federal Reserve Bank of St. Louis)* p1 Spr 2017

Loggers

THE JOY OF AX A. ZALESKI cartoon color *Men's Health* v32 no8 p100 O 2017

Logging

Forests of the Future G. POPKIN color map *Discover* v27 no10 p28 D 2016

History Lessons and Future Dreams M. BRUNE *Sierra* v102 no3 p6 My/Je 2017

Logic

See also

Counterfactuals (Logic)

Dilemma

Presupposition (Logic)

Question (Logic)

THE Punch List A. PEELE bw *GQ: Gentlemen's Quarterly* v86 no11 p69 N 2016

Logistics

See also

Military supplies

The Challenge of Renovating Historic Aquatic Facilities: How the Dallas Park & Recreation Department is preserving community history and memories R. Steinshnider and D. Mills *Parks & Recreation* v52 no9 p104 S 2017

Global Supply Chains Are About to Get Better, Thanks to Blockchain M. J. Casey and P. Wong *Harvard Business Review Digital Articles* p2 Mr 13 2017

HOW TO GET 3,000 POUNDS OF BEEF JERKY from Reno to Seattle M. Lenehan cartoon *Chicago* v66 no5 p98 My 2017

Logitech International SA

LOGITECH CIRCLE 2 HOME SECURITY CAMERA M. ANSALDO color *Macworld - Digital Edition* v34 no10 p37 O 2017

Logitech Craft hands-on: This keyboard's mini-Surface Dial is truly innovative M. HACHMAN color *PCWorld* v35 no10 p67 O 2017

A Mouse (Maker) Roars At the Industry's Giants A. Ricadela color *Bloomberg Businessweek* no4515 p30 Mr 20 2017

Logo design

Canadaversaries! E. NAWOTKA color *Publishers Weekly* v264 no41 p14 O 9 2017

MASCOT MATH T. Keith color *Sports Illustrated* v127 no8 p20 S 18 2017

THE MOST IMPORTANT QUARTER-INCH IN BUSINESS LOGO R. Walker color *Fortune* v175 no8 p210 Je 15 2017

THE WYOMING COWBOY B. Welch color *Spin to Win Rodeo* v21 no1 p96 Mr 2017

Logo design—Social aspects

Brand Management S. Rushin color *Sports Illustrated* v126 no4 p76 Ja 30 2017

Logos (Symbols)

See also

Logo design

LOGO-A-GO-GO C. O'CONNOR *Forbes* v200 no3 p88 S 28 2017

Mighty Peculiar M. W. SCHWARTZ bw color *Missouri Life* v44 no3 p62 My 2017

PERSONALLY BRANDED T. Keith color *Sports Illustrated* v127 no9 p15 S 25 2017

Logos (Symbols) in art

Canadaversaries! E. NAWOTKA color *Publishers Weekly* v264 no41 p14 O 9 2017

Logos (Symbols)—Charts, diagrams, etc.

THE SHAPE WE'RE IN *Texas Monthly* v45 no3 p62 Mr 2017

Logothetis, Leon

A Life-Changing Vacation–To the Slums L. LOGOTHETIS *Reader's Digest* v189 no1127 p118 F 2017

Logwood Co. LLC

MAKING A BEELINE TO SELF-EMPLOYMENT C. M. BROWN color *Black Enterprise* v47 no5 p13 Ja/F 2017

Loh, Edward

FJORD EXPLORER chart color *Motor Trend* v69 no11 p100 N 2017

GALA OF THE YEAR! color *Motor Trend* v69 no2 p10 F 2017

GROUNDBREAKING PERFORMANCE color *Motor Trend* v69 no9 p12 S 2017

Kaizen Of The Year color *Motor Trend* v69 no1 p12 Ja 2017

Lightning in a Bottle color *Motor Trend* v69 no5 p8 My 2017

Live from Pebble Beach color *Motor Trend* v68 no12 p12 D 2016

Luck of the half Irish *Motor Trend* v69 no6 p8 Je 2017

The Moral Cost of Dieselgate color *Motor Trend* v69 no4 p14 Ap 2017

Mr. Toyoda, please bring back MR2 *Motor Trend* v69 no7 p12 Jl 2017

NOTES ON BDC 2017 color *Motor Trend* v69 no11 p14 N 2017

PUT UP OR SHUT UP color *Motor Trend* v69 no10 p12 O 2017

TURNING OVER A NEW LEAF chart color *Motor Trend* v69 no8 p16 Ag 2017

Wait up, not so fast color *Motor Trend* v69 no3 p14 Mr 2017

What's On Demand This Month? *Motor Trend* v69 no11 p14 N 2017

World's Greatest Drag Race color graph *Motor Trend* v69 no11 p84 N 2017

Loh, Huanqian
Second-scale nuclear spin coherence time of ultracold 23Na40K molecules diag *Science* v357 no6349 p372 Jl 28 2017

Loh, Kyle M.
Thirst-associated preoptic neurons encode an aversive motivational drive diag *Science* v357 no6356 p1149 S 15 2017

LOH, SANDRA TSING
Sisyphus Shrugged *New York Times Book Review* p10 Ap 2 2017

Loh, Tim
Another Border Clash for Trump color *Bloomberg Businessweek* no4507 p22 Ja 16 2017

The Coming War On Gas color graph *Bloomberg Businessweek* no4519 p51 Ap 24 2017

In Coal Country, Signing Bonuses Are the Buzz color graph *Bloomberg Businessweek* no4521 p28 My 8 2017

Thanks to Ivanka, We May Always Have Paris color *Bloomberg Businessweek* no4519 p50 Ap 24 2017

Loh, Yong-Hwee Eddie
Early life stress confers lifelong stress susceptibility in mice via ventral tegmental area OTX2 diag *Science* v356 no6343 p1185 Je 16 2017

Lohengrin (Theatrical production)
Lohengrin S. Mudge *Opera News* v81 no10 p40 Ap 2017

Lohmann, Jan U.
RETINOBLASTOMA RELATED1 mediates germline entry in Arabidopsis color diag *Science* v356 no6336 p396 Ap 28 2017

Lohmann, Ulrike
A cirrus cloud climate dial? map *Science* v357 no6348 p248 Jl 21 2017

Lohnes, Rosmarie—Interviews
A Growing Concern color *Canadian Wildlife* v22 no5 p44 N/D 2016

Lohse, Ansgar W.
A pathogenic role for T cell–derived IL-22BP in inflammatory bowel disease bibl graph *Science* v354 no6310 p358 O 21 2016

LOI, BECKY
Fix It Up *Alternatives Journal (AJ) - Canada's Environmental Voice* v42 no2 p52 2016

Loiseau, Chloé
Red squirrels in the British Isles are infected with leprosy bacilli bibl color diag map *Science* v354 no6313 p744 N 11 2016

Loju (Company)
MASTER THE SPACE-TIME CONTINUUM IN CAUSALITY, A UNIQUE PUZZLE GAME FOR iPHONE S. J. PUREWAL color *Macworld - Digital Edition* v34 no10 p51 O 2017

Loke, Yoon—Interviews
Hidden Side Effects R. F. Mandelbaum color *Scientific American* v316 no1 p18 Ja 2017

Loken, Eric
Measurement error and the replication crisis bibl graph *Science* v355 no6325 p584 F 10 2017

Lokken, Kristen L.
Microbiota-activated PPAR-γ signaling inhibits dysbiotic Enterobacteriaceae expansion graph *Science* v357 no6351 p570 Ag 11 2017

Lollapalooza (Festival)
Lollapalooza Legends bw color *Rolling Stone* no1293 p14 Ag 10 2017

Lolley, Pam
CUT TO THE CAKES color *Southern Living* v51 no12 p156 D 2016

FAMILY TREES color *Southern Living* v52 no9 p82 S 2017

A Great Pot of Gumbo color *Southern Living* v52 no3 p126 Mr 2017

Homemade Oatmeal Pies color *Southern Living* v52 no10 p130 O 2017

OYSTER CASSEROLE color *Southern Living* v51 no12 p188 D 2016

The Scoop on Cobbler color *Southern Living* v52 no9 p142 S 2017

Lollipops
Mixing Bowl color *O, The Oprah Magazine* p134 Ap 2017

What In The World? color *National Geographic Kids* no471 p29 Je/Jl 2017

Lolo National Forest (Mont.)
The Great Wide Open E. KWAK-HEFFERAN color map *Backpacker* p12 Je 2017

Lomas, Daniel W. B.
Cold War Clem: Fiercely anti-Communist, Clement Attlee found Britain's intelligence agencies to be invaluable tools *History Today* v67 no9 p16 S 2017

LOMAX, JOHN NOVA
And the Walls Came Tumbling Down *Texas Monthly* v45 no7 p48 Jl 2017

THE HUNGRY TIDE *Texas Monthly* v45 no5 p80 My 2017

The Monument MEN *Texas Monthly* v45 no8 p31 Ag 2017

ORANGE CRUSH *Texas Monthly* v44 no11 p112 N 2016

"Racehorse" Haynes, 1927-2017 *Texas Monthly* v45 no6 p54 Je 2017

THE SECRET Agent *Texas Monthly* v45 no5 p60 My 2017

WELCOME TO THE GREEN MACHINE *Texas Monthly* v45 no6 p126 Je 2017

Where Everybody *Texas Monthly* v45 no1 p97 Ja 2017

Lomax, Michael
THE GREAT CHARTER SCHOOL DEBATE R. W. GOODE color *Black Enterprise* v47 no5 p32 Ja/F 2017

Lombard, Carole
SWAN SONG T. B. BROWNE *Indianapolis Monthly* v40 no5 p16 Ja 2017

Lombard, Joanna
Designing Parks for Health *Parks & Recreation* v51 no10 p77 O 2016

Lombardi, Joelle
A POSITION OF STRENGTH *Interview* v47 no2 p132 Mr 2017

view MARCH *Interview* v47 no2 p62 Mr 2017

Lombardi, Kristine A.
Mr. Biddles *Publishers Weekly* v264 no25 p109 Je 19 2017

Lombardi, Lisa
Jennifer Aniston on Dry Eye: "I Was Addicted to Eye Drops" color *Health* v30 no9 p80 N 2016

Lombardi, Vince, 1913-1970
LIVE AND LEARN P. King color *Sports Illustrated* v127 no10 p34 O 2 2017

Lombardo, Elizabeth
LET IT GO [Cover story] J. K. LINDLEY color *Redbook* p91 Je 2017

LOMBREGLIA, RALPH
Alphaland *American Scholar* v86 no3 p91 Summ 2017

Lomsadze, Bachana
Frequency combs enable rapid and high-resolution multidimensional coherent spectroscopy diag graph *Science* v357 no6358 p1389 S 29 2017

Lončar, M.
An integrated diamond nanophotonics platform for quantum-optical networks bibl graph *Science* v354 no6314 p847 N 18 2016

Londner, Renee
The Missing Letters: A Dreidel Story *Publishers Weekly* v264 no36 p99 S 4 2017

London (England)
Allies and Morrison C. Foges *Architectural Record* v205 no4 p120 Ap 2017

AROUND LONDON J. THATCHER cartoon color *ARTnews* v116 no1 p118 Spr 2017

CITY OF GILT T. Gold *Harper's Magazine* v334 no2002 p67 Mr 2017

Knightsbridge Residence K. L. Beamon *Architectural Record* v205 no9 p148 S 2017

Only If It SUITS YOU A. Bilmes bw color *Esquire* p66 BigBlack-Book

London (England) art scene
london, england A. SESSA color *Architectural Digest* no5 p88 My 2017

London (England)—Description & travel
48 Hours in ...London D. POINTDUJOUR color *Ebony* v72 no3 p82 D 2016/Ja 2017

The Esquire Travel Dossier 2017 S. CLEMENCE color *Esquire* v166 no5 p42 D 2016/Ja 2017

Happy Hijinks in Hampstead S. Lawrence *British Heritage Travel* v38 no2 p22 Mr/Ap 2017

It's Eccentric Glamor in Regents Park S. Lawrence color *British Heritage Travel* v38 no5 p24 S/O 2017

London C. JUDUA and E. WINDING color *Conde Nast Traveler* v52 no2 p64 F 2017

london, england A. SESSA color *Architectural Digest* no5 p88 My 2017

London (England)—Economic conditions
The Fog Lifts M. Campbell and S. Morris color *Bloomberg Businessweek* no4525 p18 Je 5 2017

London (England)—History
Take a Walk on the South Side S. Lawrence *British Heritage Travel* v38 no3 p26 My/Je 2017

London, A. J.
Direct observation of individual hydrogen atoms at trapping sites in a ferritic steel bibl diag *Science* v355 no6330 p1196 Mr 17 2017

London, Jack, 1876-1916
The Summit of Life P. BAUER bw color *Weekly Standard* v22 no11 p40 N 21 2016

London, Jackie
DO-IT-ALL DIETITIAN color *Good Housekeeping* v265 no3 p10 S 2017

MONEY SAVING GUIDE [Cover story] cartoon color *Good Housekeeping* v264 no2 p79 F 2017

London, Jaclyn
ASK JACKIE color *Good Housekeeping* v264 no5 p104 My 2017

CRUNCHY MUNCHIES color *Good Housekeeping* v264 no6 p92 Je 2017

EAT LIKE A MONKEY! J. London color *Good Housekeeping* v264 no6 p81 Je 2017

Freeze Your Wine color *Good Housekeeping* v265 no1 p89 Jl 2017

GROCERY SHOPPING MADE EASY color *Good Housekeeping* v263 no5 p152 N 2016

OUR GH DO DIET PROMISE TO YOU color *Good Housekeeping* v264 no3 p99 Mr 2017

London, Laura—Interviews
This New Animal Planet Show Will Make You Weep C. Collis color *Entertainment Weekly* no1478 / 1479 p90 Ag 18-25 2017

London, Robert E.
ZATT (ZNF451)-mediated resolution of topoisomerase 2 DNA-protein cross-links diag *Science* v357 no6358 p1412 S 29 2017

London, Stacy
Q: What is the most significant fad of all time? color *Atlantic* v319 no3 p96 Ap 2017

London Symphony Orchestra
CLASSICAL MUSIC *New Yorker* v92 no35 p13 O 31 2016

London (England)—Buildings, structures, etc.
Grenfell Tower Fire Tragedy Sparks Safety Dispute P. REINA and A. WRIGHT color *Architectural Record* v205 no8 p17 Ag 2017

Saving the Skyline D. STEWART *America* v215 no12 p11 O 24 2016

London (England)—History—1951-
LONDON CALLING T. Rohan and S. Kwak color *Sports Illustrated* v127 no11 p14 O 9 2017

London Terrorist Attack, London, England, 2017
Britain Keeps Calm and Carries on After Parliament Attack T. John color *Time* v189 no13 p12 Ap 10 2017

Lone Star Arabians LLC

PERFORMANCE HORSE AWARD PROGRAM RECIPIENTS RECOGNIZED AT THE 2016 EGYPTIAN EVENT *Arabian Horse World* v57 no3 p115 D 2016

Lone Star Geyser (Wyo.)
You Never Forget Your First Time M. Hittle, C. Lyons et al diag il *Backpacker* v45 no2 p64 Mr 2017

Lone Survivor (Film)
Military Dramas on FXM J. HOGAN *TV Guide* v65 no27 p38 Je 26 2017

Lone wolves (Terrorists)
Battling Lone-Wolf Terrorists at Home N. Rasmussen color *Time* v188 no16/17 p34 O 24 2016

Loneliness
Burnout at Work Isn't Just About Exhaustion. It's Also About Loneliness E. Seppala and M. King *Harvard Business Review Digital Articles* p? Je 29 2017

Dealing with Loneliness While Traveling for Work A. Gallo *Harvard Business Review Digital Articles* p2 N 19 2015

"FOR THE FIRST TIME IN MY LIFE, I didn't have any friends" R. Whippman bw color *Good Housekeeping* v264 no3 p75 Mr 2017

Loneliness and the Digital Workplace L. Amico *Harvard Business Review Digital Articles* p2 S 29 2017

The Social Muscle J. T. Cacioppo and S. Cacioppo *Harvard Business Review Digital Articles* p2 O 2 2017

The Strange Relationship Between Power and Loneliness A. Waytz *Harvard Business Review Digital Articles* p2 Ap 27 2016

What Do We Know About Loneliness and Work? S. Berinato *Harvard Business Review Digital Articles* p2 S 28 2017

Loneliness—Prevention
Solutions For the Solitary: Loneliness requires courage and altered perception to escape, but it is possible G. WINCH *Psychology Today* v50 no4 p32 Ag 2017

Lonely Planet (Company)
Urban Planning D. Dilworth color *Publishers Weekly* v264 no35 p32 Ag 28 2017

Lonergan, Eric
Fixing the Euro Zone and Reducing Inequality, Without Fleecing the Rich *Harvard Business Review Digital Articles* p2 Ja 9 2015

Lonergan, Kenneth, 1962-
BEST DIRECTOR CONTENDER KENNETH LONERGAN N. Sperling color *Entertainment Weekly* no1441 p40 N 25 2016

Bleak Houses J. PODHORETZ *Weekly Standard* v22 no15 p39 D 19 2016

LOST TIME R. MEAD cartoon *New Yorker* v92 no36 p46 N 7 2016

Manchester by the Sea C. Nashawaty color *Entertainment Weekly* no1441 p39 N 25 2016

MANCHESTER BY THE SEA J. Krebs color *Sound & Vision* v82 no6 p71 Jl/Ag 2017

Manchester by the Sea *New Yorker* v92 no47 p9 Ja 30 2017

No. 3 MANCHESTER BY THE SEA L. Greenblatt color *Entertainment Weekly* no1444/1445 p51 D 16 2016

The WORLD is FULL of WEEPING M. KORESKY color *Film Comment* v52 no6 p48 N/D 2016

Lonergan, Kenneth, 1962——Awards
Best Movies for Grownups B. NEWCOTT bw color *AARP: The Magazine* v60 no2A p54 F/Mr 2017

Lonergan, Kenneth—Interviews
Kenneth LONERGAN T. GEVINSON *Interview* v46 no9 p40 N 2016

Lonesome Dove (TV program)
At Home With... B. Welch bw *American Cowboy* v23 no5 p17 F/Mr 2017

TV'S BEST WESTERNS M. ROUSH *TV Guide* v65 no14 p23 Ap 3 2017

Loney, Andrea J.
Bunnybear cartoon *Publishers Weekly* v263 no45 p58 N 7 2016

LONEY, SYDNEY
The Delirium Diagnosis color *Walrus* v14 no9 p17 N 2017

Our New Home on the Water color *Walrus* v14 no9 p44 N 2017

Rediscovering Canada by Canoe color *Walrus* v14 no9 p42 N 2017

Long, Barney
Saving the saola from extinction color *Science* v357 no6357 p1248 S 22 2017

Wildlife-snaring crisis in Asian forests color *Science* v355 no6322 p255 Ja 20 2017

LONG, BEN

LAND CLAIMS color *Outdoor Life* v224 no4 p10 My 2017

Long, Elizabeth

β2-Adrenoreceptor is a regulator of the a-synuclein gene driving risk of Parkinson's disease cartoon chart graph *Science* v357 no6354 p891 S 1 2017

Long, Greg

Lining Up color *Surfer* v58 no4 p18 Ag 2017

Long, Gus

HIGHER GROUND color *American History* v52 no4 p71 O 2017

Long, Hayley

Sophie Someone *Publishers Weekly* v264 no1 p56 Ja 2 2017

Long, Heidi

A Day in the Life at Lone Mountain Ranch [Cover story] color *Log Home Living* v34 no3 p24 Ap 2017

Long, Henry W.

Rb1 and Trp53 cooperate to suppress prostate cancer lineage plasticity, metastasis, and antiandrogen resistance bibl graph *Science* v355 no6320 p1 Ja 6 2017

Long, Jake

Luke Brown & Jake Long Master the BFI Mountain [Cover story] K. Santos color *Spin to Win Rodeo* v21 no6 p56 Ag 2017

Long, Jake—Interviews

Patience and Perseverance Pay for Long K. Santos color *Spin to Win Rodeo* v21 no4 p28 Je 2017

LONG, JANE C. S.

Coordinated Action Against Climate Change A New World Symphony *Issues in Science & Technology* v33 no3 p78 Spr 2017

Long, Jeffrey W.

Rechargeable nickel–3D zinc batteries: An energy-dense, safer alternative to lithium-ion bw chart diag *Science* v356 no6336 p415 Ap 28 2017

Long, Jessica

PHOTO OF LASTING INTEREST color *Reader's Digest* v190 no1133 p26 S 2017

Long, John A.

The first jaws bibl color *Science* v354 no6310 p280 O 21 2016

Long, Kat

Home Sweet Dome color *Scientific American* v316 no5 p16 My 2017

SIX HUNDRED MILES WITH SKIS, KITES, AND WIND color *National Geographic* v231 no3 p14 Mr 2017

Tension in Taxonomy cartoon *Scientific American* v315 no5 p13 N 2016

LONG, KERRI

Benkelman hero PLUGGED INTO HIS DESTINY color *Nebraska Life* v20 no6 p45 N/D 2016

Long, Kyle—Interviews

Q+A J. BALL *Indianapolis Monthly* p46 My 2017

Long, Nia

NCIS: Los Angeles A. Bacle, D. Coggan et al *Entertainment Weekly* no1482/1483 p38 S 22 2017

Long, Rachel

Rachel Long Is Making a Splash L. Taylor *In Stride* v12 no2 p49 Mr 2017

Long, Ray

Body of knowledge color *Yoga Journal* no287 p40 N 2016

Body of knowledge [Cover story] color *Yoga Journal* no290 p54 Mr 2017

Get to know... Shoulderstand color *Yoga Journal* p28 2017 SpecialIssue

Get to know... your hips color *Yoga Journal* p68 2017 SpecialIssue

Get to know... your knee color *Yoga Journal* p96 2017 SpecialIssue

Get to know... your neck color *Yoga Journal* p22 2017 SpecialIssue

Get to know... your wrists color *Yoga Journal* p44 2017 SpecialIssue

Long, Richard—Exhibitions

Rock Steady S. COCHRAN color *Architectural Digest* v74 no8 p110 Ag 2017

LONG, ROB

Catching Up With Hillary Clinton *National Review* v69 no11 p34 Je 12 2017

CRAIGSLIST MISSED CONNECTIONS, Protest Edition il *National Review* v69 no3 p42 F 20 2017

Farewell, Obama? color *National Review* v69 no2 p23 F 6 2017

FOR IMMEDIATE RELEASE *National Review* v69 no18 p34 O 2 2017

From the Twitter feed of Kim Jong Un, @youthcaptain il *National Review* v69 no1 p34 Ja 23 2017

The Long View il *National Review* v69 no6 p38 Ap 3 2017

The Long View *National Review* v68 no21 p38 N 21 2016

The Long View *National Review* v69 no12 p34 Je 26 2017

The Long View *National Review* v69 no16 p38 Ag 28 2017

Memorandum il *National Review* v69 no5 p38 Mr 20 2017

Memorandum *National Review* v69 no19 p50 O 16 2017

NSA DOCUMENT EXTRACT 111016: 00:45GMT *National Review* v68 no22 p50 D 5 2016

NSA SURVEILLANCE INTERCEPT *National Review* v69 no8 p34 My 2017

NSA SURVEILLANCE TRANSCRIPT *National Review* v69 no9 p34 My 15 2017

OFFICIAL TRANSCRIPTS *National Review* v69 no15 p36 Ag 14 2017

"The Kellyanne Conway Show" il *National Review* v69 no4 p34 Mr 6 2017

Long, Sandra

THE LOOK BOOK A. SWERDLOFF img *New York* v50 no9 p61 My 1 2017

Long, Stephen P.

Improving photosynthesis and crop productivity by accelerating recovery from photoprotection bibl chart color graph *Science* v354 no6314 p857 N 18 2016

Long, Thomas G.

Out of unbelief color *Christian Century* v134 no15 p30 Jl 19 2017

Long, Vu

Poor fisheries struggle with U.S. import rule bibl color *Science* v355 no6329 p1031 Mr 10 2017

Long Beach (Calif.)—Description & travel

THE NEXT WAVE A. Preiser color *Sunset* v237 no5 p19 N 2016

Long Day's Journey Into Night (Theatrical production)

6 — LONG DAY'S JOURNEY INTO NIGHT M. R. Bernardo *Entertainment Weekly* no1444/1445 p118 D 16 2016

Long-distance runners

ASK THE EXPERTS H. North, M. Merlino et al color *Runner's World* v52 no2 p36 Mr 2017

BELFAST N. M. Wulfhart color *Runner's World* v52 no2 p64 Mr 2017

BREAKFASTS OF CHAMPIONS A. GORIN color *Runner's World* v52 no8 p26 S 2017

CRUSH IT. THEN COOL IT [Cover story] C. Kuzma color *Runner's World* v52 no2 p28 Mr 2017

EAT TO REMEMBER L. APPLEGATE color *Runner's World* v52 no2 p41 Mr 2017

THE FAST BREAK S. Douglas cartoon *Runner's World* v52 no2 p33 Mr 2017

HOW TO GO GREEN [Cover story] S. Jurek cartoon color *Runner's World* v52 no2 p38 Mr 2017

NATURAL ENERGY J. MIGALA color *Runner's World* v52 no8 p30 S 2017

THE NEW RELIGION R. Nelson *Virginia Living* v15 no3 p5 Ap 2017

RAPID DESCENT A. HUTCHINSON color *Runner's World* v52 no2 p32 Mr 2017

THE STARTING LINE [Cover story] J. GALLOWAY cartoon *Runner's World* v52 no2 p30 Mr 2017

WHEN YONKERS WAS BONKERS B. DONAHUE bw color *Runner's World* v51 no10 p82 N 2016

Long-distance running

See also

Marathon running

ASK MILES MILES cartoon *Runner's World* v52 no1 p32 Ja/F 2017

HOW TO EAT P. SAGAL cartoon *Runner's World* v52 no2 p18 Mr 2017

HYPERSPACE RACE [Cover story] M. PARENT cartoon color *Runner's World* v52 no2 p58 Mr 2017

RACE TO THE AFTER-PARTY [Cover story] A. C. SHILTON color *Runner's World* v52 no2 p86 Mr 2017

reviews. EAT AND RUN: MY UNLIKELY JOURNEY TO UL-TRAMARATHON GREATNESS S. Lawrence *Vegetarian Journal* v36 no3 p31 2017

Long-distance running—Training
SOMETHING OLD, SOMETHING NEW [Cover story] B. COOPER cartoon *Runner's World* v51 no10 p78 N 2016

Long distance swimming—Competitions
SEA OF DREAMS L. J. Wertheim color map *Sports Illustrated* v126 no18 p54 Je 26 2017

Long distance walking
The Never-Ending Journey C. LYONS color *Backpacker* v45 no1 p20 Ja 2017

Long hair
HAIRSTORY M. Leuchter color *Popular Photography* v81 no1 p106 Ja/F 2017

Long Island (N.Y.)
Beginnings: A Restaurant with A Literary Bent J. Maher color *Publishers Weekly* v263 no43 p6 O 24 2016

Long Strange Trip (Film)
Dark Side of the Dead D. BROWNE bw color *Rolling Stone* no1285 p11 Ap 20 2017
DEAD RECKONING B. HANDY bw *Vanity Fair* v59 no6 p72 My 2017
THE FOUR-HOUR GRATEFUL DEAD FILM... REVIEWED BY A DEADHEAD E. R. Brown color *Entertainment Weekly* no1468/1469 p89 Je 2-9 2017
The Must List color *Entertainment Weekly* no1468/1469 p3 Je 2-9 2017

Long-term care of the sick
We Can Improve Our Long-Term Care E. J. Schneidewind *AARP: The Magazine* v60 no2A p79 F/Mr 2017

Long-term debt
Why a Lower Car Payment Can Be a Costly Mistake C. Fried color graph *Consumer Reports* v82 no12 p60 D 2017

Long-term potentiation
Gliogenic LTP spreads widely in nociceptive pathways M. T. Kronschläger, R. Drdla-Schutting et al bibl graph *Science* v354 no6316 p1144 D 2 2016

Long-term potentiation—Research
How the body learns to hurt E. Underwood color *Science* v354 no6313 p694 N 11 2016

Long Trail (Vt.)
Distance Dreaming R. WICHELNS color graph map *Backpacker* v45 no1 p26 Ja 2017

Long Zhang
Realization of two-dimensional spin-orbit coupling for Bose-Einstein condensates bibl graph *Science* v354 no6308 p83 O 7 2016

Longacre, Doris Janzen
Recipes for a revolution L. H. Moses color *Christian Century* v133 no25 p32 D 7 2016

Longair, Malcolm
Maxwell's Enduring Legacy: A Scientific History of the Cavendish Laboratory A. Zangwill *Physics Today* v70 no8 p60 Ag 2017

Longaker, Michael T.
Fibroblasts become fat to reduce scarring bibl diag *Science* v355 no6326 p693 F 17 2017

Longboards
CRUISE CONTROL E. WALLIS *Cincinnati Magazine* v50 no3 p48 D 2016
Dope Runners [Cover story] D. Page color *Powder* v46 no2 p62 O 2017
LET THEM LOG A. GOGGANS bw color *Surfer* v57 no12 p62 Ja/F 2017

Longevity
See also
    Aging
The dying of the blue zones C. ROCA color *Maclean's* v129 no48/49 p30 D 5 2016
ENERGY IN THE RAW T. Rubert color *Amazing Wellness* v9 no4 p42 Summ 2017
THE GOD PILL T. FRIEND cartoon color *New Yorker* v93 no7 p54 Ap 3 2017
How Work Will Change When Most of Us Live to 100 L. Gratton and A. Scott *Harvard Business Review Digital Articles* p2 Je 27 2016

Rock-Solid Foundation B. HEINRICH *Natural History* v125 no2 p14 F 2017
Tracking Telomeres: Short telomeres are bad. Can you lengthen yours? D. SCHARDT *Nutrition Action Health Letter* v44 no4 p7 My 2017
Younger every year C. Gorrell *Yoga Journal* p4 2017 Special Issue

Longevity—Charts, diagrams, etc.
A Cure for the Ages M. Fabry color *Time* v189 no7/8 p86 F 27 2017

Longevity—Economic aspects
How Can I Afford to Live to 100? R. T. Beckwith color *Time* v189 no7/8 p96 F 27 2017

Longevity—Research
Burning Questions M. Oaklander, J. Worland et al color *Time* v189 no7/8 p88 F 27 2017
Death, Disrupted A. Sifferlin color *Time* v189 no7/8 p80 F 27 2017
The Sleep Cure A. Park color *Time* v189 no7/8 p70 F 27 2017

Longhurst, Henry
TEEING OFF color *Golf Magazine* v59 no11 p16 N 2017

Long Island City (New York, N.Y.)
All Those Cranes in Queens C. Swanson img *New York* v50 no18 p64 S 4 2017
Long Island City's Slow Sizzle C. Bonanos img *New York* v50 no18 p12 S 4 2017

Longleaf pine
Jeff Lerner, Vice President of Conservation Program *American Forests* v122 no3 p8 Fall 2016
A Long and Bright Future for Longleaf Pine M. Friedel *American Forests* v123 no3 p6 Fall 2017

LONGLEY, MARTIN
Immersive Listening color *Downbeat* v84 no3 p58 Mr 2017
Leadership Premieres color *Downbeat* v84 no1 p69 Ja 2017
Magic on the Bandstand bw *Downbeat* v84 no5 p64 My 2017
The Orbit of Ra color *Downbeat* v83 no11 p64 N 2016

Longlong Si
Generation of influenza A viruses as live but replication-incompetent virus vaccines bibl graph *Science* v354 no6316 p1170 D 2 2016

Longman, Martin
How to Win Rural Voters Without Losing Liberal Values *Washington Monthly* v49 no6-8 p9 Je-Ag 2017
Language Games color *Downbeat* v84 no6 p66 Je 2017

Longman, Phillip
How to Make Conservatism Great Again color *Washington Monthly* p3 N/D 2016

Longman, Roger
We Need More Transparency on the Cost of Specialty Drugs *Harvard Business Review Digital Articles* p2 N 4 2014
Who Has the Power to Cut Drug Prices? Employers *Harvard Business Review Digital Articles* p2 D 1 2015

LONGO, GIANLUCA
Remote Argentina color *Conde Nast Traveler* v52 no7 p16 Ag 2017

Longo, Regina
Imagining Hollywood from the Outside In: A Conversation with Celestino Deleyto on From Tinseltown to Bordertown: Los Angeles on Film *Film Quarterly* v70 no4 p118 Summ 2017
Of World Wars and Cold Wars and Hollywood Classics: Noah Isenberg onWe'll Always Have Casablanca: The Life, Legend, and Afterlife of Hollywood's Most Beloved Movie and Glenn Frankel on High Noon: The Hollywood Blacklist and the Making of an American... *Film Quarterly* v70 no3 p84 Spr 2017
Queering the Globe: A conversation with Rosalind Galt and Karl Schoonover on Queer Cinema in the World *Film Quarterly* v70 no2 p94 Wint 2016

Longo, Steve
Driving Home the Safety Discussion il *Consumer Reports* v82 no9 p6 S 2017

Longobardo, A.
Localized aliphatic organic material on the surface of Ceres bibl graph *Science* v355 no6326 p719 F 17 2017
Seasonal exposure of carbon dioxide ice on the nucleus of comet 67P/Churyumov-Gerasimenko bibl bw graph *Science* v354 no6319 p1563 D 23 2016

LONGOBUCCO, ALYSSA

12 DAYS of DECORATING color *Good Housekeeping* v263 no6 p124 D 2016

17 WAYS TO ADD COLOR TO EVERY ROOM color *Good Housekeeping* v264 no4 p50 Ap 2017

FIND MORE ROOM IN EVERY ROOM color diag *Good Housekeeping* v264 no3 p60 Mr 2017

GIVE THANKS UNDER THE STARS [Cover story] color *Good Housekeeping* v263 no5 p76 N 2016

MAKE OVER your haven color *Good Housekeeping* v264 no1 p54 Ja 1 2017

SMALL SPACE, BIG STYLE color diag *Good Housekeeping* v264 no5 p64 My 2017

top design QUESTIONS ANSWERED! chart color *Good Housekeeping* v264 no2 p41 F 2017

Longoria, Eva, 1975-
I Love My Kitchen L. BERGER color *House Beautiful* v159 no1 p104 F 2017

Longoria, Eva, 1975-—Interviews
EVA [Cover story] L. BERGER color *Redbook* p102 D 2016

Longoria, Jaime
TRUMP'S TROOPS *Mother Jones* v41 no6 p31 N/D 2016

LONGSTRETH, CAROLYN K.
The Otter, the Salmon, and the Bittern color *Natural History* v125 no4 p18 Ap 2017

Longstreth, David, 1982-
GOING SOLO J. Weiner *New York Times Magazine* p26 F 19 2017

IN THE ROOM J. LARSON img *New York* p69 F 20 2017

Long War, The (Poem)
THE LONG WAR L. Bai *MHQ: Quarterly Journal of Military History* v29 no4 p89 Summ 2017

OF SOLDIERS AND GENERALS color *MHQ: Quarterly Journal of Military History* v29 no4 p89 Summ 2017

Longwood Gardens (Kennett Square, Pa.)
A Natural Collaboration S. STEPHENS color *Architectural Record* v205 no8 p22 Ag 2017

Longworth, Karina—Interviews
You Must Remember This D. Franich color *Entertainment Weekly* no1451/1452 p16 F 3-10 2017

Lönnell, Cecilia
Basic Training Principles for Sport Horse Soundness color *Practical Horseman* v45 no11 p52 N 2017

LONSDALE, JOHN
Home Audio's New High Bar color *Rolling Stone* no1287 p15 My 18 2017

Loo, Aaron
Metal-catalyzed electrochemical diazidation of alkenes diag *Science* v357 no6351 p575 Ag 11 2017

Loo, Yueh-Lin (Loo)
Advancing clean energy *Issues in Science & Technology* v33 no3 p5 Spr 2017

Looker, Dan
HOW STRONG IS YOUR BANK? EVEN WITH LOW COMMODITY PRICES, BANKS THAT LEND TO AGRICULTURE CONTIUNE TO STRENGTHEN *Successful Farming* v115 no12 p24 O 2017

STAYING AFLOAT: MANAGING FINANCIAL UNCERTAINTY IS KEY *Successful Farming* v115 no12 p14 O 2017

THE SUCCESSFUL INTERVIEW *Successful Farming* v114 no13 p10 D 2016

Looking Out, Anytime (Poem)
LOOKING OUT, ANYTIME M. Ponsot *Commonweal* v143 no18 p27 N 11 2016

Loom Co.
YES LIST S. Marikar cartoon *New Yorker* v93 no28 p19 S 18 2017

LOOMIS, F. A.
Ditch Rider *Idaho Magazine* v16 no1 p28 O 2016

Loomis, Ilima
HOUSE OF THE SUN color map *Science* v357 no6350 p444 Ag 4 2017

The past, present, and future of ASTRONOMY IN JAPAN color *Astronomy* v45 no3 p44 Mr 2017

LOONEY, KRISTEN
China Gambles on Modernizing Through Urbanization *Current History* v116 no791 p203 S 2017

Loopholes
See also
Tax loopholes
LAUNCH color *Wired* v25 no6 p3 Je 2017

Looser, Devoney
The Making of Jane Austen *Publishers Weekly* v264 no14 p64 Ap 3. 2017

Looy, Cindy
Merging paleobiology with conservation biology to guide the future of terrestrial ecosystems color *Science* v355 no6325 p594 F 10 2017

Lopate, Phillip, 1943-
'Just Make Sure You Don't Forget' R. Franklin color *New York Review of Books* v64 no8 p46 My 11 2017

Rocking, Twirling, Happy, Silent... cartoon color *New York Review of Books* v64 no3 p48 F 23 2017

'RASHOMON' REDUX *New York Times Book Review* p30 D 4 2016

The Umpire of the Quality Lit Game bw *New York Review of Books* v63 no17 p35 N 10 2016

LOPATO, DAVID
East-West Fusions: A Delicate Balance color *Downbeat* v84 no9 p88 S 2017

East-West Fusions: A Delicate Balance D. LOPATO color *Downbeat* v84 no9 p88 S 2017

LOPER, BRETT
OBAMA'S AMERICA img *New York* v49 no20 p12 O 3 2016

Lopes, Ariadna V.
Ten policies for pollinators bibl color *Science* v354 no6315 p975 N 25 2016

Lopes, L.
Observation of a large-scale anisotropy in the arrival directions of cosmic rays above 8×1018 eV *Science* v357 no6357 p1266 S 22 2017

Lopes, Nayara
A Cinderella STORY *Dance Spirit* v21 no3 p26 Mr 2017

Lopes, Raphael
Two- and three-body contacts in the unitary Bose gas bibl diag graph *Science* v355 no6323 p377 Ja 27 2017

Lopez, Alexander E.
Distribution and clinical impact of functional variants in 50,726 whole-exome sequences from the DiscovEHR study chart graph *Science* v354 no6319 paaf6814-1 D 23 2016

Lopez, Alexandra
Dancing Through the Dog Days K. HOLMES *Dance Magazine* v91 no1 p130 Ja 2017

Lopez, Antonio, 1943-1987
ANTONIO LOPEZ B. Droitcour cartoon *Art in America* v104 no11 p120 D 2016

Lopez, Bobby—Interviews
THE GENESIS OF THE BOOK OF MORMON T. Parker, M. Stone et al *Cincinnati Magazine* v50 no8 p24 My 2017

Lopez, Carmen
between the LINES E. STUART *Virginia Living* v15 no3 p37 Ap 2017

Lopez, Christopher A.
Microbiota-activated PPAR-γ signaling inhibits dysbiotic Enterobacteriaceae expansion graph *Science* v357 no6351 p570 Ag 11 2017

López, D. Cárdenas
Persistent effects of pre-Columbian plant domestication on Amazonian forest composition bibl chart graph map *Science* v355 no6328 p925 Mr 3 2017

Lopez, Ditas
Philippine Leader Scares Off Investors color *Bloomberg Businessweek* no4493 p23 O 3 2016

Lopez, Donald S., 1952-
THE LIFE OF THE LOTUS SUTRA color *Tricycle: The Buddhist Review* v26 no2 p70 Wint 2016

Lopez, Eric D.
HAT-P-26b: A Neptune-mass exoplanet with a well-constrained heavy element abundance chart diag graph *Science* v356 no6338 p628 My 12 2017

Lopez, George, 1961-—Interviews
Let's Play It By Ear *Los Angeles Magazine* v62 no6 p50 Je 2017

Lopez, Gina

Dora Explores the Philippines? color *Earth Island Journal* v32 no1 p11 Spr 2017

Lopez, Jennifer, 1970-
THE 50 BEST DRESSED IN HOLLYWOOD E. Wilson color *InStyle* v23 no12 p266 N 2016

The Dance of Being a Judge D. HOUGH and M. Roffman *TV Guide* v65 no25 p12 Je 2017

Feeling Blue M. Logan *TV Guide* v65 no6 p9 Ja 30 2017

IN THE LINE OF FIRE M. LOGAN *TV Guide* v65 no8 p18 F 27 2017

Jennifer Lopez HER BEST EVER E. Wilson color *InStyle* v24 no8 p78 Ag 2017

THE JLO DOWN L. McCarthy color *Harper's Bazaar* no3649 p310 D 2016/Ja 2017

Shades of Blue M. Logan *TV Guide* v65 no14 p34 Ap 3 2017

Team Players E. Wilson color *InStyle* v24 no10 p92 O 2017

Lopez, Jennifer, 1970— Interviews
WORLD OF DANCE C. M. Smith color *Entertainment Weekly* no1468/1469 p64 Je 2-9 2017

Lopez, John
FROM PARTS TO ART L. F. Prater *Successful Farming* v115 no3 p56 Mid-F 2017

The Last Stand *South Dakota Magazine* v33 no2 p46 Jl/Ag 2017

Saving the Kokomo Inn *South Dakota Magazine* v33 no2 p72 Jl/Ag 2017

Lopez, Kathryn Jean
The Powerhouse On Fifth color *National Review* v69 no7 p43 Ap 17 2017

Providence And a Pope *National Review* v69 no19 p53 O 16 2017

Sanctifying the Acela color *America* v216 no8 p54 Ap 17 2017

Lopez, Marie
Dispersals and genetic adaptation of Bantu-speaking populations in Africa and North America diag *Science* v356 no6337 p543 My 5 2017

Lopez, Mario, 1973— Interviews
Candy Crush M. Roffman *TV Guide* v65 no23 p26 My 29 2017

Lopez, Nancy
Hitting the Sweet Spot color *AARP: The Magazine* v30 no6A p64 O/N 2017

Lopez, R.
Observation of a large-scale anisotropy in the arrival directions of cosmic rays above 8 × 1018 eV *Science* v357 no6357 p1266 S 22 2017

Lopez, Robert
All Back Full bw *Publishers Weekly* v263 no47 p78 N 21 2016

WORKINGMAN'S BLUE M. EMERY color *Dirt Sports + Off-Road* v51 no6 p16 Je 2017

LOPEZ, STEVE
Did You Call 911? *Reader's Digest* v189 no1128 p8 Mr 2017

López-Bao, José Vicente
Conserving the World's Megafauna and Biodiversity: The Fierce Urgency of Now *BioScience* v67 no3 p197 Mr 2017

Europe's biodiversity avoids fatal setback color *Science* v355 no6321 p140 Ja 13 2017

International Wildlife Law: Understanding and Enhancing Its Role in Conservation *BioScience* v67 no9 p784 S 2017

Modernization, Risk, and Conservation of the World's Largest Carnivores *BioScience* v67 no7 p646 Jl 2017

Saving the World's Terrestrial Megafauna color *BioScience* v66 no10 p807 O 1 2016

Lopez Casado, A.
Observation of a large-scale anisotropy in the arrival directions of cosmic rays above 8 × 1018 eV *Science* v357 no6357 p1266 S 22 2017

LÓPEZ-HOFFMAN, LAURA
Conserving Transborder Migratory Bats, Preserving Nature's Benefits to Humans: The Lesson from North America's Bird Conservation Treaties *BioScience* v67 no4 p321 Ap 2017

Lopez-Iglesias, Carmen
Fibril structure of amyloid-β(1–42) by cryo–electron microscopy color diag *Science* v357 no6359 p116 O 6 2017

Lopez-Martinez, G.
Hawkmoths use nectar sugar to reduce oxidative damage from flight bibl graph *Science* v355 no6326 p733 F 17 2017

Lopez Moreno, J. J.
Surface changes on comet 67P/Churyumov-Gerasimenko suggest

a more active past bw graph *Science* v355 no6332 p1392 Mr 31 2017

López Obrador, Andrés Manuel, 1952—— Political & social views
Is the third time the charm for Mexico's 'eternal candidate'? Hootsen color *America* v216 no10 p17 My 1 2017

Let's Make Mexico Great Again N. Cattan color *Bloomberg Businessweek* no4510 p15 F 6 2017

Lopez Ochoa, Annabelle, 1973-
Annabelle LOPEZ OCHOA N. Loeffler-Gladstone color *Dance Spirit* v20 no10 p28 D 2016

López Rioja, Alba
Tubular clathrin/AP-2 lattices pinch collagen fibers to support 3D cell migration color *Science* v356 no6343 p1138 Je 16 2017

Lopiano, Gabrielle R.
Case Study: Should He Be Fired for That Facebook Post? *Harvard Business Review Digital Articles* p2 D 11 2015

Lo Presti, D.
Observation of a large-scale anisotropy in the arrival directions of cosmic rays above 8 × 1018 eV *Science* v357 no6357 p1266 S 22 2017

Lorbeer, Franziska K.
Mutations in the promoter of the telomerase gene TERT contribute to tumorigenesis by a two-step mechanism diag *Science* v357 no6358 p1416 S 29 2017

Lorca, Federico García
Retrieving Bones, Reviving Memories N. Stockwell color *Progressive* v81 no2 p32 F 2017

Lorcan O'Herlihy Architects (Company)
K-Pop C. A. PEARSON *Architectural Record* v205 no10 p108 O 2017

MLK1101 *Architectural Record* v205 no4 p195 Ap 2017

Lord, Carnes
MANIFEST QUAGMIRE *Claremont Review of Books* v16 no4 p59 Fall 2016

Lord, Christopher J.
PARP inhibitors: Synthetic lethality in the clinic bibl diag *Science* v355 no6330 p1152 Mr 17 2017

Lord, Dana M.
Trispecific broadly neutralizing HIV antibodies mediate potent SHIV protection in macaques color graph *Science* v357 no6359 p85 O 6 2017

Lord, Phil
Solo Loses Duo A. Breznican color *Entertainment Weekly* no1472 p14 Je 30 2017

Lord of the Rings films
STRATEGIC HUMOR il *Harvard Business Review* v94 no12 p21 D 2016

Lorde, 1996-
APPROACHING AUTHENTICITY C. BATTAN cartoon color *New Yorker* v93 no18 p60 Je 26 2017

Hot Tracks color *Vanity Fair* v59 no7 p52 Summ 2017

Life of the Party S. Lansky color *Time* v189 no23 p44 Je 19 2017

Lorde N. Feeney color *Entertainment Weekly* no1471 p62 Je 23 2017

LORDE: POP'S REIGNING DRAMA QUEEN N. Feeney color *Entertainment Weekly* no1468/1469 p102 Je 2-9 2017

Lorde Returns With the Year's First Great Pop Anthem N. Feeney color *Entertainment Weekly* no1457/1458 p93 Mr 17 2017

LORDE'S GROWING PAINS A. MORRIS bw color *Rolling Stone* no1288 p32 Je 1 2017

Lorde Throws an Epic House Party W. HERMES color *Rolling Stone* no1290 p53 Je 29 2017

New Sentences N. Abebe *New York Times Magazine* p13 Jl 2 2017

A Royal Return: Lorde avoids the dreaded second-album jitters by hunkering down in New York City img *New York* v50 no13 p83 Je 26 2017

SINGING IN THE DARK S. BURT color *Nation* v305 no6 p35 S 11 2017

Sound Bites color *Entertainment Weekly* no1440 p9 N 18 2016

Lorde, Audre, 1934-1992
Demoting Shakespeare *Weekly Standard* v22 no16 p2 D 26 2016

Lordi, Emily
Q: What is the most significant fad of all time? color *Atlantic* v319 no3 p96 Ap 2017

Lord Might Have Given Him Wings, The (Poem)
The Lord Might Have Given Him Wings R. D. BETTS *Progres-*

sive v81 no4 p69 Ap/My 2017

Lord's Resistance Army

People F. Nzwili color *Christian Century* v134 no4 p18 F 15 2017

Lord's Supper

Holy crumbs M. Florer-Bixler color *Christian Century* v134 no1 p10 Ja 4 2017

One bread? J. P. Kelly color *U.S. Catholic* v82 no6 p28 Je 2017

What's new? The Eucharist may not immediately transform the faithful into better Christians, but stick around for a lifetime and see what happens A. Camille il *U.S. Catholic* v82 no8 p47 Ag 2017

Lord's Supper—Catholic Church

'Amoris' opens the door to Communion for Catholics in irregular unions G. O'Connell color *America* v216 no6 p17 Mr 20 2017

L'Oréal SA

6 mind-blowing mascaras M. OLIVA color *Redbook* p62 F 2017

ANTI-AGING DAY CREAMS color *Good Housekeeping* v264 no3 p31 Mr 2017

Cur Power [Cover story] D. Pai color *Women's Health* v13 no10 p47 D 2016

The IT Girl C. SORVINO color *Forbes* v199 no6 p80 Je 13 2017

L'Oreal SA—Officials & employees

L'Oréal's Problem With Men L. Colby cartoon graph *Bloomberg Businessweek* no4537 p19 S 11 2017

MANAGING L'ORÉAL'S 'ORGANIZED CHAOS' E. Griffith color *Fortune* v175 no4 p26 Mr 15 2017

Loree, James M.

AN OPEN LETTER TO THE MAN WHO BOUGHT CRAFTS-MAN R. Berendsohn color *Popular Mechanics* p81 Jl 2017

LOREN, KATY

5 WAYS... To Hit the Clute-Ham Tie-In color *Muscle & Performance* v9 no7 p66 Jl 2017

Bodyweight Fat Blast chart color *Muscle & Performance* v9 no7 p20 Jl 2017

Four Weeks to the Finish Line chart color *Muscle & Performance* v9 no9 p30 S 2017

Get Hydrated ... With Coffee? chart color *Muscle & Performance* v9 no11 p36 N 2017

GO LONG chart color *Muscle & Performance* v9 no5 p20 My 2017

SCULL YOUR WAY SLIM chart color *Muscle & Performance* v9 no4 p18 Ap 2017

Lorence, Sterling

light fall n. formosa color *Bike Magazine* v24 no6 p34 Ag 2017

Lorentz force

Breaking Lorentz reciprocity to overcome the time-bandwidth limit in physics and engineering K. L. Tsakmakidis, L. Shen et al bw diag graph *Science* v356 no6344 p1260 Je 23 2017

Lorentzen, Christian

The Amazing Adventures of Wernher von Braun img *New York* v49 no24 p142 N 28 2016

The Apathy of J. M. Coetzee img *New York* p73 F 20 2017

Art Brute il *New Republic* v248 no11 p50 N 2017

Big City Burnout img *New York* v49 no15 p89 Jl 25 2016

The Conundrum of Percival Everett: His fiction is major, his audience not img *New York* v50 no11 p125 My 29 2017

The Novel in the Age of Obama img *New York* p69 Ja 9 2017

OBAMA'S AMERICA img *New York* v49 no20 p12 O 3 2016

The Outsider *New Republic* v248 no10 p60 O 2017

The Passive Voice: In this smart novel, the narrator strives to matter img *New York* v50 no15 p71 Jl 24 2017

Phantom Pains *New Republic* v248 no8/9 p64 Ag/S 2017

The Ten Best Books of the Year img *New York* v49 no25 p122 D 12 2016

Things Fall Apart img *New York* v49 no20 p131 O 3 2016

We Can Be Heroes: A new novel engages the post-Occupy moment img *New York* v50 no13 p81 Je 26 2017

What Happened to Paul Auster? A decade ago, he was a Nobel contender img *New York* p68 Ja 23 2017

What Is Fame For? *New York* v49 no22 p107 O 31 2016

Lorenzen, Fred

13 DAYS ON OAHE: Three friends' odyssey on a 22-foot sailboat B. HUNHOFF *South Dakota Magazine* v33 no2 p74 Jl/Ag 2017

Lorenzi, Peter

A Different Carbon Tax: The Sustainable Green Tariff *Society* v54 no4 p342 Ag 2017

What if We Are Wrong about Rights? *Society* v54 no1 p6 F 2017

LORENZI, ROSSELLA

NOT BY BREAD ALONE color *Archaeology* v70 no5 p22 S/O 2017

WHILE YOU ARE WAITING color *Archaeology* v70 no4 p12 Je-Ag 2017

Lorenzo, Jorge

FORZA LORENZO! color *Cycle World* v56 no2 p74 Mr 2017

L'orfeo (Theatrical production)

L'Orfeo Ascending P. DEITZ color *Weekly Standard* v22 no30 p36 Ap 10 2017

Lorimer, Sally E.

Are Sales Incentives Becoming Obsolete? *Harvard Business Review Digital Articles* p2 Ag 3 2017

Can Your Sales Team Actually Achieve Their Stretch Goals? *Harvard Business Review Digital Articles* p2 Jl 11 2016

Despite Dire Predictions, Salespeople Aren't Going Away *Harvard Business Review Digital Articles* p2 Mr 31 2016

Driving Sales Success This Quarter, This Year, and Beyond *Harvard Business Review Digital Articles* p2 D 1 2016

Great Salespeople Are Born, but Great Sales Forces Are Made *Harvard Business Review Digital Articles* p2 My 20 2016

Help Your Salespeople Spend Time on the Right Things *Harvard Business Review Digital Articles* p2 F 15 2016

How More Accessible Information Is Forcing B2B Sales to Adapt *Harvard Business Review Digital Articles* p2 Ja 6 2016

How to Spot Hidden Opportunities for Sales Growth *Harvard Business Review Digital Articles* p2 S 17 2015

Ineffective Sales Leaders Can Cause Lasting Damage color *Harvard Business Review Digital Articles* p2 Ja 30 2017

Sales Bonuses Are Supposed to Motivate, So Don't Waste Them on Easy Targets *Harvard Business Review Digital Articles* p2 S 14 2017

The Technology Trends That Matter to Sales Teams *Harvard Business Review Digital Articles* p2 My 7 2015

There's No One System for Paying Your Global Sales Force *Harvard Business Review Digital Articles* p2 N 13 2015

When Sales Incentives Should Be Based on Profit, Not Revenue *Harvard Business Review Digital Articles* p2 Je 10 2015

Why Sales Ops Is So Hard to Get Right *Harvard Business Review Digital Articles* p2 D 29 2014

Why Sales Teams Should Reexamine Territory Design *Harvard Business Review Digital Articles* p2 Ag 7 2015

Lorin, Janet

Gifts The Rising Price of B-School Glory color *Bloomberg Businessweek* no4522 p51 My 15 2017

A GOP Plan to Tax Gifts For Wealthy Schools *Bloomberg Businessweek* no4506 p23 Ja 9 2017

Student Loans color graph *Bloomberg Businessweek* no4509 p33 Ja 30 2017

Things Go Better With 67 Million Coke Shares color *Bloomberg Businessweek* no4519 p46 Ap 24 2017

Why Yale Owns a Forest color *Bloomberg Businessweek* no4536 p28 S 4 2017

LORINC, JACOB

Scrounging for sustenance color graph *Maclean's* v129 no44 p64 N 7 2016

LORINC, JOHN

Rental Breakdown color *Walrus* v14 no7 p16 S 2017

Loriot, Frantz

Empire State of Mind P. MARGASAK color *Downbeat* v84 no1 p16 Ja 2017

Lorises

BORN TO BE WILD J. Actman color *National Geographic* v232 no4 p22 O 2017

Lormeau, Claude

β-cell–mimetic designer cells provide closed-loop glycemic control bibl graph *Science* v354 no6317 p1296 D 9 2016

Lorr, Ree

Caring for Aging Loved Ones color *Consumer Reports* v82 no12 p6 D 2017

Los, Fraser

IN SEARCH OF THE WOLVERINE color map *Canadian Geographic* v136 no6 p46 D 2016

Park It! color *Canadian Wildlife* v23 no2 p19 My/Je 2017

A plan comes together color map *Canadian Geographic* v135 no6

p60 D 2015

Los Angeles (Calif.)

the arts district T. HARLANDER color *Los Angeles Magazine* v62 no7 p63 Jl 2017

BEST (AND WORST) CITIES TO GOTO THE HOOP *USA Today Magazine* v146 no2868 p8 S 2017

A City On the Move M. SEGAL *Los Angeles Magazine* v62 no7 p10 Jl 2017

GOD, GUNS, AND OIL B. SMIETANA color *Christianity Today* v61 no7 p46 S 2017

A Great Foundation M. S. Eddy *Stage Directions* v30 no8 p12 Ag 2017

THE HOT LIST *Los Angeles Magazine* p148 Mr 2017

Kosher Cool P. KUH color *Los Angeles Magazine* v62 no7 p36 Jl 2017

Not Curry In a Hurry S. Marikar cartoon color *Bloomberg Businessweek* no4499 p84 N 14 2016

Play Hard at ROW DTLA L. IMMEDIATO color *Los Angeles Magazine* v62 no7 p66 Jl 2017

RECREATION STATIONS color *Los Angeles Magazine* v62 no7 p67 Jl 2017

Roast of the Town color *Los Angeles Magazine* v62 no7 p73 Jl 2017

Sign of the Times S. AMELAR *Architectural Record* v205 no7 p88 Jl 2017

south park & historic core color *Los Angeles Magazine* v62 no7 p72 Jl 2017

Los Angeles (Calif.)—Description & travel

FOLLOW YOUR GUT J. Battilana chart color *Sunset* v238 no6 p30 Je 2017

ITALIAN OASIS S. SHIBATA *Sea Magazine* v108 no12 pCA-1 D 2016

LOCAL MOTION J. Scatena color *Sunset* v238 no4 p23 Ap 2017

Los Angeles L. DeCarlo and C. Rainey color map *Conde Nast Traveler* v51 no10 p64 N 2016

Mapping It Out: Downtown L.A B. HENNEMUTH cartoon *Vanity Fair* p98 Hollywood 2017 Supplement

My Place color *Vanity Fair* p91 Hollywood 2017 Supplement

The Wonder Years M. MELTON *Los Angeles Magazine* p24 D 2016

Los Angeles (Calif.)—History

Get Your Kicks *Los Angeles Magazine* p28 Mr 2017

Hit or Miss *Los Angeles Magazine* v62 no6 p16 Je 2017

PRIDE OF PLACE D. PENER *Los Angeles Magazine* v62 no6 p80 Je 2017

Los Angeles (Calif.)—History—21st century

City of Angles W. Leitch and T. Keith color *Sports Illustrated* v126 no3 p14 Ja 23 2017

Los Angeles (Calif.)—Social conditions

More Reasons To Roam M. SEGAL *Los Angeles Magazine* p10 Ag 2017

Los Angeles (Music)

The Playlist color *Rolling Stone* no1297 p8 O 5 2017

Los Angeles Angels of Anaheim (Baseball team)

4 ANGELS color *Sports Illustrated* v126 no9 p92 Mr 27 2017

Los Angeles Aqueduct (Calif.)

ICONIC L. A *Los Angeles Magazine* p100 D 2016

Los Angeles Chargers (Football team)

3 Los Angeles Chargers color *Sports Illustrated* v127 no7 p82 S 4 2017

DEAN OF IMPUDENCE M. Rosenberg color *Sports Illustrated* v127 no12 p108 O 16 2017

Los Angeles Clippers (Basketball team)

3 Clippers B. Golliver, R. Nadkarni et al color *Sports Illustrated* v125 no14 p99 O 24-31 2016

Los Angeles Clippers (Basketball team)—History—21st century

7 CLIPPERS color *Sports Illustrated* v127 no12 p87 O 16 2017

L.A. Story B. Golliver color *Sports Illustrated* v125 no19 p106 D 12 2016

Los Angeles County Museum of Art

Fairgroup color *Vanity Fair* v59 no2 p43 F 2017

LACMA Unveils Latest Zumthor Scheme S. AMELAR color *Architectural Record* v205 no5 p25 My 2017

Los Angeles Dodgers (Baseball team)

1 DODGERS color *Sports Illustrated* v126 no9 p108 Mr 27 2017

Go West, Young Men M. GOLDBERG bw color *Weekly Standard*

v22 no34 p38 My 15 2017

HOT | NOT T. Keith color *Sports Illustrated* v127 no8 p20 S 18 2017

Julio Urias M. Hagan *Current Biography* v78 no4 p86 Ap 2017

SCOUTING REPORTS chart color *Sports Illustrated* v126 no9 p74 Mr 27 2017

SIX PLAYOFF QUESTIONS S. Apstein color *Sports Illustrated* v127 no10 p42 O 2 2017

Los Angeles Dodgers (Baseball team)—History

BLUE BLAZES S. Apstein chart color *Sports Illustrated* v127 no6 p24 Ag 28 2017

Los Angeles International Airport

All Eyes On the Next Flight P. FLAX *Los Angeles Magazine* p14 My 2017

Project Runway D. C. Vock *Governing* v30 no3 p48 D 2016

Los Angeles Kings (Hockey team)—History—20th century

WHAT IF? ... WAYNE GRETZKY HADN'T SKATED OUT WEST? J. Fuchs and J. Feldman color *Sports Illustrated* v126 no11 p59 Ap 17-24 2017

Los Angeles Lakers (Basketball team)

13 LAKERS color *Sports Illustrated* v127 no12 p95 O 16 2017

15 Lakers B. Golliver, R. Mahoney et al color *Sports Illustrated* v125 no14 p116 O 24-31 2016

Los Angeles Modern Auctions

BOOMERS CASH OUT ART COLLECTIONS L. GERSTNER color *Kiplinger's Personal Finance* v71 no2 p14 F 2017

Los Angeles Rams (Football team)

3 Los Angeles Rams color *Sports Illustrated* v127 no7 p102 S 4 2017

GO FIGURE T. Keith color *Sports Illustrated* v125 no17 p24 N 21 2016 Double Issue

I'm a Football Fan. I Just Didn't Know It J. Stein color *Time* v188 no15 p63 O 17 2016

NFC + WEST color *Sports Illustrated* v126 no5 p51 F 13 2017

Los Angeles River (Calif.)

A Data-Driven Approach to Revitalizing the L.A. River A. FIXSEN *Architectural Record* v205 no4 p34 Ap 2017

Los Angeles River (Calif.)—Environmental conditions

Whitewashing the Los Angeles River? Gente-fication not Gentrification: Green displacement threatens communities of color and low-income communities R. García and T. Mok *Parks & Recreation* v52 no9 p50 S 2017

Los Angeles Times (Newspaper)

Hard Times At The L.A. Times E. LEIBOWITZ *Los Angeles Magazine* p104 Ja 2017

Point/Counterpoint *Los Angeles Magazine* p14 Mr 2017

Los Angeles Unified School District

Where Making Matters J. Lovelace and M. R. Leach color *American Craft* v76 no6 p66 D 2016-Ja 2017

Los Elementos (Theatrical production)

For the People R. Platt cartoon *New Yorker* v93 no12 p8 My 8 2017

Los Padres National Forest (Calif.)

SOARING UNDER THE RADAR C. GRAHAM *American Forests* v123 no2 p42 Summ 2017

Losacker, Nancy

Born on the River *South Dakota Magazine* v32 no4 p61 N/D 2016

Los Angeles (Calif.)—Buildings, structures, etc.

MLK1101 *Architectural Record* v205 no4 p195 Ap 2017

THE SIX J. Zara *Architectural Record* v205 no4 p194 Ap 2017

Los Cabos (Baja California Sur, Mexico)—Description & travel

LOS CABOS, MEXICO color *Power & Motoryacht* v33 no1 p52 Ja 2017

Loschelder, David D.

Having Too Many Options Can Make You a Worse Negotiator *Harvard Business Review Digital Articles* p2 My 24 2017

Lose, David

In Appreciation of David Lose R. J. Dolesh *Parks & Recreation* v52 no8 p64 Ag 2017

Losers—History

VALIANT LOSERS K. Weikert *History Today* v66 no10 p34 O 2016

Losey, Joseph

Modesty Blaise *New Yorker* v92 no46 p11 Ja 23 2017

LOSGAR, MAXWELL

THE BERET BUNCH color *Vanity Fair* v59 no6 p66 My 2017

A TALE OF TUPAC color *Vanity Fair* v59 no7 p115 Summ 2017

LOSLEBEN, BILLY

How to Make a... CONCRETE FRAME chart color *Popular Mechanics* p82 S 2017

How to Make a... CONCRETE FRAME chart color *Popular Mechanics* v193 no7 p82 S 2016

Losos, Jonathan B.

Improbable Replications color *Natural History* v125 no7 p16 Jl/Ag 2017

Inevitable or improbable? A. Woolfson color *Science* v357 no6349 p362 Jl 28 2017

Winter storms drive rapid phenotypic, regulatory, and genomic shifts in the green anole lizard graph *Science* v357 no6350 p495 Ag 4 2017

Loss (Psychology)

See also

Grief

Separation (Psychology)

LOSING STREAK K. SCHULZ cartoon *New Yorker* v92 no49 p66 F 13 2017

Loss (Psychology)—Religious aspects—Christianity

LIVING BY The Word *Christian Century* v134 no7 p20 Mr 29 2017

Loss aversion

How Loss Aversion and Conformity Threaten Organizational Change S. Ryan *Harvard Business Review Digital Articles* p2 N 15 2016

Lossaint, Gérald

TZAP or not to zap telomeres bibl diag *Science* v355 no6325 p578 F 10 2017

Lössl, Philip

Structures of the cyanobacterial circadian oscillator frozen in a fully assembled state bibl diag *Science* v355 no6330 p1181 Mr 17 2017

Lost (TV program)

WHATEVER HAPPENED TO THAT VOLCANO ON LOST? J. Jensen color *Entertainment Weekly* no1460/1461 p101 Ap 7-17 2017

WHY YOU'LL (PROBABLY) NEVER SEE A LOST REBOOT S. Highfill color *Entertainment Weekly* no1450 p15 Ja 27 2017

Lost architecture

JULIA STREET WITH POYDRAS THE PARROT J. STREET bw *New Orleans Magazine* v51 no4 p22 F 2017

Lost Body (Poem)

Lost Body J. Rice *New York Times Magazine* p17 F 12 2017

Lost continents

See also

Atlantis (Legendary place)

SUPERCONTINENT SUPERPUZZLE [Cover story] A. Witze color map *Science News* v191 no1 p18 Ja 21 2017

Lost Distillery Co.

MR. DAVIS & HIS FANTASTIC RUM ACCELERATOR W. CURTIS color diag *Wired* v25 no6 p68 Je 2017

Lost in Emotion (Music)

1987 L. Greenblatt color *Entertainment Weekly* no1486 p59 O 13 2017

Lost in Oz (TV program)

STREAMING A. D'ARMINIO *TV Guide* v65 no31 p38 Jl 24 2017

Lost on You (Music)

LOST ON U.S.? LP is a bonafide star with a #1 hit single—in Europe. When will America catch on? J. ANDERSON-MINSHALL bw *Advocate* no1091 p32 Je/Jl 2017

Lost River Range (Idaho)

The Bighorns Are Back K. MILLGATE *Idaho Magazine* v16 no5 p20 F 2017

Lost City of Z, The (Film)

An Explorer Pursues a Jungle Dream In The Lost City of Z S. Zacharek color *Time* v189 no15 p53 Ap 24 2017

Jungle Fever R. DOUTHAT color *National Review* v69 no9 p42 My 15 2017

The Land Before GPS img *New York* v50 no7 p82 Ap 3 2017

The Lost City of Z C. Nashawaty color *Entertainment Weekly* no1462 p45 Ap 21 2017

THE LOST CITY OF Z K. P. Sullivan color *Entertainment Weekly* no1446/1447 p57 D 2016/Ja 2017

MEN ON MISSIONS A. LANE cartoon *New Yorker* v93 no9 p78 Ap 17 2017

Spring Preview R. Brody cartoon *New Yorker* v93 no4 p6 Mr 13 2017

Tropical Malady J. Gray color *Film Comment* v52 no6 p6 N/D 2016

Lost Moment, The (Film)

Magnificent Obsessive N. DAVIS bw *Film Comment* v53 no3 p20 My/Je 2017

LOTT, JEREMY

FROM THE ARCHIVES bw cartoon *Reason* v48 no11 p70 Ap 2017

Lott, Marilyn

Discussion *Smithsonian* v48 no4 p6 Jl/Ag 2017

Lott, Melissa C.

Green Hydrogen color *Scientific American* v316 no5 p21 My 2017

Lott, Sandy

TALK TO US color graph *Chicago* v66 no8 p17 Ag 2017

Lotteries—United States

It Could Be You ... Twice K. Samuelson color *Time* v190 no4 p13 Jl 24 2017

Lötters, Stefan

De-extinction, nomenclature, and the law color *Science* v356 no6342 p1016 Je 9 2017

Lottery proceeds

It Could Be You ... Twice K. Samuelson color *Time* v190 no4 p13 Jl 24 2017

Lottery tickets

Finders Keepers, Losers Weepers J. SerVaas *Saturday Evening Post* v289 no2 p23 Mr/Ap 2017

Life IN THESE UNITED STATES color *Reader's Digest* v190 no1135 p32 N 2017

Lotus, Elizabeth F.

TO ENHANCE JUSTICE: The Risk and Reward of Studying Memory E. F. Loftus *Humanist* v76 no6 p29 N/D 2016

LOTUS, FLYING

ANDERSON Paak *Interview* v47 no2 p68 Mr 2017

Lotz, Caity, 1987-

DC'S LEGENDS OF TOMORROW *TV Guide* v65 no35 p22 Ag 21 2017

Lou, Liza

Studio Bedfellows color *Art in America* v105 no1 p35 Ja 2017

Lou, Runnan

Scalable-manufactured randomized glass-polymer hybrid metamaterial for daytime radiative cooling bibl diag *Science* v355 no6329 p1062 Mr 10 2017

Lou, Zhenkun

A conserved NAD+ binding pocket that regulates protein-protein interactions during aging bibl graph *Science* v355 no6331 p1312 Mr 24 2017

Lou Reed: The RCA & Arista Album Collection (Music)

Lou Reed's Final Look Back W. HERMES bw *Rolling Stone* no1272 p19 O 20 2016

Loubeyre, P.

Synthesis of FeH5: A layered structure with atomic hydrogen slabs diag graph *Science* v357 no6349 p382 Jl 28 2017

Loud Hailer (Music)

Strings: Shredded & Bowed B. MILKOWSKI color *Downbeat* v83 no11 p58 N 2016

Louder, Mark

Trispecific broadly neutralizing HIV antibodies mediate potent SHIV protection in macaques color graph *Science* v357 no6359 p85 O 6 2017

Loudon, Andrew

Immunity around the clock bibl diag graph *Science* v354 no6315 p999 N 25 2016

LOUDON, CHRISTOPHER

LIGHT COME SHINING: THE TRANSFORMATIONS OF BOB DYLAN color *Maclean's* no1 p62 F 17 2017

Loudoun County (Va.)—Economic conditions

A TALE OF TWO COUNTIES R. NELSON *Virginia Living* v15 no2 p112 F 2017

Loudspeakers

See also

Headphones

Smart speakers (Wireless technology)

EAT, MEMORY *Harper's Magazine* no2007 p39 Ag 2017

Louie, Sharon M.

Lysosomal cholesterol activates mTORC1 via an SLC38A9–Niemann-Pick C1 signaling complex bibl diag graph *Science* v355 no6331 p1306 Mr 24 2017

Louis, Brian

The Battle of the Microwave Antennas color *Bloomberg Businessweek* no4523 p40 My 22 2017

A Wall Street Legend Flops in Sports Betting *Bloomberg Businessweek* no4515 p35 Mr 20 2017

Louis, David N.

Decoupling genetics, lineages, and microenvironment in IDH-mutant gliomas by single-cell RNA-seq diag *Science* v355 no6332 p1391 Mr 31 2017

Louis, Édouard

The Class Renegade C. Tóibín color *New York Review of Books* v64 no12 p21 Jl 13 2017

GET OUT OF TOWN G. GREENWELL color *New Yorker* v93 no12 p62 My 8 2017

Louis, Jenn

The Book of Greens: A Cook's Compendium of 40 Varieties, from Arugula to Watercress, with More Than 150 Recipes color *Publishers Weekly* v263 no50 p59 D 5 2016

Louis, Karen Seashore

Positive school leadership color *Phi Delta Kappan* v99 no1 p21 S 2017

Louis Garneau Sports (Company)

LOUIS GARNEAU CARBON LS-100 II J. Lindsey color *Bicycling* v58 no4 p89 My 2017

Louis Riel (Theatrical production)

A Rebel Returns *Opera News* v81 no9 p16 Mr 2017

Louis Vuitton Malletier SA

Bag Lover's Dream! color *Glamour* v115 no10 p83 O 2017

code RED *Interview* v47 no5 p38 Je/Jl 2017

Different Strokes color *Los Angeles Magazine* v62 no7 p26 Jl 2017

Exude The Exotic *Los Angeles Magazine* p30 Ja 2017

Fashion Masterpiece color *Glamour* v115 no7 p34 Jl 2017

GHESQUIÈRE'S VIEW E. Wilson color *InStyle* v23 no13 p238 D 2016

HELLO! L. Brown color *InStyle* v23 no13 p30 D 2016

La-Di-Dots E. Wilson color *InStyle* v24 no3 p142 Mr 2017

MARRAKECH, MOROCCO R. MISNER color *Conde Nast Traveler* v52 no2 p22 F 2017

Mobile Home H. MARTIN color *Architectural Digest* no5 p118 My 2017

Sickest Collaborations on the Planet, Part 2 > Louis Vuitton x Supreme M. A. Green color *GQ: Gentlemen's Quarterly* v97 no6 p36 Je 2017

this Way In bw color *Esquire* p5 Je/Jl 2017

UNCOMMON TREAD bw color *Esquire* v167 no2 p72 Mr 2017

Wait LIST color *Harper's Bazaar* no3655 p60 Ag 2017

Louis-Dreyfus, Julia, 1961-

Out of Office S. MARSHALL il *New Republic* v248 no6 p56 Je 2017

Veep A. D'Arminio *TV Guide* v65 no25 p35 Je 2017

'Veep' in the Age of Trump R. SHEFFIELD color *Rolling Stone* no1285 p17 Ap 20 2017

Louis-Dreyfus, Julia, 1961-—Interviews

Julia Louis-Dreyfus R. SHEFFIELD color *Rolling Stone* no1287 p20 My 18 2017

Louise, Geez

A Luxury Bath of 1924 cartoon color *Old House Journal* v45 no2 p72 Ap 2017

LOUISE, REGINA

"I Want to Make You My Daughter" [Cover story] *Reader's Digest* v188 no1126 p75 D 2016/Ja 2017

Louisiana

The Abby Effect P. PERRETTE *TV Guide* p18 D 19 2016

BEST OF LOUISIANA OUTDOORS C. HOLMES color *Louisiana Life* v38 no1 p30 S/O 2017

BIG DEVELOPMENTS K. FINN color *Louisiana Life* v37 no4 p8 Mr/Ap 2017

LOCA VORE F. Esker *Louisiana Life* v38 no1 p14 S/O 2017

NATURAL EDUCATION P. F. J. Stahls color *Louisiana Life* v38 no1 p44 S/O 2017

PUT YOUR CARDS ON THE DINING TABLE B. VAN ZANDT bw color *Louisiana Life* v38 no1 p36 S/O 2017

Louisiana. Dept. of Economic Development

GROWING STRONG K. FINN color *Louisiana Life* v37 no2 p10 N/D 2016

Louisiana Philharmonic Orchestra (Performer)

OUR TOP PICKS F. ESKER color *New Orleans Magazine* v51 no3 p24 Ja 2017

Louisiana State Penitentiary

Faith at Angola Prison M. Hallett bw *Commonweal* v144 no7 p10 Ap 14 2017

Louisiana—Antiquities

See also

Presidio de Nuestra Señora del Pilar de Los Adaes Site (La.)

OFF THE GRID M. GRUNBERG-BANYASZ color *Archaeology* v70 no5 p10 S/O 2017

Louisiana—Description & travel

Adventures in Acadiana H. Hayes color map *Southern Living* v52 no5 p77 My 2017

THE DUCKS STOP HERE G. BETHGE color *Outdoor Life* v224 no1 p70 D 2016/Ja 2017

HAPPY (HEALTHY) TRAILS F. Esker *Louisiana Life* v37 no6 p11 Jl/Ag 2017

HOPPY TRAILS M. P. SPENCER bw color *Louisiana Life* v37 no5 p32 My/Je 2017

RENAISSANCE RAMBLE P. F. STAHLS JR. color *Louisiana Life* v37 no2 p36 N/D 2016

THE TIME IS RIGHT J. BENSON color *Louisiana Life* v37 no2 p22 N/D 2016

Waterscapes W. Kalec bw color *Louisiana Life* v37 no4 p40 Mr/Ap 2017

Louisiana—Economic conditions

Purge the Surge C. ROSE color *New Orleans Magazine* v51 no12 p52 O 2017

Louisiana—Economic conditions—21st century

Oil Boom and Bust K. Finn color *New Orleans Magazine* v51 no7 p30 My 2017

Louisiana—Environmental conditions

The Incredible Shrinking State C. Flavelle color *Bloomberg Businessweek* no4509 p23 Ja 30 2017

Louisiana—News briefs

PELICAN BRIEFS L. LeBlanc-Berry bw color *Louisiana Life* v38 no1 p12 S/O 2017

PELICAN BRIEFS L. LeBlanc-Berry color *Louisiana Life* v37 no6 p10 Jl/Ag 2017

Louisiana State Capitol (Baton Rouge, La.)

QUIET TIMES AT THE CAPITOL P. F. STAHLS JR. cartoon color *Louisiana Life* v37 no4 p36 Mr/Ap 2017

Louisiana State University (Baton Rouge, La.)

PELICAN BRIEFS L. LeBlanc-Berry color *Louisiana Life* v37 no5 p10 My/Je 2017

Louisiana State University (Baton Rouge, La.)—Sports

13 LSU color *Sports Illustrated* v127 no5 p101 Ag 14 2017

Louisville & Nashville Railroad Co.

Variety from a second-hand Rose T. Koester *Model Railroader* v84 no10 p78 O 2017

Louisville (Ky.)

A Kentucky Classic A. G. BRAKE *Architectural Record* v205 no7 p86 Jl 2017

The Parklands of Floyds Fork: Louisville's 21st Century Legacy Park C. B. Neer *Parks & Recreation* v52 no9 p16 S 2017

Louisville (Ky.)—Description & travel

Heartland GETAWAYS A. S. ECKERT and C. IANZITO color *AARP: The Magazine* v30 no6A p44 O/N 2017

A Maker's Guide to... LOUISVILLE color *Popular Mechanics* v193 no7 p22 S 2016

Loukola, Olli J.

Bumblebees show cognitive flexibility by improving on an observed complex behavior bibl diag *Science* v355 no6327 p833 F 24 2017

Lounge music

MIDWEST color *Downbeat* v84 no2 p55 F 2017

Lount, Robert B., Jr.

The Biases That Punish Racially Diverse Teams *Harvard Business Review Digital Articles* p2 F 22 2016

Lous, Rianne S.
Ultrafast many-body interferometry of impurities coupled to a Fermi sea bibl diag graph *Science* v354 no6308 p96 O 7 2016

Louv, Richard, 1949-
Forward to Nature color *Canadian Wildlife* v23 no1 p12 Mr/Ap 2017

Louw, Leon
Meet Johannesburg's New Libertarian Mayor color *Reason* v48 no7 p36 D 2016

Lovano, Joe
Lovano, Valdés Explore Common Language B. Milkowski color *Downbeat* v84 no3 p16 Mr 2017

Lovato, Demi, 1992-
Damn, Demi! L. Donnenfeld color *Glamour* v115 no1 p12 Ja 2017
DEMI LOVATO M. Vain color *Entertainment Weekly* no1485 p56 O 6 2017

Lovato, Demi, 1992—Interviews
Demi Lovato R. Bruner color *Time* v190 no14 p54 O 9 2017
Demi Soars Away [Cover story] E. Mahaney color *Glamour* v114 no11 p160 N 2016
Q&A: Demi Lovato A. GREENE color *Rolling Stone* no1298 p18 O 19 2017

Lovato, Kimberley
THE FOUR-DAY REBOOT color *Sunset* v238 no2 p15 F 2017

Lovchinsky, I.
Magnetic resonance spectroscopy of an atomically thin material using a single-spin qubit bibl color diag graph *Science* v355 no6324 p503 F 3 2017

Love
See also
Marriage
50 Reasons to Love Being 50+ color *AARP: The Magazine* v60 no3A p61 Ap/My 2017
A Brief, Alphabetical Love Affair L. MERIWETHER *New York* v49 no15 p16 Jl 25 2016
Can You Really Power an Organization with Love? D. Coombe *Harvard Business Review Digital Articles* p2 Ag 1 2016
Crazy Like an Ex L. A. PHILLIPS *Psychology Today* v49 no5 p27 S/O 2016
Dear Readers B. Kelley *Reader's Digest* v189 no1127 p4 F 2017
does love end? M. BUSSOLA color *Parents* v92 no6 p106 Je 2017
DON'T SETTLE, BOO: HOLD OUT FOR MR. RIGHT INSTEAD OF MR. RIGHT NOW S. E. JAMISON color *Ebony* v72/73 no12/1 p67 O/N 2017
Dump the Emotional Manure E. TAYLOR *USA Today Magazine* v145 no2860 p61 Ja 2017
FIRST COMES LOVE... A. Breslaw color *Women's Health* v14 no6 p114 Jl 2017
Go Wild M. BECK cartoon *O, The Oprah Magazine* p37 F 2017
"His parents wouldn't attend our wedding" M. Mertens color *Glamour* v115 no6 p100 Je 2017
How I Grew Five Mothers M. PEYSER color *Reader's Digest* v189 no1130 p17 My 2017
Jennifer MacNeill bw *National Geographic* v232 no4 p6 O 2017
Live Your Best Life color *O, The Oprah Magazine* p23 My 2017
LOVE LIKE A WOMAN L. E. Royal color *Essence* v47 no7 p101 N 2016
Love Quest S. MILAN *USA Today Magazine* v145 no2860 p58 Ja 2017
The Moment I Knew I Was in Love *Reader's Digest* v189 no1127 p86 F 2017
Populism Needs Place-ism B. KAUFFMAN *American Conservative* v15 no6 p45 N/D 2016
RELATIONSHIP MATH H. ESTROFF MARANO *Psychology Today* v50 no1 p25 Ja/F 2017
The truth about love *Redbook* p140 F 2017
Wait, Maybe True Love Does Exist M. Mertens color *Glamour* v115 no9 p121 S 2017
THE WORLD ACCORDING TO Gayle color *O, The Oprah Magazine* p32 F 2017
The yoga of give & take S. Kempton color *Yoga Journal* no288 p28 D 2016

Love & Diane (Film)
Love & Diane N. DAVIS bw *Film Comment* v53 no1 p62 Ja/F 2017

Love & Friendship (Film)

Love & Friendship F. S. Nehme *Film Comment* v53 no1 p51 Ja/F 2017

Love & War (Music)
BRAD PAISLEY M. Vain *Entertainment Weekly* no1446/1447 p73 D 2016/Ja 2017

Love (Music)
The Playlist color *Rolling Stone* no1283 p8 Mr 23 2017

Love, a Prairie Discourse (Poem)
Love, a Prairie Discourse J. N. Harrington *Orion Magazine* v35 no6 p57 N/D 2016

Love, Charmian
Bringing an Entrepreneurial Mindset to the World's Failing Systems *Harvard Business Review Digital Articles* p2 F 2 2015

Love, Courtney, 1965-
Random Notes color *Rolling Stone* no1272 p30 O 20 2016

Love, Darlene
Kicking Butt color *AARP: The Magazine* v59 no6A p70 O/N 2016

Love, David K.
Kepler and the Universe O. Gingerich *Physics Today* v69 no10 p55 O 2016

Love, Davis, III, 1964-
Smokin' With Love J. Passov color *Golf Magazine* v59 no11 p94 N 2017

Love, Erica
VIEWER POSITIONING SYSTEM *Art in America* v104 no9 p122 O 2016

Love, Gary
LABOR OF LOVE L. CUTRONE color *Louisiana Life* v37 no2 p28 N/D 2016

Love, J. R.
Entrepreneurship and Economic Development Fueled by Students and Faculty *Bridges (Federal Reserve Bank of St. Louis)* p10 Summ 2016

LOVE, JAMES
Better With Time color *Ebony* v72 no4 p57 F 2017
The Blueprint color *Ebony* v72 no5 p50 Mr 2017
Great Innovators color *Ebony* v72 no5 p44 Mr 2017
A GUIDE TO THE SUMMER'S HOTTEST SNEAKERS color *Ebony* v72 no6 p48 Ap/My 2017
LEADERS OF THE NEW COOL bw color *Ebony* v72 no6 p35 Ap/My 2017

Love, Kevin, 1988-
The Stopper L. Jenkins color *Sports Illustrated* v125 no14 p64 O 24-31 2016

Love, Loni, 1971-
PARTY OF ONE color *Essence* v48 no2 p101 Je 2017

Love, Love, Love (Theatrical production)
The 10 Best Shows R. Zoglin color *Time* v188 no25-26 p156 D 19 2016 Double Issue

Love, Mike, 1941-
Mike Love: Brian Took His T-Bird Away I. Guzmán color *Time* v188 no14 p59 O 10 2016

Love, Reggie—Interviews
Obama's Former "Body Man" on Being the Ultimate Assistant D. McGinn *Harvard Business Review Digital Articles* p2 Jl 30 2015

Love, Robert
7 Cool Things I Learned Editing This Issue *AARP: The Magazine* v59 no4A p2 Je/Jl 2016
Celebrating the 50th Anniversary of the SUMMER OF LOVE 1967-2017 *AARP: The Magazine* v60 no5A p29 Ag/S 2017
A Cruise for All Reasons color *AARP: The Magazine* v59 no2A p38 F/Mr 2016
Dinner With Don—and AARP color *AARP: The Magazine* v30 no6A p4 O/N 2017
Dion and the Disrupters color *AARP: The Magazine* v59 no2A p4 F/Mr 2016
Funny Never Gets Old color *AARP: The Magazine* v60 no4A p2 Je/Jl 2017
Helen Mirren in LIGHT & SHADOW color *AARP: The Magazine* v60 no1A p26 D 2016/Ja 2017
Let's Strengthen Social Security color *AARP: The Magazine* v59 no5A p2 Ag/S 2017
Peter Max: An American Artist bw color *AARP: The Magazine* v60 no5A p6 Ag/S 2017
Rock 'n' Roll, Medicare and Me cartoon color *AARP: The Maga-*

zine v60 no1A p2 D 2016/Ja 2017

The Stars Are Out color *AARP: The Magazine* v59 no3A p4 Ap/My 2016

This Is How We Do color *AARP: The Magazine* v59 no1A p5 D 2015/Ja 2016

A Warning on Medicare color *AARP: The Magazine* v60 no2A p4 F/Mr 2017

You've Got the Power color *AARP: The Magazine* v59 no6A p4 O/N 2016

Love, Tim—Interviews

COMMON GROUND A. ROBINSON color *Outdoor Life* v224 no5 p70 Je/Jl 2017

Love, Yeardley, 1987-2010

Love Lessons A. Fenwick and T. Keith color *Sports Illustrated* v125 no20 p26 D 19 2016

Love Actually (Film)

LOVE ACTUALLY J. McGovern color *Entertainment Weekly* no1460/1461 p86 Ap 7-17 2017

Sequel With a Cause J. McGovern color *Entertainment Weekly* no1460/1461 p92 Ap 7-17 2017

Streaming S. Li color *Entertainment Weekly* no1441 p44 N 25 2016

Love Connection (TV program)

LOVE CONNECTION T. Stack color *Entertainment Weekly* no1468/1469 p49 Je 2-9 2017

TV's Silly Season: A Guide D. D'addario color *Time* v189 no24 p48 Je 26 2017

Love-hate relationships

CONFESSIONS OF DIVORCED MEN E. M. Brown color *Essence* v48 no6 p115 O 2017

Research: Love-Hate Relationships at Work Might Be Good for You S. Melwani and N. Rothman *Harvard Business Review Digital Articles* p2 Ja 20 2015

WHAT YOUR TV CRUSH SAYS ABOUT YOU E. Spitznagel color *Men's Health* v32 no3 p83 Ap 2017

Love in a Time of Madness (Music)

JOSÉ JAMES 'TORNADO OF CREATIVITY' [Cover story] P. Lutz color *Downbeat* v84 no5 p28 My 2017

Love letters

Love's Labor color *O, The Oprah Magazine* p24 F 2017

Love Poems in the Time of Climate Change (Poem)

Love Poems in the Time of Climate Change C. S. PEREZ *New Republic* v248 no3 p59 Mr 2017

Love songs

Article So Long Love Songs H. Prestwood, L. Bormel et al *Commentary* v140 no2 p5 S 2015

TONY BENNETT E. SPITZNAGEL bw *Men's Health* v31 no10 p120 D 2016

Love This Way (Music)

The Playlist bw color *Rolling Stone* no1295 p10 S 7 2017

Love Boat, The (TV program)

THE LOVE BOAT: LIFE ON THE (VERY) HIGH SEAS color *Entertainment Weekly* no1460/1461 p21 Ap 7-17 2017

Lovecraft, H. P. (Howard Phillips), 1890-1937

WEIRD TALES H. P. Lovecraft *Lapham's Quarterly* v10 no3 p54 Summ 2017

Lovegrove, Nick

Career Bankers Alone Can't Solve the Financial Industry's Problems *Harvard Business Review Digital Articles* p2 O 31 2016

The Danger of Having Too Many Experts *Time* v188 no19 p17 N 7 2016

Lovelace, Ada King, Countess of, 1815-1852

Ada Lovelace color *Discover* v38 no4 p46 My 2017

FOR YOUR CONSID-HER-ATION bw color *O, The Oprah Magazine* p22 Ja 2017

Lovelace, Joyce

Art Without Art School color *American Craft* v76 no6 p88 D 2016-Ja 2017

Common Good color *American Craft* v77 no3 p26 Je/Jl 2017

Ephemeral Is Beautiful color *American Craft* v77 no3 p56 Je/Jl 2017

Fashion Forward color *American Craft* v76 no6 p40 D 2016-Ja 2017

Gather Round bw color *American Craft* v77 no2 p36 Ap/My 2017

Slices of the World il *American Craft* v77 no3 p38 Je/Jl 2017

Tender Tribute bw color *American Craft* v77 no2 p28 Ap/My 2017

Where Making Matters color *American Craft* v76 no6 p66 D 2016-Ja 2017

Lovelace, Ryan

BEACH PEOPLE color *Popular Mechanics* p76 Ap 2017

Loveless (Film)

A Fraught Cannes, Inside Screening Rooms and Out S. Zacharek color *Time* v189 no22 p55 Je 12 2017

Lovell, Colby

FIVE FLAT B. Welch color *Spin to Win Rodeo* v20 no9 p29 N 2016

Lovell, Colby—Interviews

Lovell Kisses Full-Time Rodeo Trail Goodbye K. Santos color *Spin to Win Rodeo* v20 no12 p24 F 2017

Lovell, Joel

NATURE LOVER bw color *Conde Nast Traveler* v52 no4 p54 Ap 2017

Lovell, Mary S.

Let the Bon Temps Roll: How a villa on the Riviera became the year-round playground of the superrich S. STEIN *New York Times Book Review* p20 O 15 2017

The Riviera Set: Glitz, Glamour, and the Hidden World of High Society color *Publishers Weekly* v264 no30 p54 Jl 24 2017

Lovell, William

MAVS-dependent host species range and pathogenicity of human hepatitis A virus bibl graph *Science* v353 no6307 p1541 S 30 2016

Lovely, Lynne

The Brilliance of Colored Light A. GRAVES and A. TUCKER color *Yankee* v80 no6 p38 N/D 2016

Loverdo, Claude

Inflammation boosts bacteriophage transfer between Salmonella spp bibl diag *Science* v355 no6330 p1211 Mr 17 2017

Love—Religious aspects—Christianity

FOUR ASPECTS of RECOVERY [Cover story] M. LOFTUS cartoon *Christianity Today* v60 no10 p40 D 2016

LIVING BY The Word *Christian Century* v134 no3 p18 F 2017

LOVERING, JESSICA

Why carbon capture is not enough *Issues in Science & Technology* v33 no4 p12 Summ 2017

Lovers, The (Film)

THE 8-SECOND REVIEW J. Nolfi color *Entertainment Weekly* no1465 p40 My 12 2017

Aging Gracefully, If Not Always Smoothly, In the Lovers S. Zacharek color *Time* v189 no19 p53 My 22 2017

NOW PLAYING color *Entertainment Weekly* no1470 p43 Je 16 2017

Q&A: DEBRA WINGER J. McGovern color *Entertainment Weekly* no1463/1464 p38 Ap/My 2017

Lovesey, Peter

The Usual Santas: A Collection of Soho Crime Christmas Capers color *Publishers Weekly* v264 no35 p98 Ag 28 2017

Lovesick (TV program)

STREAMING A. D'ARMINIO *TV Guide* v64 no46 p38 N 7 2016

Love—Social aspects

The President Who Loved A. Patchett color *Time* v189 no3 p47 Ja 30 2017

Real Love S. Salzberg color *Tricycle: The Buddhist Review* v26 no4 p26 Summ 2017

Love Song, A (Music)

Matthew Garrison D. OUELLETTE color *Downbeat* v84 no8 p98 Ag 2017

Love Story, A (Short story)

A LOVE STORY S. HUNT cartoon *New Yorker* v93 no14 p70 My 22 2017

Love Supreme, A (Theatrical production)

Fall Preview M. Harss color *New Yorker* v93 no25 p20 Ag 28 2017

Love Supreme: The Complete Masters, A (Music)

HISTORICAL ALBUM OF THE YEAR bw color *Downbeat* v83 no12 p40 D 2016

LOVETT, BRIAN

CUTT AND RUN 2.0 color *Outdoor Life* v224 no3 pT1 Ap 2017

Lovett, Diana

Cocoa for a Cause A. Paturel color *Good Housekeeping* v264 no2 p59 F 2017

Lovett, Jon

CARRY A BIG SHTICK cartoon *Wired* v25 no4 p72 Ap 2017

Lovette, Lauren

All-Around arTiST M. Fuhrer color *Dance Spirit* v21 no1 p44 Ja 2017

letter to my teenage self color *Dance Spirit* v21 no8 p40 O 2017

Love Witch, The (Film)

The Love Witch V. LUCCA color *Film Comment* v52 no6 p87 N/D 2016

Lövin, Isabella

Climate Change Poses a Threat to Our Oceans *UN Chronicle* v54 no1/2 p1 2017

Loving (Film)

The 10 Best Movies S. Zacharek color *Time* v188 no25-26 p132 D 19 2016 Double Issue

ALL IN A. WINTOUR bw color *Vogue* v206 no11 p68 N 2016

Best Movies for Grownups B. NEWCOTT bw color *AARP: The Magazine* v60 no2A p54 F/Mr 2017

GOOD FIGHTS A. LANE cartoon *New Yorker* v92 no36 p82 N 7 2016

Labor of Loving J. McGovern color *Entertainment Weekly* no1439 p14 N 11 2016

LOVE & MARRIAGE R. R. Robertson color *Essence* v47 no7 p47 N 2016

Love STORY D. Senna bw color *Vogue* v206 no11 p189 N 2016

Loving C. Nashawaty color *Entertainment Weekly* no1439 p44 N 11 2016

One Couple's 'Criminal' Marriage Y. VILLARREAL *Advocate* no1088 p17 D 2016/Ja 2017

PORTRAITS OF AMERICA J. ANDERSON color *America* v215 no16 p29 N 21 2016

The Rights of the Heart, Interpreted With Beauty by Loving S. Zacharek color *Time* v188 no20 p49 N 14 2016

RUTH on the RISE G. Wood bw color *Vogue* v207 no1 p80 Ja 2017

Slow Burn D. EDELSTEIN img *New York* v49 no23 p82 N 14 2016

Stay-at-Home Heroes R. Alleva color *Commonweal* v144 no1 p26 Ja 6 2017

Telling the Lovings' Story In 1966 L. Rothman color *Time* v188 no20 p50 N 14 2016

Loving, Oliver

It Happened Here: Weatherford bw map *American Cowboy* p70 LEGENDS OF TEXAS Special Issue 2017

Loving, Richard

THE Loving STORY M. KELLY *Washingtonian Magazine* v52 no2 p92 N 2016

Loving, Richard—Trials, litigation, etc.

The Right to LOVE B. BROWN *New York Times Upfront* v149 no7 p18 Ja 9 2017

Loving v. Virginia (Supreme Court case)

The Right to LOVE B. BROWN *New York Times Upfront* v149 no7 p18 Ja 9 2017

Loving Vincent (Film)

Loving Vincent J. McGovern color *Entertainment Weekly* no1485 p41 O 6 2017

NOW PLAYING color *Entertainment Weekly* no1486 p46 O 13 2017

Lovins, Amory B.

Nuclear power: Deployment speed color *Science* v354 no6316 p1112 D 2 2016

Low, Cheryl

Vanity in Dust *Publishers Weekly* v264 no26 p161 Je 26 2017

Low, Evan

Off-Limits A. Greenblatt *Governing* v30 no12 p12 S 2017

Low, Ivy

Mapping the human DC lineage through the integration of high-dimensional techniques diag *Science* v356 no6342 p1044 Je 9 2017

Low, Jackson Mac

Pie color *Art in America* v105 no1 p43 Ja 2017

Low, John N.

Imprints: The Pokagon Band of Potawatomi Indians and the City of Chicago R. E. Walls *American Indian Quarterly* v41 no3 p292 Summ 2017

LOW, NATALIE H.

The Resilience of Marine Ecosystems to Climatic Disturbances *BioScience* v67 no3 p208 Mr 2017

Low, Tim

Extravagant, Aggressive Birds Down Under T. Flannery color *New York Review of Books* v64 no4 p27 Mr 9 2017

When Unequal Pay Is Actually Fair *Harvard Business Review Digital Articles* p2 Mr 31 2016

Why It's So Hard to Figure Out What to Pay Top Talent *Harvard Business Review Digital Articles* p2 F 19 2015

Low calorie foods

FAFQ (FREQUENTLY ASKED FOOD QUESTIONS) K. Patel and J. WUEBBEN color *Muscle & Performance* v9 no10 p20 O 2017

Low-carbohydrate diet

HOW CYCLING WORKS A. C. Shilton, S. Yeager et al cartoon diag *Bicycling* v58 no9 p21 O 2017

On the A-List J. Bowden and V. TWEED color *Better Nutrition* p16 My 2017

Low density lipoproteins

Blood Levels of Trans Fats Among American Adults Fell from 1999 to 2010 B. Restrepo *Amber Waves: The Economics of Food, Farming, Natural Resources, & Rural America* p39 Je 2017

Dr. Oz's favorite superfoods M. TAYLOR color *Redbook* p96 O 2017

Rethinking 'Good' Cholesterol *Saturday Evening Post* v289 no1 p76 Ja/F 2017

Low earth orbit satellites

Minisatellite surge spurs downlink infrastructure J. Sokol color graph *Science* v357 no6358 p1342 S 29 2017

Low-fat diet

NUTRITION HOTLINE R. MANGELS *Vegetarian Journal* v35 no1 p2 2016

Low-income housing—Design & construction

Speaking Volumes S. AMELAR *Architectural Record* v205 no10 p96 O 2017

Low-income mothers

Real life R. McCarty *U.S. Catholic* v82 no4 p4 Ap 2017

Low-income mothers—Social conditions

Orange swaddling cloths P. W. Marty *Christian Century* v133 no26 p3 D 21 2016

Low-income students

AMERICA'S BEST BANG FOR THE BUCK COLLEGES 2017 R. Kelchen *Washington Monthly* v49 no9/10 p46 S/O 2017

Backtalk J. H. Lytle *Phi Delta Kappan* v98 no4 p80 D 2016/Ja 2017

ROOM TO GROW: A private school with a noble mission gets a new lease on life--and a new building F. REDDY *Atlanta* v57 no3 p24 Jl 2017

Low-income students—Education

THE Nearly Impossible DREAM C. N. MASON *Ms.* v26 no4 p30 Wint 2016

Low noise amplifiers—Evaluation

Like a Rock color *Sound & Vision* v82 no3 p63 Ap 2017

Low temperature (Weather)

HOT | NOT T. Keith color *Sports Illustrated* v126 no1 p15 Ja 9 2017

Low temperature superconductivity

Evidence for bulk superconductivity in pure bismuth single crystals at ambient pressure O. Prakash, A. Kumar et al bibl color graph *Science* v355 no6320 p1 Ja 6 2017

Low temperatures

See also

Spin waves

Superfluidity

Zones, spots, and planetary-scale waves beating in brown dwarf atmospheres D. Apai, T. Karalidi et al color graph *Science* v357 no6352 p683 Ag 18 2017

Lowden, Jack

Jack LOWDEN G. BANKS *Interview* v47 no3 p20 Ap 2017

Low Dog, Tieraona

Dr. Low Dog [Cover story] color *Prevention* p26 Mr 2017

Dr. Low Dog [Cover story] color *Prevention* v69 no1 p26 Ja 2017

Fighting Fungus [Cover story] color *Prevention* v69 no9 p28 O 2017

First Aid on the Go color *Prevention* v69 no6 p26 Je 2017

Growing Natural Cures [Cover story] color *Prevention* v69 no5 p26 My 2017

How can I soothe my sore throat? [Cover story] color *Prevention* v69 no2 p26 F 2017

A Natural Remedy for Cuts and Scrapes color *Prevention* v69 no4 p28 Ap 2017

Soothe a Sunburn color *Prevention* v69 no7 p24 Jl 2017

Soothe Your Stomach color *Prevention* v69 no11 p24 N 2017

What's the healthiest herbal tea? color *Prevention* v68 no12 p28 D 2016

YOUR SUPPLEMENT QUESTIONS, ANSWERED! color *Amazing Wellness* p50 Fall 2017

Lowe (Company)

Lowe Infinity 250 RFL *Boating World* v38 no1 p61 Ja 2017

Lowe, Alice, 1977-

One Scary Mother C. Collis color *Entertainment Weekly* no1459 p50 Mr 31 2017

Lowe, Andrew J.

The extent of forest in dryland biomes [Cover story] chart map *Science* v356 no6338 p635 My 12 2017

Opportunities for Improved Transparency in the Timber Trade through Scientific Verification *BioScience* v66 no11 p990 N 1 2016

Publish openly but responsibly color *Science* v357 no6347 p141 Jl 14 2017

Lowe, Elisha

Work Grind Killing You? color *Black Enterprise* v47 no4 p28 N/D 2016

Lowe, Jacques

WHERE & WHEN: 18 THINGS YOU REALLY OUGHT TO DO THIS MONTH B. Freed, C. Jackson et al *Washingtonian Magazine* v52 no12 p29 S 2017

Lowe, Jaime

The Delivery Driver *New York Times Magazine* p42 F 26 2017

IN THE LINE OF FIRE *New York Times Magazine* p40 S 3 2017

LOST AND FOUND *New York Times Magazine* p53 O 30 2016

Shark Tank *New York Times Magazine* p24 O 1 2017

UKRAINE *New York Times Magazine* p22 S 24 2017

Voyages *New York Times Magazine* p16 F 26 2017

Voyages *New York Times Magazine* p24 N 6 2016

Lowe, Keith

The Fear and the Freedom: How the Second World War Changed Us J. Davis *Military History* v34 no5 p71 Ja 2018

Lowe, Laurence

AHOY, CITIZENS! cartoon *Bloomberg Businessweek* no4515 p66 Mr 20 2017

STREET FIGHTING MAN color *Esquire* p112 BigBlackBook

Lowe, Luther

City Governments Are Using Yelp to Tell You Where Not to Eat *Harvard Business Review Digital Articles* p2 F 12 2015

Lowe, Rob, 1964-

The Lowe Files M. Roffman *TV Guide* v65 no31 p36 Jl 24 2017

Lowe, Scott W.

SOX2 promotes lineage plasticity and antiandrogen resistance in TP53- and RB1-deficient prostate cancer bibl graph *Science* v355 no6320 p1 Ja 6 2017

Lowe, Terry

Hey... What Are You Doing Next January? *Stage Directions* v30 no8 p2 Ag 2017

The Parnelli Awards and NAMM: Industry Convergence K. M. Mitchell *Stage Directions* v30 no6 p16 Je 2017

Lowe Boats Inc.

Advanced Retreat A. JONES *Boating World* v38 no2 p36 F 2017

Lowe Files, The (TV program)

The Lowe Files M. Roffman *TV Guide* v65 no31 p36 Jl 24 2017

Lowell, Percival, 1855-1916

PERCIVAL LOWELL A life in astronomy K. Schindler bw color map *Astronomy* v45 no4 p44 Ap 2017

Lowell, Robert, 1917-1977

'This Suffering Business' B. D. McClay bw *Commonweal* v144 no8 p23 My 5 2017

Lowell Observatory

America's observatory D. J. Eicher color *Astronomy* v45 no4 p6 Ap 2017

Lowenstein, Roger

BREAKING THE CEO PAY CYCLE diag *Fortune* v175 no6 p58 My 1 2017

THE STORIES WE FALL FOR color *Fortune* v175 no4 p28 Mr

15 2017

Why Colleges Are Getting a C in Investing color *Fortune* v174 no8 p120 D 15 2016

Lowenthal, David

In Praise of Forgetting *History Today* v67 no3 p64 Mr 2017

Lower Brule Sioux Tribe

A Tribe's Bad Deal with Wall Street A. Ganesan color *Progressive* v81 no10 p14 N 2016

Lowery, Christopher

The formation of peak rings in large impact craters bibl color graph *Science* v354 no6314 p878 N 18 2016

Lowery, David

A Ghost Story Chills-and Makes You Wonder S. Zacharek color *Time* v190 no4 p49 Jl 24 2017

A GHOST STORY K. P. Sullivan color *Entertainment Weekly* no1463/1464 p68 Ap/My 2017

Hauntingly Lovely T. MARKATOS color *Weekly Standard* v22 no44 p36 Jl 31 2017

Phantom Pains C. LORENTZEN *New Republic* v248 no8/9 p64 Ag/S 2017

SHEET MUSIC I. Sara Smith color *Film Comment* v53 no4 p36 Jl/Ag 2017

Summer Preview R. Brody cartoon *New Yorker* v93 no14 p20 My 22 2017

Lowery, Wesley

The Activist Minds color *Sports Illustrated* v125 no20 p52 D 19 2016

Lowery, Wesley, 1990-

Black Deaths Matter REID *New York Times Book Review* p9 N 20 2016

Into the abyss of black deaths A. DOMISE cartoon color *Maclean's* v129 no46 p62 N 21 2016

ORIGINS OF A MOVEMENT N. BAPTISTE bw *Nation* v304 no6 p35 F 27 2017

Lowe's (Company)

LOWE'S GOES HIGH ON INNOVATION P. Wahba color *Fortune* v176 no1 p29 Jl 1 2017

LOWMAN, DIANE

Let it go! [Cover story] color *O, The Oprah Magazine* p92 Ag 2017

LOWMAN, MARGARET D.

Can the Spiritual Values of Forests Inspire Effective Conservation? *BioScience* v67 no8 p688 Ag 2017

Lowman, Sonia

TRANSFORMING THE NARRATIVE: The director and producer of Teach Us All on literacy's role in the fight for educational equity *Literacy Today (2411-7862)* v35 no1 p10 Jl/Ag 2017

Lownds, Sue—Interviews

WHERE ARE THEY NOW? *People Management* p36 N 2016

Lownie, Andrew

The Weird Success of Guy Burgess I. Buruma bw *New York Review of Books* v63 no20 p77 D 22 2016

Lowrance, P.

Zones, spots, and planetary-scale waves beating in brown dwarf atmospheres color graph *Science* v357 no6352 p683 Ag 18 2017

LOWREY, ANNIE

AS GLOBAL INEQUALITY GROWS, SOME SILICON VALLEY EXECUTIVES THINK A UNIVERSAL INCOME WILL BE THE ANSWER—AND THE BETA TEST IS HAPPENING IN KENYA *New York Times Magazine* p52 F 26 2017

Bitch *New York* v49 no15 p18 Jl 25 2016

Lowriders

Keeping His Fingers Crossed P. GREEN *Los Angeles Magazine* v61 no11 p30 N 2016

Slow Roll M. WAKIM *Los Angeles Magazine* p96 My 2017

Lowriders (Film)

LOWRIDERS C. M. Smith color *Entertainment Weekly* no1463/1464 p38 Ap/My 2017

Lowry, Beverly

A Cold Case in Texas E. D. NAWOTKA *Publishers Weekly* v263 no40 p92 O 3 2016

Lowry, Dave

Cinematic Sword Fighters and the Mistakes They Make color *Black Belt* v55 no5 p26 Ag/S 2017

FINE-TUNE YOUR KARATE! color *Black Belt* v55 no6 p40 O/N 2017

How to Correct Your Teacher color *Black Belt* v55 no3 p24 Ap/My 2017

The Intricacies of Power color *Black Belt* v55 no4 p26 Je/Jl 2017

PTSD and the Samurai color *Black Belt* v55 no1 p20 D 2016/Ja 2017

Some Things You Should Know About Sumo [Cover story] color *Black Belt* v55 no2 p24 F/Mr 2017

A Toothpick When You're Hungry color *Black Belt* v55 no6 p26 O/N 2017

Lowry, Kyle, 1986-

Kyle Lowry C. Cullen color *Current Biography* v77 no10 p77 O 2016

LOWRY, LOIS

'Lord of the Flies' 60 Years Later *New York Times Book Review* p29 O 30 2016

Lowry, Mary Pauline

STRANGE BREW color *O, The Oprah Magazine* p32 My 2017

LOWRY, RICHARD

For Love of Country color *National Review* v69 no3 p33 F 20 2017

The War over Enforcement [Cover story] diag *National Review* v69 no5 p30 Mr 20 2017

LOWRY, VICKY

ART OF WAR color *Architectural Digest* v73 no11 p92 N 2016

BLOM COUNTY color *Architectural Digest* v74 no3 p126 Mr 2017

COLLECTED WISDOM color *Architectural Digest* v73 no12 p96 D 2016

FRENCH FLAIR color *Architectural Digest* v73 no12 p56 D 2016

Like Minds color *Architectural Digest* v74 no3 p56 Mr 2017

Lowry, William

Park politics color *Science* v357 no6353 p762 Ag 25 2017

Lowry, Younghee—Interviews

Climbing for Mental Health H. MOORE color *Climbing* no352 p10 Ap 2017

Lows (Meteorology)

Mod squad S. Scoles and M. HONGOLTZ-HETLING cartoon *Popular Science* v289 no4 p42 Jl/Ag 2017

LOY, DAVID

IN SEARCH OF THE SACRED cartoon *Tricycle: The Buddhist Review* v26 no3 p82 Spr 2017

Loyalty

See also
> Brand loyalty
> Customer loyalty
> Patriotism

If You're Loyal to a Group, Does It Compromise Your Ethics? F. Gino *Harvard Business Review Digital Articles* p2 Ja 6 2016

Loyalty Day (U.S.)

The Loyalty Freak J. B. JUDIS color *New Republic* v248 no7 p14 Jl 2017

Loyn, David

Poster Boys of Afghan History *History Today* v67 no1 p39 Ja 2017

LOYOLA, ROMAN

7 hidden features in macOS Sierra you may have missed color *Macworld - Digital Edition* v33 no11 p27 N 2016

Apple discontinues iPod nano and iPod shuffle color *Macworld - Digital Edition* v34 no9 p87 S 2017

Apple's new Swift Playgrounds 1.5 includes controls for robots color *Macworld - Digital Edition* p16 Je 13 2017

Apple will allow developers to respond to App Store user reviews color *Macworld - Digital Edition* p19 Mr 2017

Consumer Reports updates its MacBook Pro review color *PC-World* v35 no2 p41 F 2017

HENGE DOCKS TETHERED DOCKING STATION color *Macworld - Digital Edition* p39 F 2017

How to adjust macOS Sierra 10.12.4's Night Shift settings color *Macworld - Digital Edition* v34 no4 p7 My 2017

How to bring back a physical Escape key on the new MacBook Pro with Touch Bar color *Macworld - Digital Edition* p108 D 2016

How to configure a software RAID in macOS Sierra's Disk Utility color *Macworld - Digital Edition* v33 no11 p130 N 2016

How to downgrade to iOS 9 if you don't like iOS 10 *PCWorld* p157 O 2016

How To: Get a Touch Bar without buying a MacBook color *Mac-*

world - Digital Edition p106 Ja 2017

How to open Microsoft Excel spreadsheets in Apple Numbers on a Mac color *Macworld - Digital Edition* v34 no11 p114 N 2017

How to stop autoplay videos in Safari 11 color *Macworld - Digital Edition* v34 no11 p7 N 2017

How to turn on/off read receipts in macOS Sierra's Messages cartoon color *Macworld - Digital Edition* v33 no11 p127 N 2016

How to use iCloud Drive's new Desktop and Documents access in macOS Sierra color *Macworld - Digital Edition* v33 no11 p135 N 2016

iMAC KABY LAKE (2017): THE iMAC'S EXCELLENCE CONTINUES ON color graph *Macworld - Digital Edition* v34 no8 p27 Ag 2017

LOFREE KEYBOARD: THE FEELING OF A TYPEWRITER ON YOUR MAC OR iOS DEVICE color *Macworld - Digital Edition* v34 no4 p23 My 2017

MACBOOK 2017: THE BANG FOR YOUR BUCK GETS BETTER color graph *Macworld - Digital Edition* v34 no8 p32 Ag 2017

MACBOOK PRO (2017): THE FUTURE STARTS WITH KABY LAKE color graph *Macworld - Digital Edition* v34 no8 p37 Ag 2017

macOS HIGH SIERRA: FEATURES, SYSTEM REQUIREMENTS, RELEASE DATE, AND MORE color *Macworld - Digital Edition* p72 Je 13 2017

MACOS HIGH SIERRA REVIEW: INCREMENTAL UPDATE WORTHY OF YOUR TIME, EVENTUALLY color *Macworld - Digital Edition* v34 no11 p99 N 2017

macOS Sierra: Mixing iOS with OS X to make a better Mac color *Macworld - Digital Edition* v33 no11 p7 N 2016

News: Apple to support automation in Sierra color *Macworld - Digital Edition* p16 Ja 2017

NIKE DAY TO NIGHT APPLE WATCH BANDS color *Macworld - Digital Edition* p32 Je 13 2017

Report: Security hole in macOS Keychain puts passwords at risk color *Macworld - Digital Edition* v34 no11 p22 N 2017

SATECHI ALUMINUM USB 3.0 HUB + CARD READER: EASY ACCESS TO USB 3 PORTS FOR YOUR MAC color *Macworld - Digital Edition* p29 Mr 2017

Ta-dah! Touch Bar is the highlight of Apple's newest MacBook Pro color *Macworld - Digital Edition* p7 D 2016

Wish list: What I'd like to see in a new iMac color *Macworld - Digital Edition* v34 no6 p7 Je 2017

Loyola Marymount University

WELCOME TO SILICON BEACH AT LMU *Los Angeles Magazine* p63 F 2017

Lozano, Rafael

BINGE C. Agard color *Entertainment Weekly* no1449 p51 Ja 20 2017

LOZANO, TATIANA

Open to Belief *Weekly Standard* v22 no8 p38 O 31 2016

LP (Performer)—Interviews

LOST ON U.S.? LP is a bonafide star with a #1 hit single—in Europe. When will America catch on? J. ANDERSON-MINSHALL bw *Advocate* no1091 p32 Je/Jl 2017

LPGA Tour (Golf)

ON PAR WITH NONE A. M. I. GRÍMSSON *Iceland Review* v55 no2 p14 Mr/Ap 2017

LRG (Company)

GEARBOX color *Dirt Sports + Off-Road* v51 no3 p68 Mr 2017

LSD (Drug)

Brain protein's grip on LSD imaged M. ROSEN *Science News* v191 no4 p16 Mr 4 2017

LSD (Drug)—Physiological effect

Your Boss Is Gonna Love Your New Drug Habit J. DEAN color *GQ: Gentlemen's Quarterly* v87 no1 p26 Ja 2017

Lu, Albert L.

A selective insecticidal protein from Pseudomonas for controlling corn rootworms bibl chart graph *Science* v354 no6312 p634 N 4 2016

Lu, Catherine P.

Spatiotemporal antagonism in mesenchymal-epithelial signaling in sweat versus hair fate decision graph *Science* v354 no6319 paah6102-1 D 23 2016

Lu, Chao-Yang

Satellite-based entanglement distribution over 1200 kilometers diag graph *Science* v356 no6343 p1140 Je 16 2017

Lu, Chenggang

Blocking promiscuous activation at cryptic promoters directs cell type–specific gene expression diag *Science* v356 no6339 p717 My 19 2017

Lu, Jackson G.

To Be More Creative, Schedule Your Breaks *Harvard Business Review Digital Articles* p2 My 10 2017

Lu, Jennifer

Fabrication of fillable microparticles and other complex 3D microstructures color diag *Science* v357 no6356 p1138 S 15 2017

Lu, K.

Grain boundary stability governs hardening and softening in extremely fine nanograined metals bibl color graph *Science* v355 no6331 p1292 Mr 24 2017

Lu, Ku

Systemic pan-AMPK activator MK-8722 improves glucose homeostasis but induces cardiac hypertrophy graph *Science* v357 no6350 p507 Ag 4 2017

Lu, Li

Atomic-layered Au clusters on α-MoC as catalysts for the low-temperature water-gas shift reaction chart diag graph *Science* v357 no6349 p389 Jl 28 2017

Identification of single-site gold catalysis in acetylene hydrochlorination bw diag graph *Science* v355 no6332 p1399 Mr 31 2017

Lu, Lu

Role for migratory wild birds in the global spread of avian influenza H5N8 bibl graph map *Science* v354 no6309 p213 O 14 2016

Lu, Marie

FROM REALITY TO THE PAGE— AND BACK AGAIN bw color *Literacy Today (2411-7862)* v34 no5 p16 Mr/Ap 2017

GAME CHANGER: A NEW PANTHEON OF SUPERHEROES C. HARRINGTON *Wired* v25 no9 p20 S 2017

Lu, Peiwen

Ephrin B1–mediated repulsion and signaling control germinal center T cell territoriality and function color *Science* v356 no6339 p716 My 19 2017

Lu, Qi-Ming

Satellite-based entanglement distribution over 1200 kilometers diag graph *Science* v356 no6343 p1140 Je 16 2017

Lu, Rachel

Beyond Getting Tough color *National Review* v69 no3 p46 F 20 2017

A GOOD JOB IS HARD TO FIND color *America* v217 no4 p26 Ag 21 2017

Tradition's Comeback color *National Review* v68 no19 p48 O 24 2016

Lu, Steve

Mismatch repair deficiency predicts response of solid tumors to PD-1 blockade chart graph *Science* v357 no6349 p409 Jl 28 2017

Lu, W.

Observation of coherent elastic neutrino-nucleus scattering diag *Science* v357 no6356 p1123 S 15 2017

Lu, Wan-Jin

Stromal Gli2 activity coordinates a niche signaling program for mammary epithelial stem cells color *Science* v356 no6335 p284 Ap 21 2017

Lü, Wei

Cryo-EM structures of the triheteromeric NMDA receptor and its allosteric modulation graph *Science* v355 no6331 p1282 Mr 24 2017

Lu, Ying

Interacting amino acid replacements allow poison frogs to evolve epibatidine resistance chart diag graph *Science* v357 no6357 p1261 S 22 2017

Lu, You

RETINOBLASTOMA RELATED1 mediates germline entry in Arabidopsis color diag *Science* v356 no6336 p396 Ap 28 2017

Lu, Zheng-Hong

Efficient and stable solution-processed planar perovskite solar cells via contact passivation bibl graph *Science* v355 no6326 p722 F 17 2017

Lu Liu

A selective insecticidal protein from Pseudomonas for controlling corn rootworms bibl chart graph *Science* v354 no6312 p634 N

4 2016

Lu Sun

MAVS-dependent host species range and pathogenicity of human hepatitis A virus bibl graph *Science* v353 no6307 p1541 S 30 2016

Lu Yang

Exploring genetic suppression interactions on a global scale diag *Science* v354 no6312 p599 N 4 2016

Luang Pu Thuat

THE CASE OF THE DISEMBODIED MONK M. SCARLES color *Tricycle: The Buddhist Review* v26 no2 p18 Wint 2016

Lubar, Steven D.

Beyond the museum's mandate P. D. Brinkman color *Science* v357 no6352 p652 Ag 18 2017

Lubbel, Sam

Mid-Century Modern Architecture Travel Guide *Treasures* v6 no4 p6 F/Mr 2017

LUBBEN, ALEX

A PORTRAIT IN SPEED color *Climbing* no356 p72 S/O 2017

Lubenow, William C.

Talking Heads A. VAN LOON color *Weekly Standard* v22 no16 p31 D 26 2016

Luber, Brandon S.

Mismatch repair deficiency predicts response of solid tumors to PD-1 blockade chart graph *Science* v357 no6349 p409 Jl 28 2017

Lubetzky, Daniel

How Did I Get Here? DANIEL LUBETZKY color *Bloomberg Businessweek* no4501 p64 N 28 2016

Lubezki, Emmanuel

VIRTUOUS REALITY color *Vanity Fair* v59 no8 p47 Ag 2017

Lubitsch, Ernst, 1892-1947

To Do: Twenty-five things to see, hear, watch, and read img *New York* v50 no11 p128 My 29 2017

Lubofsky, Evan

BACK TO BIKINI: SCIENTISTS STUDY LINGERING RADIOACTIVITY AT 'GROUND ZERO' FOR NUCLEAR WEAPONS TESTING AFTER WORLD WAR II *Oceanus* v52 no2 p32 Spr 2017

The Hunt for Fresh Water Below the Seafloor *Oceanus* v52 no2 p40 Spr 2017

Lubovitch, Lar

LAR LUBOVITCH M. Schrock *Dance Magazine* v90 no12 p48 D 2016

LUBOW, ARTHUR

Artistic Retreat color *Architectural Digest* v73 no12 p134 D 2016

Photography and Paradox C. Westerbeck *Art in America* v104 no9 p65 O 2016

Lubrication & lubricants

DON'T OVERLOOK THE OUTBOARD D. HISLOP *Sea Magazine* v108 no10 p30 O 2016

HARMONIC BALANCER REPAIR SLEEVE: MAKE IT A POINT TO CHECK THE BALANCER FOR WEAR R. Bohacz *Successful Farming* v115 no12 p40 O 2017

OIL VISCOSITY DEBATE R. Bohacz *Successful Farming* v115 no3 p29 Mid-F 2017

Lubrication & lubricants—Equipment & supplies—Evaluation

GEARBOX color *Dirt Sports + Off-Road* v51 no1 p68 Ja 2017

Luby, Kevin

SHINY, TASTY THINGS color *Skiing* p32 Wint 2017

Luby, Victoria

7 Tenets of a Good CEO Succession Process *Harvard Business Review Digital Articles* p2 D 7 2016

Luca, Michael

City Governments Are Using Yelp to Tell You Where Not to Eat *Harvard Business Review Digital Articles* p2 F 12 2015

FIXING DISCRIMINATION IN ONLINE MARKETPLACES color *Harvard Business Review* v94 no12 p88 D 2016

Good Communication Requires Experimenting with Your Language *Harvard Business Review Digital Articles* p2 F 4 2016

How Netflix's Content Strategy Is Reshaping Movie Culture *Harvard Business Review Digital Articles* p2 Ag 31 2017

How Streaming Is Changing Music (Again) *Harvard Business Review Digital Articles* p2 D 12 2016

How to Design (and Analyze) a Business Experiment *Harvard Business Review Digital Articles* p2 O 29 2015

Lessons from Yelp's Empirical Approach to Diversity *Harvard Business Review Digital Articles* p2 S 20 2017

Your Company Is Full of Good Experiments (You Just Have to Recognize Them) *Harvard Business Review Digital Articles* p2 N 23 2015

Luca, Mike

DO SEARCH ADS REALLY WORK?: INTERACTION color *Harvard Business Review* v95 no3 p20 My/Je 2017

Luca, Vincent C.

Notch-Jagged complex structure implicates a catch bond in tuning ligand sensitivity bibl diag graph *Science* v355 no6331 p1320 Mr 24 2017

Luca Laser Workshop (Company)

SPARKLE PLENTY *Cincinnati Magazine* v50 no5 p32 F 2017

Lucas, Ashley—Interviews

Actors on the inside Λ. Frykholm color *Christian Century* v134 no1 p28 Ja 4 2017

LUCAS, AYOKA

Adorned Beauty color *Ebony* v72 no6 p40 Ap/My 2017

BEAUTY & THE BEAT color *Ebony* v72 no6 p44 Ap/My 2017

DADDY'S DAY GIFT GUIDE color *Ebony* v72 no8 p46 Je 2017

FLAWLESS BEAUTY bw color *Ebony* v72 no6 p42 Ap/My 2017

GENT SCENTS color *Ebony* v72 no6 p45 Ap/My 2017

A GUIDE TO THE SUMMER'S HOTTEST SNEAKERS color *Ebony* v72 no6 p48 Ap/My 2017

July/August T. Ebony color *Ebony* v72 no9 p18 Jl/Ag 2017

LEADERS OF THE NEW COOL bw color *Ebony* v72 no6 p35 Ap/My 2017

YOU WANT YOUR MTV? color *Ebony* v72 no8 p35 Je 2017

Lucas, Brian J.

Giving Up Is the Enemy of Creativity *Harvard Business Review Digital Articles* p2 D 1 2015

Lucas, Forrest

LUCAS OIL OFF-ROAD RACING PUSHES EAST [Cover story] S. OCHSNER color *Dirt Sports + Off-Road* v51 no12 p24 D 2017

LUCAS, FRED

The Democrats' Last Hope cartoon *Weekly Standard* v22 no25 p21 Mr 6 2017

The Evolution of Matt Bevin color *Weekly Standard* v22 no32 p24 My 1 2017

Winning Again in Space color *Weekly Standard* v22 no42 p14 Jl 17 2017

Lucas, George R., 1949-

Ethics and Cyber Warfare: The Quest for Responsible Security in the Age of Digital Warfare K. H. Potts *Christian Century* v134 no18 p41 Ag 30 2017

Lucas, George, 1944-

The Lucas Museum of Lucas Arts Invites You to Appreciate George Lucas D. Leonard color *Bloomberg Businessweek* no4506 p42 Ja 9 2017

MUSEUM WARS A. Greenblatt *Governing* v30 no6 p9 Mr 2017

'Star Wars' at 40 D. Wallace and B. Burton bw color *AARP: The Magazine* v60 no3A p10 Ap/My 2017

"Star Wars" Goes Rogue W. D. Gehring *USA Today Magazine* v145 no2858 p63 N 2016

Lucas, H.

Improving global integration of crop research color *Science* v357 no6349 p359 Jl 28 2017

Lucas, James

Arabian Nights color *Climbing* no357 p48 N 2017

Better Kneebars color *Climbing* no350 p48 D 2016/Ja 2017

Beyond the Bolt color *Climbing* no357 p60 N 2017

Climber's Little Helper color *Climbing* no351 p44 F/Mr 2017

THE DESCENT color *Climbing* no351 p80 F/Mr 2017

The Freerider color *Climbing* no355 p18 Ag 2017

Good Cybersecurity Can Be Good Marketing *Harvard Business Review Digital Articles* p2 S 23 2016

Gypsy Kitchen color *Climbing* no356 p28 S/O 2017

Inflating Grades and Egos color *Climbing* no351 p22 F/Mr 2017

LEGAL FOR A DAY color *Climbing* no350 p64 D 2016/Ja 2017

Moose's Tooth color *Climbing* no355 p28 Ag 2017

NEW DAWN color *Climbing* no351 p72 F/Mr 2017

Scary (and true) tales from a crag near you *Climbing* no350 p19 D 2016/Ja 2017

A Study in Contrast color *Climbing* no354 p22 Jl 2017

Tag-Line Rappels color *Climbing* no351 p50 F/Mr 2017

Lucas, Joe

Sea Change C. KELLY color *House Beautiful* p86 Jl 2017

LUCAS, JOSH

Kaari UPSON: THE MONUMENTAL WORK OF THE LOS ANGELES MIXED-MEDIA ARTIST TURNS THE AMERICAN DREAM INSIDE OUT AND LETS ALL THE MESSY PARTS SPILL OUT KAARI UPSON MAY JUST BE THE ARTIST OF OUR AGE *Interview* v47 no3 p101 Ap 2017

Lucas, Julian

Beyond Genealogy: On the wealth of stories that family novels leave behind *New York Times Book Review* p18 S 3 2017

Southern Sublime color *New York Review of Books* v64 no6 p8 Ap 6 2017

They Had a Dream *New York Times Book Review* p13 N 27 2016

Lucas, Lisa, 1980-

Lisa Lucas: Executive Director, National Book Foundation C. Reid *Publishers Weekly* v263 no52 p29 D 19 2016

Lisa Lucas J. Crelin color *Current Biography* v78 no3 p40 Mr 2017

Lucas, Lisa, 1980-—Interviews

Lisa Lucas S. Begley color *Time* v189 no3 p60 Ja 30 2017

LUCAS, MARTYN C.

Envisioning the Future of Aquatic Animal Tracking: Technology, Science, and Application *BioScience* v67 no10 p884 O 2017

Lucas, Sydney

The Son M. ROUSH *TV Guide* v65 no14 p19 Ap 3 2017

Lucas Oil Products Inc.

2016 LUCAS OIL OFF-ROAD RACING SERIES FINISHES STRONG AT WILD HORSE PASS M. EMERY color *Dirt Sports + Off-Road* v51 no4 p34 Ap 2017

LOORRS TO ADD SXSs TO NATIONAL SCHEDULE color *Dirt Sports + Off-Road* v51 no4 p8 Ap 2017

OILED UP J. Pearley Huffman color *Car & Driver* v63 no4 p28 O 2017

LUCCA, VIOLET

Beatriz at Dinner color *Film Comment* v53 no3 p68 My/Je 2017

The Challenge color *Film Comment* v53 no5 p71 S/O 2017

THE CLEANING CREW color *Film Comment* v52 no6 p60 N/D 2016

Contemporary Color color *Film Comment* v53 no2 p69 Mr/Ap 2017

Fashion in Film bw *Film Comment* v52 no6 p94 N/D 2016

The Founder color *Film Comment* v53 no1 p83 Ja/F 2017

FRAME TO FRAME *Film Comment* v53 no3 p54 My/Je 2017

Intimations: The Cinema of Wojciech Has color *Film Comment* v53 no4 p78 Jl/Ag 2017

The Love Witch color *Film Comment* v52 no6 p87 N/D 2016

MOVING BEYOND bw *Film Comment* v53 no4 p42 Jl/Ag 2017

Next Steps color *Film Comment* v53 no1 p10 Ja/F 2017

NO JOKE color *Film Comment* v53 no2 p52 Mr/Ap 2017

Scene Missing color *Film Comment* v53 no3 p78 My/Je 2017

Luce, Carolyn Buck

The Health Care Industry Needs to Start Taking Women Seriously *Harvard Business Review Digital Articles* p2 My 28 2015

Luce, Edward

Failing to Deliver: Edward Luce argues that the tradition of liberty is now under mortal threat F. ZAKARIA *New York Times Book Review* p9 Jl 30 2017

Luce, Henry Robinson, 1898-1967

March 1, 1948: A Fortunate Time A. BROWN bw color *Forbes* v199 no5 p36 My 16 2017

LUCE, KELLY

MEMENTO cartoon color *O, The Oprah Magazine* p100 F 2017

Luce, Kirsten

North of the Border, South of the Wall color *Bloomberg Businessweek* no4518 p62 Ap 10 2017

Luce, Q.

Observation of a large-scale anisotropy in the arrival directions of cosmic rays above 8×1018 eV *Science* v357 no6357 p1266 S 22 2017

Lucerne Lake (Switzerland)

Lucerne is 'Essence of Switzerland' D. Heimburger color *Christianity Today* v61 no5 p7 Je 2017

Lucero, A.

Observation of a large-scale anisotropy in the arrival directions

of cosmic rays above 8×1018 eV *Science* v357 no6357 p1266 S 22 2017

Lucero, Jacinta
Single-cell methylomes identify neuronal subtypes and regulatory elements in mammalian cortex diag *Science* v357 no6351 p600 Ag 11 2017

Lucey, Donna M., 1951-
Painted Ladies: A panorama of the Gilded Age, seen through Sargent's art A. BLOOM *New York Times Book Review* p10 S 3 2017

LUCHETTE, CLAIRE
Dog Years color *O, The Oprah Magazine* p98 O 2017
LIGHT CARRIERS color *O, The Oprah Magazine* p109 N 2017
WHAT A BOOK CAN DO [Cover story] color *O, The Oprah Magazine* p76 Jl 2017

Lucia di Lammermoor (Theatrical production)
Lucia di Lammermoor M. T. Ketterson *Opera News* v81 no7 p34 Ja 2017
Operapedia: Lucia di Lammermoor G. DONIZETTI *Opera News* v81 no10 p14 Ap 2017

Luciano, Joe
TESTING? TESTING? B. CROWDER *Virginia Living* v15 no1 p27 D 2016

Lucid VR (Company)
LUCIDCAM: STEREOSCOPIC 3D VR CREATION COMES TO THE MASSES J. DOVE color *Macworld - Digital Edition* v34 no10 p102 O 2017

Lucifer (TV program)
Ask Matt M. Roush *TV Guide* v65 no11 p4 Mr 6 2017
CHEERS & JEERS D. HOLBROOK *TV Guide* v64 no46 p88 N 7 2016
Lucifer D. Holbrook *TV Guide* v65 no19 p32 My 1 2017
Lucifer N. Abrams, C. Holub et al *Entertainment Weekly* no1482/1483 p48 S 22 2017

Lucinda Childs Dance Company (Performer)
Winter Preview M. Harss cartoon *New Yorker* v92 no37 p22 N 14 2016

Luck, Andrew, 1989-
No Dumb Luck J. GUSKEY color diag *Indianapolis Monthly* v41 no2 p17 S 2017

LUCK, BARRY
CHANGING GEARS: Cycling for Social Change color *Earth Island Journal* v32 no3 p15 Aut 2017

Luck, Taylor
Christians, Muslims stump together in Jordan color *Christian Century* v133 no22 p14 O 26 2016
Christian writer's murder in Jordan reveals conflict on free speech, religion *Christian Century* v133 no22 p15 O 26 2016
A Jordanian city offers lessons on peace among Christians and Muslims *Christian Century* v134 no14 p17 Jl 5 2017
Moroccans protest after monarchy, Muslim party fail to deliver on reform *Christian Century* v134 no1 p16 Ja 4 2017

Luckett, Josslyn
DIGGING AND BLUING WITH BILLY WOODBERRY *Film Quarterly* v70 no4 p67 Summ 2017

Luckett, Karen
How My Horse De-Stresses Me color *Horse & Rider* v55 no12 p72 D 2016

LUCKETT, THOMAS
SUPERVOID *Scientific American* v315 no6 p9 D 2016

Luckie, Douglas B.
Updating the Two Cultures: How Structures Can Promote Interdisciplinary Cultures *Change* v48 no6 p28 N/D 2016

Lucky (Film)
Lucky C. Nashawaty color *Entertainment Weekly* no1485 p43 O 6 2017
A Sublime Farewell to Stanton In Lucky S. Zacharek color *Time* v190 no14 p51 O 9 2017

Lucky One, The (Theatrical production)
THE THEATRE *New Yorker* v93 no11 p8 My 1 2017

Lucy (Prehistoric hominid)
Why We Still Love 'Lucy' L. Pyne *History Today* v66 no12 p7 D 2016

Luddites—History—19th century
Rage Against the Machines C. THOMPSON *Smithsonian* v47 no9 p21 Ja/F 2017

Ludendorff, Erich, 1865-1937
What We Learned From... Operation Michael, 1918 D. T. Zabecki bw *Military History* v34 no2 p18 Jl 2017

Ludes, Bertrand
Ancient genomic changes associated with domestication of the horse color diag *Science* v356 no6336 p442 Ap 28 2017

Ludlam, Scott
For the Record color *Time* v190 no5 p9 Jl 31 2017

Ludwig, Alexander
VIKINGS D. Franich color *Entertainment Weekly* no1474/1475 p70 Jl 21-28 2017

Ludwig, Arne
Ancient genomic changes associated with domestication of the horse color diag *Science* v356 no6336 p442 Ap 28 2017

Ludwig, Benjamin
GINNY MOON J. Stuart *New York Times Book Review* p26 Je 18 2017

Ludwig, Chris
Smart Plants: The Flora of Virginia's new mobile app is the 21st century version of the classic botany card B. CROWDER *Virginia Living* v15 no6 p67 O 2017

Ludwig, David
advice every new mom needs [Cover story] color *Parents* v92 no7 p32 Jl 2017

Ludwig, Hans
618" color *Powder* p70 S 2017
RIP: TELEMARK color *Powder* v45 no6 p40 F 2017
SEE YOU IN JUNE color *Powder* p48 S 2017
Voyageur [Cover story] color *Powder* v45 no6 p60 F 2017

Ludwig, Jens
A Guide to Solving Social Problems with Machine Learning *Harvard Business Review Digital Articles* p2 D 8 2016

Ludwig, Jon
A DREADFUL TIME T. MALONE *Atlanta* v57 no6 p36 O 2017

Ludwig, Michael
You Never Forget Your First Time diag il *Backpacker* v45 no2 p64 Mr 2017

Lue, Tyronn, 1977-
Tyronn Lue C. Cullen color *Current Biography* v78 no3 p45 Mr 2017

Lueders, Bill
Barack Obama, By the Numbers *Progressive* p14 D 2016/Ja 2017
Climate Change, What Climate Change? color *Progressive* v81 no5 p43 Je/Jl 2017
Fake News chart *Progressive* v81 no4 p14 Ap/My 2017
It's a Conspiracy! color *Progressive* v81 no3 p12 Mr 2017
The Lying Golfer-in-Chief color *Progressive* v81 no7 p14 O/N 2017
'No Suits for You!' color *Progressive* p19 D 2016/Ja 2017
The Right Stuff: Charlie Sykes and the Practice of Sane Conservatism color *Progressive* v81 no7 p63 O/N 2017
'Shut Up, Already!': The New Battle Over Campus Free Speech color *Progressive* v81 no6 p52 Ag/S 2017
Spiral: Trapped in the Forever War/America's War for the Greater Middle East: A Military History/Lies, Incorporated: The World of Post-Truth Politics... color *Progressive* p60 D 2016/Ja 2017
Steve Bannon, Trump's Right-Hand Batterer cartoon *Progressive* v81 no2 p14 F 2017
Stick Up for the Press *Progressive* v81 no4 p8 Ap/My 2017
A Time to Fight *Progressive* p8 D 2016/Ja 2017
Trump and Russia: Nothing to See Here? color *Progressive* v81 no6 p14 Ag/S 2017
Trumping Trumpism *Progressive* v81 no7 p6 O/N 2017
Truth-Testing in the Post-Truth Era *Progressive* v81 no3 p40 Mr 2017
Walker Used Group to Snare Corporate Cash diag *Progressive* v81 no10 p12 N 2016
With Friends Like These... color graph *Progressive* v81 no5 p14 Je/Jl 2017

Lueneburger, Christoph
A Company's Good Deeds Can Energize Employees *Harvard Business Review Digital Articles* p2 D 3 2014

Luesse, Valerie Fraser
Florida's Unsung Beach Towns color map *Southern Living* v52 no6 p63 Je 2017
My Aunt, the Beauty Icon color *Southern Living* v52 no4 p64 Ap

2017

Old Rose for a New Garden color *Southern Living* v52 no4 p15 Ap 2017

Secrets of South Florida color map *Southern Living* v52 no1 p45 Ja 2017

SOUTH'S BEST HOTEL color *Southern Living* v52 no4 p78 Ap 2017

SPRINGTIME IN HORSE COUNTRY color *Southern Living* v52 no3 p100 Mr 2017

Luetkemeyer, Molly

PURSUIT OF BEAUTY S. DONELSON color *House Beautiful* v159 no3 p94 Ap 2017

Luetmer, Sadie

Pushing Back on Pipelines color *Progressive* v81 no10 p24 N 2016

Luety, Ali

GLEANINGS *Successful Farming* v115 no2 p8 F 2017

Luftman, Debra

FLAWLESS SKIN STARTS HERE *Redbook* p21a S 2017

Luger, Karolin

Structure of histone-based chromatin in Archaea diag *Science* v357 no6351 p609 Ag 11 2017

Luggage

See also

Suitcases

Trunks (Luggage)

AHEAD OF THE PACK S. Feinstein color *Consumer Reports* v81 no12 p12 D 2016

Back to the Future color *Conde Nast Traveler* v52 no7 p21 Ag 2017

The Duffel Shuffle color *Climbing* no357 p15 N 2017

"I EAT HEALTHY AT MOST AIRPORTS. BUT AT CDG, I'LL SNIFF OUT THE FOIE GRAS" C. TATTOLI color *Conde Nast Traveler* v52 no1 p41 Ja 2017

Luggage—Evaluation

FASTRAX BACKROADS LUGGAGE D. Canet color *Cycle World* v56 no2 p20 Mr 2017

HONOR ROLL D. FOX color *Men's Health* v32 no7 p(Sp)9 S 2017

On a Roll color *AARP: The Magazine* v60 no5A p12 Ag/S 2017

Luggage—Packing

PACKING color *Women's Health* v13 no10 p148 D 2016

Luginbuehl, Leonie H.

Fatty acids in arbuscular mycorrhizal fungi are synthesized by the host plant diag graph *Science* v356 no6343 p1175 Je 16 2017

Luginbuhl, Christian

How FLAGSTAFF is preserving DARK SKIES color graph *Astronomy* v45 no9 p54 S 2017

Lugo, Dave

Click chemistry enables preclinical evaluation of targeted epigenetic therapies diag *Science* v356 no6345 p1397 Je 30 2017

Luhan, Mabel Dodge, 1879-1962

A tastemaker and her rediscovered treasures L. Beach bw cartoon color *Magazine Antiques* v184 no2 p42 Mr/Ap 2017

Luhn, Alec

Putin's Children color *Time* v189 no23 p30 Je 19 2017

Luhrmann, Baz, 1962-

PARTY LINES [Cover story] img *New York* p85 Ja 9 2017

WELCOME TO THE BOOGIE DOWN O. SEGURA *America* v215 no10 p42 O 10 2016

Luik, Jüri

A plausible scenario of nuclear war in Europe, and how to deter it: A perspective from Estonia bibl *Bulletin of the Atomic Scientists* v73 no4 p233 Jl 2017

Luiselli, Valeria

Origin Stories: Encounters with undocumented migrant children and the circumstances that produced them D. MENGESTU *New York Times Book Review* p12 Ap 30 2017

TERRORIST AND ALIEN *Harper's Magazine* v334 no2001 p32 F 2017

Luisi, Fabio

Dec/2016 M. M. AZZARO *Opera News* v81 no6 p6 D 2016

Luiz Gasparini, João

Fringe on the brink: Intertidal reefs at risk color *Science* v357 no6348 p261 Jl 21 2017

Lukas, Emil

Liquid Lens color *Art in America* v105 no1 p18 Ja 2017

Luke, the Apostle, Saint

"Incredible Things Today" M. R. Simone *America* v216 no8 p52 Ap 17 2017

Luke Cage (TV program)

The First Black Lives Matter Superhero R. SHEFFIELD color *Rolling Stone* no1272 p29 O 20 2016

MARVELOUS MAHERSHALA S. Li color *Entertainment Weekly* no1434 p30 O 7 2016

Marvel's Luke Cage M. Logan *TV Guide* v64 no40 p31 O 3 2016

Lukić, Zarija

Measurement of the small-scale structure of the intergalactic medium using close quasar pairs diag graph *Science* v356 no6336 p418 Ap 28 2017

Lukin, Mikhail D.

An integrated diamond nanophotonics platform for quantum-optical networks bibl graph *Science* v354 no6314 p847 N 18 2016

Atom-by-atom assembly of defect-free one-dimensional cold atom arrays bibl diag graph *Science* v354 no6315 p1024 N 25 2016

Magnetic resonance spectroscopy of an atomically thin material using a single-spin qubit bibl color diag graph *Science* v355 no6324 p503 F 3 2017

Luk'yanchuk, Boris

Optically resonant dielectric nanostructures bibl graph *Science* v354 no6314 paag2472-1 N 18 2016

Lula, 1945-

Americas K. Stock color graph *Bloomberg Businessweek* no4530 p8 Jl 17 2017

Lullabies

Rock-a-Bye Baby's Rocky Roots LAW and G. Tarlach color *Discover* v38 no5 p66 Je 2017

Lulu Yilun Chen

K-Pop Eyes Its 'Michael Jackson Moment' bw color *Bloomberg Businessweek* no4535 p31 Ag 28 2017

Lululemon Athletica Inc.

And... Action! color *Women's Health* v13 no10 p18 D 2016

Founder's Remorse A. BROWN color *Forbes* v198 no9 p40 D 30 2016

Lululemon Athletica Inc.—Officials & employees

LAURENT POTDEVIN bw color *Bloomberg Businessweek* no4508 p64 Ja 23 2017

Lum, Josephine

Mapping the human DC lineage through the integration of high-dimensional techniques diag *Science* v356 no6342 p1044 Je 9 2017

Lum, Kenneth

FROM OUR READERS *Sky & Telescope* v133 no1 p6 Ja 2017

Lumax Software LLC

Drafting Made 'Easier than Pencil and Paper' *Stage Directions* v30 no5 p7 My 2017

Lumbar pain

Ache, Throb, Hurt A. Stafford *Dance Magazine* v91 no1 p83 Ja 2017

Lumbar pain—Prevention

A home practice to nix low-back pain A. Ferretti color *Yoga Journal* p63 2017 SpecialIssue

Lumber

Reclaimed Wood Tables B. D. Coleman color *Old House Journal* v45 no3 p56 My 2017

Subbing Materials for Wood R. Tschoepe diag *Old House Journal* v45 no3 p58 My 2017

Lumber drying

SEASONING your firewood [Cover story] color *Cabin Living* p56 O 2017

Lumber industry

A tale of two cities H. Wilson bw *Canadian Geographic* v137 no3 p24 My 2017

Lumber industry—Economic aspects

THE AGE OF WOOD *Vital Speeches of the Day* v83 no6 p170 Je 2017

Lumer, Yaakov

Observation of Anderson localization in disordered nanophotonic structures diag graph *Science* v356 no6341 p953 Je 1 2017

Lumineers (Performer)

Random Notes color *Rolling Stone* no1273 p24 N 3 2016

Formation of the Orientale lunar multiring basin B. C. Johnson, D. M. Blair et al bibl graph *Science* v354 no6311 p441 O 28 2016

Lunar surface

See also

Lunar craters

Changes Real and (Mostly) Imagined: Even renowned lunar observers have sometimes been fooled by tricks of lighting and resolution C. A. Wood color *Sky & Telescope* v134 no2 p52 Ag 2017

Lunar water

OUR MOON'S MANTLE IS WETTER THAN WE THOUGHT A. Klesman bw *Astronomy* v45 no11 p12 N 2017

Lunch breaks (Business)

Lunch Is Dead J. Kell color *Fortune* v175 no5 p12 Ap 1 2017

THE REAL MOST IMPORTANT MEAL OF THE DAY J. Dean color *Bloomberg Businessweek* no4493 p82 O 3 2016

WHERE SHOULD I GO? diag *Bloomberg Businessweek* no4493 p83 O 3 2016

Lunchbox cooking

EATING LUNCH AT YOUR DESK N. Richardson color *Bloomberg Businessweek* no4493 p86 O 3 2016

LUNCH BOXES [Cover story] J. Waldbieser color *Women's Health* v14 no6 p87 Jl 2017

Lunchboxes

CASE STUDIES F. VIGNA color *Martha Stewart Living* p120 S 2017

Joe Jonas' Low-Key Chic S. EXPOSITO color *Rolling Stone* no1275 p24 D 1 2016

OFF LINE color *Bike Magazine* v24 no1 p146 Ja/F 2017

Re-Think Your Choices and Reduce Your Waste! *New York State Conservationist* v71 no4 p5 F 2017

Lunchboxes—Evaluation

must-buys M. Santos color *Working Mother* v40 no3 p16 Ag/S 2017

PACK IT UP, PACK IT IN M. Khemsurov color *Bloomberg Businessweek* no4493 p84 O 3 2016

Luncheons

BEAT-THE-BUS SCHOOL LUNCHES K. Cicero color *Parents* v92 no9 p78 S 2017

Better Brown-Bag Lunches: Lunches you pack for yourself or your family can be healthier than meals purchased away from home, but only if you plan food choices wisely *Tufts University Health & Nutrition Letter* v35 no8 p7 O 2017

Bowl, PREP SCHOOL Salad, Sammy! J. Levy color *Health* v31 no7 p122 S 2017

Cousins, Tacos & Cover Babies color *Parents* v92 no9 p10 S 2017

THE EVERYTHING GUIDE TO: A Better Desk Lunch img *New York* v49 no20 p100 O 3 2016

have a better morning G. O'CONNOR *Parents* v91 no9 p86 S 2016

Martha's Winter chart color *Martha Stewart Living* no271 p2 Ja/F 2017

Resistol Hosts Second Annual Rookie of the Year Luncheon color *Spin to Win Rodeo* v20 no12 p20 F 2017

SCHEDULE OF EVENTS *Cincinnati Magazine* p90 Je 2017

simplify your lunch strategy K. CICERO *Parents* v91 no9 p92 S 2016

So, You Want a Grain Bowl M. J. WEEDMAN img *New York* v49 no20 p110 O 3 2016

Super Summer Chefs M. Espinoza *Parks & Recreation* v51 no10 p56 O 2016

Take Back Your Lunch Break color *Health* v31 no7 p20 S 2017

Luncheons—History—21st century

EATING LUNCH AT YOUR DESK N. Richardson color *Bloomberg Businessweek* no4493 p86 O 3 2016

Lund, Elizabeth

Underwater *Christian Century* v133 no22 p13 O 26 2016

LUND, NICK

Bouncing Back in Yosemite: After flirting with extinction, Sierra Nevada yellow-legged frogs are staging a remarkable—and unexpected—comeback *National Parks* v91 no3 p24 Summ 2017

Game On color *Audubon* v119 no3 p45 Fall 2017

Killer Commodes *National Parks* v91 no1 p22 Wint 2017

My Maine *National Parks* v91 no2 p12 Spr 2017

Lund, Susan

As European Banks Retreat from the World Stage, China Is Step-

ping Up *Harvard Business Review Digital Articles* p2 S 25 2017

Globalization Is Becoming More About Data and Less About Stuff *Harvard Business Review Digital Articles* p2 Mr 14 2016

Lundberg, Emma

A pathology atlas of the human cancer transcriptome diag *Science* v357 no6352 p660 Ag 18 2017

A subcellular map of the human proteome color *Science* v356 no6340 p820 My 26 2017

Lundblad, Vicki

Gender discrimination lawsuit at Salk ignites controversy M. Wadman color *Science* v357 no6348 p237 Jl 21 2017

Lundbom, Jon

Glimpses into a Grand Vision B. MILKOWSKI color *Downbeat* v83 no12 p69 D 2016

Lundeberg, Mark B.

Tuning quantum nonlocal effects in graphene plasmonics bw diag *Science* v357 no6347 p187 Jl 14 2017

Lundell, John Jeffrey

Get Beyond Your Troubled Past: You're Not Looking for a Job, You're Looking for a Person color *Publishers Weekly* v263 no46 p48 N 14 2016

LUNDERS, KATELYN

Calling All Cars *D: The Magazine of Dallas* v43 no10 p50 O 2016

LUNDGREN, CARLY

r.s.v.p color *Bon Appetit* no8 p14 Ag 2017

Lundin, Connery

CONNERY LUNDIN S. DAVIS bw *Powder* p134 S 2017

Lundquist, Verne

The Voice color *Sports Illustrated* v125 no18 p64 D 5 2016

Lundy, Carmen

Code Noir J. Mcdonough color *Downbeat* v84 no4 p49 Ap 2017

Lundy Island (England)—Description & travel

Lundy Island: A Wildlife Oasis in the Bristol Channel *British Heritage Travel* v38 no4 p62 Jl/Ag 2017

Lung diseases

See also

Obstructive lung diseases

Tuberculosis

IT'S ALL ABOUT BREATHING D. Lynkowski color *Maclean's* v129 no47 p42 N 28 2016

Lung diseases—Diagnosis

Don't Let COPD Take Your Breath Away K. Donohue bw color *Maclean's* v129 no47 p44 N 28 2016

Lung diseases—Treatment

Challenging the Status Quo with Stem Cells C. TOMPOT bw color *National Review* v68 no20 p9 N 7 2016

Lung immunology

The balance between immunity and inflammation D. L. Wiesner and B. S. Klein diag *Science* v357 no6355 p973 S 8 2017

In the lungs, mold cells self-destruct L. HAMERS color *Science News* v192 no5 p16 S 30 2017

Lung tumors—Risk factors

Is secondhand cigarette smoke dangerous to health? *Mayo Clinic Health Letter* v35 no1 p8 Ja 2017

Lungeing (Horsemanship)

Ground Work at Liberty J. GOODNIGHT and H. MELOCCO color *Trail Rider* v29 no1 p40 Ja/F 2017

Longeing Needs to Come Full Circle L. Taylor *In Stride* v12 no4 p14 Jl 2017

Overcome 5 Cold-Weather Challenges E. M. Kellon color *Trail Rider* v29 no1 p28 Ja/F 2017

The Risks and Benefits of Longeing J. F. J. Davis color *Dressage Today* v24 no1 p20 O 2017

Lungs

Protein detects when lungs fill with air R. EHRENBERG *Science News* v191 no2 p7 F 4 2017

Lungs—Cancer—Prevention

Reduce Cancer Risk E. A. Kane color *Amazing Wellness* v9 no1 p28 Wint 2017

Lungs—Infections

See also

Pneumococcal pneumonia

PNEUMONIA D. F. McCourt color *Maclean's* v129 no50 p55 D 19 2016

Lunine, J.

Jupiter's interior and deep atmosphere: The initial pole-to-pole passes with the Juno spacecraft [Cover story] color graph *Science* v356 no6340 p821 My 26 2017

Lunine, Jonathan I.

Cassini finds molecular hydrogen in the Enceladus plume: Evidence for hydrothermal processes chart graph *Science* v356 no6334 p155 Ap 14 2017

Lunken, Ebby

STAGGERWINGS AND SODA BOTTLES M. Lunken color *Flying* v144 no8 p67 Ag 2017

Lunken, Martha

ACS MAKES MY HEAD ACHE chart graph *Flying* v144 no4 p74 Ap 2017

BELONGING *Flying* v144 no11 p66 N 2017

FLIGHTS OF THE CONDOR color *Flying* v144 no5 p66 My 2017

A GLORIOUS LIFE color *Flying* v144 no1 p60 Ja 2017

IS THE FA A PULLING A FAST ONE? *Flying* v144 no10 p67 O 2017

NICKNAMES, DESERVED OR NOT! *Flying* v144 no9 p67 S 2017

PETER PAN AND WENDY *Flying* v143 no12 p64 D 2016

THE PRIVILEGE OF BEING A PILOT color *Flying* v144 no7 p64 Jl 2017

SAINTS, RABBITS' FEET, GARTERS AND BOOMERANGS bw color *Flying* v144 no2 p62 F 2017

SHAKING THINGS UP AT BRISTOL VILLAGE color *Flying* v144 no6 p66 Je 2017

STAGGERWINGS AND SODA BOTTLES color *Flying* v144 no8 p67 Ag 2017

WASN'T THAT A TIME color *Flying* v144 no3 p76 Mr 2017

Lunnan, R.

iPTF16geu: A multiply imaged, gravitationally lensed type Ia supernova color diag graph *Science* v356 no6335 p291 Ap 21 2017

Lunson, Lian

LEONARD COHEN: I'M YOUR MAN J. Krebs color *Sound & Vision* v82 no5 p69 Je 2017

Luntz, Frank

The High Middle Ground on Social Security color *Time* v188 no16/17 p55 O 24 2016

Now What? color *Time* v188 no21 p42 N 21 2016

Luo, Chongyuan

Single-cell methylomes identify neuronal subtypes and regulatory elements in mammalian cortex diag *Science* v357 no6351 p600 Ag 11 2017

Luo, Christina C.

Decoupling genetics, lineages, and microenvironment in IDH-mutant gliomas by single-cell RNA-seq diag *Science* v355 no6332 p1391 Mr 31 2017

Luo, De

Formation of matter-wave soliton trains by modulational instability diag *Science* v356 no6336 p422 Ap 28 2017

Luo, H. W.

High dislocation density–induced large ductility in deformed and partitioned steels bw color diag *Science* v357 no6355 p1029 S 8 2017

Luo, Jian

Segregation-induced ordered superstructures at general grain boundaries in a nickel-bismuth alloy color *Science* v357 no6359 p97 O 6 2017

Luo, Jun

Robust epitaxial growth of two-dimensional heterostructures, multiheterostructures, and superlattices color *Science* v357 no6353 p788 Ag 25 2017

Luo, Langli

Direction-specific van der Waals attraction between rutile TiO2 nanocrystals diag *Science* v356 no6336 p434 Ap 28 2017

Luo, Liqun

Breathing control center neurons that promote arousal in mice diag graph *Science* v355 no6332 p1411 Mr 31 2017

Gating of social reward by oxytocin in the ventral tegmental area color graph *Science* v357 no6358 p1406 S 29 2017

Lineage-dependent spatial and functional organization of the mammalian enteric nervous system color graph *Science* v356 no6339 p722 My 19 2017

Thirst-associated preoptic neurons encode an aversive motivation-al drive diag *Science* v357 no6356 p1149 S 15 2017

Luo, Xin-Yu

Deterministic entanglement generation from driving through quantum phase transitions bibl color graph *Science* v355 no6325 p620 F 10 2017

Luo, Ya-Wei

The complex effects of ocean acidification on the prominent N2-fixing cyanobacterium Trichodesmium graph *Science* v356 no6337 p527 My 5 2017

Luo, Yisha

3D organization of synthetic and scrambled chromosomes diag *Science* v355 no6329 p1050 Mr 10 2017

Bug mapping and fitness testing of chemically synthesized chromosome X diag *Science* v355 no6329 p1048 Mr 10 2017

Deep functional analysis of synII, a 770-kilobase synthetic yeast chromosome diag *Science* v355 no6329 p1047 Mr 10 2017

Engineering the ribosomal DNA in a megabase synthetic chromosome diag *Science* v355 no6329 p1049 Mr 10 2017

"Perfect" designer chromosome V and behavior of a ring derivative diag *Science* v355 no6329 p1046 Mr 10 2017

Synthesis, debugging, and effects of synthetic chromosome consolidation: synVI and beyond color *Science* v355 no6329 p1045 Mr 10 2017

Luo, Yonglun

Inactivation of porcine endogenous retrovirus in pigs using CRISPR-Cas9 diag *Science* v357 no6357 p1303 S 22 2017

Luo, Zhouqing

3D organization of synthetic and scrambled chromosomes diag *Science* v355 no6329 p1050 Mr 10 2017

Deep functional analysis of synII, a 770-kilobase synthetic yeast chromosome diag *Science* v355 no6329 p1047 Mr 10 2017

Engineering the ribosomal DNA in a megabase synthetic chromosome diag *Science* v355 no6329 p1049 Mr 10 2017

Luong, Tom

Metal-catalyzed reductive coupling of olefin-derived nucleophiles: Reinventing carbonyl addition diag *Science* v354 no6310 paah5133-1 O 21 2016

Lupia, A.

Fostering reproducibility in industry-academia research color *Science* v357 no6353 p759 Ag 25 2017

Lupia, Arthur

Inequality is Always in the Room: Language & Power in Deliberative Democracy *Daedalus* v146 no3 p64 Summ 2017

Lupo, Sarah

RIGOR VS. EASE color *Literacy Today (2411-7862)* v34 no4 p30 Ja/F 2017

LuPone, Patti, 1949-

BEAUTY QUEENS A. F. COLLINS color *Vanity Fair* v59 no4 p200 Mr 2017

GOINGS ON ABOUT TOWN bw *New Yorker* v93 no6 p4 Mr 27 2017

Scattered Brushstrokes of Beauty J. GREEN img *New York* v50 no8 p134 Ap 17 2017

LuPone, Patti, 1949—Interviews

KISS AND MAKEUP C. Collis color *Entertainment Weekly* no1459 p66 Mr 31 2017

Luray Caverns (Va.)

What Lies Beneath: THE VALLEY'S BEAUTY ISN'T ALL ABOVE GROUND D. Leatherman *Washingtonian Magazine* v53 no1 p102 O 2017

Lure fishing

See also

Fly fishing

ALIVE AND FISHING M. VINCENT and G. BETHGE color *Outdoor Life* v224 no3 p67 Ap 2017

Lure fishing—Equipment & supplies

New electronic lure may catch too many fish; one state bans it M. Butler and N. KREBS color *Outdoor Life* v224 no3 p6 Ap 2017

SPACE-AGE LURES THAT LOOK, SOUND, ACT—AND EVEN SMELL—LIKE LIVE BAIT J. BRANDT color *Outdoor Life* v224 no2 p44 F/Mr 2017

Lurie, Alison, 1926-

Boldly Going! K. ARNOLD-RATLIFF color *O, The Oprah Magazine* p84 Ja 2017

She Escaped to Become Original bw *New York Review of Books* v64 no4 p16 Mr 9 2017

LURIE, JOHN
PARKER POSEY *Interview* v46 no8 p88 O 2016
Lurie, Joshua
5 More Morning Mezes *Los Angeles Magazine* p108 Ap 2017
WATER GRILL *Los Angeles Magazine* p4 Ap 2017
Lurie, Julia
LEFT BEHIND color graph *Mother Jones* v42 no4 p50 Jl/Ag 2017
A SHOT IN THE DARK color graph *Mother Jones* v42 no2 p6 Mr/Ap 2017
TAKING PAINS cartoon *Mother Jones* v42 no5 p66 S/O 2017
LURIE, ROBERT DEAN
Bridge Across the Atlantic *National Review* v69 no15 p44 Ag 14 2017
Working Man's Bard bw *National Review* v68 no24 p40 D 31 2016
Luscombe, Belinda
Ai Weiwei color *Time* v190 no16/17 p112 O 23 2017
The Best 25 Inventions of 2016 color *Time* v188 no22-23 p43 N/D 2016
David Brown color *Time* v189 no23 p56 Je 19 2017
Debra Winger color *Time* v189 no18 p54 My 15 2017
Glenn Beck color *Time* v189 no3 p64 Ja 16 2017
Gretchen Carlson's Next Fight [Cover story] color *Time* v188 no18 p26 O 31 2016
The Growing Case for Shared Parenting After Divorce color *Time* v188 no14 p21 O 10 2016
Growing Up In Public color *Time* v189 no20 p42 My 29 2017
Ivana Trump Has Her Say color *Time* v190 no16/17 p94 O 23 2017
Jen Hatmaker color *Time* v190 no8 p60 Ag 28 2017
Life After Death [Cover story] color *Time* v189 no15 p38 Ap 24 2017
Marina Abramovic color *Time* v188 no21 p74 N 21 2016
Patty Jenkins color *Time* v189 no24 p56 Je 26 2017
Street Cred color *Time* v189 no14 p44 Ap 17 2017
Twilight Cowboy or (Why Michael Keaton Would Rather Be a Dog) color *Time* v188 no24 p56 D 12 2016
The University-Bound Mother Who Killed Her Child Deserves Forgiveness color *Time* v190 no13 p21 O 2 2017
Why Marriage Is Harder Than Ever-and Maybe Better Too color *Time* v190 no12 p25 S 25 2017
Lussier, Nancy
Pencil Pusher's Day Out *New York State Conservationist* v72 no1 p40 Ag 2017
Lust
FLEE THE RIGHTEOUS LUST T. OLSEN color *Christianity Today* v61 no7 p25 S 2017
LUST LESSONS A. Burroughs cartoon *Men's Health* v32 no3 p25 Ap 2017
Quenching Your Thirst R. Gay color *InStyle* v24 no9 p214 S 2017
SEX AFTER 40 L. Turner color *Amazing Wellness* v9 no2 p30 Spr 2017
LUST, JILL
NEW WAYS WITH WALNUTS color *Better Homes & Gardens* v95 no3 p88 Mr 2017
Lust, Ulli
VISUALIZING THE THIRD REICH B. ALVERSON color *Publishers Weekly* v264 no39 p55 S 25 2017
Lust for Life (Music)
REY OF LIGHT N. Feeney color *Entertainment Weekly* no1474/1475 p114 Jl 21-28 2017
Lustig, Jessica
Anger Management *New York Times Magazine* p15 O 30 2016
LUSTIG, JOSHUA
Anguished Echoes of Empire *Current History* v115 no783 p284 O 2016
LUT, BROBSON
LOOKING FOR HELP color *New Orleans Magazine* v51 no3 p30 Ja 2017
Lut Desert (Iran)
SOME LIKE IT HOT R. Stone color map *Science* v354 no6318 p1366 D 16 2016
Lute
ODE TO THE UKULEFE color *Women's Health* v14 no9 p40 N 2017

Lutein
Protein Surprises in The Produce Section J. SCHMID and M. SAUER color *Reader's Digest* v190 no1133 p38 S 2017
Luterbacher, Jeremy S.
Formaldehyde stabilization facilitates lignin monomer production during biomass depolymerization bibl diag graph *Science* v354 no6310 p329 O 21 2016
Lutermann, Heike
Fructose-driven glycolysis supports anoxia resistance in the naked mole-rat diag graph *Science* v356 no6335 p307 Ap 21 2017
Lutes, Brendan
2017 HONDA CRF450R color *Cycle World* v56 no1 p12 Ja/F 2017
TORTURE TEST color *Cycle World* v56 no4 p58 My 2017
Luth, Diane
Born to be Wild C. Wood color diag *Log Home Living* v34 no3 p52 Ap 2017
Luther, Joseph M.
Quantum dot–induced phase stabilization of α-CsPbI3 perovskite for high-efficiency photovoltaics bibl chart graph *Science* v354 no6308 p92 O 7 2016
Luther, Kem
CONNECTIONS BETWEEN THE UNCONNECTED C. HENDRICKSON color *Alternatives Journal (AJ) - Canada's Environmental Voice* v42 no3 p75 2016
Luther, Martin, 1483-1546
EDITOR'S NOTE T. OLSEN color *Christianity Today* v61 no1 p7 Ja/F 2017
Justify Yourself D. ZAHL bw cartoon *Christianity Today* v61 no1 p34 Ja/F 2017
KNOCK ON WOOD P. SCHJELDAHL cartoon *New Yorker* v92 no37 p92 N 14 2016
A Luther Renaissance in Catholic Thought W. W. MacDonald *America* v217 no3 p33 Ag 7 2017
LUTHER'S MONEY REFORMATION M. FOUST cartoon *Christianity Today* p30 Mr 2017
MARTIN LUTHER AND THE GERMAN REFORMATION B. Heal *History Today* v67 no3 p28 Mr 2017
On Luther and his lies N. E. Marans *Christian Century* v134 no22 p10 O 25 2017
Purgatory now! P. R. Hinlicky *Christian Century* v134 no14 p30 Jl 5 2017
Refugees and the Reformation J. WILLIS color *Christianity Today* v61 no7 p68 S 2017
A toast to Ramanuja C. Zaleski *Christian Century* v134 no6 p37 Mr 15 2017
A toy figure of Luther sparked accusations of anti-Semitism T. Heneghan color *Christian Century* v134 no3 p14 F 2017
Luther, Martin, 1483-1546—Exhibitions
Landmark Luther exhibits explore his technological and theological legacy D. Gibson color *Christian Century* v133 no23 p16 N 9 2016
Martin Luther's Burning Questions [Cover story] I. D. Rowland color *New York Review of Books* v64 no10 p10 Je 8 2017
Luther, Martin, 1483-1546—Political & social views
The Invention of Individual Freedom F. Furedi *History Today* v67 no4 p7 Ap 2017
Lutheran Church
Reformed churches affirm Catholic-Lutheran accord T. Heneghan *Christian Century* v134 no16 p12 Ag 2 2017
Lutheran Church—United States
Supreme Court may lean toward Lutheran school in public funds dispute R. Wolf color *Christian Century* v134 no11 p15 My 24 2017
Lutherans
Still reckoning with Luther S. H. Wilson *Christian Century* v134 no6 p22 Mr 15 2017
Luthman, Johanna
Love, Madness, and Scandal: The Life of Frances Coke Villiers, Viscountess Purbeck color *Publishers Weekly* v264 no21 p85 My 22 2017
LUTHRA, SHEFALI
Patients Get the Personal Touch cartoon *Kiplinger's Personal Finance* v71 no1 p68 Ja 2017
Lutolf, Matthias P.
Decoding of position in the developing neural tube from antipar-

allel morphogen gradients diag *Science* v356 no6345 p1379 Je 30 2017

Luttun, Aernout

De novo design of a biologically active amyloid bibl graph *Science* v354 no6313 paah4949-1 N 11 2016

Lutyens, Edwin Landseer, Sir, 1869-1944

Bench Mark H. MARTIN bw color *Architectural Digest* no6 p30 Je 1 2017

LUTZ, BOB

Art and Seoul color *Road & Track* v68 no6 p92 F 2017

Changing Tides *Road & Track* v68 no9 p100 Je 2017

Count Our Blessings color *Road & Track* v68 no10 p112 Jl 2017

Easy Rider color *Road & Track* v68 no8 p108 My 2017

Far Afield color *Road & Track* v69 no2 p104 S 2017

Go Lutz Yourself color *Road & Track* v68 no5 p126 D 2016/Ja 2017

Just Don't Ask *Road & Track* v69 no4 p100 N 2017

Let's Cancel *Road & Track* v69 no3 p108 O 2017

Mustang Mutability color *Road & Track* v69 no1 p108 Ag 2017

Winter of Discontent color *Road & Track* v68 no7 p104 Mr/Ap 2017

Lutz, Brobson

CRANBERRIES AND HEALTH color *New Orleans Magazine* v51 no1 p36 N 2016

Forecasting the Flu color *New Orleans Magazine* v52 no1 p40 S 2017

Good for What Ails You color *New Orleans Magazine* v51 no7 p34 My 2017

HANGOVER color *New Orleans Magazine* v51 no2 p36 D 2016

HEART TO HEART conversation with a cardiologist color *New Orleans Magazine* v51 no4 p76 F 2017

Help in the Office: The Physician Extender Will See You Now color *New Orleans Magazine* v51 no10 p46 Ag 2017

Melodies in the Mind color *New Orleans Magazine* v51 no6 p34 Ap 2017

Pipe Dreams color *New Orleans Magazine* v51 no12 p42 O 2017

Recipe for Disaster color *New Orleans Magazine* v51 no9 p34 Jl 2017

Roach Buster color *New Orleans Magazine* v51 no5 p34 Mr 2017

Swimming with Bacteria color *New Orleans Magazine* v51 no8 p34 Je 2017

LUTZ, DEBORAH

The Wilde Bunch *New York Times Book Review* p20 D 11 2016

Lutz, Eleanor

GRAPHIC SCIENCE M. RHODES color *Wired* v25 no3 p30 Mr 2017

Lutz, James A.

Plant diversity increases with the strength of negative density dependence at the global scale diag *Science* v356 no6345 p1389 Je 30 2017

Lutz, Matilda

MATILDA LUTZ K. SMITH color *Vanity Fair* v59 no2 p29 F 2017

Lutz, Phillip

Cécile McLorin Salvant: True Character [Cover story] color *Downbeat* v84 no10 p34 O 2017

DAVID L. HARRIS color *Downbeat* v84 no7 p27 Jl 2017

DIANA KRALL For Tommy [Cover story] color *Downbeat* v84 no6 p34 Je 2017

DON CHERRY: ORGANIC FLOW bw *Downbeat* v84 no8 p32 Ag 2017

FRED HERSCH TRUTH TELLER color *Downbeat* v84 no9 p34 S 2017

INGRID & CHRISTINE JENSEN: 'Our Gift Is What We Do' color *Downbeat* v84 no3 p32 Mr 2017

JAZZ AT LINCOLN CENTER ORCHESTRA color *Downbeat* v83 no12 p50 D 2016

Jazz Essential at Oberlin color *Downbeat* v84 no1 p110 Ja 2017

Jazz Studies Thrives at New Jersey's MSU color *Downbeat* v83 no12 p110 D 2016

JONATHAN FINLAYSON color *Downbeat* v84 no1 p46 Ja 2017

JOSÉ JAMES 'TORNADO OF CREATIVITY' [Cover story] color *Downbeat* v84 no5 p28 My 2017

KAMASI WASHINGTON color *Downbeat* v83 no12 p42 D 2016

NATIONAL TREASURE [Cover story] color *Downbeat* v83 no11 p30 N 2016

NO BARRIERS. NO LIMITS. NO FEAR [Cover story] color *Downbeat* v84 no2 p24 F 2017

SAYING 'YES' TO THE AVANT-GARDE color *Downbeat* v84 no3 p50 Mr 2017

Sonic Portrait of Evans in '68 bw *Downbeat* v84 no10 p13 O 2017

Syracuse Music Students Keep Options Wide Open color *Downbeat* v84 no4 p94 Ap 2017

Tepfer's Mathematical Ingenuity color *Downbeat* v84 no9 p14 S 2017

TERRACE MARTIN 'I DON'T WANT TO BE IN A BOX.' color *Downbeat* v84 no2 p30 F 2017

VARIED SKILLS YIELD REWARDS color *Downbeat* v84 no6 p100 Je 2017

Luu, Jansen

Structural basis of the day-night transition in a bacterial circadian clock bibl diag *Science* v355 no6330 p1174 Mr 17 2017

Luu, Kim

ESCAPE FROM VIETNAM *Saturday Evening Post* v289 no2 p16 Mr/Ap 2017

Luukkonen, Sami

It Might Be Time to Spill Your Corporate Secrets S. G. Carmichael *Harvard Business Review Digital Articles* p2 Ap 13 2015

Luu-Van, Melissa

How Facebook Uses Empathy to Keep User Data Safe *Harvard Business Review Digital Articles* p2 Ap 28 2016

Luxoticca Group SpA

MEANS TO A LENS S. Horaczek color *Popular Science* v289 no4 p36 Jl/Ag 2017

Luxuries

See also

Luxury cars

JUST ADD WATER K. RENDA and H. BROWN color *House Beautiful* v159 no1 p47 F 2017

THE STRUGGLE OF THE BLACK DESIGNER Q. SMITH-BRUNETEAU bw color *Ebony* v72 no11 p44 S 2017

Wearing Luxury Brands Makes You Seem More Qualified for the Job J. M. Olejarz *Harvard Business Review Digital Articles* p2 Ap 9 2015

Luxuries—Economic aspects

YEA BOXY BRONCOS, NAY BEATNIK BOLSHEVIKS W. CARINI, A. BRENNER et al bw color *Forbes* v200 no2 p31 S 5 2017

Luxury cars

Cheap's No Longer Chic For China's Carmakers color graph *Bloomberg Businessweek* no4502 p29 D 5 2016

eins, zwei, drei, quattros! C. Walton chart color *Motor Trend* v69 no8 p76 Ag 2017

THE FAST AND THE LUXURIOUS J. GORZELANY color *Forbes* v200 no4 p60 O 24 2017

Flip Your Ride: Jaguar on Wednesday, Lexus on Thursday, Porsche on Friday--welcome to Clutch! S. FENNESSY *Atlanta* v57 no3 p44 Jl 2017

Luck of the half Irish E. Loh *Motor Trend* v69 no6 p8 Je 2017

Road Test chart *Consumer Reports* v82 no11 p62 N 2017

SAME SWAGGER R. PINTO color *Road & Track* v68 no9 p82 Je 2017

Silky Sophisticate *Consumer Reports* v82 no7 p63 Jl 2017

Tesla Shows How Traditional Business Metrics Are Outdated E. Yoon *Harvard Business Review Digital Articles* p2 Ag 8 2017

Luxury cars—Evaluation

THE $399 LEASE-DEAL SPECIAL [Cover story] chart color *Motor Trend* v69 no6 p34 Je 2017

FIVE-SEAT FURY J. Cammisa color *Motor Trend* v69 no6 p54 Je 2017

Ratings chart *Consumer Reports* v81 no12 p76 D 2016

Luxury Elves (Short story)

LUXURY ELVES E. Allen cartoon *New Yorker* v92 no43 p19 Ja 2 2017

Luxury goods industry

The Best Luxury Services Are Customized, Not Standardized A. Brant *Harvard Business Review Digital Articles* p2 Mr 2 2016

Case Study: How Should an Understated Luxury Brand Compete Against Bling? S. Nason, J. Salvacruz et al color *Harvard Business Review Digital Articles* p2 F 28 2017

The Chinese Rediscover Luxury B. Einhorn, D. Wei et al color *Bloomberg Businessweek* no4509 p15 Ja 30 2017

COACH THINKS OUTSIDE THE BAG P. Wahba color diag *Fortune* v175 no7 p80 Je 1 2017

A Fashion Empire's New Clothes R. Williams and C. Matlack color graph *Bloomberg Businessweek* no4535 p17 Ag 28 2017

Luxury Brands Can No Longer Ignore Sustainability A. Winston *Harvard Business Review Digital Articles* p2 F 8 2016

The Second Time Around R. NAAS color *Forbes* v199 no6 p106 Je 13 2017

Luxury hotels

A Fresh Slice of Orange County A. ABEL color *Forbes* v198 no8 p106 D 20 2016

Take Us to Church R. MISNER color *Conde Nast Traveler* v52 no1 p46 Ja 2017

Luxury hotels—Customer services

How Our Hotel Used Data to Make Our Laundry Service Glamorous A. Brant color *Harvard Business Review Digital Articles* p2 Mr 1 2017

Luxury hotels—Evaluation

THE Beaches WE RETURN TO AGAIN AND AGAIN... bw color *Conde Nast Traveler* v52 no1 p70 Ja 2017

An ODE to HOTELS in Marrakech R. MISNER bw color *Conde Nast Traveler* v52 no1 p78 Ja 2017

An ODE to HOTELS on the Amalfi Coast P. GUZMÁN color *Conde Nast Traveler* v52 no1 p74 Ja 2017

OUR Favorite HOTELS IN FIVE OF THE WORLD'S GREATEST CITIES color *Conde Nast Traveler* v52 no1 p76 Ja 2017

THE SPIRIT OF '17 A. ABEL color *Forbes* v199 no2 p66 F 28 2017

the start color *InStyle* v24 no4 p41 Ap 2017

Luxury hotels—Sales & prices

Selling Trump's D.C. Hotel Wouldn't Be Easy Yu and B. Brody *Bloomberg Businessweek* no4505 p40 D 26 2016

Luxury housing

A HOUSE TO SAVOR L. Christensen color *Harper's Bazaar* no3652 p171 Ap 2017

OFF THE MARKET! *Washingtonian Magazine* v52 no6 p173 Mr 2017

A Resort for the Apocalypse B. ROWEN bw cartoon color diag map *Atlantic* v319 no2 p30 Mr 2017

When the President Is Your Landlord N. TABOR img *New York* p52 F 20 2017

When Trump Tower Was Luxurious C. Bonanos img *New York* p10 F 20 2017

Luxury housing—Design & construction

Inside the Most Expensive Home in America color *Money* v46 no4 p12 My 2017

Luxury housing—Evaluation

GILDED PLATEAU M. LAWLER color *Chicago* v66 no3 p27 Mr 2017

Luxury housing—Sales & prices

American Riviera S. SHARF color *Forbes* v198 no8 p20 D 20 2016

Inside the Most Expensive Home in America color *Money* v46 no4 p12 My 2017

SQUARE FEET: THE WAITING GAME M. LAWLER color *Chicago* v66 no9 p36 S 2017

Luxury travel

9 Secrets to Scoring First-Class Upgrades on the Cheap J. Calfas color *Money* v46 no9 p30 O 2017

Down and Out in FIRST CLASS D. Garner color *Esquire* p56 N 2017

SHATTERING THE STATUS QUO M. KERN *USA Today Magazine* v146 no2866 p72 Jl 2017

The Way It Was G. Hamilton *New York Times Magazine* p24 O 23 2016

Lv, Jia-Fei

"Perfect" designer chromosome V and behavior of a ring derivative diag *Science* v355 no6329 p1046 Mr 10 2017

LVL UP (Performer)

Hot Band Lvl Up J. DOLAN color *Rolling Stone* no1274 p36 N 17 2016

LVMH Moët Hennessy Louis Vuitton SA

An Inside View of How LVMH Makes Luxury More Sustainable A. Winston color *Harvard Business Review Digital Articles* p2 Ja 11 2017

Wait LIST color *Harper's Bazaar* no3651 p216 Mr 2017

L Word, The (TV program)

The L Word Returns! T. Stack color *Entertainment Weekly* no1474/1475 p18 Jl 21-28 2017

Ly, Fernanda, 1996-

FUNNY VALENTINE S. Trong color *InStyle* v24 no2 p43 F 2017

Lyall, Sarah

Rogue Britannia *New York Times Book Review* p16 F 19 2017

Spies Like Us [Cover story] *New York Times Book Review* p1 Ag 27 2017

TRESS RELIEF color *New York Times Book Review* p14 D 4 2016

Lycett, Andrew

Intelligence Matters *History Today* v67 no4 p64 Ap 2017

STRIPPING DOWN THE BUTTONED UP: An examination of the 'fleeting, fine-grained intimacies' of letters, diaries and memoirs produces a witty and scholarly account of Victorian attitudes to the body *History Today* v67 no9 p96 S 2017

Lycett, Samantha J.

Role for migratory wild birds in the global spread of avian influenza H5N8 bibl graph map *Science* v354 no6309 p213 O 14 2016

LYDERSEN, KARI

DOWN AND OUT AT THE BULLFROG HOTEL *In These Times* v41 no8 p42 Ag 2017

THE HEROIN CRISIS WE'VE IGNORED *In These Times* v41 no5 p44 My 2017

Lye

MAKE SOAP the Old-Fashioned Way S. Verberg *Mother Earth News* no279 p40 D/Ja 2017

Lyft Inc.

Movers K. Stock color *Bloomberg Businessweek* no4523 p13 My 22 2017

THE PECULIAR PARABLE OF THE LYFT LOT J. Brustein cartoon *Bloomberg Businessweek* no4534 p58 Ag 14 2017

Lykins, Kenneth

Exposing Unfair Pricing in Auto Insurance Rates color *Consumer Reports* v82 no5 p6 My 2017

Lykins, Tara

COURT of APPEALS WITH REBEL GOOD *Tennis* v52 no6 p6 N/D 2016

Lyle, Adrienne

DRESSAGE SNAPSHOT color *Dressage Today* v23 no11 p14 Ag 2017

A Rising STAR N. Jaffer color *Dressage Today* v24 no1 p42 O 2017

Lyle, Erica Dawn

MFA QUALITY color *Art in America* v105 no8 p88 S 2017

Lyle, Erick

BEATRIZ SANTIAGO MUÑOZ *Art in America* v104 no9 p156 O 2016

Rafa Esparza color *Art in America* v105 no4 p23 Ap 2017

Lyle, Michael

ENEMY color *Christian Century* v134 no5 p20 Mr 1 2017

Lyman, Edwin

Nuclear safety regulation in the post-Fukushima era color *Science* v356 no6340 p808 My 26 2017

Lyme disease

The Bugs of Summer color *Prevention* v69 no8 p9 Ag 2017

Homegrown Medical Mystery M. LALIBERTE color map *Reader's Digest* v190 no1132 p42 Jl/Ag 2017

Lyme LESSONS M. OZ cartoon *O, The Oprah Magazine* p106 My 2017

Lyme disease diagnosis

Lyme diagnostics could get an upgrade A. CUNNINGHAM *Science News* v192 no4 p8 S 16 2017

Target: LYME DISEASE [Cover story] A. PATUREL color *Prevention* v69 no6 p50 Je 2017

What Should I Do About A Physician Who May Be a Quack? K. A. Appiah *New York Times Magazine* p26 Ja 15 2017

Lyme disease prevention

HOW TO PREVENT & TREAT LYME DISEASE L. Krieger color *Harper's Bazaar* no3653 p242 My 2017

Lyme Disease Facts V. TWEED color *Better Nutrition* v79 no6 p64 Je 2017

Lyme disease treatment

HOW TO PREVENT & TREAT LYME DISEASE L. Krieger color *Harper's Bazaar* no3653 p242 My 2017

Target: LYME DISEASE [Cover story] A. PATUREL color *Pre-*

vention v69 no6 p50 Je 2017

Lymph nodes

Cancer bypasses the lymph nodes S. D. Markowitz diag *Science* v357 no6346 p35 Jl 7 2017

Lymph nodes—Tumors

Your Horse's Lumps & Bumps B. CRABBE color *Horse & Rider* v56 no10 p86 O 2017

Lymphoblastic leukemia—Patients

SURVIVING THE CURE J. Cohen color diag *Science* v357 no6347 p122 Jl 14 2017

Lymphocyte transformation

Pathological α-synuclein transmission initiated by binding lymphocyte-activation gene 3 M. T. Ou, S. S. Karuppagounder et al bibl graph *Science* v353 no6307 paah3374-1 S 30 2016

Lynam, Antony J.

Wildlife-snaring crisis in Asian forests bibl color *Science* v355 no6322 p255 Ja 20 2017

Lynch, Alessandra

Daylily Called It a Dangerous Moment color *Publishers Weekly* v264 no20 p34 My 15 2017

Lynch, Amy

49th & Penn color *Indianapolis Monthly* v42 no2 p38 O 2017

BEST NEW Breweries *Indianapolis Monthly* v40 no11 p57 Jl 2017

best of Indy *Indianapolis Monthly* v40 no4 p73 D 2016

Broad Ripple Avenue *Indianapolis Monthly* p32 My 2017

ISLAND TIME: On Mackinac, clocks seem to run more slowly —that's why visitors rush there color *Indianapolis Monthly* v41 no2 p37 S 2017

QUILT TO LAST *Indianapolis Monthly* v40 no3 p48 N 2016

Lynch, Ann

Off-Grid on Rainy Lake [Cover story] F. SIGURDSSON color *Cabin Living* p24 Ag 2017

Lynch, Brian

The Hot Box chart *Downbeat* v84 no1 p67 Ja 2017

Madera Latino P. de Barros color *Downbeat* v84 no1 p65 Ja 2017

Lynch, Catherine

People and posts: Who's making HR headlines? *People Management* p54 Ap 2017

Lynch, Christopher

Christopher Lynch and Jonathan Marks, Eds., Principle and Prudence in Western Political Thought Frost *Society* v54 no3 p303 Je 2017

Lynch, Courtney

How the U.S. Marines Encourage Service-Based Leadership color *Harvard Business Review Digital Articles* p2 F 2 2017

Lynch, David

Can Twin Peaks Make a Comeback? C. R. MORGAN bw *American Conservative* v16 no3 p52 My/Je 2017

DAVID LYNCH'S DARK ART L. ANOLIK color *Vanity Fair* p118 Hollywood 2017 Supplement

Deep in the Forest N. PINKERTON color *Film Comment* v53 no3 p18 My/Je 2017

HORROR SHOW: The nightmare logic of Twin Peaks M. Dean *Harper's Magazine* p86 O 2017

How Twin Peaks Changed TV Forever E. Dockterman color *Time* v189 no19 p51 My 22 2017

HOW TWIN PEAKS INFLUENCED MY WORK: Fargo and Legion creator Noah Hawley pays homage to Peaks' mastermind, David Lynch N. HAWLEY and A. D'Arminio *TV Guide* v65 no35 p10 Ag 21 2017

How Twin Peaks Invented Modern Television J. PARKER color *Atlantic* v319 no5 p28 Je 2017

PEACEMAKER J. R. GRITZ *Smithsonian* v47 no8 p50 D 2016

The Season's Peak [Cover story] R. SHEFFIELD color *Rolling Stone* no1289 p29 Je 15 2017

The Slowness of 'Twin Peaks' A. Kleeman *New York Times Magazine* p38 O 8 2017

Strange Seer R. SYME color *New Republic* v248 no8/9 p66 Ag/S 2017

WELCOME BACK TO TWIN PEAKS S. O'NEAL bw color *GQ: Gentlemen's Quarterly* v97 no4 p128 Ap 2017

You Were Expecting Pie? In his scalding Twin Peaks revisit, David Lynch doubles down on being David Lynch M. Z. SEITZ img *New York* v50 no11 p124 My 29 2017

Lynch, David—Interviews

A DAMN FINE REBOOT DAVID LYNCH RETURNS TO TWIN PEAKS B. R. REYNOLDS color *Wired* v25 no5 p20 My 2017

David Lynch Is Rolling Off a Log D. Marchese img *New York* v50 no10 p94 My 15 2017

DAVID LYNCH'S MIND GAMES J. Jensen color *Entertainment Weekly* no1468/1469 p90 Je 2-9 2017

LYNCH, HEATHER J.

Listing Foreign Species under the Endangered Species Act: A Primer for Conservation Biologists *BioScience* v67 no7 p627 Jl 2017

Response to "Listing Foreign Species Under the Endangered Species Act" *BioScience* v67 no10 p873 O 2017

LYNCH, JAMES

BREAK THROUGH AWARDS 2017 [Cover story] bw color *Popular Mechanics* p56 N 2017

EVERY NIGHT PERFECT bw color *Popular Mechanics* p84 O 2017

GREAT MOMENTS IN VIDEO TUTORIALS color *Popular Mechanics* p94 O 2017

HOW TO MAKE ICE CREAM bw color diag *Popular Mechanics* p80 S 2017

New Myths, New Busters color *Popular Mechanics* p22 N 2017

SNOWSHOEING color *Popular Mechanics* p49 D 2016/Ja 2017

VINYL color *Popular Mechanics* p35 My 2017

WATER BOTTLES color *Popular Mechanics* p28 Jl 2017

Lynch, Jane, 1960-

PUT ON YOUR GAME FACE! M. Roffman *TV Guide* v65 no31 p8 Jl 24 2017

Lynch, John Carroll, 1963-

Lucky C. Nashawaty color *Entertainment Weekly* no1485 p43 O 6 2017

A Sublime Farewell to Stanton In Lucky S. Zacharek color *Time* v190 no14 p51 O 9 2017

Lynch, John Terrence, 1971-

GOLD MINED P. King color *Sports Illustrated* v126 no13 p42 My 8 2017

Lynch, Joseph H.

Emission of volatile organic compounds from petunia flowers is facilitated by an ABC transporter diag *Science* v356 no6345 p1386 Je 30 2017

Lynch, Loretta, 1959-

TIPPED SCALES J. Toobin cartoon *New Yorker* v93 no2 p22 F 27 2017

When Loretta Met Bill T. Joscelyn color *Weekly Standard* v22 no47 p6 Ag 21 2017

Lynch, Lori

An Economic Perspective on Soil Health *Amber Waves: The Economics of Food, Farming, Natural Resources, & Rural America* p18 S 2016

Gathering Experimental Evidence To Improve the Design of Agricultural Programs *Amber Waves: The Economics of Food, Farming, Natural Resources, & Rural America* p1 Ag 2017

Lynch, Lorrie

Blythe Danner color *AARP: The Magazine* v59 no1A p13 D 2015/ Ja 2016

To Be Real bw color *AARP: The Magazine* v60 no2A p13 F/Mr 2017

Lynch, Mary Elizabeth

Mary Elizabeth Lynch: 1933 — 2016 E. SENGER color *Maclean's* v129 no46 p66 N 21 2016

LYNCH, MATTHEW

THE DEFINING ONES color *Vanity Fair* v59 no7 p108 Summ 2017

Lynch, Maura

Editors Tell All! bw color *Women's Health* v14 no2 p60 Mr 2017

SMOKE SIGNALS color *Women's Health* v14 no8 p43 O 2017

TAKE IT OFF [Cover story] color *Women's Health* v14 no7 p64 S 2017

Wrap. Me. Up [Cover story] color *Women's Health* v13 no10 p110 D 2016

LYNCH, MAUREEN A.

Listing Foreign Species under the Endangered Species Act: A Primer for Conservation Biologists *BioScience* v67 no7 p627 Jl 2017

Response to "Listing Foreign Species Under the Endangered Species Act" *BioScience* v67 no10 p873 O 2017

Lynch, Mike

Do as I Say, Not What I'm Accused Of M. Campbell bw *Bloomberg Businessweek* no4494 p34 O 10 2016

Lynch, Paul

On the Road to Nowhere: In the midst of the Irish famine, two children venture from home K. GRANT *New York Times Book Review* p16 S 3 2017

Lynch, Shaun G.

Patriotism in the pews color *U.S. Catholic* v82 no11 p5 N 2017

Lynch, Stacy

Modern Aquatic Therapy and a New Clientele *Parks & Recreation* v51 no11 p58 N 2016

Lynch, Thomas

The Weight of Bodies color *Commonweal* v143 no20 p28 D 16 2016

Lynch, Wayne

The Genius of the Frigatebird color *Canadian Wildlife* v23 no4 p46 S/O 2017

Nothing to Fear color *Canadian Wildlife* v22 no5 p46 N/D 2016

The Truth About Frog Spit color *Canadian Wildlife* v23 no2 p46 My/Je 2017

Vultures and their neighbours color *Canadian Wildlife* v23 no1 p46 Mr/Ap 2017

Lynch Law (Short story)

Lynch Law M. ENDICOTT color *Walrus* v14 no9 p62 N 2017

Lynching

Hanged, Burned, Shot, Drowned, Beaten K. CAPPS color *Atlantic* v320 no4 p30 N 2017

IN MEMORY OF THESE [Cover story] D. L. MAYFIELD and A. Olsen bw color *Christianity Today* v61 no7 p34 S 2017

A Presumption of Guilt B. Stevenson color *New York Review of Books* v64 no12 p8 Jl 13 2017

REMEMBER WHEN A. OLSEN *Christianity Today* v61 no7 p7 S 2017

UNWRITTEN LAW I. B. Wells *Lapham's Quarterly* v10 no3 p43 Summ 2017

Lynching—History

Lynchings Remembered S. Richardson color *American History* v52 no3 p10 Ag 2017

Lynd, Staughton, 1929——Interviews

Socialism in the Basement M. Z. MARVIT *In These Times* v41 no4 p44 Ap 2017

Lynda.com Inc.

THE PM GUIDE TO Video learning: Video is one of the most effective ways to deliver learning. So where do L&D professionals go for resources? We asked readers for their tips E. BURT *People Management* p46 Jl 2017

Lyndon State College (Lyndonville, Vt.)

ZERO DEGREES OF SEPERATION P. Bridges cartoon color *Snowboarder* v29 no4 p26 D 2016

Lyndsey, Anna

TWILIGHT E. D. CAESAR cartoon color *New Yorker* v92 no30 p48 S 26 2016

Lynen, Stefanie

The Fine Print M. OZAWA color *Martha Stewart Living* no275 p48 Je 2017

Lynes, Russell

SCHOOL SURVIVAL GUIDE *Harper's Magazine* p43 S 2017

Lynk & Co.

Lynk & Co 01 A. MacKenzie color *Motor Trend* v69 no2 p16 F 2017

Lynkowski, Debra

IT'S ALL ABOUT BREATHING color *Maclean's* v129 no47 p42 N 28 2016

Lynn, Barry C.

Democrats Must Become the Party of Freedom *Washington Monthly* p4 Ja/F 2017

The Do-Not-Think Tank C. ROSEN color *Weekly Standard* v23 no2 p24 S 18 2017

Lynn, Barry W.

People color *Christian Century* v134 no10 p21 My 10 2017

Lynn, Brenda

Fresh, Homemade SALAD DRESSINGS *Mother Earth News* no281 p36 Ap/My 2017

LYNN, BROOK

ROAR OF THE CROWD *Texas Monthly* v45 no1 p8 Ja 2017

Lynn, Holly

ASK THE EXPERTS color *Runner's World* v52 no3 p42 Ap 2017

Lynn, Jamie

ENDER ENDER color *Snowboarder* v29 no5 p123 Ja 2017

Lynn, Loretta, 1932-

Country Strong A. Nash color *AARP: The Magazine* v59 no3A p62 Ap/My 2016

MERLE HAGGARD color *Entertainment Weekly* no1446/1447 p93 D 2016/Ja 2017

Lynn, Murray

WITNESS TO DARKNESS S. FENNESSY *Atlanta* v57 no1 p22 My 2017

Lynn, Samara

5 Black-Owned Startups to Watch [Cover story] cartoon color *Black Enterprise* v47 no3 p29 O 2016

And the Award Goes to ... color *Black Enterprise* v47 no2 p22 S 2016

THE BUSINESS OF BLACK COMIC BOOKS bw cartoon color *Black Enterprise* v47 no8 p56 Jl/Ag 2017

CAN BLACKS AIRBNB THEIR WAY TO ECONOMIC EMPOWERMENT? color *Black Enterprise* v47 no8 p27 Jl/Ag 2017

KEEPING IT LOCAL color *Black Enterprise* v47 no8 p13 Jl/Ag 2017

Out From the Shadow of the Valley color *Black Enterprise* v47 no4 p18 N/D 2016

The Patent Troll Hunter: Jonathan Waldrop color *Black Enterprise* v47 no3 p28 O 2016

Rashida Hodge: A Woman in STEM color *Black Enterprise* v47 no5 p50 Ja/F 2017

TECH TRENDS CHANGING OUR WORLD color *Black Enterprise* v47 no2 p46 S 2016

THIS MAN WANTS TO DISRUPT YOUR DOWNLOAD color *Black Enterprise* v47 no5 p25 Ja/F 2017

Lynn, Troy

SADDLE CHAT bw color graph *Horse & Rider* v56 no11 p21 N 2017

Lynne, Jeff

THE TRAVELING WILBURYS M. Mettler color *Sound & Vision* v81 no9 p72 N 2016

Lynne, Nana

Popular piety color *U.S. Catholic* v82 no2 p5 F 2017

Lynx (Genus)

See also

Bobcat

HERE, KITTY C. KETTLEWELL *Virginia Living* v15 no2 p15 F 2017

Lynx—Behavior

Ghost Cat [Cover story] J. KIFFEL-ALCHEH color map *National Geographic Kids* no475 p12 N 2017

Shadow Cats C. Dell'Amore color diag map *National Geographic* v231 no2 p104 F 2017

LYON, BUD

Reiner to Ranch Rider bw color *Horse & Rider* v56 no10 p72 O 2017

Lyon, Danny

Danny Lyon D. Markus *Art in America* v104 no9 p149 O 2016

A TALE OF TWO BIKERS P. D'ORLEANS bw *Cycle World* v55 no10 p22 N 2016

Lyon, Erin

I Love You Subject to the Following Terms and Conditions: A Contract Killers Novel *Publishers Weekly* v263 no47 p97 N 21 2016

LYON, JARED

WE ARE THE RIGHTFUL HEIRS *Vital Speeches of the Day* v83 no3 p82 Mr 2017

Lyon, Shauna

Atla color *New Yorker* v93 no16 p32 Je 5 2017

The Beatrice Inn color *New Yorker* v93 no22 p15 Jl 31 2017

Chumley's color *New Yorker* v92 no42 p40 D 19 2016

Fries with That? color *New Yorker* v92 no47 p15 Ja 30 2017

Gloria color *New Yorker* v93 no25 p22 Ag 28 2017

GOLDEN TICKET cartoon *New Yorker* v93 no3 p24 Mr 6 2017

Harold's Meat + Three color *New Yorker* v92 no36 p13 N 7 2016

King color *New Yorker* v93 no10 p33 Ap 24 2017

Le Coucou color *New Yorker* v92 no30 p19 S 26 2016

THE NEW BRUNCH cartoon *New Yorker* v93 no6 p17 Mr 27 2017

Otway color *New Yorker* v93 no18 p15 Je 26 2017

Paowalla color *New Yorker* v93 no29 p33 S 25 2017

TABLES FOR TWO: The Aviary color *New Yorker* v93 no33 p31 O 23 2017

Union Square Café cartoon *New Yorker* v93 no5 p27 Mr 20 2017

LYONNE, NATASHA

Katherine WATERSTON: EMERGING, AS SHE HAS, FROM PRESTIGIOUS DIRECTOR-DRIVEN FILMS AND BEFORE THAT, A WHOLE LOT OF HUSTLE AND TOIL. THE FIERCELY TALENTED ACTRESS IS BRINGING A LITTLE SCRAPPINESS BACK TO THE BLOCKBUSTER *Interview* v47 no3 p80 My 2017

Lyons, Brandi

'Now' Exercise Makes Safety a Habit [Cover story] color *Horse & Rider* v56 no5 p42 My 2017

LYONS, CASEY

A Bandana color *Backpacker* p38 Je 2017

Discovery color *Backpacker* p70 Je 2017

Editors' Choice Awards color *Backpacker* p45 N 2017

Lonely at the Top color *Backpacker* p16 O 2017

The Never-Ending Journey color *Backpacker* v45 no1 p20 Ja 2017

Snow Day: Winter Sunsets color *Backpacker* v45 no2 p29 Mr 2017

You Never Forget Your First Time diag il *Backpacker* v45 no2 p64 Mr 2017

Lyons, Chuck

Valor Heroic Hellfighter *Military History* v33 no6 p12 Mr 2017

Valor Remarkable Exploits *Military History* v33 no5 p16 Ja 2017

What We Learned From… Nagashino, 1575 color *Military History* v34 no4 p18 N 2017

Lyons, Dan

AI'S KILLER APP? DUH … MARKETING color *Fortune* v175 no5 p40 Ap 1 2017

HOW TO MASTER CHANGE color *Fortune* v174 no7 p50 D 1 2016

JOB HUNTING? ERASE YOUR PAST color *Fortune* v175 no2 p46 F 1 2017

LOOK BEFORE YOU LEAP color *Fortune* v174 no6 p34 N 1 2016

NEW-TECH'S PROFIT BLACK HOLE color *Fortune* v174 no8 p82 D 15 2016

SNAP IS CLOWN CAR 2.0 color *Fortune* v175 no4 p72 Mr 15 2017

TYING VCs TO SHAREHOLDERS color *Fortune* v75 no1 p51 Ja 1 2017

WHO ARE YOU CALLING 'BORING'? color *Fortune* v175 no3 p52 Mr 1 2017

Lyons, Elizabeth

The Blessing of Dark Water *Publishers Weekly* v264 no13 p73 Mr 27 2017

Lyons, Jenna, 1969-

BAND OF SISTERS color *Glamour* v115 no9 p164 S 2017

Hey, Jenna! color *Glamour* v115 no2 p42 F 2017

If You Want a Pop of Color E. Velluto color *Glamour* v115 no9 p52 S 2017

JENNA LYONS K. MOLVAR bw color *Conde Nast Traveler* v52 no3 p30 Mr 2017

What Advice Would You Give Your Middle-School Self? color *Glamour* v115 no2 p22 F 2017

Lyons, Jon

COME TOGETHER A. NOLAN color *Runner's World* v52 no2 p15 Mr 2017

Lyons, Juliet

Dating the Undead *Publishers Weekly* v264 no13 p88 Mr 27 2017

Romancing the Undead: V-Date.com, Book 2 color *Publishers Weekly* v264 no33 p57 Ag 14 2017

Lyons, Justin D.

MASTER OF THE CONQUEST *Military History* v33 no6 p30 Mr 2017

Lyons, Karen

A genetic signature of the evolution of loss of flight in the Galapagos cormorant color diag *Science* v356 no6341 p921 Je 1 2017

Lyons, Patrick

How Life Insurers Can Bring Their Business into the 21st Century *Harvard Business Review Digital Articles* p2 Mr 25 2015

Lyons, Walter

Photographing Weather in the Dark bw color diag *Weatherwise* v70 no4 p20 Jl/Ag 2017

The Vedur of Iceland *Weatherwise* v70 no1 p20 Ja/F 2017

Lyric Fury (Music)

CYNTHIA HILTS K. Micallef color *Downbeat* v84 no5 p26 My 2017

Lyric Opera of Chicago

American Classic F. P. DRISCOLL *Opera News* v81 no9 p4 Mr 2017

Das Rheingold M. T. Ketterson *Opera News* v81 no6 p39 D 2016

John Neumeier: Hamburg Ballet's artistic director brings his work back to the Midwest L. WARNECKE *Dance Magazine* v91 no9 p22 S 2017

Lyricists

See also

Singer-songwriters

AMERICAN ANYONE A. PETRUSICH color *New Yorker* v93 no20 p88 Jl 10 2017

Beth DITTO *Interview* v47 no5 p20 Je/Jl 2017

BØRNS M. MULLEN *Interview* v46 no8 p40 O 2016

Broadway's Tiny Giant *Commentary* v143 no4 p4 Ap 2017

Broadway's Tiny Giant T. TEACHOUT *Commentary* v143 no4 p49 Ap 2017

Charlie Daniels Explores the Sound Quality Trail on Night Hawk M. METTLER and C. Crowley bw color *Sound & Vision* v82 no1 p22 Ja 2017

Star Time for Julia Michaels At 23, she's written smashes for Bieber and Britney. Now she's ready for some of her own J. LEVY color *Rolling Stone* no1294 p16 Ag 24 2017

Lyricists—Interviews

THE INTERVIEW M. BARCLAY color *Maclean's* v129 no46 p10 N 21 2016

Lys, Thomas Z.

More Reasons Women Need to Negotiate Their Salaries *Harvard Business Review Digital Articles* p2 Je 29 2015

Lyseggen, Jorn

Google Slayer Z. O'MALLEY GREENBURG and T. YOON color *Forbes* v199 no6 p54 Je 13 2017

Lyson, Tyler

Built for Stability L. E. Ogden *Natural History* v124 no10 p8 N 2016

Lysosomes

Lysosomal cholesterol activates mTORC1 via an SLC38A9–Niemann-Pick C1 signaling complex B. M. Castellano, A. M. Thelen et al bibl diag graph *Science* v355 no6331 p1306 Mr 24 2017

Organelle Overhaul M. Brouillette *Scientific American* v315 no6 p18 D 2016

Lyssenko, Konstantin A.

Density functional theory is straying from the path toward the exact functional bibl chart graph *Science* v355 no6320 p1 Ja 6 2017

Lyster, Rosa

Anxiety Dreams color *New York Times Magazine* p30 D 11 2016

LYTH, DAVID H.

A COSMIC CONTROVERSY color *Scientific American* v317 no1 p5 Jl 2017

Lythcott-Haims, Julie

life lessons *Parents* v91 no10 p48 O 2016

Real American: A Memoir *Publishers Weekly* v264 no26 p166 Je 26 2017

Lythgoe, Nigel, 1949-

Sound Bites color *Entertainment Weekly* no1471 p12 Je 23 2017

Lytle, James H.

Backtalk *Phi Delta Kappan* v98 no4 p80 D 2016/Ja 2017

Lyu, Dong

China Challenges the Giants With Low Fares color graph *Bloomberg Businessweek* no4504 p22 D 19 2016

China—With Western Help—Finds Its Wings diag *Bloomberg Businessweek* no4522 p25 My 15 2017

Everything Is Fine at Cathay Pacific cartoon graph *Bloomberg Businessweek* no4516 p17 Mr 27 2017

Lyu, Zhixin

GTPase activity-coupled treadmilling of the bacterial tubulin FtsZ organizes septal cell wall synthesis bibl graph *Science* v355 no6326 p744 F 17 2017

Lyumkis, Dmitry

Cryo-EM structures and atomic model of the HIV-1 strand transfer complex intasome bibl color *Science* v355 no6320 p1 Ja 6 2017

Lyver, Phil O'B.

Indigenous peoples: Conservation paradox color *Science* v357 no6347 p142 Jl 14 2017

M

M & J Trimming Co.

TRY THE TREND color *Better Homes & Gardens* v95 no10 p18 O 2017

M. Butterfly (Theatrical production)

BUTTERFLY STROKE D. STUMPF color *Vanity Fair* v59 no11 p142 N 2017

Julie Taymor Flies Again R. MILZOFF img *New York* v50 no17 p130 Ag 21 2017

M3 tank

The Reader Page R. G. Elmendorf and B. Porter color *Popular Mechanics* p8 D 2016/Ja 2017

M60 machine gun

Keep Your Powder Dry bw *Military History* v34 no2 p80 Jl 2017

M83 (Performer)

Opening Doors Z. CRAIN *D: The Magazine of Dallas* v43 no10 p60 O 2016

M87 (Galaxy)

Portrait of a giant D. J. Eicher color *Astronomy* v45 no11 p8 N 2017

MA, ALIZA

FELLOW FEELING color *Film Comment* v53 no3 p58 My/Je 2017

Ma, Chao

All-oxide–based synthetic antiferromagnets exhibiting layer-resolved magnetization reversal diag *Science* v357 no6347 p191 Jl 14 2017

Ma, Chelsea

FASHION'S WONDER GIRL! J. ABIDOR color *Seventeen* v76 no3 p98 My 2017

Ma, Ding

Atomic-layered Au clusters on α-MoC as catalysts for the low-temperature water-gas shift reaction chart diag graph *Science* v357 no6349 p389 Jl 28 2017

Ma, Helen

What It Will Take to Make the Tech Industry More Diverse *Harvard Business Review Digital Articles* p2 Mr 15 2016

Ma, Jean

Days of Heaven: Il Cinema Ritrovato on Its Thirtieth Anniversary *Film Quarterly* v70 no2 p68 Wint 2016

Ma, Jie

Deal Snapshot: Takata Corp chart *Bloomberg Businessweek* no4529 p21 Jl 3 2017

Globalism Is Alive and Well: Just Ask Carlos Ghosn color *Bloomberg Businessweek* no4531 p50 Jl 24 2017

Ma, Jun

Structure and assembly mechanism of plant C2S2M2-type PSII-LHCII supercomplex color *Science* v357 no6353 p815 Ag 25 2017

Ma, Mingguo

Reform China's fisheries subsidies color *Science* v356 no6345 p1343 Je 30 2017

Ma, Ping-Sheng

Bug mapping and fitness testing of chemically synthesized chromosome X diag *Science* v355 no6329 p1048 Mr 10 2017

"Perfect" designer chromosome V and behavior of a ring derivative diag *Science* v355 no6329 p1046 Mr 10 2017

Ma, Rujun

Highly efficient electrocaloric cooling with electrostatic actuation bw diag *Science* v357 no6356 p1130 S 15 2017

Ma, Tammy—Awards

Patents and Awards *Science & Technology Review* p23 Ja/F 2017

Ma, Yaoguang

Scalable-manufactured randomized glass-polymer hybrid metamaterial for daytime radiative cooling bibl diag *Science* v355 no6329 p1062 Mr 10 2017

Ma, Yun, 1964-

10 JACK MA S. Cendrowski color *Fortune* v174 no7 p85 D 1 2016

YOU DON'T KNOW JACK NO.2 [Cover story] A. Lashinsky color *Fortune* v175 no5 p66 Ap 1 2017

Ma, Yun, 1964—Finance

China's Richest K. A. DOLAN color map *Forbes* v198 no7 p28 N 29 2016

Ma, Zhenchuan

A paralogous decoy protects Phytophthora sojae apoplastic effector PsXEG1 from a host inhibitor bibl graph *Science* v355 no6326 p710 F 17 2017

Ma-Yi Theater Co.

GOINGS ON ABOUT TOWN color *New Yorker* v93 no26 p6 S 4 2017

Maag, Ashley

Forward: A Memoir/Redskins: Insult and Brand color *Progressive* p60 D 2016/Ja 2017

Maas, D. J. H. C.

Dual-comb spectroscopy of water vapor with a free-running semiconductor disk laser diag *Science* v356 no6343 p1164 Je 16 2017

Maas, Emily

Kal Penn Is a Deadbeat *TV Guide* v64 no15 p15 Ap 4 2016

Maas, Mirte

EYE OF THE BEHOLDER J. Ferrise and A. Syrett color *InStyle* v24 no5 p218 My 2017

Maas, P.

Persistent effects of pre-Columbian plant domestication on Amazonian forest composition bibl chart graph map *Science* v355 no6328 p925 Mr 3 2017

Maasai (African people)

Once We Were Lions S. Butler *Sierra* v101 no5 p16 S/O 2016

Maat, Margaret Morgan

ENEMY color *Christian Century* v134 no5 p20 Mr 1 2017

MAAZEL, FIONA

DEAR ME color *O, The Oprah Magazine* p80 Je 2017

Name That Tune *New York Times Book Review* p18 F 12 2017

Psychic Friend Network: A novel about mind reading, repressed memories and the self-styled superhero Brainstorm T. LeCLAIR *New York Times Book Review* p11 Je 18 2017

Mabanckou, Alain

THE APPROVAL MATRIX img *New York* v50 no13 p140 Je 26 2017

No Promised Land: After a Dickensian childhood, an orphan in Congo must contend with poverty, political instability and tribal rivalries J. HAMMER *New York Times Book Review* p18 Jl 23 2017

Maberry, Jonathan

Joe Ledger: Unstoppable *Publishers Weekly* v264 no33 p50 Ag 14 2017

MABIE, CRAIG

You Never Forget Your First Time diag il *Backpacker* v45 no2 p64 Mr 2017

Mabry, Samantha

All the Wind in the World *Publishers Weekly* v264 no31 p90 Jl 31 2017

Mac, Jimmy

Liquefied gas electrolytes for electrochemical energy storage devices graph *Science* v356 no6345 p1351 Je 30 2017

MAC, RYAN

CAN CRAIGSLIST BE KILLED? color *Forbes* v199 no5 p80 My 16 2017

THE WORLD'S BILLIONAIRES bw color diag graph map *Forbes* v199 no3 p84 Mr 28 2017

MAC Cosmetics Inc.

VELVET REVOLUTION color *O, The Oprah Magazine* p83 N 2017

Mac Mini (Computer)

Hoping for a small Mac mini revival J. SNELL color *Macworld - Digital Edition* v34 no9 p7 S 2017

What the Mac needs in 2017 J. SNELL color *Macworld - Digital Edition* p10 F 2017

Mac OS (Operating system)

Hey, Apple Fixed This! K. MCELHEARN color *Macworld - Digi-*

tal Edition v34 no8 p24 Ag 2017

How to adjust macOS Sierra 10.12.4's Night Shift settings R. LOYOLA color *Macworld - Digital Edition* v34 no4 p7 My 2017

How to configure a software RAID in macOS Sierra's Disk Utility R. LOYOLA color *Macworld - Digital Edition* v33 no11 p130 N 2016

How to stop spam emails from reaching your inbox G. FLEISH-MAN color *Macworld - Digital Edition* v34 no11 p111 N 2017

How to turn on/off read receipts in macOS Sierra's Messages R. LOYOLA cartoon color *Macworld - Digital Edition* v33 no11 p127 N 2016

How to use iCloud Drive's new Desktop and Documents access in macOS Sierra R. LOYOLA color *Macworld - Digital Edition* v33 no11 p135 N 2016

How to use the advanced Calendar Service features in macOS Sierra Server J. BATTERSBY color *Macworld - Digital Edition* p103 D 2016

Mac 911 G. FLEISHMAN and M. CONNELL color *Macworld - Digital Edition* p131 F 2017

Mac 911 G. FLEISHMAN bw color *Macworld - Digital Edition* v34 no8 p127 Ag 2017

TripMode 2 review: Utility manages, blocks, and caps macOS Internet use K. MCELHEARN color *Macworld - Digital Edition* v34 no8 p106 Ag 2017

Mac OS (Operating system)—Evaluation

6 Photos features that are worth the upgrade to macOS Sierra J. SNELL color map *Macworld - Digital Edition* v33 no11 p21 N 2016

7 hidden features in macOS Sierra you may have missed R. LOYOLA color *Macworld - Digital Edition* v33 no11 p27 N 2016

macOS Sierra: Mixing iOS with OS X to make a better Mac R. LOYOLA color *Macworld - Digital Edition* v33 no11 p7 N 2016

Maca (Plant)

SEX AFTER 40 L. Turner color *Amazing Wellness* v9 no2 p30 Spr 2017

Suprfood cocktails T. Darlington and A. Darlington color *Rodale's Organic Life* v3 no1 p85 Ja 2017

Macaca nigra

A Fight to Survive J. S. Holland color map *National Geographic* v231 no3 p86 Mr 2017

MacAdam, Charles

RUN, JUMP, EXPLORE P. Moscovitch color *American Craft* v77 no3 p48 Je/Jl 2017

MacAdam, Toshiko Horiuchi

RUN, JUMP, EXPLORE P. Moscovitch color *American Craft* v77 no3 p48 Je/Jl 2017

Macal, Charles

THE DOOMSDAY SQUAD B. Smith color *Chicago* v66 no2 p84 F 2017

MacAlister, Emory

The Thread *New York Times Magazine* p10 O 23 2016

Macao (Film)

RUNNING DEEP I. S. SMITH bw *Film Comment* v53 no5 p38 S/O 2017

Macaques

See also

Macaca nigra

A dedicated network for social interaction processing in the primate brain J. Sliwa and W. A. Freiwald color diag *Science* v356 no6339 p745 My 19 2017

A Fight to Survive J. S. Holland color map *National Geographic* v231 no3 p86 Mr 2017

Macareo, Louis R.

Dengue diversity across spatial and temporal scales: Local structure and the effect of host population size bibl graph *Science* v355 no6331 p1302 Mr 24 2017

Macaroons

Down-to-Earth Decadence S. Hackman color *Missouri Life* v44 no4 p74 Je 2017

MacArthur, Douglas, 1880-1964

Cheating Death D. Sears *American History* v51 no6 p60 F 2017

OUR MAN IN MANILA: HIS CLANDESTINE MISSIONS WERE VITAL TO MACARTHUR'S FAMED RETURN TO

THE PHILIPPINES, YET THE FULL STORY OF CHICK PARSONS' DARING FEATS HAS NOT BEEN TOLD--UNTIL NOW P. EISNER *Smithsonian* v48 no5 p42 S 2017

The Price Of FREEDOM B. MONTGOMERY bw color *Reader's Digest* v190 no1132 p80 Jl/Ag 2017

Macarthur, Robert H., 1930-1972

Island biogeography: Taking the long view of nature's laboratories R. J. Whittaker, J. María Fernández-Palacios et al map *Science* v357 no6354 p885 S 1 2017

MACAULAY, LORI WYMAN

my miracle log home color map *Cabin Living* p13 O 2017

Macaws

From The Pages Of Quiz Whiz: Stump Your Parents color *National Geographic Kids* no473 p38 S 2017

Macaws—Behavior

Elusive blue-throated macaw nests discovered color *Science* v355 no6332 p1356 Mr 31 2017

Macbeth (Play : Shakespeare)

GHOST STORY W. Shakespeare *Lapham's Quarterly* v10 no3 p126 Summ 2017

Macbeth (Theatrical production)

Macbeth S. Williams *Opera News* v81 no6 p40 D 2016

Macbird, Bonnie

Is Holmes Where the Heart Is? L. PICKER *Publishers Weekly* v264 no34 p89 Ag 21 2017

Unquiet Spirits: A Sherlock Holmes Adventure color *Publishers Weekly* v264 no33 p49 Ag 14 2017

MacBook (Computer)

See also

MacBook Pro (Computer)

HIGH or LOW? color *Good Housekeeping* v265 no3 p50 S 2017

How to bring back a physical Escape key on the new MacBook Pro with Touch Bar R. LOYOLA color *Macworld - Digital Edition* p108 D 2016

How To: Get a Touch Bar without buying a MacBook R. Loyola color *Macworld - Digital Edition* p106 Ja 2017

MACBOOK 2017: THE BANG FOR YOUR BUCK GETS BETTER R. LOYOLA color graph *Macworld - Digital Edition* v34 no8 p32 Ag 2017

TECH THE HALLS S. Grobart color *Bloomberg Businessweek* no4500 p78 N 21 2016

Why the new Mac Pro might never come D. MOREN color *Macworld - Digital Edition* v34 no4 p10 My 2017

MacBook (Computer)—Equipment & supplies

CABLE MATTERS 72W 4-PORT USB CHARGER WITH USB-C POWER DELIVERY: HIGHWATTAGE USB-C CHARGER DELIVERS THE GOODS G. FLEISHMAN color *Macworld - Digital Edition* v34 no10 p29 O 2017

FINSIX DART-C CHARGER: TINY, POWERFUL, AND WORTH THE EXPENSE G. MAH UNG chart color *Macworld - Digital Edition* v34 no6 p33 Je 2017

MacBook Air (Computer)—Evaluation

Meet Apple's complete MacBook lineup L. YAMSHON color *Macworld - Digital Edition* p13 D 2016

MacBook Pro (Computer)

Ask the iTunes Guy: iTunes libraries on the new MacBook Pro K. MCELHEARN cartoon color *Macworld - Digital Edition* p116 Mr 2017

The case for a touchscreen Mac D. Moren color *Macworld - Digital Edition* p130 Ap 2017

MACBOOK PRO (2017): THE FUTURE STARTS WITH KABY LAKE R. LOYOLA color graph *Macworld - Digital Edition* v34 no8 p37 Ag 2017

MacBook Pro's 'terrible' battery life tested G. M. Ung color graph *Macworld - Digital Edition* p20 Ap 2017

Welcome... *Macworld - Digital Edition* p3 Ap 2017

MacBook Pro (Computer)—Evaluation

7 technologies killed in Apple's new MacBook Pro B. CHACOS color *Macworld - Digital Edition* p19 D 2016

Bringing Touch Bar to desktop Macs J. Snell color *Macworld - Digital Edition* p36 Ap 2017

Consumer Reports updates its MacBook Pro review R. LOYOLA color *PCWorld* v35 no2 p41 F 2017

HANDS-ON: THE MACBOOK PRO'S INNOVATIVE TOUCH BAR GRAB YOU S. OCHS color *Macworld - Digital Edition* p79 D 2016

MacBook Pro with Touch Bar: The best bits of iOS in a really great Mac S. OCHS color graph *PCWorld* p80 D 2016

Meet Apple's complete MacBook lineup L. YAMSHON color *Macworld - Digital Edition* p13 D 2016

Review: MacBook Pro (2016) S. Ochs color graph *Macworld - Digital Edition* p18 Ja 2017

SURFACE BOOK i7 vs. MACBOOK PRO: FIGHT! G. MAH UNG color graph *PCWorld* v35 no1 p155 Ja 2017

Ta-dah! Touch Bar is the highlight of Apple's newest MacBook Pro R. LOYOLA color *Macworld - Digital Edition* p7 D 2016

Tested: The truth behind the MacBook Pro's 'terrible' battery life G. MAH UNG color graph *PCWorld* p53 Mr 2017

TESTED: THE TRUTH BEHIND THE MACBOOK PRO'S TERRIBLE BATTERY LIFE G. M. UNG cartoon color graph *Macworld - Digital Edition* p68 Mr 2017

MacCachren, Rob

ROB MAC: DRIVER OF THE YEAR M. Emery color *Dirt Sports + Off-Road* v51 no9 p6 S 2017

MacCachren, Rob—Interviews

ROB MACCACHREN M. EMERY color *Dirt Sports + Off-Road* v51 no9 p20 S 2017

Maccaferri, Marco

Wild emmer genome architecture and diversity elucidate wheat evolution and domestication color *Science* v357 no6346 p93 Jl 7 2017

MacCarald, Clara

Coyote Nation color *National Wildlife (World Edition)* v55 no1 p40 D/Ja 2016

Maccarone, Grace

The Nutcracker *Publishers Weekly* v263 no39 p91 S 26 2016

Maccarrone, Mauro

Activity-based protein profiling reveals off-target proteins of the FAAH inhibitor BIA 10-2474 chart color graph *Science* v356 no6342 p1084 Je 9 2017

MacCarthy, Fiona

City in the Dark cartoon *New York Review of Books* v64 no2 p32 F 9 2017

MacCharles, Joel

Sweet Somethings color *O, The Oprah Magazine* p38 D 2016

Macchi, Leandro

Forest conservation: Remember Gran Chaco bibl color *Science* v355 no6324 p465 F 3 2017

Macchiarini, Paolo

Paolo Macchiarini's academic afterlife in Russia ends A. Astakhova and M. Enserink color *Science* v356 no6339 p672 My 19 2017

Maccoby, Michael

Why People Are Drawn to Narcissists Like Donald Trump *Harvard Business Review Digital Articles* p2 Ag 26 2015

MacColl, Andrew D. C.

Precipitation drives global variation in natural selection bibl chart diag map *Science* v355 no6328 p959 Mr 3 2017

MacConnell, Kristen

Getting better together color il *Phi Delta Kappan* v98 no3 p16 N 2016

MacCoun, Robert J.

Brains, environments, and policy responses to addiction color *Science* v356 no6344 p1237 Je 23 2017

MacCulloch, Diarmaid

ALL THINGS MADE NEW B. BETHUNE color *Maclean's* v129 no41 p56 O 17 2016

From Wittenberg to Brexit W. Storrar cartoon *Commonweal* v143 no18 p34 N 11 2016

Great Awakening A. Pettegree color *Weekly Standard* v22 no24 p34 F 27 2017

MACDIARMID, CAMPBELL

'I came to fight for all Iraqis' color *Maclean's* v129 no44 p32 N 7 2016

MacDonal, Bruce

KEEP THAT WRECKING BALL AT BAY *Yankee* v81 no1 p48 Ja/F 2017

MacDonald, Alexander

The Surprisingly Long History of Private Space Exploration R. SIMBERG color *Reason* v49 no4 p70 Ag/S 2017

MacDonald, Allan H.

Observation of a nematic quantum Hall liquid on the surface of bismuth bibl graph *Science* v354 no6310 p316 O 21 2016

MACDONALD, CLARE

Restoration drama color *House Beautiful* p40 Ag 2017

MacDonald, Connor

HIRED! T. SPIKER cartoon color graph *Men's Health* v32 no3 p96 Ap 2017

Macdonald, Danielle

A Jersey Girl Dreams Big S. Zacharek color *Time* v190 no8 p50 Ag 28 2017

MACDONALD, DAVID W.

Conserving the World's Megafauna and Biodiversity: The Fierce Urgency of Now *BioScience* v67 no3 p197 Mr 2017

International Wildlife Law: Understanding and Enhancing Its Role in Conservation *BioScience* v67 no9 p784 S 2017

Saving the World's Terrestrial Megafauna color *BioScience* v66 no10 p807 O 1 2016

Some Animals Are More Equal than Others: Wild Animal Welfare in the Media *BioScience* v67 no1 p62 Ja 2017

Macdonald, Emma K.

What Really Makes Customers Buy a Product *Harvard Business Review Digital Articles* p2 N 9 2015

MacDonald, Eric

Multiprocess 3D printing for increasing component functionality bibl bw color *Science* v353 no6307 paaf2093-1 S 30 2016

MacDonald, G. Jeffrey

Churches see benefits in sponsoring art shows *Christian Century* v134 no13 p16 Je 21 2017

The Methodists after unity color *Christian Century* v133 no24 p28 N 23 2016

Mac Donald, Heather

The Fainting Couch at Columbia: A new 'sexual-respect initiative' puts another stake into the heart of academic seriousness *Commentary* v140 no2 p37 S 2015

In Defense of Jeff Sessions *National Review* v69 no16 p27 Ag 28 2017

Is free speech under threat IN THE UNITED STATES? WE RECEIVED TWENTY-SEVEN RESPONSES. WE PUBLISH THEM HERE, IN ALPHABETICAL ORDER *Commentary* v144 no1 p13 Jl/Ag 2017

Let the Police Police *National Review* v69 no9 p28 My 15 2017

'She Said What?' J. LILEKS *National Review* v69 no8 p33 My 2017

MacDonald, Heidi

Comics & Graphic Novels bw color *Publishers Weekly* v263 no51 p31 D 12 2016

Comics & Graphic Novels color *Publishers Weekly* v264 no26 p34 Je 26 2017

Library Demand for Graphic Novels Keeps Growing color *Publishers Weekly* v264 no20 p19 My 15 2017

R.L. Stine's First Comics Work Is on Marvel's Man-Thing color *Publishers Weekly* v263 no51 p8 D 12 2016

SAN DIEGO COMIC-CON 2017: Debut Books and Highlights color *Publishers Weekly* v264 no28 p56 Jl 10 2017

STAYING SAFE AT SAN DIEGO COMIC-CON 2017 color *Publishers Weekly* v264 no28 p48 Jl 10 2017

MacDonald, Helen

A BESTIARY OF THE MIND bw *New York Times Magazine* p40 My 21 2017

Bless the Beasts *New York Times Book Review* p11 Mr 19 2017

H Is for Hike J. Mark *Sierra* v101 no4 p10 Jl/Ag 2016

SWAN SONG *New York Times Magazine* p24 Ja 8 2017

MacDonald, James M.

Large Family Farms Continue To Dominate U.S. Agricultural Production *Amber Waves: The Economics of Food, Farming, Natural Resources, & Rural America* p1 Mr 2017

Mergers and Competition in Seed and Agricultural Chemical Markets *Amber Waves: The Economics of Food, Farming, Natural Resources, & Rural America* p1 Ap 2017

MACDONALD, JOHN

LUCKY AND GOOD *Sea Magazine* v109 no4 p12 Ap 2017

MACDONALD, KATIE

BORN THIS WAY color *Popular Mechanics* p88 My 2017

Macdonald, Maritza

What does it take to sustain a productive partnership in education? color *Phi Delta Kappan* v99 no1 p15 S 2017

MACDONALD, NANCY

1,560 DAYS [Cover story] color *Maclean's* v129 no45 p16 N 14 2016

ABOUT THAT TATTOO color *Maclean's* v129 no44 p25 N 7 2016

Agony and hope in the ashes color *Maclean's* v130 no8 p11 S 2017

Big money, big problems color *Maclean's* v130 no2 p32 Mr 2017

Confronting its biggest crisis color *Maclean's* v129 no42 p29 O 24 2016

'Death, death—day in, day out' *Maclean's* no1 p12 F 17 2017

Down on the border color *Maclean's* v130 no7 p24 Ag 2017

Escape from Winterpeg color *Maclean's* no1 p14 F 17 2017

FROM HOPE TO FURY IN 12 MONTHS color *Maclean's* v129 no42 p24 O 24 2016

The grittiest royal tour color map *Maclean's* v129 no40 p44 O 10 2016

THE INTERVIEW color *Maclean's* v130 no6 p24 Jl 2017

Lost and broken [Cover story] color *Maclean's* v130 no9 p24 O 2017

Rebranding Canada 150 *Maclean's* v130 no3 p14 Ap 2017

Recouping their losses *Maclean's* v130 no4 p15 My 2017

A RIVER OF TEARS [Cover story] color *Maclean's* v130 no7 p38 Ag 2017

A SEARCH FOR ANSWERS color *Maclean's* v129 no51/52 p31 D 26 2016

Veering off script color *Maclean's* v129 no41 p42 O 17 2016

Macdonald, Neil

Changing climate shifts timing of European floods color graph *Science* v357 no6351 p588 Ag 11 2017

Macdonald, Norm

Deadpan Walking G. MUNROE cartoon *Walrus* v13 no9 p63 N 2016

TEMPS PERDU I. Parker cartoon *New Yorker* v92 no33 p28 O 17 2016

Macdonald, Ross, 1915-1983

True Detective N. DAWIDOFF *New Republic* v248 no10 p56 O 2017

MACDONALD, SALLY

LUCKY AND GOOD *Sea Magazine* v109 no4 p12 Ap 2017

MacDonald, Sean

2017 DUCATI MONSTER 1200 S color *Cycle World* v56 no2 p10 Mr 2017

2017 DUCATI SUPERSPORT AND SUPERSPORT S color *Cycle World* v56 no4 p16 My 2017

2017 TRIUMPH BONNEVILLE BOBBER color *Cycle World* v56 no2 p58 Mr 2017

2017 TRIUMPH STREET SCRAMBLER color *Cycle World* v56 no3 p32 Ap 2017

2018 BMW R nineT URBAN G/S color *Cycle World* v56 no8 p10 S 2017

2018 INDIAN SCOUT BOBBER color *Cycle World* v56 no9 p20 O 2017

93 OCTANE color *Cycle World* v56 no2 p36 Mr 2017

ARAI QUANTUM-X AND SIGNET-X HELMETS cartoon color *Cycle World* v55 no11 p14 D 2016

CHASING A FEELING chart color *Cycle World* v56 no6 p42 Jl 2017

LEARNING FROM A MASTER color *Cycle World* v56 no1 p48 Ja/F 2017

MAKING IT chart color *Cycle World* v55 no10 p38 N 2016

OF STYLE AND SUBSTANCE chart color *Cycle World* v56 no8 p38 S 2017

PICKING THE RIGHT PACK color *Cycle World* v56 no2 p16 Mr 2017

RIDING IN THE CLOUDS color *Cycle World* v56 no5 p50 Je 2017

THE UNNECESSARY EXPRESS [Cover story] color *Cycle World* v56 no5 p32 Je 2017

VISION OF THE FUTURE? color *Cycle World* v56 no9 p22 O 2017

MacDonald, William W.

A Luther Renaissance in Catholic Thought *America* v217 no3 p33 Ag 7 2017

MacDonogh, Giles

HISTOIRE AVEC MODÉRATION *History Today* v67 no5 p94 My 2017

MacDougall, Clair

A Plague Year: An American doctor's account of his work at an Ebola treatment unit in rural Liberia color *New York Times Book Review* p18 Ap 23 2017

What Trump Got Right About The UN color *Bloomberg Businessweek* no4516 p6 Mr 27 2017

MACEK, MARTIN

Combining Biodiversity Resurveys across Regions to Advance Global Change Research *BioScience* v67 no1 p73 Ja 2017

Macfarlan, Todd S.

Deficiency of microRNA miR-34a expands cell fate potential in pluripotent stem cells diag *Science* v355 no6325 p596 F 10 2017

A placental growth factor is silenced in mouse embryos by the zinc finger protein ZFP568 color graph *Science* v356 no6339 p757 My 19 2017

Macfarlane, Allison

Déjà vu for U.S. nuclear waste color *Science* v356 no6345 p1313 Je 30 2017

Macfarlane, Robert

GIFT WORDS L. Collins cartoon *New Yorker* v93 no9 p21 Ap 17 2017

MacFarlane, Seth, 1973-

5 THINGS TO KNOW ABOUT THE ORVILLE D. Holbrook *TV Guide* v65 no37 p44 S 4 2017

I can put an IMAX in your house S. Horaczek color *Popular Science* v289 no6 p86 N/D 2017

The Orville N. Abrams, B. L. Heldman et al *Entertainment Weekly* no1482/1483 p85 S 22 2017

MacFarquhar, Larissa

OUT AND UP cartoon *New Yorker* v92 no41 p54 D 12 2016

THE SEPARATION cartoon *New Yorker* v93 no23 p36 Ag 7 2017

A Stranger Morality C. MARTIN color *Tricycle: The Buddhist Review* v26 no2 p84 Wint 2016

TRUMPTOWN cartoon color *New Yorker* v92 no32 p56 O 10 2016

MacFarquhar, Roderick

China's Astounding Religious Revival [Cover story] color *New York Review of Books* v64 no10 p36 Je 8 2017

MacGahan, Januarius Aloysius

A PICTURE OF WAR J. A. MacGahan *MHQ: Quarterly Journal of Military History* v29 no3 p86 Spr 2017

MacGillis, Alec

FRIENDS IN HIGH PLACES cartoon *New Yorker* v92 no37 p36 N 14 2016

Is Anybody Home at HUD? img *New York* v50 no17 p40 Ag 21 2017

Ohio *New York Times Magazine* p41 N 20 2016

MacGillivray, Greg

HUMPBACK WHALES D. Vaughn color *Sound & Vision* v81 no10 p69 D 2016

MacGregor, Gordon

Emergence and spread of a human-transmissible multidrug-resistant nontuberculous mycobacterium bibl diag graph *Science* v354 no6313 p751 N 11 2016

MACGREGOR, HILARY

LOST IN TRANSLATION *Los Angeles Magazine* v61 no11 p140 N 2016

MacGregor, Jeff

Chariot of Fire *Smithsonian* v48 no3 p26 Je 2017

Escape Artist *Smithsonian* v47 no7 p13 N 2016

HIGH FLIERS *Smithsonian* v47 no8 p52 D 2016

When Fonzie Lost His Cool: He was the epitome of '50s chill on TV's family-friendly "Happy Days." And then he went over the top *Smithsonian* v48 no5 p20 S 2017

MACGREGOR, ROY

THE CALL OF Algonquin color map *Canadian Geographic* v137 no1 p64 F 2017

Macgregor, Sandra

GETTING PERSONAL WITH CANCER bw *Maclean's* v130 no6 p82 Jl 2017

How Ageism Is Robbing Seniors of Their Independence color *Maclean's* v129 no40 p62 O 10 2016

NUCLEAR POWER *Maclean's* v129 no50 p53 D 19 2016

PROMOTING WOMEN IN LEADERSHIP BENEFITS ALL color *Maclean's* v130 no3 p58 Ap 2017

Macgyver (TV program)

Mac Attack! I. Rudolph color *TV Guide* v64 no42 p11 O 10 2016

MacGyver J. Halterman color *TV Guide* v65 no7 p42 F 13 2017

MacGyver N. Abrams, S. Highfill et al *Entertainment Weekly* no1482/1483 p99 S 22 2017

Mach, Katharine J.

Rightsizing carbon dioxide removal chart color *Science* v356 no6339 p706 My 19 2017

Machado, Ivens

IVENS MACHADO A. Pechman color *Art in America* v104 no11 p127 D 2016

Machado, Justina

Latina faith and family S. B. Plate *Christian Century* v134 no13 p43 Je 21 2017

Machado Silva, Hesiley

Intelligent design endangers education color *Science* v357 no6354 p880 S 1 2017

Machaqueiro, John

CHEVROLET GT4.R CAMARO color *Hot Rod* v70 no11 p78 N 2017

One of None color *Hot Rod* v70 no10 p36 O 2017

A WEDGED BLUE OVAL color *Hot Rod* v70 no4 p46 Ap 2017

Machaty, Gustav

Bohemian Rhapsody M. Nelson bw *Film Comment* v53 no3 p11 My/Je 2017

Machelska, H.

A nontoxic pain killer designed by modeling of pathological receptor conformations bibl diag graph *Science* v355 no6328 p966 Mr 3 2017

Machiah, Deepa

mTOR regulates metabolic adaptation of APCs in the lung and controls the outcome of allergic inflammation graph *Science* v357 no6355 p1014 S 8 2017

Machiavelli, Niccolò, 1469-1527

YES TO FEAR, NO TO HATRED N. Machiavelli *Lapham's Quarterly* v10 no3 p153 Summ 2017

Machida, Yuya

Recurring and triggered slow-slip events near the trench at the Nankai Trough subduction megathrust diag graph *Science* v356 no6343 p1157 Je 16 2017

Machin, Amanda

Trusting the Climate: Catastrophe Vs. Stability graph *Society* v53 no6 p573 D 2016

Machinalia (Theatrical production)

17. See Machinalia *New York* v50 no16 p113 Ag 7 2017

Machine bearing design & construction

BABBITT BEARINGS S. SMITH color *Road & Track* v69 no1 p94 Ag 2017

Machine Gun Kelly (Performer)

Machine Gun Kelly A. GREENE color *Rolling Stone* no1285 p16 Ap 20 2017

Machine guns

LEWIS GUN C. McNab *MHQ: Quarterly Journal of Military History* v29 no2 p23 Wint 2017

WEAPONS CHECK: MG 42 C. McNab color *MHQ: Quarterly Journal of Military History* v30 no1 p27 Aut 2017

Machine learning

See also

Computational learning theory

Deep learning (Machine learning)

8 Ways Machine Learning Is Improving Companie's Work Processes D. Wellers, T. Elliott et al *Harvard Business Review Digital Articles* p2 My 31 2017

Agility in the Arsenal: Technology makes for better weapons--but only until our foes catch up. Why the Pentagon needs to move faster J. Felter *Hoover Digest: Research & Opinion on Public Policy* no3 p65 Summ 2017

Algorithm of the Enlightenment E. FINN *Issues in Science & Technology* v33 no3 p21 Spr 2017

AlphaGo and the Declining Advantage of Big Companies H. Yu *Harvard Business Review Digital Articles* p2 Mr 24 2016

Artificial intelligence in research J. Sills, M. Musib et al color *Science* v357 no6346 p28 Jl 7 2017

Artificial intelligence needs smart senses to be useful *Science News* v190 no10 p2 N 12 2016

Artificial Intelligence: Not Your Father's Toolbox: Some new artificial intelligence business tools to help park and rec agencies J.

Dysart *Parks & Recreation* v52 no8 p72 Ag 2017

Business Processes Are Learning to Hack Themselves H. J. Wilson, A. Alter et al *Harvard Business Review Digital Articles* p2 Je 27 2016

A Guide to Solving Social Problems with Machine Learning J. Kleinberg, J. Ludwig et al *Harvard Business Review Digital Articles* p2 D 8 2016

How Companies Are Using Machine Learning to Get Faster and More Efficient H. J. Wilson, S. Sachdev et al *Harvard Business Review Digital Articles* p2 My 3 2016

How Machine Learning Is Helping Morgan Stanley Better Understand Client Needs T. H. Davenport and R. Bean *Harvard Business Review Digital Articles* p2 Ag 3 2017

How Machine Learning Is Helping Us Predict Heart Disease and Diabetes Y. Paschalidis *Harvard Business Review Digital Articles* p2 My 30 2017

How to Make Your Company Machine Learning Ready J. Hodson *Harvard Business Review Digital Articles* p2 N 7 2016

How to Tell If Machine Learning Can Solve Your Business Problem A. Fedyk *Harvard Business Review Digital Articles* p2 N 15 2016

Machine learning for quantum physics M. R. Hush bibl diag *Science* v355 no6325 p580 F 10 2017

Move Your Analytics Operation from Artisanal to Autonomous T. H. Davenport *Harvard Business Review Digital Articles* p2 D 2 2016

Predicting human behavior: The next frontiers V. S. Subrahmanian and S. Kumar bibl color *Science* v355 no6324 p489 F 3 2017

Real or Fake? AI Is Making It Very Hard to Know W. Knight il *MIT Technology Review* v120 no4 p26 Jl/Ag 2017

The Rise of AI Makes Emotional Intelligence More Important M. Beck and B. Libert *Harvard Business Review Digital Articles* p2 F 15 2017

What Every Manager Should Know About Machine Learning M. Yeomans *Harvard Business Review Digital Articles* p2 Jl 7 2015

What's Driving the Machine Learning Explosion? E. Brynjolfsson and A. McAfee *Harvard Business Review Digital Articles* p2 Jl 18 2017

WHAT'S DRIVING THE MACHINE LEARNING EXPLOSION? Three factors make this AI's moment E. Brynjolfsson and A. McAfee *Harvard Business Review Digital Articles* p12 Jl 1 2017

WHY AI CAN'T WRITE THIS ARTICLE (YET) W. Frick *Harvard Business Review Digital Articles* p24 Jl 1 2017

Why Machines Still Can't Learn So Good N. Kumar and T. Hall cartoon *Bloomberg Businessweek* no4499 p55 N 14 2016

Why You're Not Getting Value from Your Data Science K. Veeramachaneni *Harvard Business Review Digital Articles* p2 D 7 2016

Will Make AI Smarter For Cash M. Hutson *Bloomberg Businessweek* no4537 p23 S 11 2017

Your Algorithms Are Not Safe from Hackers K. Radinsky *Harvard Business Review Digital Articles* p2 Ja 5 2016

Machine learning research

AI Software Learns to Make AI Software T. Simonite *MIT Technology Review* v120 no3 p16 My/Je 2017

Machine learning—Congresses

LIVE WEBINAR DEEP LEARNING'S NEXT FRONTIER: Watch the recorded event here *Harvard Business Review Digital Articles* p29 Jl 1 2017

Machine learning—Moral & ethical aspects

Teaching an Algorithm to Understand Right and Wrong G. Satell *Harvard Business Review Digital Articles* p2 N 15 2016

Machine learning—Software

AI Software Learns to Make AI Software T. Simonite *MIT Technology Review* v120 no3 p16 My/Je 2017

Machine theory

See also

Artificial intelligence

Machine learning

In the AI Age, "Being Smart" Will Mean Something Completely Different E. Hess *Harvard Business Review Digital Articles* p2 Je 19 2017

Machine-to-machine communications

Make the Internet of Things More Human-Friendly H. J. Wilson *Harvard Business Review Digital Articles* p2 O 16 2014

Biodiversity in the City: Fundamental Questions for Understanding the Ecology of Urban Green Spaces for Biodiversity Conservation *BioScience* v67 no9 p799 S 2017

Mack, Alex

CENTER STAGE G. A. Bedard color *Sports Illustrated* v125 no16 p38 N 14 2016

Mack, Andre Hueston

Meet "The Wine Maker" André Hueston Mack D. Pressley and K. MEEKS chart color *Black Enterprise* v47 no4 p33 N/D 2016

Mack, Eric Nathaniel

Eric MACK S. N. PRICKETT *Interview* v46 no10 p112 D 2016/Ja 2017

Mack, Korrie L.

Ratchet-like polypeptide translocation mechanism of the AAA+ disaggregase Hsp104 diag *Science* v357 no6348 p273 Jl 21 2017

Mack, Louise

CLASSIC DISPATCHES: THE HORRORS OF AERSCHOT bw *MHQ: Quarterly Journal of Military History* v30 no1 p82 Aut 2017

Mack, Ronald

One church? *U.S. Catholic* v82 no7 p5 Jl 2017

Mackay, James

Errata *American Indian Quarterly* v40 no3 p292 Summ 2016

MacKay, Jim

Out of The Loop S. Zak and T. Keith color *Sports Illustrated* v127 no1 p16 Jl 3 2017

Mackay, Joel

Site-specific phosphorylation of tau inhibits amyloid-β toxicity in Alzheimer's mice bibl graph *Science* v354 no6314 p904 N 18 2016

MacKay, Julian

Julian MacKay L. CAPPELLE *Dance Magazine* v91 no9 p26 S 2017

MacKay, Malcolm

Every Night I Dream of Hell *Publishers Weekly* v264 no6 p46 F 6 2017

MacKay, Malcolm—Interviews

Crime and Power J. FOSTER color *Publishers Weekly* v264 no8 p65 F 20 2017

MACKAY, MARY

SHARJAH INTERNATIONAL BOOK FAIR/AMERICAN LIBRARY ASSOCIATION LIBRARY CONFERENCE NOW IN ITS THIRD YEAR color *Publishers Weekly* v263 no43 p(Sp)6 O 24 2016

MacKechnie, Johan

Justifying Slavery *History Today* v67 no5 p18 My 2017

MACKEITH, PETER

Going to the Chape *Architectural Record* v205 no1 p62 Ja 2017

MacKendrick, Karmen

The Matter of Voice: Sensual Soundings P. Jothen *Christian Century* v134 no2 p38 Ja 18 2017

Mackenzie, Andrew P.

Strong peak in Tc of Sr2RuO4 under uniaxial pressure bibl color graph *Science* v355 no6321 p1 Ja 13 2017

MacKenzie, Angus

2017 Mercedes-Benz E400 4Matic color *Motor Trend* v69 no2 p66 F 2017

2018 Volvo V90 DOING WHAT VOLVO DOES BEST color *Motor Trend* v69 no2 p64 F 2017

AXLES OF EVIL? color *Motor Trend* v69 no9 p118 S 2017

THE BENCHMARK chart color *Motor Trend* v69 no7 p94 Jl 2017

BIRTH OF A NOTION bw *Motor Trend* v69 no8 p114 Ag 2017

CHEVY CHANGES THE GAME. AGAIN chart color *Motor Trend* v69 no1 p150 Ja 2017

CONVERGENCE THEORY color *Motor Trend* v69 no7 p118 Jl 2017

Dieter Zetsche color *Motor Trend* v69 no6 p30 Je 2017

THE ESCALADE DILEMMA color *Motor Trend* v69 no11 p120 N 2017

EVERYDAY HEROES [Cover story] chart color *Motor Trend* v69 no5 p34 My 2017

GAME THEORY color *Motor Trend* v69 no3 p98 Mr 2017

GLOBAL MOTORS color *Motor Trend* v69 no4 p98 Ap 2017

HIGH RANGE color *Motor Trend* v69 no5 p102 My 2017

IDENTITY CRISIS color *Motor Trend* v69 no10 p117 O 2017

JEKYLL & HYDE chart color *Motor Trend* v69 no2 p68 F 2017

Lynk & Co 01 color *Motor Trend* v69 no2 p16 F 2017

Mark Fields out as Ford CEO color *Motor Trend* v69 no8 p24 Ag 2017

Mats Fägerhag color *Motor Trend* v69 no2 p24 F 2017

maximum mini chart color *Motor Trend* v69 no6 p92 Je 2017

Mercedes-Benz Vision Van Concept color *Motor Trend* v68 no12 p20 D 2016

Porsche 911 GT3 color *Motor Trend* v69 no5 p18 My 2017

POWER LIST cartoon *Motor Trend* v69 no1 p100 Ja 2017

PROVING A POINT color *Motor Trend* v69 no1 p177 Ja 2017

Range Rover Velar color *Motor Trend* v69 no5 p14 My 2017

RECALIBRATING THE SUPERCAR [Cover story] chart color *Motor Trend* v69 no5 p28 My 2017

THE RIGHT STUFF chart color *Motor Trend* v69 no8 p90 Ag 2017

SACRE BLEU! color *Motor Trend* v69 no2 p102 F 2017

Sergio Marchionne: CEO, FERRARI AND FCA color *Motor Trend* v69 no9 p30 S 2017

TEACHER'S PET chart color *Motor Trend* v69 no8 p80 Ag 2017

TRUE NORTH color *Motor Trend* v69 no6 p117 Je 2017

TRUTH IN ADVERTISING chart color *Motor Trend* v69 no11 p92 N 2017

THE VALUE OF NOTHING color *Motor Trend* v68 no12 p118 D 2016

WAGONS, HO! color *Motor Trend* v69 no2 p62 F 2017

MacKenzie, David

Hell or High Water *New Yorker* v92 no32 p28 O 10 2016

No. 5 HELL OR HIGH WATER C. Nashawaty color *Entertainment Weekly* no1444/1445 p53 D 16 2016

Mackenzie, Lori

To Succeed in Tech, Women Need More Visibility *Harvard Business Review Digital Articles* p2 S 13 2016

Mackenzie, Sasho

PRESS HERE! color *Golf Magazine* v59 no8 p54 Ag 2017

Mackenzie, Susan Houge

Stay on Your Smartphone! *Parks & Recreation* v51 no11 p14 N 2016

Mackenzie, Vicki

The Making of Mummy-la J. D. OLIVER color *Tricycle: The Buddhist Review* v26 no3 p86 Spr 2017

Mackenzie King Estate (Gatineau & Chelsea, Québec)

Gardens of Delight S. Coulber color *Canadian Wildlife* v23 no1 p32 Mr/Ap 2017

Mackerels

THE TASTIEST WAY TO SAVE THE PLANET chart color *GQ: Gentlemen's Quarterly* v97 no3 p122 Mr 2017

MacKerron, Gordon

Nuclear power: Serious risks *Science* v354 no6316 p1112 D 2 2016

Mackey, Charles

THOUGHTS ON BUBBLES bw color *Forbes* v200 no1 p112 Jl 27 2017

Mackey, John, 1954-

EDITOR'S LETTER T. TALIAFERRO *Texas Monthly* v45 no7 p20 Jl 2017

The Whole Foods Diet: The Lifesaving Plan for Health and Longevity *Publishers Weekly* v264 no12 p69 Mr 20 2017

WHOLE FOODS' eccentric founder changed the way Americans consume food T. FOSTER *Texas Monthly* v45 no7 p66 Jl 2017

WHOLE FOODS MARKET'S Identity Crisis C. Giammona color diag *Bloomberg Businessweek* no4519 p22 Ap 24 2017

Mackey, Katie

Find Your Focus color *Runner's World* v52 no6 p17 Jl 2017

Mackey, Nathaniel

COMEBACK CITY *Harper's Magazine* v334 no2001 p20 F 2017

Mackie, Bob

How Bob Mackie's Dazzling Designs Connected the Stars I. Biedenharn color *Entertainment Weekly* no1460/1461 p20 Ap 7-17 2017

Mackie, Douglas

HARVEST HUES M. B. EYERS color *Better Homes & Gardens* v95 no11 p34 N 2017

Mackie, Pearl

A DOCTOR WHO CHARACTER COMES OUT OF THE TAR-

DIS C. Collis color *Entertainment Weekly* no1462 p12 Ap 21 2017

EW PULLS DOUBLE PARTY DUTY AT NY COMIC CON R. Kinane color *Entertainment Weekly* no1436/1437 p18 O 21 2016

MEET THE DOCTOR'S NEW COMPANION! PEARL MACK-IE C. Collis color *Entertainment Weekly* no1446/1447 p64 D 2016/Ja 2017

Mackin, Eileen
A districtwide commitment to arts integration color il *Phi Delta Kappan* v98 no7 p29 Ap 2017

Mackin, George
Farm Team *Tennis* v52 no6 p33 N/D 2016

Mackin, Robert
A districtwide commitment to arts integration color il *Phi Delta Kappan* v98 no7 p29 Ap 2017

MACKIN, WILL
CROSSING THE RIVER NO NAME bw *New Yorker* v93 no16 p55 Je 5 2017

Mackinac Island (Mich. : Island)
ISLAND TIME: On Mackinac, clocks seem to run more slowly —that's why visitors rush there A. LYNCH color *Indianapolis Monthly* v41 no2 p37 S 2017
MICHIGAN C. Mills color map *Canadian Geographic* v135 no6 p28 D 2015

MacKinnon, Ian
Merging Their Money and Their Goals J. BENNETT CLARK color *Kiplinger's Personal Finance* v71 no5 p72 My 2017

MACKINTOSH, BARRY
Not So Fast, Golden State *American Scholar* v86 no3 p3 Summ 2017

Mackintosh, Clare
Deals R. DEAHL color *Publishers Weekly* v264 no24 p9 Je 12 2017

MACKNIK, STEPHEN L.
Misperceptions bw color *Natural History* v125 no10 p16 O 2017

Mackowiak, Matt, 1979-
HOW TED CAN GET HIS CRUZ BACK *Texas Monthly* v44 no12 p60 D 2016

Mackrell, Judith
A Mansion of Her Own: Three wealthy women and their Italian rooms J. MARTIN *New York Times Book Review* p21 O 15 2017

MacLachlan, Kyle, 1959-
Kyle MACLACHLAN B. Handy bw *Esquire* p124 My 2017
So Far, Twin Peaks' Mysteries Remain Unsatisfying D. D'Addario color *Time* v189 no21 p62 Je 5 2017
TWIN PEAKS A to Z [Cover story] D. HOLBROOK *TV Guide* v65 no21 p18 My 15 2017
Twin Peaks Cheat Sheet: Showtime's revival has (finally!) ended--here's a guide to the essential episodes J. Clark *TV Guide* v65 no39 p18 S 18 2017
Uncompromised J. Podhoretz *Weekly Standard* v22 no37 p39 Je 5 2017
AN UNRIVALED REVIVAL color *Entertainment Weekly* no1480 p42 S 1 2017
The Who's Who of Summer J. Harman bw color *Glamour* v115 no6 p29 Je 2017
YOUR GUIDE TO (ALMOST) UNDERSTANDING TWIN PEAKS J. Jensen and D. Franich color *Entertainment Weekly* no1466 p32 My 19 2017

MacLachlan, Matthew
Why Leadership Training Fails—and What to Do About It: Interaction *Harvard Business Review* v94 no12 p19 D 2016

MacLachlan, Ron P.
Wild emmer genome architecture and diversity elucidate wheat evolution and domestication color *Science* v357 no6346 p93 Jl 7 2017

MacLaine, Shirley, 1934-
A Heavenly Christmas A. D'Arminio *TV Guide* v64 no48 p37 N 21 2016

MacLauchlan, Susan
Clonal hematopoiesis associated with TET2 deficiency accelerates atherosclerosis development in mice bibl diag *Science* v355 no6327 p842 F 24 2017

MacLaughlin, Nina
In Your Hands bw *Men's Health* v32 no2 p(Sp)30 Mr 2017

MacLean, Aaron
Ron Chernow *Humanities* v37 no4 p1 Fall 2016

Maclean, Alison
Class Act N. Rapold color *Film Comment* v53 no1 p8 Ja/F 2017

MacLean, Catherine H.
Health Care Providers Need a Value Management Office *Harvard Business Review Digital Articles* p2 D 2 2015

MACLEAN, EMILY SCHULTHEIS
Hillingdon Street Blues *Weekly Standard* v22 no5 p5 O 10 2016

MacLean, Nancy
The Great James Buchanan Conspiracy B. Doherty color *Reason* v49 no5 p66 O 2017
Minority Rule: How the economist James McGill Buchanan laid out the game plan for the radical right H. BOUSHEY *New York Times Book Review* p19 Ag 20 2017
MONT PELERIN IN VIRGINIA K. PHILLIPS-FEIN bw *Nation* v305 no7 p27 S 25 2017
Rules for Radicals A. WOLFE color il *New Republic* v248 no10 p46 O 2017

Maclean's (Periodical)
Measuring excellence M. DWYER color *Maclean's* v130 no10 p108 N 2017

Maclean's (Periodical)—History
MACLEAN'S ON CANADA bw color *Maclean's* v130 no6 p85 Jl 2017

MacLeod, Ainslie
Job openings, hires, and separations return to prerecession levels in 2015 bibl chart color graph *Monthly Labor Review* p1 S 2016

MacLEOD, GILLIAN
GIFTS that UPLIFT! cartoon *O, The Oprah Magazine* p148 D 2016

Macleod Ale Brewing Co.
HOPS OVER THE HILL J. M. VERIVE *Los Angeles Magazine* p46 My 2017

Maclin, Amy
I Feel Bad About Paula Deen *O, The Oprah Magazine* p145 My 2017
No Place Like Home M. Zucca bw cartoon color *O, The Oprah Magazine* p162 D 2016

Mac Low, Jackson
THE MUSIC OF CHANCE B. Brown color *Art in America* v105 no1 p54 Ja 2017

MacMahon, Sarah Jane
Sarah Jane McMahon A. McLellan color *New Orleans Magazine* v51 no7 p28 My 2017

Macmillan, Alexander
Site-specific phosphorylation of tau inhibits amyloid-β toxicity in Alzheimer's mice bibl graph *Science* v354 no6314 p904 N 18 2016

MacMillan, Amanda
6 More Reasons to Get Up and Move color *Time* v190 no4 p40 Jl 24 2017
8 Mistakes That Mess with Your Eyes color *Health* v31 no3 p66 Ap 2017
COFFEE PERKS color *Runner's World* v52 no5 p29 Je 2017
A Dumpling Through the Digestive Tract img *New York* v49 no25 p108 D 12 2016
EAT, DRINK, AND BE SPEEDY color *Runner's World* v52 no9 p16 O 2017
New Ways to Become Happier—and Healthier color *Time* v190 no13 p30 O 2 2017
TRAINING TABLE [Cover story] bw color *Runner's World* v51 no10 p52 N 2016
What's That Cough? color *Health* v30 no9 p86 N 2016

MacMillan, David W. C.
Photosensitized, energy transfer-mediated organometallic catalysis through electronically excited nickel(II) bibl diag graph *Science* v355 no6323 p380 Ja 27 2017

MacMillan, Duncan
Every Brilliant Thing *New York* v49 no25 p143 D 12 2016

Macmillan, Gilly
Odd Child Out *Publishers Weekly* v264 no35 p103 Ag 28 2017

MACMILLAN, IAN C.
HOW TO GET ECOSYSTEM BUY-IN chart img *Harvard Business Review* v95 no2 p102 Mr/Ap 2017

MacMillan, Kyle

PROPELLER GROUP *Art in America* v104 no9 p157 O 2016

WOLF VOSTELL bw color *Art in America* v105 no5 p133 My 2017

ZAK PREKOP cartoon *Art in America* v104 no11 p124 D 2016

ZHANG PEILI color *Art in America* v105 no8 p125 S 2017

MACMILLAN, MARGARET

Neither War Nor Peace *New York Times Book Review* p16 D 11 2016

MACMILLAN, THOMAS

The Urbanist: The Teens of Havana img *New York* v49 no21 p30 O 17 2016

MacNair, Erin

Thin Crust cartoon *Walrus* v14 no2 p48 Mr 2017

Thin Crust E. MACNAIR cartoon *Walrus* v14 no2 p48 Mr 2017

MacNeal, David

Bugged N. F. Quinn color *Science* v356 no6342 p1007 Je 9 2017

Bugged: The Insects Who Rule the World and the People Obsessed with Them A. Gawrylewski color *Scientific American* v317 no1 p72 Jl 2017

Macnicol, Glynnis

PAT McGRATH'S Golden Touch color *InStyle* v24 no2 p110 F 2017

MacNicol, L. Glen

Hump Days *MHQ: Quarterly Journal of Military History* v29 no3 p10 Spr 2017

Macnie, Jim

All These Hands color *Downbeat* v84 no3 p53 Mr 2017

The Hot Box chart *Downbeat* v84 no2 p71 F 2017

The Hot Box chart *Downbeat* v84 no5 p51 My 2017

The Hot Box chart *Downbeat* v84 no7 p49 Jl 2017

Music Inspired By The Poetry Of Carl Sandburg color *Downbeat* v84 no8 p67 Ag 2017

Macomber, Debbie, 1948-

Licensing Expo 2017 Highlights Synergies Between Books and Tie-in Products K. Raugust color *Publishers Weekly* v264 no24 p20 Je 12 2017

Macomber, John D.

The 4 Types of Cities and How to Prepare Them for the Future *Harvard Business Review Digital Articles* p2 Ja 18 2016

The Future of Cities Depends on Innovative Financing *Harvard Business Review Digital Articles* p2 Ja 11 2016

Macomber, John—Interviews

The Right Way to Rebuild America's Infrastructure E. Harrell *Harvard Business Review Digital Articles* p2 D 16 2016

Macor, Alison

Rewrite Man: The Life and Career of Screenwriter Warren Skaaren *Publishers Weekly* v264 no4 p69 Ja 23 2017

Macosko, Christopher W.

Combining polyethylene and polypropylene: Enhanced performance with PE/iPP multiblock polymers bibl chart graph *Science* v355 no6327 p814 F 24 2017

MacPherson, Anna

What does it take to sustain a productive partnership in education? color *Phi Delta Kappan* v99 no1 p15 S 2017

Macpherson, Elle, 1964-

So What Do You Do, ELLE MACPHERSON? color *InStyle* v24 no3 p284 Mr 2017

MacPherson, Laura

Click chemistry enables preclinical evaluation of targeted epigenetic therapies diag *Science* v356 no6345 p1397 Je 30 2017

MacPherson, Skye

Priming HIV-1 broadly neutralizing antibody precursors in human Ig loci transgenic mice bibl graph *Science* v353 no6307 p1557 S 30 2016

MacPhun Software LLC

LUMINAR: A SERIOUS CHALLENGER TO THE REIGNING PRO APPS FOR PHOTO EDITING MASTERY J. DOVE color *Macworld - Digital Edition* p25 F 2017

Macramé—Patterns

READY or KNOT *Better Homes & Gardens* v95 no1 p14 Ja 2017

Macri, Mauricio, 1959-

Argentina's Mauricio Macri on the Challenge of Change I. Bremmer color *Time* v188 no18 p12 O 31 2016

MacroAir (Company)

CREATIVELY COOL J. von Geldern color *Horse & Rider* v56 no6 p57 Je 2017

MacRobert, Alan

A Deep Penumbral Lunar Eclipse *Sky & Telescope* v133 no2 p48 F 2017

The Drama-Ridden Couple of R Aquarii *Sky & Telescope* v134 no4 p48 O 2017

The Fast Pulse of the RR Lyraes *Sky & Telescope* v133 no6 p48 Je 2017

Help Verify a Giant Ringed Exoplanet: For about 25 days in September, its ring system should cross an easily watched star *Sky & Telescope* v134 no3 p48 S 2017

Jupiter Enters the Evening Sky *Sky & Telescope* v133 no4 p48 Ap 2017

Pluto in 2017: Don't look now, but a proposed sizing scheme would make it a planet again *Sky & Telescope* v134 no1 p48 Jl 2017

The Poleward Trek of Comet ASASSN1 color *Sky & Telescope* v134 no5 p48 N 2017

RW Tauri, an Action-Packed Eclipser *Sky & Telescope* v133 no1 p48 Ja 2017

Saturn Has a Southern Apparition *Sky & Telescope* v133 no5 p48 My 2017

The Solar Eclipse for the Rest of Us bw color *Sky & Telescope* v134 no2 p48 Ag 2017

To Build A Really Loud Hailer *Sky & Telescope* v134 no3 p40 S 2017

Volcanic Skies color *Sky & Telescope* v134 no2 p73 Ag 2017

Macrocyclic compounds

Macrocyclic bis-thioureas catalyze stereospecific glycosylation reactions Yongho Park, K. C. Harper et al bibl diag *Science* v355 no6321 p1 Ja 13 2017

Macroeconomics

CHAPTER 3 THE GLOBAL MACROECONOMIC SITUATION *Economic Indicators* p119 O 2016

THE GLOBAL MACROECONOMIC SITUATION *Economic Indicators* p119 S 2016

Macromolecular synthesis

Self-assembly of genetically encoded DNA-protein hybrid nanoscale shapes F. Praetorius and H. Dietz *Science* v355 no6331 p1283 Mr 24 2017

Macron, Emmanuel, 1977-

Après le Champagne, More Campaign G. Viscusi, H. Fouquet et al color graph *Bloomberg Businessweek* no4522 p34 My 15 2017

Brave New Europe M. Leonard color *New York Review of Books* v64 no17 p46 N 9 2017

Does Macron Hold the Key to Merkel's Heart? C. Matlack and M. Deen color *Bloomberg Businessweek* no4515 p26 Mr 20 2017

A FINE BROMANCE J. WOLCOTT color *Vanity Fair* v59 no9 p148 S 2017

For the Record color *Time* v189 no23 p8 Je 19 2017

France Picks a Novice C. CALDWELL color *Weekly Standard* v22 no35 p23 My 22 2017

France's Golden Boy Loses His Luster T. John color *Time* v190 no9 p10 S 4 2017

France's Youngest Leader Since Napoleon Takes the Stage V. Walt color *Time* v189 no19 p9 My 22 2017

French Adoption G. SCHMITT and R. BURGESS color *Weekly Standard* v22 no44 p19 Jl 31 2017

Give This Man A Party M. Champion, H. Fouquet et al color *Bloomberg Businessweek* no4520 p27 My 1 2017

I'LL DEFEND FRANCE. I'LL DEFEND EUROPE E. FRÉDÉRIC *Vital Speeches of the Day* v83 no7 p201 Jl 2017

An Insider's Outsider C. Caldwell color *Weekly Standard* v22 no33 p8 My 8 2017

Invite annoys French scientists *Science* v356 no6343 p1104 Je 16 2017

Macron Economics G. Smith color *Fortune* v175 no7 p13 Je 1 2017

Macron, Le Terminator MOUTET color *Weekly Standard* v22 no39 p18 Je 19 2017

MACRON ON THE MARCH IN FRANCE A. GOLDHAMMER color *Nation* v305 no2 p22 Jl 17 2017

Macron's Opportunity To Change France *Bloomberg Businessweek* no4527 p18 Je 19 2017

Macron's Victory Does Not Mean Liberalism Is Safe B. Emmott *NPQ: New Perspectives Quarterly* v34 no3 p43 Jl 2017

Macron vs. The Unions C. Matlack and G. Viscusi graph *Bloom-*

berg Businessweek no4529 p30 Jl 3 2017

Movers C. Winter color graph *Bloomberg Businessweek* no4522 p13 My 15 2017

The World Won't Ignore Chechnya's Purge of Gay Men T. John color *Time* v189 no22 p9 Je 12 2017

YOUTH REVOLT V. Walt, A. Vandermey et al color *Fortune* v176 no3 p64 S 1 2017

Macrophages

Immune cells give the heart a boost E. S. EATON color *Science News* v191 no10 p8 My 27 2017

Inflammation by way of macrophage metabolism A. M. Kabat and E. J. Pearce diag *Science* v356 no6337 p488 My 5 2017

IN SCIENCE JOURNALS color *Science* v355 no6331 p1277 Mr 24 2017

Local amplifiers of IL-4Rα-mediated macrophage activation promote repair in lung and liver C. M. Minutti, L. H. Jackson-Jones et al diag *Science* v356 no6342 p1076 Je 9 2017

Macrophage, a long-distance middleman M. Guilliams bibl color *Science* v355 no6331 p1258 Mr 24 2017

Macrophage function in tissue repair and remodeling requires IL-4 or IL-13 with apoptotic cells L. Bosurgi, Y. Grace Cao et al diag *Science* v356 no6342 p1072 Je 9 2017

A macrophage relay for long-distance signaling during postembryonic tissue remodeling D. Seok Eom and D. M. Parichy bibl color graph *Science* v355 no6331 p1317 Mr 24 2017

Specific repair by discerning macrophages T. Bouchery and N. L. Harris diag *Science* v356 no6342 p1014 Je 9 2017

Macsai, Dan

The Best 25 Inventions of 2016 color *Time* v188 no22-23 p43 N/D 2016

MACSWEENEY, EVE

Feast Your Eyes color *Vogue* v207 no11 p66 N 2017

Garden District color *Vogue* v207 no11 p202 N 2017

PHOEBE PHILO color *Vogue* v207 no3 p412 Mr 2017

MacVeagh, Ted

The Blue Marauders *Publishers Weekly* v264 no26 p180 Je 26 2017

MACVEAN, MARY

A Plot To Feed The Homeless *Los Angeles Magazine* p30 D 2016

Macvie, Meagan

The Ocean in My Ears *Publishers Weekly* v264 no40 p141 O 2 2017

MACWELCH, TIM

SURVIVE ANYWHERE bw cartoon color diag *Outdoor Life* v224 no3 p33 Ap 2017

Macy, Beth

THE AMAZING STORY OF EKO AND IKO B. MACY *Washingtonian Magazine* v52 no1 p80 O 2016

Sideshow Glances E. E. BAPTIST *New York Times Book Review* p13 O 23 2016

Macy, Dayna

EAT LIKE A YOGI color *Yoga Journal* p100 2017 Special Issue

EMBRACE YOUR NATURAL BEAUTY color *Yoga Journal* no294 p27 S 2017

Macy, Meg

Bearly Departed: A Teddy Bear Mystery color *Publishers Weekly* v264 no16 p48 Ap 17 2017

Macy, William H., 1950-

Out & About *TV Guide* v65 no23 p4 My 29 2017

Shameless M. Snetiker, A. Bacle et al color *Entertainment Weekly* no1482/1483 p30 S 22 2017

Shameless *TV Guide* p45 D 5 2016

Macy's Inc.

ABOVE & BEYOND cartoon *New Yorker* v93 no6 p12 Mr 27 2017

TRUMP'S STOCK SCORECARD color *Fortune* v175 no3 p18 Mr 1 2017

What Hudson's Bay Likes About Macy's L. Rupp graph *Bloomberg Businessweek* no4511 p21 F 13 2017

Macys.com Inc.

Cloud Nine color *O, The Oprah Magazine* p111 D 2016

SCENT OF STYLE M. Deem color *O, The Oprah Magazine* p67 S 2017

Mad Architects (Company)

snapshot A. Klimoski *Architectural Record* v205 no10 p172 O 2017

Mad Men (TV program)

Ad Nauseam M. Rubino *Indianapolis Monthly* p12 F 2017

I AM HAMM color *InStyle* v24 no7 p118 Jl 2017

Madagascar—Description & travel

MADAGASCAR S. ROBERTS bw color *Conde Nast Traveler* v52 no4 p74 Ap 2017

Madalinski, Mathias

Root diffusion barrier control by a vasculature-derived peptide binding to the SGN3 receptor color *Science* v355 no6322 p280 Ja 20 2017

Madam Secretary (TV program)

DOMESTIC AFFAIRS: Madam Secretary's Elizabeth McCord handles global crises on a daily basis. So challenges at home must be a cakewalk. Right? M. LOGAN *TV Guide* v65 no41 p26 O 2 2017

Madam Secretary A. Bacle, D. Coggan et al color *Entertainment Weekly* no1482/1483 p39 S 22 2017

Madam Secretary M. Logan *TV Guide* v65 no19 p27 My 1 2017

Who runs the world? P. H. Nettleton color *U.S. Catholic* v82 no6 p38 Je 2017

Madama Butterfly (Theatrical production)

Madama Butterfly S. Hastings *Opera News* v81 no9 p41 Mr 2017

ROAD SHOW: Bryan Hymel in New Orleans M. R. MERCADO *Opera News* v81 no6 p16 D 2016

Sherry Lansing color *Vanity Fair* p153 Hollywood 2017 Supplement

Madani, Tala—Exhibitions

AROUND BOSTON S. ADAMS cartoon color *ARTnews* v115 no3 p147 Fall 2016

Madannavar, Harsha

To Survive, Health Care Data Providers Need to Stop Selling Data *Harvard Business Review Digital Articles* p2 Je 14 2017

Madaras, Larry

From Jonathan Edwards to Billy Graham *America* v217 no3 p46 Ag 7 2017

Madda, Mary Jo

Eliminating Grade Levels *Education Digest* v83 no2 p61 O 2017

Madden, Beezie

Listen to Your Horse S. Oliynyk *Practical Horseman* v45 no4 p10 Ap 2017

Madden, Deanna

The World Beyond *Publishers Weekly* v264 no38 p49 S 18 2017

Madden, Debbie

4 Tips for Launching Minimum Viable Products Inside Big Companies *Harvard Business Review Digital Articles* p2 S 30 2015

Your Agile Project Needs a Budget, Not an Estimate *Harvard Business Review Digital Articles* p2 D 29 2014

Madden, Kevin A.

HACKER CRACK-UP color *Wired* v25 no6 p10 Je 2017

Madden, Pete

Bank On Him color *Golf Magazine* v59 no3 p25 Mr 2017

FIRST GOLFER color *Sports Illustrated* v127 no4 p48 Ag 7 2017

Hats Off to Ollie color *Golf Magazine* v59 no5 p27 My 2017

THE HEARTBREAK KID color *Golf Magazine* v58 no12 p49 D 2016

"I Need to Win" color *Golf Magazine* v59 no4 p29 Ap 2017

Spanish Class color *Golf Magazine* v59 no2 p25 F 2017

Madden, Thomas F.

A Megacity Old and New C. BERLINSKI color *National Review* v68 no24 p38 D 31 2016

Maddow, Rachel, 1973-

THE STORYTELLER J. MALCOLM bw cartoon *New Yorker* v93 no31 p38 O 9 2017

WINNING! O. Nuzzi color *Glamour* v115 no9 p204 S 2017

Maddow, Rachel, 1973-—Interviews

Rachel After Dark S. Smith color *Entertainment Weekly* no1435 p32 O 14 2016

THE ROLLING STONE INTERVIEW: Rachel Maddow [Cover story] J. REITMAN bw color *Rolling Stone* no1290 p34 Je 29 2017

Maddox, Marjorie

Cracks color *U.S. Catholic* v82 no8 p11 Ag 2017

Made-for-TV movies—Reviews

REAGAN REVISITED I. RUDOLPH color *TV Guide* v64 no42 p26 O 10 2016

Made Goods (Company)

Roped In H. BROWN color *House Beautiful* v159 no3 p38 Ap 2017

Made in America (Music)
BOBBY WATSON G. Himes color *Downbeat* v84 no7 p34 Jl 2017

Made in China (Poem)
MADE IN CHINA K. COX *Humanist* v77 no4 p35 Jl/Ag 2017

MADER, JACKIE
DOE Removes Requirements Around Selectivity to Diversify the Teaching Force cartoon *Education Digest* v82 no6 p30 F 2017

Madera Latino (Music)
The Hot Box chart *Downbeat* v84 no1 p67 Ja 2017
Madera Latino P. de Barros color *Downbeat* v84 no1 p65 Ja 2017
NIGHT LIFE *New Yorker* v92 no43 p11 Ja 2 2017

MADERO, ELI
2017 SXS/UTV BUYER'S GUIDE [Cover story] color *Dirt Sports + Off-Road* v51 no1 p30 Ja 2017

Madeson, Frances
Frack Attack color *Progressive* p48 D 2016/Ja 2017
'It's Indian Time!' color *Progressive* v81 no10 p19 N 2016

Made Thing Considers Itself, The (Poem)
The Made Thing Considers Itself D. BEACHY-QUICK *Nation* v305 no6 p31 S 11 2017

Madey, John Michael Julius
John Michael Julius Madey Pui Lam, V. Shiltsev et al *Physics Today* v70 no1 p70 Ja 2017

Madhvapathy, Surabhi R.
MoS2 transistors with 1-nanometer gate lengths bibl color graph *Science* v354 no6308 p99 O 7 2016

Madigan, Daniel J.
East not least for Pacific bluefin tuna color diag *Science* v357 no6349 p356 Jl 28 2017

Madigan, Michael
LAST MADIGAN STANDING E. McCLELLAND color *Chicago* v66 no11 p19 N 2017

Madill, Rebecca
Making Math Count More for Young Latinos bw *Education Digest* v83 no1 p8 S 2017

Madin, Kate
Can Animals Live Without Oxygen? *Oceanus* v52 no1 p4 Summ 2016
Communicating Under Sea Ice: ENGINEERS USE OCEAN CHANNEL TO RELAY SOUND EFFICIENTLY *Oceanus* v52 no2 p48 Spr 2017
A Drastic Decline of River Herring: TINY STONES IN FISH HOLD CLUES TO HELP RESTORE POPULATIONS *Oceanus* v52 no2 p2 Spr 2017
Eavesdropping on Whales off New York City: BUOY DETECTS WHALES AND ALERTS SHIPS TO SLOW DOWN *Oceanus* v52 no2 p14 Spr 2017
New Device Reveals What Ocean Microbes Do: INSTRUMENT MAY HELP MONITOR SEWAGE TREATMENT PLANTS *Oceanus* v52 no2 p20 Spr 2017
A New Tsunami Warning System *Oceanus* v52 no2 p53 Spr 2017
Not Just Another Lovely Summer Day on the Water *Oceanus* v52 no1 p30 Summ 2016
PlankZooka & SUPR-REMUS *Oceanus* v52 no1 p22 Summ 2016

Madisch, Ijad
The Pace of Scientific Research Is Picking Up *Harvard Business Review Digital Articles* p2 Ag 3 2015

Madison (Ind.)
DESTINATION MADISON ANTIQUES color *Indianapolis Monthly* v42 no2 p68 O 2017

Madison, Deborah
In My Kitchen: A Collection of New and Favorite Vegetarian Recipes color *Publishers Weekly* v263 no47 p101 N 21 2016

Madison, James, 1751-1836
Giving Madison His Due R. BURGESS color *Weekly Standard* v22 no30 p14 Ap 10 2017
Misquoting Madison R. R. Reilly *Claremont Review of Books* v17 no3 p45 Summ 2017
THOUGHTS ON Property *Forbes* v199 no5 p124 My 16 2017
"WHERE ARE MY PEOPLE?" At Montpelier, descendants of James Madison's slaves are reviving their ancestors' history G WEBER *Washingtonian Magazine* v52 no12 p19 S 2017

Madison Drug Co.

MADISON DRUG CO. MADISON 59 MILES EAST OF ATLANTA J. GREEN *Atlanta* v56 no10 p144 F 2017

Madison River Valley (Wyo. & Mont.)
out alive: mauled by a grizzly. twice C. Webber color diag *Backpacker* p35 Je 2017

Madison Square Garden (New York, N.Y.)
GARDEN PARTY L. J. Wertheim color *Sports Illustrated* v125 no17 p102 N 21 2016 Double Issue

Madl, Tobias
Patchy proteins form a perfect lens color *Science* v357 no6351 p546 Ag 11 2017

Madnick, Stuart
Preparing for the Cyberattack That Will Knock Out U.S. Power Grids *Harvard Business Review Digital Articles* p2 My 10 2017

Madonna, 1958-
Madonna: Rebel Heart Tour *TV Guide* p43 D 5 2016
SEX AGE MADONNA S. WELLER and J. NEWMAN cartoon color *AARP: The Magazine* v60 no2A p60 F/Mr 2017
SPRING REVIVAL bw *Harper's Bazaar* no3650 p147 F 2017

Madonna, 1958—Interviews
MADONNA R. Gay bw *Harper's Bazaar* no3650 p148 F 2017
My Obsessions J. Larkworthy color *InStyle* v24 no10 p226 O 2017

Madrick, Jeff
America: The Forgotten Poor bw *New York Review of Books* v64 no11 p49 Je 22 2017
BY THE SEAT OF HIS PANTS bw *Nation* v303 no22 p31 N 28 2016

Madrid (Spain)
VIVA PRIDE! Celebrate LGBT Life at World Pride in Gay Madrid J. ANDERSON-MINSHALL color *Advocate* no1091 p116 Je/Jl 2017

Madrid (Spain)—Description & travel
MADRID UNCLASSIFIED E. ANDERSEN color *Conde Nast Traveler* v51 no10 p144 N 2016
MASTERS OF CEREMONY P. Guzmán color *Conde Nast Traveler* v51 no10 p138 N 2016

MADSEN, DEANE
Triple Play *Architectural Record* v205 no10 p114 O 2017

Madsen, Ole Jacob
Social norms as solutions bibl color *Science* v354 no6308 p42 O 7 2016

Maduro, Nicolás, 1962-
Distorted News from Venezuela R. Erlich color *Progressive* v81 no7 p48 O/N 2017
Down And Almost Out in Latin America T. Padgett color *Bloomberg Businessweek* no4520 p10 My 1 2017
Food for Thought M. Nandini Mitra *Earth Island Journal* v32 no3 p2 Aut 2017
Lightbox color *Time* v189 no23 p16 Je 19 2017
Lightbox I. Grillo and J. Benezra color *Time* v190 no7 p14 Ag 21 2017
PHOTO color *Reason* v49 no6 p9 N 2017
Venezuela Abandons Any Claim to Democracy *Bloomberg Businessweek* no4533 p10 Ag 7 2017
Venezuela Nears a Tipping Point, and a Violent Endgame I. Bremmer color *Time* v189 no18 p14 My 15 2017

Madwar, Samia
Shape Shifters color *Walrus* v14 no6 p75 Jl/Ag 2017

Mady, Edward
Getting an Intricate Operation Back in Sync *Harvard Business Review Digital Articles* p2 My 20 2016
How Luxury Brands Can Motivate Service Employees *Harvard Business Review Digital Articles* p2 N 2 2015
How Smart Business Travelers Get More from Hotels *Harvard Business Review Digital Articles* p2 Ja 7 2016

Maehara, Kazumitsu
Crystal structure of the overlapping dinucleosome composed of hexasome and octasome graph *Science* v356 no6334 p205 Ap 14 2017

Maekawa, Takaki
Caught in the jump color *Science* v357 no6346 p31 Jl 7 2017

Maerz, Melissa
Where the Women Were bw color *Glamour* no8 p142 Ag 2017

MAES, JOACHIM
National Ecosystem Assessments in Europe: A Review chart *BioScience* v66 no10 p813 O 1 2016

MAES, SYBRYN L.
Combining Biodiversity Resurveys across Regions to Advance Global Change Research *BioScience* v67 no1 p73 Ja 2017

Maestro, Vittorio
Long Ago and Far Away color *Natural History* v125 no9 p2 S 2017

Maeve, Stella
The Magicians J. Jensen color *Entertainment Weekly* no1450 p52 Ja 27 2017

Mafessoni, Fabrizio
Neandertal and Denisovan DNA from Pleistocene sediments bw color *Science* v356 no6338 p605 My 12 2017

Mafi, Tahereh
DOUBLE VISION A. Breznican color *Entertainment Weekly* no1434 p60 O 7 2016

Mafic rocks
See also
Peridotite
Experimental constraints on the damp peridotite solidus and oceanic mantle potential temperature E. Sarafian, G. A. Gaetani et al bibl diag *Science* v355 no6328 p942 Mr 3 2017

Mag Bay Yachts Inc.
EXPOSURE D. j. Harding color *Power & Motoryacht* v32 no11 p70 N 2016
MEET BARRETT HOWARTH *Sea Magazine* v108 no9 pCA-5 S 2016

Magaña, Alex
More time for learning color *Phi Delta Kappan* v98 no4 p26 D 2016/Ja 2017

Magargle, Nancy
A Time to Live, a Time to Die *Publishers Weekly* v264 no35 p77d Ag 28 2017

Magariel, Daniel
Papa Don't Preach: Two sons watch as their post-divorce father drifts into addiction A. RUIZ-CAMACHO color *New York Times Book Review* p10 Ap 23 2017

MAGARY, DREW
Do Real Men Emoji? color *GQ: Gentlemen's Quarterly* v97 no5 p66 My 2017
The Fifty Greatest Living Athletes bw color *GQ: Gentlemen's Quarterly* v97 no11 p96 N 2017
I GOT YOU, BABE bw color *GQ: Gentlemen's Quarterly* v97 no6 p96 Je 2017
OFF the BEATEN PATH color *GQ: Gentlemen's Quarterly* v97 no9 p154 S 2017
The Ten Who'll Be Next color *GQ: Gentlemen's Quarterly* v97 no11 p114 N 2017
Trump TV color *GQ: Gentlemen's Quarterly* v86 no11 p138 N 2016

Magasinski, Alexandre
Transformation of bulk alloys to oxide nanowires bibl color graph *Science* v355 no6322 p267 Ja 20 2017

Magazine advertising
See also
Special advertising sections
A NOTE FROM OUR PUBLISHER S. Katz *Mother Jones* v42 no6 p16 N/D 2017
Storytelling Adapts To Media's New Era L. D'VORKIN *Forbes* v199 no4 p10 Ap 25 2017
TRUMP: THE ART OF THE SPIEL D. ALEXANDER bw color *Forbes* v200 no3 p98 S 28 2017

Magazine cover design
ARTIFICIAL INTELLIGENCE, FOR REAL; YOU'VE BEEN TOLD IT WILL TRANSFORM EVERYTHING. YOU'VE BEEN TOLD YOU NEED TO INVEST IN IT. BUT YOU HAVEN'T BEEN TOLD HOW. START HERE E. BRYNJOLFSSON and A. MCAFEE *Harvard Business Review Digital Articles* p1 Jl 1 2017

Magazine covers
COVERING OURSELVES D. WILLEY color *Runner's World* v51 no10 p14 N 2016
FAKE NEWSSTAND! M. SOLOMON color *Forbes* v200 no3 p92 S 28 2017
THE GREAT KATE color *Harper's Bazaar* no3649 p120 D 2016/Ja 2017
IL BRUTO color *MHQ: Quarterly Journal of Military History*

v30 no1 p96 Aut 2017
Leading Off color *Sports Illustrated* v125 no21 p12 D 26 2016
Seeing Is Believing N. Gibbs color *Time* v190 no10/11 p4 S 18 2017
Self-Portrait / Stump color *Art in America* v104 no10 pCover N 2016
That Thing with Feathers M. JANNOT *Audubon* v118 no6 p7 Wint 2016
Yes, Queen! color *Glamour* v114 no7 p28 Jl 2016

Magazine covers—History—20th century
Chuck Redux T. Keith color *Sports Illustrated* v126 no13 p22 My 8 2017
February 1, 1935: America's Secret Strength A. BROWN color *Forbes* v198 no7 p34 N 29 2016

Magazine design
See also
Periodicals—Format
DEAR ROPER B. Welch *Spin to Win Rodeo* v20 no10 p14 D 2016

Magazine Luiza (Company)
The Lady Teaching Brazilians How to Shop Online F. Moura and P. Sambo *Bloomberg Businessweek* no4536 p21 S.4 2017

Magazine photography
Adventure Starts Here! N. McGOVERN color *O, The Oprah Magazine* p12 Je 2017

Magdoff, Fred
TALKIN' 'BOUT AN ECOLOGICAL REVOLUTION *In These Times* v41 no8 p38 Ag 2017

Magee, Brian A.
Cassini finds molecular hydrogen in the Enceladus plume: Evidence for hydrothermal processes chart graph *Science* v356 no6334 p155 Ap 14 2017

Magee, Jeffrey C.
Behavioral time scale synaptic plasticity underlies CA1 place fields diag *Science* v357 no6355 p1033 S 8 2017

Magellan (Spacecraft)
More Evidence for Volcanoes on Venus J. K. BEATTY *Sky & Telescope* v133 no2 p11 F 2017

Magellanic clouds
See also
Large magellanic cloud
GALLERY *Sky & Telescope* v134 no4 p72 O 2017
Magnetic Bridge Found Between Magellanic Clouds S. Ash color *Sky & Telescope* v134 no2 p13 Ag 2017
METEORITE ORIGINS P. Mane, A. Klesman et al color *Astronomy* v45 no11 p44 N 2017

Magenheim, Aaron—Interviews
MATCH MAKING L. Bedord *Successful Farming* v115 no2 p10 F 2017

Magén Pardo, Jaime
MAGÉN ARCHITECTS D. Cohn bw color *Architectural Record* v204 no12 p46 D 2016

MAGERL, ELLA
#Climbing Training color *Climbing* no352 p9 Ap 2017

Maggard, Kaylin
WALKIN' ON SUNSHINE O. Manno color *Dance Spirit* v21 no8 p54 O 2017

Maggioni, Paul
HEARTS AND MINDS IN MINDANAO [Cover story] bw color map *Military History* v34 no4 p48 N 2017

Maggiore, Elizabeth
One church? *U.S. Catholic* v82 no7 p5 Jl 2017

Maggor, Noam
THE CONTINENTAL REVOLUTION E. FONER color *Nation* v304 no18 p24 Je 19 2017

Magi
Reflections on the lectionary M. Earley *Christian Century* v133 no25 p21 D 7 2016
To Show the Way M. R. SIMONE *America* v216 no1 p42 Ja 2 2017

Magic
Jules Fisher's Work with Derek DelGaudio *Stage Directions* v30 no8 p19 Ag 2017
Magic Show T. Groneberg bw *American Cowboy* v23 no6 p21 Ap/My 2017
Psychic Roundup: 'Psychics' Convicted B. RADFORD *Skeptical Inquirer* v41 no5 p9 S/O 2017

Technology as Magic D. Pogue color *Scientific American* v317 no2 p26 Ag 2017

Magic Leap Inc.
CONVERSATION A. WILSON color graph *Forbes* v198 no8 p36 D 20 2016

Magic Leap Inc.—Finance
DISRUPTION MACHINE [Cover story] D. M. EWALT color *Forbes* v198 no7 p76 N 29 2016

Magic shows
ABOVE & BEYOND cartoon *New Yorker* v92 no40 p18 D 5 2016
TOP PICKS F. Esker bw color *New Orleans Magazine* v51 no9 p26 Jl 2017

Magic tricks
Be Your Own Magician B. Doherty img *New York* v49 no19 p86 S 19 2016

Magic Flute, The (Theatrical production)
Operapedia: The Magic Flute W. A. MOZART *Opera News* v81 no7 p12 Ja 2017

Magicians
DAVID COPPERFIELD J. APATOW *Interview* v47 no1 p84 F 2017

Magicians, The (TV program)
The Magicians J. Jensen color *Entertainment Weekly* no1450 p52 Ja 27 2017

Magic Negro, The (Theatrical production)
"THE MAGIC NEGRO" G. GODFREY *Atlanta* v56 no11 p40 Mr 2017

Magids, Scott
What Separates the Best Customers from the Merely Satisfied *Harvard Business Review Digital Articles* p2 D 3 2015

Magie, Elizabeth
Monopoly's Feminist History J. Lance bw color *Glamour* v115 no5 p20 My 2017

Maglente, Shanon
Hope for Moms Who Need it Most color *Parents* v92 no7 p31 Jl 2017

MAGLIOZZI, RAY
What I Learned AT MY Summer Job cartoon *Popular Mechanics* p64 Je 2017

Magloire, Miro
Dancing in Space C. Atamian color *Weekly Standard* v22 no29 p37 Ap 3 2017

Magmas
Magma under volcanoes is largely solid M. TEMMING *Science News* v191 no13 p11 Jl 8 2017
Mars may feature a stagnant interior T. SUMNER color *Science News* v191 no4 p12 Mr 4 2017
Rapid cooling and cold storage in a silicic magma reservoir recorded in individual crystals A. E. Rubin, K. M. Cooper et al color diag graph *Science* v356 no6343 p1154 Je 16 2017

Magmatism
Vertically extensive and unstable magmatic systems: A unified view of igneous processes K. V. Cashman, R. S. J. Sparks et al color *Science* v355 no6331 p1280 Mr 24 2017

Magnanimity
The Magnanimity of the Gospel K. Alys Robinson color *America* v217 no5 p54 S 4 2017

Magnes, W.
Structure, force balance, and topology of Earth's magnetopause diag graph *Science* v356 no6341 p960 Je 1 2017

Magnesium
3 nutrients your body craves J. R. Marquez color *Health* v31 no8 p63 O 2017
MAGNESIUM: SUPERSTAR SUPPLEMENT V. Tweed color *Amazing Wellness* v9 no6 p26 EarlyWint 2017

Magnesium metabolism
Magnesium: Superstar Rising V. TWEED chart color diag *Better Nutrition* v79 no4 p24 Ap 2017

Magnesium—Physiological effect
Eat These, Lower Blood Pressure color *Prevention* v68 no11 p15 N 2016

Magness, Jodi
AIA Welcomes New President, Officers, and Trustees at Annual Meeting in Toronto color *Archaeology* v70 no2 p65 Mr/Ap 2017
BY WAY OF INTRODUCTION color *Archaeology* v70 no2 p6 Mr/Ap 2017

NEXT STEPS AT THE AIA bw *Archaeology* v70 no3 p6 My/Je 2017
OUR HUMAN STORY color *Archaeology* v70 no5 p6 S/O 2017
A SOBERING MOMENT FOR PUBLIC OUTREACH color *Archaeology* v70 no4 p6 Je-Ag 2017

Magness, Steve
The 7 HABITS OF HIGHLY EFFECTIVE MARATHONERS cartoon color *Runner's World* v52 no6 p62 Jl 2017

Magnet schools
CHANCES OF ACCEPTANCE: The number-one high school in America is less than 5 percent African-American and Latino. Does that make it racist? L. Rab *Washingtonian Magazine* v52 no8 p48 My 2017

Magnetic balances
THE RELIC HUNTER B. Underwood color *MHQ: Quarterly Journal of Military History* v29 no4 p24 Summ 2017

Magnetic circular dichroism
X rays peer inside a magnet: Submicron spin textures in bulk magnetic materials have been stubbornly hard to detect J. Miller *Physics Today* v70 no9 p17 S 2017

Magnetic field measurements
Classical-quantum sensors keep better time A. N. Jordan graph *Science* v356 no6340 p802 My 26 2017

Magnetic field measurements—Equipment & supplies
MEASURING THE MAGNETIC FIELD color graph *Astronomy* v45 no7 p18 Jl 2017

Magnetic fields
Aurora in a bottle *Physics Today* v69 no10 p88 O 2016
LASER EXPERIMENTS ILLUMINATE THE COSMOS *Science & Technology Review* p4 D 2016
Magnetic Bridge Found Between Magellanic Clouds S. Ash color *Sky & Telescope* v134 no2 p13 Ag 2017
The magnetic field and turbulence of the cosmic web measured using a brilliant fast radio burst V. Ravi, R. M. Shannon et al bibl chart graph *Science* v354 no6317 p1249 D 9 2016
Moon's magnetism was long-lasting A. YEAGER color *Science News* v192 no4 p10 S 16 2017

Magnetic flux
BETWEEN RESEARCH AND DEVELOPMENT: IBM AND JOSEPHSON COMPUTING C. C. M. Mody *Physics Today* v69 no10 p32 O 2016

Magnetic insulators
Control and local measurement of the spin chemical potential in a magnetic insulator C. Du, T. van der Sar et al bw diag *Science* v357 no6347 p195 Jl 14 2017

Magnetic materials synthesis
All-oxide–based synthetic antiferromagnets exhibiting layer-resolved magnetization reversal B. Chen, H. Xu et al diag *Science* v357 no6347 p191 Jl 14 2017

Magnetic monopoles
Magnetic monopole search, past and present C. Harrison *Physics Today* v70 no6 p13 Je 2017

Magnetic pole
Masako Tominaga P. HESS cartoon *Popular Science* p52 Ja/F 2017

Magnetic properties of the Moon
Moon's magnetism was long-lasting A. YEAGER color *Science News* v192 no4 p10 S 16 2017

Magnetic resonance imaging
BABY STEPS C. Zuckerman bw *National Geographic* v231 no6 pC21 Je 2017
A Better Prostate Screening color *Prevention* v69 no5 p9 My 2017
Diagnosis L. Sanders *New York Times Magazine* p26 N 20 2016
DREAM CATCHERS N. Strochlic color *National Geographic* v231 no5 p22 My 2017
This Old Brain [Cover story] J. WHEELWRIGHT bw color *Discover* v38 no8 p26 O 2017

Magnetic storms
Auroras E. BETZ color diag *Discover* v38 no6 p30 Jl/Ag 2017

Magnetism
   See also
   Magnetic fields
   Magnetic pole
Odd computer zips through knotty tasks A. Cho color *Science* v354 no6310 p269 O 21 2016
The search for MAGNETIC MONOPOLES A. Rajantie *Physics*

Today v69 no10 p40 O 2016

Structure, force balance, and topology of Earth's magnetopause C. T. Russell, R. J. Strangeway et al diag graph *Science* v356 no6341 p960 Je 1 2017

US academic fusion researchers sound alarm T. Feder *Physics Today* v70 no5 p32 My 2017

Magnetization

X rays peer inside a magnet: Submicron spin textures in bulk magnetic materials have been stubbornly hard to detect J. Miller *Physics Today* v70 no9 p17 S 2017

Magneto

The Greatest Villains of All Time D. Franich color *Entertainment Weekly* no1436/1437 p66 O 21 2016

Magnetometers

MEASURING THE MAGNETIC FIELD color graph *Astronomy* v45 no7 p18 Jl 2017

Magnets

SAM TING'S LAST TEASE J. Sokol color *Science* v356 no6335 p240 Ap 21 2017

SHOP NOTES D. Owen color *Popular Mechanics* p92 S 2017

Magnets—Evaluation

NEW PRODUCTS color *Astronomy* v45 no4 p69 Ap 2017

Magni, G.

Localized aliphatic organic material on the surface of Ceres bibl graph *Science* v355 no6326 p719 F 17 2017

Seasonal exposure of carbon dioxide ice on the nucleus of comet 67P/Churyumov-Gerasimenko bibl bw graph *Science* v354 no6319 p1563 D 23 2016

Magnificent Seven, The (Film)

THE MAGFINICENT SEVEN (2016) D. Vaughn color *Sound & Vision* v82 no4 p68 My 2017

Magnifying glasses

SHOP NOTES cartoon color *Popular Mechanics* p112 Ap 2017

Magnifying glasses—Evaluation

DOCK BOX *Sea Magazine* v109 no1 p28 Ja 2017

Magnolfi, Jennifer

Why Apple's New HQ Is Nothing Like the Rest of Silicon Valley *Harvard Business Review Digital Articles* p2 Je 26 2017

Magnúsdóttir, Erna

Why the rest of the world is marching color *Science* v356 no6334 p119 Ap 14 2017

Magnusdottir, Helga Lilja

HAILING HELICOPTER J. GOTTLIEB *Iceland Review* v55 no1 p10 Ja/F 2017

Magnuson, Jim

A Serious Writer M. AGRBSTA *Texas Monthly* v45 no4 p58 Ap 2017

Magnusson, Niklas

THE MAYOR IS IN color *Bloomberg Businessweek* no4534 p66 Ag 14 2017

Magnusson, W. E.

Persistent effects of pre-Columbian plant domestication on Amazonian forest composition bibl chart graph map *Science* v355 no6328 p925 Mr 3 2017

Magor, Liz

LIZ MAGOR P. Rafferty color *Art in America* v105 no5 p137 My 2017

Magsamen, Meg

CLASS IS IN SESSION Z. KUMOK *Indianapolis Monthly* p142 My 2017

Maguire, Bevin

4 Ways for B2B Businesses to Keep Their Customers *Harvard Business Review Digital Articles* p2 D 6 2016

MAGUIRE, GREGORY

Where the Wild Things Come From *New York Times Book Review* p13 O 30 2016

Mah, Evan

50 Best, Refreshed *Atlanta* v56 no11 p2 Mr 2017

BANH MI BREAKDOWN *Atlanta* v56 no7 p88 N 2016

BEST OF ATLANTA *Atlanta* v56 no8 p106 D 2016

SANDWICHES! *Atlanta* v56 no7 p78 N 2016

Mah, Suyun

What 100,000 Tweets About the Volkswagen Scandal Tell Us About Angry Customers *Harvard Business Review Digital Articles* p2 S 2 2016

Mahadevaiah, Shantha K.

Fertile offspring from sterile sex chromosome trisomic mice chart diag *Science* v357 no6354 p932 S 1 2017

Mahadevan, L.

Avian egg shape: Form, function, and evolution color diag *Science* v356 no6344 p1249 Je 23 2017

Controlled growth and form of precipitating microsculptures bw color diag graph *Science* v355 no6332 p1395 Mr 31 2017

Mahaffey, James

Atomic Adventures I. Ockert color *Science* v356 no6342 p1008 Je 9 2017

Mahaffy, P.

Mars' atmospheric history derived from upper-atmosphere measurements of 38 Ar/36Ar diag *Science* v355 no6332 p1408 Mr 31 2017

Mahajan, Karan, 1984-

Come Together *New York Times Book Review* p1 Je 11 2017

Conjugal Dread *New York Times Book Review* p17 N 27 2016

Karan Mahajan M. Hagan color *Current Biography* v78 no1 p37 Ja 2017

Mahajan, Vijay

How Unilever Reaches Rural Consumers in Emerging Markets *Harvard Business Review Digital Articles* p2 D 14 2016

Mahallati, Jafar

Just friends: Is friendship the key to strengthening global relationships? color *U.S. Catholic* v82 no8 p34 Ag 2017

MaHan, Sydney

19 THINGS YOU REALLY OUGHT TO 00 THIS MONTH *Washingtonian Magazine* v52 no3 p31 D 2016

CAMP AVID *Washingtonian Magazine* v52 no5 p117 F 2017

FOTOWEEKDC *Washingtonian Magazine* v52 no2 p35 N 2016

THE PET-SITTING SIDE HUSTLE *Washingtonian Magazine* v52 no4 p204 Ja 2017

WHERE & WHEN color *Washingtonian Magazine* v52 no7 p31 Ap 2017

WHERE & WHEN *Washingtonian Magazine* v52 no8 p35 My 2017

Mahaney, Emily

Demi Soars Away [Cover story] color *Glamour* v114 no11 p160 N 2016

How I Survived the Worst Depression of My Life color *Glamour* v114 no11 p144 N 2016

Is It Safe to Talk Politics Yet? bw color *Glamour* v115 no2 p77 F 2017

"Kiss all the people you want to kiss" color *Glamour* v115 no2 p82 F 2017

The Loving Legacy bw color *Glamour* v114 no11 p141 N 2016

The Most Infamously Accused Female Villain color *Glamour* v114 no11 p143 N 2016

"My self-confidence was shattered overnight" bw color *Glamour* v115 no6 p108 Je 2017

The Power of an Outsider color *Glamour* v115 no1 p62 Ja 2017

The Power of the Pink Ranger color *Glamour* v115 no4 p50 Ap 2017

The Superhero We've Been Waiting For color *Glamour* v115 no6 p110 Je 2017

"The suffragettes would not back down" color *Glamour* v115 no2 p80 F 2017

"True badassery has no gender" color diag *Glamour* v115 no1 p60 Ja 2017

The Voices of Truth color *Glamour* v115 no5 p179 My 2017

Woman Warrior color *Glamour* v115 no6 p106 Je 2017

THE Work Wives color *Glamour* v115 no10 p162 O 2017

"You have to tell yourself you're enough" bw *Glamour* v115 no9 p142 S 2017

Mahaney, Patrick

All Ears color *Amazing Wellness* v9 no1 p82 Wint 2017

MAHANTA, SIDDHARTHA

Dark Horses *Texas Monthly* v45 no9 p46 S 2017

Mahany, Barbara

Boyhood on a Shelf *New York Times Book Review* p13 Ap 9 2017

Maharidge, Dale

AMERICAN BALLAD *Smithsonian* v47 no8 p66 D 2016

SNOWDEN'S BOX *Harper's Magazine* v334 no2004 p25 My 2017

MAHARY, GRACE

WHERE FASHION GETS PERSONAL color *Harper's Bazaar*

no3648 p139 N 2016

Mahbubani, Kishore—Interviews

It's A Problem That America Is Still Unable To Admit It Will Become #2 To China K. Mahbubani *NPQ: New Perspectives Quarterly* v34 no3 p34 Jl 2017

MEANING OF New American Leadership FOR Asia color *Foreign Affairs* v95 no6 p64a N/D 2016

Mahdara, Moj—Interviews

The New Beauty Pioneers B. Meyer and Ying Chu color *Glamour* v115 no4 p110 Ap 2017

Mahdessian, Diana

A subcellular map of the human proteome color *Science* v356 no6340 p820 My 26 2017

Mahdi, Wael

Help Wanted in Saudi Arabia: Savvy Investors color graph *Bloomberg Businessweek* no4513 p41 Mr 6 2017

Mahenderkar, Naveen K.

Epitaxial lift-off of electrodeposited single-crystal gold foils for flexible electronics bibl bw diag *Science* v355 no6330 p1203 Mr 17 2017

Maher, Bill, 1956-

GARRY SHANDLING color *Entertainment Weekly* no1446/1447 p98 D 2016/Ja 2017

Sound Bites color *Entertainment Weekly* no1478 / 1479 p6 Ag 18-25 2017

THE UNKILLABLE TWO-PARTY SYSTEM M. WELCH *Reason* v48 no8 p7 Ja 2017

Maher, Daniel R.

Mythic Frontiers: Remembering, Forgetting, and Profiting with Cultural Heritage Tourism J. L. Taylor *American Indian Quarterly* v41 no2 p187 Spr 2017

Maher, James

TOP DOCTORS 2017 *Cincinnati Magazine* v51 no1 p96 O 2017

Maher, Jan

Earth As It Is *Publishers Weekly* v263 no46 p29 N 14 2016

Maher, John

At 30, the Writers Studio Gets an Anthology chart *Publishers Weekly* v264 no19 p7 My 8 2017

At Quirk Books, Quirk's the Name and the Game color *Publishers Weekly* v264 no17 p7 Ap 24 2017

AUDIO BESTSELLERS chart color *Publishers Weekly* v263 no51 p14 D 12 2016

AUDIO BESTSELLERS chart color *Publishers Weekly* v264 no15 p24 Ap 10 2017

AUDIO BESTSELLERS chart color *Publishers Weekly* v264 no33 p20 Ag 14 2017

Beginnings: A Restaurant with A Literary Bent color *Publishers Weekly* v263 no43 p6 O 24 2016

The Bestsellers of 2017 (So Far) *Publishers Weekly* v264 no28 p5 Jl 10 2017

Books on Politics, Trump Rise After Election chart *Publishers Weekly* v263 no47 p5 N 21 2016

Britain's Hottest Digital Publisher *Publishers Weekly* v263 no39 p8 S 26 2016

Brooklyn Arts Press, Indie Publishing's NBA Champion color *Publishers Weekly* v263 no51 p3 D 12 2016

Covering The World of Children's Publishing color *Publishers Weekly* v263 no51 p1 D 12 2016

Denis Johnson: An Editor's Love Story color *Publishers Weekly* v264 no41 p5 O 9 2017

Ferrante Hits in Germany, Sweden *Publishers Weekly* v263 no39 p22 S 26 2016

FRANKFURT BRIEFCASE 2016 *Publishers Weekly* v263 no39 p34 S 26 2016

FRANKFURT BRIEFCASE 2017 bw color *Publishers Weekly* v264 no39 p34 S 25 2017

The Goddard Riverside Book Fair, 30 Years In *Publishers Weekly* v263 no42 p10 O 17 2016

iBOOKS AUDIO TOP 10 chart color *Publishers Weekly* v264 no11 p15 Mr 13 2017

iBOOKS AUDIO TOP 10 chart color *Publishers Weekly* v264 no19 p17 My 8 2017

iBooks Bestsellers *Publishers Weekly* v263 no41 p19 O 10 2016

Indie House Rides the Pulitzer Wave color *Publishers Weekly* v264 no22 p7 My 29 2017

In 'Lincoln in the Bardo,' Saunders's Fiction Becomes Virtual Re-

ality color *Publishers Weekly* v264 no9 p8 F 27 2017

Inside the 'New York Times' Books Desk color *Publishers Weekly* v264 no34 p6 Ag 21 2017

An International Press Looks to 2017 color *Publishers Weekly* v263 no50 p15 D 5 2016

Jailed Palestinian Poet's Work Gets New Life in Parallel Translation chart color *Publishers Weekly* v263 no44 p11 O 31 2016

Knopf to Print 200,000 Copies of Nobel Winner Ishiguro's Works color *Publishers Weekly* v264 no41 p10 O 9 2017

Knopf to Publish Memoir of a Father's Loss color *Publishers Weekly* v264 no7 p5 F 13 2017

Least Heat-Moon Makes His Fiction Debut with Three Rooms color *Publishers Weekly* v264 no15 p12 Ap 10 2017

Leftist Indies Put Politics First color *Publishers Weekly* v264 no26 p3 Je 26 2017

Local Favorites Top in Italy, Spain, Sweden chart color *Publishers Weekly* v264 no5 p13 Ja 30 2017

A Night for Winners color *Publishers Weekly* v263 no47 p4 N 21 2016

Nonpartisan Nonprofits Fight for Free Expression, Part 2 *Publishers Weekly* v264 no14 p5 Ap 3 2017

Nonpartisan Nonprofits Fight For Free Expression *Publishers Weekly* v264 no13 p5 Mr 27 2017

Penguin Mixes Art, Books for a Cause color *Publishers Weekly* v264 no24 p10 Je 12 2017

Potter Tops Print, 'Girl' Rides E-book Train chart *Publishers Weekly* v264 no2 p5 Ja 9 2017

Prize Winners On Top in France, Spain chart *Publishers Weekly* v264 no1 p14 Ja 2 2017

The Publisher with All of Speculative Fiction in Its Orbit color *Publishers Weekly* v264 no38 p12 S 18 2017

REAPING A SECOND HARVEST color *Publishers Weekly* v264 no6 p38 F 6 2017

Rowling, O'Reilly, Hawkins All Soared in 2016 *Publishers Weekly* v264 no4 p6 Ja 23 2017

ROYAL RECEPTION chart graph *Publishers Weekly* v264 no2 p14 Ja 9 2017

SELECT BOOK CONFERENCES, FESTIVALS, AND FAIRS IN 2017 *Publishers Weekly* v264 no1 p23 Ja 2 2017

Suzanne Nossel: PEN Executive Director color *Publishers Weekly* v263 no52 p30 D 19 2016

With '1984' All the Rage, Is Dystopian Backlist a Publishing Utopia? *Publishers Weekly* v264 no29 p3 Jl 17 2017

Maher, L. James III

Cyclin A2 is an RNA binding protein that controls Mre11 mRNA translation bibl graph *Science* v353 no6307 p1549 S 30 2016

Maher, Michael—Interviews

GARDEN STATE OF MIND D. BRENNER color *House Beautiful* v159 no4 p80 My 2017

Maherali, Hafiz

Plant-soil feedbacks and mycorrhizal type influence temperate forest population dynamics bibl graph map *Science* v355 no6321 p1 Ja 13 2017

MAHFOUZ, SABRINA

Muslim Women Speak Out *Publishers Weekly* v264 no36 p104 S 4 2017

Mahfuz, Najib, 1911-2006

Portrait of the Author as a Historian A. Lee *History Today* v67 no1 p54 Ja 2017

Mahin, Jeff

JOIN THE RIDE L. FLICKINGER color *Bicycling* v58 no6 p12 Jl 2017

Mahindra Aerospace (Company)

MAHINDRA'S AIRVAN 10 GETS CERTIFIED color *Flying* v144 no9 p18 S 2017

Mahindra Group of Cos.

Let Go of What Made Your Company Great V. Govindarajan *Harvard Business Review Digital Articles* p2 Ap 13 2016

Mahler, Daniel

Zero-Based Budgeting Is Not a Wonder Diet for Companies *Harvard Business Review Digital Articles* p2 Je 30 2016

Mahler, Jonathan

ALL THE PRESIDENT'S LAWYERS: DONALD TRUMP'S LIFE AND CAREER HAVE BEEN DEFINED BY HIS LEGAL BATTLES. BUT DO THE ATTORNEYS WHO GUIDED HIM THROUGH THE COURTROOMS OF NEW YORK

AND NEW JERSEY KNOW HOW TO NAVIGATE WASH-INGTON? *New York Times Magazine* p28 Jl 9 2017

For Richer, for Poorer *New York Times Book Review* p21 My 7 2017

Search Party *New York Times Magazine* p9 Ja 1 2017

'You Want It Darker' bw *New York Times Magazine* p20 Mr 12 2017

Mahlum, Anne

Anne Mahlum's Battles C. RUBIN *Washingtonian Magazine* v52 no3 p54 D 2016

Mahmood, Rezaul

Land's complex role in climate change [Cover story] *Physics Today* v69 no11 p40 N 2016

Mahmoud, Ahmed M.

Photonic doping of epsilon-near-zero media bibl diag *Science* v355 no6329 p1058 Mr 10 2017

Mahmud, Adnan

Looking Beyond H-1B Visas to Find Tech Talent *Harvard Business Review Digital Articles* p1 Je 22 2017

Mahnke, Aaron

6 — LORE N. Serrao *Entertainment Weekly* no1444/1445 p114 D 16 2016

Mahomes, Patrick

INTO THE FIRE A. Benoit color *Sports Illustrated* v126 no13 p40 My 8 2017

Leading Men G. Baumgaertner and C. Becht color *Sports Illustrated* v125 no14 p54 O 24-31 2016

UPSIDE-DOWNSIDE A. Benoit color *Sports Illustrated* v126 no11 p40 Ap 17-24 2017

MAHON-ADAMS, TRISH

SEEING THE LIGHT color *O, The Oprah Magazine* p18 Ag 2017

Mahoney, Anne Marie

Patriotism in the pews color *U.S. Catholic* v82 no11 p5 N 2017

Mahoney, Ben

OPENING ACT color *Sports Illustrated* v126 no13 p52 My 8 2017

MAHONEY, BRENNA

Long-Term Studies Contribute Disproportionately to Ecology and Policy *BioScience* v67 no3 p271 Mr 2017

Mahoney, Brian K.

Creature Comforts color *American Craft* v76 no6 p58 D 2016-Ja 2017

Mahoney, Daniel J.

HERE THE PEOPLE RULE *Claremont Review of Books* v17 no1 p49 Wint 2016/2017

PETER AUGUSTINE LAWLER, 1951-2017 *Claremont Review of Books* v17 no3 p83 Summ 2017

Mahoney, Frank

A meal for many color *U.S. Catholic* v82 no6 p5 Je 2017

Mahoney, Joe

As the Free World Turns *Commentary* v144 no2 p4 S 2017

A Time and a Place *Publishers Weekly* v264 no27 p56 Jl 3 2017

Mahoney, Rob

10 Bucks color *Sports Illustrated* v125 no14 p84 O 24-31 2016

10 Mavericks color *Sports Illustrated* v125 no14 p110 O 24-31 2016

11 Bulls color *Sports Illustrated* v125 no14 p86 O 24-31 2016

11 Pelicans color *Sports Illustrated* v125 no14 p111 O 24-31 2016

12 Heat color *Sports Illustrated* v125 no14 p88 O 24-31 2016

12 Suns color *Sports Illustrated* v125 no14 p112 O 24-31 2016

13 Magic color *Sports Illustrated* v125 no14 p89 O 24-31 2016

13 Nuggets color *Sports Illustrated* v125 no14 p113 O 24-31 2016

14 76ers color *Sports Illustrated* v125 no14 p90 O 24-31 2016

14 Kings color *Sports Illustrated* v125 no14 p114 O 24-31 2016

15 Lakers color *Sports Illustrated* v125 no14 p116 O 24-31 2016

15 Nets color *Sports Illustrated* v125 no14 p92 O 24-31 2016

1 Cavaliers color *Sports Illustrated* v125 no14 p72 O 24-31 2016

1 Warriors color *Sports Illustrated* v125 no14 p96 O 24-31 2016

2 Celtics *Sports Illustrated* v125 no14 p74 O 24-31 2016

2 Spurs color *Sports Illustrated* v125 no14 p98 O 24-31 2016

3 Clippers color *Sports Illustrated* v125 no14 p99 O 24-31 2016

3 Raptors color *Sports Illustrated* v125 no14 p75 O 24-31 2016

4 Pistons color *Sports Illustrated* v125 no14 p76 O 24-31 2016

4 Trail Blazers color *Sports Illustrated* v125 no14 p100 O 24-31 2016

5 Hornets color *Sports Illustrated* v125 no14 p78 O 24-31 2016

5 Thunder color *Sports Illustrated* v125 no14 p102 O 24-31 2016

6 Hawks color *Sports Illustrated* v125 no14 p80 O 24-31 2016

6 Jazz color *Sports Illustrated* v125 no14 p103 O 24-31 2016

7 Grizzlies color *Sports Illustrated* v125 no14 p104 O 24-31 2016

7 Pacers color *Sports Illustrated* v125 no14 p81 O 24-31 2016

8 Rockets color *Sports Illustrated* v125 no14 p106 O 24-31 2016

8 Wizards color *Sports Illustrated* v125 no14 p82 O 24-31 2016

9 Knicks color *Sports Illustrated* v125 no14 p83 O 24-31 2016

9 Timberwolves color *Sports Illustrated* v125 no14 p108 O 24-31 2016

Scouting Reports color *Sports Illustrated* v125 no14 p70 O 24-31 2016

SI's Top 100 color *Sports Illustrated* v125 no14 p94 O 24-31 2016

MAHONEY, SARAH

The Good Life on $40,000 a year color map *AARP: The Magazine* v59 no6A p58 O/N 2016

How to Defy Your Genes color *AARP: The Magazine* v59 no4A p46 Je/Jl 2016

When Getting the Gear Isn't a Given color *Parents* v92 no11 p92 N 2017

Mahonia

AROUND THE GARDEN S. Bender color *Southern Living* v52 no3 p42 Mr 2017

MAHONY, RHONA

FROM THE ARCHIVES bw *Reason* v49 no1 p70 My 2017

Mahro, A. K.

Revealing the subfemtosecond dynamics of orbital angular momentum in nanoplasmonic vortices bibl diag *Science* v355 no6330 p1187 Mr 17 2017

Mahroum, Sami

Research: Arab Inventors Make the U.S. More Innovative *Harvard Business Review Digital Articles* p2 F 23 2017

MAH UNG, GORDON

HP Omen 17: Great gaming performance at a great price color graph *PCWorld* v35 no11 p90 N 2016

HP's Spectre x360 puts Kaby Lake and Thunderbolt into a thinner, faster package color *PCWorld* v35 no11 p8 N 2016

Surface Book i7: Still unique and still blazing fast color graph *PCWorld* p64 D 2016

Mai-Anh Le Tran

Reset the Heart: Unlearning Violence, Relearning Hope K. Banakis *Christian Century* v134 no20 p38 S 27 2017

Maiato, Helder

Actin divides to conquer color diag *Science* v357 no6353 p756 Ag 25 2017

Maier, Charles S.

Once Within Borders: Territories of Power, Wealth, and Belonging Since 1500 G. J. Ikenberry *Foreign Affairs* v96 no1 p157 Ja/F 2017

Maier, Em Dzhali

Shared history *Science* v356 no6338 p591 My 12 2017

Maier, Thomas

Writers and truth tellers, defined by war bw *America* v217 no7 p46 O 2 2017

Mail receiving & forwarding services

Help Desk G. Fleishman color *Macworld - Digital Edition* p57 Ap 2017

Mailboxes

NO-TILL OR NEVER-TILL? STORY ON THE EFFECT OF TILLAGE GETS READER REACTIONS D. KURNS *Successful Farming* v115 no11 p4 S 2017

your DECLUTTERING CALENDAR *Good Housekeeping* v264 no3 p82 Mr 2017

Mailboxes—Evaluation

Finds in Metalwork M. E. Polson color *Old House Journal* v45 no5 p68 Ag 2017

Mailchimp (Company)

Going Ape for Local Art: Thanks to a key hire, MailChimp has quietly become one of the city's biggest corporate supporters of local art S. DAZEY *Atlanta* v57 no6 p77 O 2017

Mailer, Norman, 1923-2007

SONNY NIGHTS, NORMAN DAYS P. CARLSON *American History* v51 no6 p14 F 2017

Mailrooms—Officials & employees

THE MAILROOM J. M. Laskas *New York Times Magazine* p30 Ja 22 2017

Maimon, Amit

How Self-Managed Teams Can Resolve Conflict *Harvard Business Review Digital Articles* p2 Ap 17 2017

MAIN, STEPHANIE

5 WAYS: ...to Use a Sandbag color *Muscle & Performance* v9 no8 p66 Ag 2017

Performance Yoga color *Muscle & Performance* v9 no8 p24 Ag 2017

Pilates to Improve Your Lifts color *Muscle & Performance* v9 no7 p22 Jl 2017

Mainardi, Cesare

The 3 Elements of a Strong Corporate Identity *Harvard Business Review Digital Articles* p2 D 9 2014

5 Ways to Close the Strategy-to-Execution Gap *Harvard Business Review Digital Articles* p2 D 22 2015

Connect Your Firm's Strategy to Its Identity *Harvard Business Review Digital Articles* p2 S 28 2016

Develop Your Company's Cross-Functional Capabilities *Harvard Business Review Digital Articles* p2 F 2 2016

Growth Needs to Come from the Entire Company *Harvard Business Review Digital Articles* p2 Je 17 2016

Only 8% of Leaders Are Good at Both Strategy and Execution *Harvard Business Review Digital Articles* p2 D 30 2015

Your Whole Company Needs to Be Distinctive, Not Just Your Product *Harvard Business Review Digital Articles* p2 My 19 2016

Main Attraction, The (Short story)

READINGS *Harper's Magazine* v333 no1998 p13 N 2016

Maine

Autumn's Bounty *Saturday Evening Post* v289 no5 p100 S/O 2017

Maine Energy Systems (Company)

Pellet Boilers for Off-Grid Living *Mother Earth News* no280 p9 F/Mr 2017

Maine—Description & travel

FRUITS OF THE FOREST: PHOTOGRAPHER TURNED FORAGER JAMIE SALOMON SETS HIS SIGHTS ON WILD MUSHROOMS K. PANDOLFI *Yankee* v81 no5 p58 S/O 2017

THE GREAT LOBSTER ROLL ADVENTURE: WE SENT FOOD EDITOR UP THE MAINE COAST, FROM KITTERY TO EASTPORT, TO SAMPLE NEARLY TWO | DOZEN ROLLS AND CROWN A CHAMPION A. TRAVERSO chart color *Yankee* p78 Jl 2017

Hut to Hut G. Vercesi *Sierra* v101 no6 p17 N/D 2016

The Long Run B. PIKE color *Power & Motoryacht* v33 no1 p84 Ja 2017

MAINE *Yankee* p108 My/Je 2017

Marvellous Maine S. Doyle map *Canadian Geographic* v135 no6 p16 D 2015

Tour de Maine: An unforgettable bike trip into the heart of a famous landscape and the lives of its people P. GRODINSKY *Yankee* v81 no5 p20 S/O 2017

Mainelli, Michael

Blockchain Could Help Us Reclaim Control of Our Personal Data *Harvard Business Review Digital Articles* p2 O 5 2017

Blockchain Will Help Us Prove Our Identities in a Digital World *Harvard Business Review Digital Articles* p2 Mr 16 2017

Maine—Politics & government

Wind From Down East H. HERTZBERG *Nation* v303 no20 p4 N 14 2016

Maine—Politics & government—1951-

Maine Divided E. JOHNSON il *National Review* v68 no20 p16 N 7 2016

Mainland, Joel D.

Predicting human olfactory perception from chemical features of odor molecules bibl diag graph *Science* v355 no6327 p820 F 24 2017

Mainpal, Rana

Control of meiotic pairing and recombination by chromosomally tethered 26S proteasome bibl graph *Science* v355 no6323 p408 Ja 27 2017

Mainsails

LOFTY THOUGHTS ALL ABOUT MAINSAILS B. Hancock color *Sail* v48 no3 p48 Mr 2017

Sail Care P. Nielsen color *Sail* v48 no1 p44 Ja 2017

Maintainability (Engineering)

See also

Maintenance

Year-Round Trailer Maintenance C. CASWELL *Boating World* v38 no1 p18 Ja 2017

Maintenance

See also

Automobile repair

Buildings—Repair & reconstruction

Oh No! Your Car Got Scratched! E. DYER color *Popular Mechanics* v193 no7 p52 S 2016

REPAIR MAKE-DOs D. Mowitz *Successful Farming* v115 no2 p24 F 2017

Maintenance & repair of wood floors

Fixing Sagging Floor Joists R. Tschoepe diag *Old House Journal* v45 no7 p56 O 2017

Maintenance costs

DYING TO KNOW S. STALL color *Indianapolis Monthly* p17 Ap 2017

Year-Round, Paved-Trail Surface Maintenance T. Houck *Parks & Recreation* v51 no11 p22 N 2016

Maintenance—Equipment & supplies—Evaluation

TAGGED A. McConnell and L. Bedord *Successful Farming* v115 no2 p32 F 2017

Maio, Caren

What I Look for in Candidates Interviewing at My Startup *Harvard Business Review Digital Articles* p2 N 15 2016

Maiolo, Joseph A.

RETHINKING ROCKET SCIENCE: A study of the early history of jet engines transforms the way we should think about technological change *History Today* v67 no9 p102 S 2017

Mair, Aaron

EARLY CONNECTION TO NATURE FUELS PASSION FOR ENVIRONMENT *New York State Conservationist* v71 no6 p27 Je 2017

Maire, Vincent

Global climatic drivers of leaf size [Cover story] graph *Science* v357 no6354 p917 S 1 2017

Mairs & Power Inc.

The New Bond King Is Stressing Safety N. S. HUANG chart *Kiplinger's Personal Finance* v71 no3 p61 Mr 2017

MAISELS, FIONA

Conserving the World's Megafauna and Biodiversity: The Fierce Urgency of Now *BioScience* v67 no3 p197 Mr 2017

Saving the World's Terrestrial Megafauna color *BioScience* v66 no10 p807 O 1 2016

Maisenbacher, Lothar

The Rydberg constant and proton size from atomic hydrogen bw chart color diag graph *Science* v357 no6359 p79 O 6 2017

Maisonneuve, Etienne

Mechanisms of bacterial persistence during stress and antibiotic exposure bibl diag graph *Science* v354 no6318 paaf4268-1 D 16 2016

Mait, Sandy

HIGHWAY RUN bw color *Skiing* p30 Wint 2017

HOLD, PLEASE color *Skiing* p16 D 2016

TETHERED color *Skiing* p36 D 2016

WEATHER HOLD bw *Skiing* p8 Wint 2017

Maitra, Anirban

Potential role of intratumor bacteria in mediating tumor resistance to the chemotherapeutic drug gemcitabine diag *Science* v357 no6356 p1156 S 15 2017

Maize, Jimmy

THE TEMPLE BOMBING D. SCHECHTER *Atlanta* v56 no10 p41 F 2017

Majchrzak, Yasmine Nicole

Research night owls color *Science* v354 no6315 p964 N 25 2016

Majdalani, Charif

Long Haul S. JOINSON *New York Times Book Review* p14 Je 4 2017

Majdalawi, Flora

CHANGING attitudes color *Literacy Today (2411-7862)* v34 no4 p44 Ja/F 2017

Maje (Company)

The NEWS color *Harper's Bazaar* no3656 p320 S 2017

MAJEROL, VERONICA

The Cultural Revolution *New York Times Upfront* v149 no5 p18

N 21 2016

Emmett Till Revisited img *New York Times Upfront* v149 no11 p16 Ap 3 2017

Majewski, Lori

DAMN, SOFIA! [Cover story] color *Women's Health* v14 no7 p49 S 2017

HOT YOGA HOT BOD [Cover story] cartoon color *Women's Health* v13 no10 p65 D 2016

true beauties inside & out color *Good Housekeeping* v264 no5 p44 My 2017

MAJIA, JIDI

I, SNOW LEOPARD *Orion Magazine* v35 no4/5 p82 Jl-O 2016

Majmudar, Amit

Astereognosis *America* v216 no12 p47 My 29 2017

THE BEARD *New Yorker* v93 no19 p44 Jl 3 2017

Majolica

Nicolaus Boston H. MARTIN color *Architectural Digest* v74 no8 p18 Ag 2017

Major, Brenda

Diversity Policies Rarely Make Companies Fairer, and They Feel Threatening to White Men *Harvard Business Review Digital Articles* p2 Ja 4 2016

Major, Devorah

And then We Became color *Publishers Weekly* v263 no42 p47 O 17 2016

Major Crimes (TV program)

Major Crimes N. Abrams, A. Bacle et al *Entertainment Weekly* no1482/1483 p66 S 22 2017

Major League Baseball (Organization)

12 ETA: RIGHT NOW J. Tayler color *Sports Illustrated* v126 no9 p60 Mr 27 2017

17 MACRO MANAGING T. Verducci color *Sports Illustrated* v126 no9 p70 Mr 27 2017

1 ASTROS color *Sports Illustrated* v126 no9 p88 Mr 27 2017

1 CUBS color *Sports Illustrated* v126 no9 p102 Mr 27 2017

1 DODGERS color *Sports Illustrated* v126 no9 p108 Mr 27 2017

1 INDIANS color *Sports Illustrated* v126 no9 p82 Mr 27 2017

1 NATIONALS color *Sports Illustrated* v126 no9 p94 Mr 27 2017

1 RED SOX color *Sports Illustrated* v126 no9 p76 Mr 27 2017

2 BLUEJAYS color *Sports Illustrated* v126 no9 p78 Mr 27 2017

2 CARDINALS color *Sports Illustrated* v126 no9 p104 Mr 27 2017

2 GIANTS color *Sports Illustrated* v126 no9 p110 Mr 27 2017

2 METS color *Sports Illustrated* v126 no9 p96 Mr 27 2017

2 RANGERS color *Sports Illustrated* v126 no9 p90 Mr 27 2017

2 TIGERS color *Sports Illustrated* v126 no9 p84 Mr 27 2017

3 BRAVES color *Sports Illustrated* v126 no9 p97 Mr 27 2017

3 MARINERS color *Sports Illustrated* v126 no9 p91 Mr 27 2017

3 PIRATES color *Sports Illustrated* v126 no9 p105 Mr 27 2017

3 ROCKIES color *Sports Illustrated* v126 no9 p111 Mr 27 2017

3 ROYALS color *Sports Illustrated* v126 no9 p85 Mr 27 2017

3 YANKEES color *Sports Illustrated* v126 no9 p79 Mr 27 2017

4 ANGELS color *Sports Illustrated* v126 no9 p92 Mr 27 2017

4 A QUEST CALLED TRIBE J. Dickey color *Sports Illustrated* v126 no9 p46 Mr 27 2017

4 BREWERS color *Sports Illustrated* v126 no9 p106 Mr 27 2017

4 DIAMONDBACKS color *Sports Illustrated* v126 no9 p112 Mr 27 2017

4 MARLINS color *Sports Illustrated* v126 no9 p98 Mr 27 2017

4 RAYS color *Sports Illustrated* v126 no9 p80 Mr 27 2017

4 TWINS color *Sports Illustrated* v126 no9 p86 Mr 27 2017

5 ATHLETICS color *Sports Illustrated* v126 no9 p93 Mr 27 2017

5 ORIOLES color *Sports Illustrated* v126 no9 p81 Mr 27 2017

5 PADRES color *Sports Illustrated* v126 no9 p114 Mr 27 2017

5 PHILLIES color *Sports Illustrated* v126 no9 p100 Mr 27 2017

5 REDS color *Sports Illustrated* v126 no9 p107 Mr 27 2017

5 WHITE SOX color *Sports Illustrated* v126 no9 p87 Mr 27 2017

7 AFTER BIG PAPI, THE LITTLE THINGS T. Verducci color *Sports Illustrated* v126 no9 p49 Mr 27 2017

African-Americans and the Diamond M. CAMPBELL color *Ebony* v72 no6 p88 Ap/My 2017

AT LAST E. CRAWFORD PEYTON color *New Orleans Magazine* v51 no2 p50 D 2016

Baseball Wants A Home Run in China color *Bloomberg Businessweek* no4498 p31 N 7 2016

In Tom We Trust color *Sports Illustrated* v126 no9 p12 Mr 27 2017

Leading Off B. Reiter color *Sports Illustrated* v125 no13 p6 O 17 2016

MLB'S "SURREAL" SEASON OPENER R. A. BERENZ *TV Guide* v65 no13 p48 Mr 20 2017

The Most Valuable Baseball Teams M. K. OZANIAN, K. BADENHAUSEN et al chart color *Forbes* v199 no5 p28 My 16 2017

TREND SPOTTING J. Sheehan chart color *Sports Illustrated* v126 no16 p44 Je 5 2017

WHAT ON EARTH IS IT? J. BERNHARD chart *Phi Kappa Phi Forum* v97 no1 p32 Spr 2017

Major League Baseball (Organization)—History

PEAK CONCERN M. Bechtel and T. Keith color *Sports Illustrated* v127 no9 p12 S 25 2017

Present Moment J. Fuchs and T. Keith color *Sports Illustrated* v126 no13 p20 My 8 2017

Major League Baseball (Organization)—History—21st century

5 BOLD PREDICTIONS FOR MLB'S SECOND HALF B. Reiter color *Sports Illustrated* v127 no2 p39 Jl 17 2017

Gray Area J. Dickey and T. Keith color *Sports Illustrated* v126 no14 p20 My 15-22 2017

Leading Off B. Reiter color *Sports Illustrated* v126 no10 p10 Ap 10 2017

Thrones of Their Own B. Marks and T. Keith color *Sports Illustrated* v127 no2 p22 Jl 17 2017

Major League Baseball (Organization)—Management

Actionable Offenses T. Verducci, T. Keith et al color diag *Sports Illustrated* v126 no7 p20 Mr 6 2017

Major League Baseball Advanced Media LP

CAN THE EMERGENCE OF A HIGH-TECH TOOL BRING BASE BALL'S STATISTICAL REVOLUTION TO FIELDING? B. SCHOENFELD *New York Times Magazine* p48 O 2 2016

Major League Soccer (Organization)

GOAL ORIENTED J. A. MILLER *Cincinnati Magazine* v50 no7 p24 Ap 2017

JUST FOR KICKS J. DUGDALE color *Chicago* v66 no8 p24 Ag 2017

Majorana fermions

Chiral Majorana fermion modes in a quantum anomalous Hall insulator–superconductor structure Q. Lin He, L. Pan et al diag *Science* v357 no6348 p294 Jl 21 2017

Signs of Majorana fermion detected E. CONOVER color *Science News* v192 no2 p8 Ag 19 2017

Majors, Katie Davis

Daring to Hope: Finding God's Goodness in the Broken and the Beautiful *Publishers Weekly* v264 no33 p72 Ag 14 2017

MAJUMDAR, ARUN

Advancing clean energy *Issues in Science & Technology* v33 no3 p5 Spr 2017

Majumder, Mary A.

Myriad take two: Can genomic databases remain secret? color *Science* v356 no6338 p586 My 12 2017

MAJURE, LUCAS C.

The Role of Botanical Gardens in the Conservation of Cactaceae *BioScience* v66 no12 p1057 D 1 2016

Makarenko, Adam

Imagining Exoplanets A. Tesar color *Walrus* v14 no5 p59 Je 2017

Makari, George

Mind the Gap T. EHRENFELD cartoon *Weekly Standard* v22 no14 p36 D 12 2016

Makarova, Ekaterina, 1988-

HOT | NOT T. Keith color *Sports Illustrated* v126 no16 p30 Je 5 2017

Make Me (Cry) (Music)

17 Questions With Noah Cyrus color *Seventeen* v76 no3 p16 My 2017

Make Noise! (Music)

The Hot Box chart *Downbeat* v84 no4 p51 Ap 2017

Make Them Die Slowly (Music)

'Make Them Die Slowly (John George Haigh)' J. DARNIELLE color *New York Times Magazine* p34 Mr 12 2017

Make-up brushes

Make your brushes work harder P. STABLES color *Redbook* p10 My 2017

Make-up brushes—Evaluation
   Fabulous Gifts [Cover story] color *Good Housekeeping* v263 no6 p59 D 2016
   Fara Homidi color *InStyle* v24 no10 p190 O 2017
   Inspector Gadget color *InStyle* v24 no9 p339 S 2017
   MAKEUP BRUSHES color *InStyle* v23 no13 p211 D 2016
   NOT-SO-BASIC BRUSHES A. Jordan color *Essence* v47 no9 p34 Ja 2017
   ON MAKEUP AND MEDITATION [Cover story] color *Women's Health* v14 no5 p50 Je 2017
MakeMusic Inc.
   Finale Notation Software M. Kern color *Downbeat* v83 no12 p107 D 2016
Maker, Thon
   DIFFERENCE MAKER R. Nadkarni color *Sports Illustrated* v126 no12 p34 My 1 2017
Makerspaces
   Makerspaces and Design Thinking: Perfect Together! K. JARRETT *Education Digest* v82 no4 p50 D 2016
Makeup artists
   About Face E. Graves *Martha Stewart Living* p8 O 2017
   BACK to the Future C. ELLENBERG color *Vogue* v207 no3 p366 Mr 2017
   Bold Always Wins A. Steinherr bw color *Glamour* v115 no11 p150 N 2017
   Kodo Nishimura M. Scarles color *Tricycle: The Buddhist Review* v27 no1 p22 Fall 2017
   Meet Michelle Obama's Secret Weapon T. Williams and Ying Chu color *Glamour* v115 no2 p54 F 2017
   MODEL MOMENTS BEST LIP LOOKS color *Harper's Bazaar* no3656 p385 S 2017
   Pop-tastic! bw cartoon color *Martha Stewart Living* p25 O 2017
   the RUN-DOWN N. Spradley color *Essence* v47 no11 p33 Mr 2017
   Sir John K. B. Brown color *InStyle* v24 no6 p86 Je 2017
   Smoky EYES D. Gluck color *InStyle* v23 no12 p223 N 2016
Makhmutov, Vladimir
   Global atmospheric particle formation from CERN CLOUD measurements bibl graph map *Science* v354 no6316 p1119 D 2 2016
Maki, Sydney
   Hass Avocado color graph *Bloomberg Businessweek* no4533 p31 Ag 7 2017
Makina Yabashi
   A three-dimensional movie of structural changes in bacteriorhodopsin bibl diag graph *Science* v354 no6319 p1552 D 23 2016
Making History (TV program)
   Blast from the Past D. Snierson color *Entertainment Weekly* no1456 p38 Mr 10 2017
   Making History D. Holbrook *TV Guide* v65 no8 p34 F 27 2017
Makiya, Kanan
   The Rope J. Waterbury *Foreign Affairs* v96 no1 p173 Ja/F 2017
Makkai, Rebecca
   THE SEEKERS color *O, The Oprah Magazine* p96 O 2017
MAKOFF-CLARK, ANNIE
   'No.' Is that all you're telling unsuccessful applicants? Most employers have given up on offering interview feedback - but if you handle it carefully, there s no reason to stay silent *People Management* p14 Jl 2017
Makoha, Nick
   FROM THE KING *New York Times Magazine* p15 Jl 16 2017
Makoto, Azuma, 1976-
   WELCOME TO THE ISSUE color *Harper's Bazaar* no3652 p40 Ap 2017
Makoto Araki
   Mind the gap: Neural coding of species identity in birdsong prosody bibl graph *Science* v354 no6317 p1282 D 9 2016
Makoto Kurachi
   The epigenetic landscape of T cell exhaustion bibl graph *Science* v354 no6316 p1165 D 2 2016
   Epigenetic stability of exhausted T cells limits durability of reinvigoration by PD-1 blockade bibl graph *Science* v354 no6316 p1160 D 2 2016
Makri, Anita
   Back to the future color *Science* v355 no6323 p355 Ja 27 2017
Maksik, Alexander
   If He Writes It, She Will Come D. VANN *New York Times Book*

Review p18 O 16 2016
Malacari, M.
   Observation of a large-scale anisotropy in the arrival directions of cosmic rays above 8×1018 eV *Science* v357 no6357 p1266 S 22 2017
Malachi, Carolyn—Interviews
   THE RISE OF CAROLYN MALACHI *Washingtonian Magazine* v52 no5 p18 F 2017
Malafronte, Judith
   American Identity: Tenor Nicholas Phan, who sings Berlioz's Roméo et Juliette with San Francisco Symphony this month, thrives on exploring an eclectic repertoire *Opera News* v81 no12 p1 Je 2017
   Berlioz: Roméo et Juliette *Opera News* v81 no9 p52 Mr 2017
   Handel: Alcina *Opera News* v81 no6 p53 D 2016
   La Clemenza di Tito *Opera News* v81 no9 p36 Mr 2017
   Nabucco *Opera News* v81 no9 p33 Mr 2017
Malakoff, David
   A battle over the 'best science' color *Science* v355 no6330 p1108 Mr 17 2017
   Lawmakers balk at most Trump cuts color *Science* v357 no6346 p11 Jl 7 2017
   Machines are getting much, much smarter color *Science* v354 no6310 p278 O 21 2016
   A MATTER OF FACT color *Science* v355 no6325 p562 F 10 2017
   Record storm puts gulf resilience to the test color *Science* v357 no6355 p954 S 8 2017
   Republicans ready a regulatory rollback color *Science* v354 no6315 p951 N 25 2016
   SCIENCE LESSONS FOR THE NEXT PRESIDENT *Science* v354 no6310 p274 O 21 2016
   Trump targets environmental science for cuts color graph *Science* v355 no6329 p1000 Mr 10 2017
   Trump team targets key climate metric color *Science* v354 no6318 p1364 D 16 2016
Malamut, Adam
   HOW WORK STYLES INFORM LEADERSHIP [Cover story] A. BEARD color *Harvard Business Review* v95 no2 p58 Mr/Ap 2017
Malamut, Melissa
   Out of Left Field color *Rodale's Organic Life* v3 no1 p84 Ja 2017
Malamuth, Neil
   Men Who Buy Sex Prove Sexually Coercive *USA Today Magazine* v145 no2859 p10 D 2016
Malanowski, Jamie
   Bright Idea *Smithsonian* v47 no8 p11 D 2016
Malaria
   50, 100 & 150 YEARS AGO color *Scientific American* v317 no4 p93 O 2017
Malaria diagnosis
   Revolutionary malaria tests have unexpected downsides L. Roberts color *Science* v357 no6351 p536 Ag 11 2017
Malaria prevention
   Africa's CDC Can End Malaria C. Manlan color *Scientific American* v317 no3 p10 S 2017
   Glycophorin alleles link to malaria protection E. A. Winzeler diag *Science* v356 no6343 p1122 Je 16 2017
   Malaria Dollars and Sense D. L. SMITH and J. M. COHEN bw color *Natural History* v125 no9 p28 S 2017
   Tomorrow: Carl Swanson: Where's Our Laser-Shooting Mosquito Death Machine? Nathan Myhrvold said he was making just that in 2010. We re still waiting img *New York* v50 no15 p8 Jl 24 2017
Malaria—Transmission
   Malaria molecule lures mosquitoes L. HAMERS color *Science News* v191 no5 p10 Mr 18 2017
   The 'Super-Malaria' on the Rise In Southeast Asia T. John color *Time* v190 no14 p11 O 9 2017
Malarkey, Nadia
   From Weedy to Wonderful J. Marinelli color *National Wildlife (World Edition)* v55 no3 p22 Ap/My 2017
Malaska, Mike
   AID FOR WHAT AILS YOU color *Golf Magazine* v59 no1 p39 Ja 2017
Malatesta, Martina
   CRISPRi-based genome-scale identification of functional long

noncoding RNA loci in human cells bibl graph *Science* v355 no6320 p1 Ja 6 2017

Malawi—Environmental conditions

How the church can prevent climate displacement T. Pulaski *America* v216 no6 p10 Mr 20 2017

Malaysia Airlines Flight 17 Crash, 2014

Disinformation Technology J. Pollock bw diag *MIT Technology Review* v120 no3 p64 My/Je 2017

Malaysia Airlines Flight 370 Incident, 2014

Uncharted Territory T. Cook color *Scientific American* v317 no1 p23 Jl 2017

Malaysia—Foreign relations

WATER K. ATHERTON *Popular Science* v289 no2 p64 Mr/Ap 2017

MALCHIK, ANTONIA

Uncertain Weather *Orion Magazine* v36 no1 p11 Ja/F 2017

MALCOLM, CANDICE

A Jihadist Hits the Jackpot color *Weekly Standard* v22 no43 p16 Jl 24 2017

The Merit System color *Weekly Standard* v23 no1 p11 S 11 2017

MALCOLM, JANET

Robert B. Silvers (1929–2017) [Cover story] bw color *New York Review of Books* v64 no8 p31 My 11 2017

THE STORYTELLER bw cartoon *New Yorker* v93 no31 p38 O 9 2017

Malcolm, Noel

Passions for the Past: The Aubrey Story color *New York Review of Books* v63 no19 p36 D 8 2016

Malcolm, Philippe

Fast exoskeleton optimization color graph *Science* v356 no6344 p1230 Je 23 2017

Malcolm, Scott

Dedicating Agricultural Land to Energy Crops Would Shift Land Use *Amber Waves: The Economics of Food, Farming, Natural Resources, & Rural America* p33 Ap 2017

Malcom, Shawna

TV's HOTTEST COUPLES *TV Guide* v64 no15 p28 Ap 4 2016

Maldacena, Juan

BLACK HOLES, WORMHO LES AND THE SECRETS OF QUANTUM SPACETIME color diag *Scientific American* v315 no5 p26 N 2016

A COSMIC CONTROVERSY color *Scientific American* v317 no1 p5 Jl 2017

Maldarelli, Claire

battling a waterborne plague cartoon *Popular Science* v289 no2 p78 Mr/Ap 2017

breast reconstruction, on my own time color *Popular Science* v289 no6 p78 N/D 2017

Cells that kill cancer [Cover story] color *Popular Science* v289 no6 p12 N/D 2017

clock-stoppers color *Popular Science* v289 no5 p88 S/O 2017

Finally, a Vaccine for Dengue [Cover story] color *Popular Science* v288 no6 p36 N/D 2016

I WISH SOMEONE WOULD INVENT... cartoon *Popular Science* v289 no2 p98 Mr/Ap 2017

I WISH SOMEONE WOULD INVENT... cartoon *Popular Science* v289 no5 p98 S/O 2017

the thirsty body cartoon diag *Popular Science* v289 no2 p18 Mr/Ap 2017

through the looking glass bw *Popular Science* v289 no2 p86 Mr/Ap 2017

upside-down lightning color *Popular Science* v289 no4 p90 Jl/Ag 2017

WE WISH SOMEONE WOULD INVENT... color *Popular Science* v289 no6 p98 N/D 2017

THE WORST PLACES LIFE LOVES TO LIVE cartoon *Popular Science* p30 Ja/F 2017

YOUR BRAIN ON DRUGS cartoon *Popular Science* p28 Ja/F 2017

your brain: time machine color *Popular Science* v289 no5 p6 S/O 2017

Maldives

Island Time A. SESSA color *Architectural Digest* v74 no4 p80 Ap 2017

Maldives—Description & travel

5 Romantic Destinations for a Baecation D. POINTDUJOUR

color *Ebony* v72 no4 p66 F 2017

In the Name of Love R. Cusk color *Conde Nast Traveler* v52 no2 p60 F 2017

Maldon Salt Co.

SALT OF THE EARTH N. Paumgarten color *Bon Appetit* v62 no4 p84 Ap 2017

Maldonado, Paula

A switch from canonical to noncanonical autophagy shapes B cell responses bibl graph *Science* v355 no6325 p641 F 10 2017

Male, Timothy David

Quantify endangered species listings color *Science* v356 no6345 p1342 Je 30 2017

Male actors

See also

Bisexual actors

Mad, Democrats? Blame the Iran Deal *Commentary* p1 Ja 2017

Mad, Democrats? Blame the Iran Deal *Commentary* v143 no1 p1 Ja 2017

Patrick GIBSON *Interview* v47 no5 p71 Je/Jl 2017

Star Wars' Secret Weapon J. WEINER color *Rolling Stone* no1278/1279 p20 Ja 12 2017

Male authors—Interviews

GQHQ bw color *GQ: Gentlemen's Quarterly* v97 no7 p8 Jl 2017

Richard Holmes *New York Times Book Review* p6 Mr 5 2017

Male comedians

Super-Bright (and Pretty Dark) Future J. Carmichael cartoon color *GQ: Gentlemen's Quarterly* v97 no5 p51 My 2017

Male contraception

Male contraceptives

See also

Condoms

Contraception mans up A. KINGSTON color *Maclean's* v130 no4 p8 My 2017

The Elusive Male Pill E. Lissner *MIT Technology Review* v120 no3 p10 My/Je 2017

A Miracle Drug Big Pharma Doesn't Want A. Altstedter, J. S. Hopkins et al color graph *Bloomberg Businessweek* no4517 p22 Ap 3 2017

WHAT DO WE HAVE TO DO TO GET THE MALE PILL? E. Anthes color *Bloomberg Businessweek* no4533 p44 Ag 7 2017

Male cooks

YOTAM OTTOLENGHI C. BARBOUR color *Architectural Digest* v73 no11 p112 N 2016

Male dancers

ALEXANDER MARYIANOWSKI H. Rolfe *Dance Spirit* v21 no3 p40 Mr 2017

An American in Tel Aviv B. BARRY *Dance Magazine* v91 no1 p101 Ja 2017

THE BOYS OF BALLET M. Fuhrer *Dance Spirit* v21 no3 p36 Mr 2017

CHRISTOPHER GRANT *Dance Spirit* v21 no3 p39 Mr 2017

ESTEBAN HERNÁNDEZ N. Loeffler-Gladstone *Dance Spirit* v21 no3 p40 Mr 2017

Male domination (Social structure)

Does Your Company Come Across as Too Male? A. Wittenberg-Cox *Harvard Business Review Digital Articles* p2 Ja 25 2016

Of Meat and Men A. Chen color *Scientific American* v316 no5 p22 My 2017

Male employees

Does Your Company Come Across as Too Male? A. Wittenberg-Cox *Harvard Business Review Digital Articles* p2 Ja 25 2016

Flex Time Doesn't Need to Be an HR Policy S. Behson *Harvard Business Review Digital Articles* p2 D 4 2014

Why Some Men Pretend to Work 80-Hour Weeks E. Reid *Harvard Business Review Digital Articles* p2 Ap 28 2015

Male friendship

A FINE BROMANCE J. WOLCOTT color *Vanity Fair* v59 no9 p148 S 2017

TIME FOR A MAN-CATION! D. Sax, J. GORDINIER et al color *Esquire* p114 O 2017

Male infertility

THE QUESTION K. TATUSKO HENRY *Washingtonian Magazine* v52 no5 p192 F 2017

Male infertility—Treatment

THE RED LINE S. S. Hall color diag *Scientific American* v315 no3 p54 S 2016

Speedy Delivery C. Zuckerman color *National Geographic* v230 no4 p18 O 2016

Male musicians

James Rivers and the 'Pipes E. Laborde *New Orleans Magazine* v51 no8 p16 Je 2017

Male reproductive organs

Female embryos dismantle male tissue T. HESMAN SAEY color *Science News* v192 no4 p10 S 16 2017

Male singers

Chris Cornell 1964-2017 [Cover story] D. Fricke, K. Grow et al bw color *Rolling Stone* no1289 p40 Je 15 2017

Willie Nelson P. DOYLE *Rolling Stone* no1288 p18 Je 1 2017

Male singers—Interviews

Bubbles comes back to life E. IANNACCI color *Maclean's* v129 no41 p50 O 17 2016

Q&A Robert Plant P. DOYLE color *Rolling Stone* no1297 p19 O 5 2017

Male teachers

THE ULTIMATE MEN'S HEALTH GUY M. SAGER bw cartoon color *Men's Health* v32 no9 p96 N 2017

Male-to-female transsexuals

BLAQUE OUT: BEING OUTED AS TRANS DIDN'T RUIN THIS YOUTUBE STAR. IT GAVE HER MORE FREEDOM D. GUERRERO color graph *Advocate* no1091 p78 Je/Jl 2017

SHE'S ALL THAT: LESBIAN SENSATION GIGI GORGEOUS IS ALSO A MODEL, SPOKESPERSON, ACTIVIST, AND A TRANS WOMAN IN LOVE D. GUERRERO color *Advocate* no1091 p77 Je/Jl 2017

Malech, Dora

I NOW PRONOUNCE YOU *New Yorker* v93 no15 p52 My 29 2017

Male employees—Charts, diagrams, etc.

MIND THE GAP A. Montañez graph *Scientific American* v317 no3 p78 S 2017

Malek, Alia

The Home That Was Our Country: A Memoir of Syria color *Publishers Weekly* v264 no2 p59 Ja 9 2017

Malek, Rami, 1981-

THE GOLDEN GLOBES: Who Should Win? M. ROUSH *TV Guide* v65 no2 p8 Ja 2 2017

MAVERICKS OF STYLE D. ROOKWOOD color *Esquire* v166 no5 p98 D 2016/Ja 2017

Mr. Robot 1. Ratledge *TV Guide* v65 no41 p37 O 2 2017

Mr. Robot Killed the Hollywood Hacker C. Doctorow color *MIT Technology Review* v120 no1 p100 Ja/F 2017

Malek, Rami, 1981—Interviews

6 loaded questions for Rami Malek J. Harman bw *Glamour* v115 no9 p44 S 2017

Malena, D. A.

Chronic exposure to neonicotinoids reduces honey bee health near corn crops diag *Science* v356 no6345 p1395 Je 30 2017

Malenka, Robert C.

Brains, environments, and policy responses to addiction color *Science* v356 no6344 p1237 Je 23 2017

Gating of social reward by oxytocin in the ventral tegmental area color graph *Science* v357 no6358 p1406 S 29 2017

Maléombho, Loza—Interviews

COUTURE CURATOR M. BOBO color *Ebony* v72 no4 p56 F 2017

Malesic, Jonathan

FIELD OF VISION color *America* v215 no11 p29 O 17 2016

FROM GOWN TO TOWN color *America* v215 no13 p34 O 31 2016

The Rich We Will Always Have With Us color *America* v216 no11 p50 My 15 2017

Searching for George W. Bush in his portraits of soldiers he sent to war color *America* v216 no7 p48 Ap 3 2017

Malespina, Elissa

Teachers and librarians talk favorite classroom purchases color *Publishers Weekly* v264 no34 p70 Ag 21 2017

MALETZKY, BARRY

LEARNING CODE color *Scientific American* v317 no4 p8 O 2017

Malheur National Wildlife Refuge (Or.)

HINDSIGHT I. Frazier cartoon *New Yorker* v93 no12 p17 My 8 2017

Malheur Refuge on the Rebound P. Tolmé color *National Wildlife (World Edition)* v55 no1 p14 D/Ja 2016

Malhi, Y.

Persistent effects of pre-Columbian plant domestication on Amazonian forest composition bibl chart graph map *Science* v355 no6328 p925 Mr 3 2017

Malhotra, Deepak

A Definitive Guide to the Brexit Negotiations *Harvard Business Review Digital Articles* p2 Ag 5 2016

How to Negotiate After a Staggering Defeat: A Playbook for Democrats *Harvard Business Review Digital Articles* p2 N 16 2016

What Donald Trump Doesn't Understand About Negotiation *Harvard Business Review Digital Articles* p2 Ap 8 2016

Malhotra, Neil

Research: Political Polarization Is Changing How Americans Work and Shop *Harvard Business Review Digital Articles* p2 My 19 2017

Malhotra, Saira

Critical consciousness A key to student achievement bw il *Phi Delta Kappan* v98 no5 p18 F 2017

Mali, Anaïs

State of Undress bw color *Glamour* v115 no6 p122 Je 2017

Malibu (Calif.)—Description & travel

Carbon Beach P. GUZMÁN color *Conde Nast Traveler* v52 no7 p32 Ag 2017

Malibu Boats LLC

Malibu Did What? Malibu's new 21 VLX is the boat many people wanted to own but didn't think they could afford A. JONES *Boating World* v38 no6 p34 Je 2017

Malibu Corp.

Malibu M235 *Boating World* v38 no1 p70 Ja 2017

Malicious accusation

I Came Here for an Argument G. NORMAN color *Weekly Standard* v22 no16 p16 D 26 2016

Malick, Courtney

Institute for New Feeling color *Art in America* v104 no10 p25 N 2016

Malick, Terrence, 1945-

18. See Voyage of Time *New York* v49 no21 p121 O 17 2016

Form and Void E. HYNES color *Film Comment* v53 no1 p14 Ja/F 2017

THE NOT-SO-SECRET LIFE OF TERRENCE MALICK E. BENSON *Texas Monthly* v45 no4 p114 Ap 2017

Tiny Dancers Abound In Song to Song S. Zacharek color *Time* v189 no12 p57 Ap 3 2017

Voyage of Time more art film than documentary E. Wayman color *Science News* v190 no9 p29 O 29 2016

Maligres, Peter

A multifunctional catalyst that stereoselectively assembles prodrugs diag *Science* v356 no6336 p426 Ap 28 2017

Malik, Naureen S.

Q&A color *Bloomberg Businessweek* no4496 p85 O 24 2016

A Shock From Cheap Gas color map *Bloomberg Businessweek* no4524 p38 My 29 2017

The U.S. unleashes the full power of shale, as a wave of its LNG exports hits the market color map *Bloomberg Businessweek* no4496 p76 O 24 2016

Malik, Rubina

Why Men Have More Help Getting to the C-Suite *Harvard Business Review Digital Articles* p2 N 16 2015

Malik, Veena

Where Artists Fall Afoul of Blasphemy Laws T. John color *Time* v189 no19 p13 My 22 2017

Malin, Gray

TURN AN UNUSED GARAGE INTO A Guest Retreat A. CHANTIM color diag *Good Housekeeping* v265 no1 p44 Jl 2017

Malin, Zoe

Show Up. Be You color *Glamour* v115 no5 p18 My 2017

Malina, Joshua

7 — THE WEST WING WEEKLY C. Everett *Entertainment Weekly* no1444/1445 p114 D 16 2016

Maling, George C. Jr

Leo Leroy Beranek *Physics Today* v70 no10 p74 O 2017

Maling, Jeff

Are You Accurately Measuring Your Company's Digital Strength?

Harvard Business Review Digital Articles p2 S 7 2017

Malinovska, Liliana
ATP as a biological hydrotrope color graph *Science* v356 no6339 p753 My 19 2017

Malins, Greg—Interviews
Friends: The One With the Giant Turkey A. Wilkinson color *Entertainment Weekly* no1441 p48 N 25 2016

Máliš, František
Combining Biodiversity Resurveys across Regions to Advance Global Change Research *BioScience* v67 no1 p73 Ja 2017

Maljkovic Berry, Irina
Dengue diversity across spatial and temporal scales: Local structure and the effect of host population size bibl graph *Science* v355 no6331 p1302 Mr 24 2017

Malkiel, Nancy Weiss
How Smart Women Got the Chance L. Greenhouse bw *New York Review of Books* v64 no6 p21 Ap 6 2017

Mälkki, Susanna, 1969-
360 DEGREES J. DUCHEN *Opera News* v81 no6 p34 D 2016
Susanna Mälkki J. Crelin color *Current Biography* v78 no5 p53 My 2017

Malkoc, Selin
Free up your "me time" color *Redbook* p93 Mr 2017
Planning Events Make Them Seem Like Work *USA Today Magazine* v145 no2863 p7 Ap 2017

Malkowski, Jennifer
Dying in Full Detail: Mortality and Digital Documentary K. CUMMINGS *Film Quarterly* v71 no1 p113 Fall 2017

MALKUS, PHILIP
GRANDMA USED TO MAKE *Atlanta* v56 no9 p76 Ja 2017

Mall, The (Washington, D.C.)
At Last, a Black History Museum E. Ball bw color *New York Review of Books* v63 no18 p14 N 24 2016

Mall, U.
Xenon isotopes in 67P/Churyumov-Gerasimenko show that comets contributed to Earth's atmosphere diag *Science* v356 no6342 p1069 Je 9 2017

Mallaby, Sebastian
Alan Shrugged J. FOX *New York Times Book Review* p14 N 6 2016
BY THE SEAT OF HIS PANTS J. MADRICK bw *Nation* v303 no22 p31 N 28 2016
The Man Who Knew Better R. Alcaly bw cartoon *New York Review of Books* v64 no3 p24 F 23 2017
The Man Who Knew: The Life and Times of Alan Greenspan R. N. Cooper *Foreign Affairs* v95 no6 p174 N/D 2016
A New Look at Greenspan Shows the Economic Perils of Trusting Oracles R. Foroohar color *Time* v188 no18 p24 O 31 2016
One for the Money R. Cooper *Washington Monthly* p5 N/D 2016
WHAT HATH GREENSPAN WROUGHT R. J. Samuelson *Claremont Review of Books* v17 no1 p70 Wint 2016/2017
Will Trump Destroy the Dollar? color *Atlantic* v319 no5 p15 Je 2017

Mallaby, Sebastian—Interviews
Charlie Rose talks to... Sebastian Mallaby A. Greenspan bw *Bloomberg Businessweek* no4501 p16 N 28 2016

Mallakpour, Iman
Lessons from the Oroville dam bibl *Science* v355 no6330 p1139 Mr 17 2017

Mallamaci, M.
Observation of a large-scale anisotropy in the arrival directions of cosmic rays above 8×10^{18} eV *Science* v357 no6357 p1266 S 22 2017

Mallard
wildlife quiz cartoon color *Cabin Living* p11 Je 2017

Malle, Chloe
BowWow color *Vogue* v207 no9 p450 S 2017
DOMINICAN DREAM color *Architectural Digest* no6 p124 Je 1 2017
GIRL TALK color *Vogue* v207 no1 p76 Ja 2017
IN FULL BLOOM color *Vogue* v207 no6 p114 Je 2017

Malle, Frédéric, 1962-
Sacred Spaces W. ROBINSON color *Esquire* p126 BigBlackBook
SPLASH of the TITANS H. Bowles and C. ELLENBERG bw color *Vogue* v207 no3 p372 Mr 2017

Malleret, Benoit

Mapping the human DC lineage through the integration of high-dimensional techniques diag *Science* v356 no6342 p1044 Je 9 2017

Mallery, Susan
Second Chance Girl *Publishers Weekly* v264 no34 p97 Ag 21 2017
You Say It First: Happily Inc., Book 1 color *Publishers Weekly* v264 no24 p47 Je 12 2017

Mallet, G. M.
Devil's Breath: A Max Tudor Mystery color *Publishers Weekly* v264 no8 p68 F 20 2017

Mallet, Robert
Earthquakes G. TARLACH color *Discover* v38 no4 p74 My 2017

Mallet, Veronique
Keeping history close K. INGRAM color *Maclean's* v130 no8 p13 S 2017

Malliakas, Christos D.
Bottom-up construction of a superstructure in a porous uranium-organic crystal color graph *Science* v356 no6338 p624 My 12 2017

MallinCam (Company)
Get started in VIDEO ASTRONOMY J. Thompson color *Astronomy* v45 no11 p62 N 2017

Mallinson, Allan
Muddled thinking on the Western Front T. Downing *History Today* v67 no1 p65 Ja 2017
The Permanent Stain of the Somme *History Today* v66 no11 p72 N 2016

Mallo, Ernesto
Buenos Aires Noir *Publishers Weekly* v264 no39 p86 S 25 2017

Mallon, Thomas
'Amid All This Emotional Upheaval' *New York Times Book Review* p27 D 11 2016
The Best of Words bw *New York Times Book Review* p17 S 25 2016
Bookends T. Mallon and L. Schillinger *New York Times Book Review* p27 S 3 2017
GO TO HIS GRAVE cartoon *New Yorker* v92 no49 p89 F 13 2017
JACK BE NIMBLE bw cartoon *New Yorker* v93 no14 p81 My 22 2017
LEAST LIKELY TO SUCCEED T. MALLON cartoon *New Yorker* v93 no27 p72 S 11 2017
PRESUMPTIVE cartoon color *New Yorker* v92 no35 p36 O 31 2016
What's the best book, new or old, you read this year? *New York Times Book Review* p27 D 25 2016

Mallory, Mark
LETTER FROM THE EDITOR J. STOWE *Cincinnati Magazine* v50 no7 p14 Ap 2017

Mallory LLC
PARTS & STUFF color *Hot Rod* v70 no9 p108 S 2017

Mallory Kotz, Vanessa
LEAVING A MARK bw color *Popular Photography* v81 no1 p24 Ja/F 2017

Mallowan, Max
REVIVING A RUINED CITY A. R. Williams bw color *National Geographic* v232 no1 p28 Jl 2017

Malloy, Timothy F.
Policy reforms to update chemical safety testing bibl color *Science* v355 no6329 p1016 Mr 10 2017

MALLUE, HANK
READERS' THOUGHTS ON PAST ISSUES color *Motor Trend* v69 no2 p26 F 2017

Malmberg, Jeff
All the World's Their Stage M. ATKINSON *In These Times* v41 no10 p44 O 2017

Malmedy Massacre, 1944-1945
Remember Malmedy G. SCHOENFELD bw *Weekly Standard* v22 no39 p36 Je 19 2017

Malmi, Joni
JONI MALMI T. Bird bw cartoon *Snowboarder* v29 no4 p38 D 2016

MALMO, KATHERINE
How to Be an Islander *Sierra* v102 no4 p60 Jl/Ag 2017
"THE LAST THING I EXPECTED when I was expecting was breast cancer." color *Good Housekeeping* v265 no4 p95 O 2017

Malmstrom, Malin

We Recorded VCs' Conversations and Analyzed How Differently They Talk About Female Entrepreneurs *Harvard Business Review Digital Articles* p2 My 17 2017

Malnight, Thomas

The Best Companies Aren't Afraid to Replace Their Most Profitable Products *Harvard Business Review Digital Articles* p2 Jl 14 2016

Malnutrition

Can you, should you, have medically tailored food delivered to your home? *Harvard Health Letter* v42 no10 pCover Ag 2017

More Than Skin Deep J. M. BRUCKNER color *Discover* v38 no10 p20 D 2017

The Slow-Motion Disaster M. Chan *Nutrition Action Health Letter* v44 no3 p7 Ap 2017

Malnutrition—Prevention

MULTI-TASKING [Cover story] D. SCHARDT *Nutrition Action Health Letter* v43 no9 p3 N 2016

Malone, Alexander K.

Community network for deaf scientists color *Science* v356 no6336 p386 Ap 28 2017

Malone, Jo

Jo Malone's secrets to picking a fragrance V. Kirby bw color *Redbook* p59 D 2016

Malone, John, 1941-

The Example Larry and Sergey Should Follow (It's Not Buffett) T. R. Eisenmann *Harvard Business Review Digital Articles* p2 Ag 12 2015

Malone, Matt

All the Way With J.F.K *America* v216 no12 p3 My 29 2017

Alternative facts and the coming constitutional crisis *America* v216 no3 p3 F 6 2017

Civil Society and a Public Argument *America* v217 no7 p3 O 2 2017

Here are the "America Jeopardy!" questions, er, answers *America* v217 no2 p3 Jl 24 2017

It's gut-check time *America* v216 no5 p3 Mr 6 2017

Living Waters *America* v217 no6 p3 S 18 2017

OF MANY THINGS *America* v215 no10 p2 O 10 2016

OF MANY THINGS *America* v215 no19 p2 D 19 2016

Out of Many, One *America* v217 no5 p3 S 4 2017

President Trump's ties to Russia matter. Here's why *America* v216 no4 p3 F 20 2017

Short attention spans, short news cycles and short form Gospels *America* v216 no7 p3 Ap 3 2017

A Tree Grows on the Marne *America* v216 no10 p3 My 1 2017

The virtue of a Catholic journalist *America* v217 no3 p3 Ag 7 2017

What to Think of the Reverend Graham *America* v216 no8 p3 Ap 17 2017

The women who marched *America* v216 no11 p3 My 15 2017

Malone, Michael J.

A Suitable Lie *Publishers Weekly* v263 no47 p93 N 21 2016

Malone, Michael S.

How New Technologies Push Us Toward the Past *Harvard Business Review Digital Articles* p2 My 8 2015

What Happens to Society When Robots Replace Workers? *Harvard Business Review Digital Articles* p2 D 10 2014

Malone, Mike

garden SMART J. A. BAGGETT color *Better Homes & Gardens* v95 no8 p92 Ag 2017

Malone, Noreen

Cosby's Accusers On the Mistrial: "We wanted to stand witness." img *New York* v50 no13 p10 Je 26 2017

Hillary Clinton Thought Brooklyn Could Be the Capital of America img *New York* v49 no25 p86 D 12 2016

OBAMA'S AMERICA img *New York* v49 no20 p12 O 3 2016

TO UNDERSTAND THIS NEW RIGHT, IT HELPS TO SEE IT NOT AS A FRINGE MOVEMENT, BUT A POWERFUL COUNTERCULTURE img *New York* v50 no9 p24 My 1 2017

Zoë and the Trolls img *New York* v50 no15 p21 Jl 24 2017

Malone, Sean W.

Will OpenBazaar Succeed Where Silk Road Failed? color *Reason* v48 no7 p46 D 2016

MALONE, TESS

ASHEVILLE *Atlanta* v56 no7 p56 N 2016

ATLANTA IN 50 OBJECTS *Atlanta* v56 no8 p50 D 2016

BEST OF ATLANTA *Atlanta* v56 no8 p106 D 2016

Bread WINNERS *Atlanta* v56 no7 p85 N 2016

DECK THE PAWS *Atlanta* v56 no8 p45 D 2016

A DREADFUL TIME *Atlanta* v57 no6 p36 O 2017

DREAM WEAVERS *Atlanta* v57 no4 p28 Ag 2017

THE HENDERSON *Atlanta* v57 no1 p97 My 2017

HOLDING ON *Atlanta* v57 no2 p30 Je 2017

How to be Funny *Atlanta* v57 no6 p81 O 2017

IN PERFECT HARMONY *Atlanta* v56 no12 p40 Ap 2017

Maya Penn *Atlanta* v56 no12 p46 Ap 2017

OH, CANADA! *Atlanta* v56 no11 p36 Mr 2017

Play by Play: Lawrenceville's Aurora Theatre finds inspiration in the diversity of its audience *Atlanta* v57 no6 p82 O 2017

THE PLAY'S THE THIHG *Atlanta* v56 no7 p38 N 2016

RURAL RETROSPECTIVE *Atlanta* v56 no10 p40 F 2017

St. Beauty *Atlanta* v57 no4 p30 Ag 2017

Maloney, Carolyn, 1946-

Honorable Carolyn Maloney *Congressional Digest* v95 no9 p28 N 2016

Maloney, Clare

Eight Things We Love About Gene Luen Yang: The ILA 2017 Featured Speaker is a literacy advocate on a mission to diversify children's literature color *Literacy Today (2411-7862)* v34 no6 p32 My/Je 2017

VALUING THEIR CHOICES: Fuel students' love for literature with their own reading picks map *Literacy Today (2411-7862)* v34 no6 p12 My/Je 2017

MALONEY, CLIFF JR.

Speak Your Piece *USA Today Magazine* v146 no2868 p31 S 2017

Maloney, Margaret

Letters to the Editor color *Prevention* p4 Mr 2017

MALONEY, SUZANNE

Bomb Scares *New York Times Book Review* p10 O 2 2016

Maloney, Tim

HOW TO REMAKE A CITY J. WILLIAMS *Cincinnati Magazine* v50 no7 p46 Ap 2017

Maloof, Nikki

Fair Thee Well K. McMAHON color *ARTnews* v116 no1 p48 Spr 2017

MALOUF, JUMAN

Big Books for Small People color *New York Times Book Review* p32 D 4 2016

Malpas, Jodi Ellen

The Forbidden *Publishers Weekly* v264 no20 p43 My 15 2017

Malpass, David

DEMOCRACIES IN UPHEAVAL *Forbes* v198 no9 p32 D 30 2016

DON'T LET THE FED BE ANOTHER OBAMACARE color *Forbes* v199 no4 p13 Ap 25 2017

REVOLUTION AT LABOR *Forbes* v199 no1 p32 Ja 24 2017

TRUMP–CLINTON 9.0 EARTHQUAKE *Forbes* v198 no7 p42 N 29 2016

Malpractice—Prevention

Fact Checking the 'Fact Checkers' *Weekly Standard* v22 no6 p2 O 17 2016

Malsin, Jared

Al-Qaeda Is Gathering Strength As Yemen Burns color *Time* v189 no6 p11 F 20 2017

The Beginning of the End color map *Time* v189 no15 p30 Ap 24 2017

The Fighters In the Battle for Mosul color *Time* v188 no18 p10 O 31 2016

Hamas Takes a Step Away from Isolation color *Time* v190 no13 p15 O 2 2017

Hot Spots and Double-Talk color *Time* v188 no22-23 p29 N/D 2016

Iraq Takes on ISIS color map *Time* v188 no19 p32 N 7 2016

Lebanon's New Leader Aims to Keep 'Regional Fires' at Bay color *Time* v188 no20 p9 N 14 2016

Lightbox color *Time* v189 no15 p14 Ap 24 2017

Lightbox color *Time* v189 no3 p12 Ja 16 2017

New Travel Ban Helps U.S.-Iraq Relations but Still Stings Elsewhere color *Time* v189 no10 p7 Mr 20 2017

Next Generation Leaders color *Time* v190 no16/17 p74 O 23 2017

Qatar Settles In for a Long Standoff color *Time* v190 no6 p10 Ag 7 2017

Recep Tayyip Erdogan color *Time* v188 no25-26 p106 D 19 2016

Double Issue

The Referendum Vote That Could Fracture Iraq map *Time* v190 no12 p13 S 25 2017

TIME's Foreign Correspondents on How the World Sees the U.S. Election *Time* v188 no16/17 p34 O 24 2016

Turkey's Controversial Referendum color *Time* v189 no11 p11 Mr 27 2017

A U.S. Commander's Year on the Front Line Against ISIS In Iraq and Syria color *Time* v190 no10/11 p14 S 18 2017

The White Helmets of Syria [Cover story] color *Time* v188 no15 p20 O 17 2016

Will Turkey Vote to Give Erdogan Even More Power? color *Time* v189 no4 p11 F 6 2017

With Aleppo's Fall, Syria's Civil War Reaches a Grim Turning Point color diag *Time* v188 no27-28 p11 D 26 2016

Yemen's Tragic Civil War Reaches a New Level of Violence color *Time* v188 no16/17 p7 O 24 2016

Malt liquors

See also

Beer

STARTING A PODCAST J. SCOTT *Successful Farming* v115 no6 p16 Ap 2017

Malta

At Home in a Strange Land J. McDermott color *America* v216 no4 p28 F 20 2017

Malta, Grazia

Identification of single-site gold catalysis in acetylene hydrochlorination bw diag graph *Science* v355 no6332 p1399 Mr 31 2017

Maltby, Richard E., Jr.

BY THE NUMBERS *Harper's Magazine* v334 no2001 p95 F 2017

Malter, Emily

MODERN ROYALS color *Sunset* v239 no1 p36 Jl 2017

ROAD WARRIORS color *Sunset* v239 no1 p24 Jl 2017

What's the Beef? Do the Math *Sierra* v102 no2 p38 Mr/Ap 2017

Maltese dog

SUGAR Taylor *Interview* v46 no8 p128 O 2016

Maltzan, Michael

Sixth Street Viaduct D. S. Glenn *Architectural Record* v205 no4 p207 Ap 2017

Malware (Computer software)

See also

Computer viruses

Ransomware

7 Ways to Block Computer Viruses D. SHADEL color *AARP: The Magazine* v60 no5A p26 Ag/S 2017

BOTNETS of Things B. SCHNEIER chart color map *MIT Technology Review* v120 no2 p88 Mr/Ap 2017

CYBERCRIME GETS PERSONAL A. Rock color diag *Money* v46 no2 p66 Mr 2017

Froth on the daydream C. Day *Physics Today* v69 no10 p8 O 2016

New macOS ransomware spotted L. Constantin color *Macworld - Digital Edition* p8 Ap 2017

News: Corrupt video link causes iPhones to crash O. Raymundo color *Macworld - Digital Edition* p8 Ja 2017

Malware (Computer software)—Prevention

How to remove ransomware: Use this battle plan to fight back M. HACHMAN color *PCWorld* v35 no4 p129 Ap 2017

Malygina, Anastasia

Amid high tensions, an urgent need for nuclear restraint bibl *Bulletin of the Atomic Scientists* v73 no4 p279 Jl 2017

Mamane, Bako

The extent of forest in dryland biomes [Cover story] chart map *Science* v356 no6338 p635 My 12 2017

Mamelukes

NAPOLÉON'S EGYPTIAN RIDDLE J. W. Shosenberg cartoon color map *Military History* v34 no1 p22 My 2017

MAMELUND, SVENN-ERIK

Profiling a Pandemic bw color *Natural History* v125 no9 p6 S 2017

Mamet, David, 1947-

David Mamet's Prescience G. HILLARD *National Review* v69 no18 p20 O 2 2017

PARODY color *Weekly Standard* v22 no34 p48 My 15 2017

Mamet, Zosia, 1988-

Short Stories E. Wilson color *InStyle* v24 no5 p70 My 2017

Mamihlapinatapai (Poem)

Mamihlapinatapai D. Barber *American Scholar* v86 no1 p53 Wint 2017

Mammal conservation

See also

Rhinoceroses—Conservation

Can we protect island flying foxes? C. E. Vincenot, F. B. Vincent Florens et al color *Science* v355 no6332 p1368 Mr 31 2017

Mammal diversity

DNA bucks tale of horse taming T. HESMAN SAEY color *Science News* v191 no10 p10 My 27 2017

Mammal ecology

Saving the World's Terrestrial Megafauna W. J. RIPPLE, R. L. BESCHTA et al color *BioScience* v66 no10 p807 O 1 2016

Mammal populations

See also

Bear populations

Deer populations

Moose populations

Muskox populations

The impact of hunting on tropical mammal and bird populations A. Benítez-López, R. Alkemade et al graph map *Science* v356 no6334 p180 Ap 14 2017

Mammalian embryos

A microtubule-organizing center directing intracellular transport in the early mouse embryo J. Zenker, M. D. White et al diag *Science* v357 no6354 p925 S 1 2017

Mammalogy

Calendar of meetings *BioScience* v67 no3 p313 Mr 2017

Mammals

See also

Bats

Primates

Rodents

BATS' EARS MAY SOLVE AN EVOLUTIONARY PUZZLE *Physics Today* v70 no3 p22 Mr 2017

Charting a Century of Climate Change A. MURDOCK *USA Today Magazine* v145 no2860 p72 Ja 2017

Closing the loop B. Levine bibl bw *Science* v354 no6315 p968 N 25 2016

SCALY SUPERHEROES D. BROWN color map *National Geographic Kids* no470 p22 My 2017

Mammals—Extinction

Hunting driving many mammals to edge color *Science* v354 no6310 p266 O 21 2016

Saving the World's Terrestrial Megafauna W. J. RIPPLE, R. L. BESCHTA et al color *BioScience* v66 no10 p807 O 1 2016

Mammals—Hibernation

THE RETURN OF THE GRIZZLY A. TEASDALE *Sierra* v102 no1 p38 Ja/F 2017

Mammals—Locomotion

PEDALS THE BEAR J. MOOALLEM *New York Times Magazine* p22 D 25 2016

Mammals—United States

Up to Speed: Two Months, One Page P. Rauber *Sierra* v101 no5 p19 S/O 2016

Mammaplasty

See also

Augmentation mammaplasty

THE BENEFITS D. L. Colgan *Washingtonian Magazine* v52 no1 p117 O 2016

breast reconstruction, on my own time C. Maldarelli color *Popular Science* v289 no6 p78 N/D 2017

Mammary gland physiology

Decoding hormones for a stem cell niche C. Robertson color *Science* v356 no6335 p250 Ap 21 2017

Mammary gland secretions

Decoding hormones for a stem cell niche C. Robertson color *Science* v356 no6335 p250 Ap 21 2017

Mammograms

An Individual Approach to Breast Cancer A. Park color *Time* v190 no15 p40 O 16 2017

Lest We Forget *Ms.* v27 no2 p6 Summ 2017

NEW THINK ON MAMMOGRAMS *Health* v30 no10 p16 D 2016

Why do mammograms squeeze my breasts between two x-ray

Grote color *Harvard Business Review Digital Articles* p2 Ja 2 2017

How Overfocusing on Goals Can Hold Us Back A. J. Smart *Harvard Business Review Digital Articles* p2 Mr 17 2016

Management committees—Congresses

Why Excom Meetings Are the Wrong Place to Make Decisions J. Neatby *Harvard Business Review Digital Articles* p2 Jl 8 2015

Management of charities

"Cybersecurity is now an essential part of our values": How a growing charity secured its data by changing behaviours C. NEWBERRY *People Management* p23 Mr 2017

"I used to spend half my time on candidates' complaints": How the charity revamped its applicant experience as part of an ambitious HR transformation project *People Management* p22 S 2017

"We trained the whole organisation - and it didn't cost us anything": Britain's biggest nature charity shows how everyone can benefit from leadership training - not just leaders R. JEFFERY *People Management* p18 Mr 2017

Management of government agencies

Advice on Running a Government Agency Like a Startup, from Someone Who's Tried It M. Hoch *Harvard Business Review Digital Articles* p2 Ap 12 2017

Management of public records

BUILDING BLOCKS: BLOCKCHAIN TECHNOLOGY COULD REMAKE GOVERNMENT SERVICES FROM THE GROUND UP L. Farmer *Governing* v30 no12 p44 S 2017

Management of teams in the workplace

What to Do About Mediocrity on Your Team J. Grenny *Harvard Business Review Digital Articles* p2 Ap 20 2017

Management research

What Is Management Research Actually Good For? G. F. Davis *Harvard Business Review Digital Articles* p2 My 28 2015

Management styles

Google's Secret Formula for Management? Doing the Basics Well R. Sadun *Harvard Business Review Digital Articles* p2 2017

How Overfocusing on Goals Can Hold Us Back A. J. Smart *Harvard Business Review Digital Articles* p2 Mr 17 2016

Old Management Systems Stifle New Business Models M. Wessel, J. Allworth et al *Harvard Business Review Digital Articles* p2 Ap 28 2015

Research on Delegating Shows How Uncomfortable We Are Making Choices for Others M. Steffel, E. F. Williams et al *Harvard Business Review Digital Articles* p2 Ag 30 2016

Security Software, Insecurity Culture L. Chapman and S. McBride color *Bloomberg Businessweek* no4519 p38 Ap 24 2017

What Peter Drucker Knew About 2020 R. Wartzman *Harvard Business Review Digital Articles* p2 O 16 2014

Why Is Micromanagement So Infectious? N. Canner and E. Bernstein *Harvard Business Review Digital Articles* p2 Ag 17 2016

Management—Employee participation

See also

Employee empowerment

Overcome Resistance to Change by Enlisting the Right People T. Warner *Harvard Business Review Digital Articles* p2 S 13 2016

What Great Managers Do to Engage Employees J. Harter and A. Adkins *Harvard Business Review Digital Articles* p2 Ap 2 2015

Management—Moral & ethical aspects

Keep a List of Unethical Things You'll Never Do M. Chussil *Harvard Business Review Digital Articles* p2 My 30 2016

Management—Philosophy

See also

Theory of constraints (Management)

HOW TO TURN SECOND PLACE INTO A WIN M. Heimer *Fortune* v176 no2 p72 Ag 1 2017

What If Management Ideas Actually Mattered? G. Petriglieri *Harvard Business Review Digital Articles* p2 N 5 2015

Management—United States

Managing Expectations for 2047: Here are the five trends we predict will unfold over the next three decades K. Barrett and R. Greene *Governing* v31 no1 p58 O 2017

Managerial economics

Most On-Demand Businesses Aren't Actually Disruptive S. Sachdev and M. Wessel *Harvard Business Review Digital Articles* p2 S 29 2015

Managing your boss

How to Earn Your Manager's Respect R. Knight *Harvard Business Review Digital Articles* p2 D 2 2016

To Boost Your Career, Get to Know Your Boss's Boss R. Knight *Harvard Business Review Digital Articles* p2 S 2 2016

What to Do When Your Boss Has a Favorite (and It's Not You) R. Knight *Harvard Business Review Digital Articles* p2 Je 16 2016

Manasseh, Tamar

CHICAGOANS OF THE YEAR [Cover story] R. Babcock, A. Samuels Gibbs et al color *Chicago* v65 no12 p74 D 2016

Manatees

The Quiz T. BALAZO color *Maclean's* v130 no7 p65 Ag 2017

Man Called Ove, A (Film)

A Swedish curmudgeon, redeemed by children and cats J. Anderson color *America* v216 no4 p50 F 20 2017

Mancarella, F.

Seasonal exposure of carbon dioxide ice on the nucleus of comet 67P/Churyumov-Gerasimenko bibl bw graph *Science* v354 no6319 p1563 D 23 2016

Mance, Steven M.

Reconstruction of CES time series: implementing the 2010 OMB metropolitan area delineations bibl chart color graph *Monthly Labor Review* p1 O 2016

Manchess, Gregory

Above the Timberline C. CUINN color *Publishers Weekly* v264 no39 p90 S 25 2017

Manchester (England)

Green House Effect C. FOGES *Architectural Record* v205 no7 p109 Jl 2017

Manchester by the Sea (Film)

BEST DIRECTOR CONTENDER KENNETH LONERGAN N. Sperling color *Entertainment Weekly* no1441 p40 N 25 2016

Bleak Houses J. PODHORETZ *Weekly Standard* v22 no15 p39 D 19 2016

A Boy's LIFE N. HELLER color *Vogue* v206 no12 p204 D 2016

Character Studies R. Alleva color *Commonweal* v144 no3 p21 F 10 2017

Dark Journey R. DOUTHAT color *National Review* v68 no24 p43 D 31 2016

FIGHTING DEMONS A. LANE cartoon *New Yorker* v92 no39 p96 N 28 2016

In a Tragedy, Casey Affleck Finds Triumph S. Lansky color *Time* v188 no22-23 p98 N/D 2016

MANCHESTER BY THE SEA J. Krebs color *Sound & Vision* v82 no6 p71 Jl/Ag 2017

Manchester by the Sea *New Yorker* v92 no49 p15 F 13 2017

MANCHESTER by the SEA S. Vilkomerson color *Entertainment Weekly* no1438 p43 N 4 2016

MOVIES OF THE YEAR P. TRAVERS color *Rolling Stone* no1276 p24 D 15 2016

No. 3 MANCHESTER BY THE SEA L. Greenblatt color *Entertainment Weekly* no1444/1445 p51 D 16 2016

NOW PLAYING color *Entertainment Weekly* no1448 p50 Ja 13 2017

NOW PLAYING color *Entertainment Weekly* no1450 p47 Ja 27 2017

The Real Best Pictures of 2016 M. ATKINSON *In These Times* v41 no2 p38 F 2017

Slow Burn D. EDELSTEIN img *New York* v49 no23 p82 N 14 2016

Winter Preview R. Brody cartoon *New Yorker* v92 no37 p18 N 14 2016

The WORLD is FULL of WEEPING M. KORESKY color *Film Comment* v52 no6 p48 N/D 2016

Manchester City Football Club

BRIGHT LIGHTS, BIG CITY G. Wahl color *Sports Illustrated* v126 no14 p60 My 15-22 2017

Manchester United (Soccer team)

BRIGHT LIGHTS, BIG CITY G. Wahl color *Sports Illustrated* v126 no14 p60 My 15-22 2017

THE CITY'S OTHER FOOTBALL FANS C. PENDLEY *Atlanta* v56 no11 p98 Mr 2017

THE WORLD'S MOST VALUABLE SOCCER TEAMS M. K. OZANIAN and C. SETTIMI chart color *Forbes* v199 no7 p32 Je 29 2017

Manchester Arena Bombing, Manchester, England, 2017

An Attack on Girlhood C. Alter color *Time* v189 no21 p37 Je 5

2017

HOW SAFE ARE CONCERTS? K. O'Donnell, S. Helling et al color *Entertainment Weekly* no1468/1469 p16 Je 2-9 2017

MANCHESTER UNITED A. Bacle color *Entertainment Weekly* no1470 p11 Je 16 2017

Music's Scary New Reality S. KNOPPER, S. Hewitt et al color *Rolling Stone* no1289 p13 Je 15 2017

Savagery In the U.K. Britain Comes Under Attack at a Turning Point D. Stewart, T. John et al color *Time* v189 no21 p34 Je 5 2017

Manchurian Candidate, The (Film)
Classics of Conspiracy P. TONGUETTE color *National Review* v69 no19 p56 O 16 2017

Manco, Alicia
SIMPLY PERFECT S. SMITH color *House Beautiful* p122 Ag 2017

Mandaeans
A Refugee Without a River R. MELLEN color *Foreign Policy* no226 p12 S/O 2017

Mandala
Power Poses N. HORVATH color *Prevention* v69 no4 p96 Ap 2017

Mandat, D.
Observation of a large-scale anisotropy in the arrival directions of cosmic rays above 8 × 1018 eV *Science* v357 no6357 p1266 S 22 2017

Mandatory minimum sentences
JEFF SESSIONS, GLUTTON FOR PUNISHMENT J. Sullum *Reason* v49 no5 p6 O 2017

Mandatory retirement
Should Older CEOs Be Forced to Retire? W. Frick *Harvard Business Review Digital Articles* p2 F 15 2016

Mande, Joe
12. See Joe Mande *New York* v50 no16 p112 Ag 7 2017
FOLLOW THE MONEY cartoon *New Yorker* v92 no39 p50 N 28 2016

Mandegar, Mohammad A.
CRISPRi-based genome-scale identification of functional long noncoding RNA loci in human cells bibl graph *Science* v355 no6320 p1 Ja 6 2017

MANDEL, BETHANY
No Help for the Weary *Commentary* v142 no3 p46 O 2016

Mandel, Emily St. John, 1979-
Brave New World *New York Times Book Review* p9 O 30 2016
FEBRUARY'S COOLEST EVENTS *Indianapolis Monthly* p22 F 2017

Mandel, Howard
Hungarian Jazz Showcase: 10 Years in the Spotlight color *Downbeat* v84 no5 p14 My 2017
The Musician color *Downbeat* v84 no8 p71 Ag 2017

Mandel, Howie
CARAOKE SHOWDOWN L. ACKEN *TV Guide* v65 no4 p45 Ja 16 2017

Mandel, Howie—Interviews
AGING GRACEFULLY WITH HOWIE MANDEL B. Keyes-Bevan color *Maclean's* v129 no40 p58 O 10 2016

Mandel, James
How to Better Manage Your Company's Utility Bills *Harvard Business Review Digital Articles* p2 N 24 2015
A New Way to Think About Office Lighting *Harvard Business Review Digital Articles* p2 Je 27 2017

Mandel, Mark
Puccini/Hao: Turandot *Opera News* v81 no9 p50 Mr 2017

Mandel, Michael
Factories 2.0 *MIT Technology Review* v119 no6 p10 N/D 2016

Mandel, Seth
The Cautionary Tale of Samantha Power color *Commentary* v143 no2 p1 F 2017
The Cautionary Tale of Samantha Power *Commentary* v143 no2 p28 F 2017
Grave Matter; The desecration of Jewish cemeteries has a long history—one that has nothing to do with the election of Donald Trump *Commentary* v143 no4 p27 Ap 2017
Netanyahu, the Almost-American: Bibi's unique feel for the United States hasn't always paid off *Commentary* v142 no2 p40 S 2016

Mandelbaum, Ryan F.
Beat the Lines at the Polls color *Popular Science* v288 no6 p96 N/D 2016
The Death and Life of the Great Lakes color *Scientific American* v316 no3 p76 Mr 2017
Hidden Side Effects color *Scientific American* v316 no1 p18 Ja 2017
How to Go Sonic Without a Boom color *Popular Science* v288 no6 p56 N/D 2016
Icy Retreat diag *Scientific American* v316 no2 p17 F 2017
Telltale Sounds of Tsunamis color *Scientific American* v316 no4 p18 Ap 2017

MANDEL-CAMPBELL, ANDREA
Old Growth, New Shoots cartoon *Walrus* v13 no10 p44 D 2016

Mandelis, Andreas
Focus on analytical equipment, sensors, and detectors *Physics Today* v70 no2 p63 F 2017
Focus on lasers and imaging *Physics Today* v70 no4 p61 Ap 2017
Focus on lasers, imaging, and microscopy *Physics Today* v69 no11 p64 N 2016
Focus on materials, semiconductors, vacuum, and cryogenics *Physics Today* v69 no10 p62 O 2016
Focus on microscopy, imaging, and nanotechnology *Physics Today* v70 no9 p64 S 2017
Focus on test and measurement *Physics Today* v70 no3 p68 Mr 2017
Focus on test, measurement, and analytical equipment *Physics Today* v70 no8 p66 Ag 2017
Imaging cancer with PHOTOACOUSTIC RADAR *Physics Today* v70 no5 p42 My 2017

Mandell, Avi M.
HAT-P-26b: A Neptune-mass exoplanet with a well-constrained heavy element abundance chart diag graph *Science* v356 no6338 p628 My 12 2017

MANDELLA, RICHARD
Buckets Of Horse Sense *Los Angeles Magazine* v61 no11 p96 N 2016

Mandelstam, Stanley
Stanley Mandelstam Ling-Lie Chau *Physics Today* v70 no5 p69 My 2017

Mandiberg, Michael—Exhibitions
BANK SHOT M. Singer cartoon *New Yorker* v92 no30 p22 S 26 2016

Mandibular fractures—Case studies
A tale of two mandibles T. Moates bw cartoon *Equus* no474 p20 Mr 2017

Mandibular joint
See also
Temporomandibular joint
WHY IS MY JAW CLICKING AND POPPING? P. Marzban *Washingtonian Magazine* v52 no12 p116 S 2017

Mandinova, Anna
Potential role of intratumor bacteria in mediating tumor resistance to the chemotherapeutic drug gemcitabine diag *Science* v357 no6356 p1156 S 15 2017

Mandis, Steven G.
What It Will Take to Change the Culture of Wall Street *Harvard Business Review Digital Articles* p2 O 24 2014

Mandorla Awakening II: Emerging Worlds (Music)
The Hot Box J. McDonough, J. Corbett et al chart *Downbeat* v84 no7 p49 Jl 2017

Mandrus, David G.
Neutron scattering in the proximate quantum spin liquid a-RuCl3 bw diag *Science* v356 no6342 p1055 Je 9 2017
A parity-breaking electronic nematic phase transition in the spin-orbit coupled metal Cd2Re2O7 diag *Science* v356 no6335 p295 Ap 21 2017

Manduca, Robert
The fading American dream: Trends in absolute income mobility since 1940 bw graph *Science* v356 no6336 p398 Ap 28 2017

Mandvi, Aasif—Interviews
Aasif Mandvi Knows How To Make America Great Again A. M. Cox color *New York Times Magazine* p86 O 9 2016

Mane, Gucci
TRAP TO RICHES C. Lee *Atlanta* v57 no5 p32 S 2017

Mane, Prajkta

METEORITE ORIGINS color *Astronomy* v45 no11 p44 N 2017

Manent, Pierre

FRENCH RESISTANCE T. Anderson *Claremont Review of Books* v17 no1 p16 Wint 2016/2017

Making Room A. ORWIN *Weekly Standard* v22 no10 p39 N 14 2016

Maner, Jon

Good Bosses Switch Between Two Leadership Styles *Harvard Business Review Digital Articles* p2 D 5 2016

Man for All Seasons, A (Film)

A Man for All Seasons At 50 P. TONGUETTE bw *National Review* v68 no21 p45 N 21 2016

MANFREDO, MICHAEL J.

Modernization, Risk, and Conservation of the World's Largest Carnivores *BioScience* v67 no7 p646 Jl 2017

Manfrino, Carrie

Can We Save Coral Reefs? *UN Chronicle* v54 no1/2 p1 2017

Manga (Art)

Manga Mania A. Foxwell-Barajas color *Christianity Today* v60 no8 p24 O 2016

Manga (Art)—Sales & prices

NINE REASONS MANGA PUBLISHERS CAN SMILE IN 2017 D. AOKI color *Publishers Weekly* v264 no25 p80 Je 19 2017

MANGAN, ANNA M.

Addressing the Gender Gap in Distinguished Speakers at Professional Ecology Conferences *BioScience* v67 no5 p464 My 2017

MANGAN, CHUCK

FITTING TACK, PART 1: HALTER AND WESTERN *Arabian Horse World* v57 no1 p89 O 2016

Mangan, Scott A.

Plant diversity increases with the strength of negative density dependence at the global scale diag *Science* v356 no6345 p1389 Je 30 2017

Manganese oxides

Minerals Made by Microbes E. Estes color *Oceanus* v51 no2 p72 Wint 2016

Manganiello, Joe, 1976-

Joe Manganiello C. Mari color *Current Biography* v78 no3 p50 Mr 2017

Mangano, Joy

The Joy of Giving color *Good Housekeeping* v265 no5 p55 N 2017

Mangano, Michelangelo

Anniversaries for particle physics color *Science* v356 no6344 p1213 Je 23 2017

Mangano, Valentina D.

Resistance to malaria through structural variation of red blood cell invasion receptors diag *Science* v356 no6343 p1139 Je 16 2017

MANGEL, MARC

A UNIFIED VIEW OF DEVELOPMENT: MAKING EVO-DEVO OPERATIONAL *BioScience* v67 no5 p478 My 2017

Mangels, Reed

NUTRITION HOTLINE *Vegetarian Journal* v35 no2 p2 2016

NUTRITION HOTLINE *Vegetarian Journal* v35 no4 p2 2016

NUTRITION HOTLINE *Vegetarian Journal* v36 no2 p2 2017

NUTRITION HOTLINE *Vegetarian Journal* v36 no3 p2 2017

reviews. SUPERFOODS FOR LIFE, CACAO *Vegetarian Journal* v35 no1 p31 2016

SCIENTIFIC UPDATE. Long-Term Studies of Vegetarians in the Past 35 Years *Vegetarian Journal* v36 no3 p28 2017

SCIENTIFIC UPDATE *Vegetarian Journal* v35 no4 p6 2016

SCIENTIFIC UPDATE *Vegetarian Journal* v36 no1 p12 2017

SCIENTIFIC UPDATE *Vegetarian Journal* v36 no2 p10 2017

Mangeon, S.

A human-driven decline in global burned area chart graph map *Science* v356 no6345 p1356 Je 30 2017

Manges, Chuck

TAKE A SWIM IN THE LAGOON *Sky & Telescope* v133 no6 p74 Je 2017

Mangi, Faseeh

Brands Pump Up the Volume in Pakistan color graph *Bloomberg Businessweek* no4530 p34 Jl 17 2017

Mangin, John—Interviews

JOHN MANGIN J. Chen color *Bloomberg Businessweek* no4512 p83 F 20 2017

Manginis, George

Mount Sinai A. Cameron *History Today* v66 no10 p64 O 2016

Mangione, Marco

snapshot A. Klimoski color *Architectural Record* v205 no3 p144 Mr 2017

Mangla, Ismat Sarah

THE BEST PLACES TO LIVE IN AMERICA [Cover story] chart color map *Money* v46 no9 p54 O 2017

Mango

ALLERGY BUSTER [Cover story] color *Prevention* v69 no6 p13 Je 2017

Fruit with huge health benefits M. TAYLOR color *Redbook* p72 Jl/Ag 2017

Mango, Ruiz

Exposing Unfair Pricing in Auto Insurance Rates color *Consumer Reports* v82 no5 p6 My 2017

Mango growing

India in an Instant: The secret to an amazing mango kulfi comes in a can T. Rao *New York Times Magazine* p34 S 17 2017

Mango varieties

India in an Instant: The secret to an amazing mango kulfi comes in a can T. Rao *New York Times Magazine* p34 S 17 2017

Mangold, James

Logan C. Nashawaty color *Entertainment Weekly* no1456 p56 Mr 10 2017

Old Man Wolverine P. Travers color *Rolling Stone* no1283 p54 Mr 23 2017

Mangold, Peter

What the British Did R. Carver *History Today* v67 no3 p57 Mr 2017

Mangrove forests

Panama's impotent mangrove laws G. A. Castellanos-Galindo, L. C. Kluger et al bibl *Science* v355 no6328 p918 Mr 3 2017

Mangrove plants

The Caribbean's Crown Jewels color *National Geographic* v230 no5 p96 N 2016

Mangrum, Nicole—Interviews

Happy HAIR DAYS! color *O, The Oprah Magazine* p82 Mr 2017

Manguel, Alberto

1996: Toronto *Lapham's Quarterly* v10 no2 p99 Spr 2017

Mangum, Aja

BETTER WITH AGE color *Bloomberg Businessweek* no4507 p62 Ja 16 2017

NOT YOUR DAD'S AFTER-SHAVE color *Bloomberg Businessweek* no4523 p62 My 22 2017

The Right Kind of Shine color *Bloomberg Businessweek* no4512 p79 F 20 2017

SOAK IT ALL IN color *Bloomberg Businessweek* no4498 p84 N 7 2016

Manguso, Sarah

The Big Short R. SYME *New Republic* v248 no3 p66 Mr 2017

Choir *New York Times Magazine* p22 O 23 2016

IGNORANCE WAS BLISS bw *O, The Oprah Magazine* p32 D 2016

Paper Trail diag *New York Times Book Review* p9 Ag 6 2017

A QUIET DISCONTENT C. SHANE color *Nation* v304 no18 p42 Je 19 2017

MANGU-WARD, KATHERINE

ARMLESS DROID CALLS COPS AFTER BEING ASSAULTED BY DRUNKEN MAN color *Reason* v49 no3 p4 Jl 2017

A BIG FAT FREAK-OUT OVER DONALD TRUMP'S 'SKINNY' BUDGET color *Reason* v49 no2 p4 Je 2017

THE CARROT, THE STICK, AND THE BUGGY WHIP *Reason* v48 no10 p4 Mr 2017

COMMISSARY KITCHEN color *Reason* v48 no10 p65 Mr 2017

Cory Doctorow's 'FULLY AUTOMATED LUXURY COMMUNIST CIVILIZATION' bw color *Reason* v49 no4 p54 Ag/S 2017

Free Speech Gave Us Trump *Reason* v48 no7 p2 D 2016

GIANT ZIPLOCK BAGGIES FULL OF LAMBS ARE GOING TO CHANGE EVERYTHING color *Reason* v49 no4 p4 Ag/S 2017

GOOD NEIGHBORS CAN MAKE GOOD FENCES color *Reason* v49 no1 p4 My 2017

INTERVIEW: KENNEDY color *Reason* v49 no5 p46 O 2017

IT'S TIME TO PRIVATIZE THE V.A color *Reason* v49 no6 p4 N 2017

SHIV protection in macaques color graph *Science* v357 no6359 p85 O 6 2017

Manlan, Carl

Africa's CDC Can End Malaria color *Scientific American* v317 no3 p10 S 2017

MANLEY, ANDREA

LUXURY LOOK color *House Beautiful* p127 Ag 2017

STREAMLINE YOUR SPACE color *House Beautiful* p134 Ag 2017

Manley, Brendan

AMERICANS MARK CENTENNIAL OF U.S. ENTRY INTO WORLD WAR I bw *Military History* v34 no2 p8 Jl 2017

ASSOCIATED PRESS ADMITS WARTIME DEAL WITH NAZIS bw *Military History* v34 no4 p8 N 2017

CLUES SURFACE TO LOCATION OF ILL-FATED INDIANAPOLIS *Military History* v33 no5 p10 Ja 2017

FIRST SHIP BUILT IN NORTH AMERICA? *Military History* v33 no6 p10 Mr 2017

H.L. HUNLEY SUBMARINERS' DEATHS STILL A MYSTERY color *Military History* v34 no5 p10 Ja 2018

MUSEUM OF THE AMERICAN REVOLUTION OPENS IN PHILLY color *Military History* v34 no2 p10 Jl 2017

NAVY MARKS 75TH ANNIVERSARY OF PIVOTAL BATTLE OF MIDWAY bw *Military History* v34 no4 p10 N 2017

News color *Military History* v34 no5 p8 Ja 2018

News *Military History* v33 no6 p8 Mr 2017

OSS VETERANS RECEIVE CONGRESSIONAL GOLD MEDAL bw *Military History* v34 no1 p10 My 2017

PAUL ALLEN PINPOINTS WRECK OF USS INDIANAPOLIS bw *Military History* v34 no5 p8 Ja 2018

RESEARCHERS SEEK TO ID MEXICAN WAR REMAINS *Military History* v33 no6 p8 Mr 2017

VETERANS MARK 75 YEARS SINCE PEARL HARBOR STRIKE color *Military History* v34 no1 p8 My 2017

Manley, Ray

PHOTOGENIC CANYON DE CHELLY *Arizona Highways* v93 no10 p33 O 2017

Mann, Adam

Hunt for Planet Nine heats up diag *Science* v354 no6311 p399 O 28 2016

TRIAL BALLOONS color diag *Science* v356 no6344 p1227 Je 23 2017

Mann, Chris

APOLO OHNO color *Amazing Wellness* v8 no6 p20 Early Winter2016

In the Spotlight: Tia Mowry color *Better Nutrition* v79 no9 p16 S 2017

LINDA EVANS color *Amazing Wellness* v9 no6 p22 EarlyWint 2017

SPREADING HER WINGS color *Amazing Wellness* v9 no2 p20 Spr 2017

MANN, DAVE

Capitol Crisis *Texas Monthly* v45 no1 p18 Ja 2017

flush with power *Texas Monthly* v45 no2 p84 F 2017

Party Hopping *Texas Monthly* v45 no5 p18 My 2017

Right Aid *Texas Monthly* v44 no11 p26 N 2016

MANN, DENISE

I Survived! [Cover story] *Reader's Digest* v189 no1128 p62 Mr 2017

Mann, Edie

RENOVATION MADE EASIER color *Cabin Living* p64 S 2017

Mann, Gideon

Hiring Algorithms Are Not Neutral *Harvard Business Review Digital Articles* p2 D 9 2016

Mann, Graham

Global atmospheric particle formation from CERN CLOUD measurements bibl graph map *Science* v354 no6316 p1119 D 2 2016

Mann, Horace, 1796-1859

1783: London H. Walpole *Lapham's Quarterly* v10 no2 p157 Spr 2017

The Citified Origins of Summer Vacation O. B. Waxman *Time* v190 no5 p27 Jl 31 2017

Mann, James

The Adults in the Room [Cover story] *New York Review of Books* v64 no16 p6 O 26 2017

MANN, JENNIFER

class wars *Parents* v92 no1 p78 Ja 2017

Mann, Jennifer K.

Sam and Jump *Publishers Weekly* v263 no49 p24 D 7 2016

Mann, K.

Observation of coherent elastic neutrino-nucleus scattering diag *Science* v357 no6356 p1123 S 15 2017

Mann, M. Everett

Seismic constraints on caldera dynamics from the 2015 Axial Seamount eruption bibl color graph *Science* v354 no6318 p1395 D 16 2016

MANN, MARK

The Dead Zone color diag map *Walrus* v14 no6 p38 Jl/Ag 2017

Mann, Mary

Yawn: Adventures in Boredom *Publishers Weekly* v264 no7 p61 F 13 2017

Mann, Michael (Michael Kenneth), 1943-—Interviews

RE-PACKING HEAT D. Franich color *Entertainment Weekly* no1466 p42 My 19 2017

Mann, Michael E.

A Brilliant Climate Collaboration R. LADENDORF *Skeptical Inquirer* v41 no5 p60 S/O 2017

Climate Trumps Everything color *Scientific American* v316 no2 p8 F 2017

Doctor Doom I. TUTTLE *National Review* v69 no3 p23 F 20 2017

Public Debate, Scientific Skepticism, and Science Denial *Skeptical Inquirer* v41 no1 p40 Ja/F 2017

Mann, Michael—Interviews

Michael Mann and the Climate Wars M. BOSLOUGH *Skeptical Inquirer* v40 no6 p17 N/D 2016

Mann, Rebecca

Making Microfinance More Effective *Harvard Business Review Digital Articles* p2 O 5 2016

Mann, Richard

2016 BEST OF THE BEST bw color *Field & Stream* v121 no7 p96 D 2016/Ja 2017

CENTERFIRE SHOOTOUT 2017 color *Field & Stream* v122 no5 p74 O 2017

CONCENTRICITY color *Outdoor Life* v224 no5 pR4 Je/Jl 2017

FIELD TEST color *Field & Stream* v122 no2 p99 Je/Jl 2017

HOLSTER IT RIGHT color *Outdoor Life* v224 no4 pP8 My 2017

LONG-RANGE SHOOTOUT color *Field & Stream* v121 no6 p28 N 2016

LONG-RANGE/TACTICAL RIFLES color *Field & Stream* v122 no5 p80 O 2017

PEAK GLASS color *Field & Stream* v122 no4 p69 S 2017

SELF-DEFENSE FLASH-LIGHTS color *Outdoor Life* v224 no8 pP1 O 2017

SHOT TIMERS color *Outdoor Life* v224 no5 pR10 Je/Jl 2017

THE SLIDE STOP color *Outdoor Life* v224 no8 pP5 O 2017

TERMINAL BALLISTICS PRIMER color *Outdoor Life* v224 no4 pP6 My 2017

Mann, Susan

The Librarian and the Spy *Publishers Weekly* v264 no11 p65 Mr 13 2017

Mann, Terrence

Becoming a Cats Cat R. MILZOFF img *New York* v49 no15 p82 Jl 25 2016

Mann, Thomas E.

Play Hardball in Congress *New Republic* v248 no3 p32 Mr 2017

Mann, William J.

The Wars of the Roosevelts: The Ruthless Rise of America's Greatest Political Family W. Russell Mead *Foreign Affairs* v96 no3 p161 My/Je 2017

Mannarino, Melanie

1925 VERTICAL GARDENS color *Better Homes & Gardens* v95 no6 p168 Je 2017

eat your way to GORGEOUS color *Seventeen* p144 Ja 1 2017

ORGANIZE YOUR HEALTH RECORDS color *Better Homes & Gardens* v95 no8 p174 Ag 2017

Self-care for grown-ups color *Health* v31 no4 p98 My 2017

YOUR CHEAT SHEET TO... The Perfect Prom Night color *Seventeen* p208 Ja 1 2017

YO, YOGURT! color *Better Homes & Gardens* v95 no6 p166 Je 2017

Manne, Sasikanth

Epigenetic stability of exhausted T cells limits durability of reinvigoration by PD-1 blockade bibl graph *Science* v354 no6316 p1160 D 2 2016

Manned space flight

Apollo Astronauts Claimed to Hear 'Space Music' B. RADFORD *Skeptical Inquirer* v40 no6 p13 N/D 2016

Mannequins (Figures)

Ivan Lesica color *National Geographic* v230 no4 p15 O 2016

Mannerheim, Carl Gustaf Emil, friherre, 1867-1951

Start to Finnish C. Caldwell bw color *Weekly Standard* v22 no47 p44 Ag 21 2017

Manners & customs

See also

Award presentations
Cannibalism
Clothing & dress
Costume
Dating (Social customs)
Fairs
Festivals
Food habits
Frontier & pioneer life
Funerals
Gifts
Halloween
Handshaking
Holidays
Lifestyles
Necklaces
Nightlife
Recreation
Rings (Jewelry)
Salutations
Sleeping customs
Social norms
Special events
Tattooing
Tips & tipping (Gratuities)

30 Cool THINGS ABOUT HOLIDAYS J. BEER *National Geographic Kids* no466 p24 D 2016/Ja 2017

GREENLAND'S VANISHED VIKINGS Z. Zorich color map *Scientific American* v316 no6 p66 Je 2017

IN THIS CORNER... J. FIELDEN bw *Esquire* v166 no5 p28 D 2016/Ja 2017

UNDER CONSTRUCTION J. FRANZEN color *New Yorker* v93 no33 p50 O 23 2017

We always do that A. Scobey color *U.S. Catholic* v81 no11 p36 N 2016

MANNERS, IVETTE

On the Road color *Vogue* v207 no3 p390 Mr 2017

Manney, John

The Family Telescope: Even though I'd conceived of and built it, who was I to consider it my instrument? *Sky & Telescope* v134 no6 p84 D 2017

Manning, Chelsea, 1987-

Covering the Past A. WINTOUR bw color *Vogue* v207 no9 p232 S 2017

Free Radical N. Heller color *Vogue* v207 no9 p714 S 2017

PARODY color *Weekly Standard* v23 no4 p40 O 2 2017

Manning, Christie

Beyond the roots of human inaction: Fostering collective effort toward ecosystem conservation color diag *Science* v356 no6335 p275 Ap 21 2017

MANNING, DAN R.

TELL ME A STORY color *Missouri Life* v44 no4 p24 Je 2017

Manning, Kathleen

Upstart from Assisi: St. Francis is probably our most popular saint. But do we know who he really is? [Cover story] color *U.S. Catholic* v82 no10 p12 O 2017

Manning, Peyton, 1976-

PEYTON'S (OTHER) PLACE L. Jenkins and J. Feldman color *Sports Illustrated* v126 no11 p48 Ap 17-24 2017

Manning, Richard

OVER THE RIVER *Harper's Magazine* v334 no2000 p36 Ja 2017

POLITICAL CLIMBERS *Harper's Magazine* no2007 p45 Ag 2017

Manning, Tom

THIS IS THE STORY OF AMERICA'S FIRST PENIS TRANSPLANT J. DEAN cartoon color *Esquire* v167 no2 p122 Mr 2017

Mannion, Niccolo

IN THE MIDDLE C. Ballard color *Sports Illustrated* v126 no5 p100 F 13 2017

Manno, Bruno V.

Improve governance for charters *Phi Delta Kappan* v98 no6 p63 Mr 2017

The Schools We Deserve *Hoover Digest: Research & Opinion on Public Policy* no1 p146 Wint 2017

Manno, Olivia

Caffeine 101 color *Dance Spirit* v21 no2 p30 F 2017

DAMMIEL CRVZ *Dance Spirit* v21 no3 p38 Mr 2017

DID YOU KNOW? color *Dance Spirit* v20 no9 p32 N 2016

Eat YOUR HEART OUT color *Dance Spirit* v20 no9 p32 N 2016

Head CASE *Dance Spirit* v21 no4 p26 Ap 2017

NUTRITION LABEL Breakdown chart img *Dance Spirit* v21 no3 p28 Mr 2017

ON A Roll *Dance Spirit* v21 no4 p28 Ap 2017

PORT DE Bras *Dance Spirit* v21 no1 p32 Ja 2017

Split-sational *Dance Spirit* v21 no3 p34 Mr 2017

SUGAR, SPICE AND Everything Nice *Dance Spirit* v20 no10 p32 D 2016

WALKIN' ON SUNSHINE color *Dance Spirit* v21 no8 p54 O 2017

Mannon, Melissa

Hospitals Are Finally Starting to Put Real-Time Data to Use *Harvard Business Review Digital Articles* p2 N 12 2014

Mannor, Mike

How Anxiety Affects CEO Decision Making *Harvard Business Review Digital Articles* p2 Jl 19 2016

Mano, D. Keith, 1942-2016

The Gimlet-Eyed R. BROOKHISER bw color *National Review* v68 no20 p24 N 7 2016

Man of Good Hope, A (Theatrical production)

FIELD TRIP R. Mead cartoon *New Yorker* v93 no4 p30 Mr 13 2017

Man of Limited, A (Poem)

A MAN OF LIMITED *Harper's Magazine* v333 no1999 p22 D 2016

Manolo Blahnik International Ltd.

Heart and Sole L. Yaeger, M. HOLGATE et al color *Vogue* v207 no9 p388 S 2017

Party On (in Flats) E. Velluto color *Glamour* v115 no4 p68 Ap 2017

Manon Lescaut (Theatrical production)

Manon Lescaut A. J. Goldmann *Opera News* v81 no9 p45 Mr 2017

Manor houses

bentota, sri lanka F. A. BERNSTEIN color *Architectural Digest* no5 p84 My 2017

Manor houses—Design & construction

Cloud Nine S. WALLIS color *Architectural Digest* v74 no1 p224 Ja 2017

Manor houses—England

LIVING THE DREAM [Cover story] J. K. DE VALLE color *Architectural Digest* v74 no9 p114 S 2017

Manos, Merlyn

A Deadly New Front for ISIS color map *Time* v190 no1 p36 Jl 3 2017

Manrai, A.

Fostering reproducibility in industry-academia research color *Science* v357 no6353 p759 Ag 25 2017

Manring, Teresa

QUEENS FOR A DAY [Cover story] color *Chicago* v66 no9 p112 S 2017

Mansbridge, Jane

Introduction *Daedalus* v146 no3 p6 Summ 2017

Manseau, Peter

The Apparitionists: A Tale of Phantoms, Fraud, Photography, and the Man Who Captured Lincoln's Ghost *Publishers Weekly* v264 no29 p206 Jl 17 2017

Mansel, Philip

From Levantine glory to dystopian wreck R. Carver *History Today* v66 no10 p65 O 2016

MANSFIELD, GREGG

BOARDING PASS *Sea Magazine* v109 no4 p46 Ap 2017

DINGHIES DONE RIGHT *Sea Magazine* v109 no1 p50 Ja 2017

Sweat the Details: It's a great time to sell a boat. Here's how to get it ready color *Sea Magazine* v109 no8 p52 Ag 2017

Trailers Get Personal *Boating World* v38 no4 p12 Ap 2017

MANSFIELD, HARVEY

The Suicide of Meritocracy bw *Weekly Standard* v22 no46 p12 Ag 14 2017

The Vulgar Manliness of Donald Trump: The Greeks and the Founders feared men like the president, and with good reason *Commentary* v144 no2 p23 S 2017

Mansfield, Harvey C.

WHY WE WON'T AGREE *Claremont Review of Books* v17 no3 p40 Summ 2017

Mansion design & construction

The Jewelry Queen's Castle color *Forbes* v199 no6 p16 Je 13 2017

Mansions

5 WAYS TO LOVE OLD HOUSES *Yankee* v81 no1 p30 Ja/F 2017

The House That Changed Everything J. GOODRICH and B. MORGAN bw color *Yankee* p30 Mr 2017

McMANSIONS TO SPARE A. HOAK and L. WILLIAMSON color *Chicago* v66 no11 p22 N 2017

A NIGHT AT THE OLD MANSION E. Laborde *Louisiana Life* v37 no6 p4 Jl/Ag 2017

Mansions—California

Rosetta's THRONE E. Wilson color *InStyle* v24 no3 p344 Mr 2017

Mansions—Conservation & restoration

Saving Selma: After years of neglect from an absentee owner and decay significant enough to threaten its survival, historic Selma Mansion in Loudoun County is getting a second chance R. NELSON *Virginia Living* v15 no4 p45 Je 2017

Mansions—Design & construction

The Urbanist: The Rise of the Frankenmansion S. J. ROBLEDO img *New York* v49 no24 p41 N 28 2016

Mansions—Interior decoration

ROYALE MESS A. AMBROSIUS color *Chicago* v65 no11 p22 N 2016

Mansions—Sales & prices

On the Market G. MONTES color *Architectural Digest* v73 no11 p138 N 2016

This Mansion Just Took a $66 Million Price Cut R. Wile color diag map *Money* v46 no5 p18 Je 2017

Manso, Peter

A LEAD-FOOT'S LIBRARY color *Car & Driver* v63 no1 p26 Jl 2017

Manson, Charles, 1934-

DENNIS, CHARLIE... CHARLIE, DENNIS P. CARLSON *American History* v52 no1 p14 Ap 2017

Manson, Marilyn, 1969——Interviews

Marilyn Manson A. GREENE bw *Rolling Stone* no1298 p55 O 19 2017

Manson, Mark

The Steady Rise of 'Not Giving a F*ck' J. Boog bw color *Publishers Weekly* v264 no31 p6 Jl 31 2017

Manson, Shirley, 1966-

The Return of a Grunge Goddess: Shirley Manson, lead singer of '90s band Garbage, heads back on the road with Blondie D. Evans img *New York* v50 no11 p87 My 29 2017

Manson, Shirley, 1966——Interviews

Two Rock Icons Hop on a Conference Call... N. Feeney color *Entertainment Weekly* no1473 p56 Jl 7 2017

Mansoor, Lesila

Vaginal bacteria modify HIV tenofovir microbicide efficacy in African women chart graph *Science* v356 no6341 p938 Je 1 2017

Mansoorabadi, Steven O.

The biosynthetic pathway of coenzyme F430 in methanogenic and methanotrophic archaea bibl diag graph *Science* v354 no6310 p339 O 21 2016

MANSOUR, ALI

2017 CHEVY COLORADO ZR2 [Cover story] color *Dirt Sports + Off-Road* v51 no10 p42 O 2017

Mansouri, Reza

Iran's science landscape in context *Science* v354 no6319 p1542 D 23 2016

Mansur Gavriel LLC

Mansur Gavriel Coats R. WALDMAN, M. HOLGATE et al color *Vogue* v207 no9 p386 S 2017

Mantchev, Lisa

Someday, Narwhal *Publishers Weekly* v264 no34 p108 Ag 21 2017

Manteith, James

Great Scientists Against Terrible Odds J. Bernstein bw *New York Review of Books* v63 no19 p52 D 8 2016

Mantel, Hilary

AFTERMATH bw cartoon *New Yorker* v92 no38 p48 N 21 2016

FROM THE EDITOR FACTS AND FICTIONS *History Today* v67 no7 p3 Jl 2017

The Year in Reading [Cover story] *New York Times Book Review* p8 D 25 2016

Mantello, Joe—Interviews

TENNESSEE TITANS C. Collis color *Entertainment Weekly* no1454/1455 p70 F 24 2017

Mantels

MANTELPIECE THEATER color *Timber Home Living* v27 no6 p24 D 2017

Three Ways To Style a Mantel K. Owen color *Southern Living* v51 no12 p50 D 2016

Mantidae—Behavior

Birds as Prey for Praying Mantises M. NYFFELER color *Natural History* v125 no11 p14 N 2017

Mantsch, P.

Observation of a large-scale anisotropy in the arrival directions of cosmic rays above 8×1018 eV *Science* v357 no6357 p1266 S 22 2017

Mantua Metal Products Co.

Mantua's 4-4-0 Belle was a plain Jane K. Wills color *Model Railroader* v83 no12 p26 D 2016

Mantzoukas, Jason—Interviews

Jason Mantzoukas Bets On The House C. Collis color *Entertainment Weekly* no1473 p48 Jl 7 2017

Manual labor

YOU'RE OVER-DOING IT S. ROSEN color *GQ: Gentlemen's Quarterly* v97 no3 p138 Mr 2017

Manuel, Kanahus

Tiny houses for a big battle K. EDWARDS color *Maclean's* v130 no10 p11 N 2017

Manuel, Simone, 1996-

Beauty is Strength K. Greenidge color *Glamour* v115 no6 p134 Je 2017

Simone Manuel B. Muteba color *Current Biography* v78 no3 p54 Mr 2017

Manufactures

    See also

    Candle manufacturing

    Textile industry

    Toy manufacturing

foreword P. POORE *Old House Journal* v44 p8 2016 Design Center source Book

THE INNOVATORS *Los Angeles Magazine* p110 Mr 2017

The Limits of 3D Printing M. Holweg *Harvard Business Review Digital Articles* p2 Je 23 2015

MAKER CITY: BALTIMORE F. MAROUKIAN color *Popular Mechanics* p28 S 2017

Multiprocess 3D printing for increasing component functionality E. MacDonald and R. Wicker bibl bw color *Science* v353 no6307 paaf2093-1 S 30 2016

Manufactures—Charts, diagrams, etc.

PRODUCTION AND BUSINESS ACTIVITY *Economic Indicators* p17 Je 2017

Manufactures—France

France's Industrial Past Haunts Macron H. Fouquet, A. Nussbaum et al color *Bloomberg Businessweek* no4536 p44 S 4 2017

Manufactures—Sales & prices

U.S. Dental Labs Are Gritting Their Teeth J. S. Hopkins color *Bloomberg Businessweek* no4519 p24 Ap 24 2017

Manufactures—United States

MADE in the USA F. Maroukian and K. Dupzyk color *Popular Mechanics* p64 Jl 2017

THIS "BUY AMERICAN" THING *Popular Mechanics* p4 Jl 2017

We Can't Undo Globalization, but We Can Improve It color *Harvard Business Review Digital Articles* p2 Ja 10 2017

Manzatto, A. G.
Persistent effects of pre-Columbian plant domestication on Amazonian forest composition bibl chart graph map *Science* v355 no6328 p925 Mr 3 2017

Manzella, Brian
Why Can't I Get My Pitches to Bite? *Golf Magazine* v59 no11 p54 N 2017
Why Can't I Hit Long Bunker Shots? *Golf Magazine* v59 no2 p52 F 2017

Manzi, Jenelle
The Foodie Ballerina G. HENDERSON *Dance Magazine* v91 no8 p42 Ag 2017

Manzie, Johnny
FIELD OF NIGHTMARES B. BURROUGH color *Vanity Fair* v58 no11 p164 N 2016

Manziel, Johnny, 1992-
THE YEAR IN BUM STEERS Sports *Texas Monthly* v45 no1 p90 Ja 2017

Manzke, Margarita
HALO-HALO REMIX L. BURUM *Los Angeles Magazine* v61 no11 p133 N 2016

Manzoni, Jean-François
Dealing with a Hands-Off Boss *Harvard Business Review Digital Articles* p2 D 17 2014
To Get More Feedback, Act More Coachable *Harvard Business Review Digital Articles* p2 S 22 2016

Mao, Bizeng
Epigenetic regulation of antagonistic receptors confers rice blast resistance with yield balance bibl diag *Science* v355 no6328 p962 Mr 3 2017

Mao, Chengde
Reconfiguration of DNA molecular arrays driven by information relay diag *Science* v357 no6349 p371 Jl 28 2017

MAO, ELAINE
THE WORLD'S BILLIONAIRES bw color diag graph map *Forbes* v199 no3 p84 Mr 28 2017

Mao, M. Y.
Molecular gas in the halo fuels the growth of a massive cluster galaxy at high redshift bibl graph *Science* v354 no6316 p1128 D 2 2016

Mao, Qun-Quan
A central neural circuit for itch sensation color graph *Science* v357 no6352 p695 Ag 18 2017

Mao, Scott X.
Direction-specific van der Waals attraction between rutile TiO2 nanocrystals diag *Science* v356 no6336 p434 Ap 28 2017

Maochun Yu, Miles
China's Deep Logic *Hoover Digest: Research & Opinion on Public Policy* no4 p128 Fall 2016

Maor, Eli
1925 AN ECLIPSE LIKE NO OTHER *Sky & Telescope* v133 no1 p66 Ja 2017

Maori (New Zealand people)
MAORI MARTIAL ARTS J. Guttman *Military History* v33 no5 p48 Ja 2017

Maori (New Zealand people)—Religion
The Maori: separate and equal? P. Jenkins *Christian Century* v133 no22 p45 O 26 2016

Maori art
MAORI MARTIAL ARTS J. Guttman *Military History* v33 no5 p48 Ja 2017

Mapa, Lorina
Duran Duran, Imelda Marcos, and Me *Publishers Weekly* v264 no24 p49 Je 12 2017

Mapelli, Claudio
Formation of α-chiral centers by asymmetric β-C(sp3)–H arylation, alkenylation, and alkynylation bibl diag *Science* v355 no6324 p499 F 3 2017

MAPES, JAMES
One Sting Too Many *USA Today Magazine* v145 no2858 p37 N 2016

Mapes, Lynda V.
Witness Tree: Seasons of Change with a Century-Old Oak L. A. MARSCHALL color *Natural History* v125 no4 p47 Ap 2017

Maple
The Gratitude Meter Z. Donaldson color *O, The Oprah Magazine* p20 Mr 2017
TAP IT YOURSELF J. Nick cartoon *Rodale's Organic Life* v3 no1 p92 Ja 2017
Winner, Winner, Turkey Dinner J. Bober color *InStyle* v23 no12 p283 N 2016

Maple sap
What's On Tap? S. FORBES color *Rodale's Organic Life* v3 no1 p46 Ja 2017

Maple syrup
GREAT GIFTS UNDER $20 color *Better Homes & Gardens* v95 no11 p16 N 2017
MAKE HEALTHY COME TO YOU *Los Angeles Magazine* p113 Ap 2017
MMM...MORNING color *Good Housekeeping* v265 no2 p125 Ag 2017
Out & About J. B. ills color *Yankee* p80 Mr 2017
A TRIO OF WEAPONS TO FIGHT BACTERIA... color *Prevention* v69 no8 p11 Ag 2017

Maple syrup industry—Québec (Province)
STICKY BUSINESS R. COHEN color *Vanity Fair* v59 no1 p162 Holiday 2017

Maple syrup—Therapeutic use
A NEW LEAF color *Women's Health* v14 no7 p38 S 2017

Maplebear Inc.
$400 Million Richer By Pinching Pennies E. Huet *Bloomberg Businessweek* no4515 p29 Mr 20 2017

Maplewood (Mo.)
P.I.Y.: POUR-IT-YOURSELF J. B. Patton color *Missouri Life* v44 no6 p21 S 2017

Mapp, Rue
Healing Through Hikes M. C. O'Connor *Sierra* v102 no1 p25 Ja/F 2017

Mappes, Johanna
The biology of color color *Science* v357 no6350 p470 Ag 4 2017

Mapplethorpe, Robert, 1946-1989
Sexual Racism and Reckoning with Robert Mapplethorpe C. STEPHENS bw *Advocate* no1091 p44 Je/Jl 2017

Maps
    See also
    Atlases
    Historical geography—Maps
    Meteorological charts
    Military maps
    Nautical charts
    Oceanographic maps
    Wind power maps
    World maps
The 2015–2016 U.S. Snow Report: A Slim Year with A Few Surprises D. A. Robinson chart color map *Weatherwise* v69 no6 p21 N-D 2016
Arctic odysseys H. Wilson cartoon map *Canadian Geographic* v137 no2 p22 Mr/Ap 2017
The Artists' Bugout Bag J. Duckworth *Stage Directions* v30 no6 p36 Je 2017
Ask Smithsonian K. Nodjimbadem *Smithsonian* v47 no7 p104 N 2016
'Atlantis at its Prime', 1896 K. Wiles *History Today* v66 no12 p18 D 2016
BERING STRAIT, 1860S K. Wiles *History Today* v67 no8 p4 Ag 2017
Charting the Unseen Sky L. SCHLEY color *Discover* v38 no9 p19 N 2017
Global roadless areas: Hidden roads A. C. Hughes color *Science* v355 no6332 p1381 Mr 31 2017
Map Quest color map *Publishers Weekly* v264 no35 p40 Ag 28 2017
On the move A. POPE color *Canadian Geographic* v136 no6 p32 D 2016
Predicting where victims of Mexico's violence are buried L. Wade color map *Science* v356 no6345 p1317 Je 30 2017
Putting Canada on the map S. Nemis color map *Canadian Geographic* v137 no4 p24 Jl/Ag 2017
STORMY WATERS: The fight over New York City's flood lines R. Elliott and E. Rush map *Harper's Magazine* v335 no2005

p46 Je 2017

A tale of two cities H. Wilson bw *Canadian Geographic* v137 no3 p24 My 2017

Their native land N. Walker map *Canadian Geographic* v135 no6 p26 D 2015

Window Shades from Vintage Maps B. D. Coleman color *Old House Journal* v45 no5 p56 Ag 2017

Worldly Possessions *Martha Stewart Living* no267 p26 S 2016

Maps for people with visual disabilities
See also
Tactile maps

Navigating by Touch A. Marks color *Scientific American* v317 no3 p22 S 2017

Maps—Computer network resources—Evaluation

Interactive map reveals universe's hidden details C. Crockett color *Science News* v190 no11 p29 N 26 2016

Maps—Design & construction

A pattern most fowl H. Wilson map *Canadian Geographic* v136 no6 p24 D 2016

Maps—Evaluation

SCOUTING PARTY color *Popular Science* p12 Ja/F 2017

Maquat, Lynne E.

Tudor-SN–mediated endonucleolytic decay of human cell microRNAs promotes G1/S phase transition graph *Science* v356 no6340 p859 My 26 2017

Maquet, A.

Attosecond dynamics through a Fano resonance: Monitoring the birth of a photoelectron bibl graph *Science* v354 no6313 p734 N 11 2016

Mar, Jessica C.

Self-renewal of a purified Tie2+ hematopoietic stem cell population relies on mitochondrial clearance bibl graph *Science* v354 no6316 p1156 D 2 2016

Mara, Kate, 1983-

Kate Mara J. ZAMBRANO color *O, The Oprah Magazine* p23 Je 2017

Mara, Michael W.

Metalloprotein entatic control of ligand-metal bonds quantified by ultrafast x-ray spectroscopy diag *Science* v356 no6344 p1276 Je 23 2017

Mara, Rooney, 1985-

Rooney on the Move [Cover story] N. Heller color *Vogue* v207 no10 p243 O 2017

Marable, Karen Good

BLACK WOMEN IN HOLLYWOOD color *Essence* v47 no11 p87 Mr 2017

TO THE MOON color *Essence* v47 no10 p78 F 2017

Maracaibo Lake (Venezuela)

FLASH POINTS C. Zuckerman graph map *National Geographic* v230 no6 p8 D 2016

Maracaibo Lake (Venezuela)—Environmental conditions

Venezuelan lake is a lightning hot spot color *Science* v355 no6320 p10 Ja 6 2017

Maracle, Jonathan

The Indigenous Worship War M. LEE *Christianity Today* v61 no7 p20 S 2017

Mar-A-Lago National Historic Site (Palm Beach, Fla.)

Winter White House Z. J. Miller color *Time* v189 no7/8 p50 F 27 2017

Marandi, Alireza

A coherent Ising machine for 2000-node optimization problems bibl diag graph *Science* v354 no6312 p603 N 4 2016

A fully programmable 100-spin coherent Ising machine with all-to-all connections bibl diag graph *Science* v354 no6312 p614 N 4 2016

MARANO, HARA ESTROFF

BEHIND MY PEERS *Psychology Today* v49 no5 p22 S/O 2016

A Bug in the System *Psychology Today* v50 no3 p31 My/Je 2017

The Case for Choline *Psychology Today* v50 no1 p31 Ja/F 2017

A CHILD VOID? *Psychology Today* v50 no4 p21 Ag 2017

CRUISE CONTROL *Psychology Today* v50 no5 p22 S/O 2017

A DIAGNOSTIC DILEMMA *Psychology Today* v50 no2 p22 Mr/Ap 2017

E-ssential! Vitamin E is as necessary as oxygen, but just how much we need is still up in the air *Psychology Today* v50 no2 p31 Mr/Ap 2017

From Food to Mood: The bugs in your gut have hidden ways of helping you master your emotions *Psychology Today* v50 no5 p31 S/O 2017

How Dog Brains Work: DOGS USE THE SAME NEURAL PATHWAYS WE DO TO GET WHERE THEY CANT GO *Psychology Today* v50 no5 p78 S/O 2017

JOE NAVARRO AGENT PROVOCATEUR *Psychology Today* v50 no2 p56 Mr/Ap 2017

Palate and Possibility *Psychology Today* v50 no1 p34 Ja/F 2017

Please Pass the Algae *Psychology Today* v50 no2 p34 Mr/Ap 2017

RELATIONSHIP MATH *Psychology Today* v50 no1 p25 Ja/F 2017

TIME FOR TRUST *Psychology Today* v50 no3 p22 My/Je 2017

Marans, Noam E.

On Luther and his lies *Christian Century* v134 no22 p10 O 25 2017

Marantz, Andrew

AGAINST THE CURRENT cartoon *New Yorker* v93 no22 p18 Jl 31 2017

ALT DANCE-OFF cartoon *New Yorker* v93 no13 p34 My 15 2017

BALANCING ACT cartoon *New Yorker* v92 no41 p26 D 12 2016

BELLE cartoon *New Yorker* v92 no48 p16 F 6 2017

THE BEST MEDICINE cartoon color *New Yorker* v93 no12 p28 My 8 2017

THE BIONIC CANDIDATE cartoon *New Yorker* v92 no37 p34 N 14 2016

BIRTH OF A SUPREMACIST cartoon color *New Yorker* v93 no32 p26 O 16 2017

CAPTURE THE FLAG cartoon *New Yorker* v93 no7 p34 Ap 3 2017

CRASH LANDING cartoon *New Yorker* v92 no47 p21 Ja 30 2017

DOODLES cartoon *New Yorker* v93 no30 p20 O 2 2017

EMBEDDED cartoon *New Yorker* v93 no2 p23 F 27 2017

GATEKEEPERS cartoon *New Yorker* v93 no25 p32 Ag 28 2017

HECKLERS FOR HIRE cartoon *New Yorker* v93 no4 p29 Mr 13 2017

NEWS BLUES cartoon *New Yorker* v92 no42 p44 D 19 2016

PRESIDENT BANNON'S BANNON color *New Yorker* v92 no49 p30 F 13 2017

Q. & A cartoon *New Yorker* v93 no3 p22 Mr 6 2017

TALKING HEADS cartoon *New Yorker* v92 no32 p36 O 10 2016

TROLLING THE PRESS CORPS cartoon color *New Yorker* v93 no5 p52 Mr 20 2017

TROLLS FOR TRUMP cartoon *New Yorker* v92 no35 p42 O 31 2016

VIGIL cartoon *New Yorker* v92 no43 p18 Ja 2 2017

Marantz, Melissa

Turning loss into something beautiful J. PRESS color *Redbook* p110 Mr 2017

Marantz audio equipment—Evaluation

Big Box Meets Little Speakers M. Fleischmann chart color graph *Sound & Vision* v82 no4 p38 My 2017

Marat, Andrea L.

mTORC1 activity repression by late endosomal phosphatidylinositol 3,4-bisphosphate diag *Science* v356 no6341 p968 Je 1 2017

Maratha (Indic people)

GLOSSARY *History Today* v67 no8 p110 Ag 2017

Marathon running
See also
Berlin Marathon

56 MILES OF FREEDOM R. Lenora Brown color *Runner's World* v52 no9 p84 O 2017

The 7 HABITS OF HIGHLY EFFECTIVE MARATHONERS B. Stulberg and S. Magness cartoon color *Runner's World* v52 no6 p62 Jl 2017

AGONY—AND ECSTASY [Cover story] H. M. IRVINE color *Runner's World* v52 no5 p17 Je 2017

ALISON O'BRIEN M. HAMILTON color *Runner's World* v52 no2 p21 Mr 2017

ASK MILES bw *Runner's World* v51 no10 p30 N 2016

BRIDGE TO BREWS 10K & 8K RUN color *Runner's World* v52 no3 p90 Ap 2017

Chicago Style C. KUZMA color *Runner's World* v52 no9 p50 O 2017

Chin Losers N. WELDON color *Runner's World* v52 no9 p45 O 2017

COUCH TO 50K E. Strout color *Runner's World* v52 no3 p34 Ap 2017

EAT, DRINK, AND BE SPEEDY A. MACMILLAN and J. GAL-LOWAY color *Runner's World* v52 no9 p16 O 2017

Fast on a Different Track C. BETHEA color *Runner's World* v52 no9 p56 O 2017

Front Row at the Revolution [Cover story] T. HAMILTON bw color *Runner's World* v51 no10 p72 N 2016

THE GALLERY color *Runner's World* v52 no9 p12 O 2017

Game Changer bw *Yankee* p144 Mr 2017

The Great Escape: Bill Sycalik walked away from an unfulfilling corporate job. Now he is on a quest to complete marathons in all 59 national parks K. SIBER *National Parks* v91 no3 p16 Summ 2017

GROUND BREAKERS J. Dengate and M. Shorten color *Runner's World* v52 no9 p71 O 2017

HOW HAVE MARATHONS CHANGED OVER TIME? A. HUTCHINSON graph *Runner's World* v51 no10 p86 N 2016

HYPERSPACE RACE [Cover story] M. PARENT cartoon color *Runner's World* v52 no2 p58 Mr 2017

The Intersection color *Runner's World* v52 no9 p58 O 2017

IT'S MARATHON TIME. HERE'S WHO'S WINNING P. Wahba color diag *Fortune* v174 no6 p12 N 1 2016

JINGLE ALL THE WAY K. Massicot cartoon *New Orleans Magazine* v51 no1 p38 N 2016

LA SOCIAL *Los Angeles Magazine* p139 D 2016

LET'S RUN TOGETHER B. Wong Ortiz color *Runner's World* v52 no9 p10 O 2017

THE MASOCHIST'S MARATHON G. PENDLE bw color *Esquire* p90 Ag 2017

Mile Markers bw color *Runner's World* v52 no9 p48 O 2017

NO DOGS ALLOWED K. FOX color map *Runner's World* v52 no3 p76 Ap 2017

NOT FADE AWAY [Cover story] T. Hamilton bw color *Runner's World* v52 no5 p80 Je 2017

Outracing the Reaper P. SAGAL cartoon color *Runner's World* v52 no6 p46 Jl 2017

PEAK 26.2 PLAN [Cover story] chart *Runner's World* v52 no6 p66 Jl 2017

PLANTATION COUNTRY J. FROIS color *Louisiana Life* v37 no3 p99 Ja/F 2017

QUAD GOALS A. HUTCHINSON color *Runner's World* v52 no8 p16 S 2017

READY, SET, SNOOZE C. ZULKEY color *Runner's World* v52 no9 p24 O 2017

A RUNNER REBORN P. SAGAL color *Runner's World* v51 no10 p34 N 2016

Runner's Digest K. FOX color *Runner's World* v52 no8 p48 S 2017

THE RUN TO THE RACE J. BEVERLY cartoon *Runner's World* v52 no2 p24 Mr 2017

SAM RYAN N. Weldon color *Runner's World* v52 no4 p78 My 2017

SECOND CHANCE [Cover story] J. Galloway cartoon *Runner's World* v52 no5 p24 Je 2017

STILL GOING STRONG [Cover story] J. GALLOWAY cartoon *Runner's World* v51 no10 p42 N 2016

STREET SMARTS L. Haney color *Runner's World* v51 no10 p40 N 2016

SWEAT THE DETAILS A. HUTCHINSON color *Runner's World* v51 no10 p44 N 2016

A TACTICAL TAPER A. HUTCHINSON color *Runner's World* v52 no9 p22 O 2017

TALK YOURSELF UP A. HUTCHINSON color *Runner's World* v52 no5 p26 Je 2017

THAT MAGIC MOMENT K. ARNOLD cartoon *Runner's World* v52 no3 p22 Ap 2017

THREE RABBITS AND A GUINEA PIG D. WILLEY color *Runner's World* v52 no2 p10 Mr 2017

Tough or Stupid? M. REMY color *Runner's World* v52 no9 p52 O 2017

ULTRA MARATHON color *Women's Health* v14 no5 p70 Je 2017

Use It Or Lose It A. Burfoot bw color *Runner's World* v52 no5 p84 Je 2017

WE RUN THE STREETS [Cover story] M. Gross color *Runner's World* v52 no9 p62 O 2017

When Roads Are Closed for Marathons, More Elderly People Die of Heart Attacks A. Olenski and A. B. Jena *Harvard Business Review Digital Articles* p2 Ap 12 2017

When the Race Wins J. BEVERLY color *Runner's World* v52 no9 p60 O 2017

YOU CAN FLY! C. KUZMA chart color *Runner's World* v52 no5 p18 Je 2017

ZOOM, ZOOM! H. Higdon color *Runner's World* v52 no3 p38 Ap 2017

Marathon running training

Find Your Focus color *Runner's World* v52 no6 p17 Jl 2017

Gatherings *Los Angeles Magazine* v62 no9 p164 S 2017

Going the Distance B. Marston and T. Keith color *Sports Illustrated* v126 no11 p26 Ap 17-24 2017

MARATHON MAN (AND WOMAN) V. Tweed chart color *Amazing Wellness* v8 no2 p80 Spr 2016

Marathon running—Competitions

Love on the Run A. SPENCER color *Good Housekeeping* v264 no3 p151 Mr 2017

Marathon running—Marketing

RUNNERS WITH H(e)ART [Cover story] K. Fox color map *Runner's World* v51 no10 p64 N 2016

Marathon running—New York (State)

WHEN YONKERS WAS BONKERS B. DONAHUE bw color *Runner's World* v51 no10 p82 N 2016

Marathon running—Physiological aspects

SAVE THE DAY L. BEDOSKY color *Runner's World* v52 no9 p28 O 2017

STRIDE WITH PRIDE C. KUZMA color *Runner's World* v52 no9 p26 O 2017

Marathon running—Records

Great Barrier Reach C. Chavez and T. Keith color *Sports Illustrated* v126 no8 p22 Mr 20 2017

Running Man Challenge C. Chavez and T. Keith color *Sports Illustrated* v126 no5 p20 F 13 2017

Marathon running—Charts, diagrams, etc.

ASK A FLOWCHART R. CAPPS diag *Wired* v25 no7 p96 Jl 2017

Marathons (Sports)

See also

    Marathon running

ALIA GRAY C. KUZMA color *Runner's World* v52 no1 p21 Ja/F 2017

ASK MILES cartoon *Runner's World* v51 no11 p27 D 2016

BARCELONA SPAIN M. Pucurull and S. Gearhart color *Runner's World* v52 no8 p85 S 2017

BE SELFIE-AWARE C. Kuzma cartoon *Runner's World* v52 no3 p32 Ap 2017

BRIDGE TO BREWS 10K & 8K RUN color *Runner's World* v52 no3 p90 Ap 2017

Case Study: When You Have to Choose Between Core and New Customers M. Bertini and N. Tavassoli *Harvard Business Review Digital Articles* p2 Je 26 2017

CATCH HIM IF YOU CAN M. Rosenberg and S. Kwak color *Sports Illustrated* v127 no12 p18 O 16 2017

DON'T MISS LIST NOVEMBER 2016 *Sea Magazine* v108 no10 pCA-11 O 2016

Give Yourself a Break G. Reynolds *New York Times Magazine* p36 O 30 2016

The Intersection color *Runner's World* v52 no6 p58 Jl 2017

IT'S NEVER TOO LATE TO START RUNNING M. NASSER *UN Chronicle* v53 no2 p36 2016

MARATHON MAN (AND WOMAN) V. Tweed chart color *Amazing Wellness* v8 no2 p80 Spr 2016

THE MASOCHIST'S MARATHON G. PENDLE bw color *Esquire* p90 Ag 2017

A RACE FOR EVERY PACE [Cover story] A. C. SHILTON cartoon color *Runner's World* v52 no1 p97 Ja/F 2017

RUN AROUND H. BRANDSTETTER *Cincinnati Magazine* v50 no8 p20 My 2017

THE RUNNING DEAD K. ARNOLD cartoon *Runner's World* v52 no1 p30 Ja/F 2017

THAT MAGIC MOMENT K. ARNOLD cartoon *Runner's World* v52 no3 p22 Ap 2017

USA HALF MARATHON INVITATIONAL B. McANENY, W. O'DWYER et al color *Runner's World* v51 no11 p98 D 2016

Marble

WHITE GOLD S. ANDERSON *New York Times Magazine* p34
Jl 30 2017

Marble, Alice, 1913-1990
LONG SERVE M. BRANDSTETTER *Cincinnati Magazine* v50
no11 p24 Ag 2017

Marble sculpture—Exhibitions
NOT VITAL W. Saunders and A. Rochette bw *Art in America*
v105 no4 p124 Ap 2017

Marble—Evaluation
rock of ages bw color *Architectural Digest* v74 no4 p98 Ap 2017

Marburger, Joey—Interviews
The revolution at The Washington Post K. Pope color *Columbia
Journalism Review* p94 Fall/Wint 2016

Marbury v. Madison (Supreme Court case)
WHY MARBURY MATTERS D. B. MOSKOWITZ color *American History* v52 no4 p24 O 2017

Marc Jacobs International LLC
BARELY THERE *Interview* v47 no2 p110 Mr 2017
FIND YOUR PERFECT Army Jacket & Fancy Dress color *In-
Style* v23 no13 p139 D 2016

Marcelis, Carlo L.
Neurodevelopmental protein Musashi-1 interacts with the Zika
genome and promotes viral replication diag *Science* v357
no6346 p83 Jl 7 2017

Marcelis, Sabine
Power Bloc H. MARTIN color *Architectural Digest* no6 p46 Je
1 2017

Marcella, Kenneth L.
3 STEPS TO STRONGER STIFLES color diag *Practical Horseman* v45 no4 p48 Ap 2017
Cellulitis in Your Dressage Partner color *Dressage Today* v23
no10 p20 Jl 2017

Marcellini, Paul
MONOCHROME *Popular Photography* v80 no11 p29 D 2016

Marcellus Shale
A PIPELINE RUNS THROUGH IT R. DOUGHTEN *Sierra* v102
no3 p32 My/Je 2017

March (Month)
MARCH BADNESS P. Gulley *Saturday Evening Post* v289 no2
p14 Mr/Ap 2017
MARCH color *Martha Stewart Living* p75 Mr 2017

March (Poem)
March L. Kasischke *New York Times Magazine* p20 Mr 26 2017

March, Charlotte
In the SUNSET KITCHEN color *Sunset* v238 no3 p82 Mr 2017
PEAR POWER color *Sunset* v238 no1 p77 Ja 2017
SUMMER CRUSH color *Sunset* v238 no6 p87 Je 2017
WEEKNIGHT COOKING color *Sunset* v238 no3 p80 Mr 2017
WEEKNIGHT COOKING color *Sunset* v239 no4 p90 O 2017

March of Dimes Foundation
mommy & me *Atlanta* v56 no7 p220 N 2016

Marchand, Donald A.
Firms Need a Blueprint for Building Their IT Systems *Harvard
Business Review Digital Articles* p2 Je 18 2015
Technology Isn't Enough to Empower Employees, Even in a
Digital World *Harvard Business Review Digital Articles* p2 F
17 2016

Marchant, Fred
Said Not Said *Publishers Weekly* v264 no16 p42 Ap 17 2017

Marchant, Gary E.
Soft law: New tools for governing emerging technologies bibl
Bulletin of the Atomic Scientists v73 no2 p108 Mr 2017

MARCHANT, JO
THE GOLDEN WARRIOR *Smithsonian* v47 no9 p38 Ja/F 2017
Think Yourself Healthy cartoon *Prevention* v69 no1 p28 Ja 2017

MARCHANT, LESLEY
YOUR CHEAT SHEET TO... Cramming Your Way to an A color
Seventeen v75 no11 p102 N 2016

MARCHE, STEPHEN
Canada in the Age of Donald Trump bw *Walrus* p20 Ja\F 2017
The Entertainer cartoon color *Esquire* v166 no5 p45 D 2016/Ja
2017
The Other Worst President bw *Walrus* v14 no9 p78 N 2017
This American Carnage color *Walrus* v14 no3 p36 Ap 2017

Marche, Stephen—Interviews
The problem with men A. KINGSTON color *Maclean's* v130 no3

p66 Ap 2017

Marchegger, Marcus
After a Few Do-Overs, Success J. B. CLARK color *Kiplinger's
Personal Finance* v71 no2 p72 F 2017

Marchesan, Silvia
Nanomaterials for stimulating nerve growth color *Science* v356
no6342 p1010 Je 9 2017

Marchese, Anna
'Act justly, love goodness': Black Catholics in America color
America v217 no3 p14 Ag 7 2017
CHRISTIAN POETRY VS 'CHRISTIAN POETRY' bw *America*
v217 no4 p46 Ag 21 2017

Marchese, David
THE Chef of the Future MAKES ONLY ONE DISH CRAB
BISQUE à la robot img *New York* p40 Ja 9 2017
THE Chef of the Future MARES ONLY ONE DISH CRAB
BISQUE à la robot img *New York* p40 F 9 2017
DAVID LETTERMAN img *New York* p28 Mr 6 2017
David Lynch Is Rolling Off a Log img *New York* v50 no10 p94
My 15 2017
THE EVERYTHING GUIDE TO: Sucking at Stuff img *New York*
v49 no23 p64 N 14 2016
THE EVERYTHING GUIDE TO: The Great Mattress Buyer's
Dilemma: Open-cell foam, Hyper-Elastic Polymers, 100-day
return policies: sorting through the sleep world's latest layers
of innovation—and confusion img *New York* v50 no9 p66 My
1 2017
Get Serious img *New York* v50 no8 p120 Ap 17 2017
Have Flute, Will Rock: Political reporter David Weigel outs himself as a different kind of progressive img *New York* v50 no11
p121 My 29 2017
HOW TO: Write a Perfect Pop Song *New York* v50 no13 p78 Je
26 2017
"People Need a Villain": T. J. Miller knows you think he's crazy
for leaving HBO's Silicon Valley, and he cares not in the least
img *New York* v50 no15 p57 Jl 24 2017
The Self-Made Screenwriter: Taylor Sheridan has a two-step approach to becoming an Oscar-nominated writer: One: Read lots
of bad scripts. Two: Do better img *New York* v50 no15 p62 Jl
24 2017
Someone Great Is Back img *New York* v50 no17 p112 Ag 21 2017
SPACE JAM img *New York* v49 no24 p133 N 28 2016
Swimming Upstream: The advent of streaming film and television
has brought untold freedom and opportunity to creators--and an
unprecedented chance to get lost in the Peak TV shuffle img
New York v50 no11 p111 My 29 2017
UNDER THE INFLUENCE img *New York* v49 no24 p120 N 28
2016

MARCHETTI, DOMENICA
Viva ZUCCHINI color *Better Homes & Gardens* v95 no8 p148
Ag 2017

Marchi, Giulio
The extent of forest in dryland biomes [Cover story] chart map
Science v356 no6338 p635 My 12 2017

Marchi, S.
Extensive water ice within Ceres' aqueously altered regolith:
Evidence from nuclear spectroscopy bibl graph *Science* v355
no6320 p1 Ja 6 2017
Localized aliphatic organic material on the surface of Ceres bibl
graph *Science* v355 no6326 p719 F 17 2017
Surface changes on comet 67P/Churyumov-Gerasimenko suggest
a more active past bw graph *Science* v355 no6332 p1392 Mr
31 2017

Marching
Climate Justice Marchers Bring the Heat J. COMER color *Progressive* v81 no5 p12 Je/Jl 2017

Marching bands
HIT PARADE A. BRANDT *Cincinnati Magazine* v50 no5 p26
F 2017
MOOD MUSIC B. Stephen cartoon *New Yorker* v93 no5 p33 Mr
20 2017

Marchionne, Sergio, 1952—Interviews
Sergio Marchionne: CEO, FERRARI AND FCA A. MacKenzie
color *Motor Trend* v69 no9 p30 S 2017

Marchuk, Kyle
Visualizing dynamic microvillar search and stabilization during

ligand detection by T cells color *Science* v356 no6338 p598 My 12 2017

Marciano (Company)
Collared! color *Women's Health* v13 no10 p59 D 2016

Marciano, Maurice
PICTURE PERFECT color *Vanity Fair* v59 no6 p53 My 2017

MARCIN, DIANA
USA HALF MARATHON INVITATIONAL color *Runner's World* v51 no11 p98 D 2016

Marcketta, Anthony
Distribution and clinical impact of functional variants in 50,726 whole-exome sequences from the DiscovEHR study chart graph *Science* v354 no6319 paaf6814-1 D 23 2016

Marco Island (Fla. : Island)—Description & travel
The Perfect Day S. Murray color *Power & Motoryacht* v34 no9 p56 S 2017

Marco Polo (TV program)
Wall and Polo and Wick - Oh, My! C. D. Reid color *Black Belt* v55 no4 p28 Je/Jl 2017

Marco-Izquierdo, José Antonio
CEOs Don't Care Enough About Capital Allocation *Harvard Business Review Digital Articles* p2 Ap 16 2015
Profit Is Less About Good Management than You Think *Harvard Business Review Digital Articles* p2 S 28 2015

Marcos, Enrique
Principles for designing proteins with cavities formed by curved β sheets bibl color graph *Science* v355 no6321 p1 Ja 13 2017

Marcos, Subcomandante
WHAT ARE THEY AFRAID OF? *Lapham's Quarterly* v10 no3 p179 Summ 2017

Marco's Pizza (Company)
BUILDING A FRANCHISE EMPIRE J. McKinney color *Black Enterprise* v47 no7 p13 My/Je 2017

Marcotte, Brian J.
U.S. Health Care Reform Can't Wait for Quality Measures to Be Perfect *Harvard Business Review Digital Articles* p2 O 4 2017

Marcus, Adam
Pay up or retract? Drug survey spurs conflict color *Science* v357 no6356 p1085 S 15 2017

Marcus, Aubrey
Make Your Workouts Pay S. MESTEL cartoon color *Men's Health* v32 no8 p25 O 2017

Marcus, Ben, 1967-
Blueprints for St. Louis B. Marcus cartoon *New Yorker* v93 no30 p56 O 2 2017

Marcus, C. M.
Majorana bound state in a coupled quantum-dot hybrid-nanowire system bibl graph *Science* v354 no6319 p1557 D 23 2016

Marcus, Calvin
Clearing T. Istomina color *Art in America* v105 no1 p81 Ja 2017
Me With Tongue color *ARTnews* v115 no4 p4 Wint 2016/2017

MARCUS, DAVID
THE POWER HISTORIAN bw *Nation* v305 no11 p43 O 30 2017

Marcus, Gary
AM I HUMAN? [Cover story] color *Scientific American* v316 no3 p58 Mr 2017

Marcus, Greil
The Brotherhood of Rock bw color *New York Review of Books* v64 no5 p45 Mr 23 2017

Marcus, James
EDITOR'S NOTEBOOK *Harper's Magazine* v334 no2000 p5 Ja 2017
INTO THE WILD: Henry David Thoreau as prophet, naturalist, and stealth comedian *Harper's Magazine* p90 O 2017

Marcus, Jon
THE LOOMING DECLINE OF THE PUBLIC RESEARCH UNIVERSITY cartoon *Washington Monthly* v49 no9/10 p71 S/O 2017

MARCUS, LEONARD S.
On With the Snow! *New York Times Book Review* p18 D 18 2016

Marcus, Leonard S., 1950—Interviews
A Q&A and D. Muldrow cartoon color *Publishers Weekly* v264 no7 pc3 F 13 2017

Marcus, Lilit
Permission to Leave the Airport cartoon *Conde Nast Traveler* v51 no11 p126 D 2016

Marcus Aurelius, Emperor of Rome, 121-180
THE OTHER WALL color *Archaeology* v70 no3 p32 My/Je 2017

Marcuse, Herbert, 1898-1979
Malign Marcuse D. FRENCH il *National Review* v69 no7 p32 Ap 17 2017

Marcy, Mary B.
BEYOND MERE SURVIVAL: Transforming Independent Colleges and Universities *Change* v49 no3 p36 My/Je 2017

Marczak, Bill
INVADING APPLE B. BURROUGH color *Vanity Fair* v59 no1 p144 Holiday 2017

Marczak, Jason
Latin America and the Caribbean 2030: Future Scenarios R. Feinberg *Foreign Affairs* v96 no2 p179 Mr/Ap 2017

Marden, Matthew
Strip It Down color *Esquire* v167 no1 p32 F 2017
THE TIP SHEET color *Esquire* p52 Je/Jl 2017
THE TIP SHEET color *Esquire* v167 no2 p74 Mr 2017

Marder, Eve
Not just Salk color *Science* v357 no6356 p1105 S 15 2017

Marder, Michael
Marder, Patzek, and Tinker reply *Physics Today* v70 no2 p13 F 2017

Mardi Gras Indians
Big Chiefs Coming J. Berry color *New Orleans Magazine* v51 no4 p52 F 2017

Mardi Gras World (Company)
Laissez Les Bon Temps Roulez! J. DeBold color *New Orleans Magazine* v51 no4 p142 F 2017

Mardini, Yusra
Free Style J. di Giovanni color *Vogue* v207 no4 p218 Ap 2017

Mardinoglu, Adil
A pathology atlas of the human cancer transcriptome diag *Science* v357 no6352 p660 Ag 18 2017
A subcellular map of the human proteome color *Science* v356 no6340 p820 My 26 2017

Mare Orientale (Moon)
On the shoals of a rainy sea M. RATCLIFFE and A. LING color *Astronomy* v45 no4 p37 Ap 2017

Marech, Rona
Behind the Story *National Parks* v91 no4 p4 Fall 2017
Escape, Breathe, Fight *National Parks* v91 no3 p4 Summ 2017
The Long Haul *National Parks* v91 no1 p18 Wint 2017
Off The Grid *National Parks* v91 no2 p4 Spr 2017
Special Delivery *National Parks* v91 no1 p4 Wint 2017

Marelli, Martino
An accreting pulsar with extreme properties drives an ultraluminous x-ray source in NGC 5907 bibl chart graph *Science* v355 no6327 p817 F 24 2017

Maremma sheepdog
There for ewe A. HUTCHINS color *Maclean's* v130 no9 p13 O 2017

Mares
2015 NATIONAL CHAMPION MARES *Arabian Horse World* v56 no12 p160 S 2016
ARISTOCRAT MARES *Arabian Horse World* v56 no12 p146 S 2016
ARISTOCRAT MARES M. J. Parkinson *Arabian Horse World* v57 no12 p74 S 2017
The Clinic PHOTO CRITIQUES S. von Dietze *Dressage Today* v23 no4 p20 D 2016
CONFORMATION CLINIC color *Horse & Rider* v55 no11 p33 N 2016
CONSULTANTS L. Horrigan and B. A. Connally bw *Equus* no474 p67 Mr 2017
DAMS OF DISTINCTION *Arabian Horse World* v56 no12 p162 S 2016
December M. Moore *Arabian Horse World* v57 no3 p10 D 2016
THE DOWAGER CLUB *Arabian Horse World* v56 no12 p155 S 2016
EQ CONSULTANTS K. A. Houpt color *Equus* no471 p66 D 2016
A Gelding, a Mare, a Lesson D. Robertson color *Horse & Rider* v56 no4 p16 Ap 2017
Help for a lonely mare J. Williams color *Equus* no477 p80 Je 2017
I Wish My Horse's Mentor Could Be... B. Nutter, A. Tuominen et al color *Horse & Rider* v56 no6 p88 Je 2017

The Other Mare B. FINKE *Arabian Horse World* v57 no2 p132 N 2016

The second time around H. Ellis-Ashburn color *Equus* no473 p72 F 2017

TEVIS journey D. Whyte *Arabian Horse World* v56 no12 p178 S 2016

This Month's online Exclusives. AND MORE! *Arabian Horse World* v57 no1 p8 O 2016

TO BREED OR NOT TO BREED? B. Crabbe bw color *Horse & Rider* v56 no4 p56 Ap 2017

When I Was a Horse-Crazy Kid, I... L. Prentiss, C. Zundel et al color *Horse & Rider* v56 no2 p72 F 2017

Mares, David R.

Aspirational Power: Brazil on the Long Road to Global Influence R. Feinberg *Foreign Affairs* v95 no6 p185 N/D 2016

Mares—Awards

aerc National Awards: Endurance riders and horses honored at the 2016 AERC Convention G. Stewart-Spears *Arabian Horse World* v57 no10 p58 Jl 2017

Mares—Behavior

Mare Won't Use Her Paddock J. BERGER *Horse & Rider* v56 no4 p14 Ap 2017

STUD FARM DIARIES C. Reich color *Arabian Horse World* v57 no7 p134 Ap 2017

Maresca, Marshall Ryan

An Import of Intrigue *Publishers Weekly* v263 no40 p104 O 3 2016

Marescaux, Elise

How to Allow Flexible Work Without Playing Favorites *Harvard Business Review Digital Articles* p2 2017

Mares—Diseases

A danger in the water K. Henderson color *Equus* no478 p80 Jl 2017

Mares—Physiology

CONFORMATION CLINIC K. McCuistion color *Horse & Rider* v56 no2 p29 F 2017

STUD FARM DIARIES C. Reich color *Arabian Horse World* v57 no7 p134 Ap 2017

Mares—Reproduction

Enhancing Embryo-Transfer Effectiveness S. Dulai Wenholz color *Practical Horseman* v45 no2 p69 F 2017

Marfan syndrome

Targeting nitric oxide to treat aneurysm *Science* v355 no6324 p492 F 3 2017

Margalit, Avishai

Betrayal in Jerusalem bw *New York Review of Books* v64 no4 p35 Mr 9 2017

Does Betrayal Still Matter? M. Walzer color *New York Review of Books* v64 no8 p52 My 11 2017

On Betrayal D. O'Brien color *Christian Century* v134 no10 p49 My 10 2017

Margalit, Ruth

SETTLING SCORES *New York Times Magazine* p36 O 23 2016

So When Are You Getting Married? color *New York Review of Books* v64 no16 p12 O 26 2017

There's Too Much Speech in Israel! *Commentary* v142 no2 p1 S 2016

Margalit, Yotam

Research: Political Polarization Is Changing How Americans Work and Shop *Harvard Business Review Digital Articles* p2 My 19 2017

MARGARONIS, MARIA

Labour's Revival diag *Nation* v305 no1 p3 Jl 3 2017

Margasak, Peter

Bimhuis Eschews Trends color *Downbeat* v84 no2 p63 F 2017

Chrome/Vertical color *Downbeat* v84 no10 p61 O 2017

Convergence Factor color *Downbeat* v84 no7 p19 Jl 2017

Empire State of Mind color *Downbeat* v84 no1 p16 Ja 2017

Eremite Preserves Past, Shapes Future of Free-Jazz color *Downbeat* v84 no8 p18 Ag 2017

Good for Circulation color *Downbeat* v84 no2 p16 F 2017

Graphic Designs bw *Downbeat* v84 no5 p18 My 2017

Record Store Day's Spring Awakening color *Downbeat* v84 no6 p22 Je 2017

Studio Improv bw *Downbeat* v84 no3 p19 Mr 2017

Swivel color *Downbeat* v83 no11 p52 N 2016

Trost Records Fuses Punk Ethos with Jazz Artistry bw *Downbeat* v83 no11 p18 N 2016

Margay cat

OUT ON A LIMB A. E. HURT color *National Geographic Kids* no465 p18 N 2016

Marglin, Elizabeth

Forest to face color *Yoga Journal* no290 p26 Mr 2017

The gift of meditation color *Yoga Journal* no288 p17 D 2016

Good buys color *Yoga Journal* no295 p22 O 2017

INQUIRE WITHIN color diag *Yoga Journal* no289 p28 F 2017

Mask appeal color *Yoga Journal* no289 p20 F 2017

THE panchakarma PRESCRIPTION color *Yoga Journal* no296 p32 N 2017

Q: What do you consistently do to boost happiness? color *Yoga Journal* no296 p12 N 2017

refresh your soul retreat color *Yoga Journal* no287 p14 N 2016

Sit in style color *Yoga Journal* no291 p24 My 2017

SUPPLEMENTAL KNOWLEDGE color *Yoga Journal* no293 p29 Ag 2017

take OM HOME color *Yoga Journal* no293 p104 Ag 2017

MARGOLICK, DAVID

"Get Me Marty Singer!" color *Vanity Fair* p154 Hollywood 2017 Supplement

Vaporized bw color *Weekly Standard* v22 no17 p24 Ja 2 2017

V.C. FOR VENDETTA color *Vanity Fair* v59 no1 p108 Holiday 2017

Margolin, Malcolm

Our Family is Growing color *Earth Island Journal* v32 no1 p18 Spr 2017

Margolis, Joshua D.

Advice and Credibility Go Hand-in-Hand for Managers *Harvard Business Review Digital Articles* p2 Ja 13 2015

Margolis, Robert

Terawatt-scale photovoltaics: Trajectories and challenges chart graph *Science* v356 no6334 p141 Ap 14 2017

Margolis, Seth

Presidents' Day *Publishers Weekly* v263 no51 p126 D 12 2016

Margulies, Julianna, 1966-

Fancy a Nightcap With These Folks? R. Kinane color *Entertainment Weekly* no1470 p49 Je 16 2017

Julianna Margulies C. Ianzito color *AARP: The Magazine* v59 no4A p76 Je/Jl 2016

Margulis, Arianna

COMIC S. Marikar cartoon *New Yorker* v93 no27 p27 S 11 2017

Mari, Christopher

Adam Curtis color *Current Biography* v78 no4 p17 Ap 2017

Allison Tolman color *Current Biography* v78 no3 p82 Mr 2017

Angela Flournoy color *Current Biography* v78 no4 p21 Ap 2017

Chris Bachelder color *Current Biography* v78 no2 p8 F 2017

Claire Foy color *Current Biography* v78 no5 p30 My 2017

David Szalay color *Current Biography* v78 no1 p81 Ja 2017

Dorit Rabinyan color *Current Biography* v78 no9 p71 S 2017

Javaka Steptoe *Current Biography* v78 no8 p78 Ag 2017

Joe Manganiello color *Current Biography* v78 no3 p50 Mr 2017

Matt de la Peña color *Current Biography* v78 no6 p35 Je 2017

Mike Colter color *Current Biography* v78 no6 p30 Je 2017

Simon Helberg color *Current Biography* v78 no5 p35 My 2017

Yaa Gyasi color *Current Biography* v78 no8 p40 Ag 2017

Zara Larsson color *Current Biography* v78 no2 p39 F 2017

Mari, Frisco

Wit and Wisdom From our Early Breeders M. J. PARKINSON *Arabian Horse World* v57 no4 p36 Ja 2017

Mari., I. C.

Observation of a large-scale anisotropy in the arrival directions of cosmic rays above 8 × 1018 eV *Science* v357 no6357 p1266 S 22 2017

María Fernández-Palacios, José

Island biogeography: Taking the long view of nature's laboratories map *Science* v357 no6354 p885 S 1 2017

Mariana Trench

Expedition probes ocean trench's deepest secrets J. Qiu color *Science* v355 no6321 p115 Ja 13 2017

Mariani, Mike

The Antisocial Network *Psychology Today* v49 no5 p80 S/O 2016

IN TRUMP'S AMERIKA color *Vanity Fair* v59 no5 p96 Ap 2017

Mariani, Paul

Benedict's Daughter: Poems *Christian Century* v134 no14 p42 Jl 5 2017

The Whole Harmonium: The Life of Wallace Stevens J. Johnson *Christian Century* v134 no9 p36 Ap 26 2017

Marías, Javier, 1951-

Conjugal Dread K. MAHAJAN *New York Times Book Review* p17 N 27 2016

Crimes of the Heart S. Begley color *Time* v188 no20 p55 N 14 2016

THE CURSE J. Marias *Harper's Magazine* v333 no1999 p11 D 2016

LIKELY STORY C. Tayler *Harper's Magazine* v333 no1999 p84 D 2016

Mariash, Jax

JAX MARIASH M. REMY color *Runner's World* v52 no3 p29 Ap 2017

Mariazzi, A. G.

Observation of a large-scale anisotropy in the arrival directions of cosmic rays above 8 × 1018 eV *Science* v357 no6357 p1266 S 22 2017

Marie & Rosetta (Theatrical production)

'A HEAVEN SOMEWHERE' R. WEINERT-KENDT color *America* v215 no12 p30 O 24 2016

Marigolds

Flowers with Flavor K. Hammonds color *Southern Living* v52 no3 p36 Mr 2017

Marijuana

Bay Urea M. HEMINGWAY color *Weekly Standard* v23 no6 p6 O 16 2017

EVERYTHING WORTH KNOWING color *Discover* v38 no6 p28 Jl/Ag 2017

THE GREEN RUSH R. Hale color *Earth Island Journal* v32 no4 p41 Wint 2017

Marijuana L. SCHLEY color diag *Discover* v38 no6 p56 Jl/Ag 2017

Should I Tell Uber My Driver Was High? K. A. Appiah *New York Times Magazine* p20 Mr 5 2017

A TIMELINE OF MARIJUANA IN THE NEW YORK TIMES J. SULLUM bw color *Reason* v49 no4 p52 Ag/S 2017

UP IN SMOKE Z. LOFTUS-FARREN *Earth Island Journal* v32 no4 p44 Wint 2017

Marijuana abuse

DOES LEGALIZATION BOOST TEEN MARIJUANA USE? J. SULLUM cartoon *Reason* v49 no1 p12 My 2017

Gratitude for a Femme Fatale *American Scholar* v86 no1 p15 Wint 2017

Marijuana abuse—History—20th century

MARIJUANA ON CAMPUS: By the '60s, this former street drug had become the sacrament of the youth generation. Here, a recent college graduate describes the phenomenon and the attraction R. GOLDSTEIN *Saturday Evening Post* v289 no4 p42 Jl/Ag 2017

Marijuana growing

Hot Weed Mogul Balram Vaswani D. BROWNE color *Rolling Stone* no1274 p44 N 17 2016

IN BLUEGRASS COUNTRY K. Dobie *Harper's Magazine* v333 no1998 p61 N 2016

Marijuana industry

THE Great POT MONOPOLY Mystery A. Chicago Lewis color *GQ: Gentlemen's Quarterly* v97 no9 p164 S 2017

Here Comes the "Green Rush" D. Slater *Sierra* v102 no2 p20 Mr/Ap 2017

MARIJUANA MOMS [Cover story] C. MOSCATELLO color *Working Mother* v40 no3 p20 Ag/S 2017

Not So Picture Perfect color *Working Mother* v40 no3 p5 Ag/S 2017

Peddling Weed Like It's Coca-Cola J. Kaplan color *Bloomberg Businessweek* no4509 p18 Ja 30 2017

Marijuana industry—Canada

Canada Plans to Be the Leader in Legal Weed B. Popplewell color *Bloomberg Businessweek* no4519 p32 Ap 24 2017

Marijuana industry—Officials & employees

THE WEED WARRIORS E. GARBER-PAUL color *Rolling Stone* no1295 p45 S 7 2017

Marijuana legalization

A BUD-TO-BLUNT PATH TO LEGAL WEED J. WARNER

chart color *Wired* v25 no3 p24 Mr 2017

Canada Plans to Be the Leader in Legal Weed B. Popplewell color *Bloomberg Businessweek* no4519 p32 Ap 24 2017

Cannabiz Hype Is About to Go Up in Smoke J. Alsever color *Fortune* v174 no8 p15 D 15 2016

IN NEVADA, WEED IS NEWLY LEGAL, BUT HARD TO COME BY G. Donnelly color *Fortune* v176 no2 p19 Ag 1 2017

IN THE WEEDS H. Wallace color *Vogue* v206 no12 p181 D 2016

MARIJUANA D. C. Vock, M. Quinn et al *Governing* v30 no4 p34 Ja 2017

MEDICAL USE VS. ABUSE T. W. FILARDO *Scientific American* v316 no2 p5 F 2017

THE SEARCH FOR A PLACE TO TOKE UP J. SULLUM color *Reason* v49 no3 p6 Jl 2017

Marijuana legalization—Social aspects

FRIENDS IN HIGH PLACES M. CAMPBELL color *Maclean's* p32 Je 2017

Marijuana—Economic aspects

IN NEVADA, WEED IS NEWLY LEGAL, BUT HARD TO COME BY G. Donnelly color *Fortune* v176 no2 p19 Ag 1 2017

Marijuana—Environmental aspects

Here Comes the "Green Rush" D. Slater *Sierra* v102 no2 p20 Mr/Ap 2017

Marijuana—Equipment & supplies

BONG SHOW N. Paumgarten cartoon *New Yorker* v93 no13 p36 My 15 2017

Marijuana—Government policy

Doobs of hazard C. GILLIS color *Maclean's* v129 no41 p14 O 17 2016

MARIJUANA D. C. Vock, M. Quinn et al *Governing* v30 no4 p34 Ja 2017

Marijuana—Law & legislation

See also

Marijuana legalization

The Golden State's Big Green Bet K. Steinmetz color *Time* v188 no20 p38 N 14 2016

High Stakes M. A. R. Kleiman color *Foreign Affairs* v96 no2 p130 Mr/Ap 2017

ISRAEL DECRIMINALIZES POT POSSESSION J. SULLUM color *Reason* v49 no2 p8 Je 2017

Marijuana Inc J. B. Wogan color *Governing* v30 no11 p24 Ag 2017

MEDICAL USE VS. ABUSE T. W. FILARDO *Scientific American* v316 no2 p5 F 2017

Nip It in the Bud J. Caulkins *Washington Monthly* p10 Ja/F 2017

Reefer Madness at The New York Times J. SULLUM color *Reason* v49 no4 p42 Ag/S 2017

Marijuana—Law & legislation—California

A BUD-TO-BLUNT PATH TO LEGAL WEED J. WARNER chart color *Wired* v25 no3 p24 Mr 2017

Is Recreational Pot Coming to Cali? Z. Weissmueller color *Reason* v48 no7 p11 D 2016

Marijuana—Law & legislation—Canada

Sinking like stoners B. HUTCHINSON color *Maclean's* v130 no4 p11 My 2017

Marijuana—Marketing

Peddling Weed Like It's Coca-Cola J. Kaplan color *Bloomberg Businessweek* no4509 p18 Ja 30 2017

Marijuana—Research

Obama's Belated Drug War Retreat J. SULLUM *Reason* v48 no9 p6 F 2017

Marijuana—Sales & prices

Is Recreational Pot Coming to Cali? Z. Weissmueller color *Reason* v48 no7 p11 D 2016

Marikar, Sheila

ABE BURNS, CELEBRITY TECHSPLAINER color *Bloomberg Businessweek* no4519 p82 Ap 24 2017

BOOMING cartoon *New Yorker* v92 no37 p33 N 14 2016

COMIC cartoon *New Yorker* v93 no27 p27 S 11 2017

DR. GWYNETH WILL SEE YOU cartoon *New Yorker* v93 no6 p16 Mr 27 2017

GETTING IT OUT cartoon *New Yorker* v93 no2 p24 F 27 2017

HOME IS WHERE THE PERCALE IS color *Bloomberg Businessweek* no4525 p58 Je 5 2017

INCLUSION cartoon *New Yorker* v93 no31 p22 O 9 2017

MADE TO MEASURE color *Fortune* v176 no4 p55 S 15 2017

Not Curry In a Hurry cartoon color *Bloomberg Businessweek* no4499 p84 N 14 2016

OFF THE MAT cartoon *New Yorker* v93 no14 p31 My 22 2017

REPRESENTATION cartoon *New Yorker* v93 no4 p30 Mr 13 2017

Serenbe Now! color *Bloomberg Businessweek* no4511 p59 F 13 2017

TRADING VS. TRUMP cartoon *New Yorker* v92 no33 p24 O 17 2016

WOLFGANG GOES ROGUE color *Bloomberg Businessweek* no4520 p71 My 1 2017

YES LIST cartoon *New Yorker* v93 no28 p19 S 18 2017

MARILL, MICHELE COHEN

LESS IS MORE *Atlanta* v56 no8 p32 D 2016

TRACE OF HOPE *Atlanta* v56 no8 p144 D 2016

Marimon, B. S.

Persistent effects of pre-Columbian plant domestication on Amazonian forest composition bibl chart graph map *Science* v355 no6328 p925 Mr 3 2017

Marimon, B.-H.

Persistent effects of pre-Columbian plant domestication on Amazonian forest composition bibl chart graph map *Science* v355 no6328 p925 Mr 3 2017

Marin, Guy B.

Super-dry reforming of methane intensifies CO_2 utilization via Le Chatelier's principle bibl diag graph *Science* v354 no6311 p449 O 28 2016

MARÍN, VICTOR H.

Global Disparity in Ecological Science: A Complex Systems Perspective *BioScience* v67 no2 p105 F 2017

Human Well-Being and Historical Ecosystems: The Environmentalist's Paradox Revisited *BioScience* v67 no1 p5 Ja 2017

Marin Mountain Bikes Inc.

MARIN WOLF RIDGE PRO M. Phillips color *Bicycling* v58 no9 p80 O 2017

Marinas

BREMERTON IS BOOMING: AN INTERESTING AND LIKABLE PORT OF CALL FOR PUGET SOUND BOATERS IS NOT FAR FROM SEATTLE D. HISLOP color map *Sea Magazine* v109 no8 pPNW-1 Ag 2017

A CENTURY OLD & NEW AGAIN: ROSARIO RESORT GOT A FACELIFT, A NEW MARINA CONFIGURATION AND MUCH MORE D. HISLOP color map *Sea Magazine* v109 no7 pPNW-1 Jl 2017

Marinas—Management

THE LAST HARBOR BOSS R. J. NELSON bw cartoon color *Chicago* v65 no11 p110 N 2016

Marinas—Washington (State)

MEET ANDY GREGORY color *Sea Magazine* v109 no7 pPNW-8 Jl 2017

Marine accidents

See also

Boating accidents

Shipwrecks

Tanker accidents

DOOMED N. HEIL *Reader's Digest* v188 no1125 p128 N 2016

Marine algae

Gifts of the Sea M. ALLEN *Yankee* v81 no1 p12 Ja/F 2017

Seaweed Dreaming R. Jacobsen *Yankee* v81 no1 p120 Ja/F 2017

Marine algae culture

KELP IS ON THE WAY C. Zuckerman color *National Geographic* v232 no5 p14 N 2017

Marine algae—Harvesting

TENANTS HARBOR, MAINE S. Mumford *Harper's Magazine* p30 O 2017

Marine animals

See also

Marine mammals

Sea monsters

Debris arrivals divvied up M. Quintanilla color map *Science News* v192 no7 p32 O 28 2017

From Alaska, a Lesson on the Value of Conservation Partnerships With Indigenous Communities H. P. Huntington color *Environment* v59 no1 p34 2017

Marine animals—Pacific Ocean

Castaway critters rafted to U.S. shores on Japan tsunami debris

[Cover story] M. Quintanilla color *Science News* v192 no7 p4 O 28 2017

Marine art

The Art of Sailing A. Wisch color *Sail* v47 no12 p34 D 2016

Marine bacteria

Seagrasses combat harmful bacteria L. HAMERS *Science News* v191 no5 p14 Mr 18 2017

Marine batteries

CRUISING TIPS T. Cunliffe color *Sail* v48 no7 p46 Jl 2017

Divide and Conquer B. Pike color *Power & Motoryacht* v34 no9 p112 S 2017

When stuff happens... K. Westman cartoon *Sail* v48 no4 p30 Ap 2017

Marine biodiversity

Illegal fishing on the Galápagos high seas J. José Alava and F. Paladines color *Science* v357 no6358 p1362 S 29 2017

LONG LIVE THE BEACH color *Women's Health* v14 no5 p144 Je 2017

Marine Biodiversity and Ecosystems Underpin a Healthy Planet and Social Well-Being C. P. Palmer *UN Chronicle* v54 no1/2 p1 2017

Marine biologists

Life on Ice E. B. RUSBY color *Earth Island Journal* v32 no2 p27 Summ 2017

Marine biology

Atlantic ocean gets its first U.S. national monument T. Sumner map *Science News* v190 no8 p5 O 15 2016

DARE to EXPLORE C. M. TOMLIN *National Geographic Kids* no468 p6 Mr 2017

Marine biology—Exhibitions

ABOARD THE POURQUOI-PAS? K. Murray-Bergquist *Iceland Review* v55 no2 p71 Mr/Ap 2017

UNDER THE WAVES color *National Geographic* v232 no4 p138 O 2017

Marine chemical ecology

Mummified Microbes L. Lippsett *Oceanus* v52 no1 p18 Summ 2016

Marine Corp.

Leatherneck Ladies color *Weekly Standard* v22 no37 p2 Je 5 2017

Marine debris

Garbage In, Garbage Out S. C. P. WILLIAMS *National Parks* v91 no4 p22 Fall 2017

GARBAGE SWELL C. Zuckerman color *National Geographic* v231 no4 p14 Ap 2017

Marine debris—Cleanup

Taking In the Trash E. Strickland *Sierra* v102 no1 p24 Ja/F 2017

Marine ecology

See also

Kelp bed ecology

Reef ecology

RESEARCH color *Science* v357 no6358 p1366 S 29 2017

The Resilience of Marine Ecosystems to Climatic Disturbances J. K. O'LEARY, F. MICHELI et al *BioScience* v67 no3 p208 Mr 2017

Tsunami debris spells trouble S. L. Chown map *Science* v357 no6358 p1356 S 29 2017

Underwater Barrens D. SIMPSON *Natural History* v125 no2 p24 F 2017

Marine ecology—Antarctica

Responses of Antarctic Marine and Freshwater Ecosystems to Changing Ice Conditions M. K. OBRYK, S. E. STAMMERJOHN et al color graph *BioScience* v66 no10 p864 O 1 2016

Marine ecology—California

Invasion of the Kelp Snatchers A. DOUGLAS color *Surfer* v58 no1 p38 Ap 2017

Marine ecology—Chesapeake Bay (Md. & Va.)

Submersed Aquatic Vegetation in Chesapeake Bay: Sentinel Species in a Changing World R. J. ORTH, W. C. DENNISON et al *BioScience* v67 no8 p698 Ag 2017

Marine engines

A Good Book and a Very Big Wrench B. PIKE color *Power & Motoryacht* v33 no2 p136 F 2017

The Roving Mechanic B. PIKE *Power & Motoryacht* v34 no6 p78 Je 2017

Marine engines—Maintenance & repair

Engine Emergency: DOA! Part 1 M. SMITH color *Power & Mo-*

toryacht v33 no3 p113 Mr 2017

Marine equipment

PlankZooka & SUPR-REMUS K. Madin *Oceanus* v52 no1 p22 Summ 2016

Stay Grounded (In a Good Way) M. SMITH *Power & Motoryacht* v32 no11 p150 N 2016

Marine equipment—Evaluation

gear *Boating World* v38 no6 p30 Je 2017

NEW ELECTRONICS J. Y. WOOD color *Power & Motoryacht* v33 no2 p54 F 2017

Marine food chain

A Mighty & Mysterious Molecule W. Johnson color *Oceanus* v51 no2 p76 Wint 2016

Marine geophysics

See also

Sea ice

Giant undersea craters were blown out by decomposing methane hydrates: Although the craters likely formed about 12 000 years ago, methane is still leaking profusely around and between them M. Wilson *Physics Today* v70 no8 p21 Ag 2017

Marine mammals

DEEP LISTENING D. Fox *National Parks* v91 no1 p36 Wint 2017

FEEDING FRENZY *Sierra* v102 no1 p2 Ja/F 2017

Quick Hits A. Marks map *Scientific American* v316 no5 p20 My 2017

UNICORNS OF THE SEA A. SHAW *National Geographic Kids* no467 p24 F 2017

AN UNRAVELING WEB J. Miller color *Earth Island Journal* v32 no3 p49 Aut 2017

Vaquitas on the Brink color *Earth Island Journal* v32 no1 p7 Spr 2017

Whale calves "whisper" to help them stay safe color *National Wildlife (World Edition)* v55 no6 p8 O/N 2017

Marine microbiology—Research

Mummified Microbes L. Lippsett *Oceanus* v52 no1 p18 Summ 2016

Marine microorganisms

Big Questions About Tiny Bacteria? J. McNichol color *Oceanus* v51 no2 p78 Wint 2016

How microbes survive in the open ocean J. P. Zehr, J. S. Weitz et al color diag *Science* v357 no6352 p646 Ag 18 2017

Marine One (Presidential aircraft)

TRUMP FORCE ONE G. M. Graff bw color *Bloomberg Businessweek* no4515 p48 Mr 20 2017

Marine organisms

See also

Marine animals

Giant Shape-Shifters A. Sneed color *Scientific American* v317 no4 p20 O 2017

Marine painters

The Art of Sailing A. Wisch color *Sail* v47 no12 p34 D 2016

Marine parks & reserves

Australian plan would roll back marine protections color *Science* v357 no6349 p338 Jl 28 2017

OCEAN PRESERVATION TAKES SHAPE M. WERLING *Sea Magazine* v109 no2 p4 F 2017

Saving an Arctic oasis E. HOLLAND color map *Canadian Geographic* v137 no1 p57 F 2017

WORTH NOTING K. A. GAJEWSKI *Humanist* v77 no2 p48 Mr/Ap 2017

Marine parks & reserves—Antarctica

Nations agree to create world's largest marine reserve in Antarctica color *Science* v354 no6312 p530 N 4 2016

Marine parks & reserves—Australia

A Happy Feat for Antarctica G. TARLACH color *Discover* v38 no1 p75 Ja/F 2017

Marine parks & reserves—California

A Fishing Massacree M. PETERS color *Power & Motoryacht* v33 no1 p36 Ja 2017

Marine parks & reserves—Washington (State)

See also

Blake Island State Park (Wash.)

COMPACT CRUISING D. Hislop color map *Sea Magazine* v109 no7 p16 Jl 2017

FIRE AND ICE D. HISLOP *Sea Magazine* v108 no12 pPNW-1

D 2016

Marine phytoplankton

A Green Thumb for Synechococcus K. Hunter-Cevera color *Oceanus* v51 no2 p64 Wint 2016

Marine pollution—Prevention

Ways to Rid the World's Oceans of Plastic Trash T. John color *Time* v189 no24 p9 Je 26 2017

Marine refrigeration

Ice Boxes & Refrigeration D. Everitt color *Sail* v48 no7 p47 Jl 2017

Keeping Your Cool P. Gutowski color diag *Sail* v48 no4 p64 Ap 2017

Marine resources

See also

Ocean engineering

Achieving SDG 14: the Role of the United Nations Convention on the Law of the Sea M. d. S. Soares *UN Chronicle* v54 no1/2 p1 2017

Maintaining Healthy Ocean Fisheries to Support Livelihoods: Achieving SDG 14 in Europe K. Vella *UN Chronicle* v54 no1/2 p1 2017

Making the Ocean a Partner in Our Quest for a Sustainable Future J. G. d. Silva *UN Chronicle* v54 no1/2 p1 2017

Mobilizing the Global Community to Achieve SDG 14 A. J. Mohammed *UN Chronicle* v54 no1/2 p1 2017

Portugal and the Ocean Economy A. P. Vitorino *UN Chronicle* v54 no1/2 p1 2017

Marine resources conservation

See also

Marine parks & reserves

3D Printing Reaches the Ocean Floor L. SOROKANICH color *Popular Mechanics* p18 Mr 2017

Atlantic ocean gets its first U.S. national monument T. Sumner map *Science News* v190 no8 p5 O 15 2016

Engaging Youth to Conserve Coastal and Marine Environments K. Forsberg *UN Chronicle* v54 no1/2 p1 2017

Marine Biodiversity and Ecosystems Underpin a Healthy Planet and Social Well-Being C. P. Palmer *UN Chronicle* v54 no1/2 p1 2017

SAVING OCEAN SPECIES, FROM TOP TO BOTTOM D. Stone color *National Geographic* v231 no6 p12 Je 2017

SAVING THE SEAS C. BARNETT color map *National Geographic* v231 no2 p54 F 2017

School of tides R. Stuart color *Canadian Geographic* v137 no5 p24 S/O 2017

Science-based management in decline in the Southern Ocean C. M. Brooks, L. B. Crowder et al bibl map *Science* v354 no6309 p185 O 14 2016

Snorkeling With the President C. Welch color *National Geographic* v231 no2 p76 F 2017

U.S. seafood import restriction presents opportunity and risk R. Williams, M. G. Burgess et al bibl color map *Science* v354 no6318 p1372 D 16 2016

Marine sciences

Committing to socially responsible seafood J. N. Kittinger, L. C. L. Teh et al color *Science* v356 no6341 p912 Je 1 2017

Marine scientists

See also

Marine biologists

Ocean Research Priorities: Similarities and Differences among Scientists, Policymakers, and Fishermen in the United States J. G. MASON, M. A. RUDD et al *BioScience* v67 no5 p418 My 2017

Marine species diversity

Tsunami-driven rafting: Transoceanic species dispersal and implications for marine biogeography J. T. Carlton, J. W. Chapman et al color graph *Science* v357 no6358 p1402 S 29 2017

Marine surveyors

ASKABROKER color *Sea Magazine* v109 no8 p69 Ag 2017

Marine Technologies International Adventurewear (Company)

MTI ADVENTUREWEAR: ALL IN THE FAMILY J. MOAG color *Canoe & Kayak Magazine* v45 no1 p92 Wint 2017

Marine Biological Laboratory (Woods Hole, Mass.)

As Bay Warms, Harmful Algae Bloom V. LaCapra *Oceanus* v52 no1 p9 Summ 2016

Marinelli, Janet

Creating a Haven for Beneficial Bugs color *National Wildlife (World Edition)* v55 no2 p12 F/Mr 2017

From Weedy to Wonderful color *National Wildlife (World Edition)* v55 no3 p22 Ap/My 2017

A Helping Hand for Early Bees color *National Wildlife (World Edition)* v55 no6 p16 O/N 2017

Peril at Journey's End color *National Wildlife (World Edition)* v55 no1 p34 D/Ja 2016

Mariner 9 (Spacecraft)

Mars and Our Expectations D. GRINSPOON *Sky & Telescope* v133 no1 p20 Ja 2017

Marines

HARD CORPS A. French color *Esquire* v167 no2 p142 Mr 2017

Humor in Uniform E. WHITEHOUSE and T. BATCHELOR *Reader's Digest* v189 no1127 p135 F 2017

James M. Perry, 1927-2016 R. W. MERRY *American Conservative* v16 no1 p8 Ja/F 2017

Marinkovich, M. Peter

Microtubules acquire resistance from mechanical breakage through intralumenal acetylation diag graph *Science* v356 no6335 p328 Ap 21 2017

Marino, Dan, 1961-

Dan Marino's Coaching Success color *AARP: The Magazine* v59 no4A p68 Je/Jl 2016

Marino, Fabio

A large fraction of HLA class I ligands are proteasome-generated spliced peptides bibl graph *Science* v354 no6310 p354 O 21 2016

Marino, Gordon

Blind Spots color *Commonweal* v143 no17 p38 O 21 2016

Marino, Lori—Interviews

"Scientists Make the Best Advocates" M. N. MITRA *Earth Island Journal* v32 no2 p45 Summ 2017

MARINO, NICK

BEST NEW STORES 2017 color diag *GQ: Gentlemen's Quarterly* v97 no4 p92 Ap 2017

EVERY DAY I'M SIDE-HUSTLIN' cartoon color *GQ: Gentlemen's Quarterly* v97 no4 p60 Ap 2017

Labels We Love: The Three Kings of Streetwear color *GQ: Gentlemen's Quarterly* v97 no9 p66 S 2017

Manual cartoon color *GQ: Gentlemen's Quarterly* v97 no7 p11 Jl 2017

OFF the BEATEN PATH color *GQ: Gentlemen's Quarterly* v97 no9 p154 S 2017

Three Young Designers Bring Back Custom Suits—and They're Actually Affordable bw color *GQ: Gentlemen's Quarterly* v97 no4 p42 Ap 2017

Marino, Peter

PETER MARINO'S SOFTER SIDE color *Harper's Bazaar* no3653 p134 My 2017

Marino, Vinnie

A home practice for open, happy hips color *Yoga Journal* p73 2017 SpecialIssue

A home practice for open, happy hips [Cover story] color *Yoga Journal* no291 p61 My 2017

Marinova, Polina

100 BEST COMPANIES TO WORK FOR 2017 [Cover story] color diag map *Fortune* v175 no4 p79 Mr 15 2017

THE 2017 Fortune Crystal Ball color diag *Fortune* v174 no7 p11 D 1 2016

50 BEST WORKPLACES FOR DIVERSITY color *Fortune* v174 no8 p45 D 15 2016

DREAM WEAVER color *Fortune* v176 no3 p74 S 1 2017

FORTY UNDER FORTY 2017 color *Fortune* v176 no3 p62 S 1 2017

HOW A TACO TRUCK GETS STALLED color *Fortune* v174 no6 p86 N 1 2016

"I PASSED ON TESLA" Regrets of the VCs *Fortune* v174 no8 p36 D 15 2016

LEARNING NOT TO LEAD color *Fortune* v176 no2 p38 Ag 1 2017

MINING COMEDY GOLD color *Fortune* v176 no3 p70 S 1 2017

MOST POWERFUL WOMEN INTERNATIONAL color *Fortune* v176 no5 p111 O 1 2017

SEEKING NEW HIRES, INFOR GOES STRAIGHT TO THE SOURCE color *Fortune* v175 no4 p16 Mr 15 2017

YOUTH REVOLT color *Fortune* v176 no3 p64 S 1 2017

Mario (Fictitious character)

Mario on an iPhone? It Works M. Peckham color *Time* v189 no3 p59 Ja 16 2017

Marión, Rosa M.

Tissue damage and senescence provide critical signals for cellular reprogramming in vivo bibl chart graph *Science* v354 no6315 paaf4445-1 N 25 2016

Marion, Tucker J.

4 Factors That Predict Startup Success, and One That Doesn't *Harvard Business Review Digital Articles* p2 My 3 2016

The 4 Main Ways to Innovate in a Digital Economy *Harvard Business Review Digital Articles* p2 Je 2 2016

A Case Study of Crowdsourcing Gone Wrong *Harvard Business Review Digital Articles* p2 D 15 2016

Marioni, John C.

Aging increases cell-to-cell transcriptional variability upon immune stimulation color diag graph *Science* v355 no6332 p1433 Mr 31 2017

Mariotti, Shannon L.

Liberalism and memory B. J. Dueholm *Christian Century* v134 no19 p30 S 13 2017

Maritain, Raïssa

We Have Been Friends Together & Adventures in Grace L. T. Johnson bw *Commonweal* v144 no3 p36 F 10 2017

Marital communication

A Girl, a Guy & a Coma color *Glamour* no8 p105 Ag 2017

Marital conflict—Physiological aspects

Your Body on an Argument color *Prevention* v68 no11 p17 N 2016

Marital conflict—Prevention

ON GOING TO BED ANGRY J. Jetsohn *Saturday Evening Post* v289 no3 p26 My/Je 2017

Marital relations

How to Not Fight with Your Spouse When You Get Home from Work E. Batista *Harvard Business Review Digital Articles* p2 Ap 12 2016

THE INTERVIEW B. D. JOHNSON color *Maclean's* v129 no42 p12 O 24 2016

Moving Beyond Betrayal I. Kerner color *Prevention* v69 no5 p28 My 2017

Maritime history—17th century

The Civil Wars' Troubled Waters R. Blakemore *History Today* v67 no2 p29 F 2017

Maritime museums

MEET GREG GORGA *Sea Magazine* v109 no5 pCA-6 My 2017

Maritime terrorism—Prevention

Terrorists Have Been All Too Effective by Air and Land. What If They Hit by Sea? J. Stavridis color *Time* v190 no2/3 p29 Jl 10-17 2017

Maritimo (Company)

Maritimo X60 S. Murray color *Power & Motoryacht* v34 no11 p82 N 2017

Maritimo Australia (Company)

Aussie Rules D. J. HARDING chart color *Power & Motoryacht* v32 no11 p122 N 2016

Marius (Film)

To Do img *New York* v49 no26 p96 D 26 2016

Mariutto, Craig

Branching Out S. KROWIAK *Indianapolis Monthly* v40 no3 p54 N 2016

Marjorie Prime (Film)

Disrupting Widowhood: Dead loved ones come back as holograms in Marjorie Prime D. EDELSTEIN img *New York* v50 no16 p108 Ag 7 2017

HAPPY RETURNS A. LANE cartoon *New Yorker* v93 no25 p86 Ag 28 2017

Marjorie Prime E. Taylor color *Film Comment* v53 no4 p72 Jl/Ag 2017

Mark, Jason

Climate Change Heretics *Sierra* v101 no6 p6 N/D 2016

Common Ground *Sierra* v101 no4 p6 Jl/Ag 2016

Happy Trails: Scientists examine the benefits of forests and birdsong *New York Times Book Review* p14 Mr 5 2017

H Is for Hike *Sierra* v101 no4 p10 Jl/Ag 2016

KIDS GET THEIR DAY IN COURT *Sierra* v101 no5 p42 S/O

2016

MIGRANTS *Sierra* v102 no5 p30 St/O 2017

Profiles in Courage *Sierra* v102 no4 p4 Jl/Ag 2017

Seeds of the Future *Sierra* v102 no2 p45 Mr/Ap 2017

Share & Share Alike *Sierra* v102 no1 p4 Ja/F 2017

Tear Down These Walls *Sierra* v102 no3 p4 My/Je 2017

The View Is Made by Walking *Sierra* v102 no2 p14 Mr/Ap 2017

Weaponized Wilderness *Sierra* v102 no5 p4 St/O 2017

What's the Beef? Do the Math *Sierra* v102 no2 p38 Mr/Ap 2017

The Worst Environment Money Can Buy *Sierra* v101 no5 p6 S/O 2016

Mark, Kristen

Crowdsource This color *Glamour* v115 no9 p124 S 2017

MARK, ROB

550 ONE AVIATION'S ECLIPSE bw chart color *Flying* v144 no2 p38 F 2017

ATC PRIVATIZATION bw *Flying* v144 no8 p60 Ag 2017

AUTO-THROTTLES color *Flying* v144 no9 p20 S 2017

BOMBARDIER SAFETY STANDDOWN bw color *Flying* v144 no3 p70 Mr 2017

CESSNA 206 [Cover story] chart color *Flying* v144 no9 p42 S 2017

CHART WISE map *Flying* v144 no11 p25 N 2017

CONSIDER THE OPERATING ENVIRONMENT AROUND AN ILS APPROACH color *Flying* v144 no10 p27 O 2017

ENHANCED VISION SYSTEM color *Flying* v144 no7 p22 Jl 2017

EVEN AN ILS APPROACH DEMANDS ATTENTION bw *Flying* v144 no7 p25 Jl 2017

FALCON 8X chart color *Flying* v144 no5 p42 My 2017

FLIGHT MANAGEMENT SYSTEMS color *Flying* v144 no11 p22 N 2017

The Go-Around color *Flying* v143 no12 p56 D 2016

HEAD-UP DISPLAY color *Flying* v144 no4 p26 Ap 2017

KING AIR MODS color *Flying* v144 no10 p52 O 2017

A NEW GPS PROCEDURE DEMANDS SOME STUDY map *Flying* v144 no9 p23 S 2017

PILOTS OF THE CARIBBEAN color *Flying* v144 no11 p58 N 2017

RUNWAY VISUAL RANGE color diag *Flying* v144 no5 p20 My 2017

STEMME S12 [Cover story] chart color *Flying* v144 no6 p52 Je 2017

STICK SHAKER/PUSHER diag *Flying* v144 no8 p20 Ag 2017

TRAILING-LINK LANDING GEAR color *Flying* v144 no3 p20 Mr 2017

THE UPS AND DOWNS OF VISUAL APPROACHES map *Flying* v144 no8 p23 Ag 2017

WE FLY: REMOS GXiS [Cover story] chart color *Flying* v144 no4 p50 Ap 2017

YAW DAMPER diag *Flying* v144 no10 p24 O 2017

Mark, Tyler

Historical Analysis of MPP-Dairy Suggests Limited Impact on Average Margins but Considerable Potential for Risk Reduction *Amber Waves: The Economics of Food, Farming, Natural Resources, & Rural America* p7 F 2017

Mark Morris Dance Group (Performer)

The Not Too Hard Nut J. Acocella cartoon *New Yorker* v92 no41 p19 D 12 2016

Spring Preview M. Harss cartoon *New Yorker* v93 no4 p20 Mr 13 2017

MARKATOS, TIM

Corpse in the Snow color *Weekly Standard* v22 no48 p42 S 4 2017

Hauntingly Lovely color *Weekly Standard* v22 no44 p36 Jl 31 2017

To Love Another *Weekly Standard* v22 no46 p36 Ag 14 2017

What Are Libraries For? bw color *Weekly Standard* v23 no6 p36 O 16 2017

Markel, Howard

The Man Who Invented Wellness S. Berfield bw color *Bloomberg Businessweek* no4533 p62 Ag 7 2017

Markel, Liz Farina

Life's work: Building the church takes everyone [Cover story] color *U.S. Catholic* v82 no8 p22 Ag 2017

Marker, Chris, 1921-2012

Memory Bank M. Joshua Rowin color *Film Comment* v53 no4

p34 Jl/Ag 2017

Marker, Mile

RUN THE RIVERFRONT color map *Runner's World* v52 no1 p80 Ja/F 2017

Markers (Pens)—Evaluation

must-buys M. Santos color *Working Mother* v40 no3 p16 Ag/S 2017

Market entry

7 Myths About Doing Business in Sub-Saharan Africa A. Rosenberg *Harvard Business Review Digital Articles* p2 Jl 3 2015

The Most Common Mistakes Companies Make with Global Marketing N. Kelly *Harvard Business Review Digital Articles* p2 S 7 2015

Market failure

What Economists Know That Managers Don't (and Vice Versa) P. Ghemawat *Harvard Business Review Digital Articles* p2 N 6 2014

Market prices

Is This Steak Worth $700? K. Krader color *Bloomberg Businessweek* no4536 p68 S 4 2017

Market repositioning

Repositioning Is Not a New Business Model G. Kenny *Harvard Business Review Digital Articles* p2 Ap 12 2016

Market segmentation

4 Strategies for Reaching the Chinese Consumer L. Keely *Harvard Business Review Digital Articles* p2 Jl 22 2015

Labels Like "Millennial" and "Boomer" Are Obsolete N. Dawar *Harvard Business Review Digital Articles* p2 N 18 2016

Market share

Question What You "Know" About Strategy M. Chussil *Harvard Business Review Digital Articles* p2 Jl 30 2015

Research: Perhaps Market Forces Do Work in Health Care After All A. Chandra, A. Finkelstein et al *Harvard Business Review Digital Articles* p2 D 5 2014

There Are Still Only Two Ways to Compete R. L. Martin *Harvard Business Review Digital Articles* p2 Ap 21 2015

T-MOBILE'S CEO ON WINNING MARKET SHARE BY TRASH-TALKING RIVALS J. Legere color graph img *Harvard Business Review* v95 no1 p37 Ja/F 2017

Why Companies Should Measure "Share of Growth," Not Just Market Share Eddie Yoon, S. Burchman et al color *Harvard Business Review Digital Articles* p1 Je 2 2017

Why More M&As Is a Sign That Scale Is No Longer an Advantage N. Mele *Harvard Business Review Digital Articles* p2 O 26 2015

Why Startups Are More Successful than Ever at Unbundling Incumbents H. Taneja *Harvard Business Review Digital Articles* p2 Je 18 2015

Market Spectrum (Company)

Bilge Pump 2.0 D. HARDING color *Power & Motoryacht* v33 no2 p125 F 2017

Market surveys

See also

Consumers—Attitudes

Ask Your Customers for Predictions, Not Preferences J. W. Schlack *Harvard Business Review Digital Articles* p2 Ja 5 2015

Market value

East not least for Pacific bluefin tuna D. J. Madigan, A. Boustany et al color diag *Science* v357 no6349 p356 Jl 28 2017

MARKET VALUE H. SAMPLE *Cincinnati Magazine* p112 Ja 2017

OCTOBER'S QUESTION *Sea Magazine* v108 no10 p65 O 2016

WHAT IS YOUR CMV? A. Kluis *Successful Farming* v114 no13 p22 D 2016

Market capitalization—Charts, diagrams, etc.

APPLE CLIMBS TOWARD $1 TRILLION B. O'keefe diag *Fortune* v176 no5 p124 O 1 2017

Marketing

See also

Bundling (Marketing)

Conjoint analysis (Marketing)

Customer loyalty programs

Internet marketing

Marketing strategy

New product development

Pricing

able Products H. Yu and T. Malnight *Harvard Business Review Digital Articles* p2 Jl 14 2016

EDUCATE YOURSELF M. McGinnis *Successful Farming* v114 no13 p30 D 2016

Fix Your Social Media Strategy by Taking It Back to Basics K. A. Quesenberry *Harvard Business Review Digital Articles* p2 Jl 25 2016

The Go-to-Market Approach Startups Need to Adopt R. Ashkenas and P. Finn *Harvard Business Review Digital Articles* p2 Je 10 2016

How Marketers Can Personalize at Scale M. Ariker, J. Heller et al *Harvard Business Review Digital Articles* p2 N 23 2015

How Subscriptions Are Creating Winners and Losers in Retail C. Randall, A. Lewis et al *Harvard Business Review Digital Articles* p2 Ja 8 2016

How to Craft an Agile Marketing Campaign J. DeMers *Harvard Business Review Digital Articles* p2 Ja 21 2015

How to Market to the iGeneration J. Schneider *Harvard Business Review Digital Articles* p2 My 6 2015

Is Insulting Your Rival's Supporters Ever a Good Idea? C. Graves and S. Simpson *Harvard Business Review Digital Articles* p2 O 7 2016

LATE-MODEL ROUND BALERS: 2014 MODEL YEAR BALERS OFFER A SWEET SPOT OF POTENTIAL DEALER PRICING D. Mowitz *Successful Farming* v115 no6 p22 Ap 2017

Making Sense of Owned Media M. Bonchek *Harvard Business Review Digital Articles* p2 O 10 2014

Marketers Don't Need to Be Data Scientists D. Spitz *Harvard Business Review Digital Articles* p2 O 6 2014

Marketing Is Dead, and Loyalty Killed It A. Jutkowitz *Harvard Business Review Digital Articles* p2 F 16 2015

The Mistake Companies Make When Marketing to Different Cultures Eddie Yoon *Harvard Business Review Digital Articles* p2 F 17 2015

The Problems with Jet.com's Pricing Model R. Mohammed *Harvard Business Review Digital Articles* p2 Jl 22 2015

Psychographics Are Just as Important for Marketers as Demographics A. Samuel *Harvard Business Review Digital Articles* p2 Mr 11 2016

Put the "and" Back in "Sales and Marketing" J. Cermak, M. Hancock et al *Harvard Business Review Digital Articles* p2 O 30 2014

A Refresher on Marketing Myopia A. Gallo *Harvard Business Review Digital Articles* p2 Ag 22 2016

Research: Writing a Business Plan Makes Your Startup More Likely to Succeed F. J. Greene and C. Hopp *Harvard Business Review Digital Articles* p2 Jl 14 2017

Selling to Customers Who Do Their Homework Online F. V. Cespedes and J. Hamilton *Harvard Business Review Digital Articles* p2 Mr 16 2016

Stop Designing for Millennials T. Morey and A. Schoop *Harvard Business Review Digital Articles* p2 Je 10 2015

To Increase Sales, Get Customers to Commit a Little at a Time F. V. Cespedes and D. Hoffeld *Harvard Business Review Digital Articles* p2 Jl 20 2016

What Creativity in Marketing Looks Like Today M. Bonchek and C. France *Harvard Business Review Digital Articles* p2 Mr 22 2017

What Lilly Pulitzer Learned About Marketing to Millennials O. Artun and M. Kelly *Harvard Business Review Digital Articles* p2 Mr 31 2016

What Trump Understands About Using Social Media to Drive Attention B. Bickart, S. Fournier et al color *Harvard Business Review Digital Articles* p2 Mr 1 2017

When It's Smart to Copy Your Competitor's Brand Promise Yi Zhu and A. Dukes *Harvard Business Review Digital Articles* p2 Mr 23 2017

When Sensory Marketing Works and When it Backfires A. Sundar and T. J. Noseworthy *Harvard Business Review Digital Articles* p2 My 19 2016

Why New Consumer Brands Must Scale Faster E. Yoon and S. Hughes *Harvard Business Review Digital Articles* p2 Jl 8 2016

Your Digital Strategy Shouldn't Be About Attention U. Haque *Harvard Business Review Digital Articles* p2 Ja 15 2015

Marketing strategy—Developing countries

How Unilever Reaches Rural Consumers in Emerging Markets V. Mahajan *Harvard Business Review Digital Articles* p2 D 14 2016

Marketing strategy—Study & teaching

How a Cartoon Caption Contest Can Make You a Better Writer P. Boumgarden *Harvard Business Review Digital Articles* p2 Jl 21 2015

Marketing—China

Case Study: Competing Against Bling S. NASON, J. SALVACRUZ et al il *Harvard Business Review* v95 no3 p155 My/Je 2017

Social Media Marketing Takes Center Stage T. TAN color *Publishers Weekly* v264 no12 p30 Mr 20 2017

Marketing—Computer network resources

PLAN FOR 2017 SUCCESS M. McGinnis *Successful Farming* v115 no2 p56 F 2017

Marketing—Equipment & supplies

Marketers Should Pay Attention to fMRI U. R. Karmarkar, C. Yoon et al *Harvard Business Review Digital Articles* p2 N 3 2015

Marketing—Latin America

How Marketing Is Evolving in Latin America N. Kelly *Harvard Business Review Digital Articles* p2 Je 1 2015

Marketing—Psychological aspects

Why Nudging Your Customers Can Backfire U. M. Dholakia *Harvard Business Review Digital Articles* p2 Ap 15 2016

Marketing—Software

7 Marketing Technologies Every Company Must Use L. Gudema *Harvard Business Review Digital Articles* p2 N 3 2014

Quantifying the Impact of Marketing Analytics M. Ariker, A. Diaz et al *Harvard Business Review Digital Articles* p2 N 5 2015

Marketplaces—Competitions

Selling Anything from Anywhere: It's not easy to prosper in a rootless economy. Some people are figuring it out A. Marshall color *Governing* v30 no11 p22 Ag 2017

Marketplaces—History

Selling Anything from Anywhere: It's not easy to prosper in a rootless economy. Some people are figuring it out A. Marshall color *Governing* v30 no11 p22 Ag 2017

Markets

   See also

   Emerging markets

   Farmers' markets

   Flea markets

   Labor market

   Securities markets

   Stock exchanges

ALBANIA *History Today* v67 no6 p84 Je 2016

GET YOUR FARMERS MARKET FIX: Alexandria has no fewer than five outdoor farmers markets--two open through October, three year-round *Washingtonian Magazine* v53 no1 p190 O 2017

MARKET VALUE H. SAMPLE *Cincinnati Magazine* p112 Je 2017

South MEETS Southwest: Atlantans discover Texas's mammoth Round Top Antiques Week B. RILEY *Atlanta* v57 no3 p87 Jl 2017

Markets—California

A Changing Grand Central Market *Los Angeles Magazine* p18 D 2016

Markets—United States

WHY ARE MARKETS REJOICING AT TRUMP'S WIN? V. DE RUGY *Reason* v48 no11 p10 Ap 2017

Markey, Eileen

PORTRAIT OF A MARTYR E. K. CAHILL *America* v216 no1 p37 Ja 2 2017

A RADICAL FAITH N. Ripatrazone color *U.S. Catholic* v82 no3 p41 Mr 2017

Reporting the facts does not make the press "the opposition." *America* v216 no8 p10 Ap 17 2017

The Truth That Set Her Free A. DORFMAN *New York Times Book Review* p18 D 25 2016

Markey, Rob

Run B2B Sales on Data, Not Hunches *Harvard Business Review Digital Articles* p2 S 12 2016

MARKHAM, LAUREN

THE FAR AWAY BROTHERS E. Sanna *U.S. Catholic* v82 no10 p41 O 2017

OUR SCHOOL: An Arctic community prepares its young people for the future color *Orion Magazine* v35 no6 p20 N/D 2016

Markham, Matthew

Entanglement distillation between solid-state quantum network nodes diag *Science* v356 no6341 p928 Je 1 2017

Submillihertz magnetic spectroscopy performed with a nanoscale quantum sensor diag *Science* v356 no6340 p832 My 26 2017

Markle, Meghan, 1981-

10 Women Who Changed My Life color *Glamour* v115 no9 p36 S 2017

Wild About Harry! S. KASHNER bw color *Vanity Fair* v59 no10 p148 O 2017

Märklin GmbH

How Märklin's 19th century Gauge 1 became the 20th century's LGB large scale K. Wills *Model Railroader* v84 no10 p20 O 2017

Marklund, Ulrika

Multipotent peripheral glial cells generate neuroendocrine cells of the adrenal medulla color *Science* v357 no6346 p46 Jl 7 2017

Markman, Art

16 LIFE LESSONS *Psychology Today* v49 no5 p62 S/O 2016

Coworkers Should Be Like Neighbors, Not Like Family *Harvard Business Review Digital Articles* p2 O 31 2014

Getting an Audience to Remember Your Presentation *Harvard Business Review Digital Articles* p2 S 21 2015

How to Forget About Work When You're Not Working *Harvard Business Review Digital Articles* p2 2017

How You Define the Problem Determines Whether You Solve It color *Harvard Business Review Digital Articles* p2 Je 6 2017

Influence People by Leveraging the Brain's Laziness *Harvard Business Review Digital Articles* p2 My 29 2015

"Poor Communication" Is Often a Symptom of a Different Problem *Harvard Business Review Digital Articles* p2 F 22 2017

The Problem-Solving Process That Prevents Groupthink *Harvard Business Review Digital Articles* p2 N 25 2015

Stress Is Your Brain Trying to Avoid Something *Harvard Business Review Digital Articles* p2 Ag 26 2015

Things Are Looking Down *Psychology Today* v50 no3 p18 My/Je 2017

To Achieve a Major Goal, First Tackle a Few Small Ones *Harvard Business Review Digital Articles* p2 F 24 2017

To Get More Creative, Become Less Productive *Harvard Business Review Digital Articles* p2 N 30 2015

Two Ways to Keep Your Data from Tricking You *Harvard Business Review Digital Articles* p2 O 20 2015

When You Should Worry About Failure, and When You Shouldn't *Harvard Business Review Digital Articles* p2 Ja 5 2016

Why Some of Us Dread Going on Vacation *Harvard Business Review Digital Articles* p2 Je 16 2015

You Can't Manage Emotions Without Knowing What They Really Are *Harvard Business Review Digital Articles* p2 D 23 2015

Your Employees' Emotions Are Clues to What Motivates Them *Harvard Business Review Digital Articles* p2 My 18 2015

Your Team Is Brainstorming All Wrong *Harvard Business Review Digital Articles* p2 My 18 2017

MARKMAN, JON D.

Honda Opens Its Doors color *Forbes* v199 no2 p46 F 28 2017

Lightbulb Moment color *Forbes* v199 no6 p58 Je 13 2017

T MINUS ZERO FOR INVESTING IN MARS *Forbes* v198 no7 p63 N 29 2016

Marko, Eve

NOW WHAT? color *Tricycle: The Buddhist Review* v26 no4 p68 Summ 2017

Markoe, Lauren

Christians among higher educated, though not in U.S color *Christian Century* v134 no2 p14 Ja 18 2017

Clashes over security at Jerusalem Temple Mount *Christian Century* v134 no17 p14 Ag 16 2017

Conservative synagogues can now officially accept non-Jews as members *Christian Century* v134 no8 p1 Ap 12 2017

Exhibit at Smithsonian captures art of the Qur'an color *Christian Century* v133 no24 p18 N 23 2016

FBI report shows surge in anti-Muslim attacks, rise in hate crimes *Christian Century* v133 no26 p15 D 21 2016

Hospitals with church ties win Supreme Court case on employee pensions *Christian Century* v134 no14 p17 Jl 5 2017

Interfaith support rises along with attacks color *Christian Century* v134 no7 p12 Mr 29 2017

In Uganda, a new synagogue for tiny Jewish community color *Christian Century* v133 no21 p16 O 12 2016

Lutheran church wins Supreme Court case to get public funding *Christian Century* v134 no15 p13 Jl 19 2017

Mosque wins $3.25 million in legal settlement from New Jersey township *Christian Century* v134 no14 p16 Jl 5 2017

People color *Christian Century* v134 no15 p19 Jl 19 2017

People color *Christian Century* v134 no19 p17 S 13 2017

Persecution in Russia and Kazakhstan worsens for Jehovah's Witnesses *Christian Century* v134 no13 p13 Je 21 2017

Religious groups rally around issues after election color *Christian Century* v133 no25 p12 D 7 2016

Survey: Americans accept contraception, divide over LGBT rights *Christian Century* v133 no23 p18 N 9 2016

U.S. commission: Russia among worst violators of religious freedom *Christian Century* v134 no11 p15 My 24 2017

U.S. religion worth $1.2 trillion graph *Christian Century* v133 no21 p14 O 12 2016

Markoff, D. M.

Observation of coherent elastic neutrino-nucleus scattering diag *Science* v357 no6356 p1123 S 15 2017

Markoff, Katrina

KATRINA MARKOFF J. BERG color *Chicago* v66 no1 p50 Ja 2017

Markoff, Katrina—Interviews

CHIC CHEFS bw color *Harper's Bazaar* no3654 p99 Je/Jl 2017

Markogiannakis, Despina M.

BEST DENTISTS *Washingtonian Magazine* v52 no6 p116 Mr 2017

Markova, Dawna

Reconcilable Differences: Connecting in a Disconnected World color *Publishers Weekly* v264 no25 p101 Je 19 2017

Markovich, Alexandra

Greek hospitality is put to a religious test color *Christian Century* v133 no25 p15 D 7 2016

MARKOVITS, BENJAMIN

Literature by Degree *New York Times Book Review* p15 Mr 12 2017

Living the Blues: After a family tragedy, two Scots seek solace in the American South *New York Times Book Review* p21 S 10 2017

Stranger as Fiction *New York Times Book Review* p9 Ap 2 2017

Markovitz, Daniel

How Visual Systems Make It Easier to Track Knowledge Work *Harvard Business Review Digital Articles* p2 S 24 2015

MARKOWITZ, EZRA M.

What's That Buzzing Noise? Public Opinion on the Use of Drones for Conservation Science *BioScience* v67 no4 p382 Ap 2017

MARKOWITZ, MIRIAM

Unstuck in Time *New York Times Book Review* p18 F 26 2017

Markowitz, Sanford D.

Cancer bypasses the lymph nodes diag *Science* v357 no6346 p35 Jl 7 2017

Marks, Alyssa

ALL THAT GLITTERS... color *Dance Spirit* v20 no9 p59 N 2016

COSTUME Conundrum color *Dance Spirit* v21 no8 p92 O 2017

RESIST THE Rivalry *Dance Spirit* v21 no3 p62 Mr 2017

Marks, Andrea

FOTOWEEKDC *Washingtonian Magazine* v52 no2 p35 N 2016

If I Understood You, Would I Have This Look on My Face? color *Scientific American* v316 no6 p74 Je 2017

LET THERE BE LIGHTS (AND MORE LIGHTS) *Washingtonian Magazine* v52 no3 p92 D 2016

Living Large color *Scientific American* v317 no3 p18 S 2017

The Mouse Parent Trap color *Scientific American* v317 no1 p16 Jl 2017

Navigating by Touch color *Scientific American* v317 no3 p22 S 2017

Quick Hits map *Scientific American* v316 no4 p20 Ap 2017

Quick Hits map *Scientific American* v317 no1 p22 Jl 2017

Marks, Brendan

Churn and Burn color *Sports Illustrated* v127 no2 p20 Jl 17 2017

MARR, RON

CHASING THE GHOSTS OF APRIL color *Missouri Life* v44 no2 p62 Ap 2017

HERE COMES THE SUN cartoon *Missouri Life* v44 no5 p64 Ag 2017

MODERN PROBLEMS color *Missouri Life* v44 no4 p60 Je 2017

PUTTING THE HELL BACK IN HEALTH *Missouri Life* v43 no6 p79 O/N 2016

Quaking in My Boots color *Missouri Life* v44 no6 p62 S 2017

SANTA'S SURVEILLANCE *Missouri Life* v43 no7 p65 D 2016/ Ja 2017

THIS TOO SHALL PASS cartoon *Missouri Life* v44 no3 p66 My 2017

Marr, Sharon K.

Mutation of a nucleosome compaction region disrupts Polycomb-mediated axial patterning bibl chart diag *Science* v355 no6329 p1081 Mr 10 2017

MARRA, ANTHONY

Powered UP color *Vogue* v207 no4 p130 Ap 2017

Marra, Christopher M.

Teaching music in the flat world: Reflections on the work of Darling-Hammond and Rothman bibl *Arts Education Policy Review* v118 no2 p123 2017

Marrakech (Morocco)

MARRAKECH Moderne N. Hass color *Conde Nast Traveler* v52 no8 p102 S 2017

Marrakech (Morocco)—Description & travel

THE SWEET SPOT TRIP S. Clemence cartoon color *Esquire* v167 no2 p39 Mr 2017

Marranazo, Avi

Speak up color *U.S. Catholic* v82 no4 p5 Ap 2017

Marriage

See also

Divorce

Weddings

5 JUICY QUESTIONS J. Holloway color *Women's Health* v14 no1 p148 Ja/F 2017

Every marriage needs... a meeting? A. S. GRANT and A. GRANT color *Redbook* p110 Ap 2017

Going Bare... A. GRAHAM, P. LOCKWOOD et al color *Glamour* v115 no6 p138 Je 2017

GOING TO THE COURTHOUSE C. PENDLEY *Atlanta* v56 no10 p19 F 2017

How to Be Divorceproof T. S. YOUNG and S. TIABROWN cartoon *Ebony* v72 no4 p74 F 2017

if you ask me... or me S. JAMES and A. TRAISTER *Parents* v91 no6 p108 Je 2016

My boyfriend of four years doesn't want to move in together K. Van Kirk, H. Havrilesky et al color *Glamour* v115 no3 p144 Mr 2017

My Wife Is a Trump Zealot. What's a Liberal to Do? K. A. Appiah *New York Times Magazine* p16 F 19 2017

The temporary gift of marriage M. C. Barnes *Christian Century* v134 no13 p33 Je 21 2017

Tightening Your Bond With Boo S. TIABROWN color *Ebony* v72 no4 p76 F 2017

Till Dinner Do Us Part A. GOPNIK color *Walrus* v14 no8 p36 O 2017

"We keep choosing each other" L. Brody bw color *Glamour* v115 no3 p159 Mr 2017

What Really Motivates Workers in Their 20s J. Arnett *Harvard Business Review Digital Articles* p2 Ag 25 2015

Marriage counseling

How did the church help to prepare you for marriage? graph *America* v217 no2 p6 Jl 24 2017

ON GOING TO BED ANGRY J. Jetsohn *Saturday Evening Post* v289 no3 p26 My/Je 2017

Marriage customs & rites

See also

Bachelorette parties

Wedding costume

The Truth About That White Dress (and 7 Other Wedding Traditions) B. SPECKTOR color *Reader's Digest* v189 no1131 p130 Je 2017

Marriage in motion pictures

Love Takes Bravery Too S. Zacharek color *Time* v190 no16/17

p103 O 23 2017

Marriage law

See also

Parental consent (Marriage)

Same-sex marriage—Law & legislation

Too Young to Say 'I Do'? Underage teens can still get married in most states. But some lawmakers and advocacy groups are trying to change that P. SMITH and L. W. Foderaro *New York Times Upfront* v149 no12 p6 Ap 24 2017

Marriage law—United States

Getting the State Out of Marriage S. HORWITZ and S. SKWIRE color *Reason* v49 no6 p56 N 2017

Why It's Still Legal for Underage Girls to Marry in the U.S C. Alter color *Time* v189 no22 p15 Je 12 2017

Marriage service

REAL WEDDINGS *Virginia Living* v15 no2 p77 F 2017

Marriage—China

LICENSE-PLATE MARRIAGES B. Carlson color *Atlantic* v320 no3 p22 O 2017

THE THIRD PERSON J. FAN cartoon *New Yorker* v93 no18 p22 Je 26 2017

Marriage—Government policy

The Thread A. Kaufman, M. Arjomand et al *New York Times Magazine* p9 F 12 2017

Marriage—Humor

Laughter cartoon color diag *Reader's Digest* v190 no1132 p74 Jl/ Ag 2017

Marriage of Figaro, The (Theatrical production)

Mozart: Le Nozze di Figaro F. Colin *Opera News* v81 no6 p51 D 2016

Marriage—Psychological aspects

LOVE BEYOND GENDER A. Abbott *Psychology Today* v49 no5 p72 S/O 2016

Marriage—Social aspects

FROM THE ARCHIVES bw color *Reason* v49 no5 p78 O 2017

THE MARRIAGE BIAS J. NELSON color *GQ: Gentlemen's Quarterly* v86 no12 p40 D 2016

Marriage—United States

Getting the State Out of Marriage S. HORWITZ and S. SKWIRE color *Reason* v49 no6 p56 N 2017

Married people

See also

Wives

Head toward the Island B. Wagner map *Sail* v48 no9 p26 S 2017

How did the church help to prepare you for marriage? graph *America* v217 no2 p6 Jl 24 2017

Love in an Age of Alzheimer's J. Ruck color *America* v216 no6 p32 Mr 20 2017

Moving Beyond Betrayal I. Kerner color *Prevention* v69 no5 p28 My 2017

Mr. Know-it-All J. MOOALLEM cartoon *Wired* v25 no4 p26 Ap 2017

THE THIRD PERSON J. FAN cartoon *New Yorker* v93 no18 p22 Je 26 2017

Married people—Finance

The Ultimate Guide to Retirement: Couples Edition [Cover story] P. Wang, E. O'Brien et al color diag *Money* v45 no10 p48 N 2016

Married people—Interviews

FAMILY-VACATION BREAKDOWN J. SPYRA cartoon *New Yorker* v93 no25 p41 Ag 28 2017

Married to the Mob (Film)

Jonathan Demme C. Nashawaty color *Entertainment Weekly* no1465 p44 My 12 2017

Marriner, Neville, 1924-2016

Obituaries *Opera News* v81 no6 p63 D 2016

The Old Master S. BOSE *American Scholar* v86 no1 p103 Wint 2017

Marriott International Inc.

INN THE MONEY A. WHITING *Washingtonian Magazine* v52 no8 p20 My 2017

MARRIOTT GOES ALL IN S. Tully chart color diag *Fortune* v175 no8 p200 Je 15 2017

MARRITZ, ILYA

Supermall, Superstalled color *Bloomberg Businessweek* no4504 p44 D 19 2016

Who Solved the Mystery of a 270-Million-Year-Old Fossil color *Natural History* v125 no3 p46 Mr 2017

The Seeds of Life: From Aristotle to da Vinci, from Shark's Teeth to Frog's Pants, the Long and Strange Quest to Discover Where Babies Come From color *Natural History* v125 no5 p46 My 2017

Why Time Flies: A Mostly Scientific Investigation color *Natural History* v125 no3 p47 Mr 2017

Wild Horse Country: The History, Myth, and Future of the Mustang color *Natural History* v125 no10 p46 O 2017

Witness Tree: Seasons of Change with a Century-Old Oak color *Natural History* v125 no4 p47 Ap 2017

Marschke, Melissa

Committing to socially responsible seafood color *Science* v356 no6341 p912 Je 1 2017

Marsden, James

HBO Offers a West-Ward Expansion of the Mind D. D'addario color *Time* v188 no14 p61 O 10 2016

Robots of the West K. Reklis color *Christian Century* v134 no1 p43 Ja 4 2017

Westworld J. Jensen color *Entertainment Weekly* no1434 p46 O 7 2016

Marseille (Music)

The Hot Box *Downbeat* v84 no9 p61 S 2017

Marseille M. Mercer color *Downbeat* v84 no9 p59 S 2017

Marsella, G.

Observation of a large-scale anisotropy in the arrival directions of cosmic rays above 8 × 1018 eV *Science* v357 no6357 p1266 S 22 2017

Marsh, Abigail

The Fear Factor K. E. Himes *Science* v357 no6355 p964 S 8 2017

Marsh, Bob

Find the Right Metrics for Your Sales Team *Harvard Business Review Digital Articles* p2 2017

MARSH, GERALD E.

Initiating a New Social Contract *USA Today Magazine* v145 no2860 p22 Ja 2017

STICKS "TRUMP" CARROTS FOR NORTH KOREA *USA Today Magazine* v146 no2868 p24 S 2017

Marsh, Heidi

GIFT GUIDE *South Dakota Magazine* v32 no4 p67 N/D 2016

MARSH, JASON

When It's Not Quite A Wonderful Life *Reader's Digest* v188 no1126 p43 D 2016/Ja 2017

Marsh, Kevin

Resistance to malaria through structural variation of red blood cell invasion receptors diag *Science* v356 no6343 p1139 Je 16 2017

MARSH, LAURA

A Theory of Everything il *New Republic* v247 no12 p6 D 2016

Marsh, Louise

kids' stuff P. GUGLIELMETTI color *Better Homes & Gardens* v95 no8 p16 Ag 2017

Marsh, Richard

CAN'T ANYONE HEAR ME? T. HALLMAN color *Reader's Digest* v190 no1133 p98 S 2017

MARSH, STEVE

The Ten Who'll Be Next color *GQ: Gentlemen's Quarterly* v97 no11 p114 N 2017

Marshall (Film)

Fall Preview R. Brody color *New Yorker* v93 no25 p16 Ag 28 2017

HIS MARSHALL PLAN K. SMITH color *Vanity Fair* v59 no11 p122 N 2017

MARSHALL C. Agard color *Entertainment Weekly* no1478 / 1479 p55 Ag 18-25 2017

MARSHALL, AARIAN

FETISH: SKULL CADDY color *Wired* v25 no10 p47 O 2017

GEARHEAD: OK, COMMUTER color *Wired* v25 no10 p50 O 2017

PERKS FOR THE 99% cartoon chart *Wired* v24 no12 p86 D 2016

SURVIVAL TRAINING ENTER THE CHAMBER color *Wired* v25 no5 p38 My 2017

WE FEEL IT TOO cartoon color *Wired* v25 no9 p56 S 2017

WISH LIST 2016 color *Wired* v24 no12 p45 D 2016

Marshall, Alex

5 Simple Urban Fixes *Governing* v30 no5 p24 F 2017

Cities and the People Left Behind: What should we be doing for the casualties of 'winner-take-all urbanism'? *Governing* v30 no9 p22 Je 2017

Lessons from Venice *Governing* v30 no7 p22 Ap 2017

The March of the Machines: Automation seems cold, but it's actually a sign that society is getting richer *Governing* v31 no1 p24 O 2017

No Cars Allowed *Governing* v30 no3 p22 D 2016

Our Two-Wheel Transformation *Governing* v30 no1 p22 O 2016

Selling Anything from Anywhere: It's not easy to prosper in a rootless economy. Some people are figuring it out color *Governing* v30 no11 p22 Ag 2017

MARSHALL, ALEXANDRA

RISE & SHINE color *Architectural Digest* v74 no8 p88 Ag 2017

Marshall, Andrew R.

Positive biodiversity-productivity relationship predominant in global forests bibl chart graph map *Science* v354 no6309 paaf8957-1 O 14 2016

Marshall, Ashley R.

Quantum dot–induced phase stabilization of α-CsPbI3 perovskite for high-efficiency photovoltaics bibl chart graph *Science* v354 no6308 p92 O 7 2016

Marshall, Brad

Frame-Draggin' Brat Rod P. Thomas color *Hot Rod* v70 no9 p12 S 2017

Marshall, Caleb—Interviews

DANCE REVOLUTION R. SHELLABARGER *Indianapolis Monthly* p32 F 2017

Marshall, Charles R.

Merging paleobiology with conservation biology to guide the future of terrestrial ecosystems color *Science* v355 no6325 p594 F 10 2017

Marshall, David Weston

A Guide to Discovery A. Henderson bw *Weekly Standard* v22 no33 p40 My 8 2017

Marshall, Donyell

The New Marshall Plan J. Fuchs and T. Keith color diag *Sports Illustrated* v125 no15 p20 N 7 2016

Marshall, Eliot

Tweak makes U.S. nukes more precise—and deadlier color diag *Science* v355 no6331 p1252 Mr 24 2017

Marshall, Elizabeth

Farmers Employ Strategies To Reduce Risk of Drought Damages *Amber Waves: The Economics of Food, Farming, Natural Resources, & Rural America* p57 Je 2017

Marshall, Garry, 1934-2016

GARRY MARSHALL H. Winkler and D. Snierson color *Entertainment Weekly* no1446/1447 p86 D 2016/Ja 2017

Marshall, Jim

Classic Images B. Zimmerman bw *Downbeat* v83 no12 p86 D 2016

Marshall, Justin

The biology of color color *Science* v357 no6350 p470 Ag 4 2017

Marshall, Kandice K.

Voluntary Labeling of Chicken "Raised Without Antibiotics" Has Posed Challenges for Firms and Consumers *Amber Waves: The Economics of Food, Farming, Natural Resources, & Rural America* p35 S 2016

Marshall, Kerry James, 1955-

HOW TO BUY ART [Cover story] J. FOUMBERG bw color *Chicago* v66 no9 p128 S 2017

Lynne Cooke R. Simonini color *Art in America* v105 no1 p25 Ja 2017

Marshall, Kerry James, 1955-—Exhibitions

ART cartoon *New Yorker* v92 no39 p12 N 28 2016

THE BETTER LIFE P. SCHJELDAHL cartoon *New Yorker* v92 no36 p78 N 7 2016

COLOR AS CODE B. SCHWABSKY *Nation* v304 no4 p31 F 6 2017

KERRY JAMES MARSHALL T. Istomina cartoon *Art in America* v105 no4 p109 Ap 2017

NO ORDINARY LIFE K. S. SMITH color *America* v215 p30 N 28 2016

Now You See Me M. WAKIM *Los Angeles Magazine* p70 Mr 2017

The Painting Our Art Critic Can't Stop Thinking About J. SALTZ img *New York* v49 no22 p102 O 31 2016

Marshall, Kim
  The big picture chart color diag *Phi Delta Kappan* v99 no2 p42 O 2017

Marshall, Laura
  Friend Request *Publishers Weekly* v264 no31 p63 Jl 31 2017

MARSHALL, LISA
  Best Moves for Menopause [Cover story] color *Prevention* v69 no4 p76 Ap 2017
  The POWER of the Aha! MOMENT color *Prevention* v68 no12 p60 D 2016

MARSHALL, MAX
  Great Expectations *Texas Monthly* v45 no2 p78 F 2017

Marshall, Megan
  In Her Waiting Room: A biography-memoir by a former student of Elizabeth Bishop's looks to the life behind the poems L. HAMMER *New York Times Book Review* p12 Mr 5 2017
  THE ISLAND WITHIN C. R. PIERPONT bw cartoon *New Yorker* v93 no3 p72 Mr 6 2017
  Life Studies M. Marshall bw *Vogue* v207 no3 p288 Mr 2017
  Time to Plant Tears D. Gioia *American Scholar* v86 no2 p120 Spr 2017

Marshall, Melinda
  Getting More Black Women into the C-Suite *Harvard Business Review Digital Articles* p2 Jl 1 2016
  People Suffer at Work When They Can't Discuss the Racial Bias They Face Outside of It *Harvard Business Review Digital Articles* p2 Jl 10 2017

MARSHALL, MICHAEL
  Skeptical Activism from the Bottom Up *Skeptical Inquirer* v40 no6 p49 N/D 2016

Marshall, Nate
  WHY We LOVE CHICAGO bw cartoon color *Chicago* v66 no3 p75 Mr 2017

Marshall, Patricia L.
  Less is more diag graph *Phi Delta Kappan* v98 no7 p55 Ap 2017

MARSHALL, PAUL
  Political Islam in Indonesia color *Weekly Standard* v22 no38 p22 Je 12 2017
  Year of the Sword: The Assyrian Christian Genocide, A History *Christian Century* v134 no15 p38 Jl 19 2017

Marshall, Richard
  Ethics at 3 AM: Questions and Answers on How to Live Well *Publishers Weekly* v264 no19 p49 My 8 2017
  Memories on Ice color *Money* v46 no2 p88 Mr 2017

MARSHALL, SARAH
  Girls, Interrupted *New Republic* v248 no4 p50 Ap 2017
  Out of Office il *New Republic* v248 no6 p56 Je 2017
  Queens of the Stone Age color *New Republic* v247 no12 p64 D 2016
  The Rise of the Telenovela color *New Republic* v248 no1/2 p64 Ja/F 2017

Marshall, Stacy A.
  PAF1 regulation of promoter-proximal pause release via enhancer activation color *Science* v357 no6357 p1294 S 22 2017

Marshall, Stephen A.
  Cooperative Undertaking B. HEINRICH color *Natural History* v125 no6 p14 Je 2017

Marshall, Thurgood, 1908-1993
  THURGOOD MARSHALL Z. HILL bw *Ebony* v72/73 no12/1 p98 O/N 2017

Marshall, Tim
  Silk on a Stick: The world's flags and what they mean A. RETICA *New York Times Book Review* p16 Jl 2 2017

Marshall, Wallace F.
  Self-repairing cells: How single cells heal membrane ruptures and restore lost structures diag *Science* v356 no6342 p1022 Je 9 2017

Marshall, William
  Ultrastructural evidence for synaptic scaling across the wake/sleep cycle bibl diag graph *Science* v355 no6324 p507 F 3 2017

Marshall Islands
  TheMap K. Wiles *History Today* v66 no11 p32 N 2016

Marshall Islands—Social conditions—21st century
  Islands Stranded Offline T. John color *Time* v189 no4 p12 Ja 23 2017

Marshes

Preserving a Marsh for People and Wildlife: The Dotson Family Marsh A. M. Alvarez and E. Pfuehler *Parks & Recreation* v52 no2 p28 F 2017
U.S.-Mexico water pact aims for a greener Colorado delta W. Cornwall color *Science* v357 no6352 p635 Ag 18 2017

Marshmallow (Confectionery)
  home made MARSHMALLOWS color *Good Housekeeping* v264 no5 p68M My 2017
  Hungry for S'more? R. Kinane color *Entertainment Weekly* no1486 p52 O 13 2017
  Mermaid Marshmallow Pie R. Kinane color *Entertainment Weekly* no1466 p20 My 19 2017
  Mixing Bowl color *O, The Oprah Magazine* p108 Jl 2017
  POWER PUFFS color *Rodale's Organic Life* v2 no7 p30 D 2016/Ja 2017
  Who's the Wise One? Ask the Marshmallow Bunny S. CARR *Idaho Magazine* v16 no9 p54 Je 2017

Marshmallow (Confectionery)—Evaluation
  The S'more, the Merrier color *Martha Stewart Living* p32 Jl/Ag 2017

Marsili, Francesco
  Nanophotonic rare-earth quantum memory with optically controlled retrieval diag graph *Science* v357 no6358 p1392 S 29 2017

Marske, Katharine A.
  An Anthropocene map of genetic diversity bibl graph map *Science* v353 no6307 p1532 S 30 2016

Marston, Adele L.
  Deep functional analysis of synII, a 770-kilobase synthetic yeast chromosome diag *Science* v355 no6329 p1047 Mr 10 2017

Marston, Bette
  Going the Distance color *Sports Illustrated* v126 no11 p26 Ap 17-24 2017
  Liquid Crunch color *Sports Illustrated* v127 no1 p20 Jl 3 2017

Marston, Stephanie
  Type R: Transformative Resilience for Thriving in a Turbulent World *Publishers Weekly* v264 no40 p126 O 2 2017

Marszalek, John F., 1939-
  The ghost that haunts the book of Grant T. J. Stiles *New York Times Book Review* p15 O 15 2017

MARSZEWSKI, ED
  Everything I Know About Bartending I Learned from My Korean Mother color *Bon Appetit* v62 no2 p73 Mr 2017

Martell & Co. SA
  BEYOND HENNESSY J. Clarke color *Bloomberg Businessweek* no4503 p68 D 12 2016

Martello, D.
  Observation of a large-scale anisotropy in the arrival directions of cosmic rays above 8×1018 eV *Science* v357 no6357 p1266 S 22 2017

Marten, Helen, 1985-
  Helen Marten M. Rich color *Current Biography* v78 no4 p52 Ap 2017

Martén, Linna
  Protecting unauthorized immigrant mothers improves their children's mental health diag *Science* v357 no6355 p1041 S 8 2017

Martens, Doreen
  People color *Christian Century* v134 no3 p17 F 2017

Martens, Eric C.
  Neonatal acquisition of Clostridia species protects against colonization by bacterial pathogens diag *Science* v356 no6335 p315 Ap 21 2017

Martens, Helle Juel
  Characterization of a dynamic metabolon producing the defense compound dhurrin in sorghum bibl graph *Science* v354 no6314 p890 N 18 2016

MARTENS, JOHN W.
  Get to Work il *America* v215 no14 p39 N 7 2016
  Kingdom of the Son *America* v215 no15 p38 N 14 2016
  Prepare for Battle il *America* v215 no10 p47 O 10 2016
  The Righteous Ones *America* v215 no11 p38 O 17 2016
  Seek Out and Save il *America* v215 no12 p39 O 24 2016
  Witnesses to Life color *America* v215 no13 p39 O 31 2016

Martha & Snoop's Potluck Dinner Party (TV program)
  What to Watch R. Rahman, J. Nolfi et al color *Entertainment Weekly* no1456 p62 Mr 10 2017

Martha Graham Dance Co.

whyidance L. Knight color *Dance Magazine* v91 no3 p72 Mr 2017

Martha Stewart's Cooking School (TV program)

A Feast for the Senses color *Martha Stewart Living* p13 My 2017

Marthy, William

Positive biodiversity-productivity relationship predominant in global forests bibl chart graph map *Science* v354 no6309 paaf8957-1 O 14 2016

Marti, C.

pontoon mania color *Cabin Living* p60 Je 2017

Marti, G. E.

A Fermi-degenerate three-dimensional optical lattice clock color diag graph *Science* v357 no6359 p90 O 6 2017

Martial artists

See also

Women martial artists

ADVICE FOR NOOBS C. Morgan color *Black Belt* v55 no2 p33 F/Mr 2017

ANY DAMN FOOL R. W. Young color *Black Belt* v55 no2 p8 F/Mr 2017

The Ascendancy of Tracy Kenpo B. Mornar color *Black Belt* v55 no4 p74 Je/Jl 2017

BILL WALLACE [Cover story] F. BURK color *Black Belt* v55 no2 p40 F/Mr 2017

BIOHACKING FOR MARTIAL ARTISTS M. BENJAMIN color *Black Belt* v55 no1 p39 D 2016/Ja 2017

CAITLIN DECHELLE color *Black Belt* v55 no5 p10 Ag/S 2017

CEASE AND DESIST, PLEASE R. W. Young color *Black Belt* v55 no3 p8 Ap/My 2017

Conor McGregor M. Hagan color *Current Biography* v78 no3 p64 Mr 2017

Cynthia Rothrock [Cover story] T. L. WILSON bw color *Black Belt* v55 no2 p26 F/Mr 2017

FOR SHAOLIN MONK WANG BO, THE MESSAGE REMAINS THE SAME color *Black Belt* v55 no1 p12 D 2016/Ja 2017

From the Archives color *Black Belt* v55 no1 p66 D 2016/Ja 2017

FUMIO DEMURA [Cover story] C. COCKRELL bw color *Black Belt* v55 no2 p34 F/Mr 2017

Gene LeBell [Cover story] T. L. WILSON color *Black Belt* v55 no2 p46 F/Mr 2017

HOW A SENIOR SALVAGED HIS MARTIAL ARTS CAREER — TWICE! F. Burk color *Black Belt* v55 no3 p14 Ap/My 2017

A MARTIAL ARTIST'S GUIDE TO HIP HEALTH [Cover story] T. CALLOS bw color *Black Belt* v55 no2 p54 F/Mr 2017

MARTIAL ARTS COMMUNITY BIDS FAREWELL TO RICHARD BUSTILLO bw color *Black Belt* v55 no4 p10 Je/Jl 2017

MARTIAL ARTS DISCIPLINE DRIVES GLOBAL EXPEDITION LEADER W. J. Thomas Smith color *Black Belt* v55 no6 p10 O/N 2017

NEWS BITES color *Black Belt* v55 no5 p14 Ag/S 2017

On the Magazine's Archives L. Fleury bw *Black Belt* v55 no4 p17 Je/Jl 2017

REMEMBER OUR ROOTS R. W. Young *Black Belt* v55 no6 p8 O/N 2017

RICHARD BUSTILLO (1942-2017) M. JACOBS bw color *Black Belt* v55 no5 p42 Ag/S 2017

That's "Combatives" Spelled With Four C's M. Jacobs color *Black Belt* v55 no2 p22 F/Mr 2017

Martial artists—Health

A MARTIAL ARTIST'S GUIDE TO HIP HEALTH T. CALLOS color *Black Belt* v55 no1 p32 D 2016/Ja 2017

Martial artists—Interviews

THE NEXT JCVD? R. CARTER color *Black Belt* v55 no1 p52 D 2016/Ja 2017

REFLECTIONS ON A LIFETIME OF MARTIAL ARTS bw *Black Belt* v55 no2 p44 F/Mr 2017

STILL KICKING! (and Punching and Grappling) [Cover story] M. CHENG bw color *Black Belt* v55 no1 p26 D 2016/Ja 2017

Martial artists—Training of

Pros and Cons of Randomized Training for Martial Artists M. Hatmaker bw *Black Belt* v55 no6 p20 O/N 2017

Your Fighting Skills Are First-Rate, But Is Your Physical Training Sufficient? M. Hatmaker color *Black Belt* v55 no1 p24 D 2016/Ja 2017

Martial artists—United States

KIMBO SLICE C. ROTELLA *New York Times Magazine* p30 D 25 2016

Martial arts

See also

Kickboxing

Mixed martial arts

ALL THE RIGHT MOVES *Los Angeles Magazine* p168 Mr 2017

Dropping Bombs, Kuntaw Style A. Graceffo color *Black Belt* v55 no4 p22 Je/Jl 2017

Former Kickboxing Champ Lou Neglia Is Proof of the Power of Martial Arts F. Vallejo color *Black Belt* v55 no3 p22 Ap/My 2017

From the Archives color *Black Belt* v55 no1 p66 D 2016/Ja 2017

From the Archives color *Black Belt* v55 no5 p82 Ag/S 2017

How to Correct Your Teacher D. Lowry color *Black Belt* v55 no3 p24 Ap/My 2017

HUMILITY & EMPOWERMENT S. RAVITS color *New Orleans Magazine* v51 no3 p167 Ja 2017

I Am a Weapon: Her Martial Art of Choice A. SERRA *Idaho Magazine* v16 no8 p23 My 2017

LEARN KOBUDO WEAPONRY FROM FUMIO DEMURA USING YOUR DIGITAL DEVICE! color *Black Belt* v55 no1 p13 D 2016/Ja 2017

LET THE EXPERIMENTS BEGIN! A. TAYLOR and C. THOMAS color *Black Belt* v55 no4 p66 Je/Jl 2017

Martial Arts the Old-Fashioned Way M. Jacobs bw color *Black Belt* v55 no5 p24 Ag/S 2017

MARTIAL LAWS J. VRABEL *Indianapolis Monthly* p34 My 2017

Martial Ops Ups the Ante S. D. Seong color *Black Belt* v55 no1 p60 D 2016/Ja 2017

On Putting Our Leaders in a Cage bw *Black Belt* v55 no5 p16 Ag/S 2017

Some Things You Should Know About Sumo [Cover story] D. Lowry color *Black Belt* v55 no2 p24 F/Mr 2017

WHEN OLYMPIC GAMES MEET MARTIAL ARTS R. W. Young color *Black Belt* v55 no1 p8 D 2016/Ja 2017

Martial arts equipment

ESSENTIAL GEAR color *Black Belt* v55 no4 p72 Je/Jl 2017

ESSENTIAL GEAR color *Black Belt* v55 no6 p72 O/N 2017

On the Magazine's Archives L. Fleury bw *Black Belt* v55 no4 p17 Je/Jl 2017

Martial arts equipment—Evaluation

ESSENTIAL GEAR color *Black Belt* v55 no1 p58 D 2016/Ja 2017

ESSENTIAL GEAR color *Black Belt* v55 no3 p60 Ap/My 2017

Martial arts in motion pictures

JOE LEWIS' LAST MOVIE RELEASED ON DVD, VOD color *Black Belt* v55 no6 p13 O/N 2017

WHEN EASTERN MOVIES MEET WESTERN MUSIC M. Jacobs color *Black Belt* v55 no1 p12 D 2016/Ja 2017

Martial arts injuries

Hard Training and Inevitable Injuries K. McCann color *Black Belt* v55 no1 p22 D 2016/Ja 2017

Martial arts injuries—Prevention

Safety on the Martial-Arts Mat S. SEA GOLD color *Parents* v92 no5 p28 My 2017

Martial arts on television

A BIGGER AND BETTER BLACK BELT! R. W. Young bw *Black Belt* v55 no4 p8 Je/Jl 2017

Martial arts schools

A BIGGER AND BETTER BLACK BELT! R. W. Young bw *Black Belt* v55 no4 p8 Je/Jl 2017

Martial arts techniques

See also

Martial arts—Striking

7 SILAT SOLUTIONS B. RICHARDSON color *Black Belt* v55 no3 p46 Ap/My 2017

ARNIS BACKUP PLAN [Cover story] J. MELEGRITO color *Black Belt* v55 no3 p26 Ap/My 2017

BIOHACKING FOR MARTIAL ARTISTS M. BENJAMIN color *Black Belt* v55 no1 p39 D 2016/Ja 2017

KARATE STRONG S. LENZI color *Black Belt* v55 no3 p34 Ap/My 2017

Martial Ops Ups the Ante S. D. Seong color *Black Belt* v55 no1 p60 D 2016/Ja 2017

SELF-TAUGHT MMA THUGS, PART 1 P. BAMBURAK bw

Ja/F 2017

TIME EXPOSURE bw color *Popular Photography* v81 no2 p87 Mr/Ap 2017

Martin, Harold T.

By Assuming Snowden's Guilt, NYT Indicts Itself—and Journalism J. Naureckas *Extra!* v29 no9 p4 N 2016

Martin, Henrike

De-extinction, nomenclature, and the law color *Science* v356 no6342 p1016 Je 9 2017

Martin, Hosea L.

Discussion *Smithsonian* v47 no7 p10 N 2016

Martin, J. Andrew

"Perfect" designer chromosome V and behavior of a ring derivative diag *Science* v355 no6329 p1046 Mr 10 2017

MARTIN, J. J.

FENDI'S FAIRY TALE color *Harper's Bazaar* no3648 p272 N 2016

ode to beauty bw color *Architectural Digest* v74 no3 p120 Mr 2017

Martin, Jake

American atheist is hated, murdered, revived in new film color *America* v216 no11 p57 My 15 2017

John Oliver is good for the Republic. Or not color *America* v216 no6 p47 Mr 20 2017

What '13 Reasons Why' gets wrong about suicide color *America* v216 no12 p53 My 29 2017

Martin, James

BUILDING A BRIDGE L. Lefebvre *U.S. Catholic* v82 no10 p41 O 2017

THE CHURCH AND THE L.G.B.T. PERSON: A MINISTRY OF 'RESPECT, COMPASSION & SENSITIVITY' color *America* v216 no12 p18 My 29 2017

Creating 'Silence' *America* v215 no19 p16 D 19 2016

Hate confession? *America* v216 no5 p70 Mr 6 2017

Hate.Net *America* v215 no13 p14 O 31 2016

The Ignatian Option D. Cloutier color *Commonweal* v144 no13 p24 Ag 11 2017

In Aleppo, finding God among the ruins color *America* v216 no7 p15 Ap 3 2017

A journey of healing N. P. Cafardi color *America* v217 no5 p49 S 4 2017

Not Yet a Saint color *America* v215 no12 p27 O 24 2016

The Riches of the Church *America* v216 no1 p12 Ja 2 2017

MARTIN, JASON D.

Belay Extensions bw *Climbing* no351 p52 F/Mr 2017

Martin, Jennifer

DON'T BE SAD [Cover story] color *Amazing Wellness* v9 no6 p28 EarlyWint 2017

FAST FIXES FOR FLAKES color *Amazing Wellness* p24 Fall 2017

HAVE A GOOD HAIR DAY color *Amazing Wellness* v8 no2 p74 Spr 2016

LOVE YOUR LIPS color *Amazing Wellness* v8 no6 p78 Early Winter2016

RELIEVE EYE STRAIN color *Amazing Wellness* v9 no3 p28 EarlySumm 2017

RX FOR FOOD POISONING color *Better Nutrition* v78 no11 p26 N 2016

SOS FOR PMS color *Amazing Wellness* v8 no2 p26 Spr 2016

Treat TMJ Naturally color *Amazing Wellness* v9 no1 p26 Wint 2017

Martin, Jim

Feature: Your consumer rights this Christmas bw color *Macworld - Digital Edition* p68 Ja 2017

Martin, John H.

Control of species-dependent cortico-motoneuronal connections underlying manual dexterity diag graph *Science* v357 no6349 p400 Jl 28 2017

MARTIN, JONATHAN

'Something Massive Underway' *New York Times Book Review* p21 N 20 2016

Martin, Joseph

Promoting LGBT Inclusion and Awareness in Programs and Facilities *Parks & Recreation* v52 no6 p28 Je 2017

MARTIN, JUDITH

A Mansion of Her Own: Three wealthy women and their Italian

rooms *New York Times Book Review* p21 O 15 2017

Martin, Justin

When We Don't Blame People for Their Bad Deeds *Harvard Business Review Digital Articles* p2 F 16 2016

Martin, Kathleen A.

Clonal hematopoiesis associated with TET2 deficiency accelerates atherosclerosis development in mice bibl diag *Science* v355 no6327 p842 F 24 2017

MARTIN, LINDA

Life *Reader's Digest* v188 no1124 p40 O 2016

Martin, Lindsay A.

Large Employers Are Key to Reforming Health Care *Harvard Business Review Digital Articles* p2 Jl 27 2016

This Coalition of 20 Companies Thinks It Can Change U.S. Health Care *Harvard Business Review Digital Articles* p2 F 24 2016

The Value of Teaching Patients to Administer Their Own Care color *Harvard Business Review Digital Articles* p1 Je 2 2017

Martin, Lisa

BULLISH ON BOOKS *Virginia Living* v15 no3 p27 Ap 2017

Martin, Matthew

A Building Collapse in the Desert color *Bloomberg Businessweek* no4538 p32 S 18 2017

Help Wanted in Saudi Arabia: Savvy Investors color graph *Bloomberg Businessweek* no4513 p41 Mr 6 2017

MARTIN, MICHAEL

Alden EHRENREICH *Interview* v46 no9 p86 N 2016

Ben SCHNETZER *Interview* v46 no8 p30 O 2016

Lucas HEDGES *Interview* v46 no10 p30 D 2016/Ja 2017

Martin, Paul

Inflammation and metabolism in tissue repair and regeneration diag *Science* v356 no6342 p1026 Je 9 2017

Martin, Peggy

Old Rose for a New Garden V. F. Luesse color *Southern Living* v52 no4 p15 Ap 2017

Martin, Pete

LEARNING TO WORK THE NIGHT SHIFT: With the war effort, suddenly many more factories were working around the clock to fulfill their defense contracts *Saturday Evening Post* v289 no4 p96 Jl/Ag 2017

Martin, Peter

AYESHA AND STEPH CURRY color *Bon Appetit* no1 p108 F 2017

THE BREAK-OUTS 2016 color *GQ: Gentlemen's Quarterly* v86 no12 p198 D 2016

A FRAGILE BORDER color *Bloomberg Businessweek* no4539 p33 S 25 2017

LADY GUGU color *GQ: Gentlemen's Quarterly* v97 no3 p144 Mr 2017

THE MAN IN THE TIGHT GLOWING SHORTS color *Popular Mechanics* p74 My 2017

THE PERFECT FINISH color *Popular Mechanics* p100 Jl 2017

Martin, Philis

Popular piety color *U.S. Catholic* v82 no2 p5 F 2017

MARTIN, PHILLIP

Trump Theory *Commentary* v142 no1 p9 Jl/Ag 2016

Martin, R. E.

Airborne laser-guided imaging spectroscopy to map forest trait diversity and guide conservation bibl chart graph *Science* v355 no6323 p385 Ja 27 2017

Martin, Rebecca

DIRT, CHEAP *Mother Earth News* no279 p55 D/Ja 2017

Higher Education, The Road to American Success: An Open Letter to the Presidential Nominees *Change* v48 no5 p6 S/O 2016

Taking Student Success to Scale *Change* v49 no1 p38 Ja/F 2017

Martin, Ricci, 1953-

FRANK SINATRA JR. & RICCI MARTIN E. McCRACKEN *New York Times Magazine* p26 D 25 2016

Martin, Richard

THE ONE AND ONLY TEXAS WIND BOOM color *MIT Technology Review* v119 no6 p40 N/D 2016

Why We Still Don't Have Better Batteries il *MIT Technology Review* v119 no6 p22 N/D 2016

Martin, Roger L.

The 3 Simple Rules of Managing Top Talent *Harvard Business Review Digital Articles* p2 F 24 2017

Are Americans Enamored with the Wrong Kinds of Entrepreneurs? *Harvard Business Review Digital Articles* p2 N 11 2016

Capitalism Needs Design Thinking *Harvard Business Review Digital Articles* p2 D 8 2014

CUSTOMER LOYALTY IS OVERRATED [Cover story] color *Harvard Business Review* v95 no1 p45 Ja/F 2017

The Dark Side of Efficient Markets *Harvard Business Review Digital Articles* p2 O 15 2014

The False Premise of the Shareholder Value Debate *Harvard Business Review Digital Articles* p2 S 26 2016

The First Question to Ask of Any Strategy *Harvard Business Review Digital Articles* p2 My 5 2015

How Social Entrepreneurs Make Change Happen *Harvard Business Review Digital Articles* p2 O 14 2015

How Talent Pulls One Over on the Capitalists *Harvard Business Review Digital Articles* p2 Ag 4 2015

How the Attacks on Trump Reinforce His Strategy color *Harvard Business Review Digital Articles* p2 Ja 12 2017

A Little Competition Could Improve Your HR, IT, and Legal Departments *Harvard Business Review Digital Articles* p2 F 21 2017

MANAGEMENT IS MUCH MORE THAN A SCIENCE: THE LIMITS OF DATA-DRIVEN DECISION MAKING il *Harvard Business Review* v95 no5 p128 S/O 2017

Stop Distinguishing Between Execution and Strategy *Harvard Business Review Digital Articles* p2 Mr 13 2015

Strategic Choices Need to Be Made Simultaneously, Not Sequentially color diag *Harvard Business Review Digital Articles* p2 Ap 3 2017

Strong Dollar, Weak Thinking *Harvard Business Review Digital Articles* p2 O 13 2015

There Are Still Only Two Ways to Compete *Harvard Business Review Digital Articles* p2 Ap 21 2015

Two Words That Kill Innovation *Harvard Business Review Digital Articles* p2 D 9 2014

The UK's Snap Election Reminds Us That Proposing a Change Forces People to Ask New Questions About You *Harvard Business Review Digital Articles* p2 Je 13 2017

What Economists Get Wrong About Measuring Productivity *Harvard Business Review Digital Articles* p2 S 14 2015

Why Monopolistic Pension Funds Undermine Capitalism *Harvard Business Review Digital Articles* p2 O 6 2014

Why Talking About Strategy "Execution" Is Still Dangerous *Harvard Business Review Digital Articles* p2 S 15 2015

Yes, Short-Termism Really Is a Problem *Harvard Business Review Digital Articles* p2 O 9 2015

Martin, Roger—Interviews

Worries About Short-Termism Are 40 Years Old, but Are They Overblown? W. Frick *Harvard Business Review Digital Articles* p2 2017

Martin, Ryan A.

Precipitation drives global variation in natural selection bibl chart diag map *Science* v355 no6328 p959 Mr 3 2017

Martin, Stacy, 1991-

ON THE CONTRARY C. ROITFELD and R. SIEGEL color *Harper's Bazaar* no3650 p118 F 2017

Martin, Steve, 1945-

3 — BRIGHT STAR M. Snetiker *Entertainment Weekly* no1444/1445 p118 D 16 2016

The Three Stages of STEVE MARTIN'S Journey to HAPPINESS J. NEWMAN bw color *AARP: The Magazine* v60 no4A p36 Je/Jl 2017

Martin, Steve W.

6 Reasons Salespeople Win or Lose a Sale *Harvard Business Review Digital Articles* p2 Je 23 2017

The 7 Attributes of the Most Effective Sales Leaders *Harvard Business Review Digital Articles* p2 S 11 2015

7 Reasons Salespeople Don't Close the Deal *Harvard Business Review Digital Articles* p2 Ag 2 2017

Get Your Message Across to a Skeptical Audience *Harvard Business Review Digital Articles* p2 My 28 2015

How Doctors (or Anyone) Can Craft a More Persuasive Message *Harvard Business Review Digital Articles* p2 Ja 29 2015

A Portrait of the Overperforming Salesperson *Harvard Business Review Digital Articles* p2 Je 20 2016

To Persuade Others, Give Them Options *Harvard Business Review Digital Articles* p2 D 2 2014

What Separates the Strongest Salespeople from the Weakest *Harvard Business Review Digital Articles* p2 Mr 18 2015

What Top Sales Teams Have in Common, in 5 Charts *Harvard Business Review Digital Articles* p2 Ja 20 2015

When to Set Rigid Goals, and When to Be Flexible bw *Harvard Business Review Digital Articles* p2 Ja 27 2017

When You Give Your Team a Goal, Make It a Range *Harvard Business Review Digital Articles* p2 N 21 2014

Martin, Steve W.—Interviews

Why the Remain Campaign's Persuasion Strategy Backfired S. Berinato *Harvard Business Review Digital Articles* p2 Je 24 2016

Martin, T. J.

Past Tense R. Brody color *New Yorker* v93 no10 p22 Ap 24 2017

Martin, Tara G.

The broad footprint of climate change from genes to biomes to people bibl chart color *Science* v354 no6313 paaf7671-1 N 11 2016

Martin, Terrace

Building Bridges B. ZIMMERMAN color *Downbeat* v84 no2 p8 F 2017

NO BARRIERS. NO LIMITS. NO FEAR [Cover story] P. Lutz color *Downbeat* v84 no2 p24 F 2017

TERRACE MARTIN 'I DON'T WANT TO BE IN A BOX.' P. Lutz color *Downbeat* v84 no2 p30 F 2017

Martin, Thomas

DON'T OVERSHARE YOUR MOBILE NUMBER R. STINSON color *Kiplinger's Personal Finance* v71 no10 p12 O 2017

MARTIN, THOMAS J.

SCIENCE JOURNALISM color *Scientific American* v316 no2 p5 F 2017

MARTIN, TOVAH

A GARDEN DOWNEAST color *Old House Journal* v45 no4 p14 Je 2017

The Prettiest VEGETABLE GARDEN IN NEW ENGLAND: WHEN FASHION DESIGNER LINDA ALLARD MOVED TO LITCHFIELD COUNTY, EVERYONE FIGURED THERE'D BE A GORGEOUS GARDEN IN HER FUTURE. THEY DIDN'T SUSPECT VEGETABLES, THOUGH... color *Yankee* p28 Jl 2017

THE SHAPE OF THINGS bw color *Better Homes & Gardens* v95 no11 p118 N 2017

MARTIN, TRACY

Bright Ideas *Indianapolis Monthly* p38 My 2017

Outside the Box *Indianapolis Monthly* p42 My 2017

Martin, Tracy—Interviews

Sybrina Fulton and Tracy Martin E. Dias color *Time* v189 no4 p60 F 6 2017

MARTIN, VANCE

An Ecoregion-Based Approach to Protecting Half the Terrestrial Realm *BioScience* v67 no6 p534 Je 2017

Martin, Victoria Y.

Biodiversity redistribution under climate change: Impacts on ecosystems and human well-being color *Science* v355 no6332 p1389 Mr 31 2017

Martin, Will

GOINGS ON ABOUT TOWN color *New Yorker* v93 no24 p4 Ag 21 2017

Martin, Xavier

Lightbox K. Reilly color *Time* v190 no1 p14 Jl 3 2017

Martin Co.

July 1, 1958: Rocket Men A. BROWN bw color *Forbes* v199 no1 p30 Ja 24 2017

Martin Miller's Gin (Company)

Why a Gin Company Hired Musicians as Part-Time Salespeople C. Huyghe *Harvard Business Review Digital Articles* p2 S 10 2015

Martin Wine Cellar (Company)

WINE TIME K. MASSICOT color *New Orleans Magazine* v51 no1 p183 N 2016

Martinborough (N.Z.)—Description & travel

Goes Down Easy E. FLORIO color *Conde Nast Traveler* v52 no2 p54 F 2017

The Strategy color *Conde Nast Traveler* v52 no2 p58 F 2017

MARTÍN-COLLADO, DANIEL

New Zealand Shouldn't Ignore Feral Cats *BioScience* v67 no8

p686 Ag 2017

Martincorena, Iñigo

Mutational signatures associated with tobacco smoking in human cancer bibl graph *Science* v354 no6312 p618 N 4 2016

MARTINDALE, DAYTON

Defending the Commons bw cartoon color *In These Times* v40 no11 p18 N 2016

Don't Mine What's Ours *In These Times* v41 no6 p5 Je 2017

Still Defiant at Standing Rock *In These Times* v40 no12 p32 D 2016

What's Good for the Goose *In These Times* v41 no4 p50 Ap 2017

Martindale, Kyle

PLUGGING THE PAST *New York State Conservationist* v71 no3 p18 D 2016

MARTINEAU, HARRIET

THOUGHTS ON Property *Forbes* v199 no5 p124 My 16 2017

Martineau-Corcos, Charlotte

Hydrolytically stable fluorinated metal-organic frameworks for energy-efficient dehydration diag *Science* v356 no6339 p731 My 19 2017

Martinelli, Paolo

The Man Who Spewed Too Much B. WOODIWISS cartoon *Cincinnati Magazine* v51 no1 p70 O 2017

Martinez, Antonio

What a Changing NAFTA Could Mean for Doing Business in Mexico *Harvard Business Review Digital Articles* p2 Je 20 2017

Martínez, Antonio García

VIVA EL INTERNET color map *Wired* v25 no8 p68 Ag 2017

Martinez, Barbara

How I Solved My Horse's Problem cartoon *Horse & Rider* v56 no1 p72 Ja 2017

MARTINEZ, DOMINGO

GROUNDHOG Deus *Texas Monthly* v45 no4 p74 Ap 2017

Martinez, H.

Observation of a large-scale anisotropy in the arrival directions of cosmic rays above 8 × 1018 eV *Science* v357 no6357 p1266 S 22 2017

Martinez, Jennifer

My Five...: Tips for Staying Organized All Year Long *Literacy Today (2411-7862)* v35 no1 p4 Jl/Ag 2017

Martinez, Maurice

Big Chiefs Coming J. Berry color *New Orleans Magazine* v51 no4 p52 F 2017

Martinez, Natalia

THE EXPEDITIONS color map *Canadian Geographic* v137 no4 p49 Jl/Ag 2017

Martinez, Natalie

Beauty and the Beast Mode M. SAGER cartoon color *Men's Health* v32 no3 p19 Ap 2017

MARTINEZ, NICHOLAS

A Change of Venue *Los Angeles Magazine* v62 no6 p85 Je 2017

Martinez, Oscar

Chronicles of Everyday Lawlessness S. WOLF *Current History* v116 no787 p77 F 2017

Martinez, Rick

Have Your Fruitcake color *Bon Appetit* v61 no12 p94 D 2016 / Jan2017

Home Shucked color *Bon Appetit* no11 p36 N 2017

Straight from the Orchard color *Bon Appetit* p72 S 2017

SUMMER on a PLATE color *Bon Appetit* no8 p82 Ag 2017

Martinez, Rodolfo II

A second charge of falling to put his dirty plate in the dishwasher is pending *Texas Monthly* v45 no1 p87 Ja 2017

Martinez, Rodolfo—Trials, litigation, etc.

A second charge of falling to put his dirty plate in the dishwasher is pending R. Martinez II *Texas Monthly* v45 no1 p87 Ja 2017

Martinez, Sandra

Martinez Studio A. Ranallo color *American Craft* v77 no3 p46 Je/Jl 2017

Martinez, Steve

Let Fly the Loop S. BUTCHER *Texas Monthly* v44 no11 p70 N 2016

Martinez, Todd J.

Mechanochemical unzipping of insulating polyladderene to semiconducting polyacetylene [Cover story] diag *Science* v357 no6350 p475 Ag 4 2017

Martinez, Xiuhtezcatl, ca. 2000-

Could His Hip-Hop Save the Earth? C. GRISE and J. Shotz *Scholastic Choices* v32 no6 p22 Mr 2017

Martinez, Xiuhtezcatl, ca. 2000——Interviews

Youth Voices Are Powerful Z. LOFTUS-FARREN color *Earth Island Journal* v32 no1 p47 Spr 2017

Martinez Bravo, O.

Observation of a large-scale anisotropy in the arrival directions of cosmic rays above 8 × 1018 eV *Science* v357 no6357 p1266 S 22 2017

Martinez-Canales, Miguel

Quantum and isotope effects in lithium metal color diag graph *Science* v356 no6344 p1254 Je 23 2017

MARTINEZ-CONDE, SUSANA

Misperceptions bw color *Natural History* v125 no10 p16 O 2017

Martinez-Corral, Rosa

Coupling between distant biofilms and emergence of nutrient time-sharing bw color graph *Science* v356 no6338 p638 My 12 2017

Martínez-del Campo, A.

A prominent glycyl radical enzyme in human gut microbiomes metabolizes trans-4-hydroxy-L-proline diag *Science* v355 no6325 p595 F 10 2017

Martinez-Delgado, David

Amateur Astrophotographers Wanted *Sky & Telescope* v133 no4 p29 Ap 2017

Martinez de Salas, Karla

Karla Martinez de Salas J. K. DE VALLE color *Architectural Digest* no5 p44 My 2017

Martínez-Gordillo, Martha

Mexico's ambiguous invasive species plan bibl *Science* v355 no6329 p1033 Mr 10 2017

Martinez-Harms, Maria Jose

After Chile's fires, reforest private land color *Science* v356 no6334 p147 Ap 14 2017

Martinez-Martin, Nuria

A switch from canonical to noncanonical autophagy shapes B cell responses bibl graph *Science* v355 no6325 p641 F 10 2017

Martinez-Redondo, Paloma

Integration of CpG-free DNA induces de novo methylation of CpG islands in pluripotent stem cells diag *Science* v356 no6337 p503 My 5 2017

Martínez-Sykora, J.

On the generation of solar spicules and Alfvénic waves diag *Science* v356 no6344 p1269 Je 23 2017

Martin-Green, Sonequa, 1985-

In a Quantum Leap, Star Trek Becomes a Female Enterprise E. Dockterman color *Time* v190 no13 p59 O 2 2017

Los Angeles 03/17 *Los Angeles Magazine* p6 Mr 2017

STARFLEET RISING: The new prequel goes where no Star Trek series has gone before: gay romance, major crew conflicts and a Spock sister M. LOGAN *TV Guide* v65 no35 p18 Ag 21 2017

Star Trek: Discovery D. Franich color *Entertainment Weekly* no1485 p46 O 6 2017

Martinho, Antone

Lee Rubin: Our mentor and role model *Science* v355 no6327 p806 F 24 2017

Martini, Emanuele

Reticulon 3–dependent ER-PM contact sites control EGFR non-clathrin endocytosis color diag graph *Science* v356 no6338 p617 My 12 2017

Martini, Stefanie

Killer Instinct J. POWERS color *Vogue* v207 no6 p81 Je 2017

Martinis

The Cocktail Justification Matrix S. Dreisbach and S. G. Levy cartoon chart color *Glamour* v114 no12 p153 D 2016

THE NEW APERITIF S. Schneider color *Sunset* v238 no2 p90 F 2017

Martin Luther King, Jr., Day

Calendar DECEMBER/JANUARY bw cartoon chart color *Popular Mechanics* p10 D 2016/Ja 2017

Martin Luther King, Jr., Day—History

BIRTHDAY WISHES J. Cobb bw cartoon *New Yorker* v92 no45 p21 Ja 16 2017

Martin-McAuliffe, Samantha L.

Tasty or Tasteless? C. A. Pearson color *Architectural Record* v205

no3 p55 Mr 2017

MARTINS, ANA
Building Blocks *Architectural Record* v205 no6 p68 Je 2017
Color Theory *Architectural Record* v205 no9 p98 S 2017
Go With the Flow color *Architectural Record* v205 no8 p84 Ag 2017
Mirror Image *Architectural Record* v204 no10 p108 O 2016
Puro Hotel *Architectural Record* v205 no9 p145 S 2017

Martins, Catarina Fernandes
Mothers imprisoned under El Salvador's abortion ban spark debate about reform color *Christian Century* v134 no19 p14 S 13 2017

MARTINS, CHRIS
Dr. Strange Brew color *Los Angeles Magazine* v62 no10 p42 O 2017
Super Sonic color *Los Angeles Magazine* v62 no10 p82 O 2017

Martins, Heitor
What Makes Some Silicon Valley Companies So Successful *Harvard Business Review Digital Articles* p2 Ap 26 2016

Martins, Mark S.
Stay the Hand of Justice? Evaluating Claims that War Crimes Trials Do More Harm than Good *Daedalus* v146 no1 p83 Wint 2017

Martins, Peter, 1946-
Moments in Time *Dance Magazine* v91 no7 p67 Jl 2017

Martinson, Ernest
Popular piety color *U.S. Catholic* v82 no2 p5 F 2017

Martinuzzi, Elisa
HOW TO MAKE A €367 MILLION LOSS DISAPPEAR *Bloomberg Businessweek* no4508 p36 Ja 23 2017

Martland, Samuel J.
Fire and Faith: The coverage of a disaster in Chile revealed religious divisions among the world's press *History Today* v67 no7 p14 Jl 2017

Marton, Kati
Dark Loyalties R. RADOSH color *National Review* v68 no20 p40 N 7 2016
Stalin's Second String H. KLEHR *Weekly Standard* v22 no4 p31 O 3 2016

Martsch, Doug
Spilling Over M. Trammell cartoon *New Yorker* v92 no32 p25 O 10 2016

Marty, B.
Xenon isotopes in 67P/Churyumov-Gerasimenko show that comets contributed to Earth's atmosphere diag *Science* v356 no6342 p1069 Je 9 2017

Marty, Martin E., 1928-
The Revolution, Then and Now L. GARRETT color *Publishers Weekly* v263 no45 p8 N 7 2016
A theologian of unmatched influence color *America* v216 no10 p49 My 1 2017

Marty, Olivier
Statement Piece J. LEVINE color *Architectural Digest* v74 no9 p85p S 2017

Marty, Peter W.
Ask the pastor *Christian Century* v134 no11 p3 My 24 2017
Caught by surprise *Christian Century* v134 no12 p3 Je 7 2017
A child leads *Christian Century* v134 no7 p3 Mr 29 2017
Consumed by the news *Christian Century* v133 no24 p3 N 23 2016
Don't be bored *Christian Century* v134 no20 p3 S 27 2017
From the publisher *Christian Century* v134 no13 p3 Je 21 2017
From the publisher *Christian Century* v134 no5 p3 Mr 1 2017
The gospel for Trump *Christian Century* v133 no25 p3 D 7 2016
Habit forming *Christian Century* v134 no4 p3 F 15 2017
Identity search *Christian Century* v134 no2 p3 Ja 18 2017
In praise of poetry *Christian Century* v134 no9 p3 Ap 26 2017
Make today great again *Christian Century* v133 no22 p3 O 26 2016
On being white *Christian Century* v134 no17 p3 Ag 16 2017
Orange swaddling cloths *Christian Century* v133 no26 p3 D 21 2016
Pronoun tensions *Christian Century* v134 no14 p3 Jl 5 2017
A prosecutor's shame *Christian Century* v133 no21 p3 O 12 2016
A refugee's gift *Christian Century* v134 no6 p3 Mr 15 2017
Shaping a conscience *Christian Century* v134 no18 p3 Ag 30 2017

The slow creep of hate *Christian Century* v134 no19 p3 S 13 2017
The truth about lies *Christian Century* v133 no23 p3 N 9 2016
Truth-shaped living *Christian Century* v134 no10 p3 My 10 2017
An undivided life *Christian Century* v134 no16 p3 Ag 2 2017
What drives hate? *Christian Century* v134 no1 p3 Ja 4 2017
What makes a patriot? *Christian Century* v134 no22 p3 O 25 2017
Wishing and hoping *Christian Century* v134 no15 p3 Jl 19 2017

Martyn, Torren
TORREN MARTYN A. DOUGLAS color *Surfer* v58 no3 p42 Je 2017

Maru, Duncan
Fixing Health Care Will Require More than a New Payment System *Harvard Business Review Digital Articles* p2 Ap 10 2015

Maruyama, Benji
Harvesting electrical energy from carbon nanotube yarn twist diag graph *Science* v357 no6353 p773 Ag 25 2017

Maruyama, Daisuke
RETINOBLASTOMA RELATED1 mediates germline entry in Arabidopsis color diag *Science* v356 no6336 p396 Ap 28 2017

Marvel, Elizabeth
Homeland I. Rudolph *TV Guide* v65 no11 p42 Mr 6 2017
Lend Me Your Ears M. Schulman color *New Yorker* v93 no15 p10 My 29 2017

Marvel, Kevin B.
A Survival Guide to the Misinformation Age *Physics Today* v69 no12 p56 D 2016

Marvel Universe
    See also
    Cage, Luke (Fictitious character)
    Captain America (Fictitious character)
    Daredevil (Fictitious character)
    Deadpool (Fictitious character)
    Fury, Nick (Fictitious character)
    Hulk (Fictitious character)
    Iron Man (Fictitious character)
    Ms. Marvel (Fictitious character)
    Phoenix (Fictitious character)
    Silver Surfer (Fictitious character)
    Spider-Man (Fictitious character)
    Strange, Stephen (Fictitious character)
    Thor (Fictitious character : Marvel)
    Wolverine (Fictitious character)
THE (MS. AND CAPTAIN) MARVEL UNIVERSE C. Agard color *Entertainment Weekly* no1436/1437 p65 O 21 2016

Marvel Comics (New York, N.Y.)
MEET MARVEL'S CHIEF MYTHMAKER R. Hackett color *Fortune* v175 no3 p24 Mr 1 2017
NO. 2 SPIDER-MAN D. Franich color *Entertainment Weekly* no1436/1437 p45 O 21 2016
R.L. Stine's First Comics Work Is on Marvel's Man-Thing H. MacDonald color *Publishers Weekly* v263 no51 p8 D 12 2016
STAR SEARCH C. Collis color *Entertainment Weekly* no1463/1464 p28 Ap/My 2017

Marvel's Iron Fist (TV program)
Marvel's Iron Fist M. ROUSH *TV Guide* v65 no13 p19 Mr 20 2017

Marvin's Room (Theatrical production)
THE SICK ROOM H. ALS color *New Yorker* v93 no20 p90 Jl 10 2017
THE THEATRE cartoon *New Yorker* v93 no17 p14 Je 19 2017

MARVIT, MOSHE Z.
Socialism in the Basement *In These Times* v41 no4 p44 Ap 2017

Marwell, Evan
Why Social Ventures Need Systems Thinking V. Kirsch, J. Bildner et al *Harvard Business Review Digital Articles* p2 Jl 25 2016

Marwick, Ben
Academia's failure to retain data scientists bibl *Science* v355 no6323 p357 Ja 27 2017

Marx, Patricia
AIRING YOUR GRIEVANCES color *O, The Oprah Magazine* p102 Ap 2017
Let's Be Less Stupid *Reader's Digest* v189 no1128 p108 Mr 2017
OUT WITH THE OLD cartoon *New Yorker* v92 no44 p22 Ja 9 2017

Mary, Blessed Virgin, Saint
Keep and Ponder M. R. SIMONE *America* v215 no19 p39 D 19

2016

Why was Mary a virgin? A. Camille *U.S. Catholic* v81 no12 p49 D 2016

Mary + Jane (TV program)

Queens of the Stone Age S. MARSHALL color *New Republic* v247 no12 p64 D 2016

Mary Jane (Theatrical production)

Post-Ingénue M. Schulman color *New Yorker* v93 no29 p12 S 25 2017

Mary Kay Inc.

lovely LIPS color *Better Homes & Gardens* v95 no6 p22 Je 2017

SEMI-MATTE LIP COLOR color *Good Housekeeping* v264 no6 p132 Je 2017

Mary Poppins (Film)

LIVING BY The Word N. L. Parish *Christian Century* v134 no4 p23 F 15 2017

Mary Poppins Returns (Film)

Mary Poppins Returns M. Snetiker color *Entertainment Weekly* no1457/1458 p22 Mr 17 2017

UP TO THE Highest HEIGHT [Cover story] M. Snetiker color *Entertainment Weekly* no1470 p18 Je 16 2017

WHAT DOES JULIE THINK? M. Snetiker color *Entertainment Weekly* no1470 p23 Je 16 2017

Marya, Rupa K.—Interviews

Doctor on Call D. Kupfer color *Progressive* p24 D 2016/Ja 2017

Maryianowski, Alexander—Interviews

ALEXANDER MARYIANOWSKI H. Rolfe *Dance Spirit* v21 no3 p40 Mr 2017

Maryland, My Maryland (Music)

Warlike Thrust A. SARGEANT color *Weekly Standard* v22 no48 p39 S 4 2017

Maryland—Description & travel

Hit the Trail: Perhaps nothing helps clear the head more than an exhilarating day of exertion--such as a 41-mile hike across Maryland J. SUGARMAN *Washingtonian Magazine* v52 no11 p98 Ag 2017

WORKING FOR THE WEEKEND A. Poe *Washingtonian Magazine* v52 no5 p161 F 2017

MARYLES, DAISY

THE YEAR IN BESTSELLERS chart color *Publishers Weekly* v264 no3 p23 Ja 16 2017

Marymount Manhattan College

A Moment and a Space T. H. Freeman *Stage Directions* v30 no1 p6 Ja 2017

Marz, Leigh

The Busier You Are, the More You Need Quiet Time *Harvard Business Review Digital Articles* p2 Mr 17 2017

Marzano-Lesnevich, Alexandria

Facing Her Monsters: A law intern finds unexpected connections when her firm takes on the case of a pedophile J. van der LEUN *New York Times Book Review* p25 Jl 23 2017

The Fact of a Body I. Biedenharn color *Entertainment Weekly* no1468/1469 p109 Je 2-9 2017

Marzari, F.

Rosetta's comet 67P/Churyumov-Gerasimenko sheds its dusty mantle to reveal its icy nature bibl graph *Science* v354 no6319 p1566 D 23 2016

Surface changes on comet 67P/Churyumov-Gerasimenko suggest a more active past bw graph *Science* v355 no6332 p1392 Mr 31 2017

Marzban, Pamela

WHY IS MY JAW CLICKING AND POPPING? *Washingtonian Magazine* v52 no12 p116 S 2017

Marzorati, Gerald

Green Is Gold bw color *Bloomberg Businessweek* no4529 p71 Jl 3 2017

Masafumi Takubo

Forty years of impasse: The United States, Japan, and the plutonium problem bibl *Bulletin of the Atomic Scientists* v73 no5 p337 2017

Masahiro Fukuda

A three-dimensional movie of structural changes in bacteriorhodopsin bibl diag graph *Science* v354 no6319 p1552 D 23 2016

Masakazu Hamada

Cyclin A2 is an RNA binding protein that controls Mre11 mRNA translation bibl graph *Science* v353 no6307 p1549 S 30 2016

Masakazu Iwai

Improving photosynthesis and crop productivity by accelerating recovery from photoprotection bibl chart color graph *Science* v354 no6314 p857 N 18 2016

Masaki Hori

Buffer-gas cooling of antiprotonic helium to 1.5 to 1.7 K, and antiproton-to-electron mass ratio bibl chart diag graph *Science* v354 no6312 p610 N 4 2016

Masaki Takeda

Causal neural network of metamemory for retrospection in primates bibl diag graph *Science* v355 no6321 p1 Ja 13 2017

Masakiyo Sasahara

Overlapping memory trace indispensable for linking, but not recalling, individual memories bibl graph *Science* v355 no6323 p398 Ja 27 2017

Masakowski, Sasha

Hot Jazz Festival Sizzles in New York B. Milkowski color *Downbeat* v83 no12 p17 D 2016

Masani, Zareer

A Grand Delusion? *History Today* v67 no4 p62 Ap 2017

The TIGER of Mysore *History Today* v66 no12 p11 D 2016

Masanori Nomoto

Overlapping memory trace indispensable for linking, but not recalling, individual memories bibl graph *Science* v355 no6323 p398 Ja 27 2017

Masaoka, Dan

6 ACCESSORIES that make the iPhone an even BETTER VIDEO CAMERA [Cover story] color *Macworld - Digital Edition* v34 no6 p83 Je 2017

Masaoka, Miya

MIYA MASAOKA T. Panken color *Downbeat* v84 no7 p26 Jl 2017

Masashi Nagase

Overlapping memory trace indispensable for linking, but not recalling, individual memories bibl graph *Science* v355 no6323 p398 Ja 27 2017

Masataka Kasai

Depleting dietary valine permits nonmyeloablative mouse hematopoietic stem cell transplantation bibl graph *Science* v354 no6316 p1152 D 2 2016

Masato Koike

The ATG conjugation systems are important for degradation of the inner autophagosomal membrane bibl graph *Science* v354 no6315 p1036 N 25 2016

Masatsugu Horie

Globalism Is Alive and Well: Just Ask Carlos Ghosn color *Bloomberg Businessweek* no4531 p50 Jl 24 2017

Mascara

BLACK INK CREW T. M. FERGUSON color *Ebony* v72/73 no12/1 p46 O/N 2017

Eye-Makeup Lookbook! color *Glamour* v114 no11 p100 N 2016

Mascara done exactly right M. Roncal color *Redbook* p26 My 2017

Mermaid Eyes J. Mulrow and Y. Chu color *Glamour* v115 no1 p36 Ja 2017

NEW YEAR NEW YOU Guarnieri color *Harper's Bazaar* no3649 p256 D 2016/Ja 2017

Your Cat Eye, Customized E. Reimel and Ying Chu color *Glamour* v115 no3 p108 Mr 2017

Mascara—Evaluation

100 BEST BEAUTY EDITION A. FRANZINO color *Good Housekeeping* v264 no5 p23 My 2017

6 mind-blowing mascaras M. OLIVA color *Redbook* p62 F 2017

The A-LIST G. Hadid color *Harper's Bazaar* no3654 p58 Je/Jl 2017

All Night Long S. Kitchens color *Glamour* v115 no7 p84 Jl 2017

Beauty for the Anime-Obsessed J. Mulrow and Ying Chu cartoon color *Glamour* v115 no2 p58 F 2017

BEAUTY NEWS bw color *Harper's Bazaar* no3648 p218 N 2016

cheap THRILLS E. STOVALL color *Seventeen* v76 no12 p54 D 2016/Ja 2017

Does It Really Work? color *InStyle* v24 no6 p99 Je 2017

DRY GOODS: Stay cooler and more collected with these hair and skin faves H. G. Phillips *Washingtonian Magazine* v52 no11 p106 Ag 2017

EYE CANDY color *Harper's Bazaar* no3651 p430 Mr 2017

AN EYE FOR STYLE color *Martha Stewart Living* p50 Ap 2017
FIND YOUR WINNING STYLE! [Cover story] color *Redbook* p56 S 2017
GAME ON! color *O, The Oprah Magazine* p59 Je 2017
GET YOUNGER LOOKING EYES Guarnieri color *Harper's Bazaar* no3657 p189 O 2017
International RELATIONS color *Vogue* v207 no10 p206 O 2017
Mermaid Eyes E. Reimel color *Glamour* v115 no9 p84 S 2017
My Aunt, the Beauty Icon V. F. Luesse color *Southern Living* v52 no4 p64 Ap 2017
MY GRANDMOTHER, THE BEAUTY ICON H. Hayes color *Southern Living* v51 no11 p68 N 2016
RAD'80s Makeup M. ABERMAN color *Seventeen* v76 no3 p50 My 2017
Simple EYELASH Hacks I. VAN LOTRINGEN color *Seventeen* v76 no12 p52 D 2016/Ja 2017
Spring BEAUTY O-WARDS 2017 M. Goldberg color *O, The Oprah Magazine* p69 My 2017
'tis the season... TO SPARKLE *Better Homes & Gardens* v94 no12 p24 D 2016
UPDATE YOUR LOOK Guarnieri color *Harper's Bazaar* no3655 p89 Ag 2017
Women's Health 2017 BEAUTY AWARDS A. FINNEY color graph *Women's Health* v14 no5 p116 Je 2017

MASCARELLI, AMANDA
Feel better—starting today color *Yoga Journal* p10 2016 Special Issue

Mascareñas, Dolly
How Castro Will Be Trump's First Foreign Policy Test color *Time* v188 no24 p46 D 12 2016

Mascher, Martin
Wild emmer genome architecture and diversity elucidate wheat evolution and domestication color *Science* v357 no6346 p93 Jl 7 2017

MASCHINOT, BETH
The Democrats Went Down to Georgia *In These Times* v41 no5 p8 My 2017

Masci, F.
iPTF16geu: A multiply imaged, gravitationally lensed type Ia supernova color diag graph *Science* v356 no6335 p291 Ap 21 2017

MASCIO, BRYAN
True Teaching Expertise cartoon *Education Digest* v82 no4 p17 D 2016

Mascola, John R.
Rapid development of a DNA vaccine for Zika virus bibl graph *Science* v354 no6309 p237 O 14 2016
Trispecific broadly neutralizing HIV antibodies mediate potent SHIV protection in macaques color graph *Science* v357 no6359 p85 O 6 2017

Mascots
See also
Sports team mascots

Mascots (Film)
Mascots D. Coggan color *Entertainment Weekly* no1435 p44 O 14 2016
Under the Giant Heads of Mascots Live Absurd Humans Just Like Us E. Berman color *Time* v188 no16/17 p85 O 24 2016

Masculinity
Even the Thought of Earning Less than Their Wives Changes How Men Behave D. Cassino *Harvard Business Review Digital Articles* p2 Ap 19 2016
Rethinking What Masculinity Means at the Office A. Wittenberg-Cox *Harvard Business Review Digital Articles* p2 Je 16 2017
SEXUAL HEALING L. BLADES and S. TIABROWN color *Ebony* v72 no4 p77 F 2017
STYLED to the MAX(WELL) bw *Ebony* v72/73 no12/1 p32 O/N 2017
What Happens When Men Don't Conform to Masculine Clothing Norms at Work? B. Barry *Harvard Business Review Digital Articles* p2 Ag 31 2017

Masculinity in motion pictures
MOONLIGHT AND MANHOOD B. McGARVEY *America* v216 no1 p36 Ja 2 2017

Masculinity on television
The Unfunny Fall of TV's Manly Men color *Entertainment Week-*

ly no1438 p50 N 4 2016

Masculinity—United States
Revenge of the Trolls J. M. COLÓN *In These Times* v41 no8 p34 Ag 2017

Mase, Michael
Driving Home the Safety Discussion il *Consumer Reports* v82 no9 p6 S 2017

Masekela, Hugh
Tribute to Satchmo J. Berry color *New Orleans Magazine* v51 no7 p54 My 2017

Mäser, P.
Inhibitors of PEX14 disrupt protein import into glycosomes and kill Trypanosoma parasites chart color diag graph *Science* v355 no6332 p1416 Mr 31 2017

Maserati automobiles—Evaluation
Ghost of the White Dame J. Jacquot color diag *Car & Driver* v62 no8 p60 F 2017
MONSTER-ATI C. Walton chart color *Motor Trend* v69 no5 p56 My 2017

Maserati SpA
Ghost of the White Dame J. Jacquot color diag *Car & Driver* v62 no8 p60 F 2017
MONSTER-ATI C. Walton chart color *Motor Trend* v69 no5 p56 My 2017

M.A.S.H. (TV program)
1932-2016 William Christopher L. Rice color *Entertainment Weekly* no1448 p53 Ja 13 2017

Mashaba, Herman—Interviews
Meet Johannesburg's New Libertarian Mayor L. Louw color *Reason* v48 no7 p36 D 2016

Mashburn, Ann—Interviews
FASHION TO PHOTOS: Atlanta style icons Sid and Ann Mashburn shine a light on photography F. FEASTER *Atlanta* v57 no6 p34 O 2017

Mashburn, Sid—Interviews
FASHION TO PHOTOS: Atlanta style icons Sid and Ann Mashburn shine a light on photography F. FEASTER *Atlanta* v57 no6 p34 O 2017

Masi, Gianluca
BARELY THERE ECLIPSE *Sky & Telescope* v133 no6 p76 Je 2017

Masi Bikes (Company)
"SHOULD I GET A DROP-BAR OR A FLAT-BAR ROAD BIKE?" E. Furia and B. STRICKLAND color *Bicycling* v58 no3 p108 Ap 2017
"WHAT'S A GOOD FIRST ROAD BIKE?" L. Flickinger and B. STRICKLAND color *Bicycling* v58 no3 p18 Ap 2017

Masias Meza, J. J.
Observation of a large-scale anisotropy in the arrival directions of cosmic rays above 8×1018 eV *Science* v357 no6357 p1266 S 22 2017

MASICH, MATT
MCCOOK HAS THE WRIGHT LOOK color *Nebraska Life* v21 no2 p34 Mr/Ap 2017
Nebraska AND THE GREAT WAR bw color *Nebraska Life* v21 no6 p22 N/D 2017
Time travel through the Haymarket color *Nebraska Life* v21 no2 p60 Mr/Ap 2017

Mask making
THE MASK B. L. Heldman color *Entertainment Weekly* no1460/1461 p43 Ap 7-17 2017

Mask Off (Music)
'MASK OFF' A. BARSHAD color *New York Times Magazine* p21 Mr 12 2017

Maskell, Brian
A Simple Way to Involve Frontline Clinicians in Managing Costs *Harvard Business Review Digital Articles* p2 O 11 2017

Maskell, Daniel P.
A supramolecular assembly mediates lentiviral DNA integration bibl color *Science* v355 no6320 p1 Ja 6 2017

MASKIEWICZ, APRIL CORDERO
Succeeding in Science *BioScience* v67 no4 p392 Ap 2017

Maskin, Eric
A Better Way to Choose Presidents color *New York Review of Books* v64 no10 p61 Je 8 2017
The Rules of the Game: A New Electoral System cartoon chart

New York Review of Books v64 no1 p8 Ja 19 2017

Masks

Face Time P. BRADY color *Conde Nast Traveler* v52 no4 p102 Ap 2017

Who Was That Masked Man? E. Epstein color *Weekly Standard* v22 no23 p8 F 20 2017

Masks—Evaluation

PRACTICAL PRODUCTS L. BACK color *Trail Rider* v29 no4 p52 My 2017

Masks—Exhibitions

SIMON STARLING C. M. Schultz color *Art in America* v105 no3 p125 Mr 2017

Masks—Mexico

Benjamin Booker's L.A. Punk Chic P. DOYLE bw color *Rolling Stone* no1287 p16 My 18 2017

Maslany, Tatiana, 1985-

CLONES, TWINS & DOPPELGÄNGERS: TV'S BEST DOUBLE FEATURES D. BIANCULLI *TV Guide* v65 no27 p8 Je 26 2017

HOW TO: Play 11 Different Characters (And Counting) on One TV Show E. A. JUNG img *New York* v50 no11 p118 My 29 2017

ORPHAN BLACK A TO Z N. Clark, J. Derschowitz et al color *Entertainment Weekly* no1470 p24 Je 16 2017

MASLIN, JANET

John Grisham *New York Times Book Review* p30 Je 4 2017

MASLIN, SARAH ESTHER

El Salvador's Ghost Town color *Nation* v304 no13 p20 Ap 17 2017

Maslow, Abraham H. (Abraham Harold), 1908-1970

HOW POVERTY KILLS wondeR and what we can do about it R. BELL *Humanist* v77 no5 p16 S/O 2017

Maslow, Nick

THE 8-SECOND REVIEW color *Entertainment Weekly* no1466 p46 My 19 2017

CLIVE DAVIS color *Entertainment Weekly* no1486 p59 O 13 2017

A GAY Old Timeline color diag *Entertainment Weekly* no1471 p32 Je 23 2017

VEEP'S SAM RICHARDSON GETS OUR VOTE color *Entertainment Weekly* no1467 p52 My 26 2017

What to Watch color *Entertainment Weekly* no1463/1464 p99 Ap/My 2017

What to Watch color *Entertainment Weekly* no1485 p52 O 6 2017

Mason, Arthur

To The Editor color *American Craft* v76 no6 p10 D 2016-Ja 2017

Mason, Ashley

Aloha, Poke color *Bon Appetit* p89 S 2017

THE ART of SIMPLICITY color *Bon Appetit* no8 p56 Ag 2017

Baker's Choice color *Bon Appetit* v61 no11 p23 N 2016

A Berry Good Idea color *Bon Appetit* no8 p28 Ag 2017

Cheers for Tiers color *Bon Appetit* v62 no7 p20 Jl 2017

Cook Like a Pro: Summer Edition [Cover story] bw color diag *Bon Appetit* v62 no7 p56 Jl 2017

FERMENTATION NATION color *Bon Appetit* no1 p66 F 2017

OLD CHINESE IS THE NEW CHINESE [Cover story] color *Bon Appetit* p114 S 2017

PREP SCHOOL bw color *Bon Appetit* v61 no11 p153 N 2016

prep school bw color *Bon Appetit* v62 no10 p105 O 2017

prep school bw color *Bon Appetit* v62 no4 p112 Ap 2017

prep school bw color *Bon Appetit* v62 no7 p97 Jl 2017

r.s.v.p bw *Bon Appetit* v62 no4 p10 Ap 2017

SO FRESH AND SO CLEAN color *Bon Appetit* v62 no2 p99 Mr 2017

starters color *Bon Appetit* p25 S 2017

starters color *Bon Appetit* v62 no6 p17 Je 2017

Thanksgiving LESSONS [Cover story] color *Bon Appetit* no11 p82 N 2017

Mason, Betsy

New Zealand temblor points to threat of compound quakes color map *Science* v355 no6331 p1250 Mr 24 2017

REAL SICK [Cover story] color *Science News* v191 no5 p24 Mr 18 2017

Virtual reality raises nausea risk color *Science News* v191 no1 p7 Ja 21 2017

Mason, Biddy, 1818-1891

In Our Cities B. DANIELLE bw color *Ebony* v72 no5 p32 Mr 2017

MASON, C. NICOLE

THE Nearly Impossible DREAM *Ms.* v26 no4 p30 Wint 2016

Mason, Cory

The Little School District That Could E. Gunn bw color *Progressive* v81 no3 p20 Mr 2017

Mason, Darrell

FROM OUR READERS color *Sky & Telescope* v134 no2 p6 Ag 2017

Mason, Debbie

Primrose Lane *Publishers Weekly* v264 no20 p44 My 15 2017

Mason, Frank

Leading Off color *Sports Illustrated* v126 no9 p6 Mr 27 2017

TWO OF A KIND L. Winn color *Sports Illustrated* v126 no1 p48 Ja 9 2017

Mason, Haley

BROKEN Barriers C. Hutchison bw color *American Cowboy* v24 no1 p52 Je/Jl 2017

Mason, Hilary—Interviews

How AI Fits into Your Data Science Team H. Mason *Harvard Business Review Digital Articles* p2 Jl 21 2017

HOW AI FITS INTO YOUR DATA SCIENCE TEAM: It helps to know the three things data scientists do *Harvard Business Review Digital Articles* p22 Jl 1 2017

Mason, Jack

The Valentine's Day Wine Survival Guide bw *Esquire* v167 no1 p17 F 2017

Mason, Julia G.

Committing to socially responsible seafood color *Science* v356 no6341 p912 Je 1 2017

Ocean Research Priorities: Similarities and Differences among Scientists, Policymakers, and Fishermen in the United States *BioScience* v67 no5 p418 My 2017

Mason, Malia

To Be More Creative, Schedule Your Breaks *Harvard Business Review Digital Articles* p2 My 10 2017

Mason, Martin

Who I am: Martin Mason *People Management* p49 My 2017

MASON, NICHOLAS A.

Longitudinal Analysis of a Diversity Support Program in Biology: A National Call for Further Assessment *BioScience* v67 no4 p367 Ap 2017

Mason, Nicolette

I Am Not an Hourglass color *Glamour* v115 no6 p46 Je 2017

Mason, Paul

EXIT LEFT bw color *Nation* v304 no16 p16 My 22 2017

Mason, Perry, 1899-1964

Introducing: TV for Grownups color *AARP: The Magazine* v60 no5A p14 Ag/S 2017

MASON, RICHARD K.

Assessing Spinoza *Commentary* v142 no2 p13 S 2016

Mason, Royal

How America Lost Its Mind color *Atlantic* v320 no4 p12 N 2017

Mason, Steve—Interviews

Pyrex and Pickle Jars E. GAUKEL *Treasures* v6 no2 p6 O/N 2016

Mason, Taylor

BROKEN Barriers C. Hutchison bw color *American Cowboy* v24 no1 p52 Je/Jl 2017

Mason, Wyatt

Telling the Truth *New York Times Magazine* p50 Mr 5 2017

A TO Z color *Esquire* p112 Je/Jl 2017

Violence and Creativity [Cover story] bw color *New York Review of Books* v64 no14 p47 S 28 2017

Mason, Zachary

Void Star *Publishers Weekly* v264 no7 p44 F 13 2017

Mason-Dixon Line

In Our Cities M. Starks bw color *Ebony* v72 no9 p32 Jl/Ag 2017

MASONER, RICHARD

THANKS FOR THE RIDE color *Bicycling* v58 no10 p15 N/D 2017

Mason-Suares, Heather M.

Distribution and clinical impact of functional variants in 50,726 whole-exome sequences from the DiscovEHR study chart graph *Science* v354 no6319 paaf6814-1 D 23 2016

Masood, Khalid, d. 2017

Britain Keeps Calm and Carries on After Parliament Attack T. John color *Time* v189 no13 p12 Ap 10 2017

Masotti, Perry

A CANINE ASSIST color *New York State Conservationist* v71 no2 p10 O 2016

Masri, Bashar

If You Build It, Will Peace Come? J. Ferziger and D. Rocks color *Bloomberg Businessweek* no4519 p19 Ap 24 2017

Masri, Maher

Your Company Should Be Helping Customers on Social *Harvard Business Review Digital Articles* p2 Jl 15 2015

Mass (Liturgy)

and the survey says *U.S. Catholic* v82 no9 p33 S 2017

Did God bless America? Patriotic songs should be approached carefully at church P. Gallagher color *U.S. Catholic* v82 no9 p31 S 2017

Hall Mass B. Doyle color *U.S. Catholic* v82 no9 p36 S 2017

KEEP THE MISSALETTES! A. J. Distefano *Commonweal* v144 no5 p2 Mr 10 2017

MORE ON THE MASS D. W. Byers *Commonweal* v144 no5 p2 Mr 10 2017

No 'Reform of the Reform' G. O'CONNELL *America* v215 no19 p24 D 19 2016

The Special Collection B. Doyle color *U.S. Catholic* v82 no5 p34 My 2017

Sunday Crybaby V. Schultz *America* v216 no4 p58 F 20 2017

They Only Look like Zombies F. Nonomen color *Commonweal* v144 no17 p8 O 20 2017

What Not to Do at Mass W. J. BAUSCH bw *Commonweal* v143 no20 p2 D 16 2016

Where do hosts come from? V. M. Tufano *U.S. Catholic* v82 no6 p49 Je 2017

Mass (Liturgy)—Celebration

Such Great Heights B. DOYLE color *America* v215 p25 N 28 2016

Mass (Physics)—Measurement

The Kilogram Makeover K. Sheikh color graph *Scientific American* v315 no3 p18 S 2016

Mass budget (Geophysics)

Antarctic Snowfall May Offset Sea-Level Rise *USA Today Magazine* v145 no2865 p5 Je 2017

Mass burials

LAST STAND OF THE BLUE BRIGADE D. WEISS color *Archaeology* v70 no5 p14 S/O 2017

Mass customization

What Stitch Fix Figured Out About Mass Customization S. Ahuja *Harvard Business Review Digital Articles* p2 My 26 2015

Mass Design Group (Company)

LESSON PLAN F. A. BERNSTEIN color *Architectural Digest* v73 no11 p84 N 2016

Mass extinctions

As Mass Extinction Threatens, Are Catholics Listening to 'Laudato Si"? K. CLARKE color *America* v215 no15 p9 N 14 2016

Mass incarceration

AMERICA'S TOXIC PRISONS C. Bernd, Z. Loftus-Farren et al color map *Earth Island Journal* v32 no2 p17 Summ 2017

NO WAY OUT T. RUSSELL bw *Reason* v48 no9 p58 F 2017

Unofficial Paths: Memories of Poston N. ISHIYAMA and J. KAMATA *Orion Magazine* v35 no4/5 p51 Jl-O 2016

Mass markets

Is Mass Market Dying, Or Just Evolving—Again? R. Deahl color *Publishers Weekly* v264 no21 p4 My 22 2017

Mass media

See also

Debates & debating in mass media

Digital media

Environmentalism in mass media

Mass media & culture

Mass media & education

Motion pictures

Multiculturalism in mass media

Periodicals

Television broadcasting

Television programs

Women in mass media

Donald Trump, Media Darling M. CONTINETTI *Commentary*

v142 no4 p56 N 2016

From Bias to Disruption for New Administration *USA Today Magazine* v145 no2863 p1 Ap 2017

Game, Set, Match E. Alterman *Nation* v304 no13 p6 Ap 17 2017

The Industries That Are Being Disrupted the Most by Digital R. Grossman *Harvard Business Review Digital Articles* p2 Mr 21 2016

Kodak Courage J. ELLISON color *Climbing* no354 p18 Jl 2017

Make Medicine Great Again K. S. HELD *USA Today Magazine* v145 no2860 p65 Ja 2017

My Red Carpet Diary M. Mullally color *InStyle* v24 no9 p216 S 2017

SCREEN GRAB M. BRADY *Psychology Today* v50 no3 p20 My/Je 2017

Sniffing Out Dog Whistles K. Steinmetz *Time* v188 no16/17 p65 O 24 2016

Some Animals Are More Equal than Others: Wild Animal Welfare in the Media R. E. FEBER, E. M. RAEBEL et al *BioScience* v67 no1 p62 Ja 2017

When the Media Covers Gender Inequality, the CSuite Listens L. Gaines-Ross *Harvard Business Review Digital Articles* p2 O 21 2015

Mass media & body image

Horsepower Shaming D. Freiburger color *Hot Rod* v70 no7 p122 Jl 2017

STOP THE PRESSES E. Bazelon *New York Times Magazine* p50 N 27 2016

Mass media & business

Corporate Media Threatens Our Democracy B. SANDERS *In These Times* v41 no2 p28 F 2017

Mass media & children

What It Feels Like When All Your Parental Nightmares Are Rolled Into One TV Series S. Schrobsdorff color *Time* v189 no19 p56 My 22 2017

Mass media & culture

Gone but Not Forgotten L. SMITH color *Weekly Standard* v23 no2 p5 S 18 2017

Mass media & democracy

There's Too Much Speech in Israel! M. CONTINETTI *Commentary* v142 no2 p72 S 2016

Mass media & education

The Editor's Note J. Richardson *Phi Delta Kappan* v99 no2 p4 O 2017

Mass media & history

FROM THE EDITOR P. Lay *History Today* v67 no1 p2 Ja 2017

Mass media & politics

"ADORE ME, MEDIA SCUM, OR ELSE!" G. TRUDEAU *Nation* v304 no9 p30 Mr 20 2017

The Art of Thinking in Other People's Heads A. Stern *Humanities* v38 no1 p1 Wint 2017

Bromance News E. Alterman il *Nation* v303 no20 p6 N 14 2016

CANADA'S ANTI-MEDIA MOGUL J. MARKUSOFF color *Maclean's* v130 no2 p28 Mr 2017

THE CORRUPTION CONUNDRUM J. Surowiecki cartoon *New Yorker* v92 no48 p19 F 6 2017

The Counterpuncher F. BARNES cartoon *Weekly Standard* v22 no19 p9 Ja 23 2017

How to Fight Fox and Friends M. HERTSGAARD color *Nation* v304 no9 p14 Mr 20 2017

HOW TRUMP PLAYED THE MEDIA M. BAUERLEIN *Mother Jones* v42 no1 p4 Ja/F 2017

INFO WARS S. Coll cartoon *New Yorker* v92 no48 p15 F 6 2017

The Jared bubble K. Pope color *Columbia Journalism Review* v56 no2 p34 Fall 2017

The limits of story cartoon *Christian Century* v133 no22 p7 O 26 2016

THE PRESIDENT VS. THE PRESS B. BROWN *New York Times Upfront* v149 no10 p18 Mr 13 2017

ROAR OF THE CROWD *Texas Monthly* v45 no3 p10 Mr 2017

The Serfdom of the Press E. Alterman il *Nation* v304 no3 p10 Ja 30 2017

Speak for Yourselves E. Alterman il *Nation* v303 no16 p6 O 17 2016

When a Cough Is Not Just a Cough M. CONTINETTI *Commentary* v142 no3 p56 O 2016

The White House briefing room gets its 15 minutes J. Friedman color *Columbia Journalism Review* v56 no2 p84 Fall 2017

Mass media & propaganda

HOW LIES SPREAD M. Hertsgaard and D. Grant color *Nation* v304 no9 p19 Mr 20 2017

Mass media & technology

The tech/editorial culture clash E. Bell cartoon *Columbia Journalism Review* p24 Fall/Wint 2016

Mass media censorship

BAD NEWS color *Maclean's* v129 no48/49 p9 D 5 2016

Mass media criticism

Pioneering Press Critic P. Terzian bw *Weekly Standard* v22 no26 p14 Mr 13 2017

Mass media industry

3 Strategic Questions the Media Industry's Future Depends On J. Balis *Harvard Business Review Digital Articles* p2 O 5 2015

Don't Try to Be a Publisher and a Platform at the Same Time L. Laurenson *Harvard Business Review Digital Articles* p2 Ja 19 2015

Driver's Seat C. Baker *New York Times Magazine* p58 O 8 2017

The Future of Fox News I. RUDOLPH *TV Guide* v65 no19 p16 My 1 2017

Innovation gone bad E. Wemple *Columbia Journalism Review* p30 Fall/Wint 2016

Syrian Airstrikes Rekindle Media's Love Affair With US Violence [Cover story] J. Jackson *Extra!* v30 no4 p1 My 2017

The tech/editorial culture clash E. Bell cartoon *Columbia Journalism Review* p24 Fall/Wint 2016

WHAT'S NEXT FOR O'REILLY? D. BIANCULLI *TV Guide* v65 no19 p16 My 1 2017

Your tax dollars at work L. Zagare and B. Smith color *Columbia Journalism Review* v56 no1 p30 Spr 2017

Mass media industry—United States

Donald Trump, Media Darling *Commentary* v141 no9 p1 N 2016

Donald Trump, Media Darling *Commentary* v142 no4 p1 N 2016

THE TRUMPTOWN TRIBUNES *Washingtonian Magazine* v52 no9 p76 Je 2017

Mass media influence

The Making of an American Terrorist A. ROBB chart color il *New Republic* v248 no1/2 p34 Ja/F 2017

Mass media—Finance

Where Did All the Investigative Journalism Go? J. SHAFER bw cartoon *Reason* v48 no11 p64 Ap 2017

Mass media—Moral & ethical aspects

SWAT TEAM [Cover story] T. Frank *Harper's Magazine* v333 no1998 p26 N 2016

Mass media—Political aspects

How the Media Got Smarter About Calling Elections H. S. Edwards chart color *Time* v188 no20 p17 N 14 2016

THE TORIES WHO SHOULD NOT BE NAMED [Cover story] S. GILMORE *Maclean's* v129 no51/52 p14 D 26 2016

Trump's New Enemy J. COST cartoon *Weekly Standard* v22 no25 p19 Mr 6 2017

Mass media—Political aspects—United States

THE CASE AGAINST THE MEDIA BY THE MEDIA *New York* v49 no15 p40 Jl 25 2016

More Panic from Politico and the Post *Weekly Standard* v22 no16 p2 D 26 2016

Mass media—Russia

Much media ado about a SETI nothing color *Astronomy* v44 no12 p9 D 2016

Mass media—Software

APP TO EXCELLENCE Z. HILL bw *Ebony* v72/73 no12/1 p92 O/N 2017

Mass media—United States

Ages of Argus J. NORDLINGER color *National Review* v69 no6 p21 Ap 3 2017

Attention Is Our Business cartoon *Wired* v25 no3 p60 Mr 2017

The Crime of Obama's Cool E. Alterman il *Nation* v304 no1 p10 Ja 2 2017 The Obama Years

A crisis of relevance J. Gibson color *Columbia Journalism Review* v56 no2 p23 Fall 2017

Is There a Business Model for Real Journalism? K. POPE color il *Nation* v304 no9 p32 Mr 20 2017

The Kiss-Up That Wasn't A. FERGUSON color *Weekly Standard* v22 no40 p8 Je 26 2017

Making media literacy great again M. Rosenwald color *Columbia*

Journalism Review v56 no2 p94 Fall 2017

The Making of an American Terrorist A. ROBB chart color il *New Republic* v248 no1/2 p34 Ja/F 2017

The Monuments: Demythifying the "Cult" bw *New Orleans Magazine* v51 no10 p32 Ag 2017

Nyet to the American Media J. M. ORIENT *USA Today Magazine* v146 no2866 p17 Jl 2017

Soundbites *Extra!* v29 no9 p2 N 2016

Soundbites *Extra!* v30 no4 p2 My 2017

Trump and trickle-down press persecution J. Peters color *Columbia Journalism Review* v56 no1 p27 Spr 2017

The U.S. Media's Problems Are Much Bigger than Fake News and Filter Bubbles B. N. Anand color *Harvard Business Review Digital Articles* p2 Ja 5 2017

VIEWFINDER V. M. Gezari color *Columbia Journalism Review* v56 no2 p40 Fall 2017

What if the right-wing media wins? M. Coppins and P. Vernon bw color *Columbia Journalism Review* v56 no2 p52 Fall 2017

Woefully Out of Touch *Weekly Standard* v22 no14 p3 D 12 2016

Mass Merchandisers Inc.

Sales at Mass Merchandisers Continue to Bounce Back *Publishers Weekly* v264 no18 p5 My 1 2017

Mass production

Is the Era of Mass Manufacturing Coming to an End? P. Acton *Harvard Business Review Digital Articles* p2 D 5 2014

Mass shootings

See also

Las Vegas Strip shooting, Las Vegas, Nev., 2017

ALL-AMERICAN KILLER T. DICKINSON color *Rolling Stone* no1275 p50 D 1 2016

The Color of Terrorism L. Lalami *Nation* v305 no11 p12 O 30 2017

It's Always Men J. Filipovic *Time* v190 no15 p29 O 16 2017

Let's Have a Real Gun Debate color *Weekly Standard* v23 no6 p7 O 16 2017

A Mass Shooting S. Frappier cartoon *Men's Health* v32 no4 p82 My 2017

PRODIGY OF HATE J. COBB cartoon *New Yorker* v92 no48 p20 F 6 2017

A Shooting and the Risks of Political Outrage M. Scherer color *Time* v189 no24 p12 Je 26 2017

WMDs in Las Vegas [Cover story] G. ZORNICK *Nation* v305 no10 p3 O 23 2017

Mass shootings—Florida

See also

Orlando Nightclub Massacre, Orlando, Fla., 2016

Mass shootings—Louisiana

BULLETS ON BOURBON A. J. JOHNSON color *New Orleans Magazine* v51 no3 p34 Ja 2017

Mass shootings—Prevention

Bulletproofing W. BRENNAN bw color *Atlantic* v319 no1 p26 Ja/F 2017

Mass shootings—Social aspects

One Nation, Up In Arms E. Barone color diag map *Time* v188 no16/17 p64 O 24 2016

Mass spectrometry

See also

Matrix-assisted laser desorption-ionization

Time-of-flight mass spectrometry

Exploring mass spectrometry in the precision medicine field *Science* v354 no6319 p4 D 23 2016

Mass spectrometry—Scientific applications

LION Hunts for Nuclear Forensics Clues A. Chen color graph *Science & Technology Review* p19 Ja/F 2017

Mass surveillance

SURVEILLANCE R. Hackett color *Fortune* v175 no4 p114 Mr 15 2017

THENMOZHI SOUNDARARAJAN T. SOUNDARARAJAN il *Nation* v304 no11 p5 Ap 3 2017

Massa, Annie

A China Moonshot for Chicago's Exchange *Bloomberg Businessweek* no4514 p40 Mr 13 2017

ETFs Are Hot. So's 3D Printing... I Got an Idea! color *Bloomberg Businessweek* no4497 p43 O 31 2016

Everybody Into The Dark Pool color *Bloomberg Businessweek* no4519 p45 Ap 24 2017

Maybe a Good Manager Can't Run Everything *Bloomberg Businessweek* no4510 p32 F 6 2017

Trying to Make Active Funds Cool Again cartoon diag *Bloomberg Businessweek* no4518 p40 Ap 10 2017

Massachusetts

Natasha Rizopoulos color *Yoga Journal* no296 p83 N 2017

Massachusetts. General Court. House of Representatives

The Sacred Cod H. TOURGEE color *Yankee* v80 no6 p30 N/D 2016

Massachusetts Institute of Technology

THE EDISON OF MEDICINE S. PROKESCH color img *Harvard Business Review* v95 no2 p134 Mr/Ap 2017

Income Inequality and Export "Complexity" *USA Today Magazine* v145 no2863 p12 Ap 2017

Speeding Up Nuclear Research color *MIT Technology Review* v120 no3 p24 My/Je 2017

Massachusetts Museum of Contemporary Art

ART FACTORY: MASS MOCA BULKS UP M. PHODES diag *Wired* v25 no7 p24 Jl 2017

ARTIST-GRADE CONSTRUCTION color *Popular Mechanics* p44 N 2017

Factory Made J. GONCHAR *Architectural Record* v205 no7 p82 Jl 2017

Massachusetts—Description & travel

From the Forest to the Sea J. Stringfellow *Yankee* p99 Mr 2017

Great Barrington, Massachusetts A. GRAVES and J. BIDWELL color *Yankee* v80 no6 p88 N/D 2016

MASSACHUSETTS *Yankee* p146 My/Je 2017

Massachusetts—Economic conditions

WE NEED A DAYCARE REVOLUTION [Cover story] S. E. PFEFFER chart color *Working Mother* v40 no2 p52 Je/Jl 2017

Massacre Bay (Alaska)

What's in a Name? S. SHIBATA color *Sea Magazine* v109 no8 p12 Ag 2017

Massacre survivors

El Salvador's Ghost Town S. ESTHER MASLIN color *Nation* v304 no13 p20 Ap 17 2017

Massacre: Variations on a Theme (Theatrical production)

DANCE *New Yorker* v92 no47 p8 Ja 30 2017

Massacres

THE MAKING OF A MASSACRE G. Thompson color *National Geographic* v232 no1 p120 Jl 2017

Massacres—History

LAMBS TO SLAUGHTER W. D. Howells *Lapham's Quarterly* v10 no3 p148 Summ 2017

Massage

See also
   Massage therapy
   Scalp massage

5 WAYS: ...To get a massage L. McGLASHAN color *Muscle & Performance* v9 no10 p66 O 2017

Lost in Translation color *Consumer Reports* v82 no2 p59 F 2017

The most intimate of ubers R. COUNTER color *Maclean's* v129 no41 p53 O 17 2016

my style color *InStyle* v24 no7 p70 Jl 2017

ON-TRACK MIND [Cover story] A. HUTCHINSON color *Runner's World* v52 no6 p28 Jl 2017

So What Do You Do, JASMINE TOOKES? color *InStyle* v24 no4 p158 Ap 2017

Massage therapy

5 WAYS: ...To get a massage L. McGLASHAN color *Muscle & Performance* v9 no10 p66 O 2017

The best medicine S. Sexton color *Yoga Journal* p108 2017 Special Issue

THE Magic OF Massage A. P. Taylor color *Dance Spirit* v21 no2 p32 F 2017

massage AWAY PAIN color *Good Housekeeping* v264 no4 p98 Ap 2017

take OM HOME T. Eichenseher color *Yoga Journal* no292 p96 Je 2017

TAKE OM HOME T. Eichenseher color *Yoga Journal* no295 p104 O 2017

Massage—Equipment & supplies

MORE PRESSURE, LESS PAIN M. Reinold color *Men's Health* v32 no5 p56 Je 2017

Massage—Equipment & supplies—Evaluation

ON A ROLL(ER) J. DENGATE color *Runner's World* v52 no8 p32 S 2017

Massage—Physiological aspects

RADICAL REMEDIES C. VAN DUSEN, K. JORDAN et al *Atlanta* v56 no9 p43 Ja 2017

Massaly, N.

A nontoxic pain killer designed by modeling of pathological receptor conformations bibl diag graph *Science* v355 no6328 p966 Mr 3 2017

Massasa, Efi E.

Global mRNA polarization regulates translation efficiency in the intestinal epithelium diag *Science* v357 no6357 p1299 S 22 2017

Massenet, Jules, 1842-1912

Werther *Opera News* v81 no9 p57 Mr 2017

Massey, Aaron R.

Zika virus produces noncoding RNAs using a multi-pseudoknot structure that confounds a cellular exonuclease bibl color graph *Science* v354 no6316 p1148 D 2 2016

Massey, Alana

All the Lives I Want: Essays About My Best Friends Who Happen to Be Famous Strangers *Publishers Weekly* v263 no52 p113 D 19 2016

"I get orgasm headaches" color *Glamour* v115 no3 p132 Mr 2017

Massey, James

HORSE POWER bw color *Esquire* p104 2017 BigBlackBook

Massey, James C.

EASEMENTS EXPLAINED color *Old House Journal* v45 no1 p30 F 2017

Monrovia/Greater Los Angeles, California bw color *Old House Journal* v45 no6 p34 S 2017

Tenleytown/Washington, D.C bw color *Old House Journal* v45 no3 p34 My 2017

Massey, Niki

NIKI MASSEY, AND WHY SOME HUMANIST VOICES DON'T GET HEARD G. CHRISTINA *Humanist* v76 no6 p40 N/D 2016

Massey, Tracey

How Did I Get Here?: TRACEY MASSEY *Bloomberg Businessweek* no4495 p76 O 17 2016

Massey, Wyatt

Cardinal Tobin calls on church leaders to 'put a face' on deportation crisis color *America* v216 no13 p17 Je 12 2017

CATHOLIC BETWEEN THE COASTS color *America* v216 no5 p24 Mr 6 2017

The ebb and flow of a life with depression color *America* v216 no5 p42 Mr 6 2017

Faith that grows color *U.S. Catholic* v82 no6 p22 Je 2017

IS IT A SPIRITUAL OR A MENTAL HEALTH CRISIS? bw *America* v216 no6 p12 Mr 20 2017

Learning on the Margins color *America* v216 no3 p17 F 6 2017

No hate, no fear color *U.S. Catholic* v82 no4 p12 Ap 2017

What 'S-Town' misses about life in rural America color *America* v216 no13 p57 Je 12 2017

Massicot, Kelly

Aching In The Rain color *New Orleans Magazine* v51 no8 p36 Je 2017

Archers Make Ready color *New Orleans Magazine* v51 no8 p150 Je 2017

Face Off color *New Orleans Magazine* v52 no1 p166 S 2017

Good To Go-To color *New Orleans Magazine* v51 no7 p36 My 2017

JANUARY/FEBRUARY color *Louisiana Life* v37 no3 p108 Ja/F 2017

JINGLE ALL THE WAY cartoon *New Orleans Magazine* v51 no1 p38 N 2016

JULY/AUGUST color *Louisiana Life* v37 no6 p62 Jl/Ag 2017

Libation Situation color *New Orleans Magazine* v51 no4 p34 F 2017

MAY/JUNE color *Louisiana Life* v37 no5 p62 My/Je 2017

The New Quiet Time color *New Orleans Magazine* v51 no5 p36 Mr 2017

NOVEMBER/DECEMBER color *Louisiana Life* v37 no2 p100 N/D 2016

OTTER THIS WORLD color *New Orleans Magazine* v51 no2 p151 D 2016

Paging Dr. Right: Finding the perfect M.D. for you color *New Orleans Magazine* v51 no10 p48 Ag 2017

Playing with Fire: Glass blowing at YAYA Studios color *New Orleans Magazine* v51 no10 p214 Ag 2017

REVAMPING RESOLUTIONS color *New Orleans Magazine* v51 no3 p32 Ja 2017

Rosé All Day color *New Orleans Magazine* v51 no12 p166 O 2017

Say Hay! color *New Orleans Magazine* v51 no6 p158 Ap 2017

SEPTEMBER/OCTOBER bw color *Louisiana Life* v38 no1 p62 S/O 2017

Skin Deep color *New Orleans Magazine* v51 no6 p36 Ap 2017

STICK IT TO ME color *New Orleans Magazine* v51 no2 p38 D 2016

Take Me To Church color *New Orleans Magazine* v51 no9 p134 Jl 2017

Water Fall color *New Orleans Magazine* v51 no9 p36 Jl 2017

WINE TIME color *New Orleans Magazine* v51 no1 p183 N 2016

Massie, Thomas, 1971-
A Bill With Few Friends *Bloomberg Businessweek* no4514 p30 Mr 13 2017

MASSING, MICHAEL
Journalism in Trump's America color diag *Nation* v304 no4 p24 F 6 2017

Massingale, Bryan
Bread for the world color *U.S. Catholic* v82 no6 p10 Je 2017

A church where Black lives matter color *U.S. Catholic* v81 no12 p8 D 2016

Live on the margins color *U.S. Catholic* v82 no9 p10 S 2017

The sound of silence color *U.S. Catholic* v82 no3 p10 Mr 2017

Massinger, Kate
Keep Them Poor & Tired color *Commonweal* v144 no15 p41 S 22 2017

Need a Good Parental Leave Policy? Here It Is *Harvard Business Review Digital Articles* p2 N 23 2015

Nose to the Glass [Cover story] color *Commonweal* v144 no10 p24 Je 2 2017

Present in His Grace color *Commonweal* v144 no8 p32 My 5 2017

Massironi, M.
Rosetta's comet 67P/Churyumov-Gerasimenko sheds its dusty mantle to reveal its icy nature bibl graph *Science* v354 no6319 p1566 D 23 2016

Massive open online courses
3 Ways to Use MOOCs to Advance Your Career W. Frick *Harvard Business Review Digital Articles* p2 Jl 26 2016

Closing global achievement gaps in MOOCs R. F. Kizilcec, A. J. Saltarelli et al bibl graph *Science* v355 no6322 p251 Ja 20 2017

DEFINING MOMENTS il *Phi Kappa Phi Forum* v97 no2 p5 Summ 2017

From MOOC to Bestseller A. Green color *Publishers Weekly* v264 no24 p6 Je 12 2017

The Real Revolution in Online Education Isn't MOOCs M. Weise *Harvard Business Review Digital Articles* p2 O 17 2014

Who's Benefiting from MOOCs, and Why Chen Zhenghao, B. Alcorn et al *Harvard Business Review Digital Articles* p2 S 22 2015

Massolia, William
COMING TO AMERICA N. PARSI bw color *Chicago* v66 no3 p47 Mr 2017

Masson, Charles
The French Are Coming! A. KNOWLTON, N. RICHARDSON et al bw color *Bon Appetit* v62 no4 p15 Ap 2017

Massonnet, François
Using climate models to estimate the quality of global observational data sets bibl graph *Science* v354 no6311 p452 O 28 2016

Massougbodji, Achille
Dispersals and genetic adaptation of Bantu-speaking populations in Africa and North America diag *Science* v356 no6337 p543 My 5 2017

MASSY, PERRINE
Balancing Act: Morocco's circus school takes women to new heights--though many in the country may not approve *Ms.* v27 no3 p18 Fall 2017

MAST, KATHERINE
The Desert's Living Skin color *Discover* v38 no6 p22 Jl/Ag 2017

The Future of Food bw color *Discover* v38 no6 p38 Jl/Ag 2017

Mastai, Elan

ALL OUR WRONG TODAYS M. DOHERTY color *Maclean's* v130 no2 p69 Mr 2017

Mastectomy
THE CUT-OFF POINT S. Sea Gold color *O, The Oprah Magazine* p86 O 2017

A STRANGER in My House color *Vogue* v207 no6 p42 Je 2017

WHEN LESS IS MORE L. Goldman bw *O, The Oprah Magazine* p89 O 2017

Why More Women Are Getting a Double Mastectomy A. Sifferlin diag *Time* v190 no15 p41 O 16 2017

Master & Commander (Film)
WHAT YOU SHOULD KNOW ABOUT PAUL BETTANY L. STRAUSS bw *Vanity Fair* v59 no9 p142 S 2017

Master of arts degree
Florida State University *Dance Magazine* v90 p63 2016/2017 Supplement College Guide

Goucher College *Dance Magazine* v90 p67 2016/2017 Supplement College Guide

Institute of the Arts Barcelona *Dance Magazine* v90 p76 2016/2017 Supplement College Guide

Master of business administration degree
Business Education Gets Personal G. Bauer color *Maclean's* v129 no43 p40 O 31 2016

How Having an MBA vs. a Law Degree Shapes Your Network A. Sterling *Harvard Business Review Digital Articles* p2 F 19 2016

MBAs Need to Stop Assuming That Markets Always Work P. Ghemawat *Harvard Business Review Digital Articles* p2 N 21 2014

New MBAs Should Start Their Careers in Frontier Markets J. Berman *Harvard Business Review Digital Articles* p2 Ap 28 2015

The Real Cost Of an MBA L. Lambert graph *Bloomberg Businessweek* no4500 p41 N 21 2016

Why More MBAs Should Buy Small Businesses R. S. Ruback and R. Yudkoff *Harvard Business Review Digital Articles* p2 Mr 25 2016

Master of fine arts degree
'I Don't Want That Crap in My Gallery' D. Grant cartoon *Commonweal* v144 no5 p24 Mr 10 2017

Jacksonville University *Dance Magazine* v90 p77 2016/2017 Supplement College Guide

PART-TIME POST-GRAD A. Brandt *Dance Magazine* p27 2016/2017

PART-TIME POST-GRAD A. Brandt *Dance Magazine* v90 p27 2016/2017 Supplement College Guide

scratching the MFA itch: Considering an advanced degree in dance? Learn how to choose the program that's right for you M. E. HUNT *Dance Magazine* v90 p26 2016/2017 Supplement College Guide

scratching the MFA itch M. E. HUNT *Dance Magazine* p26 2016/2017

To BA or to BFA? L. Wingenroth color *Dance Magazine* v91 no3 p48 Mr 2017

The University of Arizona *Dance Magazine* v90 p43 2016/2017 Supplement College Guide

University of Iowa *Dance Magazine* v90 p76 2016/2017 Supplement College Guide

Master of None (TV program)
ALAN YANG A. D'ARMINIO *TV Guide* v65 no23 p10 My 29 2017

Aziz Ansari's Masterpiece R. Rahman color *Entertainment Weekly* no1466 p36 My 19 2017

Master of None: A delicious new season of the slice-of-life comedy M. ROUSH *TV Guide* v65 no21 p16 My 15 2017

Master of None J. Jensen color *Entertainment Weekly* no1465 p46 My 12 2017

The Triumph of Aziz Ansari R. SHEFFIELD color *Rolling Stone* no1288 p19 Je 1 2017

Master of the Drunken Fist: Beggar So (Film)
HBO ASIA RELEASES ITS FIRST CHINESE-LANGUAGE FILMS color *Black Belt* v55 no4 p12 Je/Jl 2017

MasterChef Junior (TV program)
MasterChef Junior M. Logan *TV Guide* v65 no6 p41 Ja 30 2017

Mastercraft Boat Co.
Hitting the Spot A. JONES *Boating World* v38 no6 p42 Je 2017

MasterCraft X26 *Boating World* v38 no1 p71 Ja 2017

Ski Boats Take Control A. JONES *Boating World* v38 no5 p22

Matagorda Bay (Tex.)
Wave GOODBYE A. HANNAFORD *Texas Monthly* v45 no6 p35 Je 2017

Mata Hari, 1876-1917
The Sultry Spy and the Coverup M. Solly *Smithsonian* v48 no5 p19 S 2017

Matalon, Or
Young phosphorylation is functionally silent bibl diag *Science* v354 no6309 p176 O 14 2016

Matanock, Aila M.
The Colombian Paradox: Peace Processes, Elite Divisions & Popular Plebiscites graph *Daedalus* v146 no4 p152 Fall 2017

Matar, Hisham
The Empire in the Mirror [Cover story] *New York Times Book Review* p1 S 3 2017
Libyan Ghosts R. F. Worth color *Foreign Affairs* v96 no3 p127 My/Je 2017

Match Point (Film)
The Remarkable Laziness of Woody Allen C. ORR cartoon *Atlantic* v320 no3 p34 O 2017

Matchboxes
POP CULTURE *Indianapolis Monthly* v40 no4 p34 D 2016

Matchboxes—Evaluation
Ignite Delight color *House Beautiful* v159 no1 p32 F 2017

Matches—Evaluation
THE HOME FRONT color *Esquire* p50 N 2017

Matching games
Name Game O. B. Waxman *Time* v189 no16/17 p152 My 1-8 2017
THE WORST — WIG GAME! K. P. Sullivan color *Entertainment Weekly* no1444/1445 p60 D 16 2016

Mate, Bence
BOBBLED THE CATCH K. MOORE color *Natural History* v125 no6 p2 Je 2017

Mate, Kedar S.
4 Steps to Sustaining Improvement in Health Care *Harvard Business Review Digital Articles* p2 N 9 2016
The Antidote to Fragmented Health Care *Harvard Business Review Digital Articles* p2 D 15 2014
A Simple Way to Involve Frontline Clinicians in Managing Costs *Harvard Business Review Digital Articles* p2 O 11 2017
The Value of Teaching Patients to Administer Their Own Care color *Harvard Business Review Digital Articles* p1 Je 2 2017

Mate selection
Males Show Their True Colors [Cover story] J. OTTO, D. KNOWLES et al color *Natural History* v125 no4 p10 Ap 2017

Matell, Matthew
Why does time seem to fly when we're having fun? bibl color *Science* v354 no6317 p1231 D 9 2016

Matenaar, Daniela
De-extinction, nomenclature, and the law color *Science* v356 no6342 p1016 Je 9 2017

Mateo, Meg J.
CELEBRATING THE SEASON color *Sunset* v237 no6 p88 D 2016

Material balances
Acceptable, Not Acceptable or Preferable G. H. Morris color *Practical Horseman* v45 no11 p10 N 2017

Material culture
See also
Antiquities
Flint, Feather, and Other Material Selves M. Jones and N. Ferris *American Indian Quarterly* v41 no2 p125 Spr 2017
Material Culture color *Vogue* v207 no6 p76 Je 2017

Material culture in art
Old Kentucky Home styles at the Frazier cartoon *Magazine Antiques* v184 no1 p34 Ja/F 2017

Material safety data sheets
Protect Yourself A. JONES *Boating World* v38 no5 p24 My 2017

Materialism
EXPANDING THE REAL P. E. DINTER *Commonweal* v144 no11 p2 Je 16 2017
Getting and Spending S. MILLER *Weekly Standard* v22 no21 p38 F 6 2017

Materials for the Arts (Organization)
ART WITH A (Re)Purpose: Sloan Award Winner, Harriet Taub from Materials for the Arts L. Mulcahy *Stage Directions* v30 no9 p19 S 2017

Materials handling
See also
Automated guided vehicle systems
Bins
Freight & freightage
Storage racks
Trucks
ALL AROUND THE FARM *Successful Farming* v114 no10 p76 O 2016

Materials science
See also
Magnetic materials synthesis
Computation BOOSTS Materials Discovery A. Chen *Science & Technology Review* p16 Jl/Ag 2017
Notes on the New Big Science P. Foukal *Physics Today* v70 no3 p12 Mr 2017

Materials—Environmental aspects
Improving Environmental Outcomes at the State Level *Governing* v30 no4 p10 Ja 2017

Maternal age
it's twins! L. Vaccariello color *Parents* v92 no4 p8 Ap 2017
Older Mom, Better Memory? *Health* v31 no4 p16 My 2017

Maternal health services—United States
How Mayo Clinic Is Simplifying Prenatal Care for Low-Risk Patients Y. B. Tobah and A. Famuyide *Harvard Business Review Digital Articles* p2 Je 19 2017
PORTRAIT OF A Country Doctor J. R. MARQUEZ *Atlanta* v57 no3 p80 Jl 2017

Maternal mortality
Maternity Crisis: Texas is the most dangerous place in America to have a baby. There are many reasons why M. Quinn *Governing* v30 no8 p50 My 2017

Maternity benefits
See also
Maternity leave
What Nursing Parents Need to Know About Pumping During Work Travel J. Beck *Harvard Business Review Digital Articles* p2 Je 14 2017

Maternity leave
career coach J. Barberio color *Working Mother* v40 no3 p6 Ag/S 2017
CATASTROPHE: Sharon is in meltdown over her return from maternity leave *People Management* p58 Mr 2017
Parental Leave Can't Just Be for Mothers A. Wittenberg-Cox *Harvard Business Review Digital Articles* p2 Mr 18 2015
Planning Maternity or Paternity Leave: A Professional's Guide R. Knight *Harvard Business Review Digital Articles* p2 My 29 2015
THE REPLACEMENT: A dedicated high-flier is worried her maternity cover is trying to take *People Management* p66 My 2017
Stalled Numbers Do Not Bode Well *USA Today Magazine* v145 no2863 p6 Ap 2017
What Nursing Parents Need to Know About Pumping During Work Travel J. Beck *Harvard Business Review Digital Articles* p2 Je 14 2017

Mathematical ability
Degrees of Separation L. SCHLEY *Discover* v38 no10 p14 D 2017

Mathematical constants
Constant Connections E. Conover chart color diag *Science News* v190 no10 p24 N 12 2016

Mathematical instruments
See also
Abacus
WIRED color *Wired* v25 no7 p51 Jl 2017

Mathematical models
See also
Computer simulation
Forecasting—Mathematical models
Believe It J. LOGAN *USA Today Magazine* v145 no2864 p31 My 2017
Fairy circle origin stories may merge S. MILIUS color *Science News* v191 no3 p17 F 18 2017

Mathematical optimization
See also

Combinatorial optimization

A coherent Ising machine for 2000-node optimization problems Takahiro Inagaki, Yoshitaka Haribara et al bibl diag graph *Science* v354 no6312 p603 N 4 2016

Mathematicians

See also

Statisticians

Father (and Son) Knows Best D. FISHER color *Forbes* v199 no5 p62 My 16 2017

Maryam Mirzakhani (1977–2017) A. Wright color *Science* v357 no6353 p758 Ag 25 2017

Mathematics

See also

Equilibrium

Mathematical models

Measurement

Quantitative research

Statistics

ANIMAL MATH [Cover story] S. Milius cartoon color graph *Science News* v190 no12 p22 D 10 2016

Let Your Fingers Do The Counting M. PEYSER color *Reader's Digest* v189 no1129 p130 Ap 2017

math word problems for today's parents J. VICK color *Parents* v92 no5 p124 My 2017

Recalculating the Climate Math B. McKIBBEN il *New Republic* v247 no11 p16 N 2016

SAFETY IN NUMBERS? The mathematics of predicting war G. Greenberg chart color *Harper's Magazine* v335 no2005 p67 Je 2017

The Tech Visionary You've Never Heard Of G. Jacobs color *Glamour* v115 no5 p186 My 2017

WEAPONS OF MATH DESTRUCTION C. O'NEIL *Saturday Evening Post* v289 no2 p40 Mr/Ap 2017

Mathematics education

GRAPHIC LITERATURE M. PELL *Scientific American* v316 no6 p5 Je 2017

Scruffy Bohemianism J. Epstein *Claremont Review of Books* v17 no3 p65 Summ 2017

Mathematics in art

GRAPHIC LITERATURE M. PELL *Scientific American* v316 no6 p5 Je 2017

Mathematics—Humor

PI A LA MOAN *Reader's Digest* v189 no1131 p97 Je 2017

Mathematics—Study & teaching

Less is more V. Faulkner, P. L. Marshall et al diag graph *Phi Delta Kappan* v98 no7 p55 Ap 2017

Mathematics—Study & teaching (Early childhood)—Research

NO EASY ANSWERS J. Mervis color *Science* v355 no6325 p568 F 10 2017

Matheny, Jason—Interviews

IARPA Director Jason Matheny advances tech tools for US espionage E. Eaves color *Bulletin of the Atomic Scientists* v73 no2 p67 Mr 2017

Mather, Carolyn

CAROLYN MATHER A. BURFOOT color *Runner's World* v52 no2 p25 Mr 2017

MATHER, JOHN C.

A COSMIC CONTROVERSY color *Scientific American* v317 no1 p5 Jl 2017

Mathers, Gary

TOAST K. CAMERON *Cycle World* v56 no1 p22 Ja/F 2017

Mathes, Darrell

DARRELL MATHES bw color *Snowboarder* v29 no2 p144 O 2016

Mathes, H. J.

Observation of a large-scale anisotropy in the arrival directions of cosmic rays above 8 × 1018 eV *Science* v357 no6357 p1266 S 22 2017

Matheson, Christie

Plant the Tiny Seed color *Publishers Weekly* v263 no52 p123 D 19 2016

MATHESON, ROB

A JOLT TO THE SENSES *USA Today Magazine* v145 no2860 p66 Ja 2017

Mathevon, Nicolas

When croc babies become teenagers N. Strochlic color *National*

Geographic v230 no4 p24 O 2016

Mathew, Rose

A multifunctional catalyst that stereoselectively assembles prodrugs diag *Science* v356 no6336 p426 Ap 28 2017

MATHEW, SHAJ

Unwelcome Guests *New York Times Book Review* p18 Mr 26 2017

Mathews, Alice

Giving Gifted Women a Chance in the Church H. Anderson color *Christianity Today* v61 no6 p88 Jl/Ag 2017

Mathews, Brendan

The Plot in America: Two brothers fleeing their Irish captivities get embroiled in a wild assassination plot at the 1939 World's Fair in New York K. BAKER *New York Times Book Review* p15 S 17 2017

Mathews, Jessica T.

Can China Replace the West? [Cover story] color *New York Review of Books* v64 no8 p14 My 11 2017

What Trump Is Throwing Out the Window cartoon *New York Review of Books* v64 no2 p11 F 9 2017

MATHEWS, LAURA

Transitioning in Life And Literature color *Publishers Weekly* v264 no13 p37 Mr 27 2017

Mathews, Nicolas

Mitigating coastal landslide damage color *Science* v357 no6355 p981 S 8 2017

Mathews, Stanley

THE FUN PALACE AT FIFTY *Art in America* v104 no9 p114 O 2016

Mathews, William B.

Chemogenetics revealed: DREADD occupancy and activation via converted clozapine graph *Science* v357 no6350 p503 Ag 4 2017

Mathews Archery Inc.

BOW TEST 2017 T. HANSEN and A. McKEAN chart color *Outdoor Life* v224 no6 p17 Ag 2017

Mathewson, Tara García

Building on Diversity *America* v215 no13 p12 O 31 2016

Sub Shortage Leaves Schools Scrambling *Education Digest* v83 no3 p24 N 2017

MATHIAS, GERALDINE

RIVERSIDE: WEST OF THE WILD SNAKE *Idaho Magazine* v16 no12 p32 S 2017

Mathias, S.

Revealing the subfemtosecond dynamics of orbital angular momentum in nanoplasmonic vortices bibl diag *Science* v355 no6330 p1187 Mr 17 2017

Mathiesen, Peter B.

2016 BEST OF THE BEST bw color *Field & Stream* v121 no7 p96 D 2016/Ja 2017

RAPALA SKITTER V color *Field & Stream* v121 no8 p92 F/Mr 2017

Mathieson, Peter

Popular HKU president resigns *Science* v355 no6325 p553 F 10 2017

Mathieu, Jennifer

Moxie *Publishers Weekly* v264 no28 p89 Jl 10 2017

Mathis, Ayana

Misconceptions *New York Times Book Review* p19 F 19 2017

Not Even Past: A racist murder and the legacy of Jim Crow haunt generations of a family in Eleanor Henderson's novel *New York Times Book Review* p21 O 8 2017

What's the best book, new or old, you read this year? *New York Times Book Review* p27 D 25 2016

Mathis, Callan

To Lose Weight, Put Your Home on a Diet color *AARP: The Magazine* v60 no4A p14 Je/Jl 2017

Mathis, Jeremy T.

Darkness Falls in the Arctic color *Wilson Quarterly* p1 Summ 2017

Mathis, Joel

CONSTRUCTION SIMULATOR 2 color *Macworld - Digital Edition* v34 no4 p59 My 2017

ELAGO M4 STAND FOR iPHONE 7 color *Macworld - Digital Edition* v34 no6 p45 Je 2017

iOS Accessories color *Macworld - Digital Edition* p58 Je 13 2017

iOS Accessories color *Macworld - Digital Edition* p62 Mr 2017 iOS Accessories color *Macworld - Digital Edition* p74 D 2016

iOS Accessories color *Macworld - Digital Edition* v34 no8 p80 Ag 2017

iOS Games: THAT YOU SHOULD BE PLAYING RIGHT NOW color *Macworld - Digital Edition* v34 no11 p80 N 2017

iPhone and iPad Cases color *Macworld - Digital Edition* v33 no11 p96 N 2016

LIP SYNC BATTLE color *Macworld - Digital Edition* p73 D 2016

MY MIGGO PICTAR FOR iPHONE 7 color *Macworld - Digital Edition* p34 Je 13 2017

WHAT'S NEW AT THE APP STORE cartoon *Macworld - Digital Edition* p61 Mr 2017

What's new at the App Store cartoon *Macworld - Digital Edition* v33 no11 p95 N 2016

WHAT'S NEW AT THE APP STORE color *Macworld - Digital Edition* v34 no11 p79 N 2017

WHAT'S NEW AT THE APP STORE color *Macworld - Digital Edition* v34 no6 p75 Je 2017

Mathis, Johnny, 1935-

Longevity bw color *Forbes* v199 no2 p110 F 28 2017

MATHIS, WILLIAM J.

The Effectiveness of Class Size Reduction *Education Digest* v82 no5 p60 Ja 2017

Mathison, Cameron—Interviews

CAMERON MATHISON M. LOGAN *TV Guide* v64 no46 p42 N 7 2016

Mathot, Serge

Global atmospheric particle formation from CERN CLOUD measurements bibl graph map *Science* v354 no6316 p1119 D 2 2016

Mathur, Ambika

My second acts color *Science* v357 no6358 p1430 S 29 2017

Using Longitudinal Data on Career Outcomes to Promote Improvements and Diversity in Graduate Education *Change* v48 no6 p42 N/D 2016

Mathys, C.

Pavlovian conditioning–induced hallucinations result from overweighting of perceptual priors diag *Science* v357 no6351 p596 Ag 11 2017

Mathys, S.

Observation of a large-scale anisotropy in the arrival directions of cosmic rays above 8×1018 eV *Science* v357 no6357 p1266 S 22 2017

Mathys, Vanessa

Reversion of antibiotic resistance in Mycobacterium tuberculosis by spiroisoxazoline SMARt-420 bibl diag *Science* v355 no6330 p1206 Mr 17 2017

Mating grounds

exposure color *Canadian Geographic* v137 no2 p12 Mr/Ap 2017

Matisse, Henri, 1869-1954

By the Book with Henri Matisse *USA Today Magazine* v145 no2858 p77 N 2016

Deux Pêches color *Art in America* v105 no1 p28 Ja 2017

Guiding Light A. CRAWFORD color *Smithsonian* v47 no10 p12 Mr 2017

Object Lessons D. Green color *Weekly Standard* v22 no37 p37 Je 5 2017

MatLab (Computer software)—Evaluation

NEW PRODUCTS *Physics Today* v69 no12 p64 D 2016

Matlack, Carol

A continent divided color *Bloomberg Businessweek* no4496 p20 O 24 2016

Does Macron Hold the Key to Merkel's Heart? color *Bloomberg Businessweek* no4515 p26 Mr 20 2017

A Fashion Empire's New Clothes color graph *Bloomberg Businessweek* no4535 p17 Ag 28 2017

A Fresh Breath for Czech Glass color *Bloomberg Businessweek* no4535 p42 Ag 28 2017

Germany Builds An Election Firewall *Bloomberg Businessweek* no4527 p48 Je 19 2017

Germany's Maternity Wards Are Booked color graph *Bloomberg Businessweek* no4504 p16 D 19 2016

In France, an Election Veers Off the Rails graph *Bloomberg Businessweek* no4511 p17 F 13 2017

The Kremlin's New Disinformation Machine *Bloomberg Businessweek* no4512 p27 F 20 2017

Macron vs. The Unions graph *Bloomberg Businessweek* no4529 p30 Jl 3 2017

MEAT MARKETER [Cover story] color graph map *Bloomberg Businessweek* no4511 p42 F 13 2017

The No. 1 Airline Gets Its Wings Clipped bw color *Bloomberg Businessweek* no4531 p13 Jl 24 2017

Russia's Deadly Mideast Game *Bloomberg Businessweek* no4505 p16 D 26 2016

Severance à la Française color *Bloomberg Businessweek* no4540 p34 O 2 2017

Stand By...Scanning for Viruses and Secrets cartoon *Bloomberg Businessweek* no4530 p21 Jl 17 2017

Thatcherism Redux in France bw color *Bloomberg Businessweek* no4502 p21 D 5 2016

Toys 'R' Russia? Retailer Detsky Mir Says, 'Da' color *Bloomberg Businessweek* no4512 p23 F 20 2017

Matlock, Audrey

Relaxed Fit J. GONCHAR *Architectural Record* v205 no6 p106 Je 2017

Matlosz, Michael

Head of France's main funding body resigns amid acrimony E. Pain *Science* v357 no6349 p341 Jl 28 2017

Matos, Juliana L.

Mobile MUTE specifies subsidiary cells to build physiologically improved grass stomata bibl diag *Science* v355 no6330 p1215 Mr 17 2017

Matous, Filip

3 Ways to Get More Out of Your Web Analytics *Harvard Business Review Digital Articles* p2 O 19 2015

MATOUSEK, MARK

The Writing Cure *Saturday Evening Post* v289 no1 p48 Ja/F 2017

Matovski, Aleksandr

All Quiet on the Balkan Front? *Hoover Digest: Research & Opinion on Public Policy* no1 p120 Wint 2017

Matoza, Robin S.

Volcanic tremor and plume height hysteresis from Pavlof Volcano, Alaska bibl graph *Science* v355 no6320 p1 Ja 6 2017

Matriarchy

The Mothers color *Foreign Policy* no222 p10 Ja/F 2017

Matricaria

Pineapple Weed M. WALWYN color *Canadian Wildlife* v23 no2 p37 My/Je 2017

Matrix-assisted laser desorption-ionization

Application of MALDI-TOF mass spectrometry for identifying clinical microorganisms Xiaowei Zhan, Jun Yang et al bibl *Science* v354 no6319 p58 D 23 2016

A brief overview of matrix-assisted laser desorption/ionization time-of-flight mass spectrometry (MALDI-TOF MS) applications in clinical microbiology in China Meng Xiao, T. Kudinha et al *Science* v354 no6319 p55 D 23 2016

Matson, Ellen M.

A bioinspired iron catalyst for nitrate and perchlorate reduction bibl diag *Science* v354 no6313 p741 N 11 2016

Matson, Erik

The Sympathetic Formation of Reason and the Limits of Science *Society* v54 no3 p246 Je 2017

Matson, Pamela

Pursuing Sustainability: A Guide to the Science and Practice T. O'Riordan *Environment* v58 no6 p34 N/D 2016

Matson, R. G.

Genomic estimation of complex traits reveals ancient maize adaptation to temperate North America diag *Science* v357 no6350 p512 Ag 4 2017

Matsoukas, Melina

IMAGE CONSULTANT A. OKEOWO cartoon color *New Yorker* v93 no3 p34 Mr 6 2017

Matsoukas, Melina, 1981—Interviews

THE Work Wives E. Mahaney color *Glamour* v115 no10 p162 O 2017

Matsubara, Koji

Terawatt-scale photovoltaics: Trajectories and challenges chart graph *Science* v356 no6334 p141 Ap 14 2017

Matsubayashi, Yoshikatsu

A peptide hormone required for Casparian strip diffusion barrier formation in Arabidopsis roots bibl color graph *Science* v355 no6322 p284 Ja 20 2017

Matsuda, Seiko
Matsuda Embraces Challenge K. Micallef color *Downbeat* v84 no8 p15 Ag 2017

Matsuhisa, Nobu
Nobu: A Memoir color *Publishers Weekly* v264 no41 p59 O 9 2017

Matsumoto, Atsushi
Crystal structure of the overlapping dinucleosome composed of hexasome and octasome graph *Science* v356 no6334 p205 Ap 14 2017

Matsumoto, Nancy
Love Story, With Lettuce color *AARP: The Magazine* v60 no4A p59 Je/Jl 2017

MATSUMOTO, TAKUYA
Our Ramen Changed Texas... ...and Texas Changed Our Ramen color *Bon Appetit* v62 no2 p66 Mr 2017

Matsuoka, Yoky
RETURNING TO THE NEST A. Lashinsky color *Fortune* v175 no5 p22 Ap 1 2017

Matsushita, Kosei
The SAILING SCENE color *Sail* v48 no6 p6 Je 2017

Matsuura, Bryan S.
Synthesis of resveratrol tetramers via a stereoconvergent radical equilibrium bibl diag graph *Science* v354 no6317 p1260 D 9 2016

Matsuyama, Kanoko
THE PRICE OF A DIGITAL WORLD color *Bloomberg Businessweek* no4527 p58 Je 19 2017

Matt, Manuel
Quantized thermal transport in single-atom junctions bibl diag graph *Science* v355 no6330 p1192 Mr 17 2017

Matt Wilson's Honey & Salt (Performer)
Music Inspired By The Poetry Of Carl Sandburg J. Macnie color *Downbeat* v84 no8 p67 Ag 2017

Mattauch, Stefan
All-oxide–based synthetic antiferromagnets exhibiting layer-resolved magnetization reversal diag *Science* v357 no6347 p191 Jl 14 2017

Mattei, Simone
The structure and flexibility of conical HIV-1 capsids determined within intact virions bibl color *Science* v354 no6318 p1434 D 16 2016

Mattel Inc.
Baby's First Virtual Assistant F. Gillette color *Bloomberg Businessweek* no4506 p27 Ja 9 2017
TECH TAKEOVER IN TOYLAND M. Lev-ram, K. Bellstrom et al color diag *Fortune* v176 no5 p76 O 1 2017

Matter, Jordan
Photobombing the City img *New York* v49 no21 p108 O 17 2016

Matternet (Company)
Switzerland's New Medical Drones J. Zorthian color *Time* v190 no14 p23 O 9 2017

Matteson, John
Amid the Wreckage of World War I, Avoiding the Impulse to Despair bw diag *America* v216 no9 p20 Ap 24 2017
Fixing the capitalist system *America* v217 no3 p47 Ag 7 2017

Matteucci, Silvia D.
Forest conservation: Remember Gran Chaco bibl color *Science* v355 no6324 p465 F 3 2017

MATTHEW, ZOIE
Hot Wings color *Los Angeles Magazine* v62 no10 p20 O 2017
PANIC ROOMS color *Los Angeles Magazine* v62 no10 p90 O 2017
Secret Gardens color *Los Angeles Magazine* v62 no10 p88 O 2017
What Lurks Beneath: CONTAMINATED SOIL AND THE PUSH TO REVITALIZE PORTIONS OF THE LOS ANGELES RIVER *Los Angeles Magazine* v62 no9 p19 S 2017

Matthews, Anne
Commonplace Book *American Scholar* v86 no2 p126 Spr 2017

Matthews, Auston
AUSTON'S POWERS A. Prewitt color diag *Sports Illustrated* v127 no11 p38 O 9 2017
The Case for ... Showing Off the Kids A. Prewitt and T. Keith color *Sports Illustrated* v125 no14 p31 O 24-31 2016
Dear Auston ... W. Clark color *Sports Illustrated* v125 no12 p60 O 10 2016

Matthews, Candace
6-STEP RECIPE FOR SUCCESS C. V. CLARKE color *Black Enterprise* v47 no8 p38 Jl/Ag 2017

Matthews, Carol
When I Was a Horse-Crazy Kid, I... color *Horse & Rider* v56 no2 p72 F 2017

Matthews, Chris
THE 2017 Fortune Crystal Ball color diag *Fortune* v174 no7 p11 D 1 2016
ANATOMY OF A TRUMP TAX CUT diag *Fortune* v174 no8 p17 D 15 2016
Canada's Brain Gain Strategy color *Fortune* v174 no6 p12 N 1 2016
Here's How Donald Trump Can Win a Trade War With China color diag *Fortune* v75 no1 p22 Ja 1 2017
METALS' TIME TO SHINE diag *Fortune* v174 no8 p22 D 15 2016

Matthews, J.
Observation of a large-scale anisotropy in the arrival directions of cosmic rays above 8 × 1018 eV *Science* v357 no6357 p1266 S 22 2017

Matthews, J. A. J.
Observation of a large-scale anisotropy in the arrival directions of cosmic rays above 8 × 1018 eV *Science* v357 no6357 p1266 S 22 2017

Matthews, Jessica O.—Interviews
POWERING THE FUTURE J. Thompson color *Essence* v47 no9 p56 Ja 2017

Matthews, Kirstin R. W.
Science advice in the Trump White House [Cover story] bibl color *Science* v355 no6325 p574 F 10 2017

Matthews, Manyalibo—Awards
Patents and Awards *Science & Technology Review* p24 Ap/My 2017

Matthews, Mary
Time-resolved x-ray absorption spectroscopy with a water window high-harmonic source graph *Science* v355 no6322 p264 Ja 20 2017

Matthews, Nik
last doug standing bw *Bike Magazine* v23 no9 p46 D 2016
The linker histone H1.0 generates epigenetic and functional intra-tumor heterogeneity bibl graph *Science* v353 no6307 paaf1644-1 S 30 2016

MATTHEWS, OWEN
Front Row to Revolution *New York Times Book Review* p8 F 26 2017

Matthews, Steve
Job Switchers Solve An Inflation Mystery diag *Bloomberg Businessweek* no4513 p22 Mr 6 2017
Migration The Sun Belt Rises Again graph map *Bloomberg Businessweek* no4521 p15 My 8 2017
Trump And Yellen: Besties? color *Bloomberg Businessweek* no4502 p12 D 5 2016

Matthews, Thomas J.
Island biogeography: Taking the long view of nature's laboratories map *Science* v357 no6354 p885 S 1 2017

MATTHEWS, VIRGINIA
FIT FOR WORK *People Management* p48 N 2016
Will your best staff take flight? *People Management* p32 D 2016/Ja 2017

Matthews, Zoe
Making SDGs Work for Climate Change Hotspots bibl *Environment* v58 no6 p24 N/D 2016

Matthiae, G.
Observation of a large-scale anisotropy in the arrival directions of cosmic rays above 8 × 1018 eV *Science* v357 no6357 p1266 S 22 2017

Matthijs, Matthias
Europe After Brexit color *Foreign Affairs* v96 no1 p85 Ja/F 2017
Is the Liberal Order in Peril? color graph *Foreign Affairs* v96 no3 p178 My/Je 2017

Matti, Ibrahim
Freed Iraqi Christians tell of life under the IS K. Chick color *Christian Century* v134 no1 p12 Ja 4 2017

Mattingly, Justin
Where a Bad World Means Good Business color *Bloomberg Busi-*

nessweek no4533 p16 Ag 7 2017

Mattingly, Marybeth J.

Underemployment among Hispanics: the case of involuntary part-time work *Monthly Labor Review* p1 D 2016

Mattingly, Ted

2017 NRPA Annual Conference Exhibit Hall Highlights *Parks & Recreation* v52 no8 p54 Ag 2017

Mattingsdal, R.

Massive blow-out craters formed by hydrate-controlled methane expulsion from the Arctic seafloor graph map *Science* v356 no6341 p948 Je 1 2017

Mattiroli, Francesca

Structure of histone-based chromatin in Archaea diag *Science* v357 no6351 p609 Ag 11 2017

Mattis, James N., 1950-

The Creative, Unpredictable, and Terrifying (to Enemies) Genius That Is Mad Dog *USA Today Magazine* v145 no2860 p17 Ja 2017

General Mattis Advances on Washington J. Mattis *Hoover Digest: Research & Opinion on Public Policy* no1 p84 Wint 2017

THE WARRIOR MONK D. FILKINS cartoon *New Yorker* v93 no15 p34 My 29 2017

MATTIX, MICAH

Bard for Life color *Weekly Standard* v22 no10 p37 N 14 2016

Birds of Paradise cartoon *Weekly Standard* v22 no27 p36 Mr 20 2017

Cracks in Language bw *Weekly Standard* v23 no2 p44 S 18 2017

The Hero As Actor color *Weekly Standard* v22 no32 p34 My 1 2017

The Long Haul cartoon *Weekly Standard* v22 no12 p5 N 28 2016

MATTOCKS, STEVEN

Damming, Lost Connectivity, and the Historical Role of Anadromous Fish in Freshwater Ecosystem Dynamics *BioScience* v67 no8 p713 Ag 2017

Mattos, Ignacio

CHEF'S SALAD A. RAPOPORT *Bon Appetit* v62 no7 p10 Jl 2017

Small Plates, Big Ambition A. PLATT img *New York* p62 F 9 2017

Mattress industry

THE EVERYTHING GUIDE TO: The Great Mattress Buyer's Dilemma: Open-cell foam, Hyper-Elastic Polymers, 100-day return policies: sorting through the sleep world's latest layers of innovation—and confusion D. MARCHESE img *New York* v50 no9 p66 My 1 2017

Mattresses

Empty Promises C. HILTON ANDERSEN color *Reader's Digest* v190 no1133 p52 S 2017

It's Been Over a Year, and I Still Can't Decide on a Mattress J. YUAN *New York* v50 no9 p73 My 1 2017

I want to buy my husband a laptop that comes with great tech support because he always has a million questions. Who has the best? il *Consumer Reports* v81 no12 p16 D 2016

A Legacy of Safety Lives On M. L. Tellado color *Consumer Reports* v82 no2 p5 F 2017

Secrets to a Great Night's sleep M. H. J. Farrell chart color *Consumer Reports* v82 no2 p16 F 2017

SOLVE THE MATTRESS MAZE cartoon *Men's Health* v32 no8 p75 O 2017

Soothing Sleep Solutions color *Good Housekeeping* v265 no2 p90 Ag 2017

Two Buzzwords, Same Meaning? 'Zero waste' and 'circular economy' are often used together E. Daigneau *Governing* v30 no10 p20 Jl 2017

Mattresses—Evaluation

Airweave Traveler color *Bloomberg Businessweek* no4533 p63 Ag 7 2017

... And 15 Other Casper Types *New York* v50 no9 p70 My 1 2017

BEST BETS img *New York* v50 no15 p42 Jl 24 2017

Do You Want to Buy One Online? A comparison of the four major start-ups img *New York* v50 no9 p70 My 1 2017

Do You Want to Try One Out in Person? Here's how you can, following the bring-your-own-pillow-and-rest-for-at-least-seven-minutes advice of clinical psychologist and sleep expert Dr. Michael Breus L. SCHWARTZBERG *New York* v50 no9 p69 My 1 2017

THE INTERNET OF THINGS ... IN BED C. Kane color *Fortune*

v174 no6 p72 N 1 2016

Need a New Bed? Sleep on It J. Vrabel color *GQ: Gentlemen's Quarterly* v86 no11 p52 N 2016

Odd Couples Can Find Happiness, Too color *Consumer Reports* v82 no2 p26 F 2017

SLEEP SAVERS color *Good Housekeeping* v265 no1 p124 Jl 2017

Slosh, Slosh, Zzzzz: The hot (if you turned on the heater) mattress craze of 1970 C. Bonanos img *New York* v50 no9 p10 My 1 2017

Sweet Talk on TV Ads *Consumer Reports* v82 no2 p25 F 2017

Mattresses—Sales & prices

DREAM WEAVER E. Griffith, A. Vandermey et al color *Fortune* v176 no3 p74 S 1 2017

MATTSSON, ANETTE

ARABIAN HORSE DAYS POLAND 2016 *Arabian Horse World* v57 no2 p108 N 2016

Mattsson, Johanna

A pathology atlas of the human cancer transcriptome diag *Science* v357 no6352 p660 Ag 18 2017

Mattu, Surya

A World Apart color *Consumer Reports* v82 no7 p52 Jl 2017

Mattus, Matt

rare BEAUTIES M. OZAWA *Martha Stewart Living* no269 p120 N 2016

Maturation (Psychology)

Shakespeare's Characters Show Us How Personal Growth Should Happen D. Fitzsimons color *Harvard Business Review Digital Articles* p2 Ja 30 2017

Maturo, Hernán M.

Forest conservation: Remember Gran Chaco bibl color *Science* v355 no6324 p465 F 3 2017

MATUS, VICTORINO

The Clean-Plate Club *Weekly Standard* v22 no4 p5 O 3 2016

Paper, Plastic—or prime? color *Weekly Standard* v23 no1 p38 S 11 2017

Matussek, Karin

Can You Say Class Action in German? Nein color *Bloomberg Businessweek* no4505 p39 D 26 2016

MATUSZEWSKI, ERIK

The Long Game color *Forbes* v200 no1 p108 Jl 27 2017

Matveev, Arthur

The Rydberg constant and proton size from atomic hydrogen bw chart color diag graph *Science* v357 no6359 p79 O 6 2017

Matz, Joshua

GUEST LIST: A monthly roundup of people we'd like to have over for drinks, food, and conversation *Washingtonian Magazine* v52 no8 p26 My 2017

Matzos

matzo's makeover M. GLISAN color *Better Homes & Gardens* v95 no4 p106 Ap 2017

MMM... MORNING color *Good Housekeeping* v264 no4 p118 Ap 2017

Mauborgne, Renee

Closing the Gap Between Blue Ocean Strategy and Execution *Harvard Business Review Digital Articles* p2 F 5 2015

Identify Blue Oceans by Mapping Your Product Portfolio *Harvard Business Review Digital Articles* p2 F 12 2015

Mauborgne, Renée—Interviews

FINDING AN 'OCEAN' FREE FROM RIVALS L. Gallagher color *Fortune* v176 no5 p34 O 1 2017

Mauboussin, Michael J.

Reclaiming the Idea of Shareholder Value *Harvard Business Review Digital Articles* p2 Jl 1 2016

Mauck, Jason

10 UP & COMERS: JASON MAUCK A. McConnell *Successful Farming* v115 no8 p40 Je/Jl 2017

Maug, Ernst

CEOs Earn Less at More-Prestigious Firms color *Harvard Business Review Digital Articles* p2 F 2 2017

Maughan, Shannon

All Ears on APAC color *Publishers Weekly* v264 no20 p(Sp)22 My 15 2017

Brave New World color *Publishers Weekly* v264 no14 p30 Ap 3, 2017

EveryLibrary, Follett Partner to Save School Librarians color *Pub-*

lishers Weekly v264 no34 p56 Ag 21 2017

The Evolution Of RBmedia *Publishers Weekly* v264 no22 p11 My 29 2017

FALL 2017 AUDIO ANNOUNCEMENTS color *Publishers Weekly* v264 no27 p21 Jl 3 2017

Funding Teachers' Dreams for Their Students color *Publishers Weekly* v264 no34 p64 Ag 21 2017

How to Maximize ALA Midwinter color *Publishers Weekly* v263 no52 p62 D 19 2016

Inside the Audio Department color *Publishers Weekly* v264 no19 p18 My 8 2017

In the Studio bw color *Publishers Weekly* v264 no11 p19 Mr 13 2017

In The Studio bw color *Publishers Weekly* v264 no15 p25 Ap 10 2017

In the Studio color *Publishers Weekly* v263 no46 p22 N 14 2016

In the Studio color *Publishers Weekly* v264 no24 p22 Je 12 2017

In the Studio color *Publishers Weekly* v264 no33 p21 Ag 14 2017

Library Advocacy Efforts Gaining Steam color *Publishers Weekly* v264 no25 p64 Je 19 2017

More Originals from Audible *Publishers Weekly* v263 no41 p21 O 10 2016

Publishers See More Good Times Ahead for Audiobooks color *Publishers Weekly* v264 no3 p6 Ja 16 2017

PW TALKS WITH LIBRARIAN OF CONGRESS CARLA HAYDEN color *Publishers Weekly* v263 no52 p54 D 19 2016

PW talks with Nina Lindsay color *Publishers Weekly* v264 no14 p28 Ap 3. 2017

Reflections on a "Busy and Wonderful Year" *Publishers Weekly* v264 no25 p75 Je 19 2017

SPRING 2017 AUDIO ANNOUNCEMENTS color *Publishers Weekly* v264 no6 p20 F 6 2017

Teaching Digital Citizenship color *Publishers Weekly* v264 no34 p35 Ag 21 2017

THE TOP 10: MOST CHALLENGED BOOKS OF 2016 color *Publishers Weekly* v264 no25 p60 Je 19 2017

Who Will Win the Newbery Medal? color *Publishers Weekly* v263 no52 p56 D 19 2016

Maughan, Steve

4 Ways to Build a Productive Sales Culture *Harvard Business Review Digital Articles* p2 Je 16 2015

Maui (Hawaii)

ISLANDS color *Conde Nast Traveler* v52 no10 p96 N 2017

Maui (Hawaii)—Description & travel

STRANDED... AND LOVING IT R. Levin color *Sunset* v238 no3 p13 Mr 2017

Maui's dolphin

New Zealand's endemic dolphins are hanging by a thread C. Pala *Science* v355 no6325 p559 F 10 2017

Mauk, B.

Jupiter's magnetosphere and aurorae observed by the Juno spacecraft during its first polar orbits diag graph *Science* v356 no6340 p826 My 26 2017

Mauk, Ben

STATES OF DECAY: A journey through America's nuclear heartland *Harper's Magazine* p48 O 2017

Maum, Courtney

Publishing's Bright Future (Really!) *Publishers Weekly* v264 no22 p72 My 29 2017

Swipe Write: Courtney Maum's exuberant novel sends up the world of techie consumerism A. QUINN *New York Times Book Review* p17 Je 11 2017

Tom BURR *Interview* v46 no10 p143 D 2016/Ja 2017

Mauna Kea (Hawaii)

WHAT IT TAKES TO RIDE... MAUNA KEA S. Yeager color *Bicycling* v58 no10 p30 N/D 2017

Maunder minimum (Solar cycle)

Another Maunder Minimum? M. YOUNG *Sky & Telescope* v133 no6 p9 Je 2017

Mauntel, Michael

Families BEHIND the BADGE G. M. GRAFF color *AARP: The Magazine* v60 no1A p38 D 2016/Ja 2017

Maupin, Caroline

BROOKLYN CF *Arabian Horse World* v57 no9 p35 Je 2017

The Varian Way Weekend *Arabian Horse World* v57 no12 p60 S 2017

MAURER, BRIAN T.

Thoreau for the Ages *American Scholar* v86 no4 p3 Aut 2017

Maurer, John H.

THIS IS SPARTA *Claremont Review of Books* v16 no4 p61 Fall 2016

MAURER, ROBERT

What Are You Afraid Of? *Psychology Today* v49 no5 p50 S/O 2016

Mauri, Alessandra

Drosophila insulin release is triggered by adipose Stunted ligand to brain Methuselah receptor bibl graph *Science* v353 no6307 p1553 S 30 2016

Maurice (Film)

MERCHANT'S IVORY: James Ivory sails on without his partner Ismail Merchant, lovingly restoring the films that were their lives's work, like the newly re-released Maurice T. RING color *Advocate* no1091 p28 Je/Jl 2017

Maurice, Mark—Interviews

THE LOOK BOOK A. SWERDLOFF img *New York* p51 F 20 2017

Maurin, Guillaume

Hydrolytically stable fluorinated metal-organic frameworks for energy-efficient dehydration diag *Science* v356 no6339 p731 My 19 2017

Mauritius

Mauritius invites primate research labs to set up shop M. Wadman chart color *Science* v356 no6337 p472 My 5 2017

Mauro, Buzz

NEITHER GUYS NOR DOLLS: A theater's experiment in gender-blind casting C. JACKSON *Washingtonian Magazine* v52 no12 p23 S 2017

Mauser rifle

PISTOL ENVY *MHQ: Quarterly Journal of Military History* v29 no3 p62 Spr 2017

Mausoleums

RENEWING THE PAST color *Louisiana Life* v37 no5 p6 My/Je 2017

Maverick automobile—Evaluation

Appetite for Destruction J. Jacquot color *Car & Driver* v62 no10 p90 Ap 2017

Mavhunga, Clapperton Chakanetsa

Acknowledging Africa G. Emeagwali color *Science* v357 no6348 p258 Jl 21 2017

Mavic (Company)

MAVIC ECHAPPÉE W SHOE G. Liu color *Bicycling* v58 no4 p89 My 2017

MAVIC KSYRIUM PRO DISC J. Lindsey color *Bicycling* v58 no9 p73 O 2017

Mavroudis, Orestis

"THE EQUILIBRISTS" W. S. Smith *Art in America* v104 no9 p164 O 2016

Mavrova-Guirguinova, Maria

Changing climate shifts timing of European floods color graph *Science* v357 no6351 p588 Ag 11 2017

Mawad, Marie

THE MAYOR IS IN color *Bloomberg Businessweek* no4534 p66 Ag 14 2017

Mawdsley, Jonathan

Words alone will not protect pollinators bibl color *Science* v355 no6323 p357 Ja 27 2017

Mawritz, Mary

We're All Capable of Being an Abusive Boss [Cover story] *Harvard Business Review Digital Articles* p2 O 14 2016

Max, D. T.

BEYOND HUMAN cartoon *National Geographic* v231 no4 p40 Ap 2017

FASHION'S ATTICS cartoon color *New Yorker* v93 no5 p62 Mr 20 2017

For the Love of Lovecraft *New York Times Book Review* p14 Mr 12 2017

SOMBRE COLORS cartoon color *New Yorker* v92 no40 p42 D 5 2016

WHALES AND DINOSAURS cartoon *New Yorker* v93 no13 p32 My 15 2017

Max, Peter, 1937-

Peter Max: An American Artist R. Love bw color *AARP: The*

Magazine v60 no5A p6 Ag/S 2017

Max, Sarah
ASK THE EXPERT diag *Money* v45 no10 p31 N 2016
ASK THE EXPERT diag *Money* v46 no2 p31 Mr 2017
BEST IN TRAVEL 2017 color *Money* v46 no3 p58 Ap 2017
Best Places to Retire color *Money* v45 no10 p64 N 2016

Max, Tucker
The One Unbreakable Rule in Business Writing *Harvard Business Review Digital Articles* p2 S 13 2016

Max Mara
FASHION'S ATTICS D. T. Max cartoon color *New Yorker* v93 no5 p62 Mr 20 2017

Max-Planck-Gesellschaft zur Förderung der Wissenschaften e.V.
Germany to probe Nazi-era medical science M. Gannon bw *Science* v355 no6320 p13 Ja 6 2017

Maxfield, David
How a Culture of Silence Eats Away at Your Company *Harvard Business Review Digital Articles* p2 D 7 2016
How to React to Biased Comments at Work *Harvard Business Review Digital Articles* p2 My 3 2017
How to Talk Politics at Work Without Alienating People *Harvard Business Review Digital Articles* p2 S 14 2016

Maximus, Bobby
Bench Your Best J. Gilpatrick chart color *Men's Health* v32 no1 p52 Ja/F 2017
Forge the Maximus Body bw *Men's Health* v32 no3 p40 Ap 2017

Maxwell, Brandon
BRANDON MAXWELL Simply Irresistible E. Wilson color *InStyle* v24 no6 p136 Je 2017
Wham GLAM L. YAEGER color *Vogue* v206 no11 p108 N 2016

Maxwell, Glyn, 1962-
Derek Walcott: 'What the Twilight Says' M. Ford bw color *New York Review of Books* v63 no17 p44 N 10 2016

Maxwell, Sammie
ENEMY color *Christian Century* v134 no5 p20 Mr 1 2017

Maxwell, Shirley
Monrovia/Greater Los Angeles, California bw color *Old House Journal* v45 no6 p34 S 2017
Tenleytown/Washington, D.C bw color *Old House Journal* v45 no3 p34 My 2017

Maxwell, Steve
The Bison Deep Well Hand Pump *Mother Earth News* no280 p78 F/Mr 2017

Maxwell's demon
Maxwell's demon's memory tested E. CONOVER *Science News* v192 no2 p14 Ag 19 2017

MAY, DANIEL
HOW TO REVIVE THE PEACE MOVEMENT color diag *Nation* v304 no11 p12 Ap 3 2017

May, Melissa
Laying the Groundwork for Park Metrics *Parks & Recreation* v52 no1 p12 Ja 2017
Wild and Wonderful *Parks & Recreation* v52 no3 p14 Mr 2017

May, Michael M.
Safety first: The future of nuclear energy outside the United States bibl *Bulletin of the Atomic Scientists* v73 no1 p38 Ja 2017

May, Mike
Big data, big picture: Metabolomics meets systems biology color *Science* v356 no6338 p646 My 12 2017
Companies in the cloud: Digitizing lab operations color *Science* v355 no6324 p532 F 3 2017

May, Richard
Perovskite-perovskite tandem photovoltaics with optimized band gaps bibl chart graph *Science* v354 no6314 p861 N 18 2016

May, Scott A.
Kilogram-scale prexasertib monolactate monohydrate synthesis under continuous-flow CGMP conditions chart diag *Science* v356 no6343 p1144 Je 16 2017

May, Shannon
THE BRIDGE P. TYRE *New York Times Magazine* p40 Jl 2 2017

May, Theresa, 1956-
BREXIT: NO PARTIAL MEMBERSHIP IN THE EUROPEAN UNION T. MAY *Vital Speeches of the Day* v83 no3 p68 Mr 2017
BRITAIN UNITED, FOR THE GOOD OF THE WORLD *Vital*

Speeches of the Day v83 no5 p151 My 2017
Delusions of Power G. Younge *Nation* v304 no16 p10 My 22 2017
May Day G. Wood color *Vogue* v207 no4 p204 Ap 2017
May Poll C. CALDWELL color *Weekly Standard* v22 no32 p16 My 1 2017
May Should Go Easy On Brexit Promises color *Bloomberg Businessweek* no4521 p8 My 8 2017
May Spells Out Her Ambitious Wish List T. Ross *Bloomberg Businessweek* no4508 p14 Ja 23 2017
May's Small-Town Brexit Strategy T. Penny color *Bloomberg Businessweek* no4522 p18 My 15 2017
Mistaken Names T. John color *Time* v188 no20 p10 N 14 2016
A More Imperfect Union: Britain's separation from the EU: not merely a new political and legal arrangement but a deep and permanent schism N. Ferguson *Hoover Digest: Research & Opinion on Public Policy* no3 p88 Summ 2017
The Not-So-Darling Buds of Theresa May S. DAISLEY *Commentary* v143 no6 p20 Je 2017
No Way Out T. Ross bw *Bloomberg Businessweek* no4539 p41 S 25 2017
Oh, Snap! R. Hutton, A. Morales et al color diag *Bloomberg Businessweek* no4519 p31 Ap 24 2017
OUR VALUES WILL ALWAYS PREVAIL T. MAY *Vital Speeches of the Day* v83 no7 p196 Jl 2017
OUR VISION FOR BRITAIN AFTER THE BREXIT *Vital Speeches of the Day* v82 no12 p378 D 2016
The Prime Minister Goes All In D. GREEN color *Weekly Standard* v22 no20 p14 Ja 30 2017
The Scrooges in Charge J. MILLER *In These Times* v41 no5 p41 My 2017
Six Months In, Is Britain's Theresa May Bungling Brexit? T. John color *Time* v189 no4 p10 Ja 23 2017
SOMETHING THAT I CALL THE SHARED SOCIETY T. MAY *Vital Speeches of the Day* v83 no3 p86 Mr 2017
Theresa May and the EU Square Off Over Brexit T. Ross and I. Wishart color *Bloomberg Businessweek* no4515 p16 Mr 20 2017
Theresa May's Losing Gamble J. Freedland color *New York Review of Books* v64 no12 p42 Jl 13 2017
TOMORROW, LET THE HOUSE OF COMMONS VOTE FOR AN ELECTION *Vital Speeches of the Day* v83 no6 p186 Je 2017

May, Theresa, 1956-—Political & social views
Britain's Theresa May Is All-In on Brexit With Lousy Cards I. Bremmer *Time* v189 no4 p12 F 6 2017
FOR BUSINESS AFTER BREXIT, A NEW APPROACH T. MAY *Vital Speeches of the Day* v83 no1 p15 Ja 2017

May-December romances
When One Spouse Reaches Retirement First K. A. Renzulli color diag *Money* v46 no8 p25 S 2017

May Jeong
THE PATIENT WAR *Harper's Magazine* v334 no2001 p51 F 2017

May Kwok
Outfits for Days F. Kane, S. P. Nadella et al color *Glamour* v115 no3 p78 Mr 2017

Maya Angelou: And Still I Rise (Film)
HISTORICALLY SPEAKING L. Kennedy color *Essence* v47 no10 p56 F 2017

Maya Romanoff Corp.
OFF THE WALL E. EICHINGER color *Chicago* v66 no9 p92 S 2017

Mayas—Antiquities
ARTIFACT J. A. LOBELL color *Archaeology* v70 no3 p68 My/Je 2017
Maya codex real, analysis claims B. BOWER cartoon *Science News* v190 no9 p16 O 29 2016

Mayassi, Toufic
Reovirus infection triggers inflammatory responses to dietary antigens and development of celiac disease color diag *Science* v356 no6333 p44 Ap 7 2017

Maybach automobile
Mercedes-Maybach: Vision 6 Cabriolet S. Evans color *Motor Trend* v69 no11 p17 N 2017

Maybach automobile—Evaluation
CONCEPT CARS D. Pund color *Car & Driver* v62 no7 p24 Ja 2017

Maybellene (Music)
THE ESSENTIAL CHUCK BERRY J. Farber *Entertainment Weekly* no1459 p15 Mr 31 2017

Maybelline LLC
A Classic Reimagined A. Serrano color *InStyle* v24 no9 p325 S 2017
Model G Z. RUFFNER color *Vogue* v207 no11 p159 N 2017
The Shining color *Women's Health* v13 no10 p52 D 2016
Staying Power L. Camhi color *Vogue* v207 no11 p212 N 2017

Mayeda, Andrew
Bombardier's Painful Double Whammy *Bloomberg Businessweek* no4540 p23 O 2 2017
How Rational Are Rational Expectations? *Bloomberg Businessweek* no4501 p13 N 28 2016
Now It's Revamp, Not Replace color graph *Bloomberg Businessweek* no4531 p29 Jl 24 2017
PETER NAVARRO, TRADE WARRIOR color *Bloomberg Businessweek* no4521 p54 My 8 2017
A Raise for Mexican Workers? graph *Bloomberg Businessweek* no4534 p29 Ag 14 2017
The World Owes Too Much Money cartoon *Bloomberg Businessweek* no4495 p13 O 17 2016

Mayeda, Cassidy
teach AI when to say hi diag *Popular Science* v289 no5 p8 S/O 2017

Mayega, Roy William
Applying Deliberative Democracy in Africa: Uganda's First Deliberative Polls *Daedalus* v146 no3 p140 Summ 2017

Mayell, Sarah
Emergence and spread of a human-transmissible multidrug-resistant nontuberculous mycobacterium bibl diag graph *Science* v354 no6313 p751 N 11 2016

Mayer, Audrey L.
A scientist on any schedule color *Science* v355 no6323 p426 Ja 27 2017
Stormwater: A Resource for Scientists, Engineers, and Policy Makers *BioScience* v67 no2 p179 F 2017

Mayer, David M.
How Not to Advocate for a Woman at Work *Harvard Business Review Digital Articles* p2 Jl 26 2017
Why Are Some Whistleblowers Vilified and Others Celebrated? *Harvard Business Review Digital Articles* p2 S 1 2016

Mayer, Jack
New Titles from Self-Publishers color *Publishers Weekly* v264 no17 p48 Ap 24 2017

Mayer, Jane
AFTERMATH bw cartoon *New Yorker* v92 no38 p48 N 21 2016
THE GOLDWATER RULE cartoon *New Yorker* v93 no14 p28 My 22 2017
OBAMA'S AMERICA img *New York* v49 no20 p12 O 3 2016
THE PRESIDENT PENCE DELUSION bw color *New Yorker* v93 no33 p54 O 23 2017
TRUMP REBOOT cartoon *New Yorker* v92 no34 p20 O 24 2016
TRUMP'S MONEY MAN cartoon color *New Yorker* v93 no6 p34 Mr 27 2017

Mayer, John, 1977-
Mayer's Heartbreak Diary J. ELISCU bw *Rolling Stone* no1281/1282 p18 F 23 2017

Mayer, John, 1977——Interviews
Q&A: John Mayer P. DOYLE color *Rolling Stone* no1291/1292 p30 Jl 13 2017

Mayer, Klaus F.X.
Wild emmer genome architecture and diversity elucidate wheat evolution and domestication color *Science* v357 no6346 p93 Jl 7 2017

Mayer, Lawrence
THE EMPTY "CHOICE" ARGUMENT B. SHUCART *Advocate* no1088 p18 D 2016/Ja 2017

MAYER, LISA READIE
Party TIME color *Cabin Living* p58 D 2016

Mayer, Louis B. (Louis Burt), 1885-1957
WILLIAM HAINES DESIGNS: The legacy of a silent film star *Virginia Living* p140 2017 Best 20of Virginia

Mayer, Marissa, 1975-
GOLDEN PARACHUTE, MEET GLASS CLIFF G. Colvin color *Fortune* v175 no5 p14 Ap 1 2017

Marissa Mayer's Departure from Yahoo and the Challenge of Drawing Lessons from an N of 1 T. Chamorro-Premuzic *Harvard Business Review Digital Articles* p2 Je 15 2017
Marissa Mayer Was Right to Ask Executives to Commit to Staying at Yahoo R. Hoffman, B. Casnocha et al *Harvard Business Review Digital Articles* p2 N 11 2015

Mayer, Matthew
CIRCLE CITY AERODROME A. SHULER *Indianapolis Monthly* p21 My 2017

Mayer, Rosemary—Exhibitions
ROSEMARY MAYER T. Ballard color *Art in America* v105 no3 p130 Mr 2017

Mayer, Sophie
GIRL POWER: BACK TO THE FUTURE OF FEMINIST SCIENCE FICTION WITH INTO THE FOREST AND ARRIVAL *Film Quarterly* v70 no3 p32 Spr 2017
"WE CAN MAKE SOMETHING OUT OF ANYTHING": SALLY POTTER'S THRILLER AND LONDON'S HISTORY OF QUEER FEMINIST FILM SPACES *Film Quarterly* v70 no4 p39 Summ 2017

Mayer, Tony
Addressing scientific integrity scientifically *Science* v357 no6357 p1248 S 22 2017

Mayercak, Jim
ASTRO LETTERS color *Astronomy* v45 no5 p11 My 2017

MAYER-FOULKES, DAVID
The Crumbs of Capitalism *Commentary* v142 no2 p11 S 2016

Mayes, Ashley
i did it! J. GARLOCK color *Better Homes & Gardens* v95 no5 p72 My 2017

MAYES, FRANCES
Trailblazing *New York Times Book Review* p14 Je 4 2017

MAYES, JOSEPH
Humor in Uniform cartoon *Reader's Digest* v190 no1132 p138 Jl/Ag 2017

Mayeux, Ashley
Ashley Mayeux G. HENDERSON *Dance Magazine* v91 no6 p46 Je 2017

MAYFIELD, D. L.
Assimilate or Go Home: Notes from a Failed Missionary K. W. Pershey *Christian Century* v134 no2 p39 Ja 18 2017
IN MEMORY OF THESE [Cover story] bw color *Christianity Today* v61 no7 p34 S 2017

Mayfield, Vernita
The burden of inequity — AND WHAT SCHOOLS CAN DO ABOUT IT color *Phi Delta Kappan* v98 no5 p8 F 2017

Mayflies
HATCH OF THE MAYFLIES C. Beers *South Dakota Magazine* v33 no2 p94 Jl/Ag 2017

Mayflower (Ship)
MAYFLOWER IN LONDON: Where the famous voyage really began in Rotherhithe J. Wade *British Heritage Travel* v38 no2 p44 Mr/Ap 2017

Mayhew, Julie
The Big Lie *Publishers Weekly* v264 no40 p140 O 2 2017

Maynard, Frances
The Seven Rules of Elvira Carr *Publishers Weekly* v264 no20 p32 My 15 2017

Maynard, Joyce
The Confessionalist C. FLANAGAN color *Atlantic* v320 no3 p30 O 2017
Strangers in the House color *AARP: The Magazine* v30 no6A p68 O/N 2017

Mayne, Ann E.
Sustained virologic control in SIV+ macaques after antiretroviral and α4β7 antibody therapy bibl graph *Science* v354 no6309 p197 O 14 2016

Mayntz, Melissa
Bird Feeding: No Feeders Required color *National Wildlife (World Edition)* v55 no1 p12 D/Ja 2016

Mayo, Margarita
Don't Call It the "End of the Siesta": What Spain's New Work Hours Really Mean *Harvard Business Review Digital Articles* p2 Ap 13 2016
The Gender Gap in Feedback and Self-Perception *Harvard Business Review Digital Articles* p2 Ag 31 2016

If Humble People Make the Best Leaders, Why Do We Fall for Charismatic Narcissists? *Harvard Business Review Digital Articles* p2 Ap 7 2017

To Seem Confident, Women Have to Be Seen as Warm *Harvard Business Review Digital Articles* p2 Jl 8 2016

Mayo, Tony

Why Leadership Development Has to Happen on the Job M. Daimler *Harvard Business Review Digital Articles* p2 Mr 16 2016

Mayo Clinic

Getting Rid of "Never Events" in Hospitals T. Morgenthaler and C. M. Harper *Harvard Business Review Digital Articles* p2 O 20 2015

Mayonnaise

THE BEST BET img *New York* v49 no20 p97 O 3 2016

Mayor, The (TV program)

Breaking Big BRANDON MICHEAL HALL D. Franich, N. Abrams et al color *Entertainment Weekly* no1482/1483 p65 S 22 2017

THE MAYOR J. Russell *TV Guide* v65 no37 p29 S 4 2017

The Must Watch New Shows J. Jensen color *Entertainment Weekly* no1482/1483 p110 S 22 2017

A Very Familiar New-Old Season M. ROUSH *TV Guide* v65 no37 p18 S 4 2017

Mayors

See also

Women mayors

THE MAYOR IS IN M. Mawad, E. Chrepa et al color *Bloomberg Businessweek* no4534 p66 Ag 14 2017

Mayor Trump C. Rose color *New Orleans Magazine* v51 no7 p44 My 2017

Placing People at the Centre of Our Sustainable Urban Future A. Hidalgo *UN Chronicle* v53 no3 p13 2016

Reflections on a Career T. Dellner *Parks & Recreation* v52 no3 p44 Mr 2017

Roffignac E. LABORDE cartoon *New Orleans Magazine* v51 no12 p168 O 2017

Sadiq Khan J. Crelin color *Current Biography* v77 no10 p72 O 2016

Mayors—Attitudes

The Spirit of'76 D. COURTNEY *Texas Monthly* v44 no11 p220 N 2016

Mayors—Elections

The Battle for the Soul of Black Politics M. CUNNINGHAM-COOK *In These Times* v41 no5 p15 My 2017

Changing Course A. Greenblatt *Governing* v30 no3 p17 D 2016

DEMOCRATS STUMBLE OVER ABORTION POLITICS IN OMAHA R. D. Sullivan color graph *America* v216 no11 p12 My 15 2017

If Elected [Cover story] C. ROSE color *New Orleans Magazine* v52 no1 p50 S 2017

Mayoral Roller Coaster: Why can't Seattle find leaders it wants to keep? A. Greenblatt *Governing* v31 no1 p17 O 2017

The Political Revolution's Southern Front K. WEBB-HEHN *In These Times* v41 no10 p6 O 2017

Mayors—Interviews

Meet Johannesburg's New Libertarian Mayor L. Louw color *Reason* v48 no7 p36 D 2016

Mayors—United States

ACROSS THE AISLE A. Greenblatt *Governing* v30 no7 p12 Ap 2017

The URBAN OPPOSITION A. Greenblatt *Governing* v30 no5 p26 F 2017

When Millennials Rule C. Alter color *Time* v190 no16/17 p88 O 23 2017

Mayors—United States—Elections

Mayors, Promises and Reality A. Ehrenhalt *Governing* v30 no2 p14 N 2016

Mayotte, E.

Observation of a large-scale anisotropy in the arrival directions of cosmic rays above 8 × 1018 eV *Science* v357 no6357 p1266 S 22 2017

Mays, Malcolm

Snowfall J. Jensen color *Entertainment Weekly* no1473 p50 Jl 7 2017

MAYSH, JEFF

THE COP WHO BECAME A ROBBER *Los Angeles Magazine* v62 no9 p100 S 2017

Mayville, Luke

Orders of Merit J. COST *Weekly Standard* v22 no17 p32 Ja 2 2017

Mayweather, Floyd, Jr., 1977-

Games: Will Leitch: The Unseemly Science Is it possible for sports to sink lower than Mayweather-McGregor? img *New York* v50 no15 p13 Jl 24 2017

Leading Off B. Baskin color *Sports Illustrated* v127 no7 p6 S 4 2017

The Making of a Cynical Sporting Spectacle In the Desert S. Gregory color *Time* v190 no8 p54 Ag 28 2017

SHADOWBOXING G. Bishop color *Sports Illustrated* v127 no6 p52 Ag 28 2017

Sideshow Effect C. P. Pierce and T. Keith color *Sports Illustrated* v127 no3 p16 Jl 24 2017

Mazar, Debi

BEYOND-EASY, COMPLETELY SURPRISING ITALIAN color *Redbook* p144 O 2017

Easiest Ever THANKSGIVING [Cover story] color *Good Housekeeping* v265 no5 p10 N 2017

Mazarico, Erwan

Gravity field of the Orientale basin from the Gravity Recovery and Interior Laboratory Mission bibl graph *Science* v354 no6311 p438 O 28 2016

Mazarr, Michael J.

The Once and Future Order color *Foreign Affairs* v96 no1 p25 Ja/F 2017

MAZATAUD, VALÉRIAN

A Dangerous Place for Women: Honduras is an epicenter of violence against women *Ms.* v27 no2 p14 Summ 2017

Mazatlan (Sinaloa, Mexico)

Where we go A. Kylie color *Canadian Geographic* v135 no6 p4 D 2015

Mazatlan (Sinaloa, Mexico)—Description & Travel

Savouring SINALOA T. BURKE color map *Canadian Geographic* v135 no6 p34 D 2015

Mazda automobile—Evaluation

THE BEST NEVER REST C. Walton chart color *Motor Trend* v69 no6 p76 Je 2017

Changing Times C. Seabaugh chart color *Motor Trend* v68 no12 p82 D 2016

Fleet Files D. Beard, J. Gall et al color *Car & Driver* v63 no4 p90 O 2017

Mazda CX-9 chart color *Motor Trend* v69 no1 p67 Ja 2017

REALITY CHECK D. ZENLEA color *Road & Track* v68 no5 p106 D 2016/Ja 2017

REVIEWS E. DYER color *Popular Mechanics* p42 F 2017

Spruced Up and Sporty color *Consumer Reports* v82 no8 p58 Ag 2017

Sui Generis J. Capparella cartoon color *Car & Driver* v62 no7 p88 Ja 2017

UNSPOILED B. MCALEER color *Road & Track* v69 no2 p76 S 2017

Mazda Motor Corp.

2016 MAZDA MX-5 MIATA CLUB D. Pund color graph *Car & Driver* v63 no4 p84 O 2017

Mazda CX-9 chart color *Motor Trend* v69 no1 p67 Ja 2017

On our summer vacation, we took a bunch of new three-row SUVs to camp. You guys want to see the slideshow? J. Sabatini chart color *Car & Driver* v63 no2 p54 Ag 2017

RAISE THE ROOF color *Esquire* p18 Ap 2017

REALITY CHECK D. ZENLEA color *Road & Track* v68 no5 p106 D 2016/Ja 2017

Spruced Up and Sporty color *Consumer Reports* v82 no8 p58 Ag 2017

Mazda3 automobile

Ratings chart *Consumer Reports* v82 no7 p64 Jl 2017

Mazda3 automobile—Evaluation

THE INCUMBENTS D. GRANGER color diag *Car & Driver* v62 no7 p62 Ja 2017

Mazda MX-5 automobile

THE 10 BEST CARS FOR 2017 color *Car & Driver* v62 no7 p114 Ja 2017

Mazda MX-5 automobile—Evaluation

10 Top Picks J. S. Bartlett color *Consumer Reports* v82 no4 p22

Ap 2017

Mazda RX-7 automobile

ROTARY INTERNATIONAL S. SMITH bw color *Road & Track* v69 no2 p44 S 2017

MAZE, ALLISON

CREATIVE CLASS color *Better Homes & Gardens* v95 no2 p40 F 2016

dive into summer color *Better Homes & Gardens* v95 no7 p49 Jl 2017

HEADS UP color *Better Homes & Gardens* v95 no7 p41 Jl 2017

HOME, sweet HOME color *Better Homes & Gardens* v95 no10 p70 O 2017

IN PRAISE of VIOLAS color *Better Homes & Gardens* v95 no4 p126 Ap 2017

into the light color *Better Homes & Gardens* v95 no3 p30 Mr 2017

OBSESSED WITH GRAPHIC GAMES color *Better Homes & Gardens* v95 no8 p12 Ag 2017

OBSESSED WITH NAUTICAL color *Better Homes & Gardens* v95 no7 p14 Jl 2017

organize your DROP ZONE color *Better Homes & Gardens* v95 no11 p62 N 2017

PARTY ON... THE CHEAP color *Better Homes & Gardens* v95 no6 p46 Je 2017

SHAY spaniola color *Better Homes & Gardens* v95 no4 p34 Ap 2017

Maze puzzles

THE GREAT ESCAPE R. O'CONNOR color *Chicago* v65 no12 p40 D 2016

Mazlin, Steve

The Name Game: Have a go at this celestial sport. You might just win gold *Sky & Telescope* v134 no4 p84 O 2017

READER GALLERY bw color *Astronomy* v45 no11 p72 N 2017

READER GALLERY color *Astronomy* v45 no1 p72 Ja 2017

Mazouni, Khalil

Self-organized Notch dynamics generate stereotyped sensory organ patterns in Drosophila color *Science* v356 no6337 p501 My 5 2017

Mazower, Mark

The Historian Who Was Not Baffled by the Nazis bw *New York Review of Books* v63 no20 p70 D 22 2016

Mazumder, Robin

Robin Mazumder S. DOYLE color *Canadian Geographic* v137 no3 p19 My 2017

Mazur, P. O.

Observation of a large-scale anisotropy in the arrival directions of cosmic rays above 8 × 1018 eV *Science* v357 no6357 p1266 S 22 2017

Mazurek, Brooke

Best-Dressed LIST color *Harper's Bazaar* no3653 p100 My 2017

DINING IN STYLE WITH SARA STORY color *Harper's Bazaar* no3654 p98 Je/Jl 2017

My LIST bw color *Harper's Bazaar* no3654 p66 Je/Jl 2017

WEEKND UPDATE bw *Harper's Bazaar* no3656 p398 S 2017

Mazza, Davide

Reticulon 3–dependent ER-PM contact sites control EGFR nonclathrin endocytosis color diag graph *Science* v356 no6338 p617 My 12 2017

Mazzaferri, Marcus

out alive: stranded M. B. Skylis bw *Backpacker* p37 O 2017

Mazzalai, Christian—Interviews

PHOENIX A. Bacle color *Entertainment Weekly* no1470 p55 Je 16 2017

Mazzante, Louis

"I WANT TO TAKE MORE RISKS." color *Bicycling* v58 no3 p70 Ap 2017

Mazzarella, Nick

Mazzarella's Instrumental Voice Evolves B. Meyer color *Downbeat* v84 no8 p19 Ag 2017

Mazzaro, Maria

April/2017 *Opera News* v81 no10 p8 Ap 2017

Jakub Józef Orliński *Opera News* v81 no6 p10 D 2016

Jan/2017 *Opera News* v81 no7 p6 Ja 2017

March/2017 *Opera News* v81 no9 p6 Mr 2017

MATTHEW POLENZANI *Opera News* v81 no10 p24 Ap 2017

Metropolitan Opera *Opera News* v81 no9 p64 Mr 2017

Natasha, Pierre and the Great Comet of 1812 *Opera News* v81

no10 p48 Ap 2017

Nov/2016 *Opera News* v81 no5 p8 N 2016

Summer Holiday: OPERA NEWS's spotlights the best of the U.S. Festival scene *Opera News* v81 no12 p27 Je 2017

Mazzei, Chris

How CEOs Can Keep Their Analytics Programs from Being a Waste of Time *Harvard Business Review Digital Articles* p2 Jl 21 2016

The Reason So Many Analytics Efforts Fall Short *Harvard Business Review Digital Articles* p2 Ag 29 2016

Mazzio, Mary

TRAFFIC T. Friend cartoon *New Yorker* v92 no45 p24 Ja 16 2017

Mazzola, Tony

FREE LOVE AND FASHION S. Mooallem color *Harper's Bazaar* no3655 p142 Ag 2017

Mazzoli, Missy

Breaking the Waves D. Shengold *Opera News* v81 no6 p42 D 2016

Mazzone, Dianna

Best Face Forward color *InStyle* v24 no11 p125 N 2017

Fresh Face color *InStyle* v24 no3 p259 Mr 2017

IN TREATMENT WITH Hannah Bronfman color *InStyle* v24 no4 p146 Ap 2017

Mazzotta, Benjamin

The Countries That Would Profit Most from a Cashless World *Harvard Business Review Digital Articles* p2 My 31 2016

Mazzucato, Mariana

An Entrepreneurial Society Needs an Entrepreneurial State *Harvard Business Review Digital Articles* p1 O 25 2016

Mazzulli, Joseph R.

Dopamine oxidation mediates mitochondrial and lysosomal dysfunction in Parkinson's disease graph *Science* v357 no6357 p1255 S 22 2017

Mbatha-Raw, Gugu, 1983-

Gugu Mbatha-Raw J. Crelin color *Current Biography* v78 no5 p58 My 2017

LADY GUGU P. MARTIN color *GQ: Gentlemen's Quarterly* v97 no3 p144 Mr 2017

Mbatha-Raw, Gugu—Interviews

"True badassery has no gender" K. Branch and E. Mahaney color diag *Glamour* v115 no1 p60 Ja 2017

Mbue, Imbolo

IMBOLO MBUE L. N. Williams color map *Essence* v47 no10 p68 F 2017

A TALE OF Two Christmases cartoon color *Good Housekeeping* v263 no6 p81 D 2016

Mbue, Imbolo—Interviews

Once Upon a Time in America color *O, The Oprah Magazine* p88 Ag 2017

McAdams, David

A Wall Won't Secure the U.S.-Mexico Border, but Economic Policy Could *Harvard Business Review Digital Articles* p2 F 14 2017

McAdams, Rachel

Calling the Night Nurse C. Collis color *Entertainment Weekly* no1436/1437 p37 O 21 2016

McAfee, Andrew

ARTIFICIAL INTELLIGENCE, FOR REAL: YOU'VE BEEN TOLD IT WILL TRANSFORM EVERYTHING. YOU'VE BEEN TOLD YOU NEED TO INVEST IN IT. BUT YOU HAVEN'T BEEN TOLD HOW. START HERE *Harvard Business Review Digital Articles* p1 Jl 1 2017

THE BUSINESS OF ARTIFICIAL INTELLIGENCE: WHAT IT CAN—AND CANNOT—DO FOR YOUR ORGANIZATION *Harvard Business Review Digital Articles* p3 Jl 1 2017

The Human Mind Is Overrated P. Coy cartoon color *Bloomberg Businessweek* no4529 p78 Jl 3 2017

Machine, Platform, Crowd *People Management* p46 Ag 2017

THREE SUMMARIES: HUMAN, EXTRACTIVE, AND ABSTRACTIVE *Harvard Business Review Digital Articles* p26 Jl 1 2017

What's Driving the Machine Learning Explosion? *Harvard Business Review Digital Articles* p2 Jl 18 2017

WHAT'S DRIVING THE MACHINE LEARNING EXPLOSION? Three factors make this AI's moment *Harvard Business Review Digital Articles* p12 Jl 1 2017

McAfee, Annalena
Annalena McAfee, Author of Hame, on Her Love Letter to Scotland S. Gutierrez color *British Heritage Travel* v38 no5 p71 S/O 2017

McAfee, Felesha
DIY cabin remodel M. MYLCHREEST color *Cabin Living* p30 D 2016

McAfee, Preston
Where Predictive Analytics Is Having the Biggest Impact *Harvard Business Review Digital Articles* p2 My 25 2016

McAFEE, ROGER
ALL ABOUT ANODES: WOULD A "ZINC" MADE OF ANOTHER MATERIAL STILL WORK AS WELL? OR PERHAPS BETTER? *Sea Magazine* v109 no5 p24 My 2017
RANGER TUGS R-23 *Sea Magazine* v108 no10 p48 O 2016
REGAL 42 FLY: WHO KNEW A GREAT PACIFIC NORTHWEST BOAT WOULD BE DESIGNED AND BUILT IN FLORIDA? color *Sea Magazine* v109 no7 p32 Jl 2017
REGENCY: P65 MOTOR YACHT color *Sea Magazine* v109 no8 p34 Ag 2017
RIVIERA 6000 SPORT YACHT *Sea Magazine* v108 no10 p44 O 2016

McAfee Inc.
SECURING MCAFEE M. Lev-Ram color *Fortune* v175 no6 p24 My 1 2017

MCALEER, BRENDAN
CLASH OF CLANS chart color *Road & Track* v69 no2 p28 S 2017
POWER HITTER color *Road & Track* v68 no7 p84 Mr/Ap 2017
UNSPOILED color *Road & Track* v69 no2 p76 S 2017

McAlester, Virginia Savage
A FIELD GUIDE TO AMERICAN HOUSES P. Poore bw cartoon color *Arts & Crafts Homes & the Revival* v11 no5 p18 Wint 2017

McAlevey, Jane—Interviews
POWER PLAYERS D. D. GUTTENPLAN bw color *Nation* v304 no6 p21 F 27 2017

McAllen, Earl
Statin Denialism? *Skeptical Inquirer* v41 no5 p63 S/O 2017

McAlley, John
DOCTOR IN THE HOUSE color *Golf Magazine* v58 no12 p58 D 2016

McAllister, Nicole
Reovirus infection triggers inflammatory responses to dietary antigens and development of celiac disease color diag *Science* v356 no6333 p44 Ap 7 2017

McAlpine, Clive
Land's complex role in climate change [Cover story] *Physics Today* v69 no11 p40 N 2016

McAlpine, Skye
India Full-On bw color *Conde Nast Traveler* v52 no10 p100 N 2017

McAnally, John R.
Control of muscle formation by the fusogenic micropeptide myomixer diag *Science* v356 no6335 p323 Ap 21 2017

McANENY, BRIAN
USA HALF MARATHON INVITATIONAL color *Runner's World* v51 no11 p98 D 2016

McANINCH, DAVID
WHY We LOVE CHICAGO bw cartoon color *Chicago* v66 no3 p75 Mr 2017

McAnulty, Sarah J.
Survival of the spineless color *Science* v357 no6359 p53 O 6 2017

McArthur, Damian
FUN & GAMES color *Backpacker* p71 Je 2017

McArthur, Douglas
He Has Returned *Commentary* v142 no1 p1 Jl/Ag 2016

McAuliffe, Mary
Crazy Years K. BETTS *New York Times Book Review* p11 O 16 2016

McAuliffe, Terry, 1957-
EXECUTIVE ORDER: How Virginia Governs Cybersecurity *Governing* v30 no1 p1 O 2016

McAvoy, James, 1979-
Split *New Yorker* v92 no48 p10 F 6 2017

McBath, Lucy—Interviews

TRIUMPH THROUGH TRAGEDY J. Harris color *Essence* v47 no7 p96 N 2016

McBride, Connie
Understanding Set and Drift graph *Sail* v47 no12 p44 D 2016

McBride, Danny, 1976-
HORROR SHOW T. Friend cartoon *New Yorker* v93 no16 p40 Je 5 2017

McBride, Danny, 1976-—Interviews
DANNY McBRIDE S. Vilkomerson color *Entertainment Weekly* no1467 p45 My 26 2017

McBride, Eimear, 1976-
Interiority Complex J. WINTERSON *New York Times Book Review* p21 O 23 2016
THE LESSER BOHEMIANS E. BETH LANGILLE color *Maclean's* v129 no42 p61 O 24 2016

McBride, James, 1957-
James McBride D. Skinner *Humanities* v37 no4 p1 Fall 2016
The Salt Line *Publishers Weekly* v264 no30 p34 Jl 24 2017
The Year in Reading [Cover story] *New York Times Book Review* p8 D 25 2016

McBride, Jason
Dennis Cooper's Change of Heart: As a novelist, he's been called the "most dangerous writer in America." But what kind of filmmaker will he be? img *New York* v50 no16 p104 Ag 7 2017
Dick Comes to Marfa img *New York* v49 no15 p80 Jl 25 2016

McBride, Jennifer
Homeless bodies *Christian Century* v134 no6 p28 Mr 15 2017

McBride, Joseph
A Pen Is a Tool J. Rosenbaum color *Film Comment* v53 no4 p79 Jl/Ag 2017

McBride, Melissa
THE WALKING DEAD D. Ross color *Entertainment Weekly* no1474/1475 p68 Jl 21-28 2017

McBride, Michael
Subhuman: Unit 51, Book 1 color *Publishers Weekly* v264 no39 p90 S 25 2017

McBride, Pete
THE PEOPLE'S POWER LIST *Sierra* v102 no3 p48 My/Je 2017

McBride, Sarah
Code School's Out color *Bloomberg Businessweek* no4504 p29 D 19 2016
Cracking the Bro Code cartoon *Bloomberg Businessweek* no4533 p18 Ag 7 2017
Don't Let Your Data Sleep With the Enemy bw color *Bloomberg Businessweek* no4498 p55 N 7 2016
Elon Musk's Hyperloop Surprise *Bloomberg Businessweek* no4534 p19 Ag 14 2017
Security Software, Insecurity Culture color *Bloomberg Businessweek* no4519 p38 Ap 24 2017
Skeptical Speculators Swoon for Socks color *Bloomberg Businessweek* no4541 p21 O 9 2017
Survival of the Fitted graph *Bloomberg Businessweek* no4511 p31 F 13 2017
That Seventies Startup color *Bloomberg Businessweek* no4532 p21 Jl 31 2017
Toto, I've a Feeling We're Still In Kansas (or Missouri) color *Bloomberg Businessweek* no4514 p33 Mr 13 2017

McBride, Terry—Interviews
Where the Women Were M. Maerz and I. Kaplan bw color *Glamour* no8 p142 Ag 2017

McBurney, Christian
THE PLOT TO KIDNAP WASHINGTON [Cover story] color map *MHQ: Quarterly Journal of Military History* v29 no4 p30 Summ 2017

McCabe & Mrs. Miller (Film)
MCCABE & MRS. MILLER F. Kaplan color *Sound & Vision* v82 no5 p67 Je 2017

McCabe, Bhrett
MEDIC! color *Golf Magazine* v58 no11 p47 N 2016
REALITY BITES color *Golf Magazine* v59 no4 p64 Ap 2017
TAKE A CHANT! color *Golf Magazine* v59 no10 p44 O 2017

McCabe, Jarrod
OUR READERS RESPOND *Yankee* p10 My/Je 2017

MCCAFFERTY, KEITH
Papa's Lost Treasure *Publishers Weekly* v264 no22 p44 My 29 2017

THE WISHING TREE color *Field & Stream* v122 no2 p56 Je/
Jl 2017

McCAFFERY, JEN

35 All-Time Favorite Natural Remedies color *Prevention* v69 no8
p38 Ag 2017

5 Myths About Aging [Cover story] cartoon *Prevention* v69 no4
p34 Ap 2017

5 Myths About WEIGHT LOSS [Cover story] cartoon *Prevention*
v69 no7 p30 Jl 2017

Danielle's Heart color *Prevention* v69 no5 p32 My 2017

Keep Them Moving! color *Prevention* v69 no4 p92 Ap 2017

The Secret Language of Pets [Cover story] color *Prevention* v69
no2 p92 F 2017

Watch the Pet's Meds color *Prevention* p92 Mr 2017

MCCAFFREY, LARA

SWING TIME *Psychology Today* v50 no4 p20 Ag 2017

WHAT CAN I DO? GLOBAL WARMING SEEMS MORE LIKE
A MORAL ISSUE IF WE FEEL WE CAN FIGHT IT *Psychology Today* v50 no3 p16 My/Je 2017

MCCAIG, AMY

The god of Science *USA Today Magazine* v145 no2860 p70 Ja
2017

McCain, John

McCain, John, 1936-

Falling In and Out of Love--Again--with John McCain A. FER-
GUSON *Commentary* v144 no2 p9 S 2017

A Good Resister G. NORMAN bw color *Weekly Standard* v22
no9 p17 N 7 2016

HOW MANY CHANGES DO YOU GET TO BE AN AMERI-
CAN HERO? [Cover story] G. SHERMAN img *New York* p22
F 20 2017

It's O.K. to Be a Coward About Cancer J. Friedman color *Time*
v190 no6 p21 Ag 7 2017

Leaders color *Time* v189 no16/17 p64 My 1-8 2017

LET'S TRUST EACH OTHER. LET'S RETURN TO REGU-
LAR ORDER *Vital Speeches of the Day* v83 no9 p254 S 2017

The Pros and Cons of the President's Immigrant Travel Ban J. Mc-
Cain *Congressional Digest* v96 no3 p15 Mr 2017

True American Greatness W. Kristol color *Weekly Standard* v22
no44 p8 Jl 31 2017

Try, Try Again *National Review* v69 no16 p12 Ag 28 2017

McCain, John, 1936-　Political & social views

JOHN MCCAIN: THE ANTI-TRUMP M. Welch color *Reason*
v49 no5 p10 O 2017

McCALL, BRUCE

EMERGENCY CANADIAN RESIDENCE APPLICATION cartoon *New Yorker* v92 no39 p45 N 28 2016

KIM JONG-UN NO PATSY cartoon *New Yorker* v93 no6 p29 Mr
27 2017

KNOW YOUR COCONUTS color *New Yorker* v93 no10 p60 Ap
24 2017

NOT SO FAST, CANADA! cartoon *New Yorker* v93 no22 p27
Jl 31 2017

McCall, Cheryl

IGNITING A Love of Literature: How ILA's Choices project inspires the next generation of lifelong readers *Literacy Today*
(2411-7862) v35 no2 p44 S/O 2017

McCall, Donald D.

CHARACTER *Christian Century* v134 no17 p22 Ag 16 2017

McCall, Elizabeth Kaye

SYLVIA ZERBINI AND RAJALI KA—a conversation *Arabian
Horse World* v57 no9 p34 Je 2017

McCall, Rosie

My Immune System Attacked My Hair color *Health* v31 no2 p91
Mr 2017

McCallister, S. Leigh

Dissolved organic sulfur in the ocean: Biogeochemistry of a petagram inventory bibl chart diag graph *Science* v354 no6311
p456 O 28 2016

Genomic databases: A WHO affair *Science* v356 no6340 p812 My
26 2017

McCall Smith, Alexander, 1948-

The House of Unexpected Sisters *Publishers Weekly* v264 no38
p54 S 18 2017

Trailblazing F. MAYES *New York Times Book Review* p14 Je 4
2017

The Year in Reading [Cover story] *New York Times Book Review*
p8 D 25 2016

McCallum, Jack

CONNIE HAWKINS color *Sports Illustrated* v127 no12 p18 O
16 2017

GOLDEN DAYS color *Sports Illustrated* v127 no12 p98 O 16
2017

Tom MESCHERY color *Sports Illustrated* v127 no1 p84 Jl 3 2017

MCCALLUM, JAN

THE WORLD'S BILLIONAIRES bw color diag graph map
Forbes v199 no3 p84 Mr 28 2017

McCallum, Sarah

Lineage-dependent spatial and functional organization of the
mammalian enteric nervous system color graph *Science* v356
no6339 p722 My 19 2017

McCallum, Scott

FROM Forest TO Table color *Canadian Wildlife* v22 no5 p30 N/D
2016

McCallum, Shara

Madwoman color *Publishers Weekly* v263 no47 p82 N 21 2016

MCCAMLEY, URSULENE

ALL IN A Day's Work cartoon *Reader's Digest* v190 no1132 p54
Jl/Ag 2017

McCAMMON, ROSS

Drink Bitter Than You're Used To color *GQ: Gentlemen's Quarterly* v97 no9 p88 S 2017

How to Be a Holiday Boozetender color *GQ: Gentlemen's Quarterly* v97 no11 p50 N 2017

Mike Judge color *GQ: Gentlemen's Quarterly* v97 no6 p128 Je
2017

Musicals! (Now for Men!) bw color *GQ: Gentlemen's Quarterly*
v97 no9 p116 S 2017

McCampbell, Beth—Interviews

FINDING PURPOSE IN PLASTIC SURGERY S. Floyd and A.
GUMBS color *Black Enterprise* v47 no5 p29 Ja/F 2017

McCann, Kelly

Avoid Rather Than Fight color *Black Belt* v55 no6 p18 O/N 2017

A Down-and-Dirty Guide to Striking [Cover story] color *Black
Belt* v55 no2 p16 F/Mr 2017

Hard Training and Inevitable Injuries color *Black Belt* v55 no1
p22 D 2016/Ja 2017

The Light at the End of the Tunnel color *Black Belt* v55 no4 p18
Je/Jl 2017

Self-Defense or Self-Offense? color *Black Belt* v55 no5 p18 Ag/S
2017

Training, Not Trinkets color *Black Belt* v55 no3 p16 Ap/My 2017

McCann, Michael

LEGAL BRIEF *Sports Illustrated* v127 no11 p24 O 9 2017

TIME TO BE RELEASED? color *Sports Illustrated* v126 no5 p70
F 13 2017

Wheels of Justice color *Sports Illustrated* v126 no15 p13 My 29
2017

McCannon, Joe

A Guide to Managing a Volunteer Workforce *Harvard Business
Review Digital Articles* p2 Mr 2 2016

McCarraher, Eugene

The West Point of Capitalism color *Commonweal* v114 no14 p26
S 8 2017

McCarroll, Steven

Schizophrenia's Genetic Spark P. SMAGLIK cartoon *Discover*
v38 no1 p60 Ja/F 2017

McCarron, Andrew

LIGHT COME SHINING: THE TRANSFORMATIONS OF
BOB DYLAN C. LOUDON color *Maclean's* no1 p62 F 17 2017

MCCARRON, ANTHONY

Build Muscle at Any Age—Like This Guy color *Men's Health* v32
no7 p52 S 2017

THE WORLD IS YOUR GYM bw color *Men's Health* v32 no6
p114 Ag 2017

Your New Travel Workouts cartoon chart color *Men's Health* v32
no9 p48 N 2017

McCartan, Anne-Marie

THE CONVERSATION color *Atlantic* v319 no1 p10 Ja/F 2017

McCarter, Jeremy

EUGENE O'NEILL color *New York Times Book Review* p27 D
4 2016

Five Who Shook the World: A group biography of young Americans who embraced reform, socialism and woman suffrage G. SCIALABBA *New York Times Book Review* p21 Jl 23 2017

Rebels With Causes S. Begley color *Time* v189 no22 p53 Je 12 2017

McCarthy, Abby—Interviews

Girlfriends' Guide to Divorce *TV Guide* v65 no4 p36 Ja 16 2017

MCCARTHY, ANDREW C.

Attorney General Sessions il *National Review* v68 no23 p20 D 19 2016

Collusion Confusion *National Review* v69 no15 p26 Ag 14 2017

The Curious Case of the Disappearing Laptop *National Review* v69 no18 p16 O 2 2017

His Own Worst Enemy *National Review* v69 no12 p15 Je 26 2017

James Comey's Dereliction [Cover story] color *National Review* v68 no19 p21 O 24 2016

McCarthy, Andrew C., 1959-—Interviews

ANDREW McCARTHY I. Biedenharn color *Entertainment Weekly* no1459 p64 Mr 31 2017

McCarthy, Bailey—Interviews

A LABOR OF LOVE K. RENDA color *House Beautiful* v159 no1 p66 F 2017

McCarthy, Brian

Integrate Analytics Across Your Entire Business *Harvard Business Review Digital Articles* p2 O 3 2014

A Survey of 3,000 Executives Reveals How Businesses Succeed with AI *Harvard Business Review Digital Articles* p2 Ag 28 2017

McCARTHY, CARRIE

The Question *O, The Oprah Magazine* p14 F 2017

McCarthy, Christine E.

Cosmic meditations from Sufjan Stevens color *America* v217 no3 p49 Ag 7 2017

MCCARTHY, CORMAC

THOUGHTS ON Property *Forbes* v199 no5 p124 My 16 2017

McCarthy, Daniel

Reviving Libertarianism *American Conservative* v16 no2 p25 Mr/Ap 2017

That Old-Time Civil Religion color *Reason* v49 no2 p64 Je 2017

A Time of Transition *American Conservative* v16 no1 p5 Ja/F 2017

McCarthy, Dillon

It all started with partying *Scholastic Choices* v32 no3 p10 N/D 2016

MCCARTHY, GINA

Lean In to Climate Change color *Foreign Policy* no224 p76 My/Je 2017

McCARTHY, JESSE

Disenchanting Optimism: Three generations of a New Orleans family struggle and endure *New York Times Book Review* p15 S 10 2017

IN THE ZONE color *Nation* v305 no6 p27 S 11 2017

WIDEMAN'S GHOSTS color *Nation* v303 no25/26 p27 D 19 2016

McCarthy, Lauren

Best-Dressed LIST color *Harper's Bazaar* no3649 p140 D 2016/Ja 2017

CARA'S COMEBACK color *Harper's Bazaar* no3651 p283 Mr 2017

CHIC PICKS color *Harper's Bazaar* no3651 p269 Mr 2017

DARE TO WEAR COLOR color *Harper's Bazaar* no3648 p146 N 2016

HOME FOR THE HOLIDAYS color *Harper's Bazaar* no3649 p245 D 2016/Ja 2017

THE JLO DOWN color *Harper's Bazaar* no3649 p310 D 2016/Ja 2017

My LIST cartoon color *Harper's Bazaar* no3653 p102 My 2017

My LIST color *Harper's Bazaar* no3650 p80 F 2017

WHAT MEN THINK ABOUT WHAT WOMEN WEAR color *Harper's Bazaar* no3648 p194 N 2016

WHAT'S NEW IN LINGERIE color *Harper's Bazaar* no3650 p196 F 2017

WILD THINGS color *Harper's Bazaar* no3648 p187 N 2016

McCarthy, Linda

Feed a Child's Urge to Bird color *Audubon* v119 no3 p44 Fall 2017

MCCARTHY, MARIA

ON THE ROAD color *House Beautiful* p162 Ag 2017

SUMMER MOTORING color *House Beautiful* p156 Ag 2017

McCarthy, Mark I.

Detection of human adaptation during the past 2000 years bibl graph *Science* v354 no6313 p760 N 11 2016

Exposing the exposures responsible for type 2 diabetes and obesity bibl diag *Science* v354 no6308 p69 O 7 2016

McCarthy, Mary Jane

Lee Rubin: Our mentor and role model *Science* v355 no6327 p806 F 24 2017

McCarthy, Mary, 1912-1989

BEHIND THE FIG LEAF E. Blair *Harper's Magazine* p94 Ap 2017

MCCARTHY, MATT

My Patient Benny color *Reader's Digest* v189 no1131 p78 Je 2017

McCarthy, Melissa, 1969-

The Boss M. FELL *TV Guide* v65 no4 p47 Ja 16 2017

Sound Bites color *Entertainment Weekly* no1453 p8 F 17 2017

McCarthy, Michael

Saving Nature, for the Joy of It A. WULF *New York Times Book Review* p23 O 23 2016

What's Happening to the Bees and Butterflies? V. Klinkenborg color *New York Review of Books* v63 no20 p68 D 22 2016

A World of Wounds P. Connors color *Commonweal* v143 no20 p22 D 16 2016

MCCARTHY, MICHAEL A.

Metaresearch for Evaluating Reproducibility in Ecology and Evolution *BioScience* v67 no3 p282 Mr 2017

McCARTHY, MICHAEL C.

SETTING THE WORLD'S AGENDA *America* v215 no15 p35 N 14 2016

MCCARTHY, MICHAEL M.

Venezuela's Manmade Disaster *Current History* v116 no787 p61 F 2017

McCarthy, Mike

It's Not Easy Being Green A. Murphy color *Sports Illustrated* v125 no19 p60 D 12 2016

McCarthy, Patrick

PATRICK MCCARTHY T. Bird cartoon color *Snowboarder* v29 no5 p32 Ja 2017

McCarthy, Paul

YOU'VE GOTTA SEE THIS! B. POLLACK cartoon color *ARTnews* v116 no1 p72 Spr 2017

McCarthy, Sean

THE CINCINNATI STRONGMAN IS HERE TO PUMP YOU UP J. WILLIAMS *Cincinnati Magazine* v50 no10 p62 Jl 2017

LETTER FROM THE EDITOR J. STOWE *Cincinnati Magazine* v50 no10 p18 Jl 2017

McCarthy, Tom

THE BIG QUESTION cartoon *Atlantic* v319 no2 p100 Mr 2017

MODEL BEHAVIOR cartoon *New Yorker* v92 no32 p72 O 10 2016

McCarthy, Tom, 1969-

Typewriters, Bombs, Jellyfish G. HABASH color *Publishers Weekly* v264 no11 p69 Mr 13 2017

McCarthyism

It's Not McCarthyism K. Pollitt diag il *Nation* v304 no15 p6 My 8 2017

McCartin, James P.

Prayer Cards & Holy Dirt color *Commonweal* v144 no7 p34 Ap 14 2017

McCartney, Alistair

The Disintegrations *Publishers Weekly* v264 no25 p87 Je 19 2017

MCCARTNEY, JENNIFER

ART Therapy color *Publishers Weekly* v263 no42 p31 O 17 2016

Crowdfunding American Protest bw color *Publishers Weekly* v264 no39 p59 S 25 2017

Empire Building color *Publishers Weekly* v264 no21 p45 My 22 2017

The Game Changer color *Publishers Weekly* v263 no43 p41 O 24 2016

Me, Myself, and I color *Publishers Weekly* v264 no17 p38 Ap 24 2017

Move over Lonely Planet color *Publishers Weekly* v264 no26 p131 Je 26 2017

The World Needs More Sheroes cartoon color *Publishers Weekly* v264 no9 p41 F 27 2017

A Zombie Success Story bw color *Publishers Weekly* v264 no13 p41 Mr 27 2017

McCartney, Linda, 1941-1998

Women. Power. Love. Stella! color *Glamour* v115 no11 p20 N 2017

McCartney, Paul

TECH QUIZ *Popular Mechanics* p72 O 2017

McCartney, Paul, 1942-

Cracking the Voice img *New York* v49 no20 p113 O 3 2016

GEORGE MARTIN color *Entertainment Weekly* no1446/1447 p88 D 2016/Ja 2017

Paul and Elvis: The Fab Two B. HIATT bw *Rolling Stone* no1283 p16 Mr 23 2017

PAUL MCCARTNEY M. Mettler bw color *Sound & Vision* v82 no5 p72 Je 2017

Random Notes color *Rolling Stone* no1298 p22 O 19 2017

Rock's All-Star Weekend D. FRICKE color *Rolling Stone* no1273 p13 N 3 2016

McCartney, Paul, 1942-—Interviews

McCartney Shares His Touring Secrets K. GROW color *Rolling Stone* no1291/1292 p26 Jl 13 2017

McCartney, Stella, 1971-

ALICIA KEYS & STELLA McCARTNEY TEAM UP FOR BREAST CANCER AWARENESS color *Harper's Bazaar* no3657 p202 O 2017

RUNWAY REPORT color *Harper's Bazaar* no3654 p144 Je/Jl 2017

STELLA McCARTNEY P. SYKES color *Vogue* v207 no3 p402 Mr 2017

Women. Power. Love. Stella! color *Glamour* v115 no11 p20 N 2017

McCartney, Stella, 1971-—Interviews

THE NEXT BRITISH INVASION J. von Sothen bw color *Esquire* p62 S 2017

Stella McCARTNEY *Interview* v46 no10 p56 D 2016/Ja 2017

McCarty, Matthew W.

A Few Planes for China: The Birth of The Flying Tigers *Military History* v34 no5 p74 Ja 2018

McCarty, Rosie

Age is just a number *U.S. Catholic* v82 no10 p4 O 2017

It takes a parish color *U.S. Catholic* v82 no5 p23 My 2017

A not so cookie-cutter Christmas color *U.S. Catholic* v81 no12 p33 D 2016

O come, Emmanuel *U.S. Catholic* v81 no12 p4 D 2016

Real life *U.S. Catholic* v82 no4 p4 Ap 2017

McCary, Dave

BRAIN TRUST T. Friend cartoon *New Yorker* v93 no22 p19 Jl 31 2017

Brigsby Bear C. Nashawaty color *Entertainment Weekly* no1476 p46 Ag 4 2017

Dude Nostalgia Done Right S. Zacharek color *Time* v190 no6 p54 Ag 7 2017

McCaslin, Donny

Donny McCaslin's Tenor Sax Solo on 'Faceplant' J. DURSO bw color *Downbeat* v84 no6 p84 Je 2017

The Hot Box chart *Downbeat* v83 no11 p51 N 2016

Mccausland, Jim

Your CHECKLIST color *Sunset* v238 no1 p46 Ja 2017

Your CHECKLIST color *Sunset* v238 no4 p58 Ap 2017

McCavitt, John

The Man Who Captured Washington: Major General Robert Ross and the War of 1812 *Military History* v33 no5 p68 Ja 2017

McCharen, Becca

Our Relationship, in 7 Pictures bw color *Glamour* v114 no11 p128 N 2016

McCharen, Christine

Our Relationship, in 7 Pictures bw color *Glamour* v114 no11 p128 N 2016

McChrystal, Stan

Staying the Course in Afghanistan color *Foreign Affairs* v96 no6 p2 N/D 2017

McChrystal, Stanley A., 1954-

COMBAT CONSULTANT R. KARLGAARD color *Forbes* v200 no4 p26 O 24 2017

McChrystal, Stanley A., 1954-—Interviews

What Companies Can Learn from Military Teams D. McGinn *Harvard Business Review Digital Articles* p2 Ag 6 2015

Mcchrystal Group (Company)

COMBAT CONSULTANT R. KARLGAARD color *Forbes* v200 no4 p26 O 24 2017

McCLAIN, DANI

FIGHTING FOR A HEALTHY BLACK PREGNANCY bw color *Nation* v304 no7 p17 Mr 6 2017

THE FUTURE OF BLM [Cover story] color *Nation* v305 no8 p12 O 9 2017

McClanahan, Fred

COWBOY DOWNHILL color *Spin to Win Rodeo* v21 no1 p16 Mr 2017

McClarnon, Zahn

At Home With... D. BRISBY color *American Cowboy* v23 no6 p16 Ap/My 2017

McClary Groh, Jennifer

Kilogram-scale prexasertib monolactate monohydrate synthesis under continuous-flow CGMP conditions chart diag *Science* v356 no6343 p1144 Je 16 2017

MCCLAUGHRY, JOHN

The Decentralist color *Reason* v49 no1 p66 My 2017

McClay, B. D.

'This Suffering Business' bw *Commonweal* v144 no8 p23 My 5 2017

McCleary, Badir

West Adams J. HERDST *Los Angeles Magazine* p62 My 2017

McClellan, Chris

The No-Mortgage NATURAL COTTAGE *Mother Earth News* no281 p42 Ap/My 2017

McClellan, George Brinton, 1826-1885

MCCLELLAN'S BIG MISS R. Soodalter *MHQ: Quarterly Journal of Military History* v29 no2 p76 Wint 2017

McClellan, Joseph

A Controversial Orientation? JAM color *Advocate* no1091 p111 Je/Jl 2017

McCLELLAND, EDWARD

A BEE IN TRUMP'S BONNET color *Chicago* v66 no5 p25 My 2017

LAST MADIGAN STANDING color *Chicago* v66 no11 p19 N 2017

MR. NICER GUY color *Chicago* v66 no9 p33 S 2017

OBAMA'S CHICAGO BREAKUP cartoon color *Chicago* v66 no1 p23 Ja 2017

McClelland, Grant B.

Rewiring metabolism under oxygen deprivation color *Science* v356 no6335 p248 Ap 21 2017

McCLELLAND, MAC

THE BATHROOM AND THE BALLOT BOX color *Mother Jones* v41 no6 p38 N/D 2016

The Psychedelic Miracle cartoon color *Rolling Stone* no1283 p40 Mr 23 2017

THEY'LL BE HERE TILL THEY DIE *New York Times Magazine* p34 O 1 2017

MCCLELLAND, SUSAN

No Safe Haven *Ms.* v26 no4 p14 Wint 2016

McClenachan, Loren

Committing to socially responsible seafood color *Science* v356 no6341 p912 Je 1 2017

McCleneghan, Bromleigh

Good Christian Sex: Why Chastity Isn't the Only Option—And Other Things the Bible Says about Sex P. Boumgarden color *Christian Century* v133 no21 p48 O 12 2016

Ruined *Christian Century* v134 no7 p38 Mr 29 2017

McClintock, Barbara, 1955-

Emma and Julia Love Ballet *Publishers Weekly* v263 no49 p20 D 7 2016

McClintock, Harry

BIG BARACK CANDY MOUNTAIN C. R. Kesler *Claremont Review of Books* v17 no1 p5 Wint 2016/2017

MCCLINTOCK, TOM

SEDENTARY SENATE *USA Today Magazine* v145 no2864 p22 My 2017

McCLOSKEY, ABBY M.

Moving Beyond the Gender Gap color *National Review* v68 no22

p47 D 5 2016

McCloskey, Deirdre Nansen

AN ECONOMIST GOES TO SHANGHAI color *Reason* v49 no2 p10 Je 2017

THE GREAT ENRICHMENT P. McNamara *Claremont Review of Books* v17 no2 p82 Spr 2017

HOW DO YOU HOLD TOGETHER YOUR TRANS IDENTITY AND YOUR LIFE OF FAITH? color *Christian Century* v134 no2 p22 Ja 18 2017

THE MYTH OF TECHNOLOGICAL UNEMPLOYMENT color *Reason* v49 no4 p8 Ag/S 2017

Rich With Ideas C. WOLF JR. *Weekly Standard* v22 no5 p36 O 10 2016

SEX, SHRINKS, AND THE STATE bw *Reason* v48 no11 p12 Ap 2017

THREE BIG IDEAS: TWO BAD, ONE GOOD cartoon *Reason* v48 no9 p8 F 2017

McCloud River (Calif.)

McCloud Falls, Shasta-Trinity National Forest, California [Cover story] diag *Backpacker* p96 My 2017

McClung, Jen

Whereas *Orion Magazine* v36 no2 p61 Mr/Ap 2017

McClure, Gwen

'First you survive' color *U.S. Catholic* v82 no11 p18 N 2017

Pet-Safe Halloween Treats color *Good Housekeeping* v265 no4 p134 O 2017

McClure, Marissa

Defining quality in visual art education for young children: Building on the position statement of the Early Childhood Art Educators bibl *Arts Education Policy Review* v118 no3 p154 2017

McClure, Nikki

Waiting for High Tide T. Brorby *Orion Magazine* v35 no3 p57 My/Je 2016

McCluskey, Megan

Eddie Redmayne Wants to Make You Believe In Magic Again color *Time* v188 no22-23 p106 N/D 2016

Pop Chart color *Time* v188 no15 p62 O 17 2016

Pop Chart color *Time* v188 no21 p72 N 21 2016

Pop Chart color *Time* v189 no10 p58 Mr 20 2017

Pop Chart color *Time* v189 no21 p66 Je 5 2017

Pop Chart color *Time* v189 no4 p58 F 6 2017

Pop Chart color *Time* v190 no16/17 p110 O 23 2017

Pop Chart color *Time* v190 no7 p54 Ag 21 2017

Things color *Time* v188 no25-26 p20 D 19 2016 Double Issue

The Universe color *Time* v190 no2/3 p76 Jl 10-17 2017

The Walking Dead Deals a Grisly Blow color *Time* v188 no16/17 p91 O 24 2016

What's In Eddie Redmayne's Library color *Time* v188 no22-23 p108 N/D 2016

McCluskey, Mick

ADDITIONAL APPROVAL FOR LEPTOSPIROSIS VACCINE *Equus* no471 p12 D 2016

ADVANCES MADE IN FOAL SURVIVAL RATES color *Equus* no475 p26 Ap 2017

THE BEST WAY TO TREAT SAND COLIC color *Equus* no474 p11 Mr 2017

BEWARE BIOFILM FORMATION color *Equus* no480 p14 S 2017

BLOOD TEST HELPS MONITOR JOINT INFECTIONS color *Equus* no480 p16 S 2017

CHALLENGES OF DETECTING EARLY LAMINITIS *Equus* no482 p14 N 2017

DIET, MORE THAN WEIGHT, CRUCIAL IN INSULIN RESISTANCE color *Equus* no470 p19 N 2016

DISAPPOINTING RESULTS FOR ULCER BLOOD TEST color *Equus* no477 p17 Je 2017

DRUG SHOWS PROMISE IN PREVENTING NEUROLOGICAL COMPLICATION *Equus* no476 p20 My 2017

EATING ON THE GO AIDS WEIGHT LOSS color *Equus* no472 p12 Ja 2017

EFFECTS OF DIET ON ULCER TREATMENT STUDIED color *Equus* no472 p11 Ja 2017

EHV-1 VIABILITY HAS IMPLICATIONS FOR BIOSECURITY color *Equus* no478 p16 Jl 2017

EVIDENCE SUGGESTS EQUINE INFLUENZA VIRUS IS ZOONOTIC color *Equus* no470 p18 N 2016

EYE IMPLANTS CARRY RISKS color *Equus* no481 p13 O 2017

FEED-BASED ALLERGY TREATMENT SHOWS PROMISE color *Equus* no475 p28 Ap 2017

GENE THERAPY FOR LAMINITIS? color diag *Equus* no474 p10 Mr 2017

GENETIC BASIS FOR "TIGER EYE" IDENTIFIED color *Equus* no480 p15 S 2017

GENETIC TEST NOW AVAILABLE FOR "NAKED FOAL" SYNDROME color *Equus* no476 p19 My 2017

GOOD NEWS ABOUT CUTTING HORSE INJURIES color *Equus* no482 p12 N 2017

GOOD NEWS ABOUT LIFE AFTER COLIC SURGERY color *Equus* no476 p18 My 2017

HIGH-TECH BOOST FOR RAINROT DIAGNOSIS color *Equus* no471 p11 D 2016

HIP-SAVING STRATEGIES color *Equus* no471 p16 D 2016

HOW COAT COLOR PREFERENCES CHANGED THROUGH TIME color *Equus* no475 p24 Ap 2017

HOW MUCH DOES DENTAL WORK HELP? color *Equus* no481 p17 O 2017

HOW YOUR HORSE LEARNS BY WATCHING YOU color *Equus* no473 p10 F 2017

HYDRATION VITAL FOR SHIPPING FEVER RECOVERY color *Equus* no477 p18 Je 2017

INJECTABLE ULCER DRUG MAY SOON BE AVAILABLE color *Equus* no478 p17 Jl 2017

KEEP YOUR HANDS CLEAN color *Equus* no480 p18 S 2017

LIDOCAINE NERVE BLOCKS CAN BE TRICKY *Equus* no482 p12 N 2017

A LONG-LASTING EFFECT OF PREMATURITY color *Equus* no480 p14 S 2017

MAINTAIN FITNESS THROUGH CANTERING color *Equus* no477 p16 Je 2017

MORE EVIDENCE THAT HELMETS PROTECT AGAINST BRAIN TRAUMA color *Equus* no478 p16 Jl 2017

NAHMS SNAPSHOT: HOW WE FIGHT FLIES chart color *Equus* no478 p20 Jl 2017

NAHMS SNAPSHOT: HOW WE MANAGE MANURE chart color *Equus* no477 p20 Je 2017

NAHMS SNAPSHOT: WHERE THE BREEDS ARE chart color *Equus* no476 p22 My 2017

NERVE'S ROLE IN HEADSHAKING INVESTIGATED color *Equus* no481 p12 O 2017

NEW DEWORMING AGENT SHOWS PROMISE color *Equus* no473 p11 F 2017

NEW FLY REPELLENT IN THE WORKS color *Equus* no471 p10 D 2016

NEW LIFESTYLE FOR PRZEWALSKI'S HORSES color *Equus* no481 p14 O 2017

NEW TEST FOR TAPEWORMS color *Equus* no481 p14 O 2017

NEW WAY TO ASSESS PAIN color *Equus* no473 p12 F 2017

NIACIN DEFICIENCY RULED OUT AS GRASS SICKNESS CAUSE *Equus* no470 p20 N 2016

NOTHING BORING ABOUT YAWNING color *Equus* no470 p21 N 2016

ORIGINS OF AMBLING HORSES TRACED bw color *Equus* no471 p13 D 2016

OUTCOMES FOR ESOPHAGEAL SURGERY REVIEWED *Equus* no475 p25 Ap 2017

A POSITIVE FOR PEER PRESSURE color *Equus* no471 p12 D 2016

REASSURING FINDINGS ABOUT PREDNISOLONE color *Equus* no476 p18 My 2017

REASSURING STUDY OF CARRIAGE HORSES color *Equus* no475 p25 Ap 2017

SOME SMALL SARCOIDS GO AWAY ON THEIR OWN color *Equus* no473 p11 F 2017

STEM CELLS MAY HELP HEAL SOFT-TISSUE INJURIES AND ARTHRITIS color *Equus* no477 p16 Je 2017

STUDY CONFIRMS EFFECTIVENESS OF THE "SQUEEZE TECHNIQUE" color *Equus* no482 p13 N 2017

STUDY: GAS IS IMPORTANT SIGN IN SAND COLIC CASES *Equus* no481 p12 O 2017

SUSCEPTIBILITY TO SWEET ITCH INVESTIGATED color *Equus* no478 p18 Jl 2017

TRAINING TECHNIQUE HELPS HORSES "TALK" color

Equus no472 p10 Ja 2017
A WAY TO GET MORE FROM HOCK INJECTIONS color *Equus* no472 p12 Ja 2017
WHICH BEDDING HARBORS MORE BACTERIA? color *Equus* no471 p11 D 2016
WHIRLS AND HAIR WHORLS color *Equus* no470 p18 N 2016

McClusky, Jeff
Update Your First Aid Kit N. MONSON color *AARP: The Magazine* v60 no4A p18 Je/Jl 2017

McCollum, Allan
SIGHTLINES color *Art in America* v105 no5 p45 My 2017

McCollum, Sean
30 Cool Things About Cities color *National Geographic Kids* no472 p28 Ag 2017
DOG NABS THIEF *National Geographic Kids* no467 p13 F 2017
Expelling Islamophobia *Education Digest* v82 no8 p14 Ap 2017
MEXICO IMAGE vs. REALITY *New York Times Upfront* v149 no4 p8 O 31 2016

McComas, D. J.
Jupiter's magnetosphere and aurorae observed by the Juno spacecraft during its first polar orbits diag graph *Science* v356 no6340 p826 My 26 2017

MCCOMAS, SUZANNE
THE WALLS ARE BULGING *USA Today Magazine* v145 no2858 p24 N 2016

McComsey, Tim
POWER PLANTS V. Tweed color *Amazing Wellness* v9 no2 p72 Spr 2017

McConaughey, Matthew, 1969-
THE MALIBU MYSTIC [Cover story] M. POTTER color *Esquire* v166 no4 p92 N 2016
THE McCONAISSANCE color diag *Entertainment Weekly* no1477 p39 Ag 11 2017
Timothée CHALAMET M. Mcconaughey *Interview* v47 no5 p42 Je/Jl 2017

MCCONNACHIE, DAVID
Foundations of Belonging *Alternatives Journal (AJ) - Canada's Environmental Voice* v42 no3 p7 2016
Our Team color *Alternatives Journal (AJ) - Canada's Environmental Voice* v42 no3 p56 2016

McConnell, Anna
10 SUCCESSFUL FARMERS: ANNE WHITMAN ONGSTAD *Successful Farming* v115 no8 p20 Je/Jl 2017
10 UP & COMERS: JASON MAUCK *Successful Farming* v115 no8 p40 Je/Jl 2017
BEEF IS BOUNCING BACK *Successful Farming* v114 no10 p31 O 2016
A COMFORTABLY LARGE FARM SHOP *Successful Farming* v115 no5 p25 Mid-Mr 2017
A FARM SHOP ON-THE-GO *Successful Farming* v115 no3 p49 Mid-F 2017
THE GREAT BALANCING ACT *Successful Farming* v115 no5 p26 Mid-Mr 2017
I AM A WOMAN FARMER *Successful Farming* v115 no3 p35 Mid-F 2017
KRYSTA HARDEN *Successful Farming* v115 no3 p8 Mid-F 2017
NEW AND IMPROVED *Successful Farming* v115 no3 p24 Mid-F 2017
ONE MASSIVE MACHINE *Successful Farming* v115 no2 p32 F 2017
RECEIVER REBOOT *Successful Farming* v115 no1 p32 Ja 2017
SEPARATING CLEAN AND DIRTY *Successful Farming* v115 no4 p61 Mr 2017
SHOOT STARTER WITH SEED *Successful Farming* v114 no10 p30 O 2016
SIDEDRESS AND SEED COVER CROPS *Successful Farming* v115 no1 p32 Ja 2017
THE SUCCESSFUL INTERVIEW *Successful Farming* v115 no4 p12 Mr 2017
TAGGED *Successful Farming* v115 no2 p32 F 2017
TERRY BRANSTAND *Successful Farming* v115 no8 p8 Je/Jl 2017
THOUGHTFULLY DESIGNED FARM SHOP *Successful Farming* v115 no2 p57 F 2017
WIRELESS WATCHDOG *Successful Farming* v115 no3 p25 Mid-F 2017

McConnell, Christopher
Research: Political Polarization Is Changing How Americans Work and Shop *Harvard Business Review Digital Articles* p2 My 19 2017

McConnell, Jane
The Company Cultures That Help (or Hinder) Digital Transformation *Harvard Business Review Digital Articles* p2 Ag 28 2015
Tracking the Trends in Bringing Our Own Devices to Work *Harvard Business Review Digital Articles* p2 My 4 2016

McConnell, Jon
Big Daddies chart color *Team Roping Journal* p36 S 2017

McConnell, Kate Drezek
Big Progress in Authentic Assessment, But by Itself Not Enough *Change* v49 no1 p14 Ja/F 2017

McConnell, L.
Fostering reproducibility in industry-academia research color *Science* v357 no6353 p759 Ag 25 2017

McConnell, Michael J.
Intersection of diverse neuronal genomes and neuropsychiatric disease: The Brain Somatic Mosaicism Network color *Science* v356 no6336 p395 Ap 28 2017

McConnell, Mitch, 1942-
FEELING WORSE A. Davidson bw *New Yorker* v93 no19 p17 Jl 3 2017
For the Record color *Time* v188 no27-28 p10 D 26 2016
McConnell's Coup *Nation* v305 no4 p3 Ag 14 2017
Missouri's Political Phenom F. BARNES cartoon color *Weekly Standard* v22 no42 p16 Jl 17 2017
RIP, Repeal and Replace? The GOP Faces a New Crossroads P. Elliott, H. S. Edwards et al color *Time* v190 no5 p13 Jl 31 2017
Trump's Attacks Sow Chaos In Washington Z. J. Miller and A. Altman color *Time* v190 no6 p7 Ag 7 2017
The Vision Thing J. COST color *Weekly Standard* v22 no44 p13 Jl 31 2017

McCONNELL, SCOTT
France at the Epicenter diag *American Conservative* v16 no3 p12 My/Je 2017
Rise of the Alt-Right *American Conservative* v15 no6 p12 N/D 2016

McConnon, Shaun—Finance
The Septuagenarian Whiz Kid A. FELDMAN color *Forbes* v198 no9 p44 D 30 2016

McConville, J. G. (J. Gordon), ca. 1951-
Being Human in God's World: An Old Testament Theology of Humanity color *Publishers Weekly* v263 no45 p26 N 7 2016

McCook, Alison
Cash incentives for papers go global graph *Science* v357 no6351 p541 Ag 11 2017
OUT OF BOUNDS color *Science* v355 no6323 p339 Ja 27 2017

McCord, Patty
Meaningful Work Beats Over-the-Top Perks Every Time *Harvard Business Review Digital Articles* p2 F 18 2016

McCord, Patty—Interviews
What to Do If You Feel Stuck in the Wrong Career D. Rousmaniere *Harvard Business Review Digital Articles* p2 Ap 6 2015

McCord, T.
Seasonal exposure of carbon dioxide ice on the nucleus of comet 67P/Churyumov-Gerasimenko bibl bw graph *Science* v354 no6319 p1563 D 23 2016

McCormack, Eric, 1963-
STREAMING A. D'ARMINIO *TV Guide* p42 D 19 2016
Will & Grace Hasn't Changed Much. And That's Just Fine D. D'addario color *Time* v190 no15 p57 O 16 2017
Will & Grace L. Rice, N. Abrams et al color *Entertainment Weekly* no1482/1483 p80 S 22 2017

MCCORMACK, J. W.
The Shortlist *New York Times Book Review* p30 N 6 2016
SINGING THE BLUES bw color *Publishers Weekly* v263 no51 p117 D 12 2016

McCormack, Joe
Advice for Dealing with a Long-Winded Leader *Harvard Business Review Digital Articles* p2 Ja 9 2015

MCCORMACK, JOHN
Chilly Trade Winds color *Weekly Standard* v22 no21 p10 F 6 2017
Cracked Foundation color *Weekly Standard* v22 no34 p8 My 15 2017

Drawing Boundaries *Weekly Standard* v22 no25 p8 Mr 6 2017

Foxconned? cartoon *Weekly Standard* v22 no48 p17 S 4 2017

The 'Hail Mary' Candidate color *Weekly Standard* v22 no9 p13 N 7 2016

Moore Unmoored color *Weekly Standard* v23 no5 p12 O 9 2017

Obamacare Lives cartoon *Weekly Standard* v22 no44 p9 Jl 31 2017

Prime-Time Conspiracy Theory [Cover story] color *Weekly Standard* v22 no37 p11 Je 5 2017

A Promise the GOP Can Still Keep *Weekly Standard* v22 no46 p9 Ag 14 2017

'Too Complicated'? color *Weekly Standard* v22 no23 p12 F 20 2017

Which Side Is Gen. Mattis On? color *Weekly Standard* v22 no27 p15 Mr 20 2017

McCormack, Mike

The Day the Dead Come Back M. SEIDEL color *Publishers Weekly* v264 no31 p32 Jl 31 2017

McCormack, Phillipa C.

Biodiversity redistribution under climate change: Impacts on ecosystems and human well-being color *Science* v355 no6332 p1389 Mr 31 2017

McCormack, Terri—Interviews

Haven Custom Furnishing P. Marquis *New Orleans Homes & Lifestyles* v20 no2 p84 Spr 2017

McCORMACK, WIN

Created Equal color *New Republic* v248 no8/9 p74 Ag/S 2017

The Populist Ploy il *New Republic* v248 no3 p8 Mr 2017

McCORMALLY, KEVIN

SOCIAL SECURITY: The Real Crisis cartoon graph *Kiplinger's Personal Finance* v71 no6 p26 Je 2017

MCCORMICK, BILL

AN INTERVIEW WITH ROD DREHER color *America* v216 no8 p24 Ap 17 2017

McCormick, Colin

Soonish *Science* v357 no6355 p965 S 8 2017

McCormick, John

All the President's LLCs color *Bloomberg Businessweek* no4534 p24 Ag 14 2017

A Georgia Election Is a TV Ad Bonanza bw *Bloomberg Businessweek* no4527 p50 Je 19 2017

Illinois Budget Woes Head From Bad to Junk graph map *Bloomberg Businessweek* no4529 p36 Jl 3 2017

The Queen of Trump Swag color *Bloomberg Businessweek* no4528 p36 Je 26 2017

McCormick, Katherine Dexter, 1875-1967

PATRON OF THE PILL S. RICHARDSON *American History* v51 no6 p24 F 2017

McCormick, Liz Capo

Is the Dollar in a Trump Slump? graph *Bloomberg Businessweek* no4533 p30 Ag 7 2017

Mnuchin Ponders Locking in Low Rates *Bloomberg Businessweek* no4521 p39 My 8 2017

Mccormick, Maureen

A Wellspring of Comfort color *Time* v188 no24 p70 D 12 2016

McCormick, Norman J.

Paul Frederick Zweifel *Physics Today* v70 no8 p73 Ag 2017

McCormick, Sabrina

Science in litigation, the third branch of U.S. climate policy graph *Science* v357 no6355 p979 S 8 2017

MCCORMICK, TY

HIGHWAY THROUGH HELL color *Foreign Policy* no226 p34 S/O 2017

McCoughtry, Angel, 1986-

Angel McCoughtry J. Crelin color *Current Biography* v78 no6 p64 Je 2017

McCourt, D. F.

Biosimilars, Patient Choice, and Health Care Sustainability color *Maclean's* v130 no6 p53 Jl 2017

Canada Leads by Example with World's First National HPV Prevention Week color *Maclean's* v130 no6 p76 Jl 2017

CANADA'S ELITE VISION-IMPAIRED ATHLETES ARE RAISING AWARENESS FOR UNIVERSAL EYE HEALTH bw *Maclean's* v129 no42 p33 O 24 2016

CANNABIS AND ITS ROLE IN CANCER CARE bw *Maclean's* v130 no6 p83 Jl 2017

Collaboration Is Essential to Revitalizing Health Care in Canada map *Maclean's* v130 no6 p58 Jl 2017

COPD CANADA'S EPIDEMIC *Maclean's* v129 no47 p46 N 28 2016

Finding the Best Path with Incurable Breast Cancer bw color *Maclean's* v130 no6 p80 Jl 2017

GREEN LEADERSHIP GROWING AMONG CANADIAN BUSINESSES color *Maclean's* v129 no50 p40 D 19 2016

HOW HIGH-TECH KITCHENS ARE LEVERAGING THE INTERNET OF THINGS color *Maclean's* v129 no40 p21 O 10 2016

HOW NEW CLOUD TECH IS CHANGING THE FACE OF DIABETES MANAGEMENT *Maclean's* v129 no48/49 p44 D 5 2016

Innovations Improving Lives in Canada's Hemophilia Community *Maclean's* v130 no9 p33 O 2017

PNEUMONIA color *Maclean's* v129 no50 p55 D 19 2016

Probiotics: Good Bacteria and Your Digestive Health cartoon color *Maclean's* v129 no48/49 p80 D 5 2016

Revolutionizing Adult Leukemia Treatment with Targeted Therapies color *Maclean's* v130 no6 p77 Jl 2017

TAKING THE INFORMATION AGE ON THE ROAD color *Maclean's* v129 no51/52 p15 D 26 2016

THE TRANSITION OF CANNABIS TO MAINSTREAM PAIN MEDICATION *Maclean's* v130 no3 p48 Ap 2017

When High Drug Costs Hurt Private Insurers color *Maclean's* v130 no6 p56 Jl 2017

With Rare Diseases, a New Treatment Can Change Everything color *Maclean's* v130 no6 p54 Jl 2017

McCowan, Molly

Change & Continuity color *American Craft* v77 no3 p72 Je/Jl 2017

Hand in Hand color map *American Craft* v76 no6 p82 D 2016-Ja 2017

McCown, Josh, 1979-

WHAT IF? ... A JOURNEYMAN QB'S DESPERATE PASS HADN'T SHAPED THE 2004 NFL DRAFT? D. Greene and J. Feldman color *Sports Illustrated* v126 no11 p48 Ap 17-24 2017

McCoy, Alfred W.

In the Shadows of the American Century: The Rise and Decline of US Global Power color *Publishers Weekly* v264 no31 p77 Jl 31 2017

McCoy, Anne B.

Spectroscopic snapshots of the proton-transfer mechanism in water bibl diag graph *Science* v354 no6316 p1131 D 2 2016

McCoy, Bill

The King of Rum Row C. J. Doane bw *Sail* v48 no1 p88 Ja 2017

McCoy, Elin

Bordeaux's Fresh Fantasy bw color *Bloomberg Businessweek* no4538 p55 S 18 2017

McCoy, Jennifer

Postmasters D. Markus color *Art in America* v105 no1 p79 Ja 2017

McCOY, JENNY

Magic Bullets color *Runner's World* v52 no4 p56 My 2017

McCoy, Michel

Platforms, Codes, and Facilities Form a Three-Pronged Supercomputing Strategy *Science & Technology Review* p3 Mr 2017

McCoy, Mike

Posthole color *Powder* v45 no4 p146 D 2016

McCoy, Shirlee

Bittersweet: Home Sweet Home, Book 3 *Publishers Weekly* v264 no24 p48 Je 12 2017

McCoy, Victoria

The Tully Monster Mystery E. BETZ color *Discover* v38 no1 p56 Ja/F 2017

MCCRACKEN, BRETT

OLD, BORING WAYS OF DOING CHURCH cartoon color *Christianity Today* v61 no1 p69 Ja/F 2017

McCRACKEN, ELIZABETH

FRANK SINATRA JR. & RICCI MARTIN *New York Times Magazine* p26 D 25 2016

McCracken, John

GOINGS ON ABOUT TOWN color *New Yorker* v93 no2 p7 F 27 2017

McCracken, Ruth

Eliminating poverty in the 21st century: using entrepreneurship,

innovation, and technology to help the poor help themselves H.
O'Lawrence color *Monthly Labor Review* p1 Mr 2017

MCCRACKEN, SANDRA

Our Two Spiritual Time Zones *Christianity Today* v61 no7 p30
S 2017

McCraine, Kathy

The Boss Lady's View bw *American Cowboy* v23 no5 p10 F/Mr
2017

McCRARY, LEWIS

Bring Back Penn Station *American Conservative* v15 no6 p36
N/D 2016

Golden Age of Classicism: Notre Dame's architecture school is
rebuilding the traditional city il *American Conservative* v16 no4
p48 Jl/Ag 2017

McCrary, Meagan

consider this *Yoga Journal* no293 p12 Ag 2017

Poses of the month [Cover story] color *Yoga Journal* no293 p53
Ag 2017

McCray, Chirlane

The Meaning of Michelle bw color *Glamour* v114 no12 p198 D
2016

McCRAY, CRYSTA PARKS

The Way Forward color *O, The Oprah Magazine* p18 My 2017

Mccrea, Megan

BEST OF THE WEST color *Sunset* v237 no5 p11 N 2016

BEST OF THE WEST color *Sunset* v238 no3 p7 Mr 2017

POWDER PLAY chart color diag *Sunset* v238 no1 p22 Ja 2017

McCreary, Kelly

The Cast of Grey's Anatomy H. Goldblatt, A. Writing et al color
Entertainment Weekly no1439 p23 N 11 2016

McCreary, Lew

How to Handle Your First Meeting With a New Boss *Harvard
Business Review Digital Articles* p2 D 10 2014

McCreight, Matthew

Stop Trying to Please Everyone *Harvard Business Review Digital
Articles* p2 Jl 29 2015

McCrory, Cass

When Less Is More Money F. TORABI cartoon *O, The Oprah
Magazine* p40 Mr 2017

McCrory, Pat, 1956-

SOCIAL ISSUES A. Greenblatt *Governing* v30 no4 p37 Ja 2017

McCue, Kevin

New Zealand earthquake rattles experts color *Science* v354
no6314 p808 N 18 2016

McCue, T. J.

3D Printing Is Changing the Way We Think *Harvard Business Review Digital Articles* p2 Jl 21 2015

McCuistion, Karen

CONFORMATION CLINIC color *Horse & Rider* v56 no2 p29
F 2017

MCCULLAR, EMILY

REVENGE OF THE FILM NERDS *Texas Monthly* v45 no7 p70
Jl 2017

McCuller, Megan I.

Tsunami-driven rafting: Transoceanic species dispersal and implications for marine biogeography color graph *Science* v357
no6358 p1402 S 29 2017

McCullers, Carson, 1917-1967

The Poet of Freakiness [Cover story] J. C. Oates bw *New York
Review of Books* v64 no14 p78 S 28 2017

McCULLOUGH, J. J.

Mr. Wonderful Goes to Ottawa? color *National Review* v69 no3
p25 F 20 2017

McCULLOUGH, ROSS

THIRD PARTY REVOLUTION color *America* v215 no12 p24
O 24 2016

McCULLUM, JENNIFER

Seattle color *Martha Stewart Living* p140 O 2017

McCusker, James K.

Photosensitized, energy transfer-mediated organometallic catalysis through electronically excited nickel(II) bibl diag graph *Science* v355 no6323 p380 Ja 27 2017

McCusker, Lynne B.

Electron diffraction and the hydrogen atom bibl diag *Science* v355
no6321 p136 Ja 13 2017

McCutcheon, Patti

WPRA MOVES TO WELCOME 18 & UNDER ROPERS C. Toy
color *Spin to Win Rodeo* v20 no12 p28 F 2017

McDaniel, Gary

French Court A. Aguillard color *Southern Living* v52 no5 p15 My
2017

McDaniel, JoBeth

Easy-Peasy color *AARP: The Magazine* v59 no2A p70 F/Mr 2016

McDargh, John

Patriotism in the pews color *U.S. Catholic* v82 no11 p5 N 2017

McDavid, Connor, 1997-

The Arrival A. Prewitt color *Sports Illustrated* v126 no7 p70 Mr
6 2017

McDean, Craig

POLAROIDS BY WARHOL color *GQ: Gentlemen's Quarterly*
v97 no4 p138 Ap 2017

McDERMOT, JIM

HEAVEN HELP US color *America* v215 no14 p37 N 7 2016

McDermott, Alice

Binding Wounds N. RIPATRAZONE color *National Review* v69
no19 p55 O 16 2017

Desired Things *Commonweal* v143 no18 p24 N 11 2016

Grace and Gumption In Irish-Catholic Brooklyn S. Begley color
Time v190 no13 p67 O 2 2017

Illuminations *Commonweal* v144 no12 p26 Jl 7 2017

In the old neighborhoods of Brooklyn, Sister knows best J. Shank
graph *America* v217 no6 p52 S 18 2017

Mea Culpa: A Brooklyn convent provides a fragile refuge from
a family's shame M. GORDON *New York Times Book Review*
p11 O 8 2017

McDermott, Amy

REBUILDING Reefs cartoon color *Science News* v190 no9 p18
O 29 2016

SENTINELS OF FOREST HEALTH [Cover story] color graph
map *Science News* v190 no11 p20 N 26 2016

McDermott, Bill

SAP's CEO on Being the American Head of a German Multinational bw graph img *Harvard Business Review* v94 no11 p35
N 2016

McDermott, Charlie

THE MIDDLE A. D'Arminio *TV Guide* v65 no43 p28 O 16 2017

McDermott, Fergal

Red squirrels in the British Isles are infected with leprosy bacilli
bibl color diag map *Science* v354 no6313 p744 N 11 2016

McDermott, Gerald R.

Christian Zionism color *Christian Century* v134 no20 p6 S 27
2017

McDermott, Jason

Drawing connections color *Science* v356 no6343 p1202 Je 16
2017

McDermott, Jim

At Home in a Strange Land color *America* v216 no4 p28 F 20
2017

A Concrete Vision *America* v216 no1 p11 Ja 2 2017

A drive to thrive: energy and innovation in the Catholic schools of
Los Angeles color *America* v217 no7 p16 O 2 2017

Forsaken at the Border? *America* v215 no11 p11 O 17 2016

The Leave-Taking of Jesus Christ (and Richard Simmons) color
America v216 no8 p49 Ap 17 2017

A mass murder every day *America* v216 no3 p46 F 6 2017

Our Election, Our President *America* v215 no18 p18 D 5 2016

San Diego's Bishop McElroy encourages Catholics to be hope-
filled 'disruptors' color *America* v216 no6 p16 Mr 20 2017

TIDINGS OF GREAT JOY *America* v215 no19 p29 D 19 2016

With Kimmy Schmidt in the land of the happy fools color *America*
v217 no2 p48 Jl 24 2017

Mcdermott, Nancie

LOST PIES OF THE SOUTH color *Southern Living* v52 no11
p104 N 2017

McDermott, Shane

The Big Pictures: CANYON DE CHELLY *Arizona Highways* v93
no10 p16 O 2017

McDermott, Shane—Interviews

Q&A: Shane McDermott *Arizona Highways* v93 no3 p9 Mr 2017

McDermott, W. P.

Selective oxidative dehydrogenation of propane to propene using
boron nitride catalysts bibl diag graph *Science* v354 no6319

p1570 D 23 2016

MCDEVITT, ANDREW L.

Insights into Student Gains from Undergraduate Research Using Pre- and Post-Assessments *BioScience* v66 no12 p1070 D 1 2016

McDevitt, Kim—Interviews

POWER PLANTS M. FARRAR color *Muscle & Performance* v9 no6 p30 Je 2017

McDonagh, Martin

ALLIES H. ALS cartoon *New Yorker* v92 no47 p74 Ja 30 2017

McDonald, Arthur B., 1943-

Arthur B. McDonald R. Means *Current Biography* v78 no4 p57 Ap 2017

McDonald, Brenda

SIMPLE LIVING in Santa Barbara B. D. COLEMAN chart color *Arts & Crafts Homes & the Revival* v11 no5 p38 Wint 2017

McDonald, Brien

BookCon 2017: More of the Same, but Better L. HARTMAN color *Publishers Weekly* v264 no20 p(Sp)32 My 15 2017

Finding the Right Balance J. Milliot color *Publishers Weekly* v264 no24 p5 Je 12 2017

McDONALD, COBY

His Room-Size Computer Plays Tic-Tac-Toe color *Popular Science* v288 no6 p98 N/D 2016

Zero-Casualty Mine Sweeping cartoon color *Popular Science* p82 Ja/F 2017

McDonald, David

Single-cell RNA-seq reveals new types of human blood dendritic cells, monocytes, and progenitors color *Science* v356 no6335 p283 Ap 21 2017

McDonald, Duff

Profit or Loss: How Harvard Business School has reshaped American capitalism J. B. STEWART *New York Times Book Review* p11 Ap 30 2017

The West Point of Capitalism E. McCarraher color *Commonweal* v114 no14 p26 S 8 2017

McDonald, Erroll

Erroll McDonald D. Patrick color *Publishers Weekly* v264 no30 p8 Jl 24 2017

McDonald, Gary

OUR LIFE WITH Arabian Horses *Arabian Horse World* v57 no3 p18 D 2016

McDonald, Jan

Biodiversity redistribution under climate change: Impacts on ecosystems and human well-being color *Science* v355 no6332 p1389 Mr 31 2017

McDonald, Marie

Hollywood's ORIGINAL GONE GIRL J. McGovern color *Entertainment Weekly* no1485 p30 O 6 2017

MARIE IN THE MOVIES J. McGovern color *Entertainment Weekly* no1485 p34 O 6 2017

McDonald, Mark J.

A selective insecticidal protein from Pseudomonas for controlling corn rootworms bibl chart graph *Science* v354 no6312 p634 N 4 2016

McDonald, Michael

Jagdeep Bachher color *Bloomberg Businessweek* no4538 p64 S 18 2017

Little Good News For the Little Ivies graph *Bloomberg Businessweek* no4505 p41 D 26 2016

No Use for Old School Ties color *Bloomberg Businessweek* no4526 p32 Je 12 2017

Research: Executives Who Flatter Their CEOs Are More Likely to Criticize Them to the Press bw *Harvard Business Review Digital Articles* p2 Ap 5 2017

McDonald, Rick

California ease B. D. COLEMAN color diag *Arts & Crafts Homes & the Revival* v12 no2 p58 Spr 2017

McDONALD, ROBBIE A.

Using Social Network Measures in Wildlife Disease Ecology, Epidemiology, and Management *BioScience* v67 no3 p245 Mr 2017

McDonald, Robert, 1953-

A Transformation Is Underway at U.S. Veterans Affairs. We Got an Inside Look R. W. Buell *Harvard Business Review Digital Articles* p2 D 22 2014

McDonald, Siobhán—Exhibitions

Deep exposures D. Dixon color *Science* v355 no6328 p916 Mr 3 2017

McDonald, Steve

The Line King T. JOKINEN cartoon *Walrus* v14 no6 p12 Jl/Ag 2017

McDonald-Gibson, Charlotte

The E.U.'s Chief Executive on Trump, Populism and Russia color *Time* v189 no7/8 p19 F 27 2017

Ever More Divided Union color *Time* v189 no10 p36 Mr 20 2017

The Next Fake-News War color *Time* v190 no10/11 p48 S 18 2017

Next Generation Leaders color *Time* v190 no16/17 p74 O 23 2017

McDonald's Corp.

BEHIND THE BUNS S. WATTS bw *Chicago* v65 no11 p26 N 2016

BIG MAC ATTACK C. Suddath color *Bloomberg Businessweek* no4508 p62 Ja 23 2017

McDonald's and the Challenges of a Modern Supply Chain S. New *Harvard Business Review Digital Articles* p2 F 4 2015

McDonald's Has to Do More than Manipulate Its Stock Price W. Lazonick, M. Hopkins et al *Harvard Business Review Digital Articles* p2 My 14 2015

Milestones *Time* v188 no20 p11 N 14 2016

McDonald's Corp.—History

Putting the Fast In Fast Food E. Berman color *Time* v189 no3 p53 Ja 30 2017

McDonel, Patrick

Xist recruits the X chromosome to the nuclear lamina to enable chromosome-wide silencing bibl graph *Science* v354 no6311 p468 O 28 2016

MCDONELL-PARRY, AMELIA

Janet Mock color *Rolling Stone* no1295 p42 S 7 2017

McDonnell, Jeffrey J.

Paper writing gone Hollywood cartoon *Science* v355 no6320 p102 Ja 6 2017

The sustainable scientist color *Science* v357 no6356 p1202 S 15 2017

McDonnell, Mary-Hunter

It's Harder to Empathize with People If You've Been in Their Shoes *Harvard Business Review Digital Articles* p2 O 20 2015

McDonnell, Patrick

Tek color *Publishers Weekly* v263 no49 p41 D 7 2016

McDonnell, Peter J.—Interviews

Save Your Eyesight G. DEGROOT REDFORD color *AARP: The Magazine* v60 no2A p26 F/Mr 2017

McDonough, Frank, 1957-

Jackboots on the Ground P. FRITZSCHE *New York Times Book Review* p21 Mr 12 2017

McDonough, James Lee

FAITHFUL AND HONORABLE M. T. Owens *Claremont Review of Books* v17 no2 p74 Spr 2017

The Hell General Sherman Made S. DONOGHUE bw *American Conservative* v15 no6 p48 N/D 2016

McDonough, Jill

My Sister Wants to Buy My Dad A Drone for Father's Day *New York Times Magazine* p22 Ap 23 2017

McDonough, Jimmy

Soul Survivor: A Biography of Al Green *Publishers Weekly* v264 no26 p171 Je 26 2017

Mcdonough, John

1917 [Cover story] bw color *Downbeat* v84 no1 p27 Ja 2017

Bohemian Rhapsodies color *Downbeat* v84 no4 p67 Ap 2017

Buddy Rich bw *Downbeat* v84 no1 p42 Ja 2017

Code Noir color *Downbeat* v84 no4 p49 Ap 2017

Ella Fitzgerald bw *Downbeat* v84 no1 p38 Ja 2017

GEORGE GERSHWIN: HERE TO STAY bw *Downbeat* v84 no8 p38 Ag 2017

Harlem On My Mind color *Downbeat* v83 no11 p49 N 2016

The Hot Box chart *Downbeat* v84 no2 p71 F 2017

The Hot Box chart *Downbeat* v84 no5 p51 My 2017

The Hot Box chart *Downbeat* v84 no7 p49 Jl 2017

The Many Rosebuds of Citizen Bix color *Downbeat* v84 no5 p68 My 2017

Sassy's Story color *Downbeat* v84 no9 p72 S 2017

Sinatra Keeps on Ticking color *Downbeat* v84 no8 p79 Ag 2017

Unlimited 1 color *Downbeat* v84 no2 p69 F 2017

McDonough, Myles

CRACK M. MCDONOUGH *Saturday Evening Post* v289 no1 p62 Ja/F 2017

FRESH BEGINNINGS S. Slon *Saturday Evening Post* v289 no1 p5 Ja/F 2017

PROFILES 2017 GREAT AMERICAN FICTION CONTEST *Saturday Evening Post* v289 no1 p68 Ja/F 2017

McDonough, William

HOW CITIES COULD SAVE US color *Scientific American* v317 no1 p44 Jl 2017

McDormand, Frances, 1957-

The Natural: Frances McDormand has built a career, and a passionate fan base, playing supporting roles; now, at 60, she has become an unconventional star J. Kisner *New York Times Magazine* p44 O 8 2017

McDormand, Frances, 1957—Interviews

FRANCES McDORMAND IN Three Billboards Outside Ebbing, Missouri J. McGovern color *Entertainment Weekly* no1478 / 1479 p66 Ag 18-25 2017

McDOUGAL, DARRON

BIG GAME, SMALL BUDGETS color *Outdoor Life* v224 no8 pH1 O 2017

MAKE THIS YOUR FUNNEST DEER SEASON EVER cartoon color *Outdoor Life* v224 no8 p35 O 2017

McDougall, Amy

Help Your Team Spend Time on the Right Things *Harvard Business Review Digital Articles* p2 O 23 2014

MCDOUGALL, JESSE

CARBON FARMING WILL (HELP) SAVE THE PLANET color *Rodale's Organic Life* v3 no1 p68 Ja 2017

McDougall, Walter

Nation-Building's Siren Song D. E. SANGER *New York Times Book Review* p8 Ja 1 2017

That Old-Time Civil Religion D. MCCARTHY color *Reason* v49 no2 p64 Je 2017

The Tragedy of Foreign Policy: Walter McDougall produces another gem of a book A. J. BACEVICH *American Conservative* v16 no4 p10 Jl/Ag 2017

McDougall, Walter A.

American Civil Religion *Claremont Review of Books* v17 no3 p6 Summ 2017

NEITHER AMERICAN, NOR CIVIL, NOR A RELIGION D. P. Goldman *Claremont Review of Books* v17 no2 p64 Spr 2017

Remaking the World R. Munch bw *Commonweal* v144 no1 p34 Ja 6 2017

The Tragedy of U.S. Foreign Policy: How America's Civil Religion Betrayed the National Interest *Publishers Weekly* v263 no43 p72 O 24 2016

MCDOWALL, KERILIE

Dispatches from the Great White North color *Downbeat* v84 no7 p53 Jl 2017

Mcdowell, Coleman

BY THE NUMBERS color *Golf Magazine* v59 no4 p84 Ap 2017

McDowell, Cyd Raftus

Contributors color *InStyle* v23 no12 p24 N 2016

McDowell, Erin Jeanne

The Fearless Baker: Simple Secrets for Baking Like a Pro color *Publishers Weekly* v264 no40 p130 O 2 2017

McDowell, Linda

Who Had It So Good? L. Delap *History Today* v67 no3 p56 Mr 2017

McDowell, Malcolm

LIFE ON A TORPEDO BOAT *MHQ: Quarterly Journal of Military History* v29 no2 p84 Wint 2017

McDowell, Marta

The World of Laura Ingalls Wilder: The Frontier Landscapes That Inspired the Little House Books *Publishers Weekly* v264 no20 p52 My 15 2017

McDowell County (W. Va.)—Economic conditions

STUCK R. BAILEY bw color *Reason* v48 no8 p18 Ja 2017

McDowell County (W. Va.)—Social conditions

STUCK R. BAILEY bw color *Reason* v48 no8 p18 Ja 2017

MCELHANY, SEAN

r.s.v.p bw color *Bon Appetit* v62 no7 p12 Jl 2017

McElhearn, Kirk

Apple Music in iTunes just got more enjoyable and easier to use color *Macworld - Digital Edition* v33 no11 p147 N 2016

Apple's confusing method of device authorization and association bw color *Macworld - Digital Edition* v34 no6 p14 Je 2017

Ask the iTunes Guy: A look at new features in iTunes 12.6 cartoon color *Macworld - Digital Edition* v34 no4 p101 My 2017

Ask the iTunes Guy cartoon diag *Macworld - Digital Edition* p108 Ap 2017

Ask the iTunes Guy: iTunes libraries on the new MacBook Pro cartoon color *Macworld - Digital Edition* p116 Mr 2017

Ask the iTunes Guy: Your questions about the iOS 10 Music app cartoon color *Macworld - Digital Edition* v33 no11 p151 N 2016

Feature: Ask the iTunes Guy cartoon color *Macworld - Digital Edition* p102 Ja 2017

Feature: Help Desk color *Macworld - Digital Edition* p82 Ja 2017

The future of the Finder color *Macworld - Digital Edition* v34 no9 p11 S 2017

Hackintosh: Build a DIY Mac mini color *Macworld - Digital Edition* v34 no8 p16 Ag 2017

Hey, Apple Fixed This! color *Macworld - Digital Edition* v34 no8 p24 Ag 2017

How to personalize your own radio stations in Apple Music color *Macworld - Digital Edition* v34 no6 p120 Je 2017

How to rip DVDs and Blu-ray discs with MakeMKV and HandBrake color *Macworld - Digital Edition* v34 no4 p105 My 2017

No Internet connection? Be prepared for iTunes to drive you crazy color *Macworld - Digital Edition* p113 Mr 2017

NUANCE DRAGON PROFESSIONAL INDIVIDUAL FOR MAC 6.0: BETTER PERFORMANCE AND ACCURACY cartoon color *Macworld - Digital Edition* v33 no11 p43 N 2016

Timing 2.0 review: Mac software for professionals to track billable time color *Macworld - Digital Edition* p83 Je 13 2017

TripMode 2 review: Utility manages, blocks, and caps macOS Internet use color *Macworld - Digital Edition* v34 no8 p106 Ag 2017

McElheran, Kristina

The Rise of Data-Driven Decision Making Is Real but Uneven *Harvard Business Review Digital Articles* p2 F 3 2016

MCELIECE, JESSIKA ANSPACH

FOREIGN FOODS *Dance Magazine* v91 no4 p50 Ap 2017

McElmurray, Bruce

AGING GRACEFULLY on the Homestead *Mother Earth News* no280 p34 F/Mr 2017

Country Lore *Mother Earth News* no281 p84 Ap/My 2017

McElroy, David

Discussion *Smithsonian* v48 no4 p6 Jl/Ag 2017

McElroy, Mark W.

A Better Scorecard for Your Company's Sustainability Efforts *Harvard Business Review Digital Articles* p2 D 10 2015

McElroy, Robert W.

San Diego's Bishop McElroy encourages Catholics to be hope-filled 'disruptors' J. McDermott color *America* v216 no6 p16 Mr 20 2017

The Soul of Our Nation [Cover story] color *America* v216 no3 p18 F 6 2017

McElwee, John

The Art of Selling Movies J. Stewart bw *Film Comment* v53 no1 p92 Ja/F 2017

MCELWEE, PAMELA

Vietnam's Urgent Task: Adapting to Climate Change *Current History* v116 no791 p223 S 2017

McEnroe, John, 1959—Interviews

John McENROE A. Belth color *Esquire* p104 Ag 2017

McEntyre, John

Varieties of Gifts: Multiplicity and the Well-Lived Pastoral Life *Christian Century* v133 no24 p38 N 23 2016

McEntyre, Marilyn Chandler

Denying to the Grave: Why We Ignore the Facts that Will Save Us *Christian Century* v134 no9 p35 Ap 26 2017

McEvoy, Trish

BEAUTY LESSONS FROM AMAZING-LOOKING WOMEN [Cover story] G. Way color *Redbook* p38 Mr 2017

McEwan, Ian, 1942-

BABY HAMLET J. BIGGS il *Nation* v33 no21 p37 N 21 2016

It's Cold Outside G. HILLARD *Weekly Standard* v22 no7 p34 O 24 2016

Nutshell H. SCHNEIDER *Humanist* v77 no1 p40 Ja/F 2017

McEwen, Adam

Provocative Statements J. L. BELCOVE color *Architectural Digest* v74 no2 p22 F 2017

McFadden, Craig
How Streaming Is Changing Music (Again) *Harvard Business Review Digital Articles* p2 D 12 2016

McFadden, Jonathan
Although Small, Markets Have Been Expanding for GE Crops With Traits That Increase Nutrient Content or Improve Taste *Amber Waves: The Economics of Food, Farming, Natural Resources, & Rural America* p19 Ag 2017

McFadden, Joshua
In the SUNSET GARDEN color *Sunset* v238 no3 p38 Mr 2017
spring awakening E. Johnson and J. Mcfadden color *Sunset* v238 no4 p76 Ap 2017

McFadden, L. A.
Localized aliphatic organic material on the surface of Ceres bibl graph *Science* v355 no6326 p719 F 17 2017

McFadden, Reginald
I PARDONED A CONVICT WHO KILLED AGAIN M. S. Singel color *America* v217 no3 p34 Ag 7 2017

McFadden, Tatyana, 1989-
TATYANA MCFADDEN L. EMERY color *Runner's World* v52 no1 p86 Ja/F 2017
Tatyana McFadden M. Hagan color *Current Biography* v78 no3 p59 Mr 2017

McFarlan, F. Warren
China Still Isn't Ready to Be a True Global Leader *Harvard Business Review Digital Articles* p2 Ja 5 2015

McFarland, Billy
Pants on Fyre P. Mosendz, K. Bhasin et al color *Bloomberg Businessweek* no4524 p33 My 29 2017

MCFARLAND, CYNTHIA
Splash in the Sunshine State color *Trail Rider* v29 no3 p50 Ap 2017

McFARLAND, DENNIS
Darkspur *American Scholar* v86 no2 p91 Spr 2017

McFarland, Erika
THE STORIES WE TELL C. Paxton cartoon *Louisiana Life* v37 no2 p50 N/D 2016

MCFARLAND, K. M.
BIRTH OF A MARTIAN cartoon *Wired* v24 no12 p34 D 2016
CHOOSE YOUR OWN SCI-FI ADVENTURE cartoon chart *Wired* v25 no3 p28 Mr 2017
WISH LIST 2016 color *Wired* v24 no12 p45 D 2016

McFarland, Kim
NORTHLAKE MALL 1993 T. WHEATLEY *Atlanta* v57 no6 p144 O 2017

McFARLAND, RON
The Beautiful Game: Coming at UI from Everywhere *Idaho Magazine* v16 no7 p48 Ap 2017
BOOKS ALL OVER *Idaho Magazine* v16 no11 p40 Ag 2017

McFarland, Sabrina
We Say Goodbye to One of Our Own color *Entertainment Weekly* no1480 p3 S 1 2017

McFarland, Sarah E.
Producing Predators: Wolves, Work, and Conquest in the Northern Rockies *American Indian Quarterly* v41 no3 p289 Summ 2017

McFarland, Walter
Managers in the Digital Age Need to Stay Human *Harvard Business Review Digital Articles* p2 Je 17 2015

McFarlane, Fiona
GOD TALK WITH IRONY D. SCHARPER *America* v215 no15 p34 N 14 2016

McFarlane, Sheldon
50 SECONDS FROM DEATH R. KIENER color *Reader's Digest* v189 no1131 p88 Je 2017

McFate, Sean
Deep Black *Publishers Weekly* v264 no23 p30 Je 5 2017

McFaul, Michael A.
Allies First, Mr. President *Hoover Digest: Research & Opinion on Public Policy* no1 p77 Wint 2017
Break Up the Bromance: Just getting along with Russia isn't going to be good enough. If the new administration wants a "reset" of its own, it will need to demonstrate clarity and strength *Hoover Digest: Research & Opinion on Public Policy* no2 p86 Spr 2017
Peace as Cold as Siberia *Hoover Digest: Research & Opinion on*
Public Policy no4 p110 Fall 2016
"There's No Optimism": Hoover fellow Michael A. McFaul, former ambassador to Moscow, reflects on fading democratic hopes for Russia T. Varadarajan *Hoover Digest: Research & Opinion on Public Policy* no3 p97 Summ 2017

MCFERRAN, MEGHAN
Strong and Spirited: What it takes to be a member of a college dance team *Dance Magazine* v91 no10 p44 O 2017

McFetridge, Geoff
GEOFF McFETRIDGE color *Bicycling* v58 no4 p104 My 2017

McFetridge, John
Montreal Noir *Publishers Weekly* v264 no39 p87 S 25 2017

McGaha, Chris
Take 5 With CHRIS MCGAHA color *Hot Rod* v70 no10 p18 O 2017

McGahan, Anita
Expanding the Reach of Primary Care in Developing Countries color *Harvard Business Review Digital Articles* p2 Je 6 2017

McGahn, Don
BETTER CALL DON [Cover story] A. KROLL color *Mother Jones* v42 no3 p24 My/Je 2017

McGahn, Donald
Amid Chaos, Trump Needs a Strong Lawyer P. M. Barrett color *Bloomberg Businessweek* no4512 p26 F 20 2017

McGann, John P.
Poor human olfaction is a 19th-century myth color *Science* v356 no6338 p597 My 12 2017
WE'VE GOT A DOG'S SENSE OF SMELL color *Women's Health* v14 no8 p38 O 2017

McGarry, Caitlin
AirPods wish list: 3 ways Apple can make its Bluetooth earphones even better color *Macworld - Digital Edition* p39 Mr 2017
Apple invests $200 million in Corning to innovate on Gorilla Glass color *Macworld - Digital Edition* p46 Je 13 2017
Apple Music in iOS 10: Smart, simple, but still imperfect color *Macworld - Digital Edition* v33 no11 p141 N 2016
Apple's AirPods survive tough workouts with no sweat color *Macworld - Digital Edition* p49 F 2017
Apple sets a new environmental goal: No more mining color *Macworld - Digital Edition* v34 no6 p12 Je 2017
Apple set to open new headquarters in April color *Macworld - Digital Edition* p4 Ap 2017
APPLE WATCH SERIES 2 REVIEW: A FASTER, BRIGHTER FITNESS MACHINE color map *Macworld - Digital Edition* v33 no11 p113 N 2016
ELGATO'S EVE HOMEKIT LIGHTSWITCH color *Macworld - Digital Edition* p45 D 2016
Evernote overhauls its iOS app with focus on speed and simplicity color *Macworld - Digital Edition* p49 Mr 2017
Feature: 2017 could see just one OLED iPhone color *Macworld - Digital Edition* p100 Ja 2017
Hands-on with Apple Clips: How to use the iOS videoediting app and why you'd want to color *Macworld - Digital Edition* v34 no6 p49 Je 2017
How switching to Macs is paying off for IBM color *Macworld - Digital Edition* p95 D 2016
How Uber ran afoul of Apple's privacy rules color *Macworld - Digital Edition* v34 no6 p63 Je 2017
iPhone 7 and 7 Plus FAQ: Everything you need to know about Apple's new phones bw color *PCWorld* p8 O 2016
New Apple Watch buyers face limited band selection color *Macworld - Digital Edition* v34 no4 p49 My 2017
News: Apple's latest product is a £249 book color *Macworld - Digital Edition* p6 Ja 2017
Tim Cook reaffirms Apple's commitment to the Mac, in response to growing doubt color *Macworld - Digital Edition* p7 F 2017
VI AI PERSONAL TRAINER: HEART RATE-TRACKING BLUETOOTH EARBUDS WITH SERIOUS POTENTIAL color *Macworld - Digital Edition* v34 no6 p68 Je 2017
WatchOS 3 guide: 15 essential tips to transform your Apple Watch color *Macworld - Digital Edition* v33 no11 p75 N 2016
WWDC17 heading to San Jose color *Macworld - Digital Edition* p6 Ap 2017

McGartland, Al
Estimating the health benefits of environmental regulations color *Science* v357 no6350 p457 Ag 4 2017

McGarvey, Bill

The 'Al Franken moment' color *America* v217 no4 p53 Ag 21 2017

MOONLIGHT AND MANHOOD *America* v216 no1 p36 Ja 2 2017

Radical Reconciliation *America* v216 no11 p62 My 15 2017

YOU DON'T DO GOD ALONE bw *America* v215 no12 p32 O 24 2016

Mcgee, Earyn

Without inclusion, diversity initiatives may not be enough color *Science* v357 no6356 p1101 S 15 2017

McGee, Glenn W. "Max"

Confronting Student Suicide cartoon *Education Digest* v82 no8 p4 Ap 2017

McGee, Kristin

Yoga Moves We All Get Wrong color *Health* v31 no7 p69 S 2017

Yoga vs. Back Pain color *Health* v31 no4 p49 My 2017

McGee, Liam

CEOs, Stop Trying to Manage the Board *Harvard Business Review Digital Articles* p2 Ap 24 2015

McGee, Mary—Interviews

in the pink C. BARBOUR color *House Beautiful* v159 no7 p104 S 2017

McGee, Nikki—Interviews

Climbing Missionaries B. BLANCHARD color *Climbing* no350 p18 D 2016/Ja 2017

McGee, Patti

Gang's All Here J. Harman color *Glamour* v115 no5 p178 My 2017

McGehee, Michael D.

Perovskite-perovskite tandem photovoltaics with optimized band gaps bibl chart graph *Science* v354 no6314 p861 N 18 2016

McGhee, Heather

FIRST-TIME CALLER D. Smith cartoon *New Yorker* v92 no43 p20 Ja 2 2017

McGhee, Holly M.

Matylda, Bright and Tender *Publishers Weekly* v264 no2 p68 Ja 9 2017

McGhee, Scott

BLADE OF GLORY T. E. Nickens color *Field & Stream* v122 no2 p24 Je/Jl 2017

MCGILCHRIST, IAIN

Examining Attention cartoon *Tricycle: The Buddhist Review* v26 no3 p24 Spr 2017

MCGILL, BRYANT

THOUGHTS ON Conflict *Forbes* v199 no4 p112 Ap 25 2017

McGill, Dion

TALK TO US color graph *Chicago* v65 no12 p24 D 2016

McGill, Stuart

FIX IT WITH THE BACK MECHANIC L. Schuler cartoon color *Men's Health* v32 no1 p43 Ja/F 2017

McGill University

An audience with the Prime Minister M. HEMMADI color *Maclean's* v130 no10 p18 N 2017

McGinley, Hayley

Against the Grain S. KROWIAK *Indianapolis Monthly* v40 no7 p39 Mr 2017

McGinley, Ryan

THE LOOK BOOK img *New York* v50 no11 p95 My 29 2017

McGinley, Ryan—Interviews

RYAN McGINLEY M. MILLS *Interview* v46 no10 p128 D 2016/Ja 2017

McGinn, Bob

Bitcoin for Bohemians H. RUSTAD cartoon *Walrus* v13 no10 p24 D 2016

McGinn, Brian—Interviews

The Most Infamously Accused Female Villain L. Brody and E. Mahaney color *Glamour* v114 no11 p143 N 2016

McGinn, Daniel

CEOs Face Off Against Trump (or Not) bw *Harvard Business Review Digital Articles* p2 Ja 31 2017

Income Inequality, by Chance or by Choice *Harvard Business Review Digital Articles* p2 Mr 28 2017

Is There a Connection Between Entrepreneurship and Mental Health Conditions? *Harvard Business Review Digital Articles* p2 F 22 2016

Ken Burns on "The Roosevelts" and American Leadership *Harvard Business Review Digital Articles* p2 S 18 2017

Life's Work: An Interview with JERRY SEINFELD bw *Harvard Business Review* v95 no1 p172 Ja/F 2017

Newsweek's Decline and Why Companies Need Rivals *Harvard Business Review Digital Articles* p2 My 7 2017

Obama's Former "Body Man" on Being the Ultimate Assistant *Harvard Business Review Digital Articles* p2 Jl 30 2015

REFLECTIONS OF A SIX-TIME CMO: A CONVERSATION WITH JOE TRIPODI color *Harvard Business Review* v95 no4 p56 Jl/Ag 2017

Resisting the Lure of Short-Termism [Cover story] *Harvard Business Review* v94 no11 p42 N 2016

THE SCIENCE OF PEP TALKS: TO FIRE UP YOUR TEAM, DRAW ON A RESEARCH-PROVEN, THREE-PART FORMULA il *Harvard Business Review* v95 no4 p133 Jl/Ag 2017

What Companies Can Learn from Military Teams *Harvard Business Review Digital Articles* p2 Ag 6 2015

When a Mid-Career Move Falls Flat: The Story of Stripedshirt *Harvard Business Review Digital Articles* p2 Je 1 2015

When Personal Tragedy Strikes, Downshifting at Work Doesn't Always Help *Harvard Business Review Digital Articles* p2 My 15 2015

Why Uber and Airbnb Needed a Different Kind of CEO color *Harvard Business Review Digital Articles* p2 Ja 31 2017

McGinnis, Mike

10 SUCCESSFUL FARMERS: DOUG MARTIN *Successful Farming* v115 no8 p18 Jo/Jl 2017

ADD THIS MARKETING TOOL *Successful Farming* v114 no11 p29 N 2016

BASIS MANAGEMENT *Successful Farming* v115 no4 p25 Mr 2017

BLUE SKY IN AGRICULTURE *Successful Farming* v115 no1 p34 Ja 2017

EDUCATE YOURSELF *Successful Farming* v114 no13 p30 D 2016

McGinnis Crafts 'Dream' Project D. Ouellette color *Downbeat* v84 no8 p13 Ag 2017

ODDS FAVOR HIGHER PRICES FOR 2017 *Successful Farming* v115 no4 p18 Mr 2017

ONE BIG FIELD *Successful Farming* v114 no10 p22 O 2016

PLAN FOR 2017 SUCCESS *Successful Farming* v115 no2 p56 F 2017

REWARDING THE MARKET: FACE VOLATILITY WITH DISCIPLINE *Successful Farming* v115 no11 p45 S 2017

THE SUCCESSFUL INTERVIEW *Successful Farming* v114 no11 p12 N 2016

McGinnis, Robert

The McGinnis Look M. CALLAHAN cartoon color *Vanity Fair* v59 no5 p134 Ap 2017

McGinnis, Sean

FROM THE PUBLISHER *Atlanta* v57 no2 p91 Je 2017

GIVE ATLANTA *Atlanta* v57 no6 p20 O 2017

McGinniss, Joe, 1942-2014

The Loudest Voice in 'New York' C. Bonanos img *New York* v49 no15 p10 Jl 25 2016

McGirt, Ellen

THE BLACK CEILING color *Fortune* v176 no5 p94 O 1 2017

GOOGLE SEARCHES ITS SOUL color diag *Fortune* v175 no2 p48 F 1 2017

TIM RYAN'S AWAKENING color diag *Fortune* v175 no2 p58 F 1 2017

McGirt, William

William McGirt C. Barrett color *Golf Magazine* v58 no11 p27 N 2016

McGivern, David R.

MAVS-dependent host species range and pathogenicity of human hepatitis A virus bibl graph *Science* v353 no6307 p1541 S 30 2016

McGivney, Annette

Arizona Nordic Village. Yurts are cool. Period. But they're even better when they're located in an alpine meadow that's alive with wildflowers, songbirds and browsing elk *Arizona Highways* v93 no6 p14 Je 2017

Crescent Moon Ranch color *Arizona Highways* v93 no5 p14 My 2017

DIG THIS! *Arizona Highways* v93 no2 p44 F 2017

El Rancho Robles *Arizona Highways* v93 no1 p14 Ja 2017

Hikes Gone Wrong: We all love the trail. Sometimes love hurts color il *Backpacker* p69 S 2017

Kendrick Cabin: Built around 1960, this rustic, three-bedroom cabin features pine flooring, mugh-hewn pine ceiling beams and, best of all, a front porch adorned with Adirondack chairs aimed at distant mountains *Arizona Highways* v96 no7 p14 Jl 2017

SAN FRANCISCO PEAKS LOOP *Arizona Highways* v93 no10 p52 O 2017

SPRING VALLEY LOOP: Historic Route 66, the National Old Trails Road, the Beale Wagon Road ... some of the state's most iconic routes can be experienced along the Spring Valley Loop in Northern Arizona *Arizona Highways* v96 no7 p52 Jl 2017

The Toasted Owl *Arizona Highways* v93 no8 p12 Ag 2017

WE SET UP SHOP IN THE MIDDLE OF A NATURAL WONDER *Arizona Highways* v92 no11 p43 N 2016

WHERE THE WILD ORCHID GROWS *Arizona Highways* v93 no8 p38 Ag 2017

McGLASHAN, LARA

The 20-Minute Turkey Buster color *Muscle & Performance* v9 no11 p24 N 2017

30 MUST-DO MOVES for 2017 color *Muscle & Performance* v9 no1 p44 Ja 2017

3 GYM-FRIENDLY EXERCISE TECHNIQUES FOR GREAT GLUTES color *Muscle & Performance* v9 no5 p28 My 2017

5 WAYS: ...To get a massage color *Muscle & Performance* v9 no10 p66 O 2017

5 WAYS... To Warm Up color *Muscle & Performance* v9 no9 p66 S 2017

Abs Anywhere color *Muscle & Performance* v9 no11 p26 N 2017

BE ECCENTRIC color *Muscle & Performance* v8 no12 p20 D 2016

Braking Muscle chart color *Muscle & Performance* v9 no10 p26 O 2017

BUZZ WORTHY color *Muscle & Performance* v9 no6 p26 Je 2017

COMPLEX MOBILITY color *Muscle & Performance* v9 no5 p24 My 2017

Design Your Own Metcon chart color *Muscle & Performance* v9 no5 p48 My 2017

Establish Your Dominance color *Muscle & Performance* v9 no9 p24 S 2017

The Flexibility Factor color *Muscle & Performance* v9 no11 p28 N 2017

GET LIFTED color *Muscle & Performance* v9 no6 p16 Je 2017

Grease Your Wheels color *Muscle & Performance* v9 no8 p26 Ag 2017

GUT CHECK color diag *Muscle & Performance* v9 no7 p57 Jl 2017

HOLIDAY HIIT cartoon chart *Muscle & Performance* v8 no12 p54 D 2016

IN THE BEGINNING... color *Muscle & Performance* v9 no1 p30 Ja 2017

It's All in the Wrists color *Muscle & Performance* v9 no9 p26 S 2017

JOIN THE BIG LEAGUES color *Muscle & Performance* v9 no4 p46 Ap 2017

THE LEG PRESS, PERFECTED chart color *Muscle & Performance* v8 no12 p18 D 2016

LOW BACK ON TRACK color *Muscle & Performance* v9 no4 p22 Ap 2017

MAKING THE CUT chart color *Muscle & Performance* v9 no4 p34 Ap 2017

MASTERING YOUR BODY color *Muscle & Performance* v9 no6 p28 Je 2017

THE NEW CARDIO cartoon *Muscle & Performance* v8 no12 p30 D 2016

THE NFL WORKOUT [Cover story] chart color *Muscle & Performance* v9 no11 p52 N 2017

POW(D)ER UP YOUR MEALS color *Muscle & Performance* v9 no7 p51 Jl 2017

THE POWER OF NEGATIVITY color *Muscle & Performance* v9 no4 p16 Ap 2017

PRE-HABILITATION color *Muscle & Performance* v9 no1 p26

Ja 2017

The Queen of Pain color *Muscle & Performance* v9 no9 p36 S 2017

Roll for the Flow color *Muscle & Performance* v9 no11 p21 N 2017

THE SCIENCE OF SLEEP color *Muscle & Performance* v9 no7 p46 Jl 2017

SPARTAN UP color *Muscle & Performance* v9 no9 p44 S 2017

Sports Support color *Muscle & Performance* v9 no7 p26 Jl 2017

SQUAT TO GET LEAN? YEP cartoon chart *Muscle & Performance* v8 no12 p22 D 2016

Surf's Up bw color *Muscle & Performance* v9 no7 p34 Jl 2017

Take 5 color *Muscle & Performance* v9 no10 p32 O 2017

The Three-B Workout chart color *Muscle & Performance* v9 no8 p16 Ag 2017

TOP 5: ... Healthy Ways to Cook Thanksgiving Turkey color *Muscle & Performance* v9 no11 p66 N 2017

The Totally Trail-Ready Workout chart color *Muscle & Performance* v9 no9 p20 S 2017

TRX, REDEFINED chart color *Muscle & Performance* v9 no1 p22 Ja 2017

Turn & Burn chart color *Muscle & Performance* v9 no7 p16 Jl 2017

THE ULTIMATE PHA FAT BLAST chart color *Muscle & Performance* v9 no5 p16 My 2017

Yoga For Strength color *Muscle & Performance* v9 no1 p38 Ja 2017

McGloin, Maggy

What You Miss When You Take Notes on Your Laptop *Harvard Business Review Digital Articles* p2 Jl 31 2015

McGlynn, Catherine

FLOATING IN PLAIN SIGHT: Invasive Aquatic Garden Plants *New York State Conservationist* v71 no5 p32 Ap 2017

McGLYNN, DAVID

SMALL HOUSE, BIG LIFE color *O, The Oprah Magazine* p26 Jl 2017

McGonegal, Ro

The HOT ROD Archives D. Wallace color *Hot Rod* v70 no2 p12 F 2017

McGonigal, Kelly

SHINE ON ME color *Yoga Journal* p8 2017 Special Issue

YOUR BRAIN ON MEDITATION color *Yoga Journal* p36 2017 Special Issue

McGough, Nellah Bailey

Canine Campers color *Southern Living* v52 no7 p35 Jl 2017

Dogs on the Town color *Southern Living* v52 no6 p43 Je 2017

Get Your Dog To Behave Around Company color *Southern Living* v52 no4 p50 Ap 2017

Gracious Guests color *Southern Living* v52 no11 p47 N 2017

Hitting the Trails color *Southern Living* v52 no10 p42 O 2017

Pups & Personal Space color *Southern Living* v52 no3 p26 Mr 2017

Small-Space Living color *Southern Living* v52 no9 p33 S 2017

McGOUGH, WILL

Backpack with a Stranger il *Backpacker* p28 O 2017

McGovern, Elizabeth, 1961-

GOINGS ON ABOUT TOWN bw *New Yorker* v93 no28 p4 S 18 2017

McGovern, Joe

13TH color *Entertainment Weekly* no1435 p43 O 14 2016

THE 25 MOST PATRIOTIC MOVIES OF ALL TIME color *Entertainment Weekly* no1472 p30 Je 30 2017

3 Generations color *Entertainment Weekly* no1465 p41 My 12 2017

4 — OPENING CREDITS *Entertainment Weekly* no1444/1445 p60 D 16 2016

7 — THE ACTING CLASS *Entertainment Weekly* no1444/1445 p60 D 16 2016

Adam West color *Entertainment Weekly* no1471 p20 Je 23 2017

Also In MEMORIAM color *Entertainment Weekly* no1453 p39 F 17 2017

Ben Stiller's True Crime color *Entertainment Weekly* no1486 p50 O 13 2017

BEST ACTOR color diag *Entertainment Weekly* no1451/1452 p54 F 3-10 2017

BEST ACTRESS color diag *Entertainment Weekly* no1451/1452

p32 Jl 2017

HUMANIST PROFILE K. Winston *Humanist* v77 no5 p2 S/O 2017

McGowan, Jo

The Euphoria of the Dying color *Commonweal* v144 no7 p6 Ap 14 2017

India's Trump *Commonweal* v144 no2 p6 Ja 27 2017

'Still She Is a Wonderful Girl' color *Commonweal* v144 no12 p6 Jl 7 2017

Unpaid Bills color *Commonweal* v144 no15 p6 S 22 2017

McGowan, John Joseph

Staying Sharp color *AARP: The Magazine* v30 no6A p65 O/N 2017

MCGOWAN, KAT

WHERE DID IT ALL BEGIN? color map *Popular Science* v289 no5 p38 S/O 2017

McGowan, Steve

BRIGHT EYES: BLINK aims to establish the city's artistic vision J. WILLIAMS diag *Cincinnati Magazine* v51 no1 p19 O 2017

MCGOWAN, SUZANNE

The Arctic in the Twenty-First Century: Changing Biogeochemical Linkages across a Paraglacial Landscape of Greenland *BioScience* v67 no2 p118 F 2017

McGowan, Traci

You Never Forget Your First Time diag il *Backpacker* v45 no2 p64 Mr 2017

McGowan, Wendy

KITCHEN-TESTED TIPS color *Vegetarian Today* no1 p4 F 2017

McGrail, Laura

Blue Dust Days *Publishers Weekly* v264 no25 p113 Je 19 2017

McGrath, Ben

ON THE MAP cartoon *New Yorker* v92 no38 p31 N 21 2016

Mcgrath, Brid

Q: What was the most important letter in history? color *Atlantic* v320 no2 p104 S 2017

McGrath, Charles

The Case for Shirley Jackson *New York Times Book Review* p15 O 2 2016

CHECK, PLEASE! cartoon *New Yorker* v93 no31 p18 O 9 2017

Class Act T. TEACHOUT color *National Review* v68 no19 p46 O 24 2016

THE LAND OF LOST CONTENT cartoon *New Yorker* v93 no18 p63 Je 26 2017

What's the best book, new or old, you read this year? *New York Times Book Review* p27 D 25 2016

When Past Is Present *New York Times Book Review* p1 My 7 2017

McGrath, Dan

Adrift Upon the Open Sea *Earth Island Journal* v32 no3 p5 Aut 2017

MCGRATH, DOUGLAS

THE PENCES VISIT MANHATTAN cartoon *New Yorker* v92 no32 p47 O 10 2016

McGrath, Gabrielle—Interviews

At Work With U.S. Coast Guard Ice Patrol C. Suddath color *Bloomberg Businessweek* no4528 p37 Je 26 2017

MCGRATH, MAGGIE

A Cut Above color *Forbes* v199 no2 p104 F 28 2017

The Fintech 50 color *Forbes* v198 no7 p90 N 29 2016

McGrath, Pat

Legend Status M. KIM and C. ELLENBERG color *Vogue* v207 no9 p442 S 2017

Mogul Matchup R. Nussbaum color *Glamour* v115 no11 p88 N 2017

PAT McGRATH'S Golden Touch G. Macnicol color *InStyle* v24 no2 p110 F 2017

Supermodel Makeup School S. Kitchens and Y. Chu color *Glamour* v114 no12 p119 D 2016

McGRATH, PATRICK

'A Safe Place to Go Mad' *New York Times Book Review* p12 O 30 2016

Forty Whacks? *New York Times Book Review* p12 Ag 27 2017

McGrath, Rita Gunther

Can Nokia Reinvent Itself Again? *Harvard Business Review Digital Articles* p2 Ap 16 2015

How to Set More-Realistic Growth Targets *Harvard Business Review Digital Articles* p2 Jl 12 2017

Investors Fawning over Uber Should Recall AOL's Stumbles *Harvard Business Review Digital Articles* p2 Ja 9 2015

OLD HABITS DIE HARD, BUT THEY DO DIE [Cover story] color *Harvard Business Review* v95 no1 p54 Ja/F 2017

To Reduce Complexity in Your Company, Start with Pen and Paper *Harvard Business Review Digital Articles* p2 Ag 22 2016

McGrath, Tom

CHILD IN CHARGE D. Walters color *Bloomberg Businessweek* no4517 p71 Ap 3 2017

McGraw, David J.

Hunting for a Summer SM Job *Stage Directions* v30 no1 p16 Ja 2017

STAGE DOOR CLANDESTINE LEARNING *Stage Directions* v30 no3 p66 Mr 2017

McGraw, Eliza

Let us now praise famous horses bw color *Equus* no472 p72 Ja 2017

McGraw, Phillip C., 1950-

Dr. Phil McGraw color *AARP: The Magazine* v59 no3A p18 Ap/My 2016

McGraw, Tim, 1967-

ON THE ROAD WITH TIM AND FAITH M. Vain color *Entertainment Weekly* no1471 p63 Je 23 2017

Tim McGraw C. Ianzito color *AARP: The Magazine* v60 no3A p74 Ap/My 2017

McGreevey, Jim

The redemption of ex-prisoners is a duty of the church *America* v217 no7 p10 O 2 2017

McGreevy, John T.

All the Pope's Men J. F. Keenan cartoon *Commonweal* v143 no18 p36 N 11 2016

Destructive Solidarity color *Commonweal* v144 no8 p34 My 5 2017

FORDHAM: A NEW YORK STORY color *America* v216 no9 p41 Ap 24 2017

JESUIT MIGRATION R. E. CURRAN color *America* v215 no10 p32 O 10 2016

Looking Outward P. ALLITT bw *Weekly Standard* v22 no13 p39 D 5 2016

Mcgreger, April

SWEET ON SWEET POTATOES color *Southern Living* v51 no11 p116 N 2016

McGregor, Conor, 1988-

BLACK BELT HALL OF FAME [Cover story] cartoon color *Black Belt* v55 no5 p32 Ag/S 2017

Conor McGregor M. Hagan color *Current Biography* v78 no3 p64 Mr 2017

Games: Will Leitch: The Unseemly Science Is it possible for sports to sink lower than Mayweather-McGregor? img *New York* v50 no15 p13 Jl 24 2017

Keys to a McGregor upset ... B. Baskin color *Sports Illustrated* v127 no6 p54 Ag 28 2017

Leading Off B. Baskin color *Sports Illustrated* v127 no7 p6 S 4 2017

The Making of a Cynical Sporting Spectacle In the Desert S. Gregory color *Time* v190 no8 p54 Ag 28 2017

REMEMBER OUR ROOTS R. W. Young *Black Belt* v55 no6 p8 O/N 2017

SHADOWBOXING G. Bishop color *Sports Illustrated* v127 no6 p52 Ag 28 2017

McGregor, Ewan, 1971-

DOUBLE TROUBLE J. Hibberd color *Entertainment Weekly* no1462 p42 Ap 21 2017

Fargo A. D'Arminio *TV Guide* p36 Ap 17 2017

HEARTLAND OF DARKNESS J. Hibberd color *Entertainment Weekly* no1462 p38 Ap 21 2017

T2's Beloved Hooligans Get Older, but Not Wiser S. Zacharek color *Time* v189 no11 p59 Mr 27 2017

McGregor, Ewan, 1971—Interviews

BLOOD BROTHERS: Ewan McGregor on his dual acting triumph in Fargo-and why they're the role(s) of a lifetime A. D'ARMINIO *TV Guide* v65 no25 p26 Je 2017

Ewan McGregor E. Berman color *Time* v189 no11 p59 Mr 27 2017

McGregor, Jon

Reservoir 13 J. ROSEN color *Publishers Weekly* v264 no35 p47

Ag 28 2017

McGregor, Lindsay
How Company Culture Shapes Employee Motivation *Harvard Business Review Digital Articles* p2 N 25 2015
There Are Two Types of Performance—but Most Organizations Only Focus on One *Harvard Business Review Digital Articles* p2 O 10 2017

McGregor, Richard
Asia's Reckoning: China, Japan, and the Fate of U.S. Power in the Pacific Century *Publishers Weekly* v264 no23 p40 Je 5 2017

McGROGAN, E. D.
Another Transformation in Queens *Tennis* v52 no6 p64 N/D 2016
Best of the Rest *Tennis* v53 no1 p64 Ja/F 2017
From POW to SW19 *Tennis* v52 no6 p70 N/D 2016
HEART OF THE CITY: Roger Federer's connection to New York is unmistakable, both on and off the court color *Tennis* v53 no5 p42 S/O 2017
Tour Guide: ATP *Tennis* v53 no1 p70 Ja/F 2017
Tour Guide chart *Tennis* v53 no3 p32 My/Je 2017
Tour Guide: WTA *Tennis* v53 no1 p72 Ja/F 2017
A Tradition Unlike Any Other *Tennis* v53 no4 p58 Jl/Ag 2017

McGuigan, Cathleen
Aga Khan Bestows Architecture Awards in Dubai color *Architectural Record* v204 no12 p20 D 2016
Architecture and the Future of the Public Realm *Architectural Record* v205 no4 p24 Ap 2017
Architecture and the History of Race *Architectural Record* v204 no10 p21 O 2016
Back to the Land color *Architectural Record* v205 no8 p58 Ag 2017
Being There *Architectural Record* v205 no6 p18 Je 2017
Day in Court color diag *Architectural Record* v205 no3 p92 Mr 2017
Design for Social Animals *Architectural Record* v204 no11 p21 N 2016
Detroit: The Remix *Architectural Record* v205 no4 p84 Ap 2017
Diplomacy in Design color *Architectural Record* v205 no3 p44 Mr 2017
Equal Opportunity *Architectural Record* v205 no9 p24 S 2017
Everyone's a Winner! color *Architectural Record* v205 no3 p18 Mr 2017
Shelter from the Storm: Architects must continue to explore new forms for urban living *Architectural Record* v205 no10 p14 O 2017
Social Infrastructure *Architectural Record* v205 no1 p16 Ja 2017
What It Means to be Modern *Architectural Record* v205 no7 p24 Jl 2017

mcguiness, laura
Aquafabulous *Vegetarian Journal* v36 no2 p19 2017
Let Them Eat veGan Cake *Vegetarian Journal* v35 no4 p16 2016

McGuiness, Pete
Big Band Arranging: Reinventing Stephen Foster's 'Beautiful Dreamer' bw color *Downbeat* v83 no12 p100 D 2016
Vocal Identity T. Panken color *Downbeat* v83 no11 p26 N 2016

McGuinness, Liam P.
Submillihertz magnetic spectroscopy performed with a nanoscale quantum sensor diag *Science* v356 no6340 p832 My 26 2017

McGuinness, Martin, 1950-2017
Milestones color *Time* v189 no12 p18 Ap 3 2017

McGuire, A. David
Positive biodiversity-productivity relationship predominant in global forests bibl chart graph map *Science* v354 no6309 paaf8957-1 O 14 2016

McGuire, Amy L.
Myriad take two: Can genomic databases remain secret? color *Science* v356 no6338 p586 My 12 2017

McGuire, Ashley
Boys Will Be... M. EBERSTADT color *Weekly Standard* v22 no32 p39 My 1 2017

McGuire, Brett A.
Mirror asymmetry in life and in space *Physics Today* v69 no11 p86 N 2016

McGuire, Gene
God Remembered Me in Prison color *Christianity Today* v61 no5 p79 Je 2017

McGuire, Hugh

How Making Time for Books Made Me Feel Less Busy *Harvard Business Review Digital Articles* p2 S 1 2015

Mcguire, Ian
Frozen *New York Times Book Review* p12 Ap 9 2017

Mcguire, Kathleen
BUILDING A Fitness Empire color *Dance Spirit* v21 no2 p58 F 2017
Dance Moms--and Dads *Dance Magazine* v91 no8 p46 Ag 2017
DIGGING DEEP color *Dance Spirit* v20 no9 p47 N 2016
LEARNING Fearlessness *Dance Spirit* v21 no7 p62 S 2017
MAKING Photos DANCE bw color *Dance Spirit* v20 no9 p72 N 2016
POINTE SHOE #Hacks color *Dance Spirit* v20 no10 p56 D 2016
Tackling Depression *Dance Magazine* v90 no11 p46 N 2016
Variation Variations *Dance Spirit* v21 no3 p48 Mr 2017

McGuire, Larry
HOW I GOT MY STYLE: LARRY McGUIRE P. L. Underwood color *Esquire* p55 N 2017
A Texas Fiesta J. B. Hager color *Southern Living* v52 no9 p17 S 2017

McGuire, Nancy
THE NOME NUGGET C. Spike color *Columbia Journalism Review* v56 no1 p63 Spr 2017

McGuire, Richard
LITTLE MOMENTS J. YEH *New York Times Book Review* p44 D 4 2016

McGurl, Mark
Your Writing Tools Aren't Mine V. T. NGUYEN *New York Times Book Review* p13 Ap 30 2017

MCHENRY, JACKSON
72 minutes with ... Laurie Metcalf img *New York* v50 no11 p18 My 29 2017
Turning a Theater Inside Out: Problem No. 1: Move your musical from a cabaret into a Broadway theater. Problem No. 2: Make that theater feel like a cabaret img *New York* v50 no11 p114 My 29 2017

McHugh, Clare
Eating well—and loving it! color *Health* v31 no8 p6 O 2017
Found! A Simple Way to Slim Down color *Health* v31 no1 p4 Ja 2017
Go Ahead and Really Relax color *Health* v31 no6 p6 Jl 2017
How Do You Stay Powered Up? color *Health* v31 no4 p6 My 2017
How to Eat Healthy—and Love It color *Health* v31 no5 p4 Je 2017
It's Time to Be Good to Yourself color *Health* v30 no10 p6 D 2016
Looking Out for Small Joys color *Health* v31 no3 p8 Ap 2017
Master the Brown Bag Lunch color *Health* v31 no7 p12 S 2017
Play Hard and Still Stay Safe color *Health* v30 no9 p8 N 2016
Power Days Start Here color *Health* v31 no2 p8 Mr 2017

Mchugh, Kevin J.
Fabrication of fillable microparticles and other complex 3D microstructures color diag *Science* v357 no6356 p1138 S 15 2017

McHugh, Laura
HACKER CRACK-UP color *Wired* v25 no6 p10 Je 2017

McHugh, Rosemary
Speak up color *U.S. Catholic* v82 no4 p5 Ap 2017

McIlroy, Rory, 1989-
GO ON A BLENDER E. Rothman and D. DeNunzio chart color *Golf Magazine* v59 no8 p55 Ag 2017
Watch + Learn T. Sones and C. Barrett color *Golf Magazine* v59 no1 p30 Ja 2017

McInerney, Colette
LOST IN TOKYO color *Climbing* no349 p48 N 2016
PLANES, TRAINS, AND BROKEN LUGGAGE: A Year in the Life of a Climbing Photographer color *Climbing* no354 p70 Jl 2017

McInerney, Jay
BARBARESCO bw color *Esquire* p32 2017 BigBlackBook
Big City Burnout C. LORENTZEN img *New York* v49 no15 p89 Jl 25 2016
SETTLING DOWN M. DEAN bw il *Nation* v303 no18 p33 O 31 2016

McInerny, Austin
THE FUTURE STARTS IN A MUDDY FIELD F. BURES color *Bicycling* v58 no4 p52 My 2017

McINTOSH, CLAIRE

Secrets of Single Super color *AARP: The Magazine* v30 no6A p20 O/N 2017

MCINTOSH, KEVIN

Chords & Discords bw color *Downbeat* v84 no2 p10 F 2017

McIntosh, Matthew

TheMystery.doc *Publishers Weekly* v264 no36 p61 S 4 2017

McIntosh Laboratory Inc.

IT'S THE SOFTWARE, STUPID R. SABIN *Sound & Vision* v82 no5 p8 Je 2017

McIntosh RS100 Wireless Speaker R. Sabin color graph *Sound & Vision* v82 no5 p48 Je 2017

Spinning with Style B. Ankosko color *Sound & Vision* v82 no3 p74 Ap 2017

MCINTYRE, CATHERINE

Compliments for fishing color *Maclean's* v130 no10 p48 N 2017

DAYCARE MADE SIMPLE color *Maclean's* v130 no7 p50 Ag 2017

The embattled swastika color *Maclean's* v130 no10 p15 N 2017

On the road to saving the world color *Maclean's* p48 Je 2017

Our home and pest-ridden land color map *Maclean's* p17 Je 2017

Pizza to go. And go. And go color *Maclean's* v130 no9 p70 O 2017

A place to run color *Maclean's* v130 no8 p50 S 2017

Those flighty millennials color *Maclean's* v130 no8 p14 S 2017

When the hive mind is wrong color *Maclean's* v130 no9 p16 O 2017

YOUR PAL HARRY color *Maclean's* v130 no2 p46 Mr 2017

McIntyre, Dale

Cheers & Jeers color *Field & Stream* v121 no7 p14 D 2016/Ja 2017

McINTYRE, ERIN

Measuring the Impact: Rising opioid abuse puts pressure on schools *Education Digest* v82 no5 p4 Ja 2017

McIntyre, Hunter

BE A BACKYARD BADASS J. CSATARI color *Men's Health* v32 no6 p100 Ag 2017

McIntyre, Thomas

2016 BEST OF THE BEST bw color *Field & Stream* v121 no7 p96 D 2016/Ja 2017

FIELD TEST color *Field & Stream* v122 no2 p99 Je/Jl 2017

McKay, Adam, 1968-

THE MAVERICKS OF HOLLYWOOD 2017 J. Black, K. Sintumuang et al bw color *Esquire* v167 no2 p89 Mr 2017

McKay, Ami

THE WITCHES OF NEW YORK E. DONALDSON color *Maclean's* v129 no44 p113 N 7 2016

McKay, Chris

The LEGO Batman Movie C. Nashawaty color *Entertainment Weekly* no1453 p44 F 17 2017

THE LEGO BATMAN MOVIE M. Snetiker color *Entertainment Weekly* no1446/1447 p55 D 2016/Ja 2017

Not So Super R. DOUTHAT color *National Review* v69 no5 p46 Mr 20 2017

so you want to terraform Mars M. B. Griggs color *Popular Science* v289 no4 p14 Jl/Ag 2017

McKay, Chris—Interviews

ALL ABOUT LEGO BATMAN'S ROGUES' GALLERY M. Snetiker color *Entertainment Weekly* no1454/1455 p19 F 24 2017

McKay, Claude, 1890-1948

A Found Novel of Harlem Works As a Time Capsule S. Begley color *Time* v189 no5 p53 F 13 2017

The Harlem He Knew D. Pinckney bw color *New York Review of Books* v64 no11 p18 Je 22 2017

Prophet of Harlem G. Oleynick bw *Commonweal* v144 no12 p21 Jl 7 2017

McKAY, DEAN

Superstition Masquerading as Science *Skeptical Inquirer* v40 no6 p14 N/D 2016

McKay, Erin

Revealing Rorschach color *Science* v355 no6325 p588 F 10 2017

McKAY, TIMOTHY

BUILDING A COMMUNITY OF LIFELONG LEARNING color *Phi Kappa Phi Forum* v97 no2 p10 Summ 2017

McKEAN, ANDREW

ACCESS AGENTS color *Outdoor Life* v224 no1 p32 D 2016/Ja 2017

BOOK SMARTS color *Outdoor Life* v224 no2 p76 F/Mr 2017

BORDER BUNNIES color *Outdoor Life* v224 no1 p34 D 2016/

Ja 2017

BOW TEST 2017 chart color *Outdoor Life* v224 no6 p17 Ag 2017

BUCKS' BEDROOMS color *Outdoor Life* v223 no9 p34 N 2016

THE COYOTE SCALE color *Outdoor Life* v224 no2 p78 F/Mr 2017

Cutting Edges *Outdoor Life* v224 no2 p11 F/Mr 2017

DIY 3-D color diag *Outdoor Life* v224 no5 p92 Je/Jl 2017

DUCKING THE GREAT SALT LAKE cartoon color *Outdoor Life* v223 no9 p31 N 2016

THE FINDERS color *Outdoor Life* v224 no9 p11 N 2017

FIRST-PLANE REVOLUTION chart color *Outdoor Life* v224 no5 p15 Je/Jl 2017

FIXED FOCUS color *Outdoor Life* v224 no9 p34 N 2017

FREE-RANGE color *Outdoor Life* v224 no3 p43 Ap 2017

Full Circles *Outdoor Life* v224 no5 p10 Je/Jl 2017

A House Divided *Outdoor Life* v224 no1 p12 D 2016/Ja 2017

INLINE OPTICS color *Outdoor Life* v223 no9 p28 N 2016

JUNGLE LORE Redux bw color *Outdoor Life* v224 no2 p58 F/Mr 2017

KRYLON CAMO bw color *Outdoor Life* v224 no5 p94 Je/Jl 2017

LOOKING GLASSES chart color *Outdoor Life* v224 no5 p22 Je/Jl 2017

LOST + FOUND color *Outdoor Life* v224 no9 p54 N 2017

LUNAR BUCKS color graph *Outdoor Life* v224 no5 p87 Je/Jl 2017

ODE TO THE SPOON color *Outdoor Life* v224 no6 p29 Ag 2017

AN OPEN LETTER TO OUR NEXT PRESIDENT cartoon color *Outdoor Life* v224 no1 p56 D 2016/Ja 2017

OVER, UNDER, AND IN-BETWEEN color *Outdoor Life* v224 no5 p90 Je/Jl 2017

PARADISE FOUND color *Outdoor Life* v224 no1 p60 D 2016/Ja 2017

PUBLIC DOMAINS color map *Outdoor Life* v224 no5 p64 Je/Jl 2017

RANGE MASTERS chart color *Outdoor Life* v224 no8 p11 O 2017

SECRETS OF THE SHED MASTERS color *Outdoor Life* v224 no2 p80 F/Mr 2017

THE SLOUGH color *Outdoor Life* v224 no6 p48 Ag 2017

STRAPPED color *Outdoor Life* v224 no9 p19 N 2017

SWAMP GOBBLERS color map *Outdoor Life* v224 no2 p73 F/Mr 2017

Trusty Bargains color *Outdoor Life* v224 no4 p8 My 2017

URSUS MAJOR color *Outdoor Life* v224 no5 p89 Je/Jl 2017

USING ENGINEERED PLASTICS INSTEAD OF GLASS, A NEW GENERATION OF SPORTING OPTICS WILL BE LIGHTER, CLEARER, AND STRONGER color *Outdoor Life* v224 no2 p48 F/Mr 2017

THE WAGER color *Outdoor Life* v224 no8 p57 O 2017

WAYPOINT color *Outdoor Life* v224 no6 p7 Ag 2017

WAYPOINT N. KREBS color *Outdoor Life* v224 no3 p5 Ap 2017

McKean, Michael, 1947-

Better Call Saul J. Halterman *TV Guide* v65 no25 p32 Je 2017

McKee, Annie

A 3-Step Process to Break a Cycle of Frustration, Stress, and Fighting at Work *Harvard Business Review Digital Articles* p2 Jl 12 2017

Being Happy at Work Matters *Harvard Business Review Digital Articles* p2 N 14 2014

Don't Let Your Stressed- Out Boss Stress You Out *Harvard Business Review Digital Articles* p2 S 11 2015

The Emotional Impulses That Poison Healthy Teams *Harvard Business Review Digital Articles* p2 Jl 16 2015

Empathy Is Key to a Great Meeting *Harvard Business Review Digital Articles* p2 Mr 23 2015

HAPPINESS TRAPS: HOW WE SABOTAGE OURSELVES AT WORK color *Harvard Business Review* v95 no5 p66 S/O 2017

How Power Affects Your Productivity *Harvard Business Review Digital Articles* p2 F 9 2015

How to Free Your Innate Creativity *Harvard Business Review Digital Articles* p2 D 11 2015

How to Help Someone Develop Emotional Intelligence *Harvard Business Review Digital Articles* p2 Ap 24 2015

How to Hire for Emotional Intelligence *Harvard Business Review Digital Articles* p2 F 5 2016

If You Can't Empathize with Your Employees, You'd Better Learn

To *Harvard Business Review Digital Articles* p2 N 16 2016

Office Politics Is Just Influence by Another Name *Harvard Business Review Digital Articles* p2 Ja 16 2015

Prevent Burnout by Making Compassion a Habit *Harvard Business Review Digital Articles* p1 My 11 2017

Shifting from Star Performer to Star Manager *Harvard Business Review Digital Articles* p2 O 20 2015

What You Can Do to Improve Ethics at Your Company *Harvard Business Review Digital Articles* p2 D 29 2016

Why It's Dangerous to Love Your Boss *Harvard Business Review Digital Articles* p2 D 4 2014

Why Some People Get Burned Out and Others Don't *Harvard Business Review Digital Articles* p2 N 23 2016

McKee, Jim

Nebraska at 150 A. J. BARTELS bw color map *Nebraska Life* v21 no2 p50 Mr/Ap 2017

McKee, Krisha

Trispecific broadly neutralizing HIV antibodies mediate potent SHIV protection in macaques color graph *Science* v357 no6359 p85 O 6 2017

McKee, Martin

A plan for U.K. science after the European Union referendum bibl color *Science* v355 no6320 p31 Ja 6 2017

McKee, Paul

A Second Chance *Governing* v30 no2 p12 N 2016

McKee, Rebecca A.

Let's Talk TAPE N. Chirico color *Horse & Rider* v56 no1 p58 Ja 2017

McKeever, Karl

OUT-SMART THE SUPER-MARKET P. FLAX color *Prevention* v69 no8 p60 Ag 2017

McKellar, Bruce H. J.

International Union of Pure and Applied Physics and you *Physics Today* v70 no10 p9 O 2017

McKellen, Ian, 1939-

Family Guy A. Bacle, D. Coggan et al *Entertainment Weekly* no1482/1483 p34 S 22 2017

McKelvey, Chris

PLUGGING THE PAST *New York State Conservationist* v71 no3 p18 D 2016

McKelvey, Paul

My loved ones would describe me as... color map *Reader's Digest* v189 no1130 p34 My 2017

MCKENDRY, JOE

Tunneling to Brooklyn: The first rapid-transit tunnel linking the teeming waterfronts of Manhattan and Brooklyn was completed in January 1908. A century on, the Lexington Avenue subway lines still use the tunnel, carrying tens of thousands of riders daily *Smithsonian* v48 no2 p42 My 2017

McKendry-Smith, Emily

The Health Benefits of a Bicycle-Pedestrian Trail *Parks & Recreation* v51 no12 p16 D 2016

McKenna, Eileen

Beginning French: Lessons from a Stone Farmhouse *Publishers Weekly* v264 no13 p64c Mr 27 2017

MCKENNA, JASON

The Meaning of Scalia *Commentary* v142 no1 p13 Jl/Ag 2016

McKenna, Josephine

After 500 years, a new synagogue opens in Sicily color *Christian Century* v134 no4 p15 F 15 2017

Chief rabbi of Venice works for return of Jewish community *Christian Century* v134 no7 p15 Mr 29 2017

Lasers reveal long-hidden catacomb frescoes that have biblical themes color *Christian Century* v134 no15 p16 Jl 19 2017

McKenna, Lindsay

Wind River Rancher *Publishers Weekly* v263 no50 p55 D 5 2016

Wrangler's Challenge: Wind River Valley, Book 4 *Publishers Weekly* v264 no39 p91 S 25 2017

McKenna, Maryn

AIR SICKNESS *New York Times Magazine* p42 Ap 23 2017

COULD THE ANSWER TO OUR MOST URGENT HEALTH CRISIS BE FOUND ON A TOILET SEAT? color *Atlantic* v320 no1 p88 Jl/Ag 2017

Farm tale warns against antibiotics C. Vanchieri color *Science News* v192 no5 p30 S 30 2017

Industrializing animals T. C. Smith color *Science* v357 no6358

p1360 S 29 2017

McKenna, Megan F.

Noise pollution is pervasive in U.S. protected areas graph map *Science* v356 no6337 p531 My 5 2017

McKenna, Tom

WONDER BREADS J. DRILLING *Cincinnati Magazine* v50 no10 p124 Jl 2017

McKenny, Rachel Mans

For crying out loud color *U.S. Catholic* v82 no4 p36 Ap 2017

McKenzie, Ben

Gotham N. Abrams, B. L. Heldman et al *Entertainment Weekly* no1482/1483 p84 S 22 2017

Our Reporter Heads to Gotham D. Holbrook *TV Guide* p8 Ap 17 2017

Out & About *TV Guide* p4 D 19 2016

Mckenzie, Caroline

2017 Southern Beauties color *Southern Living* v52 no10 p53 O 2017

McKenzie, David

Teaching personal initiative beats traditional training in boosting small business in West Africa chart graph *Science* v357 no6357 p1287 S 22 2017

McKENZIE, ELIZABETH

Fox and Friend *New York Times Book Review* p13 Je 25 2017

Smokers Only *New York Times Book Review* p141 N 13 2016

McKenzie, Melissa

Human brains teach us a surprising lesson bibl color *Science* v354 no6308 p38 O 7 2016

McKenzie, Rebecca E.

CRISPR-Cas: Adapting to change color *Science* v356 no6333 p40 Ap 7 2017

MCKENZIE, WILLIAM

Liquid Assets *Weekly Standard* v22 no8 p37 O 31 2016

Sharing the Wealth *Weekly Standard* v22 no38 p35 Je 12 2017

McKenzie-Jones, Paul R.

Clyde Warrior: Tradition, Community, and Red Power D. M. Cobb *American Indian Quarterly* v41 no1 p93 Wint 2017

McKeon, Belinda

GUCCI'S URBAN GARDEN color *Harper's Bazaar* no3655 p124 Ag 2017

MCKEON, LAUREN

Whose Side Are You On, Anyway? cartoon *Walrus* v13 no10 p32 D 2016

MCKEON, ROBIN

Your True Stories IN 100 WORDS color *Reader's Digest* v189 no1129 p25 Ap 2017

McKEOUGH, TIM

#4: In a New York apartment, Bachman Brown Clem performs an about-face: The moldings and trim—not walls—are in gleaming blue, framing a neutral backdrop filled with antiques and treasures color *House Beautiful* v159 no2 p108 Mr 2017

columbus, indiana color *Architectural Digest* no5 p90 My 2017

GET PLASTERED color *Architectural Digest* v73 no11 p68 N 2016

north adams, massachusetts bw color *Architectural Digest* no5 p82 My 2017

McKeown, Greg

99% of Networking Is a Waste of Time *Harvard Business Review Digital Articles* p2 Ja 22 2015

An Exercise to Become a More Powerful Listener *Harvard Business Review Digital Articles* p2 N 6 2014

Prioritize Your Life Before Your Manager Does It for You *Harvard Business Review Digital Articles* p2 Je 1 2015

MCKESSON, DERAY

Chatter bw color *Advocate* no1089 p10 F/Mr 2017

OBAMA'S AMERICA img *New York* v49 no20 p12 O 3 2016

McKevett, G. A.

Every Body on Deck: A Savannah Reid Mystery *Publishers Weekly* v264 no11 p60 Mr 13 2017

MCKIBBEN, BETH

Field to Vase *Atlanta* v57 no1 p55 My 2017

HEY, SHORTY *Atlanta* v56 no12 p79 Ap 2017

McKibben, Bill

"A BOOK I'D LIKE MY ELECTED OFFICIALS TO READ" color *Christian Century* v133 no21 p28 O 12 2016

CLIMATE CRISIS: A NEW BATTLE PLAN *Rolling Stone*

no1280 p32 F 9 2017

THE CLIMATE TEST *Rolling Stone* no1291/1292 p43 Jl 13 2017

Climate Warriors R. CONNIFF bw *Progressive* v81 no5 p6 Je/Jl 2017

THE END OF ICE color *New Republic* v247 no12 p32 D 2016

IN CONVERSATION R. W. Emory Jr., B. Emerick et al *In These Times* v41 no10 p4 O 2017

A MARCH FOR THE FUTURE PEOPLE'S CLIMATE MOBILIZATION color *Nation* v304 no15 p12 My 8 2017

The New Nation-States color *New Republic* v248 no8/9 p14 Ag/S 2017

Pause! We Can Go Back! bw *New York Review of Books* v64 no2 p4 F 9 2017

POWER BROKERS bw cartoon color *New Yorker* v93 no18 p46 Je 26 2017

Recalculating the Climate Math il *New Republic* v247 no11 p16 N 2016

"THE ACTIVE MANY CAN OVERCOME THE RUTHLESS FEW" bw color il *Nation* v303 no25/26 p10 D 19 2016

McKibben, Kalyn

Cow College B. Welch color *American Cowboy* v23 no4 p24 D 2016/Ja 2017

McKibben, Theresa

pontoon mania color *Cabin Living* p60 Je 2017

McKie, Katherine

A districtwide commitment to arts integration color il *Phi Delta Kappan* v98 no7 p29 Ap 2017

McKiernan, Andrew

Smashing Debuts chart color *Sports Illustrated* v127 no9 p14 S 25 2017

McKINLESS, ASHLEY

OF MANY THINGS *America* v215 no15 p2 N 14 2016

McKINLEY, PETER S.

Mapping Conservation Strategies under a Changing Climate *BioScience* v67 no6 p494 Je 2017

McKinley, William

Don't Treat Innovation as a Cure-All *Harvard Business Review Digital Articles* p2 D 8 2014

McKINNEY, ANDREA

Financial Life color *Missouri Life* v44 no5 p82 Ag 2017

McKinney, Brian

BRINGING SILICON VALLEY TO DETROIT K. Johnson color *Black Enterprise* v47 no7 p21 My/Je 2017

MCKINNEY, JEFFREY

50 TOP COMPANIES FOR SUPPLIER DIVERSITY color *Black Enterprise* v47 no7 p32 My/Je 2017

ASH CASH'S LAWS FOR FINANCIAL SUCCESS color *Black Enterprise* v47 no8 p24 Jl/Ag 2017

BUILDING A FRANCHISE EMPIRE color *Black Enterprise* v47 no7 p13 My/Je 2017

EVOLUTION color diag graph *Black Enterprise* v47 no7 p46 My/Je 2017

GIVING BACK WITH IMPACT CHRISTAL JACKSON'S color *Black Enterprise* v47 no5 p22 Ja/F 2017

HOW LIFE INSURANCE CAN BUILD WEALTH FOR BLACKS color *Black Enterprise* v47 no8 p19 Jl/Ag 2017

INVESTING IN THE TRUMP ERA color *Black Enterprise* v47 no5 p19 Ja/F 2017

MID-YEAR FINANCIAL CHECKUP diag graph *Black Enterprise* v47 no8 p52 Jl/Ag 2017

MOLDING HBCU STUDENTS INTO TECH INVESTORS color *Black Enterprise* v47 no7 p20 My/Je 2017

McKinney, Joe

'TO LIVE AND LET LIVE' B. DOHERTY color map *Reason* v49 no2 p36 Je 2017

MCKINNEY, KATHERINE

For Love and Trains *National Parks* v91 no4 p16 Fall 2017

The Retirement Cure *National Parks* v91 no1 p10 Wint 2017

Mckinney, Kelsey

The Case for ... Monica Abbott color *Sports Illustrated* v126 no18 p22 Je 26 2017

McKinney, Larry

Record storm puts gulf resilience to the test E. Pennisi and D. Malakoff color *Science* v357 no6355 p954 S 8 2017

McKinney, Mark

Superstore M. Roffman *TV Guide* v65 no19 p39 My 1 2017

McKinney-Whetstone, Diane

THE ONE & ONLY QUEEN color *Essence* v48 no6 p112 O 2017

McKinnon, Arlo

Pen: Arlington *Opera News* v81 no7 p48 Ja 2017

McKinnon, Denver

FOR YOUR 'EYES ONLY B. RUZZO and G. BETHGE color map *Outdoor Life* v224 no2 p30 F/Mr 2017

McKINNON, JENNIFER

Paying Our Respects color *O, The Oprah Magazine* p15 Je 2017

McKinnon, Kate, 1984-

Kate McKinnon Didn't Make a Joke R. TRAISTER img *New York* v49 no25 p50 D 12 2016

KATE McKINNON N. Sperling color *Entertainment Weekly* no1444/1445 p24 D 16 2016

THE McKinnon Report L. ANOLIK color *Vanity Fair* v59 no11 p112 N 2017

Saturday Night Live's Weirdo in Chief A. MORRIS color *Rolling Stone* no1272 p26 O 20 2016

McKinnon, Lyle R.

Sustained virologic control in SIV+ macaques after antiretroviral and α4β7 antibody therapy bibl graph *Science* v354 no6309 p197 O 14 2016

Vaginal bacteria modify HIV tenofovir microbicide efficacy in African women chart graph *Science* v356 no6341 p938 Je 1 2017

McKinnon, Mika

MEET THE MASTER OF THE LUSH (PLANT) LIFE color *Rodale's Organic Life* v3 no1 p71 Ja 2017

McKinnon, William

Could life lurk within Pluto's ocean? A. Klesman color *Astronomy* v45 no4 p13 Ap 2017

McKinsey & Co. Inc.

This one's on the house J. GEDDES color *Maclean's* v129 no45 p22 N 14 2016

McKinsey Awards

2016 HBR MCKINSEY AWARDS color *Harvard Business Review* v95 no3 p46 My/Je 2017

McKinty, Adrian

Police at the Station and They Don't Look Friendly: A Detective Sean Duffy Novel *Publishers Weekly* v264 no2 p41 Ja 9 2017

McKinty, Adrian—Interviews

Luck and Book Sales J. FOSTER *Publishers Weekly* v264 no3 p41 Ja 16 2017

McKinty, Colin

The C-Suite and IT Need to Get on the Same Page on Cybersecurity *Harvard Business Review Digital Articles* p2 Ap 26 2017

McKnight, Carolyn—Interviews

Member Spotlight: Carolyn McKnight S. Bartram *Parks & Recreation* v51 no10 p84 O 2016

McKnight, Jenna M.

Francis Kéré Envisions House of Parliament for Burkina Faso *Architectural Record* v204 no11 p25 N 2016

Gensler *Architectural Record* v205 no4 p118 Ap 2017

Raising the Grade *Architectural Record* v205 no1 p96 Ja 2017

McKnight, Michael

38,000 CUTS (GIVE OR TAKE) color *Sports Illustrated* v126 no16 p50 Je 5 2017

FOOTBALL IN AMERICA [Cover story] color *Sports Illustrated* v125 no17 p40 N 21 2016 Double Issue

Stayin' Hollywood color *Sports Illustrated* v126 no17 p20 Je 19 2017

WHY DO I FEEL SO EMPTY INSIDE? color *Sports Illustrated* v127 no10 p16 O 2 2017

ZIMMER OF HOPE color *Sports Illustrated* v127 no7 p56 S 4 2017

McKNIGHT, REN

MASTER CLASS WITH bw cartoon color *Esquire* v166 no5 p69 D 2016/Ja 2017

A New Mecca of Cool color *Esquire* v167 no1 p44 F 2017

McKnight, Sam—Interviews

SAM MCKNIGHT L. Brown color *InStyle* v24 no1 p72 Ja 2017

The Sexiest Waves Ever B. Shapiro color *Glamour* v114 no12 p134 D 2016

McKnight, Tyler

$50K A MAN CHANGES EVERYTHING color *Team Roping Journal* p24 S 2017

MCKNIGHT, ZOE

A Free Spirit color *New Orleans Magazine* v52 no1 p30 S 2017

FROM THE SOUL color *Louisiana Life* v37 no6 p52 Jl/Ag 2017

Jimmy Buffett color *New Orleans Magazine* v51 no12 p32 O 2017

LOCAL FLAVOR color *Louisiana Life* v38 no1 p52 S/O 2017

Sarah Jane McMahon color *New Orleans Magazine* v51 no7 p28 My 2017

top female achievers color *New Orleans Magazine* v51 no8 p70 Je 2017

Zach Strief: Brewing success, both on the field and off color *New Orleans Magazine* v51 no10 p40 Ag 2017

McLellan, Karen

Karen McLellan *American Forests* v123 no1 p10 Wint/Spr 2017

McLellan, Marissa

Karen McLellan *American Forests* v123 no1 p10 Wint/Spr 2017

McLemore, Laura Lyons

GREATER NEW ORLEANS J. FROIS color *Louisiana Life* v37 no3 p101 Ja/F 2017

McLendon, Terre Gaines

Did you receive support from your faith community while you were experiencing depression and/or anxiety? graph *America* v216 no12 p6 My 29 2017

McLendon-Covey, Wendi

The Goldbergs N. Abrams, B. L. Heldman et al color *Entertainment Weekly* no1482/1483 p74 S 22 2017

McLennan, Don

DOWN MEXICO WAY color *Sail* v48 no10 p64 O 2017

McLennan, S. M.

Redox stratification of an ancient lake in Gale crater, Mars color *Science* v356 no6341 p922 Je 1 2017

McLeod, Alexus

Early and Modern Views on Celestial Events G. Aldana *Physics Today* v70 no9 p61 S 2017

McLeod, Brett

IF I HAD AN AXE R. Wiedeman cartoon *New Yorker* v92 no48 p17 F 6 2017

MAKE SYRUP from Birch, Walnut, and Sycamore Trees *Mother Earth News* no280 p60 F/Mr 2017

McLeod, Donald

Division of net assets M. FRISCOLANTI color *Maclean's* v130 no10 p13 N 2017

McLeod, Euan

MICROSCOPY without lenses: Lens-free on-chip imaging devices provide cost-effective, compact, and wide-field microscopy solutions for fieldwork and global health applications *Physics Today* v70 no9 p50 S 2017

MCLEOD, KEN

WHERE THE THINKING STOPS color *Tricycle: The Buddhist Review* v26 no2 p66 Wint 2016

McINTOSH, KERRI HANLEY

Getting It Done *Idaho Magazine* v17 no1 p50 Ja 2017

McLoughlin, Tommy

Last Band Standing D. Dudley color *AARP: The Magazine* v59 no4A p55 Je/Jl 2016

McLuckie, Joyce

Red squirrels in the British Isles are infected with leprosy bacilli bibl color diag map *Science* v354 no6313 p744 N 11 2016

McLuhan, Marshall, 1911-1980

The Editor's Note J. Richardson *Phi Delta Kappan* v99 no2 p4 O 2017

McMahan, Ian

Trail Mix color *Sports Illustrated* v126 no17 p22 Je 19 2017

McMahan, Mary

Around the Campfire color *Trail Rider* v29 no1 p6 Ja/F 2017

McMahon, Dave

THE PILOTS WHO CRASHED INTO THE SEA N. HUNE-BROWN color map *Reader's Digest* v189 no1129 p84 Ap 2017

McMahon, Jim

WHAT IF? ... THESE FIVE CAREERS HADN'T BEEN ALTERED BY INJURY? J. Feldman color *Sports Illustrated* v126 no11 p53 Ap 17-24 2017

McMahon, John

CAKEWALK TO NOVA SCOTIA A. CORT color map *Sail* v48 no11 p44 N 2017

McMAHON, KATHERINE

Fair Thee Well color *ARTnews* v116 no1 p48 Spr 2017

HABITAT Moonlighting color *ARTnews* v115 no4 p38 Wint 2016/2017

Obsessions bw color *ARTnews* v115 no3 p54 Fall 2016

MCMAHON, KATHRYN

Accelerating Tropicalization and the Transformation of Temperate Seagrass Meadows *BioScience* v66 no11 p938 N 1 2016

MCMAHON, MELISSA

THE REAL BELOW DECKS color *Power & Motoryacht* v33 no3 p80 Mr 2017

McMahon, Patrice C.

The NGO Game: Postconflict Peacebuilding in the Balkans and Beyond R. Legvold *Foreign Affairs* v96 no6 p164 N/D 2017

McMahon, Peter L.

A coherent Ising machine for 2000-node optimization problems bibl diag graph *Science* v354 no6312 p603 N 4 2016

A fully programmable 100-spin coherent Ising machine with all-to-all connections bibl diag graph *Science* v354 no6312 p614 N 4 2016

McMahon, Sean M.

Plant diversity increases with the strength of negative density dependence at the global scale diag *Science* v356 no6345 p1389 Je 30 2017

McManus, Bob

Hiroshima, His Amour *Commentary* v142 no1 p32 Jl/Ag 2016

A Riot, Not an Uprising *Commentary* v142 no4 p41 N 2016

McManus, John

SAVING THE SOUTH CHINA SEA D. LAWRENCE and W. FAN color map *Bloomberg Businessweek* no4505 p78 D 26 2016

MCMANUS, MELANIE RADZICKI

Secret Garden: Big Cypress National Preserve, Florida color *Backpacker* p16 N 2017

McManus, Patrick F.

THE QUOTABLE CURMUDGEON cartoon *Outdoor Life* v224 no1 p14 D 2016/Ja 2017

McMaster, Gerald

UNDER INDIGENOUS EYES color *Art in America* p64 O 2017

McMaster, H. R., 1962-

Should McMaster Get the Boot? If so, here's how his successor should operate W. S. LIND *American Conservative* v16 no5 p11 S/O 2017

Take Two at the NSC T. JOSCELYN cartoon *Weekly Standard* v22 no25 p11 Mr 6 2017

They Deserve Our Gratitude J. V. Last color *Weekly Standard* v22 no37 p13 Je 5 2017

McMeekin, David P.

Perovskite-perovskite tandem photovoltaics with optimized band gaps bibl chart graph *Science* v354 no6314 p861 N 18 2016

McMeekin, Sean

The Best-Laid Plans: A new history argues that the Bolshevik Revolution was largely a matter of chance G. FEIFER *New York Times Book Review* p14 Je 11 2017

The Russian Revolution: A New History *Publishers Weekly* v264 no16 p59 Ap 17 2017

McMichael, Anthony J.

Back to the future A. Makri color *Science* v355 no6323 p355 Ja 27 2017

CLIMATE CHANGE AND THE HEALTH OF NATIONS B. BETHUNE color *Maclean's* no1 p60 F 17 2017

McMillan, Cecily

An Occupy Protester's Emancipation Proclamation W. Meyer cartoon color *Progressive* v81 no10 p39 N 2016

McMillan, Chase

How to Talk Politics at Work Without Alienating People *Harvard Business Review Digital Articles* p2 S 14 2016

McMillan, Chris

The A-LIST J. Aniston bw color *Harper's Bazaar* no3657 p118 O 2017

McMillan, Chris—Interviews

Chris McMillan K. Diamond color *InStyle* v24 no3 p266 Mr 2017

McMillan, Greg

RUN YOUR BEST 5K J. B. Polloreno color *Men's Health* v32 no3 p30 Ap 2017

MCMILLAN, JEFFERY S.

THE PURSUIT OF THE ROSE *Opera News* v81 no10 p36 Ap 2017

McMillan, Tressie—Interviews

Bad Education R. M. COHEN color *New Republic* v248 no1/2 p11 Ja/F 2017

MCMILLEN, DANISE
snowbound but beautiful color map *Cabin Living* p18 Je 2017

McMillen, David
Centennial *Prologue* v48 no3 p6 Fall 2016
JFK IN CONGRESS *Prologue* v49 no1 p36 Spr 2017
MOVING OUT, MOVING IN *Prologue* v48 no4 p36 Wint 2016
When the World Went to War [Cover story] *Prologue* v49 no2 p6 Summ 2017

McMillin, Andy
LEGACY LEGITIMIZATION S. RICHARDS color *Dirt Sports + Off-Road* v51 no11 p10 N 2017

McMillon, C. Douglas, 1967——Interviews
"WE NEED PEOPLE TO LEAN INTO THE FUTURE" A. IGNATIUS color img *Harvard Business Review* v95 no2 p94 Mr/Ap 2017

McMillon, Joi
MAKING THE CUT J. Thompson color *Essence* v48 no2 p74 Je 2017

Mcminn, Mark R.
THE SCIENCE OF humility *Christianity Today* v61 no6 p80 Jl/Ag 2017

McMinnville (Or.)
OREGON'S McMINNVILLE K. Newberry color map *Sunset* v239 no4 p28 O 2017

McMORRIS, BILL
Union Republicans il *National Review* v69 no6 p31 Ap 3 2017

McMorrow, Christine
The Thread color *New York Times Magazine* p12 D 4 2016
The Thread *New York Times Magazine* p9 Ja 22 2017

McMullan, Patrick
PARTY LINES img *New York* v50 no10 p104 My 15 2017

Mcmullen, Steven
Hope in the Humanless Economy color *Christianity Today* v61 no6 p30 Jl/Ag 2017

McMullin, Evan
The Defector M. COPPINS cartoon *Atlantic* v320 no1 p20 Jl/Ag 2017
Grand New Party? J. V. LAST *Weekly Standard* v22 no4 p13 O 3 2016
The 'Hail Mary' Candidate J. MCCORMACK color *Weekly Standard* v22 no9 p13 N 7 2016

McMullin, Evan—Interviews
Evan McMullin Is Very Concerned A. M. Cox *New York Times Magazine* p62 Mr 5 2017
The Utah Surprise E. Dias color *Time* v188 no19 p11 N 7 2016

McMurdo Dry Valleys (Antarctica)—Environmental conditions
Microbial Community Dynamics in Two Polar Extremes: The Lakes of the McMurdo Dry Valleys and the West Antarctic Peninsula Marine Ecosystem J. S. BOWMAN, J. C. PRISCU et al chart color graph *BioScience* v66 no10 p829 O 1 2016

McMurdo Station (Antarctica)
Air Waves Over Antarctica H. Leifert *Natural History* v125 no2 p8 F 2017

McMURRAY, JOHN
WINDS OF CHANGE color map *Outdoor Life* v224 no5 p33 Je/Jl 2017

McMurtry, James
'COPPER CANTEEN' R. GRAHAM bw *New York Times Magazine* p47 Mr 12 2017

McMurtry, Larry, 1936-
After the hurricane, Larry McMurtry's Houston trilogy lives on D. Brinkley *New York Times Book Review* p22 O 8 2017

McNab, Chris
ANTI-ZEPPELIN DART color *MHQ: Quarterly Journal of Military History* v29 no4 p27 Summ 2017
DISCUS HAND GRENADE *MHQ: Quarterly Journal of Military History* v29 no3 p25 Spr 2017
LEWIS GUN *MHQ: Quarterly Journal of Military History* v29 no2 p23 Wint 2017
WEAPONS CHECK: MG 42 color *MHQ: Quarterly Journal of Military History* v30 no1 p27 Aut 2017

McNab, James
LARGE INDUSTRIES IN LIMITED SPACE color diag *Model Railroader* v83 no12 p52 D 2016

McNabb, Frederick William
A Mutual Fund Giant Flexes Its Muscles E. Fry color diag *Fortune* v174 no8 p126 D 15 2016

McNair-Landry, Sarah
SIX HUNDRED MILES WITH SKIS, KITES, AND WIND K. Long color *National Geographic* v231 no3 p14 Mr 2017

McNally, Janet
Girls in the Moon *Publishers Weekly* v263 no40 p126 O 3 2016

McNally, R. L.
A Fermi-degenerate three-dimensional optical lattice clock color diag graph *Science* v357 no6359 p90 O 6 2017

McNally, Tim
Attitude color *New Orleans Magazine* v51 no5 p94 Mr 2017
BAR EXAM [Cover story] color *New Orleans Magazine* v51 no3 p56 Ja 2017
Blueberry Hill color *New Orleans Magazine* v52 no1 p110 S 2017
By Any Measurement color *New Orleans Magazine* v51 no4 p90 F 2017
Café Giovanni color *New Orleans Magazine* v51 no2 p80 D 2016
Coming Around Again color *New Orleans Magazine* v51 no9 p86 Jl 2017
EAT. DRINK. ENJOY color *New Orleans Magazine* v51 no9 p56 Jl 2017
Halloween Spirits color *New Orleans Magazine* v51 no12 p116 O 2017
May Showers Bring... color *New Orleans Magazine* v51 no7 p88 My 2017
McClure's Barbecue color *New Orleans Magazine* v51 no2 p80 D 2016
Mike Gulotta [Cover story] color *New Orleans Magazine* v51 no2 p64 D 2016
OUT THE BOX color *New Orleans Magazine* v51 no1 p118 N 2016
Paul Gustings color *New Orleans Magazine* v51 no2 p76 D 2016
Pop the corks! color *New Orleans Magazine* v51 no8 p106 Je 2017
Seaworthy color *New Orleans Magazine* v51 no2 p79 D 2016
Shake, Pour and Chill Out: The Saltwater color *New Orleans Magazine* v51 no10 p178 Ag 2017
SIPPING FOR THE SEASON color *New Orleans Magazine* v51 no2 p90 D 2016
Spring Goes Fancy color *New Orleans Magazine* v51 no6 p90 Ap 2017
State of the Market *New Orleans Magazine* v51 no2 p69 D 2016
TOAST TO TRÉO color *New Orleans Magazine* v51 no3 p118 Ja 2017

McNamara, Bill
Life without Kay: Love defies death color *U.S. Catholic* v82 no10 p23 O 2017

McNamara, Charles
Report from the Afterlife color *Commonweal* v144 no1 p32 Ja 6 2017
The Resurrection Will Be a Remix color *Commonweal* v143 no18 p46 N 11 2016

McNamara, Eddie
MAC AND CHEESE color *Women's Health* v14 no5 p36 Je 2017
Toss Your Own Salad *Publishers Weekly* v264 no16 p61 Ap 17 2017

McNAMARA, JAMES
Falling Through Time: Three men, separated by three centuries, witness an Australian miracle *New York Times Book Review* p14 S 10 2017
Swift Beyond Satire *New York Times Book Review* p20 F 26 2017

McNamara, Kerry
A day at the races bw color *Equus* no477 p77 Je 2017

McNamara, Kevin J.
THE BATTLE FOR BAIKAL [Cover story] bw color map *MHQ: Quarterly Journal of Military History* v29 no4 p76 Summ 2017

Mcnamara, Maggie
CATCHING THE Ballet Bug *Dance Spirit* v21 no3 p42 Mr 2017
C'mon, Get Happy bw color *Dance Spirit* v20 no10 p44 D 2016
FROM THE PAGE TO THE STAGE color *Dance Spirit* v20 no9 p55 N 2016
Tate TALK color *Dance Spirit* v21 no4 p30 Ap 2017
Transatlantic TRAINING *Dance Spirit* v21 no7 p80 S 2017

McNamara, Peter
THE GREAT ENRICHMENT *Claremont Review of Books* v17

no2 p82 Spr 2017

TEAM OF RIVALS *Claremont Review of Books* v16 no4 p28 Fall 2016

McNamara, Robert S., 1916-2009

McNAMARA'S BOYS H. Gregory *MHQ: Quarterly Journal of Military History* v29 no3 p70 Spr 2017

McNamee, Mark

Navigating the Complexities of Doing Business in Russia *Harvard Business Review Digital Articles* p2 My 29 2017

McNearney, Allison

Which Would You Rather: a Million Dollars or True Love? color diag *Money* v46 no4 p18 My 2017

McNease, Mark

Last Room at the Cliff's Edge: A Detective Linda Mystery *Publishers Weekly* v264 no13 p64a Mr 27 2017

Last Room at the Cliff's Edge: A Detective Linda Mystery *Publishers Weekly* v264 no8 p69 F 20 2017

McNee, Margaret

Exploring genetic suppression interactions on a global scale diag *Science* v354 no6312 p599 N 4 2016

McNeely, Aaron

FROM OUR READERS *Sky & Telescope* v133 no5 p6 My 2017

McNeely, Nina

RITUAL WORK T. J. Rosenthal bw color *Art in America* v105 no3 p82 Mr 2017

McNeely, Stephen

Moon Rivers Naturals L. S. FORD *Texas Monthly* v45 no7 p25 Jl 2017

McNeil, Barbara

The Harvard Contest That's Trying to Improve Health Care Delivery *Harvard Business Review Digital Articles* p2 O 2 2015

McNeil, Rupert—Interviews

HR should stand for humane rigour R. JEFFERY *People Management* p42 N 2016

McNeill, Helen

Drosophila insulin release is triggered by adipose Stunted ligand to brain Methuselah receptor bibl graph *Science* v353 no6307 p1553 S 30 2016

McNeill, John

THE RIVER AT SPRINGFIELD B. Hunhoff *South Dakota Magazine* v32 no4 p28 N/D 2016

McNeill, Lisa C.

Release of mineral-bound water prior to subduction tied to shallow seismogenic slip off Sumatra graph *Science* v356 no6340 p841 My 26 2017

McNeill, Serayah

Yeah, Bra E. Wilson color *InStyle* v24 no9 p182 S 2017

McNichol, Jesse

Big Questions About Tiny Bacteria? color *Oceanus* v51 no2 p78 Wint 2016

McNickle, Chris

Bloomberg: A Billionaire's Ambition *Publishers Weekly* v264 no24 p51 Je 12 2017

Mayor Mike and His Data: How Bloomberg used facts and analysis to successfully transform New York City D. LEONHARDT *New York Times Book Review* p17 S 17 2017

McNicol, Ewan

Gone Fishin'; Fishin' Gone W. FERGUSON *Texas Monthly* v45 no5 p52 My 2017

McNish, Allan

CURRENT AFFAIRS A. Lindberg color *Car & Driver* v63 no5 p24 N 2017

McNulty, Amybeth

In the new adaptation of Anne of Green Gables, hope is replaced by horror H. Stewart color *America* v216 no13 p56 Je 12 2017

Reimagining Anne A. Wilkinson color *Entertainment Weekly* no1465 p47 My 12 2017

Mcnulty, Eric J.

U.S. Health Care Reform Will Require Politicians to Change Their Attitude *Harvard Business Review Digital Articles* p2 F 2 2017

McNulty, Stacy

PHENOLOGY *New York State Conservationist* v71 no4 p24 F 2017

McNutt, Crystal—Awards

the WAY WE WERE: THE YEAR WAS 1993 *Arabian Horse World* v57 no10 p53 Jl 2017

McNutt, Jennifer Powell

Division is not necessarily Scandal color *Christianity Today* v61 no1 p42 Ja/F 2017

The plain, difficult sense of scripture M. Labberton *Christian Century* v134 no8 p1 Ap 12 2017

McNutt, M.

Fostering reproducibility in industry-academia research color *Science* v357 no6353 p759 Ag 25 2017

McNutt, Marcia

Enhancing reproducibility for computational methods bibl color *Science* v354 no6317 p1240 D 9 2016

Ralph J. Cicerone (1943–2016) color *Science* v354 no6316 p1107 D 2 2016

Research integrity revisited color *Science* v356 no6334 p115 Ap 14 2017

McNutt, Nick

THE DOWNSLIDE color *Skiing* p10 Wint 2017

MCNUTT, RYAN

Least Coast color *Walrus* v14 no8 p17 O 2017

McPHAIL, WILL

GENIUS color *Esquire* p29 O 2017

N.Y.C.'S MOST ELIGIBLE PIGEONS color *New Yorker* v93 no24 p49 Ag 21 2017

PRIVATE SELVES, PUBLIC LIES cartoon *Esquire* p40 S 2017

McPhee, John, 1931-

The Agony of Writing D. HEITMAN color *Weekly Standard* v23 no6 p41 O 16 2017

THE ANGLER: John McPhee's radical structures S. Anderson *New York Times Magazine* p28 O 1 2017

McPhee, Scott A.

Polymeric peptide pigments with sequence-encoded properties color graph *Science* v356 no6342 p1064 Je 9 2017

MCPHERSON, BILL

Graying America in Search of a Solution *USA Today Magazine* v145 no2860 p30 Ja 2017

McPherson, Cindy

TOUGH CALL C. COLIN color *O, The Oprah Magazine* p30 F 2017

McPherson, James M.

America's Greatest Movement cartoon *New York Review of Books* v63 no16 p63 O 27 2016

McPherson, Tamu

Diamond in the Ruffle color *Vogue* v206 no12 p160 D 2016

McQuade, Aidan

Icons color *Time* v189 no16/17 p122 My 1-8 2017

McQUADE, PETER D.

Tangled Lines *Idaho Magazine* v16 no2 p6 N 2016

MCQUAID, JOHN

WHISTLEBLOWERS *Smithsonian* v47 no8 p48 D 2016

McQuaid, Maggie

I JUST STARTED READING THE *Arizona Highways* v92 no11 p4 N 2016

McQueen, Alexander, 1969-2010

The List color *InStyle* v23 no12 p28 N 2016

McQueen, Dan

Mayor Meltdown *Texas Monthly* v45 no3 p66 Mr 2017

McQueen, Mina—Interviews

MAKING THAT KITTY PURR D. ARTAVIA color *Advocate* no1090 p44 Ap 2017

McQuillen, Patrick S.

Extensive migration of young neurons into the infant human frontal lobe color diag graph *Science* v354 no6308 paaf7073-1 O 7 2016

McQuillen, Ryan

GTPase activity-coupled treadmilling of the bacterial tubulin FtsZ organizes septal cell wall synthesis bibl graph *Science* v355 no6326 p744 F 17 2017

McQuivey, James—Interviews

What HoloLens Has That Google Glass Didn't S. Berinato *Harvard Business Review Digital Articles* p2 Ja 29 2015

MCRAE, MICHAEL

Life *Reader's Digest* v188 no1126 p36 D 2016/Ja 2017

McRAE, ROBIN

IDAHO'S POMPELL: A GOLD RUSH TOWN DROWNED *Idaho Magazine* v16 no7 p42 Ap 2017

McRae, Tate—Interviews

American Power and Liberal Order: A Conservative Internationalist Grand Strategy *Foreign Affairs* v96 no1 p164 Ja/F 2017

The Complacent Class: The Self-Defeating Quest for the American Dream *Foreign Affairs* v96 no2 p175 Mr/Ap 2017

Devil's Bargain: Steve Bannon, Donald Trump, and the Storming of the Presidency *Foreign Affairs* v96 no6 p158 N/D 2017

Great Again: How to Fix Our Crippled America/The Field of Fight *Foreign Affairs* v96 no2 p174 Mr/Ap 2017

The Jacksonian Revolt color *Foreign Affairs* v96 no2 p2 Mr/Ap 2017

Keeper of the Flame *New York Times Book Review* p14 My 7 2017

Learning From Experience *Foreign Affairs* v96 no2 p176 Mr/Ap 2017

Stanton: Lincoln's War Secretary *Foreign Affairs* v96 no6 p159 N/D 2017

The Voice of America: Lowell Thomas and the Invention of Twentieth-Century Journalism *Foreign Affairs* v96 no6 p158 N/D 2017

Meade, Angela
GOINGS ON ABOUT TOWN bw *New Yorker* v93 no20 p5 Jl 10 2017

Meade, Birgit
International Food Security Assessment, 2017-2027 *Amber Waves: The Economics of Food, Farming, Natural Resources, & Rural America* p26 Je 2017

Meade, Norman
Contingent valuation: Flawed logic? color *Science* v357 no6349 p363 Jl 28 2017

Putting a value on injuries to natural assets: The BP oil spill chart *Science* v356 no6335 p253 Ap 21 2017

MEADOR, MICHAEL
THE THING THAT CHANGED IT ALL bw *Bicycling* v58 no6 p15 Jl 2017

Meadows
See also
Mountain meadows
Accelerating Tropicalization and the Transformation of Temperate Seagrass Meadows G. A. HYNDES, K. L. HECK, Jr. et al *BioScience* v66 no11 p938 N 1 2016

MEADOWS, AMY
The Right Decision *Atlanta* v56 no9 p139 Ja 2017

Meadows, Susannah—Interviews
SELF-HEALTH M. Bryan cartoon *O, The Oprah Magazine* p97 My 2017

Meadows, Tim
DIVE INTO Brooklyn Nine-Nine D. Snierson, N. Abrams et al color *Entertainment Weekly* no1482/1483 p67 S 22 2017

Meadows—California
Finding Home: What happens when a desert baby visits the meadows of Yosemite? M. BRANCH *National Parks* v91 no3 p18 Summ 2017

MEAGAN, CAMPBELL
The incredible journey color *Maclean's* v129 no43 p39 O 31 2016

MEAGHER, THOMAS R.
Synthesis Centers as Critical Research Infrastructure *BioScience* v67 no8 p750 Ag 2017

Meal
Exactly how to FILL your PLATE M. TAYLOR color *Redbook* p90 Ap 2017

KAISEKI GOES CALIFORNIAN *Los Angeles Magazine* p64 D 2016

Meal assembly stores—Evaluation
MEN'S HEALTH color *New Orleans Magazine* v51 no5 p130 Mr 2017

Mealing, David
Soul of the World *Publishers Weekly* v264 no21 p77 My 22 2017

Mean Girls (Theatrical production)
ARTS GUIDE: Among all the plays, exhibits, concerts, and other arts events ahead, here are 12 we most want to see in the fall and beyond M. J. GAYNOR *Washingtonian Magazine* v52 no12 p40 S 2017

Meaning (Philosophy)
Donald Trump, James Comey, and the Ambiguity of "Hope" R. T. Lakoff *Harvard Business Review Digital Articles* p2 Je 13 2017

Means, David
FISTFIGHT, SACRAMENTO, AUGUST 1950 *Harper's Magazine* p77 O 2017

Two Ruminations on a Homeless Brother cartoon color *New Yorker* v93 no11 p56 My 1 2017

Wishes From the Wings *New York Times Book Review* p12 Ja 22 2017

MEANS, HOWARD
"YOU GOING TO THE MARCH?" *Washingtonian Magazine* v52 no6 p58 Mr 2017

Means, Macho
RAP SESSION A. KONERMANN *Cincinnati Magazine* v50 no7 p19 Ap 2017

Means, Richard
Alexander Skarsgård color *Current Biography* v78 no1 p78 Ja 2017

Ali Benjamin color *Current Biography* v78 no5 p16 My 2017

Arthur B. McDonald *Current Biography* v78 no4 p57 Ap 2017

John Green *Current Biography* v78 no8 p38 Ag 2017

Means, Sam
Out & About *TV Guide* p4 D 5 2016

Mearns, Sara, 1986-
POINTE OF PERFECTION L. JACOBS color *Vanity Fair* v59 no10 p172 O 2017

Sara Mearns J. Johnson color *Current Biography* v78 no9 p57 S 2017

Mearns, Sara, 1986-—Interviews
A Film Classic, Reimagined color *Dance Spirit* v21 no8 p35 O 2017

Mears, Steven
The Little Guy color *Film Comment* v53 no4 p18 Jl/Ag 2017

The Long Way Home bw color *Film Comment* v53 no3 p74 My/Je 2017

Manchester by the Sea *Film Comment* v53 no1 p47 Ja/F 2017

Measles
Measles surges in Europe *Science* v355 no6332 p1355 Mr 31 2017

Measurement
See also
Gravitational field measurements
Organizational performance—Measurement
Units of measurement
Weights & measures
4 Steps for Thinking Critically About Data Measurements T. C. Redman *Harvard Business Review Digital Articles* p2 Mr 17 2016

Don't Be Tyrannized by Old Metrics R. C. Wolcott *Harvard Business Review Digital Articles* p2 S 23 2016

A GRAVITATIONAL-LENSING MEASUREMENT OF THE HUBBLE CONSTANT *Physics Today* v70 no4 p24 Ap 2017

Measurement errors
Measurement error and the replication crisis E. Loken and A. Gelman bibl graph *Science* v355 no6325 p584 F 10 2017

Measurement of angles (Geometry)
ANGLE OF ATTACK INDICATOR diag *Flying* v144 no6 p20 Je 2017

Measurement—Equipment & supplies
Focus on test and measurement A. Mandelis *Physics Today* v70 no3 p68 Mr 2017

Measuring instruments
See also
Balancing machines
Mini Measure L. SCHLEY color *Discover* v38 no9 p22 N 2017

My Collection T. Johnson color *Horse & Rider* v56 no11 p136 N 2017

Measuring instruments—Evaluation
Keep It Legal: Think that fish you caught is a keeper? Not so fast A. JONES *Boating World* v38 no5 p18 My 2017

Meat
See also
Beef
Ground meat
Meat cuts
BET THE FARM color *Chicago* v66 no3 p61 Mr 2017

Burrito on My Plate J. Yacoubou *Vegetarian Journal* v36 no2 p15 2017

Energy Essential V. TWEED chart color *Better Nutrition* p22 My 2017

feel-good feasts C. Nash color *Health* v30 no10 p110 D 2016 ground (meat) rules! L. PERRI color *Parents* v92 no5 p102 My 2017

HERE'S HOW YOU MAKE AN "AUTHENTIC" AMERICAN TACO W. AVILA color *Bon Appetit* v62 no2 p68 Mr 2017

How Can I Get My Toddler to Eat Meat? *Parents* v92 no2 p28 F 2017

Know Your Ribs: A guide to the perfect rack *Virginia Living* p53 2017 Smoke & Salt

Let's Eat Pig's Feet R. Bragg color *Southern Living* v52 no4 p150 Ap 2017

MAN VS. WILD BOAR R. O'CONNOR color *Chicago* v66 no7 p22 Jl 2017

Our Vegan Polish Spot Is So Polish, Polish-Americans Don't Think It's Polish T. SKOWRONSKI color *Bon Appetit* v62 no2 p69 Mr 2017

Regulation, Market Signals, and the Provision of Food Safety in Meat and Poultry M. Ollinger and M. Taylor Rhodes *Amber Waves: The Economics of Food, Farming, Natural Resources, & Rural America* p1 My 2017

RICH & SKINNY D. Wise color *Health* v31 no8 p102 O 2017

Roast onions J. Iserloh color *Yoga Journal* no291 p34 My 2017

SWEET (AND SALTY) DREAMS [Cover story] K. Ansel color *Women's Health* v14 no7 p108 S 2017

THE TRIUMPHANT RETURN OF RED MEAT M. Heid color *Men's Health* v32 no2 p88 Mr 2017

THE TWO WAYS TO COOK MEAT F. MAROUKIAN color *Popular Mechanics* p68 S 2017

Meat animals—Health

Meat Depressed color *Weekly Standard* v22 no41 p2 Jl 3 2017

Meat cuts

See also

Ribs (Cooking)

Steak (Beef)

Sandra Lee Favorites *TV Guide* v64 no40 p18 O 3 2016

SHARPEN YOUR KNIVES [Cover story] C. BOERS, P. POL-LACK et al color *Chicago* v66 no11 p60 N 2017

Meat grinders—Evaluation

MEAT EATERS A. ROBINSON color *Outdoor Life* v224 no1 p21 D 2016/Ja 2017

Meat industry

See also

Butchers

Factory farms

Slaughtering & slaughterhouses

CLOSE TO THE BONE T. GENOWAYS *New York Times Magazine* p59 O 9 2016

SERVING UP JACKFRUIT S. Stukin color *National Geographic* v230 no6 p14 D 2016

Meat industry accidents

How safe are the workers who process our food? S. M. Smith bibl *Monthly Labor Review* p1 Jl 2017

Meat industry—United States

THE NEXT MEAT MAESTROS J. Gordinier color *Esquire* p20 Je/Jl 2017

Meat loaf

The Swedish Season S. Sifton *New York Times Magazine* p26 Mr 5 2017

Meat markets

LOST CITY A. Flango *Cincinnati Magazine* v50 no5 p58 F 2017

Meat markets—Evaluation

GHENTING TO KNOW YOU *Virginia Living* v15 no2 p17 F 2017

Meat packing

GET IT ALL OUT T. WALRATH color *Outdoor Life* v224 no7 pH12 S 2017

Meat quality

CALL OF THE WILD: No need for camo. Catch these beasts at your local butcher shop J. BALL *Indianapolis Monthly* v12 no40 p75 Ag 2017

Meatballs

Meatball Makeovers B. P. KATZ and C. SULLIVAN color *Martha Stewart Living* p83 O 2017

Tiers of JOY A. Guarnaschelli color *O, The Oprah Magazine* p140 O 2017

WEEKNIGHT EASY color *Good Housekeeping* v264 no1 p117 Ja 1 2017

Meat—Evaluation

Mail Models A. HALPERN color *Bon Appetit* v61 no12 p69 D 2016 /Jan2017

Meat—Export & import trade

Feeding Extinction color *Earth Island Journal* v32 no4 p6 Wint 2017

MECH, L. DAVID

An Unparalleled Opportunity for an Important Ecological Study *BioScience* v67 no10 p875 O 2017

Mechanic, Michael

Debugging the Planet cartoon *Mother Jones* v42 no5 p49 S/O 2017

FLIGHT 1040 color *Mother Jones* v42 no3 p46 My/Je 2017

MAN IN THE MIRROR color *Mother Jones* v41 no6 p57 N/D 2016

SCHOOL OF ROCK color *Mother Jones* v42 no4 p58 Jl/Ag 2017

A WONDERFUL WORLD color *Mother Jones* v42 no6 p64 N/D 2017

Mechanical ability

Sky's the Limit Festus Z. Glasgow color *Missouri Life* v44 no5 p14 Ag 2017

Mechanical chemistry

Experimentally realized mechanochemistry distinct from force-accelerated scission of loaded bonds S. Akbulatov, Y. Tian et al diag graph *Science* v357 no6348 p299 Jl 21 2017

RESEARCH color *Science* v357 no6350 p467 Ag 4 2017

Mechanical drawing

See also

Automotive drafting

Thom On Design BDR T. Taylor bw color *Hot Rod* v70 no7 p96 Jl 2017

Mechanical efficiency

Locked synchronous rotor motion in a molecular motor P. Štacko, J. C. M. Kistemaker et al diag *Science* v356 no6341 p964 Je 1 2017

Mechanical engineering

See also

Diffusers (Fluid dynamics)

APPLIANCE ANALYST S. Bogdan color *Good Housekeeping* v264 no6 p6 Je 2017

Mechanical engineers

APPLIANCE ANALYST S. Bogdan color *Good Housekeeping* v264 no6 p6 Je 2017

Mechanical organs

See also

Calliope

Tool Sweet E. STYRON color *Missouri Life* v44 no2 p40 Ap 2017

Mechanics (Persons)

Dealer vs. Mechanic Showdown E. DYER color *Popular Mechanics* p40 F 2017

Not Sinking In G. MICHAL *Boating World* v38 no8 p47 S/O 2017

POPULAR MECHANICS EVERYWHERE color *Popular Mechanics* p10 N 2017

Mechanics (Physics)

See also

Acceleration (Mechanics)

Classical mechanics

Quantum mechanics

Viscosity

SHEDDING LIGHT (AND DARK) ON QUANTUM PROBABILITIES *Physics Today* v70 no6 p24 Je 2017

Mechanism of action (Biochemistry)

Closing the loop B. Levine bibl bw *Science* v354 no6315 p968 N 25 2016

Mechler, Reinhard

Identifying the policy space for climate loss and damage bibl color diag *Science* v354 no6310 p290 O 21 2016

MECIA, TONY

Chicken Among Bulls color *Weekly Standard* v22 no45 p33 Ag 7 2017

Feel-Good Investing color *Weekly Standard* v22 no30 p12 Ap 10 2017

A Glimpse Inside a Violent Gang color *Weekly Standard* v22 no46 p19 Ag 14 2017

The Immigration Frontlines color graph *Weekly Standard* v22 no42 p18 Jl 17 2017

It's the Corporate Tax Rate, Stupid graph *Weekly Standard* v23 no4 p10 O 2 2017

Manufacturing Optimism color *Weekly Standard* v22 no25 p30 Mr 6 2017

One Seat That Should Be Safe color *Weekly Standard* v22 no39 p12 Je 19 2017

Plowed Under color *Weekly Standard* v22 no47 p10 Ag 21 2017

Rolling Back the Obama Rules map *Weekly Standard* v22 no38 p14 Je 12 2017

Simply Unpalatable color diag *Weekly Standard* v22 no31 p20 Ap 17 2017

Teen Tech Times color *Weekly Standard* v22 no33 p22 My 8 2017

Mecklenburg, Robert S.

A Better Way for Employers to Procure Health Care *Harvard Business Review Digital Articles* p2 N 17 2016

How the EMR Is Increasing Innovation and Creativity in Health Care *Harvard Business Review Digital Articles* p1 O 10 2017

Large Employers Are Key to Reforming Health Care *Harvard Business Review Digital Articles* p2 Jl 27 2016

This Coalition of 20 Companies Thinks It Can Change U.S. Health Care *Harvard Business Review Digital Articles* p2 F 24 2016

What Employers Can Do to Accelerate Health Care Reform *Harvard Business Review Digital Articles* p2 O 16 2015

Mecklin, John

Introduction: International security in the age of renewables *Bulletin of the Atomic Scientists* v72 no6 p377 N 2016

Introduction: Into the aftermath *Bulletin of the Atomic Scientists* v73 no4 p210 Jl 2017

Introduction: Nuclear power and the urgent threat of climate change *Bulletin of the Atomic Scientists* v73 no1 p1 Ja 2017

Introduction: The evolving threat of hybrid war bibl *Bulletin of the Atomic Scientists* v73 no5 p298 2017

Medal of Honor

50 Reasons to Love Being 50+ M. Morris color *AARP: The Magazine* v30 no6A p63 O/N 2017

Valor Heroic Hellfighter C. Lyons *Military History* v33 no6 p12 Mr 2017

Medallions (Decorative arts)

MINT CONDITION C. FEHRMAN *Cincinnati Magazine* v50 no4 p28 Ja 2017

Medals

See also

Olympic medals

Three U.S. Medals at Youth Sailing Worlds A. Cort color *Sail* v48 no3 p16 Mr 2017

Medals—Great Britain

Tokens of friendship, tools of diplomacy: Presentation medals in the Age of Exploration R. M. Peck bw color *Magazine Antiques* v184 no5 p64 S/O 2017

Medals—United States

HOT | NOT T. Keith color *Sports Illustrated* v126 no2 p17 Ja 16 2017

Medefind, Jedd

THE ACTIVIST SOUL color *Christianity Today* v61 no6 p70 Jl/Ag 2017

MEDEIROS, GAYLE BURKHART

Laughter: THE BEST MEDICINE color *Reader's Digest* v190 no1135 p100 N 2017

Medeiros, João M.

In situ architecture, function, and evolution of a contractile injection system color diag *Science* v357 no6352 p713 Ag 18 2017

MEDELLIN, RODRIGO A.

Bats and human health *Issues in Science & Technology* v33 no4 p16 Summ 2017

Medford, Sarah

fertile imagination color *Architectural Digest* v74 no9 p138 S 2017

where life meets art color *InStyle* p38 Home & Design 2016

Media art

The Soft Warrior Spreads Her Wings S. SURFTONE *USA Today Magazine* v146 no2868 p60 S 2017

Media buying services

Is Programmatic Advertising the Future of Marketing? J. F. Rayport *Harvard Business Review Digital Articles* p2 Je 22 2015

Media consultants

Pulling the Strings F. Barnes *New Republic* v247 no11 p4 N 2016

Media literacy

Making media literacy great again M. Rosenwald color *Columbia Journalism Review* v56 no2 p94 Fall 2017

MEDIATI, NICK

How to use your iPhone or iPad as a wireless hotspot color *Macworld - Digital Edition* v34 no6 p105 Je 2017

Mediation—Study & teaching

TAKE A DEEP BREATH J. Miller color *Bloomberg Businessweek* no4523 p66 My 22 2017

Mediators (Persons)

Antagonistic Mediators Can Make Resolving Disputes Easier F. Gino *Harvard Business Review Digital Articles* p2 Ag 19 2016

Medic, The (Poem)

The Medic E. KHALIL WILSON *Progressive* v81 no6 p69 Ag/S 2017

Medicaid

Beyond Repeal and Replace P. Elliott, A. Park et al color diag map *Time* v190 no2/3 p30 Jl 10-17 2017

Block Grant Jitters A. Greenblatt *Governing* v30 no7 p10 Ap 2017

Health Care & the Gospel T. S. Jost color *Commonweal* v144 no8 p10 My 5 2017

Reinventing the Way Medicaid Delivers Care S. H. Jain and L. Lessin *Harvard Business Review Digital Articles* p2 Mr 31 2015

The War on Women's Health: Trumpcare leaves 23 million more people uninsured and slashes $834 billion from Medicaid, rewarding the wealthy while penalizing low-income women J. GEORGE and G. BURROUGHS *Ms.* v27 no2 p36 Summ 2017

We Can Improve Our Long-Term Care E. J. Schneidewind *AARP: The Magazine* v60 no2A p79 F/Mr 2017

Medicaid costs

HOW YOU'RE DRIVING DOWN COSTS—AND IMPROVING LIVES *Governing* v30 no1 p12 O 2016

THE MEDICAID DISASTER WHAT THE GOP MUST DO NOW S. FORBES *Forbes* v199 no7 p15 Je 29 2017

Medicaid eligibility

The Medicaid Effect M. Quinn *Governing* v30 no5 p20 F 2017

Medicaid—Finance

THE MEDICAID DISASTER WHAT THE GOP MUST DO NOW S. FORBES *Forbes* v199 no7 p15 Je 29 2017

The United Patients of America C. Alter, H. S. Edwards et al color *Time* v190 no4 p28 Jl 24 2017

Medical appointments & schedules

Health Care Providers Can Use Design Thinking to Improve Patient Experiences S. H. Kim, C. G. Myers et al *Harvard Business Review Digital Articles* p2 Ag 31 2017

Making Appointments Fast and Easy Must Be Health Care's Top Priority J. Bush *Harvard Business Review Digital Articles* p2 Je 4 2015

Your Fall Feel-Great Checklist L. Oster *Health* v31 no7 p100 S 2017

Medical assistance

THE ISLAND DOCTOR I. ALDRICH and M. FLEMING bw color *Yankee* p98 My/Je 2017

Medical care

See also

Child health services

Dental care

Diagnosis

Elder care

Health self-care

Medical screening

Prenatal care

Preventive medicine

Primary care (Medicine)

Reproductive health services

Treatment duration (Medical care)

Wound care

11 Things the Health Care Sector Must Do to Improve Cybersecurity R. Weintraub and J. Borenstein *Harvard Business Review Digital Articles* p2 Je 1 2017

34 Leaders Who Are Changing Health Care F. Staff color *Fortune* v175 no6 p46 My 1 2017

6 ways to stay on your medication plan *Harvard Health Letter* v42 no5 p7 Mr 2017

The Best Health Care Money Can't Buy S. J. Keyser bw color *Washington Monthly* v49 no6-8 p55 Je-Ag 2017

The Best Medicine M. Rubino *Indianapolis Monthly* p12 N 2017

Bureaucracy Is Keeping Health Care from Getting Better K. T. Segel *Harvard Business Review Digital Articles* p2 O 13 2017

CHOICE TREATMENTS: Central Indiana doctors share an elective or cutting-edge procedure in their field M. FERNANDEZ *Indianapolis Monthly* p80 N 2017

DEAR GOP: TAX CREDITS ARE NOT THE ANSWER V. DE RUGY *Reason* v49 no2 p13 Je 2017

The Delirium Diagnosis S. LONEY color *Walrus* v14 no9 p17 N 2017

FINDING YOUR REAL VOICE S. Hostin color *Essence* v48 no2 p118 Je 2017

Getting Buy-In for Predictive Analytics in Health Care M. Kakad, R. Rozenblum et al *Harvard Business Review Digital Articles* p2 Je 20 2017

Giving Seriously Ill Patients More Choices About Their Care B. Stuart and L. L. Berry *Harvard Business Review Digital Articles* p2 My 23 2017

The Harvard Contest That's Trying to Improve Health Care Delivery R. G. Hamermesh, R. Huckman et al *Harvard Business Review Digital Articles* p2 O 2 2015

Health Care Providers Should Publish Physician Ratings A. K. Jha *Harvard Business Review Digital Articles* p2 O 23 2015

How the EMR Is Increasing Innovation and Creativity in Health Care A. James Bender and R. S. Mecklenburg *Harvard Business Review Digital Articles* p1 O 10 2017

How to Hire In-Home Help D. Rosato *Consumer Reports* v82 no12 p50 D 2017

Innovating in a Highly Regulated Industry Like Health Care N. Fried *Harvard Business Review Digital Articles* p2 Je 12 2017

IS HEALTH CARE A RIGHT? A. GAWANDE cartoon *New Yorker* v93 no30 p48 O 2 2017

Multipurpose Pools D. Berkshire *Parks & Recreation* v52 no3 p56 Mr 2017

One More Thing J. MICHIE BRUCKNER color *Discover* v38 no5 p22 Je 2017

One Way to Prevent Clinician Burnout D. E. Mylod *Harvard Business Review Digital Articles* p2 O 12 2017

Paging Dr. Right: Finding the perfect M.D. for you K. Massicot color *New Orleans Magazine* v51 no10 p48 Ag 2017

Patient in Training L. TEDESCO color *Women's Health* v14 no9 p78 N 2017

Patients Make Better Medical Choices with Coaching J. Belkora *Harvard Business Review Digital Articles* p2 N 11 2016

PERSONAL AID A. GARCEAU *Indianapolis Monthly* p71 N 2017

Personalized Technology Will Upend the Doctor-Patient Relationship S. Subramanian, C. Dumont et al *Harvard Business Review Digital Articles* p2 Je 19 2015

PLAYING DOCTOR T. GERBER HOPE color *Prevention* v69 no8 p48 Ag 2017

Precision medicine development in Beijing Qian Li, Ke Huang et al *Science* v354 no6319 p61 D 23 2016

PREPARE FOR THE DIGITAL HEALTH REVOLUTION [Cover story] S. Mukherjee color diag *Fortune* v175 no6 p36 My 1 2017

A prescription for human dignity M. Clark color *U.S. Catholic* v82 no1 p8 Ja 2017

Prevention. Stronger Barbara *Prevention* v69 no8 p3 Ag 2017

Should you take a drug holiday? *Harvard Health Letter* v42 no1 p1 N 2016

TELEMEDICINE TROUBLE AHEAD J. M. ORIENT *USA Today Magazine* v145 no2858 p36 N 2016

Tell Congress: Don't Mess With Medicare E. J. Schneidewind *AARP: The Magazine* v60 no3A p71 Ap/My 2017

Thank You for Caring So Much P. DEMARCO color *Reader's Digest* v190 no1135 p42 N 2017

This Coalition of 20 Companies Thinks It Can Change U.S. Health Care L. A. Martin, A. H. Anderson et al *Harvard Business Review Digital Articles* p2 F 24 2016

To Radically Redesign Health Care, Start with One Unit J. S. Toussaint *Harvard Business Review Digital Articles* p2 D 9 2015

Transforming Health Care Takes Continuity and Consistency M. Britnell *Harvard Business Review Digital Articles* p2 D 28 2015

We Can Do More J. English *AARP: The Magazine* v59 no3A p91 Ap/My 2016

WELLNESS Q+A J. Willis *Atlanta* v57 no5 p119 S 2017

What nurses tell their friends L. MULCAHY and L. Rosenthal color *Redbook* p82 My 2017

What ob/gyns tell their friends J. DEMELO cartoon *Redbook* p82 O 2017

When a Health Department Fails: Is a growing focus on community factors coming at the expense of basic care? M. Quinn color *Governing* v30 no11 p18 Ag 2017

When Everyone Is Doing Design Thinking, Is It Still a Competitive Advantage? T. Brown *Harvard Business Review Digital Articles* p2 Ag 27 2015

When Health Care Providers Look at Problems from Multiple Perspectives, Patients Benefit J. A. Frimpong, C. G. Myers et al *Harvard Business Review Digital Articles* p2 Je 23 2017

Medical care conferences

"Right" You Aren't A. ECK *USA Today Magazine* v146 no2868 p17 S 2017

Medical care cost control

HOW TO MAKE HEALTH CARE BETTER AND CHEAPER S. FORBES color *Forbes* v199 no6 p11 Je 13 2017

Rehumanizing Birth and Death in America L. Hall *Society* v54 no3 p226 Je 2017

Medical care costs

See also

Medical fees

4 Ways to Cut Your Medical Bills E. O'Brien color *Money* v46 no6 p22 Jl 2017

BEST DEAL ON HEALTH CARE: exercise V. TWEED color *Better Nutrition* v78 no11 p14 N 2016

Convergence: The future of health P. Sharp and S. Hockfield bibl color *Science* v355 no6325 p589 F 10 2017

Delivering Higher Value Care Means Spending More Time with Patients D. A. Haas, Y. C. Krosner et al *Harvard Business Review Digital Articles* p2 D 26 2014

Fixing Health Care Will Require More than a New Payment System D. Maru *Harvard Business Review Digital Articles* p2 Ap 10 2015

Giving Seriously Ill Patients More Choices About Their Care B. Stuart and L. L. Berry *Harvard Business Review Digital Articles* p2 My 23 2017

Health Care Needs Real Competition L. S. DAFNY and T. H. LEE color diag graph img *Harvard Business Review* v94 no12 p76 D 2016

Health Care Providers Need a Value Management Office R. S. Kaplan, C. H. MacLean et al *Harvard Business Review Digital Articles* p2 D 2 2015

Helping Primary Care Doctors Contain Costs M. Ferguson *Harvard Business Review Digital Articles* p2 D 30 2015

Home Remedy A. Gorman color *Washington Monthly* v49 no3-5 p43 Mr-My 2017

How to Survive a High-Deductible Health Plan D. Rosato color *Consumer Reports* v82 no1 p16 Ja 2017

The 'Informed Consumer' & Other Myths C. R. Morris *Commonweal* v144 no13 p6 Ag 11 2017

A Payment Model That Prevents Unnecessary Medical Treatment D. J. Jacofsky and D. A. Haas *Harvard Business Review Digital Articles* p2 D 19 2016

Stanford's Big Health Care Idea H. Boerner color *Washington Monthly* v49 no3-5 p48 Mr-My 2017

Value-Based Care Alone Won't Reduce Health Spending and Improve Patient Outcomes D. J. Bailey *Harvard Business Review Digital Articles* p2 Je 16 2017

Medical care costs—Management

It's Absurd That Health Care Costs Are So Confusing J. Pinder *Harvard Business Review Digital Articles* p2 N 26 2014

What to Do When Health Care Costs Start to Rise Again J. Antos *Harvard Business Review Digital Articles* p2 N 28 2014

Medical care costs—United States

50 WAYS TO SAVE ON HEALTH CARE K. LANKFORD color *Kiplinger's Personal Finance* v71 no11 p26 N 2017

THE CODE RUSH E. Rosenthal *New York Times Magazine* p42 Ap 2 2017

THE High Cost OF Coping E. O'Brien and T. Tepper color diag *Money* v45 no11 p72 D 2016

How to Teach People About Health Care Pricing J. T. Kullgren

Harvard Business Review Digital Articles p2 S 29 2015

Introduction: A Cure for High Health Care Costs S. Brownlee color *Washington Monthly* v49 no3-5 p38 Mr-My 2017

The Price Is Right P. LAAKMANN *National Review* v69 no19 p18 O 16 2017

Rehumanizing Birth and Death in America L. Hall *Society* v54 no3 p226 Je 2017

ROBBING THE MIDDLE CLASS A. ECK *USA Today Magazine* v145 no2864 p26 My 2017

Start-Ups Are Helping Consumers Make Better Health Care Purchases S. H. Jain *Harvard Business Review Digital Articles* p2 Ja 13 2015

Taking Patients for a Ride D. Rosato color graph *Consumer Reports* v82 no5 p52 My 2017

Together in the risk pool *Christian Century* v134 no12 p7 Je 7 2017

U.S. Health Care Is on the Cusp of Bundled Payments F. de Brantes *Harvard Business Review Digital Articles* p2 D 11 2015

What the Cost of a Trip to the Vet Tells Us About Why Human Health Care Is So Expensive L. Einav and A. Finkelstein color *Harvard Business Review Digital Articles* p2 Ja 10 2017

Why Health Care Mergers Can Be Good for Patients J. D. Birkmeyer *Harvard Business Review Digital Articles* p2 S 30 2015

Worried Sick *Prevention* v69 no7 p9 Jl 2017

Medical care for the aged

"DON'T TOUCH MY MEDICARE!" T. Lieberman *Harper's Magazine* v333 no1998 p45 N 2016

Help With Home-Care Bills T. Stanger *Consumer Reports* v82 no12 p46 D 2017

How Atrius Health Is Making the Shift from Volume to Value T. Toussaint, K. DaSilva et al *Harvard Business Review Digital Articles* p2 D 13 2016

Medical care of veterans

See also

Veterans—Mental health services

Medical care of veterans—United States

IT'S TIME TO PRIVATIZE THE V.A K. MANGU-WARD color *Reason* v49 no6 p4 N 2017

Medical care use

See also

Drug utilization

How to Stop the Overconsumption of Health Care E. A. Kerr and J. Z. Ayanian *Harvard Business Review Digital Articles* p2 D 11 2014

Medical care—Awards

IMAGING HONORS POINT TO BEST-QUALITY PRACTICES AND DIAGNOSTIC CARE V. Prevish *Cincinnati Magazine* v50 no12 p78 S 2017

Medical care—California

A Very Expensive Free lunch M. M. SINGLETON *USA Today Magazine* v146 no2868 p16 S 2017

Medical care—China

Cancer precision medicine in China Yuankai Shi bibl *Science* v354 no6319 p20 D 23 2016

Exploring mass spectrometry in the precision medicine field *Science* v354 no6319 p4 D 23 2016

Precision medicine in the 21st century S. Sanders *Science* v354 no6319 p3 D 23 2016

Quality management for precision medicine clinical applications: A consensus from the China Precision Medicine Clinical Research and Application Association Chen Wang, Shukun Yao et al bibl *Science* v354 no6319 p11 D 23 2016

Medical care—Cost shifting

Travel Abroad for Low-Cost Care M. CROSS bw color *Kiplinger's Personal Finance* v71 no1 p62 Ja 2017

Medical care—Equipment & supplies

STRATEGIST img *New York* p53 F 9 2017

Medical care—Evaluation

See also

Outcome assessment (Medical care)

Better Value in Health Care Requires Focusing on Outcomes C. Stowell and C. Akerman *Harvard Business Review Digital Articles* p2 S 17 2015

it's twins! L. Vaccariello color *Parents* v92 no4 p8 Ap 2017

A Simple Way to Measure Health Care Outcomes J. Schupbach, A. Chandra et al *Harvard Business Review Digital Articles* p2

D 8 2016

Medical care—Finance

See also

Single-payer health care

How to Pay for Health Care/The Case for Capitation: Interaction B. Beauvais, C. Habig et al *Harvard Business Review* v94 no11 p20 N 2016

Medical care—Kentucky

Community Corps M. Quinn *Governing* v30 no6 p44 Mr 2017

Medical care—Law & legislation

HEALTH CARE AND THE POLITICS OF DISRUPTION P. SUDERMAN color *Reason* v49 no4 p7 Ag/S 2017

A Very Expensive Free lunch M. M. SINGLETON *USA Today Magazine* v146 no2868 p16 S 2017

We're All in Kansas Now K. Wright il *Nation* v304 no12 p10 Ap 10 2017

Medical care—Law & legislation—United States

Devil's Choice K. Wright *Nation* v305 no2 p10 Jl 17 2017

Healthcare Debate Has Room for Critics From the Right Only M. Corcoran *Extra!* v30 no4 p3 My 2017

Health Care & the Gospel T. S. Jost color *Commonweal* v144 no8 p10 My 5 2017

The National Interest: Jonathan Chait img *New York* v50 no11 p15 My 29 2017

Pay up or retract? Drug survey spurs conflict A. Marcus color *Science* v357 no6356 p1085 S 15 2017

Sand in the Gears F. Barnes color *Weekly Standard* v22 no29 p10 Ap 3 2017

Scoring the GOP Health-Care Plan Y. LEVIN color *National Review* v69 no6 p14 Ap 3 2017

Ticked Off B. PARKER color *Weekly Standard* v22 no43 p26 Jl 24 2017

Together in the risk pool *Christian Century* v134 no12 p7 Je 7 2017

YOUR LIFE *USA Today Magazine* v145 no2864 p6 My 2017

Medical care—Methodology

BACK TO THE (DIGITAL) DRAWING BOARD N. UNDERWOOD bw color *Maclean's* v129 no42 p48 O 24 2017

Code Comfort: A Code Blue Alternative for Patients with DNRs M. P. Phipps and J. D. Phipps *Harvard Business Review Digital Articles* p2 D 9 2014

TELL ME WHERE IT HURTS A. GAWANDE cartoon *New Yorker* v92 no46 p36 Ja 23 2017

Medical care—Ontario

Community Medicine B. Lauckner cartoon diag *Alternatives Journal (AJ) - Canada's Environmental Voice* v42 no3 p36 2016

Medical care—Psychological aspects

Innovation Starts with the Heart, Not the Head G. Hamel *Harvard Business Review Digital Articles* p2 Je 12 2015

Medical care—Quality control

How to Stop the Overconsumption of Health Care E. A. Kerr and J. Z. Ayanian *Harvard Business Review Digital Articles* p2 D 11 2014

The impact of training informal health care providers in India: A randomized controlled trial J. Das, A. Chowdhury et al chart diag *Science* v354 no6308 paaf7384-1 O 7 2016

Measuring Quality of Care for the Sickest Patients D. E. Meier *Harvard Business Review Digital Articles* p2 S 18 2015

The Next Wave of Hospital Innovation to Make Patients Safer A. A. Ghaferi, C. G. Myers et al *Harvard Business Review Digital Articles* p2 Ag 8 2016

Medical care—Religious aspects

Reaching out with Care: When it comes to providing health care, one's religion is irrelevant [Cover story] *Islamic Horizons* v46 no3 p26 My/Je 2017

Medical care—Safety measures

How U.S. Health Care Got Safer by Focusing on the Patient Experience T. H. Lee *Harvard Business Review Digital Articles* p2 My 31 2017

Medical care—Software

THE DOCTOR IS IN... YOUR POCKET *Prevention* v69 no5 p10 My 2017

Medical care—Uganda

Filling a Void L. RASKIN *Architectural Record* v205 no7 p65 Jl 2017

Medical care—United States

3 Keys to Shifting How We Pay for Health Care T. Rothenhaus and J. Fox *Harvard Business Review Digital Articles* p2 S 25 2015

50 WAYS TO SAVE ON HEALTH CARE K. LANKFORD color *Kiplinger's Personal Finance* v71 no11 p26 N 2017

The Antidote to Fragmented Health Care K. S. Mate and A. L. Compton-Phillips *Harvard Business Review Digital Articles* p2 D 15 2014

ARE THEY WITH HIM? A. D. Sorkin cartoon *New Yorker* v93 no22 p17 Jl 31 2017

As Congress Fights, Thousands Camp Out for Free Health Care S. Schrobsdorff color *Time* v190 no6 p14 Ag 7 2017

AT THE FOREFRONT OF INNOVATION M. O. SIMINGTON il *Phi Kappa Phi Forum* v97 no2 p9 Summ 2017

Bernie's Bad Medicine C. POPE color *National Review* v69 no19 p26 O 16 2017

A Case for Why Health Systems Should Partner with Pharmacies W. H. Shrank *Harvard Business Review Digital Articles* p2 O 14 2015

The Critical Skills for Leading Major Change in America's Health System D. Blumenthal *Harvard Business Review Digital Articles* p2 O 3 2017

HEALTH CARE AND THE POLITICS OF DISRUPTION P. SU-DERMAN color *Reason* v49 no4 p7 Ag/S 2017

How Analytics Can Guide Patient Care and Health Policy J. Gray *Harvard Business Review Digital Articles* p2 D 4 2014

How Bundled Health Care Payments Are Working in the Netherlands J. N. Struijs *Harvard Business Review Digital Articles* p2 O 12 2015

Making Appointments Fast and Easy Must Be Health Care's Top Priority J. Bush *Harvard Business Review Digital Articles* p2 Je 4 2015

Measuring and Communicating Health Care Value with Charts R. S. Kaplan, R. P. Blackstone et al *Harvard Business Review Digital Articles* p2 O 26 2015

OH, WHAT A TANGLED WEB WE WEAVE... A. ECK *USA Today Magazine* v146 no2866 p18 Jl 2017

PARODY color *Weekly Standard* v22 no36 p40 My 29 2017

PARODY J. Chaffetz color *Weekly Standard* v22 no27 p44 Mr 20 2017

PRICE FIX A. Davidson cartoon *New Yorker* v93 no15 p19 My 29 2017

THE PROGNOSIS S. FENNESSY *Atlanta* v57 no3 p20 Jl 2017

Remedies for Our Ailing Health Care System T. J. Donohue *Weekly Standard* v22 no7 p9 O 24 2016

Right at Home: Seniors want doctors to come to them. States are still working out how to pay for it M. Quinn *Governing* v30 no10 p18 Jl 2017

Telemedicine Is Vital to Reforming Health Care Delivery J. C. Kvedar *Harvard Business Review Digital Articles* p2 O 7 2015

TOP DOCS 2017: Every year we present a roster of the best metro Atlanta doctors, as chosen by their peers. On the following pages, find 720 of the area's most trusted physicians--our biggest list ever C. VAN DUSEN, J. GREEN et al *Atlanta* v57 no3 p65 Jl 2017

Understanding Health Care's Short-Termism Problem A. Chandra and D. Goldman *Harvard Business Review Digital Articles* p2 S 28 2015

The United Patients of America C. Alter, H. S. Edwards et al color *Time* v190 no4 p28 Jl 24 2017

What Health Care Can Learn from the Transformation of Financial Services Yuhgo Yamaguchi *Harvard Business Review Digital Articles* p2 D 16 2016

Worried Sick *Prevention* v69 no7 p9 Jl 2017

Medical care—United States—Finance
Getting Bundled Payments Right in Health Care D. A. Haas, R. S. Kaplan et al *Harvard Business Review Digital Articles* p2 O 19 2015

Medical care—United States—History—21st century
HOW TO MAKE HEALTH CARE BETTER AND CHEAPER S. FORBES color *Forbes* v199 no6 p11 Je 13 2017

Medical care—United States—Law & legislation
'Have You Read the Bill?' *Weekly Standard* v22 no41 p6 Jl 3 2017

Medical care—United States—News briefs
national: SHORT TAKES *Ms.* v27 no3 p13 Fall 2017

Medical case management

A pragmatic way forward? T. Powell-Jackson bibl color *Science* v354 no6308 p34 O 7 2016

Medical centers
CALL US EARLY--CALL US FIRST DECREASES EMERGENCY ROOM VISITS V. Prevish *Cincinnati Magazine* v50 no12 p76 S 2017

WHAT IS A MICROHOSPITAL? St. Vincent and Franciscan introduce a new type of treatment center A. GARCEAU *Indianapolis Monthly* p83 N 2017

Medical centers—Evaluation
MEN'S HEALTH color *New Orleans Magazine* v51 no5 p130 Mr 2017

SPECIALTY MEDICINE color *New Orleans Magazine* v51 no5 p131 Mr 2017

What Does the Fox Say? G. HAND *Cincinnati Magazine* v50 no6 p56 Mr 2017

Medical centers—United States
ETC M. Cameran color *New Orleans Magazine* v51 no8 p151 Je 2017

Missouri, Compromised S. Crute color *Washington Monthly* v49 no3-5 p40 Mr-My 2017

TOP HOSPITALS 2017 *Louisiana Life* v37 no6 p39 Jl/Ag 2017

Medical climatology
See also
Climatic changes—Health aspects
Predict When You'll Get Sick color *Time* v189 no3 p22 Ja 30 2017

Medical decision making
How to Teach People About Health Care Pricing J. T. Kullgren *Harvard Business Review Digital Articles* p2 S 29 2015

Patient-Reported Data Can Help People Make Better Health Care Choices W. B. Weeks and J. N. Weinstein *Harvard Business Review Digital Articles* p2 S 21 2015

Using Big Data to Make Wiser Medical Decisions J. D. Halamka *Harvard Business Review Digital Articles* p2 D 14 2015

Medical economics—United States
How the U.S. Can Reduce Waste in Health Care Spending by $1 Trillion N. Sahni, A. Chigurupati et al *Harvard Business Review Digital Articles* p2 O 13 2015

Medical education—United States
Campus Chaos M. S. GOLDMAN *Commentary* v142 no1 p14 Jl/Ag 2016

Medical emergencies
See also
Wounds & injuries
Did You Call 911? S. LOPEZ *Reader's Digest* v189 no1128 p8 Mr 2017

Embrace the Tough Stuff C. KUZMA color *Runner's World* v52 no8 p56 S 2017

Pharmacists Can Reduce Elderly Mishaps *USA Today Magazine* v145 no2861 p2 F 2017

THE VOMIT COMET L. Abend color *Flying* v144 no11 p70 N 2017

Medical emergencies—Economic aspects
families, finances, and the future *Parents* v91 no10 p118 O 2016

Medical equipment
See also
Lasers in medicine
Innovation M. Belfiore color *Bloomberg Businessweek* no4505 p37 D 26 2016

Medical equipment design
Innovation M. Belfiore bw color *Bloomberg Businessweek* no4524 p37 My 29 2017

Medical equipment industry
See also
Dental instruments & apparatus industry
41 *Prevention* v69 no7 p10 Jl 2017

Medical equipment—Evaluation
A SURGICAL ALTERNATIVE TO PRESCRIPTION BLOOD THINNERS V. Prevish *Cincinnati Magazine* v50 no12 p84 S 2017

Medical equipment—Security measures
Medical Systems Hacks Are Scary, but Medical Device Hacks Could Be Even Worse D. Nickelson *Harvard Business Review Digital Articles* p2 My 15 2017

Medical equipment—Transportation
ZIP LINE: Help from Above J. W. Rosen color *MIT Technology*

Review v120 no4 p36 Jl/Ag 2017

Medical errors

FATAL MISTAKES S. KLIFF *Reader's Digest* v189 no1128 p100 Mr 2017

THE HIGH PRICE OF MEDICAL ERRORS-DON'T LET IT COST YOU YOUR LIFE *Vital Speeches of the Day* v82 no12 p381 D 2016

Wrong! R. SHARPE cartoon *Prevention* v69 no7 p48 Jl 2017

Medical errors—Prevention

Getting Rid of "Never Events" in Hospitals T. Morgenthaler and C. M. Harper *Harvard Business Review Digital Articles* p2 O 20 2015

Medical ethics

See also

Euthanasia

Defining Doctors Down W. J. SMITH color *Weekly Standard* v22 no30 p16 Ap 10 2017

Dr. Dare Kill *Weekly Standard* v23 no4 p3 O 2 2017

Medical ethics—Religious aspects—Catholic Church

Treatment of transgender people poses new health care challenge M. O'Loughlin color *America* v216 no5 p16 Mr 6 2017

Medical examinations of air pilots

FIVE BASICMED MYTHS DEBUNKED S. Pope color *Flying* v144 no7 p8 Jl 2017

ON TENTERHOOKS D. Karl bw *Flying* v144 no8 p70 Ag 2017

Medical fees

A Proven New Model for Reimbursing Physicians G. D. Steele Jr. *Harvard Business Review Digital Articles* p2 S 15 2015

What to Do If You Get Medical Bills You Can't Pay Off Promptly A. Adamczyk color *Money* v46 no8 p18 S 2017

Medical fees—United States

OH, WHAT A TANGLED WEB WE WEAVE... A. ECK *USA Today Magazine* v146 no2866 p18 Jl 2017

Medical genetics

What Your Family History Reveals J. Migala color diag *Health* v31 no3 p59 Ap 2017

Medical history

1571: Seville N. Monardes *Lapham's Quarterly* v10 no2 p175 Spr 2017

ALL IN A Day's Work color *Reader's Digest* v189 no1129 p60 Ap 2017

Magic, medicine and the Viking way of war B. Burfield *History Today* v67 no4 p19 Ap 2017

ORGANIZE YOUR HEALTH RECORDS M. MANNARINO color *Better Homes & Gardens* v95 no8 p174 Ag 2017

Medical informatics

See also

Information storage & retrieval systems—Medical care

Bringing the Power of Platforms to Health Care J. Bush and J. Fox *Harvard Business Review Digital Articles* p2 N 10 2016

Hospitals Are Finally Starting to Put Real-Time Data to Use J. S. Toussaint and M. Mannon *Harvard Business Review Digital Articles* p2 N 12 2014

How Physicians Can Keep Up with the Knowledge Explosion in Medicine L. Chin and G. Satell *Harvard Business Review Digital Articles* p2 D 19 2016

To Survive, Health Care Data Providers Need to Stop Selling Data H. Madannavar, T. Clark et al *Harvard Business Review Digital Articles* p2 Je 14 2017

Why Health Care May Finally Be Ready for Big Data N. D. Shah and J. Pathak *Harvard Business Review Digital Articles* p2 D 3 2014

Medical informatics security

To Survive, Health Care Data Providers Need to Stop Selling Data H. Madannavar, T. Clark et al *Harvard Business Review Digital Articles* p2 Je 14 2017

Medical innovations

3D Printing Is Already Changing Health Care D. Hendricks *Harvard Business Review Digital Articles* p2 Mr 4 2016

Are New Anti-Abuse Technologies Enough? *USA Today Magazine* v145 no2861 p8 F 2017

THE BIG QUESTION cartoon *Atlantic* v320 no1 p104 Jl/Ag 2017

Canadian Innovations in Organ Donation and Transplantation A. Humar color *Maclean's* v130 no9 p34 O 2017

INNOVATIONS IN DRUG DELIVERY S. Mukherjee *Fortune* v174 no8 p20 D 15 2016

IT CAN'T ALL BE ENERGY M. SWARTZ *Texas Monthly* v45 no5 p79 My 2017

LIFE ON THE EDGE 3,822 MILES R. BASS *Texas Monthly* v45 no5 p73 My 2017

Living Life to the Fullest with a Rare Blood Disorder, Thanks to Innovative Therapies M. Sponagle *Maclean's* v130 no9 p37 O 2017

The Next Wave of Hospital Innovation to Make Patients Safer A. A. Ghaferi, C. G. Myers et al *Harvard Business Review Digital Articles* p2 Ag 8 2016

Personalized Recommendation Engines Are Coming to Health Care S. Glick *Harvard Business Review Digital Articles* p2 Jl 6 2016

The Soundtrack of Our Lives T. Golson color *Dressage Today* v24 no1 p60 O 2017

Medical laws & legislation

See also

Abortion—Law & legislation

Assisted suicide—Law & legislation

Euthanasia—Law & legislation

Physicians—Malpractice

D.C. Affirms Assisted Suicide color *America* v215 no16 p9 N 21 2016

Medical laws & legislation—United States

3 Health Care Trends That Don't Hinge on the ACA F. Baitman and K. Karpay *Harvard Business Review Digital Articles* p2 My 25 2017

States Must Face Their "Pain" *USA Today Magazine* v146 no2866 p18 Jl 2017

To Live and Die in Colorado *Weekly Standard* v22 no5 p2 O 10 2016

Medical literature

Remedies Against the Devil and Dementia: The medical advice in Bald's Leechbook outlasted the language in which it was written C. Voth *History Today* v67 no10 p18 O 2017

Medical malpractice

TRUST ME: A nurse posing as a qualified A&E doctor is putting patients at risk *People Management* p62 S 2017

Medical marijuana

Can Medical Cannabis Break the Painkiller Epidemic? J. Hsu color *Scientific American* v315 no3 p10 S 2016

Coming Around on Cannabis [Cover story] S. BARRY color *Working Mother* v40 no3 p24 Ag/S 2017

FROM THE ARCHIVES B. DOHERTY, J. SULLUM et al bw *Reason* v49 no1 p70 My 2017

GROWING PAINS FOR ILLINOIS CANNABIS FARM G. Johnston *Successful Farming* v115 no1 p56 Ja 2017

THE MARIJUANA REVIVAL: A LOOK AT WEED'S CHANGING DEMOGRAPHIC S. E. JAMISON color *Ebony* v72/73 no12/1 p66 O/N 2017

The Meaning of Scalia M. KENNEDY *Commentary* v142 no1 p12 Jl/Ag 2016

NAS: Pot does help chronic pain color *Science* v355 no6322 p228 Ja 20 2017

POT AND PAIN G. Miller color map *Science* v354 no6312 p566 N 4 2016

THE TRANSITION OF CANNABIS TO MAINSTREAM PAIN MEDICATION D. F. MCCOURT *Maclean's* v130 no3 p48 Ap 2017

Medical missionaries—Awards

People A. M. Banks color *Christian Century* v134 no2 p19 Ja 18 2017

Medical model

Doctor Direct M. TURNLUND *Idaho Magazine* v16 no5 p26 F 2017

Medical offices

See also

Medical appointments & schedules

Medical secretaries

ETC M. CAMERAN color *New Orleans Magazine* v51 no12 p167 O 2017

Medical partnership

Making Hospital Partnerships Work P. Pawlak and R. Colby *Harvard Business Review Digital Articles* p2 D 10 2015

Medical payments insurance

Taking Patients for a Ride D. Rosato color graph *Consumer Re-*

We Have Ways to Make You Conform J. V. LAST color *Weekly Standard* v22 no31 p27 Ap 17 2017

Medical sciences

    See also

    Biophysics

    Neurosciences

Call to restore NIH's cap on grant funding M. Peifer *Science* v357 no6349 p364 Jl 28 2017

Choose a program, have a life S. H. Jones color *Science* v357 no6355 p1058 S 8 2017

Medical sciences—News Briefs

NEWS FROM THE World of Medicine S. RIDEOUT *Reader's Digest* v189 no1128 p57 Mr 2017

Medical screening

Opening the Door For Future Drug Sales A. Altstedter and J. S. Hopkins color *Bloomberg Businessweek* no4533 p15 Ag 7 2017

Save Your Butt J. Stewart cartoon *Men's Health* v32 no1 p88 Ja/F 2017

STD Results in Minutes E. Biba color *Scientific American* v316 no3 p18 Mr 2017

Medical secretaries

Department of Wit Paging Dr. Malaprop! M. WOLFE cartoon *Reader's Digest* v190 no1134 p19 O 2017

Medical social work

Why Big Health Systems Are Investing in Community Health T. Hussein and M. Collins *Harvard Business Review Digital Articles* p2 D 6 2016

Medical societies

Reaching out with Care: When it comes to providing health care, one's religion is irrelevant [Cover story] *Islamic Horizons* v46 no3 p26 My/Je 2017

A Supportive Advisor: The IMANA Medical Ethics Committee reaches out to physicians, patients and all those who want Islamic answers to crucial life issues [Cover story] S. ATHAR *Islamic Horizons* v46 no3 p28 My/Je 2017

Taking Care *Islamic Horizons* v46 no3 p6 My/Je 2017

Medical spas

CLEAN SLATE [Cover story] H. MITCHELL color *Chicago* v66 no9 p73 S 2017

Medical spas—Evaluation

BEST OF ATLANTA K. Abney, B. Addison et al *Atlanta* v56 no8 p106 D 2016

Medical supplies

    See also

    Biologicals

    Drugs

The Afghan Field Medic M. LIUHTO color *Foreign Policy* no225 p14 Jl/Ag 2017

Medical technology

    See also

    Human reproductive technology

    Information technology in medicine

    Medical innovations

    Point-of-care testing

BLIND MEDICINE M. Peplow color graph *Scientific American* v316 no2 p68 F 2017

THE RISE AND FALL OF THERANOS S. VOLK color *Discover* v38 no1 p44 Ja/F 2017

Medical technology—Congresses

THE REVOLUTION STARTS HERE J. Vanian, K. Fehrenbacher et al color *Fortune* v174 no7 p26 D 1 2016

Medical thermography

ASK DR. ZIPES D. Zipes *Saturday Evening Post* v288 no6 p81 N/D 2016

Medical tourism

Can China Make Hainan A Medical Paradise? L. Hui and J. Y. de Morel *Bloomberg Businessweek* no4522 p20 My 15 2017

Travel Abroad for Low-Cost Care M. CROSS bw color *Kiplinger's Personal Finance* v71 no1 p62 Ja 2017

Medical waste disposal—Equipment & supplies

Innovation: Needle Grinder C. Winter color *Bloomberg Businessweek* no4531 p21 Jl 24 2017

Medical ethics—Societies, etc.

A Supportive Advisor: The IMANA Medical Ethics Committee reaches out to physicians, patients and all those who want Islamic answers to crucial life issues [Cover story] S. ATHAR

Islamic Horizons v46 no3 p28 My/Je 2017

Medical formulae, receipts, prescriptions

PHARM TO TABLE M. OATMAN color *Mother Jones* v42 no6 p72 N/D 2017

Medically unexplained symptoms

Diagnosis L. Sanders color *New York Times Magazine* p30 My 21 2017

Medically uninsured persons

the FACES of OBAMACARE M. HALL *Texas Monthly* v45 no3 p116 Mr 2017

Medical self-examination

Check You Out! K. LAWLER and S. PERRINE cartoon *AARP: The Magazine* v60 no5A p20 Ag/S 2017

Medicare

    See also

    Medicare Part D

"DON'T TOUCH MY MEDICARE!" T. Lieberman *Harper's Magazine* v333 no1998 p45 N 2016

Happy Warrior A. STILES *National Review* v69 no6 p48 Ap 3 2017

Health Coverage Is No Slam Dunk *Kiplinger's Personal Finance* v71 no12 p22 D 2017

Palliative Care: A Key to Living With Dignity J. English *AARP: The Magazine* v59 no1A p61 D 2015/Ja 2016

Ready or not color *U.S. Catholic* v82 no5 p5 My 2017

Tell Congress: Don't Mess With Medicare E. J. Schneidewind *AARP: The Magazine* v60 no3A p71 Ap/My 2017

Urgent Care T. Castañares *Harper's Magazine* v334 no2000 p3 Ja 2017

U.S. Health Care Is on the Cusp of Bundled Payments F. de Brantes *Harvard Business Review Digital Articles* p2 D 11 2015

A Warning on Medicare R. Love color *AARP: The Magazine* v60 no2A p4 F/Mr 2017

Will ObamaCare Kill Medicare? E. L. VLIET *USA Today Magazine* v145 no2858 p30 N 2016

Medicare Part A

Your Medicare FAQs K. LANKFORD color *Kiplinger's Personal Finance* v71 no5 p34 My 2017

Medicare Part D

CALENDAR R. ERMEY color *Kiplinger's Personal Finance* v71 no10 p16 O 2017

Medicare—Government policy

Arise, Ye Boomers of the Nation S. J. DOUGLAS *In These Times* v41 no2 p16 F 2017

Medication abuse

TEEN SUBSTANCE USE SHOWS DECLINE *USA Today Magazine* v145 no2862 p6 Mr 2017

Medication errors—Prevention

Prevent Medication Mix-Ups K. Rockwood *Parents* v91 no12 p30 D 2016

Medicinal plants

    See also

    Aloe

    Medical marijuana

Beauty Secrets of the Desert S. Strausfogel color *Better Nutrition* v79 no11 p38 N 2017

Black COHOSH D. Kalmansohn color *Vegetarian Times* v43 no2 p30 N/D 2016

IS KRATOM A DEADLY DRUG Or A Life-Saving Medicine? B. GRULEY cartoon color *Bloomberg Businessweek* no4503 p54 D 12 2016

The Whole Earth Is Medicine W. JOHNSON color *Tricycle: The Buddhist Review* v27 no1 p29 Fall 2017

Medicinal plants—History

Ashwagandha V. TWEED color *Better Nutrition* v79 no10 p26 O 2017

Medicinal plants—Therapeutic use

Ayurvedic HERB GUIDE V. Tweed color *Better Nutrition* p34 My 2017

RX FOR FOOD POISONING J. Martin color *Better Nutrition* v78 no11 p26 N 2016

Medicine

    See also

    Alternative medicine

    Diagnosis

    Health

Tool? C. Lieberman *Harvard Business Review Digital Articles* p2 Ag 25 2015

THE JOY OF YOGA [Cover story] M. Stacey cartoon color *Women's Health* v14 no1 p77 Ja/F 2017

JUST FIVE MINUTES [Cover story] J. GALLOWAY cartoon *Runner's World* v52 no4 p24 My 2017

Keep Calm and Shine On *O, The Oprah Magazine* p89 Mr 2017

Learn to listen to your emotions R. Miller *Yoga Journal* no287 p26 N 2016

LET IT GO! color *Good Housekeeping* v265 no3 p110 S 2017

meaningful MUDRAS M. RABBITT color *Yoga Journal* no287 p31 N 2016

Meddy Teddy color *Yoga Journal* no289 p18 F 2017

Meet your next teacher: Shiva Rea [Cover story] color *Yoga Journal* no292 p83 Je 2017

MENTAL CHILLNESS [Cover story] B. Stulberg cartoon color *Runner's World* v52 no3 p46 Ap 2017

Mindfulness, demystified bw *Yoga Journal* p8 2016 Special Issue

Mindfulness Mitigates Biases You May Not Know You Have N. Torres *Harvard Business Review Digital Articles* p2 D 24 2014

Mindfulness Takes Flight J. HERGENRADER color *Women's Health* v14 no9 p102 N 2017

Mind Over Mascot D. Leung and T. Keith color *Sports Illustrated* v125 no13 p23 O 17 2016

Move into meditation color *Yoga Journal* p76 2016 Special Issue

Neither Fight nor Flight C. DEDERER color *Rodale's Organic Life* v3 no1 p40 Ja 2017

On the road again C. Gorrell color *Yoga Journal* no291 p12 My 2017

peace of mind J. Gates cartoon color *Yoga Journal* p86 2017 Special Issue

peace of mind N. Isaacs cartoon *Yoga Journal* p96 2017 Special Issue

petal POWER D. KERN color *Yoga Journal* no293 p17 Ag 2017

POST-PRACTICE PAUSE H. Dowdle color *Yoga Journal* p112 2017 Special Issue

SAGE MOVES FOR MEDITATION N. Isaacs color *Yoga Journal* p54 2017 Special Issue

sitting pretty color *Yoga Journal* p106 2017 Special Issue

Snow Days S. KLEIN bw color *Prevention* v69 no1 p96 Ja 2017

TAKE A CHILL C. Van Dusen color *Tricycle: The Buddhist Review* v26 no3 p90 Spr 2017

Take it all in R. Miller cartoon *Yoga Journal* no288 p38 D 2016

take OM HOME T. Eichenseher color *Yoga Journal* no292 p96 Je 2017

Take the 21-Day Challenge *Yoga Journal* p7 2017 Special Issue

Think Yourself Healthy J. Marchant cartoon *Prevention* v69 no1 p28 Ja 2017

This Just In J. Zorthian *Time* v190 no15 p19 O 16 2017

To Stay Focused, Manage Your Emotions E. Batista *Harvard Business Review Digital Articles* p2 F 2 2015

Walk This Way S. ALTSHUL color *AARP: The Magazine* v60 no4A p17 Je/Jl 2017

What matters most C. Gorrell color *Yoga Journal* no294 p12 S 2017

Why Not... Master Meditation? color *Health* v30 no9 p10 N 2016

write your mind M. RABBITT color *Yoga Journal* no294 p53 S 2017

You can't help being overly critical of others S. Kempton bw *Yoga Journal* p40 2016 Special Issue

You just broke a resolution M. S. Kraftsow color *Yoga Journal* p42 2016 Special Issue

Your starter toolkit color *Yoga Journal* p118 2016 Special Issue

ZEN FOR MEN [Cover story] M. EASTER cartoon color *Men's Health* v32 no1 p118 Ja/F 2017

Zen Palace A. Jones img *New York* p46 F 9 2017

Meditation & psychology

Of Mice and Mindfulness: Putting mice into something like a meditative state may shed light on the human brain G. Reynolds color *New York Times Magazine* p24 My 21 2017

YOUR BRAIN ON MEDITATION K. McGonigal and N. ISAACS color *Yoga Journal* p36 2017 Special Issue

Meditation in Buddhism

FOCUSING: A PRACTICE TO COMPLEMENT MEDITATION D. ROME color *Tricycle: The Buddhist Review* v27 no1 p40 Fall 2017

The Great Divide M. Caine-Barrett and Shonin color *Tricycle: The Buddhist Review* v26 no4 p80 Summ 2017

Meditation App Roundup C. VAN DUSEN color *Tricycle: The Buddhist Review* v27 no1 p98 Fall 2017

Meditation—Buddhism

Meditation App Roundup C. VAN DUSEN color *Tricycle: The Buddhist Review* v26 no2 p88 Wint 2016

Meditation—Evaluation

The long game [Cover story] R. Miller *Yoga Journal* no291 p26 My 2017

Meditation—Physiological aspects

PERLE BESSERMAN AND MANFRED STEGER *Tricycle: The Buddhist Review* v26 no4 p19 Summ 2017

Meditation—Psychological aspects

How I Survived the Worst Depression of My Life E. Mahaney color *Glamour* v114 no11 p144 N 2016

Meditation/Resurrection (Music)

William Parker: A Sonic Trisection B. MEYER bw *Downbeat* v84 no9 p64 S 2017

Meditations

Piece of Cake [Cover story] A. Gurwitch cartoon *Prevention* v68 no11 p26 N 2016

VALERIE MASON-JOHN cartoon *Tricycle: The Buddhist Review* v26 no3 p20 Spr 2017

Méditations (Music)

FREE AT LAST A. SHATZ color graph *Nation* v305 no4 p32 Ag 14 2017

Meditations on Freedom (Music)

NOAH PREMINGER: Distinctive Character K. Micallef color *Downbeat* v84 no8 p50 Ag 2017

Meditation—Software

Meditation App Roundup C. Van Dusen color *Tricycle: The Buddhist Review* v26 no4 p92 Summ 2017

Meditation—Study & teaching

HEAD REST: Nap rooms, self-care seminars-the art of slowing down is a fast-growing business. The latest: meditation boutiques. We tested three new meditation-only centers. Here's how they compare C. Cunningham *Washingtonian Magazine* v52 no12 p109 S 2017

Mediterranean cooking

5 More Morning Mezes J. LURIE *Los Angeles Magazine* p108 Ap 2017

REVAMPING RESOLUTIONS K. Massicot color *New Orleans Magazine* v51 no3 p32 Ja 2017

Mediterranean diet

3 Mediterranean Diet Myths, Busted V. TWEED color *Better Nutrition* p8 My 2017

GOOD EGGS *Amazing Wellness* v8 no2 p8 Spr 2016

More Mediterranean Diet Magic color *Prevention* v69 no4 p10 Ap 2017

SMARTER FATS J. Bowden color *Amazing Wellness* v8 no2 p36 Spr 2016

This Just In J. Zorthian *Time* v190 no12 p23 S 25 2017

Mediterranean Region—History—476-1517

Justifying Slavery J. MacKechnie *History Today* v67 no5 p18 My 2017

Medley, Graham F.

When an emerging disease becomes endemic color *Science* v357 no6347 p156 Jl 14 2017

Medley, Tom, 1920-2014

TOM MEDLEY T. Taylor bw cartoon color *Hot Rod* v70 no3 p74 Mr 2017

MEDRESS, AMANDA

Double Take *Psychology Today* v50 no4 p36 Ag 2017

Medrzycki, Machi—Interviews

MLM Incorporated P. Marquis *New Orleans Homes & Lifestyles* v20 no2 p85 Spr 2017

Medshape Inc.

FIT TO PRINT B. YEOMAN *Atlanta* v56 no7 p90 N 2016

Medstar Health Inc.

What to Do When Your Future Strategy Clashes with Your Present M. W. Johnson *Harvard Business Review Digital Articles* p2 Ap 29 2015

Medved, Edward

Absolutely some trespassing C. GILLIS color *Maclean's* v129 no43 p26 O 31 2016

Medved, Michael

Providence and Predestination *Commentary* v141 no10 p1 D 2016

Providence and Predestination *Commentary* v142 no5 p1 D 2016

Medvedev, D. A. (Dmitrii Anatolevich), 1965-

Does Putin Still Favor His Sidekick? H. Meyer, I. Arkhipov et al color graph *Bloomberg Businessweek* no4520 p28 My 1 2017

TEACHABLE MOMENT *Harper's Magazine* no2007 p16 Ag 2017

Medvedev, Michael G.

Density functional theory is straying from the path toward the exact functional bibl chart graph *Science* v355 no6320 p1 Ja 6 2017

Medwinter-Faulkner, Carol

Q: If you had an extra hour in your day, what would you do with it? color *O, The Oprah Magazine* p18 O 2017

Medzhitov, Ruslan

Anti-inflammatory effect of IL-10 mediated by metabolic repro gramming of macrophages diag *Science* v356 no6337 p513 My 5 2017

Medzihradszky, Anna

RETINOBLASTOMA RELATED1 mediates germline entry in Arabidopsis color diag *Science* v356 no6336 p396 Ap 28 2017

Meehan, Patrick

The 5 Paradoxes of Digital Business Leadership *Harvard Business Review Digital Articles* p2 Jl 2 2015

MEEHAN, SUMAYYAH

Distorted Feminism *Islamic Horizons* v45 no6 p54 N/D 2016

Hijabi Fits: A tween is creating a rainbow of hijabs for girls of all ages *Islamic Horizons* v46 no4 p36 Jl/Ag 2017

Meehan, Thomas, 1929-2017

Milestones *Time* v190 no9 p17 S 4 2017

Meeker, Jason

LISTEN, LAUGH, LEARN L. F. Prater *Successful Farming* v115 no11 p60 S 2017

Meeks, Catherine

A beloved community: Christian churches can address racism through spiritual formation color *U.S. Catholic* v82 no10 p18 O 2017

Change the conversation *U.S. Catholic* v82 no10 p20 O 2017

MEEKS, CHAD

VASTER THAN THE ANCIENTS IMAGINED color *Christianity Today* v60 no8 p70 O 2016

Meeks, Kenneth

Blazing New Trails [Cover story] color *Black Enterprise* v47 no4 p12 N/D 2016

BRICK BY BRICK color graph *Black Enterprise* v47 no7 p56 My/Je 2017

Daring To Be Different color *Black Enterprise* v47 no3 p19 O 2016

Meet 'Mr. Diversity' James E. Taylor chart color *Black Enterprise* v47 no3 p43 O 2016

Meet "The Wine Maker" André Hueston Mack chart color *Black Enterprise* v47 no4 p33 N/D 2016

Meeks, Stephanie

The New Urban Renewal A. Shapiro color *Architectural Record* v205 no2 p43 F 2017

Meer, Whitney

My thyroid went totally haywire color *Health* v31 no9 p77 N 2017

Meerkat

Awesome Animals! R. A. MUSGRAVE color *National Geographic Kids* no471 p35A Je/Jl 2017

Meerkat—Behavior

THROWING HER WEIGHT AROUND P. Edmonds color *National Geographic* v231 no2 p29 F 2017

Meeropol, Rachel

THE TERRE HAUTE EXPERIMENT A. WREN *Indianapolis Monthly* p76 My 2017

Meester, Leighton, 1986-

LEIGHTON MEESTER FIGHTS HUNGER M. L. Lenker color *Entertainment Weekly* no1477 p17 Ag 11 2017

Meet Joe (Poem)

MEET JOE J. GRILLO *Atlanta* v56 no7 p98 N 2016

Meet the Press (TV program)

Chuck Todd Thinks It's Important to Stay Neutral A. M. Cox *New York Times Magazine* p70 O 8 2017

Meeter, Daniel

Refugee work *Christian Century* v134 no2 p6 Ja 18 2017

Meeting minutes (Documentation)

Two Things to Do After Every Meeting P. Axtell *Harvard Business Review Digital Articles* p2 N 26 2015

Meetings

See also

Summit meetings

3 Reasons Your Strategy Meetings Irritate Your Team D. Sundheim *Harvard Business Review Digital Articles* p2 Mr 1 2016

7 Ways to Stop a Meeting from Dragging On J. Grenny *Harvard Business Review Digital Articles* p2 Ap 25 2016

Global church leaders hold historic meeting *Christian Century* v134 no14 p15 Jl 5 2017

How to Design an Agenda for an Effective Meeting R. Schwarz *Harvard Business Review Digital Articles* p2 Mr 19 2015

How to Do Walking Meetings Right R. Clayton, C. Thomas et al *Harvard Business Review Digital Articles* p2 Ag 5 2015

How to Establish a Meeting-Free Day Each Week E. G. Saunders color *Harvard Business Review Digital Articles* p2 F 28 2017

How to Raise Sensitive Issues During a Virtual Meeting J. Grenny *Harvard Business Review Digital Articles* p2 Mr 14 2017

ILA—an Evolving Organization and Conference Experience M. Craig Post *Literacy Today (2411-7862)* v34 no5 p6 Mr/Ap 2017

Keeping Meetings on Track When You're Not in Charge R. Ashkenas *Harvard Business Review Digital Articles* p2 Ap 22 2016

The literacy scene color *Literacy Today (2411-7862)* v34 no5 p5 Mr/Ap 2017

NOISY BY NATURE *Harper's Magazine* v335 no2006 p17 Jl 2017

Polite Ways to Decline a Meeting Invitation L. Davey *Harvard Business Review Digital Articles* p2 My 17 2016

A P P E N D I X A REPORT TO THE PRESIDENT ON THE ACTIVITIES OF THE COUNCIL OF ECONOMIC ADVISERS DURING 2015 *Economic Indicators* p381 S 2016

PRH Employees Unite for Company Week J. Milliot color *Publishers Weekly* v264 no7 p10 F 13 2017

Stand-Up Meetings Don't Work for Everybody B. Frisch *Harvard Business Review Digital Articles* p2 My 27 2016

A Step-by-Step Guide to Structuring Better Meetings L. Davey *Harvard Business Review Digital Articles* p2 Ap 20 2016

We're rolling! map *Yoga Journal* no293 p14 Ag 2017

When It's Worth Having a Meeting Before Your Meeting A. Molinsky color *Harvard Business Review Digital Articles* p2 O 28 2016

Meetings—Equipment & supplies

Meetings Need a Shot Clock B. Frisch and C. Greene *Harvard Business Review Digital Articles* p2 Mr 16 2016

Meetings—Management

How to Run a Meeting of People from Different Cultures R. Knight *Harvard Business Review Digital Articles* p2 D 4 2015

Meetings—Methodology

How to Run a Great Virtual Meeting K. Ferrazzi *Harvard Business Review Digital Articles* p2 Mr 27 2015

Meetings—Planning

Before a Meeting, Tell Your Team That Silence Denotes Agreement B. Frisch and C. Greene *Harvard Business Review Digital Articles* p2 F 3 2016

A Checklist for Planning Your Next Big Meeting *Harvard Business Review Digital Articles* p2 Mr 26 2015

How to Know If There Are Too Many People in Your Meeting *Harvard Business Review Digital Articles* p2 Mr 18 2015

If You Can't Say What Your Meeting Will Accomplish, You Shouldn't Have It B. Frisch and C. Greene *Harvard Business Review Digital Articles* p2 Ap 18 2016

Meetings That Work for Both Managers and Makers S. Harmon *Harvard Business Review Digital Articles* p2 Jl 4 2016

The Two Things Killing Your Ability to Focus W. Treseder *Harvard Business Review Digital Articles* p2 Ag 3 2016

Meetings—Psychological aspects

Empathy Is Key to a Great Meeting A. McKee *Harvard Business Review Digital Articles* p2 Mr 23 2015

Meets

Harry "Hand Grenade" Hibler at the 1971 March Meet T. Taylor color *Hot Rod* v70 no1 p14 Ja 2017

Megabots Inc.

IRON GIANT: GET READY TO ROBO-RUMBLE! D. FERRY

color diag *Wired* v25 no8 p24 Ag 2017

Megas, Natalia

WHERE & WHEN *Washingtonian Magazine* v52 no8 p35 My 2017

Meghie, Stella

AMANDLA STENBERG A. Breznican color *Entertainment Weekly* no1463/1464 p34 Ap/My 2017

MEGIDO, RUDY CAPARROS

The Odor of Death: An Overview of Current Knowledge on Characterization and Applications *BioScience* v67 no7 p600 Jl 2017

Megoran, Nick

Broken Ties in the Ferghana Valley M. KAMP *Current History* v116 no792 p285 O 2017

Megroz, Gordy

ONE LOVE color *Bloomberg Businessweek* no4524 p66 My 29 2017

STRANGE BREW color *Bloomberg Businessweek* no4514 p74 Mr 13 2017

Meharanagarha Durga (Jodhpur, India)

India Full-On S. McAlpine bw color *Conde Nast Traveler* v52 no10 p100 N 2017

Meharenna, Ruth

Wage and employment fluctuations during the housing market cycle *Monthly Labor Review* p1 D 2016

Mehari, Hermon

FORGING HIS OWN PATH D. Ouellette color *Downbeat* v84 no6 p56 Je 2017

MEHDI, SABINA

There's More to Haya Than the Hijab: To understand hijab as an act of worship, it is first crucial to consider other common acts of worship and see the correlation between them *Islamic Horizons* v46 no4 p38 Jl/Ag 2017

Mehl, Tom

FROM OUR READERS *Sky & Telescope* v133 no4 p6 Ap 2017

Mehldau, Brad

FLOATING & FLYING J. WOODARD color *Downbeat* v83 no11 p36 N 2016

Mehle, Aileen, 1918-2016

SUZY HAD THE SCOOP! B. COLACELLO bw color *Vanity Fair* v59 no2 p106 F 2017

Mehmedinović, Harun

Epic Effort to Save the Night J. K. Beatty *Sky & Telescope* v134 no4 p67 O 2017

Mehrabi, Pedram

The role of dimer asymmetry and protomer dynamics in enzyme catalysis diag *Science* v355 no6322 p262 Ja 20 2017

Mehrotra, Kartikay

Blue State AGs: The Dems' New Resistance bw *Bloomberg Businessweek* no4516 p25 Mr 27 2017

Prisonville Could Soon Be Back in Business color *Bloomberg Businessweek* no4520 p18 My 1 2017

Saving Face color *Bloomberg Businessweek* no4531 p42 Jl 24 2017

The Unmaking Of American Dreams chart *Bloomberg Businessweek* no4537 p36 S 11 2017

Will Bosch Choke on VW's Exhaust? bw color *Bloomberg Businessweek* no4534 p12 Ag 14 2017

Mehta, Allison

Barn Parties *Arabian Horse World* v57 no11 p48 Ag 2017

Mehta, Deepa, 1949-

THE DISCOMFORTING LEGACY OF DEEPA MEHTA'S EARTH B. Qureshi *Film Quarterly* v70 no4 p77 Summ 2017

WORDS FROM THE FILMMAKERS color *Walrus* v14 no3 p1 Ap 2017

Mehta, Mayank R.

Dynamics of cortical dendritic membrane potential and spikes in freely behaving rats diag *Science* v355 no6331 p1281 Mr 24 2017

Mehta, Rita

BH&G throwback 1956 HANDMADE CERAMICS K. K. CONDON color *Better Homes & Gardens* v95 no9 p172 S 2017

Mehta, Satish

The Bitterest Pill N. VARDI and N. KARMALI cartoon color *Forbes* v199 no4 p38 Ap 25 2017

MEHTA, STEPHANIE

KEEPING IT 100 color *Vanity Fair* v58 no11 p42 N 2016

MEHTA, SUKETU

THIS LAND IS THEIR LAND color *Foreign Policy* no226 p26 S/O 2017

Mei, Lin

Three-dimensional holey-graphene/niobia composite architectures for ultrahigh-rate energy storage color diag graph *Science* v356 no6338 p599 My 12 2017

Mei-Ling Chen

Precision medicine for nasopharyngeal carcinoma bibl diag *Science* v354 no6319 p24 D 23 2016

Meidl, Tynisha

PRINCIPLES FOR ELEMENTARY PRINCIPALS: Keys to remember when it comes to being a literacy leader *Literacy Today (2411-7862)* v35 no2 p24 S/O 2017

Meier, Ana

Bright Eyes S. COCHRAN color *Architectural Digest* v74 no3 p44 Mr 2017

MEIER, ANDREW

So Close to Russia *New York Times Book Review* p20 N 27 2016

Meier, Brian—Interviews

MEET COMMANDER BRIAN MEIER *Sea Magazine* v108 no9 pPNW-10 S 2016

Meier, Diane E.

Measuring Quality of Care for the Sickest Patients *Harvard Business Review Digital Articles* p2 S 18 2015

Meier, Heinrich

THE TRUE MIRACLE K. Whitaker *Claremont Review of Books* v17 no1 p41 Wint 2016/2017

Meier, M.-A.

The hidden simplicity of subduction megathrust earthquakes graph *Science* v357 no6357 p1277 S 22 2017

Meier, Richard, 1934-

Spanning the Ages D. SNOONIAN GLENN *Architectural Record* v205 no9 p48 S 2017

Meier, Wayne—Awards

Patents and Awards *Science & Technology Review* p24 Mr 2017

Meijer, Hugo

Trading with the Enemy: The Making of U.S. Export Control Policy Toward the People's Republic of China A. J. Nathan *Foreign Affairs* v95 no6 p193 N/D 2016

Meijer, Jan

Submillihertz magnetic spectroscopy performed with a nanoscale quantum sensor diag *Science* v356 no6340 p832 My 26 2017

Meikle, Meridy

Q&A: High-Level Help color *Maclean's* v130 no9 p64 O 2017

Meilaender, Gilbert

Is Caution Enough? color *Commonweal* v144 no7 p12 Ap 14 2017

More Bathos than Pathos color *Commonweal* v144 no13 p14 Ag 11 2017

QUESTIONS AT THE END color *Commonweal* v144 no15 p2 S 22 2017

What makes a family? T. D. Kennedy color *Christian Century* v134 no7 p36 Mr 29 2017

Meilan, Richard

Formaldehyde stabilization facilitates lignin monomer production during biomass depolymerization bibl diag graph *Science* v354 no6310 p329 O 21 2016

MEINBERG, STEPHANIE

BEYOND BASIC BREWS *Cincinnati Magazine* v50 no6 p143 Mr 2017

SUMMER SUDS *Cincinnati Magazine* v50 p142 Ag 2017 Supplement

Meiners, Jens

ACE OF AN 8 color *Car & Driver* v63 no2 p19 Ag 2017

Meinert, Florian

Bloch oscillations in the absence of a lattice graph *Science* v356 no6341 p945 Je 1 2017

Meininger, Cynthia

Visualizing the function and fate of neutrophils in sterile injury and repair color graph *Science* v357 no6359 p111 O 6 2017

Meinshausen, Malte

A roadmap for rapid decarbonization bibl color graph *Science* v355 no6331 p1269 Mr 24 2017

Meiosis

Control of meiotic pairing and recombination by chromosomally tethered 26S proteasome J. S. Ahuja, R. Sandhu et al bibl graph

Science v355 no6323 p408 Ja 27 2017

A global view of meiotic double-strand break end resection E. P. Mimitou, Shintaro Yamada et al bibl graph *Science* v355 no6320 p1 Ja 6 2017

Meiri, Karina

Lee Rubin: Our mentor and role model *Science* v355 no6327 p806 F 24 2017

Meisel, Joseph W.

Friendship *Science* v354 no6308 p46 O 7 2016

Meisel, Marlies

Reovirus infection triggers inflammatory responses to dietary antigens and development of celiac disease color diag *Science* v356 no6333 p44 Ap 7 2017

MEISTER, KATHLEEN A.

FROM THE ARCHIVES bw *Reason* v49 no1 p70 My 2017

Meister, Torrey

IF YOU BUILD IT, They Will Surf T. PRODANOVICH color *Surfer* v58 no6 p48 O 2017

Taking Off color *Surfer* v57 no12 p12 Ja/F 2017

Mejia, Eva M.

The right network for the right problem color diag *Phi Delta Kappan* v98 no3 p8 N 2016

Mejia, Paula

The Love Doctor Is In img *New York* v50 no18 p71 S 4 2017

Mekong River Delta (Vietnam & Cambodia)—Environmental conditions

Dam-building threatens Mekong fisheries R. Stone color map *Science* v354 no6316 p1084 D 2 2016

Dams threaten rare Mekong dolphins R. L. J. Brownell, R. R. Reeves et al bibl color *Science* v355 no6327 p805 F 24 2017

Protecting water resources calls for international efforts A. Q. Hoy color *Science* v356 no6340 p814 My 26 2017

Melamed, Jennie

Let Me Go: Women and girls eke out an existence in a patriarchal dystopia C. JARVIS *New York Times Book Review* p18 O 15 2017

Melancon, Desiree

DESIRE MELANCON B. Merrill color *Snowboarder* v29 no3 p40 N 2016

SALMON SNOWBOARDS cartoon *Snowboarder* v29 no4 p8 D 2016

Melanins

Drawing on the Past M. Jones *Natural History* v124 no10 p16 N 2016

To Boldly Go M. DiChristina color *Scientific American* v316 no3 p4 Mr 2017

THE True Colors OF DINOSAURS [Cover story] J. Vinther color *Scientific American* v316 no3 p50 Mr 2017

Melanism

Polluted reefs may favor dark snakes S. MILIUS color graph *Science News* v192 no4 p14 S 16 2017

Melanoma

Dramatic rise of deadly skin cancer in older adults *Mayo Clinic Health Letter* v35 no4 p4 Ap 2017

Getting OUTSIDE J. Francisco color *Good Housekeeping* v264 no6 p8 Je 2017

"I'LL NEVER FORGET WHERE I WAS the moment I learned I had melanoma." N. O'DONNELL color *Good Housekeeping* v264 no6 p89 Je 2017

New insights into melanoma development J. W. Shay diag *Science* v357 no6358 p1358 S 29 2017

WHAT REALLY MATTERS M. Hansen color *Powder* v45 no5 p34 Ja 2017

Melanoma diagnosis

Should I see a doctor for a mole that bleeds on occasion? *Mayo Clinic Health Letter* v35 no7 p8 Jl 2017

This Will Sting & Burn W. M. ROBINSON *Reader's Digest* v189 no1127 p96 F 2017

Melanoma treatment

deserted [Cover story] M. W. Moyer color map *Women's Health* v14 no7 p150 S 2017

Melanoma—Prevention

Don't Get Burned! J. PRESS *Scholastic Choices* v32 no8 p12 My 2017

more than skin deep K. LEDGER *Parents* v91 no6 p80 Je 2016

sun care by the numbers A. MENCEL color *Parents* v92 no6 p91

Je 2017

Top screenings to avoid cancer *Harvard Health Letter* v42 no2 p6 D 2016

Melanoma—Risk factors

more than skin deep K. LEDGER *Parents* v91 no6 p80 Je 2016

sun care by the numbers A. MENCEL color *Parents* v92 no6 p91 Je 2017

Sun Smarts *Parents* v91 no6 p26 Je 2016

A Surprising Danger in Your Wineglass color *Health* v31 no3 p13 Ap 2017

Melatonin

Does It Work? Melatonin [Cover story] S. KLEIN color *Prevention* v69 no9 p22 O 2017

Don't Sleep on MELATONIN J. WUEBBEN color *Muscle & Performance* v9 no6 p11 Je 2017

INSOMNIAC'S LITTLE HELPER S. MICHAELS *Mother Jones* v42 no6 p70 N/D 2017

Melatonin makes the midshipman hum S. Milius color *Science News* v190 no9 p4 O 29 2016

sleep under the stars for better zzz's color *Good Housekeeping* v264 no6 p83 Je 2017

Melatonin—Physiological effect—Research

'Natural' Sleep Supplements Carry Serious Safety Concerns G. Skinner *Consumer Reports* v82 no2 p25 F 2017

Melatonin—Physiology

HUNGRY FOR SLEEP V. Clayton and A. Wolfe bw color *Yoga Journal* p114 2017 Special Issue

Melbourne (Vic.)

Walk a Thin Line T. DAVIDGE color *Architectural Record* v205 no8 p77 Ag 2017

Melby, Caleb

THE BEST YARD SALE color *Bloomberg Businessweek* no4501 p22 N 28 2016

Cost of 666 Fifth Avenue color diag graph *Bloomberg Businessweek* no4537 p39 S 11 2017

Deutsche Bank Is in a Bind Over Trump Debt color *Bloomberg Businessweek* no4517 p39 Ap 3 2017

The Most Expensive Building in NYC color *Bloomberg Businessweek* no4515 p27 Mr 20 2017

The Rich Refugees Who Saved Trump cartoon *Bloomberg Businessweek* no4515 p14 Mr 20 2017

The Trump Effect Cuts Both Ways color *Bloomberg Businessweek* no4523 p27 My 22 2017

TRUMP'S SECRET SANTAS color *Bloomberg Businessweek* no4505 p84 D 26 2016

Until Donald Trump, U.S. presidents and vice presidents went to extremes to avoid conflicts of interest... real or apparent bw color *Bloomberg Businessweek* no4503 p22 D 12 2016

When the President's A Billionaire cartoon *Bloomberg Businessweek* no4499 p24 N 14 2016

Who'll Pay to Protect Trump's Towers? *Bloomberg Businessweek* no4503 p35 D 12 2016

Melcher, David F.

Board Members Benefit from Becoming Mentors *Harvard Business Review Digital Articles* p2 D 16 2014

HOW IMPORTANT SPACE IS *Vital Speeches of the Day* v83 no7 p211 Jl 2017

MAKING OUR COUNTRY STRONGER MORE ECONOMICALLY ROBUST AND INNOVATIVE *Vital Speeches of the Day* v83 no2 p50 F 2017

MELCHIOR, JAN

REASON IN BRONZE: CLARENCE DARROW to Reunite with WILLIAM JENNINGS BRYAN at Dayton Courthouse *Humanist* v77 no4 p32 Jl/Ag 2017

Melchiore, Ron

Communications on a SASKATCHEWAN HOMESTEAD: Two remote homesteaders try a variety of methods to reach out to society *Mother Earth News* no284 p10 O/N 2017

Melde, Merri

Artist Designs New Wendell Robie Trophy for Tevis Cup *Arabian Horse World* v57 no11 p163 Ag 2017

Mele, Nicco

The Secret to Smartphone Marketing Is Still Email *Harvard Business Review Digital Articles* p2 N 2 2015

Why More M&As Is a Sign That Scale Is No Longer an Advantage *Harvard Business Review Digital Articles* p2 O 26 2015

MELEGRITO, JULIUS
ARNIS BACKUP PLAN [Cover story] color *Black Belt* v55 no3 p26 Ap/My 2017

Mélenchon, Jean-Luc, 1951-
The Wild Cards of the French Election Z. Rahim color *Time* v189 no15 p9 Ap 24 2017

Melendrez, Melanie C.
Dengue diversity across spatial and temporal scales: Local structure and the effect of host population size bibl graph *Science* v355 no6331 p1302 Mr 24 2017

Meles, Dee
Representation Matters color *Glamour* v115 no11 p22 N 2017

Melfi, Theodore
The BRIGHT Stuff T. Stack color *Entertainment Weekly* no1446/1447 p34 D 2016/Ja 2017
HIDDEN FIGURES C. Chiarella color *Sound & Vision* v82 no7 p69 S 2017
Liftoff Uplift J. PODHORETZ *Weekly Standard* v22 no22 p39 F 13 2017

Melford, Myra
MIYA MASAOKA T. Panken color *Downbeat* v84 no7 p26 Jl 2017

MELIA, THOMAS O.
FROM THE ARCHIVES color *Reason* v49 no4 p78 Ag/S 2017

MELICK, JENNIFER
Bravura STYLE *Opera News* v81 no6 p24 D 2016
The People's Opera *Opera News* v81 no6 p62 D 2016

Méliès, Georges, 1861-1938
Final CUT: WHEN TEXAS'S FILM INCENTIVES PROGRAM COMES UP FOR RENEWAL, POLITICIANS AND MOVIE BIZZERS GIVE PERFORMANCES THAT MATTHEW MC-CONAUGHEY WOULD ENVY C. HOOKS *Texas Monthly* v45 no7 p39 Jl 2017

Melillo, J. M.
Long-term pattern and magnitude of soil carbon feedback to the climate system in a warming world chart graph *Science* v357 no6359 p101 O 6 2017

Melin, Anders
How Well Is Vanguard's Boss Paid? graph *Bloomberg Businessweek* no4508 p33 Ja 23 2017
Letting Workers Have a Share bw color *Bloomberg Businessweek* no4527 p37 Je 19 2017
Monetizing Lost Vacation Time color *Bloomberg Businessweek* no4495 p33 O 17 2016
Nelson Peltz Makes Nice bw *Bloomberg Businessweek* no4536 p30 S 4 2017

Mellace, Jennifer
Bodies in Motion *Dressage Today* v23 no6 p10 F 2017
Dressage Riders Have More Fun *Dressage Today* v23 no9 p12 Je 2017
Happy New Year! *Dressage Today* v23 no5 p1 Ja 2017
Journey Through Germany *Dressage Today* v23 no7 p12 Mr 2017
Lessons In Listening *Dressage Today* p12 My 2017
Praising the Horsey Parents *Dressage Today* v24 no2 p10 N 2017
The Priceless School Horse *Dressage Today* v23 no4 p8 D 2016
Stronger Than You Think *Dressage Today* v23 no12 p10 S 2017
Trust the Journey *Dressage Today* v23 no8 p10 Ap 2017

Mellander, Charlotta
Hip, Cool & Unaffordable R. FLORIDA chart color *Alternatives Journal (AJ) - Canada's Environmental Voice* v42 no2 p42 2016

Mellen, Joan
LBJ'S DEVIOUS DANCE R. Culyer *American History* v51 no6 p68 F 2017

MELLEN, RUBY
The Rapist's Loophole: Marriage map *Foreign Policy* no223 p20 Mr/Ap 2017
A Refugee Without a River color *Foreign Policy* no226 p12 S/O 2017

Mellencamp, John, 1951—Interviews
John Mellencamp B. HIATT bw *Rolling Stone* no1286 p18 My 4 2017
John Mellencamp Continues to Explore His American Roots With Sad Clowns & Hillbillies M. METTLER bw color *Sound & Vision* v82 no7 p30 S 2017

MELLER, NANCY
SEEING THE LIGHT color *O, The Oprah Magazine* p18 Ag 2017

Mellers, Barbara A.
Bringing probability judgments into policy debates via forecasting tournaments bibl color *Science* v355 no6324 p481 F 3 2017

Mellett, Claire
The formation of peak rings in large impact craters bibl color graph *Science* v354 no6314 p878 N 18 2016

Mellis, Scott
Distribution and clinical impact of functional variants in 50,726 whole-exome sequences from the DiscovEHR study chart graph *Science* v354 no6319 paaf6814-1 D 23 2016

Mellman, Ira
T cell costimulatory receptor CD28 is a primary target for PD-1–mediated inhibition color diag graph *Science* v355 no6332 p1428 Mr 31 2017

MELLO, MARCO A. R.
Using Plant-Animal Interactions to Inform Tree Selection in Tree-Based Agroecosystems for Enhanced Biodiversity *BioScience* v66 no12 p1046 D 1 2016

Melloan, George
Tracing the WSJ's Editorial Page Journey S. LIPSKY *American Conservative* v16 no5 p58 S/O 2017

Mellon, Liz
How to Turn Around a Failing School *Harvard Business Review Digital Articles* p2 Ag 5 2016
The One Type of Leader Who Can Turn Around a Failing School bw color *Harvard Business Review Digital Articles* p2 O 20 2016
Research: How the Best School Leaders Create Enduring Change *Harvard Business Review Digital Articles* p2 S 14 2017

Mellon, Paul, 1907-1999
THE MELLON LEGACY B. Swenson *Virginia Living* v15 no2 p66 F 2017

Mellon, Rachel, 1910-2014
THE MELLON LEGACY B. Swenson *Virginia Living* v15 no2 p66 F 2017
WHEN JACKIE MET BUNNY M. GORDON color *Vanity Fair* v59 no10 p144 O 2017

Mellon, Tamara—Interviews
THE QUEEN OF HEELS TALKS SHOP(S) color *Fortune* v175 no7 p12 Je 1 2017

Mellor, Andrew
Dead Man Walking *Opera News* v81 no10 p45 Ap 2017

Mellor, Joseph C.
Exploring genetic suppression interactions on a global scale diag *Science* v354 no6312 p599 N 4 2016

Mellott, Jeff
Help for a Nervous Pattern Horse color *Horse & Rider* v56 no4 p73 Ap 2017

Melman, Rich
RICH MELMAN B. Zehme *Chicago* v66 no7 p104 Jl 2017

Melngailis, Sarma
THE RUNAWAY VEGAN A. SALKIN bw color *Vanity Fair* v58 no12 p106 D 2016

Melnikov, Igor
Mechanism of transmembrane signaling by sensor histidine kinases color *Science* v356 no6342 p1043 Je 9 2017

Melnikov, Lior
Lior MELNIKOV N. Loeffler-Gladstone *Dance Spirit* v20 no10 p71 D 2016

Melo, D.
Observation of a large-scale anisotropy in the arrival directions of cosmic rays above 8×10^{18} eV *Science* v357 no6357 p1266 S 22 2017

Melocco, Heidi
Alone on the Trail color *Horse & Rider* v56 no11 p46 N 2017
Be Trail-Tack Savvy color *Horse & Rider* v56 no9 p51 S 2017
Canter with Confidence color *Trail Rider* v29 no4 p44 My 2017
Ground Work at Liberty color *Trail Rider* v29 no1 p40 Ja/F 2017
Horse Owner's Spring Notebook color *Trail Rider* v29 no4 p38 My 2017
ON-TRAIL FIRST-AID KIT color *Trail Rider* v29 no3 p64 Ap 2017
Open a Trail Gate color *Horse & Rider* v56 no8 p46 Ag 2017
Safety in Numbers color *Trail Rider* v29 no3 p24 Ap 2017
Settle Your Cinchy Horse color *Trail Rider* v29 no2 p42 Mr 2017
Take Charge color *Horse & Rider* v56 no7 p51 Jl 2017

Trip Tips color *Trail Rider* v29 no3 p6 Ap 2017

Turn Back for Safety color *Horse & Rider* v56 no10 p48 O 2017

Melodrama (Music)

Lorde N. Feeney color *Entertainment Weekly* no1471 p62 Je 23 2017

LORDE: POP'S REIGNING DRAMA QUEEN N. Feeney color *Entertainment Weekly* no1468/1469 p102 Je 2-9 2017

Lorde Returns With the Year's First Great Pop Anthem N. Feeney color *Entertainment Weekly* no1457/1458 p93 Mr 17 2017

Lorde Throws an Epic House Party W. HERMES color *Rolling Stone* no1290 p53 Je 29 2017

The Must List color *Entertainment Weekly* no1471 p5 Je 23 2017

New Sentences N. Abebe *New York Times Magazine* p13 Jl 2 2017

A Royal Return: Lorde avoids the dreaded second-album jitters by hunkering down in New York City img *New York* v50 no13 p83 Jo 26 2017

Meloni, Christopher, 1961-

HAPPY! C. Collis color *Entertainment Weekly* no1474/1475 p70 Jl 21-28 2017

Melons

See also

Muskmelon

Watermelons

How Fresh! P. Grandjean color *Health* v31 no5 p105 Je 2017

Melons—Therapeutic use

Big SPLASH Z. RUFFNER color *Vogue* v207 no6 p74 Je 2017

NATIONAL WATERMELON DAY S. LIAO color *Better Homes & Gardens* v95 no8 p167 Ag 2017

Melosh, H. Jay

Formation of the Orientale lunar multiring basin bibl graph *Science* v354 no6311 p441 O 28 2016

Gravity field of the Orientale basin from the Gravity Recovery and Interior Laboratory Mission bibl graph *Science* v354 no6311 p438 O 28 2016

Meloy, Colin

The Whiz Mob and the Grenadine Kid *Publishers Weekly* v264 no33 p79 Ag 14 2017

Meloy, Maile

Do Not Become Alarmed L. Greenblatt color *Entertainment Weekly* no1468/1469 p108 Je 2-9 2017

Epic Quests: A graphic novel with a wandering hero raises questions about honor and social codes in medieval society *New York Times Book Review* p23 My 14 2017

Leaving the Faith *New York Times Book Review* p15 O 16 2016

Melrose Credit Union (Company)

Deposit Insurance Has Your Back L. GERSTNER chart *Kiplinger's Personal Finance* v71 no5 p49 My 2017

Melson, Eric

THE LIGHTNING ROD D. O'Neil color *Bike Magazine* v24 no8 p58 N 2017

Melton, Alex

U.S. Agricultural Trade in 2016: Major Commodities and Trends *Amber Waves: The Economics of Food, Farming, Natural Resources, & Rural America* p1 My 2017

Melton, Doris

Keep On Rockin' in the Free World color *Weekly Standard* v22 no42 p2 Jl 17 2017

Melton, Glennon Doyle

Come Out, Come Out, Whoever You Are G. Doyle color *O, The Oprah Magazine* p41 O 2017

DISMISS the Dis cartoon *O, The Oprah Magazine* p37 My 2017

Good Grief cartoon *O, The Oprah Magazine* p36 Mr 2017

Here We Go! O. Winfrey color *O, The Oprah Magazine* p19 F 2017

Hurts So Good cartoon *O, The Oprah Magazine* p48 F 2017

My husband's been totally focused on our baby color *Glamour* v115 no1 p52 Ja 2017

PRAYING ATTENTION color *O, The Oprah Magazine* p34 Ag 2017

Q: What is the most interesting family in history? color *Atlantic* v318 no5 p96 D 2016

Valley Girl color *O, The Oprah Magazine* p36 Je 2017

We're Not Fine, and We Do CARE color *O, The Oprah Magazine* p31 Jl 2017

Your Best Cyberself cartoon *O, The Oprah Magazine* p35 Ap 2017

Melton, J. R.

A human-driven decline in global burned area chart graph map *Science* v356 no6345 p1356 Je 30 2017

Melton, Jill

MOTORCYCLE ROAD: The making of a photo essay color *Virginia Living* v15 no5 p13 Ag 2017

MELTON, MARY

Get The Lead Out *Los Angeles Magazine* v61 no11 p20 N 2016

Good Night, And Good Luck *Los Angeles Magazine* p16 Ap 2017

Is There An App for That? *Los Angeles Magazine* p12 F 2017

Power And the Press *Los Angeles Magazine* p14 Ja 2017

The Wonder Years *Los Angeles Magazine* p24 D 2016

Meltwater (Company)

Google Slayer Z. O'MALLEY GREENBURG and T. YOON color *Forbes* v199 no6 p54 Je 13 2017

Meltwater Group (Company)

ANDREW HERMAN J. Chen color *Bloomberg Businessweek* no4508 p63 Ja 23 2017

Meltzer, David E.

The past and future of PHYSICS EDUCATION REFORM *Physics Today* v70 no5 p50 My 2017

Meltzer, David J.

A composite window into human history color map *Science* v356 no6343 p1118 Je 16 2017

Meltzer, Karl

2,190 MILES, 1,102 HOURS, 348,000 CALORIES, AND 1 WORLD RECORD B. HANSEN-BUNDY bw color *GQ: Gentlemen's Quarterly* v86 no12 p152 D 2016

MORE ENERGY NOW! J. LEHRER color *Men's Health* v32 no6 p108 Ag 2017

Meltzer, Marisa

The Body Electric color *Vogue* v207 no4 p170 Ap 2017

Body Work: A memoir recounts a lifelong addiction to dieting *New York Times Book Review* p21 S 10 2017

Match Me If You Can chart color graph il *Consumer Reports* v82 no2 p38 F 2017

Quest for Fire color *Walrus* v14 no4 p63 My 2017

#SHOPNOW cartoon *Wired* v24 no12 p28 D 2016

STORY TIME cartoon *New Yorker* v92 no38 p33 N 21 2016

TECH MIRROR, TECH MIRROR ON THE WALL color *Women's Health* v14 no6 p50 Jl 2017

Meltzer-Warren, Rachel

Meltzer Zepeda, Dana

JENNIFER WEINER color *Runner's World* v52 no7 p92 Ag 2017

Melursus ursinus

Sloth Bear Rescue A. SHAW color *National Geographic Kids* no473 p22 S 2017

Melville, Jean-Pierre, 1917-1973

KEEPING COOL A. LANE bw color *New Yorker* v93 no11 p70 My 1 2017

Melville, Martin

Midnight Omen *Publishers Weekly* v264 no7 p54 F 13 2017

Melville, Patrick

CAN THIS HAIRCUT BE SAVED? color *O, The Oprah Magazine* p120 Ap 2017

Melville, Sarah C.

The Campaigns of Sargon II, King of Assyria, 721-705 BC R. A. Gabriel *Military History* v33 no5 p69 Ja 2017

Melvin, Mungo

Sevastopol's Wars: Crimea From Potemkin to Putin D. T. Zabecki *Military History* v34 no4 p73 N 2017

Melvin, Robby

Caprese with a Twist color *Southern Living* v52 no7 p122 Jl 2017

Chili Out! color *Health* v31 no1 p113 Ja 2017

Eat Your Greens color *Southern Living* v52 no4 p119 Ap 2017

Pasta Night! color *Southern Living* v52 no5 p123 My 2017

Sizzling Steak Tacos color *Southern Living* v52 no7 p112 Jl 2017

TORTILLAS TONIGHT color *Southern Living* v52 no1 p115 Ja 2017

Melvin, Ted

The SAILING SCENE color *Sail* v48 no11 p6 N 2017

Melwani, Shimul

Research: Love-Hate Relationships at Work Might Be Good for You *Harvard Business Review Digital Articles* p2 Ja 20 2015

Membere, Ashley

Two Types of Diversity Training That Really Work *Harvard Business Review Digital Articles* p1 Jl 28 2017

Membership
See also
Membership in associations, institutions, etc.
2017 NRPA Annual Conference Exhibit Hall Highlights T. Mattingly *Parks & Recreation* v52 no8 p54 Ag 2017
Case Study: When You Have to Choose Between Core and New Customers M. Bertini and N. Tavassoli *Harvard Business Review Digital Articles* p2 Je 26 2017
LAKE ASSOCIATION SPOTLIGHT color *Cabin Living* p10 Ag 2017
Meet the NRPA Conservation Advisory Panel S. Ozbenian *Parks & Recreation* v52 no4 p48 Ap 2017
MEMBERS IN MOTION *Arabian Horse World* v57 no3 p50 D 2016
More Bang for Your Membership Buck color *AARP: The Magazine* v30 no6A p72 O/N 2017
Where Do You Stand? M. Babick *In Stride* v12 no2 p8 Mr 2017

Membership in associations, institutions, etc.
LAKE ASSOCIATION SPOTLIGHT color *Cabin Living* p11 S 2017

Membrane permeability (Biology)
Maximizing the right stuff: The trade-off between membrane permeability and selectivity H. B. Park, J. Kamcev et al color *Science* v356 no6343 p1137 Je 16 2017

Membrane proteins
Ephrin B1–mediated repulsion and signaling control germinal center T cell territoriality and function P. Lu, C. Shih et al color *Science* v356 no6339 p716 My 19 2017
Membrane proteins scrambling through a folding landscape D. J. Müller and H. E. Gaub bibl diag *Science* v355 no6328 p907 Mr 3 2017
Repulsive behavior in germinal centers G. Leandros Moschovakis and R. Förster diag *Science* v356 no6339 p703 My 19 2017

Membranes (Technology)
Maximizing the right stuff: The trade-off between membrane permeability and selectivity H. B. Park, J. Kamcev et al color *Science* v356 no6343 p1137 Je 16 2017

Memczak, Sebastian
Loss of a mammalian circular RNA locus causes miRNA deregulation and affects brain function color *Science* v357 no6357 p1254 S 22 2017

Memes
Bitch A. LOWREY *New York* v49 no15 p18 Jl 25 2016
How the Internet Is Getting a Little Nicer, One Meme at a Time L. Eadicicco color *Time* v189 no23 p19 Je 19 2017
Memewear J. Fisher *New York Times Magazine* p22 Ag 20 2017
STOP TRYING TO MAKE HIDDEN FENCES HAPPEN color *Entertainment Weekly* no1449 p16 Ja 20 2017
THE YEAR IN MEMES M. MALONE KIRCHER, B. FELDMAN et al img *New York* v49 no26 p38 D 26 2016

Memes—Social aspects
A New 'Hate Symbol' color *Time* v188 no14 p22 O 10 2016

Memiaghe, Hervé R.
Plant diversity increases with the strength of negative density dependence at the global scale diag *Science* v356 no6345 p1389 Je 30 2017

Memic, Fatima
Multipotent peripheral glial cells generate neuroendocrine cells of the adrenal medulla color *Science* v357 no6346 p46 Jl 7 2017

Memoirs
After The Fall M. KNOX BERAN *National Review* v69 no1 p19 Ja 23 2017
Gratitude for a Femme Fatale *American Scholar* v86 no1 p15 Wint 2017
Most-Wanted List I. Biedenharn color *Entertainment Weekly* no1438 p64 N 4 2016
One for the Books J. Hibberd color *Entertainment Weekly* no1457/1458 p18 Mr 17 2017
PLAYING THE TRUMP CARD C. Hollub color *Entertainment Weekly* no1470 p12 Je 16 2017
SHAGGY DOG STORY E. Myles *Harper's Magazine* p17 O 2017
Sketchbook G. Snider *New York Times Book Review* p27 N 20 2016
WHY ROCK MEMOIRS RULE I. Biedenharn color *Entertainment Weekly* no1438 p64 N 4 2016

Memoli, Matthew J.
IgG antibodies to dengue enhanced for FcγRIIIA binding determine disease severity bibl graph *Science* v355 no6323 p395 Ja 27 2017

Memorandums
What Trump Can Learn from Nixon A. FERGUSON bw *Weekly Standard* v22 no12 p9 N 28 2016

Memorial Day
ANCHORED IN A SMALL TOWN L. MYERS cartoon *Missouri Life* v44 no3 p68 My 2017
He Shoots! He Scores! D. SINGER *Texas Monthly* v45 no8 p36 Ag 2017
Panel 42W, Row 39 R. Brown color *Commonweal* v114 no14 p38 S 8 2017
Why Argue About a Day Off? P. TERZIAN color *Weekly Standard* v23 no2 p19 S 18 2017

Memorial design & construction
Hanged, Burned, Shot, Drowned, Beaten K. CAPPS color *Atlantic* v320 no4 p30 N 2017
A Nose for History bw *Reader's Digest* v190 no1132 p26 Jl/Ag 2017

Memorial gardens
Mixed Blessings: In the Month of May D. AGUIRRE *Idaho Magazine* v16 no11 p24 Ag 2017

Memorialization—Political aspects
The Price of Silence: Family Memory of Stalin's Repressions I. Tabarovsky *Wilson Quarterly* v40 no4 p5 Fall 2016

Memorialization—Religious aspects
The Selfie, Medieval Style E. Goodwin *History Today* v67 no2 p6 F 2017

Memorials
See also
Anniversaries
Holidays
AMERICANS MARK CENTENNIAL OF U.S. ENTRY INTO WORLD WAR I B. Manley bw *Military History* v34 no2 p8 Jl 2017
ECHOES OF THIOKOL: Survivors and their descendants seek a memorial to a forgotten tragedy on the Georgia coast J. GRILLO *Atlanta* v57 no4 p18 Ag 2017
Foundering Fathers J. COST color *Weekly Standard* v22 no39 p21 Je 19 2017
Monumentally Naïve K. SMITH *National Review* v69 no17 p30 S 11 2017
Solemn Beauty *Arizona Highways* v93 no8 p56 Ag 2017
They vs. Them R. J. SMITH *Cincinnati Magazine* v50 no7 p42 Ap 2017

Memorials—Computer network resources
EVERYONE'S A CRITIC *Washingtonian Magazine* v52 no1 p20 O 2016

Memorials—Design & construction
A Monument to Trump Hatred color *Weekly Standard* v22 no31 p2 Ap 17 2017
NYC Unveils AIDS Memorial A. FIXSEN *Architectural Record* v205 no1 p22 Ja 2017

Memorials—United States
6 CONFEDERATE MEMORIALS THAT ARE STILL HERE M. Blitz *Washingtonian Magazine* v52 no2 p22 N 2016
A GATEWAY to the West K. N. Ried *Prologue* v48 no3 p20 Fall 2016
IN MEMORY OF THESE [Cover story] D. L. MAYFIELD and A. Olsen bw color *Christianity Today* v61 no7 p34 S 2017
A Missing Memorial C. ALESSIO bw color *America* v215 no19 p21 D 19 2016

Memorization
SOUP UP YOUR RECALL A. AU LEVITT color *Reader's Digest* v190 no1133 p106 S 2017
YOUR CHEAT SHEET TO... Cramming Your Way to an A L. MARCHANT and A. STANLEY color *Seventeen* v75 no11 p102 N 2016

Memory
See also
Attention
Early memories
Cognitive Offloading L. SCHLEY cartoon *Discover* v27 no10 p14 D 2016

THE DATA DELUGE A. S. RUMSEY *Saturday Evening Post* v289 no5 p44 S/O 2017

Eat Well to Keep Mind Sharp [Cover story] *Tufts University Health & Nutrition Letter* v34 no12 p1 F 2017

The End of Forgetting B. ROWEN color *Atlantic* v319 no5 p24 Je 2017

IMPROVE YOUR MEMORY WHILE YOU SLEEP color *Prevention* v69 no8 p6 Ag 2017

Keep Your Memory Sharp K. PITSKER cartoon color *Kiplinger's Personal Finance* v71 no4 p64 Ap 2017

KEEP YOUR MIND SHARP J. Challem color *Amazing Wellness* v8 no2 p32 Spr 2016

Make it stick S. Gaidos color *Science News* v192 no4 p30 S 16 2017

MEMORY'S INTRICATE WEB A. J. Silva color diag *Scientific American* v317 no1 p30 Jl 2017

Multitask Better V. Tweed color *Amazing Wellness* v9 no1 p20 Wint 2017

Older Mom, Better Memory? *Health* v31 no4 p16 My 2017

Open your mind to calm color *Redbook* p95 N 2017

photographic memories color *Parents* v92 no6 p55 Je 2017

Retrieval practice protects memory against acute stress A. M. Smith, V. A. Floerke et al bibl chart graph *Science* v354 no6315 p1046 N 25 2016

SMARTY PLANTS M. ZARASKA color diag *Discover* v38 no4 p52 My 2017

This Just In J. Zorthian *Time* v190 no2/3 p23 Jl 10-17 2017

Ultrastructural evidence for synaptic scaling across the wake/sleep cycle L. de Vivo, M. Bellesi et al bibl diag graph *Science* v355 no6324 p507 F 3 2017

Why You Need Your Feed color *Seventeen* v76 no3 p71 My 2017

Memory Card (Film)

The Memory Card R. Brody color *New Yorker* v92 no42 p30 D 19 2016

Memory disorders

Minor Memory Lapse... or Something More? V. TWEED *Better Nutrition* v79 no9 p72 S 2017

Memory disorders in old age—Psychological aspects

You Must Remember This B. HOWARD color *AARP: The Magazine* v59 no5A p24 Ag/S 2016

Memory disorders—Prevention

HUMAN BRAIN NO KNOWN EXPIRATION DATE *Psychology Today* v49 no6 p60 N/D 2016

Memory in old age

Speak, Memory color *AARP: The Magazine* v59 no2A p74 F/Mr 2016

Memory loss

DOING GOOD S. Pulia color *InStyle* v24 no11 p66 N 2017

One Simple Trick to Reversing Memory Loss S. Wuzubia *Saturday Evening Post* v288 no6 p93 N/D 2016

One Simple Trick to Reversing Memory Loss: World's Leading Brain Expert and Winner of the Prestigious Kennedy Award, Unveils Exciting News For the Scattered, Unfocused and Forgetful S. Wuzubia *Saturday Evening Post* v289 no4 p70 Jl/Ag 2017

silver linings J. Francisco *Good Housekeeping* v264 no4 p16 Ap 2017

Memory trace (Psychology)

Engrams and circuits crucial for systems consolidation of a memory T. Kitamura, S. K. Ogawa et al diag *Science* v356 no6333 p73 Ap 7 2017

Overlapping memory trace indispensable for linking, but not recalling, individual memories J. Yokose, Reiko Okubo-Suzuki et al bibl graph *Science* v355 no6323 p398 Ja 27 2017

Memory—Competitions

FEATS OF THE MIND L. Goldman color *Women's Health* v14 no8 p86 O 2017

Memory—Nutritional aspects

MINDING YOUR MEMORY S. WADYKA *Martha Stewart Living* no269 p62 N 2016

Memory—Physiological aspects

MINDING YOUR MEMORY S. WADYKA *Martha Stewart Living* no269 p62 N 2016

Multiple mechanisms for memory replay? R. J. Gardner and Moser bibl diag *Science* v355 no6321 p131 Ja 13 2017

Social memory goes viral K. Saxena and R. G. M. Morris bibl diag *Science* v353 no6307 p1496 S 30 2016

Memory—Research

Overlapping memory trace indispensable for linking, but not recalling, individual memories J. Yokose, Reiko Okubo-Suzuki et al bibl graph *Science* v355 no6323 p398 Ja 27 2017

Memory—Social aspects

EATING YOUR FEELINGS A. GLOCK *Atlanta* v56 no9 p68 Ja 2017

Memphis (Music)

Seeds Sown and Grown HADLEY color *Downbeat* v84 no9 p66 S 2017

Memphis (Tenn.)—Description & travel

THE MEMPHIS BEAT D. HARRISON *Virginia Living* v15 no1 p56 D 2016

Memphis Gets Its Groove Back H. Hayes color *Southern Living* v52 no11 p69 N 2017

MEMPHIS, TN J. R. MARQUEZ *Atlanta* v56 no11 p52 Mr 2017

Memphis Grizzlies (Basketball team)

10 GRIZZLIES color *Sports Illustrated* v127 no12 p90 O 16 2017

7 Grizzlies R. Nadkarni, B. Golliver et al color *Sports Illustrated* v125 no14 p104 O 24-31 2016

Memran, Michelle

CANDID CAMERA *Harper's Magazine* v333 no1999 p15 D 2016

Men

> See also
>
> Bisexual men
> Brothers
> Businessmen
> Fathers
> Great men & women
> Grooming for men
> Husbands
> Male actors
> Male teachers
> Photography of men
> Sons

Ciao Napoli! D. COGGINS bw color *Esquire* p142 BigBlackBook

MAKE MINE NEAT J. Barger *Washingtonian Magazine* v52 no3 p119 D 2016

What (Real) Men (Really) Want D. T. PUTERBAUGH *USA Today Magazine* v145 no2862 p82 Mr 2017

Men in advertising

Dads in Ads J. LILEKS *National Review* v69 no15 p37 Ag 14 2017

Men in popular culture

Men Behaving Fretfully J. Pontuso *Society* v54 no1 p42 F 2017

Men on television

The Unfunny Fall of TV's Manly Men color *Entertainment Weekly* no1438 p50 N 4 2016

Mena, Addie

A documentary on abortion that fails the women it portrays color *America* v216 no10 p51 My 1 2017

MENAKER, DANIEL

Bloody Thursday color *Esquire* v166 no4 p13 N 2016

Express Yourself *New York Times Book Review* p19 Je 25 2017

Menaker, Steve

READER GALLERY color *Astronomy* v44 no12 p70 D 2016

Menand, Louis

THE DEFENSE OF POETRY cartoon *New Yorker* v93 no22 p64 Jl 31 2017

DROP YOUR WEAPONS cartoon color *New Yorker* v93 no28 p61 S 18 2017

HE'S BACK cartoon *New Yorker* v92 no32 p90 O 10 2016

Louis Menand C. Lambert *Humanities* v37 no4 p1 Fall 2016

OP DE STEZ cartoon *New Yorker* v93 no11 p63 My 1 2017

PEOPLE OF THE BOOK cartoon color *New Yorker* v92 no41 p78 D 12 2016

THE STONE GUEST cartoon *New Yorker* v93 no25 p75 Ag 28 2017

Menard, Guillaume N.

Fatty acids in arbuscular mycorrhizal fungi are synthesized by the host plant diag graph *Science* v356 no6343 p1175 Je 16 2017

Menards Inc.

Menards HO scale Red Owl grocery store C. Grivno color *Model Railroader* v84 no8 p64 Ag 2017

MENARNDT, AUBREY

A Steppe Forward: Women for Change advances women's rights in Mongolia *Ms.* v27 no2 p15 Summ 2017

Menashe (Film)

So When Are You Getting Married? R. Margalit color *New York Review of Books* v64 no16 p12 O 26 2017

Men—Attitudes

Men Choose Differently When They Choose with Other Men H. Nikolova and C. Lamberton *Harvard Business Review Digital Articles* p2 S 14 2016

Too Many Men Are Silent Bystanders to Sexual Harassment W. B. Johnson and D. G. Smith *Harvard Business Review Digital Articles* p2 Mr 13 2017

Mencel, Aleksandra

4 Skills to Teach Him Before Cold Season color *Parents* v92 no11 p19 N 2017

Help an Introverted Child Make Friends color *Parents* v92 no9 p32 S 2017

pet perks color *Parents* v92 no8 p25 Ag 2017

sun care by the numbers color *Parents* v92 no6 p91 Je 2017

The Truth About Twins color *Parents* v92 no8 p26 Ag 2017

When Your Kid Is Sick and You're Tired color *Parents* v92 no8 p28 Ag 2017

Menchaca-Bagnulo, Ashleen

I'M A CONSERVATIVE LATINA [Cover story] color *America* v217 no6 p28 S 18 2017

MENCIMER, STEPHANIE

COLORBLIND JUSTICE color *Mother Jones* v41 no6 p45 N/D 2016

Mencken, H. L. (Henry Louis), 1880-1956

1925: Baltimore H. L. Mencken *Lapham's Quarterly* v10 no1 p185 Wint 2017

Mendal, Monica

Outdoor Adventure color *Glamour* v115 no6 p36 Je 2017

Twice? Nice! color *Glamour* v115 no4 p70 Ap 2017

Mendel, Harrison

BUZZ color *Bike Magazine* v24 no2 p26 Mr 2017

MENDELL, DAVID

CHICAGO'S POPULATION PROBLEM color *Chicago* v66 no6 p19 Je 2017

Mendelsohn, Ben, 1969-

Ben Mendelsohn J. Crelin color *Current Biography* v78 no2 p48 F 2017

PARTY LINES img *New York* v49 no26 p92 D 26 2016

Mendelsohn, Daniel

A Family Cruise P. Green color diag *New York Review of Books* v64 no16 p28 O 26 2017

AN ODYSSEY cartoon color *New Yorker* v93 no10 p54 Ap 24 2017

QUEEN MOTHER cartoon color *New Yorker* v93 no22 p70 Jl 31 2017

QUEEN MOTHER D. MENDELSOHN cartoon color *New Yorker* v93 no22 p70 Jl 31 2017

Robert B. Silvers (1929-2017) bw *New York Review of Books* v64 no7 p8 Ap 20 2017

Mendelsohn, Richard

Biological control of aragonite formation in stony corals bw color graph *Science* v356 no6341 p933 Je 1 2017

Mendelson, Charles

HEALTH CARE NEEDS REAL COMPETITION: INTERACTION img *Harvard Business Review* v95 no2 p19 Mr/Ap 2017

Mendelson, Cheryl

1999: New York City *Lapham's Quarterly* v10 no1 p156 Wint 2017

Mendelson, Edward

The Genius and Generosity of Jimmy Merrill bw *New York Review of Books* v63 no20 p73 D 22 2016

What Is the Critic's Job? [Cover story] bw color *New York Review of Books* v64 no14 p39 S 28 2017

Mendelson, Joseph R. III

The call of the wild color *Science* v357 no6348 p326 Jl 21 2017

MENDENHALL, ALLEN

The Circuitous Path of Papa and Ezra bw *American Conservative* v16 no2 p52 Mr/Ap 2017

Mendenhall, Chase

Harmonizing Biodiversity Conservation and Productivity in the Context of Increasing Demands on Landscapes graph *BioScience* v66 no10 p890 O 1 2016

Merging paleobiology with conservation biology to guide the future of terrestrial ecosystems color *Science* v355 no6325 p594 F 10 2017

Mendenhall, Mary

Global Refugee Study Highlights a Gap Between Policy and Practices C. M. Rubin *Education Digest* v83 no3 p51 N 2017

Mendes, Camila

FAKE I.D.'S E. NUSSBAUM cartoon *New Yorker* v93 no7 p100 Ap 3 2017

Mendes, Shawn, 1998-

Shawn Mendes D. Kiper color *Current Biography* v78 no4 p59 Ap 2017

Mendez, Federico

Mexico's invasive species plan in context bw *Science* v356 no6336 p386 Ap 28 2017

Méndez, Rosa

ENVIRONMENTAL JUSTICE--RIGHT FOR ALL *New York State Conservationist* v71 no6 p26 Je 2017

Men—Diseases

Men, and Mortality R. G. Bribiescas *Natural History* v124 no10 p28 N 2016

Mendl, Michael T.

Bee happy bibl color diag *Science* v353 no6307 p1499 S 30 2016

Mendocino County (Calif.)

BACK TO THE LAND A. Scott color *Sunset* v239 no4 p60 O 2017

Into the Woods J. MINUTILLO *Architectural Record* v205 no6 p74 Je 2017

Mendoza, A. M.

Persistent effects of pre-Columbian plant domestication on Amazonian forest composition bibl chart graph map *Science* v355 no6328 p925 Mr 3 2017

Mendoza, C.

Persistent effects of pre-Columbian plant domestication on Amazonian forest composition bibl chart graph map *Science* v355 no6328 p925 Mr 3 2017

Mendoza, Fernando

Protecting unauthorized immigrant mothers improves their children's mental health diag *Science* v357 no6355 p1041 S 8 2017

Mendoza, Jessica

Jews and Muslims partner in efforts to defend religious minorities *Christian Century* v134 no2 p17 Ja 18 2017

Mendoza, Paola

Kerry's Got This [Cover story] color *Glamour* v115 no5 p156 My 2017

Mendoza, Roberto

Mexico's invasive species plan in context bw *Science* v356 no6336 p386 Ap 28 2017

Mendoza, Susana

Woman on Fire [Cover story] T. C. Fishman color *Chicago* v66 no7 p64 Jl 2017

Men—Employment

The Entry-Level Health Care Jobs Men Are (and Are Not) Taking J. Dill *Harvard Business Review Digital Articles* p2 F 24 2017

Menendez, Erik, 1971-

After the Verdict D. Franich, N. Abrams et al color *Entertainment Weekly* no1482/1483 p62 S 22 2017

Menendez, Lyle, 1968-

After the Verdict D. Franich, N. Abrams et al color *Entertainment Weekly* no1482/1483 p62 S 22 2017

Menendez: Blood Brothers (Film)

Revisiting the Menendez Murders A. D'Arminio *TV Guide* v65 no23 p9 My 29 2017

Meng, Rachel

Research: Being in a Group Makes Us Less Likely to Fact-Check *Harvard Business Review Digital Articles* p2 Ag 1 2017

Meng, Si

Measuring Your Employees' Invisible Forms of Influence *Harvard Business Review Digital Articles* p2 N 7 2016

Meng, Y. Shirley

Liquefied gas electrolytes for electrochemical energy storage devices graph *Science* v356 no6345 p1351 Je 30 2017

Meng Khoon Tey

Deterministic entanglement generation from driving through

quantum phase transitions bibl color graph *Science* v355 no6325 p620 F 10 2017

Meng Xiao

Application of MALDI-TOF mass spectrometry for identifying clinical microorganisms bibl *Science* v354 no6319 p58 D 23 2016

A brief overview of matrix-assisted laser desorption/ionization time-of-flight mass spectrometry (MALDI-TOF MS) applications in clinical microbiology in China *Science* v354 no6319 p55 D 23 2016

Meng Zhang

Bifurcating electron-transfer pathways in DNA photolyases determine the repair quantum yield bibl graph *Science* v354 no6309 p209 O 14 2016

MENGE, BRUCE A.

Long-Term Studies Contribute Disproportionately to Ecology and Policy *BioScience* v67 no3 p271 Mr 2017

Mengel, Dave

FEEDING CROPS IN TOUGH TIMES: FRUGAL AND FER-TILIZER ARE TWO WORDS THAT GO TOGETHER IN TO-DAY'S FARM ECONOMY G. Johnston *Successful Farming* v115 no12 p50 O 2017

Mengelberg, Misha

Misha Mengelberg Dies at 81 T. Panken bw *Downbeat* v84 no5 p19 My 2017

Mengelkoch, Kelly

SISTER ACT G. FREKING *Cincinnati Magazine* v50 no4 p24 Ja 2017

MENGES, JOCHEN

Reclaim Your Commute color *Harvard Business Review* v95 no3 p149 My/Je 2017

MENGESTU, DINAW

The First Exile *New York Times Book Review* p15 N 6 2016

Origin Stories: Encounters with undocumented migrant children and the circumstances that produced them *New York Times Magazine* p12 Ap 30 2017

Men—Health

Ask Men's Health color *Men's Health* v32 no2 p14 Mr 2017

CREATE A PERSONALIZED PLAN A. Nix color *Amazing Wellness* v9 no3 p8 EarlySumm 2017

MEN'S HEALTH GUIDE I. Eliaz color *Amazing Wellness* v9 no3 p46 EarlySumm 2017

MH WORLD color *Men's Health* v32 no4 p6 My 2017

Men—History

Men, and Mortality R. G. Bribiescas *Natural History* v124 no10 p28 N 2016

Menis, Sergey

Priming HIV-1 broadly neutralizing antibody precursors in human Ig loci transgenic mice bibl graph *Science* v353 no6307 p1557 S 30 2016

Menken, Alan, 1949-

MUSICAL MAESTRO M. Lassell *Cincinnati Magazine* v50 no8 p20 My 2017

MENKHAUS, KEN

Saints and Sinners in Somalia *Current History* v116 no790 p197 My 2017

Mennella, V.

Seasonal exposure of carbon dioxide ice on the nucleus of comet 67P/Churyumov-Gerasimenko bibl bw graph *Science* v354 no6319 p1563 D 23 2016

MENNIES, LEAH

Sour Patch Citrus color *Bon Appetit* no11 p22 N 2017

starters bw color diag *Bon Appetit* v62 no2 p19 Mr 2017

starters color *Bon Appetit* no1 p13 F 2017

starters color *Bon Appetit* p25 S 2017

Mennitt, Daniel

Noise pollution is pervasive in U.S. protected areas graph map *Science* v356 no6337 p531 My 5 2017

Mennonites

Mennonite Pride J. NEUFELD cartoon *Walrus* v13 no9 p48 N 2016

Menologium (Poem)

Out of the Margins E. Parker *History Today* v67 no1 p25 Ja 2017

Menon, Anand

Why the British Chose Brexit *Foreign Affairs* v96 no6 p122 N/D 2017

Menon, Anil S.

How NASA Uses Telemedicine to Care for Astronauts in Space *Harvard Business Review Digital Articles* p2 Jl 6 2017

Menon, Archita V.

Restored iron transport by a small molecule promotes absorption and hemoglobinization in animals color graph *Science* v356 no6338 p608 My 12 2017

Menon, M. G. K. (Mambillikalathil Govind Kumar), 1928-2016

M. G. K. Menon (1928–2016) B. Venkatasubba Sreekantan and R. Cowsik color *Science* v355 no6325 p586 F 10 2017

Menon, Priyanka

Black Money *History Today* v67 no2 p7 F 2017

MENON, RAJAN

Why Humanitarian Intervention Still Isn't a Global Norm *Current History* v116 no786 p35 Ja 2017

Menon, Sunand

Can We Quantify the Value of Connected Devices? *Harvard Business Review Digital Articles* p2 O 20 2014

Menon, Tanya

How to Hire Without Getting Fooled by First Impressions *Harvard Business Review Digital Articles* p2 F 15 2016

How to Make Better Decisions with Less Data *Harvard Business Review Digital Articles* p2 N 7 2016

Putting a Price on People Problems at Work *Harvard Business Review Digital Articles* p2 Ag 23 2016

Why You Should Always Go Off-Script in a Job Interview *Harvard Business Review Digital Articles* p2 Jl 14 2016

Menopause

Best Moves for Menopause [Cover story] L. MARSHALL color *Prevention* v69 no4 p76 Ap 2017

Let go and allow C. Gorrell *Yoga Journal* no288 p12 D 2016

NEWS FROM THE World of Medicine color *Reader's Digest* v190 no1135 p52 N 2017

Menopause—Hormone therapy

Dr. Weil [Cover story] A. Weil color *Prevention* v69 no1 p24 Ja 2017

Menorah

Chanukah around the South *Successful Farming* v115 no1 p20 Ja 2017

Men—Physiological aspects

MANSPREADERS OF THE YEAR L. FINCK cartoon chart *New Yorker* v93 no17 p40 Je 19 2017

Men's attitudes

Can a Manly Man Wear Makeup? S. HOTCHKISS color *GQ: Gentlemen's Quarterly* v97 no10 p72 O 2017

The Cure for Everything (Seriously) A. SCOTT cartoon map *Men's Health* v32 no9 p67 N 2017

Orgasm Pressure: Why?! C. Drell cartoon color graph *Glamour* v115 no11 p108 N 2017

Men' attitudes—History—20th century

WAR! WOMEN! WEASELS! M. LAFAVORE bw color *Men's Health* v32 no5 p120 Je 2017

Men's clothing

See also

Men's shirts

AN AIRPLANE HANGER-ON D. Karl color *Flying* v144 no7 p68 Jl 2017

BEST BETS img *New York* p50 F 20 2017

The Best of The Information bw color *Esquire* p132 BigBlack-Book

BLACK IS THE NEW BLACK K. Soller color *Bloomberg Businessweek* no4521 p63 My 8 2017

THE CHINO GETS ITS BALLS BACK N. Sullivan bw color *Esquire* p44 Je/Jl 2017

Daveed Diggs' Dad-Chic A. LICATA color *Rolling Stone* no1273 p20 N 3 2016

Dress Down, Look Sharp D. MICHEL cartoon color *Men's Health* v32 no9 p75 N 2017

A FEW GOOD FINDS N. SULLIVAN color *Esquire* p58 Ap 2017

Get the Look O. J. WILLIAMS color *Ebony* v72 no11 p46 S 2017

GQ STYLE FASHION DIRECTOR MOBOLAJI DAWODU A. WHITTLE color *Conde Nast Traveler* v52 no8 p30 S 2017

HOW I DISCOVERED MY STYLE M. JACOBSON and J. Roth cartoon color *Esquire* p48 My 2017

I Surrendered My Wardrobe S. HOTCHKISS color *GQ: Gentlemen's Quarterly* v87 no1 p30 Ja 2017

LOOK BETTER INSTANTLY B. BOYÉ cartoon color *Men's Health* v32 no2 p(Sp)12 Mr 2017

Manual J. MOORE, N. MARINO et al cartoon color *GQ: Gentlemen's Quarterly* v97 no7 p11 Jl 2017

Martine Rose color *Vogue* v207 no11 p118 N 2017

MAXWELL RYAN J. Chen color *Bloomberg Businessweek* no4524 p71 My 29 2017

New York R. Roye *New York Times Magazine* p39 N 20 2016

THE NIGHT MANAGER color *Esquire* p108 O 2017

Out of the Warehouse S. Eide color *Weekly Standard* v22 no33 p45 My 8 2017

Q: What's the right way to cover DWYANE WADE? J. Roth color *Esquire* p110 Ap 2017

RESTRAIN YOURSELF N. Sullivan bw color *Esquire* p46 N 2017

THE SQUARE-TOE SHOE MUST DIE! cartoon color *GQ: Gentlemen's Quarterly* v97 no4 p118 Ap 2017

The Style Guy cartoon *GQ: Gentlemen's Quarterly* v97 no5 p34 My 2017

The Style Guy M. A. Green cartoon color *GQ: Gentlemen's Quarterly* v97 no3 p66 Mr 2017

The Style Guy M. A. Green color *GQ: Gentlemen's Quarterly* v86 no11 p44 N 2016

The Style Guy M. Anthony Green bw color *GQ: Gentlemen's Quarterly* v97 no9 p76 S 2017

Three Young Designers Bring Back Custom Suits—and They're Actually Affordable M. A. GREEN and N. MARINO bw color *GQ: Gentlemen's Quarterly* v97 no4 p42 Ap 2017

TURN A CORNER J. Roth color *Esquire* p37 N 2017

VESTING OPTIONS D. STEVENS color *GQ: Gentlemen's Quarterly* v97 no4 p106 Ap 2017

What Happens When Men Don't Conform to Masculine Clothing Norms at Work? B. Barry *Harvard Business Review Digital Articles* p2 Ag 31 2017

What I Wear to Work J. Chen color *Bloomberg Businessweek* no4501 p63 N 28 2016

What I Wear to Work: NOA SANTOS J. Chen color *Bloomberg Businessweek* no4520 p75 My 1 2017

What I Wear to Work: REIHAN SALAM J. Chen color *Bloomberg Businessweek* no4495 p75 O 17 2016

WORTH EVERY PENNY color *GQ: Gentlemen's Quarterly* v87 no1 p66 Ja 2017

You're gonna want some plaid B. Goreski color *Redbook* p18 N 2017

Men's clothing stores

Party Animals F. SUN *Atlanta* v56 no7 p47 N 2016

Men's clothing—Computer network resources

FASHION FORWARD M. Berlinger color *Bloomberg Businessweek* no4510 p60 F 6 2017

Men's clothing—Evaluation

BECKHAM THE YOUNGER S. BALL color *GQ: Gentlemen's Quarterly* v97 no9 p160 S 2017

Booster Shots color *GQ: Gentlemen's Quarterly* v97 no5 p96 My 2017

Call It the Neck Tie of Winter color *GQ: Gentlemen's Quarterly* v86 no12 p88 D 2016

THE CURE FOR THE COMMON KHAKI color *Esquire* p94 2017 BigBlackBook

Double Vision T. Patterson chart color *Bloomberg Businessweek* no4535 p61 Ag 28 2017

Dressed to Chill N. SULLIVAN bw color *Esquire* v166 no5 p64 D 2016/Ja 2017

Give Up Your Boring Gray Suit S. Kennedy color *Bloomberg Businessweek* no4513 p69 Mr 6 2017

The GQ x Gap Collaboration 2017: Finally, the Clothes Are Here! color *GQ: Gentlemen's Quarterly* v97 no9 p64 S 2017

The Great Escape B. HANSEN-BUNDY color *GQ: Gentlemen's Quarterly* v97 no5 p114 My 2017

Hand SOME *Interview* v47 no2 p158 Mr 2017

The IRL Guide to Dries Van Noten color *Esquire* v166 no4 p55 N 2016

Labels We Love: The Three Kings of Streetwear N. Marino color *GQ: Gentlemen's Quarterly* v97 no9 p66 S 2017

LEADING MAN C. Heath bw color *GQ: Gentlemen's Quarterly* v87 no1 p40 Ja 2017

Living on the Edge S. HOTCHKISS color *Esquire* v166 no5 p60 D 2016/Ja 2017

The LOOK *Interview* v47 no2 p96 Mr 2017

Make the Vertical Leap color *GQ: Gentlemen's Quarterly* v97 no3 p64 Mr 2017

THE MAN IN MONO S. GOLDSTEIN color *GQ: Gentlemen's Quarterly* v97 no9 p180 S 2017

MASTER CLASS WITH R. McKNIGHT bw cartoon color *Esquire* v166 no5 p69 D 2016/Ja 2017

NOT Business as USUAL color *Esquire* p92 Ap 2017

PULLING IT OFF color *Esquire* p55 My 2017

Pull Yourself Together, Man! J. CHEN color *Esquire* v166 no4 p65 N 2016

Radical Chinos J. MOORE color *GQ: Gentlemen's Quarterly* v97 no5 p29 My 2017

THE SEASON OF RETRO-FUTURISM D. PATEL color *GQ: Gentlemen's Quarterly* v87 no1 p52 Ja 2017

SHORT STORY color *Esquire* p47 N 2017

Space Race N. SULLIVAN bw color *Esquire* v166 no4 p60 N 2016

'SUCKER, PUNCHED UP color *Esquire* p44 My 2017

The Suited Man color *GQ: Gentlemen's Quarterly* v86 no11 p42 N 2016

Take Summer into Winter color *Esquire* v166 no5 p68 D 2016/Ja 2017

WELCOME TO PEAK STYLE SEASON N. SULLIVAN color *Esquire* p61 S 2017

WHEN WE GO LOW. ALSO GO HIGH L. SABBAT color *GQ: Gentlemen's Quarterly* v97 no4 p120 Ap 2017

WHO WEARS THE PANTS? color *Esquire* p96 N 2017

YOUR TWO-STEP SUMMER UPGRADE color *Esquire* p34 Ag 2017

Your Utility Layer S. Nygaard color *Men's Health* v32 no2 p(Sp)28 Mr 2017

Men's clothing—Sales & prices

Arrival Instincts J. Lisanti and T. Keith color *Sports Illustrated* v125 no14 p24 O 24-31 2016

Men's dreams

For the Record color *Time* v189 no9 p6 Mr 13 2017

Mens' health

    See also

    Exercise for men

    Physical fitness for men

THE EXCHANGE B. Boyé and A. Eaves bw cartoon color graph *Men's Health* v32 no5 p16 Je 2017

GAME PLAN M. Zimmerman color graph *Men's Health* v32 no9 p8 N 2017

How Strong Is Your Sperm? D. CRANE bw cartoon graph *Men's Health* v32 no5 p81 Je 2017

MH WORLD color *Men's Health* v32 no5 p6 Je 2017

Power to Transform M. Bean bw *Men's Health* v32 no9 p6 N 2017

TOP THREE HERBS FOR MEN K. P. S. Khalsa color *Amazing Wellness* v8 no2 p22 Spr 2016

Men's magazines

GQ HQ color *GQ: Gentlemen's Quarterly* v97 no6 p20 Je 2017

Men's products—Evaluation

BUILT TO LAST color *Esquire* v166 no4 p128 N 2016

The Dirt on Clean Skin S. Nygaard color *Men's Health* v32 no1 p83 Ja/F 2017

PACKING LIGHT color *Ebony* v72 no3 p66 D 2016/Ja 2017

Men's sexual behavior

The Best Vanilla Sex of Your Life J. Berkowitz color *Glamour* v115 no6 p102 Je 2017

Is It "Manopause"? I. Kerner color *Prevention* v69 no11 p26 N 2017

Men's shirt design

Turtleneck 2.0 T. Patterson color *Bloomberg Businessweek* no4529 p76 Jl 3 2017

Men's shirts

9 Steps to a New Look S. NYGAARD cartoon color *Men's Health* v32 no8 p63 O 2017

NO COLLAR, NO PROBLEM color *Esquire* p53 Ap 2017

Who Said a Collared Shirt Needs a Collar? color *GQ: Gentlemen's Quarterly* v97 no4 p46 Ap 2017

Men's shirts—Evaluation

COLLAR THEM BAD color *Esquire* v167 no1 p78 F 2017

COUNTRY ROOTS J. Amay color *Ebony* v72 no9 p46 Jl/Ag

2017

Field Notes color *Climbing* no351 p46 F/Mr 2017

THE GEAR A. Shoalts *Canadian Geographic* v136 no6 p35 D 2016

HOW TO SUMMER IN STYLE J. ROTH color *Esquire* p54 2017 BigBlackBook

It's UNCOMPLICATED *Interview* v47 no6 p29 Ag 2017

PACKING LIGHT color *Ebony* v72 no3 p66 D 2016/Ja 2017

PULLING IT OFF color *Esquire* p55 My 2017

Save or Splurge? color *Horse & Rider* v55 no11 p22 N 2016

STAND OUT IN CAMO J. Roth bw color *Esquire* v167 no2 p114 Mr 2017

Street Style: FITNESS EDITION color *Women's Health* v14 no7 p20 S 2017

The Sweater Abides C. WEAVER color *GQ: Gentlemen's Quarterly* v97 no10 p160 O 2017

TEAM O.J color *GQ: Gentlemen's Quarterly* v86 no12 p180 D 2016

Tree Huggers, Unite! A Guide to Sustainable Style J. GROFF color *GQ: Gentlemen's Quarterly* v97 no10 p59 O 2017

VISION QUEST color *Esquire* v167 no1 p96 F 2017

WHAT SHE KNOWS ABOUT YOU J. von Sothen bw color *Esquire* v167 no2 p76 Mr 2017

THE WORLD ACCORDING TO Gayle Gayle color *O, The Oprah Magazine* p32 Ag 2017

Men's shoes

The Anatomy of the Shoe color *Esquire* p134 BigBlackBook

Men's shoes—Evaluation

easily suede color *GQ: Gentlemen's Quarterly* v97 no3 p128 Mr 2017

An Entire Shoe Closet for (About) a Grand chart color *GQ: Gentlemen's Quarterly* v87 no1 p12 Ja 2017

Ground Control N. SULLIVAN color *Esquire* v166 no4 p66 N 2016

THE LOOP K. B. GROSS, C. GAFFNEY et al bw color *Runner's World* v51 no11 p18 D 2016

ON-THE-GO GEAR L. BACK color *Trail Rider* v29 no4 p50 My 2017

Put Your Sole Into It *Los Angeles Magazine* p32 Ja 2017

Slip into Something More Colorful color *GQ: Gentlemen's Quarterly* v97 no11 p44 N 2017

WORTH EVERY PENNY color *GQ: Gentlemen's Quarterly* v87 no1 p66 Ja 2017

Men's toiletries

The 27-Year-Old Cologne Virgin C. Skipper bw *GQ: Gentlemen's Quarterly* v97 no5 p43 My 2017

Men's wrist watches

TIMELESS color *Road & Track* v69 no2 p96 S 2017

Men's wrist watches—Evaluation

Better With Time J. LOVE and M. BOBO color *Ebony* v72 no4 p57 F 2017

Bold-Faced Time J. MOORE color *GQ: Gentlemen's Quarterly* v97 no9 p63 S 2017

The Forward Way to Go Back in Time chart color *GQ: Gentlemen's Quarterly* v97 no3 p62 Mr 2017

Going Green T. Patterson color *Bloomberg Businessweek* no4533 p60 Ag 7 2017

LEATHER-BOUND S. Zlotnick *Washingtonian Magazine* v52 no2 p228 N 2016

Market: HIS OR HERS bw color *Vanity Fair* v59 no11 p60 N 2017

Power Tools D. Michel color *Men's Health* v32 no2 p(Sp)26 Mr 2017

Mensah, Peter

Midnight, Texas I. Rudolph *TV Guide* v65 no23 p30 My 29 2017

Men—Sexual behavior

No-Fly Zones: A New Model for Male Sexuality B. Fleming *Society* v54 no1 p34 F 2017

Men—Sexual behavior—History

LAST TABOO W. Morris *New York Times Magazine* p48 O 30 2016

Mensh, Brett D.

Deconstructing behavioral neuropharmacology with cellular specificity color *Science* v356 no6333 p42 Ap 7 2017

Menshikov, A.

Observation of a large-scale anisotropy in the arrival directions

of cosmic rays above 8×1018 eV *Science* v357 no6357 p1266 S 22 2017

Mensmann, Mona

Teaching personal initiative beats traditional training in boosting small business in West Africa chart graph *Science* v357 no6357 p1287 S 22 2017

Men—Social conditions

MALE GAZE J. WOOD cartoon *New Yorker* v92 no32 p98 O 10 2016

Menstrual cycle

See also

Menstruation

Is It "Manopause"? I. Kerner color *Prevention* v69 no11 p26 N 2017

Menstruation

Can Food Help You Feel Better? A. STANLEY color *Seventeen* v75 no11 p62 N 2016

Do You Have PERIOD BRAIN? L. SAXTON color *Seventeen* v76 no3 p66 My 2017

GOING TO the Gyno R. Zar color *Dance Spirit* v20 no9 p34 N 2016

HOW TO Talk About Periods M. COHEN *Parents* v92 no11 p122 N 2017

Is Your Period Making YOU SICK? S. Colino cartoon *O, The Oprah Magazine* p101 My 2017

PERIOD OF ADJUSTMENT A. MASTROMONACO color *Washingtonian Magazine* v52 no7 p200 Ap 2017

Period Pieces *Parents* v91 no9 p16 S 2016

Protection. PERIOD W. L. Wilson color *Essence* v48 no5 p112 S 2017

SOS FOR PMS J. Martin color *Amazing Wellness* v8 no2 p26 Spr 2016

Sync With Your Cycle W. L. Wilson *Essence* v48 no5 p112 S 2017

The WH Menses Society [Cover story] M. Devash cartoon color graph *Women's Health* v14 no1 p94 Ja/F 2017

Menstruation disorders

See also

Dysmenorrhea

Why Am I Bleeding? [Cover story] C. S. Grant color *Glamour* v114 no11 p116 N 2016

Mental accounting (Economic theory)

Behavior management I. Cingl, L. Wang et al color *Science* v356 no6335 p244 Ap 21 2017

Mental depression

BEHIND MY PEERS H. ESTROFF MARANO *Psychology Today* v49 no5 p22 S/O 2016

Did you receive support from your faith community while you were experiencing depression and/or anxiety? B. Collier, T. Trinko et al graph *America* v216 no12 p6 My 29 2017

DON'T BE SAD [Cover story] J. Martin color *Amazing Wellness* v9 no6 p28 EarlyWint 2017

For a Better Mood chart color *AARP: The Magazine* v59 no3A p36 Ap/My 2016

HERBAL SUPPORT for Wintertime Blues M. Adelmann *Mother Earth News* no280 p56 F/Mr 2017

Hit Refresh N. Spradley color *Essence* v47 no12 p29 Ap 2017

Homeopathic Mood Boosters A. CONSTANTINIDES color *Better Nutrition* v78 no12 p34 D 2016

Hovering Can Hinder Transition to Adulthood *USA Today Magazine* v145 no2859 p11 D 2016

How depression affects your thinking skills *Harvard Health Letter* v42 no7 p3 My 2017

How I Survived the Worst Depression of My Life E. Mahaney color *Glamour* v114 no11 p144 N 2016

How Pop Culture Depicts Mental Illness J. M. Goldstein and S. G. Levy color *Glamour* v115 no4 p120 Ap 2017

How Signals Get Skewed An imbalance of omega-3 and omega-6 fatty acids may be a stealth cause of depression and other disorders K. GOLDYNIA *Psychology Today* v50 no4 p29 Ag 2017

"I Had Depression": About one in five teens grapple with symptoms of depression, anxiety, or other emotional health issues--yet few talk about it. These kids are dedicated to changing that S. M. FERNÁNDEZ *Scholastic Choices* p18 O 2017

"I had no idea I had an illness" C. Enlow and S. G. Levy color *Glamour* v115 no4 p120 Ap 2017

"I made this decision for her" H. Kelly and S. G. Levy color

Glamour v115 no4 p126 Ap 2017

"I wouldn't put 'I have mental illnesses' in my Tinder profile" M. Yagoda and S. G. Levy color *Glamour* v115 no4 p124 Ap 2017

Lasting mental health may be unusual B. BOWER chart graph *Science News* v191 no4 p7 Mr 4 2017

low tide k. butcher color *Bike Magazine* v24 no2 p44 Mr 2017

OPRAH'S BLISS J. Van Meter color *Vogue* v207 no9 p666 S 2017

Our Mental Health Now S. G. Levy color *Glamour* v115 no4 p119 Ap 2017

THE REAL NARCISSISTS [Cover story] R. WEBBER *Psychology Today* v49 no5 p52 S/O 2016

The Secret Behind Chronic Pain [Cover story] S. Colino cartoon *Prevention* v69 no4 p68 Ap 2017

Stop Worrying About How Much You Matter P. Bregman *Harvard Business Review Digital Articles* p2 Je 25 2015

The Undepressing News About Depression C. Flora color *O, The Oprah Magazine* p80 Ap 2017

A Vitamin for Depression? color *O, The Oprah Magazine* p71 Jl 2017

THE VLOGGING CURE C. Lanning *Psychology Today* v50 no3 p68 My/Je 2017

WHERE ARE YOU GOING? color *O, The Oprah Magazine* p104 Ap 2017

Why Managers Are More Likely to Be Depressed D. Burkus *Harvard Business Review Digital Articles* p2 S 23 2015

Wild Women Do L. B. Ray color *InStyle* v24 no9 p208 S 2017

Mental depression genetics

Nerve cell miswiring tied to depression E. S. EATON color *Science News* v191 no10 p12 My 27 2017

Mental depression risk factors

Early life stress confers lifelong stress susceptibility in mice via ventral tegmental area OTX2 C. J. Peña, H. G. Kronman et al diag *Science* v356 no6343 p1185 Je 16 2017

Tackling Depression K. MCGUIRE *Dance Magazine* v90 no11 p46 N 2016

WEIGHT LOSS SURGERY CONFIDENTIAL J. Nathan and C. N. Pagán color *Health* v31 no7 p134 S 2017

Mental depression—Diagnosis

What's holding you back from better hearing? *Harvard Health Letter* v42 no5 p3 Mr 2017

Mental depression—Drug therapy

Time for a Brake S. POLAN *Psychology Today* v49 no5 p31 S/O 2016

treating depression J. MONINGER *Parents* v91 no11 p137 N 2016

Mental depression—Prevention

How Counseling About Work Reduces Depression G. Gavett *Harvard Business Review Digital Articles* p2 Mr 6 2015

How Founders Can Recognize and Combat Depression J. Valencia *Harvard Business Review Digital Articles* p2 F 17 2017

Start a Gratitude Habit J. Andriakos color *Health* v30 no9 p26 N 2016

Mental depression—Psychological aspects

Depressed Without Knowing It: Even when we know what depression looks like, we can miss it in ourselves S. J. GILLIHAN *Psychology Today* v50 no5 p50 S/O 2017

Fighting through the darkness C. G. Hoogstraten color *Science* v357 no6350 p522 Ag 4 2017

Mental depression—Treatment

Homeopathic Mood Boosters A. CONSTANTINIDES color *Better Nutrition* v78 no12 p34 D 2016

Is my medication causing these side effects, or is it just aging? *Harvard Health Letter* v42 no3 p6 Ja 2017

women struggling… "smiling depression" C. ARNOLD bw color *Women's Health* v14 no4 p144 My 2017

Mental depression—Treatment—Research

The Club Drug Ketamine May Treat Depression-but the Risks Could Be Big M. Oaklander color *Time* v189 no10 p19 Mr 20 2017

Mental disabilities—Religious aspects

MY DAUGHTER HAS A DISABILITY. I DON'T WANT JESUS TO 'FIX' HER [Cover story] H. K. Lanier il *America* v216 no11 p36 My 15 2017

Mental disabilities—Treatment

MY DAUGHTER HAS A DISABILITY. I DON'T WANT JESUS TO 'FIX' HER [Cover story] H. K. Lanier il *America* v216 no11

p36 My 15 2017

Mental fatigue

  See also

  Boredom

FEEL THE BURNOUT K. Schaefer cartoon *Bloomberg Businessweek* no4516 p68 Mr 27 2017

Your High-Intensity Feelings May Be Tiring You Out E. Seppala *Harvard Business Review Digital Articles* p2 F 1 2016

Mental healing

The ENERGY for HEALING [Cover story] B. ANDREWS color *Prevention* v69 no1 p64 Ja 2017

Mental health

  See also

  Personality

  Relaxation (Health)

  Stress (Psychology)

  Stress management

Always LEARNING J. Francisco color *Good Housekeeping* v265 no1 p10 Jl 2017

Audio Therapy: How Music Improved One Man's Mental Health A. HARDY and D. POINTDUJOUR color *Ebony* v72 no5 p64 Mr 2017

BUILD A BETTER BRAIN D. G. Amen and T. Amen cartoon color *Amazing Wellness* v9 no2 p60 Spr 2017

De-Stress Your Life S. BLOCK cartoon *Kiplinger's Personal Finance* v71 no2 p64 F 2017

editor's note. ON SILENCE THAT IS DEAFENING *Psychology Today* v50 no2 p3 Mr/Ap 2017

Fitness News Young Brains Can Use S. SEA GOLD color *Parents* v92 no5 p20 My 2017

Forgive: Your Life Could Depend on It G. Roberts-Grey color *Essence* v48 no2 p111 Je 2017

Get Fit Without Working Out! C. THORP color *Seventeen* v76 no3 p64 My 2017

THE HARDEST WORD [Cover story] C. FLORA *Psychology Today* v50 no5 p52 S/O 2017

Head, Fingers, Knees, and Toes K. LAMBERT *Climbing* no355 p30 Ag 2017

"I Had Depression": About one in five teens grapple with symptoms of depression, anxiety, or other emotional health issues-yet few talk about it. These kids are dedicated to changing that S. M. FERNÁNDEZ *Scholastic Choices* p18 O 2017

Lasting mental health may be unusual B. BOWER chart graph *Science News* v191 no4 p7 Mr 4 2017

The Long Reach of Popularity… Mitch Prinstein C. Park *Psychology Today* v50 no3 p12 My/Je 2017

MOOD MAKEOVER L. Turner color *Amazing Wellness* v9 no4 p28 Summ 2017

The Nature Cure F. WILLIAMS color *Reader's Digest* v189 no1129 p106 Ap 2017

NEWS FROM THE World of Medicine S. RIDEOUT color *Reader's Digest* v189 no1130 p65 My 2017

ONE IN FIVE color *Better Homes & Gardens* v95 no5 p156 My 2017

PICTURES OF MENTAL HEALTH N. Strochlic color *National Geographic* v232 no3 p16 S 2017

REVIVE YOUR Soul V. Burton color *Essence* v47 no9 p72 Ja 2017

Self-care for grown-ups M. Mannarino color *Health* v31 no4 p98 My 2017

Speak of the devil P. Jenkins *Christian Century* v134 no20 p44 S 27 2017

Stressing mental health M. Notaras color *Science* v356 no6340 p878 My 26 2017

Sweat Out Your Blahs J. SAVIN and A. STANLEY color *Seventeen* v76 no12 p65 D 2016/Ja 2017

UNDER(PROM) PRESSURE A. STANLEY cartoon *Seventeen* v76 no3 p68 My 2017

UNSOLICITED BETA S. Thomas, K. Lewandowski et al *Climbing* no355 p14 Ag 2017

What's on Your Mind? *Dance Magazine* v91 no10 p6 O 2017

When Things Aren't 'OK' A. TILLERY and D. POINTDUJOUR color *Ebony* v72 no3 p90 D 2016/Ja 2017

Mental health counseling

Provoking Thoughts V. DANIELS, M. LOUISE LIUCCI-SMITH et al color *O, The Oprah Magazine* p18 N 2017

p100 N 29 2016

Overcoming the Toughest Common Coaching Challenges A. Gallo *Harvard Business Review Digital Articles* p2 Ap 15 2015

Sign up now to become a mentor P. CROFTS *People Management* p62 O 2016

Strengths-Based Coaching Can Actually Weaken You T. Chamorro-Premuzic *Harvard Business Review Digital Articles* p2 Ja 4 2016

What the Best Mentors Do A. K. Tjan bw *Harvard Business Review Digital Articles* p2 F 27 2017

Mentoring in business—Psychological aspects

Being Experienced Doesn't Automatically Make You a Great Mentor A. Molinsky *Harvard Business Review Digital Articles* p2 Ja 28 2015

Mentoring in education

Video Links Professors to Far-Flung Student Teachers B. IASEVOLI *Education Digest* v82 no9 p14 My 2017

Mentoring in science

Lee Rubin: Our mentor and role model C. Bazenet, H. Desmond et al *Science* v355 no6327 p806 F 24 2017

Mentoring in the professions

Men Can Improve How They Mentor Women. Here's How D. G. Smith and W. B. Johnson *Harvard Business Review Digital Articles* p2 D 5 2016

THE PD NEXT DOOR: The impact of observation in our own schools S. Valter *Literacy Today (2411-7862)* v35 no2 p18 S/O 2017

Your Career Needs Many Mentors, Not Just One D. Clark color *Harvard Business Review Digital Articles* p2 Ja 19 2017

Mentors

An Ambassador of Dressage J. Pescatrice color *Dressage Today* v23 no5 p60 Ja 2017

Living up to my mentors B. Gastel cartoon *Science* v354 no6318 p1494 D 16 2016

Male Mentors Shouldn't Hesitate to Challenge Their Female Mentees D. G. Smith and W. B. Johnson *Harvard Business Review Digital Articles* p2 My 29 2017

My Professor, My Mentor, My Rock E. RAPP BLACKK *Reader's Digest* v189 no1129 p44 Ap 2017

What the Best Mentors Do A. K. Tjan bw *Harvard Business Review Digital Articles* p2 F 27 2017

Mentzer, Alexander J.

A Neolithic expansion, but strong genetic structure, in the independent history of New Guinea diag *Science* v357 no6356 p1160 S 15 2017

Menu planning

BEGINNER'S GUIDELINES TO MEAL PREP D. BACKSTROM color *Ebony* v72 no11 p64 S 2017

Better Brown-Bag Lunches: Lunches you pack for yourself or your family can be healthier than meals purchased away from home, but only if you plan food choices wisely *Tufts University Health & Nutrition Letter* v35 no8 p7 O 2017

IT'S COCKTAIL O'CLOCK! E. N. GAGE *Martha Stewart Living* no270 p128 D 2016

Who's Using Meal Kits? M. Leonhardt chart *Money* v46 no8 p72 S 2017

Men—United States

BEARDED MEN DISCOVER BEAUTY PRODUCTS J. J. Roberts diag *Fortune* v75 no1 p24 Ja 1 2017

Menus

See also

Breakfasts

Desserts

Luncheons

Restaurant menus

Salads

Soups

COOK BY NUMBERS J. Gordinier bw color *Esquire* p22 Ag 2017

From Far and Wide P. SHARPE *Texas Monthly* v45 no8 p22 Ag 2017

The Grill img *New York* v50 no9 p76 My 1 2017

HACKING THE GRAIN M. OSTRANDER color *Nation* v305 no11 p18 O 30 2017

HIT REFRESH E. Graves *Martha Stewart Living* no267 p8 S 2016

Menyoung Lee

Ballistic miniband conduction in a graphene superlattice bibl graph *Science* v353 no6307 p1526 S 30 2016

MENZ, MYLES M. H.

From Agricultural Benefits to Aviation Safety: Realizing the Potential of Continent-Wide Radar Networks *BioScience* v67 no10 p912 O 2017

Menzel, Clare

Jail Break color *Powder* p42 S 2017

NEW STAR color *Powder* v45 no4 p144 D 2016

QUIET THE MIND bw color *Powder* v45 no3 p64 N 2016

The Skis of the Year color *Powder* p82 S 2017

Menzel, Dietrich

Robert Gomer *Physics Today* v70 no5 p67 My 2017

Menzel, Idina, 1971-

Life's a BEACH D. HOLBROOK *TV Guide* v65 no4 p30 Ja 16 2017

Menzel, Idina, 1971—Interviews

Idina Menzel S. STALL *Indianapolis Monthly* v12 no40 p25 Ag 2017

Menzies LLP

"Your employees are your best ambassadors": An HR-marketing marriage was the secret to changing perceptions of a 100-year-old accountancy firm *People Management* p22 Jl 2017

Meo, Sultan Ayoub

Stop Pakistan's polio vaccination tax bibl *Science* v354 no6310 p295 O 21 2016

Meow Global Networks Inc.

Ready For the Next Phase A. ROSENBLUM *Los Angeles Magazine* v62 no9 p17 S 2017

Mer, Georges

Cyclin A2 is an RNA binding protein that controls Mre11 mRNA translation bibl graph *Science* v353 no6307 p1549 S 30 2016

MERCADO, ERIC

On the March *Los Angeles Magazine* v61 no11 p180 N 2016

Stand to Reason *Los Angeles Magazine* p156 D 2016

Mercado, Mario R.

The Hills Are Alive: The Berkshires make a spectacular setting for a variety of cultural offerings all summer long *Opera News* v81 no12 p60 Je 2017

open house *Opera News* v81 no6 p29 D 2016

ROAD SHOW: Bryan Hymel in New Orleans *Opera News* v81 no6 p16 D 2016

ROAD SHOW: Paulo Szot in Marseilles *Opera News* v81 no9 p18 Mr 2017

Mercedes-AMG GmbH

A BIGGER HAMMER J. Lieberman chart color *Motor Trend* v69 no5 p62 My 2017

CAPTURING THE LIFE AT SPEED color *Road & Track* v69 no4 p6 N 2017

EASY E B. BARRY color *Road & Track* v68 no5 p104 D 2016/Ja 2017

MEET THE NEW E43 E. Ayapana chart color *Motor Trend* v69 no5 p66 My 2017

ONE MAN, ONE ENGINE bw *Road & Track* v69 no4 p8 N 2017

Poster Boy J. Gall color *Car & Driver* v63 no1 p98 Jl 2017

RACING color *Road & Track* v69 no4 p10 N 2017

Mercedes automobiles

EDITOR'S LETTER K. WOLFKILL color *Road & Track* v68 no6 p19 F 2017

Thom On Design The Most Notorious Custom Paint Job Ever Sprayed T. Taylor bw *Hot Rod* v70 no1 p90 Ja 2017

War can be fought with many things, sometimes even sandwiches M. Duff color *Car & Driver* v62 no11 p70 My 2017

Mercedes automobiles—Awards

SECOND TIME'S A CHARMER [Cover story] J. Lieberman chart color *Motor Trend* v69 no1 p70 Ja 2017

Mercedes automobiles—Design & construction

Editor's Letter E. Alterman *Car & Driver* v62 no11 p12 My 2017

Mercedes automobiles—Evaluation

2017 Mercedes-Benz E400 4Matic A. MacKenzie color *Motor Trend* v69 no2 p66 F 2017

2018 Mercedes-AMG GT Roadster and GT C Roadster J. Lieberman color *Motor Trend* v69 no3 p26 Mr 2017

4-DOORS, 6-WHEELERS, AND GULLWINGS color *Road & Track* v69 no4 p12 N 2017

5 CARS THAT PUT AMG AT THE HEAD OF THE PACK C. PERKINS color *Esquire* p52 2017 BigBlackBook

CROSSBREEDING D. ZENLEA color *Road & Track* v69 no1 p88 Ag 2017

EASY E B. BARRY color *Road & Track* v68 no5 p104 D 2016/Ja 2017

Enemy of the Estate J. Sabatini bw chart color diag *Car & Driver* v63 no4 p74 O 2017

EVERYDAY HEROES [Cover story] C. Seabaugh, A. MacKenzie et al chart color *Motor Trend* v69 no5 p34 My 2017

THE FAST AND THE LUXURIOUS J. GORZELANY color *Forbes* v200 no4 p60 O 24 2017

FROM PIGS TO HAMMERS AND NOW... THIS color *Road & Track* v69 no4 p14 N 2017

THE GREAT ESCAPE [Cover story] J. BARUTH chart color diag graph *Road & Track* v69 no3 p30 O 2017

GREEN HELLION C. CHILTON color *Road & Track* v68 no7 p80 Mr/Ap 2017

GRIP AND GRIN J. DEMATIO color *Road & Track* v68 no8 p90 My 2017

Haymaker M. Sutton color *Car & Driver* v62 no8 p84 F 2017

LETTER OF INTENT M. PRINCE color *Road & Track* v69 no1 p80 Ag 2017

Mercedes-Benz C300 Coupe 4Matic chart color *Motor Trend* v69 no1 p130 Ja 2017

Mercedes-Benz Concept A Sedan A. Nishimoto color *Motor Trend* v69 no8 p22 Ag 2017

Mercedes-Benz E300 chart color *Motor Trend* v69 no1 p131 Ja 2017

Mercedes-Benz Generation EQ Concept A. Priddle color *Motor Trend* v69 no1 p18 Ja 2017

Mercedes-Benz GLS-Class chart color *Motor Trend* v69 no1 p54 Ja 2017

Mercedes-Maybach: Vision 6 Cabriolet S. Evans color *Motor Trend* v69 no11 p17 N 2017

NAMING RITES J. Jacquot bw chart color *Car & Driver* v63 no5 p48 N 2017

PLEASURE CRUISE K. Sintumuang color *Esquire* p35 N 2017

REVIEWS E. DYER color *Popular Mechanics* v193 no7 p54 S 2016

ROAD TEST SUMMARY cartoon chart *Road & Track* v69 no4 p94 N 2017

SECOND TIME'S A CHARMER [Cover story] J. Lieberman chart color *Motor Trend* v69 no1 p70 Ja 2017

The Smart Appliance E. Alterman color graph *Car & Driver* v62 no7 p76 Ja 2017

The SUV Just Went Topless D. DEMURO color *GQ: Gentlemen's Quarterly* v86 no11 p54 N 2016

Theater of the Absurd J. Zoellter bw color diag *Car & Driver* v62 no11 p106 My 2017

Tuned to THRILL K. Sintumuang bw *Esquire* p52 2017 BigBlackBook

YACHT ROCK T. Quiroga chart color *Car & Driver* v62 no6 p64 D 2016

Zee Über Trück E. DYER cartoon color *Popular Mechanics* v193 no7 p47 S 2016

Zee Über Trück E. DYER color *Popular Mechanics* p47 S 2017

Mercedes automobiles—Sales & prices

Editor's Letter E. Alterman *Car & Driver* v62 no11 p12 My 2017

Mercedes-Benz AG

2017 Mercedes-Benz E400 4Matic A. MacKenzie color *Motor Trend* v69 no2 p66 F 2017

2018 Mercedes-AMG GT Roadster and GT C Roadster J. Lieberman color *Motor Trend* v69 no3 p26 Mr 2017

Mercedes-Benz Concept A Sedan A. Nishimoto color *Motor Trend* v69 no8 p22 Ag 2017

THE MERCEDES-BENZ G-WAGEN B. Berk color *Car & Driver* v63 no2 p24 Ag 2017

PLEASURE CRUISE K. Sintumuang color *Esquire* p35 N 2017

Zee Über Trück E. DYER color *Popular Mechanics* p47 S 2017

Zee Über Trück E. DYER color *Popular Mechanics* v193 no7 p47 S 2016

Mercedes C-Class automobile—Evaluation

Tuned to THRILL K. Sintumuang bw *Esquire* p52 2017 BigBlackBook

Mercer, Christia

ABOVE & BEYOND bw *New Yorker* v93 no11 p14 My 1 2017

Mercer, James, 1970-——Interviews

JAMES MERCER'S NEW FRONTIER M. Vain color *Entertainment Weekly* no1457/1458 p92 Mr 17 2017

Mercer, Jaron A. M.

Mechanochemical unzipping of insulating polyladderene to semiconducting polyacetylene [Cover story] diag *Science* v357 no6350 p475 Ag 4 2017

Mercer, John

RETHINKING MASCULINITY: A new study shows that gay porn is even driving how straight guys see themselves—and that's a good thing J. ANDERSON-MINSHALL *Advocate* no1093 p59 O/N 2017

Mercer, Joyce Ann

Old, frail, called by God *Christian Century* v134 no14 p26 Jl 5 2017

Mercer, Michelle

Marseille color *Downbeat* v84 no9 p59 S 2017

Mercer, Rachel

EYE ON PARADISE *Iceland Review* v54 no6 p52 N/D 2016

MANY BRANCHES MAKE THE TREE color *Iceland Review* v54 no5 p38 S-O 2016

OUT OF THE WOMB AND INTO THE POOL color *Iceland Review* v54 no5 p68 S-O 2016

PRESSING IDEAS *Iceland Review* v54 no6 p24 N/D 2016

THERMAL BLISS *Iceland Review* v55 no3 p106 My/Je 2017

Mercer, Robert

SUPPORT FROM THE RICH FRINGE SHOWS NO SIGNS OF DRYING UP img *New York* v50 no9 p48 My 1 2017

TRUMP'S MONEY MAN J. MAYER cartoon color *New Yorker* v93 no6 p34 Mr 27 2017

Mercer, Robert—Finance

Silent Partners A. Altman and P. Rebala color diag *Time* v188 no14 p40 O 10 2016

Merchant, Brian

The Inevitability of the iPhone S. Begley color *Time* v189 no24 p18 Je 26 2017

Resistance Is Futile L. Grossman *New York Times Book Review* p1 Je 25 2017

Merchant, Carolyn

Birdman of America C. IRMSCHER bw color *Weekly Standard* v22 no13 p30 D 5 2016

Merchant, Nilofer

How to Invent the Future *Harvard Business Review Digital Articles* p2 O 17 2014

Merchant, Nilofer—Interviews

Advice from a Serial Life Reinventor S. G. Carmichael *Harvard Business Review Digital Articles* p2 Ap 2 2015

Merchant ships—History

Norse Knarr J. Guttman cartoon *Military History* v34 no1 p20 My 2017

Merchant of Venice, The (Play : Shakespeare)

IF YOU PRICK US S. GREENBLATT cartoon color *New Yorker* v93 no20 p34 Jl 10 2017

Mercier, Hugo

Faulty logic D. Frey bw color *Science* v356 no6338 p589 My 12 2017

Merckx, Eddy

The EDDY MERCKX Alphabet cartoon color *Bicycling* v58 no1 p40 Ja/F 2017

Mercola, Joseph M., 1954-

In a Quiet Week, Hardcover Gains Offset Declines in Audio, Mass Market Paperback chart *Publishers Weekly* v264 no22 p7 My 29 2017

Mercury

3 hidden food sources of mercury (besides fish) V. Tweed color *Amazing Wellness* p14 Fall 2017

Getting Back to Our Roots A. H. McGowan *Environment* v59 no4 p2 Jl-Ag 2017

A New Pollution Problem S. Novick bw chart color *Environment* v59 no4 p14 Jl-Ag 2017

Mercury (Planet)

August 2017: Totality comes to America M. RATCLIFFE and A. LING color *Astronomy* v45 no8 p44 Ag 2017

Four Out of Five: Whether you're a night owl or an early riser, you can observe a bright planet this month F. Schaaf *Sky & Tele-*

MIDNIGHT EXPRESS: A black Lesbian's play tackles her time in a Turkish prison *Advocate* no1093 p29 O/N 2017

Merkin, Daphne

Descent Into Darkness A. Solomon *New York Times Book Review* p1 F 5 2017

The ebb and flow of a life with depression W. Massey color *America* v216 no5 p42 Mr 6 2017

The Jewish Thread *New York Times Book Review* p17 F 12 2017

The Land Before GPS img *New York* v50 no7 p82 Ap 3 2017

SUICIDE NOTES *Harper's Magazine* v334 no2000 p17 Ja 2017

The Tolerable Stranger: A memoir explores the relationship between a woman and her therapist as she struggles with, and eventually overcomes, self-abuse *New York Times Book Review* p12 Jl 30 2017

Merkin, Daphne—Interviews

A Family Affair P. VOLK bw color *Publishers Weekly* v264 no2 p36 Ja 9 2017

Merkley, Jeff, 1956-

Senator Jeff Merkley, Working-Class Hero Z. CARPENTER color *Nation* v304 no17 p22 Je 5 2017

Merkury Innovations (Company)

Geeni Surge: This smart surge protector falls short on automation and documentation G. FLEISHMAN color *Macworld - Digital Edition* v34 no10 p92 O 2017

Merlin, F.

Seasonal exposure of carbon dioxide ice on the nucleus of comet 67P/Churyumov-Gerasimenko bibl bw graph *Science* v354 no6319 p1563 D 23 2016

Merlino, Michael

ASK THE EXPERTS color *Runner's World* v52 no2 p36 Mr 2017

Merluzzi, Andrew

Human health color *Science* v356 no6338 p590 My 12 2017

Merluzzi, Jennifer

Research: Black Employees Are More Likely to Be Promoted When They Were Referred by Another Employee color *Harvard Business Review Digital Articles* p2 F 28 2017

Mermaid, The (Film)

The Mermaid C. Chiarella chart color *Sound & Vision* v81 no10 p68 D 2016

Mermaids

50 Reasons to Love Being 50+ color *AARP: The Magazine* v60 no4A p57 Je/Jl 2017

SHE SELLS SEA SHELLS C. Winter color *Bloomberg Businessweek* no4497 p68 O 31 2016

Mermin, N. David

Why Quark Rhymes with Pork And Other Scientific Diversions S. Hossenfelder *Physics Today* v69 no11 p57 N 2016

MERNILD, SEBASTIAN H.

The Arctic in the Twenty-First Century: Changing Biogeochemical Linkages across a Paraglacial Landscape of Greenland *BioScience* v67 no2 p118 F 2017

MERRIAM, CHRIS

Turning Capital Against Capitalism *In These Times* v41 no6 p10 Je 2017

Merriam, Dee

Creating Safe Routes to Parks *Parks & Recreation* v52 no9 p46 S 2017

Merridale, Catherine

Fast-Tracking the Revolution: A history highlights the impact of Lenin's return to Russia from political exile in Switzerland J. RUBENSTEIN *New York Times Book Review* p15 Je 11 2017

Running a Red Light P. Waldron *History Today* v67 no3 p62 Mr 2017

Merrifield, Andy

The Amateur: The Pleasures of Doing What You Love color *Publishers Weekly* v264 no11 p70 Mr 13 2017

OVERCOMING AGORA-PHOBIA *In These Times* v41 no7 p38 Jl 2017

Merrifield, Ric

Customer-Tracking Technology Can Work Without Being Creepy *Harvard Business Review Digital Articles* p2 Ja 11 2016

The Internet of Things Is Changing How We Manage Customer Relationships *Harvard Business Review Digital Articles* p2 Je 5 2015

Too Much Profit Can Doom Your Company *Harvard Business Review Digital Articles* p2 Je 1 2015

Merrild, Paul

The Biggest U.S. Health Care Challenges Are Management Challenges *Harvard Business Review Digital Articles* p2 F 6 2015

Reflections on Leadership from Gettysburg *Harvard Business Review Digital Articles* p2 O 12 2015

MERRILL, AUSTIN

DAKAR color *Conde Nast Traveler* v52 no4 p30 Ap 2017

Merrill, Bode

ALEX SHERMAN color *Snowboarder* v29 no3 p48 N 2016

AV CLUB WITH color *Snowboarder* v29 no3 p33 N 2016

BODE MERRILL GUEST EDITOR ISSUE color *Snowboarder* v29 no3 p26 N 2016

CHRISTIAN HOBUSH color *Snowboarder* v29 no3 p50 N 2016

COLDFRONT color *Snowboarder* v29 no3 p14 N 2016

DESIRE MELANCON color *Snowboarder* v29 no3 p40 N 2016

GARAGE BRANDS color *Snowboarder* v29 no3 p32 N 2016

GORDON HARRISON color *Snowboarder* v29 no3 p42 N 2016

SALT LAKE CITY, UT bw color *Snowboarder* v29 no3 p98 N 2016

SCOTTY ARNOLD color *Snowboarder* v29 no3 p38 N 2016

SEQUENCE & DESTROY color *Snowboarder* v29 no2 p42 O 2016

SICK DAYS color *Snowboarder* v29 no3 p92 N 2016

Merrill, Charles

THOUGHTS FROM Our Readers bw *Forbes* v200 no3 p180 S 28 2017

Merrill, Dave

We're Going To Need More Lithium diag graph map *Bloomberg Businessweek* no4537 p60 S 11 2017

MERRILL, DOUG

ELEANOR MERRILL, 1933-2016 *Washingtonian Magazine* v52 no1 p12 O 2016

Merrill, Eleanor

ELEANOR MERRILL, 1933-2016 D. MERRILL *Washingtonian Magazine* v52 no1 p12 O 2016

Merrill, Richard

The biology of color color *Science* v357 no6350 p470 Ag 4 2017

Merrill Edge (Company)

We Pick the Best Online Brokers D. FONDA chart color *Kiplinger's Personal Finance* v71 no10 p48 O 2017

Merriman, John M., 1946-

Ballad of the Anarchist Bandits: The Crime Spree That Gripped Belle Époque Paris *Publishers Weekly* v264 no35 p116 Ag 28 2017

Merriman, Joseph

Lactobacillus reuteri induces gut intraepithelial CD4+CD8αα+ T cells diag graph *Science* v357 no6353 p806 Ag 25 2017

Merritt, Carol Howard

IN SEARCH OF SPIRITUAL HEALING K. Oakes color *America* v217 no7 p28 O 2 2017

New rituals for new realities *Christian Century* v133 no21 p61 O 12 2016

Pregnant with hope color *Christian Century* v133 no26 p10 D 21 2016

Shared space, shared vision *Christian Century* v134 no1 p45 Ja 4 2017

Taking risks to heal hurt *Christian Century* v133 no23 p45 N 9 2016

What to know before you plant *Christian Century* v133 no25 p45 D 7 2016

Merritt, Connie

How My Horse De-Stresses Me color *Horse & Rider* v55 no12 p72 D 2016

MERRITT, DAVID M.

Applying Functional Traits to Ecogeomorphic Processes in Riparian Ecosystems *BioScience* v67 no8 p729 Ag 2017

Merritt, Eileen G.

Going outdoors color *Phi Delta Kappan* v99 no2 p21 O 2017

Time for teacher learning, planning critical for school reform color *Phi Delta Kappan* v98 no4 p31 D 2016/Ja 2017

Merritt, Keri Leigh

'Elites Not Only Benefit From Racism, but Use Racism to Their Advantage" J. Jackson *Extra!* v30 no8 p4 O 2017

Merritt, Marilyn

Imagine this color *Science* v356 no6344 p1240 Je 23 2017

Merritt, Sandra—Trials, litigation, etc.

Journalists in the Dock C. ALLEN color *Weekly Standard* v22 no31 p14 Ap 17 2017

Merrow, John

Has D.C. Teacher Reform Been Successful? *Washington Monthly* v49 no9/10 p16 S/O 2017

MERRY, ROBERT W.

Andy Jackson's Populism il *American Conservative* v16 no3 p23 My/Je 2017

David Stockman's Latest Target: The feisty contrarian takes on the 'War Party' *American Conservative* v16 no5 p9 S/O 2017

The Fate of Republics: Does the Roman story pose lessons for America? *American Conservative* v16 no4 p13 Jl/Ag 2017

James M. Perry, 1927-2016 *American Conservative* v16 no1 p8 Ja/F 2017

The Meaning of Trump bw *American Conservative* v16 no2 p20 Mr/Ap 2017

Mertens, Maggie

Chayce Doesn't Want to Be One of Them color *Glamour* v115 no10 p149 O 2017

Girl Runs Away, Joins Circus color *Glamour* v114 no12 p180 D 2016

"His parents wouldn't attend our wedding" color *Glamour* v115 no6 p100 Je 2017

She Makes More (Way More) color *Glamour* v114 no12 p168 D 2016

(The Big)Salary Reveal [Cover story] bw color *Glamour* v115 no3 p146 Mr 2017

Wait, Maybe True Love Does Exist color *Glamour* v115 no9 p121 S 2017

"We never expected cancer to be part of our marriage" bw color *Glamour* v115 no10 p130 O 2017

When Your Paycheck Is Bigger Than His color *Glamour* v114 no12 p165 D 2016

Merton, Nicholas

Was the FIRST CRUSADE really a war against ISLAM? *History Today* v67 no3 p11 Mr 2017

Merton, Thomas, 1915-1968

Breathe color *Prevention* v68 no12 p20 D 2016

Sally Quinn *New York Times Book Review* p7 S 17 2017

Merton College (Oxford, England)

And The Winning Photo Is.... S. Saxby *British Heritage Travel* v37 no6 p88 N/D 2016

Mertyl, Moaning

TRENDING NOW color *Wired* v25 no4 p12 Ap 2017

Merullo, Roland

The Delight of Being Ordinary: A Road Trip with the Pope and the Dalai Lama *Publishers Weekly* v264 no7 p46 F 13 2017

Mervis, Jeffrey

AFTER THE FALL color *Science* v354 no6311 p408 O 28 2016

California rules U.S. corporate research graph *Science* v354 no6312 p537 N 4 2016

Congress trumps president in backing science chart color *Science* v356 no6337 p470 My 5 2017

Congress votes on sweeping biomedical bill color *Science* v354 no6316 p1085 D 2 2016

DATA FOR ALL? color *Science* v355 no6325 p573 F 10 2017

DOE freezes millions in awards color *Science* v356 no6337 p471 My 5 2017

Drop in foreign applicants worries engineering schools color *Science* v355 no6326 p676 F 17 2017

Faster Higher Smarter color *Science* v354 no6317 p1224 D 9 2016

Federal share of basic research hits new low graph *Science* v355 no6329 p1005 Mr 10 2017

Lawmakers balk at most Trump cuts color *Science* v357 no6346 p11 Jl 7 2017

Mexican scientists feel the Trump effect color *Science* v355 no6324 p440 F 3 2017

NO EASY ANSWERS color *Science* v355 no6325 p568 F 10 2017

Panel urges steps to boost evidence-based policy color *Science* v357 no6355 p959 S 8 2017

SCIENCE LESSONS FOR THE NEXT PRESIDENT *Science* v354 no6310 p274 O 21 2016

Scientists fear pending attack on federal statistics collection color *Science* v355 no6320 p16 Ja 6 2017

Scientists start to parse a Trump presidency color *Science* v354

no6314 p811 N 18 2016

Spy agencies team up with National Academies color *Science* v354 no6309 p155 O 14 2016

Strike disrupts research at Puerto Rico's top university color *Science* v356 no6340 p793 My 26 2017

The Trump era: 10 questions color *Science* v355 no6323 p333 Ja 27 2017

Trump's 2018 budget proposal 'devalues' science color graph *Science* v355 no6331 p1246 Mr 24 2017

Trump's science shop is small and waiting for leadership color *Science* v357 no6347 p117 Jl 14 2017

U.S. report calls for research integrity board diag *Science* v356 no6334 p123 Ap 14 2017

Merwin, Alyssa

A Guide to Finding and Hiring the Best Contractors *Harvard Business Review Digital Articles* p2 Jl 17 2017

Merwin, W. S. (William Stanley), 1927-

THE ASCETIC D. CHIASSON bw *New Yorker* v93 no28 p67 S 18 2017

Merz, Bruno

Changing climate shifts timing of European floods color graph *Science* v357 no6351 p588 Ag 11 2017

Merz, Janina

AT THE WATERHOLE N. Valaithan *Arabian Horse World* v56 no12 p244 S 2016

Merz, Marisa, 1931-

ART color *New Yorker* v93 no10 p14 Ap 24 2017

ART *New Yorker* v92 no48 p9 F 6 2017

Editor's Letter L. POLLOCK color *Art in America* v105 no5 p16 My 2017

EVERYDAY ALCHEMY A. H. Merjian bw color *Art in America* v105 no5 p94 My 2017

Merz, Marisa, 1931—Exhibitions

A WOMAN'S VIEW P. SCHJELDAHL color *New Yorker* v92 no47 p72 Ja 30 2017

Merz, Ralf

Changing climate shifts timing of European floods color graph *Science* v357 no6351 p588 Ag 11 2017

Mesa Verde National Park (Colo.)

AN UNCERTAIN FUTURE K. Siber *National Parks* v91 no4 p36 Fall 2017

Mescal

See also

Tequila

NOT NEW (MEXICAN!) DRINK ALERT! MEZCAL J. Kaplan, T. Buckley et al color *Bloomberg Businessweek* no4496 p66 O 24 2016

Meschenmoser, Sebastian

Pug Man's 3 Wishes color *Publishers Weekly* v263 no49 p39 D 7 2016

Meschery, Tom

Tom MESCHERY J. McCallum color *Sports Illustrated* v127 no1 p84 Jl 3 2017

Meschi, Eleonora

Drosophila insulin release is triggered by adipose Stunted ligand to brain Methuselah receptor bibl graph *Science* v353 no6307 p1553 S 30 2016

Mesenchymal stem cells

See also

Hematopoietic stem cells

Spatiotemporal antagonism in mesenchymal-epithelial signaling in sweat versus hair fate decision C. P. Lu, L. Polak et al graph *Science* v354 no6319 paah6102-1 D 23 2016

Meshorer, Eran

The linker histone H1.0 generates epigenetic and functional intra-tumor heterogeneity bibl graph *Science* v353 no6307 paaf1644-1 S 30 2016

Mesko, Sarah

Sarah Mesko B. KELLOW *Opera News* v81 no5 p12 N 2016

Meslier, Jean

The Poisoned Will of Jean Meslier: A French priest's shocking attack on religion called for the fall of altars and the heads of kings M. Guinard *History Today* v67 no10 p12 O 2017

Mesman Griffith, Jessica

Life's work: Building the church takes everyone [Cover story] color *U.S. Catholic* v82 no8 p22 Ag 2017

Mesoamerican Reef
When Nature Gets An Insurance Policy C. Flavelle color *Bloomberg Businessweek* no4531 p26 Jl 24 2017

Mesoamerican region
UNEARTHING DEMOCRACY'S ROOTS L. Wade color diag *Science* v355 no6330 p1114 Mr 17 2017

Meson decay
In familiar decays, a whiff of new physics A. Cho color diag *Science* v356 no6335 p229 Ap 21 2017

Mesones, I.
Persistent effects of pre-Columbian plant domestication on Amazonian forest composition bibl chart graph map *Science* v355 no6328 p925 Mr 3 2017

Messa, Mirko
Lipid transport by TMEM24 at ER-plasma membrane contacts regulates pulsatile insulin secretion diag *Science* v355 no6326 p709 F 17 2017

Messel, Hal
Act of Faith C. STOCKS color *Architectural Digest* v74 no4 p76 Ap 2017

Messenger (Poem)
MESSENGER M. Karr *Commonweal* v144 no5 p23 Mr 10 2017

Messenger RNA
Global mRNA polarization regulates translation efficiency in the intestinal epithelium A. E. Moor, M. Golan et al diag *Science* v357 no6357 p1299 S 22 2017
ON MESSAGE K. Servick color diag graph *Science* v355 no6324 p446 F 3 2017

Messenger RNA—Research
Moderna's Mystery Medicines N. VARDI and M. HERPER color *Forbes* v198 no9 p46 D 30 2016

Messer, Ryan
RYAN MESSER & JIMMY MUSURACA 992 MARION AVE., NORTH AVONDALE A. FLANGO *Cincinnati Magazine* v50 no11 p76 Ag 2017

Messeri, Lisa
Placing Outer Space An Earthly Ethnography of Other Worlds M. Shindell *Physics Today* v70 no3 p59 Mr 2017

Messerschmidt, Daniel M.
ELABELA deficiency promotes preeclampsia and cardiovascular malformations in mice color diag graph *Science* v357 no6352 p707 Ag 18 2017

Messersmith, Phillip B.
From sequence to color diag *Science* v356 no6342 p1011 Je 9 2017

Messiah
WHO AWAITS THE MESSIAH MOST? MUSLIMS J. CASPER cartoon *Christianity Today* v61 no1 p17 Ja/F 2017

Messiah (Theatrical production)
Hastings traditions inspire ageless symphonic voices E. Case color *Nebraska Life* v20 no6 p64 N/D 2016

Messier, Charles, 1730-1817
Celebrate with Charles G. CHAPLE color *Astronomy* v45 no2 p20 F 2017
Going deep for Andromeda P. HARRINGTON color *Astronomy* v44 no12 p68 D 2016
The obsessive comet hunter R. Jakiel bw color *Astronomy* v45 no2 p54 F 2017

MESSIMER, JENNIFER
America's Most Adventurous Cities color *Men's Health* v32 no6 p42 Ag 2017

Messin, Gaétan
Anti-coalescence of bosons on a lossy beam splitter bw chart diag graph *Science* v356 no6345 p1373 Je 30 2017

Messina, Chris
THE HASHTAG L. PANDELL color *Wired* v25 no6 p25 Je 2017

Messing, Debra, 1968-
Will & Grace L. Rice color *Entertainment Weekly* no1471 p44 Je 23 2017

Messing, Emma
The Emma Messing Story: The remarkable life of a rabbi's daughter from Indianapolis M. Lasswell *Commentary* v143 no4 p36 Ap 2017

MESSNER, KATE
The Littlest Frenemies: Elementary-school social life has its perils in this middle-grade graphic memoir *New York Times Book Review* p26 My 14 2017

Messud, Claire
Anticipation Index: What we're excited about right now *New York* v50 no13 p77 Je 26 2017
THE BURNING GIRL E. DONALDSON color *Maclean's* v130 no8 p62 S 2017
The Dancer & the Dance bw color *New York Review of Books* v63 no19 p6 D 8 2016
Fierce, She Got Outside the Moment color *New York Review of Books* v64 no5 p28 Mr 23 2017
Friends Without Benefits: In Claire Messud's new novel, a teenage girl takes a dangerous path to adulthood L. LIPPMAN *New York Times Book Review* p12 S 10 2017
THE HUNGER ARTIST R. FRANKLIN *New York Times Magazine* p24 Ag 13 2017

Mestas, Maureen
To prevent collapsing your body when riding corners and turns... color *Dressage Today* v23 no11 p72 Ag 2017

Mestel, Rosie
The Original CRISPR [Cover story] color diag graph *Science News* v191 no7 p22 Ap 15 2017

MESTEL, SPENSER
Make Your Workouts Pay cartoon color *Men's Health* v32 no8 p25 O 2017
The Prison Workout: Can You Survive? cartoon color *Men's Health* v32 no8 p43 O 2017

Meston, Cindy
SEX TONIGHT J. BENJAMIN color *Good Housekeeping* v264 no5 p107 My 2017

Mesure, Charles
The Magicians *TV Guide* v65 no4 p39 Ja 16 2017

Metabolic detoxification
MEET METABOLIC RESISTANCE G. Gullickson *Successful Farming* v115 no5 p44 Mid-Mr 2017
Spring Clean Your Life [Cover story] S. Sims color *Prevention* v69 no4 p40 Ap 2017
SUMMER "TEA-TOX" J. Bowden color *Amazing Wellness* v9 no4 p47 Summ 2017

Metabolic disorders
   See also
     Obesity
     Wasting syndrome
The New War on Obesity C. Roberts and T. Germain chart color diag *Consumer Reports* v82 no10 p48 O 2017

Metabolic disorders—Risk factors
Sweet Drinks: Bad for Your Brain? *Tufts University Health & Nutrition Letter* v35 no5 p6 Jl 2017

Metabolic disorders—Treatment
Diagnosis and treatment of inherited metabolic diseases in China Zhi-Chun Feng, Yan Wang et al bibl *Science* v354 no6319 p52 D 23 2016

Metabolic flux analysis
Systems-level analysis of mechanisms regulating yeast metabolic flux S. R. Hackett, V. R. T. Zanotelli et al bibl diag graph *Science* v354 no6311 paaf2786-1 O 28 2016

Metabolic syndrome—Risk factors
20 Things You Didn't Know About... Metabolism G. TARLACH color *Discover* v38 no2 p74 Mr 2017

Metabolism
   See also
     Cell metabolism
     Ketogenic diet
     Plant metabolism
The 20-Minute Turkey Buster L. MCGLASHAN color *Muscle & Performance* v9 no11 p24 N 2017
20 Things You Didn't Know About... Metabolism G. TARLACH color *Discover* v38 no2 p74 Mr 2017
ASK THE DOCTOR A. L. KOMAROFF *Harvard Health Letter* v42 no7 p2 My 2017
Circadian physiology of metabolism S. Panda bibl diag *Science* v354 no6315 p1008 N 25 2016
Design Your Own Metcon L. McGlashan chart color *Muscle & Performance* v9 no5 p48 My 2017
THE LARD IS YOUR SAVIOR? C. MOHR color *Men's Health* v32 no7 p102 S 2017
Metabolic cues for hematopoietic stem cells P. Sommerkamp and

A. Trumpp bibl diag *Science* v354 no6316 p1103 D 2 2016

This Just In J. Zorthian *Time* v189 no18 p25 My 15 2017

Young Horse Life J. Paulson *Horse & Rider* v56 no9 p14 S 2017

Metabolomics

Big data, big picture: Metabolomics meets systems biology M. May color *Science* v356 no6338 p646 My 12 2017

Metacarpus injuries

GOOD NEWS ABOUT CUTTING HORSE INJURIES C. Barakat and M. McCluskey color *Equus* no482 p12 N 2017

Metacognition

Causal neural network of metamemory for retrospection in primates Kentaro Miyamoto, Takahiro Osada et al bibl diag graph *Science* v355 no6321 p1 Ja 13 2017

Get More Innovative by Rethinking the Way You Think M. Schrage *Harvard Business Review Digital Articles* p2 N 5 2015

Metadata

See also

Tags (Metadata)

Reflections on Metadata R. Beardsley *Publishers Weekly* v263 no41 p8 O 10 2016

Metagenomics

Big-data approaches to protein structure prediction J. Söding bibl color diag graph *Science* v355 no6322 p248 Ja 20 2017

Finding enzymes in the gut metagenome M. E. Glasner color *Science* v355 no6325 p577 F 10 2017

Giant viruses with an expanded complement of translation system components F. Schulz, N. Yutin et al diag *Science* v356 no6333 p82 Ap 7 2017

Metal analysis

Lasers expose hidden electronic order J. Steven Dodge diag *Science* v356 no6335 p246 Ap 21 2017

Metal detectors

Broken Bow bricks hide buried treasure A. J. BARTELS color *Nebraska Life* v21 no4 p15 Jl/Ag 2017

Metal fabrication

Photolithography based on nanocrystals M. Striccoli color *Science* v357 no6349 p353 Jl 28 2017

SHEETMETAL WITH A FLARE [Cover story] J. KOPYCINSKI color *Dirt Sports + Off-Road* v51 no1 p64 Ja 2017

SHOP TIPS J. KOPYCINSKI color *Dirt Sports + Off-Road* v51 no10 p66 O 2017

Metal fatigue

Identify Bad Bolts B. HILDENBRAND color *Climbing* no354 p40 Jl 2017

Metal in interior decoration

Jean Prouvé B. LIBBY *Treasures* v6 no2 p18 O/N 2016

Metal industry

Bedding Hardware B. Pike color *Power & Motoryacht* v34 no10 p120 O 2017

Metal ions

Charged Atmosphere H. Leifert color *Natural History* v125 no7 p7 Jl/Ag 2017

Metal-organic frameworks

Hydrolytically stable fluorinated metal-organic frameworks for energy-efficient dehydration A. Cadiau, Y. Belmabkhout et al diag *Science* v356 no6339 p731 My 19 2017

Metal-organic framework extracts water from thin air J. Miller *Physics Today* v70 no6 p16 Je 2017

Metal polishes—Evaluation

16 ways to do COPPER S. Walter color *Good Housekeeping* v264 no4 p76E Ap 2017

Metal roofing

circle j lodge P. JACOT color *Cabin Living* p16 D 2016

Resources *Old House Journal* v45 no4 p87 Je 2017

Metal sculpture

See also

Aluminum sculpture

LIVING WITH FLOWERS *Martha Stewart Living* no268 p114 O 2016

Metal tableware

ART + CRAFT color *Arts & Crafts Homes & the Revival* v12 no4 p11 Fall 2017

Metal Bowl, The (Short story)

The Metal Bowl M. July cartoon color *New Yorker* v93 no26 p72 S 4 2017

Metal industry—Charts, diagrams, etc.

METALS' TIME TO SHINE C. Matthews diag *Fortune* v174 no8 p22 D 15 2016

Metallic textiles

Nasa's New 'Space Fabric' J. Zorthian color *Time* v189 no19 p19 My 22 2017

Metallica (Performer)

METALLICA'S LARS ULRICH D. Snierson color *Entertainment Weekly* no1442 p58 D 2 2016 Rebellious Special Issue

Metallica's Monster Summer K. GROW color *Rolling Stone* no1290 p13 Je 29 2017

YOU PLAY YOU S. Hyden color *New York Times Magazine* p82 Mr 12 2017

Metalloenzymes

An artificial metalloenzyme with the kinetics of native enzymes P. Dydio, H. M. Key et al bibl diag graph *Science* v354 no6308 p102 O 7 2016

Metalloproteins

See also

Zinc proteins

Metalloprotein entatic control of ligand-metal bonds quantified by ultrafast x-ray spectroscopy M. W. Mara, R. G. Hadt et al diag *Science* v356 no6344 p1276 Je 23 2017

Metals

See also

Lead

Solder & soldering

Tin

Metallic air may have swaddled moon L. GROSSMAN *Science News* v192 no1 p7 Ag 5 2017

Rio Tinto and the Mines A. LEDERER bw color *Natural History* v125 no5 p36 My 2017

Metals—Fatigue—Research

Bone-like crack resistance in hierarchical metastable nanolaminate steels M. Koyama, Z. Zhang et al bibl color diag *Science* v355 no6329 p1055 Mr 10 2017

Metals—Hardenability

Grain boundary stability governs hardening and softening in extremely fine nanograined metals J. Hu, Y. N. Shi et al bibl color graph *Science* v355 no6331 p1292 Mr 24 2017

Metals—Physiological effect

IMPLANTS color *Prevention* v69 no9 p10 O 2017

Metalwork

See also

Copperwork

HARDWARE & METALWORK color *Old House Journal* v44 p101 2016 Design Center source Book

METALHEAD A. BRANDT *Cincinnati Magazine* v50 no4 p42 Ja 2017

Metalworkers

A Family Affair color *Log Home Living* v33 no9 p20 D 2016

Metalworkers—France

The ancien régime's master of precious metals B. Laurence Scherer color *Magazine Antiques* v183 no6 p90 N/D 2016

Metamaterials

See also

Cloaking devices

Hall-effect metamaterials and "anti-Hall bars" M. Wegener, M. Kadic et al *Physics Today* v70 no10 p14 O 2017

Metalenses, megapromise R. F. Service color *Science* v354 no6319 p1523 D 23 2016

Metamaterials—Dielectric properties

Scalable-manufactured randomized glass-polymer hybrid metamaterial for daytime radiative cooling Y. Zhai, Y. Ma et al bibl diag *Science* v355 no6329 p1062 Mr 10 2017

Metamaterials—Optical properties

Metamaterials for perpetual cooling at large scales X. Zhang bibl color *Science* v355 no6329 p1023 Mr 10 2017

Metaphor

Finding the Right Metaphor for Your Presentation N. Duarte *Harvard Business Review Digital Articles* p2 N 17 2014

"Rally the Troops" and Other Business Metaphors You Can Do Without M. Chussil *Harvard Business Review Digital Articles* p2 N 24 2016

which way to tomorrow? M. B. Griggs color *Popular Science* v289 no5 p11 S/O 2017

You Are the Manure of the Earth A. B. BRADLEY bw color

Christianity Today v60 no8 p72 O 2016

Metaphor—Religious aspects

Beyond black and white: To make conversations about race more productive, try using different metaphors for God G. Ji-Sun Kim color *U.S. Catholic* v82 no10 p25 O 2017

Metapopulation (Ecology)

Effects of network modularity on the spread of perturbation impact in experimental metapopulations L. J. Gilarranz, B. Rayfield et al diag graph *Science* v357 no6347 p199 Jl 14 2017

Metarhizium

Root wars N. Walker color *Canadian Geographic* v137 no5 p26 S/O 2017

Metastable states

Bone-like crack resistance in hierarchical metastable nanolaminate steels M. Koyama, Z. Zhang et al bibl color diag *Science* v355 no6329 p1055 Mr 10 2017

Metastasis

Chemo Causes Disease to Spread to Lungs *USA Today Magazine* v146 no2869 p14 O 2017

FRONTIERS IN CANCER THERAPY P. A. Kiberstis and J. Travis *Science* v355 no6330 p1143 Mr 17 2017

Metaxatos, Paul

The Internet of Things Needs Design, Not Just Technology *Harvard Business Review Digital Articles* p2 Ap 29 2016

Metcalf, Ben

2015: Goochland, VA *Lapham's Quarterly* v10 no1 p57 Wint 2017

Metcalf, C. Jessica E.

Opportunities and challenges in modeling emerging infectious diseases diag graph *Science* v357 no6347 p149 Jl 14 2017

Metcalf, Carol

Rehab Done Right color *Horse & Rider* v55 no11 p66 N 2016

Metcalf, John

THE MUSEUM AT THE END OF THE WORLD M. DOHERTY color *Maclean's* v129 no41 p57 O 17 2016

Metcalf, Laurie

72 minutes with ... Laurie Metcalf J. MCHENRY img *New York* v50 no11 p18 My 29 2017

Metcalf, Linsey

Q&A *Texas Monthly* v45 no6 p24 Je 2017

Metcalf, Steve

Kids Will Ruin Your Life color *Powder* v46 no2 p36 O 2017

My Collection color *Horse & Rider* v56 no9 p104 S 2017

Metcalf, Tom

Could Puerto Rico Be the Next Tax Haven? color *Bloomberg Businessweek* no4535 p28 Ag 28 2017

E-Z Auto Loans Are A Tough Business color graph *Bloomberg Businessweek* no4521 p37 My 8 2017

Metcalfe, Anna

Common Good J. Lovelace color *American Craft* v77 no3 p26 Je/Jl 2017

Metcalfe, Daniel B.

Microbial change in warming soils diag *Science* v357 no6359 p41 O 6 2017

Metcalfe, Gayden

Mind Your Manners color *Southern Living* v52 no11 p26 N 2017

Metcalfe, Robert

Virgin Atlantic Tested 3 Ways to Change Employee Behavior *Harvard Business Review Digital Articles* p2 Ag 1 2016

Metchev, S.

Zones, spots, and planetary-scale waves beating in brown dwarf atmospheres color graph *Science* v357 no6352 p683 Ag 18 2017

Meteor showers

See also

Geminids (Meteors)

Calendar: Discovery L. Eadicicco color *Time* v188 no27-28 p84 D 26 2016

Perseid Forecast: Partly Moony color *Sky & Telescope* v134 no2 p51 Ag 2017

READER GALLERY color *Astronomy* v45 no5 p70 My 2017

The Taurids Are Back color *Sky & Telescope* v134 no5 p50 N 2017

Meteorite craters

EXPLORE THE IMPACT that killed the dinosaurs M. Alexander color map *Astronomy* v44 no12 p26 D 2016

A SHOCKING IMPACT: DISGUISED BY VOLCANOES AND CHALLIS S. WILLSEY *Idaho Magazine* v16 no12 p18 S 2017

Meteorite craters—Nunavut

Deep impact J. BENNETT color *Canadian Geographic* v137 no2 p29 Mr/Ap 2017

Meteorites

See also

Meteorite craters

Asteroid barrage not linked to boom in ancient marine life T. Sumner *Science News* v191 no3 p18 F 18 2017

Meteorite magnetism in the early solar system *Science* v355 no6325 p591 F 10 2017

METEORITE ORIGINS P. Mane, A. Klesman et al color *Astronomy* v45 no11 p44 N 2017

PLANETARY WEIGHT LOSS M. E. Bakich, R. Talcott et al color *Astronomy* v45 no4 p34 Ap 2017

Meteorites—Age

75, 50 & 25 YEARS AGO R. W. Sinnott *Sky & Telescope* v133 no5 p6 My 2017

Meteorological charts

See also

Wind power maps

"A MASS RESCUE OPERATION" *Smithsonian* v48 no4 p68 Jl/Ag 2017

Forecast Center T. Vasquez color map *Weatherwise* v69 no6 p62 N-D 2016

Forecast Center T. Vasquez *Weatherwise* v70 no2 p54 Mr/Ap 2017

On Our Radar K. PEEK color *Audubon* v119 no3 p16 Fall 2017

Meteorological instruments

See also

Altimeters

Weather vanes

Rooster Weathervane from the Gibbel-Kreider Farm in Lancaster County Pennsylvania color *Magazine Antiques* v183 no6 p7 N/D 2016

Meteorological observations

Stormy skies and starry nights R. Shubinski color graph *Astronomy* v45 no4 p52 Ap 2017

Meteorological photography

From the Editor M. Benner Smidt color *Weatherwise* v70 no4 p4 Jl/Ag 2017

Meteorological stations—Evaluation

STORM BRAIN R. Verger color *Popular Science* v289 no4 p30 Jl/Ag 2017

Meteorologists

Carl-Gustaf Rossby J. R. Fleming *Physics Today* v70 no1 p50 Ja 2017

David Bernard A. McLellan color *New Orleans Magazine* v51 no8 p30 Je 2017

Mod squad S. Scoles and M. HONGOLTZ-HETLING cartoon *Popular Science* v289 no4 p42 Jl/Ag 2017

supersize supercell supersimulation R. Verger color *Popular Science* v289 no4 p16 Jl/Ag 2017

Meteorology

See also

Atmospheric nucleation

Climatology

Clouds

Radar meteorology

Seasons

Weather

Chains of Connection: Alexander Von Humboldt's Meteorological Legacy Lives On S. Vermette color map *Weatherwise* v69 no6 p32 N-D 2016

The Curious Case of Concentric Craters C. Wood *Sky & Telescope* v133 no4 p52 Ap 2017

From the Editor M. Benner Smidt *Weatherwise* v70 no2 p4 Mr/Ap 2017

Meteorology education

not a weather girl R. Feltman cartoon *Popular Science* v289 no4 p81 Jl/Ag 2017

Meteorology—Computer network resources

A new cloud atlas, now with contrails color *Science* v355 no6332 p1354 Mr 31 2017

Meteors

See also

Meteor showers

Meteorites

FROM OUR READERS J. Lockwood, A. Whitman et al *Sky &*

Telescope v134 no4 p6 O 2017

READER GALLERY C. E. Fairbairn, L. Kuhn et al color *Astronomy* v45 no1 p72 Ja 2017

Metformin—Therapeutic use

Potential new benefits from an old drug *Mayo Clinic Health Letter* v35 no4 p7 Ap 2017

METH, DAN

GIFTS that UPLIFT! cartoon *O, The Oprah Magazine* p148 D 2016

Methane

See also

Bromotrifluoromethane

Low-temperature activation of methane on the IrO2(110) surface Z. Liang, T. Li et al bw diag graph *Science* v356 no6335 p299 Ap 21 2017

Massive blow-out craters formed by hydrate-controlled methane expulsion from the Arctic seafloor K. Andreassen, A. Hubbard et al graph map *Science* v356 no6341 p948 Je 1 2017

The methanogenic CO2 reducing-and-fixing enzyme is bifunctional and contains 46 [4Fe-4S] clusters T. Wagner, U. Ermler et al bibl diag *Science* v354 no6308 p114 O 7 2016

Playing marble run to make methane H. Dobbek color diag *Science* v357 no6352 p642 Ag 18 2017

Scientists flag new causes for surge in methane levels P. Voosen color *Science* v354 no6319 p1513 D 23 2016

Selective anaerobic oxidation of methane enables direct synthesis of methanol V. L. Sushkevich, D. Palagin et al diag graph *Science* v356 no6337 p523 My 5 2017

Super-dry reforming of methane intensifies CO2 utilization via Le Chatelier's principle L. C. Buelens, V. V. Galvita et al bibl diag graph *Science* v354 no6311 p449 O 28 2016

Methane & the environment

Senate upholds methane control rule color *Science* v356 no6339 p668 My 19 2017

Methane—Environmental aspects

Data show no sign of methane boost T. SUMNER *Science News* v191 no1 p15 Ja 21 2017

Much More Methane color *Earth Island Journal* v32 no4 p11 Wint 2017

Methanol

what the frack K. Pierre-Louis cartoon *Popular Science* v289 no2 p12 Mr/Ap 2017

Methanosarcina

The biosynthetic pathway of coenzyme F430 in methanogenic and methanotrophic archaea Kaiyuan Zheng, P. D. Ngo et al bibl diag graph *Science* v354 no6310 p339 O 21 2016

Methicillin-resistant staphylococcus aureus

Fighting the enemy within E. Tacconelli, I. B. Autenrieth et al bibl diag *Science* v355 no6326 p689 F 17 2017

Methionine

Redox-based reagents for chemoselective methionine bioconjugation S. Lin, X. Yang et al bibl diag graph *Science* v355 no6325 p597 F 10 2017

Methodist missions

THE SPEARS OF PEACE: The arrival of a Christian mission on the island of Dobu in Papua New Guinea was met with ambivalence, but it resulted in a mixing of cultures and the development of new traditions D. Lee-Talbot *History Today* v67 no10 p50 O 2017

Methyl groups

Pyocyanin degradation by a tautomerizing demethylase inhibits Pseudomonas aeruginosa biofilms K. C. Costa, N. R. Glasser et al bibl diag graph *Science* v355 no6321 p1 Ja 13 2017

Methyl isocyanate

ALMA uncovers more ingredients for life color *Astronomy* v45 no10 p14 O 2017

Methyl radicals

Magnetic trap snares methyl radicals A. G. Smart *Physics Today* v70 no4 p18 Ap 2017

Methylation

See also

DNA methylation

A modular and enantioselective synthesis of the pleuromutilin antibiotics S. K. Murphy, M. Zeng et al diag graph *Science* v356 no6341 p956 Je 1 2017

Métis artists

Christi Belcourt N. WALKER color *Canadian Geographic* v135 no6 p23 D 2015

Metivier, Michael

Dim Sum color *U.S. Catholic* v82 no6 p11 Je 2017

Metler, Chris

GOING GREEN4GOOD IS ABOUT MORE THAN THE ENVIRONMENT *Maclean's* v129 no50 p42 D 19 2016

Reid's Heritage Homes on Constructing Residential to the Net-Zero Standard color *Maclean's* v129 no50 p43 D 19 2016

Metpally, Raghu

Distribution and clinical impact of functional variants in 50,726 whole-exome sequences from the DiscovEHR study chart graph *Science* v354 no6319 paaf6814-1 D 23 2016

Genetic identification of familial hypercholesterolemia within a single U.S. health care system chart graph *Science* v354 no6319 paaf7000-1 D 23 2016

Metra Rail (Company)

Making Trains Run on Time J. Sanburn color diag *Time* v189 no13 p38 Ap 10 2017

Metres, Philip

For Leila Means Night and Night Is Beautiful to the Desert Mind *America* v216 no4 p41 F 20 2017

Metro Bank PLC

We want all our staff to be recruiters *People Management* p22 D 2016/Ja 2017

Metro Boomin (Performer)

Introducing the Man You've Been Listening to All Year D. FRIEDMAN color *GQ: Gentlemen's Quarterly* v86 no12 p104 D 2016

Metrology

Cold molecules: Progress in quantum engineering of chemistry and quantum matter J. L. Bohn, A. Maria Rey et al bw color *Science* v357 no6355 p1002 S 8 2017

Metropolitan (Film)

Metropolitan *New Yorker* v92 no39 p20 N 28 2016

The Witty, Wistful Films of Whit Stillman A. PALETTA *American Conservative* v16 no5 p46 S/O 2017

Metropolitan areas

See also

Urban renewal

METROPOLIS M. Roemers color *National Geographic* v231 no3 p120 Mr 2017

NEWSBITES [Cover story] *Tufts University Health & Nutrition Letter* v34 no12 p1 F 2017

Metropolitan areas—Canada

CITY WIDE B. BANKS map *Canadian Geographic* v137 no3 p62 My 2017

THE ULTIMATE CANADIAN GEOGRAPHY QUIZ CITIES EDITION N. WALKER color map *Canadian Geographic* v137 no3 p41 My 2017

Metropolitan areas—Economic aspects

Urban Wealth K. Peek color *Scientific American* v315 no3 p92 S 2016

Metropolitan areas—Ratings & rankings

So You Want to Be Like Silicon Valley? D. Gambrell and P. Coy *Bloomberg Businessweek* no4537 p48 S 11 2017

Metropolitan areas—United States

Analyzing OMB classification of regions: three case studies E. S. Baker *Monthly Labor Review* p1 N 2016

Metropolitan areas—United States—Economic conditions

AMERICA'S LARGEST EXPORTING CITIES map *Fortune* v175 no3 p11 Mr 1 2017

Metropolitan Atlanta Rapid Transit Authority

THE CONNECTOR J. GREEN *Atlanta* v56 no12 p19 Ap 2017

Mass Transit, Mass Art: MARTA finds new ways to use its vast spaces as a canvas for local artists J. HOWARD *Atlanta* v57 no6 p80 O 2017

Metropolitan Life Insurance Co.—Finance

METLIFE TAKES THE LEAD A. SHLAES color *Forbes* v198 no6 p42 N 8 2016

Metropolitan Opera Guild Inc.

Luncheon/2016 *Opera News* v81 no9 p8 Mr 2017

Metropolitan Life Insurance Co.—Trials, litigation, etc.

METLIFE TAKES THE LEAD A. SHLAES color *Forbes* v198 no6 p42 N 8 2016

Metropolitan Museum of Art (New York, N.Y.)

ART color *New Yorker* v93 no29 p15 S 25 2017

ART *New Yorker* v93 no19 p11 Jl 3 2017

Crashing the Party A. HASLETT color *Vogue* v206 no12 p132 D 2016

Fragonard: The Heights of Drawing C. B. Bailey cartoon *New York Review of Books* v64 no2 p19 F 9 2017

GOINGS ON ABOUT TOWN color *New Yorker* v92 no46 p5 Ja 23 2017

Hand in Glove R. Platt cartoon *New Yorker* v92 no47 p13 Ja 30 2017

Her Brilliant CAREER bw *Vogue* v207 no6 p50 Je 2017

KIMBERLY DREW J. Wilson color *Essence* v47 no11 p30 Mr 2017

The MET'S POWER FAILURE W. D. COHAN color *Vanity Fair* v59 no5 p122 Ap 2017

MUSE R. Mead cartoon *New Yorker* v92 no45 p24 Ja 16 2017

Plus Ça Change P. Schjeldahl cartoon *New Yorker* v92 no35 p14 O 31 2016

SHOWCASE P. DUKOVIC color *New Yorker* v93 no11 p52 My 1 2017

Sources *Lapham's Quarterly* v10 no3 p220 Summ 2017

the start color *InStyle* v24 no5 p41 My 2017

WHAT BROKE THE MET? B. KACHKA img *New York* v50 no8 p44 Ap 17 2017

Metropolitan Opera (New York, N.Y.)

6. See Der Rosenkavalier J. DAVIDSON *New York* v50 no7 p88 Ap 3 2017

CLASSICAL MUSIC *New Yorker* v92 no37 p16 N 14 2016

DEPARTURES AND ARRIVALS A. ROSS cartoon *New Yorker* v93 no19 p72 Jl 3 2017

The Sound of Love R. Platt cartoon *New Yorker* v92 no40 p11 D 5 2016

METTES, SUSAN

WAIT, WHAT IS MONEY? color *Christianity Today* v61 no1 p30 Ja/F 2017

METTI, LAURA

Life cartoon *Reader's Digest* v190 no1132 p30 Jl/Ag 2017

Mettler, Mike

THE BAND bw color *Sound & Vision* v82 no3 p72 Ap 2017

THE BRAIN BOX bw color *Sound & Vision* v82 no6 p72 Jl/Ag 2017

Charlie Daniels Explores the Sound Quality Trail on Night Hawk bw color *Sound & Vision* v82 no1 p22 Ja 2017

EMERSON, LAKE & PALMER color *Sound & Vision* v81 no10 p72 D 2016

FULL TANK: THE COMPLETE ALBUM COLLECTION color *Sound & Vision* v82 no8 p72 O 2017

Gary Brooker and Procol Harum Fuse Sonic Shades of Both Past and Present With Novum color *Sound & Vision* v82 no6 p24 Jl/Ag 2017

Greg Lake and ELP Welcome Us Back to the Hi-Fi Show That Never Ends bw color *Sound & Vision* v81 no10 p24 D 2016

John Mellencamp Continues to Explore His American Roots With Sad Clowns & Hillbillies bw color *Sound & Vision* v82 no7 p30 S 2017

THE JOSHUA TREE – SUPER DELUXE EDITION color *Sound & Vision* v82 no7 p72 S 2017

Lee Loughnane and Chicago Assert Their 4.0 Authority on Blu-ray bw color *Sound & Vision* v81 no9 p22 N 2016

Little Steven Heads Back to the Garage, Emerges With the Eclectic Sounds of Soulfire color *Sound & Vision* v82 no8 p30 O 2017

The Neal Morse Band Progresses Into the Realization of a Fine Sonic Dream color *Sound & Vision* v82 no5 p24 Je 2017

Now Here This color *Sound & Vision* v81 no9 p18 N 2016

PAUL MCCARTNEY bw color *Sound & Vision* v82 no5 p72 Je 2017

PINK FLOYD bw color *Sound & Vision* v82 no2 p72 F/Mr 2017

Prince Movie Collection color *Sound & Vision* v82 no2 p68 F/Mr 2017

THE RCA & ARISTA ALBUM COLLECTION LOU REED bw color *Sound & Vision* v82 no4 p72 My 2017

Rik Emmett on the Allied Forces Behind the Sound of RESolution9 bw color *Sound & Vision* v82 no2 p22 F/Mr 2017

SATURDAY NIGHT FEVER DIRECTOR'S CUT color *Sound & Vision* v82 no8 p70 O 2017

The Sonic Wonder of Elvis and the Royal Philharmonic Orchestra

bw color *Sound & Vision* v82 no3 p28 Ap 2017

TEMPLE OF THE DOG bw color *Sound & Vision* v82 no1 p72 Ja 2017

THE TRAVELING WILBURYS color *Sound & Vision* v81 no9 p72 N 2016

Van der Graaf Generator Disturbs the Sonic Wavelength (But in a Good Way) bw color *Sound & Vision* v82 no4 p26 My 2017

Mettler, Suzanne

Democracy on the Brink color *Foreign Affairs* v96 no3 p121 My/Je 2017

Metz, Cade

NEXT LIST 2017 bw graph *Wired* v25 no5 p63 My 2017

SAFE color diag *Wired* v24 no12 p106 D 2016

SPAWN OF BITCOIN: BLOCKCHAIN-FUELED STARTUPS color graph *Wired* v25 no7 p18 Jl 2017

Metz, Chrissy

"Always be grateful" [Cover story] A. Morris color *Glamour* v115 no3 p192 Mr 2017

THIS IS US D. Snierson color *Entertainment Weekly* no1477 p28 Ag 11 2017

Metz, Landon

Fair Thee Well K. McMAHON color *ARTnews* v116 no1 p48 Spr 2017

Metz, Pete—Interviews

RIDE ALONG C. ROSE *Cincinnati Magazine* v50 no4 p22 Ja 2017

Metz, Rachel

Growing Up with Alexa color graph il *MIT Technology Review* v120 no5 p70 S/O 2017

INVENTORS color il *MIT Technology Review* v120 no5 p56 S/O 2017

Virtual Reality's Missing Element: Other People color *MIT Technology Review* v120 no4 p84 Jl/Ag 2017

VISIONARIES color il *MIT Technology Review* v120 no5 p42 S/O 2017

METZ, TRACY

perspective: interiors color map *Architectural Record* v205 no8 p33 Ag 2017

Metzger, Daniel

Regeneration of fat cells from myofibroblasts during wound healing bibl color graph *Science* v355 no6326 p748 F 17 2017

Metzger, Erica

CURL power *Better Homes & Gardens* v94 no11 p24 N 2016

erica explores CONCEALERS color *Better Homes & Gardens* v95 no7 p18 Jl 2017

erica explores MICELLAR WATER color *Better Homes & Gardens* v95 no9 p24 S 2017

HEALTHY SKIN WINS color *Better Homes & Gardens* v95 no10 p28 O 2017

pretty COOL color *Better Homes & Gardens* v95 no7 p22 Jl 2017

the secret to FOUNDATION color *Better Homes & Gardens* v95 no9 p26 S 2017

SPICE MARKET *Better Homes & Gardens* v94 no11 p22 N 2016

winter skin SURVIVAL *Better Homes & Gardens* v94 no12 p22 D 2016

Metzl, Jordan

HIIT PLAN [Cover story] color *Runner's World* v52 no1 p58 Ja/F 2017

Meuche, Lou

SADDLE CHAT bw color graph *Horse & Rider* v56 no9 p21 S 2017

Meuwly, C.

An integrated diamond nanophotonics platform for quantum-optical networks bibl graph *Science* v354 no6314 p847 N 18 2016

Mevers, Emily

Unequivocal determination of complex molecular structures using anisotropic NMR measurements color *Science* v356 no6333 p43 Ap 7 2017

Mewborn, Stephen

How Customers Perceive a Price Is as Important as the Price Itself color *Harvard Business Review Digital Articles* p2 Ja 3 2017

Mexican-American Border Region

Activists Work to Stop Militarization of the Border J. WEST color *Progressive* p12 D 2016/Ja 2017

Borderlands R. MISRACH color *National Geographic* v232 no3 p128 S 2017

DRUG SMUGGLERS HAVE ALREADY BEATEN TRUMP'S WALL T. C. BROWN color *Reason* v49 no1 p32 My 2017

Mexican Americans—Political activity

Mexican Americans J. R. RANGEL and P. SKERRY color *Weekly Standard* v22 no22 p16 F 13 2017

Mexican Americans—Social conditions—21st century

Mexicans in the United States: In Pursuit of Inclusion A. D. ALONSO *Current History* v115 no784 p305 N 2016

Mexican art

Wall to Wall: A PAIR OF EXHIBITIONS PLUMBS THE HISTORY OF MEXICAN MURALISM IN LOS ANGELES *Los Angeles Magazine* v62 no9 p61 S 2017

Mexican athletes

FACES IN THE CROWD T. Keith color *Sports Illustrated* v127 no4 p20 Ag 7 2017

Mexican cooking

See also

Salsas (Cooking)

The Apprentice P. SHARPE *Texas Monthly* v45 no4 p40 Ap 2017

The Harder They Come: The hard-shell tacos of childhood still bring joy to the dinner table S. Sifton *New York Times Magazine* p26 My 14 2017

Mexican restaurants

Fish Milanese img *New York* v50 no9 p75 My 1 2017

La Paloma Restaurant K. MONTGOMERY *Arizona Highways* v93 no10 p12 O 2017

RENÉ REDZEPI'S MEXICO J. Gordinier color *Esquire* p28 My 2017

Mexican restaurants—Evaluation

The Apprentice P. SHARPE *Texas Monthly* v45 no4 p40 Ap 2017

Hola Again J. SPALDING color *Indianapolis Monthly* p44 Ap 2017

MEXICAN *Cincinnati Magazine* v50 no8 p123 My 2017

Mexican wolf

Critics pan wolf plan C. Carswell color map *Science* v357 no6358 p1341 S 29 2017

Mexicans

Mexican and U.S. scientists: Partners A. Lazcano, A. Ortiz Ortega et al bibl color *Science* v355 no6330 p1139 Mr 17 2017

Mexicans—Attitudes

A Random Act Of Roadside Assistance [Cover story] J. HORNER *Reader's Digest* v188 no1125 p93 N 2016

Mexicans—California

Lightbox color *Time* v188 no14 p18 O 10 2016

Mexicans—United States

No Wall to Stop Migrant Cash From Going South N. Cattan and I. Cota color *Bloomberg Businessweek* no4502 p23 D 5 2016

Mexicans—United States—History

Mexicans in the United States: In Pursuit of Inclusion A. D. ALONSO *Current History* v115 no784 p305 N 2016

Mexicans—United States—Social conditions

THE COURTESY OF THE OPPRESSED R. CONNIFF color *Progressive* v81 no7 p15 O/N 2017

Mexican War, 1846-1848

Mad, Democrats? Blame the Iran Deal *Commentary* p1 Ja 2017

Mad, Democrats? Blame the Iran Deal *Commentary* v143 no1 p1 Ja 2017

Mexico City (Mexico)—Maps—History—16th century

Tenochtitlan, 1524 K. Wiles *History Today* v66 no10 p22 O 2016

Mexico City Policy (U.S.)

MERCY DENIED S. JONES *Ms.* v27 no3 p26 Fall 2017

SIN OF OMISSION J. FILIPOVIC color *Foreign Policy* no223 p50 Mr/Ap 2017

Mexico—Boundaries—United States

Another Border Clash for Trump L. Etter, A. Navarro et al color *Bloomberg Businessweek* no4507 p22 Ja 16 2017

Trump's Priorities *New York Times Upfront* v149 no9 p9 F 20 2017

Mexico—Commerce—United States

Another Border Clash for Trump L. Etter, A. Navarro et al color *Bloomberg Businessweek* no4507 p22 Ja 16 2017

Mexico—Description & travel

BAJA ON FIRE S. Schneider color *Sunset* v239 no4 p70 O 2017

BE MORE METICULOUS A. JENKINS *Sea Magazine* v109 no1 p24 Ja 2017

HOST FOR THE HOLIDAYS P. RAINS *Sea Magazine* v108 no12 p16 D 2016

OAXACA P. Guzmán bw color *Conde Nast Traveler* v52 no8 p84 S 2017

PICK YOUR MEXICO PARADISE C. Ciarmello, E. Ehmsen et al color *Sunset* v237 no5 p29 N 2016

RENÉ REDZEPI'S MEXICO J. Gordinier color *Esquire* p28 My 2017

TRAVEL Mexico color *Sports Illustrated* v126 no6 p82 F 20 2017

UP IN THE AIR C. Pfeuffer color *Sunset* v238 no1 p28 Ja 2017

Mexico—Economic conditions

North America img *New York Times Upfront* v149 no6 p32 D 12 2016

Mexico—Economic conditions—21st century

Trump Hurts the Peso. That Helps Mexicans I. Cota color graph *Bloomberg Businessweek* no4494 p20 O 10 2016

Mexico—Economic conditions—1994-

Why Mexico's Economy Doesn't Depend on the Next U.S. President A. Ruelas-Gossi *Harvard Business Review Digital Articles* p2 N 9 2016

Mexico—Emigration & immigration—Government policy

A New Migration Agenda between the United States and Mexico A. Selee *Wilson Quarterly* p1 Wint 2017

Mexico—Foreign economic relations—United States

GOOD NEIGHBORS CAN MAKE GOOD FENCES K. MANGU-WARD color *Reason* v49 no1 p4 My 2017

A Wall Won't Secure the U.S.-Mexico Border, but Economic Policy Could D. McAdams *Harvard Business Review Digital Articles* p2 F 14 2017

Mexico—Foreign relations—United States

Bad neighbor policy? Mexico's President Peña Nieto struggles to respond to Trump administration Hootsen color *America* v216 no8 p16 Ap 17 2017

BOUNDARY ISSUES J. L. ANDERSON cartoon color *New Yorker* v93 no31 p24 O 9 2017

EDITOR'S NOTE J. WORSHAM *Prologue* v48 no4 p1 Wint 2016

Examining the Mexican-American Book Connection L. Ahuile color *Publishers Weekly* v264 no32 p16 Ag 7 2017

Keep Out! How the U.S. Is Militarizing Mexico's Southern Border J. Abbott color *Progressive* v81 no7 p40 O/N 2017

Over the Wall R. CONNIFF *Progressive* v81 no7 p5 O/N 2017

The Scotosis in the U.S.-Mexico Relationship S. Aguayo *Wilson Quarterly* p3 Spr 2017

U.S.-Mexico Energy and Climate Collaboration D. Wood *Wilson Quarterly* p1 Wint 2017

Mexico—History—21st century

In Mexico, Pricier Gas Lures the Gangs N. Cattan and E. Martin color *Bloomberg Businessweek* no4507 p16 Ja 16 2017

Mexico—Maps

THE URBAN PILEUP S. TRUBETSKOY *Texas Monthly* v45 no5 p46 My 2017

Mexico—Politics & government—2000-

In Mexico, Pricier Gas Lures the Gangs N. Cattan and E. Martin color *Bloomberg Businessweek* no4507 p16 Ja 16 2017

Who Gets to Drill Here? A. Williams color *Bloomberg Businessweek* no4517 p15 Ap 3 2017

Mexico—Relations—United States

A Bipartisan Wall C. DEATON *Weekly Standard* v22 no19 p15 Ja 23 2017

WHAT ARE THEY AFRAID OF? S. Marcos *Lapham's Quarterly* v10 no3 p179 Summ 2017

Meyer, Bill

Matters of Experience color *Downbeat* v84 no1 p77 Ja 2017

Mazzarella's Instrumental Voice Evolves color *Downbeat* v84 no8 p19 Ag 2017

Not Two color *Downbeat* v84 no7 p63 Jl 2017

Unplugged color *Downbeat* v84 no6 p72 Je 2017

William Parker: A Sonic Trisection bw *Downbeat* v84 no9 p64 S 2017

Meyer, Bunny

The New Beauty Pioneers color *Glamour* v115 no4 p110 Ap 2017

Meyer, Carson

CARSON MEYER K. SMITH color *Vanity Fair* v59 no4 p101 Mr 2017

Meyer, Christian

Mismatch repair deficiency predicts response of solid tumors to PD-1 blockade chart graph *Science* v357 no6349 p409 Jl 28

2017

Meyer, Claus

CLAUS MEYER bw color *Bloomberg Businessweek* no4510 p64 F 6 2017

Meyer, Danny

Danny MEYER M. Hainey color *Esquire* p74 Je/Jl 2017

Salted-Caraway-Rye-With-Strawberry-Cheesecake Ice Cream img *New York* v50 no10 p77 My 15 2017

Meyer, Danny—Interviews

Q&A: DANNY MEYER A. Lappé *Nation* v305 no11 p5 O 30 2017

Meyer, Deon—Interviews

The Death of One Man Is a Tragedy L. PICKER color *Publishers Weekly* v264 no29 p196 Jl 17 2017

Meyer, Ellen

Operations. Recreational Water Disinfection: Avoiding disease outbreaks *Parks & Recreation* v52 no6 p46 Je 2017

Meyer, Erin

BEING THE BOSS IN BRUSSELS, BOSTON, AND BEIJING: IF YOU WANT TO SUCCEED, YOU'LL NEED TO ADAPT color graph il img *Harvard Business Review* v95 no4 p70 Jl/Ag 2017

Tailor Your Presentation to Fit the Culture *Harvard Business Review Digital Articles* p2 O 29 2014

What Makes a Boss Too Formal? *Harvard Business Review Digital Articles* p2 Ja 6 2015

Meyer, Esther da Costa, 1947-

Pierre Chareau: Modern Architecture and Design color *Publishers Weekly* v263 no48 p57 N 28 2016

Meyer, G. J.

The World Remade: America in World War I *Publishers Weekly* v264 no1 p50 Ja 2 2017

MEYER, GRAHAM

54 GREAT THINGS TO DO THIS MONTH color *Chicago* v66 no1 p117 Ja 2017

58 GREAT THINGS TO DO THIS MONTH color *Chicago* v66 no2 p101 F 2017

63 GREAT THINGS TO DO THIS MONTH color *Chicago* v66 no8 p105 Ag 2017

65 GREAT THINGS TO DO THIS MONTH color *Chicago* v65 no11 p115 N 2016

66 GREAT THINGS TO DO THIS MONTH color *Chicago* v66 no9 p139 S 2017

67 GREAT THINGS TO DO THIS MONTH color *Chicago* v66 no3 p129 Mr 2017

68 GREAT THINGS TO DO THIS MONTH color *Chicago* v66 no5 p119 My 2017

GO: 69 GREAT THINGS TO DO THIS MONTH color *Chicago* v66 no11 p103 N 2017

GO bw color *Chicago* v66 no10 p105 O 2017

GO color *Chicago* v65 no12 p119 D 2016

GO color *Chicago* v66 no4 p113 Ap 2017

MUSICAL MARATHON cartoon *Chicago* v66 no3 p54 Mr 2017

Meyer, Henry

Does Putin Still Favor His Sidekick? color graph *Bloomberg Businessweek* no4520 p28 My 1 2017

The Fight for Syria's Future Has Only Begun map *Bloomberg Businessweek* no4525 p28 Je 5 2017

From Russia, With Debt color *Bloomberg Businessweek* no4517 p42 Ap 3 2017

FROM RUSSIA WITH LATTES color *Bloomberg Businessweek* no4534 p42 Ag 14 2017

The Game Putin Plays color *Bloomberg Businessweek* no4506 p6 Ja 9 2017

The Kremlin's New Disinformation Machine *Bloomberg Businessweek* no4512 p27 F 20 2017

Moscow Confidential: Private Jets for Dogs bw color *Bloomberg Businessweek* no4498 p24 N 7 2016

A Putin Fixer Claims Success With Turkey color *Bloomberg Businessweek* no4512 p15 F 20 2017

Putin Isn't So Sure Trump's a Pal color *Bloomberg Businessweek* no4509 p13 Ja 30 2017

Russia's Deadly Mideast Game *Bloomberg Businessweek* no4505 p16 D 26 2016

The Trouble Brewing In Putin's Heartland color graph *Bloomberg Businessweek* no4538 p36 S 18 2017

Will Beijing Also Have A Friend at State? bw *Bloomberg Businessweek* no4504 p26 D 19 2016

MEYER, HERBERT E.

How Intelligence Works (When It Does) *USA Today Magazine* v145 no2864 p10 My 2017

Meyer, Holly

People *Christian Century* v134 no17 p19 Ag 16 2017

Meyer, Jennifer Forsberg

Change It Up! color *Horse & Rider* v56 no9 p55 S 2017

Create a Confident Mindset [Cover story] color *Horse & Rider* v56 no3 p32 Mr 2017

Curing a Stumbler color *Horse & Rider* v56 no4 p64 Ap 2017

Feel-Good Work for your Senior Horse [Cover story] color *Horse & Rider* v56 no2 p34 F 2017

Get Moving! color *Horse & Rider* v56 no11 p48 N 2017

Loping 'Out Loud' bw color *Horse & Rider* v56 no7 p54 Jl 2017

Master Log (& Other) Obstacles color *Horse & Rider* v56 no11 p96 N 2017

'Now' Exercise Makes Safety a Habit [Cover story] color *Horse & Rider* v56 no5 p42 My 2017

REFORMING A Jigger [Cover story] color *Horse & Rider* v56 no1 p52 Ja 2017

'Stop and Drop' for Ultimate Control color *Horse & Rider* v55 no11 p36 N 2016

THOROUGHLY, MODERN, COWGIRL color *Horse & Rider* v56 no7 p60 Jl 2017

Why Kids Should Ride color *Horse & Rider* v56 no9 p62 S 2017

Yes—You Can Develop Feel [Cover story] color *Horse & Rider* v56 no1 p34 Ja 2017

Meyer, John

A Veteran's Voice: John Meyer's Odyssey in service and on stage H. Sherman *Stage Directions* v30 no6 p32 Je 2017

Meyer, Julien

THE whistled WORD color graph map *Scientific American* v316 no2 p60 F 2017

Meyer, Justin R.

Ecological speciation of bacteriophage lambda in allopatry and sympatry bibl graph *Science* v354 no6317 p1301 D 9 2016

Meyer, Kelsey

How We Rewrote Our Company's Mental Health Policy *Harvard Business Review Digital Articles* p2 Jl 11 2016

Meyer, M. C.

Permanent human occupation of the central Tibetan Plateau in the early Holocene bibl bw color diag *Science* v355 no6320 p1 Ja 6 2017

Meyer, Matthias

Neandertal and Denisovan DNA from Pleistocene sediments bw color *Science* v356 no6338 p605 My 12 2017

Meyer, Melissa

Heartless J. Goodman color *Entertainment Weekly* no1440 p62 N 18 2016

Meyer, Nicole

How 'Golden Visas' Work T. John color *Time* v189 no19 p10 My 22 2017

Meyer, Pablo

Predicting human olfactory perception from chemical features of odor molecules bibl diag graph *Science* v355 no6327 p820 F 24 2017

Meyer, Pamela

What to Do If You Catch Your Boss in a Lie *Harvard Business Review Digital Articles* p2 Mr 28 2017

Meyer, Philip—Interviews

Philipp Meyer *New York Times Book Review* p8 Ap 2 2017

MEYER, ROBINSON

A Year on Ice bw color map *Atlantic* v320 no3 p28 O 2017

Meyer, Stephenie, 1973-

STEPHENIE MEYER color *Entertainment Weekly* no1439 p61 N 11 2016

Meyer, Travis

Reconfiguration of DNA molecular arrays driven by information relay diag *Science* v357 no6349 p371 Jl 28 2017

Meyer, Will

An Occupy Protester's Emancipation Proclamation cartoon color *Progressive* v81 no10 p39 N 2016

'Tech Is a New Place to Have an Old Battle' color *Progressive* p30 D 2016/Ja 2017

Meyering, Emma E.
Reactivation of latent working memories with transcranial magnetic stimulation bibl graph *Science* v354 no6316 p1136 D 2 2016

Meyerowitz Stories, The (Film)
ACROSS THE AGES A. LANE color *New Yorker* v93 no33 p98 O 23 2017

Meyers, Jeffrey
His Bleak Materials bw *Commonweal* v144 no12 p18 Jl 7 2017
Hurt into Literature bw *Commonweal* v144 no6 p27 Mr 24 2017

MEYERS, NATHAN
THE PROXIMITY TAPES bw color *Surfer* v58 no3 p56 Je 2017

Meyers, Seth, 1973-
The Intersection color *Runner's World* v52 no4 p50 My 2017
LADIES' NIGHT WITH SETH MEYERS F. Penn color *InStyle* v24 no6 p150 Je 2017

Meyers, Susie
GOLF Magazine's Top 100 Teachers in America D. DeNunzio color *Golf Magazine* v59 no3 p56 Mr 2017

Meyers, William
The Last Dalai Lama D. ZIGMOND color *Tricycle: The Buddhist Review* v27 no1 p94 Fall 2017

Meyerson, Collier
Black Lives Matter color *Glamour* v114 no12 p218 D 2016
Covering a country where race is everywhere bw *Columbia Journalism Review* v56 no2 p31 Fall 2017

Meyers-Shyer, Hallie, 1987-
HOME AGAIN R. Kinane color *Entertainment Weekly* no1478 / 1479 p44 Ag 18-25 2017

Meyersson, Erik
Turkey and the Economics of Coups *Harvard Business Review Digital Articles* p2 Jl 22 2016

Meyersson, Erik—Interviews
Industrial Espionage Is More Effective Than R&D C. Nickisch il img *Harvard Business Review* v94 no11 p30 N 2016

Meyer zu Heringdorf, F.-J.
Revealing the subfemtosecond dynamics of orbital angular momentum in nanoplasmonic vortices bibl diag *Science* v355 no6330 p1187 Mr 17 2017

Meyhofer, Edgar
Quantized thermal transport in single-atom junctions bibl diag graph *Science* v355 no6330 p1192 Mr 17 2017

Meyler, Dennis
Caring for Aging Loved Ones color *Consumer Reports* v82 no12 p6 D 2017

Meyohas, Sarah
Bazaar GARDENS Glenda color *Harper's Bazaar* no3653 p132 My 2017

Meyohas, Sarah—Exhibitions
SARAH MEYOHAS color *Harper's Bazaar* no3653 p140 My 2017

Meystre, Pierre
Cavity Optomechanics Nano- and Micromechanical Resonators Interacting with Light/Quantum Optomechanics *Physics Today* v70 no2 p58 F 2017

Meze Headphones (Company)
This One Goes to 99 S. Guttenberg and C. Crowley color *Sound & Vision* v81 no9 p28 N 2016

Mezer, Aviv
Microstructural proliferation in human cortex is coupled with the development of face processing bibl graph *Science* v355 no6320 p1 Ja 6 2017

Mezouar, M.
Synthesis of FeH5: A layered structure with atomic hydrogen slabs diag graph *Science* v357 no6349 p382 Jl 28 2017

Mezrich, Ben
Woolly: The True Story of the Quest to Revive One of History's Most Iconic Extinct Creatures A. Gawrylewski color *Scientific American* v317 no2 p80 Ag 2017

Mezue, Bryan
The Type of Innovation That Builds Nations *Harvard Business Review Digital Articles* p2 Ja 7 2015

Mezzo-sopranos
ALL NATURAL W. R. BRAUN and F. FOX *Opera News* v81 no7 p22 Ja 2017
Avery Amereau M. Rich color *Current Biography* v78 no8 p3 Ag

2017
FREDERICA VON STADE L. T. Guinther *Opera News* v81 no10 p22 Ap 2017
Sarah Mesko B. KELLOW *Opera News* v81 no5 p12 N 2016

MGK, 1990-
THE WOUNDED HEART OF MACHINE GUN KELLY B. HIATT color *Rolling Stone* no1290 p40 Je 29 2017

MGMT (Performer)
Panoramic View M. Trammell *New Yorker* v93 no22 p11 Jl 31 2017

MHP (Company)
SPRING SWAG color *Amazing Wellness* v8 no2 p92 Spr 2016

Mi, X.
Strong coupling of a single electron in silicon to a microwave photon bibl graph *Science* v355 no6321 p1 Ja 13 2017

Miami (Fla.)
THE PERFECT GIRLS' GETAWAY color *Good Housekeeping* v263 no5 p202 N 2016

Miami (Fla.)—Description & travel
the buzz color *InStyle* v24 no9 p358 S 2017
Secrets of South Florida S. Granada and V. F. Luesse color map *Southern Living* v52 no1 p45 Ja 2017

Miami Beach (Fla.)
Artful Living M. SLENSKE color *Architectural Digest* v74 no7 p88 Jl 2017

Miami Dolphins (Football team)
2 Miami Dolphins color *Sports Illustrated* v127 no7 p66 S 4 2017
CSI: MIAMI M. Rosenberg and J. Feldman color *Sports Illustrated* v126 no11 p52 Ap 17-24 2017

Miami Heat (Basketball team)
12 Heat R. Mahoney, B. Golliver et al color *Sports Illustrated* v125 no14 p88 O 24-31 2016
7 HEAT color *Sports Illustrated* v127 no12 p64 O 16 2017

Miami Herald (Newspaper)
MY HOMETOWN PAPER: Dexter Filkins D. Filkins color *Columbia Journalism Review* v56 no1 p41 Spr 2017

Miami Marlins (Baseball team)
4 MARLINS color *Sports Illustrated* v126 no9 p98 Mr 27 2017
Who's the Boss? M. Rosenberg color *Sports Illustrated* v126 no13 p68 My 8 2017

Miami University (Oxford, Ohio)
The Campus Sex-Crime Tribunals Are Losing: How the courts are intervening to block some of the most unjust punishments of our time K. C. Johnson *Commentary* v144 no3 p20 O 2017

Mian Biz
Site-specific phosphorylation of tau inhibits amyloid-β toxicity in Alzheimer's mice bibl graph *Science* v354 no6314 p904 N 18 2016

Miani, Guglielmo—Interviews
Guglielmo Miani J. Roth color *Esquire* p134 2017 BigBlackBook

Miata automobile
2016 MAZDA MX-5 MIATA CLUB D. Pund color graph *Car & Driver* v63 no4 p84 O 2017
Miata, People S. SMITH cartoon *Road & Track* v68 no7 p26 Mr/ Ap 2017

Miata automobile—Evaluation
RAISE THE ROOF color *Esquire* p18 Ap 2017

Micachu, 1987-
'BAROK MAIN' R. BRADLEY color *New York Times Magazine* p36 Mr 12 2017

Micallef, Ken
ArkivMusic Launches ArkivJazz color *Downbeat* v84 no10 p19 O 2017
Copeland Taps Cosmic Vibes for Aardvarks' Disc color *Downbeat* v84 no8 p16 Ag 2017
CRAIG TABORN: 'GO INSIDE THE SOUND' [Cover story] color *Downbeat* v84 no3 p26 Mr 2017
CYNTHIA HILTS color *Downbeat* v84 no5 p26 My 2017
Cyrille's Brilliant Gamesmanship color *Downbeat* v84 no1 p17 Ja 2017
Exploring Musical Branches color *Downbeat* v84 no10 p31 O 2017
FOSTERING WIDESPREAD COLLABORATION bw color *Downbeat* v84 no9 p48 S 2017
Giordano's Future in the Past color *Downbeat* v83 no11 p20 N 2016

HUNTERTONES color *Downbeat* v83 no12 p22 D 2016

THE INSIDE STORIES OF CLASSIC JAZZ RECORDINGS color *Downbeat* v84 no2 p95 F 2017

JEN SHYU: Perpetually Compelling color *Downbeat* v84 no8 p53 Ag 2017

Matsuda Embraces Challenge color *Downbeat* v84 no8 p15 Ag 2017

Monk & Coltrane Reissue Unites Architects of Jazz bw *Downbeat* v84 no10 p24 O 2017

NATALIE CRESSMAN & MIKE BONO color *Downbeat* v84 no1 p24 Ja 2017

NATE SMITH color *Downbeat* v84 no5 p24 My 2017

Nettwerk, Justin Time Records Resurrect Rising Sun bw *Downbeat* v83 no12 p16 D 2016

NOAH PREMINGER: Distinctive Character color *Downbeat* v84 no8 p50 Ag 2017

Recalling Generations color *Downbeat* v84 no6 p31 Je 2017

Ron Rambach's Music Matters Closes Shop color *Downbeat* v84 no4 p17 Ap 2017

Mice (Computers)—Evaluation

WORKS FOR US! M. Santos color *Working Mother* p19 F/Mr 2017

Mice as laboratory animals

Bones tell other organs a thing or two C. MARTIN chart color *Science News* v191 no13 p12 Jl 8 2017

Boom Box A. Hadhazy *Natural History* v125 no1 p8 D 2016/Ja 2017

Multicluster Pcdh diversity is required for mouse olfactory neural circuit assembly G. Mountoufaris, W. V. Chen et al diag *Science* v356 no6336 p411 Ap 28 2017

Parkinson's may begin in the gut L. SANDERS color *Science News* v190 no12 p12 D 10 2016

Scratching is catching in mice S. MILIUS *Science News* v191 no7 p8 Ap 15 2017

Mice as laboratory animals—Behavior

Chemogenetics revealed: DREADD occupancy and activation via converted clozapine J. L. Gomez, J. Bonaventura et al graph *Science* v357 no6350 p503 Ag 4 2017

Mice—Behavior

Mouse with a milkshake: Behavioral windows into brain function C. Smith color *Science* v354 no6312 p638 N 4 2016

Mice—Behavior—Research

Two brain circuits help mice hunt L. HAMERS *Science News* v191 no3 p8 F 18 2017

Michael, Alicia K.

Structural basis of the day-night transition in a bacterial circadian clock bibl diag *Science* v355 no6330 p1174 Mr 17 2017

Michael, David J.

What Hipsters and Monks Share color *America* v217 no2 p40 Jl 24 2017

Michael, Gene, 1938-2017

GENE MICHAEL (1938-2017) J. Fuchs and T. Keith color *Sports Illustrated* v127 no8 p22 S 18 2017

Michael, George, 1963-2016

1963 - 2016 GEORGE MICHAEL N. Feeney color *Entertainment Weekly* no1448 p28 Ja 13 2017

The Genius of George Michael R. SHEFFIELD bw *Rolling Stone* no1280 p16 F 9 2017

George Michael M. Johnston color *Time* v189 no3 p11 Ja 16 2017

AN ICON REMEMBERED J. Goodman and K. O'Donnell color *Entertainment Weekly* no1448 p33 Ja 13 2017

In the Future, Everyone Will Be Dead for 15 Minutes C. Rosen color *Commentary* v143 no2 p1 F 2017

SONGS OF A LIFETIME L. Greenblatt color *Entertainment Weekly* no1448 p31 Ja 13 2017

Michael, Joseph

FLEETING GRACE D. Grossman color *Popular Photography* v81 no2 p32 Mr/Ap 2017

Michael, Kevin—Interviews

Driving the Boat *Boating World* v38 no2 p16 F 2017

Michael, Lucas

Nine Cool Girls img *New York* v50 no10 p60 My 15 2017

Michael, Michele

Into the Woods color *Good Housekeeping* v265 no3 p54 S 2017

Michael Che Matters (Film)

STREAMING A. D'ARMINIO *TV Guide* v64 no48 p42 N 21

2016

Michael Clayton (Film)

The Bonfire of Humanity J. PARKER color *Atlantic* v320 no4 p32 N 2017

Michael Kors (USA) Inc.

Michael Kors Collection messenger bag V. SMITH color *Vogue* v207 no3 p512 Mr 2017

Michael Maltzan Architecture Inc.

Speaking Volumes S. AMELAR *Architectural Record* v205 no10 p96 O 2017

Michael Werner Gallery (Company)

OHNE ANDERE GESELLSCHAFT (DEVOID OF ANOTHER PARTY) color *Art in America* v105 no1 p7 Ja 2017

Michael Bolton's Big, Sexy Valentine's Day Special (TV program)

Michael Bolton's Funny Valentine R. Rahman color *Entertainment Weekly* no1453 p52 F 17 2017

Michael Hanemann, W.

Putting a value on injuries to natural assets: The BP oil spill chart *Science* v356 no6335 p253 Ap 21 2017

Michaelides, Angelos

Active sites in heterogeneous ice nucleation—the example of K-rich feldspars bibl bw diag *Science* v355 no6323 p367 Ja 27 2017

Michaelides, Michael

Chemogenetics revealed: DREADD occupancy and activation via converted clozapine graph *Science* v357 no6350 p503 Ag 4 2017

Michaels, David

The dishonest HONEST Act color *Science* v356 no6342 p989 Je 9 2017

Michaels, Jillian—Interviews

JILLIAN MICHAELS [Cover story] M. C. HAREL color *Redbook* p88 F 2017

Michaels, Jim

THE POETRY OF JIM MICHAELS R. LANE bw *Forbes* v200 no3 p60 S 28 2017

Michaels, Julia

JULIA MICHAELS N. Feeney color *Entertainment Weekly* no1446/1447 p74 D 2016/Ja 2017

Star Time for Julia Michaels At 23, she's written smashes for Bieber and Britney. Now she's ready for some of her own J. LEVY color *Rolling Stone* no1294 p16 Ag 24 2017

Michaels, Lori J.

When I Was a Horse-Crazy Kid, I... color *Horse & Rider* v56 no2 p72 F 2017

Michaels, Samantha

CLEAN SLATE CLUB color *Mother Jones* v42 no6 p11 N/D 2017

IF THE SUIT FITS color *Mother Jones* v42 no3 p5 My/Je 2017

INSOMNIAC'S LITTLE HELPER *Mother Jones* v42 no6 p70 N/D 2017

LIFE AFTER LIFE color *Mother Jones* v42 no4 p10 Jl/Ag 2017

Michal, Grid

Are You Ready? *Boating World* v38 no4 p18 Ap 2017

Batteries and Boom *Boating World* v37 no9 p28 N/D 2016

The Difference Matters *Boating World* v38 no2 p30 F 2017

Directionally Challenged *Boating World* v38 no6 p45 Je 2017

A Draining Experience *Boating World* v38 no1 p36 Ja 2017

Forever Oil *Boating World* v38 no3 p47 Mr 2017

No Good Deed... color *Boating World* v38 no7 p45 Jl 2017

Not Sinking In *Boating World* v38 no8 p47 S/O 2017

Oy of the Hurricane *Boating World* v38 no4 p46 Ap 2017

POWER PROGRESSION *Boating World* v38 no2 p48 F 2017

Q+A *Boating World* v37 no9 p24 N/D 2016

Q+A *Boating World* v38 no5 p26 My 2017

Q+A *Boating World* v38 no8 p24 S/O 2017

STAY SAFE FROM SILENT DANGER *Sea Magazine* v108 no12 p24 D 2016

Think First *Boating World* v38 no6 p22 Je 2017

Ticket to Ride *Boating World* v38 no5 p46 My 2017

Michal, S.

Observation of a large-scale anisotropy in the arrival directions of cosmic rays above 8 × 1018 eV *Science* v357 no6357 p1266 S 22 2017

Michalak, A. M.

Eutrophication will increase during the 21st century as a result of precipitation changes map *Science* v357 no6349 p405 Jl 28 2017

Michalopoulos, James

AMERICAN PLACES *American Scholar* v86 no4 p128 Aut 2017

MICHAUD, DEBBIE

MORE THAN MURALS *Atlanta* v57 no5 p28 S 2017

Next Gen Arts *Atlanta* v57 no6 p73 O 2017

Michaud, Monia

Potential role of intratumor bacteria in mediating tumor resistance to the chemotherapeutic drug gemcitabine diag *Science* v357 no6356 p1156 S 15 2017

Michaud, Robert

Father (and Son) Knows Best D. FISHER color *Forbes* v199 no5 p62 My 16 2017

Micheaux, Oscar, 1884-1951

Art and Artifact: Pioneers of African-American Cinema and Its Contemporary Relevance R. Gates *Film Quarterly* v70 no2 p88 Wint 2016

Micheel, Shaun

An Inconvenient Truth A. Shipnuck and J. Marksbury color *Golf Magazine* v59 no11 p24 N 2017

Michel, Anna

Girls Just Wanna Be Engineers L. Lippsett *Oceanus* v52 no2 p29 Spr 2017

MICHEL, CHRISTOPHER

Finding Grace cartoon color *Runner's World* v52 no6 p52 Jl 2017

Michel, Dan

ACTIVE STYLE AWARDS bw color *Men's Health* v32 no7 p(Sp)17 S 2017

ALL YOU NEED FOR SPRING cartoon color *Men's Health* v32 no3 p47 Ap 2017

Dress Down, Look Sharp cartoon color *Men's Health* v32 no9 p75 N 2017

FACES OF INNOVATION color *Men's Health* v32 no7 p(Sp)14 S 2017

How to Smell Like a Wild Man color *Men's Health* v32 no9 p78 N 2017

Look Good Half Naked color *Men's Health* v32 no6 p80 Ag 2017

Look Your Best color *Men's Health* v32 no5 p99 Je 2017

Power Tools color *Men's Health* v32 no2 p(Sp)26 Mr 2017

Save $500 on a Single Outfit bw color *Men's Health* v31 no10 p74 D 2016

SMALL BATCH, HIGH YIELD color *Men's Health* v32 no2 p(Sp)14 Mr 2017

The Sneaker Selector cartoon color *Men's Health* v32 no4 p60 My 2017

You: Weatherproofed! color *Men's Health* v32 no6 p82 Ag 2017

Michel, François

Crystal structures of a group II intron lariat primed for reverse splicing color diag *Science* v354 no6316 paaf9258-1 D 2 2016

Michel, Jen Pollock

God Is a Homemaker A. J. SWOBODA bw color *Christianity Today* v61 no4 p62 My 2017

Michel, John

A Military Leader's Approach to Dealing with Complexity *Harvard Business Review Digital Articles* p2 O 23 2014

Michel, Stefan

8 Reasons Companies Don't Capture More Value *Harvard Business Review Digital Articles* p2 Ap 8 2015

Let Your Customers Segment Themselves by What They're Willing to Pay *Harvard Business Review Digital Articles* p2 Mr 11 2015

Michel, Susan

A LEGACY WORTH WORKING FOR R. Derousseau color *Fortune* v75 no1 p36 Ja 1 2017

Michel, Thomas

Turkey's Witch Hunt color *Commonweal* v143 no18 p10 N 11 2016

Michele, Alessandro

GUCCI'S MAIN MAN Z. BARON color *GQ: Gentlemen's Quarterly* v86 no12 p216 D 2016

GUCCI'S URBAN GARDEN B. McKeon color *Harper's Bazaar* no3655 p124 Ag 2017

JARED LETO TELLS ALL R. Oltuski color *Harper's Bazaar* no3648 p192 N 2016

Wild Things color *Architectural Digest* v74 no9 p60 S 2017

Michele, Lea, 1986-

SERENE QUEEN [Cover story] J. Bober color *InStyle* p4 Home & Design 2016

Micheletti, M. I.

Observation of a large-scale anisotropy in the arrival directions of cosmic rays above 8 × 1018 eV *Science* v357 no6357 p1266 S 22 2017

Micheli, Fiorenza

Committing to socially responsible seafood color *Science* v356 no6341 p912 Je 1 2017

The Resilience of Marine Ecosystems to Climatic Disturbances *BioScience* v67 no3 p208 Mr 2017

Micheli, Jason

Cancer Is Funny: Keeping Faith in Stage-Serious Chemo D. A. Thompson color *Christian Century* v134 no10 p34 My 10 2017

Michelle Lawing, A.

Merging paleobiology with conservation biology to guide the future of terrestrial ecosystems color *Science* v355 no6325 p594 F 10 2017

Michelson, Annette

Scene Missing V. LUCCA color *Film Comment* v53 no3 p78 My/Je 2017

Michelson, Megan

CHICKEN WINGS color *Skiing* p38 D 2016

Claire Smallwood is a Champion for Women color *Powder* v46 no2 p26 O 2017

Resilience bw color *Powder* p54 S 2017

RIP: TELEMARK H. Ludwig color *Powder* v45 no6 p40 F 2017

SHELTERED bw color *Powder* v45 no4 p102 D 2016

Michelson, Richard

The Language of Angels: A Story About the Reinvention of Hebrew *Publishers Weekly* v263 no48 p70 N 28 2016

Michelson, Robert

The Circle of Life: Spawning Behaviors of Smallmouth Bass *New York State Conservationist* v71 no6 p22 Je 2017

Michie, Allen

Chords & Discords color *Downbeat* v84 no4 p10 Ap 2017

Chords & Discords color *Downbeat* v84 no9 p10 S 2017

MICHIE BRUCKNER, JULIA

One More Thing color *Discover* v38 no5 p22 Je 2017

Michigan

Michigan E. Spitznagel *New York Times Magazine* p24 Ap 23 2017

Michigan, Lake

OPEN SEASON E. Graves *Martha Stewart Living* p14 Jl/Ag 2017

Michigan. Court of Appeals

PubPeer wins comments battle *Science* v354 no6318 p1357 D 16 2016

Michigan Opera Theatre (Company)

Community Organizer *Opera News* v81 no9 p14 Mr 2017

Michigan State University

Getting Real with Detroit's Myya D. Jones S. E. Jamison color *Ebony* v72 no8 p24 Je 2017

Michigan—Description & travel

MICHIGAN C. Mills color map *Canadian Geographic* v135 no6 p28 D 2015

Test the Waters R. SAYERS map *Backpacker* p23 Ag 2017

Water's Edge: Pictured Rocks National Lakeshore, Michigan E. KWAK-HEFFERAN color *Backpacker* p12 S 2017

Michihiro Sugahara

A three-dimensional movie of structural changes in bacteriorhodopsin bibl diag graph *Science* v354 no6319 p1552 D 23 2016

Michio Murata

A three-dimensional movie of structural changes in bacteriorhodopsin bibl diag graph *Science* v354 no6319 p1552 D 23 2016

Michna-Bales, Jeanine

Through Darkness to Light T. Brorby color *Orion Magazine* v36 no2 p62 Mr/Ap 2017

Michôd, David, 1967-

Brad Pitt Takes on the Runaway General In War Machine S. Zacharek color *Time* v189 no21 p58 Je 5 2017

WAR MACHINE T. Stack color *Entertainment Weekly* no1463/1464 p34 Ap/My 2017

Mick, Sara

You Never Forget Your First Time diag il *Backpacker* v45 no2

Microbreweries
99 Cans Of Beer On the Wall J. M. VERIVE *Los Angeles Magazine* p48 Ja 2017
The Founder of Dogfish Head on Flouting a 500- Year-Old Beer Law S. Calagione *Harvard Business Review Digital Articles* p2 My 5 2016
The Great BEER MIGRATION T. PILKINGTON *Virginia Living* v15 no2 p62 F 2017
The NATION of FLYING DOG A. WHITING *Washingtonian Magazine* v52 no4 p68 Ja 2017

Microcephaly
Concern grows over Zika birth defects M. ROSEN color diag *Science News* v190 no9 p14 O 29 2016
Microcephaly rises in Colombia M. Rosen graph *Science News* v191 no1 p17 Ja 21 2017
Neurodevelopmental protein Musashi-1 interacts with the Zika genome and promotes viral replication P. L. Chavali, L. Stojic et al diag *Science* v357 no6346 p83 Jl 7 2017
RESEARCH color *Science* v357 no6346 p43 Jl 7 2017
ZIKA M. Quinn *Governing* v30 no4 p33 Ja 2017

Microcephaly—Genetic aspects
Zika mutation linked to microcephaly T. H. SAEY color *Science News* v192 no7 p9 O 28 2017

Microclusters
See also
Water clusters
Spying on the neighbors' pool S. S. Xantheas bibl diag *Science* v354 no6316 p1101 D 2 2016

Microcomputer workstations (Computers)
i did it! K. SELZER color *Better Homes & Gardens* v95 no10 p82 O 2017

Microcomputer workstations (Computers)—Evaluation
Wish list: What I'd like to see in a new iMac R. LOYOLA color *Macworld - Digital Edition* v34 no6 p7 Je 2017

Microeconomics
MONEY, CREDIT, AND SECURITY MARKETS *Economic Indicators* p26 Mr 2017

Microfabrica Inc.
Metal Devices, in Miniature M. Belfiore bw *Scientific American* v316 no3 p16 Mr 2017

Microfabrication—Methodology
Fabrication of fillable microparticles and other complex 3D microstructures K. J. Mchugh, T. D. Nguyen et al color diag *Science* v357 no6356 p1138 S 15 2017

Microfibrils
Stretching and Loosening K. Moore color *Natural History* v125 no7 p7 Jl/Ag 2017

Microfinance
Making Microfinance More Effective D. Karlan, R. Mann et al *Harvard Business Review Digital Articles* p2 O 5 2016
Nearly 14,000 USDA Microloans Issued Between 2013 and 2015 S. Tulman *Amber Waves: The Economics of Food, Farming, Natural Resources, & Rural America* p12 Mr 2017
The Unique Value of Crowdfunding Is Not Money—It's Community E. Mollick *Harvard Business Review Digital Articles* p2 Ap 21 2016

Microfluidics
How boundaries shape chemical delivery in microfluidics M. Aminian, F. Bernardi et al bibl diag graph *Science* v354 no6317 p1252 D 9 2016

Microglia
Deciphering microglial diversity in Alzheimer's disease G. C. Brown and P. H. St George-Hyslop color *Science* v356 no6343 p1123 Je 16 2017
An environment-dependent transcriptional network specifies human microglia identity D. Gosselin, D. Skola et al color *Science* v356 no6344 p1248 Je 23 2017

Microirrigation—Equipment & supplies
THE FRONT-YARD FIX J. Silver color *Sunset* v238 no4 p42 Ap 2017
PMDI SUCCESS T. Gaines *Successful Farming* v115 no4 p50 Mr 2017

Microlensing (Astrophysics)
Distant galaxy setting star-formation record color *Astronomy* v45 no4 p16 Ap 2017
Hubble uses galactic lens to study universe's first stars D. Clery

color *Science* v354 no6316 p1087 D 2 2016

Micronations
'TO LIVE AND LET LIVE' B. DOHERTY color map *Reason* v49 no2 p36 Je 2017

Microorganism identification
new products: microbiome color *Science* v356 no6339 p764 My 19 2017

Microorganisms
See also
Marine microorganisms
Pathogenic microorganisms
Viruses
Beetle manipulates microbes to benefit young color *Science* v357 no6354 p851 S 1 2017
CAN BACTERIA Help Us Understand RELIGION? V. TARICO *Humanist* v77 no3 p16 My/Je 2017
Catching a Criminal J. KEATS color diag *Discover* v38 no6 p40 Jl/Ag 2017
Food for microbes seen on Enceladus A. YEAGER color *Science News* v191 no9 p6 My 13 2017
Gut Check S. SCHENCK cartoon *Rodale's Organic Life* v3 no1 p34 Ja 2017
How do gut microbes help herbivores? Counting the ways E. Pennisi color *Science* v355 no6322 p236 Ja 20 2017
I AM PLURAL C. CARLSON cartoon *Christianity Today* v60 no9 p60 N 2016
A microbial route from coal to gas C. U. Welte bibl color *Science* v354 no6309 p184 O 14 2016
The Subterraneans T. C. Onstott *Natural History* v125 no1 p16 D 2016/Ja 2017

Microorganisms—Behavior
high–flying microbes D. Schmale and S. Ross color *Scientific American* v316 no2 p40 F 2017
Microbial mass movements Zhu, M. Gillings et al color *Science* v357 no6356 p1099 S 15 2017

Microorganisms—Detection
high–flying microbes D. Schmale and S. Ross color *Scientific American* v316 no2 p40 F 2017

Microorganisms—Identification
Oral precision medicine: Identification of microbes from saliva by mass spectrometry Yifei Zhang, Chong Ding et al bibl *Science* v354 no6319 p60 D 23 2016

Microorganisms—Research
Tiny fossils could be oldest signs of life M. ROSEN color *Science News* v191 no6 p6 Ap 1 2017

Microorganisms—Therapeutic use
RESEARCH bw color *Science* v357 no6356 p1108 S 15 2017

Microphone
Audio Alternatives B. Reesman *Stage Directions* v30 no1 p8 Ja 2017
An Engineer's Approach to Modern Big Band Recording F. BREITBERG color *Downbeat* v84 no2 p92 F 2017
NEVER A DULL MOMENT L. Abend color *Flying* v144 no10 p74 O 2017
Scientists snoop to check on kelp R. EHRENBERG *Science News* v192 no1 p10 Ag 5 2017
Your Security Cam Is Watching You D. Pogue color *Scientific American* v317 no4 p30 O 2017

Microphone—Evaluation
Buyer's Guide J. Coakley *Stage Directions* v30 no1 p12 Ja 2017
A history of precision and perfection continues to define DPA Microphones *Stage Directions* v30 no3 p15 Mr 2017
Mojave Audio MA-50 M. Kern color *Downbeat* v84 no2 p99 F 2017
MUSICIANS' GEAR GUIDE BEST OF THE 2017 NAMM SHOW Ž. Čuntova, E. Enright et al color *Downbeat* v84 no4 p70 Ap 2017
Product Hits of AES 2016 G. Petersen *Stage Directions* v29 no12 p11 D 2016

Microprocessors—Design & construction
AMD busts Ryzen performance myths, clearing Windows 10 from blame G. M. UNG color graph *PCWorld* v35 no4 p9 Ap 2017
Dual-processor Fusion Mac makes sense D. Moren color *Macworld - Digital Edition* p125 Ap 2017

Microprocessors—Performance
Ryzen review: AMD is back [Cover story] G. M. UNG chart color

diag graph map *PCWorld* v35 no4 p49 Ap 2017

MicroRNA

Activity-dependent spatially localized miRNA maturation in neuronal dendrites S. Sambandan, G. Akbalik et al bibl graph *Science* v355 no6325 p634 F 10 2017

Loss of a mammalian circular RNA locus causes miRNA deregulation and affects brain function M. Piwecka, P. Glažar et al color *Science* v357 no6357 p1254 S 22 2017

miR-183 cluster scales mechanical pain sensitivity by regulating basal and neuropathic pain genes C. Peng, L. Li et al diag graph *Science* v356 no6343 p1168 Je 16 2017

Scaling pain threshold with microRNAs L. Cassels and Barde diag *Science* v356 no6343 p1124 Je 16 2017

MicroRNA genetics

Tudor-SN–mediated endonucleolytic decay of human cell microRNAs promotes G1/S phase transition R. A. Elbarbary, K. Miyoshi et al graph *Science* v356 no6340 p859 My 26 2017

Microscopes

MICROSCOPY without lenses: Lens-free on-chip imaging devices provide cost-effective, compact, and wide-field microscopy solutions for fieldwork and global health applications E. McLeod and A. Ozcan *Physics Today* v70 no9 p50 S 2017

A water window on surface chemistry J. Hunger and S. H. Parekh diag *Science* v357 no6353 p755 Ag 25 2017

Microscopes—Design & construction

EYES IN THE DEEP J. Fischman color diag *Scientific American* v315 no6 p80 D 2016

Microscopes—Evaluation

NEW PRODUCTS: MICROSCOPY/IMAGING color *Science* v354 no6313 p775 N 11 2016

Microscopical technique

MICROSCOPY without lenses: Lens-free on-chip imaging devices provide cost-effective, compact, and wide-field microscopy solutions for fieldwork and global health applications E. McLeod and A. Ozcan *Physics Today* v70 no9 p50 S 2017

Microscopy

See also

Electron microscopy

Biological eigenstrokes *Physics Today* v70 no3 p84 Mr 2017

First Glance Into the Gut P. SMAGLIK cartoon color *Discover* v38 no1 p63 Ja/F 2017

Flipping nanoscopy on its head J. Xiao and T. Ha bibl diag graph *Science* v355 no6325 p582 F 10 2017

Microscopy—Equipment & supplies—Evaluation

LIFE SCIENCE TECHNOLOGIES color *Science* v355 no6322 p313 Ja 20 2017

Microsoft Corp.

7 Ways Microsoft Can Make LinkedIn Worth $26 Billion T. H. Davenport *Harvard Business Review Digital Articles* p2 Je 13 2016

Another 40 million people bolt from Microsoft's browsers as mass exodus continues G. KEIZER color graph *PCWorld* p58 D 2016

The Disease Detectives C. GRABER color *New Republic* v248 no1/2 p10 Ja/F 2017

Do M&A Deals Ever Really Create Synergies? T. Zenger *Harvard Business Review Digital Articles* p2 Jl 6 2016

Everything Microsoft revealed: Surface Studio, Windows 10 Creators Update, and more B. CHACOS color *PCWorld* p8 D 2016

Fixing Tech's "Loss Points" G. B. White *Atlantic* v319 no5 p11 Je 2017

Great Dividends, Fair Prices T. PETRUNO color *Kiplinger's Personal Finance* v71 no10 p56 O 2017

The great equalizer P. NOWAK color *Maclean's* v130 no4 p60 My 2017

Hands-on: Microsoft's Surface Studio is a Windows PC for the Mac crowd M. HACHMAN color *PCWorld* p28 D 2016

How Microsoft Uses a Growth Mindset to Develop Leaders C. Dweck and K. Hogan *Harvard Business Review Digital Articles* p2 O 7 2016

How to force Cortana to use your default browser I. PAUL color *PCWorld* v35 no4 p141 Ap 2017

How to stop Windows 10 from rebooting after updates J. NOREM color *PCWorld* p163 Mr 2017

How to use Microsoft's Paint 3D app color *PCWorld* p174 Mr 2017

How We Built a Virtual Scheduling Assistant at Microsoft A.

Monroy-Hernández and J. Cranshaw *Harvard Business Review Digital Articles* p1 Jl 28 2017

Identify Blue Oceans by Mapping Your Product Portfolio W. C. Kim and R. Mauborgne *Harvard Business Review Digital Articles* p2 F 12 2015

Is the LinkedIn Acquisition Microsoft's Attempt to Build Its Own Alphabet? B. Gomes-Casseres *Harvard Business Review Digital Articles* p2 Je 15 2016

Meet the new Wunderlist: Microsoft's To-Do task manager takes over M. SIMON color *Macworld - Digital Edition* v34 no6 p103 Je 2017

Microsoft announces Office 2019 for customers who don't want to pay forever for Office 365 M. HACHMAN color *Macworld - Digital Edition* v34 no11 p109 N 2017

Microsoft: Don't worry, MS-DOS will live on after all S. J. VAUGHAN-NICHOLS color *PCWorld* v35 no1 p29 Ja 2017

Microsoft's Bid to Make Outlook More than Email Feng Zhu *Harvard Business Review Digital Articles* p2 Ag 18 2015

Microsoft seems ready to give up on Windows phones, if not Windows 10 Mobile M. HACHMAN color *PCWorld* p48 D 2016

Microsoft Surface Pro (2017): More power for more money M. HACHMAN color graph *PCWorld* v35 no7 p57 Jl 2017

Microsoft Surfaces D. Bass and M. Gurman color graph *Bloomberg Businessweek* no4521 p31 My 8 2017

Microsoft Surface Studio: Creativity is a sublime, pricey experience M. HACHMAN color graph *PCWorld* v35 no7 p87 Jl 2017

Microsoft teases Windows 10's sleek new look for the future I. PAUL color *PCWorld* p9 Mr 2017

Office for Mac gets Touch Bar support O. Raymundo color *Macworld - Digital Edition* p10 Ap 2017

STRONG TO THE HOOP J. BIEN-KAHN cartoon *Wired* v25 no3 p22 Mr 2017

Sunrise calendar is dead, and only some features live on in Outlook M. HACHMAN color *PCWorld* p26 O 2016

A Surface all-in-one PC may lead a Microsoft hardware refresh in October M. HACHMAN color *PCWorld* p16 O 2016

Surface Laptop: Microsoft's MacBook Air killer nails what students need M. HACHMAN color graph *PCWorld* v35 no8 p62 Ag 2017

WHAT'S NEW AT THE APP STORE color *Macworld - Digital Edition* v34 no9 p54 S 2017

The Windows 10 Anniversary Update is breaking webcams I. PAUL color *PCWorld* p50 O 2016

Windows 10 Build 16241 gives the best sneak peek yet at the Fall Creators Update M. HACHMAN color *PCWorld* v35 no8 p16 Ag 2017

WINDOWS 3.1: 25 YEARS LATER, IT'S STILL A MILESTONE B. EDWARDS color *PCWorld* v35 no5 p157 My 2017

Windows Vista has just days to live M. HACHMAN color *PCWorld* v35 no4 p42 Ap 2017

Microsoft Corp.—Congresses

Microsoft Build's biggest reveals: building the future B. CHACOS color *PCWorld* v35 no6 p14 Je 2017

Microsoft Corp.—Management

5 SATYA NADELLA A. Nusca color diag *Fortune* v174 no7 p76 D 1 2016

Microsoft Excel (Computer software)

7 Excel tips for huge spreadsheets: Split Screen, Freeze Panes, Format Painter and more J. D. SARTAIN color *PCWorld* v35 no8 p154 Ag 2017

Excel tips: 6 slick shortcuts, handy functions, and random-number generators J. D. SARTAIN diag *PCWorld* v35 no11 p148 N 2016

How to open Microsoft Excel spreadsheets in Apple Numbers on a Mac R. LOYOLA color *Macworld - Digital Edition* v34 no11 p114 N 2017

Microsoft Internet explorer (Computer software)

Microsoft ads invade Windows 10's File Explorer I. PAUL color *PCWorld* v35 no5 p61 My 2017

Microsoft Office (Computer software)

Microsoft tells some Mac Office users to pass on Apple's High Sierra G. KEIZER color *Macworld - Digital Edition* v34 no10 p86 O 2017

Office for Mac gets Touch Bar support O. Raymundo color *Macworld - Digital Edition* p10 Ap 2017

Microsoft Office (Computer software)—Evaluation

2016

The Middle East *New York Times Upfront* p2 S 18 2017 Supplement

Middle East—Politics & government

Before Push Comes to Shove: What the president needs to learn--fast P. Berkowitz *Hoover Digest: Research & Opinion on Public Policy* no2 p70 Spr 2017

Qatar Settles In for a Long Standoff J. Malsin color *Time* v190 no6 p10 Ag 7 2017

Ten Ways to Rescue Mideast Policy: In the Middle East the previous administration established neither democracy nor security--and now Russia is on the scene R. A. Berman and C. Hill *Hoover Digest: Research & Opinion on Public Policy* no2 p62 Spr 2017

Middle East—Politics & government—21st century

Middle East Rifts Are Widening Amid a Global Power Vacuum I. Bremmer *Time* v189 no24 p10 Je 26 2017

Middle East—Social conditions

MINDING THE MIDDLE EAST E. PEPPERS *USA Today Magazine* v146 no2866 p32 Jl 2017

Middle managers

See also

Sales executives

Despite What Zappos Says, Middle Managers Still Matter J. Whitehurst *Harvard Business Review Digital Articles* p2 My 28 2015

The Key to Change Is Middle Management B. Tabrizi *Harvard Business Review Digital Articles* p2 O 27 2014

What Middle Managers Can Learn from Agents, Brokers, and Other Middlemen M. Krakovsky *Harvard Business Review Digital Articles* p2 My 6 2016

Why Being a Middle Manager Is So Exhausting E. M. Anicich and J. B. Hirsh *Harvard Business Review Digital Articles* p2 Mr 22 2017

Middle managers—Psychology

Why Managers Are More Likely to Be Depressed D. Burkus *Harvard Business Review Digital Articles* p2 S 23 2015

Middle school curriculum

Inside out: Can social emotional learning prevent bullying in Catholic middle schools? [Cover story] C. Zulkey color *U.S. Catholic* v82 no9 p26 S 2017

Middle school education

See also

Language arts (Middle school)

How Five Lost Minutes Altered Our Class Culture K. HODGSON *Education Digest* v82 no4 p30 D 2016

Why Johnny Can't Sing, Dance, Saw, or Bake J. BERCKEMEYER *Education Digest* v82 no4 p25 D 2016

Middle school teachers

Helping Teachers Teach Evolution in the United States B. VAZQUEZ *Skeptical Inquirer* v41 no3 p49 My/Je 2017

Middle schools

LEADERSHIP BY COMMITTEE: Our middle school's journey to create a culture of literacy A. Osborn *Literacy Today (2411-7862)* v35 no2 p20 S/O 2017

Northern Hills Middle School *American Forests* v123 no3 p10 Fall 2017

Middle West Spirits (Company)

Bourbon. In Ohio F. MAROUKIAN color *Popular Mechanics* v193 no7 p16 S 2016

Middlebury College

Campus Cowardice *Weekly Standard* v23 no4 p3 O 2 2017

Is "Intersectionality" a Religion? img *New York* v50 no6 p11 Mr 20 2017

One Campus Arena Where Free Speech Is Not Up for Debate: Law Schools H. Gerken color *Time* v190 no4 p20 Jl 24 2017

Middle East history—1979-

The Six-Day War at 50 D. PRYCE-JONES *National Review* v69 no11 p17 Je 12 2017

Middleton, Dan

THE STORY TELLER R. D'Agostino color *Popular Mechanics* p68 O 2017

MIDDLETON, SUSAN

Lion's Mane Jelly (Cyanea capillata) color *Issues in Science & Technology* v33 no2 p96 Wint 2017

Middleton, Susie

HOLIDAY Roasts [Cover story] color *Vegetarian Times* v43 no2 p76 N/D 2016

Middleton, Tracy

THIS COULD HAPPEN IN YOUR HOMETOWN bw color *Women's Health* v14 no7 p88 S 2017

Wrap. Me. Up [Cover story] color *Women's Health* v13 no10 p110 D 2016

Mider, Zachary

Carl 'I can' bw color graph *Bloomberg Businessweek* no4515 p23 Mr 20 2017

A Climate Hawk Among the Deniers color *Bloomberg Businessweek* no4498 p70 N 7 2016

HELLO, AMERICAN color *Bloomberg Businessweek* no4503 p50 D 12 2016

How to Win Congress With a Polar Bear Outfit, Cheez-Its, and a Bunch of iPads color *Bloomberg Businessweek* no4495 p20 O 17 2016

Long Shots That May Pay Off Big bw *Bloomberg Businessweek* no4499 p23 N 14 2016

The Mess Steven Mnuchin Left Behind bw *Bloomberg Businessweek* no4504 p34 D 19 2016

Mnuchin's Conflicting Hollywood Roles *Bloomberg Businessweek* no4507 p24 Ja 16 2017

Mystery Deal *Bloomberg Businessweek* no4510 p33 F 6 2017

Private Prisons Get A Boost From Trump color *Bloomberg Businessweek* no4500 p28 N 21 2016

Washington's New Most Powerful People color *Bloomberg Businessweek* no4500 p27 N 21 2016

Midewin National Tallgrass Prairie (Ill.)

Greetings from MIDEWIN NATIONAL TALLGRASS PRAIRIE D. Newman color *Practical Horseman* v44 no12 p62 D 2016

Midland (Performer)

Back in the Old Country M. Vain color *Entertainment Weekly* no1478 / 1479 p104 Ag 18-25 2017

Midler, Bette, 1945-

Sound Bites color *Entertainment Weekly* no1454/1455 p11 F 24 2017

Sound Bites color *Entertainment Weekly* no1471 p12 Je 23 2017

THE STAR H. ALS color *New Yorker* v93 no11 p60 My 1 2017

Midler, Bette, 1945-—Interviews

Bette Midler E. Berman color *Time* v188 no27-28 p117 D 26 2016

BE TTE MIDLER K. O'Donnell color *Entertainment Weekly* no1436/1437 p100 O 21 2016

Midnight

MIDNIGHT P. STEFÁNSSON *Iceland Review* v55 no4 p92 Jl/Ag 2017

Midnight, Texas (TV program)

Midnight, Texas I. Rudolph *TV Guide* v65 no23 p30 My 29 2017

Midnight Oil (Performer)

FULL TANK: THE COMPLETE ALBUM COLLECTION M. Mettler color *Sound & Vision* v82 no8 p72 O 2017

Midnight Special (Film)

JOEL EDGERTON Z. BARON bw color *GQ: Gentlemen's Quarterly* v86 no12 p218 D 2016

No. 7 MIDNIGHT SPECIAL L. Greenblatt color *Entertainment Weekly* no1444/1445 p55 D 16 2016

Midsummer Night's Dream, A (Play)

THE THEATRE *New Yorker* v93 no20 p12 Jl 10 2017

Midtbøen, Arnfinn H.

Hiring Discrimination Against Black Americans Hasn't Declined in 25 Years *Harvard Business Review Digital Articles* p2 O 11 2017

Midwest (U.S.)—Economic conditions

Wind Is the New Corn J. Oldham chart color *Bloomberg Businessweek* no4494 p16 O 10 2016

Midwest (U.S.)—Environmental conditions

Wind Is the New Corn J. Oldham chart color *Bloomberg Businessweek* no4494 p16 O 10 2016

Mie scattering

Grape balls of fire! *Physics Today* v70 no10 p96 O 2017

Miele, Matthew

A Star-Studded Tribute to a Lovable Lensman I. Guzmán color *Time* v188 no24 p64 D 12 2016

Mienert, J.

Massive blow-out craters formed by hydrate-controlled methane expulsion from the Arctic seafloor graph map *Science* v356

Migratory locust
Madagascar color *National Geographic* v231 no5 pC12 My 2017
Miguel, Amanda
GTPase activity-coupled treadmilling of the bacterial tubulin FtsZ organizes septal cell wall synthesis bibl graph *Science* v355 no6326 p744 F 17 2017
Miguel, Y.
Jupiter's interior and deep atmosphere: The initial pole-to-pole passes with the Juno spacecraft [Cover story] color graph *Science* v356 no6340 p821 My 26 2017
Mihelich, Ed
Seeing Through the Dust: Turning to technology can improve your resolution of globular clusters *Sky & Telescope* v134 no1 p57 Jl 2017
MIHELL, CONOR
BORDERLINE WILDERNESS *Sierra* v101 no6 p28 N/D 2016
EXPANDING THE REALM color *Canoe & Kayak Magazine* v45 no1 p28 Wint 2017
Fungus of Youth [Cover story] color *Walrus* v14 no4 p20 My 2017
THE NEW KAYAKTIVISM color *Canoe & Kayak Magazine* v45 no1 p34 Wint 2017
MIHM, STEPHEN
When Europe Sneezed: A new history of the Depression looks beyond Wall Street to the global roots of the crisis bw *New York Times Book Review* p14 Ap 23 2017
Mihoub, Mouadh
Guanine glycation repair by DJ-1/Park7 and its bacterial homologs chart color diag graph *Science* v357 no6347 p208 Jl 14 2017
Mii, Horng-Sheng
21st-century rise in anthropogenic nitrogen deposition on a remote coral reef diag graph *Science* v356 no6339 p749 My 19 2017
Mijac, Corey Michael
Corey Michael Mijac A. HUTCHINS color *Maclean's* v129 no47 p66 N 28 2016
MIKACICH, TARAH
High and Dry *Boating World* v38 no3 p16 Mr 2017
Start Strong: Make sure the first session of the season goes well *Boating World* v38 no5 p16 My 2017
Mikado, The (Theatrical production)
The Mikado *New York* v49 no25 p144 D 12 2016
Mike & the Mad Dog (Film)
Short Circuit J. Fuchs and T. Keith color *Sports Illustrated* v126 no13 p22 My 8 2017
Mike Judge Presents: Tales From the Tour Bus (TV program)
Season of the Weird R. SHEFFIELD color *Rolling Stone* no1297 p21 O 5 2017
Mike Will Made It (Performer)
Mike WiLL Made-It J. Black color *Esquire* p46 Ag 2017
Mike D, 1965-
Mike D's Endless Summer J. WEINER bw *Rolling Stone* no1275 p20 D 1 2016
Mikel, Mark A.
Wild emmer genome architecture and diversity elucidate wheat evolution and domestication color *Science* v357 no6346 p93 Jl 7 2017
MIKHAIL, ALAN
Old World Order *New York Times Book Review* p19 My 7 2017
Mikkelsen, Kenneth
The Best Leaders Are Constant Learners *Harvard Business Review Digital Articles* p2 O 16 2015
Mikkelsen, Mads, 1965-
Rogue One Rewinds-and Rewrites-the Star Wars Legacy E. Dockterman color diag *Time* v188 no22-23 p100 N/D 2016
Star Wars' Secret Weapon J. WEINER color *Rolling Stone* no1278/1279 p20 Ja 12 2017
Mikkelsen, Mads, 1965-—Interviews
Strange-r Danger: Mads Mikkelsen Evils Up C. Collis color *Entertainment Weekly* no1439 p41 N 11 2016
MIKULAN, STEVEN
SOMETHING WITCHY THIS WAY COMES *Los Angeles Magazine* p128 D 2016
Mikulich, Alex
The problem of mass incarceration is more complicated than we thought color *America* v216 no4 p44 F 20 2017
Milam, Benny—Interviews

BENNY MILAM P. G. Strout color *Snowboarder* v29 no2 p46 O 2016
Milam, Erika Lorraine
Idiosyncratic desires color *Science* v356 no6341 p915 Je 1 2017
Milan (Italy)
MILAN rising H. MARTIN bw color *Architectural Digest* v74 no8 p80 Ag 2017
When in Milan L. Ermelino color *Publishers Weekly* v264 no28 p20 Jl 10 2017
MILAN, SOFIA
Love Quest *USA Today Magazine* v145 no2860 p58 Ja 2017
Milanovic, Branko
Why the Global 1% and the Asian Middle Class Have Gained the Most from Globalization *Harvard Business Review Digital Articles* p2 My 13 2016
Milazzo, Joëlle
Epigenetic regulation of antagonistic receptors confers rice blast resistance with yield balance bibl diag *Science* v355 no6328 p962 Mr 3 2017
Milazzo, Marzia
Mestizaje and Globalization: Transformations of Identity and Power *American Indian Quarterly* v40 no4 p379 Fall 2016
Milbank (S.D.)
The Entertainers of MILBANK: The Grant County city's downtown has become a fun place to visit and shop R. Jensen and B. Hunhoff *South Dakota Magazine* v33 no3 p20 S/O 2017
Milbank, John, 1952-
The Politics of Virtue: Post-Liberalism and the Human Future S. Wells color *Christian Century* v134 no10 p45 My 10 2017
Milbank Tweed Hadley & McCloy LLP
THE CHEESEMAKERS *South Dakota Magazine* v33 no3 p22 S/O 2017
MILBOURN, TODD
COMP TARGETS THAT WORK: HOW TO KEEP EXECUTIVES FROM GAMING THE SYSTEM color graph img *Harvard Business Review* v95 no5 p102 S/O 2017
Milbradt, Brandon
"I've always loved stories about women" bw color *Glamour* v114 no12 p68 D 2016
Mile (Unit of length)
Going the Extra Mile: Why a rural New England ramble always takes a bit longer than you'd think *Yankee* v81 no5 p26 S/O 2017
Miles, Barbara Curtin
A domestic whodunit color *America* v216 no13 p55 Je 12 2017
Miles, David
The Tale of the Axe A. Robinson *History Today* v66 no10 p57 O 2016
Miles, Jack
Play of Passions *New York Times Book Review* p13 F 26 2017
Shop Talk bw *Commonweal* v144 no12 p31 Jl 7 2017
Miles, Jonathan
BASS AND HAM CAKES color *Field & Stream* v122 no2 p28 Je/Jl 2017
BLACK & BLUE CHILI color *Field & Stream* v122 no4 p24 S 2017
BRAISED AND SMOKED BOAR RIBS color *Field & Stream* v122 no6 p24 Jl 2017
THE DEER STANDWICH color *Field & Stream* v121 no6 p20 N 2016
PASTRAMI TROUT color *Field & Stream* v121 no9 p20 Ap 2017
Sex Under the Dome *New York Times Book Review* p11 N 13 2016
THIN-POUNDED VENISON STEAKS color *Field & Stream* v122 no3 p20 Ag 2017
VENISON LOK LAK color *Field & Stream* v121 no8 p26 F/Mr 2017
VENISON POYHA *Field & Stream* v121 no7 p34 D 2016/Ja 2017
WILD TURKEY TONNATO cartoon color *Field & Stream* v122 no1 p20 My 2017
Miles, Kathryn
America Is Not Ready for the Earthquakes Ahead color map *Time* v190 no14 p21 O 9 2017
The Earth Moving Under Us N. Hopper color *Time* v190 no8 p58 Ag 28 2017
Miles, Margaret R.
Theodora: Actress, Empress, Saint *Christian Century* v133 no25

p39 D 7 2016

Miles, Matt

Publish openly but responsibly color *Science* v357 no6347 p141 Jl 14 2017

Miles, Terry

log cabin tranquility N. E. OATES color diag *Cabin Living* p32 S 2017

MILES, TIYA

Spooky *New York Times Book Review* p12 O 30 2016

Miles, Valerie

Literatura *New York Times Book Review* p38 D 11 2016

Miles Redd (Company)

Color Geniuses color *Architectural Digest* v74 no1 p144 Ja 2017

Miletic, Natalija

Promised Land color *Time* v190 no14 p40 O 9 2017

Milevski, Lukas

The Evolution of Modern Grand Strategic Thought L. D. Freedman *Foreign Affairs* v96 no1 p161 Ja/F 2017

Miley, G. K.

Molecular gas in the halo fuels the growth of a massive cluster galaxy at high redshift bibl graph *Science* v354 no6316 p1128 D 2 2016

Miley, Mary

Murder in Disguise: A Roaring Twenties Mystery *Publishers Weekly* v264 no25 p95 Je 19 2017

Milgrom, Judith

Perfect Match N. Silverstein bw color *Glamour* v115 no5 p54 My 2017

Milgrom, Judith—Interviews

SISTER ACT color *Harper's Bazaar* no3649 p186 D 2016/Ja 2017

MILHAN, AHAMED

The Unbreakable Relationship *Islamic Horizons* v45 no6 p48 N/D 2016

Milhaud, Darius, 1892-1974

Family Dynamics R. Platt color *New Yorker* v93 no18 p8 Je 26 2017

Milinkovitch, Michel

Skin-Deep Evolutionary Link B. ALEX color *Discover* v38 no1 p58 Ja/F 2017

Militare, Jessica

60 Years of Campus Changemakers color *Glamour* v115 no5 p138 My 2017

(The Big)Salary Reveal [Cover story] bw color *Glamour* v115 no3 p146 Mr 2017

This Is My Job bw cartoon color *Glamour* v115 no4 p146 Ap 2017

This Is My Job color *Glamour* no8 p114 Ag 2017

This Is My Job color *Glamour* v114 no11 p137 N 2016

When Beauty Is Your 9-to-5 color *Glamour* v115 no10 p108 O 2017

Militarism—United States

Weaponized Wilderness J. Mark *Sierra* v102 no5 p4 St/O 2017

Military advisors

LESSONS FROM AN ASSASSIN color *Popular Mechanics* p22 S 2017

Military aeronautics—United States

The Green line E. Moreno *Parks & Recreation* v51 no11 p44 N 2016

Military air pilots

A Fighter Pilot's New Career Takes Off K. LANKFORD color *Kiplinger's Personal Finance* v71 no4 p72 Ap 2017

Military airplanes

In Harm's Way G. NORMAN color *Weekly Standard* v22 no27 p24 Mr 20 2017

Military art & science

See also

Asymmetric warfare

Battles

Cyberspace operations (Military science)

Fortification

Information warfare

Military readiness

Military strategy

Paramilitary forces

ARE WE PREPARED FOR CYBERWAR? A. GREENBERG cartoon *Wired* v25 no9 p77 S 2017

What Is Russia's Military Up To? B. Bender *Hoover Digest: Research & Opinion on Public Policy* no4 p119 Fall 2016

What the U.S. Military Can Teach Companies About Supporting Employees' Families D. Wademan Dowling *Harvard Business Review Digital Articles* p1 My 11 2017

Military art & science—United States

How to Sustain Our Military G. Roughead *Hoover Digest: Research & Opinion on Public Policy* no4 p90 Fall 2016

Military chaplains

Father Hood W. E. Mueller bw *Commonweal* v144 no2 p31 Ja 27 2017

Military education

Land of the Hermit King J. H. LEE *New Republic* v248 no10 p38 O 2017

Military education—United States

THE MAKING—AND BREAKING—OF MARINES: THE DEATH OF A MUSLIM RECRUIT LAST YEAR HAS DRAWN SCRUTINY TO THE U.S. MARINES' TRAINING BASE AT PARRIS ISLAND, WHERE BRUTAL HAZING HAS FLOURISHED. IS THIS REALLY THE ONLY WAY TO CREATE A WARRIOR? J. Reitman *New York Times Magazine* p32 Jl 9 2017

Showing-Up Ribbon cartoon color *Weekly Standard* v22 no41 p3 Jl 3 2017

Military government

Thailand: The Permanent Coup R. Bernstein color *New York Review of Books* v64 no14 p69 S 28 2017

Military governors

World War I CENTENNIAL B. ALTOBELLO bw *New Orleans Magazine* v51 no12 p92 O 2017

Military helicopters

NAVIGATE NORTHWARD M. Gaffney *Washingtonian Magazine* v52 no8 p223 My 2017

Military history

See also

Battles

The battles inside the battle B. BETHUNE bw *Maclean's* v130 no3 p54 Ap 2017

FLASHBACK color *MHQ: Quarterly Journal of Military History* v29 no4 p4 Summ 2017

How Americans Lost Faith in the Presidency K. BURNS and L. NOVICK bw *Atlantic* v320 no3 p24 O 2017

ON THE INSIDE UNDER FIRE R. Soodalter bw color *Military History* v34 no2 p62 Jl 2017

SHADOWS OF WAR color *MHQ: Quarterly Journal of Military History* v29 no4 p50 Summ 2017

THE TWO HORSEMEN OF THE REVOLUTION E. S. Rafuse bw color *MHQ: Quarterly Journal of Military History* v30 no1 p40 Aut 2017

WAR IN HISTORY AND MEMORY J. E. Talbott *History Today* v67 no3 p18 Mr 2017

Military journalism

A PICTURE OF WAR J. A. MacGahan *MHQ: Quarterly Journal of Military History* v29 no3 p86 Spr 2017

WAR REPORTER FOR A DAY E. DYER color *Popular Mechanics* p24 O 2017

Military law

What Good Is Military Force? J. BERGNER *Weekly Standard* v22 no6 p16 O 17 2016

Military maneuvers

Russia's Rehearsal for World War S. Shuster color *Time* v190 no10/11 p12 S 18 2017

Military maps

BATTLE SCHEMES: BATTERY INCLUDED map *MHQ: Quarterly Journal of Military History* v30 no1 p20 Aut 2017

DON'T FIRE UNTIL YOU SEE... *MHQ: Quarterly Journal of Military History* v29 no2 p16 Wint 2017

Military medical personnel

The Afghan Field Medic M. LIUHTO color *Foreign Policy* no225 p14 Jl/Ag 2017

The Cat Named Morphine S. Jaszberenyi *New York Times Magazine* p23 F 19 2017

Medics on a mission A. R. KHAN color *Maclean's* v130 no3 p39 Ap 2017

Military modernization (Equipment)

Adapting nuclear modernization to the new administration A.

Mount bibl *Bulletin of the Atomic Scientists* v73 no3 p167 My 2017

Rising tensions, nuclear modernizations: How Washington can turn down the heat L. J. Korb bibl *Bulletin of the Atomic Scientists* v73 no3 p173 My 2017

Military museums

NEXT EXIT: AMERICANA: FROM FIBERGLASS DINO-SAURS TO STONEWALL JACKSON'S STUFFED HORSE TO PATSY CLINE'S ICE-CREAM SCOOP, SHENANDOAH IS HOME TO SOME PARTICULARLY AMERICAN AT-TRACTIONS B. Jensen *Washingtonian Magazine* v53 no1 p104 O 2017

Military museums—Evaluation

THE GOOD WAR C. R. Kesler *Claremont Review of Books* v16 no4 p5 Fall 2016

Military officers

See also
  Generals
  Non-commissioned officers

BEHIND THE LINES: TRAIN MAN M. G. DeSantis color map *MHQ: Quarterly Journal of Military History* v30 no1 p24 Aut 2017

EDITOR'S NOTE J. WORSHAM *Prologue* v49 no2 p2 Summ 2017

THE MAN IN CARRIAGE NO.2013: Leo Steveni was a British officer based in St Petersburg at the time of the Russian Revolution. He became an active eyewitness to the chaos of the Civil War that followed C. Boylan *History Today* v67 no10 p68 O 2017

Manuel Antonio Noriega K. Samuelson color *Time* v189 no22 p11 Je 12 2017

Where Our WWII Leaders Spent WWI J. WORSHAM *Prologue* v49 no2 p18 Summ 2017

Military officers—History

Limiting Civilian Casualties as Part of a Winning Strategy: The Case of Courageous Restraint J. H. Felter and J. N. Shapiro *Daedalus* v146 no1 p44 Wint 2017

Military officers—History—21st century

When the Commander in Chief Disrespects His Commanders J. Stavridis color *Time* v190 no16/17 p36 O 23 2017

Military parks—North Carolina

Hallowed Ground Moores Creek National Battlefield W. J. Shepherd *Military History* v33 no6 p75 Mr 2017

Military personnel

See also
  Generals
  Military advisors
  Military officers
  Women military personnel

THE BATTLE OF NEW YORK C. Buzzell color *Popular Mechanics* p80 My 2017

Captured! bw *Military History* v34 no4 p80 N 2017

December 1941 T. CLARK and E. INGRAHAM bw *Yankee* v80 no6 p20 N/D 2016

DRAWN & QUARTERED color *MHQ: Quarterly Journal of Military History* v29 no4 p96 Summ 2017

THE FLAWED PERFECT GENERAL Tang Long *Military History* v33 no6 p48 Mr 2017

FROM OUR READERS D. Phillips, H. E. Came et al *Archaeology* v70 no4 p8 Je-Ag 2017

THE GRAND ARMY DIET M. BROWN color *Archaeology* v70 no4 p22 Je-Ag 2017

Hot Seat bw *Military History* v34 no5 p80 Ja 2018

Humor in Uniform R. L. DOW, D. HETLAND *Reader's Digest* v190 no1134 p136 O 2017

Nebraska at 150 A. J. BARTELS bw color *Nebraska Life* v21 no4 p56 Jl/Ag 2017

On the Brink *Nation* v305 no4 p11 Ag 14 2017

PHOTO color *Reason* v49 no6 p9 N 2017

SKY ABOVE, MUD BELOW A. Brandt bw color *Military History* v34 no1 p32 My 2017

A SOLDIER'S STORY G. MILLER JR. *Cincinnati Magazine* v50 no2 p76 N 2016

Vegetarian Action. Vegan in the Army: Specialist Brianna Kearney S. Gendler *Vegetarian Journal* v35 no2 p35 2016

WELCOME TO THE GREEN MACHINE J. N. LOMAX *Texas*

Monthly v45 no6 p126 Je 2017

What Companies Can Learn from Military Teams D. McGinn *Harvard Business Review Digital Articles* p2 Ag 6 2015

Military personnel's injuries

Still On a Mission J. Vrabel bw *Men's Health* v32 no9 p10 N 2017

Military personnel—Attitudes

MY LONGEST DAY J. LIENHARD *Humanist* v77 no1 p34 Ja/F 2017

Military personnel—Books & reading

PATTON'S REQUIRED READING B. A. Patton *MHQ: Quarterly Journal of Military History* v29 no3 p22 Spr 2017

Military personnel—Crimes against

Breach of Faith R. WILSON *American Scholar* v86 no3 p2 Summ 2017

Dishonorable Behavior: THE SCOURGE OF MILITARY SEXU-AL ASSAULT AND THE WARRIOR'S MASCULINE CODE E. D. SAMET *American Scholar* v86 no3 p30 Summ 2017

Military personnel—Germany

GERMANY'S LION OF THE DEFENSIVE D. T. Zabecki bw color *MHQ: Quarterly Journal of Military History* v29 no4 p58 Summ 2017

Military personnel—Health

THE THINGS THEY BURNED J. PERCY bw color *New Republic* v247 no12 p22 D 2016

Military personnel—History

HIS OWN WORST ENEMY R. A. Gabriel color *Military History* v34 no2 p30 Jl 2017

Just War Theory & the Conduct of Asymmetric Warfare A. S. Weiner *Daedalus* v146 no1 p59 Wint 2017

Military personnel—Humor

Humor in Uniform J. MAYES cartoon *Reader's Digest* v190 no1132 p138 Jl/Ag 2017

Humor in Uniform *Reader's Digest* v188 no1125 p147 N 2016

Military personnel—News briefs

Humor in Uniform bw *Reader's Digest* v189 no1130 p139 My 2017

Military personnel—Physiology

WWI'S WONDER DRUG Ł. Kamiński *MHQ: Quarterly Journal of Military History* v29 no2 p44 Wint 2017

Military personnel—Religious life

Army now allows soldiers to wear turbans, beards, and heads-carves A. M. Banks color *Christian Century* v134 no4 p14 F 15 2017

Military personnel—Soviet Union

Death Battalions S. Wong and J. GUTTMAN *MHQ: Quarterly Journal of Military History* v29 no3 p11 Spr 2017

Military personnel—Training of

LESSONS FROM AN ASSASSIN color *Popular Mechanics* p22 S 2017

Military personnel—United States

See also
  African American military personnel

BRINGING BANDAR HOME J. COON color *Reason* v49 no6 p26 N 2017

Under the shade of a thirsty cottonwood C. Amundson *Nebraska Life* v21 no4 p9 Jl/Ag 2017

Warriors and Citizens R. Brooks *Hoover Digest: Research & Opinion on Public Policy* no4 p73 Fall 2016

Military personnel—United States—History

HOME OF THE BRAVE: THE NATION'S ONLY TOWN FOUNDED BY AFRICAN-AMERICAN CIVIL WAR SOL-DIERS REMAINS A BASTION OF RESILIENCE 150 YEARS LATER N. HOPKINSON *Smithsonian* v48 no5 p56 S 2017

Military policy—United States

Doctrine of Decline T. C. DONNELLY *National Review* v69 no1 p17 Ja 23 2017

The Limits of Spending More M. Thompson color *Time* v188 no22-23 p31 N/D 2016

Military readiness

See also
  Air power (Military science)

A Missile Defense Agenda T. KARAKO *National Review* v69 no18 p29 O 2 2017

The Permanent Stain of the Somme A. Mallinson *History Today* v66 no11 p72 N 2016

Take Nukes Off a Short Fuse color *Scientific American* v316 no3

p10 Mr 2017

Military readiness—History

DEFENSIVE STRATEGY AND THE CONSTRUCTION OF THE WALL color *Archaeology* v70 no3 p30 My/Je 2017

Military reform

Make Your Team Less Hierarchical C. Fussell *Harvard Business Review Digital Articles* p2 Jl 15 2015

Military reserve forces

UNDERCOVER WITH A BORDER MILITIA S. BAUER bw color graph map *Mother Jones* v41 no6 p18 N/D 2016

Military reserve forces—Employment

Research: Companies Are Less Likely to Hire Current Military Reservists T. F. Figinski *Harvard Business Review Digital Articles* p2 O 13 2017

Military retirements

LOOK FORWARD TO RETIREMENT *Washingtonian Magazine* v52 no1 p173 O 2016

The Military's Got a New Spin on Retirement D. Kadlec color diag *Money* v46 no6 p28 Jl 2017

Military service

George Goes to the Trenches of France C. Amundson bw *Nebraska Life* v21 no6 p8 N/D 2017

Military spending

As technology goes democratic, nations lose military control B. FitzGerald and J. Parziale bibl *Bulletin of the Atomic Scientists* v73 no2 p102 Mr 2017

A BLOOD-SOAKED MONEY-WASTING SCANDAL color *Forbes* v199 no5 p15 My 16 2017

Check the budget K. Clarke *U.S. Catholic* v82 no7 p42 Jl 2017

The third offset strategy: A misleading slogan L. J. Korb and C. Evans bibl *Bulletin of the Atomic Scientists* v73 no2 p92 Mr 2017

Military strategy

See also

Arctic regions—Strategic aspects

Deployment (Military strategy)

Deterrence (Military strategy)

Naval strategy

What We Learned From... Operation Michael, 1918 D. T. Zabecki bw *Military History* v34 no2 p18 Jl 2017

Why Military Assistance Programs Disappoint M. Karlin color *Foreign Affairs* v96 no6 p111 N/D 2017

Military strategy—History—20th century

GERMANY'S LION OF THE DEFENSIVE D. T. Zabecki bw color *MHQ: Quarterly Journal of Military History* v29 no4 p58 Summ 2017

Military strategy—History—21st century

Staying the Course in Afghanistan K. Sadat and S. McChrystal color *Foreign Affairs* v96 no6 p2 N/D 2017

Military supplies

'Demilitarize' the Police? A. RIZER color *Weekly Standard* v22 no7 p17 O 24 2016

Military Gear for Police *Congressional Digest* v96 no8 p31 O 2017

Military technology

Agility in the Arsenal: Technology makes for better weapons--but only until our foes catch up. Why the Pentagon needs to move faster J. Felter *Hoover Digest: Research & Opinion on Public Policy* no3 p65 Summ 2017

The upside and downside of swarming drones I. Lachow bibl *Bulletin of the Atomic Scientists* v73 no2 p96 Mr 2017

Military technology—History

Procuring Innovation F. Kaplan color il *MIT Technology Review* v120 no1 p64 Ja/F 2017

Military technology—Research

Japanese military entices academics to break taboo D. Normile color *Science* v355 no6323 p338 Ja 27 2017

Military trucks

Buried Treasure in Backyard R. Brutt color *Hot Rod* v70 no9 p22 S 2017

Military uniforms

Berets Berated color *Weekly Standard* v22 no24 p2 F 27 2017

Humor in Uniform R. L. DOW, D. HETLAND *Reader's Digest* v190 no1134 p136 O 2017

Military vehicles—Evaluation

THE MILITARY'S NEW WORKHORSE E. TEGLER chart col-

or *Popular Mechanics* p8 Jl 2017

Military weapons

See also

Biological weapons

Hardware Type 94 Infantry Mortar J. Guttman *Military History* v33 no5 p20 Ja 2017

Military weapons—Exhibitions

The Military-Industrial Party R. F. JOHNSON color *Weekly Standard* v22 no11 p28 N 21 2016

Militia

THE MOST DANGEROUS ARMY IN IRAQ A. R. KHAN color *Maclean's* no1 p44 F 17 2017

This Land Is Was Your Land D. Slater *Sierra* v101 no4 p24 Jl/Ag 2016

UNDERCOVER WITH A BORDER MILITIA S. BAUER bw color graph map *Mother Jones* v41 no6 p18 N/D 2016

Militia—Charts, diagrams, etc.

PATRIOT GAMES S. Rathod bw cartoon color *Mother Jones* v41 no6 p21 N/D 2016

Milius, Susan

Aardvarks: a new face of climate change color *Science News* v192 no4 p4 S 16 2017

ANIMAL MATH [Cover story] cartoon color graph *Science News* v190 no12 p22 D 10 2016

Brainpower aids guppy mate choice *Science News* v191 no7 p12 Ap 15 2017

Bulletins from the TICK WARS color diag map *Science News* v192 no2 p16 Ag 19 2017

Case builds for another Zika vector *Science News* v190 no9 p13 O 29 2016

Climate change may worsen nutrition graph map *Science News* v191 no6 p14 Ap 1 2017

DNA edits boost photosynthesis [Cover story] color *Science News* v190 no13 p6 D 24 2016

Don't shake hands with this crab color *Science News* v191 no4 p4 Mr 4 2017

Elephants may set new sleep record color *Science News* v191 no6 p10 Ap 1 2017

Extreme bird nests bring comforts, catastrophe color *Science News* v190 no8 p4 O 15 2016

Fairy circle origin stories may merge color *Science News* v191 no3 p17 F 18 2017

Flamingos' bones favor one-leg stance color *Science News* v191 no12 p15 Je 24 2017

Flower hosts its own war of the sexes color *Science News* v192 no1 p10 Ag 5 2017

Glass frog moms do care after all color *Science News* v191 no8 p16 Ap 29 2017

The green art of the deathtrap ambush color *Science News* v191 no1 p4 Ja 21 2017

Hot nests a major sea turtle threat color *Science News* v191 no4 p16 Mr 4 2017

How plants hunt water color *Science News* v192 no6 p24 O 14 2017

Jumping spider hears distant sounds color *Science News* v190 no10 p9 N 12 2016

Killer drillers got bigger over time color graph *Science News* v192 no1 p16 Ag 5 2017

The life and times of dodos revealed color *Science News* v192 no4 p6 S 16 2017

Light pollution foils plant pollinators color *Science News* v192 no3 p10 S 2 2017

The Lucky Ones cartoon diag *Science News* v191 no2 p26 F 4 2017

Melatonin makes the midshipman hum color *Science News* v190 no9 p4 O 29 2016

Mixed-up mammal mixes soil Down Under color *Science News* v190 no11 p4 N 26 2016

'Mucus houses' catch sea carbon fast color *Science News* v191 no11 p13 Je 10 2017

Nitrogen fixers may be at risk *Science News* v191 no10 p11 My 27 2017

Opening Arctic passageways will shake up ecosystems color *Science News* v190 no13 p23 D 24 2016

Overlooked mass migration spotted cartoon color *Science News* v191 no2 p12 F 4 2017

Polluted reefs may favor dark snakes color graph *Science News* v192 no4 p14 S 16 2017

real vampires of planet earth [Cover story] color graph *Science News* v192 no7 p22 O 28 2017

Scratching is catching in mice *Science News* v191 no7 p8 Ap 15 2017

Selfish DNA fooled scientists for years bw *Science News* v191 no12 p10 Je 24 2017

Shrinking sea ice threatens mobility bw color *Science News* v190 no9 p8 O 29 2016

Some woolly rhinos grew odd neck ribs color *Science News* v192 no5 p10 S 30 2017

The strangest insect wings bw color *Science News* v191 no13 p4 Jl 8 2017

Tastier tomatoes through chemistry color *Science News* v191 no3 p12 F 18 2017

To fight skeeters, disrupt their sex lives color *Science News* v191 no11 p10 Je 10 2017

Twilight of the fluorescent frogs color *Science News* v191 no7 p4 Ap 15 2017

Unusually loose skin protects hagfish color *Science News* v191 no2 p13 F 4 2017

Warming alters ant turnovers color *Science News* v190 no11 p17 N 26 2016

Wasps are experts at crypt escape color *Science News* v191 no6 p4 Ap 1 2017

What big fangs you have, little blenny color *Science News* v191 no10 p4 My 27 2017

What gives frogs the gift of grab color *Science News* v191 no4 p11 Mr 4 2017

When mom has favorite, blame all the swimming color *Science News* v190 no13 p4 D 24 2016

Who's (sort of) counting? color *Science News* v190 no12 p25 D 10 2016

Wild orangutans set nursing record color *Science News* v191 no12 p8 Je 24 2017

Miljković, Katarina

Formation of the Orientale lunar multiring basin bibl graph *Science* v354 no6311 p441 O 28 2016

Gravity field of the Orientale basin from the Gravity Recovery and Interior Laboratory Mission bibl graph *Science* v354 no6311 p438 O 28 2016

Milk

See also
Breast milk

High on CottonHi L. RABINOVITCH *Los Angeles Magazine* v61 no11 p132 N 2016

KNOW WHEN TO FOLD 'EM color *Men's Health* v32 no3 p57 Ap 2017

there's NO CREAM like snow CREAM color *Cabin Living* p62 D 2016

Milk, Leslie

MOST POWERFUL WOMEN: More than 100 of the area's most influential women in government, business, law, education, media, nonprofits, and the arts *Washingtonian Magazine* v53 no1 p50 O 2017

THE Quints HAVE Kids color *Washingtonian Magazine* v52 no7 p76 Ap 2017

TRADE SECRETS *Washingtonian Magazine* v52 no2 p63 N 2016

WASHINGTONIANS OF THE YEAR *Washingtonian Magazine* v52 no4 p54 Ja 2017

WELCOME TO MY WORLD: Living with a disability, I'm the one my peers call when their bodies start to fail. How sympathetic, or surprised, should I be? *Washingtonian Magazine* v52 no12 p176 S 2017

WOMEN TO WATCH *Washingtonian Magazine* v53 no1 p62 O 2017

Milk proteins

See also
Whey proteins

GO ALL OUT color *Muscle & Performance* v9 no1 p64 Ja 2017

Milk Your Inflammation! J. WUEBBEN and D. JACKSON color *Muscle & Performance* v9 no11 p32 N 2017

Milking

Keep It Simple J. SUGARMAN *Washingtonian Magazine* v52

no11 p88 Ag 2017

Milkove, Daniel

Genetically Modified Alfalfa Production in the United States *Amber Waves: The Economics of Food, Farming, Natural Resources, & Rural America* p1 My 2017

Milkowski, Bill

1954 color *Downbeat* v84 no3 p65 Mr 2017

6-String Sidestream color *Downbeat* v84 no8 p73 Ag 2017

BILL FRISELL [Cover story] color *Downbeat* v84 no7 p28 Jl 2017

DOMINIC MILLER color *Downbeat* v84 no7 p25 Jl 2017

Electrifying Saga color *Downbeat* v83 no12 p93 D 2016

For the Love of Jimi color *Downbeat* v84 no9 p24 S 2017

Glimpses into a Grand Vision color *Downbeat* v83 no12 p69 D 2016

Hot Jazz Festival Sizzles in New York color *Downbeat* v83 no12 p17 D 2016

Kurt Rosenwinkel Goes DIY, Forms New Label color *Downbeat* v83 no12 p15 D 2016

LAP OF LUXURY FOR MONK TRIBUTE color *Downbeat* v84 no6 p58 Je 2017

LARRY CORYELL BACK FROM THE BRINK [Cover story] color *Downbeat* v84 no2 p34 F 2017

Lovano, Valdés Explore Common Language color *Downbeat* v84 no3 p16 Mr 2017

Memorable Tributes Enliven Newport Sets color *Downbeat* v84 no10 p14 O 2017

Metal Guitarist Skolnick Gets Jazzy on Trio Project color *Downbeat* v84 no1 p15 Ja 2017

MICHAËL ATTIAS color *Downbeat* v84 no4 p22 Ap 2017

Outside the Box color *Downbeat* v84 no6 p32 Je 2017

Remembering Allan Holdsworth bw *Downbeat* v84 no7 p22 Jl 2017

Remembering Alphonse Mouzon bw color *Downbeat* v84 no4 p18 Ap 2017

Strings: Shredded & Bowed color *Downbeat* v83 no11 p58 N 2016

Tribute to a Maestro color *Downbeat* v84 no5 p8 My 2017

YOTAM SILBERSTEIN Burning Brightly color *Downbeat* v84 no2 p20 F 2017

Milk—Physiological aspects

Pick the Right Food for Every Task S. FEIEREISEN color *Reader's Digest* v190 no1135 p35 N 2017

Milkshakes

Milking It N. H. Reeder color *Ebony* v72 no9 p51 Jl/Ag 2017

Milkweeds

Long-Term Trends in Midwestern Milkweed Abundances and Their Relevance to Monarch Butterfly Declines D. N. ZAYA, I. S. PEARSE et al *BioScience* v67 no4 p343 Ap 2017

Pod Cast color *National Wildlife (World Edition)* v54 no6 p50 O/N 2016

Milky Way

See also
Solar system

Black holes may make good neighbors A. YEAGER *Science News* v191 no4 p8 Mr 4 2017

Cosmic rays raid the Milky Way L. GROSSMAN color *Science News* v192 no6 p7 O 14 2017

A Dark Milky Way L. KRUESI color *Discover* v38 no1 p78 Ja/F 2017

Gaia mission maps over 1 billion stars C. CROCKETT color *Science News* v190 no8 p16 O 15 2016

GALLERY *Sky & Telescope* v134 no4 p72 O 2017

How high-speed stars escape the galaxy [Cover story] B. Dorminey color *Astronomy* v45 no3 p22 Mr 2017

Milky Way May Be Made with Swapped Gas C. M. CARLISLE color *Sky & Telescope* v134 no5 p10 N 2017

MILKY WAY MEGAMOSAIC T. O'Donoghue *Sky & Telescope* v133 no6 p75 Je 2017

Milky Way's black hole may hurl galactic spitballs our way C. Crockett color *Science News* v191 no2 p11 F 4 2017

Ml7: The Nebula With Too Many Names: Follow this observers guide to find one of the best H II regions in the night sky H. Banich *Sky & Telescope* v134 no3 p57 S 2017

My Stars! *Arizona Highways* v93 no4 p5 Ap 2017

New survey strikes gold color *Astronomy* v45 no2 p74 F 2017

No new stellar births in the galaxy's center color *Astronomy* v44 no12 p12 D 2016

PLANETS OF THE MILKY WAY E. BETZ diag *Discover* v38 no1 p40 Ja/F 2017

READER GALLERY C. Eduardo Fairbairn, D. Crowson et al bw color *Astronomy* v45 no11 p72 N 2017

READER GALLERY color *Astronomy* v45 no3 p70 Mr 2017

'Runaway' stars fled nearby galaxy color *Science* v357 no6346 p8 Jl 7 2017

Seven dwarfs of winter S. J. O'MEARA color *Astronomy* v44 no12 p18 D 2016

SIZING UP PLANETARY NEBULAE R. Talcott color *Astronomy* v45 no1 p44 Ja 2017

Spirits of Our Galaxy's Past M. Young *Sky & Telescope* v133 no4 p22 Ap 2017

The star clusters of Puppis P. HARRINGTON color *Astronomy* v45 no3 p68 Mr 2017

To Build A Really Loud Hailer A. MACROBERT *Sky & Telescope* v134 no3 p40 S 2017

Treasures of the Tarantula G. Bryant color graph *Sky & Telescope* v134 no5 p24 N 2017

Void "Repels" Milky Way's Galaxy Group C. M. CARLISLE *Sky & Telescope* v133 no5 p8 My 2017

When galaxies become CANNIBALS [Cover story] M. West color *Astronomy* v44 no12 p20 D 2016

Milky Way—Atlases

The Milky Way, Transformed S. Hall and S. Goudarzi color *Scientific American* v315 no6 p14 D 2016

Milky Way—History

Amateur Astrophotographers Wanted D. Martinez-Delgado *Sky & Telescope* v133 no4 p29 Ap 2017

Mill, John Stuart, 1806-1873

A New Us W. Voegeli *Claremont Review of Books* v17 no3 p12 Summ 2017

Psychological Harm and Free Speech on Campus A. Cohen *Society* v54 no4 p320 Ag 2017

Millar, Michael

Emergence and spread of a human-transmissible multidrug-resistant nontuberculous mycobacterium bibl diag graph *Science* v354 no6313 p751 N 11 2016

Millar, Sarah E.

Regeneration of fat cells from myofibroblasts during wound healing bibl color graph *Science* v355 no6326 p748 F 17 2017

Millard, Candice

Hero of the Empire: The Boer War, a Daring Escape and the Making of Winston Churchill D. Saunders *Military History* v33 no6 p72 Mr 2017

An Indomitable Young Man A. VON TUNZELMANN *New York Times Book Review* p14 O 9 2016

Millard, Drew

High-Visibility Golf Balls *New York Times Magazine* p24 S 3 2017

Millard, Elizabeth

Bonfire Basics color *Log Home Living* v33 no9 p38 D 2016

Companion Planting color *Log Home Living* v34 no1 p24 F 2017

Coop It Up color *Log Home Living* v34 no2 p36 Mr 2017

Garden Variety color *Log Home Living* v34 no9 p34 D 2017

Good Enough to Eat color *Log Home Living* v34 no4 p36 My 2017

Grow Up color *Log Home Living* v34 no6 p36 Ag 2017

How Does Your Garden Glow? Creating a moon garden is easy and affordable. The result is an unexpected delight on a balmy summer night color *Log Home Living* v34 no5 p34 Jl 2017

Made in the Shade color map *Log Home Living* v34 no3 p34 Ap 2017

Plant Now for Winter (Really!) color *Log Home Living* v33 no7 p38 S 2016

MILLARD, PAUL

Life cartoon *Reader's Digest* v190 no1132 p30 Jl/Ag 2017

Millay, Edna St. Vincent

c. 1945: Austerlitz, NY *Lapham's Quarterly* v10 no2 p176 Spr 2017

Mille Lacs Lake (Minn.)

snowbound but beautiful D. MCMILLEN color map *Cabin Living* p18 Je 2017

MILLEA, HOLLY

STEP RIGHT UP! SEE THE REINVENTION OF THE GREAT AMERICAN CIRCUS *Smithsonian* v48 no4 p38 Jl/Ag 2017

Millepied, Benjamin, 1977-

California Dreaming: Benjamin Millepied is taking L.A. Dance Project to new horizons C. BAUER *Dance Magazine* v91 no6 p31 Je 2017

Miller, A. A.

iPTF16geu: A multiply imaged, gravitationally lensed type Ia supernova color diag graph *Science* v356 no6335 p291 Ap 21 2017

Miller, Alexander Christie

In Turkey, Erdogan builds a megamosque that outdoes the sultans color *Christian Century* v133 no21 p15 O 12 2016

MILLER, ALEXIS K.

My Late Term Abortion *Washingtonian Magazine* v52 no9 p64 Je 2017

Miller, Allan

FIRED UP M. Singer cartoon *New Yorker* v92 no48 p18 F 6 2017

Miller, Andrea

connect color *Dance Spirit* v21 no2 p20 F 2017

Miller, Andrew, 1961-

She's Come Unmoored C. MESSUD color *New York Times Book Review* p16 Ja 29 2017

MILLER, ANTHONY G.

An Ecoregion-Based Approach to Protecting Half the Terrestrial Realm *BioScience* v67 no6 p534 Je 2017

MILLER, ARTHUR

THOUGHTS ON Property *Forbes* v199 no5 p124 My 16 2017

Miller, B. J.

THE HOUSE AT THE END OF THE WORLD J. Mooallem *New York Times Magazine* p38 Ja 8 2017

Miller, Ben

A Bustle in the Hedgerow *Publishers Weekly* v264 no22 p48 My 29 2017

Is anyone out there? M. Huerta color *Science* v354 no6311 p424 O 28 2016

Miller, Bill

The Unreformed Stock Picker A. GARA color *Forbes* v200 no1 p56 Jl 27 2017

MILLER, BLAKE

5 Myths About Exercise color *Prevention* v69 no11 p30 N 2017

Miller, Bode, 1977-

COMEBACK KID? T. Neville color *Skiing* p15 Wint 2017

MILLER, BRIAN

We Need a Biologically Sound North American Conservation Plan *BioScience* v67 no8 p685 Ag 2017

Miller, Bryan

Mystery, Adventure, and Julia color *Climbing* no357 p28 N 2017

Miller, Buffy Hargett

All Set for Thanksgiving color *Southern Living* v51 no11 p19 N 2016

MILLER, C. CHET

The Stretch Goal Paradox color diag il img *Harvard Business Review* v95 no1 p92 Ja/F 2017

Miller, Chuck

Posthole color *Powder* v45 no4 p146 D 2016

MILLER, CLARK A.

It's Not a War on Science *Issues in Science & Technology* v33 no3 p26 Spr 2017

Miller, Corin

Systemic pan-AMPK activator MK-8722 improves glucose homeostasis but induces cardiac hypertrophy graph *Science* v357 no6350 p507 Ag 4 2017

Miller, D. A., 1948-

Hidden Hitchcock B. PARKER *Film Quarterly* v70 no4 p135 Summ 2017

Miller, Dana

back at the ranch color *Better Homes & Gardens* v95 no2 p29 F 2016

Miller, Danica

Understanding Louise Erdrich *American Indian Quarterly* v41 no3 p287 Summ 2017

Miller, Danny—Interviews

MBAS ARE MORE SELF-SERVING THAN OTHER CEOS N. Torres color *Harvard Business Review* v94 no12 p32 D 2016

Miller, Darcy

sue

Get to know ... Your hamstrings color *Yoga Journal* no294 p62 S 2017

Get to know ... Your IT band [Cover story] color *Yoga Journal* no295 p62 O 2017

Get to know ... Your thoracic spine color *Yoga Journal* no296 p64 N 2017

The shoulder girdle [Cover story] color *Yoga Journal* no291 p56 My 2017

Your glutes [Cover story] color *Yoga Journal* no292 p62 Je 2017

Miller, Johanna

Antihydrogen gives way to spectroscopic study *Physics Today* v70 no2 p16 F 2017

Chemistry Nobel honors mechanical bonds, molecular machines *Physics Today* v69 no12 p18 D 2016

Electron diffraction sees hydrogen atoms *Physics Today* v70 no3 p16 Mr 2017

Exceptional points make for exceptional sensors *Physics Today* v70 no10 p23 O 2017

Force spectroscopy unveils hidden protein-folding states *Physics Today* v70 no5 p16 My 2017

Metal-organic framework extracts water from thin air *Physics Today* v70 no6 p16 Je 2017

Ocean currents respond to climate change in unexpected ways *Physics Today* v70 no1 p17 Ja 2017

Passive cooling doesn't cost the planet *Physics Today* v70 no4 p16 Ap 2017

Quantum gases cooled to long-range antiferromagnetic order: The observation of a checkerboard pattern in a lattice of ultracold atoms is a sign of even more exciting experiments to come *Physics Today* v70 no8 p17 Ag 2017

Radar reveals new hot spots on Enceladus *Physics Today* v70 no5 p18 My 2017

Rapid data exchange helps keep a secret for 24 hours *Physics Today* v69 no11 p19 N 2016

Semiconductor metamaterial fools the Hall effect *Physics Today* v70 no2 p21 F 2017

Solar steam generator needs no lenses or mirrors *Physics Today* v69 no11 p17 N 2016

Solid-state NMR resolves protein structures-no deuteration required *Physics Today* v69 no10 p19 O 2016

X rays peer inside a magnet: Submicron spin textures in bulk magnetic materials have been stubbornly hard to detect *Physics Today* v70 no9 p17 S 2017

Miller, John F.

ATMOSPHERIC ELECTRICAL PHENOMENA: A Pilot's View il *Weatherwise* v70 no5 p32 S/O 2017

Miller, John G.

Hold Yourself Accountable-You'll Be Happier *Time* v188 no22-23 p20 N/D 2016

MILLER, JOHN J.

California's Bilingual-Ed Mistake il *National Review* v69 no6 p19 Ap 3 2017

Digging Politics *National Review* v69 no8 p42 My 2017

Familiar Fictions color *National Review* v69 no15 p22 Ag 14 2017

Fifty Flags color *National Review* v69 no12 p22 Je 26 2017

Introducing Jim Banks color *National Review* v68 no23 p24 D 19 2016

It Didn't Happen Here *National Review* v69 no1 p40 Ja 23 2017

The Many-Sided Sci-Fi Master color *National Review* v69 no19 p52 O 16 2017

Master of The Surreal color *National Review* v69 no11 p38 Je 12 2017

Miller, Johnny

THE BEST GRIP IN THE GAME color *Golf Magazine* v58 no12 p71 D 2016

BIG BEAR, CALIFORNIA bw color *Snowboarder* v29 no4 p96 D 2016

Miller, Jo—Interviews

FULL-FRONTAL ASSAULT V. HEFFERNAN cartoon color *Wired* v25 no4 p68 Ap 2017

MILLER, JOSHUA A.

GOAL ORIENTED *Cincinnati Magazine* v50 no7 p24 Ap 2017

INK TENT *Cincinnati Magazine* v50 no8 p32 My 2017

Life Coach *Cincinnati Magazine* v50 no4 p56 Ja 2017

Miller, Joyce

WHERE HAVE ALL THE GOOD DIVES GONE? K. WOLFE *Cincinnati Magazine* v50 no2 p53 N 2016

Miller, Julie

KUMAIL NANJIANI color *Vanity Fair* v59 no7 p60 Summ 2017

THE NEW ESTABLISHMENT 2017 bw color *Vanity Fair* v59 no11 p87 N 2017

NEW ESTABLISHMENT bw cartoon color *Vanity Fair* v58 no11 p124 N 2016

Star Without a Script bw color *Vanity Fair* v59 no1 p136 Holiday 2017

MILLER, JUSTIN

Battle of the Plutocrats *New Republic* v248 no11 p8 N 2017

Chicago's Plan to Stop Wage Theft *In These Times* v41 no4 p10 Ap 2017

Miller, K.

Observation of coherent elastic neutrino-nucleus scattering diag *Science* v357 no6356 p1123 S 15 2017

MILLER, KARA

KEEPING THE FAITH in Seminary color *Christianity Today* v60 no8 p87 O 2016

Miller, Karen Maezen

On Garden Time color *AARP: The Magazine* v59 no6A p69 O/N 2016

Miller, Kei

FLY AWAY L. MILLER color *New Yorker* v93 no14 p88 My 22 2017

MILLER, KELLEY

Naughty PETS *National Geographic Kids* no466 p7 D 2016/Ja 2017

sports funnies color *National Geographic Kids* no465 p9 N 2016

Sports Funnies color *National Geographic Kids* no472 p9 Ag 2017

Sports Funnies color *National Geographic Kids* no475 p6 N 2017

Miller, Kelly E.

Cassini finds molecular hydrogen in the Enceladus plume: Evidence for hydrothermal processes chart graph *Science* v356 no6334 p155 Ap 14 2017

Miller, Kelsey

Brides Above Size 14, Read This! color *Glamour* v115 no5 p60 My 2017

stretch your limits color *Good Housekeeping* v264 no5 p97 My 2017

"WHY I LOVE not dieting" color *Good Housekeeping* v263 no5 p159 N 2016

MILLER, KEN

A MOUNTAIN OF TROUBLE *Reader's Digest* v188 no1124 p108 O 2016

Miller, Kenneth

AFTER THE ICU color *Prevention* v69 no1 p84 Ja 2017

THE BRAIN OF BEN BARRES color diag *Discover* v38 no7 p58 S 2017

FIDO'S NO FOODIE [Cover story] color *Prevention* v69 no5 p84 My 2017

Jessica Lange Can Finally Relax color *AARP: The Magazine* v60 no5A p40 Ag/S 2017

A SOLDIER'S LAST BEDTIME Story *Reader's Digest* v189 no1128 p80 Mr 2017

Miller, Kim F.

14 TRAINING TIPS FROM OLYMPIAN CARL HESTER [Cover story] color *Practical Horseman* v45 no7 p42 Jl 2017

Business with a Cause color *Practical Horseman* v45 no10 p72 O 2017

CLASSIC MEETS CUTTING-EDGE [Cover story] color *Practical Horseman* v45 no7 p26 Jl 2017

COLLEGIATE EVENTING COMES OF AGE color *Practical Horseman* v44 no12 p24 D 2016

Giving Back to the SPORT [Cover story] color diag *Dressage Today* v24 no2 p38 N 2017

MAKING THEIR HORSES — AND THEIR MARK color *Practical Horseman* v45 no3 p28 Mr 2017

New Challenge Off to a Successful Start color *Practical Horseman* v45 no9 p70 S 2017

Riding with "GOD" color *Dressage Today* v23 no10 p46 Jl 2017

Taking on the Big-Sister Role color *Practical Horseman* v45 no6 p80 Je 2017

USHJA Focuses on Growth and Sport Integrity color *Practical*

Horseman v45 no3 p66 Mr 2017

Miller, Kimberly Rae
Body Work: A memoir recounts a lifelong addiction to dieting M. MELTZER *New York Times Book Review* p21 S 10 2017

Miller, Kirk
Q: What is the most significant fad of all time? color *Atlantic* v319 no3 p96 Ap 2017

Miller, Klancy
CHIC CHEFS bw color *Harper's Bazaar* no3654 p99 Je/Jl 2017

Miller, Kristi
The thing I wanted to say ... S. PROUDFOOT color *Maclean's* no1 p23 F 17 2017

Miller, Laura
A FAMILY AFFAIR cartoon *New Yorker* v93 no23 p75 Ag 7 2017
FLY AWAY color *New Yorker* v93 no14 p88 My 22 2017
FORK YOU cartoon *New Yorker* v92 no47 p68 Ja 30 2017
A LITTLE STRANGER color *New Yorker* v93 no10 p96 Ap 24 2017
MANHATTAN TRANSFER cartoon *New Yorker* v93 no19 p67 Jl 3 2017
OFF TO SEE THE WIZARDS A. S. GREER color *New York Times Book Review* p69 D 4 2016

MILLER, LAURA MARJORIE
The Wolves of Winter *Yankee* v81 no1 p20 Ja/F 2017

Miller, Laurel
Lost Skills of the cattle drive bw *American Cowboy* p66 LEGENDS OF TEXAS Special Issue 2017

Miller, Lee E.
Getting People to Believe in Something They Can't Yet Imagine *Harvard Business Review Digital Articles* p2 O 10 2014

Miller, Leigh Anne
Center Stage bw *Art in America* v105 no5 p51 My 2017
Character Study bw *Art in America* v105 no3 p57 Mr 2017
DESERT OASIS color *Art in America* v105 no8 p51 S 2017
Family Circus bw *Art in America* v104 no10 p79 N 2016
Going the Distance bw *Art in America* v104 no11 p59 D 2016
Snow Day bw *Art in America* v105 no4 p55 Ap 2017
Street Smarts *Art in America* v104 no9 p61 O 2016

Miller, Lisa
"A Girl Can't Be President" *New York* v49 no23 p18 N 14 2016
FORD COUNTRY, TRUMP'S AMERICA img *New York* v50 no10 p32 My 15 2017
THE GUN EXCHANGE img *New York* v49 no26 p22 D 26 2016
"I Don't Know if He Knows How Lucky He Was" [Cover story] *Reader's Digest* v188 no1126 p67 D 2016/Ja 2017
John Hinckley Left the Mental Hospital Seven Months Ago img *New York* v50 no6 p42 Mr 20 2017
What to Do About Getting Old img *New York* p32 Ja 23 2017
Who Is Betsy DeVos? And how did she get to be head of our schools? img *New York* v50 no15 p28 Jl 24 2017

Miller, Lynne
Popular piety color *U.S. Catholic* v82 no2 p5 F 2017

MILLER, M. H.
DON'T CALL IT A COMEBACK bw cartoon color *ARTnews* v115 no3 p118 Fall 2016

Miller, Mac, 1992——Interviews
Q&A Mac Miller B. HIATT color *Rolling Stone* no1273 p22 N 3 2016

MILLER, MARY
GIFTS that UPLIFT! cartoon *O, The Oprah Magazine* p148 D 2016

Miller, Matt
Beck Goes Pop (Again) color *Esquire* p24 N 2017
FITZGERALD & ME color *Esquire* p32 Je/Jl 2017

Miller, Meredith
Temp workers, permanent effects: how temps changed the nature of the U.S. workforce *Monthly Labor Review* p1 D 2016

MILLER, MERRILL
WHO WILL WE SPEAK FOR? *Humanist* v77 no1 p17 Ja/F 2017

Miller, Miriam
TALK TO US color *Dance Spirit* v20 no9 p20 N 2016

Miller, Paddy
Get More Actionable Ideas from Your Employees *Harvard Business Review Digital Articles* p2 N 25 2014

Miller, Patina, 1984-
MADAM SECRETARY DECLASSIFIED M. LOGAN *TV Guide*

v64 no15 p42 Ap 4 2016

Miller, Paul D.
American Power and Liberal Order: A Conservative Internationalist Grand Strategy W. R. Mead *Foreign Affairs* v96 no1 p164 Ja/F 2017

MILLER, PETER H.
LAKE OR POND... color *Cabin Living* p80 Ag 2017

Miller, Randy
MEET IAN ANDREWES *Sea Magazine* v108 no10 pPNW-8 O 2016

Miller, Rebecca
Neandertal and Denisovan DNA from Pleistocene sediments bw color *Science* v356 no6338 p605 My 12 2017

Miller, Rich
'Chairman Cohn' Has a Nice Ring to It color graph *Bloomberg Businessweek* no4533 p32 Ag 7 2017

Miller, Richard
Find lasting peace [Cover story] *Yoga Journal* no290 p28 Mr 2017
Learn to listen to your emotions *Yoga Journal* no287 p26 N 2016
Let joy in [Cover story] *Yoga Journal* no289 p22 F 2017
The long game [Cover story] *Yoga Journal* no291 p26 My 2017
Take it all in cartoon *Yoga Journal* no288 p38 D 2016

Miller, Richard D.
Kilogram-scale prexasertib monolactate monohydrate synthesis under continuous-flow CGMP conditions chart diag *Science* v356 no6343 p1144 Je 16 2017

Miller, Robert
'GRAND SLAM' EVOLUTION D. Ouellette color *Downbeat* v84 no3 p45 Mr 2017

Miller, Sam
Applied Thermodynamics for Meteorologists J. Knox *Physics Today* v69 no12 p58 D 2016

Miller, Sarah
My Horse Minya *Arabian Horse World* v57 no11 p39 Ag 2017

Miller, Scott
Work in Progress J. Y. WOOD color *Power & Motoryacht* v34 no8 p58 Ag 2017

Miller, Shannon McClintock
Building a Digital Toolbox color *Publishers Weekly* v264 no34 p46 Ag 21 2017

Miller, Sienna, 1981-
HER BEST EVER! Sienna Miller E. Wilson color *InStyle* v24 no1 p36 Ja 2017

Miller, Stacia C.
Movement and learning in elementary school color *Phi Delta Kappan* v98 no7 p34 Ap 2017

Miller, Stephen
Getting and Spending *Weekly Standard* v22 no21 p38 F 6 2017
Invisible Handler bw color *Weekly Standard* v22 no23 p30 F 20 2017
A Modest Proposal *Weekly Standard* v22 no35 p38 My 22 2017
ONE. HUNDRED. PERCENT J. GREEN bw color *Bloomberg Businessweek* no4513 p50 Mr 6 2017
The Spirit of '45 color *Weekly Standard* v22 no14 p34 D 12 2016
STEPHEN MILLER'S WHITE RAGE W. D. COHAN bw color *Vanity Fair* v59 no7 p102 Summ 2017
Survival of the Pithiest color *Weekly Standard* v22 no30 p30 Ap 10 2017
Word Inflation *Weekly Standard* v22 no34 p47 My 15 2017

Miller, Susan
Ask anything [Cover story] color *Women's Health* v14 no1 p24 Ja/F 2017

Miller, T. J.
"People Need a Villain": T. J. Miller knows you think he's crazy for leaving HBO's Silicon Valley, and he cares not in the least D. Marchese img *New York* v50 no15 p57 Jl 24 2017
T. J. MILLER color *Esquire* v166 no5 p156 D 2016/Ja 2017
T.J. MILLER D. Snierson color *Entertainment Weekly* no1442 p50 D 2 2016 Rebellious Special Issue
True Masculinity Is Grooming Your Elbows T. J. MILLER color *GQ: Gentlemen's Quarterly* v86 no11 p66 N 2016
WHY We LOVE CHICAGO bw cartoon color *Chicago* v66 no3 p75 Mr 2017

Miller, T. J.——Interviews
DISRUPTION BY DESIGN S. NYGAARD color *Men's Health* v32 no7 p(Sp)28 S 2017

HAVE YOURSELF A FILTHY LITTLE CHRISTMAS [Cover story] D. Snierson color diag *Entertainment Weekly* no1443 p28 D 9 2016

Miller, Tory
Burn 40 Pounds of Fat B. GREGORY color *Men's Health* v32 no7 p64 S 2017

Miller, Trisha
DEAR ROPER B. Welch *Spin to Win Rodeo* v20 no10 p14 D 2016

MILLER, VINCENT J.
The Geography of Mercy color *America* v215 no11 p14 O 17 2016

Miller, Von, 1989-
Von Miller: How an MVP Gets Better J. Nosek color *Men's Health* v31 no10 p54 D 2016
Von Miller M. Rich color *Current Biography* v78 no3 p68 Mr 2017

Miller, Wentworth, 1972-
ON THE RUN AGAIN N. Abrams color *Entertainment Weekly* no1459 p54 Mr 31 2017

Miller, Wentworth, 1972—Interviews
Brothers in ARMS M. ROFFMAN *TV Guide* p30 Ap 17 2017

Miller, Zachary D.
Enantioselective photochemistry through Lewis acid–catalyzed triplet energy transfer bibl chart diag graph *Science* v354 no6318 p1391 D 16 2016

Miller, Zeke J.
After the Massacre [Cover story] color diag *Time* v190 no15 p22 O 16 2017
The Angels of Irma [Cover story] color map *Time* v190 no12 p34 S 25 2017
As the White House Turns: A Guide to the Shifting Power Centers Among Trump's Top Advisers color *Time* v189 no15 p10 Ap 24 2017
Beyond Repeal and Replace color diag map *Time* v190 no2/3 p30 Jl 10-17 2017
Bigots, Boosted by the Bully Pulpit color *Time* v190 no8 p30 Ag 28 2017
The Budget Battle Shows That Trump Needs to Read the Fine Print color *Time* v189 no18 p11 My 15 2017
Can He Be Tamed? color *Time* v189 no24 p36 Je 26 2017
Can Trump Handle the Truth? [Cover story] color *Time* v189 no12 p32 Ap 3 2017
Chaos Theory [Cover story] color *Time* v189 no7/8 p32 F 27 2017
The Comey Misfire color *Time* v189 no19 p20 My 22 2017
Country First [Cover story] color *Time* v190 no7 p26 Ag 21 2017
Dark Secrets, Dirty Bombs [Cover story] color map *Time* v189 no14 p28 Ap 17 2017
The Face of the Opposition [Cover story] color *Time* v189 no6 p26 F 20 2017
Family First [Cover story] color *Time* v189 no22 p24 Je 12 2017
Houston After Harvey color *Time* v190 no10/11 p38 S 18 2017
How Donald Trump Jr.'s Emails Have Cranked Up the Heat on His Family [Cover story] color *Time* v190 no4 p22 Jl 24 2017
How He Won color *Time* v188 no21 p48 N 21 2016
How President Trump Is Trampling Precedent color *Time* v189 no4 p9 F 6 2017
How Trump Is Restocking the Washington Swamp color *Time* v188 no27-28 p14 D 26 2016
How Trump Plans to Win-Even If He Loses the Election color diag *Time* v188 no18 p9 O 31 2016
The Inner Circle of Trump's Inner Circle color *Time* v189 no3 p34 Ja 30 2017
Inside Donald Trump's War Against the State [Cover story] color *Time* v189 no10 p26 Mr 20 2017
Kim Jong Un Isn't the Only Wild Card In the North Korea Crisis color *Time* v190 no10/11 p11 S 18 2017
The Lost Colony color *Time* v190 no15 p32 O 16 2017
Message Delivered [Cover story] color *Time* v188 no21 p28 N 21 2016
Modernize the Skies color *Time* v189 no13 p28 Ap 10 2017
Money In Politics color *Time* v188 no21 p56 N 21 2016
The Person of the Year [Cover story] color diag map *Time* v188 no25-26 p46 D 19 2016 Double Issue
RIP, Repeal and Replace? The GOP Faces a New Crossroads color *Time* v190 no5 p13 Jl 31 2017
Russia and the Trump Campaign color *Time* v189 no12 p36 Ap 3 2017

The Second Most Powerful Man In the World? [Cover story] color *Time* v189 no5 p24 F 13 2017
The Straight Story N. Gibbs color *Time* v189 no4 p4 F 6 2017
The Suite of Power [Cover story] color *Time* v189 no23 p22 Je 19 2017
The Troublemaker color *Time* v189 no3 p22 Ja 16 2017
The Trouble With Russia color map *Time* v189 no7/8 p44 F 27 2017
Trump After Hours [Cover story] color *Time* v189 no19 p28 My 22 2017
Trump and His Allies Stumble As Russia Probe Moves Closer to the White House color *Time* v189 no21 p9 Je 5 2017
Trump Goes to War [Cover story] color *Time* v188 no16/17 p20 O 24 2016
Trump's American Vision [Cover story] color *Time* v189 no3 p24 Ja 30 2017
Trump's Attacks Sow Chaos In Washington color *Time* v190 no6 p7 Ag 7 2017
Trump's Loyalty Test [Cover story] color *Time* v189 no20 p24 My 29 2017
Trump's Offensive Playbook [Cover story] color *Time* v190 no14 p32 O 9 2017
Trump Takes Over color *Time* v188 no22-23 p24 N/D 2016
The Truth Is Out There color *Time* v188 no15 p28 O 17 2016
An Unlikely Salesman for the Republican Party's Tax Plan color *Time* v190 no14 p9 O 9 2017
What It Will Take to Rebuild America [Cover story] color *Time* v189 no13 p22 Ap 10 2017
The White House Survival Guide color *Time* v189 no4 p30 Ja 23 2017
Why President Trump Is Struggling to Staff His Government color *Time* v189 no11 p9 Mr 27 2017
Why the U.S. Is Cracking Down on Gadgets In Airplane Cabins color *Time* v189 no12 p11 Ap 3 2017
Will Bob Mueller Separate Fact from Fiction? [Cover story] color *Time* v190 no1 p24 Jl 3 2017
Winter White House color *Time* v189 no7/8 p50 F 27 2017

Miller Electric Manufacturing Co.
GEAR BOX color *Dirt Sports + Off-Road* v51 no9 p70 S 2017

Millets
Super BOWLS [Cover story] K. HYMORE color *Prevention* v69 no2 p82 F 2017

Millett, Kate, 1934-2017
Kate Millett L. Rothman color *Time* v190 no12 p15 S 25 2017

Millgate, Kris
2016 BEST OF THE BEST bw color *Field & Stream* v121 no7 p96 D 2016/Ja 2017
The Bighorns Are Back *Idaho Magazine* v16 no5 p20 F 2017
Cheers & Jeers cartoon color *Field & Stream* v121 no9 p14 Ap 2017
Cisco Time *Idaho Magazine* v17 no1 p18 Ja 2017
Let Go: Gliding over the Tetons *Idaho Magazine* v16 no8 p40 My 2017

Millhauser, Steven
1883: New York City *Lapham's Quarterly* v10 no2 p39 Spr 2017

Milligan, James A.
Systemic pan-AMPK activator MK-8722 improves glucose homeostasis but induces cardiac hypertrophy graph *Science* v357 no6350 p507 Ag 4 2017

MILLIKEN, DOUGLAS W.
INTEGERS *Humanist* v77 no3 p41 My/Je 2017

MILLIKEN, GARY
Chords & Discords bw color *Downbeat* v84 no2 p10 F 2017

MILLIKEN, GRENNAN
GEAR FOR THE LONG HAUL color *Popular Science* p18 Ja/F 2017
A Shoe Sole That Won't Slip on Ice color *Popular Science* v288 no6 p58 N/D 2016

Milliken, Kirsten
PlayDHD: Permission to Play; A Prescription for Adults with ADHD color *Publishers Weekly* v263 no52 p75 D 19 2016

Milliken, Kitty L.
Release of mineral-bound water prior to subduction tied to shallow seismogenic slip off Sumatra graph *Science* v356 no6340 p841 My 26 2017

Milliken, R. E.

Redox stratification of an ancient lake in Gale crater, Mars color *Science* v356 no6341 p922 Je 1 2017

Milliken, Ralph

OUR MOON'S MANTLE IS WETTER THAN WE THOUGHT A. Klesman bw *Astronomy* v45 no11 p12 N 2017

Milliken, W.

Persistent effects of pre-Columbian plant domestication on Amazonian forest composition bibl chart graph map *Science* v355 no6328 p925 Mr 3 2017

MILLIKIN, PATRICK

A Tragic Hero color *Publishers Weekly* v264 no19 p31 My 8 2017

Millinery

Life at the top S. Kelly cartoon *Magazine Antiques* v184 no1 p124 Ja/F 2017

Millini, Roberto

Beyond trial and error for zeolite catalysts bibl diag *Science* v355 no6329 p1028 Mr 10 2017

Millionaires—Charts, diagrams, etc.

THE MILLIONAIRES CLUB color diag map *Money* v46 no8 p50 S 2017

Millionaires—United States

CITIES OF GOLD B. O'keefe diag *Fortune* v176 no2 p116 Ag 1 2017

Government By Gazzillionaires N. Tabor and J. D. Walsh img *New York* p30 Ja 23 2017

HOW THEY DID IT K. Bahler color *Money* v46 no8 p52 S 2017

THE MILLIONAIRES CLUB color diag map *Money* v46 no8 p50 S 2017

Milliot, Jim

Adult Nonfiction Stayed Hot in 2016 chart *Publishers Weekly* v264 no3 p4 Ja 16 2017

Amazon Books Spreads Out *Publishers Weekly* v264 no13 p4 Mr 27 2017

Amazon Books Will Be the Nation's Fifth-Largest Bookstore Chain chart color *Publishers Weekly* v264 no23 p6 Je 5 2017

Amazon Buy-Button Change Raises Alarms, Questions *Publishers Weekly* v264 no20 p4 My 15 2017

Amazon Is the Big First-Quarter Winner chart *Publishers Weekly* v264 no15 p16 Ap 10 2017

The Answer is... Scholastic *Publishers Weekly* v264 no9 p4 F 27 2017

The Bad News About E-books graph *Publishers Weekly* v264 no4 p4 Ja 23 2017

The Big Stories of 2016 color *Publishers Weekly* v263 no52 p6 D 19 2016

B&N Keeps Its Focus On Revenue Growth chart *Publishers Weekly* v264 no26 p2 Je 26 2017

B&N Looking for a Sales Rebound chart color *Publishers Weekly* v263 no48 p4 N 28 2016

B&N Still Searching For "Magic Bullet" to Stop Sales Slide chart *Publishers Weekly* v264 no10 p4 Mr 6 2017

BolognaFiere Confirms 2018 N.Y.C. Rights Show *Publishers Weekly* v264 no15 p13 Ap 10 2017

Bookstore Sales Rose Again in 2016 chart color *Publishers Weekly* v264 no8 p10 F 20 2017

Business & Economics bw color *Publishers Weekly* v263 no51 p25 D 12 2016

Business & Economics color *Publishers Weekly* v264 no26 p28 Je 26 2017

A Different Feel at BookExpo 2017 color *Publishers Weekly* v264 no23 p4 Je 5 2017

Diversification Drives Gains at Abrams color *Publishers Weekly* v264 no35 p8 Ag 28 2017

DOMINIQUE RACCAH color *Publishers Weekly* v263 no52 p20 D 19 2016

Estimates Show a 6.6% Decline in Industry chart *Publishers Weekly* v264 no25 p5 Je 19 2017

E-tailers Widen Bookselling Edge chart graph *Publishers Weekly* v264 no18 p4 My 1 2017

Fast-Growing Independent Publishers, 2017 chart color *Publishers Weekly* v264 no15 p36 Ap 10 2017

Fiction Most Popular Category on Audiobooks.com graph *Publishers Weekly* v264 no11 p20 Mr 13 2017

Finding the Right Balance color *Publishers Weekly* v264 no24 p5 Je 12 2017

Flat Sales Identified as Top Industry Problem graph *Publishers*

Weekly v264 no40 p5 O 2 2017

France Loves Calendar Girl chart map *Publishers Weekly* v264 no12 p22 Mr 20 2017

Getting the Measure of Downloadable Audio chart *Publishers Weekly* v264 no38 p5 S 18 2017

'GOTT' Was Tops In 2016 *Publishers Weekly* v264 no33 p12 Ag 14 2017

HarperCollins Marks Its 200th Anniversary bw color *Publishers Weekly* v264 no10 p9 Mr 6 2017

HC Eyes More Global Expansion, Physical Distribution chart *Publishers Weekly* v264 no33 p5 Ag 14 2017

Industry Stocks Were Mixed in 2016 chart *Publishers Weekly* v264 no2 p11 Ja 9 2017

Is This Indigo's Moment? chart *Publishers Weekly* v264 no30 p4 Jl 24 2017

Knopf to Print 200,000 Copies of Nobel Winner Ishiguro's Works color *Publishers Weekly* v264 no41 p10 O 9 2017

Marcus Leaver: CEO, Quarto Group color *Publishers Weekly* v263 no52 p28 D 19 2016

Mel Shapiro Calls It a Career color *Publishers Weekly* v263 no43 p12 O 24 2016

A New Look For New York color *Publishers Weekly* v264 no20 p(Sp)6 My 15 2017

Obama Deal Sparks $65 Million Mystery *Publishers Weekly* v264 no10 p8 Mr 6 2017

O'Leary Takes the Reins at BISG *Publishers Weekly* v263 no39 p5 S 26 2016

Parneros Charged with Reversing B&N Sales Slide chart *Publishers Weekly* v264 no18 p5 My 1 2017

PEARSON RISES ABOVE chart *Publishers Weekly* v264 no35 p56 Ag 28 2017

Penguin Random House Rules The Children's Book Market chart *Publishers Weekly* v263 no45 p4 N 7 2016

Politics, Biography Hot Categories So Far in 2017: With the adult coloring book phenomenon on the decline, other categories step up chart *Publishers Weekly* v264 no29 p1 Jl 17 2017

PRH Employees Unite for Company Week color *Publishers Weekly* v264 no7 p10 F 13 2017

Print, Audio Keep Publishers Moving Ahead chart *Publishers Weekly* v264 no36 p4 S 4 2017

Print Sales Slowed in Third Quarter chart *Publishers Weekly* v263 no42 p4 O 17 2016

Print Units Through September Up 2% chart *Publishers Weekly* v264 no41 p4 O 9 2017

Publishers Did Marginally Better in 2016 chart *Publishers Weekly* v264 no14 p4 Ap 3. 2017

Publishers Find Themselves Enmeshed in Greenpeace–Paper Company Fight *Publishers Weekly* v264 no25 p6 Je 19 2017

Publishers Plan for Future Without Family Christian *Publishers Weekly* v264 no9 p5 F 27 2017

Publishers Post Good Start to 2017 chart *Publishers Weekly* v264 no22 p6 My 29 2017

Publishers See Third-Quarter Bounce chart *Publishers Weekly* v263 no46 p4 N 14 2016

Readerlink Rules *Publishers Weekly* v263 no40 p5 O 3 2016

Reed Sets a New Direction for BEA color *Publishers Weekly* v263 no44 p5 O 31 2016

Regnery Publishing: More Than Just Politics color *Publishers Weekly* v264 no12 p10 Mr 20 2017

The Rise in Print Continues chart *Publishers Weekly* v264 no28 p4 Jl 10 2017

Scholastic Aims to Improve Profits chart color *Publishers Weekly* v264 no30 p5 Jl 24 2017

Search Begins for Raab's Successor at Grand Central color *Publishers Weekly* v263 no52 p12 D 19 2016

The Sky's the Limit for Amazon's Stock chart *Publishers Weekly* v264 no28 p11 Jl 10 2017

Standing Up to President Trump *Publishers Weekly* v264 no5 p7 Ja 30 2017

Trade a Bright Spot In a Down Year for Book Sales chart *Publishers Weekly* v264 no32 p4 Ag 7 2017

Trade Publishers Focused on Strategic Deals In 2016 chart *Publishers Weekly* v264 no1 p7 Ja 2 2017

'Trees' Takes Root in France, Germany chart color *Publishers Weekly* v264 no39 p21 S 25 2017

Waterhouse Press Prepares for Misadventures chart color *Publish-*

ers Weekly v264 no18 p6 My 1 2017

The Year in Children's Bestsellers chart color *Publishers Weekly* v264 no6 p34 F 6 2017

MILLMAN, NOAH

Pondering Prospects for a U.S.-China War *American Conservative* v16 no4 p60 Jl/Ag 2017

What's the Big Idea? *New York Times Book Review* p26 My 7 2017

Whence Comes Legitimacy? il *American Conservative* v16 no2 p12 Mr/Ap 2017

Millner, Denene

Rides a Bike, Runs for Congress color *Glamour* v115 no11 p120 N 2017

MILLS, AMY

What Champion Pitmasters Pack cartoon color *Men's Health* v32 no5 p44 Je 2017

Mills, Carys

MICHIGAN color map *Canadian Geographic* v135 no6 p28 D 2015

Mills, D. J.

Architecture of a transcribing-translating expressome diag graph map *Science* v356 no6334 p194 Ap 14 2017

Mills, David

2 + 2 Can Equal 5 color *Commonweal* v144 no3 p8 F 10 2017

The Challenge of Renovating Historic Aquatic Facilities: How the Dallas Park & Recreation Department is preserving community history and memories *Parks & Recreation* v52 no9 p104 S 2017

What If? color *Commonweal* v144 no7 p39 Ap 14 2017

Mills, Erez

Host cell attachment elicits posttranscriptional regulation in infecting enteropathogenic bacteria bibl graph *Science* v355 no6326 p735 F 17 2017

Mills, Karen

The 4 Types of Small Businesses, and Why Each One Matters *Harvard Business Review Digital Articles* p2 Ap 30 2015

How Companies Can Help Rebuild America's Common Resources *Harvard Business Review Digital Articles* p2 S 21 2015

A Playbook for Making America More Entrepreneurial *Harvard Business Review Digital Articles* p2 My 27 2015

Mills, Kyle

Vince Flynn: Enemy of the State; A Mitch Rapp Novel *Publishers Weekly* v264 no27 p52 Jl 3 2017

Mills, Mark

Where Dead Men Meet *Publishers Weekly* v264 no12 p58 Mr 20 2017

Where Dead Men Meet *Publishers Weekly* v264 no26 p173 Je 26 2017

Mills, Michael

Counter-Counter-Programming M. BERG color *Forbes* v199 no4 p50 Ap 25 2017

Synthesis of mixed hypermetallic oxide BaOCa+ from laser-cooled reagents in an atom-ion hybrid trap diag graph *Science* v357 no6358 p1370 S 29 2017

Mills, Mike

20th Century Women L. Greenblatt color *Entertainment Weekly* no1446/1447 p105 D 2016/Ja 2017

CALIFORNIA DREAMIN' T. FRIEND cartoon color *New Yorker* v92 no44 p32 Ja 9 2017

RYAN McGINLEY *Interview* v46 no10 p128 D 2016/Ja 2017

What Champion Pitmasters Pack cartoon color *Men's Health* v32 no5 p44 Je 2017

When Life Imitates Artifacts C. CHOCANO img *New York* p75 F 9 2017

Mills, Ryan E.

Intersection of diverse neuronal genomes and neuropsychiatric disease: The Brain Somatic Mosaicism Network color *Science* v356 no6336 p395 Ap 28 2017

Millsaps College (Jackson, Miss.)

Millsaps starts Jewish studies minor, Professor James Bowley honored L. J. Green *Successful Farming* v115 no1 p37 Ja 2017

Mills & mill-work

See also

Sawmills

Saving the Family Business A. Reliford color *Good Housekeeping* v265 no1 p63 Jl 2017

Wales for The Weekend E. WINDING color map *Conde Nast*

Traveler v52 no6 p43 Je/Jl 2017

MILMAN, JOELLE

10 TITLES TO PICK UP NOW color *O, The Oprah Magazine* p92 S 2017

Milne, Damian

Publish openly but responsibly color *Science* v357 no6347 p141 Jl 14 2017

Milne, Sol

Higher predation risk for insect prey at low latitudes and elevations graph *Science* v356 no6339 p742 My 19 2017

Milner, Alice M.

Toward pesticidovigilance chart color *Science* v357 no6357 p1232 S 22 2017

Milner, Cas

Issues that pushed the SSC's demise *Physics Today* v70 no8 p12 Ag 2017

Milner, Greg

TUNNEL VISION color *Bloomberg Businessweek* no4534 p52 Ag 14 2017

Milner, Yuri

Breakthrough to the Stars S. NADIS chart color *Discover* v38 no1 p92 Ja/F 2017

Milner, Yuri—Interviews

Yuri Milner S. NADIS color *Discover* v38 no3 p16 Ap 2017

MILORD, CHRISTIAN

Those '60s Flashbacks *Commentary* v142 no4 p10 N 2016

Milos America Inc.

Platforms, Risers & Stage Lifts *Stage Directions* v30 no7 p45 Jl 1 2017

Milosevic, Slobodan, 1941-2006

Is Donald Trump America's Milosevic? P. Glastris *Washington Monthly* p8 Ja/F 2017

Milot, Rebecca L.

Perovskite-perovskite tandem photovoltaics with optimized band gaps bibl chart graph *Science* v354 no6314 p861 N 18 2016

Milsom, Jefrey W.

Taking On Colon Cancer *AARP: The Magazine* v59 no5A p22 Ag/S 2016

Milstein, Aaron D.

Behavioral time scale synaptic plasticity underlies CA1 place fields diag *Science* v357 no6355 p1033 S 8 2017

Milstein, Jeffery

Small Dreams *Treasures* v6 no4 p6 F/Mr 2017

Miltenburg, Sanne

AUTUMN SPLENDOR: Five books celebrate fall in all of its vibrancy color *Publishers Weekly* v264 no29 p216 Jl 17 2017

Milton, Giles

Plotting Hitler's defeat C. Mulley *History Today* v67 no1 p64 Ja 2017

Milton, Grant

Rallying For Grant L. Flynn and T. Keith color *Sports Illustrated* v125 no21 p25 D 26 2016

Milton, John, 1608-1674

Stand & Wait K. S. Franklin cartoon *Commonweal* v144 no3 p39 F 10 2017

Milton, Trevor

HAULIN' JUICE C. Atiyeh color *Car & Driver* v62 no11 p24 My 2017

Milwaukee (Wis.)—Description & travel

Heartland GETAWAYS A. S. ECKERT and C. IANZITO color *AARP: The Magazine* v30 no6A p44 O/N 2017

Milwaukee (Wis.)—Social conditions

Collars on the Corner offers prayers on the streets of Milwaukee D. Paulsen *Christian Century* v134 no17 p18 Ag 16 2017

Milwaukee Brewers (Baseball team)

4 BREWERS color *Sports Illustrated* v126 no9 p106 Mr 27 2017

Milwaukee Bucks (Basketball team)

10 Bucks A. Sharp, B. Golliver et al color *Sports Illustrated* v125 no14 p84 O 24-31 2016

5 BUCKS color *Sports Illustrated* v127 no12 p61 O 16 2017

Milway, Katie Smith

Connecting Unemployed Youth with Organizations That Need Talent *Harvard Business Review Digital Articles* p2 N 3 2016

Don't Wait Until After the Meeting to Start Your Action Items *Harvard Business Review Digital Articles* p2 Ap 28 2016

Nonprofits Can't Keep Ignoring Talent Development *Harvard*

Business Review Digital Articles p2 D 17 2015

Prevent Email Horror with a 2-Minute Send Delay *Harvard Business Review Digital Articles* p2 Jl 23 2015

You Don't Need a Promotion to Grow at Work *Harvard Business Review Digital Articles* p2 Je 24 2015

Milzoff, Rebecca

All the Way Back img *New York* v50 no10 p81 My 15 2017

Becoming a Cats Cat img *New York* v49 no15 p82 Jl 25 2016

Finding the Little Prince img *New York* v49 no15 p84 Jl 25 2016

Julie Taymor Flies Again img *New York* v50 no17 p130 Ag 21 2017

Mimitou, Eleni P.

A global view of meiotic double-strand break end resection bibl graph *Science* v355 no6320 p1 Ja 6 2017

Mimosa

Happy Grandmother's Day S. Evans color *Southern Living* v52 no5 p12 My 2017

Min, Mingwei

UBE2O remodels the proteome during terminal erythroid differentiation diag *Science* v357 no6350 p471 Ag 4 2017

Min Li

Cryo-EM structures and atomic model of the HIV-1 strand transfer complex intasome bibl color *Science* v355 no6320 p1 Ja 6 2017

Quality management for precision medicine clinical applications: A consensus from the China Precision Medicine Clinical Research and Application Association bibl *Science* v354 no6319 p11 D 23 2016

Min Peng

Aerobic glycolysis promotes T helper 1 cell differentiation through an epigenetic mechanism bibl graph *Science* v354 no6311 p481 O 28 2016

Min Zhu

A Silurian maxillate placoderm illuminates jaw evolution bibl color *Science* v354 no6310 p334 O 21 2016

Mina, Denise, 1966-

Scots on the Rocks M. Stasio *New York Times Book Review* p13 My 21 2017

Mina, Denise, 1966—Interviews

All the Shades of Guilt J. FOSTER color *Publishers Weekly* v264 no12 p54 Mr 20 2017

Mina Matsuo

Overlapping memory trace indispensable for linking, but not recalling, individual memories bibl graph *Science* v355 no6323 p398 Ja 27 2017

Minaj, Nicki, 1982-

PARTY LINES S. W. Hunt, J. Yuan et al img *New York* v50 no10 p104 My 15 2017

Minaldi, Patricia

A Judge's DWI Arrest A. Johnson color *New Orleans Magazine* v51 no8 p38 Je 2017

Minami Matsui

Photoactivation and inactivation of Arabidopsis cryptochrome 2 bibl graph *Science* v354 no6310 p343 O 21 2016

Minchin, Tim, 1975-

It's Like Broadway, But for Your Ears M. M. Kircher img *New York* v50 no11 p117 My 29 2017

Mind & body

See also

    Body image

    Consciousness

AGE PROOF YOUR BRAIN [Cover story] J. VanTine cartoon chart *Prevention* v69 no5 p60 My 2017

THE CHECKUP CHECKLIST S. WADYKA *Martha Stewart Living* no268 p70 O 2016

Extended Mind and Embodied Social Psychology: Contemporary Perspectives D. Shalin *Society* v54 no3 p279 Je 2017

MORE ENERGY NOW! J. LEHRER color *Men's Health* v32 no6 p108 Ag 2017

Stay Sharp this Semester M. AIRHART *USA Today Magazine* v146 no2868 p45 S 2017

Mind & body therapies

Cultivate a steady mind color *Yoga Journal* p94 2016 Special Issue

IN THIS SECTION color *Yoga Journal* p92 2017 Special Issue

Mindell, Jodi

advice every new mom needs [Cover story] color *Parents* v92 no7

p32 Jl 2017

Minder, Raphael

Homage to Catalonia? O. G. Encarnación color *New York Review of Books* v64 no17 p37 N 9 2017

Mindfulness (Psychology)

The Busier You Are, the More You Need Mindfulness S. Achor and M. Gielan *Harvard Business Review Digital Articles* p2 D 18 2015

Calming Your Brain During Conflict D. M. Hamilton *Harvard Business Review Digital Articles* p2 D 22 2015

Can 10 Minutes of Meditation Make You More Creative? E. Schootstra, D. Deichmann et al *Harvard Business Review Digital Articles* p2 Ag 29 2017

Don't Let Frustration Make You Say the Wrong Thing T. Healey and J. Roberts *Harvard Business Review Digital Articles* p2 D 24 2015

FINAL THOUGHT color *Yoga Journal* p120 2016 Special Issue

Finding Your Mind B. DiDomenico color *Prevention* v69 no9 p3 O 2017

FOCUSING: A PRACTICE TO COMPLEMENT MEDITATION D. ROME color *Tricycle: The Buddhist Review* v27 no1 p40 Fall 2017

Here's What Mindfulness Is (and Isn't) Good For D. Goleman *Harvard Business Review Digital Articles* p2 S 28 2017

How Mindfulness Improves Executive Coaching D. Brendel and E. R. Stamell *Harvard Business Review Digital Articles* p2 Ja 29 2016

How to Bring Mindfulness to Your Company's Leadership M. Reitz and M. Chaskalson *Harvard Business Review Digital Articles* p2 D 1 2016

How to introduce mindfulness at work M. Reitz *People Management* p48 D 2016/Ja 2017

How to Practice Mindfulness Throughout Your Work Day R. Hougaard and J. Carter *Harvard Business Review Digital Articles* p2 Mr 4 2016

If Mindfulness Makes You Uncomfortable, It's Working A. J. Su *Harvard Business Review Digital Articles* p2 D 29 2015

Is Something Lost When We Use Mindfulness as a Productivity Tool? C. Lieberman *Harvard Business Review Digital Articles* p2 Ag 25 2015

Just 6 Seconds of Mindfulness Can Make You More Effective Chade-Meng Tan *Harvard Business Review Digital Articles* p2 D 30 2015

A Mental Trick to Help with Challenging Conversations L. Davey *Harvard Business Review Digital Articles* p2 D 16 2015

Mindfulness Can Improve Strategy, Too J. Talbot-Zorn and F. Edgette *Harvard Business Review Digital Articles* p2 My 2 2016

Mindfulness Can Literally Change Your Brain C. Congleton, B. K. Hölzel et al *Harvard Business Review Digital Articles* p2 Ja 8 2015

Mindfulness for the Hedge Fund Set S. Yoon color *Bloomberg Businessweek* no4494 p41 O 10 2016

Mindfulness Isn't Much Harder than Mindlessness E. Langer *Harvard Business Review Digital Articles* p2 Ja 13 2016

Mindfulness Mitigates Biases You May Not Know You Have N. Torres *Harvard Business Review Digital Articles* p2 D 24 2014

The Mindfulness Movement M. NISBET *Skeptical Inquirer* v41 no3 p24 My/Je 2017

Mindfulness Works but Only If You Work at It M. Reitz and M. Chaskalson *Harvard Business Review Digital Articles* p2 N 4 2016

NUCLEAR MINDFULNESS E. KUPERBERG cartoon *New Yorker* v93 no31 p31 O 9 2017

pretty CALM M. RABBITT color *Yoga Journal* no287 p13 N 2016

See Colleagues as They Are, Not as They Were D. Coombe *Harvard Business Review Digital Articles* p2 Ja 14 2016

A Simple Way to Stay Grounded in Stressful Moments L. Weiss *Harvard Business Review Digital Articles* p2 N 18 2016

Spending 10 Minutes a Day on Mindfulness Subtly Changes the Way You React to Everything R. Hougaard, J. Carter et al color *Harvard Business Review Digital Articles* p2 Ja 18 2017

Stress Is Your Brain Trying to Avoid Something A. Markman *Harvard Business Review Digital Articles* p2 Ag 26 2015

There Are Risks to Mindfulness at Work D. Brendel *Harvard Business Review Digital Articles* p2 F 11 2015

Think Yourself Healthy J. Marchant cartoon *Prevention* v69 no1 p28 Ja 2017

What's So Wrong with Mindfulness? N. GAJAWEERA color *Tricycle: The Buddhist Review* v26 no2 p27 Wint 2016

Why Google, Target, and General Mills Are Investing in Mindfulness K. Schaufenbuel *Harvard Business Review Digital Articles* p2 D 28 2015

Why NYU's B-School Teaches Mindfulness C. Kim and Y. Shy *Harvard Business Review Digital Articles* p2 D 31 2015

Women Need Mindfulness Even More than Men Do B. Cabrera *Harvard Business Review Digital Articles* p2 Je 21 2016

You are struggling to feel sympathy S. Kempton color *Yoga Journal* p41 2016 Special Issue

Your Car Commute Is a Chance to Practice Mindfulness M. Gonzalez *Harvard Business Review Digital Articles* p2 N 13 2014

You're in a funk S. Kempton color *Yoga Journal* p39 2016 Special Issue

You're jealous of a colleague or friend S. Kempton color *Yoga Journal* p45 2016 Special Issue

Your energy is flagging S. Kempton color *Yoga Journal* p48 2016 Special Issue

Your Mindful Day [Cover story] C. Gregoire color *Prevention* v69 no9 p80 O 2017

You worry constantly K. Holcombe color *Yoga Journal* p46 2016 Special Issue

Zen Master J. Barberio color *Working Mother* v40 no3 p47 Ag/S 2017

Mindfulness (Psychology)—Economic aspects

How Mindfulness Can Save You Money C. Hammond *Time* v188 no15 p15 O 17 2016

Mindfulness (Psychology)—Software

Meditation App Roundup C. Van Dusen color *Tricycle: The Buddhist Review* v26 no4 p92 Summ 2017

Mindheim, Lance

THE FUTURE OF MODEL RAILROADING color diag *Model Railroader* v84 no4 p52 Ap 2017

REALISM TIPS for beginners color diag *Model Railroader* v84 no3 p28 Mr 2017

Mindhunter (TV program)

Mindhunter T. Stack, A. Bacle et al color *Entertainment Weekly* no1482/1483 p107 S 22 2017

With Mindhunter, Fincher Perfects the Art of Darkness D. D'addario color *Time* v190 no16/17 p99 O 23 2017

Mindnich, Hans—Interviews

BROTHERS FROM THE SAME MOTHER [Cover story] color *Snowboarder* v29 no3 p56 N 2016

Mindnich, Nils, 1993—Interviews

BROTHERS FROM THE SAME MOTHER [Cover story] color *Snowboarder* v29 no3 p56 N 2016

Mindy Project, The (TV program)

THE MINDY PROJECT A. Bacle color *Entertainment Weekly* no1477 p32 Ag 11 2017

THE MINDY PROJECT R. Moynihan *TV Guide* v64 no15 p53 Ap 4 2016

THE SHOWS WILL GO ON J. Hibberd color *Entertainment Weekly* no1465 p8 My 12 2017

STREAMING A. D'ARMINIO *TV Guide* v64 no40 p64 O 3 2016

Mine shafts

FEAR OF ARRIVAL I. Vladislavić *Lapham's Quarterly* v10 no3 p193 Summ 2017

Minecraft (Game)

MINECRAFT APPLE TV EDITION: BLOCK BUILDING ON THE BIG SCREEN A. HAYWARD color *Macworld - Digital Edition* p59 F 2017

Mineral content of food

Square Meal G. SNYDER *Los Angeles Magazine* v62 no9 p107 S 2017

Mineral industries

See also
Ceramics
Petroleum industry

LIFE AFTER COAL A. GREENBLATT *Governing* v30 no3 p44 D 2016

Recycling Isn't Enough D. K. Finn color *Commonweal* v144 no8 p12 My 5 2017

Mineral industries—Canada

Canadian Mining's Dark Heart R. POPLAK color *Walrus* v13 no9 p26 N 2016

Mineral industries—Corrupt practices

Battling for Blood Jade H. Beech and S. Nang color map *Time* v189 no10 p40 Mr 20 2017

Mineral industries—Environmental aspects

OUT OF SIGHT J. GAMBLE color map *Canadian Geographic* v137 no2 p38 Mr/Ap 2017

Mineral pigments

NO.9, CAROUSEL: TIME TO CHANGE THE GODS color *Art in America* v105 no1 p33 Ja 2017

Mineral supplements

BEFORE THEY'RE BORN G. Johnston *Successful Farming* v115 no3 p54 Mid-F 2017

Mineral waters—Evaluation

That Fizzy Feeling J. BAINBRIDGE *Atlanta* v57 no6 p54 O 2017

Mineral industries—Finance—Charts, diagrams, etc.

METALS' TIME TO SHINE C. Matthews diag *Fortune* v174 no8 p22 D 15 2016

Mineralization (Geology)

Carbon Dioxide and the New Stone Age S. VOLK color *Discover* v38 no1 p74 Ja/F 2017

Minerals

See also
Metals

Best Ways to Take Mineral Supplements V. TWEED color *Better Nutrition* v79 no3 p10 Mr 2017

Digging Carbon [Cover story] S. Perkins chart color graph map *Science News* v190 no8 p18 O 15 2016

HOW TO READ A Multivitamin Label [Cover story] *Nutrition Action Health Letter* v43 no9 p6 N 2016

Sometimes failure is the springboard to success E. Emerson *Science News* v190 no8 p2 O 15 2016

What's in that kibble? A. Levi color *Health* v31 no8 p86 O 2017

Minerals in human nutrition

minerals V. Tweed color *Amazing Wellness* v9 no3 p12 Early-Summ 2017

Minerals in nutrition

See also
Minerals in human nutrition

MICROMINERALS FOR MAXIMUM PERFORMANCE D. N. JACKSON color *Muscle & Performance* v9 no4 p58 Ap 2017

minerals V. Tweed color *Amazing Wellness* v9 no3 p12 Early-Summ 2017

Minerals—Analysis

Animal, Vegetable, or Mineral? P. J. HEANEY *Natural History* v125 no2 p32 F 2017

Minerals—Exhibitions

Minerals in Medicine Prove a Perfect Prescription *USA Today Magazine* v145 no2865 p16 Je 2017

Minerals—Export & import trade

MOST WANTED MINERALS B. O'keefe color map *Fortune* v176 no1 p96 Jl 1 2017

Miners

See also
Gold miners

Recycling Isn't Enough D. K. Finn color *Commonweal* v144 no8 p12 My 5 2017

Miners—Employment

LIFE AFTER COAL A. GREENBLATT *Governing* v30 no3 p44 D 2016

Mines & mineral resources

See also
Gas fields
Gold mines & mining
Lithium mines & mining
Silver mines & mining
Uranium mines & mining

ARC OF DESPERATION B. Ebus color *Earth Island Journal* v32 no3 p25 Aut 2017

BITCOIN MINING R. Chun color *Atlantic* v320 no2 p26 S 2017

Copper Queen Mine: Over the course of nearly 100 years, the Copper Queen Mine produced billions of pounds of copper. The mining operation closed in 1975, but the mine itself is still open to tourists who aren't afraid to take a train 1,500 feet into... N. AUSTIN *Arizona Highways* v93 no6 p8 Je 2017

MOST WANTED MINERALS B. O'keefe color map *Fortune*
v176 no1 p96 Jl 1 2017

Mines & mineral resources & the environment
Apple sets a new environmental goal: No more mining C. MC-
GARRY color *Macworld - Digital Edition* v34 no6 p12 Je 2017

Mines & mineral resources—Idaho
THE MAMMOTH MINE R. BROOKS *Idaho Magazine* v16 no5
p12 F 2017

Mines & mineral resources—Research
Mining Without Miners T. Simonite color *MIT Technology Review*
v120 no1 p94 Ja/F 2017

Minetor, Randi
Art Meets Organization *Stage Directions* v30 no3 p28 Mr 2017
Making Christmas Magic *Stage Directions* v29 no10 p8 O 2016
More Room More Seats More Money *Stage Directions* v29 no12
p14 D 2016
SWeeNey ToDD *Stage Directions* v29 no11 p40 N 2016
Teaching Aesthetics *Stage Directions* v30 no4 p10 Ap 2017
Visualizing "Aggressive Precision": World Premiere of Other
Than Honorable at Geva Theatre Center *Stage Directions* v30
no6 p8 Je 2017

Ming, D. W.
Redox stratification of an ancient lake in Gale crater, Mars color
Science v356 no6341 p922 Je 1 2017

Ming Cho Lee
Ming Cho Lee to step down from teaching postion at Yale *Stage
Directions* v30 no3 p4 Mr 2017

Ming Lu
Synthesis and characterization of the pentazolate anion cyclo-N_5^-
in (N5)6(H3O)3(NH4)4Cl bibl diag graph *Science* v355 no6323
p374 Ja 27 2017

Ming Wong
EVERYTHING IS ABOUT TO BEGIN A. H. Merjian bw cartoon
color *Art in America* v104 no11 p80 D 2016

Mingardon, Stephanie
A Way to Assess and Prioritize Your Change Efforts *Harvard
Business Review Digital Articles* p2 Jl 9 2015

Mingchao Xiao
Quality management for precision medicine clinical applications:
A consensus from the China Precision Medicine Clinical Research and Application Association bibl *Science* v354 no6319
p11 D 23 2016

Mingjun Gao
Phytochromes function as thermosensors in Arabidopsis bibl
graph *Science* v354 no6314 p886 N 18 2016

Mingqi Xie
β-cell–mimetic designer cells provide closed-loop glycemic control bibl graph *Science* v354 no6317 p1296 D 9 2016

Mingzhu Li
Gene expression profiling–guided clinical precision treatment for
patients with endometrial carcinoma bibl color diag *Science*
v354 no6319 p33 D 23 2016

Minhaj, Hasan
THE BIG QUESTION cartoon *Atlantic* v318 no4 p112 N 2016

Minhaj, Hasan, 1985——Interviews
Hasan Minhaj Thinks Comedy Is for Weirdos S. Dominus *New
York Times Magazine* p66 Je 25 2017

Mini (Company)
Mini Clubman chart color *Motor Trend* v69 no1 p132 Ja 2017
A Mini That Aspires to Be Mighty color *Consumer Reports* v82
no8 p58 Ag 2017

Mini automobiles
A Mini That Aspires to Be Mighty color *Consumer Reports* v82
no8 p58 Ag 2017
ON THE ROAD C. BLOOR and M. MCCARTHY color *House
Beautiful* p162 Ag 2017

Mini automobiles—Evaluation
Crosshatch Patterns M. Duff color *Car & Driver* v62 no10 p80
Ap 2017
GARRAGE cartoon chart color *Motor Trend* v69 no1 p166 Ja
2017
maximum mini A. MacKenzie chart color *Motor Trend* v69 no6
p92 Je 2017
Mini Clubman chart color *Motor Trend* v69 no1 p132 Ja 2017

Mini-Cooper automobiles—Evaluation
Crosshatch Patterns M. Duff color *Car & Driver* v62 no10 p80

Ap 2017

Miniature art
Nose to the Glass [Cover story] K. Massinger color *Commonweal*
v144 no10 p24 Je 2 2017

Miniature food
Tiny Food J. Leigh Hester color *Atlantic* v319 no1 p19 Ja/F 2017

Miniature horses
Miniature Horse Completes Endurance Ride color *Trail Rider* v29
no1 p12 Ja/F 2017

Miniature objects
See also
Miniature food
ORNAMENTAL C. HONG *Martha Stewart Living* no270 p122
D 2016

Miniature painters
LITTLE THINGS A. Gregory *Harper's Magazine* v334 no2001
p41 F 2017

Miniature painting
See also
Icon painting

Miniature plants
See also
Bonsai
Grow Your Own Miniature Fruit Trees M. L. Shaw *Mother Earth
News* no282 p89 Je/Jl 2017

Miniature railroads
ABCs of DCC power district management [Cover story] L. Puckett color diag *Model Railroader* v84 no10 p50 O 2017

Minibars—Design & construction
CLUB ROOM L. MOWRY *Atlanta* v56 no8 p64 D 2016

Minich, Aubrey
I Wish My Horse's Mentor Could Be... color *Horse & Rider* v56
no6 p88 Je 2017

Minichromosome maintenance proteins
Bidirectional eukaryotic DNA replication is established by quasi-symmetrical helicase loading G. Coster and J. F. X. Diffley
graph *Science* v357 no6348 p314 Jl 21 2017

Minimal art
GOINGS ON ABOUT TOWN color *New Yorker* v93 no2 p7 F
27 2017

Minimal design
RESTRAIN YOURSELF N. Sullivan bw color *Esquire* p46 N
2017
SIMPLY SHAKER D. DICKINSON color *Better Homes & Gardens* v95 no11 p112 N 2017

Minimum wage
THE OTHER NRA S. JAYARAMAN *Nation* v305 no11 p15 O
30 2017
THE PROBLEMS WITH FAIR TRADE R. PATEL *Nation* v305
no11 p16 O 30 2017
Should Teens Earn Less Than Adults? Some lawmakers believe
that lowering the minimum wage for young people will encourage more businesses to hire them. Would you say this is a smart
move to help teens get jobs—or is it fundamentally unfair?
Scholastic Choices v32 no5 p2 F 2017
Side Effects of 'The Great Inversion': Low pay and long, pricey
commutes often go hand in hand W. Fulton *Governing* v30 no9
p23 Je 2017

Minimum wage laws
Venezuela Nears a Tipping Point, and a Violent Endgame I. Bremmer color *Time* v189 no18 p14 My 15 2017

Minimum wage—Government policy
IN THE "FIGHT FOR 15," LABOR MAY LAND A PYRRHIC
VICTORY A. Vandermey color *Fortune* v176 no2 p17 Ag 1
2017
Raising the minimum wage in three different ways: what are the
effects? R. Hernandez *Monthly Labor Review* p30 Jl 2017

Minimum wage—Great Britain
She only makes tea and sweeps the floors *People Management*
p10 F 2017

Minimum wage—United States
Cartoons *New York Times Upfront* v150 no1 p24 S 4 2017
How Low-Paying Retailers Can Adapt to Higher Minimum Wages
Z. Ton *Harvard Business Review Digital Articles* p2 Ag 23 2016
Not So Fast, Blue Cities C. CHANG il *New Republic* v248 no6
p12 Je 2017

Raising the minimum wage in three different ways: what are the effects? R. Hernandez *Monthly Labor Review* p30 Jl 2017

Should We Raise the Minimum Wage? *New York Times Upfront* v150 no1 p22 S 4 2017

Survival of the Hippest color *Weekly Standard* v22 no33 p4 My 8 2017

Mining towns

GHOSTS OF THE GORGE: COAL, CULTURE AND THE TRANSFORMATION OF NEW RIVER GORGE NATIONAL RIVER D. FOX *National Parks* v91 no3 p26 Summ 2017

Miniskirts

IT HAPPENED IN 1967 S. WELLER bw color *Vanity Fair* v59 no4 p192 Mr 2017

Ministry & Christian union

God in Iran (Still) K. A. Ellis *Christianity Today* v61 no6 p26 Jl/ Ag 2017

MINITER, FRANK

THE BUCK PROFILE bw color *Outdoor Life* v224 no7 p43 S 2017

Minivans

Ratings chart *Consumer Reports* v82 no10 p64 O 2017

Minivans—Evaluation

2017 Chrysler Pacifica Hybrid A. Priddle color *Motor Trend* v69 no3 p29 Mr 2017

Connected Comfort for the Long Haul color *Consumer Reports* v82 no10 p63 O 2017

A Frugal Family-Friendly Ride color *Consumer Reports* v82 no10 p63 O 2017

Minivans—Social aspects

OLD FAITHFUL H. Peterson color *O, The Oprah Magazine* p34 O 2017

Mink, Bob

Aging Matters: Finding Your Calling for the Rest of Your Life *Christian Century* v133 no23 p41 N 9 2016

Minka Lighting Inc.

Summer Style color *Timber Home Living* v27 no4 p14 Ag 2017

Minkin, Jane

What doctors tell their friends about birth control S. WOOD color *Redbook* p86 F 2017

Minkoff, Rebecca

the life C. Stern color *InStyle* v24 no6 p159 Je 2017

Minneapolis (Minn.)—Description & travel

A Maker's Guide to... MINNEAPOLIS-ST. PAUL F. MAROUKI-AN color map *Popular Mechanics* p26 D 2016/Ja 2017

Minnesota

GLEANINGS *Successful Farming* v115 no8 p10 Je/Jl 2017

Minnesota C. Homans *New York Times Magazine* p46 N 20 2016

Minnesota Lynx (Basketball team)

VIEW SOME TWOSOME R. Deitsch and S. Kwak color *Sports Illustrated* v127 no11 p18 O 9 2017

Minnesota Orchestra

KPMB Architects A. Bozikovic *Architectural Record* v205 no4 p108 Ap 2017

Minnesota Timberwolves (Basketball team)

5 TIMBERWOLVES color *Sports Illustrated* v127 no12 p84 O 16 2017

9 Timberwolves R. Nadkarni, B. Golliver et al color *Sports Illustrated* v125 no14 p108 O 24-31 2016

JIMMY BUTLER [Cover story] L. Jenkins color *Sports Illustrated* v127 no12 p34 O 16 2017

WORDS WITH... Ricky Rubio A. Sharp and T. Keith color *Sports Illustrated* v126 no3 p20 Ja 23 2017

Minnesota Twins (Baseball team)

4 TWINS color *Sports Illustrated* v126 no9 p86 Mr 27 2017

Minnesota Twins (Baseball team)—History—20th century

STILL A SERIES TO SAVOR S. Rushin color *Sports Illustrated* v125 no14 p44 O 24-31 2016

Minnesota Vikings (Football team)

1 Minnesota Vikings color *Sports Illustrated* v127 no7 p92 S 4 2017

ZIMMER OF HOPE M. McKnight color *Sports Illustrated* v127 no7 p56 S 4 2017

Minnesota Wild (Hockey team)

WHEN SPRING HAS STUNG C. P. Pierce color *Sports Illustrated* v126 no11 p90 Ap 17-24 2017

WILDEST Dreams A. Prewitt color *Sports Illustrated* v126 no11

p84 Ap 17-24 2017

Minnesota—Description & travel

In the Deep Dark: Stargazing F. BURES color *Backpacker* p18 My 2017

Minnesota State University, Mankato—Students

Rise Up J. Fuchs and T. Keith color *Sports Illustrated* v126 no17 p28 Je 19 2017

Minnette, Dylan, 1996-

13 REASONS WHY: INSIDE THE MOST DARING SHOW ON TELEVISION [Cover story] S. Highfill color *Entertainment Weekly* no1466 p24 My 19 2017

Minnich, Elizabeth

An Appeal for Thoughtfulness N. Stockwell bw cartoon color *Progressive* v81 no4 p63 Ap/My 2017

Minnick, Jerad

Improving Natural Grass Field Quality *Parks & Recreation* v52 no5 p72 My 2017

minnigh, brice

AGNOSTIC AGGRESSION color *Bike Magazine* v24 no1 p106 Ja/F 2017

chemtrails bw *Bike Magazine* v24 no5 p42 Jl 2017

clutch move color *Bike Magazine* v24 no3 p54 My 2017

DOUBLE DUTY color *Bike Magazine* v24 no1 p88 Ja/F 2017

EVEN FLOW bw color *Bike Magazine* v24 no1 p94 Ja/F 2017

guilty as charged color *Bike Magazine* v24 no3 p21 My 2017

lines in the sand color *Bike Magazine* v24 no4 p48 Je 2017

METHOD TO THE MADNESS bw color *Bike Magazine* v24 no1 p42 Ja/F 2017

no free rides color *Bike Magazine* v23 no9 p19 D 2016

one more climb color *Bike Magazine* v24 no2 p21 Mr 2017

santa cruz tallboy c color *Bike Magazine* v24 no3 p108 My 2017

see the forest color *Bike Magazine* v24 no4 p19 Je 2017

SPECIALIZED S-WORKS ENDURO 29 color *Bike Magazine* v23 no9 p88 D 2016

turning the page color *Bike Magazine* v24 no5 p19 Jl 2017

Minniti, Maria

Starting a Business Can Increase Older Workers' Quality of Life (Even When It Doesn't Pay Well) *Harvard Business Review Digital Articles* p2 S 19 2017

Minocha, Vimal

NEW LIFE FOR DEAD BATTERIES *New York State Conservationist* v71 no3 p26 D 2016

Minor, Brady

ALL IN THE FAMILY C. Toy color *Spin to Win Rodeo* v21 no2 p54 Ap 2017

Minor, Dylan

CEOs with Lots of Stock Options Are More Likely to Break Laws *Harvard Business Review Digital Articles* p2 My 26 2016

Want to Be More Productive? Sit Next to Someone Who Is *Harvard Business Review Digital Articles* p2 F 14 2017

Minor, Jake

BFI BOUND color *Spin to Win Rodeo* v21 no3 p12 My 2017

GOING LEFT color *Spin to Win Rodeo* v21 no3 p14 My 2017

Minor, Libby Monteith

Pretty Pots of Spring Color color *Southern Living* v52 no4 p18 Ap 2017

The Ultimate Plot Twist color *Southern Living* v52 no3 p28 Mr 2017

Minor, Riley

ALL IN THE FAMILY C. Toy color *Spin to Win Rodeo* v21 no2 p54 Ap 2017

Freeze Frame K. Gustave color *Team Roping Journal* p74 S 2017

Minor, Travis

Newly Updated ERS Data Show 2016 Production, Trade Volume, and Per Capita Availability of Vegetables and Pulses *Amber Waves: The Economics of Food, Farming, Natural Resources, & Rural America* p11 Ag 2017

Minor league baseball

8 BRAVE NEW WORLD S. Apstein color *Sports Illustrated* v126 no9 p50 Mr 27 2017

Leading Off color *Sports Illustrated* v127 no6 p4 Ag 28 2017

Should Minor-League Ballplayers Get a Big Pay Raise? color *Kiplinger's Personal Finance* v71 no7 p16 Jl 2017

TIM TEBOW BELIEVES. DO YOU? T. Rohan color *Sports Illustrated* v126 no14 p40 My 15-22 2017

Total Eclipse of the Park T. Keith and S. Kwak color map *Sports*

Illustrated v127 no5 p24 Ag 14 2017

Minor league baseball—Marketing

How Lo Can They Go T. Keith chart color *Sports Illustrated* v125 no18 p20 D 5 2016

Minor league football

FOR THE LOVE OF THE GAME R. BASS *Texas Monthly* v45 no9 p68 S 2017

Minorities

Segregation on the Charles K. SMITH *National Review* v69 no12 p44 Je 26 2017

Minorities in motion pictures

OSCARS SO RIGHT? [Cover story] N. Sperling color *Entertainment Weekly* no1451/1452 p40 F 3-10 2017

Minorities—Canada

WHY FEAR AND DIVISION REMAIN UNDEFEATED A. DOMISE color *Maclean's* v129 no41 p11 O 17 2016

Minorities—Crimes against

See also

     African Americans—Crimes against

Minorities—Employment

Evidence That Minorities Perform Worse Under Biased Managers A. Pallais color *Harvard Business Review Digital Articles* p2 Ja 13 2017

The Unintended Consequences of Diversity Statements S. Kang, K. DeCelles et al *Harvard Business Review Digital Articles* p2 Mr 29 2016

Minorities—United States

BEYOND BLACK AND WHITE C. M. Smith and D. Lawrence *Entertainment Weekly* no1451/1452 p43 F 3-10 2017

Toward a More Diverse Research Community Models of Success: A forward-looking group of colleges and universities are demonstrating effective ways to educate underrepresented minorities for careers in science and engineering F. A. HRABOWSKI III and P. H. HENDERSON *Issues in Science & Technology* v33 no3 p33 Spr 2017

Minorities—United States—Social conditions

EASY CHAIR R. Solnit *Harper's Magazine* v334 no2002 p5 Mr 2017

"WE JUST FEEL LIKE WE DON'T BELONG HERE ANYMORE" B. Andrews color *Mother Jones* v42 no6 p14 N/D 2017

Minority students

See also

     African American students

Backtalk J. H. Lytle *Phi Delta Kappan* v98 no4 p80 D 2016/Ja 2017

Minority students—Attitudes

Getting students to believe in themselves J. Saphier color diag il *Phi Delta Kappan* v98 no5 p48 F 2017

Minoru Kubo

A three-dimensional movie of structural changes in bacteriorhodopsin bibl diag graph *Science* v354 no6319 p1552 D 23 2016

MINOT, SUSAN

My Mentor: Grand Street editor Ben Sonnenberg was a great enthusiast *American Scholar* v86 no3 p16 Summ 2017

Minoux, Maryline

Gene bivalency at Polycomb domains regulates cranial neural crest positional identity diag *Science* v355 no6332 p1390 Mr 31 2017

Minozzi, William

The need for a translational science of democracy bibl color *Science* v355 no6328 p914 Mr 3 2017

Minshall, Richard D.

Fructose-driven glycolysis supports anoxia resistance in the naked mole-rat diag graph *Science* v356 no6335 p307 Ap 21 2017

Minsky, Laurence

Good Cybersecurity Can Be Good Marketing *Harvard Business Review Digital Articles* p2 S 23 2016

How B2B Marketers Can Get Started with Social Media *Harvard Business Review Digital Articles* p2 D 24 2015

How B2B Sales Can Benefit from Social Selling *Harvard Business Review Digital Articles* p2 N 8 2016

How You Make Decisions Is as Important as What You Decide *Harvard Business Review Digital Articles* p2 Ap 28 2015

Minter, Drew

René Jacobs: The Countertenor, The Accent Recordings, 1978-1982 *Opera News* v81 no10 p56 Ap 2017

Minter, Marilyn—Interviews

Marilyn Minter Finds Art In the Female Form J. Wortham *New York Times Magazine* p58 F 19 2017

Mintova, S.

Hydrogen positions in single nanocrystals revealed by electron diffraction bibl color *Science* v355 no6321 p1 Ja 13 2017

Mints (Plants)

JUST CHILL M. C. Cairns color *Southern Living* v52 no6 p106 Je 2017

Mint's Moment K. O'SHEA-EVANS color *House Beautiful* v159 no3 p73 Ap 2017

Minturn, Kent Mitchell

Mad scientist: The strange, protean artistry of Eugen Gabritschevsky bw cartoon color *Magazine Antiques* v184 no2 p118 Mr/Ap 2017

Mintz, Dan

Bob's Burgers A. Bacle, D. Coggan et al *Entertainment Weekly* no1482/1483 p34 S 22 2017

Mintzberg, Henry

Managers Are More Connected, But Not For The Better *Harvard Business Review Digital Articles* p2 Jl 20 2015

Rescuing Capitalism from Itself *Harvard Business Review Digital Articles* p2 D 3 2015

The U.S. Cannot Be Run Like a Business *Harvard Business Review Digital Articles* p2 Mr 31 2017

We Need Both Networks and Communities *Harvard Business Review Digital Articles* p2 O 5 2015

Mintzker, Yair

The Many Deaths of Jew Süss: The Notorious Trial and Execution of an Eighteenth-Century Court Jew A. Frykholm color *Christian Century* v134 no18 p37 Ag 30 2017

Minujin, Marta—Exhibitions

A Triumph Over Censorship J. Zorthian color *Time* v190 no6 p25 Ag 7 2017

Minutillo, Josephine

Beacon of Health *Architectural Record* v205 no7 p94 Jl 2017

Cave Dweller *Architectural Record* v205 no4 p142 Ap 2017

Complexity and Candor in Architecture *Architectural Record* v205 no10 p43 O 2017

Crowning Achievement *Architectural Record* v204 no11 p70 N 2016

Edible Schoolyard New York *Architectural Record* v205 no4 p186 Ap 2017

Euroluce: The biennial lighting trade show, which took place alongside the Salone del Mobile last month, spanned four large pavilions at Milan's sprawling fairgrounds. Additional exhibitors showcased their introductions at off-site venues throughout... color *Architectural Record* v205 no5 p137 My 2017

exhibition color *Architectural Record* v204 no12 p31 D 2016

Fresh Start color diag *Architectural Record* v205 no2 p86 F 2017

The Hangover color diag *Architectural Record* v204 no12 p69 D 2016

High Note color diag *Architectural Record* v204 no12 p96 D 2016

house of the month *Architectural Record* v205 no9 p39 S 2017

house of the month color diag *Architectural Record* v205 no2 p31 F 2017

In the House *Architectural Record* v204 no10 p53 O 2016

Into the Woods *Architectural Record* v205 no6 p74 Je 2017

The Italian Job *Architectural Record* v204 no10 p84 O 2016

Jewel Box *Architectural Record* v204 no10 p96 O 2016

Out of the Ruins *Architectural Record* v205 no9 p116 S 2017

Paired Off *Architectural Record* v204 no11 p110 N 2016

Ramped Up color diag *Architectural Record* v205 no3 p100 Mr 2017

Salone del Mobile 2017: With over 2,000 exhibitors and nearly 350,000 visitors last month, Milan's furniture fair still proves to be the best in the world color *Architectural Record* v205 no5 p65 My 2017

Times Square Reconstruction New York *Architectural Record* v205 no4 p210 Ap 2017

Turn the Page *Architectural Record* v205 no10 p66 O 2017

The X Factor color diag *Architectural Record* v205 no3 p112 Mr 2017

Minutti, Carlos M.

Local amplifiers of IL-4Rα-mediated macrophage activation promote repair in lung and liver diag *Science* v356 no6342 p1076

Je 9 2017

Minxin Pei

Dirty Deeds D. Yang color *Foreign Affairs* v96 no4 p149 Jl/Ag 2017

Miłosz, Czesław, 1911-2004

Milosz: A Biography R. Legvold *Foreign Affairs* v96 no3 p169 My/Je 2017

A Polish poet's 'Brave New World' F. Freeman color *America* v216 no8 p47 Ap 17 2017

Mir (Space station)

Lessons of Mir B. BERMAN color *Astronomy* v45 no4 p10 Ap 2017

MIR, ABDUL RAUF

A Merciless Occupation *Islamic Horizons* v45 no6 p60 N/D 2016

Miracles

See also

Miracles (Judaism)

Saints—Legends

A Critical Care Surgeon Meets the Great Physician K. L. Butler color *Christianity Today* p80 Mr 2017

"I Don't Know if He Knows How Lucky He Was" [Cover story] L. MILLER *Reader's Digest* v188 no1126 p67 D 2016/Ja 2017

Miracle Tableau: Knock, Ireland, 1879 J. NICKELL *Skeptical Inquirer* v41 no2 p26 Mr/Ap 2017

Miracles (Judaism)

Saving Conservative Judaism *Commentary* v143 no4 p24 Ap 2017

Miracle Worker, The (TV program)

PATTY DUKE M. Gilbert and L. Rice color *Entertainment Weekly* no1446/1447 p92 D 2016/Ja 2017

Miral (Film)

Freida & a Pinto M. Heyman color *InStyle* v24 no5 p234 My 2017

Miraldo, Andreia

An Anthropocene map of genetic diversity bibl graph map *Science* v353 no6307 p1532 S 30 2016

Miralles, Diego G.

Satellites reveal contrasting responses of regional climate to the widespread greening of Earth diag *Science* v356 no6343 p1180 Je 16 2017

Miralles, Francesc

Opposing effects of Elk-1 multisite phosphorylation shape its response to ERK activation bibl graph *Science* v354 no6309 p233 O 14 2016

Miralles Fusté, Javier

TZAP: A telomere-associated protein involved in telomere length control bibl diag graph *Science* v355 no6325 p638 F 10 2017

Miramonti, L.

Observation of a large-scale anisotropy in the arrival directions of cosmic rays above 8×1018 eV *Science* v357 no6357 p1266 S 22 2017

MIRANDA, COTY DOLORES

PRETTY IN PLATINUM *Sea Magazine* v108 no10 pCA-4 O 2016

Miranda, Lin-Manuel, 1980-

Christian hope in Hamilton B. F. Jones color *Christian Century* v134 no7 p45 Mr 29 2017

Hamilton Goes to High School W. D'Orio *Education Digest* v83 no2 p4 O 2017

HAMILTON REINVENTED I. Biedenharn color *Entertainment Weekly* no1442 p20 D 2 2016 Rebellious Special Issue

THE HAMILTON SATISFACTION SCALE M. Snetiker color *Entertainment Weekly* no1444/1445 p119 D 16 2016

John LEGUIZAMO color *Vanity Fair* p144 Hollywood 2017 Supplement

Lin-Manuel MIRANDA color *Vanity Fair* v59 no1 p128 Holiday 2017

Pioneers [Cover story] color *Time* v189 no16/17 p14 My 1-8 2017

Salvation Song M. Snetiker color *Entertainment Weekly* no1486 p23 O 13 2017

Sound Bites color *Entertainment Weekly* no1456 p5 Mr 10 2017

The Summer Job I'll Never Forget color *Time* v190 no2/3 p55 Jl 10-17 2017

Miranda, Lin-Manuel, 1980-—Interviews

LIN-MANUEL MIRANDA color *GQ: Gentlemen's Quarterly* v97 no9 p121 S 2017

Lin-Manuel Miranda M. Snetiker color *Entertainment Weekly* no1444/1445 p18 D 16 2016

Miranda, Megan

The Perfect Stranger *Publishers Weekly* v264 no13 p66 Mr 27 2017

Miranda, Tricia

Not Just a YouTube Star A. Feller color *Dance Magazine* v91 no3 p26 Mr 2017

TRICIA MIRANDA'S TOP 10 WAYS TO OWN YOUR CAREER N. Loeffler-Gladstone color *Dance Spirit* v21 no2 p46 F 2017

MIRANDA ALCAZAR, MAGALLY A.

Female Privilege *Nation* v304 no10 p4 Mr 27 2017

Mirani, Leo

YOU SAY SLOVAKIA cartoon *New Yorker* v93 no15 p16 My 29 2017

Mirchandani, Akshay

2016-17 Viewers' Guide color *Sports Illustrated* v125 no14 p118 O 24-31 2016

Mire, Muna

"I just don't have any qualms about looking different" cartoon color *Glamour* v115 no2 p60 F 2017

Miremadi, Mehdi

The Age of Smart, Safe, Cheap Robots Is Already Here *Harvard Business Review Digital Articles* p2 Je 15 2015

The Countries Most (and Least) Likely to be Affected by Automation *Harvard Business Review Digital Articles* p2 Ap 12 2017

Mirkin, Chad A.

Clathrate colloidal crystals bibl color *Science* v355 no6328 p931 Mr 3 2017

Mironov, Vladimir

Where's the Beef? M. STONE color *Discover* v38 no4 p17 My 2017

Miroshnichenko, Andrey E.

Optically resonant dielectric nanostructures bibl graph *Science* v354 no6314 paag2472-1 N 18 2016

Mirren, Helen

Artists color *Time* v189 no16/17 p40 My 1-8 2017

Mirren, Helen, 1945-—Interviews

Helen Mirren E. Berman color *Time* v188 no24 p64 D 12 2016

Helen Mirren in LIGHT & SHADOW R. LOVE color *AARP: The Magazine* v60 no1A p26 D 2016/Ja 2017

Mirrors

NAVY + OCHRE color *Martha Stewart Living* p33 S 2017

TWO BATHS FROM A REVIVAL craftsman P. POORE color *Arts & Crafts Homes & the Revival* v12 no5 p24 Wint 2018

Mirrors—Evaluation

the best of THE BEST 120 K. O'SHEA-EVANS and H. BROWN color *House Beautiful* v158 no9 p57 N 2016

Casual Glam cartoon color *Seventeen* v76 no12 p43 D 2016/Ja 2017

Fit for a Bath M. E. Polson color *Old House Journal* v45 no1 p76 F 2017

INDIAN SUMMER L. BIRCH color *House Beautiful* p10 Ag 2017

In the ROUND A. FORD color *House Beautiful* p120 Ag 2017

MOODBOARD MASTERCLASS color *House Beautiful* p81 Ag 2017

Mirsky, Jonathan

How Tibet Is Being Crushed—While the Dalai Lama Survives color *New York Review of Books* v63 no20 p95 D 22 2016

Mirsky, Steve

23 and Pee color *Scientific American* v316 no3 p78 Mr 2017

Citrus Be the Place color *Scientific American* v315 no6 p85 D 2016

Data Deliver in the Clutch color *Scientific American* v316 no1 p70 Ja 2017

Don't Pass the Weed or Say "Guns" color *Scientific American* v316 no5 p78 My 2017

Drilling for Fossil Gold color *Scientific American* v317 no1 p74 Jl 2017

The Face of Evil color *Scientific American* v317 no3 p92 S 2017

Floor Plan color *Scientific American* v316 no4 p80 Ap 2017

Food Fright! color *Scientific American* v316 no6 p76 Je 2017

In Favor of Feline Felicity color *Scientific American* v315 no3 p90 S 2016

Muddying the Waters cartoon *Scientific American* v315 no5 p78 N 2016

None So Blind color *Scientific American* v316 no2 p74 F 2017
What's the Deal? color *Scientific American* v317 no2 p82 Ag 2017
What the Heck Is That Thing? color *Scientific American* v317 no4 p90 O 2017

Mirvis, Philip

The 3 Ways People React to Career Disasters *Harvard Business Review Digital Articles* p2 Je 18 2015
SURVIVING M&A color il *Harvard Business Review* v95 no2 p145 Mr/Ap 2017

Mirvis, Tova

The Book of Separation: A Memoir *Publishers Weekly* v264 no24 p52 Je 12 2017

Mirza, Fawzia

A STUDY ON MODERN LOVE color *Chicago* v66 no10 p82 O 2017

Mirza, Joe—Interviews

AAU'S ROLE IN OLYMPIC KARATE TO BE DETERMINED color *Black Belt* v55 no1 p50 D 2016/Ja 2017

MIRZA, MISBAHUDDIN

Democracy Besieged *Islamic Horizons* v46 no2 p56 Mr/Ap 2017
Interfaith Marriages: Do Muslims realize that interfaith unions could be an existential threat to their community? *Islamic Horizons* v46 no3 p34 My/Je 2017
Jerusalem 1000 - 1400: Every People Under Heaven *Islamic Horizons* v45 no6 p52 N/D 2016
Osmania University: A Century of Exceptional Learning: India gnarls the character of an institution created by a caring Muslim ruler *Islamic Horizons* v46 no3 p58 My/Je 2017
Strokes of Love: New York City's Metropolitan Museum of Arts Islamic displays are the largest in the world *Islamic Horizons* v46 no4 p32 Jl/Ag 2017
There is Much in a Name: A good name will have a positive impact on a growing child's manners and outlook on life *Islamic Horizons* v46 no4 p42 Jl/Ag 2017

MIRZA, UZMA

Designing Green Mosques *Islamic Horizons* v46 no1 p42 Ja/F 2017

Mirzakhani, Maryam, 1977-2017

Maryam Mirzakhani (1977–2017) A. Wright color *Science* v357 no6353 p758 Ag 25 2017

Miscarriage

A liturgy for families suffering a miscarriage E. Sanna *U.S. Catholic* v81 no11 p35 N 2016

Miscavige, Ron

The Church Militant C. ALLEN *Weekly Standard* v22 no8 p34 O 31 2016

Mischke, Jan

The World's Housing Crisis Doesn't Need a Revolutionary Solution *Harvard Business Review Digital Articles* p2 D 25 2014

Mischner, Jessica

Frame of Reference color *House Beautiful* v159 no9 p76 N 2017
SOUTH'S BEST CITY color *Southern Living* v52 no4 p74 Ap 2017

Miscik, Jami

Intelligence and the Presidency color *Foreign Affairs* v96 no3 p57 My/Je 2017

Miscommunication

When Saying Something Nice Is the Only Way to Change Someone's Mind C. Graves color *Harvard Business Review Digital Articles* p2 O 10 2016

Miserez, Ali

Preventing mussel adhesion using lubricant-infused materials color diag graph *Science* v357 no6352 p668 Ag 18 2017

Misery (Film)

KATHY BATES L. Rice color *Entertainment Weekly* no1478 / 1479 p92 Ag 18-25 2017

Mishan, Ligaya

A Strange Way to the Promised Land color *New York Review of Books* v63 no18 p35 N 24 2016

Mishchenko, A.

High-temperature quantum oscillations caused by recurring Bloch states in graphene superlattices color *Science* v357 no6347 p181 Jl 14 2017

Mishell, Bruce

All About Color E. GAUKEL *Treasures* v6 no3 p14 D 2016/Ja 2017

Mishima, Yukio, 1925-1970

Portrait of the Author as a Historian A. Lee *History Today* v67 no4 p54 Ap 2017

Mishler, Stephanie

"I Help GIRLS GET PROM-READY" M. ABERMAN color *Seventeen* p124 Ja 1 2017

Mishra, Pankaj

ALMOST EVERYONE LEFT BEHIND W. SMITH bw color *Publishers Weekly* v264 no4 p36 Ja 23 2017
As the Anglo-American right adopts the slogans of the left, it sounds the death knell of the neoliberal economic order it built. But what comes next? *New York Times Magazine* p14 Je 25 2017
BLOOD AND SOIL J. E. H. Smith *Harper's Magazine* v334 no2001 p84 F 2017
Destructive Solidarity J. T. McGreevy color *Commonweal* v144 no8 p34 My 5 2017
The Globalization of Rage color *Foreign Affairs* v95 no6 p46 N/D 2016
How the Enlightenment Predicted Modern Populism B. Walsh color *Time* v189 no6 p19 F 20 2017
Leaders color *Time* v189 no16/17 p64 My 1-8 2017
Look Back in Anger S. MOYN *New Republic* v248 no3 p60 Mr 2017
Mutually Assured Resentment D. Oppenheimer color *Washington Monthly* v49 no6-8 p68 Je-Ag 2017
Pankaj Mishra *New York Times Book Review* p31 Ja 8 2017
The price of modernity R. Westbrook *Christian Century* v134 no22 p33 O 25 2017
THE ROOTS OF OUR RAGE P. Coy cartoon *Bloomberg Businessweek* no4510 p62 F 6 2017
The Strangers in Their Midst: Two new books examine Europe's current and divisive debates over immigration, refugees and Western values *New York Times Book Review* p20 S 17 2017
Voltaire at Davos F. FOER *New York Times Book Review* p15 F 19 2017
What's the best book, new or old, you read this year? *New York Times Book Review* p27 D 25 2016
Which Way Are We Going? M. Ignatieff color *New York Review of Books* v64 no6 p4 Ap 6 2017

Mishra, Pankaj—Interviews

A Mutiny Against Modernizing Elites Has Erupted In The West P. Mishra *NPQ: New Perspectives Quarterly* v34 no2 p21 My 2017

Mishra, Saurabh

To Improve Sales, Pay More Attention to Presales *Harvard Business Review Digital Articles* p2 F 17 2015

Mishto, Michele

A large fraction of HLA class I ligands are proteasome-generated spliced peptides bibl graph *Science* v354 no6310 p354 O 21 2016

Miska, Eric A.

Transgenerational inheritance: Models and mechanisms of non–DNA sequence–based inheritance bibl color diag *Science* v354 no6308 p59 O 7 2016

Miska, Rhonda

Annunciation color *U.S. Catholic* v81 no12 p11 D 2016
Grieving with Brahms color *U.S. Catholic* v82 no3 p19 Mr 2017
Hope for all color *U.S. Catholic* v82 no2 p45 F 2017
Sacred lines color *U.S. Catholic* v82 no1 p45 Ja 2017

Miskimen, Mel

Apple Pie, Solo *Saturday Evening Post* v288 no6 p62 N/D 2016

Misner, Rebecca

3 COUPLES, ONE 45-FOOT CATAMARAN, 9 MEDITERRANEAN ISLANDS, 6 PORTS, COUNTLESS EMPTY BEACHES, AND 7 NIGHTS SPENT SIPPING ROSÉ AND BLASTING THE SMITHS UNDER THE STARS [Cover story] color *Conde Nast Traveler* v52 no7 p60 Ag 2017
MARRAKECH, MOROCCO color *Conde Nast Traveler* v52 no2 p22 F 2017
An ODE to HOTELS in Marrakech bw color *Conde Nast Traveler* v52 no1 p78 Ja 2017
SANTA BARBARA color *Conde Nast Traveler* v52 no5 p32 My 2017
SOMEWHERE NEW color *Conde Nast Traveler* v52 no5 p34 My 2017

Take Us to Church color *Conde Nast Traveler* v52 no1 p46 Ja 2017

VIENNA BOTH THE CLASSIC AND MODERN SIDES color *Conde Nast Traveler* v52 no8 p32 S 2017

WE'RE TURNING 30 bw chart color *Conde Nast Traveler* v52 no8 p55 S 2017

Misogyny

Bullied out of research R. Poole color *Science* v354 no6311 p514 O 28 2016

They're With Him K. POLLITT color il *Nation* v303 no23/24 p15 D 5 2016

Mison, Tom

A Hollow Reunion *TV Guide* v65 no4 p10 Ja 16 2017

Misra, Kanishka

Even a 14-Cent Food Tax Could Lead to Healthier Choices *Harvard Business Review Digital Articles* p2 S 29 2016

MISRACH, RICHARD

Borderlands color *National Geographic* v232 no3 p128 S 2017

Miss America Pageant

Kira Kazantsev J. Marksbury and C. Barrett color *Golf Magazine* v59 no2 p41 F 2017

Miss Peregrine's Home for Peculiar Children (Film)

The Bullseye M. Snetiker color *Entertainment Weekly* no1434 p64 O 7 2016

Burton Loses the Plot In Peregrine S. Zacharek color *Time* v188 no14 p56 O 10 2016

ELLA'S A-POPPIN' D. BLASBERG color *Vanity Fair* v59 no5 p142 Ap 2017

Grossed Out J. PODHORETZ *Weekly Standard* v22 no6 p39 O 17 2016

Miss Peregrine's Home for Peculiar Children B. Diones *New Yorker* v92 no35 p24 O 31 2016

Miss Saigon (Theatrical production)

Why Are We in Miss Saigon? img *New York* v50 no7 p83 Ap 3 2017

Miss Sloane (Film)

REALITY BITES D. Walters color *Bloomberg Businessweek* no4501 p62 N 28 2016

Miss Universe Inc.

Ms-Speaking color *Weekly Standard* v22 no43 p2 Jl 24 2017

Miss Cleo, 1962-2016

MISS CLEO J. WORTHAM *New York Times Magazine* p17 D 25 2016

MISSEL, RILEY

ADIDAS PROTEAN color *Bicycling* v58 no9 p64 O 2017

ELITE DIRETO color *Bicycling* v58 no9 p89 O 2017

Fast and Happy cartoon color *Bicycling* v58 no8 p24 S 2017

GAZELLE GAZELLENL C7 HMB color *Bicycling* v58 no9 p82 O 2017

HOW CYCLING WORKS cartoon diag *Bicycling* v58 no9 p21 O 2017

THANKS FOR THE RIDE color *Bicycling* v58 no10 p15 N/D 2017

Missick, Simone

Simone Missick N. Habtezghi color *Essence* v47 no12 p44 Ap 2017

Missing, The (TV program)

The Missing J. Russell *TV Guide* v65 no6 p40 Ja 30 2017

Missing children

99, 100, 101...FULL STOP S. Fennessy *Atlanta* v57 no5 p18 S 2017

Missing persons

See also

Missing children

AFTER THE VANISHING L. Wade bw color graph *Science* v354 no6318 p1369 D 16 2016

An Investigation of the Missing411 Conspiracy K. POUCH *Skeptical Inquirer* v41 no4 p54 Jl/Ag 2017

THE MISSING *Harper's Magazine* v335 no2005 p20 Je 2017

Where Is My Brother? E. Reidy color map *Wired* v25 no4 p84 Ap 2017

Missing persons investigation

99, 100, 101...FULL STOP S. Fennessy *Atlanta* v57 no5 p18 S 2017

Lost and broken [Cover story] N. Macdonald and M. Campbell color *Maclean's* v130 no9 p24 O 2017

Missing persons—California

The Fire Season K. Steinmetz and M. Chan color map *Time* v190 no16/17 p40 O 23 2017

Missing persons—Canada

'Psychic Detective' Noreen Renier: The Grinch Who Stole Christmas from a Grieving Family: Newly obtained recordings provide a unique opportunity to assess the sessions of a genuine "psychic detective" police case G. P. POSNER *Skeptical Inquirer* v41 no4 p46 Jl/Ag 2017

Mission, The (Film)

What We Can & Cannot Fix J. Guhin bw *Commonweal* v144 no9 p22 My 19 2017

Mission of the church

What would you like your parish to make a higher priority? graph *America* v216 no7 p6 Ap 3 2017

Mission statements

4 Hard Questions to Ask About Your Company's Purpose D. Houlder and N. Nandkishore *Harvard Business Review Digital Articles* p2 Mr 22 2016

6 Rules for Building and Scaling Company Culture A. K. Tjan *Harvard Business Review Digital Articles* p2 Mr 23 2015

Backtalk B. Sevier *Phi Delta Kappan* v99 no1 p48 S 2017

How an Accounting Firm Convinced Its Employees They Could Change the World B. N. Pfau *Harvard Business Review Digital Articles* p2 O 6 2015

The Path Ahead S. STEEN *American Forests* v123 no1 p2 Wint/Spr 2017

Stop Using Battle Metaphors in Your Company Strategy F. V. Cespedes *Harvard Business Review Digital Articles* p2 D 19 2014

Successful Startups Don't Make Money Their Primary Mission K. Laws *Harvard Business Review Digital Articles* p2 Jl 10 2015

Thinking Clearly About Your Company's Purpose G. Kenny *Harvard Business Review Digital Articles* p2 S 8 2016

Use Storytelling to Explain Your Company's Purpose J. Coleman *Harvard Business Review Digital Articles* p2 N 24 2015

What Mark Zuckerberg Understands About Corporate Purpose G. Serafeim *Harvard Business Review Digital Articles* p2 F 22 2017

Why Twitter's Mission Statement Matters J. Fox *Harvard Business Review Digital Articles* p2 N 13 2014

Mission Workshop (Company)

DISTRICT HENLEY R. Palmer color *Bike Magazine* v24 no4 p102 Je 2017

Missionaries

THE SPEARS OF PEACE: The arrival of a Christian mission on the island of Dobu in Papua New Guinea was met with ambivalence, but it resulted in a mixing of cultures and the development of new traditions D. Lee-Talbot *History Today* v67 no10 p50 O 2017

Missionaries—Societies, etc.

THE MIGRANT MISSIONARIES A. Olsen color *Christianity Today* v61 no6 p38 Jl/Ag 2017

Mission High School (San Francisco, Calif.)

Bully Pulpit K. RIZGA cartoon *Mother Jones* v42 no1 p13 Ja/F 2017

Mississippi River—Discovery & exploration

1673: Keokuk, IA J. Marquette *Lapham's Quarterly* v10 no2 p72 Spr 2017

Missoni, Angela

the life C. Stern color *InStyle* v24 no5 p249 My 2017

Missoni, Margherita Maccapani

Margherita Missoni J. K. DE VALLE color *Architectural Digest* v74 no2 p26 F 2017

Missoula (Mont.)

Welcome to Missoula A. Frykholm color *Christian Century* v133 no26 p22 D 21 2016

Missouri

BREAKOUT! R. SOODALTER *Missouri Life* v43 no6 p42 O/N 2016

Wandering into the Past G. WOOD color *Missouri Life* v44 no6 p90 S 2017

Missouri. Dept. of Natural Resources

State Playground Program Disqualified Religious Organizations J. C. Kozlowski *Parks & Recreation* v52 no9 p32 S 2017

Missouri—Description & travel

ALL AROUND Missouri S. LOUIS *Missouri Life* v43 no6 p95

O/N 2016

AMAZING MAIZE MAZES A. Stewart *Missouri Life* v43 no6 p50 O/N 2016

COURT APPEAL J. BENNER *Missouri Life* v43 no6 p34 O/N 2016

FALL HIKINGS & BIKING P. N. MORAN *Missouri Life* v43 no6 p63 O/N 2016

FROM THE COURTHOUSE STEPS *Missouri Life* v43 no6 p10 O/N 2016

A GROWING TREND A. STEWART *Missouri Life* v43 no6 p84 O/N 2016

Guide to Missouri Bed-and-Breakfasts Unique Hotels *Missouri Life* v43 no6 p92 O/N 2016

HIKES BIKES *Missouri Life* v43 no6 p64 O/N 2016

PUTTING THE HELL BACK IN HEALTH R. MARR *Missouri Life* v43 no6 p79 O/N 2016

Travel Like Truman J. AGGEN *Missouri Life* v43 no6 p54 O/N 2016

Mist, The (Film)

CHEERS & JEERS D. HOLBROOK *TV Guide* v65 no31 p76 Jl 24 2017

Mistaken identity

MISTAKEN IDENTITIES J. Hicks and M. Stroud *Harper's Magazine* v334 no2001 p48 F 2017

Misteli, Tom

The genome—seeing it clearly now diag *Science* v357 no6349 p354 Jl 28 2017

The linker histone H1.0 generates epigenetic and functional intratumor heterogeneity bibl graph *Science* v353 no6307 paaf1644-1 S 30 2016

Mistick, Barbara

How to Get Feedback When No One Is Volunteering It *Harvard Business Review Digital Articles* p2 Ag 14 2015

Mistry, Palloji

India's Richest People color *Forbes* v198 no6 p34 N 8 2016

Misumi, Osami

Holliday junction resolvases mediate chloroplast nucleoid segregation diag *Science* v356 no6338 p631 My 12 2017

Mitarai, Fujio

A Sharper Focus on Constant Transformation M. Foster and D. W. Russell color *Forbes* v199 no1 p(Sp)6 Ja 24 2017

Mitcham, Carl

Are We All Scientific Experts Now? color *Issues in Science & Technology* v33 no1 p89 Fall 2016

Mitchel, O. M. (Ormsby MacKnight), 1809-1862

Heavenly Host L. VACCARIELLO *Cincinnati Magazine* v50 no7 p168 Ap 2017

Mitchell, Alanna

100 MICROPLASTIC THREADS. WHAT DOES THAT DO TO YOU? UNKNOWN color *Canadian Geographic* v136 no6 p61 D 2016

Eye of the Beholder? Not Quite cartoon *Canadian Wildlife* v22 no5 p15 N/D 2016

Tale from the Land of Oz color *Canadian Wildlife* v23 no4 p14 S/O 2017

Toxic Mystery color *Canadian Wildlife* v23 no2 p16 My/Je 2017

Water Damage color *Canadian Wildlife* v23 no1 p15 Mr/Ap 2017

MITCHELL, ALISON

Understanding Academic Language and Its Connection to School Success *Education Digest* v82 no6 p58 F 2017

MITCHELL, BRIAN PATRICK

Benedict Option I: Dreher's Plaintive Call bw *American Conservative* v16 no3 p44 My/Je 2017

Mitchell, Brian Stokes, 1958-

17. See Brian Stokes Mitchell *New York* v50 no12 p115 Je 12 2017

Mitchell, Cassie

NO LIMITS S. COLLINS *Atlanta* v56 no9 p110 Ja 2017

Mitchell, Ceasar

OFF TO THE RACES S. HENRY *Atlanta* v56 no10 p32 F 2017

Mitchell, Dan

Are You and Your Builder Speaking the Same Language? color *Log Home Living* v34 no2 p22 Mr 2017

Builder or General Contractor? color *Log Home Living* v34 no9 p22 D 2017

Great Panes color *Log Home Living* v34 no7 p26 S 2017

Laying the Groundwork for Success color *Log Home Living* v34

no3 p22 Ap 2017

A Lesson in Addition color *Log Home Living* v33 no7 p28 S 2016

The Light Stuff color *Log Home Living* v34 no1 p22 F 2017

Master of the House bw color *Log Home Living* v34 no4 p24 My 2017

Money Saving Design Tips: A Builder's Point of View color *Log Home Living* v33 no9 p26 D 2016

Perfect Pitch color *Log Home Living* v34 no6 p24 Ag 2017

The Quest for H2O color *Log Home Living* v34 no5 p24 Jl 2017

MITCHELL, DANIEL J.

FROM THE ARCHIVES bw *Reason* v49 no1 p70 My 2017

Mitchell, David

Kilogram-scale prexasertib monolactate monohydrate synthesis under continuous-flow CGMP conditions chart diag *Science* v356 no6343 p1144 Je 16 2017

Mitchell, Derek

Looking race in the face bw *Phi Delta Kappan* v98 no5 p24 F 2017

Mitchell, E. A. D.

A worldwide survey of neonicotinoids in honey graph *Science* v357 no6359 p109 O 6 2017

Mitchell, Edgar D., 1930-2016

EDGAR MITCHELL C. HOMANS *New York Times Magazine* p16 D 25 2016

Mitchell, Elizabeth

America's Dimming Stars: Our nation has always depended on public intellectuals to guide us. How come we no longer see the light? *Smithsonian* v48 no4 p31 Jl/Ag 2017

The Surprising Power of 400-Year-Old Paintings *Smithsonian* v48 no3 p28 Je 2017

MITCHELL, FRASER J. G.

Combining Biodiversity Resurveys across Regions to Advance Global Change Research *BioScience* v67 no1 p73 Ja 2017

Mitchell, George J. (George John), 1933-

Grappling with the Gordian knot A. J. Bacevich *America* v216 no7 p46 Ap 3 2017

Our American Union color *America* v216 no6 p54 Mr 20 2017

A Path to Peace: A Brief History of Israeli-Palestinian Negotiations and a Way Forward in the Middle East J. Waterbury *Foreign Affairs* v96 no1 p172 Ja/F 2017

Mitchell, Grace

THE HEIRS APPARENT N. Feeney color *Entertainment Weekly* no1471 p63 Je 23 2017

the storyteller P. P. FISCHER color *Better Homes & Gardens* v95 no8 p132 Ag 2017

Mitchell, Greg

Escape From East Berlin N. KULISH *New York Times Book Review* p10 N 20 2016

Palace Diner: With the greatest tuna melt in lunch counter history, a 15-seat dining car becomes an anchor for a Maine mill town's revival A. TRAVERSO color *Yankee* p50 Jl 2017

MITCHELL, HEIDI

ANGELA BRANTLEY color *Chicago* v66 no11 p44 N 2017

CAPPIE PONDEXTER color *Chicago* v66 no8 p46 Ag 2017

CLEAN SLATE [Cover story] color *Chicago* v66 no9 p73 S 2017

JOSÉ ESPARZA CHONG CUY color *Chicago* v66 no10 p44 O 2017

NIGHT AND DEY color *Chicago* v66 no4 p63 Ap 2017

TASTEMAKER: CHRISTINA MONLEY color *Chicago* v66 no9 p58 S 2017

Mitchell, Jill

California BREEDERS AND TRAINERS California BREEDERS AND TRAINERS California BREEDERS AND TRAINERS *Arabian Horse World* v57 no10 p93 Jl 2017

Mitchell, Jo

When I Was a Horse-Crazy Kid, I... color *Horse & Rider* v56 no2 p72 F 2017

Mitchell, John Cameron

DAVID BOWIE color *Entertainment Weekly* no1446/1447 p88 D 2016/Ja 2017

Ruth WILSON *Interview* v46 no9 p34 N 2016

Mitchell, Jonathan

Today's radio dramas M. M. Dana color *Christian Century* v133 no25 p43 D 7 2016

Mitchell, Joni, 1943-

10 Women Who Changed My Life M. Markle color *Glamour* v115

no9 p36 S 2017

Mitchell, Joshua

SAVOIR 'FAIR' J. Roedel color *Louisiana Life* v37 no6 p14 Jl/
Ag 2017

Mitchell, Katie, 1964-

Handel: Alcina J. Malafroute *Opera News* v81 no6 p53 D 2016

Mitchell, Kelsey

OFF TO THE RACES L. Schnell color *Sports Illustrated* v125
no15 p48 N 7 2016

Mitchell, Kevin M.

The Evolving World of Fabrics and Soft Goods *Stage Directions*
v29 no11 p32 N 2016

"Failing" in the Classroom *Stage Directions* v29 no10 p34 O 2016

The Good Fight *Stage Directions* v30 no10 p12 O 2017

The Parnelli Awards and NAMM: Industry Convergence *Stage
Directions* v30 no6 p16 Je 2017

We Can't Remain Silent *Stage Directions* v30 no4 p4 Ap 2017

Mitchell, Leila

PROTECTING LIVES AND PROPERTY--DEC's Dam Safety
Program *New York State Conservationist* v71 no5 p21 Ap 2017

Mitchell, Leslie A.

3D organization of synthetic and scrambled chromosomes diag
Science v355 no6329 p1050 Mr 10 2017

Bug mapping and fitness testing of chemically synthesized chromosome X diag *Science* v355 no6329 p1048 Mr 10 2017

Deep functional analysis of synII, a 770-kilobase synthetic yeast
chromosome diag *Science* v355 no6329 p1047 Mr 10 2017

Design of a synthetic yeast genome bibl chart color graph *Science*
v355 no6329 p1040 Mr 10 2017

Engineering the ribosomal DNA in a megabase synthetic chromosome diag *Science* v355 no6329 p1049 Mr 10 2017

"Perfect" designer chromosome V and behavior of a ring derivative diag *Science* v355 no6329 p1046 Mr 10 2017

Synthesis, debugging, and effects of synthetic chromosome consolidation: synVI and beyond color *Science* v355 no6329 p1045
Mr 10 2017

Mitchell, Mardeene

When Time is Brain K. RIDDERBUSCH *Atlanta* v56 no7 p215
N 2016

MITCHELL, MARGARET

THOUGHTS ON Property *Forbes* v199 no5 p124 My 16 2017

Mitchell, Mike

Trolls L. Greenblatt color *Entertainment Weekly* no1439 p44 N
11 2016

Mitchell, Mitch

THREE DAYS IN AMERICA color *Wired* v24 no12 p114 D 2016

MITCHELL, MOLLY

r.s.v.p bw *Bon Appetit* v62 no4 p10 Ap 2017

Mitchell, Nicola J.

Biodiversity redistribution under climate change: Impacts on
ecosystems and human well-being color *Science* v355 no6332
p1389 Mr 31 2017

Mitchell, Nicole

The Hot Box J. McDonough, J. Corbett et al chart *Downbeat* v84
no7 p49 Jl 2017

The Importance of Scholarship *Publishers Weekly* v264 no38 p76
S 18 2017

Mitchell, Roscoe

Bells For The South Side B. Bambarger color *Downbeat* v84 no10
p65 O 2017

ROSCOE MITCHELL: 'PEOPLE DON'T WANT TO BE CAT-
EGORIZED' T. Panken color *Downbeat* v84 no9 p40 S 2017

Mitchell, Shay, 1987-

Pretty Little Likes color *InStyle* v24 no6 p60 Je 2017

Mitchell, Spencer

NOT TOO SHABBY color *Spin to Win Rodeo* v20 no12 p15 F
2017

Mitchell, Thomas

Evolution of the wheat blast fungus through functional losses in
a host specificity determinant diag map *Science* v357 no6346
p80 Jl 7 2017

Mitchell, Will

Expanding the Reach of Primary Care in Developing Countries
color *Harvard Business Review Digital Articles* p2 Je 6 2017

Mitchell, William, 1879-1936

COMMENTS KICKIN' BACK T. Kuhlmeier and R. Miller *MHQ:*

Quarterly Journal of Military History v29 no2 p10 Wint 2017

Mitchison, Freya L.

Release of mineral-bound water prior to subduction tied to shallow seismogenic slip off Sumatra graph *Science* v356 no6340
p841 My 26 2017

Mitchum, Robert

That man Robert Mitchum: remembering an enigmatic American
original C. Sandford bw *America* v217 no5 p38 S 4 2017

Mite ecology

The Truth About Ticks E. Laborde *New Orleans Magazine* v51
no10 p22 Ag 2017

Miter saws

BASKETBALL CATAPULT! chart color diag *Popular Mechanics* p96 My 2017

Miter saws—Evaluation

THE COMPLETE CORDLESS ARSENAL color *Popular Mechanics* p32 My 2017

Mithen, Steven

Our 86 Billion Neurons: She Showed It color *New York Review of
Books* v63 no18 p42 N 24 2016

Mitimingi, Taonga Clifford

To Talk About Sex to Teens In Zambia, Play the Diva color
Bloomberg Businessweek no4494 p42 O 10 2016

Mitman, Tammalene

My little barn color *Equus* no475 p77 Ap 2017

Mitnaul, Lyndon J.

Distribution and clinical impact of functional variants in 50,726
whole-exome sequences from the DiscovEHR study chart graph
Science v354 no6319 paaf6814-1 D 23 2016

Mitochondria

Dopamine oxidation mediates mitochondrial and lysosomal dysfunction in Parkinson's disease L. F. Burbulla, P. Song et al
graph *Science* v357 no6357 p1255 S 22 2017

Metabolic cues for hematopoietic stem cells P. Sommerkamp and
A. Trumpp bibl diag *Science* v354 no6316 p1103 D 2 2016

Mitochondrial DNA

Birth of 'three-parent baby' prompts hope and concern T. H. Saey
color *Science News* v190 no13 p22 D 24 2016

Charting genetic diversity around the world K. Travis map *Science
News* v190 no9 p32 O 29 2016

Mitochondrial DNA—Therapeutic use

License for three-parent babies *Science* v355 no6331 p1244 Mr
24 2017

Mitochondrial RNA

The structure of the yeast mitochondrial ribosome N. Desai, A.
Brown et al bibl color *Science* v355 no6324 p528 F 3 2017

Mitra, Ananda

Overcoming the Flaws of Needs Assessments: The new realm of
big data *Parks & Recreation* v52 no9 p24 S 2017

Mitra, Debayan

Spin-imbalance in a 2D Fermi-Hubbard system diag graph *Science* v357 no6358 p1385 S 29 2017

Mitra, Maureen Nandini

AMERICA'S TOXIC PRISONS color map *Earth Island Journal*
v32 no2 p17 Summ 2017

Built-in Peril color *Earth Island Journal* v32 no1 p27 Spr 2017

Food for Thought *Earth Island Journal* v32 no3 p2 Aut 2017

NATIONS RISING color *Earth Island Journal* v32 no4 p18 Wint
2017

Remediation Art cartoon color *Earth Island Journal* v32 no4 p27
Wint 2017

"Scientists Make the Best Advocates" *Earth Island Journal* v32
no2 p45 Summ 2017

There's a Crack in Everything *Earth Island Journal* v32 no4 p2
Wint 2017

Mitral valve insufficiency—Treatment

Clipped In *Virginia Living* v15 no1 p95 D 2016

Mitrica, B.

Observation of a large-scale anisotropy in the arrival directions
of cosmic rays above 8×1018 eV *Science* v357 no6357 p1266
S 22 2017

Mitski (Performer)

'YOUR BEST AMERICAN GIRL' J. ZHANG color *New York
Times Magazine* p62 Mr 12 2017

Mitsubishi Electric Corp.

The New Gold Rush for Our e-Waste T. John color *Time* v190

no15 p10 O 16 2017

Mitsubishi Estate Co. Ltd.

A PIECE OF THE ROCK A. GARA color *Forbes* v200 no1 p28 Jl 27 2017

Mitsuoka, Chikako

Evolution of the wheat blast fungus through functional losses in a host specificity determinant diag map *Science* v357 no6346 p80 Jl 7 2017

Mitsuru Osaki

Time for responsible peatland agriculture bibl *Science* v354 no6312 p562 N 4 2016

Mittal, Shuchi

β2-Adrenoreceptor is a regulator of the a-synuclein gene driving risk of Parkinson's disease cartoon chart graph *Science* v357 no6354 p891 S 1 2017

Mittelman, Melissa

Letting Workers Have a Share bw color *Bloomberg Businessweek* no4527 p37 Je 19 2017

Private Equity Is Eyeing Your Nest Egg *Bloomberg Businessweek* no4519 p47 Ap 24 2017

Mittens—Evaluation

The O List: BACK TO SCHOOL color *O, The Oprah Magazine* p49 S 2017

Mittler, Eva

A "Trojan horse" bispecific-antibody strategy for broad protection against ebolaviruses bibl graph *Science* v354 no6310 p350 O 21 2016

Mitton, Simon

Your Guide to the 2017 Total Solar Eclipse *Physics Today* v70 no8 p59 Ag 2017

MITTRA, SONALI

Can South Asia Share Its Rivers? *Current History* v116 no789 p148 Ap 2017

Miu Miu (Company)

Fresh SQUEEZED: THE SEASON'S RUBBERY SLIDE SANDAL FROM MIU MIU IS A JUICED-UP REFRESH OF A SUMMER STAPLE *Interview* v47 no3 p45 Ap 2017

Miwa, Yoko

ONE FAN AT A TIME J. Garelick color *Downbeat* v84 no9 p50 S 2017

Mixed-income housing

Parkside of Oldtown, Phase Mb A. Fixsen *Architectural Record* v205 no4 p197 Ap 2017

Mixed martial arts

7 SILAT SOLUTIONS B. RICHARDSON color *Black Belt* v55 no3 p46 Ap/My 2017

Cage Match A. SHEPHARD il *New Republic* v247 no11 p11 N 2016

COMMON GROUND T. KOCH bw color *Black Belt* v55 no5 p54 Ag/S 2017

LESSONS LEARNED! J. BEASLEY color *Black Belt* v55 no6 p46 O/N 2017

On a Question of the Day S. Marlow, J. Cordova et al color *Black Belt* v55 no6 p16 O/N 2017

SECRETS OF SYSTEMA K. SECOURS color *Black Belt* v55 no5 p66 Ag/S 2017

TAI CHI VS. MMA MATCH ANGERS CHINA *Black Belt* v55 no5 p8 Ag/S 2017

Mixed martial arts—Competitions

Fading Fast L. J. Wertheim and T. Keith color *Sports Illustrated* v127 no1 p14 Jl 3 2017

Mixed martial arts—Study & teaching

A One-Stop Hit Shop J. Kelly bw *Bloomberg Businessweek* no4538 p61 S 18 2017

Mixed media (Art)

Bibliophile R. J. Ritzel bw color *American Craft* v76 no6 p42 D 2016-Ja 2017

Mixed media (Art)—Exhibitions

HOLDING ON T. MALONE *Atlanta* v57 no2 p30 Je 2017

The Makeup Artist J. ORTVED color *Vogue* v207 no11 p136 N 2017

Mixed reality

See also

Augmented reality

DISRUPTION MACHINE [Cover story] D. M. EWALT color *Forbes* v198 no7 p76 N 29 2016

HOLO BONES N. Strochlic color *National Geographic* v231 no6 p4 Je 2017

Mixed-use developments

PIER PRESSURE: Who said building a gigantic, ambitious retail-and-residential project like the Wharf would be easy? *Washingtonian Magazine* v53 no1 p22 O 2017

Mixed-use developments—New Jersey

Teachers Village L. Allen *Architectural Record* v205 no4 p198 Ap 2017

Mixers (Kitchen appliances)

HANDY MIXERS M. XERAKIA color *Better Homes & Gardens* v95 no6 p124 Je 2017

Mixers (Kitchen appliances)—Design & Construction

Ask Martha *Martha Stewart Living* no269 p70 N 2016

Mixers (Kitchen appliances)—Sales & prices

Ask Martha *Martha Stewart Living* no269 p70 N 2016

Mixing machinery

See also

Blenders (Cooking)

How to Make a... SPINDLE SANDER FROM A BLENDER J. SCHADEWALD color *Popular Mechanics* p71 S 2017

How to Make a... SPINDLE SANDER FROM A BLENDER J. SCHADEWALD color *Popular Mechanics* v193 no7 p71 S 2016

Mixing machinery—Evaluation

new products color *Science* v357 no6355 p1053 S 8 2017

Mixing—Equipment & supplies

It's Electric—With the Right Mix A. Sneed color diag *Scientific American* v316 no3 p24 Mr 2017

Mixon, Katy, 1981-

American Housewife N. Abrams, B. L. Heldman et al *Entertainment Weekly* no1482/1483 p79 S 22 2017

KATY MIXON M. Snetiker color *Entertainment Weekly* no1434 p47 O 7 2016

Mixtec (Mexican people)—Antiquities

Codex Subtext Z. ZORICH color *Archaeology* v69 no6 p12 N/D 2016

Miyabi (Company)

Miyabi Knife color *Bloomberg Businessweek* no4532 p67 Jl 31 2017

Miyagawa, K.

Electronic crystal growth bw diag graph *Science* v357 no6358 p1378 S 29 2017

Miyagawa, Kōzan, 1842-1916—Exhibitions

"MIYAGAWA KOZAN RETROSPECTIVE" P. NAGY color *ARTnews* v115 no4 p136 Wint 2016/2017

Miyamoto, Kentaro

Conversion of object identity to object-general semantic value in the primate temporal cortex color graph *Science* v357 no6352 p687 Ag 18 2017

Miyashita, Yasushi

Conversion of object identity to object-general semantic value in the primate temporal cortex color graph *Science* v357 no6352 p687 Ag 18 2017

Miyauchi, Yuhei

Synthesis of a carbon nanobelt diag graph *Science* v356 no6334 p172 Ap 14 2017

Miyazono, Evan

Nanophotonic rare-earth quantum memory with optically controlled retrieval diag graph *Science* v357 no6358 p1392 S 29 2017

Miyoko Sakashita

Ready to Resist *Earth Island Journal* v32 no1 p56 Spr 2017

Miyoshi, Keita

Tudor-SN-mediated endonucleolytic decay of human cell microRNAs promotes G1/S phase transition graph *Science* v356 no6340 p859 My 26 2017

Mi-Young, Ahn

South Korea's nuclear U-turn draws praise and darts color graph *Science* v357 no6346 p15 Jl 7 2017

Mizrahi, Isaac, 1961-

FUN HOME E. Wilson color *InStyle* p60 Home & Design 2016

Mizrahi, Jamie

Jamie Does Juicy L. Chan color *Glamour* v115 no9 p76 S 2017

Mizrahi, Orel

Global mRNA polarization regulates translation efficiency in the

intestinal epithelium diag *Science* v357 no6357 p1299 S 22
2017

Mizu Inc.

WATER BOTTLES J. LYNCH color *Popular Mechanics* p28 Jl
2017

Mizukami, Yuka

Crystal structure of the overlapping dinucleosome composed of
hexasome and octasome graph *Science* v356 no6334 p205 Ap
14 2017

Mizumura, Minae, 1951-

Inheritance from Mother color *Publishers Weekly* v264 no11 p52
Mr 13 2017

MUST EVERYONE WRITE ENGLISH? M. A. Heberle *Claremont Review of Books* v16 no4 p76 Fall 2016

Parental Controls J. FAN *New York Times Book Review* p12 Je
11 2017

Mizuno Corp.

SMOOTH OPERATORS M. Chwasky color *Golf Magazine* v59
no11 p88 N 2017

Mlinko, Ange

MERRY WAR D. CHIASSON cartoon *New Yorker* v93 no26 p88
S 4 2017

Møller, Birger Lindberg

Characterization of a dynamic metabolon producing the defense
compound dhurrin in sorghum bibl graph *Science* v354 no6314
p890 N 18 2016

Mlod, Anne

Teachers and librarians talk favorite classroom purchases color
Publishers Weekly v264 no34 p70 Ag 21 2017

Mlotek, Haley

The Shortlist: Feminist Essays *New York Times Book Review* p26
S 17 2017

MLYNOWSKI, SARAH

Opening a New Chapter *New York Times Book Review* p19 D 18
2016

M&M candies (Trademark)

Brand new HUE M. WOLLAN *New York Times Magazine* p51
O 9 2016

Mmoh, Michael—Political & social views

American Voices Michael Mmoh J. Lisanti and T. Keith color
Sports Illustrated v125 no18 p22 D 5 2016

Mnemonics

Memory training rejiggers the brain L. SANDERS diag *Science
News* v191 no6 p7 Ap 1 2017

SOUP UP YOUR RECALL A. AU LEVITT color *Reader's Digest*
v190 no1133 p106 S 2017

MNOOKIN, SETH

High Anxiety *New York Times Book Review* p20 Mr 12 2017

Mnuchin, Steven T., 1962-

CAN STEVE MNUCHIN MAKE THE IRS GREAT AGAIN? J.
Wieczner color *Fortune* v175 no5 p13 Ap 1 2017

FROM WALL STREET TO PENNSYLVANIA AVENUE color
Fortune v175 no2 p16 F 1 2017

The Mess Steven Mnuchin Left Behind Z. Mider and S. Mohsin
bw *Bloomberg Businessweek* no4504 p34 D 19 2016

Mnuchin's Conflicting Hollywood Roles Z. Mider and S. Mohsin
Bloomberg Businessweek no4507 p24 Ja 16 2017 TRUMP'S
KEY ADVISERS BY THE NUMBERS T. Newmyer *Fortune*
v174 no8 p17 D 15 2016

An Unlikely Salesman for the Republican Party's Tax Plan Z. J.
Miller color *Time* v190 no14 p9 O 9 2017

Mnyanda, Lukanyo

A Serious Pounding color *Bloomberg Businessweek* no4497 p17
O 31 2016

Mo Zhou

Forest value: More than commercial *Science* v354 no6319 p1541
D 23 2016

Positive biodiversity-productivity relationship predominant
in global forests bibl chart graph map *Science* v354 no6309
paaf8957-1 O 14 2016

Moab (Utah)—Description & travel

RUN AWAY! [Cover story] E. STROUT, M. PRELLE et al color
Runner's World v52 no7 p54 Ag 2017

MOAG, JEFF

The Battle Within color *Canoe & Kayak Magazine* v45 no1 p4
Wint 2017

MTI ADVENTUREWEAR: ALL IN THE FAMILY color *Canoe
& Kayak Magazine* v45 no1 p92 Wint 2017

Moah, Michael

Ones to Watch N. PANTIC *Tennis* v53 no1 p34 Ja/F 2017

Moana (Film)

6 — "YOU'RE WELCOME" D. Coggan *Entertainment Weekly*
no1444/1445 p60 D 16 2016

Disney Makes Its Maiden Voyage to the South Pacific E. Berman
color *Time* v188 no20 p52 N 14 2016

Healing presence J. M. Griffith *U.S. Catholic* v82 no4 p38 Ap
2017

McConaughey Goes Carly Rae In Animated Sing E. Berman color
Time v188 no22-23 p109 N/D 2016

MOANA C. Chiarella color *Sound & Vision* v82 no6 p70 Jl/Ag
2017

MOANA M. Snetiker color *Entertainment Weekly* no1438 p44 N
4 2016

Streaming S. Li color *Entertainment Weekly* no1470 p44 Je 16
2017

The Truth Behind 3 AWESOME MOVIES J. RIZZO *National
Geographic Kids* no466 p22 D 2016/Ja 2017

MOAR, BRENDA

SMART PEOPLE DO THE Dumbest THINGS! [Cover story]
Reader's Digest v190 no1134 p62 O 2017

Moates, Tom

A tale of two mandibles bw cartoon *Equus* no474 p20 Mr 2017

Moatti, Sophie-Charlotte

3 Things to Watch as the Digital Side of the U.S. Presidential
Campaigns Unfold *Harvard Business Review Digital Articles*
p2 Jl 14 2016

The Sharing Economy's New Middlemen *Harvard Business Review Digital Articles* p2 Mr 5 2015

Why Mega-Mergers Are Back in Vogue for Internet Companies
Harvard Business Review Digital Articles p2 Je 1 2015

MOAVENI, AZADEH

A Sufi's Second Act *New York Times Book Review* p18 Ja 22 2017

MOAZAMI, JESSICA

CAT'S MEOW color *Chicago* v66 no6 p42 Je 2017

CITRUS SPLASH color *Chicago* v66 no7 p32 Jl 2017

DEEP PURPLE color *Chicago* v66 no10 p42 O 2017

ELIXIR, ELEVATED bw color *Chicago* v66 no11 p46 N 2017

MODERN ROMANCE color *Chicago* v66 no2 p34 F 2017

ON THE BREEZE color *Chicago* v66 no5 p52 My 2017

PEARLY WHITES color *Chicago* v66 no8 p48 Ag 2017

ROCK STEADY color *Chicago* v66 no4 p48 Ap 2017

SLOPE STYLE color *Chicago* v66 no1 p48 Ja 2017

Moazed, Danesh

DNA sequence-dependent epigenetic inheritance of gene silencing and histone H3K9 methylation diag *Science* v356 no6333
p88 Ap 7 2017

MOBERG, DAVID

Fighting the Bosses color *In These Times* v40 no11 p24 N 2016

Mobike (Company)

IDEAS KNOW NO BORDERS C. Leaf color *Fortune* v176 no2
p10 Ag 1 2017

Mobile (Ala.)

SOUTH'S BEST BAR H. Hayes color *Southern Living* v52 no4
p68 Ap 2017

Mobile app development

The Changing Economics of App Development P. A. Salz *Harvard Business Review Digital Articles* p2 N 4 2015

MONKEY DO C. Bethea cartoon *New Yorker* v92 no45 p23 Ja
16 2017

THE MOST TRUSTED NAME IN NEWS M. Belloni bw color
Popular Mechanics p52 O 2017

THE NEW CITIZEN JOURNALISTS cartoon color *Popular Mechanics* p38 O 2017

TREATING ADDICTION WITH AN APP N. Byrnes color *MIT
Technology Review* v120 no3 p34 My/Je 2017

Mobile apps

See also

Social networking mobile apps

Weather forecasting mobile apps

10 THINGS WE'RE TALKING ABOUT T. A. Christian color
map *Essence* v48 no5 p71 S 2017

5 AWESOME YOUTUBE APP FEATURES R. WHITWAM col-

or *PCWorld* v35 no10 p107 O 2017

6 more ways to make the most of Mail for iOS 10 B. PATTERSON color *Macworld - Digital Edition* p55 D 2016

9 free ways to get the most out of Google's Play Music app B. PATTERSON color *PCWorld* v35 no1 p201 Ja 2017

AI TEST DRIVE: IS ALEXA ON YOUR PHONE AS GOOD AS IT IS IN YOUR HOME? M. SIMON color *PCWorld* v35 no5 p149 My 2017

Ask the iTunes Guy: Your questions about the iOS 10 Music app K. McELHEARN cartoon color *Macworld - Digital Edition* v33 no11 p151 N 2016

Duolingo A. Fitzpatrick *New York Times Magazine* p20 Jl 30 2017

Evaluating EdTech: A Strategy for Selecting Digital Tools J. LINDL bw *Education Digest* v83 no1 p44 S 2017

Every Website Is a Monument A. Plessas *Art in America* v104 no9 p130 O 2016

Getting Youth to Focus on Nature C. Bolt color *National Wildlife (World Edition)* v55 no4 p14 Je/Jl 2017

Google makes the best Android apps easier to find with Android Excellence M. SIMON color *PCWorld* v35 no7 p47 Jl 2017

How a Food-Ordering App Broke into a Crowded Market B. Gilad *Harvard Business Review Digital Articles* p2 N 25 2015

Is There An App for That? M. MELTON *Los Angeles Magazine* p12 F 2017

JEPP CHARTS COME TO FOREFLIGHT color *Flying* v144 no7 p15 Jl 2017

Meditation App Roundup C. VAN DUSEN color *Tricycle: The Buddhist Review* v27 no1 p98 Fall 2017

A Modest Proposal B. Eichner color *GQ: Gentlemen's Quarterly* v97 no4 p56 Ap 2017

A NEW MIND-SET H. Clancy color *Fortune* v75 no1 p30 Ja 1 2017

Our Mobile World At Lightning Speed L. D'VORKIN *Forbes* v198 no6 p20 N 8 2016

Play On color *Sports Illustrated* v127 no6 p10 Ag 28 2017

Put Down the Reading Glasses color *Prevention* v69 no4 p8 Ap 2017

Redefining Journalism In a Mobile World L. D'VORKIN *Forbes* v199 no5 p12 My 16 2017

R.I.P. VINE: THE SIX-SECOND OBITUARY K. P. Sullivan color *Entertainment Weekly* no1439 p11 N 11 2016

rise and strrretch color *Parents* v92 no3 p15 Mr 2017

Smart Plants: The Flora of Virginia's new mobile app is the 21st century version of the classic botany card B. CROWDER *Virginia Living* v15 no6 p67 O 2017

Sync With Your Cycle W. L. Wilson *Essence* v48 no5 p112 S 2017

There Is a First Time for Everything K. Witte *Parks & Recreation* v51 no10 p52 O 2016

toys for future coders *Parents* v92 no2 p60 F 2017

WhatsApp Grew to One Billion Users by Focusing on Product, Not Technology Baculard *Harvard Business Review Digital Articles* p2 Jl 1 2016

What's Hot Now R. Mosely color *Seventeen* v76 no5 p16 S 2017

WHAT'S WRONG WITH MICROSOFT TO-DO: 8 THINGS LACKING IN WUNDERLIST'S REPLACEMENT J. NEWMAN color *PCWorld* v35 no6 p127 Je 2017

Mobile apps in business

The Productivity Payoff of Mobile Apps at Work J. Panepinto *Harvard Business Review Digital Articles* p2 N 13 2014

TECH TAKES THE FIELD H. Clancy color *Fortune* v175 no3 p32 Mr 1 2017

Traders' New Favorite Way to Swap Secrets L. J. Keller color *Bloomberg Businessweek* no4518 p41 Ap 10 2017

Mobile apps in education

TECHNOLOGY-SUPPORTED LEARNING R. Karchmer-Klein color *Literacy Today (2411-7862)* v34 no3 p8 N/D 2016

Mobile apps in education—Evaluation

MARBOTIC SMART LETTERS AND SMART NUMBERS: TOYS + TABLETS = EDUCATIONAL FUN J. R. BOOKWALTER color *Macworld - Digital Edition* p53 Mr 2017

Mobile apps—Evaluation

10 Apps to Make You Productive K. V. Syckle color *Money* v46 no9 p22 O 2017

3.15 P.M. ON PERISCOPE color *Popular Mechanics* p50 O 2017

36 APPS THAT WILL SAVE YOU MONEY M. Leonhardt, K. Mulhere et al color *Money* v46 no4 p46 My 2017

Apple Music in iOS 10: Smart, simple, but still imperfect C. McGARRY color *Macworld - Digital Edition* v33 no11 p141 N 2016

Apple Music in iTunes just got more enjoyable and easier to use K. McELHEARN color *Macworld - Digital Edition* v33 no11 p147 N 2016

APP TO EXCELLENCE Z. HILL bw *Ebony* v72/73 no12/1 p92 O/N 2017

Avoid Social Security Screwups J. B. CLARK *Kiplinger's Personal Finance* v71 no1 p32 Ja 2017

BUSYCAL 3: THE BETTER MAC CALENDAR EXPERIENCE, NOW ON iOS J. R. BOOKWALTER color *Macworld - Digital Edition* v33 no11 p33 N 2016

Digit review: Online account service needs better controls J. BATTERSBY color *Macworld - Digital Edition* p88 Je 13 2017

THE DOCTOR IS IN... YOUR POCKET *Prevention* v69 no5 p10 My 2017

Don't Let's Roll cartoon *Weekly Standard* v22 no18 p3 Ja 16 2017

Easy Family Reunions D. Pogue color *AARP: The Magazine* v59 no6A p12 O/N 2016

emporium color *Dressage Today* v23 no6 p62 F 2017

Evernote overhauls its iOS app with focus on speed and simplicity C. McGARRY color *Macworld - Digital Edition* p49 Mr 2017

A Garage Sale on Your Phone A. GEORGE cartoon chart color *Popular Mechanics* p24 My 2017

Get to the Heart of Fitness A. Koch color *Men's Health* v32 no2 p12 Mr 2017

Hands-on with Apple Clips: How to use the iOS videoediting app and why you'd want to C. McGARRY color *Macworld - Digital Edition* v34 no6 p49 Je 2017

Hands on with Setapp: Getting started with the Netflix of Mac apps J. DOVE color *Macworld - Digital Edition* p7 Mr 2017

HEART HEALTH F. ESKER color *Louisiana Life* v37 no3 p10 Ja/F 2017

Interactive map reveals universe's hidden details C. Crockett color *Science News* v190 no11 p29 N 26 2016

It's football season! These second-screen apps make NFL games even more fun M. ANSALDO color *PCWorld* p34 O 2016

Keep It Legal: Think that fish you caught is a keeper? Not so fast A. JONES *Boating World* v38 no5 p18 My 2017

Logitech ZeroTouch: This Android smartphone holder puts Amazon's Alexa in your car M. BROWN color map *PCWorld* v35 no5 p132 My 2017

LOOKING GLASS K. SHEIKH cartoon *Popular Science* p14 Ja/F 2017

Meditation App Roundup C. VAN DUSEN color *Tricycle: The Buddhist Review* v26 no2 p88 Wint 2016

Meet the new Wunderlist: Microsoft's To-Do task manager takes over M. SIMON color *Macworld - Digital Edition* v34 no6 p103 Je 2017

"MOM, I CAN'T READ!" color *Good Housekeeping* v265 no4 p132 O 2017

NEW PRODUCTS color map *Astronomy* v45 no5 p68 My 2017

new products: software/data analysis color *Science* v357 no6348 p319 Jl 21 2017

New Tools for Working Smarter K. PALMER cartoon *AARP: The Magazine* v59 no6A p24 O/N 2016

photo school: Get Serial G. FULLERTON color *Backpacker* p36 S 2017

Running with Apps M. ANTONOFF color *Sound & Vision* v82 no1 p24 Ja 2017

SECRETS FOR MAC AND SECRETS TOUCH: A SIMPLE, NO-FRILLS PASSWORD MANAGER J. R. BOOKWALTER color *Macworld - Digital Edition* p21 Mr 2017

Sky Guide: Here's a great app for casual and experienced stargazers alike S. Walker color *Sky & Telescope* v134 no2 p62 Ag 2017

SMART APP TELLS WHEN TO IRRIGATE: INTERNET PROGRAM TAPS INTO NATIONAL WEATHER SERVICE AND OTHER DATA TO GUIDE IRRIGATION SCHEDULING FOR MISSOURI FARMERS G. Johnston *Successful Farming* v115 no9 p56 Ag 2017

TAKE A CHILL C. Van Dusen color *Tricycle: The Buddhist Review* v26 no3 p90 Spr 2017

Tap Our App for Medical Records color *AARP: The Magazine* v59 no1A p60 D 2015/Ja 2016

There's An Ag App For That J. WALTER *Successful Farming* v114 no12 p70 Mid-N 2016

Tools: Products for your Consideration *Stage Directions* v30 no10 p6 O 2017

TREATING ADDICTION WITH AN APP N. Byrnes color *MIT Technology Review* v120 no3 p34 My/Je 2017

VIEWER POSITIONING SYSTEM J. Enxuto and E. Love *Art in America* v104 no9 p122 O 2016

Walk the Walk K. Stock color *Bloomberg Businessweek* no4503 p72 D 12 2016

WANT TO TREAT YOUR KID LIKE A FELON ON PAROLE? THERE'S AN APP FOR THAT L. SKENAZY color *Reason* v49 no4 p12 Ag/S 2017

Watching Your DVR From Anywhere M. ANTONOFF and C. Crowley color *Sound & Vision* v81 no9 p24 N 2016

WHAT'S NEW AT THE APP STORE color *Macworld - Digital Edition* v34 no8 p79 Ag 2017

WHAT'S NEW AT THE APP STORE J. MATHIS cartoon *Macworld - Digital Edition* p61 Mr 2017

What's new at the App Store J. MATHIS cartoon *Macworld - Digital Edition* v33 no11 p95 N 2016

WHAT'S NEW AT THE APP STORE J. MATHIS color *Macworld - Digital Edition* v34 no11 p79 N 2017

WHAT'S NEW AT THE APP STORE J. MATHIS color *Macworld - Digital Edition* v34 no6 p75 Je 2017

Mobile apps—Government policy

THE APPROVAL MATRIX img *New York* p96 Ja 23 2017

Mobile apps—History

apps we wish existed S. GIVEN color *Parents* v92 no4 p102 Ap 2017

Mobile apps—Management

VINE'S FATAL LESSON FOR THE TECH WORLD A. DOMISE *Maclean's* v129 no45 p12 N 14 2016

Mobile apps—Marketing

WHAT'S NEW AT THE APP STORE color *Macworld - Digital Edition* v34 no9 p54 S 2017

Mobile apps—Security measures

HERE COMES EVERYBODY *Harper's Magazine* p19 O 2017

Mobile apps—Social aspects

Using Tech to Feed Hungry People P. M. ESSWEIN color *Kiplinger's Personal Finance* v71 no1 p22 Ja 2017

Mobile apps—Software

Teen Tech Times T. Mecia color *Weekly Standard* v22 no33 p22 My 8 2017

Mobile banking industry

Mobile Phones Promise to Bring Banking to the World's Poorest R. Voorhies *Harvard Business Review Digital Articles* p2 Ap 4 2016

Mobile commerce

Apple Pay Is Just a Big Giveaway to Credit Card Companies J. P. V. Sampere *Harvard Business Review Digital Articles* p2 Ap 14 2015

Get Smart About Mobile Payments A. Cao color *Money* v46 no2 p34 Mr 2017

m-Commerce Growth in Sales and Fraud *USA Today Magazine* v145 no2858 p6 N 2016

Paying with YOUR FACE W. KNIGHT color *MIT Technology Review* v120 no2 p72 Mr/Ap 2017

Mobile communication systems

BLACK MARKET B. I. KOERNER cartoon color *Wired* v25 no10 p106 O 2017

The Golden Age of Podcasting M. ANTONOFF color *Sound & Vision* v82 no5 p26 Je 2017

The Greatest Generation Is Around the Corner O. Kharif and S. Moritz chart color *Bloomberg Businessweek* no4512 p41 F 20 2017

Ick! Clean Your Touch Screen! K. MURPHY *Reader's Digest* v188 no1125 p72 N 2016

Mobile Phones Promise to Bring Banking to the World's Poorest R. Voorhies *Harvard Business Review Digital Articles* p2 Ap 4 2016

Relax, Turn Off Your Phone, and Go to Sleep L. Rosen *Harvard Business Review Digital Articles* p2 Ag 31 2015

Mobile communication systems in education

We wanted to prove learning can be fun M. CALNAN *People Management* p25 O 2016

Mobile food services

BLOCK PARTY A. BROWNLEE *Cincinnati Magazine* v50 no2 p62 N 2016

LA SOCIAL color *Los Angeles Magazine* v62 no7 p125 Jl 2017

Park Bench. Nomadic Nourishment in NorCal C. Jones *Parks & Recreation* v52 no6 p56 Je 2017

A Taste of the Far East in the Northeast K. Krichko color *Powder* v46 no2 p32 O 2017

Mobile food services—Law & legislation

HOW A TACO TRUCK GETS STALLED P. Marinova color *Fortune* v174 no6 p86 N 1 2016

Mobile games

LIGHTSEEKERS SMART FIGURES A. HAYWARD color *Macworld - Digital Edition* v34 no8 p47 Ag 2017

See Mario. See Mario Run B. Einhorn and Y. Nakamura color graph *Bloomberg Businessweek* no4503 p29 D 12 2016

Turn your iPhone 7 into a handheld console A. Hayward color *Macworld - Digital Edition* p97 Ap 2017

Mobile games industry

Avenging MySpace K. CHAYKOWSKI color *Forbes* v199 no7 p46 Je 29 2017

Mobile games—Evaluation

10 great, older games that you can still play on iOS 11 A. HAYWARD color *Macworld - Digital Edition* v34 no11 p59 N 2017

Mobile home parks—Economic aspects

The Home of the Future K. Vick color *Time* v189 no12 p46 Ap 3 2017

Mobile homes

Model a TRAILER HOME scene B. Bennett color *Model Railroader* v84 no9 p36 S 2017

Mobile music

Outta Obsolescence M. ANTONOFF color *Sound & Vision* v82 no3 p19 Ap 2017

Mobile operating systems

See also

Android (Operating system)

iOS (Operating system)

How to downgrade to iOS 9 if you don't like iOS 10 R. LOYOLA *PCWorld* p157 O 2016

Report: Security hole in macOS Keychain puts passwords at risk R. LOYOLA color *Macworld - Digital Edition* v34 no11 p22 N 2017

Mobile operating systems—Evaluation

iOS 11 FAQ: EVERYTHING WE KNOW ABOUT NEW SIRI, PHOTOS, APPLE PAY, & MESSAGES [Cover story] O. Raymundo color *Macworld - Digital Edition* p65 Je 13 2017

Mobileye NV

Deal Snapshot Intel + Mobileye I. King and G. Coppola diag graph *Bloomberg Businessweek* no4515 p21 Mr 20 2017

Intel buys Mobileye for $15 billion to challenge Nvidia for the future of self-driving cars I. PAUL color *PCWorld* v35 no4 p27 Ap 2017

MOBILIO, ALBERT

FRANCIS PICABIA color *New York Times Book Review* p64 D 4 2016

Mobility (Structural dynamics)

The fading American dream: Trends in absolute income mobility since 1940 R. Chetty, D. Grusky et al bw graph *Science* v356 no6336 p398 Ap 28 2017

Mobilization (Social action)

CALIFORNIA STUDENT SUSTAIN ABILITY COALITION: Complacency Is Not an Option D. ADEL color *Earth Island Journal* v32 no1 p16 Spr 2017

Mobisson, Jidenna

Jidenna's Redemption Songs B. HIATT color *Rolling Stone* no1284 p42 Ap 6 2017

Möbius, Matthias E.

Sensitive electromechanical sensors using viscoelastic graphene-polymer nanocomposites bibl graph *Science* v354 no6317 p1257 D 9 2016

Mobley, Miller

July/August T. Ebony color *Ebony* v72 no9 p18 Jl/Ag 2017

Mobulidae

SAVING OCEAN SPECIES, FROM TOP TO BOTTOM D. Stone color *National Geographic* v231 no6 p12 Je 2017

MOBY

The Year in Reading [Cover story] *New York Times Book Review* p8 D 25 2016

Moccasins
How to Make Your Own MOCCASINS D. Biswell *Mother Earth News* no280 p26 F/Mr 2017

Mochica art
Painted Worlds [Cover story] J. A. LOBELL color *Archaeology* v70 no5 p26 S/O 2017

MOCHON, DANIEL
WHAT'S THE VALUE OF A LIKE? color *Harvard Business Review* v95 no2 p108 Mr/Ap 2017

Mock, Elliot D.
Activity-based protein profiling reveals off-target proteins of the FAAH inhibitor BIA 10-2474 chart color graph *Science* v356 no6342 p1084 Je 9 2017

Mock, Janet
Going Bare... color *Glamour* v115 no6 p138 Je 2017
Janet Mock A. MCDONELL-PARRY color *Rolling Stone* no1295 p42 S 7 2017
Lest We Forget *Ms.* v27 no1 p4 Spr 2017
Pioneers [Cover story] color *Time* v189 no16/17 p14 My 1-8 2017

Mock trials
A Day in Court D. SHERRIN *Education Digest* v82 no8 p28 Ap 2017

MOCKAITIS, THOMAS
Are We Winning the Battle Against Terrorism? *New York Times Upfront* v149 no7 p22 Ja 9 2017

MOCKENHAUPT, BRIAN
The Honor Guard color *Atlantic* v318 no5 p20 D 2016
LETTING A Wildfire BURN OVER YOU color *Reader's Digest* v189 no1131 p112 Je 2017

MOCKER, MARTIN
The Problem with Product Proliferation color *Harvard Business Review* v95 no3 p104 My/Je 2017
THE PROBLEM WITH PRODUCT PROLIFERATION: INTERACTION color graph *Harvard Business Review* v95 no5 p16 S/O 2017

Mockingbirds
Songs on the Wing E. A. WCELA *America* v216 no1 p29 Ja 2 2017

Mockler, D.
Observation of a large-scale anisotropy in the arrival directions of cosmic rays above 8×1018 eV *Science* v357 no6357 p1266 S 22 2017

Moda Operandi Inc.
LAUREN SANTO DOMINGO J. KELTNER DE VALLE color *Architectural Digest* v73 no12 p60 D 2016

Modahl, Bruce K.
A preacher builds bridges color *Christian Century* v134 no3 p24 F 2017

ModCloth Inc.
Corrections & Clarifications *Bloomberg Businessweek* no4522 p6 My 15 2017

Model airplanes
See also
Paper airplanes
THE PRIVILEGE OF BEING A PILOT M. Lunken color *Flying* v144 no7 p64 Jl 2017

Model airplanes—Evaluation
BENCHMARK: SAFE PASSAGE J. KEATS color *Wired* v25 no10 p52 O 2017

Model cars (Toys)
See also
Model racing automobiles (Toys)
Slot cars
Woodland Scenics HO Just Plug vehicles S. Otte *Model Railroader* v84 no7 p65 Jl 2017

Model cars (Toys)—Evaluation
TAKE YOUR KID FOR A RIDE color *Men's Health* v31 no10 p(Sp)26 D 2016

Model homes (Housing development)—Design & construction
It's a Small World After All JOHNSON color *Treasures* v5 no5 p53 Ap/My 2016

Model homes (Housing development)—Evaluation
It's a Small World After All JOHNSON color *Treasures* v5 no5 p53 Ap/My 2016

Model racing automobiles (Toys)
140-MPH, Slot-Car Drag Racing P. Thomas color *Hot Rod* v70 no7 p12 Jl 2017

Model railroad stations
British Columbia Ry.'s FORT ST. JOHN SUB C. Javier color diag *Model Railroader* v84 no11 p55 N 2017
Model a LARGE STATION using 3-D PRINTING B. Kingsnorth color *Model Railroader* v84 no8 p24 Ag 2017
TRACKS IN THE STREET [Cover story] P. Dolkos color *Model Railroader* v84 no10 p30 O 2017

Model Railroader (Periodical)
A modeling ambassador T. Koester color *Model Railroader* v84 no2 p90 F 2017
Trackside Photos bw color *Model Railroader* v84 no4 p102 Ap 2017

Model railroads
See also
Photography of model railroads
1940s cement mixers from 3-D printed parts E. White color *Model Railroader* v84 no6 p24 Je 2017
50 years and 2 houses [Cover story] L. Sassi and D. Elwell color map *Model Railroader* v84 no8 p40 Ag 2017
ABCs of DCC power district management [Cover story] L. Puckett color diag *Model Railroader* v84 no10 p50 O 2017
Adding onto a SECOND DECK B. Foltz color diag *Model Railroader* v84 no8 p48 Ag 2017
Adding sound to a vintage Kato locomotive [Cover story] L. Puckett color *Model Railroader* v84 no10 p56 O 2017
Ask MR S. Otte bw color *Model Railroader* v84 no6 p20 Je 2017
ASK MR S. Otte color *Model Railroader* v83 no12 p20 D 2016
BALLASTING main lines & sidings [Cover story] L. Sassi color *Model Railroader* v84 no7 p36 Jl 2017
BUILD A LAYOUT IN A WEEKEND P. Boehlert color *Model Railroader* v84 no9 p26 S 2017
Build: DISPATCHER AND OPERATOR DESKS [Cover story] D. Ball color diag *Model Railroader* v84 no10 p45 O 2017
CAPTURING THE MIDWEST in HO scale [Cover story] P. K. Søeborg color diag *Model Railroader* v84 no5 p40 My 2017
CASTING PLASTER WALLS for a scratchbuilt structure [Cover story] R. Howard color diag *Model Railroader* v84 no10 p24 O 2017
CSX up on Rocky Top B. Sprague color diag map *Model Railroader* v84 no8 p34 Ag 2017
Derailments of the curious kind J. Kelly color *Model Railroader* v84 no7 p22 Jl 2017
DIGITAL MR D. Kawala color il *Model Railroader* v84 no3 p6 Mr 2017
Enough theory; where do I put the wires? N. Besougloff *Model Railroader* v84 no9 p8 S 2017
Fighting the clicker wars T. Koester *Model Railroader* v84 no9 p78 S 2017
Finding your comfort zone T. Koester color *Model Railroader* v84 no11 p82 N 2017
From the Editor H. Miller *Model Railroader* v84 no10 p8 O 2017
THE FUTURE OF MODEL RAILROADING L. Mindheim color diag *Model Railroader* v84 no4 p52 Ap 2017
HO scale locomotives C. Grivno color *Model Railroader* v84 no7 p10 Jl 2017
How Märklin's 19th century Gauge 1 became the 20th century's LGB large scale K. Wills *Model Railroader* v84 no10 p20 O 2017
How to build an operating switch stand [Cover story] G. Butts diag *Model Railroader* v84 no7 p52 Jl 2017
How to model realistic rock outcroppings R. Nulton color *Model Railroader* v84 no6 p50 Je 2017
Keeping short circuits at bay with DCC L. Puckett color *Model Railroader* v84 no6 p60 Je 2017
Keeping your hobby hoard manageable [Cover story] N. Besougloff color *Model Railroader* v84 no7 p8 Jl 2017
LAYOUT IN A WEEKEND UPDATE [Cover story] P. Boehlert color diag *Model Railroader* v84 no10 p40 O 2017
'Layout In A Weekend,' we hardly knew ye H. Miller *Model Railroader* v84 no11 p8 N 2017
Make a hill from foam peanuts C. Grivno color *Model Railroader* v84 no10 p22 O 2017
Making a multimedia HIGHWAY OVERPASS D. Kawala color

p90 Ja 2017

Two railroads in one bedroom B. Sprague color diag *Model Railroader* v84 no1 p62 Ja 2017

Use natural soil and rocks in scenery A. Dodge color *Model Railroader* v84 no9 p52 S 2017

Z SCALE IN A CLOSET V. Sargent color *Model Railroader* v84 no11 p50 N 2017

Model railroads—Design & construction—Equipment & supplies

Mantua's 4-4-0 Belle was a plain Jane K. Wills color *Model Railroader* v83 no12 p26 D 2016

Model railroads—Electric equipment

Making the DCC suitcase connection L. Puckett color diag *Model Railroader* v83 no12 p62 D 2016

The next game changer? N. Besougloff *Model Railroader* v83 no12 p8 D 2016

Model railroads—Electric equipment—Evaluation

Athearn HO Southern Pacific EMD SD40 S. Otte color *Model Railroader* v84 no6 p64 Je 2017

Digitrax Evolution advanced DCC starter set L. Puckett color *Model Railroader* v84 no5 p62 My 2017

TrainClap 2000 audio DCC controller N. Besougloff color *Model Railroader* v84 no4 p98 Ap 2017

Model railroads—Electronic equipment—Evaluation

Digitrax DCS240 advanced command station provides more power and upgrades L. Puckett diag *Model Railroader* v83 no12 p70 D 2016

Model railroads—Equipment & supplies

5 ways to interchange freight cars T. Koester color *Model Railroader* v83 no12 p38 D 2016

Accurately modeled HO EMD GP38-2 features powerful motor and sound S. Otte color *Model Railroader* v84 no1 p70 Ja 2017

ANE Model Lococruiser DCC decoder color *Model Railroader* v84 no1 p75 Ja 2017

Bachmann introduces new N scale lighted streamlined passenger cars E. White color *Model Railroader* v84 no1 p72 Ja 2017

Build a signal system with Arduino microcontrollers D. Kurpanek color diag *Model Railroader* v83 no12 p42 D 2016

HO scale details and accessories C. Grivno color *Model Railroader* v84 no7 p14 Jl 2017

MOUNTAIN RAILROADING, NEW YORK STYLE S. Colabufo color il *Model Railroader* v83 no12 p56 D 2016

NEWS & PRODUCTS C. Grivno color diag *Model Railroader* v84 no1 p10 Ja 2017

Rivarossi HO scale 50-foot boxcar C. Grivno color *Model Railroader* v84 no1 p74 Ja 2017

ScaleTrains.com HO Union Pacific GTEL lives up to Museum Quality expectations D. Kawala color *Model Railroader* v84 no1 p68 Ja 2017

SCRATCHBUILD A DIESEL SHELL from styrene B. Stover color diag *Model Railroader* v84 no1 p54 Ja 2017

Showcase C. Grivno color *Model Railroader* v84 no7 p13 Jl 2017

Model railroads—Equipment & supplies—Evaluation

Athearn HO scale GP39-2 diesel features accurate details and realistic sound D. Kawala chart color diag *Model Railroader* v84 no3 p64 Mr 2017

Micro-Trains True-Scale couplers color *Model Railroader* v84 no3 p70 Mr 2017

NEWS & PRODUCTS C. Grivno color *Model Railroader* v83 no12 p10 D 2016

Rivarossi adds upgraded ESU LokSound DCC decoder in impressive HO Big Boy S. Otte chart color *Model Railroader* v84 no3 p66 Mr 2017

TrainClap 2000 audio DCC controller N. Besougloff color *Model Railroader* v84 no4 p98 Ap 2017

Model railroads—Evaluation

Atlas N scale FMC boxcar color *Model Railroader* v84 no2 p75 F 2017

Atlas O Pullman troop sleeper S. Otte *Model Railroader* v84 no10 p63 O 2017

Bachmann HO scale lighted passenger cars E. White *Model Railroader* v84 no10 p62 O 2017

Bachmann HO SoundValue USRA light 4-6-2 D. Kawala chart color *Model Railroader* v84 no4 p92 Ap 2017

Broadway Limited Imports HO scale P70 D. Kawala color *Model Railroader* v84 no11 p66 N 2017

Detailed SD45 from Walthers rumbles to life in HO scale with SoundTraxx DCC D. Kawala chart color diag *Model Railroader* v83 no12 p66 D 2016

ExactRail HO scale SP gondola C. Grivno *Model Railroader* v84 no11 p67 N 2017

InterMountain HO scale GP10 diesel C. Grivno color *Model Railroader* v84 no10 p60 O 2017

Kato HO scale Dash 9 features upgraded mechanism and roadname-specific detail D. Kawala chart color diag *Model Railroader* v84 no2 p68 F 2017

Kato N scale SDP40F with ESU LokSound D. Kawala *Model Railroader* v84 no10 p63 O 2017

Model Power N scale 2-6-0 Mogul D. Kawala chart color *Model Railroader* v84 no11 p64 N 2017

Moloco HO General American 50-foot insulated boxcar C. Grivno color *Model Railroader* v83 no12 p72 D 2016

MTH HO scale New York City subway cars E. White chart color *Model Railroader* v84 no4 p94 Ap 2017

New paint schemes for smooth-running Atlas N scale General Electric B36-7 E. White bw color *Model Railroader* v83 no12 p68 D 2016

News & Products bw color *Model Railroader* v84 no9 p10 S 2017

NEWS & PRODUCTS C. Grivno color *Model Railroader* v83 no12 p10 D 2016

News & Products color *Model Railroader* v84 no10 p10 O 2017

Rapido brings feature-packed New Haven FL9 commuter locomotive to N scale E. White chart color diag *Model Railroader* v84 no2 p70 F 2017

ScaleTrains.com HO scale SD40-2 E. White chart color *Model Railroader* v84 no11 p62 N 2017

WalthersMainline 40-foot AAR boxcar S. Otte *Model Railroader* v84 no11 p67 N 2017

WalthersProto HO scale PRR BR70n RPO-baggage car S. Otte color *Model Railroader* v84 no4 p96 Ap 2017

Model railroads—Flatcars

Easier access to an N scale sneak track J. Kelly color *Model Railroader* v84 no3 p24 Mr 2017

Model railroads—Flatcars—Evaluation

NEWS & PRODUCTS C. Grivno color *Model Railroader* v84 no3 p10 Mr 2017

Model railroads—Hopper cars

Model an aluminum billet load M. R. Snell color diag *Model Railroader* v84 no3 p35 Mr 2017

Model railroads—Hopper cars—Evaluation

Atlas N Dry-Flo covered hopper C. Grivno *Model Railroader* v84 no6 p68 Je 2017

Micro-Trains N scale Airslide hopper C. Grivno color *Model Railroader* v84 no3 p69 Mr 2017

Spring Mills Depot HO wagontop hopper E. White color *Model Railroader* v84 no6 p66 Je 2017

Model railroads—Landscapes

CHANGING SEASONS on a finished layout B. Stover color *Model Railroader* v83 no12 p32 D 2016

TRACKSIDE PHOTOS S. Otte color *Model Railroader* v84 no3 p72 Mr 2017

Model railroads—Layouts

Appalachian scenes along the B&O D. Ridgeway color diag map *Model Railroader* v84 no3 p44 Mr 2017

Ask MR S. Otte color *Model Railroader* v84 no5 p18 My 2017

Build a WIRING HARNESS P. Birdsong color diag *Model Railroader* v84 no2 p54 F 2017

CHANGING SEASONS on a finished layout B. Stover color *Model Railroader* v83 no12 p32 D 2016

Chasing the MR&T J. ". Pete Jr. color map *Model Railroader* v84 no4 p40 Ap 2017

Finding ghosts in old layout photos K. Wills bw *Model Railroader* v84 no4 p33 Ap 2017

FOUR ERAS OVER WP'S FEATHER RIVER ROUTE R. W. Scott color diag *Model Railroader* v83 no12 p46 D 2016

Horseshoe curves work better in N scale J. Kelly color *Model Railroader* v84 no5 p20 My 2017

A hybrid DCC system D. Kawala *Model Railroader* v84 no4 p47 Ap 2017

LARGE INDUSTRIES IN LIMITED SPACE J. McNab color diag *Model Railroader* v83 no12 p52 D 2016

Model railroading present, past, and future N. Besougloff *Model*

Railroader v84 no4 p8 Ap 2017

MOUNTAIN RAILROADING, NEW YORK STYLE S. Co-labufo color il *Model Railroader* v83 no12 p56 D 2016

NEW ENGLAND RAIL ROADING IN A SMALL SPACE D. Kirkpatrick color diag *Model Railroader* v84 no3 p58 Mr 2017

Pragmatic prototype modeling T. Koester color *Model Railroader* v84 no5 p78 My 2017

REALISM TIPS for beginners L. Mindheim color diag *Model Railroader* v84 no3 p28 Mr 2017

Rio Grande through the West D. Rickaby color map *Model Railroader* v84 no2 p58 F 2017

TRACKSIDE PHOTOS S. Otte color *Model Railroader* v84 no3 p72 Mr 2017

UPSTATE NEW YORK IN 1948 J. Heidt color map *Model Railroader* v84 no2 p46 F 2017

Was Al Kalmbach a railroader? J. Dziedzic color *Model Railroader* v84 no4 p100 Ap 2017

Model railroads—Maintenance & repair

Bringing engines back from the dead J. Kelly color *Model Railroader* v84 no1 p26 Ja 2017

Model partial loads to enrich operations D. Popp color diag *Model Railroader* v84 no3 p26 Mr 2017

Model railroads—News briefs

News & Products C. Grivno color *Model Railroader* v84 no8 p10 Ag 2017

Model railroads—Operation

Model railroads are a time machine T. Koester color *Model Railroader* v84 no4 p118 Ap 2017

Model railroads—Painting

DIGITALMR D. Kawala color *Model Railroader* v83 no12 p6 D 2016

FREELANCED PAINT SCHEMES from factory-painted models B. Kingsnorth color *Model Railroader* v84 no2 p42 F 2017

Paint, decal, and weather a locomotive C. Grivno color diag *Model Railroader* v83 no12 p28 D 2016

Model railroads—Periodicals

Another round: MR returns to the Beer Line E. White color diag *Model Railroader* v84 no1 p32 Ja 2017

"Are you Tony?" T. Koester *Model Railroader* v84 no6 p82 Je 2017

Model railroading present, past, and future N. Besougloff *Model Railroader* v84 no4 p8 Ap 2017

Model Rectifier Corp.

Model Power N scale 2-6-0 Mogul D. Kawala chart color *Model Railroader* v84 no11 p64 N 2017

Modeling (Sculpture)—Equipment & supplies

Electronic Play Dough J. Zorthian color *Time* v189 no24 p19 Je 26 2017

Models & modelmaking

See also

Patternmaking

How to model REPAIRED HOPPERS M. R. Snell color *Model Railroader* v84 no9 p32 S 2017

LAYOUT IN A WEEKEND UPDATE [Cover story] P. Boehlert color diag *Model Railroader* v84 no10 p40 O 2017

Making better-looking foreground trees P. K. Søeborg color diag *Model Railroader* v84 no8 p22 Ag 2017

Model a TRAILER HOME scene B. Bennett color *Model Railroader* v84 no9 p36 S 2017

MODEL: SIMPLE UTILITY POLES M. Tylick color *Model Railroader* v84 no10 p38 O 2017

Re-enacting Rio Grande narrow gauge [Cover story] B. Hamm color diag *Model Railroader* v84 no9 p40 S 2017

Use natural soil and rocks in scenery A. Dodge color *Model Railroader* v84 no9 p52 S 2017

When O scale traction was popular K. Wills bw diag *Model Railroader* v84 no8 p20 Ag 2017

Models & modelmaking—Methodology

MODEL STOCK PENS along a fascia A. Dodge color *Model Railroader* v84 no5 p36 My 2017

Models (Persons)

See also

Photography of models (Persons)

Plus-sized models (Persons)

'80s Strong K. Erickson color *Glamour* v115 no2 p120 F 2017

AM I TOO OLD FOR THIS? S. Cristobal color *InStyle* v24 no9

p422 S 2017

BARE Essential color *Seventeen* v76 no4 p13 Jl/Ag 2017

BAZAAR THINGS S. Doonan color *Harper's Bazaar* no3656 p462 S 2017

Bella Hadid K. B. Brown color *InStyle* v24 no6 p102 Je 2017

CARA'S COMEBACK L. McCarthy color *Harper's Bazaar* no3651 p283 Mr 2017

Chaos Theory color *Vogue* v207 no7 p61 Jl 2017

COLOR THERAPY color *Harper's Bazaar* no3656 p448 S 2017

EYE OF THE BEHOLDER J. Ferrise and A. Syrett color *InStyle* v24 no5 p218 My 2017

A FASHIONABLE ESCAPE L. Christensen color *Harper's Bazaar* no3653 p280 My 2017

GIRLS *Interview* v47 no2 p178 Mr 2017

THE GOLD STANDARD color *Harper's Bazaar* no3656 p458 S 2017

GOOD GOLLY, MISS MARLEY! D. BLASBERG color *Vanity Fair* v59 no11 p132 N 2017

Good Jeans color *Vogue* v207 no9 p640 S 2017

GRACE JONES color *Ebony* v72 no11 p98 S 2017

The Great Beauty Shake-Up M. Singer bw color *Vogue* v207 no3 p436 Mr 2017

THE GUARDIAN E. S. ARNARSDÓTTIR *Iceland Review* v55 no3 p40 My/Je 2017

Home of the Brave R. Sullivan bw color *Vogue* v207 no1 p60 Ja 2017

How fro can you go? J. Wilson color *InStyle* v24 no5 p242 My 2017

I Am Iman I. Abdulmajid bw color *Vogue* v207 no9 p302 S 2017

Jordan Barrett L. SCHWARTZBERG img *New York* v49 no19 p18 S 19 2016

KARLIE KLOSS SUPER MODEL [Cover story] L. Brown color *InStyle* v24 no6 p118 Je 2017

Kate Moss color *InStyle* v24 no11 p140 N 2017

Levi DYLAN G. SIEFF *Interview* v47 no1 p14 F 2017

THE LOOK BOOK A. SWERDLOFF and B. Doherty img *New York* v49 no15 p65 Jl 25 2016

Making HISTORY color *Vogue* v206 no11 p106 N 2016

Making Magic color *Vogue* v207 no7 p108 Jl 2017

Model BEHAVIOR R. Sullivan, M. HOLGATE et al color *Vogue* v207 no1 p30 Ja 2017

THE MODERN GIRL A. Syrett color *InStyle* v24 no7 p110 Jl 2017

MODESTY BLAZES! L. Camhi color *Vogue* v207 no7 p90 Jl 2017

My LIST L. McCarthy cartoon color *Harper's Bazaar* no3653 p102 My 2017

"My Mom Taught Me Less Is More" K. Gerber and F. Valdesolo color *Glamour* v115 no5 p69 My 2017

THE NEW BODY SCULPTORS E. Listfield color *Harper's Bazaar* no3654 p152 Je/Jl 2017

THE NEW CLASSICS color *Harper's Bazaar* no3656 p416 S 2017

Our Bodies. No Shame S. Altopp-Miller, G. Thomas et al color *Glamour* v115 no9 p32 S 2017

PAUL HAMELINE *Interview* v47 no1 p50 F 2017

The Photo That Changed My Life color *Vanity Fair* v58 no12 p70 D 2016

PRECIOUS LEE J. Wilson color *Essence* v47 no8 p38 D 2016

PURE A WHITE CANVAS OF MODERN SHAPES AND TEXTURES. AN ARTISTIC STUDY OF LINEAR STROKES AND WASHED-OER FABRICATIONS THAT GIVES THE CHALKY COLOR A NEW ROMANTIC WARMTH AND TOUCH *Interview* v47 no3 p88 Ap 2017

SAM MCKNIGHT L. Brown color *InStyle* v24 no1 p72 Ja 2017

Scarlett COSTELLO *Interview* v47 no2 p94 Mr 2017

THE SECRETS OF THE EI8HTY YEAR OLD CHINESE RUNWAY MODEL M. PATERNITI bw color *GQ: Gentlemen's Quarterly* v97 no4 p112 Ap 2017

Sister Act K. Lafferty color *Glamour* v115 no5 p188 My 2017

So What Do You Do, HAILEY BALDWIN? color *InStyle* v24 no6 p90 Je 2017

SUKI WATERHOUSE K. SMITH color *Vanity Fair* v59 no5 p45 Ap 2017

THE TAO OF LAIRD HAMILTON J. Roth color *Esquire* p54 O 2017

view MARCH *Interview* v47 no2 p62 Mr 2017

WE ARE HERE L. Chan color map *Glamour* v115 no9 p206 S 2017

What you don't know about... me [Cover story] bw color *Glamour* v115 no4 p160 Ap 2017

Models (Persons)—Competitions

Model Search Body Paint ANGUILLA color *Sports Illustrated* v126 no6 p140 F 20 2017

Models (Persons)—Interviews

Date with DIANE color *InStyle* v24 no5 p118 My 2017

Taylor Hill K. B. Brown color *InStyle* v24 no4 p148 Ap 2017

Models of railroad passenger cars

Upgrade a Varney gondola kit [Cover story] C. Grivno color *Model Railroader* v84 no7 p24 Jl 2017

Modern art

The CONVERSATION of Art J. H. Richardson and D. Salle bw color *Esquire* p76 Je/Jl 2017

Palazzo Intrigue M. ESTEROW bw color *Vanity Fair* v59 no2 p90 F 2017

Modern art—20th century

See also

Abstract art

Computer art

Conceptual art

Cubism

Installation art

Institutional Critique (Art movement)

Video art

What Picasso inspired in Prague R. Pepall bw color *Magazine Antiques* v183 no6 p108 N/D 2016

YOU CAN ALWAYS GO DOWNTOWN bw color *ARTnews* v115 no4 p142 Wint 2016/2017

Modern art—21st century

See also

Computer art

Conceptual art

Institutional Critique (Art movement)

CONTEMPORARY CRAFT color *American Craft* v77 no3 p97 Je/Jl 2017

The Identitarians *Commentary* v141 no9 p1 N 2016

The Identitarians *Commentary* v142 no4 p1 N 2016

Palace of Power color *Art in America* v105 no1 p103 Ja 2017

Modern art—21st century—Exhibitions

RACING MAGPIE *South Dakota Magazine* v32 no6 p77 Mr/Ap 2017

Modern art—Exhibitions

ART *New Yorker* v93 no25 p12 Ag 28 2017

Picabia's Big Moment S. Schwartz color *New York Review of Books* v64 no3 p12 F 23 2017

RURAL RETROSPECTIVE T. MALONE *Atlanta* v56 no10 p40 F 2017

Modern dance—Study & teaching

Marygrove College *Dance Magazine* v90 p81 2016/2017 Supplement College Guide

Washington University in St. Louis *Dance Magazine* v90 p122 2016/2017 Supplement College Guide

Modern Family (TV program)

Modern Family N. Abrams, B. L. Heldman et al *Entertainment Weekly* no1482/1483 p75 S 22 2017

Modern Family's Graduation Day *TV Guide* v65 no19 p10 My 1 2017

Modern furniture

Fine Art, Furniture, and Fun *Treasures* v6 no5 p6 Ap/My 2017

Modern history—21st century

The 2017 Quiz on News-to-Be color *Time* v188 no27-28 p122 D 26 2016

Modern literature—Social aspects

A CLASSIC DEBATE E. Chiariello color *Literacy Today (2411-7862)* v34 no6 p26 My/Je 2017

Modern movement (Architecture)

See also

Midcentury modern (Architecture)

Columbus Begins a New Conversation About Modernism D. A. CIAMPAGLIA *Architectural Record* v205 no9 p36 S 2017

Home Again M. ROZZO color *Architectural Digest* no6 p82 Je 1 2017

Modern Primitive (Music)

Strings: Shredded & Bowed B. MILKOWSKI color *Downbeat* v83 no11 p58 N 2016

Modern society

A Changing World: Expectations of Higher Education J. Daniel *Change* v49 no4 p8 Jl/Ag 2017

Moderna Therapeutics Inc.

ON MESSAGE K. Servick color diag graph *Science* v355 no6324 p446 F 3 2017

Moderna Therapeutics Inc.—Finance

Moderna's Mystery Medicines N. VARDI and M. HERPER color *Forbes* v198 no9 p46 D 30 2016

Modernism (Art)

See also

Abstract art

Cubism

My Living Room *Indianapolis Monthly* v40 no5 p33 Ja 2017

Modernism (Art)—Exhibitions

At Vanderbilt: an influential artist and teacher remembered color *Magazine Antiques* v184 no4 p32 Jl/Ag 2017

Mile-High Modern E. GAUKEL color *Treasures* v5 no5 p14 Ap/My 2016

Modernism (Art)—Social aspects

West Coast Modern color *Treasures* v5 no5 p24 Ap/My 2016

Modernism (Literature)

Postmodernism vs. Science M. Shermer color *Scientific American* v317 no3 p90 S 2017

Modernization (Social science)

The 1900 World's Fair Helped Shape How We Talk About Tech Today A. MOLELLA *NPQ: New Perspectives Quarterly* v33 no4 p31 O 2016

Modersohn, Bob

GROWING GARLIC *Successful Farming* v114 no11 p48 N 2016

Modest Mouse (Performer)

After Live M. Trammell color *New Yorker* v93 no32 p10 O 16 2017

Modesta, Viktoria

Better Than Ever M. Walker color *Wired* v24 no11 p48 N 2016

Modestini, Eddie

LIVE JOY color *Yoga Journal* p66 2017 Special Issue

MODESTINO, ALICIA SASSER

The Importance of Middle-Skill Jobs *Issues in Science & Technology* v33 no1 p41 Fall 2016

Modesty

Life without Kay: Love defies death B. McNamara color *U.S. Catholic* v82 no10 p23 O 2017

Modesty Blaise (Film)

Modesty Blaise *New Yorker* v92 no46 p11 Ja 23 2017

Modha, Deborah

Emergence and spread of a human-transmissible multidrug-resistant nontuberculous mycobacterium bibl diag graph *Science* v354 no6313 p751 N 11 2016

Modi, Narendra, 1950-

India Pays Steep Price for Cash Withdrawal N. Kumar color *Time* v188 no22-23 p11 N/D 2016

India's Trump J. McGowan *Commonweal* v144 no2 p6 Ja 27 2017

India's Weakened Unions Face a Push for Reform E. TEITELBAUM *Current History* v116 no789 p142 Ap 2017

We Hope That All Stakeholders Can Work Together to Find a Solution in Myanmar *Vital Speeches of the Day* v83 no10 p287 O 2017

Modi, Narendra, 1950-—Political & social views

Black Money P. Menon *History Today* v67 no2 p7 F 2017

Modi's Turbulent Priest Signals Change In Approach N. Kumar color *Time* v189 no13 p9 Ap 10 2017

A State Election In India Reinforces Narendra Modi's Grip on Power N. Kumar color map *Time* v189 no11 p12 Mr 27 2017

Modiano, David

Resistance to malaria through structural variation of red blood cell invasion receptors diag *Science* v356 no6343 p1139 Je 16 2017

Modiano, Patrick, 1945-

LE RÉVEILLON *Harper's Magazine* no2007 p20 Ag 2017

THE NOTES OF PATRICK MODIANO P. de Jonge *Harper's Magazine* v334 no2000 p77 Ja 2017

Modifications

Essential Framework for Adaptive Aquatics R. Barley, I. Hausknecht et al *Parks & Recreation* v52 no10 p54 O 2017

Modified Newtonian dynamics

Can dark matter vanquish controversial rival theory? A. Cho color *Science* v355 no6323 p337 Ja 27 2017

Modigliani, Amedeo, 1884-1920

THE MODIGLIANI CODE M. ESTEROW, J. Harris et al bw color *Vanity Fair* v59 no6 p110 My 2017

Modigliani, Amedeo, 1884-1920—Exhibitions

Why the long face: The Jewish Museum explores Modigliani's lonely sense of self D. Ebony bw color *Magazine Antiques* v184 no5 p72 S/O 2017

Modoski, Mark

2016 BEST OF THE BEST bw color *Field & Stream* v121 no7 p96 D 2016/Ja 2017

All Spun Up color *Field & Stream* v121 no9 pF5 Ap 2017

BREAK OUT! cartoon color *Field & Stream* v121 no9 p35 Ap 2017

BURNING RUBBER cartoon color *Field & Stream* v121 no8 p72 F/Mr 2017

FROST BITES color *Field & Stream* v121 no7 p70 D 2016/Ja 2017

HELL ON REELS 2017 color *Field & Stream* v121 no9 p67 Ap 2017

HOT RODS 2017 cartoon color *Field & Stream* v122 no1 p59 My 2017

THE NATURALS cartoon *Field & Stream* v121 no9 p24 Ap 2017

SEASON'S EATINGS bw color *Field & Stream* v122 no5 p20 O 2017

SLAB WORK color *Field & Stream* v122 no3 p24 Ag 2017

THE TAGGED-OUT DEER HUNTER'S GUIDE TO FALL [Cover story] color *Field & Stream* v122 no6 p59 N 2017

WHAT'S THAT SMELL? color *Field & Stream* v122 no2 p30 Je/Jl 2017

Modshop (Company)

Back to Mid-century M. E. Polson color *Old House Journal* v45 no3 p76 My 2017

Modular construction

Robots Will Build Your Next House P. Gopal and H. Perlberg color *Bloomberg Businessweek* no4519 p43 Ap 24 2017

Modulational instability

Formation of matter-wave soliton trains by modulational instability J. H. V. Nguyen, D. Luo et al diag *Science* v356 no6336 p422 Ap 28 2017

Mody, Cyrus C. M.

BETWEEN RESEARCH AND DEVELOPMENT: IBM AND JOSEPHSON COMPUTING *Physics Today* v69 no10 p32 O 2016

Moe, Terry—Interviews

A Miracle or a Relic P. Robinson *Hoover Digest: Research & Opinion on Public Policy* no1 p165 Wint 2017

Moelleken, Brent

L.A. LUMINARIES *Los Angeles Magazine* p116 F 2017

MOELLER, AMY

OUT SIDE THE BOX: THESE NINE TRENDSETTERS ARE STEPPING UP WASHINGTON STYLE WITH UNEXPECTED PAIRINGS, BOLD PRINTS, AND PERFECT TAILORING *Washingtonian Magazine* v52 no12 p78 S 2017

WHERE & WHEN: 18 THINGS YOU REALLY OUGHT TO DO THIS MONTH *Washingtonian Magazine* v52 no11 p31 Ag 2017

Moeller, Martin

VITAL SIGNS: Amid Washington's visual cacophony, some signage stands out. An expert weighs in on a few of the area's significant images C. VINOPAL *Washingtonian Magazine* v53 no1 p18 O 2017

Moen, Sharon

protect your watershed color *Cabin Living* p13 Ag 2017

Moesslang, Denise

The SAILING SCENE color *Sail* v48 no11 p6 N 2017

Moesslang, Peter

The SAILING SCENE color *Sail* v48 no11 p6 N 2017

Moessner, Roderich

Neutron scattering in the proximate quantum spin liquid a-RuCl3 bw diag *Science* v356 no6342 p1055 Je 9 2017

Moesta, Bob

Know the Job Your Product Was Hired for (with Help from Cus-

tomer Selfies) *Harvard Business Review Digital Articles* p2 Je 6 2016

Moffett, Jane

How to retain women after maternity leave *People Management* p48 S 2017

MOFFIC, H. STEVEN

Chords & Discords color *Downbeat* v84 no9 p10 S 2017

Moffitt, Andrea Turner

The Financial Services Industry's Untapped Market *Harvard Business Review Digital Articles* p2 D 8 2014

Women in Asia Are More Financially Savvy than Women in the U.S *Harvard Business Review Digital Articles* p2 Ag 25 2015

Moffitt, Nancy

Rethinking the BOX STALL color *Equus* no478 p34 Jl 2017

Moffitt, Phillip

You just woke up and already feel behind color *Yoga Journal* p38 2016 Special Issue

Mofokeng, Santu

Through blur, shadow and drift, the photographer Santu Mofokeng shows that black South Africans were more than their suffering T. Cole *New York Times Magazine* p12 Ag 13 2017

Mogavero, Damian

INDUSTRY INSIDER A. Orr color *Louisiana Life* v37 no5 p14 My/Je 2017

Mogel, Wendy

advice every new mom needs [Cover story] color *Parents* v92 no7 p32 Jl 2017

MOGELSON, LUKE

THE AVENGERS OF MOSUL bw cartoon map *New Yorker* v92 no48 p34 F 6 2017

Mogessie, Binyam

Actin protects mammalian eggs against chromosome segregation errors color *Science* v357 no6353 p772 Ag 25 2017

Mogg, Brian

STOP YOUR DROP color *Golf Magazine* v58 no12 p83 D 2016

Moghadam, Farhad

Perovskite-perovskite tandem photovoltaics with optimized band gaps bibl chart graph *Science* v354 no6314 p861 N 18 2016

Moghul, Haroon

How to be an American Muslim *Christian Century* v134 no11 p26 My 24 2017

Mogi, Yuzaburo, 1935-

Healthy, Sustainable Growth on the Menu M. Foster and D. W. Russell color *Forbes* v199 no1 p(Sp)5 Ja 24 2017

Mogil, H. Michael

The Weather and Climate of Nebraska: The Heartland of Extremes bw chart color diag graph map *Weatherwise* v70 no4 p12 Jl/Ag 2017

Mogilner, Cassie

When Multitasking Makes You Happy and When It Doesn't *Harvard Business Review Digital Articles* p2 F 26 2015

Mogni, Virginia

Forest conservation: Remember Gran Chaco bibl color *Science* v355 no6324 p465 F 3 2017

Mogollón, H. F.

Persistent effects of pre-Columbian plant domestication on Amazonian forest composition bibl chart graph map *Science* v355 no6328 p925 Mr 3 2017

Mogollon Rim (Ariz.)

editor's LETTER R. STIEVE *Arizona Highways* v92 no7 p2 Jl 2016

THE LEGEND OF PEARL GREY E. H. PEPLOW JR. *Arizona Highways* v92 no7 p34 Jl 2016

Mogollon Rim (Ariz.)—Description & travel

A RIM COUNTRY ALMANAC E. LIERLE *Arizona Highways* v92 no7 p28 Jl 2016

RIMCOUNTRY E. H. Peplow Jr. *Arizona Highways* v92 no7 p16 Jl 2016

Mogwai (Performer)

Pop img *New York* v50 no17 p116 Ag 21 2017

Mohabir, Rajiv

The Cowherd's Son color *Publishers Weekly* v264 no16 p41 Ap 17 2017

Mo Hailong—Trials, litigation, etc.

Chinese scientist jailed over theft of hybrid corn M. Hvistendahl color *Science* v354 no6309 p160 O 14 2016

Mohamed, Abdinasir
How Immigrant Workers Are Reviving the Labor Movement J. Rosenblum color *Progressive* v81 no4 p42 Ap/My 2017
MOHAMED, FEISAL G.
Occupational Hazards *American Scholar* v86 no4 p6 Aut 2017
MOHAMED, NADIFA
Foreign Correspondence: A journalist's account of his long fascination with Africa *New York Times Book Review* p17 Jl 9 2017
Mohammad, Hanif, 1934-2016
IN MEMORIAM *Islamic Horizons* v45 no6 p56 N/D 2016
Mohammad, Sohail
Muslims in the Halls of Justice J. KOZAK *Islamic Horizons* v45 no6 p46 N/D 2016
Mohammad bin Salman, 1980-
Help Wanted in Saudi Arabia: Savvy Investors M. Martin, G. Carey et al color graph *Bloomberg Businessweek* no4513 p41 Mr 6 2017
To Reinvent Itself, Saudi Arabia Must Empower Its Women I. Bremmer *Time* v189 no10 p10 Mr 20 2017
Mohammed, Amina J.
Mobilizing the Global Community to Achieve SDG 14 *UN Chronicle* v54 no1/2 p1 2017
Mohammed, Jameel—Interviews
JAMEEL MOHAMMED J. Wilson color *Essence* v47 no12 p24 Ap 2017
Mohammed, Omar F.
Powering up perovskite photoresponse bibl color *Science* v355 no6331 p1260 Mr 24 2017
Mohammed, Rafi
Airlines Like United Can Underpay Bumped Passengers Because of a Government Rule *Harvard Business Review Digital Articles* p2 Ap 12 2017
Airlines' New Basic Economy Fares Show the Power of No-Frills Pricing color *Harvard Business Review Digital Articles* p2 Mr 3 2017
The Apple Watch's Big Pricing Problem *Harvard Business Review Digital Articles* p2 Ap 10 2015
Are You Really Getting a Discount, or Is It Just a Pricing Trick? *Harvard Business Review Digital Articles* p2 Mr 23 2016
Bed Bath & Beyond's Persistent Coupons and the Return of Thrifty Consumers *Harvard Business Review Digital Articles* p2 O 6 2015
Cheap Drugs from Canada Won't Reduce U.S. Drug Prices *Harvard Business Review Digital Articles* p2 F 12 2016
Falling Oil Prices Don't Make OPEC Irrelevant *Harvard Business Review Digital Articles* p2 D 11 2014
Hamilton's $849 Tickets Are Priced Too Low *Harvard Business Review Digital Articles* p2 Je 24 2016
How Retailers Should Think About Online Versus In-Store Pricing bw *Harvard Business Review Digital Articles* p2 Ja 26 2017
How to Stay in Premium Hotels Without Blowing Your Expense Account *Harvard Business Review Digital Articles* p2 Ag 2 2016
How Walmart Can Start Competing Online *Harvard Business Review Digital Articles* p2 O 21 2015
It's Time to Rein in Exorbitant Pharmaceutical Prices *Harvard Business Review Digital Articles* p2 S 22 2015
The Logic Behind Amazon's Prime Day *Harvard Business Review Digital Articles* p2 Jl 13 2015
Of Course Disney Should Use Surge Pricing at Its Theme Parks *Harvard Business Review Digital Articles* p2 Je 4 2015
Price-Sensitive Customers Will Tolerate Uncertainty *Harvard Business Review Digital Articles* p2 Mr 26 2015
The Problems with Jet.com's Pricing Model *Harvard Business Review Digital Articles* p2 Jl 22 2015
The Psychology Behind the New iPhone's Four-Digit Price *Harvard Business Review Digital Articles* p2 S 21 2017
Retailers' Holiday Strategy Doesn't Have to Be "Discount Everything" *Harvard Business Review Digital Articles* p2 N 29 2016
The Taxi Industry Can Innovate, Too *Harvard Business Review Digital Articles* p2 F 13 2015
Uber's New Tipping Policy Is a Mistake *Harvard Business Review Digital Articles* p2 My 5 2016
What Amazon Risks by Eliminating List Prices *Harvard Business Review Digital Articles* p2 Jl 13 2016
What America's Best BBQ Joint Can Teach You About Pricing *Harvard Business Review Digital Articles* p2 N 12 2015
Whole Foods Needs a More Consistent Pricing Message *Harvard Business Review Digital Articles* p2 Ag 20 2015
Why Apple's New iPhone Upgrade Plan Is Driving Growth *Harvard Business Review Digital Articles* p2 S 28 2015
Why Businesses Should Lower Prices During Natural Disasters *Harvard Business Review Digital Articles* p2 S 11 2017
You Can Charge Women More, but Should You? *Harvard Business Review Digital Articles* p2 Ja 29 2016
Mohammed, Shabaz
Posttranslational mutagenesis: A chemical strategy for exploring protein side-chain diversity diag *Science* v354 no6312 p597 N 4 2016
Mohammed VI, King of Morocco, 1963-
Glaring Paradoxes: PROGRESS, BUT DISAPPOINTMENT *Vital Speeches of the Day* v83 no9 p265 S 2017
Mohan, Shashank
Estimating economic damage from climate change in the United States color graph *Science* v356 no6345 p1362 Je 30 2017
Mohawk General Store (Company)
We Found the Perfect Fall Sweater J. MOORE bw *GQ: Gentlemen's Quarterly* v97 no10 p66 O 2017
Moher, David
Promote scientific integrity via journal peer review data color *Science* v357 no6348 p256 Jl 21 2017
Mohite, A. D.
Extremely efficient internal exciton dissociation through edge states in layered 2D perovskites bibl graph *Science* v355 no6331 p1288 Mr 24 2017
MOHLENBROCK, ROBERT H.
Accessible Serenity color *Natural History* v125 no6 p42 Je 2017
Kelso Dunes *Natural History* v125 no2 p40 F 2017
Land Between the Lakes color map *Natural History* v125 no11 p42 N 2017
The Meandering Poultney River *Natural History* v125 no1 p36 D 2016/Ja 2017
Paulk's Pasture color map *Natural History* v125 no4 p42 Ap 2017
Pipestone and Prairies color map *Natural History* v125 no5 p42 My 2017
Sosebee Cove, Georgia *Natural History* v124 no10 p42 N 2016
Theodore Roosevelt National Park color map *Natural History* v125 no3 p42 Mr 2017
Waterfront Property color map *Natural History* v125 no7 p40 Jl/Ag 2017
Where Whooping Cranes Winter color *Natural History* v125 no10 p42 O 2017
Mohliver, Aharon
CEOs Who Began Their Careers During Booms Tend to Be Less Ethical *Harvard Business Review Digital Articles* p2 My 12 2017
Mohney, Curran
Mitigating coastal landslide damage color *Science* v357 no6355 p981 S 8 2017
Moholy-Nagy, László, 1895-1946
LÁSZLÓ MOHOLY-NAGY A. Considine color *Art in America* v104 no10 p147 N 2016
Mohorovicic discontinuity
The Quest for the Moho G. Schanker and L. Lippsett *Oceanus* v52 no1 p44 Summ 2016
MOHR, CHRIS
THE LARD IS YOUR SAVIOR? color *Men's Health* v32 no7 p102 S 2017
Mohr, Jay—Interviews
Hello Again T. Keith color *Sports Illustrated* v125 no21 p24 D 26 2014
Mohr, Robert D.
Wage and job-skill distributions in the National Compensation Survey bibl chart color graph *Monthly Labor Review* p1 F 2017
Mohr, Tara Sophia
Helping an Employee Overcome Their Self-Doubt *Harvard Business Review Digital Articles* p2 O 1 2015
Mohsin, Saleha
Hellllp! color *Bloomberg Businessweek* no4526 p22 Je 12 2017
It's Hard to Label China A Currency Manipulator *Bloomberg Businessweek* no4500 p17 N 21 2016
The Mess Steven Mnuchin Left Behind bw *Bloomberg Business-*

week no4504 p34 D 19 2016

Mnuchin Ponders Locking in Low Rates *Bloomberg Businessweek* no4521 p39 My 8 2017

Mnuchin's Conflicting Hollywood Roles *Bloomberg Businessweek* no4507 p24 Ja 16 2017

The World Owes Too Much Money cartoon *Bloomberg Businessweek* no4495 p13 O 17 2016

Moisture

Cabin Condensation D. Everitt cartoon *Sail* v48 no11 p58 N 2017

Moisture meters—Evaluation

HAY MOISTURE TESTERS G. Gullickson *Successful Farming* v115 no4 p57 Mr 2017

Mojarad, Sarah

Social media: More scientists needed *Science* v357 no6358 p1362 S 29 2017

Mojave Audio (Company)

Mojave Audio MA-50 M. Kern color *Downbeat* v84 no2 p99 F 2017

Mojave Desert

lost borders j. murren bw color *Bike Magazine* v24 no4 p38 Je 2017

Moji (Company)

ON A ROLL(ER) J. DENGATE color *Runner's World* v52 no8 p32 S 2017

MOJOLA, SANYU A.

AIDS in Africa: Progress and Obstacles *Current History* v116 no790 p170 My 2017

Mok, Aurelia

If You Feel Left Out at Work, Visualize Money *Harvard Business Review Digital Articles* p2 O 22 2015

Mok, Tim

Whitewashing the Los Angeles River? Gente-fication not Gentrification: Green displacement threatens communities of color and low-income communities *Parks & Recreation* v52 no9 p50 S 2017

Mok, Wendy W. K.

Biased inheritance protects older bacteria from harm diag *Science* v356 no6335 p247 Ap 21 2017

Mokalled, Mayssa H.

Injury-induced ctgfa directs glial bridging and spinal cord regeneration in zebrafish bibl graph *Science* v354 no6312 p630 N 4 2016

Moksha (Performer)

MOKSHA J. Ephland color *Downbeat* v84 no1 p25 Ja 2017

Mokyr, Joel

REFRAMING THE GREAT DIVERGENCE: A detailed study of the Enlightenment and the Great Divergence displays admirable depth of knowledge and subtlety of argument N. Crafts *History Today* v67 no6 p102 Je 2016

Mol, Gretchen

Chance D. Franich color *Entertainment Weekly* no1436/1437 p90 O 21 2016

Mola, Maria

Sparkle Boy *Publishers Weekly* v264 no19 p60 My 8 2017

Moland, Eryn Norton—Interviews

Real-World Wind Power W. Becktold *Sierra* v101 no5 p63 S/O 2016

Molaro, Steven—Interviews

STEVEN MOLARO J. HALTERMAN color *TV Guide* v64 no42 p12 O 10 2016

Moldavski, Ofer

Lysosomal cholesterol activates mTORC1 via an SLC38A9–Niemann-Pick C1 signaling complex bibl diag graph *Science* v355 no6331 p1306 Mr 24 2017

Molds (Fungi)

Here's How [Cover story] S. Coles and L. Thompson color *Practical Horseman* v45 no7 p62 Jl 2017

The Lowdown on Mold M. E. Polson color *Old House Journal* v45 no3 p52 My 2017

Mole (Dermatology)

5 EYE SYMPTOMS YOU SHOULDN'T IGNORE color *Prevention* v69 no2 p9 F 2017

Mole (Dermatology)—Diagnosis

Talk to the hand(s) C. T. Burns color *Health* v31 no9 p33 N 2017

Molecular beams

Footnote on femtochemistry Yang Gan *Physics Today* v70 no4

p14 Ap 2017

Molecular biology

See also

Aging—Molecular aspects

Bringing proteins into the fold [Cover story] S. M. Douglas bibl color *Science* v355 no6331 p1261 Mr 24 2017

Molecular cloning

GENE GENIES A. VLASITS color *Wired* v25 no6 p18 Je 2017

Molecular clouds

Phantoms of the Deep Sky R. Jakiel *Sky & Telescope* v133 no6 p70 Je 2017

Molecular genetics

See also

Gene expression

Genes

Genetic regulation

Genomics

Protein genetics

Ancient genomic changes associated with domestication of the horse P. Librado, C. Gamba et al color diag *Science* v356 no6336 p442 Ap 28 2017

A FANTASTIC VOYAGE IN GENOMICS L. M. Zahn color *Science* v357 no6359 p56 O 6 2017

Molecular machinery (Technology)

See also

Molecular switches

The architecture of transcription elongation T. Fouqueau and F. Werner diag *Science* v357 no6354 p871 S 1 2017

A cargo-sorting DNA robot A. J. Thubagere, W. Li et al color *Science* v357 no6356 p1112 S 15 2017

Chemistry Nobel heralds age of molecular machines R. F. Service color *Science* v354 no6309 p158 O 14 2016

Crystal-clear memories of a bacterium R. Globus and U. Qimron diag *Science* v357 no6356 p1096 S 15 2017

Gearing up molecular rotary motors M. Baroncini and A. Credi color *Science* v356 no6341 p906 Je 1 2017

Molecular motor proteins

Locked synchronous rotor motion in a molecular motor P. Štacko, J. C. M. Kistemaker et al diag *Science* v356 no6341 p964 Je 1 2017

Molecular physics—Congresses

Gordon Research Conferences [Cover story] color *Science* v355 no6327 p848 F 24 2017

Molecular shapes

Braiding a molecular knot with eight crossings J. J. Danon, A. Krüger et al bibl diag graph *Science* v355 no6321 p1 Ja 13 2017

Molecular spectroscopy

Molecular force spectroscopy with a DNA origami–based nanoscopic force clamp P. C. Nickels, B. Wünsch et al bibl diag graph *Science* v354 no6310 p305 O 21 2016

Molecular structure of hemoglobin

RESOLVING SMALLER MOLECULES WITH CRYO-EM *Physics Today* v70 no9 p22 S 2017

Molecular switches

The architecture of transcription elongation T. Fouqueau and F. Werner diag *Science* v357 no6354 p871 S 1 2017

Molecular self-assembly

Reconfiguration of DNA molecular arrays driven by information relay J. Song, Z. Li et al diag *Science* v357 no6349 p371 Jl 28 2017

Molecular structure of amyloid beta-protein

Fibril structure of amyloid-β(1–42) by cryo–electron microscopy L. Gremer, D. Schölzel et al color diag *Science* v357 no6359 p116 O 6 2017

Molecule trapping

Magnetic trap snares methyl radicals A. G. Smart *Physics Today* v70 no4 p18 Ap 2017

Molecules

See also

Molecular switches

The atom, the molecule, and the covalent organic framework C. S. Diercks and O. M. Yaghi diag *Science* v355 no6328 p923 Mr 3 2017

IN SCIENCE JOURNALS color *Science* v355 no6327 p808 F 24 2017

Molecules face the biggest chill E. CONOVER color *Science*

News v192 no4 p18 S 16 2017

A moonshot for chemistry R. F. Service color *Science* v356 no6335 p231 Ap 21 2017

Neural networks learn the art of chemical synthesis R. F. Service *Science* v357 no6346 p27 Jl 7 2017

Predicting human olfactory perception from chemical features of odor molecules A. Keller, R. C. Gerkin et al bibl diag graph *Science* v355 no6327 p820 F 24 2017

Restored iron transport by a small molecule promotes absorption and hemoglobinization in animals A. S. Grillo, A. M. SantaMaria et al color graph *Science* v356 no6338 p608 My 12 2017

Single-particle mapping of nonequilibrium nanocrystal transformations Xingchen Ye, M. R. Jones et al bibl bw graph *Science* v354 no6314 p874 N 18 2016

Molecules—Research

Molecular knot is most complex yet M. ROSEN color *Science News* v191 no3 p8 F 18 2017

MOLELLA, ARTHUR

The 1900 World's Fair Helped Shape How We Talk About Tech Today *NPQ: New Perspectives Quarterly* v33 no4 p31 O 2016

Moles (Animals)

Pest Control D. Howland *Cabin Living* p15 Ag 2017

Molesworth, Helen

The Genius of Blackness D. Pinckney cartoon *New York Review of Books* v64 no1 p40 Ja 19 2017

Moley Robotics (Company)

THE Chef of the Future MAKES ONLY ONE DISH CRAB BISQUE à la robot D. MARCHESE img *New York* p40 Ja 9 2017

Molin, Anna

The Taming of a Teen Emporium color *Bloomberg Businessweek* no4518 p26 Ap 10 2017

Molina, Nelson

Lost and Found M. SIMMS color *O, The Oprah Magazine* p21 Ja 2017

Molina, Rocio

Defying Tradition J. BAYOD ESPOZ *Dance Magazine* v90 no11 p58 N 2016

Molina-Morales, Agustin

Determinants of Child Health Inequalities in Developing Countries: a New Perspective chart diag *Society* v53 no6 p641 D 2016

Molinaro, Vince

Why a Corporate Scandal Will Follow You Even If You Weren't Involved *Harvard Business Review Digital Articles* p2 D 4 2014

MOLINE, PEG

Spice of Life color *Rodale's Organic Life* v2 no7 p38 D 2016/Ja 2017

Moliner, Manuel

"Ab initio" synthesis of zeolites for preestablished catalytic reactions bibl chart diag *Science* v355 no6329 p1051 Mr 10 2017

Molino, J.-F.

Persistent effects of pre-Columbian plant domestication on Amazonian forest composition bibl chart graph map *Science* v355 no6328 p925 Mr 3 2017

Molinsky, Andy

The 4 Types of Ineffective Apologies *Harvard Business Review Digital Articles* p2 N 15 2016

5 Tips for Managing Successful Overseas Assignments *Harvard Business Review Digital Articles* p2 Mr 16 2016

Adapting Your Organizational Processes to a New Culture *Harvard Business Review Digital Articles* p2 O 7 2016

Becoming a Manager in a New Country *Harvard Business Review Digital Articles* p2 S 14 2015

Being a Successful Entrepreneur Isn't Only About Having the Best Ideas *Harvard Business Review Digital Articles* p2 Ag 30 2016

Being Experienced Doesn't Automatically Make You a Great Mentor *Harvard Business Review Digital Articles* p2 Ja 28 2015

Building Relationships in Cultures That Don't Do Small Talk *Harvard Business Review Digital Articles* p2 Ap 8 2015

Cultural Differences Are More Complicated than What Country You're From *Harvard Business Review Digital Articles* p2 Ja 14 2016

Don't Let Inexperience Stop You from Participating in Meetings color *Harvard Business Review Digital Articles* p2 Ja 4 2017

Emotional Intelligence Doesn't Translate Across Borders *Harvard Business Review Digital Articles* p2 Ap 20 2015

Everyone Suffers from Impostor Syndrome—Here's How to Handle It *Harvard Business Review Digital Articles* p2 Jl 7 2016

Free Yourself from What You "Should" Be Doing color *Harvard Business Review Digital Articles* p2 Ja 18 2017

Having a Difficult Conversation with Someone from a Different Culture *Harvard Business Review Digital Articles* p2 Mr 25 2016

The Hidden Benefits of Short-Term Business Travel *Harvard Business Review Digital Articles* p2 Je 13 2016

How to Build Trust on Your Cross-Cultural Team *Harvard Business Review Digital Articles* p2 Je 28 2016

If You're Not Outside Your Comfort Zone, You Won't Learn Anything *Harvard Business Review Digital Articles* p2 Jl 29 2016

Learning the Language of Indirectness *Harvard Business Review Digital Articles* p2 My 6 2015

Managing Vacations When Your Team Is Global *Harvard Business Review Digital Articles* p2 S 25 2015

The Mistake Most Managers Make with Cross-Cultural Training *Harvard Business Review Digital Articles* p2 Ja 15 2015

Practice for Tough Situations as You'd Practice a Sport *Harvard Business Review Digital Articles* p2 F 18 2016

A Simple Way to Be More Assertive (Without Being Pushy) *Harvard Business Review Digital Articles* p2 Ag 31 2017

To Connect Across Cultures, Find Out What You Have in Common *Harvard Business Review Digital Articles* p2 Ja 20 2016

The Two Conversations You're Having When You Negotiate *Harvard Business Review Digital Articles* p2 Ap 5 2016

What to Do When Your Heart Isn't in Your Work Anymore *Harvard Business Review Digital Articles* p2 Jl 10 2017

When Cultural Differences Interfere with Your Time *Harvard Business Review Digital Articles* p2 Ap 14 2015

When It's Worth Having a Meeting Before Your Meeting color *Harvard Business Review Digital Articles* p2 O 28 2016

When to Stay Inside Your Comfort Zone *Harvard Business Review Digital Articles* p2 S 7 2016

Will That Cross-Cultural Coach Really Help Your Team? *Harvard Business Review Digital Articles* p2 Ap 29 2015

You're More Resilient Than You Give Yourself Credit For bw *Harvard Business Review Digital Articles* p2 Ja 25 2017

Molitor, Daniel

Faith and Science at a Crossroad *Sky & Telescope* v134 no3 p6 S 2017

Moll, Rob

CURING OUR MISPLACED FAITH IN MEDICINE color *Christianity Today* v60 no8 p79 O 2016

A Thousand Religions Bloom Again bw color *Christianity Today* p70 Ap 2017

MOLLENKAMP, BECKY

backyard hideaway color *Better Homes & Gardens* v95 no8 p84 Ag 2017

up to the CHALLENGE color diag *Better Homes & Gardens* v95 no11 p40 N 2017

Mollerach, S.

Observation of a large-scale anisotropy in the arrival directions of cosmic rays above 8 × 1018 eV *Science* v357 no6357 p1266 S 22 2017

Mollick, Ethan

The Unique Value of Crowdfunding Is Not Money—It's Community *Harvard Business Review Digital Articles* p2 Ap 21 2016

Mollicone, Danilo

The extent of forest in dryland biomes [Cover story] chart map *Science* v356 no6338 p635 My 12 2017

Mollise, Rod

MallinCarrVs SkyRaider DS2.3 Plus: This device promises to be three cameras in one convenient package *Sky & Telescope* v134 no4 p58 O 2017

Smart Astronomy: The NexStar Evolution 9,25 *Sky & Telescope* v133 no5 p60 My 2017

Molloy, Margaret

Why Simple Brands Win *Harvard Business Review Digital Articles* p2 N 9 2015

Mollusks

See also

Cephalopoda

We Are Not Alone G. DREVITCH *Psychology Today* v49 no6 p47

N/D 2016

Molly's Game (Film)
MOLLY'S GAME R. Rahman color *Entertainment Weekly* no1478 / 1479 p67 Ag 18-25 2017

Molnar, Lawrence
Paired Stars in Cygnus En Route to Merger? C. M. CARLISLE *Sky & Telescope* v133 no4 p11 Ap 2017
Red nova explosion predicted for 2022 color *Astronomy* v45 no5 p13 My 2017

Molnar, Peter
Changing climate shifts timing of European floods color graph *Science* v357 no6351 p588 Ag 11 2017

Moloco Trains (Company)
Moloco HO General American 50-foot insulated boxcar C. Grivno color *Model Railroader* v83 no12 p72 D 2016

Moloney, Ciara
356 Mission color *Art in America* v105 no1 p87 Ja 2017
Château Shatto color *Art in America* v105 no6 p142 Je/Jl 2017
THE HARRISONS color *Art in America* v105 no5 p136 My 2017
HENRY TAYLOR cartoon *Art in America* v104 no11 p125 D 2016
LLYN FOULKES cartoon *Art in America* v105 no4 p117 Ap 2017
SAM PULITZER AND PETER WÄCHTLER color *Art in America* v105 no3 p136 Mr 2017

Molster, Janie
Retail Therapy M. HERMANSON *Virginia Living* v15 no1 p45 D 2016

MOLTENI, MEGAN
NONBINARY CODE cartoon *Wired* v25 no6 p20 Je 2017

Molvar, Kari
AERIN LAUDER color *Conde Nast Traveler* v52 no7 p22 Ag 2017
CAROLINA HERRERA bw color *Conde Nast Traveler* v52 no1 p42 Ja 2017
Fresh COAT color *Vogue* v207 no7 p56 Jl 2017
GUCCI WESTMAN color *Conde Nast Traveler* v52 no8 p24 S 2017
HAPPY RETURNS color *Conde Nast Traveler* v52 no7 p26 Ag 2017
Heir TRANSPARENT color *Vogue* v207 no4 p174 Ap 2017
JENNA LYONS bw color *Conde Nast Traveler* v52 no3 p30 Mr 2017
Northern Exposure color *Vogue* v207 no11 p152 N 2017
PALE Fire color *Vogue* v206 no12 p198 D 2016

Molyneux, John
Walk of life *U.S. Catholic* v82 no8 p4 Ag 2017
"We welcomed them" *U.S. Catholic* v81 no12 p17 D 2016

Molyneux, Malcolm
Resistance to malaria through structural variation of red blood cell invasion receptors diag *Science* v356 no6343 p1139 Je 16 2017

Mom (TV program)
Chris Pratt on Mom! M. Roffman *TV Guide* v65 no4 p10 Ja 16 2017
Comedies Get Serious J. HALTERMAN *TV Guide* v64 no48 p7 N 21 2016
MOM L. Rice color *Entertainment Weekly* no1446/1447 p62 D 2016/Ja 2017
Mom N. Abrams, B. L. Heldman et al color *Entertainment Weekly* no1482/1483 p85 S 22 2017
MOM STIRS THE POT L. Rice color *Entertainment Weekly* no1435 p10 O 14 2016

Moments Captured (Music)
Sipiagin Assembles Elite Sextet for New Album of Original Music T. Panken color *Downbeat* v84 no6 p16 Je 2017

Moments in Time (Music)
Moments In Time J. Potter color *Downbeat* v84 no2 p77 F 2017

Momentum (Mechanics)
Angular momentum–induced delays in solid-state photoemission enhanced by intra-atomic interactions F. Siek, S. Neb et al chart color graph *Science* v357 no6357 p1274 S 22 2017

Momentum distributions
Bloch oscillations in the absence of a lattice F. Meinert, M. Knap et al graph *Science* v356 no6341 p945 Je 1 2017

Momoa, Jason, 1979-
The Bad Batch L. Greenblatt color *Entertainment Weekly* no1472 p43 Je 30 2017

Momosan Restaurant LLC
Pickled Napa Cabbage M. J. WEEDMAN and B. Doherty img *New York* v49 no15 p67 Jl 25 2016

Momose, Julia
Make the Perfect Summer Drink color *Chicago* v66 no7 p62 Jl 2017

Monachello, Dario
Crystal structures of a group II intron lariat primed for reverse splicing color diag *Science* v354 no6316 paaf9258-1 D 2 2016

MONACO, C. S.
Whose War Was It? *American Indian Quarterly* v41 no1 p31 Wint 2017

Monaco, Lisa
Preventing the Next Attack color *Foreign Affairs* v96 no6 p23 N/D 2017

Monáe, Janelle, 1985-
Black & White, Amirite? color *Glamour* v115 no5 p196 My 2017
Hidden Figures Proves There's Power In Numbers S. Zacharek color *Time* v189 no3 p56 Ja 16 2017
WE LOVE HEARING FROM YOU! color diag *Essence* v47 no12 p14 Ap 2017

Monáe, Janelle, 1985—Interviews
JANELLE MONÁE R. L. ELDREDGE *Atlanta* v56 no9 p24 Ja 2017

Monaghan, Jacqueline
The receptor kinase FER is a RALF-regulated scaffold controlling plant immune signaling graph *Science* v355 no6322 p287 Ja 20 2017

Monaghan, Keegan
KEEGAN MONAGHAN J. Wolkoff color *Art in America* v104 no10 p150 N 2016

Monaghan, Michelle, 1976-
THE COUNTRY color *InStyle* p14 Home & Design 2016
good morning, sunshine D. Pener color *InStyle* p16 Home & Design 2016

Monahan, Gretta
New Shape, New Style [Cover story] color *Women's Health* v14 no1 p65 Ja/F 2017

Monahan, Jay
A "Dear Jay" Letter A. Shipnuck and C. Barrett color *Golf Magazine* v59 no1 p24 Ja 2017

MONAHAN, PATRICK
A HITCHCOCK FANTASY color *Vanity Fair* v58 no12 p146 D 2016

Monahan, Patrick—Interviews
Patrick Monahan S. Stall *Indianapolis Monthly* v40 no10 p23 Je 2017

Monahan, Tom
Your Company Needs a More-Radical Board of Directors *Harvard Business Review Digital Articles* p2 Je 20 2016

Monarch butterfly
ENDANGERED! B. Banks color *Canadian Wildlife* v23 no1 p26 Mr/Ap 2017
FLIGHT OF FANCY M. REAGIN color *Louisiana Life* v37 no5 p28 My/Je 2017
MONARCHS J. Jelly-Schapiro cartoon *New Yorker* v93 no31 p20 O 9 2017
Monarchs Visit NRPA Waystation R. J. Dolesh *Parks & Recreation* v51 no10 p96 O 2016
on a wing and a prayer B. BUTLER and L. Heck color *Missouri Life* v44 no6 p38 S 2017

Monarch butterfly—Research
A Call to Action R. Bates *Canadian Wildlife* v23 no1 p5 Mr/Ap 2017
Peril at Journey's End J. Marinelli color *National Wildlife (World Edition)* v55 no1 p34 D/Ja 2016

Monarchy
Moroccans protest after monarchy, Muslim party fail to deliver on reform T. Luck *Christian Century* v134 no1 p16 Ja 4 2017

Monardes, Nicolás
1571: Seville *Lapham's Quarterly* v10 no2 p175 Spr 2017

Monarth, Harrison
Evaluate Your Leadership Development Program *Harvard Business Review Digital Articles* p2 Ja 22 2015
How Upworthy Gets Its Staff to Bond *Harvard Business Review Digital Articles* p2 N 11 2015

Monashee Mountains (B.C.)
ALL TIME color *Powder* v45 no6 p8 F 2017

Monasteries
China color *National Geographic* v232 no1 p12 Jl 2017
Prophet Elias' Chapel N. AUSTIN color *Arizona Highways* v93 no5 p6 My 2017

Monasteries—United States
Hermitage sees surge in laypeople who want a monastic experience K. Olson color *Christian Century* v134 no10 p18 My 10 2017

Monastic life
What Hipsters and Monks Share D. J. Michael color *America* v217 no2 p40 Jl 24 2017

Moncler SpA
REMO RUFFINI color *Esquire* v167 no1 p112 F 2017

Moncrief, Clare
The New Orleans Shakespeare Festival at Tulane color *New Orleans Magazine* v51 no8 p29 Je 2017

Mondalek, Alexandra
ASK THE EXPERT chart *Money* v46 no4 p20 My 2017

MONDAY, NICOLE
TIBBS DRIVE-IN THEATRE *Indianapolis Monthly* v12 no40 p20 Ag 2017

Monday Night Brewing (Company)
BeltLine BREWERS S. Henry *Atlanta* v56 no11 p114 Mr 2017

Monday Night Football (TV program)
THE BEST ØF TELEVISION R. Deitsch color *Sports Illustrated* v125 no18 p33 D 5 2016

Mondi, Donna
SPRING FORTH E. EICHINGER color *Chicago* v66 no4 p74 Ap 2017

Monemar, Bo
Jacques Isaac Pankove *Physics Today* v70 no4 p64 Ap 2017

MONET, AJA
We're On: A June Jordan Reader color *Publishers Weekly* v264 no34 p86 Ag 21 2017

Monet, Jenni
Covering Standing Rock color *Columbia Journalism Review* v56 no1 p86 Spr 2017

Monetary incentives
Are Sales Incentives Becoming Obsolete? A. A. Zoltners, P. K. Sinha et al *Harvard Business Review Digital Articles* p2 Ag 3 2017
CENTURY marks *Christian Century* v134 no7 p8 Mr 29 2017

Monetary policy
See also
Federal Reserve monetary policy
SCALING BACK ECONOMIC ACCOMMODATION *Vital Speeches of the Day* v83 no5 p153 My 2017

Monetary policy—India
A Cash Crackdown Hits Gold Pawners B. Einhorn and A. Antony color *Bloomberg Businessweek* no4502 p46 D 5 2016
India's Cash-Canceling Experiment B. Einhorn, V. Beniwal et al color *Bloomberg Businessweek* no4501 p12 N 28 2016

Monetary policy—Japan
What's Behind Shinzo Abe's Plummeting Popularity C. Campbell color *Time* v190 no6 p9 Ag 7 2017

Monetary policy—United States
Our Approach to Economic Growth Isn't Working R. D. Atkinson *Harvard Business Review Digital Articles* p2 F 16 2017

Monetary policy—United States—Economic aspects
A Technology-Based Growth Policy G. TASSEY graph *Issues in Science & Technology* v33 no2 p80 Wint 2017

Monetary theory
DEBT IS NOT THE END A. A. ABRAHAMIAN color *Nation* v304 no16 p12 My 22 2017

Monetary unions
See also
European Union
Eurozone
A Marxist Manifesto J. LOCONTE *Weekly Standard* v22 no5 p20 O 10 2016

Money
See also
Paper money
Prices

10 GENIUS WAYS TO make money in your $pare time [Cover story] N. SAPORITA color *Good Housekeeping* v265 no2 p79 Ag 2017

ALL About MONEY! K. B. RATTINI color *National Geographic Kids* no465 p8 N 2016

If You Feel Left Out at Work, Visualize Money A. Mok and D. De Cremer *Harvard Business Review Digital Articles* p2 O 22 2015

Meet the New Money Experts L. B. West-Rosenthal color *Glamour* v115 no9 p134 S 2017

WAIT, WHAT IS MONEY? S. METTES color *Christianity Today* v61 no1 p30 Ja/F 2017

What I'd Do with It cartoon *GQ: Gentlemen's Quarterly* v87 no1 p17 Ja 2017

Your secret weapon for saving more N. Lapin color *Redbook* p32 O 2017

Money (Periodical)—Officials & employees
A Few More Words—Before I Go D. Harris color *Money* v46 no3 p9 Ap 2017

Money for Nothing (Music)
1985 L. Greenblatt color *Entertainment Weekly* no1434 p57 O 7 2016

Money laundering
The Great Indian Tax Dodge of 2016 A. Antony *Bloomberg Businessweek* no4503 p14 D 12 2016
IN THE DARK A. Greenblatt *Governing* v30 no1 p26 O 2016

Money laundering—Economic aspects
Demonetization in India: One More Rock in the River A. KRISHNA *Current History* v116 no789 p154 Ap 2017

Money laundering—Law & legislation
Dirty Money: I FOUGHT THE LAW. AND I WON. SORT OF J. GILBERT *Cincinnati Magazine* v50 no10 p46 Jl 2017

Money laundering—Prevention
Demonetization in India: One More Rock in the River A. KRISHNA *Current History* v116 no789 p154 Ap 2017

Money laundering—Prevention—Government policy
India's Trump J. McGowan *Commonweal* v144 no2 p6 Ja 27 2017

Money—Canada
Bitcoin for Bohemians H. RUSTAD cartoon *Walrus* v13 no10 p24 D 2016

Money—Charts, diagrams, etc.
MONEY, CREDIT, AND SECURITY MARKETS *Economic Indicators* p26 Je 2017

Money—Government policy
How India Broke Its Economy Overnight (on Purpose) E. Fry color *Fortune* v75 no1 p18 Ja 1 2017

Money—India
How India Broke Its Economy Overnight (on Purpose) E. Fry color *Fortune* v75 no1 p18 Ja 1 2017
How India Tripped Itself Up A. Nag, I. Marlow et al graph *Bloomberg Businessweek* no4538 p30 S 18 2017

Money market—Charts, diagrams, etc.
MONEY, CREDIT, AND SECURITY MARKETS *Economic Indicators* p26 O 2016

Money—Security measures
SMART MONEY A. Davidson cartoon *New Yorker* v93 no26 p23 S 4 2017

Money—Social aspects
Money In Politics Z. J. Miller color *Time* v188 no21 p56 N 21 2016
Our Emotional Attachment to Local Currencies C. de Anca *Harvard Business Review Digital Articles* p2 N 5 2014

Money supply—Charts, diagrams, etc.
MONEY, CREDIT, AND SECURITY MARKETS *Economic Indicators* p26 Ag 2017
MONEY, CREDIT, AND SECURITY MARKETS *Economic Indicators* p26 F 2017

Money—United States
See also
Dollar (United States currency)

Monfils, Gaël, 1986-
Gael Monfils' Swinging Forehand Volley J. YANDELL chart color *Tennis* v53 no5 p72 S/O 2017
Gael Monfils *Tennis* v53 no1 p24 Ja/F 2017
MIRACLe MAN B. Austen *New York Times Magazine* p44 Ag 27 2017

MONFORT, STEVE

Society Is Ready for a New Kind of Science--Is Academia? *Bio-Science* v67 no7 p591 Jl 2017

Monforte, Antonio

A chemical genetic roadmap to improved tomato flavor bibl graph *Science* v355 no6323 p391 Ja 27 2017

MONFORTON, DOUG

Chatter color graph *Indianapolis Monthly* v42 no2 p11 O 2017

Monfregola, Jlenia

Transcriptional activation of RagD GTPase controls mTORC1 and promotes cancer growth diag *Science* v356 no6343 p1188 Je 16 2017

Mongiardino, Renzo

A Lasting Memory M. MONDADORI SARTOGO color *Architectural Digest* v74 no10 p168 O 1 2017

La Vita Brandolini J. REGINATO bw color *Vanity Fair* v59 no7 p128 Summ 2017

Mongodin, Emmanuel F.

Changes in the microbiota cause genetically modified *Anopheles* to spread in a population graph *Science* v357 no6358 p1396 S 29 2017

Mongolia

EN ROUTE S. Cravatts color *Popular Photography* v80 no11 p86 D 2016

Mongolia—Description & travel

IN HIS ELEMENT BRUNELLO CUCINELLI FINDS CASHMERE AND PEACE IN MONGOLIA A. WHITTLE color *Conde Nast Traveler* v52 no10 p44 N 2017

Mongolia—Economic conditions

Lessons From Mongolia's Bust cartoon *Bloomberg Businessweek* no4512 p8 F 20 2017

Mongolian spot

My Mongolian Spot: AN EPHEMERAL BIRTHMARK IS A RARE GIFT, CONNECTING ME TO GENERATIONS SPANNING THE CENTURIES J. H. CHOI *American Scholar* v86 no3 p62 Summ 2017

Mongolia—Social conditions

A Steppe Forward: Women for Change advances women's rights in Mongolia A. MENARNDT *Ms.* v27 no2 p15 Summ 2017

Monier, Jean-Hugues

Who's Better at Strategy: CFOs or CSOs? *Harvard Business Review Digital Articles* p2 Ja 11 2016

MONINGER, JEANNETTE

fireproof your family *Parents* v92 no1 p62 Ja 2017

make room for dad *Parents* v91 no6 p135 Je 2016

the skinny on thin kids *Parents* v91 no9 p46 S 2016

treating depression *Parents* v91 no11 p137 N 2016

Moniot, Sébastien

A conserved NAD+ binding pocket that regulates protein-protein interactions during aging bibl graph *Science* v355 no6331 p1312 Mr 24 2017

MONIZ, ERNEST

OBAMA'S AMERICA img *New York* v49 no20 p12 O 3 2016

Moniz, Ernest J.

A comprehensive nuclear test ban bibl color *Science* v354 no6316 p1081 D 2 2016

Moniz, Ernest J., 1944—Interviews

Obama's Energy Secretary Addresses Trump's Attacks on His Legacy J. Temple il *MIT Technology Review* v120 no5 p15 S/O 2017

Moniz, Jill—Interviews

Art Without Art School J. Lovelace color *American Craft* v76 no6 p88 D 2016-Ja 2017

Moniz, Seth, 1997-

MOST PROGRESSIVE color *Surfing Magazine* v53 no1 p48 Ja 2017

Monje, Michelle

Decoupling genetics, lineages, and microenvironment in IDH-mutant gliomas by single-cell RNA-seq diag *Science* v355 no6332 p1391 Mr 31 2017

Monk, Ray

'One of the Great Intellects of His Time' bw *New York Review of Books* v63 no20 p80 D 22 2016

Monk, Thelonious, 1917-1982

Centennial for Jazz B. ZIMMERMAN color *Downbeat* v84 no1 p8 Ja 2017

Dharmawan Promotes Indonesian Culture J. Ephland color *Down-*

beat v84 no7 p21 Jl 2017

Monk & Coltrane Reissue Unites Architects of Jazz K. MICALLEF bw *Downbeat* v84 no10 p24 O 2017

Revealing Liaisons J. Hale bw *Downbeat* v84 no1 p32 Ja 2017

THELONIOUS MONK J. Hale bw *Downbeat* v84 no1 p30 Ja 2017

Monk Dreams, Hallucinations & Nightmares (Music)

Monk Dreams, Hallucinations And Nightmares F. Bouchard bw *Downbeat* v84 no5 p57 My 2017

Monkeys

Ancient Monkey Teeth Change Evolutionary Timeline G. TARLACH bw color diag *Discover* v38 no1 p76 Ja/F 2017

The Grass-Eating Monkeys of Ethiopia C. Welch cartoon color map *National Geographic* v231 no4 p72 Ap 2017

Monkeys—Behavior

Mind the Monkey Business E. UNDERWOOD *Smithsonian* v47 no8 p21 D 2016

Monkeys—Physiology

Vocalizations channeled by developmental affordances color *Science* v355 no6326 p708 F 17 2017

Monkeys—Psychology

Brains encode faces piece by piece L. HAMERS bw *Science News* v191 no13 p9 Jl 8 2017

Monkkonen, Pentti—Exhibitions

PENTTI MONKKONEN J. Griffin *Art in America* v104 no9 p160 O 2016

Monks

Hold to the Center! W. Egyoku Nakao Roshi color *Tricycle: The Buddhist Review* v26 no4 p36 Summ 2017

Laughter THE BEST MEDICINE color *Reader's Digest* v189 no1130 p86 My 2017

WHEN MY SON BECAME A MONK S. CONOVER color *Tricycle: The Buddhist Review* v27 no1 p72 Fall 2017

Will the Hulk Save Buddhism? *New York Times Upfront* v149 no11 p2 Ap 3 2017

Monks, Matthew

Another Border Clash for Trump color *Bloomberg Businessweek* no4507 p22 Ja 16 2017

Deal Snapshot: Oncor Electric Delivery Co bw graph *Bloomberg Businessweek* no4530 p19 Jl 17 2017

Monks—Attitudes

Hermitage sees surge in laypeople who want a monastic experience K. Olson color *Christian Century* v134 no10 p18 My 10 2017

Monks—Crimes against

Ethiopia's martyred monks P. Jenkins *Christian Century* v134 no2 p45 Ja 18 2017

Monmaney, Terence

LIFE ON THE EDGE *Smithsonian* v48 no1 p56 Ap 2017

Monne, Isabella

Role for migratory wild birds in the global spread of avian influenza H5N8 bibl graph map *Science* v354 no6309 p213 O 14 2016

MONNIER, MIA NAKAJI

THE BEGINNER'S GUIDE TO Making a Difference cartoon color diag *O, The Oprah Magazine* p114 S 2017

Monochrome art

Dominique Lévy R. Wetzler color *Art in America* v105 no1 p78 Ja 2017

Monochrome painting

COLOR IS A BOUNDARY W. S. Smith color *Art in America* v105 no3 p74 Mr 2017

Monocle (Periodical)

Nowhere Mag K. CHAYKA *New Republic* v248 no7 p64 Jl 2017

Monoclonal antibodies

Making a difference, differently M. Tuthill cartoon *Science* v354 no6316 p1194 D 2 2016

Monoclonal antibodies—Therapeutic use

Surprising treatment 'cures' monkey HIV infection J. Cohen color *Science* v354 no6309 p157 O 14 2016

Monod, Tatum

TATUM MONOD T. W. Strokes color *Skiing* p34 D 2016

Monomolecular films

Large, valley-exclusive Bloch-Siegert shift in monolayer WS2 E. J. Sie, C. Hung Lui et al bibl diag *Science* v355 no6329 p1066 Mr 10 2017

SPLIT-SECOND REACTIONS P. Fromme and J. C. H. Spence

color *Scientific American* v316 no5 p62 My 2017

Monopolies

See also

Cartels

The Next Battle in Antitrust Will Be About Whether One Company Knows Everything About You B. Iyer, M. Subramaniam et al *Harvard Business Review Digital Articles* p2 Jl 6 2017

Monopolies—Government policy

GOOD NEWS color *Maclean's* v129 no46 p8 N 21 2016

Monopolies—United States

Democrats Must Become the Party of Freedom B. C. Lynn *Washington Monthly* p4 Ja/F 2017

Monopolies—United States—Social aspects

How About a Bit More Room For Competition? P. Dwyer, D. McLaughlin et al *Bloomberg Businessweek* no4531 p8 Jl 24 2017

Monopolistic competition

How to Make Conservatism Great Again P. Longman color *Washington Monthly* p3 N/D 2016

Making Sense of Our Very Competitive, Super Monopolistic Economy W. Frick *Harvard Business Review Digital Articles* p1 Jl 25 2017

Monopoly (Game)

The Quiz T. BALAZO color *Maclean's* v129 no46 p64 N 21 2016

WHO REALLY INVENTED MONOPOLY? M. Pilon *Saturday Evening Post* v289 no5 p80 S/O 2017

Monopoly capitalism

THE CONTENT OF NO CONTENT E. KOLBERT cartoon *New Yorker* v93 no25 p42 Ag 28 2017

Hillary Opens the Overton Window P. Glastris *Washington Monthly* p2 N/D 2016

THE RETURN OF MONOPOLY M. STOLLER color *New Republic* v248 no8/9 p18 Ag/S 2017

Monosson, Emily

Evolution in a Toxic World F. W. ALLENDORF *BioScience* v67 no6 p476 Je 2017

Toxic textiles bibl bw color *Science* v354 no6315 p977 N 25 2016

Unlikely allies D. Schar color *Science* v356 no6343 p1130 Je 16 2017

Working with Nature L. FABIANI color *Earth Island Journal* v32 no3 p54 Aut 2017

Monounsaturated fatty acids

Dr. Oz's favorite superfoods M. TAYLOR color *Redbook* p96 O 2017

Monroe, Jamison

RICH KIDS ANONYMOUS R. KOLKER color *Bloomberg Businessweek* no4500 p48 N 21 2016

MONROE, RACHEL

Don't Mess With Texas color *New Republic* v248 no5 p10 My 2017

GONE BABY GONE color *New Republic* v248 no10 p34 O 2017

Prime Opportunity *Texas Monthly* v45 no5 p56 My 2017

SOMETHING IN THE AIR bw cartoon *New Yorker* v93 no31 p32 O 9 2017

#VANLIFE cartoon color *New Yorker* v93 no10 p40 Ap 24 2017

Monroe, Valerie

THE Skinny with Val *O, The Oprah Magazine* p64 Je 2017

Val's Guide to GORGEOUS color *O, The Oprah Magazine* p116 D 2016

Val's Guide to GORGEOUS color *O, The Oprah Magazine* p50 Ja 2017

Val's Guide to GORGEOUS color *O, The Oprah Magazine* p68 Ag 2017

Val's Guide to GORGEOUS color *O, The Oprah Magazine* p83 Mr 2017

Val's Guide to GORGEOUS O's beauty director, Valerie Monroe, finds a new way to appreciate April showers, and more... color *O, The Oprah Magazine* p64 Ap 2017

Monroy-Hernández, Andrés

How We Built a Virtual Scheduling Assistant at Microsoft *Harvard Business Review Digital Articles* p1 Jl 28 2017

Monsanto Co.

GMOs J. HIRSCH color *Popular Mechanics* p108 S 2017

GROW YOUR TRIBE J. Scott *Successful Farming* v115 no5 p16 Mid-Mr 2017

Unsavory Alliance *Earth Island Journal* v32 no4 p12 Wint 2017

Monsanto Co.—Trials, litigation, etc.

Roundup: The Usual Suspect P. WALDMAN, L. MULVANY et al color graph *Bloomberg Businessweek* no4530 p42 Jl 17 2017

Monsef, Maryam

One mother's brave choice T. GLAVIN color *Maclean's* v129 no40 p28 O 10 2016

MONSMA, GENEVIEVE

BE YOUR OWN COLORIST cartoon color *Better Homes & Gardens* v95 no4 p12 Ap 2017

your good-hair GAME PLAN color *Better Homes & Gardens* v95 no10 p24 O 2017

MONSON, NANCY

Update Your First Aid Kit color *AARP: The Magazine* v60 no4A p18 Je/Jl 2017

Monster, The (Film)

The Monster C. Collis color *Entertainment Weekly* no1440 p45 N 18 2016

THE Punch List cartoon color *GQ: Gentlemen's Quarterly* v87 no1 p18 Ja 2017

Monster Beverage Corp.

9 RODNEY SACKS L. Entis color *Fortune* v174 no7 p85 D 1 2016

Monster Energy Co.

BRINGING THE 'SHINE BACK J. Jacquot cartoon *Car & Driver* v62 no10 p16 Ap 2017

Monster-In-Law (Film)

MOTHER'S DAY WEEKEND M. FELL *TV Guide* v65 no19 p44 My 1 2017

Monster of Florence

The Monster of Florence: Case Closed? The Terrifying Story of the Most Infamous Ritual Murders in Italian History, Part 1 M. POLIDORO *Skeptical Inquirer* v41 no4 p16 Jl/Ag 2017

Monster trucks—Competitions

MARCH/APRIL K. MASSICOT color *Louisiana Life* v37 no4 p108 Mr/Ap 2017

Monster Calls, A (Film)

A MONSTER CALLS N. Sperling color *Entertainment Weekly* no1438 p39 N 4 2016

A Monster Calls Offers a Big, Less-Friendly Giant S. Zacharek color *Time* v189 no3 p57 Ja 16 2017

Monsters

See also

Gorgons (Greek mythology)

Sea monsters

Bogeyman Hunt *Lapham's Quarterly* v10 no3 p178 Summ 2017

Woman Dies Searching for Monster B. RADFORD *Skeptical Inquirer* v40 no6 p12 N/D 2016

Monsters in motion pictures

Hey, These Beasts Are Fantastic! K. P. Sullivan color *Entertainment Weekly* no1441 p37 N 25 2016

Mont-Tremblant (Québec)—Description & travel

Where to go in 2017 S. Kelso color *Money* v46 no1 p124 Ja/F 2017

Monta, Robert

Railway Post Office color *Model Railroader* v84 no8 p16 Ag 2017

Montagnac, Guillaume

Tubular clathrin/AP-2 lattices pinch collagen fibers to support 3D cell migration color *Science* v356 no6343 p1138 Je 16 2017

Montague, Atoya—Interviews

Confronting its biggest crisis N. MACDONALD color *Maclean's* v129 no42 p29 O 24 2016

MONTAGUE, DENA

ÉNERGIERICH: Sowing Seeds of Solar color *Earth Island Journal* v32 no3 p16 Aut 2017

MONTAIGNE, FEN

American Surveyor: A new life of Thoreau on his 200th birthday shows that his time at Walden Pond was far from solitary *New York Times Book Review* p17 Jl 23 2017

Sand Walker *New York Times Book Review* p52 Je 4 2017

Montaigne, Michel de, 1533-1592

Montaigne: What Was Truly Courageous? T. Parks cartoon *New York Review of Books* v63 no18 p59 N 24 2016

MONTALVO, JACKIE

The Dayhiker's Triple Crown color *Backpacker* v45 no1 p14 Ja 2017

Love at First Sight color *Backpacker* v45 no2 p54 Mr 2017

STAY AWHILE color *Backpacker* v45 no1 p85 Ja 2017

Montana

High on the Edge D. PENCE *Idaho Magazine* v16 no3 p47 D 2016

PAYDAY MAYDAY L. Farmer *Governing* v30 no6 p32 Mr 2017

WILDERNESS Wonderland M. MYLCHREEST color diag *Cabin Living* p42 Ap 2017

MONTANA, KELLEY

WEST COUNTY DIGS: Sowing Stewardship color *Earth Island Journal* v32 no1 p15 Spr 2017

Montana—Description & travel

BIG SKY, MONTANA color *Runner's World* v52 no4 p8 My 2017

Discover the Wonder of Winter in Montana *Texas Monthly* v44 no11 p40 N 2016

ROAD TRIP G. R. SCHIAVINO color *American Cowboy* v24 no1 p39 Je/Jl 2017

Montana—Politics & government

THE BATTLE FOR MONTANA T. Dickinson color *Rolling Stone* no1288 p26 Je 1 2017

Montanari, Alberto

Changing climate shifts timing of European floods color graph *Science* v357 no6351 p588 Ag 11 2017

MONTANARI, SHAENA

Old World, Young Promise color *Forbes* v199 no1 p20 Ja 24 2017

Montaner, Beatriz

A switch from canonical to noncanonical autophagy shapes B cell responses bibl graph *Science* v355 no6325 p641 F 10 2017

Montanet, F.

Observation of a large-scale anisotropy in the arrival directions of cosmic rays above 8 × 1018 eV *Science* v357 no6357 p1266 S 22 2017

Montañez, Amanda

BEYOND XX AND XY diag *Scientific American* v317 no3 p50 S 2017

MIND THE GAP graph *Scientific American* v317 no3 p78 S 2017

Montano, Tom

2017 KAWASAKI NINJA 650 color *Cycle World* v56 no3 p14 Ap 2017

Montblanc International GmbH

Leather Heads N. SULLIVAN color *Esquire* v166 no4 p52 N 2016

Montclair State University (Montclair, N.J.)

Jazz Studies Thrives at New Jersey's MSU P. Lutz color *Downbeat* v83 no12 p110 D 2016

Monte Carlo Yachts SpA

The Power of Proportion J. Y. WOOD chart color *Power & Motoryacht* v33 no4 p92 Ap 2017

Montecito (Calif.)—Economic conditions—21st century

American Riviera S. SHARF color *Forbes* v198 no8 p20 D 20 2016

MONTEFIORE, SIMON SEBAG

Stalin Goes Atomic: The Soviet leader's terror tactics extended even to the men driving his technology program *New York Times Book Review* p16 Mr 5 2017

Montelione, Gaetano T.

Principles for designing proteins with cavities formed by curved β sheets bibl color graph *Science* v355 no6321 p1 Ja 13 2017

Montemaggi, Vittorio

Taking It Personally G. Oleynick cartoon *Commonweal* v144 no5 p34 Mr 10 2017

Monterde, Stephan

How We Think About Innovation at Cisco *Harvard Business Review Digital Articles* p2 Je 8 2016

Montero, J. C.

Persistent effects of pre-Columbian plant domestication on Amazonian forest composition bibl chart graph map *Science* v355 no6328 p925 Mr 3 2017

Montero, Miguel

Leading Off color *Sports Illustrated* v125 no14 p10 O 24-31 2016

Montero-Luque, Carlos

Humans Can Make the Internet of Things Smarter *Harvard Business Review Digital Articles* p2 O 28 2014

Monterosso, Tom

2017 ACCESSORIES GUIDE color *Snowboarder* v29 no3 p104 N 2016

2017 HOLIDAY GIFT GUIDE bw *Snowboarder* v29 no4 p108 D 2016

2017 OUTERWEAR BUYER'S GUIDE color *Snowboarder* v29 no2 p114 O 2016

2017 RESORT GUIDE color map *Snowboarder* v29 no5 p90 Ja 2017

BEN FERGUSON cartoon color *Snowboarder* v29 no4 p40 D 2016

CHRIS BRADSHAW color *Snowboarder* v29 no2 p39 O 2016

DAN BRISSE color *Snowboarder* v29 no2 p38 O 2016

JAKE KUZYK cartoon color *Snowboarder* v29 no4 p42 D 2016

JP WALKER color *Snowboarder* v29 no5 p33 Ja 2017

SCOTT BLUM color *Snowboarder* v29 no5 p34 Ja 2017

MONTES, GEOFFREY

On the Market color *Architectural Digest* v73 no11 p138 N 2016

PERMANENT COLLECTION color *Architectural Digest* v73 no12 p66 D 2016

Montet, Benjamin

The Most Mysterious Star in the Galaxy *Sky & Telescope* v133 no6 p16 Je 2017

Montezuma Castle (Ariz.)

REVISITING MONTEZUMA CASTLE E. A. POWELL color *Archaeology* v70 no2 p12 Mr/Ap 2017

MONTGOMERY, BEN

The Price Of FREEDOM bw color *Reader's Digest* v190 no1132 p80 Jl/Ag 2017

Montgomery, Clark

DRESSAGE SNAPSHOT color *Dressage Today* v23 no10 p16 Jl 2017

Montgomery, Denise

The rise of creative youth development bibl *Arts Education Policy Review* v118 no1 p1 2017

Montgomery, Evan Braden

In the Hegemon's Shadow: Leading States and the Rise of Regional Powers G. J. Ikenberry *Foreign Affairs* v95 no6 p173 N/D 2016

Montgomery, Georgina M.

Conceptions of Good Science in Our Data-Rich World chart *BioScience* v66 no10 p1 O 1 2016

ESTABLISHING PRIMATE SCIENCE L. BARRETT *BioScience* v67 no3 p309 Mr 2017

Updating the Two Cultures: How Structures Can Promote Interdisciplinary Cultures *Change* v48 no6 p28 N/D 2016

Montgomery, John A. Jr.

Synthesis of mixed hypermetallic oxide BaOCa+ from laser-cooled reagents in an atom-ion hybrid trap diag graph *Science* v357 no6358 p1370 S 29 2017

MONTGOMERY, KATHY

Alpine Inn Bed & Breakfast *Arizona Highways* v93 no8 p14 Ag 2017

Augie's *Arizona Highways* v93 no9 p14 S 2017

CONTROL ROAD color map *Arizona Highways* v93 no5 p52 My 2017

Cotton Fields in Scottsdale *Arizona Highways* v93 no2 p8 F 2017

Gourmet Girls *Arizona Highways* v93 no3 p12 Mr 2017

HART IS WHERE THE HOME IS *Arizona Highways* v93 no8 p46 Ag 2017

Hotel San Ramón *Arizona Highways* v93 no3 p14 Mr 2017

Humble Pie *Arizona Highways* v93 no4 p12 Ap 2017

The Inn at Castle Rock: Like so many things in Bisbee, this old hotel has its quirks, including 14 funky guest rooms with names such as Crying Shame and Last Chance, a "Ghost Book" and a "moat." *Arizona Highways* v93 no11 p14 N 2017

La Paloma Restaurant *Arizona Highways* v93 no10 p12 O 2017

The Mission in the Sun *Arizona Highways* v92 no11 p8 N 2016

Paradise Point Café: Known as "Old Town's sweet retreat," Paradise Point Café has built a loyal following with its baked goods, including a signature carrot cake and salted caramel apple pie that's made with house-made caramel. Mmmm ... *Arizona Highways* v96 no7 p12 Jl 2017

A PLACE INN THE SUN *Arizona Highways* v93 no2 p34 F 2017

PRESCOTT LAKES LOOP *Arizona Highways* v93 no4 p52 Ap 2017

Rancho de la Osa *Arizona Highways* v92 no7 p8 Jl 2016

Simpson Hotel *Arizona Highways* v93 no10 p14 O 2017

Table 10 *Arizona Highways* v93 no1 p12 Ja 2017

TAKING THE TOUR 2017 *Arizona Highways* v93 no11 p40 N 2017

THIS LAND IS YOUR LAND *Arizona Highways* v92 no8 p12 Ag 2016

Verde Brewing Co *Arizona Highways* v93 no2 p12 F 2017

WITH A 10-FEET POLE *Arizona Highways* v93 no3 p38 Mr 2017

Montgomery, L. M. (Lucy Maud), 1874-1942

THE OTHER SIDE OF ANNE W. PASKIN *New York Times Magazine* p32 Ap 30 2017

Montgomery, Lisa Kennedy

INTERVIEW: KENNEDY K. Mangu-Ward color *Reason* v49 no5 p46 O 2017

Montgomery, Monk

Opening Chords T. B. BROWNE *Indianapolis Monthly* v40 no7 p22 Mr 2017

Montgomery, Scott

Are We Civilized Yet? *Society* v54 no2 p133 Ap 2017

Montgomery, Stephanie

MAVS-dependent host species range and pathogenicity of human hepatitis A virus bibl graph *Science* v353 no6307 p1541 S 30 2016

MONTGOMERY, SY

Pass the Fava Beans *New York Times Book Review* p20 F 26 2017

Montgomery, Wes, 1925-1968

Opening Chords T. B. BROWNE *Indianapolis Monthly* v40 no7 p22 Mr 2017

Montgomery County (Md.)

BIKE LANES, SUBURBAN STYLE: While city dwellers were bickering, Montgomery County launched a surprisingly smart initiative D. Reed *Washingtonian Magazine* v52 no11 p50 Ag 2017

Montgomery Kovacs, Debbonnaire

Discussion *Smithsonian* v47 no7 p10 N 2016

MONTICELLO, JUSTIN

'EGYPT'S JON STEWART' IN EXILE color *Reason* v49 no6 p44 N 2017

Monticello, Mike

Cars That Owners Love and Hate chart color *Consumer Reports* v82 no2 p46 F 2017

A Decision That Could Save Your Life color graph *Consumer Reports* v82 no8 p52 Ag 2017

Passing the Screen Test chart color graph il *Consumer Reports* v82 no10 p54 O 2017

The People's Choice color diag graph *Consumer Reports* v82 no4 p7 Ap 2017

Reinventing the Wheel chart color *Consumer Reports* v82 no1 p52 Ja 2017

Winter Driving: Your Survival Guide chart color *Consumer Reports* v82 no11 p52 N 2017

Montiel, Anya

AFTER COLUMBUS color *Art in America* p86 O 2017

MONTOYA, ANDY

The Question color *O, The Oprah Magazine* p14 N 2017

Montpelier Hunt Races, Montpelier Station, Va.

Living & Recreation *Virginia Living* p35 2017 Best 20of Virginia

Montréal (Québec)

MEANWHILE, ELSEWHERE IN CANADA ... R. King *Fortune* v176 no2 p31 Ag 1 2017

Out of the Ruins J. MINUTILLO *Architectural Record* v205 no9 p116 S 2017

Montréal (Québec)—Description & travel

Bonjour, Montréal R. WALLWORK *Tennis* v53 no4 p30 Jl/Ag 2017

Montréal (Québec)—History

Bright lights, big history A. Gunadie and H. Wilson color *Canadian Geographic* v137 no3 p26 My 2017

Montreal Canadiens (Hockey team)

THE FORGOTTEN HABS A. ABEL bw color *Maclean's* v130 no10 p122 N 2017

HOT | NOT T. Keith color *Sports Illustrated* v125 no15 p22 N 7 2016

Montreuil, Ricardo de, 1974-

LOWRIDERS C. M. Smith color *Entertainment Weekly* no1463/1464 p38 Ap/My 2017

Monument design & construction

Needed, A Public Monuments Plan cartoon *New Orleans Magazine* v51 no8 p22 Je 2017

Monument Valley Navajo Tribal Park (Ariz. & Utah)

In the Frame *Arizona Highways* v93 no1 p5 Ja 2017

Monumento ao Christo Redemptor (Rio de Janeiro, Brazil)

Brazil's iconic statue Christ the Redeemer is in need of restoration J. T. Coelho color *Christian Century* v134 no3 p14 F 2017

Monuments

See also

Historic buildings

National monuments

Soldiers' monuments

African Renaissance Monument R. Griffiths *History Today* v66 no10 p70 O 2016

Decommissioning Lee: The controversial removal of a prominent New Orleans statue W. CURTIS *American Scholar* v86 no4 p97 Aut 2017

DUNGEONS AND DRAGONS D. Goodyear cartoon *New Yorker* v93 no15 p18 My 29 2017

Every Website Is a Monument A. Plessas *Art in America* v104 no9 p130 O 2016

The Fred & Karl Show K. SMITH *National Review* v69 no16 p48 Ag 28 2017

Inclusion Is the Solution G. MULLINS-COHEN *Parks & Recreation* v52 no10 p10 O 2017

The Monuments bw *New Orleans Magazine* v51 no6 p20 Ap 2017

The Monuments bw *New Orleans Magazine* v52 no1 p20 S 2017

Southwest Solitude K. KRONE and C. KRONE color *Horse & Rider* v56 no9 p94 S 2017

THESE LANDS ARE NOW YOUR LANDS *National Parks* v91 no2 p10 Spr 2017

Monuments—California

They Don't Know When They're Licked color *Weekly Standard* v23 no6 p3 O 16 2017

Will Women Ever Break the Bronze Ceiling? M. Rhodan color *Time* v190 no9 p28 S 4 2017

Monuments—Conservation & restoration

White Supremacist Monument Ditched S. Richardson *American History* v51 no6 p6 F 2017

Monuments—Design & construction

ADVENTURES WITH ZIOLKOWSKI *South Dakota Magazine* v32 no6 p53 Mr/Ap 2017

WASHINGTON GHOST STORIES M. Blitz *Washingtonian Magazine* v52 no1 p24 O 2016

Monuments—Egypt

Buried Secrets S. W. DRIMMER bw color map *National Geographic Kids* no470 p26 My 2017

Monuments—Evaluation

EVERYONE'S A CRITIC *Washingtonian Magazine* v52 no1 p20 O 2016

JACK POOLE PLAZA *Sea Magazine* v108 no8 pPNW-13 Ag 2016

Monuments—Great Britain

THE BRITISH HERITAGE TRAVEL PUZZLER T. Allen, M. Trinder et al color *British Heritage Travel* v38 no5 p78 S/O 2017

Monuments—Social aspects

The Monuments cartoon *New Orleans Magazine* v51 no9 p20 Jl 2017

Monuments—Washington (D.C.)

WASHINGTON GHOST STORIES M. Blitz *Washingtonian Magazine* v52 no1 p24 O 2016

Monvoisin, Raymond Quinsac

The Tax Collector and the Pharisee bw *Christian Century* v133 no21 p63 O 12 2016

Monzon-Palma, Tina

Do Journalists Still Matter? *Vital Speeches of the Day* v83 no10 p293 O 2017

Moo-Young Han

Moo-Young Han W. T. Chu and Kwang-Je Kim *Physics Today* v69 no11 p70 N 2016

Mooallem, Jon

THE DELUGE *New York Times Magazine* p36 Ap 23 2017

THE HOUSE AT THE END OF THE WORLD *New York Times Magazine* p38 Ja 8 2017

Mr. Know-it-All cartoon *Wired* v25 no4 p26 Ap 2017

MR. KNOW-IT-ALL cartoon *Wired* v25 no7 p28 Jl 2017

MR. KNOW-IT-ALL cartoon *Wired* v25 no8 p28 Ag 2017

MY PAL WON'T TEXT ME BECAUSE I DON'T USE SIGNAL.

BUT HE'LL SAY ANYTHING ON SOCIAL MEDIA. HE'S BEING ANNOYING, RIGHT? cartoon *Wired* v25 no5 p30 My 2017

OBAMA'S AMERICA img *New York* v49 no20 p12 O 3 2016

PEDALS THE BEAR *New York Times Magazine* p22 D 25 2016

Q: MY 7-YEAR-OLD TOOK PICTURES OF MY NAKED 3-YEAR-OLD AND ALMOST PUT THEM ON FACEBOOK. HOW DO I EXPLAIN THIS IS A BAD IDEA? cartoon *Wired* v24 no12 p32 D 2016

US AND THEM *New York Times Magazine* p40 Ja 15 2017

VOYAGES *New York Times Magazine* p37 Mr 26 2017

Mooallem, Stephen

150 YEARS OF BAZAR cartoon *Harper's Bazaar* no3649 p326 D 2016/Ja 2017

THE 1940S bw color *Harper's Bazaar* no3652 p228 Ap 2017

THE ALLURE OF JACKIE bw color *Harper's Bazaar* no3650 p184 F 2017

ASTONISH ME bw color *Harper's Bazaar* no3651 p436 Mr 2017

THE BALLAD OF SEAN & YOKO bw color *Harper's Bazaar* no3655 p162 Ag 2017

BAZAAR: THE DEFINITION OF FASHION bw *Harper's Bazaar* no3653 p268 My 2017

THE BIG '80S bw color *Harper's Bazaar* no3656 p326 S 2017

FREE LOVE AND FASHION color *Harper's Bazaar* no3655 p142 Ag 2017

THE LEGEND OF LIZ TILBERIS bw color *Harper's Bazaar* no3657 p222 O 2017

MICK TALKS bw color *Harper's Bazaar* no3649 p336 D 2016/Ja 2017

POP GOES BAZAAR color *Harper's Bazaar* no3654 p132 Je/Jl 2017

Moochin' About (Company)

Abundance of Amram B. Reed bw *Downbeat* v83 no12 p95 D 2016

Mood (Psychology)

4 Steps to Dispel a Bad Mood A. Caillet, J. Hirshberg et al *Harvard Business Review Digital Articles* p2 Ap 6 2015

All the Feels A. E. Walker color *Glamour* v115 no6 p142 Je 2017

Go SPLAT! On the Tee Box E. A. Tischler and D. DeNunzio color *Golf Magazine* v58 no12 p82 D 2016

How Your Morning Mood Affects Your Whole Workday N. Rothbard *Harvard Business Review Digital Articles* p2 Jl 21 2016

RAGING BRAIN A. BARTZ *Scholastic Choices* v32 no3 p20 N/D 2016

This Just In J. Zorthian color *Time* v190 no14 p23 O 9 2017

Moods (Dance)

Business Trip A. FORTINI color *Esquire* v167 no1 p28 F 2017

Moody, A. David

A LEGACY CORRUPTED J. T. KEANE color *America* v215 no10 p38 O 10 2016

MOODY, ELYSE

CANVAS SHOWER CURTAINS color *Martha Stewart Living* p38 Ap 2017

COOL AND COLLECTED color *Martha Stewart Living* p40 Jl/Ag 2017

GIFTS that UPLIFT! cartoon *O, The Oprah Magazine* p148 D 2016

Go With the Grain chart color *Martha Stewart Living* p36 Mr 2017

HOW TO BUILD CHARACTER color *Martha Stewart Living* p76 My 2017

LAUNDRY QUANDARIES color *Martha Stewart Living* p34 S 2017

MEET AND GREET color *Martha Stewart Living* p28 My 2017

O's 2017 HEALTH HEROES color *O, The Oprah Magazine* p57 Ja 2017

PEEL-OFF WALLPAPER color *Martha Stewart Living* p29 Mr 2017

TRUE-BLUE WINNERS color *Martha Stewart Living* no271 p76 Ja/F 2017

Moody, James—Interviews

A Desert Classic W. Becktold *Sierra* v102 no3 p68 My/Je 2017

Moody, Lynn

DIFFERENTIATED AND MEANINGFUL INSTRUCTION: Turning around districtwide performance by immersing students in an engaging, literacy-rich environment *Literacy Today (2411-7862)* v35 no1 p18 Jl/Ag 2017

Moody, M. P.

Direct observation of individual hydrogen atoms at trapping sites in a ferritic steel bibl diag *Science* v355 no6330 p1196 Mr 17 2017

Moody Boats (Company)

Moody DS54 Z. Prochazka cartoon color *Sail* v48 no2 p34 F 2017

Mooers, Arne

Adapting to the Anthropocene color *Science* v357 no6354 p878 S 1 2017

Moon

See also

Space flight to the moon

Bad Moon Rising K. HAYNES color *Discover* v38 no1 p48 Ja/F 2017

Celebrating S&T's 75th Anniversary T. Sales, P. Wiggins et al *Sky & Telescope* v133 no2 p6 F 2017

December Delights: The Moon occults Aldebaran, and Mars and Jupiter dance with a star F. Schaaf *Sky & Telescope* v134 no6 p46 D 2017

February 2017: Venus blazes after sunset M. RATCLIFFE and A. LING color *Astronomy* v45 no2 p36 F 2017

Fossil Moon S. R. Das color *Scientific American* v317 no4 p18 O 2017

GALLERY *Sky & Telescope* v134 no6 p70 D 2017

The Great American Eclipse E. Barone color diag map *Time* v190 no2/3 p14 Jl 10-17 2017

Hello, Moon S. J. O'MEARA color *Astronomy* v45 no10 p66 O 2017

How Earth Got its MOON T. Sumner color *Science News* v191 no7 p18 Ap 15 2017

Lunar Birth H. Leifert bw *Natural History* v125 no4 p6 Ap 2017

Moonlighting in May J. RAO color *Natural History* v125 no5 p45 My 2017

READER GALLERY J. Fisanotti, D. Crowson et al color *Astronomy* v44 no12 p70 D 2016

STAR DOME chart map *Astronomy* v45 no10 p38 O 2017

Surprising number of craters, splotches mark the moon E. DeMarco bw *Science News* v190 no11 p32 N 26 2016

WHERE THE SUN DON'T SHINE E. MASTROIANNI bw *Discover* v38 no9 p17 N 2017

Moon, Eileen

EVERYDAY HEROES color *Runner's World* v51 no11 p16 D 2016

Moon, Elizabeth

Cold Welcome color *Publishers Weekly* v264 no2 p45 Ja 9 2017

Moon, J.

Quantized Faraday and Kerr rotation and axion electrodynamics of a 3D topological insulator bibl graph *Science* v354 no6316 p1124 D 2 2016

Moon, Twila

Saying goodbye to glaciers color *Science* v356 no6338 p580 My 12 2017

Moon, Wesley—Interviews

MAKE IT HUM C. BARBOUR color *House Beautiful* v159 no1 p76 F 2017

Moon light

MEANT TO BE L. MYERS *Missouri Life* v43 no6 p80 O/N 2016

Moonan, Wendy

Industrial Evolution color *Architectural Record* v205 no3 p53 Mr 2017

A Landmark Restaurant Redux *Architectural Record* v205 no9 p52 S 2017

On the Home Front color *Architectural Record* v205 no5 p61 My 2017

Second Course *Architectural Record* v205 no4 p166 Ap 2017

Moondog (Performer)

Howlin' at the Moondog M. BARCLAY bw *Maclean's* v129 no48/49 p36 D 5 2016

Mooney, D. J.

Tough adhesives for diverse wet surfaces diag *Science* v357 no6349 p378 Jl 28 2017

MOONEY, HAROLD

Invasion Dynamics: From Invasion Biology to Invasion Science *BioScience* v67 no9 p860 S 2017

Mooney, Harold A.

Toward a national, sustained U.S. ecosystem assessment bibl color

Science v354 no6314 p838 N 18 2016

MOONEY, JESSIE

Mating bw color *GQ: Gentlemen's Quarterly* v86 no11 p58 N 2016

Mooney, John

DISH OF THE MONTH J. SIDMAN *Washingtonian Magazine* v52 no8 p135 My 2017

Mooney, Julie

THE 33 YEAR SEARCH FOR MY BIRTH MOTHER J. BIGLEY II *Reader's Digest* v189 no1127 p77 F 2017

MOONEY, MICHAEL J.

America's QB color *GQ: Gentlemen's Quarterly* v97 no9 p168 S 2017

CANDID Cameraman: JASON LEE EXPLAINS WHY HE LEFT LOS ANGELES FOR DENTON AND WHY, RIGHT NOW, HE PREFERS TAKING PHOTOGRAPHS TO ACTING *Texas Monthly* v45 no7 p52 Jl 2017

The Empathy of David Brown *Texas Monthly* v45 no6 p122 Je 2017

The Future of Humanitarianism [Cover story] bw color *Popular Mechanics* p13 S 2017

The Future of Humanitarianism [Cover story] bw color *Popular Mechanics* v193 no7 p13 S 2016

Mooney, R. A.

Architecture of a transcribing-translating expressome diag graph map *Science* v356 no6334 p194 Ap 14 2017

Mooney airplanes

IMMACULATE PROTECTION P. BERGQVIST color *Flying* v144 no4 p60 Ap 2017

Moon Jae-in, 1953-

A New President Aims to Change South Korea's Course D. C. KANG *Current History* v116 no791 p217 S 2017

Pop Chart R. Bruner, C. Lang et al color *Time* v189 no21 p66 Je 5 2017

South Korea's nuclear U-turn draws praise and darts D. Normile and A. Mi-Young color graph *Science* v357 no6346 p15 Jl 7 2017

Moon—Libration

Pickin' up good librations M. RATCLIFFE and A. LING bw *Astronomy* v45 no5 p37 My 2017

Moonlight (Film)

The 10 Best Movies S. Zacharek color *Time* v188 no25-26 p132 D 19 2016 Double Issue

Black and blue J. SEMLEY color *Maclean's* v129 no43 p56 O 31 2016

BLACK POWER H. ALS color *New Yorker* v92 no34 p70 O 24 2016

CRITICAL MASS chart color *Entertainment Weekly* no1444/1445 p64 D 16 2016

The Culturati Caucus img *New York* v49 no25 p124 D 12 2016

JANELLE MONÁE R. L. ELDREDGE *Atlanta* v56 no9 p24 Ja 2017

Limelight [Cover story] C. Wallace color *GQ: Gentlemen's Quarterly* v97 no7 p48 Jl 2017

MAKING THE CUT J. Thompson color *Essence* v48 no2 p74 Je 2017

MOONLIGHT AND MANHOOD B. McGARVEY *America* v216 no1 p36 Ja 2 2017

Moonlight B. A. DuHamel chart color *Sound & Vision* v82 no6 p68 Jl/Ag 2017

Moonlight color *New Yorker* v93 no5 p14 Mr 20 2017

Moonlight Enchants by Revealing Itself In a Thousand Facets S. Zacharek color *Time* v188 no18 p43 O 31 2016

Moonlight *New Yorker* v92 no40 p17 D 5 2016

'Moonlight' Sonata J. Podhoretz color *Weekly Standard* v22 no26 p39 Mr 13 2017

Moon Over Miami D. Pinckney color *New York Review of Books* v64 no7 p24 Ap 20 2017

The MORNING AFTER N. Sperling color *Entertainment Weekly* no1456 p52 Mr 10 2017

No. 2 MOONLIGHT L. Greenblatt color *Entertainment Weekly* no1444/1445 p50 D 16 2016

No Refuge R. Alleva color *Commonweal* v143 no20 p18 D 16 2016

NOW PLAYING color *Entertainment Weekly* no1439 p47 N 11 2016

One Part, Three Breakouts J. Yuan img *New York* v49 no21 p104 O 17 2016

ONE STEP AHEAD: A CONVERSATION WITH BARRY JENKINS M. Boyce Gillespie *Film Quarterly* v70 no3 p52 Spr 2017

PICTURE J. McGovern, D. Franich et al color diag *Entertainment Weekly* no1451/1452 p70 F 3-10 2017

Portrait of a Hustler T. CHATTERTON WILLIAMS color *Esquire* v166 no4 p40 N 2016

The Real Best Pictures of 2016 M. ATKINSON *In These Times* v41 no2 p38 F 2017

SHOCK of MOONLIGHT N. Sperling, D. Coggan et al color *Entertainment Weekly* no1456 p42 Mr 10 2017

Streaming S. Li color *Entertainment Weekly* no1463/1464 p91 Ap/My 2017

SUPPORTING ACTOR CONTENDER ASHTON SANDERS N. Sperling color *Entertainment Weekly* no1438 p48 N 4 2016

Total Eclipse img *New York* v49 no21 p114 O 17 2016

Moonlight International Academy (Little Sands, P.E.I.)

Little monks of Little Sands M. CAMPBELL color *Maclean's* v130 no7 p16 Ag 2017

Moon—Observations

FROM OUR READERS M. Lewicki, T. Sales et al *Sky & Telescope* v133 no1 p6 Ja 2017

Mercury Maxes Out F. Schaaf *Sky & Telescope* v133 no4 p46 Ap 2017

Mystery Ray in Serenitatis C. A. Wood *Sky & Telescope* v132 no6 p52 D 2016

OBSERVING April 2017r M. Wedel *Sky & Telescope* v133 no4 p41 Ap 2017

Year-End Extravaganza *Sky & Telescope* v132 no6 p46 D 2016

Moon—Phases

See also

Full moon

The pulsing Moon S. J. O'MEARA color *Astronomy* v45 no1 p64 Ja 2017

Moon—Pictorial works

Lightbox color *Time* v188 no22-23 p14 N/D 2016

Moon—Research

Lunar Almanac: Northern Hemisphere Sky Chart *Sky & Telescope* v133 no6 p42 Je 2017

Peaks of "Eternal" Light C. Wood *Sky & Telescope* v133 no6 p52 Je 2017

Retracing Origins of Massive Moon Crater *USA Today Magazine* v145 no2865 p13 Je 2017

Moor, Andreas E.

Global mRNA polarization regulates translation efficiency in the intestinal epithelium diag *Science* v357 no6357 p1299 S 22 2017

Moor, Kathrin

Inflammation boosts bacteriophage transfer between Salmonella spp bibl diag *Science* v355 no6330 p1211 Mr 17 2017

Moor, Robert

THE APPROVAL MATRIX img *New York* v49 no15 p100 Jl 25 2016

Five Alive *New York Times Book Review* p12 My 28 2017

HOW TO CROSS A FIELD OF SNOW *Lapham's Quarterly* v10 no2 p181 Spr 2017

Paths Forged by Man and Beast B. BUCK color *Earth Island Journal* v32 no4 p54 Wint 2017

WHAT HAPPENS TO AMERICAN MYTH WHEN YOU TAKE THE DRIVER OUT OF IT? *New York* v49 no21 p36 O 17 2016

Moore, Alan, 1953-

Epic of the Midlands K. J. TORRANCE *National Review* v69 no2 p45 F 6 2017

Wild in the Streets D. WOLK *New York Times Book Review* p23 O 16 2016

Moore, Alison

The Circles of Hellhaus: A lonely British hiker goes dangerously walkabout in Germany S. WYNDHAM *New York Times Book Review* p19 S 10 2017

Moore, Amanda

YOU LOSE, YOU WIN color *Women's Health* v14 no4 p118 My 2017

Moore, Andrew

THE AIA TODAY AND TOMORROW *Archaeology* v70 no1 p8 Ja/F 2017

The Past in the Present color *Archaeology* v69 no6 p6 N/D 2016

PAWPAW MEAD: Foraged fruit + fermentation = funky firewater *Mother Earth News* no283 p28 Ag/S 2017

Moore, Andrew W.

How to Prepare the Next Generation for Jobs in the AI Economy color *Harvard Business Review Digital Articles* p2 Je 5 2017

Moore, Anne Elizabeth—Interviews

THE WAR ON WOMEN H. NYHART color *Chicago* v66 no4 p24 Ap 2017

Moore, Arthur Cotton

A BRILLIANT PROPOSAL TO SOLVE OUR AIRPORT PROBLEMS A. WHITING *Washingtonian Magazine* v52 no2 p12 N 2016

Moore, Bill

ON Art L. Copan *Christian Century* v134 no16 p39 Ag 2 2017

Moore, Blake

alaskan weather *Weatherwise* v70 no5 p48 S/O 2017

Weatherwatch color map *Weatherwise* v70 no4 p38 Jl/Ag 2017

Weatherwatch *Weatherwise* v70 no1 p50 Ja/F 2017

Weatherwatch *Weatherwise* v70 no2 p38 Mr/Ap 2017

Moore, Booth

HELLO, TOKYO A. WHITTLE color *Conde Nast Traveler* v52 no4 p24 Ap 2017

Moore, Brian

The SAILING SCENE color *Sail* v48 no9 p6 S 2017

Moore, Cara

WOMEN WORKERS IN WARTIME *Prologue* v48 no3 p60 Fall 2016

Moore, Celia

Does Doing the Same Work Over and Over Again Make You Less Ethical? *Harvard Business Review Digital Articles* p2 Mr 28 2017

Moore, Charles

HEAR HER ROAR F. Gray *Claremont Review of Books* v16 no4 p25 Fall 2016

MOORE, CHIVVIS

To Arms Over LGBT? *USA Today Magazine* v145 no2860 p54 Ja 2017

Moore, Clement C.

The Night Before Christmas *Publishers Weekly* v264 no36 p97 S 4 2017

Moore, David J.

Don Wilson Is Playing a Hit Man? color *Black Belt* v55 no6 p24 O/N 2017

Moore, David T.

Quantum dot–induced phase stabilization of α-CsPbI3 perovskite for high-efficiency photovoltaics bibl chart graph *Science* v354 no6308 p92 O 7 2016

Moore, Deborah

Indianola Promise Community: Improving Academic Outcomes in the Delta *Bridges (Federal Reserve Bank of St. Louis)* p1 Wint 2016/2017

Moore, Deborah Dash

Jewish New York: The Remarkable Story of a City and a People *Publishers Weekly* v264 no33 p66 Ag 14 2017

Moore, Demi, 1962-

Best-Dressed LIST color *Harper's Bazaar* no3655 p64 Ag 2017

Dear Diana, You Still Rule. Love, Everyone J. Kantor and J. Harman color *Glamour* v115 no9 p42 S 2017

Moore, Demi, 1962—Interviews

DEMI MOORE OF Empire T. Stack, N. Abrams et al color *Entertainment Weekly* no1482/1483 p78 S 22 2017

Moore, Don

Smart Leaders Are OK with Seeming Uncertain *Harvard Business Review Digital Articles* p2 F 10 2015

Moore, Fernanda

Bad Sexpectations *Commentary* v140 no2 p8 S 2015

MOORE, GRAHAM

The Fabulous Baker Street Boys color *New York Times Book Review* p8 Ja 29 2017

The Last Days of Night color *Publishers Weekly* v263 no44 p70 O 31 2016

MOORE, HAILEY

Climbing for Mental Health color *Climbing* no352 p10 Ap 2017

Proper Hydration chart *Climbing* no351 p51 F/Mr 2017

Rotating-Wall Workouts bw *Climbing* no353 p47 My/Je 2017

Sending Southern Smoke chart color *Climbing* no351 p32 F/Mr 2017

Moore, Henry, 1898-1986

Monumental Offenses K. Samuelson color *Time* v188 no18 p13 O 31 2016

Moore, J.

MEN OF HONOR D. HOLBROOK *TV Guide* v65 no4 p28 Ja 16 2017

MOORE, JAMES

ROAR OF THE CROWD *Texas Monthly* v45 no9 p8 S 2017

Moore, James D. P.

Imaging the distribution of transient viscosity after the 2016 Mw 7.1 Kumamoto earthquake map *Science* v356 no6334 p163 Ap 14 2017

MOORE, JANICE

My Nearest and Dearest Enemy *BioScience* v66 no10 p907 O 1 2016

Moore, Jason J.

Dynamics of cortical dendritic membrane potential and spikes in freely behaving rats diag *Science* v355 no6331 p1281 Mr 24 2017

Moore, Jennifer

Miss Leslie's Secret *Publishers Weekly* v264 no30 p46 Jl 24 2017

MOORE, JIM

Bold-Faced Time color *GQ: Gentlemen's Quarterly* v97 no9 p63 S 2017

Golden Goose Sneakers *GQ: Gentlemen's Quarterly* v86 no11 p35 N 2016

The High-Fashion Varsity Jacket color *GQ: Gentlemen's Quarterly* v97 no3 p59 Mr 2017

THE LONG SOLO FLIGHT OF HARRISON FORD [Cover story] bw color *GQ: Gentlemen's Quarterly* v97 no10 p116 O 2017

Manual cartoon color *GQ: Gentlemen's Quarterly* v97 no7 p11 Jl 2017

The New Velcro Sneaker color *GQ: Gentlemen's Quarterly* v97 no4 p41 Ap 2017

The New Vows of Wedding Style color *GQ: Gentlemen's Quarterly* v97 no6 p23 Je 2017

Our Favorite Designer Collections (as Worn by Our Favorite Human Collections) bw color *GQ: Gentlemen's Quarterly* v97 no11 p33 N 2017

Radical Chinos color *GQ: Gentlemen's Quarterly* v97 no5 p29 My 2017

The Thousand-Dollar Pair of Jeans color *GQ: Gentlemen's Quarterly* v87 no1 p9 Ja 2017

We Found the Perfect Fall Sweater bw *GQ: Gentlemen's Quarterly* v97 no10 p66 O 2017

MOORE, JINA

A Woman in Charge *New York Times Book Review* p20 Mr 19 2017

Moore, John

FINDING YOUR NERVE IN FINDING NEVERLAND *Cincinnati Magazine* v50 no8 p8 My 2017

Moore, John P.

HIV's ACHILLES' HEEL color diag *Scientific American* v315 no6 p50 D 2016

Moore, Jonni S.

Peter C. Nowell (1928–2016) color *Science* v355 no6328 p913 Mr 3 2017

Moore, Julianne, 1960-

THE 50 BEST DRESSED IN HOLLYWOOD E. Wilson color *InStyle* v23 no12 p266 N 2016

Flip the Script M. RUS color *Architectural Digest* no11 p104 N 1 2017

InSTYLE October 2017 color *InStyle* v24 no10 p205 O 2017

To Be Real L. Lynch bw color *AARP: The Magazine* v60 no2A p13 F/Mr 2017

The Woman of Many Faces [Cover story] L. B. Ray color *InStyle* v24 no10 p206 O 2017

Moore, Julie L.

Three questions *Christian Century* v133 no23 p12 N 9 2016

MOORE, KATE

These Shining Women *Publishers Weekly* v264 no16 p60 Ap 17 2017

Moore, Kate—Interviews

Lower Your Expectations color *Kiplinger's Personal Finance* v71

no1 p45 Ja 2017

Moore, Kathleen Dean

Dangerous Years color *Orion Magazine* v36 no1 p59 Ja/F 2017

The Moral Urgency of Action to Protect the World's Megafauna *BioScience* v66 no12 p1009 D 1 2016

MOORE, KATHLEEN M. T.

Google Haul Out: Earth Observation Imagery and Digital Aerial Surveys in Coastal Wildlife Management and Abundance Estimation *BioScience* v67 no8 p760 Ag 2017

MOORE, KATI

Ancient Algae color *Natural History* v125 no6 p6 Je 2017

Ants in Your Plants color *Natural History* v125 no11 p6 N 2017

BOARD GAMES *Natural History* v124 no10 p2 N 2016

BOBBLED THE CATCH color *Natural History* v125 no6 p2 Je 2017

Clean Combustion *Natural History* v124 no10 p8 N 2016

Deep Relationships color *Natural History* v125 no10 p6 O 2017

Diet Change color *Natural History* v125 no3 p6 Mr 2017

Dividing the Spoils color *Natural History* v125 no5 p7 My 2017

Every Tree, an Island *Natural History* v125 no2 p8 F 2017

FED UP color *Natural History* v125 no11 p2 N 2017

FOR DEAR LIFE color *Natural History* v125 no5 p2 My 2017

Humanity for Habitat *Natural History* v125 no1 p6 D 2016/Ja 2017

THE NATURAL EXPLANATION color *Natural History* v125 no7 p4 Jl/Ag 2017

SEX APPEAL color *Natural History* v125 no4 p2 Ap 2017

STRESSED OUT *Natural History* v125 no1 p2 D 2016/Ja 2017

Stretching and Loosening color *Natural History* v125 no7 p7 Jl/Ag 2017

Viral Decisions color *Natural History* v125 no4 p8 Ap 2017

WATER BREAK color *Natural History* v125 no3 p2 Mr 2017

MOORE, KENNETH A.

Submersed Aquatic Vegetation in Chesapeake Bay: Sentinel Species in a Changing World *BioScience* v67 no8 p698 Ag 2017

Moore, Lane

Am I the Last Romantic Millennial? bw color *Glamour* v115 no5 p120 My 2017

Moore, Laura

Making Waves: Beach Lane, Book 1 color *Publishers Weekly* v264 no11 p64 Mr 13 2017

MOORE, LINDA MCCULLOUGH

Before I Go *Saturday Evening Post* v289 no2 p60 Mr/Ap 2017

Moore, Lisa

Bold Push to Save Wildlife—and Inspire Kids color *National Wildlife (World Edition)* v55 no3 p18 Ap/My 2017

Flag a Fence, Save a Sage-Grouse color *National Wildlife (World Edition)* v55 no5 p18 Ag/S 2017

Mammals in Motion bw color *National Wildlife (World Edition)* v55 no4 p30 Je/Jl 2017

MOTHER AND MONSTER color *Walrus* v14 no6 p48 Jl/Ag 2017

Nature's Ambassador Hits the Big 5-0 color *National Wildlife (World Edition)* v55 no1 p18 D/Ja 2016

Safeguarding Summer's Bounty *National Wildlife (World Edition)* v55 no5 p4 Ag/S 2017

Moore, Lorrie

The Case of O.J. Simpson bw color *New York Review of Books* v63 no16 p75 O 27 2016

Moore, Mandy, 1984-

Tangled Before Ever After M. Logan *TV Guide* v65 no11 p39 Mr 6 2017

This Is Us: Before They Met D. Snierson color *Entertainment Weekly* no1457/1458 p83 Mr 17 2017

Moore, Mandy, 1984——Interviews

Mandy Moore M. Gajanan color *Time* v189 no24 p50 Je 26 2017

MOORE, MARCUS J.

THE DONALD GLOVER EXPERIMENT color *Nation* v304 no3 p37 Ja 30 2017

TWIN PEAKS color *Nation* v304 no4 p35 F 6 2017

Moore, Marianne, 1887-1972

'A Place for the Genuine'; A new volume does justice to one of the 20th century's most singular poets S. Burt *New York Times Book Review* p12 Ag 13 2017

Moore, Mary Tyler, 1936-2017

The MARY MARY MARY MARY MARY MARY MARY I

Knew E. Asner and D. Snierson color *Entertainment Weekly* no1453 p34 F 17 2017

Mary Tyler Moore M. Roush color *TV Guide* v65 no7 p6 F 13 2017

Moore, Matt

The South's Best Butts color *Southern Living* v52 no4 p134 Ap 2017

MOORE, MATTHEW

Presidents and Parliaments *Commentary* v142 no4 p13 N 2016

Moore, Melanie, 1991-

Melanie MOORE C. Bowers *Dance Spirit* v21 no7 p46 S 2017

Moore, Michael

Research *Oceanus* v52 no2 p1 Spr 2017

Moore, Michael, 1954——Interviews

Michael MOORE H. FIERSTEIN *Interview* v47 no6 p14 Ag 2017

Moore, Michael, 1954——Political & social views

THE THANKLESS TASK OF BEING MICHAEL MOORE J. PRESSLER img *New York* v50 no18 p40 S 4 2017

Moore, Mike

SMOKE'EM OUT [Cover story] E. E. Deprez and P. M. Barrett bw color *Bloomberg Businessweek* no4541 p40 O 9 2017

Moore, Morgan

11th Annual twenty seventeen Las Vegas: ARABIAN BREEDERS WORLD CUP SHOW color *Arabian Horse World* v57 no7 p70 Ap 2017

BIG RESULTS *Arabian Horse World* v57 no6 p146 Mr 2017

December *Arabian Horse World* v57 no3 p10 D 2016

Dr. Karlan Downing's Trail Stars *Arabian Horse World* v57 no3 p68 D 2016

THE JOURNEY TO NAMPA *Arabian Horse World* v57 no4 p84 Ja 2017

Small Breeders BIG RESULTS *Arabian Horse World* v56 no12 p74 S 2016

Small Breeders BIG RESULTS *Arabian Horse World* v57 no4 p150 Ja 2017

SPORT HORSE NATIONALS AND THE RALVON ELIJAH INFLUENCE *Arabian Horse World* v57 no4 p102 Ja 2017

Moore, Natalie——Interviews

Home equity? color *U.S. Catholic* v82 no4 p32 Ap 2017

MOORE, NICOLE

The Shark in the Shallows *Reader's Digest* v189 no1127 p110 F 2017

Moore, Paul

Roll Out the Green Carpet S. Bender color *Southern Living* v51 no11 p38 N 2016

Moore, Peter

Four Wise Moves cartoon *AARP: The Magazine* v30 no6A p13 O/N 2017

Moore, R. G.

Femtosecond electron-phonon lock-in by photoemission and x-ray free-electron laser chart diag *Science* v357 no6346 p71 Jl 7 2017

Moore, Raymond

Equal Measures N. Pantic color *Tennis* v53 no2 p6 Mr/Ap 2017

MOORE, REBECCA

An Ecoregion-Based Approach to Protecting Half the Terrestrial Realm *BioScience* v67 no6 p534 Je 2017

The extent of forest in dryland biomes [Cover story] chart map *Science* v356 no6338 p635 My 12 2017

Moore, Reginald

Blood and SUGAR M. HARDY *Texas Monthly* v45 no1 p47 Ja 2017

Moore, Renee

Learning from our elders bw *Phi Delta Kappan* v98 no5 p45 F 2017

Moore, Roger, 1927-2017

Milestones color *Time* v189 no21 p14 Je 5 2017

MOORE THAN BOND C. Nashawaty color *Entertainment Weekly* no1468/1469 p81 Je 2-9 2017

ROGER MOORE C. Nashawaty color *Entertainment Weekly* no1468/1469 p80 Je 2-9 2017

Moore, Roy S.

NO MOORE: ALABAMA IS FINALLY RID OF THE WORST JUDGE IN AMERICA R. BOSTON *Humanist* v76 no6 p38 N/D 2016

Moore, Roy Stewart, 1947-

Firebrand Moore wins GOP primary runoff K. Chandler, B. Barrow et al color *Christian Century* v134 no22 p15 O 25 2017

Moore Unmoored J. McCORMACK color *Weekly Standard* v23 no5 p12 O 9 2017

Moore, Russell

AMAZING DISGRACE S. POSNER *New Republic* v248 no4 p34 Ap 2017

Fragmentation Of the Soul color *National Review* v68 no22 p45 D 5 2016

The Reformation At 500 color *National Review* v69 no12 p35 Je 26 2017

Moore, Russell—Interviews

Russell Moore Can't Support Either Candidate A. M. Cox *New York Times Magazine* p66 O 16 2016

Moore, Shemar, 1970-

S.W.A.T A. D'Arminio *TV Guide* v65 no37 p36 S 4 2017

Moore, Shemar, 1970—Interviews

Criminal Minds A. D'Arminio *TV Guide* v65 no19 p29 My 1 2017

Moore, Stephen

The Big 4 F. BARNES color *Weekly Standard* v23 no2 p14 S 18 2017

If They Only Had a Brain color *Weekly Standard* v22 no36 p16 My 29 2017

The Trump Plan for Boom Times color *Time* v189 no3 p46 Ja 30 2017

Untapped Revenue color *Weekly Standard* v22 no29 p16 Ap 3 2017

Moore, T. E.

Structure, force balance, and topology of Earth's magnetopause diag graph *Science* v356 no6341 p960 Je 1 2017

Moore, Tirin

Selective modulation of cortical state during spatial attention bibl graph *Science* v354 no6316 p1140 D 2 2016

Moore, Tobin

The Point of All Returns S. ADAMS color *Forbes* v200 no4 p75 O 24 2017

Moore, Veronica Morris—Interviews

THE ORGANIZER J. R. Hawkins color *Essence* v47 no7 p60 N 2016

MOORE, WAYNE

Q: Who's your trusty sidekick for summer adventures, and why? color *O, The Oprah Magazine* p14 Je 2017

Moore, Wendy

ANIMAL MAGNETISM IN VICTORIAN LONDON: Mesmerism was a short-lived medical phenomenon, but its most celebrated British exponent, John Elliotson, attracted large crowds, which incensed his rivals J. Peakman *History Today* v67 no9 p98 S 2017

Crown of Blood *History Today* v67 no3 p59 Mr 2017

Moore's law

Why the Public Utility Model Is the Wrong Approach for Internet Regulation L. Downes *Harvard Business Review Digital Articles* p2 N 11 2014

Moore y Medina, Scott

Design, Place and Indigenous Ways: Working with Local Communities *Parks & Recreation* v51 no12 p30 D 2016

Mooring of ships

See also

Anchorage

ANCHORING 201: SOMETIMES, SIMPLY FIGURING OUT SCOPE AND DROPPING THE HOOK ISN'T ENOUGH F. LANIER color *Sea Magazine* v109 no6 p52 Je 2017

ART AND CULTURE PIT STOPS IN PUGET SOUND: LEARN THE RICH HISTORY OF THE SAN JUAN ISLANDS AT ONE OF THESE MUSEUMS ON PUGET SOUND D. HISLOP *Sea Magazine* v109 no9 pPNW-8 S 2017

Moorman, Antoon F. M.

An interactive three-dimensional digital atlas and quantitative database of human development bibl color graph *Science* v354 no6315 paag0053-1 N 25 2016

Moorman, Christine

Quantifying the Impact of Marketing Analytics *Harvard Business Review Digital Articles* p2 N 5 2015

MOOS, MARKUS

Evicted color *Alternatives Journal (AJ) - Canada's Environmental Voice* v42 no2 p16 2016

Welcome Home *Alternatives Journal (AJ) - Canada's Environmental Voice* v42 no2 p7 2016

Moose

At Home with Moose J. KEEBLE color *Natural History* v125 no7 p48 Jl/Ag 2017

Moose Amour J. WARBURTON *Idaho Magazine* v17 no1 p24 Ja 2017

Moose hunting

BIG GAME, SMALL BUDGETS D. McDOUGAL color *Outdoor Life* v224 no8 pH1 O 2017

YOUR Wildest DREAMS W. Brantley, B. Fenson et al color *Field & Stream* v122 no5 p38 O 2017

Moose populations

Helping moose get it on R. COUNTER color *Maclean's* v130 no4 p16 My 2017

The Mystery of Our Disappearing Moose B. Banks color *Canadian Wildlife* v23 no4 p18 S/O 2017

MooseBooties (Company)

Pitter Patter A. LAMAN *Indianapolis Monthly* v40 no4 p38 D 2016

Moosehead Lake (Me.)

Think big color *Backpacker* p20 O 2017

Moostash Joe Tours (Company)

Sandhill Crane Tour color *Nebraska Life* v20 no6 p70 N/D 2016

Moothart, Bonnie

Around the Campfire color *Trail Rider* v29 no4 p8 My 2017

Mopane tree

Cohabitating with Elephants B. HEINRICH color *Natural History* v125 no5 p16 My 2017

Mopar Performance Parts (Company)

Mopar Sacrifice R. Brutt color *Hot Rod* v70 no5 p14 My 2017

Mophie Inc.

MOPHIE WIRELESS CHARGING BASE L. YAMSHON color *Macworld - Digital Edition* v34 no11 p36 N 2017

Mor, Shira

Why Some Women Negotiate Better Than Others *Harvard Business Review Digital Articles* p2 O 8 2014

Mora, Camilo

The broad footprint of climate change from genes to biomes to people bibl chart color *Science* v354 no6313 paaf7671-1 N 11 2016

The interaction of human population, food production, and biodiversity protection color diag graph *Science* v356 no6335 p260 Ap 21 2017

Mora, M. C. Peñuela

Persistent effects of pre-Columbian plant domestication on Amazonian forest composition bibl chart graph map *Science* v355 no6328 p925 Mr 3 2017

Morabito, Kaitlyn M.

Rapid development of a DNA vaccine for Zika virus bibl graph *Science* v354 no6309 p237 O 14 2016

Moraceae

See also

Osage orange

Osage Orange *American Forests* v123 no3 p11 Fall 2017

Morais, Alécia

How fro can you go? J. Wilson color *InStyle* v24 no5 p242 My 2017

Moral courage

LEARNING Fearlessness K. Mcguire *Dance Spirit* v21 no7 p62 S 2017

Moral education—United States

The 2016 Election as a 'Sputnik' Moment for Character Education J. VALENT *Education Digest* v82 no7 p57 Mr 2017

Character Qualities in a 21st Century Curriculum C. M. RUBIN *Education Digest* v82 no5 p17 Ja 2017

Moral panics

America's New Clown Panic M. Chan color *Time* v188 no15 p9 O 17 2016

Moral relativism

DIFFERENTLY MORAL T. OLSEN cartoon *Christianity Today* p23 Ap 2017

Morale

See also

Employee morale

Crispy Duck *New Republic* v247 no12 p4 D 2016

Morales, Aaron

2 — DISHONORED 2 color *Entertainment Weekly* no1444/1445 p122 D 16 2016

3 — THE LAST GUARDIAN color diag *Entertainment Weekly* no1444/1445 p122 D 16 2016

4 — TITANFALL 2 *Entertainment Weekly* no1444/1445 p122 D 16 2016

6 — UNCHARTED 4: A THIEF'S END *Entertainment Weekly* no1444/1445 p122 D 16 2016

7 — REZ INFINITE color *Entertainment Weekly* no1444/1445 p122 D 16 2016

9 — DOOM color *Entertainment Weekly* no1444/1445 p123 D 16 2016

No. 1 INSIDE color *Entertainment Weekly* no1444/1445 p120 D 16 2016

Morales, Alex

Oh, Snap! color diag *Bloomberg Businessweek* no4519 p31 Ap 24 2017

MORALES, BONNIE

WE'RE GONNA PARTY LIKE WE'RE IN POST-SOVIET RUSSIA color *Bon Appetit* v62 no2 p64 Mr 2017

Morales, Bonnie Frumkin

Kachka: A Return to Russian Cooking color *Publishers Weekly* v264 no34 p100 Ag 21 2017

Morales, David J.

The microbial metabolite desaminotyrosine protects from influenza through type I interferon graph *Science* v357 no6350 p498 Ag 4 2017

MORALES, ED.

Puerto Rico in Crisis *Nation* v305 no9 p4 O 16 2017

Morales, Esai, 1962-

OZARK D. Snierson color *Entertainment Weekly* no1468/1469 p66 Je 2-9 2017

Morales, Narkis S.

Chile unprepared for Ph.D. influx *Science* v356 no6343 p1131 Je 16 2017

Morales, Natalie, 1972-

THE INTERSECTION color *Runner's World* v52 no2 p19 Mr 2017

Morales, Natalie, 1972----Interviews

HOST STORIES I. RATLEDGE *TV Guide* v65 no14 p28 Ap 3 2017

Morales, Nicolas

Crossing borders along an endless frontier color *Science* v356 no6339 p694 My 19 2017

Morales, Peter

Unitarian Universalist head resigns amid controversy about staff diversity A. M. Banks color *Christian Century* v134 no9 p15 Ap 26 2017

Morales Ayma, Evo, 1959-

Indigenous Empowerment in Evo Morales's Bolivia J. CRABTREE *Current History* v116 no787 p55 F 2017

Morales Torres, Cristina

The linker histone H1.0 generates epigenetic and functional intratumor heterogeneity bibl graph *Science* v353 no6307 paaf1644-1 S 30 2016

Moralioglu, Erdem

DRESS TO IMPRESS R. WALDMAN color *Vogue* v206 no12 p268 D 2016

Moran, Britt

NEW OPULENCE H. MARTIN color *Architectural Digest* v74 no1 p186 Ja 2017

Moran, Caitlin

Mad Futures A. ZEISLER *New York Times Book Review* p15 D 11 2016

MORAN, DANIEL THOMAS

THE Arts FOR HUMANISTS *Humanist* v77 no2 p24 Mr/Ap 2017

BOB DYLAN, NOBEL LAUREATE *Humanist* v77 no1 p36 Ja/F 2017

IT WAS FIFTY YEARS AGO TODAY. . *Humanist* v77 no3 p28 My/Je 2017

Leonardo Flies Home *Humanist* v77 no1 p28 Ja/F 2017

POETRY & PAINT *Humanist* v77 no5 p40 S/O 2017

Moran, Greg

BREAK THE RULES bw color *Tennis* v53 no2 p66 Mr/Ap 2017

Hold Strong *Tennis* v53 no4 p72 Jl/Ag 2017

How to Cover a Lob *Tennis* v53 no3 p72 My/Je 2017

Moran, John

Trident *Publishers Weekly* v264 no4 p50d Ja 23 2017

Moran, John V.

Intersection of diverse neuronal genomes and neuropsychiatric disease: The Brain Somatic Mosaicism Network color *Science* v356 no6336 p395 Ap 28 2017

MORAN, PORCHSEN N.

FALL HIKINGS & BIKING *Missouri Life* v43 no6 p63 O/N 2016

MORAN, ROBBIN

Sex and the Single Gametophyte: Revising the Homosporous Vascular Plant Life Cycle in Light of Contemporary Research *BioScience* v66 no11 p928 N 1 2016

Moran, Tyler

Study: Firms with More Women in the C-Suite Are More Profitable *Harvard Business Review Digital Articles* p2 F 8 2016

Morandi, Bill

Palladium-catalyzed carbon-sulfur or carbon-phosphorus bond metathesis by reversible arylation diag *Science* v356 no6342 p1059 Je 9 2017

Morash, Marian

the producers P. DICKEY color *Better Homes & Gardens* v95 no5 p136 My 2017

Moravčík, Matej

DeepStack: Expert-level artificial intelligence in heads-up no-limit poker [Cover story] chart diag *Science* v356 no6337 p508 My 5 2017

Moravcsik, Andrew

After Europe *Foreign Affairs* v96 no6 p161 N/D 2017

Architects of the Euro: Intellectuals in the Making of European Monetary Union/The Euro and the Battle of Ideas *Foreign Affairs* v95 no6 p182 N/D 2016

Europe's Ugly Future bw *Foreign Affairs* v95 no6 p139 N/D 2016

The Face of Britain: The History of the Nation Through Its Portraits *Foreign Affairs* v96 no2 p178 Mr/Ap 2017

Four Princes: Henry VIII, Francis I, Charles V, Suleiman the Magnificent, and the Obsessions That Forged Modern Europe *Foreign Affairs* v96 no3 p163 My/Je 2017

From Convergence to Crisis: Labor Markets and the Instability of the Euro *Foreign Affairs* v96 no1 p165 Ja/F 2017

The Global Chancellor: Helmut Schmidt and the Reshaping of the International Order *Foreign Affairs* v96 no1 p165 Ja/F 2017

A History of the Iraq Crisis: France, the United States, and Iraq, 1991–2003 *Foreign Affairs* v96 no3 p162 My/Je 2017

Hitler: Ascent, 1889-1939 *Foreign Affairs* v96 no2 p176 Mr/Ap 2017

Holocaust Angst: The Federal Republic of Germany and American Holocaust Memory Since the 1970s *Foreign Affairs* v96 no2 p177 Mr/Ap 2017

Karl Polanyi: A Life on the Left *Foreign Affairs* v95 no6 p180 N/D 2016

Laid Low: Inside the Crisis That Overwhelmed Europe and the IMF *Foreign Affairs* v96 no2 p177 Mr/Ap 2017

The Nordic Theory of Everything: In Search of a Better Life *Foreign Affairs* v95 no6 p181 N/D 2016

The Pursuit of Power: Europe 1815–1914 *Foreign Affairs* v96 no3 p164 My/Je 2017

Tangled Governance: International Regime Complexity, the Troika, and the Euro Crisis *Foreign Affairs* v96 no6 p160 N/D 2017

Why the UK Voted for Brexit: David Cameron's Great Miscalculation *Foreign Affairs* v96 no3 p164 My/Je 2017

Morawska, Lidia

Emergence and spread of a human-transmissible multidrug-resistant nontuberculous mycobacterium bibl diag graph *Science* v354 no6313 p751 N 11 2016

Morbid obesity—Patients

Dr. Kismet's Cure J. Queenan *Weekly Standard* v22 no23 p38 F 20 2017

Morbidelli, Alessandro

Identification of a primordial asteroid family constrains the original planetesimal population diag graph *Science* v357 no6355 p1026 S 8 2017

Morby, Kevin

66 GREAT THINGS TO DO THIS MONTH J. FOUMBERG, J. HARDBERGER et al color *Chicago* v66 no9 p139 S 2017

Mordden, Ethan

When Broadway Went to Hollywood C. RICKEY *Film Quarterly* v70 no2 p101 Wint 2016

Morduch, Jonathan

We Tracked Every Dollar 235 U.S. Households Spent for a Year, and Found Widespread Financial Vulnerability *Harvard Business Review Digital Articles* p2 Ap 12 2017

More, Karren L.

Direct atomic-level insight into the active sites of a high-performance PGM-free ORR catalyst diag graph *Science* v357 no6350 p479 Ag 4 2017

More Life (Music)

Drake's Playful World Tour R. SHEFFIELD color *Rolling Stone* no1285 p52 Ap 20 2017

New Music Containing Multitudes R. Bruner color *Time* v189 no14 p50 Ap 17 2017

What to Stream color *Entertainment Weekly* no1459 p59 Mr 31 2017

MOREAU, NICK

COPPER BRACELETS color *Popular Mechanics* p97 Mr 2017

HOW TO MAKE ANYTHING [Cover story] color diag *Popular Mechanics* p56 S 2017

Morehouse, Macon

Astronomy's unsung heroines get their due *Science News* v190 no12 p28 D 10 2016

Morel, François M. M.

The complex effects of ocean acidification on the prominent N2-fixing cyanobacterium Trichodesmium graph *Science* v356 no6337 p527 My 5 2017

Moreland, John

AMERICAN ANYONE A. PETRUSICH color *New Yorker* v93 no20 p88 Jl 10 2017

Moreland, Nancy

Old Town bw cartoon color *Old House Journal* v45 no2 p34 Ap 2017

Morell, Benedict

Serious Lawyers, Serious Results S. Stonefield img *New York* v49 no25 p19 D 12 2016

Morell, Ellen

Welcome Home *Washingtonian Magazine* v52 no1 p188 O 2016

Morell, Katie

Cures for the business travel blues color *Bloomberg Businessweek* no4522 p89 My 15 2017

Don't Wake Me Unless There's Snacks *Bloomberg Businessweek* no4504 p63 D 19 2016

Fix It Faster with Food bw cartoon *Men's Health* v32 no3 p62 Ap 2017

How Do You Handle an Office Romance? color *Bloomberg Businessweek* no4511 p62 F 13 2017

How Do You Waste Time at Work? color *Bloomberg Businessweek* no4494 p70 O 10 2016

What's Your Most Awkward Team-Building Experience? cartoon *Bloomberg Businessweek* no4518 p78 Ap 10 2017

Morell, Virginia

Mind-reading great apes color *Science* v354 no6319 p1520 D 23 2016

World's most endangered marine mammal down to 30 color graph *Science* v355 no6325 p558 F 10 2017

Morelli, Lauren

I would like to try dating women bw *Glamour* v115 no6 p98 Je 2017

Morelli Law Firm PLLC

Serious Lawyers, Serious Results S. Stonefield img *New York* v49 no25 p19 D 12 2016

Morello, C.

Observation of a large-scale anisotropy in the arrival directions of cosmic rays above 8 × 1018 eV *Science* v357 no6357 p1266 S 22 2017

Morelock, Jerry D.

Tet Turnaround color *Military History* v34 no4 p70 N 2017

Morels

Hunting for Nebraska spring treasure S. W. Kansteiner color *Nebraska Life* v21 no2 p16 Mr/Ap 2017

Unseen Fruit H. HAWORTH color *Orion Magazine* v35 no6 p7 N/D 2016

Moremi Wildlife Reserve (Botswana)

The Hunt B. HEINRICH color *Natural History* v125 no3 p12 Mr 2017

Moren, Dan

3 FEATURES: Apple's HomePod needs to hit the smartphone sweet spot color *Macworld - Digital Edition* v34 no9 p66 S 2017

AFTER 10 YEARS, WHERE DOES THE iPHONE GO NEXT? color *Macworld - Digital Edition* v34 no8 p91 Ag 2017

Apple's acquisition of Workflow could bring automation to iOS color *Macworld - Digital Edition* v34 no4 p45 My 2017

The case for a touchscreen Mac color *Macworld - Digital Edition* p130 Ap 2017

Dual-processor Fusion Mac makes sense color *Macworld - Digital Edition* p125 Ap 2017

How Apple's wearable tech could and should help your health color *Macworld - Digital Edition* v34 no8 p65 Ag 2017

How making its iWork and iLife apps free could hurt Apple and its users color *Macworld - Digital Edition* v34 no6 p17 Je 2017

The iPad's popularity is on the rise, and it's all thanks to cheaper prices color *Macworld - Digital Edition* v34 no10 p42 O 2017

The iPhone's Home button is gone: What's next to go? color *Macworld - Digital Edition* v34 no11 p56 N 2017

Is iPhone set to get facial recognition? color *Macworld - Digital Edition* p93 Ap 2017

iTunes needs to go (well, the name, anyway) color *Macworld - Digital Edition* v34 no6 p123 Je 2017

Opinion: Why Apple is smart to pursue AR color *Macworld - Digital Edition* p111 Ja 2017

Waiting on Apple's podcast recording app—or for better Garage-Band features color *Macworld - Digital Edition* v34 no9 p89 S 2017

Why the Mac needs iCloud backup color *Macworld - Digital Edition* v34 no10 p20 O 2017

Why the new Mac Pro might never come color *Macworld - Digital Edition* v34 no4 p10 My 2017

With an impressive lineup of Macs, it's time to return to the desktop color *Macworld - Digital Edition* v34 no9 p14 S 2017

Moreno, Berta

DRIVEN & DETERMINED B. Bambarger color *Downbeat* v84 no9 p54 S 2017

Moreno, Clara

A Foot In Two Worlds A. Morrison color *Downbeat* v83 no11 p27 N 2016

Moreno, Eric

The Green line *Parks & Recreation* v51 no11 p44 N 2016

Member Spotlight: Laura Bauernfeind *Parks & Recreation* v52 no8 p68 Ag 2017

Planning a Park From Concept to Reality *Parks & Recreation* v52 no3 p36 Mr 2017

Moreno, Gaby

Mara Davis *Atlanta* v56 no10 p46 F 2017

Moreno, Gean

Flotsam from the Future color *Art in America* v104 no11 p31 D 2016

From the Margins bw color *Art in America* v105 no6 p53 Je/Jl 2017

Place Markers bw color *Art in America* v105 no3 p33 Mr 2017

POSTCOMMODITY color *Art in America* p96 O 2017

Moreno, H.

Observation of coherent elastic neutrino-nucleus scattering diag *Science* v357 no6356 p1123 S 15 2017

Moreno, J. J. Lopez

Rosetta's comet 67P/Churyumov-Gerasimenko sheds its dusty mantle to reveal its icy nature bibl graph *Science* v354 no6319 p1566 D 23 2016

Moreno, Jonathan

Managing cell and human identity cartoon *Science* v356 no6334 p139 Ap 14 2017

Moreno, Pablo

Emergence and spread of a human-transmissible multidrug-resistant nontuberculous mycobacterium bibl diag graph *Science* v354 no6313 p751 N 11 2016

Moreno, Rita, 1931-

Telling a Family Story S. Wloszczyna color *AARP: The Magazine* v60 no1A p9 D 2016/Ja 2017

Moreno, Rita, 1931——Interviews

MAKING WEST SIDE STORY'S "AMERICA" J. McGovern

color *Entertainment Weekly* no1473 p46 Jl 7 2017

MORENO, SHONQUIS
The Ripple Effect: Concealing a straightforward office tower within, a curvilinear exterior commands attention, color map *Architectural Record* v205 no5 p98 My 2017

Moreno, Zerka
ZERKA MORENO B. DENIZET-LEWIS *New York Times Magazine* p32 D 25 2016

MORETTI, ANTHONY
ACADEMIA ON THE MOVE *Phi Kappa Phi Forum* v96 no4 p10 Wint 2016
A SACRED BOND il *Phi Kappa Phi Forum* v97 no1 p10 Spr 2017
SANCTUARY CONUNDRUM color *Phi Kappa Phi Forum* v97 no2 p8 Summ 2017

Moretti, David
GET THE PICTURE color *Wired* v25 no6 p8 Je 2017

Moretti, Mia, 1984-
UPDATE YOUR LOOK Guarnieri color *Harper's Bazaar* no3651 p311 Mr 2017
WOMEN ON THE GO color *Harper's Bazaar* no3651 p305 Mr 2017

Moretti, Nanni
Revolutions per Minute R. Brody color *New Yorker* v93 no33 p16 O 23 2017

Moretz, Chloë, 1997——Interviews
Chloë Grace Moretz S. Zuckerman color *InStyle* v23 no12 p200 N 2016

Morewedge, Carey K.
How a Video Game Helped People Make Better Decisions *Harvard Business Review Digital Articles* p2 O 13 2015
Why Buyers and Sellers Inherently Disagree on What Things Are Worth *Harvard Business Review Digital Articles* p2 My 13 2016

Morey, Timothy
Stop Designing for Millennials *Harvard Business Review Digital Articles* p2 Je 10 2015

Morey, Tom
TOM MOREY 1971 M. Warshaw cartoon *Surfer* v57 no12 p36 Ja/F 2017

Morfit, Cameron
HE'S THE alpha dog color *Golf Magazine* v59 no2 p58 F 2017
TEEING OFF color *Golf Magazine* v58 no11 p16 N 2016
What a Journey, Man! color *Golf Magazine* v59 no1 p21 Ja 2017

MORFORD, KATIE SULLIVAN
5 minute breakfasts *Parents* v91 no9 p150 S 2016
true colors *Parents* v92 no2 p48 F 2017

MORFORD, STACY
A River Runs Through It *USA Today Magazine* v146 no2866 p66 Jl 2017

MORGAN, ADAM
THE DREAM WEAVER bw *Chicago* v66 no10 p80 O 2017

Morgan, Angie
How the U.S. Marines Encourage Service-Based Leadership color *Harvard Business Review Digital Articles* p2 F 2 2017

MORGAN, BARBARA
Memorial Hike color *Idaho Magazine* v16 no1 p24 O 2016

Morgan, Blake
AI Can Comb Through Your Data to Create More Compelling Customer Experiences *Harvard Business Review Digital Articles* p2 Je 14 2017

MORGAN, BRET
The House That Changed Everything bw color *Yankee* p30 Mr 2017

MORGAN, BRUCE
Is There a Doctor on the Boat? *USA Today Magazine* v146 no2866 p69 Jl 2017

Morgan, C. E., 1976-
The Sport of Kings: A Novel W. Bassett *Christian Century* v134 no7 p41 Mr 29 2017

Morgan, Candice
What We Learned from Improving Diversity Rates at Pinterest *Harvard Business Review Digital Articles* p2 Jl 11 2017

Morgan, Candice——Interviews
A More Colorful Picture color *Black Enterprise* v47 no2 p25 S 2016

MORGAN, CHRIS R.

Can Twin Peaks Make a Comeback? bw *American Conservative* v16 no3 p52 My/Je 2017

Morgan, Clay
ADVICE FOR NOOBS color *Black Belt* v55 no2 p33 F/Mr 2017

Morgan, David J.
Identification of single-site gold catalysis in acetylene hydrochlorination bw diag graph *Science* v355 no6332 p1399 Mr 31 2017

Morgan, Greg
Rescue Mission A. OPAR *Audubon* v118 no6 p32 Wint 2016

Morgan, Iwan
Bold Enough to Compromise *History Today* v66 no12 p72 D 2016
Reagan's Most Convincing Role A. Brown *History Today* v67 no2 p63 F 2017

Morgan, Jacob
How Senior Executives Stay Passionate About Their Work *Harvard Business Review Digital Articles* p2 2017

Morgan, Jason
The Pro-Life Movement in Japan *Society* v54 no3 p238 Je 2017

Morgan, Jeffrey Dean
The Walking Dead A. Bacle, D. Coggan et al color *Entertainment Weekly* no1482/1483 p38 S 22 2017
The Walking Dead's Brutal Return E. Lewis *TV Guide* v64 no46 p11 N 7 2016

Morgan, Joanna V.
The formation of peak rings in large impact craters bibl color graph *Science* v354 no6314 p878 N 18 2016

MORGAN, JOHN
WOMEN IN SCIENCE *Scientific American* v316 no4 p6 Ap 2017

Morgan, John A.
Emission of volatile organic compounds from petunia flowers is facilitated by an ABC transporter diag *Science* v356 no6345 p1386 Je 30 2017

Morgan, Joseph
The Originals I. Rudolph *TV Guide* v65 no25 p38 Je 2017

Morgan, Kathryn
letter to my teenage self color *Dance Spirit* v21 no2 p24 F 2017

Morgan, Laura
Lauren's Confessions color *Parents* v92 no7 p36 Jl 2017
TV Moms Breaking the Mold *Parents* v91 no10 p22 O 2016

Morgan, Louisa
A Secret History of Witches *Publishers Weekly* v264 no31 p61 Jl 31 2017

MORGAN, M. GRANGER
Rethinking the Social Cost of Carbon Dioxide: The standard benefit-cost methodology that is used to calculate marginal costs of environmental regulations should not be used for long-lasting greenhouse gases *Issues in Science & Technology* v33 no4 p43 Summ 2017

MORGAN, NEIL
EXECUTIVE SUMMARIES bw color *Harvard Business Review* v95 no4 p146 Jl/Ag 2017
THE POWER PARTNERSHIP: CMO & CIO *Harvard Business Review* v95 no4 p55 Jl/Ag 2017
WHY CMOs NEVER LAST AND WHAT TO DO ABOUT IT chart color graph img *Harvard Business Review* v95 no4 p46 Jl/Ag 2017

Morgan, Nick
Understand the 4 Components of Influence *Harvard Business Review Digital Articles* p2 My 19 2015

Morgan, Peter, 1963-
A Great Family Business J. Freedland color *New York Review of Books* v64 no5 p16 Mr 23 2017

MORGAN, RICHARD
The Urbanist: The Teens of Havana img *New York* v49 no21 p30 O 17 2016

MORGAN, TIMOTHY C.
Aren't Anglicans Protestant? *Christianity Today* p19 Mr 2017
BLESSED ARE THE LAWYERS color *Christianity Today* v61 no5 p54 Je 2017

Morgan, Tracy, 1968-
FIRST LOOK: FIST FIGHT N. PARKER and L. CROSS color *Ebony* v72 no4 p40 F 2017
Tracy Morgan What's your favorite restaurant in the world? S. Z. WEXLER cartoon color *Bon Appetit* v62 no2 p104 Mr 2017

Morgan, Tracy, 1968——Interviews
Tracy Morgan Z. BARON color *GQ: Gentlemen's Quarterly* v97

Fossils push back origin of humans B. BOWER color *Science News* v191 no13 p6 Jl 8 2017

Morocco—Description & travel

MARRAKECH Moderne N. Hass color *Conde Nast Traveler* v52 no8 p102 S 2017

NORTHERN MOROCCO Y. EDWARDS and A. WHITTLE color map *Conde Nast Traveler* v52 no4 p64 Ap 2017

Morocco—Politics & government—1999-

Moroccan Rules U. LINDSEY color *Nation* v303 no22 p20 N 28 2016

Morocco—Social conditions—21st century

Moroccans protest after monarchy, Muslim party fail to deliver on reform T. Luck *Christian Century* v134 no1 p16 Ja 4 2017

MORONE, JAMES A.

SCARFACE *New York Times Book Review* p36 D 4 2016

Moroney, Bill

Bill Moroney Sets Sail for New Challenges N. Jaffer *In Stride* v11 no6 p50 N 2016

Thank You for the Honor *In Stride* v11 no6 p8 N 2016

Moroz, L.

Seasonal exposure of carbon dioxide ice on the nucleus of comet 67P/Churyumov-Gerasimenko bibl bw graph *Science* v354 no6319 p1563 D 23 2016

Morozov, Alexander

From chaos to order in active fluids bibl color *Science* v355 no6331 p1262 Mr 24 2017

Morozov, S. V.

High-temperature quantum oscillations caused by recurring Bloch states in graphene superlattices color *Science* v357 no6347 p181 Jl 14 2017

Morphology (Grammar)

SO MANY WORDS, SO LITTLE TIME: How morphological awareness can help young learners with their vocabulary comprehension S. L. Hall *Literacy Today (2411-7862)* v35 no1 p26 Jl/Ag 2017

Morrill, Dustin

DeepStack: Expert-level artificial intelligence in heads-up no-limit poker [Cover story] chart diag *Science* v356 no6337 p508 My 5 2017

Morrill, Hannah

the new girl color *InStyle* v24 no2 p146 F 2017

Morris, Adele

Reforming the U.S. coal leasing program color graph *Science* v354 no6316 p1096 D 2 2016

Morris, Alex

"Always be grateful" [Cover story] color *Glamour* v115 no3 p192 Mr 2017

The Awakening of Evan Rachel Wood color *Rolling Stone* no1275 p46 D 1 2016

Even Our Protesters Are Precocious img *New York* v49 no25 p46 D 12 2016

Hot Actress Haley Bennett color *Rolling Stone* no1274 p40 N 17 2016

Laid Bare img *New York* v50 no17 p94 Ag 21 2017

LORDE'S GROWING PAINS bw color *Rolling Stone* no1288 p32 Je 1 2017

The Pill Freaks of Silicon Valley img *New York* v49 no21 p56 O 17 2016

The Queen of Dragons Tells All color *Rolling Stone* no1291/1292 p46 Jl 13 2017

Saturday Night Live's Weirdo in Chief color *Rolling Stone* no1272 p26 O 20 2016

THIS PICTURE IS PERFECT. BLAKE LIVELY IS NOT color *Glamour* v115 no9 p188 S 2017

Trump and the Pathology of Narcissism color *Rolling Stone* no1285 p42 Ap 20 2017

The Wonder of Gal Gadot [Cover story] color *Rolling Stone* no1295 p36 S 7 2017

Zendaya color *Glamour* v114 no12 p216 D 2016

Morris, Annie

ACTIVATE YOUR HORSE'S MOTOR color *Dressage Today* v23 no7 p22 Mr 2017

Basic Horse Behavior for Dressage Success color *Dressage Today* v24 no1 p24 O 2017

Develop Your Feel and Find Harmony color *Dressage Today* v23 no10 p26 Jl 2017

Finding the Ideal Free Walk color *Dressage Today* v23 no12 p28 S 2017

A GUIDE TO ACCURACY AND BALANCE color diag *Dressage Today* v23 no5 p24 Ja 2017

Improve Body Awareness for a Better Seat color *Dressage Today* v23 no8 p24 Ap 2017

LET THE LEG YIELD WORK FOR YOU color *Dressage Today* v23 no6 p22 F 2017

LIPICA: The Original Home of the LIPIZZANER color *Dressage Today* v23 no11 p44 Ag 2017

Monte Velho: AN EQUESTRIAN PARADISE color *Dressage Today* v23 no11 p36 Ag 2017

Organize, Plan and Structure Your Ride color *Dressage Today* p30 My 2017

The Secret to Free, Forward Collection color *Dressage Today* v23 no9 p24 Je 2017

To ride the walk in balance by being grounded to the earth and in harmony with the movement of your horse's barrel... color *Dressage Today* v23 no12 p72 S 2017

Tune Your Riding Position to Put Your Horse into "Drive" [Cover story] color diag *Dressage Today* v24 no2 p26 N 2017

Uncover the Mystery of "On the Bit" color diag *Dressage Today* v23 no11 p24 Ag 2017

Morris, Carolyn

AN IDEAL SETTING: JEWELRY ARTIST CAROLYN MORRIS BACH TRANSFORMS AN OVERGROWN 18TH-CENTURY CAPE INTO A POLISHED WORK-AND-LIVING SPACE A. GRAVES *Yankee* v81 no5 p32 S/O 2017

Morris, Catherine Avril

Marry Me Twice: Rose Quartz, Book 1 *Publishers Weekly* v264 no9 p66e F 27 2017

Morris, Charles R.

Backlash [Cover story] *Commonweal* v144 no1 p6 Ja 6 2017

The 'Informed Consumer' & Other Myths *Commonweal* v144 no13 p6 Ag 11 2017

Misdirected Investment color *Commonweal* v143 no18 p6 N 11 2016

Republican Heaven cartoon *Commonweal* v144 no9 p6 My 19 2017

Top Heavy chart *Commonweal* v144 no5 p6 Mr 10 2017

What Econ 101 gets wrong color *America* v216 no7 p47 Ap 3 2017

When Europe Sneezed: A new history of the Depression looks beyond Wall Street to the global roots of the crisis S. MIHM bw *New York Times Book Review* p14 Ap 23 2017

Morris, Chris

COLLEGES RECRUIT A NEW KIND OF ATHLETE: VIDEO GAMERS color *Fortune* v176 no5 p23 O 1 2017

The Rise of the Room-Service Robots color *Fortune* v175 no7 p16 Je 1 2017

UBISOFT'S CEO ISN'T PLAYING GAMES color *Fortune* v176 no3 p21 S 1 2017

Morris, David Z.

Nintendo Bets Big on the Switch color *Fortune* v175 no3 p18 Mr 1 2017

MORRIS, EDMUND

History's FIRST DRAFT color *Vanity Fair* v59 no10 p158 O 2017

MORRIS, ERROL

Who's Asking? color *Film Comment* v53 no3 p14 My/Je 2017

Morris, George

Celebrating Four Decades of Fame N. Jaffer *In Stride* v12 no2 p53 Mr 2017

Morris, George H.

Acceptable, Not Acceptable or Preferable color *Practical Horseman* v45 no11 p10 N 2017

Clean is What Horse-Keeping is All About color *Practical Horseman* v45 no9 p14 S 2017

Close the Legs to Go Forward color *Practical Horseman* v44 no12 p10 D 2016

Four Good Legs, Two Faulty Releases color *Practical Horseman* v45 no8 p10 Ag 2017

Four Riders with Good Legs color *Practical Horseman* v45 no7 p8 Jl 2017

Invite Your Horse to Be Round color *Practical Horseman* v45 no10 p12 O 2017

Judging Rider Angles color *Practical Horseman* v45 no6 p14 Je

2017

Three Good Seats, One Jumping Ahead color *Practical Horseman* v45 no1 p10 Ja 2017

Three Solid Leg Positions color *Practical Horseman* v45 no3 p10 Mr 2017

Two Good Legs; Two That Have Slipped Back color *Practical Horseman* v45 no2 p10 F 2017

'What the Horse Takes, the Rider Gives' color *Practical Horseman* v45 no4 p12 Ap 2017

Which Rider Is Not Jumping Ahead? color *Practical Horseman* v45 no5 p14 My 2017

Morris, Gillian

Traveling the World Made Me a Better Entrepreneur *Harvard Business Review Digital Articles* p2 My 26 2015

Morris, Ian

A Brief History of Britain's Relationship with Europe, Starting in 6000 BCE *Harvard Business Review Digital Articles* p2 Je 24 2016

Morris, James McGrath

The Ambulance Drivers: Hemingway, Dos Passos, and a Friendship Made and Lost in War *Publishers Weekly* v264 no5 p189 Ja 30 2017

MORRIS, JAN

The Raj Duet: An account of Queen Victoria's late-life bond with an Indian Muslim *New York Times Book Review* p26 O 8 2017

Morris, Jay Hunter

The Redneck Tenor M. HARDY *Texas Monthly* v44 no11 p82 N 2016

Morris, Jeannine

Jennifer Lopez color *InStyle* v24 no6 p94 Je 2017

Morris, Jennalyn

How I Solved My Horse's Problem cartoon *Horse & Rider* v56 no1 p72 Ja 2017

MORRIS, JEREMY

Working-Class Resilience in Russia *Current History* v115 no783 p264 O 2016

Morris, Joe

Mary Halvorson D. OUELLETTE color *Downbeat* v84 no7 p90 Jl 2017

Morris, John

THE FAST AND THE FILTHY RICH J. DEAN color *Bloomberg Businessweek* no4510 p55 F 6 2017

Nature's Bounty S. SCHAEFER color *Forbes* v199 no2 p34 F 28 2017

Morris, Julie

Permeable savior *Christian Century* v134 no2 p12 Ja 18 2017

MORRIS, LACY

In Colombia, You'll Get Beach and Then Some color *Conde Nast Traveler* v52 no1 p51 Ja 2017

Morris, Liz

Keeping Work Flexible, Even with Changes to U.S. Overtime Rules *Harvard Business Review Digital Articles* p2 F 12 2016

Pregnant Workers Have Rights, No Matter What the Supreme Court Says About UPS *Harvard Business Review Digital Articles* p2 D 18 2014

What Young vs. UPS Means for Pregnant Workers and Their Bosses *Harvard Business Review Digital Articles* p2 Mr 26 2015

Morris, Marc

The Conqueror Reassessed *History Today* v66 no10 p43 O 2016

Morris, Maren, 1990——Interviews

Maren Morris D. BROWNE color *Rolling Stone* no1280 p20 F 9 2017

Morris, Mark—Interviews

10 MINUTES WITH . . . Mark Morris Z. WHITTENBURG *Dance Magazine* v90 no12 p30 D 2016

Morris, Melvin

50 Reasons to Love Being 50+ color *AARP: The Magazine* v30 no6A p63 O/N 2017

Morris, Nate

Trash Tech A. KONRAD and M. COHEN color *Forbes* v199 no1 p46 Ja 24 2017

Morris, Nathaniel P.

Keep Hospitals Weapons-Free color *Scientific American* v316 no1 p8 Ja 2017

Morris, Richard G. M.

Social memory goes viral bibl diag *Science* v353 no6307 p1496 S 30 2016

Morris, Sarah—Interviews

Sarah MORRIS P. PARRENO *Interview* v47 no2 p78 Mr 2017

Morris, Stephen

Diamonds Aren't A Bank's Best Friend color *Bloomberg Businessweek* no4537 p26 S 11 2017

The Fog Lifts color *Bloomberg Businessweek* no4525 p48 Je 5 2017

Morris, Tony

A Simple Observing Stool, Plus: Build the Swiss Army Knife of observing stools J. Oltion *Sky & Telescope* v134 no3 p70 S 2017

Morris, Wesley

16 ACTORS color *New York Times Magazine* p52 D 11 2016

ALISA BELLETTINI *New York Times Magazine* p52 D 25 2016

Arm's Length *New York Times Magazine* p11 Ja 22 2017

Guilt Free *New York Times Magazine* p11 Jl 30 2017

L. A. NOIR bw *New York Times Magazine* p64 D 11 2016

LAST TABOO *New York Times Magazine* p48 O 30 2016

The Others *New York Times Magazine* p15 N 20 2016

'Send My Love (to Your New Lover)' color *New York Times Magazine* p18 Mr 12 2017

Voices in My Head: I listened to only female singers all summer. Here's What I learned *New York Times Magazine* p27 O 8 2017

Morris, William, 1834-1896

AT HOME WITH MORRIS: PATTERNS NEVER OUT OF STYLE bw color *Old House Journal* v45 no6 p22 S 2017

furniture & art color *Arts & Crafts Homes & the Revival* v12 no1 p22 2017 Resouce Guide

Morris Brown College

SAVING MORRIS BROWN T. WHEATLEY *Atlanta* v56 no12 p92 Ap 2017

Morrisey, Will

Dominique Schnapper: The Democratic Spirit of Law *Society* v53 no6 p672 D 2016

James L. Nolan, Jr.: What they Saw in America: Alexis de Tocqueville, Max Weber, G. K. Chesterton, and Sayyid Qutb *Society* v54 no2 p204 Ap 2017

Statesmanship and Geopolitics J. Muller *Society* v54 no2 p188 Ap 2017

Waller R. Newell: Tyrants: A History of Power, Injustice, and Terror *Society* v54 no4 p383 Ag 2017

Morrison, Alix

A Passion for Horses and Horsemanship Lead Alix Morrison to Gold L. Taylor *In Stride* v12 no1 p26 Ja 2017

Morrison, Allen

All The Dreams/Dream In The Blue color *Downbeat* v83 no11 p60 N 2016

Anat Cohen color *Downbeat* v84 no7 p38 Jl 2017

The Beautiful Sound bw *Downbeat* v84 no7 p59 Jl 2017

BECCA STEVENS: Regal Strength color *Downbeat* v84 no8 p52 Ag 2017

Eliane Elias Returns to Samba color *Downbeat* v84 no6 p18 Je 2017

A Foot In Two Worlds color *Downbeat* v83 no11 p27 N 2016

JON BATISTE: 'Reservoir of Positivity' [Cover story] color *Downbeat* v84 no4 p28 Ap 2017

MARIA SCHNEIDER ATTACKING THE 'DATA LORDS' [Cover story] color *Downbeat* v83 no12 p26 D 2016

Memorable Melodies color *Downbeat* v84 no6 p30 Je 2017

Revisiting Sinatra's Bossa Gems color *Downbeat* v84 no9 p13 S 2017

Singer-Songwriters Follow Their Muses color *Downbeat* v84 no5 p60 My 2017

Morrison, Bill, 1965-

Dawson City: Frozen Time *New Yorker* v93 no18 p13 Je 26 2017

Morrison, Curt

Framus Mayfield Pro 16-3106 color *Downbeat* v84 no7 p82 Jl 2017

Santa Cruz Guitar Co. FS Model color *Downbeat* v84 no7 p80 Jl 2017

Morrison, Dianne

SURPRISE *Christian Century* v134 no12 p22 Je 7 2017

Morrison, Ernestine

SECOND ACT C. JAY color *Louisiana Life* v37 no3 p18 Ja/F 2017

Morrison, James
   JAMES MORRISON THE ADVENTURER M. Jackson color *Downbeat* v84 no10 p176 O 2017

Morrison, Jennifer, 1979-
   Once Upon a Time M. Logan *TV Guide* v65 no19 p36 My 1 2017

MORRISON, JOHN C.
   Conserving the World's Megafauna and Biodiversity: The Fierce Urgency of Now *BioScience* v67 no3 p197 Mr 2017
   Saving the World's Terrestrial Megafauna color *BioScience* v66 no10 p807 O 1 2016

Morrison, Judith
   Putting paraeducators on the path to teacher certification color *Phi Delta Kappan* v98 no8 p43 My 2017

Morrison, Keith—Interviews
   DATELINE DATE NIGHT color *Entertainment Weekly* no1457/1458 p56 Mr 17 2017

Morrison, Rosanna Mentzer
   Increased Consumer Sensitivity to Food Safety Raised Financial Costs of Ground Beef Recalls *Amber Waves: The Economics of Food, Farming, Natural Resources, & Rural America* p1 O 2016

Morrison, Sigourney—Interviews
   IN STITCHES J. ROEDEL color *Louisiana Life* v37 no2 p16 N/D 2016

Morrison, Simon
   Russia's dance of history P. SHAWN TAYLOR color *Maclean's* v129 no43 p60 O 31 2016

Morrison, Susan
   Sweet Dreams Are Made of This M. GOLDBERG color *O, The Oprah Magazine* p30 D 2016

Morrison, Toni, 1931-
   1927: Harlem T. Morrison *Lapham's Quarterly* v10 no1 p124 Wint 2017
   AFTERMATH bw cartoon *New Yorker* v92 no38 p48 N 21 2016
   HOW TO TURN THE PAGE color *Entertainment Weekly* no1446/1447 p120 D 2016/Ja 2017
   Long Divisions N. IRVIN PAINTER bw color il *New Republic* v248 no11 p44 N 2017
   The Origin of Others color *Publishers Weekly* v264 no29 p211 Jl 17 2017
   THE WORK YOU DO, THE PERSON YOU ARE cartoon *New Yorker* v93 no16 p66 Je 5 2017

Morrison, Toni, 1931-—Political & social views
   Portrait of the Author as a Historian A. Lee *History Today* v67 no2 p54 F 2017

Morrison, William
   OUTWARD BOUND J. CROWN cartoon graph *Chicago* v66 no2 p13 F 2017

Morriss, Anne—Interviews
   Yes, Your Uber Driver Is Judging You S. G. Carmichael *Harvard Business Review Digital Articles* p2 F 20 2015

Morrissey, Mark D.
   Engrams and circuits crucial for systems consolidation of a memory diag *Science* v356 no6333 p73 Ap 7 2017

Morrissey, Michael B.
   Precipitation drives global variation in natural selection bibl chart diag map *Science* v355 no6328 p959 Mr 3 2017

Morrone, Anthony
   RAISING BOYS WHO'LL NEVER GROW UP color *Men's Health* v32 no5 p114 Je 2017

Morrow, Alex
   no-fly zone [Cover story] R. Feltman color *Popular Science* v289 no6 p76 N/D 2017

Morrow, Ann
   Portraying and Parodying Patroons bw *American History* v52 no3 p54 Ag 2017
   What's in a Name? bw color *American History* v52 no3 p48 Ag 2017

Morrow, Bradford
   The Prague Sonata color *Publishers Weekly* v264 no32 p46 Ag 7 2017

Morrow, John Andrew
   Interfaith Understanding *Islamic Horizons* v45 no6 p21 N/D 2016

Morrow, Joshua—Interviews
   THE YOUNG AND THE RESTLESS M. LOGAN *TV Guide* v65 no14 p44 Ap 3 2017

Morrow, Julie
   DIFFERENTIATED AND MEANINGFUL INSTRUCTION: Turning around districtwide performance by immersing students in an engaging, literacy-rich environment *Literacy Today (2411-7862)* v35 no1 p18 Jl/Ag 2017

Morrow, Leon
   POWER [Cover story] color *Christian Century* v134 no1 p22 Ja 4 2017

MORROW, SARA
   FALL INTO PLACE *Martha Stewart Living* no269 p27 N 2016
   HOLIDAY UP YOUR HOME *Martha Stewart Living* no270 p56 D 2016
   PERSONAL EFFECTS color *Martha Stewart Living* no271 p96 Ja/F 2017
   ROOMS FOR IMPROVEMENT *Martha Stewart Living* no267 p100 S 2016

Morrow, Selma
   DIY Delicious [Cover story] color *Vegetarian Times* v43 no2 p45 N/D 2016

Morrow, Shauna
   Social status alters immune regulation and response to infection in macaques bibl graph *Science* v354 no6315 p1041 N 25 2016

Morrow, Susan Brind
   THE TURNING SKY *Lapham's Quarterly* v10 no2 p199 Spr 2017

MORROW, SYLVIA
   20 Things You Didn't Know About … Color color *Discover* v38 no9 p74 N 2017
   FANCY FOOTWORK color *Discover* v38 no9 p9 N 2017

Mors, Marie Louise
   What Board Directors Really Think of Gender Quotas *Harvard Business Review Digital Articles* p2 N 14 2016

Morsch, Gary
   Encounters with a saint D. Nelson *Christian Century* v133 no24 p10 N 23 2016

Morse, Gardiner
   When Customers Will (Willingly) Pay More for Less *Harvard Business Review Digital Articles* p2 F 24 2015

Morse, Jim
   PACIFIC NORTHWEST EMPIRE color *Model Railroader* v84 no6 p28 Je 2017

Morse, Lynn
   Q: What was the most important letter in history? color *Atlantic* v320 no2 p104 S 2017

Morse, Neal
   The Neal Morse Band Progresses Into the Realization of a Fine Sonic Dream M. METTLER and C. Crowley color *Sound & Vision* v82 no5 p24 Je 2017

Morson, Gary Saul
   Herzen: The Hero of Skeptical Idealism bw *New York Review of Books* v63 no18 p45 N 24 2016
   Will We Ever Pin Down Pushkin? bw color *New York Review of Books* v64 no5 p43 Mr 23 2017

MORSON, JENN
   Whom Do We Trust? color *Reader's Digest* v189 no1131 p36 Je 2017

MORT, TERRY
   THE HEMINGWAY PATROLS: THE ENEMY IN THE MACHINE bw *Power & Motoryacht* v33 no2 p110 F 2017

Mortada, Dalia
   fulCan Stories About Food Upend Familiar Narratives of War? K. SURANA bw *Foreign Policy* no225 p16 Jl/Ag 2017
   WHAT IS THE RECIPE FOR HOME? color *Nation* v305 no11 p24 O 30 2017

Mortal sin
   What is sin? K. Considine *U.S. Catholic* v82 no7 p49 Jl 2017

Mortali, Micah
   Q: What do you consistently do to boost happiness? color *Yoga Journal* no296 p12 N 2017

Mortality
   See also
     Child mortality
     Women's mortality
   Death March of 1918 G. CHOWELL, L. SIMONSEN et al bw color *Natural History* v125 no9 p11 S 2017
   SOW PROLAPSE SYNDROME: AN INCREASE IN THIS

MYSTERIOUS PROBLEM HAS THE INDUSTRY SEARCHING FOR ANSWERS B. Freese *Successful Farming* v115 no6 p40 Ap 2017

White Americans' Mortality Rates Are Rising. Something Similar Happened in Russia from 1965 to 2005 D. A. Squires and D. Blumenthal *Harvard Business Review Digital Articles* p2 Je 26 2017

Mortality—Computer network resources

Online Tool Shows City-by-City Health Impacts *USA Today Magazine* v145 no2861 p6 F 2017

Mortality—Prevention

Drink Coffee, Live Longer? Growing evidence suggests enjoying a daily cup (or more) of this popular beverage may help decrease risk of an early death *Tufts University Health & Nutrition Letter* v35 no8 p6 O 2017

Mortality—Risk factors

Longevity Dietary Pattern: Fruits, Vegetables, Fish *Tufts University Health & Nutrition Letter* v34 no9 p7 N 2016

Making sense of numbers *Mayo Clinic Health Letter* v35 no2 p4 F 2017

New Evidence for the Benefits of Whole Grains *Tufts University Health & Nutrition Letter* v34 no9 p4 N 2016

Mortality—Statistics

The Opioid Crisis D. W. MURRAY, B. BLAKE et al color graph *Weekly Standard* v22 no9 p19 N 7 2016

Mortality—United States

Diet Causing 300,000 + Annual Cardiovascular & Diabetes Deaths [Cover story] *Tufts University Health & Nutrition Letter* v35 no5 p1 Jl 2017

Lost in Storyland M. Phillips color *Commonweal* v143 no17 p23 O 21 2016

Mortazavi, Ali

Regeneration of fat cells from myofibroblasts during wound healing bibl color graph *Science* v355 no6326 p748 F 17 2017

MORTENSEN, DAVID A.

Agriculture in 2050: Recalibrating Targets for Sustainable Intensification *BioScience* v67 no4 p386 Ap 2017

Mortensen, Mark

Collaborating Well in Large Global Teams *Harvard Business Review Digital Articles* p2 Jl 1 2015

A First-Time Manager's Guide to Leading Virtual Teams *Harvard Business Review Digital Articles* p2 S 25 2015

THE OVERCOMMITTED ORGANIZATION: WHY IT'S HARD TO SHARE PEOPLE ACROSS MULTIPLE TEAMS—AND WHAT TO DO ABOUT IT [Cover story] chart graph il img *Harvard Business Review* v95 no5 p58 S/O 2017

Technology Alone Won't Solve Our Collaboration Problems *Harvard Business Review Digital Articles* p2 Mr 26 2015

When You Have to Coach Remotely *Harvard Business Review Digital Articles* p2 Ap 20 2015

Mortgage banks—Corrupt practices

BANKING ON THE BUBBLE J. CASTALDO color *Maclean's* p44 Je 2017

Mortgage loans

After a Few Do-Overs, Success J. B. CLARK color *Kiplinger's Personal Finance* v71 no2 p72 F 2017

Deutsche Bank Is in a Bind Over Trump Debt G. Farrell and C. Melby color *Bloomberg Businessweek* no4517 p39 Ap 3 2017

JPMorgan Traders Get Into Property Deals S. Mulholland and H. Son *Bloomberg Businessweek* no4504 p35 D 19 2016

MORTGAGE HELP FOR DEBT-SADDLED GRADS P. MERTZ ESSWEIN color graph *Kiplinger's Personal Finance* v71 no8 p15 Ag 2017

Thriving After an Early Retirement K. LANKFORD color *Kiplinger's Personal Finance* v71 no7 p72 Jl 2017

Mortgage loans—Refinancing

Pull Down the Best Rate B. Braverman chart color *Money* v46 no3 p21 Ap 2017

Mortgage loans—United States

MORTGAGE OUTLOOK: MOSTLY GOOD NEWS P. M. ESSWEIN color *Kiplinger's Personal Finance* v71 no1 p14 Ja 2017

Mortgage rates

Home Prices Keep Climbing P. M. ESSWEIN cartoon chart *Kiplinger's Personal Finance* v71 no4 p40 Ap 2017

Mortgages

ASK THE EXPERT K. Close, S. Max et al diag *Money* v45 no10 p31 N 2016

THE BIG SHORT color *Alternatives Journal (AJ) - Canada's Environmental Voice* v42 no2 p18 2016

Our Mortgaged Future A. WALKS color graph *Alternatives Journal (AJ) - Canada's Environmental Voice* v42 no2 p22 2016

Pull Down the Best Rate B. Braverman chart color *Money* v46 no3 p21 Ap 2017

Mortgages—Canada

TOUGH LOVE REQUIRED J. CASTALDO color *Maclean's* v130 no10 p46 N 2017

Mortgages—United States

Time to Fix Fannie and Freddie I. BRANNON color *Weekly Standard* v22 no30 p18 Ap 10 2017

MORTICE, ZACH

MCA Renovation Aims to Bring Chicago into the Museum color *Architectural Record* v205 no3 p21 Mr 2017

Mortier, Frédéric

Positive biodiversity-productivity relationship predominant in global forests bibl chart graph map *Science* v354 no6309 paaf8957-1 O 14 2016

Mortimer, Ian

BACK IN TIME TO AN ICE AGE AND A GREAT FIRE W. Gibson *History Today* v67 no8 p98 Ag 2017

Mortimer, Jeylan

How Unemployment Affects Twentysomethings' Self-Worth *Harvard Business Review Digital Articles* p2 D 22 2016

Morton, Burke

Dubble Bath *Cincinnati Magazine* v50 no3 p136 D 2016

Cru Cut *Cincinnati Magazine* v50 no12 p104 S 2017

Morton, D. C.

A human-driven decline in global burned area chart graph map *Science* v356 no6345 p1356 Je 30 2017

Morton, Donna Gentry

Seeking the Shore *Publishers Weekly* v264 no33 p58 Ag 14 2017

Morton, Mandy

Cat Among the Pumpkins: A Hettie Bagshot Mystery *Publishers Weekly* v264 no33 p52 Ag 14 2017

Morton, Mary

DAN ABOUT TOWN: Party photographer Dan Swartz's monthly roundup of bashes, balls, and benefits *Washingtonian Magazine* v52 no12 p26 S 2017

Morton, Zander

CONFIRMATION color *Surfing Magazine* v53 no2 p18 F 2017

Don't Call It "Alternative" color *Surfer* v58 no3 p32 Je 2017

The Featherweight Future color *Surfer* v58 no4 p40 Ag 2017

Gut Check color *Surfer* v58 no5 p28 S 2017

KAI LENNY color *Surfer* v58 no3 p40 Je 2017

LAGUNDRI BAY NIAS, INDONESIA color *Surfer* v58 no4 p56 Ag 2017

MASON HO color *Surfer* v58 no3 p38 Je 2017

NEW PIER DURBAN, SOUTH AFRICA color *Surfer* v58 no4 p60 Ag 2017

On the Nose color *Surfer* v58 no5 p44 S 2017

THE PATH OF MOST RESISTANCE color *Surfing Magazine* v53 no2 p10 F 2017

Rizal Tanjung, 42 color *Surfer* v58 no4 p36 Ag 2017

SEBASTIAN INLET FLORIDA, UNITED STATES OF AMERICA color *Surfer* v58 no4 p62 Ag 2017

SKELETON BAY NAMIBIA color *Surfer* v58 no4 p58 Ag 2017

UNNAMED SLAB NORTHERN ITALY color *Surfer* v58 no4 p64 Ag 2017

YOUTH-FUL EXUBERANCE color *Surfing Magazine* v53 no1 p12 Ja 2017

MORTON-KEITHLEY, LINDA

This Good Old Building: A Place Full of History *Idaho Magazine* v16 no12 p25 S 2017

Mörtsell, E.

iPTF16geu: A multiply imaged, gravitationally lensed type Ia supernova color diag graph *Science* v356 no6335 p291 Ap 21 2017

Morus, Iwan Rhys

Images help tell story of science T. Siegfried color *Science News* v192 no1 p26 Ag 5 2017

Mosaddeq, Mohammad, 1880-1967

The Myths of 1953 R. TAKEYH bw *Weekly Standard* v22 no43 p21 Jl 24 2017

Mosaics (Art)
A Mosaic Tile Floor M. E. Polson color *Arts & Crafts Homes & the Revival* v12 no2 p34 Spr 2017
People Watching S. COCHRAN color *Architectural Digest* v74 no3 p146 Mr 2017
wall & floor tiles *Design Center Sourcebook* p36 2017

Mosaics (Art)—Evaluation
MOSAIC PATTERNS for Serviceable Floors B. D. COLEMAN color *Arts & Crafts Homes & the Revival* v12 no2 p29 Spr 2017

Mosaics (Art)—History
And They're Off! J. A. LOBELL color *Archaeology* v69 no6 p20 N/D 2016

Mosby, Marilyn J., 1980-
IN THE MIDST OF A NATIONAL CRISIS OF POLICE VIOLENCE, SHE GAMBLED THAT PROSECUTING SIX OFFICERS WOULD HELP HEAL HER CITY. SHE LOST MUCH MORE THAN JUST THE CASE W. S. Hylton *New York Times Magazine* p42 O 2 2016

Mosca, August
POETRY & PAINT D. T. MORAN *Humanist* v77 no5 p40 S/O 2017

MOSCATELLO, CAITLIN
MARIJUANA MOMS [Cover story] color *Working Mother* v40 no3 p20 Ag/S 2017

Moschella, Mary Clark
Caring for Joy: Narrative, Theology and Practice A. B. Robinson *Christian Century* v134 no14 p39 Jl 5 2017

Moschella, Melissa
TEACH YOUR CHILDREN WELL J. R. Stoner Jr. *Claremont Review of Books* v17 no2 p91 Spr 2017

Moscovitch, Philip
RUN, JUMP, EXPLORE color *American Craft* v77 no3 p48 Je/Jl 2017

Moscow (Russia)
THE EMBARGO DIET N. Sneider color *Atlantic* v319 no5 p18 Je 2017

Moscow (Russia)—Description & travel
FROM RUSSIA WITH LOVE C. TATTOLI color *Conde Nast Traveler* v52 no2 p26 F 2017

Moscow (Russia)—Politics & government
FROM RUSSIA WITH LATTES V. Stivers, H. Meyer et al color *Bloomberg Businessweek* no4534 p42 Ag 14 2017

Mos Def (Performer), 1973-
NIGHT LIFE cartoon *New Yorker* v92 no42 p18 D 19 2016

Moseley, Annabelle
The Peacock Pin *America* v217 no6 p51 S 18 2017

Moseley, Gina E.
Response to Comments on "Reconciliation of the Devils Hole climate record with orbital forcing" bibl chart graph *Science* v354 no6310 p296-e O 21 2016

Moseley, Jane
WHOLLY MOSELEY D. BLASBERG color *Vanity Fair* v58 no12 p160 D 2016

Mosely, Rachel
The Fab Four color *Seventeen* v76 no5 p80 S 2017
Things to Do! color *Seventeen* v76 no4 p8 Jl/Ag 2017
What's Hot Now color *Seventeen* v76 no5 p16 S 2017

Mosendz, Polly
Pants on Fyre color *Bloomberg Businessweek* no4524 p33 My 29 2017
The Rich Refugees Who Saved Trump cartoon *Bloomberg Businessweek* no4515 p14 Mr 20 2017

Moser, Benjamin
Bookends: Do grants, professorships and other forms of institutional support help writers but hurt writing? *New York Times Book Review* p23 Jl 9 2017
What's the best book, new or old, you read this year? *New York Times Book Review* p27 D 25 2016

MOSER, BOB
Trump's Vanishing Base il *New Republic* v248 no1/2 p6 Ja/F 2017

Moser, Edvard I.
Stellate cells drive maturation of the entorhinal-hippocampal circuit diag *Science* v355 no6330 p1172 Mr 17 2017

Moser, Eric
Cutest Garden Shed Ever Z. Gowen color diag *Southern Living* v51 no11 p44 N 2016

MOSER, JEFF
The Doctor Is In color *Power & Motoryacht* v34 no10 p44 O 2017
Seeing into the Future [Cover story] color *Power & Motoryacht* v34 no6 p22 Je 2017
Who's Driving? color *Power & Motoryacht* v34 no8 p24 Ag 2017

Moser, Koloman, 1868-1918
"Pleasure in the beautiful 'thing as such'": Fashion and the Wiener Werkstätte J. Staggs bw color *Magazine Antiques* v184 no5 p96 S/O 2017

Moser, May-Britt
Multiple mechanisms for memory replay? bibl diag *Science* v355 no6321 p131 Ja 13 2017
Stellate cells drive maturation of the entorhinal-hippocampal circuit diag *Science* v355 no6330 p1172 Mr 17 2017

MOSER, WHET
THE SOX'S NEW VOICE color *Chicago* v66 no8 p26 Ag 2017
WHY We LOVE CHICAGO bw cartoon color *Chicago* v66 no3 p75 Mr 2017

Moses (Biblical leader)
Becoming the Body of Christ M. R. Simone *America* v216 no13 p58 Je 12 2017

Moses, Grandma, 1860-1961
Thoroughly modern Moses: What did Grandma Moses have in common with the likes of Jackson Pollock? Arguably, plenty J. Franklin color *Magazine Antiques* v184 no4 p74 Jl/Ag 2017

Moses, Lee Hull
The ethics of excess color *Christian Century* v134 no1 p36 Ja 4 2017
Limits of a feel-good movie *Christian Century* v134 no4 p10 F 15 2017
Recipes for a revolution color *Christian Century* v133 no25 p32 D 7 2016

Moses, Monica
Bringing Vision to Life color *American Craft* v77 no3 p20 Je/Jl 2017
On the Horizon color *American Craft* v76 no6 p36 D 2016-Ja 2017
Small Victories bw color *American Craft* v77 no3 p24 Je/Jl 2017

Moses, Paul
Dispatches from America's ethnic enclaves color *America* v217 no3 p44 Ag 7 2017

Moses, Robert, 1888-1981
Global Ambition A. Rogers *Smithsonian* v48 no3 p11 Je 2017

Moses, Sarah
The Good Death: An Exploration of Dying in America *Christian Century* v134 no1 p39 Ja 4 2017

Moshammer, R.
Ultrafast electron diffraction imaging of bond breaking in di-ionized acetylene bibl graph *Science* v354 no6310 p308 O 21 2016

Moshe, Asher
The cytotoxic Staphylococcus aureus PSMα3 reveals a cross-α amyloid-like fibril bibl color diag graph *Science* v355 no6327 p831 F 24 2017

Mosheim, Roberto
Productivity Growth Is Still the Major Driver in Growing U.S. Agricultural Output *Amber Waves: The Economics of Food, Farming, Natural Resources, & Rural America* p5 S 2016

Moshenska, Gabriel
THE MYTH OF MUMMY WHEAT: Despite a total lack of evidence, the belief that grains of wheat found in Ancient Egyptian tombs could produce bountiful crops was surprisingly hardy *History Today* v67 no9 p36 S 2017

Mosher, Carrie M.
Potential role of intratumor bacteria in mediating tumor resistance to the chemotherapeutic drug gemcitabine diag *Science* v357 no6356 p1156 S 15 2017

Moshfegh, Ottessa, 1981-
An Honest Woman O. Moshfegh cartoon color *New Yorker* v92 no34 p62 O 24 2016
"I Love My Characters, But I Don't Like Them" C. PETACCIO color *Publishers Weekly* v263 no44 p46 O 31 2016
Not Totally Deplorable S. Begley color *Time* v188 no27-28 p110 D 26 2016
Ordinary Monsters J. LIVINGSTONE color *New Republic* v248 no1/2 p59 Ja/F 2017
Ottessa Moshfegh J. Johnson color *Current Biography* v78 no2

p53 F 2017

Wishes From the Wings D. MEANS *New York Times Book Review* p12 Ja 22 2017

Moskowitz, Clara

The Beautiful Brain: The Drawings of Santiago Ramón y Cajal color *Scientific American* v316 no1 p68 Ja 2017

Citizen Scientist color *Scientific American* v315 no6 p82 D 2016

Curators: Behind the Scenes of Natural History Museums color *Scientific American* v316 no3 p76 Mr 2017

The Death and Life of the Great Lakes color *Scientific American* v316 no3 p76 Mr 2017

The Enigma of the Owl: An Illustrated Natural History color *Scientific American* v316 no3 p76 Mr 2017

The Neutrino Puzzle [Cover story] color diag map *Scientific American* v317 no4 p32 O 2017

Never Out of Season: How Having the Food We Want When We Want It Threatens Our Food Supply and Our Future color *Scientific American* v316 no3 p76 Mr 2017

Seeds on Ice: Svalbard and the Global Seed Vault color *Scientific American* v315 no3 p86 S 2016

Tangled Up in Spacetime color *Scientific American* v316 no1 p32 Ja 2017

MOSKOWITZ, DANIEL B.

A MATTER OF PRIVACY bw *American History* v52 no3 p22 Ag 2017

No, I Will Not Move to the Back of the Bus bw color *American History* v52 no3 p40 Ag 2017

PRAYING FOR CLARITY bw *American History* v52 no2 p26 Je 2017

WHY MARBURY MATTERS color *American History* v52 no4 p24 O 2017

Moskowitz, Eva—Interviews

Why Charter School Leader Eva Moskowitz Endorses Betsy DeVos C. Feldman *Education Digest* v83 no1 p15 S 2017

Moskowitz, Gabi

Inside the Hot Mess Kitchen color *Glamour* v115 no9 p111 S 2017

Moskwa, Wojciech

Christ, King, and Corporate Savior bw *Bloomberg Businessweek* no4531 p33 Jl 24 2017

MOSLE, SARA

Gimme Shelter *New York Times Book Review* p23 Ag 27 2017

GWEN IFILL *New York Times Magazine* p56 D 25 2016

Mosley, Adam

Missions Unmasked: What I Never Knew About Missionary Life color *Publishers Weekly* v263 no52 p74 D 19 2016

Mosley, Eric

Creating an Effective Peer Review System *Harvard Business Review Digital Articles* p2 Ag 19 2015

MOSLEY, LAYNA

Labor Rights in the Age of Global Supply Chains *Current History* v116 no786 p17 Ja 2017

Mosley, Richard

CEOs Need to Pay Attention to Employer Branding *Harvard Business Review Digital Articles* p2 My 11 2015

Mosley, Walter, 1952-

Live Your Best Life color *O, The Oprah Magazine* p23 My 2017

My Call for "Untopia" *Nation* v33 no21 p6 N 21 2016

Mosow, Julie

Help Your Overwhelmed, Stressed-Out Team *Harvard Business Review Digital Articles* p2 Ja 16 2015

How to Motivate Yourself When Your Boss Doesn't *Harvard Business Review Digital Articles* p2 N 14 2014

Mosqueda, Juan Garcia

Juan Garcia Mosqueda H. MARTIN color *Architectural Digest* v74 no1 p44 Ja 2017

Mosques

The Science of Giving I. BAGBY *Islamic Horizons* v46 no2 p44 Mr/Ap 2017

Mosques—Canada

Little mosque on Lake Erie A. HUTCHINS color *Maclean's* v130 no10 p14 N 2017

Mosques—Design & construction

Construction of mosque gives Greek Muslims hope of greater religious parity U. Farooq *Christian Century* v133 no25 p14 D 7 2016

Designing Green Mosques U. MIRZA *Islamic Horizons* v46 no1

p42 Ja/F 2017

In Turkey, Erdogan builds a megamosque that outdoes the sultans A. C. Miller color *Christian Century* v133 no21 p15 O 12 2016

Mosques—Social aspects

Our Model Mosque: Muslims have a model for shaping their institutions: the way that the Prophet nurtured his Mosque I. BAGBY *Islamic Horizons* v46 no4 p46 Jl/Ag 2017

Mosques—United States

Masjid Muhammad: The Nation's Mosque S. SWETZOFF *Islamic Horizons* v46 no1 p26 Ja/F 2017

Mosquito (Poem)

MOSQUITO M. Cadnum *Commonweal* v144 no12 p25 Jl 7 2017

Mosquito control

The enforcer J. LEDERMAN color *Popular Science* v289 no6 p28 N/D 2017

I WISH SOMEONE WOULD INVENT... color *Popular Science* v288 no6 p114 N/D 2016

Nonnative Fish to Control Aedes Mosquitoes: A Controversial, Harmful Tool V. M. AZEVEDO-SANTOS, J. R. S. VITULE et al *BioScience* v67 no1 p84 Ja 2017

To fight skeeters, disrupt their sex lives S. MILIUS color *Science News* v191 no11 p10 Je 10 2017

U.S.-Cuba scientific collaboration advances M. Jarvis color *Science* v357 no6358 p1364 S 29 2017

WINGED WARRIORS K. Servick color diag *Science* v354 no6309 p164 O 14 2016

Mosquito genetics research

DEPARTMENT OF DEFENSE TARGETS MOSQUITOES *USA Today Magazine* v146 no2868 p6 S 2017

Mosquitoes

See also

Anopheles

Bet you didn't know M. HARRIS color *National Geographic Kids* no470 p10 My 2017

BITING BACK M. Enserink and L. Roberts color *Science* v354 no6309 p162 O 14 2016

BLOOD-SUCKING VISITORS: BUGS IN THE PNW CAN BE VORACIOUS, SO DON'T BECOME THEIR NEXT VICTIM D. HISLOP *Sea Magazine* v109 no5 pCA-10 My 2017

BUGS, BEGONE! *Health* v31 no5 p13 Je 2017

Changes in the microbiota cause genetically modified Anopheles to spread in a population A. Pike, Y. Dong et al graph *Science* v357 no6358 p1396 S 29 2017

The enforcer J. LEDERMAN color *Popular Science* v289 no6 p28 N/D 2017

They're Taking Our Tires! K. N. SMITH color *Discover* v38 no9 p12 N 2017

TRENDING L. SCHLEY color diag graph *Discover* v38 no6 p12 Jl/Ag 2017

Mosquitoes as carriers of disease

AIR SICKNESS M. McKenna *New York Times Magazine* p42 Ap 23 2017

WINGED WARRIORS K. Servick color diag *Science* v354 no6309 p164 O 14 2016

Mosquitoes—Biological control

Bacterial genes sterilize mosquitoes E. S. EATON color *Science News* v191 no6 p10 Ap 1 2017

Moss, Arthur

My President Was Black *Atlantic* v319 no2 p8 Mr 2017

Moss, Charlotte

BEING PRESENT color *House Beautiful* v159 no2 p57 Mr 2017

A PATCH OF BEAUTY color *House Beautiful* v159 no4 p52 My 2017

A VERY CHARLOTTE CHRISTMAS K. O'SHEA-EVANS color *House Beautiful* v158 no10 p54 D 2016/Ja 2017

Moss, Elisabeth, 1982-

THE Anticipation Index *New York* p61 Ja 23 2017

ELISABETH MOSS'S MAD WORLD M. Tedder color *Esquire* p26 My 2017

Elisabeth Moss: The Handmaid's Tale's star can't help turning her characters into feminist heroes, even if she's just trying to play a human J. YUAN img *New York* v50 no9 p16 My 1 2017

The Handmaid's Tale M. ROUSH *TV Guide* p18 Ap 17 2017

The Handmaid's Tale S. Vilkomerson color *Entertainment Weekly* no1442 p13 D 2 2016 Rebellious Special Issue

MY LIFE ON TV J. RUSSELL *TV Guide* p28 Ap 17 2017

Real Housewives S. JONES *New Republic* v248 no5 p58 My 2017

A Strait-Laced America S. ERICKSON *Los Angeles Magazine* p64 My 2017

TV's Great New Heroine Is Born In The Handmaid's Tale D. D'Addario color *Time* v189 no18 p53 My 15 2017

The Who's Who of Summer J. Harman bw color *Glamour* v115 no6 p29 Je 2017

Why I Love DAN-AH KIM'S ARTWORK color *InStyle* v24 no9 p440 S 2017

Women's Work C. Wren color *Commonweal* v144 no12 p30 Jl 7 2017

Moss, Elliott

The Secrets of Southern Comfort S. NYGAARD color *Men's Health* v32 no6 p73 Ag 2017

Moss, Jennifer

Happiness Isn't the Absence of Negative Feelings *Harvard Business Review Digital Articles* p2 Ag 20 2015

Making Your Workplace Safe for Grief color *Harvard Business Review Digital Articles* p2 Je 6 2017

Moss, Jeremiah

Vanishing New York: How a Great City Lost Its Soul color *Publishers Weekly* v264 no22 p59 My 29 2017

The Way We Were: The creator of the blog 'Jeremiah's Vanishing New York' tracks hyper-gentrification and its discontents G. BELLAFANTE *New York Times Book Review* p15 O 1 2017

Moss, Kate, 1974-

Fashion Moments A. ASTLEY color *Architectural Digest* v74 no9 p28 S 2017

THE GREAT KATE color *Harper's Bazaar* no3649 p120 D 2016/Ja 2017

IN FULL FLOWER J. K. DE VALLE color *Architectural Digest* v74 no9 p146 S 2017

Kate Moss color *InStyle* v24 no11 p140 N 2017

KATE'S NEW OBSESSION M. Heyman bw color *Harper's Bazaar* no3656 p442 S 2017

Moss, Kevin

Solving the Twin Crises of Energy and Water Scarcity *Harvard Business Review Digital Articles* p2 Ja 25 2016

Moss, Lottie

My LIST L. McCarthy color *Harper's Bazaar* no3651 p224 Mr 2017

MOSS, N. WEST

THE ABSENCE OF SOUND *Saturday Evening Post* v289 no4 p62 Jl/Ag 2017

Moss, Robert

THE CONVERSATION color *Atlantic* v319 no3 p12 Ap 2017

SOUTH'S BEST BARBECUE color *Southern Living* v52 no4 p70 Ap 2017

Moss, Sherry

When Work Satisfaction Comes from Having 4 Jobs *Harvard Business Review Digital Articles* p2 My 4 2015

Moss, Stanley

Collecting Himself S. BURT *New York Times Book Review* p21 F 26 2017

Moss, Todd

The Shadow List *Publishers Weekly* v264 no25 p90 Je 19 2017

Moss, Todd—Interviews

MURDER CALLS L. ACKEN *TV Guide* v65 no2 p45 Ja 2 2017

Moss gardening

Roll Out the Green Carpet S. Bender color *Southern Living* v51 no11 p38 N 2016

Mosscreek Designs (Company)

Renovation Re-imagined [Cover story] S. Logan color *Log Home Living* v34 no7 p28 S 2017

Mosses

ASK OLD HOUSE JOURNAL P. Poore color *Old House Journal* v45 no2 p60 Ap 2017

Gather color *Rodale's Organic Life* v3 no1 p15 Ja 2017

GREEN GODDESS A. WALL color *Rodale's Organic Life* v3 no1 p43 Ja 2017

Mossett, Kandi—Interviews

Still Defiant at Standing Rock D. MARTINDALE *In These Times* v40 no12 p32 D 2016

Mossey, Mary

Virtual Trolls il *MIT Technology Review* v120 no4 p10 Jl/Ag 2017

MOSSLER, JULIE

OBAMA'S AMERICA img *New York* v49 no20 p12 O 3 2016

Mossman, Kathryn

Expanding the Reach of Primary Care in Developing Countries color *Harvard Business Review Digital Articles* p2 Je 6 2017

Mossman, Matt

How Offshore Is All That Overseas Cash? color *Bloomberg Businessweek* no4541 p28 O 9 2017

Mossop, Dave

Kestrel mystery J. BENNETT color *Canadian Geographic* v137 no3 p31 My 2017

Mossop, Elizabeth

Time & Again L. CUTRONE *New Orleans Homes & Lifestyles* v20 no1 p42 Wint 2016

Most Die Young (Short story)

Most Die Young cartoon color *New Yorker* v92 no43 p56 Ja 2 2017

Most Valuable Player Award (Baseball)—History—21st century

The Case for ... KLUBOT AS MVP G. Baumgaertner and S. Kwak color *Sports Illustrated* v127 no10 p24 O 2 2017

Mostacedo, B.

Persistent effects of pre-Columbian plant domestication on Amazonian forest composition bibl chart graph map *Science* v355 no6328 p925 Mr 3 2017

Mostafa, M.

Observation of a large-scale anisotropy in the arrival directions of cosmic rays above 8×10^{18} eV *Science* v357 no6357 p1266 S 22 2017

Mostafa, Meraz

Climate adaptation funding: Getting the money to those who need it bibl *Bulletin of the Atomic Scientists* v72 no6 p396 N 2016

Mosteiro, Lluc

Tissue damage and senescence provide critical signals for cellular reprogramming in vivo bibl chart graph *Science* v354 no6315 paaf4445-1 N 25 2016

Most Hated Woman in America, The (Film)

American atheist is hated, murdered, revived in new film J. Martin color *America* v216 no11 p57 My 15 2017

Mostue, Anne

Doctors Without Patients *Bloomberg Businessweek* no4537 p34 S 11 2017

Mosul (Iraq)

THE AVENGERS OF MOSUL L. MOGELSON bw cartoon map *New Yorker* v92 no48 p34 F 6 2017

The Iraqis Who Fled Mosul C. YAR color *Foreign Policy* no226 p5 S/O 2017

snapshot *In These Times* v41 no6 p7 Je 2017

Mosul (Iraq)—History

INSIDE MOSUL A. R. KHAN color *Maclean's* v129 no50 p14 D 19 2016

Mosul (Iraq)—Military history—21st century

The Beginning of the End J. Malsin color map *Time* v189 no15 p30 Ap 24 2017

Iraq Takes on ISIS J. Malsin and M. Thompson color map *Time* v188 no19 p32 N 7 2016

Motamed, Mesbah

Managing Agricultural Risk Under Different Scenarios: Selected 2014 Farm Act Programs *Amber Waves: The Economics of Food, Farming, Natural Resources, & Rural America* p22 F 2017

Mota Neumage, Monica

Lee Rubin: Our mentor and role model *Science* v355 no6327 p806 F 24 2017

Motavalli, Jim

2017 EV BUYERS' GUIDE *Sierra* v102 no5 p40 St/O 2017

Motawia, Mohammed Saddik

Characterization of a dynamic metabolon producing the defense compound dhurrin in sorghum bibl graph *Science* v354 no6314 p890 N 18 2016

Motels

Road Hawgs D. DRAPER bw color *Field & Stream* v122 no2 p39 Je/Jl 2017

WHAT'S GOING DOWN IN ROOM 312 A. E. Ward *Texas Monthly* v45 no2 p52 F 2017

Motels—Design & construction

BEST OF THE WEST J. Sexton color *Sunset* v238 no2 p7 F 2017

Motels—Evaluation

BEST OF THE WEST L. Ladoceour and A. Young color *Sunset*

v239 no4 p13 O 2017

The Downtown Clifton N. B. TRULSSON *Arizona Highways* v93 no2 p14 F 2017

Motes, Ryan

Riding an Offensive Corner with Ryan Motes color *Team Roping Journal* p73 S 2017

Motevalli, Golnar

Iran Has a 1 Percent Too, and It's Pro-West cartoon *Bloomberg Businessweek* no4495 p14 O 17 2016

Iranian Voters Want a Share of the Wealth color *Bloomberg Businessweek* no4521 p14 My 8 2017

Mother & child

See also

Mothers & daughters

Am I Obliged To Support My Elderly Mother? K. A. Appiah *New York Times Magazine* p30 N 20 2016

EVERYDAY HEROES Raising Grateful Kids A. Reliford color *Good Housekeeping* v265 no5 p82 N 2017

the fun one B. BROYARD color *Parents* v92 no8 p102 Ag 2017

Good Grief G. D. MELTON cartoon *O, The Oprah Magazine* p36 Mr 2017

if you ask me... S. JAMES color *Parents* v92 no6 p100 Je 2017

In Her Wake: A few words about my mom, whom I wish were here to read them P. GULLEY *Indianapolis Monthly* p56 N 2017

a letter to my child about growing up in the dark ages R. D'APICE *Parents* v92 no1 p38 Ja 2017

MAKING moonlight MEMORIES S. Piecuch *New York State Conservationist* v71 no3 p22 D 2016

Mama Loves Me Anyway R. Bragg color *Southern Living* v52 no5 p154 My 2017

MY BADASS MOM M. EASTER bw *Men's Health* v32 no4 p122 My 2017

PLAYING OUR SONG color *O, The Oprah Magazine* p24 Ja 2017

The Power of Language G. Bastidas *Parents* v91 no10 p16 O 2016

Rock On, Single Moms S. S. GOLD *Parents* v92 no1 p16 Ja 2017

SCREEN TIME RULES L. GOLDMAN *Better Homes & Gardens* v95 no6 p165 Je 2017

the wackiest advice my kid ever gave me... *Parents* v91 no9 p176 S 2016

Mother & infant

See also

Breastfeeding (Humans)

Birth of 'three-parent baby' prompts hope and concern T. H. Saey color *Science News* v190 no13 p22 D 24 2016

Mother! (Film)

2017 Fall Performances *Time* v190 no10/11 p101 S 18 2017

Appetite for Creation R. DOUTHAT color *National Review* v69 no19 p58 O 16 2017

Fall Preview R. Brody color *New Yorker* v93 no25 p16 Ag 28 2017

Michelle Pfeiffer As a Nefarious House Guest E. Dockterman color *Time* v190 no10/11 p102 S 18 2017

MOTHER! S. Vilkomerson color *Entertainment Weekly* no1478 / 1479 p40 Ag 18-25 2017

Oh, mother! J. Nolfi and S. Vilkomerson color *Entertainment Weekly* no1484 p16 S 29 2017

Sight Unseen A. RIESMAN img *New York* v50 no17 p102 Ag 21 2017

A WOMAN'S WORK A. LANE color *New Yorker* v93 no29 p104 S 25 2017

Mother Nature's Quilt (Poem)

Mother Nature's Quilt T. Krysl color *Nebraska Life* v21 no5 p45 S/O 2017

Motherboards (Microcomputers)—Equipment & supplies

Facepalm: Intel's upcoming Coffee Lake CPUs won't work with today's motherboards G. M. UNG color *PCWorld* v35 no9 p11 S 2017

Motherboards (Microcomputers)—Evaluation

Official Intel 7th-gen Kaby Lake: One big change makes up for smaller ones G. MAHUNG chart color diag graph *PCWorld* v35 no2 p49 F 2017

Ryzen 5 vs. Core i5: Ryzen 5 1600X wins for best mainstream power CPU G. MAH UNG chart color graph *PCWorld* v35 no5 p107 My 2017

Ryzen Threadripper: AMD's monster stomps on other CPUs G. M. UNG chart color graph *PCWorld* v35 no9 p27 S 2017

Motherhood

See also

Surrogate motherhood

4 "Mom" Things People Insult That Are Actually Pretty Darn Awesome S. James *Parents* v92 no1 p7 Ja 2017

9 parent click-bait headlines you never see online M. DUBIN cartoon *Parents* v92 no7 p94 Jl 2017

Actress Reshma Shetty is busy being a mom at the moment. The baby monitor in her Manhattan *Virginia Living* v15 no4 p17 Je 2017

Bridget Jones's Baby *Parents* v91 no9 p18 S 2016

the fun one B. BROYARD color *Parents* v92 no8 p102 Ag 2017

Gold-Medal Moms L. Krieger *Parents* v91 no9 p22 S 2016

guess my power move L. Vaccariello *Parents* v92 no3 p6 Mr 2017

ha! *Parents* v91 no12 p76 D 2016

The journey of a scientist mother P. de Tezanos Pinto color *Science* v356 no6339 p774 My 19 2017

Lauren's Confessions L. Morgan color *Parents* v92 no7 p36 Jl 2017

"OUR BIG SISTER is our guardian angel" J. SAGER bw color *Good Housekeeping* v265 no2 p71 Ag 2017

PARENT CRUSH S. James *Parents* v91 no9 p15 S 2016

parents last laugh *Parents* v91 no11 p152 N 2016

Phone Home L. SMITH cartoon *Weekly Standard* v22 no13 p5 D 5 2016

Savannah Guthrie Looks Back at 2016 M. LaScala *Parents* v91 no12 p12 D 2016

strong /not-strong D. Points *Parents* v91 no9 p10 S 2016

TV Moms Breaking the Mold L. Morgan *Parents* v91 no10 p22 O 2016

where does the time go? C. HOLECKO cartoon *Parents* v92 no7 p80 Jl 2017

Motherhood—Moral & ethical aspects

QUEER THEOREM S. Hunt *Lapham's Quarterly* v10 no2 p210 Spr 2017

Motherhood—Psychological aspects

baby no. 2 C. W. DINEEN *Parents* v91 no11 p90 N 2016

love times two L. IANNOTTI *Parents* v91 no9 p134 S 2016

mothering with a migraine L. McMULLAN ABRAMSON color *Parents* v92 no4 p94 Ap 2017

when a parent is about to snap [Cover story] K. LEDGER cartoon *Parents* v92 no3 p76 Mr 2017

Mothers

See also

Birthmothers

Single mothers

Stepmothers

Surrogate mothers

Working mothers

The Drinking Game, Ladies Who Lunch, Mother's Day L. KOGAN color *O, The Oprah Magazine* p35 Jl 2017

Families Don't Have to "Match" L. L. Tharps *Parents* v91 no10 p24 O 2016

Family Is What You Make It A. Davies *Parents* v91 no10 p24 O 2016

get a fresh start *Parents* v91 no10 p85 O 2016

Heart problems tied to mom's diet L. BEIL cartoon *Science News* v190 no12 p14 D 10 2016

Here We Go! Oprah color *O, The Oprah Magazine* p18 Ap 2017

How I really met my mother G. SORELL color *Good Housekeeping* v264 no5 p73 My 2017

HOW TO GET PREGNANT (AGAIN) L. Murray color *Health* v31 no1 p73 Ja 2017

Kids Should Be Part of Mom's Treatment *USA Today Magazine* v146 no2867 p13 Ag 2017

Let's celebrate AMAZING MOMS J. PRESS bw color *Redbook* p110 My 2017

LIKE MOTHER, LIKE DAUGHTER A. KELLER LAIRD *Women's Health* v14 no4 p8 My 2017

'ME TIME' FOR MOMS Z. HUGHES and S. T. BROWN cartoon *Ebony* v72 no6 p66 Ap/My 2017

Mom's Dinner Party Diaries A. SEAN GREER *Reader's Digest* v188 no1125 p62 N 2016

MY MOTHER, SEWING V. HARTMAN *Washingtonian Magazine* v52 no3 p192 D 2016

ROCK STAR MOM S. COLL *Washingtonian Magazine* v52 no8

p84 My 2017

Royalty Gets a Rethink M. LaScala color *Parents* v92 no8 p15 Ag 2017

sign up for fun I. COHEN *Parents* v92 no6 p134 Je 2017

Style in Store M. Tamte color *Working Mother* v40 no4 p14 O/N 2017

that time i won parenting L. Vaccariello *Parents* v92 no5 p6 My 2017

TV Moms Breaking the Mold L. Morgan *Parents* v91 no10 p22 O 2016

Want to feel less guilty? bw diag *Redbook* p150 S 2017

When the weather gets hotter, so do your choices at the multiplex M. LaScala color *Parents* v92 no7 p14 Jl 2017

Mothers & daughters

"A Girl Can't Be President" L. Miller *New York* v49 no23 p18 N 14 2016

Bye-Bye Baby: Sentiment and relief E. C. Peyton color *New Orleans Magazine* v51 no10 p58 Ag 2017

family matters J. Barberio color *Working Mother* v40 no3 p38 Ag/S 2017

From One Horse Parent To Another A. Costello color *Dressage Today* v24 no2 p60 N 2017

LET'S DO THIS E. Graves color *Martha Stewart Living* p6 My 2017

LIKE MOTHER, LIKE DAUGHTER A. KELLER LAIRD *Women's Health* v14 no4 p8 My 2017

MOTHERS DAUGHTERS STRANGERS A. ROSS color *Women's Health* v14 no2 p152 Mr 2017

"OUR BIG SISTER is our guardian angel" J. SAGER bw color *Good Housekeeping* v265 no2 p71 Ag 2017

STRONG GENES color *Women's Health* v14 no4 p162 My 2017

THE TROUBLE WITH MIA: At what point do our adult children cease to be the adoring babies we once knew? K. W. Reyes *Saturday Evening Post* v289 no5 p18 S/O 2017

The Unexpected Benefits of Ending Up at the Back of the Pack S. Schrobsdorff color *Time* v189 no3 p63 Ja 16 2017

Mothers & daughters—United States

INTRODUCING WASHINGTONIAN'S Best Moms *Washingtonian Magazine* v52 no9 p116 Je 2017

Mothers & sons

How I Grew Five Mothers M. PEYSER color *Reader's Digest* v189 no1130 p17 My 2017

Laugh Lines K. WHITEHORN, K. HALL et al color *Reader's Digest* v189 no1130 p107 My 2017

A Letter of Apology to a Son Graduating from College K. Van Ogtrop color *Time* v189 no15 p55 Ap 24 2017

My Swimming Instructor K. BURGE bw color *Reader's Digest* v189 no1129 p18 Ap 2017

THE RAW, REAL, AND UTTERLY INSPIRING STORY OF A NEW YORK KID WHO MADE HIS OWN RULES FOR LIVING, 10 TILLETT WRIGHT'S NEW MEMOIR IS A TRIBAL CRY FOR A WHOLE GENERATION N. GOLDIN *Interview* v46 no8 p116 O 2016

The Roses of Fairhope R. BRAGG color *Reader's Digest* v189 no1130 p22 My 2017

The Seven Words I Cannot Say Around My Children J. WOLF *Reader's Digest* v189 no1127 p52 F 2017

Mother's Day

The Forgotten Parent Behind Mother's Day O. B. Waxman *Time* v189 no19 p19 My 22 2017

Mama Loves Me Anyway R. Bragg color *Southern Living* v52 no5 p154 My 2017

mothers' DAY J. YONAN color *Better Homes & Gardens* v95 no5 p122 My 2017

What's your superpower? M. Rollins color *Redbook* p10 My 2017

Mother's Day (Film)

Mother's Day R. Brody color *New Yorker* v93 no16 p26 Je 5 2017

Mothers-in-law

The Euphoria of the Dying J. McGowan color *Commonweal* v144 no7 p6 Ap 14 2017

'Still She Is a Wonderful Girl' J. McGowan color *Commonweal* v144 no12 p6 Jl 7 2017

Mothers—Attitudes

let's get real *Parents* v91 no9 p79 S 2016

My Mother Gives the Weirdest Gifts I. OLUO *Reader's Digest* v188 no1126 p14 D 2016/Ja 2017

PARENTS POLL *Parents* v92 no2 p18 F 2017

Mothers—Death

THE TEACHER J. WOOD cartoon *New Yorker* v92 no40 p28 D 5 2016

Mothers—Psychology

beauty reboot T. PEREZ *Parents* v91 no10 p86 O 2016

Mothers—Religious life

The Church Is Not a Single-Parent Family J. WILKIN *Christianity Today* v60 no10 p30 D 2016

Mothers—United States—Political activity

MOTHERS OF THE WORLD, UNITE! S. DOYLE *In These Times* v41 no6 p44 Je 2017

Moths

> *See also*
> Caterpillars

Motion

> *See also*
> Acceleration (Mechanics)
> Rotational motion
> Speed

Quantum correlations from a room-temperature optomechanical cavity T. P. Purdy, K. E. Grutter et al color diag graph *Science* v356 no6344 p1265 Je 23 2017

Motion, Andrew

Fells Point Songs *American Scholar* v86 no4 p59 Aut 2017

Hawthorn *American Scholar* v86 no4 p53 Aut 2017

He Saw the Marches Differently on the March color *New York Review of Books* v64 no5 p49 Mr 23 2017

The Last of England *American Scholar* v86 no4 p52 Aut 2017

Surveillance *American Scholar* v86 no4 p55 Aut 2017

Too Much Poetic License *American Scholar* v86 no1 p118 Wint 2017

WADERS A. Motion *New Yorker* v93 no9 p54 Ap 17 2017

WADERS *New Yorker* v93 no9 p54 Ap 17 2017

Motion control devices

> *See also*
> Brakes

Creative Motion M. S. Eddy *Stage Directions* v30 no2 p22 F 2017

Motion picture acting

THE RIDE OF HIS LIFE M. POTTER bw color *Esquire* p100 S 2017

Motion picture actors & actresses

Bulletproof! J. Roth color *Esquire* p66 Ag 2017

CARSON MEYER K. SMITH color *Vanity Fair* v59 no4 p101 Mr 2017

The Celebrity We Need [Cover story] D. FRENCH color *National Review* v69 no9 p21 My 15 2017

DONNA REED: FIRE AND NICE *Saturday Evening Post* v289 no5 p95 S/O 2017

ELBA'S EASE [Cover story] M. POTTER bw color *Esquire* p50 Ag 2017

HOUSE OF SHADOWS A. GREEN color *Vogue* v207 no7 p96 Jl 2017

Motion picture actors & actresses—Awards

RED CARPET INTELLIGENCE I. Biedenharn color *Entertainment Weekly* no1456 p50 Mr 10 2017

WHO WILL WIN N. Sperling color *Entertainment Weekly* no1454/1455 p44 F 24 2017

Motion picture actors & actresses—Interviews

Helen Mirren E. Berman color *Time* v188 no24 p64 D 12 2016

Motion picture actors & actresses—United States

92 MINUTES WITH ... Glenn Close C. SWANSON img *New York* p16 F 20 2017

Glass Ceiling J. Yuan img *New York* p63 F 20 2017

THE MALIBU MYSTIC [Cover story] M. POTTER color *Esquire* v166 no4 p92 N 2016

Runaway Starlets K. Buchanan img *New York* p71 F 20 2017

Motion picture audiences

HOLLYWOOD WRAPS ONE OF ITS WORST SUMMERS EVER T. J. Huddleston color *Fortune* v176 no4 p27 S 15 2017

Motion picture authorship

SE7EN J. Hibberd color *Entertainment Weekly* no1460/1461 p62 Ap 7-17 2017

Motion picture authorship—Software

FINAL DRAFT 10: NEW WAYS TO PLOT YOUR NEXT OSCAR-WORTHY SCREENPLAY J. R. BOOKWALTER color

Ja 2 2017

Motion pictures—Setting & scenery
See also
Stage props
How to Make an American Pie! C. Agard color *Entertainment Weekly* no1460/1461 p66 Ap 7-17 2017
Original Scenesters img *New York* v49 no22 p98 O 31 2016

Motion pictures—Social aspects
Film Adaptation color *MIT Technology Review* v119 no6 p108 N/D 2016
The movie is the message J. WEINMAN bw color *Maclean's* v129 no45 p52 N 14 2016

Motion pictures—Social aspects—History
THE BIG QUESTION A. Schroeder, A. Biller et al cartoon *Atlantic* v319 no2 p100 Mr 2017

Motion pictures—Software
REELGOOD: ONE APP, SO MANY STREAMING OR THEATRICAL MOVIES TO DISCOVER J. R. BOOKWALTER color *Macworld - Digital Edition* p69 D 2016

Motion pictures—United States
Fix the Fixer J. Podhoretz color *Weekly Standard* v22 no33 p47 My 8 2017
STILL LOOKING M. HARRIS color *Film Comment* v52 no6 p66 N/D 2016

Motion Pro Inc.
A NATION'S DATEBOOK *Dirt Sports + Off-Road* v51 no7 p72 Jl 2017

Motion sickness
How to Combat Car Sickness *Catnip* v24 no10 p3 O 2016
REAL SICK [Cover story] B. Mason color *Science News* v191 no5 p24 Mr 18 2017
Virtual reality raises nausea risk B. MASON color *Science News* v191 no1 p7 Ja 21 2017

Motion sickness—Risk factors
Queasy Street Riding in autonomous cars without losing our lunch F. Markus color *Motor Trend* v69 no6 p28 Je 2017

Motion picture industry—Trials, litigation, etc.
THIS CAWSUIT GOES TO 11 R. KOLKER bw color *Bloomberg Businessweek* no4519 p72 Ap 24 2017

Motion pictures—Awards—Charts, diagrams, etc.
OSCAR SECRET BALLOT N. Sperling color *Entertainment Weekly* no1454/1455 p52 F 24 2017

Motion pictures—Charts, diagrams, etc.
Fast & Furious: The Completist's Guide E. Dockterman and M. Vella color *Time* v189 no14 p54 Ap 17 2017

Motion pictures—Evaluation—Charts, diagrams, etc.
CRITICAL MASS chart color *Entertainment Weekly* no1444/1445 p64 D 16 2016
THE McCONAISSANCE color diag *Entertainment Weekly* no1477 p39 Ag 11 2017

Motion pictures—History—1901-1930
50, 100 & 150 YEARS AGO bw color *Scientific American* v315 no3 p91 S 2016

Motion pictures—Plots, themes, etc.
FROZEN J. Hibberd color *Entertainment Weekly* no1460/1461 p97 Ap 7-17 2017

Motion pictures—Reviews—Charts, diagrams, etc.
TIM BURTON'S SCORE CARD color *Entertainment Weekly* no1434 p42 O 7 2016

Motivation (Psychology)
See also
Ambition
Burnout (Psychology)
Competition (Psychology)
Employee motivation
Goal (Psychology)
Motivation in education
Reading motivation
Social desirability
10 SUCCESSFUL FARMERS: DALE REICKS B. Freese *Successful Farming* v115 no8 p16 Je/Jl 2017
7 Ways to Capture Someone's Attention B. Parr *Harvard Business Review Digital Articles* p2 Mr 3 2015
Avoid Burnout by Asking This Question N. Pasricha *Harvard Business Review Digital Articles* p2 Je 21 2016
BEAT THE HEAT *Health* v31 no5 p14 Je 2017

BEHIND MY PEERS H. ESTROFF MARANO *Psychology Today* v49 no5 p22 S/O 2016
Feel better—starting today A. MASCARELLI color *Yoga Journal* p10 2016 Special Issue
From the Editor J. Paulson *Horse & Rider* v55 no12 p7 D 2016
GET FIT WITH A FRENEMY *Health* v31 no2 p15 Mr 2017
How to Get Excited About Topics That Bore You B. Oakley *Harvard Business Review Digital Articles* p2 Jl 3 2017
I CAN MAKE LEOPARDS CHANGE THEIR SPOTS R. BAIN *People Management* p26 O 2016
Live Your Best Life bw *O, The Oprah Magazine* p19 Mr 2017
Live Your Best Life color *O, The Oprah Magazine* p21 F 2017
Live Your Best Life color *O, The Oprah Magazine* p25 S 2017
THE LURE OF CHARISMA: COLORFUL LEADERS INSPIRE, BUT THEY MAY HAVE UNEXPECTED LIMITS M. Huston *Psychology Today* v50 no5 p9 S/O 2017
Match Your Motivational Tactic to the Situation J. Schroeder and A. Fishbach *Harvard Business Review Digital Articles* p2 Ja 8 2016
A MONDAY J. Migala color *Women's Health* v14 no3 p86 Ap 2017
Motivate Me C. NEWMAN *USA Today Magazine* v145 no2864 p63 My 2017
THE MYSTERY OF MOTIVATION G. DREVITCH *Psychology Today* v50 no1 p54 Ja/F 2017
The POWER of the Aha! MOMENT L. MARSHALL color *Prevention* v68 no12 p60 D 2016
Put some pep in your step! *Harvard Health Letter* v42 no8 p1 Je 2017
Quotable Quotes color *Reader's Digest* v190 no1135 p136 N 2017
Safety Pins For Slackers: Does the like button impede social change? D. FELDMAN *Psychology Today* v50 no4 p40 Ag 2017
Should You Give Up on Your New Dream? W. Johnson *Harvard Business Review Digital Articles* p2 Ja 28 2016
SLAY YOUR SETBACKS M. NICOLE NAZZARO color *Runner's World* v52 no8 p24 S 2017
THE STARTING LINE [Cover story] J. GALLOWAY cartoon *Runner's World* v52 no2 p30 Mr 2017
Staying Motivated After a Major Achievement R. Friedman *Harvard Business Review Digital Articles* p2 F 3 2015
Talk It Out color *Dance Spirit* v21 no8 p48 O 2017
What Maslow's Hierarchy Won't Tell You About Motivation S. Fowler *Harvard Business Review Digital Articles* p2 N 26 2014

Motivation in education
Engage Students' Creativity Through Animated Whiteboard Video Project M. O'SHEA *Education Digest* v82 no7 p61 Mr 2017
To engage students, give them meaningful choices in the classroom F. Parker, J. Novak et al il *Phi Delta Kappan* v99 no2 p37 O 2017

Motivation in religious education
Making Religious Education Work F. Nonomen bw *Commonweal* v143 no18 p8 N 11 2016

Motivational speakers
Fredricka Whitfield *Atlanta* v57 no2 p96 Je 2017

Moto Guzzi motorcycle—Evaluation
2017 MOTO GUZZI MGX-21 FLYING FORTRESS B. Adams color *Cycle World* v55 no10 p10 N 2016
A Cruiser for a Superhero D. CURCURITO color *Popular Mechanics* p46 F 2017
PERPENDICULAR TWINS D. Canet chart color *Cycle World* v56 no2 p42 Mr 2017

Moto Guzzi SpA
2017 MOTO GUZZI MGX-21 FLYING FORTRESS B. Adams color *Cycle World* v55 no10 p10 N 2016

Motocross
ROCZEN ROLL B. Smith color *Cycle World* v55 no10 p60 N 2016

Motor ability
The Best Strategic Leaders Balance Agility and Consistency J. Coleman bw color *Harvard Business Review Digital Articles* p2 Ja 4 2017
Control of species-dependent cortico-motoneuronal connections underlying manual dexterity Z. Gu, J. Kalamboglas et al diag graph *Science* v357 no6349 p400 Jl 28 2017
Introduce Team Sports L. Anastasia *Parents* v92 no9 p168 S 2017

Motor failure
VECTORS TO ZMB P. Garrison *Flying* v144 no10 p36 O 2017
Motor gliders
STEMME S12 [Cover story] R. MARK chart color *Flying* v144 no6 p52 Je 2017
Motor Trend Car of the Year Awards
Danger and deliberation in the desert color *Motor Trend* v69 no1 p120 Ja 2017
The finalist round F. Markus color *Motor Trend* v69 no1 p136 Ja 2017
Kaizen Of The Year E. Loh color *Motor Trend* v69 no1 p12 Ja 2017
THE NUMBER GAME K. Reynolds color *Motor Trend* v69 no1 p116 Ja 2017
PROVING A POINT A. MacKenzie color *Motor Trend* v69 no1 p177 Ja 2017
Sand and Deliver Three contests, six weeks, and a river of Gatorade M. Rechtin color *Motor Trend* v69 no1 p24 Ja 2017
Motor Trend Truck of the Year Awards
BACK TO WORK B. Kong color map *Motor Trend* v69 no1 p80 Ja 2017
Dodging monsoons and haboobs M. Rechtin color *Motor Trend* v69 no1 p84 Ja 2017
Motor vehicle brakes
WORLD DOMINATION M. EMERY color *Dirt Sports + Off-Road* v51 no10 p20 O 2017
Motor vehicle design & construction
See also
Motorcycle design & construction
GROUNDBREAKING PERFORMANCE E. Loh color *Motor Trend* v69 no9 p12 S 2017
Motor vehicle drivers
See also
Automobile drivers
Motorcyclists
Truck drivers
6 DRIVES TO TAKE YOUR BREATH AWAY G. HERBERT color *House Beautiful* p158 Ag 2017
The best of the west with Nebraska Life color *Nebraska Life* v21 no4 p89 Jl/Ag 2017
Motor vehicle driving
See also
Automobile driving
Distracted driving
You're Busted: And It's a Laugh C. WHITE *Idaho Magazine* v16 no8 p43 My 2017
Motor vehicle springs & suspension
SPRINGTIME FOR HITTING AND G-OUTS [Cover story] M. EMERY color *Dirt Sports + Off-Road* v51 no10 p36 O 2017
Motor vehicle testing
EATON COUNTY, MI T. Hansen color *Outdoor Life* v224 no7 p7 S 2017
Motor vehicle vandalism
Vulture Vandals N. BRULLIARD *National Parks* v91 no4 p24 Fall 2017
Motor vehicles
See also
Automobiles
Electric vehicles
Golf carts
Lowriders
Motorcycles
Off-road vehicles
Sport utility vehicles
Trucks
The Desert Monster E. DYER color *Popular Mechanics* p59 D 2016/Ja 2017
Motor vehicles—Bearings
BEARING TIPS & TRICKS J. KOPYCINSKI color *Dirt Sports + Off-Road* v51 no5 p64 My 2017
Motor vehicles—Brakes
Service R. NIERLICH cartoon color *Cycle World* v56 no3 p58 Ap 2017
Motor vehicles—Environmental aspects
The Great Cities of Britain Can't Breathe bw *Bloomberg Businessweek* no4509 p9 Ja 30 2017

Motor vehicles—Evaluation
THE MECHANICS OF FUN E. DYER chart color *Popular Mechanics* p84 Mr 2017
Motor vehicles—Fuel systems
Service R. NIERLICH cartoon color *Cycle World* v56 no3 p58 Ap 2017
Motor vehicles—Research
Aaron Robinson A. Robinson *Car & Driver* v62 no8 p26 F 2017
Motor vehicles—Steering gear
Service R. NIERLICH color *Cycle World* v55 no10 p56 N 2016
Motor vehicles—Tires—Evaluation
Where the Rubber Meets the Road J. Linkov chart color graph *Consumer Reports* v82 no4 p17 Ap 2017
Motorboat repair
A Timely Save B. PIKE color *Power & Motoryacht* v32 no11 p156 N 2016
Motorboats
See also
Outboard motorboats
DON'T MISS LIST MAY 2017 *Sea Magazine* v109 no5 pPNW-6 My 2017
Going Big A. JONES *Boating World* v38 no8 p4 S/O 2017
Grand Opening A. JONES *Boating World* v38 no3 p32 Mr 2017
HECK OF A COMMUTE P. RAINS *Sea Magazine* v109 no2 p14 F 2017
WESTCOASTFOCUS *Sea Magazine* v109 no1 p12 Ja 2017
Motorboats—Equipment & supplies
Spar Check D. Kent color *Sail* v48 no5 p46 My 2017
Motorboats—Evaluation
Beneteau Gran Turismo 46 J. Y. Wood color *Power & Motoryacht* v33 no2 p44 F 2017
Cutwater 302 Sport Coupe B. Pike color *Power & Motoryacht* v33 no2 p42 F 2017
Diamond Setting: The first-class cabin at G3 pontoons just got a lot more plush and stylish A. JONES *Boating World* v38 no8 p44 S/O 2017
Flexible Formula: The 310 BR is a bowrider that can cruise to the sandbar ... or the Bahamas ... in style A. JONES *Boating World* v38 no8 p40 S/O 2017
GALEON 420 FLY: THE POLISH BUILDER PREMIERES A SOLID BOAT WITH A FEW NEAT TRICKS UP ITS SLEEVE Z. PROCHAZKA *Sea Magazine* v109 no5 p40 My 2017
INSIDE OUT: THE NEW BENETEAU GRAN TURISMO 46 BLENDS OUTSIDE AND INSIDE SEAMLESSLY Z. PROCHAZKA *Sea Magazine* v109 no5 p36 My 2017
SHOWCASE *Sea Magazine* v109 no1 p61 Ja 2017
Wakesports For Working Sorts: Heyday's WT-2 allows boaters to have their wake and eat it too ... for a lot less money A. JONES *Boating World* v38 no8 p36 S/O 2017
WAKE UP: MONTEREY UTILIZES FORWARD DRIVE TO LAUNCH A SURFING BOAT WITH PIZZAZZ S. SHIBATA *Boating World* v38 no8 p6 S/O 2017
Motorboats—Maintenance & repair
Q+A F. Lanier, G. Michal et al *Boating World* v38 no8 p24 S/O 2017
Spar Check D. Kent color *Sail* v48 no5 p46 My 2017
TLC FOR YOUR BOAT color *Cabin Living* p74 Mr 2017
Motorboats—Motors
See also
Inboard-outboard engines
Outboard motors
TLC FOR YOUR BOAT color *Cabin Living* p74 Mr 2017
Motorcycle boots—Evaluation
CHARACTER ADJUSTMENT D. Canet color *Cycle World* v56 no2 p18 Mr 2017
Motorcycle customizing
DYNAMIC CHANGES ATHARLEY-DAVIDSON: ADIOS, DYNA! K. Cameron color *Cycle World* v56 no9 p30 O 2017
Motorcycle design & construction
CHOOSING MATERIALS K. CAMERON color *Cycle World* v56 no8 p20 S 2017
CRAZY IS THE NEW NORMAL [Cover story] P. d'Orléans color *Cycle World* v56 no6 p32 Jl 2017
HIGH-PERFORMANCE ATTACHÉ P. d'Orléans color *Cycle World* v56 no8 p48 S 2017
A MAD, MONSTROUS MOTUS P. Jones color *Cycle World* v56

2017 BMW HP4 RACER B. Conner color *Cycle World* v56 no8 p34 S 2017

2017 DUCATI SUPERSPORT AND SUPERSPORT S S. Mac-Donald color *Cycle World* v56 no4 p16 My 2017

2017 HARLEY-DAVIDSON STREET GLIDE SPECIAL J. Gustafson color *Cycle World* v55 no11 p8 D 2016

2017 INDIAN ROADMASTER CLASSIC D. Canet color *Cycle World* v56 no3 p16 Ap 2017

2017 TRIUMPH STREET TRIPLE RS D. Canet color *Cycle World* v56 no4 p10 My 2017

2018 BMW K1600B P. Jones color *Cycle World* v56 no10 p12 N 2017

2018 BMW R nineT URBAN G/S S. MacDonald color *Cycle World* v56 no8 p10 S 2017

2018 INDIAN SCOUT BOBBER S. Macdonald color *Cycle World* v56 no9 p20 O 2017

2018 SUZUKI GSX-S750 D. Canet color *Cycle World* v56 no10 p16 N 2017

ANSWERING THE R QUESTION D. Canet chart color diag *Cycle World* v56 no10 p44 N 2017

AT PLAY M. Hoyer color *Cycle World* v56 no3 p52 Ap 2017

Built for War, Just as Fun on a Trip to the Coffee Shop D. CURCURITO color *Popular Mechanics* p58 My 2017

DADDY, WHAT'S A CARBURETOR? K. CAMERON color *Cycle World* v56 no10 p22 N 2017

HIGHWAY TO HELL B. Catterson chart color *Cycle World* v56 no1 p36 Ja/F 2017

Indian FTR750 Is On Track C. Texter color *Cycle World* v55 no11 p34 D 2016

Little Bike, Big Promise J. Gustafson color *Cycle World* v55 no11 p44 D 2016

LOW AND SLOW THROUGH FLYOVER COUNTRY J. Gustafson color *Cycle World* v56 no4 p50 My 2017

THE NORTH RIM Z. Bowman color *Cycle World* v56 no10 p24 N 2017

NOT AGAIN! color *Cycle World* v56 no8 p6 S 2017

OF STYLE AND SUBSTANCE S. MacDonald chart color *Cycle World* v56 no8 p38 S 2017

RIDING WITH THE KING D. Canet cartoon chart color *Cycle World* v56 no8 p22 S 2017

RUBBER SOUL *Cycle World* v56 no9 p8 O 2017

SCRAMBLER PARADOX color *Cycle World* v56 no3 p30 Ap 2017

A Silent Road Warrior H. Elliott color *Bloomberg Businessweek* no4533 p59 Ag 7 2017

SOFTAILS P. Egan color *Cycle World* v56 no9 p38 O 2017

TRIUMPH BONNEVILLE T120 P. Egan bw chart color graph *Cycle World* v55 no11 p46 D 2016

UNPLUG + PLAY S. Anderson color *Cycle World* v56 no3 p46 Ap 2017

The Very Long-Term Buell P. Egan bw color *Cycle World* v55 no10 p48 N 2016

ZAETA 530 SE B. Adams color *Cycle World* v56 no2 p34 Mr 2017

Motorcycles—Exhibitions

Old Iron Shows *South Dakota Magazine* v33 no2 p13 Jl/Ag 2017

Motorcycles—Maintenance & repair

Old Is the New New D. CURCURITO color *Popular Mechanics* p67 D 2016/Ja 2017

Service R. NIERLICH color *Cycle World* v56 no2 p62 Mr 2017

Motorcycles—Motors

VIRTUAL COMBUSTION P. JONES *Cycle World* v55 no11 p20 D 2016

Motorcycles—Motors—Exhaust systems

Service R. NIERLICH color *Cycle World* v56 no4 p62 My 2017

Motorcycles—Motors—Exhaust systems—Evaluation

YOSHIMURA SIGNATURE SERIES ALPHA SLIP-ON D. Canet color *Cycle World* v56 no1 p19 Ja/F 2017

Motorcycles—Seats

GENUINE ACCESSORIES D. Canet color *Cycle World* v56 no5 p22 Je 2017

Motorcycles—Testing

TORTURE TEST B. Lutes color *Cycle World* v56 no4 p58 My 2017

Motorcycling

See also

Motorcycle touring

Motorcycle track days

1-PERCENT FASTER J. L. Stein color *Cycle World* v56 no4 p30 My 2017

AN ALL-AMERICAN STREET RACE D. CURCURITO color *Popular Mechanics* p48 Jl 2017

CRASHING DOWN M. HOYER *Cycle World* v56 no6 p8 Jl 2017

FLAT-LAND PROBLEM: FREEWAY ON- AND OFF-RAMPS N. Ienatsch color *Cycle World* v55 no10 p20 N 2016

NO PARTICULAR NIGHT OR MORNING P. JONES color *Cycle World* v56 no6 p24 Jl 2017

A QUESTION OF BALANCE P. JONES color *Cycle World* v56 no8 p18 S 2017

SAY WHAT? J. L. Stein cartoon *Cycle World* v55 no11 p16 D 2016

SIMPLE AND STRAIGHT-FORWARD K. CAMERON *Cycle World* v56 no2 p26 Mr 2017

THE UNNECESSARY EXPRESS [Cover story] Z. Bowman, S. Smith et al color *Cycle World* v56 no5 p32 Je 2017

Motorcycling accidents

THE ACCIDENT: When a car struck a young biker, it produced a surprising melange of kindness, chaos, and serendipity K. Budd *Saturday Evening Post* v289 no4 p20 Jl/Ag 2017

Motorcycling accidents—Prevention

CAN YOU SEE ME NOW? J. L. Stein color *Cycle World* v56 no8 p16 S 2017

Motorcycling techniques

BODY POSITION, AN OVERVIEW N. Ienatsch cartoon *Cycle World* v56 no3 p24 Ap 2017

FOCUS, FOOL! J. L. Stein color *Cycle World* v56 no6 p22 Jl 2017

LOOK NOW. DON'T LOOK NOW N. Ienatsch color *Cycle World* v56 no1 p20 Ja/F 2017

A QUESTION OF BALANCE P. JONES color *Cycle World* v56 no8 p18 S 2017

SIMPLE AND STRAIGHT-FORWARD K. CAMERON *Cycle World* v56 no2 p26 Mr 2017

Motorcycling—Competitions

2017 CAN-AM RACING TEAM AND X-TEAM CONTINGENCY PROGRAM color *Dirt Sports + Off-Road* v51 no8 p8 Ag 2017

HARLEY VS. INDIAN M. Hoyer color *Cycle World* v56 no5 p8 Je 2017

STUDYING ABROAD B. Adams color *Cycle World* v56 no1 p14 Ja/F 2017

Motorcycling—Equipment & supplies

The Inflatable Man D. CURCURITO color *Popular Mechanics* p46 S 2017

Motorcycling—Safety measures

MONEY FOR SOMETHING J. L. Stein color *Cycle World* v56 no9 p24 O 2017

Motorcyclists

CANNONBALLS DEEP P. D'ORLÉANS *Cycle World* v56 no1 p21 Ja/F 2017

CRASHING AND LEARNING N. Ienatsch color *Cycle World* v56 no7 p24 Ag 2017

FLAT-LAND PROBLEM: FREEWAY ON- AND OFF-RAMPS N. Ienatsch color *Cycle World* v55 no10 p20 N 2016

FORZA LORENZO! color *Cycle World* v56 no2 p74 Mr 2017

HURRICANES, POOP, AND FLAT-TRACKS P. JONES color *Cycle World* v56 no2 p24 Mr 2017

KICK THE DUST UP color *Cycle World* v56 no5 p74 Je 2017

LIGHTING IT UP color *Cycle World* v56 no7 p70 Ag 2017

LOOK NOW. DON'T LOOK NOW N. Ienatsch color *Cycle World* v56 no1 p20 Ja/F 2017

MOTORCYCLE ROAD: The making of a photo essay E. Parkhurst, K. Volman et al color *Virginia Living* v15 no5 p13 Ag 2017

NOT AGAIN! color *Cycle World* v56 no8 p6 S 2017

ON BEING A FAN K. Cameron color *Cycle World* v56 no1 p58 Ja/F 2017

SLIPSTREAM color *Cycle World* v56 no4 p74 My 2017

VICTORY! color *Cycle World* v56 no1 p66 Ja/F 2017

Motorcyclists—Clothing

The Inflatable Man D. CURCURITO color *Popular Mechanics* p46 S 2017

Motorcyclists—Clothing—Evaluation

RIDERS ON THE STORM D. Canet color *Cycle World* v55 no11 p12 D 2016

Motorcyclists—Equipment & supplies

CHARACTER ADJUSTMENT D. Canet color *Cycle World* v56 no2 p18 Mr 2017

PICKING THE RIGHT PACK S. MacDonald color *Cycle World* v56 no2 p16 Mr 2017

Motorcyclists—Health

THAT TWIST OF YOUR WRIST J. L. Stein color *Cycle World* v56 no2 p22 Mr 2017

Motorcyclists—Training of

MONEY FOR SOMETHING J. L. Stein color *Cycle World* v56 no9 p24 O 2017

Motorman's Son, The (Music)

Recalling Generations K. Micallef color *Downbeat* v84 no6 p31 Je 2017

Motorola Inc.

Moto Z Play: Long-lasting, affordable, and modular too J. CROSS color graph *PCWorld* p114 O 2016

Motors—Maintenance & repair

cabin capers P. SULLIVAN cartoon *Cabin Living* p88 Ap 2017

Motorsports

See also

Automobile racing

Motorcycle racing

Mud racing

Off-road racing

2017 SCHEDULE chart *Dirt Sports + Off-Road* v51 no5 p72 My 2017

2017 SCHEDULE chart *Dirt Sports + Off-Road* v51 no8 p72 Ag 2017

2017 SCHEDULE *Dirt Sports + Off-Road* v51 no11 p72 N 2017

Best Pit Stop Ever J. SCHWARB *Indianapolis Monthly* p15 My 2017

Go color *Road & Track* v68 no10 p9 Jl 2017

A HALF CENTURY OF PENSKE M. PRINCE color *Road & Track* v68 no5 p14 D 2016/Ja 2017

Race to the Bottom S. SMITH color *Road & Track* v68 no9 p22 Je 2017

RUNWAY MODEL C. Csere diag *Car & Driver* v62 no10 p20 Ap 2017

TURNING POINTS P. LERNER color *Road & Track* v68 no10 p98 Jl 2017

Motorsports instruction

OVERLAND AFFAIR M. PRINCE color *Road & Track* v68 no9 p92 Je 2017

Motorsports—Competitions

MOTORSPORT | BEST OF 2016 color *Road & Track* v68 no6 p8 F 2017

A NATION'S DATEBOOK color *Dirt Sports + Off-Road* v51 no12 p72 D 2017

Motorsports—News Briefs

REIGNED OUT color *Road & Track* v68 no6 p10 F 2017

Mott, Catherine

Lulu and the Shadow Catcher bw color *Magazine Antiques* v184 no3 p82 My/Je 2017

Mott, Jessie

ECCENTRIC BEASTS J. FOUMBERG cartoon *Chicago* v66 no2 p28 F 2017

Mott, Lucretia, 1793-1880

"The suffragettes would not back down" A. Haglage and E. Mahaney color *Glamour* v115 no2 p80 F 2017

Mott, Mary

Dream Buddy on a Trail Ride cartoon *Horse & Rider* v56 no3 p72 Mr 2017

Mott, N. F. (Nevill Francis), Sir, 1905-1996

50, 100 & 150 YEARS AGO bw color *Scientific American* v317 no3 p94 S 2017

Motta, Mario

Amateurs Track a DISINTEGRATING Planet *Sky & Telescope* v133 no4 p66 Ap 2017

Evolution of Astroimaging *Sky & Telescope* v132 no6 p57 D 2016

Motter, Adilson E.

THE UNFOLDING AND CONTROL OF NETWORK CASCADES *Physics Today* v70 no1 p32 Ja 2017

Mottola, Greg

The Joneses Tries to Shake Up the 'Hood S. Zacharek color *Time* v188 no18 p44 O 31 2016

Mottola, S.

Rosetta's comet 67P/Churyumov-Gerasimenko sheds its dusty mantle to reveal its icy nature bibl graph *Science* v354 no6319 p1566 D 23 2016

Seasonal exposure of carbon dioxide ice on the nucleus of comet 67P/Churyumov-Gerasimenko bibl bw graph *Science* v354 no6319 p1563 D 23 2016

Surface changes on comet 67P/Churyumov-Gerasimenko suggest a more active past bw graph *Science* v355 no6332 p1392 Mr 31 2017

Mouchawar, Ronaldo

SOUQ.COM'S CEO ON BUILDING AN E-COMMERCE POWERHOUSE IN THE MIDDLE EAST: Winning trust in regions where payments are made in cash color *Harvard Business Review* v95 no5 p35 S/O 2017

Mouguiama-Daouda, Patrick

Dispersals and genetic adaptation of Bantu-speaking populations in Africa and North America diag *Science* v356 no6337 p543 My 5 2017

Moukarbel, Chris

Lady Gaga, Brought Low D. D'addario color *Time* v190 no14 p54 O 9 2017

MOUKHEIBER, ZINA

THE WORLD'S BILLIONAIRES bw color diag graph map *Forbes* v199 no3 p84 Mr 28 2017

Mould, Arne

PCGF3/5–PRC1 initiates Polycomb recruitment in X chromosome inactivation color *Science* v356 no6342 p1081 Je 9 2017

Moulet, A.

Soft x-ray excitonics bw diag *Science* v357 no6356 p1134 S 15 2017

Moulin, Solène

An algal photoenzyme converts fatty acids to hydrocarbons color graph *Science* v357 no6354 p903 S 1 2017

Moulton, David

PHOTO FINISH color *Backpacker* v45 no1 p96 Ja 2017

Moulton, Melissa

The Riddle of Rip Currents color *Oceanus* v51 no2 p44 Wint 2016

Moultrie, Autumn

for the Win N. Spradley color *Essence* v47 no12 p57 Ap 2017

Mounds (Archaeology)

Breaking Cahokia's Glass Ceiling E. A. POWELL bw color *Archaeology* v69 no6 p16 N/D 2016

Mounds (Archaeology)—Sweden

OFF THE GRID M. GRUNBERG-BANYASZ color *Archaeology* v70 no4 p10 Je-Ag 2017

Moune, Martin

Reversion of antibiotic resistance in Mycobacterium tuberculosis by spiroisoxazoline SMARt-420 bibl diag *Science* v355 no6330 p1206 Mr 17 2017

Mounk, Yascha

ECHT DEUTSCH *Harper's Magazine* p66 Ap 2017

European Disunion color *New Republic* v248 no8/9 p58 Ag/S 2017

What Your Country Should Do for You W. A. Galston color *Washington Monthly* v49 no9/10 p126 S/O 2017

Mount, Adam

Adapting nuclear modernization to the new administration bibl *Bulletin of the Atomic Scientists* v73 no3 p167 My 2017

Mount, Anson

Marvel's Inhumans N. Abrams, S. Highfill et al color *Entertainment Weekly* no1482/1483 p99 S 22 2017

Mount, Christopher

Decoupling genetics, lineages, and microenvironment in IDH-mutant gliomas by single-cell RNA-seq diag *Science* v355 no6332 p1391 Mr 31 2017

MOUNT, EMILY

Silversword Fight *National Parks* v91 no2 p28 Spr 2017

Mount, Ferdinand

Good Lord color *New York Review of Books* v64 no16 p66 O 26 2017

Mount, Nick

Blinking like moles B. BETHUNE bw *Maclean's* v130 no8 p60 S 2017

Mount Baker Wilderness (Wash.)
the play list color diag il *Backpacker* v45 no2 p14 Mr 2017
Mount Baldy Wilderness (Ariz.)—Description & travel
Change of Pace Q. HARPER color *Backpacker* p24 My 2017
Mount Holyoke College
Womanhood Redefined N. VARGAS-COOPER *American Conservative* v16 no1 p27 Ja/F 2017
Mount Kimbie (Performer)
Step Out M. Trammell cartoon *New Yorker* v93 no16 p22 Je 5 2017
Winter Preview M. Trammell cartoon *New Yorker* v92 no37 p12 N 14 2016
Mount of Olives (Jerusalem)
Center of The World R. BROOKHISER bw *National Review* v69 no7 p47 Ap 17 2017
Mount Rushmore National Memorial (S.D.)
A Nose for History bw *Reader's Digest* v190 no1132 p26 Jl/Ag 2017
PRESIDENTIAL TRAIL *South Dakota Magazine* v32 no4 p109 N/D 2016
VOYAGES S. ANDERSON, J. L. KEILES et al *New York Times Magazine* p37 Mr 26 2017
Mount Yasur (Vanuatu)
Volcanic carbon dioxide seen from space color *Science* v354 no6319 p1508 D 23 2016
Mountain bikes
BUZZ bw color *Bike Magazine* v24 no3 p30 My 2017
dream builds R. Palmer color *Bike Magazine* v23 no9 p82 D 2016
dreams of youth b. gavelda color *Bike Magazine* v23 no9 p44 D 2016
full circle r. palmer color *Bike Magazine* v24 no5 p96 Jl 2017
missed connections d. tolnai color *Bike Magazine* v24 no7 p40 S 2017
momentum r. palmer color *Bike Magazine* v24 no7 p46 S 2017
OFFLINE color *Bike Magazine* v24 no7 p122 S 2017
room with a pew c. reid color *Bike Magazine* v24 no7 p36 S 2017
scratch and sniff m. ferrentino color *Bike Magazine* v24 no6 p60 Ag 2017
turning the page b. minnigh color *Bike Magazine* v24 no5 p19 Jl 2017
Mountain bikes—Design & construction
made rad l. kemp color *Bike Magazine* v24 no2 p38 Mr 2017
solid as steel t. w. strokes bw color *Bike Magazine* v24 no6 p42 Ag 2017
Mountain bikes—Equipment & supplies
OFF LINE color *Bike Magazine* v24 no2 p90 Mr 2017
Mountain bikes—Equipment & supplies—Evaluation
9POINT8 FALL LINE T. Engel color *Bike Magazine* v24 no2 p84 Mr 2017
BEATDOWN t. engel color *Bike Magazine* v24 no5 p102 Jl 2017
breadwinner color *Bike Magazine* v24 no2 p77 Mr 2017
CRANKBROTHERS HIGHLINE color *Bike Magazine* v24 no2 p86 Mr 2017
DOUBLE DOWN: BETTING ON THE VERSATILE MAXXIS AGGRESSOR color *Bike Magazine* v24 no2 p88 Mr 2017
FOX TRANSFER PERFORMANCE N. Formosa color *Bike Magazine* v24 no2 p85 Mr 2017
full service r. cleek color *Bike Magazine* v24 no6 p126 Ag 2017
KS LEV CI R. Palmer color *Bike Magazine* v24 no2 p84 Mr 2017
ROCKSHOX REVERB STEALTH color *Bike Magazine* v24 no2 p85 Mr 2017
WHAT'S IN THE BOX? A SHIFT IN PERSPECTIVE t. engel color *Bike Magazine* v24 no6 p134 Ag 2017
X-FUSION MANIC J. Weber color *Bike Magazine* v24 no2 p86 Mr 2017
Mountain bikes—Evaluation
AGNOSTIC AGGRESSION A. Smith, R. Palmer et al color *Bike Magazine* v24 no1 p106 Ja/F 2017
asylum M. Ferrentino color *Bike Magazine* v24 no2 p76 Mr 2017
Cannondale R. Cleek color *Bike Magazine* v24 no7 p108 S 2017
chromag T. Engel color *Bike Magazine* v24 no2 p78 Mr 2017
Commencal J. Weber color *Bike Magazine* v24 no4 p98 Je 2017
Diamondback Clutch N. Formosa and S. Westover color *Bike Magazine* v24 no6 p122 Ag 2017
DOUBLE DUTY J. Weber, R. Palmer et al color *Bike Magazine* v24 no1 p88 Ja/F 2017

Ellsworth T. Engel color *Bike Magazine* v24 no7 p104 S 2017
EVEN FLOW T. Engel, R. Cleek et al bw color *Bike Magazine* v24 no1 p94 Ja/F 2017
EVIL'S THE FOLLOWING T. Engel color *Bike Magazine* v23 no9 p94 D 2016
FORWARD MOMENTUM L. Kemp, K. Butcher et al color *Bike Magazine* v24 no1 p116 Ja/F 2017
IBIS RIPLEY LS J. Weber color *Bike Magazine* v23 no9 p92 D 2016
"I JUST SIGNED UP FOR DIRTY KANZA. WTF DO I DO NOW?!" S. Yeager and B. STRICKLAND color *Bicycling* v58 no3 p88 Ap 2017
jamis R. Palmer color *Bike Magazine* v24 no2 p82 Mr 2017
Kona Honzo J. Weber and I. Schmitt color *Bike Magazine* v24 no6 p118 Ag 2017
Niner RIP 9 R. Cleek and B. Cole color *Bike Magazine* v24 no6 p114 Ag 2017
Norco Sight R. Palmer color *Bike Magazine* v24 no5 p88 Jl 2017
Reinventing the Wheels color *Men's Health* v32 no6 p57 Ag 2017
Rocky Mountain R. Palmer color *Bike Magazine* v24 no7 p100 S 2017
Salsa Deadwood J. Weber color *Bike Magazine* v24 no5 p84 Jl 2017
SALSA REDPOINT color *Bike Magazine* v23 no9 p84 D 2016
Scott T. Engel color *Bike Magazine* v24 no4 p90 Je 2017
"SHOULD I GET A FULL-SUSPENSION OR HARDTAIL MOUNTAIN BIKE?" M. Yozell and B. STRICKLAND color *Bicycling* v58 no3 p28 Ap 2017
"SHOULD I GET A PLUS BIKE OR A 29ER?" J. Lindsey and B. STRICKLAND color *Bicycling* v58 no3 p100 Ap 2017
SPECIALIZED S-WORKS ENDURO 29 B. Minnigh color *Bike Magazine* v23 no9 p88 D 2016
TAKE WINTER BY STORM color *Men's Health* v31 no10 p(Sp)14 D 2016
TRANSITION PATROL CARBON A. Smith color *Bike Magazine* v23 no9 p86 D 2016
trek color *Bike Magazine* v24 no2 p80 Mr 2017
TREK FUEL EX 9.8 WOMEN'S N. Formosa color *Bike Magazine* v23 no9 p90 D 2016
Turbo Levo color *Bike Magazine* v24 no5 p6 Jl 2017
Why Cycles R. Palmer color *Bike Magazine* v24 no4 p94 Je 2017
Mountain bikes—Maintenance & repair
master of (dis)repair k. butcher color *Bike Magazine* v24 no1 p60 Ja/F 2017
Mountain biking
AFTER THE FLOOD M. COTÉ bw color *Bike Magazine* v24 no4 p58 Je 2017
all access A. FINDLAY bw color *Bike Magazine* v24 no5 p70 Jl 2017
ARE YOU A BELIEVER IN SUFFERING? BELIEVING YOU AREN'T ALLOWED TO HAVE FUN UNTIL YOU'VE PUT IN SOME SOLID WORK? G. AVERILL bw color *Bike Magazine* v24 no4 p76 Je 2017
ask me no questions... k. butcher color *Bike Magazine* v23 no9 p50 D 2016
aspirations of mediocrity k. butcher color *Bike Magazine* v24 no7 p48 S 2017
awes8me EXTREME SPORTS J. AGRESTA *National Geographic Kids* no467 p9 F 2017
bogged down n. formosa bw *Bike Magazine* v24 no3 p56 My 2017
BUZZ bw color *Bike Magazine* v23 no9 p24 D 2016
BUZZ color *Bike Magazine* v24 no2 p26 Mr 2017
BUZZ color *Bike Magazine* v24 no4 p26 Je 2017
COLNAGO C60 DISC M. Phillips color *Bicycling* v58 no6 p58 Jl 2017
a cross to air: EL BRUC, SPAIN | MAY 14, 2017 | 3:01 P.M n. formosa cartoon *Bike Magazine* v24 no8 p34 N 2017
dirty in dodge r. stuart color *Bike Magazine* v24 no6 p36 Ag 2017
divide and conquer b. welch bw color *Bike Magazine* v23 no9 p36 D 2016
front lines n. formosa bw *Bike Magazine* v24 no7 p23 S 2017
GEOFF McFETRIDGE color *Bicycling* v58 no4 p104 My 2017
ICE CYCLE A. HALPERN color *Wired* v25 no6 p26 Je 2017
It's all in the hips c. brown color *Bike Magazine* v23 no9 p98 D 2016
light fall n. formosa color *Bike Magazine* v24 no6 p34 Ag 2017

PLANES, TRAINS, AND BROKEN LUGGAGE: A Year in the Life of a Climbing Photographer C. McInerney color *Climbing* no354 p70 Jl 2017

THE PUSH T. CALDWELL color *Climbing* no353 p52 My/Je 2017

Safe Foraging d. mother il *Backpacker* p48 Ag 2017

A Storied Isle S. Turrentine color *Climbing* no351 p34 F/Mr 2017

A Study in Contrast J. Lucas color *Climbing* no354 p22 Jl 2017

Thunder Thighs D. ALLFREY color *Climbing* no354 p27 Jl 2017

Trail of Memories C. WOODSIDE and J. BIDWELL bw color *Yankee* p20 Mr 2017

UNSOLICITED BETA M. Hook, M. Bourguignon et al color *Climbing* no351 p18 F/Mr 2017

UNSOLICITED BETA S. Thomas, K. Lewandowski et al *Climbing* no355 p14 Ag 2017

UNSOLICITED BETA T. Blasucci, S. Taylor et al color *Climbing* no352 p8 Ap 2017

WEIRD PEP TALKS WHILE OVERCOMING MY FEAR OF THE OVERHANGING WALL cartoon *Climbing* no357 p14 N 2017

Where the Waves Meet the Rock A. BURR color *Climbing* no354 p46 Jl 2017

The Winter Maestro M. Rossi bw color *Climbing* no350 p52 D 2016/Ja 2017

YES, YOU CAN! CLIMB A MOUNTAIN J. Ator color *Women's Health* v14 no8 p69 O 2017

You Are Not a Salt Lick M. TERRA-BERNS *Idaho Magazine* v16 no3 p6 D 2016

Z L. Hittmeier color *Skiing* p58 D 2016

Mountaineering accidents

THE DEADLY VALLEY A. Flower and M. Oakley bw color *Climbing* no356 p44 S/O 2017

Kodak Courage J. ELLISON color *Climbing* no354 p18 Jl 2017

SCARY (AND TRUE) TALES FROM A CRAG NEAR YOU *Climbing* no351 p21 F/Mr 2017

Mountaineering equipment

The Carabiner A. DENNIS color graph *Climbing* no350 p28 D 2016/Ja 2017

Contact High A. WHITTLE color *Conde Nast Traveler* v51 no10 p182 N 2016

THE DESCENT A. BURR color *Climbing* no353 p80 My/Je 2017

Field Notes color *Climbing* no354 p36 Jl 2017

The LSD Lower R. COPPOLILLO and M. CHAUVIN color *Climbing* no353 p50 My/Je 2017

A Theoretical Climbing Rope B. BLANCHARD *Climbing* no349 p10 N 2016

Mountaineering equipment—Evaluation

Climber's Little Helper J. LUCAS color *Climbing* no351 p44 F/Mr 2017

Field Notes color *Climbing* no351 p46 F/Mr 2017

Field Notes color *Climbing* no357 p26 N 2017

Mountaineering guides (Persons)

Opening Season B. HOINESS color *Climbing* no355 p32 Ag 2017

Mountaineering in art

Climber Art color *Climbing* no349 p9 N 2016

Mountaineering instruction

Break Through Ceilings C. VULTAGGIO color *Climbing* no351 p48 F/Mr 2017

Proper Hydration H. MOORE chart *Climbing* no351 p51 F/Mr 2017

Tag-Line Rappels J. LUCAS color *Climbing* no351 p50 F/Mr 2017

Mountaineering techniques

Belay Extensions J. D. MARTIN bw *Climbing* no351 p52 F/Mr 2017

Better Kneebars J. LUCAS color *Climbing* no350 p48 D 2016/Ja 2017

Break Through Ceilings C. VULTAGGIO color *Climbing* no351 p48 F/Mr 2017

Cross a Talus Field C. BUHAY color *Backpacker* p33 Ag 2017

TRAIN SMART B. BLANCHARD color *Climbing* no351 p54 F/Mr 2017

Mountaineering—Everest, Mount (China & Nepal)

EVEREST PEAK Performer [Cover story] A. Murphy color *Sports Illustrated* v126 no13 p26 My 8 2017

Mountaineering—Safety measures

Rap Smart A. FLOWER and M. OAKLEY color *Climbing* no356 p40 S/O 2017

Mountaineering—Search & rescue operations

Mountain Rescue S. VanLaer *New York State Conservationist* v71 no4 p2 F 2017

Mountaineers

    See also

    Women mountaineers

Abysmal Belay L. SHERMAN *Sierra* v102 no5 p16 St/O 2017

Approach the altar color *Backpacker* p20 My 2017

The Art and Science of LAYERING E. Larsen color diag *Backpacker* p71 My 2017

Being There D. Copeland bw color *Climbing* no355 p22 Ag 2017

Belay Extensions J. D. MARTIN bw *Climbing* no351 p52 F/Mr 2017

#ClimberBivy color *Climbing* no353 p19 My/Je 2017

The Curated Image K. LAMBERT color *Climbing* no350 p38 D 2016/Ja 2017

The Duffel Shuffle color *Climbing* no357 p15 N 2017

#Dynos color *Climbing* no351 p19 F/Mr 2017

Fast, Safe, and Easy Anchoring R. COPPOLILLO and M. CHAUVIN color *Climbing* no355 p50 Ag 2017

FLASH color *Climbing* no351 p8 F/Mr 2017

FLASH color *Climbing* no354 p6 Jl 2017

FLASH color *Climbing* no356 p8 S/O 2017

For the most determined R. STIEVE *Arizona Highways* v93 no8 p2 Ag 2017

The Freerider J. LUCAS color *Climbing* no355 p18 Ag 2017

Hero Shot M. SAMET color *Climbing* no354 p13 Jl 2017

How Not to Climb a Mountain J. MUIR *Sierra* v102 no3 p16 My/Je 2017

Mind the Gap *Arizona Highways* v92 no7 p5 Jl 2016

#NightClimbing color *Climbing* no354 p15 Jl 2017

A PORTRAIT IN SPEED A. LUBBEN color *Climbing* no356 p72 S/O 2017

The Prison Workout: Can You Survive? S. MESTEL cartoon color *Men's Health* v32 no8 p43 O 2017

Scary (and true) tales from a crag near you Mark and T. Jenkin *Climbing* no352 p11 Ap 2017

Thunder Thighs D. ALLFREY color *Climbing* no354 p27 Jl 2017

TRANSITIONS J. ELLISON color *Climbing* no356 p66 S/O 2017

UNSOLICITED BETA T. Blasucci, S. Taylor et al color *Climbing* no352 p8 Ap 2017

Van Mouse K. CORRIGAN color *Climbing* no351 p24 F/Mr 2017

WEIRD PEP TALKS WHILE OVERCOMING MY FEAR OF THE OVERHANGING WALL cartoon *Climbing* no357 p14 N 2017

Mountaineers—Attitudes

Climbr: Climbing Partner Reviews K. CORRIGAN*Climbing* no356 p32 S/O 2017

Ego Kills A. TOWER color *Climbing* no350 p30 D 2016/Ja 2017

No Man's Land N. PHILLIPS color *Climbing* no356 p22 S/O 2017

The Onsight Gamble H. WEIDNER color *Climbing* no356 p42 S/O 2017

Mountaineers—Charts, diagrams, etc.

Sending Southern Smoke H. MOORE chart color *Climbing* no351 p32 F/Mr 2017

Mountaineers—Equipment & supplies

A Climber's Guide to Food K. CORRIGAN color *Climbing* no350 p36 D 2016/Ja 2017

Protect Your Belay, Protect Your Belayer R. COPPOLILLO and M. CHAUVIN color *Climbing* no354 p42 Jl 2017

Sending Snacks K. CORRIGAN and J. ELLISON color *Climbing* no350 p42 D 2016/Ja 2017

Mountaineers—Health

Proper Hydration H. MOORE chart *Climbing* no351 p51 F/Mr 2017

Mountaineers—Societies, etc.

The Givers J. Abegg color *Climbing* no355 p52 Ag 2017

Mountaineers—Travel

LOST IN TOKYO C. MCINERNEY color *Climbing* no349 p48 N 2016

Mountains

BUZZ color *Bike Magazine* v24 no4 p26 Je 2017

cloud encounters of the third kind Cici Zhang color *Popular Sci-*

ence v289 no4 p92 Jl/Ag 2017

Double your fun: Trail Running C. BUHAY *Backpacker* p22 O 2017

EXPERIENCE THE PEAK OF MAGNIFICENCE *Iceland Review* v55 no3 p105 My/Je 2017

Forge ahead! A. Camille color *U.S. Catholic* v82 no5 p47 My 2017

The International Seabed Authority and Deep Seabed Mining M. Lodge *UN Chronicle* v54 no1/2 p1 2017

LAST PAGE P. STEFÁNSSON color *Iceland Review* v54 no5 p128 S-O 2016

LAST PAGE P. STEFÁNSSON *Iceland Review* v55 no4 p111 Jl/Ag 2017

LOOK EAST *Iceland Review* v55 no4 p102 Jl/Ag 2017

MIDDLEMARCH ROAD N. AUSTIN *Arizona Highways* v93 no11 p52 N 2017

Rock of Ages color *Log Home Living* v34 no6 p16 Ag 2017

SECRET MOUNTAIN TRAIL R. STIEVE *Arizona Highways* v93 no9 p54 S 2017

Mountains-to-Sea Trail (N.C.)—Description & travel

Mountains to Sea R. WICHELNS color map *Backpacker* v45 no1 p17 Ja 2017

Mountains—Alaska

Moose's Tooth J. LUCAS color *Climbing* no355 p28 Ag 2017

Mountains—Arizona

See also

    Chiricahua Mountains (Ariz.)

    Dos Cabezas Mountains (Ariz.)

    Rincon Mountains (Ariz.)

    San Francisco Peaks (Ariz.)

AT HOME IN THE WOODS J. Baeza *Arizona Highways* v96 no7 p48 Jl 2017

JUNIPER SPRINGS TRAIL R. STIEVE *Arizona Highways* v93 no11 p54 N 2017

LIKE A MOUNTAIN K. VAUGHN *Arizona Highways* v96 no7 p30 Jl 2017

SAN FRANCISCO PEAKS LOOP A. MCGIVNEY *Arizona Highways* v93 no10 p52 O 2017

Mountains—Arkansas

Accessible Serenity R. H. MOHLENBROCK color *Natural History* v125 no6 p42 Je 2017

Mountains—Asia

See also

    Himalaya Mountains

Mountains—British Columbia

See also

    Coast Mountains (B.C. & Alaska)

    North Cascades (B.C. & Wash.)

Coast Mountains of British Columbia—Wilderness of Sky and Ice E. Darack *Weatherwise* v70 no5 p8 S/O 2017

Mountains—Charts, diagrams, etc.

THE PRINCIPAL MOUNTAINS AND RIVERS OF THE WORLD, 1829 K. Wiles *History Today* v67 no5 p4 My 2017

Mountains—Colorado

OXYGEN IS OVERRATED J. Sumner color *Bicycling* v58 no8 p22 S 2017

Mountains—Georgia

The First Steps J. P. Davis *Backpacker* p71 Je 2017

Mountains—Idaho

See also

    Pioneer Mountains (Idaho)

    Seven Devils Mountains (Idaho)

ACROSS THE DEVILS BACK IN 1973 L. ADDINGTON *Idaho Magazine* v16 no10 p12 Jl 2017

A Dream Shared [Cover story] J. LEONARD *Idaho Magazine* v16 no6 p11 Mr 2017

Mountains—Italy

The Peaks of PERFECTION J. Murphy color *Esquire* p54 Big-BlackBook

Mountains—Japan

EATING CAKE L. Hittmeier color *Skiing* p64 D 2016

Mountains—Michigan

decay [Cover story] J. C. Davies color *Powder* v45 no6 p66 F 2017

Mountains—New Hampshire

EATON, NEW HAMPSHIRE color *Runner's World* v52 no8 p8

S 2017

Link 10 Peaks in a Day B. TARAZI il *Backpacker* p36 Ag 2017

Mountains—New York (State)

Easy Summits R. WICHELNS map *Backpacker* p26 My 2017

Mountains—North America

All 50 Classics, for Your Pleasure Z. GATES *Climbing* no355 p66 Ag 2017

Mountains—Oregon

WILD EAST N. FORMOSA bw color *Bike Magazine* v24 no7 p80 S 2017

Mountains—Pakistan

Home on the Range M. PALEY color map *National Geographic* v231 no4 p64 Ap 2017

Mountains—South Dakota

See also

    Black Hills (S.D. & Wyo.)

The Legendary Black Hills A. Radke color *American Cowboy* v23 no4 p28 D 2016/Ja 2017

Plan It: Black Hills Adventure *American Cowboy* v23 no4 p39 D 2016/Ja 2017

TOP 7 Things Craig Howe Loves About South Dakota *South Dakota Magazine* v33 no2 p17 Jl/Ag 2017

A Town Every 10 Miles: Trains don't stop in most Corson County towns today, but that doesn't mean you shouldn't B. HUNHOFF *South Dakota Magazine* v33 no2 p20 Jl/Ag 2017

Mountains—Switzerland

#NGMADVENTURE color *National Geographic* v232 no1 p14 Jl 2017

Mountains—Utah

"NEVER LOOK LIKE A TOURIST. ACT LIKE YOU KNOW WHERE YOU ARE." A. WHITTLE color *Conde Nast Traveler* v52 no3 p32 Mr 2017

Mountains—Uzbekistan

Into the Deep M. Synnott color map *National Geographic* v231 no3 p104 Mr 2017

Mountains—Wales

See also

    Snowdon (Wales)

And the Winning Photo Is... D. Tura *British Heritage Travel* v38 no4 p80 Jl/Ag 2017

Mountain yellow-legged frog

Bouncing Back in Yosemite: After flirting with extinction, Sierra Nevada yellow-legged frogs are staging a remarkable—and unexpected—comeback N. LUND *National Parks* v91 no3 p24 Summ 2017

Mounting of cameras—Equipment & supplies

Make a tripod holder for your smart phone L. Sassi color diag *Model Railroader* v84 no5 p56 My 2017

THEN SPEED IT UP color *Popular Science* v289 no5 p31 S/O 2017

Mountoufaris, George

Multicluster Pcdh diversity is required for mouse olfactory neural circuit assembly diag *Science* v356 no6336 p411 Ap 28 2017

Pcdhαc2 is required for axonal tiling and assembly of serotonergic circuitries in mice diag *Science* v356 no6336 p406 Ap 28 2017

Mount Vesuvius Eruption, 79 AD

The Lost City Of Pompeii K. B. RATTINI cartoon color map *National Geographic Kids* no471 p20 Je/Jl 2017

Moura, Fabiola

Brazil Has a School Problem diag *Bloomberg Businessweek* no4513 p24 Mr 6 2017

In Brazil, It's Now Beer—Without the Babes color *Bloomberg Businessweek* no4508 p20 Ja 23 2017

The Lady Teaching Brazilians How to Shop Online *Bloomberg Businessweek* no4536 p21 S 4 2017

MOURE, ERÍN

And What Of *Walrus* v14 no2 p40 Mr 2017

Mourn at Night (Music)

'MOURN AT NIGHT' J. ROSEN color *New York Times Magazine* p40 Mr 12 2017

Mourning dove shooting

FIVE REASONS YOU MISSED THAT DOVE P. Bourjaily color *Field & Stream* v122 no4 p34 S 2017

Mourning What We Thought We Were (Poem)

MOURNING WHAT WE THOUGHT WE WERE F. Bidart *New Yorker* v92 no46 p40 Ja 23 2017

Mourshed, Mona

A Better Metric for the Value of a Worker Training Program *Harvard Business Review Digital Articles* p2 F 14 2017

To Better Train Workers, Figure Out Where They Struggle *Harvard Business Review Digital Articles* p2 Je 30 2017

MOUSA, ABBAS

Home of the Brave cartoon *Reader's Digest* v190 no1132 p99 Jl/Ag 2017

Mousavian, Seyed Hossein

Winning Iran's Election Is Just The Beginning Of Rouhani's Political Struggles *NPQ: New Perspectives Quarterly* v34 no3 p22 Jl 2017

Mouse pads

free the mouse S. Horaczek color *Popular Science* v289 no6 p84 N/D 2017

MOUSHABECK, MICHEL

DATING IN SHARJAH *Publishers Weekly* v263 no43 p(Sp)16 O 24 2016

Mousis, O.

Xenon isotopes in 67P/Churyumov-Gerasimenko show that comets contributed to Earth's atmosphere diag *Science* v356 no6342 p1069 Je 9 2017

Moussi, Alain—Interviews

THE NEXT JCVD? R. CARTER color *Black Belt* v55 no1 p52 D 2016/Ja 2017

Moussouris, Katie

BUG BARONESS AND LUTA SECURITY CEO KATIE MOUSSOURIS EXPLAINS THE ECONOMY OF EXPLOITS R. Hackett color *Fortune* v176 no1 p65 Jl 1 2017

Moustakas, Leonidas

In the Dark About Dark Matter color diag graph *Sky & Telescope* v134 no2 p28 Ag 2017

Moustakas, Theodore D.

Jacques Isaac Pankove *Physics Today* v70 no4 p64 Ap 2017

MOUTET, ANNE-ELISABETH

Macron, Le Terminator color *Weekly Standard* v22 no39 p18 Je 19 2017

Mouth in literature

Bookends J. Parker and R. Galchen *New York Times Book Review* p31 O 30 2016

Mouthpieces (Musical instruments)—Evaluation

D'Addario Select Jazz Tenor Saxophone Mouthpiece J. Bowes color *Downbeat* v84 no5 p86 My 2017

JodyJazz Super Jet Alto Saxophone Mouthpiece B. Gibson color *Downbeat* v84 no5 p86 My 2017

Theo Wanne Slant Sig B. Gibson color *Downbeat* v84 no1 p106 Ja 2017

Mouths of Babes (Performer)

OUT OF THE MOUTHS OF BABES JAM color *Advocate* no1091 p34 Je/Jl 2017

Mouthwashes

Good for What Ails You B. Lutz color *New Orleans Magazine* v51 no7 p34 My 2017

PLAY DIRTY R. Dunn bw color *Men's Health* v32 no2 p108 Mr 2017

TRUSTED BRAND *Reader's Digest* v188 no1124 p50 O 2016

Mouzon, Alphonse, 1948-2016

Remembering Alphonse Mouzon B. Milkowski bw color *Downbeat* v84 no4 p18 Ap 2017

Movement disorders—Prevention

Good old-fashioned mobility insurance: Protecting your feet and ankles *Harvard Health Letter* v41 no12 p1 O 2016

Movement education

Movement and learning in elementary school S. F. Lindt and S. C. Miller color *Phi Delta Kappan* v98 no7 p34 Ap 2017

Moverman, Oren

THE DINNER J. McGovern color *Entertainment Weekly* no1463/1464 p34 Ap/My 2017

Dysfunction by the Plateful In The Dinner S. Zacharek color *Time* v189 no18 p55 My 15 2017

Movidius (Company)

Innovation M. Belfiore color *Bloomberg Businessweek* no4511 p33 F 13 2017

Movimento 5 stelle (Political party : Italy)

Participate. Don't Delegate D. Casaleggio *NPQ: New Perspectives Quarterly* v34 no2 p14 My 2017

When La Dolce Vita Starts to Sour J. Follain color *Bloomberg Businessweek* no4536 p33 S 4 2017

Moving on up a Little Higher (Music)

Shared Vision, Common Spirit Hadley bw *Downbeat* v84 no4 p61 Ap 2017

Moving of buildings, bridges, etc.

Historic Bargains color *Old House Journal* v45 no2 p36 Ap 2017

Mowatt, J.

Trap Karaoke Lets Fans Take Center Stage B. Danielle color *Ebony* v72 no9 p22 Jl/Ag 2017

Mowe, Sam

100 BEST Climate Solutions—And Why They're Going to Work color *Tricycle: The Buddhist Review* v26 no4 p44 Summ 2017

Mowen, Andrew J.

Local Officials' Opinions About Local Park and Recreation Services *Parks & Recreation* v52 no8 p48 Ag 2017

Mower, Sarah

High Time bw *Vogue* v207 no11 p117 N 2017

MARIA GRAZIA CHIURI cartoon color *Vogue* v207 no3 p415 Mr 2017

Sparkles FLY color *Vogue* v207 no3 p314 Mr 2017

Mowitz, Dave

10 SUCCESSFUL FARMERS: PEOPLE TO WATCH IN AGRICULTURE *Successful Farming* v115 no8 p12 Je/Jl 2017

THE APPEAL OF ROUGH-TERRAIN FORKLIFTS *Successful Farming* v114 no11 p24 N 2016

BATTERY CHARGERS: THE NEED FOR SPEED TO JUMP-START AN ENGINE DETERMINES WHICH CHARGER TO GET *Successful Farming* v115 no12 p41 O 2017

BLUE SKY IN AGRICULTURE *Successful Farming* v115 no1 p34 Ja 2017

BUYING USED PRECISION AG GEAR *Successful Farming* v115 no1 p26 Ja 2017

COMBAT HEAT STRESS WITH A QUICK RUN AROUND WITH THE PIVOT *Successful Farming* v115 no1 p58 Ja 2017

COMBINE TLC: HOW TO SCRUTINIZE YOUR COMBINE TO SHORT-CIRCUIT BREAKDOWNS *Successful Farming* v115 no11 p28 S 2017

DEALER DEALS FOR LARGE FWDs *Successful Farming* v114 no13 p38 D 2016

DEERE DEALERS' DEALS ON 4WDs *Successful Farming* v115 no3 p20 Mid-F 2017

FALL TILLAGE VALUES: THERE ARE OPPORTUNITIES TO BUY LITTLE-USED TILLAGE IMPLEMENTS AT MUCH-USED PRICES *Successful Farming* v115 no12 p36 O 2017

HEAVY-DUTY PICKUP REVIEW *Successful Farming* v115 no2 p38 F 2017

HOPPER-BOTTOM BUYING: SOFTNESS IN LATE-MODEL HOPPER-BOTTOM TRAILER VALUES OFFERS BUYING OPPORTUNITY *Successful Farming* v115 no11 p21 S 2017

INSPECTION CAMERAS: MECHANIC'S BORESCOPE HAS ENDLESS USES *Successful Farming* v115 no6 p30 Ap 2017

IRRIGATION ADVANCES *Successful Farming* v114 no13 p70 D 2016

IT'S A DISCOUNT MARKET ON CLASS 7 COMBINES: EXPECT FURTHER DISCOUNTS ON LATE-MODEL HARVESTERS THIS SUMMER AS WE WORK THROUGH A GLUT OF MACHINES *Successful Farming* v115 no9 p26 Ag 2017

LARGE SPLIT-ROW PLANTER PRICES ARE UP *Successful Farming* v115 no4 p28 Mr 2017

LATE-MODEL CULTIVATOR PRICES RISE *Successful Farming* v115 no5 p21 Mid-Mr 2017

LATE-MODEL ROUND BALERS: 2014 MODEL YEAR BALERS OFFER A SWEET SPOT OF POTENTIAL DEALER PRICING *Successful Farming* v115 no6 p22 Ap 2017

LEAKY PIPE CAN COST YOU $32 PER ACRE: A THIRD OF PUMPED WATER CAN LEAK OUT OF WORN GATES AND GASKETS *Successful Farming* v115 no12 p58 O 2017

LET'S MAKE A DEAL *Successful Farming* v114 no13 p32 D 2016

MECHANIC MAKE-DOs *Successful Farming* v114 no13 p40 D 2016

PAINTING TIPS, TRICKS: HERE ARE FOUR HOMEMADE IDEAS THAT CAN STREAMLINE YOUR PAINTING CHORES *Successful Farming* v115 no9 p36 Ag 2017

Moyo, Dambisa

Does Your Board Need a Tech Expert? *Harvard Business Review Digital Articles* p2 Mr 10 2016

Mozambique

Mozambique color *National Geographic* v231 no3 p8 Mr 2017

Mozart, Wolfgang Amadeus, 1756-1791

Idomeneo *Opera News* v81 no9 p60 Mr 2017

Operapedia: The Magic Flute W. A. MOZART *Opera News* v81 no7 p12 Ja 2017

Mozart in the Jungle (TV program)

Armed & Musical C. Wren color *Commonweal* v144 no6 p22 Mr 24 2017

Mozart in the Jungle M. ROUSH *TV Guide* p22 D 5 2016

Mozartiana (Theatrical production)

DANCE *New Yorker* v93 no20 p15 Jl 10 2017

Mozilla Firefox (Computer software)

Best web browsers of 2017: Chrome, Edge, Firefox, and Opera go head-to-head I. PAUL color graph *PCWorld* v35 no9 p43 S 2017

Mozilla promises a next-gen Firefox engine that will deliver huge improvements M. HACHMAN color *PCWorld* p61 D 2016

Mozuraitis, Raimondas

A key malaria metabolite modulates vector blood seeking, feeding, and susceptibility to infection bibl chart diag *Science* v355 no6329 p1076 Mr 10 2017

Mozzarella cheese

BUILD A BETTER SANDWICH color *Redbook* p125 S 2017

Get the Party Started! R. Meltzer Warren color *Consumer Reports* v82 no1 p9 Ja 2017

Mozziconacci, Julien

3D organization of synthetic and scrambled chromosomes diag *Science* v355 no6329 p1050 Mr 10 2017

MP3 players

Ode to MP3 K. C. POHLMANN color *Sound & Vision* v82 no8 p26 O 2017

Mpinja, Baze

No-Makeup Makeup for Women of Color color *Glamour* v115 no9 p79 S 2017

Mr. Gaga (Film)

Gaga for Mr. Gaga color *Dance Spirit* v21 no2 p18 F 2017

Mr. Mercedes (TV program)

Mr. Mercedes J. Jensen color *Entertainment Weekly* no1477 p46 Ag 11 2017

MR PORTER (Company)

STATE OF MIND L. IMMEDIATO *Los Angeles Magazine* v62 no6 p28 Je 2017

Mr. Robot (TV program)

6 loaded questions for Rami Malek J. Harman bw *Glamour* v115 no9 p44 S 2017

Mr. Robot Killed the Hollywood Hacker C. Doctorow color *MIT Technology Review* v120 no1 p100 Ja/F 2017

Mr. Robot K. P. Sullivan, N. Abrams et al color *Entertainment Weekly* no1482/1483 p77 S 22 2017

The Year of the Detail J. Harman color *Glamour* v114 no12 p77 D 2016

Mraz, Jason, 1977-

SPARC OF GENIUS J. TUPPONCE *Virginia Living* v15 no3 p33 Ap 2017

Mrazek, Michael

You're stronger than you think color *Redbook* p81 D 2016

MrSpeakers (Company)

MrSpeakers Aeon Headphones S. Guttenberg color *Sound & Vision* v82 no8 p20 O 2017

This Year's Model S. Guttenberg and C. Crowley color *Sound & Vision* v82 no5 p18 Je 2017

Ms. (Periodical)

ROOTS IN THE GROUND: The idea was simple but revolutionary: a magazine for women that was owned and controlled by women G. STEINEM *Ms.* v27 no3 p38 Fall 2017

MS-DOS (Operating system)

Microsoft: Don't worry, MS-DOS will live on after all S. J. VAUGHAN-NICHOLS color *PCWorld* v35 no1 p29 Ja 2017

Ms. Marvel (Fictitious character)

THE (MS. AND CAPTAIN) MARVEL UNIVERSE C. Agard color *Entertainment Weekly* no1436/1437 p65 O 21 2016

Mtingwa, Sekazi K.

SESAME and beyond color *Science* v356 no6340 p785 My 26

2017

MTV Movie Awards

ADAM DEVINE D. Franich color *Entertainment Weekly* no1465 p16 My 12 2017

MTV Networks

Dora Explores the Philippines? color *Earth Island Journal* v32 no1 p11 Spr 2017

Queens of the Stone Age S. MARSHALL color *New Republic* v247 no12 p64 D 2016

Should Awards Shows Be Gender-Neutral? N. Sperling color *Entertainment Weekly* no1466 p16 My 19 2017

Mu, Di

A central neural circuit for itch sensation color graph *Science* v357 no6352 p695 Ag 18 2017

Mu-Sheng Zeng

Precision medicine for nasopharyngeal carcinoma bibl diag *Science* v354 no6319 p24 D 23 2016

Muay Thai

A One-Stop Hit Shop J. Kelly bw *Bloomberg Businessweek* no4538 p61 S 18 2017

PRADAL SEREY M. ANDERSON, L. ELLIOTT et al bw color *Black Belt* v55 no5 p48 Ag/S 2017

MUBARAK, SALEH

Technology and Decorum inside the Mosque *Islamic Horizons* v46 no1 p52 Ja/F 2017

Mubili, Betiana Namambwe

Betiana Namambwe Mubili: 1988 – 2017 A. A. DAVIS color *Maclean's* v130 no10 p130 N 2017

Mück-Lichtenfeld, Christian

Radical-polar crossover reactions of vinylboron ate complexes bibl diag *Science* v355 no6328 p936 Mr 3 2017

Mucklow, Liam

TAPE-MEASURE TEE SHOTS! chart color *Golf Magazine* v58 no12 p75 D 2016

Mucocutaneous leishmaniasis

Microbial Mystery C. P. DUNAVAN bw color diag *Discover* v27 no10 p22 D 2016

Mucus

'Mucus houses' catch sea carbon fast S. MILIUS color *Science News* v191 no11 p13 Je 10 2017

Mud

MUD TROUBLES C. Barakat and M. Freckleton *Equus* no472 p14 Ja 2017

VET'S TOP MUD TIPS B. Crabbe color *Horse & Rider* v55 no12 p48 D 2016

Mud mounds

UNCONVENTIONAL GARDENING METHODS Pros and Cons S. Stonebrook *Mother Earth News* no280 p14 F/Mr 2017

Mud racing

ADD WATER TO DIRT AND YOU GET MUD. ADD BEER, WEED, AND 15,000 PEOPLE TO MUD AND YOU GET MICHIGAN MUD JAM M. DUFF color *Car & Driver* v63 no5 p106 N 2017

Mudambi, Ram

Local R&D Won't Help You Go Global *Harvard Business Review Digital Articles* p2 Je 25 2015

Sometimes Cutting R&D Spending Can Yield More Innovation *Harvard Business Review Digital Articles* p2 Ja 8 2015

Mudbound (Film)

MARY J. BLIGE IN Mudbound K. P. Sullivan color *Entertainment Weekly* no1478 / 1479 p61 Ag 18-25 2017

Mudde, Cas

Europe's Populist Surge color *Foreign Affairs* v95 no6 p25 N/D 2016

Mudge, Margaret

911 ACTION PLAN color *Practical Horseman* v45 no11 p42 N 2017

Mudge, Stephen J.

Cavalleria Rusticana/Sancta Susanna *Opera News* v81 no9 p47 Mr 2017

Così Fan Tutte *Opera News* v81 no10 p41 Ap 2017

Eliogabalo *Opera News* v81 no6 p48 D 2016

Lohengrin *Opera News* v81 no10 p40 Ap 2017

Manon *Opera News* v81 no6 p49 D 2016

Orange *Opera News* v81 no5 p52 N 2016

Samson et Dalila *Opera News* v81 no7 p45 Ja 2017

MudLOVE (Company)
Handsome Mug *Indianapolis Monthly* p25 F 2017
Mudstone
Dragon dinosaur met a muddy end M. Rosen cartoon *Science News* v190 no12 p5 D 10 2016
Redox stratification of an ancient lake in Gale crater, Mars J. A. Hurowitz, J. P. Grotzinger et al color *Science* v356 no6341 p922 Je 1 2017
Muehlhoff, Timothy M.
The gospel in a violent culture *Christian Century* v134 no12 p30 Je 7 2017
Mueller, Christof
Complex multifault rupture during the 2016 Mw 7.8 Kaikōura earthquake, New Zealand color map *Science* v356 no6334 p154 Ap 14 2017
MUELLER, COREY
SHOULD I REPLACE MY LAPTOP WITH A TABLET? color *Popular Science* v288 no6 p18 N/D 2016
Mueller, Cristina
6 Annoying Winter Skin Issues, Solved color *Glamour* v114 no12 p144 D 2016
the exact SKIN-CARE ROUTINE for you color *Redbook* p24 My 2017
How to Look Less Tired bw color *Glamour* v115 no3 p120 Mr 2017
ICONS bw color *Glamour* v115 no5 p190 My 2017
Pick your perfect serum color *Redbook* p54 Ap 2017
Mueller, Daren
SCOUT FOR SUDDEN DEATH SYNDROME: IOWA STATE UNIVERSITY EXTENSION PLANT PATHOLOGIST DAREN MUELLER ANSWERS FIVE QUESTIONS WITH THE LATEST RESEARCH RESULTS ON SDS G. Johnston color *Successful Farming* v115 no7 p34 My 2017
Mueller, Geoffrey A.
ZATT (ZNF451)–mediated resolution of topoisomerase 2 DNA-protein cross-links diag *Science* v357 no6358 p1412 S 29 2017
Mueller, Jakob
A Hero's Welcome *Tennis* v52 no6 p14 N/D 2016
Mueller, Jennifer
Chinese and American Consumers Have Different Ideas About What Makes a Product Creative *Harvard Business Review Digital Articles* p2 F 23 2017
Mueller, Jessie, 1983-
8 — WAITRESS M. Snetiker *Entertainment Weekly* no1444/1445 p118 D 16 2016
Jessie Mueller D. Kiper color *Current Biography* v78 no1 p41 Ja 2017
Mueller, Martin
Coker Fosters Customized Learning at New School J. Hale color *Downbeat* v84 no7 p86 Jl 2017
Mueller, Nicolas
ELEMENTS color *Snowboarder* v29 no2 p98 O 2016
Mueller, P.
Selective oxidative dehydrogenation of propane to propene using boron nitride catalysts bibl diag graph *Science* v354 no6319 p1570 D 23 2016
Mueller, P. E.
Observation of coherent elastic neutrino-nucleus scattering diag *Science* v357 no6356 p1123 S 15 2017
Mueller, Robert S., 1944-
Collusion Confusion A. C. MCCARTHY *National Review* v69 no15 p26 Ag 14 2017
Impatient for Impeachment F. BARNES color *Weekly Standard* v22 no40 p11 Je 26 2017
It's Mueller Time [Cover story] M. WARREN and J. LIFHITS color *Weekly Standard* v22 no36 p18 My 29 2017
Mueller's Dream Team Gears Up T. Schoenberg and D. Voreacos bw *Bloomberg Businessweek* no4527 p46 Je 19 2017
NO QUESTIONS ASKED A. DAVIDSON cartoon color *New Yorker* v93 no24 p20 Ag 21 2017
Special Counsel Named In Russia Probe M. Duffy color *Time* v189 no20 p29 My 29 2017
SURPRISE OUTCOMES TO THE MUELLER PROBE Y. BRENNER cartoon *New Yorker* v93 no20 p33 Jl 10 2017
Will Bob Mueller Separate Fact from Fiction? [Cover story] D. V. Drehle, T. Berenson et al color *Time* v190 no1 p24 Jl 3 2017

MUELLER, SHERI
Life cartoon *Reader's Digest* v190 no1132 p30 Jl/Ag 2017
Mueller, W. E.
Father Hood bw *Commonweal* v144 no2 p31 Ja 27 2017
MUENCH, JOYCE ROCKWOOD
White Mountain Country *Arizona Highways* v96 no7 p40 Jl 2017
Mufan Li
Ultrafine jagged platinum nanowires enable ultrahigh mass activity for the oxygen reduction reaction bibl chart graph *Science* v354 no6318 p1414 D 16 2016
Muffins
20-MINUTE SUPPERS A. Stewart color *Good Housekeeping* v265 no4 p117 O 2017
Blueberry Muffin Parfait color *Prevention* v69 no2 p17 F 2017
THE HANDBOOK *Martha Stewart Living* no267 p123 S 2016
MMM...MORNING color *Good Housekeeping* v265 no1 p110 Jl 2017
muffins remixed *Martha Stewart Living* no267 p88 S 2016
Pastries Galore J. RITZ *Los Angeles Magazine* v61 no11 p126 N 2016
Muffins—Evaluation
HYBRID *Washingtonian Magazine* v52 no1 p96 O 2016
Mufleh, Nina
What a Year of Job Rejections Taught Me About Pitching Myself *Harvard Business Review Digital Articles* p2 S 9 2015
Mugs
Essentials diag *Backpacker* v45 no3 p97 Ap 2017
Guten Co L. S. FORD *Texas Monthly* v45 no8 p17 Ag 2017
starters J. BAINBRIDGE, E. WARTZMAN et al color *Bon Appetit* p25 S 2017
WINNER'S CUP: A local potter sends fans on a hunt for free mugs around the city K. FRANZMAN *Indianapolis Monthly* v12 no40 p36 Ag 2017
Mugs—Evaluation
Adam's Home STYLE SHEET Adam color *O, The Oprah Magazine* p44 Ja 2017
The List color *O, The Oprah Magazine* p59 D 2016
OUR HOLIDAY GIFT GUIDE E. N. GAGE *Martha Stewart Living* no270 p31 D 2016
Muguruza, Garbiñe, 1993-
Garbiñe Muguruza C. Cullen color *Current Biography* v78 no1 p46 Ja 2017
GARBINE MUGURUZA'S FOREHAND SWING J. YANDELL *Tennis* v53 no1 p57 Ja/F 2017
Garbiñe Muguruza S. Gregory color *Time* v190 no9 p64 S 4 2017
Garbine Muguruza *Tennis* v53 no1 p56 Ja/F 2017
Holding Court G. WOOD and C. SCHAMA bw color *Vogue* v207 no9 p618 S 2017
Muhammad, Ibtihaj, 1985-
Ibtihaj Muhammad M. Hagan color *Current Biography* v78 no1 p51 Ja 2017
Ibtihaj Muhammad Redefining the Muslim American Image [Cover story] R. FATIMA *Islamic Horizons* v45 no6 p28 N/D 2016
A Letter to the President color *Time* v189 no12 p31 Ap 3 2017
Muhammad, Prophet, d. 632
'I'm Not Willing to Sacrifice Freedom of Expression on the Altar of Cultural Diversity' N. GILLESPIE color *Reason* v49 no1 p44 My 2017
Our Model Mosque: Muslims have a model for shaping their institutions: the way that the Prophet nurtured his Mosque I. BAGBY *Islamic Horizons* v46 no4 p46 Jl/Ag 2017
Muhammad ibn Sa'd, Abu Abdullah
c. 700: Medina *Lapham's Quarterly* v10 no1 p118 Wint 2017
Muhanna, Elias
Recipes for Aphrodisiacs Included K. THAROOR *New York Times Book Review* p21 O 9 2016
MUHLBAUM, DAVID
Buy the Gas Your Car Deserves *Kiplinger's Personal Finance* v71 no11 p71 N 2017
How to Get a Great Deal on a Lease *Kiplinger's Personal Finance* v71 no1 p38 Ja 2017
How to Get a Great Deal on a New Car color *Kiplinger's Personal Finance* v71 no5 p48 My 2017
Muhlenberg College (Allentown, Pa.)
Muhlenberg College *Dance Magazine* v90 p86 2016/2017 Sup-

plement College Guide

MUHLKE, CHRISTINE

APie fROM The SkY color *Bon Appetit* p140 S 2017

The Coffeeization of Tea color *GQ: Gentlemen's Quarterly* v86 no12 p108 D 2016

The Great British Day Off color *Bon Appetit* v62 no7 p70 Jl 2017

IN BLOOM bw color *Bon Appetit* v62 no6 p74 Je 2017

starters bw color diag *Bon Appetit* v62 no2 p19 Mr 2017

SUNNY SIDE UP color *Bon Appetit* v61 no12 p146 D 2016 / Jan2017

Muhlstein, Anka

A Marvelous Moment for French Writers and Artists J. Barnes color *New York Review of Books* v64 no6 p25 Ap 6 2017

A Marvelous Writer in a Hopeless Situation bw *New York Review of Books* v63 no20 p40 D 22 2016

Painters and Writers: When Something New Happens color *New York Review of Books* v64 no1 p33 Ja 19 2017

Muilenburg, Cheryl

Pretty Farmhouse on Medicine Creek color *Nebraska Life* v21 no2 p18 Mr/Ap 2017

Muir, David

2017 MaVeRicks OF Style J. Roth, N. Zarinsky et al bw color *Esquire* p81 S 2017

Muir, John, 1838-1914

7 BEARDS FROM THE CONSERVATION HALL OF FAME L. TONINO *Orion Magazine* v35 no4/5 p6 Jl-O 2016

How Not to Climb a Mountain *Sierra* v102 no3 p16 My/Je 2017

A Scotsman's Homecoming J. Miller *Sierra* v102 no3 p14 My/Je 2017

MUIR, SHARONA

6 FREQUENTLY ASKED QUESTIONS BY THE TIME-TRAVELING NATURE LOVER *Orion Magazine* v35 no6 p6 N/D 2016

Muir, T. Frank

The Meating Room: A DCI Gilchrist Investigation *Publishers Weekly* v264 no9 p80 F 27 2017

Muir, Vita

LITCHFIELD FOSTERS 'LIFETIME CONNECTIONS' J. Hale color *Downbeat* v84 no3 p72 Mr 2017

Muirhead, Russell

Rhapsody in Blue and Red: "We don't need less partisanship. We need better partisanship." Russell Muirhead shows how political parties get things done P. Robinson *Hoover Digest: Research & Opinion on Public Policy* no3 p153 Summ 2017

Muir-Wood, Robert

Estimating economic damage from climate change in the United States color graph *Science* v356 no6345 p1362 Je 30 2017

MUJAHID, ABDUL MALIK

What She Did Not Tell Me Was the Story *Islamic Horizons* v46 no2 p50 Mr/Ap 2017

Mujhid, Hadiyah

MOLDING HBCU STUDENTS INTO TECH INVESTORS J. McKinney color *Black Enterprise* v47 no7 p20 My/Je 2017

Mukamel, Eran A.

Single-cell methylomes identify neuronal subtypes and regulatory elements in mammalian cortex diag *Science* v357 no6351 p600 Ag 11 2017

Mukerji, Nirvan

Delivering Higher Value Care Means Spending More Time with Patients *Harvard Business Review Digital Articles* p2 D 26 2014

Mukharlyamov, Vladimir

What Private Equity Investors Think They Do for the Companies They Buy *Harvard Business Review Digital Articles* p2 Je 18 2015

Mukherjee, Abir—Interviews

"At Least We Gave Them the Railways" L. PICKER color *Publishers Weekly* v264 no11 p58 Mr 13 2017

Mukherjee, Amit S.

Why We're Seeing So Many Corporate Scandals *Harvard Business Review Digital Articles* p2 D 28 2016

MUKHERJEE, BHARATI

I AM an AMERICAN, NOT an ASIAN-AMERICAN *O, The Oprah Magazine* p137 My 2017

Mukherjee, Pranab, 1935-

I Am a Creation of This Parliament: IT SHAPED MY POLITICAL OUTLOOK AND PERSONA *Vital Speeches of the Day*

v83 no9 p256 S 2017

MUKHERJEE, RAHUL

The Act of Documenting: Documentary Film in the 21st Century *Film Quarterly* v71 no1 p115 Fall 2017

Mukherjee, S.

Discovery of orbital-selective Cooper pairing in FeSe diag *Science* v357 no6346 p75 Jl 7 2017

Mukherjee, Semanti

Distribution and clinical impact of functional variants in 50,726 whole-exome sequences from the DiscovEHR study chart graph *Science* v354 no6319 paaf6814-1 D 23 2016

Mukherjee, Siddhartha

THE ALGORITHM WILL SEE YOU NOW cartoon *New Yorker* v93 no7 p46 Ap 3 2017

The Gene: An Intimate History C. PELFREY KANNENGIESER *Humanist* v76 no6 p44 N/D 2016

THE INVASION EQUATION cartoon color *New Yorker* v93 no27 p40 S 11 2017

New, Improved, Obsolete *New York Times Book Review* p12 Mr 19 2017

The Story of the Gene H. HALL *Skeptical Inquirer* v41 no1 p59 Ja/F 2017

What we learn when two killers, heart disease and cancer, collide and reveal a common root *New York Times Magazine* p14 O 1 2017

Mukherjee, Sy

CHANGE THE WORLD !!!! color diag map *Fortune* v176 no4 p74 S 15 2017

DREAM WEAVER color *Fortune* v176 no3 p74 S 1 2017

FORTY UNDER FORTY 2017 color *Fortune* v176 no3 p62 S 1 2017

HOW AMERICANS LEARNED TO STOP WORRYING AND LOVE THE ACA diag *Fortune* v175 no8 p46 Je 15 2017

INNOVATIONS IN DRUG DELIVERY *Fortune* v174 no8 p20 D 15 2016

MINING COMEDY GOLD color *Fortune* v176 no3 p70 S 1 2017

Next Up for FDA Approval: Fewer FDA Rules color *Fortune* v175 no5 p14 Ap 1 2017

Obamacare's Thousand Cuts color *Fortune* v176 no3 p13 S 1 2017

PREPARE FOR THE DIGITAL HEALTH REVOLUTION [Cover story] color diag *Fortune* v175 no6 p36 My 1 2017

WORLD'S 50 GREATEST LEADERS [Cover story] color *Fortune* v175 no5 p46 Ap 1 2017

YOUTH REVOLT color *Fortune* v176 no3 p64 S 1 2017

Mukoyoshi, Hideki

Release of mineral-bound water prior to subduction tied to shallow seismogenic slip off Sumatra graph *Science* v356 no6340 p841 My 26 2017

Mukunda, Gautam

If Democrats Want to Challenge Trump, They Need a New Strategy *Harvard Business Review Digital Articles* p2 F 23 2017

Trump Is About to Test Our Theory of When Leaders Actually Matter *Harvard Business Review Digital Articles* p2 N 9 2016

The Values Crisis Shaking the Republican Party *Harvard Business Review Digital Articles* p2 Jl 27 2016

What Brexit Means for the Openness of the World Economy *Harvard Business Review Digital Articles* p2 Je 24 2016

Will President Trump Learn on the Job? *Harvard Business Review Digital Articles* p2 My 4 2017

Mulan (Film : 2018)

Disney's Renaissance Revival E. Berman color *Time* v189 no11 p58 Mr 27 2017

MULAN RIDES BACK INTO BATTLE—FOR REAL D. Coggan color *Entertainment Weekly* no1435 p10 O 14 2016

Mulani, Narendra

Simplify Your Analytics Strategy *Harvard Business Review Digital Articles* p2 Je 15 2015

Mulcahy, Diane

Don't Take Money from VCs Until You've Asked 4 Questions *Harvard Business Review Digital Articles* p2 F 26 2016

Repealing Obamacare Would Be Bad News for the Gig Economy *Harvard Business Review Digital Articles* p2 F 13 2017

Will the Gig Economy Make the Office Obsolete? *Harvard Business Review Digital Articles* p2 Mr 17 2017

Mulcahy, Lisa

The 411 On Curtain Clean-Up *Stage Directions* v30 no4 p16 Ap

2017

The Activist ARTIST *Stage Directions* v30 no3 p56 Mr 2017

ART WITH A (Re)Purpose: Sloan Award Winner, Harriet Taub from Materials for the Arts *Stage Directions* v30 no9 p19 S 2017

Color and Light *Stage Directions* v30 no2 p20 F 2017

The Costumer Is Thriving At 100 Years Young *Stage Directions* v30 no8 p23 Ag 2017

Director Kate Whoriskey brings intellect and compassion to Sweat *Stage Directions* v30 no5 p8 My 2017

Everything Old Is New Again *Stage Directions* v30 no1 p20 Ja 2017

The Gilded Cage *Stage Directions* v29 no12 p28 D 2016

HIGH SCHOOL THEATRE HONORS PROGRAM *Stage Directions* v29 no11 p24 N 2016

Historic and Thriving: Ford's Theatre: A hallowed past meets a modern aesthetic *Stage Directions* v30 no6 p11 Je 2017

Making Art Accessible *Stage Directions* v29 no10 p28 O 2016

Present to Past *Stage Directions* v30 no10 p60 O 2017

What doctors tell their friends about energy [Cover story] color *Redbook* p66 Jl/Ag 2017

What doctors tell their friends about weight loss [Cover story] color *Redbook* p72 Mr 2017

What nurses tell their friends color *Redbook* p82 My 2017

Mulcair, Tom, 1954-

PARLIAMENTARIAN OF THE YEAR J. GEDDES color *Maclean's* v129 no47 p18 N 28 2016

Mulch, Andreas

Merging paleobiology with conservation biology to guide the future of terrestrial ecosystems color *Science* v355 no6325 p594 F 10 2017

MULDER, CHRISTA P. H.

Validating Herbarium-Based Phenology Models Using Citizen-Science Data chart graph *BioScience* v66 no10 p897 O 1 2016

Mulder, Jan

A subcellular map of the human proteome color *Science* v356 no6340 p820 My 26 2017

MULDER, MARK

Geographic Justice bw color *Christianity Today* v61 no1 p72 Ja/F 2017

MULDER, MONIQUE BORGERHOFF

The Consequences of Internal Migration in Sub-Saharan Africa: A Case Study *BioScience* v67 no7 p664 Jl 2017

Muldoon, Paul, 1951-

Selected Poems 1968-2014 *Publishers Weekly* v263 no47 p84 N 21 2016

SUPERIOR ALOESWOOD P. Muldoon *New York Review of Books* v64 no1 p30 Ja 19 2017

Muldoon, Ryan

Free Speech and Learning from Difference *Society* v54 no4 p331 Ag 2017

Muldoon, Sean

Raising The Bar K. Tablang color *Forbes* v198 no9 p51 D 30 2016

Muldowney, Shirley, 1940-

Shirley Muldowney's Top Gas Dragster T. Taylor bw *Hot Rod* v70 no5 p10 My 2017

Muldrow, Diane

A Q&A cartoon color *Publishers Weekly* v264 no7 pc3 F 13 2017

Muldrow, Diane—Interviews

A Q&A L. S. Marcus and D. Muldrow cartoon color *Publishers Weekly* v264 no7 pc3 F 13 2017

Mule deer

MULE DEER color *Nebraska Life* v21 no5 p35 S/O 2017

Mule deer behavior

MAPPING MULEYS A. ISBERG color *Outdoor Life* v224 no8 p18 O 2017

MULE DEER color *Nebraska Life* v21 no5 p35 S/O 2017

Mule deer hunting

FEEL THE BURN T. WALRATH color *Outdoor Life* v224 no7 pH5 S 2017

MAPPING MULEYS A. ISBERG color *Outdoor Life* v224 no8 p18 O 2017

MULEYS ON YOUR OWN T. Walrath color *Outdoor Life* v223 no9 pH5 N 2016

Q & A D. E. Petzal cartoon *Field & Stream* v122 no5 p35 O 2017

Mulfinger, Dale

Adding On diag *Cabin Living* p22 Je 2017

Building at the Water's Edge bw color *Cabin Living* p20 Ap 2017

Cabin Details [Cover story] color *Cabin Living* p18 O 2017

Cabin Patterns color *Cabin Living* p20 Mr 2017

Carpenter Logic color *Cabin Living* p20 D 2016

Color Your World color *Cabin Living* p18 S 2017

Designing for Guests [Cover story] color *Cabin Living* p20 Ag 2017

Linkages color diag *Cabin Living* p36 Ja/F 2017

making the connection [Cover story] G. C. GRENSING color diag *Cabin Living* p38 O 2017

Mulhauser, B.

A worldwide survey of neonicotinoids in honey graph *Science* v357 no6359 p109 O 6 2017

Mulhere, Kaitlin

33 WAYS TO CUT YOUR TAXES [Cover story] color diag *Money* v46 no2 p52 Mr 2017

36 APPS THAT WILL SAVE YOU MONEY color *Money* v46 no4 p46 My 2017

5 Things to Know About the New FAFSA *Money* v45 no10 p37 N 2016

ALL THE PLACES YOU CAN GO TO COLLEGE FOR FREE color *Money* v46 no9 p82 O 2017

ASK THE EXPERT chart *Money* v46 no1 p29 Ja/F 2017

The Best Cell Phone Plan for You color diag *Money* v46 no6 p64 Jl 2017

Best Colleges for Sports Lovers chart *Money* v46 no3 p24 Ap 2017

THE BEST COLLEGES FOR YOUR MONEY 2017 chart color *Money* v46 no7 p52 Ag 2017

Climb Out of Student Debt chart color *Money* v45 no10 p29 N 2016

A Guide to Borrowing for Your Kid's College Degree color *Money* v46 no7 p20 Ag 2017

Lending Giant Gets Sued color *Money* v46 no2 p21 Mr 2017

Score a Great Summer Internship chart color *Money* v46 no1 p34 Ja/F 2017

Your Home Could Be a Star! color *Money* v46 no5 p14 Je 2017

Mulholland, Sarah

JPMorgan Traders Get Into Property Deals *Bloomberg Businessweek* no4504 p35 D 19 2016

Mulholland Drive (Film)

DAVID LYNCH'S DARK ART L. ANOLIK color *Vanity Fair* p118 Hollywood 2017 Supplement

Mullainathan, Sendhil

A Guide to Solving Social Problems with Machine Learning *Harvard Business Review Digital Articles* p2 D 8 2016

MULLALLY, ERIN

SAMHAIN REVIVAL color *Archaeology* v69 no6 p34 N/D 2016

Mullally, Megan

CONTRIBUTORS color *InStyle* v24 no9 p100 S 2017

THE FANTASTIC FOUR RETURN: Will. Grace. Karen. Jack. Need we say more? Behind the scenes of NBC's must-see revival [Cover story] J. HALTERMAN *TV Guide* v65 no41 p16 O 2 2017

MEGAN MULLALLY D. KAMP color *Vanity Fair* v59 no6 p60 My 2017

My Red Carpet Diary color *InStyle* v24 no9 p216 S 2017

Sound Bites color *Entertainment Weekly* no1451/1452 p2 F 3-10 2017

Mullally, Megan—Interviews

Megan Mullally color *O, The Oprah Magazine* p32 O 2017

Megan Mullally: How to Meet Your In-Laws C. M. Smith color *Entertainment Weekly* no1446/1447 p102 D 2016/Ja 2017

QUESTIONS FOR MEGAN MULLALLY D. ANDERSON-MINSHALL color *Advocate* no1090 p58 Ap 2017

Will & Grace Reunion! L. Beard color *Entertainment Weekly* no1434 p15 O 7 2016

With The Band M. WAKIM *Los Angeles Magazine* p84 Ap 2017

Mullaney, James

FROM OUR READERS *Sky & Telescope* v134 no6 p6 D 2017

Mullaney, Kathleen

BEST DENTISTS *Washingtonian Magazine* v52 no6 p116 Mr 2017

MULLARKEY, MAUREEN

Crosses to Bear color *Weekly Standard* v22 no39 p40 Je 19 2017

Mulleavy, Kate

The Dreamers E. Wilson color *InStyle* v24 no6 p38 Je 2017

Mulleavy, Laura

The Dreamers E. Wilson color *InStyle* v24 no6 p38 Je 2017

KATE AND LAURA MULLEAVY J. FELSENTHAL color *Vogue* v207 no3 p418 Mr 2017

MULLEN, MATT

Benoit DELHOMME *Interview* v47 no2 p70 Mr 2017

BØRNS *Interview* v46 no8 p40 O 2016

Francesco RAGAZZI *Interview* v47 no1 p20 F 2017

GHETTO GASTRO *Interview* v46 no8 p42 O 2016

Sarah SUTHERLAND *Interview* v47 no3 p18 Ap 2017

Steven SHEARER *Interview* v46 no9 p38 N 2016

Visionaire *Interview* v46 no9 p42 N 2016

MULLEN, SEAMUS

Hit the Grill Mark color *Bon Appetit* no8 p46 Ag 2017

Mullen, Thomas—Interviews

Totalitarian Noir: It Happened Here L. PICKER color *Publishers Weekly* v264 no31 p63 Jl 31 2017

Muller, A. L.

Observation of a large-scale anisotropy in the arrival directions of cosmic rays above 8 × 1018 eV *Science* v357 no6357 p1266 S 22 2017

Müller, Carolin A.

Deep functional analysis of synII, a 770-kilobase synthetic yeast chromosome diag *Science* v355 no6329 p1047 Mr 10 2017

Müller, Christoph

Submillihertz magnetic spectroscopy performed with a nanoscale quantum sensor diag *Science* v356 no6340 p832 My 26 2017

Müller, Daniel J.

Membrane proteins scrambling through a folding landscape bibl diag *Science* v355 no6328 p907 Mr 3 2017

Muller, G.

Observation of a large-scale anisotropy in the arrival directions of cosmic rays above 8 × 1018 eV *Science* v357 no6357 p1266 S 22 2017

Muller, Héloïse

3D organization of synthetic and scrambled chromosomes diag *Science* v355 no6329 p1050 Mr 10 2017

Müller, J.

Crystallization and vitrification of electrons in a glass-forming charge liquid bw *Science* v357 no6358 p1381 S 29 2017

Muller, James

Statesmanship and Geopolitics *Society* v54 no2 p188 Ap 2017

MÜLLER, JAN-WERNER

BLAMING THE PEOPLE color *Nation* v305 no8 p31 O 9 2017

MULLER, JOANN

Peugeot on the Go color *Forbes* v200 no2 p48 S 5 2017

THE WORLD'S BILLIONAIRES bw color diag graph map *Forbes* v199 no3 p84 Mr 28 2017

Müller, Jürg

Propagation of Polycomb-repressed chromatin requires sequence-specific recruitment to DNA diag *Science* v356 no6333 p85 Ap 7 2017

Muller, M. A.

Observation of a large-scale anisotropy in the arrival directions of cosmic rays above 8 × 1018 eV *Science* v357 no6357 p1266 S 22 2017

Muller, Monica

Driving Home the Safety Discussion il *Consumer Reports* v82 no9 p6 S 2017

Müller, Nicolas

GORDON HARRISON color *Snowboarder* v29 no3 p42 N 2016

HARMONIC CONVERGENCE O. Gagnon bw *Snowboarder* v29 no4 p14 D 2016

Müller, Norbert

Angular momentum–induced delays in solid-state photoemission enhanced by intra-atomic interactions chart color graph *Science* v357 no6357 p1274 S 22 2017

Müller, Pavel

An algal photoenzyme converts fatty acids to hydrocarbons color graph *Science* v357 no6354 p903 S 1 2017

Müller, Rainer

mTORC1 activity repression by late endosomal phosphatidylino-sitol 3,4-bisphosphate diag *Science* v356 no6341 p968 Je 1 2017

Muller, Richard A., 1944-

Now The Physics of Time M. Bojowald *Physics Today* v70 no2 p57 F 2017

Rethinking the arrow of time L. Jardine-Wright color *Science* v353 no6307 p1504 S 30 2016

Muller, S.

Observation of a large-scale anisotropy in the arrival directions of cosmic rays above 8 × 1018 eV *Science* v357 no6357 p1266 S 22 2017

Mulley, Clare

NO HUSBAND NEEDED - I FLY A SPITFIRE: The memoir of a pioneering woman pilot who delivered vital fi ghter aircraft and bombers around Britain during the war *History Today* v67 no6 p100 Je 2016

Plotting Hitler's defeat *History Today* v67 no1 p64 Ja 2017

MULLICH, JOE

Donor-Advised Funds: The Fastest-Growing Vehicle For Charitable Giving color *Forbes* v200 no5 p88 N 14 2017

How Three Top CIOs Turn IT Into "Empowerment Organizations" color *Forbes* v200 no1 p92 Jl 27 2017

SMART MOTION: The New Body Language color diag *Forbes* v200 no4 p78 O 24 2017

Mullie, Tom

Reducing Noise in Decision Making: Interaction color *Harvard Business Review* v94 no12 p18 D 2016

Mulligan, Joseph E.

Did you receive support from your faith community while you were experiencing depression and/or anxiety? graph *America* v216 no12 p6 My 29 2017

Mulligan, Vikram K.

Global analysis of protein folding using massively parallel design, synthesis, and testing color diag *Science* v357 no6347 p168 Jl 14 2017

Mullikin, Tom

MARTIAL ARTS DISCIPLINE DRIVES GLOBAL EXPEDITION LEADER W. J. Thomas Smith color *Black Belt* v55 no6 p10 O/N 2017

Mullin, Emily

Edible CRISPR Could Precisely Target Dangerous Germs color *MIT Technology Review* v120 no4 p23 Jl/Ag 2017

Gene Therapy 2.0 bw color *MIT Technology Review* v120 no2 p48 Mr/Ap 2017

HUMANITARIANS color il *MIT Technology Review* v120 no5 p62 S/O 2017

A Mind-Reading Device Gives Words to "Locked In" Patients color *MIT Technology Review* v120 no3 p18 My/Je 2017

PIONEERS color il *MIT Technology Review* v120 no5 p50 S/O 2017

Mullin, Vinny

UNSOLICITED BETA color *Climbing* no353 p18 My/Je 2017

Mullins, Alyssa

How Stable is the Condition of Family Homelessness? chart *Society* v54 no1 p46 F 2017

Mullins, Dyche

Not just Salk color *Science* v357 no6356 p1105 S 15 2017

Mullins, John

Shutting Down Your Business Gracefully *Harvard Business Review Digital Articles* p2 Mr 20 2017

Mullins, Luke

BREITBART'S (OTHER) MAN IN THE WHITE HOUSE *Washingtonian Magazine* v52 no9 p70 Je 2017

FOTOWEEKDC *Washingtonian Magazine* v52 no2 p35 N 2016

I'M PROBABLY THE ONLY PERSON ON THE PLANET THAT'S KIND OF HAPPY THE NEW COLD WAR IS HAPPENING. I'VE BEEN WAITING 25 YEARS *Washingtonian Magazine* v52 no12 p68 S 2017

LARRY HOGAN IS HAVING A GRAND OLD TIME AS GOVERNOR *Washingtonian Magazine* v52 no5 p52 F 2017

My Mr. Chemotherapy Contest *Washingtonian Magazine* v52 no3 p60 D 2016

WHAT A COUNTRY! (AGAIN!): WHO'D HAVE THOUGHT THERE'D COME A TIME WHEN THE KING OF COLD WAR COMEDY, YAKOV SIMIRNOFF, JUST MIGHT MAKE A COMEBACK? AN ONLY-IN-AMERICA-RIGHT-NOW STORY *Washingtonian Magazine* v52 no12 p64 S 2017

WHERE & WHEN: 18 THINGS YOU REALLY OUGHT TO DO THIS MONTH *Washingtonian Magazine* v52 no12 p29 S 2017

Mullins, Sarah M.

Cooking Up New Ideas *Cincinnati Magazine* v50 no8 p83 My 2017

Fabulous Finds *Cincinnati Magazine* v50 no2 pH4 N 2016

MULLINS-COHEN, GINA

Another Year of Progress *Parks & Recreation* v51 no10 p12 O 2016

Arts and Parks: A Natural Fit *Parks & Recreation* v52 no8 p10 Ag 2017

Celebrating Community and People *Parks & Recreation* v51 no12 p8 D 2016

A Guiding Hand *Parks & Recreation* v52 no2 p10 F 2017

Hate Has No Place Here *Parks & Recreation* v52 no9 p10 S 2017

Inclusion Is the Solution *Parks & Recreation* v52 no10 p10 O 2017

It's All in the Details *Parks & Recreation* v52 no3 p10 Mr 2017

Keep On Moving *Parks & Recreation* v52 no1 p10 Ja 2017

A Path to Leadership *Parks & Recreation* v52 no5 p10 My 2017

Think Healthy Across the Board *Parks & Recreation* v52 no6 p10 Je 2017

A Threat to Our Legacy *Parks & Recreation* v52 no4 p10 Ap 2017

United We Serve *Parks & Recreation* v51 no11 p8 N 2016

Mulot, M.

A worldwide survey of neonicotinoids in honey graph *Science* v357 no6359 p109 O 6 2017

Mulrain, Ed

The SAILING SCENE color *Sail* v48 no7 p6 Jl 2017

Mulrow, Jennifer

THE 2017 GLAMOUR BEAUTY AWARD color *Glamour* v115 no4 p81 Ap 2017

Beauty for the Anime-Obsessed cartoon color *Glamour* v115 no2 p58 F 2017

Eye-Makeup Lookbook color *Glamour* v115 no5 p72 My 2017

Mermaid Eyes color *Glamour* v115 no1 p36 Ja 2017

The Most Fun Makeup to Wear This Spring color *Glamour* v115 no3 p99 Mr 2017

My Beauty Passport to Paris color *Glamour* v115 no9 p100 S 2017

Our Most-Loved Hair & Makeup Looks for Fall color *Glamour* no8 p73 Ag 2017

Party-Hair Lookbook color *Glamour* v114 no12 p142 D 2016

Your Hair Lookbook color *Glamour* v115 no10 p90 O 2017

Your Hair Lookbook color *Glamour* v115 no4 p104 Ap 2017

Your Hair Lookbook color *Glamour* v115 no7 p50 Jl 2017

Your Ponytail Lookbook color *Glamour* v115 no3 p106 Mr 2017

Multhaup, Marina

How the Imagined "Rationality" of Engineering Is Hurting Diversity—and Engineering *Harvard Business Review Digital Articles* p2 Ag 10 2017

Uber and Other Tech Companies Could Make Simple Changes to Avoid Driving Away Their Female Engineers color *Harvard Business Review Digital Articles* p2 F 28 2017

Multi-sided platform businesses

3 Questions to Ask Before Adopting a Platform Business Model C. Brown *Harvard Business Review Digital Articles* p2 Ap 5 2016

FINDING THE PLATFORM IN YOUR PRODUCT: FOUR STRATEGIES THAT CAN REVEAL HIDDEN VALUE A. HAGIU and E. J. ALTMAN il *Harvard Business Review* v95 no4 p94 Jl/Ag 2017

Platforms might soon consume huge swaths of our economy—but what do they want to do with their power? J. Herrman *New York Times Magazine* p16 Mr 26 2017

Transitioning Your Company from Product to Platform N. Furr *Harvard Business Review Digital Articles* p2 Ap 7 2016

Multicellular life

Can Animals Live Without Oxygen? K. Madin *Oceanus* v52 no1 p4 Summ 2016

Multicore processors (Computers)

HP's 15-inch Spectre x360 features upgraded hardware and a new look A. YEE color *PCWorld* p30 Mr 2017

Multiculturalism

See also

Diversity in organizations

Diversity in the workplace

Autopsies W. Voegeli *Claremont Review of Books* v17 no3 p8 Summ 2017

Deloitte's Radical Attempt to Reframe Diversity A. Wittenberg-

Cox *Harvard Business Review Digital Articles* p2 Ag 3 2017

First Line of Diversity K. R. LEWIS color *Working Mother* v40 no2 p32 Je/Jl 2017

Sadiq Khan T. Penny color *Bloomberg Businessweek* no4540 p80 O 2 2017

What It Will Take to Make the Tech Industry More Diverse S. Colby, H. Ma et al *Harvard Business Review Digital Articles* p2 Mr 15 2016

Why Diverse Teams Are Smarter D. Rock and H. Grant *Harvard Business Review Digital Articles* p2 N 4 2016

Multiculturalism in mass media

The Woman Changing the Face of Hollywood D. Coggan color *Entertainment Weekly* no1476 p46 Ag 4 2017

Multiculturalism—Canada

Canada in the Age of Donald Trump S. MARCHE bw *Walrus* p20 Ja\F 2017

Multiculturalism—United States

LOVE IN BLACK & WHITE L. L. Joiner color *Essence* v47 no8 p129 D 2016

WORKING WITH The Donald S. SMITH *Texas Monthly* v45 no3 p82 Mr 2017

Multidrug tolerance (Microbiology)

Mechanisms of bacterial persistence during stress and antibiotic exposure A. Harms, E. Maisonneuve et al bibl diag graph *Science* v354 no6318 paaf4268-1 D 16 2016

Multihull sailboats

See also

Catamarans

Herdin' Cats color *Sail* v48 no7 p8 Jl 2017

Multilingual education

WORLD OF WORDS P. STEFÁNSSON *Iceland Review* v55 no4 p78 Jl/Ag 2017

Multilingualism

See also

Multilingual education

WORLD OF WORDS P. STEFÁNSSON *Iceland Review* v55 no4 p78 Jl/Ag 2017

Multimatic Inc.

SPOOL SAMPLE K. C. Colwell color *Car & Driver* v63 no5 p20 N 2017

Multimedia (Art)—Exhibitions

The Multimedia Artwork of Doug Aitken D. AITKEN bw color *Issues in Science & Technology* v33 no2 p73 Wint 2017

TOXIC DUST IN THE WIND T. NASSAR *In These Times* v41 no6 p39 Je 2017

Multimode-mode optical fibers

Spatiotemporal mode-locking in multimode fiber lasers L. G. Wright, D. N. Christodoulides et al color *Science* v357 no6359 p94 O 6 2017

Multiple choice examinations

Recruiters urged to rethink testing after tribunal win: EAT agrees multiple-choice test discriminated against applicant with Asperger's syndrome *People Management* p16 Je 2017

Multiple human abnormalities—Psychological aspects

a rare condition, a beautiful legacy M. ZUCKER *Parents* v92 no2 p80 F 2017

Multiple intelligences

See also

Emotional intelligence

Emotional Intelligence Has 12 Elements. Which Do You Need to Work On? D. Goleman and R. E. Boyatzis color graph *Harvard Business Review Digital Articles* p2 F 6 2017

Multiple Maniacs (Film)

John Waters: Multiple Maniacs Relaunch C. Holmlund *Film Quarterly* v71 no1 p98 Fall 2017

Multiple sclerosis

A Fresh Approach to Fighting MS D. Ferry color *AARP: The Magazine* v30 no6A p29 O/N 2017

Multiple sclerosis risk factors

Europe's top court alarms vaccine experts G. Vogel color *Science* v356 no6345 p1320 Je 30 2017

Multiple sclerosis—Diagnosis

Bickell Brave A. Prewitt and T. Keith color *Sports Illustrated* v126 no11 p21 Ap 17-24 2017

Multiple sclerosis—Patients

Unstoppable S. DEZIEL color *Maclean's* v130 no6 p60 Jl 2017

Dunkirk and Us W. Kristol bw *Weekly Standard* v22 no45 p7 Ag 7 2017

Municipal accounting

KEEPING TABS M. Maciag *Governing* v30 no2 p56 N 2016

Municipal bonds

ASK THE EXPERT K. Close, S. Max et al diag *Money* v45 no10 p31 N 2016

Municipal bonds—Rate of return

If It's Good Enough for the Gherkin ...: The biggest of big investors see less risk in government than Main Street does J. Marlowe color *Governing* v30 no11 p61 Ag 2017

Municipal bonds—United States

Doing Good While Doing Well J. Marlowe *Governing* v30 no7 p62 Ap 2017

If It's Good Enough for the Gherkin ...: The biggest of big investors see less risk in government than Main Street does J. Marlowe color *Governing* v30 no11 p61 Ag 2017

Municipal finance—United States

KEEPING TABS M. Maciag *Governing* v30 no2 p56 N 2016

Taking Socialism to the Bank D. DAYEN *In These Times* v41 no5 p27 My 2017

Municipal government—Canada

Reckless sanctuary *Maclean's* v130 no3 p5 Ap 2017

Municipal government—United States

G2G: Why don't more governments with big IT budgets assist their smaller peers? T. Newcombe *Governing* v30 no10 p60 Jl 2017

Isles of Debris B. BRASSAW color *Natural History* v125 no11 p18 N 2017

Municipal lighting

See also

Street lighting

ICONIC L. A *Los Angeles Magazine* p100 D 2016

Municipal services

See also

Homeowners' associations

How Local Governments Are Using Technology to Serve Citizens Better S. Ressler *Harvard Business Review Digital Articles* p2 Ja 12 2016

Municipal services—United States

Lone Country: Navajos in Utah are used to having to fight for basic government services. But they'd at least like to see some roads that don't turn every trip into an endurance test D. C. Vock *Governing* v30 no10 p48 Jl 2017

The Really Hard Stuff M. Funkhouser *Governing* v30 no10 p4 Jl 2017

Municipal water supply

Working with Strong Service Providers to Address the Urban Water and Sanitation Challenge S. Ramanantsoa *UN Chronicle* v53 no3 p28 2016

Munier, Vincent

THE BEAUTY BELOW THE ICE L. BALLESTA color *National Geographic* v232 no1 p50 Jl 2017

Munn, Olivia, 1980-

X-Men: Apocalypse M. FELL *TV Guide* v65 no8 p37 F 27 2017

Munoz, Marco A.

A better research-practice partnership color *Phi Delta Kappan* v98 no3 p23 N 2016

Munoz, Oscar, 1959-

20 OSCAR MUNOZ S. Tully color diag *Fortune* v174 no7 p90 D 1 2016

CORPORATE CONTRITION: WHO GROVELED BEST? color *Fortune* v175 no6 p15 My 1 2017

THE MUNOZ WAY J. CROWN cartoon color *Chicago* v65 no11 p19 N 2016

OSCAR MUNOZ'S NEW DIGS M. LAWLER color *Chicago* v66 no8 p28 Ag 2017

Muñoz, William

Layer-specific modulation of neocortical dendritic inhibition during active wakefulness bibl diag *Science* v355 no6328 p954 Mr 3 2017

Muñoz-Cabello, Ana M.

ZATT (ZNF451)–mediated resolution of topoisomerase 2 DNA-protein cross-links diag *Science* v357 no6358 p1412 S 29 2017

Muñoz-Martin, Maribel

Tissue damage and senescence provide critical signals for cellular

reprogramming in vivo bibl chart graph *Science* v354 no6315 paaf4445-1 N 25 2016

Munro, Alice, 1931-

1962: Vancouver *Lapham's Quarterly* v10 no1 p158 Wint 2017

Munro, Burt, 1899-1978

HONORING BURT MUNRO, CELEBRATING SPEED K. Cameron bw color *Cycle World* v56 no10 p52 N 2017

SLIPSTREAM color *Cycle World* v56 no9 p66 O 2017

Munro, William J.

Optical circulators reach the quantum level bibl diag *Science* v354 no6319 p1532 D 23 2016

MUNROE, GRANT

Deadpan Walking cartoon *Walrus* v13 no9 p63 N 2016

The Lovebirds color *Walrus* v14 no7 p62 S 2017

Munroe, Scott

5 WAYS TO GET A PERFECT READ color *Golf Magazine* v59 no8 p48 Ag 2017

CHIP WITH YOUR 3-WOOD color *Golf Magazine* v59 no4 p60 Ap 2017

A FAULT-FREE BACKSWING color *Golf Magazine* v59 no9 p50 S 2017

Flight School color *Golf Magazine* v59 no1 p52 Ja 2017

STARE WAY TO HEAVEN color *Golf Magazine* v59 no6 p49 Je 2017

TRY THIS! STRONG & LONG color *Golf Magazine* v59 no11 p50 N 2017

WRISTS OF FURY color *Golf Magazine* v58 no12 p83 D 2016

Muns, Scott

DAN ABOUT TOWN *Washingtonian Magazine* v52 no3 p28 D 2016

Munschauer, Mathias

Systematic mapping of functional enhancer–promoter connections with CRISPR interference bibl graph *Science* v354 no6313 p769 N 11 2016

Munsel, Patrice, 1925-2016

PATRICE MUNSEL. SPOKANE, WA, MAY 14, 1925-SCHROON LAKE, NY, AUGUST 4, 2016 B. Kellow *Opera News* v81 no5 p62 N 2016

Munson, Glen

Systematic mapping of functional enhancer–promoter connections with CRISPR interference bibl graph *Science* v354 no6313 p769 N 11 2016

Munson, Marty

CAN YOU POP PILLS FOR BETTER LOOKS? color *Esquire* p52 N 2017

A Cure for Diabetes? color *O, The Oprah Magazine* p104 N 2017

Munster, Pamela

I Treated Breast Cancer for Years As a Doctor. Then I Was Diagnosed color *Time* v190 no15 p46 O 16 2017

Munz, Tania

The Bee's Needs D. GOLDMAN *Weekly Standard* v22 no4 p34 O 3 2016

Muons

Muon surplus may reveal new physics E. CONOVER *Science News* v190 no11 p15 N 26 2016

Mura, A.

Jupiter's interior and deep atmosphere: The initial pole-to-pole passes with the Juno spacecraft [Cover story] color graph *Science* v356 no6340 p821 My 26 2017

Jupiter's magnetosphere and aurorae observed by the Juno spacecraft during its first polar orbits diag graph *Science* v356 no6340 p826 My 26 2017

Murad, Nadia

the advocates bw *Foreign Policy* no221 p72 N/D 2016

People K. Chick and K. L. Gilbert color *Christian Century* v134 no22 p20 O 25 2017

Murad, Nadia—Interviews

Nadia MURAD E. Griswold color *Glamour* v114 no12 p206 D 2016

Murad, Rabi

Regeneration of fat cells from myofibroblasts during wound healing bibl color graph *Science* v355 no6326 p748 F 17 2017

Murakami, Haruki, 1949-

The Art of Conversation F. Cohn *Opera News* v81 no10 p62 Ap 2017

Fish Without Bicycles: In seven stories from Haruki Murakami, wounded men can't hold on to the women they love J. Fielden *New York Times Book Review* p12 My 21 2017

Murakami, Takashi, 1962-
Pop Tech A. Popescu color *Bloomberg Businessweek* no4502 p41 D 5 2016

Murakami, Y.
Crystallization and vitrification of electrons in a glass-forming charge liquid bw *Science* v357 no6358 p1381 S 29 2017

Mural painting & decoration
See also
American mural painting & decoration
CONCRETE History [Cover story] M. DURÓN bw cartoon color *ARTnews* v116 no1 p78 Spr 2017
Good Medicine S. COCHRAN color *Architectural Digest* no6 p154 Je 1 2017
The Heart of the Florida Keys color *Flying* v144 no3 p90 Mr 2017
If These Walls Could Talk color *Bon Appetit* v62 no7 p21 Jl 2017
Motor Works *Indianapolis Monthly* v40 no5 p20 Ja 2017
OFF THE WALL E. EICHINGER color *Chicago* v66 no9 p92 S 2017
Oshkosh: Heart of Garden County A. J. BARTELS and D. CARPENTER-NOLTING color *Nebraska Life* v21 no5 p52 S/O 2017
PERSIMMON + SAND color *Martha Stewart Living* p27 My 2017
Pop Chart R. Bruner, C. Lang et al color *Time* v190 no13 p69 O 2 2017
Power of Art L. Judge cartoon *Alternatives Journal (AJ) - Canada's Environmental Voice* v42 no3 p68 2016
RUSTIC CEDAR PICKET SIGN D. Kuczynski color *Cabin Living* p62 Ag 2017
SOUTH SIDE STORY J. FOUMBERG color *Chicago* v66 no11 p42 N 2017
SPORTS CANVAS ART GETS A BIG RA-RAH-RAH! *USA Today Magazine* v146 no2866 p78 Jl 2017
THE WALL C. Shafaieh cartoon *New Yorker* v93 no26 p21 S 4 2017
WALLS & CEILINGS color *Old House Journal* v44 p47 2016 Design Center source Book
We'll Get Write on That *Los Angeles Magazine* p6 Ag 2017
The White Shaman Mural *Texas Monthly* v45 no2 p34 F 2017
XAVIER GONZALEZ J. R. KEMP cartoon *Louisiana Life* v37 no2 p32 N/D 2016

Mural painting & decoration—Competitions
Refreshing an Entrance D. Sanford *Parks & Recreation* v52 no2 p56 F 2017

Mural painting & decoration—History
A Short History of Muralism cartoon *Alternatives Journal (AJ) - Canada's Environmental Voice* v42 no3 p70 2016

Mural painting & decoration—Social aspects
THE MOBRIDGE ART COLLECTION B. Hunhoff *South Dakota Magazine* v33 no3 p64 S/O 2017
The Muralist color *Alternatives Journal (AJ) - Canada's Environmental Voice* v42 no3 p14 2016

Murali, Nagarajan
Biological control of aragonite formation in stony corals bw color graph *Science* v356 no6341 p933 Je 1 2017

Muralidhar, Varsha
Clonal hematopoiesis associated with TET2 deficiency accelerates atherosclerosis development in mice bibl diag *Science* v355 no6327 p842 F 24 2017

Muralidharan, Sujatha
Clonal hematopoiesis associated with TET2 deficiency accelerates atherosclerosis development in mice bibl diag *Science* v355 no6327 p842 F 24 2017

Murarik, Thomas
We're Number One! color *Backpacker* v45 no1 p8 Ja 2017

Murata, Koichi
Chiral Majorana fermion modes in a quantum anomalous Hall insulator–superconductor structure diag *Science* v357 no6348 p294 Jl 21 2017

Muravchik, Joshua
The Truth About Black Lives Matter: The movement paints a false and disturbing portrait of America in order to justify its even more disturbing aims *Commentary* v142 no5 p20 D 2016

Murawski, Sara Michelle

A Tall TALE color *Dance Spirit* v21 no8 p44 O 2017

Murder
See also
Assassination
Trials (Murder)
THE APPROVAL MATRIX Our deliberately oversimplified guide to who falls where on our taste hierarchies img *New York* v50 no9 p124 My 1 2017
THE CASE OF BIRNA Z. ROBERT *Iceland Review* v55 no2 p42 Mr/Ap 2017
In Mexico, journalists become targets Hootsen color *America* v216 no11 p15 My 15 2017
The Monster of Florence: Case Closed? The Terrifying Story of the Most Infamous Ritual Murders in Italian History, Part 2 M. POLIDORO *Skeptical Inquirer* v41 no5 p20 S/O 2017
The Monuments bw *New Orleans Magazine* v51 no6 p20 Ap 2017
Murder in the Sandhills S. SCHMECKPEPER bw color *Nebraska Life* v21 no5 p36 S/O 2017
Not Without My Brothers [Cover story] J. C. Kang *New York Times Magazine* p30 Ag 13 2017
OLD MURDER CASE REVIVED V. HAFSTAÐ *Iceland Review* v55 no3 p10 My/Je 2017
Prime-Time Conspiracy Theory [Cover story] J. Mccormack color *Weekly Standard* v22 no37 p11 Je 5 2017
Sandhills murders solved after 80 years A. J. BARTELS bw color *Nebraska Life* v21 no6 p18 N/D 2017
SAY HER NAME: As one murder case is closed, another begins, marking 16 trans women killed before August N. BROVERMAN and D. GUERRERO *Advocate* no1093 p8 O/N 2017

Murder Calls (TV program)
MURDER CALLS L. ACKEN *TV Guide* v65 no2 p45 Ja 2 2017

Murder in Space (Film)
Home Invasion M. BARTON-FUMO color *Film Comment* v52 no6 p93 N/D 2016

Murder investigation
COLD CASE J. WILLIAMS *Cincinnati Magazine* v50 no3 p30 D 2016
THE MURDER OF ROGER ACKROYED L. Pham *New York Times Book Review* p27 Ja 22 2017
A SEARCH FOR ANSWERS N. MACDONALD color *Maclean's* v129 no51/52 p31 D 26 2016
Why Marcus? M. Bamberger color *Golf Magazine* v59 no3 p128 Mr 2017
The Worst Case: Husband-and-wife private detectives work their saddest investigation yet: the murder of their own daughter A. WREN *Indianapolis Monthly* v40 no11 p52 Jl 2017

Murder on the Orient Express (Film)
Back on the Train T. Appelo color *AARP: The Magazine* v30 no6A p14 O/N 2017
How to GET AWAY WITH MURDER ON THE ORIENT EXPRESS [Cover story] C. Collis color *Entertainment Weekly* no1465 p22 My 12 2017
MURDER ON THE ORIENT EXPRESS C. Collis color *Entertainment Weekly* no1478 / 1479 p69 Ag 18-25 2017

Murder victims
People D. Paulsen color *Christian Century* v133 no26 p19 D 21 2016

Murdered Out (Music)
KIM GORDON K. O'Donnell color *Entertainment Weekly* no1440 p59 N 18 2016

Murderers
THE HUNTING ACCIDENT N. PARSI bw color *Chicago* v66 no9 p124 S 2017
OLD MURDER CASE REVIVED V. HAFSTAÐ *Iceland Review* v55 no3 p10 My/Je 2017

Murderers in motion pictures
Disney Darlings Who Kill J. McGovern color *Entertainment Weekly* no1467 p16 My 26 2017

Murderers—Psychology
NYT's Killer Logic color *Weekly Standard* v22 no47 p2 Ag 21 2017

Murder—History
Big Viking families nurtured murder B. BOWER *Science News* v190 no10 p16 N 12 2016

Murder—History—21st century
Murder at Terminal 2 C. Campbell color *Time* v189 no9 p34 Mr

13 2017

Murder—Lawsuits & claims

GUILT BY OMISSION E. BAZELON color *New York Times Magazine* p40 Ag 6 2017

Kafka in Vegas M. ROSE bw color *Vanity Fair* v59 no7 p116 Summ 2017

Simplify The Law B. H. BARTON and S. BIBAS color *National Review* v69 no15 p20 Ag 14 2017

Murder—Social aspects

A DEATH IN THE ANDES M. Reel color *Bloomberg Businessweek* no4513 p62 Mr 6 2017

Murder—United States—Lawsuits & claims

Your Echo Is Listening D. Pogue color *Scientific American* v316 no3 p28 Mr 2017

MURDIN, PAUL

Picturing the Universe color *Natural History* v125 no11 p24 N 2017

Murdoch, Rupert, 1931——Finance

Paper Chase S. SCHAEFER cartoon *Forbes* v198 no5 p42 O 25 2016

Murdoch, Rupert, 1931——Interviews

Château Murdoch J. Stein bw *Bloomberg Businessweek* no4530 p63 Jl 17 2017

Murdoch, Wendi

Pioneers [Cover story] color *Time* v189 no16/17 p14 My 1-8 2017

MURDOCK, ANDY

Charting a Century of Climate Change *USA Today Magazine* v145 no2860 p72 Ja 2017

Murdock, David H., 1923-

MAN OF THE HOUSE P. HALDEMAN *Los Angeles Magazine* v61 no11 p134 N 2016

Murfett, Malcolm

The Sinking of JAPAN *History Today* v66 no12 p20 D 2016

Murff, Zora

OMAHA, NEBRASKA *Harper's Magazine* p33 O 2017

Murkowski, Lisa, 1957-

The Pros and Cons of the Obama Era Federal Lands Policy: Should Congress Repeal the Obama Administration's Public Land Management Rule? *Congressional Digest* v96 no6 p10 Je 2017

Murmann, Boris

Highly stretchable polymer semiconductor films through the nanoconfinement effect bibl graph *Science* v355 no6320 p1 Ja 6 2017

MURN, CHARLES

ASK WHAT YOU CAN DO FOR YOUR CLIMATE *Humanist* v77 no3 p25 My/Je 2017

Murnane, Richard J.

American movers and shakers bw color *Science* v357 no6351 p555 Ag 11 2017

Muro, Mark

Entrepreneurs Take On Manufacturing *Harvard Business Review Digital Articles* p2 F 22 2016

It's the Jobs, Stupid il *MIT Technology Review* v120 no1 p10 Ja/F 2017

Robots Seem to Be Improving Productivity, Not Costing Jobs *Harvard Business Review Digital Articles* p2 Je 16 2015

Murph, John

Artists Collaborate, Celebrate at Jazz Day Events in Havana color *Downbeat* v84 no7 p14 Jl 2017

DAYMÉ AROCENA color *Downbeat* v84 no4 p26 Ap 2017

Fonseca Explores Cuban Styles color *Downbeat* v84 no4 p14 Ap 2017

Friendship Through Mentorship color *Downbeat* v84 no10 p30 O 2017

The Hot Box *Downbeat* v84 no8 p69 Ag 2017

In Praise of $%!#?! cartoon chart *AARP: The Magazine* v60 no1A p12 D 2016/Ja 2017

JAZZMEIA HORN color *Downbeat* v84 no7 p24 Jl 2017

Jersey solo *Downbeat* v84 no10 p55 O 2017

VICTOR GOULD color *Downbeat* v83 no12 p20 D 2016

VICTOR PROVOST color *Downbeat* v84 no3 p23 Mr 2017

Murphey, David

Making Math Count More for Young Latinos bw *Education Digest* v83 no1 p8 S 2017

Murphree, Michael

What the U.S. Should Be Doing to Protect Intellectual Property *Harvard Business Review Digital Articles* p2 Ja 27 2016

Murphy, Alyssa

Impacting Homelessness in Missouri *Bridges (Federal Reserve Bank of St. Louis)* p12 Summ 2016

Murphy, Amanda

Breaking New Ground S. Murphy color *Log Home Living* v33 no9 p24 D 2016

MURPHY, ANDREA

The Expense of Exclusive Living color graph *Forbes* v198 no5 p46 O 25 2016

THE PRICE OF THE GOOD LIFE color graph *Forbes* v200 no5 p32 N 14 2017

Murphy, Andrew

Distribution and clinical impact of functional variants in 50,726 whole-exome sequences from the DiscovEHR study chart graph *Science* v354 no6319 paaf6814-1 D 23 2016

Murphy, Asia

Scientists stand with Standing Rock bibl color *Science* v353 no6307 p1506 S 30 2016

Murphy, Austin

BELL EPOCH color *Sports Illustrated* v126 no3 p30 Ja 23 2017

BREATH OF FRESH HEIR color *Sports Illustrated* v126 no2 p34 Ja 16 2017

EVEREST PEAK Performer [Cover story] color *Sports Illustrated* v126 no13 p26 My 8 2017

FADE TO BLACK? color *Sports Illustrated* v125 no17 p70 N 21 2016 Double Issue

FREE VERSE color *Sports Illustrated* v126 no15 p52 My 29 2017

It's Not Easy Being Green color *Sports Illustrated* v125 no19 p60 D 12 2016

LIVE STRONGISH color *Sports Illustrated* v126 no11 p54 Ap 17-24 2017

O.K. • CALL IT A • COME BACK color *Sports Illustrated* v125 no14 p32 O 24-31 2016

VELOCI-RAPTURE color *Sports Illustrated* v127 no3 p98 Jl 24 2017

WILDER. CRAZIER. FASTER! bw color *Men's Health* v32 no8 p116 O 2017

Murphy, Brian K.

Hot Date N. Abrams, B. L. Heldman et al *Entertainment Weekly* no1482/1483 p74 S 22 2017

Murphy, Clarke

When Leaders Are Hired for Talent but Fired for Not Fitting In *Harvard Business Review Digital Articles* p2 Je 14 2017

Murphy, Conor

Changing climate shifts timing of European floods color graph *Science* v357 no6351 p588 Ag 11 2017

MURPHY, CULLEN

Cartoon County: My Father and His Friends in the Golden Age of Make-Believe *Publishers Weekly* v264 no30 p49 Jl 24 2017

CARTOON COUNTY, U.S.A bw cartoon color *Vanity Fair* v59 no9 p158 S 2017

John le CARRÉ color *Vanity Fair* v59 no10 p156 O 2017

TEAMWORK CITY OF HOPE color *Vanity Fair* v59 no8 p83 Ag 2017

Murphy, Debra Dean

An invitation to wonder bw *Christian Century* v134 no9 p20 Ap 26 2017

Murphy, Emily Bain

The Disappearances color *Publishers Weekly* v264 no19 p61 My 8 2017

Murphy, Emily F. (Emily Ferguson), 1868-1933

The First Lady of Reefer Madness M. GREEN cartoon *Walrus* p36 Ja\F 2017

MURPHY, G. RONALD

HUMBLE AND HAUGHTY *America* v215 no11 p36 O 17 2016

Murphy, Harlan

The everything-proof house color *Popular Science* v289 no4 p56 Jl/Ag 2017

Light Hammer Heavy Hitter color *Popular Science* v288 no6 p68 N/D 2016

RAIN, RAIN, STOW AWAY cartoon *Popular Science* v289 no2 p30 Mr/Ap 2017

Smartest. Cooker. Ever [Cover story] color diag *Popular Science* v289 no6 p60 N/D 2017

MURPHY, JAMES

MEN BEHAVING BADLY color *Vanity Fair* v59 no11 p54 N 2017

OVER IT HUA HSU cartoon *New Yorker* v93 no26 p90 S 4 2017

Someone Great Is Back D. MARCHESE img *New York* v50 no17 p112 Ag 21 2017

MURPHY, JARRETT

NYC vs. TRUMP [Cover story] color *Nation* v304 no3 p12 Ja 30 2017

MURPHY, JEN

6 MORE LIFE-CHANGING TRIPS cartoon *Men's Health* v32 no6 p31 Ag 2017

Get Some Alone Time color *Conde Nast Traveler* v51 no11 p72 D 2016

Peak Lunching color *Conde Nast Traveler* v52 no2 p42 F 2017

The Peaks of PERFECTION color *Esquire* p54 BigBlackBook

Playing (High-Design) House color *Conde Nast Traveler* v52 no8 p44 S 2017

Start Your ADVENTURE color *Men's Health* v32 no1 p20 Ja/F 2017

UPPER CRUST [Cover story] color *Runner's World* v52 no4 p28 My 2017

Murphy, Jim

PURE GENIUS color *Golf Magazine* v58 no11 p50 N 2016

Revenge of the Green Banana *Publishers Weekly* v263 no44 p76 O 31 2016

Watch + Learn color *Golf Magazine* v59 no4 p36 Ap 2017

Murphy, Joseph

Positive school leadership color *Phi Delta Kappan* v99 no1 p21 S 2017

MURPHY, KATE

Ick! Clean Your Touch Screen! *Reader's Digest* v188 no1125 p72 N 2016

Murphy, Liza

Should You Try a Yoni Egg? color *Glamour* v115 no7 p67 Jl 2017

Murphy, Mary

My Obsessions. . *TV Guide* v65 no31 p7 Jl 24 2017

Murphy, Mary Jo

Have You Met Miss Jane?: Test your Austen I.Q.—from family scandals to a wet-shirted Colin Firth *New York Times Book Review* p15 Jl 16 2017

Murphy, Mary—Interviews

So You Think You Can Dance M. Logan *TV Guide* v65 no25 p34 Je 2017

Murphy, Matthew

How a Startup Accelerator at Boston Children's Hospital Helps Launch Companies color *Harvard Business Review Digital Articles* p2 Je 5 2017

MURPHY, MEG

The Question *O, The Oprah Magazine* p16 Ap 2017

Murphy, Megan

'Bill and I are impatient optimists' color *Bloomberg Businessweek* no4512 p46 F 20 2017

EDITOR'S LETTER *Bloomberg Businessweek* no4527 p6 Je 19 2017

Ginni Rometty: CEO, IBM color *Bloomberg Businessweek* no4539 p62 S 25 2017

'He knew how to get things done, but he managed by chaos' color *Bloomberg Businessweek* no4526 p42 Je 12 2017

'If you can duplicate what they've done in Detroit around the country, you're going to have a huge renaissance' color *Bloomberg Businessweek* no4505 p46 D 26 2016

'If you're in a partnership, you're only as good as your weakest partners' color *Bloomberg Businessweek* no4522 p54 My 15 2017

Tim Cook CEO, Apple: "I am so excited about it, I just want to yell out and scream" [Cover story] color *Bloomberg Businessweek* no4527 p52 Je 19 2017

You Talkin; to us? color *Bloomberg Businessweek* no4519 p68 Ap 24 2017

Murphy, Michael

ALL DAT NEW ORLEANS A. McLellan color *New Orleans Magazine* v51 no12 p60 O 2017

On Interventions that Catalyze Greater Change *Architectural Record* v205 no4 p212 Ap 2017

MURPHY, MYATT

IN THE RIGHT FIELD color *Muscle & Performance* v9 no8 p36 Ag 2017

Murphy, Patrick

AT LAST, SHE SPEAKS! C. Connors color *Women's Health* v14 no5 p142 Je 2017

Murphy, Patrick J.

Examining Columbus's Complicated Leadership Legacy *Harvard Business Review Digital Articles* p2 O 13 2014

Murphy, Paul

Contractions: Slowing Down Research chart graph *Bloomberg Businessweek* no4534 p39 Ag 14 2017

Miami's Mayor Climbs Aboard the Trump Train color *Bloomberg Businessweek* no4512 p28 F 20 2017

MURPHY, REBECCA R.

Submersed Aquatic Vegetation in Chesapeake Bay: Sentinel Species in a Changing World *BioScience* v67 no8 p698 Ag 2017

Murphy, Roland G.

AMERICAN RENAISSANCE J. BROWN color *Popular Science* v289 no5 p66 S/O 2017

MURPHY, RYAN

LIVING THE DREAM color *Architectural Digest* v74 no2 p60 F 2017

Murphy, Ryan, 1965-

ALL ABOUT FEUD A. D'ARMINIO and J. Halterman *TV Guide* v65 no8 p8 F 27 2017

Feud: Bette and Joan M. ROUSH *TV Guide* v65 no11 p20 Mr 6 2017

Hollywood Horror Story img *New York* p124 Mr 6 2017

Murphy, Ryan, 1995-

FIGHT CLUB [Cover story] J. Cagle color *Entertainment Weekly* no1450 p22 Ja 27 2017

MURPHY, SAMANTHA RAZOOK

that's so cool! *Parents* v92 no1 p32 Ja 2017

Murphy, Sean

Breaking New Ground color *Log Home Living* v33 no9 p24 D 2016

Home (Be)Coming color *Log Home Living* v34 no7 p22 S 2017

It's Going Up! color *Log Home Living* v34 no1 p20 F 2017

Kitchen Creativity color *Log Home Living* v34 no4 p22 My 2017

Money Matters color *Log Home Living* v33 no7 p22 S 2016

Roughin' It color *Log Home Living* v34 no2 p20 Mr 2017

Sentimental Journey color diag *Log Home Living* v34 no9 p24 D 2017

Small Sacrifices color *Log Home Living* v34 no6 p22 Ag 2017

Sweat Equity color *Log Home Living* v34 no3 p20 Ap 2017

Murphy, Stephanie

Milestones *Ms.* v27 no1 p5 Spr 2017

Why Did the El Faro Sink?: DEEP-SEA VEHICLES LOCATE DATA RECORDER ON THE SEAFLOOR *Oceanus* v52 no2 p12 Spr 2017

Murphy, Stephen K.

A modular and enantioselective synthesis of the pleuromutilin antibiotics diag graph *Science* v356 no6341 p956 Je 1 2017

MURPHY, STEVE

ASTEROID MISSION *Scientific American* v315 no6 p8 D 2016

Murphy, Tim

BANNED TOGETHER color *Mother Jones* v42 no4 p39 Jl/Ag 2017

CONSPIRACY THEORIST IN CHIEF cartoon *Mother Jones* v41 no6 p5 N/D 2016

FABLES OF THE RECONSTRUCTION bw *Mother Jones* v42 no4 p55 Jl/Ag 2017

THE GHOSTS OF GEORGE SAUNDERS bw *Mother Jones* v42 no2 p53 Mr/Ap 2017

HOUSTON, WE HAVE PROGRESS color graph map *Mother Jones* v42 no5 p24 S/O 2017

Iron Man bw *Mother Jones* v42 no6 p32 N/D 2017

THE Radically INTERNATIONAL History of AMERICA'S BEST IDEA color *Foreign Policy* no224 p66 My/Je 2017

RED DAWN *Mother Jones* v42 no3 p10 My/Je 2017

Return to the Dark Side bw *Mother Jones* v42 no1 p22 Ja/F 2017

RULES FOR RADICALS bw cartoon color *Mother Jones* v42 no2 p44 Mr/Ap 2017

Murphy, Wendy

The Benefits of Virtual Mentors *Harvard Business Review Digital Articles* p2 Ap 26 2016

How Women (and Men) Can Find Role Models When None Are Obvious *Harvard Business Review Digital Articles* p2 Je 1 2016

Murphy-Gill, Meghan
As I have loved you bw *U.S. Catholic* v82 no4 p45 Ap 2017
Let there be peace *U.S. Catholic* v82 no2 p4 F 2017
A place at the table color *U.S. Catholic* v82 no6 p31 Je 2017
Thank God for the stars *U.S. Catholic* v81 no11 p4 N 2016

MURR, SCOTT
CRUSH ANY GOAL color *Runner's World* v52 no8 p74 S 2017

Murrah, Philip
DROP IT LIKE IT'S HOT J. Mankin color *Team Roping Journal* p76 O 2017

Murray, Adam Patrick
Photo shootout: We tested Portrait mode with an iPhone 7 Plus fashion shoot color *Macworld - Digital Edition* p47 D 2016
TESTED: GALAXY NOTE 8 LIVE FOCUS VS. iPHONE 7 PLUS PORTRAIT MODE color *Macworld - Digital Edition* v34 no10 p75 O 2017

Murray, Alan
THE CASE FOR OPTIMISM color *Fortune* v175 no3 p6 Mr 1 2017
CEO SOOTHSAYERS diag *Fortune* v175 no8 p340 Je 15 2017
Free Trade Can't Get a Break color *Fortune* v175 no4 p16 Mr 15 2017
A HEDGE FUND TITAN'S PLAYBOOK color *Fortune* v176 no4 p126 S 15 2017
HOPE FOR THE DAY AFTER color *Fortune* v174 no6 p6 N 1 2016
THE MORAL IMPERATIVE FOR LEADERS color *Fortune* v174 no7 p6 D 1 2016
A PATH THROUGH THE GRIDLOCK color *Fortune* v75 no1 p6 Ja 1 2017
A SMART INVESTMENT IN AMERICA color *Fortune* v175 no4 p8 Mr 15 2017
Trump's Break With CEOs Is a Big Deal color *Fortune* v176 no4 p28 S 15 2017

Murray, Andrew
Exploring genetic suppression interactions on a global scale diag *Science* v354 no6312 p599 N 4 2016

Murray, Andy, 1987-
Andy Murray *Tennis* v53 no1 p12 Ja/F 2017

Murray, Benjamin J.
Cracking the problem of ice nucleation bibl color diag *Science* v355 no6323 p346 Ja 27 2017

Murray, Bill, 1950-
The Full-Court Parent Trap T. Keith chart color *Sports Illustrated* v126 no8 p24 Mr 20 2017
Pop Chart R. Bruner, C. Lang et al color *Time* v188 no19 p62 N 7 2016

Murray, Brad
"IF YOU PACK EVERYTHING IN ONE COLOR PALETTE, YOU'LL BRING 30 PERCENT LESS" A. WHITTLE color *Conde Nast Traveler* v52 no2 p24 F 2017

Murray, Brian H.
Crushing It in Apartments and Commercial Real Estate: How a Small Investor Can Make It Big color *Publishers Weekly* v264 no38 p64 S 18 2017

Murray, Charles, 1943-
Charles Murray's Attackers *Commentary* v143 no4 p10 Ap 2017
Charles Murray's Attackers M. CONTINETTI *Commentary* v143 no4 p56 Ap 2017
Good News at Harvard! color *Weekly Standard* v23 no2 p2 S 18 2017

Murray, Chris
WINNING LIGHT color *Popular Photography* v81 no1 p42 Ja/F 2017

Murray, Christopher
The Garden of the Great Spirit: A Photo Essay of the Thousand Islands *New York State Conservationist* v72 no1 p2 Ag 2017

Murray, Cori
10 YEARS TEN STORIES color *Essence* v47 no11 p96 Mr 2017
THE ARTIST WAY color *Essence* v48 no2 p57 Je 2017
BOYFRIEND MATERIAL color *Essence* v47 no7 p48 N 2016
GROWING UP NICELY color *Essence* v48 no3 p52 Jl 2017
HEY, MISS DJ color *Essence* v48 no2 p58 Je 2017
ONE NIGHT ONLY color *Essence* v47 no8 p70 D 2016

STATE OF THE UNION [Cover story] color *Essence* v47 no7 p76 N 2016
STILL ON & ON color *Essence* v47 no11 p60 Mr 2017
THEN AND NOW Drama Queens color *Essence* v48 no5 p64 S 2017

MURRAY, DAVID W.
The Opioid Crisis color graph *Weekly Standard* v22 no9 p19 N 7 2016

Murray, Douglas
Can Europe Be Saved? S. AHMARI *Commentary* v144 no2 p42 S 2017
The Party of Left-Wing Anti-Semitism: The shocking decline and fall of Labour *Commentary* v142 no4 p29 N 2016
When Was It Better? [Cover story] J. J. Sheehan bw *Commonweal* v144 no17 p22 O 20 2017

Murray, Jason
OF WAVES AND WHITE ELEPHANTS K. TAYLOR color *Surfer* v58 no4 p86 Ag 2017

Murray, John
PRELUDE TO REVOLUTION J. Bertrand *Military History* v33 no5 p61 Ja 2017

Murray, John Courtney, 1904-1967
FOR GOD AND COUNTRY R. R. Reilly *Claremont Review of Books* v17 no3 p44 Summ 2017

Murray, Kirsty
Eat the Sky, Drink the Ocean color *Publishers Weekly* v263 no52 p126 D 19 2016

Murray, Latavius
Pictures of the Year color *Sports Illustrated* v125 no20 p74 D 19 2016

MURRAY, LAURA RENA
TEEN, TRANS AND HOMELESS: ON THE STREETS OF NEW YORK WITH AMERICA'S MOST VULNERABLE POPULATION color *Rolling Stone* no1297 p44 O 5 2017

Murray, Lindsey
The Best Apps for Pet Lovers color *Health* v30 no10 p91 D 2016
Decode Your Pet's Body Language color *Health* v31 no3 p71 Ap 2017
First Aid for Your Pet color *Health* v30 no9 p106 N 2016
GAME-CHANGING GIFTS color *Health* v30 no10 p116 D 2016
How I Shed 72 Pounds color *Health* v31 no2 p58 Mr 2017
HOW TO GET PREGNANT (AGAIN) color *Health* v31 no1 p73 Ja 2017
I Got Back into Athlete Shape color *Health* v30 no10 p58 D 2016
Losing Big Saved My Life color *Health* v30 no9 p54 N 2016
My Shape-Up Secret? The Buddy System! color *Health* v31 no1 p46 Ja 2017
Start Your Day Strong color *Health* v31 no2 p69 Mr 2017
Why So Itchy? color *Health* v31 no2 p94 Mr 2017
Winterproof Your Pup color *Health* v31 no1 p70 Ja 2017

Murray, Martine
Molly & Pim and the Millions of Stars *Publishers Weekly* v263 no45 p61 N 7 2016

Murray, Michael F.
Distribution and clinical impact of functional variants in 50,726 whole-exome sequences from the DiscovEHR study chart graph *Science* v354 no6319 paaf6814-1 D 23 2016
Genetic identification of familial hypercholesterolemia within a single U.S. health care system chart graph *Science* v354 no6319 paaf7000-1 D 23 2016

Murray, Michael T.
DIGESTION AND AGING color *Amazing Wellness* v8 no2 p64 Spr 2016
FOOD ALLERGY RESCUE color *Amazing Wellness* p66 Fall 2017

Murray, Patrick J.
CRISIS MANAGEMENT FOR FEEDING THE POOR: England's population boomed between the 11th and 16th centuries. It became increasingly difficult to feed a hungry nation *History Today* v67 no7 p92 Jl 2017

Murray, Patty
The Pros and Cons of Federally Funded School Choice Programs *Congressional Digest* v96 no7 p12 S 2017

Murray, Patty—Interviews
Making the Grade? A. G. Kingo color *Working Mother* v40 no3 p44 Ag/S 2017

Murray, Pauli, 1910-1985
SAINT PAULI K. SCHULZ bw cartoon *New Yorker* v93 no9 p67 Ap 17 2017

Murray, Sabina
Love and Revolution D. LEAVITT *New York Times Book Review* p20 N 20 2016

Murray, Sean
10 — NO MAN'S SKY D. Franich color *Entertainment Weekly* no1444/1445 p123 D 16 2016
AGENT OF CHANGE A. D'ARMINIO *TV Guide* v65 no11 p30 Mr 6 2017

Murray, Simon
Because It's There [Cover story] color *Power & Motoryacht* v34 no6 p54 Je 2017
Bertram 60 color *Power & Motoryacht* v34 no9 p52 S 2017
Big Memories, Small Drone color *Power & Motoryacht* v34 no10 p66 O 2017
Breathe Easy color *Power & Motoryacht* v34 no7 p39 Jl 2017
Concrete Jungle color *Power & Motoryacht* v34 no10 p68 O 2017
Cut 'Em Loose color *Power & Motoryacht* v34 no11 p84 N 2017
Duffield 58 color *Power & Motoryacht* v34 no8 p28 Ag 2017
EXPOSURE color *Power & Motoryacht* v33 no4 p48 Ap 2017
EXPOSURE color *Power & Motoryacht* v34 no8 p38 Ag 2017
Flash Forward color *Power & Motoryacht* v34 no8 p36 Ag 2017
Go West, Young Men color *Power & Motoryacht* v34 no11 p72 N 2017
Gym with a View color *Power & Motoryacht* v33 no3 p32 Mr 2017
Havana, Cuba color *Power & Motoryacht* v33 no2 p60 F 2017
Hell and High Water color *Power & Motoryacht* v34 no11 p46 N 2017
Lexus Sport Yacht 42 color *Power & Motoryacht* v33 no4 p44 Ap 2017
Maritimo X60 color *Power & Motoryacht* v34 no11 p82 N 2017
One Man's MISSION bw color *Power & Motoryacht* v34 no9 p96 S 2017
Palmer Johnson 63 Sport color *Power & Motoryacht* v33 no3 p58 Mr 2017
The Perfect Day color *Power & Motoryacht* v34 no9 p56 S 2017
"Pig Beach," Bahamas color *Power & Motoryacht* v33 no3 p60 Mr 2017
Private Party color *Power & Motoryacht* v33 no2 p32 F 2017
Put Your Best Foot Forward color *Power & Motoryacht* v34 no6 p36 Je 2017
Suit Yourself bw *Power & Motoryacht* v34 no9 p54 S 2017
Ten ADVENTURES color *Power & Motoryacht* v34 no9 p64 S 2017
Viking 93 MY color *Power & Motoryacht* v34 no11 p76 N 2017
A World Apart bw color *Power & Motoryacht* v33 no4 p56 Ap 2017

Murray, Soraya
RACE, GENDER, AND GENRE IN SPEC OPS: THE LINE *Film Quarterly* v70 no2 p38 Wint 2016

Murray, William
Three Centuries, One Scope *Sky & Telescope* v132 no6 p84 D 2016

Murray, Williamson
A Savage War: A Military History of the Civil War L. D. Freedman *Foreign Affairs* v96 no1 p162 Ja/F 2017

Murray-Bergquist, Karin
ABOARD THE POURQUOI-PAS? *Iceland Review* v55 no2 p71 Mr/Ap 2017
GRAND (I) PALACE *Iceland Review* v55 no3 p52 My/Je 2017

murren, james
lost borders bw color *Bike Magazine* v24 no4 p38 Je 2017

MURRISON, TERI TORELL
COWBOY NINJA: THE RANCHER AS OBSTACLE RACER *Idaho Magazine* v16 no10 p6 Jl 2017

MURROW, LAUREN
COP TALK: THE SOUND OF BIAS color *Wired* v25 no8 p20 Ag 2017
CRASH COURSE cartoon *Wired* v25 no6 p24 Je 2017
THE GRAND iOPERA: STEVE JOBS, ULTIMATE DIVA color *Wired* v25 no7 p22 Jl 2017
NEXT LIST 2017 bw graph *Wired* v25 no5 p63 My 2017
THE QUEEN OF CLEAN CLAPS BACK cartoon color *Wired*

v25 no4 p73 Ap 2017

Murtaugh, Dan
Finally, Some Good News for Shipyards *Bloomberg Businessweek* no4518 p23 Ap 10 2017

MURTHA, LISA
ALL IN A ROW *Cincinnati Magazine* v50 no7 p34 Ap 2017
BORN USERS *Cincinnati Magazine* v50 no4 p68 Ja 2017
CURVES AHEAD *Cincinnati Magazine* v50 no2 p34 N 2016
ELEMENTS OF STYLES *Cincinnati Magazine* p36 Je 2017
A FAIRY TALE color *Cincinnati Magazine* v51 no1 p30 O 2017
THE FIGHT OF THEIR LIVES *Cincinnati Magazine* v50 no2 p66 N 2016
HEX APPEAL *Cincinnati Magazine* v50 no8 p30 My 2017
HOME IS WHERE YOU MAKE IT *Cincinnati Magazine* v50 no6 p23 Mr 2017
THE ILLUMINATI *Cincinnati Magazine* v50 no5 p36 F 2017
Lords of Newport *Cincinnati Magazine* v50 no8 p56 My 2017
NAME GAME *Cincinnati Magazine* v50 no6 p42 Mr 2017
No Place Like Home *Cincinnati Magazine* v50 no2 p40 N 2016
PENTHOUSE VIEWS: A TIP-TOP CONDO IN THE HEART OF DOWNTOWN *Cincinnati Magazine* v50 no11 p36 Ag 2017
PRIMING THE PUMP *Cincinnati Magazine* v50 no4 p66 Ja 2017
REBUILD THE NEIGHBORHOOD *Cincinnati Magazine* v50 no5 p34 F 2017
RETOOLED JEWEL *Cincinnati Magazine* v50 no4 p38 Ja 2017
SECRET PASSAGE *Cincinnati Magazine* v50 no3 p46 D 2016
SEE YVETTEY RUN *Cincinnati Magazine* v50 no4 p82 Ja 2017
Shopping Spree *Cincinnati Magazine* v50 no5 p66 F 2017
Those Old Houses: 8K Construction is out to save Cincinnati's historic fabric, one home at a time *Cincinnati Magazine* v50 no11 p78 Ag 2017

Murthy, Neil
Telltale 'Bathtub Rings' Reveal Ancient Rainfall *Oceanus* v52 no1 p30 Summ 2016

Murthy, Vivek
Our Addiction Crisis Can Be Solved-With Hard Work color *Time* v188 no16/17 p53 O 24 2016

Murthy, Vivek, 1977-—Interviews
America's Opioid Crisis (Might Be Different Than You Think) V. Murthy and S. KLEIN color *Prevention* p32 Mr 2017
Vivek Murthy Thinks We Need to Learn How to Deal With Stress A. M. Cox *New York Times Magazine* p58 Ja 1 2017
WHAT IT MEANS TO BE HEALTHY color *National Geographic* v232 no3 p8 S 2017

MURTUZA, IRFAN
Living with Autism: Early intervention is critical to helping children diagnosed with autism reach their full potential *Islamic Horizons* v46 no3 p44 My/Je 2017

Muruganantham, Arunachalam
PAD LAUNCH Y. BHATTACHARJEE color *New York Times Magazine* p78 N 13 2016

MUSACCHIO, ALDO
MAPPING FRONTIER ECONOMIES [Cover story] chart color diag graph il img *Harvard Business Review* v94 no12 p40 D 2016

Musacchio, Andrew J.
Catalytic intermolecular hydroaminations of unactivated olefins with secondary alkyl amines bibl diag *Science* v355 no6326 p727 F 17 2017

Muschietti, Andrés
IT A. Breznican color *Entertainment Weekly* no1446/1447 p48 D 2016/Ja 2017
Sunlit Horror R. DOUTHAT color *National Review* v69 no18 p43 O 2 2017

Muschietti, Andy
IT A. Breznican color *Entertainment Weekly* no1474/1475 p46 Jl 21-28 2017
It Takes All Kinds J. PODHORETZ color *Weekly Standard* v23 no3 p39 S 25 2017

Muscle cars
More Doors, More Fun E. Perkins, B. Gillogly et al color *Hot Rod* v70 no5 p8 My 2017

Muscle cars—Evaluation
GONE IN 2.3 SECONDS S. Horaczek color *Popular Science* v289 no5 p32 S/O 2017

Muscle contraction

Crowning Achievement J. MINUTILLO *Architectural Record* v204 no11 p70 N 2016

Design Museum Redux C. FOGES *Architectural Record* v205 no1 p44 Ja 2017

FXFOWLE Museum Breaks Ground on Liberty Island A. FIXSEN *Architectural Record* v204 no11 p28 N 2016

The Good Earth C. A. PEARSON *Architectural Record* v205 no4 p134 Ap 2017

LANDFORMS *Architectural Record* v205 no4 p133 Ap 2017

LANDMARKS *Architectural Record* v204 no11 p69 N 2016

MCA Renovation Aims to Bring Chicago into the Museum Z. MORTICE color *Architectural Record* v205 no3 p21 Mr 2017

Museum closings

Mom & Popped N. FREEMAN bw color *ARTnews* v115 no4 p116 Wint 2016/2017

Museum curators

Avant Guards L. CAMHI color *Vogue* v207 no10 p190 O 2017

The Curator L. GRANDE color *Natural History* v125 no11 p48 N 2017

Curator resigns after sexual misconduct investigations A. Gibbons color *Science* v354 no6317 p1216 D 9 2016

JOSÉ ESPARZA CHONG CUY H. MITCHELL color *Chicago* v66 no10 p44 O 2017

RUJEKO HOCKLEY: Whitney Museum of American Art K. DREW color *Vogue* v207 no10 p192 O 2017

TIME TRAVEL J. Blitzer cartoon *New Yorker* v92 no42 p46 D 19 2016

Museum curatorship

Autocorrect R. WETZLER color *ARTnews* v115 no3 p38 Fall 2016

Museum exhibits

ART cartoon *New Yorker* v92 no39 p12 N 28 2016

HOT SEATS L. VACCARIELLO *Indianapolis Monthly* p34 F 2017

LIGHTING UP REYKJAVÍK J. GOTTLIEB *Iceland Review* v55 no2 p6 Mr/Ap 2017

Provocative Statements J. L. BELCOVE color *Architectural Digest* v74 no2 p22 F 2017

What to Do and See in DC *New York* v50 no17 p147 Ag 21 2017

Museum exhibits—Evaluation

Museums Lighting Up A. Popescu color *Bloomberg Businessweek* no4522 p39 My 15 2017

Museum maintenance & repair

Engaging the third solitude J. GEDDES *Maclean's* v130 no7 p14 Ag 2017

Museum podcasts

Voices of America M. DEAN *New Republic* v248 no4 p56 Ap 2017

Museum stores

Shopping for Kids this Holiday Season L. PETERSON *Atlanta* v56 no7 p48 N 2016

Museum of African-American History (Detroit, Mich.)

I, TOO, AM AMERICA M. Norris bw color *National Geographic* v230 no4 p116 O 2016

Museum of Contemporary Art (Chicago, Ill.)

MCA Renovation Aims to Bring Chicago into the Museum Z. MORTICE color *Architectural Record* v205 no3 p21 Mr 2017

Museum of Contemporary Art (Los Angeles, Calif.)

"R. H. Quaytman, Morning: Chapter 30" A. Doran color *ARTnews* v115 no3 p33 Fall 2016

Museum of Modern Art (New York, N.Y.)

A Different Slant on Frank Lloyd Wright S. STEPHENS *Architectural Record* v205 no7 p54 Jl 2017

DO THE WRIGHT THING P. GOLDBERGER color *Vanity Fair* v59 no7 p126 Summ 2017

PICABIA'S MONSTERS B. SCHWABSKY color il *Nation* v304 no8 p35 Mr 13 2017

REVIVALS AND FESTIVALS bw *New Yorker* v92 no40 p17 D 5 2016

The Wright Stuff B. Bergdoll bw color diag *Architectural Digest* no6 p65 Je 1 2017

Museum of Modern Art (New York, N.Y.)—Computer network resources

PERSONAL VOICE L. Schwulst *Art in America* v104 no9 p108 O 2016

Museums

See also

Art museums

Best Pit Stop Ever J. SCHWARB *Indianapolis Monthly* p15 My 2017

COMMEMORATIVE AIR FORCE DIXIE WING PEACHTREE CITY 36 MILES SOUTHWEST OF ATLANTA J. GREEN *Atlanta* v56 no12 p144 Ap 2017

Discussion D. Montgomery Kovacs, C. J. WOODRING et al *Smithsonian* v47 no7 p10 N 2016

Editor's Letter L. POLLOCK *Art in America* v104 no9 p16 O 2016

Funny Fill-In E. WHITMER cartoon *National Geographic Kids* no471 p31 Je/Jl 2017

Getting Warmer E. FLORIO color *Conde Nast Traveler* v52 no4 p14 Ap 2017

Historic District / Old Wethersfield, Conn D. J. Silber bw color *Old House Journal* v45 no1 p34 F 2017

HUMBOLDT PARK J. REESE cartoon color *Chicago* v66 no4 p31 Ap 2017

Juan Garcia Mosqueda H. MARTIN color *Architectural Digest* v74 no1 p44 Ja 2017

A Museum That Overcomes Its Correctness: In Philadelphia, the American Revolution comes alive despite contemporary curatorial ideology M. J. Lewis *Commentary* v144 no1 p39 Jl/Ag 2017

NAME-DROPPERS S. STALL *Indianapolis Monthly* v40 no3 p22 N 2016

News B. Manley color *Military History* v34 no4 p9 N 2017

ON THE WAY *Cincinnati Magazine* p55 Je 2017

Route 66 J. BREAL *Texas Monthly* v45 no3 p38 Mr 2017

SO SAINT LAURENT bw *Harper's Bazaar* no3656 p184 S 2017

SOUTHERN AFRICA S. KHAN color *Conde Nast Traveler* v52 no4 p38 Ap 2017

This Good Old Building: A Place Full of History M. COOK WYLIE and L. MORTON-KEITHLEY *Idaho Magazine* v16 no12 p25 S 2017

WELCOME TO CARTERSVILLE H. S. PHILBRICK *Atlanta* v56 no7 p18 N 2016

We Remember J. BILLS and M. SEAMANS color *Yankee* v80 no6 p96 N/D 2016

Museums & women

A Museum of Our Own: Congress takes steps to turn the longtime dream of a national women's history museum into reality C. RIOS *Ms.* v27 no3 p10 Fall 2017

Museums—California

An Abundance Of Bones M. SEGAL color *Los Angeles Magazine* v62 no7 p18 Jl 2017

A New House of Worship D. PENER *Los Angeles Magazine* p70 My 2017

Renovated Nixon Library Reopening *Prologue* v48 no3 p68 Fall 2016

Museums—Canada

FEATURED FELLOW: GEORGE JACOB M. Rosano color *Canadian Geographic* v136 no6 p78 D 2016

Lady Gaga-ntuan C. Schuknecht *Sierra* v101 no4 p23 Jl/Ag 2016

Museums—China

Taiping Heavenly Kingdom History Museum, Nanjing, China S. M. Johnson cartoon color *Military History* v34 no1 p76 My 2017

Museums—Computer network resources

OBJECTS OF OUR AFFECTION J. BREAL *Texas Monthly* v44 no11 p99 N 2016

Museums—England

London C. JUDUA and E. WINDING color *Conde Nast Traveler* v52 no2 p64 F 2017

Museums—England—Evaluation

SIMPLY THE WORLD'S GREATEST RAILWAY MUSEUM D. Huntley *British Heritage Travel* v38 no2 p54 Mr/Ap 2017

Museums—Evaluation

See also

Art museums—Evaluation

ALL ABOUT YVES A. F. COLLINS color *Vanity Fair* v59 no10 p189 O 2017

BATON ROUGE AND THE VISUAL ARTS J. R. KEMP cartoon color *Louisiana Life* v37 no4 p32 Mr/Ap 2017

Connected by Canoe color *Walrus* v14 no9 p39 N 2017

CROSS PURPOSES: The Museum of the Bible will bring religion

near the Mall. Does it belong there? R. Brunner *Washingtonian Magazine* v53 no1 p15 O 2017

Louvre of Arabia R. COUNTER color *Maclean's* v129 no51/52 p71 D 26 2016

LYFORD'SR TOWER, TIBURON, CALIF *Sea Magazine* v109 no1 pCA-4 Ja 2017

A New House of Worship D. PENER *Los Angeles Magazine* p70 My 2017

Plan It: A Prairie Weekend *American Cowboy* v24 no1 p37 Je/Jl 2017

PLAN IT: San Antonio, Texas *American Cowboy* v23 no6 p33 Ap/My 2017

POINTS of INTEREST *Texas Monthly* v45 no3 p110 Mr 2017

PUNK FINDS A HOME A. M. I. GRÍMSSON *Iceland Review* v55 no1 p8 Ja/F 2017

A Record of Time J. BERRY color *New Orleans Magazine* v52 no1 p60 S 2017

SEA OF LOUVRE ABU DHABI'S NEW ISLAND MUSEUM A. VLASITS bw color *Wired* v25 no5 p28 My 2017

SOUTH'S BEST MUSEUM V. Gregory color *Southern Living* v52 no4 p84 Ap 2017

Start to Finnish C. Caldwell bw color *Weekly Standard* v22 no47 p44 Ag 21 2017

Summer School *Atlanta* v57 no2 p148 Je 2017

Taiping Heavenly Kingdom History Museum, Nanjing, China S. M. Johnson cartoon color *Military History* v34 no1 p76 My 2017

THOSE MAGNIFICENT BRITISH FLYING MACHINES S. Reeves *British Heritage Travel* v38 no2 p48 Mr/Ap 2017

WRIGHT'S MASTERWORK F. L. Wright *Saturday Evening Post* v289 no3 p43 My/Je 2017

Museums—Great Britain

THOSE MAGNIFICENT BRITISH FLYING MACHINES S. Reeves *British Heritage Travel* v38 no2 p48 Mr/Ap 2017

Museums—Great Britain—Evaluation

TAKE TEN *British Heritage Travel* v38 no2 p12 Mr/Ap 2017

Museums—Italy

Florence's gift to the people, believers and nonbelievers alike E. W. Schmidt color *America* v217 no4 p52 Ag 21 2017

Museums—Maintenance & repair

New Looks for Museums At Presidential Libraries *Prologue* v49 no1 p69 Spr 2017

Museums—Massachusetts

Beyond Camelot J. BILLS color *Yankee* p76 Mr 2017

The Day Our Ship Came In J. Johnson bw *Yankee* p184 My/Je 2017

A new look for the Davis at Wellesley E. H. Gustafson color *Magazine Antiques* v183 no6 p136 N/D 2016

Museums—Societies, etc.

MUSEUMS FOR EVERYONE IN BRITISH COLUMBIA *Sea Magazine* v108 no9 pPNW-1 S 2016

Museums—United Arab Emirates

THE GULF ART WAR N. AZIMI cartoon color *New Yorker* v92 no42 p74 D 19 2016

Museums—United States

Battle of the War Museums C. H. STAPEN *Washingtonian Magazine* v52 no11 p90 Ag 2017

AN EVEN GREATER NATION FOR GENERATIONS TO COME G. W. BUSH *Vital Speeches of the Day* v82 no11 p349 N 2016

Grand Island's FORGOTTEN BIRTHPLACE B. SASS bw color *Nebraska Life* v21 no4 p44 Jl/Ag 2017

Living & Recreation *Virginia Living* p143 2017 Best 20of Virginia

Made-in-America—The Colony S. Richardson color *American History* v52 no2 p8 Je 2017

Prairie celebration casts warm glow over Wahoo color *Nebraska Life* v20 no6 p63 N/D 2016

Museums—United States—Evaluation

Immerse Yourself in 1776 and All That A. FERGUSON color *Weekly Standard* v22 no32 p10 My 1 2017

Lonnie G. BUNCH III bw *Vanity Fair* v59 no1 p126 Holiday 2017

Permanent February J. NORDLINGER color *National Review* v69 no4 p22 Mr 6 2017

Museums—Washington Metropolitan Area

Lights, Camera, Peacocks: A unique Smithsonian museum devoted to Asian arts reopens with an innovative new film that turns the building inside out A. Diamond *Smithsonian* v48 no6 p22 O 2017

Museum Workout, The (Theatrical production)

DANCE *New Yorker* v92 no47 p8 Ja 30 2017

MUSGRAVE, RUTH A.

Amazing Animals color map *National Geographic Kids* no472 p10 Ag 2017

Awesome Animals! color *National Geographic Kids* no471 p35A Je/Jl 2017

Awesome Animals! *National Geographic Kids* no466 p42 D 2016/Ja 2017

Sea Otters: Supercute, Supertough color *National Geographic Kids* no475 p24 N 2017

Musgraves, Kacey, 1988-

Paying Respect to Country Music's Original Rebel W. HERMES color *Rolling Stone* no1285 p54 Ap 20 2017

MUSHABEN, JOYCE MARIE

Angela Merkel's Leadership in the Refugee Crisis *Current History* v116 no788 p95 Mr 2017

Mushers

The Great White Hope B. Braverman *Smithsonian* v47 no10 p11 Mr 2017

Mushroom culture

CSA CONFIDENTIAL: If you've splurged on a COMMUNITY SUPPORTED AGRICULTURE membership, take these simple steps to protect your investment. Because thyme is money S. KROWIAK *Indianapolis Monthly* v12 no40 p65 Ag 2017

Mushroom harvesting

KING TRUMPET MUSHROOM *South Dakota Magazine* v33 no3 p36 S/O 2017

Mushroom poisoning

Second Helpings D. DAVIS *Sierra* v102 no2 p17 Mr/Ap 2017

Mushroom Gatherers, The (Poem)

The Mushroom Gatherers Y. KOMUNYAKAA *Progressive* p69 D 2016/Ja 2017

Mushrooms

    See also

    Edible mushrooms

Do Not Fear Gene-Edited Food J. SCHWARTZ color *Popular Science* v288 no6 p82 N/D 2016

Forest to face E. Marglin color *Yoga Journal* no290 p26 Mr 2017

FRUITS OF THE FOREST: PHOTOGRAPHER TURNED FORAGER JAMIE SALOMON SETS HIS SIGHTS ON WILD MUSHROOMS K. PANDOLFI *Yankee* v81 no5 p58 S/O 2017

Lighter Manicotti color *Vegetarian Today* no1 p28 F 2017

new ways with CHARD M. XERAKIA *Better Homes & Gardens* v94 no12 p92 D 2016

Quick Hits L. Nemo map *Scientific American* v317 no2 p18 Ag 2017

Quick Meals color *Vegetarian Today* no1 p42 F 2017

RAY OF HOPE S. STALL *Indianapolis Monthly* p17 My 2017

SL cooking school K. Hammonds color *Southern Living* v52 no1 p130 Ja 2017

Warm Winter Menus For Two color *Vegetarian Today* no1 p16 F 2017

Mushrooms—Harvesting

Hunting for Nebraska spring treasure S. W. Kansteiner color *Nebraska Life* v21 no2 p16 Mr/Ap 2017

Mushrooms—Therapeutic use

Fungus of Youth [Cover story] C. MIHELL color *Walrus* v14 no4 p20 My 2017

MUSIAL, J. F.

200-MPH TRICKLE-DOWN color *Road & Track* v69 no4 p66 N 2017

MUSIAL, JOHANNES

THE WORLD'S BILLIONAIRES bw color diag graph map *Forbes* v199 no3 p84 Mr 28 2017

Musib, Mrinal

Artificial intelligence in research color *Science* v357 no6346 p28 Jl 7 2017

Music

    See also

    Fashion & music

    Jazz

    Music & society

    Music psychology

ticles p2 N 6 2014

Music industry—Finance

Inside the War Over Album Exclusives S. KNOPPER color *Rolling Stone* no1272 p13 O 20 2016

Music industry—News briefs

NIGHT LIFE *New Yorker* v92 no44 p15 Ja 9 2017

Music industry—United States

ABE BURNS, CELEBRITY TECHSPLAINER S. MARIKAR color *Bloomberg Businessweek* no4519 p82 Ap 24 2017

Keep On Rockin' in the Free World color *Weekly Standard* v22 no42 p2 Jl 17 2017

Let's Play It By Ear *Los Angeles Magazine* v62 no6 p50 Je 2017

Music Inspired by the Poetry of Carl Sandburg (Music)

Music Inspired By The Poetry Of Carl Sandburg J. Macnie color *Downbeat* v84 no8 p67 Ag 2017

Music literacy

Acquiring "Perfect" Pitch Now Possible *USA Today Magazine* v145 no2865 p8 Je 2017

Music museums

That'll Be the Day bw *Weekly Standard* v22 no39 p2 Je 19 2017

Music Of Miles Davis & Original Compositions (Music)

Music Of Miles Davis & Original Compositions Y. Kato color *Downbeat* v84 no7 p58 Jl 2017

Music psychology

PULSE color *Prevention* v69 no11 p8 N 2017

Smooth Operators color *Prevention* v69 no11 p9 N 2017

Music rehearsals

STRANGE BANDFELLOWS J. KNAPP *Washingtonian Magazine* v52 no5 p19 F 2017

Music software

Ask the iTunes Guy: A look at new features in iTunes 12.6 K. McELHEARN cartoon color *Macworld - Digital Edition* v34 no4 p101 My 2017

Music software—Evaluation

Steinberg Dorico M. Kern color *Downbeat* v84 no3 p114 Mr 2017

Music teachers

Theological muscle memory S. Paulsell *Christian Century* v134 no20 p35 S 27 2017

Music teachers—Awards

Kelly Stomps S. RAVITS color *Louisiana Life* v37 no3 p58 Ja/F 2017

Music television programs

Facebook poll: What did you think of Fox's rock-infused adaptation of The Passion? *TV Guide* v64 no15 p4 Ap 4 2016

Music therapy

The Beat Goes On color *Prevention* v68 no11 p12 N 2016

Intersections between music education and music therapy: Education reform, arts education, exceptionality, and policy at the local level K. Salvador and V. Pasiali bibl *Arts Education Policy Review* v118 no2 p93 2017

Music videos

Berg: Wozzeck W. R. Braun *Opera News* v81 no10 p54 Ap 2017

Elīna Garanča: Revive H. Keys *Opera News* v81 no10 p56 Ap 2017

"Express Yourself" R. Kinane color *Entertainment Weekly* no1460/1461 p47 Ap 7-17 2017

Glinka: Ruslan and Lyudmila R. Pines *Opera News* v81 no10 p52 Ap 2017

Jenkins: Cantata Memoria S. F. Vasta *Opera News* v81 no10 p55 Ap 2017

More Than Backup L. WINGENROTH *Dance Magazine* v91 no1 p78 Ja 2017

Pluhar: Orfeo Chamán J. Cadagin *Opera News* v81 no10 p53 Ap 2017

René Jacobs: The Countertenor, The Accent Recordings, 1978-1982 D. Minter *Opera News* v81 no10 p56 Ap 2017

"Video Killed the Radio Star" E. R. Brown color *Entertainment Weekly* no1460/1461 p45 Ap 7-17 2017

A VR SPACE ODYSSEY color *Entertainment Weekly* no1441 p54 N 25 2016

Music videos—Production & direction

Eli Russell LINNETZ: ONE OF KANYE'S CLOSEST CREATIVE COLLABORATORS HAS ALREADY ANNOUNCED HIMSELF AS SOMETHING OF A WUNDERKIND WITH HIS VIDEO WORK FOR THE RAPPER E. RUTBERG *Interview* v47 no3 p28 Ap 2017

IMAGE CONSULTANT A. OKEOWO cartoon color *New Yorker* v93 no3 p34 Mr 6 2017

Music—21st century

Random Notes color *Rolling Stone* no1272 p30 O 20 2016

Musical collaboration

Timbaland N. Feeney color *Entertainment Weekly* no1460/1461 p96 Ap 7-17 2017

Musical criticism

For the Record J. LEVY bw color *Rolling Stone* no1285 p18 Ap 20 2017

Musical films

The MUSICAL That CHANGED MOVIES J. Mcgovern color *Entertainment Weekly* no1451/1452 p82 F 3-10 2017

Musical freestyle rides (Dressage)

Bound For Omaha! N. Jaffer color *Dressage Today* v23 no7 p48 Mr 2017

Musical groups

See also

Bands (Musical groups)

Quintets

Rock groups

COMPLETE RESULTS color *Downbeat* v84 no8 p54 Ag 2017

GREAT ODIN'S RAVEN! *Cincinnati Magazine* v50 no11 p31 Ag 2017

Keeping It Classic: GROUPMUSE TAKES MOZART, STRAVINSKY, AND HANDEL OUT OF THE CONCERT HALL AND PUTS THEM IN THE MIDDLE OF YOUR LIVING ROOM M. WAKIM *Los Angeles Magazine* v62 no9 p64 S 2017

Odradek's Juried Art T. Staudter bw *Downbeat* v84 no3 p18 Mr 2017

STRENGTH IN DIVERSITY Y. Kato color *Downbeat* v84 no6 p106 Je 2017

Musical instruments

See also

Percussion instruments

EXTRA CREDIT I. Frazier cartoon *New Yorker* v93 no23 p21 Ag 7 2017

HOW TO: Write a Perfect Pop Song D. Marchese *New York* v50 no13 p78 Je 26 2017

THE MYSTIC C. Daly bw *Downbeat* v83 no11 p40 N 2016

SOUNDS OF SCIENCE J. R. MARQUEZ *Atlanta* v56 no11 p34 Mr 2017

Musical instruments—Evaluation

GEAR BOX color *Downbeat* v84 no10 p196 O 2017

GEAR BOX color *Downbeat* v84 no3 p116 Mr 2017

Korg monologue C. Neville color *Downbeat* v84 no3 p114 Mr 2017

Roland Aerophone AE-10 E. Enright color *Downbeat* v84 no6 p88 Je 2017

UA Apollo Twin MkII K. Baumann color *Downbeat* v84 no6 p89 Je 2017

Vic Firth Modern Jazz Collection R. Bennett color *Downbeat* v84 no6 p86 Je 2017

Musical notation—Software—Evaluation

Finale Notation Software M. Kern color *Downbeat* v83 no12 p107 D 2016

Musical performance

See also

Concerts

Flute playing

Singing

After Live M. Trammell color *New Yorker* v93 no32 p10 O 16 2017

AUGUST'S HOTTEST EVENTS *Indianapolis Monthly* v12 no40 p24 Ag 2017

CLASSICAL MUSIC *New Yorker* v93 no15 p9 My 29 2017

CLASSICAL MUSIC *New Yorker* v93 no23 p14 Ag 7 2017

Deep Freeze R. Platt color *New Yorker* v93 no23 p14 Ag 7 2017

EVENT CALENDAR *Washingtonian Magazine* v52 no12 p165 S 2017

Events *Virginia Living* v15 no6 p39 O 2017

Junkies get their fix at Junkstock festival O. SNOW color *Nebraska Life* v21 no5 p84 S/O 2017

Making Music Bounce J. BERRY color *New Orleans Magazine* v51 no12 p62 O 2017

NIGHT LIFE *New Yorker* v93 no15 p8 My 29 2017

NIGHT LIFE *New Yorker* v93 no23 p7 Ag 7 2017

Present in His Grace K. Massinger color *Commonweal* v144 no8 p32 My 5 2017

ROAD TRIP G. R. SCHIAVINO color *American Cowboy* v24 no1 p39 Je/Jl 2017

Summer Preview M. Schulman cartoon *New Yorker* v93 no14 p8 My 22 2017

Super Sonic C. MARTINS color *Los Angeles Magazine* v62 no10 p82 O 2017

Under Cover Bands Go as Greats St. Louis A. Burger color *Missouri Life* v44 no5 p24 Ag 2017

Musical performance—Reviews

CLASSICAL MUSIC *New Yorker* v93 no20 p10 Jl 10 2017

NIGHT LIFE *New Yorker* v93 no20 p6 Jl 10 2017

Musical theater

    See also

    Musicals

5 Guys 2 Coasts *Stage Directions* v30 no9 p20 S 2017

Dancing with the Stars S. Gold color *Dance Magazine* v91 no3 p20 Mr 2017

From BFA to Broadway L. WINGENROTH *Dance Magazine* v91 no8 p48 Ag 2017

Musical theater producers & directors

17 Shows, 1 Legend S. GOLD *Dance Magazine* v91 no8 p20 Ag 2017

Musical theater—Evaluation

Welcoming the Most Famous Reindeer of All *USA Today Magazine* v145 no2859 p16 D 2016

Musical theater—Reviews

A BRILLIANT PAIRING R. L. ELDREDGE *Atlanta* v56 no9 p78 Ja 2017

Choreographing Cyberspace S. GOLD *Dance Magazine* v90 no12 p32 D 2016

Musicals! (Now for Men!) R. McCAMMON and J. WILLIS bw color *GQ: Gentlemen's Quarterly* v97 no9 p116 S 2017

Musical theater—Study & teaching

Institute of the Arts Barcelona *Dance Magazine* v90 p116 2016/2017 Supplement College Guide

Valdosta State University *Dance Magazine* v90 p106 2016/2017 Supplement College Guide

Western Michigan University *Dance Magazine* v90 p109 2016/2017 Supplement College Guide

Musicals

'Annie Hall' Is No 'Groundhog Day' img *New York* v50 no7 p10 Ap 3 2017

THE KEYS TO MARGARITAVILLE J. BUFFETT color *Vanity Fair* v59 no11 p151 N 2017

Let the Sunshine In H. Als color *New Yorker* v92 no46 p8 Ja 23 2017

The Musicality Question G. BERARDI *Dance Magazine* v91 no8 p30 Ag 2017

POKÉMANIA! M. WELLS *Atlanta* v56 no7 p44 N 2016

Welcoming the Most Famous Reindeer of All *USA Today Magazine* v145 no2859 p16 D 2016

Musicals—Humor

CLASSIC MUSICALS, UPDATED S. REED cartoon *New Yorker* v93 no5 p43 Mr 20 2017

Musicals—Production & direction

RISKY BUSINESS C. Brody, I. Biedenharn et al color *Entertainment Weekly* no1449 p38 Ja 20 2017

Musicals—Reviews

2 — FALSETTOS M. R. Bernardo color *Entertainment Weekly* no1444/1445 p118 D 16 2016

On Broadway, It's Déjà Vu All Over-and Not Just for Groundhog Day E. Berman color *Time* v189 no18 p51 My 15 2017

Spring Awakening S. GOLD *Dance Magazine* v91 no4 p20 Ap 2017

Musicals—Social aspects

Hamilton Nation E. Berman color *Time* v188 no14 p50 O 10 2016

Music—Awards

Student Music Award Listings color *Downbeat* v84 no6 p96 Je 2017

Music—Charts, diagrams, etc.

The Hot Box J. McDonough, P. de Barros et al chart *Downbeat* v84 no5 p51 My 2017

Songs That Won the Summer R. Bruner color *Time* v190 no9 p54

S 4 2017

Music—Computer network resources

ArkivMusic Launches ArkivJazz K. Micallef color *Downbeat* v84 no10 p19 O 2017

Music—Congresses

Parnelli Awards to Relocate to the 2018 NAMM Show *Stage Directions* v30 no5 p4 My 2017

Studio Improv P. MARGASAK bw *Downbeat* v84 no3 p19 Mr 2017

Music—Equipment & supplies—Evaluation

GEAR BOX color *Downbeat* v84 no1 p108 Ja 2017

Music halls (Variety-theaters, cabarets, etc.)

FABLES OF THE RECONSTRUCTION R. J. SMITH *Cincinnati Magazine* v50 no11 p86 Ag 2017

GROOVE M. GRIFFITH color *New Orleans Magazine* v51 no8 p58 Je 2017

Q + A cartoon *Cincinnati Magazine* v51 no1 p26 O 2017

WITH POYDRAS THE PARROT J. STREET bw *New Orleans Magazine* v51 no8 p24 Je 2017

Music halls (Variety-theaters, cabarets, etc.)—Design & construction

KPMB Architects A. Bozikovic *Architectural Record* v205 no4 p108 Ap 2017

Music halls (Variety-theaters, cabarets, etc.)—Law & legislation

DANCE OUTLAWS E. Witt cartoon *New Yorker* v93 no20 p24 Jl 10 2017

Musician, The (Music)

The Musician H. Mandel color *Downbeat* v84 no8 p71 Ag 2017

Musicians

    See also

    Composers

    Conductors (Musicians)

    Country musicians

    Disc jockeys

    Jazz musicians

    Rap musicians

    Rock groups

    Rock musicians

    Singers

    Women musicians

10 ARTISTS WHO WILL RULE 2017 E. R. Brown, N. Feeney et al color *Entertainment Weekly* no1450 p56 Ja 27 2017

Aldous HARDING A. WEISS *Interview* v47 no6 p24 Ag 2017

ANDERSON Paak F. LOTUS *Interview* v47 no2 p68 Mr 2017

At Home With... B. Welch color *American Cowboy* v23 no4 p16 D 2016/Ja 2017

Big Band Arranging: Reinventing Stephen Foster's 'Beautiful Dreamer' P. MCGUINNESS bw color *Downbeat* v83 no12 p100 D 2016

Blockchain Could Help Musicians Make Money Again I. Heap color *Harvard Business Review Digital Articles* p2 Je 5 2017

The Case of The Violent Rap Lyrics V. GLEMBOCKI color *Reader's Digest* v189 no1129 p23 Ap 2017

Chords & Discords L. THOMAS, R. JONES et al color *Downbeat* v84 no3 p10 Mr 2017

Clarity: The Art Behind Artistry N. Finzer bw *Downbeat* v84 no4 p86 Ap 2017

COMPLETE RESULTS color *Downbeat* v84 no8 p54 Ag 2017

Following WISE MEN J. EPHLAND color *Downbeat* v83 no12 p54 D 2016

Genius at Work J. Johnson color *Downbeat* v83 no12 p91 D 2016

Gregg Allman S. Lansky color *Time* v189 no22 p11 Je 12 2017

KAMASI WASHINGTON P. Lutz color *Downbeat* v83 no12 p42 D 2016

Lured to New Orleans J. Berry color *New Orleans Magazine* v51 no6 p52 Ap 2017

Mac DeMarco D. Kiper color *Current Biography* v77 no11 p35 N 2016

A new kind of music J. M. Griffith color *U.S. Catholic* v82 no3 p45 Mr 2017

Next Stop: 0tis in 1966 J. Johnson color *Downbeat* v83 no12 p90 D 2016

NILS ØKLAND J. Woodard color *Downbeat* v84 no1 p20 Ja 2017

PERSONA color *New Orleans Magazine* v51 no12 p27 O 2017

Random Notes color *Rolling Stone* no1281/1282 p26 F 23 2017

SAD 13 D. HYMAN *Interview* v46 no9 p24 N 2016

Salomon FAYE D. HYMAN *Interview* v47 no3 p24 My 2017

Saying Goodbye B. REED color *Downbeat* v84 no3 p8 Mr 2017

Speed Read J. BALL *Indianapolis Monthly* p18 N 2017

Staying Sharp J. J. McGowan color *AARP: The Magazine* v30 no6A p65 O/N 2017

St. Beauty T. MALONE *Atlanta* v57 no4 p30 Ag 2017

STREET FIGHTING MAN L. LOWE color *Esquire* p112 Big-BlackBook

WHAT YOU SHOULD KNOW ABOUT BECK D. KAMP bw *Vanity Fair* v59 no11 p78 N 2017

Why a Gin Company Hired Musicians as Part-Time Salespeople C. Huyghe *Harvard Business Review Digital Articles* p2 S 10 2015

Musicians as authors

Most-Wanted List I. Biedenharn color *Entertainment Weekly* no1438 p64 N 4 2016

WHY ROCK MEMOIRS RULE I. Biedenharn color *Entertainment Weekly* no1438 p64 N 4 2016

Musicians—Awards

DownBeat Celebrates 40 Years of SMAs F. Alkyer color *Downbeat* v84 no6 p97 Je 2017

Musicians—Canada

The Real Ex-Husband of Beverly Hills E. KONIGSBERG color diag *Vanity Fair* p164 Hollywood 2017 Supplement

Musicians—Clothing

Gary Clark Jr.'s Juke-Joint Couture P. DOYLE color *Rolling Stone* no1278/1279 p16 Ja 12 2017

Musicians—Congresses

Bimhuis Eschews Trends P. Margasak color *Downbeat* v84 no2 p63 F 2017

Musicians—Employment

THE Theme Park LIFE M. Benjamin color *Dance Spirit* v21 no2 p56 F 2017

Musicians—History

THICH NHAT HANH color *Tricycle: The Buddhist Review* v26 no4 p20 Summ 2017

Musicians—Interviews

Blanchard Helps Fans Process Anger B. Reed color *Downbeat* v84 no10 p20 O 2017

Carlos Santana D. BROWNE bw *Rolling Stone* no1291/1292 p70 Jl 13 2017

Don't Miss Steven Curtis Chapman's Point S. TURNER bw *Christianity Today* p60 Mr 2017

Hot Tracks: JASON ISBELL L. ROBINSON color *Vanity Fair* v59 no11 p76 N 2017

Iggy Pop A. GREENE bw *Rolling Stone* no1278/1279 p58 Ja 12 2017

Jazzie B L. BRADLEY *Interview* v47 no1 p74 F 2017

Joe Walsh A. GREENE bw *Rolling Stone* no1293 p58 Ag 10 2017

Musicians—Political activity

MOOD MUSIC B. Stephen cartoon *New Yorker* v93 no5 p33 Mr 20 2017

Musicians—Salaries, etc.

TOP-EARNING DJs color *Forbes* v200 no2 p26 S 5 2017

Musicians—United States

Anderson .Paak M. Hagan color *Current Biography* v78 no6 p88 Je 2017

AND THEN SHE APPEARED M. SUMELL color *Popular Mechanics* p32 O 2017

Beck Goes Pop (Again) M. Miller color *Esquire* p24 N 2017

FAMILY TRADITION: Roanoke's Rutledge is a little bit country, a little bit rock 'n' roll D. HARRISON *Virginia Living* v15 no4 p31 Je 2017

Henry Threadgill M. Hagan color *Current Biography* v77 no10 p87 O 2016

Julien Baker M. Rich color *Current Biography* v77 no11 p17 N 2016

King Records Month, CITY-WIDE *Cincinnati Magazine* v50 no12 p60 S 2017

Lightbox M. Johnston color *Time* v190 no15 p14 O 16 2017

Orchestrating a new approach to learning M. Kaplan color *Phi Delta Kappan* v98 no7 p23 Ap 2017

The Piano Man's Apprentice A. GREENE color *Rolling Stone* no1272 p24 O 20 2016

THE POLYMATH A. WILKINSON bw cartoon *New Yorker* v93 no4 p42 Mr 13 2017

Musicians—United States—Interviews

Little Steven Heads Back to the Garage, Emerges With the Eclectic Sounds of Soulfire M. METTLER color *Sound & Vision* v82 no8 p30 O 2017

Musicians—United States—Political activity

Rock's New Protest Era S. KNOPPER color *Rolling Stone* no1281/1282 p13 F 23 2017

Music—Iceland

NORDIC FIRE A. ROSS color *New Yorker* v93 no11 p78 My 1 2017

Music—Instruction & study

   See also

     Music conservatories

FOCUSYEAR BASEL GOES DEEP J. Hale color *Downbeat* v84 no3 p105 Mr 2017

Intersections between music education and music therapy: Education reform, arts education, exceptionality, and policy at the local level K. Salvador and V. Pasiali bibl *Arts Education Policy Review* v118 no2 p93 2017

Teaching music in the flat world: Reflections on the work of Darling-Hammond and Rothman J. C. Vaughan-Marra and C. M. Marra bibl *Arts Education Policy Review* v118 no2 p123 2017

University of the Pacific Fosters Collaborations Y. Kato color *Downbeat* v83 no11 p102 N 2016

Music—Instruction & study—United States

Why music matters in urban school districts: The perspectives of students and parents of the Celia Cruz High School of Music, Bronx, New York N. A. Dosman bibl chart *Arts Education Policy Review* v118 no2 p67 2017

Music—Korea

K-Pop's Global Success Didn't Happen by Accident Won-Yong Oh and M. Rhee *Harvard Business Review Digital Articles* p2 N 10 2016

Music—News briefs

Random Notes color *Rolling Stone* no1295 p26 S 7 2017

Music—Performance

   See also

     Concerts

     Improvisation in music

     Music rehearsals

19 THINGS YOU REALLY OUGHT TO DO THIS MONTH M. J. Gaynor, B. Freed et al *Washingtonian Magazine* v52 no1 p33 O 2016

April Events F. Esker color *New Orleans Magazine* v51 no6 p26 Ap 2017

The Biggest Tours of 2017, From GNR to Bieber S. KNOPPER color *Rolling Stone* no1278/1279 p14 Ja 12 2017

CELEBRATING THE HOLIDAYS cartoon *New Yorker* v92 no39 p10 N 28 2016

CLASSICAL MUSIC *New Yorker* v92 no44 p12 Ja 9 2017

Dancing in the Field C. Rose color *New Orleans Magazine* v51 no6 p42 Ap 2017

GIFTS THAT STIR THE SOUL T. Marks color *Consumer Reports* v81 no12 p57 D 2016

THE GUIDE / 11.16 M. WAKIM *Los Angeles Magazine* v61 no11 p84 N 2017

MARCH'S COOLEST EVENTS *Indianapolis Monthly* v40 no7 p24 Mr 2017

March! T. PAYNE color *Ebony* v72 no5 p24 Mr 2017

The New York Philharmonic *New York* v49 no25 p145 D 12 2016

NIGHT LIFE cartoon *New Yorker* v92 no42 p18 D 19 2016

TAKE ME OUT TO THE "SONG" PARK *USA Today Magazine* v145 no2862 p42 Mr 2017

The Ten Best Classical Music Performances of the Year J. Davidson img *New York* v49 no25 p130 D 12 2016

Music—Performance—Reviews

CLASSICAL MUSIC *New Yorker* v92 no30 p15 S 26 2016

Kenny Rogers Is Walkin' Away A. Nash color *AARP: The Magazine* v59 no4A p14 Je/Jl 2017

NIGHT LIFE *New Yorker* v92 no41 p16 D 12 2016

Music—Performance—Social aspects

CHRISTMAS PRESENTS M. GRIFFITH bw *New Orleans Magazine* v51 no2 p52 D 2016

Music—Periodicals—History

Making the First Issue A. GREENE bw color *Rolling Stone* no1278/1279 p24 Ja 12 2017

Music—Political aspects
See also
Popular music—Political aspects
4 THINGS YOU DIDN'T SEE AT THE GRAMMYS N. Feeney
color *Entertainment Weekly* no1454/1455 p16 F 24 2017
Chords & Discords L. Coryell, A. Michie et al color *Downbeat*
v84 no4 p10 Ap 2017

Music—Religious aspects
THE MUSIC OF TIME NO 2: ANGELIC CHOIRS AND DEV-
ILISH VOICES A. Lee *History Today* v67 no8 p86 Ag 2017

Music—Religious aspects—Christianity
Kanye, Kendrick, Chance & the Surprising Christian Language of
Rap Z. Davis color *America* v216 no5 p34 Mr 6 2017

Music—Reviews
Signs of Changing Times K. GOTTSCHALK bw *Downbeat* v84
no10 p72 O 2017

Music—Societies, etc.
195 Clubs Where Music Thrives [Cover story] color *Downbeat*
v84 no2 p45 F 2017
EAST color *Downbeat* v84 no2 p47 F 2017
JEN Grows Up F. Alkyer color *Downbeat* v84 no4 p19 Ap 2017

Music—Societies, etc.—Evaluation
Rock 'n' Roll 'n' Romance at (le) Poisson Rouge K. Gottschalk
color *Downbeat* v84 no2 p46 F 2017

Music—United States
See also
African American music
Elvis In the Heart of America J. Meacham and A. Rumer color
Time v190 no7 p38 Ag 21 2017

Music—United States—Reviews
NIGHT LIFE *New Yorker* v92 no41 p16 D 12 2016

Musiek, Erik S.
Mechanisms linking circadian clocks, sleep, and neurodegeneration bibl diag *Science* v354 no6315 p1004 N 25 2016

MUSIWA, ELAINE
The Bare ESSENTIALS color *Ebony* v72 no11 p54 S 2017
LASER-SHARP FAT REDUCTION color *Ebony* v72 no11 p56
S 2017
TIKA SUMPTER color *Ebony* v72 no11 p57 S 2017

Musk, Elon, 1971-
Elon Musk's FUTURE SHOCK M. DOWD bw color *Vanity Fair*
v59 no5 p116 Ap 2017
Elon Musk's House of Giga-cards P. Burrows graph il *MIT Tech-
nology Review* v119 no6 p58 N/D 2016
Elon Musk's Hyperloop Surprise S. McBride *Bloomberg Busi-
nessweek* no4534 p19 Ag 14 2017
THE FLOATING WORLD M. BRANDSTETTER *Cincinnati
Magazine* v50 no5 p24 F 2017
THE FUTURE ACCORDING TO MUSK T. Randall bw color
Bloomberg Businessweek no4529 p48 Jl 3 2017
A Humongous Rocket That Just Might Work B. FERDOWSI color
diag *Popular Mechanics* p12 S 2017
Inching Ahead With Hyperloop B. R. REYNOLDS *Los Angeles
Magazine* p18 Ja 2017
Lightning in a Bottle E. Loh color *Motor Trend* v69 no5 p8 My
2017
Mars J. Achenbach chart color *National Geographic* v230 no5 p31
N 2016
Rocket plan C. SORENSEN cartoon color *Maclean's* v129
no48/49 p64 D 5 2016
Stock X-Ray: Tesla T. Tepper color diag *Money* v46 no7 p36 Ag
2017
Tech Industry, Meet Donald color *Popular Mechanics* p18 S 2017
THE TROLLS ARE COMING P. M. Barrett color *Bloomberg
Businessweek* no4501 p27 N 28 2016
TUNNEL VISION M. CHAFKIN color *Bloomberg Businessweek*
no4512 p52 F 20 2017
Why Elon Musk's New Strategy Makes Sense J. Gans *Harvard
Business Review Digital Articles* p2 Jl 25 2016
the year in review *Car & Driver* v62 no7 p17 Ja 2017

Musk, Elon, 1971-—Awards
Elon Musk CEO TESLA MOTORS cartoon *Motor Trend* v69 no1
p108 Ja 2017

Musk, Elon, 1971-—Interviews
What I'd Do Differently Fake Elon Musk, not 45 J. P. HUFFMAN
cartoon *Car & Driver* v62 no7 p120 Ja 2017

Musk, Kimbal
LOCAL FLAVOR: Kimbal Musk considers Indy fertile ground
for continuing his food fight S. Krowiak *Indianapolis Monthly*
v40 no10 p42 Je 2017

Musk, Maye
MAYE IN AUTUMN D. BLASBERG color *Vanity Fair* v59 no4
p172 Mr 2017

Muskellunge
THE ABYSS S. HEITING and G. BETHGE color *Outdoor Life*
v224 no3 pF1 Ap 2017

Muskellunge fishing
THE WEATHER RULES B. RUZZO and G. BETHGE color *Outdoor Life* v224 no4 p67 My 2017

Musker, John—Interviews
MAKING WAVES WITH MOANA M. Snetiker color *Entertainment Weekly* no1442 p12 D 2 2016 Rebellious Special Issue

Muskmelon
Fruit with huge health benefits M. TAYLOR color *Redbook* p72
Jl/Ag 2017
Mixing Bowl color *O, The Oprah Magazine* p134 Ap 2017

Muskox populations
Umingmak in danger J. BENNETT color *Canadian Geographic*
v137 no4 p31 Jl/Ag 2017

Muskus, Jeff
CHINA'S ROBOT REVOLUTION color graph *Bloomberg Businessweek* no4520 p32 My 1 2017
Why Japan's Idemitsu Isn't Feeling Blue color *Bloomberg Businessweek* no4520 p34 My 1 2017

Muslim artists
The Modern Hamzanama: A epic project in memory of a departed
son *Islamic Horizons* v46 no4 p40 Jl/Ag 2017

Muslim athletes
Ibtihaj Muhammad Redefining the Muslim American Image
[Cover story] R. FATIMA *Islamic Horizons* v45 no6 p28 N/D
2016

Muslim businesspeople—History—20th century
Cambodian Cham Muslims and the Quran: A shattered communi-
ty continues to rebuild its foundations of faith S. NAZY *Islamic
Horizons* v46 no4 p34 Jl/Ag 2017

Muslim children
Timeless Teachings for Young Readers G. HENRY *Islamic Horizons* v45 no6 p34 N/D 2016

Muslim diaspora
Misperceptions of the 'Muslim Diaspora' S. SILVESTRI *Current
History* v115 no784 p319 N 2016

Muslim physicians
HALF A CENTURY OF CARE [Cover story] *Islamic Horizons*
v46 no3 p22 My/Je 2017
Medicine for the Heart and Mind *Islamic Horizons* v45 no6 p26
N/D 2016

Muslim students
American Muslim Students Need Understanding and Support F.
N. Shah *Education Digest* v83 no2 p33 O 2017

Muslim Students' Association of the United States & Canada
Countering Violence in DC and Baltimore S. SWETZOFF *Islamic
Horizons* v46 no1 p28 Ja/F 2017
The Deen Chasers N. RIAZ *Islamic Horizons* v45 no6 p23 N/D
2016

Muslim teachers
With More Than a Prayer N. ZAKI *Islamic Horizons* v46 no1 p38
Ja/F 2017

Muslim teenagers
Hijabi Fits: A tween is creating a rainbow of hijabs for girls of all
ages S. MEEHAN *Islamic Horizons* v46 no4 p36 Jl/Ag 2017

Muslim women
Distorted Feminism S. MEEHAN *Islamic Horizons* v45 no6 p54
N/D 2016
Geert Goes Down color *Nation* v304 no12 p11 Ap 10 2017
JOKING WHILE MUSLIM N. FARSAD cartoon *Wired* v25 no4
p75 Ap 2017
Muslim Women Speak Out S. MAHFOUZ *Publishers Weekly*
v264 no36 p104 S 4 2017

Muslim women—Civil rights
Why Did France Ban A Bathing Suit? P. SMITH and A. J. Rubin
New York Times Upfront v149 no3 p6 O 10 2016

Muslim women—Clothing

American communities geared to supporting childless couples? M. B. AHMED *Islamic Horizons* v46 no3 p40 My/Je 2017

Empowerment through the Quran *Islamic Horizons* v46 no4 p6 Jl/Ag 2017

Muslims in America R. MARC GERECHT color *Weekly Standard* v22 no9 p23 N 7 2016

Muslims on the Front Lines: Countering violent Islamophobia with knowledge and organizing I. QAIYIM *Islamic Horizons* v46 no4 p44 Jl/Ag 2017

New Ban, No Relief J. HING color *Nation* v304 no10 p4 Mr 27 2017

Muslims—United States—Social conditions—21st century
Which religion's liberty is most threatened in the United States? graph *America* v216 no6 p6 Mr 20 2017

MUSMECI, CECILIA
TINARIWEN *Interview* v47 no2 p76 Mr 2017

Mussa, R.
Observation of a large-scale anisotropy in the arrival directions of cosmic rays above 8×1018 eV *Science* v357 no6357 p1266 S 22 2017

Mussels
Preventing mussel adhesion using lubricant-infused materials S. Amini, S. Kolle et al color diag graph *Science* v357 no6352 p668 Ag 18 2017

A Tougher Tooth Thanks to Mussels *USA Today Magazine* v146 no2869 p7 O 2017

Musser, Charles
Politicking and Emergent Media: US Presidential Elections of the 1890s J. COPPOLA *Film Quarterly* v71 no1 p123 Fall 2017

Musser, George
Something Faster Than Light? What Is It? J. Holt color *New York Review of Books* v63 no17 p50 N 10 2016

Spooky Physics Up Close: An Exchange J. Bernstein bw *New York Review of Books* v63 no19 p62 D 8 2016

Mussett, Mickey
The Right Step L. Feldman color *American Cowboy* v24 no1 p48 Je/Jl 2017

Mussolini, Benito, 1883-1945
IL BRUTO color *MHQ: Quarterly Journal of Military History* v30 no1 p96 Aut 2017

Must Farm site (England)
FIRE IN THE FENS J. URBANUS color *Archaeology* v70 no1 p34 Ja/F 2017

Mustaches
MY MUSTACHE AND ME M. Hansen color *Powder* v45 no6 p48 F 2017

Mustafa, Nujeen
The incredible journey C. MEAGAN color *Maclean's* v129 no43 p39 O 31 2016

Mustafa, Rana
Migration today: Displaced scientists color *Science* v356 no6339 p698 My 19 2017

Mustang
MUSTANGS ON A MISSION: THESE FIVE WOMEN PLAN TO SPREAD INSPIRATION FROM MEXICO TO CANADA L. F. Prater *Successful Farming* v115 no6 p62 Ap 2017

Spirit of the Black Hills A. PAVIA color *Trail Rider* v29 no1 p44 Ja/F 2017

Mustang automobile
Bowling Green's Variable-Cam Brawler P. Thomas color graph *Hot Rod* v70 no7 p34 Jl 2017

Every Year (Almost) of "Ohio" George Montgomery's Iconic Willys Gasser T. Taylor bw *Hot Rod* v70 no8 p94 Ag 2017

Fleet Files D. Beard, J. Gall et al color *Car & Driver* v63 no4 p90 O 2017

The HOT ROD Archives D. Wallace color *Hot Rod* v70 no1 p18 Ja 2017

Ken Zimmer Swapped a Modern Ford AOD Trans into His 1967 Mustang. Now it Has a Shift-Timing Problem. We're Gonna Fix It M. Davis chart color *Hot Rod* v70 no1 p94 Ja 2017

Mustang ROUSH P-51 B. Gillogly color *Hot Rod* v70 no11 p30 N 2017

Under Pressure P. Thomas color *Hot Rod* v70 no12 p26 D 2017

Upped Ante M. Gearhart color diag graph *Hot Rod* v70 no7 p54 Jl 2017

Vicious B. Gillogly color *Hot Rod* v70 no8 p32 Ag 2017

Mustang automobile—Evaluation
MANO A MANO T. Quiroga cartoon color *Car & Driver* v62 no7 p70 Ja 2017

Mustard
ALL THE THINGS S. KROWIAK *Indianapolis Monthly* v40 no4 p54 D 2016

RIDE THE WAVE J. CISSIK color *Muscle & Performance* v9 no6 p22 Je 2017

UP IN SMOKE BOURGEOIS color *Field & Stream* v122 no2 p66 Je/Jl 2017

Musto, Michael
DOUG WRIGHT *Advocate* no1088 p30 D 2016/Ja 2017

home & help img *New York* p96 Mr 6 2017

Musto, Russ
'Ella 100' Celebrates First Lady of Song color *Downbeat* v84 no1 p18 Ja 2017

Stars Salute Ella at Lincoln Center color *Downbeat* v84 no7 p13 Jl 2017

Mustonen, Tero
Biodiversity redistribution under climate change: Impacts on ecosystems and human well-being color *Science* v355 no6332 p1389 Mr 31 2017

Mutabazi, A.
A worldwide survey of neonicotinoids in honey graph *Science* v357 no6359 p109 O 6 2017

Mutation (Biology)
See also
DNA damage
Somatic mutation

GENETIC TEST NOW AVAILABLE FOR "NAKED FOAL" SYNDROME C. Barakat and M. McCluskey color *Equus* no476 p19 My 2017

Human knockouts provide drug clues T. H. SAEY graph *Science News* v191 no9 p10 My 13 2017

Night Owl Genes V. Greenwood color *Scientific American* v317 no3 p21 S 2017

Muteba, Bertha
Alessia Cara color *Current Biography* v77 no11 p26 N 2016
Cam color *Current Biography* v78 no6 p20 Je 2017
Camila Cabello color *Current Biography* v78 no9 p7 S 2017
Charlie Puth color *Current Biography* v78 no1 p64 Ja 2017
Cynthia Erivo color *Current Biography* v77 no11 p40 N 2016
Danai Gurira color *Current Biography* v77 no10 p44 O 2016
Jordan Spieth color *Current Biography* v78 no5 p82 My 2017
Lalah Hathaway color *Current Biography* v77 no10 p53 O 2016
Nneka Ogwumike color *Current Biography* v78 no8 p68 Ag 2017
Simone Manuel color *Current Biography* v78 no3 p54 Mr 2017
Solange Knowles color *Current Biography* v78 no4 p47 Ap 2017
Thomas Rhett color *Current Biography* v78 no2 p70 F 2017

Muth, Lisa
CANOVA *South Dakota Magazine* v33 no3 p40 S/O 2017

Muthiah, Rob
How spiritual practices can foster creativity *Christian Century* v134 no8 p1 Ap 12 2017

Muthspiel, Wolfgang, 1965-
Muthspiel Assembles All-Star Ensemble T. Panken bw *Downbeat* v83 no12 p18 D 2016

Wolfgang Muthspiel's 5/4 Guitar Solo on 'Boogaloo' J. DURSO bw diag *Downbeat* v84 no7 p78 Jl 2017

Muthupalaniappan, Arun
Are You Accurately Measuring Your Company's Digital Strength? *Harvard Business Review Digital Articles* p2 S 7 2017

Mutism
SMART PEOPLE DO THE Dumbest THINGS! [Cover story] A. MARIE, S. CONNOR et al *Reader's Digest* v190 no1134 p62 O 2017

Mutsuga, Tatsuya
Photoinduced decarboxylative borylation of carboxylic acids diag *Science* v357 no6348 p283 Jl 21 2017

Mutual fund fees
Fidelity Fires a Shot in The Fund Price War C. Stein *Bloomberg Businessweek* no4533 p26 Ag 7 2017

Mutual funds
See also
Index mutual funds
Stock funds

She was 94, and all signs pointed to a stroke. But when tests came back negative, the doctors had to explore more unusual possibilities L. Sanders *New York Times Magazine* p20 O 1 2017

Mycelium

See also

Hyphae of fungi

Deep Relationships K. Moore color *Natural History* v125 no10 p6 O 2017

Unseen Fruit H. HAWORTH color *Orion Magazine* v35 no6 p7 N/D 2016

Mycenaean antiquities

THE GOLDEN WARRIOR J. MARCHANT *Smithsonian* v47 no9 p38 Ja/F 2017

Mychajliw, Alexis M.

Merging paleobiology with conservation biology to guide the future of terrestrial ecosystems color *Science* v355 no6325 p594 F 10 2017

Mycobacterial diseases

Study suggests hidden epidemic in CF patients K. Kupferschmidt color *Science* v354 no6313 p695 N 11 2016

Mycobacterium

See also

Mycobacterium leprae

Mycobacterium tuberculosis

Emergence and spread of a human-transmissible multidrug-resistant nontuberculous mycobacterium J. M. Bryant, D. M. Grogono et al bibl diag graph *Science* v354 no6313 p751 N 11 2016

Red squirrels in the British Isles are infected with leprosy bacilli C. Avanzi, J. del-Pozo et al bibl color diag map *Science* v354 no6313 p744 N 11 2016

Mycobacterium avium—Genetics

Study suggests hidden epidemic in CF patients K. Kupferschmidt color *Science* v354 no6313 p695 N 11 2016

Mycobacterium leprae

Leprosy in red squirrels R. Brosch and T. P. Stinear bibl color diag *Science* v354 no6313 p702 N 11 2016

Mycobacterium smegmatis

Intercellular communication and conjugation are mediated by ESX secretion systems in mycobacteria T. A. Gray, R. R. Clark et al bibl diag graph *Science* v354 no6310 p347 O 21 2016

Mycobacterium tuberculosis

Killing the Unkillable K. LOUGHEED color *Natural History* v125 no7 p34 Jl/Ag 2017

Reversion of antibiotic resistance in Mycobacterium tuberculosis by spiroisoxazoline SMARt-420 N. Blondiaux, M. Moune et al bibl diag *Science* v355 no6330 p1206 Mr 17 2017

TB exploits zombie cells *Science* v356 no6334 p150 Ap 14 2017

Mycobacterium tuberculosis—Treatment

Eclipse, Epidemic, Evolution, Ecology *Natural History* v125 no7 p5 Jl/Ag 2017

Mycoplasma

Biologists Create Organism With Smallest Genome J. KEATS chart color graph *Discover* v38 no1 p15 Ja/F 2017

Mycorrhizal fungi

Plant-soil feedbacks and mycorrhizal type influence temperate forest population dynamics J. A. Bennett, H. Maherali et al bibl graph map *Science* v355 no6321 p1 Ja 13 2017

Mycoses

Fighting Fungus [Cover story] T. L. Dog color *Prevention* v69 no9 p28 O 2017

SAVING EUROPE'S SALAMANDERS E. Stokstad color map *Science* v357 no6348 p242 Jl 21 2017

Mycoses—Diagnosis

Which DIY Health Tests Are Worth It? S. S. Gold color *Health* v31 no2 p77 Mr 2017

Mycoses—Prevention

Fungal pneumonia: Unusual suspects *Mayo Clinic Health Letter* v35 no11 p4 N 2017

Put Your Best Foot Forward J. Stewart color *Men's Health* v32 no2 p78 Mr 2017

Mycoskie, Blake

THE CHANGE MAKER M. Goldstein color *Sunset* v238 no1 p17 Ja 2017

My Crazy Ex-Girlfriend (TV program)

The Must List color *Entertainment Weekly* no1436/1437 p1 O 21 2016

Mydock-McGrane, Laurel

Lysosomal cholesterol activates mTORC1 via an SLC38A9–Niemann-Pick C1 signaling complex bibl diag graph *Science* v355 no6331 p1306 Mr 24 2017

Myelin

BUNDLED UP E. MASTROIANNI color *Discover* v38 no6 p14 Jl/Ag 2017

Myeloid leukemia

Sterilizing immunity in the lung relies on targeting fungal apoptosis-like programmed cell death N. Shlezinger, H. Irmer et al color diag *Science* v357 no6355 p1037 S 8 2017

Myeong-Gu Seo

Why Certain Managers Thrive in Tough New Jobs While Others Get Fed Up *Harvard Business Review Digital Articles* p2 Ap 22 2015

Myers, Alexandra

Reflections on the Meaning of Horsemanship *In Stride* v12 no1 p33 Ja 2017

MYERS, B. R.

Oswald Spengler: Pessimism's Prophet *American Conservative* v15 no6 p51 N/D 2016

Myers, Ben

Theology color *Christian Century* v134 no10 p27 My 10 2017

Myers, Blanca

21st-Century Exodus graph map *Wired* v25 no4 p90 Ap 2017

WISH LIST 2016 color *Wired* v24 no12 p45 D 2016

Myers, Cash

BUCKLE UP B. Welch color *Spin to Win Rodeo* v20 no9 p19 N 2016

Myers, Chad L.

Exploring genetic suppression interactions on a global scale diag *Science* v354 no6312 p599 N 4 2016

Myers, Christopher G.

Health Care Providers Can Use Design Thinking to Improve Patient Experiences *Harvard Business Review Digital Articles* p2 Ag 31 2017

Is Your Company Encouraging Employees to Share What They Know? *Harvard Business Review Digital Articles* p2 N 6 2015

The Next Wave of Hospital Innovation to Make Patients Safer *Harvard Business Review Digital Articles* p2 Ag 8 2016

When Health Care Providers Look at Problems from Multiple Perspectives, Patients Benefit *Harvard Business Review Digital Articles* p2 Je 23 2017

Why Companies Are Becoming B Corporations *Harvard Business Review Digital Articles* p2 Je 17 2016

Myers, David P.

Kilogram-scale prexasertib monolactate monohydrate synthesis under continuous-flow CGMP conditions chart diag *Science* v356 no6343 p1144 Je 16 2017

Myers, Drew

The Call of the Wild color *Field & Stream* v121 no7 p50 D 2016/ Ja 2017

Myers, Eddie L.

Photoinduced decarboxylative borylation of carboxylic acids diag *Science* v357 no6348 p283 Jl 21 2017

Myers, Jason R.

Tudor-SN–mediated endonucleolytic decay of human cell microRNAs promotes G1/S phase transition graph *Science* v356 no6340 p859 My 26 2017

Myers, Jonathan A.

Plant diversity increases with the strength of negative density dependence at the global scale diag *Science* v356 no6345 p1389 Je 30 2017

Myers, Kirk

A Gym of Angels E. SULLIVAN cartoon color *Esquire* v167 no1 p48 F 2017

Myers, Lorry

ANCHORED IN A SMALL TOWN cartoon *Missouri Life* v44 no3 p68 My 2017

THE BUNNY CAKE BAKE-OFF color *Missouri Life* v44 no2 p64 Ap 2017

GO TEAM! color *Missouri Life* v44 no4 p62 Je 2017

Happy Birthday to Me! color *Missouri Life* v44 no6 p64 S 2017

HOME FOR THE HOLIDAY *Missouri Life* v43 no7 p67 D 2016/ Ja 2017

MEAN TO BE *Missouri Life* v43 no6 p80 O/N 2016

THE SOUNDS OF VACATION cartoon *Missouri Life* v44 no5 p66 Ag 2017

Myers, Marc
GOLDEN OLDIES A. DeCURTIS color *New York Times Book Review* p37 D 4 2016
A Story Benind Every Song S. YANOW color *Downbeat* v84 no2 p82 F 2017

Myers, Margaret
The Political Economy of China-Latin America Relations in the New Millennium: Brave New World R. Feinberg *Foreign Affairs* v96 no2 p179 Mr/Ap 2017

Myers, Matthew Ward
Braised Pork Shoulder *Indianapolis Monthly* p45 My 2017

Myers, Michael
What the U.S. Can Learn From India and Brazil About Preventive Health Care *Harvard Business Review Digital Articles* p2 N 14 2014

Myers, Mike, 1963—Interviews
Meet The Gong Show's New Host J. Russell *TV Guide* v65 no27 p4 Je 26 2017

Myers, Robert W.
Systemic pan-AMPK activator MK-8722 improves glucose homeostasis but induces cardiac hypertrophy graph *Science* v357 no6350 p507 Ag 4 2017

Myers, Roy—Interviews
Trendy Touches *Indianapolis Monthly* p104 F 2017

MYERS, STEVEN LEE
Frozen Souls *New York Times Book Review* p12 Ja 8 2017

Myers, Steven S.
Kilogram-scale prexasertib monolactate monohydrate synthesis under continuous-flow CGMP conditions chart diag *Science* v356 no6343 p1144 Je 16 2017

MYERSON, JESSE A.
WHITE, BLACK, & RED bw color *Nation* v304 no16 p21 My 22 2017

Myerson, Julie
Mind Games: Two young men sink deep into an online fantasy world, pitting the virtual against the real *New York Times Book Review* p7 Ag 13 2017

Myers-Powell, Brenda
REBIRTHED AFTER A LIFE IN THE SEX TRADE A. EMMANUEL color *Ebony* v72 no6 p86 Ap/My 2017

Myhrvold, Cameron
Nucleic acid detection with CRISPR-Cas13a/C2c2 color diag *Science* v356 no6336 p438 Ap 28 2017

Mykonos Island (Greece)—Description & travel
FROM RUNWAY TO (ESCAPING) REALITY color *Esquire* p23 2017 BigBlackBook

Mylan NV
You'll Feel a Little Pinch M. W. O'Reilly color *Commonweal* v143 no17 p6 O 21 2016

Mylan NV—Finance
EPIPEN PANIC J. Wieczner color *Fortune* v174 no8 p21 D 15 2016

MYLCHREEST, MELISSA
BIG SKY LIVING color diag *Cabin Living* p38 Ag 2017
cozy MOUNTAIN CABIN [Cover story] color *Cabin Living* p42 D 2016
DIY cabin remodel color *Cabin Living* p30 D 2016
forest TLC color *Cabin Living* p52 O 2017
WILDERNESS Wonderland color diag *Cabin Living* p42 Ap 2017

Myles, Eileen
Dog Years C. Luchette color *O, The Oprah Magazine* p98 O 2017
Jack PIERSON *Interview* v47 no1 p114 F 2017
PUBLIC DISPLAY *Harper's Magazine* v334 no2001 p15 F 2017
SHAGGY DOG STORY *Harper's Magazine* p17 O 2017
To Do img *New York* v50 no18 p88 S 4 2017

Mylod, Deirdre E.
One Way to Prevent Clinician Burnout *Harvard Business Review Digital Articles* p2 O 12 2017
What Makes Doctors Value Patient Feedback *Harvard Business Review Digital Articles* p2 N 30 2015

Mylona, Anastasia
Opposing effects of Elk-1 multisite phosphorylation shape its response to ERK activation bibl graph *Science* v354 no6309 p233 O 14 2016

Mylvaganam, Ravindra
Decoupling genetics, lineages, and microenvironment in IDH-mutant gliomas by single-cell RNA-seq diag *Science* v355 no6332 p1391 Mr 31 2017

Mynatt, Lyndsay
PICKLE RECIPES for the Picking: Ferment or quick-pickle your harvest with this assortment of ideas from Mother Earth News bloggers *Mother Earth News* no282 p56 Je/Jl 2017

Myocardial infarction
ALL IN A Day's Work S. JESTER and S. HARVEY *Reader's Digest* v190 no1135 p56 N 2017
Danielle's Heart J. MCCAFFERY color *Prevention* v69 no5 p32 My 2017
Data back ban of artificial trans fats A. CUNNINGHAM *Science News* v191 no9 p8 My 13 2017
How to (Safely) Let Off Steam *Saturday Evening Post* v289 no2 p72 Mr/Ap 2017
How to Survive Your First Heart Attack *AARP: The Magazine* v59 no2A p18 F/Mr 2016
The man had suffered two strokes and was on medication to prevent more. Was this another stroke? Or something else? L. Sanders *New York Times Magazine* p20 My 14 2017
When Roads Are Closed for Marathons, More Elderly People Die of Heart Attacks A. Olenski and A. B. Jena *Harvard Business Review Digital Articles* p2 Ap 12 2017

Myocardial infarction treatment
Photosynthesis treats ailing hearts T. HESMAN SAEY *Science News* v192 no1 p8 Ag 5 2017

Myocardial infarction—Mortality
Blood Levels of 0mega-3s from Fish, Plants Linked to Lower Fatal Heart Risk *Tufts University Health & Nutrition Letter* v34 no8 p3 O 2016

Myocardial infarction—Patients
Women at Higher Risk of Silent Heart Attack D. Zipes *Saturday Evening Post* v289 no3 p74 My/Je 2017

Myocardial infarction—Prevention
Are You Smarter Than a HEART ATTACK? K. Rockwood cartoon *O, The Oprah Magazine* p90 F 2017
ASK THE DOCTOR A. L. KOMAROFF *Harvard Health Letter* v42 no3 p2 Ja 2017
A Chile Pepper a Day... color graph *Prevention* v69 no6 p11 Je 2017
heart therapy [Cover story] G. Rubanyi color *Scientific American* v316 no1 p38 Ja 2017
June/July color *AARP: The Magazine* v59 no4A p9 Je/Jl 2016

Myocardial infarction—Risk factors
ASK THE DOCTOR A. L. KOMAROFF *Harvard Health Letter* v42 no4 p2 F 2017

Myofibroblasts
Fibroblasts become fat to reduce scarring C. K. F. Chan and M. T. Longaker bibl diag *Science* v355 no6326 p693 F 17 2017

Myopia—Prevention
Let There Be Light G. Reynolds *New York Times Magazine* p16 Ja 22 2017

Myopia—Treatment
Let There Be Light G. Reynolds *New York Times Magazine* p16 Ja 22 2017

Myoung-Gyun Suh
Microresonator soliton dual-comb spectroscopy bibl diag graph *Science* v354 no6312 p600 N 4 2016

MyPillow Inc.
Are You There God? It's Me, the Pillow King J. Dean color *Bloomberg Businessweek* no4507 p52 Ja 16 2017

Myrick, Sonia
Back to School *Parks & Recreation* v52 no9 p120 S 2017
Environmental Career Forecasting *Parks & Recreation* v52 no4 p16 Ap 2017
Go Healthy STL *Parks & Recreation* v52 no2 p30 F 2017
How the City of Keller, Texas, Built a Dog Agility Course *Parks & Recreation* v52 no2 p49 F 2017
Member Spotlight: Kristina K. Adams *Parks & Recreation* v51 no11 p54 N 2016
Movable Chairs *Parks & Recreation* v51 no11 p64 N 2016
Passport to Fun! *Parks & Recreation* v51 no12 p56 D 2016
Story Stroll *Parks & Recreation* v52 no10 p64 O 2017
Terry Hershey: 'A Force of Nature for Nature' *Parks & Recreation*

v52 no3 p50 Mr 2017

Myrick, Svante

Hot Do-Gooder Svante Myrick R. WIEDEMAN color *Rolling Stone* no1274 p46 N 17 2016

Mystere (Theatrical production)

CIRQUE Queen C. Bowers *Dance Spirit* v21 no7 p52 S 2017

Mystére á la Tour Eiffel (Film)

Victorian Lust D. GUERRERO color *Advocate* no1091 p30 Je/Jl 2017

Mystery

Mystery of the Paulding Light B. RADFORD *Skeptical Inquirer* v41 no2 p36 Mr/Ap 2017

Some Queensland Mysteries J. NICKELL *Skeptical Inquirer* v41 no3 p14 My/Je 2017

Mystery in literature

iBook Bestsellers chart color *Publishers Weekly* v264 no20 p17 My 15 2017

Mystery shopping

Everyone Says They Listen to Their Customers— Here's How to Really Do It A. Brant *Harvard Business Review Digital Articles* p2 O 28 2015

Mysticism

THE RIGHT PATH I. RUDOLPH *TV Guide* v65 no6 p28 Ja 30 2017

Walking Backward Toward the Future J. BRICKLIN cartoon *Tricycle: The Buddhist Review* v26 no3 p26 Spr 2017

Myth

THE GREAT "PERSECUTION OF CHRISTIANS" MYTH R. BOSTON *Humanist* v77 no3 p34 My/Je 2017

TRACKING MYTHS J. R. HALE, E. CHIASSON et al color *Scientific American* v316 no4 p6 Ap 2017

Mythbusters (TV program)

New Myths, New Busters J. LYNCH color *Popular Mechanics* p22 N 2017

Mytho? Lure of Wildness? (Theatrical production)

Time Flies H. Als cartoon *New Yorker* v92 no42 p20 D 19 2016

Mythology

TRACKING MYTHS J. R. HALE, E. CHIASSON et al color *Scientific American* v316 no4 p6 Ap 2017

Mythology—Research

THE EVOLUTION OF MYTHS J. d'Huy color diag *Scientific American* v315 no6 p62 D 2016

N

Na Yin

Aerobic glycolysis promotes T helper 1 cell differentiation through an epigenetic mechanism bibl graph *Science* v354 no6311 p481 O 28 2016

NAAF, TOBIAS

Combining Biodiversity Resurveys across Regions to Advance Global Change Research *BioScience* v67 no1 p73 Ja 2017

Naar, Devin

Mad, Democrats? Blame the Iran Deal *Commentary* p1 Ja 2017

A Proto-Zion A. Apostolou *Commentary* v143 no1 p56 Ja 2017

Naar, Nancy

Q: If you had an extra hour in your day, what would you do with it? color *O, The Oprah Magazine* p18 O 2017

NAAS, ROBERTA

The Second Time Around color *Forbes* v199 no6 p106 Je 13 2017

NABAUM, ALEX

Copy the Tea Party *New Republic* v248 no3 p32 Mr 2017

Don't Give In to Despair *New Republic* v248 no3 p37 Mr 2017

Organize a Moral Resistance *New Republic* v248 no3 p36 Mr 2017

Reinvent Labor *New Republic* v248 no3 p35 Mr 2017

Revamp the Democratic Party *New Republic* v248 no3 p35 Mr 2017

Use Vivid Language color *New Republic* v248 no3 p34 Mr 2017

Utilize the Courts *New Republic* v248 no3 p36 Mr 2017

Nabeel, Gilgamesh

Displaced Iraqi Christians await return to Mosul color *Christian Century* v133 no24 p14 N 23 2016

Nabel, Gary J.

Trispecific broadly neutralizing HIV antibodies mediate potent SHIV protection in macaques color graph *Science* v357 no6359 p85 O 6 2017

Nabokov, Peter

Indians, Slaves, and Mass Murder: The Hidden History bw *New York Review of Books* v63 no18 p70 N 24 2016

Nabokov, Vladimir Vladimirovich, 1899-1977

Commonplace Book A. Matthews *American Scholar* v86 no2 p126 Spr 2017

Nabors, Rachel

Real News, Fake Panic J. LILEKS *National Review* v69 no5 p39 Mr 20 2017

Nabucco (Theatrical production)

Nabucco G. VERDI and T. SOLERA *Opera News* v81 no7 p54 Ja 2017

Nabucco J. Malafronte *Opera News* v81 no9 p33 Mr 2017

Nabuurs, Gert-Jan

Positive biodiversity-productivity relationship predominant in global forests bibl chart graph map *Science* v354 no6309 paaf8957-1 O 14 2016

Nacci, Diane

The genomic landscape of rapid repeated evolutionary adaptation to toxic pollution in wild fish bibl graph *Science* v354 no6317 p1305 D 9 2016

Nace, Arben

Regeneration of fat cells from myofibroblasts during wound healing bibl color graph *Science* v355 no6326 p748 F 17 2017

Nachbagauer, Raffael

Enhancement of Zika virus pathogenesis by preexisting antiflavivirus immunity graph *Science* v356 no6334 p175 Ap 14 2017

Nachev, Vladislav

Cognition-mediated evolution of low-quality floral nectars bibl graph *Science* v355 no6320 p1 Ja 6 2017

Nachos

NACHO NIRVANA M. HENNESSY color *Chicago* v66 no2 p52 F 2017

Sizzlin' Campfire Nachos P. KITA bw color *Men's Health* v32 no6 p36 Ag 2017

Nachury, Maxence V.

Microtubules acquire resistance from mechanical breakage through intralumenal acetylation diag graph *Science* v356 no6335 p328 Ap 21 2017

Nacogdoches (Tex.)

It Happened Here: Nacogdoches, Texas G. R. Schiavino color *American Cowboy* v23 no6 p36 Ap/My 2017

NAD Electronics International (Company)

MQA Is Coming to NAD's M. Fleischmann and C. Crowley color *Sound & Vision* v81 no9 p17 N 2016

Nadal, Marc

Guanine glycation repair by DJ-1/Park7 and its bacterial homologs chart color diag graph *Science* v357 no6347 p208 Jl 14 2017

Nadal, Rafael, 1986-

The Fifty Greatest Living Athletes D. MAGARY, Z. BARON et al bw color *GQ: Gentlemen's Quarterly* v97 no11 p96 N 2017

Leading Off K. Kahler color *Sports Illustrated* v126 no17 p8 Je 19 2017

Lightbox S. Gregory color *Time* v189 no24 p14 Je 26 2017

RAFAEL NADAL'S FOREHAND EXTENSION J. YANDELL *Tennis* v53 no1 p29 Ja/F 2017

Rafael Nadal *Tennis* v53 no1 p28 Ja/F 2017

Nadar, Félix, 1820-1910

A Wink and a Nod: The French artist Nadar at his most subversive and sly A. BEGLEY *American Scholar* v86 no3 p102 Summ 2017

Nadeau, Marie-Claude

How CMOs and CROs Can Be Allies *Harvard Business Review Digital Articles* p2 Mr 26 2015

Nadel, Dan

IN THE STUDIO: NANCY SHAVER bw color *Art in America* v105 no6 p118 Je/Jl 2017

Precision Drawing and Useless Categories color *Art in America* v104 no10 p29 N 2016

NADELLA, ANU

A Mother's Journey color *Good Housekeeping* v265 no5 p62 N 2017

Nadella, Satya, 1967-

5 SATYA NADELLA A. Nusca color diag *Fortune* v174 no7 p76 D 1 2016

"The moment that CHANGED OUR LIVES FOREVER" J. Francisco color *Good Housekeeping* v265 no5 p58 N 2017

Nadella, Shilpa Prabhakar

The 2017 Essentials color *Glamour* v115 no1 p23 Ja 2017

All the Ruffles color *Glamour* no8 p50 Ag 2017

Amazing Lace color *Glamour* v114 no12 p96 D 2016

Define Yourself color *Glamour* v115 no3 p60 Mr 2017

Do You Know These Labels? bw color *Glamour* v115 no3 p86 Mr 2017

The Evening Suit color *Glamour* v114 no12 p94 D 2016

Find Your Passion bw color *Glamour* v115 no3 p194 Mr 2017

Flowers, Girl color *Glamour* v115 no2 p32 F 2017

A Fresh Coat color *Glamour* no8 p48 Ag 2017

Give Good Gift color *Glamour* v114 no12 p183 D 2016

Hey, Jenna! color *Glamour* v115 no3 p92 Mr 2017

If You Like to Rework the Classics color *Glamour* v115 no9 p54 S 2017

If You Love a Good Throwback color *Glamour* v115 no9 p58 S 2017

If You're Gearing Up for Date Night color *Glamour* v115 no9 p48 S 2017

If You're Getting Your Girlboss On color *Glamour* v115 no9 p50 S 2017

If You're Living for the Weekend color *Glamour* v115 no9 p56 S 2017

Katy's Got Sole color *Glamour* v115 no2 p25 F 2017

The Man Who Loves Women color *Glamour* v115 no3 p94 Mr 2017

One Suit, Two Ways color *Glamour* v115 no9 p62 S 2017

Outfits for Days color *Glamour* v115 no3 p78 Mr 2017

Pack Your Bags color *Glamour* v115 no3 p206 Mr 2017

Purple's Reign color *Glamour* v115 no3 p212 Mr 2017

Red-Carpet Revolution color *Glamour* v115 no3 p82 Mr 2017

Sleeve Game Strong color *Glamour* v115 no3 p62 Mr 2017

Start Here color *Glamour* v115 no1 p24 Ja 2017

Stripe Hype color *Glamour* v115 no2 p28 F 2017

That Robe Life color *Glamour* v115 no3 p64 Mr 2017

Twice? Nice! color *Glamour* no8 p58 Ag 2017

Twice? Nice! color *Glamour* v115 no3 p74 Mr 2017

Va-Va-Va Velvet color *Glamour* v114 no12 p92 D 2016

What to Know NOW color *Glamour* v114 no11 p72 N 2016

Wide-Leg Wonders color *Glamour* no8 p46 Ag 2017

Work Your Look color *Glamour* v115 no3 p166 Mr 2017

Your Spring Look Is Here color *Glamour* v115 no3 p59 Mr 2017

Nader, Mina

Egyptian Copts finally fulfilling dream of Jerusalem pilgrimage color *Christian Century* v134 no9 p15 Ap 26 2017

Egypt's Copts face rising fears, divisions color *Christian Century* v134 no10 p14 My 10 2017

Nadir Kaplan, C.

Controlled growth and form of precipitating microsculptures bw color diag graph *Science* v355 no6332 p1395 Mr 31 2017

NADIS, STEVE

Black Holes and Revelations color *Discover* v38 no9 p70 N 2017

Breakthrough to the Stars chart color *Discover* v38 no1 p92 Ja/F 2017

The Universe According to Emmy Noether color diag *Discover* v38 no5 p48 Je 2017

Yuri Milner color *Discover* v38 no3 p16 Ap 2017

Nadkarni, Rohan

10 Bucks color *Sports Illustrated* v125 no14 p84 O 24-31 2016

10 Mavericks color *Sports Illustrated* v125 no14 p110 O 24-31 2016

11 Bulls color *Sports Illustrated* v125 no14 p86 O 24-31 2016

11 Pelicans color *Sports Illustrated* v125 no14 p111 O 24-31 2016

12 Heat color *Sports Illustrated* v125 no14 p88 O 24-31 2016

12 Suns color *Sports Illustrated* v125 no14 p112 O 24-31 2016

13 Magic color *Sports Illustrated* v125 no14 p89 O 24-31 2016

13 Nuggets color *Sports Illustrated* v125 no14 p113 O 24-31 2016

14 76ers color *Sports Illustrated* v125 no14 p90 O 24-31 2016

14 Kings color *Sports Illustrated* v125 no14 p114 O 24-31 2016

15 Lakers color *Sports Illustrated* v125 no14 p116 O 24-31 2016

15 Nets color *Sports Illustrated* v125 no14 p92 O 24-31 2016

1 Cavaliers color *Sports Illustrated* v125 no14 p72 O 24-31 2016

1 Warriors color *Sports Illustrated* v125 no14 p96 O 24-31 2016

2 Celtics *Sports Illustrated* v125 no14 p74 O 24-31 2016

2 Spurs color *Sports Illustrated* v125 no14 p98 O 24-31 2016

3 Clippers color *Sports Illustrated* v125 no14 p99 O 24-31 2016

3 Raptors color *Sports Illustrated* v125 no14 p75 O 24-31 2016

4 Pistons color *Sports Illustrated* v125 no14 p76 O 24-31 2016

4 Trail Blazers color *Sports Illustrated* v125 no14 p100 O 24-31 2016

5 Hornets color *Sports Illustrated* v125 no14 p78 O 24-31 2016

5 Thunder color *Sports Illustrated* v125 no14 p102 O 24-31 2016

6 Hawks color *Sports Illustrated* v125 no14 p80 O 24-31 2016

6 Jazz color *Sports Illustrated* v125 no14 p103 O 24-31 2016

7 Grizzlies color *Sports Illustrated* v125 no14 p104 O 24-31 2016

7 Pacers color *Sports Illustrated* v125 no14 p81 O 24-31 2016

8 Rockets color *Sports Illustrated* v125 no14 p106 O 24-31 2016

8 Wizards color *Sports Illustrated* v125 no14 p82 O 24-31 2016

9 Knicks color *Sports Illustrated* v125 no14 p83 O 24-31 2016

9 Timberwolves color *Sports Illustrated* v125 no14 p108 O 24-31 2016

DIFFERENCE MAKER color *Sports Illustrated* v126 no12 p34 My 1 2017

FASHIONABLE 50 [Cover story] color *Sports Illustrated* v127 no3 p26 Jl 24 2017

GOING GREEN color *Sports Illustrated* v126 no12 p37 My 1 2017

OPENING ACT color *Sports Illustrated* v126 no13 p52 My 8 2017

RESERVE AND PROTECT color *Sports Illustrated* v126 no12 p33 My 1 2017

Scouting Reports color *Sports Illustrated* v125 no14 p70 O 24-31 2016

SCOUTING REPORTS color *Sports Illustrated* v127 no12 p54 O 16 2017

SI's Top 100 color *Sports Illustrated* v125 no14 p94 O 24-31 2016

TAKE THAT! color *Sports Illustrated* v126 no12 p35 My 1 2017

WHOSE TROPHY IS IT? color *Sports Illustrated* v126 no5 p56 F 13 2017

WORDS WITH... Dwyane Wade color *Sports Illustrated* v125 no14 p120 O 24-31 2016

Nadler, Jerrold, 1947

Honorable Jerrold Nadler *Congressional Digest* v95 no9 p20 N 2016

NADOLSKY, SPENCER

4 Steps to REVERSE DIABETES Naturally [Cover story] color *Prevention* p78 Mr 2017

NADON, CHRISTOPHER

Self-Restraint in the Executive bw *Weekly Standard* v22 no28 p28 Mr 27 2017

NADP (Coenzyme)

A conserved NAD+ binding pocket that regulates protein-protein interactions during aging J. Li, M. S. Bonkowski et al bibl graph *Science* v355 no6331 p1312 Mr 24 2017

Naeye, Robert

GRAVITATIONAL WAVES: From novelty to science [Cover story] color diag *Astronomy* v45 no11 p18 N 2017

Making sense of the exoplanetary zoo color *Astronomy* v45 no6 p24 Je 2017

Naff, Clay Farris

THE FUTURE OF SEX: How technology, morality, and politics are reshaping human sexuality *Humanist* v77 no4 p12 Jl/Ag 2017

MAKE AMERICA KIND AGAIN *Humanist* v77 no1 p12 Ja/F 2017

Prepare to March for Science and the Climate *Humanist* v77 no3 p9 My/Je 2017

Naficy, Mariam

"I EAT HEALTHY AT MOST AIRPORTS. BUT AT CDG, I'LL SNIFF OUT THE FOIE GRAS" C. TATTOLI color *Conde Nast Traveler* v52 no1 p41 Ja 2017

Naftulin, Julia

EMILY SKYE A New Kind of Fit Chick color *Health* v31 no1 p56 Ja 2017

ISKRA LAWRENCE "BODY POSITIVE IS A CHOICE" color *Health* v31 no7 p26 S 2017

MANDY MOORE "I'm never going to deprive myself" color

Health v31 no9 p25 N 2017

Nag, Anirban

How India Tripped Itself Up graph *Bloomberg Businessweek* no4538 p30 S 18 2017

Nagai, Mariko

Irradiated Cities *Publishers Weekly* v264 no26 p152 Je 26 2017

NAGANO, AARON

Trump Theory *Commentary* v142 no1 p11 Jl/Ag 2016

NAGEEB, SAMIYAH

Navigating Challenges and Seizing Opportunities *Islamic Horizons* v45 no6 p16 N/D 2016

Nagel, Greg

FIFTY Favorites *Los Angeles Magazine* p8 Ap 2017

Nagel, Sarah

Neandertal and Denisovan DNA from Pleistocene sediments bw color *Science* v356 no6338 p605 My 12 2017

Nagel, Thomas

A Gruesome Ghost Dance bw *New York Review of Books* v64 no14 p50 S 28 2017

Is Consciousness an Illusion? bw color *New York Review of Books* v64 no4 p32 Mr 9 2017

Nagele, S.

Observing the ultrafast buildup of a Fano resonance in the time domain bibl graph *Science* v354 no6313 p738 N 11 2016

Nagendra, Harini

Ecosystem management as a wicked problem chart color diag *Science* v356 no6335 p265 Ap 21 2017

Nägerl, Hanns-Christoph

Bloch oscillations in the absence of a lattice graph *Science* v356 no6341 p945 Je 1 2017

Nagle, Angela

Kill All the Normies: Online Culture Wars From 4Chan And Tumblr To Trump And The Alt-Right M. DUNBAR *Humanist* v77 no5 p45 S/O 2017

Nagle, Ron

Turkish Hairlines color *Art in America* v105 no1 pC1 Ja 2017

Nagle, Tadhg

Only 3% of Companies' Data Meets Basic Quality Standards *Harvard Business Review Digital Articles* p2 S 11 2017

Nagler, Cathryn R.

Neonatal acquisition of Clostridia species protects against colonization by bacterial pathogens diag *Science* v356 no6335 p315 Ap 21 2017

Nagler, Stephen E.

Neutron scattering in the proximate quantum spin liquid a-RuCl3 bw diag *Science* v356 no6342 p1055 Je 9 2017

Naguib, Saeed G.

Catalytic intermolecular hydroaminations of unactivated olefins with secondary alkyl amines bibl diag *Science* v355 no6326 p727 F 17 2017

NAGY, PETER

"MIYAGAWA KOZAN RETROSPECTIVE" color *ARTnews* v115 no4 p136 Wint 2016/2017

Nahai, Nathalie

Why We're So Hypocritical About Online Privacy *Harvard Business Review Digital Articles* p1 My 1 2017

Nahalka, Igor

Optical imaging of surface chemistry and dynamics in confinement color *Science* v357 no6353 p784 Ag 25 2017

Naharin, Ohad

Gaga for Mr. Gaga color *Dance Spirit* v21 no2 p18 F 2017

Nahed, Brian V.

Decoupling genetics, lineages, and microenvironment in IDH-mutant gliomas by single-cell RNA-seq diag *Science* v355 no6332 p1391 Mr 31 2017

NAHIGIAN, KENNETH

BEHAVIORISM *Humanist* v77 no2 p36 Mr/Ap 2017

Nahorski, Michael S.

Neurodevelopmental protein Musashi-1 interacts with the Zika genome and promotes viral replication diag *Science* v357 no6346 p83 Jl 7 2017

Naidu, M. Venkaiah, 1949-

All That I Can and Would Like to Do Is to Make You All Speak and Act to Enable Effective Functioning of the House: I CERTAINLY CAN'T BE LIKE A HEADMASTER HERDING THE ERRANT STUDENTS ON THE PATH OF DISCIPLINE *Vital*

Speeches of the Day v83 no9 p261 S 2017

Nail art (Manicuring)

Insider Tips N. Spradley color *Essence* v47 no7 p23 N 2016

Nail art (Manicuring)—Evaluation

MANICURE MASTER CLASS color *Martha Stewart Living* p46 Jl/Ag 2017

Nail care

See also

Manicuring

GH BEAUTY LAB M. OZ and B. ARAL color *Good Housekeeping* v265 no4 p30 O 2017

Got MANI Game? K. FOSTER color *Seventeen* v76 no12 p56 D 2016/Ja 2017

manicure makeover *Parents* v92 no1 p15 Ja 2017

Snap the Ultimate NAILFIE M. OLIVA color *Seventeen* v76 no5 p46 S 2017

Nail care equipment

THE ODD Couples color *O, The Oprah Magazine* p61 Je 2017

Nail care—Equipment & supplies—Evaluation

Got MANI Game? K. FOSTER color *Seventeen* v76 no12 p56 D 2016/Ja 2017

Nail polish

Fresh COAT K. MOLVAR color *Vogue* v207 no7 p56 Jl 2017

Give It a Swirl color *Martha Stewart Living* no275 p20 Je 2017

Organize Like a VLOGGER E. STOVALL color *Seventeen* v76 no2 p74 Mr 2017

The Price of Fear M. Gunch cartoon *New Orleans Magazine* v51 no8 p46 Je 2017

Shelf Awareness J. W. Blaschke cartoon *O, The Oprah Magazine* p63 Ap 2017

Nail polish—Evaluation

16 ways to do CREAMSICLE color *Good Housekeeping* v265 no1 p48D Jl 2017

Amazing Lace S. P. Nadella color *Glamour* v114 no12 p96 D 2016

BEAUTY UNDER $25 P. STABLES bw color *Redbook* p34 N 2017

cheap THRILLS K. FOSTER color *Seventeen* v75 no11 p50 N 2016

CHERRY PICKED A. B. RAYA color *Chicago* v65 no11 p48 N 2016

Colors of Summer A. R. Williams color *Southern Living* v52 no6 p52 Je 2017

Does It Really Work? color *Southern Living* v52 no6 p59 Je 2017

DOPE STUFF ON MY DESK J. Wilson color *Essence* v47 no10 p28 F 2017

Give Good Gift S. P. Nadella and E. Velluto color *Glamour* v114 no12 p183 D 2016

GLAM BY TONIGHT Guarnieri color *Harper's Bazaar* no3649 p251 D 2016/Ja 2017

LUXE BEAUTY color *Harper's Bazaar* no3649 p174 D 2016/Ja 2017

MANICURE MASTER CLASS color *Martha Stewart Living* p46 Jl/Ag 2017

Meet Us at the Beach C. Solomon color *Glamour* v114 no7 p74 Jl 2016

My Aunt, the Beauty Icon V. F. Luesse color *Southern Living* v52 no4 p64 Ap 2017

No-Makeup Makeup for Women of Color B. Mpinja color *Glamour* v115 no9 p79 S 2017

NUDE NAIL POLISH color *Women's Health* v14 no7 p172 S 2017

THE ODD Couples color *O, The Oprah Magazine* p61 Je 2017

O, THE OPRAH MAGAZINE Fall BEAUTY O-WARDS 2017 color *O, The Oprah Magazine* pC5 S 2017

Our Holiday Faves color *Prevention* v68 no12 p5 D 2016

Perfectly quiet polishes color *Redbook* p35 O 2017

the pick color *InStyle* v24 no3 p270 Mr 2017

POP STARS color *Vogue* v206 no12 p230 D 2016

SEEING GREEN M. BOBO color *Ebony* v72 no5 p40 Mr 2017

Sunny Side Up! E. Reimel color *Glamour* v115 no7 p52 Jl 2017

'tis the season... TO SPARKLE *Better Homes & Gardens* v94 no12 p24 D 2016

Try a pretty jewel-tone mani color *Redbook* p45 F 2017

UPDATE YOUR LOOK Guarnieri color *Harper's Bazaar* no3655 p89 Ag 2017

VIP TREATMENT color *O, The Oprah Magazine* p47 Ja 2017

Nail salons
Great moments in local journalism A. Hiatt bw color *Columbia Journalism Review* v56 no1 p112 Spr 2017

Nails & spikes
Letting it be C. Barakat bw color *Equus* no472 p20 Ja 2017

Nails (Anatomy)
earthly delights T. PEREZ *Parents* v91 no11 p76 N 2016
A MANI WITH CRYSTAL POWER color *Health* v31 no1 p14 Ja 2017

Nails, Jen
One Hundred Spaghetti Strings *Publishers Weekly* v264 no7 p76 F 13 2017

Naim Audio Ltd.
Naim Mu-so Qb Wireless Music System B. Ankosko color graph *Sound & Vision* v82 no5 p60 Je 2017

Naimark, Norman M.
All Quiet on the Balkan Front? *Hoover Digest: Research & Opinion on Public Policy* no1 p120 Wint 2017
The Future of Genocide: International law changes, but human nature doesn't. Hoover fellow Norman M. Naimark on the ancient and persistent crime of genocide K. Davidson *Hoover Digest: Research & Opinion on Public Policy* no3 p164 Summ 2017
The Many Lives of Babi Yar *Hoover Digest: Research & Opinion on Public Policy* no2 p176 Spr 2017

Naipaul, V. S. (Vidiadhar Surajprasad), 1932-
c. 1935: Trinidad *Lapham's Quarterly* v10 no1 p34 Wint 2017

Nair, Anita
Chain of Custody: An Inspector Gowda Novel *Publishers Weekly* v263 no39 p68 S 26 2016

Nair, Dinesh
Help Wanted in Saudi Arabia: Savvy Investors color graph *Bloomberg Businessweek* no4513 p41 Mr 6 2017
Rockwell Collins Inc *Bloomberg Businessweek* no4537 p29 S 11 2017

Nair, Nisha
Release of mineral-bound water prior to subduction tied to shallow seismogenic slip off Sumatra graph *Science* v356 no6340 p841 My 26 2017

Nair, Raj, 1965——Interviews
Mark Fields and Raj Nair A. Priddle color *Motor Trend* v69 no4 p32 Ap 2017

Nair, Usha
A switch from canonical to noncanonical autophagy shapes B cell responses bibl graph *Science* v355 no6325 p641 F 10 2017

Nairoukh, Zackaria
Hydrogenation of fluoroarenes: Direct access to all-cis-(multi)fluorinated cycloalkanes diag *Science* v357 no6354 p908 S 1 2017

Najar, Bernie
Find Your Personal Power Move color *Golf Magazine* v59 no7 p54 Jl 2017

Naji, Zohrehsadat
Creating a culture of ethics in Iran bibl *Science* v354 no6310 p296 O 21 2016

Najib Tun Razak, Datuk, 1953-
Our Economy Continues to Prosper: MALAYSIA IS STRONGER THAN EVER AS A RESULT OF REFORMS *Vital Speeches of the Day* v83 no9 p252 S 2017

NAKADATE, LAUREL
Mary GAITSKILL: ONE OF OUR MOST ORIGINAL FICTION WRITERS TURNS HER WIT AND WISDOM TOWARD THE REAL WORLD, RIGHT WHEN WE NEED IT MOST *Interview* v47 no3 p34 Ap 2017

Nakagawa, H.
Structural basis of the redox switches in the NAD+-reducing soluble [NiFe]-hydrogenase diag *Science* v357 no6354 p928 S 1 2017

Nakagawa, Hiroyuki
Laundroid color *Bloomberg Businessweek* no4510 p28 F 6 2017

Nakai, Patti
Confronting the Heart of Darkness bw *Tricycle: The Buddhist Review* v26 no4 p28 Summ 2017

Nakajima, F.
Coseismic rupturing stopped by Aso volcano during the 2016 Mw 7.1 Kumamoto earthquake, Japan bibl color graph *Science* v354 no6314 p869 N 18 2016

Nakajima, Haruo, 1929-2017

Milestones *Time* v190 no7 p13 Ag 21 2017

Nakajima, Kazunori
A crossroad of neuronal diversity to build circuitry color *Science* v356 no6336 p376 Ap 28 2017

Nakamoto, David
FROM OUR READERS *Sky & Telescope* v133 no6 p6 Je 2017

Nakamoto, Satoshi, 1975-
THE SECRET, DANGEROUS WORLD OF VENEZUELAN BITCOIN MINING J. EPSTEIN *Reason* v48 no8 p27 Ja 2017

Nakamura, Akihiro
Higher predation risk for insect prey at low latitudes and elevations graph *Science* v356 no6339 p742 My 19 2017

Nakamura, Fuminori
The Boy in the Earth *Publishers Weekly* v264 no9 p76 F 27 2017

Nakamura, Hiroki
TRUE GRIT bw color *Esquire* p80 2017 BigBlackBook

Nakamura, Hiroshi, 1974-
On a Clear Day N. R. POLLOCK color *Architectural Record* v205 no8 p102 Ag 2017

Nakamura, Junji
TECHNICAL COMMENT ABSTRACTS *Science* v357 no6354 p881 S 1 2017

Nakamura, Katrina
Committing to socially responsible seafood color *Science* v356 no6341 p912 Je 1 2017

Nakamura, R.
Structure, force balance, and topology of Earth's magnetopause diag graph *Science* v356 no6341 p960 Je 1 2017

Nakamura, Toshikazu
Two-dimensional sp2 carbon-conjugated covalent organic frameworks diag graph *Science* v357 no6352 p673 Ag 18 2017

Nakamura, Yuji
How to Lose $6 Billion color graph *Bloomberg Businessweek* no4512 p19 F 20 2017
Laundroid color *Bloomberg Businessweek* no4510 p28 F 6 2017
Nintendo's New Guard Tries to Switch It Up color *Bloomberg Businessweek* no4514 p35 Mr 13 2017
See Mario. See Mario Run color graph *Bloomberg Businessweek* no4503 p29 D 12 2016

NAKANISHI, LAUREL
A Private Wild *Orion Magazine* v35 no4/5 p102 Jl-O 2016

Nakao, Wendy Egyoku
Hold to the Center! color *Tricycle: The Buddhist Review* v26 no4 p36 Summ 2017

Nakashima, H.
Structural basis of the redox switches in the NAD+-reducing soluble [NiFe]-hydrogenase diag *Science* v357 no6354 p928 S 1 2017

Nakayama, Manabu
PCGF3/5–PRC1 initiates Polycomb recruitment in X chromosome inactivation color *Science* v356 no6342 p1081 Je 9 2017

Nakayama, Niki
Niki Nakayama G. SNYDER *Los Angeles Magazine* v62 no9 p98 S 2017

Nakayama, Takuya
A peptide hormone required for Casparian strip diffusion barrier formation in Arabidopsis roots bibl color graph *Science* v355 no6322 p284 Ja 20 2017

Naked singularities (Cosmology)
Singularities may reveal themselves E. CONOVER *Science News* v191 no11 p12 Je 10 2017

Naked Magicians, The (Theatrical production)
67 GREAT THINGS TO DO THIS MONTH J. FOUMBERG, J. HARDERGER et al color *Chicago* v66 no3 p129 Mr 2017

Nakicenovic, Nebojsa
A roadmap for rapid decarbonization bibl color graph *Science* v355 no6331 p1269 Mr 24 2017

Nakintu, Sarah——Interviews
SARAH NAKINTU J. Wilson color *Essence* v47 no8 p40 D 2016

Naldoni, Alberto
Applying plasmonics to a sustainable future color *Science* v356 no6341 p908 Je 1 2017

Nalebuff, Barry
Priceless color *Science* v354 no6312 p560 N 4 2016

Nalesso, Valérie
The DNA methyltransferase DNMT3C protects male germ cells

from transposon activity bibl diag graph *Science* v354 no6314 p909 N 18 2016

Naletto, G.

Rosetta's comet 67P/Churyumov-Gerasimenko sheds its dusty mantle to reveal its icy nature bibl graph *Science* v354 no6319 p1566 D 23 2016

Surface changes on comet 67P/Churyumov-Gerasimenko suggest a more active past bw graph *Science* v355 no6332 p1392 Mr 31 2017

Naloxone

The Resurrection Drug F. Gillette color graph *Bloomberg Businessweek* no4499 p42 N 14 2016

Naloxone—Therapeutic use

Where County Lines Mean Life and Death J. Tozzi and J. S. Hopkins graph *Bloomberg Businessweek* no4538 p31 S 18 2017

Naltrexone—Therapeutic use

Inspired Health *Psychology Today* v49 no5 p16 S/O 2016

NPR Talks Smack color *Weekly Standard* v22 no40 p3 Je 26 2017

Nam, Sooji

Double-heterojunction nanorod light-responsive LEDs for display applications bibl color graph *Science* v355 no6325 p616 F 10 2017

NAM, SUZANNE

THE WORLD'S BILLIONAIRES bw color diag graph map *Forbes* v199 no3 p84 Mr 28 2017

Namane, Abdelkader

The cryo-EM structure of a ribosome–Ski2-Ski3-Ski8 helicase complex bibl color graph *Science* v354 no6318 p1431 D 16 2016

Nambiar, Kalyani

A nuclease that mediates cell death induced by DNA damage and poly(ADP-ribose) polymerase-1 bw graph *Science* v354 no6308 paad6872-1 O 7 2016

NAMDAR, RUBY

SACRED CITY color *New York Times Book Review* p67 D 4 2016

Name tags

Letter Perfect B. PIKE color *Power & Motoryacht* v32 no12 p68 D 2016

Names

HELLO MY NAME IS JANE J. Bernstein *Saturday Evening Post* v289 no1 p18 Ja/F 2017

Mislabeled *Lapham's Quarterly* v10 no2 p48 Spr 2017

Position Change A. Staples and T. Keith color *Sports Illustrated* v126 no8 p20 Mr 20 2017

Names of stars

NAME THAT STAR C. Zuckerman color *National Geographic* v232 no2 p16 Ag 2017

Say Betelgeuse B. BERMAN color *Astronomy* v45 no10 p10 O 2017

NAMI MUN

What the Dead Know *New York Times Book Review* p12 Ja 15 2017

Namib-Naukluft Park (Namibia)

72 Hours in ... Namibia D. POINTDUJOUR color *Ebony* v72 no6 p60 Ap/My 2017

Namibia—Description & travel

72 Hours in ... Namibia D. POINTDUJOUR color *Ebony* v72 no6 p60 Ap/My 2017

Naming rights

From Laps to Lap Bands T. Keith color *Sports Illustrated* v126 no11 p22 Ap 17-24 2017

Gifts The Rising Price of B-School Glory J. Lorin color *Bloomberg Businessweek* no4522 p51 My 15 2017

MINT 400 STILL GOING STRONG S. OCHSNER chart color *Dirt Sports + Off-Road* v51 no8 p10 Ag 2017

Namou, Weam

Healing Wisdom for a Wounded World: My Life-Changing Journey Through a Shamanic School (Book 2) *Publishers Weekly* v264 no4 p50e Ja 23 2017

Nan Zhang

Biaxially strained PtPb/Pt core/shell nanoplate boosts oxygen reduction catalysis bibl color graph *Science* v354 no6318 p1410 D 16 2016

Nance, Erik

Milking It N. H. Reeder color *Ebony* v72 no9 p51 Jl/Ag 2017

Nance, Michelle

HOOKED ON HER color *Essence* v47 no7 p48 N 2016

Nancherla, Aparna

Ask anything bw color *Women's Health* v14 no2 p18 Mr 2017

GET UP Stand Up [Cover story] A. Breslaw bw color *Women's Health* v13 no10 p103 D 2016

Laugh Lines A. NANCHERLA, J. KELLY et al color *Reader's Digest* v190 no1132 p86 Jl/Ag 2017

Nandgaon (India)

Lightbox color *Time* v189 no10 p16 Mr 20 2017

Nandkishore, Nandu

4 Hard Questions to Ask About Your Company's Purpose *Harvard Business Review Digital Articles* p2 Mr 22 2016

All Hail Medium-Term Planning *Harvard Business Review Digital Articles* p2 Je 23 2016

Corporate Governance Should Combine the Best of Private Equity and Family Firms *Harvard Business Review Digital Articles* p2 D 22 2016

NANDUDU, SARAH

Transforming Settlements in Africa *UN Chronicle* v53 no3 p23 2016

Nang, Saw

Battling for Blood Jade color map *Time* v189 no10 p40 Mr 20 2017

Nango, Eriko

A three-dimensional movie of structural changes in bacteriorhodopsin bibl diag graph *Science* v354 no6319 p1552 D 23 2016

Nanibush, Wanda

SHARED AUTHORITY bw *Art in America* p76 O 2017

Nanjiani, Kumail

BEING A FISH OUT OF WATER IS TOUGH, BUT IT'S HOW YOU EVOLVE *Vital Speeches of the Day* v83 no8 p234 Ag 2017

THE BEST MEDICINE A. MARANTZ cartoon color *New Yorker* v93 no12 p28 My 8 2017

KUMAIL NANJIANI J. MILLER color *Vanity Fair* v59 no7 p60 Summ 2017

The Romantic Comedian E. Berman color *Time* v190 no1 p49 Jl 3 2017

Nanjiani, Kumail—Interviews

12 Questions for Kumail Nanjiani A. RAPOPORT bw *Bon Appetit* v62 no7 p24 Jl 2017

This Man Is the Future of Funny Kumail Nanjiani can see what's coming in comedy—including everything that's in this issue A. PEELE color *GQ: Gentlemen's Quarterly* v97 no6 p44 Je 2017

Nanjundiah, Priyamvada

Imaging the distribution of transient viscosity after the 2016 Mw 7.1 Kumamoto earthquake map *Science* v356 no6334 p163 Ap 14 2017

Nanmadol (Extinct city)

Monumental Feats A. Braun *Natural History* v125 no2 p7 F 2017

Nannies

The Ethicist K. A. Appiah *New York Times Magazine* p22 S 3 2017

Nannies—History

Things Sweet to Taste: MUCH TO MY REGRET, I NEVER TRULY KNEW THE WOMAN WHO HELPED RAISE ME L. STAINTON *American Scholar* v86 no3 p72 Summ 2017

Nanobelts

Synthesis of a carbon nanobelt G. Povie, Y. Segawa et al diag graph *Science* v356 no6334 p172 Ap 14 2017

Nanocrystals

Clathrates grow up D. Samanta and R. Klajn bibl color *Science* v355 no6328 p912 Mr 3 2017

Hydrogen positions in single nanocrystals revealed by electron diffraction L. Palatinus, P. Brázda et al bibl color *Science* v355 no6321 p1 Ja 13 2017

Nanocrystalline copper films are never flat X. Zhang, J. Han et al diag graph *Science* v357 no6349 p397 Jl 28 2017

Photolithography based on nanocrystals M. Striccoli color *Science* v357 no6349 p353 Jl 28 2017

Nanocrystals manufacturing

Growing anisotropic crystals at the nanoscale L. M. Liz-Marzán and M. Grzelczak color diag *Science* v356 no6343 p1120 Je 16 2017

Nanoelectromechanical systems

Quantized thermal transport in single-atom junctions L. Cui, W. Jeong et al bibl diag graph *Science* v355 no6330 p1192 Mr 17

Nanoelectronics

    See also

      Nanoelectromechanical systems

    Applying plasmonics to a sustainable future A. Naldoni, V. M. Shalaev et al color *Science* v356 no6341 p908 Je 1 2017

    Quantized thermal transport in single-atom junctions L. Cui, W. Jeong et al bibl diag graph *Science* v355 no6330 p1192 Mr 17 2017

Nanoparticles

    See also

      Nanocrystals

    Clathrates grow up D. Samanta and R. Klajn bibl color *Science* v355 no6328 p912 Mr 3 2017

    Emergence of hierarchical structural complexities in nanoparticles and their assembly Chenjie Zeng, Yuxiang Chen et al bibl color *Science* v354 no6319 p1580 D 23 2016

    A whole new (tiny) ball game for color L. Hamers color *Science News* v192 no6 p32 O 14 2017

Nanoparticles—Research

    Laser-driven nanoparticle motion in liquids P. Baum bibl color *Science* v355 no6324 p458 F 3 2017

Nanophotonics

    Diamond defects cooperate via light R. Hanson bibl diag *Science* v354 no6314 p835 N 18 2016

    Long-distance operator for energy transfer F. J. Garcia-Vidal and J. Feist diag *Science* v357 no6358 p1357 S 29 2017

    Nanophotonic rare-earth quantum memory with optically controlled retrieval T. Zhong, J. M. Kindem et al diag graph *Science* v357 no6358 p1392 S 29 2017

    Optically resonant dielectric nanostructures A. I. Kuznetsov, A. E. Miroshnichenko et al bibl graph *Science* v354 no6314 paag2472-1 N 18 2016

    Visionary wrangles light E. Conover color *Science News* v192 no6 p23 O 14 2017

Nanopores

    Improving on aquaporins Z. Siwy and F. Fornasiero diag *Science* v357 no6353 p753 Ag 25 2017

Nanoscience

    Flipping nanoscopy on its head J. Xiao and T. Ha bibl diag graph *Science* v355 no6325 p582 F 10 2017

Nanostructured materials

    See also

      Nanoparticles

      Nanopores

    All-printed thin-film transistors from networks of liquid-exfoliated nanosheets A. G. Kelly, T. Hallam et al diag *Science* v356 no6333 p69 Ap 7 2017

    Directing reconfigurable DNA nanoarrays Y. Yang and C. Lin color *Science* v357 no6349 p352 Jl 28 2017

    Emergence of hierarchical structural complexities in nanoparticles and their assembly Chenjie Zeng, Yuxiang Chen et al bibl color *Science* v354 no6319 p1580 D 23 2016

    Multiscale measurements for materials modeling R. Suter diag *Science* v356 no6339 p704 My 19 2017

    Nanomaterials for stimulating nerve growth S. Marchesan, L. Ballerini et al color *Science* v356 no6342 p1010 Je 9 2017

Nanostructures

    See also

      Nanoelectromechanical systems

    BLUE BY DESIGN E. MASTROIANNI color *Discover* v38 no4 p15 My 2017

    Braiding a molecular knot with eight crossings J. J. Danon, A. Krüger et al bibl diag graph *Science* v355 no6321 p1 Ja 13 2017

    Bringing proteins into the fold [Cover story] S. M. Douglas bibl color *Science* v355 no6331 p1261 Mr 24 2017

    Charge delivery goes the distance Cheng and F. Li color *Science* v356 no6338 p582 My 12 2017

    Dynamic creation and evolution of gradient nanostructure in single-crystal metallic microcubes R. Thevamaran, O. Lawal et al bibl bw *Science* v354 no6310 p312 O 21 2016

    Optically resonant dielectric nanostructures A. I. Kuznetsov, A. E. Miroshnichenko et al bibl graph *Science* v354 no6314 paag2472-1 N 18 2016

    Single-molecule optomechanics in "picocavities" F. Benz, M. K. Schmidt et al bibl graph *Science* v354 no6313 p726 N 11 2016

Nanotechnology

    See also

      DNA nanotechnology

      Nanostructured materials

    Gearing up molecular rotary motors M. Baroncini and A. Credi color *Science* v356 no6341 p906 Je 1 2017

    Soft x-ray excitonics A. Moulet, J. B. Bertrand et al bw diag *Science* v357 no6356 p1134 S 15 2017

Nanowires

    Transformation of bulk alloys to oxide nanowires D. Lei, J. Benson et al bibl color graph *Science* v355 no6322 p267 Ja 20 2017

    Ultrafine jagged platinum nanowires enable ultrahigh mass activity for the oxygen reduction reaction Mufan Li, Zipeng Zhao et al bibl chart graph *Science* v354 no6318 p1414 D 16 2016

Nantier Beall Minoustchine Publishing Inc.

    Pioneering NBM Marks 40 Years of Graphic Novels B. Alverson color *Publishers Weekly* v264 no21 p12 My 22 2017

Nantucket (Mass.)—Description & travel

    ISLAND TIME S. COCHRAN bw color *Architectural Digest* v73 no11 p94 N 2016

Nantz, Jim

    NFL PLAYOFFS K. ROSEN *TV Guide* v65 no2 p48 Ja 2 2017

Nao (Performer)

    NIGHT LIFE *New Yorker* v93 no12 p9 My 8 2017

Naotaka Tomioka

    The formation of peak rings in large impact craters bibl color graph *Science* v354 no6314 p878 N 18 2016

Naoya Takahashi

    Active cortical dendrites modulate perception bibl graph *Science* v354 no6319 p1587 D 23 2016

Napa (Calif.)

    Blue Note Takes Root in Napa Y. Kato color *Downbeat* v84 no2 p57 F 2017

Napa Valley (Calif.)—Description & travel

    IN Season L. RAMZI color *Vogue* v206 no12 p212 D 2016

    NAPA VALLEY, A CONNOISSEUR'S PARADISE O. J. WILLIAMS color *Ebony* v72 no11 p62 S 2017

Napkin rings—Evaluation

    Setting the Rustic Table color *Log Home Living* v33 no9 p40 D 2016

Napkins

    A BUSHEL AND A PECK E. N. GAGE color *Martha Stewart Living* p23 Ap 2017

    COLOR US HAPPY *Better Homes & Gardens* v94 no11 p18 N 2016

    In the SUNSET GARDEN color *Sunset* v239 no1 p56 Jl 2017

    to dye for L. HEDRICK *Better Homes & Gardens* v94 no11 p16 N 2016

Napkins—Evaluation

    BAYOU BEAUTY color *House Beautiful* v159 no8 p122 O 2017

    BHG throw back 1953 UPDATED HEIRLOOMS K. K. CONDON *Better Homes & Gardens* v94 no11 p168 N 2016

    THE BIG MIX-UP [Cover story] H. BROWN color *House Beautiful* v159 no8 p57 O 2017

    Have a Ball color *House Beautiful* v159 no2 p34 Mr 2017

    june & DECEMBER M. POLLITT color *Better Homes & Gardens* v95 no7 p60 Jl 2017

    PACK A PRETTY PICNIC: No yard? No problem. Turn one of Washington's beautiful parks into your own outdoor dining room H. Kelly *Washingtonian Magazine* v52 no8 p169 My 2017

    SUMMER MAGIC G. Sohr color *House Beautiful* v159 no5 p56 Je 2017

Naples (Italy)

    Ciao Napoli! D. COGGINS bw color *Esquire* p142 BigBlackBook

    First, a Note About Napoli... D. COGGINS color *Esquire* p158 BigBlackBook

Naples (Italy)—Description & travel

    NAPOLI DI NUOVO color *Conde Nast Traveler* v51 no10 p166 N 2016

Naplin, Denise

    Chics Smart Lena N. Chirico color *Horse & Rider* v56 no1 p17 Ja 2017

Napoléon (Film : 1927)

    Man of Action F. S. NEHME bw *Film Comment* v53 no1 p88 Ja/F 2017

Napoléon I, Emperor of the French, 1769-1821

Napoleon's Comets R. Jakiel *Sky & Telescope* v133 no5 p52 My 2017

NAPOLÉON'S EGYPTIAN RIDDLE J. W. Shosenberg cartoon color map *Military History* v34 no1 p22 My 2017

Napoli, Eleonora
Microbiota-activated PPAR-γ signaling inhibits dysbiotic Enterobacteriaceae expansion graph *Science* v357 no6351 p570 Ag 11 2017

NAPOLI, TONI
The Question *O, The Oprah Magazine* p14 F 2017

Napoli Bern (Company)
HELL IS OTHER LAWYERS P. M. Barrett color *Bloomberg Businessweek* no4499 p72 N 14 2016

Napolitano, Simone
Staying conductive in the stretch bibl diag *Science* v355 no6320 p24 Ja 6 2017

Nappo, Gilda
Reticulon 3-dependent ER-PM contact sites control EGFR non-clathrin endocytosis color diag graph *Science* v356 no6338 p617 My 12 2017

Naps (Sleep)
SLEEP LIKE A BABY? C. Barakat and M. Freckleton color *Equus* no477 p22 Je 2017

Naps (Sleep)—Research
This Just In J. Zorthian *Time* v189 no7/8 p27 F 27 2017

Naragon, Kristin
Email Is the Best Way to Reach Millennials *Harvard Business Review Digital Articles* p2 N 12 2015

Naragon, Lee
AN HEIRLOOM PROJECT color *Popular Mechanics* p8 Mr 2017

Narang, Jimmy
The fading American dream: Trends in absolute income mobility since 1940 bw graph *Science* v356 no6336 p398 Ap 28 2017

Naranjo, I.
Observation of a large-scale anisotropy in the arrival directions of cosmic rays above 8 × 1018 eV *Science* v357 no6357 p1266 S 22 2017

Naranjo, Michelle
Coming to a Dashboard Near You chart color *Consumer Reports* v82 no3 p58 Mr 2017

The Safest Car Seat for Your Child chart color *Consumer Reports* v82 no1 p56 Ja 2017

Staying Power chart color diag *Consumer Reports* v81 no12 p66 D 2016

Narayanamurti, Venkatesh
The End of the Line: Cycles of Invention and Discovery: Rethinking the Endless Frontier G. P. Zachary *Issues in Science & Technology* v33 no4 p87 Summ 2017

Narayanan, Archana
The Plucky Little Emirate Vs. Old Foes color *Bloomberg Businessweek* no4535 p36 Ag 28 2017

Narayanan, Arvind
Semantics derived automatically from language corpora contain human-like biases chart graph *Science* v356 no6334 p183 Ap 14 2017

Narayanan, Badri
Quantitative 3D evolution of colloidal nanoparticle oxidation in solution diag graph *Science* v356 no6335 p303 Ap 21 2017

Narayanan, Shankar
Water harvesting from air with metal-organic frameworks powered by natural sunlight diag *Science* v356 no6336 p430 Ap 28 2017

Narayanan, Subu
The Age of Smart, Safe, Cheap Robots Is Already Here *Harvard Business Review Digital Articles* p2 Je 15 2015

Narayanan, V. G.
What Harvard Business School Has Learned About Online Collaboration From HBX *Harvard Business Review Digital Articles* p2 Ap 14 2015

Narayanan, Vijay K.
Where Predictive Analytics Is Having the Biggest Impact *Harvard Business Review Digital Articles* p2 My 25 2016

Narayandas, Das
Study: More Frequent Sales Quotas Help Volume but Hurt Profits *Harvard Business Review Digital Articles* p2 2017

What's the Right Kind of Bonus to Motivate Your Sales Force? *Harvard Business Review Digital Articles* p2 S 12 2017

Narayen, Shantanu
FLASH FORWARD J. Vanian color *Fortune* v175 no8 p60 Je 15 2017

Narcissism
CARTOONS *In These Times* v40 no12 p34 D 2016

How to Manage a Narcissist M. F. R. Kets de Vries *Harvard Business Review Digital Articles* p2 My 10 2017

How to Work for a Narcissistic Boss R. Knight *Harvard Business Review Digital Articles* p2 Ap 1 2016

Narcissistic Students Get Better Grades from Narcissistic Professors N. Torres *Harvard Business Review Digital Articles* p2 Mr 4 2016

None of the Above C. J. Cook *Commentary* v141 no10 p1 D 2016
None of the Above C. J. Cook *Commentary* v142 no5 p1 D 2016

Research: Narcissists Don't Like Flat Organizations E. Zitek and A. Jordan *Harvard Business Review Digital Articles* p2 Jl 27 2016

Why Bad Guys Win at Work T. Chamorro-Premuzic *Harvard Business Review Digital Articles* p2 N 2 2015

Why People Are Drawn to Narcissists Like Donald Trump M. Maccoby *Harvard Business Review Digital Articles* p2 Ag 26 2015

Why We Keep Hiring Narcissistic CEOs T. Chamorro-Premuzic *Harvard Business Review Digital Articles* p2 N 29 2016

Zadie SMITH cartoon *Vanity Fair* v58 no12 p184 D 2016

Narcissists
How to Mentor a Narcissist W. B. Johnson and D. G. Smith *Harvard Business Review Digital Articles* p2 S 19 2017

Narcos (TV program)
Must List color diag *Entertainment Weekly* no1480 p7 S 1 2017
STREAMING A. D'ARMINIO *TV Guide* v65 no35 p38 Ag 21 2017

Narcotics
See also
Heroin
Oxycodone

AMERICA'S OLDEST LIVING DRUG ADVICE GOLUMNIST TELLS ALL E. Dean *Washingtonian Magazine* v52 no11 p64 Ag 2017

Nardi, Maria
Member Spotlight: Maria Nardi C. Jones *Parks & Recreation* v52 no9 p97 S 2017

Nardini, Sadie
A home practice to Boost heart health color *Yoga Journal* p33 2017 Special Issue

A home practice to get strong and empowered [Cover story] color *Yoga Journal* no290 p59 Mr 2017

Nardone, Christopher
Restored iron transport by a small molecule promotes absorption and hemoglobinization in animals color graph *Science* v356 no6338 p608 My 12 2017

NAREA, NICOLE
The Democrats' Biggest Disaster color *New Republic* v248 no1/2 p8 Ja/F 2017

NARGI, LELA
Flex Equity diag *Working Mother* v40 no3 p26 Ag/S 2017
PASS THE PACIFIER color *Publishers Weekly* v264 no2 p26 Ja 9 2017
quiet child *Parents* v92 no2 p104 F 2017

Narlikar, Geeta J.
Distortion of histone octamer core promotes nucleosome mobilization by a chromatin remodeler diag *Science* v355 no6322 p263 Ja 20 2017

Narration (Motion pictures)
Choose Wisely T. KUBOTA color *Film Comment* v52 no6 p20 N/D 2016

Narration (Rhetoric)
See also
First person narrative

THE STORIES WE FALL FOR R. Lowenstein color *Fortune* v175 no4 p28 Mr 15 2017

Twilight of the Narratives M. CONTINETTI *Commentary* v143 no2 p56 F 2017

Narrative art

THE 25 MOST PATRIOTIC MOVIES OF ALL TIME color *Entertainment Weekly* no1472 p30 Je 30 2017

ALAN RICKMAN color *Entertainment Weekly* no1446/1447 p92 D 2016/Ja 2017

Allied color *Entertainment Weekly* no1442 p40 D 2 2016 Rebellious Special Issue

THE ALL-TIME GREATEST TOM CRUISE PERFORMANCES color *Entertainment Weekly* no1485 p39 O 6 2017

Also In MEMORIAM color *Entertainment Weekly* no1453 p39 F 17 2017

American Made color *Entertainment Weekly* no1485 p38 O 6 2017

Atomic Blonde color *Entertainment Weekly* no1476 p48 Ag 4 2017

Baywatch color *Entertainment Weekly* no1468/1469 p88 Je 2-9 2017

The BEST OF Elba color *Entertainment Weekly* no1486 p30 O 13 2017

The Best of Sundance color *Entertainment Weekly* no1451/1452 p90 F 3-10 2017

THE BIGGEST SUMMER BREAKOUTS (SO FAR) color diag *Entertainment Weekly* no1474/1475 p15 Jl 21-28 2017

The Big Sick color *Entertainment Weekly* no1472 p42 Je 30 2017

Bokeh color *Entertainment Weekly* no1459 p48 Mr 31 2017

The Book of Love color *Entertainment Weekly* no1449 p45 Ja 20 2017

Brigsby Bear color *Entertainment Weekly* no1476 p46 Ag 4 2017

By Sidney Lumet color *Entertainment Weekly* no1438 p49 N 4 2016

Casting JonBenét color *Entertainment Weekly* no1463/1464 p88 Ap/My 2017

City of Ghosts color *Entertainment Weekly* no1473 p47 Jl 7 2017

A Cure for Wellness color *Entertainment Weekly* no1454/1455 p82 F 24 2017

Death Note color *Entertainment Weekly* no1480 p35 S 1 2017

Desierto color *Entertainment Weekly* no1436/1437 p84 O 21 2016

The Dinner color *Entertainment Weekly* no1465 p42 My 12 2017

Doctor Strange color *Entertainment Weekly* no1439 p40 N 11 2016

EDWARD ALBEE color *Entertainment Weekly* no1446/1447 p96 D 2016/Ja 2017

Elle color *Entertainment Weekly* no1440 p47 N 18 2016

Fantastic Beasts and Where to Find Them color *Entertainment Weekly* no1441 p36 N 25 2016

Fences color *Entertainment Weekly* no1446/1447 p100 D 2016/Ja 2017

Free Fire color *Entertainment Weekly* no1463/1464 p89 Ap/My 2017

A Ghost Story color *Entertainment Weekly* no1473 p43 Jl 7 2017

THE GREATEST DISNEY SONGS OF ALL TIME color *Entertainment Weekly* no1454/1455 p36 F 24 2017

GUARDIANS OF THE GALAXY VOL.2 color *Entertainment Weekly* no1465 p40 My 12 2017

I Am Not Your Negro color *Entertainment Weekly* no1451/1452 p92 F 3-10 2017

I, Daniel Blake color *Entertainment Weekly* no1448 p50 Ja 13 2017

An Inconvenient Sequel: Truth to Power color *Entertainment Weekly* no1476 p47 Ag 4 2017

In Honor of Atticus color *Entertainment Weekly* no1470 p40 Je 16 2017

It Comes at Night color *Entertainment Weekly* no1470 p41 Je 16 2017

JERRY-RIGGED ESSENTIALS color *Entertainment Weekly* no1480 p17 S 1 2017

John Wick: Chapter 2 color *Entertainment Weekly* no1453 p45 F 17 2017

Jonathan Demme color *Entertainment Weekly* no1465 p44 My 12 2017

King Arthur: Legend of the Sword color *Entertainment Weekly* no1466 p40 My 19 2017

Kingsman: The Golden Circle color *Entertainment Weekly* no1484 p42 S 29 2017

Lady Macbeth color *Entertainment Weekly* no1474/1475 p98 Jl 21-28 2017

THE LAST PICTURE SHOW color *Entertainment Weekly* no1460/1461 p14 Ap 7-17 2017

The LEGO Batman Movie color *Entertainment Weekly* no1453 p44 F 17 2017

Logan color *Entertainment Weekly* no1456 p56 Mr 10 2017

Logan Lucky color *Entertainment Weekly* no1478 / 1479 p82 Ag 18-25 2017

The Lost City of Z color *Entertainment Weekly* no1462 p45 Ap 21 2017

Loving color *Entertainment Weekly* no1439 p44 N 11 2016

Lucky color *Entertainment Weekly* no1485 p43 O 6 2017

Manchester by the Sea color *Entertainment Weekly* no1441 p39 N 25 2016

A MAN FOR ALL REASONS [Cover story] color *Entertainment Weekly* no1486 p26 O 13 2017

Manifesto color *Entertainment Weekly* no1466 p43 My 19 2017

Moonlight color *Entertainment Weekly* no1436/1437 p82 O 21 2016

MOORE THAN BOND color *Entertainment Weekly* no1468/1469 p81 Je 2-9 2017

No. 10 CAPTAIN AMERICA: CIVIL WAR color diag *Entertainment Weekly* no1444/1445 p56 D 16 2016

No. 1 LA LA LAND color *Entertainment Weekly* no1444/1445 p48 D 16 2016

No. 4 THE LOBSTER color *Entertainment Weekly* no1444/1445 p51 D 16 2016

No. 5 HELL OR HIGH WATER color *Entertainment Weekly* no1444/1445 p53 D 16 2016

No. 8 WEINER color *Entertainment Weekly* no1444/1445 p55 D 16 2016

Raw color *Entertainment Weekly* no1457/1458 p74 Mr 17 2017

ROGER MOORE color *Entertainment Weekly* no1468/1469 p80 Je 2-9 2017

The Sundance Must List color *Entertainment Weekly* no1449 p42 Ja 20 2017

Super Dark Times color *Entertainment Weekly* no1485 p42 O 6 2017

T2 Trainspotting color *Entertainment Weekly* no1457/1458 p72 Mr 17 2017

Table 19 color *Entertainment Weekly* no1456 p56 Mr 10 2017

The Trip to Spain color *Entertainment Weekly* no1478 / 1479 p85 Ag 18-25 2017

True Memoirs of an International Assassin color *Entertainment Weekly* no1440 p44 N 18 2016

Wakefield color *Entertainment Weekly* no1467 p48 My 26 2017

War for the Planet of the Apes color *Entertainment Weekly* no1474/1475 p95 Jl 21-28 2017

War Machine color *Entertainment Weekly* no1468/1469 p89 Je 2-9 2017

WarReN BEAtty An ORAL HISTORY color *Entertainment Weekly* no1440 p30 N 18 2016

We Say Goodbye to One of Our Own color *Entertainment Weekly* no1480 p3 S 1 2017

Wilson color *Entertainment Weekly* no1459 p47 Mr 31 2017

THE WORST FILMS OF THE YEAR color *Entertainment Weekly* no1444/1445 p62 D 16 2016

Nashville (Poem)

NASHVILLE T. Clark *New Yorker* v93 no31 p42 O 9 2017

Nashville (Tenn.)

SOUTH'S BEST RESORT A. Nash color *Southern Living* v52 no4 p86 Ap 2017

Nashville (Tenn.)—Description & travel

Music Lovers' Mecca M. WHITE color *AARP: The Magazine* v59 no5A p59 Ag/S 2016

Nashville E. LEIBOWITZ color *Los Angeles Magazine* v62 no7 p48 Jl 2017

NASHVILLE... FOR WASHINGTONIANS A. Cochran *Washingtonian Magazine* v52 no1 p111 O 2016

STAR TREK: Prime viewing of a rare celestial phenomenon puts a different kind of spotlight on Nashville R. ANNIS *Indianapolis Monthly* v12 no40 p40 Ag 2017

Nashville (TV program)

ALSO COMING... A. D'Arminio and J. Russell *TV Guide* v65 no23 p25 My 29 2017

America's top TV critic Matt Roush answers your burning questions M. Roush *TV Guide* v65 no13 p4 Mr 20 2017

Ask Matt *TV Guide* v65 no6 p5 Ja 30 2017

Meet Nashville's Newbies S. Highfill color *Entertainment Weekly*

no1468/1469 p91 Je 2-9 2017
Nashville M. ROUSH *TV Guide* v65 no2 p19 Ja 2 2017
Nashville's Life After Death S. Highfill color *Entertainment Weekly* no1456 p16 Mr 10 2017

Nashville Opera (Performer)
Nashville Opera W. WEISMAN *Opera News* v81 no5 p16 N 2016

Nashville Predators (Hockey team)
PRED ALERT A. Prewitt color *Sports Illustrated* v126 no15 p46 My 29 2017
WESTERN CONFERENCE POWER RANKINGS S. Page color *Sports Illustrated* v125 no12 p58 O 10 2016

Nasir, Adnan
THE EXCHANGE cartoon chart color graph *Men's Health* v32 no9 p16 N 2017

Nasiripour, Shahien
Defrauded For-Profit Grads Seek Relief bw color *Bloomberg Businessweek* no4505 p30 D 26 2016
Pants on Fyre color *Bloomberg Businessweek* no4524 p33 My 29 2017
Student Lenders Get a Chance to Cut Loose *Bloomberg Businessweek* no4500 p37 N 21 2016
Student Loans color graph *Bloomberg Businessweek* no4509 p33 Ja 30 2017

Nason, Martha C.
Rapid development of a DNA vaccine for Zika virus bibl graph *Science* v354 no6309 p237 O 14 2016

Nason, Stephen
Case Study: Competing Against Bling II *Harvard Business Review* v95 no3 p155 My/Je 2017
Case Study: How Should an Understated Luxury Brand Compete Against Bling? color *Harvard Business Review Digital Articles* p2 F 28 2017

Nasopharynx—Cancer—Treatment
Precision medicine for nasopharyngeal carcinoma Lin-Quan Tang, Hua Zhang et al bibl diag *Science* v354 no6319 p24 D 23 2016

Nassar, Lawrence—Trials, litigation, etc.
Protect and Serve L. Green, T. Keith et al color *Sports Illustrated* v126 no7 p17 Mr 6 2017

NASSAR, TAMARA
TOXIC DUST IN THE WIND *In These Times* v41 no6 p39 Je 2017

Nasser, Maher
FOREWORD *UN Chronicle* v53 no2 p4 2016
Foreword *UN Chronicle* v53 no4 p1 2016
FOREWORD *UN Chronicle* v54 no4 p5 2017
IT'S NEVER TOO LATE TO START RUNNING *UN Chronicle* v53 no2 p36 2016

Nasseri, Ladane
Iranian Voters Want a Share of the Wealth color *Bloomberg Businessweek* no4521 p14 My 8 2017
Iran's Islamic Evolution color *Bloomberg Businessweek* no4524 p14 My 29 2017

NASSIF, TOM
Greens Make Green *Weekly Standard* v22 no5 p21 O 10 2016

Nasti, Tahseen
Rescue of exhausted CD8 T cells by PD-1–targeted therapies is CD28-dependent bw diag graph *Science* v355 no6332 p1423 Mr 31 2017

Nastri, Carmine
Nastri Sets Records at First Frontier Circuit Finals color *Spin to Win Rodeo* v21 no1 p22 Mr 2017

Nasty Gal Inc.
Starting Over color *InStyle* v24 no5 p101 My 2017

Nat Turner in Jerusalem (Theatrical production)
'A HEAVEN SOMEWHERE' R. WEINERT-KENDT color *America* v215 no12 p30 O 24 2016
THE THEATRE *New Yorker* v92 no30 p12 S 26 2016

Natale, Simone
Supernatural Entertainments: Victorian Spiritualism and the Rise of Modern Media Culture M. SOLOMON *Film Quarterly* v71 no1 p121 Fall 2017

Natalie, Emily
letter to my teenage self color *Dance Spirit* v21 no2 p24 F 2017

Natalio, Filipe
Biological fabrication of cellulose fibers with tailored properties color *Science* v357 no6356 p1118 S 15 2017

Natarajan, Chandrasekhar
Predictable convergence in hemoglobin function has unpredictable molecular underpinnings bibl graph *Science* v354 no6310 p336 O 21 2016

Natarajan, Priyamvada
Calculating Women color *New York Review of Books* v64 no9 p38 My 25 2017

Natarajan, Sridhar
Deal Snapshot: Oncor Electric Delivery Co bw graph *Bloomberg Businessweek* no4530 p19 Jl 17 2017
Payless Flops, But the Owners Get a Payday graph *Bloomberg Businessweek* no4516 p35 Mr 27 2017

Natasha, Pierre & the Great Comet of 1812 (Theatrical production)
Natasha, Pierre and the Great Comet of 1812 M. Mazzaro *Opera News* v81 no10 p48 Ap 2017
Russian Unorthodox M. Schulman cartoon *New Yorker* v92 no34 p9 O 24 2016

Natel Energy (Company)
AN ENERGY-GENERATING BEAVER DAM J. Leslie *Harper's Magazine* v333 no1998 p72 N 2016

Nath, Ishani
BREATHING NEW LIFE INTO IPF TREATMENTS *Maclean's* v129 no47 p44 N 28 2016
Shingles A Pain That Lasts color *Maclean's* v129 no40 p64 O 10 2016
S-ICD The Life-Saving Device That's Made to Last color *Maclean's* v129 no40 p65 O 10 2016

Nathalang, Anuttara
Plant diversity increases with the strength of negative density dependence at the global scale diag *Science* v356 no6345 p1389 Je 30 2017

Nathan, Andrew J.
Assignment: China *Foreign Affairs* v96 no6 p170 N/D 2017
China's Governance Puzzle: Enabling Transparency and Participation in a Single-Party State *Foreign Affairs* v96 no6 p172 N/D 2017
China: The Struggle at the Top color *New York Review of Books* v64 no2 p34 F 9 2017
Chinese Politics in the Xi Jinping Era: Reassessing Collective Leadership *Foreign Affairs* v96 no1 p177 Ja/F 2017
The Chinese World Order color *New York Review of Books* v64 no15 p31 O 12 2017
Easternization: Asia's Rise and America's Decline, From Obama to Trump and Beyond *Foreign Affairs* v96 no3 p172 My/Je 2017
The Great East Asian War and the Birth of the Korean Nation/South Korea's New Nationalism: The End of "One Korea"? *Foreign Affairs* v95 no6 p191 N/D 2016
How China Escaped the Poverty Trap/Centrifugal Empire: Central-Local Relations in China/Unlikely Partners: Chinese Reformers, Western Economists, and the Making of Global China *Foreign Affairs* v96 no2 p186 Mr/Ap 2017
Information for Autocrats: Representation in Chinese Local Congresses *Foreign Affairs* v95 no6 p192 N/D 2016
A Most Enterprising Country: North Korea in the Global Economy *Foreign Affairs* v96 no3 p174 My/Je 2017
Park Chung Hee and Modern Korea: The Roots of Militarism *Foreign Affairs* v96 no1 p175 Ja/F 2017
Populist Authoritarianism: Chinese Political Culture and Regime Sustainability *Foreign Affairs* v96 no3 p173 My/Je 2017
Powerplay: The Origins of the American Alliance System in Asia *Foreign Affairs* v95 no6 p190 N/D 2016
Purifying the Land of the Pure: A History of Pakistan's Religious Minorities *Foreign Affairs* v96 no6 p171 N/D 2017
Rising China's Influence in Developing Asia *Foreign Affairs* v96 no6 p169 N/D 2017
The Souls of China: The Return of Religion After Mao *Foreign Affairs* v96 no3 p172 My/Je 2017
Trading With the Enemy: The Making of U.S. Export Control Policy Toward the People's Republic of China *Foreign Affairs* v95 no6 p193 N/D 2016
Turn of the Tortoise: The Challenge and Promise of India's Future *Foreign Affairs* v95 no6 p191 N/D 2016
Vietnam's Communist Revolution: The Power and Limits of Ideology *Foreign Affairs* v96 no3 p173 My/Je 2017

Nathan, Aparna

I WISH SOMEONE WOULD INVENT... cartoon *Popular Science* v289 no5 p98 S/O 2017

Nathan, Arokia

Subthreshold Schottky-barrier thin-film transistors with ultralow power and high intrinsic gain bibl graph *Science* v354 no6310 p302 O 21 2016

NATHAN, JAMES A.

TRUMPING OBAMA ON CUBA *USA Today Magazine* v145 no2862 p30 Mr 2017

Nathan, Joan—Interviews

MAKING HISTORY S. Wildman color *Washingtonian Magazine* v52 no7 p147 Ap 2017

Nathan, Julia

WEIGHT LOSS SURGERY CONFIDENTIAL color *Health* v31 no7 p134 S 2017

Nathan, Syd

King Records Month, CITY-WIDE *Cincinnati Magazine* v50 no12 p60 S 2017

Nathans, Sydney

This Is the Place J. M. BANNER JR. color *Weekly Standard* v22 no28 p37 Mr 27 2017

Nathanson, Charles G.

What If Socially Useful Jobs Were Taxed Less Than Other Jobs? *Harvard Business Review Digital Articles* p2 O 11 2017

NATHANSON, MICHAEL E.

The Growing Lone Wolf Threat from ISIS and Other Players *USA Today Magazine* v145 no2860 p48 Ja 2017

Nathanson, Rebecca

Denver's Crackdown on Being Homeless color *Progressive* v81 no7 p30 O/N 2017

Educating Homeless Kids in New York City color *Progressive* v81 no4 p38 Ap/My 2017

Nation building—Social aspects

The Nationalist Origins of Political Islam J. CESARI *Current History* v116 no786 p31 Ja 2017

National (Performer)

CORNERED AT THE PARTY A. PETRUSICH color *New Yorker* v93 no27 p80 S 11 2017

National Academies (U.S.)

Spy agencies team up with National Academies J. Mervis color *Science* v354 no6309 p155 O 14 2016

National Academy of Engineering

Building the future D. Riley bibl color *Science* v355 no6326 p702 F 17 2017

National Academy of Sciences (U.S.)

Is Caution Enough? G. Meilaender color *Commonweal* v144 no7 p12 Ap 14 2017

PANDORA'S UMBRELLA J. Gertner *New York Times Magazine* p58 Ap 23 2017

U.S. report calls for research integrity board J. Mervis diag *Science* v356 no6334 p123 Ap 14 2017

National Arbor Day

REPLANTING OUR NATIONAL FORESTS *Log Home Living* v34 no3 p14 Ap 2017

National archives

'GENERAL CONDITION: FAIRLY GOOD': RESEARCHING TUBERCULOSIS PATIENTS AT AN ARMY HOSPITAL IN NEW MEXICO C. White *Prologue* v49 no2 p56 Summ 2017

National Archives (U.S.)

The FIRST RECORDS J. Kratz *Prologue* v49 no2 p40 Summ 2017

Looking Ahead A. Bundles *Prologue* v49 no2 p70 Summ 2017

The National Archives' ROLE IN Amending the Constitution J. Kratz *Prologue* v49 no1 p32 Spr 2017

National Assessment of Educational Progress (Project)

CHASING A MOVING TARGET D. R. WILSON cartoon *New Orleans Magazine* v51 no1 p34 N 2016

U.S. science test shows gains *Science* v354 no6312 p530 N 4 2016

National Association for Female Executives (U.S.)

BY THE NUMBERS chart *Working Mother* p26 F/Mr 2017

Step Up and Lead S. BARRY cartoon *Working Mother* p49 F/Mr 2017

TOP 60 COMPANIES FOR EXECUTIVE WOMEN 2017 *Working Mother* p28 F/Mr 2017

National Association for the Advancement of Colored People

CAN BLACKS AIRBNB THEIR WAY TO ECONOMIC EM-POWERMENT? S. Lynn color *Black Enterprise* v47 no8 p27 Jl/Ag 2017

THE GREAT CHARTER SCHOOL DEBATE R. W. GOODE color *Black Enterprise* v47 no5 p32 Ja/F 2017

The NAACP And the GOP K. D. WILLIAMSON *National Review* v69 no12 p16 Je 26 2017

National Association of College Stores (U.S.)

National Association of College Stores Gears Up to Fight for Indies J. Rosen color *Publishers Weekly* v264 no11 p4 Mr 13 2017

National Association of Fleet Administrators (U.S.)

The Next Stage of Sustainability D. Gould color *Bloomberg Businessweek* no4502 p10 D 5 2016

National Association of Home Builders (U.S.)

Celebrate Our Log Home Heritage in July C. Bevier color *Log Home Living* v34 no5 p14 Jl 2017

INVEST WISELY color *Cabin Living* p11 Ag 2017

Seal Your Deal D. PERRY color *Log Home Living* v34 no9 p71 D 2017

National Association of Music Merchants (U.S.)—Congresses

Hey... What Are You Doing Next January? T. Lowe *Stage Directions* v30 no8 p2 Ag 2017

Parnelli Awards to Relocate to the 2018 NAMM Show *Stage Directions* v30 no5 p4 My 2017

National Association of Realtors

Homebuyers Show Greater Interest in Green Living *Mother Earth News* no284 p7 O/N 2017

National Automobile Dealers Association

Aaron Robinson A. Robinson color *Car & Driver* v62 no11 p30 My 2017

National Ballet of Canada (Company)

30 Years Ago This Month color *Dance Magazine* v91 no3 p67 Mr 2017

National Bank of Canada

Enlightened Workplaces: Illuminated ceilings are at the heart of the design strategies for two corporate office projects—the National Bank of Canada Trading Floor by Architecture49 and Osram Americas Headquarters by Sasaki—resulting in... D. Sokol color map *Architectural Record* v205 no5 p127 My 2017

National Baseball Hall of Fame & Museum

JUST MY TYPE D. Patrick and T. Keith color *Sports Illustrated* v125 no15 p27 N 7 2016

National Basketball Association

Austin Power D. Gardner and T. Keith color *Sports Illustrated* v125 no19 p22 D 12 2016

BASKETBALL SALARIES GET SOME AIR M. Heimer color diag *Fortune* v75 no1 p24 Ja 1 2017

BILLIONAIRES PLAY BALL color *Fortune* v175 no7 p14 Je 1 2017

The future of basketball as both sport and marketing enterprise can be glimpsed in the moves of seven-foot wonder athletes who handle the ball like point guards J. C. Kang *New York Times Magazine* p17 Ja 22 2017

The Golden State Warriors As 2017 NBA Champions S. Gregory color *Time* v189 no24 p11 Je 26 2017

HOT | NOT T. Keith color *Sports Illustrated* v125 no13 p19 O 17 2016

THE JUSTICE LEAGUE B. SCHOENFELD bw color *Esquire* p90 N 2017

Leap Year [Cover story] color *GQ: Gentlemen's Quarterly* v86 no11 p106 N 2016

LOOKING FOR REVENGE N. SANTOS color *Ebony* v72 no11 p88 S 2017

NBA JUMPSTART R. A. BERENZ *TV Guide* v65 no43 p45 O 16 2017

PHIL JACKSON E. SPITZNAGEL color *Men's Health* v32 no2 p120 Mr 2017

That's Shoe Business L. Jenkins color *Sports Illustrated* v125 no21 p68 D 26 2016

TOAST TO TRÉO T. MCNALLY color *New Orleans Magazine* v51 no3 p118 Ja 2017

WHO IS RUSSELL WESTBROOK? B. DANIELLE color *Ebony* v72 no6 p76 Ap/My 2017

National Basketball Association—History—20th century

SCOUTING REPORTS R. Nadkarni and A. Sharp color *Sports Illustrated* v127 no12 p54 O 16 2017

National Basketball Association—History—21st century

2017-18 ENTERTAINMENT VALUE GUIDE B. Golliver color *Sports Illustrated* v127 no12 p76 O 16 2017

The Case for ... Peak NBA L. J. Wertheim and T. Keith color *Sports Illustrated* v127 no2 p27 Jl 17 2017

NOVEMBER Blues B. Golliver color *Sports Illustrated* v125 no17 p88 N 21 2016 Double Issue

National Basketball Association—Management

The Case for ... LOWERING THE NBA AGE MINIMUM J. Woo and S. Kwak color *Sports Illustrated* v127 no12 p24 O 16 2017

The Case for ... The High School Combine B. Hamilton and T. Keith color *Sports Illustrated* v126 no14 p31 My 15-22 2017

Virtually Yours M. Burns and T. Keith color *Sports Illustrated* v125 no17 p30 N 21 2016 Double Issue

National Black Catholic Congress (Organization)

'Act justly, love goodness': Black Catholics in America A. Marchese color *America* v217 no3 p14 Ag 7 2017

National Book Awards

A Night for Winners J. Maher color *Publishers Weekly* v263 no47 p4 N 21 2016

National Book Foundation (U.S.)—Officials & employees

Lisa Lucas S. Begley color *Time* v189 no3 p60 Ja 30 2017

National Broadcasting Co. Inc.

Freedom of Speech Doesn't Guarantee the Right to a Megaphone J. Jackson *Extra!* v30 no7 p4 S 2017

THE PEACOCK THRONE S. ELLISON color *Vanity Fair* v59 no4 p184 Mr 2017

The Voices of Truth E. Mahaney color *Glamour* v115 no5 p179 My 2017

National Brotherhood of Skiers (Organization)

Posthole B. Finley, L. Joseph et al color *Powder* v45 no5 p108 Ja 2017

National Building Museum (U.S.)

EVENT CALENDAR *Washingtonian Magazine* v52 no4 p206 Ja 2017

Seeking asylum G. Adamson bw color *Magazine Antiques* v184 no5 p22 S/O 2017

National Bureau of Economic Research

How Software Could Help Judges Reduce Crime T. Simonite il *MIT Technology Review* v120 no3 p15 My/Je 2017

National Cancer Institute (U.S.)

HIGH-PERFORMANCE COMPUTING TAKES AIM AT CANCER A. Heller color *Science & Technology Review* p4 O/N 2016

"Home-Grown" Efforts Thrive at Livermore color *Science & Technology Review* p11 O/N 2016

THE INFORMATION CURE T. CHIARELLA cartoon color *Chicago* v66 no1 p74 Ja 2017

National Capital Region (Ont. & Québec)

Capital considerations B. BANKS map *Canadian Geographic* v137 no3 p32 My 2017

National Cattlemen's Beef Association (U.S.)

SOIL BUILDERS R. Nickel *Successful Farming* v115 no5 p55 Mid-Mr 2017

National cemeteries

SERVICE & SACRIFICE M. W. SCHWARTZ color *Missouri Life* v44 no3 p56 My 2017

National Center for Atmospheric Research (U.S.)

Atmospheric research in the Rocky Mountain foothills: As an NSF-funded center approaches its 60th birthday, scientific and fiscal challenges lie ahead D. Kramer *Physics Today* v70 no8 p32 Ag 2017

National Championship Air Races

Reno Gains a Powerful Sponsor color *Flying* v143 no12 p82 D 2016

National championships

Jita Kyoei: Mutual Welfare and Benefit in Judo M. Jacobs color *Black Belt* v55 no4 p24 Je/Jl 2017

National championships—History—20th century

Past Perfect L. Flynn and T. Keith color *Sports Illustrated* v125 no14 p22 O 24-31 2016

National Civil Rights Museum

Memphis Gets Its Groove Back H. Hayes color *Southern Living* v52 no11 p69 N 2017

National Collegiate Athletic Association

Hometown Hero J. SCOTT *Tennis* v52 no6 p38 N/D 2016

LET'S MAKE FOOTBALL A COLLEGE MAJOR D. V. Johnson *Saturday Evening Post* v288 no6 p12 N/D 2016

NCEA Works to Keep Riding Relevant for COLLEGIATE EQUESTRIANS J. Pierce color *Practical Horseman* v44 no12 p63 D 2016

Off-Court Issues C. FEHRMAN *Indianapolis Monthly* v40 no7 p51 Mr 2017

She Got Game N. Santos color *Ebony* v72 no9 p31 Jl/Ag 2017

UNEVEN PLAYING FIELD M. CAMPBELL color *Ebony* v72 no5 p92 Mr 2017

Winning Season: VIRGINIA WESLEYAN SOFTBALL STAFF NAMED COACHES OF THE YEAR *Virginia Living* v15 no6 p107 O 2017

National Collegiate Athletic Association—History—21st century

The Case for ... CHANGING THE TRANSFER RULE D. Greene and T. Keith color *Sports Illustrated* v127 no8 p26 S 18 2017

National Council of Teachers of English

Choices Are Here! color *Literacy Today (2411-7862)* v34 no6 p4 My/Je 2017

National Council of the Churches of Christ in the United States of America

Creation stories S. R. Alonso bw color *U.S. Catholic* v82 no11 p32 N 2017

National Economic Council (U.S.)

The Swamp: Jessica Pressler: Gary Cohn's Gamble: Watching a risky career move unfold in real time img *New York* v50 no12 p24 Je 12 2017

A Tax with a Twist: A novel idea to distribute carbon dividends that's both fair and workable G. P. Shultz and T. Halstead *Hoover Digest: Research & Opinion on Public Policy* no3 p73 Summ 2017

National emblems

Fifty Flags J. J. MILLER color *National Review* v69 no12 p22 Je 26 2017

National Endowment for the Arts

ARCHIE SHEPP PROUD PIONEER [Cover story] J. EPHLAND bw color *Downbeat* v84 no5 p36 My 2017

ARTLESS T. Genoways cartoon chart *Mother Jones* v42 no5 p60 S/O 2017

National Endowment for the Arts—Finance

Modern Medicis A. CLINE *Weekly Standard* v22 no34 p18 My 15 2017

National Endowment for the Humanities

The Great Destroyer: Donald Trump's Contempt for Aesthetics W. Vaillancourt color *Progressive* v81 no6 p24 Ag/S 2017

If Odysseus Started a Book Club *Humanities* v37 no4 p1 Fall 2016

Oh, the Humanities! color *Weekly Standard* v22 no41 p2 Jl 3 2017

A SOBERING MOMENT FOR PUBLIC OUTREACH J. Magness color *Archaeology* v70 no4 p6 Je-Ag 2017

National Flood Insurance Program (U.S.)

Flood Insurance Had Problems Before Harvey C. Flavelle color *Bloomberg Businessweek* no4536 p38 S 4 2017

UNDER WATER B. Jarvis *New York Times Magazine* p64 Ap 23 2017

National Football Conference

NFC + EAST color *Sports Illustrated* v126 no5 p48 F 13 2017

NFC + NORTH color *Sports Illustrated* v126 no5 p49 F 13 2017

NFC + SOUTH color *Sports Illustrated* v126 no5 p50 F 13 2017

NFC + WEST color *Sports Illustrated* v126 no5 p51 F 13 2017

National Football League

Ambassadors of Defiance D. ZIRIN color *Progressive* v81 no4 p68 Ap/My 2017

BEST AND WORST CITIES FOR FOOTBALL ENTHUSIASTS *USA Today Magazine* v146 no2867 p15 Ag 2017

Boycotts and Brain Damage Cast a Dark Shadow Over Football Season S. Gregory color *Time* v190 no10/11 p25 S 18 2017

Developing Story T. Keith chart color *Sports Illustrated* v126 no3 p16 Ja 23 2017

FIELD OF NIGHTMARES B. BURROUGH color *Vanity Fair* v58 no11 p164 N 2016

GRIDIRON GRIDLOCK N. SANTOS color *Ebony* v72/73 no12/1 p90 O/N 2017

Here Comes Another Round of Everyone's favorites *USA Today Magazine* v145 no2860 p78 Ja 2017

Meet the NFL's Newest Stadium L. SOROKANICH color *Popular Mechanics* p20 S 2017

Meet the NFL's Newest Stadium L. SOROKANICH color *Popular Mechanics* v193 no7 p20 S 2016

Milestones *Time* v188 no18 p13 O 31 2016

Muscle Secrets of NFL Vets M. EASTER color *Men's Health* v32 no8 p48 O 2017

NFL DRAFT T. WORGO *TV Guide* p48 Ap 17 2017

The NFL in Decline G. NORMAN *Weekly Standard* v22 no8 p16 O 31 2016

NFL WARM-UP R. A. BERENZ *TV Guide* v65 no31 p43 Jl 24 2017

THE NFL WORKOUT [Cover story] L. MCGLASHAN chart color *Muscle & Performance* v9 no11 p52 N 2017

Political Football R. Deitsch and T. Keith color *Sports Illustrated* v125 no13 p18 O 17 2016

Politics [Cover story] F. Gillette, S. Banjo et al color graph *Bloomberg Businessweek* no4498 p60 N 7 2016

SAINTS PHOTO OF THE HALF-CENTURY (NOT COUNTING ANYTHING SUPER BOWL-RELATED) color *New Orleans Magazine* v51 no1 p78 N 2016

THE SCIENCE OF SLEEP L. McGLASHAN color *Muscle & Performance* v9 no7 p46 Jl 2017

SPORTS K. ROSEN *TV Guide* v64 no48 p48 N 21 2016

Star-Spangled PROTEST [Cover story] C. STOFFERS and S. Borden *New York Times Upfront* v149 no3 p8 O 10 2016

Trump's Offensive Playbook [Cover story] A. Altman, S. Gregory et al color *Time* v190 no14 p32 O 9 2017

Why Is the NFL's Brand More Valuable than Ever? W. Anson *Harvard Business Review Digital Articles* p2 N 26 2015

National Football League Players Association

Greener Pastures E. Kaplan and T. Keith color *Sports Illustrated* v126 no12 p14 My 1 2017

National Football League—History

JUST RELOCATE, BABY! J. Feldman color map *Sports Illustrated* v126 no11 p66 Ap 17-24 2017

THE TAO OF Z P. Zimmerman color *Sports Illustrated* v127 no7 p120 S 4 2017

WHAT IF? ... GEORGE HALAS—AND THE NFL—HAD SUNK IN LAKE MICHIGAN? K. Kahler and J. Feldman color *Sports Illustrated* v126 no11 p51 Ap 17-24 2017

National Football League—History—21st century

The 'Boys Are Back J. Dickey and T. Keith color *Sports Illustrated* v126 no1 p12 Ja 9 2017

THE GOOD BOOK S. Rushin color *Sports Illustrated* v125 no17 p76 N 21 2016 Double Issue

Masquerade Ball M. Rosenberg color *Sports Illustrated* v127 no6 p60 Ag 28 2017

O.K. • CALL IT A • COME BACK A. Murphy color *Sports Illustrated* v125 no14 p32 O 24-31 2016

Sane Old Story J. Dickey and T. Keith color *Sports Illustrated* v127 no6 p14 Ag 28 2017

SCOUTING Reports A. Benoit color *Sports Illustrated* v127 no7 p62 S 4 2017

National Football League—Management

The Case for ... Killing TNF J. Dickey and T. Keith color *Sports Illustrated* v125 no18 p26 D 5 2016

Foul Language J. Jones and T. Keith color *Sports Illustrated* v125 no14 p19 O 24-31 2016

LONDON CALLING T. Rohan and S. Kwak color *Sports Illustrated* v127 no11 p14 O 9 2017

National Football League—Officials & employees

CHIEF CONCERNS FOOTBALL IS... color *Sports Illustrated* v125 no17 p57 N 21 2016 Double Issue

National Gallery of Art (U.S.)

SECOND IMPRESSIONS P. SCHJELDAHL cartoon *New Yorker* v93 no9 p74 Ap 17 2017

National Geographic (Periodical)

ON THE SIDE OF SCIENCE S. Goldberg color *National Geographic* v231 no3 p4 Mr 2017

National Geographic (TV program)

Dare To Explore C. M. TOMLIN color *National Geographic Kids* no473 p28 S 2017

National Geographic Society (U.S.)

FEATURED FELLOW: MILBRY POLK M. Rosano color *Canadian Geographic* v135 no6 p82 D 2015

Tap Twice to Like color *National Geographic* v230 no4 p16 O 2016

To Mars, by Multimedia S. Goldberg color *National Geographic* v230 no5 pC5 N 2016

TRUE DISCOVERY K. Broad color *National Geographic* v232 no1 p26 Jl 2017

WE ARE ALLIES IN EARTH'S CARE G. E. Knell *National Geographic* v230 no6 pc7 D 2016

National Geographic Society Kids Network (Computer network)

Jungle Jam color *National Geographic Kids* no473 p32 S 2017

National health services

Is Laughter the Best Medicine? J. Crane *History Today* v66 no11 p19 N 2016

National Hockey League

Betting on Ice In the Desert P. Brownfield color *Bloomberg Businessweek* no4540 p64 O 2 2017

THE BIG BANG A. Prewitt and J. Fuchs color *Sports Illustrated* v125 no12 p50 O 10 2016

THE EDITORIAL *Maclean's* v129 no43 p5 O 31 2016

GREENING YOUR HOME + BUSINESS R. Druzin color *Maclean's* v129 no50 p37 D 19 2016

Hockey year in Canada J. GATEHOUSE color *Maclean's* v129 no51/52 p57 D 26 2016

HOT | NOT T. Keith color *Sports Illustrated* v125 no13 p19 O 17 2016

OCTOBER MAGIC R. A. BERENZ *TV Guide* v65 no41 p43 O 2 2017

Pushback to NHL records demand *Science* v355 no6326 p671 F 17 2017

STRENGTH VS. STRENGTH A. Prewitt color *Sports Illustrated* v126 no16 p62 Je 5 2017

National Hockey League—History

17 ICONIC MOMENTS IN NHL HISTORY J. Fuchs and S. Page color *Sports Illustrated* v126 no4 p56 Ja 30 2017

Chunk of Change T. Keith chart color *Sports Illustrated* v126 no10 p26 Ap 10 2017

National Hockey League—Management

ALL IN A. Prewitt color *Sports Illustrated* v125 no19 p92 D 12 2016

HOT ICE A. Prewitt color *Sports Illustrated* v126 no10 p64 Ap 10 2017

National Hot Rod Association

Gone Gassers T. Taylor bw *Hot Rod* v70 no3 p8 Mr 2017

The HOT ROD Archives D. Wallace color *Hot Rod* v70 no3 p12 Mr 2017

Take 5 With SHIRLEY SHAHAN T. Taylor bw color *Hot Rod* v70 no4 p16 Ap 2017

National Humanities Medal

The 2015 National Humanities Medalists *Humanities* v37 no4 p1 Fall 2016

Abraham Verghese E. W. Gutting *Humanities* v37 no4 p1 Fall 2016

National Institute of Allergy & Infectious Diseases (U.S.)

GO NUTS S. Shelley *Virginia Living* v15 no3 p9 Ap 2017

National Institute of Mental Health (U.S.)

Panic Attack N. Abebe *New York Times Magazine* p13 Ap 23 2017

Quaking in My Boots R. Marr color *Missouri Life* v44 no6 p62 S 2017

National Institute on Drug Abuse

STRESSED OUT? *New York Times Upfront* v149 no8 p20 Ja 30 2017

National Institutes of Health (U.S.)

The applied value of public investments in biomedical research D. Li, P. Azoulay et al diag graph *Science* v356 no6333 p78 Ap 7 2017

Call to restore NIH's cap on grant funding M. Peifer *Science* v357 no6349 p364 Jl 28 2017

Congress trumps president in backing science J. Mervis chart color *Science* v356 no6337 p470 My 5 2017

An extra $2 billion for NIH? *Science* v357 no6356 p1078 S 15 2017

Minority investigators lack NIH funding J. J. Guers, J. Gwathmey et al color *Science* v356 no6342 p1018 Je 9 2017

NIH abandons grant cap, offers new help to younger scientists J. Kaiser *Science* v356 no6343 p1108 Je 16 2017

NIH overhead plan draws fire J. Kaiser color *Science* v356 no6341 p893 Je 1 2017

NIH quietly shelves gun research program M. Wadman *Science* v357 no6356 p1082 S 15 2017

NIH redefines clinical trials, attracting critics J. Kaiser color *Science* v357 no6348 p236 Jl 21 2017

NIH's ineffective funding policies W. P. Wahls *Science* v356 no6343 p1132 Je 16 2017

NIH's massive health study is off to a slow start J. Kaiser color *Science* v357 no6355 p955 S 8 2017

NIH tests blind reviews *Science* v356 no6342 p990 Je 9 2017

NIH to cap grants for well-funded investigators J. Kaiser graph *Science* v356 no6338 p574 My 12 2017

Revisit NIH biosafety guidelines K. A. Oye, M. O'Leary et al color *Science* v357 no6352 p627 Ag 18 2017

National interest

American Interests and Obligations D. C. Frazier and J. NORDLINGER map *National Review* v68 no23 p2 D 19 2016

National Marine Manufacturers Association (Organization)

Best Boating Week A. JONES *Boating World* v38 no4 p4 Ap 2017

National missile defense

Homeland missile defense: How the United States got here T. Karako bibl chart diag *Bulletin of the Atomic Scientists* v73 no3 p159 My 2017

National Model Railroad Association (U.S.)

Layout names from a more playful era N. Besougloff color *Model Railroader* v84 no8 p8 Ag 2017

National monuments

Monumental Achievements... and Controversy L. Davis and P. Jacoby-Garrett *Parks & Recreation* v52 no4 p32 Ap 2017

Native Americans press to keep Bears Ears land a national monument H. Gass *Christian Century* v134 no12 p17 Je 7 2017

Obama's Monuments T. STRAKA *Commentary* v143 no2 p6 F 2017

POWERFUL MEMORIES S. Evans color *Southern Living* v52 no2 p14 F 2017

Saving our unique places color map *National Wildlife (World Edition)* v55 no1 p44 D/Ja 2016

A Threat to Our Legacy G. MULLINS-COHEN *Parks & Recreation* v52 no4 p10 Ap 2017

U.S. monuments at risk color *Science* v357 no6357 p1216 S 22 2017

What to do about the Monuments cartoon *New Orleans Magazine* v51 no7 p20 My 2017

WITH POYDRAS THE PARROT J. STREET color *New Orleans Magazine* v51 no7 p22 My 2017

National monuments—Alabama

A PEOPLE'S HISTORY color *Mother Jones* v42 no4 p57 Jl/Ag 2017

National monuments—Arizona

See also
   Canyon de Chelly National Monument (Ariz.)
   Casa Grande Ruins National Monument (Ariz.)
   Ironwood Forest National Monument (Ariz.)

Canyon de Chelly National Monument K. FROST *Arizona Highways* v92 no7 p7 Jl 2016

I watched the sun set with one R. STIEVE *Arizona Highways* v92 no8 p3 Ag 2016

National monuments—California

See also
   Death Valley National Park (Calif. & Nev.)

Desert Guardian W. Becktold *Sierra* v101 no4 p67 Jl/Ag 2016

National monuments—Evaluation

IRONWOOD FOREST N. AUSTIN *Arizona Highways* v93 no1 p52 Ja 2017

National monuments—Government policy

A Monumental Fight K. Steinmetz color *Time* v190 no9 p30 S 4 2017

National monuments—Law & legislation

Trump Delays a Fight On Presidential Power E. E. Deprez and A. Natter color *Bloomberg Businessweek* no4520 p29 My 1 2017

National monuments—Minnesota

See also
   Pipestone National Monument (Minn.)

Pipestone and Prairies R. H. MOHLENBROCK color map *Natural History* v125 no5 p42 My 2017

National monuments—Nevada

New National Monuments *Congressional Digest* v96 no2 p10 F 1 2017

New protected area in Utah includes land that's sacred for Native

Americans H. Bruinius and H. Gass color *Christian Century* v134 no3 p13 F 2017

National monuments—South Carolina

Remembering Reconstruction S. Richardson color *American History* v52 no2 p9 Je 2017

National monuments—Utah

See also
   Bears Ears National Monument (Utah)

New National Monuments *Congressional Digest* v96 no2 p10 F 1 2017

National Museum of African American History & Culture (U.S.)

Admission is free. Exit is not A. ABEL bw color *Maclean's* v129 no40 p36 O 10 2016

AN AMERICAN PLACE R. Smith bw color *American History* v52 no3 p72 Ag 2017

At Last, a Black History Museum E. Ball bw color *New York Review of Books* v63 no18 p14 N 24 2016

BEST OF WASHINGTON *Washingtonian Magazine* v52 no9 p80 Je 2017

Crowning Achievement J. MINUTILLO *Architectural Record* v204 no11 p70 N 2016

THE CRUCIBLE OF A CULTURE L. J. O'DONOVAN bw color *America* v216 no1 p32 Ja 2 2017

FULL ATTIC? B. Freed *Washingtonian Magazine* v52 no2 p17 N 2016

Lonnie G. BUNCH III bw *Vanity Fair* v59 no1 p126 Holiday 2017

Memorial for the Future E. RUSH color *Orion Magazine* v36 no1 p9 Ja/F 2017

National Museum of African American History & Culture A. KONERMANN *Cincinnati Magazine* p56 Je 2017

Never Forget B. Dufresne bw color *Commonweal* v144 no7 p20 Ap 14 2017

OF MANY THINGS M. MALONE *America* v215 no10 p2 O 10 2016

Out&About color *Martha Stewart Living* no271 p10 Ja/F 2017

Permanent February J. NORDLINGER color *National Review* v69 no4 p22 Mr 6 2017

Redoubting Thomas color *Weekly Standard* v23 no5 p4 O 9 2017

RINGING THE FREEDOM BELL E. A. DUNBAR color *Nation* v303 no25/26 p22 D 19 2016

National Museum of Natural History (U.S.)

The Preservation of a Naturalist S. Bartram *Parks & Recreation* v52 no5 p20 My 2017

National museums—Evaluation

riga, latvia M. OWENS bw color *Architectural Digest* no5 p80 My 2017

National museums—United States

A RICHER STORY OF WHO WE ARE B. OBAMA *Vital Speeches of the Day* v82 no11 p345 N 2016

THIS IS A GREAT ACHIEVEMENT J. LEWIS *Vital Speeches of the Day* v82 no11 p348 N 2016

National Nurses United (Organization)

Nurses Lead the Way S. Johnson color *Progressive* v81 no4 p47 Ap/My 2017

National parks & reserves

See also
   Marine parks & reserves
   National monuments
   Wilderness areas

100% Clean National Park P. Rauber *Sierra* v101 no4 p30 Jl/Ag 2016

Better in Winter O. DWYER color *Backpacker* p34 N 2017

Celebrating Three Years of Healthy Out-of-School Time A. Colman *Parks & Recreation* v52 no3 p32 Mr 2017

Echoes *National Parks* v91 no2 p8 Spr 2017

Escape, Breathe, Fight R. Marech *National Parks* v91 no3 p4 Summ 2017

IN HIS ELEMENT BRUNELLO CUCINELLI FINDS CASHMERE AND PEACE IN MONGOLIA A. WHITTLE color *Conde Nast Traveler* v52 no10 p44 N 2017

It's Background Screening Season *Parks & Recreation* v52 no3 p54 Mr 2017

Jump Start Data-Driven Parks Management *Parks & Recreation* v52 no5 p49 My 2017

Land Between the Lakes R. H. MOHLENBROCK color map *Natural History* v125 no11 p42 N 2017

Los Angeles Innovation Lab Tackles Homelessness H. Williams *Parks & Recreation* v52 no3 p48 Mr 2017

Making Memories C. Ianzito color *AARP: The Magazine* v59 no3A p75 Ap/My 2016

Member Spotlight: M. Jean Keller V. Paynich *Parks & Recreation* v52 no3 p51 Mr 2017

MY LADY OF THE DESERT K. VAUGHN *Arizona Highways* v93 no6 p28 Je 2017

A Parks Bucket List: We'll Visit All 59! C. Ianzito color *AARP: The Magazine* v59 no3A p84 Ap/My 2016

PEAK EXPERIENCE *Iceland Review* v55 no3 p98 My/Je 2017

A PIPELINE RUNS THROUGH IT T. CLYNES *Audubon* v118 no6 p18 Wint 2016

Preamble H. E. Blake *Orion Magazine* v35 no4/5 p1 Jl-O 2016

Public Spaces and Social Equity M. A. Currie *Parks & Recreation* v52 no3 p34 Mr 2017

Spectacle of Lights G. Versed *Sierra* v102 no4 p14 Jl/Ag 2017

Spring Has Sprung--Way Too Early *USA Today Magazine* v145 no2863 p14 Ap 2017

THE WILDERNESS OUT YOUR FRONT DOOR G. KAMIYA *Sierra* v102 no3 p42 My/Je 2017

Wildlife Explorers: Connecting Kids to Nature *Parks & Recreation* v52 no3 p46 Mr 2017

National parks & reserves—Alaska
See also
Arctic National Wildlife Refuge (Alaska)
Denali National Park & Preserve (Alaska)
Garbage In, Garbage Out S. C. P. WILLIAMS *National Parks* v91 no4 p22 Fall 2017

National parks & reserves—Arizona
See also
Coconino National Forest (Ariz.)
Grand Canyon National Park (Ariz.)
Petrified Forest National Park (Ariz.)
Saguaro National Park (Ariz.)
CAPE ROYAL ROAD Cape Royal offers one of the best overlooks in Grand Canyon National Park. It's impressive, and so is the narrow, winding road that takes you there N. AUSTIN *Arizona Highways* v93 no6 p52 Je 2017

from our archives [July 1946] *Arizona Highways* v93 no1 p10 Ja 2017

GREEN GIANTS I. Cobb color *Sunset* v237 no6 p32 D 2016

National Parks Guide *Arizona Highways* v92 no8 p52 Ag 2016

THIS LAND IS YOUR LAND K. MONTGOMERY *Arizona Highways* v92 no8 p12 Ag 2016

WHAT'S NEW? K. FROST *Arizona Highways* v92 no8 p8 Ag 2016

National parks & reserves—California
See also
Yosemite National Park (Calif.)
BATTLE GROUND P. Fish color *Sunset* v238 no5 p70 My 2017

Sierra Solitude M. HORJUS color graph map *Backpacker* p20 Je 2017

National parks & reserves—Canada
Avoid the crowds J. KIRBY map *Maclean's* v130 no4 p17 My 2017

Canada's indigenous peoples are crashing its 150th birthday D. Dettloff color *America* v217 no4 p15 Ag 21 2017

Cory Trépanier S. DOYLE color *Canadian Geographic* v137 no1 p19 F 2017

exposure color *Canadian Geographic* v137 no1 p14 F 2017

Park It! F. Los color *Canadian Wildlife* v23 no2 p19 My/Je 2017

National parks & reserves—Conservation & restoration
National Moments *Natural History* v125 no2 p5 F 2017

SERVICE *Sierra* v102 no1 p83 Ja/F 2017

National parks & reserves—Description & travel
UNPLUGGING THE SELFIE GENERATION [Cover story] T. Egan and C. Egan color graph map *National Geographic* v230 no4 p34 O 2016

National parks & reserves—Economic aspects
Yellowstone 2.0 J. ABRAHAMSON *Sierra* v101 no4 p36 Jl/Ag 2016

National parks & reserves—Fees
Grab This $10 Parks Bargain ... Quick! J. Calfas color *Money* v46 no7 p26 Ag 2017

National parks & reserves—History

America's Evolving Idea T. T. Williams *Sierra* v101 no4 p31 Jl/Ag 2016

National parks & reserves—Iceland
NORÐUR-pINGEYJARSÝSLA P. STEFÁNSSON *Iceland Review* v55 no4 p26 Jl/Ag 2017

SAGALAND *Iceland Review* v54 no6 p100 N/D 2016

National parks & reserves—Interpretive programs
Interview with a ... Park interpreter E. Torpey *Career Outlook* p1 Jl 2017

National parks & reserves—Law & legislation
To preserve and protect N. WALKER graph map *Canadian Geographic* v137 no1 p32 F 2017

National parks & reserves—Madagascar
Stone Forest K. B. RATTINI color map *National Geographic Kids* no473 p20 S 2017

National parks & reserves—Maine
My Maine N. LUND *National Parks* v91 no2 p12 Spr 2017

Terra Incognita R. WICHELNS color *Backpacker* p14 My 2017

National parks & reserves—Management
Centennial D. McMillen *Prologue* v48 no3 p6 Fall 2016

National parks & reserves—North Carolina
Hallowed Ground Moores Creek National Battlefield W. J. Shepherd *Military History* v33 no6 p75 Mr 2017

National parks & reserves—Periodicals
Special Delivery R. Marech *National Parks* v91 no1 p4 Wint 2017

National parks & reserves—Public use
Nature Fix J. SCHARPER *National Parks* v91 no4 p14 Fall 2017

National parks & reserves—Puerto Rico
See also
Vieques National Wildlife Refuge (P.R.)
Vieques refuge: Not for sale color *National Wildlife (World Edition)* v54 no6 p44 O/N 2016

National parks & reserves—South Dakota
See also
Badlands National Park (S.D.)
Bittersweet in the Preserve W. K. Stoos *South Dakota Magazine* v33 no3 p93 S/O 2017

National parks & reserves—Texas
DESERT HISTORIES H. HAWORTH *Orion Magazine* v35 no3 p64 My/Je 2016

National parks & reserves—United States
THE BURRO QUANDARY N. Brulliard *National Parks* v91 no1 p28 Wint 2017

Estamos Aquí J. G. GONZÁLEZ *Orion Magazine* v35 no4/5 p49 Jl-O 2016

A Fare Deal M. Haiken *Sierra* v101 no4 p47 Jl/Ag 2016

Hoover and the Great Outdoors J. M. Cannon *Hoover Digest: Research & Opinion on Public Policy* no2 p187 Spr 2017

An Invitation C. FINNEY *Orion Magazine* v35 no4/5 p46 Jl-O 2016

My Life, Before and After National Parks A. PETERMAN *Orion Magazine* v35 no4/5 p54 Jl-O 2016

OUR CHANGING ROLE IN PARKS S. Goldberg color *National Geographic* v230 no6 pc9 D 2016

Our Disappearing Wildlife: What Parks Can Do About It R. J. Dolesh *Parks & Recreation* v52 no1 p26 Ja 2017

THE PARKS OF TOMORROW M. Nijhuis and K. Ladzinski color diag graph map *National Geographic* v230 no6 p102 D 2016

Protecting America's Last Dark Skies E. BETZ cartoon color map *Discover* v38 no4 p60 My 2017

SERVICE *Sierra* v102 no1 p83 Ja/F 2017

THESE LANDS ARE NOW YOUR LANDS *National Parks* v91 no2 p10 Spr 2017

THIS LAND WAS MADE FOR YOU AND ME [Cover story] T. TEMPEST WILLIAMS color *O, The Oprah Magazine* p78 Ja 2017

UNPLUGGING THE SELFIE GENERATION [Cover story] T. Egan and C. Egan color graph map *National Geographic* v230 no4 p34 O 2016

What Unites Us T. Pierno *National Parks* v91 no2 p3 Spr 2017

National Parks Conservation Association
NPCA AT WORK: TRASH SOLUTIONS J. VARNER *National Parks* v91 no1 p19 Wint 2017

REAPPEARING ACT K. SIBER *National Parks* v91 no2 p20 Spr 2017

Trash Talk T. Pierno *National Parks* v91 no1 p3 Wint 2017

A Consistently Erroneous Technology J. RANDI *Skeptical Inquirer* v41 no5 p16 S/O 2017

National Restaurant Association (U.S.)

THE OTHER NRA S. JAYARAMAN *Nation* v305 no11 p15 O 30 2017

Up Against the Other NRA: Trump Could Help Restaurant Group Eat Away at Workers' Rights E. Popp cartoon *Progressive* v81 no7 p35 O/N 2017

National Review (Periodical)

Conservatism In Dissent K. D. WILLIAMSON *National Review* v68 no22 p42 D 5 2016

National Rifle Association of America

Gunning for Hillary F. BARNES color *Weekly Standard* v22 no25 p14 Mr 6 2017

The NRA's New Scare Tactics L. RESTON il *New Republic* v248 no11 p6 N 2017

National Rifle Association of America—Political activity

TRUMP AND THE NRA [Cover story] G. ZORNICK color *Nation* v305 no2 p12 Jl 17 2017

National school lunch program

Simply Unpalatable T. MECIA color diag *Weekly Standard* v22 no31 p20 Ap 17 2017

USDA's National School Lunch Program Reduces Food Insecurity K. Ralston and A. Coleman-Jensen *Amber Waves: The Economics of Food, Farming, Natural Resources, & Rural America* p38 Ag 2017

National Science Foundation (U.S.)

Federal share of basic research hits new low J. Mervis graph *Science* v355 no6329 p1005 Mr 10 2017

Green Bank Goes Independent M. TEMMING *Sky & Telescope* v133 no2 p12 F 2017

The Internet As You Know It Does Not Exist B. FELDMAN *New York* v49 no21 p54 O 17 2016

THE LOOMING DECLINE OF THE PUBLIC RESEARCH UNIVERSITY J. Marcus cartoon *Washington Monthly* v49 no9/10 p71 S/O 2017

NSF says: Out with the old telescopes, in with the new D. Clery chart color *Science* v354 no6313 p693 N 11 2016

NSF: Time for Big Ideas R. E. GROPP *BioScience* v66 no11 p920 N 1 2016

U.S. observers seek a more perfect union D. Clery chart color *Science* v355 no6324 p442 F 3 2017

National Science Foundation (U.S.)—Officials & employees

NSF requests salary cost-sharing *Science* v354 no6311 p394 O 28 2016

National security

See also

    Biosecurity

    Refugee screening

Homeland missile defense: How the United States got here T. Karako bibl chart diag *Bulletin of the Atomic Scientists* v73 no3 p159 My 2017

Hot Air E. Alterman il *Nation* v303 no18 p8 O 31 2016

THE NEW RED SCARE A. Cockburn *Harper's Magazine* v333 no1999 p25 D 2016

Sakharov, Gorbachev, and nuclear reductions F. N. von Hippel *Physics Today* v70 no4 p48 Ap 2017

A Stellar Experimental Facility for Stockpile Sustainment and Fundamental Science C. Verdon *Science & Technology Review* p3 D 2016

National Security Council (U.S.)

TQ TECH QUOTIENT M. SMITH *Foreign Policy* no221 p104 N/D 2016

National Security Council (U.S.)—Officials & employees

Take Two at the NSC T. JOSCELYN cartoon *Weekly Standard* v22 no25 p11 Mr 6 2017

National security—Finance

HOMELAND SECURITY M. Robespierre *Lapham's Quarterly* v10 no3 p159 Summ 2017

National security—United States

AMERICA IN AFGHANISTAN: THREE FUNDAMENTAL CONCLUSIONS *Vital Speeches of the Day* v83 no10 p282 O 2017

Exposing Shabby Intelligence P. GIRALDI bw *American Conservative* v16 no2 p6 Mr/Ap 2017

HATE SPEECH W. Wilson *Lapham's Quarterly* v10 no3 p60 Summ 2017

How To Address Strategic Insecurity In A Turbulent Age Z. Brzezinski *NPQ: New Perspectives Quarterly* v34 no2 p29 My 2017

Red Herring M. Y. Omelicheva *Harper's Magazine* v334 no2001 p2 F 2017

Restoring Solvency H. BRANDS and E. EDELMAN color *Weekly Standard* v22 no25 p23 Mr 6 2017

Secret Wars L. DeJonge Schulman *Harper's Magazine* no2007 p2 Ag 2017

Trump's Travel Bans—Look Beyond the Text [Cover story] D. Cole color *New York Review of Books* v64 no8 p4 My 11 2017

National security—United States—History—21st century

U.S. Security Hinges on Getting Foggy Bottom Back In the Game A. J. Stavridis color *Time* v189 no11 p32 Mr 27 2017

National Sleep Foundation

BETTER SLEEP A to Z L. KRIEGER color *Good Housekeeping* v264 no3 p107 Mr 2017

National socialism & medicine

Germany to probe Nazi-era medical science M. Gannon bw *Science* v355 no6320 p13 Ja 6 2017

National socialism & sex

Was National Socialism Anti-Sex? On Left-Wing Fantasies and Sex as the Dark Matter of Politics G. Adamson *Society* v54 no1 p23 F 2017

National socialism—Social aspects

Was National Socialism Anti-Sex? On Left-Wing Fantasies and Sex as the Dark Matter of Politics G. Adamson *Society* v54 no1 p23 F 2017

National songs

Comments img *New York* p12 Mr 6 2017

The Season for Dissent D. ZIRIN *Progressive* v81 no10 p44 N 2016

What Kaepernick Started E. Thomas bw *Progressive* v81 no10 p29 N 2016

National songs—Canada

"O Canada, Beloved Country, Thou!" P. KUITENBROUWER cartoon *Walrus* v14 no6 p23 Jl/Ag 2017

National songs—United States

Off Key J. Connor *American History* v51 no6 p42 F 2017

National songs—United States—History

Hail to the Chieftain A. Tucker *Smithsonian* v47 no9 p11 Ja/F 2017

National songs—United States—Social aspects

Leading Off color *Sports Illustrated* v127 no10 p6 O 2 2017

PROTEST SONG C. P. Pierce color *Sports Illustrated* v127 no10 p30 O 2 2017

National sports teams

THE AWAY TEAM A. OKEOWO cartoon color *New Yorker* v92 no41 p42 D 12 2016

National Trails Day

#trailchat R. Bovee, S. West et al color il map *Backpacker* p6 Je 2017

National trees

The Extinction Risk and Conservation Status of Most National Plants Are Unknown K. J. FEELEY *BioScience* v67 no9 p782 S 2017

National Trust for Historic Preservation in the United States

Fund supports historic congregations C. Kennel-Shank color *Christian Century* v134 no4 p12 F 15 2017

National University of Singapore

Biological tissue can behave like a liquid crystal M. Wilson *Physics Today* v70 no6 p19 Je 2017

It's A Problem That America Is Still Unable To Admit It Will Become #2 To China K. Mahbubani *NPQ: New Perspectives Quarterly* v34 no3 p34 Jl 2017

National Wildlife Federation

20 million sustainability leaders by 2025 color *National Wildlife (World Edition)* v55 no2 p44 F/Mr 2017

Bison welcomed home on Wind River Reservation color map *National Wildlife (World Edition)* v55 no2 p44 F/Mr 2017

Connecting forest habitat for wildlife and people color *National Wildlife (World Edition)* v55 no2 p46 F/Mr 2017

Honoring those who go above and beyond for conservation color *National Wildlife (World Edition)* v55 no4 p46 Je/Jl 2017

Keeping Illinois waters clean color *National Wildlife (World Edition)* v55 no2 p46 F/Mr 2017

Nature's Ambassador Hits the Big 5-0 L. Moore color *National Wildlife (World Edition)* v55 no1 p18 D/Ja 2016

NWF names 100th certified community color *National Wildlife (World Edition)* v55 no3 p44 Ap/My 2017

Protecting the Delaware River Basin color *National Wildlife (World Edition)* v55 no5 p44 Ag/S 2017

Providing havens for pollinators color *National Wildlife (World Edition)* v55 no1 p46 D/Ja 2016

Ranger Rick Helps Teach a Love of Nature C. O'MARA color *National Wildlife (World Edition)* v55 no2 p6 F/Mr 2017

Regional wins for people and wildlife in 2016 color *National Wildlife (World Edition)* v55 no1 p48 D/Ja 2016

Saving our unique places color map *National Wildlife (World Edition)* v55 no1 p44 D/Ja 2016

Showing that every elephant—and every voice—counts color *National Wildlife (World Edition)* v55 no6 p48 O/N 2017

Unexpected Bounties A. Bolen color *National Wildlife (World Edition)* v55 no2 p18 F/Mr 2017

U.S. offshore wind power gains force color *National Wildlife (World Edition)* v55 no1 p46 D/Ja 2016

A vision to save wildlife in crisis color *National Wildlife (World Edition)* v55 no6 p44 O/N 2017

Vital wetlands saved from proposed levee color *National Wildlife (World Edition)* v55 no4 p44 Je/Jl 2017

National Wildlife Federation—Congresses

Adopting a New Vision for Wildlife C. O'MARA color *National Wildlife (World Edition)* v54 no6 p6 O/N 2016

National Women's History Project

A Museum of Our Own: Congress takes steps to turn the longtime dream of a national women's history museum into reality C. RIOS *Ms.* v27 no3 p10 Fall 2017

National Women's Studies Association

Transformation of Consciousness: The National Women's Studies Association and the Combahee River Collective's "Black Feminist Statement" turn 40 J. HOBSON and K. JOLNA *Ms.* v27 no3 p48 Fall 2017

National Zoological Park (U.S.)

THE CAT GAME BACK B. Freed *Washingtonian Magazine* v52 no6 p13 Mr 2017

Trivia T. TROY *Washingtonian Magazine* v52 no4 p104 Ja 2017

National Agrarian University of the Jungle (Tingo Maria, Peru)

Ollanta Humala B. Lightner *Current Biography* v78 no3 p34 Mr 2017

National Football League—Charts, diagrams, etc.

HOT | NOT T. Keith color *Sports Illustrated* v126 no16 p30 Je 5 2017

National income—Charts, diagrams, etc.

FEDERAL FINANCE *Economic Indicators* p32 Ag 2017

FEDERAL FINANCE *Economic Indicators* p32 Ja 2017

FEDERAL FINANCE *Economic Indicators* p32 S 2016

TOTAL OUTPUT, INCOME, AND SPENDING *Economic Indicators* p1 Ja 2017

TOTAL OUTPUT, INCOME, AND SPENDING *Economic Indicators* p1 Je 2017

Nationalism

See also

Cultural nationalism

In Defense of Cosmopolitanism G. Petriglieri *Harvard Business Review Digital Articles* p2 D 15 2016

Out of Many, One M. Malone *America* v217 no5 p3 S 4 2017

The Wave to Come I. Bremmer color *Time* v189 no19 p38 My 22 2017

Nationalism & art

African Renaissance Monument R. Griffiths *History Today* v66 no10 p70 O 2016

Nationalism—Eastern Europe

Shape-Shifting Illiberalism in East-Central Europe H. CASE *Current History* v116 no788 p112 Mr 2017

Nationalism—Europe

Pump Up the Geopolitical Volume T. Rogers color *Bloomberg Businessweek* no4526 p52 Je 12 2017

Nationalism—Religious aspects—Christianity

The rise and fall (and rise?) of Christian nationalism D. Briggs color *Christian Century* v133 no26 p16 D 21 2016

Nationalism—Russia

Is Nationalism a Force for Change in Russia? M. Laruelle *Daedalus* v146 no2 p89 Spr 2017

Nationalism—Social aspects

Pronoun tensions P. W. Marty *Christian Century* v134 no14 p3 Jl 5 2017

Nationalism—United States

American Hate, a History J. Meacham and A. Abrams color *Time* v190 no8 p36 Ag 28 2017

The Fight for the Meaning of America D. Von Drehle color *Time* v188 no16/17 p82 O 24 2016

For Love of Country R. PONNURU and R. LOWRY color *National Review* v69 no3 p33 F 20 2017

Nationalism And Patriotism, Cont'd R. PONNURU *National Review* v69 no6 p18 Ap 3 2017

President Trump's dangerous nationalism *America* v216 no3 p8 F 6 2017

The rise and fall (and rise?) of Christian nationalism D. Briggs color *Christian Century* v133 no26 p16 D 21 2016

The Soul of Our Nation [Cover story] R. W. McElroy color *America* v216 no3 p18 F 6 2017

Taking on the Bully Empire cartoon *Progressive* v81 no10 p6 N 2016

To the University, with Love P. J. Griffiths color *Commonweal* v144 no11 p39 Je 16 2017

What Makes America Great? [Cover story] D. Krauthammer color *Weekly Standard* v22 no33 p26 My 8 2017

Nationalism—Vietnam

Vietnam before the War C. Goscha *History Today* v67 no2 p20 F 2017

Nationalists

BEYOND LE PEN: The world's nationalists J. LARSON img *New York* v50 no9 p32 My 1 2017

HIS KAMPF G. WOOD bw *Atlantic* v319 no5 p40 Je 2017

THE RETURN OF FASCISM S. BENHABIB color *New Republic* v248 no11 p36 N 2017

THEIR THOUGHT LEADERS ARE OBSESSED WITH THE PAST—BUT SAW A WAY TO WIN THE FUTURE img *New York* v50 no9 p31 My 1 2017

Nationalists—Attitudes

It's Putin's World F. FOER cartoon color *Atlantic* v319 no2 p13 Mr 2017

Nationalists—Congresses

League of nationalists K. ENGELHART color *Maclean's* v130 no2 p35 Mr 2017

National parks & reserves—Charts, diagrams, etc.

NATIONAL PARKS TIMELINE E. LIERLE *Arizona Highways* v92 no8 p10 Ag 2016

National parks & reserves—Societies, etc.

The Big Pictures: SAGUARO NATIONAL PARK *Arizona Highways* v93 no3 p16 Mr 2017

Nationalsozialistische Deutsche Arbeiter-Partei

National World War II Museum hosting USHMM exhibit on Nazi propaganda *Successful Farming* v115 no1 p17 Ja 2017

Q + A *Cincinnati Magazine* p28 Je 2017

Nationwide Window Cleaning (Company)

WINDOW WASHING BUCKHEAD 6 MILES NORTH OF DOWNTOWN J. GREEN *Atlanta* v56 no7 p236 N 2016

Native American activists

THE SEVENTH GENERATION S. Elbein *New York Times Magazine* p24 F 5 2017

Native American antiquities

See also

Banner stones

Native American art—Exhibitions

ART cartoon *New Yorker* v92 no43 p8 Ja 2 2017

Native American artists

Ahmoo Angeconeb A. A. DAVIS color *Maclean's* v130 no8 p66 S 2017

Bethany Yellowtail L. IMMEDIATO *Los Angeles Magazine* v62 no9 p95 S 2017

Native American college students

Truth and education J. LEWINGTON color *Maclean's* v130 no10 p52 N 2017

Native American languages

IT PAYS TO INCREASE YOUR Word Power E. COX and H. RATHVON *Reader's Digest* v190 no1132 p135 Jl/Ag 2017

Native American women

This Is My Job K. Schmitt color *Glamour* v115 no10 p132 O 2017

Native Americans

See also

Native American women

Design, Place and Indigenous Ways: Working with Local Communities P. Droz, D. Jaber et al *Parks & Recreation* v51 no12 p30 D 2016

Double Life L. Feldman bw cartoon *American Cowboy* v23 no4 p20 D 2016/Ja 2017

Go West, Young Man map *Weekly Standard* v22 no47 p3 Ag 21 2017

The Indian Wars Have Never Ended M. A. Rolo bw *Progressive* v81 no2 p35 F 2017

Invasive Species, Indigenous Stewards, and Vulnerability Discourse N. J. REO, K. WHYTE et al chart diag map *American Indian Quarterly* v41 no3 p201 Summ 2017

Mislabeled *Lapham's Quarterly* v10 no2 p48 Spr 2017

NATIONS RISING R. Johnson, M. N. Mitra et al color *Earth Island Journal* v32 no4 p18 Wint 2017

Timbisha... M. Dolan color *American History* v52 no2 p72 Je 2017

Native Americans—Agriculture

Hard Times at Mid-Continent S. Richardson color *American History* v52 no2 p10 Je 2017

Native Americans—Alaska

Alaska's Close-Up N. KIRSCHNER *American Scholar* v86 no2 p16 Spr 2017

Native Americans—Arizona—History—14th century

REVISITING MONTEZUMA CASTLE E. A. POWELL color *Archaeology* v70 no2 p12 Mr/Ap 2017

Native Americans—Education

LEFT BEHIND R. Clarren color *Nation* v305 no4 p12 Ag 14 2017

Native Americans—Ethnic identity

Who gets to be Indigenous? J. Boyden bw color *Maclean's* v130 no8 p36 S 2017

Native Americans—Government relations

See also

First Nations (Canada)—Government relations

The Big Black Box of Indian Country V. LAMBERT *American Indian Quarterly* v40 no4 p333 Fall 2016

Native Americans—History

Unofficial Paths: Memories of Poston N. ISHIYAMA and J. KAMATA *Orion Magazine* v35 no4/5 p51 Jl-O 2016

Native Americans—Pictorial works

Lulu and the Shadow Catcher C. Mott and J. A. Hayner bw color *Magazine Antiques* v184 no3 p82 My/Je 2017

Native Americans—Reservations—North Dakota

See also

Standing Rock Indian Reservation (N.D. & S.D.)

The Indian Wars Have Never Ended M. A. Rolo bw *Progressive* v81 no2 p35 F 2017

'It's Indian Time!' F. Madeson color *Progressive* v81 no10 p19 N 2016

Standing Rock Says No to the Dakota Access Pipeline E. CASSIDY color *Progressive* v81 no10 p10 N 2016

Native Americans—Reservations—South Dakota

See also

Great Sioux Reservation (N.D. & S.D.)

SOUTH DAKOTA TRIVIA *South Dakota Magazine* v32 no6 p16 Mr/Ap 2017

Native Americans—Reservations—United States

OIL AND WATER D. GRANN color *Mother Jones* v42 no3 p59 My/Je 2017

Native Americans—Reservations—Wisconsin

My Tribe's Stand Against Corporate Mining M. A. ROLO *Progressive* v81 no10 p22 N 2016

Native Americans—South Dakota

A Case Study of Descriptive Representation: The Experience of Native American Elected Officials in South Dakota J. R. SCHROEDEL and A. ASLANIAN *American Indian Quarterly* v41 no3 p250 Summ 2017

Native Americans—Washington (State)—History—20th century

OFF THE GRID M. GRUNBERG BANYASZ color *Archaeology* v70 no3 p10 My/Je 2017

Native language

My Forgotten Language S. SUBRAMANIAN color *Discover* v38 no9 p28 N 2017

SPEAKING OF NATURE: Finding language that affirms our kinship with the natural world R. W. KIMMERER color *Orion Magazine* v36 no2 p14 Mr/Ap 2017

TO SPEAK IS TO BLUNDER YIYUN LI cartoon *New Yorker* v92 no43 p30 Ja 2 2017

Native plant gardening

the dirt M. HUGHES *Better Homes & Gardens* v94 no11 p68 N 2016

Native Union (Company)

Somebody Solved the Ugly-Cord-and-Charger Thing G. MUNCE color *GQ: Gentlemen's Quarterly* v97 no10 p76 O 2017

Nativism

Quiet Time P. Beinart *New Republic* v248 no4 p4 Ap 2017

Natsume, Sōseki, 1867-1916

Meiji Modernist C. Harding *History Today* v67 no1 p28 Ja 2017

Natter, Ari

A Cloud Hangs Over a Clean-Energy Fund color graph *Bloomberg Businessweek* no4513 p33 Mr 6 2017

Thanks to Ivanka, We May Always Have Paris color *Bloomberg Businessweek* no4519 p50 Ap 24 2017

Trump Delays a Fight On Presidential Power color *Bloomberg Businessweek* no4520 p29 My 1 2017

Natterer, Fabian D.

An on/off Berry phase switch in circular graphene resonators diag graph *Science* v356 no6340 p845 My 26 2017

Natu, Vaidehi

Microstructural proliferation in human cortex is coupled with the development of face processing bibl graph *Science* v355 no6320 p1 Ja 6 2017

Natural areas

See also

Wilderness areas

Wildlife refuges

Gold Rush H. B. ROCHFORT color map *Backpacker* p18 O 2017

In Praise of Sandstone T. Flannery color *New York Review of Books* v64 no11 p28 Je 22 2017

KOMO MAI E AI L. ANTHONY color map *Canadian Geographic* v137 p24 2017 Travel

Lundy Island: A Wildlife Oasis in the Bristol Channel *British Heritage Travel* v38 no4 p62 Jl/Ag 2017

TINT AND TONE P. STEFÁNSSON color *Iceland Review* v54 no5 p86 S-O 2016

WHERE'S THIS? color *Canadian Geographic* v135 no6 p77 D 2015

Wonder Beyond Words R. GRIJALVA *Sierra* v101 no4 p68 Jl/Ag 2016

Natural areas—Ohio

Enter fantasyland color *Backpacker* p22 Ag 2017

Natural areas—Russia

Pleistocene Park R. ANDERSEN color *Atlantic* v319 no3 p74 Ap 2017

Natural areas—Wales

Lapwing Get a Life Raft *British Heritage Travel* v38 no1 p6 Ja/F 2017

Natural Born Juicers (Company)

Pro Bowl *Indianapolis Monthly* p42 F 2017

Natural bridges

Last Look E. Daigneau *Governing* v30 no1 p64 O 2016

Natural disasters

See also

Droughts

Earth movements

Earthquakes

Environmental degradation

Floods

Hurricanes

Impact of asteroids with Earth

Storms

Volcanic eruptions

10 FREAKY FORCES OF NATURE D. E. RICHARDS color *National Geographic Kids* no465 p26 N 2016

The Angels of Irma [Cover story] J. Kluger, H. S. Edwards et al color map *Time* v190 no12 p34 S 25 2017

Cleaning Up: After a natural disaster, environmental agencies are among the first on the ground E. Daigneau *Governing* v30 no8

p20 My 2017

The Deluge *Commonweal* v144 no15 p5 S 22 2017

Fire and Flood *Change* v82 no3 p5 Mr 2017

GREAT UNKNOWNS cartoon *Popular Mechanics* p26 Mr 2017

Houston After Harvey J. Kluger, C. Alter et al color *Time* v190 no10/11 p38 S 18 2017

MAKE THE MOST OF YOUR DONOR DOLLARS S. BLOCK color *Kiplinger's Personal Finance* v71 no12 p9 D 2017

Q+A *Cincinnati Magazine* v50 no6 p32 Mr 2017

Science of preparedness J. Berg color *Science* v357 no6356 p1073 S 15 2017

Using Animals to Predict the Future A. Popescu color *Bloomberg Businessweek* no4533 p19 Ag 7 2017

Why Businesses Should Lower Prices During Natural Disasters R. Mohammed *Harvard Business Review Digital Articles* p2 S 11 2017

WORTH NOTING K. A. GAJEWSKi *Humanist* v76 no6 p46 N/D 2016

Natural disasters—Economic aspects

As Oceans Rise, Insurers Flee B. Kowitt, P. Wahba et al color *Fortune* v176 no2 p18 Ag 1 2017

The effect of natural disasters on local economies M. Brown *Monthly Labor Review* p1 Jl 2017

Natural disasters—History

Recovering from Disaster, Reinventing Japan? S. KLIEN *Current History* v116 no791 p241 S 2017

Natural disasters—United States

Tomorrow: David Wallace-Wells C. Bonanos img *New York* v50 no18 p15 S 4 2017

Natural dyes & dyeing

Gather I. Edwards color *Sunset* v237 no5 p54 N 2016

Jussara Lee R. Gollin bw *Rodale's Organic Life* v3 no1 p54 Ja 2017

Natural Element Homes (Company)

BEST FLOORING color *Timber Home Living* p28 2017 SpecialIssue

BEST GREAT ROOM color *Timber Home Living* p18 2017 SpecialIssue

Big Sky Beauty color *Timber Home Living* p38 2017 SpecialIssue

Right on the MONEY color diag *Log Home Living* p50 2017 SpecialIssue

Taking Stock color diag *Log Home Living* p16 2017 SpecialIssue

Natural fibers

Historical Emporium Brings High Quality to Both Customer Service and Period Costumes *Stage Directions* v30 no3 p63 Mr 2017

Natural foods

AMAZING NEWS V. Tweed color *Amazing Wellness* v9 no4 p12 Summ 2017

Americans Want Healthier Food and Drink Options *Parks & Recreation* v51 no12 p14 D 2016

BEAT-THE-BUS SCHOOL LUNCHES K. Cicero color *Parents* v92 no9 p78 S 2017

DEPRIVATION IS OUT. GOOD NUTRITION IS IN. EMBRACE THE NEW HEALTHY *Los Angeles Magazine* p112 Ap 2017

Eating well—and loving it! C. McHugh color *Health* v31 no8 p6 O 2017

Foodie Fun in the Sun L. TURNER color *Better Nutrition* v79 no7 p58 Jl 2017

Food of THE GODS M. BECK color *O, The Oprah Magazine* p36 Jl 2017

GO NATURAL IN 90 days V. Tweed color *Better Nutrition* v79 no6 p32 Je 2017

GQHQ cartoon color *GQ: Gentlemen's Quarterly* v97 no3 p54 Mr 2017

GRAB & GO! [Cover story] color *Yoga Journal* no293 p18 Ag 2017

How to Eat Well-and Still Feel Full A. Sifferlin color *Time* v189 no12 p26 Ap 3 2017

LIGHT, FRESH, FAST C. Ferreira color *Yoga Journal* p104 2017 Special Issue

Make healthy eating easy H. Powell color *Redbook* p95 O 2017

Make That Change Nicole color *Better Nutrition* v79 no7 p6 Jl 2017

nourish your practice *Yoga Journal* p110 2017 Special Issue

Nutritional and Brewer's Yeasts: What's the Difference? V.

TWEED chart color *Better Nutrition* v79 no3 p24 Mr 2017

Quinn Popcorn cofounder Kristy Lewis Z. Verbit *Parents* v91 no6 p18 Je 2016

The Scoop on Ice Cream's Health-Food Origins O. B. Waxman *Time* v190 no8 p21 Ag 28 2017

Second opinion *Mayo Clinic Health Letter* v358 no8 p8 Ag 2017

Simply Irresistible color *Better Nutrition* v79 no11 p24 N 2017

SMARTEN UP TO SHRINK YOUR GUT C. HANSEN color *Men's Health* v32 no4 p52 My 2017

The truth about your takeout color *Health* v31 no8 p49 O 2017

VEGAN Meat ALTERNATIVES A. Custer *Vegetarian Journal* v35 no1 p24 2016

veggie bits *Vegetarian Journal* v36 no2 p28 2017

What experts tell their friends about EATING HEALTHY J. DEMELO color *Redbook* p82 Ap 2017

Natural foods—Economic aspects

Want Fries With That Kale Salad? L. Patton color graph *Bloomberg Businessweek* no4499 p45 N 14 2016

Natural foods—History

Want Fries With That Kale Salad? L. Patton color graph *Bloomberg Businessweek* no4499 p45 N 14 2016

Natural gas

DIESEL NATURAL GAS CONVERSION: DUAL-FUEL CONVERSION KITS SLASH LARRY URWILLER'S IRRIGATION FUEL COSTS BY 25% TO 30% T. Gaines *Successful Farming* v115 no6 p52 Ap 2017

Methane production from coal by a single methanogen Daisuke Mayumi, Hanako Mochimaru et al bibl graph *Science* v354 no6309 p222 O 14 2016

WILL FLORIDA BAN FRACKING? R. BAILEY color *Reason* v49 no2 p8 Je 2017

Natural gas pipeline design & construction

Pennsylvania nuns sue federal agency over natural gas pipeline M. Cusick color *Christian Century* v134 no18 p15 Ag 30 2017

Natural gas sales & prices

The Future of Yesterday's Fuel B. H. Potts color *Weekly Standard* v22 no29 p14 Ap 3 2017

The Relationship Between Energy Prices and Food-Related Energy Use in the United States P. Canning and S. Rehkamp *Amber Waves: The Economics of Food, Farming, Natural Resources, & Rural America* p17 Je 2017

Natural gas—Economic aspects

From Scarcity to Abundance: The New Geopolitics of Energy M. T. KLARE *Current History* v116 no786 p3 Ja 2017

Natural gas—United States—Government policy

There's a Crack in Everything M. N. Mitra *Earth Island Journal* v32 no4 p2 Wint 2017

Natural history museums

Around the Country color *Natural History* v125 no6 p40 Je 2017

Natural history—Exhibitions

Around the Country color *Natural History* v125 no10 p40 O 2017

Around the Country *Natural History* v125 no2 p38 F 2017

Natural history—Periodicals

OUR SOCIAL MEDIA MISSION S. Goldberg color *National Geographic* v231 no4 p4 Ap 2017

Natural language processing (Computer science)

Bots That Can Talk Will Help Us Get More Value from Analytics S. Frankel *Harvard Business Review Digital Articles* p2 N 24 2016

Natural law

See also

Liberty

The Legal Rights of Nature T. John color *Time* v189 no14 p14 Ap 17 2017

Natural products

See also

Natural sweeteners

Nature's best beauty secrets K. D. HODES color *Redbook* p48 Ap 2017

Promises, PROMISES chart color *O, The Oprah Magazine* p79 Mr 2017

Natural products—Marketing

Supermarket Dot Com K. FINN color *New Orleans Magazine* v51 no12 p36 O 2017

Natural products—Therapeutic use

"My body was telling me to go back to basics—and stop straightening my hair" S. Kitchens color *Glamour* v115 no6 p74 Je 2017

Natural resources

　　See also

　　　Forests & forestry

　　　Metals

　　　Mines & mineral resources

　　　Resource exploitation

　　　Water supply

Cartoons *New York Times Upfront* v149 no9 p24 F 20 2017

Contingent valuation: Flawed logic? J. Baron, R. C. Bishop et al color *Science* v357 no6349 p363 Jl 28 2017

COSMOS CONSENSUS? J. A. SCLATER *Scientific American* v317 no4 p8 O 2017

How the Natural Resources Business Is Turning into a Technology Industry J. Woetzel and S. Nyquist color *Harvard Business Review Digital Articles* p1 Je 2 2017

A looming tragedy of the sand commons A. Torres, J. Brandt et al color *Science* v357 no6355 p970 S 8 2017

PHOTOGRAPHS OF ALASKA K. LAWRENCE *Prologue* v49 no2 p28 Summ 2017

PUTTING A PRICE ON NATURE H. Lárusson *Iceland Review* v54 no6 p58 N/D 2016

Natural resources conservation areas

　　See also

　　　Natural areas

THE HEROIC WORK OF THIN GREEN LINE GAME WARDENS J. A. SWAN *American Forests* v122 no3 p32 Fall 2016

Natural resources management

　　See also

　　　Coastal zone management

　　　Forest management

　　　Wildlife management

Pipe Dreams B. LUTZ color *New Orleans Magazine* v51 no12 p42 O 2017

A plan comes together F. LOS color map *Canadian Geographic* v135 no6 p60 D 2015

Why Waste Our Energy? T. J. Donohue *Weekly Standard* v22 no24 p17 F 27 2017

Natural resources—United States

The Preservation and Use of America's Natural Resources *Congressional Digest* v96 no6 p2 Je 2017

Natural satellite orbits

PATH OF THE PLANETS chart color diag graph *Astronomy* v45 no9 p40 S 2017

Natural satellites

　　See also

　　　Moon

　　　Planetary rings

AROUND THE WORLD *Science* v357 no6358 p1332 S 29 2017

OBSERVING July 2017 *Sky & Telescope* v134 no1 p41 Jl 2017

Spring Tide J. RAO *Natural History* v124 no10 p45 N 2016

Natural satellites—Atmospheres—Research

IO'S ATMOSPHERE PERIODICALLY COLLAPSES J. Rice color *Astronomy* v44 no12 p8 D 2016

Natural selection

　　See also

　　　Biological fitness

BEAUTY HAPPENS R. O. Prum bw color *Natural History* v125 no4 p24 Ap 2017

BEYOND HUMAN D. T. MAX cartoon *National Geographic* v231 no4 p40 Ap 2017

Negative selection in humans and fruit flies involves synergistic epistasis M. Sohai, O. A. Vakhrusheva et al chart graph *Science* v356 no6337 p539 My 5 2017

Natural sweeteners

　　See also

　　　Honey

　　　Sugar

CAN YOU BUILD A BETTER SUGAR? M. Stacey color *Women's Health* v14 no4 p112 My 2017

Natural ventilation

Breath of Fresh Air K. Logan *Architectural Record* v205 no7 p126 Jl 2017

Natural Vitality (Company)

THE EVOLUTION OF THE MULTIVITAMIN V. Tweed chart

color *Amazing Wellness* v9 no3 p62 EarlySumm 2017

Natural wines

THE WILD THINGS: AN UNFILTERED GUIDE TO THE CITY'S BEST PURVEYORS OF NATURAL WINE M. BUSICO color *Los Angeles Magazine* v62 no7 p39 Jl 2017

WINE GONE WILD J. Gordinier color *Esquire* p98 My 2017

Naturalists

　　See also

　　　Biologists

　　　Zoologists

Lichen Adventure N. CONROY color *Canadian Wildlife* v23 no1 p7 Mr/Ap 2017

Off The Grid R. Marech *National Parks* v91 no2 p4 Spr 2017

Outstanding in the Fields bw *Canadian Wildlife* v23 no1 p9 Mr/Ap 2017

Naturalists—Interviews

PODCAST EARTH K. DOANE *Cincinnati Magazine* v50 no8 p18 My 2017

Naturalization—United States

America Is Still the Future A. Sullivan img *New York* p16 Ja 23 2017

Becoming An American A. M. AHSAN *Islamic Horizons* v45 no6 p42 N/D 2016

NEWBIES Jiayang Fan cartoon *New Yorker* v92 no34 p24 O 24 2016

Nature

　　See also

　　　Nature appreciation

25 best vacation spots for big kids [Cover story] K. CICERO color *Parents* v92 no6 p66 Je 2017

BE THE SKY F. J. Boccio color *Yoga Journal* p110 2017 Special Issue

BETTER FOR IT P. Fox bw *Powder* v45 no4 p36 D 2016

BREATHE color *Prevention* v69 no4 p38 Ap 2017

Estamos Aquí J. G. GONZÁLEZ *Orion Magazine* v35 no4/5 p49 Jl-O 2016

The Lasting Images of Wayne Trimm *New York State Conservationist* v72 no1 p10 Ag 2017

LEARNING FROM NATURE D. Zipes *Saturday Evening Post* v289 no4 p76 Jl/Ag 2017

Let it RAIN color *Yoga Journal* p34 2016 Special Issue

MAKING moonlight MEMORIES S. Piecuch *New York State Conservationist* v71 no3 p22 D 2016

My Shot *National Geographic Kids* no467 p34 F 2017

THE NATURAL ORDER OF THINGS T. CHRISTOPHER color *Martha Stewart Living* p108 Jl/Ag 2017

The Nature Cure F. WILLIAMS color *Reader's Digest* v189 no1129 p106 Ap 2017

Our Family is Growing color *Earth Island Journal* v32 no1 p18 Spr 2017

PILGRIMAGE TO INDIA [Cover story] M. RABBITT color *Yoga Journal* no290 p34 Mr 2017

Recollections of Wayne Trimm W. Jones *New York State Conservationist* v72 no1 p14 Ag 2017

SOME OF THE BEST PLACES IN THE BIOSPHERE *Sierra* v102 no1 p30 Ja/F 2017

Something Very Clear color *Arizona Highways* v93 no5 p5 My 2017

take it outside *Parents* v92 no2 p27 F 2017

Try the nature cure color *Parents* v92 no5 p80 My 2017

Using History to Activate a Neighborhood Green Space C. G. Wallace *Parks & Recreation* v52 no10 p24 O 2017

Veggie Meals in (or near!) National Parks C. Brown and H. Francis *Vegetarian Journal* v36 no1 p25 2017

weekend getaways: nature *Washingtonian Magazine* v52 no11 p93 Ag 2017

Nature & nurture

BLESSED INHERITANCE S. CRANE-MURDOCH *Orion Magazine* v35 no4/5 p94 Jl-O 2016

Flawed environmental justice analyses R. E. Emanuel color *Science* v357 no6348 p260 Jl 21 2017

A place of first permission J. WILKINS *Orion Magazine* v35 no4/5 p73 Jl-O 2016

Nature (Aesthetics)

Legacy of Nature C. Kolb color *New Orleans Magazine* v51 no9 p38 Jl 2017

tra! v29 no8 p3 O 2016

Schoolhouse Rock Won't Stop Fascism *Extra!* v29 no10 p4 D 2016

To NYT, Trump's 'Populism' Still an 'Open Question' *Extra!* v30 no2 p1 Mr 2017

WaPo Spun Scoop to Shelter Sessions *Extra!* v30 no3 p4 Ap 2017

When Journalism Gets a Jail Threat, Most Media Respond With Silence [Cover story] *Extra!* v29 no8 p1 O 2016

Why Advocating Torture Is OK, but Single-Payer Is Beyond the Pale *Extra!* v30 no5 p3 Je 2017

Why the Revolution Will Not (but Must) Be Televised *Extra!* v30 no7 p1 S 2017

Nautical astronomy

The Name Game: Have a go at this celestial sport. You might just win gold S. Mazlin *Sky & Telescope* v134 no4 p84 O 2017

Nautical charts

At a Glance *Sea Magazine* v108 no8 p42 Ag 2016

C-MAP Genesis Edge Premium Marine-Mapping Service J. Y. WOOD color *Power & Motoryacht* v34 no10 p58 O 2017

Cuba On the Rocks A. Chan color *Sail* v48 no10 p34 O 2017

Intro to Electronic Charts F. LANIER *Sea Magazine* v108 no8 p40 Ag 2016

JEPP CHARTS COME TO FOREFLIGHT color *Flying* v144 no7 p15 Jl 2017

MEXICO MADE EASIER C. P. RAINS *Sea Magazine* v109 no1 p18 Ja 2017

Off the Charts B. ELLISON color map *Power & Motoryacht* v33 no4 p32 Ap 2017

Nautical instruments

Make a Sextant from Junk S. BUSHWICK color *Popular Science* p84 Ja/F 2017

Nautitech (Company)

Nautitech 46 Fly [Cover story] T. Dove color *Sail* v48 no8 p22 Ag 2017

Navajo (North American people)

Lone Country: Navajos in Utah are used to having to fight for basic government services. But they'd at least like to see some roads that don't turn every trip into an endurance test D. C. Vock *Governing* v30 no10 p48 Jl 2017

Navajo Nation, Arizona, New Mexico & Utah

The Development of a Gaming Enterprise for the Navajo Nation S. F. CARDER *American Indian Quarterly* v40 no4 p295 Fall 2016

Naval architecture

See also

Boatbuilding

Trim of ships (Equilibrium)

Shipshape and Well-Equipped K. Kostel *Oceanus* v52 no1 p38 Summ 2016

Naval aviation

In Harm's Way G. NORMAN color *Weekly Standard* v22 no27 p24 Mr 20 2017

Naval bases—History—20th century

THE THIRD REICH'S ARCTIC OUTPOST E. A. POWELL bw color *Archaeology* v70 no3 p22 My/Je 2017

Naval battles

In Praise of the Aircraft Carrier G. Norman color *Weekly Standard* v22 no37 p20 Je 5 2017

WAR LIST: MILITARY MAXIMS B. Quintin color *MHQ: Quarterly Journal of Military History* v30 no1 p22 Aut 2017

Naval Criminal Investigative Service (TV program)

Pauley Perrette's Shocking Exit: What It Means for NCIS A. D'Arminio *TV Guide* v65 no43 p6 O 16 2017

Naval History & Heritage Command (U.S.)

CLUES SURFACE TO LOCATION OF ILL-FATED INDIANAPOLIS B. Manley *Military History* v33 no5 p10 Ja 2017

Naval officers

CHURCHILL'S IMPROBABLE ARMY J. A. Raymond *MHQ: Quarterly Journal of Military History* v29 no3 p78 Spr 2017

Humor in Uniform color *Reader's Digest* v189 no1131 p135 Je 2017

Pete Buttigieg A. WREN color *Indianapolis Monthly* p48 Ap 2017

Naval strategy

Thinking clearly about China's layered Indo-Pacific strategy Z. Cooper and A. Shearer bibl *Bulletin of the Atomic Scientists* v73 no5 p305 2017

Navales, Eric

Manufacturing Companies Need to Sell Outcomes, Not Products *Harvard Business Review Digital Articles* p2 Je 2 2016

Navalny, Alexei, 1976-

Moscow Confidential: Private Jets for Dogs H. Meyer, I. Reznik et al bw color *Bloomberg Businessweek* no4498 p24 N 7 2016

Opposing Forces: Plotting the New Russia R. Legvold *Foreign Affairs* v96 no1 p170 Ja/F 2017

Putin's Rival Targets Provincial Russians L. Ragozin, I. Arkhipov et al color *Bloomberg Businessweek* no4517 p28 Ap 3 2017

TEACHABLE MOMENT *Harper's Magazine* no2007 p16 Ag 2017

Navarra, Katie

Chaps by Discipline color *Horse & Rider* v55 no12 p58 D 2016

The Long Haul to a New Home color *Horse & Rider* v56 no11 p126 N 2017

PLAN. WORK. ACHIEVE color *Horse & Rider* v56 no8 p71 Ag 2017

Trailer Innovations bw color *Horse & Rider* v56 no7 p78 Jl 2017

Navarro, Ana—Interviews

Ana Navarro Wants the G.O.P. to Stand Up to Trump A. M. Cox *New York Times Magazine* p62 O 2 2016

Navarro, Andrea

Another Border Clash for Trump color *Bloomberg Businessweek* no4507 p22 Ja 16 2017

Give Us Your Coders Yearning to Be Free color graph *Bloomberg Businessweek* no4518 p16 Ap 10 2017

NOT NEW (MEXICAN!) DRINK ALERT! MEZCAL color *Bloomberg Businessweek* no4496 p66 O 24 2016

Navarro, Arcadi

Chimpanzee genomic diversity reveals ancient admixture with bonobos bibl diag graph map *Science* v354 no6311 p477 O 28 2016

Navarro, Eduardo

SÃO PAULO BIENAL B. Droitcour cartoon *Art in America* v104 no11 p128 D 2016

Navarro, Joe

16 LIFE LESSONS *Psychology Today* v49 no5 p62 S/O 2016

Navarro, Peter

PETER NAVARRO, TRADE WARRIOR P. COY, M. Jamrisko et al color *Bloomberg Businessweek* no4521 p54 My 8 2017

Professor Propaganda K. D. WILLIAMSON color *National Review* v69 no6 p28 Ap 3 2017

Trump's Economic Brain Trust color diag *Bloomberg Businessweek* no4507 p17 Ja 16 2017

Navarro, Ronald

Health Care Providers Must Stop Wasting Patients' Time *Harvard Business Review Digital Articles* p2 My 24 2017

NAVAS, CARLOS A.

Anesthesia and Euthanasia of Amphibians and Reptiles Used in Scientific Research: Should Hypothermia and Freezing Be Prohibited? *BioScience* v67 no1 p53 Ja 2017

Nave, Moran

Wild emmer genome architecture and diversity elucidate wheat evolution and domestication color *Science* v357 no6346 p93 Jl 7 2017

Navet, Eric

CLASSIC MEETS CUTTING-EDGE [Cover story] K. F. Miller color *Practical Horseman* v45 no7 p26 Jl 2017

Navico Holding AS

Pulling Back the Curtain J. Y. WOOD color *Power & Motoryacht* v34 no7 p26 Jl 2017

Navicular disease—Treatment

Q&A: Navicular Syndrome [Cover story] color *Horse & Rider* v56 no3 p19 Mr 2017

Navient Corp.—Trials, litigation, etc.

Lending Giant Gets Sued K. Mulhere color *Money* v46 no2 p21 Mr 2017

Navigation

See also

Aids to navigation

Artificial satellites in navigation

FINDING THAT SILVER LINING A. ROSS color *Flying* v144 no1 p20 Ja 2017

TRAINING & TECHNIQUE cartoon *Flying* v144 no1 p19 Ja 2017

Weekly v264 no29 p4 Jl 17 2017

University Presses: More Relevant than Ever color *Publishers Weekly* v264 no25 p12 Je 19 2017

The World Needs More Canada *Publishers Weekly* v263 no39 p3 S 26 2016

Naxerova, Kamila

Origins of lymphatic and distant metastases in human colorectal cancer diag graph *Science* v357 no6346 p55 Jl 7 2017

Naxi (Chinese people)

The Mothers color *Foreign Policy* no222 p10 Ja/F 2017

Nayar, Shree

THE CAMERA MAN C. Iozzio color *Popular Photography* v81 no1 p76 Ja/F 2017

Nayar, Vineet

3 Traps That Block Corporate Transformation *Harvard Business Review Digital Articles* p2 N 5 2014

The Costs of India's Annual Budget Guessing Game *Harvard Business Review Digital Articles* p2 Ap 6 2016

Don't Let Outdated Management Structures Kill Your Company *Harvard Business Review Digital Articles* p2 F 10 2016

Managing 3 Types of Bad Bosses *Harvard Business Review Digital Articles* p2 D 1 2014

Naydenov, Boris

Submillihertz magnetic spectroscopy performed with a nanoscale quantum sensor diag *Science* v356 no6340 p832 My 26 2017

Nayel, Fouad

The wheels of injustice M. FRISCOLANTI color *Maclean's* v130 no3 p35 Ap 2017

Nayeri, Dina

Death of a Dream *New York Times Book Review* p12 Je 25 2017

Great Reads for Summer 2017 *Ms.* v27 no2 p46 Summ 2017

Out of Touch *New York Times Magazine* p35 O 16 2016

Naylor, Glenn

COMMENT color *Canadian Geographic* v137 no4 p72 Jl/Ag 2017

Naylor, June

KNIVES OUT *Texas Monthly* v44 no12 p90 D 2016

Naylor, Quentin

PEREGRINE BLOODSTOCK *Arabian Horse World* v57 no5 p1 F 2017

Naylor, Ryan M.

Cyclin A2 is an RNA binding protein that controls Mre11 mRNA translation bibl graph *Science* v353 no6307 p1549 S 30 2016

Naylor-Leyland, Alice

how sweet it is A. BROOKS color *Architectural Digest* v74 no9 p166 S 2017

NAYMAN, ADAM

UNHOLY FOOLS AND BEAUTIFUL LOSERS color *Film Comment* v53 no3 p62 My/Je 2017

Nayman, Samuel J.

Madam Secretary, help us improve social-emotional learning color *Phi Delta Kappan* v98 no8 p64 My 2017

Nayyeri, H.

iPTF16geu: A multiply imaged, gravitationally lensed type Ia supernova color diag graph *Science* v356 no6335 p291 Ap 21 2017

Nazaré (Portugal)

EMBRACING COLOSSUS J. HOUSMAN bw color *Surfer* v58 no4 p96 Ag 2017

Nazarenko, A.

An artificial metalloenzyme with the kinetics of native enzymes bibl diag graph *Science* v354 no6308 p102 O 7 2016

Nazareno, Lori

4 steps for redesigning time for student and teacher learning diag il *Phi Delta Kappan* v98 no4 p21 D 2016/Ja 2017

Taking care of ourselves and others color *Phi Delta Kappan* v98 no6 p25 Mr 2017

Nazaryan, Alexander

'Mason & Dixon' and Me: A personal foray into the long-lost Pynchon tapes *New York Times Book Review* p18 My 21 2017

Nazi propaganda—Exhibitions

National World War II Museum hosting USHMM exhibit on Nazi propaganda *Successful Farming* v115 no1 p17 Ja 2017

Nazis

IT HAPPENED HERE D. Goodyear diag *New Yorker* v93 no29 p40 S 25 2017

WAR! WOMEN! WEASELS! M. LAFAVORE bw color *Men's Health* v32 no5 p120 Je 2017

NAZY, SLES

Cambodian Cham Muslims and the Quran: A shattered community continues to rebuild its foundations of faith *Islamic Horizons* v46 no4 p34 Jl/Ag 2017

NAZZARO, M. NICOLE

SLAY YOUR SETBACKS color *Runner's World* v52 no8 p24 S 2017

NBA 2K (Game)

FACE OF THE FRANCHISE S. Kwak color *Sports Illustrated* v127 no11 p20 O 9 2017

XBOX WIZARD: We challenged NBA star Bradley Beal to a game of basketball--on his couch J. KNAPP *Washingtonian Magazine* v53 no1 p19 O 2017

NBA JAM (Game)

NBA JAM D. Greene and A. Abnos color *Sports Illustrated* v127 no1 p90 Jl 3 2017

NBBJ LP

Meridian Center for Health J. Bittle *Architectural Record* v205 no4 p188 Ap 2017

NBC Nightly News (TV program)

NBC's Fake News Show color *Weekly Standard* v22 no40 p2 Je 26 2017

NCAA Basketball Tournament

COMPLETE MADNESS R. A. BERENZ *TV Guide* v65 no11 p50 Mr 6 2017

Ha to the Chief T. Keith color *Sports Illustrated* v125 no13 p19 O 17 2016

ONE TO CROW ON S. Davis color *Sports Illustrated* v126 no9 p35 Mr 27 2017

Should Catholics be feeling March Madness? P. Kelly color *America* v216 no6 p36 Mr 20 2017

STRONG TO THE HOOP J. BIEN-KAHN cartoon *Wired* v25 no3 p22 Mr 2017

NCAA Basketball Tournament—History

First DANCE [Cover story] L. Winn color *Sports Illustrated* v126 no8 p52 Mr 20 2017

NCAA Basketball Tournament—History—21st century

5 MINUTE GUIDE D. Greene color *Sports Illustrated* v126 no8 p58 Mr 20 2017

Big SHOTS B. Hamilton, L. Winn et al color *Sports Illustrated* v126 no8 p32 Mr 20 2017

Full SWING [Cover story] M. Rosenberg color *Sports Illustrated* v126 no10 p36 Ap 10 2017

HOW TO WATCH R. Deitsch color *Sports Illustrated* v126 no8 p61 Mr 20 2017

Inside LOOK L. Winn color diag *Sports Illustrated* v126 no8 p42 Mr 20 2017

Lightbox color *Time* v189 no14 p16 Ap 17 2017

New VIBRATIONS R. Deitsch color *Sports Illustrated* v126 no10 p48 Ap 10 2017

The Power Of Three K. Jenkins color *Sports Illustrated* v125 no15 p76 N 7 2016

WHO CAN BEAT UCONN? R. Deitsch color *Sports Illustrated* v126 no8 p65 Mr 20 2017

NCAA Basketball Tournament—Charts, diagrams, etc.

THE BRACKETS D. Greene and L. Winn *Sports Illustrated* v126 no8 p40 Mr 20 2017

NCIS (TV program)

The Abby Effect P. PERRETTE *TV Guide* p18 D 19 2016

AGENT OF CHANGE A. D'ARMINIO *TV Guide* v65 no11 p30 Mr 6 2017

America's top TV critic Matt Roush answers your burning questions M. ROUSH *TV Guide* v65 no23 p3 My 29 2017

NCIS A. D'Arminio color *TV Guide* v64 no42 p34 O 10 2016

NCIS A. D'Arminio *TV Guide* v65 no21 p32 My 15 2017

NCIS N. Abrams, A. Bacle et al *Entertainment Weekly* no1482/1483 p60 S 22 2017

NCIS: Los Angeles (TV program)

Callen Gets in the Spirit on NCIS: Los Angeles A. D'Arminio *TV Guide* p13 D 5 2016

NCIS: Los Angeles A. D'Arminio *TV Guide* v64 no46 p32 N 7 2016

NCIS: Los Angeles A. D'Arminio *TV Guide* v65 no14 p32 Ap 3 2017

NCIS: Los Angeles A. D'Arminio *TV Guide* v65 no41 p30 O 2 2017

NCIS: New Orleans (TV program)

NCIS: New Orleans A. D'Arminio *TV Guide* p34 Ap 17 2017

"NCIS: NEW ORLEANS" A. JOHNSON JR. color *New Orleans Magazine* v51 no1 p40 N 2016

NCIS: NEW ORLEANS *TV Guide* v65 no39 p41 S 18 2017

NCL Corp. Ltd.

Every Fast-Growing Company Has to Combat Overload C. Zook *Harvard Business Review Digital Articles* p2 Je 21 2016

NCsoft Corp.

How the West Was Won D. M. EWALT and W. BALDWIN color *Forbes* v199 no6 p44 Je 13 2017

Ndegéocello, Meshell, 1969-

Stoking the Fire H. Als cartoon *New Yorker* v92 no40 p13 D 5 2016

Ndila, Carolyne M.

Resistance to malaria through structural variation of red blood cell invasion receptors diag *Science* v356 no6343 p1139 Je 16 2017

Ndour, Oumy

New Comfort Zones P. Guzmán bw *Conde Nast Traveler* v52 no4 p12 Ap 2017

Neal, Jim—Interviews

Hope and Change A. RICHARD ALBANESE color *Publishers Weekly* v264 no25 p47 Je 19 2017

Neal, Larry

An Organization-Wide Approach to Good Decision Making *Harvard Business Review Digital Articles* p2 My 27 2015

Neal, Terri Brown

Speak up color *U.S. Catholic* v82 no4 p5 Ap 2017

Neale, Margaret A.

More Reasons Women Need to Negotiate Their Salaries *Harvard Business Review Digital Articles* p2 Je 29 2015

NEALON, KEVIN

Laugh Lines color *Reader's Digest* v190 no1132 p86 Jl/Ag 2017

Neander, Joachim, 1650-1680

US AND THEM J. Mooallem *New York Times Magazine* p40 Ja 15 2017

Neanderthals

The growth pattern of Neandertals, reconstructed from a juvenile skeleton from El Sidrón (Spain) A. Rosas, L. Ríos et al color graph *Science* v357 no6357 p1282 S 22 2017

Late Pleistocene archaic human crania from Xuchang, China Li, Wu et al bibl color diag graph *Science* v355 no6328 p969 Mr 3 2017

Layers of Hominin History A. Hadhazy color *Natural History* v125 no10 p8 O 2017

Neandertal and Denisovan DNA from Pleistocene sediments V. Slon, C. Hopfe et al bw color *Science* v356 no6338 p605 My 12 2017

Neandertal genome reveals greater legacy in the living A. Gibbons *Science* v357 no6359 p21 O 6 2017

Neandertals mated early with modern humans A. Gibbons color *Science* v357 no6346 p14 Jl 7 2017

Neandertal tar-making reconstructed B. BOWER color *Science News* v192 no5 p13 S 30 2017

Our First Date Out of Africa? B. ALEX color *Discover* v38 no1 p70 Ja/F 2017

Stone Age injuries lack modern analog B. BOWER color *Science News* v191 no10 p13 My 27 2017

A TRADITIONAL NEANDERTHAL HOME Z. ZORICH color *Archaeology* v70 no2 p23 Mr/Ap 2017

Neanderthals—Physiology

The new Neanderthals B. BETHUNE color *Maclean's* v130 no4 p68 My 2017

Near Death (Film)

THE PRE-SHOW color *Film Comment* v53 no4 p6 Jl/Ag 2017

Near-death experiences

THE GRAVE IS A GATEWAY C. W. KEGLEY and D. J. KEGLEY *USA Today Magazine* v145 no2862 p48 Mr 2017

I Survived! [Cover story] J. RIOS, C. S. GRANT et al *Reader's Digest* v189 no1128 p62 Mr 2017

The luckiest man in Canada M. CAMPBELL color *Maclean's* v130 no2 p14 Mr 2017

Near infrared radiation

HEALING With Light A. PATUREL and A. Jung color *Prevention*

v69 no11 p72 N 2017

Near misses (Aeronautics)

A NEAR MISS D. FRANCIS color map *Flying* v144 no10 p28 O 2017

Neason, Alexandria

CLASS DISMISSED: When a state divests from public education *Harper's Magazine* p35 S 2017

NEASON, AMY

On the SIDE color *House Beautiful* p169 Ag 2017

Woven WORKS color *House Beautiful* p126 Ag 2017

Neatby, Jacques

The Ballooning Executive Team *Harvard Business Review Digital Articles* p2 Jl 21 2016

How to Break into Your CEO's Inner Circle *Harvard Business Review Digital Articles* p2 Ja 12 2015

Why Excom Meetings Are the Wrong Place to Make Decisions *Harvard Business Review Digital Articles* p2 Jl 8 2015

Neb, Sergej

Angular momentum–induced delays in solid-state photoemission enhanced by intra-atomic interactions chart color graph *Science* v357 no6357 p1274 S 22 2017

NEBER, JACQUELINE

10 TITLES TO PICK UP NOW color *O, The Oprah Magazine* p110 N 2017

Neblo, Michael A.

The need for a translational science of democracy bibl color *Science* v355 no6328 p914 Mr 3 2017

NEDOZENKO, MARC

Chords & Discords bw color *Downbeat* v84 no10 p10 O 2017

Nebraska

1867 - The Time of our Birth C. Amundson *Nebraska Life* v21 no1 p9 Ja/F 2017

NEBRASKA'S Public Servants color *Nebraska Life* v21 no2 p19 Mr/Ap 2017

NEBRASKA'S Wild West bw color *Nebraska Life* v21 no1 p17 Ja/F 2017

SHOWCASE SHOTS color *Nebraska Life* v21 no1 p80 Ja/F 2017

Nebraska in art

Nebraskans' bridge past and present with photography J. Boschen color *Nebraska Life* v21 no1 p14 Ja/F 2017

Nebraska Life (Periodical)

Happy Birthday to us! color *Nebraska Life* v21 no2 p56 Mr/Ap 2017

NEBRASKA'S Wild West bw color *Nebraska Life* v21 no1 p17 Ja/F 2017

New Nebraska threads for 2017 color *Nebraska Life* v21 no2 p11 Mr/Ap 2017

Pretty Farmhouse on the Hill color *Nebraska Life* v21 no1 p16 Ja/F 2017

See the sights color *Nebraska Life* v21 no2 p66 Mr/Ap 2017

SHOWCASE SHOTS color *Nebraska Life* v21 no2 p80 Mr/Ap 2017

Sweepstakes color *Nebraska Life* v21 no1 p13 Ja/F 2017

Nebraska state history

Nebraska at 150 A. J. BARTELS bw color map *Nebraska Life* v21 no6 p50 N/D 2017

Politics and murder C. Amundson *Nebraska Life* v21 no5 p11 S/O 2017

Nebraska—Description & travel

Hit the Road in 2017 color *Nebraska Life* v21 no1 p68 Ja/F 2017

NEBRASKA TRAVELER *Nebraska Life* v20 no6 p63 N/D 2016

Sandhill Crane Tour color *Nebraska Life* v21 no1 p65 Ja/F 2017

Time travel through the Haymarket M. Masich color *Nebraska Life* v21 no2 p60 Mr/Ap 2017

Winter fun heats up in Bellevue S. W. Kansteiner color *Nebraska Life* v21 no1 p66 Ja/F 2017

Nebraska—Environmental conditions

The Weather and Climate of Nebraska: The Heartland of Extremes K. Dewey and H. M. Mogil bw chart color diag graph map *Weatherwise* v70 no4 p12 Jl/Ag 2017

Nebraska—History

Nebraska at 150 A. J. BARTELS bw color map *Nebraska Life* v21 no2 p50 Mr/Ap 2017

Nebraska at 150 A. J. BARTELS bw color *Nebraska Life* v21 no1 p50 Ja/F 2017

Nebraska—Politics & government

A Final Fight for the Keystone Pipeline S. ELBEIN color *Rolling Stone* no1298 p24 O 19 2017

Nebulae

See also
Orion Nebula

A colorful crustacean color *Astronomy* v45 no10 p74 O 2017

Cosmic cats and crustaceans color *Astronomy* v45 no6 p74 Je 2017

The Dark Wolf of Summer R. P. Wilds *Sky & Telescope* v133 no6 p64 Je 2017

Discover 10 weird emission nebulae S. J. O'Meara color *Astronomy* v45 no5 p44 My 2017

Float like a butterfly color *Astronomy* v45 no4 p74 Ap 2017

GALLERY color *Sky & Telescope* v134 no5 p74 N 2017

GALLERY *Sky & Telescope* v133 no1 p71 Ja 2017

GALLERY *Sky & Telescope* v133 no5 p74 My 2017

GALLERY *Sky & Telescope* v134 no1 p74 Jl 2017

Herschel's Ghosts M. Bartels *Sky & Telescope* v133 no4 p30 Ap 2017

Lifetime of the solar nebula constrained by meteorite paleomagnetism H. Wang, B. P. Weiss et al bibl graph *Science* v355 no6325 p623 F 10 2017

MYSTERY SPOT J. O. Johnson *Sky & Telescope* v133 no6 p76 Je 2017

READER GALLERY color *Astronomy* v45 no2 p72 F 2017

READER GALLERY color *Astronomy* v45 no5 p70 My 2017

TAKE A SWIM IN THE LAGOON C. Manges *Sky & Telescope* v133 no6 p74 Je 2017

Necessary Driving Skills (Short story)

NECESSARY DRIVING SKILLS N. Segnit *Harper's Magazine* p79 Ap 2017

Necessity (Philosophy)

The Truth About Black Lives Matter *Commentary* v141 no10 p1 D 2016

The Truth About Black Lives Matter *Commentary* v142 no5 p1 D 2016

Neck anatomy

Body of knowledge R. Long color *Yoga Journal* no287 p40 N 2016

Get to know... your neck R. Long color *Yoga Journal* p22 2017 SpecialIssue

Neck pain

Is your workout giving you a stiff neck? *Harvard Health Letter* v42 no11 p5 S 2017

Neck pain treatment

Get to know... your neck R. Long color *Yoga Journal* p22 2017 SpecialIssue

Head & neck pain color *Yoga Journal* p21 2017 SpecialIssue

A healing sequence to ease neck & shoulder pain G. Kraftsow color *Yoga Journal* p25 2017 SpecialIssue

Neck Scarves (Poem)

NECK SCARVES M. Eden *Commonweal* v144 no11 p10 Je 16 2017

NECKAR, ELISA

Our Personal Favorites bw *Discover* v38 no4 p44 My 2017

Necklaces

THE DO-GOOD DESIGNER L. B. LAUREN color *Martha Stewart Living* p42 Mr 2017

MARRAKECH, MOROCCO R. MISNER color *Conde Nast Traveler* v52 no2 p22 F 2017

The NEW STRONG *Interview* v46 no10 p90 D 2016/Ja 2017

QUEENS FOR A DAY [Cover story] T. Manring color *Chicago* v66 no9 p112 S 2017

Russell SIMMONS color *Esquire* p128 Ap 2017

Necklaces—Design & construction

Why I Love P. Chopra color *InStyle* v24 no1 p104 Ja 2017

Necklaces—Evaluation

BASIC INSTINCT color *Harper's Bazaar* no3650 p91 F 2017

CADET CHIC color *Harper's Bazaar* no3648 p156 N 2016

CAFÉ SOCIETY color *Conde Nast Traveler* v52 no9 p19 O 2017

CHAIN REACTION color *O, The Oprah Magazine* p45 Jl 2017

Check LIST color *Harper's Bazaar* no3653 p88 My 2017

DIAMONDS IN THE SKY color *Harper's Bazaar* no3653 p288 My 2017

DIGITAL CRAFT: LASER CUTTING. COMPUTER MODELING. THREE DIMENSIONS. A NEW AGE OF DESIGN IS

UPON US *Cincinnati Magazine* v50 no11 p32 Ag 2017

FABULOUS at Every Age color *Harper's Bazaar* no3653 p183 My 2017

FABULOUS at Every Age color *Harper's Bazaar* no3654 p103 Je/Jl 2017

FORCES OF NATURE color *Harper's Bazaar* no3649 p170 D 2016/Ja 2017

GARDEN PARTY color *Harper's Bazaar* no3649 p168 D 2016/Ja 2017

getting ready with DR. KIM NICHOLS K. NICHOLS color *Better Homes & Gardens* v95 no3 p20 Mr 2017

GREAT BUYS UNDER $100 color *O, The Oprah Magazine* p104 D 2016

The In/Out LIST color *Harper's Bazaar* no3657 p122 O 2017

IN TO THE WILD C. ROITFELD color *Harper's Bazaar* no3649 p273 D 2016/Ja 2017

It's Spring! color *InStyle* v24 no3 p225 Mr 2017

The LIST color *Harper's Bazaar* no3655 p57 Ag 2017

Market bw color *Vanity Fair* p90 Hollywood 2017 Supplement

Meet your new favorite basics B. Goreski color *Redbook* p12 Mr 2017

MIX IT UP color *Seventeen* v76 no3 p84 My 2017

The Moon & Stars E. Velluto color *Glamour* v115 no2 p36 F 2017

my style color *InStyle* v24 no6 p79 Je 2017

Necklace Party E. Velluto color *Glamour* v115 no6 p50 Je 2017

The New Blooms J. J. CONDON color *House Beautiful* v159 no4 p35 My 2017

NEW PRODUCTS color *Astronomy* v45 no3 p67 Mr 2017

Nice ICE color *Seventeen* p56 Ja 1 2017

off the chain A. Syrett color *InStyle* v24 no1 p82 Ja 2017

The O List cartoon color *O, The Oprah Magazine* p51 My 2017

on demand color *InStyle* v24 no2 p39 F 2017

on demand color *InStyle* v24 no5 p51 My 2017

ORANGE CRUSH *Cincinnati Magazine* v50 no12 p34 S 2017

PLAID TO THE BONE: A fall trend as versatile as it is classic E. STUART *Virginia Living* v15 no6 p37 O 2017

RANCH DRESSING: Styles that are right at home on the range (and beyond) L. WALTERS *Indianapolis Monthly* v12 no40 p32 Ag 2017

Shop & Do Good color *Seventeen* v75 no11 p34 N 2016

Sleeve Game Strong F. Kane, S. P. Nadella et al color *Glamour* v115 no3 p62 Mr 2017

SO BAZAAR color *Harper's Bazaar* no3655 p170 Ag 2017

STAND TO ATTENTION color *Harper's Bazaar* no3648 p138 N 2016

SWING LOW SEXY PENDANT NECKLACES YOU CAN WEAR ANYWHERE, WITH ANYTHING (OR NOTHING AT ALL) color *Conde Nast Traveler* v52 no10 p42 N 2017

TAKE THE PLUNGE color *Harper's Bazaar* no3649 p213 D 2016/Ja 2017

VENICE, ITALY color *Conde Nast Traveler* v51 no10 p40 N 2016

Wait LIST color *Harper's Bazaar* no3657 p120 O 2017

WEEKEND GETAWAY color *Essence* v48 no3 p20 Jl 2017

WHERE FASHION GETS PERSONAL color *Harper's Bazaar* no3650 p95 F 2017

WHY I LOVE MY CUSTOM PEARL NECKLACE M. Kaling color *InStyle* v24 no10 p254 O 2017

Necks (Performer)

Something From Nothing: My obsession with the Necks, the greatest trio on earth G. Dyer *New York Times Magazine* p52 O 8 2017

Neckties

See also
Bolo ties

The Style Guy M. Anthony Green bw color *GQ: Gentlemen's Quarterly* v97 no9 p76 S 2017

Neckties—Evaluation

60 FOR 60 color *GQ: Gentlemen's Quarterly* v97 no10 p134 O 2017

Business Class S. YEUN color *GQ: Gentlemen's Quarterly* v86 no11 p148 N 2016

THE CURE FOR THE COMMON KHAKI color *Esquire* p94 2017 BigBlackBook

Huge coaster, one thin rail M. B. Griggs and A. Rosenblum color diag *Popular Science* v289 no6 p24 N/D 2017

PETAL TO THE METAL *Cincinnati Magazine* v50 no6 p38 Mr

Former Kickboxing Champ Lou Neglia Is Proof of the Power of Martial Arts F. Vallejo color *Black Belt* v55 no3 p22 Ap/My 2017

Negotiation

    See also
      Brinkmanship
      Conflict management
      Deals
      International arbitration

The Best Path to Brexit Is Painful for Both Sides bw *Bloomberg Businessweek* no4503 p8 D 12 2016

Get the money you deserve N. Lapin color *Redbook* p26 S 2017

Having Too Many Options Can Make You a Worse Negotiator M. Schaerer, D. D. Loschelder et al *Harvard Business Review Digital Articles* p2 My 24 2017

How to Bounce Back After a Failed Negotiation C. O'Hara *Harvard Business Review Digital Articles* p2 Ap 21 2016

How to Cool Down a Heated Negotiation J. Weiss *Harvard Business Review Digital Articles* p2 F 16 2016

How to Negotiate After a Staggering Defeat: A Playbook for Democrats D. Malhotra *Harvard Business Review Digital Articles* p2 N 16 2016

I Don't Want a Bargain J. BOTTUM cartoon *Weekly Standard* v22 no38 p5 Je 12 2017

LET'S NEGOTIATE E. L. FERNANDEZ *USA Today Magazine* v145 no2862 p72 Mr 2017

The Personality Traits of Good Negotiators T. Chamorro-Premuzic *Harvard Business Review Digital Articles* p2 Ag 7 2017

The Two Conversations You're Having When You Negotiate A. Molinsky *Harvard Business Review Digital Articles* p2 Ap 5 2016

What Donald Trump Doesn't Understand About Negotiation D. Malhotra and J. Powell *Harvard Business Review Digital Articles* p2 Ap 8 2016

Negotiation in business

Having Too Many Options Can Make You a Worse Negotiator M. Schaerer, D. D. Loschelder et al *Harvard Business Review Digital Articles* p2 My 24 2017

How to Deal with the Irrational Parts of a Negotiation J. Grenny *Harvard Business Review Digital Articles* p2 Je 6 2016

How to Negotiate for Vacation Time D. M. Kolb and S. M. Brady *Harvard Business Review Digital Articles* p2 Je 19 2015

How to Negotiate Nicely Without Being a Pushover C. O'Hara *Harvard Business Review Digital Articles* p2 Ap 9 2015

Negotiating with Clients You Can't Afford to Lose R. K. Holden *Harvard Business Review Digital Articles* p2 Je 10 2016

Setting the Record Straight on Negotiating Your Salary A. Gallo *Harvard Business Review Digital Articles* p2 Mr 9 2015

Setting the Record Straight: Using an Outside Offer to Get a Raise A. Gallo *Harvard Business Review Digital Articles* p2 Jl 5 2016

Negotiation in business—Psychological aspects

The Secret to Negotiating Is Reading People's Faces K. Wezowski *Harvard Business Review Digital Articles* p2 Je 16 2016

Win Over the Person Blocking Your Deal P. V. Weinstein *Harvard Business Review Digital Articles* p2 N 4 2014

Negotiation—Moral & ethical aspects

Cultural Stereotypes May Make You a Less Ethical Negotiator Yu Yang and D. De Cremer *Harvard Business Review Digital Articles* p2 Ja 8 2016

Negotiation—Psychological aspects

Get in the Right State of Mind for Any Negotiation M. Wheeler *Harvard Business Review Digital Articles* p2 My 5 2015

Negotiation—United States

Uncommon Cooperation A. Greenblatt *Governing* v30 no12 p9 S 2017

Negron, Julia

A SHOT IN THE DARK J. Lurie color graph *Mother Jones* v42 no2 p6 Mr/Ap 2017

Negron-Almodovar, Ricardo J.

To Vegas, With Love from Orlando *Time* v190 no15 p26 O 16 2017

Negroponte, Diana Villiers

The Hesitant U.S. Rescue of the Soviet Economy *Wilson Quarterly* v40 no4 p4 Fall 2016

Nehamas, Alexander

BAD COMPANY D. Schaub *Claremont Review of Books* v16 no4

p81 Fall 2016

Character Counts T. EHRENFELD cartoon *Weekly Standard* v22 no19 p35 Ja 23 2017

Nehme, Farran Smith

Love & Friendship *Film Comment* v53 no1 p51 Ja/F 2017

Man of Action bw *Film Comment* v53 no1 p88 Ja/F 2017

Nehring, James

What real high performance looks like chart diag *Phi Delta Kappan* v98 no7 p38 Ap 2017

Nehring, Richard

Productivity Growth Is Still the Major Driver in Growing U.S. Agricultural Output *Amber Waves: The Economics of Food, Farming, Natural Resources, & Rural America* p5 S 2016

Neibart, Sam

GET YOUR BEST HAIR EVER color *Harper's Bazaar* no3656 p374 S 2017

Neiberg, Michael S.

Brothers at Arms: American Independence and the Men of France and Spain Who Saved It *Military History* v33 no6 p71 Mr 2017

Neidell, Matthew

Air Pollution Is Making Office Workers Less Productive *Harvard Business Review Digital Articles* p2 S 29 2016

Neiderman, Amihai

Hacker shows how easy it is to take over a city's public Wi-Fi network L. CONSTANTIN color *PCWorld* v35 no1 p51 Ja 2017

NEIDL, PHOEBE

Masha Gessen color *Rolling Stone* no1295 p46 S 7 2017

NEIER, ARYEH

SPECIAL Letters color *Nation* v303 no17 p8 O 24 2016

Neifert, Stewart

A nuclease that mediates cell death induced by DNA damage and poly(ADP-ribose) polymerase-1 bw graph *Science* v354 no6308 paad6872-1 O 7 2016

Neighborhood change

BEST FOOT FORWARD *Atlanta* v57 no5 p103 S 2017

Civic Lesson D. LIND *Architectural Record* v205 no4 p176 Ap 2017

Neighborhood planning

Walking the Walk: In creating walkable neighborhoods, a little audacity goes a long way A. Ehrenhalt *Governing* v30 no10 p14 Jl 2017

Neighborhood Youth Corps (U.S.)

MAKE-WORK R. FORD cartoon *New Yorker* v93 no16 p58 Je 5 2017

Neighborhoods

ALL THAT And More *Atlanta* v57 no2 p134 Je 2017

CAMPUS POLITICS D. Reed *Washingtonian Magazine* v52 no5 p49 F 2017

THE COP NEXT DOOR: Can police rebuild trust by moving into the neighborhood? J. Buntin *Governing* v30 no10 p24 Jl 2017

Dear Readers *Reader's Digest* v190 no1132 p4 Jl/Ag 2017

Elisabeth Moss: The Handmaid's Tale's star can't help turning her characters into feminist heroes, even if she's just trying to play a human J. YUAN img *New York* v50 no9 p16 My 1 2017

Front-Yard Friends C. Kopaczewski color *Good Housekeeping* v264 no6 p59 Je 2017

THE HALFWAY HOUSE J. C. Henriquez color *O, The Oprah Magazine* p25 Mr 2017

MISSISSIPPI'S JUMP-OUT BOYS C. J. Ciaramella color *Reason* v49 no5 p8 O 2017

The Neighborhood Naming Game: What people call a community can have a big impact on its self-image A. Ehrenhalt *Governing* v31 no1 p14 O 2017

The Right Mix: Portland's Eastside neighborhoods offer easy living and shopping S. Beyer *Governing* v30 no10 p23 Jl 2017

A Shooting in the Neighborhood D. SKINNER color *Weekly Standard* v22 no41 p5 Jl 3 2017

Walking the Walk: In creating walkable neighborhoods, a little audacity goes a long way A. Ehrenhalt *Governing* v30 no10 p14 Jl 2017

Neighborhoods—Design & construction

A Rose is A Rose: Bayou Road Renaissance C. Kolb color *New Orleans Magazine* v51 no10 p50 Ag 2017

Neighbors

Down These Lonely Streets R. BROOKHISER bw *National Review* v69 no17 p43 S 11 2017

AN HEIRLOOM PROJECT L. Naragon color *Popular Mechanics* p8 Mr 2017

Neighbors family

My Social Butterfly C. HEITGER-EWING color *Cabin Living* p16 Ap 2017

Neighbors—Societies, etc.

My Social Butterfly C. HEITGER-EWING color *Cabin Living* p16 Ap 2017

Neihardt, John G.

PREMONITION *Lapham's Quarterly* v10 no3 p91 Summ 2017

Neill, D.

Persistent effects of pre-Columbian plant domestication on Amazonian forest composition bibl chart graph map *Science* v355 no6328 p925 Mr 3 2017

Neill, J. D.

iPTF16geu: A multiply imaged, gravitationally lensed type Ia supernova color diag graph *Science* v356 no6335 p291 Ap 21 2017

NEILSON, LAURA

RUNWAY *Interview* v46 no8 p38 O 2016

Neimann, Andrew

SURFER OF THE MONTH: ANDREW NEIMANN M. Ciaramella color *Surfing Magazine* v53 no3 p84 Mr 2017

Neimark, Jill

Rum Country *Atlanta* v57 no5 p57 S 2017

NEIRENE, RAHEL

50 FOR 50: EVERY STATE HAS ITS OWN LGBT LEADERS AND HEROES. 50 CURRENT LGBT LEADERS SHARE THEIR STATE'S HEROES map *Advocate* no1091 p98 Je/Jl 2017

Know Thyself (And Try to Understand Everyone Else): Our 101 guide to gender identities and sexual orientations *Advocate* no1093 p17 O/N 2017

SISTERS ARE DOING IT FOR THEMSELVES: BLACK QUEER WOMEN TAKE SEXUAL HEALTH INTO THIER OWN HANDS color *Advocate* no1091 p112 Je/Jl 2017

Neisess, Debi

The Body's Repair Kit at Work K. RIDDERBUSCH *Atlanta* v56 no7 p212 N 2016

Neistat, Casey

SAVE THIS ISSUE *Popular Mechanics* p8 O 2017

Neistat, Casey—Interviews

THE MOST TRUSTED NAME IN NEWS M. Belloni bw color *Popular Mechanics* p52 O 2017

NEITZ, KATIE

CHANDRA POINTER color *Runner's World* v51 no10 p23 N 2016

Fit for a Fashion Pro color *Runner's World* v52 no8 p41 S 2017

RW 2016 COVER SEARCH [Cover story] color *Runner's World* v51 no11 p62 D 2016

TRENDING FRIENDS color *Runner's World* v52 no1 p28 Ja/F 2017

Neitzel, Molly Moon—Interviews

Get the Scoop on Seattle P. M. ESSWEIN cartoon color *Kiplinger's Personal Finance* v71 no7 p22 Jl 2017

Neiwert, David

MAKE AMERICA HATE AGAIN bw cartoon *Mother Jones* v42 no1 p24 Ja/F 2017

TRUMP'S TROOPS *Mother Jones* v41 no6 p31 N/D 2016

Nejman, Deborah

Potential role of intratumor bacteria in mediating tumor resistance to the chemotherapeutic drug gemcitabine diag *Science* v357 no6356 p1156 S 15 2017

Nel, Andre E.

Policy reforms to update chemical safety testing bibl color *Science* v355 no6329 p1016 Mr 10 2017

Nel, Philip

The Hidden (and Not-So-Hidden) Racism In Kids' Lit S. Begley color *Time* v190 no6 p56 Ag 7 2017

Nelan, Edmund P.

Relativistic deflection of background starlight measures the mass of a nearby white dwarf star chart color graph *Science* v356 no6342 p1046 Je 9 2017

Neldner, Victor J.

Positive biodiversity-productivity relationship predominant in global forests bibl chart graph map *Science* v354 no6309

paaf8957-1 O 14 2016

Nell, Colleen S.

Higher predation risk for insect prey at low latitudes and elevations graph *Science* v356 no6339 p742 My 19 2017

Nellen, L.

Observation of a large-scale anisotropy in the arrival directions of cosmic rays above 8×1018 eV *Science* v357 no6357 p1266 S 22 2017

NELSEN, AARON

Before THE FLOOD *Texas Monthly* v45 no5 p43 My 2017

Nelson, Andrew Tobias

HOW DO YOU HOLD TOGETHER YOUR TRANS IDENTITY AND YOUR LIFE OF FAITH? color *Christian Century* v134 no2 p22 Ja 18 2017

Nelson, Ann

Diversity in physics: Are you part of the problem? *Physics Today* v70 no5 p10 My 2017

Nelson, Anthony

FOOD-TRIPPING: The tiny hunt country town of Marshall may not be top of your list for a food-centric day trip, but it should be W. PIPKIN *Virginia Living* v15 no6 p33 O 2017

Nelson, Battling, 1882-1954

Battling Nelson and the Scissor Punch M. Hatmaker bw *Black Belt* v55 no3 p18 Ap/My 2017

NELSON, BROOKE

6 Things You Should Never Park in Your Garage color *Reader's Digest* v190 no1133 p44 S 2017

Nelson, Candace

THE SWEET SPOT color *InStyle* v23 no13 p274 D 2016

Nelson, Cassandra

Losing His Way bw *Commonweal* v144 no12 p33 Jl 7 2017

Seeing Is Believing bw *Commonweal* v143 no18 p14 N 11 2016

Nelson, Craig

Pearl Harbor: From Infamy to Greatness L. D. Freedman *Foreign Affairs* v95 no6 p177 N/D 2016

Nelson, Cristin

Amber Waves OF GRAINS color *Vegetarian Times* v43 no2 p38 N/D 2016

Nelson, Dave

RESTORING LEAN-TOS, VOLUNTEERS WORK TO SAVE THESE HISTORIC STRUCTURES *New York State Conservationist* v72 no1 p34 Ag 2017

Nelson, Dean

Encounters with a saint *Christian Century* v133 no24 p10 N 23 2016

Nelson, Dennis

A COMFORTABLY LARGE FARM SHOP A. McConnell *Successful Farming* v115 no5 p25 Mid-Mr 2017

Nelson, Derek R.

The ministry of convening *Christian Century* v134 no20 p12 S 27 2017

Nelson, Hosea M.

Arylation of hydrocarbons enabled by organosilicon reagents and weakly coordinating anions diag *Science* v355 no6332 p1403 Mr 31 2017

Nelson, J.

Improving global integration of crop research color *Science* v357 no6349 p359 Jl 28 2017

Nelson, Jane

No Company Can Solve a Massive Global Problem on Its Own *Harvard Business Review Digital Articles* p2 Ja 21 2016

NELSON, JAY J.

FONTAGENT 7 AND FONTAGENT SYNC: ALL-NEW INTERFACE AND FONT SYNCING ACROSS USERS AND MACS color *Macworld - Digital Edition* p31 D 2016

Nelson, Jen

The Power of Bare color *Glamour* no8 p28 Ag 2017

NELSON, JIM

THE CULT OF THE GOOD GUY *GQ: Gentlemen's Quarterly* v97 no10 p50 O 2017

Hack Trump *GQ: Gentlemen's Quarterly* v86 no11 p22 N 2016

Louder Than Bombs color *GQ: Gentlemen's Quarterly* v97 no6 p16 Je 2017

THE MARRIAGE BIAS color *GQ: Gentlemen's Quarterly* v86 no12 p40 D 2016

OFF the BEATEN PATH color *GQ: Gentlemen's Quarterly* v97

no9 p154 S 2017

NELSON, KADIR

MAKING THE COVER bw color *Ebony* v72 no4 p20 F 2017

Nelson, Kari

To The Editor color *American Craft* v76 no6 p10 D 2016-Ja 2017

Nelson, Kristin Bratton

Culture Research: The Vaccine Race: Science, Politics, and the Human Costs of Defeating Disease *Issues in Science & Technology* v33 no4 p85 Summ 2017

Nelson, Larry

TEEING OFF J. Sens color *Golf Magazine* v59 no8 p16 Ag 2017

Nelson, Linda

Pleasure of a Good Ride color *Horse & Rider* v56 no6 p18 Je 2017

Nelson, Lukas, 1989-

Music Royalty's Next Generation E. R. Brown color *Entertainment Weekly* no1457/1458 p96 Mr 17 2017

Nelson, Lusha

AN EYE TO REMEMBER S. WALDRON bw *Vanity Fair* v59 no2 p69 F 2017

Nelson, Maggie, 1973-

Maggie Nelson D. Kiper color *Current Biography* v78 no5 p68 My 2017

Nelson, Marcia Z.

Fresh Lenses color *Publishers Weekly* v263 no45 p17 N 7 2016

Islamic Studies Picking Up Momentum color *Publishers Weekly* v263 no45 p6 N 7 2016

Something Old, Something New color *Publishers Weekly* v264 no34 p23 Ag 21 2017

Way of Love: Recovering the Heart of Christianity color *Christian Century* v133 no25 p38 D 7 2016

Nelson, Max

Between Two Fires bw *Film Comment* v53 no1 p11 Ja/F 2017

Bohemian Rhapsody bw *Film Comment* v53 no3 p11 My/Je 2017

Day of the Dead color *Film Comment* v53 no2 p11 Mr/Ap 2017

Everybody Wants Some!! *Film Comment* v53 no1 p52 Ja/F 2017

First-World Problems bw *Film Comment* v53 no5 p11 S/O 2017

Heart in a Cage color *Film Comment* v52 no6 p11 N/D 2016

The Human Surge color *Film Comment* v53 no1 p82 Ja/F 2017

READING INTO IT bw color *Film Comment* v53 no2 p48 Mr/Ap 2017

Stir Crazy color *Film Comment* v53 no4 p11 Jl/Ag 2017

Nelson, Merle

OUR 'COUSIN' MERLE K. Hunlioff *South Dakota Magazine* v32 no6 p8 Mr/Ap 2017

NELSON, MICHAEL

Patience Rewarded color *Weekly Standard* v22 no41 p38 Jl 3 2017

Running on Empty color *Weekly Standard* v22 no13 p32 D 5 2016

NELSON, MICHAEL PAUL

Conserving the World's Megafauna and Biodiversity: The Fierce Urgency of Now *BioScience* v67 no3 p197 Mr 2017

The Moral Urgency of Action to Protect the World's Megafauna *BioScience* v66 no12 p1009 D 1 2016

Saving the World's Terrestrial Megafauna color *BioScience* v66 no10 p807 O 1 2016

NELSON, R. J.

THE LAST HARBOR BOSS bw cartoon color *Chicago* v65 no11 p110 N 2016

Nelson, Rebecca

Meet Yr Match! color *Glamour* v115 no5 p116 My 2017

Nelson, Richard, 1950-

Real-Time Results J. GREEN *New York* v49 no23 p86 N 14 2016

NELSON, ROBERT

ALMOST FAMOUS: Waterfront the Blue Ridge hasn't won any contests--yet *Virginia Living* v15 no6 p112 O 2017

FOOD FOR THOUGHT color *Virginia Living* v15 no5 p96 Ag 2017

GENEALOGY BUG BITE: Alt-facts, fake news, obsession and wasted days in the land of the dead *Virginia Living* v15 no4 p112 Je 2017

HARD BALL *Virginia Living* v15 no3 p100 Ap 2017

THE NEW RELIGION *Virginia Living* v15 no3 p5 Ap 2017

Saving Selma: After years of neglect from an absentee owner and decay significant enough to threaten its survival, historic Selma Mansion in Loudoun County is getting a second chance *Virginia Living* v15 no4 p45 Je 2017

A TALE OF TWO COUNTIES *Virginia Living* v15 no2 p112 F

2017

VEHICULAR VANITY RUN AMUCK *Virginia Living* v15 no1 p112 D 2016

Nelson, S.

Femtosecond electron-phonon lock-in by photoemission and x-ray free-electron laser chart diag *Science* v357 no6346 p71 Jl 7 2017

Nelson, S. D.

RED CLOUD'S STORIES: The Lcikota leader knew when to fight, and when to stop *South Dakota Magazine* v33 no2 p69 Jl/Ag 2017

Nelson, Sara D.

What Do YOU Think Should Be Hot? color *Literacy Today (2411-7862)* v34 no4 p43 Ja/F 2017

Nelson, Scott A.

The Internet of Things Needs Design, Not Just Technology *Harvard Business Review Digital Articles* p2 Ap 29 2016

Nelson, Silke

Metalloprotein entatic control of ligand-metal bonds quantified by ultrafast x-ray spectroscopy diag *Science* v356 no6344 p1276 Je 23 2017

Nelson, Sophia A.

President vs. Press *USA Today Magazine* v145 no2864 p14 My 2017

Nelson, Susan

MAKE A SPLASH: Bathrooms done up in unexpected colors, patterns, and accessories will make you forget basic, boring white M. M. Kashino *Washingtonian Magazine* v52 no12 p130 S 2017

Nelson, Tara-Nicholle

Obsess Over Your Customers, Not Your Rivals *Harvard Business Review Digital Articles* p1 My 11 2017

Nelson, Tia

Climate Change, What Climate Change? B. Lueders color *Progressive* v81 no5 p43 Je/Jl 2017

Nelson, Tom

A Matter of Taste: The concerns and conflicts that shape our approach to food L. ABEND *New York Times Book Review* p14 Mr 5 2017

Nelson, Willie, 1933-

Singers and Songwriters bw cartoon color *American Cowboy* p22 LEGENDS OF TEXAS Special Issue 2017

STEM CELL THERAPY AND WILLIE NELSON: Rebels by Their Own Rules M. Reinstetle *Saturday Evening Post* v289 no2 p92 Mr/Ap 2017

Nelson, Willie, 1933----Interviews

Willie Nelson P. DOYLE *Rolling Stone* no1288 p18 Je 1 2017

Nelson Byrd Woltz Landscape Architects (Company)

Buckhead Park Over GA400 *Architectural Record* v205 no4 p214 Ap 2017

Nelsons, Andris, 1978-

Contemporary Boston R. Platt cartoon *New Yorker* v93 no3 p15 Mr 6 2017

Nelson-Selby, Carol

Driving Home the Safety Discussion il *Consumer Reports* v82 no9 p6 S 2017

Nemcova, Petra

WOMEN ON THE GO color *Harper's Bazaar* no3651 p305 Mr 2017

Neme, Maximiliano

Phytochrome B integrates light and temperature signals in Arabidopsis bibl graph *Science* v354 no6314 p897 N 18 2016

Nemer, Mona

NEWSMAKERS *Science* v357 no6358 p1333 S 29 2017

Nemeth, P.

An unusual white dwarf star may be a surviving remnant of a subluminous Type Ia supernova chart diag *Science* v357 no6352 p680 Ag 18 2017

Nemeth, Zoltan

People B. Dooley *Christian Century* v134 no12 p19 Je 7 2017

Nemis, Sabrina

MOST COLLEGIAL color *Maclean's* v129 no47 p23 N 28 2016

Putting Canada on the map color map *Canadian Geographic* v137 no4 p24 Jl/Ag 2017

NEMKO, MARTY

The Accidental Career Coach *Psychology Today* v49 no5 p48 S/O 2016

Nemmers, Adam

Imagining Sovereignty: Self- Determination in American Indian Law and Literature *American Indian Quarterly* v41 no2 p195 Spr 2017

Nemo, Leslie

Change of Heartbeat diag *Scientific American* v317 no3 p17 S 2017

Moving a Giant color *Scientific American* v317 no4 p26 O 2017

Quick Hits map *Scientific American* v317 no3 p20 S 2017

Nemtsov, Boris, 1959-2015

A Defender Of His Country J. NORDLINGER color *National Review* v69 no7 p22 Ap 17 2017

Nenes, Athanasios

Global atmospheric particle formation from CERN CLOUD measurements bibl graph map *Science* v354 no6316 p1119 D 2 2016

Nengudi, Senga

Center Stage bw *Art in America* v105 no5 p51 My 2017

Neo-Nazis—Computer network resources

Don't Kick Neo-Nazis Off the Internet *Bloomberg Businessweek* no4537 p14 S 11 2017

Neo-Nazism

The 'N' Word K. D. WILLIAMSON color *National Review* v69 no17 p22 S 11 2017

TO UNDERSTAND THIS NEW RIGHT, IT HELPS TO SEE IT NOT AS A FRINGE MOVEMENT, BUT A POWERFUL COUNTERCULTURE N. MALONE, M. Read et al img *New York* v50 no9 p24 My 1 2017

WHAT ARE THE ROOTS OF THIS RAGE?: A few theories, not all of them having to do entirely with race *New York* v50 no9 p42 My 1 2017

WHICH IS WHY THE MOVEMENT EXPRESSES ITSELF IS WAY: Memes of the alt-right img *New York* v50 no9 p36 My 1 2017

Neo-Nazism—Social aspects

Denouncing the evil lie of white supremacy *Christian Century* v134 no19 p7 S 13 2017

Neoarchaean

Building Archean cratons from Hadean mafic crust J. O'Neil and R. W. Carlson bibl graph *Science* v355 no6330 p1199 Mr 17 2017

Neoclassicism (Architecture)

Golden Age of Classicism: Notre Dame's architecture school is rebuilding the traditional city L. MCCRARY il *American Conservative* v16 no4 p48 Jl/Ag 2017

Neodymium

Nanophotonic rare-earth quantum memory with optically controlled retrieval T. Zhong, J. M. Kindem et al diag graph *Science* v357 no6358 p1392 S 29 2017

Neodymium isotopes

Rocks retain bits of Earth's early crust T. SUMNER color *Science News* v191 no7 p8 Ap 15 2017

Neoliberalism

As the Anglo-American right adopts the slogans of the left, it sounds the death knell of the neoliberal economic order it built. But what comes next? P. Mishra *New York Times Magazine* p14 Je 25 2017

Zombie Ideology S. LEONARD *Nation* v304 no16 p3 My 22 2017

Neoliberalism—Latin America

Indigenous Empowerment in Evo Morales's Bolivia J. CRABTREE *Current History* v116 no787 p55 F 2017

Neolithic period—Europe

The Temple Builders of Malta E. A. POWELL color *Archaeology* v69 no6 p38 N/D 2016

Neolithic period—Italy

ARTIFACT J. A. LOBELL color *Archaeology* v70 no1 p68 Ja/F 2017

Neon lighting

LAS VEGAS REVISITED B. O'Doherty bw color *Art in America* v104 no11 p96 D 2016

Neonatal abstinence syndrome

HOOKED AT BIRTH color *National Geographic* v232 no3 p54 S 2017

SHAKY START [Cover story] M. Rosen color graph map *Science News* v191 no11 p16 Je 10 2017

Neonatal intensive care

Ask the Expert R. Allen *Atlanta* v56 no7 p220 N 2016

Neonicotinoids

CHAIN REACTION E. Royte *Audubon* v119 no1 p38 Spr 2017

A cocktail of toxins J. T. Kerr color diag map *Science* v356 no6345 p1331 Je 30 2017

European bee study fuels debate over pesticide ban E. Stokstad color *Science* v356 no6345 p1321 Je 30 2017

Neonicotinoids found in honey globally [Cover story] L. HAMERS *Science News* v192 no7 p16 O 28 2017

'Neonics' and Other Pesticides C. CALLAGHAN color *Canadian Wildlife* v23 no2 p44 My/Je 2017

Nerve agents in honey C. N. Connolly color diag *Science* v357 no6359 p38 O 6 2017

A worldwide survey of neonicotinoids in honey E. A. D. Mitchell, B. Mulhauser et al graph *Science* v357 no6359 p109 O 6 2017

Neonicotinoids—Environmental aspects

Chronic exposure to neonicotinoids reduces honey bee health near corn crops N. Tsvetkov, O. Samson-Robert et al diag *Science* v356 no6345 p1395 Je 30 2017

Country-specific effects of neonicotinoid pesticides on honey bees and wild bees B. A. Woodcock, J. M. Bullock et al diag map *Science* v356 no6345 p1393 Je 30 2017

Neoplatonism

AWAITING ARMAGEDDON A. Wallach color *Art in America* v104 no10 p108 N 2016

Nephew, Tim

Targeting TRACTORS *Mother Earth News* no284 p18 O/N 2017

Nephews

Learning CURVE C. Kitchener color *Vogue* v207 no4 p116 Ap 2017

Your True Stories IN 100 WORDS L. LESHAW, L. ALBRECHT et al color *Reader's Digest* v189 no1129 p25 Ap 2017

NEPORADNY, JOHN, JR.

float & live color *Cabin Living* p80 Ja/F 2017

Nepotism

FIRST FAMILIES R. BROOKHISER bw color *American History* v52 no4 p20 O 2017

Is it acceptable to hire your sister? *People Management* p53 My 2017

Neptune (Planet)

HAT-P-26b: A Neptune-mass exoplanet with a well-constrained heavy element abundance H. R. Wakeford, D. K. Sing et al chart diag graph *Science* v356 no6338 p628 My 12 2017

The unsolved mysteries of the ICE GIANTS K. Haynes bw color *Astronomy* v45 no10 p46 O 2017

Nerds (Persons)

Geek Love K. PATTERSON cartoon *Walrus* v13 no10 p54 D 2016

MOST LIKELY TO NERD OUT M. Devash bw color *Women's Health* v14 no6 p107 Jl 2017

Nereim, Vivian

A Building Collapse in the Desert color *Bloomberg Businessweek* no4538 p32 S 18 2017

THE HIJACKING OF THE BRILLANTE VIRTUOSO color map *Bloomberg Businessweek* no4532 p48 Jl 31 2017

Nerem, Robert M.

Research integrity revisited color *Science* v356 no6334 p115 Ap 14 2017

Neren, Uri

How Avaya Turned Around Its Customer Ratings *Harvard Business Review Digital Articles* p2 O 25 2016

NERF toys

#SQUAD GOALS C. VAN BUSEN *Atlanta* v56 no9 p118 Ja 2017

Nero, Patrick

THE CATCH AT McNENNY: Where South Dakota hatches trout, salmon and researchers P. HIGBEE *South Dakota Magazine* v33 no2 p48 Jl/Ag 2017

Neruda (Film)

BETWEEN the LINES A. CHAN color *Film Comment* v52 no6 p72 N/D 2016

A Love Poem to Neruda M. ATKINSON *In These Times* v41 no1 p37 Ja 2017

THE STATE THAT I AM IN J. TEODORO bw color *Film Comment* v52 no6 p42 N/D 2016

Nerve block

LIDOCAINE NERVE BLOCKS CAN BE TRICKY C. Barakat and M. McCluskey *Equus* no482 p12 N 2017

Nerve Growth Factor

Nanomaterials for stimulating nerve growth S. Marchesan, L. Ballerini et al color *Science* v356 no6342 p1010 Je 9 2017

Nerves

See also

Neuroglia

Synapses

RESURRECTION R. Story bw color *Skiing* p66 Wint 2017

Nervous system

See also

Neural circuitry

Neurons

MEET YOUR CHAKRAS Zya color *Essence* v48 no5 p116 S 2017

Nervous system—Diseases—Treatment

Antisense rescues babies from killer disease M. Wadman color diag *Science* v354 no6318 p1359 D 16 2016

Injectable Wires for Fixing the Brain J. Sklar bw color *MIT Technology Review* v119 no6 p104 N/D 2016

Nervous system—Wounds & injuries—Treatment

REVERSING Paralysis A. REGALADO color *MIT Technology Review* v120 no2 p82 Mr/Ap 2017

Nery, Joseph R.

Single-cell methylomes identify neuronal subtypes and regulatory elements in mammalian cortex diag *Science* v357 no6351 p600 Ag 11 2017

A transcription factor hierarchy defines an environmental stress response network diag *Science* v354 no6312 p598 N 4 2016

Nery, Scot

Secret Circus D. ROTHBART *Los Angeles Magazine* p86 Ap 2017

Nesbø, Jo—Interviews

Jo Nesbø *New York Times Book Review* p8 My 14 2017

NESBIT, JOANNA

baring it all *Parents* v91 no10 p138 O 2016

Nesbitt, Brenda

How My Horse De-Stresses Me color *Horse & Rider* v55 no12 p72 D 2016

NESELOVSKYI, VADIM

Improvising Freely Over Complex Left-Hand Keyboard Figures color *Downbeat* v84 no9 p92 S 2017

Nesmith, Michael, 1942-

Infinite Tuesday: An Autobiographical Riff *Publishers Weekly* v264 no5 p190 Ja 30 2017

Ness, Erik

Communities Take the Lead in Battling Frac Sand Mines color *Progressive* v81 no5 p19 Je/Jl 2017

Ness, Patti

Around the Campfire color *Trail Rider* v29 no1 p6 Ja/F 2017

Nest building

MONITORING NESTING BIRDS *New York State Conservationist* v71 no5 p10 Ap 2017

The Mouse Parent Trap A. Marks color *Scientific American* v317 no1 p16 Jl 2017

MURRAY M. TERRA-BERNS *Idaho Magazine* v16 no6 p32 Mr 2017

Nest Labs Inc.

RETURNING TO THE NEST A. Lashinsky color *Fortune* v175 no5 p22 Ap 1 2017

A Smarter Way to Heat and Cool Your Home P. M. ESSWEIN color *Kiplinger's Personal Finance* v70 no12 p39 D 2016

Nester, William R.

Titan: The Art of British Power in the Age of Revolution and Napoléon T. Zacharis *Military History* v33 no5 p74 Ja 2017

Nesterova, Tatyana B.

PCGF3/5–PRC1 initiates Polycomb recruitment in X chromosome inactivation color *Science* v356 no6342 p1081 Je 9 2017

Nestlé SA

emporium color *Dressage Today* v24 no1 p64 O 2017

The Nestlé Bottled Water Cycle C. Winter cartoon color *Bloomberg Businessweek* no4539 p56 S 25 2017

Purina Donates Timely Feed color *Trail Rider* v29 no2 p10 Mr 2017

Nestler, Eric J.

Early life stress confers lifelong stress susceptibility in mice via ventral tegmental area OTX2 diag *Science* v356 no6343 p1185

Je 16 2017

Nestola, Fabrizio

Large gem diamonds from metallic liquid in Earth's deep mantle bibl color *Science* v354 no6318 p1403 D 16 2016

Nestor, Danny

A Trip West bw color *American Cowboy* v23 no6 p10 Ap/My 2017

Nestor, James

GET CLEAN or DIE TRYING color diag *Scientific American* v315 no5 p62 N 2016

Net Irrigate LLC

WIRELESS WATCHDOG A. McConnell and L. Bedord *Successful Farming* v115 no3 p25 Mid-F 2017

NET Power LLC

FOSSIL POWER, GUILT FREE R. F. Service color diag *Science* v356 no6340 p796 My 26 2017

Net present value

A Refresher on Internal Rate of Return A. Gallo *Harvard Business Review Digital Articles* p2 Mr 17 2016

A Refresher on Net Present Value A. Gallo *Harvard Business Review Digital Articles* p2 N 19 2014

What Net Present Value Can't Tell You M. Wessel *Harvard Business Review Digital Articles* p2 N 20 2014

Net worth

CONVERSATION A. WILSON color *Forbes* v199 no4 p30 Ap 25 2017

NO COMMENT cartoon *Progressive* v81 no10 p8 N 2016

Net worth—News briefs

LeaderBoard color *Forbes* v198 no7 p28 N 29 2016

Netanel, Neil Weinstock

Thou Shalt Not Reprint R. R. KWALL *Commentary* v142 no2 p58 S 2016

Netanyahu, Binyamin, 1949-

After Netanyahu N. ROGACHEVSKY color *Weekly Standard* v23 no6 p32 O 16 2017

Assessing Bibi S. CHESTER *Commentary* v142 no4 p14 N 2016

Bibi the Strategist: A close look at Benjamin Netanyahu's foreign policy reveals an underappreciated and misunderstood record of accomplishment L. Berman *Commentary* v142 no2 p33 S 2016

Bibi the Strategist *Commentary* v142 no1 p1 Jl/Ag 2016

A Big Deal? E. Abrams color *Weekly Standard* v22 no24 p9 F 27 2017

Cigars, Bubbly, and Subs Haunt Netanyahu J. Ferziger and D. Wainer *Bloomberg Businessweek* no4540 p35 O 2 2017

ISRAEL HAS A BRIGHT FUTURE AT THE UNITED NATIONS *Vital Speeches of the Day* v82 no12 p368 D 2016

Netanyahu, the Almost-American: Bibi's unique feel for the United States hasn't always paid off S. Mandel *Commentary* v142 no2 p40 S 2016

Netanyahu, the Almost-American *Commentary* v142 no1 p1 Jl/Ag 2016

Netanyahu, the AlmostAmerican *Commentary* v142 no2 p1 S 2016

There's Too Much Speech in Israel! *Commentary* v142 no2 p1 S 2016

There Will Be Nothing Found Because There Is Nothing There: AN UNPRECEDENTED, OBSESSIVE WITCH HUNT *Vital Speeches of the Day* v83 no9 p260 S 2017

THIS CONFLICT IS NOT ABOUT HOUSES *Vital Speeches of the Day* v83 no2 p40 F 2017

TURNING WORDS INTO POLICIES: THE TRUMP ADMINISTRATION IS SHOWING ITS COMMITMENT TO ISRAEL *Vital Speeches of the Day* v83 no5 p146 My 2017

Netessine, Serguei

A Lean Startup Approach to International Development *Harvard Business Review Digital Articles* p2 D 11 2014

Netflix Inc.

13 REED HASTINGS M. Lev-Ram color *Fortune* v174 no7 p87 D 1 2016

Apple TV gets cozy with Amazon Prime, so where does that leave Netflix? J. NEWMAN color *PCWorld* v35 no7 p50 Jl 2017

The Download on Netflix M. ANTONOFF color *Sound & Vision* v82 no4 p25 My 2017

FULLER HOUSE GETS FESTIVE A. D'ARMINIO *TV Guide* p24 D 5 2016

How Netflix's Content Strategy Is Reshaping Movie Culture D. Gilchrist and M. Luca *Harvard Business Review Digital Articles* p2 Ag 31 2017

How to watch Netflix offline on your PC I. PAUL color *PCWorld* v35 no6 p155 Je 2017

The Intersection color *Runner's World* v52 no8 p54 S 2017

NETFLIX PRESENTS BUILDING A WORLD OF BINGE-WATCHERS L. Shaw and F. Gillette color *Bloomberg Businessweek* no4507 p40 Ja 16 2017

Netflix Zombies N. ROBEHMED bw *Forbes* v199 no7 p98 Je 29 2017

What Netflix and Starbucks Know About Cash Flow Eddie Yoon *Harvard Business Review Digital Articles* p2 Ja 22 2015

Netflix Inc.—Charts, diagrams, etc.

Stand-Up Finds a Home on Netflix A. Hoffman color *Time* v189 no10 p52 Mr 20 2017

Netherlands

Ever More Divided Union color *Time* v189 no10 p36 Mr 20 2017

Rare Gems Stand Out at North Sea Fest D. Ouellette color *Downbeat* v84 no9 p21 S 2017

Netherlands—Politics & government—21st century

Blame Automation, Not Immigration M. Champion and A. van der Schoot color *Bloomberg Businessweek* no4513 p30 Mr 6 2017

Netrebko, Anna, 1971-

Anna Netrebko: Verismo J. S. Lessner *Opera News* v81 no9 p54 Mr 2017

Nets—Evaluation

Playing It Safe: Orchestra Pit Safety Net Systems from InCord. Ltd *Stage Directions* v30 no3 p38 Mr 2017

Netter, Sarah

Cajun Son: A Louisiana native has spent his career working to save the state's coastline and the communities he loves *Sierra* v102 no4 p24 Jl/Ag 2017

Nettleton, Pamela Hill

A good critic: Film critic Roger Ebert made himself his own life project color *U.S. Catholic* v82 no8 p45 Ag 2017

Table for two color *U.S. Catholic* v81 no12 p38 D 2016

Urban presence [Cover story] color *U.S. Catholic* v82 no1 p25 Ja 2017

Who runs the world? color *U.S. Catholic* v82 no6 p38 Je 2017

A woman at last: In Wonder Woman, accomplishment trumps beauty color *U.S. Catholic* v82 no9 p38 S 2017

Women's work color *U.S. Catholic* v82 no3 p38 Mr 2017

NETTO, DAVID

Kitchens color *Architectural Digest* no11 p73 N 1 2017

Perfect Fit color *Architectural Digest* v74 no10 p120 O 1 2017

WARM WELCOME color *Architectural Digest* v73 no11 p182 N 2016

Network-attached storage

Back up all your data—and we mean all of it—to your NAS box without installing any software J. L. JACOBI color *Macworld - Digital Edition* v34 no4 p86 My 2017

Network hubs

DODOCOOL DC30 7-IN-1 USB-C HUB: AFFORDABLE HUB WITH PASSTHROUGH POWER ALONGSIDE THREE USB TYPE-A PORTS G. FLEISHMAN color *Macworld - Digital Edition* p30 Je 13 2017

MANAGING OUR HUB ECONOMY: STRATEGY, ETHICS, AND NETWORK COMPETITION IN THE AGE OF DIGITAL SUPERPOWERS M. IANSITI and K. R. LAKHANI color diag graph img *Harvard Business Review* v95 no5 p84 S/O 2017

SATECHI ALUMINUM USB 3.0 HUB + CARD READER: EASY ACCESS TO USB 3 PORTS FOR YOUR MAC R. LOYOLA color *Macworld - Digital Edition* p29 Mr 2017

Network neutrality

Net Neutrality Rules Will Make Winners and Losers Out of Businesses S. Greenstein, M. Peitz et al *Harvard Business Review Digital Articles* p2 Je 27 2016

The Tangled Web of Net Neutrality and Regulation L. Downes *Harvard Business Review Digital Articles* p2 Mr 31 2017

Network neutrality—Government policy

Time for Some Traffic Problems on Netflix? J. Brustein *Bloomberg Businessweek* no4500 p34 N 21 2016

Net worth—Charts, diagrams, etc.

THE BIGGEST chart *Money* v46 no1 p115 Ja/F 2017

Trump's Gilded Team A. Abrams color diag *Time* v189 no3 p37 Ja 30 2017

Neu, Brad

THE SECRETS TO Floor Plan Perfection diag *Log Home Living* v34 no1 p44 F 2017

Neubert, Michael G.

Physiological and ecological drivers of early spring blooms of a coastal phytoplankter bibl graph *Science* v354 no6310 p326 O 21 2016

Neubig, Megan E.

A catalytic fluoride-rebound mechanism for C(sp3)-CF3 bond formation diag *Science* v356 no6344 p1272 Je 23 2017

NEUDING, PAULINA

See No Evil color *Weekly Standard* v22 no20 p18 Ja 30 2017

The Truth About Sweden color *Weekly Standard* v22 no26 p27 Mr 13 2017

Neuditschko, Markus

Ancient genomic changes associated with domestication of the horse color diag *Science* v356 no6336 p442 Ap 28 2017

Neuer, Manuel, 1986-

Manuel Neuer M. Hagan color *Current Biography* v78 no5 p73 My 2017

Neufeld, Josh

THE TRUMP-RUSSIA MEMOS cartoon *Columbia Journalism Review* v56 no2 p89 Fall 2017

NEUFELD, JOSIAH

Mennonite Pride cartoon *Walrus* v13 no9 p48 N 2016

Neufeld, Michael J.

How to Make a Spaceship *Physics Today* v70 no6 p62 Je 2017

Neugeboren, Jay

Take Me to Bellevue color *New York Review of Books* v64 no1 p19 Ja 19 2017

The Ultimate Pawn Sacrifice *American Scholar* v86 no2 p86 Spr 2017

Neugeboren, Robert, 1943-2015

The Ultimate Pawn Sacrifice J. NEUGEBOREN *American Scholar* v86 no2 p86 Spr 2017

Neuhaus, Cable

BOOKS OF KNOWLEDGE *Saturday Evening Post* v289 no5 p14 S/O 2017

THE COLLECTORS *Saturday Evening Post* v289 no3 p14 My/Je 2017

Love and Haight: In the brief span of a summer, an effervescent cultural revolution based on sex, drugs, rock 'n' roll, and, you know, pure love, was taking place in the tiny pocket of San Francisco known as Haight-Ashbury. By October of '67, the... *Saturday Evening Post* v289 no4 p32 Jl/Ag 2017

THE ME PROJECT *Saturday Evening Post* v289 no2 p12 Mr/Ap 2017

THE PICKUP TRUCK MYSTIQUE *Saturday Evening Post* v288 no6 p16 N/D 2016

SMARTPHONE DENIERS *Saturday Evening Post* v289 no1 p14 Ja/F 2017

TV SKILLS: Ever dream of being on television? Here's where you go to learn how to sound like an expert *Saturday Evening Post* v289 no4 p16 Jl/Ag 2017

Neumann, Ann

The Good Death: An Exploration of Dying in America S. Moses *Christian Century* v134 no1 p39 Ja 4 2017

Neumann, Barbara

Making SDGs Work for Climate Change Hotspots bibl *Environment* v58 no6 p24 N/D 2016

Neumann, Gregory A.

Gravity field of the Orientale basin from the Gravity Recovery and Interior Laboratory Mission bibl graph *Science* v354 no6311 p438 O 28 2016

Neumann, Peter R.

Can Bankers Fight Terrorism? *Foreign Affairs* v96 no6 p144 N/D 2017

Don't Follow the Money color *Foreign Affairs* v96 no4 p93 Jl/Ag 2017

Neumann, Philipp

Nanoscale nuclear magnetic resonance with chemical resolution diag *Science* v357 no6346 p67 Jl 7 2017

NEUMANN, SCOTT

Rhythmic Approaches To Improvisation color diag *Downbeat* v83 no11 p74 N 2016

Neumark, Heidi

My incarcerated nephew, the guest of honor color *Christian Century* v134 no8 p1 Ap 12 2017

Neumeier, John—Interviews

John Neumeier: Hamburg Ballet's artistic director brings his work back to the Midwest L. WARNECKE *Dance Magazine* v91 no9 p22 S 2017

Neumont, Maurice, 1868-1930

ARMS RACE map *MHQ: Quarterly Journal of Military History* v29 no4 p22 Summ 2017

Neuner, Sophie

Gating of social reward by oxytocin in the ventral tegmental area color graph *Science* v357 no6358 p1406 S 29 2017

Neupert, Titus

Robust spin-polarized midgap states at step edges of topological crystalline insulators bibl graph *Science* v354 no6317 p1269 D 9 2016

Neural circuitry

AI's early proving ground: the hunt for new particles A. Cho color *Science* v357 no6346 p20 Jl 7 2017

A central neural circuit for itch sensation D. Mu, J. Deng et al color graph *Science* v357 no6352 p695 Ag 18 2017

Encoding vocal culture O. Tchernichovski and D. Lipkind bibl color *Science* v354 no6317 p1234 D 9 2016

Engrams and circuits crucial for systems consolidation of a memory T. Kitamura, S. K. Ogawa et al diag *Science* v356 no6333 p73 Ap 7 2017

Fired Up A. PATUREL color *Discover* v38 no3 p26 Ap 2017

Mental health chief to stress neural circuits M. Wadman color *Science* v354 no6311 p405 O 28 2016

Neural circuits for pain: Recent advances and current views C. Peirs and R. P. Seal bibl diag *Science* v354 no6312 p578 N 4 2016

Neural codes

Saving Face K. Sheikh bw color *Scientific American* v317 no2 p12 Ag 2017

Neural conduction

Wire together, fire apart J. Krupic diag *Science* v357 no6355 p974 S 8 2017

Neural development

Adding depth to cell culture K. Powell color *Science* v356 no6333 p96 Ap 7 2017

Brain Trust [Cover story] K. G. Noble color graph *Scientific American* v316 no3 p44 Mr 2017

Extensive migration of young neurons into the infant human frontal lobe M. F. Paredes, D. James et al color diag graph *Science* v354 no6308 paaf7073-1 O 7 2016

LAB-BUILT BRAINS [Cover story] J. A. Knoblich color *Scientific American* v316 no1 p26 Ja 2017

MAPPING THE BRAIN *New York Times Upfront* v149 no4 p20 O 31 2016

Microstructural proliferation in human cortex is coupled with the development of face processing J. Gomez, M. A. Barnett et al bibl graph *Science* v355 no6320 p1 Ja 6 2017

Sensory overload hurts young brains L. SANDERS *Science News* v190 no12 p12 D 10 2016

Neural networks (Computer science)

Machine learning for quantum physics M. R. Hush bibl diag *Science* v355 no6325 p580 F 10 2017

Solving the quantum many-body problem with artificial neural networks G. Carleo and M. Troyer bibl diag *Science* v355 no6325 p602 F 10 2017

US AND HIS KINGDOM OF THE FLUBBINGS OF SHADOWS J. SHANE cartoon color *Wired* v25 no10 p22 O 2017

Neural networks (Neurobiology)

Causal neural network of metamemory for retrospection in primates Kentaro Miyamoto, Takahiro Osada et al bibl diag graph *Science* v355 no6321 p1 Ja 13 2017

Interactions between brain and spinal cord mediate value effects in nocebo hyperalgesia A. Tinnermann, S. Geuter et al color *Science* v357 no6359 p105 O 6 2017

Neural stem cells

Hypothalamic regulation of regionally distinct adult neural stem cells and neurogenesis A. Paul, Z. Chaker et al diag *Science* v356 no6345 p1383 Je 30 2017

On the Brain's Path B. Lang *Discover* v38 no8 p6 O 2017

Neural stem cells—Therapeutic use

What Once Was Lost L. MARSA color *Discover* v38 no8 p32 O 2017

Neural transmission

See also

Synapses

Cryo-EM structures of the triheteromeric NMDA receptor and its allosteric modulation W. Lü, J. Du et al graph *Science* v355 no6331 p1282 Mr 24 2017

Neural tube

Decoding of position in the developing neural tube from antiparallel morphogen gradients M. Zagorski, Y. Tabata et al diag *Science* v356 no6345 p1379 Je 30 2017

Neurobehavioral disorders

HIDDEN INVADERS P. WEINTRAUB cartoon color diag *Discover* v38 no3 p46 Ap 2017

Intersection of diverse neuronal genomes and neuropsychiatric disease: The Brain Somatic Mosaicism Network M. J. McConnell, J. V. Moran et al color *Science* v356 no6336 p395 Ap 28 2017

Neurobehavioral disorders—Research

Target for Preventing Long-Term Effects *USA Today Magazine* v145 no2861 p13 F 2017

Neurobiologists

Howard Eichenbaum (1947–2017) M. Hasselmo and C. Stern color *Science* v357 no6354 p875 S 1 2017

Neurodegeneration

The Body Electric S. ORNES color diag *Discover* v38 no6 p94 Jl/Ag 2017

THE BRAIN OF BEN BARRES K. MILLER color diag *Discover* v38 no7 p58 S 2017

Vitamin B3 modulates mitochondrial vulnerability and prevents glaucoma in aged mice P. A. Williams, J. M. Harder et al bibl graph *Science* v355 no6326 p756 F 17 2017

Neurofibromatosis 2—Patients

HACK YOUR DNA AND 19 OTHER WAYS TO BE YOUR OWN DOCTOR G. RUBENSTEIN cartoon color *Men's Health* v32 no9 p114 N 2017

Neuroglia

Building bridges to regenerate axons P. R. Williams and Zhigang He bibl color diag *Science* v354 no6312 p544 N 4 2016

Glia put visual map in sync J. Isaacman-Beck and T. R. Clandinin color *Science* v357 no6354 p867 S 1 2017

Glia relay differentiation cues to coordinate neuronal development in Drosophila V. M. Fernandes, Z. Chen et al color *Science* v357 no6354 p886 S 1 2017

HOW TO DELETE PORN FROM YOUR BRAIN T. WILES color *Christianity Today* p11 Ap 2017

Neurological research

Giving Proof: It turns out that generosity really can make us happier G. Reynolds *New York Times Magazine* p16 S 17 2017

Neurologists

I sometimes call my children by other family members' names S. Yeager cartoon *AARP: The Magazine* v60 no3A p18 Ap/My 2017

Is the Pain in Your BRAIN? J. Thompson color *O, The Oprah Magazine* p86 F 2017

Neurology

See also

Electrophysiology

Inhibition

CAN NUTRITION CHANGE YOUR PERSONALITY? K. James chart color *Amazing Wellness* v9 no1 p48 Wint 2017

Screen Savers *Virginia Living* v15 no1 p105 D 2016

Neuron analysis

Neurons that drive and quench thirst C. Gizowski and C. W. Bourque color diag *Science* v357 no6356 p1092 S 15 2017

Neurons

See also

Neural stem cells

30 Cool THINGS ABOUT SOUND A. SILEN *National Geographic Kids* no468 p22 Mr 2017

Active cortical dendrites modulate perception Naoya Takahashi, T. G. Oertner et al bibl graph *Science* v354 no6319 p1587 D 23 2016

BOOST YOUR BRAIN POWER [Cover story] S. Klein color *Prevention* v69 no9 p68 O 2017

Brain waves fight Alzheimer's protein L. SANDERS color *Science News* v191 no1 p13 Ja 21 2017

Branch-specific plasticity of a bifunctional dopamine circuit encodes protein hunger Q. Liu, M. Tabuchi et al graph *Science* v356 no6337 p534 My 5 2017

BUNDLED UP E. MASTROIANNI color *Discover* v38 no6 p14 Jl/Ag 2017

BURST THE HEALTH BUBBLE! G. Hamadey color *Women's Health* v14 no8 p102 O 2017

Clearing Memory A. Braun color *Natural History* v125 no4 p8 Ap 2017

Conversion of object identity to object-general semantic value in the primate temporal cortex K. Tamura, M. Takeda et al color graph *Science* v357 no6352 p687 Ag 18 2017

How the body learns to hurt E. Underwood color *Science* v354 no6313 p694 N 11 2016

Human brains teach us a surprising lesson M. McKenzie and G. Fishell bibl color *Science* v354 no6308 p38 O 7 2016

Midbrain dopamine neurons control judgment of time S. Soares, B. V. Atallah et al bibl graph *Science* v354 no6317 p1273 D 9 2016

RESEARCH color *Science* v356 no6336 p392 Ap 28 2017

Ring attractor dynamics in the Drosophila central brain S. S. Kim, H. Rouault et al diag graph *Science* v356 no6340 p849 My 26 2017

Single-cell methylomes identify neuronal subtypes and regulatory elements in mammalian cortex C. Luo, C. L. Keown et al diag *Science* v357 no6351 p600 Ag 11 2017

Thirst-associated preoptic neurons encode an aversive motivational drive W. E. Allen, L. A. Denardo et al diag *Science* v357 no6356 p1149 S 15 2017

Wire together, fire apart J. Krupic diag *Science* v357 no6355 p974 S 8 2017

Neuropharmacology

Deconstructing behavioral neuropharmacology with cellular specificity B. C. Shields, E. Kahuno et al color *Science* v356 no6333 p42 Ap 7 2017

Neurophysiology

See also

Brain physiology

Neural conduction

Neuroplasticity

Improvisation helps reveal our inner lives L. Sanders color *Science News* v192 no6 p21 O 14 2017

Mouse with a milkshake: Behavioral windows into brain function C. Smith color *Science* v354 no6312 p638 N 4 2016

Neuroplasticity

Flex Time [Cover story] L. Sanders color diag graph *Science News* v192 no4 p22 S 16 2017

RESEARCH color *Science* v356 no6340 p816 My 26 2017

Neuroscience equipment

new products color *Science* v356 no6345 p1402 Je 30 2017

Neurosciences

Completing a career G. Andrew Mickley color *Science* v356 no6337 p554 My 5 2017

Deconstructing behavioral neuropharmacology with cellular specificity B. C. Shields, E. Kahuno et al color *Science* v356 no6333 p42 Ap 7 2017

Love on the Mind D. HOWARD color *Prevention* v69 no6 p30 Je 2017

The mystery of faith and science color *U.S. Catholic* v81 no11 p18 N 2016

Scratching is catching in mice S. MILIUS *Science News* v191 no7 p8 Ap 15 2017

A Sense of Our Own B. Lang *Discover* v38 no9 p6 N 2017

WHAT THE REVOLUTION IN NEUROSCIENCE WILL MEAN FOR M. REIMERS *Humanist* v77 no2 p27 Mr/Ap 2017

Neurosciences—Equipment & supplies—Evaluation

NEW PRODUCTS: NEUROTECHNIQUES color *Science* v354 no6312 p641 N 4 2016

Neurosciences—Research

CAN NEUROSCIENCE HELP US UNDERSTAND TRUST AT WORK?: INTERACTION P. J. ZAK, B. Henderson et al color *Harvard Business Review* v95 no2 p18 Mr/Ap 2017

Gene bivalency at Polycomb domains regulates cranial neural crest positional identity M. Minoux, S. Holwerda et al diag *Sci-*

ence v355 no6332 p1390 Mr 31 2017

Memory training rejiggers the brain L. SANDERS diag *Science News* v191 no6 p7 Ap 1 2017

Neuroscientists

Robin Mazumder S. DOYLE color *Canadian Geographic* v137 no3 p19 My 2017

"Scientists Make the Best Advocates" M. N. MITRA *Earth Island Journal* v32 no2 p45 Summ 2017

Who's influencing brain science? *Science* v354 no6314 p809 N 18 2016

Neuroses—History

Welcome to Dottyville E. Turner *History Today* v67 no4 p6 Ap 2017

Neurotechnology (Bioengineering)

The White House BRAIN Initiative *Congressional Digest* v96 no2 p5 F 1 2017

Neurotics—Medical care

Welcome to Dottyville E. Turner *History Today* v67 no4 p6 Ap 2017

Neurotoxic agents

Asymmetric synthesis of batrachotoxin: Enantiomeric toxins show functional divergence against NaV M. M. Logan, Tatsuya Toma et al bibl diag graph *Science* v354 no6314 p865 N 18 2016

RESEARCH color *Science* v357 no6357 p1250 S 22 2017

Neurotransmitters

Cryo-EM structures of the triheteromeric NMDA receptor and its allosteric modulation W. Lü, J. Du et al graph *Science* v355 no6331 p1282 Mr 24 2017

Peering into the Brain with Chemical Biosensors A. Chen color *Science & Technology Review* p16 O/N 2016

Problem Solved! [Cover story] R. LALIBERTE cartoon *Prevention* v69 no1 p18 Ja 2017

Neutrino detectors

NEUTRINO DETECTION GOES SMALL *Physics Today* v70 no10 p29 O 2017

Waiting for a Supernova E. Conover color diag *Science News* v191 no3 p24 F 18 2017

Neutrino mass

Massive machine gears up to weigh nearly massless particles: An experiment in Germany looks for missing electron energy to infer neutrino rest mass T. Feder *Physics Today* v70 no8 p26 Ag 2017

THE UNBEARABLE LIGHTNESS OF NEUTRINOS A. Cho color diag map *Science* v356 no6345 p1322 Je 30 2017

Neutrino scattering

Neutrinos caught bouncing off nuclei E. CONOVER color *Science News* v192 no3 p7 S 2 2017

Observation of coherent elastic neutrino-nucleus scattering D. Akimov, J. B. Albert et al diag *Science* v357 no6356 p1123 S 15 2017

Scattering neutrinos caught in the act [Cover story] J. M. Link color *Science* v357 no6356 p1098 S 15 2017

Neutrinos

AROUND THE WORLD color *Science* v357 no6349 p336 Jl 28 2017

Scattering neutrinos caught in the act [Cover story] J. M. Link color *Science* v357 no6356 p1098 S 15 2017

Triplet of high-energy neutrinos detected from unknown source E. Conover *Science News* v191 no6 p16 Ap 1 2017

Neutrogena Corp.

SKINFESSIONS color *Women's Health* v13 no10 p55 D 2016

When Eating "Healthy" MESSES WITH YOUR SKIN F. EMBLETON color *Seventeen* v76 no4 p48 Jl/Ag 2017

Neutron scattering

Neutron scattering in the proximate quantum spin liquid a-RuCl3 A. Banerjee, J. Yan et al bw diag *Science* v356 no6342 p1055 Je 9 2017

Neutron stars

In Good Company M. BARTUSIAK color *Natural History* v125 no10 p10 O 2017

The Inside Story of Neutron Stars F. Özel *Sky & Telescope* v134 no1 p16 Jl 2017

Pulsars at 50 still going strong [Cover story] C. R. James bw color diag graph *Astronomy* v45 no5 p22 My 2017

Neutrons

See also
Neutrinos

Neutron longevity remains elusive E. CONOVER *Science News* v191 no4 p13 Mr 4 2017

Nothin' But Neutrons S. PALUS color *Discover* v38 no1 p52 Ja/F 2017

Neutrophil immunology

Visualizing the function and fate of neutrophils in sterile injury and repair J. Wang, M. Hossain et al color graph *Science* v357 no6359 p111 O 6 2017

Neutrophils

Neutrophils take a round-trip H. Garner and K. E. de Visser diag *Science* v357 no6359 p42 O 6 2017

Neutze, Richard

A three-dimensional movie of structural changes in bacteriorhodopsin bibl diag graph *Science* v354 no6319 p1552 D 23 2016

NEUZIL, MARK

A BRIEF HISTORY OF THE CANOE: From postwar 'canoedling' to unplugging from our smartphones, the elegantly simple and efficient conveyance takes us back to simpler days *Saturday Evening Post* v289 no4 p82 Jl/Ag 2017

Nevada—Description & travel

NEVADA A. Kylie color *Canadian Geographic* v135 no6 p30 D 2015

Northern Nevada's Cowboy Culture G. R. SCHIAVINO map *American Cowboy* v23 no5 p45 F/Mr 2017

Nevada—Politics & government

Nevada Says ERA Yes!: Propelled by a record number of women lawmakers, the state becomes the 36th to ratify the Equal Rights Amendment--and the first in 40 years C. N. BAKER *Ms.* v27 no2 p8 Summ 2017

Nevada—Politics & government—21st century

Nevada voted twice for President Obama, but Republicans have spent millions trying to win its U.S. Senate seat—and perhaps the state I. Brekken color *Bloomberg Businessweek* no4498 p39 N 7 2016

Neve, Rachael L.

Early life stress confers lifelong stress susceptibility in mice via ventral tegmental area OTX2 diag *Science* v356 no6343 p1185 Je 16 2017

Never Gonna Give You Up (Music)

GREAT MOMENTS IN RICKROLLING C. Collis *Entertainment Weekly* no1435 p38 O 14 2016

Neves, E. G.

Persistent effects of pre-Columbian plant domestication on Amazonian forest composition bibl chart graph map *Science* v355 no6328 p925 Mr 3 2017

Neville, Chris

Korg monologue color *Downbeat* v84 no3 p114 Mr 2017

Roland RD-2000 color *Downbeat* v84 no9 p98 S 2017

ROLI Seaboard Rise color *Downbeat* v83 no12 p107 D 2016

Neville, Tim

COMEBACK KID? color *Skiing* p15 Wint 2017

A GIRL ON THE ROAD color *Skiing* p42 D 2016

Nevins, Dan

A home practice to awaken your inner warrior [Cover story] color *Yoga Journal* no293 p65 Ag 2017

Nevins, Sheila

Defending My Mother S. Nevins bw color *AARP: The Magazine* v60 no5A p61 Ag/S 2017

Nevinson, C. R. W. (Christopher Richard Wynne), 1889-1946

THE HARVEST OF BATTLE D. Stadtler cartoon *Military History* v34 no1 p56 My 2017

Nevsehir (Turkey)

HIDDEN FROM VIEW B. DONAHUE color *Archaeology* v70 no2 p48 Mr/Ap 2017

New, Mark

Making SDGs Work for Climate Change Hotspots bibl *Environment* v58 no6 p24 N/D 2016

New, Steve

Don't Set Process Without Input from Frontline Workers *Harvard Business Review Digital Articles* p2 Je 26 2015

McDonald's and the Challenges of a Modern Supply Chain *Harvard Business Review Digital Articles* p2 F 4 2015

New Atlantic Independent Booksellers Association

FALL REGIONALS NAVIGATE TURBULENT TIMES J.

ROSEN color *Publishers Weekly* v264 no36 p28 S 4 2017

New Audio LLC

FETISH ART ROCK L. STINSON color *Wired* v25 no4 p35 Ap 2017

New Balance Athletic Shoe Inc.

Day Glow color *Glamour* v115 no7 p26 Jl 2017

FOR YOUR FEET ONLY T. Newcomb color *Runner's World* v52 no4 p16 My 2017

SHOP TILL THEY DROP J. Surowiecki cartoon *New Yorker* v92 no44 p23 Ja 9 2017

SPEED RACERS J. DENGATE color *Runner's World* v52 no5 p36 Je 2017

New Belgium Brewing Co. Inc.

Growing Pains S. ADAMS color *Forbes* v200 no1 p35 Jl 27 2017

New business enterprises

4 Factors That Predict Startup Success, and One That Doesn't T. J. Marion *Harvard Business Review Digital Articles* p2 My 3 2016

THE 5 HOTTEST BLACK-OWNED BEAUTY TECH START-UPS S. Blodgett color *Black Enterprise* v47 no8 p28 Jl/Ag 2017

5 THINGS SILICON VALLEY START-UP SHOULD KNOW ABOUT FARMERS *Successful Farming* v115 no3 p33 Mid-F 2017

AFRICA'S NEW GENERATION OF INNOVATORS C. M. CHRISTENSEN, E. OJOMO et al color il img *Harvard Business Review* v95 no1 p128 Ja/F 2017

THE ANTI-UBER S. KOLHATKAR cartoon *New Yorker* v92 no32 p40 O 10 2016

The Barriers Big Companies Face When They Try to Act Like Lean Startups S. Kirsner *Harvard Business Review Digital Articles* p2 Ag 16 2016

Battling Giants A. TILLEY chart color *Forbes* v200 no1 p50 Jl 27 2017

BETTING ON AG L. Bedord *Successful Farming* v115 no3 p30 Mid-F 2017

Can Lemonade Lure Insurance Skeptics? R. Walker *Bloomberg Businessweek* no4503 p40 D 12 2016

Can You Predict a Startup's Success Based on the Concept Alone? W. Frick *Harvard Business Review Digital Articles* p2 S 10 2015

CHASING RAINBOWS E. Griffith color *Fortune* v175 no5 p39 Ap 1 2017

COME ON AND SHINE E. Griffith color *Fortune* v174 no6 p29 N 1 2016

The Different Reasons Men and Women Leave Their Successful Startups R. Justo color *Harvard Business Review Digital Articles* p2 F 8 2017

A Different Story from the Middle East: Entrepreneurs Building an Arab Tech Economy C. M. Schroeder bw *MIT Technology Review* v120 no5 p64 S/O 2017

Do Startups Really Create Lots of Good Jobs? D. Isenberg *Harvard Business Review Digital Articles* p2 Je 6 2016

EVERY PIVOT NEEDS A STORY il *Harvard Business Review* v95 no4 p24 Jl/Ag 2017

Fintech Companies Could Give Billions of People More Banking Options J. Kendall color *Harvard Business Review Digital Articles* p2 Ja 20 2017

Holla for Challah! J. Miller color *Bloomberg Businessweek* no4517 p67 Ap 3 2017

How a Startup Accelerator at Boston Children's Hospital Helps Launch Companies C. E. Small, M. Murphy et al color *Harvard Business Review Digital Articles* p2 Je 5 2017

How Decision Making Evolves as a Startup Grows B. Halligan *Harvard Business Review Digital Articles* p2 Mr 23 2016

How I Built a $2 Billion Company by Thinking Small J. Rodman *Harvard Business Review Digital Articles* p2 S 7 2016

How Israeli Startups Can Scale J. Bussgang and O. Stern *Harvard Business Review Digital Articles* p2 S 10 2015

How Morale Changes as a Startup Grows D. Niu and M. Roberge *Harvard Business Review Digital Articles* p2 Mr 24 2017

How Startup "Joiners" Are (and Aren't) Like Founders W. Frick *Harvard Business Review Digital Articles* p2 Jl 20 2015

How to Bring in a New CEO for Your Startup S. Dutia *Harvard Business Review Digital Articles* p2 F 29 2016

How to Know If Joining a Startup Is Right for You R. Knight *Harvard Business Review Digital Articles* p2 My 16 2016

Improving Innovation in Africa N. Ekekwe *Harvard Business Re-*

view *Digital Articles* p2 F 18 2015

Keep Austin ... Tough To Get Around? J. Brustein *Bloomberg Businessweek* no4515 p31 Mr 20 2017

The Limits of the Lean Startup Method T. Ladd *Harvard Business Review Digital Articles* p2 Mr 7 2016

Namaste Now try my herbal toothpaste P. R. Sanjai and B. Pradhan color graph *Bloomberg Businessweek* no4502 p27 D 5 2016

The Pill Freaks of Silicon Valley A. MORRIS img *New York* v49 no21 p56 O 17 2016

Private fusion machines aim to beat massive global effort D. Clery chart color *Science* v356 no6336 p360 Ap 28 2017

The Problem of Bolt-On Acquisitions in a Digital World J. Kolko *Harvard Business Review Digital Articles* p2 Jl 5 2016

A Recession Doesn't Mean Your Startup Can't Grow M. Roberge *Harvard Business Review Digital Articles* p2 F 24 2016

Research: The Gender Gap in Startup Success Disappears When Women Fund Women S. Raina *Harvard Business Review Digital Articles* p2 Jl 19 2016

RIDING THE WAVE [Cover story] B. R. REYNOLDS *Los Angeles Magazine* p88 F 2017

Scaling Customer Service as Your Startup Grows M. Redbord *Harvard Business Review Digital Articles* p2 S 11 2017

Self STARTERS *Atlanta* v57 no2 p118 Je 2017

Silicon Valley, USA V. Vara bw diag graph map *Wired* v25 no6 p76 Je 2017

A SOBERING REALIZATION L. Entis color *Fortune* v176 no5 p32 O 1 2017

Stalking the Next Zuckerberg L. Chapman color *Bloomberg Businessweek* no4502 p39 D 5 2016

Start Me Up ... or not *USA Today Magazine* v145 no2863 p12 Ap 2017

A STARTUP ON THE INSIDE I. Lapowsky color *Wired* v24 no11 p42 N 2016

Startups Can't Revolve Around Their Founders If They Want to Succeed R. Gulati and A. DeSantola *Harvard Business Review Digital Articles* p2 Mr 4 2016

Successful Startups Don't Make Money Their Primary Mission K. Laws *Harvard Business Review Digital Articles* p2 Jl 10 2015

Tech's Royal Kingmaker P. OLSON *Forbes* v199 no4 p42 Ap 25 2017

To Grow a Digital Business, Learn from the Startup Community J. Birkinshaw *Harvard Business Review Digital Articles* p2 Je 11 2015

The Top 20 Start-Up Accelerators in the U.S Y. Hochberg, S. Cohen et al *Harvard Business Review Digital Articles* p2 Mr 31 2015

TYING VCs TO SHAREHOLDERS D. Lyons color *Fortune* v75 no1 p51 Ja 1 2017

WARDENSVILLE TOWN CRIERS K. OLSEN *Washingtonian Magazine* v52 no12 p12 S 2017

"We're always glad it's Monday morning": Keeping things positive is key for the co-working start-up. But how can it stay happy as it goes global? *People Management* p20 Jl 2017

What Airbnb, Uber, and Alibaba Have in Common B. Libert, Y. (. Wind et al *Harvard Business Review Digital Articles* p2 N 20 2014

What It Takes to Build a Startup into a Brand M. J. Silverstein *Harvard Business Review Digital Articles* p2 Mr 9 2016

When Large Companies Are Better at Entrepreneurship than Startups C. Zook *Harvard Business Review Digital Articles* p2 D 27 2016

When Start-ups Should (and Shouldn't) Partner with Industry Leaders T. Bartman *Harvard Business Review Digital Articles* p2 O 9 2014

Why Are Startup Founders So Bad at Changing Their Own Companies? T. Klein *Harvard Business Review Digital Articles* p2 O 13 2017

Why Buying a Company Can Be Better than Starting One R. S. Ruback and R. Yudkoff *Harvard Business Review Digital Articles* p2 Ap 5 2016

Why Lawyers Make Good Early-Stage Startup Hires D. Doktori and S. Reed *Harvard Business Review Digital Articles* p2 My 2 2016

Why Startups Shouldn't Chase Media Buzz A. Zacharakis and A. Jno-Charles color *Harvard Business Review Digital Articles* p2 Je 5 2017

Why You Can't Just Tell a Company "Be More Like a Startup" S. Blank *Harvard Business Review Digital Articles* p2 Je 19 2017

YOU'LL LAUGH! CRY! (MAYBE BUY.) E. Griffith color *Fortune* v175 no8 p94 Je 15 2017

New business enterprises—California—Santa Clara Valley

SATELLITE PICS FOR CHEAP!! A. Vance bw *Bloomberg Businessweek* no4522 p37 My 15 2017

New business enterprises—China

Hong Kong and Shenzhen Band Together to Lure Startups N. Khan and E. Curran color *Bloomberg Businessweek* no4527 p44 Je 19 2017

New business enterprises—Finance

BETTING ON AI B. O'Keefe diag *Fortune* v175 no3 p144 Mr 1 2017

Brand Boys A. FELDMAN and J. BUCKINGHAM color *Forbes* v199 no2 p58 F 28 2017

Corporate VCs Are Moving the Goalposts il img *Harvard Business Review* v94 no11 p24 N 2016

Don't Expect New Crowdfunding Rules to Create a Startup Boom W. Frick *Harvard Business Review Digital Articles* p2 My 16 2016

LOOK BEFORE YOU LEAP D. Lyons color *Fortune* v174 no6 p34 N 1 2016

NEXT BILLION-DOLLAR STARTUPS color *Forbes* v198 no6 p94 N 8 2016

Startups Need Relationships Before They Ask for Money E. Baehr *Harvard Business Review Digital Articles* p2 Mr 3 2016

Why Every Startup Should Bootstrap R. Smith *Harvard Business Review Digital Articles* p2 Mr 2 2016

New business enterprises—France

How France Used Unemployment Benefits to Kickstart Entrepreneurship W. Frick *Harvard Business Review Digital Articles* p2 Ja 8 2015

Jump-starting French startups *Science* v355 no6327 p778 F 24 2017

New business enterprises—Management

Making Your Business Marriage Work color *Ebony* v72 no9 p70 Jl/Ag 2017

ONCE CODDLED, NOW CURBED E. Griffith color *Fortune* v176 no3 p40 S 1 2017

Start-ups Should Sell to Small Businesses, Not Big Enterprises T. Bartman *Harvard Business Review Digital Articles* p2 Ja 27 2015

Why Startups Are More Successful than Ever at Unbundling Incumbents H. Taneja *Harvard Business Review Digital Articles* p2 Je 18 2015

New business enterprises—New York (State)—New York

BEST BETS img *New York* p40 Ja 23 2017

New business enterprises—Officials & employees

Driven S. ADAMS and K. KAM color *Forbes* v199 no5 p46 My 16 2017

New business enterprises—Planning

Empowering Woman J. Caplin color *Money* v46 no1 p24 Ja/F 2017

New business enterprises—Research

NEXT BILLION-DOLLAR STARTUPS color *Forbes* v198 no6 p94 N 8 2016

New business enterprises—Social aspects

LOOK BEFORE YOU LEAP D. Lyons color *Fortune* v174 no6 p34 N 1 2016

New business enterprises—Strategic planning

Keeping the Zeal of a Startup as You Scale J. Allen *Harvard Business Review Digital Articles* p2 Jl 5 2016

New business enterprises—Study & teaching

BRINGING SILICON VALLEY TO DETROIT K. Johnson color *Black Enterprise* v47 no7 p21 My/Je 2017

New business enterprises—United States

5 Black-Owned Startups to Watch [Cover story] S. Blodgett, S. Lynn cartoon color *Black Enterprise* v47 no3 p29 O 2016

6 Things New Grads Should Know Before Joining a Startup L. Berger *Harvard Business Review Digital Articles* p1 My 1 2017

The Fintech 50 S. SHARF, L. SHIN et al color *Forbes* v198 no7 p90 N 29 2016

FROM BOOM TO DOOM E. Griffith color *Fortune* v176 no4 p68 S 15 2017

ON MESSAGE, OFF TARGET E. Griffith color *Fortune* v176

no1 p44 Jl 1 2017

Start-Ups Are Helping Consumers Make Better Health Care Purchases S. H. Jain *Harvard Business Review Digital Articles* p2 Ja 13 2015

Titans of Business Think Small V. Zarya color *Fortune* v175 no8 p44 Je 15 2017

The U.S. Startup Economy Is in Both Better and Worse Shape than We Thought W. Frick *Harvard Business Review Digital Articles* p2 Mr 11 2016

What Startup Accelerators Really Do I. Hathaway *Harvard Business Review Digital Articles* p2 Mr 1 2016

New business enterprises—United States—Finance

AGE OF DISSONANCE E. Griffith color *Fortune* v174 no7 p49 D 1 2016

Start-Up Capital Is Spreading Across the U.S I. Hathaway *Harvard Business Review Digital Articles* p2 F 23 2015

New Chamber Ballet (Performer)

DANCE *New Yorker* v93 no31 p11 O 9 2017

Dancing in Space C. Atamian color *Weekly Standard* v22 no29 p37 Ap 3 2017

New Democratic Party (Political party : Canada)

BEST ORATOR D. SMITH color *Maclean's* v129 no47 p22 N 28 2016

LIFETIME ACHIEVEMENT AWARD J. GEDDES color *Maclean's* v129 no47 p24 N 28 2016

Midterm crises S. PROUDFOOT color *Maclean's* v129 no51/52 p30 D 26 2016

A party with a cover charge J. MARKUSOFF color diag *Maclean's* p13 Je 2017

The newest new NDP P. WELLS color *Maclean's* v130 no10 p8 N 2017

THE NEW ORANGE CRUSH N. KÖHLER color *Maclean's* v130 no8 p26 S 2017

PARLIAMENTARIAN OF THE YEAR J. GEDDES color *Maclean's* v129 no47 p18 N 28 2016

REGRETS? THEY HAVE A FEW J. MARKUSOFF color *Maclean's* v130 no10 p30 N 2017

Socialism Is Back I. WELLS color *Walrus* v14 no7 p14 S 2017

New Edition (Performer)

'90S Till Infinity J. HARRIS bw color *Ebony* v72 no4 p96 F 2017

New employees

New Hires Create More Anxiety at a Midsized Company K. Firestone *Harvard Business Review Digital Articles* p2 Ap 23 2015

Why We Ask Every New Employee to Code an App Their First Week on the Job M. Nowack *Harvard Business Review Digital Articles* p2 D 23 2016

Your New Hires Won't Succeed Unless You Onboard Them Properly A. M. Ellis, S. S. Nifadkar et al *Harvard Business Review Digital Articles* p2 Je 20 2017

New Energy Works (Company)

BEST KITCHEN color *Timber Home Living* p20 2017 SpecialIssue

New Energy Works Timberframers (Company)

The Great Escape color *Timber Home Living* p54 2017 SpecialIssue

New England

Stone by Stone J. E. DAVIS color *Orion Magazine* v36 no2 p8 Mr/Ap 2017

New England Conservatory of Music

NEC TEACHES JAZZ BY EXAMPLE J. Garelick bw color *Downbeat* v84 no10 p82 O 2017

New England Patriots (Football team)

AFC + EAST color *Sports Illustrated* v126 no5 p44 F 13 2017

HATERS GONNA FLUCTUATE P. King color *Sports Illustrated* v127 no7 p40 S 4 2017

How to Beat THE PATS color *Sports Illustrated* v127 no7 p35 S 4 2017

NFL PREVIEW TOP 10 CONTENDERS R. A. BERENZ *TV Guide* v65 no37 p55 S 4 2017

OUR TIME? NOT THIS TIME J. KOVAC JR. *Atlanta* v56 no11 p19 Mr 2017

SUPER BOWL LI: THE PICK G. A. Bedard color *Sports Illustrated* v126 no4 p39 Ja 30 2017

SUSPENDED DISBELIEF [Cover story] G. Bishop, B. Baskin et al color *Sports Illustrated* v126 no5 p26 F 13 2017

Tom Brady S. Gregory color *Time* v189 no6 p13 F 20 2017

New England Patriots (Football team)—History—21st century

1 New England Patriots color *Sports Illustrated* v127 no7 p64 S 4 2017

PATFALLS A. Benoit color *Sports Illustrated* v127 no7 p43 S 4 2017

THE PATRIOTS PROBLEM [Cover story] A. Benoit color *Sports Illustrated* v127 no7 p32 S 4 2017

WIN ONE MORE? ROGER T. Layden color *Sports Illustrated* v126 no4 p31 Ja 30 2017

New England—Description & travel

Fall Foliage Trains: All aboard for autumn thrills on New England's historic rails K. K. BECKIUS *Yankee* v81 no5 p76 S/O 2017

LEAF PEQPLE: A WEEK ON A GUIDED FOLIAGE TOUR SHOWS OFF NOT ONLY NEW ENGLAND BUT A BIT OF HUMAN NATURE, TOO I. ALDRICH *Yankee* v81 no5 p110 S/O 2017

Winter Ocean Weekends K. K. BECKIUS *Yankee* v81 no1 p74 Ja/F 2017

YOUR PERFECT WEEKEND color *Yankee* p97 Mr 2017

New Hampshire—Description & travel

HANOVER, NEW HAMPSHIRE A. GRAVES *Yankee* v81 no1 p68 Ja/F 2017

NEW HAMPSHIRE *Yankee* p120 My/Je 2017

A 'Very Impressive Rock' J. SHIPLEY and M. SEAMANS bw color *Yankee* p20 My/Je 2017

New Horizons (Spacecraft)

A double target for a distant probe? color *Science* v357 no6351 p532 Ag 11 2017

Is New Horizons' Next Target a Binary Body? J. K. BEATTY color *Sky & Telescope* v134 no5 p9 N 2017

X-ray mystery shrouds Pluto C. CROCKETT color *Science News* v190 no11 p15 N 26 2016

New Jersey. Supreme Court

New Jersey case tests whether historic churches can get state grants B. Allen *Christian Century* v134 no17 p16 Ag 16 2017

New Jersey—Description & travel

GHOSTS IN WINTER V. M. Kotz color *Popular Photography* v80 no11 p20 D 2016

New left (Politics)

From Old to New C. R. Kesler *Claremont Review of Books* v17 no3 p36 Summ 2017

The Old New Left C. R. Kesler *Claremont Review of Books* v17 no3 p32 Summ 2017

New Mexico

Falling in love with New Mexico B. Jo Lieberman color *Equus* no477 p46 Je 2017

New Mexico whiptail

All Moms, No Dads P. Edmonds color *National Geographic* v230 no5 p30 N 2016

New Mexico—Description & travel

Middle of Somewhere O. Summerscales color *Climbing* no357 p36 N 2017

ROAD TRIP J. Wignall bw *Popular Photography* v80 no11 p38 D 2016

New Order (Performer)

Spring Preview M. Trammell cartoon *New Yorker* v93 no4 p10 Mr 13 2017

New Orleans (La.)

2016 TOP LAWYERS color *New Orleans Magazine* v51 no1 p80 N 2016

Acalli Chocolate J. Forman color *New Orleans Magazine* v51 no2 p71 D 2016

Carnival Clash M. Griffith bw *New Orleans Magazine* v51 no4 p48 F 2017

Clean Eats: A new wave transforms health food from bland to bold [Cover story] J. Forman color *New Orleans Magazine* v51 no10 p172 Ag 2017

Follow Us to Jazz Fest H. Hayes color *Southern Living* v52 no3 p78 Mr 2017

Fountain Fancy L. Tudor *New Orleans Homes & Lifestyles* v20 no2 p33 Spr 2017

Got Orange? J. DeBold color *New Orleans Magazine* v51 no7 p150 My 2017

Harrison Avenue Boom K. Finn color *New Orleans Magazine* v51 no9 p30 Jl 2017

HOUSE MUSIC M. ROMER color *Louisiana Life* v37 no4 p110 Mr/Ap 2017

JULIA STREET: WITH POYDRAS THE PARROT bw color *New Orleans Magazine* v51 no10 p34 Ag 2017

JULIA STREET WITH POYDRAS THE PARROT J. STREET bw *New Orleans Magazine* v51 no5 p22 Mr 2017

Kitchens *New Orleans Homes & Lifestyles* v20 no2 p58 Spr 2017

Middle Ground V. Hart *New Orleans Homes & Lifestyles* v20 no2 p52 Spr 2017

Mr. Rose's wild ride C. Rose color *New Orleans Magazine* v51 no9 p74 Jl 2017

New Orleans Cake Café & Bakery R. Peyton color *New Orleans Magazine* v51 no2 p76 D 2016

NEWS FROM THE KITCHENS R. PEYTON color *New Orleans Magazine* v51 no1 p114 N 2016

News From the Kitchens R. Peyton color *New Orleans Magazine* v51 no7 p86 My 2017

Old Men Behaving Badly R. Bragg color *Southern Living* v52 no2 p146 F 2017

SEPTEMBER/OCTOBER K. Massicot bw color *Louisiana Life* v38 no1 p62 S/O 2017

Small Hotels, Big Restaurants J. Forman color *New Orleans Magazine* v51 no5 p88 Mr 2017

SPECIAL SANDWICH J. FORMAN color *New Orleans Magazine* v51 no2 p84 D 2016

Starcation: New Orleans O. I. Williams color *Ebony* v72 no9 p58 Jl/Ag 2017

Tchoup Yard J. Forman color *New Orleans Magazine* v51 no2 p74 D 2016

Understanding New Orleans C. Rose color *New Orleans Magazine* v51 no5 p44 Mr 2017

New Orleans (La.)—Description & travel

In Our Cities M. Starks bw color *Ebony* v72 no9 p32 Jl/Ag 2017

Just Wait Till Next Year S. Kelso color *Money* v45 no11 p17 D 2016

New Orleans B. P. KATZ color *Martha Stewart Living* p136 Ap 2017

New Orleans: Notable Local Places *Parks & Recreation* v52 no9 p84 S 2017

NEW ORLEANS N. Weldon bw color map *Runner's World* v52 no1 p76 Ja/F 2017

We're Headed to the Big Eassy P. M. Jacoby-Garrett *Parks & Recreation* v52 no9 p78 S 2017

WICKED GOOD TIME: New Orleans is a decadent location to spend Halloween D. ARTAVIA *Advocate* no1093 p62 O/N 2017

New Orleans (La.)—Economic conditions

What Makes New Orleans a Startup City to Rival the "Big Three" T. Williamson *Harvard Business Review Digital Articles* p2 Mr 8 2016

New Orleans (La.)—History

FACING HISTORY R. Sullivan cartoon *New Yorker* v93 no17 p20 Je 19 2017

The Monuments bw *New Orleans Magazine* v52 no1 p20 S 2017

The QUIZ J. R. KEMP bw color diag *New Orleans Magazine* v51 no12 p68 O 2017

New Orleans (La.)—In literature

DYLAN IN STOCKHOLM J. BERRY bw *New Orleans Magazine* v51 no2 p56 D 2016

New Orleans (La.)—Social conditions

Last Days Of Storyville S. ASHER bw color *New Orleans Magazine* v51 no12 p78 O 2017

New Orleans (La.)—Social conditions—21st century

State of the Market J. FORMAN, T. MCNALLY et al *New Orleans Magazine* v51 no2 p69 D 2016

New Orleans (La.)—Social life & customs

CHRISTMAS PRESENTS M. GRIFFITH bw *New Orleans Magazine* v51 no2 p52 D 2016

A Free Spirit A. MCLELLAN color *New Orleans Magazine* v52 no1 p30 S 2017

Keeping it in the Family C. KOLB bw *New Orleans Magazine* v52 no1 p46 S 2017

New Orleans International Airport

BIG DEVELOPMENTS K. FINN color *Louisiana Life* v37 no4 p8 Mr/Ap 2017

New Orleans Pelicans (Basketball team)

11 PELICANS color *Sports Illustrated* v127 no12 p92 O 16 2017

11 Pelicans R. Nadkarni, B. Golliver et al color *Sports Illustrated* v125 no14 p111 O 24-31 2016

New Orleans Saints (Football team)

4 New Orleans Saints color *Sports Illustrated* v127 no7 p99 S 4 2017

New Press (Organization)

Diversity in Publishing D. WACHTELL *Publishers Weekly* v263 no51 p152 D 12 2016

New product development

6 Ways to Keep Good Ideas from Dying at Your Company S. Kirsner *Harvard Business Review Digital Articles* p2 S 10 2015

The Benefits of Taking a Slower Approach to Innovation S. Ford and F. R. Tarditi *Harvard Business Review Digital Articles* p2 Je 26 2017

The Best Digital Companies Are Set Up to Never Stop Innovating B. Power *Harvard Business Review Digital Articles* p2 My 17 2016

Deciding to Fix or Kill a Problem Product M. Kelley *Harvard Business Review Digital Articles* p2 Je 19 2015

Every Company Needs a Growth Manager J. Bussgang and N. Benbarak *Harvard Business Review Digital Articles* p2 F 19 2016

The Goldilocks Theory of Product Success J. Berger *Harvard Business Review Digital Articles* p2 Jl 7 2016

How Gatorade Invented New Products by Revisiting Old Ones D. Robertson *Harvard Business Review Digital Articles* p2 2017

In Product Development, Let Your Customers Define Perfection M. Ramanujam and G. Tacke *Harvard Business Review Digital Articles* p2 My 9 2016

Packaging Salmon Jerky for the Masses C. Giammona color *Bloomberg Businessweek* no4495 p36 O 17 2016

The Problem with Product Proliferation M. MOCKER and J. W. ROSS color *Harvard Business Review* v95 no3 p104 My/Je 2017

Retooling the HONG KONG & CHINA Print Business T. TAN color *Publishers Weekly* v264 no35 p78 Ag 28 2017

So Many M&A Deals Fail Because Companies Overlook This Simple Strategy A. Lewis and D. McKone *Harvard Business Review Digital Articles* p2 My 10 2016

This Winter, Be Ready for Anything color *Consumer Reports* v81 no12 p9 D 2016

Use Your Customers as Ethnographers J. W. Schlack *Harvard Business Review Digital Articles* p2 Ag 17 2015

What we know about AMD's Ryzen so far G. MAH UNG chart color graph *PCWorld* v35 no1 p18 Ja 2017

When First Movers Are Rewarded, and When They're Not R. Klingebiel and J. Joseph *Harvard Business Review Digital Articles* p2 Ag 11 2015

Why We Are So Careless with the Things We Own S. Bellezza and F. Gino *Harvard Business Review Digital Articles* p2 D 2 2016

Win Over Executives by Proving Customers Support Your Idea R. Ashkenas and D. Dworkin *Harvard Business Review Digital Articles* p2 Jl 14 2015

Yes, A/B Testing Is Still Necessary K. Fung *Harvard Business Review Digital Articles* p2 D 10 2014

Your Boss Won't Say Yes If Emotions Are Running High J. R. Detert and S. J. Ashford *Harvard Business Review Digital Articles* p2 D 19 2014

Your New Hit Product Might Be Underpriced M. Ramanujam and G. Tacke *Harvard Business Review Digital Articles* p2 My 24 2016

New product development—Congresses

Microsoft Build's biggest reveals: building the future B. CHACOS color *PCWorld* v35 no6 p14 Je 2017

New product development—Management

When Not to Celebrate Failure R. Ashkenas *Harvard Business Review Digital Articles* p2 D 11 2014

New product development—Marketing

Crowdsourced Products Sell Better When They're Marketed That Way M. Schreier, H. Nishikawa et al *Harvard Business Review Digital Articles* p2 N 8 2016

New product development—Psychological aspects

DON'T LAUNCH YOUR PRODUCT IN 2020 graph img *Harvard Business Review* v95 no3 p30 My/Je 2017

For Any Product to be Successful, Empathy Is Key J. Kolko *Harvard Business Review Digital Articles* p2 N 20 2014

New product development—Social aspects
Chinese and American Consumers Have Different Ideas About What Makes a Product Creative J. Mueller *Harvard Business Review Digital Articles* p2 F 23 2017

New Skin (Music)
New RIDE H. WEISS *Interview* v46 no9 p45 N 2016

New urbanism
An Affordable-Housing Fix J. JEWELL *American Conservative* v16 no3 p36 My/Je 2017

New wave music—Reviews
DREAMCAR K. O'Donnell *Entertainment Weekly* no1446/1447 p77 D 2016/Ja 2017

New words
Out of the margins E. Parker *History Today* v67 no3 p25 Mr 2017

New World (Short story)
NEW WORLD A. Kumarasamy *Harper's Magazine* no2007 p77 Ag 2017

New Year
See also
Chinese New Year
13 Resolutions Other People Really Need to Make This Year K. Bonnell and P. R. Satran color *Glamour* v115 no1 p99 Ja 2017
Beginner's mind A. Camille color *U.S. Catholic* v82 no1 p47 Ja 2017
THE GOODS C. COX *Atlanta* v56 no9 p41 Ja 2017
HAPPY(?) NEW YEAR *Sea Magazine* v109 no2 p32 F 2017
How to meet your goals bw color *Redbook* p152 D 2016
January! T. PAYNE and L. CROSS bw color *Ebony* v72 no3 p36 D 2016/Ja 2017
On Your Way to Your New Year's Self G. Hamilton *New York Times Magazine* p20 Ja 1 2017
"Party-Hop" Around the World chart color *Good Housekeeping* v264 no1 p131 Ja 1 2017
TENDER IS THE NIGHT A. RAPOPORT color *Bon Appetit* v61 no12 p18 D 2016 /Jan2017
WHO WILL YOU SPEND NEW YEAR'S EVE WITH? M. Snetiker color *Entertainment Weekly* no1446/1447 p109 D 2016/Ja 2017

New Year's decorations
START THE NEW YEAR WITH A TWINKLE color *Entertainment Weekly* no1443 p24 D 9 2016

New Year's entertaining
PARTY HEARTY A. Vorrasi color *InStyle* v24 no1 p98 Ja 2017

New Year's resolutions
Become more prayerful this year A. Scobey color *U.S. Catholic* v82 no1 p43 Ja 2017
Feminist Force S. Whitlock, A. Taylor et al color *Glamour* v115 no3 p38 Mr 2017
For a Fabulous 2016, One Tip: Take It Slow T. SPIKER color *AARP: The Magazine* v59 no1A p22 D 2015/Ja 2016
NEW New Year's Resolutions color *Prevention* v69 no1 p13 Ja 2017
A Picture of the Future F. P. DRISCOLL *Opera News* v81 no7 p4 Ja 2017
To Hell With Resolutions S. Dreisbach and S. G. Levy color *Glamour* v115 no1 p44 Ja 2017

New York (N.Y.)
1633 N. Niarchos color *New Yorker* v92 no33 p20 O 17 2016
Agern C. Kormann color *New Yorker* v92 no45 p19 Ja 16 2017
ART cartoon *New Yorker* v92 no45 p8 Ja 16 2017
ART *New Yorker* v93 no4 p19 Mr 13 2017
Augustine B. Cooper color *New Yorker* v93 no7 p27 Ap 3 2017
THE BETTER LIFE P. SCHJELDAHL cartoon *New Yorker* v92 no36 p78 N 7 2016
BULL'S-EYE E. Allen cartoon *New Yorker* v92 no47 p19 Ja 30 2017
Chinese Tuxedo Jiayang Fan color *New Yorker* v92 no49 p27 F 13 2017
CITIES color *Conde Nast Traveler* v52 no10 p76 N 2017
Comments img *New York* v49 no26 p8 D 26 2016
DANCE *New Yorker* v92 no46 p9 Ja 23 2017
DANCE *New Yorker* v93 no11 p12 My 1 2017
DANCE *New Yorker* v93 no5 p20 Mr 20 2017
Déjeuner sur l'Herbe J. Acocella cartoon *New Yorker* v92 no34 p14 O 24 2016
Dinner in a Dumpster J. LABIANCA *Reader's Digest* v188

no1125 p12 N 2016
DK Kitchen A. PLATT img *New York* p50 Ja 23 2017
Dokebi Bar & Grill J. Fan color *New Yorker* v93 no4 p22 Mr 13 2017
Flora Bar D. Wenger color *New Yorker* v93 no11 p15 My 1 2017
THE FORBES 2016 ALL-STAR EATERIES IN NEW YORK S. FORBES color *Forbes* v198 no9 p12 D 30 2016
Fries with That? S. Lyon color *New Yorker* v92 no47 p15 Ja 30 2017
Go Get Your Gown! color *Glamour* v115 no5 p62 My 2017
GOINGS ON ABOUT TOWN bw *New Yorker* v92 no38 p9 N 21 2016
Günter Seeger D. Wenger color *New Yorker* v92 no40 p19 D 5 2016
Ikinari Steak R. RAISFELD and R. PATRONITE img *New York* v50 no7 p68 Ap 3 2017
Italian Flair in Sheridan Square img *New York* v50 no17 p74 Ag 21 2017
IT'S NEVER TOO LATE TO START RUNNING M. NASSER *UN Chronicle* v53 no2 p36 2016
The Lucky Bee Jiayang Fan color *New Yorker* v92 no35 p29 O 31 2016
Mermaid Spa B. Cooper color *New Yorker* v93 no3 p19 Mr 6 2017
Modern Mexican: Atla is designed for how New Yorkers eat now R. RAISFELD and R. PATRONITE img *New York* v50 no15 p50 Jl 24 2017
NIGHT LIFE cartoon *New Yorker* v92 no40 p10 D 5 2016
NIGHT LIFE cartoon *New Yorker* v93 no7 p25 Ap 3 2017
NIGHT LIFE *New Yorker* v93 no11 p13 My 1 2017
No Boys Allowed D. EVANS img *New York* v49 no21 p67 O 17 2016
Olmsted B. Cooper color *New Yorker* v92 no32 p31 O 10 2016
Once Upon A Time bw color *Architectural Digest* v74 no7 p24 Jl 2017
Paowalla S. Lyon color *New Yorker* v93 no29 p33 S 25 2017
Pith E. Allen color *New Yorker* v93 no14 p23 My 22 2017
Pondicheri D. Wenger color *New Yorker* v92 no34 p17 O 24 2016
REVIVALS AND FESTIVALS color *New Yorker* v92 no32 p29 O 10 2016
Second Home W. GOODMAN img *New York* p43 Ja 23 2017
Sen Sakana C. Kormann color *New Yorker* v93 no32 p18 O 16 2017
Setting the Mood O. Strand color *Vogue* v207 no7 p112 Jl 2017
SNAPCHAT C. WARE cartoon *New Yorker* v92 no37 p44 N 14 2016
Spaghetti and Meatballs for the Masses R. RAISFELD and R. PATRONITE img *New York* v50 no17 p72 Ag 21 2017
StairMaster to Heaven C. BATTAN color *GQ: Gentlemen's Quarterly* v86 no11 p76 N 2016
Stores K. Schneider img *New York* v50 no17 p80 Ag 21 2017
Sunday in Brooklyn B. Cooper color *New Yorker* v92 no46 p15 Ja 23 2017
TABLES FOR TWO: The Aviary S. Lyon color *New Yorker* v93 no33 p31 O 23 2017
Tighten Up F. VALDESOLO color *Vogue* v207 no4 p172 Ap 2017
To Do M. Z. SEITZ, J. SALTZ et al img *New York* p72 Ja 23 2017
Union Square Café S. Lyon cartoon *New Yorker* v93 no5 p27 Mr 20 2017
Yemen Café N. Niarchos color *New Yorker* v92 no38 p27 N 21 2016

New York (N.Y.) art scene—Exhibitions
WHEN DOWNTOWN WAS UP B. SCHWABSKY *Nation* v304 no11 p35 Ap 3 2017

New York (N.Y.) art scene—History—20th century
WHEN DOWNTOWN WAS UP B. SCHWABSKY *Nation* v304 no11 p35 Ap 3 2017

New York (N.Y.) on television
Risky Business A. Bhattacharji color *Bloomberg Businessweek* no4538 p62 S 18 2017

New York (N.Y.). Dept. of Environmental Conservation
THE air THAT WE BREATHE J. Sheppard *New York State Conservationist* v72 no1 p26 Ag 2017
BRIEFLY color *New York State Conservationist* v71 no2 p28 O 2016
New Visitor Center at Five Rivers *New York State Conservationist* v72 no1 p36 Ag 2017

New York (N.Y.). Housing Authority
ASPHALT GARDENS S. James *Harper's Magazine* p50 Ap 2017
New York (N.Y.). Police Dept.
A SHOT TO THE HEART S. CLIFFORD cartoon *New Yorker* v92 no34 p26 O 24 2016
New York (N.Y.)—Description & travel
NEW YORK STATE OF MIND A. BARRONIAN color *Powder* v46 no2 p42 O 2017
Your $1,000 New York Weekend color map *GQ: Gentlemen's Quarterly* v87 no1 p14 Ja 2017
New York (N.Y.)—Economic conditions
The City Is Still Ours D. Wallace-Wells img *New York* v49 no25 p40 D 12 2016
New York (N.Y.)—Economic conditions—21st century
DEFENDER OF THE COMMUNITY A. Feuer *Harper's Magazine* p41 Ap 2017
New York (N.Y.)—Environmental conditions
The Joys of autumn color *New York State Conservationist* v71 no2 p2 O 2016
New York (N.Y.)—Maps
TUNNEL VISION G. Milner color *Bloomberg Businessweek* no4534 p52 Ag 14 2017
New York (N.Y.)—News briefs
BEST BETS img *New York* p40 Ja 23 2017
New York (N.Y.)—Politics & government
NYC vs. TRUMP [Cover story] J. MURPHY color *Nation* v304 no3 p12 Ja 30 2017
The Quiz T. BALAZO color *Maclean's* v129 no40 p80 O 10 2016
New York (N.Y.)—Social conditions
WE RUN THE STREETS [Cover story] M. Gross color *Runner's World* v52 no9 p62 O 2017
New York (N.Y.)—Social conditions—21st century
Even Our Protesters Are Precocious A. MORRIS img *New York* v49 no25 p46 D 12 2016
TEEN, TRANS AND HOMELESS: ON THE STREETS OF NEW YORK WITH AMERICA'S MOST VULNERABLE POPULATION L. R. MURRAY color *Rolling Stone* no1297 p44 O 5 2017
New York (N.Y.)—Social life & customs—19th century
New York Would Never Dream of Building a Wall A. STERNBERGH img *New York* v49 no25 p62 D 12 2016
New York (Periodical)
the absolute best R. PATRONITE and R. RAISFELD *New York* p74 Mr 6 2017
BEST OF NEW YORK *New York* p67 Mr 6 2017
New York (State). Dept. of Environmental Conservation
Report Bear Dens *New York State Conservationist* v71 no4 p28 F 2017
New York (State). Metropolitan Transportation Authority
MILLION-DOLLAR SUBWAY FIXES E. WAITE and R. CLEGG cartoon *New Yorker* v93 no24 p29 Ag 21 2017
New York (State)—Description & travel
Easy Summits R. WICHELNS map *Backpacker* p26 My 2017
NEW YORK H. Wilson color map *Canadian Geographic* v135 no6 p22 D 2015
ON THE MAP B. McGrath cartoon *New Yorker* v92 no38 p31 N 21 2016
New York (State)—Politics & government
Constitutional Inertia A. Greenblatt *Governing* v30 no4 p12 Ja 2017
New York Botanical Garden
ABOVE & BEYOND cartoon *New Yorker* v93 no8 p14 Ap 10 2017
New York City Ballet
ABOVE & BEYOND cartoon *New Yorker* v93 no12 p12 My 8 2017
All-Around arTiST M. Fuhrer color *Dance Spirit* v21 no1 p44 Ja 2017
CULTURE Club E. ELWICK-BATES color *Vogue* v206 no12 p280 D 2016
DANCE *New Yorker* v92 no30 p10 S 26 2016
DANCE *New Yorker* v92 no48 p12 F 6 2017
DANCE *New Yorker* v93 no10 p31 Ap 24 2017
DANCE *New Yorker* v92 no51 p11 O 9 2017
Troy Schumacher: The choreographer is premiering three ballets in a span of four weeks M. HARSS *Dance Magazine* v91 no10

p18 O 2017
New York City Center
A Film Classic, Reimagined color *Dance Spirit* v21 no8 p35 O 2017
New York City Dance Alliance (Company)
NEW YORK CITY DANCE ALLIANCE *Dance Spirit* v20 no10 p20 D 2016
Stretch Yourself K. SCHWAB *Dance Magazine* v91 no1 p138 Ja 2017
New York City Marathon
CURATOR OF CUTE A. NOLAN color *Runner's World* v52 no3 p17 Ap 2017
New York city mayors
IN CONVERSATION Bill de Blasio C. SMITH img *New York* v50 no18 p24 S 4 2017
The Minimal Mayor [Cover story] K. SMITH color *National Review* v69 no18 p22 O 2 2017
WEATHERING THE STORM S. KNIGHT bw cartoon *New Yorker* v93 no22 p34 Jl 31 2017
New York City nightclubs
ABOVE & BEYOND bw *New Yorker* v93 no33 p30 O 23 2017
New York Civil Liberties Union (Organization)—Congresses
THE NEW BRUNCH S. Lyon cartoon *New Yorker* v93 no6 p17 Mr 27 2017
New York Fashion Week
American Fashion Confronts America C. HORYN img *New York* p43 F 20 2017
New York Giants (Football team)
1 New York Giants color *Sports Illustrated* v127 no7 p86 S 4 2017
New York Herald Tribune (Newspaper)
REALITY SHOW D. Thompson *Lapham's Quarterly* v10 no3 p70 Summ 2017
New-York Historical Society
Silver Prints *American History* v51 no6 p52 F 2017
New York Is My Home (Music)
Dion and the Disrupters R. Love color *AARP: The Magazine* v59 no2A p4 F/Mr 2016
New York Jets (Football team)
4 New York Jets color *Sports Illustrated* v127 no7 p68 S 4 2017
New York Knickerbockers (Basketball team)
10 KNICKS color *Sports Illustrated* v127 no12 p68 O 16 2017
9 Knicks R. Nadkarni, B. Golliver et al color *Sports Illustrated* v125 no14 p83 O 24-31 2016
HOT | NOT T. Keith color *Sports Illustrated* v126 no3 p17 Ja 23 2017
New York Liberty (Basketball team)
The New York Liberty's Dancers, the Timeless Torches, Are All 40-Plus A. TSOULIS-REAY img *New York* v49 no25 p54 D 12 2016
New York Mets (Baseball team)
2 METS color *Sports Illustrated* v126 no9 p96 Mr 27 2017
Games: Will Leitch B. Doherty img *New York* v50 no10 p30 My 15 2017
Mr. Met S. Stein color *New York Times Magazine* p34 My 21 2017
New York Philharmonic
CLASSICAL MUSIC cartoon *New Yorker* v92 no32 p14 O 10 2016
CLASSICAL MUSIC color *New Yorker* v93 no28 p9 S 18 2017
CLASSICAL MUSIC *New Yorker* v93 no17 p10 Je 19 2017
The New York Philharmonic *New Yorker* v49 no25 p145 D 12 2016
On the Town A. Ross cartoon *New Yorker* v93 no31 p12 O 9 2017
SOUND WAVES A. ROSS cartoon *New Yorker* v92 no35 p96 O 31 2016
Voice of the Viola A. Ross cartoon *New Yorker* v92 no38 p20 N 21 2016
New York Public Library
How Citizen Action Saved the New York Public Library S. SHERMAN color *Nation* v305 no9 p20 O 16 2017
How Employees Shaped Strategy at the New York Public Library B. A. Strong and M. L. Kennedy *Harvard Business Review Digital Articles* p2 D 5 2016
Open Book S. STEPHENS *Architectural Record* v204 no10 p102 O 2016
What Are Libraries For? T. MARKATOS bw color *Weekly Standard* v23 no6 p36 O 16 2017
New York Public Library (Film)

BOOKISH A. LANE color *New Yorker* v93 no28 p72 S 18 2017

New York Public Library—Congresses

Comics in Libraries and Schools at the New York Public Library color *Publishers Weekly* v264 no38 p33 S 18 2017

New York Standards Quartet (Performer)

The Long Run J. Potter color *Downbeat* v84 no9 p26 S 2017

New York Times Co. v. Sullivan (Supreme Court case)

"The Power of the Thought":Contempt for freedom of speech reflects impoverished minds. Colleges that reject intellectual diversity are much to blame R. A. Epstein *Hoover Digest: Research & Opinion on Public Policy* no3 p120 Summ 2017

New York University

Derek Cianfrance M. Hagan color *Current Biography* v78 no3 p15 Mr 2017

New York University. Stern School of Business

A DEAN FOR ALL SEASONS T. J. Huddleston color *Fortune* v174 no7 p38 D 1 2016

New York Yankees (Baseball team)

3 YANKEES color *Sports Illustrated* v126 no9 p79 Mr 27 2017

6 THE LONG GAME B. Reiter color *Sports Illustrated* v126 no9 p48 Mr 27 2017

Aaron Judge Sizes Up As Baseball's Best New Hope S. Gregory color *Time* v190 no8 p22 Ag 28 2017

GO FIGURE T. Keith color *Sports Illustrated* v126 no14 p22 My 15-22 2017

New York Yankees (Baseball team)—History

GENE MICHAEL (1938-2017) J. Fuchs and T. Keith color *Sports Illustrated* v127 no8 p22 S 18 2017

New Yorkers

New Yorkers I. M. STELZER bw *Weekly Standard* v22 no46 p5 Ag 14 2017

New York Would Never Dream of Building a Wall A. STERNBERGH img *New York* v49 no25 p62 D 12 2016

New Zealand—Description & travel

The Southern Wild M. Shipstead bw *Conde Nast Traveler* v52 no7 p46 Ag 2017

Newark (N.J.)—Politics & government

Schumer's Losing This One F. Barnes color *Weekly Standard* v22 no47 p14 Ag 21 2017

Newbegin, Hall

Beauty J. Chamberlain color *Sunset* v237 no5 p60 N 2016

Newberger, Stuart H.

Terror & Slow Justice A. MARLOWE color *Weekly Standard* v23 no1 p40 S 11 2017

NEWBERRY, JUDY

Life IN THESE UNITED STATES *Reader's Digest* v189 no1128 p38 Mr 2017

Newberry, Kerry

OREGON'S McMINNVILLE color map *Sunset* v239 no4 p28 O 2017

NEWBERY, CATHRYN

"Bad bosses are the cause of so much misery": Author Kim Scott on how honesty at work can make us happier and more productive *People Management* p13 Mr 2017

"Cybersecurity is now an essential part of our values": How a growing charity secured its data by changing behaviours *People Management* p23 Mr 2017

HR should be the experts in managing and leading change *People Management* p13 O 2016

People tell us this is the best thing we've ever done *People Management* p22 O 2016

Women leaders still need to be trailblazers *People Management* p40 F 2017

"YOU DON'T HAVE TO PRETEND TO KNOW EVERYTHING": Organisational psychologist Dr Tasha Eurich on the power of self-awareness—and why Uber is getting it badly wrong *People Management* p40 Jl 2017

Newbery Medal

Who Will Win the Newbery Medal? S. MAUGHAN color *Publishers Weekly* v263 no52 p56 D 19 2016

NEWBOLD, TIM

Harmonizing Biodiversity Conservation and Productivity in the Context of Increasing Demands on Landscapes graph *BioScience* v66 no10 p890 O 1 2016

Newborn infant physiology

A newborn's pain registers in the brain L. SANDERS color *Science News* v191 no11 p8 Je 10 2017

Newborn infants

See also

Premature infants

There is Much in a Name: A good name will have a positive impact on a growing child's manners and outlook on life M. MIRZA *Islamic Horizons* v46 no4 p42 Jl/Ag 2017

Newborn infants—Medical examinations

See also

Apgar score

Speeding Up Baby's First Test M. Quinn *Governing* v30 no2 p18 N 2016

Newby, J.

Observation of coherent elastic neutrino-nucleus scattering diag *Science* v357 no6356 p1123 S 15 2017

New Career in a New Town: 1977-1982, A (Music)

THE BEST OF BOWIE'S NEW BOX SET E. R. Brown color *Entertainment Weekly* no1485 p59 O 6 2017

Newcastle, Margaret Cavendish, Duchess of, ca. 1624-1674

1666: Blazing World M. Cavendish *Lapham's Quarterly* v10 no2 p117 Spr 2017

New Celebrity Apprentice, The (TV program)

Arnold Takes the Boardroom: Schwarzenegger inherits Donald Trump's role as chairman of NBC's rebooted Celebrity Apprentice I. RATLEDGE *TV Guide* v65 no2 p20 Ja 2 2017

Trump Learned Lessons About Reality TV That The Apprentice Hasn't D. D'Addario color *Time* v189 no4 p47 Ja 23 2017

Who's Hired? Schwarzenegger shares his performance reviews of this season's standouts *TV Guide* v65 no2 p23 Ja 2 2017

New Colonialism, The (Poem)

The New Colonialism J. HAYSOM *Walrus* v13 no10 p65 D 2016

New Colossus, The (Poem : Lazarus)

Wretched Refuse, Indeed K. D. WILLIAMSON bw *National Review* v69 no16 p14 Ag 28 2017

NEWCOMB, CLAY

URSUS MAJOR color *Outdoor Life* v224 no5 p89 Je/Jl 2017

Newcomb, Jill

Back-Through Gate color *Horse & Rider* v56 no6 p35 Je 2017

Precise Circles color *Horse & Rider* v56 no2 p23 F 2017

Newcomb, Tim

Best in Shoe: 2017 *Tennis* v53 no3 p16 My/Je 2017

FOR YOUR FEET ONLY color *Runner's World* v52 no4 p16 My 2017

Newcomb College

Tulane University Newcomb College Dance Program *Dance Magazine* v90 p105 2016/2017 Supplement College Guide

Newcombe, Tod

30 Years of Disruption: Technology evolves rapidly, but that's not always true for states and localities *Governing* v31 no1 p60 O 2017

Busing In Wi-Fi *Governing* v30 no4 p60 Ja 2017

Chicago Gets a Fitbit *Governing* v30 no2 p60 N 2016

Cyber-Regulating Banks *Governing* v30 no3 p62 D 2016

Dislike: Are state ethics rules keeping up with social media? *Governing* v30 no8 p60 My 2017

Disrupted Government: Florida wants to cut IT costs. But is the state going about it all wrong? *Governing* v30 no9 p62 Je 2017

G2G: Why don't more governments with big IT budgets assist their smaller peers? *Governing* v30 no10 p60 Jl 2017

The Heat Is On: To succeed, a new first responder network needs most states to opt in *Governing* v30 no12 p62 S 2017

Letting the Little Guy In *Governing* v30 no6 p60 Mr 2017

Lurking in the Shadows *Governing* v30 no7 p60 Ap 2017

Nudged Out *Governing* v30 no5 p62 F 2017

Robocops (and Roboinspectors) *Governing* v30 no1 p62 O 2016

You Don't Have to Be an Expert: As cities become inundated with data, they're turning to citizens for help color *Governing* v30 no11 p60 Ag 2017

Newcomer, Eric

¿Cómo se dice 'Uber'? color *Bloomberg Businessweek* no4495 p25 O 17 2016

Deactivated color *Bloomberg Businessweek* no4527 p27 Je 19 2017

Uber's Campsites color *Bloomberg Businessweek* no4510 p24 F 6 2017

Uber's Taxicab Confessions color *Bloomberg Businessweek*

no4513 p26 Mr 6 2017

Uber Without the Smartphone color *Bloomberg Businessweek* no4530 p22 Jl 17 2017

Newcomers (Sociology)

Why Your Team Needs Rookies L. Wiseman *Harvard Business Review Digital Articles* p2 O 2 2014

NEWCOTT, BILL

Best Movies for Grownups bw color *AARP: The Magazine* v60 no2A p54 F/Mr 2017

The Caribbean With a Twang color *AARP: The Magazine* v59 no2A p44 F/Mr 2016

David Hyde Pierce color *AARP: The Magazine* v60 no3A p13 Ap/My 2017

Movies for Grownups color *AARP: The Magazine* v59 no2A p61 F/Mr 2016

Pacific Coast Highway color map *AARP: The Magazine* v60 no3A p48 Ap/My 2017

William Shatner: Still Beaming After All These Years color *AARP: The Magazine* v59 no5A p14 Ag/S 2016

New Deal, 1933-1939

THE HUNDRED DAYS HUSTLE C. R. Kesler *Claremont Review of Books* v17 no2 p5 Spr 2017

Newdealdesign (Company)

Reinventions: Scrip J. Brustein color *Bloomberg Businessweek* no4494 p46 O 10 2016

Newell, Evan W.

Mapping the human DC lineage through the integration of high-dimensional techniques diag *Science* v356 no6342 p1044 Je 9 2017

Newell, Gabe

Gabe Newell's Reddit Q&A: on Half-Life 3, Steam support, and more H. DINGMAN color *PCWorld* v35 no2 p25 F 2017

Newell, Waller R.

THE FACE OF TYRANNY T. Lindberg *Claremont Review of Books* v17 no1 p59 Wint 2016/2017

Waller R. Newell: Tyrants: A History of Power, Injustice, and Terror W. Morrisey *Society* v54 no4 p383 Ag 2017

Newell Brands Inc.

Investors Go Long on Slime J. Wieczner color *Fortune* v175 no7 p12 Je 1 2017

Newfoundland & Labrador—Description & travel

In the easternmost reaches of Canada, looking for where the cold waters of the Labrador Current and the warmth of the Gulf Stream create the foggiest place in the world color *New York Times Magazine* p24 D 11 2016

Newgarden, Josef

GOOD AS NEW M. Harris and S Kwak color *Sports Illustrated* v127 no10 p20 O 2 2017

STAR POWER P. LERNER color *Road & Track* v68 no9 p66 Je 2017

NEWHOUSE, ALANA

Along for the Ride *New York Times Book Review* p23 My 7 2017

Newhouse, Joseph P.

Do Doctors Get Worse as They Get Older? *Harvard Business Review Digital Articles* p2 My 23 2017

The Harvard Contest That's Trying to Improve Health Care Delivery *Harvard Business Review Digital Articles* p2 O 2 2015

Newhouse, Ryan

Grow Together color *Log Home Living* p90 2018 Annual Buyers Guide

Newhouse, S. I., Jr., 1927-2017

Milestones *Time* v190 no15 p13 O 16 2017

S. I. Newhouse, JR D. Remnick cartoon *New Yorker* v93 no32 p24 O 16 2017

S. I. Newhouse T. Brown color *Time* v190 no15 p13 O 16 2017

Newhouse, Victoria

Beyond Architecture P. Goldberger color *Architectural Record* v205 no8 p49 Ag 2017

Newkirk, Margaret

Faces of the Venezuelan Exodus color *Bloomberg Businessweek* no4522 p15 My 15 2017

A Georgia Election Is a TV Ad Bonanza bw *Bloomberg Businessweek* no4527 p50 Je 19 2017

Houston and the Politics of Immigration color *Bloomberg Businessweek* no4537 p31 S 11 2017

Newlyweds

FOR NEWLYWEDS WHO HAVE EVERYTHING L. GERSTNER color *Kiplinger's Personal Finance* v71 no6 p15 Je 2017

The Newlyweds' Guide to Financial Success K. A. Renzulli color diag *Money* v46 no5 p54 Je 2017

NEWMAN, CAROLINE

Motivate Me *USA Today Magazine* v145 no2864 p63 My 2017

Newman, Catherine

RAISE A TOUGH COOKIE color *Parents* v92 no9 p48 S 2017

Newman, Cathy

Whose Moors Are They? color map *National Geographic* v231 no5 p84 My 2017

The Wisdom of TREES color *National Geographic* v231 no3 p52 Mr 2017

Newman, Daniel—Interviews

GINGER SNAPS: The Walking Dead's bi star on being the change he wants to see in Hollywood D. ARTAVIA *Advocate* no1093 p28 O/N 2017

Newman, Darley

Greetings from JACKSON HOLE, WYOMING *Practical Horseman* v45 no2 p62 F 2017

Greetings from MIDEWIN NATIONAL TALLGRASS PRAIRIE color *Practical Horseman* v44 no12 p62 D 2016

Newman, Dianne K.

Dianne Newman J. Crelin color *Current Biography* v78 no6 p68 Je 2017

Pyocyanin degradation by a tautomerizing demethylase inhibits Pseudomonas aeruginosa biofilms bibl diag graph *Science* v355 no6321 p1 Ju 13 2017

Newman, Dianne—Awards

Three Society alumni named MacArthur Fellows color *Science News* v190 no12 p29 D 10 2016

Newman, Emma

Brother's Ruin: Industrial Magic *Publishers Weekly* v264 no4 p61 Ja 23 2017

Newman, Griffin

GRIFFIN NEWMAN S. Li color *Entertainment Weekly* no1468/1469 p39 Je 2-9 2017

Newman, Isabella

RECIPES *Virginia Living* v15 no1 p71 D 2016

NEWMAN, J. H.

BUZZWORTHY *Indianapolis Monthly* p14 N 2017

Newman, James

His Room-Size Computer Plays Tic-Tac-Toe C. McDONALD color *Popular Science* v288 no6 p98 N/D 2016

NEWMAN, JARED

Apple TV gets cozy with Amazon Prime, so where does that leave Netflix? color *PCWorld* v35 no7 p50 Jl 2017

Cord cutting is a bigger bargain than ever cartoon color *PCWorld* p123 O 2016

How streaming TV services are coping with ISP data caps color *Macworld - Digital Edition* v34 no8 p120 Ag 2017

How to cut the cord without resorting to a pricey streaming-TV bundle color *PCWorld* v35 no6 p47 Je 2017

How to watch the news without cable TV: 2017 edition color *PCWorld* v35 no5 p197 My 2017

iPAD PRO SMART KEYBOARD VS. LOGITECH SLIM COMBO: WHICH iPAD PRO KEYBOARD SHOULD YOU BUY? color *Macworld - Digital Edition* v34 no8 p75 Ag 2017

The new Apple TV update is no friend to cord cutters color *PCWorld* v35 no1 p35 Ja 2017

USING CROSSOVER ANDROID TO RUN WINDOWS APPS ON A CHROME-BOOK color *PCWorld* p148 D 2016

WHAT'S WRONG WITH MICROSOFT TO-DO: 8 THINGS LACKING IN WUNDERLIST'S REPLACEMENT color *PCWorld* v35 no6 p127 Je 2017

Why AMD FreeSync is beating Nvidia G-Sync on monitor selection and price color *PCWorld* v35 no11 p118 N 2016

Why Google plans to stop supporting your Chromebook after five years color *PCWorld* p43 O 2016

NEWMAN, JASON

Sharon Jones color *Rolling Stone* no1276 p30 D 15 2016

Newman, Judith

Doctors Say the Darnedest Things [Cover story] cartoon *Prevention* v69 no6 p90 Je 2017

Help Desk color *New York Times Book Review* p27 Ap 23 2017

Help Desk *New York Times Book Review* p31 N 6 2016

How-To and Self-Help *New York Times Book Review* p27 F 26 2017

How-To and Self-Help *New York Times Book Review* p27 Ja 1 2017

The Joy of Gardening color *AARP: The Magazine* v59 no4A p63 Je/Jl 2016

New books use the language of empowerment to advise women on their careers, love lives and cars *New York Times Book Review* p31 O 8 2017

OPENING DOORS FOR MY AUTISTIC SON color *Reader's Digest* v190 no1134 p78 O 2017

Self-Improvement: Parenting books on how to ignore bad behavior and yet be fully present for your kids *New York Times Book Review* p27 Ag 13 2017

SEX AGE MADONNA cartoon color *AARP: The Magazine* v60 no2A p60 F/Mr 2017

Still Having FUN! color *AARP: The Magazine* v59 no5A p42 Ag/S 2016

The Three Stages of STEVE MARTIN'S Journey to HAPPINESS bw color *AARP: The Magazine* v60 no4A p36 Je/Jl 2017

Where the #@$%! Have You Been, Warren Beatty? color *AARP: The Magazine* v59 no6A p42 O/N 2016

Newman, Katherine S.

Make America Make Again color *Foreign Affairs* v96 no1 p114 Ja/F 2017

Newman, Kurt

The CEO of Children's National Health System on Leadership, Innovation, and Delivering Specialized Care K. Bell *Harvard Business Review Digital Articles* p1 Je 22 2017

NEWMAN, LILY HAY

ESCAPE THE MATRIX: THE INTERNET IS THE UNCANNIEST VALLEY. DON'T GET TRAPPED THERE *Wired* v25 no9 p92 S 2017

PARENT TRAP: YOUR KIDS WILL SEE INTERNET PORN. DEAL WITH IT. A CONVERSATION WITH PEGGY ORENSTEIN cartoon *Wired* v25 no9 p78 S 2017

NEWMAN, M. SOPHIA

THE BUDDHIST HISTORY OF MOVABLE TYPE color *Tricycle: The Buddhist Review* v26 no2 p46 Wint 2016

Newman, Paul, 1925-2008

How Do You Sell A Priceless Watch? K. Kazakina color *Bloomberg Businessweek* no4535 p66 Ag 28 2017

THE POSTHUMOUS RETURN OF PAUL NEWMAN M. Snetiker color *Entertainment Weekly* no1471 p49 Je 23 2017

Newman, Randy, 1943-

HIGH CEILINGS J. Seabrook cartoon *New Yorker* v93 no24 p17 Ag 21 2017

Randy Newman Makes Irony Great Again J. DOLAN color *Rolling Stone* no1293 p54 Ag 10 2017

THE RANDY NEWMAN SONGBOOK N. Liao bw *U.S. Catholic* v82 no6 p40 Je 2017

New Mexico—History—Civil War, 1861-1865

It Happened Here: Pinos Altos, N.M G. R. Schiavino color *American Cowboy* v23 no5 p43 F/Mr 2017

New Museum of Contemporary Art (New York, N.Y.)

The Art-History Straitjacket J. SALTZ img *New York* v49 no19 p96 S 19 2016

ART *New Yorker* v93 no2 p8 F 27 2017

MAN OF MANY WORDS P. SCHJELDAHL cartoon *New Yorker* v92 no49 p96 F 13 2017

SILICON VALUES M. Pepi *Art in America* v104 no9 p90 O 2016

Newmyer, Tory

THE 2017 Fortune Crystal Ball color diag *Fortune* v174 no7 p11 D 1 2016

Business Waits in Limbo color *Fortune* v175 no3 p9 Mr 1 2017

Repeal Is Easy. Replace? Not So Much color *Fortune* v175 no2 p9 F 1 2017

TALE OF THE TAPE: CLINTON VS. TRUMP color *Fortune* v174 no6 p79 N 1 2016

That 'Huge' Tax Cut May Take a While color *Fortune* v175 no4 p19 Mr 15 2017

TRADING WITH AMERICA diag *Fortune* v174 no6 p132 N 1 2016

TRUMP'S KEY ADVISERS BY THE NUMBERS *Fortune* v174 no8 p17 D 15 2016

What Happens After the Election color *Fortune* v174 no6 p9 N 1 2016

WHAT TO WATCH FOR IN TRUMP'S TAX PLAN *Fortune* v75 no1 p14 Ja 1 2017

WORLD'S 50 GREATEST LEADERS [Cover story] color *Fortune* v175 no5 p46 Ap 1 2017

Newport, Cal

Deep Work: Rules for Focused Success in a Distracted World A. Frykholm *Christian Century* v134 no3 p33 F 2017

A Modest Proposal: Eliminate Email *Harvard Business Review Digital Articles* p2 F 18 2016

New Republic, The (Periodical)

The New Republic's New Tilt: The magazine repudiates its 'neoliberal' past T. DAVIDSON *American Conservative* v16 no5 p6 S/O 2017

News agencies

The AP's Pronoun Decree A. FERGUSON color *Weekly Standard* v22 no31 p10 Ap 17 2017

Finding common ground over barbecue S. Blanchard color *Columbia Journalism Review* v56 no1 p42 Spr 2017

Islamophobia in Focus E. ABDELKADER *Islamic Horizons* v46 no1 p32 Ja/F 2017

News briefs on crime

BRICKBATS C. OLIVER color *Reason* v49 no4 p80 Ag/S 2017

News gathering

SKYWITNESS NEWS C. R. JOYNT *Washingtonian Magazine* v52 no2 p26 N 2016

News periodicals

Power And the Press M. MELTON *Los Angeles Magazine* p14 Ja 2017

News websites

Consumed by the news P. W. Marty *Christian Century* v133 no24 p3 N 23 2016

How local is the local news at Gannett? L. Bastien and S. Blaskey diag *Columbia Journalism Review* v56 no1 p69 Spr 2017

How to watch the news without cable TV: 2017 edition J. NEWMAN color *PCWorld* v35 no5 p197 My 2017

Inside (The) Information M. Marr color *Columbia Journalism Review* p62 Fall/Wint 2016

Past Blast color *Sports Illustrated* v127 no1 p112 Jl 3 2017

Newseum (Washington, D.C.)

BEST OF WASHINGTON HALL OF FAME *Washingtonian Magazine* v52 no1 p206 O 2016

BEST OF WASHINGTON HALL OF FAME *Washingtonian Magazine* v52 no6 p186 Mr 2017

Newsies: The Broadway Musical! (Film)

Extra! C. Bowers color *Dance Spirit* v21 no2 p17 F 2017

Newsletters

See also

Electronic newsletters

ADD THIS MARKETING TOOL M. McGinnis *Successful Farming* v114 no11 p29 N 2016

Newsom, Gavin

Look to Cities and States *New Republic* v248 no3 p33 Mr 2017

NEWSOME, THOMAS M.

Conserving the World's Megafauna and Biodiversity: The Fierce Urgency of Now *BioScience* v67 no3 p197 Mr 2017

Making a New Dog? *BioScience* v67 no4 p374 Ap 2017

Saving the World's Terrestrial Megafauna color *BioScience* v66 no10 p807 O 1 2016

Newspaper publishing

A note from the editor K. Pope color *Columbia Journalism Review* v56 no1 p12 Spr 2017

Point/Counterpoint *Los Angeles Magazine* p14 Mr 2017

The Write Stuff T. EASTLAND *Weekly Standard* v22 no6 p5 O 17 2016

Newspaper reading

Use the News to Teach Reading Comprehension M. Zalaznick bw *Education Digest* v83 no3 p12 N 2017

Newspaper subscriptions

Power And the Press M. MELTON *Los Angeles Magazine* p14 Ja 2017

Newspapers

See also

News agencies

Newspaper sections, columns, etc.

Reporters & reporting

IN COUNTRY K. Vongkiatkajorn color *Mother Jones* v42 no1 p54 Ja/F 2017

Viet Thanh Nguyen *New York Times Book Review* p6 F 5 2017

Viet Thanh Nguyen writes about the refugees we don't remember anymore Q. D. Tran color *America* v216 no4 p38 F 20 2017

NGUYEN, VIVIAN M.

Envisioning the Future of Aquatic Animal Tracking: Technology, Science, and Application *BioScience* v67 no10 p884 O 2017

Nguyen, Vy

Evolutionary drivers of thermoadaptation in enzyme catalysis [Cover story] color graph *Science* v355 no6322 p289 Ja 20 2017

Nguyen Diep

Role for migratory wild birds in the global spread of avian influenza H5N8 bibl graph map *Science* v354 no6309 p213 O 14 2016

Nhamire, Borges

China's Troubles Down on the Farm color *Bloomberg Businessweek* no4525 p16 Je 5 2017

NHS London

NHS 'struggling with staff shortages and high workloads' *People Management* p11 F 2017

We're serious about putting patients at the heart of learning M. CALNAN *People Management* p22 F 2017

NI, WENFEI

Ecological Forecasting and the Science of Hypoxia in Chesapeake Bay *BioScience* v67 no7 p614 Jl 2017

Niacin

NIACIN DEFICIENCY RULED OUT AS GRASS SICKNESS CAUSE C. Barakat and M. McCluskey *Equus* no470 p20 N 2016

Nian, Xiao-Mei

Late Pleistocene archaic human crania from Xuchang, China bibl color diag graph *Science* v355 no6328 p969 Mr 3 2017

Niarchos, Eugenie

The INTERNATIONAL BEST-DRESSED List color *Vanity Fair* v59 no10 p97 O 2017

Niarchos, Nicolas

1633 color *New Yorker* v92 no33 p20 O 17 2016

Bunna Café color *New Yorker* v93 no6 p13 Mr 27 2017

By Chloe color *New Yorker* v93 no12 p13 My 8 2017

The Grill color *New Yorker* v93 no19 p15 Jl 3 2017

La Morada color *New Yorker* v93 no30 p15 O 2 2017

Lenox Saphire color *New Yorker* v92 no43 p15 Ja 2 2017

Pho Real color *New Yorker* v93 no23 p17 Ag 7 2017

Safari color *New Yorker* v93 no26 p17 S 4 2017

Sexy Taco/Dirty Cash color *New Yorker* v92 no48 p13 F 6 2017

Yemen Café color *New Yorker* v92 no38 p27 N 21 2016

Nibbering, Erik T. J.

Large-amplitude transfer motion of hydrated excess protons mapped by ultrafast 2D IR spectroscopy graph *Science* v357 no6350 p491 Ag 4 2017

Niblett, Robin

Liberalism in Retreat color *Foreign Affairs* v96 no1 p17 Ja/F 2017

Nicaragua—Description & travel

5 Romantic Destinations for a Baecation D. POINTDUJOUR color *Ebony* v72 no4 p66 F 2017

Nice Guys, The (Film)

THE NICE GUYS C. Gunnestad color *Sound & Vision* v82 no1 p71 Ja 2017

NICELY, JENNIFER

#Climbing Training color *Climbing* no352 p9 Ap 2017

Nichanian, Véronique—Interviews

WHAT SHE KNOWS ABOUT YOU J. von Sothen bw color *Esquire* v167 no2 p76 Mr 2017

Nichiporuk, Rita V.

Redox-based reagents for chemoselective methionine bioconjugation bibl diag graph *Science* v355 no6325 p597 F 10 2017

Nichol, Doug

The Soul of an Old Machine S. Zacharek color *Time* v190 no9 p56 S 4 2017

Nicholas, Johnny, 1948-

Cream of the Crop HADLEY color *Downbeat* v84 no1 p73 Ja 2017

Nicholas, Milton Claiborne

TESTING THE 15TH AMENDMENT H. Glasby *Prologue* v48 no4 p51 Wint 2016

Nicholas, Tom

When America Was Most Innovative, and Why bw graph *Harvard Business Review Digital Articles* p2 Mr 6 2017

Nicholas, Tsar

KNOW YOUR COCONUTS B. McCALL color *New Yorker* v93 no10 p60 Ap 24 2017

Nicholas II, Emperor of Russia, 1868-1918

A gift from the czar, and a puzzle solved T. Adams color *Magazine Antiques* v184 no4 p46 Jl/Ag 2017

Nicholes, Victoria

Psychic Arrested in Exorcism Scam B. RADFORD *Skeptical Inquirer* v41 no1 p12 Ja/F 2017

Nicholls, Miles

Publish openly but responsibly color *Science* v357 no6347 p141 Jl 14 2017

Nicholls, Robert J.

Making SDGs Work for Climate Change Hotspots bibl *Environment* v58 no6 p24 N/D 2016

Nichols, Annika L. A.

A global brain state underlies C. elegans sleep behavior diag *Science* v356 no6344 p1247 Je 23 2017

NICHOLS, ASHTON

home to roost color map *Cabin Living* p19 Je 2017

Nichols, Betty Lou

HEADS UP JOHNSON *Treasures* v6 no5 p38 Ap/My 2017

NICHOLS, CHRIS

Compound Interest color *Los Angeles Magazine* v62 no10 p128 O 2017

Double Vision in South Park. RISING UP OUT OF NOWHERE NEAR STAPLES CENTER, THE TWIN CIRCA TOWERS HAVE ALREADY ALTERED HOW WE SEE DOWNTOWN *Los Angeles Magazine* v62 no9 p24 S 2017

The Gilded Age color *Los Angeles Magazine* v62 no7 p74 Jl 2017

Hallowed Grounds color *Los Angeles Magazine* v62 no10 p131 O 2017

Homes Below $760K color *Los Angeles Magazine* v62 no10 p120 O 2017

The Wrecking Crew *Los Angeles Magazine* v62 no6 p18 Je 2017

Nichols, Elizabeth

Higher predation risk for insect prey at low latitudes and elevations graph *Science* v356 no6339 p742 My 19 2017

Nichols, Frederick W.

A life with loss color *U.S. Catholic* v82 no1 p5 Ja 2017

Nichols, Herbie

Deserving Honorees B. REED bw *Downbeat* v84 no8 p8 Ag 2017

HERBIE NICHOLS: RIGHTFUL HONOR J. Hale bw *Downbeat* v84 no8 p36 Ag 2017

Nichols, Jack—Interviews

50 YEARS AFTER THE HOMOSEXUALS B. CONNELLY bw *Advocate* no1089 p12 F/Mr 2017

Nichols, Jeff, 1978-

Loving C. Nashawaty color *Entertainment Weekly* no1439 p44 N 11 2016

No. 7 MIDNIGHT SPECIAL L. Greenblatt color *Entertainment Weekly* no1444/1445 p55 D 16 2016

The Rights of the Heart, Interpreted With Beauty by Loving S. Zacharek color *Time* v188 no20 p49 N 14 2016

RUTH on the RISE G. Wood bw color *Vogue* v207 no1 p80 Ja 2017

Nichols, John

100 Days of Resistance color *Nation* v304 no15 p3 My 8 2017

The Battle for the DNC *Nation* v304 no9 p10 Mr 20 2017

Betsy DeVos: The Investor Who Got a High Return color *Progressive* v81 no7 p57 O/N 2017

The Case for Impeachment color *Progressive* v81 no6 p18 Ag/S 2017

DEMOCRACY DENIED bw map *Progressive* p15 D 2016/Ja 2017

Down-Ballot Hopefuls *Nation* v303 no18 p6 O 31 2016

Drop the College color *Nation* v303 no25/26 p3 D 19 2016

For Impeachment *Nation* v304 no18 p4 Je 19 2017

Harvard's Shame *Nation* v305 no8 p4 O 9 2017

HORSEMEN of the TRUMPOCALYPSE color il *Nation* v305 no6 p18 S 11 2017

How to Fight Back il *Nation* v304 no10 p3 Mr 27 2017

How to Revive Democracy *Nation* v305 no3 p3 Jl 31 2017

HOW TO TAKE BACK RURAL AMERICA color *Nation* v305

p26 S 2017

HAPPY MEAL color *Field & Stream* v121 no8 p38 F/Mr 2017

HERE THEY COME color *Field & Stream* v122 no5 p27 O 2017

HIGHS AND LOW COUNTRY color *Field & Stream* v121 no9 p58 Ap 2017

The Locals color *Field & Stream* v122 no4 p60 S 2017

LOCKJAW LESSONS color *Field & Stream* v122 no4 p32 S 2017

NO SMALL MATTER color *Field & Stream* v122 no6 p20 N 2017

ONE LASTING CAST color *Field & Stream* v121 no9 p22 Ap 2017

THIS LAND WAS YOUR LAND cartoon color diag map *Field & Stream* v122 no1 p40 My 2017

THE TRUE North color *Field & Stream* v122 no5 p66 O 2017

THE WILDERNESS WAY cartoon *Field & Stream* v122 no1 p26 My 2017

WILD FIRES color *Field & Stream* v121 no8 p44 F/Mr 2017

Nickerson, Brittany Wood

Recipes from the Herbalist's Kitchen: Delicious, Nourishing Food for Lifelong Health and Well-Being *Publishers Weekly* v264 no18 p53 My 1 2017

Nickerson, N. H.

Entanglement distillation between solid-state quantum network nodes diag *Science* v356 no6341 p928 Je 1 2017

Nickisch, Curt

Industrial Espionage Is More Effective Than R&D il img *Harvard Business Review* v94 no11 p30 N 2016

Leaders Who Get How to Give color *Harvard Business Review Digital Articles* p2 Ja 24 2017

LEADERS WHO GET HOW TO GIVE *Harvard Business Review Digital Articles* p12 Ja 1 2017

The Market Punished "Panama Papers" Firms to the Tune of $230 Billion *Harvard Business Review Digital Articles* p2 My 16 2016

The Olympics Needs a New Business Model *Harvard Business Review Digital Articles* p2 Ag 5 2016

Outsider CEOs Are on the Rise at the World's Biggest Companies *Harvard Business Review Digital Articles* p2 Ap 19 2016

Nick Lai, Kuan-Yu

A placental growth factor is silenced in mouse embryos by the zinc finger protein ZFP568 color graph *Science* v356 no6339 p757 My 19 2017

Nicklaus, Jack, 1940-

JACK ON ARNIE color *Golf Magazine* v58 no12 p28 D 2016

TEEING OFF J. Sens color *Golf Magazine* v59 no7 p18 Jl 2017

You're Up! color *Golf Magazine* v59 no5 p13 My 2017

Nicklen, Paul

Life on Ice E. B. RUSBY color *Earth Island Journal* v32 no2 p27 Summ 2017

The Seal who Loved Me MY UNDERWATER ADVENTURE ANTARCTICA *National Geographic Kids* no466 p28 D 2016/Ja 2017

NICKLIN, MARY WINSTON

Euro Star color *Conde Nast Traveler* v52 no3 p42 Mr 2017

Nicknames

CALL OF THE WILD C. ROSE color *New Orleans Magazine* v51 no3 p40 Ja 2017

"IT'S FOR YOU, JACKIE" J. CURRY *Washingtonian Magazine* v52 no2 p312 N 2016

NICKOLS, KERRY J.

The Resilience of Marine Ecosystems to Climatic Disturbances *BioScience* v67 no3 p208 Mr 2017

Nicks, Stevie, 1948-

Random Notes bw color *Rolling Stone* no1289 p32 Je 15 2017

Nicks, Stevie, 1948——Interviews

Stevie Nicks A. GREENE bw *Rolling Stone* no1283 p58 Mr 23 2017

Nicky Jam, 1981-

Nicky Jam D. Kiper color *Current Biography* v78 no3 p36 Mr 2017

NICODEMO, ALLIE

Putting Peer Pressure in Its Place *USA Today Magazine* v146 no2868 p38 S 2017

TWEETING TERROR *USA Today Magazine* v145 no2860 p46 Ja 2017

Nicol, Andrew

Complex multifault rupture during the 2016 Mw 7.8 Kaikōura earthquake, New Zealand color map *Science* v356 no6334 p154 Ap 14 2017

Nicola, Stefan

Achtung, Berlin: Your Flight Is Five Years Late color *Bloomberg Businessweek* no4517 p18 Ap 3 2017

Europe's Startup Factory Sputters color *Bloomberg Businessweek* no4495 p31 O 17 2016

Germany Builds An Election Firewall *Bloomberg Businessweek* no4527 p48 Je 19 2017

How Facebook Could Stop bw color *Bloomberg Businessweek* no4524 p56 My 29 2017

The Kremlin's New Disinformation Machine *Bloomberg Businessweek* no4512 p27 F 20 2017

Spread Your Wings and Fly, Penguin color graph *Bloomberg Businessweek* no4509 p17 Ja 30 2017

Where YouTube Meets The Boob Tube graph *Bloomberg Businessweek* no4512 p44 F 20 2017

NICOLAKIS, THEO

Astell&Kern AK XB10 Bluetooth DAC and amp: Wireless, hi-res audio for any headphones color *Macworld - Digital Edition* v34 no11 p129 N 2017

BEYERDYNAMIC AMIRON HOME HEADPHONES color *Macworld - Digital Edition* p35 Mr 2017

JBL E55BT review: These modestly priced cans deliver strong features color *Macworld - Digital Edition* p102 Je 13 2017

ULTIMATE EARS MEGABOOM BLUETOOTH SPEAKER: BUILT TO BE THE LIFE OF THE PARTY color *Macworld Digital Edition* v33 no11 p48 N 2016

Nicolas-Troyan, Cedric

THE HUNTSMAN: WINTER'S WAR D. Vaughn color *Sound & Vision* v82 no1 p69 Ja 2017

Nicolau, Bruno G.

Restored iron transport by a small molecule promotes absorption and hemoglobinization in animals color graph *Science* v356 no6338 p608 My 12 2017

NICOLAY, FRANZ

Satisfaction: How does this country acknowledge the power of sexuality? Through music, Ann Powers says *New York Times Book Review* p11 S 3 2017

Nicolaÿ, Renaud

High-performance vitrimers from commodity thermoplastics through dioxaborolane metathesis color diag *Science* v356 no6333 p62 Ap 7 2017

Nicole, Fred

Swiss Precision Instrument B. BLANCHARD color *Climbing* no353 p40 My/Je 2017

Nicolosi, Valeria

All-printed thin-film transistors from networks of liquid-exfoliated nanosheets diag *Science* v356 no6333 p69 Ap 7 2017

Nicotine—Metabolism

Nicotine Metabolism Makes Smokers Crave *USA Today Magazine* v145 no2861 p16 F 2017

Niculescu-Oglinzanu, M.

Observation of a large-scale anisotropy in the arrival directions of cosmic rays above 8×10^{18} eV *Science* v357 no6357 p1266 S 22 2017

Nides, Thomas R.

FRIENDS IN HIGH PLACES A. MACGILLIS cartoon *New Yorker* v92 no37 p36 N 14 2016

Nido-Russo, Alexis

ALEXIS NIDO-RUSSO J. BERG cartoon color *Chicago* v66 no3 p56 Mr 2017

Nie, Tianxiao

Chiral Majorana fermion modes in a quantum anomalous Hall insulator–superconductor structure diag *Science* v357 no6348 p294 Jl 21 2017

Nie, W.

Extremely efficient internal exciton dissociation through edge states in layered 2D perovskites bibl graph *Science* v355 no6331 p1288 Mr 24 2017

Niebuhr, Carsten

THE GREAT EXPEDITION: A Danish-German survey sought to unearth the roots of the Hebrew Bible in Arabia. It became the first to comprehend a new Islamic ideology, which now threatens the West M. Ronan *History Today* v67 no6 p72 Je 2016

Niebuhr, Reinhold, 1892-1971
Realism without despair J. Sabella *Christian Century* v134 no18 p10 Ag 30 2017
Shaping a conscience P. W. Marty *Christian Century* v134 no18 p3 Ag 30 2017
Why Niebuhr mattered J. Byassee *Christian Century* v134 no7 p44 Mr 29 2017

Niebuhr, Richard Reinhold
People A. M. Banks color *Christian Century* v134 no7 p17 Mr 29 2017

Niechciol, M.
Observation of a large-scale anisotropy in the arrival directions of cosmic rays above 8×10^{18} eV *Science* v357 no6357 p1266 S 22 2017

Niederle, Muriel
New Research: Women Who Don't Negotiate Might Have a Good Reason *Harvard Business Review Digital Articles* p2 Ap 12 2016

NIEDOBA, SARAH
For beer drinkers, by beer drinkers color *Maclean's* v130 no4 p56 My 2017

Nieduszynski, Conrad A.
Deep functional analysis of synII, a 770-kilobase synthetic yeast chromosome diag *Science* v355 no6329 p1047 Mr 10 2017

Niedzviecki, Hal
THE ARCHAEOLOGISTS B. BETHUNE bw color *Maclean's* v129 no44 p112 N 7 2016

Niehardt, John
PREMONITION J. G. Neihardt *Lapham's Quarterly* v10 no3 p91 Summ 2017

Nielaba, Peter
Quantized thermal transport in single-atom junctions bibl diag graph *Science* v355 no6330 p1192 Mr 17 2017

Nielsen, Chantrelle
Measuring Your Employees' Invisible Forms of Influence *Harvard Business Review Digital Articles* p2 N 7 2016
What Work Email Can Reveal About Performance and Potential *Harvard Business Review Digital Articles* p2 F 10 2016

NIELSEN, ELIZABETH CONNELL
Opera Omaha *Opera News* v81 no7 p60 Ja 2017

Nielsen, Jenny
Amid high tensions, an urgent need for nuclear restraint bibl *Bulletin of the Atomic Scientists* v73 no4 p279 Jl 2017

NIELSEN, JULIUS
Dating a Greenland Shark *Natural History* v125 no2 p10 F 2017

Nielsen, Karina
Research: How Incentive Pay Affects Employee Engagement, Satisfaction, and Trust *Harvard Business Review Digital Articles* p2 Mr 15 2017

NIELSEN, KIRK
Bad Vibes in Big Cypress *Sierra* v101 no4 p50 Jl/Ag 2016

Nielsen, Peter
Beneteau Foiler Makes its Debut color diag *Sail* v48 no10 p26 O 2017
Big, Bold and Classy color *Sail* v48 no2 p28 F 2017
Breaking the Mold color *Sail* v48 no7 p20 Jl 2017
Catalina 425 cartoon color *Sail* v48 no1 p26 Ja 2017
COASTAL CRUISING Gear color *Sail* v48 no5 p26 My 2017
Crazy Times at Sea *Sail* v48 no3 p4 Mr 2017
Distance isn't Everything color *Sail* v48 no6 p4 Je 2017
Doing it By the Book *Sail* v47 no12 p6 D 2016
Drawing from Life cartoon *Sail* v48 no4 p6 Ap 2017
European Newcomers color *Sail* v48 no6 p24 Je 2017
Following the Dream *Sail* v48 no2 p4 F 2017
Gear color *Sail* v48 no11 p30 N 2017
Gear color *Sail* v48 no1 p22 Ja 2017
Gear color *Sail* v48 no4 p32 Ap 2017
Gear color *Sail* v48 no6 p30 Je 2017
Gear color *Sail* v48 no8 p28 Ag 2017
Ghost in the machine *Sail* v48 no7 p4 Jl 2017
HH66 cartoon color *Sail* v48 no2 p32 F 2017
Higher Tech color *Sail* v48 no7 p48 Jl 2017
HOME IS WHERE THE BOAT IS color map *Sail* v48 no3 p38 Mr 2017
Informational overload? color *Sail* v48 no5 p4 My 2017
The Kraken Awakes color *Sail* v48 no11 p20 N 2017

Light Refreshment color *Sail* v48 no3 p56 Mr 2017
MATTHEW'S AFTERMATH color *Sail* v47 no12 p13 D 2016
NATURE'S WRATH color *Sail* v48 no11 p10 N 2017
ORIENT Excess color map *Sail* v48 no10 p44 O 2017
Raymarine EV-100 Wheelpilot color *Sail* v48 no4 p70 Ap 2017
Rigged for Success *Sail* v48 no1 p6 Ja 2017
Sail Care color *Sail* v48 no1 p44 Ja 2017
The Show Goes On color *Sail* v48 no4 p24 Ap 2017
Slow Track to Havana color *Sail* v48 no6 p20 Je 2017
A Solid Half-Century *Sail* v48 no10 p6 O 2017
Star Struck *Sail* v48 no9 p4 S 2017
STAYING ALIVE color *Sail* v48 no7 p42 Jl 2017
Taking it all with you *Sail* v48 no8 p4 Ag 2017
Tender Touch-Up [Cover story] color *Sail* v48 no8 p58 Ag 2017
Triumph of Will [Cover story] color *Sail* v48 no8 p10 Ag 2017

Nielsen, Robin
Raising Canes L. VACCARIELLO *Cincinnati Magazine* v50 no2 p136 N 2016

Nielsen, Tomas
The 5 Paradoxes of Digital Business Leadership *Harvard Business Review Digital Articles* p2 Jl 2 2015

Niemann, Christoph
Gap Life *Publishers Weekly* v263 no40 p125 O 3 2016
MR. KNOW-IT-ALL cartoon *Wired* v25 no3 p26 Mr 2017

Niemann, Michael
Illicit Trade: A Valentin Vermeulen Thriller *Publishers Weekly* v264 no1 p39 Ja 2 2017

Niemeier, Ulrike
Sulfur injections for a cooler planet color graph *Science* v357 no6348 p246 Jl 21 2017

Niemeijer, Andre R.
Understanding induced seismicity bibl color graph *Science* v354 no6318 p1380 D 16 2016

Niemeyer, Simon
Twelve Key Findings in Deliberative Democracy Research *Daedalus* v146 no3 p28 Summ 2017

NIEMI, MATTHEW DAVID ABDULHAQQ
Navigating Challenges and Seizing Opportunities *Islamic Horizons* v45 no6 p16 N/D 2016

Niemietz, L.
Observation of a large-scale anisotropy in the arrival directions of cosmic rays above 8×10^{18} eV *Science* v357 no6357 p1266 S 22 2017

NIEMTUS, ZOFIA
THE URBANIST: Lisbon: Why the European expats are coming by the EasyJet-ful img *New York* v50 no9 p62 My 1 2017

Nienaber, Suzanne
Place-Based Desing and Civic Health: New findings from the Center for Active Design's Assembly Civic Engagement Survey *Parks & Recreation* v52 no9 p62 S 2017

Nieng Yan
Structural basis for the gating mechanism of the type 2 ryanodine receptor RyR2 bibl color graph *Science* v354 no6310 paah5324-1 O 21 2016

Nierenberg, George
Tap Masters J. Acocella bw *New Yorker* v93 no20 p14 Jl 10 2017

Nierlich, Ray
Service cartoon color *Cycle World* v56 no3 p58 Ap 2017
Service color *Cycle World* v56 no2 p62 Mr 2017
Service color *Cycle World* v56 no5 p63 Je 2017
SERVICE color *Cycle World* v56 no7 p54 Ag 2017
Service color *Cycle World* v56 no8 p60 S 2017
Service color *Cycle World* v56 no9 p58 O 2017

Niesen, Joan
THE AGONY AND ECSTASY OF OT color *Sports Illustrated* v125 no16 p48 N 14 2016
PRO MOTION chart color *Sports Illustrated* v127 no5 p71 Ag 14 2017
W STARTS WITH D color *Sports Illustrated* v125 no13 p36 O 17 2016

Niessen-Ruenzi, Alexandra
CEOs Earn Less at More-Prestigious Firms color *Harvard Business Review Digital Articles* p2 F 2 2017

NIETO, PEÑA
MEXICO DOES NOT BELIEVE IN WALLS *Vital Speeches of the Day* v83 no3 p78 Mr 2017

Nieto-Rodriguez, Antonio
  How to Prioritize Your Company's Projects *Harvard Business Review Digital Articles* p2 D 13 2016

Nietzsche, Friedrich Wilhelm, 1844-1900
  1888: Turin *Lapham's Quarterly* v10 no2 p64 Spr 2017
  THOUGHTS ON Conflict *Forbes* v199 no4 p112 Ap 25 2017

NIEUWESTEEG, TARA
  Sea Change *D: The Magazine of Dallas* v43 no10 p78 O 2016

Nifadkar, Sushil S.
  Your New Hires Won't Succeed Unless You Onboard Them Properly *Harvard Business Review Digital Articles* p2 Je 20 2017

Nigeria—Economic conditions
  NIGERIA'S INVISIBLE CRISIS [Cover story] L. Roberts color map *Science* v356 no6333 p18 Ap 7 2017

Nigerian novelists
  FROM NIGERIA TO AMERICA AND BACK A. Frykholm *Christian Century* v133 no24 p33 N 23 2016

Nigerian Civil War, 1967-1970
  BIAFRA 50 YEARS ON: The civil war that resulted from the division of Nigeria was a major human disaster that should not be forgotten R. T. Howard *History Today* v67 no6 p36 Je 2016

Nigerians—Social conditions—21st century
  WE HAVE NO CHOICE B. TAUB cartoon color map *New Yorker* v93 no8 p36 Ap 10 2017

Nigeria—Officials & employees
  Nigeria's Unity Is Settled and Not Negotiable *Vital Speeches of the Day* v83 no10 p292 O 2017

Nigeria—Politics & government
  A Nigerian President's Disappointing Return E. OBADARE *Current History* v116 no790 p194 My 2017

Nigeria—Religion
  The Hand of Iran In Nigeria D. Abu-Nasr color *Bloomberg Businessweek* no4514 p17 Mr 13 2017

Nigeria—Social conditions—21st century
  The Hand of Iran In Nigeria D. Abu-Nasr color *Bloomberg Businessweek* no4514 p17 Mr 13 2017

Nigg, Joseph, 1782-1863
  Birds of Paradise M. MATTIX cartoon *Weekly Standard* v22 no27 p36 Mr 20 2017

Niggemann, T.
  Observation of a large-scale anisotropy in the arrival directions of cosmic rays above 8×1018 eV *Science* v357 no6357 p1266 S 22 2017

Nighan, Michael J.
  Q: Who Is the Worst Leader of All Time? color *Atlantic* v319 no1 p100 Ja/F 2017

Night
  Encounters with the Other Side *Reader's Digest* v188 no1124 p116 O 2016
  Ghost Hunters in the Dark B. RADFORD *Skeptical Inquirer* v41 no1 p32 Ja/F 2017

Night blindness
  OUR FAMILY'S TOP DOG B. STUMP color *Men's Health* v32 no6 p127 Ag 2017

Night fishing
  BRING ON THE NIGHT D. KARCZYNSKI and G. BETHGE color *Outdoor Life* v224 no5 p36 Je/Jl 2017
  SPORTING LIFE *Cincinnati Magazine* v50 no8 p50 My 2017

Night lamps—Design & construction
  Solar-Powered Night-Light chart color diag *Popular Mechanics* p90 F 2017

Night photography
  All of the lights M. HEMMADI color *Maclean's* v130 no4 p18 My 2017
  Q&A: Shane McDermott *Arizona Highways* v93 no3 p9 Mr 2017

Night School (Film)
  WONDER WOMEN S. KLAWANS color *Nation* v305 no1 p44 Jl 3 2017

Night work
  Research night owls Y. N. Majchrzak, M. Soták et al color *Science* v354 no6315 p964 N 25 2016

Night work—Physiological aspects
  THE SCIENTIFIC NIGHT SHIFT S. Kean color *Science* v354 no6315 p988 N 25 2016

Nightcap (TV program)
  Ali Wentworth Talks the Talk D. Coggan color *Entertainment Weekly* no1440 p16 N 18 2016
  Fancy a Nightcap With These Folks? R. Kinane color *Entertainment Weekly* no1470 p49 Je 16 2017

Nightclubs
  NIGHT CLUBBING G. HAND *Cincinnati Magazine* v50 no8 p51 My 2017
  THEY OWNED THE NIGHT M. THOMAS bw color *Chicago* v66 no11 p96 N 2017

Nightclubs—Evaluation
  THE AFTER-AFTER-PARTY *Indianapolis Monthly* p67 F 2017
  It Takes TWO M. SWANN bw color *Conde Nast Traveler* v52 no10 p114 N 2017
  A Little Slice Of Havana D. ROTHBART *Los Angeles Magazine* p55 F 2017

Nightclubs—Social aspects
  DANCERS AT EL CHISPAS K. GOODRICH *Indianapolis Monthly* v40 no11 p18 Jl 2017

Nightcrawler (Film)
  FIGHT THE POWER A. Carter color *Esquire* p32 N 2017

Nightforce Optics Inc.
  NIGHTFORCE 4-16X42 F1 ATACR J. B. SNOW color *Outdoor Life* v224 no1 pR16 D 2016/Ja 2017

Nighthawks (Music)
  Erik Friedlander's Cello Solo on '26 Gasoline Stations' J. DURSO bw color *Downbeat* v84 no1 p104 Ja 2017

Nightlife
  NIGHT CLUBBING G. HAND *Cincinnati Magazine* v50 no8 p51 My 2017
  NIGHT LIFE *New Yorker* v93 no27 p8 S 11 2017
  NIGHT MOVES A. BERNSTEIN, M. BRANDSTETTER et al *Cincinnati Magazine* v50 no8 p40 My 2017
  ON THE FLY color *Vanity Fair* v58 no12 p83 D 2016

Night Manager, The (TV program)
  The Night Manager J. Krebs chart color *Sound & Vision* v82 no1 p68 Ja 2017

Nightmares—Humor
  Humor in Uniform color *Reader's Digest* v190 no1133 p139 S 2017

Night Of, The (TV program)
  The 3-Minute Interview K. Branch and J. Harman color *Glamour* v115 no1 p18 Ja 2017
  Episodes in hell B. F. Jones color *Christian Century* v133 no23 p43 N 9 2016

Night Shift, The (TV program)
  Night Shift's New Nurse A. D'Arminio *TV Guide* v65 no25 p8 Je 2017

Nightshirts—Evaluation
  Quirky Chic cartoon color *Seventeen* v76 no12 p45 D 2016/Ja 2017

Nightstands (Furniture)—Evaluation
  TEEN DREAM L. MOWRY *Atlanta* v56 no10 p48 F 2017

NIGRO, RICHARD
  Chords & Discords bw *Downbeat* v84 no1 p10 Ja 2017

Nihilism
  THE YEAR OF LIVING HOPELESSLY R. CLARK cartoon *Christianity Today* v60 no9 p25 N 2016

Niikura, Hiromichi
  Coherent imaging of an attosecond electron wave packet bw chart diag *Science* v356 no6343 p1150 Je 16 2017

Niinemets, Ülo
  Global climatic drivers of leaf size [Cover story] graph *Science* v357 no6354 p917 S 1 2017

Nijhawan, Deepak
  Anticancer sulfonamides target splicing by inducing RBM39 degradation via recruitment to DCAF15 color diag *Science* v356 no6336 p397 Ap 28 2017

Nijhuis, Michelle
  THE PARKS OF TOMORROW color diag graph map *National Geographic* v230 no6 p102 D 2016
  When Cooking Kills color map *National Geographic* v232 no3 p76 S 2017

Nike Inc.
  Can Lean Manufacturing Put an End to Sweatshops? G. Distelhorst *Harvard Business Review Digital Articles* p2 My 26 2016
  GET YOUR KICKS color *Wired* v24 no12 p18 D 2016
  GIVE ME TWO PAIR *Cincinnati Magazine* v50 no8 p27 My

2017

JUST DO IT REDO IT TRY NOT TO UNDO IT DON'T LOSE TO ADIDAS I. Boudway, K. Stock et al color *Bloomberg Businessweek* no4523 p42 My 22 2017

Movers K. Stock color graph *Bloomberg Businessweek* no4505 p11 D 26 2016

NIKE DAY TO NIGHT APPLE WATCH BANDS R. LOYOLA color *Macworld - Digital Edition* p32 Je 13 2017

OFF THE MAT S. Marikar cartoon *New Yorker* v93 no14 p31 My 22 2017

Paloma Elsesser S. DRUMMOND color *Vogue* v207 no11 p126 N 2017

Setting Big Hairy Goals—and Missing P. Wahba color *Fortune* v176 no2 p16 Ag 1 2017

TEST OF TIME J. Dengate and M. Shorten color *Runner's World* v52 no4 p14 My 2017

THREE RABBITS AND A GUINEA PIG D. WILLEY color *Runner's World* v52 no2 p10 Mr 2017

winter SHOE GUIDE J. DENGATE and M. SHORTEN cartoon chart color diag graph *Runner's World* v51 no11 p87 D 2016

Niki, Shigeru

Terawatt-scale photovoltaics: Trajectories and challenges chart graph *Science* v356 no6334 p141 Ap 14 2017

Nikitas, Theano

RAW TO GO color *Popular Photography* v80 no11 p40 D 2016

Tin Works bw *Popular Photography* v81 no1 p68 Ja/F 2017

Niklas, Karl

THE EVOLUTION OF PLANTS J. PRESTON *BioScience* v67 no6 p577 Je 2017

Niklaus, Pascal A.

Positive biodiversity-productivity relationship predominant in global forests bibl chart graph map *Science* v354 no6309 paaf8957-1 O 14 2016

Nikola Motor Co.

HAULIN' JUICE C. Atiyeh color *Car & Driver* v62 no11 p24 My 2017

Nikolov, Nikolay

HAT-P-26b: A Neptune-mass exoplanet with a well-constrained heavy element abundance chart diag graph *Science* v356 no6338 p628 My 12 2017

Nikolova, Hristina

Men Choose Differently When They Choose with Other Men *Harvard Business Review Digital Articles* p2 S 14 2016

Nikon camera

Best Bins for Your Buck *Audubon* v118 no6 p44 Wint 2016

Nikon camera—Evaluation

NIKON KEYMISSION 360 color *Flying* v144 no3 p15 Mr 2017

THEATER IN THE ROUND A. Ryder color *Popular Photography* v81 no1 p20 Ja/F 2017

ULTIMATE "IT" Gifts color *Good Housekeeping* v263 no6 p71 D 2016

Nikon Corp.

ENTER HERE P. Ryan bw color graph *Popular Photography* v81 no1 p92 Ja/F 2017

EYES IN THE SKIES P. Saha color *Audubon* v119 no3 p46 Fall 2017

NIKON KEYMISSION 360 color *Flying* v144 no3 p15 Mr 2017

Nik-Zainal, Serena

Mutational signatures associated with tobacco smoking in human cancer bibl graph *Science* v354 no6312 p618 N 4 2016

Nile Hilton Incident, The (Film)

A Dirty Business N. Rapold color *Film Comment* v53 no2 p8 Mr/Ap 2017

Nilekani, Nandan

Titans color *Time* v189 no16/17 p94 My 1-8 2017

Nilgiri Biosphere Reserve (India)

THE TIGER WATCHERS M. BENANAV *Sierra* v102 no4 p36 Jl/Ag 2017

NILON, CHARLES H.

Planning for the Future of Urban Biodiversity: A Global Review of City-Scale Initiatives *BioScience* v67 no4 p332 Ap 2017

Nilsen, Anders

Sketchbook *New York Times Book Review* p27 Je 25 2017

Nilsson, Emil

Single-cell RNA-seq reveals new types of human blood dendritic cells, monocytes, and progenitors color *Science* v356 no6335 p283 Ap 21 2017

Nilsson, Gladys—Exhibitions

GLADYS NILSSON J. Kreimer cartoon *Art in America* v105 no4 p112 Ap 2017

Nilsson, Jeff

Crowd-Sourced *Saturday Evening Post* v288 no6 p114 N/D 2016

FROM THE ARCHIVE *Saturday Evening Post* v289 no2 p94 Mr/Ap 2017

Notice Anything Unusual? *Saturday Evening Post* v289 no2 p102 Mr/Ap 2017

Psst! Wanna Hear a Secret? *Saturday Evening Post* v289 no1 p106 Ja/F 2017

Stepping in for Gls *Saturday Evening Post* v289 no4 p98 Jl/Ag 2017

Sweet Memories *Saturday Evening Post* v289 no5 p99 S/O 2017

Willie Gillis Comes Home *Saturday Evening Post* v289 no3 p102 My/Je 2017

Nilsson, K. Peter R.

De novo design of a biologically active amyloid bibl graph *Science* v354 no6313 paah4949-1 N 11 2016

Nilsson, Lennart, 1922-2017

Lennart Nilsson's Unborn Beauties B. SEITZ color *National Review* v69 no5 p36 Mr 20 2017

Nilsson, Peter

A pathology atlas of the human cancer transcriptome diag *Science* v357 no6352 p660 Ag 18 2017

A subcellular map of the human proteome color *Science* v356 no6340 p820 My 26 2017

Nimbus Boats AB

NIMBUS 365 COUPE: A SWEDISH BUILDER COOKS UP A WEST COAST-WORTHY FAMILY COASTAL CRUISER color *Sea Magazine* v109 no7 p38 Jl 2017

NIMEN, THOMAS ROYAL

Home of the Brave cartoon *Reader's Digest* v190 no1132 p99 Jl/Ag 2017

Nîmes (France)—History

MEMENTO MORI J. A. LOBELL color *Archaeology* v70 no2 p38 Mr/Ap 2017

Nimmo, Francis

Formation of the Orientale lunar multiring basin bibl graph *Science* v354 no6311 p441 O 28 2016

Global drainage patterns and the origins of topographic relief on Earth, Mars, and Titan diag graph *Science* v356 no6339 p727 My 19 2017

Gravity field of the Orientale basin from the Gravity Recovery and Interior Laboratory Mission bibl graph *Science* v354 no6311 p438 O 28 2016

Nimoy, Julie—Interviews

Leonard's Lasting Legacy bw *Maclean's* v129 no47 p41 N 28 2016

Nimoy, Leonard, 1931-2015

Leonard's Lasting Legacy bw *Maclean's* v129 no47 p41 N 28 2016

Nimura, Tsuyoshi

Fashion Cares For Its Own A. RONAN img *New York* v49 no25 p84 D 12 2016

Nin, Anais, 1903-1977—Diaries

A DREAM PREFERRED A. Nin *Harper's Magazine* v334 no2004 p18 My 2017

Ninan, T. N.

Turn of the Tortoise: The Challenge and Promise of India's Future A. J. Nathan *Foreign Affairs* v95 no6 p191 N/D 2016

Nine Inch Nails (Performer)

The Playlist color *Rolling Stone* no1293 p8 Ag 10 2017

Nine West Group Inc.

FASHION UNDER $100 color *Redbook* p60 Ap 2017

KICK IT! color *InStyle* v24 no10 p143 O 2017

Petal Pumps color *Good Housekeeping* v264 no3 p15 Mr 2017

Niner Bikes (Company)

niner jet 9 T. Engel color *Bike Magazine* v24 no3 p104 My 2017

Niner RIP 9 R. Cleek and B. Cole color *Bike Magazine* v24 no6 p114 Ag 2017

Nineteen sixties

Hope I Die Before I Get Young J. Epstein *Commentary* v143 no2 p34 F 2017

Nineteen eighty-nine, A.D.

CHRISTMAS OF '89 E. LABORDE bw *New Orleans Magazine* v51 no2 p152 D 2016

Ninety-five Theses

KNOCK ON WOOD P. SCHJELDAHL cartoon *New Yorker* v92 no37 p92 N 14 2016

Purgatory now! P. R. Hinlicky *Christian Century* v134 no14 p30 Jl 5 2017

Ning Li

Team Leaders Should Play Favorites (but Only in Moderation) *Harvard Business Review Digital Articles* p2 Ja 13 2016

Teamwork Works Best When Top Performers Are Rewarded *Harvard Business Review Digital Articles* p2 Mr 14 2016

Ninja

NINJA GIRAFFES D. BROWN *National Geographic Kids* no468 p24 Mr 2017

NINTEMANN, TERRI

Blowin' in the Wind *USA Today Magazine* v146 no2868 p73 S 2017

Nintendo Co. Ltd.

An Ancient Power Awakens, and Evolves, In New Zelda M. Peckham color *Time* v189 no9 p54 Mr 13 2017

Disney, Mario, and Yo-Kai Prove a Delight *USA Today Magazine* v145 no2858 p80 N 2016

How to use the Nintendo Switch's Joy-Cons with your Mac—and why you'd want to A. HAYWARD color *Macworld - Digital Edition* v34 no4 p13 My 2017

The New Zen of Playing Old Video Games M. Peckham color *Time* v190 no16/17 p109 O 23 2017

Nintendo Bets Big on the Switch D. Z. Morris color *Fortune* v175 no3 p18 Mr 1 2017

Nintendo's New Guard Tries to Switch It Up Y. Nakamura and S. Stapczynski color *Bloomberg Businessweek* no4514 p35 Mr 13 2017

Nintendo Switches Up Mobile Gaming With a Novel Console M. Peckham color *Time* v189 no9 p55 Mr 13 2017

Nintendo Switch Launches This month *USA Today Magazine* v145 no2862 p80 Mr 2017

See Mario. See Mario Run B. Einhorn and Y. Nakamura color graph *Bloomberg Businessweek* no4503 p29 D 12 2016

TOO FUN TO FAIL K. Sintumuang cartoon color *Esquire* p32 Ap 2017

With Arms, Nintendo Wants to Rekindle Excitement for Motion Controls M. Peckham color *Time* v189 no24 p53 Je 26 2017

Nintendo video game consoles

Nintendo Bets Big on the Switch D. Z. Morris color *Fortune* v175 no3 p18 Mr 1 2017

A real console, really mobile S. Horazcek and A. Smith color *Popular Science* v289 no6 p18 N/D 2017

Nintendo video game consoles—Evaluation

Gadgets to Gift C. Everett color *Entertainment Weekly* no1441 p15 N 25 2016

Nintendo Switch console details revealed H. DINGMAN color *PCWorld* v35 no2 p28 F 2017

Nintendo Switches Up Mobile Gaming With a Novel Console M. Peckham color *Time* v189 no9 p55 Mr 13 2017

Nintendo video games

Mario on an iPhone? It Works M. Peckham color *Time* v189 no3 p59 Ja 16 2017

The New Zen of Playing Old Video Games M. Peckham color *Time* v190 no16/17 p109 O 23 2017

With Arms, Nintendo Wants to Rekindle Excitement for Motion Controls M. Peckham color *Time* v189 no24 p53 Je 26 2017

Nintendo video games—Evaluation

Disney, Mario, and Yo-Kai Prove a Delight *USA Today Magazine* v145 no2858 p80 N 2016

There's No Match for Nintendo Gameplay *USA Today Magazine* v146 no2866 p79 Jl 2017

Nipkow, Kim

Model tracks in dirt and cinders color *Model Railroader* v84 no7 p40 Jl 2017

Nipple (Anatomy)—Anatomy

Our Doc Will See You Now R. Rajapaksa color *Health* v31 no2 p86 Mr 2017

This Is You on Sex A. Levi color *Health* v31 no6 p86 Jl 2017

Nipton (Calif.)

THE PROMISED LAND D. Slater color *Sunset* v238 no4 p68

Ap 2017

Niquette, Mark

An Infrastructure Plan From Down Under diag *Bloomberg Businessweek* no4534 p37 Ag 14 2017

In Ohio, the Ground War Goes Door-to-Door color *Bloomberg Businessweek* no4494 p26 O 10 2016

Is Trump's Plan Shovel - Ready??? color *Bloomberg Businessweek* no4513 p45 Mr 6 2017

Raising Private Money For Public Projects *Bloomberg Businessweek* no4513 p46 Mr 6 2017

Nirav Modi (Company)

The BUY Jewelry color *Harper's Bazaar* no3648 p88 N 2016

Nirenberg, Ron—Interviews

CHANGING The Conversation C. HOOKS *Texas Monthly* v45 no8 p44 Ag 2017

Nirujogi, Raja S.

Homer1a drives homeostatic scaling-down of excitatory synapses during sleep bibl graph *Science* v355 no6324 p511 F 3 2017

Nisalak, Ananda

Dengue diversity across spatial and temporal scales: Local structure and the effect of host population size bibl graph *Science* v355 no6331 p1302 Mr 24 2017

NISBET, MATTHEW

Evolution in the College Classroom Facilitating Conversations about Science and Religion *Skeptical Inquirer* v41 no5 p22 S/O 2017

The March for Science: Partisan Protests Put Public Trust in Scientists at Risk *Skeptical Inquirer* v41 no4 p18 Jl/Ag 2017

The Mindfulness Movement *Skeptical Inquirer* v41 no3 p24 My/Je 2017

The Superbug Crisis *Skeptical Inquirer* v41 no1 p27 Ja/F 2017

Winning the Vaccine War *Skeptical Inquirer* v40 no6 p27 N/D 2016

NISBET, MATTHEW C.

What's That Buzzing Noise? Public Opinion on the Use of Drones for Conservation Science *BioScience* v67 no4 p382 Ap 2017

Nisbet, Roger M.

Chemical safety must extend to ecosystems *Science* v356 no6341 p917 Je 1 2017

Nisenholtz, Martin

What Trump Understands About Using Social Media to Drive Attention color *Harvard Business Review Digital Articles* p2 Mr 1 2017

Nishi, Toshio

At Fukushima, Still More Heat than Light: Six years after a tsunami struck the Honshu coast, the ruins of the nuclear power plant seethe and the Japanese still await honest answers *Hoover Digest: Research & Opinion on Public Policy* no3 p102 Summ 2017

Nishihara, H.

Structural basis of the redox switches in the NAD+-reducing soluble [NiFe]-hydrogenase diag *Science* v357 no6354 p928 S 1 2017

Nishihara, Taishi

Synthesis of a carbon nanobelt diag graph *Science* v356 no6334 p172 Ap 14 2017

Nishikawa, Hidehiko

Crowdsourced Products Sell Better When They're Marketed That Way *Harvard Business Review Digital Articles* p2 N 8 2016

Nishikori, Kei, 1989-

KEI NISHIKORI'S TWO-HANDED BACKHAND J. YANDELL *Tennis* v53 no1 p21 Ja/F 2017

Kei Nishikori *Tennis* v53 no1 p20 Ja/F 2017

Nishimoto, Alex

2018 Chevrolet Camaro ZL1 1LE color *Motor Trend* v69 no6 p20 Je 2017

Attack of the Cute Utes color *Motor Trend* v69 no2 p14 F 2017

GARAGE chart color diag *Motor Trend* v69 no9 p104 S 2017

GARAGE cartoon chart color *Motor Trend* v69 no3 p86 Mr 2017

Mercedes-Benz Concept A Sedan color *Motor Trend* v69 no8 p22 Ag 2017

New Teslas Get Autonomous Tech with a Temporary Catch color *Motor Trend* v69 no2 p18 F 2017

TRUCK TIRE TECH color *Motor Trend* v69 no10 p80 O 2017

Nishimura, Kodo

Kodo Nishimura M. Scarles color *Tricycle: The Buddhist Review* v27 no1 p22 Fall 2017

Nishimura, Yoshifumi
Crystal structure of the overlapping dinucleosome composed of hexasome and octasome graph *Science* v356 no6334 p205 Ap 14 2017

Nishimura, Yoshiki
Holliday junction resolvases mediate chloroplast nucleoid segregation diag *Science* v356 no6338 p631 My 12 2017

Nishio, Y.
Crystallization and vitrification of electrons in a glass-forming charge liquid bw *Science* v357 no6358 p1381 S 29 2017

NISHIOKA, HAYWARD
Judo Back in the Day bw *Black Belt* v55 no4 p54 Je/Jl 2017

NISSAN, COLIN
STEVE AT THE PARTY cartoon *New Yorker* v93 no19 p29 Jl 3 2017

Nissan 240SX automobile
V8 Anything D. Freiburger color *Hot Rod* v70 no5 p114 My 2017

Nissan Armada sport utility vehicle—Evaluation
THE 2017 AUTOMOTIVE EXCELLENCE AWARDS chart color *Popular Mechanics* p46 My 2017
Nissan Armada chart color *Motor Trend* v69 no1 p56 Ja 2017

Nissan automobile
See also
Infiniti automobile
Nissan Leaf automobile
1991 Nissan Skyline GTS-t Type M color *Popular Mechanics* p40 N 2017

Nissan automobile—Evaluation
FROM THE ROAD & TRACK ARCHIVES color *Road & Track* v69 no4 p90 N 2017

Nissan Leaf automobile
The New Nissan Leaf Is Fun. Can It Transform the Electric-Vehicle Market? J. Worland color *Time* v190 no13 p24 O 2 2017
Nissan Tries Turning Over a New Leaf Jie Ma and Masatsugu Horie *Bloomberg Businessweek* no4536 p18 S 4 2017
TURNING OVER A NEW LEAF E. Loh chart color *Motor Trend* v69 no8 p16 Ag 2017

Nissan Motor Co. Ltd.
1970-1973 DATSUN 240Z C. COMER color *Road & Track* v69 no2 p92 S 2017
The Ambitious Business Goals Aiming to Change the World A. Winston *Harvard Business Review Digital Articles* p2 F 5 2015
DIFFERENT STROKES color *Road & Track* v68 no6 p90 F 2017
Nissan Armada chart color *Motor Trend* v69 no1 p56 Ja 2017
On the Shoulders of Giants J. Gall color *Car & Driver* v62 no11 p118 My 2017
Rental Cars to The Rescue J. Butters, J. Lippert et al cartoon graph *Bloomberg Businessweek* no4526 p18 Je 12 2017
TURNING OVER A NEW LEAF E. Loh chart color *Motor Trend* v69 no8 p16 Ag 2017

Nissan Titan truck—Evaluation
Nissan Titan chart color *Motor Trend* v69 no1 p86 Ja 2017
Nissan Titan XD chart color *Motor Trend* v69 no1 p87 Ja 2017

Nissan trucks—Evaluation
GARRAGE S. Evans, A. Nishimoto et al cartoon chart color *Motor Trend* v69 no3 p86 Mr 2017

Nissan GT-R automobile—Evaluation
SUPERCAR SLAYER SEEKS WORTHY OPPONENT J. Cammisa chart color *Motor Trend* v68 no12 p52 D 2016

Nistoroiu, Alexandra
Romanian researchers decry sudden power grab color *Science* v356 no6342 p994 Je 9 2017

Nitori Holdings Co. Ltd.
Japan's Furniture King Caters to the Plebes J. Clenfield; M. Horie et al color *Bloomberg Businessweek* no4526 p19 Je 12 2017

Nitrates
A bioinspired iron catalyst for nitrate and perchlorate reduction C. L. Ford, Yun Ji Park et al bibl diag *Science* v354 no6313 p741 N 11 2016

Nitric oxide
nitric oxide V. Tweed color *Amazing Wellness* v9 no6 p13 EarlyWint 2017

Nitrogen
See also

Polynitrogens
Quantum sensing with arbitrary frequency resolution J. M. Boss, K. S. Cujia et al diag graph *Science* v356 no6340 p837 My 26 2017
Synthesis and characterization of the pentazolate anion cyclo-N_5^- in $(N5)6(H3O)3(NH4)4Cl$ Chong Zhang, Chengguo Sun et al bibl diag graph *Science* v355 no6323 p374 Ja 27 2017

Nitrogen & the environment
21st-century rise in anthropogenic nitrogen deposition on a remote coral reef H. Ren, Chen et al diag graph *Science* v356 no6339 p749 My 19 2017
Nitrogen fixers may be at risk S. MILIUS *Science News* v191 no10 p11 My 27 2017
Nitrogen pollution knows no bounds E. Boyle color *Science* v356 no6339 p700 My 19 2017

Nitrogen compounds
See also
Nitric oxide
Nitrogen stewardship in the Anthropocene S. P. Seitzinger and L. Phillips color *Science* v357 no6349 p350 Jl 28 2017

Nitrogen oxides—Environmental aspects
STAY SAFE FROM SILENT DANGER G. MICHAL *Sea Magazine* v108 no12 p24 D 2016

Nitrogen—Environmental aspects
THE DOs & DON'Ts OF APPLICATIONS K. BIRCHMIER *Successful Farming* v114 no11 p34 N 2016

Nitrous oxide
HOT SIP: NITRO COFFEE color *Health* v31 no8 p10 O 2017
A molecular dance to cleaner air T. V. W. Janssens and P. N. R. Vennestrøm color *Science* v357 no6354 p866 S 1 2017

Nitta, Kazuhiro R.
Impact of cytosine methylation on DNA binding specificities of human transcription factors diag *Science* v356 no6337 p502 My 5 2017

Nitto Tire (Company)
FROM NAPKIN NOTES TO WORLD PHENOMENA C. COLLARD color *Dirt Sports + Off-Road* v51 no7 p20 Jl 2017

Nityanandam, Ramya
Rapid development of a DNA vaccine for Zika virus bibl graph *Science* v354 no6309 p237 O 14 2016

Nitz, D.
Observation of a large-scale anisotropy in the arrival directions of cosmic rays above 8×1018 eV *Science* v357 no6357 p1266 S 22 2017

Niu, David
How Morale Changes as a Startup Grows *Harvard Business Review Digital Articles* p2 Mr 24 2017
Measuring Your Employees' Invisible Forms of Influence *Harvard Business Review Digital Articles* p2 N 7 2016

Niu, Dong
Inactivation of porcine endogenous retrovirus in pigs using CRISPR-Cas9 diag *Science* v357 no6357 p1303 S 22 2017

Niu, Shuping
China's Troubles Down on the Farm color *Bloomberg Businessweek* no4525 p16 Je 5 2017

Niu, Xianghong
An organic-inorganic perovskite ferroelectric with large piezoelectric response graph *Science* v357 no6348 p306 Jl 21 2017

Niu, Xiaoda
Systemic pan-AMPK activator MK-8722 improves glucose homeostasis but induces cardiac hypertrophy graph *Science* v357 no6350 p507 Ag 4 2017

Niven, Jennifer
Holding Up the Universe color *Publishers Weekly* v263 no49 p96 D 7 2016

Niven, Karen
When Tough Performance Goals Lead to Cheating *Harvard Business Review Digital Articles* p2 S 8 2016

Nix, Ann
CREATE A PERSONALIZED PLAN color *Amazing Wellness* v9 no3 p8 EarlySumm 2017
EXPERT ADVICE *Amazing Wellness* p8 Fall 2017
Get Real *Amazing Wellness* v9 no1 p8 Wint 2017
HIT REFRESH! *Amazing Wellness* v9 no2 p8 Spr 2017
THE PALEO VEGAN color *Amazing Wellness* v8 no2 p84 Spr 2016

J. Miller *Physics Today* v69 no12 p18 D 2016

Nobel Prize in Economics

Movers K. Stock cartoon color diag *Bloomberg Businessweek* no4495 p11 O 17 2016

Nobel Prize in Literature

Bob Dylan, Nobelist A. FERGUSON cartoon *Weekly Standard* v22 no7 p11 O 24 2016

BOB DYLAN, NOBEL LAUREATE D. T. MORAN *Humanist* v77 no1 p36 Ja/F 2017

Bob the Bard D. HAJDU *Nation* v303 no19 p6 N 7 2016

Ring Them Bells A. GREENE bw color *Rolling Stone* no1274 p13 N 17 2016

Nobel Prize in Physics

Foundational theories in topological physics garner Nobel Prize Sung Chang *Physics Today* v69 no12 p14 D 2016

Nobels honor the small and exotic E. Conover, C. Crockett et al cartoon color *Science News* v190 no9 p6 O 29 2016

Trio surfs gravitational waves to Nobel glory A. Cho color *Science* v357 no6359 p17 O 6 2017

Trio wins Nobel for effects of topology on exotic matter A. Cho color *Science* v354 no6308 p21 O 7 2016

Will Nobel Prize overlook LIGO's master builder? A. Cho color *Science* v353 no6307 p1478 S 30 2016

Nobel Prize in Physiology or Medicine

Nobel honors discoveries in how cells eat themselves M. Enserink and E. Pennisi color *Science* v354 no6308 p20 O 7 2016

Nobels honor the small and exotic E. Conover, C. Crockett et al cartoon color *Science News* v190 no9 p6 O 29 2016

Revelations about rhythm of life rewarded E. Stokstad and G. Vogel color *Science* v357 no6359 p18 O 6 2017

Nobel Prize winners

A corner turned D. D. Collum bw *U.S. Catholic* v82 no2 p38 F 2017

The International Campaign to Abolish Nuclear Weapons M. Douglas *Time* v190 no16/17 p20 O 23 2017

James W. Cronin (1931–2016) A. A. Watson bw *Science* v353 no6307 p1501 S 30 2016

Nobel by the Numbers L. SCHLEY color graph *Discover* v38 no9 p16 N 2017

The prize, it is a-changing J. J. WEINMAN bw *Maclean's* v129 no43 p59 O 31 2016

Nobel Prizes

See also

Nobel Peace Prize

Nobel Prize in Physics

Nobel Prize in Physiology or Medicine

New views snag science Nobels B. Bower, E. Conover et al bw *Science News* v192 no7 p6 O 28 2017

Nobility (Social class)

c. 1550: Moscow *Lapham's Quarterly* v10 no1 p104 Wint 2017

Noble, Andy

How to Make Agile Work for the C-Suite *Harvard Business Review Digital Articles* p2 Jl 19 2017

Noble, Kimberly G.

Brain Trust [Cover story] color graph *Scientific American* v316 no3 p44 Mr 2017

Noble, Mary Heather

Coast Range bw *Orion Magazine* v36 no1 p61 Ja/F 2017

Noble Group Ltd.

The Rise and Fall of a Trading Giant in Asia A. Hoffman color graph map *Bloomberg Businessweek* no4525 p39 Je 5 2017

Noble Outfitters LLC

Tack Room color *Practical Horseman* v45 no3 p70 Mr 2017

Nobles, Gregory

BIRD MAN OF AMERICA L. Bradner color *American History* v52 no4 p68 O 2017

Nobodies (TV program)

Nobodies J. Russell *TV Guide* p38 Ap 17 2017

Nobodies L. Greenblatt color *Entertainment Weekly* no1459 p52 Mr 31 2017

Nobody's Gonna Love You Better (Music)

Gentlemen Prefer Song K. SILSBEE color *Downbeat* v83 no11 p54 N 2016

Noboru Mizushima

The ATG conjugation systems are important for degradation of the inner autophagosomal membrane bibl graph *Science* v354

no6315 p1036 N 25 2016

Nocebos (Medicine)

Interactions between brain and spinal cord mediate value effects in nocebo hyperalgesia A. Tinnermann, S. Geuter et al color *Science* v357 no6359 p105 O 6 2017

Nocebo effects can make you feel pain L. Colloca color *Science* v357 no6359 p44 O 6 2017

NOCERA, JOE

Should College Athletes Be Paid? *New York Times Upfront* v149 no10 p22 Mr 13 2017

Nochlin, Lina

Move Over, Michelangelo S. BOXER color *Atlantic* v318 no5 p44 D 2016

Nocturama (Film)

DESPERADOES A. LANE color *New Yorker* v93 no24 p82 Ag 21 2017

EDITOR'S LETTER N. Rapold bw *Film Comment* v53 no3 p4 My/Je 2017

FRAME TO FRAME V. LUCCA *Film Comment* v53 no3 p54 My/Je 2017

Nocturnal animals

FOOD-PLOT Rx NOCTURNAL BUCKS G. Almy color *Field & Stream* v122 no4 pW8 S 2017

Nocturnal Animals (Film)

ALSO PLAYING D. Coggan color *Entertainment Weekly* no1438 p44 N 4 2016

THE MAN IN THE MIRROR J. McGovern color *Entertainment Weekly* no1439 p36 N 11 2016

NOCTURNAL ANIMALS J. Krebs color *Sound & Vision* v82 no6 p71 Jl/Ag 2017

Nocturnal Animals L. Greenblatt color *Entertainment Weekly* no1441 p38 N 25 2016

PREDATORS A. LANE cartoon *New Yorker* v92 no38 p92 N 21 2016

A Writer's Story J. DeBROSSE *Cincinnati Magazine* v50 no4 p50 Ja 2017

Nodjimbadem, Katie

Ask Smithsonian color *Smithsonian* v47 no10 p96 Mr 2017

Ask Smithsonian *Smithsonian* v47 no8 p104 D 2016

Born to Be Wild *Smithsonian* v48 no1 p19 Ap 2017

The Judgment *Smithsonian* v47 no9 p12 Ja/F 2017

The Unexpected Beauty of Tearing Things Apart: Grammy Award-winning musician Esperanza Spalding puts her spin on the history of design at Smithsonian's Cooper Hewitt museum in a show about transformation, the motif of her latest Interview by Katie... *Smithsonian* v48 no5 p22 S 2017

Why were electric cars of the early 1900s advertised as "ladies' cars"? *Smithsonian* v47 no9 p140 Ja/F 2017

Noël, Alyson

Five Days of Famous *Publishers Weekly* v263 no41 p78 O 10 2016

Noel, Felisha

FE NOEL A. Dorsey color *Essence* v48 no3 p22 Jl 2017

NOEL, NIREE

Knitting Classes *Los Angeles Magazine* p60 F 2017

Noël-Romas, Laura

Vaginal bacteria modify HIV tenofovir microbicide efficacy in African women chart graph *Science* v356 no6341 p938 Je 1 2017

NOER, MICHAEL

AMERICA'S TOP 50 COMPANIES 1917-2017 chart graph *Forbes* v200 no3 p38 S 28 2017

LESSONS AND IDEAS BY THE 100 GREATEST LIVING BUSINESS MINDS bw color *Forbes* v200 no3 p115 S 28 2017

POSTCARDS FROM THE PAST color *Forbes* v200 no3 p76 S 28 2017

Noether, Emmy, 1882-1935

The Universe According to Emmy Noether S. NADIS color diag *Discover* v38 no5 p48 Je 2017

Noga, Markus

8 Ways Machine Learning Is Improving Companie's Work Processes *Harvard Business Review Digital Articles* p2 My 31 2017

Nogales, Eva

Structures of the CRISPR genome integration complex color *Science* v357 no6356 p1113 S 15 2017

Nogami, Jumpei

Crystal structure of the overlapping dinucleosome composed of hexasome and octasome graph *Science* v356 no6334 p205 Ap

14 2017

NOGEIRE-MCRAE, THERESA

Addressing the Gender Gap in Distinguished Speakers at Professional Ecology Conferences *BioScience* v67 no5 p464 My 2017

Nogly, Przemyslaw

A three-dimensional movie of structural changes in bacteriorhodopsin bibl diag graph *Science* v354 no6319 p1552 D 23 2016

Noguchi, Hiroshi

Bone-like crack resistance in hierarchical metastable nanolaminate steels bibl color diag *Science* v355 no6329 p1055 Mr 10 2017

Noguchi, Isamu, 1904-1988

Paper Chase H. MARTIN color *Architectural Digest* v74 no7 p12 Jl 2017

Nogueira, Junior

The ALL-NEW RACE for the ULTIMATE CROWN in Cowboy Town [Cover story] K. SANTOS color *Spin to Win Rodeo* v20 no10 p62 D 2016

Driggers and Nogueira Roll Through July color *Team Roping Journal* p28 S 2017

Freeze Frame color *Team Roping Journal* p70 O 2017

More of the Same B. Welch color *Spin to Win Rodeo* v21 no2 p70 Ap 2017

Nogués-Bravo, David

An Anthropocene map of genetic diversity bibl graph map *Science* v353 no6307 p1532 S 30 2016

Noh, Jun Hong

Colloidally prepared La doped BaSnO3 electrodes for efficient, photostable perovskite solar cells graph *Science* v356 no6334 p167 Ap 14 2017

Iodide management in formamidinium-lead-halide-based perovskite layers for efficient solar cells bw diag *Science* v356 no6345 p1376 Je 30 2017

Noise

See also

Noise control

Run SILENT, Run DEEP D. Garner bw *Esquire* p58 O 2017

Noise control

Go to bed with Alexa color *Health* v31 no9 p18 N 2017

let's pretend H. GOWEN WALSH *Parents* p136 2015

Muting Unwanted Noise in an Open Office J. Beckerman *Harvard Business Review Digital Articles* p2 D 17 2015

Stop Noise from Ruining Your Open Office C. Calisi and J. Stout *Harvard Business Review Digital Articles* p2 Mr 16 2015

Noise control equipment

The Art Of Noise K. L. Beamon color *Architectural Record* v205 no8 p69 Ag 2017

Noise pollution

50, 100 & 150 YEARS AGO bw color *Scientific American* v315 no6 p86 D 2016

Human noises invade wilderness L. HAMERS color map *Science News* v191 no11 p14 Je 10 2017

Noise pollution is pervasive in U.S. protected areas R. T. Buxton, M. F. McKenna et al graph map *Science* v356 no6337 p531 My 5 2017

RESEARCH color *Science* v356 no6337 p497 My 5 2017

Noise pollution—Research

Coping with Chronic Clamor M. Wexler color *National Wildlife (World Edition)* v55 no2 p40 F/Mr 2017

Noise pollution—Social aspects

Is it religious freedom or noise disturbance? Israelis debate call to prayer J. Greenberg color *Christian Century* v134 no10 p17 My 10 2017

Noise research

Arousing Performance A. Hadhazy bw *Natural History* v125 no11 p7 N 2017

Noise—Charts, diagrams, etc.

Sounds Like Trouble M. Fischetti diag graph *Scientific American* v316 no6 p78 Je 2017

Noises Off (Theatrical production)

4 — NOISES OFF M. R. Bernardo *Entertainment Weekly* no1444/1445 p118 D 16 2016

Nokia Corp.

Can Nokia Reinvent Itself Again? R. G. McGrath *Harvard Business Review Digital Articles* p2 Ap 16 2015

REMEMBER NOKIA? D. Bennett and K. Pohjanpalo color

Bloomberg Businessweek no4529 p66 Jl 3 2017

NOLAN, ALI

COME TOGETHER color *Runner's World* v52 no2 p15 Mr 2017

CURATOR OF CUTE color *Runner's World* v52 no3 p17 Ap 2017

LOST AND FOUND color *Runner's World* v52 no8 p80 S 2017

Running Ink bw color *Runner's World* v52 no6 p43 Jl 2017

RW 2016 COVER SEARCH [Cover story] color *Runner's World* v51 no11 p62 D 2016

Nolan, Britt

Britt Nolan R. O'CONNOR color *Chicago* v66 no6 p90 Je 2017

Nolan, Christopher, 1970-

DUNKIRK K. P. Sullivan color *Entertainment Weekly* no1446/1447 p50 D 2016/Ja 2017

DUNKIRK K. P. Sullivan color *Entertainment Weekly* no1463/1464 p66 Ap/My 2017

Dunkirk Undone A. ROBERTS *Commentary* v144 no2 p51 S 2017

The Miracle of Dunkirk S. Zacharek color *Time* v190 no5 p48 Jl 31 2017

On the Beach R. DOUTHAT color *National Review* v69 no16 p47 Ag 28 2017

Splendid Isolation [Cover story] M. Hastings bw color *New York Review of Books* v64 no15 p14 O 12 2017

THE TEENY-TINY NOLAN MOVIE K. P. Sullivan color *Entertainment Weekly* no1474/1475 p60 Jl 21-28 2017

Undone Dunkirk J. PODHORETZ color *Weekly Standard* v22 no45 p38 Ag 7 2017

Will Dunkirk Score Nolan His First Oscar? K. P. Sullivan color *Entertainment Weekly* no1476 p16 Ag 4 2017

Nolan, Christopher, 1970-—Interviews

THE BATTLE OF CHRISTOPHER NOLAN K. P. Sullivan color *Entertainment Weekly* no1474/1475 p56 Jl 21-28 2017

Christopher Nolan's Great War E. Berman color *Time* v190 no5 p53 Jl 31 2017

CHRISTOPHER NOLAN Wants You to Silence Your Phones A. Grant color *Esquire* p48 Ag 2017

Nolan, Daniel

dream scape M. Silva color *Martha Stewart Living* p116 O 2017

Nolan, Greg

Car Shades for Household Windows *Mother Earth News* no282 p85 Je/Jl 2017

Nolan, James L.

James L. Nolan, Jr.: What they Saw in America: Alexis de Tocqueville, Max Weber, G. K. Chesterton, and Sayyid Qutb W. Morrisey *Society* v54 no2 p204 Ap 2017

Nolan, Janne E.

Cold combat: The memoir of a nuclear convert *Bulletin of the Atomic Scientists* v73 no3 p192 My 2017

What Comes Next *Daedalus* v146 no1 p125 Wint 2017

Nolan, Jonathan

Westworld M. ROUSH *TV Guide* v64 no40 p22 O 3 2016

Nolan, Joy

Growing mastery in NYC chart color il *Phi Delta Kappan* v98 no3 p41 N 2016

Nolan, Kevin

How GE Appliances Built an Innovation Lab to Rapidly Prototype Products *Harvard Business Review Digital Articles* p2 Jl 18 2017

Nolan, Lisa S.

Community network for deaf scientists color *Science* v356 no6336 p386 Ap 28 2017

Nolan, Paul Alexander

THE KEYS TO MARGARITAVILLE J. BUFFETT color *Vanity Fair* v59 no11 p151 N 2017

Nolan, Richard

Leading in a World Without Secrets *Harvard Business Review Digital Articles* p2 D 2 2016

Nolan, Tom

True Detective N. DAWIDOFF bw color *New Republic* v248 no10 p56 O 2017

Nolan, Tracy—Interviews

Ministry with trans people E. Palmer color *Christian Century* v134 no2 p28 Ja 18 2017

Noland, Marcus

Study: Firms with More Women in the C-Suite Are More Profitable *Harvard Business Review Digital Articles* p2 F 8 2016

NOLAND, TERRANCE

WHY We LOVE CHICAGO bw cartoon color *Chicago* v66 no3 p75 Mr 2017

Nolde, Emil, 1867-1956

Der Jäger (The Hunter) color *ARTnews* v115 no4 p15 Wint 2016/2017

Nole Hall, Fadocia Annette

My Deluxe Dream Barn Will Have... color *Horse & Rider* v56 no4 p80 Ap 2017

Nolf, Pamela

Sitting pretty color *Equus* no480 p80 S 2017

Nolfi, Joey

THE 25 MOST PATRIOTIC MOVIES OF ALL TIME color *Entertainment Weekly* no1472 p30 Je 30 2017

3 GENERATIONS color *Entertainment Weekly* no1463/1464 p37 Ap/My 2017

THE 8-SECOND REVIEW color *Entertainment Weekly* no1465 p40 My 12 2017

ALSO PLAYING: JULY color *Entertainment Weekly* no1463/1464 p66 Ap/My 2017

ALSO PLAYING: JUNE color *Entertainment Weekly* no1463/1464 p53 Ap/My 2017

ALSO PLAYING: MAY color *Entertainment Weekly* no1463/1464 p40 Ap/My 2017

AMERICAN MADE color *Entertainment Weekly* no1478 / 1479 p43 Ag 18-25 2017

CALL ME BY YOUR NAME color *Entertainment Weekly* no1478 / 1479 p63 Ag 18-25 2017

DOWNSIZING color *Entertainment Weekly* no1478 / 1479 p79 Ag 18-25 2017

The Eagle Huntress color *Entertainment Weekly* no1438 p47 N 4 2016

Gaga Hitches a Ride on Drag Race color *Entertainment Weekly* no1457/1458 p17 Mr 17 2017

A GAY Old Timeline color diag *Entertainment Weekly* no1471 p32 Je 23 2017

GET OUT BREAKS OUT color *Entertainment Weekly* no1456 p16 Mr 10 2017

Leah Remini's Divine Intervention color *Entertainment Weekly* no1472 p52 Je 30 2017

A MAN IN FULL color *Entertainment Weekly* no1477 p14 Ag 11 2017

Oh, mother! color *Entertainment Weekly* no1484 p16 S 29 2017

Risky Business color *Entertainment Weekly* no1480 p15 S 1 2017

SEPARATION ANXIETY color *Entertainment Weekly* no1478 / 1479 p14 Ag 18-25 2017

STEVIE NICKS' SHOW STARTER color *Entertainment Weekly* no1472 p49 Je 30 2017

SUMMER'S WINNERS AND LOSERS color *Entertainment Weekly* no1477 p18 Ag 11 2017

"WE NEED TO CONTINUE TO TELL THESE STORIES" color *Entertainment Weekly* no1459 p44 Mr 31 2017

What to Watch color *Entertainment Weekly* no1456 p62 Mr 10 2017

WHAT TO WATCH color *Entertainment Weekly* no1468/1469 p68 Je 2-9 2017

WINNING STREEP *Entertainment Weekly* no1449 p14 Ja 20 2017

Your LGBTQ Pop Preview color *Entertainment Weekly* no1471 p44 Je 23 2017

Noll, Angela

Sustained virologic control in SIV+ macaques after antiretroviral and α4β7 antibody therapy bibl graph *Science* v354 no6309 p197 O 14 2016

Noll, Brandi

Buyer — Be informed color il *Phi Delta Kappan* v98 no4 p60 D 2016/Ja 2017

Noll, Mark A., 1946-—Interviews

Sola Scriptura M. GALLI bw *Christianity Today* v61 no5 p50 Je 2017

Nolte, Nick, 1941-

Graves J. Halterman color *TV Guide* v64 no42 p37 O 10 2016

Nomads—Kenya

Live on the margins B. Massingale color *U.S. Catholic* v82 no9 p10 S 2017

Nome Nugget (Newspaper)

THE NOME NUGGET C. Spike color *Columbia Journalism Review* v56 no1 p63 Spr 2017

Nominations for office

Seventh-Circuit Shakedown C. Kaveny color *Commonweal* v144 no16 p8 O 6 2017

Nomura, Daniel K.

Lysosomal cholesterol activates mTORC1 via an SLC38A9–Niemann-Pick C1 signaling complex bibl diag graph *Science* v355 no6331 p1306 Mr 24 2017

NOMURA, YASUNORI

A COSMIC CONTROVERSY color *Scientific American* v317 no1 p5 Jl 2017

THE QUANTUM MULTIVERSE [Cover story] color *Scientific American* v316 no6 p28 Je 2017

Non-alcoholic beer

LOW ALCOHOL COULD MEAN HIGH PERCENTAGE GROWTH B. Kowitt color *Fortune* v176 no5 p33 O 1 2017

Non-alcoholic beverages

103 MINUTES WITH ... Amanda Chantal Bacon J. PRESSLER img *New York* v49 no25 p24 D 12 2016

Kid-Friendly Fare E. HARE cartoon color *Cabin Living* p62 Je 2017

Non-alcoholic beverages—Marketing

LOW ALCOHOL COULD MEAN HIGH PERCENTAGE GROWTH B. Kowitt color *Fortune* v176 no5 p33 O 1 2017

Non-alcoholic cocktails

A SOBERING REALIZATION L. Entis color *Fortune* v176 no5 p32 O 1 2017

Non-coding DNA

Decoding the evolution of species K. L. Cooper color *Science* v356 no6341 p904 Je 1 2017

High-resolution interrogation of functional elements in the non-coding genome N. E. Sanjana, J. Wright et al bibl graph *Science* v353 no6307 p1545 S 30 2016

Non-coding RNA

See also
Circular RNA
MicroRNA

Making the cut in the dark genome J. M. Einstein and G. W. Yeo bibl diag *Science* v354 no6313 p705 N 11 2016

Non-commissioned officers

Life Lessons From Boot Camp J. MARK JACKSON color *Reader's Digest* v190 no1135 p26 N 2017

Non-communicable diseases

Green Spaces: An Invaluable Resource for Delivering Sustainable Urban Health N. Röbbel *UN Chronicle* v53 no3 p6 2016

Non-insulin-dependent diabetes

Exposing the exposures responsible for type 2 diabetes and obesity P. W. Franks and M. I. McCarthy bibl diag *Science* v354 no6308 p69 O 7 2016

Let's get granular about SUGAR S. KUZEMCHAK color *Redbook* p96 Ap 2017

OPERATION: DIABETES F. Rubino color *Scientific American* v317 no1 p60 Jl 2017

recent study correlates multi-strain probiotics with blood sugar benefit K. James and V. TWEED color *Better Nutrition* v79 no10 p18 O 2017

Sick and Tired P. GULLEY *Indianapolis Monthly* v40 no4 p63 D 2016

Non-insulin-dependent diabetes prevention

5 tiny bits of health wisdom color *Redbook* p92 N 2017

6 Strategies for Better Blood Sugar After Meals *Tufts University Health & Nutrition Letter* v35 no3 p7 My 2017

7 WAYS TO LOWER BLOOD SUGAR V. Tweed color diag graph *Amazing Wellness* v8 no6 p58 Early Winter2016

Cinnamon and Blood Sugar *Tufts University Health & Nutrition Letter* v35 no8 p3 O 2017

FIGHTING DIABETES WITH FOOD L. Entis color *Fortune* v176 no1 p33 Jl 1 2017

QUICK STUDIES *Nutrition Action Health Letter* v44 no5 p10 Je 2017

Sugar Swings [Cover story] E. A. Kane color *Better Nutrition* v79 no11 p30 N 2017

Non-insulin-dependent diabetes risk factors

DIABETES DEFENSE B. LIEBMAN *Nutrition Action Health Letter* v44 no1 p3 Ja/F 2017

no4 p65 O 2017

Do Over A. BROWNLEE *Cincinnati Magazine* v50 p152 Ag 2017 Supplement

Filling the Void in Spanish-language Islamic Material W. DÍAZ *Islamic Horizons* v46 no1 p40 Ja/F 2017

Foundations of Belonging D. MCCONNACHIE *Alternatives Journal (AJ) - Canada's Environmental Voice* v42 no3 p7 2016

GIVING BACK R. Cartagena *Washingtonian Magazine* v52 no3 p106 D 2016

GIVING GIRLS A FUTURE color *Good Housekeeping* v263 no5 p99 N 2016

THE GOOD IDEA FUND *Governing* v30 no2 p10 N 2016

Harm reduction underused *Science* v354 no6315 p948 N 25 2016

Helping Kids Cope T. ANDERSON and D. POINTDUJOUR color *Ebony* v72 no4 p70 F 2017

HOW SENIORS SUPPORT EACH OTHER D. Rosato color *Consumer Reports* v82 no12 p48 D 2017

HOW TO CHECK UP ON "CHARITABLE" DEALS K. A. Renzulli color *Money* v46 no1 p21 Ja/F 2017

How WE Is Making a Difference color *Good Housekeeping* v265 no3 p20 S 2017

Memphis Fights Blight: Collaborating to Win the Battle Against Vacant and Abandoned Property S. Barlow *Bridges (Federal Reserve Bank of St. Louis)* p8 Fall 2016

Mending Their Lives: Through sewing and design, survivors of Israel's sex industry begin anew S. T. STUB *Ms.* v27 no2 p12 Summ 2017

Monster Splash color *Field & Stream* v122 no2 p12 Je/Jl 2017

The New Assault on Privacy J. PIERESON cartoon *Weekly Standard* v22 no27 p20 Mr 20 2017

New Heart, New Mission color *Men's Health* v32 no1 p8 Ja/F 2017

NEW PARK SMELL: 3CDC is investing nearly $32 million in the new Ziegler Park. So what's all the fuss about? J. WILLIAMS *Cincinnati Magazine* p19 Je 2017

Nonpartisan Nonprofits Fight For Free Expression J. Maher *Publishers Weekly* v264 no13 p5 Mr 27 2017

Overhead Overhaul K. Shellnutt color *Christianity Today* v60 no8 p25 O 2016

PDK Connection *Phi Delta Kappan* v98 no6 p79 Mr 2017

Poverty and the Controversial Work of Nonprofits M. Jindra and I. Jindra *Society* v53 no6 p634 D 2016

Restoring Dignity S. QURAESHI *Islamic Horizons* v46 no1 p34 Ja/F 2017

SAN ANTONIO STOCK SHOW & RODEO *Texas Monthly* v45 no1 p72 Ja 2017

Saving the planet starts here color *Redbook* p100 Je 2017

Turning loss into something beautiful J. PRESS color *Redbook* p110 Mr 2017

UNSUNG SAVIORS *Atlanta* v56 no9 p122 Ja 2017

WARDENSVILLE TOWN CRIERS K. OLSEN *Washingtonian Magazine* v52 no12 p12 S 2017

What Next? Succession Planning for Nonprofits A. Fraizer *Bridges (Federal Reserve Bank of St. Louis)* p5 Fall 2016

What the Nonprofit Sector Needs to Reach Its Full Potential D. Pallotta *Harvard Business Review Digital Articles* p2 My 13 2016

THE WOMEN'S FUND – A CONVERSATION WITH ABBY WAMBACH *Cincinnati Magazine* p42 Je 2017

YAMAHA CONTINUES TO SUPPORT SEAL-NAVAL SPECIAL WARFARE FAMILY color *Dirt Sports + Off-Road* v51 no10 p8 O 2017

Nonprofit organizations—Awards

Honoring those who go above and beyond for conservation color *National Wildlife (World Edition)* v55 no4 p46 Je/Jl 2017

Nonprofit organizations—California

When a Startup Means A Fresh Start A. Popescu color *Bloomberg Businessweek* no4507 p28 Ja 16 2017

Nonprofit organizations—Canada

Stronger Together J. Glave color *Alternatives Journal (AJ) - Canada's Environmental Voice* v42 no3 p48 2016

Nonprofit organizations—Finance

The 2016 Magnolia Designer Show House B. Baribault, J. Rothman et al *Atlanta* v56 no7 p2 N 2016

Nonprofit organizations—Finance—Government policy

A Promise the GOP Can Still Keep J. McCormack *Weekly Standard* v22 no46 p9 Ag 14 2017

Nonprofit organizations—Finance—Social aspects

Liberal Nonprofits Ride The Anti-Trump Wave I. Boudway, C. Suddath et al color *Bloomberg Businessweek* no4500 p30 N 21 2016

Nonprofit organizations—History

35 Year of Vegan Activism *Vegetarian Journal* v36 no3 p18 2017

Nonprofit organizations—Officials & employees

MIRY WHITEHILL-BEN ATAR: THE FOUNDER OF MIRY'S LIST HAS HELPED MORE THAN 100 RESETTLED FAMILIES MAKE A LIFE IN THE U.S. HERE'S WHERE HER INSPIRATION CAME FROM L. B. SUTER *Los Angeles Magazine* v62 no9 p94 S 2017

WE ARE THE RIGHTFUL HEIRS J. LYON *Vital Speeches of the Day* v83 no3 p82 Mr 2017

Nonprofit organizations—Officials & employees—Interviews

Latino Outdoors J. ELLISON color *Climbing* no353 p20 My/Je 2017

Nonprofit organizations—Political activity

Takin' It To the STREETS R. ROSS *Texas Monthly* v44 no11 p53 N 2016

Nonprofit organizations—United States

Bad at Doing Good L. Featherstone color *Nation* v304 no16 p5 My 22 2017

CODE CRACKING YIREN LU color *New York Times Magazine* p39 N 13 2016

Don't Stop Now! Give, Give! K. Pollitt color diag *Nation* v304 no2 p10 Ja 16 2017

FOXFIRE AT 50 S. HANSELL *Atlanta* v56 no8 p27 D 2016

RECOVERY MISSION H. G. Philllips *Washingtonian Magazine* v52 no2 p299 N 2016

Teach For America: An Economic Boost for Rural Mississippi Delta Communities C. King *Bridges (Federal Reserve Bank of St. Louis)* p10 Fall 2016

Thank You Greetings To Our Special Partners A. Bundles *Prologue* v48 no3 p70 Fall 2016

Nonprofit sector

See also

Nonprofit organizations

How the Social Sector Can Attract More Young Talent K. Sanders and D. Thompson *Harvard Business Review Digital Articles* p2 D 7 2016

Nonsteroidal anti-inflammatory agents

See also

Aspirin

Celebrex's risk to heart debated L. BEIL color *Science News* v190 no12 p6 D 10 2016

EASE ARTHRITIS IN PETS J. Szabo color *Amazing Wellness* p82 Fall 2017

POP QUIZ C. Barakat and M. Freckleton color *Equus* no471 p14 D 2016

Nonsteroidal anti-inflammatory agents—Therapeutic use

Gout [Cover story] *Mayo Clinic Health Letter* v35 no4 p1 Ap 2017

Medications for rheumatoid arthritis *Harvard Health Letter* v42 no6 p3 Ap 2017

Nontraded goods

Tradable and nontradable inflation indexes: replicating New Zealand's tradable indexes with BLS CPI data N. N. Johnson bibl *Monthly Labor Review* p1 My 2017

Nonverbal communication

See also

Laughter

Nonverbal communication in the workplace

Don't Look Now M. HUSTON *Psychology Today* v50 no2 p18 Mr/Ap 2017

Nonverbal communication in the workplace

When Giving Critical Feedback, Focus on Your Nonverbal Cues E. Seppala color *Harvard Business Review Digital Articles* p2 Ja 20 2017

Nonviolence

How Nonviolent Resistance Can Change the World G. Sharp color *Progressive* v81 no4 p54 Ap/My 2017

Just War? G. W. Schlabach bw *Commonweal* v144 no11 p11 Je 16 2017

LIVING BY The Word *Christian Century* v134 no1 p20 Ja 4 2017

The War against Just War P. Steinfels color *Commonweal* v144

no11 p15 Je 16 2017

Nonwoven fabric wipes

the COMPACT J. Wilson color *Essence* v48 no2 p46 Je 2017

Nonwoven fabric wipes—Evaluation

A Natural Start A. Andrews *Sierra* v102 no1 p9 Ja/F 2017

Noodle soups

Chicken Noodle Soup L. REGE color *Martha Stewart Living* no271 p61 Ja/F 2017

A TIME TO START E. Graves *Martha Stewart Living* no271 p8 Ja/F 2017

Noodles

See also

Ramen

Soba (Noodles)

At my house J. Francisco *Good Housekeeping* v264 no2 p8 F 2017

GLASS ACT N. Appleman color *Runner's World* v52 no2 p42 Mr 2017

Healthyish C. SAFFITZ color *Bon Appetit* v62 no6 p35 Je 2017

Hot-Weather Comfort Food: Cold pork noodles dressed in vinegar, from the East Village by way of Yunnan T. Rao *New York Times Magazine* p28 Jl 23 2017

A New Twist on Pasta R. Meltzer-Warren chart color *Consumer Reports* v82 no5 p14 My 2017

Novel Noodles: Two new shops shine a light on the seldom-seen Yunnanese rice variety R. RAISFELD and R. PATRONITE img *New York* v50 no9 p74 My 1 2017

r.s.v.p R. SODERSTROM, E. EISEN et al bw *Bon Appetit* v61 no12 p20 D 2016 /Jan2017

Using All That Squash V. Willis color *Southern Living* v52 no7 p114 Jl 2017

Viva ZUCCHINI D. MARCHETTI color *Better Homes & Gardens* v95 no8 p148 Ag 2017

WHEAT MONTANA NOODLES *South Dakota Magazine* v33 no3 p31 S/O 2017

Noodles—Evaluation

MARKET WATCH *Los Angeles Magazine* v62 no9 p112 S 2017

Noonan, David

The Epilepsy Dilemma color *Scientific American* v316 no4 p28 Ap 2017

Noonan, K.

Fostering reproducibility in industry-academia research color *Science* v357 no6353 p759 Ag 25 2017

NOONAN, PEGGY

Points to Ponder *Reader's Digest* v188 no1124 p39 O 2016

Noone, Peadar G.

Emergence and spread of a human-transmissible multidrug-resistant nontuberculous mycobacterium bibl diag graph *Science* v354 no6313 p751 N 11 2016

Nooner, Scott L.

Inflation-predictable behavior and co-eruption deformation at Axial Seamount bibl graph map *Science* v354 no6318 p1399 D 16 2016

Noorani, Ali—Interviews

Talking together about immigration A. Frykholm *Christian Century* v134 no17 p10 Ag 16 2017

Noorduin, Wim L.

Controlled growth and form of precipitating microsculptures bw color diag graph *Science* v355 no6332 p1395 Mr 31 2017

Nootrobox Inc.

The Pill Freaks of Silicon Valley A. MORRIS img *New York* v49 no21 p56 O 17 2016

Nootropic agents

See also

Phosphatidylserines

Like It or Not, "Smart Drugs" Are Coming to the Office C. Cederström *Harvard Business Review Digital Articles* p2 My 19 2016

Nooyi, Indra K., 1955-—Interviews

THE QUEEN OF POP [Cover story] B. Kowitt, K. Bellstrom et al color diag *Fortune* v176 no5 p70 O 1 2017

Noradrenergic neurons

Breathing to inspire and arouse S. Sheikhbahaei and J. C. Smith bw *Science* v355 no6332 p1370 Mr 31 2017

Norco Bicycles (Company)

#BIKECRUSH M. Phillips, T. Rojek et al color *Bicycling* v58 no7 p65 Ag 2017

Norco Sight R. Palmer color *Bike Magazine* v24 no5 p88 Jl 2017

ON THE MOUNTAIN G. Liu and B. STRICKLAND color *Bicycling* v58 no3 p84 Ap 2017

Norcross, John

To Hell With Resolutions S. Dreisbach and S. G. Levy color *Glamour* v115 no1 p44 Ja 2017

Nord, Douglas C.

The Challenge of Arctic Governance color *Wilson Quarterly* p1 Summ 2017

NORD, DYLAN

GET IN THE VAN! color *Bicycling* v58 no8 p18 S 2017

Nordgren, Loran

Giving Up Is the Enemy of Creativity *Harvard Business Review Digital Articles* p2 D 1 2015

It's Harder to Empathize with People If You've Been in Their Shoes *Harvard Business Review Digital Articles* p2 O 20 2015

NORDGREN, SARAH ROSE

LIFE WITHOUT A SPINE *Humanist* v77 no3 p33 My/Je 2017

Nordgren, Tyler

BOOKSHELF L. A. MARSCHALL *Natural History* v124 no10 p46 N 2016

Darkness Is Coming color map *Discover* v38 no7 p36 S 2017

Totality Changes Everything S. N. Johnson-Roehr *Sky & Telescope* v133 no2 p57 F 2017

Nordhaus, Hannah

CORNBOY VS. THE BILLION-DOLLAR BUG [Cover story] color *Scientific American* v316 no3 p64 Mr 2017

Dj Cavem bw *Rodale's Organic Life* v3 no1 p76 Ja 2017

The Fastest Nun in the West *Smithsonian* v47 no7 p35 N 2016

NORDHAUS, TED

The Energy Rebound Battle: An embattled economist's research shows that energy efficiency cant solve climate change. But it is an important contributor to human progress *Issues in Science & Technology* v33 no4 p51 Summ 2017

Nordhavn (Company)

NORDHAVN 59 COASTAL PILOT M. WERLING *Sea Magazine* v108 no8 p30 Ag 2016

Nordic Naturals Inc.

Get to Know: Nordic Naturals J. SCHILDHOUSE color *Muscle & Performance* v9 no9 p34 S 2017

PREMIER PROVISIONS color *Muscle & Performance* v9 no5 p64 My 2017

Nordic Tugs Inc.

Nordic Tug 44 B. Pike color *Power & Motoryacht* v32 no11 p66 N 2016

NORDLAND, ROD

Afghanistan's Romeo & Juliet: The true story of two young Afghans who risked death by defying their families and their culture to be together *New York Times Upfront* v150 no1 p14 S 4 2017

NORDLINGER, JAY

Act of Love color *National Review* v69 no3 p27 F 20 2017

Ages of Argus color *National Review* v69 no6 p21 Ap 3 2017

American Interests and Obligations map *National Review* v68 no23 p2 D 19 2016

An American Outsider *National Review* v69 no9 p40 My 15 2017

Calls To Arms color *National Review* v68 no24 p20 D 31 2016

A Defender Of His Country color *National Review* v69 no7 p22 Ap 17 2017

Drops from A Niagara color *National Review* v68 no23 p40 D 19 2016

Getting to Peace in Colombia color *National Review* v68 no23 p30 D 19 2016

Girl, Misplaced color *National Review* v69 no8 p18 My 2017

The Grave Hunter, Hunted color *National Review* v69 no19 p24 O 16 2017

A Hero's Daughter color *National Review* v69 no12 p20 Je 26 2017

Jared and Other Sons-In-Law color *National Review* v69 no16 p19 Ag 28 2017

Killing Aida color *National Review* v68 no21 p22 N 21 2016

Maestrissimo bw *National Review* v69 no15 p39 Ag 14 2017

Notes, Asides, And Memories color *National Review* v69 no18 p31 O 2 2017

Permanent February color *National Review* v69 no4 p22 Mr 6 2017

A Salzburg Trio color *National Review* v69 no17 p40 S 11 2017

A POWERFUL VOICE P. RUHE *Atlanta* v56 no7 p42 N 2016

Norman, Matthew

HIKER LOOK BOOK M. B. ". Skylis color *Backpacker* v45 no1 p78 Ja 2017

Norman, Michael R.

Alexei Alexeyevich Abrikosov *Physics Today* v70 no10 p73 O 2017

NORMAN, PETER

Conservatives in Cruise Wear cartoon *Walrus* v14 no3 p26 Ap 2017

Norman, Ralph

One Seat That Should Be Safe T. MECIA color *Weekly Standard* v22 no39 p12 Je 19 2017

Norman, Roy

Above the Bad River *South Dakota Magazine* v32 no4 p56 N/D 2016

Normand, Andreas

Andrea Norman K. SINGLETARY color *Louisiana Life* v37 no3 p56 Ja/F 2017

Normand, Mabel

GOINGS ON ABOUT TOWN bw *New Yorker* v92 no45 p5 Ja 16 2017

Normative theory (Communication)

Twelve Key Findings in Deliberative Democracy Research N. Curato, J. S. Dryzek et al *Daedalus* v146 no3 p28 Summ 2017

NORMENT, CHRISTOPHER

A Case for Wonder: In science education, nothing is more important than developing the capacity for amazement bw color *Orion Magazine* v35 no6 p13 N/D 2016

Normile, Dennis

THE BIGGEST EAR color *Science* v353 no6307 p1488 S 30 2016

China cracks down on coastal fisheries color *Science* v356 no6338 p573 My 12 2017

China cracks down on fraud color *Science* v357 no6350 p435 Ag 4 2017

CHINA'S CHILDHOOD EXPERIMENT color diag *Science* v357 no6357 p1226 S 22 2017

China sprints ahead in CRISPR therapy race chart color *Science* v357 no6359 p20 O 6 2017

Critics assail paper claiming harm from cancer vaccine color graph *Science* v354 no6319 p1514 D 23 2016

Designers squabble over giant Chinese scope color *Science* v356 no6343 p1107 Je 16 2017

iPS cell therapy reported safe color *Science* v355 no6330 p1109 Mr 17 2017

Japanese military entices academics to break taboo color *Science* v355 no6323 p338 Ja 27 2017

Japan reboots x-ray probe— and mission management color diag *Science* v354 no6314 p814 N 18 2016

Science suffers as China plugs holes in Great Firewall color *Science* v357 no6354 p856 S 1 2017

South Korea's nuclear U-turn draws praise and darts color graph *Science* v357 no6346 p15 Jl 7 2017

Unique free electron laser laboratory opens in China color *Science* v355 no6322 p235 Ja 20 2017

Norris, David

Did you receive support from your faith community while you were experiencing depression and/or anxiety? graph *America* v216 no12 p6 My 29 2017

Norris, Ida

ask the experts color *Dressage Today* p66 My 2017

Norris, Justin

TOP TRAINERS' BEST NEW MOVES bw color diag *Men's Health* v32 no7 p98 S 2017

Norris, Kathleen

OUR FIRST LOVE *America* v216 no1 p38 Ja 2 2017

WRITERS' FEAST color *Christian Century* v134 no10 p30 My 10 2017

Norris, Michele

I, TOO, AM AMERICA bw color *National Geographic* v230 no4 p116 O 2016

Norris, R. P.

Molecular gas in the halo fuels the growth of a massive cluster galaxy at high redshift bibl graph *Science* v354 no6316 p1128 D 2 2016

Norris, Robert

HOLIDAY OPEN HOUSE J. Farmer color *Southern Living* v51 no12 p23 D 2016

NORRIS, ROBERT J.

DNA EVIDENCE FREES THE INNOCENT color *Reason* v49 no4 p34 Ag/S 2017

Norris, Robert S.

Indian nuclear forces, 2017 bibl chart *Bulletin of the Atomic Scientists* v73 no4 p205 Jl 2017

Pakistani nuclear forces, 2016 bibl chart *Bulletin of the Atomic Scientists* v72 no6 p368 N 2016

Russian nuclear forces, 2017 bibl chart *Bulletin of the Atomic Scientists* v73 no2 p115 Mr 2017

United States nuclear forces, 2017 bibl *Bulletin of the Atomic Scientists* v73 no1 p48 Ja 2017

Worldwide deployments of nuclear weapons, 2017 bibl *Bulletin of the Atomic Scientists* v73 no5 p289 2017

NORTH, ANNA

THE WORK OF EQUALITY bw *Nation* v304 no16 p39 My 22 2017

North, Bob

A CONVERSATION WITH BOB AND DIXIE NORTH D. Hearst *Arabian Horse World* v57 no9 p13 Je 2017

North, Dixie

A CONVERSATION WITH BOB AND DIXIE NORTH D. Hearst *Arabian Horse World* v57 no9 p13 Je 2017

NORTH ARABIANS *Arabian Horse World* v57 no9 p15 Je 2017

North, Heather

ASK THE EXPERTS color *Runner's World* v52 no2 p36 Mr 2017

North, Robert

NORTH ARABIANS *Arabian Horse World* v57 no9 p15 Je 2017

North Adams (Mass.)

north adams, massachusetts T. McKEOUGH bw color *Architectural Digest* no5 p82 My 2017

North America

DARKNESS FALLS E. Conant color map *National Geographic* v232 no2 p24 Ag 2017

North America—History

Losing the West A. Brandt bw color map *American History* v52 no3 p32 Ag 2017

North American Free Trade Agreement (NAFTA)

As Nafta II begins, Mexico shows cautious optimism Hootsen color *America* v217 no6 p15 S 18 2017

Bringing NAFTA Into the 21st Century T. J. DONOHUE *Weekly Standard* v22 no34 p23 My 15 2017

CALIFORNIA TRADE JUSTICE COALITION: Hope for a New Trade Agenda A. LEHMER-CHANG color *Earth Island Journal* v32 no2 p15 Summ 2017

THE DAWN OF THE STRONGMAN ERA IS HERE E. SOLOMON color *Maclean's* v129 no48/49 p12 D 5 2016

Don't Scrap Nafta, Improve It bw *Bloomberg Businessweek* no4524 p10 My 29 2017

FARMERS ARE OPTIMISTIC ABOUT NAFTA RENEGOTIATION *Successful Farming* v115 no9 p15 Ag 2017

Is Your Supply Chain Ready for a NAFTA Overhaul? J. Terino *Harvard Business Review Digital Articles* p2 Je 30 2017

Lori Wallach J. Crelin color *Current Biography* v78 no3 p86 Mr 2017

NAFTA Modernization Moves Forward T. J. DONOHUE *Weekly Standard* v22 no44 p21 Jl 31 2017

Now It's Revamp, Not Replace P. Coy, A. Mayeda et al color graph *Bloomberg Businessweek* no4531 p29 Jl 24 2017

Smashing NAFTA Apart Is Harder Than It Seems, Especially When You're Blindfolded J. SABATINI color graph *Car & Driver* v62 no11 p90 My 2017

Trudeau Pushes for a Feminist NAFTA C. Zillman color *Fortune* v176 no5 p17 O 1 2017

TRUMP'S TARGET IN NAFTA NEGOTIATIONS: MEXICO *Successful Farming* v115 no4 p15 Mr 2017

Trump Threatens to Undo Nafta's Auto Alley B. Greeley, D. Welch et al bw graph *Bloomberg Businessweek* no4509 p25 Ja 30 2017

Trump Unbound F. BARNES color *Weekly Standard* v22 no32 p18 My 1 2017

What a Changing NAFTA Could Mean for Doing Business in Mexico A. Martinez *Harvard Business Review Digital Articles* p2 Je 20 2017

Why Florida Farmers Want to Kill Nafta A. Bjerga and E. Martin

color graph *Bloomberg Businessweek* no4535 p35 Ag 28 2017

Wooing America N. TAYLOR-VAISEY color graph *Maclean's* v130 no8 p20 S 2017

North American river otter

The Otter, the Salmon, and the Bittern C. K. LONGSTRETH color *Natural History* v125 no4 p18 Ap 2017

North America—News briefs

Americas K. Stock color *Bloomberg Businessweek* no4535 p9 Ag 28 2017

North America img *New York Times Upfront* v149 no6 p32 D 12 2016

North Americans

See also

Americans

Canadians

North Atlantic Treaty Organization

Europe's nuclear woes: Mitigating the challenges of the next years U. Kühn, S. Shetty et al bibl *Bulletin of the Atomic Scientists* v73 no4 p245 Jl 2017

How will NATO's non-nuclear members handle the UN's ban on nuclear weapons? T. Sauer bibl *Bulletin of the Atomic Scientists* v73 no3 p177 My 2017

NATO Makes It Rain R. Clough color graph *Bloomberg Businessweek* no4509 p12 Ja 30 2017

THE (NEW) TROUBLE WITH RUSSIA J. Pappalardo color *Popular Mechanics* p72 Mr 2017

PARODY color *Weekly Standard* v22 no32 p44 My 1 2017

WILL NATO NOW BE 'OBSOLETE'? J. WEINMAN color *Maclean's* v129 no47 p30 N 28 2016

North Atlantic Treaty Organization—News briefs

BAD NEWS color *Maclean's* v129 no46 p9 N 21 2016

North Carolina

The Conference Skinny B. D. Coleman bw color *Arts & Crafts Homes & the Revival* v12 no5 p20 Wint 2018

WHY AREN'T YOU LAUGHING? D. SEDARIS bw cartoon *New Yorker* v93 no17 p30 Je 19 2017

North Carolina—Description & travel

Spring into action color *Backpacker* p10 My 2017

TAKE A DRIVE: THE OUTER BANKS S. Herrada *Washingtonian Magazine* v52 no9 p133 Je 2017

Winter-Riding Opportunities R. EVERSOLE color *Trail Rider* v29 no1 p22 Ja/F 2017

North Cascades (B.C. & Wash.)

See also

Baker, Mount (Wash.)

The Griz is Good for Ya E. SHAW il *Backpacker* p18 S 2017

North Cascades National Park (Wash.)

Cure summit fever color *Backpacker* p14 Ag 2017

North Dakota—Description & travel

ROAD TRIP cartoon *American Cowboy* v23 no4 p41 D 2016/Ja 2017

North Dakota—Social conditions

backstory color *New Republic* v248 no5 p72 My 2017

North Devon (England)

In Search of Lorna Doone *British Heritage Travel* v37 no6 p44 N/D 2016

North East Regional (Short story)

NORTH EAST REGIONAL E. CLINE cartoon *New Yorker* v93 no8 p58 Ap 10 2017

North Korean military history

Diplomacy; Not Doomsday W. J. Perry *Hoover Digest: Research & Opinion on Public Policy* no2 p139 Spr 2017

North Pacific Yachts Inc.

NORTH PACIFIC *Sea Magazine* v109 no5 p34 My 2017

Notebook D. HARDING color *Power & Motoryacht* v32 no11 p68 N 2016

North Pole

THE NORTH POLE F. ROOTS map *Canadian Geographic* v137 no2 p46 Mr/Ap 2017

POLAR EXPRESSED K. SCHULZ cartoon color *New Yorker* v93 no10 p88 Ap 24 2017

North Sails Group LLC

Higher Tech P. Nielsen color *Sail* v48 no7 p48 Jl 2017

North Star Editions (Company)

Shining a Light on YA, MG Fiction C. Kirch *Publishers Weekly* v264 no3 p11 Ja 16 2017

North Yorkshire (England)—Description & travel

To the Great Beyond and North Yorkshire E. D. Huntley *British Heritage Travel* v38 no1 p28 Ja/F 2017

Northam, Ralph

Blue on Blue in Virginia A. FERGUSON color *Weekly Standard* v22 no35 p15 My 22 2017

THE RUMBLE IN RICHMOND: THE BIGGEST DEMOCRATIC TITLE BOUT SINCE HILLARY VS. BERNIE A. SHEPHARD color *New Republic* v248 no6 p18 Je 2017

North American International Auto Show (Detroit, Mich.)

EDITOR'S LETTER K. WOLFKILL *Road & Track* v68 no7 p22 Mr/Ap 2017

Winter of Discontent B. LUTZ color *Road & Track* v68 no7 p104 Mr/Ap 2017

North Carolina—Politics & government—1951-

PURPLE WITH RAGE: North Carolina is narrowly split between Democratic and Republican Parties that agree on virtually nothing. Are its scorched-earth politics what the rest of us have to look forward to? J. Zengerle *New York Times Magazine* p36 Je 25 2017

Northeast Passage

The Arctic Waterway to Russia's Economic Future L. W. Brigham color map *Wilson Quarterly* p1 Summ 2017

The Navigable Northwest Passage A. Tartar graph map *Bloomberg Businessweek* no4537 p73 S 11 2017

Northern California Independent Booksellers Association (Organization)

Independent Bookstore Day 2017: A Perfect Storm for Sales E. Nawotka, J. Boog et al color map *Publishers Weekly* v264 no17 p6 Ap 24 2017

Northern California—Description & travel

WIN A MENDOCINO GETAWAY! color *Sunset* v239 no3 p110 S 2017

Northern California—History

Decalifornication S. Richardson bw *American History* v52 no4 p6 O 2017

Northern Canada—Environmental conditions

Canada ice cores suffer meltdown color *Science* v356 no6334 p116 Ap 14 2017

Northern cardinal

Cardinal Rules A. Hadhazy color *Natural History* v125 no4 p6 Ap 2017

A Day in the Life of a Teen Birder N. Koszycki color *Audubon* v119 no3 p45 Fall 2017

Northern gannet

Rescue Mission A. OPAR *Audubon* v118 no6 p32 Wint 2016

Northern Hemisphere

See also

North America

Lunar Almanac Northern Hemisphere Sky Chart *Sky & Telescope* v134 no3 p42 S 2017

Northern Italy—History—20th century

The pain behind the pleasure R. Bosworth *History Today* v67 no2 p47 F 2017

Northern Nigeria—Politics & government

THE BOYS FROM BAGA: THE FOUR OF THEM, CHILDREN FROM A FISHING VILLAGE IN NORTHEASTERN NIGERIA, WERE AMONG THOUSANDS ABDUCTED BY BOKO HARAM AND TRAINED AS CHILD SOLDIERS. THEY LEARNED TO SURVIVE, BUT ONLY BY FORGETTING WHO THEY WERE S. A. Topol *New York Times Magazine* p42 Je 25 2017

Northern right whale

Keeping Whales Free from Fishing Gear: NEW "ON-CALL" BUOY FOR LOBSTER TRAPS COULD HELP PREVENT ENTANGLEMENTS V. LaCapra *Oceanus* v52 no2 p16 Spr 2017

Northern sky (Astronomy)

Through a High Window F. Schaaf *Sky & Telescope* v132 no6 p45 D 2016

NORTHINGTON, ROBERT M.

The Arctic in the Twenty-First Century: Changing Biogeochemical Linkages across a Paraglacial Landscape of Greenland *BioScience* v67 no2 p118 F 2017

Northmen—History

DARKNESS AT THE EDGE OF THE WORLD T. Folger color

map *Smithsonian* v47 no10 p28 Mr 2017

NORTHRIDGE, SUZAN K. H.

Paying Our Respects color *O, The Oprah Magazine* p15 Je 2017

Northrop Grumman Corp.

THE BEST DEFENSE A. GARA color *Forbes* v199 no7 p30 Je 29 2017

Northumbria University (Northumbria, England)

What's the healthiest herbal tea? L. Dog color *Prevention* v68 no12 p28 D 2016

Northwest Passage

The Elusive Northwest Passage K. Peek color graph *Scientific American* v316 no5 p80 My 2017

The Navigable Northwest Passage A. Tartar graph map *Bloomberg Businessweek* no4537 p73 S 11 2017

Northwest Passage—History

THE SEARCH FOR THE NORTHWEST PASSAGE P. Hatfield *History Today* v67 no2 p10 F 2017

Northwestern University (Evanston, Ill.)

AMERICA'S BEST EMPLOYERS 2017 chart *Forbes* v199 no5 p110 My 16 2017

Northwestern University (Evanston, Ill.)—Sports

BEST OF THE BOWLS C. Johnson color *Sports Illustrated* v126 no2 p31 Ja 16 2017

First DANCE [Cover story] L. Winn color *Sports Illustrated* v126 no8 p52 Mr 20 2017

Northwest Ordinance, 1787 (U.S.)

The Preservation and Use of America's Natural Resources *Congressional Digest* v96 no6 p2 Je 2017

Norton, Anne

Inequality is Always in the Room: Language & Power in Deliberative Democracy *Daedalus* v146 no3 p64 Summ 2017

Norton, Ben

Labour's Corbyn Faced Media Attacks From Right and Center--on Both Sides of Atlantic *Extra!* v30 no6 p3 Jl/Ag 2017

Norton, Edward

We Must Protect the Bounty and Beauty of the Sea *UN Chronicle* v54 no1/2 p1 2017

Norton, Elizabeth

THE 24-WORD REVIEW T. Jordan color *Entertainment Weekly* no1474/1475 p118 Jl 21-28 2017

NORTON, ERIC

FROM RUSSIA WITH LOVE? color *Publishers Weekly* v264 no13 p25 Mr 27 2017

On the Tip of My Tongue color *Publishers Weekly* v264 no11 p71 Mr 13 2017

Revenge of the Internet color *Publishers Weekly* v264 no33 p48 Ag 14 2017

Norton, James

Grantchester *TV Guide* v65 no27 p35 Je 26 2017

Norton, Thomas J.

THE ANGRY BIRDS MOVIE cartoon *Sound & Vision* v82 no1 p69 Ja 2017

Aperion Audio Verus II Grand Speaker System color graph *Sound & Vision* v82 no3 p54 Ap 2017

BOY & THE WORLD color *Sound & Vision* v81 no10 p69 D 2016

IN THE HEART OF THE SEA color *Sound & Vision* v81 no9 p68 N 2016

Laser Lightshow color graph *Sound & Vision* v82 no4 p50 My 2017

LG OLED65E6P OLED Ultra HDTV color graph *Sound & Vision* v82 no2 p54 F/Mr 2017

LG Signature OLED65W7P OLED Ultra HDTV color graph *Sound & Vision* v82 no5 p44 Je 2017

Not Your Father's HDTV color *Sound & Vision* v82 no7 p42 S 2017

PASSENGERS color *Sound & Vision* v82 no7 p68 S 2017

Philips BDP7501/F7 Ultra HD Blu-ray Player color *Sound & Vision* v81 no10 p50 D 2016

Projection for All? color *Sound & Vision* v82 no4 p42 My 2017

Q and Me bw color graph *Sound & Vision* v82 no8 p48 O 2017

THE SECRET LIFE OF PETS color *Sound & Vision* v82 no4 p68 My 2017

SING color *Sound & Vision* v82 no7 p70 S 2017

Sony XBR-65Z9D LCD Ultra HDTV color graph *Sound & Vision* v82 no1 p36 Ja 2017

STAR TREK INTO DARKNESS color *Sound & Vision* v81 no9 p67 N 2016

TROLLS color *Sound & Vision* v82 no7 p69 S 2017

UHD Star-Lord? color *Sound & Vision* v82 no4 p54 My 2017

The Unfolding Story color *Sound & Vision* v82 no3 p66 Ap 2017

Norwich, John Julius

Four Princes: Henry VIII, Francis I, Charles V, Suleiman the Magnificent, and the Obsessions That Forged Modern Europe A. Moravcsik *Foreign Affairs* v96 no3 p163 My/Je 2017

Old World Order A. MIKHAIL *New York Times Book Review* p19 My 7 2017

Norwood, Mary

THERE'S SOMETHING ABOUT MARY: The implausible and inevitable rise of the woman who could be mayor T. WHEATLEY *Atlanta* v57 no6 p28 O 2017

Noschese, R.

Seasonal exposure of carbon dioxide ice on the nucleus of comet 67P/Churyumov-Gerasimenko bibl bw graph *Science* v354 no6319 p1563 D 23 2016

Nose

Nose's flu fighters have long memories T. HESMAN SAEY color *Science News* v191 no13 p16 Jl 8 2017

SCENTS & SENSIBILITY [Cover story] M. ZARASKA bw color diag graph *Discover* v38 no9 p42 N 2017

What in the World? *National Geographic Kids* no468 p29 Mr 2017

Nose, The (Theatrical production)

The Nose G. Hall *Opera News* v81 no7 p43 Ja 2017

Nose—Abnormalities

ITCHY NOSE K. Tatsuta *Harper's Magazine* v334 no2002 p41 Mr 2017

Nosek, D.

Observation of a large-scale anisotropy in the arrival directions of cosmic rays above 8×1018 eV *Science* v357 no6357 p1266 S 22 2017

Nosek, James

Bring the Noise cartoon color *Men's Health* v32 no4 p32 My 2017

For the Man on a Mission cartoon color *Men's Health* v32 no4 p36 My 2017

An NHL Star's Insane Muscle Moves cartoon *Men's Health* v32 no3 p44 Ap 2017

THIS IS HOW YOU ROLL cartoon *Men's Health* v32 no3 p32 Ap 2017

Von Miller: How an MVP Gets Better color *Men's Health* v31 no10 p54 D 2016

Noseworthy, Theodore J.

When Sensory Marketing Works and When it Backfires *Harvard Business Review Digital Articles* p2 My 19 2016

Nosferatu the Vampyre (Film)

GRAPHIC DETAIL A. Curry color *Film Comment* v53 no3 p80 My/Je 2017

Nosrat, Samin

IN BLOOM C. MUHLKE bw color *Bon Appetit* v62 no6 p74 Je 2017

A Matter of Taste: Perfecting gazpacho beyond a recipe's instructions by learning to trust your own palate *New York Times Magazine* p24 Jl 2 2017

The Taste of Regret: How you should—and should not—cook with garlic *New York Times Magazine* p26 O 1 2017

Ugly but Good: Cooking your vegetables long past 'done' yields a deliriously sweet and rich version *New York Times Magazine* p28 Ag 27 2017

Wrap It Up: Discovering the wonders of a Parsi-style fish in banana leaves, cooked on the grill *New York Times Magazine* p22 Jl 30 2017

Noss, Andrew

Forest conservation: Remember Gran Chaco bibl color *Science* v355 no6324 p465 F 3 2017

NOSS, REED

An Ecoregion-Based Approach to Protecting Half the Terrestrial Realm *BioScience* v67 no6 p534 Je 2017

We Need a Biologically Sound North American Conservation Plan *BioScience* v67 no8 p685 Ag 2017

Nossack, Hans Erich

SKY IS FALLING *Lapham's Quarterly* v10 no3 p184 Summ 2017

NOSSEL, SUZANNE

Suzanne Nossel: PEN Executive Director J. Maher color *Publishers Weekly* v263 no52 p30 D 19 2016

Words Matter *Publishers Weekly* v263 no48 p72 N 28 2016

Nostalgia

The End of Forgetting B. ROWEN color *Atlantic* v319 no5 p24 Je 2017

Feelings of Nostalgia Can Make Us More Patient Xun (Irene) Huang *Harvard Business Review Digital Articles* p2 N 7 2016

In the Groove D. HARSANYI color *National Review* v69 no7 p48 Ap 17 2017

Nostalgia—Social aspects

The Change Is Us R. D. SULLIVAN *America* v215 p23 N 28 2016

Share with us L. Hammett, A. Marie O'Leary et al color *House Beautiful* p8 Ag 2017

Not in Our Name (Music)

Chords & Discords P. D'RIVERA, D. ELLIS et al color *Downbeat* v84 no5 p10 My 2017

Not Two (Music)

Not Two B. Meyer color *Downbeat* v84 no7 p63 Jl 2017

Notaras, Michael

Stressing mental health color *Science* v356 no6340 p878 My 26 2017

Notaro, Tig, 1971-

SHOW AND TELL E. NUSSBAUM color *New Yorker* v93 no31 p76 O 9 2017

Notaro, Tig, 1971—Interviews

Tig Notaro A. Hoffman color *Time* v190 no10/11 p116 S 18 2017

Notch signaling pathway—Research

Notch-Jagged complex structure implicates a catch bond in tuning ligand sensitivity V. C. Luca, B. Choul Kim et al bibl diag graph *Science* v355 no6331 p1320 Mr 24 2017

Notebooks

Notable Addiction M. W. Spencer *New Orleans Homes & Lifestyles* v20 no1 p104 Wint 2016

NOTEWORTHY ADVENTURES color *Field & Stream* v122 no5 p8 O 2017

Sketchbook: 'Moby-Dick,' Part 2 S. García Sánchez *New York Times Book Review* p21 Je 11 2017

Work Wonders *Martha Stewart Living* no267 p22 S 2016

Notebooks—Evaluation

Mother's Day gift guide L. BERGAMOTTO color *Good Housekeeping* v264 no5 p68I My 2017

OFFICE UPGRADE: Work from home in style B. L. GRANT color *Chicago* v66 no9 p80 S 2017

Rethink Your Ink L. LARSON color *GQ: Gentlemen's Quarterly* v97 no11 p48 N 2017

NOTEBOOM, BEN

CASE STUDY: IS HOLACRACY FOR US? color il *Harvard Business Review* v95 no2 p151 Mr/Ap 2017

Notes From New York (Music)

BEST ALBUMS OF 2016 bw color *Downbeat* v84 no1 p51 Ja 2017

Notes From the Field (Theatrical production)

Anna Deavere Smith E. Berman color *Time* v188 no19 p64 N 7 2016

Scholars Behind Bars J. Zimmerman color *New York Review of Books* v64 no3 p43 F 23 2017

Notetaking

Become a Better Listener by Taking Notes S. Nawaz *Harvard Business Review Digital Articles* p2 Mr 24 2017

Improving Student Note-Taking Skills C. CHANDLER *Education Digest* v82 no7 p54 Mr 2017

What You Miss When You Take Notes on Your Laptop M. McGloin *Harvard Business Review Digital Articles* p2 Jl 31 2015

Notetaking—Software

Capture Your Creativity with a Digital Notebook A. Samuel *Harvard Business Review Digital Articles* p2 My 29 2015

Noth, Paul

15 QUESTIONS ABOUT BARBEQUE ANSWERED cartoon map *Esquire* p110 S 2017

Nothing (Philosophy)

Imagine No Universe M. Shermer color *Scientific American* v316 no2 p73 F 2017

Notley, Rachel, 1964-

REGRETS? THEY HAVE A FEW J. MARKUSOFF color *Maclean's* v130 no10 p30 N 2017

Notley, Rachel—Interviews

THE INTERVIEW J. MARKUSOFF color *Maclean's* v129 no51/52 p18 D 26 2016

Notre-Dame de Paris (Cathedral)

Notre Dame Cathedral Is Crumbling. Who Will Help Save It? V. Walt color *Time* v190 no6 p26 Ag 7 2017

Nottage, Lynn

CLOSE UP WITH CONDOLA RASHAD L. Cross color *Ebony* v72 no6 p22 Ap/My 2017

THE LISTENER M. SCHULMAN cartoon color *New Yorker* v93 no6 p30 Mr 27 2017

WORKED H. ALS cartoon *New Yorker* v92 no39 p94 N 28 2016

Notz, Dirk

Arctic summer may be iceless by 2050 T. SUMNER chart *Science News* v190 no12 p15 D 10 2016

Observed Arctic sea-ice loss directly follows anthropogenic CO_2 emission bibl graph *Science* v354 no6313 p747 N 11 2016

Noumair, Debra A.

How to Negotiate for Yourself When People Don't Expect You To *Harvard Business Review Digital Articles* p2 Je 17 2016

Nouvel, Jean, 1945-

SEA OF LOUVRE ABU DHABI'S NEW ISLAND MUSEUM A. VLASITS bw color *Wired* v25 no5 p28 My 2017

Nouwen, Henri J. M., 1932-1996

Priest, Writer, Mentor, Misfit M. Higgins color *Commonweal* v143 no20 p13 D 16 2016

Nova, Annie

THE BEST PLACES TO LIVE IN AMERICA [Cover story] chart color map *Money* v46 no9 p54 O 2017

"It's Going to Collapse" and Other Dire Warnings About Stocks color *Money* v46 no8 p33 S 2017

Taking Out the Meal-Kit Trash color *Money* v46 no8 p74 S 2017

Nova automobile

Automotive Archaeology: Junkyard Jewels R. Brutt color *Hot Rod* v70 no8 p22 Ag 2017

HOT ROD TO THE RESCUE chart color graph *Hot Rod* v69 no12 p92 D 2016

Sean Price's 1965 Nova 350 Nose-Dives Over 4,500 RPM. We Fixed the Cam; Now We're Gonna Fix the Heads and Valvetrain M. Davis color *Hot Rod* v69 no12 p90 D 2016

Nova automobile—Maintenance & repair

The Thumpr-Cammed 383 Small-Block in Don Kwiatkowski's 1971 Nova Hesitates and Stumbles Off Idle. We're Gonna Fix It M. Davis chart color *Hot Rod* v70 no6 p104 Je 2017

Nova Scotia—Environmental conditions

Helping moose get it on R. COUNTER color *Maclean's* v130 no4 p16 My 2017

Novack, Janet

LESSONS AND IDEAS BY THE 100 GREATEST LIVING BUSINESS MINDS bw color *Forbes* v200 no3 p115 S 28 2017

Novae (Astronomy)

The Bright One That Got Away: Fifty years ago this month, the author, then 16, came a hair's breadth from making a huge discovery S. P. Cook *Sky & Telescope* v134 no1 p84 Jl 2017

Historical Observations Reveal an Ancient Explosion J. BARBUZANO *Sky & Telescope* v134 no6 p12 D 2017

Novak, Annie

GROWING GARDENERS color *Better Homes & Gardens* v95 no3 p154 Mr 2017

Novak, B. J.

EVERY DAY I'M SIDE-HUSTLIN' cartoon color *GQ: Gentlemen's Quarterly* v97 no4 p60 Ap 2017

Novak, Celeste Allen

Innovation and Industry: Ceramic's Sustainable Story *Architectural Record* v205 no7 p164 Jl 2017

Revolutionizing Ceiling and Wall Surfaces with Parametrics and Digital Fabrication color *Architectural Record* v204 no12 p194 D 2016

Novak, David

Recognizing Employees Is the Simplest Way to Improve Morale *Harvard Business Review Digital Articles* p2 My 9 2016

Novak, Jodie

To engage students, give them meaningful choices in the classroom il *Phi Delta Kappan* v99 no2 p37 O 2017

Novák, László

CREPUSCULAR COVERLET *Sierra* v101 no4 p2 Jl/Ag 2016

NOVAK, MARK

Long-Term Studies Contribute Disproportionately to Ecology and Policy *BioScience* v67 no3 p271 Mr 2017

Novak, Michael, 1933-2017

An Extraordinary Career J. BOTTUM color *Weekly Standard* v22 no25 p15 Mr 6 2017

Friend of Freedom C. DEMUTH SR. color *Weekly Standard* v22 no25 p17 Mr 6 2017

Moral Economy R. R. RENO color *National Review* v69 no5 p25 Mr 20 2017

People A. M. Banks color *Christian Century* v134 no7 p17 Mr 29 2017

A Turn That Went a Long Way P. Steinfels *Commonweal* v144 no6 p12 Mr 24 2017

Novara, Giovanni

An accreting pulsar with extreme properties drives an ultraluminous x-ray source in NGC 5907 bibl chart graph *Science* v355 no6327 p817 F 24 2017

Novartis AG

FDA OKs cancer gene therapy *Science* v357 no6355 p952 S 8 2017

Novel ecosystems

Anthropocene has begun, group says T. SUMNER color graph *Science News* v190 no8 p14 O 15 2016

Novelists

See also

Women novelists

CanLit gets lit up B. BETHUNE color *Maclean's* v129 no48/49 p32 D 5 2016

Celeste Ng, Novelist S. Begley color *Time* v190 no12 p58 S 25 2017

Choose Your Own Rachel Cusk H. Fulavits img *New York* p101 Mr 6 2017

Emma Straub *New York Times Book Review* p8 Je 25 2017

Exile From Brooklyn: The writer Danzy Senna moved to California because New York felt like "a book party that never ended." She doesn't mean that in a good way J. Press img *New York* v50 no15 p66 Jl 24 2017

George SAUNDERS Z. SMITH *Interview* v47 no2 p72 Mr 2017

Gods and Monsters L. PICKER color *Publishers Weekly* v264 no41 p44 O 9 2017

How Is a Debut Novel Like Lizzy Bennet? K. A. FLYNN *New York Times Book Review* p29 Je 4 2017

HUMANIST PROFILE *Humanist* v77 no2 p1 Mr/Ap 2017

Jason Reynolds: The Hardest-Working Man in Washington S. CORBETT color *Publishers Weekly* v264 no29 p28 Jl 17 2017

John Berger of the Haute-Savoie J. White *Film Quarterly* v70 no4 p93 Summ 2017

Karan Mahajan M. Hagan color *Current Biography* v78 no1 p37 Ja 2017

THE MAGUS OF PARIS A. ROSS bw cartoon *New Yorker* v93 no18 p67 Je 26 2017

The Meaning of Zelda E. STONE and C. SIGAL *Commentary* v144 no1 p6 Jl/Ag 2017

Meeting Childhood Idols bw color *Publishers Weekly* v264 no29 p30 Jl 17 2017

Portrait of the Author as a Historian A. Lee *History Today* v67 no3 p54 Mr 2017

A Turn That Went a Long Way P. Steinfels *Commonweal* v144 no6 p12 Mr 24 2017

Viet Thanh Nguyen *New York Times Book Review* p6 F 5 2017

Viet Thanh Nguyen writes about the refugees we don't remember anymore Q. D. Tran color *America* v216 no4 p38 F 20 2017

Novelists—Attitudes

WATCH CLOSELY A. SCHWARTZ cartoon color map *New Yorker* v93 no32 p56 O 16 2017

Waugh's Gift A. VALIUNAS bw *Weekly Standard* v22 no16 p34 D 26 2016

Novelists—Awards

Eight Things We Love About Gene Luen Yang: The ILA 2017 Featured Speaker is a literacy advocate on a mission to diversify children's literature C. Maloney color *Literacy Today (2411-7862)* v34 no6 p32 My/Je 2017

Knopf to Print 200,000 Copies of Nobel Winner Ishiguro's Works J. Maher and J. Milliot color *Publishers Weekly* v264 no41 p10 O 9 2017

Novelists—Interviews

Q&A WITH ERIC VAN LUSTBADER bw *Publishers Weekly* v263 no43 p(Sp)13 O 24 2016

Novels of manners

THE LIVES OF OTHERS: Does the social novel have a future? J. Dee *Harper's Magazine* p86 S 2017

Novelty (Perception)

HOW HABIT BEATS NOVELTY [Cover story] S. BERINATO color diag *Harvard Business Review* v95 no1 p60 Ja/F 2017

Novembre, John

Chimpanzee genomic diversity reveals ancient admixture with bonobos bibl diag graph map *Science* v354 no6311 p477 O 28 2016

Nover, Maddi

Glitter Galore color *Dance Spirit* v20 no9 p26 N 2016

Novex Biotech LLC

Boost Your Performance color *Muscle & Performance* v9 no11 p62 N 2017

NOVICK, LYNN

How Americans Lost Faith in the Presidency bw *Atlantic* v320 no3 p24 O 2017

NEW EYES on VIETNAM A. Grant color *Esquire* p69 S 2017

Novick, Lynn—Interviews

An interview about interviewing with Lynn Novick and Sarah Botstein of The Vietnam War M. Hindley *Humanities* v38 no4 p1 Fall 2017

Novick, Peter

FREAKY FANTASTIC GEORGETOWN K. OLSEN *Washingtonian Magazine* v52 no11 p10 Ag 2017

Novick, Sheldon

A New Pollution Problem bw chart color *Environment* v59 no4 p14 Jl-Ag 2017

Novick, Tzvi

The First Christian? cartoon *Commonweal* v144 no6 p25 Mr 24 2017

Noviello, Bob

How to Get Squirrels Out of Your Attic J. BILLS and J. P. SCHMELZER color *Yankee* p28 Mr 2017

Novitskova, Katja—Exhibitions

KATJA NOVITSKOVA *Interview* v47 no5 p22 Je/Jl 2017

Novoselov, K. S.

High-temperature quantum oscillations caused by recurring Bloch states in graphene superlattices color *Science* v357 no6347 p181 Jl 14 2017

Novostroïka (Short story)

NOVOSTROÏKA M. Reva color *Atlantic* v318 no5 p80 D 2016

Novotny, V.

Observation of a large-scale anisotropy in the arrival directions of cosmic rays above 8×10^{18} eV *Science* v357 no6357 p1266 S 22 2017

Novotny, Vojtech

Higher predation risk for insect prey at low latitudes and elevations graph *Science* v356 no6339 p742 My 19 2017

Plant diversity increases with the strength of negative density dependence at the global scale diag *Science* v356 no6345 p1389 Je 30 2017

Novy-Williams, Eben

College Football's Fumble: Empty Stands color *Bloomberg Businessweek* no4506 p17 Ja 9 2017

GAME TIME DECISIONS color *Bloomberg Businessweek* no4515 p59 Mr 20 2017

Hot Tickets and Wall Street Marks *Bloomberg Businessweek* no4540 p33 O 2 2017

'Sold Out' Is for Suckers cartoon *Bloomberg Businessweek* no4495 p70 O 17 2016

Why European Soccer Is Coming To America color *Bloomberg Businessweek* no4534 p15 Ag 14 2017

Now (Music)

Nashville Rebels Try a Little Sincerity R. SHEFFIELD color *Rolling Stone* no1297 p53 O 5 2017

Now That the Light Is Fading (Music)

MAGGIE ROGERS N. Feeney color *Entertainment Weekly* no1454/1455 p95 F 24 2017

Now We Eat the Dark Vein (Poem)

NOW WE EAT THE DARK VEIN J. Seay *New Yorker* v93 no18 p42 Je 26 2017

Now You See Me 2 (Film)
NEWLY AVAILABLE MOVIES M. FELL *TV Guide* v65 no2 p46 Ja 2 2017
NOW YOU SEE ME 2 D. Vaughn color *Sound & Vision* v82 no5 p66 Je 2017

Nowack, Matt
Why We Ask Every New Employee to Code an App Their First Week on the Job *Harvard Business Review Digital Articles* p2 D 23 2016

Nowack, Moritz K.
RETINOBLASTOMA RELATED1 mediates germline entry in Arabidopsis color diag *Science* v356 no6336 p396 Ap 28 2017

Nowak, Carsten
Merging paleobiology with conservation biology to guide the future of terrestrial ecosystems color *Science* v355 no6325 p594 F 10 2017

NOWAK, CLAIRE
Couponing for Charity color *Reader's Digest* v190 no1132 p8 Jl/Ag 2017

Nowak, Martin A.
Genes, environment, and "bad luck" bibl color *Science* v355 no6331 p1266 Mr 24 2017
Origins of lymphatic and distant metastases in human colorectal cancer diag graph *Science* v357 no6346 p55 Jl 7 2017

NOWAK, PETER
The great equalizer color *Maclean's* v130 no4 p60 My 2017

Nowakowski, Kelsey
CALORIES COUNT diag *National Geographic* v232 no4 p8 O 2017
SUSTAINING OUR CITIES graph *National Geographic* v231 no5 p10 My 2017
WHERE IN THE WORLD ARE WOMEN AND MEN MOST—AND LEAST—EQUAL? graph *National Geographic* v231 no1 p28 Ja 2017
WHO'S THE FAIREST? color graph *National Geographic* v231 no1 p24 Ja 2017

Nowalk, Pete—Interviews
PETE NOWALK M. LOGAN *TV Guide* v65 no4 p12 Ja 16 2017

Nowatzki, Timothy M.
A selective insecticidal protein from Pseudomonas for controlling corn rootworms bibl chart graph *Science* v354 no6312 p634 N 4 2016

Nowell, Peter C.
Peter C. Nowell (1928–2016) M. I. Greene and J. S. Moore color *Science* v355 no6328 p913 Mr 3 2017

Nowinski, Hanna
Meg & Linus *Publishers Weekly* v264 no7 p77 F 13 2017

Nowotny, Helga
ERC—the next 10 years color *Science* v355 no6329 p997 Mr 10 2017

Noxon, Marti
Bring "Your Ugly Stuff" M. K. Schilling img *New York* v50 no13 p74 Je 26 2017
To the Bone L. Greenblatt color *Entertainment Weekly* no1474/1475 p98 Jl 21-28 2017

Noy, Aleksandr
Enhanced water permeability and tunable ion selectivity in subnanometer carbon nanotube porins chart color *Science* v357 no6353 p792 Ag 25 2017

Noyes, Frederick
Parallel LINES bw color *Esquire* p136 S 2017

Noyes, Jesse
Should Your Company Start a Podcast? *Harvard Business Review Digital Articles* p2 D 9 2014

Noyes, Lydia
Cultivating a Seed Community *Mother Earth News* no282 p9 Je/Jl 2017
Dig In: The Food Freedom Act *Mother Earth News* no282 p10 Je/Jl 2017
Energy Cooperatives Make 'Solar Gardens' Bloom *Mother Earth News* no283 p8 Ag/S 2017
Hydroponic Farming: Organic or Not? *Mother Earth News* no282 p8 Je/Jl 2017

Nozzles
See also
Spray nozzles

KNOW NOZZLES G. Guilickson *Successful Farming* v115 no2 p41 F 2017
Where Should EFI Nozzles Be Located on the Intake Runner for Best Performance? M. Davis color *Hot Rod* v70 no4 p86 Ap 2017

Nozzles—Evaluation
IRRIGATION ADVANCES D. Mowitz *Successful Farming* v114 no13 p70 D 2016

NRBQ (Performer)
At Home Anywhere C. WOLFF color *Downbeat* v84 no1 p79 Ja 2017

Nørskov, Jens K.
Combining theory and experiment in electrocatalysis: Insights into materials design bibl color graph *Science* v355 no6321 p1 Ja 13 2017
Direct and continuous strain control of catalysts with tunable battery electrode materials bibl graph *Science* v354 no6315 p1031 N 25 2016

Nseir, Ibrahim
People D. Martens and M. I. Pinsky color *Christian Century* v134 no3 p17 F 2017

N'Sonde, Wilfried
The Silence of the Spirits *Publishers Weekly* v264 no27 p50 Jl 3 2017

Ntaiya, Kakenya
FIELD NOTES color *National Geographic* v230 no6 p17 D 2016

Ntim, Christine Souffrant
Startup Queen Z. HUGHES color *Ebony* v72 no8 p72 Je 2017

NTLOKO, ZIPHO
Clear, Glowy SKIN—Now color *Seventeen* v76 no5 p38 S 2017

Nuance Communications Inc.
NUANCE DRAGON PROFESSIONAL INDIVIDUAL FOR MAC 6.0: BETTER PERFORMANCE AND ACCURACY K. McELHEARN cartoon color *Macworld - Digital Edition* v33 no11 p43 N 2016

Nubreed Nutrition (Company)
GET TO KNOW: NUBREED NUTRITION J. SCHILDHOUSE color *Muscle & Performance* v9 no5 p32 My 2017

Nuclear arms control
See also
Nuclear nonproliferation
Ban the bomb by... banning the bomb? M. Kibaroglu bibl *Bulletin of the Atomic Scientists* v73 no3 p199 My 2017
Farewell to a Citizen-Scientist D. E. Hoffman *Hoover Digest: Research & Opinion on Public Policy* no2 p160 Spr 2017
The International Campaign to Abolish Nuclear Weapons M. Douglas *Time* v190 no16/17 p20 O 23 2017

Nuclear arms control verification
Introduction: Nuclear disarmament and arms control for the next decade U. Kühn *Bulletin of the Atomic Scientists* v73 no4 p244 Jl 2017

Nuclear batteries
Celebrating Targeted Investments in Innovative Research P. Falcone *Science & Technology Review* p3 Ap/My 2017
PROLONGED POWER in Remote Places L. L. Helms *Science & Technology Review* p21 Ap/My 2017

Nuclear bomb shelters
Where a Bad World Means Good Business J. Mattingly and A. Sharp color *Bloomberg Businessweek* no4533 p16 Ag 7 2017

Nuclear counters
Nuclear Ghosts J. Emspak bw *Scientific American* v316 no5 p12 My 2017
Patents and Awards *Science & Technology Review* p24 Ap/My 2017
Revealing the Presence of Hidden Nuclear Materials A. Chen color *Science & Technology Review* p18 Ja/F 2017

Nuclear crisis control
STICKS "TRUMP" CARROTS FOR NORTH KOREA G. E. MARSH *USA Today Magazine* v146 no2868 p24 S 2017

Nuclear disarmament
Ban the bomb by... banning the bomb? J. Pretorius bibl *Bulletin of the Atomic Scientists* v73 no3 p201 My 2017
China's proper role in the global nuclear order G. Kulacki bibl *Bulletin of the Atomic Scientists* v73 no2 p131 Mr 2017
Editor's note L. Crowder *Bulletin of the Atomic Scientists* v73 no1 p58 Ja 2017

Nuclear weapons plants

Worldwide deployments of nuclear weapons, 2017 H. M. Kristensen and R. S. Norris bibl *Bulletin of the Atomic Scientists* v73 no5 p289 2017

Nuclear weapons testing

See also

Underground nuclear explosions

Amid high tensions, an urgent need for nuclear restraint A. Malygina, Fikenscher et al bibl *Bulletin of the Atomic Scientists* v73 no4 p279 Jl 2017

THE APPROVAL MATRIX img *New York* v50 no18 p124 S 4 2017

BACK TO BIKINI: SCIENTISTS STUDY LINGERING RADIOACTIVITY AT 'GROUND ZERO' FOR NUCLEAR WEAPONS TESTING AFTER WORLD WAR II E. Lubofsky *Oceanus* v52 no2 p32 Spr 2017

Nuclear weapons testing—History

A Bomb to Remember J. M. Cannon and J. Sam *Hoover Digest: Research & Opinion on Public Policy* no1 p184 Wint 2017

Nuclear weapons—Asia

Managing nuclear risk in South Asia J. Sarkar bibl *Bulletin of the Atomic Scientists* v73 no1 p59 Ja 2017

Nuclear weapons—China

China's proper role in the global nuclear order R. Rajagopalan *Bulletin of the Atomic Scientists* v73 no2 p133 Mr 2017

Nuclear weapons—Design & construction

The secret of the SOVIET HYDROGEN BOMB A. Wellerstein and E. Geist *Physics Today* v70 no4 p40 Ap 2017

Nuclear weapons—Germany

Keine Atombombe, Bitte U. Kühn and T. Volpe color *Foreign Affairs* v96 no4 p103 Jl/Ag 2017

Nuclear weapons—History

AUTUMN OF THE ATOM J. LEPORE cartoon color *New Yorker* v92 no47 p22 Ja 30 2017

Nuclear weapons—Iran

A Disaster He's Proud Of L. Smith *Weekly Standard* v22 no18 p8 Ja 16 2017

HOW RESTRAINT LEADS TO WAR H. R. NAU *Commentary* v140 no2 p13 S 2015

Mad, Democrats? Blame the Iran Deal *Commentary* p1 Ja 2017

Mad, Democrats? Blame the Iran Deal *Commentary* v143 no1 p1 Ja 2017

Notes on a Disaster J. PODHORETZ *Commentary* v140 no2 p1 S 2015

Nuclear weapons—Korea (North)

Cover *Time* v189 no12 pC1 Ap 3 2017

Expert eavesdroppers occasionally catch a break E. Quill *Science News* v192 no1 p2 Ag 5 2017

HALEIWA, HAWAII P. Theroux *Harper's Magazine* p35 O 2017

How the Kims Came to Love The Bomb M. J. Schuman color *Bloomberg Businessweek* no4537 p12 S 11 2017

STICKS "TRUMP" CARROTS FOR NORTH KOREA G. E. MARSH *USA Today Magazine* v146 no2868 p24 S 2017

Thwarting the North Korean Powder Keg *USA Today Magazine* v146 no2866 p30 Jl 2017

Nuclear weapons—Korea (North)—History

Getting Tough on North Korea J. Stanton, Lee et al color *Foreign Affairs* v96 no3 p65 My/Je 2017

Nuclear weapons—Korea (North)—Testing

A Different Kind of Crisis M. AUSLIN color *National Review* v69 no9 p19 My 15 2017

Nuclear weapons—Pakistan

Pakistani nuclear forces, 2016 H. M. Kristensen and R. S. Norris bibl chart *Bulletin of the Atomic Scientists* v72 no6 p368 N 2016

Nuclear weapons—Russia

Nonstrategic nuclear weapons in Russia's evolving military doctrine K. Zysk bibl *Bulletin of the Atomic Scientists* v73 no5 p322 2017

Nuclear weapons—United States

Adapting nuclear modernization to the new administration A. Mount bibl *Bulletin of the Atomic Scientists* v73 no3 p167 My 2017

The political and military vulnerability of America's land-based nuclear missiles J. Wolfsthal bibl *Bulletin of the Atomic Scientists* v73 no3 p150 My 2017

The right planning now will save countless lives after a nuclear attack D. Hanfling, F. M. Burkle et al bibl *Bulletin of the Atomic Scientists* v73 no4 p220 Jl 2017

Trump's Nuclear Tweets R. JOSEPH and E. EDELMAN color *Weekly Standard* v22 no18 p24 Ja 16 2017

US cities are not medically prepared for a nuclear detonation J. M. Hauer *Bulletin of the Atomic Scientists* v73 no4 p215 Jl 2017

Nuclear weapons—United States—Government policy

AUTUMN OF THE ATOM J. LEPORE cartoon color *New Yorker* v92 no47 p22 Ja 30 2017

An occurrence at Oak Ridge: Morality in an age of nuclear peril J. E. Doyle bibl *Bulletin of the Atomic Scientists* v73 no2 p135 Mr 2017

Take Nukes Off a Short Fuse color *Scientific American* v316 no3 p10 Mr 2017

Nuclear weapons—United States—Law & legislation

A comprehensive nuclear test ban E. J. Moniz bibl color *Science* v354 no6316 p1081 D 2 2016

Nuclear War Should Require a Second Opinion color *Scientific American* v317 no2 p8 Ag 2017

Nucleases

The MIFstep in parthanatos E. Jonas bibl diag *Science* v354 no6308 p36 O 7 2016

Nucleic acids

See also

DNA

RNA

Genetic Engineering through Music? D. M. STOKES *Skeptical Inquirer* v41 no5 p11 S/O 2017

Nucleic acid detection with CRISPR-Cas13a/C2c2 J. S. Gootenberg, O. O. Abudayyeh et al color diag *Science* v356 no6336 p438 Ap 28 2017

Revisit NIH biosafety guidelines K. A. Oye, M. O'Leary et al color *Science* v357 no6352 p627 Ag 18 2017

Nucleophiles

Metal-catalyzed reductive coupling of olefin-derived nucleophiles: Reinventing carbonyl addition K. D. Nguyen, B. Y. Park et al diag *Science* v354 no6310 paah5133-1 O 21 2016

Nucleoproteins—Structure

Architecture of the yeast small subunit processome M. Chaker-Margot, J. Barandun et al bibl color *Science* v355 no6321 p1 Ja 13 2017

Nucleotide sequence

See also

CRISPRs (Genetics)

The CRISPR Pioneers A. Park color *Time* v188 no25-26 p116 D 19 2016 Double Issue

DNA sequence-directed shape change of photopatterned hydrogels via high-degree swelling A. Cangialosi, C. Yoon et al color diag *Science* v357 no6356 p1126 S 15 2017

RESEARCH color *Science* v357 no6352 p656 Ag 18 2017

A transcription factor hierarchy defines an environmental stress response network Liang Song, Shao-shan Carol Huang et al diag *Science* v354 no6312 p598 N 4 2016

Nucleus accumbens

How a Song Brings Out Your Beast K. A. FETTERS cartoon *Men's Health* v32 no8 p78 O 2017

Nude in art

See also

Photography of the nude

Nudge theory

NUDGE BACKLASH B. Bower color diag graph *Science News* v191 no5 p18 Mr 18 2017

Why Nudging Your Customers Can Backfire U. M. Dholakia *Harvard Business Review Digital Articles* p2 Ap 15 2016

Women leaders still need to be trailblazers C. NEWBERY *People Management* p40 F 2017

Nudity

How They Make the Greatest Show on Earth [Cover story] D. D'addario color *Time* v190 no2/3 p66 Jl 10-17 2017

PORTRAIT OF A Naked Woman K. Dold chart color graph *Women's Health* v14 no7 p130 S 2017

NUGENT, HUGH W.

CLASH OF THE TITANS cartoon *Vanity Fair* p84 Hollywood 2017 Supplement

Nugent, P. E.

iPTF16geu: A multiply imaged, gravitationally lensed type Ia supernova color diag graph *Science* v356 no6335 p291 Ap 21 2017

Nuisances

See also

Odors

50, 100 & 150 YEARS AGO bw color *Scientific American* v315 no6 p86 D 2016

NULL, CHRISTOPHER

HEAD-TO-HEAD: BABY DRIVERS color *Wired* v25 no9 p48 S 2017

Oomi Home: Semi-smarten your home, at a steep price color *Mac-world - Digital Edition* v34 no11 p126 N 2017

Null, Jan

California's Stressed Water System: A Primer *Weatherwise* v70 no1 p12 Ja/F 2017

Null, Matthew Neill

Honey from the Lion S. B. Trout color *Orion Magazine* v35 no6 p60 N/D 2016

Nulton, Roger

How to model realistic rock outcroppings color *Model Railroader* v84 no6 p50 Je 2017

Numarine (Company)

BEST OF BOTH WORLDS C. CASWELL chart color *Power & Motoryacht* v34 no7 p54 Jl 2017

Numarine 105HT J. Y. Wood color *Power & Motoryacht* v34 no10 p60 O 2017

Number One Angel (Music)

Charli XCX Gets Down With the Robots C. R. WEINGARTEN color *Rolling Stone* no1284 p52 Ap 6 2017

Numbers of species

LOVED TO DEATH R. Conniff color graph *Scientific American* v317 no4 p40 O 2017

Numeracy

Can Data Literacy Protect Us from Misleading Political Ads? W. Frick *Harvard Business Review Digital Articles* p2 Ap 5 2016

Nunes, Paul

Is Tesla Really a Disruptor? (And Why the Answer Matters) *Harvard Business Review Digital Articles* p2 2017

NUÑEZ, ALANNA

Surprisingly Ordinary Allergy Triggers color *Reader's Digest* v189 no1129 p54 Ap 2017

Núñez, Gabriel

Neonatal acquisition of Clostridia species protects against coloni-zation by bacterial pathogens diag *Science* v356 no6335 p315 Ap 21 2017

Nunez, L. A.

Observation of a large-scale anisotropy in the arrival directions of cosmic rays above 8 × 1018 eV *Science* v357 no6357 p1266 S 22 2017

NUNEZ, SIGRID

Bow Wow Wow: When your greatest muse has four legs and pees on the furniture *New York Times Book Review* p18 O 1 2017

Nunez, Tina

How My Horse De-Stresses Me color *Horse & Rider* v55 no12 p72 D 2016

Nunley, Ian

Memphis & Beyond: Assessing the Market for CRA Investment Bridges *(Federal Reserve Bank of St. Louis)* p1 Spr 2017

Nunn, Bill, 1952-2016

Milestones color *Time* v188 no14 p12 O 10 2016

Nuns

SIEGE MENTALITY Gan *Lapham's Quarterly* v10 no3 p97 Summ 2017

TIME CAPSULE P. STEFÁNSSON *Iceland Review* v55 no2 p68 Mr/Ap 2017

Nuns as teachers

One afternoon in October B. DOYLE *Christian Century* v133 no21 p11 O 12 2016

Teachers Who Teach J. J. CONLEY *America* v215 no19 p28 D 19 2016

Nuns—United States

Pennsylvania nuns sue federal agency over natural gas pipeline M. Cusick color *Christian Century* v134 no18 p15 Ag 30 2017

Nuqingaq, Mathew

big picture color *Canadian Geographic* v137 no4 p12 Jl/Ag 2017

Nuraliev, Boris

A Billionaire Emerges On the Silicon Steppe I. Khrennikov and A. Sazonov bw *Bloomberg Businessweek* no4527 p28 Je 19 2017

Nurdjaja, Ayesha

Ayesha's Falafel img *New York* v50 no7 p66 Ap 3 2017

Nuremberg War Crime Trials, Nuremberg, Germany, 1945-1949—Influence

Don't Wait for Nuremberg C. EDELSON *In These Times* v41 no4 p13 Ap 2017

NURICK, ALBERT

ROAR OF THE CROWD *Texas Monthly* v45 no7 p12 Jl 2017

Nurizzo, Didier

An algal photoenzyme converts fatty acids to hydrocarbons color graph *Science* v357 no6354 p903 S 1 2017

Nurkka, Jaakko

How Investors React When Companies Announce They're Mov-ing to a SaaS Business Model color *Harvard Business Review Digital Articles* p2 Ja 12 2017

NURSE, DONNA BAILEY

COMMOWEALTH bw color *Maclean's* v129 no41 p56 O 17 2016

Nurse administrators

Health Care HERO K. CICERO color *Prevention* v69 no6 p34 Je 2017

Nurse practitioners

Lauren Doolittle A. BRANDT *Cincinnati Magazine* p34 Je 2017

Nurseries (Children's rooms)

UPCOMING IN 2017 *Washingtonian Magazine* v52 no2 p218 N 2016

Nurseries (Horticulture)

Your CHECKLIST E. Jardina and J. Mccausland color *Sunset* v238 no1 p46 Ja 2017

Nurseries (Horticulture)—Evaluation

GARDEN GREATS: Landscapers, nurseries, and furniture stores that can help you create your outdoor escape J. Sergent *Wash-ingtonian Magazine* v52 no8 p176 My 2017

Nursery growers

Seoul's Garden In the Sky J. Zorthian color *Time* v189 no22 p17 Je 12 2017

Nurses

ALL IN A Day's Work S. JESTER and S. HARVEY *Reader's Di-gest* v190 no1135 p56 N 2017

GETTING A GRIP ON ADVENTURE P. Edmonds color *Nation-al Geographic* v232 no1 p22 Jl 2017

LOOKING BACK C. L. HOYING, Y. WESS et al *Cincinnati Magazine* v50 no8 p73 My 2017

REMAINS OF THE DAY C. Wolf *Harper's Magazine* v334 no2002 p11 Mr 2017

Smoking Quit Rates Rise After Nurse Talk *USA Today Magazine* v146 no2869 p6 O 2017

What Nurses Know (THAT CAN SAVE YOUR LIFE) L. Pepper cartoon *Prevention* p70 Mr 2017

What nurses tell their friends L. MULCAHY and L. Rosenthal color *Redbook* p82 My 2017

Nurses—Attitudes

WITH CHILD K. Feldman *Harper's Magazine* v333 no1999 p59 D 2016

Nurses—Awards

Andrea Norman K. SINGLETARY color *Louisiana Life* v37 no3 p56 Ja/F 2017

Nurses—Employment

Flexible working 'key to solving NHS brain drain': HR profes-sionals say nurses prefer agency work *People Management* p10 Mr 2017

Nursing and the Great Recession M. L. Dolfman, M. Insco et al bibl *Monthly Labor Review* p1 Jl 2017

Reducing barriers of occupational licensing: insights from nursing Y. Ivanchev *Monthly Labor Review* p1 D 2016

Nurses—United States

Honor America's Amazing Nurses color *Prevention* v68 no12 p19 D 2016

A Nurse's Daughter Barbara *Prevention* v68 no12 p3 D 2016

Nurses We Love K. Cicero color *Prevention* v69 no5 p42 My 2017

Nursing

THE HIGHEST STANDARDS V. PREVISH *Cincinnati Maga-zine* v50 no8 p72 My 2017

LOOKING BACK C. L. HOYING, Y. WESS et al *Cincinnati*

Are These 'Healthy' Foods Really Good for You? A. Park and A. Sifferlin color *Time* v190 no10/11 p32 S 18 2017

THE audition prep TIMELINE j. Queuene color *Dance Spirit* v21 no2 p42 F 2017

Brain-Healthy Diets J. GRAHAM color *Kiplinger's Personal Finance* v71 no7 p68 Jl 2017

CAN NUTRITION CHANGE YOUR PERSONALITY? K. James chart color *Amazing Wellness* v9 no1 p48 Wint 2017

CONSTANT CRAVINGS [Cover story] L. Turner color *Amazing Wellness* v9 no6 p44 EarlyWint 2017

Dedicated Vegan Dietitian Dr. John Westerdahl H. Francis *Vegetarian Journal* v36 no1 p35 2017

A Diet of Good Information M. L. Tellado *Consumer Reports* v82 no11 p4 N 2017

Eat Smarter, Eat Healthier [Cover story] S. Wadyka, C. Roberts et al color *Consumer Reports* v82 no11 p18 N 2017

Exactly how to FILL your PLATE M. TAYLOR color *Redbook* p90 Ap 2017

THE EXCHANGE B. Boyé and A. Eaves bw cartoon color *Men's Health* v32 no6 p18 Ag 2017

Fat Fictions: Don't get fooled by the fads when it comes to this nutrient A. FELLER *Dance Magazine* v91 no9 p46 S 2017

Fixin' for a Fight M. F. Jacobson *Nutrition Action Health Letter* v44 no1 p2 Ja/F 2017

THE FOOD ISSUE J. DOWNER *New York Times Magazine* p37 O 9 2016

The Fruit Case L. MOYER and B. LIEBMAN *Nutrition Action Health Letter* v44 no4 p13 My 2017

GREAT GRAINS B. BRODY *Better Homes & Gardens* v94 no12 p152 D 2016

A GUIDE TO VEGAN CHEESE C. Brown and S. Keenan *Vegetarian Journal* v36 no2 p12 2017

the health nut A. Brightfield cartoon *Better Homes & Gardens* v95 no6 p162 Je 2017

Healthy Choices That Really Aren't P. O. BLUMBERG color *Prevention* v69 no5 p30 My 2017

The Hidden Power of Funky Foods T. CORSON color *Men's Health* v32 no4 p65 My 2017

label lingo J. Bauer and A. OGLETHORPE color *Better Homes & Gardens* v95 no8 p180 Ag 2017

Life Advice from Kids E. Spitznagel bw cartoon color *Men's Health* v32 no1 p140 Ja/F 2017

LIGHTEN UP THE GRILL G. KO color *Parents* v92 no8 p58 Ag 2017

THE NEW POWER FOOD FORMULA color *Men's Health* v31 no10 p104 D 2016

Nutrion SCHOOL [Cover story] color *Redbook* p81 Ap 2017

NUTRITION HOTLINE R. MANGELS *Vegetarian Journal* v36 no2 p2 2017

power GREENS A. TUST color *Yoga Journal* no291 p21 My 2017

Prioritizing good diets D. A. Cleveland bibl color *Science* v354 no6318 p1385 D 16 2016

THE REAL DEAL ON FIBER J. Bowden color *Amazing Wellness* v8 no6 p42 Early Winter2016

REBOOT! A. Nix *Amazing Wellness* v9 no4 p8 Summ 2017

Resolutions Nutritionists Wish You'd Make K. BRADY *Dance Magazine* v91 no1 p116 Ja 2017

Salt for the Earth C. Leu *Sierra* v101 no6 p11 N/D 2016

Scientists share 50 food facts to help you live longer (and lose weight too) [Cover story] M. CROUCH *Reader's Digest* v189 no1127 p63 F 2017

Second opinion *Mayo Clinic Health Letter* v358 no8 p8 Ag 2017

Simply Superior N. Brechka *Better Nutrition* v78 no11 p6 N 2016

sound bites L. Ladoceour color *Yoga Journal* p111 2017 Special Issue

test your nutrition IQ S. KUZEMCHAK *Parents* v92 no2 p72 F 2017

TRAIN LIKE A GIRL D. HIGGINS color *Climbing* no356 p60 S/O 2017

The truth about CALORIES color *Redbook* p88 Ap 2017

VEGAN Meat ALTERNATIVES A. Custer *Vegetarian Journal* v35 no1 p24 2016

What experts tell their friends about EATING HEALTHY J. DEMELO color *Redbook* p82 Ap 2017

What is the Nutritional Yeast *Vegetarian Journal* v36 no3 p14 2017

Nutrition disorders in children—Prevention

teaching little ones to give K. BELL *Parents* v91 no11 p48 N 2016

Nutrition disorders—Prevention

7 COMMON NUTRIENT DEFICIENCIES L. TURNER color *Better Nutrition* v79 no3 p48 Mr 2017

Nutrition in pregnancy

RESEARCH FOCUSES ON PREVENTING PRETERM BIRTHS V. Prevish *Cincinnati Magazine* v50 no12 p82 S 2017

Nutrition of athletes

See also

Cyclists—Nutrition

CITRULLINE MALATE: FUEL FOR FEMALES color *Muscle & Performance* v9 no1 p14 Ja 2017

GET TO KNOW: BEAST SPORTS NUTRITION J. SCHILDHOUSE color *Muscle & Performance* v9 no6 p32 Je 2017

Is It Better to Burn Carbs or Burn Fat? M. Rodriguez color *Black Belt* v55 no1 p18 D 2016/Ja 2017

Is This the Perfect Power Snack? *Scholastic Choices* pT8 S 2017 Supplement

Old School Food J. Lisanti and T. Keith color *Sports Illustrated* v126 no2 p18 Ja 16 2017

A WHEY BETTER (BLEND) PROTEIN M. FARRAR color *Muscle & Performance* v9 no6 p34 Je 2017

Nutrition policy

FDA Nutrition Guidelines *Congressional Digest* v95 no10 p12 D 2016

Nutrition services

See also

Diet therapy

BETTER DIETING THROUGH CHEMISTRY A. Cohen color *Bloomberg Businessweek* no4516 p70 Mr 27 2017

Nutritional assessment

AllMax Nutrition TestoFX color *Muscle & Performance* v9 no10 p64 O 2017

Nutritional requirements

3 nutrients your body craves J. R. Marquez color *Health* v31 no8 p63 O 2017

FALL INTO GREAT SKIN: 3 Supplements You Need V. TWEED chart color *Better Nutrition* v79 no10 p19 O 2017

Nutritional Yeast Dishes D. Wasserman *Vegetarian Journal* v36 no3 p13 2017

Nutritional value of bread

FAFQ K. Patel and J. WUEBBEN color *Muscle & Performance* v9 no6 p13 Je 2017

Nutritional value of food

Climate change may worsen nutrition S. MILIUS graph map *Science News* v191 no6 p14 Ap 1 2017

FOOD FOR THOUGHT *Nutrition Action Health Letter* v44 no2 p16 Mr 2017

Go Fish: Ripe, juicy tomatoes and fresh fish--could it get any better? Don't have heirlooms? Use cherry or campari tomatoes K. SHERWOOD *Nutrition Action Health Letter* v44 no7 p13 S 2017

Hit Refresh B. O'Dair color *Prevention* v69 no6 p3 Je 2017

Make Over Your Breakfast *Parents* v91 no9 p154 S 2016

Trout: The Perfect Catch J. BOWDEN and J. BESSINGER color *Better Nutrition* v79 no9 p70 S 2017

Nutrition—Economic aspects

Even a 14-Cent Food Tax Could Lead to Healthier Choices R. Khan, K. Misra et al *Harvard Business Review Digital Articles* p2 S 29 2016

Nutrition—Evaluation

DIGITAL DIET J. Kell color *Fortune* v175 no4 p38 Mr 15 2017

What Are You Missing? N. Brechka color *Better Nutrition* v79 no3 p6 Mr 2017

Nutritionists

See also

Women nutritionists

BETTER BOARDWALK BITES E. Bacharach color *Women's Health* v14 no5 p141 Je 2017

Secrets of Nutritionists J. MIGALA color *Martha Stewart Living* p56 S 2017

Nutrition—Physiological effect

SKIN DEEP color *Vogue* v207 no9 p438 S 2017

Nutrition—Requirements

Veggies du jour R. Begun chart color *Yoga Journal* no289 p70

KILL THE CHILL cartoon color *Men's Health* v32 no1 p77 Ja/F 2017

Look Your Best color *Men's Health* v32 no5 p99 Je 2017

Master the New Mixology color *Men's Health* v32 no3 p54 Ap 2017

THE RULES OF CASUAL COOL color *Men's Health* v32 no7 p(Sp)10 S 2017

The Secrets of Southern Comfort color *Men's Health* v32 no6 p73 Ag 2017

Steal Her Stuff color *Men's Health* v32 no4 p62 My 2017

Your Utility Layer color *Men's Health* v32 no2 p(Sp)28 Mr 2017

Nygård, J.

Majorana bound state in a coupled quantum-dot hybrid-nanowire system bibl graph *Science* v354 no6319 p1557 D 23 2016

Nygren, Patrick J.

Local protein kinase A action proceeds through intact holoenzymes color diag graph *Science* v356 no6344 p1288 Je 23 2017

Nygren, Steve

Serenbe Now! S. MARIKAR color *Bloomberg Businessweek* no4511 p59 F 13 2017

NYHART, HANNAH

BIRTH OF THE PICASSO bw *Chicago* v66 no5 p30 My 2017

CURATORS' SECRETS color *Chicago* v66 no3 p32 Mr 2017

Eve Ewing color *Chicago* v66 no6 p82 Je 2017

MANUSCRIPTS NO MORE cartoon *Chicago* v66 no5 p46 My 2017

SIN CITY bw *Chicago* v66 no6 p22 Je 2017

THE WAR ON WOMEN color *Chicago* v66 no4 p24 Ap 2017

Nyirongo, Vysaul

Resistance to malaria through structural variation of red blood cell invasion receptors diag *Science* v356 no6343 p1139 Je 16 2017

Nylon

As You Like It color *Martha Stewart Living* no275 p24 Je 2017

Nymphs (Insects)

The Truth About Frog Spit W. Lynch color *Canadian Wildlife* v23 no2 p46 My/Je 2017

Nyong'o, Lupita, 1983-

9 — ECLIPSED M. Snetiker color *Entertainment Weekly* no1444/1445 p118 D 16 2016

Lupita Nyong'o HER BEST EVER color *InStyle* v24 no4 p86 Ap 2017

A New Leaf color *Vogue* v207 no11 p124 N 2017

NYQUIST, JOEL

KNIVES/ACCESSORIES color *Backpacker* v45 no3 p122 Ap 2017

Nyquist, Sarah K.

De novo assembly of the Aedes aegypti genome using Hi-C yields chromosome-length scaffolds chart color diag *Science* v356 no6333 p92 Ap 7 2017

Nyquist, Scott

How the Natural Resources Business Is Turning into a Technology Industry color *Harvard Business Review Digital Articles* p1 Je 2 2017

Nyshadham, Anant

An Experiment in India Shows How Much Companies Have to Gain by Investing in Their Employees *Harvard Business Review Digital Articles* p1 Jl 25 2017

Nystrand, Joakim

ULTRAPERIPHERAL NUCLEAR COLLISIONS *Physics Today* v70 no10 p40 O 2017

Nyström, Sofie

De novo design of a biologically active amyloid bibl graph *Science* v354 no6313 paah4949-1 N 11 2016

Nyugen, Chuong

A refugee's gift P. W. Marty *Christian Century* v134 no6 p3 Mr 15 2017

NYX Cosmetics (Company)

Top Liquid Lipsticks color *Good Housekeeping* v265 no4 p32 O 2017

Nzwili, Fredrick

Aid groups seek funds as Sudan crisis worsens color *Christian Century* v134 no20 p14 S 27 2017

Muslim clerics disappearing near Kenya-Somalia border *Christian Century* v134 no1 p13 Ja 4 2017

People color *Christian Century* v134 no1 p18 Ja 4 2017

People color *Christian Century* v134 no4 p18 F 15 2017

Severe drought brings starving Kenyans to church doorsteps *Christian Century* v134 no5 p16 Mr 1 2017

O

O, My Christ (Poem)

o, my Christ *Christian Century* v134 no8 p1 Ap 12 2017

O Canada (Music)

"O Canada, Beloved Country, Thou!" P. KUITENBROUWER cartoon *Walrus* v14 no6 p23 Jl/Ag 2017

O. J.: Made in America (Film)

THE BEST ØF TELEVISION R. Deitsch color *Sports Illustrated* v125 no18 p33 D 5 2016

The Case of O.J. Simpson L. Moore bw color *New York Review of Books* v63 no16 p75 O 27 2016

Oahu (Hawaii)—Description & travel

THE GATHERING PLACE A. Erace color *Fortune* v176 no4 p64 S 15 2017

HAWAII FOR FAMILY B. VAN GORDER color *Advocate* no1089 p54 F/Mr 2017

OAHU, HAWAII J. WOGAN color *Conde Nast Traveler* v52 no6 p26 Je/Jl 2017

Oak

See also

Acorns

Coast live oak

BARREN OAKS G. Almy color *Field & Stream* v121 no6 pW4 N 2016

SAVING THE CABINET OAK W. FERGUSON *Texas Monthly* v45 no7 p46 Jl 2017

Oak Creek Canyon (Ariz.)

Levitation 29 B. BLANCHARD color *Climbing* no351 p38 F/Mr 2017

Oak Labs (Company)

Mirror, Mirror, You're the Smartest of Them All M. Townsend color *Bloomberg Businessweek* no4512 p42 F 20 2017

Oak Park (Ill.)

SPILT MILK PASTRY C. SCHEDLER color *Chicago* v66 no2 p50 F 2017

Oak wilt

BRIEFLY *New York State Conservationist* v71 no3 p28 D 2016

Oakbridge Timber Framing (Company)

Haven in a Hayfield S. LOGAN color diag *Timber Home Living* v27 no3 p34 Je 2017

Oakes, James

The Supreme Partisan bw *New York Review of Books* v64 no12 p28 Jl 13 2017

Oakes, Kaya

A Crossroads in Oakland color *America* v215 no16 p14 N 21 2016

IN SEARCH OF SPIRITUAL HEALING color *America* v217 no7 p28 O 2 2017

MEET THE "BUDDHISH" NONES cartoon *Tricycle: The Buddhist Review* v26 no3 p50 Spr 2017

NEIGHBOR TO ALL color *America* v216 no7 p18 Ap 3 2017

Oakhurst Dairy (Company)—Trials, litigation, etc.

For Want of a Comma J. Servaas *Saturday Evening Post* v289 no3 p23 My/Je 2017

Oak Knoll School (Menlo Park, Calif.)

THE SCHOOL PROJECT THAT SETS PARENTS FREE L. SKENAZY color *Reason* v48 no10 p10 Mr 2017

Oakland (Calif.)—Description & travel

Oakland J. HERBST *Los Angeles Magazine* v62 no9 p68 S 2017

Oakland Athletics (Baseball team)

5 ATHLETICS color *Sports Illustrated* v126 no9 p93 Mr 27 2017

Oakland Raiders (Football team)

1 Oakland Raiders color *Sports Illustrated* v127 no7 p80 S 4 2017

HOT | NOT T. Keith color *Sports Illustrated* v127 no1 p18 Jl 3 2017

JUST MY TYPE D. Patrick and T. Keith color *Sports Illustrated* v125 no14 p28 O 24-31 2016

Leading Off color *Sports Illustrated* v127 no10 p6 O 2 2017

When Raiders Become Traitors D. ZIRIN color *Progressive* v81 no5 p68 Je/Jl 2017

Oakland Raiders (Football team)—Management

FADE TO BLACK? A. Murphy color *Sports Illustrated* v125 no17 p70 N 21 2016 Double Issue

Oakland Spirits Co.
Drink J. Sens color *Sunset* v237 no5 p62 N 2016
Oaklander, Mandy
6 More Reasons to Get Up and Move color *Time* v190 no4 p40 Jl 24 2017
Burning Questions color *Time* v189 no7/8 p88 F 27 2017
The Club Drug Ketamine May Treat Depression-but the Risks Could Be Big color *Time* v189 no10 p19 Mr 20 2017
Go Ahead, Stop Counting Calories color *Health* v31 no5 p45 Je 2017
Hope from a Strange Source [Cover story] color *Time* v190 no6 p38 Ag 7 2017
Jessamyn Stanley, Internet Yogi color *Time* v188 no20 p22 N 14 2016
The Science of Pet Therapy Is Getting Serious color *Time* v189 no14 p24 Ap 17 2017
Simple Moves Can Lead to a Less Stressed-Out You color *Time* v189 no4 p56 F 6 2017
Surprising News About Salt color *Time* v189 no18 p26 My 15 2017
Why Fitness Trackers Aren't Making Us Healthier color *Time* v188 no18 p19 O 31 2016
Oakley, Annie, 1860-1926
MONTHS PAST AUGUST J. Pollard and S. Pollard *History Today* v67 no8 p22 Ag 2017
Oakley, Barbara
How to Get Excited About Topics That Bore You *Harvard Business Review Digital Articles* p2 Jl 3 2017
Oakley, Charles
Team of Rivals L. J. Wertheim color *Sports Illustrated* v125 no19 p100 D 12 2016
Oakley, Dan
How CEOs Can Keep Their Analytics Programs from Being a Waste of Time *Harvard Business Review Digital Articles* p2 Jl 21 2016
The Reason So Many Analytics Efforts Fall Short *Harvard Business Review Digital Articles* p2 Ag 29 2016
Oakley, Francis
Infallible Saintmakers? color *Commonweal* v144 no10 p28 Je 2 2017
Oakley, J. L.
The Jøssing Affair *Publishers Weekly* v264 no32 p55 Ag 7 2017
Oakley, Luis
Forest conservation: Remember Gran Chaco bibl color *Science* v355 no6324 p465 F 3 2017
Oakley, Miranda
THE DEADLY VALLEY bw color *Climbing* no356 p44 S/O 2017
A League of Her Own C. Kalman color *Climbing* no351 p26 F/Mr 2017
Rap Smart color *Climbing* no356 p40 S/O 2017
What Inspires You? J. ELLISON color *Climbing* no351 p17 F/Mr 2017
Oakley, Tyler, 1989-——Interviews
8 MILLION FOLLOWERS CANT BE WRONG: Why Tyler Oakley has an army of YouTube fans D. ARTAVIA *Advocate* no1093 p25 O/N 2017
Oasis Floral Products (Company)
So CLUTCH color *Seventeen* p54 Ja 1 2017
Oates, Barb
Hap and Leonard: Mucho Mojo *TV Guide* v65 no11 p42 Mr 6 2017
Princess Diana: Her Life, Her Death, the Truth *TV Guide* v65 no21 p37 My 15 2017
The White Princess *TV Guide* v65 no13 p36 Mr 20 2017
Oates, John
Change of Seasons *Publishers Weekly* v264 no2 p51 Ja 9 2017
Oates, Joyce Carol, 1938-
A Book of American Martyrs L. Greenblatt color *Entertainment Weekly* no1451/1452 p109 F 3-10 2017
A Deep American Horror Exposed R. Franklin bw color *New York Review of Books* v64 no5 p47 Mr 23 2017
Dis mem ber and Other Stories *Publishers Weekly* v264 no16 p44 Ap 17 2017
The Insiders color *O, The Oprah Magazine* p82 Ag 2017
JOYCE CAROL OATES color *Entertainment Weekly* no1473 p62 Jl 7 2017

Misconceptions A. MATHIS *New York Times Book Review* p19 F 19 2017
NOT ALL THERE cartoon *New Yorker* v92 no49 p93 F 13 2017
The Poet of Freakiness [Cover story] bw *New York Review of Books* v64 no14 p78 S 28 2017
Postcards from the Edge bw color *New York Review of Books* v64 no7 p52 Ap 20 2017
Shirley Jackson in Love & Death bw cartoon *New York Review of Books* v63 no16 p47 O 27 2016
OATES, NANCY E.
log cabin tranquility color diag *Cabin Living* p32 S 2017
OATES, SARAH
A Perfect Storm: American Media, Russian Propaganda *Current History* v116 no792 p282 O 2017
Oates, Warren
Cockfighter color *New Yorker* v93 no29 p24 S 25 2017
Oaths—History—9th century
Oaths of Strasbourg sworn *History Today* v67 no2 p8 F 2017
Oatman, Maddie
A FISH OUT OF WATER color *Mother Jones* v42 no1 p44 Ja/F 2017
THE GUST BELT color graph *Mother Jones* v42 no3 p70 My/Je 2017
HEARING VOICES color *Mother Jones* v42 no5 p59 S/O 2017
PHARM TO TABLE color *Mother Jones* v42 no6 p72 N/D 2017
Oatmeal
DINNER, UNDRESSED A. Fritch color *Women's Health* v14 no7 p99 S 2017
FOR BRAIN HEALTH chart color *AARP: The Magazine* v59 no3A p39 Ap/My 2016
Homemade Oatmeal Pies P. Lolley color *Southern Living* v52 no10 p130 O 2017
PB & J Oatmeal Cup [Cover story] color *Prevention* v69 no6 p17 Je 2017
Rise and Shine color *American Cowboy* v23 no5 p68 F/Mr 2017
Oats
Oat-standing color *Vegetarian Today* no1 p30 F 2017
Oaxaca (Mexico : State)
OAXACA P. Guzmán bw color *Conde Nast Traveler* v52 no8 p84 S 2017
Obadare, Ebenezer
Humor, Silence, and Civil Society in Nigeria N. van de Walle *Foreign Affairs* v96 no2 p190 Mr/Ap 2017
A Nigerian President's Disappointing Return *Current History* v116 no790 p194 My 2017
Obali, Ahmad
THE DOUBLE LIFE OF AHMAD OBALI B. SMITH bw color map *Chicago* v65 no11 p104 N 2016
Obama, Barack, 1961-
10 THINGS WE'RE TALKING ABOUT T. A. Christian color *Essence* v47 no10 p63 F 2017
The 2015 National Humanities Medalists *Humanities* v37 no4 p1 Fall 2016
21st Century Cures Act *Congressional Digest* v96 no2 p1 F 1 2017
9/11, 15 YEARS LATER: WE REMEMBER B. OBAMA *Vital Speeches of the Day* v82 no11 p344 N 2016
Aaron Robinson A. Robinson color *Car & Driver* v62 no10 p24 Ap 2017
After Obama W. Kristol *Weekly Standard* v22 no20 p8 Ja 30 2017
After The Fall M. KNOX BERAN *National Review* v69 no1 p19 Ja 23 2017
Amazing Grace J. Klein color *Time* v188 no25-26 p160 D 19 2016 Double Issue
America Is Finally Winning Again(TM)! F. FIORENTINI color *Nation* v304 no9 p28 Mr 20 2017
An American Emblem G. Younge il *Nation* v304 no1 p6 Ja 2 2017 The Obama Years
APPENDIX A REPORT TO THE PRESIDENT ON THE ACTIVITIES OF THE COUNCIL OF ECONOMIC ADVISERS DURING 2015 *Economic Indicators* p381 O 2016
AT THIS MOMENT WE ALL FACE A CHOICE B. OBAMA *Vital Speeches of the Day* v82 no11 p322 N 2016
BAD GUYS N. Schmidle cartoon *New Yorker* v92 no37 p32 N 14 2016
Barack Obama, By the Numbers B. LUEDERS *Progressive* p14 D 2016/Ja 2017

Barack Obama, Neo-Hawk S. F. Hayes *Weekly Standard* v22 no17 p6 Ja 2 2017

Barack Obama, the nation's first truly digital president, brought Silicon Valley ideas - and influence—to Washington. Is that a good thing? J. Wortham *New York Times Magazine* p22 O 30 2016

Barack to the Future C. CALDWELL color *Weekly Standard* v22 no18 p27 Ja 16 2017

Bare, Ruined Choirs *Commentary* v141 no10 p1 D 2016

Bare, Ruined Choirs *Commentary* v142 no5 p1 D 2016

BARE, RUINED CHOIRS: HOW BARACK OBAMA WRECKED THE DEMOCRATIC PARTY [Cover story] J. PODHORETZ and N. C. ROTHMAN *Commentary* v142 no5 p12 D 2016

Bathroom Foofaraw *Reason* v48 no7 p6 D 2016

The Better-than-Monroe Doctrine color *Weekly Standard* v22 no24 p2 F 27 2017

BIG BARACK CANDY MOUNTAIN C. R. Kesler *Claremont Review of Books* v17 no1 p5 Wint 2016/2017

BLACK LIKE WHO? C. Baker *Harper's Magazine* v334 no2002 p49 Mr 2017

BO Brummell color *Weekly Standard* v22 no39 p3 Je 19 2017

The Butcher's Bill J. COST cartoon *Weekly Standard* v22 no13 p13 D 5 2016

Celebrity in Chief P. TERZIAN color *Weekly Standard* v22 no18 p13 Ja 16 2017

CENTURY marks cartoon *Christian Century* v134 no4 p8 F 15 2017

The Change We Believed In L. Lalami il *Nation* v304 no1 p8 Ja 2 2017 The Obama Years

CLEANING UP OBAMA'S FOREIGN POLICY MESS A. GREENWALD *Commentary* v142 no4 p15 N 2016

CLEANING UP OBAMA'S HEALTH-CARE MESS T. TROY *Commentary* v142 no4 p25 N 2016

Cleaning Up Obama's Syria Mess *Commentary* v141 no9 p1 N 2016

Cleaning Up Obama's Syria Mess *Commentary* v142 no4 p1 N 2016

Climate Changed M. HERTSGAARD color il *Nation* v304 no1 p70 Ja 2 2017 The Obama Years

Comments img *New York* v49 no21 p10 O 17 2016

THE CONFIDENCE THAT MIGHT MAKES RIGHT, NOT THE OTHER WAY AROUND *Vital Speeches of the Day* v83 no2 p42 F 2017

Courtiers in Denial A. FERGUSON cartoon *Weekly Standard* v22 no18 p10 Ja 16 2017

Cover *Time* v189 no4 pC1 Ja 23 2017

Creating Communities of Change S. van Gelder *Progressive* v81 no4 p26 Ap/My 2017

The Crime of Obama's Cool E. Alterman il *Nation* v304 no1 p10 Ja 2 2017 The Obama Years

Decisions and Revisions That a Moment Will Reverse N. Rothman color *Commentary* v143 no2 p1 F 2017

DEMOCRATS DEFECT FROM OBAMACARE P. SUDERMAN bw cartoon color graph *Reason* v48 no9 p26 F 2017

Did You Ever See a Dreamer Walking? B. SWAIM color *Weekly Standard* v23 no2 p9 S 18 2017

A Disaster He's Proud Of L. Smith *Weekly Standard* v22 no18 p8 Ja 16 2017

The Disintegrating Obama Coalition J. COST color *Weekly Standard* v22 no11 p13 N 21 2016

Doctrine of Decline T. C. DONNELLY *National Review* v69 no1 p17 Ja 23 2017

Do You Hear Me Now? S. F. Hayes color *Weekly Standard* v22 no11 p7 N 21 2016

ECONOMIC REPORT OF THE PRESIDENT *Economic Indicators* p3 S 2016

An Education in Statecraft A. J. BACEVICH bw color *Nation* v304 no1 p28 Ja 2 2017 The Obama Years

The Education of Barack Obama D. GOLDSTEIN bw color diag *Nation* v304 no1 p64 Ja 2 2017 The Obama Years

'Everybody Says How Cool I Am' A. Ferguson color *Commentary* v143 no2 p1 F 2017

'Everybody Says How Cool I Am' A. FERGUSON *Commentary* v143 no2 p9 F 2017

FAREWELL D. Eggers cartoon *New Yorker* v92 no46 p20 Ja 23

2017

Farewell, Obama? R. LONG color *National Review* v69 no2 p23 F 6 2017

Farewell to the Writer-in-Chief A. KIRSCH color *Foreign Policy* no221 p100 N/D 2016

Fear and Self-Loathing color *Weekly Standard* v22 no18 p2 Ja 16 2017

The Final Obama Scandal [Cover story] S. F. HAYES and T. JOSCELYN color *Weekly Standard* v22 no21 p22 F 6 2017

The First Family of Tennis *Tennis* v52 no6 p34 N/D 2016

FIVE THINGS: OBAMA WHISTLES CONSTANTLY C. FELSENTHAL color *Chicago* v66 no9 p38 S 2017

For the Record color *Time* v189 no3 p6 Ja 30 2017

From President Obama to President-Elect Trump: Ever Forward color *Black Enterprise* v47 no4 p6 N/D 2016

FROM THE REARVIEW MIRROR R. L. BOROSAGE color *Nation* v304 no15 p35 My 8 2017

Giving Every Student a Fair Shot J. B. KING JR. *Education Digest* v82 no7 p16 Mr 2017

THE GOLDWATER RULE J. Mayer cartoon *New Yorker* v93 no14 p28 My 22 2017

Goodbye, Obama G. HEALY color *Reason* v48 no9 p18 F 2017

Gunning for the Guns G. NORMAN color *Weekly Standard* v22 no7 p24 O 24 2016

Ha to the Chief T. Keith color *Sports Illustrated* v125 no13 p19 O 17 2016

Hiroshima, His Amour B. McManus *Commentary* v142 no1 p32 Jl/Ag 2016

How Good We Had It K. Pollitt diag il *Nation* v304 no1 p12 Ja 2 2017 The Obama Years

HOW LIES SPREAD M. Hertsgaard and D. Grant color *Nation* v304 no9 p19 Mr 20 2017

How Restraint Leads to War H. R. Nau *Commentary* v140 no2 p17 S 2015

Identity Politician J. V. LAST color *Weekly Standard* v22 no18 p11 Ja 16 2017

If Given the Chance, the Dems Will Make the U.S. into a "Flabby Europe" R. J. BRESLER *USA Today Magazine* v146 no2868 p10 S 2017

The Institutionalist C. HAYES color *Nation* v304 no1 p1 Ja 2 2017 The Obama Years

INTRAMURAL POLITICS A. Beaujon *Washingtonian Magazine* v52 no2 p53 N 2016

Iowa N. Hannah-Jones *New York Times Magazine* p43 N 20 2016

The irreversible momentum of clean energy color *Science* v355 no6321 p126 Ja 13 2017

IT HAPPENED HERE D. REMNICK cartoon color *New Yorker* v92 no39 p54 N 28 2016

The Judgment K. NODJIMBADEM *Smithsonian* v47 no9 p12 Ja/F 2017

THE LAST OF THE FOUNDING GENERATION IS GONE *Vital Speeches of the Day* v82 no12 p372 D 2016

THE LAST WORD bw *Rolling Stone* no1280 p58 F 9 2017

Learn from His Mistakes F. Barnes color *Weekly Standard* v22 no15 p8 D 19 2016

Learning from Obamacare J. Ennis *Commentary* v143 no1 p9 Ja 2017

Leaving a Clean Desk J. RAUCH color *Atlantic* v318 no5 p15 D 2016

Legislative Background on the 21st Century Cures Act *Congressional Digest* v96 no2 p9 F 1 2017

THE LESSONS OF HENRY KISSINGER J. Goldberg bw color *Atlantic* v318 no5 p50 D 2016

Let's Give the Stimulus Its Due: It saved the economy, but that isn't always acknowledged P. A. Harkness *Governing* v30 no10 p16 Jl 2017

LETTER OF TRANSMITTAL J. Furman, S. E. Black et al *Economic Indicators* p9 O 2016

Liberalism's Half-Life B. COVERT and M. KONCZAL color graph *Nation* v304 no1 p14 Ja 2 2017 The Obama Years

The Long Goodbye color *Weekly Standard* v22 no20 p2 Ja 30 2017

Mad, Democrats? Blame the Iran Deal *Commentary* p1 Ja 2017

Mad, Democrats? Blame the Iran Deal *Commentary* v143 no1 p1 Ja 2017

Make Politics Boring Again D. FOSTER *National Review* v69

no5 p48 Mr 20 2017

The Maligning Of Israel D. PRYCE-JONES *National Review* v69 no1 p20 Ja 23 2017

Mandate for Confusion R. PONNURU *National Review* v69 no5 p22 Mr 20 2017

A Messy World A. SATTLER and M. SATTLER *Commentary* v143 no1 p6 Ja 2017

Monumental Achievements... and Controversy L. Davis and P. Jacoby-Garrett *Parks & Recreation* v52 no4 p32 Ap 2017

My President Was Black [Cover story] Coates bw color *Atlantic* v319 no1 p46 Ja/F 2017

My President Was Black G. Haley, J. Knoll et al *Atlantic* v319 no2 p8 Mr 2017

National GMO Labeling Bill Signed Into Law S. Stonebrook *Mother Earth News* no279 p6 D/Ja 2017

The National Interest: Jonathan Chait img *New York* p13 Ja 9 2017

THE NEGLECT OF THE IMMIGRANT CHILD: MAKING THE CASE FOR A CHILD-CENTERED APPROACH TO UNITED STATES IMMIGRATION POLICY I. PADILLA-RODRÍGUEZ bw color *Phi Kappa Phi Forum* v96 no4 p12 Wint 2016

The Night Data Died *Commentary* v141 no10 p1 D 2016

The Night Data Died *Commentary* v142 no5 p1 D 2016

NO CONGRESS? NO PROBLEM M. J. STERN *Advocate* no1088 p12 D 2016/Ja 2017

A Non-transformational President R. PONNURU il *National Review* v69 no1 p16 Ja 23 2017

Notes on a Disaster J. PODHORETZ *Commentary* v140 no2 p1 S 2015

Obamacare Doings and Undoings J. COST color *Weekly Standard* v22 no28 p12 Mr 27 2017

OBAMA FINALLY FINDS HIS CLEMENCY PEN J. SULLUM graph *Reason* v48 no11 p44 Ap 2017

Obama Goes From the White House To Wall Street M. Abelson *Bloomberg Businessweek* no4539 p42 S 25 2017

OBAMA, RACE, AND AMERICA'S FUTURE J. Goldberg color *Atlantic* v319 no1 p8 Ja/F 2017

OBAMA'S AMERICA D. AXELROD, A. SULLIVAN et al img *New York* v49 no20 p12 O 3 2016

Obama's Belated Drug War Retreat J. SULLUM *Reason* v48 no9 p6 F 2017

The Obamas' BEST POP CULTURE MOMENTS color *Entertainment Weekly* no1450 p20 Ja 27 2017

OBAMA'S BETRAYAL OF BELIEVERS S. SLADE bw cartoon *Reason* v48 no9 p12 F 2017

Obama's Book of Balderdash K. SMITH color *National Review* v69 no11 p15 Je 12 2017

Obama's broken legacy A. ABEL color *Maclean's* no1 p36 F 17 2017

OBAMA'S CHICAGO BREAKUP E. McCLELLAND cartoon color *Chicago* v66 no1 p23 Ja 2017

The OBAMAS color *Vanity Fair* v59 no1 p130 Holiday 2017

OBAMA'S DC *Washingtonian Magazine* v52 no3 p70 D 2016

Obama's Gift to Iran R. D. Wilkins *Commentary* v141 no10 p1 D 2016

Obama's Gift to Iran R. D. Wilkins *Commentary* v142 no5 p1 D 2016

Obama's Legacy W. Kristol color *Weekly Standard* v22 no32 p7 My 1 2017

OBAMA'S LOST ARMY [Cover story] M. L. SIFRY color *New Republic* v248 no3 p18 Mr 2017

Obama's Monuments T. STRAKA *Commentary* v143 no2 p6 F 2017

Obama's Post-Presidency E. J. Dionne Jr. color *Commonweal* v144 no2 p7 Ja 27 2017

Obama's Top 50 Accomplishments, Revisited P. Glastris and N. LeTourneau *Washington Monthly* p12 Ja/F 2017

Obama's Young Garden [Cover story] H. OLSEN il *National Review* v69 no1 p24 Ja 23 2017

OBAMA THE CARE OPERATION R. DRAPER *New York Times Magazine* p32 F 19 2017

Obama Wasn't No FDR S. SHEPPARD *USA Today Magazine* v145 no2862 p22 Mr 2017

THE OBAMA YEARS [Cover story] E. PLOTT *Washingtonian Magazine* v52 no3 p66 D 2016

OFFICE OF THE PRESIDENT *Weekly Standard* v23 no2 p48 S

18 2017

OUR BRAND IS FINE B. Freed *Washingtonian Magazine* v52 no8 p17 My 2017

Our Failed Cybersecurity Policy L. THOMPSON color *National Review* v69 no1 p30 Ja 23 2017

Pants on Fire *Weekly Standard* v22 no10 p3 N 14 2016

PARODY color *Weekly Standard* v22 no20 p40 Ja 30 2017

PARTING WORDS G. Packer cartoon *New Yorker* v92 no46 p17 Ja 23 2017

THE PEACE PRIZE WINNER WHO WAGED WAR E. KRAYEWSKI cartoon *Reason* v48 no9 p14 F 2017

Power Games N. Abebe *New York Times Magazine* p11 Je 25 2017

President Obama's science legacy is big on climate change and clean energy D. Kramer *Physics Today* v69 no12 p26 D 2016

A Proof, a Test, an Instruction M. ROBINSON color *Nation* v304 no1 p16 Ja 2 2017 The Obama Years

Race Against Time K. WRIGHT color *Nation* v304 no1 p46 Ja 2 2017 The Obama Years

Readers Respond color *Publishers Weekly* v264 no8 p3 F 20 2017

Reflections on a Great and Disappointing President S. MUWAK-KIL *In These Times* v41 no2 p44 F 2017

Restraint and Its Discontents R. FONTAINE *National Review* v69 no1 p26 Ja 23 2017

REVERSAL OF JUSTICE J. Cobb cartoon *New Yorker* v93 no10 p35 Ap 24 2017

A RICHER STORY OF WHO WE ARE B. OBAMA *Vital Speeches of the Day* v82 no11 p345 N 2016

The Road Not Taken P. J. WILLIAMS color *Nation* v304 no1 p56 Ja 2 2017 The Obama Years

A Rush to Regulate Before Inauguration J. A. Dlouhy color diag *Bloomberg Businessweek* no4501 p24 N 28 2016

Sand in the Gears F. Barnes color *Weekly Standard* v22 no29 p10 Ap 3 2017

Scandals Aplenty M. HEMINGWAY color *Weekly Standard* v22 no18 p14 Ja 16 2017

Secret History C. Homans *New York Times Magazine* p17 O 2 2016

The Senate Did Its Job T. Eastland *Weekly Standard* v22 no11 p8 N 21 2016

Shrinking the Gap Is Key for Democracy color *Time* v188 no16/17 p36 O 24 2016

The Silicon President S. VAIDHYANATHAN color *Nation* v304 no1 p74 Ja 2 2017 The Obama Years

Since Obama Took Office, Debt Has Nearly Doubled V. DE RUGY graph *Reason* v48 no9 p15 F 2017

Speaking Up for Standing Down M. O. Steinfels color *Commonweal* v143 no19 p6 D 2 2016

The Strange Career of American Exceptionalism G. GRANDIN color *Nation* v304 no1 p22 Ja 2 2017 The Obama Years

Teaching the History of Radicalism in the Age of Obama E. FONER color *Nation* v304 no1 p76 Ja 2 2017 The Obama Years

Tears of the Times color *Weekly Standard* v22 no34 p2 My 15 2017

'The Most Transparent Administration in History' C. J. CIARAMELLA color *Reason* v48 no9 p10 F 2017

THEY SAID WHAT? color *Maclean's* v129 no48/49 p74 D 5 2016

THIS CONFLICT IS NOT ABOUT HOUSES *Vital Speeches of the Day* v83 no2 p40 F 2017

THIS MODERN WORLD T. TOMORROW *In These Times* v41 no2 p6 F 2017

Ticked Off B. PARKER color *Weekly Standard* v22 no43 p26 Jl 24 2017

TO GET THIS NEXT GENERATION TO MOVE TOWARD LEADERSHIP *Vital Speeches of the Day* v83 no6 p178 Je 2017

'Tough Love'—The First and Last Obama Lie J. PODHORETZ *Commentary* v143 no2 p1 F 2017

The Tragedy of Obama's Foreign Policy M. J. BOYLE *Current History* v116 no786 p10 Ja 2017

Unleashing Energy Winners K. TUBB il *American Conservative* v16 no1 p20 Ja/F 2017

Unprecedented? J. Cost color *Weekly Standard* v22 no37 p19 Je 5 2017

U.S. OUT OF SPACE K. MANGU-WARD color *Reason* v48 no9 p4 F 2017

A Victory for Free Speech il *Consumer Reports* v82 no3 p8 Mr

2017

The victory lap A. ABEL color *Maclean's* v129 no43 p37 O 31 2016

VIEWFINDER V. M. Gezari color *Columbia Journalism Review* v56 no2 p16 Fall 2017

Was Barack Obama a Transformational President? R. L. BOROSAGE color *Nation* v304 no1 p40 Ja 2 2017 The Obama Years

The Week color il *National Review* v69 no1 p4 Ja 23 2017

Whitewash Interrupted color *Weekly Standard* v23 no2 p2 S 18 2017

Who Has Paid Sick Leave, Who Doesn't, and What's Changing G. Gavett *Harvard Business Review Digital Articles* p2 Ja 21 2015

Whose Neighborhood Is It Anyway? color *Weekly Standard* v22 no20 p3 Ja 30 2017

Winning the 9/11 Wars [Cover story] S. F. Hayes color *Weekly Standard* v22 no37 p6 Je 5 2017

YES, WE CAN. YES, WE DID. YES, WE CAN B. OBAMA *Vital Speeches of the Day* v83 no3 p93 Mr 2017

Yes We Did M. BRUNE *Sierra* v101 no6 p4 N/D 2016

Obama, Barack, 1961——Awards

And the Oscar Goes to... color *Weekly Standard* v22 no35 p2 My 22 2017

Obama, Barack, 1961——Interviews

BARACK OBAMA, NEURAL NETS, SELF-DRIVING CARS, AND THE FUTURE OF THE WORLD S. DADICH color *Wired* v24 no11 p124 N 2016

A Conversation With President Obama [Cover story] J. S. WENNER color *Rolling Stone* no1276 p34 D 15 2016

OFFICE POLITICS D. K. GOODWIN bw color *Vanity Fair* v58 no11 p156 N 2016

Obama, Barack, 1961——Political & social views

After Life M. Rhodan color diag *Time* v188 no19 p38 N 7 2016

Obama Says NASA Will Put a Human on Mars 'by the 2030s.' Can It? J. Kluger color *Time* v188 no16/17 p9 O 24 2017

OBAMA'S FEEBLE APOLOGIA FOR THE ECONOMY S. FORBES *Forbes* v198 no6 p23 N 8 2016

Obama's Terror 'Narrative' M. Hemingway *Weekly Standard* v22 no4 p7 O 3 2016

The Original Deplorables G. NORMAN *Weekly Standard* v22 no4 p25 O 3 2016

The Walking Dead P. R. Gregory *Hoover Digest: Research & Opinion on Public Policy* no4 p66 Fall 2016

Who We Are and Who He Is S. F. Hayes color *Weekly Standard* v22 no16 p7 D 26 2016

Obama, Barack, 1961——Psychology

The President Who Loved A. Patchett color *Time* v189 no3 p47 Ja 30 2017

Obama, Barack, 1961——Travel

PARODY color *Weekly Standard* v22 no23 p40 F 20 2017

Obama, Malia, 1998-

Dear Sasha and Malia ... J. B. Hager and B. Bush color *Time* v189 no4 p43 Ja 23 2017

Obama, Malik

CELEBRITIES ... img *New York* v50 no9 p40 My 1 2017

Obama, Michelle, 1964-

Amazing Grace J. Klein color *Time* v188 no25-26 p160 D 19 2016 Double Issue

American Woman J. GAMBLE bw *Nation* v304 no1 p60 Ja 2 2017 The Obama Years

First Among Equals A. Wintour bw color *Vogue* v206 no12 p92 D 2016

The First Family of Tennis *Tennis* v52 no6 p34 N/D 2016

FORCES TO RECKON WITH M. HOLGATE and M. GUIDUCCI bw color *Vogue* v207 no3 p357 Mr 2017

The Magic of Michelle color *Glamour* v115 no1 p100 Ja 2017

The Meaning of Michelle E. Egan, B. Little et al bw color *Glamour* v114 no12 p198 D 2016

MRS. OBAMA A. Davidson cartoon *New Yorker* v92 no43 p17 Ja 2 2017

The Obamas' BEST POP CULTURE MOMENTS color *Entertainment Weekly* no1450 p20 Ja 27 2017

OBAMA'S DC *Washingtonian Magazine* v52 no3 p70 D 2016

THE OBAMA YEARS [Cover story] E. PLOTT *Washingtonian Magazine* v52 no3 p66 D 2016

Sound Bites color *Entertainment Weekly* no1473 p8 Jl 7 2017

THE STYLIST & THE FIRST LADY L. Christensen color *Harp-*

er's Bazaar no3648 p268 N 2016

Thank You, FLOTUS! color *Glamour* v115 no1 p14 Ja 2017

THE TRUTH IS, IT HURTS *Vital Speeches of the Day* v82 no12 p358 D 2016

UNFORGETTABLE [Cover story] J. Van Meter color *Vogue* v206 no12 p219 D 2016

The victory lap A. ABEL color *Maclean's* v129 no43 p37 O 31 2016

Watching Michelle A. KENNEDY color *Nation* v304 no1 p62 Ja 2 2017 The Obama Years

Obama, Sasha, 2001-

Dear Sasha and Malia ... J. B. Hager and B. Bush color *Time* v189 no4 p43 Ja 23 2017

O'Banion, Matthew

Mitigating coastal landslide damage color *Science* v357 no6355 p981 S 8 2017

Obara, Christopher J.

Increased spatiotemporal resolution reveals highly dynamic dense tubular matrices in the peripheral ER bibl bw color graph *Science* v354 no6311 paaf3928-1 O 28 2016

Obedience

THE CASE FOR Robot Disobedience [Cover story] G. Briggs and M. Scheutz color *Scientific American* v316 no1 p44 Ja 2017

O'Beirne, Kate, 1949-2017

Kate Walsh O'Beirne, R.I.P R. Ponnuru *National Review* v69 no9 p12 My 15 2017

Wit and Witness J. V. Last color *Weekly Standard* v22 no33 p14 My 8 2017

Obejas, Achy

The Tower of Antilles *Publishers Weekly* v264 no18 p33 My 1 2017

Obel, Agnes

Agnes Obel: Citizen of Glass J. Cadagin *Opera News* v81 no6 p54 D 2016

Obelisks

FOGGY BOTTOM A. WHITING *Washingtonian Magazine* v52 no6 p24 Mr 2017

New Orleans Confronts Its Confederate History J. Sanburn color *Time* v189 no19 p12 My 22 2017

OBENOUR, GRAYDEN

Easy Rider color *Road & Track* v68 no8 p108 My 2017

OBER, JIM

1987 MINI-METAL CHAMPIONSHIP bw *Dirt Sports + Off-Road* v51 no11 p74 N 2017

A CHUNK OF BAJA color *Dirt Sports + Off-Road* v51 no8 p74 Ag 2017

THE CIRCUS COMES TO TOWN color *Dirt Sports + Off-Road* v51 no7 p74 Jl 2017

DUNE BUGGIES RACING ACROSS AMERICA bw *Dirt Sports + Off-Road* v51 no6 p74 Je 2017

EL CARMELO GRANDE color *Dirt Sports + Off-Road* v51 no12 p74 D 2017

FERRO'S FAVORITE RACE bw *Dirt Sports + Off-Road* v51 no9 p74 S 2017

GOING IN STYLE bw *Dirt Sports + Off-Road* v51 no5 p74 My 2017

HOUR GLASS color *Dirt Sports + Off-Road* v51 no2 p74 F 2017

LARRY RAGLAND FIVE BAJA WINS [Cover story] color *Dirt Sports + Off-Road* v51 no1 p74 Ja 2017

MICKEY & TRUDY THOMPSON color *Dirt Sports + Off-Road* v51 no10 p74 O 2017

NOVICE RACERS bw *Dirt Sports + Off-Road* v51 no3 p74 Mr 2017

WHEN DODGE WON THE MTEG GRAND NATIONAL SPORT TRUCK CHAMPIONSHIP bw *Dirt Sports + Off-Road* v51 no4 p74 Ap 2017

Ober Alp SpA

Footwear A. H. BIBLE color diag graph il *Backpacker* v45 no3 p43 Ap 2017

Oberdorfer, Gustav

Principles for designing proteins with cavities formed by curved β sheets bibl color graph *Science* v355 no6321 p1 Ja 13 2017

Obergefell v. Hodges (Supreme Court case)

MARRIAGE EQUALITY WAS WON BY WIDOWERS: THE LOVE STORIES BEHIND THE LANDMARK COURT CASES BOTH ENDED TRAGICALLY J. ANDERSON-MIN-

SHALL bw color *Advocate* no1091 p80 Je/Jl 2017

Oberlin College—Curricula

Jazz Essential at Oberlin P. Lutz color *Downbeat* v84 no1 p110 Ja 2017

Obermaier, Carolin D.

Dopamine oxidation mediates mitochondrial and lysosomal dysfunction in Parkinson's disease graph *Science* v357 no6357 p1255 S 22 2017

Obermeyer, Ziad

Making Predictive Analytics a Routine Part of Patient Care *Harvard Business Review Digital Articles* p2 Ap 21 2016

Oberst, Conor, 1980-

Conor Oberst Goes Home L. Goodman img *New York* v49 no19 p88 S 19 2016

OBERWEIS, JIM

EARNINGS SURPRISES IN THE HEARTLAND *Forbes* v198 no6 p70 N 8 2016

Wall Street's Robocop color *Forbes* v199 no6 p62 Je 13 2017

Obesity

See also

Obesity in children

AT HOME IN EVERY POSE [Cover story] color *Yoga Journal* no292 p72 Je 2017

The Delectable Myths of Healthy and Healthier Obesity K. W. KRAUSE *Skeptical Inquirer* v41 no2 p33 Mr/Ap 2017

Exposing the exposures responsible for type 2 diabetes and obesity P. W. Franks and M. I. McCarthy bibl diag *Science* v354 no6308 p69 O 7 2016

Gut Reaction: Bacteria to Autism in Four (Not-So-) Easy Steps M. STONE *BioScience* v66 no11 p1004 N 1 2016

How to Lose Those 10 Dang Pounds B. GREGORY color *Men's Health* v32 no8 p90 O 2017

MAN OF STYLE Kofi Siriboe F. Penn color *InStyle* v23 no12 p92 N 2016

The New War on Obesity C. Roberts and T. Germain chart color diag *Consumer Reports* v82 no10 p48 O 2017

On Obesity S. Vyse *Skeptical Inquirer* v40 no6 p64 N/D 2016

REST UP, CROSSFITTERS color *Muscle & Performance* v9 no1 p16 Ja 2017

STATES OF EMERGENCY cartoon chart color *Muscle & Performance* v9 no1 p15 Ja 2017

To Lose Weight, Put Your Home on a Diet N. Wertheimer and C. Mathis color *AARP: The Magazine* v60 no4A p14 Je/Jl 2017

Obesity in animals

POOCHED OUT R. Khamsi color *New York Times Magazine* p44 My 21 2017

Obesity in children

BATTLING CHILDHOOD OBESITY D. WERNER *USA Today Magazine* v146 no2866 p62 Jl 2017

CITYWIDE EPIDEMIC J. WUEBBEN color *Muscle & Performance* v9 no10 p19 O 2017

Obesity in children—Research

Weight Gain Occurs When School Is Out *USA Today Magazine* v145 no2861 p5 F 2017

Obesity in children—Risk factors

The Sleep-Weight Connection W. C. WINTER color *Better Nutrition* v79 no10 p56 O 2017

Obesity risk factors

Are Chemicals Contributing to the Obesity Epidemic? Although there is growing concern that everyday chemicals may contribute to weight woes, more research is needed *Tufts University Health & Nutrition Letter* v35 no7 p7 S 2017

Obesity surgery

Dramatic Changes *Virginia Living* v15 no1 p101 D 2016

KEEPING IT OFF R. GALCHEN cartoon *New Yorker* v92 no30 p32 S 26 2016

Mental Illness Does not Impede Weight Loss *USA Today Magazine* v146 no2869 p10 O 2017

Obesity—Complications

Weighing in *Mayo Clinic Health Letter* v35 no3 p4 Mr 2017

Obi, Chris

STAR TREK: DISCOVERY J. Hibberd color *Entertainment Weekly* p24 Jl 24 2017

Obioma, Chigozie

FROM NIGERIA TO AMERICA AND BACK A. Frykholm *Christian Century* v133 no24 p33 N 23 2016

Obit (Film)

The Art of Obit: A Life In 800 Words S. Zacharek color *Time* v189 no18 p55 My 15 2017

BIG NAMES EVERYWHERE S. KLAWANS *Nation* v304 no16 p44 My 22 2017

The Fundamentals R. R. Cooper color *Commonweal* v144 no12 p28 Jl 7 2017

Obituary writing

Saying Goodbye B. REED color *Downbeat* v84 no3 p8 Mr 2017

STRATEGIC HUMOR *Harvard Business Review* v94 no11 p32 N 2016

Writing on Deadline D. Skinner color *Weekly Standard* v22 no24 p5 F 27 2017

Object permanence (Psychology)

OBJECT PERMANENCE K. RUSSELL cartoon *New Yorker* v93 no26 p54 S 4 2017

Object tracking (Computer vision)

Cutting through the Fog P. Patel *Scientific American* v317 no3 p216 S 2017

Objective Development Software GmbH

Little Snitch 4 review: Mac app excels at monitoring and controlling network activity G. FLEISHMAN color *Macworld - Digital Edition* v34 no11 p117 N 2017

Objectivity

Leslie Jamison L. Jamison *New York Times Book Review* p31 Ja 8 2017

Pankaj Mishra P. Mishra *New York Times Book Review* p31 Ja 8 2017

OBLAD, BRUCE

READERS' THOUGHTS ON PAST ISSUES color *Motor Trend* v69 no2 p26 F 2017

Obreht, Téa

Balkan Ghosts: Even in exile, a Kosovan mother and son hold on to their dreams color *New York Times Book Review* p9 Ap 23 2017

DAVID ATTENBOROUGH cartoon *New Yorker* v92 no42 p104 D 19 2016

Obremski, John

A districtwide commitment to arts integration color il *Phi Delta Kappan* v98 no7 p29 Ap 2017

O'Brien, Alison

ALISON O'BRIEN M. HAMILTON color *Runner's World* v52 no2 p21 Mr 2017

O'Brien, Christopher

Emergence and spread of a human-transmissible multidrug-resistant nontuberculous mycobacterium bibl diag graph *Science* v354 no6313 p751 N 11 2016

O'Brien, Clay

MAXIMIZING THE BENEFITS of Minimal Practice color *Team Roping Journal* p56 S 2017

O'Brien, Conan, 1963-

Sound Bites color *Entertainment Weekly* no1435 p6 O 14 2016

Titans color *Time* v189 no16/17 p94 My 1-8 2017

O'Brien, Conan, 1963—Interviews

LOOKWELL D. Snierson color *Entertainment Weekly* no1460/1461 p70 Ap 7-17 2017

O'Brien, Conor

...from the farthest lands of the English *History Today* v66 no11 p44 N 2016

O'Brien, Cynthia-Marie Marmo

Community practice: Founding a community for lay members to live lives of peace and justice took years of commitment color *U.S. Catholic* v82 no9 p45 S 2017

O'Brien, Dan

Bandaged Wounds J. Matthew Wilson color *Weekly Standard* v22 no24 p37 F 27 2017

O'Brien, David

KEEPING THE FLAME LIT bw *America* v215 no10 p27 O 10 2016

Mission before Identity color *Commonweal* v144 no6 p8 Mr 24 2017

O'Brien, Deirdre

Emergence and spread of a human-transmissible multidrug-resistant nontuberculous mycobacterium bibl diag graph *Science* v354 no6313 p751 N 11 2016

O'Brien, Dennis

On Betrayal color *Christian Century* v134 no10 p49 My 10 2017

Prophecy without Contempt: Religious Discourse in the Public Square color *Christian Century* v133 no21 p45 O 12 2016

O'Brien, Ed

Stop Putting Off Fun for After You Finish All Your Work *Harvard Business Review Digital Articles* p2 Jl 7 2017

O'Brien, Edna, 1930-

TO SOFTEN A HEART OF STONE D. VELLUCCI *America* v215 no11 p33 O 17 2016

O'brien, Elizabeth

THE 2017 WASHINGTON WISH LIST color diag *Money* v46 no1 p96 Ja/F 2017

33 WAYS TO CUT YOUR TAXES [Cover story] color diag *Money* v46 no2 p52 Mr 2017

36 APPS THAT WILL SAVE YOU MONEY color *Money* v46 no4 p46 My 2017

The [4Fe4S] cluster of human DNA primase functions as a redox switch using DNA charge transport color *Science* v355 no6327 p813 F 24 2017

4 Ways to Cut Your Medical Bills color *Money* v46 no6 p22 Jl 2017

ASK THE EXPERT chart *Money* v46 no1 p29 Ja/F 2017

ASK THE EXPERT chart *Money* v46 no4 p20 My 2017

ASK THE EXPERT diag *Money* v45 no10 p31 N 2016

The End of 4%? Smarter Ways to Generate Income for Life chart color *Money* v46 no9 p38 O 2017

Four Tips for Going Solo chart color *Money* v46 no2 p41 Mr 2017

THE High Cost OF Coping color diag *Money* v45 no11 p72 D 2016

Low-Fee 401(k) Choices Are Hiding in Plain Sight color diag *Money* v46 no6 p25 Jl 2017

Moving in Retirement? How to Time It Right color diag *Money* v46 no5 p27 Je 2017

RETIRE EARLY? YES YOU CAN [Cover story] color diag *Money* v46 no3 p34 Ap 2017

The Ultimate Guide to Retirement: Couples Edition [Cover story] color diag *Money* v45 no10 p48 N 2016

You're Retiring Should Your Savings Move On Too? color diag *Money* v46 no4 p23 My 2017

O'Brien, Emily

Built On a Dream color diag *Log Home Living* v34 no6 p64 Ag 2017

Into the Woods color diag *Log Home Living* p84 2018 Annual Buyers Guide

O'Brien, Emma

China's Troubles Down on the Farm color *Bloomberg Businessweek* no4525 p16 Je 5 2017

O'brien, Geoffrey

Five Magnificent Years [Cover story] bw *New York Review of Books* v64 no14 p59 S 28 2017

Let's Face the Music and Dance color *New York Review of Books* v64 no6 p16 Ap 6 2017

Spielberg: The Inner Lives of a Genius color *New York Review of Books* v64 no3 p17 F 23 2017

O'Brien, George Dennis

STUDENTS ON THE WAY *America* v215 no18 p36 D 5 2016

Volunteers or Conscripts? color *Commonweal* v144 no1 p36 Ja 6 2017

O'Brien, Glenn

Glen O'BRIEN *Interview* v47 no5 p120 Je/Jl 2017

O'Brien, Holly

"I Knew She Was Out There" [Cover story] M. PEYSER *Reader's Digest* v188 no1126 p73 D 2016/Ja 2017

O'Brien, Jack

André BISHOP color *Vanity Fair* v58 no12 p130 D 2016

IT'S A WONKA WORLD D. KAMP color *Vanity Fair* p187 Hollywood 2017 Supplement

O'BRIEN, JEN

HOME, sweet HOME color *Better Homes & Gardens* v95 no10 p70 O 2017

O'Brien, Richard

The SAINT V. THE 'THUG' color *Sports Illustrated* v125 no13 p48 O 17 2016

WHAT IF? ... MUHAMMAD ALI HAD NEVER MET MALCOLM X? color *Sports Illustrated* v126 no11 p61 Ap 17-24 2017

O'Brien, Robyn

ROBYN O'BRIEN D. M. Zepeda color *Runner's World* v52 no3 p96 Ap 2017

O'BRIEN, SEAN

Dump the Slump: If midseason finds you stuck in a rut instead of excelling, we have nine tips to break you out color *Boating World* v38 no7 p16 Jl 2017

Get Board *Boating World* v38 no1 p12 Ja 2017

Steer Clear of Self-Sabotage *Boating World* v38 no4 p14 Ap 2017

O'Brien, Soledad

50 Reasons to Love Being 50+ color *AARP: The Magazine* v59 no5A p65 Ag/S 2016

WOMEN'S WORK S. T. BROWN color *Ebony* v72 no5 p84 Mr 2017

O'Brien, Tim

The People's Princess img *New York* v50 no10 p46 My 15 2017

O'Brien, Tim, 1946-

War and Storytelling *South Dakota Magazine* p9 S/O 2017 Supplement

O'Brien, Timothy

Positive biodiversity-productivity relationship predominant in global forests bibl chart graph map *Science* v354 no6309 paaf8957-1 O 14 2016

O'Brien, Timothy W.

THE DISCOMFORTS OF HOME color *America* v217 no3 p26 Ag 7 2017

O'Brien Steinfels, Margaret

What Doomed Clinton? color *Commonweal* v144 no15 p39 S 22 2017

O'Brien Wood, Bridget

Simply Unpalatable T. MECIA color diag *Weekly Standard* v22 no31 p20 Ap 17 2017

OBRYK, MACIEJ K.

The Impact of a Large-Scale Climate Event on Antarctic Ecosystem Processes chart graph *BioScience* v66 no10 p848 O 1 2016

Responses of Antarctic Marine and Freshwater Ecosystems to Changing Ice Conditions color graph *BioScience* v66 no10 p864 O 1 2016

Obscene words

Slanted Justice K. D. WILLIAMSON color *National Review* v68 no19 p19 O 24 2016

Obscenity (Law) in literature

X-RATED TWAIN bw *Atlantic* v319 no3 p19 Ap 2017

Obscenity (Law)—History

PEOPLE OF THE BOOK L. MENAND cartoon color *New Yorker* v92 no41 p78 D 12 2016

Observation (Educational method)

THE PD NEXT DOOR: The impact of observation in our own schools S. Valter *Literacy Today (2411-7862)* v35 no2 p18 S/O 2017

Observation (Scientific method)

Using climate models to estimate the quality of global observational data sets F. Massonnet, O. Bellprat et al bibl graph *Science* v354 no6311 p452 O 28 2016

Observation decks

Lofty Heights color *Los Angeles Magazine* v62 no7 p68 Jl 2017

Observational learning

Is Your Company Encouraging Employees to Share What They Know? C. G. Myers *Harvard Business Review Digital Articles* p2 N 6 2015

Observations of Jupiter

Juno reveals more complex Jupiter A. YEAGER color *Science News* v191 no12 p14 Je 24 2017

Jupiter's magnetosphere and aurorae observed by the Juno spacecraft during its first polar orbits J. E. P. Connerney, A. Adriani et al diag graph *Science* v356 no6340 p826 My 26 2017

A recurring rendezvous E. DeMarco color *Science News* v191 no12 p32 Je 24 2017

Observations of Mars

DRONES ON MARS M. Golombek, A. Kehoe et al color *Astronomy* v45 no7 p34 Jl 2017

Planetary Almanac *Sky & Telescope* v134 no3 p44 S 2017

Observations of the Moon

The 1794 Volcano on the Moon A. Livingston *Sky & Telescope* v134 no5 p30 N 2017

Moon motion B. Berman color *Astronomy* v45 no7 p10 Jl 2017

Shoot for the moon. Again S. Howe Verhovek color diag *National Geographic* v232 no2 p32 Ag 2017

Observations of Venus
NOVEMBER 2017 OBSERVING color *Sky & Telescope* v134 no5 p41 N 2017
November 2017: Venus meets Jupiter M. RATCLIFFE and A. LING color *Astronomy* v45 no11 p36 N 2017

Observatories
See also
Astronomical observatories
Flashes of gravitational waves? *Science* v357 no6354 p851 S 1 2017
McDonald OBSERVATORY *Texas Monthly* v45 no4 p108 Ap 2017
Star struck N. Walker color *Canadian Geographic* v137 no4 p28 Jl/Ag 2017

Obsessive-compulsive disorder
Always LEARNING J. Francisco color *Good Housekeeping* v265 no1 p10 Jl 2017
"HERE'S WHAT IT REALLY FEELS LIKE to have OCD ...welcome to my brain" C. SCHEELER color *Good Housekeeping* v265 no1 p96 Jl 2017
JUNGLE LOVE: A brief history of Cincinnati's love affair with animals, from fat-rendered soap to Fiona the hippo J. GILBERT *Cincinnati Magazine* v50 no10 p23 Jl 2017

Obsidian Entertainment Inc.
Tyranny: Obsidian's RPG ponders the nature of evil H. DINGMAN color *PCWorld* v35 no1 p137 Ja 2017

Obsolescence
Are Sales Incentives Becoming Obsolete? A. A. Zoltners, P. K. Sinha et al *Harvard Business Review Digital Articles* p2 Ag 3 2017
What Happened to User Manuals? D. Pogue color *Scientific American* v316 no4 p30 Ap 2017

Obstacle racing
Conquer Any Obstacle J. COVERT cartoon color *Men's Health* v32 no4 p23 My 2017

Obstinacy
Signs That You're Being Too Stubborn M. M. Wilkins *Harvard Business Review Digital Articles* p2 My 21 2015

Obstructive lung disease treatment
Are you at risk for COPD? *Harvard Health Letter* v42 no8 p7 Je 2017

Obstructive lung diseases
CONSULTANTS L. L. Couetil color *Equus* no475 p81 Ap 2017
COPD CANADA'S EPIDEMIC D. F. McCourt *Maclean's* v129 no47 p46 N 28 2016
Don't Let COPD Take Your Breath Away K. Donohue bw color *Maclean's* v129 no47 p44 N 28 2016

Obstructive lung diseases—Prognosis
Are you at risk for COPD? *Harvard Health Letter* v42 no8 p7 Je 2017

Obura, David
Refilling the coral reef glass color *Science* v357 no6357 p1215 S 22 2017

O'Byrne, Eamon—Interviews
MEET EAMON O'BYRNE *Sea Magazine* v108 no8 pCA-4 Ag 2016

O'Byrne, W. Ian
SCAFFOLDING DIGITAL CREATION color *Literacy Today (2411-7862)* v34 no3 p14 N/D 2016

Ocado Ltd.
The Robotic Grocery Store of the Future Is Here J. Condliffe color *MIT Technology Review* v120 no2 p22 Mr/Ap 2017

O'CAIN, PATRICK
r.s.v.p color *Bon Appetit* no8 p14 Ag 2017

Ocampo-Torres, Rubén
The formation of peak rings in large impact craters bibl color graph *Science* v354 no6314 p878 N 18 2016

Occidental (Film)
OCCIDENTAL J. Romney color *Film Comment* v53 no2 p22 Mr/Ap 2017

Occidental Petroleum Corp.—Officials & employees
Oil's Changing Face C. HELMAN color graph *Forbes* v200 no1 p38 Jl 27 2017

Occultations (Astronomy)

Get ready for E-Day [Cover story] M. E. Bakich color map *Astronomy* v45 no8 p20 Ag 2017

Occultism on television
The Awesome Pulp Sermon of 'Preacher' R. SHEFFIELD color *Rolling Stone* no1290 p25 Je 29 2017

Occupational achievement
American Identity: Tenor Nicholas Phan, who sings Berlioz's Roméo et Juliette with San Francisco Symphony this month, thrives on exploring an eclectic repertoire J. Malafronte *Opera News* v81 no12 p1 Je 2017
Fleur de Lis Forge L. S. FORD *Texas Monthly* v45 no5 p27 My 2017
Higher Power: Soprano Leah Crocetto views singing as a gift she is called to share F. Cohn *Opera News* v81 no12 p7 Je 2017
If You're Not Collecting Productivity Data, You'll Never Succeed at Work M. Schrage *Harvard Business Review Digital Articles* p2 F 4 2016
IT CAN'T ALL BE ENERGY M. SWARTZ *Texas Monthly* v45 no5 p79 My 2017
Janet Jackson C. Ianzito color *AARP: The Magazine* v59 no3A p92 Ap/My 2016
Lennart Nilsson's Unborn Beauties B. SEITZ color *National Review* v69 no5 p36 Mr 20 2017
LIFE ON THE EDGE 3,822 MILES R. BASS *Texas Monthly* v45 no5 p73 My 2017
LITTLE TOWN ON THE PRAIRIE S. HOLLANDSWORTH *Texas Monthly* v45 no5 p87 My 2017
Missy Hammond Casino Dealer: The longtime French Lick Resort employee is something of a card L. WRIGHT *Indianapolis Monthly* v12 no40 p48 Ag 2017
PIERRE-Ange CARLOTTI B. BERGMANN *Interview* v47 no3 p78 Ap 2017
The Talent Curse J. PETRIGLIERI and G. PETERIGLIERI il *Harvard Business Review* v95 no3 p88 My/Je 2017
Teach Your Team to Expect Success C. Curtis *Harvard Business Review Digital Articles* p2 Je 9 2016
WHAT MAKES A GREAT HR LEADER? We forensically examined the careers of notable HR and L&D directors to find out what makes them tick. It might just help you make it to the top too [Cover story] *People Management* p24 Mr 2017
What Sets Successful CEOs Apart [Cover story] E. L. BOTELHO, K. R. POWELL et al color *Harvard Business Review* v95 no3 p70 My/Je 2017
Why Subtle Bias Is So Often Worse than Blatant Discrimination E. King and K. Jones *Harvard Business Review Digital Articles* p2 Jl 13 2016

Occupational hazards
COPS SHOULD NOT PLAY JEOPARDY D. SPENCER *USA Today Magazine* v146 no2868 p32 S 2017

Occupational mobility
See also
Career changes
5 Signs It's Time for a New Job T. Chamorro-Premuzic *Harvard Business Review Digital Articles* p2 Ap 7 2015
Can You Really Not Afford to Change Jobs? W. Johnson *Harvard Business Review Digital Articles* p2 Ap 9 2015
The impact of business cycles on job mobility D. Wile *Monthly Labor Review* p1 Je 2017
The Truth About the Gig Economy J. Fox graph *Bloomberg Businessweek* no4528 p14 Je 26 2017

Occupational mobility—United States
Why make it hard for teachers to cross state borders? D. Goldhaber, C. Grout et al color il *Phi Delta Kappan* v98 no5 p55 F 2017

Occupational retraining—United States
What If All U.S. Coal Workers Were Retrained to Work in Solar? J. M. Pearce *Harvard Business Review Digital Articles* p2 Ag 8 2016

Occupational sociology
ALL IN A Day's Work U. MCCAMLEY, C. BUSSEY cartoon *Reader's Digest* v190 no1132 p54 Jl/Ag 2017

Occupational surveys
Occupational Requirements Survey: results from a job observation pilot test bibl chart color graph *Monthly Labor Review* p1 N 2016

Occupational training
See also

Nitrogen fixers may be at risk S. MILIUS *Science News* v191
no10 p11 My 27 2017

Ocean Alexander (Company)

ALL-AMERICAN R. THIEL chart color diag *Power & Motory-acht* v33 no3 p90 Mr 2017

Ocean Alexander *Sea Magazine* v108 no12 p50 D 2016

Ocean Alexander Marine Yacht Sales Inc.

OCEAN ALEXANDER 70 EVOLUTION M. WERLING *Sea Magazine* v108 no12 p32 D 2016

Ocean-atmosphere interaction

Oceans Drive Weather and Climate Extremes [Cover story] *USA Today Magazine* v145 no2865 p1 Je 2017

Ocean bottom

Ghostly glimpses of Earth's glacial past B. Geiger color *Science News* v191 no10 p32 My 27 2017

Massive blow-out craters formed by hydrate-controlled methane expulsion from the Arctic seafloor K. Andreassen, A. Hubbard et al graph map *Science* v356 no6341 p948 Je 1 2017

Ocean bottom temperature

Deep heat intensified mega-quake L. HAMERS *Science News* v191 no12 p7 Je 24 2017

Ocean bottom—International cooperation

An ecosystem-based deep-ocean strategy R. Danovaro, J. Aguzzi et al bibl color map *Science* v355 no6324 p452 F 3 2017

Ocean conditions (Weather)

Toxic Ocean Condition Tied to Climate Shifts *USA Today Magazine* v145 no2865 p3 Je 2017

Ocean currents

Engaging Youth to Conserve Coastal and Marine Environments K. Forsberg *UN Chronicle* v54 no1/2 p1 2017

Radar reveals new hot spots on Enceladus J. Miller *Physics Today* v70 no5 p18 My 2017

Ocean currents—Environmental aspects

Ocean currents respond to climate change in unexpected ways J. Miller *Physics Today* v70 no1 p17 Ja 2017

Ocean currents—Mathematical models

Oceanic Highway I. L. Bras color *Oceanus* v51 no2 p40 Wint 2016

Ocean engineering

Girls Just Wanna Be Engineers L. Lippsett *Oceanus* v52 no2 p29 Spr 2017

Ocean liners

OFF - BOAT & OFF BEAT T. Hill color *Sea Magazine* v109 no6 p22 Je 2017

Ocean surface topography

Radar reveals new hot spots on Enceladus J. Miller *Physics Today* v70 no5 p18 My 2017

Through the Looking-Glass of the Ocean Surface A. Bogdanoff color *Oceanus* v51 no2 p106 Wint 2016

Uncharted Territory T. Cook color *Scientific American* v317 no1 p23 Jl 2017

Ocean temperature

Regional and global sea-surface temperatures during the last interglaciation J. S. Hoffman, P. U. Clark et al bibl color graph *Science* v355 no6322 p276 Ja 20 2017

Ocean temperature—Measurement

Epiphany Among the Manta Rays D. Akkaynak color *Oceanus* v51 no2 p98 Wint 2016

Ocean travel

13 Things Cruise Lines Won't Tell You M. CROUCH *Reader's Digest* v188 no1125 p138 N 2016

ALASKA & ARCTIC CANADA *Sierra* v102 no1 p52 Ja/F 2017

The Caribbean With a Twang B. NEWCOTT color *AARP: The Magazine* v59 no2A p44 F/Mr 2016

CHOOSE YOUR Cruise P. BRADY bw color *Conde Nast Traveler* v52 no1 p72 Ja 2017

A Cruise for All Reasons R. LOVE color *AARP: The Magazine* v59 no2A p38 F/Mr 2016

A Cruising Family Reunion C. J. Doane color *Sail* v47 no12 p80 D 2016

Distance isn't Everything P. Nielsen color *Sail* v48 no6 p4 Je 2017

Doing it By the Book P. Nielsen *Sail* v47 no12 p6 D 2016

ENJOY THE CRUISING LIFE: WHEN IT'S TIME, CUT THE LINES AND GO! D. HISLOP bw color *Sea Magazine* v109 no6 pPNW-1 Je 2017

EXPEDITION CHARTERS Z. Prochazka color *Sail* v48 no11

p32 N 2017

THE FINAL FRONTIER B. SPRINGER color *Power & Motoryacht* v34 no9 p82 S 2017

From the Atlantic to the Pacific A. Wisch color *Sail* v48 no5 p17 My 2017

GETTING BETTER M. WERLING *Sea Magazine* v109 no1 p6 Ja 2017

Go West, Young Men S. Murray color *Power & Motoryacht* v34 no11 p72 N 2017

How to Choose a Cruising Crew J. Fredrick bw color *Sail* v48 no6 p10 Je 2017

Lifetime experience #19 A. White color *Canadian Geographic* v137 no4 p11 Jl/Ag 2017

Love Boat A. S. Greer color *Sunset* v238 no6 p78 Je 2017

OFF - BOAT & OFF BEAT T. Hill color *Sea Magazine* v109 no6 p22 Je 2017

Operation Vacation! J. Raycroft color *Power & Motoryacht* v34 no10 p94 O 2017

OUR OWN ODYSSEY M. BREEN bw color *Advocate* no1089 p48 F/Mr 2017

PLAYING BY HIS OWN RULES D. J. HARDING color *Power & Motoryacht* v34 no11 p100 N 2017

RAFT & SMALL BOAT *Sierra* v102 no1 p72 Ja/F 2017

Rigged for Success P. Nielsen *Sail* v48 no1 p6 Ja 2017

RIG ROULETTE J. Rasmussen color diag *Sail* v48 no11 p28 N 2017

The SAILING SCENE P. Veillette, B. Veillette et al color *Sail* v48 no6 p6 Je 2017

See aurorae in beautiful Norway D. J. EICHER color *Astronomy* v45 no6 p6 Je 2017

slow boat on a big lake M. Allen bw color map *Yankee* p70 My/Je 2017

Slow Track to Havana P. Nielsen color *Sail* v48 no6 p20 Je 2017

Summertime Slipups color *Consumer Reports* v82 no8 p63 Ag 2017

Take a River Cruise P. BRADY color *Conde Nast Traveler* v51 no11 p23 D 2016

Tall Tales on the High Seas L. ADDISON color *AARP: The Magazine* v59 no2A p42 F/Mr 2016

TNT color *Vogue* v206 no12 p172 D 2016

Tour de Seine *Boating World* v38 no3 p12 Mr 2017

Transat on a Fast Cat A. Dike color *Sail* v48 no10 p14 O 2017

Travel *D: The Magazine of Dallas* v43 no10 p100 O 2016

Ocean travel—Evaluation

Water Whirl J. Sens and J. Passov color *Golf Magazine* v58 no11 p90 N 2016

Ocean travel—Social aspects

TO BOLDLY CRUISE WHERE NO COUPLE HAS CRUISED BEFORE F. GOLDEN color *Bloomberg Businessweek* no4512 p75 F 20 2017

Ocean waves

LIQUID IDEALS color *Surfer* v58 no1 p76 Ap 2017

Ocean waves—Measurement

Turbulence in breaking waves G. B. Deane, D. Stokes et al *Physics Today* v69 no10 p86 O 2016

Ocean—Congresses

A Conference to #SaveOurOcean W. Hongbo *UN Chronicle* v54 no1/2 p1 2017

The Ocean Conference: a Game-Changer P. Thomson *UN Chronicle* v54 no1/2 p1 2017

Ocean—Environmental conditions

OCEAN PRESERVATION TAKES SHAPE M. WERLING *Sea Magazine* v109 no2 p4 F 2017

SAVING THE WORLD'S OCEANS M. FRANK *New York Times Upfront* v149 no8 p12 Ja 30 2017

TROUBLED WATERS D. Stone map *National Geographic* v231 no4 p20 Ap 2017

What's So Great About the Great Outdoors? J. HOUSMAN cartoon color *Surfer* v57 no11 p32 D 2016

Why the ocean's carbon sink has gotten stronger Sung Chang *Physics Today* v70 no4 p21 Ap 2017

Oceanic mixing

Ocean mixing and ice-sheet control of seawater 234U/238U during the last deglaciation Tianyu Chen, L. F. Robinson et al bibl graph *Science* v354 no6312 p626 N 4 2016

Oceanic Yachts (Company)

ONE STEP IN THE RIGHT DIRECTION A. HARPER chart color diag *Power & Motoryacht* v33 no3 p62 Mr 2017

Oceanographers

MAKING WAVES E. Pennisi bw color *Science* v355 no6329 p1006 Mr 10 2017

Sailing through uncertainty K. Frischkorn color *Science* v355 no6328 p986 Mr 3 2017

SEA CHANGE S. RICHARDSON bw color *American History* v52 no2 p28 Je 2017

Oceanographic maps

On the Waterfront: Millions of people live, work and play along New York's rivers and harbor. Here, a snapshot of the marine traffic on one recent day—March 22—shows the amazing range of activity H. HUSSEIN *Smithsonian* v48 no2 p36 My 2017

THE White RIVER R. Annis, S. Bahr et al diag *Indianapolis Monthly* v41 no2 p59 S 2017

Oceanographic research

Ocean Research Priorities: Similarities and Differences among Scientists, Policymakers, and Fishermen in the United States J. G. MASON, M. A. RUDD et al *BioScience* v67 no5 p418 My 2017

Warming Waters color *Earth Island Journal* v32 no2 p6 Summ 2017

Oceanographic research ships

Boaty McBoatface's Maiden Voyage color *Earth Island Journal* v32 no2 p8 Summ 2017

Oceanographic submersibles

After Overhaul, Jason Is Stronger Than Ever: DEEP-SEA VEHI-CLE IS STRIPPED DOWN, REDESIGNED, AND UPGRAD-ED E. Koenig *Oceanus* v52 no2 p14 Spr 2017

Technology *Oceanus* v52 no2 p13 Spr 2017

Oceanography—Research

It began with the four guys in the front row color *Oceanus* v51 no2 p2 Wint 2016

Ocean's Eight (Film)

Ocean's 8: Everything We Know So Far D. Coggan color *Entertainment Weekly* no1442 p10 D 2 2016 Rebellious Special Issue

Ocean's Eleven (Film : 2001)

LATE NIGHT E. ASLANIAN *TV Guide* v65 no23 p43 My 29 2017

Ocelot

COLLATERAL DAMAGE *Sierra* v102 no5 p34 St/O 2017

Ochilo, L.

Observation of a large-scale anisotropy in the arrival directions of cosmic rays above 8 × 1018 eV *Science* v357 no6357 p1266 S 22 2017

Ochoa, Christina

Valor N. Abrams, C. Holub et al color *Entertainment Weekly* no1482/1483 p52 S 22 2017

Ochoa, Lorena

TEEING OFF color *Golf Magazine* v59 no11 p16 N 2017

Ochoa-Ochoa, Leticia M.

Mexico's ambiguous invasive species plan bibl *Science* v355 no6329 p1033 Mr 10 2017

Ochola, MacLeod Baker

People F. Nzwili color *Christian Century* v134 no4 p18 F 15 2017

Ochs, Susan M.

The Leadership Blind Spots at Wells Fargo *Harvard Business Review Digital Articles* p2 O 6 2016

OCHS, SUSIE

AIRPODS REVIEW: They sound great, but Siri holds them back color *Macworld - Digital Edition* p72 F 2017

AirPods: They sound great, but Siri holds them back color *PCWorld* v35 no2 p116 F 2017

APPLE'S NIKE SPORT BAND color *Macworld - Digital Edition* v34 no4 p41 My 2017

BeatsX review: Just as magical as the AirPods, but more comfortable and convenient bw color *Macworld - Digital Edition* v34 no4 p72 My 2017

Everything you need to know about Apple's extended warranty program color *Macworld - Digital Edition* v34 no11 p10 N 2017

HANDS-ON: THE MACBOOK PRO'S INNOVATIVE TOUCH BAR GRAB YOU color *Macworld - Digital Edition* p79 D 2016

IPAD (2017) REVIEW: WITH A STRIPPED-DOWN iPAD FOR $329, YOU MAY NOT NEED TO GO PRO color *Macworld - Digital Edition* v34 no4 p67 My 2017

iPhone 7: ITS SPEED AND CAMERA ARE CRAZY-GOOD, BUT IT STILL DRIVES ME CRAZY color graph *Macworld - Digital Edition* v33 no11 p101 N 2016

iPHONE 7 PLUS REVIEW: THE DUAL-LENS CAMERA MAKES IT A WINNER color graph *Macworld - Digital Edition* p85 D 2016

KANEX GOPOWER WATCH AND ZENS POWERBANK FOR APPLE WATCH: CONVENIENT CHARGING color *Macworld - Digital Edition* p55 F 2017

LEGO BOOST CREATIVE TOOLBOX: YUP, TABLET-CONNECTED LEGO ROBOTS ARE AS COOL AS THEY SOUND color *Macworld - Digital Edition* v34 no11 p67 N 2017

MacBook Pro with Touch Bar: The best bits of iOS in a really great Mac color graph *PCWorld* p80 D 2016

News: Trump tells Apple to build iPhones in US color *Macworld - Digital Edition* p10 Ja 2017

Photo shootout: We tested Portrait mode with an iPhone 7 Plus fashion shoot color *Macworld - Digital Edition* p47 D 2016

Review: MacBook Pro (2016) color graph *Macworld - Digital Edition* p18 Ja 2017

OCHSNER, SHAUN

LUCAS OIL OFF-ROAD RACING PUSHES EAST [Cover story] color *Dirt Sports + Off-Road* v51 no12 p24 D 2017

MINT 400 STILL GOING STRONG chart color *Dirt Sports + Off-Road* v51 no8 p10 Ag 2017

RACING THE LONG WAY TO RENO [Cover story] color *Dirt Sports + Off-Road* v51 no1 p10 Ja 2017

REBELLES NAVIGATE THE ULTIMATE ADVENTURE color *Dirt Sports + Off-Road* v51 no4 p24 Ap 2017

TOYOTAS GO FULL MOON IN BAJA color *Dirt Sports + Off-Road* v51 no3 p58 Mr 2017

Ockels, Carolyn

How PwC and The Washington Post Are Finding and Hiring External Talent *Harvard Business Review Digital Articles* p2 Mr 29 2016

Ockert, Ingrid

Atomic Adventures color *Science* v356 no6342 p1008 Je 9 2017

Ocko, Ilissa B.

Unmask temporal trade-offs in climate policy debates color *Science* v356 no6337 p492 My 5 2017

O'Connell, Aaron B.

Our Latest Longest War: Losing Hearts and Minds in Afghanistan *Publishers Weekly* v264 no7 p65 F 13 2017

O'Connell, Andrew

The Pros and Cons of Doing One Thing at a Time *Harvard Business Review Digital Articles* p2 Ja 20 2015

Why Do We Get So Emotional About Brands? *Harvard Business Review Digital Articles* p2 Ap 21 2015

Why Superstars Struggle to Bond with Their Teams *Harvard Business Review Digital Articles* p2 O 27 2014

O'connell, Chris

STAR ROCKET IN FLIGHT *Texas Monthly* v45 no4 p90 Ap 2017

Watch + Learn color *Golf Magazine* v58 no11 p30 N 2016

Yes!!! *Texas Monthly* v45 no8 p48 Ag 2017

O'Connell, Gerard

'Amoris' opens the door to Communion for Catholics in irregular unions color *America* v216 no6 p17 Mr 20 2017

Beijing and Holy See near accord? color *America* v216 no5 p17 Mr 6 2017

Cardinal Bo on Myanmar's 'delicate' path to democracy color *America* v217 no4 p16 Ag 21 2017

The Ecumenical Pope *America* v215 p24 N 28 2016

Francis for the Poor *America* v215 no15 p26 N 14 2016

Francis the Preacher *America* v215 no18 p24 D 5 2016

New Leader of Jesuits Worldwide Is Latin American 'Historic Choice' color *America* v215 no13 p9 O 31 2016

No 'Reform of the Reform' *America* v215 no19 p24 D 19 2016

No Slowing Down *America* v216 no1 p28 Ja 2 2017

On Board With Peter *America* v215 no14 p22 N 7 2016

Pope Francis says Vatican II liturgical reform is 'irreversible' color *America* v217 no6 p17 S 18 2017

Pope Francis tells Colombians, 'Be slaves of peace' color *America* v217 no7 p15 O 2 2017

Springtime in Asia? *America* v215 no13 p27 O 31 2016

Steps to Hanoi *America* v215 no16 p24 N 21 2016

Vatican Power Shift *America* v215 no12 p26 O 24 2016

O'Connell, Katharine

My husband's been totally focused on our baby color *Glamour* v115 no1 p52 Ja 2017

O'Connell, Lauren A.

Interacting amino acid replacements allow poison frogs to evolve epibatidine resistance chart diag graph *Science* v357 no6357 p1261 S 22 2017

O'CONNELL, LINDSEY BENOIT

(not so) bad moms [Cover story] color *Good Housekeeping* v265 no5 p26 N 2017

O'CONNELL, MARK

THE IMMORTALITY CAMPAIGN color *New York Times Magazine* p44 F 12 2017

Only Human A. WIENER color *New Republic* v248 no3 p68 Mr 2017

To Be a Machine: Adventures Among Cyborgs, Utopians, Hackers, and the Futurists Solving the Modest Problem of Death M. DUNBAR *Humanist* v77 no3 p42 My/Je 2017

O'CONNELL, MEAGHAN

What to Do About Getting Old img *New York* p32 Ja 23 2017

O'Connell, Sean J.

Brainfeeder Showcase Fuses Enlightened Funk, Innovative Jazz color *Downbeat* v83 no12 p19 D 2016

MACY GRAY bw *Downbeat* v83 no12 p23 D 2016

Til They Bang On The Door color *Downbeat* v83 no11 p63 N 2016

Under My Skin color *Downbeat* v84 no3 p64 Mr 2017

O'conner, Patricia T.

Nova Scotia Noir *New York Times Book Review* p9 Ap 9 2017

O'Connor, Carolyn

An environment-dependent transcriptional network specifies human microglia identity color *Science* v356 no6344 p1248 Je 23 2017

O'CONNOR, CLARE

America's Richest Celebrities color *Forbes* v198 no9 p18 D 30 2016

Bangle Billionaire [Cover story] bw color *Forbes* v199 no6 p70 Je 13 2017

THE FEMINIST MYSTIQUE color *Forbes* v200 no3 p68 S 28 2017

LESSONS AND IDEAS BY THE 100 GREATEST LIVING BUSINESS MINDS bw color *Forbes* v200 no3 p115 S 28 2017

LOGO-A-GO-GO *Forbes* v200 no3 p88 S 28 2017

The Retail Whisperer color *Forbes* v198 no7 p58 N 29 2016

Social Animals color *Forbes* v199 no4 p26 Ap 25 2017

THE WORLD'S BILLIONAIRES bw color diag graph map *Forbes* v199 no3 p84 Mr 28 2017

Your Next Assistant: A Cyborg color *Forbes* v199 no4 p48 Ap 25 2017

O'Connor, Colleen

The Elements of Value: Interaction *Harvard Business Review* v94 no11 p18 N 2016

O'Connor, David

News BITS *Practical Horseman* v45 no1 p64 Ja 2017

O'Connor, Flannery, 1925-1964

Seeing Is Believing C. Nelson bw *Commonweal* v143 no18 p14 N 11 2016

O'CONNOR, GAIL

have a better morning *Parents* v91 no9 p86 S 2016

O'Connor, Gavin

THE ACCOUNTANT C. Chiarella color *Sound & Vision* v82 no5 p66 Je 2017

The Accountant L. Greenblatt color *Entertainment Weekly* no1436/1437 p83 O 21 2016

The Accountant Pays Small Dividends on Its Star S. Zacharek color *Time* v188 no16/17 p87 O 24 2016

Kind of a Drag J. PODHORETZ *Weekly Standard* v22 no8 p43 O 31 2016

O'Connor, George

UNSOLICITED BETA color *Climbing* no353 p18 My/Je 2017

O'Connor, Jason

When Real-Time Intel Still Isn't Fast Enough *Harvard Business Review Digital Articles* p2 O 30 2014

O'Connor, Jennifer

Feminist Force color *Glamour* v115 no3 p38 Mr 2017

O'Connor, Jill

O'Connor, Laurel Berger

TRAIL & CAMPING GEAR color *Trail Rider* v29 no1 p50 Ja/F 2017

TRAIL & CAMPING GEAR color *Trail Rider* v29 no2 p54 Mr 2017

TRAIL & CAMPING GEAR color *Trail Rider* v29 no4 p48 My 2017

O'Connor, M. R.

Can We Bring Back the Passenger Pigeon? T. Flannery bw color *New York Review of Books* v64 no7 p58 Ap 20 2017

Resurrection Science C. Gramling color *Science* v354 no6317 p1228 D 9 2016

O'Connor, Malachi

When Your Company Has a Problem It Can't Ignore *Harvard Business Review Digital Articles* p2 O 7 2014

O'Connor, Mark

Statistical Fallacy about Nuclear Risks *Skeptical Inquirer* v41 no5 p66 S/O 2017

O'Connor, Mary Catherine

Healing Through Hikes *Sierra* v102 no1 p25 Ja/F 2017

O'CONNOR, MAUREEN

CITY DAMES color *New York Times Book Review* p44 D 4 2016

OBAMA'S AMERICA img *New York* v49 no20 p12 O 3 2016

PORNHUB IS THE KINSEY REPORT OF OUR TIME *New York* v50 no12 p30 Je 12 2017

O'Connor, Michael P.

Is 'democratic policing' the answer to law enforcement abuses? color *America* v216 no13 p50 Je 12 2017

O'CONNOR, ROD

BESPOKEN FOR cartoon *Chicago* v66 no2 p22 F 2017

BOWLED OVER cartoon *Chicago* v66 no4 p34 Ap 2017

Britt Nolan color *Chicago* v66 no6 p90 Je 2017

THE CALL OF THE NORTH color *Chicago* v66 no7 p13 Jl 2017

Do You Know the Mushroom Man? color *Chicago* v66 no4 p100 Ap 2017

THE GREAT ESCAPE color *Chicago* v65 no12 p40 D 2016

A GURU FOR THE END OF DAYS color *Chicago* v66 no11 p32 N 2017

HACK ATTACK cartoon *Chicago* v66 no3 p40 Mr 2017

IT TAKES A VILLAGE color *Chicago* v66 no8 p32 Ag 2017

MAN VS. WILD BOAR color *Chicago* v66 no7 p22 Jl 2017

OF MICE AND MEAT color *Chicago* v66 no10 p34 O 2017

ROMANCING THE DRONE color *Chicago* v66 no6 p30 Je 2017

SAVE THE PAST LIFE FOR ME cartoon *Chicago* v66 no1 p34 Ja 2017

SHOW HIM THE MONEY color *Chicago* v65 no11 p32 N 2016

THE URBANIST: MY SUPER CLASSY SPA DAY color *Chicago* v66 no9 p44 S 2017

THE VOICE cartoon *Chicago* v66 no5 p40 My 2017

WHY We LOVE CHICAGO bw cartoon color *Chicago* v66 no3 p75 Mr 2017

O'Connor, Sandra Day, 1930-

A MATTER OF DEGREES: America's long struggle with affirmative action M. S. Collins *Harper's Magazine* p69 S 2017

O'Connor, Siobhan

The Best 25 Inventions of 2016 color *Time* v188 no22-23 p43 N/D 2016

Pioneers [Cover story] color *Time* v189 no16/17 p14 My 1-8 2017

Ocracoke Island (N.C.)

OCRACOKE OBSERVER P. Vernon bw *Columbia Journalism Review* v56 no1 p33 Spr 2017

Octopuses

Weird but true! J. SWAIN and A. E. HURT color map *National Geographic Kids* no470 p4 My 2017

Octopuses—Anatomy

The Power of Eight O. Judson chart color *National Geographic* v230 no5 p62 N 2016

Octopuses—Psychology

The Power of Eight O. Judson chart color *National Geographic* v230 no5 p62 N 2016

Octopuses—Research

Fossil Octopus Is a Jurassic Jewel B. Switek color *Scientific American* v316 no3 p21 Mr 2017

Ocular injuries—Treatment

First Aid for Eye Ouches J. Chen *Parents* v92 no8 p33 Ag 2017

Oda, Fernanda S.
Promoting human rights through science color *Science* v357 no6359 p34 O 6 2017

Oda, Nobunaga, 1534-1582
What We Learned From... Nagashino, 1575 C. Lyons color *Military History* v34 no4 p18 N 2017

ODA, STEPHANIE
Consolidation, Innovation Draw the Focus of Printers *Publishers Weekly* v264 no24 p28 Je 12 2017

Odahara, Masaki
Holliday junction resolvases mediate chloroplast nucleoid segregation diag *Science* v356 no6338 p631 My 12 2017

O'Dair, Barbara
All Yours *Prevention* v68 no11 p3 N 2016
Bright Ideas *Prevention* v69 no11 p3 N 2017
Change Is Good color *Prevention* v69 no1 p3 Ja 2017
Hit Refresh color *Prevention* v69 no6 p3 Je 2017
Let It Go *Prevention* v69 no4 p3 Ap 2017
My Energy Makeover *Prevention* v69 no2 p3 F 2017
A Really Good Year *Prevention* v69 no7 p3 Jl 2017
Save the Earth, Save Our Health color *Prevention* v69 no8 p18 Ag 2017
Walk This Way *Prevention* p3 Mr 2017

O'Daniel, Wilbert Lee
W. LEE "PAPPY" O'DANIEL P. CARLSON bw color *American History* v52 no2 p18 Je 2017

Odbadrakh, Tuguldur T.
Spectroscopic snapshots of the proton-transfer mechanism in water bibl diag graph *Science* v354 no6316 p1131 D 2 2016

Odd Mom Out (TV program)
ALSO COMING... A. D'Arminio *TV Guide* v65 no23 p35 My 29 2017

Odd Couple, The (TV program : 2015-)
The Odd Couple I. Ratledge color *TV Guide* v64 no42 p38 O 10 2016

Oddi, Nicolo
GLOBAL Warmth M. HOLGATE and M. GUIDUCCI color *Vogue* v207 no1 p34 Ja 2017

Ode to the Double "L" (Poem)
ODE TO THE DOUBLE "L" M. B. Rosado *New Yorker* v93 no5 p60 Mr 20 2017

Ode to the Office Fridge (Poem)
ODE TO THE OFFICE FRIDGE L. SKENAZY *Reader's Digest* v188 no1126 p65 D 2016/Ja 2017

Odebrecht SA
DEPT. OF SHELL COMPANIES CLANDESTINE ACCOUNTS, & BRIBERY M. SMITH, S. VALLE et al cartoon color *Bloomberg Businessweek* no4526 p46 Je 12 2017

Odeke, David E.
Positive biodiversity-productivity relationship predominant in global forests bibl chart graph map *Science* v354 no6309 paaf8957-1 O 14 2016

O'Dell, Dana
#trailchat color *Backpacker* p8 My 2017

O'Dell, Jason
A+ REVIVAL [Cover story] C. Lamers color *Sunset* v238 no4 p60 Ap 2017

Odell, Jennifer
The Hot Box *Downbeat* v84 no8 p69 Ag 2017
TROMBONE SHORTY SPIRITUAL CONNECTION color *Downbeat* v84 no6 p48 Je 2017

ODELL, KATE BACHELDER
Is free speech under threat IN THE UNITED STATES? WE RECEIVED TWENTY-SEVEN RESPONSES. WE PUBLISH THEM HERE, IN ALPHABETICAL ORDER *Commentary* v144 no1 p13 Jl/Ag 2017

O'Dell, Nancy
HOST STORIES I. RATLEDGE *TV Guide* v65 no14 p28 Ap 3 2017

O'Dell, Sijy
Trispecific broadly neutralizing HIV antibodies mediate potent SHIV protection in macaques color graph *Science* v357 no6359 p85 O 6 2017

ODENBAUGH, JAY
THINKING LIKE A WATERSHED *BioScience* v67 no9 p861 S 2017

Odenkirk, Bob
Better Call Saul J. Halterman *TV Guide* v65 no13 p31 Mr 20 2017
DRUNK HISTORY L. ACKEN *TV Guide* p49 D 5 2016
How to Pick a Tattoo B. ODENKIRK *Reader's Digest* v188 no1125 p17 N 2016
WHY We LOVE CHICAGO bw cartoon color *Chicago* v66 no3 p75 Mr 2017

Odenkirk, Bob—Interviews
Bob Odenkirk C. HOARD bw *Rolling Stone* no1285 p58 Ap 20 2017

Odessa (Mo.)
Rawhide and Java L. A. Addington color *Missouri Life* v44 no2 p18 Ap 2017

Odessa College
THE TWELVE MOST INNOVATIVE COLLEGES FOR ADULT LEARNERS J. Alvarez color *Washington Monthly* v49 no9/10 p38 S/O 2017

Odin Leather Goods (Company)
Odin Leather Goods L. S. FORD *Texas Monthly* v45 no2 p32 F 2017

O'Doherty, Brian
LAS VEGAS REVISITED bw color *Art in America* v104 no11 p96 D 2016

O'Doherty, Claudia
CLAUDIA O'DOHERTY: LOVES OF MY LIFE A. Bacle color *Entertainment Weekly* no1457/1458 p81 Mr 17 2017

Odom, Duncan T.
Aging increases cell-to-cell transcriptional variability upon immune stimulation color diag graph *Science* v355 no6332 p1433 Mr 31 2017

Odom, Ivy
Top that salmon color *Health* v31 no8 p132 O 2017

ODOM, MAYA
DOG DAZE *Cincinnati Magazine* v50 no10 p52 Jl 2017

Odom, Mel
Gene Marshall, Hollywood Fashion Icon JOHNSON *Treasures* v6 no3 p38 D 2016/Ja 2017

O'Donnel, Chris
Callen Gets in the Spirit on NCIS: Los Angeles A. D'Arminio *TV Guide* p13 D 5 2016

O'Donnell, Alina
CELEBRATING LITERACY LEADERS: ILA's awards program recognizes both rising stars and lifetime contributions [Cover story] *Literacy Today (2411-7862)* v35 no2 p26 S/O 2017
TEACHING A PEDAGOGY OF PEACE: Starting a dialogue by engaging one's differences *Literacy Today (2411-7862)* v35 no2 p38 S/O 2017

O'Donnell, Angela Alaimo
Death & Life in the Afternoon: A meditation on bullfighting color *America* v217 no7 p40 O 2 2017
A GREAT AND HARSH BEAUTY *America* v215 no13 p33 O 31 2016
Still Pilgrim: Poems C. Hughes *Christian Century* v134 no17 p41 Ag 16 2017
'They Are Not Themselves': The Lives of the English Queens color *America* v216 no7 p38 Ap 3 2017

O'Donnell, Chris
NCIS: LOS ANGELES A. D'Arminio *TV Guide* v65 no39 p54 S 18 2017

O'Donnell, Kate
gather ROUND chart color *Yoga Journal* no287 p68 N 2016

O'DONNELL, KATHERINE M.
Overcoming Challenges to the Recovery of Declining Amphibian Populations in the United States *BioScience* v67 no2 p156 F 2017

O'donnell, Kevin
10 ARTISTS WHO WILL RULE 2017 color *Entertainment Weekly* no1450 p56 Ja 27 2017
THE 26-WORD REVIEW color *Entertainment Weekly* no1465 p52 My 12 2017
THE 28-WORD REVIEW color *Entertainment Weekly* no1472 p56 Je 30 2017
And the Winner Is... chart color *Entertainment Weekly* no1451/1452 p26 F 3-10 2017
THE BEST ALBUMS OF 2017 (SO FAR) color *Entertainment*

AN ODYSSEY D. MENDELSOHN cartoon color *New Yorker* v93 no10 p54 Ap 24 2017

Odyssey, The (Theatrical production)

A Veteran's Voice: John Meyer's Odyssey in service and on stage H. Sherman *Stage Directions* v30 no6 p32 Je 2017

Odyssey van—Evaluation

2018 Honda Odyssey E. DYER color *Popular Mechanics* p40 S 2017

Oehler, Ken

What Makes Someone an Engaging Leader *Harvard Business Review Digital Articles* p2 N 7 2014

Oertner, Thomas G.

Active cortical dendrites modulate perception bibl graph *Science* v354 no6319 p1587 D 23 2016

Oesterlund, Robert

SEA OF MONEY N. Confessore *New York Times Magazine* p30 D 4 2016

Oestreich, Martin

Teaching nature the unnatural bibl diag *Science* v354 no6315 p970 N 25 2016

Oettingen, Gabriele

Stop Being So Positive *Harvard Business Review Digital Articles* p2 O 27 2014

Of Gods & Men (Film)

quick takes color *U.S. Catholic* v82 no8 p39 Ag 2017

Of the North (Film)

OF DIGITAL SELVES AND DIGITAL SOVEREIGNTY: OF THE NORTH M. Stewart *Film Quarterly* v70 no4 p23 Summ 2017

Of Windows & Doors (Short story)

Of Windows and Doors M. Hamid bw cartoon *New Yorker* v92 no37 p70 N 14 2016

O'Farill, Arturo

Arturo O'Farrill & Chucho Valdés: SONGS FOR OUR FATHERS T. Panken color *Downbeat* v84 no10 p40 O 2017

Ofek, E. O.

iPTF16geu: A multiply imaged, gravitationally lensed type Ia supernova color diag graph *Science* v356 no6335 p291 Ap 21 2017

Ofer, Sammy

One Winner, One Loser After a Fortune's Split D. Pendleton and Y. Benmeleh color *Bloomberg Businessweek* no4506 p33 Ja 9 2017

Off-label use (Drugs)

Should Drugs Do Double Duty? T. Carr il *Consumer Reports* v82 no2 p12 F 2017

Off-road racing

2016 LUCAS OIL OFF-ROAD RACING SERIES FINISHES STRONG AT WILD HORSE PASS M. EMERY color *Dirt Sports + Off-Road* v51 no4 p34 Ap 2017

FERRO'S FAVORITE RACE J. OBER bw *Dirt Sports + Off-Road* v51 no9 p74 S 2017

HOW TO FIND YOUR SELF A. Giacobbe color *Women's Health* v14 no6 p132 Jl 2017

LOORRS 2017 SEASON DEBUT REDUX [Cover story] R. JOHNSTON color *Dirt Sports + Off-Road* v51 no10 p60 O 2017

MINT 400 STILL GOING STRONG S. OCHSNER chart color *Dirt Sports + Off-Road* v51 no8 p10 Ag 2017

A NATION'S DATEBOOK color *Dirt Sports + Off-Road* v51 no12 p72 D 2017

A NATION'S DATEBOOK *Dirt Sports + Off-Road* v51 no3 p72 Mr 2017

NOVICE RACERS J. OBER bw *Dirt Sports + Off-Road* v51 no3 p74 Mr 2017

RACING THE LONG WAY TO RENO [Cover story] S. OCHSNER color *Dirt Sports + Off-Road* v51 no1 p10 Ja 2017

REBELLES NAVIGATE THE ULTIMATE ADVENTURE S. OCHSNER color *Dirt Sports + Off-Road* v51 no4 p24 Ap 2017

RETRO OFFROAD RACING TO RESTORE TEAM CAR FOR ORMHOF INDUCTEE VALENTA color *Dirt Sports + Off-Road* v51 no1 p8 Ja 2017

ROB MAC: DRIVER OF THE YEAR M. Emery color *Dirt Sports + Off-Road* v51 no9 p6 S 2017

ROB MAC RIPS TO THREE-PEAT BAJA 1000 OVERALL M. EMERY color *Dirt Sports + Off-Road* v51 no4 p10 Ap 2017

SWEEPING UP AT THE NORRA MEXICAN 1000 J. RETTIE color *Dirt Sports + Off-Road* v51 no10 p14 O 2017

VIVA LA BAJA! [Cover story] C. COLLARD color *Dirt Sports + Off-Road* v51 no10 p10 O 2017

WHEN DODGE WON THE MTEG GRAND NATIONAL SPORT TRUCK CHAMPIONSHIP J. OBER bw *Dirt Sports + Off-Road* v51 no4 p74 Ap 2017

Off-road racing—Competitions

2017 SCHEDULE chart *Dirt Sports + Off-Road* v51 no8 p72 Ag 2017

2017 SONORA RALLY J. RETTIE color *Dirt Sports + Off-Road* v51 no8 p18 Ag 2017

2017 UTV WORLD CHAMPIONSHIPS M. EMERY color *Dirt Sports + Off-Road* v51 no9 p10 S 2017

A CHUNK OF BAJA J. OBER color *Dirt Sports + Off-Road* v51 no8 p74 Ag 2017

THE CIRCUS COMES TO TOWN J. OBER color *Dirt Sports + Off-Road* v51 no7 p74 Jl 2017

DEEP IN THE HEART OF TEXAS M. KAUSCH color *Dirt Sports + Off-Road* v51 no3 p38 Mr 2017

A NATION'S DATEBOOK *Dirt Sports + Off-Road* v51 no9 p72 S 2017

RUNNING WILD M. Emery color *Dirt Sports + Off-Road* v51 no8 p6 Ag 2017

Off-road vehicle equipment

THE 50TH ANNUAL SEMA SHOW M. EMERY color *Dirt Sports + Off-Road* v51 no3 p24 Mr 2017

FLEX JOINTS J. KOPYCINSKI color *Dirt Sports + Off-Road* v51 no2 p64 F 2017

GEARBOX bw color *Dirt Sports + Off-Road* v51 no2 p68 F 2017

GEARBOX color *Dirt Sports + Off-Road* v51 no10 p70 O 2017

GEAR BOX color *Dirt Sports + Off-Road* v51 no8 p70 Ag 2017

ONE OF THOSE THINGS M. EMERY color *Dirt Sports + Off-Road* v51 no2 p60 F 2017

SXS/UTV PARTS BUYER'S GUIDE color *Dirt Sports + Off-Road* v51 no8 p24 Ag 2017

Off-road vehicle trails

FIXING TRAIL FAILURESL J. KOPYCINSKI color *Dirt Sports + Off-Road* v51 no9 p66 S 2017

NON-JEEPS INVADE EASTER JEEP SAFARI J. HEADLEE color *Dirt Sports + Off-Road* v51 no9 p40 S 2017

Off-road vehicles

See also

All terrain vehicles

Sport utility vehicles

2017 SCHEDULE: A NATION'S DATEBOOK *Dirt Sports + Off-Road* v51 no2 p72 F 2017

CLEANING UP M. EMERY color *Dirt Sports + Off-Road* v51 no10 p52 O 2017

EL CARMELO GRANDE J. OBER color *Dirt Sports + Off-Road* v51 no12 p74 D 2017

FAMILY TRADITION M. EMERY color *Dirt Sports + Off-Road* v51 no8 p40 Ag 2017

HOUR GLASS J. OBER color *Dirt Sports + Off-Road* v51 no2 p74 F 2017

HUCKING IT AT HAVOC 4 M. KAUSCH color *Dirt Sports + Off-Road* v51 no2 p54 F 2017

A NATION'S DATEBOOK *Dirt Sports + Off-Road* v51 no3 p72 Mr 2017

NOVICE RACERS J. OBER bw *Dirt Sports + Off-Road* v51 no3 p74 Mr 2017

THE NUCLEAR MARSHMALLOW M. EMERY color *Dirt Sports + Off-Road* v51 no8 p54 Ag 2017

OVERLAND AFFAIR M. PRINCE color *Road & Track* v68 no9 p92 Je 2017

SHOCK DOCTRINE B. SOROKANICH color *Road & Track* v69 no1 p84 Ag 2017

SWITCH IT UP [Cover story] B. W. SMITH color *Dirt Sports + Off-Road* v51 no10 p48 O 2017

TIME HAS COME M. Emery color *Dirt Sports + Off-Road* v51 no2 p4 F 2017

TRAIL HERO WORKS WITH UPLA TO SAVE SAND MOUNTAIN OHV ACCESS color *Dirt Sports + Off-Road* v51 no2 p6 F 2017

TWO HOUR WONDER: PUTTING THE FOX IN THE PENTHOUSE S. RICHARDS color *Dirt Sports + Off-Road* v51 no8

p62 Ag 2017

Off-road vehicles—Congresses

LUCAS OIL OFF-ROAD EXPO M. EMERY color *Dirt Sports + Off-Road* v51 no3 p10 Mr 2017

Off-road vehicles—Equipment & supplies

GEAR BOX color *Dirt Sports + Off-Road* v51 no8 p70 Ag 2017

AN INTERESTING TWIST S. RICHARDS color diag *Dirt Sports + Off-Road* v51 no11 p62 N 2017

LUCAS OIL OFF-ROAD EXPO M. EMERY color *Dirt Sports + Off-Road* v51 no3 p10 Mr 2017

SOUND MACHINE J. HEADLEE color *Dirt Sports + Off-Road* v51 no8 p48 Ag 2017

SXS/UTV PARTS BUYER'S GUIDE color *Dirt Sports + Off-Road* v51 no8 p24 Ag 2017

TWO HOUR WONDER: PUTTING THE FOX IN THE PENTHOUSE S. RICHARDS color *Dirt Sports + Off-Road* v51 no8 p62 Ag 2017

Off-road vehicles—Evaluation

2017 Land Rover Discovery E. DYER color *Popular Mechanics* p43 S 2017

The Battle of the Off-Road Beaters J. Gall bw chart color graph *Car & Driver* v62 no6 p84 D 2016

The Desert Monster E. DYER color *Popular Mechanics* p59 D 2016/Ja 2017

FIRST IMPRESSION: POLARIS RZR XP TURBO EPS color *Dirt Sports + Off-Road* v51 no5 p12 My 2017

X-FACTOR TURBO RS B. SMITH color *Dirt Sports + Off-Road* v51 no2 p48 F 2017

Off-road vehicles—Exhibitions

HAPPY WANDERERS UNITE IN FLAGSTAFF M. EMERY color *Dirt Sports + Off-Road* v51 no2 p42 F 2017

Off-the-grid living

The Basics of BATTERY POWER A. Sindelar *Mother Earth News* no279 p61 D/Ja 2017

Offe, Claus

Referendum vs. Institutionalized Deliberation: What Democratic Theorists Can Learn from the 2016 Brexit Decision *Daedalus* v146 no3 p14 Summ 2017

Offenbach, Jacques, 1819-1880

Operapedia: Tales of Hoffmann *Opera News* v81 no5 p14 N 2016

Offensive (Military science)

Another War, Another Blitzerkrieg S. J. DOUGLAS *In These Times* v41 no6 p13 Je 2017

THE "TRUMP DOCTRINE" *In These Times* v41 no6 p33 Je 2017

Trump's Great Faith In the Military Does Not a Strategy Make K. Vick color diag *Time* v190 no1 p9 Jl 3 2017

Offensive behavior

THE AGE OF RUDENESS *New York Times Magazine* p38 F 19 2017

ANTHONY BOURDAIN ON SMUG LIBERALS AND EATING DOGS A. BISLEY color *Reason* v48 no10 p67 Mr 2017

How Rudeness Stops People from Working Together C. Porath color *Harvard Business Review Digital Articles* p2 Ja 20 2017

How to Respond to an Offensive Comment at Work A. Gallo color *Harvard Business Review Digital Articles* p2 F 8 2017

Offensive players

CENTER STAGE G. A. Bedard color *Sports Illustrated* v125 no16 p38 N 14 2016

SCAR'S TO PROVE IT G. A. Bedard color *Sports Illustrated* v126 no4 p36 Ja 30 2017

Öffentliche Kunstsammlung Basel

AROUND BASEL S. DOUGLAS cartoon color *ARTnews* v115 no3 p138 Fall 2016

Offerman, Nick

IF YOU'RE NOT MAKING MISTAKES, YOU'RE NOT LIVING N. OFFERMAN *Vital Speeches of the Day* v83 no8 p239 Ag 2017

WORLD'S FUNNIEST WOODWORKER TELLS ALL M. B. CRAWFORD color *Popular Mechanics* p64 S 2017

WORLD'S FUNNIEST WOODWORKER TELLS ALL M. B. CRAWFORD color *Popular Mechanics* v193 no7 p64 S 2016

Offerman, Nick—Interviews

Big Mac Daddy M. WAKIM *Los Angeles Magazine* p54 Ja 2017

NICK OFFERMAN I. Biedenharn color *Entertainment Weekly* no1486 p61 O 13 2017

Offermanns, Stefan

Regeneration of fat cells from myofibroblasts during wound healing bibl color graph *Science* v355 no6326 p748 F 17 2017

OfferUp Inc.

CAN CRAIGSLIST BE KILLED? R. MAC color *Forbes* v199 no5 p80 My 16 2017

Office building interior decoration

THE GOOP LIFE M. RUS color *Architectural Digest* no6 p120 Je 1 2017

Office building lighting

Linear Lighting Frenzy: The lighting industry continues to seek inventive ways to make light more efficient and ultimately more appealing to vastly improve the user experience R. Empfield color diag *Architectural Record* v205 no8 p148 Ag 2017

A New Way to Think About Office Lighting I. Campbell, K. Calhoun et al *Harvard Business Review Digital Articles* p2 Je 27 2017

Office building remodeling

Enlightened Workplaces: Illuminated ceilings are at the heart of the design strategies for two corporate office projects—the National Bank of Canada Trading Floor by Architecture49 and Osram Americas Headquarters by Sasaki—resulting in... D. Sokol color map *Architectural Record* v205 no5 p127 My 2017

Our Tech Office H. COX color *Indianapolis Monthly* v42 no2 p34 O 2017

Office buildings

See also

Offices

Office buildings—China—Design & construction

Diamond Standard: A high-rise for a Chinese conglomerate showcases its distinctive structural system A. A. SENO color diag map *Architectural Record* v205 no5 p110 My 2017

Office buildings—Design & construction

Allies and Morrison C. Foges *Architectural Record* v205 no4 p120 Ap 2017

Beebe Skidmore Architects D. Sokol *Architectural Record* v205 no4 p115 Ap 2017

Gensler J. M. McKnight *Architectural Record* v205 no4 p118 Ap 2017

Home Grown M. Cockram *Architectural Record* v205 no6 p120 Je 2017

Out of the Ruins J. MINUTILLO *Architectural Record* v205 no9 p116 S 2017

Packing a Punch: A new corporate headquarters makes a big impact both inside and out B. KAMIN color map *Architectural Record* v205 no5 p104 My 2017

Page J. Krichels *Architectural Record* v205 no4 p104 Ap 2017

Skidmore, Owings & Merrill H. Corcoran *Architectural Record* v205 no4 p112 Ap 2017

Office buildings—Evaluation

Harrison Avenue Boom K. Finn color *New Orleans Magazine* v51 no9 p30 Jl 2017

Office buildings—Lighting

ESI Design with HOK and Available Light L. C. Lentz color *Architectural Record* v205 no2 p118 F 2017

Office buildings—Washington (D.C.)

THE NEW WASHINGTON OFFICE S. DALPHONSE *Washingtonian Magazine* v52 no6 p76 Mr 2017

Office Christmas Party (Film)

OFFICE CHRISTMAS PARTY D. Snierson and W. Robinson color *Entertainment Weekly* no1438 p39 N 4 2016

Office decoration

Do Look Down D. Selig color *Bloomberg Businessweek* no4495 p72 O 17 2016

Give Your Office a Raise cartoon color *GQ: Gentlemen's Quarterly* v97 no5 p70 My 2017

Miles Redd M. RUS color *Architectural Digest* v74 no8 p28 Ag 2017

Why I Love MY DAUGHTERS' ARTWORK J. Alba color *InStyle* v24 no8 p176 Ag 2017

Office design & construction

The Evolving Workplace Environment P. J. Arsenault color graph *Architectural Record* v205 no8 p138 Ag 2017

Office environment

MYSTERY NOVELS INSPIRED BY A CO-WORKING SPACE Z. KHALID cartoon *New Yorker* v93 no3 p33 Mr 6 2017

Research: Stale Office Air Is Making You Less Productive J. G.

Allen *Harvard Business Review Digital Articles* p2 Mr 21 2017

Will the Gig Economy Make the Office Obsolete? D. Mulcahy *Harvard Business Review Digital Articles* p2 Mr 17 2017

Office for Metropolitan Architecture (Company)

White Hot B. BROOME color diag *Architectural Record* v204 no12 p90 D 2016

Office layout

See also

Open plan offices

7 Factors of Great Office Design P. Bacevice, L. Burow et al *Harvard Business Review Digital Articles* p2 My 20 2016

Design a Workspace that Gives Extroverts Privacy, Too *Harvard Business Review Digital Articles* p2 O 22 2014

An Open Office Experiment That Actually Worked P. Rosenberg and K. Campbell *Harvard Business Review Digital Articles* p2 O 3 2014

Office mail procedures

THE MAILROOM J. M. Laskas *New York Times Magazine* p30 Ja 22 2017

Office management

Reclassifying Office "Housework" M. Ertman *Harvard Business Review Digital Articles* p2 Ag 17 2015

Office of the United Nations High Commissioner for Refugees

I AM THAT GIRL Cate Blanchett A. Synnott color *InStyle* v23 no13 p282 D 2016

SCIENCE, INTERRUPTED J. HATTAM bw color graph map *Discover* v38 no7 p42 S 2017

Which Refugees? N. RUSH *National Review* v69 no4 p16 Mr 6 2017

Office parties

MONEY MANNERS M. CROSS color *Kiplinger's Personal Finance* v71 no12 p37 D 2017

A Reputation for Badoo Behavior G. Turner, A. Satariano et al color *Bloomberg Businessweek* no4526 p30 Je 12 2017

Office politics

4 Strategies for Women Navigating Office Politics K. Heath *Harvard Business Review Digital Articles* p2 Ja 14 2015

Great Leaders Embrace Office Politics M. C. Wenderoth *Harvard Business Review Digital Articles* p2 Ap 11 2016

How Facebook Tries to Prevent Office Politics J. Parikh *Harvard Business Review Digital Articles* p2 Je 29 2016

How to Respond When Someone Takes Credit for Your Work A. Gallo *Harvard Business Review Digital Articles* p2 Ap 29 2015

How to Talk About Office Politics with a New Colleague K. Dillon *Harvard Business Review Digital Articles* p2 Je 17 2016

More Data Won't Turn Employees into High- Performing Machines T. Chamorro-Premuzic *Harvard Business Review Digital Articles* p2 O 30 2014

Office Politics Is Just Influence by Another Name A. McKee *Harvard Business Review Digital Articles* p2 Ja 16 2015

Office Politics Isn't Something You Can Sit Out K. K. Reardon *Harvard Business Review Digital Articles* p2 Ja 12 2015

Surviving in a Family Business When You're Not Part of the Family J. Baron and R. Lachenauer *Harvard Business Review Digital Articles* p2 Ja 15 2015

The Underlying Psychology of Office Politics T. Chamorro-Premuzic *Harvard Business Review Digital Articles* p2 D 25 2014

What Everyone Should Know About Office Politics D. Rousmaniere *Harvard Business Review Digital Articles* p2 F 13 2015

Offices

See also

Home offices

Medical offices

Newsrooms

Shared workspaces

GENIUS W. McPhail color *Esquire* p29 O 2017

A New Home for The Advocate bw *New Orleans Magazine* v51 no5 p20 Mr 2017

THE OFFICE *Interview* v46 no9 p98 N 2016

WHAT'S NEW *Sea Magazine* v109 no8 pCA-12 Ag 2017

Offices—Design & construction

7 Factors of Great Office Design P. Bacevice, L. Burow et al *Harvard Business Review Digital Articles* p2 My 20 2016

interiors C. ROUX color *Architectural Record* v205 no3 p37 Mr 2017

Mirror Image A. MARTINS *Architectural Record* v204 no10 p108

O 2016

My Desk color *Vanity Fair* p93 Hollywood 2017 Supplement

THE NEW WASHINGTON OFFICE S. DALPHONSE *Washingtonian Magazine* v52 no6 p76 Mr 2017

Rules for Designing an Engaging Workplace S. Augustin *Harvard Business Review Digital Articles* p2 O 28 2014

OFFIT, PAUL

5 THINGS WE KNOW TO BE TRUE cartoon *Scientific American* v315 no5 p46 N 2016

God's Own Medicine *Skeptical Inquirer* v41 no2 p44 Mr/Ap 2017

Pandora's Lab color diag *National Geographic* v231 no6 p136 Je 2017

Offseason (Sports)

PICK 'N' ROLL HIGH SCHOOL S. Rushin color *Sports Illustrated* v127 no12 p50 O 16 2017

Offshore gas industry

Big Gas Finds, Bigger Political Problems D. Wainer map *Bloomberg Businessweek* no4511 p37 F 13 2017

Offshore oil & gas leases

Seizing Our Energy Potential T. J. DONOHUE *Weekly Standard* v22 no14 p29 D 12 2016

Offshore oil well drilling

See also

Drilling platforms

Offshore outsourcing

France's Youngest Leader Since Napoleon Takes the Stage V. Walt color *Time* v189 no19 p9 My 22 2017

A New Caribbean Bank For Chinese Money A. Liu color *Bloomberg Businessweek* no4523 p38 My 22 2017

Offshore sailing

ACTING A LITTLE DINGHY P. BACICH and M. BACICH *Sea Magazine* v109 no1 p26 Ja 2017

BE MORE METICULOUS A. JENKINS *Sea Magazine* v109 no1 p24 Ja 2017

BOUNTY OF THE SEA: THE OCEAN PROVIDES SUSTENANCE THAT IS FRESH, NUTRITIOUS AND FUN TO HARVEST D. HISLOP color *Sea Magazine* v109 no7 pPNW-14 Jl 2017

BROKEN WINDOWS K. TENNEFOSS *Sea Magazine* v109 no1 p24 Ja 2017

CAPTIVATED BY CRUISING H. Steinberger *Sea Magazine* v108 no9 p20 S 2016

COMPACT CRUISING D. Hislop color map *Sea Magazine* v109 no7 p16 Jl 2017

CRUISING TIPS T. Cunliffe color *Sail* v48 no7 p46 Jl 2017

CRUISING TIPS T. Cunliffe color *Sail* v48 no9 p52 S 2017

Cuba On the Rocks A. Chan color *Sail* v48 no10 p34 O 2017

Deep INTO THE Delta P. RAINS *Sea Magazine* v108 no9 p40 S 2016

DISCOVER PORT SAN LUIS *Sea Magazine* v108 no9 pCA-1 S 2016

ENJOY THE CRUISING LIFE: WHEN IT'S TIME, CUT THE LINES AND GO! D. HISLOP bw color *Sea Magazine* v109 no6 pPNW-1 Je 2017

HIDDEN GEMS P. RAINS *Sea Magazine* v108 no8 p14 Ag 2016

IT'S THE LITTLE THINGS: MANY OF THE DIFFERENCES BETWEEN CRUISING IN THE U.S AND CRUISING IN MEXICO ARE SUBTLE P. RAINS color *Sea Magazine* v109 no8 p14 Ag 2017

LONG NIGHT IN FOSSIL BAY E. LEE *Sea Magazine* v109 no9 p22 S 2017

Mini-Crulse M. Werling and S. Shibata *Sea Magazine* v109 no5 p20 My 2017

NORTHERN EXPOSURE B. COOK color map *Sail* v48 no11 p40 N 2017

On The Beach B. Gray color *Sail* v48 no7 p26 Jl 2017

Pam Wall A. Schell color *Sail* v48 no5 p14 My 2017

The SAILING SCENE T. Heinz, D. Siver et al color *Sail* v48 no9 p6 S 2017

Sophia Hears the Siren's Song A. JENKINS *Sea Magazine* v108 no8 p16 Ag 2016

SUMMER GETAWAYS: IT'S POSSIBLE TO ENJOY MINI-CRUISES IN THE SEA OF CORTEZ WHILE STAYING CLOSE TO A HURRICANE HOLE P. RAINS color map *Sea Magazine* v109 no7 p12 Jl 2017

THINGS I LEARNED THIS PAST WEEK J. Kennedy *Sail* v48

no1 p16 Ja 2017

Transat on a Fast Cat A. Dike color *Sail* v48 no10 p14 O 2017

UNINTENDED ENTANGLEMENTS K. PAINTER *Sea Magazine* v109 no1 p25 Ja 2017

UP FOR A CHALLENGE? WHETHER IT'S THE GETTING THERE OR THE RELAXING ATMOSPHERE, YOU'LL FIND SOMETHING TO ENJOY AND REMEMBER ABOUT SILVA BAY *Sea Magazine* v108 no9 pPNW-12 S 2016

WAIT IT OUT AT WAKES COVE: OOZING WITH MYSTERY, HISTORY AND INTRIGUE, THE COVE IS A POPULAR STOPPING POINT BEFORE TRANSITING GABRIOLA PASSAGE D. HISLOP color *Sea Magazine* v109 no7 pPNW-10 Jl 2017

we done reach R. BERINGER color map *Sail* v48 no10 p58 O 2017

West Coast "Winterization" D. THOMPSON *Sea Magazine* v108 no10 p54 O 2016

Offshore sailing—Social aspects

Keeping Up With the Jones C. J. Doane color *Sail* v48 no9 p96 S 2017

Offshore sailing—Study & teaching

No Man's Land: SHARPENING SAILING SKILLS ON A WOMEN-ONLY COURSE A. Wisch color map *Sail* v48 no8 p41 Ag 2017

Offshore wind power plants

POPULAR MECHANICS EVERYWHERE color *Popular Mechanics* p12 Mr 2017

WIND ON THE WATER B. Dumaine color diag map *Fortune* v175 no4 p184 Mr 15 2017

Winds of Change J. Hsu color *Scientific American* v315 no5 p21 N 2016

Offshore yacht racing

ANOTHER LAP R. KOTHE color map *Sail* v48 no10 p50 O 2017

Offutt, Chris

IN THE HOLLOW *Harper's Magazine* v333 no1998 p53 N 2016

Ofili, Elizabeth

NIH's mentoring makes progress bibl *Science* v354 no6314 p840 N 18 2016

Ofis Architects (Company)

A Precarious but Picturesque Perch J. Zorthian color *Time* v188 no22-23 p20 N/D 2016

OFRI, DANIELLE

No Money, No Care *New York Times Book Review* p15 Ag 27 2017

Ogasawara, Daisuke

Activity-based protein profiling reveals off-target proteins of the FAAH inhibitor BIA 10-2474 chart color graph *Science* v356 no6342 p1084 Je 9 2017

Ogata, Issey, 1952-

Issey Ogata M. Hagan color *Current Biography* v78 no8 p64 Ag 2017

Ogawa, Aimie

Systemic pan-AMPK activator MK-8722 improves glucose homeostasis but induces cardiac hypertrophy graph *Science* v357 no6350 p507 Ag 4 2017

Ogawa, Sachie K.

Engrams and circuits crucial for systems consolidation of a memory diag *Science* v356 no6333 p73 Ap 7 2017

Ogawa, Susumu

Crowdsourced Products Sell Better When They're Marketed That Way *Harvard Business Review Digital Articles* p2 N 8 2016

Ogawa-Ohnishi, Mari

A peptide hormone required for Casparian strip diffusion barrier formation in Arabidopsis roots color graph *Science* v355 no6322 p284 Ja 20 2017

Ogbac, Stefan

NEW CARS 2018-2019 [Cover story] chart color *Motor Trend* v69 no9 p34 S 2017

NEW SUVS & TRUCKS 2018-2019 [Cover story] color *Motor Trend* v69 no10 p32 O 2017

Ram Rebel TRX Concept color *Motor Trend* v69 no1 p16 Ja 2017

Ogbonnaya, Chidiebere

Research: How Incentive Pay Affects Employee Engagement, Satisfaction, and Trust *Harvard Business Review Digital Articles* p2 Mr 15 2017

OGDEN, ELLEN ECKER

GREEN GIANT color *Better Homes & Gardens* v95 no3 p118

Mr 2017

Ogden, Katharine—Awards

Ice the Drought J. Fuchs and T. Keith color *Sports Illustrated* v126 no8 p26 Mr 20 2017

Ogden, Laura A.

Toward a national, sustained U.S. ecosystem assessment bibl color *Science* v354 no6314 p838 N 18 2016

Ogden, Lesley Evans

Adapting to Outer Space color *Natural History* v125 no5 p7 My 2017

Border Walls and Biodiversity *BioScience* v67 no6 p498 Je 2017

Brewing Big Data: The Tea-Bag Index *BioScience* v67 no7 p680 Jl 2017

Built for Stability *Natural History* v124 no10 p8 N 2016

Canada aims to rewrite environmental law color *Science* v353 no6307 p1480 S 30 2016

Colorful Language color *Natural History* v125 no4 p7 Ap 2017

The Complex Business of Sustainable Exploitation of Wildlife: Researchers grapple with the many unknowns *BioScience* v67 no8 p691 Ag 2017

Conservation Biology: A New Hope? *BioScience* v66 no12 p1088 D 1 2016

Directional Signals *Natural History* v125 no2 p6 F 2017

Fisherwomen--The Uncounted Dimension in Fisheries Management *BioScience* v67 no2 p111 F 2017

Food for Thought color *Natural History* v125 no7 p6 Jl/Ag 2017

Growing Dependency color *Natural History* v125 no6 p7 Je 2017

Lunch Breaks bw *Natural History* v125 no11 p8 N 2017

Missing Teeth color *Natural History* v125 no3 p7 Mr 2017

A modern diagnosis of an ancient cat color *Science News* v192 no7 p5 O 28 2017

Strains in a Relationship *Natural History* v125 no1 p8 D 2016/Ja 2017

Too Hot to Stomach color *Natural History* v125 no10 p7 O 2017

Ogg, Kim

Law and the New Order A. Greenblatt *Governing* v30 no7 p26 Ap 2017

Oglesby, Robert J.

Nuclear Weapons in a Changing Climate: Probability, Increasing Risks, and Perception bibl chart color graph *Environment* v59 no4 p22 Jl-Ag 2017

OGLETHORPE, ALICE

FLEX TIME color *O, The Oprah Magazine* p78 S 2017

Get a Good Night's Sleep ...Finally [Cover story] cartoon *Prevention* p52 Mr 2017

happy teeth color *Better Homes & Gardens* v95 no3 p152 Mr 2017

label lingo color *Better Homes & Gardens* v95 no8 p180 Ag 2017

shake it off color *Better Homes & Gardens* v95 no7 p168 Jl 2017

THE SKINNY ON FATS color *Better Homes & Gardens* v95 no4 p148 Ap 2017

wellness TRAILBLAZERS color *Better Homes & Gardens* v95 no9 p146 S 2017

Ogmundsdottir, Margret Helga

Transcriptional activation of RagD GTPase controls mTORC1 and promotes cancer growth diag *Science* v356 no6343 p1188 Je 16 2017

Ogo, S.

Structural basis of the redox switches in the NAD+-reducing soluble [NiFe]-hydrogenase diag *Science* v357 no6354 p928 S 1 2017

O'GRADY, JIM

BROTHERLY LOVE *America* v215 no18 p34 D 5 2016

O'GRADY, MEGAN

The Long View color *Vogue* v207 no9 p616 S 2017

PAGING Beauty bw color *Vogue* v206 no12 p214 D 2016

TWO to Tango bw color *Vogue* v206 no11 p186 N 2016

O'GRADY, SIOBHÁN

GUARDIAN OF THE GIRL-CHILD color *Foreign Policy* no223 p36 Mr/Ap 2017

OGUNJINMI, FEMI

Your Cheatin' Heart *USA Today Magazine* v145 no2862 p68 Mr 2017

Ogunnaike, Lola

RED-CARPET INTELLIGENCE Emmys Edition color *Entertainment Weekly* no1484 p22 S 29 2017

Ogunseitan, Oladele A.

A CALL FOR BETTER Toxics Policy Reform color diag *Environment* v59 no1 p30 2017

Mercury Safety Reform in the 21st Century: Advancing the New Framework for Toxic Substances Control bibl color *Environment* v59 no4 p4 Jl-Ag 2017

OGUNTOLA, SUNDAY

PUTTING PASTORS TO PASTURE cartoon *Christianity Today* p15 Ap 2017

Ogwumike, Nneka, 1990-

Nneka Ogwumike B. Muteba color *Current Biography* v78 no8 p68 Ag 2017

Ogwumike, Nneka—Political & social views

American Voices Nneka Ogwumike D. Greene and T. Keith color *Sports Illustrated* v125 no12 p20 O 10 2016

Oh, Areum

Mutations in the promoter of the telomerase gene TERT contribute to tumorigenesis by a two-step mechanism diag *Science* v357 no6358 p1416 S 29 2017

Oh, Deog-Seong

Technology assessment and the social and human impact of innovation bibl diag *Bulletin of the Atomic Scientists* v72 no6 p402 N 2016

Oh, Ellen

A Collection of Tales That Bind S. Begley color *Time* v188 no27-28 p112 D 26 2016

Oh, Hello (Theatrical production)

GOINGS ON ABOUT TOWN color *New Yorker* v92 no30 p6 S 26 2016

Oh, Ji Won

Regeneration of fat cells from myofibroblasts during wound healing bibl color graph *Science* v355 no6326 p748 F 17 2017

Oh, Leslie Hsu

Equip the Kids *Sierra* v101 no4 p20 Jl/Ag 2016

Rules, Shmoolz *Backpacker* p73 Je 2017

Oh, Linda May Han

The Hot Box chart *Downbeat* v84 no6 p63 Je 2017

Walk Against Wind J. Corbett color *Downbeat* v84 no6 p61 Je 2017

Oh, Nuri

Double-heterojunction nanorod light-responsive LEDs for display applications bibl color graph *Science* v355 no6325 p616 F 10 2017

Oh, S.

Quantized Faraday and Kerr rotation and axion electrodynamics of a 3D topological insulator bibl graph *Science* v354 no6316 p1124 D 2 2016

Oh, Steven—Interviews

Are The Young Turks Progressive Media's Rising Stars? L. FLANDERS color *Nation* v304 no9 p38 Mr 20 2017

Oh, Whistle & I'll Come to You, My Lad (Short story)

BAD MOON RISING M. R. James *Lapham's Quarterly* v10 no3 p95 Summ 2017

Oh, Young Jun

Harvesting electrical energy from carbon nanotube yarn twist diag graph *Science* v357 no6353 p773 Ag 25 2017

Oh My My (Music)

Ryan Tedder S. Lansky color *Time* v188 no15 p55 O 17 2016

Ohad, Nir

Wild emmer genome architecture and diversity elucidate wheat evolution and domestication color *Science* v357 no6346 p93 Jl 7 2017

Ohadi, Hamid

Single-molecule optomechanics in "picocavities" bibl graph *Science* v354 no6313 p726 N 11 2016

Ohanesian, Adriane

CLOSE CALL D. Owen cartoon *New Yorker* v93 no26 p22 S 4 2017

Ohanian, Alexis, 1983-

Serena's Love Match B. BUSSINGER bw color *Vanity Fair* v59 no8 p62 Ag 2017

Ohanian, Lee E.

A "Big Intellectual Risk" J. Wolf *Hoover Digest: Research & Opinion on Public Policy* no4 p195 Fall 2016

Putting Words into Action *Hoover Digest: Research & Opinion on Public Policy* no1 p36 Wint 2017

O'Hara, Austin

Popular piety color *U.S. Catholic* v82 no2 p5 F 2017

O'Hara, Carolyn

5 Ways to Work from Home More Effectively *Harvard Business Review Digital Articles* p2 O 2 2014

How to Ask for a Raise *Harvard Business Review Digital Articles* p2 Mr 5 2015

How to Bounce Back After a Failed Negotiation *Harvard Business Review Digital Articles* p2 Ap 21 2016

How to Deal with a Boss Who Behaves Unpredictably *Harvard Business Review Digital Articles* p2 N 3 2016

How to Fall Back in Love with Your Job *Harvard Business Review Digital Articles* p2 Jl 23 2015

How to Get an Employee to Work Faster color *Harvard Business Review Digital Articles* p2 Ja 3 2017

How to Get the Feedback You Need *Harvard Business Review Digital Articles* p2 My 15 2015

How to Improve Your Business Writing *Harvard Business Review Digital Articles* p2 N 20 2014

How to Negotiate Nicely Without Being a Pushover *Harvard Business Review Digital Articles* p2 Ap 9 2015

How to Overcome the Midday Slump *Harvard Business Review Digital Articles* p2 Jl 1 2015

How to Work with Someone Who Isn't a Team Player *Harvard Business Review Digital Articles* p2 Ap 21 2017

Keeping It Professional When You Work in a Family Business *Harvard Business Review Digital Articles* p2 Je 14 2016

Stop Second-Guessing Your Decisions at Work *Harvard Business Review Digital Articles* p2 N 6 2015

What to Do After a Bad Performance Review *Harvard Business Review Digital Articles* p2 O 29 2014

What to Do After You Tell Your Boss You're Leaving *Harvard Business Review Digital Articles* p2 Ag 11 2016

You Really Can Change Your Reputation at Work *Harvard Business Review Digital Articles* p2 S 11 2015

O'Hara, Catherine

GRAND MOTEL D. KAMP color *Vanity Fair* v59 no1 p166 Holiday 2017

O'Hara, John

A Timeless Observer/Writing With Sassigassity J. WILLIAMS *New York Times Book Review* p6 S 25 2016

O'Hara, John, 1905-1970

A Rage to Write J. EPSTEIN bw color *Weekly Standard* v22 no14 p30 D 12 2016

O'Hara, Robert

Westward Journey M. S. Eddy *Stage Directions* v29 no11 p36 N 2016

Ohashi, Pamela S.

Costimulation, a surprising connection for immunotherapy color diag *Science* v355 no6332 p1373 Mr 31 2017

O'HEHIR, ANDREW

Seismic Change: A mother and daughter do geologic battle for the fate of the world as a Hugo-winning trilogy ends *New York Times Book Review* p12 O 1 2017

OH-HYUN, CHO

Waves color *Tricycle: The Buddhist Review* v26 no2 p116 Wint 2016

Ohi, Debbie Ridpath

Sam & Eva *Publishers Weekly* v264 no33 p77 Ag 14 2017

Ohia lehua—Diseases & pests

Alien fungus blights Hawaii's native trees I. Vesper color *Science* v354 no6310 p273 O 21 2016

Tree-Killing Fungus Continues to Spread on Hawaii's Biggest Island M. STONE *BioScience* v67 no8 p776 Ag 2017

Ohio River

Bridge to the Future E. Barone color *Time* v189 no13 p42 Ap 10 2017

Sparkle and Dance K. LAUR *Cincinnati Magazine* v50 no7 p38 Ap 2017

Ohio State University—Sports

3 Ohio State color *Sports Illustrated* v127 no5 p91 Ag 14 2017

CASE FOR ... OHIO STATE P. Thamel color *Sports Illustrated* v125 no19 p41 D 12 2016

Week 6 color *Sports Illustrated* v127 no5 p64 Ag 14 2017

Ohio University

Ohio University Theater Division Collaboration and Critical Thinking *Stage Directions* v30 no3 p70 Mr 2017

Ohio—Description & travel

Easy Living A. M. HALLIGAN map *Backpacker* p19 O 2017

ON THE WAY *Cincinnati Magazine* p55 Je 2017

Ohio—Economic conditions—21st century

OHIO, OURSELVES E. Fry map *Fortune* v174 no6 p10 N 1 2016

Ohkawa, Yasuyuki

Crystal structure of the overlapping dinucleosome composed of hexasome and octasome graph *Science* v356 no6334 p205 Ap 14 2017

Ohler, Norman

Hitler's Little Helper D. HERZOG *New York Times Book Review* p19 Ap 2 2017

MR. BLITZED N. Paumgarten cartoon *New Yorker* v93 no5 p30 Mr 20 2017

The Very Drugged Nazis A. Beevor bw *New York Review of Books* v64 no4 p14 Mr 9 2017

WAR ON DRUGS G. Pendle color *Esquire* p40 Ap 2017

Ohlin, Alix

Quarantine A. Ohlin cartoon *New Yorker* v92 no47 p56 Ja 30 2017

A System from the North cartoon *Walrus* v13 no10 p62 D 2016

Ohlson, Kristin

The Great Forgetting *Reader's Digest* v189 no1127 p41 F 2017

More Than Dirt bw color *National Wildlife (World Edition)* v55 no3 p34 Ap/My 2017

Ohlsson, Kristina

The Chosen *Publishers Weekly* v263 no44 p54 O 31 2016

Öhman, Johannes, 1967-

Johannes Öhman M. Hagan color *Current Biography* v78 no1 p55 Ja 2017

Upheaval at Staatsballett Berlin L. Cappelle *Dance Magazine* v91 no1 p40 Ja 2017

Ohnemus, Dan

Uncovering the Ocean's Biological Pump color *Oceanus* v51 no2 p52 Wint 2016

Ohno, Apolo, 1982-—Interviews

APOLO OHNO C. Mann color *Amazing Wellness* v8 no6 p20 Early Winter2016

OHNSMAN, ALAN

EYES ON THE ROAD color *Forbes* v200 no2 p78 S 5 2017

Honda Opens Its Doors color *Forbes* v199 no2 p46 F 28 2017

The Tesla of Buses color *Forbes* v198 no8 p54 D 20 2016

UBER'S BOLD MOVE [Cover story] color *Forbes* v198 no9 p58 D 30 2016

Ohri, Chandra

Emergence and spread of a human-transmissible multidrug-resistant nontuberculous mycobacterium bibl diag graph *Science* v354 no6313 p751 N 11 2016

Ohsugi, Miho

Mitotic chromosome assembly despite nucleosome depletion in Xenopus egg extracts diag *Science* v356 no6344 p1284 Je 23 2017

Ohsumi, Keita

Mitotic chromosome assembly despite nucleosome depletion in Xenopus egg extracts diag *Science* v356 no6344 p1284 Je 23 2017

Ohsumi, Yoshinori, 1945-

WHY OUR BODY DESTROY ITSELF L. STOKES bw color *Christianity Today* v61 no1 p60 Ja/F 2017

Yoshinori Ohsumi J. Crelin color *Current Biography* v78 no6 p78 Je 2017

Ohsumi, Yoshinori, 1945-—Awards

Nobel honors discoveries in how cells eat themselves M. Enserink and E. Pennisi color *Science* v354 no6308 p20 O 7 2016

Ohta, Hiroshi

Fertile offspring from sterile sex chromosome trisomic mice chart diag *Science* v357 no6354 p932 S 1 2017

Oikonomou, F.

Observation of a large-scale anisotropy in the arrival directions of cosmic rays above 8 × 1018 eV *Science* v357 no6357 p1266 S 22 2017

Oil & gas leases—Colorado

Don't Frack on Me C. Traywick color *Bloomberg Businessweek* no4541 p24 O 9 2017

Oil changes—Equipment & supplies

Sump, dude? The 90-second oil change F. Markus color *Motor Trend* v69 no4 p30 Ap 2017

Oil fields—Iraq

A Ride Through Horror *New York Times Upfront* v149 no7 p2 Ja 9 2017

Oil fields—Texas

Despite cheap crude prices, America's best oil field, Texas' Permian Basin, is thriving A. Nussbaum color map *Bloomberg Businessweek* no4496 p77 O 24 2016

Oil sands

Tar Sands Are Coming to Wisconsin S. Taylor cartoon *Progressive* v81 no10 p28 N 2016

Oil sands—Alberta

Boom town revival color *Maclean's* p36 Je 2017

Oil sands—Alberta—Research

A sticky national debate J. MARKUSOFF color *Maclean's* no1 p11 F 17 2017

Oil shales

Fat Wallets Come To the Shale Patch J. Blas *Bloomberg Businessweek* no4516 p34 Mr 27 2017

Oil spill risk assessment

Putting a value on injuries to natural assets: The BP oil spill R. C. Bishop, K. J. Boyle et al chart *Science* v356 no6335 p253 Ap 21 2017

Oil spills

THE FIRST LINE OF DEFENSE J. NOBEL color *Audubon* v119 no3 p30 Fall 2017

Oil spills & the environment

Putting a value on injuries to natural assets: The BP oil spill R. C. Bishop, K. J. Boyle et al chart *Science* v356 no6335 p253 Ap 21 2017

Oil spills—Alaska

Sound of Silence color *Sail* v48 no8 p8 Ag 2017

Oil well drilling

Bad Vibes in Big Cypress K. NIELSEN *Sierra* v101 no4 p50 Jl/Ag 2016

Don't Mine What's Ours D. MARTINDALE *In These Times* v41 no6 p5 Je 2017

Oil well drilling rigs

See also

Drilling platforms

The Platform Paradox A. POPESCU *Los Angeles Magazine* p92 D 2016

Rigged for Tuna J. BROWNLEE color *Power & Motoryacht* v34 no6 p24 Je 2017

Oil well fires & fire prevention

The Burning Sands of Iraq K. Vick color *Time* v189 no24 p30 Je 26 2017

Oil wells

WILL FLORIDA BAN FRACKING? R. BAILEY color *Reason* v49 no2 p8 Je 2017

Ointments

See also

Facial creams (Cosmetics)

COUNTER INTELLIGENCE M. MILRAD GOLDSTEIN *Martha Stewart Living* no268 p62 O 2016

Country Lore *Mother Earth News* no279 p83 D/Ja 2017

THE DAY & NIGHT GUIDE TO GORGEOUS SKIN G. WAY color *Redbook* p1c O 2017

Dry & flaky? Put down that moisturizer! [Cover story] A. PATZ color *Prevention* v69 no2 p56 F 2017

EMILY LEY color *Better Homes & Gardens* v95 no5 p22 My 2017

FACE-SAVING CROP OF WINNERS O. J. WILLIAMS color *Ebony* v72 no11 p52 S 2017

Forest to face E. Marglin color *Yoga Journal* no290 p26 Mr 2017

HOW TO winterize your skin A. FRANZINO color *Good Housekeeping* v264 no1 p25 Ja 1 2017

Liquid Courage color *Martha Stewart Living* p52 O 2017

So What Do You Do, TEYANA TAYLOR? color *InStyle* v24 no5 p166 My 2017

Val's Guide to GORGEOUS V. Monroe color *O, The Oprah Magazine* p68 Ag 2017

Why I'm for Gym Makeup color *Glamour* no8 p88 Ag 2017

Why It's Time to Go Back to the Mall J. VRABEL cartoon *GQ: Gentlemen's Quarterly* v97 no3 p74 Mr 2017

Ointments—Evaluation

15 INSTANT SKIN FIXES Guarnieri color *Harper's Bazaar*

no3652 p177 Ap 2017

2017 Best Beauty BUYS K. D. Hodes and P. Reynoso color *InStyle* v24 no5 p169 My 2017

4 beauty tricks I just learned V. Kirby color *Redbook* p54 N 2017

ANTI-AGING DAY CREAMS color *Good Housekeeping* v264 no3 p31 Mr 2017

AWASH WITH WONDER A. Finney color *Women's Health* v14 no7 p56 S 2017

BEAUTY NEWS A. Parnass color *Harper's Bazaar* no3651 p330 Mr 2017

The Best Body Moisturizers color *InStyle* v23 no13 p200 D 2016

BLOOM BOOM color *Women's Health* v14 no3 p(Sp)14 Ap 2017

breakthrough skin reliever color *Good Housekeeping* v264 no4 p92 Ap 2017

Cold Weather FIXES K. FOSTER color *Seventeen* v76 no12 p62 D 2016/Ja 2017

CREAM BLUSH color *InStyle* v23 no12 p202 N 2016

The Decider Find Your Perfect FACIAL MOISTURIZER color diag *InStyle* v23 no12 p190 N 2016

DO-IT-YOURSELF Treasures N. BUCK color *Nebraska Life* v21 no5 p69 S/O 2017

DRY GOODS: Stay cooler and more collected with these hair and skin faves H. G. Phillips *Washingtonian Magazine* v52 no11 p106 Ag 2017

emporium color *Dressage Today* v23 no12 p64 S 2017

face savers color *Good Housekeeping* v263 no6 p34 D 2016

getting ready with DALLAS SHAW color *Better Homes & Gardens* v95 no9 p29 S 2017

GIFT GUIDE 2017 [Cover story] color *Amazing Wellness* v9 no6 p70 EarlyWint 2017

Highlighted Cheeks color *InStyle* v23 no12 p184 N 2016

HOW TO BE DARING WITH YOUR BEAUTY ROUTINE color *Harper's Bazaar* no3648 p66 N 2016

I Can't Live Without My ... color *InStyle* v24 no9 p331 S 2017

MAKING waves color *Harper's Bazaar* no3648 p226 N 2016

MAN-I-CURE! M. BOBO color *Ebony* v72 no3 p70 D 2016/Ja 2017

MOISTURIZING MATTERS A. R. Williams color *Southern Living* v52 no1 p43 Ja 2017

notebook *Martha Stewart Living* no270 p71 D 2016

ONE OF THESE INVENTIONS color *Good Housekeeping* v263 no6 p98 D 2016

ON-THE-GO MUSTS color *Good Housekeeping* v264 no2 p87 F 2017

The Pick color *InStyle* v23 no12 p206 N 2016

the pick color *InStyle* v24 no8 p116 Ag 2017

SAVE YOUR SKIN color *Harper's Bazaar* no3654 p165 Je/Jl 2017

SHINING MOMENT N. McGOVERN color *O, The Oprah Magazine* p16 S 2017

SIX WAYS TO WAKE UP BETTER-LOOKING color *Esquire* p42 Ag 2017

So What Do You Do, CINDY CRAWFORD? color *InStyle* v24 no9 p354 S 2017

STAFF SUMMER SKIN CARE PICKS T. Payne color *Ebony* v72 no8 p40 Je 2017

stellar serum color *Good Housekeeping* v265 no4 p136 O 2017

TIKA SUMPTER E. MUSIWA color *Ebony* v72 no11 p57 S 2017

Travel at a moment's notice color *Good Housekeeping* v264 no3 p20 Mr 2017

Val's Guide to GORGEOUS V. Monroe color *O, The Oprah Magazine* p67 Je 2017

White Now! color *Essence* v47 no7 p34 N 2016

You, Unfiltered S. George color *InStyle* v24 no4 p141 Ap 2017

Oiticica, Hélio, 1937-1980

FULL IMMERSION P. SCHJELDAHL color *New Yorker* v93 no22 p78 Jl 31 2017

Ojai Valley (Calif.)

OJAI VALLEY, CALIFORNIA C. Ress *Harper's Magazine* p38 O 2017

Ojarikre, Obah A.

Fertile offspring from sterile sex chromosome trisomic mice chart diag *Science* v357 no6354 p932 S 1 2017

Ojelade, Ifetayo

Killing the Competition A. LEAK and S. T. BROWN color *Ebony* v72 no5 p66 Mr 2017

Ojibwa (North American people)

Under the industrial lights M. HEMMADI color *Maclean's* p18 Je 2017

Ojibwa (North American people)—Social life & customs

"Our Hope and Our Protection": Misko-biiwaabik (Copper) and Tribal Sovereignty in Michigan E. M. REDix bw map *American Indian Quarterly* v41 no3 p224 Summ 2017

Ojibwa children

THE OTHER RUNAWAYS M. FRISCOLANTI bw color *Maclean's* v129 no43 p20 O 31 2016

Ojibway, Therese

On the Trail Of a Fairy Queen L. VACCARIELLO *Reader's Digest* v189 no1127 p32 F 2017

Ojomo, Efosa

6 Signs You're Living in an Entrepreneurial Society *Harvard Business Review Digital Articles* p2 O 4 2016

AFRICA'S NEW GENERATION OF INNOVATORS color il img *Harvard Business Review* v95 no1 p128 Ja/F 2017

Ok Computer (Music)

RADIOHEAD'S GENIUS & PARANOIA [Cover story] A. GREENE bw color *Rolling Stone* no1289 p34 Je 15 2017

OK Go (Performer)

HIGH FLIERS J. MACGREGOR *Smithsonian* v47 no8 p52 D 2016

THIS IS HOW YOU MAKE A MISIC M. Rapkin color *Popular Mechanics* p74 O 2017

Okafuji, Masahiro

Traditional Values Bring Tectonic Shift to Trading Sector M. Foster and D. W. Russell color *Forbes* v199 no1 p(Sp)3 Ja 24 2017

Okamoto, Kazuhiro

Radical-polar crossover reactions of vinylboron ate complexes bibl diag *Science* v355 no6328 p936 Mr 3 2017

Okamoto, Kihachi

Army of One I. S. SMITH bw *Film Comment* v53 no1 p16 Ja/F 2017

Okavango River Delta (Botswana)

The Mission to Save Africa's Okavango Delta D. Quammen color map *National Geographic* v232 no5 p80 N 2017

Okawa, Ryūho

The Laws of Justice. 2016 *Publishers Weekly* v263 no39 p24 S 26 2016

Okazaki, Miles

Outside the Box B. Milkowski color *Downbeat* v84 no6 p32 Je 2017

O'keefe, Brian

100 FASTEST-GROWING COMPANIES chart color diag map *Fortune* v176 no4 p157 S 15 2017

APPLE CLIMBS TOWARD $1 TRILLION diag *Fortune* v176 no5 p124 O 1 2017

AUTOMATION AHEAD diag *Fortune* v176 no3 p96 S 1 2017

BETTING ON AI diag *Fortune* v175 no3 p144 Mr 1 2017

CASH HOARDERS diag *Fortune* v174 no7 p108 D 1 2016

CHINA BUYS INTO THE U.S diag *Fortune* v175 no4 p196 Mr 15 2017

CITIES OF GOLD diag *Fortune* v176 no2 p116 Ag 1 2017

COASTS OF LIVING map *Fortune* v176 no4 p176 S 15 2017

HACKERS ARE GETTING BOLDER diag *Fortune* v75 no1 p100 Ja 1 2017

IT'S GETTING HARDER TO HIRE diag *Fortune* v175 no5 p92 Ap 1 2017

MOST WANTED MINERALS color map *Fortune* v176 no1 p96 Jl 1 2017

PICTURING AN H-1B OVERHAUL diag *Fortune* v175 no6 p88 My 1 2017

PILING UP CO[subscript 2] SAVINGS diag *Fortune* v175 no7 p88 Je 1 2017

THE RED TAPE CONUNDRUM: HOW THE WRONG KIND OF REGULATION IS STRANGLING BUSINESS—AND WHAT TO DO ABOUT IT [Cover story] color diag *Fortune* v174 no6 p76 N 1 2017

WHERE TO SPEND ON INFRASTRUCTURE diag *Fortune* v174 no8 p192 D 15 2016

O'Keefe, Georgia

Self-Made Woman R. SYME bw color *New Republic* v248 no7 p56 Jl 2017

O'Keefe, Nancy

One church? *U.S. Catholic* v82 no7 p5 Jl 2017

O'Keeffe, Georgia, 1887-1986—Exhibitions
ART cartoon *New Yorker* v93 no6 p11 Mr 27 2017

O'Keeffe, Kate
Managing Multiparty Innovation color img *Harvard Business Review* v94 no11 p76 N 2016

O'KEEFFE, LINDA
ALL the RIGHT MOVES *Better Homes & Gardens* v95 no1 p80 Ja 2017
CAMERA READY *Better Homes & Gardens* v94 no11 pN1 N 2016
FAIRY-TALE ENDING cartoon color *Better Homes & Gardens* v95 no2 p90 F 2016

O'Keeffe, Michael
Bottom-up construction of a superstructure in a porous uranium-organic crystal color graph *Science* v356 no6338 p624 My 12 2017

O'Keeffe, Sean
Multicluster Pcdh diversity is required for mouse olfactory neural circuit assembly diag *Science* v356 no6336 p411 Ap 28 2017
Pcdhαc2 is required for axonal tiling and assembly of serotonergic circuitries in mice diag *Science* v356 no6336 p406 Ap 28 2017

Okeley, Kristin
Bright Ideas T. MARTIN *Indianapolis Monthly* p38 My 2017
Outside the Box T. MARTIN *Indianapolis Monthly* p42 My 2017
Sweet Dreams L. D. ROBERTS *Indianapolis Monthly* p24 My 2017
Work Hard, Play Hard J. YOUNG *Indianapolis Monthly* p34 My 2017

Okeowo, Alexis
ARMOR AND LINGERIE cartoon color *New Yorker* v93 no29 p52 S 25 2017
THE AWAY TEAM cartoon color *New Yorker* v92 no41 p42 D 12 2016
The Dangerous Lives of Girls color *National Geographic* v231 no1 p130 Ja 2017
Darkest Night: A Moonless, Starless Sky: Ordinary Women and Men Fighting Extremism in Africa E. A. KAPLAN *Ms.* v27 no3 p51 Fall 2017
IMAGE CONSULTANT cartoon color *New Yorker* v93 no3 p34 Mr 6 2017
A Moonless, Starless Sky: Ordinary Women and Men Fighting Extremism in Africa color *Publishers Weekly* v264 no27 p65 Jl 3 2017
OUT OF BOUNDS cartoon *New Yorker* v93 no27 p34 S 11 2017

Okja (Film)
BEHIND THE DESIGN OKJA D. Franich color *Entertainment Weekly* no1446/1447 p52 D 2016/Ja 2017
Can You Love This Super-Pig? It's one thing to dream up a nonexistent creature. But just try bringing it adorably to life E. A. JUNG img *New York* v50 no13 p72 Je 26 2017
COME BACK A. LANE color *New Yorker* v93 no20 p92 Jl 10 2017
FREE RANGE A. Taubin color *Film Comment* v53 no4 p28 Jl/Ag 2017
MASTER OF STRANGE E. Poenisch bw color *Esquire* p13 Ag 2017
Okja, Super-Pig in the City M. ATKINSON *In These Times* v41 no8 p36 Ag 2017

Oklahoma (Film)
Rodgers and Hammerstein R. STIEVE *Arizona Highways* v93 no4 p2 Ap 2017

Oklahoma City (Okla.)
Dangerous Legacy: Cities get themselves into a fiscal squeeze paying bills they ran up decades ago M. Maciag *Governing* v30 no12 p58 S 2017

Oklahoma City Thunder (Basketball team)
4 THUNDER color *Sports Illustrated* v127 no12 p82 O 16 2017
5 Thunder R. Nadkarni, B. Golliver et al color *Sports Illustrated* v125 no14 p102 O 24-31 2016
BRICKTOWN Bricolage L. Jenkins color *Sports Illustrated* v126 no11 p76 Ap 17-24 2017
Confidence D. Riley color *GQ: Gentlemen's Quarterly* v86 no11 p114 N 2016
HOT | NOT T. Keith color *Sports Illustrated* v125 no19 p24 D 12 2016

HOW OKC GOT ITS MAN L. Jenkins color *Sports Illustrated* v127 no3 p50 Jl 24 2017
Staying Power [Cover story] L. Jenkins color *Sports Illustrated* v125 no14 p56 O 24-31 2016

Oklahoma Panhandle (Okla.)
John Phillips J. Phillips color *Car & Driver* v63 no5 p28 N 2017

Oklahoma State University—Sports
4 Oklahoma State color *Sports Illustrated* v127 no5 p92 Ag 14 2017

Okland, Nils
NILS ØKLAND J. Woodard color *Downbeat* v84 no1 p20 Ja 2017

Oklay, N.
Rosetta's comet 67P/Churyumov-Gerasimenko sheds its dusty mantle to reveal its icy nature bibl graph *Science* v354 no6319 p1566 D 23 2016
Surface changes on comet 67P/Churyumov-Gerasimenko suggest a more active past bw graph *Science* v355 no6332 p1392 Mr 31 2017

OKO, DAN
BORN TO BE WILD *Texas Monthly* v45 no4 p102 Ap 2017

Okonedo, Sophie
Undercover J. Russell *TV Guide* v64 no46 p36 N 7 2016

Okorafor, Nnedi
Binti: Home *Publishers Weekly* v263 no48 p52 N 28 2016
THE DREAM WEAVER A. MORGAN bw *Chicago* v66 no10 p80 O 2017

Okoro, Enuma
Reflections on the lectionary *Christian Century* v134 no9 p19 Ap 26 2017

Okpokwasili, Okwui
Body Politics H. Als color *New Yorker* v93 no10 p26 Ap 24 2017

Okrent, Abigail
Purchases of Foods by Convenience Type Driven by Prices, Income, and Advertising *Amber Waves: The Economics of Food, Farming, Natural Resources, & Rural America* p33 N 2016

Oksanen, Sofi
Norma *Publishers Weekly* v264 no31 p68 Jl 31 2017

Oksvold, Per
A pathology atlas of the human cancer transcriptome diag *Science* v357 no6352 p660 Ag 18 2017
A subcellular map of the human proteome color *Science* v356 no6340 p820 My 26 2017

ÖKTEM, KEREM
An Islamist Power Grab Derails Democracy in Turkey *Current History* v115 no785 p331 D 2016

Oktoberfest
SEPTEMBER bw chart color *Popular Mechanics* p6 S 2017
SEPTEMBER bw chart color *Popular Mechanics* v193 no7 p6 S 2017

Okumu, Fredros
the innovators bw *Foreign Policy* no221 p62 N/D 2016

Okumura, M.
Direct frequency comb measurement of OD + CO→DOCO kinetics bibl graph *Science* v354 no6311 p444 O 28 2016

Okur, Halil I.
Optical imaging of surface chemistry and dynamics in confinement color *Science* v357 no6353 p784 Ag 25 2017

Okuyama, Teruhiro
Engrams and circuits crucial for systems consolidation of a memory diag *Science* v356 no6333 p73 Ap 7 2017

Okuyemi, Kolawole
NIH's mentoring makes progress bibl *Science* v354 no6314 p840 N 18 2016

Olaf I Tryggvason, King of Norway, 968-1000
A STORM IN EVERY PORT D. Stadtler cartoon color map *Military History* v34 no1 p62 My 2017

Olaf's Frozen Adventure (Film)
A Frozen Treat M. Snetiker color *Entertainment Weekly* no1471 p18 Je 23 2017

Ólafsdóttir, Björt
TOWARDS A CLEANER CONSCIENCE Z. ROBERT *Iceland Review* v55 no4 p50 Jl/Ag 2017

OLANDER, LYDIA
Society Is Ready for a New Kind of Science--Is Academia? *BioScience* v67 no7 p591 Jl 2017

Olasky, Catherine

Older people—Employment—United States
The Grayest Professions In America C. Wilson color diag map *Time* v189 no15 p20 Ap 24 2017

Older people—Family relationships
In Middle East conflicts, families struggle to care for elderly members S. Peterson *Christian Century* v134 no3 p16 F 2017

Older people—Finance
Paying It Forward M. SOLHEIM *Kiplinger's Personal Finance* v71 no11 p4 N 2017
Self-Defense Can Ward Off Senior Financial Abuse M. Leonhardt color *Money* v46 no1 p20 Ja/F 2017

Older people—Great Britain—Government policy
Hubris in the U.K A. Stuttaford color *Weekly Standard* v22 no37 p14 Je 5 2017

Older people—Health
Older Adults M. J. Keller *Parks & Recreation* v52 no1 p36 Ja 2017
Rock 'n' Roll, Medicare and Me R. Love cartoon color *AARP: The Magazine* v60 no1A p2 D 2016/Ja 2017

Older people—Mental health
Keep On Moving G. MULLINS-COHEN *Parks & Recreation* v52 no1 p10 Ja 2017

Older people—Orientation & mobility
Mom, Dad: Your House Isn't Safe K. Clark and P. Wang color *Money* v46 no5 p22 Je 2017

Older people—Social aspects
Data on display: Senior shift: Activities change as we age K. Green *Career Outlook* p1 My 2017

Older people—Social networks
Life amid Loss K. Kilby *Commonweal* v144 no4 p13 F 24 2017

Older people—United States
Data on display: Senior shift: Activities change as we age K. Green *Career Outlook* p1 My 2017
A Home for Now and Later C. Fried chart color *Money* v45 no11 p37 D 2016
Life at Trump Pavilion M. PILON color *New Republic* v248 no7 p12 Jl 2017
Moving to Be Near the Grandkids J. BENNETT CLARK *Kiplinger's Personal Finance* v71 no5 p46 My 2017
Senior LIVING R. Bird color *Cincinnati Magazine* v51 no1 p141 O 2017
SUSPICION T. A. FRAIL *Smithsonian* v47 no9 p88 Ja/F 2017
THE TAKEOVER R. AVIV cartoon color *New Yorker* v93 no31 p48 O 9 2017
Your Medicare FAQs K. LANKFORD color *Kiplinger's Personal Finance* v71 no5 p34 My 2017

Older people—United States—Finance
Retirees Shoulder a Bigger Share of Student Debt H. S. Edwards color *Time* v189 no6 p22 F 20 2017

Older people—United States—Services for
Older Adults M. J. Keller *Parks & Recreation* v52 no1 p36 Ja 2017

Older prisoners—Medical care
WHEN PRISONS BECOME NURSING HOMES M. RIGGS bw *Reason* v49 no6 p8 N 2017

Older students
STUDENT DEBT: Good, Bad, and Misunderstood S. Baum *Change* v49 no3 p60 My/Je 2017

Older track & field athletes
FACES IN THE CROWD T. Keith color *Sports Illustrated* v127 no2 p26 Jl 17 2017

Older women
SIEGE MENTALITY Gan *Lapham's Quarterly* v10 no3 p97 Summ 2017

Older women athletes
Keep on Moving J. Fuchs and T. Keith color *Sports Illustrated* v127 no6 p20 Ag 28 2017

Older women—Employment
Older Women Are Being Forced Out of the Workforce L. S. Rikleen *Harvard Business Review Digital Articles* p2 Mr 10 2016
What Work Looks Like for Women in Their 50s A. Wittenberg-Cox *Harvard Business Review Digital Articles* p2 Ap 22 2016

Oldham, Jennifer
Wind Is the New Corn chart color *Bloomberg Businessweek* no4494 p16 O 10 2016

Oldham, Julia
The Loneliest Place color *Art in America* v105 no1 p36 Ja 2017

Oldham, Scott
The Apostate color *Car & Driver* v63 no2 p84 Ag 2017

Old Montreal (Montreal, Québec)—Description & travel
OFF THE GRID M. GRUNBERG BANYASZ color *Archaeology* v70 no2 p10 Mr/Ap 2017

Oldroyd, Giles E. D.
Fatty acids in arbuscular mycorrhizal fungi are synthesized by the host plant diag graph *Science* v356 no6343 p1175 Je 16 2017

Oldroyd, William
Lady Macbeth C. Nashawaty color *Entertainment Weekly* no1474/1475 p98 Jl 21-28 2017
LADY MACBETH R. Kinane color *Entertainment Weekly* no1463/1464 p71 Ap/My 2017

OLDS, SHARON
Letting My Hair Down *Nation* v304 no4 p37 F 6 2017
Silver Spoon Ode *Nation* v304 no4 p36 F 6 2017

Olds, Sharon, 1942-
HER BIRTHDAY AS ASHES IN SEAWATER S. Olds *New Yorker* v92 no32 p86 O 10 2016

Olds, Will
Life's work: Building the church takes everyone [Cover story] color *U.S. Catholic* v82 no8 p22 Ag 2017

Oleanna (Theatrical production)
David Mamet's Prescience G. HILLARD *National Review* v69 no18 p20 O 2 2017

O'Leary, Alan
THE BATTLE OF ALGIERS AT FIFTY: END OF EMPIRE CINEMA AND THE FIRST BANUEUE FILM *Film Quarterly* v70 no2 p17 Wint 2016

O'Leary, Brian F.
Content Discovery and Consumption Go Mobile *Publishers Weekly* v263 no39 p25 S 26 2016
O'Leary Takes the Reins at BISG J. Milliot *Publishers Weekly* v263 no39 p5 S 26 2016

O'Leary, Erin
PUTTING BOOKS TO WORK: Create lessons based on children's and YA books, side by side with the authors themselves, at ILA 2017 color *Literacy Today (2411-7862)* v34 no6 p30 My/Je 2017

O'LEARY, JENNIFER K.
The Resilience of Marine Ecosystems to Climatic Disturbances *BioScience* v67 no3 p208 Mr 2017

O'Leary, John
Do Managers and Leaders Really Do Different Things? *Harvard Business Review Digital Articles* p2 Je 20 2016

O'Leary, Kevin
Advice Worth Taking color *AARP: The Magazine* v59 no2A p30 F/Mr 2016
CANADA'S OWN TWO TINY TRUMPS S. FESCHUK color *Maclean's* v130 no2 p73 Mr 2017
Mr. Wonderful Goes to Ottawa? J. J. McCULLOUGH color *National Review* v69 no3 p25 F 20 2017

O'leary, Lizzie
The Carpet Whisperer *New York Times Magazine* p45 F 26 2017

O'Leary, Maureen
Revisit NIH biosafety guidelines color *Science* v357 no6352 p627 Ag 18 2017

O'LEARY, SHANNON
Graphic Novels Rise, Periodicals Struggle in 2016 color *Publishers Weekly* v264 no7 p36 F 13 2017

O'Leary, William
I would be remiss if I didn't consider the possibility of gratitude *America* v217 no3 p43 Ag 7 2017

Olejarz, J. M.
How Geography Affects Where Elite Consulting Firms Recruit *Harvard Business Review Digital Articles* p2 Jl 5 2016
LIBERAL ARTS IN THE DATA AGE: WHY THE HARD SCIENCES NEED THE HUMANITIES color il *Harvard Business Review* v95 no4 p144 Jl/Ag 2017
The More Experience You Have, the Worse You Are at Bootstrapping *Harvard Business Review Digital Articles* p2 Jl 22 2015
Powerful People React More Unethically to Incentives *Harvard Business Review Digital Articles* p2 Mr 9 2016
Understanding White-Collar Crime il img *Harvard Business Re-*

view v94 no11 p110 N 2016
Wearing Luxury Brands Makes You Seem More Qualified for the
    Job *Harvard Business Review Digital Articles* p2 Ap 9 2015
Why Cybersecurity Is So Difficult to Get Right *Harvard Business
    Review Digital Articles* p2 Jl 27 2015

Olekalns, Mara
Would the World Be Different with Merkel, May, and Clinton in
    Charge? *Harvard Business Review Digital Articles* p2 S 12 2016

Oleksiak, Marjorie F.
The genomic landscape of rapid repeated evolutionary adaptation
    to toxic pollution in wild fish bibl graph *Science* v354 no6317
    p1305 D 9 2016

Oleksiak, Penny
Canada's champion A. HUTCHINS color *Maclean's* v129
    no48/49 p66 D 5 2016

Oleksyn, Jacek
Positive biodiversity-productivity relationship predominant
    in global forests bibl chart graph map *Science* v354 no6309
    paaf8957-1 O 14 2016

Olendzki, Andrew
Advice for Conflict *Tricycle: The Buddhist Review* v26 no4 p29
    Summ 2017
Giving Pain the Slip color *Tricycle: The Buddhist Review* v26 no2
    p30 Wint 2016
Guardians of the World color *Tricycle: The Buddhist Review* v27
    no1 p34 Fall 2017
The Search for Meaning cartoon *Tricycle: The Buddhist Review*
    v26 no3 p28 Spr 2017
When Roads Are Closed for Marathons, More Elderly People Die
    of Heart Attacks *Harvard Business Review Digital Articles* p2
    Ap 12 2017

Olesen, Thomas Agerfeldt
Olesen: The Picture of Dorian Gray J. Rosenblum *Opera News*
    v81 no9 p53 Mr 2017

Oleynick, Griffin
Prophet of Harlem bw *Commonweal* v144 no12 p21 Jl 7 2017
Taking It Personally cartoon *Commonweal* v144 no5 p34 Mr 10
    2017

Olfactory bulb
WE'VE GOT A DOG'S SENSE OF SMELL J. McGann color
    Women's Health v14 no8 p38 O 2017

Olfactory perception
Predicting human olfactory perception from chemical features of
    odor molecules A. Keller, R. C. Gerkin et al bibl diag graph *Sci-
    ence* v355 no6327 p820 F 24 2017
WE'VE GOT A DOG'S SENSE OF SMELL J. McGann color
    Women's Health v14 no8 p38 O 2017

Oligarchy
The Administrative State on the Chopping Block J. W. EMORD
    USA Today Magazine v145 no2864 p18 My 2017
The Atlas That has Not Shrugged: Why Russia's Oligarchs are an
    Unlikely Force for Change S. Markus *Daedalus* v146 no2 p101
    Spr 2017
Conservatives in Denial C. G. RYN *American Conservative* v15
    no6 p32 N/D 2016

Oligonucleotides
A cyclic oligonucleotide signaling pathway in type III CRISPR-
    Cas systems M. Kazlauskiene, G. Kostiuk et al *Science* v357
    no6351 p605 Ag 11 2017

OLIN, KEN
From thirtysomething to This Is Us: My Pop Culture Milestones
    K. OLIN and J. Halterman *TV Guide* v65 no43 p12 O 16 2017
From thirtysomething to This Is Us: My Pop Culture Milestones
    TV Guide v65 no43 p12 O 16 2017

Olin Studio (Company)
11th Street Bridge Park Washington, D.C *Architectural Record*
    v205 no4 p212 Ap 2017

Olinto, A.
Observation of a large-scale anisotropy in the arrival directions
    of cosmic rays above 8×1018 eV *Science* v357 no6357 p1266
    S 22 2017

Olinto, Jon
How a Fast Casual Chain Shows Employees Their Work Matters
    Harvard Business Review Digital Articles p2 N 19 2015

Oliphant, Kelly—Interviews
HOW MEDICINAL CANNABIS HELPED A CANCER SURVI-

VOR LIVE AGAIN A. Yu color *Maclean's* v129 no40 p61 O
    10 2016

Oliva, Jose—Interviews
A fair deal for food workers A. Frykholm color *Christian Century*
    v134 no2 p10 Ja 18 2017

OLIVA, MARISSA
6 mind-blowing mascaras color *Redbook* p62 F 2017
Age-proof your hands color *Redbook* p36 Mr 2017
Get more from your shower! color *Redbook* p30 My 2017
Glow your own way color *Redbook* p36 Je 2017
Go light. Go dramatic. be gorgeous color *Redbook* p6 My 2017
HAIR REPAIR [Cover story] color *Redbook* p32 Je 2017
HAVE A beautiful WINTER color *Redbook* p38 N 2017
Little ways to boost your color color *Redbook* p54 O 2017
MAKEUP MAGIC color *Redbook* p42 O 2017
MAKE YOUR HAIR easy hair color *Redbook* p36 S 2017
Masks that fix everything color *Redbook* p50 S 2017
New shortcuts to flawless skin color *Redbook* p16 My 2017
THE PERFECT HAIR CUT FINDER [Cover story] bw color
    Redbook p36 Ap 2017
Put on liner perfectly cartoon *Redbook* p12 My 2017
SEXY, EASY SHORTCUTS color *Redbook* p52 D 2016
Smoother skin in seconds color *Redbook* p47 Mr 2017
Snap the Ultimate NAILFIE color *Seventeen* v76 no5 p46 S 2017
Sneaky strategies for better hair *Redbook* p50 N 2017
USE THIS MUCH for great hair color *Redbook* p22 My 2017

Olive
One-Pot Wonders C. SAFFITZ color *Bon Appetit* v61 no12 p77
    D 2016 /Jan2017

Olive, Keith
Gary Steigman *Physics Today* v70 no8 p72 Ag 2017

Olive oil
Change Your Oil color *Good Housekeeping* v265 no3 p103 S 2017
Cooking with Chia Seeds [Cover story] R. Robertson color *Amaz-
    ing Wellness* v9 no6 p90 EarlyWint 2017
Growing PAINS J. THOMPSON color *O, The Oprah Magazine*
    p62 Je 2017
Liquid GOLD color *O, The Oprah Magazine* p78 Mr 2017
Liquid Gold C. SAFFITZ and B. CUSHING color *Bon Appetit*
    no11 p60 N 2017

Olive oil industry—Italy
Bramasole Olive Oil color *Bloomberg Businessweek* no4530 p67
    Jl 17 2017

Olive oil—Evaluation
Bramasole Olive Oil color *Bloomberg Businessweek* no4530 p67
    Jl 17 2017

Oliveira, A. A.
Persistent effects of pre-Columbian plant domestication on Ama-
    zonian forest composition bibl chart graph map *Science* v355
    no6328 p925 Mr 3 2017

Oliveira, Victor
WIC Participation Continues To Decline *Amber Waves: The Eco-
    nomics of Food, Farming, Natural Resources, & Rural America*
    p53 Je 2017

Oliveira Passos, Dario
Cryo-EM structures and atomic model of the HIV-1 strand transfer
    complex intasome bibl color *Science* v355 no6320 p1 Ja 6 2017

Oliver, Abbie
Serving on Boards Helps Executives Get Promoted *Harvard Busi-
    ness Review Digital Articles* p2 My 20 2016

OLIVER, CHARLES
BEST OF BRICKBATS: THE OBAMA YEARS, 2009-2016 car-
    toon *Reason* v48 no9 p72 F 2017
BRICKBATS bw color *Reason* v49 no5 p80 O 2017
Brickbats cartoon *Reason* v48 no7 p9 D 2016
BRICKBATS cartoon *Reason* v49 no1 p72 My 2017
BRICKBATS color *Reason* v49 no4 p80 Ag/S 2017
BRICKBATS color *Reason* v49 no6 p80 N 2017
FROM THE ARCHIVES bw cartoon *Reason* v48 no11 p70 Ap
    2017

Oliver, Craig
THAT DIDN'T GO TO PLAN J. HARRIS color *Nation* v304
    no12 p27 Ap 10 2017

Oliver, Garrett
Points to Ponder color *Reader's Digest* v189 no1131 p22 Je 2017

OLIVER, JOAN DUNCAN

The Making of Mummy-la color *Tricycle: The Buddhist Review* v26 no3 p86 Spr 2017

Raising Olsen, Patrick Lettuce, Buddhist Style color *Tricycle: The Buddhist Review* v27 no1 p28 Fall 2017

Oliver, John, 1977-

Old and New Holiday Traditions D. Harris color *Money* v45 no11 p10 D 2016

THE UNKILLABLE TWO-PARTY SYSTEM M. WELCH *Reason* v48 no8 p7 Ja 2017

Oliver, John, 1977——Interviews

John Oliver R. Rahman color *Entertainment Weekly* no1453 p18 F 17 2017

OLIVER, MARY

The Year in Reading [Cover story] *New York Times Book Review* p8 D 25 2016

Oliver, Monica

Competing Against Cancer color *Practical Horseman* v45 no8 p72 Ag 2017

Oliver, Tommy

The Truth About 'Black Love' S. E. Jamison color *Ebony* v72 no9 p66 Jl/Ag 2017

Oliver, William D.

Suppressing relaxation in superconducting qubits by quasiparticle pumping bibl graph *Science* v354 no6319 p1573 D 23 2016

Oliver Twist (Book : Dickens)

MONTHS PAST JUNE *History Today* v67 no6 p22 Je 2016

Olivera-Filho, Ary

Forest conservation: Humans' handprints bibl color *Science* v355 no6324 p466 F 3 2017

Forest conservation: Remember Gran Chaco bibl color *Science* v355 no6324 p465 F 3 2017

Oliveros, Pauline, 1932-2016

The Recordings of Pauline Oliveros Bennett *New York Times Magazine* p20 F 12 2017

Olivetti, Claudia

The Average Mid-Forties Male College Graduate Earns 55% More Than His Female Counterparts *Harvard Business Review Digital Articles* p2 Je 12 2017

Olivieri, Vincent

Balancing Audio and Life *Stage Directions* v30 no3 p10 Mr 2017

Oliynyk, Sandra

Celebrate Simple *Practical Horseman* v45 no10 p10 O 2017

Control What You Can color *Practical Horseman* v45 no1 p8 Ja 2017

Equestrian Idols color *Practical Horseman* v45 no6 p8 Je 2017

Four Disciplines, Similar Themes color *Practical Horseman* v45 no7 p6 Jl 2017

Let Your Horse Figure It Out *Practical Horseman* v45 no3 p8 Mr 2017

Listen to Your Horse *Practical Horseman* v45 no4 p10 Ap 2017

Trust in the Classical System color *Practical Horseman* v45 no9 p12 S 2017

Tune In *Practical Horseman* v45 no11 p8 N 2017

Universal Appeal *Practical Horseman* v45 no8 p8 Ag 2017

Worth the Effort *Practical Horseman* v45 no2 p8 F 2017

Olken, Benjamin A.

Citywide effects of high-occupancy vehicle restrictions: Evidence from "three-in-one" in Jakarta chart graph map *Science* v357 no6346 p89 Jl 7 2017

Ollier-Malaterre, Ariane

How to Separate the Personal and Professional on Social Media *Harvard Business Review Digital Articles* p2 Mr 26 2015

Ollikainen, Noah

Xist recruits the X chromosome to the nuclear lamina to enable chromosome-wide silencing bibl graph *Science* v354 no6311 p468 O 28 2016

Ollinger, Michael

Regulation, Market Signals, and the Provision of Food Safety in Meat and Poultry *Amber Waves: The Economics of Food, Farming, Natural Resources, & Rural America* p1 My 2017

Ollman, Leah

REMATERIALIZING PHOTOGRAPHY color *Art in America* v105 no6 p102 Je/Jl 2017

Ollmann Saphire, Erica

Structural basis for antibody-mediated neutralization of Lassa virus [Cover story] color diag *Science* v356 no6341 p923 Je 1 2017

Ollokot, Nez Percé Chief, ca. 1844-1877

The Spirit of Ollokot L. B. BATEMAN *Idaho Magazine* v16 no6 p42 Mr 2017

Olmecs

KINGS OF COOPERATION [Cover story] L. WADE color *Archaeology* v70 no2 p26 Mr/Ap 2017

Olmstead, Gracy

LIFE AS LITURGY J. TURNER *American Conservative* v15 no6 p4 N/D 2016

Olmstead, Robert

Culling the Herd: A widow and her brother-in-law hunt buffalo in the 1870s R. BASS *New York Times Book Review* p18 O 15 2017

Olmsted, Frederick Law, 1822-1903

Central Parc K. LAIDLAW color *Walrus* v13 no9 p68 N 2016

OLMSTED, LARRY

Book a Last-Minute Trip—Right Now! color *Men's Health* v32 no7 p40 S 2017

Olorunnipa, Toluse

Trump's Real Jobs Crisis chart *Bloomberg Businessweek* no4528 p32 Je 26 2017

O'Loughlin, Alex

HAWAII FIVE-0 J. Halterman *TV Guide* v65 no39 p53 S 18 2017

O'Loughlin, Marina

The Last European Christmas cartoon *Bon Appetit* v61 no12 p66 D 2016 /Jan2017

O'Loughlin, Michael J.

Archbishop Coleridge: Resist 'False Clarity' *America* v216 no1 p9 Ja 2 2017

AS HISPANIC CATHOLIC NUMBERS GROW, CENTER OF GRAVITY FOR U.S. CHURCH SHIFTS TO SOUTH AND WEST bw color graph *America* v217 no7 p12 O 2 2017

As Trump Era Begins, Church Leaders Defend Health Care, Immigration, Worker Rights color *America* v216 no3 p16 F 6 2017

Bishops Await President Trump *America* v215 no18 p9 D 5 2016

Cardinal Nichols: Fight populism by appealing to what is best in people color *America* v216 no7 p16 Ap 3 2017

CATHOLIC SCHOOLS WAIT ON TRUMP SCHOOL CHOICE PROMISES color graph *America* v217 no4 p12 Ag 21 2017

Death Penalty on the Ropes? *America* v215 no11 p8 O 17 2016

Discerning a New Role color *America* v215 no14 p8 N 7 2016

El Paso bishop urges deportation halt until immigration is fixed color *America* v217 no3 p16 Ag 7 2017

In a Cape Cod fishing town, Catholic culture is a blessing color *America* v217 no2 p17 Jl 24 2017

LAWYERS LEAD, PASTORAL WORKERS LAG ON PAY SCALE IN CATHOLIC CHURCH il *America* v217 no5 p12 S 4 2017

New U.S. Cardinals Condemn Polarization Inside the Church color *America* v215 no18 p8 D 5 2016

THE POLITICS OF LIFE AND DEATH color *America* v217 no2 p18 Jl 24 2017

Treatment of transgender people poses new health care challenge color *America* v216 no5 p16 Mr 6 2017

Unprecedented Preaching *America* v215 no15 p10 N 14 2016

U.S. CHURCH WRESTLES WITH CHANGING ATTITUDES, PASTORAL PRACTICE TOWARD L.G.B.T. CATHOLICS chart color *America* v216 no12 p12 My 29 2017

Olsan, Erin E.

Microbiota-activated PPAR-γ signaling inhibits dysbiotic Enterobacteriaceae expansion graph *Science* v357 no6351 p570 Ag 11 2017

Olsen, Andy

IN MEMORY OF THESE [Cover story] bw color *Christianity Today* v61 no7 p34 S 2017

THE MIGRANT MISSIONARIES color *Christianity Today* v61 no6 p38 Jl/Ag 2017

REMEMBER WHEN *Christianity Today* v61 no7 p7 S 2017

THANKS, ROBOTS *Christianity Today* v61 no6 p7 Jl/Ag 2017

Olsen, Angel

Angel Olsen: Boss Lady S. EXPOSITO color *Rolling Stone* no1272 p18 O 20 2016

Angel Olsen [Cover story] M. Rich color *Current Biography* v78 no6 p83 Je 2017

Olsen, Ashley, 1986-

MARY-KATE & ASHLEY OLSEN E. ELWICK-BATES color *Vogue* v207 no3 p428 Mr 2017

Olsen, Carl Erik

Characterization of a dynamic metabolon producing the defense compound dhurrin in sorghum bibl graph *Science* v354 no6314 p890 N 18 2016

Olsen, Elizabeth, 1989-

CAUSE & EFFECT C. Shanahan color *InStyle* v24 no3 p138 Mr 2017

Olsen, Elizabeth, 1989—Interviews

STYLE CRUSH Elizabeth Olsen S. Simon color *InStyle* v24 no11 p86 N 2017

Olsen, Eric

Farm, Fresher K. Renda color *House Beautiful* p41 Jl 2017

Olsen, Eric Christian—Interviews

NCIS: Los Angeles A. D'Arminio *TV Guide* v64 no46 p32 N 7 2016

Olsen, Greg

Enjoy the Ride S. BROWN color *Timber Home Living* p6 2017 Annual Buyers

OLSEN, HENRY

Don't Forget High Earners *National Review* v69 no19 p32 O 16 2017

Hardly Working K. WILLIAMSON *Commentary* v144 no2 p39 S 2017

Obama's Young Garden [Cover story] il *National Review* v69 no1 p24 Ja 23 2017

Reagan Reconsidered J. COST bw *Weekly Standard* v22 no44 p30 Jl 31 2017

Tax Reform For the Working Class *National Review* v69 no9 p16 My 15 2017

Trump Democrats il *National Review* v68 no22 p22 D 5 2016

Was Ronald Reagan an FDR Republican? M. BARONE *American Conservative* v16 no5 p60 S/O 2017

Olsen, Ken

Ensuring a Moveable Feast color *National Wildlife (World Edition)* v55 no2 p14 F/Mr 2017

Railway Post Office color *Model Railroader* v84 no8 p16 Ag 2017

OLSEN, KIM

5 Tips to sell a Super-Pricey House color *Washingtonian Magazine* v52 no7 p98 Ap 2017

ALEXANDRIA: Where to eat, shop, and explore *Washingtonian Magazine* v53 no1 p176 O 2017

BEST & WORST OF WASHINGTON *Washingtonian Magazine* v52 no9 p12 Je 2017

FREAKY FANTASTIC GEORGETOWN *Washingtonian Magazine* v52 no11 p10 Ag 2017

IS DC BECOMING THE GAY CAPITAL OF AMERICA? *Washingtonian Magazine* v53 no1 p10 O 2017

NAVE-GAZING color *Washingtonian Magazine* v52 no7 p24 Ap 2017

THE SUPREMACIST NEXT DOOR: What to do about a notorious new neighbor? *Washingtonian Magazine* v52 no11 p21 Ag 2017

TAKING STOCK color *Washingtonian Magazine* v52 no7 p129 Ap 2017

WARDENSVILLE TOWN CRIERS *Washingtonian Magazine* v52 no12 p12 S 2017

WHERE & WHEN color *Washingtonian Magazine* v52 no7 p31 Ap 2017

Olsen, Mary-Kate, 1986-

MARY-KATE & ASHLEY OLSEN E. ELWICK-BATES color *Vogue* v207 no3 p428 Mr 2017

Olsen, Michael J.

Mitigating coastal landslide damage color *Science* v357 no6355 p981 S 8 2017

Olsen, Nick

#1: For a dapper New Yorker, Nick Olsen crafts a kaleidoscopic fantasia of freewheeling color, one-of a-kind auction finds, and yin-yang contrasts—plus a bedroom as handsomely tailored as a bespoke suit K. RENDA color *House Beautiful* v159 no2 p82 Mr 2017

Olsen, Patrick

Cars That Go the Distance chart color diag *Consumer Reports* v82 no12 p52 D 2017

Olsen, Roy

THE FORMAL FAÇADE IMPROVED color *Old House Journal* v45 no5 p32 Ag 2017

OLSEN, TED

DIFFERENTLY MORAL cartoon *Christianity Today* p23 Ap 2017

DO YOU KNOW THIS SONG? *Christianity Today* p7 Ap 2017

EDITOR'S NOTE color *Christianity Today* v61 no1 p7 Ja/F 2017

FLEE THE RIGHTEOUS LUST color *Christianity Today* v61 no7 p25 S 2017

THE OTHER CHRISTIANITY TODAY *Christianity Today* v60 no8 p7 O 2016

RELATED LINKS *Christianity Today* v61 no5 p9 Je 2017

WHITHER WILLPOWER? When entering disputed territory, you need a good guide color *Christianity Today* v61 no4 p7 My 2017

WHY CHRISTIANITY TODAY REVISITED color *Christianity Today* v60 no8 p46 O 2016

Olson, Aaron K.

A Story from Google Shows You Don't Need Power to Drive Strategy *Harvard Business Review Digital Articles* p2 Ap 29 2015

OLSON, BOBBI

Dairy family raises COWS AND QUADRUPLETS color *Nebraska Life* v21 no2 p44 Mr/Ap 2017

OLSON, DAVID

An Ecoregion-Based Approach to Protecting Half the Terrestrial Realm *BioScience* v67 no6 p534 Je 2017

Olson, Donald W.

The Comets of Edgar Allan Poe *Sky & Telescope* v132 no6 p30 D 2016

"The Moon Is Up . . . A Single Star Is at Her Side" bw color *Sky & Telescope* v134 no2 p68 Ag 2017

Who Discovered the Ring Nebula? [Cover story] *Sky & Telescope* v133 no6 p32 Je 2017

Olson, Eric N.

Control of muscle formation by the fusogenic micropeptide myomixer diag *Science* v356 no6335 p323 Ap 21 2017

Olson, John

FINGER PAINTING N. Daly color *National Geographic* v231 no6 p2 Je 2017

Olson, Kaitlin

ACCORDING TO: Kaitlin Olson J. DUBOFF bw *Vanity Fair* v59 no11 p72 N 2017

Cheers & Jeers D. HOLBROOK *TV Guide* v65 no2 p84 Ja 2 2017

The Mick N. Abrams, A. Bacle et al *Entertainment Weekly* no1482/1483 p67 S 22 2017

Olson, Kaitlin—Interviews

KAITLIN OLSON D. Snierson color *Entertainment Weekly* no1446/1447 p110 D 2016/Ja 2017

The Mick *TV Guide* p40 D 19 2016

OLSON, KAREN

What's your favorite work of public art? color *American Craft* v77 no3 p16 Je/Jl 2017

Olson, Karen E.

Betrayed: The Nicole Jones Series *Publishers Weekly* v264 no5 p181 Ja 30 2017

Olson, Kate

Hermitage sees surge in laypeople who want a monastic experience color *Christian Century* v134 no10 p18 My 10 2017

OLSON, KRISTINA R.

WHEN SEX AND GENDER COLLIDE color *Scientific American* v317 no3 p44 S 2017

Olson, Lauren

Oshkosh: Heart of Garden County A. J. BARTELS and D. CARPENTER-NOLTING color *Nebraska Life* v21 no5 p52 S/O 2017

OLSON, LINK E.

Transformational Principles for NEON Sampling of Mammalian Parasites and Pathogens: A Response to Springer and Colleagues *BioScience* v66 no11 p917 N 1 2016

Olson, Lynne

Last Days bw *New York Times Book Review* p11 S 25 2016

The Liberation Game H. EVANS *New York Times Book Review* p20 My 7 2017

Olson, Nels

Why CIOs Make Great Board Directors *Harvard Business Review Digital Articles* p2 Mr 15 2017

OLSON, PARMY
  Buy Now, Pay Later color *Forbes* v198 no7 p88 N 29 2016
  Dial-a-Caravan color *Forbes* v199 no7 p41 Je 29 2017
  Old World, Young Promise color *Forbes* v199 no1 p20 Ja 24 2017
  Tech's Royal Kingmaker *Forbes* v199 no4 p42 Ap 25 2017
OLSON, RICHARD
  Chinese technocracy *Issues in Science & Technology* v33 no2 p15 Wint 2017
Olson, Robert J.
  Physiological and ecological drivers of early spring blooms of a coastal phytoplankter bibl graph *Science* v354 no6310 p326 O 21 2016
OLSON, ROGER E.
  Grace stet OR Grace ALONE? bw *Christianity Today* p42 Ap 2017
OLSON, STEVE
  Dairy family raises COWS AND QUADRUPLETS color *Nebraska Life* v21 no2 p44 Mr/Ap 2017
Olson, Theodore B.
  Jill Stein's Recounts Are Destructive to Democracy *Time* v188 no24 p18 D 12 2016
OLSON, WALTER
  FROM THE ARCHIVES bw *Reason* v49 no1 p70 My 2017
Olsson, Nina
  SALAD DAYS color *House Beautiful* p164 Ag 2017
Olsson, Tjelvar S. G.
  Distinct phases of Polycomb silencing to hold epigenetic memory of cold in Arabidopsis diag *Science* v357 no6356 p1142 S 15 2017
Olstein, Lisa, 1972-
  Late Empire *Publishers Weekly* v264 no38 p51 S 18 2017
Oltion, Jerry
  Brent's Beauties *Sky & Telescope* v133 no5 p72 My 2017
  Build Your Own On-Axis Guider *Sky & Telescope* v133 no1 p72 Ja 2017
  The Craig Daniels Dogson Telescope *Sky & Telescope* v133 no2 p70 F 2017
  The Dethloff Eyepiece Shade *Sky & Telescope* v133 no4 p72 Ap 2017
  A Foolproof Analemma Box: This project practically guarantees good results *Sky & Telescope* v134 no6 p68 D 2017
  Low-Tech Eclipse Viewing: What to do if you're caught without optics on eclipse day color *Sky & Telescope* v134 no2 p66 Ag 2017
  Make a Solar Filter *Sky & Telescope* v133 no6 p38 Je 2017
  A Simple Observing Stool, Plus: Build the Swiss Army Knife of observing stools *Sky & Telescope* v134 no3 p70 S 2017
  Solar Finders: How to point out the obvious *Sky & Telescope* v134 no1 p72 Jl 2017
  State of the Art — 63 Years Ago: How amateur telescope making was done in the early days *Sky & Telescope* v134 no4 p70 O 2017
  State of the Art – Today: Here's a look at the cutting edge of telescope technology now color *Sky & Telescope* v134 no5 p72 N 2017
  Take Make a Seat *Sky & Telescope* v132 no6 p70 D 2016
  Understanding Surface Brightness *Sky & Telescope* v134 no6 p28 D 2017
Oltmanns, Marilena
  Ice, Wind & Fury color *Oceanus* v51 no2 p24 Wint 2016
Oltuski, Romy
  JARED LETO TELLS ALL color *Harper's Bazaar* no3648 p192 N 2016
  War and Peace color *InStyle* v24 no11 p94 N 2017
  YOU'RE YOUNGER. HE'S OLDER. WHY DO PEOPLE STILL CARE? color *Women's Health* v14 no5 p108 Je 2017
Olukotun, Deji Bryce
  After the Flare *Publishers Weekly* v264 no28 p62 Jl 10 2017
Olunloyo, Shola
  TOOLS THEY USE color *Popular Mechanics* p112 D 2016/Ja 2017
OLUO, IJEOMA
  My Mother Gives the Weirdest Gifts *Reader's Digest* v188 no1126 p14 D 2016/Ja 2017
Olusoga, David
  DAVID OLUSOGA *History Today* v67 no8 p112 Ag 2017

Oluwa, Moji—Interviews
  A Born Natural J. KINDELA chart color *Muscle & Performance* v9 no8 p30 Ag 2017
Olvera, Michael P.
  CRISPRi-based genome-scale identification of functional long noncoding RNA loci in human cells bibl graph *Science* v355 no6320 p1 Ja 6 2017
Olympia (Wash.)—Description & travel
  WASHINGTON'S OLYMPIA R. Denn color map *Sunset* v238 no5 p34 My 2017
Olympia oyster
  THE WILD OYSTERP ROJECT: Saving Oysters to Save Ourselves L. HUNTER color *Earth Island Journal* v32 no2 p13 Summ 2017
Olympic (Company)
  OUTDOOR PAINT color *Good Housekeeping* v264 no5 p68P My 2017
Olympic athletes
  Catching Up With Olympian Lucy Davis K. Rover *In Stride* v12 no1 p46 Ja 2017
  The first modern Olympic Games *History Today* v67 no4 p9 Ap 2017
  THE GOLD STANDARD [Cover story] T. Layden chart color *Sports Illustrated* v125 no21 p30 D 26 2016
  NEVER LOOK BACK J. KINDELA color *Muscle & Performance* v9 no4 p30 Ap 2017
Olympic athletes—Education
  The Olympian on campus A. HUTCHINS color *Maclean's* v130 no10 p58 N 2017
Olympic Games
  See also
    Olympic medals
  Fleet Geek K. FOX color *Runner's World* v52 no4 p39 My 2017
  Gold Medal C. WRIGHT color *Climbing* no351 p30 F/Mr 2017
  THE INTERSECTION color *Runner's World* v52 no2 p19 Mr 2017
  Now Arriving (Really!) on Second Avenue img *New York* v49 no25 p18 D 12 2016
  The Olympics Needs a New Business Model C. Nickisch *Harvard Business Review Digital Articles* p2 Ag 5 2016
  A SICK FINISH K. A. FETTERS color *Runner's World* v51 no10 p33 N 2016
  Sport Promoting Human Development and Well-Being: Psychological Components of Sustainability J. M. GARY and N. S. RUBIN *UN Chronicle* v53 no2 p30 2016
  WHEN OLYMPIC GAMES MEET MARTIAL ARTS R. W. Young color *Black Belt* v55 no1 p8 D 2016/Ja 2017
Olympic Games—Congresses
  Torching L.A.'s Olympic Plans L. WOODHOUSE *In These Times* v41 no10 p12 O 2017
Olympic Games—History
  The first modern Olympic Games *History Today* v67 no4 p9 Ap 2017
Olympic medals
  Simone Manuel B. Muteba color *Current Biography* v78 no3 p54 Mr 2017
Olympic Mountains (Wash.)
  SAN JUAN ISLANDS GEMS D. HISLOP *Sea Magazine* v109 no4 p1 Ap 2017
Olympic National Park (Wash.)
  Mercy Rule E. KWAK-HEFFERAN color *Backpacker* p22 My 2017
  The Most Silent Night A. Castleman *Sierra* v101 no6 p14 N/D 2016
Olympic Winter Games
  See also
    Olympic Winter Games (23rd : 2018 : Pyeongchang, South Korea)
Olympic Games (17th : 1960 : Rome, Italy)
  Original Miracle on Ice A. Fenwick and T. Keith color *Sports Illustrated* v125 no13 p20 O 17 2016
Olympic Games (31st : 2016 : Rio de Janeiro, Brazil)
  THE FEMMEPIRE STRIKES BACK bw color *GQ: Gentlemen's Quarterly* v86 no12 p160 D 2016
  Mr. Comeback *Tennis* v52 no6 p72 N/D 2016
  News BITS color *Practical Horseman* v45 no6 p70 Je 2017

Olympic Games (32nd : 2020 : Tokyo, Japan)
The American "Meh" J. HOUSMAN color *Surfer* v58 no3 p30 Je 2017
KARATE WINS ITS OLYMPIC BID F. BURK color *Black Belt* v55 no1 p44 D 2016/Ja 2017
Roads? Where We're Going ... K. Samuelson color *Time* v189 no23 p14 Je 19 2017
Veterans Aiming for 2020 Games A. Cort color *Sail* v48 no6 p16 Je 2017

Olympic Winter Games (23rd : 2018 : Pyeongchang, South Korea)
HOT IN THE COLD color *Sports Illustrated* v126 no5 p88 F 13 2017
WHAT WILL TEAM USA LOOK LIKE AT THE OLYMPICS? J. Fuchs color *Sports Illustrated* v127 no11 p44 O 9 2017

Olympus camera—Evaluation
NEW PRODUCTS *Physics Today* v70 no1 p64 Ja 2017

Olympus Corp.
TOUGH LOVE P. Ryan color graph *Popular Photography* v81 no2 p82 Mr/Ap 2017

Om
SONIC HEALING A. Russell cartoon *New Yorker* v93 no20 p26 Jl 10 2017

Om El Arab International (Company)
California BREEDERS AND TRAINERS California BREEDERS AND TRAINERS California BREEDERS AND TRAINERS *Arabian Horse World* v57 no10 p93 Jl 2017
The Other Mare B. FINKE *Arabian Horse World* v57 no2 p132 N 2016

Omaha (Neb.)
Delightful fusion of worldly food in Omaha S. W. KANSTEINER color *Nebraska Life* v21 no4 p50 Jl/Ag 2017
OMAHA, NEBRASKA Z. Murff *Harper's Magazine* p33 O 2017

O'Mahony, John
The Start of a New Legacy color *Bloomberg Businessweek* no4493 p2 O 3 2016

O'Mahony, Siobhan
A Study Shows How to Find New Ideas Inside and Outside the Company *Harvard Business Review Digital Articles* p2 Jl 18 2017

O'MALLEY, J. P.
Stefan Zweig's Ordeal bw *American Conservative* v16 no3 p39 My/Je 2017

O'Malley, John W.
The man who fought papal infallibility color *America* v217 no2 p44 Jl 24 2017

O'MALLEY, MARY NETTLETON
A Bell for the Queen: In a High-Desert Haven *Idaho Magazine* v16 no10 p24 Jl 2017

O'Malley, Maureen
TALK TO US color graph *Chicago* v66 no8 p17 Ag 2017

Omar, Ilhan
MINNESOTA NICE R. Forgrave color *Mother Jones* v42 no3 p7 My/Je 2017
Unity Will Take Generations *Time* v190 no8 p44 Ag 28 2017

O'MARA, COLLIN
Adopting a New Vision for Wildlife color *National Wildlife (World Edition)* v54 no6 p6 O/N 2016
How Do You Save a Species? Save Its Habitat *National Wildlife (World Edition)* v55 no4 p6 Je/Jl 2017
Looking Forward to New Growth color *National Wildlife (World Edition)* v55 no3 p6 Ap/My 2017
Making the Case for Conservation color *National Wildlife (World Edition)* v55 no6 p6 O/N 2017
Ranger Rick Helps Teach a Love of Nature color *National Wildlife (World Edition)* v55 no2 p6 F/Mr 2017
United in the Fight for Conservation color *National Wildlife (World Edition)* v55 no5 p6 Ag/S 2017
Uniting Americans for Wildlife color *National Wildlife (World Edition)* v55 no1 p6 D/Ja 2016

O'Mare, T. J.
Winner's CIRCLE color *Practical Horseman* v44 no12 p64 D 2016

O'Meara, Mark Linden
Let Go, Heal, Be Happy: An In-Depth Roadmap to Life-long Emotional Mastery *Publishers Weekly* v264 no7 p67 F 13 2017

O'Meara, Rachael
If You're Fed Up with Your Job, Try Working More Pauses into Your Day *Harvard Business Review Digital Articles* p2 Ap 7 2017

O'MEARA, STEPHEN JAMES
Cloudshine color *Astronomy* v45 no7 p20 Jl 2017
The color purple color *Astronomy* v45 no9 p20 S 2017
Coronal shadows color *Astronomy* v45 no8 p80 Ag 2017
Discover 10 weird emission nebulae color *Astronomy* v45 no5 p44 My 2017
FALL INTO AUTUMN GALAXIES color *Astronomy* v45 no11 p46 N 2017
A fishy tale in the fall sky color *Astronomy* v45 no11 p16 N 2017
Hello, Moon color *Astronomy* v45 no10 p66 O 2017
The pulsing Moon color *Astronomy* v45 no1 p64 Ja 2017
Seven dwarfs of winter color *Astronomy* v44 no12 p18 D 2016
Skipping through the Virgo Cluster color *Astronomy* v45 no4 p58 Ap 2017
The Sun's crystal horns color *Astronomy* v45 no2 p18 F 2017
The Sun's 'shimmering' corona color *Astronomy* v45 no6 p60 Je 2017
Telescopic sprites color *Astronomy* v45 no4 p66 Ap 2017
Twice-setting stars color *Astronomy* v45 no3 p20 Mr 2017
Uncommon bino galaxies color *Astronomy* v45 no5 p20 My 2017

Omega-3 fatty acids
A Nutrient to Avoid Early Delivery color *Parents* v92 no3 p72 Mr 2017
Potent Cancer Fighters K. Gazella *Amazing Wellness* v9 no1 p30 Wint 2017

Omega-3 fatty acids—Evaluation
CARLSON MAXIMUM OMEGA 2000 color *Muscle & Performance* v9 no6 p62 Je 2017
Get More WH bw color *Women's Health* v14 no1 p20 Ja/F 2017

Omega-3 fatty acids—Research
OIL UP For Results J. WUEBBEN color *Muscle & Performance* v8 no12 p13 D 2016

Omega-3 fatty acids—Therapeutic use
Do omega-3s protect your thinking skills? *Harvard Health Letter* v42 no1 p3 N 2016

Omega-6 fatty acids
For a Better Mood chart color *AARP: The Magazine* v59 no3A p36 Ap/My 2016

Omelets
KNOW WHEN TO FOLD 'EM color *Men's Health* v32 no3 p57 Ap 2017

Omelicheva, Mariya Y.
Red Herring *Harper's Magazine* v334 no2001 p2 F 2017

Omene, Gulia
happy teeth A. OGLETHORPE color *Better Homes & Gardens* v95 no3 p152 Mr 2017

Omens
Never Fear! There's History Behind These Superstitions B. SPECKTOR color *Reader's Digest* v190 no1134 p130 O 2017

Omeprazole
INJECTABLE ULCER DRUG MAY SOON BE AVAILABLE C. Barakat and M. McCluskey color *Equus* no478 p17 Jl 2017

Omer, Arina D.
De novo assembly of the Aedes aegypti genome using Hi-C yields chromosome-length scaffolds chart color diag *Science* v356 no6333 p92 Ap 7 2017

Omerbašić, Damir
Fructose-driven glycolysis supports anoxia resistance in the naked mole-rat diag graph *Science* v356 no6335 p307 Ap 21 2017

OMETTO, JEAN
Synthesis Centers as Critical Research Infrastructure *BioScience* v67 no8 p750 Ag 2017

OMICS Group Inc.
U.S. charges journal publisher with misleading authors J. Bohannon *Science* v354 no6308 p23 O 7 2016

Omnirange system
A REVIEW OF THE BASICS diag *Flying* v144 no4 p29 Ap 2017
THE SYNTHETIC AND THE REAL P. Garrison color *Flying* v144 no7 p80 Jl 2017

Omori, Chizu
UNWANTED *Saturday Evening Post* v289 no3 p30 My/Je 2017

Omori, Emiko

RABBIT IN AND OUT OF THE MOON: A RETROSPECTIVE OF EMIKO OMORI Ling Zhang *Film Quarterly* v71 no1 p42 Fall 2017

Omorovicza (Company)
BETTER WITH AGE A. Mangum color *Bloomberg Businessweek* no4507 p62 Ja 16 2017

Omran, Ahmed
Revealing hidden antiferromagnetic correlations in doped Hubbard chains via string correlators bw diag graph *Science* v357 no6350 p484 Ag 4 2017

On a Discharged Firework (Poem)
On a Discharged Firework J. M. Wilson *America* v217 no4 p43 Ag 21 2017

On a Shaker Admonition (Poem)
On a Shaker Admonition *American Scholar* v86 no1 p54 Wint 2017

On Distance (Quondam/Quantum Overdue Notice) (Poem)
ON DISTANCE (QUONDAM/QUANTUM OVERDUE NOTICE) L. Waldner *New Yorker* v92 no46 p63 Ja 23 2017

On Hold (Music)
NEW TUNES FOR THE NEW YEAR color *Entertainment Weekly* no1448 p60 Ja 13 2017
The Playlist color *Rolling Stone* no1275 p8 D 1 2016

On the Beach at Night Alone (Film)
Two from the Heart R. Brody color *New Yorker* v93 no30 p8 O 2 2017

On the Origin of Species (Book : Darwin)
The Surprising Origin of Canada's Thanksgiving O. B. Waxman *Time* v190 no15 p19 O 16 2017

On the Road Again (Music)
Nashville Toasts the CMAs at 50 E. Finan color *Entertainment Weekly* no1434 p18 O 7 2016

On the Street Where You Live (Short story)
ON THE STREET WHERE YOU LIVE YIYUN LI cartoon color *New Yorker* v92 no44 p60 Ja 9 2017

Onaran, Yalman
Banking Regulation color *Bloomberg Businessweek* no4502 p47 D 5 2016
How to Launder A Russian graph *Bloomberg Businessweek* no4522 p17 My 15 2017

Onassis, Jacqueline Kennedy, 1929-1994
THE ALLURE OF JACKIE S. Mooallem bw color *Harper's Bazaar* no3650 p184 F 2017
Being Jackie Kennedy color *Entertainment Weekly* no1442 p42 D 2 2016 Rebellious Special Issue

Onbasli, Mehmet C.
Control and local measurement of the spin chemical potential in a magnetic insulator bw diag *Science* v357 no6347 p195 Jl 14 2017

Onboarding (Management coaching)
Onboarding Isn't Enough M. BYFORD, M. D. WATKINS et al color diag graph il img *Harvard Business Review* v95 no3 p78 My/Je 2017
The Powerful Way Onboarding Can Encourage Authenticity D. Cable, F. Gino et al *Harvard Business Review Digital Articles* p2 N 26 2015
Technology Can Save Onboarding from Itself K. Ferrazzi *Harvard Business Review Digital Articles* p2 Mr 25 2015

Once on This Island (Theatrical production)
Fall Preview M. Schulman color *New Yorker* v93 no25 p6 Ag 28 2017

Once Upon a Time (TV program)
CHEERS & JEERS D. HOLBROOK *TV Guide* v65 no23 p84 My 29 2017
Inside Once Upon a Time's Big Reset N. Abrams color *Entertainment Weekly* no1467 p52 My 26 2017
Once Upon a Time M. Logan *TV Guide* v65 no19 p36 My 1 2017
Once Upon a Time N. Abrams, S. Highfill et al color *Entertainment Weekly* no1482/1483 p96 S 22 2017

Oncogenic DNA viruses
See also
Papillomaviruses
How DNA Can Guide Cancer Treatments A. Park color *Time* v190 no15 p46 O 16 2017

Oncologists
I Treated Breast Cancer for Years As a Doctor. Then I Was Diag-

nosed P. Munster color *Time* v190 no15 p46 O 16 2017
TOP DOCTORS 2017 *Cincinnati Magazine* p84 Je 2017

Oncology
The challenges and prospects of precision oncology Lun-Xiu Qin bibl *Science* v354 no6319 p22 D 23 2016

Oncor Electric Delivery Co. LLC
Deal Snapshot: Oncor Electric Delivery Co R. Collins, J. Polson et al bw graph *Bloomberg Businessweek* no4530 p19 Jl 17 2017

Ondaatje, Christopher
CANADA'S NATIONAL BIRD THE GRAY JAY [Cover story] N. Walker, L. Anthony et al color map *Canadian Geographic* v136 no6 p36 D 2016

Onder, Catherine
Deals R. DEAHL color *Publishers Weekly* v264 no29 p6 Jl 17 2017

Ondra, Adam, 1993-
NEW DAWN J. LUCAS color *Climbing* no351 p72 F/Mr 2017
What Inspires You? J. ELLISON color *Climbing* no351 p17 F/Mr 2017

Ondra, Adam, 1993——Interviews
Next-Gen Visualization J. FLASHMAN color *Climbing* no357 p16 N 2017

One Aviation Corp.
550 ONE AVIATION'S ECLIPSE R. MARK bw chart color *Flying* v144 no2 p38 F 2017
ECLIPSE 700 MAKES BOLD STATEMENT color *Flying* v144 no8 p16 Ag 2017

One Dance (Music)
SINGLES OF THE YEAR R. SHEFFIELD color *Rolling Stone* no1276 p18 D 15 2016

One Day at a Time (TV program)
Latina faith and family S. B. Plate *Christian Century* v134 no13 p43 Je 21 2017
LATINA LESBIAN TAKES ON NEW MEANING IN TRUMP ERA Y. VILLARREAL color *Advocate* no1090 p58 Ap 2017
One Day at a Time M. Logan *TV Guide* v65 no2 p28 Ja 2 2017
One (More) Day at a Time img *New York* v49 no26 p78 D 26 2016
Telling a Family Story S. Wloszczyna color *AARP: The Magazine* v60 no1A p9 D 2016/Ja 2017

One-design sailboats
100 years OF BOATS [Cover story] A. Cort color *Sail* v48 no8 p30 Ag 2017

One Direction (Performer)
The One Direction Solo Guide color *Rolling Stone* no1293 p21 Ag 10 2017
One Direction? Try 5 Directions A. Bacle and N. Feeney color *Entertainment Weekly* no1477 p58 Ag 11 2017

One Eight Distilling (Company)
The Great Whiskey Mash-Up F. MAROUKIAN color *Popular Mechanics* p22 Mr 2017

One Lap of America (Rally)
One Lap of America D. Freiburger color *Hot Rod* v70 no9 p114 S 2017

One Mississippi (TV program)
SHOW AND TELL E. NUSSBAUM color *New Yorker* v93 no31 p76 O 9 2017

One Night (Music)
'One Night' J. L. KEILES color *New York Times Magazine* p28 Mr 12 2017

One Ocean Expeditions (Company)
ONE OCEAN EXPEDITIONS EXPANDS FLEET TO INCLUDE RCGS RESOLUTE S. Doyle color *Canadian Geographic* v137 no5 p75 S/O 2017

One-person shows (Performing arts)——Reviews
In the Shadow Of a Bear J. Tarmy color *Bloomberg Businessweek* no4541 p66 O 9 2017

One Week & a Day (Film)
Dazed and Bereaved D. EDELSTEIN img *New York* v50 no8 p132 Ap 17 2017

One World Technologies Inc,
ELECTRIC MOWERS J. SCHADEWALD color *Popular Mechanics* p22 Je 2017

One97 Communications Ltd.
The Young and the Restless K. VINTON color *Forbes* v199 no3 p32 Mr 28 2017

O'NEAL, AMY

STREET TO STAGE *Dance Magazine* v91 no7 p42 Jl 2017

O'Neal, Blair
A BEND FOR BIG DRIVES color *Golf Magazine* v59 no1 p48 Ja 2017
GET A LEG UP ON THE TEE color *Golf Magazine* v59 no2 p56 F 2017

O'NEAL, SEAN
WELCOME BACK TO TWIN PEAKS bw color *GQ: Gentlemen's Quarterly* v97 no4 p128 Ap 2017

O'Neal, Shaquille, 1972-
I'M THE REAL SHAQUILLE A. Prewitt color diag *Sports Illustrated* v127 no1 p60 Jl 3 2017
UNQUALIFIED CATCH-UP C. Everett color *Entertainment Weekly* no1436/1437 p28 O 21 2016

O'Neal, Tatum, 1963-
Tatum O'Neal N. Sperling color *Entertainment Weekly* no1460/1461 p30 Ap 7-17 2017

Oneida Air Systems Inc.
Around the House color *Old House Journal* v45 no4 p50 Je 2017

O'Neil, Alison Linsley
Lee Rubin: Our mentor and role model *Science* v355 no6327 p806 F 24 2017

O'Neil, Anica
The Empty Bowls Soup Tale: How you can help fight hunger in New Orleans *Parks & Recreation* v52 no8 p36 Ag 2017

O'Neil, Cathy
ALGORITHM BLUES S. Kolhatkar cartoon *New Yorker* v92 no32 p38 O 10 2016
DOESN'T ADD UP J. Derbyshire *Claremont Review of Books* v17 no2 p61 Spr 2017
Hiring Algorithms Are Not Neutral *Harvard Business Review Digital Articles* p2 D 9 2016
Life in the age of the algorithm color *Science* v355 no6321 p137 Ja 13 2017
WEAPONS OF MATH DESTRUCTION *Saturday Evening Post* v289 no2 p40 Mr/Ap 2017

o'neil, devon
I SURVIVED color *Men's Health* v32 no6 p128 Ag 2017
THE LIGHTNING ROD color *Bike Magazine* v24 no8 p58 N 2017
LINES IN THE DIRT [Cover story] bw color *Bike Magazine* v24 no7 p60 S 2017
over drive bw color *Bike Magazine* v24 no7 p66 S 2017
warm front color *Bike Magazine* v24 no5 p34 Jl 2017

O'Neil, James P.
A catalytic fluoride-rebound mechanism for C(sp3)-CF3 bond formation diag *Science* v356 no6344 p1272 Je 23 2017

O'Neil, Jonathan
Building Archean cratons from Hadean mafic crust bibl graph *Science* v355 no6330 p1199 Mr 17 2017
Eureka in the Arctic M. CAMPBELL color *Maclean's* v130 no3 p18 Ap 2017

O'Neil, Joseph
THE MUSTACHE IN 2010 J. O'Neill *Harper's Magazine* v335 no2006 p77 Jl 2017
Pardon Edward Snowden J. O'Neill bw cartoon *New Yorker* v92 no41 p64 D 12 2016

O'Neil, Kathleen
S&T Policy Forum examines evolving opioid epidemic color *Science* v356 no6336 p390 Ap 28 2017

O'Neil, Shannon K.
Latin America's Populist Hangover color *Foreign Affairs* v95 no6 p31 N/D 2016

O'Neill, Deborah
If Your Company Isn't Good at Analytics, It's Not Ready for AI color *Harvard Business Review Digital Articles* p2 Je 7 2017
Using Data to Strengthen Your Connections to Customers *Harvard Business Review Digital Articles* p2 Ag 25 2016

O'Neill, Ed, 1946-
Modern Family N. Abrams, B. L. Heldman et al *Entertainment Weekly* no1482/1483 p75 S 22 2017

O'NEILL, EDDIE
BAKE TO THE FUTURE *Missouri Life* v43 no7 p46 D 2016/Ja 2017
THE BIRDMAN OF SALEM color *Missouri Life* v44 no2 p26 Ap 2017

THE PANCAKE PICASSO *Missouri Life* v43 no6 p26 O/N 2016
SUBURBAN COWBOY color *Missouri Life* v44 no5 p26 Ag 2017
Take Me Away! color *Missouri Life* v44 no3 p32 My 2017

O'Neill, Eugene, 1888-1953
THE FALL GUYS H. ALS color *New Yorker* v93 no8 p74 Ap 10 2017

O'Neill, Heather
Ms. Lonelyhearts A. FORGET color *Walrus* p60 Ja\F 2017
'Oh, DUBAI. I do not understand you' color map *Canadian Geographic* v137 p30 2017 Travel

O'Neill, J.
Superficial layers of the medial entorhinal cortex replay independently of the hippocampus bibl graph *Science* v355 no6321 p1 Ja 13 2017

O'Neill, Jack
Editor's Note color *Surfer* v58 no5 p10 S 2017

O'Neill, Joseph
THE MUSTACHE IN 2010 *Harper's Magazine* v335 no2006 p77 Jl 2017
Pardon Edward Snowden bw cartoon *New Yorker* v92 no41 p64 D 12 2016

O'NEILL, KAREN M.
Planning for the Future of Urban Biodiversity: A Global Review of City-Scale Initiatives *BioScience* v67 no4 p332 Ap 2017

O'NEILL, MICHAEL L.
KOCH-FUELED DYSTOPIA *Commonweal* v114 no14 p2 S 8 2017

O'Neill, Olivia A.
Quantifying Your Company's Emotional Culture *Harvard Business Review Digital Articles* p2 Ja 6 2016

Oneill, Therese
JIGGERY-POKERY L. PRICE color *New York Times Book Review* p40 D 4 2016

OneWest Bank (Company)
The Mess Steven Mnuchin Left Behind Z. Mider and S. Mohsin bw *Bloomberg Businessweek* no4504 p34 D 19 2016

Oneworld Publications Ltd.
Oneworld Piles Up the Wins L. Thomson color *Publishers Weekly* v264 no20 p5 My 15 2017

ONEY, STEVE
HOME AGAIN *Atlanta* v56 no8 p136 D 2016

Ong, Perry S.
Plant diversity increases with the strength of negative density dependence at the global scale diag *Science* v356 no6345 p1389 Je 30 2017

Ong, Sheena
ELABELA deficiency promotes preeclampsia and cardiovascular malformations in mice color diag graph *Science* v357 no6352 p707 Ag 18 2017

Onieal, Kathleen Hays
Getting People to Believe in Something They Can't Yet Imagine *Harvard Business Review Digital Articles* p2 O 10 2014

Onion, The (Newspaper)
NEWS-ISH C. Bethea cartoon *New Yorker* v93 no5 p32 Mr 20 2017

Onions
CHEW ON THIS SWEDISH MEATBALLS K. BOATNER *National Geographic Kids* no466 p9 D 2016/Ja 2017
Golden! C. SAFFITZ color *Bon Appetit* no8 p40 Ag 2017
LOVING ONIONS bw color *Bon Appetit* no11 p130 N 2017
THE NEW POWER FOOD FORMULA color *Men's Health* v31 no10 p104 D 2016
Words To Live (Longer & Better) By [Cover story] A. AU LEVITT color *Reader's Digest* v189 no1130 p70 My 2017

Onions—Therapeutic use
natural remedies color *Good Housekeeping* v264 no4 p104 Ap 2017

ONKA, WILLIAM W.
THE BIG CANDY APPLE img *New York* v49 no19 p21 S 19 2016

Onkyo audio equipment
Old Faithful D. Kumin color graph *Sound & Vision* v82 no8 p42 O 2017

Onkyo audio equipment—Evaluation
Onkyo TX-RZ1100 A/V Receiver D. Kumin chart color graph *Sound & Vision* v82 no2 p44 F/Mr 2017

Onkyo Corp.

Old Faithful D. Kumin color graph *Sound & Vision* v82 no8 p42 O 2017

Onkyo TX-RZ1100 A/V Receiver D. Kumin chart color graph *Sound & Vision* v82 no2 p44 F/Mr 2017

Onkyo TX-RZ610 A/V Receiver M. Fleischmann chart color graph *Sound & Vision* v81 no9 p44 N 2016

Onlamoon, Nattawat

IgG antibodies to dengue enhanced for FcγRIIIA binding determine disease severity bibl graph *Science* v355 no6323 p395 Ja 27 2017

Online business networks (Social networks)

3 Ways to Get Your Own Digital Platform B. Libert, M. Beck et al *Harvard Business Review Digital Articles* p2 Jl 22 2016

Digital Business Models Should Have to Follow the Law, Too B. Edelman *Harvard Business Review Digital Articles* p2 Ja 6 2015

Online chat

See also

Video chat services (Internet)

PARODY diag *Weekly Standard* v22 no18 p44 Ja 16 2017

Online chat software

Build, Race, Fight... and Chat K. CHAYKOWSKI color *Forbes* v200 no1 p46 Jl 27 2017

Online comments

If Only AI Could Save Us from Ourselves D. Auerbach color diag *MIT Technology Review* v120 no1 p104 Ja/F 2017

THE MOVEMENT'S NEW VANGUARD IS TEENAGE "SHIT-LORDS." THE WORLD IS THEIR MESSAGE BOARD NOW M. READ img *New York* v50 no9 p34 My 1 2017

THE PROBLEM WITH COMMENTERS cartoon *New Orleans Magazine* v51 no3 p18 Ja 2017

TROLLS ACROSS AMERICA L. BÉNICHOU map *Wired* v25 no9 p90 S 2017

Online courses

See also

Massive open online courses

Online Courses for Homestead Herbalists S. Stonebrook *Mother Earth News* no281 p9 Ap/My 2017

Ready to Launch J. FRIEDMAN color *Publishers Weekly* v264 no4 p42 Ja 23 2017

Thwarting the Grievance-Industrial Complex cartoon *Weekly Standard* v22 no28 p2 Mr 27 2017

Who's Benefiting from MOOCs, and Why Chen Zhenghao, B. Alcorn et al *Harvard Business Review Digital Articles* p2 S 22 2015

Online dating

Sex, Super Likes & Five Years of Tinder C. Drell color *Glamour* v115 no5 p113 My 2017

Online dating services

Dating While Black H. RODERIQUE color *Walrus* v14 no2 p24 Mr 2017

Match Me If You Can M. Meltzer chart color graph il *Consumer Reports* v82 no2 p38 F 2017

Online dating services—Social aspects

Love in the Time of Mass Incarceration M. Pilon color *Bloomberg Businessweek* no4531 p18 Jl 24 2017

Online dating—Humor

CRAIGSLIST MISSED CONNECTIONS, Protest Edition R. LONG il *National Review* v69 no3 p42 F 20 2017

Online dating—Safety measures

Match Me If You Can M. Meltzer chart color graph il *Consumer Reports* v82 no2 p38 F 2017

Online etiquette

See also

Online trolling

Do Real Men Emoji? D. MAGARY color *GQ: Gentlemen's Quarterly* v97 no5 p66 My 2017

The Dos and Don'ts of Work Email, from Emojis to Typos A. Brodsky *Harvard Business Review Digital Articles* p2 Ap 23 2015

MONEY MANNERS M. CROSS cartoon *Kiplinger's Personal Finance* v71 no4 p48 Ap 2017

Using Social Media Without Jeopardizing Your Career A. Samuel *Harvard Business Review Digital Articles* p2 Jl 20 2015

Online exhibitions

Revealing views of the American past, courtesy of Cornell bw

Magazine Antiques v184 no2 p38 Mr/Ap 2017

Online identity theft

Operations. The Digital Imposter: After penetrating your website, a hacker can do business as you J. Dysart *Parks & Recreation* v52 no6 p48 Je 2017

Online information services

How to replace 5 Yahoo services and delete your Yahoo account I. PAUL color *Macworld - Digital Edition* p111 F 2017

The Myth of 'Going Viral' on the Internet D. Thompson *Time* v189 no6 p21 F 20 2017

Online journalism

THE EDITORIAL *Maclean's* v129 no41 p5 O 17 2016

SI DIGITAL color *Sports Illustrated* v125 no12 p6 O 10 2016

Online marketplaces

6 Reasons Platforms Fail M. W. Van Alstyne, G. G. Parker et al *Harvard Business Review Digital Articles* p2 Mr 31 2016

Online sexual predators

The New Scarlet Letter C. Alter color *Time* v190 no2/3 p60 Jl 10-17 2017

Online shopping

13 Things Savvy Shoppers Look for in Online Reviews C. HILTON ANDERSEN *Reader's Digest* v188 no1126 p120 D 2016/Ja 2017

The Cardinal Rules of Buying on eBay color *Esquire* p111 Big-BlackBook

Great Style Has No Size color *InStyle* v23 no12 p124 N 2016

How New Technologies Push Us Toward the Past W. H. Davidow and M. S. Malone *Harvard Business Review Digital Articles* p2 My 8 2015

How to stop Google Home or Amazon Echo from making unwanted online purchases F. ION color *PCWorld* v35 no9 p107 S 2017

Laugh Lines: SHOP AROUND THE CLOCK color *Reader's Digest* v190 no1135 p114 N 2017

The Logic Behind Amazon's Prime Day R. Mohammed *Harvard Business Review Digital Articles* p2 Jl 13 2015

NEVER PAY FULL PRICE AGAIN K. Dold color *Men's Health* v31 no10 p73 D 2016

NOVEMBER @ GH color *Good Housekeeping* v265 no5 p6 N 2017

ONLINE MERCHANTS THAT DON'T DELIVER B. PEDERSEN color *Kiplinger's Personal Finance* v71 no11 p11 N 2017

Purchases, Chargebacks Are on the Rise *USA Today Magazine* v145 no2859 p7 D 2016

The Retail Whisperer C. O'CONNOR color *Forbes* v198 no7 p58 N 29 2016

Shop Online With Confidence B. Braverman, A. Giorgianni et al graph il *Consumer Reports* v82 no12 p20 D 2017

Sleuth Smarts color *Men's Health* v31 no10 p74 D 2016

Whole Foods Is Becoming Amazon's Brick-and-Mortar Pricing Lab H. Simon *Harvard Business Review Digital Articles* p2 S 12 2017

Work Those Resale Sites F. Kane color *Glamour* v115 no10 p80 O 2017

Online shopping—Social aspects

Worshipping at the Altar of Brick and Mortar K. C. POHLMANN color *Sound & Vision* v82 no3 p30 Ap 2017

Online social networks

Am I Going to Post This, or Are You? B. GREGORY cartoon graph *Men's Health* v32 no9 p80 N 2017

FOLLOW THE MONEY J. Mande cartoon *New Yorker* v92 no39 p50 N 28 2016

LETTER TO SILICON VALLEY K. Crawford *Harper's Magazine* v334 no2001 p36 F 2017

MY PAL WON'T TEXT ME BECAUSE I DON'T USE SIGNAL. BUT HE'LL SAY ANYTHING ON SOCIAL MEDIA. HE'S BEING ANNOYING, RIGHT? J. MOOALLEM cartoon *Wired* v25 no5 p30 My 2017

The Potential of Virtual Communities in the Publishing Ecosystem R. Beardsley *Publishers Weekly* v264 no3 p12 Ja 16 2017

Readers Respond T. S. Mulvaugh, K. Fain et al color *Publishers Weekly* v263 no51 pC4 D 12 2016

They launched an internal social network. What happened next will blow your mind... *People Management* p40 My 2017

Using Social Media to Build Professional Skills A. Samuel *Harvard Business Review Digital Articles* p2 Ag 4 2016

Video Metrics Every Marketer Should Be Watching K. Craft *Har-*

vard Business Review Digital Articles p2 Ap 24 2015

We Need Both Networks and Communities H. Mintzberg *Harvard Business Review Digital Articles* p2 O 5 2015

We Say We Want Privacy Online, But Our Actions Say Otherwise L. K. John *Harvard Business Review Digital Articles* p2 O 16 2015

What CEOs Have Learned About Social Media L. Gaines-Ross *Harvard Business Review Digital Articles* p2 My 18 2015

What Marketers Need to Know About Chat Apps M. W. Schaefer *Harvard Business Review Digital Articles* p2 Je 14 2016

WHICH ONE IS #FAKENEWS?* S. M. FERNÁNDEZ *Scholastic Choices* v32 no8 p6 My 2017

Why Social Networks Still Haven't Cracked the Job Search Puzzle J. P. V. Sampere *Harvard Business Review Digital Articles* p2 Ja 13 2015

Your Network's Structure Matters More than Its Size K. Libert *Harvard Business Review Digital Articles* p2 F 23 2016

Online social networks—Economic aspects

WHAT'S THE VALUE OF A LIKE? L. K. JOHN, D. MOCHON et al color *Harvard Business Review* v95 no2 p108 Mr/Ap 2017

Online social networks—Finance

WHAT'S THE VALUE OF A LIKE? L. K. JOHN, D. MOCHON et al color *Harvard Business Review* v95 no2 p108 Mr/Ap 2017

Online social networks—Management

How Bots Took Over Twitter A. Samuel *Harvard Business Review Digital Articles* p2 Je 19 2015

Online social networks—Moral & ethical aspects

A KINDER, GENTLER REDDIT J. STEIN cartoon color *Bloomberg Businessweek* no4503 p65 D 12 2016

Online trolling

Click Bait A. Hess *New York Times Magazine* p11 Mr 5 2017

If Only AI Could Save Us from Ourselves D. Auerbach color diag *MIT Technology Review* v120 no1 p104 Ja/F 2017

Secret's Problem Wasn't Trolls L. Laurenson *Harvard Business Review Digital Articles* p2 My 20 2015

THE TROLLS ARE COMING P. M. Barrett color *Bloomberg Businessweek* no4501 p27 N 28 2016

Online trolling—Prevention

Me and My Troll J. Pontin il *MIT Technology Review* v120 no3 p91 My/Je 2017

TROLL HUNTERS J. J. Roberts color *Fortune* v175 no2 p22 F 1 2017

Online trolling—Social aspects

Me and My Troll J. Pontin il *MIT Technology Review* v120 no3 p91 My/Je 2017

Online information services—Charts, diagrams, etc.

Hand Over the Data graph *MIT Technology Review* v120 no2 p26 Mr/Ap 2017

Onnela, Antti

Global atmospheric particle formation from CERN CLOUD measurements bibl graph map *Science* v354 no6316 p1119 D 2 2016

Ono, Yoko, 1933-

THE BALLAD OF SEAN & YOKO S. Mooallem bw color *Harper's Bazaar* no3655 p162 Ag 2017

The Photo Issue [Cover story] D. Browne, P. Doyle et al bw *Rolling Stone* no1299 p24 N 2 2017

Onoda, Shinobu

Nanoscale nuclear magnetic resonance with chemical resolution diag *Science* v357 no6346 p67 Jl 7 2017

Onomasiology

Make it Final with Vinyl W. SHEPPARD *Boating World* v38 no1 p28 Ja 2017

Oñorbe, Jose

Measurement of the small-scale structure of the intergalactic medium using close quasar pairs diag graph *Science* v356 no6336 p418 Ap 28 2017

Onozato, Maristela L.

Decoupling genetics, lineages, and microenvironment in IDH-mutant gliomas by single-cell RNA-seq diag *Science* v355 no6332 p1391 Mr 31 2017

Onshape (Company)

Bringing CAD To the Cloud M. Belfiore *Bloomberg Businessweek* no4511 p30 F 13 2017

Onstad, Katrina

GIVE ME A BREAK B. Begun color *Bloomberg Businessweek* no4521 p62 My 8 2017

Impossible Dream img *New York* p55 Ja 23 2017

Onstage New York (Company)

ONSTAGE NEW YORK *Dance Spirit* v20 no10 p22 D 2016

Onstott, Tullis C.

The Subterraneans *Natural History* v125 no1 p16 D 2016/Ja 2017

Ontario, Lake (N.Y. & Ont.)

The Birds in the Hand color *Canadian Wildlife* v22 no5 p7 N/D 2016

Onuki, Juri

Adrenaline Rush S. BURKE *Dance Magazine* v91 no4 p35 Ap 2017

Onyemah, Vincent

Midsize Cities Are Entrepreneurship's Real Test color *Harvard Business Review Digital Articles* p2 Ja 24 2017

Ookla (Company)

Comcast is the fastest ISP, and T-Mobile is the fastest wireless carrier, Ookla says M. HACHMAN color graph *PCWorld* v35 no10 p18 O 2017

OOOUUU (Music)

'OOOUUU' H. GIORGIS color *New York Times Magazine* p57 Mr 12 2017

Oostenbrink, Chris

Exploring genetic suppression interactions on a global scale diag *Science* v354 no6312 p599 N 4 2016

OOSTHOEK, SHARON

GAME OF THRONES [Cover story] color map *Canadian Geographic* v135 no6 p36 D 2015

Oostra, Roelof-Jan

An interactive three-dimensional digital atlas and quantitative database of human development bibl color graph *Science* v354 no6315 paag0053-1 N 25 2016

Opal, Charlotte

Committing to socially responsible seafood color *Science* v356 no6341 p912 Je 1 2017

Opal, J. M.

Avenging the People: Andrew Jackson, the Rule of Law, and the American Nation W. Russell Mead *Foreign Affairs* v96 no3 p160 My/Je 2017

Opalesky, Luisa

THE LOOK BOOK img *New York* v50 no11 p95 My 29 2017

Opar, Alisa

Choose Your Adventure *Audubon* v119 no2 p54 Summ 2017

GEAR *Audubon* v118 no6 p47 Wint 2016

Rescue Mission *Audubon* v118 no6 p32 Wint 2016

Resurgence *Audubon* v119 no1 p1 Spr 2017

Spirit of the West color *Audubon* v119 no3 p3 Fall 2017

THE ULTIMATE KIDS' KIT color *Audubon* v119 no3 p44 Fall 2017

Opelka, Reilly

Serving Notice P. Bodo *Tennis* v53 no4 p8 Jl/Ag 2017

Open & closed shop (Labor unions)—Law & legislation— United States

Labor's Last Stand J. Eidelson cartoon map *Bloomberg Businessweek* no4512 p25 F 20 2017

The Public Sector on Trial N. WALKER *In These Times* v41 no6 p15 Je 2017

Open access publishing

See also

Predatory open access publishing

The Coming Era of Open Data S. L. COLLINS and J. M. VERDIER *BioScience* v67 no3 p191 Mr 2017

Germany seeks 'big flip' in publishing model G. Vogel and K. Kupferschmidt color graph *Science* v357 no6353 p744 Ag 25 2017

A nod to public open access infrastructures B. Fecher, S. Friesike et al *Science* v356 no6344 p1242 Je 23 2017

The state of open access C. Day *Physics Today* v70 no5 p8 My 2017

Steady, strong growth is expected for open-access journals D. Kramer *Physics Today* v70 no5 p24 My 2017

Open access publishing—Europe

Science funders plunge into publishing M. Enserink color *Science* v355 no6332 p1357 Mr 31 2017

Open access publishing—Government policy

Publish openly but responsibly A. J. Lowe, A. K. Smyth et al color *Science* v357 no6347 p141 Jl 14 2017

Lebanon, NH D. Shengold *Opera News* v81 no5 p44 N 2016

Opera Omaha Inc.

Opera Omaha E. C. NIELSEN and T. Burton *Opera News* v81 no7 p60 Ja 2017

Opera singers

360 DEGREES J. DUCHEN *Opera News* v81 no6 p34 D 2016

Accidental Diva *Opera News* v81 no5 p6 N 2016

Bravura STYLE J. MELICK *Opera News* v81 no6 p24 D 2016

Das Rheingold M. T. Ketterson *Opera News* v81 no6 p39 D 2016

Dateline *Opera News* v81 no6 p8 D 2016

Diva CALIENTE D. ACOSTA *Opera News* v81 no5 p36 N 2016

Jakub Józef Orliński M. MAZZARO *Opera News* v81 no6 p10 D 2016

JOHN DEL CARLO F. P. Driscoll *Opera News* v81 no7 p58 Ja 2017

Opera Before Instagram *USA Today Magazine* v145 no2860 p38 Ja 2017

A POWERFUL VOICE P. RUHE *Atlanta* v56 no7 p42 N 2016

Room for Interpretation A. WASSERMAN *Opera News* v81 no6 p22 D 2016

Scott Conner F. P. DRISCOLL *Opera News* v81 no9 p10 Mr 2017

Soul SISTER F. COHN *Opera News* v81 no5 p26 N 2016

Sound Bites: Theo Hoffman: A native New Yorker returns to Missouri F. P. Driscoll *Opera News* v81 no12 p58 Je 2017

A Winter's Journey M. Sandor *Opera News* v81 no5 p32 N 2016

Opera singers—News briefs

Dec/2016 M. M. AZZARO *Opera News* v81 no6 p6 D 2016

Opera singers—Training of

Behind the Scenes: Liner Notes L. T. Guinther *Opera News* v81 no12 p5 Je 2017

Opera Software ASA

Meet Opera Neon, Opera's radical vision for the future of web browsers M. HACHMAN color *PCWorld* v35 no2 p17 F 2017

Opera—Chorus

IN PERFECT HARMONY T. MALONE *Atlanta* v56 no12 p40 Ap 2017

Opera—Great Britain

OPERA: FOR THE ORDINARY: Despite popular misconceptions and its aristocratic origins, for part of its history opera was inextricably linked with popular culture - no more so than in the 1920s A. Wilson *History Today* v67 no9 p58 S 2017

Opera—News briefs

EURO STARS B. KIRCHNER *Opera News* v81 no7 p20 Ja 2017

Jan/2017 M. MAZZARO *Opera News* v81 no7 p6 Ja 2017

Opera—Production & direction

ROBERT CARSEN F. P. Driscoll *Opera News* v81 no10 p26 Ap 2017

Opera—Reviews

6. See Der Rosenkavalier J. DAVIDSON *New York* v50 no7 p88 Ap 3 2017

Armide A. J. Goldmann *Opera News* v81 no7 p42 Ja 2017

CLASSICAL MUSIC *New Yorker* v92 no42 p24 D 19 2016

Così Fan Tutte S. J. Mudge *Opera News* v81 no10 p41 Ap 2017

Dead Man Walking A. Mellor *Opera News* v81 no10 p45 Ap 2017

Der Freischütz M. Wheeler *Opera News* v81 no7 p44 Ja 2017

The Dictator's Wife T. Smith *Opera News* v81 no10 p47 Ap 2017

Eugene Onegin W. Spiegelman and G. Barnett *Opera News* v81 no7 p34 Ja 2017

Gluck: Iphigénie en Tauride D. J. Baker *Opera News* v81 no7 p49 Ja 2017

Hamburg A. J. Goldmann *Opera News* v81 no10 p42 Ap 2017

Hitting the Mark W. R. Braun and D. Shengold *Opera News* v81 no7 p32 Ja 2017

King Arthur A. J. Goldmann *Opera News* v81 no10 p42 Ap 2017

King of Diamonds A. KOZINN *Opera News* v81 no10 p18 Ap 2017

La Favorite J. A. Leipsic *Opera News* v81 no7 p41 Ja 2017

Lohengrin S. Mudge *Opera News* v81 no10 p40 Ap 2017

Lucia di Lammermoor M. T. Ketterson *Opera News* v81 no7 p34 Ja 2017

Natasha, Pierre and the Great Comet of 1812 M. Mazzaro *Opera News* v81 no10 p48 Ap 2017

Nixon in China G. Barnett *Opera News* v81 no10 p50 Ap 2017

Operapedia: Lucia di Lammermoor G. DONIZETTI *Opera News* v81 no10 p14 Ap 2017

The Pearl Fishers J. Pell *Opera News* v81 no7 p38 Ja 2017

Samson et Dalila S. J. Mudge *Opera News* v81 no7 p45 Ja 2017

The Snow Maiden G. Hall *Opera News* v81 no10 p46 Ap 2017

Operas

Classical Music & Dance img *New York* v50 no17 p140 Ag 21 2017

Operas—News briefs

Nov/2016 M. MAZZARO *Opera News* v81 no5 p8 N 2016

Operas—Performances

Dateline *Opera News* v81 no7 p10 Ja 2017

Operating budgets

Your Agile Project Needs a Budget, Not an Estimate D. Madden *Harvard Business Review Digital Articles* p2 D 29 2014

Operating costs

Cost of Running Harvard K. Stock color diag *Bloomberg Businessweek* no4535 p19 Ag 28 2017

Operating costs—Management

MANAGING FOR LEAN TIMES R. Nickel *Successful Farming* v114 no11 p20 N 2016

Operating revenue

Publishers Did Marginally Better in 2016 J. Milliot chart *Publishers Weekly* v264 no14 p4 Ap 3. 2017

Workers Are Bad at Filling Out Timesheets, and It Costs Billions a Day G. Gavett *Harvard Business Review Digital Articles* p2 Ja 12 2015

Operating systems (Computers)

See also

Linux operating systems

Mobile operating systems

3 handy image tools you can use in File Explorer I. PAUL color *PCWorld* p182 D 2016

5 terminal commands every Linux newbie should know A. CAMPBELL color *PCWorld* p174 D 2016

Back up via a network without using Time Machine G. Fleishman color *Macworld - Digital Edition* p119 Ap 2017

How to pin the Recent Items folder to File Explorer in Windows 10 I. PAUL color *PCWorld* p187 D 2016

How to stop autoplay videos in Safari 11 R. LOYOLA color *Macworld - Digital Edition* v34 no11 p7 N 2017

Mac 911 G. FLEISHMAN color *Macworld - Digital Edition* v34 no6 p127 Je 2017

Microsoft tells some Mac Office users to pass on Apple's High Sierra G. KEIZER color *Macworld - Digital Edition* v34 no10 p86 O 2017

What to do when you hate Windows 10 J. NOREM color *PCWorld* v35 no11 p138 N 2016

Operating systems (Computers)—Evaluation

The 11 most intriguing Fall Creators Update features in Windows 10 Build 16215 M. HACHMAN color *PCWorld* v35 no7 p11 Jl 2017

6 Photos features that are worth the upgrade to macOS Sierra J. SNELL color map *Macworld - Digital Edition* v33 no11 p21 N 2016

7 hidden features in macOS Sierra you may have missed R. LOYOLA color *Macworld - Digital Edition* v33 no11 p27 N 2016

Google Builds Operating System From Scratch S. ORNES bw diag *Discover* v38 no1 p52 Ja/F 2017

Google's Fuchsia OS is out in the open and shrouded in mystery C. HOFFMAN color *PCWorld* p22 O 2016

MACOS HIGH SIERRA REVIEW: INCREMENTAL UPDATE WORTHY OF YOUR TIME, EVENTUALLY R. Loyola color *Macworld - Digital Edition* v34 no11 p99 N 2017

macOS Sierra: Mixing iOS with OS X to make a better Mac R. LOYOLA color *Macworld - Digital Edition* v33 no11 p7 N 2016

The Windows 10 CREATORS UPDATE'S BEST NEW FEATURES: Dynamic Lock, Game Mode, privacy tweaks B. CHACOS color *PCWorld* v35 no2 p151 F 2017

Windows 10's privacy settings will be simpler with Creators' Update M. HACHMAN color map *PCWorld* v35 no2 p36 F 2017

Operation Crossroads, Marshall Islands, 1946

A Bomb to Remember J. M. Cannon and J. Sam *Hoover Digest: Research & Opinion on Public Policy* no1 p184 Wint 2017

Operations management

8 Reasons Companies Don't Capture More Value S. Michel *Harvard Business Review Digital Articles* p2 Ap 8 2015

EUROPE'S BEST AIRPORT *Iceland Review* v55 no3 p56 My/ Je 2017

The History and Future of Operations M. Iansiti *Harvard Business Review Digital Articles* p2 Je 30 2015

The Subtle Ways Our Screens Are Pushing Us Apart K. Sobel-Lojeski *Harvard Business Review Digital Articles* p2 Ap 8 2015

What Hospitals Can Learn from Airlines About Buying Equipment P. Pronovost, S. Palmer et al *Harvard Business Review Digital Articles* p2 Je 13 2017

Operative dentistry

My Dentist 3D Printed My Crown S. Kaplan *Harvard Business Review Digital Articles* p2 O 24 2014

Opera—United States

The Best of 2016 *Opera News* v81 no7 p52 Ja 2017

Ophiurida

Living Color color *National Wildlife (World Edition)* v55 no6 p20 O/N 2017

Ophthalmic lenses

    See also

    Contact lenses

SEE Change L. REGENSDORF cartoon *Vogue* v206 no11 p162 N 2016

Ophthalmic surgery

EYE IMPLANTS CARRY RISKS C. Barakat and M. McCluskey color *Equus* no481 p13 O 2017

Opie, Catherine

PORTFOLIO color *Art in America* v104 no10 p114 N 2016

SECRET SELVES A. LEVY cartoon color *New Yorker* v93 no4 p58 Mr 13 2017

Opie, Tina R.

Our Biases Undermine Our Colleagues' Attempts to Be Authentic *Harvard Business Review Digital Articles* p2 Jl 5 2017

Opinion (Philosophy)

ON DEMONSTRATIONS AND VIRTUE SIGNALING G. CHRISTINA *Humanist* v77 no4 p38 Jl/Ag 2017

Opio, Joseph

Trevor NOAH cartoon *Vanity Fair* v58 no11 p210 N 2016

Opioid abuse

2,816 dead Canadians and counting P. Wells color *Maclean's* v130 no10 p20 N 2017

31 Women Are Killed by Opioids Each Day bw *Glamour* v115 no10 p148 O 2017

THE ADDICTS NEXT DOOR M. TALBOT bw cartoon *New Yorker* v93 no16 p74 Je 5 2017

AMERICA IN PERIL C. B. Smithers *Weekly Standard* v22 no38 p41 Je 12 2017

Chayce Doesn't Want to Be One of Them M. Mertens, W. Yakowicz et al color *Glamour* v115 no10 p149 O 2017

Clumsy Reform A. Greenblatt *Governing* v30 no3 p10 D 2016

The Drug Cascade H. S. Edwards color *Time* v190 no1 p32 Jl 3 2017

Forecasting the opioid epidemic D. S. Burke color *Science* v354 no6312 p529 N 4 2016

GENERATION: America's opioid epidemic is leaving an entire generation of children behind J. B. Wogan *Governing* v30 no10 p32 Jl 2017

How has the opioid crisis affected your community? map *America* v217 no3 p6 Ag 7 2017

A Lawsuit Deluge for Opioid Inc E. Fry color *Fortune* v176 no5 p16 O 1 2017

LEFT BEHIND J. Lurie color graph *Mother Jones* v42 no4 p50 Jl/Ag 2017

A LOOK AT THE SOCIAL ISSUES DEMANDING YOUR ATTENTION *Governing* v30 no1 p6 O 2016

Making Opioid Addiction Searchable J. Green *Bloomberg Businessweek* no4535 p22 Ag 28 2017

McKESSON FEELS THE PAIN E. Fry chart color diag map *Fortune* v175 no8 p170 Je 15 2017

MISDIAGNOSING A CRISIS A. D. Sorkin cartoon *New Yorker* v93 no24 p15 Ag 21 2017

OPIATE OF THE MASSES J. HEARN *Humanist* v77 no1 p22 Ja/F 2017

The Opioid Crisis D. W. MURRAY, B. BLAKE et al color graph *Weekly Standard* v22 no9 p19 N 7 2016

Opioid Deaths Soar M. Fischetti graph *Scientific American* v317 no4 p96 O 2017

Opioids and Paternalism: TO HELP END THE CRISIS, BOTH DOCTORS AND PATIENTS NEED TO FIND A NEW WAY TO THINK ABOUT PAIN [Cover story] D. BROWN *American Scholar* v86 no4 p22 Aut 2017

OPIOIDS AND THE OVERDOSE EPIDEMIC *New York Times Upfront* v149 no11 p20 Ap 3 2017

OPIOIDS AND THE OVERDOSE EPIDEMIC *Scholastic Choices* v32 no8 p22 My 2017

OPIOIDS M. Quinn *Governing* v30 no4 p35 Ja 2017

Our National Pain R. Chapman color *Sports Illustrated* v126 no17 p72 Je 19 2017

Some topics call for science reporting from many angles E. Quill *Science News* v191 no11 p2 Je 10 2017

Time for nonaddictive relief of pain T. Grosser, C. J. Woolf et al bibl color *Science* v355 no6329 p1026 Mr 10 2017

Tracking an Epidemic diag *Fortune* v176 no2 p15 Ag 1 2017

Opioid abuse—Economic aspects

Why the Fed Cares About America's Opioid Crisis J. Smialek graph *Bloomberg Businessweek* no4532 p34 Jl 31 2017

Opioid abuse—Law & legislation

Cons Cures Act *Congressional Digest* v96 no2 p13 F 1 2017

Opioid abuse—Prevention

Are New Anti-Abuse Technologies Enough? *USA Today Magazine* v145 no2861 p8 F 2017

ARE WE TALKING ABOUT OPIOIDS THE WAY? Officials say they're doing everything they can to stop the epidemic. But a real solution may be a lot more complicated M. Quinn *Governing* v30 no10 p38 Jl 2017

Confronting the Opioid Outbreak in Our Parks M. S. Ibrahim and C. Jones *Parks & Recreation* v52 no6 p34 Je 2017

Parishes Should Lead Efforts to Understand Opioid Addiction *America* v217 no3 p8 Ag 7 2017

TAKING PAINS J. LURIE cartoon *Mother Jones* v42 no5 p66 S/O 2017

Opioid abuse—Social aspects

Facing the opioid crisis [Cover story] A. Hearlson color *Christian Century* v133 no23 p22 N 9 2016

Seattle Breaks New Ground on Opioids A. Arnold color graph *Bloomberg Businessweek* no4494 p28 O 10 2016

The truth about lies P. W. Marty *Christian Century* v133 no23 p3 N 9 2016

Opioid abuse—Treatment

Christian recovery programs in Vancouver respond to opioid crisis A. Ambrosio color *Christian Century* v134 no15 p17 Jl 19 2017

Facing the opioid crisis [Cover story] A. Hearlson color *Christian Century* v133 no23 p22 N 9 2016

JUST SAY NO TO SHAME [Cover story] T. KING cartoon color *Christianity Today* v60 no10 p34 D 2016

A New Paradigm for Opioid Addiction: More Drugs A. Park color *Time* v188 no16/17 p48 O 24 2016

Our Addiction Crisis Can Be Solved-With Hard Work V. Murthy color *Time* v188 no16/17 p53 O 24 2016

Treating Opioid Addiction S. SATEL il *National Review* v69 no4 p26 Mr 6 2017

Opioid analgesics

PRIMED FOR PAIN K. Servick color *Science* v354 no6312 p569 N 4 2016

Opioids

    See also

    Oxycodone

Beyond Today's Opioids L. Hamers color graph *Science News* v191 no11 p22 Je 10 2017

BORN USERS L. MURTHA *Cincinnati Magazine* v50 no4 p68 Ja 2017

Does Legalized Pot Fuel Opioid Epidemic? *USA Today Magazine* v146 no2867 p12 Ag 2017

End the Epidemic color *America* v215 no13 p5 O 31 2016

"I WAS NO KIND OF MOTHER. The drugs were MY EVERYTHING" C. RUBIN color *Good Housekeeping* v265 no2 p104 Ag 2017

NEWS FROM THE World of Medicine S. RIDEOUT *Reader's Digest* v188 no1124 p66 O 2016

Pandora's Lab P. A. Offit color diag *National Geographic* v231 no6 p136 Je 2017

Sore Loser: Why the opioid crisis is personal D. Paul diag *Indianapolis Monthly* v42 no2 p128 O 2017

Opioids—Government policy
　THE ADDICTS NEXT DOOR M. TALBOT bw cartoon *New Yorker* v93 no16 p74 Je 5 2017

Opioids—Receptors
　A nontoxic pain killer designed by modeling of pathological receptor conformations V. Spahn, G. Del Vecchio et al bibl diag graph *Science* v355 no6328 p966 Mr 3 2017

Opioids—Therapeutic use
　GETTING DARK A. FLANGO and J. WILLIAMS *Cincinnati Magazine* v50 no3 p29 D 2016
　TAKING PAINS J. LURIE cartoon *Mother Jones* v42 no5 p66 S/O 2017

Opium abuse
　God's Own Medicine P. A. OFFIT *Skeptical Inquirer* v41 no2 p44 Mr/Ap 2017

Opium—Law & legislation
　The First Lady of Reefer Madness M. GREEN cartoon *Walrus* p36 Ja\F 2017

Opium—Therapeutic use
　God's Own Medicine P. A. OFFIT *Skeptical Inquirer* v41 no2 p44 Mr/Ap 2017

Opko Health Inc.
　A BOUNTIFUL MIND M. SCHIFRIN bw color *Forbes* v199 no1 p94 Ja 24 2017

Oplev, Niels Arden
　FLATLINERS J. Ganz color *Entertainment Weekly* no1478 / 1479 p41 Ag 18-25 2017

Opossums
　City Creatures G. VAN HORN *Orion Magazine* v35 no4/5 p9 Jl-O 2016
　Wild in the City color *Canadian Wildlife* v23 no2 p42 My/Je 2017

Oppenheim, Mike
　Becoming Hitler: The Making of a Nazi color *Military History* v34 no4 p71 N 2017
　Consequence: A Memoir *Military History* v33 no5 p70 Ja 2017
　THE PIGBOAT'S ORIGINS color *American History* v52 no3 p67 Ag 2017
　VERY TAXING TIMES color *American History* v52 no2 p70 Je 2017

Oppenheimer, Daniel
　Identity Crisis bw *Washington Monthly* v49 no9/10 p129 S/O 2017
　Mutually Assured Resentment color *Washington Monthly* v49 no6-8 p68 Je-Ag 2017

Oppenheimer, Jerry
　The Kardashians: An American Drama *Publishers Weekly* v264 no33 p70 Ag 14 2017

Oppenheimer, Mark
　BEYOND UNBELIEF *New York Times Magazine* p42 Ja 1 2017
　The Born-Again Scoundrel bw cartoon *GQ: Gentlemen's Quarterly* v97 no3 p140 Mr 2017
　WHEN A JEW & A CATHOLIC MARRY color *America* v217 no5 p18 S 4 2017

Oppenheimer, Michael
　Estimating economic damage from climate change in the United States color graph *Science* v356 no6345 p1362 Je 30 2017
　How high will the seas rise? bibl color graph *Science* v354 no6318 p1375 D 16 2016
　Unmask temporal trade-offs in climate policy debates color *Science* v356 no6337 p492 My 5 2017

Oppenheimer, Stephen J.
　A Neolithic expansion, but strong genetic structure, in the independent history of New Guinea diag *Science* v357 no6356 p1160 S 15 2017

Oppermann, Cait
　GOING THE DISTANCE color map *Wired* v25 no7 p8 Jl 2017

Oppo Electronics Corp.
　New Gear color *Sound & Vision* v82 no6 p26 Jl/Ag 2017
　Sonic Boom B. Ankosko and C. Crowley color *Sound & Vision* v81 no10 p2 D 2016
　UHD Star-Lord? T. J. Norton color *Sound & Vision* v82 no4 p54 My 2017

Opportunity International (Company)
　MALIN AKERMAN FIGHTS GLOBAL POVERTY R. Kinane color *Entertainment Weekly* no1465 p16 My 12 2017

Opposites Attract (Music)
　Paula Abdul's Greatest Hits A. Bacle color *Entertainment Weekly*

no1465 p55 My 12 2017

Opposition (Political science)
　America's New Opposition J. PURDY color *New Republic* v248 no3 p26 Mr 2017
　The 'Global Order' Myth A. J. BACEVICH *American Conservative* v16 no3 p19 My/Je 2017
　Just Say No to Just Say No J. B. JUDIS color *New Republic* v248 no5 p14 My 2017
　Mourn, Resist, Organize D. D. GUTTENPLAN il *Nation* v303 no22 p3 N 28 2016
　NOT ON THEIR WATCH M. PATRIQUIN and J. MARKUSOFF color *Maclean's* v129 no40 p16 O 10 2016
　The Perils of Hyperbole J. COST color *Weekly Standard* v22 no17 p12 Ja 2 2017
　Putin's Rival Targets Provincial Russians L. Ragozin, I. Arkhipov et al color *Bloomberg Businessweek* no4517 p28 Ap 3 2017
　The West Coast Fights Back Against Trump S. ABRAMSKY color il *Nation* v304 no6 p16 F 27 2017

Opposition (Political science)—History
　Learn From History S. Benhabib *New Republic* v248 no3 p33 Mr 2017

Opposition With Jordan Klepper, The (TV program)
　Fake News Tonight: Comedy Central's latest news satire show pokes fun at the right and left *TV Guide* v65 no39 p12 S 18 2017
　The Opposition With Jordan Klepper N. Abrams, C. Holub et al *Entertainment Weekly* no1482/1483 p55 S 22 2017

Oprah
　Here We Go! color *O, The Oprah Magazine* p17 Je 2017
　What I Know for Sure color *O, The Oprah Magazine* p124 Ag 2017

Oprah Magazine, The (Periodical)
　Behind the Scenes color *O, The Oprah Magazine* p12 N 2017
　Permission to Speak Freely L. Kogan color *O, The Oprah Magazine* p44 O 2017

Oprah Winfrey Show, The (TV program)
　Celebrity in Chief P. TERZIAN color *Weekly Standard* v22 no18 p13 Ja 16 2017

Optical aberrations
　The color purple S. J. O'MEARA color *Astronomy* v45 no9 p20 S 2017
　RESEARCH color *Science* v357 no6351 p560 Ag 11 2017

Optical astronomy
　Your self-driving car could kill radio astronomy D. Clery color *Science* v355 no6322 p232 Ja 20 2017

Optical character recognition software—Evaluation
　READIRIS PRO 16: OCR SOFTWARE MORE FOCUSED ON SPEED THAN ACCURACY J. R. BOOKWALTER color *Macworld - Digital Edition* v34 no6 p29 Je 2017

Optical circulators
　Optical circulators reach the quantum level W. J. Munro and Kae Nemoto bibl diag *Science* v354 no6319 p1532 D 23 2016

Optical coherence tomography
　From lab to clinic C. Day *Physics Today* v70 no8 p8 Ag 2017

Optical detectors
　Sterile neutrinos give IceCube and other experiments the cold shoulder Sung Chang *Physics Today* v69 no10 p15 O 2016

Optical disk drives
　If you've ever owned a PC with a DVD drive, you may get a $10 settlement M. HACHMAN color *PCWorld* p38 Mr 2017

Optical fibers—Joints—Evaluation
　Focus on lasers, imaging, and microscopy A. Mandelis *Physics Today* v69 no11 p64 N 2016

Optical goods stores
　SUNSET JUNCTION L. IMMEDIATO *Los Angeles Magazine* v62 no6 p68 Je 2017

Optical illusions
　coloring inside the lines color *Popular Science* v289 no2 p89 Mr/Ap 2017
　NATURAL MAGIC S. JOHNSON *New York Times Magazine* p48 N 6 2016
　snakes on a plane M. Shieh color *Popular Science* v289 no5 p84 S/O 2017
　Xtreme Illusions *National Geographic Kids* no469 p26 Ap 2017

Optical instruments—Evaluation
　LOOKING GLASSES A. McKEAN chart color *Outdoor Life* v224 no5 p22 Je/Jl 2017

Observe with both eyes open P. Harrington color *Astronomy* v45 no11 p58 N 2017

Optical lattices

A Fermi-degenerate three-dimensional optical lattice clock S. L. Campbell, R. B. Hutson et al color diag graph *Science* v357 no6359 p90 O 6 2017

RESEARCH color *Science* v357 no6359 p76 O 6 2017

Optical radar

Air Waves Over Antarctica H. Leifert *Natural History* v125 no2 p8 F 2017

Optical scanners—Evaluation

EPSON DS-320 REVIEW: PORTABLE PRODUCTIVITY SCANNER, SANS WIRELESS J. R. BOOKWALTER color *Macworld - Digital Edition* v34 no6 p42 Je 2017

EPSON FASTFOTO FF-640: QUICK, CONVENIENT PHOTO SCANS DON'T COME CHEAP J. R. BOOKWALTER color *Macworld - Digital Edition* p31 Mr 2017

Optical telescopes

75, 50 & 25 YEARS AGO R. W. Sinnott color *Sky & Telescope* v134 no2 p8 Ag 2017

Designers squabble over giant Chinese scope D. Normile color *Science* v356 no6343 p1107 Je 16 2017

Hobby-Eberly Telescope eyes sky with new capabilities T. Feder *Physics Today* v70 no6 p36 Je 2017

McDonald OBSERVATORY *Texas Monthly* v45 no4 p108 Ap 2017

Telescope design spat heats up *Science* v357 no6352 p628 Ag 18 2017

Optical head-mounted displays

See also

Google Glass

GADGETRY J. J. Roberts color *Fortune* v174 no8 p22 D 15 2016

What HoloLens Has That Google Glass Didn't S. Berinato *Harvard Business Review Digital Articles* p2 Ja 29 2015

Optics

See also

Color

Imaging systems

Spectrum analysis

LOOKING for TROUBLE on Optical Surfaces H. Auten *Science & Technology Review* p17 Ap/My 2017

Optics—Equipment & supplies

GO-TO GLASS D. Hurteau and J. Zavislan color *Field & Stream* v121 no6 p75 N 2016

Optimism

The 7 Deadly Sins of Personal Finance A. ROTH color *AARP: The Magazine* v59 no1A p16 D 2015/Ja 2016

Competing Against Cancer M. Oliver color *Practical Horseman* v45 no8 p72 Ag 2017

How the Internet Is Getting a Little Nicer, One Meme at a Time L. Eadicicco color *Time* v189 no23 p19 Je 19 2017

Optimists Are Better at Finding New Jobs M. Gielan *Harvard Business Review Digital Articles* p2 Ap 15 2016

See You in London A. R. ALBANESE *Publishers Weekly* v264 no9 p20 F 27 2017

Silence the Critical Voices in Your Head S. Nawaz *Harvard Business Review Digital Articles* p2 D 5 2016

The Silver Lining P. GULLEY *Indianapolis Monthly* v40 no3 p64 N 2016

Stop Being So Positive G. Oettingen *Harvard Business Review Digital Articles* p2 O 27 2014

This Just In J. Zorthian *Time* v189 no3 p19 Ja 16 2017

Why the Future Belongs to Tough-Minded Optimists B. Taylor *Harvard Business Review Digital Articles* p2 Mr 3 2016

Optimism—Physiological aspects

Bee happy M. T. Mendl and E. S. Paul bibl color diag *Science* v353 no6307 p1499 S 30 2016

Optimism—Social aspects

THE POWER OF POSITIVE SURVEYING bw *Harvard Business Review* v95 no1 p22 Ja/F 2017

Options (Finance)

See also

Stock options

Boost Your Income With Options D. FONDA color *Kiplinger's Personal Finance* v71 no6 p52 Je 2017

Optoelectronic devices

See also

Imaging systems

Light emitting diodes

Optical radar

Television

Quantum dot–induced phase stabilization of α-CsPbI3 perovskite for high-efficiency photovoltaics A. Swarnkar, A. R. Marshall et al bibl chart graph *Science* v354 no6308 p92 O 7 2016

Optoelectronics

See also

Optical lattices

Tailored semiconductors for high-harmonic optoelectronics M. Sivis, M. Taucer et al graph *Science* v357 no6348 p303 Jl 21 2017

Optogenetics

Trial and error N. Eshel bibl graph *Science* v354 no6316 p1108 D 2 2016

Optoma Group (Company)

Optoma HD142X 3D DLP Projector A. Griffin color graph *Sound & Vision* v81 no10 p62 D 2016

Optomechanics

Ambient quantum optomechanics J. G. E. Harris diag *Science* v356 no6344 p1232 Je 23 2017

Single-molecule optomechanics in "picocavities" F. Benz, M. K. Schmidt et al bibl graph *Science* v354 no6313 p726 N 11 2016

Opus Cactus! (Theatrical production)

DANCE *New Yorker* v93 no19 p8 Jl 3 2017

Ora, Rita, 1990-

America's Next Top Model I. Ratledge *TV Guide* p44 D 5 2016

America's Next Top Model Struts Again T. Stack color *Entertainment Weekly* no1443 p52 D 9 2016

Boy Band I. Ratledge *TV Guide* v65 no25 p38 Je 2017

Jean on Jean? Genius! color *Glamour* no8 p162 Ag 2017

MY BEAUTY MARK ... Rita Ora color *InStyle* v24 no4 p164 Ap 2017

PARTY LINES img *New York* v49 no26 p92 D 26 2016

Oral, Jarred

A selective insecticidal protein from Pseudomonas for controlling corn rootworms bibl chart graph *Science* v354 no6312 p634 N 4 2016

Oral communication

See also

Conversation

Invective

Narrators

Public speaking

Small talk

Telephone calls

Verbal ability

Whistle speech

Word-of-mouth communication

How to Know If You Talk Too Much M. Goulston *Harvard Business Review Digital Articles* p2 Je 3 2015

Oral communication—Psychological aspects

The Science of Sounding Smart J. Schroeder and N. Epley *Harvard Business Review Digital Articles* p2 O 7 2015

Oral communication—Study & teaching

ACADEMIC CONVERSATIONS S. Hamerla color *Literacy Today (2411-7862)* v34 no3 p30 N/D 2016

Oral diseases—Prevention

Advances in dental care *Mayo Clinic Health Letter* v35 p1 My 2017 Supplement

Oral diseases—Treatment

THE ORAL REPORT N. BARR color *Martha Stewart Living* p42 My 2017

Oral habits

See also

Mastication

Smoking

Good News for Thumb-Suckers *Parents* v91 no12 p28 D 2016

Oral hygiene

See also

Tooth care & hygiene

KEEP YOUR TEETH HEALTHY THIS HALLOWEEN [Cover story] *USA Today Magazine* v146 no2869 p1 O 2017

To Floss or Not to Floss J. KEATS color *Discover* v38 no1 p88 Ja/F 2017

Oral hygiene products—Evaluation
Winter Whites color *Prevention* v69 no1 p11 Ja 2017
Oral interpretation of poetry
THE BRIEF bw color *Art in America* v105 no1 p19 Ja 2017
Pick a Word, Any Word M. Zapruder *New York Times Book Review* p8 Jl 16 2017
Sacred lines R. Miska color *U.S. Catholic* v82 no1 p45 Ja 2017
Oral sex
12 Sex Things We Still Don't Understand K. Bonnell and P. R. Satran color *Glamour* v115 no7 p109 Jl 2017
Oral tradition
Creating better stories M. Dodd color *Christian Century* v134 no20 p10 S 27 2017
Orange (Fruit)
Why There's No Clean Way to Peel An Orange B. SPECKTOR color *Reader's Digest* v189 no1130 p132 My 2017
Orange Beach (Ala.)
ETC M. Cameran color *New Orleans Magazine* v51 no10 p215 Ag 2017
Orange Is the New Black (TV program)
No Break for Orange's Prisoners D. D'Addario color *Time* v189 no23 p53 Je 19 2017
Orange Is the New Black: In a riotous season, the women are no longer behind bars M. ROUSH *TV Guide* v65 no25 p14 Je 2017
RIOT GIRL E. NUSSBAUM cartoon color *New Yorker* v93 no26 p38 S 4 2017
Orange oil
TRIPLE-ACTION MACE: CRY, FRY, AND DYE C. LEU color *Wired* v25 no7 p26 Jl 2017
Orangutan behavior
HIGH ANXIETY: Daring orangutans, perfect weather, and food deserts. Ask the Hoosierist S. STALL color *Indianapolis Monthly* v41 no2 p19 S 2017
Wild orangutans set nursing record S. MILIUS color *Science News* v191 no12 p8 Je 24 2017
Orangutans
Epic Animal Fake Outs J. KIFFEL-ALCHIEH *National Geographic Kids* no469 p14 Ap 2017
ORANGUTAN WHISTLES A. Benjamin *National Geographic Kids* no466 p13 D 2016/Ja 2017
Out on a Limb M. White color map *National Geographic* v230 no6 p56 D 2016
Personality Quiz color diag *National Geographic Kids* no473 p14 S 2017
Riding in a Rickshaw With a Hostage Orangutan D. Stone color *National Geographic* v230 no5 p25 N 2016
Orators
See also
Motivational speakers
How to Give a Great Speech J. JOHNSON color *Yankee* p28 My/Je 2017
Orators—United States
Speak for America W. Kristol *Weekly Standard* v22 no7 p10 O 24 2016
Orbán, Viktor, 1963——Political & social views
Viktor Orban Is Turning Hungary Into Europe's Black Sheep I. Bremmer color *Time* v189 no15 p12 Ap 24 2017
Orbea Bicycles (Company)
ORBEA ORCA M11ILTD E. Huyett color *Bicycling* v58 no8 p70 S 2017
Orbea Occam (Company)
orbea occam R. Palmer color *Bike Magazine* v24 no3 p100 My 2017
Orbit Books (Company)
The Publisher with All of Speculative Fiction in Its Orbit J. Maher color *Publishers Weekly* v264 no38 p12 S 18 2017
Orbits
See also
Cometary orbits
Elliptical orbits
Orbits of artificial satellites
Planetary orbits
DETAILS ARRIVE ON TRAPPIST-1'S OUTERMOST PLANET N. Kiefert color *Astronomy* v45 no9 p12 S 2017
A Foolproof Analemma Box: This project practically guarantees good results J. Oltion *Sky & Telescope* v134 no6 p68 D 2017

Help Verify a Giant Ringed Exoplanet: For about 25 days in September, its ring system should cross an easily watched star A. MacRobert *Sky & Telescope* v134 no3 p48 S 2017
SPACE ODDITY P. FARSON and B. COLE *Scientific American* v315 no3 p5 S 2016
Orbits of artificial satellites
WHERE ARE YOU GOING? P. WHITSON color *O, The Oprah Magazine* p128 S 2017
Orbs
Orbs as Plasma Life B. RADFORD *Skeptical Inquirer* v41 no5 p28 S/O 2017
Orchard, Dunstan
FROM BACKYARD TO BACKCOUNTRY [Cover story] color *Sunset* v238 no5 p60 My 2017
Orchards
Country Lore *Mother Earth News* no283 p67 Ag/S 2017
I don't have a favorite place R. STIEVE *Arizona Highways* v93 no11 p2 N 2017
Orchestra
19 THINGS YOU REALLY OUGHT TO DO THIS MONTH M. J. Gaynor, A. Beaujon et al *Washingtonian Magazine* v52 no3 p31 D 2016
7 IDEAS FOR ORCHESTRATING BIG BAND BRASS M. Buselli color *Downbeat* v84 no4 p80 Ap 2017
Orchestras and Nazis: When music could not transcend evil T. TEACHOUT *Commentary* v144 no1 p58 Jl/Ag 2017
'Step, Step, Step' J. NORDLINGER *National Review* v69 no5 p26 Mr 20 2017
Woman of the Wand D. GROEN cartoon *Walrus* p44 Ja\F 2017
Orchestra of St. Luke's (Performer)
CLASSICAL MUSIC *New Yorker* v93 no10 p20 Ap 24 2017
Orchestral music
CLASSICAL MUSIC *New Yorker* v92 no39 p24 N 28 2016
CLASSICAL MUSIC *New Yorker* v93 no24 p10 Ag 21 2017
Orchid (Poem)
AN IMMIGRANT DAUGHTER'S SONG A. S. GIBBS bw *Chicago* v66 no7 p30 Jl 2017
Orchids
See also
Coralroots
Vanilla
WHERE THE WILD ORCHID GROWS A. McGIVNEY *Arizona Highways* v93 no8 p38 Ag 2017
WINTER FRESH color *Sunset* v237 no6 p46 D 2016
Orcutt, Mike
The Next Big Encryption Fight May Not Happen in Public [Cover story] il *MIT Technology Review* v120 no3 p26 My/Je 2017
PIONEERS color il *MIT Technology Review* v120 no5 p50 S/O 2017
VISIONARIES color il *MIT Technology Review* v120 no5 p42 S/O 2017
Orden Pour le Mérite
Valor The Last Blue Max D. T. Zabecki bw *Military History* v34 no5 p16 Ja 2018
Orderliness
THE ODDS AND ENDS OF ZEN L. Haney color *Women's Health* v14 no4 p121 My 2017
Order of Time, The (Music)
Why Valerie June Sings the Blues D. BROWNE bw *Rolling Stone* no1287 p18 My 18 2017
Ordinary income
Where the Living Is Easy Wei Lu map *Bloomberg Businessweek* no4514 p41 Mr 13 2017
Ordinary Miracles (Short story)
ORDINARY MIRACLES On hope, howling, and weeds S. A. RUSSELL *Orion Magazine* v35 no3 p12 My/Je 2016
Ordin-Nashchokin, Afanasiĭ Lavrent'evich ca. 1606-1680 ...
The Truce of Andrusovo is signed *History Today* v67 no1 p9 Ja 2017
Ordnance
See also
Machine guns
Nuclear weapons
Telescopic gun sights
Warheads
How to... DESTROY ANYTHING color *Popular Mechanics* p83

S 2017
JOURNEY TO GUNLAND M. Wenner Moyer color graph *Scientific American* v317 no4 p54 O 2017

Ordovician radiation (Evolution)
Asteroid barrage not linked to boom in ancient marine life T. Sumner *Science News* v191 no3 p18 F 18 2017

Ordway, Diane
Emergence and spread of a human-transmissible multidrug-resistant nontuberculous mycobacterium bibl diag graph *Science* v354 no6313 p751 N 11 2016

Ore deposits
Biological control of aragonite formation in stony corals S. Von Euw, Q. Zhang et al bw color graph *Science* v356 no6341 p933 Je 1 2017
NEVADA A. Kylie color *Canadian Geographic* v135 no6 p30 D 2015

Oregano
Speeches and Herb S. F. HAYES color *Weekly Standard* v22 no7 p5 O 24 2016

Oregon silverspot butterfly
THE BUTTERFLY EFFECT N. Hill color *Earth Island Journal* v32 no2 p30 Summ 2017

Oregon—Description & travel
CAPE COVE, OREGON color *Runner's World* v52 no6 p8 Jl 2017
High-Desert Adventure C. KAYANO color *Trail Rider* v29 no4 p58 My 2017
OREGON'S McMINNVILLE K. Newberry color map *Sunset* v239 no4 p28 O 2017
Where-to-Ride Guide map *Trail Rider* v29 no1 p58 Ja/F 2017

O'Reilly, Bill, 1949-
HIT THE ROAD, BILL T. BOSNIC *In These Times* v41 no6 p11 Je 2017
Is This Thing On? C. Collis color *Entertainment Weekly* no1436/1437 p15 O 21 2016
Unit Sales Rise 4% chart *Publishers Weekly* v264 no40 p6 O 2 2017
Super Bowl Sunday Presidential Sit-Down I. RUDOLPH *TV Guide* v65 no6 p11 Ja 30 2017

O'reilly, Finbarr
The Emotional Fallout from War color *Publishers Weekly* v264 no30 p34 Jl 24 2017

O'Reilly, Katie
Back in Style *Sierra* v102 no3 p18 My/Je 2017
Catering to the Planet *Sierra* v102 no2 p10 Mr/Ap 2017
Code of Silence *Sierra* v102 no3 p10 My/Je 2017
COOL SCHOOLS 2017 *Sierra* v102 no5 p41 St/O 2017
Don't Have a Cow *Sierra* v102 no5 p8 St/O 2017
Nature's Blockbuster *Sierra* v102 no2 p8 Mr/Ap 2017
Truth Be Told: Former vice president Al Gore returns to theaters to discuss our continuing climate crisis *Sierra* v102 no4 p10 Jl/Ag 2017

O'Reilly, Mollie Wilson
The Man Who Knew Too Little [Cover story] bw *Commonweal* v144 no17 p6 O 20 2017
Missing Nixon bw *Commonweal* v144 no8 p6 My 5 2017
Out of Luck color *Commonweal* v144 no4 p6 F 24 2017
Solidarity or Silence? color *Commonweal* v144 no12 p7 Jl 7 2017
Waiting by the Jesse Tree color *Commonweal* v143 no20 p7 D 16 2016
You'll Feel a Little Pinch color *Commonweal* v143 no17 p6 O 21 2016

O'Reilly Automotive Inc.
The Delivery Driver J. Lowe *New York Times Magazine* p42 F 26 2017

O'Reilly Media Inc.
WHAT'S NEXT FOR O'REILLY? D. BIANCULLI *TV Guide* v65 no19 p16 My 1 2017

Oren, Michael B., 1955-
The Ally That Wasn't E. Abrams *Commentary* v140 no2 p34 S 2015
The Ally That Wasn't: Michael Oren's memoir blasts Barack Obama but pulls its punches elsewhere E. ABRAMS *Commentary* v140 no2 p55 S 2015

Orenstein, M.
Revealing the subfemtosecond dynamics of orbital angular mo-

mentum in nanoplasmonic vortices bibl diag *Science* v355 no6330 p1187 Mr 17 2017

Orenstein, Peggy
NEW HAWAII color *Sunset* v237 no6 p23 D 2016

Orenstein, Peggy—Interviews
PARENT TRAP: YOUR KIDS WILL SEE INTERNET PORN. DEAL WITH IT. A CONVERSATION WITH PEGGY ORENSTEIN S. FALLON and L. H. NEWMAN cartoon *Wired* v25 no9 p78 S 2017

Oresick, Jake
NEVER GOING BACK TO MY OLD SCHOOL M. Taylor bw color *American History* v52 no4 p67 O 2017

Oreskes, Michael
When local stopped being cool color *Columbia Journalism Review* v56 no1 p15 Spr 2017

Oreskes, Naomi
Corporations Will Never Solve Climate Change *Harvard Business Review Digital Articles* p2 D 4 2015

Oresteia (Play : Aeschylus)
ORIGINAL INTENT Aeschylus *Lapham's Quarterly* v10 no3 p29 Summ 2017

Orfalea, Gregory
Self-Inflicted Carnage color *Commonweal* v144 no13 p17 Ag 11 2017

Orfield, Gary
When choice fosters inequality chart color graph il *Phi Delta Kappan* v98 no4 p49 D 2016/Ja 2017

Organa, Leia (Fictitious character)
1956 - 2016 CARRIE FISHER [Cover story] A. Breznican color *Entertainment Weekly* no1448 p18 Ja 13 2017

Organic beverages
HERB APPEAL J. BALL *Indianapolis Monthly* v12 no40 p66 Ag 2017

Organic chemistry
Allotropy by design—Carbon nanohoops J. S. Siegel diag *Science* v356 no6334 p135 Ap 14 2017
Unequivocal determination of complex molecular structures using anisotropic NMR measurements Y. Liu, J. Sauri et al color *Science* v356 no6333 p43 Ap 7 2017

Organic compounds
See also
Alcohols (Chemical class)
Methyl isocyanate
Proteins
Localized aliphatic organic material on the surface of Ceres M. C. De Sanctis, E. Ammannito et al bibl graph *Science* v355 no6326 p719 F 17 2017
MEET THE MASTER OF THE LUSH (PLANT) LIFE M. McKinnon color *Rodale's Organic Life* v3 no1 p71 Ja 2017
Organic compounds detected on Ceres color *Science* v355 no6326 p706 F 17 2017
Organic compounds found on Ceres E. S. EATON color *Science News* v191 no5 p8 Mr 18 2017
Two-dimensional sp2 carbon–conjugated covalent organic frameworks E. Jin, M. Asada et al diag graph *Science* v357 no6352 p673 Ag 18 2017

Organic design
This is how to mix prints color *Redbook* p134 O 2017

Organic farming
Case Study: How Would You Save This Farm? F. L. Reinhardt and A. Beard *Harvard Business Review Digital Articles* p2 Ag 12 2016
Nature's Cancer Sticks P. Brownfield cartoon color *Bloomberg Businessweek* no4499 p64 N 14 2016
new orleAns' new Groove B. ANDREWS color *Rodale's Organic Life* v2 no7 p66 D 2016/Ja 2017
Tea service J. M. Griffith color *U.S. Catholic* v82 no6 p45 Je 2017

Organic farming—Study & teaching
Take a Free Course on Organic Seed S. Stonebrook *Mother Earth News* no279 p7 D/Ja 2017

Organic fertilizers
BEST ORGANIC FERTILIZERS [Cover story] H. Garrett *Mother Earth News* no281 p16 Ap/My 2017

Organic foods
AMAZING NEWS V. Tweed color *Amazing Wellness* v9 no1 p14 Wint 2017

Catering to the Planet K. O'Reilly *Sierra* v102 no2 p10 Mr/Ap 2017

GROW, EAT, LOVE [Cover story] T. Karras and S. Beaucamp cartoon chart color *Yoga Journal* no291 p36 My 2017

LONG LIVE THE BEACH color *Women's Health* v14 no5 p144 Je 2017

Organic foods—Economic aspects

THE HEALTHY FOOD PRICE MYTH color *Better Nutrition* v79 no3 p18 Mr 2017

Organic gardening

Fresh From the Hills *South Dakota Magazine* v32 no6 p42 Mr/Ap 2017

Organic light emitting diode efficiency

High-performance light-emitting diodes based on carbene-metal-amides D. Di, A. S. Romanov et al chart graph *Science* v356 no6334 p159 Ap 14 2017

Organic light emitting diode manufacturing

Why Japan's Idemitsu Isn't Feeling Blue P. Alpeyev, T. Taniguchi et al color *Bloomberg Businessweek* no4520 p34 My 1 2017

Organic light emitting diodes

Feature: 2017 could see just one OLED iPhone C. McGarry color *Macworld - Digital Edition* p100 Ja 2017

OLED Turns 30 C. Crowley color *Sound & Vision* v82 no6 p16 Jl/Ag 2017

Organic light emitting diodes—Evaluation

Alienware 13 (2016): The first OLED gaming laptop has landed J. NOREM color graph *PCWorld* p102 D 2016

Organic products

Catering to the Planet K. O'Reilly *Sierra* v102 no2 p10 Mr/Ap 2017

Hey Mr. Green! Why are organics plastic-wrapped? B. Schildgen *Sierra* v101 no4 p12 Jl/Ag 2016

Into the Mild L. REGENSDORF color *Vogue* v207 no10 p220 O 2017

Promises, PROMISES chart color *O, The Oprah Magazine* p79 Mr 2017

Organic wastes

See also

Food industrial waste

TRASH NATION C. WILKINS cartoon *Canadian Geographic* v137 no3 p48 My 2017

Organic farmers—Societies, etc.

The Wild and Wonderful J. TUNG *Martha Stewart Living* no267 p54 S 2016

Organic light-emitting diode televisions

TOP PICKS OF THE TOP PICKS R. SABIN *Sound & Vision* v82 no2 p8 F/Mr 2017

Organisms

See also

Cells

Eukaryotes

Microorganisms

Transgenic organisms

Evolution of protein phosphorylation across 18 fungal species R. A. Studer, R. A. Rodriguez-Mias et al bibl graph *Science* v354 no6309 p229 O 14 2016

Synthetic cell may reveal what is necessary for life R. Ehrenberg color *Science News* v190 no13 p26 D 24 2016

Organization

See also

Community organization

Industrial organization (Management)

Organizational change

Organizational effectiveness

Organizational structure

Planning

wrap party! J. PHILLIP color *Good Housekeeping* v263 no6 p36 D 2016

Organization of Petroleum Exporting Countries

The Cartel That Failed I. M. Stelzer color *Weekly Standard* v22 no29 p11 Ap 3 2017

Falling Oil Prices Don't Make OPEC Irrelevant R. Mohammed *Harvard Business Review Digital Articles* p2 D 11 2014

How Frackers Beat OPEC V. VARA color *Atlantic* v319 no1 p20 Ja/F 2017

Milestones color *Time* v188 no24 p19 D 12 2016

A SAUDI ABOUT-FACE J. Blas graph *Bloomberg Businessweek* no4496 p82 O 24 2016

Organizational accountability

The Unsexy Fundamentals of Great HR M. Effron and M. Ort *Harvard Business Review Digital Articles* p2 Ag 19 2015

Organizational aims & objectives

Getting Employees Excited About a New Direction D. A. Ready *Harvard Business Review Digital Articles* p2 N 20 2015

How to Make Agile Work for the C-Suite E. Garton and A. Noble *Harvard Business Review Digital Articles* p2 Jl 19 2017

Organizational behavior

See also

Corporate culture

Organizational resilience

50 Years Ago an Economist Worried About Unchecked Corporate Power. Here's What His Theory Got Wrong J. Gans *Harvard Business Review Digital Articles* p2 2017

Adapting Your Organizational Processes to a New Culture A. Molinsky and R. Moriarty *Harvard Business Review Digital Articles* p2 O 7 2016

The Biggest Mistakes New Executives Make S. Nawaz *Harvard Business Review Digital Articles* p2 My 15 2017

Get Your Organization to Run in Sync G. Satell *Harvard Business Review Digital Articles* p2 N 5 2014

How Self-Managed Companies Help People Learn on the Job E. Bernstein, N. Canner et al *Harvard Business Review Digital Articles* p2 Ag 3 2016

Loyalty to a Leader Is Overrated, Even Dangerous J. Irwin *Harvard Business Review Digital Articles* p2 D 16 2014

Office Politics Is Just Influence by Another Name A. McKee *Harvard Business Review Digital Articles* p2 Ja 16 2015

Office Politics Isn't Something You Can Sit Out K. K. Reardon *Harvard Business Review Digital Articles* p2 Ja 12 2015

Research: For a Corporate Apology to Work, the CEO Should Look Sad S. G. Carmichael *Harvard Business Review Digital Articles* p2 Ag 24 2015

Signs Your Team Is Too Strong for Its Own Good J. Grenny *Harvard Business Review Digital Articles* p2 Je 29 2015

To Be More Creative, Schedule Your Breaks J. G. Lu, M. Akinola et al *Harvard Business Review Digital Articles* p2 My 10 2017

To Foster Innovation, Connect Coworkers Who Share Aspirations C. de Anca and S. Aragón *Harvard Business Review Digital Articles* p2 Jl 14 2016

Use Stories from Customers to Highlight Your Company's Purpose E. Keswin *Harvard Business Review Digital Articles* p1 Je 22 2017

When Your Boss Gives You Conflicting Messages L. Schlesinger and C. Kiefer *Harvard Business Review Digital Articles* p2 N 27 2014

You Can't Engage Employees by Copying How Other Companies Do It M. Beer *Harvard Business Review Digital Articles* p2 N 17 2015

Your New Idea Is Worthless Unless You Know How to Sell It L. Davey *Harvard Business Review Digital Articles* p2 N 26 2015

Organizational behavior—Management

Find Purpose in Even Your Most Mundane Tasks at Work V. Keller and C. Webb color graph *Harvard Business Review Digital Articles* p2 Mr 8 2017

When Your Company Has a Problem It Can't Ignore M. O'Connor and B. Dornfeld *Harvard Business Review Digital Articles* p2 O 7 2014

Why the Problem with Learning Is Unlearning M. Bonchek *Harvard Business Review Digital Articles* p2 N 3 2016

Organizational change

See also

Resistance to change

Retail store closures

3 Traps That Block Corporate Transformation V. Nayar *Harvard Business Review Digital Articles* p2 N 5 2014

ANTHEA MARRIS: Managing change can be disheartening - but it's worth sticking with *People Management* p18 S 2017

The Biggest U.S. Health Care Challenges Are Management Challenges P. Merrild *Harvard Business Review Digital Articles* p2 F 6 2015

Change Efforts Can Fail Unless They're Coordinated R. Newton *Harvard Business Review Digital Articles* p2 Ja 22 2016

Change Management and Leadership Development Have to Mesh R. W. Quinn and R. E. Quinn *Harvard Business Review Digital Articles* p2 Ja 7 2016

Changing an Organization's Culture, Without Resistance or Blame T. DiDonato and N. Gill *Harvard Business Review Digital Articles* p2 Jl 15 2015

Data Can Do for Change Management What It Did for Marketing M. L. Tushman, A. Kahn et al *Harvard Business Review Digital Articles* p2 Jl 31 2017

DAVID CLUTTERBUCK: HR must 'upcycle' outdated approaches to survive the future D. Clutterbuck *People Management* p19 Je 2017

Email and Calendar Data Are Helping Firms Understand How Employees Work M. L. Tushman, A. Kahn et al *Harvard Business Review Digital Articles* p2 Ag 28 2017

Embracing Change Means Disrupting Your Day K. Sweetman and S. Cragun *Harvard Business Review Digital Articles* p2 Jl 22 2016

EXECUTIVE SUMMARIES color *Harvard Business Review* v95 no5 p150 S/O 2017

Experiment with Organizational Change Before Going All In J. Beshears and F. Gino *Harvard Business Review Digital Articles* p2 O 13 2014

The Female Soldiers Who've Already Joined Special Ops Teams G. T. Lemmon *Harvard Business Review Digital Articles* p2 Ag 21 2015

Getting People to Believe in Something They Can't Yet Imagine L. E. Miller and K. H. Onieal *Harvard Business Review Digital Articles* p2 O 10 2014

How Domino's Pizza Reinvented Itself B. Taylor *Harvard Business Review Digital Articles* p2 N 28 2016

How I Led Change in the U.S. State Department Bureaucracy T. Cochran color *Harvard Business Review Digital Articles* p2 Ja 4 2017

How Loss Aversion and Conformity Threaten Organizational Change S. Ryan *Harvard Business Review Digital Articles* p2 N 15 2016

How to Communicate Clearly During Organizational Change E. Johnson *Harvard Business Review Digital Articles* p2 Je 13 2017

HOW TO MASTER CHANGE D. Lyons color *Fortune* v174 no7 p50 D 1 2016

The Internet of Things Will Change Your Company, Not Just Your Products J. Fitts *Harvard Business Review Digital Articles* p2 O 24 2014

Leadership in Liminal Times D. Pontefract *Harvard Business Review Digital Articles* p2 O 10 2014

Leaders Who Get Change Right Know How to Listen P. Sanchez *Harvard Business Review Digital Articles* p2 O 17 2016

Non-Discrimination Laws Make U.S. States More Innovative Huasheng Gao and Wei Zhang *Harvard Business Review Digital Articles* p2 Ag 17 2016

Overcome Resistance to Change with Two Conversations S. Blount and S. Carroll *Harvard Business Review Digital Articles* p2 My 16 2017

"People were sceptical but now we're delivering better patient care": Why an NHS Trust invested in upskilling middle managers as OD practitioners *People Management* p25 S 2017

Rethinking the Corporate Love Affair with Change Z. First *Harvard Business Review Digital Articles* p2 Mr 20 2017

Stop Using the Excuse "Organizational Change Is Hard" N. Tasler *Harvard Business Review Digital Articles* p2 Jl 19 2017

To Lead Change, Explain the Context R. Ashkenas *Harvard Business Review Digital Articles* p2 N 24 2015

To Radically Redesign Health Care, Start with One Unit J. S. Toussaint *Harvard Business Review Digital Articles* p2 D 9 2015

Transitioning Your Company from Product to Platform N. Furr *Harvard Business Review Digital Articles* p2 Ap 7 2016

A Way to Assess and Prioritize Your Change Efforts P. Keenan, S. Mingardon et al *Harvard Business Review Digital Articles* p2 Jl 9 2015

"We deliberately don't call it 'engagement'": Why HR put employees in the driving seat in its quest to reinvigorate the company's culture E. BURT *People Management* p20 Mr 2017

We Still Don't Know the Difference Between Change and Transformation R. Ashkenas *Harvard Business Review Digital Articles* p2 Ja 15 2015

What Spinning Off a GE Business Taught Me About Managing Ultra-Fast Change M. Keane *Harvard Business Review Digital Articles* p2 Jl 24 2017

What the Best Transformational Leaders Do S. Anthony and E. I. Schwartz *Harvard Business Review Digital Articles* p2 My 8 2017

What the Companies on the Right Side of the Digital Business Divide Have in Common R. Bock, M. Iansiti et al color *Harvard Business Review Digital Articles* p2 Ja 31 2017

Why Government Workers Are Harder to Motivate R. Lavigna *Harvard Business Review Digital Articles* p2 N 28 2014

You Don't Have to Be the Boss to Change How Your Company Works J. Overbeck *Harvard Business Review Digital Articles* p2 F 26 2015

Zappos and the Connection Between Structure and Strategy J. P. Vazquez Sampere *Harvard Business Review Digital Articles* p2 Je 3 2015

Organizational change—Germany

Reinventing These Wheels C. Rauwald and C. Reiter color graph *Bloomberg Businessweek* no4504 p19 D 19 2016

Organizational change—History

HOW I REMADE GE: AND WHAT I LEARNED ALONG THE WAY J. R. IMMELT color *Harvard Business Review* v95 no5 p42 S/O 2017

Organizational change—United States

Artifact: General Electric Lightbulb R. Clough and A. Ricadela color *Bloomberg Businessweek* no4527 p25 Je 19 2017

No Use for Old School Ties M. McDonald and J. Brustein color *Bloomberg Businessweek* no4526 p32 Je 12 2017

Organizational commitment

Germany's Midsize Manufacturers Outperform Its Industrial Giants W. W. Weber *Harvard Business Review Digital Articles* p2 Ag 12 2016

A Guide to Managing a Volunteer Workforce J. McCannon and H. Han *Harvard Business Review Digital Articles* p2 Mr 2 2016

How Hard Do Company Founders Really Work? K. Firestone *Harvard Business Review Digital Articles* p2 D 17 2014

Loyalty to a Leader Is Overrated, Even Dangerous J. Irwin *Harvard Business Review Digital Articles* p2 D 16 2014

Marissa Mayer Was Right to Ask Executives to Commit to Staying at Yahoo R. Hoffman, B. Casnocha et al *Harvard Business Review Digital Articles* p2 N 11 2015

You Can't Engage Employees by Copying How Other Companies Do It M. Beer *Harvard Business Review Digital Articles* p2 N 17 2015

Organizational effectiveness

See also

Organizational performance

The 15 Diseases of Leadership, According to Pope Francis G. Hamel *Harvard Business Review Digital Articles* p2 Ap 14 2015

A Brief History of the Ways Companies Compete K. Favaro *Harvard Business Review Digital Articles* p2 Ap 22 2015

Collaboration Overload Is a Symptom of a Deeper Organizational Problem M. Mankins *Harvard Business Review Digital Articles* p2 Mr 27 2017

How to Design Meetings Your Team Will Want to Attend P. Axtell color *Harvard Business Review Digital Articles* p2 Ap 5 2017

Jack Welch's Approach to Breaking Down Silos Still Works R. Ashkenas *Harvard Business Review Digital Articles* p2 S 9 2015

Why the Future Belongs to Tough-Minded Optimists B. Taylor *Harvard Business Review Digital Articles* p2 Mr 3 2016

Your Customers' Behavior Is a Competitive Advantage M. Schrage *Harvard Business Review Digital Articles* p2 Ja 16 2015

Organizational goals

Align Your Time Management with Your Goals *Harvard Business Review Digital Articles* p2 D 8 2014

Can Your Sales Team Actually Achieve Their Stretch Goals? A. A. Zoltners, P. K. Sinha et al *Harvard Business Review Digital Articles* p2 Jl 11 2016

COMPETING ON SOCIAL PURPOSE: BRANDS THAT WIN BY TYING MISSION TO GROWTH O. R. VIL&#193 and S. BHARADWAJ chart diag il img *Harvard Business Review* v95 no5 p94 S/O 2017

Downsizing Google's Dream C. Chen and M. Bergen color *Bloomberg Businessweek* no4519 p36 Ap 24 2017

How Aligned Is Your Organization? J. Trevor and B. Varcoe color *Harvard Business Review Digital Articles* p2 F 7 2017

Make Your Work Resolutions Stick R. Knight *Harvard Business Review Digital Articles* p2 D 29 2014

NEXT STEPS AT THE AIA J. Magness bw *Archaeology* v70 no3 p6 My/Je 2017

A Simple Way to Test Your Company's Strategic Alignment J. Trevor and B. Varcoe *Harvard Business Review Digital Articles* p2 My 16 2016

Staples Doesn't Want To Be Your Superstore M. Townsend color *Bloomberg Businessweek* no4517 p24 Ap 3 2017

A Way to Know If Your Corporate Goals Are Too Aggressive M. E. Raynor and D. Pankratz *Harvard Business Review Digital Articles* p2 Jl 13 2015

Organizational growth

Farm to Theater J. Peters *Dance Magazine* v91 no1 p42 Ja 2017

Organizational ideology

Does Stating What Your Company Stands for Affect Your Bottom Line? W. Frick *Harvard Business Review Digital Articles* p2 Ag 3 2015

How Corporate Values Get Hijacked and Misused R. Carucci *Harvard Business Review Digital Articles* p2 My 29 2017

LESSONS AND IDEAS BY THE 100 GREATEST LIVING BUSINESS MINDS R. Lane, S. Adams et al bw color *Forbes* v200 no3 p115 S 28 2017

Simple Ethics Rules for Better Risk Management D. Disparte *Harvard Business Review Digital Articles* p2 N 8 2016

Why Self Image Matters in B2B Sales B. Adamson, K. Schmidt et al *Harvard Business Review Digital Articles* p2 Ap 2 2015

Organizational learning

How Learning and Development Are Becoming More Agile J. Younger *Harvard Business Review Digital Articles* p2 O 11 2016

How to Support Employees' Learning Goals While Getting Day-to-Day Stuff Done N. Gidwani *Harvard Business Review Digital Articles* p2 Ag 1 2017

Increasing Student Success in STEM: Summary of A Guide to Systemic Institutional Change S. Elrod and A. Kezar *Change* v49 no4 p26 Jl/Ag 2017

Organizational learning—Management

The Most Productive Way to Develop as a Leader H. Ibarra *Harvard Business Review Digital Articles* p2 Mr 27 2015

Why the Problem with Learning Is Unlearning M. Bonchek *Harvard Business Review Digital Articles* p2 N 3 2016

Organizational name changes

See also

School name changes

Name Fights, IRL T. Keith color diag *Sports Illustrated* v127 no1 p16 Jl 3 2017

Nullifying Calhoun J. Cost *Weekly Standard* v22 no24 p16 F 27 2017

To Stay Relevant, Professional Associations Must Rebrand D. L. Yohn *Harvard Business Review Digital Articles* p2 Ja 5 2016

Organizational performance

The 3 Company Crises Boards Should Watch For P. Cebon color *Harvard Business Review Digital Articles* p2 Ja 16 2017

4 Tools to Help You Identify the Skills You Need to Grow D. Rousmaniere *Harvard Business Review Digital Articles* p2 Ag 8 2016

50 COMPANIES TO WATCH color diag graph map *Bloomberg Businessweek* no4496 p91 O 24 2016

Calculating the Market Value of Leadership A. Freed and D. Ulrich *Harvard Business Review Digital Articles* p2 Ap 3 2015

Cheap Shares, Plenty of Cash R. ERMEY chart color *Kiplinger's Personal Finance* v71 no11 p58 N 2017

Collaboration Overload Is a Symptom of a Deeper Organizational Problem M. Mankins *Harvard Business Review Digital Articles* p2 Mr 27 2017

The Curse Of Zombie Inc J. Clenfield color *Bloomberg Businessweek* no4519 p16 Ap 24 2017

Great Companies Stay True to the Spirit of Their Founders J. Allen *Harvard Business Review Digital Articles* p2 Mr 14 2016

How Shared Leadership Changes Our Relationships at Work D. Fitzsimons *Harvard Business Review Digital Articles* p2 My 12

2016

Inequality Isn't Just Due to Market Forces — It's Caused by Decisions the Boss Makes, Too A. Cobb *Harvard Business Review Digital Articles* p2 Mr 30 2017

Is It Too Late for Sears to Save Itself? D. Lee Yohn color *Harvard Business Review Digital Articles* p2 Mr 30 2017

Jack Welch's Approach to Breaking Down Silos Still Works R. Ashkenas *Harvard Business Review Digital Articles* p2 S 9 2015

Reigning Supreme R. Sullivan bw color *Vogue* v207 no9 p710 S 2017

Stop Comparing Management to Sports F. Vermeulen *Harvard Business Review Digital Articles* p2 Je 2 2016

Surviving Amazon D. FONDA color *Kiplinger's Personal Finance* v71 no7 p60 Jl 2017

To Grow as a Person, Selectively Forget the Past V. Govindarajan *Harvard Business Review Digital Articles* p2 My 12 2016

A Way to Gauge How Well Your Company Is Really Performing M. E. Raynor and D. Pankratz *Harvard Business Review Digital Articles* p2 My 8 2015

Where to Invest Now A. K. SMITH cartoon graph *Kiplinger's Personal Finance* v71 no7 p46 Jl 2017

WHY DO WE UNDERVALUE COMPETENT MANAGEMENT? NEITHER GREAT LEADERSHIP NOR BRILLIANT STRATEGY MATTERS WITHOUT OPERATIONAL EXCELLENCE R. SADUN, N. BLOOM et al graph il img *Harvard Business Review* v95 no5 p120 S/O 2017

Organizational performance—Measurement

The False Promise of the Single Metric G. Kenny *Harvard Business Review Digital Articles* p2 Ag 26 2015

Find Purpose in Even Your Most Mundane Tasks at Work V. Keller and C. Webb color graph *Harvard Business Review Digital Articles* p2 Mr 8 2017

Organizational resilience

The Better You Know Yourself, the More Resilient You'll Be R. Carucci *Harvard Business Review Digital Articles* p2 S 4 2017

What Resilience Means, and Why It Matters A. Ovans *Harvard Business Review Digital Articles* p2 Ja 5 2015

Organizational sociology

See also

Diversity in organizations

Getting Teams with Different Subcultures to Collaborate R. Schwarz *Harvard Business Review Digital Articles* p2 Jl 22 2016

The Oldest Kid on The Job B. BRODY color *Reader's Digest* v190 no1134 p22 O 2017

Organizational structure

3 Things Are Holding Back Your Analytics, and Technology Isn't One of Them T. Clark and D. Wiesenfeld *Harvard Business Review Digital Articles* p2 Je 8 2017

Don't Let Outdated Management Structures Kill Your Company V. Nayar *Harvard Business Review Digital Articles* p2 F 10 2016

Dysfunctional Products Come from Dysfunctional Organizations J. Kolko *Harvard Business Review Digital Articles* p2 Ja 21 2015

Figuring Out How IT, Analytics, and Operations Should Work Together G. Berkooz *Harvard Business Review Digital Articles* p2 Ag 3 2016

Getting Reorgs Right S. Heidari-Robinson and S. Heywood diag *Harvard Business Review* v94 no11 p84 N 2016

Making Matrix Organizations Actually Work H. Vantrappen and F. Wirtz *Harvard Business Review Digital Articles* p2 Mr 1 2016

Research: Narcissists Don't Like Flat Organizations E. Zitek and A. Jordan *Harvard Business Review Digital Articles* p2 Jl 27 2016

Top-Down Solutions Like Holacracy Won't Fix Bureaucracy G. Hamel and M. Zanini *Harvard Business Review Digital Articles* p2 Mr 22 2016

Why Being a Middle Manager Is So Exhausting E. M. Anicich and J. B. Hirsh *Harvard Business Review Digital Articles* p2 Mr 22 2017

Why Tesla Won't Be Able to Scale T. Bartman *Harvard Business Review Digital Articles* p2 Ap 23 2015

Organization—Management

Most Reorgs Aren't Ambitious Enough R. Carucci color *Harvard Business Review Digital Articles* p2 F 10 2017

Organized crime

THE NEXT-GENERATION NARCO J. EELLS color map *Rolling Stone* no1291/1292 p54 Jl 13 2017

OldFellas G. ANASTASIA color *AARP: The Magazine* v59 no1A p44 D 2015/Ja 2016

The Wild BUNCH S. HOLLANDSWORTH *Texas Monthly* v45 no4 p47 Ap 2017

Organoids

Human tissues in a dish: The research and ethical implications of organoid technology A. L. Bredenoord, H. Clevers et al diag *Science* v355 no6322 p260 Ja 20 2017

LAB-BUILT BRAINS [Cover story] J. A. Knoblich color *Scientific American* v316 no1 p26 Ja 2017

Mini-livers reveal fine details of organ development E. Pennisi color *Science* v356 no6343 p1109 Je 16 2017

THE ORGANOID ARCHITECT G. Sinha color *Science* v357 no6353 p746 Ag 25 2017

Organometallic chemistry

Improving efficiency and stability of perovskite solar cells with photocurable fluoropolymers F. Bella, G. Griffini et al bibl chart graph *Science* v354 no6309 p203 O 14 2016

Photosensitized, energy transfer-mediated organometallic catalysis through electronically excited nickel(II) E. R. Welin, D. M. Arias-Rotondo et al bibl diag graph *Science* v355 no6323 p380 Ja 27 2017

Organovo Holdings Inc.

Synthetic Tissues A. Popescu color *Bloomberg Businessweek* no4520 p35 My 1 2017

Organs (Anatomy)

The future of bionic dynamos C. Dagdeviren bibl color *Science* v354 no6316 p1109-A D 2 2016

Human-animal chimeras created T. H. SAEY color *Science News* v191 no3 p6 F 18 2017

Multipotent peripheral glial cells generate neuroendocrine cells of the adrenal medulla A. Furlan, V. Dyachuk et al color *Science* v357 no6346 p46 Jl 7 2017

ORGAN ID C. Barakat and M. Freckleton *Equus* no478 p22 Jl 2017

Orgasm

For Better Sex, Ask Her This color *Men's Health* v31 no10 p38 D 2016

Orgeron, Ed

Coach Ed Orgeron F. ESKER color *Louisiana Life* v37 no3 p66 Ja/F 2017

Orient, Jane M.

The Blight of ObamaCare Will Not Vanish *USA Today Magazine* v146 no2868 p16 S 2017

THE CASE FOR BEING UNINSURED *USA Today Magazine* v145 no2861 p4 F 2017

CHEMICAL WEAPONS CONUNDRUM *USA Today Magazine* v146 no2866 p34 Jl 2017

Nyet to the American Media *USA Today Magazine* v146 no2866 p17 Jl 2017

REPEAL VS. REALITY *USA Today Magazine* v145 no2864 p28 My 2017

TELEMEDICINE TROUBLE AHEAD *USA Today Magazine* v145 no2858 p36 N 2016

Orient Epithalamion (Poem)

ORIENT EPITHALAMION J. Galassi *New Yorker* v92 no43 p40 Ja 2 2017

Oriental fire-bellied toad

Who's (sort of) counting? S. Milius color *Science News* v190 no12 p25 D 10 2016

Orientation

What Do New Faculty Members Want From Their University? C. A. Flores and E. J. Gordon *Change* v49 no4 p52 Jl/Ag 2017

Origami

The Gilded Cage L. Mulcahy *Stage Directions* v29 no12 p28 D 2016

MONEYGAMI G. WEBER *Washingtonian Magazine* v52 no4 p23 Ja 2017

Origami outfits help bots retool M. TEMMING color *Science News* v192 no7 p13 O 28 2017

Origanum

See also
    Oregano

Majorana bound state in a coupled quantum-dot hybrid-nanowire system M. T. Deng, S. Vaitiekénas et al bibl graph *Science* v354 no6319 p1557 D 23 2016

Origin of life

If Life Can Make It Here, It Can Make It Anywhere *USA Today Magazine* v145 no2865 p11 Je 2017

Let's hear it for abiogenesis D. J. Eicher color *Astronomy* v45 no9 p8 S 2017

Many Planets, Not Much Life P. Davies color *Scientific American* v315 no3 p8 S 2016

Science's Confusion Concerning the Origin of Life M. AVERICK *USA Today Magazine* v145 no2862 p46 Mr 2017

WHERE DID IT ALL BEGIN? K. MCGOWAN color map *Popular Science* v289 no5 p38 S/O 2017

Origin of planets

Exoplanet's skies hint at origin story A. YEAGER color *Science News* v191 no11 p11 Je 10 2017

Giant solo planets are in limited supply A. YEAGER *Science News* v192 no2 p10 Ag 19 2017

New proposal reimagines Mars' origin T. SUMNER color *Science News* v191 no10 p14 My 27 2017

Solar system birthed Jupiter early on L. GROSSMAN color *Science News* v191 no13 p18 Jl 8 2017

Origin of planets—Research

BROWN DWARFS FORMING PLANETS K. Haynes color *Astronomy* v45 no1 p10 Ja 2017

Origin Story (Poem)

ORIGIN STORY B. Hicok *New Yorker* v93 no24 p46 Ag 21 2017

Original Dixieland Jazz Band (Performer)

1917 [Cover story] J. McDonough bw color *Downbeat* v84 no1 p27 Ja 2017

All That Jass *Smithsonian* v47 no9 p13 Ja/F 2017

Centennial for Jazz B. ZIMMERMAN color *Downbeat* v84 no1 p8 Ja 2017

Originalism (Constitutional interpretation)

The Meaning of Scalia J. MCKENNA *Commentary* v142 no1 p13 Jl/Ag 2016

Originals, The (TV program)

The Originals I. Rudolph *TV Guide* v65 no25 p38 Je 2017

Orihuela, Rodrigo

Injecting Data, Not Drugs, to Win the Tour color *Bloomberg Businessweek* no4515 p41 Mr 20 2017

Oriol, Estevan

Keeping His Fingers Crossed P. GREEN *Los Angeles Magazine* v61 no11 p30 N 2016

Orion (Constellation)

Orion's Sword P. HARRINGTON color *Astronomy* v45 no2 p70 F 2017

Orion Nebula

The Jewel in the Sword: An observer captures on a sketchpad the stunning details of one of the most wondrous objects in the night sky H. Banich *Sky & Telescope* v134 no6 p32 D 2017

Orion's Sword P. HARRINGTON color *Astronomy* v45 no2 p70 F 2017

Orion with a twist color *Astronomy* v44 no12 p74 D 2016

O'Riordan, Adam

The Burning Ground *Publishers Weekly* v264 no19 p33 My 8 2017

O'Riordan, Tim

The Cerrado: One of Many Cinderellas of Global Hotspots *Environment* v58 no6 p2 N/D 2016

The Fight for Beauty: Our Path to a Better Future *Environment* v58 no6 p35 N/D 2016

Knowledge, Policy, and Expertise: The UK Royal Commission on Environmental Pollution 1970–2011 color *Environment* v59 no1 p39 2017

The Precautionary Principle Under Fire bibl *Environment* v59 no5 p4 S/O 2017

Pursuing Sustainability: A Guide to the Science and Practice *Environment* v58 no6 p34 N/D 2016

Putting the Paris Agreement to the Test *Environment* v59 no2 p2 Mr/Ap 2017

Oris (Company)

The Forward Way to Go Back in Time chart color *GQ: Gentlemen's Quarterly* v97 no3 p62 Mr 2017

Oriss, Timothy

mTOR regulates metabolic adaptation of APCs in the lung and controls the outcome of allergic inflammation graph *Science* v357 no6355 p1014 S 8 2017

Orji, Yvonne
3 ROUNDS WITH INSECURE D. Franich color *Entertainment Weekly* no1468/1469 p44 Je 2-9 2017
YVONNE ORJI C. Brody color *Entertainment Weekly* no1441 p49 N 25 2016
YVONNE ORJI O. J. Williams color *Ebony* v72 no9 p44 Jl/Ag 2017

Orkaby, Asher
Yemen's Humanitarian Nightmare color *Foreign Affairs* v96 no6 p93 N/D 2017

Orkney (Scotland)—Description & travel
Lyrical Isles S. LODGE color *Weekly Standard* v22 no46 p32 Ag 14 2017

Orland, Kevin
Can Oil Sands Pay Off At $50 a Barrel? graph *Bloomberg Businessweek* no4535 p33 Ag 28 2017

Orlando (Fla.)
Nirvana with NETS C. SHMERLER color *Tennis* v53 no2 p56 Mr/Ap 2017

Orlando, Ludovic
Ancient genomic changes associated with domestication of the horse color diag *Science* v356 no6336 p442 Ap 28 2017

Orlando, Silvio
A Kangaroo in the Vatican C. Wren color *Commonweal* v144 no2 p24 Ja 27 2017

Orlando, Terry P.
Suppressing relaxation in superconducting qubits by quasiparticle pumping bibl graph *Science* v354 no6319 p1573 D 23 2016

Orlando Magic (Basketball team)
13 MAGIC color *Sports Illustrated* v127 no12 p72 O 16 2017
13 Magic R. Mahoney, B. Golliver et al color *Sports Illustrated* v125 no14 p89 O 24-31 2016

Orlando Nightclub Massacre, Orlando, Fla., 2016
ORLANDO: THE DAY AFTER S. Flynn color *GQ: Gentlemen's Quarterly* v86 no12 p190 D 2016
PEOPLE OF THE YEAR: THE HEROES OF PULSE M. LAMBERT *Advocate* no1088 p34 D 2016/Ja 2017

Orleane, Pia
Sacred Retreat: Using Natural Cycles to Recharge Your Life *Publishers Weekly* v264 no28 p84 Jl 10 2017

Orliński, Jakub Józef
Jakub Józef Orliński M. MAZZARO *Opera News* v81 no6 p10 D 2016

Orloff, Chana, 1888-1968
Accordeoniste color *Magazine Antiques* v183 no6 p8 N/D 2016
Der Judische Maler color *Magazine Antiques* v183 no6 p9 N/D 2016

Orloff, Judith
What doctors tell their friends about energy [Cover story] L. MULCAHY color *Redbook* p66 Jl/Ag 2017

Orlow, Uriel, 1973-
Sharjah Biennial W. S. Smith bw color *Art in America* v105 no5 p140 My 2017
URIEL ORLOW G. Coxhead cartoon *Art in America* v104 no11 p129 D 2016

Orlowitz, Jake
Discovery Happens Here A. R. ALBANESE color *Publishers Weekly* v264 no38 p40 S 18 2017

Orme, Nicholas
William the Wanderer *History Today* v66 no12 p32 D 2016

Orme, Seth
GARBAGE MEN C. Webber color *Backpacker* v45 no1 p63 Ja 2017
The Long Haul R. MARECH *National Parks* v91 no1 p18 Wint 2017
Packing It Out A. Carnes *Sierra* v102 no2 p25 Mr/Ap 2017

Ormiston, Margaret
We Know Female CEOs Get Paid More, But We Don't Know Why *Harvard Business Review Digital Articles* p2 Mr 13 2017

Ornamental moldings
ENRICHED & embellished: REVIVING ORNAMENTAL PLASTERWORK M. E. POLSON color diag *Old House Journal* v45 no6 p40 S 2017

Ornamental plants
Can't. Look. Away Z. Schaeffer color *Women's Health* v14 no2 p78 Mr 2017
Going Native B. Yeoman color *National Wildlife (World Edition)* v55 no3 p28 Ap/My 2017

Ornamental trees
Serbian Spruce *American Forests* v123 no2 p9 Summ 2017

Orne, Jason—Interviews
BOYS ON THE SIDE N. PARSI color *Chicago* v66 no1 p31 Ja 2017

Orner, Peter
AM I ALONE HERE? H. AKLER color *Maclean's* v129 no47 p61 N 28 2016
Two Places at Once *New York Times Book Review* p1 S 17 2017

ORNES, STEPHEN
35 Cool Things About Space color *National Geographic Kids* no471 p22 Je/Jl 2017
The Body Electric color diag *Discover* v38 no6 p94 Jl/Ag 2017
Google Builds Operating System From Scratch bw diag *Discover* v38 no1 p52 Ja/F 2017
The Perfect Battery color diag graph *Discover* v38 no6 p78 Jl/Ag 2017
THINK LIKE A HACKER bw color graph *Discover* v38 no8 p48 O 2017
Virtual Reality color *Discover* v38 no6 p48 Jl/Ag 2017

Ornithological research
A Voice You Can Trust M. JANNOT *Audubon* v119 no2 p7 Summ 2017

Ornithologist, The (Film)
Get Lost J. P. Rodrigues color *Film Comment* v53 no2 p6 Mr/Ap 2017
The Ornithologist A. CHAN color *Film Comment* v53 no3 p66 My/Je 2017

Ornithologists
The FEATHER DETECTIVE C. SWEENEY *Audubon* v118 no6 p28 Wint 2016
THE LOST BIRDS P. GREENBERG color *Audubon* v119 no3 p38 Fall 2017

Ornot (Company)
Ornot Bar Bag T. Rojek color *Bicycling* v58 no4 p79 My 2017

Oropesa, Lisette
Diva CALIENTE D. ACOSTA *Opera News* v81 no5 p36 N 2016

Orosei, R.
Seasonal exposure of carbon dioxide ice on the nucleus of comet 67P/Churyumov-Gerasimenko bibl bw graph *Science* v354 no6319 p1563 D 23 2016

Orosz, Attila
New Dawn color *Publishers Weekly* v264 no14 p51 Ap 3. 2017

O'Rourke, Beto
HOUSTON, WE HAVE PROGRESS T. MURPHY color graph map *Mother Jones* v42 no5 p24 S/O 2017

O'Rourke, Meghan
The Ethics of Watching Gymnastics img *New York* v49 no15 p54 Jl 25 2016
Self-Portrait as Myself *New York Times Magazine* p17 O 8 2017
Why can't Americans cope with trauma? color *Foreign Policy* no221 p30 N/D 2016

O'Rourke, Melissa
SOCIAL MEDIA SOUND OFF L. F. Prater *Successful Farming* v114 no10 p63 O 2016

O'ROURKE, P. J.
The Beach Is for the Birds cartoon *Reader's Digest* v190 no1132 p15 Jl/Ag 2017
Make Progress Exciting Again color *Weekly Standard* v22 no41 p20 Jl 3 2017
The Revolt Against the Elites [Cover story] *Weekly Standard* v22 no22 p26 F 13 2017

O'Rourke, P. J., 1947-—Interviews
P.J. O'Rourke: Things Are Going to Be Fine N. GILLESPIE color *Reason* v49 no2 p38 Je 2017

Oroville Dam (Calif.)
Lightbox J. Sanburn color *Time* v189 no7/8 p20 F 27 2017

Orphan, Victoria
Victoria Orphan J. Crelin color *Current Biography* v78 no4 p63 Ap 2017

Orphan Black (TV program)

ORPHAN BLACK A TO Z N. Clark, J. Derschowitz et al color *Entertainment Weekly* no1470 p24 Je 16 2017

Orphanages

ABANDONING THE ORPHANAGE S. Eekhoff Zylstra color *Christianity Today* v61 no6 p54 Jl/Ag 2017

POWER [Cover story] C. J. Rottman, W. H. Camp II et al color *Christian Century* v134 no1 p22 Ja 4 2017

Orphans

31 Days of Giving C. de Len chart color *Glamour* v114 no12 p192 D 2016

Mother of Invention L. GOLDMAN color *Better Homes & Gardens* v95 no2 p134 F 2016

Orphaned by War M. Doe color *Christianity Today* v60 no9 p95 N 2016

THANKS, ROBOTS A. Olsen *Christianity Today* v61 no6 p7 Jl/Ag 2017

Orphans—Congresses

ORPHANS 2017 / ORPHELINS DE PARIS B. Meacham *Film Quarterly* v71 no1 p80 Fall 2017

Orr, Amanda

AXED IN NEW ORLEANS color *Louisiana Life* v37 no4 p14 Mr/Ap 2017

CARNAL KNOWLEDGE color *Louisiana Life* v38 no1 p16 S/O 2017

INDUSTRY INSIDER color *Louisiana Life* v37 no5 p14 My/Je 2017

A MOTHER'S LOVE color *Louisiana Life* v37 no6 p12 Jl/Ag 2017

Orr, Bobby, 1948-

17 ICONIC MOMENTS IN NHL HISTORY J. Fuchs and S. Page color *Sports Illustrated* v126 no4 p56 Ja 30 2017

ORR, CHRISTOPHER

How Pixar Lost Its Way cartoon *Atlantic* v319 no5 p34 Je 2017

The Remarkable Laziness of Woody Allen cartoon *Atlantic* v320 no3 p34 O 2017

Orr, Curtis

OH, HOW I HAVE ENJOYED *Arizona Highways* v93 no10 p4 O 2017

ORR, DAVID

First Verses, Lasting Impressions *New York Times Book Review* p19 F 5 2017

The Lyrics Laureate *New York Times Book Review* p22 Mr 26 2017

Two new collections delve into the challenging subject of modern combat and its impacts color *New York Times Book Review* p21 Ag 6 2017

Orr, David W.

Dangerous Years K. D. Moore color *Orion Magazine* v36 no1 p59 Ja/F 2017

Orr, Niela

Humor as It's Meant to Be Heard: In W. Kamau Bell's memoir, timing is everything *New York Times Book Review* p20 My 21 2017

ORR, STEPHEN

COLOR THEORY *Better Homes & Gardens* v95 no4 p2 Ap 2017

EDITOR'S LETTER *Better Homes & Gardens* v95 no3 p4 Mr 2017

EDITOR'S LETTER *Better Homes & Gardens* v95 no7 p8 Jl 2017

FINDING BEAUTY IN THE BASICS *Better Homes & Gardens* v95 no2 p4 F 2016

FOLDING LAUNDRY *Better Homes & Gardens* v95 no11 p10 N 2017

Make It Your Own *Better Homes & Gardens* v94 no12 p4 D 2016

a place at the table *Better Homes & Gardens* v94 no11 p4 N 2016

A PLACE TO BE *Better Homes & Gardens* v95 no8 p6 Ag 2017

THE SLOWER LANE *Better Homes & Gardens* v95 no1 p2 Ja 2017

SMALL WORLD *Better Homes & Gardens* v95 no10 p10 O 2017

SOCIAL SET *Better Homes & Gardens* v95 no9 p10 S 2017

THINKING OUTSIDE *Better Homes & Gardens* v95 no6 p6 Je 2017

ORR, TODD

A BAD DAY IN BEAR COUNTRY cartoon color *Outdoor Life* v224 no8 p49 O 2017

I Survived! [Cover story] *Reader's Digest* v189 no1128 p62 Mr 2017

Orrell, J. L.

Observation of coherent elastic neutrino-nucleus scattering diag *Science* v357 no6356 p1123 S 15 2017

Orrell, Rita Catinella

The Outside Scoop *Architectural Record* v205 no6 p61 Je 2017

Radiant Materials color *Architectural Record* v205 no5 p135 My 2017

Record Products 2016 color *Architectural Record* v204 no12 p113 D 2016

Sun Blocks *Architectural Record* v205 no7 p73 Jl 2017

Surface Value *Architectural Record* v205 no6 p57 Je 2017

Topped Out: Utilize any of these basic solutions for a well-protected, beautiful, and long-lasting roof color *Architectural Record* v205 no5 p77 My 2017

The Wellness Factor *Architectural Record* v205 no7 p69 Jl 2017

Wrap It Up: These weather-tight products will seal the deal for a variety of project categories and programs color *Architectural Record* v205 no5 p71 My 2017

ORRINGER, JULIE

On the Way to a New World *New York Times Book Review* p8 Ja 22 2017

Orsak, Geoffrey C.

He's Got Nerve *D: The Magazine of Dallas* v43 no10 p122 O 2016

Orsi, Robert A.

Prayer Cards & Holy Dirt J. P. McCartin color *Commonweal* v144 no7 p34 Ap 14 2017

Ort, Miriam

The Unsexy Fundamentals of Great HR *Harvard Business Review Digital Articles* p2 Ag 19 2015

Ortega, Davi R.

Giant viruses with an expanded complement of translation system components diag *Science* v356 no6333 p82 Ap 7 2017

Ortega, Ismael K.

Global atmospheric particle formation from CERN CLOUD measurements bibl graph map *Science* v354 no6316 p1119 D 2 2016

Ortega, Ramona

How to Flip Your Money Script C. de León color *Glamour* v115 no5 p124 My 2017

Ortega Inc.

The Open-Top Submarine J. Zorthian color *Time* v188 no20 p19 N 14 2016

Ortenblad, Maddie

THE THING THAT CHANGED IT ALL color *Bicycling* v58 no4 p17 My 2017

Orth, Patrick

One Man's MISSION S. MURRAY bw color *Power & Motoryacht* v34 no9 p96 S 2017

ORTH, ROBERT J.

Accelerating Tropicalization and the Transformation of Temperate Seagrass Meadows *BioScience* v66 no11 p938 N 1 2016

Submersed Aquatic Vegetation in Chesapeake Bay: Sentinel Species in a Changing World *BioScience* v67 no8 p698 Ag 2017

Orthodontic appliances

DOG WEARS BRACES A. Shaw *National Geographic Kids* no468 p13 Mr 2017

Orthodontics

See also

Orthodontic appliances

DOG WEARS BRACES A. Shaw *National Geographic Kids* no468 p13 Mr 2017

Orthodox Eastern doctrines

Not a Novelty C. F. Frost color *Commonweal* v144 no10 p9 Je 2 2017

Orthodox Jews

See also

Ultra-Orthodox Jews

Among the Hasidim J. ROSEN cartoon *Walrus* v14 no2 p32 Mr 2017

Orthodoxos Ekklesia tes Hellados

Scholars re-create the sounds of worship at an ancient Greek church Z. Abrams color *Christian Century* v134 no10 p20 My 10 2017

Orthopedic casts (Medical device)—Evaluation

A Better Cast for Broken Bones color *Prevention* p8 Mr 2017

Orthopedics

CONSULTANTS D. Frisbie *Equus* no481 p74 O 2017

What doctors tell their friends about bones S. WOOD color *Redbook* p82 D 2016

Orthopedists

SOLDIERING ON M. HILL color *Louisiana Life* v37 no4 p112 Mr/Ap 2017

WORTH OF MOUTH: One doctor uses a DNA swab to put the chill on opioid pills T. REHAGEN *Indianapolis Monthly* p73 N 2017

Orthostatic hypotension—Diagnosis

Orthostatic hypotension *Mayo Clinic Health Letter* v35 no2 p6 F 2017

Ortiz, Betty Wong

LET'S RUN TOGETHER color *Runner's World* v52 no9 p10 O 2017

Ortiz, David, 1975-

GAME PLAN M. Zimmerman color map *Men's Health* v32 no4 p8 My 2017

THE PAPI PAPERS D. Ortiz and M. Holley color *Sports Illustrated* v126 no14 p68 My 15-22 2017

Ortiz, Jennifer

19 THINGS YOU REALLY OUGHT TO DO THIS MONTH *Washingtonian Magazine* v52 no1 p33 O 2016

Ortiz, Kristina T.

Sustained virologic control in SIV+ macaques after antiretroviral and α4β7 antibody therapy bibl graph *Science* v354 no6309 p197 O 14 2016

ORTIZ, SARENNA M.

Vaccines, Autism, and the Promotion of Irrelevant Research: A Science-Pseudoscience Analysis *Skeptical Inquirer* v41 no3 p44 My/Je 2017

Ortiz Beltran, Kristty Stephanie

A chemical genetic roadmap to improved tomato flavor bibl graph *Science* v355 no6323 p391 Ja 27 2017

Ortiz Ortega, Adriana

Mexican and U.S. scientists: Partners bibl color *Science* v355 no6330 p1139 Mr 17 2017

Orton, G.

Jupiter's interior and deep atmosphere: The initial pole-to-pole passes with the Juno spacecraft [Cover story] color graph *Science* v356 no6340 p821 My 26 2017

Ortved, John

home & help img *New York* p96 Mr 6 2017

Keir GILCHRIST *Interview* v47 no6 p10 Ag 2017

Labels We Love bw color *GQ: Gentlemen's Quarterly* v86 no12 p106 D 2016

The Makeup Artist color *Vogue* v207 no11 p136 N 2017

The New World of Old-World Tailoring bw color *GQ: Gentlemen's Quarterly* v86 no11 p38 N 2016

The Rise of Homer Sapiens *Smithsonian* v48 no1 p13 Ap 2017

ROYA SACHS: Independent Curator color *Vogue* v207 no10 p196 O 2017

Orvell, Ariana

How "you" makes meaning bibl diag graph *Science* v355 no6331 p1299 Mr 24 2017

Orville, The (TV program)

5 THINGS TO KNOW ABOUT THE ORVILLE D. Holbrook *TV Guide* v65 no37 p44 S 4 2017

J Lee C. Collis color *Entertainment Weekly* no1485 p45 O 6 2017

The Orville N. Abrams, B. L. Heldman et al *Entertainment Weekly* no1482/1483 p85 S 22 2017

SHIP HAPPENS: 25,000 square feet covering two sound-stages, with tons of high-tech touches--the spaceship on Fox's out-of-this world hit The Orville is a stunner D. HOLBROOK *TV Guide* v65 no41 p22 O 2 2017

What to Watch color *Entertainment Weekly* no1482/1483 p112 S 22 2017

Orwell, George, 1903-1950

1937: Wigan G. Orwell *Lapham's Quarterly* v10 no1 p117 Wint 2017

All's Orwell That Ends Orwell cartoon chart *Weekly Standard* v22 no29 p2 Ap 3 2017

'A Sense of Responsibility' W. Kristol *Weekly Standard* v22 no35 p8 My 22 2017

Warning: Semantic Traps Ahead: Environmental politics are littered with language that obscures meaning and hinders good policy T. L. Anderson and K. R. Leube *Hoover Digest: Research & Opinion on Public Policy* no3 p77 Summ 2017

We Are (Still) Living in an Orwellian World T. E. RICKS color *Foreign Policy* no225 p80 Jl/Ag 2017

WORST COME TO WORST *Lapham's Quarterly* v10 no3 p111 Summ 2017

Orwells, The (Performer)

The ORWELLS D. HYMAN *Interview* v47 no1 p16 F 2017

WHICH CHICACQ INDIE BAHB SHOULD YOU SEE THIS MONTH? *Washingtonian Magazine* v52 no8 p36 My 2017

Orwig, David A.

Plant diversity increases with the strength of negative density dependence at the global scale diag *Science* v356 no6345 p1389 Je 30 2017

ORWIN, ALEXANDER

Making Room *Weekly Standard* v22 no10 p39 N 14 2016

Orwoll, Mark

MY WIFE WANTS A BIDET: Plumbing is the glue that holds a marriage together *Saturday Evening Post* v289 no4 p18 Jl/Ag 2017

ON A DREAM VACATION YOU WOULD bw color *Conde Nast Traveler* v52 no7 p48 Ag 2017

Ory, Daniel S.

Lysosomal cholesterol activates mTORC1 via an SLC38A9–Niemann-Pick C1 signaling complex bibl diag graph *Science* v355 no6331 p1306 Mr 24 2017

Ory, Deborah

MAKING Photos DANCE K. McGuire bw color *Dance Spirit* v20 no9 p72 N 2016

Ory, Meghan

Chesapeake Shores K. Freeze *TV Guide* v65 no31 p34 Jl 24 2017

Oryx

Back to the Wild K. Samuelson color *Time* v190 no12 p12 S 25 2017

Born to Be Wild K. NODJIMBADEM *Smithsonian* v48 no1 p19 Ap 2017

Oryx—Behavior

Discussion P. Werner, K. MK et al *Smithsonian* v48 no2 p8 My 2017

Orza, Seth

Seth Orza G. BERARDI *Dance Magazine* v91 no8 p44 Ag 2017

Os Mutantes (Performer)

Paradise Played M. Trammell cartoon *New Yorker* v93 no2 p10 F 27 2017

Osage County (Okla.)

The Last Prairie S. C. Cooper color *American Cowboy* v24 no1 p28 Je/Jl 2017

Osage orange

Osage Orange *American Forests* v123 no3 p11 Fall 2017

Osakabe, Akihisa

Crystal structure of the overlapping dinucleosome composed of hexasome and octasome graph *Science* v356 no6334 p205 Ap 14 2017

Osakwe, Amaka

ARMOR AND LINGERIE A. OKEOWO cartoon color *New Yorker* v93 no29 p52 S 25 2017

Osamu Nureki

A three-dimensional movie of structural changes in bacteriorhodopsin bibl diag graph *Science* v354 no6319 p1552 D 23 2016

Osamu Tadanaga

A coherent Ising machine for 2000-node optimization problems bibl diag graph *Science* v354 no6312 p603 N 4 2016

Osberg, Sally R.

How Social Entrepreneurs Make Change Happen *Harvard Business Review Digital Articles* p2 O 14 2015

Osborn, Anna

LEADERSHIP BY COMMITTEE: Our middle school's journey to create a culture of literacy *Literacy Today (2411-7862)* v35 no2 p20 S/O 2017

OSBORN, ELIANA

Passing It Down *Sierra* v101 no5 p64 S/O 2016

Osborn, John

Otello S. Hastings *Opera News* v81 no9 p43 Mr 2017

Osborne, Christine

From Beanie Babies to fidget spinners, the evolution of toy fads shows how technology has thrown the consumer economy into chaos C. Duhigg *New York Times Magazine* p12 Ag 20 2017

Osborne, George Gideon Oliver, 1971-
THE BATTLE FOR BRITAIN E. CAESAR color *Esquire* p124 O 2017

Osborne, Lawrence
Beautiful Animals *Publishers Weekly* v264 no40 p133 O 2 2017
Nightmare at the Border *New York Times Book Review* p17 F 5 2017
The Stranger on the Shore K. Kitamura *New York Times Book Review* p1 Jl 9 2017

Osborne, Mark
Finding the Little Prince R. MILZOFF img *New York* v49 no15 p84 Jl 25 2016

Osborne, Robert
TRIBUTES M. Roush and M. Fell *TV Guide* v65 no13 p14 Mr 20 2017

Osborne, Shawn
Young People Need to Know Entrepreneurship Is Hard *Harvard Business Review Digital Articles* p2 Ap 6 2015

Osborne, Tom
Documentary reveals Osborne in his own words A. J. BARTELS bw color *Nebraska Life* v21 no4 p14 Jl/Ag 2017

Osbourne, Sharon, 1952-
Small Changes for a Big Difference color *Prevention* v69 no2 p4 F 2017

OSBURN, CHRISTOPHER L.
The Arctic in the Twenty-First Century: Changing Biogeochemical Linkages across a Paraglacial Landscape of Greenland *BioScience* v67 no2 p118 F 2017

Osby, Greg
Greg Osby T. PANKEN color *Downbeat* v84 no3 p122 Mr 2017

Oscar Insurance Corp.
This Kushner Likes Obamacare M. Chafkin and Z. Tracer bw *Bloomberg Businessweek* no4527 p22 Je 19 2017

Oscillations—Mathematical models
High-temperature quantum oscillations caused by recurring Bloch states in graphene superlattices R. Krishna Kumar, X. Chen et al color *Science* v357 no6347 p181 Jl 14 2017

Oseltamivir
Before You Take It S. KLEIN color *Prevention* v69 no1 p22 Ja 2017

Oseman, Alice
Radio Silence *Publishers Weekly* v264 no4 p82 Ja 23 2017

O'Shaughnessy, Laura
The High Price of Low-Cost CPMs *Harvard Business Review Digital Articles* p2 Ag 10 2016

O'Shaughnessy, Susan
WATER-SAVING SORGHUM D. Mowitz *Successful Farming* v114 no10 p47 O 2016

O'Shea, Clodagh C.
ChromEMT: Visualizing 3D chromatin structure and compaction in interphase and mitotic cells color *Science* v357 no6349 p370 Jl 28 2017

O'shea, Erin
Not just Salk color *Science* v357 no6356 p1105 S 15 2017

O'SHEA, MILES
Engage Students' Creativity Through Animated Whiteboard Video Project *Education Digest* v82 no7 p61 Mr 2017

O'Shea, Monica
Speak up color *U.S. Catholic* v82 no4 p5 Ap 2017

O'Shea-Evans, Kathryn
THE $3,000 SOFA CHALLENGE color *House Beautiful* v159 no2 p38 Mr 2017
Anniversary Punch color *House Beautiful* v158 no9 p106 N 2016
BARBARA WESTBROOK ON "FEEL" color *House Beautiful* p38 Jl 2017
The Belle Is Back color *House Beautiful* v159 no8 p53 O 2017
the best of THE BEST 120 color *House Beautiful* v158 no9 p57 N 2016
Cover Stars color *House Beautiful* v158 no9 p170 N 2016
DARRYL CARTER ON MIXING MODERN WITH TRADITIONAL color *House Beautiful* v159 no2 p56 Mr 2017
Dazzle Them! color *House Beautiful* v159 no8 p60 O 2017
Fancy Cocktails? A Breeze! color *House Beautiful* v159 no4 p65 My 2017
Homecoming Season color *House Beautiful* v159 no7 p41 S 2017
The House Always Wins color *House Beautiful* v159 no8 p35 O 2017

THE HOUSE THAT BLUE & WHITE BUILT color *House Beautiful* v158 no9 p158 N 2016
AN INVITING POOL PAVILION color *House Beautiful* v159 no4 p60 My 2017
Island Girl color *House Beautiful* v159 no4 p43 My 2017
LES ENSEMBLIERS ON TRAYS color *House Beautiful* v159 no8 p56 O 2017
LIFE AT LULU'S: A Seasonal "Sneeky" color *House Beautiful* v159 no9 p62 N 2017
Lush Life color *House Beautiful* v159 no2 p31 Mr 2017
MARTYN LAWRENCE BULLARD ON CEILINGS color *House Beautiful* v159 no7 p60 S 2017
Mint's Moment color *House Beautiful* v159 no3 p73 Ap 2017
The Natural bw color *House Beautiful* v159 no5 p51 Je 2017
Now Serving: Comfort and Joy color *House Beautiful* v158 no10 p45 D 2016/Ja 2017
Out of Africa color *House Beautiful* v159 no5 p39 Je 2017
A PATCH OF BEAUTY color *House Beautiful* v159 no4 p52 My 2017
Perk Up Your Iced Coffee color *House Beautiful* v159 no5 p64 Je 2017
P. GAYE TAPP ON ICONIC STYLE bw color *House Beautiful* v159 no4 p56 My 2017
Remaking History bw color *House Beautiful* v158 no9 p112 N 2016
Rhymes with Smiles color *House Beautiful* p26 Jl 2017
ROBERT COUTURIER ON FIRE! color *House Beautiful* v158 no10 p34 D 2016/Ja 2017
Roll the Tape color *House Beautiful* v159 no1 p25 F 2017
The Secret to Layered Lighting color *House Beautiful* p46 Jl 2017
A SERENE DRAWING ROOM color *House Beautiful* v159 no7 p65 S 2017
SERVING UP SIMPLICITY color *House Beautiful* v159 no7 p58 S 2017
shopping secrets OF THE PROS color *House Beautiful* v159 no3 p46 Ap 2017
Star-Spangled Style color *House Beautiful* p50 Jl 2017
Stocking Your Pantry Like a Pro color *House Beautiful* v159 no2 p72 Mr 2017
STRIPE RIGHT color *House Beautiful* p21 Jl 2017
Stroke of Genius color *House Beautiful* p31 Jl 2017
Sweet Corn Gazpacho color *House Beautiful* p47 Jl 2017
TOM KLIGERMAN ON CRUCIAL DETAILS bw color *House Beautiful* v159 no1 p41 F 2017
Top This Ice Cream color *House Beautiful* v159 no7 p74 S 2017
TROPICAL BRUNCH color *House Beautiful* v159 no4 p54 My 2017
True Colorist color *House Beautiful* v159 no7 p55 S 2017
VERN YIP ON PERFECT MEASUREMENTS color *House Beautiful* v159 no5 p57 Je 2017
A VERY CHARLOTTE CHRISTMAS color *House Beautiful* v158 no10 p54 D 2016/Ja 2017

OSHINSKY, DAVID
Don't You Be My Neighbor *New York Times Book Review* p15 Je 25 2017

Oshinsky, David M., 1944-
Bellevue I. Biedenharn color *Entertainment Weekly* no1440 p62 N 18 2016
None So Blind S. Mirsky color *Scientific American* v316 no2 p74 F 2017
The Past Goes to the Hospital L. Rothman color *Time* v188 no21 p70 N 21 2016

Oshita, preston
The Chosen One M. POLLOCK color *Chicago* v66 no10 p84 O 2017

Oshkosh Corp. Defense Division
THE MILITARY'S NEW WORKHORSE E. TEGLER chart color *Popular Mechanics* p8 Jl 2017

Oshodin, William
KICK-ASS CUSTOMER SERVICE: INTERACTION color *Harvard Business Review* v95 no3 p16 My/Je 2017

Osinski, Gordon
Deep impact J. BENNETT color *Canadian Geographic* v137 no2 p29 Mr/Ap 2017
The formation of peak rings in large impact craters bibl color

graph *Science* v354 no6314 p878 N 18 2016

Oslo (Theatrical production)

A False Theatrical Peace J. S. TOBIN *Commentary* v143 no2 p52 F 2017

OSLO CONFIDENTIAL M. BRENNER color *Vanity Fair* v59 no5 p133 Ap 2017

Oslo Accords (1993)

Stop Supporting Palestinian Terror E. ABRAMS *National Review* v69 no7 p20 Ap 17 2017

Osman, Najma Ali—Interviews

Is It Safe to Talk Politics Yet? S. E. Cupp, K. Ball et al bw color *Glamour* v115 no2 p77 F 2017

Osman Ali, Nizam of Hyderabad, 1886-1967

An Empowering Rule Z. PARVEZ *Islamic Horizons* v46 no1 p54 Ja/F 2017

Osmania University: A Century of Exceptional Learning: India gnarls the character of an institution created by a caring Muslim ruler M. MIRZA *Islamic Horizons* v46 no3 p58 My/Je 2017

Osmanbeyoglu, Hatice U.

PI3K pathway regulates ER-dependent transcription in breast cancer through the epigenetic regulator KMT2D bibl graph *Science* v355 no6331 p1324 Mr 24 2017

Osmania University (India)

Osmania University: A Century of Exceptional Learning: India gnarls the character of an institution created by a caring Muslim ruler M. MIRZA *Islamic Horizons* v46 no3 p58 My/Je 2017

OSNOS, EVAN

ACTIVE MEASURES cartoon color *New Yorker* v93 no3 p40 Mr 6 2017

AFTERMATH bw cartoon *New Yorker* v92 no38 p48 N 21 2016

COMMENT: FIGHTING WORDS bw *New Yorker* v93 no33 p35 O 23 2017

ENDGAMES cartoon color *New Yorker* v93 no12 p34 My 8 2017

HOMECOMING cartoon *New Yorker* v93 no19 p18 Jl 3 2017

KAINE COUNTRY bw cartoon *New Yorker* v92 no34 p40 O 24 2016

MAY DAYS cartoon *New Yorker* v93 no15 p15 My 29 2017

ON THE BRINK cartoon color *New Yorker* v93 no28 p34 S 18 2017

PRESIDENT TRUMP cartoon color *New Yorker* v92 no30 p38 S 26 2016

SURVIVAL OF THE RICHEST cartoon color *New Yorker* v92 no47 p36 Ja 30 2017

XU HONGCI cartoon *New Yorker* v92 no42 p94 D 19 2016

OSOFSKY, LULING

In Svalbard *Orion Magazine* v35 no4/5 p12 Jl-O 2016

Osorio, Daniel

The biology of color color *Science* v357 no6350 p470 Ag 4 2017

Osprey

Lessons from the Osprey Garden A. W. SEMMES color *Natural History* v125 no7 p28 Jl/Ag 2017

Q&A: John Sherman *Arizona Highways* v93 no4 p9 Ap 2017

Osprey—Behavior

Ospreys E. Balli *Arizona Highways* v96 no7 p13 Jl 2017

Ossendrijver, Mathieu

Babylonian Tablets Tracked Jupiter J. KEATS color diag *Discover* v38 no1 p54 Ja/F 2017

Ossman, Mugs

Slide into Ski Joring S. HAMILTON color *Trail Rider* v29 no1 p26 Ja/F 2017

Ossoff, Jon

The Body Politic: Rebecca Traister: Georgia's Silver Lining A new game plan for the Democratic Party emerges out of Jon Ossofrs loss img *New York* v50 no13 p17 Je 26 2017

The Democrats Went Down to Georgia B. MASCHINOT *In These Times* v41 no5 p8 My 2017

Disappointed Dems F. BARNES color *Weekly Standard* v22 no41 p9 Jl 3 2017

The Trump-Hate Weather Vane O. Nuzzi img *New York* v50 no7 p22 Ap 3 2017

Ostaseski, Frank

WASHING MY BOY'S BODY color *Tricycle: The Buddhist Review* v26 no4 p74 Summ 2017

Osteoarthritis

Don't Blame the Rain color *Prevention* v69 no5 p10 My 2017

Total knee replacement [Cover story] *Mayo Clinic Health Letter*

v35 no9 p1 S 2017

Osteoarthritis—Prevention

ARTHRITIS: What works. What doesn't [Cover story] D. Felson *Nutrition Action Health Letter* v44 no8 p3 O 2017

Best ways to cope with hand pain *Harvard Health Letter* v42 no9 p4 Jl 2017

CRAZY ABOUT COLLAGEN J. BOWDEN color *Better Nutrition* v78 no12 p40 D 2016

Osteoarthritis—Treatment

Knee Pain from Arthritis? Try Tai Chi *Tufts University Health & Nutrition Letter* v34 no9 p3 N 2016

Osteochondroma

CONSULTANTS D. Frisbie *Equus* no481 p74 O 2017

Osteochondrosis

Diet Does Matter In OCD Development S. Wenholz color *Practical Horseman* v45 no6 p76 Je 2017

Osteopenia—Prevention

Better Bones A. Weil color *Prevention* v69 no11 p22 N 2017

Osteoporosis

Reading the Bones S. C. AGARWAL bw color *Natural History* v125 no5 p26 My 2017

Osteoporosis prevention

trend WATCH V. Tweed *Better Nutrition* v79 no11 p12 N 2017

Oster, Lauren

Alternative Medicine for Your Pet color *Health* v31 no4 p70 My 2017

Your Fall Feel-Great Checklist *Health* v31 no7 p100 S 2017

OSTERBACK, ANN-MARIE K.

Long-Term Studies Contribute Disproportionately to Ecology and Policy *BioScience* v67 no3 p271 Mr 2017

Osterheldt, Jeneé

WHEN LINKEDIN ISN'T ENOUGH color *Essence* v48 no6 p86 O 2017

Ostertag, Rebecca

Plant diversity increases with the strength of negative density dependence at the global scale diag *Science* v356 no6345 p1389 Je 30 2017

Osterwalder, Alexander

The C-Suite Needs a Chief Entrepreneur *Harvard Business Review Digital Articles* p2 Je 25 2015

Don't Let Your Company Culture Just Happen *Harvard Business Review Digital Articles* p2 Jl 7 2016

Osterweis, Max

"I READ CRIME FICTION ON THE PLANE—IT TAKES MY MIND OFF MY OWN LIFE" A. HALPERN color *Conde Nast Traveler* v51 no10 p42 N 2016

Ostfeld, Jackie

Turning the Tide on a Generation Left Inside *Parks & Recreation* v52 no4 p18 Ap 2017

Östlund, Ruben, 1974-

Art Brute C. LORENTZEN il *New Republic* v248 no11 p50 N 2017

The Danish Boy J. POWERS color *Vogue* v207 no10 p228 O 2017

Ostovar, Afshon

Vanguard of the Imam: Religion, Politics, and Iran's Revolutionary Guards J. Waterbury *Foreign Affairs* v96 no1 p174 Ja/F 2017

Ostrander, Leslie

Learning to Dance in the Rain color *Horse & Rider* v56 no5 p14 My 2017

OSTRANDER, MADELINE

HACKING THE GRAIN color *Nation* v305 no11 p18 O 30 2017

OSTRIKER, ALICIA

The Glory of Cities *Progressive* v81 no10 p42 N 2016

Ostriker, Allison C.

Clonal hematopoiesis associated with TET2 deficiency accelerates atherosclerosis development in mice bibl diag *Science* v355 no6327 p842 F 24 2017

Ostrom, Tony—Interviews

Wireless Hi-Res C. Crowley color *Sound & Vision* v82 no2 p16 F/Mr 2017

Ostrow, Lonnie

Poet of the Wrong Generation *Publishers Weekly* v264 no4 p50c Ja 23 2017

Osuch, Marzena

Changing climate shifts timing of European floods color graph

2017

WalthersMainline 40-foot AAR boxcar *Model Railroader* v84 no11 p67 N 2017

WalthersMainline HO 53-foot Thrall corrugated-side gondola color *Model Railroader* v84 no2 p74 F 2017

WalthersProto HO scale PRR BR70n RPO-baggage car color *Model Railroader* v84 no4 p96 Ap 2017

Wheels of Time HO 62-foot bulkhead flatcar color *Model Railroader* v84 no5 p64 My 2017

Where is Canadian spelled with an "e"? color *Model Railroader* v84 no7 p18 Jl 2017

Woodland Scenics HO Just Plug vehicles *Model Railroader* v84 no7 p65 Jl 2017

OTTEN, CATHY

A Legacy in Ruins: What now for Iraq's Mosul Museum, recently liberated from ISIS? *American Scholar* v86 no3 p99 Summ 2017

Otten, Edwin

Locked synchronous rotor motion in a molecular motor diag *Science* v356 no6341 p964 Je 1 2017

Ottenberg, Mel

Rihanna HER BEST EVER E. Wilson color *InStyle* v24 no7 p50 Jl 2017

Otter, Anne Sofie von, 1955-

Anne Sofie von Otter: So Many Things J. Cadagin *Opera News* v81 no9 p54 Mr 2017

Otter, Jack

Fear of Finance? color *AARP: The Magazine* v60 no5A p44 Ag/S 2017

Otters

Keep Your Distance S. O'DONNELL color *Natural History* v125 no6 p48 Je 2017

Sea Otters: Supercute, Supertough R. A. MUSGRAVE color *National Geographic Kids* no475 p24 N 2017

The Two Sides of Sea Otters Sea otters I. Groc color *Canadian Wildlife* v22 no5 p24 N/D 2016

Otterson, Helen

Mergers M. Guerber color *American Craft* v76 no6 p38 D 2016-Ja 2017

Otto, Bill—Interviews

Gettin' Better M. Werling *Sea Magazine* v109 no5 p54 My 2017

OTTO, JÜRGEN

Males Show Their True Colors [Cover story] color *Natural History* v125 no4 p10 Ap 2017

Otto, Mary

THE DENTAL DIVIDE cartoon *Mother Jones* v42 no5 p68 S/O 2017

Molar Mobility S. JAFFE *New York Times Book Review* p21 Mr 26 2017

Teeth: Beauty, Inequality, and the Struggle for Oral Health in America *Publishers Weekly* v264 no2 p58 Ja 9 2017

The Teeth Gap A. GAFFNEY color il *New Republic* v248 no6 p64 Je 2017

Otto, Miranda

24: LEGACY M. ROFFMAN *TV Guide* v65 no14 p26 Ap 3 2017

24: Legacy M. Roffman *TV Guide* v65 no2 p38 Ja 2 2017

Otto, Olivia

"We Are STEM-inists" A. STANLEY color *Seventeen* v75 no11 p22 N 2016

Otto, Shawn

Crusades of the clueless: Who will win the war on science? E. Eaves bibl *Bulletin of the Atomic Scientists* v72 no6 p418 N 2016

Otto Bock North America Inc.

Page J. Krichels *Architectural Record* v205 no4 p104 Ap 2017

OTTOLENGHI, EMANUELE

The Iranian Express color map *Weekly Standard* v22 no44 p22 Jl 31 2017

Ottolenghi, Yotam

the other kind of steak night color *Bon Appetit* v62 no4 p52 Ap 2017

summer on the side color *Bon Appetit* v62 no7 p50 Jl 2017

YOTAM OTTOLENGHI C. BARBOUR color *Architectural Digest* v73 no11 p112 N 2016

Ottoman Empire, 1288-1918

DISASTER AT DJERBA: During a period of European peace, Spain sought to establish control of the Mediterranean. Yet a disastrous attempt to oust the Ottomans from North Africa threatened to accelerate the westward advance of Islam B. W. Allen *History Today* v67 no6 p24 Je 2016

'The Turkish Lawrence of Arabia': The dramatic life of the outlaw and special agent Eşref Bey epitomises the end of the Ottoman Empire B. C. Fortna *History Today* v67 no9 p8 S 2017

Ottomans (Furniture)—Evaluation

I LOVE IT E. GAUKEL *Treasures* v6 no3 p48 D 2016/Ja 2017

Otzi (Ice mummy)

Ötzi's Sartorial Splendor J. URBANUS color *Archaeology* v69 no6 p18 N/D 2016

Ou, Horng D.

ChromEMT: Visualizing 3D chromatin structure and compaction in interphase and mitotic cells color *Science* v357 no6349 p370 Jl 28 2017

Ou, Michael Tianhao

Pathological α-synuclein transmission initiated by binding lymphocyte-activation gene 3 bibl graph *Science* v353 no6307 paah3374-1 S 30 2017

Ouachita National Recreation Trail (Ark. & Okla.)

THE PATH LESS TRAVELED C. Gerard color *Backpacker* v45 no1 p86 Ja 2017

Ouellette, Dan

Akua Dixon: PLAYING WITH POWER color *Downbeat* v84 no4 p44 Ap 2017

ART HIRAHARA color *Downbeat* v84 no3 p22 Mr 2017

Christian McBride color *Downbeat* v84 no1 p114 Ja 2017

Christian Sands color *Downbeat* v84 no7 p42 Jl 2017

FORGING HIS OWN PATH color *Downbeat* v84 no6 p56 Je 2017

'GRAND SLAM' EVOLUTION color *Downbeat* v84 no3 p45 Mr 2017

JD Allen color *Downbeat* v84 no5 p146 My 2017

Joel Harrison color *Downbeat* v84 no2 p106 F 2017

JOEY DEFRANCESCO REJUVENATED MASTER [Cover story] bw color *Downbeat* v84 no5 p40 My 2017

Mary Halvorson color *Downbeat* v84 no7 p90 Jl 2017

MARY HALVORSON: 'MORE THAN I WOULD'VE HOPED FOR' color *Downbeat* v84 no8 p42 Ag 2017

Matthew Garrison color *Downbeat* v84 no8 p98 Ag 2017

MATT WILSON: LIFE'S CALLING color *Downbeat* v84 no9 p44 S 2017

McGinnis Crafts 'Dream' Project color *Downbeat* v84 no8 p13 Ag 2017

Monterey Nurtured by Music bw color *Downbeat* v84 no5 p92 My 2017

Rare Gems Stand Out at North Sea Fest color *Downbeat* v84 no9 p21 S 2017

RUDY ROYSTON: 'JUST PLAY' color *Downbeat* v84 no3 p40 Mr 2017

Saluting ELLA color *Downbeat* v84 no10 p46 O 2017

Shorter, Metheny Play it Cool at Monterey Jazz Fest color *Downbeat* v83 no12 p14 D 2016

Subversive Soul color *Downbeat* v84 no6 p28 Je 2017

Truesdell & Fresu Channel Evans & Davis color *Downbeat* v84 no10 p16 O 2017

Vocal Dynamos Add Spark to Umbria Jazz Fest color *Downbeat* v84 no10 p22 O 2017

Ouellette, Jenny

In the Books bw color *Dance Spirit* v20 no9 p50 N 2016

READY, SET—PLACES! color *Dance Spirit* v20 no10 p46 D 2016

SO YOU THINK You Want to Transfer? color *Dance Spirit* v21 no2 p54 F 2017

Ouellette, Richard

LES ENSEMBLIERS ON TRAYS K. O'SHEA-EVANS color *House Beautiful* v159 no8 p56 O 2017

Ouija boards

Conjuring God P. S. Hawkins *Christian Century* v134 no12 p12 Je 7 2017

OULLETTE, DAN

Jarrett's Pivotal Moment color *Downbeat* v84 no2 p80 F 2017

Our Kind of Traitor (Film)

OUR KIND OF TRAITOR J. Krebs color *Sound & Vision* v82 no3 p70 Ap 2017

Our Souls at Night (Film)

OUR SOULS AT NIGHT J. McGovern color *Entertainment Weekly* no1446/1447 p54 D 2016/Ja 2017

Our Souls at Night L. Greenblatt color *Entertainment Weekly* no1485 p39 O 6 2017

YOUNG AT HEART A. LANE color *New Yorker* v93 no31 p80 O 9 2017

Our Trojan War (Theatrical production)

A Warrior Chorus: Aquila Theatre, Veterans, and Our Trojan War H. Sherman *Stage Directions* v30 no6 p18 Je 2017

Ourisman, Mary

GUEST LIST *Washingtonian Magazine* v52 no4 p24 Ja 2017

Oust, Gail

Curried Away: A Spice Shop Mystery color *Publishers Weekly* v263 no44 p55 O 31 2016

Out Front Theatre Co. (Performer)

ACTING OUT W. BROCK *Atlanta* v56 no12 p38 Ap 2017

Out in the Storm (Music)

WAXAHATCHEE N. Feeney color *Entertainment Weekly* no1476 p61 Ag 4 2017

Out of the Wild (Film)

OUT OF THE WILD L. Feldman color *American Cowboy* v23 no5 p50 F/Mr 2017

Out One (Film)

The Greatest Enigma of French Film L. Sante bw color *New York Review of Books* v63 no16 p54 O 27 2016

Outboard motorboats

CUTWATER: 302 SPORT COUPE THIS OUTBOARD-POWERED CRUISER CAN HIT 50 MPH AND HOST A DOCKSIDE SUNSET DINNER M. WERLING color *Sea Magazine* v109 no6 p34 Je 2017

Monsters of the Midrange A. JONES *Boating World* v38 no3 p20 Mr 2017

POCKETS GET POPULAR M. WERLING color *Sea Magazine* v109 no8 p4 Ag 2017

Outboard motorboats—Maintenance & repair

HELP! MY OUTBOARD WON'T START! J. Tiger color *Cabin Living* p72 Mr 2017

Outboard motors

Ghost in the machine P. Nielsen *Sail* v48 no7 p4 Jl 2017

Going Big A. JONES *Boating World* v38 no8 p4 S/O 2017

HELP! MY OUTBOARD WON'T START! J. Tiger color *Cabin Living* p72 Mr 2017

Outboard motors—Evaluation

Positive Spin: Suzuki raises the bar on high-horsepower outboards with a testosterone-laced engine that has a pair … of propellers A. JONES *Boating World* v38 no8 p20 S/O 2017

You Can Have a V-8 A. Jones *Boating World* v37 no9 p20 N/D 2016

Outbuildings—Design & construction

Outside Influence color *Log Home Living* v33 no7 p10 S 2016

Outcome assessment (Medical care)

A Blueprint for Measuring Health Care Outcomes J. Arora, J. Hazelzet et al *Harvard Business Review Digital Articles* p2 D 12 2016

Health Care Providers Need a Value Management Office R. S. Kaplan, C. H. MacLean et al *Harvard Business Review Digital Articles* p2 D 2 2015

Immigrant Doctors Provide Better Care, According to a Study of 1.2 Million Hospitalizations Yusuke Tsugawa, A. B. Jena et al color *Harvard Business Review Digital Articles* p2 F 3 2017

Research: Higher U.S. Physician Spending Doesn't Lead to Better Patient Outcomes Yusuke Tsugawa and A. B. Jena *Harvard Business Review Digital Articles* p2 Mr 13 2017

A Simple Way to Measure Health Care Outcomes J. Schupbach, A. Chandra et al *Harvard Business Review Digital Articles* p2 D 8 2016

Value-Based Care Alone Won't Reduce Health Spending and Improve Patient Outcomes D. J. Bailey *Harvard Business Review Digital Articles* p2 Je 16 2017

What Health Care Leaders Need to Do to Improve Value for Patients J. Lippa, C. Pinnock et al *Harvard Business Review Digital Articles* p2 D 3 2015

Outcome assessment (Social services)

The Effort-Outcomes Relationship in Applied Ecology: Evaluation and Implications J. HONE, V. A. DRAKE et al *BioScience* v67 no9 p845 S 2017

Outcome-based education

Get it right the first time! T. Heflebower, J. Hoegh et al chart color *Phi Delta Kappan* v98 no6 p58 Mr 2017

Growing mastery in NYC J. Nolan chart color il *Phi Delta Kappan* v98 no3 p41 N 2016

Outcome Health (Company)

FEVER HIGH M. HERPER and A. KONRAD color *Forbes* v199 no7 p26 Je 29 2017

Outcrops (Geology)

How to model realistic rock outcroppings R. Nulton color *Model Railroader* v84 no6 p50 Je 2017

Outdoor Afro (Company)

Healing Through Hikes M. C. O'Connor *Sierra* v102 no1 p25 Ja/F 2017

Outdoor concerts

CANADA color *Downbeat* v84 no5 p128 My 2017

Outdoor cooking

See also

Barbecue cooking

TRAILBLAZERS E. Johnson color *Sunset* v238 no5 p74 My 2017

Outdoor cooking equipment

See also

Grills (Cooking)

Smokers (Outdoor cooking)

STAFF PICK: A-MAZE-N SMOKER bw color *Bon Appetit* v62 no6 p110 Je 2017

Outdoor cooking—Equipment & supplies

See also

Barbecue pits

Build an OUTDOOR OVEN W. Rubel *Mother Earth News* no281 p50 Ap/My 2017

Outdoor education

THE SCHOOL PROJECT THAT SETS PARENTS FREE L. SKENAZY color *Reason* v48 no10 p10 Mr 2017

Outdoor enthusiasts

THE FINDERS A. MCKEAN color *Outdoor Life* v224 no9 p11 N 2017

LOST + FOUND A. McKean color *Outdoor Life* v224 no9 p54 N 2017

OL FAMILY RECIPES N. KREBS bw color *Outdoor Life* v224 no9 p13 N 2017

A STICKY SITUATION B. HEAVEY cartoon *Field & Stream* v121 no9 p86 Ap 2017

Tents, Trails and Tranquility A. TARIQ *Islamic Horizons* v46 no1 p44 Ja/F 2017

What I Know for Sure O. Winfrey color *O, The Oprah Magazine* p152 F 2017

Outdoor exhibitions

KATJA NOVITSKOVA *Interview* v47 no5 p22 Je/Jl 2017

Outdoor fireplaces

BACKYARD BONFIRES color *Timber Home Living* v27 no4 p28 Ag 2017

Fire Away! color *Log Home Living* v34 no3 p8 Ap 2017

Outdoor furniture

my amish-built cabin D. ARMITAGE color *Cabin Living* p28 Mr 2017

PICNIC PERFECT B. RILEY *Atlanta* v57 no3 p46 Jl 2017

RESOURCES *New Orleans Homes & Lifestyles* v20 no3 p110 Summ 2017

Under the Sun color *Architectural Digest* no6 p56 Je 1 2017

Outdoor furniture industry

Under the Sun color *Architectural Digest* no6 p56 Je 1 2017

Outdoor furniture—Design & construction

Outdoor & Recreational color *Architectural Record* v204 no12 p134 D 2016

Outdoor furniture—Evaluation

Outdoor & Recreational color *Architectural Record* v204 no12 p134 D 2016

The Outside Scoop R. C. Orrell *Architectural Record* v205 no6 p61 Je 2017

Outdoor games

The Outdoor Alliance for Kids Holds Capitol Hill Briefing M. Aquino *Parks & Recreation* v52 no8 p66 Ag 2017

Outdoor kitchen design & construction

Dining Out color *Timber Home Living* v27 no4 p22 Ag 2017

Outdoor kitchens

Fire Away! color *Log Home Living* v34 no3 p8 Ap 2017

Say Hello to Summer! S. BROWN *Timber Home Living* v27 no4 p8 Ag 2017

Outdoor life

See also

Mountaineering

Picnics

5 REASONS TO GO PLAY T. ROSS color *Rodale's Organic Life* v2 no7 p95 D 2016/Ja 2017

Night Train F. Schaaf *Sky & Telescope* v133 no6 p45 Je 2017

Summer Lovin' M. W. Spencer *New Orleans Homes & Lifestyles* v20 no3 p14 Summ 2017

Outdoor life—Equipment & supplies—Evaluation

TENT WITH A VIEW *Saturday Evening Post* v288 no6 p25 N/D 2016

Outdoor life—Periodicals

GIFT OF A LIFETIME C. Kearns color *Field & Stream* v121 no7 p10 D 2016/Ja 2017

Outdoor living space design & construction

See also

Outdoor kitchen design & construction

BEST OUTDOOR SPACE color *Timber Home Living* p24 2017 SpecialIssue

EFFECTIVE DECK DESIGN color *Cabin Living* p66 Je 2017

Outdoor living spaces

See also

Outdoor kitchens

25 TRENDS ARE MAKING BOATING BETTER Z. PROCHAZKA *Sea Magazine* v109 no4 p50 Ap 2017

BEST OUTDOOR SPACE color *Log Home Living* p64 2017 SpecialIssue

Cozy Northwoods Retreat F. SIGURDSSON color *Cabin Living* p24 Mr 2017

The Great Outdoors: Creating backyard living spaces fit for your indoor style K. Wilburn *New Orleans Homes & Lifestyles* v20 no3 p100 Summ 2017

HOME STRETCH: luxe outdoor living spaces create opportunities for gracious year-round entertaining V. Hubbard *Virginia Living* v15 no4 p81 Je 2017

Poolside Video J. SCIACCA color *Sound & Vision* v81 no9 p19 N 2016

Unique Challenges of Building on an Island K. Paulsen color *Cabin Living* p51 Mr 2017

Outdoor photography

See also

Landscape photography

Picture Perfect color *Backpacker* v45 no2 p88 Mr 2017

Snow Day: Winter Sunsets C. LYONS color *Backpacker* v45 no2 p29 Mr 2017

WINNING LIGHT C. Murray color *Popular Photography* v81 no1 p42 Ja/F 2017

Your Top Shots color *Backpacker* v45 no2 p78 Mr 2017

Outdoor recreation

See also

Adventure racing

Camping

Camps

Fishing

Hunting

Outdoor games

Outdoor recreation for children

ALASKA & ARCTIC CANADA *Sierra* v102 no1 p52 Ja/F 2017

BACKPACK *Sierra* v102 no1 p58 Ja/F 2017

BREAKING BARRIERS P. Constantakes *New York State Conservationist* v71 no3 p6 D 2016

Connecting People & Nature L. DiBetta *New York State Conservationist* v72 no1 p15 Ag 2017

DITCH THE JITTERS! J. YOUNG *Indianapolis Monthly* v40 no7 p86 Mr 2017

DIVE IN THE DEEP END L. ROBERTS *Indianapolis Monthly* v40 no7 p88 Mr 2017

A DOG IN THE HUNT B. Heavey cartoon *Field & Stream* v122 no1 p46 My 2017

Don't Ask, Don't Tell P. FREDERIKSEN color *Power & Motory-*

acht v33 no1 p38 Ja 2017

Family Values [Cover story] C. DEMARTINO color *Climbing* no350 p20 D 2016/Ja 2017

THE GREAT INDOORS B. Wieners color *Bloomberg Businessweek* no4495 p71 O 17 2016

HAWAII & AMERICAN CARIBBEAN *Sierra* v102 no1 p55 Ja/F 2017

HEALTHY AGING--Older adults staying connected with the outdoors A. Hyatt *New York State Conservationist* v72 no1 p30 Ag 2017

Heather Anderson A. A. DAVIS color *Maclean's* v130 no3 p74 Ap 2017

The Highest Order M. JOHANSON color *Backpacker* p10 N 2017

A House Divided A. McKEAN *Outdoor Life* v224 no1 p12 D 2016/Ja 2017

HOW TO GET AWAY color *Popular Mechanics* p65 Mr 2017

Inspired, Recharged and Raring to Go *Parks & Recreation* v51 no11 p38 N 2016

Keep calm and adventure on P. TREBLE bw color *Maclean's* v129 no40 p56 O 10 2016

LOST + FOUND A. McKean color *Outdoor Life* v224 no9 p54 N 2017

Memories gathered by the mile in Western Nebraska color *Nebraska Life* v21 no6 p71 N/D 2017

Off-Grid in Northern Ontario F. SIGURDSSON color *Cabin Living* p22 S 2017

ON THE ROCKS L. VACCARIELLO *Indianapolis Monthly* v40 no5 p30 Ja 2017

OUT OF MY LEAGUE B. HEAVEY *Field & Stream* v122 no3 p86 Ag 2017

Performance Climbing Nutrition J. DELVES bw color graph *Climbing* no353 p48 My/Je 2017

QUEST: BACKPACKING ACROSS WESTERN NEW YORK M. Foley *New York State Conservationist* v71 no5 p14 Ap 2017

September 2017 color *O, The Oprah Magazine* p113 S 2017

Snowmen, ice skates and lights make Nebraska's holiday bucket list D. LEFEVERS color *Nebraska Life* v21 no6 p68 N/D 2017

Steal Their Weekends: Sick of your same old summer routine? Then take someone else's. We found dozens of opinionated locals to pick from K. SCHNEIDER img *New York* v50 no12 p63 Je 12 2017

The Thrill of Letting Go A. DAWSON color *Men's Health* v32 no6 p12 Ag 2017

A Walk on the Wild Side C. HEITGER-EWING color *Cabin Living* p22 Ja/F 2017

THE WILDERNESS WAY T. E. Nickens cartoon *Field & Stream* v122 no1 p26 My 2017

Outdoor recreation equipment industry

GET YOUR HUNT ON! color *Horse & Rider* v56 no11 p66 N 2017

Outdoor recreation for children

Going outdoors E. G. Merritt color *Phi Delta Kappan* v99 no2 p21 O 2017

Laundering My History: For a Cleaner America S. CARR *Idaho Magazine* v16 no11 p54 Ag 2017

Outdoor recreation for women

Campspo! A. KOZOLCHYK color *Women's Health* v14 no4 p130 My 2017

Outdoor recreation industry

Climate Change Is Changing the Face of Outdoor Recreation R. J. Dolesh *Parks & Recreation* v52 no10 p30 O 2017

Outdoor recreation—Congresses

The Outdoor Alliance for Kids Holds Capitol Hill Briefing M. Acquino *Parks & Recreation* v52 no8 p66 Ag 2017

Outdoor recreation—Equipment & supplies

Natural Selection B. Rassler *Sierra* v102 no2 p18 Mr/Ap 2017

PADDLING + fishing A WINNING COMBO D. ARMITAGE color *Cabin Living* p62 Mr 2017

Outdoor recreation—Equipment & supplies—Exhibitions

GET YOUR HUNT ON! color *Horse & Rider* v56 no11 p66 N 2017

Outdoor recreation—Physiological aspects

Let's Take This Outside M. Bean color *Men's Health* v32 no6 p8 Ag 2017

Outdoor recreation—Social aspects

Creating a Special Space for Their Buddies M. Bosack *Parks &*

p6 Ag 2017

OvaScience Inc.

Rejuvenating the Chance of Motherhood? K. Weintraub color il *MIT Technology Review* v120 no1 p44 Ja/F 2017

Ovcharuk, Valeryia

Changing climate shifts timing of European floods color graph *Science* v357 no6351 p588 Ag 11 2017

Ovchinnikov, Sergey

Protein structure determination using metagenome sequence data color graph *Science* v355 no6322 p294 Ja 20 2017

Ovechkin, Alexander, 1985-

HOT | NOT S. Kwak color *Sports Illustrated* v127 no12 p20 O 16 2017

Overachievement

Degrees of Success M. BECK color *O, The Oprah Magazine* p34 Je 2017

Overactive bladder—Treatment

BLADDER CONTROL K. P. S. Khalsa color *Amazing Wellness* v9 no4 p36 Summ 2017

Overalls—Evaluation

Jump Around S. Kennedy color *Bloomberg Businessweek* no4514 p70 Mr 13 2017

Overbeck, Jen

You Don't Have to Be the Boss to Change How Your Company Works *Harvard Business Review Digital Articles* p2 F 26 2015

Overcast Radio LLC

OVERCAST 3: iOS PODCAST APP ADDS A QUEUE AND PERKS UP ITS INTERFACE G. FLEISHMAN color *Macworld - Digital Edition* v34 no4 p56 My 2017

Overfishing

Foreword M. Nasser *UN Chronicle* v54 no1/2 p1 2017

A SEA'S FADING BOUNTY R. BALE color map *National Geographic* v231 no3 p74 Mr 2017

Overfishing—Computer network resources

Commercial Overfishing map *Discover* v38 no2 p17 Mr 2017

Overfishing—Prevention

Fishy Business E. STRICKLAND color *Foreign Policy* no222 p24 Ja/F 2017

look at this trove, treasures untold E. KELLY and P. Hess cartoon *Popular Science* v289 no2 p76 Mr/Ap 2017

Overkleeft, Herman S.

Activity-based protein profiling reveals off-target proteins of the FAAH inhibitor BIA 10-2474 chart color graph *Science* v356 no6342 p1084 Je 9 2017

Overman, C. T.

Observation of coherent elastic neutrino-nucleus scattering diag *Science* v357 no6356 p1123 S 15 2017

Overmarine USA LLC

Overmarine Mangusta Oceano 42 J. Y. Wood color *Power & Motoryacht* v32 no11 p66 N 2016

Overpopulation

Is There a Case to be Made Against Baby Making? color *Foreign Policy* no224 p26 My/Je 2017

Overproduction

INTERNATIONAL STATISTICS *Economic Indicators* p35 Mr 2017

Overproduction—Charts, diagrams, etc.

INTERNATIONAL STATISTICS *Economic Indicators* p35 S 2016

PRODUCTION AND BUSINESS ACTIVITY *Economic Indicators* p17 S 2016

Overspending

Your Foolproof Holiday Budget T. E. Holmes color *Essence* v47 no7 p69 N 2016

Overtime

The Overworked Cop: Police overtime and long hours of off-duty work come with alarming consequences M. Maciag *Governing* v31 no1 p56 O 2017

Overtime pay

Why Overtime Pay Doesn't Change How Much We Work W. Frick *Harvard Business Review Digital Articles* p2 Jl 1 2015

Why the U.S. Decided That Managers Deserve Overtime Too P. Cappelli *Harvard Business Review Digital Articles* p2 My 26 2015

Overtime pay—Government policy

CALENDAR R. ERMEY color *Kiplinger's Personal Finance* v70

no12 p17 D 2016

Overtime pay—Law & legislation

Overtime Rule *Congressional Digest* v96 no1 p17 Ja 2017

Overtime pay—Lawsuits & claims

The Case of the Missing Comma V. GLEMBOCKI *Reader's Digest* v190 no1133 p18 S 2017

Overtime play (Sports)—Psychological aspects

THE AGONY AND ECSTASY OF OT J. Niesen color *Sports Illustrated* v125 no16 p48 N 14 2016

Overtime—Law & legislation—United States

Four Decades of Court Battles and Counting T. J. DONOHUE *Weekly Standard* v22 no28 p9 Mr 27 2017

Keeping Work Flexible, Even with Changes to U.S. Overtime Rules L. Morris *Harvard Business Review Digital Articles* p2 F 12 2016

Overtime Rule *Congressional Digest* v96 no1 p17 Ja 2017

Taking DOL's Overtime Rule to Court T. J. Donohue *Weekly Standard* v22 no6 p11 O 17 2016

Overtime—Lawsuits & claims

Defeat for employee sacked for refusing Christmas overtime' *People Management* p17 D 2016/Ja 2017

Overton, John D.

Distribution and clinical impact of functional variants in 50,726 whole-exome sequences from the DiscovEHR study chart graph *Science* v354 no6319 paaf6814-1 D 23 2016

Genetic identification of familial hypercholesterolemia within a single U.S. health care system chart graph *Science* v354 no6319 paaf7000-1 D 23 2016

Overton, Joseph

A Theory of Everything L. MARSH il *New Republic* v247 no12 p6 D 2016

Overweight men

'THE BRIEF WONDROUS LIFE OF OSCAR WAO' J. DIAZ, J. Aguirre et al *New York Times Book Review* p30 Ja 8 2017

Overweight persons

Big, Bigger, Biggest *Change* v82 no3 p34 Mr 2017

The LATEST WORD on WEIGHT LOSS B. HOWARD color *Prevention* v69 no11 p36 N 2017

NO LIMITS T. ROJEK color *Bicycling* v58 no9 p34 O 2017

Overweight persons—Health

The Delectable Myths of Healthy and Healthier Obesity K. W. KRAUSE *Skeptical Inquirer* v41 no2 p33 Mr/Ap 2017

Overweight women

I Am Not an Hourglass N. Mason color *Glamour* v115 no6 p46 Je 2017

Ovide, Shira

The Mother of All Early Days cartoon *Bloomberg Businessweek* no4514 p35 Mr 13 2017

Oviedo, Juan Pablo

Harvesting electrical energy from carbon nanotube yarn twist diag graph *Science* v357 no6353 p773 Ag 25 2017

Ovis

See also
Sheep

Desert Bighorn Sheep B. Cossavella *Arizona Highways* v92 no7 p13 Jl 2016

Ovum

Actin protects mammalian eggs against chromosome segregation errors B. Mogessie and M. Schuh color *Science* v357 no6353 p772 Ag 25 2017

Mouse eggs made in the lab G. Vogel color *Science* v354 no6319 p1520 D 23 2016

Ovum donors

WHAT IT REALLY TAKES TO GET PREGNANT AT 46 color *Redbook* p93 D 2016

Ovum—Cryopreservation

Why I Froze My Eggs color *InStyle* v23 no12 p193 N 2016

Ovum—Research

Eggs grown from mouse skin cells T. H. SAEY color *Science News* v190 no10 p6 N 12 2016

Owari, Satoko

Release of mineral-bound water prior to subduction tied to shallow seismogenic slip off Sumatra graph *Science* v356 no6340 p841 My 26 2017

Owen, Adrian

Awakenings G. JOHNSON *New York Times Book Review* p13 Ag

Knowledge, Policy, and Expertise: The UK Royal Commission on Environmental Pollution 1970–2011 T. O'Riordan color *Environment* v59 no1 p39 2017

Owens, Victoria L.
The biosynthetic pathway of coenzyme F430 in methanogenic and methanotrophic archaea bibl diag graph *Science* v354 no6310 p339 O 21 2016

Owerko, Carrie
Poses of the month color *Yoga Journal* no290 p47 Mr 2017
Q: For stress relief, what is your go-to practice or pose? color *Yoga Journal* no294 p14 S 2017

Owl behavior
Tricks For Treats A. SHAW color *National Geographic Kids* no474 p12 O 2017

Owlet Baby Care Inc.
WANT TO TREAT YOUR KID LIKE A FELON ON PAROLE? THERE'S AN APP FOR THAT L. SKENAZY color *Reason* v49 no4 p12 Ag/S 2017
Warning Signs N. SPORTELLI and J. BUCKINGHAM color *Forbes* v200 no4 p46 O 24 2017

Owls
Owls J. Rowen *New York State Conservationist* v71 no4 p32 F 2017

Owls as pets
The Harry Potter Effect color *Earth Island Journal* v32 no3 p4 Aut 2017

Owls—Research
Winter recharge color *National Wildlife (World Edition)* v55 no1 p8 D/Ja 2016

Own It (Music)
Singles Swap K. O'Donnell color *Entertainment Weekly* no1459 p61 Mr 31 2017

Owonikoko, Taofeek K.
Rescue of exhausted CD8 T cells by PD-1–targeted therapies is CD28-dependent bw diag graph *Science* v355 no6332 p1423 Mr 31 2017

Oxazoline
Formation of α-chiral centers by asymmetric β-C(sp3)–H arylation, alkenylation, and alkynylation Wu, Shen et al bibl diag *Science* v355 no6324 p499 F 3 2017

Oxford, Cyril
Can We Leave Now? V. FAIRBANK cartoon *Walrus* p18 Ja\F 2017

Oxford, Kelly
THE CRYSTAL METHOD color *InStyle* v24 no3 p328 Mr 2017
Oversharing Economy S. TIEN color *Walrus* v14 no4 p59 My 2017

Oxford, Pete
Rare Encounter color *National Wildlife (World Edition)* v55 no4 p20 Je/Jl 2017

Oxford Nanopore Technologies Ltd.
Mining microbes: Creating genomic tools to fight disease A. Dance color *Science* v356 no6339 p761 My 19 2017
Oxford Nanopore A. Regalado color il *MIT Technology Review* v120 no4 p66 Jl/Ag 2017

Oxidation
Earth's big oxygen boost pushed back T. SUMNER *Science News* v191 no4 p9 Mr 4 2017
Identify Bad Bolts B. HILDENBRAND color *Climbing* no354 p40 Jl 2017
Oxidation at the atomic scale D. Cadavid and A. Cabot diag *Science* v356 no6335 p245 Ap 21 2017
RESEARCH color *Science* v356 no6342 p1040 Je 9 2017

Oxidation-reduction reaction
Redox stratification of an ancient lake in Gale crater, Mars J. A. Hurowitz, J. P. Grotzinger et al color *Science* v356 no6341 p922 Je 1 2017

Oxidative dehydrogenation
Selective oxidative dehydrogenation of propane to propene using boron nitride catalysts J. T. Grant, C. A. Carrero et al bibl diag graph *Science* v354 no6319 p1570 D 23 2016

Oxidative stress
See also
Oxidative stress in mammals
The Oxidative Cost of Reproduction: Theoretical Questions and Alternative Mechanisms C. ALONSO-ALVAREZ, T. CANELO

et al *BioScience* v67 no3 p258 Mr 2017

Oxidative stress in mammals
Sweet relief for pollinators C. M. del Rio and M. E. Dillon bibl color diag *Science* v355 no6326 p686 F 17 2017

Oximetry
Warning Signs N. SPORTELLI and J. BUCKINGHAM color *Forbes* v200 no4 p46 O 24 2017

Oximetry—Equipment & supplies
Based on his snoring, I think my husband may have sleep apnea. However, he doesn't want to get tested because he doesn't want to spend a night hooked up to a bunch of equipment. Is there an easier way to know? *Mayo Clinic Health Letter* v35 no4 p8 Ap 2017

Oxitec Ltd.
EVEN IN THE AGE OF ZIKA, THE PEOPLE OF KEY WEST WANT NOTHING TO DO WITH OXITEC'S GENETICALLY MODIFIED MOSQUITOES [Cover story] R. KOLKER color *Bloomberg Businessweek* no4494 p48 O 10 2016
Mosquitoes to the Rescue J. Hsu color diag map *Scientific American* v315 no5 p17 N 2016

Oxman, Neri
The Art of Science L. Dern color *InStyle* v24 no11 p96 N 2017

Oxnard, Thomas
How to model a river channel color diag *Model Railroader* v84 no3 p41 Mr 2017

Oxtail stew
Just Like Mom Made—But Better G. VILLAMORA color *Bon Appetit* v62 no2 p62 Mr 2017

Oxycodone
AMERICAN HIGH J. FIELDEN color *Esquire* p16 N 2017

Oxygen
Comet's oxygen may be homegrown A. YEAGER color *Science News* v191 no11 p9 Je 10 2017
Fossil Moon S. R. Das color *Scientific American* v317 no4 p18 O 2017
How Cyanobacteria went green R. E. Blankenship color *Science* v355 no6332 p1372 Mr 31 2017

Oxygen reduction
Biaxially strained PtPb/Pt core/shell nanoplate boosts oxygen reduction catalysis Lingzheng Bu, Nan Zhang et al bibl color graph *Science* v354 no6318 p1410 D 16 2016

Oxygen—Equipment & supplies—Evaluation
NEW PRODUCTS color *Science* v354 no6309 p241 O 14 2016

Oxygen—Physiological effect
DEFLATING CANCER [Cover story] L. Beil color graph *Science News* v191 no4 p24 Mr 4 2017
Science's questions rarely have clear, easy answers E. Quill *Science News* v191 no4 p2 Mr 4 2017

Oxytocin
Gating of social reward by oxytocin in the ventral tegmental area L. W. Hung, S. Neuner et al color graph *Science* v357 no6358 p1406 S 29 2017
The rewarding nature of social contact S. D. Preston color diag *Science* v357 no6358 p1353 S 29 2017
Tend and Defend C. BADCOCK and J. BLEYER *Psychology Today* v50 no2 p38 Mr/Ap 2017

Oxytocin—Psychological aspects
THE NEUROSCIENCE OF TRUST P. J. ZAK color *Harvard Business Review* v95 no1 p84 Ja/F 2017

Oyamada, Aline
Will Bad Beef Taint Brazil's Meat Master? cartoon chart *Bloomberg Businessweek* no4516 p20 Mr 27 2017

Oye, Kenneth A.
Revisit NIH biosafety guidelines color *Science* v357 no6352 p627 Ag 18 2017

Øyehaug, Gunnhild
ENTANGLEMENT THEORY J. WOOD color *New Yorker* v93 no25 p83 Ag 28 2017

Oyelowo, David, 1976-
ACTION HERO N. Sperling color *Entertainment Weekly* no1454/1455 p74 F 24 2017
The King and His Wartime Consigliere J. GREEN img *New York* v49 no26 p91 D 26 2016

OYENIYI, DOYIN
THE ONE QUESTION INTERVIEW: NICKY DRAYDEN *Texas Monthly* v45 no6 p54 Je 2017

Oyster farmers
  EDITOR'S LETTER E. PARKHURST *Virginia Living* p9 2017
    Smoke & Salt
  SHELL GAME V. HUBBARD *Virginia Living* p60 2017 Smoke
    & Salt
Oyster populations
  THE WILD OYSTERP ROJECT: Saving Oysters to Save Our-
    selves L. HUNTER color *Earth Island Journal* v32 no2 p13
    Summ 2017
Oysters
  More than Half the Fun color *Conde Nast Traveler* v52 no6 p16
    Je/Jl 2017
  Naked Lunch: Oysters on the half shell are on the menu this fall
    M. W. Spencer *New Orleans Homes & Lifestyles* v20 no4 p112
    Aut 2017
  Oysters: A Love Story T. Rao *New York Times Magazine* p24 Ag
    20 2017
  ROAR OF THE CROWD R. OWENS, C. CHESHIRE et al *Texas*
    Monthly v45 no1 p8 Ja 2017
Oysters—Shucking
  Give 'Em Shell A. HUNTER *Virginia Living* p21 2017 Smoke
    & Salt
  Home Shucked N. RICHARDSON, A. STANEK et al color *Bon*
    Appetit no11 p36 N 2017
  OH, SHUCKS! M. HILL color *Louisiana Life* v37 no2 p104 N/D
    2016
Oz (TV program)
  THE GREAT OZ A. Westenfeld color *Esquire* p?? N 2017
Oz, Amos, 1939-
  Betrayal in Jerusalem A. Margalit bw *New York Review of Books*
    v64 no4 p35 Mr 9 2017
  By the Book *New York Times Book Review* p8 N 27 2016
  The First Christian? T. Novick cartoon *Commonweal* v144 no6
    p25 Mr 24 2017
  Judas, Jesus and Politics E. BARTON *New York Times Book Re-*
    view p26 D 11 2016
  The Samaritan impulse D. Vellucci color *America* v216 no9 p52
    Ap 24 2017
Oz, Amos, 1939——Interviews
  By the Book A. Oz *New York Times Book Review* p8 N 27 2016
OZ, MEHMET
  ASK DR. OZ: How do I avoid a HOLIDAY FOOD "COMA"?
    color *Good Housekeeping* v265 no5 p71 N 2017
  BE SMART ABOUT Supplements color *O, The Oprah Magazine*
    p84 Ap 2017
  The Best Reasons to EXERCISE color *O, The Oprah Magazine*
    p67 Ja 2017
  Boost Your BRAINPOWER color *Good Housekeeping* v265 no4
    p91 O 2017
  EAT YOUR WAY TO BETTER HEALTH color *O, The Oprah*
    Magazine p86 S 2017
  GH BEAUTY LAB color *Good Housekeeping* v265 no4 p30 O
    2017
  Hearts and MINDS color *O, The Oprah Magazine* p78 Je 2017
  inside the GH BEAUTY LAB color *Good Housekeeping* v265
    no3 p34 S 2017
  Lyme LESSONS cartoon *O, The Oprah Magazine* p106 My 2017
  SPRING-CLEAN Your Kitchen cartoon *O, The Oprah Magazine*
    p99 Mr 2017
  This Is Your Heart ON STRESS cartoon *O, The Oprah Magazine*
    p96 F 2017
  YOUR YEAREND BONUS cartoon *O, The Oprah Magazine*
    p134 D 2016
Ozanian, Michael
  INSIDE THE HUDDLE color *Forbes* v200 no4 p15 O 24 2017
  LESSONS AND IDEAS BY THE 100 GREATEST LIVING
    BUSINESS MINDS bw color *Forbes* v200 no3 p115 S 28 2017
  The Most Valuable Baseball Teams chart color *Forbes* v199 no5
    p28 My 16 2017
  The Most Valuable NBA Teams chart color *Forbes* v199 no2 p30
    F 28 2017
  The Most Valuable NFL Teams color graph *Forbes* v198 no5 p32
    O 25 2016
  The Most Valuable Sports Brands chart color *Forbes* v198 no8
    p34 D 20 2016
  THE WORLD'S MOST VALUABLE SOCCER TEAMS chart

    color *Forbes* v199 no7 p32 Je 29 2017
Ozark (TV program)
  America's top TV critic Matt Roush answers your burning ques-
    tions Jodi *TV Guide* v65 no37 p9 S 4 2017
  Bateman's Stab at High Drama D. D'addario color *Time* v190 no5
    p61 Jl 31 2017
  FROM PAGE TO SCREEN color *Entertainment Weekly*
    no1468/1469 p66 Je 2-9 2017
  Laura Linney's Ozark Adventure D. Snierson color *Entertainment*
    Weekly no1476 p51 Ag 4 2017
  Ozark: A gripping thriller of money, murder and family M.
    ROUSH *TV Guide* v65 no31 p14 Jl 24 2017
  OZARK D. Snierson color *Entertainment Weekly* no1468/1469
    p66 Je 2-9 2017
  What to Watch R. Rahman, J. Jensen et al color *Entertainment*
    Weekly no1474/1475 p108 Jl 21-28 2017
Ozark, Patrick A.
  PAF1 regulation of promoter-proximal pause release via enhancer
    activation color *Science* v357 no6357 p1294 S 22 2017
Ozark Mountain Daredevils (Performer)
  Speaking of Springfield Music... M. W. Schwartz color *Missouri*
    Life v44 no3 p22 My 2017
Ozawa, Melissa
  BEYOND THE GARDEN GATE *Martha Stewart Living* no267
    p94 S 2016
  THE BOLD AND THE BEAUTIFUL *Martha Stewart Living*
    no270 p53 D 2016
  CALL OF THE WILD color *Martha Stewart Living* p40 Mr 2017
  Emerald City color *Martha Stewart Living* p92 S 2017
  The Fine Print color *Martha Stewart Living* no275 p48 Je 2017
  THE FRESH FACE OF BEAUTY color *Martha Stewart Living*
    no271 p40 Ja/F 2017
  FULL CIRCLE color *Martha Stewart Living* p60 O 2017
  HEAVEN ON EARTH color *Martha Stewart Living* no275 p86
    Je 2017
  HIT THE BOOKS! cartoon color *Martha Stewart Living* no271
    p104 Ja/F 2017
  HOW TO PLANT A VEGETABLE GARDEN cartoon chart color
    Martha Stewart Living p76 Mr 2017
  Learning the Ropes color *Martha Stewart Living* p42 S 2017
  LILIES FOR DAYS color *Martha Stewart Living* p90 My 2017
  Nailed It *Martha Stewart Living* no268 p44 O 2016
  One Stitch at a Time color *Martha Stewart Living* p34 My 2017
  rare BEAUTIES *Martha Stewart Living* no269 p120 N 2016
  SITTING PRETTY color *Martha Stewart Living* no275 p32 Je
    2017
  A Stitch in Time *Martha Stewart Living* no269 p44 N 2016
  TRUE-BLUE WINNERS color *Martha Stewart Living* no271 p76
    Ja/F 2017
Ozbenian, Serda
  Meet the NRPA Conservation Advisory Panel *Parks & Recreation*
    v52 no4 p48 Ap 2017
  Organic Parks: The challenge of managing and maintaining well-
    manicured landscapes *Parks & Recreation* v52 no10 p26 O
    2017
  Quantifying Green Infrastructure's Stormwater Capture Potential
    Parks & Recreation v52 no9 p42 S 2017
  Wild and Wonderful *Parks & Recreation* v52 no3 p14 Mr 2017
Ozcan, Aydogan
  MICROSCOPY without lenses: Lens-free on-chip imaging devic-
    es provide cost-effective, compact, and wide-field microscopy
    solutions for fieldwork and global health applications *Physics*
    Today v70 no9 p50 S 2017
Ozek, Ceren
  Lee Rubin: Our mentor and role model *Science* v355 no6327 p806
    F 24 2017
Özel, Feryal
  The Inside Story of Neutron Stars *Sky & Telescope* v134 no1 p16
    Jl 2017
Ozel, N. Bugra
  Research: Workplace Injuries Are More Common When Compa-
    nies Face Earnings Pressure *Harvard Business Review Digital*
    Articles p2 My 18 2017
Ozick, Cynthia
  The Last Road Trip *New York Times Book Review* p1 F 19 2017
Ozon, François

Frantz color *New Yorker* v93 no7 p22 Ap 3 2017

FRANTZ J. Christman *U.S. Catholic* v82 no10 p40 O 2017

Ozone layer depletion—Prevention

Antarctic ozone hole officially on the mend A. Witze color *Science News* v190 no13 p28 D 24 2016

Ozone layer protection

THE OZONE HOLE IS FINALLY HEALING N. SCHARPING color *Discover* v38 no1 p24 Ja/F 2017

Ozone—Environmental aspects

Pollution on the Move D. Stone graph map *National Geographic* v230 no4 p22 O 2016

P

P Cygni stars

Twelve Steps to Infinity M. Wedel *Sky & Telescope* v132 no6 p24 D 2016

P-N junctions (Semiconductors)

Electron optics with p-n junctions in ballistic graphene M. M. Elahi, K. M. M. Habib et al bibl graph *Science* v353 no6307 p1522 S 30 2016

Pääbo, Svante

Neandertal and Denisovan DNA from Pleistocene sediments bw color *Science* v356 no6338 p605 My 12 2017

Paalman, Koren

Bharadvajasana II [Cover story] color *Yoga Journal* no292 p53 Je 2017

Paasche, Franz W.

FinTech Is Weaving Charitable Giving into Everyday Transactions *Harvard Business Review Digital Articles* p2 Jl 11 2016

Paaso, Jackie

Resilience M. MICHELSON bw color *Powder* p54 S 2017

Paben, Steven P.

The 2018 revision of the Consumer Price Index geographic sample bibl chart color diag map *Monthly Labor Review* p1 O 2016

Pacala, Stephen W.

Unmask temporal trade-offs in climate policy debates color *Science* v356 no6337 p492 My 5 2017

Pace, Lee

Halt and Catch Fire J. Jensen color *Entertainment Weekly* no1478 / 1479 p88 Ag 18-25 2017

PACE, STEVEN

Teaching Biology in the Field: Importance, Challenges, and Solutions *BioScience* v67 no6 p558 Je 2017

PACE, TONI J.

Aligned Transitions *Education Digest* v82 no5 p12 Ja 2017

Paces Properties Inc.

Sarah Spear *Atlanta* v56 no7 p52 N 2016

Pace University (New York, N.Y.)

Pace University *Dance Magazine* v90 p91 2016/2017 Supplement College Guide

Pacewicz, Josh

Above the Fray A. Greenblatt *Governing* v30 no6 p17 Mr 2017

Pacey, Asher

OUT OF BOUNDS A. GOGGANS color *Surfer* v57 no12 p74 Ja/F 2017

Pacheco, J. L.

An integrated diamond nanophotonics platform for quantum-optical networks bibl graph *Science* v354 no6314 p847 N 18 2016

Pachico, Julianne

Colombian Exposition S. PATERNOSTRO *New York Times Book Review* p22 Mr 19 2017

Pachino, Jamie

Visualizing "Aggressive Precision": World Premiere of Other Than Honorable at Geva Theatre Center R. Minetor *Stage Directions* v30 no6 p8 Je 2017

Pachisia, Nitin

HACKING THE VISA RACKET M. Helft color *Forbes* v198 no5 p74 O 25 2016

Pachnis, Vassilis

Lineage-dependent spatial and functional organization of the mammalian enteric nervous system color graph *Science* v356 no6339 p722 My 19 2017

Pacific Area—History

Trump and the Asia-Pacific: Do the Ties Still Bind? M. BEESON

Current History v116 no791 p235 S 2017

Pacific Asian Enterprises Inc.

NORDHAVN N96: AWARD-WINNING DESIGN AND OCEAN-CROSSING RANGE FIND A HOME IN ONE NEAR-100-FOOT YACHT M. WERLING *Sea Magazine* v109 no9 p42 S 2017

Pacific Coast (North America)

Debris arrivals divvied up M. Quintanilla color map *Science News* v192 no7 p32 O 28 2017

Pacific Coast (U.S.)

GUESS THE LOCATION *Sea Magazine* v109 no4 p11 Ap 2017

NAME THE BOAT *Sea Magazine* v109 no4 p12 Ap 2017

Pacific Coast (U.S.)—History

Who Named It? S. SHIBATA *Sea Magazine* v108 no8 p12 Ag 2016

Pacific Crest Bicycle Trail

Start your engines map *Backpacker* p13 My 2017

Pacific Crest Trail

LONG TRAIL NATION map *Backpacker* v45 no1 p60 Ja 2017

THE SHARPEST TOOL IN THE SHED S. SALABERT color *Backpacker* p71 Ag 2017

STAY AWHILE J. Montalvo color *Backpacker* v45 no1 p85 Ja 2017

#trailchat A. Grieve, J. Wells et al color *Backpacker* v45 no2 p10 Mr 2017

What's the Rush? L. ". C. LANCASTER color *Backpacker* v45 no1 p28 Ja 2017

Pacific Emblem Co.

Products *Parks & Recreation* v52 no10 p56 O 2017

Pacific Grove (Calif.)

You're Up! color *Golf Magazine* v59 no4 p15 Ap 2017

Pacific herring fisheries

A Drastic Decline of River Herring: TINY STONES IN FISH HOLD CLUES TO HELP RESTORE POPULATIONS K. Madin *Oceanus* v52 no2 p2 Spr 2017

Pacific Investment Management Co.—Finance

The Bond King Gets Lost in the Crowd J. Gittelsohn bw *Bloomberg Businessweek* no4539 p29 S 25 2017

Pacific Investment Management Co.—Officials & employees

Dan Ivascyn J. Gittelsohn *Bloomberg Businessweek* no4531 p72 Jl 24 2017

Pacific madrone

A Body of Trees N. NEELY color *Orion Magazine* v35 no6 p46 N/D 2016

Pacific Northwest

What's in a Name? S. SHIBATA color *Sea Magazine* v109 no8 p12 Ag 2017

Pacific Northwest Ballet (Performer)

DAMMIEL CRVZ O. Manno *Dance Spirit* v21 no3 p38 Mr 2017

FROM THE PAGE TO THE STAGE M. McNAMARA color *Dance Spirit* v20 no9 p55 N 2016

Pacific Northwest Trail

ROOM WITH A VIEW M. Horjus color *Backpacker* v45 no1 p78 Ja 2017

Pacific Ocean

GLIMPSES B. HURD bw color *Orion Magazine* v35 no6 p38 N/D 2016

Pacific Rim Uprising (Film)

Pacific Rim Uprising A. Breznican color *Entertainment Weekly* no1486 p44 O 13 2017

Pacifica Quartet (Performer)

66 GREAT THINGS TO DO THIS MONTH J. FOUMBERG, J. HARDBERGER et al color *Chicago* v66 no9 p139 S 2017

Pacifici, Michela

The broad footprint of climate change from genes to biomes to people bibl chart color *Science* v354 no6313 paaf7671-1 N 11 2016

Pacifico, Francesco

Williamsburg, Seen From Italy: Francesco Pacifico's sharp new novel of North Brooklyn img *New York* v50 no12 p109 Je 12 2017

Pacific University (Forest Grove, Or.)

Pacific University *Dance Magazine* v90 p92 2016/2017 Supplement College Guide

Pacifism—Japan

Is Japan Ready To Abandon Pacifism? A. Sharp, Yuki Hagiwara et al color *Bloomberg Businessweek* no4536 p37 S 4 2017

Pacifists—United States

Tom Hayden E. Garcetti color *Time* v188 no19 p11 N 7 2016

Pack transportation

See also

Backpacking

A Step-by-Step Guide to Packing for a Complicated Work Trip S. G. Carmichael *Harvard Business Review Digital Articles* p2 N 18 2015

Package tours

Give-Back Getaways C. Kopaczewski color *Good Housekeeping* v264 no5 p69 My 2017

INTERNATIONAL *Sierra* v102 no1 p89 Ja/F 2017

WIN A MENDOCINO GETAWAY! color *Sunset* v239 no3 p110 S 2017

Package tours—Evaluation

Go West YOUNG MEN! (and women, too) color *Nebraska Life* v20 no6 p68 N/D 2016

Hit the Road in 2017 color *Nebraska Life* v21 no1 p68 Ja/F 2017

How You Should Really Do Cuba cartoon chart *Conde Nast Traveler* v52 no3 p100 Mr 2017

LOCAL MOTION J. Scatena color *Sunset* v238 no4 p23 Ap 2017

OUTSIDER'S PASSAGE S. Shain color *Sunset* v239 no3 p19 S 2017

Sandhill Crane Tour color *Nebraska Life* v20 no6 p70 N/D 2016

See the sights color *Nebraska Life* v21 no2 p66 Mr/Ap 2017

WIN A SOCAL BEACH GETAWAY! T. Enriquez color *Sunset* v238 no5 p106 My 2017

WIN A TRIP AND FRAME IT! color *Sunset* v237 no6 p110 D 2016

WIN A TRIP TO MAUI! color *Sunset* v238 no2 p98 F 2017

WIN A TRIP TO SOUTHERN UTAH! color *Sunset* v239 no1 p110 Jl 2017

Packaged foods—Evaluation

Plevention CLEANEST PACKAGED FOOD AWARDS 2017 [Cover story] S. Eckelkamp color *Prevention* p60 Mr 2017

Packaging

See also

Food—Packaging

Gift wrapping

Labels

Plastics in packaging

Customers Aren't Very Good at Judging Product Sizing P. Chandon *Harvard Business Review Digital Articles* p2 N 11 2015

When Sensory Marketing Works and When it Backfires A. Sundar and T. J. Noseworthy *Harvard Business Review Digital Articles* p2 My 19 2016

Packaging recycling

Molecular stitches for enhanced recycling of packaging C. Creton bibl diag *Science* v355 no6327 p797 F 24 2017

Taking Out the Meal-Kit Trash A. Nova color *Money* v46 no8 p74 S 2017

PACKARD, MORGAN

DANCIN' IN THE STREET [Cover story] color *New Orleans Magazine* v51 no4 p58 F 2017

Packer, Dominic

The Problem with Rewarding Individual Performers *Harvard Business Review Digital Articles* p2 D 27 2016

Packer, George

AFTERMATH bw cartoon *New Yorker* v92 no38 p48 N 21 2016

OFFICIAL DUTIES cartoon *New Yorker* v93 no2 p21 F 27 2017

PARTING WORDS cartoon *New Yorker* v92 no46 p17 Ja 23 2017

THE UNCONNECTED cartoon color *New Yorker* v92 no35 p48 O 31 2016

Packer, James, 1967-

JAMES AND THE GIANT BREACH W. D. COHAN color *Vanity Fair* p114 Hollywood 2017 Supplement

Packer, James, 1967——Finance

LeaderBoard color *Forbes* v198 no7 p28 N 29 2016

Packer, Jonathan S.

Comprehensive single-cell transcriptional profiling of a multicellular organism diag *Science* v357 no6352 p661 Ag 18 2017

Distribution and clinical impact of functional variants in 50,726 whole-exome sequences from the DiscovEHR study chart graph *Science* v354 no6319 paaf6814-1 D 23 2016

Packing-house workers—United States

Big Meat Braces for A Labor Shortage L. Etter and S. Singh color *Bloomberg Businessweek* no4511 p19 F 13 2017

Packing luggage

DOOMSDAY IN IGLOO R. Holtzmann *South Dakota Magazine* v33 no3 p52 S/O 2017

Packnett, Brittany

Education For Us, By Us color *Essence* v47 no12 p132 Ap 2017

Packwood, Burley

READER GALLERY bw color *Astronomy* v45 no11 p72 N 2017

PACTON, JAMIE

popular authors' favorite children's books color *Parents* v92 no5 p48 My 2017

PACZESNY, JOHN

Chatter color graph *Indianapolis Monthly* v42 no2 p11 O 2017

Padalecki, Jared, 1982-

Supernatural S. Highfill, N. Abrams et al color *Entertainment Weekly* no1482/1483 p84 S 22 2017

PADAWER, RUTH

All His Loving *New York Times Book Review* p17 Je 25 2017

Paddleboarding

EVENTS *Sea Magazine* v109 no7 pCA-10 Jl 2017

From polo to paddleboarding A. KYLIE color map *Canadian Geographic* v137 p11 2017 Travel

IN THE SHOP, ON THE WATER color *Popular Mechanics* p57 S 2017

Letters to the Editor M. Halligan, U. Heidenreich et al color *Prevention* v69 no5 p4 My 2017

Standing Alone *Arizona Highways* v93 no11 p5 N 2017

Surf's SUP! D. Wolman color *Bloomberg Businessweek* no4518 p76 Ap 10 2017

Paddleboarding—Equipment & supplies

IN THE SHOP, ON THE WATER color *Popular Mechanics* v193 no7 p57 S 2016

Paddlefish

THE DISH ON THE SPOONS B. COOPER and G. BETHGE color *Outdoor Life* v224 no3 p64 Ap 2017

Paddock, LeRoy

Science in litigation, the third branch of U.S. climate policy graph *Science* v357 no6355 p979 S 8 2017

Paddy fields

HUNGRY PLANET *Sierra* v102 no2 p4 Mr/Ap 2017

PADELA, AASIM I.

The Unbreakable Relationship *Islamic Horizons* v45 no6 p48 N/D 2016

Pademelons

PADEMELON A. KLEPEIS *National Geographic Kids* no466 p20 D 2016/Ja 2017

Padgett, Tim

BRAZIL'S CARWASH SCANDAL color *Bloomberg Businessweek* no4524 p8 My 29 2017

Can Pope Francis help Venezuela step back from the edge? color *America* v217 no3 p15 Ag 7 2017

Can statehood save Puerto Rico? color *America* v216 no13 p15 Je 12 2017

Down And Almost Out in Latin America color *Bloomberg Businessweek* no4520 p10 My 1 2017

Fidel Castro 1926-2016 [Cover story] color *Time* v188 no24 p40 D 12 2016

A lesson from Pope Francis for Miami's gridlocked streets color *America* v217 no6 p16 S 18 2017

New Respect for Haiti's Kamoken *America* v215 p12 N 28 2016

PADILLA-RODRÍGUEZ, IVÓN

THE NEGLECT OF THE IMMIGRANT CHILD: MAKING THE CASE FOR A CHILD-CENTERED APPROACH TO UNITED STATES IMMIGRATION POLICY bw color *Phi Kappa Phi Forum* v96 no4 p12 Wint 2016

Padmore, Owen

Forced Confessions B. TRAVERS color *Walrus* v14 no4 p42 My 2017

Padova, Nino

STRIP TEASE chart color *Sunset* v238 no2 p20 F 2017

Paducah (Ky.)

QUILT TO LAST A. LYNCH *Indianapolis Monthly* v40 no3 p48 N 2016

Padukone, Deepika, 1986-

the new girl H. Morrill color *InStyle* v24 no2 p146 F 2017

Padura, Leonardo, 1955-
Four Seasons in Havana R. Feinberg *Foreign Affairs* v96 no3 p166 My/Je 2017

Pae, Peter
South Korea Tries to Curb the Chaebol color *Bloomberg Businessweek* no4504 p15 D 19 2016

PAESEL, BRETT
i don't feel guilty about not feeling guilty color *Parents* v92 no5 p84 My 2017

Paetz, Hans
Key Nuclear Reaction Experiments Discoveries and Consequences C. Bertulani *Physics Today* v69 no11 p58 N 2016

Pagán, Camille Noe
WEIGHT LOSS SURGERY CONFIDENTIAL color *Health* v31 no7 p134 S 2017

Paganism in art
NOT BY BREAD ALONE R. LORENZI color *Archaeology* v70 no5 p22 S/O 2017

Page, Angelica
Paging Geraldine H. Als cartoon *New Yorker* v92 no49 p23 F 13 2017

Page, Bettie
Top-Earning Dead Celebrities color *Forbes* v198 no6 p28 N 8 2016

PAGE, CASEY
The Question *O, The Oprah Magazine* p16 Ap 2017

Page, David
Dope Runners [Cover story] color *Powder* v46 no2 p62 O 2017
THE SOLOIST [Cover story] bw *Powder* v45 no6 p78 F 2017

Page, Diamond Dallas, 1949-
Broga? D. Greene and T. Keith color *Sports Illustrated* v126 no14 p24 My 15-22 2017

Page, Dick
Read My Lips Y. Chu color *Glamour* v114 no11 p166 N 2016

Page, Elina
FoodAPS Data Now Available to the General Public chart color graph *Amber Waves: The Economics of Food, Farming, Natural Resources, & Rural America* p27 D 2016

Page, Jimmy, 1944-
Random Notes color *Rolling Stone* no1288 p24 Je 1 2017

Page, Larry, 1973-
4 LARRY PAGE L. Rao color *Fortune* v174 no7 p75 D 1 2016

Page, Lindsay
Getting More Students to College, Without Breaking School Budgets *Harvard Business Review Digital Articles* p2 F 15 2016
Small Nudges Can Improve How Students Apply to College *Harvard Business Review Digital Articles* p2 N 29 2016

Page, Max
An Authentic Argument J. Gauer color *Architectural Record* v205 no2 p41 F 2017

Page, Sam
17 ICONIC MOMENTS IN NHL HISTORY color *Sports Illustrated* v126 no4 p56 Ja 30 2017
WESTERN CONFERENCE POWER RANKINGS color *Sports Illustrated* v125 no12 p58 O 10 2016

Page, Sebastien—Interviews
What to Own in an Expensive Market color *Kiplinger's Personal Finance* v71 no7 p50 Jl 2017

Page, Susan E.
Time for responsible peatland agriculture bibl *Science* v354 no6312 p562 N 4 2016

Page, Thomas Hyde
DON'T FIRE UNTIL YOU SEE... *MHQ: Quarterly Journal of Military History* v29 no2 p16 Wint 2017

Page, Tim
An Elusive Cold War Star color *New York Review of Books* v64 no12 p40 Jl 13 2017
John Cage's Gift to Us bw *New York Review of Books* v63 no16 p42 O 27 2016
The Perfectionist bw *New York Review of Books* v64 no17 p14 N 9 2017

Pageants
See also
Parades
GOTTSCHEE QUESTION R. Corbett cartoon *New Yorker* v93 no19 p20 Jl 3 2017

Pagels, Elaine H., 1943-
Editor's Note D. Skinner *Humanities* v37 no4 p1 Fall 2016

Pager, Devah
Hiring Discrimination Against Black Americans Hasn't Declined in 25 Years *Harvard Business Review Digital Articles* p2 O 11 2017

Paglia, Camille, 1947-
A 'Fractious' Feminist Decries the Ruthless Thought Police Stifling Free Speech on Campus color *Time* v189 no12 p28 Ap 3 2017
Love and War: Camille Paglia Predicted 2017 M. FISCHER img *New York* p24 Mr 6 2017

Paglia, Vincenzo
Opposition to Óscar Romero's canonization was political J. Dueño color *America* v216 no8 p17 Ap 17 2017

Pagodas—Japan
Misty Weather color *House Beautiful* v159 no2 p26 Mr 2017

Pagrus auratus
DISH OF THE MONTH A. LIMPERT *Washingtonian Magazine* v52 no9 p142 Je 2017

Paharia, Neeru
Research: Why Americans Are So Impressed by Busyness *Harvard Business Review Digital Articles* p2 D 15 2016

Pai, Deanna
Cur Power [Cover story] color *Women's Health* v13 no10 p47 D 2016
My Hair, Lost & Found Again color *Glamour* v115 no9 p104 S 2017

Pai, Emil F.
The role of dimer asymmetry and protomer dynamics in enzyme catalysis diag *Science* v355 no6322 p262 Ja 20 2017

Paige, Jennifer
Rekindle Your Crush on Jennifer Paige N. Feeney color *Entertainment Weekly* no1462 p62 Ap 21 2017

Paige, Patricia
PROFILES *Arabian Horse World* v57 no3 p60 D 2016

Paige Denim (Company)
THE CHICEST LADY AT THE AIRPORT S. Trong color *InStyle* v24 no2 p132 F 2017

Paillole, Paul
The Spy in Hitler's Inner Circle: Hans-Thilo Schmidt and the Intelligence That Decoded Enigma T. Zacharis *Military History* v33 no5 p73 Ja 2017

Pails
HAPPY TO HOST R. DOLGIN color *Martha Stewart Living* no275 p28 Je 2017

Pails—Evaluation
Mothers Product Picks *Mother Earth News* no284 p12 O/N 2017

Pain
See also
Abdominal pain
Backache
Chronic pain
Headache
Myalgia
Neck pain
Pain management
Toothache
Diagnosis L. Sanders *New York Times Magazine* p32 O 16 2016
The Link Between Income Inequality and Physical Pain E. Y. Chou, B. L. Parmar et al *Harvard Business Review Digital Articles* p2 Mr 21 2016
PACKING FOR ETERNITY R. Holtzmann *South Dakota Magazine* v32 no6 p66 Mr/Ap 2017
Relief is here! C. Gorrell *Yoga Journal* p3 2017 SpecialIssue
Spinal T(ap) E. CALDERONE color *Muscle & Performance* v9 no10 p28 O 2017

Pain, Elisabeth
At 10, Europe's 'excellence' fund ponders changes color graph *Science* v355 no6329 p1002 Mr 10 2017
Head of France's main funding body resigns amid acrimony *Science* v357 no6349 p341 Jl 28 2017
Reports raise concerns about France's nuclear waste tomb color *Science* v357 no6354 p858 S 1 2017
A top mathematician joins the Macron revolution color *Science* v356 no6344 p1223 Je 23 2017

Unusual presidential race rattles French scientists color *Science* v356 no6333 p14 Ap 7 2017

Pain in animals

POP QUIZ C. Barakat and M. Freckleton color *Equus* no482 p16 N 2017

Pain management

ASK A FLOWCHART HOW STRONG IS MY GENETIC TOLERANCE TO PAIN? R. CAPPS diag *Wired* v25 no5 p120 My 2017

Beyond Today's Opioids L. Hamers color graph *Science News* v191 no11 p22 Je 10 2017

THE FUTURE OF PAIN RESEARCH P. Stem and L. Roberts color *Science* v354 no6312 p565 N 4 2016

"How Bad Is Your Pain?" Notes on the nature of suffering R. TELHAN *American Scholar* v86 no4 p20 Aut 2017

massage AWAY PAIN color *Good Housekeeping* v264 no4 p98 Ap 2017

NATURAL TREATMENT FOR PAIN J. Bowden color *Amazing Wellness* v9 no2 p34 Spr 2017

Opioids and Paternalism: TO HELP END THE CRISIS, BOTH DOCTORS AND PATIENTS NEED TO FIND A NEW WAY TO THINK ABOUT PAIN [Cover story] D. BROWN *American Scholar* v86 no4 p22 Aut 2017

Shoulder & wrist pain color *Yoga Journal* p35 2017 SpecialIssue

Pain perception

Deconstructing the sensation of pain: The influence of cognitive processes on pain perception K. Wiech bibl diag graph *Science* v354 no6312 p584 N 4 2016

Pain prevention

10 Foods to Tame Your Pain L. TURNER color *Better Nutrition* v79 no10 p68 O 2017

6 Rules of Recovery A. HEFFERNAN color *Men's Health* v32 no5 p54 Je 2017

Ankle arthritis [Cover story] *Mayo Clinic Health Letter* v358 no8 p1 Ag 2017

ASK TUFTS EXPERTS A. H. Lichtenstein *Tufts University Health & Nutrition Letter* v34 no10 p8 D 2016

Body of knowledge R. Long color *Yoga Journal* no287 p40 N 2016

CBD Oil: Anxiety Aid & Much More [Cover story] L. Turner color *Better Nutrition* v79 no11 p34 N 2017

Cut down on pain this way color *Redbook* p81 O 2017

Feet First E. A. KANE color *Better Nutrition* v79 no9 p26 S 2017

Get to know... your glutes J. Miller color *Yoga Journal* p76 2017 SpecialIssue

Get to know... your SI joint J. H. Lasater color *Yoga Journal* p60 2017 SpecialIssue

Giving Pain the Slip A. OLENDZKI color *Tricycle: The Buddhist Review* v26 no2 p30 Wint 2016

Hip & glute pain color *Yoga Journal* p67 2017 SpecialIssue

I promise you a pain-free life or your money back T. Lemerond color *Better Nutrition* v78 no11 p76 N 2016

Leg pain color *Yoga Journal* p89 2017 SpecialIssue

Off the mat color *Yoga Journal* p101 2017 SpecialIssue

A Salve for the Shot S. SEA GOLD color *Parents* v92 no4 p24 Ap 2017

Tight Club color *Health* v30 no9 p20 N 2016

Total knee replacement [Cover story] *Mayo Clinic Health Letter* v35 no9 p1 S 2017

Pain threshold

miR-183 cluster scales mechanical pain sensitivity by regulating basal and neuropathic pain genes C. Peng, L. Li et al diag graph *Science* v356 no6343 p1168 Je 16 2017

Scaling pain threshold with microRNAs L. Cassels and Barde diag *Science* v356 no6343 p1124 Je 16 2017

Pain tolerance

PRIMED FOR PAIN K. Servick color *Science* v354 no6312 p569 N 4 2016

Pain—Diagnosis

ERASE YOUR PAIN: A USER'S MANUAL H. Levine color *Health* v31 no2 p97 Mr 2017

PAINE, LYNN S.

The Error at the Heart of Corporate Leadership chart img *Harvard Business Review* v95 no3 p50 My/Je 2017

THE ERROR AT THE HEART OF CORPORATE LEADERSHIP: INTERACTION color *Harvard Business Review* v95

no4 p16 Jl/Ag 2017

PAINE, THOMAS

THOUGHTS ON Conflict *Forbes* v199 no4 p112 Ap 25 2017

Pain—Physiological aspects

Exploring pain pathophysiology in patients C. Sommer bibl diag *Science* v354 no6312 p588 N 4 2016

Neural circuits for pain: Recent advances and current views C. Peirs and R. P. Seal bibl diag *Science* v354 no6312 p578 N 4 2016

Pain regulation by non-neuronal cells and inflammation Ru-Rong Ji, A. Chamessian et al bibl diag *Science* v354 no6312 p572 N 4 2016

Pain—Prevention—Research

Time for nonaddictive relief of pain T. Grosser, C. J. Woolf et al bibl color *Science* v355 no6329 p1026 Mr 10 2017

Pain—Research

THE FUTURE OF PAIN RESEARCH P. Stem and L. Roberts color *Science* v354 no6312 p565 N 4 2016

Paint

6 Things You Should Never Park in Your Garage B. NELSON color *Reader's Digest* v190 no1133 p44 S 2017

H2-Whoa! color *House Beautiful* v159 no5 p34 Je 2017

PAINT: Hue New? color *House Beautiful* v159 no9 p24 N 2017

Pretty in Paint K. Janeway chart color il *Consumer Reports* v82 no5 p38 My 2017

This is how to mix prints color *Redbook* p134 O 2017

walls & ceilings *Design Center Sourcebook* p76 2017

WHAT THEY DID K. SELZER color *Better Homes & Gardens* v95 no9 p66 S 2017

Paint materials

WATCHING-PAINT-DRY CAM color *Popular Mechanics* p6 O 2017

Paint removal

THE NEVER-ENDING INSTRUCTION MANUAL color *Popular Mechanics* p41 O 2017

Paint removers—Evaluation

Winter Hot Stuff color *Old House Journal* v45 no7 p48 O 2017

Paintbrushes—Equipment & supplies

Blank Canvas color *Martha Stewart Living* p22 My 2017

Paintbrushes—Evaluation

BEST TOY AWARDS 2017 N. SAPORITA color *Good Housekeeping* v265 no5 p85 N 2017

Painted Desert (Ariz.)

Nature's Pied Piper J. I. Keith color *AARP: The Magazine* v59 no3A p82 Ap/My 2016

Painted signs & signboards

Ghost Busters B. PIKE color *Power & Motoryacht* v32 no11 p141 N 2016

Painter, George

Arrested development color *Science* v354 no6316 p1111 D 2 2016

PAINTER, KEN

UNINTENDED ENTANGLEMENTS *Sea Magazine* v109 no1 p25 Ja 2017

Painter, Kimberley

The Price of Australia's Complacency color *Bloomberg Businessweek* no4541 p33 O 9 2017

PAINTER, LUKE

Conserving the World's Megafauna and Biodiversity: The Fierce Urgency of Now *BioScience* v67 no3 p197 Mr 2017

Saving the World's Terrestrial Megafauna color *BioScience* v66 no10 p807 O 1 2016

PAINTER, NELL IRVIN

Long Divisions bw color il *New Republic* v248 no11 p44 N 2017

Painter, Nell Irvine—Interviews

BEYOND HOPE [Cover story] E. BATES color il *New Republic* v248 no1/2 p20 Ja/F 2017

WHITENESS UNDER THE MICROSCOPE A. CARP img *New York* v50 no6 p21 Mr 20 2017

Painter, Ronald E.

Systemic pan-AMPK activator MK-8722 improves glucose homeostasis but induces cardiac hypertrophy graph *Science* v357 no6350 p507 Ag 4 2017

Painters

See also

Women painters

Alex Janvier A. BRACKEN color *Canadian Geographic* v137

2016

Painting—India

The Beautiful, Magical World of Rajput Art W. Dalrymple cartoon *New York Review of Books* v63 no18 p32 N 24 2016

Painting—Study & teaching

Iconography classes draw non-Orthodox in search of spiritual images A. M. Banks color *Christian Century* v134 no4 p16 F 15 2017

Painting—Themes, motives

Q&A: Julian Schnabel B. POWERS bw color *ARTnews* v115 no4 p18 Wint 2016/2017

Paintner, Christine Valters

Lauds *U.S. Catholic* v82 no10 p51 O 2017

Vigils color *U.S. Catholic* v82 no11 p11 N 2017

Paisley, Brad, 1972-

BRAD PAISLEY M. Vain *Entertainment Weekly* no1446/1447 p73 D 2016/Ja 2017

Paisley, Brad, 1972-—Interviews

Brad Paisley: The CMA's Stand-up Guy M. Vain color *Entertainment Weekly* no1438 p21 N 4 2016

Paiva, Thereza

Spin-imbalance in a 2D Fermi-Hubbard system diag graph *Science* v357 no6358 p1385 S 29 2017

Pajak, Eirini

Q&A: Eirini Pajak *Arizona Highways* v96 no7 p9 Jl 2017

Pajamas

Pajama Party E. Wilson color *InStyle* v24 no7 p42 Jl 2017

POP CULTURE *Indianapolis Monthly* v40 no4 p34 D 2016

Scene, Not Heard L. KO *O, The Oprah Magazine* p149 My 2017

Pajamas—Evaluation

NAP TOWN L. BAILEY *Indianapolis Monthly* v40 no5 p24 Ja 2017

Pump Up the Jammies color *Good Housekeeping* v264 no2 p13 F 2017

Pajola, M.

Rosetta's comet 67P/Churyumov-Gerasimenko sheds its dusty mantle to reveal its icy nature bibl graph *Science* v354 no6319 p1566 D 23 2016

Surface changes on comet 67P/Churyumov-Gerasimenko suggest a more active past bw graph *Science* v355 no6332 p1392 Mr 31 2017

Pak, Ch'an-uk, 1963-

The Handmaiden K. P. Sullivan color *Entertainment Weekly* no1436/1437 p87 O 21 2016

No. 6 THE HANDMAIDEN L. Greenblatt color *Entertainment Weekly* no1444/1445 p54 D 16 2016

Pakenham, Thomas

What the Trees Say bw color *New York Review of Books* v63 no19 p45 D 8 2016

Pakistan—Economic conditions

PAKISTAN: A FAILED STATE? Seventy years on from its creation, crisis-ridden Pakistan is a very different country from the one envisioned by its founder, Muhammad Ali Jinnah T. Kamran *History Today* v67 no9 p24 S 2017

Pakistan—Economic conditions—21st century

Brands Pump Up the Volume in Pakistan C. Kay and F. Mangi color graph *Bloomberg Businessweek* no4530 p34 Jl 17 2017

Pakistanis—United States

NEIGHBORHOOD WATCHED J. GONNERMAN bw cartoon *New Yorker* v93 no18 p30 Je 26 2017

Pakistan—Politics & government

PAKISTAN: A FAILED STATE? Seventy years on from its creation, crisis-ridden Pakistan is a very different country from the one envisioned by its founder, Muhammad Ali Jinnah T. Kamran *History Today* v67 no9 p24 S 2017

Pal, Parneet

Battling the Physical Symptoms of Stress *Harvard Business Review Digital Articles* p2 Je 23 2016

Pal, Ritesh Ranjan

Host cell attachment elicits posttranscriptional regulation in infecting enteropathogenic bacteria bibl graph *Science* v355 no6326 p735 F 17 2017

Pala, Christopher

Corals tie stronger El Niños to climate change color *Science* v354 no6317 p1210 D 9 2016

New Zealand's endemic dolphins are hanging by a thread *Science*

v355 no6325 p559 F 10 2017

Pala, Irina R.

Rechargeable nickel-3D zinc batteries: An energy-dense, safer alternative to lithium-ion bw chart diag *Science* v356 no6336 p415 Ap 28 2017

Palace design & construction

Majestic makeover [Cover story] B. Laurence Scherer color *Magazine Antiques* v184 no3 p102 My/Je 2017

Palace of Nestor (Pylos, Greece)

THE GOLDEN WARRIOR J. MARCHANT *Smithsonian* v47 no9 p38 Ja/F 2017

Palaces in art—Exhibitions

SHATTERING EFFECT J. Gardner bw cartoon color *Magazine Antiques* v184 no2 p126 Mr/Ap 2017

Palaces—India

More Is More H. YANAGIHARA color *Conde Nast Traveler* v52 no5 p50 My 2017

Palaces—Mexico

HOUSE RULES M. BROWN color *Archaeology* v70 no4 p14 Je-Ag 2017

Palacio, Derek

The First Exile D. MENGESTU *New York Times Book Review* p15 N 6 2016

PALACIO, R. J.

Peace, Love and Understanding *New York Times Book Review* p24 Ag 27 2017

Palacio, R. J.—Interviews

A WONDERFUL WORLD M. Mechanic color *Mother Jones* v42 no6 p64 N/D 2017

Paladines, Fabrizio

Illegal fishing on the Galápagos high seas color *Science* v357 no6358 p1362 S 29 2017

Palaeologi, House of

The Grave of Ferdinando Palaiologos R. Griffiths *History Today* v67 no1 p70 Ja 2017

Palagin, Dennis

Selective anaerobic oxidation of methane enables direct synthesis of methanol diag graph *Science* v356 no6337 p523 My 5 2017

Palahniuk, Chuck, 1962-

Points to Ponder C. PALAHNIUK, P. NOONAN et al *Reader's Digest* v188 no1124 p39 O 2016

PALANJIAN, AMY

baby's position *Parents* v92 no7 p118 Jl 2017

bursting with goodness color *Parents* v92 no8 p96 Ag 2017

don't fear this test *Parents* v92 no6 p132 Je 2017

sofa table update *Better Homes & Gardens* v95 no1 pN6 Ja 2017

Palanski, Brad A.

Reovirus infection triggers inflammatory responses to dietary antigens and development of celiac disease color diag *Science* v356 no6333 p44 Ap 7 2017

Palanthir Technologies Inc.—Trials, litigation, etc.

THE APPROVAL MATRIX img *New York* v49 no20 p160 O 3 2016

Palantir Technologies Inc.

DONALD TRUMP, PALANTIR, AND THE CRAZY BATTLE TO CLEAN UP A MULTIBILLION-DOLLAR MILITARY PROCUREMENT SWAMP S. Brill color diag *Fortune* v175 no5 p78 Ap 1 2017

THE GREATEST ASSIGNMENT C. Leaf color *Fortune* v175 no5 p6 Ap 1 2017

Palatinus, L.

Hydrogen positions in single nanocrystals revealed by electron diffraction bibl color *Science* v355 no6321 p1 Ja 13 2017

Palatka, M.

Observation of a large-scale anisotropy in the arrival directions of cosmic rays above 8×1018 eV *Science* v357 no6357 p1266 S 22 2017

Palau

Whose Convenience? A. MARLOWE color map *Weekly Standard* v22 no14 p27 D 12 2016

Palau, Guido

BLUNT *Interview* v47 no1 p80 F 2017

The Bob SQUAD A. Serrano color *InStyle* v24 no6 p81 Je 2017

Palazzo apostolico (Castel Gandolfo, Italy)

CENTURY marks bw graph *Christian Century* v133 no24 p8 N 23 2016

Palenque (Chiapas, Mexico)

The Count's Temple R. Griffiths *History Today* v67 no3 p70 Mr 2017

Paleo diet

In surprise, tooth decay afflicts hunter-gatherers A. Gibbons color *Science* v356 no6336 p362 Ap 28 2017

THE PALEO VEGAN L. Turner color *Amazing Wellness* v8 no2 p84 Spr 2016

Paleo-Indians

Kennewick Man buried, along with conflict color *Science* v355 no6328 p892 Mr 3 2017

Paleoanthropologists—Interviews

THE HOMININ HUNTER L. BERGER color *National Geographic* v231 no5 pC10 My 2017

Paleoanthropology

DNA from cave soil reveals ancient human occupants L. Wade color *Science* v356 no6336 p363 Ap 28 2017

Lucy in the Sky M. Wedel color *Sky & Telescope* v134 no2 p42 Ag 2017

THE NEW ORIGINS OF TECHNOLOGY [Cover story] K. Wong color map *Scientific American* v316 no5 p28 My 2017

Paleobiology

See also

Ordovician radiation (Evolution)

Fossil data lacking for insects and fungi A. Hochkirch bibl color *Science* v355 no6329 p1032 Mr 10 2017

Merging paleobiology with conservation biology to guide the future of terrestrial ecosystems A. D. Barnosky, E. A. Hadly et al color *Science* v355 no6325 p594 F 10 2017

Paleobiology—Research

From Sand to Soil K. ELLISON color *Discover* v38 no1 p82 Ja/F 2017

Paleolithic period—Japan

JAPAN'S EARLY ANGLERS Z. ZORICH color *Archaeology* v70 no1 p18 Ja/F 2017

Paleologus, Ferdinando

The Grave of Ferdinando Palaiologos R. Griffiths *History Today* v67 no1 p70 Ja 2017

Paleologus, Theodore

Byzantine Tale J. Hall *History Today* v67 no3 p66 Mr 2017

Paleomagnetism

Lifetime of the solar nebula constrained by meteorite paleomagnetism H. Wang, B. P. Weiss et al bibl graph *Science* v355 no6325 p623 F 10 2017

Paleontological excavations

WHERE THE WILD THINGS WERE: Denali paleontologists brave blizzards and bears to find fossils that could challenge what we know about dinosaurs K. Siber *National Parks* v91 no3 p46 Summ 2017

Paleontologists

DIG THIS! A. McGivney *Arizona Highways* v93 no2 p44 F 2017

KEEPING THE FAITH R. F. Service color *Science* v357 no6356 p1088 S 15 2017

When Dinosaurs Went Bad G. TARLACH bw color *Discover* v38 no4 p66 My 2017

Paleontology

See also

Paleoanthropology

Paleontological excavations

DNA from cave soil reveals ancient human occupants L. Wade color *Science* v356 no6336 p363 Ap 28 2017

PALEON TOLOGY in Action N. BUCK color *Nebraska Life* v21 no4 p96 Jl/Ag 2017

Paleontology—Congresses

THE WANDERERS A. Gibbons bw color map *Science* v354 no6315 p958 N 25 2016

Palermo (Italy)—Description & travel

CHINA SYNDROME M. OWENS color *Architectural Digest* v73 no11 p78 N 2016

Palermo, Jaclyn

Glass Slipper (But Hipper) [Cover story] color *Glamour* v115 no4 p45 Ap 2017

Palermo, Olivia, 1986-

Contributors color *InStyle* v23 no13 p40 D 2016

Olivia, Over Here! color *InStyle* v24 no9 p256 S 2017

Palestine

EGYPT'S FINAL REDOUBT IN CANAAN [Cover story] R. ATWOOD color *Archaeology* v70 no4 p26 Je-Ag 2017

Palestine—Foreign relations—United States

Trump and the Holy Land D. H. Allin and S. N. Simon color *Foreign Affairs* v96 no2 p37 Mr/Ap 2017

Palestine—Politics & government

How to Build Middle East Peace M. Yaalon color *Foreign Affairs* v96 no1 p73 Ja/F 2017

Palestine—Social conditions

Protecting Palestine R. M. GERECHT color *Weekly Standard* v22 no18 p30 Ja 16 2017

Palestinian National Authority

Deep State of Affairs T. Troy *Commentary* v143 no4 p4 Ap 2017

The Department of Pay-for-Slay *Commentary* v143 no4 p29 Ap 2017

The Department of Pay-for-Slay: How the Palestinian Authority not only incites terrorist murder—but supports it with U.S. tax dollars D. J. Feith and S. Gerber *Commentary* v143 no4 p19 Ap 2017

Palestinians

Hanging tough N. WIART color *Maclean's* v129 no43 p50 O 31 2016

Palestinians—Attitudes

How Israel Wins M. Amitay *Commentary* v143 no3 p6 Mr 2017

Paletta, Anthony

Greatest Showman on Earth *Architectural Record* v205 no7 p59 Jl 2017

No Victory in Valhalla: The Untold Story of 3rd Battalion, 506th Parachute Infantry Regiment, From Bastogne to Berchtesgaden *Military History* v34 no1 p72 My 2017

The Struggle for Sea Power: A Naval History of the American Revolution *Military History* v34 no4 p72 N 2017

The Witty, Wistful Films of Whit Stillman *American Conservative* v16 no5 p46 S/O 2017

Palette (Color range)

THE COLOR ISSUE color *House Beautiful* v159 no2 p81 Mr 2017

EMERALD & IVORY color *Martha Stewart Living* p46 O 2017

her style color *InStyle* v24 no11 p34 N 2017

Paley, Grace, 1922-2007

BELIEVE YOU ME A. SCHWARTZ bw cartoon *New Yorker* v93 no12 p66 My 8 2017

BIG DISTURBANCES M. DOHERTY bw *Nation* v305 no2 p27 Jl 17 2017

Postmodern Mom D. Johnson bw *New York Review of Books* v64 no15 p37 O 12 2017

PALEY, MATTHIEU

Home on the Range color map *National Geographic* v231 no4 p64 Ap 2017

Pali Buddhist literature

TREADING THE PATH WITH CARE [Cover story] W. HIGGINS color *Tricycle: The Buddhist Review* v26 no2 p38 Wint 2016

Palin, Sarah, 1964-

No Smiling *Weekly Standard* v22 no13 p2 D 5 2016

PALIS, JOHN G.

Overcoming Challenges to the Recovery of Declining Amphibian Populations in the United States *BioScience* v67 no2 p156 F 2017

Palkhivala, Aadil

consider this *Yoga Journal* no293 p12 Ag 2017

Poses of the month color *Yoga Journal* no288 p47 D 2016

strike a ROYAL pose color *Yoga Journal* p64 2017 Special Issue

Pall, Alex—Interviews

5 JUICY QUESTIONS with... The Chainsmokers C. Keller color *Women's Health* v14 no3 p128 Ap 2017

Palladium catalysts

Palladium-catalyzed carbon-sulfur or carbon-phosphorus bond metathesis by reversible arylation Z. Lian, B. N. Bhawal et al diag *Science* v356 no6342 p1059 Je 9 2017

Pallais, Amanda

The Ambition-Marriage Trade-Off Too Many Single Women Face *Harvard Business Review Digital Articles* p2 My 8 2017

Evidence That Minorities Perform Worse Under Biased Managers color *Harvard Business Review Digital Articles* p2 Ja 13 2017

Pallante, Maria A., 1964-

Changes Coming To the Copyright Office? A. Albanese color *Publishers Weekly* v263 no44 p6 O 31 2016

The Pallante Era Begins at AAP A. Albanese color *Publishers Weekly* v264 no3 p5 Ja 16 2017

Pallas (Asteroid)

Track an asteroid pair G. CHAPLE color *Astronomy* v45 no10 p18 O 2017

Pallenberg, Anita, 1942-2017

Milestones *Time* v189 no24 p11 Je 26 2017

PALLER, JEFFREY W.

The Contentious Politics of African Urbanization *Current History* v116 no790 p163 My 2017

Palliative treatment

CAN WE TALK? A. BRANDT *Cincinnati Magazine* v50 no4 p72 Ja 2017

The doctor who took on death S. PROUDFOOT color *Maclean's* v130 no8 p52 S 2017

Measuring Quality of Care for the Sickest Patients D. E. Meier *Harvard Business Review Digital Articles* p2 S 18 2015

Palliative Care: A Key to Living With Dignity J. English *AARP: The Magazine* v59 no1A p61 D 2015/Ja 2016

THE POLITICS OF LIFE AND DEATH M. J. O'Loughlin color *America* v217 no2 p18 Jl 24 2017

The Ultimate Gift I. Byock color *Prevention* v69 no8 p28 Ag 2017

Pallister, Brian

Escape from Winterpeg N. MACDONALD color *Maclean's* no1 p14 F 17 2017

Pallotta, Dan

The Economics of Charity Telemarketing *Harvard Business Review Digital Articles* p2 Ap 15 2015

What the Nonprofit Sector Needs to Reach Its Full Potential *Harvard Business Review Digital Articles* p2 My 13 2016

Why Mark Zuckerberg and Priscilla Chan Should Use Their Money for Fundraising *Harvard Business Review Digital Articles* p2 D 3 2015

Pallotta, J.

Observation of a large-scale anisotropy in the arrival directions of cosmic rays above 8×10^{18} eV *Science* v357 no6357 p1266 S 22 2017

Pally, Adam

Blast from the Past D. Snierson color *Entertainment Weekly* no1456 p38 Mr 10 2017

Making History D. Holbrook *TV Guide* v65 no8 p34 F 27 2017

Palm, Angela

Riverine J. Shipley color *Orion Magazine* v36 no1 p60 Ja/F 2017

Palm, Mark

THE GOOD SAMARITAN K. TAYLOR bw color *Surfer* v57 no11 p44 D 2016

Palm Beach (Fla.)

All the President's Neighbors C. PETERSON-WITHORN color *Forbes* v199 no4 p18 Ap 25 2017

Palm Beach (Fla.)—Description & travel

From polo to paddleboarding A. KYLIE color map *Canadian Geographic* v137 p11 2017 Travel

Palm Beach County (Fla.)—Environmental conditions

Trump's Tax Bill For Global Warming M. Smith and J. Levin color *Bloomberg Businessweek* no4504 p26 D 19 2016

Palm Beach Motor Yachts (Company)

To Each His Own J. Y. WOOD cartoon chart color *Power & Motoryacht* v32 no12 p44 D 2016

Palm Desert (Calif.)

CITY OF PALM DESERT *Los Angeles Magazine* p84 F 2017

Palm-leaf manuscripts

EXTRA CREDIT I. Frazier cartoon *New Yorker* v93 no23 p21 Ag 7 2017

Palm oil—Export & import trade

Oil Change J. C. Zuckerman and C. ELLENBERG color *Vogue* v207 no9 p454 S 2017

Palm Springs (Calif.)

True to Form S. DRUCKER color *Architectural Digest* no11 p66 N 1 2017

Palma de Mallorca (Spain)

Building Blocks A. MARTINS *Architectural Record* v205 no6 p68 Je 2017

Puro Hotel A. Martins *Architectural Record* v205 no9 p145 S 2017

PALMER, ALEX W.

The Last Line of Defense *New York Times Magazine* p24 Jl 30 2017

Palmer, Arnold, 1929-2016

ACE IN THE CROWD R. Reilly color *Golf Magazine* v58 no12 p52 D 2016

Air Palmer M. Bamberger color *Golf Magazine* v58 no12 p104 D 2016

ARNIE ON JACK *Golf Magazine* v58 no12 p29 D 2016

Arnold Palmer D. Von Drehle color *Time* v188 no14 p12 O 10 2016

AUGUSTA ROYALTY K. Bense color *Golf Magazine* v58 no12 p34 D 2016

THE DRIVE THAT CHANGED EVERYTHING J. Passov color *Golf Magazine* v58 no12 p46 D 2016

EMPIRE OF THE SON J. Passov color *Golf Magazine* v58 no12 p30 D 2016

GOLF'S KING OF COOL J. Sens color *Golf Magazine* v58 no12 p42 D 2016

THE HEARTBREAK KID P. Madden color *Golf Magazine* v58 no12 p49 D 2016

IN HIS OWN WORDS C. Barrett color *Golf Magazine* v58 no12 p20 D 2016

JACK ON ARNIE color *Golf Magazine* v58 no12 p28 D 2016

THE MEANING OF ARNIE [Cover story] A. Shipnuck color *Golf Magazine* v58 no12 p16 D 2016

THE TINKERER M. Chwasky color *Golf Magazine* v58 no12 p62 D 2016

WHEN WE WERE KINGS D. M. Clarke color *Golf Magazine* v58 no12 p11 D 2016

You're Up! color *Golf Magazine* v59 no2 p12 F 2017

Palmer, Blaire

Why Leadership Training Fails—and What to Do About It: Interaction *Harvard Business Review* v94 no12 p19 D 2016

PALMER, BRIAN

Is the Endangered Species Act in Danger? *Audubon* v119 no1 p19 Spr 2017

PALMER, CHARLIE

How to Sear a Steak color *Esquire* p141 BigBlackBook

Palmer, Cristiana Paṣca

Marine Biodiversity and Ecosystems Underpin a Healthy Planet and Social Well-Being *UN Chronicle* v54 no1/2 p1 2017

PALMER, DANIEL S.

Q&A: Douglas Crimp bw color *ARTnews* v115 no4 p74 Wint 2016/2017

Palmer, Diana

Christmas with My Cowboy *Publishers Weekly* v264 no36 p74 S 4 2017

Palmer, Elizabeth

Here I Am: A Novel *Christian Century* v133 no26 p41 D 21 2016

Kierkegaard: A Single Life color *Christian Century* v134 no11 p30 My 24 2017

Ministry with trans people color *Christian Century* v134 no2 p28 Ja 18 2017

The ones that got away *Christian Century* v134 no1 p32 Ja 4 2017

POST-APOCALYPTIC NOW *Christian Century* v134 no16 p27 Ag 2 2017

PALMER, HANNAH

ATLANTA *Atlanta* v56 no10 p70 F 2017

More Than Eats *Atlanta* v56 no12 p55 Ap 2017

Palmer, Iris

The False Promise of "Free College" *Washington Monthly* p1 S/O 2016

Palmer, James

A Bodega Once Stood Here color *Foreign Policy* no224 p32 My/Je 2017

Palmer, James C.

The Community College and the Business Cycle *Change* v48 no5 p52 S/O 2016

Palmer, Jane

Chile's glacial lakes pose newly recognized flood threat color *Science* v355 no6329 p1004 Mr 10 2017

Palmer, Jesse, 1978-

Your New Travel Workouts A. McCARRON cartoon chart color *Men's Health* v32 no9 p48 N 2017

Palmer, John

Ready for Our Close-Up S. LEWSEN color *Walrus* v14 no6 p79 Jl/Ag 2017

PALMER, KIMBERLY

25 People Who Bust the Myths color *AARP: The Magazine* v59 no4A p42 Je/Jl 2016

6 Ways to Supercharge Your LinkedIn Profile color *AARP: The Magazine* v60 no4A p22 Je/Jl 2017

The Best Investment I Ever Made color *AARP: The Magazine* v59 no2A p34 F/Mr 2016

'How can I build upon a career in aerospace to become a high school teacher?' color *AARP: The Magazine* v59 no6A p28 O/N 2016

'I can help you transform a fixer-upper, but how do I go from architect to real estate agent?' color *AARP: The Magazine* v59 no5A p36 Ag/S 2016

In Search of Color color *AARP: The Magazine* v59 no4A p30 Je/Jl 2016

It's Mama's Turn! How to Start Your Second Career color *AARP: The Magazine* v59 no4A p26 Je/Jl 2016

New Tools for Working Smarter cartoon *AARP: The Magazine* v59 no6A p24 O/N 2016

PALMER, LISA

One Meal a Day color *New Republic* v248 no7 p32 Jl 2017

Palmer, Liza

The F Word *Publishers Weekly* v264 no9 p70 F 27 2017

PALMER, MEGAN J.

Rethinking biosecurity bw *Issues in Science & Technology* v33 no2 p13 Wint 2017

Palmer, Neville

Complex multifault rupture during the 2016 Mw 7.8 Kaikōura earthquake, New Zealand color map *Science* v356 no6334 p154 Ap 14 2017

Palmer, Ryan

AGNOSTIC AGGRESSION color *Bike Magazine* v24 no1 p106 Ja/F 2017

analysis paralysis color *Bike Magazine* v24 no1 p21 Ja/F 2017

Devinci: SPARTAN CARBON | X01EAGLE color *Bike Magazine* v24 no8 p70 N 2017

DISTRICT HENLEY color *Bike Magazine* v24 no4 p102 Je 2017

DOUBLE DUTY color *Bike Magazine* v24 no1 p88 Ja/F 2017

dream builds color *Bike Magazine* v23 no9 p82 D 2016

EVEN FLOW bw color *Bike Magazine* v24 no1 p94 Ja/F 2017

Face off color *Bike Magazine* v24 no7 p112 S 2017

full circle color *Bike Magazine* v24 no5 p96 Jl 2017

GET IN GEAR bw color *Bike Magazine* v24 no1 p122 Ja/F 2017

jamis color *Bike Magazine* v24 no2 p82 Mr 2017

KS LEV CI color *Bike Magazine* v24 no2 p84 Mr 2017

momentum color *Bike Magazine* v24 no7 p46 S 2017

Norco Sight color *Bike Magazine* v24 no5 p88 Jl 2017

orbea occam color *Bike Magazine* v24 no3 p100 My 2017

Rocky Mountain color *Bike Magazine* v24 no7 p100 S 2017

Why Cycles color *Bike Magazine* v24 no4 p94 Je 2017

Palmer, Sezin

What Hospitals Can Learn from Airlines About Buying Equipment *Harvard Business Review Digital Articles* p2 Je 13 2017

Palmer Johnson Yachts LLC

Palmer Johnson 63 Sport S. Murray color *Power & Motoryacht* v33 no3 p58 Mr 2017

Palmeri, Christopher

Beauty and the Bakeware Set color graph *Bloomberg Businessweek* no4515 p20 Mr 20 2017

Cruises Could Be Big Winners in Cuba color graph *Bloomberg Businessweek* no4522 p23 My 15 2017

DISNEY'S GALACTIC GAMBIT color diag *Bloomberg Businessweek* no4519 p56 Ap 24 2017

Sheldon Adelson's Not-So-Winning Year bw *Bloomberg Businessweek* no4530 p40 Jl 17 2017

A Wall Street Legend Flops in Sports Betting *Bloomberg Businessweek* no4515 p35 Mr 20 2017

What Happens in Vegas Doesn't Stay There color *Bloomberg Businessweek* no4497 p24 O 31 2016

Palm-Espling, Maria E.

Posttranslational mutagenesis: A chemical strategy for exploring protein side-chain diversity diag *Science* v354 no6312 p597 N 4 2016

PALMIERI, GRACE

TRADERS POINT HUNT *Indianapolis Monthly* p20 F 2017

Words to Live By *Indianapolis Monthly* p28 F 2017

PALMINTERI, SUZANNE

An Ecoregion-Based Approach to Protecting Half the Terrestrial Realm *BioScience* v67 no6 p534 Je 2017

Palmisano, Samuel J.—Interviews

Charlie Rose talks about... Cybersecurity C. Rose bw *Bloomberg Businessweek* no4504 p31 D 19 2016

Palms

Go Figure *Los Angeles Magazine* p16 My 2017

HERE'S THE DIRT S. STALL *Indianapolis Monthly* p18 F 2017

Palmstrom, Axel

Perovskite-perovskite tandem photovoltaics with optimized band gaps bibl chart graph *Science* v354 no6314 p861 N 18 2016

Palo Duro Canyon (Tex.)

Color Country K. BASTONE color *Backpacker* v45 no2 p16 Mr 2017

It Happened Here: Palo Duro Canyon M. Coppock color *American Cowboy* p65 LEGENDS OF TEXAS Special Issue 2017

Palomarez, Javier—Interviews

WORKING WITH The Donald S. SMITH *Texas Monthly* v45 no3 p82 Mr 2017

Palomba, E.

Localized aliphatic organic material on the surface of Ceres bibl graph *Science* v355 no6326 p719 F 17 2017

Seasonal exposure of carbon dioxide ice on the nucleus of comet 67P/Churyumov-Gerasimenko bibl bw graph *Science* v354 no6319 p1563 D 23 2016

Palombella Rossa (Film)

Revolutions per Minute R. Brody color *New Yorker* v93 no33 p16 O 23 2017

Palombo, Alyssa

The Most Beautiful Woman in Florence *Publishers Weekly* v264 no8 p58 F 20 2017

Palomero-Gallagher, Nicola

Microstructural proliferation in human cortex is coupled with the development of face processing bibl graph *Science* v355 no6320 p1 Ja 6 2017

Palozola, Katherine C.

Mitotic transcription and waves of gene reactivation during mitotic exit color graph *Science* v357 no6359 p119 O 6 2017

Pal's Sudden Service Inc.

How One Fast-Food Chain Keeps Its Turnover Rates Absurdly Low B. Taylor *Harvard Business Review Digital Articles* p2 Ja 26 2016

Palter, Robert

How to Get It Right color *Time* v189 no13 p45 Ap 10 2017

Paltrow, Bruce

Blythe Danner L. Lynch color *AARP: The Magazine* v59 no1A p13 D 2015/Ja 2016

Paltrow, Gwyneth, 1972-

The A–LIST G. Paltrow color *Harper's Bazaar* no3648 p108 N 2016

BLOND AMBITION [Cover story] C. Bagley color *InStyle* v24 no2 p120 F 2017

the cover color *InStyle* v24 no2 p20 F 2017

DR. GWYNETH WILL SEE YOU S. Marikar cartoon *New Yorker* v93 no6 p16 Mr 27 2017

editor's letter color *Architectural Digest* no6 p28 Je 1 2017

EDITOR'S LETTER G. Bailey color *Harper's Bazaar* no3648 p94 N 2016

THE GOOP LIFE M. RUS color *Architectural Digest* no6 p120 Je 1 2017

GWYNETH PALTROW'S SHOE SECRETS N. Silva-Jelly color *Harper's Bazaar* no3657 p242 O 2017

The Society PAGE *Interview* v46 no10 p72 D 2016/Ja 2017

Sound Bites color *Entertainment Weekly* no1442 p7 D 2 2016 Rebellious Special Issue

A symptom of a deeper problem A. KINGSTON color *Maclean's* v130 no7 p8 Ag 2017

The Wellness Epidemic A. LAROCCA img *New York* v50 no13 p38 Je 26 2017

Paltrow, Gwyneth, 1972-—Interviews

GWYNERGY! J. GODFREY-JUNE color *Women's Health* v14 no3 p(Sp)2 Ap 2017

THE REAL GWYNETH S. Bee color *Harper's Bazaar* no3648

p232 N 2016

Paltsev, Sergey

The complicated geopolitics of renewable energy bibl *Bulletin of the Atomic Scientists* v72 no6 p390 N 2016

PALUS, SHANNON

HUMAN-FREE HUMAN TRIALS color *Popular Science* v288 no6 p32 N/D 2016

Nothin' But Neutrons color *Discover* v38 no1 p52 Ja/F 2017

The Tsunamis of Mars bw color *Discover* v38 no1 p61 Ja/F 2017

Tunnel Through the Alps color *Popular Science* v288 no6 p78 N/D 2016

Palvin, Barbara

STYLE CRUSH Barbara Palvin S. Simon color *InStyle* v24 no1 p34 Ja 2017

Palynology—History

The fourth dimension of vegetation H. J. B. Birks, H. H. Birks et al bibl color graph *Science* v354 no6311 p412 O 28 2016

Pama-Nyungan languages

Colorful Language L. E. Ogden color *Natural History* v125 no4 p7 Ap 2017

PAMUK, ORHAN

The Year in Reading [Cover story] *New York Times Book Review* p8 D 25 2016

PAN, J. C.

The New Yuppies *New Republic* v248 no8/9 p69 Ag/S 2017

THE RESPONSIBLE HEDONISTS color *Nation* v303 no23/24 p32 D 5 2016

Pan, Jian-Wei

Satellite-based entanglement distribution over 1200 kilometers diag graph *Science* v356 no6343 p1140 Je 16 2017

Pan, Ki-mun, 1944-

Ban Ki-moon E. Dias color *Time* v188 no27-28 p70 D 26 2016

the decision–makers bw *Foreign Policy* no221 p50 N/D 2016

Pan, Lei

Chiral Majorana fermion modes in a quantum anomalous Hall insulator–superconductor structure diag *Science* v357 no6348 p294 Jl 21 2017

Pan, Xiaojing

Structure of a eukaryotic voltage-gated sodium channel at near-atomic resolution diag graph *Science* v355 no6328 p924 Mr 3 2017

Pan, Xubin

Artificial intelligence in research color *Science* v357 no6346 p28 Jl 7 2017

Panagiotopoulos, Takis

Live Well, Die Well: Does Neil Gorsuch Understand Epicurus? H. Crespo *Humanist* v77 no3 p6 My/Je 2017

Panaïotis, Frédéric

Notes from Underground M. Krigbaum color *Conde Nast Traveler* v51 no11 p118 D 2016

Panaite, Cristian Petru

Gotham Ink cartoon *Magazine Antiques* v184 no1 p154 Ja/F 2017

Panama hats

DECKED OUT: Make a splash at your next pool party with these hot summer accessories *Indianapolis Monthly* v40 no10 p28 Je 2017

Panama Papers

The Market Punished "Panama Papers" Firms to the Tune of $230 Billion C. Nickisch *Harvard Business Review Digital Articles* p2 My 16 2016

Panasonic Corp.

Panasonic DMP-UB900 Ultra HD Blu-ray Player A. Griffin color *Sound & Vision* v82 no2 p40 F/Mr 2017

Pancakes, waffles, etc.

Better-for-You Blueberry Waffles *Saturday Evening Post* v289 no3 p23 My/Je 2017

THE BETTER — THAN — EVER BREAKFAST GUIDE color *Redbook* p117 Ap 2017

BRING ON BRINNER L. REGE color *Martha Stewart Living* p64 Mr 2017

BUTTERMILK PANCAKES B. PORTER KATZ color *Martha Stewart Living* p55 My 2017

Cooking the Pinterest Way S. Dreisbach color *Glamour* v115 no6 p88 Je 2017

EASY AS PIE ACTUALLY, EASIER A. Cayne color *Redbook* p154 My 2017

Rachel Zoe A. Syrett color *InStyle* v24 no9 p197 S 2017

RANCH DRESSING color *Good Housekeeping* v265 no2 p116 Ag 2017

SANTA'S LITTLE CHEFS C. K. Jackson color *Essence* v47 no8 p133 D 2016

Socca Star A. Sullivan color *Bon Appetit* no1 p42 F 2017

Thompson Playa del Carmen, Mexico color *Conde Nast Traveler* v52 no5 p54 My 2017

WAFFLE MAKER color *Good Housekeeping* v265 no3 p148 S 2017

Waffle On A. RAMPE color *Bon Appetit* p76 S 2017

Pancakes, waffles, etc.—Evaluation

In the SUNSET KITCHEN E. Johnson color *Sunset* v237 no6 p98 D 2016

Pancratium

The Pankration Flow J. ARVANITIS bw color *Black Belt* v55 no3 p54 Ap/My 2017

Pancreas—Physiology

ASK TUFTS EXPERTS A. H. Lichtenstein *Tufts University Health & Nutrition Letter* v35 no2 p8 2017

Pancreatitis [Cover story] *Mayo Clinic Health Letter* v34 no12 p1 D 2016

Pancreatic beta cells

β-cell–mimetic designer cells provide closed-loop glycemic control Mingqi Xie, Haifeng Ye et al bibl graph *Science* v354 no6317 p1296 D 9 2016

Pancreatic cancer

Opportunities and challenges for precision medicine in pancreatic cancer prevention and treatment Chengfeng Wang bibl *Science* v354 no6319 p42 D 23 2016

Pancreatic cancer treatment

FIGHTING BACK: HOW LOCAL TEAMS ARE TREATING A CHALLENGING DISEASE J. H. REDMOND color *Cincinnati Magazine* v51 no1 p91 O 2017

A Master of Evasion D. G. ADLER color *Discover* v38 no4 p70 My 2017

Pancreatitis—Diagnosis

Pancreatitis [Cover story] *Mayo Clinic Health Letter* v34 no12 p1 D 2016

Panda (Music)

DESIIGNER T. PUSHA *Interview* v46 no8 p34 O 2016

Panda, Satchidananda

Circadian physiology of metabolism bibl diag *Science* v354 no6315 p1008 N 25 2016

Pandas

Exposed M. B. Griggs color *Popular Science* v289 no4 p70 Jl/Ag 2017

Panda Patrol J. KIFFEL-ALCHEH color map *National Geographic Kids* no472 p12 Ag 2017

PANDAS WILL FIX EVERYTHING C. SWANSON img *New York* p54 Mr 6 2017

Pande, Rohini

A Friend's Support Can Make Women Better Entrepreneurs *Harvard Business Review Digital Articles* p2 Je 19 2015

Making Microfinance More Effective *Harvard Business Review Digital Articles* p2 O 5 2016

Pandelaere, Mario

Companies Fare Worse When the Press Exposes Their Problems Before They Do *Harvard Business Review Digital Articles* p2 Ag 22 2016

Pandell, Lexi

A Body Computer to Manage Insulin color *AARP: The Magazine* v30 no6A p32 O/N 2017

ESCAPE THE MATRIX: THE INTERNET IS THE UNCANNIEST VALLEY. DON'T GET TRAPPED THERE *Wired* v25 no9 p92 S 2017

THE HASHTAG color *Wired* v25 no6 p25 Je 2017

Not-So-Gray Matter color *Wired* v24 no11 p44 N 2016

THREE DAYS IN AMERICA color *Wired* v24 no12 p114 D 2016

WISH LIST 2016 color *Wired* v24 no12 p45 D 2016

Pandemics

Civil War & the Global Threat of Pandemics P. H. Wise and M. Barry *Daedalus* v146 no4 p71 Fall 2017

If You Think Fighting Climate Change Will Be Expensive, Calculate the Cost of Letting It Happen D. Disparte *Harvard Business Review Digital Articles* p2 Je 12 2017

New bird flu strain takes human toll color *Science* v355 no6327 p778 F 24 2017

New Ebola outbreak rings alarm bells early J. Cohen and G. Vogel color map *Science* v356 no6340 p788 My 26 2017

We Can't Avoid Future Disease Outbreaks color *Scientific American* v317 no1 p9 Jl 2017

Pandemics—Government policy

U.S. Policies Informed by Science J. Worland color *Time* v189 no5 p19 F 13 2017

Pandey, Akhilesh

Homer1a drives homeostatic scaling-down of excitatory synapses during sleep bibl graph *Science* v355 no6324 p511 F 3 2017

Pandey, Sushil

Emergence and spread of a human-transmissible multidrug-resistant nontuberculous mycobacterium bibl diag graph *Science* v354 no6313 p751 N 11 2016

Pandita Bivamsa, 1921-2016—Interviews

The Best Remedy -. Clements color *Tricycle: The Buddhist Review* v26 no2 p42 Wint 2016

PANDLEY, CAMILLE

HOW CLEAN IS THE WATER REALLY? Well, it depends. But seriously, don't swallow the water *Atlanta* v57 no4 p54 Ag 2017

Pando, Karen

What Price for a Plain Pony? color *Horse & Rider* v56 no1 p10 Ja 2017

Pandolfi, John M.

Biodiversity redistribution under climate change: Impacts on ecosystems and human well-being color *Science* v355 no6332 p1389 Mr 31 2017

The broad footprint of climate change from genes to biomes to people bibl chart color *Science* v354 no6313 paaf7671-1 N 11 2016

Pandolfi, Keith

Buicks *New York Times Magazine* p28 O 30 2016

DOWN TO THE ATP *Cincinnati Magazine* p64 Je 2017

FRUITS OF THE FOREST: PHOTOGRAPHER TURNED FORAGER JAMIE SALOMON SETS HIS SIGHTS ON WILD MUSHROOMS *Yankee* v81 no5 p58 S/O 2017

Pandolfo, Gustavo

Street Smarts L. A. Miller and Otavio Pandolfo of OSGEMEOS *Art in America* v104 no9 p61 O 2016

Pandolfo, Otavio

Street Smarts *Art in America* v104 no9 p61 O 2016

Pandora A/S

The BUY Jewelry color *Harper's Bazaar* no3656 p178 S 2017

Pandya, Dhwani

Getting Mumbai On Track *Bloomberg Businessweek* no4536 p35 S 4 2017

Paneling (Interior walls)

THE Arts & Crafts ROOM B. D. Coleman and M. E. Polson color *Arts & Crafts Homes & the Revival* v12 no1 p10 2017 Resouce Guide

Paneling (Interior walls)—Evaluation

Over Our Heads J. Taraska color *Architectural Record* v205 no2 p46 F 2017

Panepinto, Joe

The Elements of an Effective Cause Marketing Campaign *Harvard Business Review Digital Articles* p2 F 19 2016

Good Leaders Aren't Afraid to Be Nice *Harvard Business Review Digital Articles* p2 Ap 8 2015

The Productivity Payoff of Mobile Apps at Work *Harvard Business Review Digital Articles* p2 N 13 2014

Panera Bread Co.

How Did I Get Here?: RON SHAICH bw color *Bloomberg Businessweek* no4493 p92 O 3 2016

Panetta, Leon E.

The Former Head of the CIA on Managing the Hunt for Bin Laden *Harvard Business Review Digital Articles* p2 My 2 2016

The Strength of a Nation *America* v216 no12 p58 My 29 2017

Panfil, Vanessa R.

The Gang's All Queer: The Lives of Gay Gang Members color *Publishers Weekly* v264 no25 p104 Je 19 2017

Panfish fishing

THE NATURALS M. Modoski cartoon *Field & Stream* v121 no9 p24 Ap 2017

Pang, Alex Soojung-Kim

The Workaholic's Case for a Four-Hour Day S. Begley color *Time* v188 no22-23 p18 N/D 2016

PANG, KEVIN

STRENGTH SERVICE cartoon color *Men's Health* v32 no4 p116 My 2017

Pangasius

Mexico's invasive species plan in context J. Golubov, A. Aguirre-Muñoz et al bw *Science* v356 no6336 p386 Ap 28 2017

Pangolin trade

Step Aside, Platypus R. Nuwer *Sierra* v101 no5 p21 S/O 2016

Pangolins

Can the Pangolin Be Saved? *New York Times Upfront* v149 no6 p2 D 12 2016

SCALY SUPERHEROES D. BROWN cartoon color map *National Geographic Kids* no470 p22 My 2017

Step Aside, Platypus R. Nuwer *Sierra* v101 no5 p21 S/O 2016

Pangolins—Behavior

SCALY SUPERHEROES D. BROWN color map *National Geographic Kids* no470 p22 My 2017

Pani, Amar

Restoring auditory cortex plasticity in adult mice by restricting thalamic adenosine signaling graph *Science* v356 no6345 p1352 Je 30 2017

Panic

See also

Moral panics

Trumpocalypse [Cover story] D. FRENCH il *National Review* v68 no23 p26 D 19 2016

Panic attacks

Anatomy of a Panic Attack N. DEVON cartoon *Seventeen* v76 no12 p70 D 2016/Ja 2017

Panic disorders

The Three Stages of STEVE MARTIN'S Journey to HAPPINESS J. NEWMAN bw color *AARP: The Magazine* v60 no4A p36 Je/Jl 2017

Panic Inc.

TRANSMIT 5: FILE TRANSFER UTILITY EXPANDS SUPPORT FOR CLOUD SERVICES G. FLEISHMAN color *Macworld - Digital Edition* v34 no9 p21 S 2017

Panic in Needle Park, The (Film)

THE WHOLE WIDE WORLD OF JOAN DIDION I. Biedenharn color map *Entertainment Weekly* no1457/1458 p104 Mr 17 2017

Panicker, Nikhil

Pathological α-synuclein transmission initiated by binding lymphocyte-activation gene 3 bibl graph *Science* v353 no6307 paah3374-1 S 30 2016

Panitch, Amanda

Never Missing, Never Found color *Publishers Weekly* v263 no49 p116 D 7 2016

Panjwani, Sachin

DO SEARCH ADS REALLY WORK?: INTERACTION color *Harvard Business Review* v95 no3 p20 My/Je 2017

Panken, Ted

Aaron Parks color *Downbeat* v83 no11 p106 N 2016

Arturo O'Farrill & Chucho Valdés: SONGS FOR OUR FATHERS color *Downbeat* v84 no10 p40 O 2017

Birthday Milestone: Corea Relives Davis Years at Blue Note color *Downbeat* v84 no1 p13 Ja 2017

Boppin' Savoy Sessions bw *Downbeat* v84 no3 p64 Mr 2017

Catherine Russell color *Downbeat* v84 no4 p98 Ap 2017

CHRIS POTTER WAKING DREAMS color *Downbeat* v84 no6 p42 Je 2017

DANIEL FREEDMAN bw *Downbeat* v84 no3 p24 Mr 2017

DIZZY GILLESPIE bw *Downbeat* v84 no1 p34 Ja 2017

EMMET COHEN Student of History color *Downbeat* v84 no2 p22 F 2017

EUBIE BLAKE: 'NOTHING STAYS THE SAME' bw *Downbeat* v84 no8 p37 Ag 2017

Festive Activism color *Downbeat* v83 no11 p99 N 2016

Frisell, Lloyd Assert Mastery in Funchal color *Downbeat* v84 no10 p25 O 2017

Greg Osby color *Downbeat* v84 no3 p122 Mr 2017

Hall of Fame PHIL WOODS 'A SOLIDER FOR JAZZ' bw color *Downbeat* v83 no12 p34 D 2016

Jimmy Greene color *Downbeat* v84 no6 p138 Je 2017

John Abercrombie color *Downbeat* v83 no12 p114 D 2016

Louis Hayes color *Downbeat* v84 no9 p106 S 2017

Manuel Valera color *Downbeat* v84 no10 p202 O 2017

Misha Mengelberg Dies at 81 bw *Downbeat* v84 no5 p19 My 2017

MIYA MASAOKA color *Downbeat* v84 no7 p26 Jl 2017

Motor City Magic color *Downbeat* v83 no11 p14 N 2016

Muthspiel Assembles All-Star Ensemble bw *Downbeat* v83 no12 p18 D 2016

OLEG BUTMAN color *Downbeat* v83 no12 p24 D 2016

Rocking Grooves, Roaring Oceans at DR Jazz Fest color *Downbeat* v84 no2 p14 F 2017

ROSCOE MITCHELL: 'PEOPLE DON'T WANT TO BE CAT-EGORIZED' color *Downbeat* v84 no9 p40 S 2017

Sipiagin Assembles Elite Sextet for New Album of Original Music color *Downbeat* v84 no6 p16 Je 2017

Treasures Abound in 'Savory Collection' bw *Downbeat* v84 no1 p19 Ja 2017

Trio 3: SURVIVAL SYNDROME color *Downbeat* v84 no4 p34 Ap 2017

Vanguard in the Spotlight color *Downbeat* v84 no6 p23 Je 2017

VINCENT GARDNER color *Downbeat* v84 no5 p25 My 2017

Vocal Identity color *Downbeat* v83 no11 p26 N 2016

WADADA Leo Smith: RISING UP IN PURITY [Cover story] color *Downbeat* v84 no8 p22 Ag 2017

WALLACE RONEY TAKING THE HARD TRAIL [Cover story] color *Downbeat* v84 no2 p40 F 2017

Weiss Explores 'Fusion-Blues' Sounds with Point of Departure color *Downbeat* v84 no7 p17 Jl 2017

Pankove, Jacques Isaac

Jacques Isaac Pankove T. D. Moustakas and B. Monemar *Physics Today* v70 no4 p64 Ap 2017

Pankratz, Derek

Performance Can't Be Measured by Company Growth Alone *Harvard Business Review Digital Articles* p2 Je 5 2015

A Way to Gauge How Well Your Company Is Really Performing *Harvard Business Review Digital Articles* p2 My 8 2015

A Way to Know If Your Corporate Goals Are Too Aggressive *Harvard Business Review Digital Articles* p2 Jl 13 2015

Panoramic photography

'Ghostly' Image at Haunted Stanley Hotel B. RADFORD *Skeptical Inquirer* v40 no6 p9 N/D 2016

Panoringan, Anne Marie

TOP CHEFS color *Los Angeles Magazine* v62 no10 p8 O 2017

PANOS, AMY

DESIGNING WOMAN color *Better Homes & Gardens* v95 no7 p54 Jl 2017

PARTY station color *Better Homes & Gardens* v95 no6 p94 Je 2017

SUPPLY & DEMAND color *Better Homes & Gardens* v95 no8 p62 Ag 2017

SWEET ON CARNATIONS color *Better Homes & Gardens* v95 no2 p96 F 2016

WITH an ARTIST'S EYE color *Better Homes & Gardens* v95 no4 p120 Ap 2017

PANOU, ATHA C.

Q: Who's your trusty sidekick for summer adventures, and why? color *O, The Oprah Magazine* p14 Je 2017

Pansini, S.

Persistent effects of pre-Columbian plant domestication on Amazonian forest composition bibl chart graph map *Science* v355 no6328 p925 Mr 3 2017

Pansino, Rosanna

THE VIEW MASTERS E. G. ELLIS color graph *Wired* v25 no4 p18 Ap 2017

Pansonato, M. P.

Persistent effects of pre-Columbian plant domestication on Amazonian forest composition bibl chart graph map *Science* v355 no6328 p925 Mr 3 2017

Pant, Rajiv

Why Data Breaches Don't Hurt Stock Prices *Harvard Business Review Digital Articles* p2 Mr 31 2015

Pantic, Nina

Center Stage color *Tennis* v53 no5 p8 S/O 2017

Equal Measures color *Tennis* v53 no2 p6 Mr/Ap 2017

The Man Behind the Cup *Tennis* v52 no6 p54 N/D 2016

Ones to Watch *Tennis* v53 no1 p66 Ja/F 2017

Sport's Centre *Tennis* v53 no4 p10 Jl/Ag 2017

Pantin, Laurel

Outfits for Days color *Glamour* v114 no11 p66 N 2016

Pantoja, Cristina

Tissue damage and senescence provide critical signals for cellular reprogramming in vivo bibl chart graph *Science* v354 no6315 paaf4445-1 N 25 2016

Pants

BACK to BLACK *Interview* v47 no1 p33 F 2017

CARE LESS, LOOK BETTER N. Sullivan bw cartoon color *Esquire* v167 no2 p66 Mr 2017

CREW UP *Interview* v46 no10 p62 D 2016/Ja 2017

THE NIGHT MANAGER color *Esquire* p108 O 2017

WHERE TO BUY color *Essence* v47 no9 p90 Ja 2017

Pants—Evaluation

2017 OUTERWEAR BUYER'S GUIDE T. Monterosso color *Snowboarder* v29 no2 p114 O 2016

$50 & Under Team Spirit color *Seventeen* v75 no11 p32 N 2016

Adam's STYLE SHEET color *O, The Oprah Magazine* p54 Ap 2017

BUCKLE UP color *Esquire* p48 N 2017

BUTTFESSIONS color *Women's Health* v14 no2 p62 Mr 2017

COOLER THREADS PREVAIL N. SULLIVAN color *Esquire* p40 Ag 2017

DON'T CALL IT ATHLEISURE J. Roth color *Esquire* p30 Ag 2017

Double Denim bw color *Glamour* v115 no5 p168 My 2017

EVERYTHING Must GO *Interview* v47 no6 p30 Ag 2017

FANCY FOOTWORK color *O, The Oprah Magazine* p114 Ap 2017

Field Notes color *Climbing* no354 p36 Jl 2017

Find Your Passion F. Kane, S. P. Nadella et al bw color *Glamour* v115 no3 p194 Mr 2017

FULL ENGLISH M. GUIDUCCI bw color *Vogue* v207 no10 p252 O 2017

GREAT BUYS UNDER $100 color *O, The Oprah Magazine* p60 My 2017

INSTANT STYLE color *InStyle* v24 no1 p46 Ja 2017

instant style color *InStyle* v24 no7 p57 Jl 2017

It's a Cinch color *Los Angeles Magazine* v62 no10 p28 O 2017

Jersey GIRL *Interview* v47 no5 p80 Je/Jl 2017

THE LADY Laura Linney E. Wilson color *InStyle* v24 no4 p92 Ap 2017

One Suit, Two Ways S. P. Nadella color *Glamour* v115 no9 p62 S 2017

Outfits for Days color *Glamour* v115 no7 p32 Jl 2017

Outfits for Days F. Kane color *Glamour* v115 no4 p74 Ap 2017

Revolutionary Love color *Essence* v47 no10 p86 F 2017

SO BAZAAR color *Harper's Bazaar* no3648 p280 N 2016

Space Race N. SULLIVAN bw color *Esquire* v166 no4 p60 N 2016

'SUCKER, PUNCHED UP color *Esquire* p44 My 2017

Take COVER: FASHION'S RECONFIGURATIONS OF THE WIND-BREAKER BREATHE A FUTURISTIC LOOK INTO THE UTILITARIAN STAPLE FOR THOSE COOL NIGHTS OUT *Interview* v47 no3 p46 Ap 2017

That Old Time Feeling B. Welch color *American Cowboy* v23 no6 p38 Ap/My 2017

TO THE MOON K. G. Marable color *Essence* v47 no10 p78 F 2017

Uptown SOUL *Interview* v46 no8 p48 O 2016

VICTORIAN REVIVAL color *Harper's Bazaar* no3657 p132 O 2017

THE WHITE STUFF J. Roth bw color *Esquire* p39 My 2017

YARA SHAHIDI C. Stern color *InStyle* v24 no8 p57 Ag 2017

Pants—Pattern design

PANTS ON FIRE color *Vogue* v207 no1 p98 Ja 2017

Pants—Social aspects

Girl in Pants L. Dunham color *Glamour* v115 no5 p164 My 2017

Pao, Caroline S.

Emergence and spread of a human-transmissible multidrug-resistant nontuberculous mycobacterium bibl diag graph *Science* v354 no6313 p751 N 11 2016

Pao, Ellen, 1969-

This Is How Sexism Works in Silicon Valley My lawsuit failed. Others won't img *New York* v50 no17 p56 Ag 21 2017

Pao, Ellen, 1969——Interviews

Ellen Pao E. Dockterman color *Time* v190 no14 p56 O 9 2017

Pao, Ellen, 1969——Trials, litigation, etc.

The Throwback Sexism of Kleiner Perkins J. C. Williams *Harvard Business Review Digital Articles* p2 Mr 12 2015

Paolucci, Christopher

Dynamic multinuclear sites formed by mobilized copper ions in NOx selective catalytic reduction bw color diag graph *Science* v357 no6354 p898 S 1 2017

Paothong, Noppadol

A Photographer on the Dance Floor M. Bartels *Audubon* v119 no1 p49 Spr 2017

Spirit of the West A. Opar color *Audubon* v119 no3 p3 Fall 2017

Pap test

Gyno Paps Aren't Just for Cis Women D. GUERRERO *Advocate* no1090 p47 Ap 2017

Why You Probably Need an Anal Pap Smear J. ANDERSON-MINSHALL color *Advocate* no1090 p47 Ap 2017

Papa John's International Inc.

JOHN SCHNATTER color *Bloomberg Businessweek* no4525 p64 Je 5 2017

Papacy

Steps to Hanoi G. O'CONNELL *America* v215 no16 p24 N 21 2016

Papadimitriou, Odysseas

Creating Smart Tools J. Caplin color *Money* v45 no11 p20 D 2016

Papadogiannakis, S.

iPTF16geu: A multiply imaged, gravitationally lensed type Ia supernova color diag graph *Science* v356 no6335 p291 Ap 21 2017

Papadopoulos, Nicklaos

Mismatch repair deficiency predicts response of solid tumors to PD-1 blockade chart graph *Science* v357 no6349 p409 Jl 28 2017

Papahānaumokuākea Marine National Monument (Hawaii)

SAVING THE SEAS C. BARNETT color map *National Geographic* v231 no2 p54 F 2017

Papal visits

No Slowing Down G. O'CONNELL *America* v216 no1 p28 Ja 2 2017

Pope Bashing *America* v217 no7 p8 O 2 2017

Pope Francis tells Colombians, 'Be slaves of peace' G. O'Connell color *America* v217 no7 p15 O 2 2017

Pope visits Egypt to join imams, Coptic church in rejecting violence C. Lamb *Christian Century* v134 no12 p14 Je 7 2017

Papandrea, Benjamin

Three-dimensional holey-graphene/niobia composite architectures for ultrahigh-rate energy storage color diag graph *Science* v356 no6338 p599 My 12 2017

Papanikolaou, Aristotle

The dance of faith color *Christian Century* v134 no4 p36 F 15 2017

Papantonio, Mike

Law and Vengeance: A Legal Thriller *Publishers Weekly* v264 no34 p90 Ag 21 2017

Telling Overlooked Stories L. PICKER color *Publishers Weekly* v264 no35 p103 Ag 28 2017

Pape, Allie

FOOD TOWN THROWDOWN color *Sunset* v238 no6 p36 Je 2017

Pape, Lygia—Exhibitions

ART color *New Yorker* v93 no9 p8 Ap 17 2017

Papenbreer, P.

Observation of a large-scale anisotropy in the arrival directions of cosmic rays above 8 × 1018 eV *Science* v357 no6357 p1266 S 22 2017

Paper

See also

Blotting paper

Decorative paper

Tissue paper

Paper Trail *Martha Stewart Living* no267 p24 S 2016

Weird But True! J. SWAIN and A. E. HURT color *National Geographic Kids* no473 p4 S 2017

Paper airplanes

PAPER AIRPLANE LAUNCHER! J. SCHADEWALD cartoon color *Popular Mechanics* p104 Je 2017

Paper airplanes—Design & construction

HOW TO MAKE ANYTHING [Cover story] B. WAINFAN, J. BOBROW et al color diag *Popular Mechanics* p56 S 2017

Paper art—Exhibitions

CHIRLITY M. Shlian color *Issues in Science & Technology* v33 no1 p64 Fall 2016

Paper bags—Evaluation

Buying Time *Cincinnati Magazine* v50 no3 p42 D 2016

Paper clips—Evaluation

Top Brass M. Khemsurov color *Bloomberg Businessweek* no4509 p58 Ja 30 2017

Paper lanterns

Paper Chase H. MARTIN color *Architectural Digest* v74 no7 p12 Jl 2017

Paper Lanterns (Music)

KUNG-FU APPALACHIAN PUNK JAM color *Advocate* no1091 p34 Je/Jl 2017

Paper money

See also

Bank notes

CASHING OUT N. HELLER cartoon *New Yorker* v92 no32 p48 O 10 2016

Paper Problem K. Rogoff *MIT Technology Review* v120 no2 p11 Mr/Ap 2017

Weird Things from the Blue K. Samuelson color *Time* v190 no6 p16 Ag 7 2017

Paper money—United States

Mind-Blowing Facts About Your Money B. SPECKTOR *Reader's Digest* v189 no1128 p128 Mr 2017

Paper Moon (Film)

Tatum O'Neal N. Sperling color *Entertainment Weekly* no1460/1461 p30 Ap 7-17 2017

Paper products

See also

Stationery

Toilet paper

mantel makers color *Good Housekeeping* v263 no6 p32 D 2016

Paper research

Print, Wipe, Rewrite M. Peplow color *Scientific American* v316 no6 p16 Je 2017

Paper towels

A House Divided L. IMMEDIATO color *Los Angeles Magazine* v62 no10 p133 O 2017

Paper wasps

wild things color *Canadian Geographic* v135 no6 p66 D 2015

Paper work

PAPER POSIES L. HEDRICK color *Better Homes & Gardens* v95 no5 p39 My 2017

Paper work—Exhibitions

TAL R D. Ebony color *Art in America* v105 no3 p126 Mr 2017

Paperbacks

Is Mass Market Dying, Or Just Evolving—Again? R. Deahl color *Publishers Weekly* v264 no21 p4 My 22 2017

Paperhanging

PLAN TO PERFECTION C. RODRIGUES color *House Beautiful* p92 Ag 2017

Papermaking

MAKE PAPER from Grasses and Leaves: Connect with an age-old process and the life cycle of plants to make fragrant, textured paper K. Quillen *Mother Earth News* no282 p28 Je/Jl 2017

Paper—Pressing

ASK ROY R. BERENDSOHN color *Popular Mechanics* p34 Ap 2017

Paperweights

WORTH THEIR WEIGHT F. VIGNA *Martha Stewart Living* no267 p132 S 2016

Paperweights—Evaluation

IN THE STARS *Better Homes & Gardens* v95 no1 p12 Ja 2017

Papillomavirus diseases—Diagnosis

HPV: THE HEALTH CRISIS WE'RE NOT TALKING ABOUT B. SYLVESTRE color *Advocate* no1089 p23 F/Mr 2017

Papillomavirus diseases—Vaccination

Critics assail paper claiming harm from cancer vaccine D. Normile color graph *Science* v354 no6319 p1514 D 23 2016

Papillomaviruses

FIVE QUESTIONS bw *Los Angeles Magazine* v62 no10 p159 O

2017

Problem Solved: Warts R. LALIBERTE *Prevention* v69 no11 p20 N 2017

The STI You Already Have J. Stewart cartoon *Men's Health* v32 no3 p78 Ap 2017

Targeting nonviral antigens in viral-driven cancer color *Science* v356 no6334 p149 Ap 14 2017

Papillomaviruses—Risk factors

About Those HPV Rumors... B. Lieberman color *Glamour* v115 no7 p57 Jl 2017

Papineau, Dominic

ROCKS THAT TALK color *Popular Science* v289 no5 p43 S/O 2017

Papineau, Louis Joseph, 1786-1871

Montebello monument N. Walker color map *Canadian Geographic* v137 no1 p26 F 2017

Papis, Max

JUST LIKE YESTERDAY color *Road & Track* v68 no7 p10 Mr/Ap 2017

WHEEL OF FORTUNE color *Road & Track* v68 no7 p98 Mr/Ap 2017

Papitto, Alessandro

An accreting pulsar with extreme properties drives an ultraluminous x-ray source in NGC 5907 bibl chart graph *Science* v355 no6327 p817 F 24 2017

Papke, Bjoern

Drugging RAS: Know the enemy bibl diag *Science* v355 no6330 p1158 Mr 17 2017

Papmehl, Anne

A Critical Gap in Cancer Care bw color *Maclean's* v130 no9 p38 O 2017

PAPPADEMAS, ALEX

STILL KICKING bw color *GQ: Gentlemen's Quarterly* v97 no10 p104 O 2017

Pappalardo, Joe

DISPOSABLE DRONES cartoon *Popular Mechanics* p9 Je 2017

HOW IT WORKS NASA's Venus Machine color *Popular Mechanics* p72 F 2017

THE (NEW) TROUBLE WITH RUSSIA color *Popular Mechanics* p72 Mr 2017

NORTH KOREA: HOW BIG A THREAT? color *Popular Mechanics* p16 Jl 2017

The Young Rocketeers color *Popular Mechanics* p26 N 2017

Pappan, Sonda Andersson

NINE LIVES AND COUNTING: Saying farewell to our art director E. PARKHURST *Virginia Living* v15 no4 p9 Je 2017

Pappas, Cynthia

Mad as Hellas at the Onassis Cultural Center color *Magazine Antiques* v184 no3 p28 My/Je 2017

Pappé, Ilan, 1954-

The Biggest Prison on Earth: A History of the Occupied Territories *Publishers Weekly* v264 no26 p169 Je 26 2017

PAPRITZ, CAREW

"Scripting" a Writing Revival *USA Today Magazine* v146 no2868 p40 S 2017

Papua New Guinea

Papua New Guinea's genetic diversity withstood farming A. Gibbons color *Science* v357 no6356 p1086 S 15 2017

Papua New Guinea—Population

A Neolithic expansion, but strong genetic structure, in the independent history of New Guinea A. Bergström, S. J. Oppenheimer et al diag *Science* v357 no6356 p1160 S 15 2017

Paquette, Alain

Positive biodiversity-productivity relationship predominant in global forests bibl chart graph map *Science* v354 no6309 paaf8957-1 O 14 2016

Paquette, Joey

COMMENT color *Canadian Geographic* v137 no1 p72 F 2017

Paquola, Apua C. M.

Intersection of diverse neuronal genomes and neuropsychiatric disease: The Brain Somatic Mosaicism Network color *Science* v356 no6336 p395 Ap 28 2017

Parables

See also

Bible—Parables

Jesus Christ—Parables

Hold your lamp high A. Camille color *U.S. Catholic* v82 no11 p47 N 2017

Parachin, Victor M.

The Franklin File bw color *American History* v52 no4 p34 O 2017

Parachutes

THE MAN WHO FELL TO EARTH N. PENN color *GQ: Gentlemen's Quarterly* v86 no12 p148 D 2016

Parades

13 Things You Didn't Know About the Macy's Thanksgiving Parade B. SPECKTOR bw color *Reader's Digest* v190 no1135 p124 N 2017

ABOVE & BEYOND cartoon *New Yorker* v92 no35 p28 O 31 2016

ABOVE & BEYOND cartoon *New Yorker* v93 no17 p16 Je 19 2017

ALL AROUND Missouri *Missouri Life* v43 no7 p79 D 2016/Ja 2017

That's a Wrap E. Crawford Peyton color *New Orleans Magazine* v51 no6 p46 Ap 2017

Parades—New York (State)

See also

Macy's Thanksgiving Day Parade

ABOVE & BEYOND cartoon *New Yorker* v92 no44 p16 Ja 9 2017

ABOVE & BEYOND cartoon *New Yorker* v93 no8 p14 Ap 10 2017

Parades—Social aspects

Carnival SOME OF OUR FAVORITE THINGS E. LABRODE color *New Orleans Magazine* v51 no4 p68 F 2017

Parades—United States

Carnival SOME OF OUR FAVORITE THINGS E. LABRODE color *New Orleans Magazine* v51 no4 p68 F 2017

JANUARY/FEBRUARY K. MASSICOT color *Louisiana Life* v37 no3 p108 Ja/F 2017

Parades—United States—History—20th century

Talk of the Town: In a city temporarily teeming with Shriners, silent-film star Harold Lloyd was the most famous man in a fez C. Zeigler *Indianapolis Monthly* v40 no10 p21 Je 2017

Paradigm (Linguistics)

From Dissemination to Propagation: A New Paradigm for Education Developers J. E. Froyd, C. Henderson et al *Change* v49 no4 p35 Jl/Ag 2017

Paradigm Electronics Inc.

Beryllium Makes It Better [Cover story] D. Wilkinson color graph *Sound & Vision* v82 no7 p48 S 2017

Paradigms (Social sciences)

Data Deliver in the Clutch S. Mirsky color *Scientific American* v316 no1 p70 Ja 2017

Paradis, Michel

Guantánamo lawyer: Military tribunals are built on American apartheid [Cover story] *America* v216 no10 p10 My 1 2017

Paradis, Pierre

STICKY BUSINESS R. COHEN color *Vanity Fair* v59 no1 p162 Holiday 2017

Paradise Island (Bahamas)—Description & travel

weekend getaways: water *Washingtonian Magazine* v52 no11 p85 Ag 2017

Paradise Reloaded (Lilith) (Music)

Eotvos: Paradise Reloaded (Lilith) J. Cadagin *Opera News* v81 no7 p47 Ja 2017

Paragon Software Group Corp.

Paragon NTFS for Mac 15: Slick, native performance for accessing NTFS Windows drives J. R. BOOKWALTER color *Macworld - Digital Edition* v34 no10 p83 O 2017

Paraguay

PERSONAL THOUGHTS ON MY DAYS IN THE ARCHIVES P. Encina *Film Quarterly* v70 no4 p47 Summ 2017

Parajka, Juraj

Changing climate shifts timing of European floods color graph *Science* v357 no6351 p588 Ag 11 2017

Parakh, Kapil

WIRED FOR SUCCESS C. Cunningham *Washingtonian Magazine* v52 no9 p119 Je 2017

Parallax View, The (Film)

Classics of Conspiracy P. TONGUETTE color *National Review* v69 no19 p56 O 16 2017

Paralympics

MIKEY BRANNIGAN J. HANC color *Runner's World* v52 no1 p88 Ja/F 2017

The Paralympic Games and the Promotion of the Rights of Persons with Disabilities P. CRAVEN *UN Chronicle* v53 no2 p10 2016

PHOTO OF LASTING INTEREST color *Reader's Digest* v190 no1133 p26 S 2017

Sport Promoting Human Development and Well-Being: Psychological Components of Sustainability J. M. GARY and N. S. RUBIN *UN Chronicle* v53 no2 p30 2016

Tatyana McFadden M. Hagan color *Current Biography* v78 no3 p59 Mr 2017

U.S. Sonar Crew Scores Paralympic Silver A. Cort color *Sail* v47 no12 p18 D 2016

Paramilitary forces

backstory color *New Republic* v247 no12 p80 D 2016

EVERYMAN'S WAR: The paramilitary fighters training to keep Russia out of the Baltics E. Zerofsky *Harper's Magazine* p69 O 2017

Paramours

Phone Home L. SMITH cartoon *Weekly Standard* v22 no13 p5 D 5 2016

Paranicas, C.

Jupiter's magnetosphere and aurorae observed by the Juno spacecraft during its first polar orbits diag graph *Science* v356 no6340 p826 My 26 2017

Paranikas, Petros

Is Your Supply Chain Ready for the Congestion Crisis? *Harvard Business Review Digital Articles* p2 Je 22 2015

Paranoid (TV program)

STREAMING A. D'ARMINIO *TV Guide* v64 no46 p38 N 7 2016

Parapsychology

See also

Karma

Mental healing

From Tiny Acorns ... C. C. FRENCH *Skeptical Inquirer* v40 no6 p39 N/D 2016

It Just Never Stops ... J. RANDI *Skeptical Inquirer* v41 no3 p18 My/Je 2017

'M' Is for Mysterious Marks B. RADFORD *Skeptical Inquirer* v40 no6 p30 N/D 2016

Skeptical about Skeptics? R. Rood *Skeptical Inquirer* v41 no3 p65 My/Je 2017

Parapsychology—Societies, etc.

Ghost Hunters in the Dark B. RADFORD *Skeptical Inquirer* v41 no1 p32 Ja/F 2017

Parasites

The Indomitable Dung Beetle Plays Key Role in Parasite Regulation J. CESSNA *BioScience* v67 no6 p583 Je 2017

Keeping Worms at Bay color *Horse & Rider* v56 no9 p38 S 2017

Parasite control L. Bonner color *Equus* no476 p37 My 2017

Transformational Principles for NEON Sampling of Mammalian Parasites and Pathogens: A Response to Springer and Colleagues J. A. COOK, S. E. GREIMAN et al *BioScience* v66 no11 p917 N 1 2016

Transient compartmentalization of RNA replicators prevents extinction due to parasites Shigeyoshi Matsumura, A. Kun et al bibl chart graph *Science* v354 no6317 p1293 D 9 2016

Parc national de la Kagera (Rwanda)

MYSTERY ON THE SAVANNA [Cover story] A. SHOUMATOFF color map *Smithsonian* v47 no10 p53 Mr 2017

Parc national de Taï (Côte d'Ivoire)

Anthrax cousin wreaks havoc in the rainforest K. Kupferschmidt color *Science* v357 no6350 p438 Ag 4 2017

Parcak, Sarah

ANCIENT SITES AS SEEN FROM SPACE A. R. Williams color *National Geographic* v232 no2 p138 Ag 2017

SPACE ARCHAEOLOGIST A. TUCKER *Smithsonian* v47 no8 p38 D 2016

Parchment—Conservation & restoration

RECOVERING ERASED WISDOM A. R. Williams color *National Geographic* v231 no3 p16 Mr 2017

PARDES, ARIELLE

FETISH: FLIGHT MANUAL color *Wired* v25 no9 p43 S 2017

Pardoll, Drew M.

Mismatch repair deficiency predicts response of solid tumors to PD-1 blockade chart graph *Science* v357 no6349 p409 Jl 28 2017

Pardon

What Does the Arpaio Pardon Mean for the Future of Civil Rights? *America* v217 no6 p8 S 18 2017

Pardon Edward Snowden (Short story)

Pardon Edward Snowden J. O'Neill bw cartoon *New Yorker* v92 no41 p64 D 12 2016

Pardon My Sarong (Film)

MARIE IN THE MOVIES J. McGovern color *Entertainment Weekly* no1485 p34 O 6 2017

Pardy, Brandon

FEATURED FELLOW: BRANDON PARDY M. Rosano color *Canadian Geographic* v137 no2 p70 Mr/Ap 2017

Paredes, M. Ríos

Persistent effects of pre-Columbian plant domestication on Amazonian forest composition bibl chart graph map *Science* v355 no6328 p925 Mr 3 2017

Paredes, Mercedes F.

Extensive migration of young neurons into the infant human frontal lobe color diag graph *Science* v354 no6308 paaf7073-1 O 7 2016

PAREINSON, MARY JANE

Wit and Wisdom From our Early Breeders: Edna and Jim Draper *Arabian Horse World* v57 no8 p152 My 2017

Parekh, Atish A.

Dynamic multinuclear sites formed by mobilized copper ions in NOx selective catalytic reduction bw color diag graph *Science* v357 no6354 p898 S 1 2017

Parekh, Sapun H.

A water window on surface chemistry diag *Science* v357 no6353 p755 Ag 25 2017

Pareles, Jon

Swept Away by Springsteen bw *New York Review of Books* v63 no20 p44 D 22 2016

Parent & adult child

PARENTS, PROTECT YOUR WEALTH [Cover story] A. Edmond Jr. cartoon color *Black Enterprise* v47 no3 p45 O 2016

Sorry, Kids: We Made You This Way S. Koslow color *AARP: The Magazine* v59 no3A p55 Ap/My 2016

Parent & child

See also

Child abuse

Father & child

Mother & child

Parental deprivation

Parenting

Parent-student relationships

Stepmothers

4 Skills to Teach Him Before Cold Season A. Mencel color *Parents* v92 no11 p19 N 2017

9 PARENTING HACKS: NOT TO FEEL GUILTY ABOUT [Cover story] J. MIGALA color *Parents* v92 no11 p26 N 2017

Baby love: Forget the stages--be present to parenting A. Scobey color *U.S. Catholic* v82 no10 p43 O 2017

BREAKING UP WITH YOUR PARENTS C. FRAZIER cartoon *New Yorker* v92 no37 p43 N 14 2016

A children's guide to parenting S. FESCHUK color *Maclean's* v130 no3 p72 Ap 2017

Comic Relief for Tired Potty Trainers color *Parents* v92 no11 p20 N 2017

A Daughter's Gratitude L. Paulsen color *Dressage Today* v24 no2 p20 N 2017

Does My Ex Owe Anything To Our Grown Kids? K. A. Appiah *New York Times Magazine* p24 Je 11 2017

drop-off jitters R. FELSENTHAL STEWART *Parents* v92 no4 p130 Ap 2017

Explaining Dangerous Situations to Kids *USA Today Magazine* v145 no2861 p1 F 2017

fooled you! K. STONEY color *Parents* v92 no4 p74 Ap 2017

Giggles *Parents* v92 no11 p124 N 2017

Hey, Mom and Dad: You Have No Idea C. Weaver color *AARP: The Magazine* v59 no3A p57 Ap/My 2016

High Marks For Fair Praise K. GOLDYNIA *Psychology Today* v50 no3 p21 My/Je 2017

How Could You? B. GRIERSON cartoon *Walrus* v13 no10 p15

D 2016

"I HAVEN'T HAD THIS MUCH FUN SINCE I WAS A KID!" J. Ketteler color *Good Housekeeping* v264 no1 p109 Ja 1 2017

IT'S COME TO THIS *Parents* v91 no6 p13 Je 2016

The Kids Will Be Fine H. WILHELM *National Review* v68 no22 p48 D 5 2016

LET US GIVE THANKS R. Holtzmann *South Dakota Magazine* v32 no4 p46 N/D 2016

Making Room at the Table T. D. Jakes and D. POINTDUJOUR color *Ebony* v72 no4 p73 F 2017

me to we J. Francisco *Good Housekeeping* v264 no3 p8 Mr 2017

oOps *Parents* v91 no6 p74 Je 2016

oops *Parents* v92 no4 p78 Ap 2017

reconnecting as a family J. WILSON *Parents* p86 2015

The Soccer Mom's Lament C. VAN DUSEN *Atlanta* v56 no11 p93 Mr 2017

A STORY AT HOME S. FENNESSY *Atlanta* v56 no7 p20 N 2016

We need to talk A. Scobey color *U.S. Catholic* v82 no1 p36 Ja 2017

What Kids Expect of Parents *USA Today Magazine* v145 no2859 p6 D 2016

What to Do If Your Parents Are Causing You Career Angst S. Friedman *Harvard Business Review Digital Articles* p2 Ag 5 2016

Parent & child—United States

RJ CYLER *Interview* v47 no5 p64 Je/Jl 2017

Women & Children First B. G. Prusak color *Commonweal* v143 no17 p19 O 21 2016

Parent & infant

The Smarter Way to Play *Parents* v91 no11 p30 N 2016

spending time apart J. MIGALA *Parents* v92 no3 p106 Mr 2017

PARENT, MARC

HYPERSPACE RACE [Cover story] cartoon color *Runner's World* v52 no2 p58 Mr 2017

Parent-child communication

How to Talk to Your Kids About Money When You Have a Lot of It J. Christianson *Harvard Business Review Digital Articles* p2 S 13 2016

Parent participation in children's reading

THE LITERACY LINK: Reading activities as a mechanism to strengthen family engagement S. Tambyraja *Literacy Today (2411-7862)* v35 no1 p12 Jl/Ag 2017

Parent participation in education

See also

Parent participation in children's reading

Dance Moms--and Dads K. MCGUIRE *Dance Magazine* v91 no8 p46 Ag 2017

Making Religious Education Work F. Nonomen bw *Commonweal* v143 no18 p8 N 11 2016

TALKING TO KIDS BOOSTS TEST SCORES, CAREERS [Cover story] *USA Today Magazine* v145 no2865 p1 Je 2017

Parent-student relationships

Dance Moms--and Dads K. MCGUIRE *Dance Magazine* v91 no8 p46 Ag 2017

THE LITERACY LINK: Reading activities as a mechanism to strengthen family engagement S. Tambyraja *Literacy Today (2411-7862)* v35 no1 p12 Jl/Ag 2017

Parent-teacher conferences

Face to face A. Scobey color *U.S. Catholic* v82 no2 p43 F 2017

Parent-teacher relationships

See also

Parent-teacher conferences

Face to face A. Scobey color *U.S. Catholic* v82 no2 p43 F 2017

Parental alienation syndrome

WHEN PARENTS ACT BADLY *USA Today Magazine* v145 no2863 p1 Ap 2017

Parental behavior in animals

Glass frog moms do care after all S. MILIUS color *Science News* v191 no8 p16 Ap 29 2017

Parental consent (Marriage)

Why It's Still Legal for Underage Girls to Marry in the U.S C. Alter color *Time* v189 no22 p15 Je 12 2017

Parental deprivation

THE SEPARATION L. MACFARQUHAR cartoon *New Yorker* v93 no23 p36 Ag 7 2017

Parental leave

See also

Maternity leave

3 Ways Tech Companies Are Offering Parental Leave J. C. Williams *Harvard Business Review Digital Articles* p2 N 19 2015

Complying with Family-Friendly Leave Policies Is Not Enough J. Beck and S. Behson *Harvard Business Review Digital Articles* p2 Ap 13 2016

The Family Leave Dilemma A. B. LLOYD color graph *Weekly Standard* v22 no48 p21 S 4 2017

Need a Good Parental Leave Policy? Here It Is J. C. Williams and K. Massinger *Harvard Business Review Digital Articles* p2 N 23 2015

Paid Parent Leave: Rare A. Adamczyk color *Money* v46 no1 p21 Ja/F 2017

Parental leave laws

Paid Parental Leave *Congressional Digest* v96 no7 p31 S 2017

Parental leave—Government policy

Bringing Up Baby, Helping the Economy color *Scientific American* v315 no6 p10 D 2016

Parental leave—Great Britain

Will shared parental leave ever work? M. STERN *People Management* p8 F 2017

Parental leave—Law & legislation

Will shared parental leave ever work? M. STERN *People Management* p8 F 2017

Parental leave—United States

Bringing Up Baby, Helping the Economy color *Scientific American* v315 no6 p10 D 2016

Parental Leave Can't Just Be for Mothers A. Wittenberg-Cox *Harvard Business Review Digital Articles* p2 Mr 18 2015

Society Needs to Care for All Our Caregivers M. Gates color *Time* v188 no16/17 p43 O 24 2016

Parental overprotection

A DISCOURAGING WORD T. Pitock *Saturday Evening Post* v289 no3 p10 My/Je 2017

Parente, G.

Observation of a large-scale anisotropy in the arrival directions of cosmic rays above 8 × 1018 eV *Science* v357 no6357 p1266 S 22 2017

Parenthood

See also

Fatherhood

10 ways to prepare your first-time-parent friends R. D'APICE cartoon *Parents* v92 no3 p116 Mr 2017

ARE YOU MY MOTHER? I. PARKER cartoon color *New Yorker* v93 no14 p46 My 22 2017

the funny factor D. Points *Parents* p12 2015

Meow or Never: Was I up to pet parenthood one more time? D. Paul color *Indianapolis Monthly* v41 no2 p168 S 2017

Parenthood (TV program)

My Obsessions... *TV Guide* v65 no14 p12 Ap 3 2017

Parenting

15 Minutes to a Simpler Day L. Fenton color *Parents* v92 no9 p158 S 2017

20 Dad Hacks for Enjoying Dadhood D. GORDON, D. Wade et al cartoon chart color *GQ: Gentlemen's Quarterly* v97 no7 p32 Jl 2017

21 ways to enjoy cooking with kids more K. CICERO color *Parents* v92 no5 p38 My 2017

2 PARENTS, 3 BOYS, 50,000 FLOWERS color *Parents* v92 no8 p114 Ag 2017

9 PARENTING HACKS: NOT TO FEEL GUILTY ABOUT [Cover story] J. MIGALA color *Parents* v92 no11 p26 N 2017

Article Sins Of The Father J. H. Reynolds and J. Ting *Commentary* v140 no2 p4 S 2015

awesome ideas for your little one's summer K. ROCKWOOD color *Parents* v92 no8 p68 Ag 2017

Baby love: Forget the stages--be present to parenting A. Scobey color *U.S. Catholic* v82 no10 p43 O 2017

Baby want a kale salad? [Cover story] A. Hutchins color *Maclean's* no1 p52 F 17 2017

"Bad Mommy" Guilt Busters J. K. Geddes cartoon color *Working Mother* p54 F/Mr 2017

Balancing Parenting and Work Stress: A Guide D. W. Dowling bw *Harvard Business Review Digital Articles* p2 Mr 9 2017

beach towns with benefits K. CICERO color *Parents* v92 no8 p74

Ag 2017

Being a Parent Made Me a Better Manager, and Vice Versa J. Zikic *Harvard Business Review Digital Articles* p2 My 9 2016

Brush Up on Mealtime Manners H. G. Walsh *Parents* v92 no9 p170 S 2017

Bye-Bye Baby: Sentiment and relief E. C. Peyton color *New Orleans Magazine* v51 no10 p58 Ag 2017

cope with the crazy J. KING LINDLEY color *Parents* v92 no5 p76 My 2017

DO INTERNATIONAL PARENTS DO IT BETTER? color *Publishers Weekly* v264 no2 p32 Ja 9 2017

eating issues E. KLEIN *Parents* v91 no6 p138 Je 2016

Giggles *Parents* v92 no9 p172 S 2017

going dark color *Parents* v92 no8 p111 Ag 2017

haikus for parents S. WATTS color *Parents* v92 no8 p108 Ag 2017

How Could You? B. GRIERSON cartoon *Walrus* v13 no10 p15 D 2016

how to teach time R. HARTMAN *Parents* v92 no8 p133 Ag 2017

i don't feel guilty about not feeling guilty B. PAESEL color *Parents* v92 no5 p84 My 2017

If Parents Were Middle-Schoolers S. Given color *Parents* v92 no5 p12 My 2017

Let's talk about bullies M. Rollins *Redbook* p12 O 2017

love shack, baby Liz color *Parents* v92 no6 p12 Je 2017

master the drop-off N. HOWEY *Parents* v91 no9 p88 S 2016

math word problems for today's parents J. VICK color *Parents* v92 no5 p124 My 2017

MISSING PARENT BLUES E. C. PEYTON cartoon *New Orleans Magazine* v51 no1 p50 N 2016

oops *Parents* v92 no5 p62 My 2017

oops *Parents* v92 no8 p140 Ag 2017

our cradle: it's ugly, but it rocks! M. DICKS color *Parents* v92 no8 p52 Ag 2017

raise a good sport E. ZAMMETT RUDDY color graph *Parents* v92 no5 p36 My 2017

THE REAL GWYNETH S. Bee color *Harper's Bazaar* no3648 p232 N 2016

Relatable Days With Rebecca Minkoff J. Hartshorn color *Parents* v92 no9 p15 S 2017

a roof over one's bed color *Parents* v92 no5 p89 My 2017

Royalty Gets a Rethink M. LaScala color *Parents* v92 no8 p15 Ag 2017

Science, Public Trust, and CSICon 2016 K. FRAZIER *Skeptical Inquirer* v41 no1 p4 Ja/F 2017

scrap the nap [Cover story] R. R. PEACHMAN *Parents* v92 no7 p124 Jl 2017

THE SECRET LIFE OF SCHOOL M. Crouch cartoon color *Parents* v92 no9 p66 S 2017

show how to share J. RAINEY MARQUEZ *Parents* v92 no6 p136 Je 2017

a sillier hide-and-seek color *Parents* v92 no5 p47 My 2017

Social Networking for Kids *USA Today Magazine* v145 no2860 p34 Ja 2017

Solve My Screen-Time Skirmishes E. Z. Ruddy color graph *Parents* v92 no9 p56 S 2017

sprinkle them with joy color *Parents* v92 no8 p67 Ag 2017

Tackling Technology Tactfully H. QUADRI *Islamic Horizons* v45 no6 p36 N/D 2016

Teddy's Wisdom Made Me Weep H. Levine color *Parents* v92 no5 p10 My 2017

that time i won parenting L. Vaccariello *Parents* v92 no5 p6 My 2017

These Celebs Win at Family Comedy J. Hartshorn color *Parents* v92 no5 p9 My 2017

tooth-fairy time R. RABKIN PEACHMAN *Parents* v91 no6 p144 Je 2016

Try These Five Fun Ideas! S. James color *Parents* v92 no8 p30 Ag 2017

Vintage Views bw *Parents* v92 no9 p18 S 2017

What Am I Thinking? M. Dicks cartoon *Parents* v92 no9 p124 S 2017

What Parents Should Tell Their Kids About Finding a Career J. M. Citrin *Harvard Business Review Digital Articles* p2 My 15 2015

WHO ASKED YOU? (WE DID!) *Parents* v91 no9 p24 S 2016

THE YEAR OF MAGICAL PARENTING P. OSWALT color *GQ: Gentlemen's Quarterly* v86 no12 p158 D 2016

Yes, I'm Playing Favorites L. Vaccariello bw *Parents* v92 no9 p8 S 2017

you're welcome! color *Parents* v92 no8 p12 Ag 2017

Parenting—United States

Parent Trap *Commentary* v142 no1 p1 Jl/Ag 2016

Parents

    See also

      Fathers

      Grandparents

      Mothers

      White parents

      Working parents

Are You Sure You Can't Eat That? color *Parents* v92 no8 p94 Ag 2017

Be not afraid A. Scobey color *U.S. Catholic* v82 no11 p25 N 2017

CONNECT WITH YOUR CHILD'S CLASSROOM J. Hartshorn and J. Tahnk color *Parents* v92 no9 p86 S 2017

Do I Get Involved When A Parent Treats a Child Badly? K. A. Appiah color *New York Times Magazine* p38 D 11 2016

future focus D. Points *Parents* v91 no10 p12 O 2016

haikus for parents S. WATTS color *Parents* v92 no8 p108 Ag 2017

Home for the Holidays S. James *Parents* p17 2015

How to Overcome Sibling Rivalry J. WILKIN *Christianity Today* v61 no4 p32 My 2017

How to Swear in Front of Your Kids R. Straetker color *Parents* v92 no4 p20 Ap 2017

If Parents Were Middle-Schoolers S. Given color *Parents* v92 no5 p12 My 2017

IT'S COME TO THIS *Parents* v91 no6 p13 Je 2016

A Letter Opener M. Schnaidt bw *Men's Health* v32 no5 p140 Je 2017

Life IN THESE UNITED STATES Y. BRODD, E. BOGAERT et al *Reader's Digest* v189 no1128 p38 Mr 2017

My Snow Angel L. Wright color *Good Housekeeping* v264 no2 p63 F 2017

A new family activism M. Walker color *U.S. Catholic* v82 no11 p12 N 2017

No-Filter Fams *Parents* v91 no10 p15 O 2016

Objects of PIN-terest color *Parents* v92 no8 p18 Ag 2017

oops *Parents* v92 no6 p140 Je 2017

OUR PARENTS ARE OUR FUTURE C. FRAZIER color *New Yorker* v93 no29 p50 S 25 2017

our weirdest family tradition is... *Parents* p144 2015

PARENTAL GUIDANCE M. M. Kashino *Washingtonian Magazine* v52 no3 p122 D 2016

RIGHT UNDER YOUR NOSE A. BAIR *USA Today Magazine* v145 no2860 p32 Ja 2017

Sex WHILE PARENTING J. Press color *Parents* v92 no9 p106 S 2017

Try These Five Fun Ideas! S. James color *Parents* v92 no8 p30 Ag 2017

What to Do About Junior B. M. WILSEY *USA Today Magazine* v145 no2864 p66 My 2017

When Big Brother Parents J. Darrow img *New York* v50 no18 p34 S 4 2017

Where Kids Get Their Political Views J. Wilkin *Christianity Today* v60 no8 p32 O 2016

you're welcome! color *Parents* v92 no8 p12 Ag 2017

YOUR FROZEN EGG HAS A QUESTION S. FOGEL cartoon *New Yorker* v93 no14 p39 My 22 2017

Parents—Attitudes

    See also

      Mothers—Attitudes

Baby genome screening needs more time to gestate J. Kaiser color *Science* v354 no6311 p398 O 28 2016

Parents—Services for

Bathroom wars 2.0 E. ALINI color *Maclean's* v129 no43 p48 O 31 2016

Parents—Societies, etc.

Explore, Enjoy--and Parent M. Brune and M. Brune *Sierra* v102 no5 p6 St/O 2017

PARET, MARCEL

South Africa's Divided Working-Class Movements *Current History* v116 no790 p176 My 2017

Pareto analysis

When a Simple Rule of Thumb Beats a Fancy Algorithm J. Fox

Harvard Business Review Digital Articles p2 O 2 2014

Pareto principle

AI Is Going to Change the 80/20 Rule M. Schrage color *Harvard Business Review Digital Articles* p2 F 28 2017

Parfenova, Elena I.

Positive biodiversity-productivity relationship predominant in global forests bibl chart graph map *Science* v354 no6309 paaf8957-1 O 14 2016

PARHAM, JASON

False Witness *New York Times Book Review* p11 F 12 2017

'Seigfried' *New York Times Magazine* p61 Mr 12 2017

Parham, Lennon, 1976-

Playing House D. Holbrook *TV Guide* v65 no23 p35 My 29 2017

Parham, Robert

Baptist ethicist and commentator dies at age 63 A. M. Banks *Christian Century* v134 no8 p1 Ap 12 2017

Parichy, David M.

A macrophage relay for long-distance signaling during postembryonic tissue remodeling bibl color graph *Science* v355 no6331 p1317 Mr 24 2017

Parija, Pratik

India's Cash-Canceling Experiment color *Bloomberg Businessweek* no4501 p12 N 28 2016

Parijs, Philippe van, 1951-

Born to Be Free B. M. Friedman bw color *New York Review of Books* v64 no15 p39 O 12 2017

Parikh, Jay

How Facebook Tries to Prevent Office Politics *Harvard Business Review Digital Articles* p2 Je 29 2016

Parikh, Jay—Interviews

An Inside Look at Facebook's Approach to Automation and Human Work J. Kirby *Harvard Business Review Digital Articles* p2 Je 12 2015

Parikh, Ravi B.

Making Predictive Analytics a Routine Part of Patient Care *Harvard Business Review Digital Articles* p2 Ap 21 2016

PARINI, JAY

Princes of Darkness *New York Times Book Review* p19 Mr 19 2017

Travels in Literary Time *American Scholar* v86 no2 p124 Spr 2017

Paris (France)

COUTURE REPORT color *Harper's Bazaar* no3656 p320 S 2017

HOW TO KNOW URINE PARIS D. Stone color *National Geographic* v232 no5 p16 N 2017

UNLUCKY JIM L. Collins cartoon *New Yorker* v93 no4 p28 Mr 13 2017

Paris (France)—Description & travel

INSTYLE [Loves] PARIS C. Pérez color *InStyle* v23 no12 p229 N 2016

Mom and Me: 4 Destinations to Explore with Your Mother O. RAYMOND and D. POINTDUJOUR color *Ebony* v72 no6 p58 Ap/My 2017

THE SEXIEST TOUR OF PARIS color *Advocate* no1091 p118 Je/Jl 2017

Paris, B. A.

The Breakdown *Publishers Weekly* v264 no22 p46 My 29 2017

Paris, Cecilia

"Ab initio" synthesis of zeolites for preestablished catalytic reactions bibl chart diag *Science* v355 no6329 p1051 Mr 10 2017

Paris, David C.

The Bargain *Change* v48 no5 p4 S/O 2016

Learning, Professionalism, and Change *Change* v49 no1 p4 Ja/F 2017

The Man in the Mirror *Change* v48 no6 p4 N/D 2016

A Tale of Two Universities *Change* v49 no3 p4 My/Je 2017

Think Globally, Act Locally *Change* v49 no4 p4 Jl/Ag 2017

Paris, Jay—Awards

2017 PITTMAN INNOVATION AWARDS color *Sail* v48 no2 p58 F 2017

Paris, Oskar

Biological fabrication of cellulose fibers with tailored properties color *Science* v357 no6356 p1118 S 15 2017

PARIS, WENDY

LAWS OF ATTRACTION: Who we desire is driven by powerful evolutionary forces, but while most of us are drawn to looks first (whether or not we admit it), human attraction is far more complex than it appears at first sight [Cover story] *Psychology Today* v50 no4 p52 Ag 2017

Paris Agreement (2016)

AT THE TOP OF THE LIST A. GUTERRES *Vital Speeches of the Day* v83 no7 p197 Jl 2017

Australia eyes clean energy goal color *Science* v356 no6343 p1105 Je 16 2017

Can U.S. states and cities overcome Paris exit? W. Cornwall graph *Science* v356 no6342 p1000 Je 9 2017

China can lead on climate change C. Wang and F. Wang color *Science* v357 no6353 p764 Ag 25 2017

A Climate of Denial E. Alterman color il *Nation* v305 no1 p6 Jl 3 2017

Design Community Reacts to Paris Agreement Withdrawal M. SITZ *Architectural Record* v205 no7 p32 Jl 2017

The Future Economy Project A. Ignatius *Harvard Business Review Digital Articles* p2 2017

The New Nation-States B. MCKIBBEN color *New Republic* v248 no8/9 p14 Ag/S 2017

The Next Standing Rock B. ADLER il *New Republic* v248 no10 p10 O 2017

Opportunities Lost? R. E. GROPP *BioScience* v67 no8 p683 Ag 2017

Out of Paris color *National Review* v69 no12 p12 Je 26 2017

Paris Isn't Burning B. Deese color *Foreign Affairs* v96 no4 p83 Jl/Ag 2017

The Perils of Pulling Out of Paris J. Worland color *Time* v189 no22 p8 Je 12 2017

POX AMERICANA M. Amis and S. Fleishman bw color *Esquire* p110 N 2017

A roadmap for rapid decarbonization J. Rockström, O. Gaffney et al bibl color graph *Science* v355 no6331 p1269 Mr 24 2017

Thanks to Ivanka, We May Always Have Paris J. A. Dlouhy, T. Loh et al color *Bloomberg Businessweek* no4519 p50 Ap 24 2017

Time for Going-Away Gifts? E. Roston and J. A. Dlouhy color *Bloomberg Businessweek* no4525 p6 Je 5 2017

Vietnam's Urgent Task: Adapting to Climate Change P. MCELWEE *Current History* v116 no791 p223 S 2017

Your Country Is Flooding? Tough Luck C. Flavelle color *Bloomberg Businessweek* no4526 p24 Je 12 2017

Paris Can Wait (Film)

Paris Can Wait L. Greenblatt color *Entertainment Weekly* no1466 p44 My 19 2017

PARISEAU, PIERRE-PAUL

visual statement color *Foreign Policy* no221 p26 N/D 2016

Paris (France)—Buildings, structures, etc.

Alley-Oop S. COCHRAN color *Architectural Digest* v74 no9 p184 S 2017

At Long Last, Labrouste: A newly restored masterwork reopens in Paris B. BERGDOLL color map *Architectural Record* v205 no8 p52 Ag 2017

snapshot color *Architectural Record* v204 no12 p208 D 2016

Parish, George

Hydraulic control of tuna fins: A role for the lymphatic system in vertebrate locomotion color *Science* v357 no6348 p310 Jl 21 2017

Parish, Meera M.

Ultrafast many-body interferometry of impurities coupled to a Fermi sea bibl diag graph *Science* v354 no6308 p96 O 7 2016

Parish, Nurya Love

LIVING BY The Word *Christian Century* v134 no4 p23 F 15 2017

Parish, Sister

editor's letter color *Architectural Digest* v74 no4 p30 Ap 2017

Parishes

and the survey says *U.S. Catholic* v82 no11 p29 N 2017

Can a parish ever have clutter? J. Ferrari *U.S. Catholic* v82 no3 p35 Mr 2017

DISPUTED MATERIAL B. A. RAGEN and E. BRENDE *Commonweal* v144 no13 p2 Ag 11 2017

Get your money in order C. Zech color graph *U.S. Catholic* v82 no1 p30 Ja 2017

How do you rate the quality of liturgy in your parish? Mary, Thomas et al graph *America* v217 no7 p6 O 2 2017

INSIDE THE CHANGING U.S. CATHOLIC CHURCH L. Libresco color diag *America* v216 no5 p12 Mr 6 2017

An Ordinary Sunday [Cover story] T. Baker, J. Schwenkler et al color *Commonweal* v144 no15 p11 S 22 2017

Shared space T. Flanigan color *U.S. Catholic* v82 no11 p28 N 2017

"We welcomed them" J. Molyneux *U.S. Catholic* v81 no12 p17 D 2016

You invited me in [Cover story] P. Feuerherd color *U.S. Catholic* v81 no12 p12 D 2016

Parishes—United States

How were your children received by your parish? graph il *America* v216 no13 p6 Je 12 2017

Parishes Should Lead Efforts to Understand Opioid Addiction *America* v217 no3 p8 Ag 7 2017

What to Measure If You're Mission Driven Z. First *Harvard Business Review Digital Articles* p2 Jl 9 2015

Parisi, M.

Jupiter's interior and deep atmosphere: The initial pole-to-pole passes with the Juno spacecraft [Cover story] color graph *Science* v356 no6340 p821 My 26 2017

Parisien, Marc

miR-183 cluster scales mechanical pain sensitivity by regulating basal and neuropathic pain genes diag graph *Science* v356 no6343 p1168 Je 16 2017

Paris Peace Conference (1919-1920)

DROP YOUR WEAPONS L. MENAND cartoon color *New Yorker* v93 no28 p61 S 18 2017

Paris Terrorist Attacks, Paris, France, 2015

After Paris, We Need More Fellowship, Not More Leadership G. Petriglieri *Harvard Business Review Digital Articles* p2 N 14 2015

Park, Alice

6 More Reasons to Get Up and Move color *Time* v190 no4 p40 Jl 24 2017

Are These 'Healthy' Foods Really Good for You? color *Time* v190 no10/11 p32 S 18 2017

Beyond Repeal and Replace color diag map *Time* v190 no2/3 p30 Jl 10-17 2017

Burning Questions color *Time* v189 no7/8 p88 F 27 2017

Cancer's Newest Miracle Cure color *Time* v190 no7 p32 Ag 21 2017

Coffee: The Latest Antidote to Aging? color *Time* v189 no3 p22 Ja 30 2017

The CRISPR Pioneers color *Time* v188 no25-26 p116 D 19 2016 Double Issue

Dr. Willie Parker color *Time* v189 no15 p56 Ap 24 2017

The Forgotten Side of Cancer Care color *Time* v188 no19 p20 N 7 2016

The Growing Fight Against Food Fraud color *Time* v189 no3 p15 Ja 16 2017

How DNA Can Guide Cancer Treatments color *Time* v190 no15 p46 O 16 2017

An Individual Approach to Breast Cancer color *Time* v190 no15 p40 O 16 2017

Inside Donald Trump's War Against the State [Cover story] color *Time* v189 no10 p26 Mr 20 2017

Meet the Class of 2016 color *Time* v188 no18 p22 O 31 2016

New Frontiers In Breast Cancer color diag *Time* v188 no15 p34 O 17 2016

A New Paradigm for Opioid Addiction: More Drugs color *Time* v188 no16/17 p48 O 24 2016

Next Generation Leaders color *Time* v188 no15 p41 O 17 2016

Next Generation Leaders color *Time* v189 no9 p38 Mr 13 2017

The Race to Zero color diag map *Time* v188 no22-23 p38 N/D 2016

Simple Drugs Stopped This Child from Getting HIV from Her Mother. Yet 400 Babies Are Born Every Day With the Disease. What Will It Take to Protect Them All? color diag map *Time* v189 no11 p40 Mr 27 2017

The Sleep Cure color *Time* v189 no7/8 p70 F 27 2017

The Test of a Lifetime color *Time* v190 no13 p52 O 2 2017

Titans color *Time* v189 no16/17 p94 My 1-8 2017

The Truth About Whole Wheat and 'Whole-Grain' Bread color *Time* v189 no4 p17 F 6 2017

When Parents and Doctors Disagree on What Futile Means color *Time* v190 no4 p17 Jl 24 2017

Park, Andrea

America's growing news deserts map *Columbia Journalism Review* v56 no1 p34 Spr 2017

Park, Boyoung Y.

Metal-catalyzed reductive coupling of olefin-derived nucleophiles: Reinventing carbonyl addition diag *Science* v354 no6310 paah5133-1 O 21 2016

Park, Byung-Wook

Iodide management in formamidinium-lead-halide–based perovskite layers for efficient solar cells bw diag *Science* v356 no6345 p1376 Je 30 2017

Park, Colleen

Can You Handle the Truth? BEING LESS THAN ACCURATE ABOUT WHAT OTHERS THINK OF YOU MAY HAVE AN UPSIDE *Psychology Today* v49 no6 p18 N/D 2016

EYES OFF THE PRIZE *Psychology Today* v49 no5 p18 S/O 2016

The Long Reach of Popularity... Mitch Prinstein *Psychology Today* v50 no3 p12 My/Je 2017

OPENING UP *Psychology Today* v50 no4 p18 Ag 2017

Park, David S.

β2-Adrenoreceptor is a regulator of the a-synuclein gene driving risk of Parkinson's disease cartoon chart graph *Science* v357 no6354 p891 S 1 2017

Park, Geun-hye, 1952-

Park in Limbo J. Lee, K. Kong et al color *Bloomberg Businessweek* no4498 p22 N 7 2016

South Korea's Familial Presidential Family Scandal I. Bremmer *Time* v188 no20 p10 N 14 2016

Troubled Seoul F. EPSTEIN color *Weekly Standard* v22 no30 p22 Ap 10 2017

Who's Who In South Korea's Widening Graft Scandal C. Campbell color *Time* v189 no3 p9 Ja 30 2017

Park, Geun-hye, 1952-—Trials, litigation, etc.

Lightbox color *Time* v189 no11 p20 Mr 27 2017

Park, H.

An integrated diamond nanophotonics platform for quantum-optical networks bibl graph *Science* v354 no6314 p847 N 18 2016

Magnetic resonance spectroscopy of an atomically thin material using a single-spin qubit bibl color diag graph *Science* v355 no6324 p503 F 3 2017

Park, Hahnbeom

Protein structure determination using metagenome sequence data bibl color graph *Science* v355 no6322 p294 Ja 20 2017

Park, Hang-Ah

Polymeric peptide pigments with sequence-encoded properties color graph *Science* v356 no6342 p1064 Je 9 2017

Park, Hluhluwe-Imfolozi

TURTLES GROOM WARTHOG color *National Geographic Kids* no465 p13 N 2016

Park, Ho Bum

Maximizing the right stuff: The trade-off between membrane permeability and selectivity color *Science* v356 no6343 p1137 Je 16 2017

Park, Inbee, 1988-

Inbee Park M. Hagan color *Current Biography* v78 no2 p58 F 2017

Park, Joonsuk

Highly stretchable polymer semiconductor films through the nanoconfinement effect bibl graph *Science* v355 no6320 p1 Ja 6 2017

Park, Junyoung O.

Systems-level analysis of mechanisms regulating yeast metabolic flux bibl diag graph *Science* v354 no6311 paaf2786-1 O 28 2016

Park, Kee B.

Korean physicians' bond defies borders *Science* v357 no6353 p764 Ag 25 2017

Park, Kyunghee

China Challenges the Giants With Low Fares color graph *Bloomberg Businessweek* no4504 p22 D 19 2016

Everything Is Fine at Cathay Pacific cartoon graph *Bloomberg Businessweek* no4516 p17 Mr 27 2017

Finally, Some Good News for Shipyards *Bloomberg Businessweek* no4518 p23 Ap 10 2017

South Korea's High-Value Targets *Bloomberg Businessweek* no4520 p17 My 1 2017

PARK, LINDA SUE

Origin of a Species *New York Times Book Review* p17 Mr 12 2017

Park, Peter J.
Intersection of diverse neuronal genomes and neuropsychiatric disease: The Brain Somatic Mosaicism Network color *Science* v356 no6336 p395 Ap 28 2017

Park, Randall, 1974—Interviews
Brothers in Comedy M. Schneider *TV Guide* v64 no15 p16 Ap 4 2016

Park, Ryan S.
Gravity field of the Orientale basin from the Gravity Recovery and Interior Laboratory Mission bibl graph *Science* v354 no6311 p438 O 28 2016

Park, Sam-Yong
Crystal structure of the overlapping dinucleosome composed of hexasome and octasome graph *Science* v356 no6334 p205 Ap 14 2017

Park, Soojin
Sliding chains keep particles together diag *Science* v357 no6348 p250 Jl 21 2017

Park, Taezoon
How We'll Stereotype Our Robot Coworkers *Harvard Business Review Digital Articles* p2 O 2 2014

Park, Thomas J.
Fructose-driven glycolysis supports anoxia resistance in the naked mole-rat diag graph *Science* v356 no6335 p307 Ap 21 2017

Park design
Another Year of Progress G. MULLINS-COHEN *Parks & Recreation* v51 no10 p12 O 2016
Design, Place and Indigenous Ways: Working with Local Communities P. Droz, D. Jaber et al *Parks & Recreation* v51 no12 p30 D 2016
The Parklands of Floyds Fork: Louisville's 21st Century Legacy Park C. B. Neer *Parks & Recreation* v52 no9 p16 S 2017
Trojan Park: Welcome to the Parks Build Community Family [Cover story] P. M. Jacoby-Garrett *Parks & Recreation* v51 no12 p36 D 2016
URBAN PASTORALS S. W. Goldhagen bw color *Art in America* v105 no3 p88 Mr 2017

Park employees
See also
Park rangers
Parks Using Technology to Engage and Inspire T. Dellner *Parks & Recreation* v52 no5 p42 My 2017

Park lodging facilities
Drainage Pipe Lodge R. DAVIDSON color *National Geographic Kids* no475 p7 N 2017

Park management
It's All in the Details G. MULLINS-COHEN *Parks & Recreation* v52 no3 p10 Mr 2017
Public Park Usage: Motives and Challenges K. Roth *Parks & Recreation* v51 no10 p16 O 2016

Park management—Awards
The 'Why' for the National Gold Medal Award M. B. Thaman *Parks & Recreation* v52 no1 p42 Ja 2017

Park rangers
See also
Women park rangers
Parks Using Technology to Engage and Inspire T. Dellner *Parks & Recreation* v52 no5 p42 My 2017

Park Tool Co.
PARK TOOL X BICYCLING PEDAL WRENCH M. Yozell color *Bicycling* v58 no9 p54 O 2017
Pocket Heroes color *Bicycling* v58 no1 p84 Ja/F 2017

Parkas—Evaluation
Peak Performance J. CHEN bw color *Esquire* v166 no5 p56 D 2016/Ja 2017

Park Bench Joke, The (Poem)
The Park Bench Joke *Commentary* v140 no2 p10 S 2015

Parker, Ann
COMPUTATIONAL Innovation Boosts MANUFACTURING color *Science & Technology Review* p4 Ja/F 2017
NEW INSIGHT INTO AN INTRIGUING MATERIAL color graph *Science & Technology Review* p12 O/N 2016
SHOCKING COLLISIONS of Cosmological Proportions *Science & Technology Review* p20 Jl/Ag 2017

Parker, Ashley
THE NEW WHITE HOUSE REPORTERS A. Beaujon *Washing-*

tonian Magazine v52 no4 p49 Ja 2017
The World Is Watching color *Glamour* v115 no11 p115 N 2017

PARKER, BEN
Hidden Hitchcock *Film Quarterly* v70 no4 p135 Summ 2017

PARKER, BENJAMIN
The Acid Test of Dissent in Russia color *Weekly Standard* v22 no40 p15 Je 26 2017
Ticked Off color *Weekly Standard* v22 no43 p26 Jl 24 2017

Parker, David
Make 'Em Laugh K. BRADY *Dance Magazine* v90 no11 p34 N 2016

Parker, Eleanor
A Nation of Regions: Modern Britain is dominated economically, culturally and politically by London, its capital city. It was not always the way, as an examination of medieval texts reveals *History Today* v67 no7 p106 Jl 2017
Out of the Margins *History Today* v66 no11 p25 N 2016
Out of the margins *History Today* v67 no3 p25 Mr 2017
Points of Interest: Even the most obscure topic can be fascinating, and fascination can be found in the most unlikely places *History Today* v67 no9 p106 S 2017
The Queen's Encomium *History Today* v67 no5 p106 My 2017

Parker, Emily
Hack Job color *Foreign Affairs* v96 no3 p133 My/Je 2017
Mark Zuckerberg's Long March to China il *MIT Technology Review* v119 no6 p100 N/D 2016

Parker, Frieda
To engage students, give them meaningful choices in the classroom il *Phi Delta Kappan* v99 no2 p37 O 2017

Parker, Geoffrey G.
6 Reasons Platforms Fail *Harvard Business Review Digital Articles* p2 Mr 31 2016
Plant diversity increases with the strength of negative density dependence at the global scale diag *Science* v356 no6345 p1389 Je 30 2017

PARKER, IAN
ARE YOU MY MOTHER? cartoon color *New Yorker* v93 no14 p46 My 22 2017
BARGAIN BASEMENT cartoon *New Yorker* v93 no23 p20 Ag 7 2017
BEAUTIFUL RUINS cartoon *New Yorker* v93 no19 p21 Jl 3 2017
CASHLESS bw *New Yorker* v93 no28 p18 S 18 2017
THE CULLING cartoon color *New Yorker* v92 no45 p42 Ja 16 2017
MR. AMERICA cartoon *New Yorker* v93 no26 p50 S 4 2017
REAL WORK cartoon *New Yorker* v93 no18 p19 Je 26 2017
REDUX cartoon *New Yorker* v93 no26 p20 S 4 2017
TEMPS PERDU cartoon *New Yorker* v92 no33 p28 O 17 2016

Parker, James
Beowulf Is Back! color *Atlantic* v319 no3 p30 Ap 2017
The Bonfire of Humanity color *Atlantic* v320 no4 p32 N 2017
Bookends *New York Times Book Review* p31 O 30 2016
Dear Diary (Volume 1 of 148) *New York Times Book Review* p23 D 11 2016
The First Troll color *Atlantic* v318 no5 p28 D 2016
How Twin Peaks Invented Modern Television color *Atlantic* v319 no5 p28 Je 2017
The Joys of Binge-Watching *New York Times Book Review* p10 O 9 2016
The Ninja Cure for Anxiety color *Atlantic* v319 no1 p30 Ja/F 2017
A Saint for Difficult People bw *Atlantic* v319 no2 p32 Mr 2017
What Inspired the Summer of Love? cartoon *Atlantic* v320 no1 p32 Jl/Ag 2017
What's the best book, new or old, you read this year? *New York Times Book Review* p27 D 25 2016
When the World Is an Arcade cartoon *Atlantic* v318 no4 p40 N 2016
The Whitest Music Ever color *Atlantic* v320 no2 p32 S 2017

Parker, Joel
Anatomy of a COMET *Sky & Telescope* v133 no5 p14 My 2017

PARKER, JOHN N.
Synthesis Centers as Critical Research Infrastructure *BioScience* v67 no8 p750 Ag 2017

Parker, Joseph
A new evolutionary classic E. Pennisi color *Science* v354 no6314 p813 N 18 2016

place *Virginia Living* v15 no6 p11 O 2017

SEA CHANGE *Virginia Living* v15 no3 p13 Ap 2017

STYLE IS ETERNAL: Yves Saint Laurent exhibition makes only East Coast stop at VMFA *Virginia Living* v15 no4 p23 Je 2017

Parkin, Brian

Christoph Gebald and Jan Wurzbacher cartoon *Bloomberg Businessweek* no4537 p76 S 11 2017

PARKIN, JONATHAN

BETTER THAN BESPOKE color *House Beautiful* p139 Ag 2017

Parkin, Simon

PIONEERS color il *MIT Technology Review* v120 no5 p50 S/O 2017

SO SUBTLE A CATCH *Harper's Magazine* v333 no1999 p67 D 2016

Parking facilities

See also

Parking garages

The Never-Ending Mosque Parking Syndrome A. N. KASIM *Islamic Horizons* v46 no1 p50 Ja/F 2017

A Parking Garage for Bikes J. Zorthian color *Time* v190 no10/11 p29 S 18 2017

Parking garages

6 Things You Should Never Park in Your Garage B. NELSON color *Reader's Digest* v190 no1133 p44 S 2017

Parking Lot Symphony (Music)

TROMBONE SHORTY SPIRITUAL CONNECTION J. ODELL color *Downbeat* v84 no6 p48 Je 2017

Parking lots

The Beach Is for the Birds P. J. O'ROURKE cartoon *Reader's Digest* v190 no1132 p15 Jl/Ag 2017

IS THIS SPACE FREE? D. Reed color *Washingtonian Magazine* v52 no7 p49 Ap 2017

Malls A New Use For Empty Spaces H. Perlberg color *Bloomberg Businessweek* no4521 p40 My 8 2017

PARK AND SIGH A. WHITING *Washingtonian Magazine* v52 no8 p12 My 2017

Parking lots—Humor

Humor in Uniform J. MAYES cartoon *Reader's Digest* v190 no1132 p138 Jl/Ag 2017

Parking violations

THE END OF PARKING TICKETS M. Maciag chart color *Governing* v30 no11 p44 Ag 2017

THE THING THAT CHANGED IT ALL K. GARRISON color *Bicycling* v58 no9 p19 O 2017

Parkinson, Andrew

Schaefer Yachts 560 color *Power & Motoryacht* v33 no3 p54 Mr 2017

Parkinson, Cody

Missing: America's middle-educated workers *Monthly Labor Review* p1 Ag 2017

Parkinson, Jack

Global Citizenship color diag *Alternatives Journal (AJ) - Canada's Environmental Voice* v42 no3 p76 2016

PARKINSON, MARY JANE

ARISTOCRAT MARES *Arabian Horse World* v57 no12 p74 S 2017

Heritage Breeder: Abbas Pasha I *Arabian Horse World* v57 no11 p84 Ag 2017

Small Breeders BIG RESULTS *Arabian Horse World* v57 no9 p82 Je 2017

Wit and Wisdom: Alexander Keene Richards color *Arabian Horse World* v57 no7 p136 Ap 2017

Wit and Wisdom From our Early Breeders *Arabian Horse World* v57 no2 p130 N 2016

Wit and Wisdom From our Early Breeders *Arabian Horse World* v57 no4 p36 Ja 2017

Wit and Wisdom from Our Early Breeders: Garth and Joe Buchanan *Arabian Horse World* v57 no9 p134 Je 2017

Wit and Wisdom From Our Early Breeders: THE ED TWEED FAMILY *Arabian Horse World* v57 no11 p94 Ag 2017

Wit & Wisdom from Our Early Breeders: The Dr. Joseph L. Doyle Family *Arabian Horse World* v57 no10 p54 Jl 2017

Parkinson, Robert

The Captive Aliens Who Remain Our Shame A. Gordon-Reed cartoon *New York Review of Books* v64 no1 p54 Ja 19 2017

PARKINSON, SHADD

Simplify the Turn color *Horse & Rider* v56 no8 p42 Ag 2017

Parkinson's disease

Finding a new purpose for old drugs E. Y. Snyder color *Science* v357 no6354 p869 S 1 2017

Gut microbes may spark Parkinson's [Cover story] L. HAMERS color *Science News* v190 no13 p10 D 24 2016

The Kid Is Alright A. CORSELLO color *AARP: The Magazine* v60 no3A p44 Ap/My 2017

Parkinson's may begin in the gut L. SANDERS color *Science News* v190 no12 p12 D 10 2016

Pathological α-synuclein transmission initiated by binding lymphocyte-activation gene 3 M. T. Ou, S. S. Karuppagounder et al bibl graph *Science* v353 no6307 paah3374-1 S 30 2016

Virtual Reality S. ORNES color *Discover* v38 no6 p48 Jl/Ag 2017

Parkinson's disease diagnosis

Probing for Parkinson's A. Pycha color *Scientific American* v316 no6 p14 Je 2017

Parkinson's disease—Etiology

Immune receptor for pathogenic α-synuclein M. Jucker and M. Heikenwalder bibl diag *Science* v353 no6307 p1498 S 30 2016

Parkinson's disease—History

Microbial Targets Can Help Make Parkinson's History M. STONE *BioScience* v67 no5 p484 My 2017

Parkinson's disease—Patients

Teen Tech Times T. Mecia color *Weekly Standard* v22 no33 p22 My 8 2017

Parkinson's disease—Physiological aspects

Parkinson's may provoke T cells A. CUNNINGHAM *Science News* v192 no1 p14 Ag 5 2017

Parkinson's disease—Treatment

Venturing for a Cure color *Forbes* v199 no4 p90 Ap 25 2017

Parkland Health & Hospital System (Company)

Health Care Innovation Doesn't Have to Be Driven by Profit F. P. Cerise *Harvard Business Review Digital Articles* p2 D 4 2015

Parks

See also

Amusement parks

Botanical gardens

Historic parks

Landscape gardening

National parks & reserves

Urban parks

Zoos

2017 Education Highlights: The Golden Thread of Parks and Recreation T. Crosley *Parks & Recreation* v52 no8 p52 Ag 2017

Additional Park and Recreation Mapping and Data Resources: A variety of tools to help in planning a new facility or assessing a community's recreation needs D. Espada *Parks & Recreation* v52 no8 p12 Ag 2017

Bringing Whitewater Kayaking to Your Community B. Bevacqua *Parks & Recreation* v52 no4 p20 Ap 2017

The Charm of Cobb *Atlanta* v57 no2 p117 Je 2017

Content-Based Park Permit Decisions Unconstitutional J. C. Kozlowski *Parks & Recreation* v52 no10 p18 O 2017

From the Director's Chair S. Bartram *Parks & Recreation* v51 no10 p30 O 2016

The Health Benefits of Small Parks and Green Spaces K. L. Wolf *Parks & Recreation* v52 no4 p28 Ap 2017

How to Leverage Geocaching to Promote Park and Recreation Events A. Frank *Parks & Recreation* v52 no10 p52 O 2017

Introducing NRPA Park Metrics K. Roth *Parks & Recreation* v51 no11 p12 N 2016

Local Officials' Opinions About Local Park and Recreation Services A. G. Barrett and A. J. Mowen *Parks & Recreation* v52 no8 p48 Ag 2017

LOOK UP T. WHEATLEY *Atlanta* v56 no11 p22 Mr 2017

Member Spotlight: Jay Tryon V. Paynich *Parks & Recreation* v52 no5 p69 My 2017

Monarchs Visit NRPA Waystation R. J. Dolesh *Parks & Recreation* v51 no10 p96 O 2016

Notable News *Parks & Recreation* v51 no10 p32 O 2016

Park Champion of the Year: Portland's Som Subedi: Promoting equity and inclusion while ensuring congressional support for parks and recreation J. Rasmussen and C. Hodgkins *Parks & Recreation* v52 no10 p16 O 2017

Parks and Rec and BMX: Alternative programming for today's

youth N. Adams *Parks & Recreation* v52 no8 p16 Ag 2017

Peace Amid Chaos *Parks & Recreation* v52 no4 p64 Ap 2017

Products *Parks & Recreation* v52 no9 p110 S 2017

Restoration and Renewal S. K. TRAUTMAN *Parks & Recreation* v51 no10 p8 O 2016

SAFETY HARBOR, FLORIDA color *Runner's World* v52 no9 p8 O 2017

Social Equity: Plays Key Role in New Braunfels' New Recreation Center S. L. Dicke and S. Springs *Parks & Recreation* v52 no10 p40 O 2017

Splash Zones *Atlanta* v57 no2 p150 Je 2017

Think Healthy Across the Board G. Mullins-Cohen *Parks & Recreation* v52 no6 p10 Je 2017

A Threat to Our Legacy G. MULLINS-COHEN *Parks & Recreation* v52 no4 p10 Ap 2017

Wildlife in Winter *South Dakota Magazine* v32 no4 p107 N/D 2016

Parks & Recreation (Periodical)

Hate Has No Place Here G. MULLINS-COHEN *Parks & Recreation* v52 no9 p10 S 2017

Parks & Recreation (TV program)

The Nicest Evil Girl in the World: Aubrey Plaza knows you want her to be mean to you, and she's happy to oblige A. P. Davis img *New York* v50 no15 p34 Jl 24 2017

NICK KROLL D. BLASBERG color *Vanity Fair* v58 no12 p92 D 2016

PLAZA SUITE B. HANDY color *Vanity Fair* v59 no8 p94 Ag 2017

Will Parks and Recreation Predict 2017? D. Snierson color *Entertainment Weekly* no1449 p50 Ja 20 2017

Parks & recreation commissions (Government)

Advocacy Through Storytelling J. Rasmussen *Parks & Recreation* v51 no12 p18 D 2016

Member Spotlight: Patty Wieliczko V. Paynich *Parks & Recreation* v51 no12 p44 D 2016

NRPA Research Year in Review K. Roth *Parks & Recreation* v51 no12 p12 D 2016

Passport to Fun! S. Myrick *Parks & Recreation* v51 no12 p56 D 2016

Research. Parks and Recreation: Meeting Community Fitness Needs at All Levels K. Roth *Parks & Recreation* v52 no6 p12 Je 2017

Rural Park and Recreation Agencies Struggle to Find Funding B. TULIPANE *Parks & Recreation* v51 no12 p6 D 2016

Setting the Table for a Successful Summer at South Burlington Recreation and Parks H. Baker and B. Leonard *Parks & Recreation* v51 no12 p28 D 2016

Parks, Aaron

Aaron Parks T. PANKEN color *Downbeat* v83 no11 p106 N 2016

Parks, Bill

Mini church replica looms large in Elgin A. J. BARTELS color *Nebraska Life* v21 no6 p44 N/D 2017

Parks, Brad

The Book That Scared Me B. PARKS color *Publishers Weekly* v264 no5 p178 Ja 30 2017

Say Nothing *Publishers Weekly* v264 no2 p40 Ja 9 2017

Parks, Donovan H.

On the origins of oxygenic photosynthesis and aerobic respiration in Cyanobacteria chart diag *Science* v355 no6332 p1436 Mr 31 2017

PARKS, JOSH

THE BIG GAMERS cartoon color *Field & Stream* v121 no7 p82 D 2016/Ja 2017

THIS LAND WAS YOUR LAND cartoon color diag map *Field & Stream* v122 no1 p40 My 2017

Parks, Phaedra

CHEERS & JEERS D. HOLBROOK *TV Guide* v65 no21 p84 My 15 2017

Sound Bites color *Entertainment Weekly* no1449 p10 Ja 20 2017

Parks, Richard

GOD, GUNS, AND OIL B. SMIETANA color *Christianity Today* v61 no7 p46 S 2017

Parks, Rosa, 1913-2005

Conscientious Consumerism: Making Black Dollars Matter E. G. Graves color *Black Enterprise* v47 no2 p6 S 2016

I, TOO, AM AMERICA M. Norris bw color *National Geographic*

v230 no4 p116 O 2016

Parks, Stella

Bravetart: Iconic American Desserts *Publishers Weekly* v264 no18 p52 My 1 2017

THE SOUTHERN LIVING COOKIE COOKBOOK color *Southern Living* v51 no12 p190 D 2016

Parks, Suzan-Lori, 1963-

MOTHER! H. ALS cartoon *New Yorker* v93 no30 p76 O 2 2017

Parks, Tim

A Game of Love and Chance bw color *New York Review of Books* v64 no10 p44 Je 8 2017

How Mary Anne Became George bw *New York Review of Books* v64 no17 p49 N 9 2017

International Literature *New York Times Book Review* p35 O 23 2016

Montaigne: What Was Truly Courageous? cartoon *New York Review of Books* v63 no18 p59 N 24 2016

Mr. Smith Goes to Rome [Cover story] bw color *New York Review of Books* v64 no15 p25 O 12 2017

Roving Eye: International Literature *New York Times Book Review* p27 D 18 2016

Roving Eye *New York Times Book Review* p27 F 12 2017

Parks Canada

Born to be wild A. Pope cartoon map *Canadian Geographic* v137 no1 p28 F 2017

Park It! F. Los color *Canadian Wildlife* v23 no2 p19 My/Je 2017

Parks for dogs

A COMMUNITY, UNLEASHED: The NoMa dog park opens this fall. It got built thanks to 400 neighbors who sneaked onto a vacant, muddy lot D. Bruno *Washingtonian Magazine* v53 no1 p213 O 2017

How the City of Keller, Texas, Built a Dog Agility Course S. Myrick *Parks & Recreation* v52 no2 p49 F 2017

The Urbanist: The Best & Worst Cities to Be a Dog img *New York* v49 no15 p22 Jl 25 2016

Parks—Arizona

And So It Grows *Arizona Highways* v93 no3 p5 Mr 2017

Climate Change, Parks and Health R. J. Dolesh *Parks & Recreation* v52 no6 p30 Je 2017

Etched in Stone *Arizona Highways* v92 no7 p56 Jl 2016

HUNTER TRAIL R. STIEVE *Arizona Highways* v93 no3 p54 Mr 2017

Solemn Beauty *Arizona Highways* v93 no8 p56 Ag 2017

Parks—Awards

National 'Meet Me at the Park' Grant Recipients Selected *Parks & Recreation* v52 no9 p100 S 2017

Parks—California—San Francisco

Boeddeker Park L. Lee *Architectural Record* v205 no4 p182 Ap 2017

Parks—Connecticut

Stepping into Another World S. SLOSBERG color *Yankee* p95 Mr 2017

Parks—Conservation & restoration

I REDISCOVERED ARMSTRONG PARK C. ROSE color *New Orleans Magazine* v51 no2 p46 D 2016

Saving Atlanta's Centennial Olympic Park from Concert Damage R. W. Cohen *Parks & Recreation* v51 no12 p48 D 2016

Parks—Economic aspects

The Economic Benefit of Downtown Parks C. Bowen *Parks & Recreation* v52 no9 p54 S 2017

Parks—Employees

Green Workers Certification May Create New Training Opportunities R. J. Dolesh *Parks & Recreation* v51 no10 p54 O 2016

Member Spotlight: Adriane Clutter V. Paynich *Parks & Recreation* v52 no4 p54 Ap 2017

Parks—England

LAKE COMPOUNCE *Yankee* p25 Jl 2017

Parks—Equipment & supplies

Products *Parks & Recreation* v51 no10 p90 O 2016

Products *Parks & Recreation* v52 no4 p58 Ap 2017

Parks—Evaluation

Creating a Vibrant Public Space on the Lafitte Greenway: Parks Build Community project to add several amenities to the southeast portion of the greenway P. Jacoby-Garrett *Parks & Recreation* v52 no8 p44 Ag 2017

HUNTER TRAIL R. STIEVE *Arizona Highways* v93 no3 p54 Mr

2017

Last Look D. Kidd *Governing* v30 no8 p64 My 2017

The Loop That Leads You Home *Yankee* p91 Mr 2017

Nathan Benderson Park: A Classic Reclamation Project R. Sullivan *Parks & Recreation* v51 no10 p28 O 2016

A PARK FOR VINE CITY S. HENRY *Atlanta* v56 no9 p24 Ja 2017

Restorative Healing at Youth Visions Relection Park S. Bartram *Parks & Recreation* v51 no10 p58 O 2016

Stepping into Another World S. SLOSBERG color *Yankee* p95 Mr 2017

Parks—Finance

What Drives Public Officials' Budget Priorities? K. Roth *Parks & Recreation* v52 no10 p12 O 2017

Parks—Florida

Key Biscayne Parks and Recreation Protects Its Citizens from Severe Weather E. Carp *Parks & Recreation* v52 no5 p47 My 2017

SEBASTIAN INLET FLORIDA, UNITED STATES OF AMERICA Z. MORTON color *Surfer* v58 no4 p62 Ag 2017

Parks—France

Take Me to the River C. FOGES color *Architectural Record* v205 no8 p96 Ag 2017

Parks—Georgia

See also

Piedmont Park (Atlanta, Ga.)

Buckhead Park Over GA400 *Architectural Record* v205 no4 p214 Ap 2017

Parks—Idaho

Packing the Tot C. BONK *Idaho Magazine* v16 no5 p23 F 2017

Parks—Indiana

See also

White River State Park (Indianapolis, Ind.)

Mounds STATE PARK R. Annis, S. Bahr et al color map *Indianapolis Monthly* v41 no2 p60 S 2017

Riverside PARK R. Annis, S. Bahr et al color map *Indianapolis Monthly* v41 no2 p68 S 2017

Parks—Law & legislation

Park Permit for Commercial Wedding Photos J. C. Kozlowski *Parks & Recreation* v52 no4 p22 Ap 2017

Parks—Louisiana

Creating a Vibrant Public Space on the Lafitte Greenway: Parks Build Community project to add several amenities to the southeast portion of the greenway P. Jacoby-Garrett *Parks & Recreation* v52 no8 p44 Ag 2017

HAPPY (HEALTHY) TRAILS F. Esker *Louisiana Life* v37 no6 p11 Jl/Ag 2017

I REDISCOVERED ARMSTRONG PARK C. ROSE color *New Orleans Magazine* v51 no2 p46 D 2016

Outliers: Is opportunity knocking in the suburbs? P. Reichard *New Orleans Homes & Lifestyles* v20 no3 p94 Summ 2017

Parks—Maintenance

Grassroots Park Stewardship: A Force of Change L. S. Boykin and K. T. Trainor *Parks & Recreation* v51 no10 p36 O 2016

Green Infrastructure R. J. Dolesh *Parks & Recreation* v52 no4 p42 Ap 2017

NWF joins The Nut Job 2 to protect our parks color *National Wildlife (World Edition)* v55 no5 p48 Ag/S 2017

Parks—Missouri

Celebrating Community and People G. MULLINS-COHEN *Parks & Recreation* v51 no12 p8 D 2016

Dark in the Parks L. A. ADDINGTON chart color map *Missouri Life* v44 no3 p28 My 2017

St. Louis Parks and Green Spaces P. M. Jacoby-Garrett *Parks & Recreation* v51 no10 p66 O 2016

Parks—New Hampshire

The Loop That Leads You Home *Yankee* p91 Mr 2017

A 'Very Impressive Rock' J. SHIPLEY and M. SEAMANS bw color *Yankee* p20 My/Je 2017

Parks—New York (State)

TINY INSECT—BIG IMPACT S. Walsh *New York State Conservationist* v71 no3 p14 D 2016

Parks—New York (State)—New York

The Lowline D. A. Ciampaglia *Architectural Record* v205 no4 p213 Ap 2017

Parks—North Carolina

Park Bench. Nomadic Nourishment in NorCal C. Jones *Parks &*

Recreation v52 no6 p56 Je 2017

Parks—Ontario

See also

Algonquin Provincial Park (Ont.)

THE CALL OF Algonquin R. MACGREGOR color map *Canadian Geographic* v137 no1 p64 F 2017

Parks—Pennsylvania

Celebrating Community and People G. MULLINS-COHEN *Parks & Recreation* v51 no12 p8 D 2016

From Steel to Green: Revitalizing Pittsburgh Through Its Park System: The Pittsburgh Parks Conservancy shares lessons learned as it celebrates 20 years S. Roller *Parks & Recreation* v52 no8 p18 Ag 2017

'Good' Times in Pennsylvania T. Herd *Parks & Recreation* v52 no2 p18 F 2017

Parks—Singapore

SUSTAINABILITY color *National Geographic* v232 no5 p10 N 2017

Parks—Social aspects

Creating Safe Routes to Parks D. Merriam, E. Sauer et al *Parks & Recreation* v52 no9 p46 S 2017

The Economic Benefit of Downtown Parks C. Bowen *Parks & Recreation* v52 no9 p54 S 2017

Unconscious Bias in Parks and Recreation A. Holliday and A. Rajagopal-Durbin *Parks & Recreation* v52 no2 p32 F 2017

Parks—Societies, etc.

Empowering Youth to Care for Local Parks and Their Neighborhoods M. Talbert *Parks & Recreation* v52 no8 p30 Ag 2017

Now Available: The Annual Summary of Key Findings from NRPA Park Metrics *Parks & Recreation* v52 no4 p53 Ap 2017

Parks—Texas

See also

Brazos Bend State Park (Tex.)

Confluence Park M. Sitz *Architectural Record* v205 no4 p208 Ap 2017

ESTERO LLANO GRANDE *Texas Monthly* v45 no4 p107 Ap 2017

Last Look D. Kidd *Governing* v30 no8 p64 My 2017

The Stars at Night F. ROSS *Texas Monthly* v45 no4 p56 Ap 2017

Parks—United States

Designing Parks for Health J. Lombard *Parks & Recreation* v51 no10 p77 O 2016

Instant Awesome M. HORJUS and R. Wichelns color map *Backpacker* p76 Je 2017

NRPA Park Pulse *Parks & Recreation* v51 no10 p85 O 2016

NRPA Park Pulse *Parks & Recreation* v52 no10 p14 O 2017

PARK YOURSELF HERE M. Graham color *Washingtonian Magazine* v52 no7 p116 Ap 2017

A Path to Leadership G. MULLINS-COHEN *Parks & Recreation* v52 no5 p10 My 2017

weekend getaways: nature *Washingtonian Magazine* v52 no11 p93 Ag 2017

Parks—Washington (D.C.)—Design & construction

11th Street Bridge Park Washington, D.C *Architectural Record* v205 no4 p212 Ap 2017

Park West Gallery (Southfield, Mich.)

To the Tipsy Guy on the Lido Deck! V. SILVER color *Bloomberg Businessweek* no4504 p50 D 19 2016

PARLA, KATIE

Rome bw chart color map *Conde Nast Traveler* v52 no3 p52 Mr 2017

Parloff, Roger

THE 2017 Fortune Crystal Ball color diag *Fortune* v174 no7 p11 D 1 2016

Parmar, Belinda

50 Companies That Get Twitter - and 50 That Don't *Harvard Business Review Digital Articles* p2 Ap 27 2015

Corporate Empathy Is Not an Oxymoron *Harvard Business Review Digital Articles* p2 Ja 8 2015

Parmar, Bidhan L.

The Link Between Income Inequality and Physical Pain *Harvard Business Review Digital Articles* p2 Mr 21 2016

PARMAR, PRIYA

VICTORIA'S SECRETS color *New York Times Book Review* p20 D 4 2016

Parmesan cheese

Eat these for healthier eyes M. TAYLOR color *Redbook* p82 S 2017

Fast and Flavorful L. TYRELL color *Martha Stewart Living* p88 O 2017

Parnass, Alexandra

BEAUTY NEWS color *Harper's Bazaar* no3653 p238 My 2017

BEAUTY NEWS color *Harper's Bazaar* no3654 p112 Je/Jl 2017

BEAUTY NEWS color *Harper's Bazaar* no3657 p194 O 2017

My LIST: 24 hours with Natalie Portman color *Harper's Bazaar* no3656 p236 S 2017

Packing LIST color *Harper's Bazaar* no3653 p93 My 2017

Parnassus Investments (Company)

Investing With a Conscience A. K. SMITH chart color *Kiplinger's Personal Finance* v71 no7 p54 Jl 2017

Parnaudeau, Miia

Severe Weather Threatens Businesses. It's Time to Measure and Disclose the Risks *Harvard Business Review Digital Articles* p2 S 14 2017

Parnell, Andrew C.

Regional and global sea-surface temperatures during the last interglaciation color graph *Science* v355 no6322 p276 Ja 20 2017

Parnes, Amie

What Doomed Clinton? M. O'Brien Steinfels color *Commonweal* v144 no15 p39 S 22 2017

Parnes, Sam

REMEMBERING PEARL HARBOR *Saturday Evening Post* v288 no6 p6 N/D 2016

Parno, D. S.

Observation of coherent elastic neutrino-nucleus scattering diag *Science* v357 no6356 p1123 S 15 2017

Parody

Portraying and Parodying Patroons A. Morrow bw *American History* v52 no3 p54 Ag 2017

Parody television programs

PBS: WHAT'S AT STAKE J. RUSSELL *TV Guide* p6 Ap 17 2017

Parole

JUVENILE LIFERS' LAST CHANCE J. PISHKO bw color *Nation* v305 no1 p18 Jl 3 2017

Paroxysmal hemoglobinuria—Treatment

Living Life to the Fullest with a Rare Blood Disorder, Thanks to Innovative Therapies M. Sponagle *Maclean's* v130 no9 p37 O 2017

PARR, AMANDA

Assessing National Biodiversity Trends for Rocky and Coral Reefs through the Integration of Citizen Science and Scientific Monitoring Programs *BioScience* v67 no2 p134 F 2017

Parr, Ben

7 Ways to Capture Someone's Attention *Harvard Business Review Digital Articles* p2 Mr 3 2015

Parra, A.

Observation of a large-scale anisotropy in the arrival directions of cosmic rays above 8 × 1018 eV *Science* v357 no6357 p1266 S 22 2017

Parren, Paul W. H. I.

Hitting Ebola, to the power of two bibl diag *Science* v354 no6310 p284 O 21 2016

PARRENO, PHILIPPE

Sarah MORRIS *Interview* v47 no2 p78 Mr 2017

Parrington, John

Tinkering with evolution A. Woolfson color *Science* v354 no6313 p712 N 11 2016

Parris, Michael

TOOLS THEY USE color *Popular Mechanics* p96 F 2017

PARRISH, JULIA K.

Teaching Biology in the Field: Importance, Challenges, and Solutions *BioScience* v67 no6 p558 Je 2017

Parrish, Susan Scott

The Flood Year 1927: A Cultural History *Publishers Weekly* v263 no45 p53 N 7 2016

Parrot behavior

A Laughing Matter color *Earth Island Journal* v32 no2 p5 Summ 2017

Parrott, Elizabeth S.

Perovskite-perovskite tandem photovoltaics with optimized band gaps bibl chart graph *Science* v354 no6314 p861 N 18 2016

Parrott, Jeff

A chance to retreat: Spiritual retreats help those who struggle with homelessness and addiction move forward color *U.S. Catholic* v82 no10 p32 O 2017

Land of plenty color *U.S. Catholic* v82 no6 p12 Je 2017

Parrott, Nicki

NIGHT LIFE *New Yorker* v93 no16 p24 Je 5 2017

Parry, Kate

You Never Forget Your First Time diag il *Backpacker* v45 no2 p64 Mr 2017

Parry, Richard Lloyd

Wave of Anguish: Could disobedience have saved a group of Japanese students? A. HOCHSCHILD *American Scholar* v86 no4 p114 Aut 2017

WHAT REMAINS R. L. Parry *Harper's Magazine* p11 O 2017

Parry, Stephen

A Lighter Mainsail color *Sail* v48 no9 p54 S 2017

Parry, Tyler D.

Man's Best Fiend *History Today* v66 no12 p50 D 2016

Parry, William Edward, 1790-1855

The Sun's crystal horns S. J. O'MEARA color *Astronomy* v45 no2 p18 F 2017

Parsegov, Sergey E.

Network science on belief system dynamics under logic constraints bibl diag graph *Science* v354 no6310 p321 O 21 2016

Parshley, Lois

ARTIFICIAL SKIN FROM THE SEA color diag *Bloomberg Businessweek* no4529 p58 Jl 3 2017

PARSI, NOVID

THE AGITATOR color *Chicago* v66 no5 p48 My 2017

ALMOST FAMOUS color *Chicago* v66 no11 p37 N 2017

BOOK OF FEARS color *Chicago* v66 no8 p42 Ag 2017

BOYS ON THE SIDE color *Chicago* v66 no1 p31 Ja 2017

COMING TO AMERICA bw color *Chicago* v66 no3 p47 Mr 2017

THE HUNTING ACCIDENT bw color *Chicago* v66 no9 p124 S 2017

A STAR IS REBORN color *Chicago* v65 no11 p37 N 2016

STEVE CONRAD bw color *Chicago* v66 no2 p30 F 2017

THE UPCYCLE ARTIST color *Chicago* v66 no7 p25 Jl 2017

WHY WE LOVE CHICAGO bw cartoon color *Chicago* v66 no3 p75 Mr 2017

Parsi, Trita

Losing an Enemy: Obama, Iran, and the Triumph of Diplomacy *Publishers Weekly* v264 no19 p48 My 8 2017

Parsifal (Theatrical production)

Bayreuth J. Leipsic *Opera News* v81 no5 p46 N 2016

Parsley

Herbs and spices with benefits A. B. Kay, A. Rumsey et al cartoon *Redbook* p87 Mr 2017

MUSSELS, REBOOTED M. HENNESSY color *Chicago* v65 no11 p60 N 2016

Parslow, Tristram G.

Sustained virologic control in SIV+ macaques after antiretroviral and α4β7 antibody therapy bibl graph *Science* v354 no6309 p197 O 14 2016

PARSON, EDWARD A.

Climate engineering *Issues in Science & Technology* v33 no4 p5 Summ 2017

Parsonages

(SUB)URBAN E. EICHINGER color *Chicago* v66 no9 p90 S 2017

Parsons, Bob

TEE FOR 'TUDE M. BURKE color *Forbes* v200 no5 p81 N 14 2017

Parsons, Bob—Interviews

Bob Parsons J. Marksbury color *Golf Magazine* v59 no9 p43 S 2017

Parsons, Charles

OUR MAN IN MANILA: HIS CLANDESTINE MISSIONS WERE VITAL TO MACARTHUR'S FAMED RETURN TO THE PHILIPPINES, YET THE FULL STORY OF CHICK PARSONS' DARING FEATS HAS NOT BEEN TOLD--UNTIL NOW P. EISNER *Smithsonian* v48 no5 p42 S 2017

Parsons, Jim, 1973-

A Tale of Two Sheldons D. Franich, N. Abrams et al color *Entertainment Weekly* no1482/1483 p44 S 22 2017

Parsons, Matthew

Adaptation *Science* v356 no6335 p243 Ap 21 2017

Parsons, Mikeal C.

Adoration of the Magi *Christian Century* v133 no25 p47 D 7 2016

Christ and the Woman of Samaria at the Well by Guercino (Giovanni Francesco Barbieri) color *Christian Century* v134 no5 p47 Mr 1 2017

Crucifixion color *Christian Century* v134 no1 p47 Ja 4 2017

Gathering Manna in the Desert color *Christian Century* v134 no19 p47 S 13 2017

The Good Shepherd, early fourth century, Museo Pio Cristiano, Vatican color *Christian Century* v134 no9 p39 Ap 26 2017

ON Art *Christian Century* v134 no13 p47 Je 21 2017

St. Peter Walking on Water color *Christian Century* v134 no15 p47 Jl 19 2017

The Supper at Emmaus color *Christian Century* v134 no7 p47 Mr 29 2017

Transfiguration color *Christian Century* v134 no3 p39 F 2017

Trinity with Saint Jerome color *Christian Century* v134 no11 p47 My 24 2017

PARSONS, WILLIAM B.

SBNR PAST & PRESENT cartoon *Tricycle: The Buddhist Review* v26 no3 p48 Spr 2017

Parsons Xtreme Golf LLC

Bob Parsons J. Marksbury color *Golf Magazine* v59 no9 p43 S 2017

Part-time employees

The Problem with Part- Time Work Is That It's Rarely Part-Time L. Vanderkam *Harvard Business Review Digital Articles* p2 My 26 2015

Part-time employees—Medical care

Repealing Obamacare Would Be Bad News for the Gig Economy D. Mulcahy *Harvard Business Review Digital Articles* p2 F 13 2017

Part-time employment—United States

LEGENDS LIST C. Zillman color *Fortune* v175 no4 p92 Mr 15 2017

The New Work J. B. Wogan *Governing* v31 no1 p50 O 2017

No Time Off M. LINDBERG *Education Digest* v82 no5 p36 Ja 2017

Part-time jobs that pay more than $20 per hour E. Torpey chart color img *Career Outlook* p1 Je 2017

Underemployment among Hispanics: the case of involuntary part-time work J. R. Young and M. J. Mattingly *Monthly Labor Review* p1 D 2016

Partanen, Anu

The Nordic Theory of Everything: In Search of a Better Life A. Moravcsik *Foreign Affairs* v95 no6 p181 N/D 2016

Partch, Carrie L.

Structural basis of the day-night transition in a bacterial circadian clock bibl diag *Science* v355 no6330 p1174 Mr 17 2017

Parthemore, Christine

The ambiguity challenge: Why the world needs a multilateral nuclear cruise missile agreement bibl *Bulletin of the Atomic Scientists* v73 no3 p154 My 2017

Parthenogenesis

A ONE-PARENT FAMILY, LITERALLY P. Edmonds color *National Geographic* v232 no5 p29 N 2017

Parti québécois

Behind the curve M. PATRIQUIN color *Maclean's* v129 no42 p28 O 24 2016

Participation

See also

Parent participation in education

School involvement

Social action

How to Prevent Bible Study Dropouts J. Wilkin *Christianity Today* v61 no6 p28 Jl/Ag 2017

Polite Ways to Decline a Meeting Invitation L. Davey *Harvard Business Review Digital Articles* p2 My 17 2016

Particle accelerators

See also

Superconducting Super Collider

Degas' Other Woman N. SCHARPING cartoon *Discover* v38 no1 p91 Ja/F 2017

THE LARGE HADRON COLLIDER: AN ORAL HISTORY E. G. ELLIS bw color *Wired* v25 no7 p20 Jl 2017

ULTRAPERIPHERAL NUCLEAR COLLISIONS S. Klein and J. Nystrand *Physics Today* v70 no10 p40 O 2017

Particle physics

See also

Collisions (Nuclear physics)

Cosmic rays

Particle accelerators

Synchrotron radiation

Anniversaries for particle physics M. Mangano color *Science* v356 no6344 p1213 Je 23 2017

HIDDEN WORLDS of fundamental particles D. Curtin and R. Sundrum *Physics Today* v70 no6 p46 Je 2017

NEW BOOKS *Physics Today* v70 no9 p62 S 2017

Notes on the New Big Science P. Foukal *Physics Today* v70 no3 p12 Mr 2017

Particles

See also

Nanoparticles

DANCING QUEEN *Iceland Review* v54 no6 p126 N/D 2016

NEW PARTICLE FIZZLES, LEAVING PHYSICISTS TO SOUL SEARCH N. SCHARPING color *Discover* v38 no1 p20 Ja/F 2017

Probing the frontiers of particle physics with tabletop-scale experiments D. DeMille, J. M. Doyle et al color graph *Science* v357 no6355 p990 S 8 2017

Particles (Nuclear physics)

See also

Bosons

Fermions

Quasiparticles (Physics)

HIDDEN WORLDS of fundamental particles D. Curtin and R. Sundrum *Physics Today* v70 no6 p46 Je 2017

Particles—Research

Uncovering the Ocean's Biological Pump D. Ohnemus color *Oceanus* v51 no2 p52 Wint 2016

Partido Comunista de España

Soviet Spain? R. Radosh *Commentary* v142 no3 p10 O 2016

Parties

See also

Halloween parties

Office parties

4 Reasons to Kill the Office Holiday Party—and One Reason to Save It J. Kirby *Harvard Business Review Digital Articles* p2 D 17 2014

ABOVE & BEYOND *New Yorker* v93 no25 p20 Ag 28 2017

THE ABROAD-ROBE N. SULLIVAN bw color *Esquire* p46 My 2017

Best-Dressed LIST color *Harper's Bazaar* no3652 p104 Ap 2017

A Bountiful Life A. SULLIVAN color *Nebraska Life* v21 no4 p76 Jl/Ag 2017

BY THE NUMBERS R. E. Maltby Jr. *Harper's Magazine* v334 no2001 p95 F 2017

Cake pops and communion wafers M. J. Rose color *U.S. Catholic* v82 no3 p22 Mr 2017

DAN ABOUT TOWN *Washingtonian Magazine* v52 no3 p28 D 2016

ENTERTAINMENT WEEKLY'S SAG-ADELIC PARTY color *Entertainment Weekly* no1453 p4 F 17 2017

How to Be a Holiday Boozetender R. McCAMMON color *GQ: Gentlemen's Quarterly* v97 no11 p50 N 2017

Inter Continental Los Angeles Downtown *Los Angeles Magazine* v62 no9 p86 S 2017

Interview 15 MINUTES *Interview* v47 no1 p19 F 2017

In the SUNSET GARDEN color *Sunset* v239 no1 p56 Jl 2017

KICK IT WITH YOUR COLLEAGUES A. Cohen, M. Koester et al color *Bloomberg Businessweek* no4525 p55 Je 5 2017

Ladies' Night R. Apodaca color *InStyle* v24 no4 p82 Ap 2017

MY RECIPE FOR SUCCESS color *Bon Appetit* v62 no10 p12 O 2017

OR BE THE FIRST TO PARTY AT ... A. SCHREIBER img *New York* v50 no12 p66 Je 12 2017

The Parties B. Fowler, J. Ferrise et al color *InStyle* v23 no12 p84 N 2016

A place at the table M. Murphy-Gill color *U.S. Catholic* v82 no6 p31 Je 2017

POUR KILL A BEER! bw color diag *Men's Health* v32 no6 p106

Ag 2017

ROCK THE BLOCK A. RAO color *Chicago* v66 no7 p52 Jl 2017

School's Over, Let's Party! C. THORP color *Seventeen* v76 no3 p106 My 2017

STATEWIDE EVENTS N. BUCK color *Nebraska Life* v21 no4 p85 Jl/Ag 2017

A Taste of Relativity P. Tyson *Sky & Telescope* v134 no1 p4 Jl 2017

TENDER IS THE NIGHT A. RAPOPORT color *Bon Appetit* v61 no12 p18 D 2016 /Jan2017

TRAUMARAMA color *Seventeen* v76 no2 p132 Mr 2017

THE ULTIMATE TAILGATE GRILL TEST M. SULA color *Popular Mechanics* p34 Jl 2017

A Western weekend M. CAMPBELL chart color *Maclean's* v130 no2 p60 Mr 2017

Parties—Equipment & supplies

PARTY station A. PANOS color *Better Homes & Gardens* v95 no6 p94 Je 2017

Parties—Management

BANGIN' BASH (On a Budget) N. M. Pittmon color *Ebony* v72 no9 p54 Jl/Ag 2017

The Tao of Hosting J. GORDINIER bw color *Esquire* v166 no5 p33 D 2016/Ja 2017

Partiia sotsialistov-revoliutsionerov (Political Party : Russia)

HOUSE OF SHADOWS J. YAFFA cartoon color *New Yorker* v93 no32 p34 O 16 2017

Parting Glances (Film)

Parting Glances M. CONNOLLY color *Film Comment* v53 no1 p64 Ja/F 2017

Partington, Richard

Digital Banks Take On The High Street Giants *Bloomberg Businessweek* no4493 p50 O 3 2016

Where Paper Checks Go—for Now cartoon *Bloomberg Businessweek* no4497 p41 O 31 2016

Partisanship

DIVIDED WE FALL G. SITARAMAN color *New Republic* v248 no5 p42 My 2017

How Unfair Is the Map? A new measurement may identify gerrymandering A. Greenblatt *Governing* v30 no8 p17 My 2017

In Praise of Politics il *America* v215 no12 p5 O 24 2016

KEN BURNS: VIETNAM J. WOLF *Saturday Evening Post* v289 no5 p32 S/O 2017

The Political Gets Personal *America* v216 no5 p8 Mr 6 2017

The Republican's Party S. Kapur *Bloomberg Businessweek* no4517 p27 Ap 3 2017

Skepticism Should Be Nonpartisan R. A. Billinghurst, W. A. Robinson et al *Skeptical Inquirer* v41 no3 p63 My/Je 2017

Partlow, Joshua

Afghanistan: Obama's Sad Legacy C. Gall color *New York Review of Books* v64 no1 p31 Ja 19 2017

Partnership (Business)

Big Companies Should Collaborate with Startups E. Yoon and S. Hughes *Harvard Business Review Digital Articles* p2 F 25 2016

Building Better Cause-Marketing Relationships T. L. Kuntz and R. B. Dieser *Parks & Recreation* v52 no5 p60 My 2017

Collaborating Well in Large Global Teams H. K. Gardner and M. Mortensen *Harvard Business Review Digital Articles* p2 Jl 1 2015

Don't Base Business Partnerships on Personal Chemistry B. Gomes-Casseres *Harvard Business Review Digital Articles* p2 O 2 2015

Don't Take Money from VCs Until You've Asked 4 Questions D. Mulcahy *Harvard Business Review Digital Articles* p2 F 26 2016

LG's Channel Plus M. Fleischmann and C. Crowley color *Sound & Vision* v81 no10 p17 D 2016

Lilly Pulitzer's Target Disaster Was Actually a Success D. Lee Yohn *Harvard Business Review Digital Articles* p2 My 22 2015

Making Hospital Partnerships Work P. Pawlak and R. Colby *Harvard Business Review Digital Articles* p2 D 10 2015

Our Colleges Are-Finally-Neighborhood shapers D. REED color *Washingtonian Magazine* v52 no7 p110 Ap 2017

The Prenup That Didn't Stick B. Einhorn, I. Marlow et al chart color *Bloomberg Businessweek* no4498 p25 N 7 2016

ROLEX PARTNERS WITH NATIONAL GEOGRAPHIC ON A VITAL MISSION G. E. Knell color *National Geographic* v232

no1 p9 Jl 2017

When Start-ups Should (and Shouldn't) Partner with Industry Leaders T. Bartman *Harvard Business Review Digital Articles* p2 O 9 2014

Whole Foods Market *American Forests* v122 no3 p10 Fall 2016

Partnership (Business)—United States

This Coalition of 20 Companies Thinks It Can Change U.S. Health Care L. A. Martin, A. H. Anderson et al *Harvard Business Review Digital Articles* p2 F 24 2016

Partnerships in education

Cultivating a school-university partnership for teacher learning C. H. Reischl, D. Khasnabis et al color *Phi Delta Kappan* v98 no8 p48 My 2017

What does it take to sustain a productive partnership in education? K. Hammerness, A. MacPherson et al color *Phi Delta Kappan* v99 no1 p15 S 2017

Partnoy, Frank

Are Index Funds Evil? color *Atlantic* v320 no2 p24 S 2017

Parton, Dolly, 1946-—Interviews

DOLLY'S TRUE COLORS I. RUDOLPH *TV Guide* v64 no48 p28 N 21 2016

Parton, R. G.

A microtubule-organizing center directing intracellular transport in the early mouse embryo diag *Science* v357 no6354 p925 S 1 2017

Parton, Raan

"NO ONE WILL HELP YOU RUSH THROUGH SECURITY IF YOU LOOK LIKE YOU JUST ROLLED OUT OF BED." A. WHITTLE color *Conde Nast Traveler* v52 no5 p28 My 2017

Parton, Shea

"NO ONE WILL HELP YOU RUSH THROUGH SECURITY IF YOU LOOK LIKE YOU JUST ROLLED OUT OF BED." A. WHITTLE color *Conde Nast Traveler* v52 no5 p28 My 2017

Parturition

Ancient marine reptile gave live birth E. S. EATON color *Science News* v191 no5 p9 Mr 18 2017

Party Down (Film)

What You Should Know About ADAM SCOTT D. KAMP bw *Vanity Fair* p108 Hollywood 2017 Supplement

Party for Freedom (Political party : Netherlands)

Dutch election highlights divisions about religion and immigration M. Richards and Z. F. Parvez *Christian Century* v134 no8 p1 Ap 12 2017

Paruelo, José

Forest conservation: Remember Gran Chaco bibl color *Science* v355 no6324 p465 F 3 2017

Parui, Subir

A molecular spin-photovoltaic device color diag *Science* v357 no6352 p677 Ag 18 2017

Paruroctonus

Nothing to Fear W. Lynch color *Canadian Wildlife* v22 no5 p46 N/D 2016

Parvez, Z. Fareen

Dutch election highlights divisions about religion and immigration *Christian Century* v134 no8 p1 Ap 12 2017

PARVEZ, ZAHEER

An Empowering Rule *Islamic Horizons* v46 no1 p54 Ja/F 2017

Parziale, Jacqueline

As technology goes democratic, nations lose military control bibl *Bulletin of the Atomic Scientists* v73 no2 p102 Mr 2017

Pasachoff, Jay M.

THE GREAT SOLAR ECLIPSE of 2017 color *Scientific American* v317 no2 p54 Ag 2017

Pascal, Blaise, 1623-1662

Blaise Pascal, blessed doubter C. Zaleski *Christian Century* v134 no18 p35 Ag 30 2017

Pascarella, Elena M.

Designing for Landscape Architecture color *Architectural Record* v204 no12 p166 D 2016

Exteriors and Outdoor Design: Design trends for exterior spaces and four-season rooms *Architectural Record* v205 no7 p146 Jl 2017

Trends in Urban Outdoor Amenity Spaces: In-demand roof deck systems add value to today's buildings color diag *Architectural Record* v205 no5 p165 My 2017

Paschalidis, Yannis

Passman, Rod—Interviews

The Connected Heart K. PEIKOFF color *Popular Mechanics* p14 F 2017

Passmore, Jo-Ann S.

Vaginal bacteria modify HIV tenofovir microbicide efficacy in African women chart graph *Science* v356 no6341 p938 Je 1 2017

Passov, Joe

The 6th Annual Travelin' Joe AWARDS color *Golf Magazine* v59 no2 p38 F 2017

All Over the Map color *Golf Magazine* v59 no10 p82 O 2017

Bet On Black color *Golf Magazine* v59 no10 p27 O 2017

Dad Trippers color *Golf Magazine* v59 no6 p102 Je 2017

DEAD AT AUGUSTA color *Golf Magazine* v59 no4 p72 Ap 2017

THE DRIVE THAT CHANGED EVERYTHING color *Golf Magazine* v58 no12 p46 D 2016

EMPIRE OF THE SON color *Golf Magazine* v58 no12 p30 D 2016

Erin Go Ah color *Golf Magazine* v59 no6 p70 Je 2017

Four-Leaf Dining and Drinking color *Golf Magazine* v59 no7 p94 Jl 2017

GIL HANSE color *Golf Magazine* v59 no1 p92 Ja 2017

Go Big & Go Home color *Golf Magazine* v59 no3 p106 Mr 2017

Going Once, Going Twice color *Golf Magazine* v59 no4 p124 Ap 2017

The Golfer's Ultimate Guide Ireland color *Golf Magazine* v59 no7 p90 Jl 2017

Grains & Beauty color *Golf Magazine* v59 no5 p42 My 2017

Island Fever color *Golf Magazine* v59 no5 p100 My 2017

King of Clubs color *Golf Magazine* v59 no7 p36 Jl 2017

Kiwi's Big Adventure color *Golf Magazine* v59 no1 p91 Ja 2017

Leaders in the Clubhouse color *Golf Magazine* v58 no11 p94 N 2016

Lifestyles of the Top 100 color *Golf Magazine* v59 no10 p88 O 2017

Lone Star Links color *Golf Magazine* v59 no11 p30 N 2017

Mississippi Queen color *Golf Magazine* v59 no1 p36 Ja 2017

Missouri Tiger color *Golf Magazine* v59 no8 p36 Ag 2017

Modern Love color *Golf Magazine* v58 no11 p36 N 2016

Multi-Flasking color *Golf Magazine* v59 no7 p95 Jl 2017

National Treasures color *Golf Magazine* v59 no4 p120 Ap 2017

North Star color *Golf Magazine* v59 no2 p40 F 2017

Not Throwin' Away My Shot color *Golf Magazine* v59 no9 p96 S 2017

Ode to Joe D. Denunzio color *Golf Magazine* v59 no10 p8 O 2017

ON THE ROAD WITH... BRANDEL CHAMBLEE color *Golf Magazine* v59 no3 p110 Mr 2017

Pebble Beach The Golfer's Ultimate Guide color *Golf Magazine* v59 no2 p84 F 2017

Small Wonder color *Golf Magazine* v59 no4 p42 Ap 2017

Smokin' With Love color *Golf Magazine* v59 no11 p94 N 2017

Soothe Moves color *Golf Magazine* v59 no5 p103 My 2017

Striking Gold—Again color *Golf Magazine* v59 no9 p38 S 2017

Tee, Ball chart color *Golf Magazine* v59 no3 p40 Mr 2017

TEEING OFF color *Golf Magazine* v59 no1 p14 Ja 2017

TEEING OFF color *Golf Magazine* v59 no9 p16 S 2017

Tee Shots & Tailgating color *Golf Magazine* v59 no11 p90 N 2017

The Tick List color *Golf Magazine* v59 no3 p108 Mr 2017

Top Golf color *Golf Magazine* v59 no9 p90 S 2017

United Steaks color *Golf Magazine* v58 no11 p96 N 2016

Untie Him color *Golf Magazine* v59 no6 p106 Je 2017

U.S. and the World Edition chart color *Golf Magazine* v59 no10 p62 O 2017

Water Whirl color *Golf Magazine* v58 no11 p90 N 2016

While You're In the Neighborhood... A Top 100 Trip Planner color *Golf Magazine* v59 no10 p92 O 2017

Wrap It Up! color *Golf Magazine* v59 no1 p88 Ja 2017

Your Ultimate Golf Bucket List color *Golf Magazine* v59 no8 p92 Ag 2017

Passover

See also

Matzos

Password software—Evaluation

Best password managers of 2017: Reviews of the top products M. ANSALDO color *PCWorld* v35 no10 p79 O 2017

Passwords (Computers)

4 easy ways to keep your iCloud password safe B. PATTERSON

color *Macworld - Digital Edition* v34 no6 p99 Je 2017

Build a Better Password D. Shadel cartoon *AARP: The Magazine* v60 no3A p24 Ap/My 2017

Equifax and the Perils of Password Protection L. Eadicicco color *Time* v190 no12 p21 S 25 2017

Get More WH color *Women's Health* v14 no2 p14 Mr 2017

LastPass password manager fixes serious password leak vulnerabilities L. CONSTANTIN color *PCWorld* v35 no5 p59 My 2017

Passwords (Computers)—Software

THE 10 MUST-HAVE UTILITIES FOR MACOS SIERRA G. Fleishman cartoon color *Macworld - Digital Edition* p82 F 2017

Passwords (Computers)—Software—Evaluation

SECRETS FOR MAC AND SECRETS TOUCH: A SIMPLE, NO-FRILLS PASSWORD MANAGER J. R. BOOKWALTER color *Macworld - Digital Edition* p21 Mr 2017

Pasta products

See also

Spaghetti

BUCATINI WITH SHRIMP, ALMOND PESTO, AND CHERRY TOMATOES *Washingtonian Magazine* v52 no9 p144 Je 2017

DINNER TONIGHT C. Morocco color *Bon Appetit* v62 no6 p40 Je 2017

how to cook PASTA M. GLISAN *Better Homes & Gardens* v95 no1 p64 Ja 2017

A Maestro Returns: AT FELIX IN VENICE, EVAN FUNKE ROLLS OUT SUBLIMELY REGIONAL ITALIAN FOOD P. KUH color *Los Angeles Magazine* v62 no7 p38 Jl 2017

A New Twist on Pasta R. Meltzer Warren chart color *Consumer Reports* v82 no5 p14 My 2017

SPRING FLING C. Stone *Saturday Evening Post* v289 no2 p74 Mr/Ap 2017

Summer Kitchen D. Curry color *New Orleans Magazine* v51 no8 p104 Je 2017

Pastel drawing—Exhibitions

SAM PULITZER AND PETER WÄCHTLER C. Moloney color *Art in America* v105 no3 p136 Mr 2017

Pastern

Scratches L. Bonner color *Equus* no474 p18 Mr 2017

Pasternak, Anna

A Grand Passion bw color *Vogue* v206 no12 p120 D 2016

Pasternak's Muse S. PINKHAM *New York Times Book Review* p13 Ja 29 2017

Somewhere, MY LOVE L. SCHILLINGER cartoon color *O, The Oprah Magazine* p99 F 2017

Pasternak, Ben

MONKEY DO C. Bethea cartoon *New Yorker* v92 no45 p23 Ja 16 2017

Pastor, Joaquin

Tissue damage and senescence provide critical signals for cellular reprogramming in vivo bibl chart graph *Science* v354 no6315 paaf4445-1 N 25 2016

Pastoral care

Hovering over the deep S. Wells *Christian Century* v134 no17 p28 Ag 16 2017

Pastoral theology

See also

Preaching

It is time to get past the snobbery against pastoral theologians J. Heft *America* v217 no2 p10 Jl 24 2017

Priest, Writer, Mentor, Misfit M. Higgins color *Commonweal* v143 no20 p13 D 16 2016

Pastore, Nunzia

Transcriptional activation of RagD GTPase controls mTORC1 and promotes cancer growth diag *Science* v356 no6343 p1188 Je 16 2017

Pastorius, Jaco

New Album Chronicles Pastorius in '82 T. Staudter color *Downbeat* v84 no6 p20 Je 2017

Pastoureau, Michel

Crimson Tidings E. POWERS color *Weekly Standard* v22 no40 p34 Je 26 2017

Pastrana, Julian—Interviews

Q&A WITH JULIAN PASTRANA *Texas Monthly* v45 no4 p30 Ap 2017

Pastry

See also

Cobblers (Cooking)
  Doughnuts
  Pies
The Chew's Surefire Party-Starters color *Entertainment Weekly* no1443 p24 D 9 2016
THE CHRISTIANE CHRONICLES *Atlanta* v56 no12 p60 Ap 2017
THE DOUGHNUT KING J. RAUSA FULLER color *Chicago* v66 no11 p50 N 2017
Sopaipillas C. BOND *Texas Monthly* v45 no3 p42 Mr 2017
TEATIME P. POLLACK color *Chicago* v66 no5 p72 My 2017

Pastry chefs
FLOUR GIRL: Head baker Jessica Flores is a rising star at Open Society Public House S. KROWIAK *Indianapolis Monthly* v40 no11 p40 Jl 2017
NEW COURSE: A fresh start awaits pastry chef Pete Schmutte after five years spent preparing finales at Cerulean S. KROWIAK *Indianapolis Monthly* p48 N 2017
A Sugar High P. KUH *Los Angeles Magazine* p50 Ap 2017

Pastry—Evaluation
HYBRID *Washingtonian Magazine* v52 no1 p96 O 2016

Pastuglia, Martine
The preprophase band of microtubules controls the robustness of division orientation in plants graph *Science* v356 no6334 p186 Ap 14 2017

Pastures
HEAVE-HO HAZARDS C. Barakat and M. Freckleton color *Equus* no473 p16 F 2017
Mare Won't Use Her Paddock J. BERGER *Horse & Rider* v56 no4 p14 Ap 2017
OLD-SCHOOL PIG FARMING: NIMAN RANCH PORK IS LOOKING FOR GROWERS TO PRODUCE PIGS IN BEDDED PENS AND PASTURES FOR HEALTH-CONSCIOUS CONSUMERS OF NATURAL PORK G. Johnston *Successful Farming* v115 no6 p40 Ap 2017
Slow feeding is best color *Horse & Rider* v56 no10 p34 O 2017
When Raiders Become Traitors D. ZIRIN color *Progressive* v81 no5 p68 Je/Jl 2017

Pasupathy, Kalyan S.
How RFID Technology Improves Hospital Care *Harvard Business Review Digital Articles* p2 D 31 2015

Pasztor, Janos
Cooling-Off Period *MIT Technology Review* v120 no3 p10 My/Je 2017
How to govern geoengineering? color *Science* v357 no6348 p231 Jl 21 2017

Patagonia (Argentina & Chile)
WORLDLY ADVICE E. FLORIO and C. TATTOLI color *Conde Nast Traveler* v52 no6 p22 Je/Jl 2017

Patagonia Inc.
Companies Are Working with Consumers to Reduce Waste M. Esposito, T. Tse et al *Harvard Business Review Digital Articles* p2 Je 7 2016

Patagonia Provisions Inc.
Patagonia: For climbing Everest, diving the Great Barrier Reef, and saving the planet on a beer run B. Wieners color *Bloomberg Businessweek* no4494 p54 O 10 2016

Patagonia-Sonoita Creek Preserve (Ariz.)
Patagonia-Sonoita Creek Preserve *Arizona Highways* v93 no4 p28 Ap 2017

PATAKI, DIANE
THIRSTY GRASS *USA Today Magazine* v146 no2866 p70 Jl 2017

Patch, Nathaniel
Silently. Quickly. By Sea, in Darkness *Prologue* v48 no4 p6 Wint 2016

Patchett, Ann, 1963-
COMMOWEALTH D. B. NURSE bw color *Maclean's* v129 no41 p56 O 17 2016
Icons color *Time* v189 no16/17 p122 My 1-8 2017
Power-Couple Breakfast, with Lesley Stahl and Ann Patchett A. Gross color *Publishers Weekly* v264 no3 p6 Ja 16 2017
The President Who Loved color *Time* v189 no3 p47 Ja 30 2017
The Year in Reading [Cover story] *New York Times Book Review* p8 D 25 2016

Patchwork

FINISHING TOUCHES H. GILBERT color *House Beautiful* p108 Ag 2017

Patchwork quilts
LOVE YOUR HOMEMADE QUILT? THANK CAPITALISM V. POSTREL color *Reason* v48 no8 p14 Ja 2017

PATEK, CAROLINE
Funny FiLL-IN *National Geographic Kids* no467 p36 F 2017

Patek Philippe SA
ALTITUDE ADJUSTMENT S. Watson color *Esquire* p29 Ag 2017

Patel, Anamika
A placental growth factor is silenced in mouse embryos by the zinc finger protein ZFP568 color graph *Science* v356 no6339 p757 My 19 2017

Patel, Anoop P.
Decoupling genetics, lineages, and microenvironment in IDH-mutant gliomas by single-cell RNA-seq diag *Science* v355 no6332 p1391 Mr 31 2017

Patel, Avinash
ATP as a biological hydrotrope color graph *Science* v356 no6339 p753 My 19 2017

Patel, Chirag H.
Warburg meets epigenetics bibl diag *Science* v354 no6311 p419 O 28 2016

Patel, Dev, 1990-
Lion's True Story of an Unlikely Homecoming C. Lang color *Time* v188 no22-23 p99 N/D 2016
THE SEASON OF RETRO-FUTURISM D. PATEL color *GQ: Gentlemen's Quarterly* v87 no1 p52 Ja 2017

Patel, Dev, 1990-—Interviews
THE MAN DEV PATEL R. Reilich color *InStyle* v23 no13 p118 D 2016

Patel, H. S.
Chronic exposure to neonicotinoids reduces honey bee health near corn crops diag *Science* v356 no6345 p1395 Je 30 2017

Patel, Harshil
The linker histone H1.0 generates epigenetic and functional intra-tumor heterogeneity bibl graph *Science* v353 no6307 paaf1644-1 S 30 2016

Patel, Jay B.
Perovskite-perovskite tandem photovoltaics with optimized band gaps bibl chart graph *Science* v354 no6314 p861 N 18 2016

Patel, Kalpesh
CASHLESS I. Parker bw *New Yorker* v93 no28 p18 S 18 2017

Patel, Kamal
FAFQ color *Muscle & Performance* v9 no6 p13 Je 2017
FAFQ (FREQUENTLY ASKED FOOD QUESTIONS) color *Muscle & Performance* v9 no10 p20 O 2017
FAFQ *Muscle & Performance* v9 no5 p14 My 2017

Patel, Ketan J.
Of sizzling steaks and DNA repair diag *Science* v357 no6347 p130 Jl 14 2017

Patel, Kiran Klaus
The Borrowers I. Katznelson bw *Foreign Affairs* v95 no6 p159 N/D 2016

PATEL, MANISHA V.
Insights into Student Gains from Undergraduate Research Using Pre- and Post-Assessments *BioScience* v66 no12 p1070 D 1 2016

Patel, Mona
Tough Love Performance Reviews, in 10 Minutes *Harvard Business Review Digital Articles* p2 Ag 3 2015

Patel, Prachi
2016 WORLD CHANGING IDEAS [Cover story] color *Scientific American* v315 no6 p32 D 2016
Bots in Your Bloodstream diag *Scientific American* v316 no2 p15 F 2017
Cutting through the Fog *Scientific American* v317 no3 p216 S 2017
Hot Rockets bw color *Scientific American* v317 no1 p20 Jl 2017

PATEL, RAJ
THE PROBLEMS WITH FAIR TRADE *Nation* v305 no11 p16 O 30 2017

PATEL, SAMIR S.
THE BLACKENER'S CAVE color *Archaeology* v70 no3 p36 My/Je 2017

THE BUDDHA OF THE LAKE color *Archaeology* v70 no3 p23 My/Je 2017

DECEMBER 7, 1941 bw color diag *Archaeology* v70 no1 p40 Ja/F 2017

DIGGING UP DIGITAL MUSIC bw color *Archaeology* v70 no2 p9 Mr/Ap 2017

Landscape of Secrets bw color *Archaeology* v70 no5 p48 S/O 2017

Piltdown's Lone Forger bw color *Archaeology* v69 no6 p9 N/D 2016

Seeing Beauty in the Mundane bw cartoon color *Archaeology* v70 no1 p46 Ja/F 2017

TOP 10 DISCOVERIES OF 2016 bw cartoon color *Archaeology* v70 no1 p26 Ja/F 2017

WORLD ROUNDUP color map *Archaeology* v69 no6 p24 N/D 2016

WORLD ROUNDUP color map *Archaeology* v70 no1 p24 Ja/F 2017

Patel, Vikram

A GLOBAL STATE OF MIND J. SILBERNER color diag *Discover* v38 no10 p30 D 2017

Patella diseases

Sticky Stifle Management J. Sobota *Dressage Today* v23 no12 p20 S 2017

Patent laws & legislation—United States

Why Congress Needs to Pass the Innovation Act This Time L. Downes *Harvard Business Review Digital Articles* p2 Mr 9 2015

Patent lawyers

Patent work blends science, business, and law T. Feder *Physics Today* v70 no10 p36 O 2017

An Unlikely Marketing Lesson from Patent Lawyers B. D. Gelb and G. M. Gelb *Harvard Business Review Digital Articles* p2 N 25 2014

Patent suits—United States

CRISPR patent ruling leaves license holders scrambling J. Cohen color *Science* v355 no6327 p786 F 24 2017

Kiss of Summer: The first families of salt water taffy stir up another season of making history by the bite A. Owens *Smithsonian* v48 no4 p9 Jl/Ag 2017

Movers K. Stock cartoon color diag *Bloomberg Businessweek* no4495 p11 O 17 2016

Patents

Astounding Tales of Science! B. RADFORD *Skeptical Inquirer* v41 no2 p66 Mr/Ap 2017

Entrepreneurs, Economic Growth, and the Enlightenment T. Sullivan *Harvard Business Review Digital Articles* p2 Ag 10 2015

MASS EXPOSURE R. EBERSOLE color *Nation* v305 no11 p34 O 30 2017

A new Microsoft foldable device patent offers more grist for the Surface phone rumor mill M. HACHMAN cartoon *PCWorld* v35 no2 p11 F 2017

AN UN-SOUND FUTURE P. D'orléans *Cycle World* v56 no9 p26 O 2017

Patents—Management

An Unlikely Marketing Lesson from Patent Lawyers B. D. Gelb and G. M. Gelb *Harvard Business Review Digital Articles* p2 N 25 2014

Patents—United States

A Biologic Problem cartoon *Weekly Standard* v22 no38 p3 Je 12 2017

The dual frontier: Patented inventions and prior scientific advance M. Ahmadpoor and B. F. Jones graph *Science* v357 no6351 p583 Ag 11 2017

Patents and Awards *Science & Technology Review* p24 Jl/Ag 2017

When America Was Most Innovative, and Why U. Akcigit, J. Grigsby et al bw graph *Harvard Business Review Digital Articles* p2 Mr 6 2017

Patents—United States—Law & legislation

Ode to MP3 K. C. POHLMANN color *Sound & Vision* v82 no8 p26 O 2017

Paterniti, Michael

JANET RENO *New York Times Magazine* p14 D 25 2016

Maine *New York Times Magazine* p36 N 20 2016

NORMAN LEAR color *GQ: Gentlemen's Quarterly* v97 no6 p120 Je 2017

THE SECRETS OF THE EI8HTY YEAR OLD CHINESE RUNWAY MODEL bw color *GQ: Gentlemen's Quarterly* v97 no4 p112 Ap 2017

Should We Kill Animals to Save Them? bw color graph *National Geographic* v232 no4 p70 O 2017

Paternity leave

Planning Maternity or Paternity Leave: A Professional's Guide R. Knight *Harvard Business Review Digital Articles* p2 My 29 2015

PATERNOSTRO, SILVANA

Colombian Exposition *New York Times Book Review* p22 Mr 19 2017

Paterson (Film)

Bard on a Bus D. EDELSTEIN img *New York* v49 no26 p88 D 26 2016

BETWEEN the LINES A. CHAN color *Film Comment* v52 no6 p72 N/D 2016

Grounded R. Alleva color *Commonweal* v144 no6 p23 Mr 24 2017

The Must List color *Entertainment Weekly* no1448 p2 Ja 13 2017

Paterson Sings the Poetry of Everyday Life In the City S. Zacharek color *Time* v189 no4 p50 Ja 23 2017

POETS' CORNER A. LANE cartoon *New Yorker* v92 no43 p76 Ja 2 2017

Two visions of creativity K. Reklis color *Christian Century* v134 no4 p59 F 15 2017

Paterson (N.J.)—History

Paterson: Alexander Hamilton's Trickle-Down City [Cover story] R. KREITNER bw color *Nation* v304 no8 p18 Mr 13 2017

Paterson, Don

The Versatile Form H. TRESELER *Weekly Standard* v22 no32 p36 My 1 2017

Paterson, Jim

A Case for Acculturation *Education Digest* v83 no1 p29 S 2017

Paterson, Katherine

My Brigadista Year *Publishers Weekly* v264 no34 p112 Ag 21 2017

Paterson, Ken

ANGLO-FILE S. Gutierrez *British Heritage Travel* v38 no3 p12 My/Je 2017

Paterson, Robert

20. Hear Three Way *New York* v50 no12 p116 Je 12 2017

Contingent valuation: Flawed logic? color *Science* v357 no6349 p363 Jl 28 2017

Putting a value on injuries to natural assets: The BP oil spill chart *Science* v356 no6335 p253 Ap 21 2017

Paterson, W. R.

Structure, force balance, and topology of Earth's magnetopause diag graph *Science* v356 no6341 p960 Je 1 2017

Pathak, Jyotishman

Why Health Care May Finally Be Ready for Big Data *Harvard Business Review Digital Articles* p2 D 3 2014

Pathberyia, Semini

Paying It Forward cartoon color *Alternatives Journal (AJ) - Canada's Environmental Voice* v42 no3 p62 2016

Pathogenic bacteria

Neonatal acquisition of Clostridia species protects against colonization by bacterial pathogens Kim, K. Sakamoto et al diag *Science* v356 no6335 p315 Ap 21 2017

Seagrass ecosystems reduce exposure to bacterial pathogens of humans, fishes, and invertebrates J. B. Lamb, J. A. J. M. van de Water et al bibl graph *Science* v355 no6326 p731 F 17 2017

Pathogenic microorganisms

Caught in the jump T. Maekawa and P. Schulze-Lefert color *Science* v357 no6346 p31 Jl 7 2017

Fungal Feedback A. Braun color *Natural History* v125 no3 p8 Mr 2017

RESEARCH bw color *Science* v357 no6355 p1011 S 8 2017

WHO's dirty dozen microbes color *Science* v355 no6328 p890 Mr 3 2017

Pathogenic microorganisms—Research

WHICH BEDDING HARBORS MORE BACTERIA? C. Barakat and M. McCluskey color *Equus* no471 p11 D 2016

Pathological physiology

Exploring pain pathophysiology in patients C. Sommer bibl diag *Science* v354 no6312 p588 N 4 2016

Pathological psychology

See also
Adjustment disorders
Affective disorders
Behavior disorders in children
Cognition disorders
Eating disorders
Mental illness
Negativism
Sleep disorders
A Streak of Madness D. TWEEDY bw color *Discover* v38 no9 p24 N 2017

Patience
lying in wait: THE LOST ART OF PATIENCE k. butcher color *Bike Magazine* v24 no8 p38 N 2017
Small Sacrifices S. Murphy color *Log Home Living* v34 no6 p22 Ag 2017
The STRENGTH Issue *Men's Health* v32 no4 p93 My 2017

Patience—Social aspects
Patience is one virtue scientists must embrace *Science News* v192 no3 p2 S 2 2017

Patient-centered care
Giving Patients an Active Role in Their Health Care L. Schlesinger and J. Fox *Harvard Business Review Digital Articles* p2 N 21 2016
Redesigning Care for High-Cost, High-Risk Patients Z. J. Eapen and S. H. Jain color *Harvard Business Review Digital Articles* p2 F 7 2017

Patient compliance
Pay up or retract? Drug survey spurs conflict A. Marcus color *Science* v357 no6356 p1085 S 15 2017

Patient education
The Value of Teaching Patients to Administer Their Own Care A. H. Anderson, L. A. Martin et al color *Harvard Business Review Digital Articles* p1 Je 2 2017

Patient monitoring
See also
Drug monitoring
Heart rate monitoring
A newborn's pain registers in the brain L. SANDERS color *Science News* v191 no11 p8 Je 10 2017

Patient monitoring equipment—Evaluation
New At-Home Health Tests—Rated K. DOLD color *Men's Health* v32 no7 p86 S 2017

Patient participation
Redesigning Care for High-Cost, High-Risk Patients Z. J. Eapen and S. H. Jain color *Harvard Business Review Digital Articles* p2 F 7 2017

Patient readmissions
30% V. Tweed color *Amazing Wellness* v9 no2 p18 Spr 2017
What Has the Biggest Impact on Hospital Readmission Rates C. Senot and A. Chandrasekaran *Harvard Business Review Digital Articles* p2 S 23 2015

Patient representatives
Help Navigating the Medical System *Kiplinger's Personal Finance* v71 no12 p70 D 2017

Patient safety
How U.S. Health Care Got Safer by Focusing on the Patient Experience T. H. Lee *Harvard Business Review Digital Articles* p2 My 31 2017

Patient satisfaction—Evaluation
Do you need a second opinion? K. Canning color *Health* v31 no9 p68 N 2017

Patients
See also
HIV-positive persons
Physician & patient
Big Daddy Medicine Man J. Kirkpatrick color *American Cowboy* v24 no1 p19 Je/Jl 2017
A Day's Work *Reader's Digest* v188 no1124 p70 O 2016
THE FUTURE IS FEMALE... INSPIRED P. Yee and W. Branch color *Women's Health* v14 no4 p38 My 2017
LISTEN UP, Doc! L. Haney chart color *O, The Oprah Magazine* p75 S 2017
Rise of the Zombie Hospitals S. RUSSELL-KRAFT il *New Republic* v247 no12 p12 D 2016
When Health Care Providers Look at Problems from Multiple

Perspectives, Patients Benefit J. A. Frimpong, C. G. Myers et al *Harvard Business Review Digital Articles* p2 Je 23 2017

Patients—Health
Code Comfort: A Code Blue Alternative for Patients with DNRs M. P. Phipps and J. D. Phipps *Harvard Business Review Digital Articles* p2 D 9 2014

Patients—Mental health
Doctors Say the Darnedest Things [Cover story] J. Newman cartoon *Prevention* v69 no6 p90 Je 2017

Patients—Psychology
AFTER THE ICU K. MILLER color *Prevention* v69 no1 p84 Ja 2017
DOCTORING THE TRUTH: The worst lies you tell your physician K. KENDALL *Indianapolis Monthly* p74 N 2017

Patients—Services for
Patients Make Better Medical Choices with Coaching J. Belkora *Harvard Business Review Digital Articles* p2 N 11 2016
The Ultimate Gift I. Byock color *Prevention* v69 no8 p28 Ag 2017

Patin, Etienne
Dispersals and genetic adaptation of Bantu-speaking populations in Africa and North America diag *Science* v356 no6337 p543 My 5 2017

Patina Restaurant Group LLC
Ask a Water Sommelier S. TISHGART *New York* p60 F 9 2017

Patios
See also
Decks (Domestic architecture)
STUFF A PLUMBER SCREWED UP P. O'Donnell cartoon *Old House Journal* v45 no5 p54 Ag 2017

Patkau Architects Inc.
Lightly on the Land A. WEDER color diag *Architectural Record* v204 no12 p84 D 2016

PATKIN, TODD
Besting The Bullies *USA Today Magazine* v145 no2860 p36 Ja 2017

Patltic, Nina
Captain Kathy *Tennis* v53 no3 p8 My/Je 2017

Patmos (Greece : Municipality)
CAROLINA HERRERA K. MOLVAR bw color *Conde Nast Traveler* v52 no1 p42 Ja 2017

Patnaik, Gayatri
Gayatri Patnaik J. Rosen color *Publishers Weekly* v263 no42 p5 O 17 2016

Paton, James
The Crazy Math Behind Drug Prices graph *Bloomberg Businessweek* no4529 p14 Jl 3 2017
J&J Plays the Spurned Suitor cartoon *Bloomberg Businessweek* no4503 p20 D 12 2016

Paton, Joseph J.
Midbrain dopamine neurons control judgment of time bibl graph *Science* v354 no6317 p1273 D 9 2016

Paton, W. R.
The Ancient Delights of the Epigram H. N. Pelliccia color *New York Review of Books* v64 no10 p52 Je 8 2017

Patra, Chinmoy
Injury-induced ctgfa directs glial bridging and spinal cord regeneration in zebrafish bibl graph *Science* v354 no6312 p630 N 4 2016

Patriarca, Chiara
The extent of forest in dryland biomes [Cover story] chart map *Science* v356 no6338 p635 My 12 2017

Patrick, Artemis
SKIN IN THE GAME L. WELLS color *Harper's Bazaar* no3651 p333 Mr 2017

Patrick, Bethanne
Victoria: A Novel *British Heritage Travel* v37 no6 p78 N/D 2016

PATRICK, CHRISTOPHER J.
Submersed Aquatic Vegetation in Chesapeake Bay: Sentinel Species in a Changing World *BioScience* v67 no8 p698 Ag 2017

Patrick, Dan
JUST MY TYPE color *Sports Illustrated* v125 no19 p27 D 12 2016

Patrick, Dan, 1950-
flush with power E. BENSON, D. MANN et al *Texas Monthly* v45 no2 p84 F 2017
ROAR OF THE CROWD *Texas Monthly* v45 no3 p10 Mr 2017

Paper Trail L. RAMZI and C. SCHAMA color *Vogue* v207 no9 p614 S 2017

PATTERSON, BEN

4 easy ways to keep your iCloud password safe color *Macworld - Digital Edition* v34 no6 p99 Je 2017

4 ways to keep from sleeping through your Android alarm color *PCWorld* v35 no2 p193 F 2017

5 alternative (and easier) ways to unlock your Android phone color *PCWorld* v35 no4 p136 Ap 2017

6 easy ways to keep your Android phone secure color *PCWorld* v35 no6 p39 Je 2017

6 more ways to make the most of Mail for iOS 10 color *Macworld - Digital Edition* p55 D 2016

6 quick ways to clear space on an overstuffed Android device color *PCWorld* v35 no9 p101 S 2017

6 settings to make your Android phone anticipate your needs color *PCWorld* p168 D 2016

8 Android gestures that speed up everyday tasks color *PCWorld* v35 no1 p192 Ja 2017

9 free ways to get the most out of Google's Play Music app color *PCWorld* v35 no1 p201 Ja 2017

Become an expert at Safari for iOS with these 8 tips and tricks color *Macworld - Digital Edition* v34 no8 p51 Ag 2017

Patterson, Bob

WORLD ON A STRING S. TIGNOR color *Tennis* v53 no2 p42 Mr/Ap 2017

PATTERSON, BRENT

An Unparalleled Opportunity for an Important Ecological Study *BioScience* v67 no10 p875 O 2017

PATTERSON, BRUCE D.

Getting Back to the Basics: Museum Collections and Satellite Imagery Are Critical to Analyzing Species Diversity *BioScience* v67 no5 p405 My 2017

Transformational Principles for NEON Sampling of Mammalian Parasites and Pathogens: A Response to Springer and Colleagues *BioScience* v66 no11 p917 N 1 2016

Patterson, Christina

Research: The Rise of Superstar Firms Has Been Better for Investors than for Employees *Harvard Business Review Digital Articles* p1 My 11 2017

Patterson, Cordarrelle—Interviews

SI NOW M. Gray color *Sports Illustrated* v126 no4 p4 Ja 30 2017

Patterson, Daniel

Ambiguous Eye C. IRMSCHER color *Weekly Standard* v22 no30 p34 Ap 10 2017

The Art of Flavor: Practices and Principles for Creating Delicious Food color *Publishers Weekly* v264 no23 p46 Je 5 2017

Patterson, Eric—Interviews

Water Wizard J. Spring *Sierra* v102 no1 p103 Ja/F 2017

Patterson, Frank

MOVIE MAN S. HENRY *Atlanta* v56 no12 p24 Ap 2017

Patterson, James, 1947-

James PATTERSON J. Black color *Esquire* p76 S 2017

The Literacy of Long-form Thinking color *Time* v188 no16/17 p77 O 24 2016

PARODY *Weekly Standard* v22 no35 p40 My 22 2017

The Summer Job I'll Never Forget color *Time* v190 no2/3 p55 Jl 10-17 2017

Word of Mouse *Publishers Weekly* v263 no40 p123 O 3 2016

Patterson, Jamie

CAUGHT L. Kern color *Film Comment* v53 no3 p24 My/Je 2017

PATTERSON, JODIE

SHE'S GOT THE LOOK *O, The Oprah Magazine* p121 Mr 2017

PATTERSON, KEVIN

Geek Love cartoon *Walrus* v13 no10 p54 D 2016

Patterson, Lorie—Interviews

WHAT'S YOUR NUMBER with LORIE PATTERSON A. Gentry color *Spin to Win Rodeo* v20 no10 p30 D 2016

PATTERSON, MARGOT

Hillary Clinton's Legacy color *America* v215 no18 p14 D 5 2016

Outlaw Nation *America* v215 no12 p12 O 24 2016

Peace Over Politics *America* v215 no19 p14 D 19 2016

Patterson, Paul

The extent of forest in dryland biomes [Cover story] chart map *Science* v356 no6338 p635 My 12 2017

Patterson, Richard North

Fever Swamp: My Journey Through the Strange Neverland of the 2016 Presidential Race *Publishers Weekly* v263 no48 p62 N 28 2016

Patterson, Rocky

TRIPPED UP color *Spin to Win Rodeo* v20 no11 p11 Ja 2017

Patterson, Sarah

Glory Bound L. VACCARIELLO *Cincinnati Magazine* v50 no6 p160 Mr 2017

Patterson, Scott

Gilmore Girls: A Year in the Life M. ROUSH *TV Guide* v64 no48 p18 N 21 2016

Patterson, Spencer

The Big Factors That Attract the Best Freelancers *Harvard Business Review Digital Articles* p2 D 10 2015

Patterson, Troy

Alexander Wang color *Bloomberg Businessweek* no4535 p72 Ag 28 2017

Beyond Basic bw color *Bloomberg Businessweek* no4541 p64 O 9 2017

Double Vision chart color *Bloomberg Businessweek* no4535 p61 Ag 28 2017

Going Green color *Bloomberg Businessweek* no4533 p60 Ag 7 2017

The Loafer Steps Out color *Bloomberg Businessweek* no4532 p64 Jl 31 2017

Made to Be Undone color *Bloomberg Businessweek* no4535 p70 Ag 28 2017

Savile Row Arrives Stateside bw color *Bloomberg Businessweek* no4530 p59 Jl 17 2017

Turtleneck 2.0 color *Bloomberg Businessweek* no4529 p76 Jl 3 2017

When Bad Things Happen to Rich People color *Bloomberg Businessweek* no4527 p90 Je 19 2017

Patti Cake$ (Film)

Mamoudou ATHIE *Interview* v47 no5 p63 Je/Jl 2017

PATTI CAKE$ C. Agard color *Entertainment Weekly* no1463/1464 p70 Ap/My 2017

STARTED FROM THE BOTTOM NOW SHE'S HERE C. Sosenko color *Entertainment Weekly* no1480 p18 S 1 2017

Summer Movie Preview: August S. Begley, E. Berman et al color *Time* v189 no20 p58 My 29 2017

PATTILLO, ALLISON

Country Trails color *Runner's World* v52 no6 p54 Jl 2017

Pattinson, Robert, 1986-

Good Time K. P. Sullivan color *Entertainment Weekly* no1478 / 1479 p84 Ag 18-25 2017

Pattinson Packs a Punch In Good Time S. Zacharek color *Time* v190 no7 p51 Ag 21 2017

The Robert Pattinson Career-Makeover Playbook K. LINCOLN img *New York* v50 no8 p128 Ap 17 2017

THE SECOND COMING OF ROBERT PATTINSON [Cover story] T. BRODESSER-AKNER bw color *GQ: Gentlemen's Quarterly* v97 no9 p142 S 2017

Pattinson, Robert, 1986-—Interviews

COMPLETELY MENTAL N. Rapold color *Film Comment* v53 no4 p27 Jl/Ag 2017

Seducing Robert Pattinson: How directors Josh and Benny Safdie landed the star for their heist thriller Good Time C. Swanson img *New York* v50 no16 p97 Ag 7 2017

Patton, Beatrice Ayer

PATTON'S REQUIRED READING *MHQ: Quarterly Journal of Military History* v29 no3 p22 Spr 2017

Patton, George S. (George Smith), 1885-1945

PATTON'S REQUIRED READING B. A. Patton *MHQ: Quarterly Journal of Military History* v29 no3 p22 Spr 2017

Patton, H.

Massive blow-out craters formed by hydrate-controlled methane expulsion from the Arctic seafloor graph map *Science* v356 no6341 p948 Je 1 2017

PATTON, JAMES L.

Transformational Principles for NEON Sampling of Mammalian Parasites and Pathogens: A Response to Springer and Colleagues *BioScience* v66 no11 p917 N 1 2016

Patton, Jerrilynn

MOOD MUSIC HUA HSU color *New Yorker* v93 no14 p92 My 22 2017

PATTON, JULIE BROWN

As the Windmill Turns St. Louis color *Missouri Life* v44 no5 p74 Ag 2017

Beef, Buns & Brews Perryville color *Missouri Life* v44 no3 p78 My 2017

Faires, Feasting & Fun chart color *Missouri Life* v44 no5 p42 Ag 2017

P.I.Y.: POUR-IT-YOURSELF color *Missouri Life* v44 no6 p21 S 2017

Patton, Leslie

Halal's Rise From Street Carts to Whole Foods color *Bloomberg Businessweek* no4494 p24 O 10 2016

The Latest Shortage: Fast-Food Workers cartoon graph *Bloomberg Businessweek* no4507 p21 Ja 16 2017

MEAT MARKETER [Cover story] color graph map *Bloomberg Businessweek* no4511 p42 F 13 2017

Want Fries With That Kale Salad? color graph *Bloomberg Businessweek* no4499 p45 N 14 2016

Patton, Paula, 1975-

Somewhere Between J. Halterman *TV Guide* v65 no31 p30 Jl 24 2017

Sound Bites color *Entertainment Weekly* no1477 p5 Ag 11 2017

Patton, Zach

No Strings Attached color *Governing* v30 no11 p32 Ag 2017

PATUREL, AMY

Cocoa for a Cause color *Good Housekeeping* v264 no2 p59 F 2017

Fired Up color *Discover* v38 no3 p26 Ap 2017

HEALING With Light color *Prevention* v69 no11 p72 N 2017

a labor to love *Parents* v91 no9 p119 S 2016

Memory Maker color *Good Housekeeping* v264 no1 p69 Ja 1 2017

Power Poses: Plus or Bust? color *Discover* v38 no2 p18 Mr 2017

Target: LYME DISEASE [Cover story] color *Prevention* v69 no6 p50 Je 2017

What you need to know about... Immuno therapy [Cover story] color *Prevention* v68 no11 p68 N 2016

PATZ, AVIVA

5 Little Ways to Detox Your Body color *Health* v31 no7 p83 S 2017

The best cold & flu fighting secrets of all time color *Health* v31 no9 p71 N 2017

Blind Spots bw color *Women's Health* v14 no9 p72 N 2017

Dry & flaky? Put down that moisturizer! [Cover story] color *Prevention* v69 no2 p56 F 2017

Got Tummy Troubles? color diag *Health* v30 no10 p85 D 2016

Great Sleep Starts Here color *Health* v30 no9 p92 N 2016

Natural Beauty Awards 2017 [Cover story] color *Prevention* v69 no7 p58 Jl 2017

Patzek, Tadeusz

Marder, Patzek, and Tinker reply *Physics Today* v70 no2 p13 F 2017

PATZELT, ANNETTE

An Ecoregion-Based Approach to Protecting Half the Terrestrial Realm *BioScience* v67 no6 p534 Je 2017

Pauken, Kristen E.

Epigenetic stability of exhausted T cells limits durability of reinvigoration by PD-1 blockade bibl graph *Science* v354 no6316 p1160 D 2 2016

PAUL, ALAN

Study Skills *New York Times Book Review* p22 Ag 27 2017

Paul, Alex

Hypothalamic regulation of regionally distinct adult neural stem cells and neurogenesis diag *Science* v356 no6345 p1383 Je 30 2017

Paul, Alice, 1885-1977

Monumental Efforts T. Pierno *National Parks* v91 no3 p3 Summ 2017

PAUL, AMANDA

Turkey's Tenuous Pivot Toward Russia *Current History* v115 no783 p277 O 2016

PAUL, ANNIE MURPHY

Not From Venus, Not From Mars *New York Times Book Review* p10 F 26 2017

Paul, Ari

Another Election Day Loser: Corporate Media [Cover story] *Extra!* v29 no10 p1 D 2016

PAUL, BILL

BORN OF THE MUD: THE STORY OF A COLLECTION color *Phi Kappa Phi Forum* v97 no1 p13 Spr 2017

Paul, Blake, 1993-

BLAKE PAUL color *Snowboarder* v29 no5 p122 Ja 2017

Paul, Carola

Forest value: More than commercial bibl color *Science* v354 no6319 p1541 D 23 2016

Paul, Chris

WHAT IF? ... THESE FOUR ENTIRELY REALISTIC TRADES HAD GONE DOWN? J. Feldman color *Sports Illustrated* v126 no11 p68 Ap 17-24 2017

Paul, Christian

#trailchat color il map *Backpacker* p6 Je 2017

Paul, Deborah

Borrowed Time bw *Indianapolis Monthly* p120 Ap 2017

Drifting Backward: The world feels more dangerous than the one I used to know *Indianapolis Monthly* v40 no11 p128 Jl 2017

Food Fright *Indianapolis Monthly* v40 no5 p132 Ja 2017

Meow or Never: Was I up to pet parenthood one more time? color *Indianapolis Monthly* v41 no2 p168 S 2017

Move Over *Indianapolis Monthly* v40 no3 p160 N 2016

Movin' on Up *Indianapolis Monthly* p136 F 2017

Puppy Love *Indianapolis Monthly* v40 no7 p144 Mr 2017

Shot in the Dark *Indianapolis Monthly* v40 no4 p160 D 2016

Sole Survivor: How I found myself at the special store for special people with broken-down feet requiring special footwear *Indianapolis Monthly* v12 no40 p192 Ag 2017

Sore Loser: Why the opioid crisis is personal diag *Indianapolis Monthly* v42 no2 p128 O 2017

Wit's End *Indianapolis Monthly* p172 My 2017

Paul, Elizabeth S.

Bee happy bibl color diag *Science* v353 no6307 p1499 S 30 2016

Paul, Gregory

Dog Behavior *Skeptical Inquirer* v41 no1 p63 Ja/F 2017

Paul, Helena

New Genetic Engineering Techniques: Precaution, Risk, and the Need to Develop Prior Societal Technology Assessment bibl *Environment* v59 no5 p38 S/O 2017

PAUL, IAN

10 ALTERNATIVE BROWSERS color *PCWorld* v35 no9 p91 S 2017

10 Best Edge (SO FAR) Extensions *PCWorld* v35 no8 p127 Ag 2017

10 powerful, obscure Windows keyboard shortcuts you should know color *PCWorld* v35 no5 p189 My 2017

3 handy image tools you can use in File Explorer color *PCWorld* p182 D 2016

AirPods teardown reveals the magic and glue that make Apple's wireless earphones work color *Macworld - Digital Edition* p52 F 2017

Any website can crash your Windows 7 or 8 PC with these four characters color *PCWorld* v35 no7 p42 Jl 2017

The best PC game recording software: 5 freeware capture tools compared color graph *PCWorld* v35 no10 p83 O 2017

Best web browsers of 2017: Chrome, Edge, Firefox, and Opera go head-to-head color graph *PCWorld* v35 no9 p43 S 2017

Comcast's 1TB data cap starts rolling out across the U.S color diag *PCWorld* v35 no11 p39 N 2016

Dell's futuristic Smart Desk PC will challenge Microsoft's Surface Studio color *PCWorld* p38 D 2016

Dell's wild 8K monitor goes on sale with a just-as-stunning price tag color *PCWorld* v35 no5 p41 My 2017

Facebook's Community Help lets you aid your neighbors in a crisis color *PCWorld* p45 Mr 2017

The free Windows 10 Creators Update will have all these upgrades color *PCWorld* p19 D 2016

Get more Edge extensions by installing beta versions color *PCWorld* v35 no11 p141 N 2016

Gmail is dumping Windows XP and Vista, now what? color *PCWorld* p165 Mr 2017

Google brands malicious websites with 'repeat offender' warnings color *PCWorld* v35 no1 p54 Ja 2017

Google combats fake news with 'Fact Check' results in search and news color *PCWorld* v35 no5 p57 My 2017

Google Drive dumps Windows XP and Vista, now what? color *PCWorld* p56 D 2016

Faith Matters *Christian Century* v134 no14 p32 Jl 5 2017

Faith Matters *Christian Century* v134 no19 p40 S 13 2017

Harry Potter, holy writ *Christian Century* v133 no22 p35 O 26 2016

Mysteries in the edgelands *Christian Century* v134 no4 p45 F 15 2017

Pilgrims together *Christian Century* v134 no16 p29 Ag 2 2017

Theological muscle memory *Christian Century* v134 no20 p35 S 27 2017

When the market is God *Christian Century* v134 no12 p35 Je 7 2017

Paulsen, David

Collars on the Corner offers prayers on the streets of Milwaukee *Christian Century* v134 no17 p18 Ag 16 2017

People color *Christian Century* v133 no26 p19 D 21 2016

St. Louis Episcopalians act against gun violence as homicide rate spikes color *Christian Century* v134 no9 p14 Ap 26 2017

PAULSEN, GARY

A BOY'S BEST FRIEND HAS A SECRET PAST color *Reader's Digest* v190 no1134 p112 O 2017

Paulsen, Kristen

Unique Challenges of Building on an Island color *Cabin Living* p51 Mr 2017

Paulsen, Lindsay

At HOME with Three of Germany's Elite Riders color *Dressage Today* v23 no7 p40 Mr 2017

A Daughter's Gratitude color *Dressage Today* v24 no2 p20 N 2017

A JOURNEY Through Germany color *Dressage Today* v23 no7 p32 Mr 2017

A Rider's Journey with Anxiety color *Dressage Today* v23 no5 p16 Ja 2017

Words of WISDOM from the West Coast color *Dressage Today* v23 no8 p44 Ap 2017

PAULSEN, MICHAEL

A TRULY Special PLACE bw color diag *Cabin Living* p46 Mr 2017

PAULSEN, STEPHEN TUCKER

LOST IN THE SUPERMARKET cartoon *Mother Jones* v42 no1 p64 Ja/F 2017

Paulson, Jennifer

Back-Through Gate color *Horse & Rider* v56 no6 p35 Je 2017

Barrel Arc and Counter-Arc [Cover story] color *Horse & Rider* v55 no12 p25 D 2016

The 'Beehive' color *Horse & Rider* v56 no10 p43 O 2017

Best Show-Halter Fit color *Horse & Rider* v56 no2 p32 F 2017

The Biggest Mistakes Nonpro Riders Make color *Horse & Rider* v56 no4 p35 Ap 2017

Body Control color *Horse & Rider* v56 no11 p44 N 2017

Broaden Your Horizons color *Horse & Rider* v56 no3 p26 Mr 2017

Cloverleaf Over Poles color diag *Horse & Rider* v56 no4 p31 Ap 2017

Corner Control Down the Fence color *Horse & Rider* v56 no3 p66 Mr 2017

Effective Transitions color *Horse & Rider* v56 no9 p43 S 2017

Fancy Barns *Horse & Rider* v56 no4 p11 Ap 2017

The Finer Points of Fencing *Horse & Rider* v56 no6 p40 Je 2017

From the Editor *Horse & Rider* v55 no12 p7 D 2016

Get Out of the Way color *Horse & Rider* v56 no10 p46 O 2017

Get Ready to Win color *Horse & Rider* v55 no12 p28 D 2016

Get Snaffle-Bit Smart color *Horse & Rider* v56 no8 p48 Ag 2017

Get Your Mojo Back color *Horse & Rider* v55 no11 p30 N 2016

The Hay Man *Horse & Rider* v56 no11 p14 N 2017

Hind-End 'L' [Cover story] color *Horse & Rider* v56 no5 p31 My 2017

Is It You? Or Your Horse? color *Horse & Rider* v56 no8 p44 Ag 2017

Lead-Change Precision color *Horse & Rider* v56 no2 p26 F 2017

Let's Fix It *Horse & Rider* v56 no1 p8 Ja 2017

Mecate Tie Rope color *Horse & Rider* v56 no10 p50 O 2017

My Soft Spot *Horse & Rider* v56 no2 p6 F 2017

New for You *Horse & Rider* v56 no7 p14 Jl 2017

Open Up *Horse & Rider* v56 no8 p15 Ag 2017

Precise Circles color *Horse & Rider* v56 no2 p23 F 2017

Ready for Fall? *Horse & Rider* v56 no10 p14 O 2017

Reiner to Ranch Rider bw color *Horse & Rider* v56 no10 p72 O 2017

Riding With a Hackamore color *Horse & Rider* v56 no11 p41 N 2017

Road-Ready Tips color *Horse & Rider* v56 no7 p47 Jl 2017

Romal Reins color *Horse & Rider* v56 no6 p46 Je 2017

Running Martingale color *Horse & Rider* v55 no12 p30 D 2016

Save a Shoe color *Horse & Rider* v56 no1 p50 Ja 2017

School With Class color *Horse & Rider* v56 no1 p28 Ja 2017

Setbacks & Comebacks *Horse & Rider* v55 no11 p6 N 2016

Show-Horse Care at Home color *Horse & Rider* v56 no5 p35 My 2017

Simplify the Turn color *Horse & Rider* v56 no8 p42 Ag 2017

Stay Free in the Stop [Cover story] color *Horse & Rider* v56 no1 p25 Ja 2017

Step Control color *Horse & Rider* v56 no7 p41 Jl 2017

TRENDS for 2017 [Cover story] color *Horse & Rider* v56 no3 p46 Mr 2017

Trend-Spotting *Horse & Rider* v56 no3 p6 Mr 2017

Warm Up for Horsemanship color *Horse & Rider* v55 no11 p25 N 2016

Young Horse Life *Horse & Rider* v56 no9 p14 S 2017

Your Health Matters, Too *Horse & Rider* v56 no5 p10 My 2017

Your Summer Savior *Horse & Rider* v56 no6 p15 Je 2017

Youth Riders Should Know... color *Horse & Rider* v56 no9 p47 S 2017

Paulson, John

Trump and the Economy color *Foreign Affairs* v96 no2 p8 Mr/Ap 2017

Paulson, John Alfred, 1955-

John Paulson's Long Bet on Trump Pays Off J. Light color graph *Bloomberg Businessweek* no4501 p33 N 28 2016

Paulson, Rocky—Awards

2017 Distinguished Achievement Winners *Stage Directions* v30 no3 p6 Mr 2017

Paulson, Sarah, 1974-

BEST DRESS E. Wilson color *InStyle* v24 no7 p41 Jl 2017

The Glamour Do: No-Polish Mani J. Harman color *Glamour* no8 p40 Ag 2017

PARTY LINES img *New York* v49 no20 p134 O 3 2016

Paulson, Sarah, 1974—Interviews

Sarah Paulson T. Stack color *Entertainment Weekly* no1444/1445 p34 D 16 2016

Paulus, Diane

FINDING YOUR NERVE IN FINDING NEVERLAND J. Moore *Cincinnati Magazine* v50 no8 p8 My 2017

Pauly, Fabian

Quantized thermal transport in single-atom junctions bibl diag graph *Science* v355 no6330 p1192 Mr 17 2017

Pauly, Madison

THE NEW MILITANTS *Mother Jones* v42 no3 p22 My/Je 2017

Paumgarten, Nick

362" color graph *Powder* p68 S 2017

ALL ABOARD cartoon *New Yorker* v92 no49 p36 F 13 2017

BIGGER cartoon *New Yorker* v93 no12 p16 My 8 2017

BONG SHOW cartoon *New Yorker* v93 no13 p36 My 15 2017

I SAY KOCH cartoon *New Yorker* v93 no8 p19 Ap 10 2017

MR. BLITZED cartoon *New Yorker* v93 no5 p30 Mr 20 2017

RAMBLING MAN cartoon color *New Yorker* v93 no18 p36 Je 26 2017

SALT OF THE EARTH color *Bon Appetit* v62 no4 p84 Ap 2017

SINGER OF SECRETS cartoon color *New Yorker* v93 no25 p60 Ag 28 2017

SING IT STRONG cartoon *New Yorker* v92 no33 p26 O 17 2016

SPIDERWEB-MAN cartoon *New Yorker* v93 no6 p18 Mr 27 2017

Pausanias, fl. ca. 150-175

PANIKON Pausanias *Lapham's Quarterly* v10 no3 p94 Summ 2017

Pauthner, Matthias

Priming HIV-1 broadly neutralizing antibody precursors in human Ig loci transgenic mice bibl graph *Science* v353 no6307 p1557 S 30 2016

Pauw, Amy Plantinga

From God-talk to God's work *Christian Century* v134 no14 p22 Jl 5 2017

A WISDOM ECCLESIOLOGY: The cosmic church on earth *Christian Century* v134 no16 p20 Ag 2 2017

Pauwels, Jim
  An Ordinary Sunday [Cover story] color *Commonweal* v144 no15 p11 S 22 2017
Pavements
  PROTECT FIDO'S FEET FROM HEAT AND BURNS *USA Today Magazine* v146 no2868 p6 S 2017
Pavements—Design & construction
  Last Look D. Kidd *Governing* v30 no6 p64 Mr 2017
Pavements—Equipment & supplies—Evaluation
  CURB APPEAL bw color *Good Housekeeping* v264 no5 p90 My 2017
Pavia, Audrey
  8 Great Gaited Getaways color *Horse & Rider* v56 no10 p80 O 2017
  Catch Fall COLOR color *Horse & Rider* v56 no9 p72 S 2017
  Handy Checklist color *Trail Rider* v29 no2 p14 Mr 2017
  Ride California's Wine Country color *Trail Rider* v29 no3 p42 Ap 2017
  Spirit of the Black Hills color *Trail Rider* v29 no1 p44 Ja/F 2017
Pavicic, Karen
  How STRETCHING Can BENEFIT Your Horse [Cover story] color *Dressage Today* p32 My 2017
  Lessons In Listening J. Mellace *Dressage Today* p12 My 2017
Pavilion design & construction
  Summer Follies C. Foges and A. Klimoski color *Architectural Record* v205 no8 p46 Ag 2017
Pavilions
  Summer Follies C. Foges and A. Klimoski color *Architectural Record* v205 no8 p46 Ag 2017
Pavilions—Design & construction
  From Vision to Reality A. PILLALAMARRI bw *American Conservative* v16 no2 p9 Mr/Ap 2017
Pavilions—England
  TWIST AND SHOUT S. COCHRAN color *Architectural Digest* no11 p138 N 1 2017
Pavillard-Cain, Francesca
  GROUNDED color *Powder* v45 no6 p94 F 2017
  GROUNDED F. Pavillard-Cain color *Powder* v45 no6 p94 F 2017
Pavitt, Charles
  CATCHING A CONSPIRACY color *Scientific American* v317 no2 p5 Ag 2017
  Discussion *Smithsonian* v47 no7 p10 N 2016
Pavlik, Mike
  Wynton Marsalis Omnibook color *Downbeat* v84 no4 p93 Ap 2017
Pavlopoulos, Georgios A.
  Protein structure determination using metagenome sequence data color graph *Science* v355 no6322 p294 Ja 20 2017
Pavlov, Vadim
  Hydraulic control of tuna fins: A role for the lymphatic system in vertebrate locomotion color *Science* v357 no6348 p310 Jl 21 2017
Pavlus, John
  2016 WORLD CHANGING IDEAS [Cover story] color *Scientific American* v315 no6 p32 D 2016
  THE NEW TURING TESTS color *Scientific American* v316 no3 p61 Mr 2017
  Postcards From The Edge color *Bloomberg Businessweek* no4494 p44 O 10 2016
Paw, Barry H.
  Restored iron transport by a small molecule promotes absorption and hemoglobinization in animals color graph *Science* v356 no6338 p608 My 12 2017
Pawar, Sunny
  JACOB TREMBLAY 2.0? S. Li color *Entertainment Weekly* no1442 p10 D 2 2016 Rebellious Special Issue
Pawlak, Paul
  Making Hospital Partnerships Work *Harvard Business Review Digital Articles* p2 D 10 2015
PAWLICK, CATHERINE
  Makhar Vaziev: The Bolshoi's ballet director talks future plans ahead of the company's Lincoln Center appearance *Dance Magazine* v91 no7 p18 Jl 2017
Pawson, John
  LIGHT FANTASTIC M. OWENS color *Architectural Digest* v74 no3 p98 Mr 2017

Paxton, Bill, 1955-2017
  Bill Paxton J. Cameron color *Time* v189 no9 p14 Mr 13 2017
  The Essential Paxton D. Franich color *Entertainment Weekly* no1456 p14 Mr 10 2017
  TRIBUTES M. Roush and M. Fell *TV Guide* v65 no13 p14 Mr 20 2017
  A True Texas Gentleman D. Franich, C. Collis et al color *Entertainment Weekly* no1456 p12 Mr 10 2017
Paxton, Charles
  THE STORIES WE TELL cartoon *Louisiana Life* v37 no2 p50 N/D 2016
Paxton, James
  So Good It's Criminal D. ANDERSON-MINSHALL *Advocate* no1088 p62 D 2016/Ja 2017
Paxton, Ken, 1962-
  Indictment? What Indictment? A. Greenblatt *Governing* v31 no1 p11 O 2017
  THE TELEVANGELISM OF KEN PAXTON R. G. RATCLIFFE *Texas Monthly* v44 no12 p118 D 2016
Paxton, Robert O.
  AMERICAN DUCE *Harper's Magazine* v334 no2004 p38 My 2017
  The Cultural Axis bw color *New York Review of Books* v64 no16 p16 O 26 2017
  A Parliament of Owls color *New York Review of Books* v64 no9 p20 My 25 2017
Pay equity
  Earning Less Than Their Wives Makes U.S. Men More Partisan D. Cassino *Harvard Business Review Digital Articles* p2 Ap 14 2017
  Equal Pay for Equal Play? C. STOFFERS and B. Rothenberg *New York Times Upfront* v149 no7 p16 Ja 9 2017
  Pay Fairness Isn't Just About Teaching Employees to Negotiate C. H. Arscott *Harvard Business Review Digital Articles* p2 My 4 2016
  Why Banning Questions About Salary History May Not Improve Pay Equity L. Frank *Harvard Business Review Digital Articles* p1 S 5 2017
Pay equity—Great Britain
  13 down, 8,987 to go...: Organisations have been slow to report their gender pay gaps. But the real question is how they will explain them when they do G. GYTON *People Management* p8 Jl 2017
  PAY GAP J. FARAGHER *People Management* p26 F 2017
Pay equity—United States
  How Female Athletes Can Help Advance the Fight for Fair Pay S. Gregory color *Time* v189 no12 p23 Ap 3 2017
PAYA, DARÍO
  An Odd Way to Discredit DeVos color *Weekly Standard* v22 no21 p12 F 6 2017
Payday loans—Law & legislation
  PAYDAY MAYDAY L. Farmer *Governing* v30 no6 p32 Mr 2017
Paying Mr. McGetty (Film)
  Don Wilson Is Playing a Hit Man? D. J. Moore color *Black Belt* v55 no6 p24 O/N 2017
Payless ShoeSource Inc.
  Payless Flops, But the Owners Get a Payday N. Ahmed and S. Natarajan graph *Bloomberg Businessweek* no4516 p35 Mr 27 2017
Payment
  See also
    Rent
  Buy Now, Pay Later P. OLSON color *Forbes* v198 no7 p88 N 29 2016
  Electronic Money Is Too Easy color *MIT Technology Review* v120 no2 p108 Mr/Ap 2017
  A Payment Model That Prevents Unnecessary Medical Treatment D. J. Jacofsky and D. A. Haas *Harvard Business Review Digital Articles* p2 D 19 2016
  What to Know Before You Sign a Payment-by-Results Contract D. Lancefield and C. Gagliardi *Harvard Business Review Digital Articles* p2 S 5 2016
Payment systems
  THE BLOCKCHAIN REVOLUTION: INTERACTION M. IANSITI, K. R. LAKHANI et al color *Harvard Business Review* v95 no2 p20 Mr/Ap 2017
  A Deep Look Inside Apple Pay's Matchmaker Economics D. S.

Evans and R. Schmalensee *Harvard Business Review Digital Articles* p2 Je 17 2016

Improve the Affordable Care Act, Don't Repeal It J. S. Toussaint *Harvard Business Review Digital Articles* p2 N 16 2016

Shop 'til Your Eyes Pop E. LAHEY *USA Today Magazine* v146 no2868 p79 S 2017

Payment systems—Evaluation

APPLE PAY FAQ: THE ULTIMATE GUIDE ON HOW AND WHERE TO USE APPLE'S PAYMENT PLATFORM color *Macworld - Digital Edition* v34 no10 p67 O 2017

Payments for ecosystem services

Cash for carbon: A randomized trial of payments for ecosystem services to reduce deforestation S. Jayachandran, J. de Laat et al bw chart *Science* v357 no6348 p267 Jl 21 2017

Payment—United States

Getting Bundled Payments Right in Health Care D. A. Haas, R. S. Kaplan et al *Harvard Business Review Digital Articles* p2 O 19 2015

The Ways Americans Pay for Things Are Woefully Out of Date J. Lampe *Harvard Business Review Digital Articles* p2 O 14 2015

Payne, Alexander, 1961-

DOWNSIZING J. Nolfi color *Entertainment Weekly* no1478 / 1479 p79 Ag 18-25 2017

PAYNE, BRIDGET WATSON

In Praise of the Coffee Table Book *Publishers Weekly* v264 no16 p72 Ap 17 2017

PAYNE, JACK

EVEN IF PEOPLE CAN'T MOVE FREELY IDEAS MUST *Vital Speeches of the Day* v83 no4 p118 Ap 2017

Payne, Jim

Cheers & Jeers color *Field & Stream* v121 no7 p14 D 2016/Ja 2017

Payne, Kate

island time color *Power & Motoryacht* v34 no10 p84 O 2017

Payne, Keith

Waking From the Dream: Most Americans assume society is more egalitarian than it is *American Scholar* v86 no3 p112 Summ 2017

Payne, Liam, 1993-

One Direction? Try 5 Directions A. Bacle and N. Feeney color *Entertainment Weekly* no1477 p58 Ag 11 2017

Payne, Nick

Written In the Stars M. WAKIM *Los Angeles Magazine* v62 no6 p48 Je 2017

Payne, Teryn

April/May color *Ebony* v72 no6 p18 Ap/My 2017

December! color *Ebony* v72 no3 p34 D 2016/Ja 2017

February! cartoon color *Ebony* v72 no4 p24 F 2017

January! bw color *Ebony* v72 no3 p36 D 2016/Ja 2017

MAKING THE COVER color *Ebony* v72 no8 p20 Je 2017

March! color *Ebony* v72 no5 p24 Mr 2017

STAFF SUMMER SKIN CARE PICKS color *Ebony* v72 no8 p40 Je 2017

TEYANA TAYLOR color *Ebony* v72 no3 p40 D 2016/Ja 2017

TRISTAN 'MACK' WILDS color *Ebony* v72 no4 p34 F 2017

YOUNG PARIS color *Ebony* v72 no5 p28 Mr 2017

Payne Caravella, Holly

THOROUGHBREDS ARE MADE FOR EVENTING color *Practical Horseman* v45 no2 p40 F 2017

Paynich, Vitisia

A Cut Above *Parks & Recreation* v52 no1 p56 Ja 2017

Member Spotlight: Adriane Clutter *Parks & Recreation* v52 no4 p54 Ap 2017

Member Spotlight: Jay Tryon *Parks & Recreation* v52 no5 p69 My 2017

Member Spotlight: John C. Staley *Parks & Recreation* v52 no2 p48 F 2017

Member Spotlight: M. Jean Keller *Parks & Recreation* v52 no3 p51 Mr 2017

Member Spotlight: Patty Wieliczko *Parks & Recreation* v51 no12 p44 D 2016

Starting a Difficult Conversation *Parks & Recreation* v52 no1 p30 Ja 2017

When Art Imitates Park Life: "The Nut Job 2: Nutty by Nature" animates land conservation *Parks & Recreation* v52 no8 p42 Ag 2017

PAYNTER, BRADLEY

Moving the Merchandise *Treasures* v6 no5 p12 Ap/My 2017

PayPal Inc.

PAYPAL'S CEO ON CREATING PRODUCTS FOR UNDER-SERVED MARKETS D. Schulman color diag graph img *Harvard Business Review* v94 no12 p35 D 2016

Payra, Syamantak

Intel ISEF students imagine the future at White House Frontiers Conference color *Science News* v191 no1 p27 Ja 21 2017

Payroll services

MISTAKES COST MONEY: If you thought payroll ran itself, recent high-profile cases mean you might need to think again. How do you avoid an expensive error? L. FARRAND *People Management* p36 Ag 2017

Payroll tax

No Help from Noah *Governing* v30 no8 p11 My 2017

Payson (Ariz.)

CONTROL ROAD K. MONTGOMERY color map *Arizona Highways* v93 no5 p52 My 2017

Paytm (Company)—Finance

TFW Your Country's Shredding Money And You Own a Payment App S. Rai bw *Bloomberg Businessweek* no4507 p30 Ja 16 2017

PAYTON, JAMES R., JR.

Luther's World color *Weekly Standard* v22 no34 p42 My 15 2017

Payton, Jennifer

CLEAN LIVING: A minimalist home for a design sophisticate has maximum impact in its downtown neighborhood *Indianapolis Monthly* p92 N 2017

SEX AND THE SUBURBS *Indianapolis Monthly* p36 My 2017

SPLASH PAD: This Lake Monroe vacation home lives in a whole different league *Indianapolis Monthly* v40 no10 p34 Je 2017

Payton, Khary

What's Next for the Survivors D. Ross color *Entertainment Weekly* no1438 p27 N 4 2016

Paz, Ignacio

DATA IS EVERYTHING color *Maclean's* v129 no51/52 p17 D 26 2016

Paz, Vinny—Health

THE DEVIL GETS HIS DUE B. Baskin color *Sports Illustrated* v125 no18 p42 D 5 2016

Pazcoguin, Georgina—Interviews

THE DIRT color *Dance Spirit* v20 no9 p24 N 2016

PAZHOOR, MOHAMED SALA'HUDDIN

The Most 25 Electrifying Minutes of My Life *Islamic Horizons* v46 no1 p60 Ja/F 2017

Pazourek, R.

Observing the ultrafast buildup of a Fano resonance in the time domain bibl graph *Science* v354 no6313 p738 N 11 2016

PBMares LLP

Services *Virginia Living* p153 2017 Best 20of Virginia

PBS Kids (TV program)

A New PBS, Just for Kids J. Halterman *TV Guide* v65 no4 p9 Ja 16 2017

PD-1 protein

Antibody combats variety of cancers T. HESMAN SAEY color *Science News* v191 no13 p7 Jl 8 2017

PDK International (Company)

PDK Connection color *Phi Delta Kappan* v98 no7 p79 Ap 2017

PDK Connection *Phi Delta Kappan* v98 no3 p79 N 2016

Show what you know D. Brown and D. E. Rhodes color *Phi Delta Kappan* v98 no8 p38 My 2017

Peabody, Maryanne

Getting Your Career Back on Track After a Catastrophic Error *Harvard Business Review Digital Articles* p2 My 12 2016

Peabody Energy Corp.

Is Coal No Longer King? A. STREEP *New Republic* v247 no12 p8 D 2016

Peabody Essex Museum

Design on the high seas at the Peabody Essex color *Magazine Antiques* v184 no3 p32 My/Je 2017

Peace

See also

International arbitration

The Best of Who We Are R. Bragg color *Southern Living* v52 no10 p136 O 2017

Calm After the Storm D. POLISH color *America* v215 no14 p19

N 7 2016

The Difficult Road to Peace in Colombia E. POSADA-CARBO *Current History* v116 no787 p74 F 2017

The Year's at the Spring W. Kristol *Weekly Standard* v22 no30 p8 Ap 10 2017

Peace, Jennifer

War and Peace R. Oltuski color *InStyle* v24 no11 p94 N 2017

Peace movements

The War against Just War P. Steinfels color *Commonweal* v144 no11 p15 Je 16 2017

Peace movements—United States

HOW TO REVIVE THE PEACE MOVEMENT D. MAY color diag *Nation* v304 no11 p12 Ap 3 2017

THIS MONTH: The U.S. Is Bombing at Least Six Countries. How Can the Anti-War Movement Step Up? P. BENNIS, V. PRA-SHAD et al *In These Times* v41 no10 p14 O 2017

Peace movements—United States—History—20th century

Our New Left Pillar E. Leanza *Nation* v303 no20 p5 N 14 2016

Peace of mind

Holiday Happiness: Will You Fake It or Make It? S. T. BROWN color *Ebony* v72 no3 p98 D 2016/Ja 2017

Soaking It All In: The woods are lovely, dark and deep—perfect for forest bathers searching for a little peace of mind N. BRUL-LIARD *National Parks* v91 no3 p12 Summ 2017

Peace officers

See also

Police

Unpardonable contempt *Christian Century* v134 no20 p7 S 27 2017

Peace treaties

How the West is winning S. GILMORE color *Maclean's* v129 no41 p32 O 17 2016

Peace treaties—History—17th century

The Truce of Andrusovo is signed *History Today* v67 no1 p9 Ja 2017

Peacebuilding

Mali's Enduring Crisis S. D. WING *Current History* v116 no790 p189 My 2017

WONDER WOMAN FOR PRESIDENT *Ms.* v27 no3 p33 Fall 2017

Peace—International cooperation

See also

International armistice cooperation

The Harm in Trying E. ABRAMS color *Weekly Standard* v22 no41 p8 Jl 3 2017

Peace process in the Arab-Israeli conflict

A Peaceless Process F. W. BRECHER *Commentary* v142 no2 p12 S 2016

Peace—Religious aspects—Catholic Church

At a time of real division, how can we help clear the air? First, breathe K. Weber *America* v216 no6 p3 Mr 20 2017

Peace—Religious aspects—Christianity

See also

Peace—Religious aspects—Catholic Church

The Right Word M. R. SIMONE il *America* v215 no19 p38 D 19 2016

Peace—Social aspects

PROMOTING PEACE: How libraries, schools, and art help in a time of crisis C. S. Klein color *Literacy Today (2411-7862)* v34 no6 p18 My/Je 2017

What's Next After the Peace Deal In Colombia T. John color *Time* v188 no14 p9 O 10 2016

Peacey, Jonathan

Committing to socially responsible seafood color *Science* v356 no6341 p912 Je 1 2017

Peach

See also

Frozen peaches

Peach, Damian

Image the GIANT planets bw color *Astronomy* v45 no10 p52 O 2017

READER GALLERY color *Astronomy* v44 no12 p70 D 2016

Peachman, Rachel Rabkin

beat the clock *Parents* v92 no2 p44 F 2017

frozen fun *Parents* p137 2015

have a nicer trip *Parents* v91 no11 p142 N 2016

scrap the nap [Cover story] *Parents* v92 no7 p124 Jl 2017

Too Many Meds? [Cover story] color *Consumer Reports* v82 no9 p24 S 2017

tooth-fairy time *Parents* v91 no6 p144 Je 2016

Peacock, Barbara

HOME TOWN bw color *Yankee* p108 Jl 2017

Summer Quests bw color *Yankee* p10 Jl 2017

Peacock, Molly, 1947-

ALTER EGO N. ALSADIR color *O, The Oprah Magazine* p72 Ja 2017

PEACOCK, RYAN

A TO Z Guide to cues [Cover story] color *Yoga Journal* no293 p71 Ag 2017

Peacock, Scott

THE KITCHEN COOKBOOK color *Better Homes & Gardens* v95 no10 p160 O 2017

POT LUCK J. YONAN color *Better Homes & Gardens* v95 no10 p146 O 2017

Peacock Pin, The (Poem)

The Peacock Pin A. Moseley *America* v217 no6 p51 S 18 2017

Peak, Donna

The 7 Kitchen Essentials color diag *Log Home Living* v34 no4 p54 My 2017

Bathing Beauties color diag *Log Home Living* v34 no4 p68 My 2017

The Beauty Within *Log Home Living* v33 no7 p8 S 2016

The Best of Both Worlds color *Log Home Living* p10 2018 Annual Buyers Guide

Boot Camp Beauty color diag *Log Home Living* v34 no2 p70 Mr 2017

Cabin Power *Log Home Living* v34 no3 p6 Ap 2017

Come Along for the Ride *Log Home Living* v34 no9 p6 D 2017

Crash & Learn color *Log Home Living* v34 no5 p18 Jl 2017

The Fix is In color *Log Home Living* v34 no7 p6 S 2017

For the Love of Logs color *Log Home Living* p10 2017 SpecialIssue

Get the Perfect Getaway! color diag *Log Home Living* v34 no3 p62 Ap 2017

An Hour Away, a World Apart color diag *Log Home Living* v34 no3 p68 Ap 2017

Log Home Fixer Upper color diag *Log Home Living* v33 no7 p24 S 2016

Make it Yours *Log Home Living* v34 no1 p8 F 2017

Map Out a Plan *Log Home Living* v34 no6 p6 Ag 2017

Nama"stay" color *Log Home Living* v33 no7 p68 S 2016

Natural Attraction [Cover story] color diag *Log Home Living* v34 no9 p64 D 2017

Playing Favorites *Log Home Living* v34 no4 p8 My 2017

Secondhand Shangri-La color *Log Home Living* v34 no7 p72 S 2017

Second Nature color diag *Log Home Living* v34 no5 p26 Jl 2017

THE SECRETS TO Floor Plan Perfection diag *Log Home Living* v34 no1 p44 F 2017

Small Talk with HGTV's Property Brothers color *Log Home Living* v34 no3 p18 Ap 2017

Tennessee Strong *Log Home Living* v34 no2 p6 Mr 2017

Things to Do Today: Make My Dreams Come True *Log Home Living* v34 no5 p6 Jl 2017

You Only Get What You Give color *Log Home Living* v33 no9 p8 D 2016

Peakman, Julie

ANIMAL MAGNETISM IN VICTORIAN LONDON: Mesmerism was a short-lived medical phenomenon, but its most celebrated British exponent, John Elliotson, attracted large crowds, which incensed his rivals *History Today* v67 no9 p98 S 2017

Peale, Charles Willson, 1741-1827

PORTRAIT OF A REVOLUTION P. Staiti *MHQ: Quarterly Journal of Military History* v29 no2 p60 Wint 2017

Peanut butter

24 WAYS TO CARRY PEANUT BUTTER IN YOUR JERSEY POCKET color *Bicycling* v58 no4 p46 My 2017

Cooking with Coconut Oil J. Bessinger color *Amazing Wellness* v9 no2 p80 Spr 2017

Critter Crudités color *Good Housekeeping* v264 no6 p129 Je 2017

Peanut Butter & Co.

24 WAYS TO CARRY PEANUT BUTTER IN YOUR JERSEY

POCKET color *Bicycling* v58 no4 p46 My 2017

Peanut butter—Evaluation

Bust Out of Your Nut Rut color *Men's Health* v31 no10 p64 D 2016

Peanut hulls

A Body of Trees N. NEELY color *Orion Magazine* v35 no6 p46 N/D 2016

Peanuts

See also

Peanut hulls

Peanut Love color *Better Nutrition* v79 no3 p58 Mr 2017

The Peanut Plague J. LEWIS color *Discover* v38 no10 p50 D 2017

Tourist Traps: Tricks for eating healthy on tour K. BRADY *Dance Magazine* v91 no10 p38 O 2017

Peanuts—Therapeutic use

17 Healthy Hacks the Food Pros Use C. Sass color *Health* v31 no2 p63 Mr 2017

Pear, Warren S.

Regeneration of fat cells from myofibroblasts during wound healing bibl color graph *Science* v355 no6326 p748 F 17 2017

PEARCE, ALAN

Accelerating Tropicalization and the Transformation of Temperate Seagrass Meadows *BioScience* v66 no11 p938 N 1 2016

Pearce, Brad—Interviews

Q&A WITH BRAD PEARCE *Texas Monthly* v44 no11 p36 N 2016

Pearce, Dalton

REED AND PEARCE CAP ROP ING ROLL WITH PENDLETON WIN K. SANTOS color *Spin to Win Rodeo* v20 no9 p54 N 2016

Pearce, Edward J.

Inflammation by way of macrophage metabolism diag *Science* v356 no6337 p488 My 5 2017

Pearce, Joanne

4,000 KILOMETRES 6,000 YEARS OF HISTORY 500 PETRO-GLYPHS 2 COLONIAL FORTS 17 STUDENTS 4 CULTURES ONE COOL TRIP color map *Canadian Geographic* v137 p47 2017 Travel

FEATURED FELLOW: JESSICA LINDSAY PHILLIPS color *Canadian Geographic* v137 no4 p78 Jl/Ag 2017

Search for the blue goose bw color *Canadian Geographic* v137 no5 p22 S/O 2017

Wildfire watch map *Canadian Geographic* v137 no5 p30 S/O 2017

Pearce, Joshua

From selfies to selfless: Managing multigenerational teams A. G. Levine color *Science* v357 no6356 p1170 S 15 2017

Pearce, Joshua M.

Solar Is Being Held Back by Regulations, Not Technology *Harvard Business Review Digital Articles* p2 D 15 2016

What If All U.S. Coal Workers Were Retrained to Work in Solar? *Harvard Business Review Digital Articles* p2 Ag 8 2016

PEARCE, MICHAEL

WHEN DOVES DON'T FLY color *Outdoor Life* v224 no7 pH1 S 2017

Pearce, Steve

How Salt Chlorination Systems Work *Parks & Recreation* p4 Aquatics Guide 2017

Pearce, Terry

Mattress Missionaries A. FELDMAN and M. GERSTEIN color *Forbes* v199 no5 p50 My 16 2017

Pearce, Tony

Mattress Missionaries A. FELDMAN and M. GERSTEIN color *Forbes* v199 no5 p50 My 16 2017

Pearce, Walter

Change AGENTS K. BERNARD color *Vogue* v206 no11 p124 N 2016

Pearce-Kelly, Paul

The broad footprint of climate change from genes to biomes to people bibl chart color *Science* v354 no6313 paaf7671-1 N 11 2016

Pearl, Nancy, 1945-

George & Lizzie *Publishers Weekly* v264 no30 p38 Jl 24 2017

Nancy Pearl's Next Chapter S. Feldman color *Publishers Weekly* v264 no34 p29 Ag 21 2017

Pearl, Robert M.

What Health Systems, Hospitals, and Physicians Need to Know About Implementing Electronic Health Records *Harvard Business Review Digital Articles* p2 Je 15 2017

Pearl jewelry—Evaluation

PEARL Crush color *InStyle* v23 no12 p136 N 2016

What I'd Do Differently Marcello Gandini, 78 color *Car & Driver* v62 no6 p108 D 2016

Pearley Huffman, John

Take 5 With DALE EARNHARDT JR color *Hot Rod* v70 no11 p14 N 2017

Take 5 With KENNY DUTTWEILER color *Hot Rod* v70 no12 p12 D 2017

Pearl Fishers, The (Theatrical production)

The Pearl Fishers J. Pell *Opera News* v81 no7 p38 Ja 2017

Pearl Harbor (Hawaii), Attack on, 1941

Countdown to Infamy S. TWOMEY *Smithsonian* v47 no8 p25 D 2016

DECEMBER 7, 1941 S. S. PATEL bw color diag *Archaeology* v70 no1 p40 Ja/F 2017

Discussion *Smithsonian* v47 no9 p6 Ja/F 2017

FROM ISOLATIONISM TO INTERVENTIONISN *Saturday Evening Post* v288 no6 p110 N/D 2016

REMEMBERING PEARL HARBOR S. Parnes, J. Steele et al *Saturday Evening Post* v288 no6 p6 N/D 2016

Pearlman, Catherine

Just Ignore It color *Parents* v92 no9 p58 S 2017

Pearlman, Isaac N.

FOREST GUARDIANS color *Earth Island Journal* v32 no4 p48 Wint 2017

Pearlman, Jeff

THE OFF SEASON color *Sports Illustrated* v125 no14 p38 O 24-31 2016

Pearlman, Wendy

THE REVOLUTION BEGAN color *Harper's Magazine* v335 no2005 p11 Je 2017

We Crossed a Bridge and It Trembled: Voices from Syria *Publishers Weekly* v264 no13 p91 Mr 27 2017

Pearlstein, Karla

A Storybook ODYSSEY D. Pizzi color *Old House Journal* v44 no8 p28 D 2016

Pearlstine, Norman

What Really Worries South Koreans: Trump color *Time* v190 no14 p24 O 9 2017

PEARMAN, HUGH

Elegant Finish *Architectural Record* v205 no7 p99 Jl 2017

Grounds for Justice color diag *Architectural Record* v205 no3 p106 Mr 2017

Last days of the Smithsons' Robin Hood Gardens *Architectural Record* v205 no9 p32 S 2017

The Past Laid Bare *Architectural Record* v205 no10 p90 O 2017

Star Ship *Architectural Record* v204 no11 p78 N 2016

Pears

Quick and Easy Pear Dishes N. Berkoff *Vegetarian Journal* v36 no1 p10 2017

Pears, Kerry

ESCAPE FROM STATEN ISLAND color *Sail* v48 no1 p42 Ja 2017

PEARSALL, TRICIA

Spires in the Sky Myanmar lifts the curtain on the Golden Land of Burma *Virginia Living* v15 no6 p52 O 2017

PEARSE, IAN S.

Long-Term Trends in Midwestern Milkweed Abundances and Their Relevance to Monarch Butterfly Declines *BioScience* v67 no4 p343 Ap 2017

Pearson, Chris

Complex multifault rupture during the 2016 Mw 7.8 Kaikōura earthquake, New Zealand color map *Science* v356 no6334 p154 Ap 14 2017

Pearson, Clifford A.

The Good Earth *Architectural Record* v205 no4 p134 Ap 2017

house of the month color diag *Architectural Record* v204 no12 p25 D 2016

interiors *Architectural Record* v205 no1 p31 Ja 2017

interiors color diag *Architectural Record* v205 no2 p33 F 2017

K-Pop *Architectural Record* v205 no10 p108 O 2017

Tasty or Tasteless? color *Architectural Record* v205 no3 p55 Mr

2017

Pearson, Helen
The Life Project: The Extraordinary Story of 70,000 Ordinary Lives L. Neff color *Christian Century* v133 no25 p41 D 7 2016

PEARSON, JOHN
DRUG ADVERTISING color *Scientific American* v315 no3 p5 S 2016

Pearson, Liz
SINGULAR Sensation color *O, The Oprah Magazine* p107 Ja 2017

Pearson, Natalie Obiko
The Best Former Whorehouse in Canada color *Bloomberg Businessweek* no4497 p28 O 31 2016
Can Oil Sands Pay Off At $50 a Barrel? graph *Bloomberg Businessweek* no4535 p33 Ag 28 2017
A First Nation For the 21st Century color *Bloomberg Businessweek* no4541 p30 O 9 2017
WHISTLER HITS A PEAK color *Bloomberg Businessweek* no4541 p62 O 9 2017

PEARSON, PATRICIA
Jagged Little Pills color *Walrus* v14 no8 p42 O 2017

PEARSON, RACHEL
No Money, No Care D. OFRI *New York Times Book Review* p15 Ag 27 2017
Seeing the Body *Texas Monthly* v45 no8 p54 Ag 2017

Pearson, Scott
CABIN art color *Cabin Living* p11 O 2017

PEARSON, STEPHANIE
HEAD-TO-HEAD: WATTS HAPPENING color *Wired* v25 no7 p38 Jl 2017

Pearson PLC
PEARSON RISES ABOVE J. MILLIOT chart *Publishers Weekly* v264 no35 p56 Ag 28 2017

Peart, Byron—Interviews
BYRON & DEXTER PEART J. Wilson color *Essence* v47 no9 p18 Ja 2017

Peart, Dexter—Interviews
BYRON & DEXTER PEART J. Wilson color *Essence* v47 no9 p18 Ja 2017

Peas
Easy-Peasy J. McDaniel color *AARP: The Magazine* v59 no2A p70 F/Mr 2016
Power Pods L. REGE color *Martha Stewart Living* no275 p74 Je 2017

Peas—Breeding
THE SWEETEST PEAS J. Silver color *Sunset* v238 no2 p33 F 2017

PEASLEY, AARON
BUILDING GREEN color *Architectural Digest* no5 p142 My 2017
creative haven bw color *Architectural Digest* v74 no2 p100 F 2017
Jesse WINE *Interview* v46 no10 p110 D 2016/Ja 2017

Peat mosses
Water-Trough Raised Beds P. Sweeney *Mother Earth News* no282 p84 Je/Jl 2017

Peatland management
Time for responsible peatland agriculture L. S. Wijedasa, S. E. Page et al bibl *Science* v354 no6312 p562 N 4 2016

Pebble Beach (Calif.)—Description & travel
Pebble Beach The Golfer's Ultimate Guide J. Passov and J. Sens color *Golf Magazine* v59 no2 p84 F 2017

Pebble Beach Golf Links (Pebble Beach, Calif.)
Major problem? Major solution! M. Bamberger color *Golf Magazine* v59 no8 p112 Ag 2017

Pecan growing
FAMILY TREES K. Owen and P. Lolley color *Southern Living* v52 no9 p82 S 2017

Pecan industry
CAJUN COUNTRY J. FROIS color *Louisiana Life* v37 no2 p91 N/D 2016

Peccaries
Javelinas N. Austin *Arizona Highways* v93 no11 p13 N 2017

Pech, M.
Observation of a large-scale anisotropy in the arrival directions of cosmic rays above 8 × 1018 eV *Science* v357 no6357 p1266 S 22 2017

Pech, Markus
The cryo-EM structure of a ribosome–Ski2–Ski3–Ski8 helicase complex bibl color graph *Science* v354 no6318 p1431 D 16 2016

PECHERSKI, KRISTAL
ROAR OF THE CROWD *Texas Monthly* v45 no9 p8 S 2017

Pechlaner, Maria
Exploring genetic suppression interactions on a global scale diag *Science* v354 no6312 p599 N 4 2016

Pechman, Alexandra
IVENS MACHADO color *Art in America* v104 no11 p127 D 2016

Peck, Annie S. (Annie Smith), 1850-1935
CAN'T KEEP HER DOWN M. WALSH bw color *Climbing* no356 p54 S/O 2017

PECK, EMILY
ALFRESCO PARTY PREP color *House Beautiful* p135 Ag 2017

Peck, Gregory, 1916-2003
COLLEGE TOWN SMACKDOWN G. A. Warner color *Sunset* v239 no3 p28 S 2017
In Honor of Atticus C. Nashawaty color *Entertainment Weekly* no1470 p40 Je 16 2017

Peck, Raoul
BALDWIN'S RENDEZVOUSWITH THE TWENTY-FIRST CENTURY: I AM NOT YOUR NEGRO W. Crichlow *Film Quarterly* v70 no4 p9 Summ 2017
Dear America, James Baldwin Is Still 'Not Your Negro' B. DANIELLE and L. CROSS bw color *Ebony* v72 no4 p22 F 2017
FADE TO BLACK H. ALS bw cartoon *New Yorker* v92 no49 p84 F 13 2017
I Am Not Your Negro C. Nashawaty color *Entertainment Weekly* no1451/1452 p92 F 3-10 2017
Language in black and white A. Frykholm bw *Christian Century* v134 no9 p10 Ap 26 2017
Under the Spell of James Baldwin D. Pinckney bw *New York Review of Books* v64 no5 p24 Mr 23 2017

Peck, Raoul—Interviews
O SAY CAN YOU SEE A. CLARK bw *Film Comment* v53 no1 p57 Ja/F 2017

Peck, Robert McCracken
Tokens of friendship, tools of diplomacy: Presentation medals in the Age of Exploration bw color *Magazine Antiques* v184 no5 p64 S/O 2017

Peck, S. C.
A prominent glycyl radical enzyme in human gut microbiomes metabolizes trans-4-hydroxy-L-proline diag *Science* v355 no6325 p595 F 10 2017

Peck, Tiler
THE 2016 DANCE MAGAZINE AWARDS color *Dance Magazine* v91 no3 p16 Mr 2017
TILER PECK M. Harss *Dance Magazine* v90 no12 p47 D 2016

Pecker, David
FEEDING THE BEAST J. TOOBIN bw cartoon *New Yorker* v93 no19 p38 Jl 3 2017

Peckham, Daniel
Emergence and spread of a human-transmissible multidrug-resistant nontuberculous mycobacterium bibl diag graph *Science* v354 no6313 p751 N 11 2016

Peckham, Matt
An Ancient Power Awakens, and Evolves, In New Zelda color *Time* v189 no9 p54 Mr 13 2017
The Best of Everything This Year-So Far color *Time* v189 no21 p61 Je 5 2017
Mario on an iPhone? It Works color *Time* v189 no3 p59 Ja 16 2017
The New Zen of Playing Old Video Games color *Time* v190 no16/17 p109 O 23 2017
Nintendo Switches Up Mobile Gaming With a Novel Console color *Time* v189 no9 p55 Mr 13 2017
With Arms, Nintendo Wants to Rekindle Excitement for Motion Controls color *Time* v189 no24 p53 Je 26 2017

Peckham, S. Hoyt
Committing to socially responsible seafood color *Science* v356 no6341 p912 Je 1 2017

PECKNOLD, C. C.
Praying for an Imperfect President color *America* v215 no18 p17 D 5 2016

Pecl, Gretta T.

Biodiversity redistribution under climate change: Impacts on ecosystems and human well-being color *Science* v355 no6332 p1389 Mr 31 2017

Péczeli, Anna

The future of US–Russian nuclear deterrence and arms control bibl *Bulletin of the Atomic Scientists* v73 no4 p271 Jl 2017

Peczuh, Mark W.

Unequivocal determination of complex molecular structures using anisotropic NMR measurements color *Science* v356 no6333 p43 Ap 7 2017

Pedagogical content knowledge

IT'S NOT THE TOOLS ...IT'S THE TEACHING B. Steckel and V. Harlow Shinas color *Literacy Today (2411-7862)* v34 no3 p22 N/D 2016

Peddada, Shyamal

Seasonal change in the gut [Cover story] color *Science* v357 no6353 p754 Ag 25 2017

Pedder, Adele

Protecting the Coral Sea–the Cradle to the Great Barrier Reef *UN Chronicle* v54 no1/2 p1 2017

PEDERSEN, BRENDAN

ONLINE MERCHANTS THAT DON'T DELIVER color *Kiplinger's Personal Finance* v71 no11 p11 N 2017

Pedersen, Carsten Lund

The 4 Types of Project Manager *Harvard Business Review Digital Articles* p2 Jl 27 2017

Pedesseau, L.

Extremely efficient internal exciton dissociation through edge states in layered 2D perovskites bibl graph *Science* v355 no6331 p1288 Mr 24 2017

Pedestrian accidents—Prevention

COUNTING DOWN TO ZERO D. C. Vock *Governing* v30 no5 p38 F 2017

Pedestrian areas

See also

Footbridges

Shopping malls

THE MORE THINGS CHANGE... D. HISLOP *Sea Magazine* v109 no2 pPNW-6 F 2017

World's Longest Suspension Footbridge J. Zorthian color *Time* v190 no8 p21 Ag 28 2017

Pedevilla, Philipp

Active sites in heterogeneous ice nucleation—the example of K-rich feldspars bibl bw diag *Science* v355 no6323 p367 Ja 27 2017

Pediatric surgeons

Close to Her Heart B. Hargrove *D: The Magazine of Dallas* v43 no10 p116 O 2016

Pediatricians

2016 Best Doctors and Pediatric Specialists *D: The Magazine of Dallas* v43 no10 p130 O 2016

2016 BEST PEDIATRIC SPECIALISTS IN DALLAS *D: The Magazine of Dallas* v43 no10 p262 O 2016

BEST DOCS: 559 PHYSICIANS IN 77 SPECIALTIES [Cover story] S. RAVITS color *New Orleans Magazine* v51 no10 p84 Ag 2017

What pediatricians tell their friends S. WOOD color *Redbook* p79 S 2017

Pediatrics

Can this trick help with ear problems? *Parents* v91 no6 p24 Je 2016

HEALING THE WHOLE CHILD A. BROWNLEE *Cincinnati Magazine* v50 no4 p70 Ja 2017

Pediculosis—Prevention

The Latest Lice Advice color *Parents* v92 no3 p20 Mr 2017

Pediculosis—Treatment

How to Get Rid of Lice M. Wollan *New York Times Magazine* p19 My 14 2017

Pedreira, F.

Observation of a large-scale anisotropy in the arrival directions of cosmic rays above 8 × 1018 eV *Science* v357 no6357 p1266 S 22 2017

Pedrick, Andrea C.

FINDING STATION 77—A piece of history is restored at Stillwater Mountain fire tower color *New York State Conservationist* v71 no2 p18 O 2016

Pedrosa, Dani

EL GANADOR color *Cycle World* v56 no6 p74 Jl 2017

Peduto, Bill

Winning the Permit Game A. Greenblatt *Governing* v30 no1 p12 O 2016

Peebles, Paul

Not Your Grandfather's Log Cabin color *Log Home Living* v34 no2 p66 Mr 2017

Stop the Rot color *Log Home Living* v34 no7 p38 S 2017

Peed, Mike

Families in Fiction *New York Times Book Review* p26 Ja 1 2017

The Shortlist *New York Times Book Review* p26 Jl 30 2017

Peek, Katie

COPING SKILLS graph map *Scientific American* v315 no3 p38 S 2016

The Elusive Northwest Passage color graph *Scientific American* v316 no5 p80 My 2017

A HISTORY IN LAYERS [Cover story] color graph *Scientific American* v315 no3 p30 S 2016

Is the Rise in Twin Births Cresting? graph *Scientific American* v315 no6 p88 D 2016

Long Live Hubble color *Scientific American* v316 no3 p80 Mr 2017

The Odyssey of the Great Frigatebird *Audubon* v118 no6 p14 Wint 2016

On Our Radar color *Audubon* v119 no3 p16 Fall 2017

Urban Wealth color *Scientific American* v315 no3 p92 S 2016

Peek, Patricia

And the Winning Photo Is... *British Heritage Travel* v38 no3 p80 My/Je 2017

PEELE, ANNA

Mating bw color *GQ: Gentlemen's Quarterly* v86 no11 p58 N 2016

Mel Brooks *GQ: Gentlemen's Quarterly* v97 no6 p130 Je 2017

MOTY DUDE FINALLY MADE IT [Cover story] color *GQ: Gentlemen's Quarterly* v86 no12 p172 D 2016

THE NEW CLASS OF CLOWNS color *GQ: Gentlemen's Quarterly* v97 no6 p106 Je 2017

OFF the BEATEN PATH color *GQ: Gentlemen's Quarterly* v97 no9 p154 S 2017

THE Punch List bw *GQ: Gentlemen's Quarterly* v86 no11 p69 N 2016

This Man Is the Future of Funny Kumail Nanjiani can see what's coming in comedy—including everything that's in this issue color *GQ: Gentlemen's Quarterly* v97 no6 p44 Je 2017

THE WORLD ACCORDING TO GOLDBLUM color *GQ: Gentlemen's Quarterly* v97 no11 p134 N 2017

Peele, Jordan, 1979-

ATTACK OF THE KILLER WHITE PEOPLE K. P. Sullivan color *Entertainment Weekly* no1454/1455 p80 F 24 2017

Bigotry is the Monster in Jordan Peele's New Film K. KYLES color *Ebony* v72 no5 p20 Mr 2017

GET OUT BREAKS OUT J. Nolfi color *Entertainment Weekly* no1456 p16 Mr 10 2017

Hollywood Signs: Mark Harris: The Get Out Effect Does Hollywood know what to do with a surprise success? img *New York* v50 no9 p13 My 1 2017

How to Sell a Crazy Idea P. Kita cartoon color *Men's Health* v32 no2 p32 Mr 2017

Jordan Peele Made Us Seriously Laugh. Now He's Going to Scare Us Silly E. Berman color *Time* v189 no7/8 p108 F 27 2017

Lost Weekend J. PODHORETZ color *Weekly Standard* v22 no28 p43 Mr 27 2017

The Response to 'Get Out' D. Lindelof *New York Times Magazine* p41 O 8 2017

SCARY PLACES A. LANE cartoon *New Yorker* v93 no3 p84 Mr 6 2017

White Fright D. EDELSTEIN img *New York* p75 F 20 2017

Peele, Jordan, 1979—Interviews

Jordan Peele Is Terrifying color *GQ: Gentlemen's Quarterly* v97 no3 p82 Mr 2017

Peelers (Utensils)

SEASONS FLEETING D. Copaken color *O, The Oprah Magazine* p35 S 2017

Peelle, Lydia

The Midnight Cool *Publishers Weekly* v263 no42 p45 O 17 2016

PEEPLES, JASE

GAY (SUPER) POWER *Advocate* no1088 p22 D 2016/Ja 2017

Peer, Amanda

The Clinic: PHOTO CRITIQUES S. von Dietze color *Dressage Today* v23 no11 p20 Ag 2017

Peer, Basharat

A Question of Order: India, Turkey, and the Return of Strongmen G. J. Ikenberry *Foreign Affairs* v96 no3 p155 My/Je 2017

Pe'er, Guy

A global map of roadless areas and their conservation status bibl color graph map *Science* v354 no6318 p1423 D 16 2016

Peer pressure

NOW THAT SOUNDS POSITIVE D. MILLER *USA Today Magazine* v146 no2868 p36 S 2017

A POSITIVE FOR PEER PRESSURE C. Barakat and M. McCluskey color *Equus* no471 p12 D 2016

Peer pressure in adolescence

Are You Following the Herd? H. CORBETT *Scholastic Choices* v32 no8 p16 My 2017

Peer pressure in children—Psychological aspects

Putting Peer Pressure in Its Place A. NICODEMO *USA Today Magazine* v146 no2868 p38 S 2017

Peer pressure—Psychological aspects

Putting Peer Pressure in Its Place A. NICODEMO *USA Today Magazine* v146 no2868 p38 S 2017

Peer relations

Observing peers develops practice, changes culture K. A. Reilly il *Phi Delta Kappan* v98 no6 p13 Mr 2017

Strategies for Working Smoothly with Your Peers R. Newton *Harvard Business Review Digital Articles* p2 Je 11 2015

Peer review (Professional performance)

Creating an Effective Peer Review System E. Mosley *Harvard Business Review Digital Articles* p2 Ag 19 2015

Peer review of academic writing

IN REFEREES WE TRUST? M. Baldwin *Physics Today* v70 no2 p44 F 2017

Peer review as collaboration T. Shinbrot *Physics Today* v70 no10 p15 O 2017

Peer review as conflict P. T. Williams *Physics Today* v70 no10 p17 O 2017

A Scientist Pushes Psychology Journals toward Open Data T. Witkowski *Skeptical Inquirer* v41 no4 p6 Jl/Ag 2017

Peer review of academic writing—Moral & ethical aspects

China cracks down on fraud D. Normile *Science* v357 no6350 p435 Ag 4 2017

Peer review of research grant proposals

A lifeline for Greek science—or living on borrowed time? E. Stokstad color *Science* v353 no6307 p1481 S 30 2016

Peer-to-peer file sharing

The iPhone switcher's guide: Move from iOS to Android and keep all your stuff M. SIMON color *PCWorld* v35 no1 p173 Ja 2017

Peer-to-peer lending

Peering Into Peer-to-Peer Loans A. GARA color *Forbes* v198 no7 p98 N 29 2016

Peerenboom, Harold—Trials, litigation, etc.

Intrigue at Sloan's Curve J. CASTALDO color *Maclean's* v130 no8 p45 S 2017

Peers

From Young Professional to Respected Leader: Navigating the park and recreation career ladder R. Fink II *Parks & Recreation* v52 no5 p34 My 2017

Peery, Janet

The Exact Nature of Our Wrongs *Publishers Weekly* v264 no32 p49 Ag 7 2017

Peet, Mal, 1947-2015

Beck *Publishers Weekly* v264 no9 p101 F 27 2017

Peeters, Clara, ca. 1590-1657

Farther afield C. C. Young bw color *Magazine Antiques* v183 no6 p36 N/D 2016

A wreath of flowers surrounding an oval medallion of the Madonna and Child, 1621 color *Magazine Antiques* v183 no6 p35 N/D 2016

Peet's Coffee & Tea Inc.

DAVE BURWICK bw color *Bloomberg Businessweek* no4517 p76 Ap 3 2017

Pegu, Amarendra

Trispecific broadly neutralizing HIV antibodies mediate potent SHIV protection in macaques color graph *Science* v357 no6359 p85 O 6 2017

Pei, I. M., 1917-

The Master J. Davidson img *New York* v50 no8 p115 Ap 17 2017

pei day P. Goldberger bw color *Architectural Digest* v74 no4 p154 Ap 2017

Pei, Qibing

Highly efficient electrocaloric cooling with electrostatic actuation bw diag *Science* v357 no6356 p1130 S 15 2017

Pei-Hsuan Chu

Engineering extrinsic disorder to control protein activity in living cells bibl color *Science* v354 no6318 p1441 D 16 2016

Pei-Yong Shi

Zika virus produces noncoding RNAs using a multi-pseudoknot structure that confounds a cellular exonuclease bibl color graph *Science* v354 no6316 p1148 D 2 2016

Peifer, Mark

Call to restore NIH's cap on grant funding *Science* v357 no6349 p364 Jl 28 2017

Peiffer, Kim

Gold Rush color *InStyle* v24 no5 p84 My 2017

HOORAY FOR Hollywood color *InStyle* v23 no12 p252 N 2016

THE INSTYLE AWARDS Fashion Goes to Hollywood color *InStyle* v24 no1 p39 Ja 2017

The Parties color *InStyle* v23 no12 p84 N 2016

SOLID GOLD color *InStyle* v24 no3 p153 Mr 2017

Peiker, E.J.

Sitting Ducks color *Audubon* v119 no3 p48 Fall 2017

PEIKOFF, KIRA

The Connected Heart color *Popular Mechanics* p14 F 2017

Peipei Zhu, Yanfang

Hematopoietic stem cells gone rogue bibl color diag *Science* v355 no6327 p798 F 24 2017

PEIRIS, HIRANYA

A COSMIC CONTROVERSY color *Scientific American* v317 no1 p5 Jl 2017

PEIROLO, STEPHANIE

WHEN INSURANCE STOPS PAYING color *Reader's Digest* v189 no1129 p116 Ap 2017

Peirs, Cedric

Neural circuits for pain: Recent advances and current views bibl diag *Science* v354 no6312 p578 N 4 2016

PEISNER, DAVID

St. Paul's Southern Soul Revival color *Rolling Stone* no1275 p16 D 1 2016

Peitz, Martin

Net Neutrality Rules Will Make Winners and Losers Out of Businesses *Harvard Business Review Digital Articles* p2 Je 27 2016

PEJCHAR, LIBA

Addressing the Gender Gap in Distinguished Speakers at Professional Ecology Conferences *BioScience* v67 no5 p464 My 2017

Pejrone, Paolo

fertile imagination S. MEDFORD color *Architectural Digest* v74 no9 p138 S 2017

Péladan, Joséphin, 1859-1918

THE MAGUS OF PARIS A. ROSS bw cartoon *New Yorker* v93 no18 p67 Je 26 2017

Pelagic red crab

Crabs Swarm on the Seafloor V. LaCapra *Oceanus* v52 no1 p6 Summ 2016

Pelargoniums

See also

Scented geraniums

SMELL-GOOD GREENERY J. Silver color *Sunset* v238 no4 p46 Ap 2017

Pelayo, R.

Observation of a large-scale anisotropy in the arrival directions of cosmic rays above 8×1018 eV *Science* v357 no6357 p1266 S 22 2017

Pelc, Rebecca S.

Rapid development of a DNA vaccine for Zika virus bibl graph *Science* v354 no6309 p237 O 14 2016

Pelczar, Penelope

A pathogenic role for T cell–derived IL-22BP in inflammatory bowel disease bibl graph *Science* v354 no6310 p358 O 21 2016

Peleg, Zvi
Wild emmer genome architecture and diversity elucidate wheat evolution and domestication color *Science* v357 no6346 p93 Jl 7 2017

PELICICE, FERNANDO M.
Nonnative Fish to Control Aedes Mosquitoes: A Controversial, Harmful Tool *BioScience* v67 no1 p84 Ja 2017

PELINI, JAKE
Unsafe at Any Speed cartoon *Atlantic* v319 no2 p22 Mr 2017
When the Mind Wanders color *Atlantic* v320 no3 p26 O 2017

Pelkmans, Mathijs
Fragile Conviction: Changing Ideological Landscapes in Urban Kyrgyzstan R. Legvold *Foreign Affairs* v96 no6 p165 N/D 2017

Pell, Jonathan
The Pearl Fishers *Opera News* v81 no7 p38 Ja 2017

PELL, MICHELLE
GRAPHIC LITERATURE *Scientific American* v316 no6 p5 Je 2017

Pelleted feed—Evaluation
STOCK & TRADE color *Equus* no475 p84 Ap 2017

PELLETIER, FRANCINE
A SUGAR CUBE BESIDE A GALLON OF COFFEE chart color *Maclean's* v130 no6 p17 Jl 2017

Pelletier, Josh
The Locals T. E. Nickens color *Field & Stream* v122 no4 p60 S 2017

Pelley, Scott
PARODY color *Weekly Standard* v22 no30 p40 Ap 10 2017

Pelli Clarke Pelli Architects (Company)
Transbay Transit Center *Architectural Record* v205 no4 p202 Ap 2017

Pelliccia, Hayden
The Art of Wrath color *New York Review of Books* v64 no15 p42 O 12 2017

Pelliccia, Hayden N.
The Ancient Delights of the Epigram color *New York Review of Books* v64 no10 p52 Je 8 2017

Pellicciotto, Jane
To The Editor color *American Craft* v76 no6 p10 D 2016-Ja 2017

Pellot, Brian
Yemen's Bahá'ís keep faith amid conflict, crackdown color *Christian Century* v134 no1 p15 Ja 4 2017

PELLY, JENN
Crutchfield Sisters color *Rolling Stone* no1295 p43 S 7 2017

Pelorosso, Facundo
Macrophage function in tissue repair and remodeling requires IL-4 or IL-13 with apoptotic cells diag *Science* v356 no6342 p1072 Je 9 2017

Pelosi, Nancy, 1940-
NYT Values Reputation for 'Balance' More Than Health of Sick Kids J. Naureckas *Extra!* v30 no5 p4 Je 2017

PELOT, CAROLE
Q: What did you let go of that changed your life? color *O, The Oprah Magazine* p16 Ag 2017

Peloton Technology Inc.
IN THE DRAFT P. LERNER color *Road & Track* v69 no4 p62 N 2017

Pelphrey, Tom
Marvel's Iron Fist M. ROUSH *TV Guide* v65 no13 p19 Mr 20 2017

Peltier, Gilles
An algal photoenzyme converts fatty acids to hydrocarbons color graph *Science* v357 no6354 p903 S 1 2017

Peltz, Nelson, 1942-
Nelson Peltz Makes Nice A. Melin and S. Deveau bw *Bloomberg Businessweek* no4536 p30 S 4 2017

Peltz, Nicola
STYLE CRUSH Nicola Peltz S. Simon color *InStyle* v24 no2 p62 F 2017

PELUSI, NANDO
Conquering the Divided Self: ONE QUESTION FOR WEIKE WANG *Psychology Today* v50 no5 p96 S/O 2017

Peluso, Michelle
How I Got Here M. Peluso color *Working Mother* v40 no4 p12 O/N 2017

Pelz, Dave

The Crisp Wedge Secret color *Golf Magazine* v59 no11 p33 N 2017
Damage Control color *Golf Magazine* v59 no10 p30 O 2017
Fly It High, Land It Softly color *Golf Magazine* v59 no5 p40 My 2017
Have No Fear! color *Golf Magazine* v59 no3 p38 Mr 2017
It's All Fun and Gains color *Golf Magazine* v59 no6 p30 Je 2017
Long-Distance Service color *Golf Magazine* v59 no4 p40 Ap 2017
No Gust, No Glory color *Golf Magazine* v59 no1 p34 Ja 2017
Pulling Out All the Flops color *Golf Magazine* v59 no7 p35 Jl 2017
(Really) Close Encounters color *Golf Magazine* v59 no9 p34 S 2017
That Hits the Spot color *Golf Magazine* v59 no2 p32 F 2017
Turn In, Plug Out color *Golf Magazine* v59 no8 p33 Ag 2017

Pemberton, Daniel, 1977-
Daniel Pemberton M. Hagan color *Current Biography* v78 no2 p62 F 2017

Pembrokeshire (Wales)—Description & travel
Wales for The Weekend E. WINDING color map *Conde Nast Traveler* v52 no6 p43 Je/Jl 2017

Pembrolizumab
New Hope at Stage 4 M. Fetterman color *AARP: The Magazine* v30 no6A p27 O/N 2017

Pemmaraju, C. D.
Femtosecond x-ray spectroscopy of an electrocyclic ring-opening reaction diag graph *Science* v356 no6333 p54 Ap 7 2017

Pen, Polly, 1953-
Pen: Arlington A. McKinnon *Opera News* v81 no7 p48 Ja 2017

Pen-based computers
iOS Accessories J. Mathis color *Macworld - Digital Edition* v34 no6 p76 Je 2017

Peña, Catherine J.
Early life stress confers lifelong stress susceptibility in mice via ventral tegmental area OTX2 diag *Science* v356 no6343 p1185 Je 16 2017

PEÑA, CHRISTINA
Needed: better labor market data *Issues in Science & Technology* v33 no2 p5 Wint 2017

Peña, Michael—Interviews
MICHAEL PEÑA D. Franich color *Entertainment Weekly* no1459 p46 Mr 31 2017

Pena, Monique
An environment-dependent transcriptional network specifies human microglia identity color *Science* v356 no6344 p1248 Je 23 2017

Pena, Salomon
On a Question of the Day color *Black Belt* v55 no6 p16 O/N 2017

Peña-Claros, Marielos
Forest conservation: Humans' handprints bibl color *Science* v355 no6324 p466 F 3 2017
Persistent effects of pre-Columbian plant domestication on Amazonian forest composition bibl chart graph map *Science* v355 no6328 p925 Mr 3 2017

Penaeus monodon
Black Tiger Shrimp C. BOND *Texas Monthly* v45 no5 p34 My 2017

Peña Nieto, Enrique, 1966-
MEXICO DOES NOT BELIEVE IN WALLS P. NIETO *Vital Speeches of the Day* v83 no3 p78 Mr 2017
Mexico's basic science funding falls short E. Frixione and J. P. Laclette *Science* v357 no6348 p260 Jl 21 2017

Pena-Rodriguez, J.
Observation of a large-scale anisotropy in the arrival directions of cosmic rays above 8×1018 eV *Science* v357 no6357 p1266 S 22 2017

PENCE, DENNIS
Giant Red color *Idaho Magazine* v16 no1 p6 O 2016
High on the Edge *Idaho Magazine* v16 no3 p47 D 2016

Pence, Mike, 1959-
Chatter J. SMOKER, R. TUNGATE et al *Indianapolis Monthly* v40 no7 p15 Mr 2017
LIFE IS WINNING IN AMERICA M. PENCE *Vital Speeches of the Day* v83 no3 p92 Mr 2017
Mike Pence Is No Ordinary Wingman P. Elliott color *Time* v188 no27-28 p52 D 26 2016

PACKING HIS BAGGAGE C. FEHRMAN *Indianapolis Monthly* v40 no5 p46 Ja 2017

THE PENCES VISIT MANHATTAN D. MCGRATH cartoon *New Yorker* v92 no32 p47 O 10 2016

The Persistent Passion of Vice President Mike Pence P. Elliott color *Time* v189 no21 p18 Je 5 2017

THE PRESIDENT PENCE DELUSION J. MAYER bw color *New Yorker* v93 no33 p54 O 23 2017

Speed Read K. KENDALL *Indianapolis Monthly* v40 no3 p18 N 2016

UNDER PRESIDENT TRUMP, AMERICA STANDS WITH IS-RAEL *Vital Speeches of the Day* v83 no5 p143 My 2017

Voter Fraud Commission *Congressional Digest* v96 no6 p31 Je 2017

WHAT WOULD BILLY DO? L. Collins cartoon *New Yorker* v93 no8 p20 Ap 10 2017

When The Vice President Is Not a Political Prop S. Pettypiece and E. Wasson color *Bloomberg Businessweek* no4535 p34 Ag 28 2017

Where's the Welcome Mat? *Weekly Standard* v22 no15 p2 D 19 2016

Who's Afraid of President Pence? J. ZENGERLE color *GQ: Gentlemen's Quarterly* v97 no9 p124 S 2017

Pence, Mike, 1959-—Political & social views

THE RADICAL CRUSADE OF MIKE PENCE S. RODRICK cartoon color *Rolling Stone* no1280 p44 F 9 2017

Running Mates from the Past Prove the Need for a New Politics of the Future J. Klein color *Time* v188 no15 p18 O 17 2016

Pencil drawing

Megan Mullally color *O, The Oprah Magazine* p32 O 2017

Pencils

THE HANDBOOK *Martha Stewart Living* no267 p123 S 2016

My Favorite Thing color *Esquire* p162 BigBlackBook

Pencils—Evaluation

Rethink Your Ink L. LARSON color *GQ: Gentlemen's Quarterly* v97 no11 p48 N 2017

Penck, A. R.

A.R. PENCK D. Ebony *Art in America* v104 no10 p148 N 2016

Pendants (Jewelry)

ARTIFACT J. A. LOBELL color *Archaeology* v70 no3 p68 My/Je 2017

ARTIFACT J. A. LOBELL color *Archaeology* v70 no4 p68 Je-Ag 2017

DIGITAL CRAFT: LASER CUTTING. COMPUTER MODEL-ING. THREE DIMENSIONS. A NEW AGE OF DESIGN IS UPON US *Cincinnati Magazine* v50 no11 p32 Ag 2017

Pendants (Jewelry)—Evaluation

Break the Mold color *Martha Stewart Living* p20 My 2017

DOPE STUFF ON MY DESK J. Wilson color *Essence* v47 no12 p22 Ap 2017

The LIST color *Harper's Bazaar* no3650 p73 F 2017

Pender, John

The Gulf Opportunity Zone Helped Affected Counties Recover Economically After Hurricane Katrina *Amber Waves: The Economics of Food, Farming, Natural Resources, & Rural America* p1 O 2016

Pendergrass, Sarah A.

Distribution and clinical impact of functional variants in 50,726 whole-exome sequences from the DiscovEHR study chart graph *Science* v354 no6319 paaf6814-1 D 23 2016

Pendergrast, Mark

LITTLE BEAN, FAIRLY BIG IMPACT D. ALEXANDER color *Alternatives Journal (AJ) - Canada's Environmental Voice* v42 no2 p77 2016

Pendle, George

THE MASOCHIST'S MARATHON bw color *Esquire* p90 Ag 2017

'ROID RAGE cartoon color *Esquire* p100 Ap 2017

SPACE COWBOY color *Esquire* p17 N 2017

WAR ON DRUGS color *Esquire* p40 Ap 2017

Pendleton, Adam, 1984-

Adam Pendleton M. Hagan color *Current Biography* v78 no9 p62 S 2017

Pendleton, Devon

One Winner, One Loser After a Fortune's Split color *Bloomberg Businessweek* no4506 p33 Ja 9 2017

Pendleton, Hadiya, 1997-2013

"I'm Doing This for Hadiya" L. Brody color *Glamour* v114 no7 p102 Jl 2016

PENDLEY, CAMILLE

THE CHIEF *Atlanta* v57 no2 p23 Je 2017

THE CITY'S OTHER FOOTBALL FANS *Atlanta* v56 no11 p98 Mr 2017

GOING TO THE COURTHOUSE *Atlanta* v56 no10 p19 F 2017

NOISES OFF *Atlanta* v56 no11 p28 Mr 2017

PLAY STATION *Atlanta* v56 no11 p95 Mr 2017

PENDLEY, MICHAEL

THE MEAT ROOM color *Field & Stream* v122 no6 p32 N 2017

Young Blood color *Field & Stream* v122 no4 p54 S 2017

Pendse, Mihir

Paneth cells secrete lysozyme via secretory autophagy during bacterial infection of the intestine color diag *Science* v357 no6355 p1047 S 8 2017

Pener, Degen

good morning, sunshine color *InStyle* p16 Home & Design 2016

A New House of Worship *Los Angeles Magazine* p70 My 2017

PRIDE OF PLACE *Los Angeles Magazine* v62 no6 p80 Je 2017

Penfold, J. L.

I've Got Mail J. V. LAST color *Weekly Standard* v22 no22 p5 F 13 2017

Peng, Changgeng

miR-183 cluster scales mechanical pain sensitivity by regulating basal and neuropathic pain genes diag graph *Science* v356 no6343 p1168 Je 16 2017

Peng, Cheng-Zhi

Satellite-based entanglement distribution over 1200 kilometers diag graph *Science* v356 no6343 p1140 Je 16 2017

Peng, Dongju

Imaging the distribution of transient viscosity after the 2016 Mw 7.1 Kumamoto earthquake map *Science* v356 no6334 p163 Ap 14 2017

Peng, Lian-Mao

Scaling carbon nanotube complementary transistors to 5-nm gate lengths chart graph *Science* v355 no6322 p271 Ja 20 2017

Peng, Sheng

Quantitative 3D evolution of colloidal nanoparticle oxidation in solution diag graph *Science* v356 no6335 p303 Ap 21 2017

Peng, Weiqun

Deficiency of microRNA miR-34a expands cell fate potential in pluripotent stem cells diag *Science* v355 no6325 p596 F 10 2017

Peng Xuejun

Peng Xuejun color *Publishers Weekly* v264 no12 p33 Mr 20 2017

Peng Zhang

Save the world's primates in peril bibl color *Science* v354 no6311 p425 O 28 2016

Penguin behavior

Weird But True! M. TERRELL color map *National Geographic Kids* no471 p4 Je/Jl 2017

Penguin Books Ltd.

Cover Girl M. FERNANDEZ *Indianapolis Monthly* v40 no4 p20 D 2016

Penguin Mixes Art, Books for a Cause J. Maher color *Publishers Weekly* v264 no24 p10 Je 12 2017

Penguin Random House

Big Books for Big Country E. NAWOTKA *Publishers Weekly* v263 no39 p20 S 26 2016

One for the Books J. Hibberd color *Entertainment Weekly* no1457/1458 p18 Mr 17 2017

PRH Employees Unite for Company Week J. Milliot color *Publishers Weekly* v264 no7 p10 F 13 2017

Penguins

Noah and Penguin *Orion Magazine* v35 no3 p1 My/Je 2016

Rebel Penguins J. KIFFEL-ALCHEH color map *National Geographic Kids* no473 p26 S 2017

Penguins—Behavior

Penguin and Human BFFs R. d. Janeiro and S. Schwartz color *National Geographic Kids* no465 p12 N 2016

THE TRUTH ABOUT PENGUINS R. Story color *Skiing* p24 D 2016

Penguins—Ecology

THE TRUTH ABOUT PENGUINS R. Story color *Skiing* p24 D 2016

Penguins—Study & teaching

See Those Black Dots? They're Penguins. Now Count Them V. LaCapra *Oceanus* v52 no1 p13 Summ 2016

Penicillin

He thought he was getting the same stomach bug that his co-worker had. But his symptoms wound up being completely different L. Sanders color *New York Times Magazine* p18 Ag 6 2017

Most penicillin allergies are off base E. DeMarco color *Science News* v190 no13 p5 D 24 2016

Penicillium

See also

Penicillium notatum

LEARNING FROM NATURE D. Zipes *Saturday Evening Post* v289 no4 p76 Jl/Ag 2017

Penicillium notatum

The Cold War's Modern Resistance M. LANDAS bw color *Discover* v38 no8 p74 O 2017

Penick, Douglas

THE ART THAT OPENS color *Tricycle: The Buddhist Review* v27 no1 p82 Fall 2017

A World Ever at Its End bw diag *Tricycle: The Buddhist Review* v26 no4 p60 Summ 2017

Penile transplantation

THIS IS THE STORY OF AMERICA'S FIRST PENIS TRANSPLANT J. DEAN cartoon color *Esquire* v167 no2 p122 Mr 2017

Peninsulas—Iceland

NORÐUR-þINGEYJARSÝSLA P. STEFÁNSSON *Iceland Review* v55 no4 p26 Jl/Ag 2017

Peninsulas—Mexico

See also

Baja California (Mexico : Peninsula)

FLOATING TOWARD ECSTASY T. PITOCK *Saturday Evening Post* v289 no1 p56 Ja/F 2017

Penitents

A Useful David J. HELBERG and D. J. FRIEDMAN *Commentary* v144 no3 p5 O 2017

Penmanship

See also

Alphabets

THE COWBOY AND THE RICE WRITER P. Higbee *South Dakota Magazine* v32 no6 p58 Mr/Ap 2017

Penn, Ben

MEAT MARKETER [Cover story] color graph map *Bloomberg Businessweek* no4511 p42 F 13 2017

Penn, Charli

Still Shining On [Cover story] color *Essence* v48 no6 p94 O 2017

WE FOUND LOVE color *Essence* v47 no9 p80 Ja 2017

Penn, Donald

Leading Off color *Sports Illustrated* v125 no15 p10 N 7 2016

Penn, Emily

Know Your Ocean. Love Your Ocean *UN Chronicle* v54 no1/2 p1 2017

Penn, Faye

LADIES' NIGHT WITH SETH MEYERS color *InStyle* v24 no6 p150 Je 2017

MAN OF STYLE Kofi Siriboe color *InStyle* v23 no12 p92 N 2016

NON-STOP Hilaria color *InStyle* v24 no1 p58 Ja 2017

Penn, Irving

Glamour Shots J. GARDNER bw color *Weekly Standard* v22 no43 p37 Jl 24 2017

Penn, Irving—Exhibitions

MIGHTY PENN bw *Vanity Fair* v59 no5 p51 Ap 2017

Object Lesson D. KAZANJIAN and V. STEIKER bw cartoon *Vogue* v207 no3 p388 Mr 2017

Penn, John

Distribution and clinical impact of functional variants in 50,726 whole-exome sequences from the DiscovEHR study chart graph *Science* v354 no6319 paaf6814-1 D 23 2016

Penn, Kal, 1977-

Kal Penn Is a Deadbeat E. Maas *TV Guide* v64 no15 p15 Ap 4 2016

MR. PENN GOES TO WASHINGTON I. RATLEDGE *TV Guide* v64 no40 p44 O 3 2016

Penn, Maya—Interviews

Maya Penn T. MALONE *Atlanta* v56 no12 p46 Ap 2017

PENN, NATHANIEL

Buried Alive: Stories from Inside Solitary Confinement color map *GQ: Gentlemen's Quarterly* v97 no3 p154 Mr 2017

THE MAN WHO FELL TO EARTH color *GQ: Gentlemen's Quarterly* v86 no12 p148 D 2016

Penn, William, 1644-1718

PENN'S PLAN for a united Europe P. SchröDer *History Today* v66 no10 p32 O 2016

Pennanen, Valerie H.

Three Stones Make a Wall: The Story of Archaeology *Christian Century* v134 no14 p40 Jl 5 2017

PENNAZ, STEVE

LOOK OUT BELOW color *Outdoor Life* v224 no5 p38 Je/Jl 2017

Penney, Alexandra

Pink Power S. Leach color *Glamour* v115 no10 p36 O 2017

Penning, David

King snake's strength is in its squeeze E. S. EATON color *Science News* v191 no7 p13 Ap 15 2017

Pennington, R. Toby

Forest conservation: Humans' handprints bibl color *Science* v355 no6324 p466 F 3 2017

Forest conservation: Remember Gran Chaco bibl color *Science* v355 no6324 p465 F 3 2017

Pennisi, Elizabeth

Birds don't need exercise to stay fit for epic flights color *Science* v355 no6321 p121 Ja 13 2017

Circular DNA throws biologists for a loop color *Science* v356 no6342 p996 Je 9 2017

Combing the genome for the roots of autism color *Science* v357 no6346 p25 Jl 7 2017

Drowned wildebeest provide ecological feast color diag *Science* v356 no6344 p1217 Je 23 2017

Evolution promises unpleasant surprises color *Science* v354 no6310 p274 O 21 2016

Fossil fishes challenge 'urban legend' of evolution color *Science* v353 no6307 p1483 S 30 2016

How do gut microbes help herbivores? Counting the ways color *Science* v355 no6322 p236 Ja 20 2017

How plants learned to breathe color *Science* v355 no6330 p1110 Mr 17 2017

In a first, natural selection defeats a biocontrol insect color *Science* v356 no6338 p570 My 12 2017

Like birds, insects may travel in sync with the seasons color *Science* v354 no6319 p1515 D 23 2016

MAKING WAVES bw color *Science* v355 no6329 p1006 Mr 10 2017

Mini-livers reveal fine details of organ development color *Science* v356 no6343 p1109 Je 16 2017

Mysterious unchanging DNA finds a purpose in life *Science* v356 no6341 p892 Je 1 2017

A new evolutionary classic color *Science* v354 no6314 p813 N 18 2016

A new neglected crop: cannabis color *Science* v356 no6335 p232 Ap 21 2017

New technologies boost genome quality chart color *Science* v357 no6346 p10 Jl 7 2017

Nobel honors discoveries in how cells eat themselves color *Science* v354 no6308 p20 O 7 2016

Pocket-sized sequencers start to pay off big color *Science* v356 no6338 p572 My 12 2017

Record storm puts gulf resilience to the test color *Science* v357 no6355 p954 S 8 2017

Researchers parse ecosystems fueled by chemistry, not light color *Science* v357 no6357 p1223 S 22 2017

SAVING THE 'GOD OF UGLY THINGS' color *Science* v356 no6342 p1001 Je 9 2017

Sequencing all life captivates biologists chart color *Science* v355 no6328 p894 Mr 3 2017

SHAKING UP THE TREE OF LIFE color diag *Science* v354 no6314 p817 N 18 2016

A shortcut to a species color *Science* v354 no6314 p818 N 18 2016

'Supergenes' drive evolution color *Science* v357 no6356 p1083 S 15 2017

Unlocking a key to maize's amazing success color *Science* v357 no6348 p240 Jl 21 2017

Pennisi, Nahuel

Pluhar: Orfeo Chamán J. Cadagin *Opera News* v81 no10 p53 Ap

Pentax's "Astro" DSLR A. Dyer *Sky & Telescope* v133 no2 p64 F 2017

Penteado, Renato

The Best of 2016 G. PEREZ, M. SCHROCK et al *Dance Magazine* v90 no12 p84 D 2016

Pentecost

From Ashes to Fire M. Simone *America* v216 no12 p54 My 29 2017

Pentericci, L.

Molecular gas in the halo fuels the growth of a massive cluster galaxy at high redshift bibl graph *Science* v354 no6316 p1128 D 2 2016

Penthouses

PENTHOUSE PEOPLE C. KOLB color *New Orleans Magazine* v51 no3 p36 Ja 2017

SEX AND THE SUBURBS J. PAYTON *Indianapolis Monthly* p36 My 2017

Penthouses—Evaluation

GLITZ ON THE RITZ B. WARREN color *New Orleans Magazine* v51 no2 p58 D 2016

Penthouses—Interior decoration

THE CITY color *InStyle* p36 Home & Design 2016

GLITZ ON THE RITZ B. WARREN color *New Orleans Magazine* v51 no2 p58 D 2016

where life meets art S. Medford color *InStyle* p38 Home & Design 2016

Pentland, Alex "Sandy"

Research: You Have Fewer Friends than You Think *Harvard Business Review Digital Articles* p2 My 12 2016

Pentón Herrera, Luis Javier

THE KEY IS DIFFERENTIATION: Recognizing the literacy and linguistic needs of indigenous Hispanic students color *Literacy Today (2411-7862)* v34 no6 p8 My/Je 2017

Pentreath, Ben

Ben Pentreath M. OWENS color *Architectural Digest* v74 no4 p56 Ap 2017

Penttila, S.

Observation of coherent elastic neutrino-nucleus scattering diag *Science* v357 no6356 p1123 S 15 2017

Penty, Charles

Anatomy of a Bad Marriage color *Bloomberg Businessweek* no4541 p10 O 9 2017

Penty, Rebecca

Racing to Run A Two-Hour Marathon color graph *Bloomberg Businessweek* no4538 p18 S 18 2017

Spread Your Wings and Fly, Penguin color graph *Bloomberg Businessweek* no4509 p17 Ja 30 2017

Penuel, William R.

Design principles for new systems of assessment color *Phi Delta Kappan* v98 no6 p47 Mr 2017

Penuelas, Josep

Microbial mass movements color *Science* v357 no6356 p1099 S 15 2017

PENZ, LEEANN

CONSTITUENTS AT THE GATES *In These Times* v41 no4 p11 Ap 2017

Penz, Thomas

In situ architecture, function, and evolution of a contractile injection system color diag *Science* v357 no6352 p713 Ag 18 2017

Penzler, Otto

Staying Alive L. PICKER color *Publishers Weekly* v263 no45 p34 N 7 2016

Penzler, Otto—Interviews

Otto Penzler *New York Times Book Review* p7 O 30 2016

People for the Ethical Treatment of Animals

Is It Best To Get a Pet From a No-Kill Shelter? K. A. Appiah *New York Times Magazine* p22 Ap 30 2017

Monkey species may be listed as 'threatened' color *Science* v355 no6330 p1104 Mr 17 2017

PETA targets early-career wildlife researcher D. Grimm color *Science* v357 no6356 p1087 S 15 2017

People of color

Nature Fix J. SCHARPER *National Parks* v91 no4 p14 Fall 2017

People of color—Attitudes

Students of Color Face a Trump Presidency C. GONZÁLEZ-ANDRIEU *America* v215 no18 p16 D 5 2016

People of color—Education

New Education Majority: Attitudes and Aspirations of Parents and Families of Color *Education Digest* v82 no4 p55 D 2016

People of Earth (TV program)

The Must List color *Entertainment Weekly* no1438 p5 N 4 2016

People of Earth A. D'Arminio *TV Guide* v65 no31 p31 Jl 24 2017

YOU'RE NOT FROM AROUND HERE, ARE YOU? S. Li color *Entertainment Weekly* no1440 p49 N 18 2016

People with disabilities

See also

Children with disabilities

Developmental disabilities

Diversity and disability . . . B. Gaventa *Christian Century* v134 no10 p6 My 10 2017

Keep On Turning: New artistic director Marc Brew has big plans for AXIS C. Bauer *Dance Magazine* v91 no10 p16 O 2017

No Vacancy S. TRICK cartoon *Walrus* v13 no10 p22 D 2016

People with disabilities—Employment

I'LL TELL YOU SOMETHING SEEMA MALHOTRA MP *People Management* p18 D 2016/Ja 2017

You don't have to lose your job if you lose your sight M. Schuman *Bloomberg Businessweek* no4508 p6 Ja 23 2017

People with disabilities—Housing

Sanctuary Cities for the Disabled *USA Today Magazine* v145 no2861 p14 F 2017

People with disabilities—Recreation

See also

Sports for people with disabilities

BREAKING BARRIERS P. Constantakes *New York State Conservationist* v71 no3 p6 D 2016

People with disabilities—Services for

Carole Fraser: All About Access *New York State Conservationist* v71 no3 p9 D 2016

Creating a Special Space for Their Buddies M. Bosack *Parks & Recreation* v51 no11 p36 N 2016

"I Help GIRLS GET PROM-READY" M. ABERMAN color *Seventeen* p124 Ja 1 2017

People with disabilities—United States

Sending a Message to Paul Ryan M. Ervin *Progressive* v81 no3 p24 Mr 2017

People with disabilities—United States—Medical care

The Young and the Vulnerable W. J. Smith bw *Weekly Standard* v22 no47 p21 Ag 21 2017

People with mental disabilities

High-Pressure Jobs and Mental Illness D. Coutu *Harvard Business Review Digital Articles* p2 Ap 2 2015

People with visual disabilities

See also

Blind

PEOPLES, LINDSAY

Ladies With Lassos: Four women known as the Cowgirls of Color have found a niche within the rodeo community img *New York* v50 no13 p46 Je 26 2017

People's Choice Awards

WINNING STREEP J. Nolfi *Entertainment Weekly* no1449 p14 Ja 20 2017

People v. O.J. Simpson: American Crime Story, The (TV program)

The 10 Best Shows D. D'Addario color *Time* v188 no25-26 p138 D 19 2016 Double Issue

CHEERS & JeeRS D. HOLBROOK *TV Guide* v64 no15 p96 Ap 4 2016

Sarah Paulson T. Stack color *Entertainment Weekly* no1444/1445 p34 D 16 2016

Sterling K. Brown A. Wilkinson color *Entertainment Weekly* no1444/1445 p30 D 16 2016

TELEVISION OF THE YEAR R. SHEFFIELD color *Rolling Stone* no1276 p22 D 15 2016

Pepall, Rosalind

What Picasso inspired in Prague bw color *Magazine Antiques* v183 no6 p108 N/D 2016

PEPCHINSKI, MARY

Hip to be Square *Architectural Record* v205 no1 p106 Ja 2017

interiors *Architectural Record* v205 no6 p33 Je 2017

A Measure of Harmony color diag *Architectural Record* v205 no3 p72 Mr 2017

Sayne Foundry *Architectural Record* v204 no11 p143 N 2016

Second Coming color diag *Architectural Record* v205 no2 p70 F 2017

Peper, Eliot

Why Business Leaders Need to Read More Science Fiction *Harvard Business Review Digital Articles* p2 Jl 14 2017

Pepi, Mike

SILICON VALUES *Art in America* v104 no9 p90 O 2016

Pépin, C. M.

Synthesis of FeH5: A layered structure with atomic hydrogen slabs diag graph *Science* v357 no6349 p382 Jl 28 2017

Pepinster, Catherine

Church of England sees its cathedrals at risk color *Christian Century* v134 no10 p19 My 10 2017

George Carey quits role as Anglicans confront sexual abuse scandal *Christian Century* v134 no16 p15 Ag 2 2017

PEPLOW, EDWARD H. JR.

THE LEGEND OF PEARL GREY *Arizona Highways* v92 no7 p34 Jl 2016

RIMCOUNTRY *Arizona Highways* v92 no7 p16 Jl 2016

Peplow, Mark

BLIND MEDICINE color graph *Scientific American* v316 no2 p68 F 2017

Enzymes offer waste-to-energy solution diag *Science* v355 no6332 p1360 Mr 31 2017

Print, Wipe, Rewrite color *Scientific American* v316 no6 p16 Je 2017

Peppard, Joe

Executives Get the IT They Deserve *Harvard Business Review Digital Articles* p2 D 1 2015

Firms Need a Blueprint for Building Their IT Systems *Harvard Business Review Digital Articles* p2 Je 18 2015

Technology Isn't Enough to Empower Employees, Even in a Digital World *Harvard Business Review Digital Articles* p2 F 17 2016

A Tool to Map Your Next Digital Initiative *Harvard Business Review Digital Articles* p2 Je 3 2016

Peppard, Michael

Negotiating Surrender bw *Commonweal* v144 no10 p30 Je 2 2017

Pepper (Spice)

Burn Your Vegetables: For this Mexican-style slaw, employ the power of fire and smoke S. Sifton color *New York Times Magazine* p26 Ag 6 2017

Herbs and spices with benefits A. B. Kay, A. Rumsey et al cartoon *Redbook* p87 Mr 2017

Shake, Pour and Chill Out: The Saltwater T. McNally color *New Orleans Magazine* v51 no10 p178 Ag 2017

Pepper, Leslie

Drip, Drip, Stop [Cover story] color *Prevention* v69 no7 p68 Jl 2017

What Nurses Know (THAT CAN SAVE YOUR LIFE) cartoon *Prevention* p70 Mr 2017

Pepper mills—Evaluation

On the SIDE A. NEASON color *House Beautiful* p169 Ag 2017

Pepper pungency

A Chile Pepper a Day... color graph *Prevention* v69 no6 p11 Je 2017

Pepper spray

BEAR NECESSITIES C. AUSTIN color *Outdoor Life* v224 no7 p30 S 2017

Peppered moth

Dark Wings Decoded C. ENGELKING color *Discover* v38 no1 p65 Ja/F 2017

Peppermint

BIG-BATCH GIFTS E. Johnson color *Sunset* v237 no6 p81 D 2016

Peppers

See also

Hot peppers

eat this now SHICHIMI TOGARASHI color *Better Homes & Gardens* v95 no2 p84 F 2016

Extreme Weirdness A. SHAW color *National Geographic Kids* no473 p7 S 2017

Power To the Pepper *Los Angeles Magazine* p57 Mr 2017

SOME LIKE IT HOT B. ESPARZA *Los Angeles Magazine* p64 Mr 2017

PEPPERS, ELLIOTT

MINDING THE MIDDLE EAST *USA Today Magazine* v146 no2866 p32 Jl 2017

Obama's JV Jibe Still Stings *USA Today Magazine* v145 no2864 p47 My 2017

"Teaching" Social Justice *USA Today Magazine* v145 no2864 p70 My 2017

PepsiCo Inc.

Progressives, Inc J. PIERESON and N. SCHAEFER RILEY color *Weekly Standard* v22 no31 p24 Ap 17 2017

Peptic ulcer—Risk factors

Our doc will see you now R. Rajapaka color *Health* v31 no9 p66 N 2017

Peptide antibiotics—Research

New Weapon Against Bacteria *USA Today Magazine* v145 no2861 p11 F 2017

Peptide hormones

See also

Insulin

Precursor processing for plant peptide hormone maturation by subtilisin-like serine proteinases K. Schardon, M. Hohl et al bibl color graph *Science* v354 no6319 p1594 D 23 2016

Peptide receptors

See also

Epidermal growth factor receptors

Keeping in touch with the ER network X. Tan and R. A. Anderson color *Science* v356 no6338 p584 My 12 2017

Peptides

See also

Growth factors

Drug Couriers for Brain Injuries T. BURRELL color *Discover* v38 no1 p33 Ja/F 2017

A large fraction of HLA class I ligands are proteasome-generated spliced peptides J. Liepe, F. Marino et al bibl graph *Science* v354 no6310 p354 O 21 2016

A peptide hormone required for Casparian strip diffusion barrier formation in Arabidopsis roots T. Nakayama, H. Shinohara et al bibl color graph *Science* v355 no6322 p284 Ja 20 2017

The receptor kinase FER is a RALF-regulated scaffold controlling plant immune signaling M. Stegmann, J. Monaghan et al bibl graph *Science* v355 no6322 p287 Ja 20 2017

Root diffusion barrier control by a vasculature-derived peptide binding to the SGN3 receptor V. G. Doblas, E. Smakowska-Luzan et al bibl color *Science* v355 no6322 p280 Ja 20 2017

Peptidoglycans—Research

Treadmilling by FtsZ filaments drives peptidoglycan synthesis and bacterial cell division A. W. Bisson-Filho, Hsu et al bibl graph *Science* v355 no6326 p739 F 17 2017

Per capita

FEED 9.75 BILLION PEOPLE? NOT AS HARD AS IT LOOKS *Successful Farming* v115 no6 p11 Ap 2017

Pera, Martin

Embryogenesis in a dish color *Science* v356 no6334 p137 Ap 14 2017

PERA, RYAN

r.s.v.p bw *Bon Appetit* v62 no4 p10 Ap 2017

Perabo, Piper

PARTY LINES img *New York* v50 no8 p138 Ap 17 2017

Peraino, Kevin

The Quarrels of '49: A history of the pivotal year that set the course of Chinese-American relations O. SCHELL *New York Times Book Review* p12 O 8 2017

Perception

See also

Consciousness

Distraction (Psychology)

Olfactory perception

Sensory stimulation

Time perception

Can You Handle the Truth? BEING LESS THAN ACCURATE ABOUT WHAT OTHERS THINK OF YOU MAY HAVE AN UPSIDE C. PARK *Psychology Today* v49 no6 p18 N/D 2016

Ecology for the Shrinking City D. L. HERRMANN, K. SCHWARZ et al *BioScience* v66 no11 p965 N 1 2016

Misperceptions S. MARTINEZ-CONDE and S. L. MACKNIK bw color *Natural History* v125 no10 p16 O 2017

p769 N 11 2016

PEREZ, GUILLERMO

The Best of 2016 *Dance Magazine* v90 no12 p84 D 2016

Pérez, Laura M.

Spiral density waves in a young protoplanetary disk bibl graph *Science* v353 no6307 p1519 S 30 2016

Perez, O.

Hydrogen positions in single nanocrystals revealed by electron diffraction bibl color *Science* v355 no6321 p1 Ja 13 2017

Perez, Pat—Health

Loud And Clear A. Shipnuck color *Sports Illustrated* v126 no4 p68 Ja 30 2017

Perez, Thomas E., 1961-

The Battle for the DNC J. NICHOLS *Nation* v304 no9 p10 Mr 20 2017

THE COLD CIVIL WAR *Claremont Review of Books* v17 no2 p24 Spr 2017

A Revolution Deferred C. STANGLER *In These Times* v41 no4 p19 Ap 2017

Perez, Tom

The Week color *National Review* v69 no5 p6 Mr 20 2017

PEREZ, TRACY

2017's top trends for moms *Parents* v92 no1 p46 Ja 2017

30 ways to wow *Parents* v91 no9 p107 S 2016

beauty reboot *Parents* v91 no10 p86 O 2016

color your hair like a pro *Parents* v91 no11 p78 N 2016

earthly delights *Parents* v91 no11 p76 N 2016

glam it up! *Parents* p82 2015

how dulce candy does the holidays *Parents* v91 no12 p72 D 2016

mask your problem color *Parents* v92 no4 p86 Ap 2017

star scents *Parents* p80 2015

swipe right! color *Parents* v92 no3 p64 Mr 2017

virtual vacation *Parents* v91 no6 p78 Je 2016

Perez-Cruz, Ligia

The formation of peak rings in large impact craters bibl color graph *Science* v354 no6314 p878 N 18 2016

Perfect Arrangement (Theatrical production)

EVENT CALENDAR *Washingtonian Magazine* v52 no9 p198 Je 2017

Perfect games (Baseball)—History—20th century

Pitch Perfect K. Olbermann and T. Keith color *Sports Illustrated* v125 no12 p18 O 10 2016

Perfect Obedience (Film)

Films against the church P. Jenkins color *Christian Century* v134 no22 p44 O 25 2017

Perfect World Co. Ltd.

Juvenile & Children Reading Experience Wonderland: A New Business Model color *Publishers Weekly* v264 no12 p4 Mr 20 2017

Perfectionism (Personality trait)

How to Mentor a Perfectionist W. B. Johnson and D. G. Smith *Harvard Business Review Digital Articles* p2 F 21 2017

The Personality Traits That Make Us Feel Like Frauds S. Berinato *Harvard Business Review Digital Articles* p2 O 22 2015

Perfluorocarbons

DON'T DRINK THE WATER C. Schmidt color map *Scientific American* v316 no4 p64 Ap 2017

Perform Group LLC

Correction: *Dance Spirit* v21 no2 p14 F 2017

Performance

See also

Academic achievement

Failure (Psychology)

Job performance

Musical performance

Organizational performance

BLUE BLAZES S. Apstein chart color *Sports Illustrated* v127 no6 p24 Ag 28 2017

DANCE *New Yorker* v93 no15 p12 My 29 2017

Leaving a Clean Desk J. RAUCH color *Atlantic* v318 no5 p15 D 2016

Research: Cracking a Joke at Work Can Make You Seem More Competent A. W. Brooks color *Harvard Business Review Digital Articles* p2 Ja 11 2017

Research: Performing a Ritual Before a Stressful Task Improves Performance A. W. Brooks color *Harvard Business Review*

Digital Articles p2 Ja 10 2017

A SIMPLE PLAN [Cover story] L. Jenkins color *Sports Illustrated* v126 no7 p36 Mr 6 2017

Summer Preview M. Harss cartoon *New Yorker* v93 no14 p6 My 22 2017

Performance art

See also

Cosplay

CURTAIN CALL A. BURGER color *Missouri Life* v44 no2 p46 Ap 2017

FAST AND FURIOUS B. Reesman *Stage Directions* v30 no9 p14 S 2017

Jasmine Nyende T. J. Rosenthal color *Art in America* v104 no11 p27 D 2016

Performance art—Exhibitions

AROUND NEW YORK A. RUSSETH bw color *ARTnews* v115 no4 p124 Wint 2016/2017

ART *New Yorker* v93 no25 p12 Ag 28 2017

Performance artists

Lindsey Stirling M. Hagan color *Current Biography* v78 no9 p76 S 2017

Performance artists—Interviews

A Talk with Andrea Fraser A. DORAN color *ARTnews* v115 no4 p98 Wint 2016/2017

Performance-enhancing drugs—Law & legislation

PUMP IT UP T. Layden and J. Feldman color *Sports Illustrated* v126 no11 p58 Ap 17-24 2017

Performance evaluation

Dopamine neurons encode performance error in singing birds V. Gadagkar, P. A. Puzerey et al bibl graph *Science* v354 no6317 p1278 D 9 2016

Fixing Performance Appraisal Is About More than Ditching Annual Reviews G. Kenny *Harvard Business Review Digital Articles* p2 F 2 2016

How Gender Bias Corrupts Performance Reviews, and What to Do About It P. Cecchi-Dimeglio *Harvard Business Review Digital Articles* p2 Ap 12 2017

Managing Performance When It's Hard to Measure J. Whitehurst *Harvard Business Review Digital Articles* p2 My 11 2015

Now Available: The Annual Summary of Key Findings from NRPA Park Metrics *Parks & Recreation* v52 no4 p53 Ap 2017

Strong Patient-Provider Relationships Drive Healthier Outcomes E. E. Sullivan and A. Ellner *Harvard Business Review Digital Articles* p2 O 9 2015

TEEN AGE *Surfing Magazine* v53 no1 p42 Ja 2017

A Way to Gauge How Well Your Company Is Really Performing M. E. Raynor and D. Pankratz *Harvard Business Review Digital Articles* p2 My 8 2015

WHY FACEBOOK IS KEEPING PERFORMANCE REVIEWS: INTERACTION F. Langness, N. Schultz et al color *Harvard Business Review* v95 no1 p18 Ja/F 2017

Performance management

Are Bad Managers Holding Back Your Best Talent? A. Behrens *Harvard Business Review Digital Articles* p2 Ap 23 2015

Bank transfer... 2 seconds Movie download... 2 minutes Grocery delivery... 1 hour Appraisal... 12 months? J. SIMMS *People Management* p44 Je 2017

How to Ask for Feedback That Will Actually Help You P. Bregman *Harvard Business Review Digital Articles* p2 D 5 2014

The Ideal Work Schedule, as Determined by Circadian Rhythms C. M. Barnes *Harvard Business Review Digital Articles* p2 Ja 28 2015

The Key to Performance Reviews Is Preparation B. Dattner *Harvard Business Review Digital Articles* p2 Je 21 2016

Performance Management in the Gig Economy J. Younger and N. Smallwood *Harvard Business Review Digital Articles* p2 Ja 11 2016

Understanding When to Give Feedback *Harvard Business Review Digital Articles* p2 D 4 2014

What Great Managers Do to Engage Employees J. Harter and A. Adkins *Harvard Business Review Digital Articles* p2 Ap 2 2015

What to Do When You Think Your Performance Review Is Wrong D. Grote bw *Harvard Business Review Digital Articles* p2 Mr 7 2017

Why More and More Companies Are Ditching Performance Ratings D. Rock and B. Jones *Harvard Business Review Digital*

editor's note. On wanting more for others than they want for themselves *Psychology Today* v49 no5 p4 S/O 2016

editor's note. THE 100-YEAR PLAN *Psychology Today* v50 no4 p3 Ag 2017

editor's note. THE MIND'S WHITE SPACE *Psychology Today* v50 no5 p3 S/O 2017

editor's note. WHAT DOES IT MEAN TO BE ON THE RIGHT SIDE OF THE FUTURE? *Psychology Today* v49 no6 p3 N/D 2016

THE MAD GENIUS MYSTERY *Psychology Today* v50 no4 p70 Ag 2017

Perina, Rubén M.

The Organization of American States as the Advocate and Guardian of Democracy R. Feinberg *Foreign Affairs* v95 no6 p183 N/D 2016

Perinatally-acquired HIV infections—Prevention

Simple Drugs Stopped This Child from Getting HIV from Her Mother. Yet 400 Babies Are Born Every Day With the Disease. What Will It Take to Protect Them All? A. Park color diag map *Time* v189 no11 p40 Mr 27 2017

Perino, Dana, 1972-

How to Reach Across the Aisle? Get a Dog L. Hartman bw *Publishers Weekly* v263 no44 p(Sp)12 O 31 2016

Period Arts Fan Co.

HOUSE & GARDEN color *Timber Home Living* p62 2017 SpecialIssue

Periodic health examinations

HOW TO CHEAT DEATH [Cover story] M. HERPER color map *Forbes* v199 no2 p74 F 28 2017

Laugh Out Loud color *National Geographic Kids* no475 p33 N 2017

TO YOUR HEALTH: Physicians and specialists recommend baseline health exams to prolong active lifestyle Rin-rin Yu *Washingtonian Magazine* v52 no8 p150 My 2017

Periodic table of the elements

THE END OF THE PERIODIC TABLE? E. BETZ color *Discover* v38 no1 p32 Ja/F 2017

Periodical archives

From the Archives color *Black Belt* v55 no4 p82 Je/Jl 2017

The HOT ROD Archives D. Wallace color *Hot Rod* v70 no6 p20 Je 2017

Periodical articles—History—20th century

March 1, 1948: A Fortunate Time A. BROWN bw color *Forbes* v199 no5 p36 My 16 2017

Periodical editors

See also

Women periodical editors

40 Years AT HOT ROD: THE MARLAN DAVIS SAGA T. Taylor bw color *Hot Rod* v70 no12 p68 D 2017

A\J CREATORS *Alternatives Journal (AJ) - Canada's Environmental Voice* v42 no3 p8 2016

EDITOR'S LETTER B. D. SWEANY *Texas Monthly* v45 no1 p14 Ja 2017

FALLING FOR TV AGAIN (AND AGAIN) H. Goldblatt color *Entertainment Weekly* no1482/1483 p20 S 22 2017

Farewell, My Friend B. PIKE color *Power & Motoryacht* v32 no11 p72 N 2016

A Few More Words—Before I Go D. Harris color *Money* v46 no3 p9 Ap 2017

GIFT OF A LIFETIME C. Kearns color *Field & Stream* v121 no7 p10 D 2016/Ja 2017

Karla Martinez de Salas J. K. DE VALLE color *Architectural Digest* no5 p44 My 2017

Leaving the Flatiron M. FLAMINI and E. BEIER bw *Publishers Weekly* v264 no35 p132 Ag 28 2017

The Literacy Scene color il *Literacy Today (2411-7862)* v34 no3 p4 N/D 2016

Mission Creep in Media D. Freiburger color *Hot Rod* v70 no11 p130 N 2017

Modest Cultural Literacy J. Epstein *Claremont Review of Books* v17 no3 p66 Summ 2017

OF MANY THINGS M. MALONE *America* v215 no11 p2 O 17 2016

PENN JILLETTE K. MANGU-WARD bw color *Reason* v48 no8 p34 Ja 2017

PETER AUGUSTINE LAWLER, 1951-2017 D. J. Mahoney *Cla-*

remont Review of Books v17 no3 p83 Summ 2017

THE POETRY OF JIM MICHAELS R. LANE bw *Forbes* v200 no3 p60 S 28 2017

Robert B. Silvers (1929–2017) [Cover story] R. Hederman, E. BLAIR et al bw color *New York Review of Books* v64 no8 p31 My 11 2017

Thomas J. Wilbanks *Environment* v59 no4 p3 Jl-Ag 2017

The virtue of a Catholic journalist M. Malone *America* v217 no3 p3 Ag 7 2017

Wit and Witness J. V. Last color *Weekly Standard* v22 no33 p14 My 8 2017

THE WORLD ACCORDING TO Gayle color *O, The Oprah Magazine* p32 Ap 2017

Periodical layout & typography

Get The Lead Out M. MELTON *Los Angeles Magazine* v61 no11 p20 N 2016

Periodical publishing

See also

Magazine design

Science periodical publishing

ELEANOR MERRILL, 1933-2016 D. MERRILL *Washingtonian Magazine* v52 no1 p12 O 2016

A HOT SPOT FOR COMICS AND GAMING cartoon color *Publishers Weekly* v263 no47 p38 N 21 2016

THE PREPRINT DILEMMA J. Kaiser chart color graph *Science* v357 no6358 p1344 S 29 2017

The Progressive N. Stockwell color *Progressive* v81 no4 p2 Ap/My 2017

Social Science and the Public Interest *Society* v54 no1 p1 F 2017

THE SUN NEVER SETS ON FORBES M. SOLOMON color *Forbes* v200 no3 p104 S 28 2017

Winter 2017 available on ISSUU *Humanities* v38 no1 p1 Wint 2017

Periodical subscriptions

Page after page T. Belcher color *Equus* no482 p65 N 2017

Periodicals

See also

Magazine advertising

Magazine covers

Medical periodicals

Television program guides

60 Minutes Turns 50 I. RUDOLPH *TV Guide* v65 no41 p4 O 2 2017

THE BOYS OF BALLET M. Fuhrer *Dance Spirit* v21 no3 p36 Mr 2017

A family analysis J. Berg color *Science* v355 no6320 p9 Ja 6 2017

The First "Best Bets" img *New York* v49 no21 p12 O 17 2016

Foreword M. Nasser *UN Chronicle* v53 no4 p1 2016

FROM THE ARCHIVES N. GILLESPIE, A. C. KORS et al bw cartoon *Reason* v48 no11 p70 Ap 2017

If I had an extra vacation day, I would... map *Reader's Digest* v189 no1131 p30 Je 2017

OF MANY THINGS M. MALONE *America* v215 no18 p2 D 5 2016

ON THE ROAD WITH... BRANDEL CHAMBLEE J. Passov color *Golf Magazine* v59 no3 p110 Mr 2017

Seeing Is Believing N. Gibbs color *Time* v190 no10/11 p4 S 18 2017

What Makes Tech Tick E. Perkins color *Hot Rod* v70 no11 p6 N 2017

Periodicals—Anniversary editions

150 YEARS OF BAZAR S. Mooallem cartoon *Harper's Bazaar* no3649 p326 D 2016/Ja 2017

THE EDITORIAL *Maclean's* v129 no51/52 p7 D 26 2016

EDITOR'S LETTER G. Bailey color *Harper's Bazaar* no3649 p118 D 2016/Ja 2017

Happy 20th Birthday, DANCESPIRIT *Dance Spirit* v21 no7 p36 S 2017

We're 20! *Dance Spirit* v21 no7 p32 S 2017

Periodicals—Canada

FEATURED FELLOW: SHELLEY AMBROSE S. Doyle color *Canadian Geographic* v137 no1 p78 F 2017

Periodicals—Computer network resources

Cheers to a New Year D. Hearst *Arabian Horse World* v57 no4 p10 Ja 2017

EDITOR'S LETTER M. Murphy *Bloomberg Businessweek*

no4527 p6 Je 19 2017

LG's robot lineup for the lazy future color *PCWorld* v35 no2 p204 F 2017

A NEW LOOK FOR A NEW ERA A. IGNATIUS img *Harvard Business Review* v95 no1 p10 Ja/F 2017

Periodicals—History

Conservatism In Dissent K. D. WILLIAMSON *National Review* v68 no22 p42 D 5 2016

FORBES @ 100 A. BROWN bw color *Forbes* v199 no2 p36 F 28 2017

OUR FIRST 100 YEARS bw color *Forbes* v200 no3 p23 S 28 2017

Sept. 13, 1982: The First Forbes 400 A. BROWN bw color *Forbes* v198 no5 p54 O 25 2016

Periodicals—History—20th century

July 1, 1968: HOUSTON, WE'VE GOT YOUR BACK A. BROWN bw color *Forbes* v200 no2 p32 S 5 2017

Periodicals—Officials & employees

1951-2017 GEORGE PITTS M. Romero color *Entertainment Weekly* no1457/1458 p17 Mr 17 2017

Good Night, And Good Luck M. MELTON *Los Angeles Magazine* p16 Ap 2017

THERE GOES THE NEIGHBORHOOD E. Plott *Washingtonian Magazine* v52 no1 p51 O 2016

We Say Goodbye to One of Our Own H. Goldblatt, D. Snierson et al color *Entertainment Weekly* no1480 p3 S 1 2017

Periodicals—Political activity

THE KNIGHT'S MOVE G. LEWIS-KRAUS il *Nation* v304 no15 p27 My 8 2017

Periodicals—Reviews

Promote scientific integrity via journal peer review data C. J. Lee and D. Moher color *Science* v357 no6348 p256 Jl 21 2017

Periodicals—United States

AMERICA'S MAGAZINE S. Slon *Saturday Evening Post* v289 no2 p4 Mr/Ap 2017

Peripheral neuropathy

See also

Spinal nerve root diseases

PAIN E. Hayasaki color *Wired* v25 no5 p84 My 2017

Peripheral vision

STARE WAY TO HEAVEN S. Munroe and D. DeNunzio color *Golf Magazine* v59 no6 p49 Je 2017

Perisoreus canadensis

Bird of a Nation D. Bird color *Canadian Wildlife* v23 no1 p40 Mr/Ap 2017

CANADA'S NATIONAL BIRD THE GRAY JAY [Cover story] N. Walker, L. Anthony et al color map *Canadian Geographic* v136 no6 p36 D 2016

COMMENT A. Abbott, Spence et al color *Canadian Geographic* v137 no1 p72 F 2017

Perkel, Jeffrey M.

Chromatin untangled: New methods map genomic structure color *Science* v354 no6308 p118 O 7 2016

Perkins, Anthony

People and posts *People Management* p60 N 2016

PERKINS, CHRIS

5 CARS THAT PUT AMG AT THE HEAD OF THE PACK color *Esquire* p52 2017 BigBlackBook

Perkins, Evan

BRAKE DOWN color *Hot Rod* v70 no5 p78 My 2017

Degrees of Separation chart color graph *Hot Rod* v70 no6 p72 Je 2017

FORCE FED color graph *Hot Rod* v69 no12 p74 D 2016

FROM ACROSS THE POND color *Hot Rod* v70 no1 p42 Ja 2017

Give the Kid a Chance color *Hot Rod* v70 no4 p8 Ap 2017

It's in Our Blood color *Hot Rod* v70 no9 p8 S 2017

Knockout Punch color *Hot Rod* v70 no7 p8 Jl 2017

Memory LANE color *Hot Rod* v70 no11 p60 N 2017

More Doors, More Fun color *Hot Rod* v70 no5 p8 My 2017

ONE RING TO RULE THEM ALL chart color graph *Hot Rod* v70 no9 p80 S 2017

Program Your Camshafts? color *Hot Rod* v70 no2 p8 F 2017

A RACER'S SENDOFF color *Hot Rod* v70 no2 p46 F 2017

RESPECT YOUR ELDERS color *Hot Rod* v70 no3 p62 Mr 2017

Running Cars are More Fun color *Hot Rod* v70 no1 p12 Ja 2017

Salt-Flat Racing Happens at a Different Pace color *Hot Rod* v69

no12 p10 D 2016

SUCKER PUNCH color *Hot Rod* v70 no3 p60 Mr 2017

Things to Come color *Hot Rod* v70 no10 p8 O 2017

The Truth About Cheap Turbos [Cover story] color graph *Hot Rod* v69 no12 p64 D 2016

Two of a Kind color *Hot Rod* v70 no3 p6 Mr 2017

Until Next Time color *Hot Rod* v70 no12 p6 D 2017

WEEKEND EFI color *Hot Rod* v70 no10 p46 O 2017

What Makes Tech Tick color *Hot Rod* v70 no11 p6 N 2017

Where's My Barn Find? color *Hot Rod* v70 no6 p8 Je 2017

Who Needs TV? color *Hot Rod* v70 no8 p8 Ag 2017

Perkins, Lynne Rae

Frank and Lucky Get Schooled color *Publishers Weekly* v263 no49 p21 D 7 2016

Perkins, Raymond

Better Questions to Ask Your Data Scientists *Harvard Business Review Digital Articles* p2 N 15 2016

Perkins, Sid

Digging Carbon [Cover story] chart color graph map *Science News* v190 no8 p18 O 15 2016

Grisly dining habit not taboo among animals color *Science News* v191 no3 p29 F 18 2017

How animals exploit physical phenomena bw *Science News* v191 no1 p29 Ja 21 2017

Radical idea could restore Arctic Ocean's sea ice color graph *Science News* v191 no9 p4 My 13 2017

Science of solar eclipses continues to amaze color *Science News* v191 no9 p28 My 13 2017

Perkins, Stephanie

Summer Days and Summer Nights: Twelve Love Stories *Publishers Weekly* v263 no49 p103 D 7 2016

PERKINS, TERRY

50 YEARS OF JAZZ CAMPS AT SHELL LAKE color *Downbeat* v84 no3 p88 Mr 2017

Breaking Jazz's Glass Ceiling color *Downbeat* v84 no7 p65 Jl 2017

CREATIVITY IN COMMON color *Downbeat* v84 no6 p122 Je 2017

Elkhart Hosts Massive Jazz Party color *Downbeat* v84 no5 p111 My 2017

FOSTERING A WINNING TEAM color *Downbeat* v84 no6 p118 Je 2017

Widner Big Band Camp Turns 30, Remains True to Kenton's Format color *Downbeat* v84 no6 p134 Je 2017

Perkins, Thomas T.

Hidden dynamics in the unfolding of individual bacteriorhodopsin proteins bibl diag *Science* v355 no6328 p945 Mr 3 2017

Perkins, Useni Eugene

Hey Black Child color *Publishers Weekly* v264 no39 p104 S 25 2017

Perkins + Will Inc.

Perkins+Will H. Corcoran *Architectural Record* v205 no4 p124 Ap 2017

Whitman-Walker Health B. Agnese *Architectural Record* v205 no4 p190 Ap 2017

PERKOWITZ, SIDNEY

Ice bw color diag *Discover* v38 no6 p66 Jl/Ag 2017

Perl, Jed

Calder's Magic Year J. PERL *Smithsonian* v48 no6 p40 O 2017

The Confidence Man of American Art [Cover story] bw color *New York Review of Books* v64 no8 p18 My 11 2017

Cool, Sublime, Idealistic Diebenkorn cartoon *New York Review of Books* v64 no1 p12 Ja 19 2017

High-Wire Act H. Spurling color *New York Review of Books* v64 no17 p20 N 9 2017

A Visionary of the Real bw color *New York Review of Books* v64 no16 p30 O 26 2017

Perlberg, Heather

Federal Agencies Play 'Not It' With Flood Insurance *Bloomberg Businessweek* no4538 p28 S 18 2017

Malls A New Use For Empty Spaces color *Bloomberg Businessweek* no4521 p40 My 8 2017

Robots Will Build Your Next House color *Bloomberg Businessweek* no4519 p43 Ap 24 2017

Perlin, M.

Observation of a large-scale anisotropy in the arrival directions

of cosmic rays above 8 × 1018 eV *Science* v357 no6357 p1266 S 22 2017

Perlis, Mike
THE TITANS VS. THE UNICORNS *Vital Speeches of the Day* v83 no6 p179 Je 2017

Perlman, David H.
Systems-level analysis of mechanisms regulating yeast metabolic flux bibl diag graph *Science* v354 no6311 paaf2786-1 O 28 2016

Perlman, Ken
How Coty Reinvigorated Its Supply Chain *Harvard Business Review Digital Articles* p2 My 19 2016

Perlmutter, Isaac—Trials, litigation, etc.
Intrigue at Sloan's Curve J. CASTALDO color *Maclean's* v130 no8 p45 S 2017

Perloff, Marjorie
The Codebreaker bw *Weekly Standard* v22 no30 p32 Ap 10 2017
Ironists of a Vanished Empire A. Kirsch bw *New York Review of Books* v64 no11 p26 Je 22 2017

PERLOW, LESLIE A.
STOP THE MEETING MADNESS: HOW TO FREE UP TIME FOR MEANINGFUL WORK chart color img *Harvard Business Review* v95 no4 p62 Jl/Ag 2017

PERLS, DANA
THE NEXT GENERATION OF GMOs *Nation* v305 no11 p17 O 30 2017

Perlstein, Rick
He's Making a List il *New Republic* v248 no1/2 p18 Ja/F 2017
John DEAN bw *Esquire* p152 S 2017
Peter's Choice cartoon *Mother Jones* v42 no1 p9 Ja/F 2017
Rick Perlstein color *Current Biography* v78 no1 p60 Ja 2017
The Trauma We Must Confront *In These Times* v40 no12 p20 D 2016

Permaculture
9 PERMACULTURE PRACTICES: Apply permaculture to your land to nurture its natural features J. Bloom *Mother Earth News* no282 p22 Je/Jl 2017
Can Modern Agriculture Be Sustainable? B. BAKER *BioScience* v67 no4 p325 Ap 2017
Natural Environment P. Marquis *New Orleans Homes & Lifestyles* v20 no2 p26 Spr 2017
Profitable PERMACULTURE PRINCIPLES: The application of permaculture design at Polyface has helped increase the farm's efficiency and functionality J. Salatin *Mother Earth News* no282 p75 Je/Jl 2017

Permafrost
Climate Change Adaptation and Traditional Cultures in Northern Russia S. CRATE *Current History* v116 no792 p277 O 2017
NASA armada targets thaw in Arctic soil P. Voosen color map *Science* v357 no6346 p12 Jl 7 2017
Water Damage A. Mitchell color *Canadian Wildlife* v23 no1 p15 Mr/Ap 2017
What Lies Beneath S. Goudarzi color *Scientific American* v315 no5 p11 N 2016

Permafrost microbiology
THE PERMAFROST PREDICTION T. Schuur color map *Scientific American* v315 no6 p56 D 2016
WHAT LIES BENEATH C. LEU bw *Wired* v24 no12 p26 D 2016

Permafrost—Research
THE PERMAFROST PREDICTION T. Schuur color map *Scientific American* v315 no6 p56 D 2016
WHAT LIES BENEATH C. LEU bw *Wired* v24 no12 p26 D 2016

Perman, Stacy
HOLY GRAILS color *Fortune* v176 no4 p59 S 15 2017
TIME FOR SOMETHING MORE color *Fortune* v176 no5 p43 O 1 2017

Permanent (Film)
ALSO PLAYING D. Heching color *Entertainment Weekly* no1478 / 1479 p78 Ag 18-25 2017

Permanent Green Light (Film)
Dennis Cooper's Change of Heart: As a novelist, he's been called the "most dangerous writer in America." But what kind of filmmaker will he be? J. McBride img *New York* v50 no16 p104 Ag 7 2017

Permeability
Enhanced water permeability and tunable ion selectivity in subnanometer carbon nanotube porins R. H. Tunuguntla, R. Y.

Henley et al chart color *Science* v357 no6353 p792 Ag 25 2017

Permian Basin (Tex. & N.M.)
Despite cheap crude prices, America's best oil field, Texas' Permian Basin, is thriving A. Nussbaum color map *Bloomberg Businessweek* no4496 p77 O 24 2016

PERMISSION, TENEICE
Q: What did you let go of that changed your life? color *O, The Oprah Magazine* p16 Ag 2017

Pernell, Kim
Research: Hiring Chief Risk Officers Led Banks to Take on Even More Risk *Harvard Business Review Digital Articles* p2 Jl 13 2017

Perner, Michelle
Vaginal bacteria modify HIV tenofovir microbicide efficacy in African women chart graph *Science* v356 no6341 p938 Je 1 2017

Pernsteiner, George
Higher Education, The Road to American Success: An Open Letter to the Presidential Nominees *Change* v48 no5 p6 S/O 2016

Perona, Elizabeth
Murder at the Male Revue *Publishers Weekly* v264 no21 p75 My 22 2017

Perone, Nicole
A Millennial walks into a church: Young qualified Catholics don't need to earn their stripes before taking on church leadership roles color *U.S. Catholic* v82 no10 p27 O 2017
A new frontier L. Eppinger color *U.S. Catholic* v81 no12 p45 D 2016

Perovskite
Incorporation of rubidium cations into perovskite solar cells improves photovoltaic performance M. Saliba, Taisuke Matsui et al bibl graph *Science* v354 no6309 p206 O 14 2016
Long-range hot-carrier transport in hybrid perovskites visualized by ultrafast microscopy Z. Guo, Y. Wan et al diag graph *Science* v356 no6333 p59 Ap 7 2017
An organic-inorganic perovskite ferroelectric with large piezoelectric response You, Liao et al graph *Science* v357 no6348 p306 Jl 21 2017
Perovskite-perovskite tandem photovoltaics with optimized band gaps G. E. Eperon, T. Leijtens et al bibl chart graph *Science* v354 no6314 p861 N 18 2016
Perovskite solar cells gear up to go commercial R. F. Service color *Science* v354 no6317 p1214 D 9 2016
Powering up perovskite photoresponse O. M. Bakr and O. F. Mohammed bibl color *Science* v355 no6331 p1260 Mr 24 2017
POWER UP L. Hamers color diag graph *Science News* v192 no1 p22 Ag 5 2017
WATCHING PEROVSKITE PHOTOEXCITATIONS, ATOM BY ATOM *Physics Today* v70 no3 p21 Mr 2017

Perovskite—Electric properties
Extremely efficient internal exciton dissociation through edge states in layered 2D perovskites Blancon, H. Tsai et al bibl graph *Science* v355 no6331 p1288 Mr 24 2017

Peroxisomes
Organelle inheritance—what players have skin in the game? U. Gruneberg and F. Barr bibl color *Science* v355 no6324 p459 F 3 2017

Perpetual motion
PERPETUAL MOTION K. Dold cartoon *Runner's World* v52 no1 p40 Ja/F 2017

Perpich, Mike
ATTACK THE FLAG color *Golf Magazine* v59 no4 p52 Ap 2017
GREEN MACHINE color *Golf Magazine* v59 no3 p50 Mr 2017
Tilt for Speed color *Golf Magazine* v59 no8 p50 Ag 2017
Watch + Learn color *Golf Magazine* v59 no11 p28 N 2017
Watch + Learn color *Golf Magazine* v59 no2 p34 F 2017
Wrap Star color *Golf Magazine* v59 no5 p58 My 2017

PERRAULT, KATELYNN A.
The Odor of Death: An Overview of Current Knowledge on Characterization and Applications *BioScience* v67 no7 p600 Jl 2017

Perrault, Tom
Digital Companies Need More Liberal Arts Majors *Harvard Business Review Digital Articles* p2 Ja 29 2016
Why Digital Companies Grow Without Adding Headcount *Harvard Business Review Digital Articles* p2 F 11 2016

Perrenoud, Christian
Neandertal and Denisovan DNA from Pleistocene sediments bw

color *Science* v356 no6338 p605 My 12 2017

PERRETTE, PAULEY

The Abby Effect *TV Guide* p18 D 19 2016

Pauley Perrette's Shocking Exit: What It Means for NCIS A. D'Arminio *TV Guide* v65 no43 p6 O 16 2017

Perrey, Jesko

How Marketers Can Personalize at Scale *Harvard Business Review Digital Articles* p2 N 23 2015

PERRI, LARAINE

ground (meat) rules! color *Parents* v92 no5 p102 My 2017

Perri, Matteo

An accreting pulsar with extreme properties drives an ultraluminous x-ray source in NGC 5907 bibl chart graph *Science* v355 no6327 p817 F 24 2017

Perriello, Tom

Is Virginia for Populists? G. ZORNICK color *Nation* v304 no17 p19 Je 5 2017

THE RUMBLE IN RICHMOND: THE BIGGEST DEMOCRATIC TITLE BOUT SINCE HILLARY VS. BERNIE A. SHEPHARD color *New Republic* v248 no6 p18 Je 2017

Perriello, Tom—Interviews

THE MONTHLY INTERVIEW: TOM PERRIELLO color *Washington Monthly* v49 no6-8 p16 Je-Ag 2017

PERRIER, NUMA

These Are Your Sexual Rights color *Glamour* v114 no7 p94 Jl 2016

Perrin, Felicity

Emergence and spread of a human-transmissible multidrug-resistant nontuberculous mycobacterium bibl diag graph *Science* v354 no6313 p751 N 11 2016

PERRINE, STEPHEN

The Bank of Mom and Dad color *AARP: The Magazine* v60 no1A p20 D 2016/Ja 2017

Check You Out! cartoon *AARP: The Magazine* v60 no5A p20 Ag/S 2017

PERRING, MICHAEL P.

Combining Biodiversity Resurveys across Regions to Advance Global Change Research *BioScience* v67 no1 p73 Ja 2017

Perrini, Guido

GLASS bw *Powder* v45 no5 p20 Ja 2017

Perrmann-Graham, Jaclyn

Research on Delegating Shows How Uncomfortable We Are Making Choices for Others *Harvard Business Review Digital Articles* p2 Ag 30 2016

Perron, Sandra—Interviews

THE INTERVIEW B. BETHUNE color *Maclean's* p20 Je 2017

Perron, Wendy

Diana Vishneva *Dance Magazine* v90 no11 p18 N 2016

MAI: Lil Buck and Jon Boogz *Dance Magazine* v91 no9 p13 S 2017

A New Nutcracker for the Joffrey *Dance Magazine* v90 no12 p26 D 2016

Perrone, L.

Observation of a large-scale anisotropy in the arrival directions of cosmic rays above 8 × 1018 eV *Science* v357 no6357 p1266 S 22 2017

Perrotta, Tom

All About Eve C. Bacheleder *New York Times Book Review* p1 Ag 13 2017

Courting Greatness color *Weekly Standard* v23 no4 p35 O 2 2017

Everyday People, Extraordinary Books D. D'addario color *Time* v190 no7 p53 Ag 21 2017

A FAMILY AFFAIR L. MILLER cartoon *New Yorker* v93 no23 p75 Ag 7 2017

Golden Opportunity *Tennis* v52 no6 p10 N/D 2016

Parallel Lives *New York Times Book Review* p8 F 5 2017

SUBURBAN SAFARI cartoon *New Yorker* v92 no41 p28 D 12 2016

Top of His Game color *Weekly Standard* v22 no44 p37 Jl 31 2017

Whole New Ballgame color *Weekly Standard* v23 no6 p44 O 16 2017

PERROTTET, TONY

The Lovers of Shanxi *Smithsonian* v47 no9 p110 Ja/F 2017

WET AND WILD: New York's waterfront, once home to pirates and robber barons, fell into dangerous decline. But with a new wave of money and creativity the city is rediscovering its mari-

time spirit *Smithsonian* v48 no2 p26 My 2017

Perry, Anne, 1938-

An Echo of Murder: A William Monk Novel *Publishers Weekly* v264 no30 p40 Jl 24 2017

Perry, Audrey

Emergence and spread of a human-transmissible multidrug-resistant nontuberculous mycobacterium bibl diag graph *Science* v354 no6313 p751 N 11 2016

Perry, Clint J.

Bumblebees show cognitive flexibility by improving on an observed complex behavior bibl diag *Science* v355 no6327 p833 F 24 2017

Unexpected rewards induce dopamine-dependent positive emotion–like state changes in bumblebees bibl graph *Science* v353 no6307 p1529 S 30 2016

PERRY, CYNTHIA BOND

RADICAL BALLET *Atlanta* v56 no9 p36 Ja 2017

TURNING POINTE *Atlanta* v56 no8 p48 D 2016

Perry, Devin

Seal Your Deal color *Log Home Living* v34 no9 p71 D 2017

Why Buy From A Log and Timber Homes Council Member? color *Log Home Living* v33 no9 p71 D 2016

Perry, George H.

Dispersals and genetic adaptation of Bantu-speaking populations in Africa and North America diag *Science* v356 no6337 p543 My 5 2017

Perry, James M.

James M. Perry, 1927-2016 R. W. MERRY *American Conservative* v16 no1 p8 Ja/F 2017

Perry, Katy, 1984-

Katy Perry color *InStyle* v24 no10 p178 O 2017

Katy Perry K. O'Donnell color *Entertainment Weekly* no1470 p54 Je 16 2017

Katy Perry Talks (and Talks...) A. Bacle color *Entertainment Weekly* no1471 p61 Je 23 2017

Random Notes color *Rolling Stone* no1290 p26 Je 29 2017

SECRET STRESS BUSTERS of the Stars C. GOYANES *Scholastic Choices* v32 no7 p16 Ap 2017

Seeing Red L. Schallon color *Glamour* v114 no11 p34 N 2016

Sound Bites color *Entertainment Weekly* no1466 p10 My 19 2017

WHO'S YOUR DREAM GRAD SPEAKER? color *Seventeen* v76 no3 p10 My 2017

THE WORLD ACCORDING TO Gayle color *O, The Oprah Magazine* p30 Mr 2017

Perry, Katy, 1984-—Interviews

Katy's Got Sole N. Silverstein, F. Kane et al color *Glamour* v115 no2 p25 F 2017

THE TRANSFORMATION OF KATY PERRY T. Stack, A. Bacle et al color *Entertainment Weekly* no1467 p28 My 26 2017

Perry, Lee

Fall Preview M. Trammell color *New Yorker* v93 no25 p14 Ag 28 2017

PERRY, LINCOLN

Some Perspective, Please *American Scholar* v86 no2 p105 Spr 2017

Perry, Lisa

THE CITY color *InStyle* p36 Home & Design 2016

OUTSIDER ART H. MARTIN color *Architectural Digest* v73 no12 p52 D 2016

where life meets art S. Medford color *InStyle* p38 Home & Design 2016

Perry, Luke

LUKE PERRY MY LIFE ON TV D. HOLBROOK *TV Guide* v65 no8 p26 F 27 2017

PERRY, MALCOLM

A COSMIC CONTROVERSY color *Scientific American* v317 no1 p5 Jl 2017

Perry, Mark E.

Cassini finds molecular hydrogen in the Enceladus plume: Evidence for hydrothermal processes chart graph *Science* v356 no6334 p155 Ap 14 2017

Perry, Mary Allen

CUT TO THE CAKES color *Southern Living* v51 no12 p156 D 2016

FOR THE LOVE OF PIE S. Evans color *Southern Living* v51 no11 p16 N 2016

THE SOUTH'S MOST STORIED PIES color *Southern Living*
v51 no11 p132 N 2016
Perry, Matthew, 1969-
The Odd Couple I. Ratledge color *TV Guide* v64 no42 p38 O 10
2016
Perry, Michael
How Your Company Can Better Retain Employees Who Are Vet-
erans *Harvard Business Review Digital Articles* p2 Jl 11 2017
Perry, Patrick
HOLIDAY GAME PLAN *Saturday Evening Post* v288 no6 p82
N/D 2016
What Makes Me Laugh: An interview with david sedaris *Saturday
Evening Post* v289 no5 p36 S/O 2017
Perry, Rick, 1950-
Governor Goodhair Goes to Washington J. HIGHTOWER cartoon
Progressive v81 no3 p46 Mr 2017
Perry, Simon
The CROWN SEASON 2 color *Entertainment Weekly* no1478 /
1479 p24 Ag 18-25 2017
Inferno color *Entertainment Weekly* no1438 p46 N 4 2016
PERRY, STACI
Frosting Flandreau: Two generations of bakers have cultivated the
taste buds of Flandreau s citizenry for 88 years *South Dakota
Magazine* v33 no2 p42 Jl/Ag 2017
Perry, Troy
FINDING FAMILY, FINDING FREEDOM D. ANDERSON-
MINSHALL color *Advocate* no1091 p94 Je/Jl 2017
Perry, William J.
Diplomacy, Not Doomsday *Hoover Digest: Research & Opinion
on Public Policy* no2 p139 Spr 2017
President Trump, There Is A Deal To Be Made With North Korea
NPQ: New Perspectives Quarterly v34 no2 p6 My 2017
Sidney David Drell *Physics Today* v70 no9 p69 S 2017
Trump Now Has A Rare Window Of Opportunity To Defuse The
North Korean Crisis *NPQ: New Perspectives Quarterly* v34 no3
p10 Jl 2017
Perry-Glass, Kasey
DRESSAGE SNAPSHOT color *Dressage Today* v23 no11 p14
Ag 2017
Perryman, Rebecca S.
Cassini finds molecular hydrogen in the Enceladus plume: Evi-
dence for hydrothermal processes chart graph *Science* v356
no6334 p155 Ap 14 2017
Persaud, Chris
From the Ground Up: Black Voters in a Florida City Become a
Potent Political Force color *Progressive* v81 no6 p28 Ag/S 2017
Persaud, Ramona
Untangling Dividend Stocks C. Taylor color diag *Fortune* v174
no8 p132 D 15 2016
Persecution
See also
Bahais—Persecutions
REDUCED TO ASHES E. S. ARNARSDÓTTIR *Iceland Review*
v54 no6 p64 N/D 2016
Persecution of Christians
THE GREAT "PERSECUTION OF CHRISTIANS" MYTH R.
BOSTON *Humanist* v77 no3 p34 My/Je 2017
Persecution of Christians—History—20th century
The Russian Orthodox Church's Conservative Crusade K.
STOECKL *Current History* v116 no792 p271 O 2017
Persecution of Jehovah's Witnesses
Persecution in Russia and Kazakhstan worsens for Jehovah's Wit-
nesses L. Markoe and F. Weir *Christian Century* v134 no13 p13
Je 21 2017
Persecution of Jews—Germany
THE FORGER J. BERGER *New York Times Upfront* v149 no8
p16 Ja 30 2017
Persecution—Soviet Union
The Price of Silence: Family Memory of Stalin's Repressions I.
Tabarovsky *Wilson Quarterly* v40 no4 p5 Fall 2016
Persecution—United States
The Persecution of Ting Xue K. STARR bw cartoon *Weekly Stan-
dard* v22 no42 p8 Jl 17 2017
Perseids (Meteors)
Perseid Forecast: Partly Moony color *Sky & Telescope* v134 no2
p51 Ag 2017

Perseverance (Ethics)
NEVER GIVE UP J. HANDEY cartoon *New Yorker* v92 no33
p37 O 17 2016
RAISING Alexander C. TURNER *Reader's Digest* v188 no1124
p124 O 2016
Pershell, Karoline
Planet Hunters *Science* v357 no6355 p969 S 8 2017
Pershey, Katherine Willis
Assimilate or Go Home: Notes from a Failed Missionary *Chris-
tian Century* v134 no2 p39 Ja 18 2017
Pershing Square Capital Management LP
SHORTING A RAINBOW S. KOLHATKAR cartoon color *New
Yorker* v93 no3 p56 Mr 6 2017
Persian Gulf War, 1991
AIR WAR: DAY 4 color *AARP: The Magazine* v59 no3A p68 Ap/
My 2016
Persian Gulf War, 1991—American participation
Getting Out of the Gulf C. L. Glaser and R. A. Kelanic color *For-
eign Affairs* v96 no1 p122 Ja/F 2017
Persimmon
FINDERS, KEEPERS: Take the hunt for fresh produce outside
with this guide to Indiana foraging. Get your hands dirty and go
wild M. MCLAUGHLIN *Indianapolis Monthly* v12 no40 p77
Ag 2017
Persistence (Personality trait)
The Connection Between Pride and Persistence D. DeSteno *Har-
vard Business Review Digital Articles* p2 Ag 22 2016
Giving Up Is the Enemy of Creativity B. J. Lucas and L. Nordgren
Harvard Business Review Digital Articles p2 D 1 2015
Persistent vegetative state—Patients
Border Line A. OWEN color *Discover* v38 no8 p18 O 2017
Persky, Aaron
Judge on Trial L. YOUNG *Ms.* v26 no4 p8 Wint 2016
PERSON, JAMES E. JR.
Recovering The Soul of Conservatism *National Review* v69 no16
p46 Ag 28 2017
Person, Thomas N.
Distribution and clinical impact of functional variants in 50,726
whole-exome sequences from the DiscovEHR study chart graph
Science v354 no6319 paaf6814-1 D 23 2016
Person of Interest (TV program)
Person of Interest M. Roush *TV Guide* v64 no15 p8 Ap 4 2016
Person of the Year (Award)
See also
Time's Person of the Year selections
GALA OF THE YEAR! E. Loh color *Motor Trend* v69 no2 p10
F 2017
Louisianians of the Year M. W. SPENCER *Louisiana Life* v37 no3
p50 Ja/F 2017
Person to Person (Film)
Person to Person *New Yorker* v93 no23 p11 Ag 7 2017
Personal assistants
Obama's Former "Body Man" on Being the Ultimate Assistant
D. McGinn *Harvard Business Review Digital Articles* p2 Jl 30
2015
Personal beauty
See also
Clothing & dress
Eyebrow care
Hair removal
Hairdressing
Manicuring
22 ways to get SUMMERLICIOUS A. FRANZINO color *Good
Housekeeping* v265 no1 p21 Jl 2017
30-second MAKEOVER color *Good Housekeeping* v265 no2 p20
Ag 2017
The 5-Minute Smoky Eye color *Health* v31 no1 p32 Ja 2017
Ace No-Makeup Makeup L. Desantis color *Health* v31 no2 p27
Mr 2017
Amber Rose Isn't Here for Your Opinions color *Glamour* v114
no11 p102 N 2016
ASK APRIL A. FRANZINO color *Good Housekeeping* v264 no1
p20 Ja 1 2017
ASK APRIL A. FRANZINO color *Good Housekeeping* v264 no3
p25 Mr 2017
batting above average color *Parents* v92 no4 p83 Ap 2017

BEAUTY BUYS color *Good Housekeeping* v265 no2 p18 Ag 2017

The Beauty Complex G. DOYLE color *O, The Oprah Magazine* p39 N 2017

Beauty Loot We Love color *Health* v31 no5 p34 Je 2017

beauty NEWSFEED K. FOSTER color *Seventeen* v76 no5 p60 S 2017

THE Beauty OF Giving M. Goldberg and H. Carter color *O, The Oprah Magazine* p76 N 2017

The Beauty of Keratin V. TWEED color *Better Nutrition* v79 no6 p22 Je 2017

Beauty Sleep A. FRANZINO color *Good Housekeeping* v265 no4 p25 O 2017

BEAUTY'S NEW EXPERIMENT A. SYNNOTT color *Women's Health* v14 no9 p124 N 2017

BEAUTY'S NEXT BIG THINGS L. Desantis color *Health* v31 no7 p35 S 2017

beauty wishes from moms M. MATTHEWS BROWN color *Parents* v92 no5 p70 My 2017

Being a Good Leader Makes You More Attractive K. Kniffin *Harvard Business Review Digital Articles* p2 D 4 2014

BEST BETS img *New York* v50 no6 p56 Mr 20 2017

Better Skin, Distilled M. MILRAD GOLDSTEIN *Martha Stewart Living* no267 p44 S 2016

Black Hair Now C. Martin color *Essence* v48 no6 p59 O 2017

BREATHE color *Prevention* v69 no11 p34 N 2017

Bring on the Bangs! color *Health* v31 no2 p18 Mr 2017

But First, SKIN CARE A. Kallor color *Women's Health* v14 no1 p54 Ja/F 2017

Celebrate Your Post-Baby Body color *Health* v30 no10 p23 D 2016

COUNTER INTELLIGENCE M. M. GOLDSTEIN color *Martha Stewart Living* p46 Mr 2017

COUNTER INTELLIGENCE M. MILRAD GOLDSTEIN *Martha Stewart Living* no267 p48 S 2016

The Cut of the Year color *Health* v30 no10 p34 D 2016

Dads Are So Hot Right Now S. James *Parents* v91 no12 p11 D 2016

drugstore beauty stars from $4 [Cover story] A. FRANZINO color v265 no3 p25 S 2017

Emma Watson K. B. Brown color *InStyle* v24 no5 p152 My 2017

EMOJIS FOR BEAUTY LOVERS color *Health* v31 no2 p12 Mr 2017

EYES OFF THE PRIZE C. PARK *Psychology Today* v49 no5 p18 S/O 2016

The Face of Evil S. Mirsky color *Scientific American* v317 no3 p92 S 2017

Face Scrubs to Leave You Glowing S. STRAUSFOGEL color *Better Nutrition* p30 My 2017

Find Your Power color *Glamour* v114 no11 p147 N 2016

FLAWLESS SKIN STARTS HERE *Redbook* p21a S 2017

Fresh Faced A. R. Williams color *Southern Living* v52 no5 p65 My 2017

Fun Gift Ideas N. Brechka *Better Nutrition* v78 no12 p6 D 2016

GABRIELLE UNION What I Love color *Health* v31 no7 p31 S 2017

GALACTIC Glam M. ABERMAN color *Seventeen* v76 no4 p34 Jl/Ag 2017

GET GORGEOUS SKIN Guarnieri color *Harper's Bazaar* no3649 p262 D 2016/Ja 2017

getting ready with ATHENA CALDERONE *Better Homes & Gardens* v94 no12 p26 D 2016

Give yourself better brows P. STABLES cartoon color *Redbook* p18 My 2017

THE GLAM GAME color *O, The Oprah Magazine* p94 Ja 2017

glam it up! T. PEREZ *Parents* p82 2015

Go light. Go dramatic. be gorgeous M. Oliva color *Redbook* p6 My 2017

HALEYBENNETT'S BEAUTY DIARY Guarnieri color *Harper's Bazaar* no3657 p192 O 2017

harness your hair envy M. MATTHEWS BROWN color *Parents* v92 no4 p88 Ap 2017

health & self img *New York* p92 Mr 6 2017

Hello! L. Brown color *InStyle* v24 no10 p28 O 2017

How to Compliment a Woman color *Esquire* p136 BigBlackBook

How to feel beautiful *Redbook* p160 My 2017

if you ask me ... S. JAMES *Parents* v91 no10 p96 O 2016

Insider Tips N. Spradley color *Essence* v47 no7 p23 N 2016

I Want Her...Coral Lips L. Desantis color *Health* v31 no6 p32 Jl 2017

I Want Her Polished Pony! L. Desantis color *Health* v31 no7 p50 S 2017

Janelle Monáe Is Our Hair Hero color *Health* v31 no5 p14 Je 2017

Kate Lee S. Zuckerman color *InStyle* v24 no5 p146 My 2017

Keira Knightley color *InStyle* v23 no13 p188 D 2016

Kerry Washington color *InStyle* v24 no5 p150 My 2017

LAWS OF ATTRACTION: Who we desire is driven by powerful evolutionary forces, but while most of us are drawn to looks first (whether or not we admit it), human attraction is far more complex than it appears at first sight [Cover story] W. PARIS *Psychology Today* v50 no4 p52 Ag 2017

MAKE YOUR EYES POP T. T. Canel color *Health* v31 no2 p116 Mr 2017

Master the Brown Bag Lunch C. McHugh color *Health* v31 no7 p12 S 2017

Melt-Proof Your Makeup C. T. Burns color *Health* v31 no5 p96 Je 2017

My Brows B. Shields and S. Cristobal color *InStyle* v24 no5 p226 My 2017

My Vanity G. Sidibe color *InStyle* v24 no5 p232 My 2017

navigate the beauty aisle [Cover story] K. S. BOX color *Parents* v92 no7 p72 Jl 2017

New Shape, New Style [Cover story] G. Monahan color *Women's Health* v14 no1 p65 Ja/F 2017

Passion's Frontier P. Thungkasemvathana *Psychology Today* v50 no1 p12 Ja/F 2017

Product Spotlights color *Better Nutrition* v79 no4 p71 Ap 2017

RADIATE BEAUTY from the Inside Out color *Better Nutrition* v79 no4 p41 Ap 2017

READY FOR YOUR CLOSE-UP? L. Turner color *Amazing Wellness* v8 no6 p82 Early Winter2016

Renaissance Fare C. ELLENBERG color *Vogue* v207 no10 p222 O 2017

Self-Made Women A. FINNEY color *Women's Health* v14 no9 p50 N 2017

Sexy as the Rock S. FESCHUK color *Maclean's* v129 no50 p65 D 19 2016

SEXY, EASY SHORTCUTS M. OLIVA color *Redbook* p52 D 2016

THE Skinny with Val color *O, The Oprah Magazine* p84 Mr 2017

Special Beauty Issue N. Brechka color *Better Nutrition* v79 no4 p6 Ap 2017

Stronger, Shinier, Silkier! S. BREAKEY color *Parents* v92 no11 p75 N 2017

Style Blogger *Indianapolis Monthly* v40 no4 p94 D 2016

Summer Beauty 911 color *O, The Oprah Magazine* p60 Je 2017

SUPERCHARGE your daily routine color *Good Housekeeping* v264 no6 p18 Je 2017

"They Said I Didn't Have the Face for Short Hair" S. Kitchens color *Glamour* v114 no7 p76 Jl 2017

TIME TO SHINE K. CASTAÑON color *Seventeen* v75 no11 p86 N 2016

To Be Real L. Lynch bw color *AARP: The Magazine* v60 no2A p13 F/Mr 2017

UNDENIABLY EVA [Cover story] A. Prato color *Health* v31 no5 p84 Je 2017

UP YOUR BEAUTY GAME L. Desantis color *Health* v31 no1 p102 Ja 2017

Welcome to Beard City M. HUSTON *Psychology Today* v50 no1 p20 Ja/F 2017

What are the best ANTI-AGING TRICKS? A. FRANZINO cartoon color *Good Housekeeping* v264 no2 p23 F 2017

What Before-and-After Pictures Don't Tell You B. Lieberman bw color *Glamour* no8 p99 Ag 2017

What Love Really Looks Like M. Huston *Psychology Today* v50 no1 p9 Ja/F 2017

What's Hot Now for Brows *Parents* v91 no12 p70 D 2016

When Do You Feel Most Beautiful? color *Glamour* v115 no4 p32 Ap 2017

WHY SO DRY? G. WAY color *Martha Stewart Living* p44 Mr 2017

WRITTEN ALL OVER YOUR FACE [Cover story] A. S.

D'Annibale color *Women's Health* v14 no5 p45 Je 2017

Your Anti-Aging Lip Kit color *Health* v31 no5 p10 Je 2017

your BEAUTY PROBLEMS solved! A. FRANZINO cartoon color *Good Housekeeping* v264 no4 p33 Ap 2017

you REALLY can wear GLITTER after 30 L. Desantis color *Health* v31 no9 p88 N 2017

Zendaya color *InStyle* v24 no7 p78 Jl 2017

Zoë Kravitz S. Zuckerman color *InStyle* v23 no13 p197 D 2016

Personal beauty—Equipment & supplies

BEAUTY BUYS UNDER $25 color *Good Housekeeping* v264 no2 p20 F 2017

Beauty S. GRINNELL cartoon color *Vanity Fair* p94 Hollywood 2017 Supplement

Beauty Tools S. STRAUSFOGEL color *Better Nutrition* v79 no4 p38 Ap 2017

COUNTER INTELLIGENCE M. MILRAD GOLDSTEIN *Martha Stewart Living* no268 p62 O 2016

Great Innovators M. BOBO, J. LOVE et al color *Ebony* v72 no5 p44 Mr 2017

Island-Inspired Skin & Hair Care S. STRAUSFOGEL color *Better Nutrition* v79 no3 p34 Mr 2017

Perfect Pare F. VALDESOLO and C. ELLENBERG color *Vogue* v207 no9 p450 S 2017

The Ultimate Beauty How-tos... F. Valdesolo, S. Kitchens et al color *Glamour* v115 no4 p204 Ap 2017

Personal beauty—Equipment & supplies—Evaluation

150 BEAUTY MUST HAVES color *Harper's Bazaar* no3653 p214 My 2017

BEAUTY NEWS A. Parnass color *Harper's Bazaar* no3653 p238 My 2017

the buzz color *InStyle* v24 no11 p156 N 2017

the buzz color *InStyle* v24 no7 p98 Jl 2017

Glow Getters color *InStyle* v24 no5 p148 My 2017

Modern GIRL Makeup color *InStyle* v24 no5 p139 My 2017

MY BEAUTY MARK ... Liya Kebede color *InStyle* v24 no11 p150 N 2017

My Grandmother, the Beauty Icon A. R. Williams color *Southern Living* v52 no7 p42 Jl 2017

SUMMER BEAUTY ESSENTIALS Guarnieri color *Harper's Bazaar* no3653 p234 My 2017

TECH MIRROR, TECH MIRROR ON THE WALL M. Meltzer color *Women's Health* v14 no6 p50 Jl 2017

THANKSGIVING WITH A VIEW C. Stern color *InStyle* v24 no11 p211 N 2017

Personal beauty—Evaluation

EMILY LEY color *Better Homes & Gardens* v95 no5 p22 My 2017

MILLIE BOBBY BROWN UPSIDE DOWN S. Cristobal color *InStyle* v24 no11 p178 N 2017

PEONY PINKS J. GARLOCK color *Better Homes & Gardens* v95 no5 p24 My 2017

Personal beauty—Psychological aspects

Welcome to Beard City M. HUSTON *Psychology Today* v50 no1 p20 Ja/F 2017

Personal beauty—Research

This Just In J. Zorthian *Time* v188 no15 p15 O 17 2016

Personal care industry

See also

Cosmetics industry

Physical fitness centers

Get more from your shower! M. OLIVA color *Redbook* p30 My 2017

Personal coaching

See also

Coaching of employees

How to Get Your Team to Coach Each Other S. Friedman *Harvard Business Review Digital Articles* p2 Mr 13 2015

Is Your Employee Coachable? M. M. Wilkins *Harvard Business Review Digital Articles* p2 F 19 2015

Mentor People Who Aren't Like You R. Farnell *Harvard Business Review Digital Articles* p2 Ap 17 2017

Once-on-Wonderful. What makes a good competition coach and how do you find one? K. BRADY *Dance Magazine* v91 no10 p42 O 2017

People Who Think They're Great Coaches Often Aren't J. Zenger and J. Folkman *Harvard Business Review Digital Articles* p2

Je 23 2016

The Questions Good Coaches Ask A. J. Su *Harvard Business Review Digital Articles* p2 D 12 2014

Tips for Coaching Someone Remotely E. Batista *Harvard Business Review Digital Articles* p2 Mr 18 2015

What I Learned About Coaching After Losing the Ability to Speak M. Rosen *Harvard Business Review Digital Articles* p2 S 20 2017

When Coaching Finds That an Executive Isn't in the Right Role B. Dattner and E. Wood *Harvard Business Review Digital Articles* p2 Jl 31 2017

When to Bring in a Professional Coach R. Wynn *Harvard Business Review Digital Articles* p2 F 20 2015

Younger and Older Executives Need Different Things from Coaching L. Tamir and L. Finfer *Harvard Business Review Digital Articles* p2 Jl 6 2017

Your Coaching Is Only as Good as Your Follow-Up Skills *Harvard Business Review Digital Articles* p2 Mr 4 2015

You're a what? Life coach K. Green *Career Outlook* p1 Ja 2017

Personal computer equipment—Evaluation

Finsix Dart-C charger: Tiny, powerful, and worth the expense G. MAH UNG chart color *PCWorld* v35 no7 p145 Jl 2017

Personal computers

See also

Apple computers

Microcomputer workstations (Computers)

10 powerful, obscure Windows keyboard shortcuts you should know I. PAUL color *PCWorld* v35 no5 p189 My 2017

Everything Microsoft revealed: Surface Studio, Windows 10 Creators Update, and more B. CHACOS color *PCWorld* p8 D 2016

How to overclock your PC's CPU T. WALSH color *PCWorld* v35 no6 p139 Je 2017

How to switch to Chrome's Material Design settings page for an easier experience I. PAUL color *PCWorld* p170 Mr 2017

Mac Pro Users Want Updates? M. Gurman color *Bloomberg Businessweek* no4505 p33 D 26 2016

Personal computers—Design & construction

7 WAYS TO SAVE MONEY WHEN YOU BUILD A PC B. CHACOS color *PCWorld* p131 Mr 2017

Personal computers—Equipment & supplies

Intel demotes PCs, giving datacenter chips first crack at new technologies M. HACHMAN color *PCWorld* p22 Mr 2017

Personal computers—Equipment & supplies—Evaluation

Official Intel 7th-gen Kaby Lake: One big change makes up for smaller ones G. MAHUNG chart color diag graph *PCWorld* v35 no2 p49 F 2017

Personal computers—Evaluation

A botnet vaccine [Cover story] K. D. Atherton and R. Feltman color *Popular Science* v289 no6 p49 N/D 2017

Dell's futuristic Smart Desk PC will challenge Microsoft's Surface Studio I. PAUL color *PCWorld* p38 D 2016

Dell XPS Tower Special Edition: It's faster than it looks J. NOREM color graph *PCWorld* p67 Mr 2017

Gigabyte PC (GB-GZ1DTi7-1070): A powerhouse PC diminished by noisy fans A. YEE color graph *PCWorld* v35 no2 p71 F 2017

Hands-on: Microsoft's Surface Studio is a Windows PC for the Mac crowd M. HACHMAN color *PCWorld* p28 D 2016

Meet the Corsair One, Corsair's 'category-defying' gaming PC debut B. CHACOS color *PCWorld* p27 Mr 2017

Microsoft Surface Studio: Creativity is a sublime, pricey experience M. HACHMAN color graph *PCWorld* v35 no7 p87 Jl 2017

Ryzen 51600X: Building a versatile work-and-play PC with AMD's 6-core CPU champion B. CHACOS color graph *PCWorld* v35 no5 p175 My 2017

Samsung's ArtPC Pulse is a cylindrical desktop PC with 360-degree sound J. PHILLIPS color *PCWorld* v35 no11 p11 N 2016

Personal computers—Sales & prices

Apple Mac shipments take a beating in the third quarter as PC shipments decline A. SHAH color *PCWorld* v35 no11 p19 N 2016

Personal computers—Upgrading

The Scariest Word C. TRILLIN *New York Times Book Review* p29 N 27 2016

Personal criticism

The Spectrum of Skepticism K. FRAZIER *Skeptical Inquirer* v41 no5 p4 S/O 2017

Personal finance

> *See also*
>> Estate planning
>> Thriftiness

10 GENIUS WAYS TO make money in your $pare time [Cover story] N. SAPORITA color *Good Housekeeping* v265 no2 p79 Ag 2017

10 WAYS TO BECOME A MONEY BADASS J. Sincero color *Money* v46 no5 p62 Je 2017

3 Tips From Millionaires That Can Improve Your Retirement W. Updegrave color diag *Money* v46 no9 p35 O 2017

The 7 Deadly Sins of Personal Finance A. ROTH color *AARP: The Magazine* v59 no1A p16 D 2015/Ja 2016

Bad Ideas Gone Good [Cover story] color *Forbes* v199 no7 p123 Je 29 2017

BEST & BRIGHTEST MONEY ADVICE OF ALL TIME [Cover story] color *Redbook* p107 Ap 2017

CA$HING IN C. WAXLER color *Publishers Weekly* v263 no50 p34 D 5 2016

The Case for Not Overstocking Your IRA B. Steverman *Bloomberg Businessweek* no4516 p41 Mr 27 2017

Credit, Debit or Cash? L. GERSTNER cartoon color *Kiplinger's Personal Finance* v71 no3 p32 Mr 2017

Crowdsource This color *Glamour* v114 no11 p126 N 2016

The Early-Bird Dividend K. Holland color diag *Money* v46 no1 p27 Ja/F 2017

The End of 4%? Smarter Ways to Generate Income for Life E. O'brien chart color *Money* v46 no9 p38 O 2017

THE FALLOUT FROM RISING RATES A. K. SMITH cartoon *Kiplinger's Personal Finance* v71 no3 p11 Mr 2017

Family + money = happiness?! L. FREEDMAN color *Redbook* p105 N 2017

Getting Women to Talk About Money J. BODNAR color *Kiplinger's Personal Finance* v71 no10 p24 O 2017

GREAT IDEAS for $1,000, $10,000 or even $100,000 color *Kiplinger's Personal Finance* v71 no2 p26 F 2017

Hello, Reader. Let's Talk *Kiplinger's Personal Finance* v71 no10 p4 O 2017

How Can I ... Save More $$$? *Scholastic Choices* v32 no7 p24 Ap 2017

How Couples (and Throuples!) Do Money J. Eidelson, E. Holland et al color *Bloomberg Businessweek* no4502 p74 D 5 2016

How Millenials Manage Their Money C. M. Brown color *Black Enterprise* v47 no3 p23 O 2016

How to Improve Your Finance Skills (Even If You Hate Numbers) R. Knight *Harvard Business Review Digital Articles* p2 Mr 31 2017

How to Talk to Your Kids About Money When You Have a Lot of It J. Christianson *Harvard Business Review Digital Articles* p2 S 13 2016

Invest in Mutual Fun B. Risher and J. Covert cartoon *Men's Health* v32 no1 p30 Ja/F 2017

Lunch Break Money Boosters J. GARSKOF and K. FIFIELD color *AARP: The Magazine* v30 no6A p19 O/N 2017

The MONEY Do List A. Cao color *Money* v46 no1 p19 Ja/F 2017

The MONEY Do List color *Money* v46 no3 p15 Ap 2017

Money Help for Aging Parents E. AMBROSE and S. BLOCK color *Kiplinger's Personal Finance* v71 no11 p34 N 2017

The Newlyweds' Guide to Financial Success K. A. Renzulli color diag *Money* v46 no5 p54 Je 2017

PACK A PLAN R. HENAGER color *Phi Kappa Phi Forum* v96 no4 p17 Wint 2016

Save your way to zero stress [Cover story] L. FREEDMAN color *Redbook* p120 My 2017

Secrets of Single Super B. HOROVITZ, D. HOCHMAN et al color *AARP: The Magazine* v30 no6A p20 O/N 2017

Secrets to being smart with money N. Lapin color *Redbook* p30 N 2017

SPENT D. Garner color *Esquire* p72 S 2017

THE THOUSAND DOLLAR PAGE M. Thakor and L. Khalfani-Cox bw color *Men's Health* v32 no7 p42 S 2017

top 10 money to-dos of 2015 *Parents* p124 2015

We Retired Before 35 A. Breslaw color *Glamour* v115 no10 p136 O 2017

What to Do If You Get Medical Bills You Can't Pay Off Promptly A. Adamczyk color *Money* v46 no8 p18 S 2017

Personal finance—Bibliographies

REFERENCES *Economic Indicators* p331 S 2016

Personal finance—Computer network resources

3 Great Podcasts About Money A. Adamczyk color *Money* v46 no7 p15 Ag 2017

Personal finance—Software—Evaluation

Let's Get Digital F. TORABI color *O, The Oprah Magazine* p33 Ja 2017

Personal finance—United States

Best Cards for College Students L. GERSTNER chart *Kiplinger's Personal Finance* v71 no10 p46 O 2017

HOW THEY DID IT K. Bahler color *Money* v46 no8 p52 S 2017

Managing a Family (and Cash Flow) K. LANKFORD color *Kiplinger's Personal Finance* v71 no10 p72 O 2017

The MONEY Do List color *Money* v46 no2 p19 Mr 2017

We Pick the Best Banks *Kiplinger's Personal Finance* v71 no7 p8 Jl 2017

YOUR 20 BEST MONEY MOVES FOR 2017 P. J. Lim, K. Bahler et al color diag *Money* v45 no11 p60 D 2016

Personal grooming

> *See also*
>> Grooming for men

How to Give an Employee Feedback About Their Appearance A. Gallo *Harvard Business Review Digital Articles* p2 My 26 2017

Is Beauty Self-Care? S. Kitchens color *Glamour* v115 no7 p55 Jl 2017

SPOT Check M. Fuhrer *Dance Spirit* v21 no3 p58 Mr 2017

Personal grooming—Equipment & supplies

In the ROUND A. FORD color *House Beautiful* p120 Ag 2017

Tack Room color *Practical Horseman* v45 no5 p78 My 2017

Personal identification numbers

SMARTPHONE SECURITY L. Bedord *Successful Farming* v114 no11 p18 N 2016

Personal information management

Help! Sharing personal problems at work is no longer taboo. People Management examines what that means for employers - and how HR can help in eight key crises [Cover story] J. FARAGHER *People Management* p26 Jl 2017

Personal loans

Entrepreneurship and Re-entry: Aspire Entrepreneurship Initiative T. Thetford *Bridges (Federal Reserve Bank of St. Louis)* p8 Spr 2017

Personal managers

COMIC STRIP E. STEED cartoon *New Yorker* v93 no14 p65 My 22 2017

Personal names

America's Buzziest Baby Names C. Wilson color *Time* v189 no20 p9 My 29 2017

CALL OF THE WILD C. ROSE color *New Orleans Magazine* v51 no3 p40 Ja 2017

First-Name Basis J. EPSTEIN cartoon *Weekly Standard* v22 no18 p5 Ja 16 2017

FRESH BEGINNINGS S. Slon *Saturday Evening Post* v289 no1 p5 Ja/F 2017

HELLO MY NAME IS JANE J. Bernstein *Saturday Evening Post* v289 no1 p18 Ja/F 2017

IDENTITY CRISIS L. COLLINS color diag *New Yorker* v93 no23 p24 Ag 7 2017

"IT'S FOR YOU, JACKIE" J. CURRY *Washingtonian Magazine* v52 no2 p312 N 2016

NAME DROPPING D. Garner cartoon color *Esquire* v166 no5 p92 D 2016/Ja 2017

Reflections on the lectionary L. A. Powery *Christian Century* v134 no16 p19 Ag 2 2017

WE LOOK LIKE OUR NAMES S. Berinato color img *Harvard Business Review* v95 no5 p32 S/O 2017

What Popular Baby Names Teach Us About Data Analytics K. Fung *Harvard Business Review Digital Articles* p2 Ap 3 2015

Personal names—African American

I'M THE REAL SHAQUILLE A. Prewitt color diag *Sports Illustrated* v127 no1 p60 Jl 3 2017

Personal names—China

Charting China's Rising Individualism in Names, Songs, and Attitudes Xi Zou and Huajian Cai *Harvard Business Review Digital Articles* p2 Mr 11 2016

Personal names—Psychological aspects

There is Much in a Name: A good name will have a positive impact on a growing child's manners and outlook on life M. MIRZA *Islamic Horizons* v46 no4 p42 Jl/Ag 2017

Personal property

glamping cabin *Cabin Living* p25 O 2017

Letting Go P. Walsh color *Prevention* v69 no4 p54 Ap 2017

The Things She'll Carry: In the event of a house fire, some of my possessions must be saved—and my wife stands ready to haul them P. GULLEY color *Indianapolis Monthly* v41 no2 p50 S 2017

Personal propulsion units

I WISH SOMEONE WOULD INVENT... S. Chodosh, M. Koziol et al cartoon *Popular Science* p98 Ja/F 2017

Personal Shopper (Film)

Kristen Stewart Sets Personal Shopper Ablaze S. Zacharek color *Time* v189 no10 p51 Mr 20 2017

THE LIVING DEAD A. LANE cartoon *New Yorker* v93 no5 p100 Mr 20 2017

THE MATERIAL WORLD J. ROMNEY color *Film Comment* v53 no2 p36 Mr/Ap 2017

Only Connect R. R. Cooper color *Commonweal* v144 no8 p30 My 5 2017

Personal Shopper L. Greenblatt color *Entertainment Weekly* no1457/1458 p73 Mr 17 2017

Separated at Death img *New York* p121 Mr 6 2017

Personal shoppers

The Lawyer, the Wife, and the Wardrobe K. WISE *D: The Magazine of Dallas* v43 no10 p68 O 2016

Personal trainers

Build a Body Like J.Lo T. Anderson color *Health* v30 no9 p59 N 2016

consider this M. Dalbec, A. Palkhivala et al *Yoga Journal* no293 p12 Ag 2017

Forge Real Fitness with Top E-Trainers L. ROSENBAUM color *Men's Health* v32 no7 p45 S 2017

GETTING IT OUT S. Marikar cartoon *New Yorker* v93 no2 p24 F 27 2017

JILLIAN MICHAELS [Cover story] M. C. HAREL color *Redbook* p88 F 2017

Listen within C. Gorrell color *Yoga Journal* no293 p10 Ag 2017

THIGH Masters M. DESANCTIS color *Vogue* v206 no12 p197a D 2016

WORK OUT LIKE A PRO C. VAN DUSEN *Atlanta* v56 no9 p112 Ja 2017

Personal training

THE LAB OF LEAN A. HEFFERNAN bw *Men's Health* v32 no7 p100 S 2017

Personal watercraft

THE right PWC J. HEMMEL color *Cabin Living* p76 Ja/F 2017

Trailers Get Personal G. MANSFIELD *Boating World* v38 no4 p12 Ap 2017

Personality

See also

Adaptability (Psychology)

Adjustment (Psychology)

Assertiveness (Psychology)

Body image

Laziness

Mood (Psychology)

Negativism

Pessimism

Resilience (Personality trait)

Sociability

Toughness (Personality trait)

CAUTION: Toxic! K. Holmes *Dance Spirit* v20 no10 p58 D 2016

COULD YOUR PERSONALITY DERAIL YOUR CAREER? DON'T TAKE THESE TRAITS TO THE EXTREME T. CHAMORRO-PREMUZIC chart il img *Harvard Business Review* v95 no5 p138 S/O 2017

Embrace Awkwardness G. DREVITCH *Psychology Today* v50 no3 p48 My/Je 2017

The Feral Test color *Surfer* v57 no11 p96 D 2016

Getting It Done M. Funkhouser *Governing* v30 no3 p4 D 2016

Great Teams Are About Personalities, Not Just Skills D. Winsborough and T. Chamorro-Premuzic color *Harvard Business Review Digital Articles* p2 Ja 25 2017

How Diana Became Britain's 'Queen of the Heart' D. Stewart color *Time* v190 no9 p23 S 4 2017

How Well Do You Know... You? Are you an assertive "eagle"? A social "parrot"? This fun--and surprisingly accurate!--quiz will help you identify the personality traits that make you special *Scholastic Choices* p12 O 2017

INQUIRE WITHIN E. Marglin color diag *Yoga Journal* no289 p28 F 2017

Jerk Logic D. HARSANYI *National Review* v68 no21 p48 N 21 2016

PERSONALITY QUIZ: WHAT IS YOUR MONEY PERSONALITY? *Scholastic Choices* p8 O 2017 Supplement

Personality Tests Can Help Balance a Team T. Chamorro-Premuzic and D. Winsborough *Harvard Business Review Digital Articles* p2 Mr 19 2015

The Personality Traits of Good Negotiators T. Chamorro-Premuzic *Harvard Business Review Digital Articles* p2 Ag 7 2017

STYLE CRUSH Alanna Arrington S. Simon color *InStyle* v24 no8 p80 Ag 2017

To Reduce Stress, Embrace Your Inner Type-B V. Lipman *Harvard Business Review Digital Articles* p2 S 22 2015

Wit's End D. Paul *Indianapolis Monthly* p172 My 2017

Personality & intelligence

PIONEERS, DRIVERS, INTEGRATORS, & GUARDIANS [Cover story] S. M. J. VICKBERG and K. CHRISTFORT bw graph il img *Harvard Business Review* v95 no2 p50 Mr/Ap 2017

Personality & motivation

How to Get Excited About Topics That Bore You B. Oakley *Harvard Business Review Digital Articles* p2 Jl 3 2017

How to Get Work Done on the Road J. Grenny *Harvard Business Review Digital Articles* p2 N 9 2015

Personality & occupation

KICK-ASS CUSTOMER SERVICE M. Dixon, L. Ponomareff et al chart color graph il img *Harvard Business Review* v95 no1 p110 Ja/F 2017

Personality & situation

Split Personality B. PIKE bw *Power & Motoryacht* v34 no10 p200 O 2017

Personality assessment

See also

Personality tests

Board Members Should Have to Take a Personality Test M. Schrage *Harvard Business Review Digital Articles* p2 N 10 2014

Employees Can't Be Summed Up by a Personality Test P. Bregman *Harvard Business Review Digital Articles* p2 Ag 19 2015

O's GO-FOR-IT GUIDE to Getting Unstuck cartoon chart *O, The Oprah Magazine* p114 F 2017

Personality disorders

See also

Antisocial personality disorders

Passive-aggressive personality

Substance abuse

Go Wild M. BECK cartoon *O, The Oprah Magazine* p37 F 2017

Personality tests

PRESSING AND PRESCIENT K. BEATY *Christianity Today* v60 no9 p9 N 2016

Personality tests—History

A BRIEF HISTORY OF PERSONALITY TESTS [Cover story] E. HARRELL *Harvard Business Review* v95 no2 p63 Mr/Ap 2017

Personality tests—Research

A BRIEF HISTORY OF PERSONALITY TESTS [Cover story] E. HARRELL *Harvard Business Review* v95 no2 p63 Mr/Ap 2017

Personally identifiable information

Bad Credit M. CHEN *Nation* v305 no9 p6 O 16 2017

Blockchain Could Help Us Reclaim Control of Our Personal Data M. Mainelli *Harvard Business Review Digital Articles* p2 O 5 2017

If Data Is Money, Why Don't Businesses Keep It Secure? T. Cooper, R. LaSalle et al *Harvard Business Review Digital Articles* p2 F 10 2015

There's No Such Thing as Anonymous Data S. Berinato *Harvard Business Review Digital Articles* p2 F 9 2015

What Cancer Researchers Can Learn from Direct-to-Consumer Companies K. Giusti and R. G. Hamermesh color *Harvard*

Work environment

The 3 Simple Rules of Managing Top Talent R. L. Martin *Harvard Business Review Digital Articles* p2 F 24 2017

3 Things Managers Should Be Doing Every Day L. A. Hill and K. Lineback *Harvard Business Review Digital Articles* p2 S 24 2015

A 4-Step Process to Help Senior Teams Prioritize Decisions P. Hopper and J. Sakuja color *Harvard Business Review Digital Articles* p2 Mr 27 2017

5 Questions Leaders Should Be Asking All the Time J. E. Ryan *Harvard Business Review Digital Articles* p2 Ap 14 2017

5 Ways to Help Employees Keep Up with Digital Transformation D. Henretta and A. Chopra-McGowan *Harvard Business Review Digital Articles* p2 S 27 2017

7 Ways People Quit Their Jobs A. C. Klotz and M. C. Bolino *Harvard Business Review Digital Articles* p2 S 15 2016

ANTHEA MARRIS: Managing change can be disheartening - but it's worth sticking with *People Management* p18 S 2017

The A-Z of BAD managment *People Management* p38 D 2016/Ja 2017

The Benefits of Peer-to-Peer Praise at Work S. Achor *Harvard Business Review Digital Articles* p2 F 19 2016

The Best Advice I Never Got N. Gibbs color *InStyle* v24 no9 p210 S 2017

The Best Companies Don't Have More Stars — They Cluster Them Together M. Mankins color *Harvard Business Review Digital Articles* p2 F 3 2017

The Big Disconnect in Your Talent Strategy and How to Fix It J. Boudreau, M. Swan et al *Harvard Business Review Digital Articles* p2 D 23 2016

Case Study: Can an Airline Cut "Turn Times" Without Adding Staff? E. Bernstein and R. Buell *Harvard Business Review Digital Articles* p2 Ja 27 2016

Case Study: Should He Be Fired for That Facebook Post? M. A. Watson and G. R. Lopiano *Harvard Business Review Digital Articles* p2 D 11 2015

CEO is full of ideas - but doesn't listen *People Management* p53 My 2017

CEOs Need to Pay Attention to Employer Branding R. Mosley *Harvard Business Review Digital Articles* p2 My 11 2015

Companies Are Bad at Identifying High-Potential Employees J. Zenger and J. Folkman *Harvard Business Review Digital Articles* p2 F 20 2017

DAVID CLUTTERBUCK: HR must 'upcycle' outdated approaches to survive the future D. Clutterbuck *People Management* p19 Je 2017

Dear Boss: Your Team Wants You to Go on Vacation R. Friedman *Harvard Business Review Digital Articles* p2 Je 18 2015

Designing the Machines That Will Design Strategy M. Reeves and D. Ueda *Harvard Business Review Digital Articles* p2 Ap 18 2016

Design Your Employee Experience as Thoughtfully as You Design Your Customer Experience D. L. Yohn *Harvard Business Review Digital Articles* p2 D 8 2016

Developing Employees' Strengths Boosts Sales, Profit, and Engagement B. Rigoni and J. Asplund *Harvard Business Review Digital Articles* p2 S 1 2016

"Diversity doesn't have to be burdensome - it's magic": Stonewall co-founder and D&I consultant Simon Fanshawe on how to bridge the gap between good intentions and real change *People Management* p15 S 2017

"Don't Take It Personally" Is Terrible Work Advice D. Coombe *Harvard Business Review Digital Articles* p2 Mr 29 2016

Do You Know How Each Person on Your Team Likes to Work? S. Nawaz *Harvard Business Review Digital Articles* p2 My 30 2017

The Easiest Thing You Can Do to Be a Great Boss D. Sturt *Harvard Business Review Digital Articles* p2 N 9 2015

Employee Engagement Depends on What Happens Outside of the Office S. LaMotte *Harvard Business Review Digital Articles* p2 Ja 13 2015

Even Tiny Rewards Can Motivate People to Go the Extra Mile G. Furtmüller, C. Garaus et al *Harvard Business Review Digital Articles* p2 Je 7 2016

FLIGHT OF THE CONCHORDS *People Management* p66 O 2016

GE's Real-Time Performance Development L. Baldassarre and B. Finken *Harvard Business Review Digital Articles* p2 Ag 12 2015

Help Employees Create Knowledge—Not Just Share It J. Hagel III and J. S. Brown *Harvard Business Review Digital Articles* p2 2017

How Age and Gender Affect Self-Improvement J. Zenger and J. Folkman *Harvard Business Review Digital Articles* p2 Ja 5 2016

How HR Can Become Agile (and Why It Needs To) J. Gothelf *Harvard Business Review Digital Articles* p2 Je 19 2017

How HR can support a new leader A. Stanley *People Management* p50 Mr 2017

How Leaders Can Let Go Without Losing Control M. Bonchek *Harvard Business Review Digital Articles* p2 Je 2 2016

How Leaders Should React When Someone Disappoints P. Bregman *Harvard Business Review Digital Articles* p2 F 20 2015

How Managers Can Avoid Playing Favorites R. Knight *Harvard Business Review Digital Articles* p2 Mr 15 2017

How Not to Advocate for a Woman at Work D. M. Mayer *Harvard Business Review Digital Articles* p2 Jl 26 2017

How Powerful, Low-Status Jobs Lead to Conflict E. M. Anicich, N. J. Fast et al *Harvard Business Review Digital Articles* p2 F 11 2016

How Some Companies Are Making Child Care Less Stressful for Their Employees J. Beck *Harvard Business Review Digital Articles* p2 Ap 14 2017

How to Become a More Well-Rounded Leader T. Schwartz *Harvard Business Review Digital Articles* p2 Jl 21 2017

How to conduct difficult conversations N. Gold *People Management* p44 Ag 2017

How to Design a Corporate Wellness Plan That Actually Works H. De La Torre and R. Goetzel *Harvard Business Review Digital Articles* p2 Mr 31 2016

How to Design Work Projects for Maximum Learning J. M. Stearn *Harvard Business Review Digital Articles* p2 Jl 22 2015

How to Finally Kill the Useless, Recurring Meeting R. Fuller *Harvard Business Review Digital Articles* p2 Mr 17 2015

How to Get a New Employee Up to Speed S. Stibitz *Harvard Business Review Digital Articles* p2 My 22 2015

How to Get Out from Under Your Boss's Shadow P. Claman *Harvard Business Review Digital Articles* p2 D 2 2014

How to Get People to Collaborate When You Don't Control Their Salary H. K. Gardner bw graph *Harvard Business Review Digital Articles* p2 Ja 23 2017

How to Handle Underperformers on a Team You Inherit R. Ashkenas *Harvard Business Review Digital Articles* p2 Je 15 2017

How to Make Raising Difficult Issues Everyone's Job R. Carucci *Harvard Business Review Digital Articles* p2 My 19 2017

How to Manage a Needy Employee R. Knight color *Harvard Business Review Digital Articles* p2 Je 5 2017

How to Manage a Toxic Employee A. Gallo *Harvard Business Review Digital Articles* p2 O 3 2016

How to Manage Managers A. Gallo *Harvard Business Review Digital Articles* p2 Ag 29 2016

How to Manage People Who Are Smarter than You R. Knight *Harvard Business Review Digital Articles* p2 Ag 6 2015

How to Manage Remote Direct Reports R. Knight *Harvard Business Review Digital Articles* p2 F 10 2015

How to Manage Someone Who Thinks Everything Is Urgent L. Kislik *Harvard Business Review Digital Articles* p2 Ag 2 2017

How to Motivate Someone You Don't Like L. Davey *Harvard Business Review Digital Articles* p2 N 4 2014

How to Respond When Your Employee Asks for a Raise A. Gallo *Harvard Business Review Digital Articles* p2 F 17 2016

How to Signal That Your Company Cares About Diversity C. Romero *Harvard Business Review Digital Articles* p2 D 3 2015

How to Stop Micromanaging Your Team R. Knight *Harvard Business Review Digital Articles* p2 Ag 21 2015

How to Support Employees' Learning Goals While Getting Day-to-Day Stuff Done N. Gidwani *Harvard Business Review Digital Articles* p2 Ag 1 2017

How to Teach Employees Skills They Don't Know They Lack U. J. Christensen *Harvard Business Review Digital Articles* p2 S 29 2017

How Tribalism Hurts Companies, and What to Do About It R. Kovach *Harvard Business Review Digital Articles* p2 Jl 26 2017

If You Can't Empathize with Your Employees, You'd Better Learn To A. McKee *Harvard Business Review Digital Articles* p2 N 16 2016

I'LL TELL YOU SOMETHING LAURA RENNIE: HR 'bad apples' value power and policy over doing good work L. Rennie *People Management* p19 Ap 2017

Internal Hires Need Just as Much Support as External Ones M. D. Watkins *Harvard Business Review Digital Articles* p2 Ap 4 2016

Internal Hires Need Orientation Too L. Sterling *Harvard Business Review Digital Articles* p2 N 4 2016

Is 'cosy' deal with ex-staff fair? PM's Fixer Samantha Sales tackles readers' big issues S. Sales *People Management* p52 Jl 2017

Isolate Toxic Employees to Reduce Their Negative Effects C. Porath *Harvard Business Review Digital Articles* p2 N 14 2016

It's not an HR thing - it's a business thing C. NFWRFRY *People Management* p20 F 2017

It's Not HR's Job to Be Strategic S. Graber *Harvard Business Review Digital Articles* p2 O 31 2014

It's the Company's Job to Help Employees Learn T. Chamorro-Premuzic and M. Swan *Harvard Business Review Digital Articles* p2 Jl 18 2016

Leading People When They Know More than You Do W. T. Wallace and D. Creelman *Harvard Business Review Digital Articles* p2 Je 18 2015

Managers in the Digital Age Need to Stay Human W. McFarland *Harvard Business Review Digital Articles* p2 Je 17 2015

Managing Up Without Sucking Up W. Johnson *Harvard Business Review Digital Articles* p2 D 15 2014

MEAN GIRLS: A committed team player is falsely accused of dealing drugs *People Management* p66 Je 2017

More Data Won't Turn Employees into High- Performing Machines T. Chamorro-Premuzic *Harvard Business Review Digital Articles* p2 O 30 2014

Most HR Data Is Bad Data M. Buckingham *Harvard Business Review Digital Articles* p2 F 9 2015

The Most Overlooked Way of Stimulating Team Creativity J. Levirne *Harvard Business Review Digital Articles* p2 My 15 2015

One Engagement Strategy Does Not Fit All N. Baumgartner *Harvard Business Review Digital Articles* p2 N 26 2014

"People don't seem so keen to move to our US offices all of a sudden...": The tricky logistics of global mobility - and HR's crucial role in getting it right J. SIMMS *People Management* p46 Mr 2017

THE PM GUIDE A. HAYES *People Management* p39 N 2016

The Portable Leader Is the New "Organization Man" G. Petriglieri *Harvard Business Review Digital Articles* p2 Ag 10 2017

Proof That Positive Work Cultures Are More Productive E. Seppala and K. Cameron *Harvard Business Review Digital Articles* p2 D 1 2015

PUTTING A PRICE ON "PEOPLE PROBLEMS" graph img *Harvard Business Review* v94 no12 p28 D 2016

Recognizing the Role of Emotional Labor in the On-Demand Economy L. Stark *Harvard Business Review Digital Articles* p2 Ag 26 2016

Setting the Record Straight on Managing Your Boss A. Gallo *Harvard Business Review Digital Articles* p2 D 18 2014

Shifting from Star Performer to Star Manager A. McKee *Harvard Business Review Digital Articles* p2 O 20 2015

Signs That You're a Micromanager M. M. Wilkins *Harvard Business Review Digital Articles* p2 N 11 2014

Small Talk Is an Overrated Way to Build Relationships with Your Employees K. Scott *Harvard Business Review Digital Articles* p1 Jl 25 2017

Stop Wasting Your Time on Work Calls D. Clark *Harvard Business Review Digital Articles* p2 Mr 31 2016

Success with the Internet of Things Requires More Than Chasing the Cool Factor M. Kranz *Harvard Business Review Digital Articles* p2 Ag 7 2017

There Is No Right Way to Unplug from Work S. Schrobsdorff color *Time* v189 no3 p19 Ja 30 2017

There's more than one way to solve a dispute: Resolving workplace differences is a fine art - and many businesses have been getting it dramatically wrong J. SIMMS *People Management* p32 Ag 2017

These are the experts deciding the future of HR......shouldn't you

know who they are? [Cover story] G. GYTON and R. JEFFSRY *People Management* p24 Ag 2017

To Fix a Chronic Problem, Try Winging It M. Lipson *Harvard Business Review Digital Articles* p2 Ja 20 2016

To Get More Creative, Become Less Productive A. Markman *Harvard Business Review Digital Articles* p2 N 30 2015

To Hold Someone Accountable, First Define What Accountable Means B. Frisch and C. Greene *Harvard Business Review Digital Articles* p2 Je 28 2016

To Understand Whether Your Company Is Inclusive, Map How Your Employees Interact B. Yamkovenko and S. Tavares *Harvard Business Review Digital Articles* p2 Jl 19 2017

Uber Is Finally Realizing HR Isn't Just for Recruiting J. Boudreau color *Harvard Business Review Digital Articles* p2 Mr 7 2017

The Unsexy Fundamentals of Great HR M. Effron and M. Ort *Harvard Business Review Digital Articles* p2 Ag 19 2015

Upbeat Music Can Make Employees More Cooperative K. Kniffin *Harvard Business Review Digital Articles* p2 Ag 30 2016

"We'd like to make you an offer" H. KIRTON *People Management* p40 Je 2017

We're All Capable of Being an Abusive Boss [Cover story] M. Mawritz, R. L. Greenbaum et al *Harvard Business Review Digital Articles* p2 O 14 2016

What Amazing Bosses Do Differently S. Finkelstein *Harvard Business Review Digital Articles* p2 N 27 2015

What Great Managers Do Daily R. Fuller and N. Shikaloff *Harvard Business Review Digital Articles* p2 D 14 2016

What HR Can Do to Fix the Gender Pay Gap D. Ashton *Harvard Business Review Digital Articles* p2 D 2 2014

What HR Needs to Do to Get a Seat at the Table C. Anderson *Harvard Business Review Digital Articles* p2 N 27 2014

What If Companies Managed People as Carefully as They Manage Money? E. Garton *Harvard Business Review Digital Articles* p2 My 24 2017

What I Learned from Transforming the U.S. Military's Approach to Talent A. Carter *Harvard Business Review Digital Articles* p2 My 23 2017

What Marissa Mayer Got Wrong (and Right) About Stack Ranking Employees C. Yeh *Harvard Business Review Digital Articles* p2 Ja 8 2015

What Ruthless Innovators Can Learn from the New England Patriots V. Govindarajan *Harvard Business Review Digital Articles* p2 Mr 9 2016

What's Worse than a Difficult Conversation? Avoiding One D. Rowland *Harvard Business Review Digital Articles* p2 Ap 8 2016

What to Do If Your Team Is Letting You Down A. Grady *Harvard Business Review Digital Articles* p2 My 4 2015

What to Do When You Don't Trust Your Team W. T. Wallace and D. Creelman *Harvard Business Review Digital Articles* p2 S 30 2015

What to Do When Your Boss Doesn't Like You L. Davey *Harvard Business Review Digital Articles* p2 D 8 2014

What to Do When Your Employee Asks for a Raise Too Soon R. Knight *Harvard Business Review Digital Articles* p2 Jl 15 2016

When an Employee Quits and You Didn't See It Coming R. Knight *Harvard Business Review Digital Articles* p2 Mr 12 2015

When Employees Think the Boss Is Unfair, They're More Likely to Disengage and Leave S. A. Hewlett, R. Rashid et al *Harvard Business Review Digital Articles* p2 Ag 1 2017

When the Competition Is Trying to Poach Your Top Employee R. Knight *Harvard Business Review Digital Articles* p2 S 29 2015

When Your Employee Doesn't Take Feedback D. G. Riegel *Harvard Business Review Digital Articles* p2 N 6 2015

When You're Worried About a Colleague's Mental Health A. Gallo *Harvard Business Review Digital Articles* p2 D 18 2015

Who I am: Martin Mason *People Management* p49 My 2017

Whose Job Is It to Manage Freelancers? J. Younger and R. Blumberg *Harvard Business Review Digital Articles* p2 Mr 14 2016

Why CEOs Can't Stay Silent in the Wake of Events Like Charlottesville N. Kteily and F. Gino *Harvard Business Review Digital Articles* p2 2017

Why More Executives Should Consider Becoming a CHRO J. Boudreau, P. Navin et al *Harvard Business Review Digital Articles* p2 My 3 2017

Why My Company Serves Free Breakfast to All Employees J.

If You Want People to Listen, Stop Talking P. Bregman *Harvard Business Review Digital Articles* p2 My 25 2015

Persuasion Depends Mostly on the Audience T. Chamorro-Premuzic *Harvard Business Review Digital Articles* p2 Je 2 2015

Research: You Have Fewer Friends than You Think A. ". Pentland *Harvard Business Review Digital Articles* p2 My 12 2016

Why the Gettysburg Address Is Still a Great Case Study in Persuasion T. David *Harvard Business Review Digital Articles* p2 Ap 9 2015

Persuasion (Rhetoric)
See also
Argument

How Doctors (or Anyone) Can Craft a More Persuasive Message S. Martin *Harvard Business Review Digital Articles* p2 Ja 29 2015

Persuasive technology
the health nut A. Brightfield color *Better Homes & Gardens* v95 no8 p178 Ag 2017

Pertot, Yoann
Time-resolved x-ray absorption spectroscopy with a water window high-harmonic source graph *Science* v355 no6322 p264 Ja 20 2017

Peru
Take and drink D. Philippart color *U.S. Catholic* v82 no6 p33 Je 2017

Peru—Economic conditions—21st century
Under new management J. Quigley and B. Bartenstein color *Bloomberg Businessweek* no4496 p18 O 24 2016

Perumpilly, G.
Observation of coherent elastic neutrino-nucleus scattering diag *Science* v357 no6356 p1123 S 15 2017

Peruzzi, Marc
Skiing Is Politics color *Powder* p38 S 2017

Pervasive child development disorders
See also
Autism spectrum disorders

Recent progress in autism spectrum disorder research in China Jinchen Li, Lin Wang et al bibl chart diag *Science* v354 no6319 p48 D 23 2016

Pervo, Marco
UNSOLICITED BETA color *Climbing* no353 p18 My/Je 2017

Pesacov, Lewis
Pesacov: The Edge of Forever D. J. Baker *Opera News* v81 no5 p55 N 2016

Pescatore, Fred
Knock Out a Cold with Pycnogenol *Amazing Wellness* v9 no6 p66 EarlyWint 2017

ON THE A-LIST J. Bowden color *Amazing Wellness* v9 no3 p22 EarlySumm 2017

Pescatrice, Jessica
An Ambassador of Dressage color *Dressage Today* v23 no5 p60 Ja 2017

PESCE, CHERYL
The Question *O, The Oprah Magazine* p16 My 2017

Pesce, Gaetano
Up Rising H. MARTIN color *Architectural Digest* v74 no10 p30 O 1 2017

Pesce, Nicolas
The Eyes of My Mother *New Yorker* v92 no40 p16 D 5 2016

Peschel, Andreas
Fighting the enemy within bibl diag *Science* v355 no6326 p689 F 17 2017

Peschel, Joseph
Inside the eager mind color *Science* v357 no6346 p42 Jl 7 2017

Peshu, Norbert
Resistance to malaria through structural variation of red blood cell invasion receptors diag *Science* v356 no6343 p1139 Je 16 2017

Peskanov, Mark
CLASSICAL MUSIC cartoon *New Yorker* v93 no26 p14 S 4 2017

PESKIN, JOY
Drawing the Line *Publishers Weekly* v264 no6 p72 F 6 2017

Peskin, Michael
Q: What was the most important letter in history? color *Atlantic* v320 no2 p104 S 2017

Peso (Mexican currency)
Trump Hurts the Peso. That Helps Mexicans I. Cota color graph *Bloomberg Businessweek* no4494 p20 O 10 2016

Pessimism
See also
Cynicism

The Cure for Everything (Seriously) A. SCOTT cartoon map *Men's Health* v32 no9 p67 N 2017

GAME PLAN M. Zimmerman color *Men's Health* v32 no8 p8 O 2017

The Silver Lining P. GULLEY *Indianapolis Monthly* v40 no3 p64 N 2016

Why Gloom Trumps Glad M. Shermer cartoon *Scientific American* v315 no5 p77 N 2016

Pessl, Marisha
Deals R. DEAHL bw color *Publishers Weekly* v264 no25 p10 Je 19 2017

EVERY DAY I'M SIDE-HUSTLIN' cartoon color *GQ: Gentlemen's Quarterly* v97 no4 p60 Ap 2017

Pessoa, Fernando, 1888-1935
The Book of Disquiet M. VALDES color *Publishers Weekly* v264 no27 p51 Jl 3 2017

VOICES FROM THE VOID A. KIRSCH color *New Yorker* v93 no26 p84 S 4 2017

Pest control
Organic Parks: The challenge of managing and maintaining well-manicured landscapes S. Ozbenian *Parks & Recreation* v52 no10 p26 O 2017

Our home and pest-ridden land C. McINTYRE color map *Maclean's* p17 Je 2017

Q+A *Boating World* v38 no6 p26 Je 2017

SECRETS OF THE GUIDES T. ALVAREZ color il *Backpacker* p75 Ag 2017

Pest control baits
Chronic exposure to neonicotinoids reduces honey bee health near corn crops N. Tsvetkov, O. Samson-Robert et al diag *Science* v356 no6345 p1395 Je 30 2017

Country-specific effects of neonicotinoid pesticides on honey bees and wild bees B. A. Woodcock, J. M. Bullock et al diag map *Science* v356 no6345 p1393 Je 30 2017

Pest control in buildings
Our home and pest-ridden land C. McINTYRE color map *Maclean's* p17 Je 2017

Pestana, Carla Gardina
Imperial Designs: Cromwell's move on Jamaica transformed Britain's early empire *History Today* v67 no6 p8 Je 2016

Peste des petits ruminants
Fatal virus felling rare antelope color *Science* v355 no6324 p436 F 3 2017

Pestel, Sabrina
mom wins… …and fails color *Working Mother* v40 no2 p8 Je/Jl 2017

Pesticide use regulations
Toward pesticidovigilance A. M. Milner and I. L. Boyd chart color *Science* v357 no6357 p1232 S 22 2017

Pesticides
See also
Herbicides

AMAZING NEWS V. Tweed color *Amazing Wellness* v9 no1 p14 Wint 2017

BACKUP BEES? C. Zuckerman color *National Geographic* v232 no4 p24 O 2017

'Neonics' and Other Pesticides C. CALLAGHAN color *Canadian Wildlife* v23 no2 p44 My/Je 2017

A New Pollution Problem S. Novick bw chart color *Environment* v59 no4 p14 Jl-Ag 2017

A Real Grass Act J. SerVaas *Saturday Evening Post* v289 no5 p25 S/O 2017

Pesticides—Environmental aspects
Ethical Evergreens Z. SCHAEFFER and T. ROSS color *Rodale's Organic Life* v2 no7 p94 D 2016/Ja 2017

Just Choose Hope H. Kincaid *Mother Earth News* no279 p3 D/Ja 2017

Pestos
BUCATINI WITH SHRIMP, ALMOND PESTO, AND CHERRY TOMATOES *Washingtonian Magazine* v52 no9 p144 Je 2017

home made PESTO color *Good Housekeeping* v265 no3 p116 S 2017

Provence in a Bowl T. Rao *New York Times Magazine* p30 Ap 30 2017

Pet adoption

See also

Dog adoption

Adopt a Critter S. Bower. chart color *Good Housekeeping* v264 no4 p140 Ap 2017

NOT-FOREVER FAMILIES D. Bruno color *Washingtonian Magazine* v52 no7 p161 Ap 2017

Pet allergy

NOTHING TO SNEEZE AT J. Szabo color *Amazing Wellness* v9 no2 p76 Spr 2017

SCRATCH AND SNIFFLE E. BATTAGLIA color *Martha Stewart Living* no275 p56 Je 2017

Pet boarding facilities—Evaluation

BEST OF HALL OF FAME *Washingtonian Magazine* v53 no1 p214 O 2017

Pet care

BEST OF WASHINGTON HALL OF FAME *Washingtonian Magazine* v52 no8 p209 My 2017

Comfort Creatures S. ECKELKAMP color *Prevention* v68 no12 p94 D 2016

CREATURE COMFORTS E. BATTAGLIA color *Martha Stewart Living* no271 p48 Ja/F 2017

Hitting the Trails N. B. McGough and P. S. York color *Southern Living* v52 no10 p42 O 2017

HOW TO SAVE A CAT M. GUNCH color *New Orleans Magazine* v51 no3 p42 Ja 2017

My golden mare S. Thompson color *Equus* no474 p64 Mr 2017

my night in the doghouse C. Alter *Washingtonian Magazine* v52 no11 p60 Ag 2017

THE PET-SITTING SIDE HUSTLE S. MaHan *Washingtonian Magazine* v52 no4 p204 Ja 2017

Pups & Personal Space N. B. McGough and P. York color *Southern Living* v52 no3 p26 Mr 2017

Pet clothing & dress

Amazing Animals A. SILEN color *National Geographic Kids* no474 p8 O 2017

Pet clothing & dress—Evaluation

BECAUSE DOGS LOVE WINTER, TOO J. Schnuer color *Rodale's Organic Life* v2 no7 p16 D 2016/Ja 2017

Pet food

13 Things Pet Stores Won't Tell You M. CROUCH color *Reader's Digest* v189 no1131 p128 Je 2017

Pet-Safe Halloween Treats G. McClure color *Good Housekeeping* v265 no4 p134 O 2017

Pet food industry

FIDO'S NO FOODIE [Cover story] K. MILLER color *Prevention* v69 no5 p84 My 2017

Pet food—Equipment & supplies

Petnet SmartFeeder: Robot pet feeder meets smartphone app with mostly good results K. STEVENSON color *PCWorld* v35 no7 p155 Jl 2017

Pet health insurance

Ask Martha Martha color *Martha Stewart Living* p50 My 2017

Need That Insurance? J. GARSKOF color *AARP: The Magazine* v60 no1A p24 D 2016/Ja 2017

Pet industry

See also

Dog industry

BEST OF HALL OF FAME *Washingtonian Magazine* v52 no11 p162 Ag 2017

Pet owners

See also

Dog owners

BONE-A FIDE ADVICE L. ROBERTS color *Indianapolis Monthly* v42 no2 p99 O 2017

Dogs on the Town N. B. McGough and P. S. York color *Southern Living* v52 no6 p43 Je 2017

The Richest PETS OF ALL TIME! J. KIFFEL *National Geographic Kids* no467 p22 F 2017

When You're Away, The Cats And Dogs Will Play E. HAMES color *Reader's Digest* v189 no1130 p43 My 2017

Pet shops

13 Things Pet Stores Won't Tell You M. CROUCH color *Reader's Digest* v189 no1131 p128 Je 2017

Incorruptible, Uncritical Devotion J. EPSTEIN color *Weekly Standard* v22 no9 p5 N 7 2016

Pet shops—Moral & ethical aspects

The Dog Factory P. Solotaroff color *Rolling Stone* no1278/1279 p42 Ja 12 2017

Pet supplies industry

Pet Food That Comes With an Oil Painting O. Zaleski color *Bloomberg Businessweek* no4501 p30 N 28 2016

Pet supplies—Evaluation

Holiday Gift Guide color *Timber Home Living* v27 no6 p10 D 2017

Petnet SmartFeeder: Robot pet feeder meets smartphone app with mostly good results K. STEVENSON color *PCWorld* v35 no7 p155 Jl 2017

Pet therapy

Comfort Creatures S. ECKELKAMP color *Prevention* v68 no12 p94 D 2016

The Science of Pet Therapy Is Getting Serious M. Oaklander color *Time* v189 no14 p24 Ap 17 2017

PETACCIO, CARMEN

"I Love My Characters, But I Don't Like Them" color *Publishers Weekly* v263 no44 p46 O 31 2016

Pete, John "Boomer", Jr.

Chasing the MR&T color map *Model Railroader* v84 no4 p40 Ap 2017

Peter, Benjamin M.

Chimpanzee genomic diversity reveals ancient admixture with bonobos bibl diag graph map *Science* v354 no6311 p477 O 28 2016

Peter, Cindy

Poor fisheries struggle with U.S. import rule bibl color *Science* v355 no6329 p1031 Mr 10 2017

Peter, G.

Seasonal exposure of carbon dioxide ice on the nucleus of comet 67P/Churyumov-Gerasimenko bibl bw graph *Science* v354 no6319 p1563 D 23 2016

Peter, the Apostle, Saint, ca. 1 B.C.-67 A.D., in art

St. Peter Walking on Water H. J. Hornik and M. C. Parsons color *Christian Century* v134 no15 p47 Jl 19 2017

Peter Bernstein Quartet (Performer)

NIGHT LIFE *New Yorker* v93 no26 p15 S 4 2017

PETERIGLIERI, GIANPIERO

The Talent Curse il *Harvard Business Review* v95 no3 p88 My/Je 2017

PETERIGLIERI, JENNIFER

The Talent Curse il *Harvard Business Review* v95 no3 p88 My/Je 2017

PETERKEN, GEORGE

Combining Biodiversity Resurveys across Regions to Advance Global Change Research *BioScience* v67 no1 p73 Ja 2017

PETERMAN, AUDREY

My Life, Before and After National Parks *Orion Magazine* v35 no4/5 p54 Jl-O 2016

Petermon, Jade D.

THE SHADOW BEHIND THE REAL: SPIKE LEE DOES CHICAGO *Film Quarterly* v70 no2 p30 Wint 2016

Peters, Benjamin T.

Dorothy Day's 'Second Conversion'? P. Jordan bw *Commonweal* v144 no11 p31 Je 16 2017

Peters, C.

Observation of a large-scale anisotropy in the arrival directions of cosmic rays above 8 × 1018 eV *Science* v357 no6357 p1266 S 22 2017

Peters, Charlie

Call of Duty P. GLASTRIS *Washington Monthly* v49 no3-5 p4 Mr-My 2017

PETERS, CLINTON CROCKETT

Beasts on the Street *Orion Magazine* v35 no3 p5 My/Je 2016

Peters, David S.

Decarboxylative borylation color *Science* v356 no6342 p1045 Je 9 2017

Peters, Evelyn

Contemporary Identities and Cultural Innovation F. Delgado *American Indian Quarterly* v40 no3 p283 Summ 2016

Peters, Frank

Exposing Unfair Pricing in Auto Insurance Rates color *Consumer*

Reports v82 no5 p6 My 2017

Peters, Glen

The promise of negative emissions bibl *Science* v354 no6313 p714 N 11 2016

The trouble with negative emissions bibl graph *Science* v354 no6309 p182 O 14 2016

PETERS, GREG M.

THE WILD CONGAREE *National Parks* v91 no4 p44 Fall 2017

PETERS, JANE SLOAN

Meeting Our Neighbors *America* v215 no18 p15 D 5 2016

Peters, Jen

Cassandre Joseph: How the STREB member conditions her body to pull off "impossible" stunts *Dance Magazine* v91 no9 p48 S 2017

Farm to Theater *Dance Magazine* v91 no1 p42 Ja 2017

The Tax-Season Dance color *Dance Magazine* v91 no3 p50 Mr 2017

Peters, John

Driving Home the Safety Discussion il *Consumer Reports* v82 no9 p6 S 2017

Peters, Jonathan

'Put the camera down' color *Columbia Journalism Review* v56 no2 p21 Fall 2017

Trump and trickle-down press persecution color *Columbia Journalism Review* v56 no1 p27 Spr 2017

Peters, Julia Tang

How You Make Decisions Is as Important as What You Decide *Harvard Business Review Digital Articles* p2 Ap 28 2015

Peters, Meike

Malta Made Me Do It color *Conde Nast Traveler* v52 no9 p45 O 2017

PETERS, MICHAEL

Boat Porn color *Power & Motoryacht* v33 no3 p36 Mr 2017

Delusions of Grandeur color *Power & Motoryacht* v32 no11 p44 N 2016

Don Aronow: The Legend in My Corner color *Power & Motoryacht* v33 no2 p36 F 2017

The Father of Modern Powerboat Design color *Power & Motoryacht* v34 no6 p20 Je 2017

A Fishing Massacree color *Power & Motoryacht* v33 no1 p36 Ja 2017

Keyboard Warriors color *Power & Motoryacht* v34 no9 p28 S 2017

A Mark in Time color *Power & Motoryacht* v34 no7 p20 Jl 2017

Permission Granted color *Power & Motoryacht* v34 no8 p22 Ag 2017

Walking the Walk color *Power & Motoryacht* v34 no10 p42 O 2017

Water Dog color *Power & Motoryacht* v33 no4 p28 Ap 2017

Peters, Ralph

Chicken Soup for the Russian Soul: A strongman with a messianic streak, Vladimir Putin might almost have stepped from the pages of Russian history *Hoover Digest: Research & Opinion on Public Policy* no2 p101 Spr 2017

Peters, Roberta, 1930-2017

ROBERTA PETERS I. Siff *Opera News* v81 no10 p64 Ap 2017

Peters, Ted

Sin Boldly! Justifying Faith for Fragile and Broken Souls M. L. Riegel color *Christian Century* v134 no11 p36 My 24 2017

Sin Bravely: A Memoir of Spiritual Disobedience *Christian Century* v134 no9 p34 Ap 26 2017

Peters, Thomas J., 1942-

REPUTATION BY . . . TOM PETERS bw *Forbes* v200 no4 p24 O 24 2017

Peters, Tom—Interviews

THE NEW RULES OF FEED ANTIBIOTICS G. Johnston *Successful Farming* v115 no1 p60 Ja 2017

PETERS, VALERIE E.

Using Plant-Animal Interactions to Inform Tree Selection in Tree-Based Agroecosystems for Enhanced Biodiversity *BioScience* v66 no12 p1046 D 1 2016

Petersen, Andrea

Show Me Where It WORRIES color *O, The Oprah Magazine* p81 Ag 2017

Petersen, Andrew

People TO WATCH [Cover story] K. SINGLETARY color *New*

Orleans Magazine v52 no1 p76 S 2017

PETERSEN, ANNE HELEN

Lives in Pieces *New York Times Book Review* p14 F 26 2017

Petersen, George

Product Hits of AES 2016 *Stage Directions* v29 no12 p11 D 2016

Sounds From Under the Sea *Stage Directions* v30 no5 p16 My 2017

Petersen, Julian

Multipotent peripheral glial cells generate neuroendocrine cells of the adrenal medulla color *Science* v357 no6346 p46 Jl 7 2017

Peterson, Adrian Lewis, 1985-

ENCORE PERFORMANCE J. Vrentas color *Sports Illustrated* v127 no7 p104 S 4 2017

PETERSON, AMBER

The Question *O, The Oprah Magazine* p12 Mr 2017

Peterson, Bethany L.

Fructose-driven glycolysis supports anoxia resistance in the naked mole-rat diag graph *Science* v356 no6335 p307 Ap 21 2017

PETERSON, BRENDA

Howling with Wolves color *Orion Magazine* v36 no2 p10 Mr/Ap 2017

Peterson, Britt

The Case Against Cats color *Atlantic* v318 no5 p40 D 2016

"LAME DUCK" /LĀM DÚK/ *Washingtonian Magazine* v52 no2 p20 N 2016

THE MATH POLYMATH *Washingtonian Magazine* v52 no4 p45 Ja 2017

"PANTSUIT" /PANT SOOT/ *Washingtonian Magazine* v52 no3 p18 D 2016

SOURCE OF DEBATE: Twitter star Claude Taylor says he has juicy inside info about Trump investigations. Should we take him seriously? *Washingtonian Magazine* v53 no1 p20 O 2017

Transcendigital color *Smithsonian* v47 no10 p14 Mr 2017

VIRGINIA TECH, TEN YEARS LATER color *Washingtonian Magazine* v52 no7 p69 Ap 2017

Peterson, Derek

TECH TRENDS CHANGING OUR WORLD color *Black Enterprise* v47 no2 p46 S 2016

Peterson, Eugene H., 1932-

The Pursuit of Happiness Is a Dead-End Street E. H. PETERSON color *Christianity Today* v61 no5 p71 Je 2017

Peterson, Gale

A SALTY TREAT color *Golf Magazine* v59 no11 p42 N 2017

PETERSON, GARRY D.

When, Where, and How Nature Matters for Ecosystem Services: Challenges for the Next Generation of Ecosystem Service Models *BioScience* v67 no9 p820 S 2017

Peterson, Gerri

HOOKER COUNTY TRIBUNE C. Spike bw *Columbia Journalism Review* v56 no1 p95 Spr 2017

Peterson, Holly

OLD FAITHFUL color *O, The Oprah Magazine* p34 O 2017

Peterson, Jessica

Ink in Her Blood L. LaBorde *New Orleans Homes & Lifestyles* v20 no1 p30 Wint 2016

Peterson, Kathleen M.

KICK-ASS CUSTOMER SERVICE: INTERACTION color *Harvard Business Review* v95 no3 p16 My/Je 2017

Peterson, Keri

Ask anything bw color *Women's Health* v14 no4 p18 My 2017

Ask anything [Cover story] cartoon color *Women's Health* v13 no10 p22 D 2016

HEALTHFESSIONS color *Women's Health* v14 no2 p86 Mr 2017

PETERSON, KOREY

The Best of Both Worlds: Gooseberry Falls and Split Rock Lighthouse State Parks, Minnesota color *Backpacker* p24 S 2017

Holiday Hike: Stephens State Forest, Iowa map *Backpacker* p15 N 2017

Pioneer Days diag *Backpacker* p22 Je 2017

The Zone of Death *Idaho Magazine* v16 no5 p45 F 2017

Peterson, Kyle

"We Ought to Be Humble" *Hoover Digest: Research & Opinion on Public Policy* no4 p180 Fall 2016

PETERSON, LESLI

Shopping for Kids this Holiday Season *Atlanta* v56 no7 p48 N 2016

Indicators p51 S 2016

Petroleum prospecting

PACHAMAMA'S BLOOD G. Raygorodetsky color *Earth Island Journal* v32 no3 p34 Aut 2017

Saudi Arabia's sell-off of Aramco: Risk or opportunity? Seznec bibl *Bulletin of the Atomic Scientists* v72 no6 p378 N 2016

Petroleum prospecting—Alaska

STALKING AN ELUSIVE PRIZE IN ALASKA B. Reiss color diag map *Fortune* v176 no4 p144 S 15 2017

Time to Debate Arctic Drilling Again A. Nussbaum color map *Bloomberg Businessweek* no4509 p36 Ja 30 2017

Petroleum refineries

"Terrible Terry" CARPENTER A. J. BARTELS color *Nebraska Life* v21 no4 p62 Jl/Ag 2017

Petroleum sales & prices

The Drop in Oil Prices Might Be Bad for Business A. Winston *Harvard Business Review Digital Articles* p2 D 3 2014

Falling Oil Prices Don't Make OPEC Irrelevant R. Mohammed *Harvard Business Review Digital Articles* p2 D 11 2014

Oil's Fall Is a Challenge for Gulf Economies, but Also an Opportunity L. El-Katiri *Harvard Business Review Digital Articles* p2 Mr 7 2016

RAW MATERIALS FOR A REBOUND diag *Fortune* v174 no8 p113 D 15 2016

THREE SQUARED G. R. Schiavino color *Team Roping Journal* p58 S 2017

What Low Oil Prices Really Mean B. Hartmann and S. Sam *Harvard Business Review Digital Articles* p2 Mr 28 2016

Why the Oil Glut Isn't Gone Yet J. Blas graph *Bloomberg Businessweek* no4514 p39 Mr 13 2017

Petroleum supply & demand

Milestones color *Time* v188 no24 p19 D 12 2016

Petroleum supply & demand forecasting

Peak Oil Could Be Here Sooner Than You Think J. Blas and J. Farchy bw *Bloomberg Businessweek* no4530 p32 Jl 17 2017

Petroleum workers—Employment

Drilling Is Back. What About the Workers? D. Wethe graph *Bloomberg Businessweek* no4509 p14 Ja 30 2017

Petroleum—Economic aspects

the 10 best new family cars [Cover story] L. ULRICH cartoon color *Parents* v92 no7 p100 Jl 2017

From Scarcity to Abundance: The New Geopolitics of Energy M. T. KLARE *Current History* v116 no786 p3 Ja 2017

The Tables Have Turned J. Blas, N. Razzouk et al cartoon graph *Bloomberg Businessweek* no4493 p47 O 3 2016

Petroleum industry—Trials, litigation, etc.

Payback, Louisiana Style A. Greenblatt *Governing* v30 no3 p9 D 2016

Petroleum pipelines—Charts, diagrams, etc.

A Tale of Two Pipelines J. Worland color map *Time* v189 no5 p13 F 13 2017

Petroleum—Sales & prices—Economic aspects

THE MANY EFFECTS OF OIL'S BIG BUST diag *Fortune* v174 no6 p11 N 1 2016

Petroleum—Sales & prices—Charts, diagrams, etc.

Oil and Equity Prices Rally chart diag *Money* v45 no10 p94 N 2016

Outlook Where the Growth Is A. Tartar and C. Saraiva map *Bloomberg Businessweek* no4517 p17 Ap 3 2017

Petronas Pacific Northwest (Company)

Pipelines imperil Canada's ecosystem J. J. Alava and N. Calle *Science* v355 no6321 p140 Ja 13 2017

Petrone, Luigi

Preventing mussel adhesion using lubricant-infused materials color diag graph *Science* v357 no6352 p668 Ag 18 2017

Petronelli, P.

Persistent effects of pre-Columbian plant domestication on Amazonian forest composition bibl chart graph map *Science* v355 no6328 p925 Mr 3 2017

Petronio, Stephen

Naked Flag Dance J. Acocella bw *New Yorker* v93 no6 p10 Mr 27 2017

Petronotis, Katerina E.

Release of mineral-bound water prior to subduction tied to shallow seismogenic slip off Sumatra graph *Science* v356 no6340 p841 My 26 2017

PETRO-ROY, FRANK J.

Life *Reader's Digest* v188 no1126 p36 D 2016/Ja 2017

Petros, Walatta

Of Saints and Kings W. L. Belcher *History Today* v66 no11 p52 N 2016

Petrov, Aleksandr

Systemic pan-AMPK activator MK-8722 improves glucose homeostasis but induces cardiac hypertrophy graph *Science* v357 no6350 p507 Ag 4 2017

Petrov, Anatoly

Gold Standard L. BAILEY *Indianapolis Monthly* v40 no3 p38 N 2016

Petrov, Stanislav, 1939-2017

Milestones *Time* v190 no13 p17 O 2 2017

Stanislav Petrov S. Shuster color *Time* v190 no13 p17 O 2 2017

Petrucelli, Leonard

UNLOCKING THE MYSTERY OF ALS color *Scientific American* v316 no6 p46 Je 2017

Petrulionis, Sandra Harbert

Mary Moody Emerson Was a Scholar, a Thinker, and an Inspiration *Humanities* v38 no1 p1 Wint 2017

PETRUNO, TOM

7 Great All-American Stocks chart color *Kiplinger's Personal Finance* v71 no5 p58 My 2017

Cheap Stocks for a Pricey Market color *Kiplinger's Personal Finance* v71 no8 p50 Ag 2017

Great Dividends, Fair Prices color *Kiplinger's Personal Finance* v71 no10 p56 O 2017

Wielding Weapons Against Cancer color *Kiplinger's Personal Finance* v71 no6 p68 Je 2017

Petrushevska, T.

iPTF16geu: A multiply imaged, gravitationally lensed type Ia supernova color diag graph *Science* v356 no6335 p291 Ap 21 2017

Petrushevskaya, Ludmilla

Red Ripening I. KAMINSKY *New York Times Book Review* p20 F 12 2017

The Wild Child of Russian Literature O. Figes color *New York Review of Books* v64 no8 p57 My 11 2017

PETRUSICH, AMANDA

ALL IN color *New Yorker* v93 no4 p80 Mr 13 2017

AMERICAN ANYONE color *New Yorker* v93 no20 p88 Jl 10 2017

BEGIN ANYWHERE color *Nation* v304 no10 p36 Mr 27 2017

CORNERED AT THE PARTY color *New Yorker* v93 no27 p80 S 11 2017

IN RETROSPECT cartoon color *New Yorker* v92 no47 p64 Ja 30 2017

THE SPARK color *Esquire* v166 no5 p106 D 2016/Ja 2017

THINK PIECES cartoon *New Yorker* v93 no24 p78 Ag 21 2017

WHAT THE HEART SAYS bw cartoon *New Yorker* v92 no39 p82 N 28 2016

Petry, Ashley

CHANGE the CITY *Indianapolis Monthly* p55 Ap 2017

Ten Directions: Lori McDonough puts your passport on display *Indianapolis Monthly* v40 no10 p30 Je 2017

Petry, William K.

Higher predation risk for insect prey at low latitudes and elevations graph *Science* v356 no6339 p742 My 19 2017

Petrzela, Natalia Mehlman

The Thread *New York Times Magazine* p12 N 6 2016

Pets

See also

Owls as pets

Salamanders as pets

Swine as pets

Animal House! color *Parents* v92 no11 p72 N 2017

Animal House color *Parents* v92 no9 p64 S 2017

The Best Apps for Pet Lovers L. Murray color *Health* v30 no10 p91 D 2016

Captive Royals & Meat MACHINES ANIMALS in AMERICA TODAY G. Sager *Vegetarian Journal* v35 no2 p18 2016

COLD-WEATHER PET-GROOMING GUIDE J. Szabo color *Amazing Wellness* v9 no6 p88 EarlyWint 2017

Dogs on the Town N. B. McGough and P. S. York color *Southern Living* v52 no6 p43 Je 2017

Blackness Is Burning: Civil Rights, Popular Culture, and the Problem of Recognition *Film Quarterly* v70 no4 p133 Summ 2017

Petty, Richard, 1937-

Petersen's Toast to "THE KING" P. Thomas color *Hot Rod* v70 no10 p60 O 2017

Petty, Richard, 1937—Interviews

Take 5 With RICHARD PETTY color *Hot Rod* v70 no9 p18 S 2017

Petty, Thomas

STUFF USE & TIME SCREWED UP cartoon *Old House Journal* v45 no3 p54 My 2017

Petty, Tom, 1950-2017

1950-2017 Tom Petty E. R. Brown color *Entertainment Weekly* no1486 p18 O 13 2017

ESSENTIAL PETTY L. Greenblatt *Entertainment Weekly* no1486 p20 O 13 2017

Inside Tom Petty's Last Big Tour S. RODRICK color *Rolling Stone* no1291/1292 p22 Jl 13 2017

Lightbox M. Johnston color *Time* v190 no15 p14 O 16 2017

Petty's 'Last Big One'? A. GREENE color *Rolling Stone* no1278/1279 p13 Ja 12 2017

Tom Petty: 1950-2017 D. Fricke bw *Rolling Stone* no1299 p12 N 2 2017

Pettypiece, Shannon

Do You Love It Now? color *Bloomberg Businessweek* no4530 p36 Jl 17 2017

How Big-Box Retailers Weaponize Old Stores color *Bloomberg Businessweek* no4503 p17 D 12 2016

LEGAL JEOPARDY bw color *Bloomberg Businessweek* no4541 p35 O 9 2017

The Other Wall Trump Hasn't Built color *Bloomberg Businessweek* no4534 p34 Ag 14 2017

The Unmaking Of American Dreams chart *Bloomberg Businessweek* no4537 p36 S 11 2017

When The Vice President Is Not a Political Prop color *Bloomberg Businessweek* no4535 p34 Ag 28 2017

Petunias

Emission of volatile organic compounds from petunia flowers is facilitated by an ABC transporter F. Adebesin, J. R. Widhalm et al diag *Science* v356 no6345 p1386 Je 30 2017

The strange case of the orange petunias K. Servick color *Science* v356 no6340 p792 My 26 2017

Petzal, David E.

THE BIG 1-5-0 color *Field & Stream* v121 no6 p64 N 2016

CENTERFIRE SHOOTOUT 2017 color *Field & Stream* v122 no5 p74 O 2017

FIELD & STREAM'S ULTIMATE GUIDE TO HUNTING RIFLES color *Field & Stream* v122 no3 p34 Ag 2017

FIELD TEST color *Field & Stream* v122 no2 p99 Je/Jl 2017

FRESH MAG color *Field & Stream* v121 no9 p26 Ap 2017

HOLIDAY GIFT GUIDE 2016 color *Field & Stream* v121 no7 p92 D 2016/Ja 2017

LONG-RANGE/TACTICAL RIFLES color *Field & Stream* v122 no5 p80 O 2017

METHANE MOUNTAIN color *Field & Stream* v121 no7 p48 D 2016/Ja 2017

Q & A cartoon *Field & Stream* v121 no7 p22 D 2016/Ja 2017

Q&A cartoon *Field & Stream* v122 no1 p18 My 2017

Q & A cartoon *Field & Stream* v122 no5 p35 O 2017

RIGHT ON TARGET C. Kearns color *Field & Stream* v122 no3 p6 Ag 2017

TOUGHING it OUT color *Field & Stream* v121 no7 p40 D 2016/Ja 2017

Peugeot automobile

My Wrench D. BRANCACCIO cartoon *Popular Mechanics* p54 D 2016/Ja 2017

Pevear, Richard

LOST IN TRANSLATION E. ALTER bw color *Publishers Weekly* v264 no1 p31 Ja 2 2017

Pevsner, Jonathan

Intersection of diverse neuronal genomes and neuropsychiatric disease: The Brain Somatic Mosaicism Network color *Science* v356 no6336 p395 Ap 28 2017

Pevzner, Holly

Breast and Bottle for the Win! color *Parents* v92 no9 p40 S 2017

complicating factors *Parents* p129 2015

Pew Research Center

More education doesn't mean less religious commitment among Christians, Pew says E. M. Miller *Christian Century* v134 no11 p17 My 24 2017

Survey: Americans accept contraception, divide over LGBT rights L. Markoe *Christian Century* v133 no23 p18 N 9 2016

Pewen, William F.

Ebola: A postmortem bibl color *Science* v355 no6324 p463 F 3 2017

Pexa, Aaron

Who is pushing the craft field forward? J. VANGOOL, D. HARROW et al color *American Craft* v76 no6 p26 D 2016-Ja 2017

Peymani, Golverdi

FLIGHTS OF THE CONDOR M. Lunken color *Flying* v144 no5 p66 My 2017

PEYSER, MARC

How I Grew Five Mothers color *Reader's Digest* v189 no1130 p17 My 2017

"I Knew She Was Out There" [Cover story] *Reader's Digest* v188 no1126 p73 D 2016/Ja 2017

Let Your Fingers Do The Counting color *Reader's Digest* v189 no1129 p130 Ap 2017

Peyton, Eve Crawford

The Aging Process color *New Orleans Magazine* v52 no1 p54 S 2017

Bye-Bye Baby: Sentiment and relief color *New Orleans Magazine* v51 no10 p58 Ag 2017

Desperately Seeking Sweet Stop E. Crawford Peyton color *New Orleans Magazine* v51 no4 p46 F 2017

Grammar School color *New Orleans Magazine* v51 no5 p48 Mr 2017

Gut Instinct cartoon *New Orleans Magazine* v51 no7 p48 My 2017

Imperfect Home cartoon *New Orleans Magazine* v51 no12 p56 O 2017

Mourning a Friend, Losing a Hero color *New Orleans Magazine* v51 no8 p48 Je 2017

War Cry color *New Orleans Magazine* v51 no9 p44 Jl 2017

Peyton, J.

Country-specific effects of neonicotinoid pesticides on honey bees and wild bees diag map *Science* v356 no6345 p1393 Je 30 2017

Peyton, Mike

Drawing from Life P. Nielsen cartoon *Sail* v48 no4 p6 Ap 2017

Peyton, Robert

Brennan's color *New Orleans Magazine* v51 no2 p66 D 2016

EAT. DRINK. ENJOY color *New Orleans Magazine* v51 no9 p56 Jl 2017

Little Korea BBQ color *New Orleans Magazine* v51 no2 p74 D 2016

New Orleans Cake Café & Bakery color *New Orleans Magazine* v51 no2 p76 D 2016

News From the Kitchen color *New Orleans Magazine* v51 no12 p112 O 2017

NEWS FROM THE KITCHENS color *New Orleans Magazine* v51 no1 p114 N 2016

News From the Kitchens color *New Orleans Magazine* v51 no6 p86 Ap 2017

News From the Kitchens color *New Orleans Magazine* v51 no7 p86 My 2017

News From the Kitchens: Public Service, Piece of Meat Butcher & Restaurant, Sprout and Press color *New Orleans Magazine* v51 no10 p174 Ag 2017

State of the Market *New Orleans Magazine* v51 no2 p69 D 2016

Pezza, Roberto J.

A SUMO-ubiquitin relay recruits proteasomes to chromosome axes to regulate meiotic recombination bibl graph *Science* v355 no6323 p403 Ja 27 2017

Pezzagna, Sebastien

Submillihertz magnetic spectroscopy performed with a nanoscale quantum sensor diag *Science* v356 no6340 p832 My 26 2017

Pfaeffle, Emma—Interviews

Candy Land C. Dowers color *Dance Spirit* v21 no4 p15 Ap 2017

Pfaff, John F.

All Criminal Justice Reform Is Local G. Edelman *Washington Monthly* p2 Ja/F 2017

Beyond Getting Tough R. LU color *National Review* v69 no3 p46 F 20 2017

The Hidden Realities of U.S. Incarceration R. VERBRUGGEN *American Conservative* v16 no3 p50 My/Je 2017

Locked In: The True Causes of Mass Incarceration and How to Achieve Real Reform A. Levad *Christian Century* v134 no17 p37 Ag 16 2017

RATTLING THE CAGE A. GOPNIK cartoon color *New Yorker* v93 no8 p71 Ap 10 2017

PFAFF, LESLIE GARISTO

10 discipline mistakes chart color *Parents* v92 no6 p48 Je 2017

powerful emotions *Parents* v91 no11 p144 N 2016

school support *Parents* v91 no11 p148 N 2016

Pfanner, Eric

Innovation Fill-Air Flow diag *Bloomberg Businessweek* no4495 p28 O 17 2016

Will Not-Quite-Fiber Make the Grade? diag *Bloomberg Businessweek* no4495 p27 O 17 2016

Pfannstiel, Jens

Precursor processing for plant peptide hormone maturation by subtilisin-like serine proteinases bibl color graph *Science* v354 no6319 p1594 D 23 2016

Pfattner, Raphael

Mechanochemical unzipping of insulating polyladderene to semi-conducting polyacetylene [Cover story] diag *Science* v357 no6350 p475 Ag 4 2017

Pfau, Bruce N.

How an Accounting Firm Convinced Its Employees They Could Change the World *Harvard Business Review Digital Articles* p2 O 6 2015

What Do Millennials Really Want at Work? The Same Things the Rest of Us Do *Harvard Business Review Digital Articles* p2 Ap 7 2016

Pfautsch, Sebastian

Positive biodiversity-productivity relationship predominant in global forests bibl chart graph map *Science* v354 no6309 paaf8957-1 O 14 2016

Pfeffer, Naomi

Insider Trading J. Keen *Science* v357 no6355 p966 S 8 2017

PFEFFER, STEPHANIE EMMA

WE NEED A DAYCARE REVOLUTION [Cover story] chart color *Working Mother* v40 no2 p52 Je/Jl 2017

Pfeifer, Gerd P.

How tobacco smoke changes the (epi)genome bibl color diag *Science* v354 no6312 p549 N 4 2016

PFEIFER, JAMISON

62 GREAT THINGS TO DO THIS MONTH color *Chicago* v66 no6 p97 Je 2017

67 GREAT THINGS TO DO THIS MONTH color *Chicago* v66 no3 p129 Mr 2017

REQUIRED READING color *Chicago* v66 no6 p36 Je 2017

SEEDS OF CHANGE cartoon map *Chicago* v66 no5 p34 My 2017

TOP CANCER DOCTORS color *Chicago* v66 no1 p84 Ja 2017

Pfeifer, T.

Observing the ultrafast buildup of a Fano resonance in the time domain bibl graph *Science* v354 no6313 p738 N 11 2016

Spectral narrowing of x-ray pulses for precision spectroscopy with nuclear resonances diag *Science* v357 no6349 p375 Jl 28 2017

Ultrafast electron diffraction imaging of bond breaking in di-ionized acetylene bibl graph *Science* v354 no6310 p308 O 21 2016

Pfeiffer, Dan—Interviews

Keepin' It 1600 With Jon Favreau & Dan Pfeiffer R. Rahman color *Entertainment Weekly* no1435 p12 O 14 2016

Pfeiffer, Jeff

Powerless *TV Guide* v65 no6 p36 Ja 30 2017

Pfeiffer, Michelle, 1957——Interviews

2017 Fall Performances *Time* v190 no10/11 p101 S 18 2017

Michelle PFEIFFER: AFTER A BRIEF HIATUS, THE ONE-TIME SO-CAL SURFER GIRL TURNED SCREEN SIREN, THE THREE-TIME OSCAR NOMINEE—AND STILL SOMEHOW WOEFULLY UNDERRATED—MICHELLE PFEIFFER IS BACK IN A BIG WAY, WITH A BEVY OF FILMS TO ADD TO HER ALREADY... D. ARONOFSKY *Interview* v47 no3 p64 Ap 2017

Michelle Pfeiffer As a Nefarious House Guest E. Dockterman color *Time* v190 no10/11 p102 S 18 2017

Pfeiffer, Tim

Pitch Perfect K. RENDA color *House Beautiful* p60 Jl 2017

TREASURE ISLAND J. Chamberlain color *Sunset* v238 no3 p29 Mr 2017

Pfeiffer, Walter

Angular momentum–induced delays in solid-state photoemission enhanced by intra-atomic interactions chart color graph *Science* v357 no6357 p1274 S 22 2017

Pfender, Matthias

Nanoscale nuclear magnetic resonance with chemical resolution diag *Science* v357 no6346 p67 Jl 7 2017

Pfeuffer, Charyn

UP IN THE AIR color *Sunset* v238 no1 p28 Ja 2017

PFISTER, DONALD H.

"What a Painfully Interesting Subject": Charles Darwin's Studies of Potato Late Blight *BioScience* v66 no12 p1035 D 1 2016

Pfitzer, Marc W.

Can Insurance Companies Incentivize Their Customers to Be Healthier? *Harvard Business Review Digital Articles* p2 Je 23 2017

Pfizer Inc.

U.S. Corporations Don't Need Tax Breaks on Foreign Profits W. Lazonick *Harvard Business Review Digital Articles* p2 D 21 2015

Pfuehler, Erich

Preserving a Marsh for People and Wildlife: The Dotson Family Marsh *Parks & Recreation* v52 no2 p28 F 2017

Pfund, Christine

NIH's mentoring makes progress bibl *Science* v354 no6314 p840 N 18 2016

Pfundstein Chamberlain, Dianne

Cheap Threats: Why the United States Struggles to Coerce Weak States G. J. Ikenberry *Foreign Affairs* v96 no1 p156 Ja/F 2017

PG & E Corp.

A BOLT OF ENERGY V. Zarya chart color *Fortune* v175 no8 p160 Je 15 2017

PGA Championship (Golf tournament)

Finishing Rush A. Shipnuck, T. Keith et al color *Sports Illustrated* v127 no5 p26 Ag 14 2017

An Inconvenient Truth A. Shipnuck and J. Marksbury color *Golf Magazine* v59 no11 p24 N 2017

Major problem? Major solution! M. Bamberger color *Golf Magazine* v59 no8 p112 Ag 2017

A Man in Full A. Shipnuck and C. Barrett color *Golf Magazine* v59 no7 p28 Jl 2017

playing with fire R. Asselta color *Golf Magazine* v59 no8 p76 Ag 2017

TEEING OFF color *Golf Magazine* v59 no3 p16 Mr 2017

PGA Tour (Association)

Brutish Empire M. Broadie and C. Barrett color *Golf Magazine* v59 no3 p36 Mr 2017

DRIVE IT A MILE! J. Sutton and D. DeNunzio color *Golf Magazine* v59 no8 p43 Ag 2017

THE LOW DOWN ON LEFT HAND LOW M. Blackburn and D. Dethier color *Golf Magazine* v59 no11 p72 N 2017

The New Kids are All Right A. Shipnuck and C. Barrett color *Golf Magazine* v59 no2 p28 F 2017

Paul Goydos J. Marksbury and C. Barrett color *Golf Magazine* v59 no5 p45 My 2017

Playing It Cool R. Asselta and C. Barrett color *Golf Magazine* v59 no8 p27 Ag 2017

Season's Readings M. Broadie and J. Marksbury chart color *Golf Magazine* v59 no11 p32 N 2017

Phadnis, Nitin

Poisons, antidotes, and selfish genes diag *Science* v356 no6342 p1013 Je 9 2017

Phair, Liz

Elizabeth WURTZEL *Interview* v47 no5 p26 Je/Jl 2017

Pham, LeUyen

THE MURDER OF ROGER ACKROYED *New York Times Book Review* p27 Ja 22 2017

Pham, Phuc

Nation Voices 2016 *Nation* v304 no2 p8 Ja 16 2017

Phan, Sébastien

ChromEMT: Visualizing 3D chromatin structure and compaction in interphase and mitotic cells color *Science* v357 no6349 p370 Jl 28 2017

Phanerozoic paleontology

Increase in predator-prey size ratios throughout the Phanerozoic history of marine ecosystems A. A. Klompmaker, M. Kowalewski et al diag *Science* v356 no6343 p1178 Je 16 2017

Phantasm: Ravager (Film)

PHANTASM: RAVAGER B. A. DuHamel color *Sound & Vision* v82 no4 p71 My 2017

Phantom automobile

KING CUSH M. Duff color *Car & Driver* v63 no4 p21 O 2017

Rolls-Royce: Phantom K. Pleskot color *Motor Trend* v69 no11 p20 N 2017

Phantom cats

30 Cool THINGS ABOUT BIG CATS J. BEER *National Geographic Kids* no467 p18 F 2017

Phantom of the Opera, The (Theatrical production)

THE MASK B. L. Heldman color *Entertainment Weekly* no1460/1461 p43 Ap 7-17 2017

Phanumartwiwath, Anuchit

Posttranslational mutagenesis: A chemical strategy for exploring protein side-chain diversity diag *Science* v354 no6312 p597 N 4 2016

Pharaohs

Inaugural undress *Successful Farming* v115 no1 p46 Ja 2017

Pharisee & the publican (Parable)

The Righteous Ones J. W. MARTENS *America* v215 no11 p38 O 17 2016

The Tax Collector and the Pharisee R. Q. Monvoisin bw *Christian Century* v133 no21 p63 O 12 2016

The Word *Christian Century* v133 no21 p20 O 12 2016

Pharmaceutical industry

See also

Dietary supplements industry

A Few Tweaks to Keep Pharma Profits Rolling N. Kresge and S. Decker *Bloomberg Businessweek* no4535 p15 Ag 28 2017

How Pharma Can Offer More than Pills S. H. Jain *Harvard Business Review Digital Articles* p2 Jl 23 2015

A Miracle Drug Big Pharma Doesn't Want A. Altstedter, J. S. Hopkins et al color graph *Bloomberg Businessweek* no4517 p22 Ap 3 2017

The Promise and Challenge of Big Data for Pharma R. Copping and M. Li *Harvard Business Review Digital Articles* p2 N 29 2016

Pharmaceutical industry employees

The new tissue culture R. L. Ruben color *Science* v356 no6335 p342 Ap 21 2017

Pharmaceutical industry—Corrupt practices

How do you maximize the profits of a drug that treats a very rare disease? [Cover story] B. Elgin, D. Bloomfield et al color *Bloomberg Businessweek* no4524 p42 My 29 2017

Pharmaceutical industry—Economic aspects

How Pharma Can Fix Its Reputation and Its Business at the Same Time D. de Felice color *Harvard Business Review Digital Articles* p2 F 3 2017

Pharmaceutical industry—European Union countries

The Greek Pharmaceutical Industry: A Strong Contributor to its Economy color *Foreign Affairs* v96 no3 p86h My/Je 2017

Pharmaceutical industry—Government policy

Next Up for FDA Approval: Fewer FDA Rules S. Mukherjee color *Fortune* v175 no5 p14 Ap 1 2017

Pharmaceutical industry—United States

Drug Costs Too High? Fire the Middleman N. Weinberg and R. Langreth *Bloomberg Businessweek* no4513 p28 Mr 6 2017

Fixing Pharma's Incentives Problem in the Wake of the U.S. Opioid Crisis C. Bowe *Harvard Business Review Digital Articles* p2 Je 13 2016

It's Time to Rein in Exorbitant Pharmaceutical Prices R. Mohammed *Harvard Business Review Digital Articles* p2 S 22 2015

McKESSON FEELS THE PAIN E. Fry chart color diag map *Fortune* v175 no8 p170 Je 15 2017

Pharma's Worst Nightmare D. Bloomfield and H. Li cartoon *Bloomberg Businessweek* no4508 p18 Ja 23 2017

Price Gouging and the Dangerous New Breed of Pharma Companies A. G. Smith *Harvard Business Review Digital Articles* p2 Jl 6 2016

Your Prescription Gets A Rebate—for Insurers R. Langreth *Bloomberg Businessweek* no4494 p23 O 10 2016

Pharmaceutical policy—United States

Available Drugs, Affordable Drugs P. HOWARD color *National Review* v69 no6 p34 Ap 3 2017

Pharmaceutical research

THE XX FACTOR: WHEN GENDER DIFFERENCES ARE IGNORED IN HEALTH STUDIES, IT'S WOMEN WHO PAY THE PRICE [Cover story] C. LEHMANN *Commentary* v143 no4 p13 Ap 2017

Pharmacists

Get Advice From a Pharmacist color *Kiplinger's Personal Finance* v71 no4 p70 Ap 2017

Moon Rivers Naturals L. S. FORD *Texas Monthly* v45 no7 p25 Jl 2017

Pharmacists—Certification

GET MORE OUT OF YOUR DRUGSTORE C. Ratcliff color *Men's Health* v32 no1 p85 Ja/F 2017

Pharmacists—Research

Pharmacists Can Reduce Elderly Mishaps *USA Today Magazine* v145 no2861 p2 F 2017

Pharmacodynamics

'Exercise pill' boosts mice's endurance L. BEIL *Science News* v191 no11 p7 Je 10 2017

Pharmacogenomics

Opportunities and advantages for the development of precision medicine in China Qimin Zhan and Haili Qian *Science* v354 no6319 p6 D 23 2016

Pharmacy

See also

Drug development

MADISON DRUG CO. MADISON 59 MILES EAST OF ATLANTA J. GREEN *Atlanta* v56 no10 p144 F 2017

Pharoah, Jay, 1987-

White Famous I. Ratledge *TV Guide* v65 no41 p34 O 2 2017

Pharyngitis—Diagnosis

kids * health news *Parents* v91 no9 p27 S 2016

Phase Technology (Company)

Phase Technology dARTS DFS-660-T Speaker System D. Wilkinson color *Sound & Vision* v82 no3 p38 Ap 2017

Phased retirement

The Same Gold Watch, It Just Arrives Later C. Hymowitz chart color *Bloomberg Businessweek* no4504 p20 D 19 2016

Phases of the planets

August Sun & Planets chart color *Sky & Telescope* v134 no2 p44 Ag 2017

Phasmida

Lady Gaga-ntuan C. Schuknecht *Sierra* v101 no4 p23 Jl/Ag 2016

Pheasant shooting

THE SLOUGH A. McKEAN color *Outdoor Life* v224 no6 p48 Ag 2017

Pheasants

FOR THE BIRDS T. KEER chart color *Outdoor Life* v224 no6 pH5 Ag 2017

SNOW BIRDS D. DRAPER color *Field & Stream* v121 no6 p14 N 2016

Pheidippides, fl. 490 B.C.

YOU DON'T KNOW PHEIDIPPIDES! [Cover story] D. KARNAZES bw cartoon color map *Runner's World* v51 no11 p72 D 2016

PHELAN, HAYLEY

Tyler HAYS *Interview* v47 no1 p24 F 2017

Phelan, J. Greg

A lover of fiction sets out to find the truth *America* v216 no3 p46 F 6 2017

Witness to suffering *America* v217 no7 p49 O 2 2017

PHELAN, MATTHEW

Trump's Brain color *New Republic* v248 no4 p14 Ap 2017

Phelan, Unity

25 to Watch *Dance Magazine* v91 no1 p50 Ja 2017

Phelps, Evans

A Mother's Nature S. Davis bw color *Powder* v45 no4 p94 D 2016

PHELPS, JOE

OBAMA'S AMERICA img *New York* v49 no20 p12 O 3 2016

Phelps, Michael, 1985-

The Flip Turn M. BURKE color *Forbes* v199 no1 p100 Ja 24 2017

For the Record color *Time* v190 no6 p6 Ag 7 2017

THE GOLD STANDARD [Cover story] T. Layden chart color

Sports Illustrated v125 no21 p30 D 26 2016

Pool Pals E. Brady and T. Keith chart color *Sports Illustrated* v127 no3 p24 Jl 24 2017

Taking on the Animal Kingdom K. Samuelson color *Time* v190 no1 p12 Jl 3 2017

PHELPS, NICOLE

VERA WANG color *Vogue* v207 no3 p419 Mr 2017

Phenicie, Carolyn

The Core of a Just Society *Hoover Digest: Research & Opinion on Public Policy* no2 p146 Spr 2017

Phenology

    See also

    Plant phenology

PHENOLOGY S. McNulty *New York State Conservationist* v71 no4 p24 F 2017

Phenology—Mathematical models

Validating Herbarium-Based Phenology Models Using Citizen-Science Data K. V. SPELLMAN and C. P. H. MULDER chart graph *BioScience* v66 no10 p897 O 1 2016

Phenomenalism

HENRY DAVID THOREAU color *Tricycle: The Buddhist Review* v26 no2 p21 Wint 2016

Phenotype

Predicting Phenotypes in a Changing Climate C. BEANS *BioScience* v67 no7 p593 Jl 2017

Phenotypic plasticity

Restoring auditory cortex plasticity in adult mice by restricting thalamic adenosine signaling J. A. Blundon, N. C. Roy et al graph *Science* v356 no6345 p1352 Je 30 2017

Phenylephrine (Drug)

13 Things Your Pharmacist Won't Tell You M. CROUCH color *Reader's Digest* v189 no1129 p124 Ap 2017

Phi Delta Kappa (Organization)

Travel to Germany with PDK color *Phi Delta Kappan* v98 no5 p79 F 2017

Phi Delta Kappa (Organization)—Officials & employees

PDK Connection color *Phi Delta Kappan* v99 no1 p46 S 2017

Phi Delta Kappan (Periodical)

Rafael Heller joins Kappan color *Phi Delta Kappan* v98 no5 p79 F 2017

Phi Kappa Phi

BENEFITS AND AWARDS *Phi Kappa Phi Forum* v97 no1 p35 Spr 2017

BENEFITS AND AWARDS *Phi Kappa Phi Forum* v97 no2 p35 Summ 2017

LOOKING BACK AT PHI KAPPA PHI'S FELLOWS B. COLVIN color *Phi Kappa Phi Forum* v97 no2 p24 Summ 2017

PHI KAPPA PHI K. WHITE color *Phi Kappa Phi Forum* v97 no1 p8 Spr 2017

Phi Kappa Phi—Congresses

CHAPTER UPDATE K. WHITE color *Phi Kappa Phi Forum* v96 no4 p8 Wint 2016

Phi Kappa Phi—News briefs

CHAPTER UPDATE K. WHITE color *Phi Kappa Phi Forum* v97 no2 p6 Summ 2017

MEMBER NEWS color *Phi Kappa Phi Forum* v97 no2 p3 Summ 2017

Phibbs, Kathy

TURN THIS MOTHER OUT K. Krichko color *Powder* v45 no4 p140 D 2016

Phifer, Thomas

Back to the Land C. MCGUIGAN color *Architectural Record* v205 no8 p58 Ag 2017

Philadelphia (Film)

A GAY Old Timeline C. Brody, H. Goldblatt et al color diag *Entertainment Weekly* no1471 p32 Je 23 2017

Philadelphia (Pa.)

1917 HOW ONE YEAR CHANGED THE WORLD *USA Today Magazine* v145 no2862 p26 Mr 2017

MUSEUM OF THE AMERICAN REVOLUTION OPENS IN PHILLY B. Manley color *Military History* v34 no2 p10 Jl 2017

Philadelphia (Pa.)—Description & travel

8 Travel Ideas for the Winter-Weary A. Fitzpatrick color *Time* v189 no7/8 p114 F 27 2017

A Philadelphia flaneur E. Pochoda cartoon color diag *Magazine Antiques* v184 no2 p92 Mr/Ap 2017

Philadelphia M. Rosano color *Canadian Geographic* v135 no6 p18 D 2015

Rocky Weekend T. Keith color *Sports Illustrated* v126 no12 p16 My 1 2017

Second Coming C. RAINEY and P. BRADY color *Conde Nast Traveler* v52 no5 p56 My 2017

Philadelphia (Pa.)—Politics & government

The Decline of the Shrug A. Greenblatt *Governing* v30 no12 p11 S 2017

Philadelphia 76ers (Basketball team)

14 76ers R. Nadkarni, B. Golliver et al color *Sports Illustrated* v125 no14 p90 O 24-31 2016

9 76ERS color *Sports Illustrated* v127 no12 p66 O 16 2017

Embiid, Indiid L. Jenkins color *Sports Illustrated* v125 no16 p42 N 14 2016

HOT | NOT T. Keith color *Sports Illustrated* v126 no4 p19 Ja 30 2017

Philadelphia Eagles (Football team)

3 Philadelphia Eagles color *Sports Illustrated* v127 no7 p89 S 4 2017

Philadelphia Orchestra

Fall Preview R. Platt color *New Yorker* v93 no25 p8 Ag 28 2017

On the Town A. Ross cartoon *New Yorker* v93 no31 p12 O 9 2017

Philadelphia Phillies (Baseball team)

5 PHILLIES color *Sports Illustrated* v126 no9 p100 Mr 27 2017

Green Day T. Keith color *Sports Illustrated* v125 no12 p19 O 10 2016

HOT | NOT T. Keith color *Sports Illustrated* v126 no10 p28 Ap 10 2017

Philanthropists

    See also

    Women philanthropists

The $150 BILLION MOMENT A. BROWN color *Forbes* v200 no5 p21 N 14 2017

AUDACIOUS PHILANTHROPY: LESSONS FROM 15 WORLD-CHANGING INITIATIVES S. W. DITKOFF and A. GRINDLE chart img *Harvard Business Review* v95 no5 p110 S/O 2017

Mega Donors' Perspectives on Philanthropy and Government Relations in Israel B. Shimoni *Society* v54 no3 p261 Je 2017

Reading Charles Darwin Utterly Changed How Charles Loring Brace Thought about Social Reform R. Fuller *Humanities* v38 no1 p1 Wint 2017

Techie Largesse N. Schaefer Riley *Weekly Standard* v22 no24 p18 F 27 2017

A Walrus Tribute G. Lazare and B. R. Bennett color *Walrus* v14 no2 p56 Mr 2017

Warren Buffett's Risky Final Bet J. Baron and R. Lachenauer *Harvard Business Review Digital Articles* p2 Ap 21 2016

Philanthropists—Interviews

'Bill and I are impatient optimists' M. Murphy color *Bloomberg Businessweek* no4512 p46 F 20 2017

Philanthropists—United States

The boldness of philanthropists D. Baltimore color *Science* v353 no6307 p1473 S 30 2016

EDITOR'S NOTE J. BARDI *Humanist* v77 no5 p3 S/O 2017

Philanthropists—United States—Charts, diagrams, etc.

America's Top Philanthropists K. SAVCHUK color graph *Forbes* v198 no5 p44 O 25 2016

THE GREATEST GIVERS J. WANG color graph *Forbes* v200 no5 p30 N 14 2017

Philbin, Ann—Interviews

Masterful mixing at the Hammer E. H. Gustafson color *Magazine Antiques* v184 no3 p136 My/Je 2017

PHILBRICK, HOPE S.

WELCOME TO CARTERSVILLE *Atlanta* v56 no7 p18 N 2016

Philbrick, Nathaniel

Honor and Glory A. J. BAKSHIAN color *Weekly Standard* v22 no16 p33 D 26 2016

Honor vs. Betrayal S. L. Hoffman bw color *Military History* v34 no1 p70 My 2017

Philip, Prince, consort of Elizabeth II, Queen of Great Britain, 1921-

Prince Philip Retires--at 95 *British Heritage Travel* v38 no4 p8 Jl/Ag 2017

Philip, Siddharth

India's Movie Industry Gets a New Script color graph *Bloomberg Businessweek* no4525 p20 Je 5 2017

Philip, Vivek M.
Vitamin B3 modulates mitochondrial vulnerability and prevents glaucoma in aged mice bibl graph *Science* v355 no6326 p756 F 17 2017

Philip Morris International Inc.
Marlboro F. Gillette, J. Kaplan et al color *Bloomberg Businessweek* no4514 p46 Mr 13 2017

Philip II, King of Macedonia, 382 B.C.-336 B.C.
Humor in Uniform bw *Reader's Digest* v189 no1130 p139 My 2017

Philippart, David
Take and drink color *U.S. Catholic* v82 no6 p33 Je 2017

Philippine cooking
Just Like Mom Made—But Better G. VILLAMORA color *Bon Appetit* v62 no2 p62 Mr 2017

Philippines—Civilization
Death Reigns on the Streets of Duterte's Philippines N. Jenkins color *Time* v189 no3 p28 Ja 16 2017

Philippines—Economic conditions—1986-
Philippine Casinos Are Cleaning Up D. Wei, B. Einhorn et al color graph *Bloomberg Businessweek* no4521 p19 My 8 2017
Philippine Leader Scares Off Investors B. Einhorn, D. Lopez et al color *Bloomberg Businessweek* no4493 p23 O 3 2016

Philippines—Foreign relations—United States
Best Friends No More? P. SMITH *New York Times Upfront* v149 no6 p6 D 12 2016
A Friendship on the Rocks C. CONDA color *Weekly Standard* v22 no10 p14 N 14 2016

Philippines—Foreign relations—United States—History—21st century
How to Stay Friends With the Philippines bw *Bloomberg Businessweek* no4497 p12 O 31 2016

Philippines—Military history
A Deadly New Front for ISIS J. Hincks and M. Manos color map *Time* v190 no1 p36 Jl 3 2017

Philippines—Politics & government
#IHeartMyDictator S. WILLIAMS *New Republic* v248 no1/2 p13 Ja/F 2017

Philippines—Politics & government—1986-
Death Reigns on the Streets of Duterte's Philippines N. Jenkins color *Time* v189 no3 p28 Ja 16 2017

Philipps, Busy
Can Fans Save The Sackett Sisters? R. Kinane color *Entertainment Weekly* no1468/1469 p92 Je 2-9 2017

Philipps, David
Wild Horse Country: The History, Myth, and Future of the Mustang L. A. MARSCHALL color *Natural History* v125 no10 p46 O 2017

Philips, Matthew
Cold Climate *Bloomberg Businessweek* no4499 p31 N 14 2016
Exit the Old Elite *Bloomberg Businessweek* no4499 p26 N 14 2016
How Climate Rules Might Fade Away color *Bloomberg Businessweek* no4504 p6 D 19 2016
North Dakota Pipe Dreams color map *Bloomberg Businessweek* no4502 p44 D 5 2016
An Oily Reset in U.S.-Russia Relations graph *Bloomberg Businessweek* no4507 p38 Ja 16 2017
Russia's Deadly Mideast Game *Bloomberg Businessweek* no4505 p16 D 26 2016
Wanted: Forklift Driver color graph *Bloomberg Businessweek* no4504 p13 D 19 2016

Philips, Peter
Peter Philips S. Cristobal color *InStyle* v24 no8 p106 Ag 2017

Philips audio equipment—Evaluation
Philips BDP7501/F7 Ultra HD Blu-ray Player T. J. Norton color *Sound & Vision* v81 no10 p50 D 2016

Philistines
A BONE TO PICK ABOUT PHILISTINES B. ALEX color *Discover* v38 no1 p36 Ja/F 2017

PHILLIP, JEFFREY
9 Tidy Resolutions color *Good Housekeeping* v264 no1 p46 Ja 1 2017
ASK JEFFREY color *Good Housekeeping* v264 no2 p54 F 2017

ASK JEFFREY color *Good Housekeeping* v264 no4 p49 Ap 2017
how to ORGANIZE EVERYTHING color *Good Housekeeping* v264 no3 p47 Mr 2017
MOVING made easy color *Good Housekeeping* v264 no5 p58 My 2017
wrap party! color *Good Housekeeping* v263 no6 p36 D 2016
YOUR GUIDE TO A Fridge Makeover (for easy party hosting!) cartoon color *Good Housekeeping* v263 no5 p62 N 2016

Phillippe, Ryan
Call Of DUTY [Cover story] I. RATLEDGE *TV Guide* v64 no46 p14 N 7 2016
SHOOTER COVER PARTY, LOS ANGELES *TV Guide* v64 no48 p3 N 21 2016
THE THINKING MAN RYAN PHILLIPPE M. Khidekel color *Women's Health* v14 no7 p128 S 2017

PHILLIPPS, KENNARD
visual statement color *Foreign Policy* no222 p20 Ja/F 2017

PHILLIPS, AMY
'Jolene' color *New York Times Magazine* p24 Mr 12 2017

PHILLIPS, ANGUS
Cup Half Empty bw color *Weekly Standard* v22 no42 p37 Jl 17 2017

PHILLIPS, ANNA J.
Transformational Principles for NEON Sampling of Mammalian Parasites and Pathogens: A Response to Springer and Colleagues *BioScience* v66 no11 p917 N 1 2016

PHILLIPS, BOB
Diamond in the Rough *Texas Monthly* v45 no6 p26 Je 2017
Dinner and a Show *Texas Monthly* v45 no8 p20 Ag 2017
Jack Huey Field *Texas Monthly* v44 no11 p38 N 2016

PHILLIPS, CARL
That It Might Save, or Drown Them *Nation* v304 no5 p31 F 20 2017

Phillips, Christina Jane
Reducing Noise in Decision Making: Interaction color *Harvard Business Review* v94 no12 p18 D 2016

Phillips, Christopher
Arab Fling P. Wood *Washington Monthly* p3 Ja/F 2017

Phillips, Christopher J.
Fun and games color *Science* v357 no6359 p54 O 6 2017
Quantifying culture color *Science* v354 no6308 p45 O 7 2016

Phillips, Craig
A Hillary Fan Inside Trump's Treasury R. Schmidt color *Bloomberg Businessweek* no4517 p30 Ap 3 2017

Phillips, Dave
MISSION: POSSIBLE! chart color *Golf Magazine* v59 no9 p76 S 2017

Phillips, David H.
Mutational signatures associated with tobacco smoking in human cancer bibl graph *Science* v354 no6312 p618 N 4 2016

Phillips, Dawa Tarchin
What to Do When You Don't Know What's Next color *Tricycle: The Buddhist Review* v26 no4 p40 Summ 2017

Phillips, Debbie
'I'm Not Giving Up my Torch, Thank You Very Much' color *Progressive* p54 D 2016/Ja 2017

Phillips, Derek
GAME OF SILENCE *TV Guide* v64 no15 p55 Ap 4 2016

Phillips, Doris
FROM OUR READERS *Archaeology* v70 no4 p8 Je-Ag 2017

Phillips, Elizabeth
Research night owls color *Science* v354 no6315 p964 N 25 2016

Phillips, Fred Young
Technology assessment and the social and human impact of innovation bibl diag *Bulletin of the Atomic Scientists* v72 no6 p402 N 2016

Phillips, Gin
Fierce Kingdom color *Publishers Weekly* v264 no18 p2 My 1 2017

Phillips, Hayley Garrison
19 THINGS YOU REALLY OUGHT TO 00 THIS MONTH *Washingtonian Magazine* v52 no3 p31 D 2016
19 THINGS YOU REALLY OUGHT TO DO THIS MONTH *Washingtonian Magazine* v52 no1 p33 O 2016
ARM CANDY: Totes used to be more function than form, but these fall bags don't sacrifice details or style *Washingtonian Magazine* v53 no1 p109 O 2017

DECK THE TABLE *Washingtonian Magazine* v52 no2 p271 N 2016

DRY GOODS: Stay cooler and more collected with these hair and skin faves *Washingtonian Magazine* v52 no11 p106 Ag 2017

FOTOWEEKDC *Washingtonian Magazine* v52 no2 p35 N 2016

In Bloom color *Washingtonian Magazine* v52 no7 p80 Ap 2017

MAKING ROOM TO GROW *Washingtonian Magazine* v52 no6 p157 Mr 2017

PACK A PUNCH *Washingtonian Magazine* v52 no9 p113 Je 2017

RECOVERY MISSION *Washingtonian Magazine* v52 no2 p299 N 2016

A TALE OF TWO BAR CARTS *Washingtonian Magazine* v52 no3 p170 D 2016

PHILLIPS, HELEN

Flash Friction: Thirty-nine offbeat stories find humor among the ruins *New York Times Magazine* p16 Ap 30 2017

PHILLIPS, HELEN R. P.

Harmonizing Biodiversity Conservation and Productivity in the Context of Increasing Demands on Landscapes graph *BioScience* v66 no10 p890 O 1 2016

PHILLIPS, IAN

the LONG VIEW color *Architectural Digest* no5 p152 My 2017

Phillips, J. F.

Persistent effects of pre-Columbian plant domestication on Amazonian forest composition bibl chart graph map *Science* v355 no6328 p925 Mr 3 2017

Phillips, Jack—Trials, litigation, etc.

The Continuing Threat to Religious Liberty R. T. ANDERSON color *National Review* v69 no15 p32 Ag 14 2017

Wicked Ways M. Hemingway color *Weekly Standard* v22 no45 p8 Ag 7 2017

Phillips, Joe

Evangelical Christian Discourse in South Korea on the LGBT: the Politics of Cross-Border Learning *Society* v54 no1 p29 F 2017

Phillips, John

BROCK YATES 1933-2016 bw *Car & Driver* v62 no7 p32 Ja 2017

Fleet Files color *Car & Driver* v63 no4 p90 O 2017

John Phillips color *Car & Driver* v62 no11 p28 My 2017

John Phillips color *Car & Driver* v62 no8 p24 F 2017

John Phillips color *Car & Driver* v63 no2 p30 Ag 2017

John Phillips color *Car & Driver* v63 no5 p28 N 2017

PHILLIPS, JON

Google Home: Google puts its A.I. on a nightstand for the win color *PCWorld* p115 D 2016

LG V20 hands-on: A 5.7-inch phablet for smartphone content creators color *PCWorld* p104 O 2016

LG V20: The Android phone for hard-core enthusiasts color *PCWorld* v35 no1 p108 Ja 2017

Nixon Mission: A hardcore Android Wear watch for surf and snow color *PCWorld* v35 no11 p104 N 2016

Samsung DeX: 7 days using the DeX dock and a Galaxy S8+ as a desktop PC color *PCWorld* v35 no6 p117 Je 2017

Samsung's ArtPC Pulse is a cylindrical desktop PC with 360-degree sound color *PCWorld* v35 no11 p11 N 2016

TAG Heuer Connected Modular 45: Hands on with the swankiest Wear watch of all color *PCWorld* v35 no5 p140 My 2017

THE WILD, WEIRD, AND POWERFUL PC HARDWARE of CES 2017 color *PCWorld* v35 no2 p127 F 2017

Phillips, Joseph L.

Kilogram-scale prexasertib monolactate monohydrate synthesis under continuous-flow CGMP conditions chart diag *Science* v356 no6343 p1144 Je 16 2017

PHILLIPS, JULIE

All Undone: Future Home of the Living God *Ms.* v27 no3 p52 Fall 2017

OUT OF BOUNDS cartoon *New Yorker* v92 no33 p38 O 17 2016

Phillips, Katherine W.

The Biases That Punish Racially Diverse Teams *Harvard Business Review Digital Articles* p2 F 22 2016

Phillips, Kevin, 1940-

Super Dark Times C. Nashawaty color *Entertainment Weekly* no1485 p42 O 6 2017

Phillips, Lawrence

Cold Truth about Cardio Safety [Cover story] color *Prevention* v69 no2 p10 F 2017

Soup's On color *Backpacker* v45 no2 p36 Mr 2017

Phillips, Leigh

Nitrogen stewardship in the Anthropocene color *Science* v357 no6349 p350 Jl 28 2017

PHILLIPS, LISA A.

Crazy Like an Ex *Psychology Today* v49 no5 p27 S/O 2016

Getting Close [Cover story] *Psychology Today* v50 no1 p44 Ja/F 2017

Phillips, Mark

Above Old Bones color *Commonweal* v114 no14 p22 S 8 2017

Lost in Storyland color *Commonweal* v143 no17 p23 O 21 2016

Phillips, Matt

THE ANSWER IS ETAP color *Bicycling* v58 no10 p58 N/D 2017

#BIKECRUSH color *Bicycling* v58 no7 p65 Ag 2017

#BIKECRUSH color *Bicycling* v58 no8 p53 S 2017

BMC TEAMMACHINE SLR01 [Cover story] color *Bicycling* v58 no10 p70 N/D 2017

CANYON ENDURAGE CF SIX 9.0 color *Bicycling* v58 no1 p74 Ja/F 2017

CERVÉLO R5 color *Bicycling* v58 no7 p88 Ag 2017

COLNAGO C60 DISC color *Bicycling* v58 no6 p58 Jl 2017

GIRO PROLIGHT TECHLACE color *Bicycling* v58 no10 p66 N/D 2017

HOW CYCLING WORKS cartoon diag *Bicycling* v58 no9 p21 O 2017

"HOW MUCH TRAVEL DO I NEED?" color *Bicycling* v58 no3 p44 Ap 2017

"I LIKE RIDING FAST, BUT I DON'T RACE." color *Bicycling* v58 no3 p20 Ap 2017

"I WANT A BIKE THAT MAKES CLIMBING EASY." color *Bicycling* v58 no3 p34 Ap 2017

"I WANT A BIKE WITH HERITAGE." color *Bicycling* v58 no3 p58 Ap 2017

"I WANT TO GET AWAY." color *Bicycling* v58 no3 p82 Ap 2017

MARIN WOLF RIDGE PRO color *Bicycling* v58 no9 p80 O 2017

Oooh... Cozy! color *Bicycling* v58 no1 p64 Ja/F 2017

PEARL IZUMI PI DRY APPAREL color *Bicycling* v58 no9 p81 O 2017

SPEEDVAGEN ROAD DISC color *Bicycling* v58 no4 p61 My 2017

SUPERCOMPUTERS color *Bicycling* v58 no6 p64 Jl 2017

SUPERDIALED color *Bicycling* v58 no4 p68 My 2017

THAT FRESH TIRE FEEL color *Bicycling* v58 no7 p84 Ag 2017

Yokozuna Motoko Road Disc Brake color *Bicycling* v58 no4 p82 My 2017

Phillips, Noah

ACROSS THE GREAT DIVIDE: On the Road in Trump's America color *Progressive* v81 no7 p18 O/N 2017

PHILLIPS, NOËL

No Man's Land color *Climbing* no356 p22 S/O 2017

Phillips, O. L.

Persistent effects of pre-Columbian plant domestication on Amazonian forest composition bibl chart graph map *Science* v355 no6328 p925 Mr 3 2017

Phillips, Patrick

American Apartheid C. ANDERSON *New York Times Book Review* p12 O 2 2016

Phillips, Richard P.

Plant diversity increases with the strength of negative density dependence at the global scale diag *Science* v356 no6345 p1389 Je 30 2017

Phillips, Robert

CONTEMPORARY CRAFT color *American Craft* v77 no3 p97 Je/Jl 2017

Distribution and clinical impact of functional variants in 50,726 whole-exome sequences from the DiscovEHR study chart graph *Science* v354 no6319 paaf6814-1 D 23 2016

Phillips, Robert Allan

PRODUCING MIRACLES IS ALL IN A DAY'S WORK FOR NAVY MEDIC *Saturday Evening Post* v289 no5 p34 S/O 2017

Phillips, Rod

HISTOIRE AVEC MODÉRATION G. MacDonogh *History Today* v67 no5 p94 My 2017

Phillips, Roger J.

Gravity field of the Orientale basin from the Gravity Recovery and Interior Laboratory Mission bibl graph *Science* v354 no6311

p438 O 28 2016

Phillips, Sam

Sun Records A. D'arminio color *TV Guide* v65 no7 p42 F 13 2017

Phillips, Sandra

THE MOST POWERFUL WOMEN IN BUSINESS [Cover story] S. Floyd, K. Wilder et al color *Black Enterprise* v47 no5 p56 Ja/F 2017

PHILLIPS, STEPHEN

Hear Here! *Smithsonian* v47 no8 p17 D 2016

Phillips, Susanna

CLASSICAL MUSIC *New Yorker* v93 no17 p10 Je 19 2017

PHILLIPS, WALLY

The Skis of the Year color *Powder* p82 S 2017

PHILLIPS, WILL

Laugh Lines color *Reader's Digest* v190 no1132 p86 Jl/Ag 2017

Phillips-Fein, Kim

The Bankers Take Manhattan M. TKACIK *In These Times* v41 no6 p34 Je 2017

For Richer, for Poorer J. MAHLER *New York Times Book Review* p21 My 7 2017

MONT PELERIN IN VIRGINIA bw *Nation* v305 no7 p27 S 25 2017

Rich Man, Poor City *New Republic* v248 no8/9 p8 Ag/S 2017

Teaching and the Bottom Line *New York Times Book Review* p21 Ag 27 2017

Trump's Big Agenda color *New Republic* v248 no3 p6 Mr 2017

THE TWO WOMEN'S MOVEMENTS bw *Nation* v304 no18 p33 Je 19 2017

Philo, Phoebe, 1973-

PHOEBE PHILO E. MACSWEENEY color *Vogue* v207 no3 p412 Mr 2017

Philosophers

See also

Aestheticians (Philosophers)

c. 60: Rome *Lapham's Quarterly* v10 no2 p27 Spr 2017

EPICTETUS E. Batuman *New Yorker* v92 no42 p84 D 19 2016

Ivory Tower J. Ryerson *New York Times Book Review* p31 Mr 12 2017

One and the Many P. Gibbon *Humanities* v37 no4 p1 Fall 2016

Philosopher and CSI Fellow Robert Carroll, Creator of Skeptics Dictionary, Dies at Seventy-One S. GERBIC *Skeptical Inquirer* v41 no1 p11 Ja/F 2017

Pop Goes German Philosophy S. JEFFRIES color *Foreign Policy* no225 p70 Jl/Ag 2017

Philosophers—United States

A SCIENCE OF THE SOUL J. ROTHMAN cartoon color *New Yorker* v93 no6 p46 Mr 27 2017

Philosophical behaviorism

BEHAVIORISM K. NAHIGIAN *Humanist* v77 no2 p36 Mr/Ap 2017

Philosophy

See also

Absurd (Philosophy)

Aesthetics

Alienation (Philosophy)

Belief & doubt

Buddhist philosophy

Consciousness

Cycles

Cynicism

Emotions (Philosophy)

Ethics

Evolutionary theories

Experience

Facts (Philosophy)

Fate & fatalism

Humanism

Ideology

Isolation (Philosophy)

Perception

Pessimism

Power (Philosophy)

Psychology

Quality (Philosophy)

Realism

Thought & thinking

CHEWING IT OVER R. Mead cartoon *New Yorker* v93 no10 p37 Ap 24 2017

Embodying the sutra N. Rizopoulos color *Yoga Journal* no296 p51 N 2017

How to Grow Your Soul K. VONNEGUT *Reader's Digest* v188 no1126 p18 D 2016/Ja 2017

Philosophy & humor

May You Be Inscribed for a Good Laugh M. Y. SOLOVEICHIK *Commentary* v144 no2 p11 S 2017

Philosophy of medicine

TELL ME WHERE IT HURTS A. GAWANDE cartoon *New Yorker* v92 no46 p36 Ja 23 2017

Philosophy of mind

Apes know what others believe F. B. M. de Waal bibl color *Science* v354 no6308 p39 O 7 2016

Great apes anticipate that other individuals will act according to false beliefs C. Krupenye, Fumihiro Kano et al bibl chart diag graph *Science* v354 no6308 p110 O 7 2016

Philosophy of nature

See also

Continuity

Nature—Religious aspects

HENRY DAVID THOREAU color *Tricycle: The Buddhist Review* v26 no2 p21 Wint 2016

Philosophy of punishment

Revenge J. Rothkopf *New York Times Magazine* p26 Je 25 2017

Philosophy of time

which way to tomorrow? M. B. Griggs color *Popular Science* v289 no5 p11 S/O 2017

Philosophy teachers

The Revolution Devours Its Children Dept color *Weekly Standard* v22 no34 p2 My 15 2017

Philosophy—Social aspects

SelfCare and the Disappearance of the Adult *Commentary* v142 no2 p1 S 2016

Philpot, Robert

THE ANGEL OF BUDAPEST *History Today* v67 no1 p21 Ja 2017

Thatcher's Jewish Brain Trust: The story of Britain's unknown neoconservatives *Commentary* v144 no2 p27 S 2017

Philpott, Karen

Lee Rubin: Our mentor and role model *Science* v355 no6327 p806 F 24 2017

PHILPOTT, TOM

BURGER WITH FLIES cartoon *Mother Jones* v42 no2 p64 Mr/Ap 2017

RUN FOR COVER color *Mother Jones* v42 no4 p68 Jl/Ag 2017

SLIM PICKINGS color *Mother Jones* v42 no3 p72 My/Je 2017

PHILYAW, DEESHA

FIRST LOOK: FENCES color *Ebony* v72 no3 p38 D 2016/Ja 2017

FIRST LOOK: SLEIGHT color *Ebony* v72 no6 p24 Ap/My 2017

Phimister, E.

Fostering reproducibility in industry-academia research color *Science* v357 no6353 p759 Ag 25 2017

Phipps, Catherine

Citrus: Recipes that Celebrate the Sour and the Sweet *Publishers Weekly* v264 no6 p63 F 6 2017

Phipps, Clayton

DINOSAUR COWBOY M. Sager *Smithsonian* v48 no4 p52 Jl/Ag 2017

Phipps, John D.

Code Comfort: A Code Blue Alternative for Patients with DNRs *Harvard Business Review Digital Articles* p2 D 9 2014

Phipps, Melissa P.

Code Comfort: A Code Blue Alternative for Patients with DNRs *Harvard Business Review Digital Articles* p2 D 9 2014

Phish (Performer)

The Jam Kings Come Down to Earth W. HERMES color *Rolling Stone* no1272 p49 O 20 2016

Phish's New Harmony P. DOYLE bw color *Rolling Stone* no1273 p40 N 3 2016

The Road Heats Up P. Doyle, D. Fricke et al bw color *Rolling Stone* no1288 p11 Je 1 2017

Phishing

What It's Really Like to... img *New York* v50 no10 p54 My 15

2017

Phlox

EARLY RISER *South Dakota Magazine* v32 no6 p92 Mr/Ap 2017

Phobias

See also

Claustrophobia

Fear of contamination

Xenophobia

FLAVOR QUEST *Better Homes & Gardens* v95 no5 p4 My 2017

Laugh Lines J. FALLON color *Reader's Digest* v190 no1134 p127 O 2017

Quaking in My Boots R. Marr color *Missouri Life* v44 no6 p62 S 2017

Phobias treatment

How to Treat Phobias T. John color *Time* v189 no6 p12 F 20 2017

NEWS FROM THE World of Medicine S. RIDEOUT color *Reader's Digest* v190 no1132 p51 Jl/Ag 2017

Phobos (Satellite)

How moon dust will put a ring around MARS J. Davis bw color diag *Astronomy* v44 no12 p46 D 2016

Phocoena sinus

Vaquitas on the Brink color *Earth Island Journal* v32 no1 p7 Spr 2017

World's most endangered marine mammal down to 30 V. Morell color graph *Science* v355 no6325 p558 F 10 2017

PHODES, MARGARET

ART FACTORY: MASS MOCA BULKS UP diag *Wired* v25 no7 p24 Jl 2017

Phoenician antiquities

DISPOSABLE GODS D. WEISS color *Archaeology* v70 no5 p16 S/O 2017

Phoenix (Ariz.)

IMMIGRATION: LET ME TELL YOU ABOUT MY PLAN *Vital Speeches of the Day* v82 no10 p286 O 2016

The Phoenix Driveway Ghost B. RADFORD *Skeptical Inquirer* v41 no4 p24 Jl/Ag 2017

SUBURBAN FUTURISM G. Kroeber bw color *Art in America* v104 no11 p106 D 2016

Phoenix (Fictitious character)

NO. 14 JEAN GREY T. Stack color *Entertainment Weekly* no1436/1437 p56 O 21 2016

Phoenix Suns (Basketball team)

12 Suns B. Golliver, R. Mahoney et al color *Sports Illustrated* v125 no14 p112 O 24-31 2016

15 SUNS color *Sports Illustrated* v127 no12 p97 O 16 2017

Leading Off color *Sports Illustrated* v127 no2 p8 Jl 17 2017

Pholcidae

OH DADDY! *Virginia Living* v15 no1 p19 D 2016

Phonesack Group Co. Ltd.

Local Leaders in the Power Industry *Foreign Affairs* v95 no6 p(Sp)7 N/D 2016

Phongsavanh Group (Company)

The Reward of Taking the Initiative *Foreign Affairs* v95 no6 p(Sp)14 N/D 2016

Phonograph

Build a Record Player Powered by Wind T. LEAVY color *Popular Science* v288 no6 p88 N/D 2016

Phonograph records

COLLECTIVE Might D. Garner color *Esquire* p70 Je/Jl 2017

RECORDS OF REBELLION N. Daly bw color *National Geographic* v231 no5 p16 My 2017

The Revenge of the Real D. SAX *Columbia Journalism Review* p36 Fall/Wint 2016

the temple K. DUPZYK color *Popular Mechanics* p82 Jl 2017

THIS "BUY AMERICAN" THING *Popular Mechanics* p4 Jl 2017

VINYL J. LYNCH color *Popular Mechanics* p35 My 2017

Phonograph turntables—Evaluation

FEEL THE SOUND S. NYGAARD color *Men's Health* v32 no2 p(Sp)13 Mr 2017

Phononic crystals

Sounding out optical phonons D. M. Juraschek and N. A. Spaldin diag *Science* v357 no6354 p873 S 1 2017

Phonons

See also

Phononic crystals

Sounding out optical phonons D. M. Juraschek and N. A. Spaldin diag *Science* v357 no6354 p873 S 1 2017

Phoo, Wint Wint

Crystal structure of unlinked NS2B-NS3 protease from Zika virus bibl color graph *Science* v354 no6319 p1597 D 23 2016

Phosphatidylserines

One Simple Trick to Reversing Memory Loss S. Wuzubia color *National Review* v68 no21 p7 N 21 2016

One Simple Trick to Reversing Memory Loss S. Wuzubia *Saturday Evening Post* v289 no2 p99 Mr/Ap 2017

Phospholipids

See also

Phosphatidylserines

SOIL HEALTH TESTS B. Spiegel *Successful Farming* v115 no1 p52 Ja 2017

Phosphoramidates

RESEARCH color *Science* v356 no6336 p392 Ap 28 2017

Phosphorus

Magic Dust from Afar *Earth Island Journal* v32 no2 p11 Summ 2017

Phosphorylation

Evolution of protein phosphorylation across 18 fungal species R. A. Studer, R. A. Rodriguez-Mias et al bibl graph *Science* v354 no6309 p229 O 14 2016

Multisite phosphorylation by MAPK A. J. Whitmarsh and R. J. Davis bibl diag *Science* v354 no6309 p179 O 14 2016

Opposing effects of Elk-1 multisite phosphorylation shape its response to ERK activation A. Mylona, Theillet et al bibl graph *Science* v354 no6309 p233 O 14 2016

Young phosphorylation is functionally silent O. Matalon, B. Dubreuil et al bibl diag *Science* v354 no6309 p176 O 14 2016

Photoacoustic effect

Imaging cancer with PHOTOACOUSTIC RADAR A. Mandelis *Physics Today* v70 no5 p42 My 2017

Photoactivation

Photoactivation and inactivation of Arabidopsis cryptochrome 2 Qin Wang, Zecheng Zuo et al bibl graph *Science* v354 no6310 p343 O 21 2016

Photobooks

the start color *InStyle* v24 no7 p27 Jl 2017

Photochemistry

See also

Photoactivation

Enantioselective photochemistry through Lewis acid–catalyzed triplet energy transfer T. R. Blum, Z. D. Miller et al bibl chart diag graph *Science* v354 no6318 p1391 D 16 2016

Photocurrents

Extremely efficient internal exciton dissociation through edge states in layered 2D perovskites Blancon, H. Tsai et al bibl graph *Science* v355 no6331 p1288 Mr 24 2017

Photodetectors—Evaluation

Focus on analytical equipment, sensors, and detectors A. Mandelis *Physics Today* v70 no2 p63 F 2017

Photoelectric devices

75, 50 & 25 YEARS AGO R. W. Sinnott *Sky & Telescope* v133 no4 p8 Ap 2017

Photoelectron spectroscopy

Angular momentum can slow down photoemission V. S. Yakovlev and N. Karpowicz color *Science* v357 no6357 p1239 S 22 2017

Photoelectrons

Attosecond dynamics through a Fano resonance: Monitoring the birth of a photoelectron V. Gruson, L. Barreau et al bibl graph *Science* v354 no6313 p734 N 11 2016

Photograph captions

Back talk *National Geographic Kids* no468 p34 Mr 2017

SIGNS OF THE TIMES *National Geographic Kids* no468 p33 Mr 2017

Photograph captions—Competitions

NAME THE BOAT S. SHIBATA color *Sea Magazine* v109 no8 p10 Ag 2017

Photograph collections

HOW TO SEE THE WORLD S. DADICH color map *Wired* v24 no12 p16 D 2016

Photographers

See also

Photojournalists

Photographs

ASSOCIATED PRESS ADMITS WARTIME DEAL WITH NA-ZIS B. Manley bw *Military History* v34 no4 p8 N 2017

Back in the Picture S. J. Smith bw color *AARP: The Magazine* v60 no5A p59 Ag/S 2017

backstory color *New Republic* v247 no12 p80 D 2016

big picture color *Canadian Geographic* v136 no6 p10 D 2016

The Big Pictures: GRAND CANYON [Cover story] *Arizona Highways* v93 no1 p17 Ja 2017

COLDFRONT B. Merrill bw *Snowboarder* v29 no3 p12 N 2016

COLORING SPACE N. Strochlic color *National Geographic* v232 no1 p152 Jl 2017

THE DESCENT D. SMITH color *Climbing* no349 p80 N 2016

DOUBLE VISION J. Paul color *Snowboarder* v29 no3 p74 N 2016

ELEMENTS color *Snowboarder* v29 no3 p80 N 2016

ENDER/ENDER color *Snowboarder* v29 no3 p136 N 2016

THE END OF ICE B. MCKIBBEN color *New Republic* v247 no12 p32 D 2016

Endpaper *New York Times Magazine* p82 S 24 2017

EVERYWHERE color *Popular Mechanics* p6 Ap 2017

Flagstaff Train Station N. AUSTIN *Arizona Highways* v93 no1 p6 Ja 2017

FLASH A. Burr bw color *Climbing* no349 p12 N 2016

GLASS color *Powder* v45 no6 p18 F 2017

GOOD CHEMISTRY A. KONERMANN *Cincinnati Magazine* v50 no6 p28 Mr 2017

A grandmother's death prompts a search for her in family snapshots. Photographs are our reservoirs of memory, our talismans of mourning T. Cole *New York Times Magazine* p12 Jl 16 2017

Hello! L. Brown color *InStyle* v24 no8 p24 Ag 2017

How I really met my mother G. SORELL color *Good Housekeeping* v264 no5 p73 My 2017

How to watermark multiple photos in Lightroom L. SNIDER color *Macworld - Digital Edition* p128 D 2016

IN FOCUS O. Gagnon color *Snowboarder* v29 no3 p66 N 2016

The "Laundromat" bw *Nation* v33 no21 p13 N 21 2016

Lightbox color *Time* v188 no20 p14 N 14 2016

My Shot color *National Geographic Kids* no470 p35 My 2017

Nail Every Photo Op M. ABERMAN bw color *Seventeen* p106 Ja 1 2017

Nebraskans' bridge past and present with photography J. Boschen color *Nebraska Life* v21 no1 p14 Ja/F 2017

NILS MINDNICH color *Snowboarder* v29 no3 p134 N 2016

Off Center M. Ryan bw color *Popular Photography* v81 no1 p82 Ja/F 2017

Photos from the Field *Mother Earth News* no281 p128 Ap/My 2017

Q&A: Jacques Barbey *Arizona Highways* v92 no7 p9 Jl 2016

SALT LAKE CITY, UT B. Merrill bw color *Snowboarder* v29 no3 p98 N 2016

SCOTTY ARNOLD B. Merrill color *Snowboarder* v29 no3 p38 N 2016

SELF-RELIANCE S. Korman color *Art in America* v104 no10 p130 N 2016

SEQUENCE & DESTROY color *Snowboarder* v29 no3 p46 N 2016

SICK DAYS B. Merrill color *Snowboarder* v29 no3 p92 N 2016

Snap Dynamite Fireworks Photos J. LABIANCA color *Reader's Digest* v190 no1132 p33 Jl/Ag 2017

A Song FOR Katie K. VAUGHN bw *Arizona Highways* v93 no5 p50 My 2017

Spacecraft eyes Great Red Spot color *Science* v357 no6348 p232 Jl 21 2017

That Thing with Feathers M. JANNOT *Audubon* v118 no6 p7 Wint 2016

Time Out color *Art in America* v104 no10 p64 N 2016

Twenty Thousand Leagues Under the Sea M. CASEY *American Scholar* v86 no4 p94 Aut 2017

Who's (sort of) counting? S. Milius color *Science News* v190 no12 p25 D 10 2016

Photographs—19th century

"B BOARD" OPERATOR bw *Magazine Antiques* v183 no6 p62 N/D 2016

Photographs—Editing

Editor's Letter M. Fell *TV Guide* v65 no37 p4 S 4 2017

Picture Perfect T. Bufete chart color diag graph *Consumer Reports* v82 no12 p14 D 2017

Secrets of Fake Photos Revealed J. KIFFEL-ALCHEH *National Geographic Kids* no469 p22 Ap 2017

Photographs—Editing—Computer network resources

FACE FACTS D. Grossman color *Popular Photography* v81 no1 p46 Ja/F 2017

Photographs—Editing—Software

4 secrets for editing images in Apple Photos L. SNIDER color *Macworld - Digital Edition* p117 F 2017

How to use Levels adjustments in Photos and how to use Copy Adjustments to tweak other images L. SNIDER diag *Macworld - Digital Edition* p122 F 2017

LUMINAR: A SERIOUS CHALLENGER TO THE REIGNING PRO APPS FOR PHOTO EDITING MASTERY J. DOVE color *Macworld - Digital Edition* p25 F 2017

Photographs—History

Picturing Mardi Gras C. Kolb bw *New Orleans Magazine* v51 no4 p38 F 2017

Photographs—Law & legislation

Ne Retouche Pas color *Weekly Standard* v23 no6 p3 O 16 2017

Photographs—Psychological aspects

What makes an image surreal is not the artful crafting of illusion but the eruption of the accidental into the everyday *New York Times Magazine* p16 O 23 2016

Photography

  See also
  Aerial photography
  Astronomical photography
  Composition (Photography)
  Digital photography
  Photography of airplanes
  Photography of animals
  Photography of food
  Photography of girls
  Photography of men
  Photography of models (Persons)
  Photography of plants
  Photography of skiing
  Photography of sports
  Photography of the nude
  Photography of women
  Portrait photography
  Space photography
  Wildlife photography

10 Frames T. Fitzharris color *Popular Photography* v81 no1 p54 Ja/F 2017

ALL MY RIVERS ARE GONE: The Prologue K. LEE color *Arizona Highways* v93 no5 p48 My 2017

the big picture bw color *Parents* v92 no3 p83 Mr 2017

BOARD GAMES K. MOORE *Natural History* v124 no10 p2 N 2016

A Bronx Tale *American Scholar* v86 no4 p14 Aut 2017

CABIN art color *Cabin Living* p11 O 2017

DANCING IN THE DARK E. WOOD bw chart color map *Missouri Life* v44 no5 p32 Ag 2017

editor's LETTER R. STIEVE *Arizona Highways* v92 no11 p2 N 2016

EN ROUTE S. Cravatts color *Popular Photography* v80 no11 p86 D 2016

Happy Snaps color *Health* v31 no1 p12 Ja 2017

HOW TO SHOOT IN 360 P. SARCONI color *Wired* v25 no5 p50 My 2017

in focus bw color *Yoga Journal* no290 p93 Mr 2017

The Inside Track A. J. BARTELS color *Nebraska Life* v21 no2 p20 Mr/Ap 2017

A LIFE IN FOCUS G. CARTER and D. JONES bw *Vanity Fair* v59 no6 p100 My 2017

lose the moment k. butcher color *Bike Magazine* v24 no6 p56 Ag 2017

Making It New M. Leuchter *Popular Photography* v81 no1 p10 Ja/F 2017

Michigan J. Dimmock *New York Times Magazine* p47 N 20 2016

OFF LINE color *Bike Magazine* v24 no6 p136 Ag 2017

One-Minute Stress Tips [Cover story] color *Prevention* v69 no1 p16 Ja 2017

Photography of athletes
   See also
      Photography of football players
   Hanging tough N. WIART color *Maclean's* v129 no43 p50 O 31
      2016
Photography of automobile racing
   A-LIST CARS, STARS color *Road & Track* v68 no7 p14 Mr/Ap
      2017
   DAYTONA GRAND PRIX color *Road & Track* v68 no7 p16 Mr/
      Ap 2017
Photography of automobiles
   DIGNIFIED DECAY color *Road & Track* v68 no8 p14 My 2017
   Go color *Road & Track* v69 no1 p10 Ag 2017
   SUNSET STRIP color *Road & Track* v68 no8 p16 My 2017
Photography of automobiles—Exhibitions
   The Power of Car Pictures B. Shapiro bw *Popular Mechanics* p19
      My 2017
Photography of baseball
   Leading Off B. Reiter color *Sports Illustrated* v127 no12 p6 O
      16 2017
   Leading Off color *Sports Illustrated* v126 no13 p6 My 8 2017
   Leading Off color *Sports Illustrated* v126 no8 p6 Mr 20 2017
Photography of bathing suits
   Curaçao color *Sports Illustrated* v126 no6 p150 F 20 2017
   EDITOR'S LETTER color *Sports Illustrated* v126 no6 p16 F 20
      2017
   Fiji [Cover story] color *Sports Illustrated* v126 no6 p32 F 20 2017
   Finland KAKSLAUTTANEN color *Sports Illustrated* v126 no6
      p92 F 20 2017
   Hot Mama TURKS & CAICOS color *Sports Illustrated* v126 no6
      p102 F 20 2017
   Mexico TULUM color *Sports Illustrated* v126 no6 p62 F 20 2017
   Pure Gold HOUSTON color *Sports Illustrated* v126 no6 p84 F
      20 2017
   Simply Smashing TURKS & CAICOS color *Sports Illustrated*
      v126 no6 p132 F 20 2017
   Sumba Island INDONESIA color *Sports Illustrated* v126 no6
      p112 F 20 2017
Photography of beaches
   Beach Life A. HEROLD *Los Angeles Magazine* p86 Ag 2017
Photography of birds
   3 Strategies for Flocks N. Bahl *Audubon* v119 no3 p49 Fall 2017
   AIM HIGH B. Zwiebel color *Audubon* v119 no3 p48 Fall 2017
   Bound for the Heavens color *National Wildlife (World Edition)*
      v55 no1 p50 D/Ja 2016
   Cooper's Hawks N. Austin *Arizona Highways* v93 no10 p13 O
      2017
   Find the Hidden Animals color *National Geographic Kids* no475
      p31 N 2017
   Go Mobile M. Furtman color *Audubon* v119 no3 p49 Fall 2017
   THE IMAGE-MAKER P. STEFÁNSSON *Iceland Review* v55
      no4 p68 Jl/Ag 2017
   PECKING ORDER color *Louisiana Life* v38 no1 p8 S/O 2017
   A Photographer on the Dance Floor M. Bartels *Audubon* v119 no1
      p49 Spr 2017
   Resurgence A. Opar *Audubon* v119 no1 p1 Spr 2017
   Romancing the Water D. Walters color *Audubon* v119 no3 p49
      Fall 2017
   Sitting Ducks E. J. Peiker color *Audubon* v119 no3 p48 Fall 2017
   Swamp Steward M. Bartels color *Audubon* v119 no3 p49 Fall
      2017
   WHERE IS THIS? *Arizona Highways* v93 no1 p56 Ja 2017
   Wood Duck color *Audubon* v119 no3 p48 Fall 2017
Photography of cats
   CAT'S MEOW J. MOAZAMI color *Chicago* v66 no6 p42 Je 2017
   INSIDE PEEK color *Chicago* v66 no6 p16 Je 2017
Photography of celebrities
   150 MOST FASHIONABLE WOMEN color *Harper's Bazaar*
      no3650 p127 F 2017
   15 MINUTES *Cincinnati Magazine* v50 no12 p39 S 2017
   THE ALLURE OF JACKIE S. Mooallem bw color *Harper's Ba-*
      zaar no3650 p184 F 2017
   Bald & Beautiful: A Timeline S. Leach bw color *Glamour* v115
      no1 p46 N 2017
   THE CHIC SHEATH color *Vogue* v207 no9 p402 S 2017
   DAN ABOUT TOWN *Washingtonian Magazine* v52 no5 p28 F

2017
   Everybody Is a Star color *Glamour* v115 no11 p158 N 2017
   Kendall Jenner color *InStyle* v24 no2 p109 F 2017
   Kristen Stewart HER BEST EVER T. Swennen and K. Stewart's
      color *InStyle* v24 no2 p60 F 2017
   Out & About *TV Guide* v64 no46 p4 N 7 2016
   Random Notes color *Rolling Stone* no1275 p34 D 1 2016
   Random Notes color *Rolling Stone* no1283 p23 Mr 23 2017
   "Style," bw color *Vanity Fair* v59 no9 p1c S 2017
   STYLE with SUBSTANCE K. SMITH color *Vanity Fair* v59 no4
      p96 Mr 2017
Photography of children
   A Ride Through Horror *New York Times Upfront* v149 no7 p2 Ja
      9 2017
Photography of churches
   And The Winning Photo Is... T. Zamboni *British Heritage Travel*
      v38 no1 p80 Ja/F 2017
   LIGHT IN THE DARKNESS, Salt of the Earth C. BEGEMAN
      South Dakota Magazine v32 no6 p30 Mr/Ap 2017
Photography of cities & towns
   THAT TOWN A. Wiener color *Mother Jones* v42 no4 p6 Jl/Ag
      2017
Photography of clothing & dress
   Lightbox color *Time* v189 no4 p14 F 6 2017
   Photographic Memory J. DEMELO color *O, The Oprah Magazine*
      p24 Jl 2017
   Slick: WITH A NOD TO '80s HAIR BANDS, PATENT LEATH-
      ER SLITHERS WITH ELECTRIC SEXUALITY *Interview* v47
      no3 p50 Ap 2017
   Sweater WEATHER H. Rolfe *Dance Spirit* v20 no10 p54 D 2016
Photography of clouds
   Cloud Control color *Backpacker* p40 My 2017
   CLOUDSCAPES P. Kolonia color *Popular Photography* v81 no1
      p36 Ja/F 2017
Photography of cycling
   BUZZ bw color *Bike Magazine* v24 no8 p22 N 2017
   It's all in the hips c. brown color *Bike Magazine* v23 no9 p98 D
      2016
Photography of dogs
   WOMAN'S BEST FRIENDS color *O, The Oprah Magazine* pC1
      Jl 2017
Photography of dwellings
   SHOW US YOUR color *Log Home Living* v33 no9 p88 D 2016
   STILL NIGHT P. STEFÁNSSON *Iceland Review* v55 no2 p58
      Mr/Ap 2017
Photography of eclipses
   The Eclipse Megamovie Project H. Hudson and M. Bender bw
      color *Sky & Telescope* v134 no2 p20 Ag 2017
   How To Shoot a Solar Eclipse chart color *Sky & Telescope* v134
      no2 p14 Ag 2017
   Leading Off color *Sports Illustrated* v127 no6 p4 Ag 28 2017
   TARGETING THE "Tutulemma" T. Tezel *Sky & Telescope* v132
      no6 p66 D 2016
Photography of families
   Lightbox color *Time* v188 no16/17 p10 O 24 2016
   On Photography G. Dyer *New York Times Magazine* p14 Ja 8 2017
   pontoon mania M. Willers, M. Sorenson et al color *Cabin Living*
      p60 Je 2017
Photography of festivals
   Lightbox color *Time* v189 no9 p16 Mr 13 2017
Photography of fireworks
   My Shot color *National Geographic Kids* no471 p32 Je/Jl 2017
Photography of fishes
   big picture color *Canadian Geographic* v135 no6 p16 D 2015
   CHALLENGE #NGMH2O bw *National Geographic* v231 no4
      p12 Ap 2017
Photography of food
   Candy Cottontail Cookies color *Good Housekeeping* v264 no4
      p137 Ap 2017
   Cocoa-Nutty Lime Tart color *Good Housekeeping* v264 no4 p111
      Ap 2017
   FLAVOR-PACKED PASTAS *Martha Stewart Living* no270 p94
      D 2016
   Home Sweet Home color *House Beautiful* v159 no8 p29 O 2017
   A ROUND OF APPLAUSE S. DIGREGORIO *Martha Stewart*
      Living no269 p90 N 2016

DEEP BLACK AND WHITE D. Grossman color *Popular Photography* v81 no2 p36 Mr/Ap 2017

Photography—Studios & dark rooms

The Darkroom A. Rossiter *Art in America* v104 no9 p50 O 2016

Photography—Studios & dark rooms—Evaluation

GOOD CHEMISTRY A. KONERMANN *Cincinnati Magazine* v50 no6 p28 Mr 2017

Photography—United States—20th century

COOL MOM R. Mead cartoon *New Yorker* v93 no7 p36 Ap 3 2017

Photojournalism

THE 360-Degree Selfie E. WOYKE color *MIT Technology Review* v120 no2 p36 Mr/Ap 2017

CLOSE CALL D. Owen cartoon *New Yorker* v93 no26 p22 S 4 2017

PASSION FOR PEOPLE P. STEFÁNSSON *Iceland Review* v55 no4 p62 Jl/Ag 2017

Photojournalists

Barbara McClatchie Andrews A. HUTCHINS color *Maclean's* v129 no43 p66 O 31 2016

This Magic Moment: For more than 50 years, photographer Jean-Pierre Laffont has proved that in New York, you never know what you might see A. STERNBERGH img *New York* v50 no15 p64 Jl 24 2017

Photolithography

Direct optical lithography of functional inorganic nanomaterials Y. Wang, I. Fedin et al diag graph *Science* v357 no6349 p385 Jl 28 2017

Photomontage

SHADOWS OF WAR color *MHQ: Quarterly Journal of Military History* v29 no4 p50 Summ 2017

Photon emission

Nanometer resolution imaging and tracking of fluorescent molecules with minimal photon fluxes F. Balzarotti, Y. Eilers et al bibl graph *Science* v355 no6325 p606 F 10 2017

Polaritons in van der Waals materials D. N. Basov, M. M. Fogler et al bibl chart color diag graph *Science* v354 no6309 paag1992-1 O 14 2016

Photon-photon scattering

Aloof light particles nudged to interact E. CONOVER color *Science News* v192 no4 p7 S 16 2017

Photons

Deterministic generation of a cluster state of entangled photons I. Schwartz, D. Cogan et al bibl diag graph *Science* v354 no6311 p434 O 28 2016

An integrated diamond nanophotonics platform for quantum-optical networks A. Sipahigil, R. E. Evans et al bibl graph *Science* v354 no6314 p847 N 18 2016

Is the Milky Way in a Void? M. YOUNG *Sky & Telescope* v134 no4 p12 O 2017

Quantum entanglement reaches new heights: The satellite-based distribution of entangled photons to cities 1200 km apart bolsters prospects for a global quantum communication network A. G. Smart *Physics Today* v70 no8 p14 Ag 2017

Quantum satellite sets distance record E. CONOVER color *Science News* v192 no1 p14 Ag 5 2017

A 'Teleportation' to Outer Space J. Kluger color *Time* v190 no4 p13 Jl 24 2017

Photoperiodism

REAL-WORLD RUT [Cover story] M. KENYON color *Outdoor Life* v224 no9 p39 N 2017

Photoreceptors

See also

    Eye

Glia put visual map in sync J. Isaacman-Beck and T. R. Clandinin color *Science* v357 no6354 p867 S 1 2017

Photoresists

Direct optical lithography of functional inorganic nanomaterials Y. Wang, I. Fedin et al diag graph *Science* v357 no6349 p385 Jl 28 2017

Photosynthesis

See also

    Photosystems (Photosynthesis)

COMBAT HEAT STRESS WITH A QUICK RUN AROUND WITH THE PIVOT D. Mowitz *Successful Farming* v115 no1 p58 Ja 2017

DNA edits boost photosynthesis [Cover story] S. MILIUS color *Science News* v190 no13 p6 D 24 2016

Engineered crops could have it made in the shade E. Stokstad color *Science* v354 no6314 p816 N 18 2016

Improving photosynthesis and crop productivity by accelerating recovery from photoprotection J. Kromdijk, K. Głowacka et al bibl chart color graph *Science* v354 no6314 p857 N 18 2016

On the origins of oxygenic photosynthesis and aerobic respiration in Cyanobacteria R. M. Soo, J. Hemp et al chart diag *Science* v355 no6332 p1436 Mr 31 2017

Photosynthesis treats ailing hearts T. HESMAN SAEY *Science News* v192 no1 p8 Ag 5 2017

Structure of a symmetric photosynthetic reaction center–photosystem C. Gisriel, I. Sarrou et al color *Science* v357 no6355 p1021 S 8 2017

The tie that binds J. Swift bibl color *Science* v355 no6326 p701 F 17 2017

Photosynthesis research

To Feed the World, Improve Photosynthesis K. Bourzac color *MIT Technology Review* v120 no5 p80 S/O 2017

Photosynthetic reaction centers

Structure of a symmetric photosynthetic reaction center–photosystem C. Gisriel, I. Sarrou et al color *Science* v357 no6355 p1021 S 8 2017

Photosystems (Photosynthesis)

See also

    Light-harvesting complex (Photosynthesis)

    Photosynthetic reaction centers

The complex that conquered the land R. Croce and H. van Amerongen diag *Science* v357 no6353 p752 Ag 25 2017

Phototherapy

The Body Electric M. Meltzer color *Vogue* v207 no4 p170 Ap 2017

COMPLEMENTARY CARE M. DEPAULO *Arabian Horse World* v57 no5 p238 F 2017

Photovoltaic power systems

The Basics of BATTERY POWER A. Sindelar *Mother Earth News* no279 p61 D/Ja 2017

Do-It-Yourself OFF-GRID SOLAR: Explore the components and considerations for creating your own off-grid photovoltaic system J. Burdick and P. Schmidt *Mother Earth News* no282 p16 Je/Jl 2017

Groundbreaking Solar Roof Panels S. Stonebrook *Mother Earth News* no281 p9 Ap/My 2017

How to Install a Solar Panel K. HARRIS color *Boating World* v38 no7 p26 Jl 2017

Imaginary futures C. Day *Physics Today* v69 no12 p8 D 2016

A molecular spin-photovoltaic device X. Sun, S. Vélez et al color diag *Science* v357 no6352 p677 Ag 18 2017

Off-Grid in the Catskills F. SIGURDSSON color *Cabin Living* p24 Ap 2017

Save Money T. Stanger, J. Blyskal et al il *Consumer Reports* v82 no3 p30 Mr 2017

Solar Energy color *Cabin Living* p68 Ja/F 2017

The Solar-Power Road J. Zorthian color *Time* v189 no4 p23 Ja 23 2017

Something New Under the Sun P. Hope color *Consumer Reports* v82 no9 p18 S 2017

sun power [Cover story] S. FREED color *Cabin Living* p34 O 2017

The Unstoppable Green Power Revolution H. Wasserman cartoon color *Progressive* v81 no5 p40 Je/Jl 2017

Zero Net Energy Ordinance *Mother Earth News* no283 p10 Ag/S 2017

Photovoltaic power systems—Government policy

ROOFTOP SOLAR CLOUDS UP B. Eckhouse and C. Martin graph *Bloomberg Businessweek* no4496 p80 O 24 2016

Phra Dhammachayo

Buddhist Bad Boys M. Scarles color *Tricycle: The Buddhist Review* v26 no4 p17 Summ 2017

PHUNTSHO, KARMA

Bridging the Gaps between Science and Policy for the Sustainable Management of Rangeland Resources in the Developing World *BioScience* v67 no7 p656 Jl 2017

Phuntsho, Karma—Interviews

BHUTAN on the Brink color *Tricycle: The Buddhist Review* v26

no3 p42 Spr 2017

Phuntsok, J.

Observation of a large-scale anisotropy in the arrival directions of cosmic rays above 8 × 1018 eV *Science* v357 no6357 p1266 S 22 2017

Phylloxera

Blame Canada J. RAPP LEARN map *Canadian Geographic* v135 no6 p34 D 2015

Phylogenetic models

Avian egg shape: Form, function, and evolution M. Caswell Stoddard, E. Hou Yong et al color diag *Science* v356 no6344 p1249 Je 23 2017

Phylogeny

Decoupled ecomorphological evolution and diversification in Neogene-Quaternary horses J. L. Cantalapiedra, J. L. Prado et al bibl graph *Science* v355 no6325 p627 F 10 2017

Empowerment P. Chakrabarty, S. Negi et al color *Science* v356 no6335 p242 Ap 21 2017

Physical & theoretical chemistry

See also

Atoms

Crystallization

Mechanical chemistry

Surface chemistry

Optical imaging of surface chemistry and dynamics in confinement C. Macias-Romero, I. Nahalka et al color *Science* v357 no6353 p784 Ag 25 2017

Physical (Music)

Olivia Newton-John's "Physical" M. Vain color *Entertainment Weekly* no1460/1461 p42 Ap 7-17 2017

Physical activity

50 Reasons to Love Being 50+ color *AARP: The Magazine* v60 no1A p53 D 2016/Ja 2017

Fat-Shame for Guys P. SAGAL color *Runner's World* v52 no8 p50 S 2017

Get Your Kid Moving *Parents* p46 2015

How to drink, relax, snack... and slim down A. Sweeney color *Redbook* p20 Jl/Ag 2017

Keep It Moving G. Reynolds color *New York Times Magazine* p36 D 11 2016

ON YOUR MARK cartoon color *Better Homes & Gardens* v95 no5 p178 My 2017

Save with NRPA-Sponsored Insurance Plans *Parks & Recreation* v52 no1 p48 Ja 2017

Senior Games: Everybody Can Play M. Stalling and T. Grodsky *Parks & Recreation* v52 no1 p16 Ja 2017

Snacking Before Exercise color *Kiplinger's Personal Finance* v71 no7 p71 Jl 2017

Physical activity—Equipment & supplies

Find Your Fitness Tracker color *Glamour* v114 no7 p56 Jl 2016

Physical activity—Psychological aspects

How Gardening Beats the Gym V. TWEED color *Better Nutrition* v79 no7 p10 Jl 2017

Physical anthropologists

Bigfoot and I: Reflections on Forty Years of Skepticism E. SCOTT *Skeptical Inquirer* v40 no6 p35 N/D 2016

Physical anthropology

See also

Forensic anthropology

Human behavior

Human evolution

Human genetics

Human skin color

Race

Bigfoot and I: Reflections on Forty Years of Skepticism E. SCOTT *Skeptical Inquirer* v40 no6 p35 N/D 2016

Physical characteristics (Human body)

WHAT DOES SHE SEE IN THAT GUY? H. HAVRILESKY bw color *Esquire* p80 Ap 2017

Physical contact

Crunch Time A. Prewitt color *Sports Illustrated* v126 no12 p44 My 1 2017

Physical cosmology

See also

Big bang theory

Cosmic background radiation

Dark energy (Astronomy)

Dark matter (Astronomy)

One frame in the cosmic movie *Astronomy* v44 no12 p6 D 2016

Physical distribution of goods

See also

Food deserts

Packaging

Product recall

Product returns

Shipment of goods

ALL AROUND THE FARM *Successful Farming* v114 no10 p76 O 2016

Physical education

See also

Drills (Practice)

Games

Movement education

Finding Time for P.E *Parents* v91 no10 p36 O 2016

Reintroducing the Game of Golf J. R. Johnson *Parks & Recreation* v52 no1 p50 Ja 2017

Physical education teacher education (Higher)

Bridgewater State University *Dance Magazine* v90 p48 2016/2017 Supplement College Guide

Physical fitness

See also

Anaerobic exercises

Bodybuilding

Muscle strength

Physical fitness for men

Physical fitness for older people

Physical fitness for women

15 MINUTE WORKOUT M. Gainsburg color *Women's Health* v14 no1 p90 Ja/F 2017

31 DAY HAPPY * LIFE MAKEOVER E. BRIED color *Good Housekeeping* v264 no1 p81 Ja 1 2017

3 GYM-FRIENDLY EXERCISE TECHNIQUES FOR GREAT GLUTES L. McGLASHAN color *Muscle & Performance* v9 no5 p28 My 2017

3 Things to Avoid as You Seek to Become a Fitter Fighter M. Hatmaker color *Black Belt* v55 no4 p20 Je/Jl 2017

5 WAYS ...TO SURVIVE THE HOLIDAYS J. CONNOR cartoon *Muscle & Performance* v8 no12 p66 D 2016

5 Weather-Proof Workout Strategies *Tufts University Health & Nutrition Letter* v34 no11 p3 Ja 2017

6 More Reasons to Get Up and Move A. Macmillan, A. Park et al color *Time* v190 no4 p40 Jl 24 2017

6-WEEK YOGA GUIDE chart color *Yoga Journal* p8 2017 Special Issue

79 IS THE NEW 29 N. HEIL bw color *Men's Health* v32 no5 p126 Je 2017

BEING MY OWN CHEERLEADER C. Alexander color *Women's Health* v14 no9 p36 N 2017

The Best Reasons to EXERCISE OZ color *O, The Oprah Magazine* p67 Ja 2017

Be your own personal trainer J. Andriakos color *Health* v31 no8 p21 O 2017

Build Mental Muscle M. SORKIN color *Climbing* no354 p44 Jl 2017

BULK SEASON L. BOYCE chart color *Muscle & Performance* v8 no12 p38 D 2016

cheat, drink, & still shrink A. Rios color *Yoga Journal* p23 2017 Special Issue

Chisel Your Back B. Gaddour bw color *Men's Health* v31 no10 p40 D 2016

CONFESSIONS OF A FITNESS EDITOR color *Women's Health* v14 no2 p132 Mr 2017

CROSSFIT V. Tweed color *Amazing Wellness* v8 no6 p86 Early Winter 2016

Design Your Own Metcon L. McGlashan chart color *Muscle & Performance* v9 no5 p48 My 2017

Don't take that seat! color *Redbook* p65 Jl/Ag 2017

Do this to meet your goals A. Sweeney color *Redbook* p19 S 2017

EMILY SKYE A New Kind of Fit Chick J. Naftulin color *Health* v31 no1 p56 Ja 2017

THE EXCHANGE B. Boyé and A. Eaves bw cartoon color *Men's Health* v32 no6 p18 Ag 2017

'Exercise pill' boosts mice's endurance L. BEIL *Science News* v191 no11 p7 Je 10 2017

Fitness, According to Superheroes J. M. Goldstein and S. G. Levy bw chart color *Glamour* v115 no2 p63 F 2017

Fitness feeds on Instagram can perpetuate harmful ideas about the perfect body—but they can also inspire us with bodies that are more like ours J. Wortham *New York Times Magazine* p14 Jl 9 2017

A Fitness Makeover A. FRIEDMAN and T. DIPACE color *Tennis* v53 no2 p60 Mr/Ap 2017

Forge the Maximus Body B. Maximus bw *Men's Health* v32 no3 p40 Ap 2017

GET A LEG UP ON THE TEE B. O'neal and D. Denunzio color *Golf Magazine* v59 no2 p56 F 2017

GET FIT THE 2017 WAY color *Black Enterprise* v47 no5 p70 Ja/F 2017

Get Real A. Nix *Amazing Wellness* v9 no1 p8 Wint 2017

Get Your Group On color *Men's Health* v32 no9 p41 N 2017

good to the CORE [Cover story] T. RUSSO color *Yoga Journal* no291 p66 My 2017

The Guru of Abs J. SCHILDHOUSE color *Muscle & Performance* v9 no11 p40 N 2017

HAPPIER, HEALTHIER, WELLTHIER K. Dold color *Women's Health* v14 no4 p89 My 2017

HAVE A BALL color *Good Housekeeping* v265 no2 p100 Ag 2017

HEART-HEALTHY WISDOM V. PREVISH *Cincinnati Magazine* v50 no5 p128 F 2017

HIIT PLAN [Cover story] J. Metzl color *Runner's World* v52 no1 p58 Ja/F 2017

HOLIDAY HIIT L. McGLASHAN cartoon chart *Muscle & Performance* v8 no12 p54 D 2016

HOP TO IT E. Graves *Martha Stewart Living* p10 Ap 2017

HOW FIT ARE YOU REALLY? K. A. Fetters chart color *Women's Health* v14 no4 p68 My 2017

HOW HEALTHY ARE YOU? J. THOMPSON color *Martha Stewart Living* p48 Mr 2017

How to Be Unbreakable L. LEICHT cartoon color *Women's Health* v14 no9 p68 N 2017

just 3 moves TOWEL TONE-UP E. Shannon color *Good Housekeeping* v264 no1 p102 Ja 1 2017

Life Advice from Kids E. Spitznagel bw cartoon color *Men's Health* v32 no1 p140 Ja/F 2017

Lifting Off S. Apstein and T. Keith color *Sports Illustrated* v126 no1 p16 Ja 9 2017

Look better in the buff T. Anderson color *Health* v31 no8 p37 O 2017

Love on the Run A. SPENCER color *Good Housekeeping* v264 no3 p151 Mr 2017

Make Your Workouts Pay S. MESTEL cartoon color *Men's Health* v32 no8 p25 O 2017

Move the Chains E. Samuel color *Men's Health* v32 no8 p10 O 2017

Moving Toward Joy K. BOLONIK color *Prevention* v69 no2 p36 F 2017

NAMASTAY AWHILE M. Gainsburg bw color diag *Women's Health* v14 no4 p78 My 2017

A New Take on Shipshape M. CROSS color *Kiplinger's Personal Finance* v71 no3 p71 Mr 2017

New Year, New Arms T. Anderson color *Health* v31 no1 p58 Ja 2017

No-Gear Total-Body Blast E. SAMUEL color *Men's Health* v32 no8 p46 O 2017

AN ODE TO RICHARD SIMMONS cartoon *Women's Health* v14 no6 p36 Jl 2017

OIL UP For Results J. WUEBBEN color *Muscle & Performance* v8 no12 p13 D 2016

On the Move Oprah color *O, The Oprah Magazine* p109b Ja 2017

POSTCARDS FROM HELL J. Roth color *Esquire* p51 BigBlack-Book

Power to Transform M. Bean bw *Men's Health* v32 no9 p6 N 2017

The Pull-Up S. Graham-Felsen *New York Times Magazine* p20 Jl 2 2017

PURE ENERGY! V. Tweed color *Amazing Wellness* v9 no4 p38 Summ 2017

Put some pep in your step! *Harvard Health Letter* v42 no8 p1 Je 2017

Redefine Holiday Fitness bw *Men's Health* v31 no10 p69 D 2016

RESOLVE TO 'AGCERCISE' L. F. Prater *Successful Farming* v115 no1 p66 Ja 2017

Rewriting a Family History color *Women's Health* v13 no10 p100 D 2016

RIP, Dreadmill M. Gainsburg cartoon chart color *Women's Health* v14 no1 p84 Ja/F 2017

Secrets of the Super Healthy [Cover story] D. HUDEPOHL cartoon color *Prevention* v69 no1 p74 Ja 2017

Self-care for grown-ups M. Mannarino color *Health* v31 no4 p98 My 2017

SETTING THE PACE C. Cunningham *Washingtonian Magazine* v52 no4 p114 Ja 2017

Show of Strength A. Hess *New York Times Magazine* p19 O 16 2016

SIX STEPS TO MAXIMUM FITNESS M. Easter bw chart color *Men's Health* v32 no3 p39 Ap 2017

SKYE HIGH CONFIDENCE [Cover story] L. Goldman color *Women's Health* v14 no6 p63 Jl 2017

SLIDE INTO A FIT NEW YEAR [Cover story] V. Tweed color *Amazing Wellness* v9 no6 p86 EarlyWint 2017

SPECIAL OPS FITNESS SECRETS [Cover story] B. COURT cartoon color *Men's Health* v32 no4 p94 My 2017

SPRING-CLEAN Your Kitchen M. OZ cartoon *O, The Oprah Magazine* p99 Mr 2017

#SQUAD GOALS C. VAN BUSEN *Atlanta* v56 no9 p118 Ja 2017

START YOUR RESOLUTIONS NOW A. Nix *Amazing Wellness* v9 no6 p8 EarlyWint 2017

The state of Health map *Prevention* v69 no9 p9 O 2017

STEP OUT OF YOUR COMFORT ZONE D. BACKSTROM color *Ebony* v72/73 no12/1 p65 O/N 2017

street style: FITNESS EDITION color *Women's Health* v14 no8 p16 O 2017

A TACTICAL TAPER A. HUTCHINSON color *Runner's World* v52 no9 p22 O 2017

The #TBT Workout E. Abbate color *Glamour* v115 no7 p58 Jl 2017

Tech for Your Fittest Year Yet J. Smith color *Health* v31 no1 p23 Ja 2017

TONE YOUR TUSH A. Reliford color *Good Housekeeping* v265 no1 p92 Jl 2017

TRACKING YOUR WEIGHT LOSS M. Farrar and J. WUEB-BEN color *Muscle & Performance* v8 no12 p15 D 2016

Tracy Anderson's Beautiful Body Secrets [Cover story] R. S. Frazier color *Health* v31 no4 p82 My 2017

Train Trendy: Boutique fitness classes are popular--but are they right for your cross-training? L. WINGENROTH *Dance Magazine* v91 no9 p44 S 2017

Turn & Burn L. McGLASHAN chart color *Muscle & Performance* v9 no7 p16 Jl 2017

THE ULTIMATE PHA FAT BLAST L. McGLASHAN chart color *Muscle & Performance* v9 no5 p16 My 2017

Von Miller: How an MVP Gets Better J. Nosek color *Men's Health* v31 no10 p54 D 2016

Walk This Way S. ALTSHUL color *AARP: The Magazine* v60 no4A p17 Je/Jl 2017

The Walt Whitman Workout Plan N. Hopper color *Time* v189 no5 p53 F 13 2017

What's My Age Again? E. Freud color *InStyle* v24 no9 p206 S 2017

#WH STRONG color *Women's Health* v14 no9 p16 N 2017

Work It Out(side) K. Casteel color *Missouri Life* v44 no6 p76 S 2017

Your Fit in 10 Plan cartoon *Prevention* v69 no2 p16 F 2017

Your Fit in 10 Plan color *Prevention* v69 no11 p15 N 2017

Your Hour-by-Hour Plan for LIVING BETTER C. Pikul cartoon *O, The Oprah Magazine* p94 Mr 2017

Physical fitness center personnel

Stay Snatched This Season Karla and Rob color *Ebony* v72 no9 p64 Jl/Ag 2017

Physical fitness centers

THE ADVENTURE ISSUE color *Men's Health* v32 no6 p99 Ag 2017

Aging Parents color *New Orleans Magazine* v51 no6 p135 Ap 2017

EGREGIOUS ACTS OF EXERCISE N. TUMMINELLO color *Muscle & Performance* v9 no10 p46 O 2017

Escape Gym Fees! A. Adamczyk color *Money* v46 no6 p21 Jl 2017

Exercise for Couch Potatoes color *Prevention* v69 no8 p16 Ag 2017

FIGHT CLUB L. SCHOLZ *Atlanta* v57 no6 p46 O 2017

A Fitness Makeover A. FRIEDMAN and T. DIPACE color *Tennis* v53 no2 p60 Mr/Ap 2017

Get Your Group On color *Men's Health* v32 no9 p41 N 2017

A Gym of Angels E. SULLIVAN cartoon color *Esquire* v167 no1 p48 F 2017

Gym with a View S. MURRAY color *Power & Motoryacht* v33 no3 p32 Mr 2017

the health nut A. Brightfield *Better Homes & Gardens* v94 no11 p158 N 2016

NINA'S GREATEST BEAUTY HITS color *Harper's Bazaar* no3656 p346 S 2017

The Rise of the Ninja Gym D. Eng color *Fortune* v75 no1 p24 Ja 1 2017

SLIDE INTO A FIT NEW YEAR [Cover story] V. Tweed color *Amazing Wellness* v9 no6 p86 EarlyWint 2017

Welcome to Sendhaus™: America's Hippest New Climbing Gym K. CORRIGAN color *Climbing* no355 p38 Ag 2017

Physical fitness centers—Equipment & supplies

THE WORLD IS YOUR GYM A. McCARRON, L. ROSEN-BAUM et al bw color *Men's Health* v32 no6 p114 Ag 2017

Physical fitness centers—Evaluation

BEST BETS img *New York* p54 Ja 9 2017

Got Orange? J. DeBold color *New Orleans Magazine* v51 no7 p150 My 2017

On the Rebound E. Batuman bw *Vogue* v207 no11 p154 N 2017

Palm Springs color *Los Angeles Magazine* v62 no10 p147 O 2017

Rent the Runway S. FITZ-GERALD *Los Angeles Magazine* p72 D 2016

StairMaster to Heaven C. BATTAN color *GQ: Gentlemen's Quarterly* v86 no11 p76 N 2016

There's No 'I' in Tone House J. Kelly color *Bloomberg Businessweek* no4528 p72 Je 26 2017

Physical fitness centers—Humor

Laugh Lines *Reader's Digest* v189 no1128 p93 Mr 2017

Physical fitness centers—Officials & employees

Ask anything V. Vlachonis, J. Blackburn et al bw color *Women's Health* v14 no4 p18 My 2017

Physical fitness centers—Social aspects

The 10 Simple Rules of Gym Etiquette M. ZIMMERMAN cartoon *Men's Health* v32 no9 p46 N 2017

Physical fitness for men

BIGGER, STRONGER, FASTER, BROKENER G. Bishop color diag *Sports Illustrated* v127 no6 p38 Ag 28 2017

THE EXCHANGE B. Boyé and A. Eaves bw cartoon color graph *Men's Health* v32 no5 p16 Je 2017

Fat-Shame for Guys P. SAGAL color *Runner's World* v52 no8 p50 S 2017

Finish Your Six-Pack in Just 10 Minutes bw color *Men's Health* v32 no2 p116 Mr 2017

Living by the Eastwood Code P. FLAX cartoon color *Men's Health* v32 no5 p27 Je 2017

MH WORLD color *Men's Health* v32 no9 p4 N 2017

Swing Shift J. Gorant and T. Keith color *Sports Illustrated* v126 no15 p22 My 29 2017

Physical fitness for older people

Endless Recess C. Ianzito color *AARP: The Magazine* v60 no5A p16 Ag/S 2017

Physical fitness for women

10-Minute Clean Meals color *Prevention* v69 no1 p58 Ja 2017

10 Minutes a Day [Cover story] J. B. SOUTHERLAND bw color *Prevention* v69 no1 p46 Ja 2017

10 Minutes to Slim & Strong [Cover story] color *Prevention* v69 no1 p56 Ja 2017

And Down 140 Pounds! color *Women's Health* v14 no3 p114 Ap 2017

BEST SHAPE OF YOUR LIFE [Cover story] M. Gainsburg color *Women's Health* v13 no10 p76 D 2016

A BODY IN MOTION & A BODY AT REST [Cover story] M. GAINSBURG color *Women's Health* v14 no4 p156 My 2017

Change Is Good B. O'Dair color *Prevention* v69 no1 p3 Ja 2017

Get More WH color *Women's Health* v13 no10 p16 D 2016

July/August All-Star color *Women's Health* v14 no6 p16 Jl 2017

Leatherneck Ladies color *Weekly Standard* v22 no37 p2 Je 5 2017

MASTERING YOUR BODY L. MCGLASHAN color *Muscle & Performance* v9 no6 p28 Je 2017

October All-Star color *Women's Health* v14 no8 p14 O 2017

SPRING CLEAN YOUR FITNESS ROUTINE [Cover story] L. LEICHT cartoon color *Women's Health* v14 no3 p130 Ap 2017

SWEATY, SANDY, SCULPTED M. Gainsburg color *Women's Health* v14 no5 p136 Je 2017

Your Fit in 10 Plan cartoon color *Prevention* v69 no5 p16 My 2017

Physical fitness for women—Equipment & supplies

HOW FAST COULD YOU RUN... HOW FAR COULD YOU GO... IF YOU TOOK OFF YOUR TRACKER AND RAN FREE? M. Easter color *Women's Health* v14 no7 p168 S 2017

Physical fitness mobile apps

Hot-Workout Alert S. G. Levy color *Glamour* v114 no11 p114 N 2016

How to Stalk Your Pet J. Kirkland color *AARP: The Magazine* v60 no4A p10 Je/Jl 2017

I Need (an App) Consult J. LANGSTON *USA Today Magazine* v145 no2862 p51 Mr 2017

TECH RX *Cincinnati Magazine* v50 no4 p73 Ja 2017

Walk This Way B. Borrell chart color diag graph *Consumer Reports* v82 no8 p8 Ag 2017

Physical fitness testing—Equipment & supplies

Walk This Way B. Borrell chart color diag graph *Consumer Reports* v82 no8 p8 Ag 2017

Physical fitness—Competitions

Welcome to the Sufferfest [Cover story] T. DASWICK color *Men's Health* v32 no4 p10 My 2017

Physical fitness—Computer network resources

Forge Real Fitness with Top E-Trainers L. ROSENBAUM color *Men's Health* v32 no7 p45 S 2017

Physical fitness—Equipment & supplies

How Accurate Is Your Fitness Tracker? L. SCHLEY color graph *Discover* v38 no7 p18 S 2017

Physical fitness—Evaluation

Get Action Star Strong color *Health* v31 no6 p14 Jl 2017

The Real Reason I Work Out N. Blades, J. Dunn et al color *Health* v31 no2 p120 Mr 2017

Wake Up and Work Out! K. Canning color *Health* v31 no6 p24 Jl 2017

Physical fitness—Genetic aspects

Do You Have SKINNY GENES? A. Synnott color *InStyle* v24 no1 p64 Ja 2017

Physical fitness—Social aspects

Stay Snatched This Season Karla and Rob color *Ebony* v72 no9 p64 Jl/Ag 2017

Physical sciences

See also

Electronics

Materials science

Physics

Approaches to studying our history M. Berry *Physics Today* v70 no3 p11 Mr 2017

Important factors in shaping physics identities E. De Pree and J. M. Grossman *Physics Today* v70 no5 p12 My 2017

Physical therapists

Are You Rolling Wrong? N. Wozny color *Dance Magazine* v91 no3 p40 Mr 2017

CHANGING THE FACE OF THERAPY J. Thompson color *O, The Oprah Magazine* p84 S 2017

Physical therapy

See also

Baths

Phototherapy

Thermotherapy

Don't shrug off shoulder pain *Harvard Health Letter* v42 no10 p6 Ag 2017

HITTING REFRESH D. WILLEY color *Runner's World* v52 no4 p10 My 2017

PRE-HABILITATION L. MCGLASHAN color *Muscle & Performance* v9 no1 p26 Ja 2017

the Black Belt Helen Ouyang color *Harper's Magazine* v335 no2005 p27 Je 2017

Who Saved Whom? W. Sheridan bw *Commonweal* v144 no4 p31 F 24 2017

Physicians (General practice)

2016 Best Doctors and Pediatric Specialists *D: The Magazine of Dallas* v43 no10 p130 O 2016

Tips to find a new doctor *Harvard Health Letter* v42 no9 p5 Jl 2017

Physicians as businesspeople

Doctors Without Patients A. Mostue *Bloomberg Businessweek* no4537 p34 S 11 2017

Physicians' assistants

Help in the Office: The Physician Extender Will See You Now B. Lutz color *New Orleans Magazine* v51 no10 p46 Ag 2017

Physicians—Attitudes

Patients Get the Personal Touch S. LUTHRA cartoon *Kiplinger's Personal Finance* v71 no1 p68 Ja 2017

Physicians—Corrupt practices

Burzynski Sanctioned by Texas Medical Board R. Blaskiewicz *Skeptical Inquirer* v41 no4 p7 Jl/Ag 2017

POST SCRIPT: HOW A SMALL-TIME CHICAGO DOCTOR CAME TO THE SOUTHEASTERN OHIO TOWN OF PORTSMOUTH AND HELPED SPUR AN EPIDEMIC P. EIL *Cincinnati Magazine* v50 no10 p66 Jl 2017

Physicians—Humor

Sketchbook / Graphic Review A. Spiegelman *New York Times Book Review* p51 N 13 2016

Physicians—Interviews

Doctor on Call D. Kupfer color *Progressive* p24 D 2016/Ja 2017

woman to woman A. Nix color *Amazing Wellness* v9 no3 p40 EarlySumm 2017

Physicians—Malpractice

Conscripting Doctors W. J. SMITH *Weekly Standard* v22 no6 p10 O 17 2016

Physicians—Moral & ethical aspects

Can a Therapist Fake His Online Reviews? K. A. Appiah *New York Times Magazine* p20 F 26 2017

Physicians—New Jersey

States Must Face Their "Pain" *USA Today Magazine* v146 no2866 p18 Jl 2017

Physicians—Societies, etc.

Ask a Doctor: A feminist-founded group of Ohio doctors is vocal in its support of health care and abortion rights C. HAHN *Ms.* v27 no3 p12 Fall 2017

Physicians—Sweden

Hans Rosling (1948–2017) B. Gates and M. Gates color *Science* v355 no6331 p1268 Mr 24 2017

Physicians—Training of

How One Hospital Turns Doctors into Leaders J. Dudley *Harvard Business Review Digital Articles* p2 D 12 2014

Physicians—United States

2017 TOP DOCTORS *Indianapolis Monthly* p69 N 2017

41 *Prevention* v69 no7 p10 Jl 2017

923,308 *Prevention* v69 no9 p8 O 2017

BEST DOCS: 559 PHYSICIANS IN 77 SPECIALTIES [Cover story] S. RAVITS color *New Orleans Magazine* v51 no10 p84 Ag 2017

BEST DOCTORS IN WASHINGTON *Washingtonian Magazine* v52 no2 p159 N 2016

BEST DOCTORS *Louisiana Life* v37 no2 p59 N/D 2016

Immigrant Doctors Provide Better Care, According to a Study of 1.2 Million Hospitalizations Yusuke Tsugawa, A. B. Jena et al color *Harvard Business Review Digital Articles* p2 F 3 2017

PHYSICIAN BURNOUT: The number of overworked, emotionally exhausted doctors has reached epidemic proportions. Stressed-out doctors have less time with patients and are more prone to making medical errors. Fixing the problem is a matter of national... N. STEDMAN *Saturday Evening Post* v289 no4 p46 Jl/Ag 2017

THE PROGNOSIS S. FENNESSY *Atlanta* v57 no3 p20 Jl 2017

Taking Care *Islamic Horizons* v46 no3 p6 My/Je 2017

Thomas Earl Starzl (1926–2017) J. J. Fung color *Science* v356 no6337 p491 My 5 2017

TOP DOCS 2017: Every year we present a roster of the best metro Atlanta doctors, as chosen by their peers. On the following

pages, find 720 of the area's most trusted physicians--our biggest list ever C. VAN DUSEN, J. GREEN et al *Atlanta* v57 no3 p65 Jl 2017

TOP DOCTORS 2016 [Cover story] *Washingtonian Magazine* v52 no2 p100 N 2016

TOP DOCTORS 2017 *Cincinnati Magazine* v51 no1 p96 O 2017

Physicians—United States—Social conditions—21st century

Dr. Dare Kill *Weekly Standard* v23 no4 p3 O 2 2017

Physicists

Abraham Szöke S. B. Libby and M. D. Rosen *Physics Today* v70 no10 p76 O 2017

Alexei Alexeyevich Abrikosov M. R. Norman and A. A. Varlamov *Physics Today* v70 no10 p73 O 2017

Anthony Philip French P. H. Fisher and C. H. Holbrow *Physics Today* v70 no6 p74 Je 2017

Arthur Hinton Rosenfeld A. Gadgil, D. B. Goldstein et al *Physics Today* v70 no9 p72 S 2017

Cornelis A. Gehrels S. B. Cenko and F. Reddy *Physics Today* v70 no10 p75 O 2017

Deborah Jin *Physics Today* v70 no1 p69 Ja 2017

Discoveries and explanations C. Day *Physics Today* v70 no3 p8 Mr 2017

Double Darkness [Cover story] T. Siegfried color *Science News* v190 no13 p30 D 24 2016

Edwin Leo Goldwasser R. A. Carrigan and R. O. Simmons *Physics Today* v70 no9 p70 S 2017

European detector 'sees' space ripples color *Science* v357 no6359 p14 O 6 2017

Gabriela González M. Hagan *Current Biography* v77 no10 p35 O 2016

Gary Steigman R. Scherrer, J. Beacom et al *Physics Today* v70 no8 p72 Ag 2017

Harassment in our community: An open letter *Physics Today* v69 no10 p12 O 2016

James Watson Cronin H. J. Frisch, J. E. Pilcher et al *Physics Today* v70 no3 p72 Mr 2017

Kerson Huang Chi Xiong *Physics Today* v70 no9 p71 S 2017

Kwok-Yung Lo P. A. Vanden Bout and A. I. Sargent *Physics Today* v70 no8 p71 Ag 2017

Leo Leroy Beranek G. C. Maling Jr and E. J. W. Wood *Physics Today* v70 no10 p74 O 2017

Leonid Keldysh F. Capasso, P. Corkum et al *Physics Today* v70 no6 p75 Je 2017

Lev Petrovich Gor'kov G. Boebinger, S. Iordansky et al *Physics Today* v70 no5 p68 My 2017

Martin Moses Block F. L. Halzen *Physics Today* v69 no10 p66 O 2016

M. G. K. Menon (1928–2016) B. Venkatasubba Sreekantan and R. Cowsik color *Science* v355 no6325 p586 F 10 2017

Mildred S. Dresselhaus M. Endo, A. Jorio et al *Physics Today* v70 no6 p73 Je 2017

Patent work blends science, business, and law T. Feder *Physics Today* v70 no10 p36 O 2017

Paul Frederick Zweifel N. J. McCormick, C. E. Siewert et al *Physics Today* v70 no8 p73 Ag 2017

Physicists without borders A. P. Gast *Physics Today* v70 no1 p10 Ja 2017

Robert Gomer D. Menzel, M. C. Tringides et al *Physics Today* v70 no5 p67 My 2017

Roger Wolfe Cohen P. Eisenberger, M. P. Fricke et al *Physics Today* v70 no8 p70 Ag 2017

Sidney David Drell J. D. Bjorken, R. L. Garwin et al *Physics Today* v70 no9 p69 S 2017

Spartak Timofeevich Belyaev A. Barabanov and V. Zelevinsky *Physics Today* v70 no6 p72 Je 2017

Stanley Mandelstam Ling-Lie Chau *Physics Today* v70 no5 p69 My 2017

Thomas Walter Bannerman Kibble E. Copeland, N. Turok et al *Physics Today* v69 no12 p68 D 2016

Physicists—Congresses

Collider data hint at new particle E. CONOVER color *Science News* v191 no9 p16 My 13 2017

Physicists—United States

Bacteria's physical playbook T. H. Saey color *Science News* v192 no6 p17 O 14 2017

David Ritz Finkelstein P. Cvitanović and L. Susskind *Physics To-*

day v70 no2 p68 F 2017

Edward Joseph Lofgren W. Barletta and J. Alonso *Physics Today* v70 no2 p69 F 2017

First physicist in Congress dies D. Kramer *Physics Today* v70 no10 p38 O 2017

Mobilizing US physics in World War I Hagmann *Physics Today* v70 no8 p44 Ag 2017

Physics

See also

Astronomy

Astrophysics

Biophysics

Electricity

Force & energy

Geophysics

Particle physics

Permeability

Radiation

Superposition principle (Physics)

Approaches to studying our history M. Berry *Physics Today* v70 no3 p11 Mr 2017

Guns on campus: Is that physics? D. A. Roberts *Physics Today* v70 no6 p15 Je 2017

NEW BOOKS *Physics Today* v70 no3 p63 Mr 2017

PHYSICS IN 2116 S. RICHARD *Physics Today* v69 no12 p39 D 2016

Quantum simulations with ultracold atoms in optical lattices C. Gross and I. Bloch cartoon color diag *Science* v357 no6355 p995 S 8 2017

Physics equipment

Focus on test, measurement, and analytical equipment A. Mandelis *Physics Today* v70 no8 p66 Ag 2017

Physics experiments

A biology journal provides a lesson in peer review R. E. Goldstein *Physics Today* v69 no12 p10 D 2016

Physics literature

The state of open access C. Day *Physics Today* v70 no5 p8 My 2017

Physics periodicals

Against the rising flood of information C. Day *Physics Today* v70 no9 p8 S 2017

Physics research

Hassani replies S. Hassani *Physics Today* v69 no11 p12 N 2016

Pseudoscience versus science M. Beauregard, N. Trent et al *Physics Today* v69 no11 p10 N 2016

Yuri Milner S. NADIS color *Discover* v38 no3 p16 Ap 2017

Physics students

Two-year colleges teach physics to widening range of students T. Feder *Physics Today* v69 no11 p26 N 2016

Physics teachers

Diversity in physics: Are you part of the problem? A. Nelson *Physics Today* v70 no5 p10 My 2017

Important factors in shaping physics identities E. De Pree and J. M. Grossman *Physics Today* v70 no5 p12 My 2017

In the digital age, physics students and professors prefer paper textbooks: Whether electronic textbooks become more popular may depend on making them more interactive and user-friendly M. Baldwin *Physics Today* v70 no8 p30 Ag 2017

Methods for teaching traditional physics K. K. Shah *Physics Today* v69 no12 p12 D 2016

The past and future of PHYSICS EDUCATION REFORM V. K. Otero and D. E. Meltzer *Physics Today* v70 no5 p50 My 2017

Physics textbooks

In the digital age, physics students and professors prefer paper textbooks: Whether electronic textbooks become more popular may depend on making them more interactive and user-friendly M. Baldwin *Physics Today* v70 no8 p30 Ag 2017

Physics—Computer network resources

Our new website C. Day *Physics Today* v70 no1 p8 Ja 2017

Physics—Information services

Against the rising flood of information C. Day *Physics Today* v70 no9 p8 S 2017

Physics—International cooperation

International Union of Pure and Applied Physics and you B. H. J. McKellar *Physics Today* v70 no10 p9 O 2017

Physics—Study & teaching

The beauty of outreach P. Riccardi cartoon *Science* v354 no6312 p674 N 4 2016

Commentary How to teach me physics: Tradition is not always a virtue R. Heras *Physics Today* v70 no3 p10 Mr 2017

Physics education research and student development J. Winfrey *Physics Today* v70 no2 p10 F 2017

Physics—Study & teaching (Higher)

A bridge between undergraduate and doctoral degrees T. Hodapp and K. S. Woodle *Physics Today* v70 no2 p50 F 2017

Two-year colleges teach physics to widening range of students T. Feder *Physics Today* v69 no11 p26 N 2016

Physiognomy

Are Facial Expressions Universal? T. BURRELL color *Discover* v38 no5 p18 Je 2017

Physiological aspects of aging

Old Money A. Hess *New York Times Magazine* p13 S 17 2017

Physiological aspects of sleep

See also

Sleep—Stages

Roughing It M. KADEY color *Muscle & Performance* v9 no9 p56 S 2017

The Stuff of Dreams T. Lewis color *Scientific American* v317 no1 p16 Jl 2017

Physiological aspects of walking

The No-Excuses Guide to Walking E. Gradwell color *Prevention* v69 no7 p82 Jl 2017

Physiological effect of glyphosate

Guess Who's Ghostwriting Monsanto's Safety Reviews P. Waldman, T. Stecker et al color *Bloomberg Businessweek* no4534 p14 Ag 14 2017

Roundup: The Usual Suspect P. WALDMAN, L. MULVANY et al color graph *Bloomberg Businessweek* no4530 p42 Jl 17 2017

Physiological effects of antidepressants

AMAZING NEWS V. Tweed *Amazing Wellness* v8 no2 p12 Spr 2016

Physiological effects of aspirin

Aspirin vs. Cancer V. Callier color *Scientific American* v316 no5 p24 My 2017

How Top Docs Avoid Cancer J. BIANCHI color *Men's Health* v32 no7 p82 S 2017

Physiological effects of blue light

EYE HEALTH IN THE DIGITAL AGE J. Stringham color *Amazing Wellness* p26 Fall 2017

Physiological effects of caffeine

BUZZ WORTHY L. MCGLASHAN color *Muscle & Performance* v9 no6 p26 Je 2017

Five to Fight Fat A. GONZALEZ color *Muscle & Performance* v9 no9 p28 S 2017

Physiological effects of chemicals

See also

Physiological effects of caffeine

Chemical safety must extend to ecosystems J. R. Rohr, C. J. Salice et al *Science* v356 no6341 p917 Je 1 2017

Physiological effects of chemotherapy

The Danger of Chromotherapy: Despite the lack of scientific evidence for its effectiveness and its use of esoteric theories to describe its mechanisms of action, chromotherapy has become popular. But is It safe? S. POINT *Skeptical Inquirer* v41 no4 p50 Jl/Ag 2017

Physiological effects of essential oils

OIL Boom J. BUNTIN color *Vogue* v207 no6 p78 Je 2017

Physiological effects of heat

See also

Heat adaptation

BEAT the HEAT A. SHAFFER color *Better Homes & Gardens* v95 no7 p161 Jl 2017

Keep Your COOL at SUMMER SHOWS K. Brittle chart color *Dressage Today* v23 no10 p58 Jl 2017

Physiological Stress and Ethanol Accumulation in Tree Stems and Woody Tissues at Sublethal Temperatures from Fire R. G. KELSEY and D. J. WESTLIND *BioScience* v67 no5 p443 My 2017

WHEN LIGHT color *Women's Health* v14 no6 p38 Jl 2017

Physiological effects of lead

Phytoremediation of Lead: What Works, What Doesn't R. BLAUSTEIN *BioScience* v67 no9 p868 S 2017

Physiological effects of leucine
MASTERING YOUR BODY L. MCGLASHAN color *Muscle & Performance* v9 no6 p28 Je 2017

Physiological effects of proteins
PICKING THE PERFECT PROTEIN D. N. JACKSON color *Muscle & Performance* v9 no6 p51 Je 2017
Protein Surprises in The Produce Section J. SCHMID and M. SAUER color *Reader's Digest* v190 no1133 p38 S 2017

Physiological effects of salt
shake it off A. OGLETHORPE, J. Brill et al color *Better Homes & Gardens* v95 no7 p168 Jl 2017

Physiological effects of sodium
Surprising News About Salt M. Oaklander color *Time* v189 no18 p26 My 15 2017

Physiological effects of ultraviolet radiation—Prevention
your get-real SUN-CARE GUIDE M. R. CHADWICK cartoon color *Better Homes & Gardens* v95 no6 p18 Je 2017

Physiological effects of vitamin D
NEWS FROM THE World of Medicine color *Reader's Digest* v190 no1135 p52 N 2017

Physiological effects of water
Delicious Hydration Tips L. DIAMOND color *Reader's Digest* v189 no1131 p52 Je 2017

Physiological research
The emergent physics of animal locomotion: Many physiological systems must work together to enable movement in animals and other organisms. Neuromechanics explores how those systems interact with each other and the environment S. Sponberg *Physics Today* v70 no9 p34 S 2017

Physiological therapeutics
See also
 Baths
 Exercise therapy
 Massage therapy
 Music therapy
 Physical therapy
 Reflexotherapy
PRE-HABILITATION L. MCGLASHAN color *Muscle & Performance* v9 no1 p26 Ja 2017

Phytic acid
FAFQ K. Patel and J. WUEBBEN color *Muscle & Performance* v9 no6 p13 Je 2017

Phytochemicals
See also
 Resveratrol
Score All Your Fruits and Vegetables cartoon chart *Men's Health* v32 no8 p56 O 2017

Phytochromes
Light-sensing phytochromes feel the heat K. J. Halliday and S. J. Davis bibl color *Science* v354 no6314 p832 N 18 2016

Phytopathogenic microorganisms—Research
Pathogens on the Move: A 100-Year Global Experiment with Planted Eucalypts T. I. BURGESS and M. J. WINGFIELD *BioScience* v67 no1 p14 Ja 2017

Phytophthora sojae
A paralogous decoy protects Phytophthora sojae apoplastic effector PsXEG1 from a host inhibitor Z. Ma, L. Zhu et al bibl graph *Science* v355 no6326 p710 F 17 2017

Phytoplankton
See also
 Algae
 Marine phytoplankton
Biological Pump B. Edwards color *Oceanus* v51 no2 p56 Wint 2016
Spring Arrives Earlier in the Ocean Too: WARMING OCEANS ARE SHIFTING MARINE ECOSYSTEMS E. Koenig *Oceanus* v52 no2 p25 Spr 2017

Phytoremediation
Phytoremediation of Lead: What Works, What Doesn't R. BLAUSTEIN *BioScience* v67 no9 p868 S 2017

Phytotherapy
See also
 Therapeutic use of coffee
Natural Skin Savers color *Health* v31 no6 p12 Jl 2017

Pi, Xiaoqing
China's Numbers Man color *Bloomberg Businessweek* no4516

p12 Mr 27 2017
China Unleashes Its Farmers color *Bloomberg Businessweek* no4540 p36 O 2 2017

Piaggio & C. SpA
A Cruiser for a Superhero D. CURCURITO color *Popular Mechanics* p46 F 2017

Piaggio Fast Forward (Company)
A Suitcase That Follows Its Owner J. Zorthian color *Time* v189 no6 p21 F 20 2017

Pianists
Aaron Parks T. PANKEN color *Downbeat* v83 no11 p106 N 2016
ART HIRAHARA D. Ouellette color *Downbeat* v84 no3 p22 Mr 2017
Deserving Honorees B. REED bw *Downbeat* v84 no8 p8 Ag 2017
ELEW Rejoins 'Jazz Republic' C. Wolff color *Downbeat* v83 no11 p19 N 2016
EMMET COHEN Student of History T. Panken color *Downbeat* v84 no2 p22 F 2017
In Your Hands N. MacLaughlin bw *Men's Health* v32 no2 p(Sp)30 Mr 2017
Leon Russell D. FRICKE bw *Rolling Stone* no1276 p28 D 15 2016
Misha Mengelberg Dies at 81 T. Panken bw *Downbeat* v84 no5 p19 My 2017
NAVIGATE NORTHWARD M. Gaffney *Washingtonian Magazine* v52 no8 p223 My 2017
NO CIGAR A. Gopnik cartoon *New Yorker* v92 no47 p20 Ja 30 2017
Revealing Liaisons J. Hale bw *Downbeat* v84 no1 p32 Ja 2017
THELONIOUS MONK J. Hale bw *Downbeat* v84 no1 p30 Ja 2017
Van Cliburn, To Russia With Love T. TEACHOUT *Commentary* v142 no3 p50 O 2016

Pianists—Biography
Yuja Wang M. Rich color *Current Biography* v78 no1 p86 Ja 2017

Pianists—United States
Leon Russell I. Guzmán color *Time* v188 no22-23 p13 N/D 2016

Piano
At Christie's M. Willoughby color *Magazine Antiques* v184 no1 p84 Ja/F 2017
'In Tune' with the Community M. Acquino *Parks & Recreation* v52 no8 p80 Ag 2017
Karl-Anthony Towns M. Hagan color *Current Biography* v78 no4 p82 Ap 2017
Liner Notes: Ruth Bader Ginsburg L. T. GUINTHER *Opera News* v81 no10 p68 Ap 2017

Piano music
GOINGS ON ABOUT TOWN color *New Yorker* v93 no8 p4 Ap 10 2017
Your True Stories IN 100 WORDS L. LESHAW, L. ALBRECHT et al color *Reader's Digest* v189 no1129 p25 Ap 2017

Piano music (1 hand)
Improvising Freely Over Complex Left-Hand Keyboard Figures V. NESELOVSKYI color *Downbeat* v84 no9 p92 S 2017

Piano students
Resolved to Play D. GUASPARI *Weekly Standard* v22 no5 p41 O 10 2016

Piano—Evaluation
Kawai ES110 Digital Piano J. Ann Daugherty color *Downbeat* v84 no9 p99 S 2017
Play Me a Tune B. Ankosko color *Sound & Vision* v82 no1 p74 Ja 2017
Roland FP-90 R. Gehrenbeck color *Downbeat* v84 no1 p107 Ja 2017
Roland RD-2000 C. Neville color *Downbeat* v84 no9 p98 S 2017
Yamaha MX88 R. Gehrenbeck color *Downbeat* v84 no9 p98 S 2017

Piano—Instruction & study
Resolved to Play D. GUASPARI *Weekly Standard* v22 no5 p41 O 10 2016

Piano—Performance
Creating a Convincing Solo Piano Performance R. PIKET and R. Piket bw color *Downbeat* v83 no12 p102 D 2016
SLEIGHT OF HAND A. ROSS cartoon *New Yorker* v92 no44 p74 Ja 9 2017

Piano Teacher's Pupil, The (Short story)

THE PIANO TEACHER'S PUPIL W. TREVOR cartoon *New Yorker* v93 no18 p56 Je 26 2017

Piatt, Adam

home & help img *New York* p96 Mr 6 2017

Piatt, Byron

IRON MAN B. COLVIN color *Phi Kappa Phi Forum* v96 no4 p3 Wint 2016

Piazza, Jo

Love Advice I Wish Would Die color *Glamour* v115 no4 p135 Ap 2017

Piazza, Roberto

Statistical Physics: A Prelude and Fugue for Engineers E. Chimowitz *Physics Today* v70 no10 p62 O 2017

Piazza, Tim

A DEATH AT PENN STATE C. FLANAGAN color *Atlantic* v320 no4 p92 N 2017

Fatal Initiation B. WALLACE color *Vanity Fair* v59 no11 p134 N 2017

Picabia, Francis, 1879-1953

PICABIA, GRASSHOPPER OF MODERN ART bw cartoon color *ARTnews* v115 no3 p159 Fall 2016

Picabia's Big Moment S. Schwartz color *New York Review of Books* v64 no3 p12 F 23 2017

Picabia, Francis, 1879-1953—Exhibitions

ART color *New Yorker* v93 no5 p10 Mr 20 2017

PICABIA'S MONSTERS B. SCHWABSKY color il *Nation* v304 no8 p35 Mr 13 2017

TROUBLE MAKER P. SCHJELDAHL cartoon *New Yorker* v92 no39 p92 N 28 2016

Winter Preview A. K. Scott cartoon *New Yorker* v92 no37 p24 N 14 2016

Picador (Company)

Deals R. DEAHL color *Publishers Weekly* v263 no47 p12 N 21 2016

Picard, Nicolas

The extent of forest in dryland biomes [Cover story] chart map *Science* v356 no6338 p635 My 12 2017

Positive biodiversity-productivity relationship predominant in global forests bibl chart graph map *Science* v354 no6309 paaf8957-1 O 14 2016

Picard, Seb—Interviews

SEB PICARD P. Harrington bw cartoon color *Snowboarder* v29 no4 p50 D 2016

Picardie, Justine

DIOR'S NEW GUARD color *Harper's Bazaar* no3651 p410 Mr 2017

INTERVIEW WITH THE MAESTRO color *Harper's Bazaar* no3657 p236 O 2017

Picasso, Pablo, 1881-1973

BIRTH OF THE PICASSO H. NYHART bw *Chicago* v66 no5 p30 My 2017

Pablo's Pots A. BROWN color *Forbes* v198 no6 p32 N 8 2016

STREET ART A. KONERMANN *Cincinnati Magazine* v50 no7 p62 Ap 2017

Picasso, Pablo, 1881-1973—Exhibitions

When Diego met Pablo, in Los Angeles cartoon *Magazine Antiques* v184 no1 p36 Ja/F 2017

Piccadilly Circus (London, England)

Piccadilly Circus Goes Dark for the Summer *British Heritage Travel* v38 no2 p7 Mr/Ap 2017

Piccard, Bertrand

Quotable Quotes *Reader's Digest* v189 no1130 p140 My 2017

Piccard, Jacques

SPECIAL EXPERIENCE K. Krause *Lapham's Quarterly* v10 no2 p192 Spr 2017

Piccinotti, Silvia

Lee Rubin: Our mentor and role model *Science* v355 no6327 p806 F 24 2017

Picciola, Manny

The New World of Mini Consumer Packaged Goods *Harvard Business Review Digital Articles* p2 S 26 2016

Piccioli, Pierpaolo—Interviews

CP WHEN CHRISTY MET PIERPAOLO L. Brown color *InStyle* v24 no3 p330 Mr 2017

Piccioni, G.

Seasonal exposure of carbon dioxide ice on the nucleus of comet 67P/Churyumov-Gerasimenko bibl bw graph *Science* v354 no6319 p1563 D 23 2016

Piccorossi, Vanessa York

Speak up color *U.S. Catholic* v82 no4 p5 Ap 2017

Pichia

Common fungus may raise asthma risk R. EHRENBERG *Science News* v191 no5 p16 Mr 18 2017

Picidae

See also

Woodpeckers

Woodpeckers THE ENGINEERS OF ECOSYSTEMS J. LLOYD *American Forests* v123 no3 p16 Fall 2017

Pick a Chair (Theatrical production)

Movement, Amplified B. GOLDEN bw *Chicago* v66 no10 p76 O 2017

Pick Your Poison (Music)

Seeds Sown and Grown HADLEY color *Downbeat* v84 no9 p66 S 2017

Pick-your-own farms

Apple-Picking Time R. BROOKHISER color il *National Review* v68 no20 p47 N 7 2016

Pickard, Joseph M.

Neonatal acquisition of Clostridia species protects against colonization by bacterial pathogens diag *Science* v356 no6335 p315 Ap 21 2017

Pickens, James

50 Reasons to Love Being 50+ color *AARP: The Magazine* v59 no1A p49 D 2015/Ja 2016

This Is How We Do R. Love color *AARP: The Magazine* v59 no1A p5 D 2015/Ja 2016

PICKER, LENNY

A 21st-Century Agatha Christie color *Publishers Weekly* v264 no25 p84 Je 19 2017

Art Noir color *Publishers Weekly* v263 no44 p50 O 31 2016

"At Least We Gave Them the Railways" color *Publishers Weekly* v264 no11 p58 Mr 13 2017

Bishop's Murder Case color *Publishers Weekly* v264 no2 p42 Ja 9 2017

A Complex Conclave *Publishers Weekly* v263 no39 p66 S 26 2016

The Death of One Man Is a Tragedy color *Publishers Weekly* v264 no29 p196 Jl 17 2017

Gods and Monsters color *Publishers Weekly* v264 no41 p44 O 9 2017

Is Holmes Where the Heart Is? *Publishers Weekly* v264 no34 p89 Ag 21 2017

Lost Memories color *Publishers Weekly* v264 no16 p44 Ap 17 2017

Masks and Murder *Publishers Weekly* v264 no19 p37 My 8 2017

Murder Analytics *Publishers Weekly* v264 no35 p116 Ag 28 2017

Murder in East Germany bw *Publishers Weekly* v264 no25 p92 Je 19 2017

Murderous Storms color *Publishers Weekly* v264 no13 p77 Mr 27 2017

Private Investigator and Redeemer color *Publishers Weekly* v263 no51 p126 D 12 2016

Pushing the Envelopes *Publishers Weekly* v264 no9 p76 F 27 2017

PW TALKS WITH BRAD RICCA bw *Publishers Weekly* v263 no46 p42 N 14 2016

Rain of Terror color *Publishers Weekly* v264 no39 p86 S 25 2017

Southern Discomfort color *Publishers Weekly* v264 no26 p129 Je 26 2017

Staying Alive color *Publishers Weekly* v263 no45 p34 N 7 2016

Telling Overlooked Stories color *Publishers Weekly* v264 no35 p103 Ag 28 2017

Totalitarian Noir: It Happened Here color *Publishers Weekly* v264 no31 p63 Jl 31 2017

Total Recall color *Publishers Weekly* v264 no4 p56 Ja 23 2017

Pickering, Kevin T.

Release of mineral-bound water prior to subduction tied to shallow seismogenic slip off Sumatra graph *Science* v356 no6340 p841 My 26 2017

Pickersgill, Annemarie

The formation of peak rings in large impact craters bibl color graph *Science* v354 no6314 p878 N 18 2016

Picket Fences (TV program)

MY LIFE ON TV J. RUSSELL *TV Guide* p28 Ap 17 2017

PICKETT, MALLORY
TIGER BALM ULTRA color *Wired* v25 no3 p21 Mr 2017

Pickleball (Game)
A GAME TO RELISH: Pickleball finds a home at a new racquet club L. BAILEY *Indianapolis Monthly* v40 no11 p32 Jl 2017
Pickleballed L. TANNER *Idaho Magazine* v16 no5 p6 F 2017

Pickles
Ask Martha *Martha Stewart Living* no267 p62 S 2016
Dill Pickle Dip A. Larson *Idaho Magazine* v16 no3 p57 D 2016
home made PICKLES color *Good Housekeeping* v263 no5 p177 N 2016
PICKLE RECIPES for the Picking: Ferment or quick-pickle your harvest with this assortment of ideas from Mother Earth News bloggers K. Quillen, K. Shockey et al *Mother Earth News* no282 p56 Je/Jl 2017
Pile On the PICKLES M. VEGA *Atlanta* v56 no7 p84 N 2016
Q + A J. Gilbert *Cincinnati Magazine* v50 no10 p32 Jl 2017
Quick-pickle anything C. Hall color *Redbook* p22 S 2017

Pickles—Evaluation
Mixing Bowl color *O, The Oprah Magazine* p120 Ag 2017

Pickrell, John
Australia to ax support for long-term ecology sites color *Science* v357 no6352 p632 Ag 18 2017

Pickup trucks
See also
Colorado truck
Ford F-Series trucks
EDITOR'S LETTER K. WOLFKILL color *Road & Track* v69 no1 p24 Ag 2017
FINNISH LINE A. Russell cartoon *New Yorker* v93 no30 p18 O 2 2017
Hauling Class J. CONDON color *Esquire* p62 BigBlackBook
The New Luxury Trucks E. DYER color *Popular Mechanics* p50 S 2017
New Tranny In Town A. Priddle color *Motor Trend* v68 no12 p66 D 2016
THE PICKUP TRUCK MYSTIQUE C. Neuhaus *Saturday Evening Post* v288 no6 p16 N/D 2016
Power Tour's TOP 5 FREAKS T. Taylor color *Hot Rod* v70 no11 p54 N 2017

Pickup trucks—Evaluation
Four Powerful Pickups A. DEL-COLLE cartoon color *Men's Health* v32 no4 p30 My 2017
HEAVY-DUTY PICKUP REVIEW D. Mowitz *Successful Farming* v115 no2 p38 F 2017
KING IN THE NORTH M. Cortina, S. Evans et al chart color map *Motor Trend* v69 no10 p68 O 2017

Pickwick Papers (Book : Dickens)
THE SECRET OF SLEEP J. GROOPMAN bw color *New Yorker* v93 no33 p88 O 23 2017

Picnic grounds
PICNIC CHIC: A vintage-inspired outdoor spread to kick your summer off in style V. HART *New Orleans Homes & Lifestyles* v20 no3 p66 Summ 2017
PICTURESQUE PICNIC *Iceland Review* v55 no4 p42 Jl/Ag 2017

Picnic tables
Benefits of a Local Lumber Mill J. Irwin *Mother Earth News* no282 p83 Je/Jl 2017
Hot Rod Anything! Motorized Picnic Table Because—Why Not? T. Kempkes color *Hot Rod* v70 no1 p16 Ja 2017
Products *Parks & Recreation* v51 no10 p90 O 2016

Picnics
See also
Tailgate parties
BY THE NUMBERS R. E. Maltby Jr. *Harper's Magazine* v334 no2001 p95 F 2017
Extra! Extra! Pie-eating contests, swimming, junk food. For years, the annual Indianapolis Recorder picnics were a summertime highlight C. ZEIGLER *Indianapolis Monthly* v12 no40 p22 Ag 2017
Front-Yard Friends C. Kopaczewski color *Good Housekeeping* v264 no6 p59 Je 2017
PICNIC CHIC: A vintage-inspired outdoor spread to kick your summer off in style V. HART *New Orleans Homes & Lifestyles* v20 no3 p66 Summ 2017
That Was Then *National Parks* v91 no3 p60 Summ 2017

Picnics in art
Lightbox C. Alter color *Time* v190 no16/17 p24 O 23 2017

Picnics—Equipment & supplies
PICNIC PERFECT B. RILEY *Atlanta* v57 no3 p46 Jl 2017

Picnics—Social aspects
No Picnic: Nothing is as good in real life as it is in theory P. Gulley *Indianapolis Monthly* v40 no10 p50 Je 2017

Picotti, Paola
Cell-wide analysis of protein thermal unfolding reveals determinants of thermostability color *Science* v355 no6327 p812 F 24 2017

Picoult, Jodi, 1966-
Black Lives Imagined R. GAY *New York Times Book Review* p10 O 16 2016

Pictorial maps
WHERE TO LIVE IN AMERICA, 2100 A.D P. HESS cartoon *Popular Science* p32 Ja/F 2017

Picture books
See also
Picture books for children & education
Celebrate a hobby journey N. Besougloff color *Model Railroader* v84 no1 p8 Ja 2017
Weirdest Places on Earth color *Entertainment Weekly* no1478 / 1479 p108 Ag 18-25 2017

Picture books for children
DISCOVERING THEIR IDENTITY: Using gender nonconforming picture books in early education classrooms S. Evans, S. Gilbert et al color *Literacy Today (2411-7862)* v34 no6 p20 My/Je 2017

Picture books for children & education
STORIES WITH VALUE: Inspiring positive student conduct with children's picture books C. A. Jones *Literacy Today (2411-7862)* v35 no1 p28 Jl/Ag 2017

Picture frames & framing
Freeze Frame: Antique and vintage frames make a comeback L. Claverie *New Orleans Homes & Lifestyles* v20 no4 p28 Aut 2017
How to Make a... CONCRETE FRAME B. LOSLEBEN chart color *Popular Mechanics* v193 no7 p82 S 2016
i did it! K. SELZER color *Better Homes & Gardens* v95 no10 p82 O 2017

Picture frames & framing—Evaluation
PUNCH LIST K. SELZER color *Better Homes & Gardens* v95 no3 p56 Mr 2017
THE ULTIMATE GUIDE TO TECH @50+ STEPHANIE CHANG color *AARP: The Magazine* v59 no1A p34 D 2015/ Ja 2016

Picture puzzles
Birthday Bash! cartoon *National Geographic Kids* no472 p30 Ag 2017
THE BRITISH HERITAGE TRAVEL PUZZLER *British Heritage Travel* v38 no1 p78 Ja/F 2017
WHAT'S THIS? color *Canadian Geographic* v136 no6 p73 D 2016
WHERE'S THIS? color *Canadian Geographic* v136 no6 p73 D 2016

Picture books—Charts, diagrams, etc.
CHILDREN'S BESTSELLERS C. JURIS chart *Publishers Weekly* v263 no42 p16 O 17 2016

Picture of Dorian Gray, The (Theatrical production)
Olesen: The Picture of Dorian Gray J. Rosenblum *Opera News* v81 no9 p53 Mr 2017

Pictures—Printing
See also
Woodcutting (Printmaking)

Piecuch, Sarah
MAKING moonlight MEMORIES *New York State Conservationist* v71 no3 p22 D 2016

Piedmont Park (Atlanta, Ga.)
TAKE IT OUTSIDE *Atlanta* v56 no11 p48 Mr 2017

Piegaia, R.
Observation of a large-scale anisotropy in the arrival directions of cosmic rays above 8 × 1018 eV *Science* v357 no6357 p1266 S 22 2017

Pielke, Roger A.
Land's complex role in climate change [Cover story] *Physics To-*

day v69 no11 p40 N 2016

Piellucci, Mike

STOP US IF YOU'VE HEARD THIS ... color *Sports Illustrated* v127 no8 p60 S 18 2017

PIERCE, BILL

CRUSH ANY GOAL color *Runner's World* v52 no8 p74 S 2017

Pierce, Charles P.

CIVIL UNREST color *Sports Illustrated* v127 no8 p16 S 18 2017

Head Games color *Sports Illustrated* v127 no4 p68 Ag 7 2017

LIVE FROM D.C.! color *Esquire* p30 Je/Jl 2017

No Exit color *Sports Illustrated* v126 no7 p30 Mr 6 2017

PROTEST SONG color *Sports Illustrated* v127 no10 p30 O 2 2017

Rearview Sharer color *Sports Illustrated* v125 no21 p20 D 26 2016

Sideshow Effect color *Sports Illustrated* v127 no3 p16 Jl 24 2017

Unbeatable color *Sports Illustrated* v126 no2 p14 Ja 16 2017

WHAT IF? ... THE PLAYERS' UNION HADN'T REJECTED A-ROD'S 2003 TRADE TO THE RED SOX? color *Sports Illustrated* v126 no11 p55 Ap 17-24 2017

WHEN SPRING HAS STUNG color *Sports Illustrated* v126 no11 p90 Ap 17-24 2017

Pierce, Chonda—Interviews

THE QUEEN OF CLEAN CLAPS BACK L. MURROW cartoon color *Wired* v25 no4 p73 Ap 2017

Pierce, David

GEARHEAD AWAY GAME bw color *Wired* v25 no6 p34 Je 2017

GEARHEAD: ROCK GROUP color *Wired* v25 no8 p42 Ag 2017

GEARHEAD SQUARE SPACE color *Wired* v25 no5 p44 My 2017

HEAD-TO-HEAD color *Wired* v25 no3 p36 Mr 2017

HOW TO WATCH IT ALL cartoon color *Wired* v25 no4 p42 Ap 2017

HOW VULNERABLE IS YOUR PHONE? diag *Wired* v25 no6 p37 Je 2017

NEXT LIST 2017 bw graph *Wired* v25 no5 p63 My 2017

OK, HOUSE. GET SMART chart color *Wired* v25 no6 p39 Je 2017

one for all color diag *Wired* v25 no8 p86 Ag 2017

TOP 3: BOOK SMARTS color *Wired* v25 no9 p44 S 2017

WISH LIST 2016 color *Wired* v24 no12 p45 D 2016

Pierce, David Hyde, 1959-

David Hyde Pierce B. Newcott color *AARP: The Magazine* v60 no3A p13 Ap/My 2017

Pierce, David Hyde, 1959—Interviews

David HYDE PIERCE cartoon *Vanity Fair* v59 no5 p166 Ap 2017

Pierce, Deborah

THE Accessible CABIN S. BROWN color *Cabin Living* p64 Ja/F 2017

Pierce, Heather H.

What do revised U.S. rules mean for human research? color *Science* v357 no6352 p650 Ag 18 2017

Pierce, Jo Carol

BAD GIRLS GET OLD J. STANFORD *Texas Monthly* v45 no7 p92 Jl 2017

Pierce, Jocelyn

Make a Checklist *Practical Horseman* v44 no12 p8 D 2016

NCEA Works to Keep Riding Relevant for COLLEGIATE EQUESTRIANS color *Practical Horseman* v44 no12 p63 D 2016

WINNING A DAY WITH WOFFORD AND WHITE color *Practical Horseman* v44 no12 p38 D 2016

Pierce, Justin R.

Mergers May Be Profitable, but Are They Good for the Economy? *Harvard Business Review Digital Articles* p2 N 15 2016

Pierce, Kristi

How My Horse De-Stresses Me color *Horse & Rider* v55 no12 p72 D 2016

Pierce, Michael

Seven Ways to Leverage Mobile Technology in Aquatics *Parks & Recreation* v52 no5 p50 My 2017

Pierce, Nancy

Esperanza ARABIANS, LLC: FOUR DECADES OF DEVOTION TO THE BREED *Arabian Horse World* v57 no12 p1 S 2017

Pierce, Thomas

The Afterlives *Publishers Weekly* v264 no41 p41 O 9 2017

CHAIRMAN SPACEMAN cartoon color *New Yorker* v92 no45 p68 Ja 16 2017

PIERCEY, NAOMI

THE GIRLS NEXT DOOR color diag *Men's Health* v32 no9 p82 N 2017

Piercey, Naomi—Interviews

Celebrating 16 Years of THE GIRL NEXT DOOR cartoon color *Men's Health* v32 no8 p94 O 2017

Piercy, Scott

Scott Piercy J. Marksbury and C. Barrett color *Golf Magazine* v59 no7 p38 Jl 2017

Piereson, James

The New Assault on Privacy cartoon *Weekly Standard* v22 no27 p20 Mr 20 2017

Progressives, Inc color *Weekly Standard* v22 no31 p24 Ap 17 2017

The Redistribution Fallacy *Commentary* v140 no2 p51 S 2015

The Redistribution Fallacy: The federal government knows how to support a welfare state. It does not know how to transfer money from the rich to the poor *Commentary* v140 no2 p27 S 2015

Ridicule Didn't Work color *Weekly Standard* v22 no20 p17 Ja 30 2017

The Tax Conundrum color *Weekly Standard* v22 no32 p30 My 1 2017

PIERI, KERRY

THE HERO color *Harper's Bazaar* no3656 p154 S 2017

Pierman, Baptiste

Emission of volatile organic compounds from petunia flowers is facilitated by an ABC transporter diag *Science* v356 no6345 p1386 Je 30 2017

Pierno, Theresa

Echoes *National Parks* v91 no1 p8 Wint 2017

Echoes *National Parks* v91 no4 p8 Fall 2017

Fighting Harder *National Parks* v91 no4 p3 Fall 2017

Monumental Efforts *National Parks* v91 no3 p3 Summ 2017

Trash Talk *National Parks* v91 no1 p3 Wint 2017

What Unites Us *National Parks* v91 no2 p3 Spr 2017

Pierog, T.

Observation of a large-scale anisotropy in the arrival directions of cosmic rays above 8 × 1018 eV *Science* v357 no6357 p1266 S 22 2017

Pieroni, P.

Observation of a large-scale anisotropy in the arrival directions of cosmic rays above 8 × 1018 eV *Science* v357 no6357 p1266 S 22 2017

PIERPONT, CLAUDIA ROTH

ANGELS AND MEN cartoon color *New Yorker* v93 no32 p87 O 16 2017

THE ISLAND WITHIN bw cartoon *New Yorker* v93 no3 p72 Mr 6 2017

Pierpont Morgan Library

A Swedish Collector in Paris [Cover story] S. Schwartz color *New York Review of Books* v64 no8 p24 My 11 2017

Pierre, Aubry

How CEOs Can Manage Strategic Tensions *Harvard Business Review Digital Articles* p2 D 19 2016

Pierre Frey Inc.

debut: On a Roll M. OWENS color *Architectural Digest* no11 p50 N 1 2017

PIERREHUMBERT, RAY

5 THINGS WE KNOW TO BE TRUE cartoon *Scientific American* v315 no5 p46 N 2016

Pierre-Louis, Kendra

Bats in the Bronx color *Scientific American* v316 no1 p15 Ja 2017

consider the caribou chart color *Popular Science* v289 no5 p10 S/O 2017

exit, pursued by bear cartoon *Popular Science* v289 no4 p83 Jl/Ag 2017

FORECAST: UNCERTAIN color *Earth Island Journal* v32 no2 p48 Summ 2017

our swiftly dimming planet color *Popular Science* v289 no4 p23 Jl/Ag 2017

The Road to Hakha *Sierra* v102 no5 p64 St/O 2017

what the frack cartoon *Popular Science* v289 no2 p12 Mr/Ap 2017

Piers

Pier Review color *Los Angeles Magazine* v62 no10 p16 O 2017

Pierson, Jack

Editor's note A. ASTLEY color *Architectural Digest* v73 no12 p32 D 2016

SECRET HISTORY D. COLMAN color *Architectural Digest* v73 no12 p120 D 2016

Pierson, Jack—Interviews

Jack PIERSON E. MYLES *Interview* v47 no1 p114 F 2017

PIERSON, LISA

ask the experts color *Dressage Today* v23 no8 p66 Ap 2017

Pierson, Theodore C.

Rapid development of a DNA vaccine for Zika virus bibl graph *Science* v354 no6309 p237 O 14 2016

PIERUCCI, ANTONE

THE ANCIENT ECOLOGY OF FIRE color *Archaeology* v70 no5 p55 S/O 2017

Pies

See also

Ice cream pies

Apple Pie, Solo M. Miskimen *Saturday Evening Post* v288 no6 p62 N/D 2016

ART OF THE TART S. PUCKET and N. W. HOPKINS color *Better Homes & Gardens* v95 no3 p124 Mr 2017

AUGUST@GH color *Good Housekeeping* v265 no2 p10 Ag 2017

BAKE ME HAPPY J. Drilling *Cincinnati Magazine* v50 no12 p102 S 2017

CHRISTMAS CREATIONS D. CURRY color *New Orleans Magazine* v51 no2 p88 D 2016

Cocoa-Nutty Lime Tart color *Good Housekeeping* v264 no4 p111 Ap 2017

EASY AS PIE *Martha Stewart Living* no269 p96 N 2016

A French-Canadian Christmas Carol S. Sifton color *New York Times Magazine* p44 D 11 2016

Fried Delights D. Wise color *Southern Living* v52 no6 p134 Je 2017

FROM NAPLES TO HOLLYWOOD L. RABINOVITCH *Los Angeles Magazine* p44 Ja 2017

Good Vibration T. Rao *New York Times Magazine* p30 O 16 2016

HOLIDAY KITCHEN A. TRAVERSO and E. CECIL color *Yankee* v80 no6 p58 N/D 2016

Homemade Oatmeal Pies P. Lolley color *Southern Living* v52 no10 p130 O 2017

How to Make an American Pie! C. Agard color *Entertainment Weekly* no1460/1461 p66 Ap 7-17 2017

Indoor S'mores color *Good Housekeeping* v264 no2 p139 F 2017

In the Kitchen with James Whiteside C. ESCOYNE *Dance Magazine* v91 no6 p44 Je 2017

THE KITCHEN COOKBOOK color *Better Homes & Gardens* v95 no3 p128 Mr 2017

LOST PIES OF THE SOUTH N. Mcdermott color *Southern Living* v52 no11 p104 N 2017

Mermaid Marshmallow Pie R. Kinane color *Entertainment Weekly* no1466 p20 My 19 2017

MIX MASTER R. Atwood *Martha Stewart Living* no268 p66 O 2016

OYSTER FEST S. DRY color *Louisiana Life* v37 no2 p24 N/D 2016

pick your finish *Martha Stewart Living* no269 p97 N 2016

A ROUND OF APPLAUSE S. DIGREGORIO *Martha Stewart Living* no269 p90 N 2016

SWEETS IN A FLASH color *Redbook* p127 Je 2017

the SWEET spot [Cover story] K. Hammonds color *Southern Living* v52 no7 p86 Jl 2017

To-Die-For Pie color *Southern Living* v52 no1 p128 Ja 2017

TOP THAT M. MCLAUGHLIN *Indianapolis Monthly* v12 no40 p70 Ag 2017

YOUR PANTRY color *Good Housekeeping* v264 no4 p127 Ap 2017

Pies—History

As American as Apple Pie? S. SETHI color *Reader's Digest* v190 no1132 p40 Jl/Ag 2017

Pies—Sales & prices

better *Better Homes & Gardens* v94 no12 p143 D 2016

Pieters, C. M.

Localized aliphatic organic material on the surface of Ceres bibl graph *Science* v355 no6326 p719 F 17 2017

Pietsch, Ted

ROMANTIC ATTACHMENT P. Edmonds color *National Geographic* v230 no6 p25 D 2016

Piety

Addicted to piety B. Haile color *U.S. Catholic* v82 no5 p10 My 2017

Popular piety R. Throm, P. Cronin et al color *U.S. Catholic* v82 no2 p5 F 2017

Piezoelectric ceramics

An organic-inorganic perovskite ferroelectric with large piezoelectric response You, Liao et al graph *Science* v357 no6348 p306 Jl 21 2017

Piezunka, Henning

Why Some Crowdsourcing Efforts Work and Others Don't *Harvard Business Review Digital Articles* p2 F 21 2017

Pig-tailed macaque

FINDINGS *Harper's Magazine* v334 no2004 p96 My 2017

Pigeon behavior

Project Pigeon J. Ingram color *Canadian Wildlife* v23 no2 p14 My/Je 2017

Pigeon shooting

WHEN DOVES DON'T FLY M. PEARCE color *Outdoor Life* v224 no7 pH1 S 2017

Pigeons

See also

Feral pigeons

Commonplace Book *American Scholar* v86 no3 p126 Summ 2017

Piglia, Ricardo, 1941-2017

The Diaries of Emilio Renzi: Formative Years *Publishers Weekly* v264 no39 p81 S 25 2017

PIGLIUCCI, MASSIMO

The Virtuous Skeptic *Skeptical Inquirer* v41 no2 p54 Mr/Ap 2017

Pigments

See also

Dyes & dyeing

CSI TOOL FROM ANCIENT EGYPT A. R. Williams color *National Geographic* v231 no5 p24 My 2017

Pigneur, Yves

Don't Let Your Company Culture Just Happen *Harvard Business Review Digital Articles* p2 Jl 7 2016

Pignol, David

An algal photoenzyme converts fatty acids to hydrocarbons color graph *Science* v357 no6354 p903 S 1 2017

Pigott-Smith, Tim, 1946-2017

ROYAL PAIN: King Charles III S. Gutierrez *British Heritage Travel* v38 no3 p70 My/Je 2017

Pigozzi, Jean C., 1952-

The Selfie Samurai A. CARTER bw *Vanity Fair* v59 no10 p182 O 2017

TANGLED UP IN BLUE D. GILMORE color *Vanity Fair* v59 no8 p52 Ag 2017

Pike, Andrew

Changes in the microbiota cause genetically modified Anopheles to spread in a population graph *Science* v357 no6358 p1396 S 29 2017

Pike, Bill

2017 A Look Ahead color map *Power & Motoryacht* v32 no12 p38 D 2016

Bedding Hardware color *Power & Motoryacht* v34 no10 p120 O 2017

Can Your Refrigerator Help? color *Power & Motoryacht* v33 no3 p120 Mr 2017

Cloak and Dagger bw *Power & Motoryacht* v34 no7 p136 Jl 2017

Clog-Free Nation cartoon *Power & Motoryacht* v33 no2 p232 F 2017

COMMAND PERFORMANCE chart color diag *Power & Motoryacht* v33 no3 p84 Mr 2017

Crunch Time *Power & Motoryacht* v33 no3 p118 Mr 2017

Cutwater 302 Sport Coupe color *Power & Motoryacht* v33 no2 p42 F 2017

Divide and Conquer color *Power & Motoryacht* v34 no9 p112 S 2017

Eye of the Hurricane cartoon *Power & Motoryacht* v32 no12 p128 D 2016

Farewell, My Friend color *Power & Motoryacht* v32 no11 p72 N 2016

Filling in the Gaps color *Power & Motoryacht* v32 no12 p72 D

2016

Ghost Busters color *Power & Motoryacht* v32 no11 p141 N 2016

A Good Book and a Very Big Wrench color *Power & Motoryacht* v33 no2 p136 F 2017

Guardian Angels cartoon *Power & Motoryacht* v33 no1 p168 Ja 2017

The Halon Tragedy bw *Power & Motoryacht* v34 no11 p264 N 2017

HIGH-TECH BOAT TESTING chart color diag *Power & Motoryacht* v33 no2 p104 F 2017

Hose Clamp Smarts color *Power & Motoryacht* v34 no6 p79 Je 2017

THE INTERPRETATION OF DREAMS bw *Power & Motoryacht* v34 no6 p144 Je 2017

LEADING LADY chart color *Power & Motoryacht* v34 no11 p86 N 2017

Letter Perfect color *Power & Motoryacht* v32 no12 p68 D 2016

Light Show color *Power & Motoryacht* v34 no6 p71 Je 2017

Little Sister chart color *Power & Motoryacht* v32 no11 p128 N 2016

A Little Tape'll Do Ya! color *Power & Motoryacht* v33 no4 p104 Ap 2017

The Long Run color *Power & Motoryacht* v33 no1 p84 Ja 2017

Look! Kangaroos? cartoon *Power & Motoryacht* v34 no8 p160 Ag 2017

The Modular Approach color *Power & Motoryacht* v34 no7 p74 Jl 2017

Move Over, Gilligan! bw *Power & Motoryacht* v33 no4 p184 Ap 2017

Nordic Tug 44 color *Power & Motoryacht* v32 no11 p66 N 2016

One Tool Box Is Never Enough color *Power & Motoryacht* v34 no11 p152 N 2017

Pirate of the Caribbean color *Power & Motoryacht* v33 no3 p68 Mr 2017

Return of a Legend chart color *Power & Motoryacht* v34 no7 p42 Jl 2017

The Roving Mechanic *Power & Motoryacht* v34 no6 p78 Je 2017

Sea Ray SLX 400 color *Power & Motoryacht* v34 no10 p64 O 2017

Shelter from the Storm color *Power & Motoryacht* v32 no12 p74 D 2016

Sorry, Mr Roboto! cartoon *Power & Motoryacht* v33 no3 p208 Mr 2017

Split Personality bw *Power & Motoryacht* v34 no10 p200 O 2017

THE STAR OF THE SHOW [Cover story] color *Power & Motoryacht* v32 no11 p76 N 2016

Take It Easy cartoon *Power & Motoryacht* v34 no9 p184 S 2017

Ten ADVENTURES color *Power & Motoryacht* v34 no9 p64 S 2017

A Timely Save color *Power & Motoryacht* v32 no11 p156 N 2016

Viking 37 Billfish color *Power & Motoryacht* v34 no6 p30 Je 2017

What's in a Name? bw *Power & Motoryacht* v32 no11 p256 N 2016

What Were They Thinking? color *Power & Motoryacht* v33 no4 p102 Ap 2017

When Nobody Else Is Around color *Power & Motoryacht* v34 no8 p90 Ag 2017

Whole New World chart color *Power & Motoryacht* v34 no8 p40 Ag 2017

XO 270 Cabin OB color *Power & Motoryacht* v34 no9 p47 S 2017

PIKE, LAURIE

House Mother: MAUREEN WOOD SPENT A LIFETIME CREATING A SENSE OF HOME FOR OTHERS *Cincinnati Magazine* v50 no11 p44 Ag 2017

PIKE, SARAH

Rewilders *Orion Magazine* v35 no4/5 p10 Jl-O 2016

Pikes & Pickerels (Short story)

Pikes and Pickerels C. FLEMING *Commentary* v142 no1 p40 Jl/Ag 2016

Piket, Roberta

Creating a Convincing Solo Piano Performance bw color *Downbeat* v83 no12 p102 D 2016

Piketty, Thomas, 1971-

When Money Talks Too Much C. Lehmann *In These Times* v41 no7 p38 Jl 2017

Pikovsky, Arkady

Lyapunov Exponents A Tool to Explore Complex Dynamics R. C. Hilborn *Physics Today* v70 no3 p62 Mr 2017

Pikul, Corrie

LEAK PROOF YOUR LIFE color *Parents* v92 no11 p86 N 2017

O's 2017 HEALTH HEROES color *O, The Oprah Magazine* p57 Ja 2017

Your Hour-by-Hour Plan for LIVING BETTER cartoon *O, The Oprah Magazine* p94 Mr 2017

You Snooze, You Spoon color *Good Housekeeping* v263 no5 p149 N 2016

Pilar Martinez-Jimenez, Celia

Aging increases cell-to-cell transcriptional variability upon immune stimulation color diag graph *Science* v355 no6332 p1433 Mr 31 2017

Pilates method

HARDER, BETTER, FASTER, STRONGER K. Schaefer color *Bloomberg Businessweek* no4511 p66 F 13 2017

Pilates to Improve Your Lifts S. MAIN color *Muscle & Performance* v9 no7 p22 Jl 2017

Pilates method—Study & teaching

Nicole Gunderman A. BRANDT *Cincinnati Magazine* v50 no3 p44 D 2016

Pilatus Aircraft Ltd.

PILATUS PC-12 NG P. BERGQVIST chart color *Flying* v144 no8 p42 Ag 2017

Pilcher, Helen

Bring Back the King: The New Science of De-extinction *Publishers Weekly* v263 no41 p66 O 10 2016

Pilcher, James E.

James Watson Cronin *Physics Today* v70 no3 p72 Mr 2017

Pilenko, Jelizawieta Juriewna, 1891-1945

True evangelical faith A. Frykholm bw *Christian Century* v133 no25 p28 D 7 2016

Pilet, Guillaume

GUILLAUME PILET A. Rosenmeyer color *Art in America* v104 no10 p162 N 2016

Pilgrim Bell (Poem)

Pilgrim Bell K. AKBAR *Nation* v305 no8 p30 O 9 2017

Pilgrimage (Film)

Dahmer, Docs, and Godfathers J. McGovern color *Entertainment Weekly* no1462 p48 Ap 21 2017

Pilgrims & pilgrimages

Laughter: THE BEST MEDICINE G. BURKHART MEDEIROS color *Reader's Digest* v190 no1135 p100 N 2017

THE LONG WAY 'ROUND E. KWAK-HEFFERAN il *Backpacker* p83 My 2017

Magnificent Thrill Machines C. C. W. COOKE color *National Review* v69 no15 p24 Ag 14 2017

Mind Over Matter E. Vance color diag *National Geographic* v230 no6 p30 D 2016

Pilgrims together S. Paulsell *Christian Century* v134 no16 p29 Ag 2 2017

Researchers open tomb believed to be the one where Jesus was buried E. Powell *Christian Century* v133 no24 p17 N 23 2016

Pilgrims (New Plymouth Colony)—History

THE MAKING OF THE PILGRIMS D. Huntley *British Heritage Travel* v38 no3 p36 My/Je 2017

Pilhofer, Martin

In situ architecture, function, and evolution of a contractile injection system color diag *Science* v357 no6352 p713 Ag 18 2017

Pilkey, Dav, 1966-

CHILDREN'S BEST SELLERS *New York Times Book Review* p25 Ap 30 2017

DAV PILKEY I. Biedenharn color *Entertainment Weekly* no1485 p61 O 6 2017

PILKINGTON, TAYLOR

THE 12 DAYS OF CHRISTMAS *Virginia Living* v15 no1 p21 D 2016

Chasing the Dream: Speed is always in style when vintage sports cars hit the track at Virginia International Raceway in Danville *Virginia Living* v15 no4 p49 Je 2017

The Great BEER MIGRATION *Virginia Living* v15 no2 p62 F 2017

MADE IN VIRGINIA 2016 AWARDS *Virginia Living* v15 no1 p82 D 2016

Pillage
> *See also*
> Destruction of cultural property

Pillai, Rathi N.
Rescue of exhausted CD8 T cells by PD-1-targeted therapies is CD28-dependent bw diag graph *Science* v355 no6332 p1423 Mr 31 2017

Pillai, Renjith S.
Hydrolytically stable fluorinated metal-organic frameworks for energy-efficient dehydration diag *Science* v356 no6339 p731 My 19 2017

PILLALAMARRI, AKHILESH
From Vision to Reality bw *American Conservative* v16 no2 p9 Mr/Ap 2017

Pillay, Srini
4 Signs That Your Focus Is Holding You Back at Work *Harvard Business Review Digital Articles* p1 Ag 30 2017
A Better Way to Think About Risk *Harvard Business Review Digital Articles* p2 D 23 2014
Having Inside Information Leads to Worse Decisions *Harvard Business Review Digital Articles* p2 Ap 2 2015
How Leaderless Groups End Up with Leaders *Harvard Business Review Digital Articles* p2 F 19 2016
The Science Behind How Leaders Connect with Their Teams *Harvard Business Review Digital Articles* p2 Mr 31 2016
The Ways Your Brain Manages Overload, and How to Improve Them color *Harvard Business Review Digital Articles* p2 Je 7 2017

Pillemer, Karl Andrew
16 LIFE LESSONS *Psychology Today* v49 no5 p62 S/O 2016

Pillot, Éric
CONCRETE JUNGLES color *Mother Jones* v42 no2 p10 Mr/Ap 2017

Pillowcases
50 Everyday Mistakes And How to Fix Them [Cover story] B. SPECKTOR color *Reader's Digest* v189 no1129 p62 Ap 2017
Silky Pillowcases L. SACHS color *Good Housekeeping* v263 no5 p133 N 2016

Pillowcases—Evaluation
CHERRY + SKY BLUE color *Martha Stewart Living* no275 p27 Je 2017
A TO Z GUIDE TO YOUR BEST NIGHT'S SLEEP D. DICKINSON *Better Homes & Gardens* v95 no1 p41 Ja 2017

Pillows
20 WAYS TO DO PLUM S. Walter color *Good Housekeeping* v263 no5 p56C N 2016
3-D PILLOWS L. HEDRICK color *Better Homes & Gardens* v95 no10 p76 O 2017
7 rules for a great room G. Schafer color *Redbook* p132 O 2017
APPLY Yourself P. GUGLIELMETTI *Martha Stewart Living* no269 p106 N 2016
Are You Using the Wrong Pillow? *Parents* v91 no10 p94 O 2016
Ask Martha color diag *Martha Stewart Living* p72 Ap 2017
MAKE YOUR BED... AMAZING S. JEAN SHELTON color *Redbook* p136 O 2017
Pillow Talk C. K. Lehrman color *Consumer Reports* v82 no2 p22 F 2017
SPRING FORTH E. EICHINGER color *Chicago* v66 no4 p74 Ap 2017

Pillows—Design & construction
RETURN TO EDEN M. K. QUINLAN color *House Beautiful* v159 no3 p84 Ap 2017

Pillows—Evaluation
2017'S HOTTEST COLOR COMBOS color *Good Housekeeping* v265 no5 p60A N 2017
THE BEST BET img *New York* p49 F 20 2017
The cure for a bland sofa S. J. SHELTON color *Redbook* p136 Ap 2017
GET OUTSIDE! S. JEAN SHELTON color *Good Housekeeping* v265 no1 p35 Jl 2017
Get the Look color *House Beautiful* v159 no1 p28 F 2017
Global Warming L. Tudor *New Orleans Homes & Lifestyles* v20 no1 p32 Wint 2016
go to your ROOM K. K. CONDON color *Better Homes & Gardens* v95 no8 p34 Ag 2017
The House Always Wins K. O'SHEA-EVANS color *House Beau-*

tiful v159 no8 p35 O 2017
IN THE STARS *Better Homes & Gardens* v95 no1 p12 Ja 2017
AN INVITING POOL PAVILION M. Braff and K. O'SHEA-EVANS color *House Beautiful* v159 no4 p60 My 2017
Mad About Plaid color *Timber Home Living* v27 no2 p10 Ap 2017
Matcha Green K. RENDA color *House Beautiful* v159 no5 p29 Je 2017
MOVE THE PARTY OUTSIDE color *House Beautiful* v159 no4 p74 My 2017
NAP TOWN L. BAILEY *Indianapolis Monthly* v40 no5 p24 Ja 2017
The New Blooms J. J. CONDON color *House Beautiful* v159 no4 p35 My 2017
Nordic White color *House Beautiful* v158 no10 p16 D 2016/Ja 2017
OBSESSED WITH TRIM & TASSELS P. GUGLIELMETTI color *Better Homes & Gardens* v95 no10 p16 O 2017
The O List: BACK TO SCHOOL color *O, The Oprah Magazine* p49 S 2017
RADAR GIFT GUIDE L. CROSS and B. DANIELLE color *Ebony* v72 no3 p46 D 2016/Ja 2017
Red, White and You color *Log Home Living* v33 no7 p40 S 2016
Sit Back, Relax M. Khemsurov color *Bloomberg Businessweek* no4512 p80 F 20 2017
Sleeping with Apps M. ANTONOFF color *Sound & Vision* v82 no8 p22 O 2017
SLEEP SAVERS color *Good Housekeeping* v265 no1 p124 Jl 2017
SO BAZAAR color *Harper's Bazaar* no3652 p250 Ap 2017
Statement Chair, 2 Ways color *Good Housekeeping* v264 no1 p45 Ja 1 2017
STYLE *New Orleans Homes & Lifestyles* v20 no1 p16 Wint 2016
Sunset Orange K. RENDA and B. REYNAERT color *House Beautiful* p15 Jl 2017
Velvet for All Seasons H. BROWN color *House Beautiful* v159 no3 p36 Ap 2017

Pillsbury, Joanne
Treasures beyond gold: A new exhibition examines the luxury arts of the ancient Americas color *Magazine Antiques* v184 no5 p108 S/O 2017

Pills—Evaluation
New Male Potency Formula Makes "The Little Blue Pill" Obsolete H. S. Waxman *Saturday Evening Post* v289 no2 p103 Mr/Ap 2017

Pilobolus (Performer)
DANCE *New Yorker* v92 no39 p28 N 28 2016

Pilobolus Dance Theatre (Performer)
SKETCHBOOK E. KERET and M. KALMAN cartoon *New Yorker* v92 no38 p73 N 21 2016

Pilon, Mary
CHUCK'S NEW CHEDDAR color *Bloomberg Businessweek* no4494 p74 O 10 2016
Life at Trump Pavilion color *New Republic* v248 no7 p12 Jl 2017
Love in the Time of Mass Incarceration color *Bloomberg Businessweek* no4531 p18 Jl 24 2017
WHO REALLY INVENTED MONOPOLY? *Saturday Evening Post* v289 no5 p80 S/O 2017

Pilot Rock Park Equipment (Company)
Products *Parks & Recreation* v52 no9 p110 S 2017

Pilot sport utility vehicle
GARAGE chart color diag *Motor Trend* v69 no7 p106 Jl 2017

Pilots & pilotage
AN ADDICT SEEKS TO CHANGE D. Karl color *Flying* v144 no1 p62 Ja 2017
Feathered Flight Attendants color *Reader's Digest* v190 no1135 p30 N 2017
FINDING THAT SILVER LINING A. ROSS color *Flying* v144 no1 p20 Ja 2017
A GLORIOUS LIFE M. Lunken color *Flying* v144 no1 p60 Ja 2017
Great Escapes P. LOBO bw color *Power & Motoryacht* v33 no3 p96 Mr 2017
HOMEWARD BOUND S. Weigel color *Flying* v143 no12 p34 D 2016
LEARNING TO RIDE A TRIKE P. Garrison *Flying* v144 no1 p30 Ja 2017

LOGBOOK D. Harding Jr. *Power & Motoryacht* v33 no3 p26 Mr 2017

MAYDAY! MAYDAY! MAYDAY! D. HABER color *Flying* v144 no5 p24 My 2017

OBSERVING A LOT JUST BY WATCHING J. King color *Flying* v144 no5 p30 My 2017

RECURRENT TRAINING WITH A FRIEND L. Abend color *Flying* v144 no5 p74 My 2017

RUNWAY VISUAL RANGE R. Mark color diag *Flying* v144 no5 p20 My 2017

A SOLID PLAN GONE AWRY S. R. DEIGNAN-SCHMIDT color *Flying* v144 no7 p26 Jl 2017

THE SPEED OF SOUND R. Lengel chart color *Flying* v144 no1 p24 Ja 2017

THE SULLENBERGER-SKILES EFFECT L. Abend color *Flying* v144 no1 p66 Ja 2017

TRAINING & TECHNIQUE cartoon *Flying* v144 no1 p19 Ja 2017

WHEREVER THE WINDS BLOW S. Weigel color *Flying* v144 no5 p38 My 2017

Pilots & pilotage—Substance use

ALMOST THERE P. Garrison *Flying* v144 no7 p36 Jl 2017

Pilots & pilotage—Training of

LEARNING TO FLY THE ICON A5 P. BERGQVIST color *Flying* v144 no1 p38 Ja 2017

PRECISION FLYING IS CRITICAL map *Flying* v144 no5 p23 My 2017

TWO BOBS P. Garrison bw *Flying* v144 no9 p80 S 2017

Pilots & pilotage—United States

Keeping America Moving E. Humes *Saturday Evening Post* v289 no3 p44 My/Je 2017

WHO BENEFITS FROM THE STATUS QUO? map *Reason* v49 no6 p24 N 2017

PILS, EVA

To Build a Free China: A Citizen's Journey *Foreign Affairs* v96 no3 p175 My/Je 2017

Piltdown forgery

Piltdown's Lone Forger S. S. PATEL bw color *Archaeology* v69 no6 p9 N/D 2016

Pimenta, M.

Observation of a large-scale anisotropy in the arrival directions of cosmic rays above 8×1018 eV *Science* v357 no6357 p1266 S 22 2017

Pimenta, Marcos A.

Mildred S. Dresselhaus *Physics Today* v70 no6 p73 Je 2017

Pimentel, Dan

In Depth color *Flying* v143 no12 p66 D 2016

InDepth color *Flying* v144 no3 p41 Mr 2017

JIM IRWIN bw color *Flying* v144 no2 p67 F 2017

THE PILOT PIPELINE color *Flying* v144 no2 p48 F 2017

Pimentel, Sasha

For Want of Water *Publishers Weekly* v264 no38 p50 S 18 2017

Pin & needle manufacturing

ADAM SMITH NEEDS A PAPER CLIP V. POSTREL cartoon *Reason* v49 no1 p14 My 2017

Pin, Carmen

Lineage-dependent spatial and functional organization of the mammalian enteric nervous system color graph *Science* v356 no6339 p722 My 19 2017

Pinarello SpA

PINARELLO DOGMA F10 DISK M. Yozell color *Bicycling* v58 no9 p84 O 2017

Pinault, David

Extremists, 'X-Men,' and an Ex-Governor color *Commonweal* v144 no12 p12 Jl 7 2017

On Mecca's Front Porch color *Commonweal* v144 no7 p8 Ap 14 2017

The Story of Islam cartoon color *Commonweal* v144 no6 p14 Mr 24 2017

Pinault, François-Henri, 1962-

François-Henri Pinault A. B. -B. bw *Vanity Fair* v58 no12 p137 D 2016

Pinault, François-Henri, 1962—Interviews

WHERE DID YOU GET THAT LOVELY SUPPLY CHAIN? K. Bhasin color *Bloomberg Businessweek* no4505 p62 D 26 2016

Pinball game competitions

Pinball Wizard J. DeMELO color *O, The Oprah Magazine* p28 D 2016

Pinches, Charles R.

How to live in hope color *Christian Century* v134 no15 p22 Jl 19 2017

PINCHIN, KAREN

Über Tuber color *Walrus* v14 no4 p18 My 2017

'We were here first' color map *Canadian Geographic* v137 no3 p34 My 2017

Pinckney, Darryl

Black Lives Matter bw color *New York Review of Books* v64 no17 p55 N 9 2017

Catching Up to James Baldwin color *New York Review of Books* v64 no9 p22 My 25 2017

The Genius of Blackness cartoon *New York Review of Books* v64 no1 p40 Ja 19 2017

The Harlem He Knew bw color *New York Review of Books* v64 no11 p18 Je 22 2017

Laughing to Keep from Crying bw color *New York Review of Books* v63 no20 p28 D 22 2016

Master Class bw *New York Review of Books* v64 no15 p19 O 12 2017

Moon Over Miami color *New York Review of Books* v64 no7 p24 Ap 20 2017

Robert B. Silvers (1929–2017) [Cover story] bw color *New York Review of Books* v64 no8 p31 My 11 2017

A SENTIMENTAL EDUCATION cartoon *New Yorker* v93 no26 p58 S 4 2017

Under the Spell of James Baldwin bw *New York Review of Books* v64 no5 p24 Mr 23 2017

Pinder, Joanne

It's Absurd That Health Care Costs Are So Confusing *Harvard Business Review Digital Articles* p2 N 26 2014

Pine

See also

Longleaf pine

Ponderosa pine

Rocky Mountain bristlecone pine

Stone pines

Whitebark pine

Arnica City: Could the Dream Be Real? J. W. DAVIS *Idaho Magazine* v16 no9 p51 Je 2017

How Long Is a Year? S. BUSHWICK bw color graph *Popular Science* v289 no5 p50 S/O 2017

ONE TREE, MANY FUTURES D. IRVIN *American Forests* v123 no3 p24 Fall 2017

the refuge R. BUDD color map *Cabin Living* p12 O 2017

Pine, B. Joseph II

The 7 Laws of Regenerative Enterprises *Harvard Business Review Digital Articles* p2 N 17 2014

Pine, Nancy

The Balance Between Humility and Confidence color *Dressage Today* v23 no8 p20 Ap 2017

Pine, Ronald H.

Specimen collection crucial to taxonomy bibl *Science* v355 no6331 p1275 Mr 24 2017

Pine bark—Therapeutic use

Knock Out a Cold with Pycnogenol F. Pescatore *Amazing Wellness* v9 no6 p66 EarlyWint 2017

Pine Street Market (Company)

FOOD TOWN THROWDOWN A. Pape color *Sunset* v238 no6 p36 Je 2017

Pineapple

SL COOKING SCHOOL color *Southern Living* v52 no5 p150 My 2017

Pineapple—Therapeutic use

More Sex Can Provide Hay Fever Relief *USA Today Magazine* v146 no2869 p3 O 2017

Pineiro, Matias

Hermia & Helena *New Yorker* v93 no16 p28 Je 5 2017

Pines, David

Lev Petrovich Gor'kov *Physics Today* v70 no5 p68 My 2017

Pines, Ehud

Large-amplitude transfer motion of hydrated excess protons mapped by ultrafast 2D IR spectroscopy graph *Science* v357 no6350 p491 Ag 4 2017

Pines, Giulia
ROYAL FLUSH color *Conde Nast Traveler* v52 no2 p96 F 2017
Pines, Roger
Glinka: Ruslan and Lyudmila *Opera News* v81 no10 p52 Ap 2017
Leoncavallo: Zazà *Opera News* v81 no5 p55 N 2016
Sullivan: H.M.S. Pinafore *Opera News* v81 no5 p57 N 2016
Pinewood Atlanta Studios (Company)
MOVIE MAN S. HENRY *Atlanta* v56 no12 p24 Ap 2017
PING Inc.
G400 Drivers and Irons M. Chwasky color *Golf Magazine* v59 no9 p84 S 2017
Ping Mu
Rb1 and Trp53 cooperate to suppress prostate cancer lineage plasticity, metastasis, and antiandrogen resistance bibl graph *Science* v355 no6320 p1 Ja 6 2017
SOX2 promotes lineage plasticity and antiandrogen resistance in TP53- and RB1-deficient prostate cancer bibl graph *Science* v355 no6320 p1 Ja 6 2017
Pingos
Pingo L. SCHLEY *Discover* v38 no7 p12 S 2017
Ping Song, Xiao
Benefits of trees in tropical cities color *Science* v356 no6344 p1241 Je 23 2017
Pinho, Sandra
Self-renewal of a purified Tie2+ hematopoietic stem cell population relies on mitochondrial clearance bibl graph *Science* v354 no6316 p1156 D 2 2016
Pink
THE LOOK BOOK A. SWERDLOFF img *New York* v50 no6 p57 Mr 20 2017
MOVE OVER, MILLENNIAL PINK color *Women's Health* v14 no7 p36 S 2017
THE POWER OF PINK J. Miller color *Bloomberg Businessweek* no4501 p55 N 28 2016
Why Hasn't Millennial Pink Faded Away? L. SCHWARTZBERG img *New York* v50 no6 p58 Mr 20 2017
Pink, 1979-
WE DON'T CHANGE *Vital Speeches of the Day* v83 no10 p307 O 2017
Pink Flamingos (Film)
John Waters: Multiple Maniacs Relaunch C. Holmlund *Film Quarterly* v71 no1 p98 Fall 2017
Pink Floyd (Performer)
A compendium of news and notes from around the state G. MARTIN *Virginia Living* v15 no4 p35 Je 2017
PINK FLOYD M. Mettler bw color *Sound & Vision* v82 no2 p72 F/Mr 2017
Roger Waters' Fight D. FRICKE color *Rolling Stone* no1295 p13 S 7 2017
Pink noise—Research
This Just In J. Zorthian *Time* v189 no11 p27 Mr 27 2017
Pink Tulip Club (Company)
BABY'S IN BLACK *Cincinnati Magazine* v50 no7 p29 Ap 2017
Pinkerton, Helen
It's a Battlefield J. M. WILSON *Weekly Standard* v22 no15 p32 D 19 2016
PINKERTON, JAMES P.
Peace Through Trump? il *American Conservative* v15 no6 p18 N/D 2016
Pinkerton, JoAnn
FADING FLOW color *Women's Health* v14 no2 p34 Mr 2017
PINKERTON, NICK
ALONE WITH YOU color *Film Comment* v53 no3 p33 My/Je 2017
The Beauty of Chaos bw color *Film Comment* v53 no5 p66 S/O 2017
Beyond the Nickel Ride color *Film Comment* v53 no2 p20 Mr/Ap 2017
Canadian Hustle color *Film Comment* v53 no2 p79 Mr/Ap 2017
Changing the Narrative bw *Film Comment* v53 no5 p78 S/O 2017
Deep in the Forest color *Film Comment* v53 no3 p18 My/Je 2017
Free Fire color *Film Comment* v53 no2 p67 Mr/Ap 2017
PLEASE SEND HELP color *Film Comment* v53 no4 p46 Jl/Ag 2017
Things to Come color *Film Comment* v52 no6 p85 N/D 2016
Through a Glass Darkly bw *Film Comment* v52 no6 p90 N/D 2016

YOU TALKIN' TO ME? color *Film Comment* v53 no1 p26 Ja/F 2017
Pinkham, Sophie
Pasternak's Muse *New York Times Book Review* p13 Ja 29 2017
THE SEALED TRAIN color *Nation* v305 no1 p40 Jl 3 2017
So Close to Russia A. MEIER *New York Times Book Review* p20 N 27 2016
War Stories color *New Republic* v248 no10 p62 O 2017
Pinkney, Andrea Davis
Supremely Retro C. Ianzito color *AARP: The Magazine* v59 no5A p69 Ag/S 2016
Pinkus, Gary
The Most Digital Companies Are Leaving All the Rest Behind *Harvard Business Review Digital Articles* p2 Ja 21 2016
We Can't Undo Globalization, but We Can Improve It color *Harvard Business Review Digital Articles* p2 Ja 10 2017
Pinky & the Brain (TV program)
'Pinky and the Brain' J. Weiner *New York Times Magazine* p22 N 6 2016
Pinn, Anthony B.
HUMANISM and the CHALLENGE of PRIVILEGE *Humanist* v77 no3 p22 My/Je 2017
When Colorblindness Isn't the Answer: Humanism and the Challenge of Race S. KIRABO *Humanist* v77 no4 p44 Jl/Ag 2017
Pinnacle Technical Resources Inc.
A Tech Entrepreneur Goes Global K. LANKFORD color *Kiplinger's Personal Finance* v71 no6 p72 Je 2017
Pinnock, Claude
What Health Care Leaders Need to Do to Improve Value for Patients *Harvard Business Review Digital Articles* p2 D 3 2015
Pinochet Porn (Film)
IS TRAGEDY A CHOICE? B. SCHWABSKY bw *Nation* v304 no2 p32 Ja 16 2017
Pornography of Power D. E. Howe *Art in America* v104 no9 p29 O 2016
Pinot gris (Wine)
THE BEST WINES OF THE YEAR S. Schneider color *Sunset* v239 no4 p94 O 2017
Pinot gris (Wine)—Evaluation
OUR 2017 GOLD & SILVER MEDAL WINNERS color *Sunset* v239 no4 p100 O 2017
Pinot noir (Wine)—Congresses
LA SOCIAL color *Los Angeles Magazine* v62 no7 p125 Jl 2017
Pinot noir (Wine)—Evaluation
Uncharted Terroir J. Clarke color *Bloomberg Businessweek* no4517 p72 Ap 3 2017
Pins & needles
Getting Started In... SEWING L. SOROKANICH color diag *Popular Mechanics* p46 N 2017
Pinsky, Benjamin A.
IgG antibodies to dengue enhanced for FcγRIIIA binding determine disease severity bibl graph *Science* v355 no6323 p395 Ja 27 2017
Pinsky, Mark I.
People color *Christian Century* v134 no18 p17 Ag 30 2017
People color *Christian Century* v134 no3 p17 F 2017
Pinsky, Robert
BRANCA *New Yorker* v93 no4 p64 Mr 13 2017
Candid Camera *New York Times Book Review* p15 Je 4 2017
'EXILE AND LIGHTNING' R. Pinsky bw *New York Times Book Review* p16 Ag 6 2017
Pintacuda, Greta
PCGF3/5–PRC1 initiates Polycomb recruitment in X chromosome inactivation color *Science* v356 no6342 p1081 Je 9 2017
PINTEA, LILIAN
An Ecoregion-Based Approach to Protecting Half the Terrestrial Realm *BioScience* v67 no6 p534 Je 2017
Pinterest (Web resource)
Cake pops and communion wafers M. J. Rose color *U.S. Catholic* v82 no3 p22 Mr 2017
A More Colorful Picture color *Black Enterprise* v47 no2 p25 S 2016
Pinto, Alberto
PORT OF CALL M. OWENS bw color *Architectural Digest* v73 no11 p192 N 2016
Pinto, Freida

Crewel Summer E. Wilson color *InStyle* v24 no8 p72 Ag 2017

Dior and Me J. Davison and S. Iglehart bw color *Glamour* no8 p66 Ag 2017

Freida & a Pinto M. Heyman color *InStyle* v24 no5 p234 My 2017

Guerrilla Chic E. JONES *In These Times* v41 no6 p38 Je 2017

Radicals In Love Go Guerrilla D. D'Addario color *Time* v189 no15 p52 Ap 24 2017

PINTO, RICHARD

RETRO, ACTIVE color *Road & Track* v69 no1 p64 Ag 2017

SAME SWAGGER color *Road & Track* v68 no9 p82 Je 2017

TIME MACHINE color *Road & Track* v69 no2 p82 S 2017

Pinto horse

From FEEDLOT to FINALS J. M. Keeler color *Dressage Today* p56 My 2017

Pinton, Paolo

Reticulon 3–dependent ER-PM contact sites control EGFR non-clathrin endocytosis color diag graph *Science* v356 no6338 p617 My 12 2017

Pinus edulis

Singleleaf Pinyon Pine *American Forests* v123 no1 p11 Wint/Spr 2017

Pioneer Mountains (Idaho)

THE LAST TREK? M. COTHERN *Idaho Magazine* v16 no12 p48 S 2017

Pioneers

Pioneering painter leaves glowing mark on Ashland S. Kansteiner cartoon *Nebraska Life* v20 no6 p58 N/D 2016

Pioneers—History

Pioneers bw color *Forbes* v199 no6 p108 Je 13 2017

Pioneers of African-American Cinema (Film)

Art and Artifact: Pioneers of African-American Cinema and Its Contemporary Relevance R. Gates *Film Quarterly* v70 no2 p88 Wint 2016

Pioneers—United States

NEBRASKA Female Pioneers bw color *Nebraska Life* v20 no6 p19 N/D 2016

Waiting on Winter A. J. BARTELS color *Nebraska Life* v20 no6 p20 N/D 2016

PIORE, ADAM

the body electrician cartoon color *Popular Science* p64 Ja/F 2017

How We Decide color diag *Discover* v38 no6 p34 Jl/Ag 2017

James Allison Has Unfinished Business with Cancer [Cover story] bw color il *MIT Technology Review* v120 no3 p78 My/Je 2017

PIOTROWSKI, JOYCE

What to Eat Now: Cranberries color *Better Nutrition* v78 no12 p58 D 2016

Piotto, Daniel

Positive biodiversity-productivity relationship predominant in global forests bibl chart graph map *Science* v354 no6309 paaf8957-1 O 14 2016

Pipe

See also

Valves

Make a pipe load from plastic and stripwood D. Popp bw color *Model Railroader* v84 no4 p36 Ap 2017

The New Café Racer Paradigm P. d 'Orléans color *Cycle World* v55 no11 p42 D 2016

Refit Tips C. Lawson color *Sail* v48 no1 p46 Ja 2017

Pipeline (Theatrical production)

THE THEATRE color *New Yorker* v93 no24 p11 Ag 21 2017

Pipeline design & construction

Bury Their Future at Standing Rock: The truth about the shutdown of the Dakota Pipeline N. Schaefer Riley *Commentary* v143 no1 p29 Ja 2017

United in Protest S. ELBEIN color map *National Geographic* v231 no5 p78 My 2017

Pipeline transportation

Pushing Back on Pipelines S. Taylor and S. Luetmer color *Progressive* v81 no10 p24 N 2016

Pipelines

See also

Petroleum pipelines

Water pipelines

Hiding DAPL Violence Behind 'Nothing to See Here' Headlines J. Naureckas *Extra!* v30 no1 p4 Ja/F 2017

Pipelines—Design & construction

Acceptable R. Gibson *Alternatives Journal (AJ) - Canada's Environmental Voice* v42 no3 p80 2016

'It's Indian Time!' F. Madeson color *Progressive* v81 no10 p19 N 2016

When Journalism Gets a Jail Threat, Most Media Respond With Silence [Cover story] J. Naureckas *Extra!* v29 no8 p1 O 2016

Why BC Is Standing Up to Kinder Morgan D. Cayley-Daoust *Alternatives Journal (AJ) - Canada's Environmental Voice* v42 no2 p10 2016

Pipelines—Government policy

A Tale of Two Protests M. Hemingway *Weekly Standard* v22 no10 p8 N 14 2016

Pipelines—Safety measures

Pressure Test M. FAWCETT diag *Walrus* v14 no2 p14 Mr 2017

PIPENBERG, NATHAN

Hike It All *Backpacker* p24 Ag 2017

Mountain Magic map *Backpacker* p24 Je 2017

Piper, Ashlee

Cozy & Cruelty-Free color *Vegetarian Times* v43 no2 p15 N/D 2016

Piper, Nicole

An AIDS Charity Fights Builders in L.A *Bloomberg Businessweek* no4513 p42 Mr 6 2017

Los Angeles's New Circus Act color *Bloomberg Businessweek* no4517 p44 Ap 3 2017

Piper airplanes

2016 FLYING EDITORS' CHOICE AWARDS color *Flying* v144 no1 p46 Ja 2017

LAST DANCE S. Weigel color *Flying* v144 no2 p36 F 2017

Pipes, Billy

CASE CLOSED color *Spin to Win Rodeo* v21 no2 p60 Ap 2017

PIPES, DANIEL

A New Strategy for Israeli Victory *Commentary* v143 no1 p13 Ja 2017

Pipes, Richard

The Sad Fate of Birobidzhan color *New York Review of Books* v63 no16 p66 O 27 2016

Pipestone National Monument (Minn.)

Pipestone and Prairies R. H. MOHLENBROCK color map *Natural History* v125 no5 p42 My 2017

Pipettes

new products: general lab equipment color *Science* v357 no6352 p721 Ag 18 2017

Pipettes—Evaluation

new products color *Science* v355 no6332 p1441 Mr 31 2017

Piping installation

REVAMP YOUR AIR SYSTEM: HERE ARE POINTERS FOR RETROFITTING A SHOP D. Mowitz chart color diag *Successful Farming* v115 no7 p21 My 2017

Pipkin, John

CONFORMATION CLINIC color *Horse & Rider* v56 no6 p43 Je 2017

Sky Fever K. A. POWERS *New York Times Book Review* p20 N 6 2016

PIPKIN, WHITNEY

FOOD-TRIPPING: The tiny hunt country town of Marshall may not be top of your list for a food-centric day trip, but it should be *Virginia Living* v15 no6 p33 O 2017

Pique-Regi, Roger

Social status alters immune regulation and response to infection in macaques bibl graph *Science* v354 no6315 p1041 N 25 2016

Piquer-Rodríguez, Maria

Forest conservation: Remember Gran Chaco bibl color *Science* v355 no6324 p465 F 3 2017

Piracy (Maritime)

See also

Hijacking of ships

Where Pirates Still Roam the Seas color *Time* v189 no18 p12 My 15 2017

Piraeus Port Authority SA

Shipping News J. PSAROPOULOS color map *Weekly Standard* v22 no45 p24 Ag 7 2017

Pirate Party (Political party : Iceland)

ON PIRATE ISLAND IN THE NORTH ATLANTIC P. HOCKENOS bw color *Nation* v303 no19 p22 N 7 2016

The Pirate Party Sets Sail for Election Victory In Iceland T. John color *Time* v188 no19 p9 N 7 2016

Pirate Radio (Film)

5 MOVIES FOR INSOMNIACS M. FELL *TV Guide* v65 no14 p45 Ap 3 2017

Pirates

A Pirate's Life for Me E. Spitznagel color *Money* v46 no7 p84 Ag 2017

Pirates of the Caribbean: Dead Men Tell No Tales (Film)

'Pirates 5' Scrapes the Franchise Bottom P. Travers color *Rolling Stone* no1289 p60 Je 15 2017

PIRATES OF THE CARIBBEAN: DEAD MEN TELL NO TALES M. Snetiker color *Entertainment Weekly* no1463/1464 p36 Ap/My 2017

WHEN ZOMBIE SHARKS ATTACK D. Coggan color *Entertainment Weekly* no1468/1469 p84 Je 2-9 2017

Pirates of the Caribbean: The Curse of the Black Pearl (Film)

Pirates of the Caribbean: The Curse of the Black Pearl M. FELL *TV Guide* v65 no21 p42 My 15 2017

Pirates—History

A Lot of What Is Known about Pirates Is Not True, and a Lot of What Is True Is Not Known M. G. Hanna *Humanities* v38 no1 p1 Wint 2017

Pirch (Company)

CATCHING FIRE color *Architectural Digest* v73 no11 p108 N 2016

Pirelli & C. SpA

REEL BEAUTY L. IMMEDIATO *Los Angeles Magazine* p36 Ap 2017

Pirelli Tire LLC

A TIRE FOR EVERY SEASON S. Horaczek color *Popular Science* v289 no4 p37 Jl/Ag 2017

Pires, Carmen

Ten policies for pollinators bibl color *Science* v354 no6315 p975 N 25 2016

Pires, Leah

KINDLING color *Art in America* v105 no6 p88 Je/Jl 2017

Piri Reis, d. ca. 1554

The Map K. Wiles *History Today* v67 no3 p26 Mr 2017

Pirronello, V.

Observation of a large-scale anisotropy in the arrival directions of cosmic rays above 8×1018 eV *Science* v357 no6357 p1266 S 22 2017

Pisani, Niccolò

The Fortune Global 500 Isn't All That Global *Harvard Business Review Digital Articles* p2 N 4 2014

Pisano, Dominic V.

Community network for deaf scientists color *Science* v356 no6336 p386 Ap 28 2017

PISANO, GARY P.

Neurodiversity as a Competitive Advantage color *Harvard Business Review* v95 no3 p96 My/Je 2017

Pisces (Astrology)

Surviving a Pisces M. ENGLISH *USA Today Magazine* v145 no2862 p70 Mr 2017

Pisces (Constellation)

A fishy tale in the fall sky S. JAMES O'MEARA color *Astronomy* v45 no11 p16 N 2017

PISCOPO, JENNIFER M.

L.A. Women LEAD THE WAY *Ms.* v27 no1 p32 Spr 2017

Pisgah National Forest (N.C.)

Instant Awesome M. HORJUS and R. Wichelns color map *Backpacker* p76 Je 2017

PISHKO, JESSICA

JUVENILE LIFERS' LAST CHANCE bw color *Nation* v305 no1 p18 Jl 3 2017

Pismennaya, Evgenia

Does Putin Still Favor His Sidekick? color graph *Bloomberg Businessweek* no4520 p28 My 1 2017

Pisner, Devin

THE Quints HAVE Kids L. MILK color *Washingtonian Magazine* v52 no7 p76 Ap 2017

Pisner family

THE Quints HAVE Kids L. MILK color *Washingtonian Magazine* v52 no7 p76 Ap 2017

Pissarro, Camille, 1830-1903—Exhibitions

The Perennial Student J. Bell color *New York Review of Books* v64 no12 p23 Jl 13 2017

Pistachio Press (Company)

POWER OF THE PRESS A. BRANDT *Cincinnati Magazine* v50 no5 p38 F 2017

Pistol shooting

POINT SHOOTING B. M. TOWSLEY color *Outdoor Life* v224 no8 pP7 O 2017

Pistols

CASE FOR THE REVOLVER B. M. TOWSLEY color *Outdoor Life* v224 no4 pP15 My 2017

SPEED & PRECISION DRILL B. M. TOWSLEY and J. B. SNOW color *Outdoor Life* v224 no5 pR1 Je/Jl 2017

TERMINAL BALLISTICS PRIMER R. MANN color *Outdoor Life* v224 no4 pP6 My 2017

Pistols—Accidents

A BACKUP PLAN K. Ainsworth color map *Outdoor Life* v223 no9 pH7 N 2016

Pistols—Design & construction

PISTOL ENVY *MHQ: Quarterly Journal of Military History* v29 no3 p62 Spr 2017

Pistols—Equipment & supplies

.38 SPECIALS J. B. SNOW color *Outdoor Life* v224 no8 pP8 O 2017

Pistols—Evaluation

ADVENTURES IN SQUIRREL COUNTRY W. BRANTLEY, T. E. NICKENS et al cartoon *Field & Stream* v122 no5 p59 O 2017

CARRY ON W. Brantley color *Field & Stream* v122 no1 p52 My 2017

RUGER LCP II Y. SUED and J. B. SNOW color *Outdoor Life* v224 no4 pP1 My 2017

STI 211 HEX TACTICAL J. B. SNOW chart color *Outdoor Life* v224 no1 pR13 D 2016/Ja 2017

Pistols—History

The Responsible Parties W. Utley and R. S. Neyland *Archaeology* v69 no6 p8 N/D 2016

Pistols—Safety measures

THE SLIDE STOP R. MANN color *Outdoor Life* v224 no8 pP5 O 2017

Piston rings—Evaluation

TESTED: TOTAL SEAL'S 110V RING FILER B. Gillogly color *Hot Rod* v70 no2 p72 F 2017

Pistons

See also

Automobile piston & piston rings

Jake Jacobs Asks... Can Pistons Be Changed on a Rotating Assembly Without Upsetting Its Balance? M. Davis color *Hot Rod* v70 no8 p112 Ag 2017

Pistrui, Joseph

How Managers Can See the Future More Clearly *Harvard Business Review Digital Articles* p2 O 2 2015

To Seize the Future, Create a Leadership Circle *Harvard Business Review Digital Articles* p2 Je 23 2016

Piłsudski, Józef, 1867-1935

MIRACLE ON THE VISTULA T. Fleming bw color map *MHQ: Quarterly Journal of Military History* v30 no1 p66 Aut 2017

Pit bull terriers

Amazing Animals K. JAZYNKA color map *National Geographic Kids* no470 p12 My 2017

Pitaevskii, Lev

Leonid Keldysh *Physics Today* v70 no6 p75 Je 2017

Lev Petrovich Gor'kov *Physics Today* v70 no5 p68 My 2017

Pitas, Jeannine M.

Idyll color *U.S. Catholic* v82 no2 p11 F 2017

Seeds color *U.S. Catholic* v82 no1 p11 Ja 2017

To an Immigrant il *U.S. Catholic* v82 no5 p11 My 2017

Pitbull, 1981-

Squabbling in the Sunshine A. Greenblatt *Governing* v30 no8 p9 My 2017

Pitch (TV program)

America's top TV critic Matt Roush answers your burning questions M. Roush *TV Guide* v65 no21 p5 My 15 2017

Can Pitch Be a Major League Success? J. HALTERMAN color *TV Guide* v64 no42 p8 O 10 2016

WATCH THIS/SORRY ABOUT THAT D. Snierson color *Entertainment Weekly* no1438 p51 N 4 2016

Pitch Perfect 3 (Film)
  PITCH PERFECT 3 R. Kinane color *Entertainment Weekly* no1478 / 1479 p78 Ag 18-25 2017

Pitchers (Baseball)
  Beyond Relief: Managers rarely use their closers—often the most dominant pitchers in baseball—for more than a few outs at the end of the game. Is that beginning to change? B. Schoenfeld *New York Times Magazine* p42 O 1 2017
  HAVE IT BOTH WAYS L. J. Wertheim color *Sports Illustrated* v126 no11 p92 Ap 17-24 2017
  Mourning After T. Verducci and T. Keith color *Sports Illustrated* v126 no4 p14 Ja 30 2017
  THE SEEKER B. Reiter color *Sports Illustrated* v127 no4 p60 Ag 7 2017
  SYNDERELLA B. Reiter color *Sports Illustrated* v126 no5 p64 F 13 2017

Pitchers (Baseball)—Awards
  MACKENZIE GORE S. Apstein color *Sports Illustrated* v127 no2 p32 Jl 17 2017

Pitchers (Baseball)—Biography
  Noah Syndergaard J. Crelin color *Current Biography* v78 no9 p85 S 2017

Pitchers (Containers)
  A "Circa '70" Pattern Silver Tea & Coffee Service color *Magazine Antiques* v184 no3 p11 My/Je 2017
  Gorham Sterling 'Japanese' Tea & Coffee Service color *Magazine Antiques* v184 no3 p137 My/Je 2017

Pitchers (Containers)—Evaluation
  All-Star Pitchers color *Treasures* v5 no5 p8 Ap/My 2016
  Beyond the Brita T. RAMI img *New York* p61 F 9 2017

Pitchers (Containers)—History
  ARTIFACT J. A. LOBELL color *Archaeology* v70 no2 p68 Mr/Ap 2017

Pitchfork Media Inc.
  PiTCHFORK GROWS UP D. Leonard color *Bloomberg Businessweek* no4521 p59 My 8 2017

Pitching (Baseball)
  16 PITCH WHISPERERS T. Verducci color *Sports Illustrated* v126 no9 p69 Mr 27 2017
  The Case for ... Banishing Beanballs J. Dickey and T. Keith color *Sports Illustrated* v126 no15 p26 My 29 2017

Pitching (Baseball)—History
  REAL MEN HAVE CURVES [Cover story] T. Verducci color *Sports Illustrated* v126 no15 p36 My 29 2017

Pitching (Golf)
  private LESSONS color *Golf Magazine* v59 no8 p99 Ag 2017
  Why Can't I Get My Pitches to Bite? B. Manzella and D. Denunzio *Golf Magazine* v59 no11 p54 N 2017

Pitici, Mircea
  The Best Writing in Mathematics 2017 *Publishers Weekly* v264 no39 p97 S 25 2017

Pitino, Rick, 1952-
  CARDINALS' SINS T. Layden color *Sports Illustrated* v127 no11 p26 O 9 2017

Pitman, N. C. A.
  Persistent effects of pre-Columbian plant domestication on Amazonian forest composition bibl chart graph map *Science* v355 no6328 p925 Mr 3 2017

Pitman, Nigel
  Forest conservation: Humans' handprints bibl color *Science* v355 no6324 p466 F 3 2017

Pitner, Gregory
  MoS2 transistors with 1-nanometer gate lengths bibl color graph *Science* v354 no6308 p99 O 7 2016

Pitney, John J. Jr.
  AMERICA'S RELENTLESS SUITOR *Claremont Review of Books* v16 no4 p22 Fall 2016

Pitock, Todd
  A DISCOURAGING WORD *Saturday Evening Post* v289 no3 p10 My/Je 2017
  FLOATING TOWARD ECSTASY *Saturday Evening Post* v289 no1 p56 Ja/F 2017

Piton, Jérémie
  Red squirrels in the British Isles are infected with leprosy bacilli bibl color diag map *Science* v354 no6313 p744 N 11 2016

Pitoniak, Anna

The Futures *Publishers Weekly* v263 no39 p62 S 26 2016

Pitsiladis, Yannis
  SWEAT THE DETAILS A. HUTCHINSON color *Runner's World* v51 no10 p44 N 2016

PITSKER, KAITLIN
  Alexa, at Your Command color *Kiplinger's Personal Finance* v71 no1 p37 Ja 2017
  Best Places to Retire [Cover story] color *Kiplinger's Personal Finance* v71 no8 p56 Ag 2017
  EMPLOYERS HELP WITH COLLEGE SAVING color *Kiplinger's Personal Finance* v71 no5 p13 My 2017
  HOME SMART HOME bw color *Kiplinger's Personal Finance* v71 no10 p64 O 2017
  Keep Your Memory Sharp cartoon color *Kiplinger's Personal Finance* v71 no4 p64 Ap 2017
  Kiplinger's Best College Values 2017 chart color *Kiplinger's Personal Finance* v71 no2 p36 F 2017
  The Lure of Virtual Reality color *Kiplinger's Personal Finance* v71 no7 p41 Jl 2017
  MONEY MADE SIMPLE [Cover story] color *Kiplinger's Personal Finance* v71 no5 p24 My 2017
  Now Hear This cartoon *Kiplinger's Personal Finance* v71 no10 p70 O 2017
  SKIRTING THE SALARY QUESTION color *Kiplinger's Personal Finance* v71 no7 p14 Jl 2017
  THERE'S MORE TO THE MALL THAN SHOPPING color *Kiplinger's Personal Finance* v70 no12 p13 D 2016
  Your Rights on Flights cartoon *Kiplinger's Personal Finance* v71 no7 p42 Jl 2017

Pitt, Brad, 1963-
  CAN ALLIED SURVIVE THE BREAKUP? N. Sperling and L. Rice color *Entertainment Weekly* no1434 p13 O 7 2016
  The Quiz T. BALAZO color *Maclean's* v129 no42 p64 O 24 2016

Pittampalli, Al
  The Best Leaders Allow Themselves to Be Persuaded *Harvard Business Review Digital Articles* p2 Mr 3 2016
  Stop Calling Every Conversation a "Meeting" *Harvard Business Review Digital Articles* p3 N 3 2015

Pittendreigh, W. Maynard
  Faith and Science at a Crossroad *Sky & Telescope* v134 no3 p6 S 2017

Pittinsky, Todd L.
  Learning from the other achievement gap *Phi Delta Kappan* v98 no5 p80 F 2017
  We're Making the Wrong Case for Diversity in Silicon Valley *Harvard Business Review Digital Articles* p2 Ap 11 2016

Pittman, Craig
  Citrus Be the Place S. Mirsky color *Scientific American* v315 no6 p85 D 2016

PITTMAN, RICHARD
  Your True Stories *Reader's Digest* v189 no1127 p28 F 2017

Pittmon, Nicole Marie
  BANGIN' BASH (On a Budget) color *Ebony* v72 no9 p54 Jl/Ag 2017

Pittock, Murray
  Blades not bullets *History Today* v67 no1 p45 Ja 2017
  The Spirit of '45 S. MILLER color *Weekly Standard* v22 no14 p34 D 12 2016

Pitts, Cherri
  Cherri Pitts: A Rose Amongst San Antonio's STARs S. HEAP *Humanist* v77 no5 p28 S/O 2017

Pitts, George
  1951-2017 GEORGE PITTS M. Romero color *Entertainment Weekly* no1457/1458 p17 Mr 17 2017

Pitts, Jake
  Storm WARNING [Cover story] color *Sail* v48 no8 p26 Ag 2017

PITTS, JAMILAH
  Don't Say Nothing *Education Digest* v82 no7 p50 Mr 2017

Pitts, Leonard
  Grant Park: A Novel L. Neff *Christian Century* v134 no2 p35 Ja 18 2017

Pittsburgh (Pa.)
  Innovative Community Celebrations in an Urban Green Space [Cover story] S. Roller *Parks & Recreation* v51 no12 p32 D 2016

Pittsburgh (Pa.)—Description & travel

Pittsburgh A. FLANGO *Cincinnati Magazine* p62 Je 2017

Steel Yourself: You're Gonna Love Pittsburgh B. HANSEN-BUNDY color *GQ: Gentlemen's Quarterly* v97 no9 p82 S 2017

Pittsburgh (Pa.)—Environmental conditions

Pittsburgh myth, Paris reality P. Gallagher color *Science* v356 no6343 p1103 Je 16 2017

Pittsburgh Penguins (Hockey team)

Emperor PENGUINS A. Prewitt color *Sports Illustrated* v126 no17 p42 Je 19 2017

Leading Off K. Kahler color *Sports Illustrated* v126 no17 p8 Je 19 2017

Lost to History T. Keith color *Sports Illustrated* v126 no17 p18 Je 19 2017

NHL HOCKEY T. WORGO color *TV Guide* v64 no42 p48 O 10 2016

WHO CAN END THE PENGUINS' REIGN? J. Fuchs color *Sports Illustrated* v127 no11 p43 O 9 2017

Pittsburgh Pirates (Baseball team)

3 PIRATES color *Sports Illustrated* v126 no9 p105 Mr 27 2017

Pittsburgh Steelers (Football team)

1 Pittsburgh Steelers color *Sports Illustrated* v127 no7 p70 S 4 2017

Pitt-Watson, David

What We Lose When Giant Investment Funds Run All Our Companies *Harvard Business Review Digital Articles* p2 Jl 19 2016

Pitz, Katie

Trouble in Tropics color *Oceanus* v51 no2 p60 Wint 2016

Pius XII, Pope, 1876-1958

JOHN CONNELLY REPLIES: J. CONNELLY *Commonweal* v144 no7 p2 Ap 14 2017

LESSONS LEARNED? J. CORNWELL *Commonweal* v144 no7 p2 Ap 14 2017

PIVEN, FRANCES FOX

The Prospects for Resistance il *Nation* v304 no4 p13 F 6 2017

Scenes from the Front Lines bw color *In These Times* v40 no11 p29 N 2016

Piven, Jeremy, 1965-

Wisdom of the Crowd A. Bacle, D. Coggan et al color *Entertainment Weekly* no1482/1483 p34 S 22 2017

Pivot Cycles (Company)

"SHOULD I GET AN ENDURO BIKE?" R. Koch and B. STRICKLAND color *Bicycling* v58 no3 p94 Ap 2017

Pivotal Corp.

Why My Company Serves Free Breakfast to All Employees J. Hum *Harvard Business Review Digital Articles* p1 My 1 2017

Piwecka, Monika

Loss of a mammalian circular RNA locus causes miRNA deregulation and affects brain function color *Science* v357 no6357 p1254 S 22 2017

Piwowar, Michael—Political & social views

SEC's Acting Chair Acts Like He Runs the Place R. Schmidt and B. Bain bw *Bloomberg Businessweek* no4512 p29 F 20 2017

Pixar (Company)

How Pixar Lost Its Way C. ORR cartoon *Atlantic* v319 no5 p34 Je 2017

Think Like an Author, Not an Owner C. A. Hidalgo *Harvard Business Review Digital Articles* p2 O 15 2015

Pixels

4 secrets for editing images in Apple Photos L. SNIDER color *Macworld - Digital Edition* p117 F 2017

Pixie Technology Inc.

PIXIE SMART TAGS J. R. BOOKWALTER color *Macworld - Digital Edition* v34 no4 p43 My 2017

Pixley, Marcella

Ready to Fall color *Publishers Weekly* v264 no38 p73 S 18 2017

Pizer, William A.

What's the damage from climate change? *Science* v356 no6345 p1330 Je 30 2017

Pizza

15-Minute All-Organic Meal Under $15 color *Prevention* v69 no5 p13 My 2017

American Pie S. Sifton *New York Times Magazine* p32 Ja 15 2017

Bonfire Pizza Chips A. Larson *Idaho Magazine* v16 no9 p56 Je 2017

BREAKFAST PIZZA *Washingtonian Magazine* v52 no1 p91 O 2016

Cabin Fever E. HARE color *Cabin Living* p84 Ja/F 2017

THE CHRISTIANE CHRONICLES *Atlanta* v56 no12 p60 Ap 2017

DISH OF THE MONTH A. SPIEGEL *Washingtonian Magazine* v52 no2 p263 N 2016

DISH OF THE MONTH J. SIDMAN *Washingtonian Magazine* v52 no8 p135 My 2017

FARM-TO-TABLE FAVES *Indianapolis Monthly* v12 no40 p79 Ag 2017

FAVORITE FLAVORS A. Limpert, A. Spiegel et al *Washingtonian Magazine* v52 no3 p154 D 2016

Happy, healthy pizza night L. Lillien color *Redbook* p87 N 2017

Inside the Hot Mess Kitchen G. Moskowitz and M. Berman color *Glamour* v115 no9 p111 S 2017

kitchen J. BEDDIA color *Bon Appetit* v62 no4 p31 Ap 2017

The Longest Meals T. John color *Time* v189 no24 p10 Je 26 2017

MAC'S ZUCCHINI-CRUST PIZZA bw color *Skiing* p22 Wint 2017

Mixing Bowl color *O, The Oprah Magazine* p172 My 2017

The NEW RULES of PIZZA cartoon color *Men's Health* v32 no8 p123 O 2017

OUR GUIDE TO THE FUTURE OF FOOD *Nation* v305 no11 p23 O 30 2017

THE PIES HAVE IT S. GOLDBERG color *Cincinnati Magazine* v51 no1 p82 O 2017

Pizza Power color *Bicycling* v58 no6 p38 Jl 2017

Q + A cartoon *Cincinnati Magazine* v51 no1 p26 O 2017

RECIPES I. Newman *Virginia Living* v15 no1 p71 D 2016

RISE TO THE OCCASION *Martha Stewart Living* no268 p88 O 2016

The Salad Pizza *Saturday Evening Post* v289 no2 p23 Mr/Ap 2017

San Antonio *Texas Monthly* v45 no3 p142 Mr 2017

SLICE OF LIFE J. COHEN *Cincinnati Magazine* v50 no2 p24 N 2016

Toss Like a Boss R. Kinane color *Entertainment Weekly* no1484 p50 S 29 2017

TRAINING TABLE [Cover story] A. MacMillan bw color *Runner's World* v51 no10 p52 N 2016

UPPER CRUST [Cover story] J. MURPHY color *Runner's World* v52 no4 p28 My 2017

What's for Dinner? R. HILMANTEL *Scholastic Choices* v32 no3 p12 N/D 2016

Year of the Square img *New York* p66 F 9 2017

Your Pooch Is Becoming A PIZZA ADDICT K. Asp color *O, The Oprah Magazine* p76 Ag 2017

PIZZA, DONNA

a perfect marriage color *Arts & Crafts Homes & the Revival* v12 no3 p40 Summ 2017

Pizza chefs

FROM PORTUGAL WITH LOVE W. BOLAND and M. SAMET bw color *Climbing* no353 p66 My/Je 2017

A Pizza-Making Robot J. Zorthian color *Time* v189 no7/8 p27 F 27 2017

Pizza dough

home made PIZZA DOUGH color *Good Housekeeping* v264 no3 p131 Mr 2017

kitchen J. BEDDIA color *Bon Appetit* v62 no4 p31 Ap 2017

Pizza Power color *Bicycling* v58 no6 p38 Jl 2017

RISE TO THE OCCASION *Martha Stewart Living* no268 p88 O 2016

Pizza—Equipment & supplies

A SLICE OF ALFRESCO EATING C. HASLAM bw color *House Beautiful* p144 Ag 2017

Pizza—Evaluation

Year of the Square img *New York* p66 Ja 9 2017

Pizzerias

Little Italy: Authentic Italian cuisine is among the last things you'd expect to find in Gila Bend, but Little Italy is the real deal. Even Prince Harry says it serves "the best pizza in the world". N. AUSTIN *Arizona Highways* v93 no6 p12 Je 2017

That's Outrageous! color *Reader's Digest* v189 no1129 p82 Ap 2017

Pizzerias—Evaluation

DINING GUIDE M. Cameran color *New Orleans Magazine* v51 no5 p96 Mr 2017

Poor Hendrix J. ZYMAN *Atlanta* v57 no1 p68 My 2017

Restaurant GUIDE *Indianapolis Monthly* p152 My 2017

Restaurant GUIDE *Indianapolis Monthly* v12 no40 p178 Ag 2017

Variety on Piety J. Forman color *New Orleans Magazine* v51 no8 p100 Je 2017

Pizzi, Donna

A CRAFTSMAN HOME in Perfect Pitch [Cover story] color *Arts & Crafts Homes & the Revival* v12 no5 p40 Wint 2018

DECO delight color *Old House Journal* v45 no2 p14 Ap 2017

Gentle Stewards for a 1908 house color *Arts & Crafts Homes & the Revival* v12 no2 p40 Spr 2017

Pleasures of TAKING IT BACK color *Arts & Crafts Homes & the Revival* v12 no3 p25 Summ 2017

A Storybook ODYSSEY color *Old House Journal* v44 no8 p28 D 2016

PJ1 (Company)

STICKY ICKY color *Road & Track* v68 no8 p100 My 2017

Pkala, J.

Observation of a large-scale anisotropy in the arrival directions of cosmic rays above 8×1018 eV *Science* v357 no6357 p1266 S 22 2017

Place (Philosophy)

Baby Center J. CASE *Orion Magazine* v35 no4/5 p38 Jl-O 2016

Place, Liz

Hind-End 'L' [Cover story] color *Horse & Rider* v56 no5 p31 My 2017

Step Control color *Horse & Rider* v56 no7 p41 Jl 2017

Place marketing

CAPITOLA, CALIF *Sea Magazine* v108 no10 pCA-10 O 2016

Place mats

Fancy Feast L. Tudor *New Orleans Homes & Lifestyles* v20 no3 p33 Summ 2017

Place mats—Evaluation

Whirlwind color *Architectural Digest* v74 no2 p19 F 2017

Placebos (Medicine)

See also

Nocebos (Medicine)

JUST LIKE MEDICINE T. G. HOPE *Prevention* v69 no5 p54 My 2017

Mind Over Matter E. Vance color diag *National Geographic* v230 no6 p30 D 2016

Nocebo effects can make you feel pain L. Colloca color *Science* v357 no6359 p44 O 6 2017

Placebos (Medicine)—History

Why I Take Fake Pills: Surprising new research shows that placebos still work even when you know they're not real R. A. SIEGEL *Smithsonian* v48 no2 p21 My 2017

Placenta

BABY'S FIRST ORGAN A. Erlebacher and S. J. Fisher color *Scientific American* v317 no4 p46 O 2017

Placenta praevia

complicating factors H. PEVZNER *Parents* p129 2015

Placenta—Development

Finding beauty in a mouse wheel of life E. S. Eaton color *Science News* v191 no7 p32 Ap 15 2017

Places of retirement

WHERE SHOULD YOU RETIRE? W. P. BARRETT and A. BROWN color *Forbes* v200 no1 p20 Jl 27 2017

Plachta, N.

A microtubule-organizing center directing intracellular transport in the early mouse embryo diag *Science* v357 no6354 p925 S 1 2017

Placodermi

The first jaws J. A. Long bibl color *Science* v354 no6310 p280 O 21 2016

Fossil find revises history of jaws M. ROSEN color *Science News* v190 no11 p12 N 26 2016

A Silurian maxillate placoderm illuminates jaw evolution Min Zhu, P. E. Ahlberg et al bibl color *Science* v354 no6310 p334 O 21 2016

Placodes

HOW VERTEBRATES GOT THEIR COATS M. GresÛo color *National Geographic* v232 no4 p14 O 2017

PLAGENS, PETER

All Seeing, If Not All Knowing *Architectural Record* v205 no7 p51 Jl 2017

Plagiarism

Creating a culture of ethics in Iran M. S. Rezaee-Zavareh, Z. Naji et al bibl *Science* v354 no6310 p296 O 21 2016

Iran's science landscape in context R. Mansouri *Science* v354 no6319 p1542 D 23 2016

Plaid

1975 PLAID L. HEDRICK color *Better Homes & Gardens* v95 no11 p156 N 2017

Adam's Home STYLE SHEET: MAD FOR PLAID A. Glassman color *O, The Oprah Magazine* p70 N 2017

You're gonna want some plaid B. Goreski color *Redbook* p18 N 2017

Plaid—Evaluation

CHECK THIS OUT S. Kennedy color *Bloomberg Businessweek* no4504 p64 D 19 2016

Mad About Plaid color *Timber Home Living* v27 no2 p10 Ap 2017

Plains bison

BACK WHERE THEY BELONG N. WILSON color map *Canadian Geographic* v137 no5 p32 S/O 2017

Planck, Max, 1858-1947

1918: Berlin A. Einstein *Lapham's Quarterly* v10 no2 p125 Spr 2017

Planet Earth II (TV program)

Nature's Blockbuster K. O'Reilly *Sierra* v102 no2 p8 Mr/Ap 2017

Planet Earth As Spectacle and Cautionary Tale J. Worland color *Time* v189 no7/8 p111 F 27 2017

Planet Earth II A. D'arminio color *TV Guide* v65 no7 p39 F 13 2017

PLANET EARTH II D. Vaughn color *Sound & Vision* v82 no7 p71 S 2017

A Trestles Taxonomy T. PRODANOVICH color *Surfer* v58 no5 p32 S 2017

TV'S WINNERS AND LOSERS BY THE NUMBERS *TV Guide* v65 no11 p16 Mr 6 2017

A View to a Kill C. DICKEY color *New Republic* v248 no3 p54 Mr 2017

Planet Nine

Citizen scientists join the hunt for Planet 9 A. Yeager color *Science News* v191 no1 p28 Je 10 2017

COULD PLANET NINE TILT OUR SOLAR SYSTEM? J. Wenz color *Astronomy* v45 no2 p12 F 2017

Hunt for Planet Nine heats up A. Mann diag *Science* v354 no6311 p399 O 28 2016

New haul of distant worlds casts doubt on Planet Nine J. Sokol *Science* v356 no6344 p1221 Je 23 2017

Planet of the Apes (Film)

Ape Overload R. DOUTHAT *National Review* v69 no15 p47 Ag 14 2017

The Hero As Actor M. MATTIX color *Weekly Standard* v22 no32 p34 My 1 2017

Planetarium (Music)

Cosmic meditations from Sufjan Stevens C. E. McCarthy color *America* v217 no3 p49 Ag 7 2017

What to Stream color *Entertainment Weekly* no1470 p58 Je 16 2017

Planetariums

WITH KIDS *Indianapolis Monthly* p61 F 2017

Planetary exploration

See also

Exploration of Jupiter

Saturn exploration

Faith and Science at a Crossroad G. Imm, D. Waters et al *Sky & Telescope* v134 no3 p6 S 2017

The Hunt for Planet X: Evidence is building that a large world lurks far beyond Pluto and the Kuiper Belt. The race to find it is on S. S. Sheppard *Sky & Telescope* v134 no4 p16 O 2017

STAR DOME R. TALCOTT color *Astronomy* v45 no11 p38 N 2017

A system of seven worlds D. J. Eicher color *Astronomy* v45 no7 p8 Jl 2017

Planetary mass

HAT-P-26b: A Neptune-mass exoplanet with a well-constrained heavy element abundance H. R. Wakeford, D. K. Sing et al chart diag graph *Science* v356 no6338 p628 My 12 2017

Planetary nebulae

GALLERY color *Sky & Telescope* v134 no2 p74 Ag 2017

George Abell's Ethereal Bubbles S. Gottlieb *Sky & Telescope*

LILIES FOR DAYS M. OZAWA color *Martha Stewart Living* p90 My 2017

SEEDING SUCCESS L. BEDORD *Successful Farming* v114 no12 p42 Mid-N 2016

Plant life cycles

Sex and the Single Gametophyte: Revising the Homosporous Vascular Plant Life Cycle in Light of Contemporary Research C. H. HAUFLER, K. M. PRYER et al *BioScience* v66 no11 p928 N 1 2016

Plant mechanics

Structure and assembly mechanism of plant C2S2M2-type PSII-LHCII supercomplex X. Su, J. Ma et al color *Science* v357 no6353 p815 Ag 25 2017 .

Plant metabolism

Plant metabolons assembled on demand M. Dastmalchi and P. J. Facchini bibl color *Science* v354 no6314 p829 N 18 2016

To Feed the World, Improve Photosynthesis K. Bourzac color *MIT Technology Review* v120 no5 p80 S/O 2017

Plant-microbe relationships

RESEARCH color *Science* v356 no6343 p1134 Je 16 2017

Plant nutrients

How microbes survive in the open ocean J. P. Zehr, J. S. Weitz et al color diag *Science* v357 no6352 p646 Ag 18 2017

SILENT ALARMS: Look closely. Your corn might be trying to tell you something. Watch for signs of the following 5 nutrient deficiencies K. Birchmier *Successful Farming* v115 no11 p38 S 2017

Plant nutrition

See also

Crops—Nutrition

Fertilizers

Ants in Your Plants K. Moore color *Natural History* v125 no11 p6 N 2017

Plant openings (Factories)

the temple K. DUPZYK color *Popular Mechanics* p82 Jl 2017

Plant pathologists

SCOUT FOR SUDDEN DEATH SYNDROME: IOWA STATE UNIVERSITY EXTENSION PLANT PATHOLOGIST DAREN MUELLER ANSWERS FIVE QUESTIONS WITH THE LATEST RESEARCH RESULTS ON SDS G. Johnston color *Successful Farming* v115 no7 p34 My 2017

Plant phenology

PHENOLOGY S. McNulty *New York State Conservationist* v71 no4 p24 F 2017

Plant photoreceptors

See also

Phytochromes

A photoreceptor's on-off switch C. Fankhauser and R. Ulm bibl diag *Science* v354 no6310 p282 O 21 2016

Plant physiology

How plants learned to breathe E. Pennisi color *Science* v355 no6330 p1110 Mr 17 2017

Releasing plant volatiles, as simple as ABC F. Eberl and J. Gershenzon color *Science* v356 no6345 p1334 Je 30 2017

Plant products

See also

Fibers

Pepper spray

Much ado about mulching T. Brockman *Christian Century* v134 no17 p32 Ag 16 2017

Plant propagation

ONE TO GROW ON L. SCARDELLI color *Rodale's Organic Life* v2 no7 p34 D 2016/Ja 2017

Plant protection

BUILDING A BETTER HARVEST M. Broadfoot color *Scientific American* v317 no2 p66 Ag 2017

Rooting for Trees *South Dakota Magazine* v32 no6 p91 Mr/Ap 2017

Plant proteins

POWER PLANTS V. Tweed color *Amazing Wellness* v9 no2 p72 Spr 2017

Plant shutdowns

Did Streaming Finally Kill Serving? J. SCIACCA color *Sound & Vision* v81 no10 p26 D 2016

Nuclear Withdrawal A. Greenblatt *Governing* v30 no9 p12 Je 2017

THE WORKERS TRUMP FORGOT S. JAFFE color *Nation* v304 no15 p18 My 8 2017

Plant shutdowns—United States

END OF THE LINE E. Fry color *Fortune* v175 no2 p80 F 1 2017

Plant-soil relationships

See also

Soil productivity

Belowground drivers of plant diversity W. H. van der Putten bibl color *Science* v355 no6321 p134 Ja 13 2017

Plant-soil feedback and the maintenance of diversity in Mediterranean-climate shrublands F. P. Teste, P. Kardol et al bibl graph *Science* v355 no6321 p1 Ja 13 2017

Plant-soil feedbacks and mycorrhizal type influence temperate forest population dynamics J. A. Bennett, H. Maherali et al bibl graph map *Science* v355 no6321 p1 Ja 13 2017

Plant species

Gulf of St Lawrence Beach Pinweed M. WALWYN color *Canadian Wildlife* v23 no4 p37 S/O 2017

IN PRAISE of VIOLAS A. MAZE color *Better Homes & Gardens* v95 no4 p126 Ap 2017

Land Between the Lakes R. H. MOHLENBROCK color map *Natural History* v125 no11 p42 N 2017

Meet the World's 'Newest' Plants T. John color *Time* v189 no21 p12 Je 5 2017

Plant stems

Aerial Picnic color *National Wildlife (World Edition)* v55 no2 p50 F/Mr 2017

How to Knot a Cherry Stem With Your Tongue M. Wollan *New York Times Magazine* p28 Je 25 2017

Plant toxins

Too Hot to Stomach L. Evans Ogden color *Natural History* v125 no10 p7 O 2017

Tough Choices for a Pygmy Rabbit L. SHIPLEY, J. FORBEY et al color map *Natural History* v125 no3 p9 Mr 2017

Plant varieties

Organic Seed Cultivars to Try This Year S. Stonebrook *Mother Earth News* no281 p8 Ap/My 2017

Precision Decisions *Successful Farming* v115 no4 p44 Mr 2017

TERRIFIC TOMATOES for Spectacular Sauces and Creative Canning C. LeHoullier *Mother Earth News* no280 p20 F/Mr 2017

Plant-water relationships

See also

Water requirements of plants

How plants hunt water S. Milius color *Science News* v192 no6 p24 O 14 2017

Plantar fasciitis

Plantar Fasciitis [Cover story] R. LALIBERTE cartoon *Prevention* v69 no4 p18 Ap 2017

Plantar fasciitis—Prevention

Feet First E. A. KANE color *Better Nutrition* v79 no9 p26 S 2017

Plantations

Barrens to Blueberries J. D. SHORTHOUSE color map *Natural History* v125 no6 p34 Je 2017

Certified Spectacular color *Canadian Wildlife* v23 no2 p38 My/Je 2017

Grow Up E. Millard color *Log Home Living* v34 no6 p36 Ag 2017

HISTORICALLY PASSIONATE P. F. Stahls Jr. color *Louisiana Life* v37 no6 p44 Jl/Ag 2017

On the Plantation color *American History* v52 no3 p30 Ag 2017

Pothos J. Hughes *New York Times Magazine* p26 Je 11 2017

Plantations—History

Belvoir's Legacy J. M. SCHABLITSKY color *Archaeology* v69 no6 p55 N/D 2016

Plantations—Louisiana

HISTORICALLY PASSIONATE P. F. Stahls Jr. color *Louisiana Life* v37 no6 p44 Jl/Ag 2017

Plantations—Maryland

Belvoir's Legacy J. M. SCHABLITSKY color *Archaeology* v69 no6 p55 N/D 2016

Plante, David

NEW BOOKS C. Smallwood *Harper's Magazine* p83 S 2017

Planters (Agricultural machinery)

THE FARM D. Gephart, G. Gunn et al *Successful Farming* v115 no11 p75 S 2017

Great Outdoors color *Old House Journal* v45 no5 p52 Ag 2017

LARGE SPLIT-ROW PLANTER PRICES ARE UP D. Mowitz *Successful Farming* v115 no4 p28 Mr 2017

Pinpoint Planting D. Mowitz *Successful Farming* v115 no4 p34 Mr 2017

THE PLANTING SQUAD L. BEDORD *Successful Farming* v115 no4 p41 Mr 2017

Planters (Agricultural machinery)—Equipment & supplies—Evaluation

SHOOT STARTER WITH SEED A. McConnell and L. Bedord *Successful Farming* v114 no10 p30 O 2016

Planters (Agricultural machinery)—Evaluation

POCKET PRICE GUIDE: Late-Model 16/31 Planters *Successful Farming* v115 no4 p31 Mr 2017

Planting (Plant culture)

See also

Tree planting

AROUND THE GARDEN S. Bender color map *Southern Living* v52 no2 p46 F 2017

AROUND THE GARDEN S. Bender color *Southern Living* v52 no10 p50 O 2017

AROUND THE GARDEN S. Bender color *Southern Living* v52 no5 p60 My 2017

Building a Good Picket Fence B. Ticineto and J. Chase color *Old House Journal* v45 no5 p48 Ag 2017

GREEN THUMB F. SUN *Atlanta* v56 no12 p44 Ap 2017

Martha's Month chart color *Martha Stewart Living* p4 Ap 2017

Planting garlic T. Brockman color *Christian Century* v133 no26 p11 D 21 2016

POT LUCK L. HEDRICK color *Better Homes & Gardens* v95 no4 p46 Ap 2017

PROVE IT ON THE FARM: ON-FARM TEST PLOTS HAVE LED TO SUCCESSFUL PRACTICE ADOPTION ON THIS FARM G. Gullickson *Successful Farming* v115 no11 p43 S 2017

The Shapely Boxwood K. Owen color *Southern Living* v52 no9 p24 S 2017

Window Boxes P. POORE and B. D. Coleman color *Old House Journal* v45 no5 p60 Ag 2017

Your CHECKLIST E. Jardina color *Sunset* v238 no3 p40 Mr 2017

Plantinga, Adam—Interviews

A cop's view from the street D. Heim *Christian Century* v134 no6 p32 Mr 15 2017

Plantronics Inc.

PLANTRONICS BACKBEAT PRO 2 S. J. PUREWAL color *Macworld - Digital Edition* p41 F 2017

Plants

See also

Aquatic plants

Endemic plants

Fire resistant plants

Flowers

Herbs

Ornamental plants

Photography of plants

Plant diversity

Plant varieties

Roots (Botany)

Seeds

Succulent plants

Weeds

7 MISSOURI DICAMBA-DAMAGE TAKEAWAYS G. Gullickson *Successful Farming* v115 no5 p42 Mid-Mr 2017

Evolution Blooms J. Wallace *Natural History* v124 no10 p34 N 2016

Life Finds a Way map *Earth Island Journal* v32 no2 p10 Summ 2017

Maple Syrup color *Vegetarian Today* no2 p14 Ap 2017

Nature's treasure hunt S. Boyer *Science* v356 no6336 p387 Ap 28 2017

SMARTY PLANTS M. ZARASKA color diag *Discover* v38 no4 p52 My 2017

Students *Oceanus* v52 no2 p21 Spr 2017

Veggies with Vision M. Zaraska color *Scientific American* v316 no1 p18 Ja 2017

WIN A GARDEN REVAMP! color *Sunset* v238 no3 p94 Mr 2017

Plants & the environment

Adaptation R. Hilleary, P. Kobina Arthur et al *Science* v356 no6335 p243 Ap 21 2017

Worth Their Weight in Gold M. Wexler color *National Wildlife (World Edition)* v55 no5 p12 Ag/S 2017

Plants in art

STUART THORNTON M. OWENS color *Architectural Digest* no6 p60 Je 1 2017

Plants in interior decoration

SHIMMER & SHINE M. HUGHES bw color *Better Homes & Gardens* v95 no6 p90 Je 2017

Plants—Adaptation

Light-sensing phytochromes feel the heat K. J. Halliday and S. J. Davis bibl color *Science* v354 no6314 p832 N 18 2016

Plants—Arctic regions

Shrinking sea ice threatens mobility S. MILIUS bw color *Science News* v190 no9 p8 O 29 2016

Plants—Canada

WHAT'S THIS? color *Canadian Geographic* v136 no6 p73 D 2016

Plants—Carbon content

The Virtual Forest V. SCHIPANI *American Scholar* v86 no2 p16 Spr 2017

Plants—India

Fruitful Endeavor N. Zevnik and V. TWEED color *Better Nutrition* v79 no10 p20 O 2017

Plaques, plaquettes

Writing on the Wall *Arizona Highways* v96 no7 p56 Jl 2017

PLA-RABÈS, SERGI

The Arctic in the Twenty-First Century: Changing Biogeochemical Linkages across a Paraglacial Landscape of Greenland *BioScience* v67 no2 p118 F 2017

Plaschke, F.

Structure, force balance, and topology of Earth's magnetopause diag graph *Science* v356 no6341 p960 Je 1 2017

Plasma Alfven waves

On the generation of solar spicules and Alfvénic waves J. Martínez-Sykora, B. De Pontieu et al diag *Science* v356 no6344 p1269 Je 23 2017

A STEP TOWARD DECIPHERING AURORAS *Physics Today* v70 no5 p22 My 2017

Plasma flow

PLASMA DISCHARGE FOR FOOD STERILIZATION *Physics Today* v69 no10 p22 O 2016

Plasma oscillations

A STEP TOWARD DECIPHERING AURORAS *Physics Today* v70 no5 p22 My 2017

Plasmodium falciparum

A key malaria metabolite modulates vector blood seeking, feeding, and susceptibility to infection S. N. Emami, B. G. Lindberg et al bibl chart diag *Science* v355 no6329 p1076 Mr 10 2017

Malaria molecule lures mosquitoes L. HAMERS color *Science News* v191 no5 p10 Mr 18 2017

Resistance to malaria through structural variation of red blood cell invasion receptors E. M. Leffler, G. Band et al diag *Science* v356 no6343 p1139 Je 16 2017

Plasmonics (Electronics)

Applying plasmonics to a sustainable future A. Naldoni, V. M. Shalaev et al color *Science* v356 no6341 p908 Je 1 2017

Plass, Mireya

Loss of a mammalian circular RNA locus causes miRNA deregulation and affects brain function color *Science* v357 no6357 p1254 S 22 2017

Plassmann, Hilke

Marketers Should Pay Attention to fMRI *Harvard Business Review Digital Articles* p2 N 3 2015

Plaster casts

A Better Cast for Broken Bones color *Prevention* p8 Mr 2017

Plastering

GET PLASTERED T. MCKEOUGH color *Architectural Digest* v73 no11 p68 N 2016

Plastic bags

Bless her, Father: For she has sinned (sort of) M. Gunch color *New Orleans Magazine* v51 no10 p56 Ag 2017

Carry-On Health B. HOWARD color *AARP: The Magazine* v60 no5A p19 Ag/S 2017

WHAT'S IN YOUR BASKET? S. LIAO color *Better Homes &*

Gardens v95 no4 p146 Ap 2017

Plastic containers
    See also
      Plastic bags
  The great plastic basket makeover J. Jones color *Redbook* p20 Mr 2017

Plastic flooring
  i did it! K. SELZER color *Better Homes & Gardens* v95 no11 p66 N 2017

Plastic flooring—Evaluation
  PUNCH LIST K. SELZER color *Better Homes & Gardens* v95 no10 p62 O 2017

Plastic marine debris
  FISHY BUSINESS M. Enserink color *Science* v355 no6331 p1254 Mr 24 2017
  Purging Plastic A. Skolnick *Sierra* v102 no3 p24 My/Je 2017
  Sea trash traps face doubts E. Stokstad *Science* v356 no6339 p671 My 19 2017

Plastic scrap
  Awash in Plastic J. Greenspan graph *Scientific American* v317 no2 p20 Ag 2017
  The Truth About Our Trash L. SCHLEY color graph *Discover* v38 no9 p18 N 2017

Plastic scrap & the environment
  Ways to Rid the World's Oceans of Plastic Trash T. John color *Time* v189 no24 p9 Je 26 2017

Plastic sculpture
  FORCE OF NATURE J. K. DE VALLE color *Architectural Digest* v74 no3 p116 Mr 2017

Plastic Soul (Music)
  What to Stream N. Feeney color *Entertainment Weekly* no1477 p57 Ag 11 2017

Plastic surgeons
  THE NEW BOTOX FACIAL E. Listfield color *Harper's Bazaar* no3656 p390 S 2017

Plastic surgeons—Interviews
  FINDING PURPOSE IN PLASTIC SURGERY S. Floyd and A. GUMBS color *Black Enterprise* v47 no5 p29 Ja/F 2017

Plastic surgery
  See also
    Breast implants
    Facelift
    Mammaplasty
  ETC M. CAMERAN color *New Orleans Magazine* v51 no12 p167 O 2017
  FACE ODYSSEY J. Dunn cartoon color *Vogue* v207 no1 p94 Ja 2017
  Top Countries for Plastic Surgery *USA Today Magazine* v146 no2869 p4 O 2017
  What Happens Between Before and After: A rarely seen side of plastic surgery L. Wells img *New York* v50 no11 p46 My 29 2017
  What your DOCTOR needs to know S. COLINO color *Good Housekeeping* v264 no6 p97 Je 2017
  Women of the World, Unite! color graph *Glamour* v115 no11 p31 N 2017

Plastic surgery—Humor
  Laughter THE BEST MEDICINE color *Reader's Digest* v189 no1131 p96 Je 2017

Plasticity
  Behavioral time scale synaptic plasticity underlies CA1 place fields K. C. Bittner, A. D. Milstein et al diag *Science* v357 no6355 p1033 S 8 2017
  Branch-specific plasticity of a bifunctional dopamine circuit encodes protein hunger Q. Liu, M. Tabuchi et al graph *Science* v356 no6337 p534 My 5 2017
  Epigenetic plasticity and the hallmarks of cancer W. A. Flavahan, E. Gaskell et al diag *Science* v357 no6348 p266 Jl 21 2017
  Specific repair by discerning macrophages T. Bouchery and N. L. Harris diag *Science* v356 no6342 p1014 Je 9 2017

Plastics
  See also
    Plastic flooring
    Thermoplastics
  EQ CONSULTANTS K. A. Houpt color *Equus* no471 p66 D 2016
  Evaluating Science's open-data policy D. G. Roche *Science* v357

no6352 p654 Ag 18 2017
  SPRING CLEAN your kitchen H. Gray color *Better Nutrition* v79 no3 p16 Mr 2017

Plastics & the environment
  Bless her, Father: For she has sinned (sort of) M. Gunch color *New Orleans Magazine* v51 no10 p56 Ag 2017

Plastics in packaging
  Hey Mr. Green! Why are organics plastic-wrapped? B. Schildgen *Sierra* v101 no4 p12 Jl/Ag 2016

Plastics—Environmental aspects
  100 MICROPLASTIC THREADS. WHAT DOES THAT DO TO YOU? UNKNOWN A. MITCHEL color *Canadian Geographic* v136 no6 p61 D 2016

Plastics—Recycling—Equipment & supplies
  Innovation 3D-Printing Recycler M. Purves color *Bloomberg Businessweek* no4498 p46 N 7 2016
  Recycle Plastic at Home M. L. CALLAGHAN cartoon color *Popular Science* p89 Ja/F 2017

Plate, S. Brent
  Latina faith and family *Christian Century* v134 no13 p43 Je 21 2017

Plate tectonics
  Heat from Earth's Core Drives Movement *USA Today Magazine* v145 no2865 p13 Je 2017
  Recurring and triggered slow-slip events near the trench at the Nankai Trough subduction megathrust E. Araki, D. M. Saffer et al diag graph *Science* v356 no6343 p1157 Je 16 2017
  Trekking the terminator G. CHAPLE color *Astronomy* v45 no4 p68 Ap 2017

Plateau of Tibet
  Ice Age Tibetans J. Qiu color *Scientific American* v316 no3 p14 Mr 2017

Plateaus—Laos
  A SINGULAR LANDSCAPE K. COATES color *Archaeology* v70 no1 p55 Ja/F 2017

Plateaus—Utah
  Is the MOON HOUSE an AMERICAN STONEHENGE? M. Boslough color map *Astronomy* v45 no7 p50 Jl 2017

Plated (Company)
  DINNER IN A BOX M. Leonhardt chart color *Money* v46 no8 p67 S 2017

Plater-Zyberk, Elizabeth
  On Architecture that Addresses the Street E. Plater-Zyberk *Architectural Record* v205 no4 p209 Ap 2017

Plates (Tableware)
  DELFT BLUE M. B. EYERS color *Better Homes & Gardens* v95 no8 p26 Ag 2017
  DOING THE DISHES *Saturday Evening Post* v289 no1 p28 Ja/F 2017
  HOME UNDER $150 color *Redbook* p108 Je 2017
  The Life Aquatic J. JONES CONDON color *House Beautiful* p24 Jl 2017

Plates (Tableware)—Evaluation
  DECK THE TABLE H. Kelly and H. G. Phillips *Washingtonian Magazine* v52 no2 p271 N 2016
  FIERCE FEMME color *House Beautiful* v159 no8 p124 O 2017
  Goldenrod color *House Beautiful* v159 no9 p19 N 2017
  Melamine Scene color *House Beautiful* v159 no3 p40 Ap 2017
  Mother's Day gifts UNDER $50 color *Redbook* p132 My 2017
  OBSESSED WITH CATS E. S. SOTO color *Better Homes & Gardens* v95 no2 p10 F 2016
  OBSESSED WITH TILE MOTIFS E. S. SOTO color *Better Homes & Gardens* v95 no4 p6 Ap 2017
  TABLESCAPE: A WELCOME BRUNCH W. M. Porter color *House Beautiful* v159 no9 p42 N 2017

Platform shoes—Evaluation
  Play Time! color *Glamour* v114 no11 p178 N 2016

Plath, Martin
  EVOLUTION AT THE LIMITS color diag map *Scientific American* v316 no4 p54 Ap 2017

Platino, M.
  Observation of a large-scale anisotropy in the arrival directions of cosmic rays above 8×10^{18} eV *Science* v357 no6357 p1266 S 22 2017

Platinum
  Cooling Element H. Leifert color *Natural History* v125 no5 p8

My 2017

Ultrafine jagged platinum nanowires enable ultrahigh mass activity for the oxygen reduction reaction Mufan Li, Zipeng Zhao et al bibl chart graph *Science* v354 no6318 p1414 D 16 2016

Platinum Drive Realty (Company)

SUBURBAN SAFARI T. Perrotta cartoon *New Yorker* v92 no41 p28 D 12 2016

Platinum Partners (Company)—Officials & employees

Red Flags Abounded On Platinum Partners Z. Faux *Bloomberg Businessweek* no4506 p31 Ja 9 2017

Plato, 428-347 B.C.

Athens as Analogy J. Borini color *Atlantic* v319 no5 p12 Je 2017

Plato, 428-347 B.C.—Political & social views

Making ATHENS GREAT AGAIN R. NEWBERGER GOLD-STEIN *Atlantic* v319 no3 p86 Ap 2017

PLATT, ADAM

Brooklyn Pastoral img *New York* v49 no23 p58 N 14 2016

Cold Fish: After declaring independence from Brushstroke, Ichimura raises its prices and loses some of its charm img *New York* v50 no10 p76 My 15 2017

DK Kitchen img *New York* p50 Ja 23 2017

An Empire Built on Tacos: With his posh new midtown Empellón, Alex Stupak means business img *New York* v50 no11 p102 My 29 2017

Floyd's New Bread Bar img *New York* v49 no21 p76 O 17 2016

I'll Get the Next One: If someone else is paying, by all means try the new version of the Four Seasons Grill Room img *New York* v50 no16 p94 Ag 7 2017

Jean-Georges's Double Life: Opening two restaurants at once yields mixed results img *New York* v50 no18 p58 S 4 2017

Phô With Soul and Style: The Vietnamese cooking at Hanoi House tastes fresh, homespun, and inventive all at once img *New York* v50 no13 p56 Je 26 2017

Progressive Chinese img *New York* v49 no15 p66 Jl 25 2016

Red Meat, Brown Liquor, Tight Squeeze img *New York* v50 no8 p109 Ap 17 2017

Small Plates, Big Ambition img *New York* p62 Ja 9 2017

Spring Has Sprung img *New York* v49 no19 p72 S 19 2016

This Meat-and-Potatoes City Is Now a Vegetarian Paradise img *New York* v49 no25 p74 D 12 2016

Two Cuisines, Two Menus, Too Much *New York* v50 no7 p64 Ap 3 2017

Union Square Cafe, Take Two img *New York* v50 no6 p66 Mr 20 2017

What'll it be FOR THE NEW YORK DINER? img *New York* v50 no13 p30 Je 26 2017

Where to EAT 2017 img *New York* v49 no26 p54 D 26 2016

Platt, Ben, 1993-

7 — DEAR EVAN HANSEN M. R. Bernardo *Entertainment Weekly* no1444/1445 p118 D 16 2016

The Anxious Man's Guide to Public Speaking color *GQ: Gentlemen's Quarterly* v97 no5 p36 My 2017

BEN PLATT M. Snetiker color *Entertainment Weekly* no1438 p69 N 4 2016

GOINGS ON ABOUT TOWN color *New Yorker* v92 no37 p11 N 14 2016

School of LIFE A. Green bw *Vogue* v206 no11 p222 N 2016

Platt, Jeff

Learning On the Fly N. KIRSCH color *Forbes* v199 no7 p60 Je 29 2017

Platt, John R.

Home Is Where They Make It color diag *Scientific American* v315 no5 p20 N 2016

PLATT, LARRY

Life Lessons of the Anti-Coach bw color *GQ: Gentlemen's Quarterly* v97 no3 p100 Mr 2017

Platt, Nick

Transcriptional activation of RagD GTPase controls mTORC1 and promotes cancer growth diag *Science* v356 no6343 p1188 Je 16 2017

Platt, Russell

Baltic Baton cartoon *New Yorker* v92 no30 p14 S 26 2016

Contemporary Boston cartoon *New Yorker* v93 no3 p15 Mr 6 2017

Deep Freeze color *New Yorker* v93 no23 p14 Ag 7 2017

Fall Preview color *New Yorker* v93 no25 p8 Ag 28 2017

Family Dynamics color *New Yorker* v93 no18 p8 Je 26 2017

For the People cartoon *New Yorker* v93 no12 p8 My 8 2017

The Good Germany cartoon *New Yorker* v92 no33 p16 O 17 2016

Hand in Glove cartoon *New Yorker* v92 no47 p13 Ja 30 2017

High Art cartoon *New Yorker* v93 no27 p12 S 11 2017

Less Is More cartoon *New Yorker* v93 no7 p20 Ap 3 2017

Power Games cartoon *New Yorker* v93 no22 p8 Jl 31 2017

The Sound of Love cartoon *New Yorker* v92 no40 p11 D 5 2016

Spring Preview cartoon *New Yorker* v93 no4 p12 Mr 13 2017

Summer Preview cartoon *New Yorker* v93 no14 p12 My 22 2017

Time Capsule cartoon *New Yorker* v93 no9 p13 Ap 17 2017

Winter Preview cartoon *New Yorker* v92 no37 p14 N 14 2016

Woman, Interrupted color *New Yorker* v93 no33 p26 O 23 2017

Platte River (Neb.)

Platte River REUNION A. J. BARTELS cartoon color *Nebraska Life* v21 no2 p70 Mr/Ap 2017

Platten, Rachel, 1981-

Rachel Platten M. Hagan color *Current Biography* v77 no11 p59 N 2016

Platters

SHINE ON color *Bon Appetit* v61 no11 p128 N 2016

Platters—Evaluation

BEAST MODE *Indianapolis Monthly* v40 no7 p28 Mr 2017

TROPICAL BRUNCH K. O'SHEA-EVANS color *House Beautiful* v159 no4 p54 My 2017

Platto, Gordon—Interviews

HOG CALLING J. Gall color *Car & Driver* v62 no10 p18 Ap 2017

Platzer, Brian

Bed-Stuy Is Burning *Publishers Weekly* v264 no18 p35 My 1 2017

There Goes the Block: A debut novel about gentrification and turmoil in a Brooklyn neighborhood M. Denzel Smith *New York Times Book Review* p20 Ag 13 2017

Platzman, Daniel

Imagine Dragons M. Tillman bw *Current Biography* v78 no9 p42 S 2017

Plawsky, Joel L.

Wickless heat pipes in microgravity *Physics Today* v70 no9 p82 S 2017

Play

See also

Hobbies

cleared for takeoff! J. HARTSHORN *Parents* v91 no11 p123 N 2016

Cute Ways to Organize Toys E. Walker color *Parents* v92 no4 p106 Ap 2017

ENJOY A NATURAL CRAFTERNOON A. KINGLOFF color *Parents* v92 no11 p108 N 2017

fooled you! K. STONEY color *Parents* v92 no4 p74 Ap 2017

Goop vs. Slime M. LaScala color *Parents* v92 no11 p16 N 2017

Handle a Sibling's Playdate J. W. Dubin *Parents* v92 no9 p169 S 2017

made in america [Cover story] color *Parents* v92 no7 p68 Jl 2017

MAKE YOUR BACKYARD more FUN! color *Parents* v92 no6 p114 Je 2017

Meddy Teddy color *Yoga Journal* no289 p18 F 2017

A Playground Hug Means Everything M. M. Brown color *Parents* v92 no7 p18 Jl 2017

playing with purpose J. HARTSHORN color *Parents* v92 no5 p60 My 2017

play school *Parents* v91 no9 p74 S 2016

The PLAY'S the THING M. ZARASKA color diag *Discover* v38 no5 p54 Je 2017

Q: Can a 2-year-old safely play on a playground without being spotted? color *Parents* v92 no6 p30 Je 2017

score more storage *Parents* p93 2015

Sensory Toys Are Having a Moment color *Parents* v92 no11 p24 N 2017

a sillier hide-and-seek color *Parents* v92 no5 p47 My 2017

a smash hit! *Parents* v91 no6 p21 Je 2016

soar indoors *Parents* v91 no10 p107 O 2016

Special Dolls for Special Kids S. Watts color *Parents* v92 no3 p18 Mr 2017

sprinkle them with joy color *Parents* v92 no8 p67 Ag 2017

TOY JOY J. HARTSHORN color *Parents* v92 no11 p56 N 2017

toys for future coders *Parents* v92 no2 p60 F 2017

the toys of childhood J. HARTSHORN color *Parents* v92 no6 p56

Je 2017

What Am I Thinking? M. Dicks cartoon *Parents* v92 no9 p124 S 2017

You're Welcome color *Parents* v92 no9 p12 S 2017

Play behavior in animals
To Play Or Not To Play? J. HARRISON color *Horse & Rider* v56 no11 p90 N 2017

Play-Doh (Toy)
Electronic Play Dough J. Zorthian color *Time* v189 no24 p19 Je 26 2017

Play equipment
Creating a Better Playground Experience for Children R. Lockhart *Parks & Recreation* p28 2017 Supplement Field Guide - Supplier and Resource Directory

Play Hawkers SL
Hey Guys, Watch This N. Leiber color *Bloomberg Businessweek* no4498 p45 N 7 2016

Playboy (Periodical)
Hugh Hefner L. Rothman color *Time* v190 no15 p13 O 16 2017

The Male-Gazer in Chief K. Pollitt *Nation* v305 no10 p6 O 23 2017

WHEN PLAYBOY MADE IT BIG L. SKENAZY *Reason* v48 no11 p6 Ap 2017

Playcraft Boats (Company)
The Good Life In the Fast Lane: You don't have to give up go-fast performance to embrace the pontoon lifestyle A. JONES *Boating World* v38 no5 p42 My 2017

Player, Simrin—Interviews
BEST ALL AROUND C. Bowers *Dance Spirit* v20 no10 p24 D 2016

Players' Tribune Inc.
DEREK JETER'S NEXT SWING M. Lev-Ram color *Fortune* v175 no3 p30 Mr 1 2017

Playground design & construction
Creating a Better Playground Experience for Children R. Lockhart *Parks & Recreation* p28 2017 Supplement Field Guide - Supplier and Resource Directory

Sensory Development Playgrounds for Parks, Schools A. Grego *Parks & Recreation* p8 2017 Supplement Field Guide - Supplier and Resource Directory

Playground equipment
See also
Swings

How to Make a... PORCH SWING cartoon chart *Popular Mechanics* v193 no7 p75 S 2016

Playground equipment—Design & construction
Playground Safety: A Shared Responsibility K. S. Kutska *Parks & Recreation* p12 2017 Supplement Field Guide - Supplier and Resource Directory

Playground equipment—Safety measures
Playground Safety: A Shared Responsibility K. S. Kutska *Parks & Recreation* p12 2017 Supplement Field Guide - Supplier and Resource Directory

Playgrounds
Central Parc K. LAIDLAW color *Walrus* v13 no9 p68 N 2016

Playgrounds—Design & construction
The Playborhood M. Thernstrom *New York Times Magazine* p42 O 23 2016

snapshot A. Klimoski color *Architectural Record* v205 no3 p144 Mr 2017

Playgrounds—Evaluation
Audubon Road K. FRANZMAN color *Indianapolis Monthly* p32 Ap 2017

Playing cards
My Parlor: Vicki Atwood hosts gatherings of history buffs in her home's Colonial-era tavern *Indianapolis Monthly* p43 N 2017

NAMED FOR A CRAZE *Saturday Evening Post* v289 no2 p98 Mr/Ap 2017

SPELL Caster: THE OCCULT ITEM OF THE SEASON: DIOR'S PETITE MINAUDIERES ADD A BEWITCHING CHIONESS TO YOUR LOOK. IT'S IN THE CARDS *Interview* v47 no3 p44 Ap 2017

Playing House (TV program)
The Must List color *Entertainment Weekly* no1471 p5 Je 23 2017

Playing House D. Holbrook *TV Guide* v65 no23 p35 My 29 2017

Plays on words

The Logophile A. Hollandbeck *Saturday Evening Post* v289 no3 p24 My/Je 2017

word play m. ferrentino color *Bike Magazine* v24 no4 p54 Je 2017

PlaySight Interactive Ltd.
The Rules of the Game *Tennis* v52 no6 p62 N/D 2016

PlayStation video game consoles
Hot Digital Psychedelia Rez Infinite and Thumper E. SHAMOON color *Rolling Stone* no1274 p47 N 17 2016

Sony's Bet on Gamers Can't Get Much Bigger B. Einhorn bw *Bloomberg Businessweek* no4499 p48 N 14 2016

VR'S CROSSOVER MOMENT? N. Abrams color *Entertainment Weekly* no1439 p12 N 11 2016

PlayStation video game consoles—Evaluation
VR GOALS N. SANTOS color *Ebony* v72/73 no12/1 p93 O/N 2017

Playwriting—Collaboration
Edgerton Foundation New Play Awards *Stage Directions* v30 no8 p4 Ag 2017

Plaza, Aubrey, 1984-
Aubrey Plaza's Status Update E. Berman color *Time* v190 no7 p47 Ag 21 2017

The Nicest Evil Girl in the World: Aubrey Plaza knows you want her to be mean to you, and she's happy to oblige A. P. Davis img *New York* v50 no15 p34 Jl 24 2017

Our bad habit: The recent film that fixates on nuns having fun isn't all that funny J. M. Griffith color *U.S. Catholic* v82 no10 p38 O 2017

PLAZA SUITE B. HANDY color *Vanity Fair* v59 no8 p94 Ag 2017

UNICORN ROOM A. Russell cartoon *New Yorker* v93 no19 p19 Jl 3 2017

Plaza-Faverola, A.
Massive blow-out craters formed by hydrate-controlled methane expulsion from the Arctic seafloor graph map *Science* v356 no6341 p948 Je 1 2017

Plazas
Intel bw chart *Conde Nast Traveler* v52 no8 p119 S 2017

Plazas—Evaluation
Innovative Community Celebrations in an Urban Green Space [Cover story] S. Roller *Parks & Recreation* v51 no12 p32 D 2016

Pleasure
See also
Sexual excitement

Looking Out for Small Joys C. McHugh color *Health* v31 no3 p8 Ap 2017

Pleasure (Music)
The Playlist color *Rolling Stone* no1285 p8 Ap 20 2017

Pleasure of Being Robbed, The (Film)
URBAN LEGENDS E. Hynes bw color *Film Comment* v53 no4 p22 Jl/Ag 2017

Pleats (Sewing)
Back from the Dead S. HINE bw color *GQ: Gentlemen's Quarterly* v97 no3 p60 Mr 2017

Plec, Julie—Interviews
JULIE PLEC I. RUDOLPH *TV Guide* v65 no13 p11 Mr 20 2017

Plecas, Darryl
A Speaker on mute B. HUTCHINSON color *Maclean's* v130 no10 p12 N 2017

Plecker, Joe
ATTACK THE BALL color diag *Golf Magazine* v59 no6 p52 Je 2017

BASKET CASE color *Golf Magazine* v59 no10 p35 O 2017

MAKE LAYUPS A SLAM DUNK color *Golf Magazine* v59 no7 p52 Jl 2017

Watch + Learn color *Golf Magazine* v59 no5 p36 My 2017

Pledge of Allegiance to the Flag
The Pledge at 125 B. BROWN *New York Times Upfront* v149 no9 p20 F 20 2017

Pleger, Ralf
In War and Peace D. Shengold *Opera News* v81 no9 p34 Mr 2017

PLEGGE, NICOLE
HOLIDAYS IN THE LITTLE HILLS *Missouri Life* v43 no7 p50 D 2016/Ja 2017

Pleiades
Cluster Shots [Cover story] J. RAO color *Natural History* v125

UNCHARTED WATERS T. REHAGEN *Indianapolis Monthly* p84 N 2017

Plumb, Eve

FLORENCE HENDERSON color *Entertainment Weekly* no1446/1447 p94 D 2016/Ja 2017

Plumb, Mike

Max Corcoran: 'Not Just the Groom' T. Conahan color *Practical Horseman* v45 no1 p24 Ja 2017

Plumb, Sean Michael

Sean Michael Plumb H. STEWART *Opera News* v81 no10 p12 Ap 2017

Plumbers

Interview with a ... K. Green color *Career Outlook* p1 O 2016

In Your Hands N. MacLaughlin bw *Men's Health* v32 no2 p(Sp)30 Mr 2017

NO PIPE DREAM S. Apstein color *Sports Illustrated* v126 no3 p40 Ja 23 2017

Plumbing

See also

Solder & soldering

Clog-Free Nation B. PIKE cartoon *Power & Motoryacht* v33 no2 p232 F 2017

MY WIFE WANTS A BIDET: Plumbing is the glue that holds a marriage together M. Orwoll *Saturday Evening Post* v289 no4 p18 Jl/Ag 2017

Running New Plumbing Lines R. Tschoepe cartoon *Old House Journal* v45 no2 p58 Ap 2017

A Second Biffy color *Cabin Living* p69 Ja/F 2017

STUFF A PLUMBER SCREWED UP P. O'Donnell cartoon *Old House Journal* v45 no5 p54 Ag 2017

Plumbing fixtures

See also

Bidets

Showers (Plumbing fixtures)

Sinks (Plumbing fixtures)

chance OF SHOWERS J. BREWSTER color *Cabin Living* p51 S 2017

Plumbing fixtures—Evaluation

Playing with Scale K. L. Beamon *Architectural Record* v205 no9 p153 S 2017

Plumbing—Safety measures

Running New Plumbing Lines R. Tschoepe cartoon *Old House Journal* v45 no2 p58 Ap 2017

Plumes (Fluid dynamics)

Cassini finds molecular hydrogen in the Enceladus plume: Evidence for hydrothermal processes J. H. Waite, C. R. Glein et al chart graph *Science* v356 no6334 p155 Ap 14 2017

PLUMMER, KATE E.

Doses of Neighborhood Nature: The Benefits for Mental Health of Living with Nature *BioScience* v67 no2 p147 F 2017

Plummer, Matt

Even Life-Saving Innovations Don't Sell Themselves *Harvard Business Review Digital Articles* p2 F 16 2017

Plungis, Jeff

Driving Into the Future color map *Consumer Reports* v82 no4 p10 Ap 2017

Shattered chart color diag graph *Consumer Reports* v82 no12 p30 D 2017

Plunkett, James

NECESSARY RISKS *Climbing* no357 p32 N 2017

Plunkett, Nandi Rose

Follow Ahead M. Trammell cartoon *New Yorker* v93 no8 p6 Ap 10 2017

Pluralism

See also

Cultural pluralism

Hoffman: U.S. Jews need to speak out on religious pluralism in Israel *Successful Farming* v115 no1 p11 Ja 2017

Plurality voting

A Better Way to Choose Presidents E. Maskin and A. Sen color *New York Review of Books* v64 no10 p61 Je 8 2017

Pluripotent stem cells

See also

Induced pluripotent stem cells

Deficiency of microRNA miR-34a expands cell fate potential in pluripotent stem cells Y. Jin Choi, Lin et al diag *Science* v355

no6325 p596 F 10 2017

Mobile elements control stem cell potency H. Hasuwa and H. Siomi bibl diag *Science* v355 no6325 p581 F 10 2017

Plus-size women's clothing

I Am Not an Hourglass N. Mason color *Glamour* v115 no6 p46 Je 2017

This Model Belongs on the Runway L. Chan color *Glamour* v115 no9 p70 S 2017

Plus-size women's clothing—Evaluation

The most versatile dress M. Handahu color *Redbook* p82 F 2017

Plus-sized models (Persons)

Ashley GRAHAM A. Prato color *Glamour* v114 no12 p222 D 2016

FALL FASHION A. LAROCCA img *New York* v50 no16 p29 Ag 7 2017

FASHION FOR THE SIXTY-SEVEN PERCENT: A revolution in the plus-size market A. C. FORD img *New York* v50 no16 p38 Ag 7 2017

NOW, THIS IS A SUPERMODEL: ASHLEY GRAHAM ISN'T A SAMPLE SIZE.: Which is exactly why she's become the face of a movement J. YUAN img *New York* v50 no16 p30 Ag 7 2017

Paloma Elsesser S. DRUMMOND color *Vogue* v207 no11 p126 N 2017

This Model Belongs on the Runway L. Chan color *Glamour* v115 no9 p70 S 2017

Plush—Evaluation

Kitted Out color *Martha Stewart Living* p25 My 2017

Plutarch, ca. 46-120

133 BC: Rome Plutarch *Lapham's Quarterly* v10 no1 p132 Wint 2017

A Few of Plutarch's Oldies but Goodies S. DONOGHUE *American Conservative* v16 no2 p55 Mr/Ap 2017

Pluto (Dwarf planet)

FROM OUR READERS F. Housel, D. Kreuer et al *Sky & Telescope* v133 no4 p6 Ap 2017

Haze may explain Pluto's red spots A. YEAGER color *Science News* v191 no7 p14 Ap 15 2017

The Hunt for Planet X: Evidence is building that a large world lurks far beyond Pluto and the Kuiper Belt. The race to find it is on S. S. Sheppard *Sky & Telescope* v134 no4 p16 O 2017

In pursuit of PLUTO R. Talcott color *Astronomy* v45 no7 p56 Jl 2017

The Next Horizon E. BETZ color *Discover* v38 no10 p44 D 2017

Pluto in 2017: Don't look now, but a proposed sizing scheme would make it a planet again A. MacRobert *Sky & Telescope* v134 no1 p48 Jl 2017

Pluto's Hidden Ocean K. HAYNES bw color *Discover* v38 no1 p46 Ja/F 2017

Pluto's slushy heart contains a large ocean bw *Astronomy* v45 no3 p13 Mr 2017

PUZZLED BY PLUTO [Cover story] S. A. Stern bw color *Astronomy* v45 no9 p22 S 2017

Separated at Birth N. T. REDD chart color diag *Discover* v38 no10 p38 D 2017

Top 10 space stories of 2016 [Cover story] L. Kruesi color *Astronomy* v45 no1 p18 Ja 2017

What's a planet? A. Yeager color *Science News* v191 no8 p4 Ap 29 2017

Pluto (Dwarf planet)—Research

Could life lurk within Pluto's ocean? A. Klesman color *Astronomy* v45 no4 p13 Ap 2017

Pluto (Dwarf planet)—Satellites—Research

Charon & Company J. K. BEATTY *Sky & Telescope* v132 no6 p36 D 2016

Plutonium

Forty years of impasse: The United States, Japan, and the plutonium problem Masafumi Takubo and F. von Hippel bibl *Bulletin of the Atomic Scientists* v73 no5 p337 2017

HOW TO MAKE PLUTONIUM K. DUPZYK color *Popular Mechanics* p64 S 2017

Plymouth automobile

See also

Barracuda automobile

DIGNIFIED DECAY color *Road & Track* v68 no8 p14 My 2017

JULY 15, 1931: DRIVING FORCE A. BROWN bw color *Forbes* v200 no1 p30 Jl 27 2017

The Entertainment Weekly Must List R. Kinane color *Entertainment Weekly* no1441 p4 N 25 2016

GOING IRL C. Everett color *Entertainment Weekly* no1465 p57 My 12 2017

The Golden Age of Podcasting M. ANTONOFF color *Sound & Vision* v82 no5 p26 Je 2017

The Gratitude Meter Z. Donaldson color *O, The Oprah Magazine* p20 Ja 2017

LISTEN, LAUGH, LEARN L. F. Prater *Successful Farming* v115 no11 p60 S 2017

LISTEN TO THIS M. Godsey color *Literacy Today (2411-7862)* v34 no3 p28 N/D 2016

The Podcast Finder E. Dockterman color *Time* v189 no13 p52 Ap 10 2017

A Podcast for Every Season C. Agard color *Entertainment Weekly* no1477 p47 Ag 11 2017

Podcasting J. PODHORETZ *Commentary* v143 no6 p1 Je 2017

POD HELP ME D. Sax cartoon *Bloomberg Businessweek* no4512 p78 F 20 2017

Rap Radar Podcast Shines as Voice of Hip-Hop Culture B. ADAMS color *Ebony* v72 no8 p22 Je 2017

REALITY BREAK C. Everett color *Entertainment Weekly* no1454/1455 p98 F 24 2017

THE RISE, RISE, AND RISE OF PODCASTS N. Quah color *Wired* v25 no10 p36 O 2017

Spending to Save F. TORABI cartoon *O, The Oprah Magazine* p48 My 2017

Still Missing Richard Simmons C. Everett color *Entertainment Weekly* no1459 p12 Mr 31 2017

Sunshine outside the ivory tower A. Welch, C. Helena et al bw *Science* v357 no6357 p1322 S 22 2017

TOP BANANA D. Franich color *Entertainment Weekly* no1436/1437 p26 O 21 2016

UNQUALIFIED CATCH-UP C. Everett color *Entertainment Weekly* no1436/1437 p28 O 21 2016

What 'S-Town' misses about life in rural America W. Massey color *America* v216 no13 p57 Je 12 2017

You Must Remember This D. Franich color *Entertainment Weekly* no1451/1452 p16 F 3-10 2017

Podcasts—Evaluation

Happy Mix J. HERBST color *Los Angeles Magazine* v62 no7 p41 Jl 2017

POPULAR MECHANICS EVERYWHERE J. Bennett color *Popular Mechanics* p6 F 2017

Today's radio dramas M. M. Dana color *Christian Century* v133 no25 p43 D 7 2016

Tune in to Our New 'Open Space Radio' Podcast *Parks & Recreation* v52 no9 p95 S 2017

Podcasts—Reviews

10 — SCIENCE VS C. Everett *Entertainment Weekly* no1444/1445 p114 D 16 2016

2 — MY FAVORITE MURDER J. Goodman color *Entertainment Weekly* no1444/1445 p114 D 16 2016

3 — KEEPIN' IT 1600 J. Goodman *Entertainment Weekly* no1444/1445 p114 D 16 2016

4 — IN THE DARK A. Sadlier *Entertainment Weekly* no1444/1445 p114 D 16 2016

5 — BI2TCH SESH: A REAL HOUSEWIVES BREAKDOWN A. Sadlier color *Entertainment Weekly* no1444/1445 p114 D 16 2016

6 — LORE N. Serrao *Entertainment Weekly* no1444/1445 p114 D 16 2016

7 — THE WEST WING WEEKLY C. Everett *Entertainment Weekly* no1444/1445 p114 D 16 2016

8 — 2 DOPE QUEENS D. Jackson color *Entertainment Weekly* no1444/1445 p114 D 16 2016

9 — BEAUTIFUL STORIES FROM ANONYMOUS PEOPLE C. Everett *Entertainment Weekly* no1444/1445 p114 D 16 2016

ANGLO-FILE *British Heritage Travel* v37 no6 p80 N/D 2016

DEATH BECOMES THEM A. Wilkinson color *Entertainment Weekly* no1457/1458 p98 Mr 17 2017

A different kind of family in Providence K. Weber color *America* v216 no3 p49 F 6 2017

No. 1 ANNA FARIS IS UNQUALIFIED C. Everett color *Entertainment Weekly* no1444/1445 p112 D 16 2016

Podcasts—Software

OVERCAST 3: iOS PODCAST APP ADDS A QUEUE AND PERKS UP ITS INTERFACE G. FLEISHMAN color *Macworld - Digital Edition* v34 no4 p56 My 2017

POCKET CASTS 6.5: iOS PODCAST APP EMPHASIZES GRAPHICS AND SIMPLICITY G. FLEISHMAN color *Macworld - Digital Edition* v34 no4 p53 My 2017

Waiting on Apple's podcast recording app—or for better GarageBand features D. MOREN color *Macworld - Digital Edition* v34 no9 p89 S 2017

Podesta, John, 1949-

'UFO Disclosure' Fizzles Again in 2016 R. SHEAFFER *Skeptical Inquirer* v41 no2 p32 Mr/Ap 2017

PODHORETZ, JOHN

BARE, RUINED CHOIRS: HOW BARACK OBAMA WRECKED THE DEMOCRATIC PARTY [Cover story] *Commentary* v142 no5 p12 D 2016

Bleak Houses *Weekly Standard* v22 no15 p39 D 19 2016

Blowed Up color *Weekly Standard* v22 no7 p39 O 24 2016

Chauvinist Racket color *Weekly Standard* v23 no5 p46 O 9 2017

Comic Critics *Weekly Standard* v22 no39 p43 Je 19 2017

Commentary on Commentary *Commentary* v143 no4 p1 Ap 2017

An Echo, Not a Choice *Commentary* v142 no3 p1 O 2016

Fix the Fixer color *Weekly Standard* v22 no33 p47 My 8 2017

Forward to the Past color *Weekly Standard* v22 no17 p39 Ja 2 2017

The Gibson Quandary *Weekly Standard* v22 no4 p38 O 3 2016

Going Theronuclear color *Weekly Standard* v22 no47 p47 Ag 21 2017

Gorilla Theater color *Weekly Standard* v22 no29 p39 Ap 3 2017

Go With It *Weekly Standard* v22 no35 p39 My 22 2017

Grossed Out *Weekly Standard* v22 no6 p39 O 17 2016

Hillary Milhous Clinton *Commentary* v142 no2 p1 S 2016

It Takes All Kinds color *Weekly Standard* v23 no3 p39 S 25 2017

Kind of a Drag *Weekly Standard* v22 no8 p43 O 31 2016

Liftoff Uplift *Weekly Standard* v22 no22 p39 F 13 2017

The Little Sick color *Weekly Standard* v22 no44 p39 Jl 31 2017

Lost Weekend color *Weekly Standard* v22 no28 p43 Mr 27 2017

Magical Kingdom *Weekly Standard* v22 no25 p43 Mr 6 2017

Market Rules color *Weekly Standard* v22 no38 p39 Je 12 2017

Measuring Up color *Weekly Standard* v23 no4 p39 O 2 2017

Meek but Mighty color *Weekly Standard* v22 no42 p39 Jl 17 2017

Money for Nothing color *Weekly Standard* v22 no30 p39 Ap 10 2017

Monster Mash color *Weekly Standard* v22 no32 p43 My 1 2017

'Moonlight' Sonata color *Weekly Standard* v22 no26 p39 Mr 13 2017

Notes on a Disaster *Commentary* v140 no2 p1 S 2015

The Other Tom *Weekly Standard* v22 no40 p39 Je 26 2017

Podcasting *Commentary* v143 no6 p1 Je 2017

Potted Kroc *Weekly Standard* v22 no21 p39 F 6 2017

Replicants' Return color *Weekly Standard* v23 no6 p46 O 16 2017

Scared Straight color *Weekly Standard* v22 no23 p39 F 20 2017

Shallow Fences *Weekly Standard* v22 no20 p39 Ja 30 2017

A Star Is Born color *Weekly Standard* v22 no16 p39 D 26 2016

Strange Interlude *Weekly Standard* v22 no11 p43 N 21 2016

Superheroes at Bay color *Weekly Standard* v22 no27 p43 Mr 20 2017

Surprise Ending color *Weekly Standard* v22 no24 p43 F 27 2017

'Tough Love'—The First and Last Obama Lie *Commentary* v143 no2 p1 F 2017

The Truly Forgotten Republican Voter *Commentary* v142 no4 p1 N 2016

Uncompromised *Weekly Standard* v22 no37 p39 Je 5 2017

Undone Dunkirk color *Weekly Standard* v22 no45 p38 Ag 7 2017

Warren and Howard *Weekly Standard* v22 no14 p39 D 12 2016

We Ain't Seen Nothin' Yet *Commentary* v143 no1 p1 Ja 2017

Welcome to the Club *Weekly Standard* v22 no18 p43 Ja 16 2017

Worlds in Collision color *Weekly Standard* v22 no12 p39 N 28 2016

Yes,'He's Your President *Commentary* v142 no5 p1 D 2016

Podhoretz, Norman

'Making It' at 50 M. CONTINETTI *Commentary* v143 no6 p56 Je 2017

OP DE STEZ L. MENAND cartoon *New Yorker* v93 no11 p63 My 1 2017

Podiatrists

FOOT SOLDIERS R. AHALT and A. ASSILI *Washingtonian*

Magazine v52 no1 p126 O 2016

Podojil, Janet

I Wish My Horse's Mentor Could Be... color *Horse & Rider* v56 no6 p88 Je 2017

Podolsky, Anne

Sticky schools color graph *Phi Delta Kappan* v98 no8 p19 My 2017

Poe, Andrea

SLEEP EASY: FIVE OF OUR FAVORITE PLACES TO STAY IN THE VALLEY *Washingtonian Magazine* v53 no1 p100 O 2017

WORKING FOR THE WEEKEND *Washingtonian Magazine* v52 no5 p161 F 2017

Poe, Edgar Allan, 1809-1849

1840: Philadelphia E. A. Poe *Lapham's Quarterly* v10 no1 p102 Wint 2017

The Comets of Edgar Allan Poe D. W. Olson and S. B. Ford *Sky & Telescope* v132 no6 p30 D 2016

DUST TO DUST *Lapham's Quarterly* v10 no3 p118 Summ 2017

Poeciliidae

EVOLUTION AT THE LIMITS R. Riesch and M. Plath color diag map *Scientific American* v316 no4 p54 Ap 2017

Poelchau, Michael

The formation of peak rings in large impact craters bibl color graph *Science* v354 no6314 p878 N 18 2016

Poelker, Tom

A meal for many color *U.S. Catholic* v82 no6 p5 Je 2017

Patriotism in the pews color *U.S. Catholic* v82 no11 p5 N 2017

Poelman, Hilde

Super-dry reforming of methane intensifies CO_2 utilization via Le Chatelier's principle bibl diag graph *Science* v354 no6311 p449 O 28 2016

Poem for a Quiet Lady at Saint Patrick's Church in Oregon (Poem)

Poem for a Quiet Lady at Saint Patrick's Church in Oregon B. Doyle color *U.S. Catholic* v82 no3 p11 Mr 2017

Poems syndrome

The Social and etalk's Lainey Lui Turns Caregiver for Her Mother M. Sponagle color *Maclean's* v130 no9 p36 O 2017

Poenisch, Emily

2017 MaVeRicks OF Style bw color *Esquire* p81 S 2017

BELLA color *Esquire* p106 N 2017

MASTER OF STRANGE bw color *Esquire* p13 Ag 2017

A WOMAN OF INFLUENCE bw color *Esquire* p120 O 2017

Poeppel, Amy

What we're reading diag *Literacy Today (2411-7862)* v34 no6 p5 My/Je 2017

Poeschl, Mark

MARK POESCHL: FFA CEO TALKS ABOUT THE ORGANI-ZATION'S UPS AND DOWNS, AND THE NEXT GENERA-TION OF AG LEADERS J. Davey *Successful Farming* v115 no12 p10 O 2017

POET, J.

Get Up, Stand Up for Reggae color *Downbeat* v84 no8 p77 Ag 2017

A Little Bit of Everything color *Downbeat* v84 no2 p78 F 2017

TOM TEASLEY color *Downbeat* v83 no11 p24 N 2016

Poetry (Literary form)

ABOVE & BEYOND cartoon *New Yorker* v92 no40 p18 D 5 2016

At Home in Baltimore L. HAMMER *American Scholar* v86 no4 p51 Aut 2017

THE DEFENSE OF POETRY L. MENAND cartoon *New Yorker* v93 no22 p64 Jl 31 2017

THE ELEGANT TRANSLATOR *Psychology Today* v49 no6 p14 N/D 2016

A Few Questions for Poetry D. HALPERN *New York Times Book Review* p25 Ja 1 2017

In praise of poetry P. W. Marty *Christian Century* v134 no9 p3 Ap 26 2017

Just Saying *American Scholar* v86 no1 p52 Wint 2017

The poet editor of West Marin B. Tsui color *Columbia Journalism Review* v56 no1 p74 Spr 2017

Portrait of Our Time A. Domestico color *Commonweal* v144 no15 p34 S 22 2017

The Russian We Need C. YOUNG bw *Weekly Standard* v22 no46 p35 Ag 14 2017

Septic Poem L. Donnellan color *Cabin Living* p71 Ja/F 2017

Theme Park Bards color *Weekly Standard* v23 no1 p4 S 11 2017

WHY POETRY?: Lee Bennett Hopkins on why we must share poetry with our students S. Knell color *Literacy Today (2411-7862)* v34 no6 p16 My/Je 2017

Poetry (Literary form)—Exhibitions

An Unquiet Belle D. R. GOODMAN color *Weekly Standard* v22 no25 p42 Mr 6 2017

Poetry (Literary form)—Publishing

Jailed Palestinian Poet's Work Gets New Life in Parallel Transla-tion J. Maher chart color *Publishers Weekly* v263 no44 p11 O 31 2016

Poetry (Literary form)—Religious aspects

Sacred lines R. Miska color *U.S. Catholic* v82 no1 p45 Ja 2017

Poetry (Literary form)—Social aspects

Finding the Catholic Voices In Social Justice Poetry L. Ampleman color *America* v216 no10 p42 My 1 2017

Poetry collections—Reviews

One Hand Slapping K. Rooney *New York Times Book Review* p18 Ap 9 2017

Poetry competitions

'Music Is Life and Life Is Poetry' J. Hoover il *America* v216 no13 p48 Je 12 2017

Poetry of Departures (Poem : Larkin)

1955: Hull P. Larkin *Lapham's Quarterly* v10 no1 p145 Wint 2017

Poetry slams

WHAT THE WHITE BOY WANTS M. POLLOCK color *Chi-cago* v66 no4 p90 Ap 2017

Poetry writing

Pick a Word, Any Word M. Zapruder *New York Times Book Re-view* p8 Jl 16 2017

Seen and Unseen R. ROSENBLATT *New York Times Book Re-view* p8 Ag 27 2017

Poets

See also

Lyricists

Women poets

The Abolitionist of Walden Pond *In These Times* v41 no8 p38 Ag 2017

Brodsky and His Muses: A new collection shows where the great émigré poet Joseph Brodsky found friendship, love, and inspira-tion C. L. Haven *Hoover Digest: Research & Opinion on Public Policy* no3 p188 Summ 2017

CHANGE IS GOOD A. Stanley bw color *Seventeen* v76 no4 p80 Jl/Ag 2017

Cracks in Language M. MATTIX bw *Weekly Standard* v23 no2 p44 S 18 2017

Derek Walcott's Timeless Fable I. Hutchinson bw *New York Times Book Review* p27 Ag 6 2017

Is Poetry "the New Adult Coloring Book"? J. Boog color *Publish-ers Weekly* v264 no35 p12 Ag 28 2017

John Ashbery (1927–2017) [Cover story] L. Sante bw *New York Review of Books* v64 no15 p4 O 12 2017

A Life in the Family K. CLINTON color *Progressive* v81 no7 p67 O/N 2017

Louise Glück S. Moyer *Humanities* v37 no4 p1 Fall 2016

No Strength in Numbers J. GURIEL cartoon *Walrus* v14 no6 p15 Jl/Ag 2017

POETRY: TO FIGHT ANOTHER DAY R. W. Service bw color *MHQ: Quarterly Journal of Military History* v30 no1 p90 Aut 2017

Poets—Interviews

The Poetic Is Political C. M. TEICHER bw color *Publishers Weekly* v264 no14 p38 Ap 3. 2017

Poets—Political activity

Leonard Cohen's Life of Poetry and Song D. COWAN bw *Ameri-can Conservative* v16 no1 p54 Ja/F 2017

Poets—United States

AMERICAN EXPANSION H. Vendler *Harper's Magazine* no2007 p68 Ag 2017

Poetz, Marion

Sometimes the Best Ideas Come from Outside Your Industry *Har-vard Business Review Digital Articles* p2 N 21 2014

Pogge, Drew

18 DAYS ON DENALI color *Skiing* p52 D 2016

Accessorize color *Skiing* p86 D 2016

p111 Wint 2016

POLAN, SHIRA

Cause for Hope *Psychology Today* v50 no1 p21 Ja/F 2017

ON THE RUN *Psychology Today* v50 no4 p16 Ag 2017

SMOOTH CRIMINALS *Psychology Today* v50 no3 p19 My/Je 2017

Time for a Brake *Psychology Today* v49 no5 p31 S/O 2016

Why Do We Lash Out? IT MIGHT BE MORE THAN A BAD MOOD *Psychology Today* v50 no5 p16 S/O 2017

Woeful Words *Psychology Today* v50 no2 p21 Mr/Ap 2017

YOU LOOKIN' AT ME? *Psychology Today* v49 no5 p21 S/O 2016

Polanco, Dascha

Orange Is the New Black: In a riotous season, the women are no longer behind bars M. ROUSH *TV Guide* v65 no25 p14 Je 2017

Poland—Politics & government—1989-

In Poland, the Stench Of Swamp Clearing M. Champion and M. Strzelecki color map *Bloomberg Businessweek* no4505 p17 D 26 2016

POLANECZKY, RONNIE

Less Is More color *Prevention* v68 no12 p34 D 2016

The Power to Transform color *Prevention* v69 no11 p82 N 2017

Polanskey, C. A.

Extensive water ice within Ceres' aqueously altered regolith: Evidence from nuclear spectroscopy bibl graph *Science* v355 no6320 p1 Ja 6 2017

Polar bear

CRITTER CHAT A. SHAW *National Geographic Kids* no467 p29 F 2017

in a snap color *Canadian Geographic* v137 no2 p14 Mr/Ap 2017

Lightbox color *Time* v190 no8 p16 Ag 28 2017

MOTHER AND MONSTER L. Moore color *Walrus* v14 no6 p48 Jl/Ag 2017

A SCENT ON THE WIND color *Canadian Geographic* v137 no4 p22 Jl/Ag 2017

STATEWIDE N. BUCK color *Nebraska Life* v21 no2 p63 Mr/Ap 2017

Polar bear hunting

WILDLIFE color *Canadian Geographic* v136 no6 p22 D 2016

Polar bear watching

Undercover Polar Bears K. DESEVE color *National Geographic Kids* no465 p22 N 2016

Polar bear—Conservation

GAME OF THRONES [Cover story] S. OOSTHOEK color map *Canadian Geographic* v135 no6 p36 D 2015

Polar bear—Research

Berries and Eggs Won't Be Enough color *Canadian Wildlife* v22 no5 p9 N/D 2016

Undercover Polar Bears K. DESEVE color *National Geographic Kids* no465 p22 N 2016

Polar regions—Discovery & exploration—Exhibitions

ABOARD THE POURQUOI-PAS? K. Murray-Bergquist *Iceland Review* v55 no2 p71 Mr/Ap 2017

Polar Express, The (Film)

HOLIDAY MOVIES M. FELL *TV Guide* p46 D 19 2016

Polaris all terrain vehicles

UTV PROTECTION J. HEADLEE color *Dirt Sports + Off-Road* v51 no6 p24 Je 2017

Polaris Industries Inc.

2017 INDIAN ROADMASTER CLASSIC D. Canet color *Cycle World* v56 no3 p16 Ap 2017

2017 RZR FACTORY RACING ROSTER *Dirt Sports + Off-Road* v51 no7 p8 Jl 2017

93 OCTANE S. MacDonald color *Cycle World* v56 no2 p36 Mr 2017

CAMP RZR WEST M. EMERY color *Dirt Sports + Off-Road* v51 no5 p10 My 2017

GMZ UTV WINTER NATIONALS/BITD PARKER 250 M. EMERY color *Dirt Sports + Off-Road* v51 no5 p28 My 2017

A NATION'S DATEBOOK *Dirt Sports + Off-Road* v51 no7 p72 Jl 2017

PASSION AND BUSINESS M. HOYER *Cycle World* v56 no3 p5 Ap 2017

WILD WEST SHOWOFF M. EMERY color *Dirt Sports + Off-Road* v51 no2 p22 F 2017

Polaritons

Plasmons that won't stick D. Faccio diag *Science* v356 no6345 p1336 Je 30 2017

Polarization (Social sciences)

Listening and Hearing L. Goodman *Society* v54 no2 p163 Ap 2017

Making Up Is Hard to Do C. FRIEDERSDORF color *Atlantic* v318 no4 p19 N 2016

New U.S. Cardinals Condemn Polarization Inside the Church M. O'LOUGHLIN and J. ZIPPLE color *America* v215 no18 p8 D 5 2016

The Polarization Trap R. J. BRESLER *USA Today Magazine* v145 no2864 p13 My 2017

POLARIZED R. M. HOGARTH and E. SOYER *USA Today Magazine* v145 no2860 p44 Ja 2017

Research: Political Polarization Is Changing How Americans Work and Shop C. McConnell, Y. Margalit et al *Harvard Business Review Digital Articles* p2 My 19 2017

Polaroid Corp.

The Golden Age of the Instant Camera... Just Got Started F. Woodward bw color *GQ: Gentlemen's Quarterly* v97 no3 p70 Mr 2017

The No-Frills, Full-Fun Snapshot Is Back A. Fitzpatrick and K. Bachor color *Time* v190 no4 p52 Jl 24 2017

Polasky, Stephen

Social norms as solutions bibl color *Science* v354 no6308 p42 O 7 2016

Polastro, Enrico

How to Know If a Spin-Off Will Succeed *Harvard Business Review Digital Articles* p2 F 24 2015

Polat, Emre Ozan

Promoting human rights through science color *Science* v357 no6359 p34 O 6 2017

Pold, G.

Long-term pattern and magnitude of soil carbon feedback to the climate system in a warming world chart graph *Science* v357 no6359 p101 O 6 2017

Poldark (TV program)

My Obsessions... *TV Guide* p10 D 19 2016

Poldark A. Bacle, D. Coggan et al *Entertainment Weekly* no1482/1483 p38 S 22 2017

POLDARK'S HEIDA REED S. Gutierrez color *British Heritage Travel* v38 no5 p48 S/O 2017

Polenta

IN THE KITCHEN: VENETIAN BITES M. HENNESSY color *Chicago* v66 no9 p68 S 2017

SINGULAR Sensation M. Kiesel cartoon color *O, The Oprah Magazine* p137 Mr 2017

Polenzani, Matthew

MATTHEW POLENZANI M. Mazzaro *Opera News* v81 no10 p24 Ap 2017

Polepalli, Jai S.

Gating of social reward by oxytocin in the ventral tegmental area color graph *Science* v357 no6358 p1406 S 29 2017

Police

See also

Border patrol agents

Border patrols

Detectives

35 Things Police Officers Want To Tell You M. CROUCH *Reader's Digest* v188 no1126 p100 D 2016/Ja 2017

BRICKBATS C. OLIVER cartoon *Reason* v49 no2 p72 Je 2017

THE COP WHO BECAME A ROBBER J. MAYSH *Los Angeles Magazine* v62 no9 p100 S 2017

Cruising on a Sunday Afternoon: In a country hamlet, everyone notices when the police chief is driving around color *Yankee* p12 Jl 2017

Just Joking *National Geographic Kids* no469 p32 Ap 2017

MISSISSIPPI'S JUMP-OUT BOYS C. J. Ciaramella color *Reason* v49 no5 p8 O 2017

The Overworked Cop: Police overtime and long hours of off-duty work come with alarming consequences M. Maciag *Governing* v31 no1 p56 O 2017

TALK TO US M. O'Malley and S. Lott color graph *Chicago* v66 no8 p17 Ag 2017

The Truth About Black Lives Matter *Commentary* v141 no10 p1 D 2016

The Truth About Black Lives Matter *Commentary* v142 no5 p1

D 2016

WHAT COPS KNOW [Cover story] P. Nickeas color *Chicago* v66 no7 p78 Jl 2017

Who Wants to be the Police? A. Johnson color *New Orleans Magazine* v51 no7 p38 My 2017

Will Alexa Take the Witness Stand? Our electronic gadgets are collecting data about us that police are using to solve When does that violate our constitutional right to privacy? [Cover story] P. SMITH *New York Times Upfront* v150 no1 p6 S 4 2017

Police & race relations

Do You See Me? J. Legend color *Time* v188 no16/17 p60 O 24 2016

What Videos Can't Show G. Gutting color *Commonweal* v143 no18 p12 N 11 2016

Police administration

CAN A CITY TAKE ON ITS POLICE? Chicago must confront the Fraternal Order of Police without backup from the feds *In These Times* v41 no6 p21 Je 2017

Police administration—United States

Managing Police Departments Post-Ferguson S. Wolfe and J. Nix *Harvard Business Review Digital Articles* p2 S 13 2016

THREE DAYS IN AMERICA B. Stole, B. Williams et al color *Wired* v24 no12 p114 D 2016

Police brutality

An anti-gay campaign turns deadly in Chechnya, and journalists are also in danger R. Denber *America* v216 no13 p10 Je 12 2017

Banlieue Battles D. Green color *Weekly Standard* v22 no24 p19 F 27 2017

The Catalonia Question [Cover story] S. FABER and B. SEGUÍN *Nation* v305 no10 p4 O 23 2017

A New American Rebellion R. CONNIFF *Progressive* v81 no10 p5 N 2016

"NONE OF US IS ENTIRELY INNOCENT" W. Greenberg bw *Mother Jones* v42 no2 p24 Mr/Ap 2017

POLICING THE COLONY [Cover story] C. HAYES color *Nation* v304 no13 p12 Ap 17 2017

What Videos Can't Show G. Gutting color *Commonweal* v143 no18 p12 N 11 2016

Police chiefs

Chief Concerns P. A. Harkness *Governing* v30 no2 p16 N 2016

Police chiefs—United States—Attitudes

Lynchings Remembered S. Richardson color *American History* v52 no3 p10 Ag 2017

Police-community relations

POLICING M. Maciag *Governing* v30 no4 p34 Ja 2017

Technology to the Rescue? A. AUMEN *USA Today Magazine* v146 no2868 p34 S 2017

Police-community relations—United States

GUERRILLA GO PROS W. ENZINNA color *Mother Jones* v42 no4 p40 Jl/Ag 2017

The Truth About Black Lives Matter: The movement paints a false and disturbing portrait of America in order to justify its even more disturbing aims J. Muravchik *Commentary* v142 no5 p20 D 2016

Police corruption

WHO PAYS FOR THE RCMP'S EPIC FAILURE? A. KINGSTON *Maclean's* v129 no43 p10 O 31 2016

Police discretion

COPS SHOULD NOT PLAY JEOPARDY D. SPENCER *USA Today Magazine* v146 no2868 p32 S 2017

Police misconduct

See also

Police brutality

ARRESTED DEVELOPMENT N. Baptiste *Mother Jones* v42 no4 p10 Jl/Ag 2017

Police on television

THE BEST ON THE BEAT M. Roush *TV Guide* v65 no8 p21 F 27 2017

Police reform

5 ROADBLOCKS TO REFORM IN CHICAGO'S POLICE UNION CONTRACT *In These Times* v41 no6 p22 Je 2017

CAN A CITY TAKE ON ITS POLICE? Chicago must confront the Fraternal Order of Police without backup from the feds *In These Times* v41 no6 p21 Je 2017

Cops May Get Freer Hand Under Trump M. Rhodan color *Time* v189 no14 p10 Ap 17 2017

The Organizational Reasons Police Departments Don't Change B. Armacost *Harvard Business Review Digital Articles* p2 Ag 19 2016

Police reports

Steve Bannon, Trump's Right-Hand Batterer B. LUEDERS cartoon *Progressive* v81 no2 p14 F 2017

Police shootings

Changing Course A. Greenblatt *Governing* v30 no3 p17 D 2016

PROFESSOR CARNAGE S. FEATHERSTONE color *New Republic* v248 no5 p20 My 2017

Police shootings—Congresses

Starting a Difficult Conversation V. Paynich *Parks & Recreation* v52 no1 p30 Ja 2017

Police training

'HOW WOULD AN ETHICAL OFFICER REACT?' S. SMITH *New York Times Magazine* p36 Ag 20 2017

Police training— United States

KILLER INSTINCTS B. SCHATZ *Mother Jones* v42 no2 p28 Mr/Ap 2017

Training Police Departments to Be Less Biased S. G. Carmichael *Harvard Business Review Digital Articles* p2 Mr 6 2015

Police unions

IMPUNITY IN THE FINE PRINT: Chicago's police union contract ensures that abuses remain in the shadows A. EMMANUEL *In These Times* v41 no7 p24 Jl 2017

Police vehicles

Blue Steel cartoon *Road & Truck* v69 no4 p24 N 2017

Police—California

A Change In the Force: A RUBBER-STAMP COMMITTEE NO MORE, THE LOS ANGELES POLICE COMMISSION HAS BEEN WORKING TO TRANSFORM LAPD POLICY. MATTHEW JOHNSON IS A BIG REASON WHY J. DOMANICK *Los Angeles Magazine* p68 Ag 2017

A cop's view from the street D. Heim *Christian Century* v134 no6 p32 Mr 15 2017

Police—Canada

INSIDE THE KEN PAGAN WITCHHUNT A. LEE color *Maclean's* v129 no42 p11 O 24 2016

Project Spade R. KOLKER bw *Walrus* v14 no7 p44 S 2017

Police—Georgia

JACKSON POLICE DEPARTMENT JACKSON 53 MILES SOUTHEAST OF ATLANTA J. GREEN *Atlanta* v57 no1 p144 My 2017

Police—Illinois—Chicago

Widening the Whistleblower's Reach G. PURDOM *American Scholar* v86 no1 p16 Wint 2017

Police—Mental health

S.O.B. STORY *Harper's Magazine* v334 no2000 p21 Ja 2017

Police—Michigan

THE FIRE LAST TIME M. BINELLI bw *New Republic* v248 no5 p28 My 2017

Police—New York (State)

A Muslim police officer sues the NYPD, citing religious harassment G. Kauffman *Christian Century* v134 no6 p15 Mr 15 2017

NYPD BLACK E. CONLON bw color *Esquire* p104 Ap 2017

Police—North Carolina

Soundbites *Extra!* v29 no9 p2 N 2016

Police—Québec (Province)

Bad boys M. PATRIQUIN color *Maclean's* v129 no46 p12 N 21 2016

Police—Trials, litigation, etc.

The Thread M. Mosby, R. Nicholson Jr. et al *New York Times Magazine* p16 O 16 2016

Police—United States

AMERICAN SEX POLICE E. N. BROWN color *Reason* v48 no11 p16 Ap 2017

THE COP NEXT DOOR: Can police rebuild trust by moving into the neighborhood? J. Buntin *Governing* v30 no10 p24 Jl 2017

'Demilitarize' the Police? A. RIZER color *Weekly Standard* v22 no7 p17 O 2017

How America Outlawed Adolescence A. RIPLEY bw color *Atlantic* v318 no4 p86 N 2016

How Do You Define Hate? color *Governing* v30 no11 p11 Ag 2017

Military Gear for Police *Congressional Digest* v96 no8 p31 O 2017

Who we are P. WELLS chart color *Maclean's* v130 no6 p10 Jl 2017

Political attitudes—United States

Asymmetric Rhetorical Warfare D. FOSTER *National Review* v68 no20 p48 N 7 2016

The California Republic Comes Roaring Back K. Steinmetz color diag map *Time* v189 no5 p34 F 13 2017

CALL AND RESPONSE K. SCHULZ cartoon color *New Yorker* v93 no3 p26 Mr 6 2017

COULD THIS GET ANY WORSE? A. ABEL color *Maclean's* v129 no41 p30 O 17 2016

The Education Gap T. ALBERTA color *National Review* v68 no19 p14 O 24 2016

Fair-Weather Originalists J. BLACKMAN color *National Review* v69 no3 p20 F 20 2017

Maine Divided E. JOHNSON il *National Review* v68 no20 p16 N 7 2016

Movie Stars and the Perils of the Podium D. Von Drehle color *Time* v189 no4 p21 Ja 23 2017

The people for Donald Trump A. ABEL color *Maclean's* v129 no46 p42 N 21 2016

TRUMP COUNTY, USA M. Binelli bw color *Rolling Stone* no1280 p26 F 9 2017

TRUMPTOWN L. MACFARQUHAR cartoon color *New Yorker* v92 no32 p56 O 10 2016

Political campaigns

CAN'T AFFORD A LAWYER? NO FREE SPEECH FOR YOU N. SIBILLA and J. KERR *Reason* v48 no8 p44 Ja 2017

Good Luck With Your Predictions N. EMERY *Weekly Standard* v22 no5 p26 O 10 2016

His Reelection Plan T. LINDBERG color *Weekly Standard* v22 no13 p18 D 5 2016

Is the Best Offense a Good Defense Lawyer? C. HOOKS *Texas Monthly* v44 no11 p62 N 2016

Men Behaving Badly K. Pollitt color *Nation* v33 no21 p10 N 21 2016

The Normal One J. GERAGHTY il *National Review* v69 no19 p13 O 16 2017

Ohio A. MacGillis *New York Times Magazine* p41 N 20 2016

Speech! Speech! T. B. BROWNE *Indianapolis Monthly* v40 no3 p26 N 2016

Political campaigns—United States

Alpha Dog Days B. Whalen *Hoover Digest: Research & Opinion on Public Policy* no4 p49 Fall 2016

THE BERNIECRATS PAINTING TRUMP COUNTRY BLUE C. BRENNAN *In These Times* v41 no7 p11 Jl 2017

CAMPAIGN SKETCHES S. Mumford *Harper's Magazine* v333 no1998 p37 N 2016

Could this get any worse? [Cover story] J. Gatehouse color *Maclean's* v129 no43 p28 O 31 2016

For Better, for Worse H. Clinton color *Vogue* v207 no10 p148 O 2017

Free Press Under Assault L. Lalami diag *Nation* v304 no18 p10 Je 19 2017

Going Off the Rails? W. S. LIND *American Conservative* v16 no3 p8 My/Je 2017

THE GREAT ABANDONMENT T. GENOWAYS bw *New Republic* v248 no1/2 p42 Ja/F 2017

GUILTY PLEASURE E. NUSSBAUM color *New Yorker* v93 no22 p22 Jl 31 2017

HER WAY M. Leibovich *New York Times Magazine* p40 O 16 2016

How Putin Plays Trump Like a Piano *Commentary* v142 no2 p1 S 2016

Is It 1968? *Commentary* v142 no2 p1 S 2016

Mayors, Promises and Reality A. Ehrenhalt *Governing* v30 no2 p14 N 2016

The New Assault on Privacy J. PIERESON cartoon *Weekly Standard* v22 no27 p20 Mr 20 2017

PROGRESSIVE 2016 Honor Role J. Nichols color *Nation* v304 no2 p20 Ja 16 2017

The Racist Movement Promoted by Trump's Campaign Chief J. Naureckas *Extra!* v29 no8 p3 O 2016

THE SECOND-STRANGEST CAMPAIGN OF THE SEASON J. ZENGERLE img *New York* v49 no15 p28 Jl 25 2016

The Spin Zone W. Robinson color *Art in America* v104 no10 p65

N 2016

Stop Trump!: A Conservative's Perspective R. Berg *Progressive* v81 no6 p23 Ag/S 2017

THANKS TRUMP! [Cover story] K. BAKER color *New Republic* v247 no12 p16 D 2016

TIME TO RESTORE THE BONDS BETWEEN CITIZENS D. TRUMP *Vital Speeches of the Day* v83 no1 p8 Ja 2017

TRUMP'S CAMPAIGN HAS BEEN SO INSANE E. LEVITZ and J. D. WALSH *New York* v49 no22 p46 O 31 2016

Political candidate recruitment

The Trump Effect A. Altman color *Time* v189 no15 p24 Ap 24 2017

Political candidates

See also

Presidential candidates

Women political candidates

AND NINE THEY NEED TO PROTECT E. Benson, M. Kinney et al *New York* v50 no7 p31 Ap 3 2017

ED RECKONING: The Republican candidate for governor of Virginia comes straight from the national GOP establishment. Not long ago, his résumé could have been a plus. These days, it might be Ed Gillespie's biggest challenge S. van Zuylen-Wood *Washingtonian Magazine* v53 no1 p84 O 2017

From Movement to Mayor K. ARONOFF *In These Times* v41 no6 p30 Je 2017

Political candidates—Canada

Running from office K. EDWARDS *Maclean's* v130 no10 p16 N 2017

Political candidates—Public opinion

TIME's Foreign Correspondents on How the World Sees the U.S. Election H. Beech, D. Stewart et al *Time* v188 no16/17 p34 O 24 2016

Political candidates—United States

Rides a Bike, Runs for Congress D. Millner color *Glamour* v115 no11 p120 N 2017

What You Said About ... chart color *Time* v190 no14 p4 O 9 2017

Political cartoons

Cartoons *New York Times Upfront* p24 S 18 2017

Cartoons *New York Times Upfront* v149 no6 p40 D 12 2016

COMICS T. LABAN, K. BABIS et al *In These Times* v41 no10 p46 O 2017

NATION NEWS: Drawing Opposition color *Nation* v305 no11 p10 O 30 2017

THIS MODERN WORLD T. TOMORROW il *Nation* v305 no8 p8 O 9 2017

THE TRUMP-RUSSIA MEMOS J. Neufeld cartoon *Columbia Journalism Review* v56 no2 p89 Fall 2017

Views From Abroad *New York Times Upfront* p1 Mr 13 2017 Supplement World Week

VOICES OF The RESISTANCE color *Progressive* v81 no4 p15 Ap/My 2017

Political change

DEMOCRACIES IN UPHEAVAL D. MALPASS *Forbes* v198 no9 p32 D 30 2016

Macron's Opportunity To Change France *Bloomberg Businessweek* no4527 p18 Je 19 2017

TGI (TPRM) R. L. FISCHER *USA Today Magazine* v145 no2864 p16 My 2017

What the Nation Can Learn from North Carolina K. Ross color *Progressive* v81 no4 p34 Ap/My 2017

Political change—History—21st century

The Ultimate Insider Who Could Still Change the Game In the Oval Office J. Klein color *Time* v188 no19 p24 N 7 2016

Political collectibles

To Be Black and Selling Trump Merch R. BROWNE *New York* v49 no15 p16 Jl 25 2016

Political communication

See also

Propaganda

WASHINGTON CONFIDENTIAL: Why a Tinseltown insider publication is suddenly a player in DC E. Plott *Washingtonian Magazine* v52 no11 p52 Ag 2017

Political communication—United States

OF MANY THINGS M. MALONE *America* v215 p2 N 28 2016

Trump as Communicator H. R. HIGGINS *National Review* v69 no4 p18 Mr 6 2017

Use Vivid Language A. NABAUM color *New Republic* v248 no3 p34 Mr 2017

Political consultants

Amid Chaos, Trump Needs a Strong Lawyer P. M. Barrett color *Bloomberg Businessweek* no4512 p26 F 20 2017

FINAL DAYS G. SHERMAN img *New York* v49 no22 p28 O 31 2016

Milestones color *Time* v189 no22 p10 Je 12 2017

The Second Most Powerful Man In the World? [Cover story] D. Von Drehle, A. Altman et al color *Time* v189 no5 p24 F 13 2017

THE WEST WING'S PHONY FOREIGN-POLICY GURU B. Dreyfuss color *Rolling Stone* no1294 p34 Ag 24 2017

Zbigniew Brzezinski P. Elliott color *Time* v189 no22 p10 Je 12 2017

Political consultants—Interviews

EXIT, LEFT A. HICKLIN color *Advocate* no1089 p30 F/Mr 2017

Political consultants—United States

As the White House Turns: A Guide to the Shifting Power Centers Among Trump's Top Advisers M. Scherer and Z. J. Miller color *Time* v189 no15 p10 Ap 24 2017

The Doomsayer M. BALL cartoon *Atlantic* v318 no4 p24 N 2016

Enter the Bannon [Cover story] J. Green color *Bloomberg Businessweek* no4540 p40 O 2 2017

Family First [Cover story] Z. J. Miller, M. Scherer et al color *Time* v189 no22 p24 Je 12 2017

The Inner Circle of Trump's Inner Circle Z. J. Miller color *Time* v189 no3 p34 Ja 30 2017

ONE. HUNDRED. PERCENT. J. GREEN bw color *Bloomberg Businessweek* no4513 p50 Mr 6 2017

OVAL OFFICE INFLUENCE MAZE color diag *Fortune* v175 no7 p14 Je 1 2017

The Selling of the Candidates, 2016 J. V. LAST color *Weekly Standard* v22 no11 p23 N 21 2016

The Ziegfeld of Political Theater A. FERGUSON color *Weekly Standard* v22 no36 p12 My 29 2017

Political consultants—United States—Attitudes

Billionaires vs. Bombardiers M. T. KLARE diag *Nation* v304 no8 p3 Mr 13 2017

Political correctness

Free Speech on College Campuses H. W. N. THOMAS III *American Scholar* v86 no3 p4 Summ 2017

Killing the Messenger: Mark Lilla's 'End of Identity Liberalism' and its Critics G. Brahm *Society* v54 no4 p326 Ag 2017

Latest Language Abuse S. BEAUCHAMP *American Conservative* v16 no3 p9 My/Je 2017

Not So Fast, Golden State B. MACKINTOSH and R. A. HARRISON *American Scholar* v86 no3 p3 Summ 2017

THE RISE OF POLITICAL CORRECTNESS A. M. Codevilla *Claremont Review of Books* v16 no4 p37 Fall 2016

A Tale of Two Universities D. C. Paris *Change* v49 no3 p4 My/Je 2017

Political correctness—United States

Guilt Free W. Morris *New York Times Magazine* p11 Jl 30 2017

On Political Correctness W. DERESIEWICZ *American Scholar* v86 no2 p30 Spr 2017

Political correctness—United States—Social aspects

The Soft Bigotry of Political Correctness: President Trump has never bowed to the culture of victimization. His lack of deference could be liberating S. Steele *Hoover Digest: Research & Opinion on Public Policy* no2 p54 Spr 2017

Political correctness—United States—Universities & colleges

A 'Fractious' Feminist Decries the Ruthless Thought Police Stifling Free Speech on Campus C. Paglia color *Time* v189 no12 p28 Ap 3 2017

Political corruption

See also

Corrupt practices in elections

Being an Ethical Business in a Corrupt Environment S. R. Velamuri, W. S. Harvey et al *Harvard Business Review Digital Articles* p2 Mr 23 2017

Election 2016 [Cover story] J. J. Sheehan, A. J. Bacevich et al color *Commonweal* v144 no1 p14 Ja 6 2017

The Kleptocracy Preps for Pennsylvania Avenue J. Chait img *New York* v49 no24 p29 N 28 2016

POLITICIANS WILL DISAPPOINT YOU M. WELCH color *Reason* v49 no4 p14 Ag/S 2017

Scandals Aplenty M. HEMINGWAY color *Weekly Standard* v22 no18 p14 Ja 16 2017

Toward a birthday etiquette *Maclean's* no1 p4 F 17 2017

Political corruption—Brazil

BRAZIL'S CARWASH SCANDAL T. Padgett color *Bloomberg Businessweek* no4524 p8 My 29 2017

Brazil's Never-Ending Corruption Crisis B. Winter color *Foreign Affairs* v96 no3 p87 My/Je 2017

Political corruption—Israel

Cigars, Bubbly, and Subs Haunt Netanyahu J. Ferziger and D. Wainer *Bloomberg Businessweek* no4540 p35 O 2 2017

Political corruption—Korea (South)

Park in Limbo J. Lee, K. Kong et al color *Bloomberg Businessweek* no4498 p22 N 7 2016

A Scandal at Korea's Retirement Giant B. Einhorn and H. Kim color *Bloomberg Businessweek* no4507 p31 Ja 16 2017

South Korea Tries to Curb the Chaebol B. Einhorn, P. Pae et al color *Bloomberg Businessweek* no4504 p15 D 19 2016

Who's Who In South Korea's Widening Graft Scandal C. Campbell color *Time* v189 no3 p9 Ja 30 2017

Political corruption—Latin America

Latin America Drains Its Political Swamp R. Colitt, C. Devereux et al bw *Bloomberg Businessweek* no4531 p38 Jl 24 2017

Political corruption—Lawsuits & claims

Latin America Drains Its Political Swamp R. Colitt, C. Devereux et al bw *Bloomberg Businessweek* no4531 p38 Jl 24 2017

Political corruption—Prevention

Lightbox T. John color *Time* v189 no6 p16 F 20 2017

Political corruption—Russia

Moscow Confidential: Private Jets for Dogs H. Meyer, I. Reznik et al bw color *Bloomberg Businessweek* no4498 p24 N 7 2016

Political corruption—United States

ALL TOGETHER NOW L. LESSIG *Sierra* v101 no5 p30 S/O 2016

Corruption as a Way of Life J. COST color map *Weekly Standard* v22 no38 p18 Je 12 2017

Political crimes & offenses

See also

Concentration camps

Corrupt practices in elections

Insurgency

Terrorism

A Shooting and the Risks of Political Outrage M. Scherer color *Time* v189 no24 p12 Je 26 2017

Political crimes & offenses—Prevention

How to Hunt a Lone Wolf D. Byman cartoon *Foreign Affairs* v96 no2 p96 Mr/Ap 2017

Political culture

Turning Blue A. Cockburn *Harper's Magazine* v334 no2004 p2 My 2017

Political culture—United States

Call of Duty P. GLASTRIS *Washington Monthly* v49 no3-5 p4 Mr-My 2017

Political culture—United States—History

A Usable Past A conversation on Politics & History with Eric Foner R. KREITNER color *Nation* v304 no15 p16 My 8 2017

Political customs & rites

Back When Everyone Knew How You Voted P. Wasley *Humanities* v37 no4 p1 Fall 2016

Political debates & debating

America's loss A. ABEL color *Maclean's* v129 no40 p32 O 10 2016

Bringing probability judgments into policy debates via forecasting tournaments P. E. Tetlock, B. A. Mellers et al bibl color *Science* v355 no6324 p481 F 3 2017

The Debate We Need W. GREIDER *Nation* v303 no17 p6 O 24 2016

Hot tips for Trump's next debate S. FESCHUK color *Maclean's* v129 no40 p81 O 10 2016

INQUIETUDE J. Lepore cartoon *New Yorker* v93 no31 p17 O 9 2017

It's not so bad. Really [Cover story] P. WELLS color *Maclean's* p24 Je 2017

Political Deliberation & the Adversarial Principle B. Manin *Daedalus* v146 no3 p39 Summ 2017

THE SMILE THAT TRUMPED THE DONALD A. KINGSTON

4 2017

Takin' It To the STREETS R. ROSS *Texas Monthly* v44 no11 p53 N 2016

What Does Trump See When He Looks Back In History? Mostly He Sees ... Trump J. Meacham color *Time* v189 no18 p31 My 15 2017

Political participation—Philippines

SUPER FANS J. Fan cartoon *New Yorker* v93 no16 p38 Je 5 2017

Political participation—United States

The Editor's Note J. Richardson *Phi Delta Kappan* v98 no6 p4 Mr 2017

How satire failed F. DEAN color *Maclean's* v129 no47 p56 N 28 2016

THE LAST WORD bw *Rolling Stone* no1280 p58 F 9 2017

New Institutions that Embrace Participation Without Populism N. Gardels and N. Berggruen *NPQ: New Perspectives Quarterly* v34 no1 p9 Ja 2017

A RECIPE J. FRIEDMAN cartoon *New Yorker* v92 no44 p31 Ja 9 2017

Reinvent Labor A. NABAUM *New Republic* v248 no3 p35 Mr 2017

SUPER FANS J. Fan cartoon *New Yorker* v93 no16 p38 Je 5 2017

WHITE SPACE T. Rehagen bw *Indianapolis Monthly* p74 Ap 2017

Political parties

30 SEATS THE DEMS COVET... *New York* v50 no7 p27 Ap 3 2017

BEYOND LE PEN: The world's nationalists J. LARSON img *New York* v50 no9 p32 My 1 2017

Leftward March R. PONNURU il *National Review* v69 no12 p13 Je 26 2017

THE TROUBLE WITH "ACTIVIST": A case for dropping the A-word J. M. SMUCKER *In These Times* v41 no6 p28 Je 2017

The Veneration of Cool P. TERZIAN *Weekly Standard* v22 no8 p12 O 31 2016

Political parties—Canada

Meanwhile, Up North K. J. TORRANCE color *Weekly Standard* v22 no36 p22 My 29 2017

Political parties—Québec (Province)

Here they go again M. PATRIQUIN color *Maclean's* v129 no51/52 p32 D 26 2016

Political parties—United States

A Heartbeat Away P. SMITH *New York Times Upfront* v149 no4 p14 O 31 2016

The Way We Were/Are R. J. BRESLER *USA Today Magazine* v145 no2858 p13 N 2016

WHITE SPACE T. Rehagen bw *Indianapolis Monthly* p74 Ap 2017

Political party leadership

The End of an Era S. Frizell and M. Rhodan color *Time* v188 no21 p62 N 21 2016

Political persecution—United States

Creative Reconstruction M. ATWOOD il *Nation* v304 no4 p15 F 6 2017

Political philosophy

See also

Dystopias

Political philosophy—History—17th century

PENN'S PLAN for a united Europe P. SchröDer *History Today* v66 no10 p32 O 2016

Political planning

See also

Political entrepreneurship

How Trump Plans to Win-Even If He Loses the Election Z. J. Miller color diag *Time* v188 no18 p9 O 31 2016

Political platforms

Democratic Party Platform: "We Are Stronger Together" *Congressional Digest* v95 no8 p6 O 2016

What Hillary Clinton's Insiders Know That Voters Don't-Yet S. Frizell and P. Elliott color *Time* v188 no18 p14 O 31 2016

Political prisoners—Russia

To Protest In Russia J. NORDLINGER color *National Review* v69 no2 p22 F 6 2017

Political psychology

See also

Propaganda

Emotional Divide K. Vick, C. Alter et al color diag *Time* v189 no7/8 p38 F 27 2017

HOW TO GET OVER IT S. KOGAN *USA Today Magazine* v146 no2866 p28 Jl 2017

Political purges

The Purge That's Paralyzed Turkey O. Ant and B. Harvey *Bloomberg Businessweek* no4506 p15 Ja 9 2017

Political realism

A New Urgent Realism Is Making Negotiations With North Korea More Likely N. Gardels *NPQ: New Perspectives Quarterly* v34 no3 p6 Jl 2017

Saving Realism from the So-Called Realists: A foreign-policy approach based in security and pragmatism is now characterized by retrenchment and radicalism H. Brands and P. Feaver *Commentary* v144 no2 p15 S 2017

Political reform

In Iraq, mercurial cleric redefines himself as a nationalist patriot J. Arraf *Christian Century* v134 no13 p14 Je 21 2017

Political refugees

Displaced Iraqi Christians await return to Mosul G. Nabeel and A. A. Shamary color *Christian Century* v133 no24 p14 N 23 2016

FLASHBACK *MHQ: Quarterly Journal of Military History* v29 no3 p4 Spr 2017

A MODERN ODYSSEY J. HAMMER *Smithsonian* v48 no1 p70 Ap 2017

A NEW UNDERGROUND RAILROAD J. HALPERN cartoon color *New Yorker* v93 no4 p32 Mr 13 2017

People B. Dooley *Christian Century* v134 no12 p19 Je 7 2017

United States of Refugees *Smithsonian* v48 no1 p76 Ap 2017

The Waiting Room D. Bonessi and M. Abunnassr color *Commonweal* v144 no5 p39 Mr 10 2017

Political refugees—Crimes against

A Catastrophic Error In Nigeria Kills Scores color *Time* v189 no3 p9 Ja 30 2017

Political refugees—Government policy

What a Just Immigration Policy Looks Like B. HELLER and B. Allen-Ebrahimian cartoon *Foreign Policy* no226 p80 S/O 2017

Why Do Some Countries Get Away With Taking Fewer Refugees? K. SURANA bw *Foreign Policy* no226 p14 S/O 2017

Political refugees—Services for

Catholic Relief Services responds to misery in Mosul K. Clarke color *America* v217 no3 p17 Ag 7 2017

Political refugees—Social conditions

A Refugee Without a River R. MELLEN color *Foreign Policy* no226 p12 S/O 2017

A VOICE IN THE NIGHT G. BEALS color *Foreign Policy* no226 p44 S/O 2017

Political rights

See also

Political participation

Half a Century of a Right to Health? J. BHABHA *UN Chronicle* v54 no4 p13 2017

The Long Road Ahead H. S. PURI *UN Chronicle* v54 no4 p28 2017

Political risk (Foreign investments)

THE 5TH RISK M. LEWIS color *Vanity Fair* v59 no9 p192 S 2017

Why Europe Tops 2015's List of Global Risks J. Kehoe *Harvard Business Review Digital Articles* p2 Ja 9 2015

Political satire

CARRY A BIG SHTICK J. Lovett cartoon *Wired* v25 no4 p72 Ap 2017

HOW YOUR: COMEDY GETS MADE D. AMIRA cartoon color *Wired* v25 no4 p70 Ap 2017

JOKING WHILE MUSLIM N. FARSAD cartoon *Wired* v25 no4 p75 Ap 2017

The Long View R. LONG il *National Review* v68 no19 p40 O 24 2016

New Sentences N. Abebe *New York Times Magazine* p16 My 21 2017

PARODY color *Weekly Standard* v22 no38 p40 Je 12 2017

PARODY *Weekly Standard* v22 no43 p40 Jl 24 2017

Translating Trump S. FESCHUK color *Maclean's* v130 no10 p128 N 2017

Political science

See also

no19 p48 S 19 2016

Moving Beyond the Gender Gap A. M. McCLOSKEY color *National Review* v68 no22 p47 D 5 2016

NEBRASKA'S Public Servants color *Nebraska Life* v21 no2 p19 Mr/Ap 2017

POLITICIANS WILL DISAPPOINT YOU M. WELCH color *Reason* v49 no4 p14 Ag/S 2017

The TRAGEDY of CHRISTOPHER BARRY H. JAFFE *Washingtonian Magazine* v52 no4 p62 Ja 2017

UNEARTHING DEMOCRACY'S ROOTS L. Wade color diag *Science* v355 no6330 p1114 Mr 17 2017

United Kingdom and Australia: the Values We Share: AFTER WE LEAVE THE EU, AUSTRALIA WILL BE AT, OR NEAR, THE FRONT OF THE QUEUE FOR A NEW FREE TRADE AGREEMENT WITH BRITAIN *Vital Speeches of the Day* v83 no9 p238 S 2017

WHAT DO YOU DO WITH THE MAD THAT YOU FEEL? [Cover story] D. Dark color *America* v216 no10 p26 My 1 2017

What to Do About Dictators? *America* v215 no15 p5 N 14 2016

Politicians' families

Jared and Other Sons-In-Law J. NORDLINGER color *National Review* v69 no16 p19 Ag 28 2017

Politicians—Attitudes

The Long View R. LONG il *National Review* v68 no23 p34 D 19 2016

Why Gloom Trumps Glad M. Shermer cartoon *Scientific American* v315 no5 p77 N 2016

Politicians—Canada

Bringing out the big guns A. HUTCHINS color *Maclean's* v130 no4 p13 My 2017

Escape from Winterpeg N. MACDONALD color *Maclean's* no1 p14 F 17 2017

THE INTERVIEW J. GEDDES color *Maclean's* v129 no43 p12 O 31 2016

Politicians—History

THE BIG QUESTION H. Minhaj, A. S. Cooper et al cartoon *Atlantic* v318 no4 p112 N 2016

The People v. Jefferson Davis: A legal showdown 150 years ago laid bare the complexities of reuniting the States T. A. FRAIL *Smithsonian* v48 no2 p18 My 2017

Q: Who Is the Worst Leader of All Time? M. Karp, L. Leamer et al color *Atlantic* v319 no1 p100 Ja/F 2017

Politicians—Humor

THE PENCES VISIT MANHATTAN D. MCGRATH cartoon *New Yorker* v92 no32 p47 O 10 2016

Politicians—Moral & ethical aspects

False equivalencies A. KINGSTON color *Maclean's* v129 no45 p35 N 14 2016

Politicians—United States

David Stockman's Latest Target: The feisty contrarian takes on the 'War Party' R. W. MERRY *American Conservative* v16 no5 p9 S/O 2017

Disappointed Dems F. BARNES color *Weekly Standard* v22 no41 p9 Jl 3 2017

A Grouse About Government D. YARNOLD color *Audubon* v119 no3 p8 Fall 2017

The Hardest Lesson of a Liberal Democracy? How to Live With Critics A. Kirsch *New York Times Book Review* p21 Je 18 2017

Is the Endangered Species Act in Danger? B. PALMER *Audubon* v119 no1 p19 Spr 2017

Jared and Other Sons-In-Law J. NORDLINGER color *National Review* v69 no16 p19 Ag 28 2017

Loyal Opposition J. COST color *Weekly Standard* v22 no41 p10 Jl 3 2017

Politicians bw cartoon color *American Cowboy* p26 LEGENDS OF TEXAS Special Issue 2017

Pundits Told Dems to Spurn Sanders for 'Electable' Clinton A. Johnson *Extra!* v29 no10 p3 D 2016

The real bubble protects elected officials R. David Sullivan *America* v216 no13 p3 Je 12 2017

The Republican Civil War in Texas K. D. WILLIAMSON *National Review* v69 no15 p17 Ag 14 2017

Resistance Is Rising in the Heartland J. NICHOLS color il *Nation* v305 no1 p30 Jl 3 2017

Save Our Science, Save Our Planet M. Hamilton *Humanist* v77 no2 p6 Mr/Ap 2017

Scott Garrett Turns to Extremists for Votes J. Green color *Bloomberg Businessweek* no4494 p29 O 10 2016

The Teddy Awards, Even In a Year That Set New Lows for Politicians J. Klein color *Time* v188 no25-26 p39 D 19 2016 Double Issue

"Terrible Terry" CARPENTER A. J. BARTELS color *Nebraska Life* v21 no4 p62 Jl/Ag 2017

WHAT'S WRONG WITH THE DEMOCRATS? F. FOER color *Atlantic* v320 no1 p48 Jl/Ag 2017

Politicians—United States—Attitudes

Falling In and Out of Love--Again--with John McCain A. FERGUSON *Commentary* v144 no2 p9 S 2017

He Was One of a Kind, Alas F. BARNES *Weekly Standard* v22 no10 p9 N 14 2016

Pledging Allegiance E. Felten color *Weekly Standard* v22 no33 p16 My 8 2017

Politicians—United States—Biography

Mike Pence Is No Ordinary Wingman P. Elliott color *Time* v188 no27-28 p52 D 26 2016

Politicians—United States—Health

ORGAN RECITAL R. BROOKHISER *American History* v51 no6 p18 F 2017

Politicians—United States—History—21st century

RULES FOR RADICALS T. MURPHY and R. Felton bw cartoon color *Mother Jones* v42 no2 p44 Mr/Ap 2017

Politics & culture—United States

Do Culture and Politics Mix? J. EPSTEIN cartoon *Weekly Standard* v22 no34 p5 My 15 2017

Politics & economics

Tricentennial: The Montreal Influence E. Laborde *New Orleans Magazine* v51 no12 p16 O 2017

WHY DON'T WE HAVE MORE BILLIONAIRES? S. FORBES color *Forbes* v199 no3 p25 Mr 28 2017

Politics & ethnic relations

"Identity Politics" Takes a Hit S. MUWAKKIL *In These Times* v41 no1 p16 Ja 2017

Politics & gender

Can women really revolutionize politics with protest? color *Foreign Policy* no223 p22 Mr/Ap 2017

Politics & humanities

The Art of the Squeal cartoon *Weekly Standard* v22 no48 p14 S 4 2017

Politics & literature

Farewell to the Writer-in-Chief A. KIRSCH color *Foreign Policy* no221 p100 N/D 2016

PRESUMPTIVE T. MALLON cartoon color *New Yorker* v92 no35 p36 O 31 2016

Roving Eye: International Literature T. Parks *New York Times Book Review* p27 D 18 2016

Politics & war

Repeal and Replace *GQ: Gentlemen's Quarterly* v97 no5 p18 My 2017

Politics on television

Election 2016: Winners & Losers I. RUDOLPH *TV Guide* v64 no46 p6 N 7 2016

LATE-NIGHT POLIT-O-METER R. Rahman color diag *Entertainment Weekly* no1457/1458 p15 Mr 17 2017

Poll Watchers: A Late-Night Guide R. Rahman color *Entertainment Weekly* no1438 p18 N 4 2016

SCANDAL WITH CARE L. Rice color *Entertainment Weekly* no1451/1452 p30 F 3-10 2017

POLITO, MICHAEL J.

Google Haul Out: Earth Observation Imagery and Digital Aerial Surveys in Coastal Wildlife Management and Abundance Estimation *BioScience* v67 no8 p760 Ag 2017

Poljak, Anne

Site-specific phosphorylation of tau inhibits amyloid-β toxicity in Alzheimer's mice bibl graph *Science* v354 no6314 p904 N 18 2016

POLJAREVIC, EMIN

Ramadan in Scandinavia: Muslims face the choice between "excessive" and "moderate" fasting *Islamic Horizons* v46 no3 p48 My/Je 2017

Polk, Milbry

FEATURED FELLOW: MILBRY POLK M. Rosano color *Canadian Geographic* v135 no6 p82 D 2015

Polk Audio Inc.
  Gallons of Sound, Pint-Sized Speaker M. Trei color *Sound & Vision* v82 no4 p46 My 2017
  Polk Signature S60 Speaker System D. Kumin color graph *Sound & Vision* v82 no6 p34 Jl/Ag 2017

POLLACK, BARBARA
  FROM PALACE TO TANK color diag *ARTnews* v115 no3 p128 Fall 2016
  YOU'VE GOTTA SEE THIS! cartoon color *ARTnews* v116 no1 p72 Spr 2017

Pollack, Eileen
  The Only Woman in the Room B. L. Whitten *Physics Today* v69 no10 p55 O 2016

Pollack, Judah
  UNLOCKING YOUR BIG IDEAS color *Fortune* v175 no4 p142 Mr 15 2017

Pollack, Kenneth M.
  Leaders color *Time* v189 no16/17 p64 My 1-8 2017

POLLACK, NEAL
  GOOD MORNING, NEAL! color *Popular Mechanics* p72 My 2017
  What I Learned AT MY Summer Job cartoon *Popular Mechanics* p64 Je 2017
  WILL IT KILL YOU? bw color *Popular Mechanics* p88 Jl 2017

Pollack, Penny
  2017 DINING GUIDE WHERE TO EAT bw color *Chicago* v65 no12 p(Sp)1 D 2016
  CAKES, PASTRIES, PIES, COOKIES, HOT FUDGE, GALATO, BROWNIES & MORE! chart color *Chicago* v65 no11 p70 N 2016
  The Hot List color *Chicago* v66 no2 p48a F 2017
  The Hot List color *Chicago* v66 no5 p74 My 2017
  The Hot List color *Chicago* v66 no7 p45 Jl 2017
  The Hot List color *Chicago* v66 no8 p53 Ag 2017
  NEW & UPDATED color *Chicago* v65 no11 p68 N 2016
  PENNY POLLACK M. Thomas color *Chicago* v66 no11 p164 N 2017
  SHARPEN YOUR KNIVES [Cover story] color *Chicago* v66 no11 p60 N 2017
  TEATIME color *Chicago* v66 no5 p72 My 2017
  TICKET TO RIDE color *Chicago* v66 no4 p51 Ap 2017
  URBAN COUNTRY CLUB color *Chicago* v66 no11 p49 N 2017

POLLAN, MICHAEL
  BIG FOOD STRIKES BACK color *New York Times Magazine* p40 O 9 2016

Pollara, Alexander
  CLIPPERS, YACHTS, and the false promise of the wave line: John Scott Russell's 19th-century theory of ship design promised speed and delivered elegance. But, ultimately, it didn't hold water *Physics Today* v70 no7 p52 Jl 2017

Pollard, Amari D.
  The Hosts of Pantsuit Politics *Parents* v91 no11 p16 N 2016

Pollard, Garland
  Treasure Map *Virginia Living* v15 no2 p35 F 2017

Pollard, Justin
  DOROTHY LAWRENCE 4 OCTOBER 1896 - 4 OCTOBER 1964 *History Today* v67 no10 p22 O 2017
  MONTHS PAST AUGUST *History Today* v67 no8 p22 Ag 2017

Pollard, Stephanie
  DOROTHY LAWRENCE 4 OCTOBER 1896 - 4 OCTOBER 1964 *History Today* v67 no10 p22 O 2017
  MONTHS PAST AUGUST *History Today* v67 no8 p22 Ag 2017
  POMPEY THE GREAT: BORN 29 SEPTEMBER 106 BC *History Today* v67 no9 p22 S 2017

POLLARD-POST, LINDSAY
  SEEING THE LIGHT color *O, The Oprah Magazine* p18 Ag 2017

Pollen
  Can Plants Hear? M. Zaraska color *Scientific American* v317 no1 p21 Jl 2017
  For the Record color *Time* v189 no20 p4 My 29 2017

Polleux, Franck
  Multicluster Pcdh diversity is required for mouse olfactory neural circuit assembly diag *Science* v356 no6336 p411 Ap 28 2017

Pollin, Irene, 1924——Interviews
  IRENE POLLIN P. O'Donnell *Washingtonian Magazine* v52 no2 p47 N 2016

Pollin, Sharon
  Kindergarten on our minds *Successful Farming* v115 no1 p4 Ja 2017

Pollination
  See also
      Pollinators
  Declines in Pollinator Forage Suitability Were Concentrated in the Midwest, the Over-Summering Grounds for Many Honeybees C. Hitaj, D. Smith et al *Amber Waves: The Economics of Food, Farming, Natural Resources, & Rural America* p1 Jl 2017
  Drones can pollinate E. S. Eaton color *Science News* v191 no5 p4 Mr 18 2017
  Light pollution foils plant pollinators S. MILIUS color *Science News* v192 no3 p10 S 2 2017
  Pollinator Drones N. Leiber bw color *Bloomberg Businessweek* no4516 p31 Mr 27 2017

Pollination by bees——Research
  The Bee Drone J. Zorthian color *Time* v189 no11 p27 Mr 27 2017

Pollination services (Commercial services)——Government policy
  Ten policies for pollinators L. V. Dicks, B. Viana et al bibl color *Science* v354 no6315 p975 N 25 2016

Pollinator (Music)
  THERE'S SOMETHING ABOUT HARRY T. Janowitz bw color *Harper's Bazaar* no3652 p244 Ap 2017

Pollinators
  Declines in Pollinator Forage Suitability Were Concentrated in the Midwest, the Over-Summering Grounds for Many Honeybees C. Hitaj, D. Smith et al *Amber Waves: The Economics of Food, Farming, Natural Resources, & Rural America* p1 Jl 2017
  Providing havens for pollinators color *National Wildlife (World Edition)* v55 no1 p46 D/Ja 2016
  Sweet relief for pollinators C. M. del Rio and M. E. Dillon bibl color diag *Science* v355 no6326 p686 F 17 2017
  Ten policies for pollinators L. V. Dicks, B. Viana et al bibl color *Science* v354 no6315 p975 N 25 2016
  Words alone will not protect pollinators D. Inouye, S. Droege et al bibl color *Science* v355 no6323 p357 Ja 27 2017
  A worldwide survey of neonicotinoids in honey E. A. D. Mitchell, B. Mulhauser et al graph *Science* v357 no6359 p109 O 6 2017

Polling places
  Where We Vote *Governing* v30 no1 p40 O 2016

Pollio, Marty
  Making grades more meaningful chart color il *Phi Delta Kappan* v98 no3 p49 N 2016

Pollitt, Katha
  42 Months to Go... *Nation* v305 no4 p6 Ag 14 2017
  The Case for Hillary il *Nation* v303 no17 p10 O 24 2016
  Don't Stop Now! Give, Give! color diag *Nation* v304 no2 p10 Ja 16 2017
  Feminism for All bw diag *Nation* v304 no8 p6 Mr 13 2017
  A Feminism of Everything diag il *Nation* v304 no12 p6 Ap 10 2017
  The Fight for Choice diag il *Nation* v304 no4 p6 F 6 2017
  Hillary Clinton Tells All *Nation* v305 no8 p6 O 9 2017
  How Good We Had It diag il *Nation* v304 no1 p12 Ja 2 2017 The Obama Years
  It's Not McCarthyism diag il *Nation* v304 no15 p6 My 8 2017
  The Male-Gazer in Chief *Nation* v305 no10 p6 O 23 2017
  Men Behaving Badly color *Nation* v33 no21 p10 N 21 2016
  Orange Julius *Nation* v305 no2 p6 Jl 17 2017
  Religious Right, Resurgent diag il *Nation* v304 no6 p6 F 27 2017
  Running From Choice *Nation* v305 no3 p12 Jl 31 2017
  They're With Him color il *Nation* v303 no23/24 p15 D 5 2016
  Too-Big-Tent Feminism diag il *Nation* v304 no10 p6 Mr 27 2017
  Under the Bus? *Nation* v304 no16 p6 My 22 2017
  Women Strike Back color *Nation* v303 no19 p10 N 7 2016

POLLITT, MIRANDA
  june & DECEMBER color *Better Homes & Gardens* v95 no7 p60 Jl 2017
  make sparks fly color *Better Homes & Gardens* v95 no7 p68 Jl 2017

Pollitt, Russell
  After decades, a dictator is overturned in Gambia color *America* v216 no4 p17 F 20 2017
  Swazi Catholics march against human trafficking and gender-based violence color *America* v217 no7 p17 O 2 2017

D 2016

DOUG CHRISTIE color *Arts & Crafts Homes & the Revival* v12 no3 p48 Summ 2017

Enduring Finish color *Old House Journal* v45 no2 p76 Ap 2017

ENRICHED & embellished: REVIVING ORNAMENTAL PLASTERWORK color diag *Old House Journal* v45 no6 p40 S 2017

Finds in Metalwork color *Old House Journal* v45 no5 p68 Ag 2017

Fit for a Bath color *Old House Journal* v45 no1 p76 F 2017

Fixing Wood Floors color *Log Home Living* v33 no7 p75 S 2016

Front Door, Back Door AND DOORS INSIDE color diag *Old House Journal* v45 no5 p40 Ag 2017

furniture FOR THE PORCH color *Arts & Crafts Homes & the Revival* v12 no3 p28 Summ 2017

house of sunshine color *Old House Journal* v45 no6 p14 S 2017

Indoor, Outdoor color *Old House Journal* v45 no4 p76 Je 2017

Kitchen Cabinets for Period Houses bw cartoon color diag *Old House Journal* v45 no2 p40 Ap 2017

lighting & METALWORK color *Arts & Crafts Homes & the Revival* v12 no1 p44 2017 Resouce Guide

The Lowdown on Mold color *Old House Journal* v45 no3 p52 My 2017

Low Key Floors color *Arts & Crafts Homes & the Revival* v12 no5 p34 Wint 2018

A Mosaic Tile Floor color *Arts & Crafts Homes & the Revival* v12 no2 p34 Spr 2017

the new lighting HIGH TECH, HISTORICAL REVIVAL chart color *Old House Journal* v45 no1 p40 F 2017

PLANNING FOR adding on color diag *Old House Journal* v45 no7 p62 O 2017

the pleasures of Handwork color *Arts & Crafts Homes & the Revival* v11 no5 p33 Wint 2017

A Porch Long Missing color diag *Arts & Crafts Homes & the Revival* v12 no3 p34 Summ 2017

Postwar Challenges color *Old House Journal* v45 no3 p40 My 2017

The Right Ladder color *Old House Journal* v45 no2 p52 Ap 2017

ROOF PREP color diag *Old House Journal* v45 no4 p39 Je 2017

Rookwood Pottery color *Arts & Crafts Homes & the Revival* v12 no2 p48 Spr 2017

Save, Repair, or Replace? color *Old House Journal* v44 no8 p44 D 2016

Tile Everywhere color *Old House Journal* v45 no6 p76 S 2017

UNDERSTANDING FIREPLACES color diag *Old House Journal* v45 no7 p38 O 2017

Ventilating an Attic color diag *Old House Journal* v45 no4 p52 Je 2017

Vintage Lighting Restored color *Arts & Crafts Homes & the Revival* v12 no4 p34 Fall 2017

WALL PANELS IN THE AGE OF PLASTICS color *Old House Journal* v45 no2 p20 Ap 2017

Polster, Christopher S.

Kilogram-scale prexasertib monolactate monohydrate synthesis under continuous-flow CGMP conditions chart diag *Science* v356 no6343 p1144 Je 16 2017

Poltava (Ukraine)

THE MAP POLTAVA, 1709 K. Wiles *History Today* v67 no10 p4 O 2017

Polumbo, Randy

A Camper on the Ceiling W. GOODMAN img *New York* v49 no19 p65 S 19 2016

Poly, Natasha

Supermodel Makeup School S. Kitchens and Y. Chu color *Glamour* v114 no12 p119 D 2016

Poly ADP ribose

A nuclease that mediates cell death induced by DNA damage and poly(ADP-ribose) polymerase-1 Yingfei Wang, Ran An et al bw graph *Science* v354 no6308 paad6872-1 O 7 2016

Polyakov, Igor V.

Greater role for Atlantic inflows on sea-ice loss in the Eurasian Basin of the Arctic Ocean chart diag graph *Science* v356 no6335 p285 Ap 21 2017

Polyandry

SEX THAT WORKS UP A LATHER P. Edmonds color *National Geographic* v231 no3 p29 Mr 2017

Polychlorinated biphenyls

Europe's insufficient pollutant remediation R. J. Law and P. D. Jepson color *Science* v356 no6334 p148 Ap 14 2017

Polycom Inc.

How I Built a $2 Billion Company by Thinking Small J. Rodman *Harvard Business Review Digital Articles* p2 S 7 2016

Polycomb group protein genetics

Distinct phases of Polycomb silencing to hold epigenetic memory of cold in Arabidopsis H. Yang, S. Berry et al diag *Science* v357 no6356 p1142 S 15 2017

Polycomb group proteins

Mutation of a nucleosome compaction region disrupts Polycomb-mediated axial patterning M. Sheng Lau, M. G. Schwartz et al bibl chart diag *Science* v355 no6329 p1081 Mr 10 2017

PCGF3/5–PRC1 initiates Polycomb recruitment in X chromosome inactivation M. Almeida, G. Pintacuda et al color *Science* v356 no6342 p1081 Je 9 2017

Propagation of Polycomb-repressed chromatin requires sequence-specific recruitment to DNA F. Laprell, K. Finkl et al diag *Science* v356 no6333 p85 Ap 7 2017

Polycrystals

Bragg coherent diffractive imaging of single-grain defect dynamics in polycrystalline films A. Yau, W. Cha et al color graph *Science* v356 no6339 p739 My 19 2017

Multiscale measurements for materials modeling R. Suter diag *Science* v356 no6339 p704 My 19 2017

Polycystic kidney disease

BROUGHT TO LIGHT color *Women's Health* v14 no3 p32 Ap 2017

Polycystic ovary syndrome

Why Am I Bleeding? [Cover story] C. S. Grant color *Glamour* v114 no11 p116 N 2016

Polyelectrolytes

Breakthroughs Advance U.S. Competitiveness B. E. Warner *Science & Technology Review* p3 Ja/F 2017

Polyethylene

Combining polyethylene and polypropylene: Enhanced performance with PE/iPP multiblock polymers J. M. Eagan, J. Xu et al bibl chart graph *Science* v355 no6327 p814 F 24 2017

Plastic-Eating Worms M. Sedacca color *Scientific American* v317 no2 p21 Ag 2017

Polyface Inc.

Profitable PERMACULTURE PRINCIPLES: The application of permaculture design at Polyface has helped increase the farm's efficiency and functionality J. Salatin *Mother Earth News* no282 p75 Je/Jl 2017

Polygamy—Religious aspects—Christianity

Christians Started the Wedding Wars S. SLADE cartoon *Reason* v48 no11 p56 Ap 2017

Polymer aggregates

Direct atomic-level insight into the active sites of a high-performance PGM-free ORR catalyst H. T. Chung, D. A. Cullen et al diag graph *Science* v357 no6350 p479 Ag 4 2017

Polymer currency

A License to Print Plastic A. Satariano color *Bloomberg Businessweek* no4498 p41 N 7 2016

Polymer films—Synthesis

Fabricating the World's Thinnest Plastic Wrap L. Casonhua color *Science & Technology Review* p16 Ja/F 2017

Polymerase chain reaction

HIGH-TECH BOOST FOR RAINROT DIAGNOSIS C. Barakat and M. McCluskey color *Equus* no471 p11 D 2016

Polymerase chain reaction—Equipment & supplies

NEW PRODUCTS color *Science* v354 no6319 p1601 D 23 2016

new products: dna/rna analysis color *Science* v357 no6357 p1317 S 22 2017

Polymerases

PAF1 regulation of promoter-proximal pause release via enhancer activation F. Xavier Chen, P. Xie et al color *Science* v357 no6357 p1294 S 22 2017

PARP inhibitors: Synthetic lethality in the clinic C. J. Lord and A. Ashworth bibl diag *Science* v355 no6330 p1152 Mr 17 2017

Polymerization

Mechanochemical unzipping of insulating polyladderene to semiconducting polyacetylene [Cover story] Z. Chen, J. A. M. Mercer et al diag *Science* v357 no6350 p475 Ag 4 2017

Polymeric peptide pigments with sequence-encoded properties A. Lampel, S. A. McPhee et al color graph *Science* v356 no6342 p1064 Je 9 2017

Polymers

See also

Elastomers

Plastics

Biological fabrication of cellulose fibers with tailored properties F. Natalio, R. Fuchs et al color *Science* v357 no6356 p1118 S 15 2017

Highly stretchable polymer semiconductor films through the nanoconfinement effect Jie Xu, Sihong Wang et al bibl graph *Science* v355 no6320 p1 Ja 6 2017

High-performance vitrimers from commodity thermoplastics through dioxaborolane metathesis M. Röttger, T. Domenech et al color diag *Science* v356 no6333 p62 Ap 7 2017

Polymer-based transistors bring fully stretchable devices within reach A. G. Smart *Physics Today* v70 no3 p14 Mr 2017

RUBBER REVOLUTION K. CAMERON *Cycle World* v55 no11 p24 D 2016

Scalable-manufactured randomized glass-polymer hybrid metamaterial for daytime radiative cooling Y. Zhai, Y. Ma et al bibl diag *Science* v355 no6329 p1062 Mr 10 2017

Sliding chains keep particles together J. Ryu and S. Park diag *Science* v357 no6348 p250 Jl 21 2017

Polymers—Bibliographies

NEW BOOKS *Physics Today* v69 no12 p60 D 2016

Polymers—Evaluation

Effetto Mariposa Zot! Nano and Caffélatex color *Bicycling* v58 no4 p80 My 2017

Polynitrogens

Polynitrogen chemistry enters the ring K. O. Christe bibl diag *Science* v355 no6323 p351 Ja 27 2017

Polynyas

Ice-free in the Arctic M. Rosano color map *Canadian Geographic* v135 no6 p30 D 2015

Polypeptides

CAT-tailing as a fail-safe mechanism for efficient degradation of stalled nascent polypeptides K. K. Kostova, K. L. Hickey et al diag *Science* v357 no6349 p414 Jl 28 2017

Ratchet-like polypeptide translocation mechanism of the AAA+ disaggregase Hsp104 S. N. Gates, A. L. Yokom et al diag *Science* v357 no6348 p273 Jl 21 2017

Poly Prep Country Day School (New York, N.Y.)—Trials, litigation, etc.

SEE NO EVIL HEAR NO EVIL SPEAK NO EVIL E. LEWIS bw color *Esquire* v166 no5 p114 D 2016/Ja 2017

Polysaccharides—Therapeutic use

Stress incontinence [Cover story] *Mayo Clinic Health Letter* v35 no2 p1 F 2017

PolyScience (Company)

Chef-spector Gadget M. Kronsberg color *Bloomberg Businessweek* no4516 p63 Mr 27 2017

Polyurethanes

THE NEWS ABOUT SHOES E. Pascoe color *Practical Horseman* v44 no12 p46 D 2016

Polyvinyl alcohol

Innovation Synthetic Cartilage M. Belfiore bw color diag *Bloomberg Businessweek* no4518 p37 Ap 10 2017

Pomat, William

A Neolithic expansion, but strong genetic structure, in the independent history of New Guinea diag *Science* v357 no6356 p1160 S 15 2017

Pomegranate

ASK SUSAN S. WESTMORELAND color *Good Housekeeping* v264 no1 p114 Ja 1 2017

EAT, DRINK, AND BE WARY C. Zuckerman color *National Geographic* v232 no3 p14 S 2017

HOLIDAYS ON ICE A. Vorrasi color *InStyle* v23 no13 p276 D 2016

IT'S THE BOMB *Martha Stewart Living* no270 p96 D 2016

Pomegranate Power D. Wise color *Health* v30 no10 p133 D 2016

POMEGRANATE PUMP J. WUEBBEN cartoon *Muscle & Performance* v9 no4 p10 Ap 2017

RACK OF LAMB WITH SMOKED HERBED POTATOES AND POMEGRANATE SAUCE: WANT A BEAUTIFUL MAIN

COURSE FOR EASTER DINNER? TRY THIS DISH *Successful Farming* v115 no6 p64 Ap 2017

Pomeroy, L. A.

50 Years of IHSA bw *Practical Horseman* v45 no4 p72 Ap 2017

Pomeroy, Naomi

A Cut Above color *Bon Appetit* v61 no11 p38 N 2016

Pomès, Régis

The role of dimer asymmetry and protomer dynamics in enzyme catalysis diag *Science* v355 no6322 p262 Ja 20 2017

Pomfret, John

Confronting China S. WINCHESTER *New York Times Book Review* p13 Ja 1 2017

Open & Shut N. Clifford color *Commonweal* v144 no5 p32 Mr 10 2017

Pommerol, A.

Rosetta's comet 67P/Churyumov-Gerasimenko sheds its dusty mantle to reveal its icy nature bibl graph *Science* v354 no6319 p1566 D 23 2016

Surface changes on comet 67P/Churyumov-Gerasimenko suggest a more active past bw graph *Science* v355 no6332 p1392 Mr 31 2017

Pommier, Rod

Observing on the edge color *Astronomy* v45 no3 p50 Mr 2017

Pomorski, Chris

THE EMPEROR OF EMPTY LOTS bw color *Bloomberg Businessweek* no4538 p42 S 18 2017

Pompa, Robin Nixon

Allergy-Free Kids: The Science-Based Approach to Preventing Food Allergies *Publishers Weekly* v264 no12 p70 Mr 20 2017

Pompeii (Extinct city)—History

The Map K. Wiles *History Today* v67 no4 p26 Ap 2017

Pompeo, Ellen, 1969-

GREY'S ANATOMY M. Logan *TV Guide* v65 no39 p48 S 18 2017

Pomper, Martin G.

Chemogenetics revealed: DREADD occupancy and activation via converted clozapine graph *Science* v357 no6350 p503 Ag 4 2017

Pompey, the Great, 106 B.C.-48 B.C.

POMPEY THE GREAT: BORN 29 SEPTEMBER 106 BC Justin and S. Pollard *History Today* v67 no9 p22 S 2017

Pompos, Arnold

On the value of carbon-ion therapy *Physics Today* v69 no11 p14 N 2016

Ponca (North American people)

Nebraska at 150 A. J. BARTELS bw color map *Nebraska Life* v21 no6 p50 N/D 2017

Poncavage, Joanna

5 Expert-Recommended TOOLS FOR NO-TILL PLOTS *Mother Earth News* no279 p43 D/Ja 2017

Ponchos

Case Study: How Do You Compete with a Goliath? J. Avery *Harvard Business Review Digital Articles* p2 Jl 7 2016

Cozy Comforts color *Martha Stewart Living* p50 O 2017

Ponciano, Jonathan

MONEY THERAPISTS color *Forbes* v200 no4 p104 O 24 2017

Ponderosa pine

The Big Pictures: THE SAN FRANCISCO PEAKS *Arizona Highways* v93 no8 p16 Ag 2017

GROWING, GROWING, GONE T. WILLIAMS *Arizona Highways* v93 no1 p44 Ja 2017

TRIPP CANYON ROAD N. AUSTIN *Arizona Highways* v93 no9 p52 S 2017

Pondexter, Cappie, 1983-

CAPPIE PONDEXTER H. MITCHELL color *Chicago* v66 no8 p46 Ag 2017

Ponds

WHAT A BILLION LOOKS LIKE color *Canadian Wildlife* v22 no5 p10 N/D 2016

Poneman, Daniel B.

The case for American nuclear leadership *Bulletin of the Atomic Scientists* v73 no1 p44 Ja 2017

Pong, Chun-ho, 1969-

BEHIND THE DESIGN OKJA D. Franich color *Entertainment Weekly* no1446/1447 p52 D 2016/Ja 2017

Can You Love This Super-Pig? It's one thing to dream up a nonexistent creature. But just try bringing it adorably to life E. A. JUNG img *New York* v50 no13 p72 Je 26 2017

MAGNIFICENT OBSESSION: A CULT AUTEUR'S NETFLIX DEBUT M. YARM color *Wired* v25 no7 p16 Jl 2017

Okja, Super-Pig in the City M. ATKINSON *In These Times* v41 no8 p36 Ag 2017

Ponge, Dirk

Bone-like crack resistance in hierarchical metastable nanolaminate steels bibl color diag *Science* v355 no6329 p1055 Mr 10 2017

PONGE, JEAN-FRANÇOIS

HIERARCHY AND COMPLEXITY *BioScience* v67 no7 p672 Jl 2017

Ponies

Half Ponies color *InStyle* v23 no12 p182 N 2016

Ponies—Research

EATING ON THE GO AIDS WEIGHT LOSS C. Barakat and M. McCluskey color *Equus* no472 p12 Ja 2017

Ponnampalam, Louisa S.

Poor fisheries struggle with U.S. import rule bibl color *Science* v355 no6329 p1031 Mr 10 2017

Ponnuru, Ramesh

The Contest For the Senate *National Review* v68 no19 p18 O 24 2016

Divided They Stand (or Fall) il *National Review* v69 no17 p12 S 11 2017

For Love of Country color *National Review* v69 no3 p33 F 20 2017

The Gorsuch Triumph il *National Review* v69 no8 p14 My 2017

The Health-Care Crack-Up il *National Review* v69 no7 p16 Ap 17 2017

Infrastructure Observations *National Review* v68 no23 p22 D 19 2016

Kate Walsh O'Beirne, R.I.P *National Review* v69 no9 p12 My 15 2017

Leftward March il *National Review* v69 no12 p13 Je 26 2017

Mandate for Confusion *National Review* v69 no5 p22 Mr 20 2017

Nationalism And Patriotism, Cont'd *National Review* v69 no6 p18 Ap 3 2017

A Non-transformational President il *National Review* v69 no1 p16 Ja 23 2017

Obamacare Unravels, Cont'd il *National Review* v68 no21 p16 N 21 2016

The Plot against The President color *National Review* v69 no11 p13 Je 12 2017

Protection Racket color *National Review* v68 no24 p17 D 31 2016

A Risky Obamacare Strategy il *National Review* v69 no2 p16 F 6 2017

System Failure *National Review* v69 no15 p14 Ag 14 2017

Trumpism And Ryanism *National Review* v68 no22 p30 D 5 2016

Trump's New Deal color *National Review* v69 no18 p13 O 2 2017

Trump Will Always Be Trump *Bloomberg Businessweek* no4535 p12 Ag 28 2017

Two Flawed Tax Plans *National Review* v68 no20 p18 N 7 2016

Untaxing the Rich color *National Review* v69 no19 p21 O 16 2017

What We Saw Is What We've Got bw *Bloomberg Businessweek* no4523 p10 My 22 2017

Ponomareff, Lara

KICK-ASS CUSTOMER SERVICE chart color graph il img *Harvard Business Review* v95 no1 p110 Ja/F 2017

Ponomarenko, L. A.

High-temperature quantum oscillations caused by recurring Bloch states in graphene superlattices color *Science* v357 no6347 p181 Jl 14 2017

Pons, Carles

Exploring genetic suppression interactions on a global scale diag *Science* v354 no6312 p599 N 4 2016

Pons, Lele

Lele Pons Is the Most Popular Girl in Hollywood: A day in the life of YouTube's reigning queen of teens A. JONES img *New York* v50 no9 p53 My 1 2017

Ponsoldt, James—Interviews

TOO MUCH INFORMATION C. Thompson color *Mother Jones* v42 no3 p66 My/Je 2017

Ponsot, Marie

Lately Blooming W. LOGAN *New York Times Book Review* p22

O 23 2016

LOOKING OUT, ANYTIME M. Ponsot *Commonweal* v143 no18 p27 N 11 2016

The World in Its Glory A. Domestico bw *Commonweal* v144 no4 p28 F 24 2017

Ponta, Victor, 1972-

Victor Ponta E. Turner *Current Biography* v78 no2 p67 F 2017

Pontchartrain, Lake (La.)

Waterscapes W. Kalec bw color *Louisiana Life* v37 no4 p40 Mr/Ap 2017

Pontecorvo, Gillo

THE BATTLE OF ALGIERS AT FIFTY: END OF EMPIRE CINEMA AND THE FIRST BANUEUE FILM A. O'Leary *Film Quarterly* v70 no2 p17 Wint 2016

Pontefract, Dan

Leadership in Liminal Times *Harvard Business Review Digital Articles* p2 O 10 2014

You're Never Done Finding Purpose at Work [Cover story] *Harvard Business Review Digital Articles* p2 Mr 20 2016

Ponten, Fredrik

A pathology atlas of the human cancer transcriptome diag *Science* v357 no6352 p660 Ag 18 2017

A subcellular map of the human proteome color *Science* v356 no6340 p820 My 26 2017

Ponti, Gio, 1891-1979

Early Signs of modernism E. Gaukel *Treasures* v6 no5 p4 Ap/My 2017

Gio Ponti B. LIBBY *Treasures* v6 no5 p16 Ap/My 2017

Pontiac Motor Co.

One of None J. Machaqueiro color *Hot Rod* v70 no10 p36 O 2017

Pontiac's Conspiracy, 1763-1765

Hallowed Ground Bushy Run Battlefield, Pennsylvania W. J. Shepherd color *Military History* v34 no2 p76 Jl 2017

Pontifical Catholic University of Puerto Rico (Ponce, P.R.)

PHI KAPPA PHI K. WHITE color *Phi Kappa Phi Forum* v97 no1 p8 Spr 2017

Pontin, Jason

Me and My Troll il *MIT Technology Review* v120 no3 p91 My/Je 2017

Q+A: Jessica Brillhart color *MIT Technology Review* v120 no2 p28 Mr/Ap 2017

Pontine Islands (Italy)

FROM RUNWAY TO (ESCAPING) REALITY color *Esquire* p23 2017 BigBlackBook

Pontoon boating

6 Must-Haves to Turn Your Pontoon Into a Fishing Machine L. Whiteley color *Cabin Living* p12 Ag 2017

KEEP PONTOON TUBES SHIPSHAPE: They keep the family afloat, so make sure the pontoon's logs are ready for action B. M. KENYON color *Boating World* v38 no7 p52 Jl 2017

Qwest For the Best A. JONES color *Boating World* v38 no7 p34 Jl 2017

Towing 'Toons color *Boating World* v38 no7 p14 Jl 2017

Pontoons

Advanced Retreat A. JONES *Boating World* v38 no2 p36 F 2017

Chasing the Sun for Less A. JONES *Boating World* v38 no2 p40 F 2017

HATCH OF THE MAYFLIES C. Beers *South Dakota Magazine* v33 no2 p94 Jl/Ag 2017

Pontoon For the Populous A. JONES *Boating World* v38 no3 p44 Mr 2017

pontoon mania M. Willers, M. Sorenson et al color *Cabin Living* p60 Je 2017

Pontoon Propping *Boating World* v38 no5 p60 My 2017

Q+A F. Lanier, G. Michal et al *Boating World* v37 no9 p24 N/D 2016

Quadroponic: Turn a pontoon into the four boats of your dreams *Boating World* v38 no5 p62 My 2017

Pontoons—Evaluation

En Vogue A. Jones *Boating World* v37 no9 p38 N/D 2016

Pontormo, Jacopo da, 1494-1556

The Supper at Emmaus H. J. Hornik and M. C. Parsons color *Christian Century* v134 no7 p47 Mr 29 2017

Pontuso, James

Men Behaving Fretfully *Society* v54 no1 p42 F 2017

Pontzer, Herman

week no4533 p19 Ag 7 2017

When a Startup Means A Fresh Start color *Bloomberg Businessweek* no4507 p28 Ja 16 2017

Popescu, Gabriel

THE POWER OF IMAGING WITH PHASE, NOT POWER *Physics Today* v70 no5 p34 My 2017

Spooky action achieved at record distance [Cover story] color *Science* v356 no6343 p1110 Je 16 2017

Popescu, Ioana

A Lean Startup Approach to International Development *Harvard Business Review Digital Articles* p2 D 11 2014

Popina, Elena

Crimea Welcomes a Flood of Putin Patriots cartoon color *Bloomberg Businessweek* no4497 p21 O 31 2016

Popina Foods (Company)

Also Opening img *New York* v50 no17 p78 Ag 21 2017

POPKIN, GABRIEL

Forests of the Future color map *Discover* v27 no10 p28 D 2016

QUEST FOR QUBITS color diag *Science* v354 no6316 p1090 D 2 2016

Popky, Linda J.

Identify the Marketing Metrics That Actually Matter *Harvard Business Review Digital Articles* p2 Jl 14 2015

POPLAK, RICHARD

Canadian Mining's Dark Heart color *Walrus* v13 no9 p26 N 2016

Popoff, Lueb

A Cut Above color *Log Home Living* v33 no7 p18 S 2016

Popoff, Peter

The Born-Again Scoundrel M. OPPENHEIMER bw cartoon *GQ: Gentlemen's Quarterly* v97 no3 p140 Mr 2017

Popolizio, Madison

Mountain Rescue S. VanLaer *New York State Conservationist* v71 no4 p2 F 2017

Popov, Alexander

Impact of cytosine methylation on DNA binding specificities of human transcription factors diag *Science* v356 no6337 p502 My 5 2017

Mechanism of transmembrane signaling by sensor histidine kinases color *Science* v356 no6342 p1043 Je 9 2017

Popov, Stasik

Arylation of hydrocarbons enabled by organosilicon reagents and weakly coordinating anions diag *Science* v355 no6332 p1403 Mr 31 2017

Popova, Ekaterina

Biodiversity redistribution under climate change: Impacts on ecosystems and human well-being color *Science* v355 no6332 p1389 Mr 31 2017

Popova, Maria

Putin-Style "Rule of Law" & the Prospects for Change *Daedalus* v146 no2 p64 Spr 2017

The Year in Reading [Cover story] *New York Times Book Review* p8 D 25 2016

Popovich, Gregg, 1949-

Coach Pop vs. Donald Trump D. ZIRIN color *Progressive* v81 no3 p45 Mr 2017

Popowicz, G. M.

Inhibitors of PEX14 disrupt protein import into glycosomes and kill Trypanosoma parasites chart color diag graph *Science* v355 no6332 p1416 Mr 31 2017

Popp, David

How to model tall grass easily color diag *Model Railroader* v84 no2 p32 F 2017

Make a pipe load from plastic and stripwood bw color *Model Railroader* v84 no4 p36 Ap 2017

Model partial loads to enrich operations color diag *Model Railroader* v84 no3 p26 Mr 2017

Popp, Evan

Up Against the Other NRA: Trump Could Help Restaurant Group Eat Away at Workers' Rights cartoon *Progressive* v81 no7 p35 O/N 2017

Popper, Nathaniel

Currency bw color *Forbes* v198 no7 p112 N 29 2016

POPPICK, LAURA

The Water Keeper's Dilemma *Audubon* v119 no3 p10 Fall 2017

Popplewell, Brett

Canada Plans to Be the Leader in Legal Weed color *Bloomberg*

Businessweek no4519 p32 Ap 24 2017

Head Games color *Walrus* v14 no7 p30 S 2017

Kill Shot cartoon *Walrus* v14 no2 p42 Mr 2017

Rookie Sensation bw *Walrus* v13 no9 p16 N 2016

POPPY, CARRIE

Survey Shows Americans Fear Ghosts, the Government, and Each Other *Skeptical Inquirer* v41 no1 p16 Ja/F 2017

Popular actions

Blowing the Whistle E. K. BOEGEL *America* v215 no13 p20 O 31 2016

Popular culture

See also

Hip-hop culture

Sports in popular culture

39 Perfect Pop Culture Presents C. Everett, D. Coggan et al color *Entertainment Weekly* no1442 p31 D 2 2016 Rebellious Special Issue

THE 67 GREATEST, CRAZIEST, AND MOST PERSISTENT POP-CULTURE CONSPIRACY THEORIES OF ALL TIME A. K. RAYMOND img *New York* v49 no23 p72 N 14 2016

BILLY EICHN ER R. Rahman color *Entertainment Weekly* no1441 p48 N 25 2016

Center Stage N. Pantic color *Tennis* v53 no5 p8 S/O 2017

COLOR CODE C. Zuckerman color *National Geographic* v231 no1 p18 Ja 2017

DAV PILKEY I. Biedenharn color *Entertainment Weekly* no1485 p61 O 6 2017

How to Take Back the Counterculture M. Hirschorn *New York* v49 no24 p34 N 28 2016

Jessica St. Clair and Lennon Parham A. Wilkinson color *Entertainment Weekly* no1473 p16 Jl 7 2017

JOYCE CAROL OATES color *Entertainment Weekly* no1473 p62 Jl 7 2017

LIZZIE BORDEN'S POP CULTURE PANOPLY I. Biedenharn color *Entertainment Weekly* no1477 p61 Ag 11 2017

Lo, and Behold J. Pressler img *New York* v49 no22 p93 O 31 2016

Pop Chart R. Bruner, C. Lang et al color *Time* v188 no18 p54 O 31 2016

The Quiz T. BALAZO color *Maclean's* v129 no41 p60 O 17 2016

R.L. STINE I. Biedenharn color *Entertainment Weekly* no1477 p62 Ag 11 2017

SHE'S YOUR LOBSTER': MEMORABLE MOMENTS IN POP CULTURE bw color *Yankee* p99 Jl 2017

T.J. MILLER D. Snierson color *Entertainment Weekly* no1442 p50 D 2 2016 Rebellious Special Issue

VERY NECESSARY BROTHAS Z. HILL color *Ebony* v72/73 no12/1 p25 O/N 2017

Which Virtual Assistant Tells the Best Jokes? B. SPECKTOR color *Reader's Digest* v189 no1129 p126 Ap 2017

WHO'S THE FAIREST? K. Nowakowski color graph *National Geographic* v231 no1 p24 Ja 2017

Your LGBTQ Pop Preview C. Agard, A. Bacle et al color *Entertainment Weekly* no1471 p44 Je 23 2017

Popular culture—Congresses

Editor's Note H. Goldblatt, A. Breznican et al color *Entertainment Weekly* no1439 p23 N 11 2016

Entertainment WEEKLY POPFEST TM color *Entertainment Weekly* no1436/1437 p8 O 21 2016

EW PULLS DOUBLE PARTY DUTY AT NY COMIC CON R. Kinane color *Entertainment Weekly* no1436/1437 p18 O 21 2016

NEW YORK COMIC CON'S GREATEST HITS S. Li color *Entertainment Weekly* no1436/1437 p18 O 21 2016

THE SCOOP, STARS & SONGS N. Abrams, A. Breznican et al color *Entertainment Weekly* no1439 p16 N 11 2016

Popular culture—Great Britain—History—20th century

OPERA: FOR THE ORDINARY: Despite popular misconceptions and its aristocratic origins, for part of its history opera was inextricably linked with popular culture - no more so than in the 1920s A. Wilson *History Today* v67 no9 p58 S 2017

Popular culture—News briefs

Milestones *Time* v189 no3 p11 Ja 16 2017

Pop Chart R. Bruner, C. Lang et al color *Time* v188 no20 p57 N 14 2016

Pop Chart R. Bruner, C. Lang et al color *Time* v189 no3 p58 Ja 30 2017

Pop Chart R. Bruner, C. Lang et al color *Time* v190 no1 p55 Jl 3 2017

Pop Chart R. Bruner, C. Lang et al color *Time* v190 no5 p63 Jl 31 2017

Popular culture—United States

See also

Hip-hop culture

The Culture Business: Mark Harris img *New York* v50 no18 p20 S 4 2017

DAVID BALDACCI color *Entertainment Weekly* no1442 p61 D 2 2016 Rebellious Special Issue

The Enduring Legacy of Diana R. Rahman and T. Stack color *Entertainment Weekly* no1476 p13 Ag 4 2017

'Masterpieces' Without Masters T. TEACHOUT *Commentary* v142 no1 p56 Jl/Ag 2016

THE SCHAEFFER EFFECT J. McGovern color *Entertainment Weekly* no1457/1458 p70 Mr 17 2017

SLEEPER HIT A. Beaujon color *Washingtonian Magazine* v52 no7 p13 Ap 2017

VERONICA ROTH color *Entertainment Weekly* no1450 p61 Ja 27 2017

Popular culture—United States—History—20th century

1908 IN REVIEW C. Agard color *Entertainment Weekly* no1440 p17 N 18 2016

Popular culture—United States—History—21st century

THE 2016 POP CULTURE CHALLENGE A. Wilkinson color *Entertainment Weekly* no1444/1445 p40 D 16 2016

The YEAR THAT WAS color *Entertainment Weekly* no1444/1445 p12 D 16 2016

Popular literature

See also

Graphic novels

BESTSELLERS C. JURIS chart *Publishers Weekly* v263 no50 p17 D 5 2016

Celebrating the Holidays With Favorite Friends K. Raugust color *Publishers Weekly* v263 no50 p21 D 5 2016

COMBINED PRINT AND E-BOOK BEST SELLERS *New York Times Book Review* p22 Jl 2 2017

PRINT/HARDCOVER BEST SELLERS *New York Times Book Review* p24 Jl 2 2017

PW'S TOP AUTHORS PICK THEIR FAVORITE BOOKS OF 2016 J. BUNTIN bw color *Publishers Weekly* v263 no50 p38 D 5 2016

Popular music

See also

Country music

Funk music

Korean pop music

Rap music

Rock music

Techno music

HOW TO: Write a Perfect Pop Song D. Marchese *New York* v50 no13 p78 Je 26 2017

NIGHT LIFE *New Yorker* v93 no30 p5 O 2 2017

Pop's Young a-Listers Look to the Past S. Lansky color *Time* v189 no21 p64 Je 5 2017

REVIVING THE PAST, DEFINING THE FUTURE K. Baumann color *Downbeat* v84 no7 p68 Jl 2017

Popular music genres

Is It Here to Stay? *Commentary* v142 no1 p1 Jl/Ag 2016

Popular music—History & criticism

THE PROG SPRING K. SANNEH bw cartoon *New Yorker* v93 no17 p67 Je 19 2017

Popular music—News briefs

Random Notes color *Rolling Stone* no1297 p24 O 5 2017

Popular music—Political aspects

Zara Larsson Is Wide A-Woke N. Feeney color *Entertainment Weekly* no1457/1458 p94 Mr 17 2017

Popular music—Social aspects

BOLD-SOUNDING THINGS D. HAJDU *Nation* v304 no17 p42 Je 5 2017

Popular music—United States

See also

Rap music

Is It Here to Stay? *Commentary* v142 no1 p1 Jl/Ag 2016

THE MUSIC ISSUE N. Abebe color *New York Times Magazine* p16 Mr 12 2017

Popular music—Writing & publishing

5 REASONS YOU CAN'T SLEEP ON SZA M. Vain color *Entertainment Weekly* no1446/1447 p73 D 2016/Ja 2017

EVANESCENCE'S AMY LEE J. Goodman color *Entertainment Weekly* no1443 p60 D 9 2016

GLENN FREY B. Seger and C. Collis color *Entertainment Weekly* no1446/1447 p91 D 2016/Ja 2017

INSIDE JACK ANTONOFF'S POP LABORATORY K. O'Donnell color *Entertainment Weekly* no1470 p56 Je 16 2017

John Mellencamp E. Gundersen color *AARP: The Magazine* v60 no4A p15 Je/Jl 2017

JULIA MICHAELS N. Feeney color *Entertainment Weekly* no1446/1447 p74 D 2016/Ja 2017

KINGS OF LEON'S CALEB FOLLOWILL M. Vain color *Entertainment Weekly* no1436/1437 p98 O 21 2016

PRINCE E. R. Brown color *Entertainment Weekly* no1446/1447 p87 D 2016/Ja 2017

SHERYL CROW REBORN M. Vain color *Entertainment Weekly* no1462 p60 Ap 21 2017

Popular vote

The National Interest: Jonathan Chait img *New York* v49 no25 p21 D 12 2016

Popular culture—Charts, diagrams, etc.

Pop Chart R. Bruner, C. Lang et al color *Time* v189 no5 p54 F 13 2017

SWIMMING WITH SHARKS C. Sosenko color *Entertainment Weekly* no1476 p19 Ag 4 2017

Popular culture—United States—Charts, diagrams, etc.

Pop Chart R. Bruner, C. Lang et al color *Time* v188 no21 p72 N 21 2016

Popularity

Becoming Barnum P. Carlson *American History* v51 no6 p26 F 2017

Gone Viral Z. WHITTENBURG and S. SKYBETTER *Dance Magazine* v90 no12 p59 D 2016

Popular music, 1991-2000

1994 L. Greenblatt color *Entertainment Weekly* no1466 p58 My 19 2017

The Nineties Rise Again R. SHEFFIELD color *Rolling Stone* no1293 p23 Ag 10 2017

Popular music—1981-1990

1983 L. Greenblatt color *Entertainment Weekly* no1449 p59 Ja 20 2017

1984 L. Greenblatt color *Entertainment Weekly* no1456 p66 Mr 10 2017

1985 L. Greenblatt color *Entertainment Weekly* no1434 p57 O 7 2016

1985 L. Greenblatt color *Entertainment Weekly* no1470 p59 Je 16 2017

1987 L. Greenblatt color *Entertainment Weekly* no1486 p59 O 13 2017

1990 L. Greenblatt color *Entertainment Weekly* no1476 p60 Ag 4 2017

CHART FLASHBACK 1989 L. Greenblatt color *Entertainment Weekly* no1439 p58 N 11 2016

Popular music—2011-2020

15 Fresh Songs for Fall color *Entertainment Weekly* no1434 p54 O 7 2016

The 2017 Album Watch List R. Bruner color *Time* v188 no27-28 p106 D 26 2016

THE BEST ALBUMS OF 2017 (SO FAR) A. Bacle, E. R. Brown et al color *Entertainment Weekly* no1468/1469 p98 Je 2-9 2017

THE BEST SONGS OF 2017 (SO FAR) color *Entertainment Weekly* no1468/1469 p100 Je 2-9 2017

Dua Lipa's Tough Love A. GOLD color *Rolling Stone* no1291/1292 p18 Jl 13 2017

MUSIC N. Feeney, K. O'Donnell et al color *Entertainment Weekly* no1444/1445 p88 D 16 2016

NEW TUNES FOR THE NEW YEAR color *Entertainment Weekly* no1448 p60 Ja 13 2017

Pop Radio Rocks Again D. BROWNE color *Rolling Stone* no1290 p18 Je 29 2017

Taylor Swift's Battle of the Brands T. J. Huddleston color *Fortune* v176 no5 p18 O 1 2017

THE ULTIMATE 2016 ALBUM SWAP E. R. Brown and N. Feeney color *Entertainment Weekly* no1446/1447 p116 D 2016/Ja 2017

THE ULTIMATE WINTER SINGLES SWAP color *Entertainment Weekly* no1451/1452 p104 F 3-10 2017

YOUR "SPRING IS COMING!" PLAYLIST color *Entertainment Weekly* no1456 p64 Mr 10 2017

Popular music—2011-2020—Reviews

THE CHAINSMOKERS J. Goodman *Entertainment Weekly* no1446/1447 p76 D 2016/Ja 2017

CHARLI XCX N. Feeney *Entertainment Weekly* no1446/1447 p75 D 2016/Ja 2017

HAIM N. Feeney color *Entertainment Weekly* no1446/1447 p70 D 2016/Ja 2017

KELLY CLARKSON N. Feeney and I. Biedenharn color *Entertainment Weekly* no1446/1447 p76 D 2016/Ja 2017

NIALL HORAN J. Goodman *Entertainment Weekly* no1446/1447 p75 D 2016/Ja 2017

Population

See also

Baby boom generation

Demographic characteristics

Emigration & immigration

Generation Y

Generation Z

Generations

Human migrations

Urban growth

ARLINGTON, VIRGINIA J. WALLJASPER color *Washington Monthly* v49 no3-5 p25 Mr-My 2017

THE CLASH OF POPULATIONS? K. Clarke color graph *America* v216 no10 p12 My 1 2017

COLLEGE TOWN SMACKDOWN G. A. Warner color *Sunset* v239 no3 p28 S 2017

Come Along Boys and Listen to My Tale... color *American Cowboy* p56 LEGENDS OF TEXAS Special Issue 2017

COUNTING AMERICANS IN REAL TIME *Saturday Evening Post* v289 no2 p96 Mr/Ap 2017

The Future of Food K. MAST bw color *Discover* v38 no6 p38 Jl/Ag 2017

Make Data a Walk in the Park *Parks & Recreation* v51 no10 p86 O 2016

The space between us J. KIRBY map *Maclean's* v130 no3 p19 Ap 2017

Split Personalities W. Fulton *Governing* v30 no3 p24 D 2016

St. Louis Bound *Parks & Recreation* v51 no10 p24 O 2016

TALK TO US chart color *Chicago* v66 no7 p11 Jl 2017

Population & the environment

Avoid the crowds J. KIRBY map *Maclean's* v130 no4 p17 My 2017

Living by the lessons of the planet J. Foley color *Science* v356 no6335 p251 Ap 21 2017

Population aging

A LOOK AT THE SOCIAL ISSUES DEMANDING YOUR ATTENTION *Governing* v30 no1 p6 O 2016

The Productivity Challenge of an Aging Global Workforce J. Manyika, J. Remes et al *Harvard Business Review Digital Articles* p2 Ja 20 2015

What a Study of 33 Countries Found About Aging Populations and Innovation A. Irmen and A. Litina bw *Harvard Business Review Digital Articles* p2 Ja 18 2017

Population density

Ask Smithsonian K. Nodjimbadem color *Smithsonian* v47 no10 p96 Mr 2017

Population density—Psychological aspects

CROWDED PLACES MAKE PEOPLE THINK MORE ABOUT THE FUTURE A. Beard graph img *Harvard Business Review* v95 no4 p34 Jl/Ag 2017

Population density—Social aspects

The Case for Density M. Funkhouser *Governing* v30 no12 p4 S 2017

Population genetics

A Neolithic expansion, but strong genetic structure, in the independent history of New Guinea A. Bergström, S. J. Oppenheimer et al diag *Science* v357 no6356 p1160 S 15 2017

Population geography

See also

Emigration & immigration

Population health

Unhealthy Habits M. Quinn *Governing* v30 no1 p18 O 2016

Why It's Hard to Measure Improved Population Health S. Galea *Harvard Business Review Digital Articles* p2 S 16 2015

Population statistics

Is Bigger Always Better? Population growth doesn't necessarily mean a city is thriving J. B. Wogan *Governing* v30 no12 p24 S 2017

A RECIPE FOR TOMORROW H. Rosner color *Wired* v24 no11 p104 N 2016

Why the Census Matters Now More Than Ever H. S. Edwards color *Time* v189 no20 p17 My 29 2017

Population transfers

For the Record color *Time* v190 no12 p8 S 25 2017

Myanmar's Shame E. Dias and F. Solomon color *Time* v190 no13 p42 O 2 2017

Population—Charts, diagrams, etc.

BY THE NUMBERS Z. Bu *Washingtonian Magazine* v52 no3 p78 D 2016

Population forecasting—Charts, diagrams, etc.

The Changing United States img *New York Times Upfront* v149 no5 p8 N 21 2016

Populism

Backlash [Cover story] C. R. Morris *Commonweal* v144 no1 p6 Ja 6 2017

European Disunion Y. MOUNK color *New Republic* v248 no8/9 p58 Ag/S 2017

How Populism May Stifle Growth bw *Bloomberg Businessweek* no4520 p12 My 1 2017

The Jacksonian Revolt W. R. Mead color *Foreign Affairs* v96 no2 p2 Mr/Ap 2017

The Original Deplorables G. NORMAN *Weekly Standard* v22 no4 p25 O 3 2016

Populism Is Not Fascism S. Berman bw *Foreign Affairs* v95 no6 p39 N/D 2016

Populism Needs Place-ism B. KAUFFMAN *American Conservative* v15 no6 p45 N/D 2016

Populism on the March F. Zakaria color *Foreign Affairs* v95 no6 p9 N/D 2016

THE POWER OF POPULISM G. Rose *Foreign Affairs* v95 no6 p1g N/D 2016

Zombie Ideology S. LEONARD *Nation* v304 no16 p3 My 22 2017

Populism—Canada

It could happen here [Cover story] C. GILLIS color *Maclean's* v129 no47 p26 N 28 2016

Populism—China

Index *NPQ: New Perspectives Quarterly* v34 no1 p80 Ja 2017

Populism—Europe

2017 Might Not Be Europe's 'Year of the Populist' After All I. Bremmer *Time* v189 no9 p12 Mr 13 2017

A Petri Dish of Populist Dissent A. Migliaccio and J. Follain cartoon *Bloomberg Businessweek* no4501 p14 N 28 2016

Populism—European Union countries

Europe's Populist Surge C. Mudde color *Foreign Affairs* v95 no6 p25 N/D 2016

Populism—History—21st century

The Power of Le Pen V. Walt color *Time* v189 no11 p34 Mr 27 2017

Populism—Latin America

Latin America's Populist Hangover S. K. O'Neil color *Foreign Affairs* v95 no6 p31 N/D 2016

Populism—Mexico

Trump's Hard Line on Mexico Gives Left-Wing Populist an Opening I. Bremmer *Time* v189 no5 p12 F 13 2017

Populism—United States

Andy Jackson's Populism R. W. MERRY il *American Conservative* v16 no3 p23 My/Je 2017

Communitarian Antidotes to Populism A. Etzioni *Society* v54 no2 p95 Ap 2017

The Conservative Case for Unions J. RAUCH color graph *Atlantic* v320 no1 p15 Jl/Ag 2017

Has Our Country Gone Nuts? J. HIGHTOWER cartoon *Progressive* p70 D 2016/Ja 2017

The Last Time New York Felt Blue C. Bonanos img *New York* v49 no24 p26 N 28 2016

New Institutions that Embrace Participation Without Populism N. Gardels and N. Berggruen *NPQ: New Perspectives Quarterly* v34 no1 p9 Ja 2017

A PEOPLE'S REVOLT D. D. GUTTENPLAN color *Nation* v303 no23/24 p10 D 5 2016

The Populist Ploy W. McCORMACK il *New Republic* v248 no3 p8 Mr 2017

Principled Populism M. LEE *National Review* v68 no22 p32 D 5 2016

The Road to Statism... J. COST color *Weekly Standard* v22 no45 p11 Ag 7 2017

Serving God and Mammon P. J. Williams il *Nation* v303 no25/26 p7 D 19 2016

Trump and the "New Nationalism": It's not new at all. Andrew Jackson, almost two centuries ago, also championed a populist style--and, in the end, strengthened American democracy K. N. Schake *Hoover Digest: Research & Opinion on Public Policy* no3 p23 Summ 2017

Populism—United States—History

Trump and American Populism M. Kazin color *Foreign Affairs* v95 no6 p17 N/D 2016

Populism—United States—History—20th century

The Thread T. Travis, C. J. Guthrie et al *New York Times Magazine* p10 Ap 30 2017

Populism—United States—History—21st century

The Patriotic Response To Populism color *Bloomberg Businessweek* no4506 p8 Ja 9 2017

PIPELINE POPULISM: Out on the prairie, unlikely alliances may hold the key to transforming the Democratic Party K. ARONOFF *In These Times* v41 no10 p18 O 2017

Populism—Venezuela

Populism in Venezuela: When Discourse Derails Institutionalized Practice V. Rodner *Society* v53 no6 p629 D 2016

Populorum progressio (Papal encyclical)

A Larger Solidarity B. Hudock bw *Commonweal* v144 no5 p11 Mr 10 2017

Porat, Ruth, 1957-

Google Returns to Earth M. Chafkin and M. Bergen color *Bloomberg Businessweek* no4503 p44 D 12 2016

Porath, Christine

Give Your Team More-Effective Positive Feedback *Harvard Business Review Digital Articles* p2 O 25 2016

Half of Employees Don't Feel Respected by Their Bosses *Harvard Business Review Digital Articles* p2 N 19 2014

How Rudeness Stops People from Working Together color *Harvard Business Review Digital Articles* p2 Ja 20 2017

How to Avoid Hiring a Toxic Employee *Harvard Business Review Digital Articles* p2 F 3 2016

How to Succeed at Work When Your Boss Doesn't Respect You *Harvard Business Review Digital Articles* p2 Je 22 2016

Isolate Toxic Employees to Reduce Their Negative Effects *Harvard Business Review Digital Articles* p2 N 14 2016

The Key to Campbell Soup's Turnaround? Civility *Harvard Business Review Digital Articles* p2 O 5 2017

The Leadership Behavior That's Most Important to Employees *Harvard Business Review Digital Articles* p2 My 11 2015

Porcaro, Gabrielle

Leggings for Days color *Women's Health* v14 no2 p72 Mr 2017

Wrap. Me. Up [Cover story] color *Women's Health* v13 no10 p110 D 2016

Porcelain

See also

Chinese porcelain

Tureens

HANDFORMS color *Indianapolis Monthly* v42 no2 p61 O 2017

Hang some plates on the wall color *Redbook* p105 Jl/Ag 2017

Porcelain—Design & construction

Made-in-America—The Colony S. Richardson color *American History* v52 no2 p8 Je 2017

Porcelain—Evaluation

Keith Kreeger Studios L. S. FORD *Texas Monthly* v45 no1 p25 Ja 2017

MADE IN THE USA color *Martha Stewart Living* no271 p46 Ja/F 2017

Porch design & construction

house & garden details *Design Center Sourcebook* p108 2017

Past and Present J. Brewster color diag *Log Home Living* v34 no7 p42 S 2017

Perfecting the Porch color *Timber Home Living* v27 no4 p16 Ag 2017

Porches

The Dethloff Eyepiece Shade J. Oltion *Sky & Telescope* v133 no4 p72 Ap 2017

furniture FOR THE PORCH M. E. POLSON color *Arts & Crafts Homes & the Revival* v12 no3 p28 Summ 2017

How to Make a... PORCH SWING chart color *Popular Mechanics* v193 no7 p75 S 2016

A Porch Long Missing M. E. Polson color diag *Arts & Crafts Homes & the Revival* v12 no3 p34 Summ 2017

Why So Blue? K. Owen color *Southern Living* v52 no5 p46 My 2017

Porches—Decoration

A WRIGHT HOUSE IN ROCHESTER M. DeFRANCO color *Old House Journal* v45 no3 p24 My 2017

Porchon-Lynch, Tyo

LIVE Long AND PROSPER [Cover story] A. GIACOBBE and J. MIGALA color *Women's Health* v14 no1 p170 Ja/F 2017

Porciatti, Vittorio

Vitamin B3 modulates mitochondrial vulnerability and prevents glaucoma in aged mice bibl graph *Science* v355 no6326 p756 F 17 2017

Porcine somatotropin

Inactivation of porcine endogenous retrovirus in pigs using CRISPR-Cas9 D. Niu, Wei et al diag *Science* v357 no6357 p1303 S 22 2017

Porcini, Mauro, 1975-—Interviews

PepsiCo's Chief Design Officer on Creating an Organization Where Design Can Thrive J. de Vries *Harvard Business Review Digital Articles* p2 Ag 11 2015

Porco, Carolyn

CASSINI AT SATURN color *Scientific American* v317 no4 p78 O 2017

Porcupine Meat (Music)

Singing on Solid Ground HADLEY color *Downbeat* v83 no11 p56 N 2016

Porcupine Mountains State Park (Mich.)

Test the Waters R. SAYERS map *Backpacker* p23 Ag 2017

Porges, Seth

2016 Holiday GIFT GUIDE color *InStyle* v23 no13 p249 D 2016

home & help img *New York* p96 Mr 6 2017

Porites lobata—Research

Coral Coring L. Lippsett *Oceanus* v52 no1 p7 Summ 2016

Poritz, Aaron

Tambour Home Bar color *Bloomberg Businessweek* no4539 p75 S 25 2017

Pork

See also

Pork chops

Braised Pork Shoulder *Indianapolis Monthly* p45 My 2017

A Passion for HERITAGE PIGS: A burgeoning pig farmer perseveres through rough patches to provide pastured pork to farm-to-table restaurants D. H. Kindler *Mother Earth News* no282 p12 Je/Jl 2017

SLOW COOKER PORK CARNITAS *Successful Farming* v115 no1 p69 Ja 2017

Pork chops

EASY WEEKNIGHTS color *Good Housekeeping* v263 no5 p181 N 2016

r.s.v.p C. DANIELS, A. REUSING et al bw color *Bon Appetit* v62 no7 p12 Jl 2017

You've Never Seen a Pork Chop Like This A. GOMEZ color *Bon Appetit* v62 no2 p71 Mr 2017

Pork-free diet

Gloria S. Lyon color *New Yorker* v93 no25 p22 Ag 28 2017

Pork industry—United States

U.S. Beef and Pork Consumption Projected To Rebound F. Badau *Amber Waves: The Economics of Food, Farming, Natural Resources, & Rural America* p1 S 2016

Pork products—Evaluation

FILIPINO BOUNTY C. SCHEDLER color *Chicago* v65 no12 p59 D 2016

Pornhub (Company)

What We Want When Nobody's Watching: A sampling of everything Pornhub has learned about its users since 2008 img *New York* v50 no12 p36 Je 12 2017

Pornographic films

PARENT TRAP: YOUR KIDS WILL SEE INTERNET PORN. DEAL WITH IT. A CONVERSATION WITH PEGGY ORENSTEIN S. FALLON and L. H. NEWMAN cartoon *Wired* v25 no9 p78 S 2017

This Isn't Fun Anymore: When Molly Haskell offered to take porn seriously, the movies didn't perform on command C. Bonanos img *New York* v50 no12 p14 Je 12 2017

Pornography

See also
Internet pornography
Pornographic films

Amateur Hour: Three stars of Pornhub Community, the site's user-contributed channel img *New York* v50 no12 p38 Je 12 2017

Comments img *New York* v50 no13 p8 Je 26 2017

PORNHUB IS THE KINSEY REPORT OF OUR TIME M. O'CONNOR *New York* v50 no12 p30 Je 12 2017

The Sexual Almanac *New York* v50 no12 p33 Je 12 2017

What We Want When Nobody's Watching: A sampling of everything Pornhub has learned about its users since 2008 img *New York* v50 no12 p36 Je 12 2017

Pornography addiction

CONFESSING MY PORN ADDICTION J. Smith color *America* v216 no7 p32 Ap 3 2017

Pornography—Psychological aspects

HOW TO DELETE PORN FROM YOUR BRAIN T. WILES color *Christianity Today* p11 Ap 2017

"Your sexuality and your naked body are not shameful." color *Glamour* v115 no7 p92 Jl 2017

Pornography—Religious aspects—Christianity

HOW PORNOGRAPHY IS PARALYZING THE CHURCH L. GIBBONS color graph *Christianity Today* v61 no7 p2 S 2017

Pornography—Research

ONE IN FIVE STRAIGHT MEN WATCHES GAY SEX B. SHUCART color *Advocate* no1089 p17 F/Mr 2017

Porosoff, Lauren

Backtalk *Phi Delta Kappan* v99 no2 p80 O 2017

Porowski, C.

Observation of a large-scale anisotropy in the arrival directions of cosmic rays above 8×10^{18} eV *Science* v357 no6357 p1266 S 22 2017

Porras, R. C.

The whole-soil carbon flux in response to warming [Cover story] chart graph *Science* v355 no6332 p1420 Mr 31 2017

Porray, Mary Elizabeth

Data Can Do for Change Management What It Did for Marketing *Harvard Business Review Digital Articles* p2 Jl 31 2017

Email and Calendar Data Are Helping Firms Understand How Employees Work *Harvard Business Review Digital Articles* p2 Ag 28 2017

Porridge

See also
Congee
Polenta

fast, easy, fresh C. MOROCCO bw color *Bon Appetit* v61 no11 p47 N 2016

The NEW L.A. BREAKFAST *Los Angeles Magazine* p106 Ap 2017

Porsche 911 automobile

Feel Lucky, Punk? [Cover story] J. Jacquot, A. Robinson et al color *Car & Driver* v63 no1 p36 Jl 2017

THE GREAT ESCAPE [Cover story] J. BARUTH chart color diag graph *Road & Track* v69 no3 p30 O 2017

RETRO, ACTIVE R. PINTO color *Road & Track* v69 no1 p64 Ag 2017

Three for the Road H. Elliott color *Bloomberg Businessweek* no4528 p70 Je 26 2017

With Porsche's transcendent new 911 GT3, you won't need any damn luck J. JACQUOT color *Car & Driver* v63 no1 p42 Jl 2017

Porsche 911 automobile—Evaluation

911 WEAPONS-GRADE EDITION C. Walton chart color *Motor Trend* v69 no5 p82 My 2017

Big T, No S T. Quiroga color *Car & Driver* v62 no8 p90 F 2017

FRATERNAL TWINS [Cover story] S. Evans chart color *Motor Trend* v68 no12 p42 D 2016

Porsche 911 chart color *Motor Trend* v69 no1 p142 Ja 2017

Porsche 911 GT3 A. MacKenzie color *Motor Trend* v69 no5 p18 My 2017

Porsche AG

2017 PORSCHE 718 BOXSTER S E. Tingwall color graph *Car & Driver* v63 no2 p78 Ag 2017

911 WEAPONS-GRADE EDITION C. Walton chart color *Motor Trend* v69 no5 p82 My 2017

BEST PORSCHE of the Year B. WASEF bw color *Esquire* v166 no4 p75 N 2016

Big T, No S T. Quiroga color *Car & Driver* v62 no8 p90 F 2017

Braking Bad E. Johnson color *Car & Driver* v62 no11 p116 My 2017

In Product Development, Let Your Customers Define Perfection M. Ramanujam and G. Tacke *Harvard Business Review Digital Articles* p2 My 9 2016

JEKYLL & HYDE A. MacKenzie chart color *Motor Trend* v69 no2 p68 F 2017

The Lapper Gets Dapper T. Quiroga color *Car & Driver* v63 no2 p94 Ag 2017

The New Heathen Porsche E. DYER bw color *Popular Mechanics* p38 F 2017

Porsche 911 chart color *Motor Trend* v69 no1 p142 Ja 2017

Porsche 911 GT3 A. MacKenzie color *Motor Trend* v69 no5 p18 My 2017

SKINNY LEGS AND ALL D. Sherman chart color graph *Car & Driver* v62 no6 p72 D 2016

With Porsche's transcendent new 911 GT3, you won't need any damn luck J. JACQUOT color *Car & Driver* v63 no1 p42 Jl 2017

Porsche Automobil Holding SE

Engineering the Sound Of Silence at Porsche C. Rauwald and D. Rocks color graph *Bloomberg Businessweek* no4499 p44 N 14 2016

Porsche automobiles

See also
Porsche 911 automobile

Esquire's 2016 CAR AWARDS color *Esquire* v166 no4 p73 N 2016

LEGEND OF THE FALL J. H. HARPER color *Road & Track* v68 no6 p24 F 2017

VERY CLOSE VANES color *Road & Track* v68 no5 p116 D 2016/Ja 2017

Porsche automobiles—Design & construction

Engineering the Sound Of Silence at Porsche C. Rauwald and D. Rocks color graph *Bloomberg Businessweek* no4499 p44 N 14 2016

Porsche automobiles—Evaluation

Beverly Hills Butt Lift E. Tingwall bw color *Car & Driver* v62 no6 p94 D 2016

FOURS TO BE RECKONED WITH J. Gall color graph *Car & Driver* v62 no7 p94 Ja 2017

THE FULL KIT K. KINARD color *Road & Track* v69 no2 p86 S 2017

The Lapper Gets Dapper T. Quiroga color *Car & Driver* v63 no2 p94 Ag 2017

NAMING RITES J. Jacquot bw chart color *Car & Driver* v63 no5 p48 N 2017

The New Heathen Porsche E. DYER bw color *Popular Mechanics* p38 F 2017

SKINNY LEGS AND ALL D. Sherman chart color graph *Car & Driver* v62 no6 p72 D 2016

SPORTS-CAR RACING 101 P. LERNER color *Road & Track* v68 no8 p50 My 2017

Sui Generis J. Capparella cartoon color *Car & Driver* v62 no7 p88 Ja 2017

Porsche Panamera automobile

Don't Call It a Wagon E. Tingwall color *Car & Driver* v63 no4 p80 O 2017

Porsche Panamera automobile—Evaluation

Beverly Hills Butt Lift E. Tingwall bw color *Car & Driver* v62 no6 p94 D 2016

Braking Bad E. Johnson color *Car & Driver* v62 no11 p116 My 2017

JEKYLL & HYDE A. MacKenzie chart color *Motor Trend* v69 no2 p68 F 2017

Port, Elisa

What doctors tell their friends about cancer S. WOOD and J. Detwiler color *Redbook* p77 N 2017

Port Aransas (Tex.)

Seeing the Body R. PEARSON *Texas Monthly* v45 no8 p54 Ag 2017

Port Bou (Music)

Dialectrical/Port Bou B. Bambarger color *Downbeat* v84 no3 p59 Mr 2017

Port of Long Beach

It's a Gusher S. SHIBATA *Sea Magazine* v108 no9 p14 S 2016

Porta Romana (Company)

The Natural K. O'SHEA-EVANS bw color *House Beautiful* v159 no5 p51 Je 2017

Portable computers—Evaluation

Best cheap laptops: We rate the best-sellers on Amazon and Best Buy G. M. UNG color *PCWorld* v35 no9 p56 S 2017

Google Home: Google puts its A.I. on a nightstand for the win J. PHILLIPS color *PCWorld* p115 D 2016

Portable food & beverage coolers—Evaluation

Chill'n A. BENNETT color *Cabin Living* p87 Ja/F 2017

Day Tripper L. BECKETT color *Power & Motoryacht* v33 no3 p50 Mr 2017

NEW PRODUCTS color *Spin to Win Rodeo* v21 no2 p26 Ap 2017

Portable planetariums—Evaluation

Rocketing off to (cyber)space T. Trusock color *Astronomy* v45 no2 p62 F 2017

Porter, Bill

The Reader Page color *Popular Mechanics* p8 D 2016/Ja 2017

Porter, Billy

SOUL GATHERING C. Arnold color *Essence* v47 no12 p68 Ap 2017

Porter, Cole, 1891-1964

Cole Mining S. Rushin color *Sports Illustrated* v126 no8 p88 Mr 20 2017

Porter, Fairfield

The Black Tree cartoon *Magazine Antiques* v184 no1 p22 Ja/F 2017

PORTER, GARETH

Another Mideast Debacle: How America armed terrorists in Syria *American Conservative* v16 no4 p20 Jl/Ag 2017

PORTER, HENRY

GILLIAN'S RAINBOW cartoon *Vanity Fair* v59 no1 p115 Holiday 2017

Porter, Jane

Back-to-School Shopping Still Exists color diag *Fortune* v176 no4 p30 S 15 2017

Q: IS SLOW WAGE GROWTH BOOMERS' FAULT? *Fortune* v176 no4 p28 S 15 2017

Porter, Jennifer

Being a Good Boss in Dark Times *Harvard Business Review Digital Articles* p2 Jl 5 2016

How to Give Negative Feedback When Your Organization Is "Nice" *Harvard Business Review Digital Articles* p2 Mr 14 2016

How to Handle the Naysayer on Your Team *Harvard Business Review Digital Articles* p2 Mr 30 2016

Why You Should Make Time for Self-Reflection (Even If You Hate Doing It) *Harvard Business Review Digital Articles* p2 Mr 21 2017

Porter, Jessica L.

"Office Housework" Gets in Women's Way *Harvard Business Review Digital Articles* p2 Ap 16 2015

Porter, Joy

The Cultural Resilience of a Continent's Dispossessed *History Today* v67 no4 p59 Ap 2017

Porter, Justin A.

Emission of volatile organic compounds from petunia flowers is facilitated by an ABC transporter diag *Science* v356 no6345 p1386 Je 30 2017

Porter, Kaitlyn Elizabeth

Promoting human rights through science color *Science* v357

no6359 p34 O 6 2017

Porter, Lauren J.S.

PICK UP HER CROWN color *Essence* v48 no3 p122 Jl 2017

Porter, Linda

Royal Renegades J. Ravenscroft *History Today* v67 no4 p57 Ap 2017

Porter, Michael

Missouri Compromise J. Fuchs and T. Keith color *Sports Illustrated* v126 no10 p32 Ap 10 2017

Porter, Michael E.

WHY POLITICS IS FAILING AMERICA color *Fortune* v175 no4 p74 Mr 15 2017

PORTER, PAMELA

thrift like a pro color *Better Homes & Gardens* v95 no3 p38 Mr 2017

Porter, Ryan

The Parties color *InStyle* v23 no12 p84 N 2016

Porter, Sarah

Deals R. DEAHL color *Publishers Weekly* v263 no42 p6 O 17 2016

Porter, Ware M.

TABLESCAPE: A WELCOME BRUNCH color *House Beautiful* v159 no9 p42 N 2017

Portfolio management (Investments)

See also

Asset allocation

Robo-advisors (Financial planning)

5 Ways Retirement Savers Put Their Dreams at Risk W. Updegrave color *Money* v46 no7 p28 Ag 2017

Active Funds Still Rule Down Under. For Now E. Cadman and R. Liew color *Bloomberg Businessweek* no4526 p33 Je 12 2017

All-Stars of the Kip 25 J. BODNAR color *Kiplinger's Personal Finance* v71 no5 p22 My 2017

THE CASE FOR INVESTING ABROAD P. J. Lim chart *Money* v46 no6 p36 Jl 2017

How Much Risk Can You Stand? A. K. SMITH color *Kiplinger's Personal Finance* v71 no2 p24 F 2017

Investing Can Be About Feelings Too M. Statman color *Money* v46 no5 p30 Je 2017

Not Your Average Utility Fund R. ERMEY chart *Kiplinger's Personal Finance* v71 no5 p63 My 2017

Shift Your Bond Gears C. Fried color diag *Money* v46 no2 p47 Mr 2017

Spring-Clean Your Portfolio J. Waggoner color diag *Money* v46 no2 p49 Mr 2017

That ETF May Not Be as Cheap as You Think P. J. Lim diag *Money* v46 no5 p36 Je 2017

Time for a Portfolio Pit Stop C. Fried color diag *Money* v46 no6 p33 Jl 2017

Why Income Investors Shouldn't Panic J. R. KOSNETT *Kiplinger's Personal Finance* v71 no11 p62 N 2017

Portfolio management (Investments)—History—21st century

Stay Cool and Stay Invested [Cover story] M. Heimer color diag *Fortune* v174 no8 p84 D 15 2016

Portilla, M. Teresa

"Ab initio" synthesis of zeolites for preestablished catalytic reactions bibl chart diag *Science* v355 no6329 p1051 Mr 10 2017

Portis, Clinton

Clinton PORTIS B. Burnsed color *Sports Illustrated* v127 no1 p98 Jl 3 2017

Portland (Me.)

Practical Magic K. Kelleher color map *American Craft* v77 no3 p86 Je/Jl 2017

Portland (Me.)—Description & travel

The Natural J. CRAIG color *Power & Motoryacht* v33 no1 p66 Ja 2017

Portland (Or.)

Beebe Skidmore Architects D. Sokol *Architectural Record* v205 no4 p115 Ap 2017

Bridging the Green Divide E. Daigneau *Governing* v30 no6 p20 Mr 2017

CHILDREN'S INSTITUTE HEADS TO PORTLAND J. ROSEN cartoon *Publishers Weekly* v264 no11 p21 Mr 13 2017

Home Grown M. Cockram *Architectural Record* v205 no6 p120 Je 2017

it's a colorful life S. BRICKELL cartoon color *Better Homes &*

Gardens v95 no4 p10 Ap 2017

THE ULTIMATE NATU RAL WINE BAR H. Wallace color *Rodale's Organic Life* v3 no1 p50 Ja 2017

Portland (Or.)—Description & travel

DOWNTOWN PORTLAND B. Collins color map *Sunset* v237 no6 p34 D 2016

FOOD TOWN THROWDOWN A. Pape color *Sunset* v238 no6 p36 Je 2017

Portland Art Museum (Or.)

Getting hitched: The St. John Altarpiece color *Magazine Antiques* v184 no3 p30 My/Je 2017

Portland cement

Of Form and Folly J. TUPPONCE *Virginia Living* v15 no1 p41 D 2016

Portland Design (Company)

WOWZA! color *Bicycling* v58 no6 p66 Jl 2017

Portland Trail Blazers (Basketball team)

6 TRAIL BLAZERS color *Sports Illustrated* v127 no12 p86 O 16 2017

WHAT IF? ... WALTON AND ODEN AND ROY HAD STAYED HEALTHY? (DON'T EVEN START ON MJ) B. Golliver and J. Feldman color *Sports Illustrated* v126 no11 p67 Ap 17-24 2017

Portland Trail Blazers (Basketball team)—Finance

4 Trail Blazers R. Nadkarni, B. Golliver et al color *Sports Illustrated* v125 no14 p100 O 24-31 2016

Portman, John

Buildings Seeking Art V. Camblin bw color *Art in America* v104 no11 p48 D 2016

Portman, Natalie, 1981-

Bald & Beautiful: A Timeline S. Leach bw color *Glamour* v115 no11 p46 N 2017

DOING GOOD C. Shanahan color *InStyle* v24 no4 p70 Ap 2017

Jackie *New Yorker* v92 no46 p10 Ja 23 2017

My LIST: 24 hours with Natalie Portman A. Parnass color *Harper's Bazaar* no3656 p236 S 2017

PARTY LINES img *New York* v49 no25 p140 D 12 2016

With Camelot Behind Her S. ERICKSON *Los Angeles Magazine* p72 Ja 2017

Portman, Natalie, 1981-—Interviews

Natalie Portman D. D'Addario color *Time* v188 no22-23 p112 N/D 2016

Portner, Emma

Easton PAYNE H. Rolfe bw *Dance Spirit* v21 no8 p119 O 2017

Emma THE ENIGMA N. Loeffler-Gladstone and J. Thornton color *Dance Spirit* v20 no9 p38 N 2016

PERFORMANCE Anxieties color *Dance Spirit* v20 no9 p18 N 2016

RENAISSANCE Woman color *Dance Spirit* v20 no9 p26 N 2016

Portrait drawing

The Gratitude Meter Z. Donaldson color *O, The Oprah Magazine* p22 Jl 2017

Portrait painters

THE PULPIT AND THE PAINTBRUSH C. M. Riley bw color *Magazine Antiques* v183 no6 p84 N/D 2016

Portrait painting

John vs. George E. Dale Santos color *MHQ: Quarterly Journal of Military History* v30 no1 p12 Aut 2017

Portrait photographers

REFLECTIONS IN A CAMERA A. LEIBOVITZ color *Vanity Fair* v59 no11 p128 N 2017

VICTOR SKREBNESKI B. Zehme color *Chicago* v66 no8 p132 Ag 2017

Who's Asking? E. MORRIS color *Film Comment* v53 no3 p14 My/Je 2017

Portrait photography

Country Trails A. PATTILLO color *Runner's World* v52 no6 p54 Jl 2017

How Art Can Fight Trump J. SALTZ img *New York* p70 Ja 23 2017

PLEASE DON'T SAY CHEESE S. Zlotnick *Washingtonian Magazine* v52 no6 p97 Mr 2017

Portraits from the Détente Era N. Farb and I. Tabarovsky *Wilson Quarterly* v40 no4 p3 Fall 2016

REFLECTIONS IN A CAMERA A. LEIBOVITZ color *Vanity Fair* v59 no11 p128 N 2017

SHOOTING STARS L. SCHNEIDER bw *Vanity Fair* v59 no11

p69 N 2017

Portrait photography—19th century

From specimens to souls B. Tannenbaum bw color *Magazine Antiques* v183 no6 p68 N/D 2016

Portrait photography—Exhibitions

See also

Portrait photography

From specimens to souls B. Tannenbaum bw color *Magazine Antiques* v183 no6 p68 N/D 2016

Portrait As Self-Portrait (Poem)

'PORTRAIT AS SELF-PORTRAIT' M. J. Bang bw *New York Times Book Review* p17 Ag 6 2017

Portrait of the Artist as a Young Man, A (Film)

Welcome to America's biannual literary review R. A. Schroth *America* v216 no9 p3 Ap 24 2017

Portraits

Christmas Gifts to Cherish bw color *Yankee* v80 no6 p26 N/D 2016

FROM THE ARTISTS Just Because VICTOR ADAM *Arabian Horse World* v57 no8 p18 My 2017

HELL ON THE RIVER KWAI P. D. Toler *MHQ: Quarterly Journal of Military History* v29 no3 p89 Spr 2017

IS THAT WHAT THEY SHOULD LOOK LIKE? T. Harris, B. Stoker et al bw color *Reader's Digest* v190 no1134 p98 O 2017

My Living Room L. BAILEY *Indianapolis Monthly* v40 no7 p33 Mr 2017

SMILE AND SAY, "MALAWI!" *Texas Monthly* v44 no12 p14 D 2016

WELCOME TO THE ISSUE *Harper's Bazaar* no3650 p36 F 2017

Portraits—Exhibitions

"ENCODED" G. Kroeber color *Art in America* v105 no4 p117 Ap 2017

Pictorialist photography at the Palmer bw *Magazine Antiques* v184 no1 p46 Ja/F 2017

WOMEN: NEW PORTRAITS A. LEIBOVITZ bw color *Vogue* v206 no11 p147 N 2016

Portran, Didier

Microtubules acquire resistance from mechanical breakage through intralumenal acetylation diag graph *Science* v356 no6335 p328 Ap 21 2017

Ports (Electronic computer system)—Evaluation

SATECHI ALUMINUM USB 3.0 HUB + CARD READER: EASY ACCESS TO USB 3 PORTS FOR YOUR MAC R. LOYOLA color *Macworld - Digital Edition* p29 Mr 2017

Portugal

Where Catcalling Is Criminalized T. John color *Time* v188 no27-28 p12 D 26 2017

Portuguese Kid, The (Theatrical production)

Serenity Now! M. Schulman color *New Yorker* v93 no33 p22 O 23 2017

Porzecanski, Katia

A Reckoning At Trump's Alma Mater color *Bloomberg Businessweek* no4502 p64 D 5 2016

Stock Investors Nervously Do the Math color *Bloomberg Businessweek* no4520 p41 My 1 2017

Porzel, Dan

HOT PROPERTY T. BRAND *Indianapolis Monthly* v40 no4 p42 D 2016

POSADA-CARBO, EDUARDO

The Difficult Road to Peace in Colombia *Current History* v116 no787 p74 F 2017

Posadas (Social custom)

Singing for shelter P. Hovey color *U.S. Catholic* v81 no12 p19 D 2016

Posada-Swafford, Angela

Amazon Atlantis color map *Scientific American* v317 no1 p12 Jl 2017

Posamentier, Jordan

How States Can Promote Local Innovation, Options, and Problem-Solving in Public Education bw *Education Digest* v83 no3 p30 N 2017

Posas, Francesc

Evolution of protein phosphorylation across 18 fungal species bibl graph *Science* v354 no6309 p229 O 14 2016

Posen, Adam—Interviews

What British, European, and American Policymakers Need to Do Now W. Frick *Harvard Business Review Digital Articles* p2 Je 24 2016

What You Should Know About Dodd-Frank and What Happens If It's Rolled Back W. Frick color *Harvard Business Review Digital Articles* p2 Mr 2 2017

Posen, Barry R.

Civil Wars & the Structure of World Power *Daedalus* v146 no4 p167 Fall 2017

POSEN, ZAC

Christine BARANSKI *Interview* v47 no1 p21 F 2017

Posey, Anna

DANISH MODERN color *Chicago* v66 no7 p37 Jl 2017

SUGAR RUSH! color *Bon Appetit* v61 no12 p136 D 2016 / Jan2017

Posey, Avery D. Jr.

CANCER KILLERS color *Scientific American* v316 no3 p38 Mr 2017

Posey, David

DANISH MODERN color *Chicago* v66 no7 p37 Jl 2017

Posey, Monica J.

Welcome *Cincinnati Magazine* v50 no8 p82 My 2017

Posey, Tyler

THE 22-WORD REVIEW D. Rovenstine color *Entertainment Weekly* no1476 p50 Ag 4 2017

Positive psychology

Make any day more vibrant color *Redbook* p99 Ap 2017

Positivity effect (Psychology)

Making Emotional and Spiritual Hijrah in the Post-Election Era T. ALVI *Islamic Horizons* v46 no1 p30 Ja/F 2017

Positrons

White dwarf mergers seen as antimatter source color *Astronomy* v45 no9 p19 S 2017

POSNANSKI, JOE

An Evening Drive *Reader's Digest* v188 no1125 p24 N 2016

POSNER, GARY P.

'Psychic Detective' Noreen Renier: The Grinch Who Stole Christmas from a Grieving Family: Newly obtained recordings provide a unique opportunity to assess the sessions of a genuine "psychic detective" police case *Skeptical Inquirer* v41 no4 p46 Jl/Ag 2017

Posner, Sarah

AMAZING DISGRACE *New Republic* v248 no4 p34 Ap 2017

MAKE AMERICA HATE AGAIN bw cartoon *Mother Jones* v42 no1 p24 Ja/F 2017

TRUMP'S TROOPS *Mother Jones* v41 no6 p31 N/D 2016

Posnick, Phyllis

RADICAL CHIC color *Vogue* v206 no11 p84 N 2016

Pospich, Sabrina

The molecular basis of Alzheimer's plaques color *Science* v357 no6359 p45 O 6 2017

Poss, Kenneth D.

Cardiac regeneration strategies: Staying young at heart diag *Science* v356 no6342 p1035 Je 9 2017

Injury-induced ctgfa directs glial bridging and spinal cord regeneration in zebrafish bibl graph *Science* v354 no6312 p630 N 4 2016

Poss, Michael A.

Formation of α-chiral centers by asymmetric β-C(sp3)–H arylation, alkenylation, and alkynylation bibl diag *Science* v355 no6324 p499 F 3 2017

Possibility

Life unexpected: When plans go awry, consider the possibilities A. Scobey color *U.S. Catholic* v82 no8 p43 Ag 2017

Possingham, Hugh P.

After Chile's fires, reforest private land color *Science* v356 no6334 p147 Ap 14 2017

Society Is Ready for a New Kind of Science--Is Academia? *BioScience* v67 no7 p591 Jl 2017

Possokhov, Yuri

Gravitas, Russian-Style *Dance Magazine* v91 no1 p38 Ja 2017

Post, Emily, 1873-1960

PRIDE AND PROTOCOL J. Goodman color *Bloomberg Businessweek* no4523 p63 My 22 2017

POST, ERIC

The Arctic in the Twenty-First Century: Changing Biogeochemi-

cal Linkages across a Paraglacial Landscape of Greenland *BioScience* v67 no2 p118 F 2017

Post, Mark

Goodbye Farm. Hello Lab K. Wong *Sierra* v102 no2 p24 Mr/Ap 2017

Post-Cold War period

Now for the Post-Post-Cold War Era T. DONNELLY color *Weekly Standard* v22 no19 p26 Ja 23 2017

Post-Elect (Poem)

Post-Elect I. ROCHA *Nation* v305 no9 p32 O 16 2017

Post-retirement employment

Planning Your Post-Retirement Career D. Clark *Harvard Business Review Digital Articles* p2 Ap 28 2016

Post roads

THE MAIL COACH TO ABERYSTWYTH: Jolts and All: How to Journey in Style--as if It Were 1835 S. Ellis *British Heritage Travel* v38 no4 p38 Jl/Ag 2017

Post-translational modification

A chemical biology route to site-specific authentic protein modifications A. Yang, S. Ha et al bibl diag graph *Science* v354 no6312 p623 N 4 2016

A radical approach to posttranslational mutagenesis R. Hofmann and J. W. Bode bibl diag *Science* v354 no6312 p553 N 4 2016

Post-traumatic stress disorder

Climate Trauma color *Earth Island Journal* v32 no2 p4 Summ 2017

The Inheritance cartoon *O. The Oprah Magazine* p134 F 2017

NEWS FROM THE World of Medicine S. RIDEOUT color *Reader's Digest* v190 no1133 p61 S 2017

Post-Traumatic Stress A. CONSTANTINIDES color *Better Nutrition* v79 no3 p32 Mr 2017

PTSD and the Samurai D. Lowry color *Black Belt* v55 no1 p20 D 2016/Ja 2017

THE SWEET SPOT J. FIELDEN color *Esquire* p8 Ag 2017

The Writing Cure M. MATOUSEK *Saturday Evening Post* v289 no1 p48 Ja/F 2017

Post-traumatic stress disorder—Alternative treatment

TANK TREATMENT J. GREEN *Atlanta* v56 no9 p19 Ja 2017

Post-traumatic stress disorder—Diagnosis

A Unique Standard of Care *Psychology Today* v49 no5 p12 S/O 2016

Post-traumatic stress disorder—Treatment

A Unique Standard of Care *Psychology Today* v49 no5 p12 S/O 2016

Postal Savings Bank of China (Company)—Finance

POSTAL SAVINGS BANK OF CHINA GOES BIG S. Cendrowski diag *Fortune* v174 no8 p24 D 15 2016

Postal service

See also

Email systems

Mailboxes

Socks, Underwear, and a Camaro R. Bragg color *Southern Living* v51 no12 p234 D 2016

Postal service—Missouri

Mighty Peculiar M. W. SCHWARTZ bw color *Missouri Life* v44 no3 p62 My 2017

Postal service—United States

The Gratitude Meter Z. Donaldson color *O, The Oprah Magazine* p26 O 2017

Postal service—United States—History—20th century

How the Rise of the Post Office Explains American Innovation W. Frick *Harvard Business Review Digital Articles* p2 F 3 2016

Postal voting

The Day America Stops Voting A. FERGUSON color *Weekly Standard* v22 no11 p22 N 21 2016

How to Bring Home Democratic Voters P. Keisling *Washington Monthly* p7 Ja/F 2017

Postcards

Notes FROM THE COAST *Texas Monthly* v45 no5 p22 My 2017

POSTCARDS FROM THE CANYON K. Vaughn *Arizona Highways* v93 no10 p28 O 2017

Postcards—Collectors & collecting

It seemed like such a simple R. STIEVE *Arizona Highways* v92 no12 p1 D 2016

Postcards—History

Golden Age of Postcards D. GIFFORD *Saturday Evening Post*

v288 no6 p52 N/D 2016

Postcommunism—Eastern Europe

Labor's Travails in Postcommunist Eastern Europe R. SIL *Current History* v116 no788 p88 Mr 2017

Postdoctoral programs

Knocking on opportunity's door D. Shao cartoon *Science* v354 no6310 p382 O 21 2016

When personal becomes professional K. F. Boehnke color *Science* v357 no6352 p726 Ag 18 2017

Postdoctoral researchers

Postdocs power research R. Wallach color *Science* v357 no6355 p951 S 8 2017

When personal becomes professional K. F. Boehnke color *Science* v357 no6352 p726 Ag 18 2017

POSTELL, JOSEPH

Excellently Foolish color *National Review* v69 no3 p52 F 20 2017

Poster Frost Mirto (Company)

Bowman Senior Residences *Architectural Record* v205 no4 p198 Ap 2017

Posters

See also

Commercial art

War posters

FOOD WILL WIN THE WAR! *Prologue* v49 no2 p72 Summ 2017

Posters—Evaluation

TEEN DREAM L. MOWRY *Atlanta* v56 no10 p48 F 2017

Posters—History—20th century

THE POSTER CRAZE: Freaky, funny, and fashionable, in the '60s, these were the signs of our times H. Gold *Saturday Evening Post* v289 no4 p41 Jl/Ag 2017

Postindustrial societies

The Urban Future We Can't See A. M. Renn *Governing* v30 no2 p22 N 2016

Postle, Bradley R.

Reactivation of latent working memories with transcranial magnetic stimulation bibl graph *Science* v354 no6316 p1136 D 2 2016

Postman, Alex

DOWN SHIFTING color map *Conde Nast Traveler* v52 no10 p122 N 2017

ETHIOPIA color *Conde Nast Traveler* v52 no4 p36 Ap 2017

LIVING IN COLOR color *Conde Nast Traveler* v51 no11 p102 D 2016

WE'RE TURNING 30 bw chart color *Conde Nast Traveler* v52 no8 p55 S 2017

Postman, Lore

Recent History color diag *Log Home Living* v34 no7 p54 S 2017

Postmasters

'Ain't Doing Right': NO MATTER YOUR AGE, BEING OPEN TO NEW LOVE IS NEVER EASY L. GOODSON color *Yankee* p122 Jl 2017

Postmodern Jukebox (Performer)

The Bandleader: Sarah Reich is bringing tap to new audiences with innovative collaborations and daring creativity R. P. CASEY *Dance Magazine* v91 no9 p58 S 2017

Postmodernism (Literature)

Postmodernism vs. Science M. Shermer color *Scientific American* v317 no3 p90 S 2017

Postnatal exercise

FLAT ABS AFTER BABY M. Gainsburg color *Women's Health* v14 no2 p76 Mr 2017

Poston, Ashley

Geekerella *Publishers Weekly* v264 no8 p86 F 20 2017

Poston, Elly

All Decked Out color *Southern Living* v51 no12 p34 D 2016

Postoperative period

THE CROWNING TOUCH K. Hobson bw color diag *O, The Oprah Magazine* p95 O 2017

THE POST-OP BRAIN M. Leslie color *Science* v356 no6341 p898 Je 1 2017

Postpartum depression

Speak Your Truth T. Eason, K. Swails bw color *Glamour* v115 no6 p22 Je 2017

Postpartum depression—Prevention

a parent's musical powers color *Parents* v92 no7 p21 Jl 2017

Postpartum depression—Treatment

HEALING A MOTHER'S PAIN [Cover story] K. Weber color il *America* v216 no11 p18 My 15 2017

Postracialism

Confronting colorblindness E. Fergus il *Phi Delta Kappan* v98 no5 p30 F 2017

Postrel, Virginia

ADAM SMITH NEEDS A PAPER CLIP cartoon *Reason* v49 no1 p14 My 2017

FROM THE ARCHIVES bw cartoon *Reason* v48 no11 p70 Ap 2017

FROM THE ARCHIVES bw color *Reason* v49 no3 p70 Jl 2017

FROM THE ARCHIVES cartoon *Reason* v48 no10 p66 Mr 2017

FROM THE ARCHIVES bw *Reason* v49 no1 p70 My 2017

LOVE YOUR HOMEMADE QUILT? THANK CAPITALISM color *Reason* v48 no8 p14 Ja 2017

Umbrellas: The iPhones of the Victorian Age bw *Reason* v48 no10 p8 Mr 2017

When Play Drives Progress color *Reason* v48 no10 p60 Mr 2017

WHEN TIN CEILINGS WERE HIGH-TECH *Reason* v49 no5 p16 O 2017

YOUR MONEY OR YOUR LIFE color *Reason* v49 no3 p8 Jl 2017

POSTREL, VIRGINIA I.

Posts & Telecommunications Press (Company)

Children's Fun Publishing Company color *Publishers Weekly* v264 no12 p14 Mr 20 2017

Postsecondary education

See also

Higher education

Merging movements: Diverse dance practices in postsecondary education K. Schupp bibl *Arts Education Policy Review* v118 no2 p104 2017

Postsecondary education—United States

Improving Alignment between Educational Supply and Labor Market Needs P. Kelly, B. T. Prescott et al *Change* v49 no1 p34 Ja/F 2017

Posttraumatic growth

Use Failure as Fuel S. Weinman color *Men's Health* v31 no10 p36 D 2016

Postural muscles

STRAIGHT UP [Cover story] L. BEDOSKY color *Runner's World* v52 no3 p48 Ap 2017

Posture

See also

Sitting position

Standing position

15 MINUTE WORKOUT M. Gainsburg color *Women's Health* v14 no3 p60 Ap 2017

4 little moves that work wonders A. Sweeney color *Redbook* p24 N 2017

ATTACK THE FLAG M. Perpich and D. DeNunzio color *Golf Magazine* v59 no4 p52 Ap 2017

BODY POSITION, AN OVERVIEW N. Ienatsch cartoon *Cycle World* v56 no3 p24 Ap 2017

Brought to You by the Letter K D. Denunzio and E. Johnson color *Golf Magazine* v58 no11 p52 N 2016

THE BUCK PROFILE F. MINITER bw color *Outdoor Life* v224 no7 p43 S 2017

Don't Let Migraines Derail Your Career M. Aarons-Mele *Harvard Business Review Digital Articles* p2 Mr 20 2017

The Dressage Seat A. Beran color *Dressage Today* v24 no1 p46 O 2017

FREEZE FRAME WITH WHITNEY DESALVO K. Gustave color *Spin to Win Rodeo* v21 no6 p42 Ag 2017

Get Yer Slalom On Z. BILAS *Boating World* v38 no6 p16 Je 2017

Get Your Posture Point A. STANLEY color *Seventeen* v76 no5 p65 S 2017

good to the CORE [Cover story] T. RUSSO color *Yoga Journal* no291 p66 My 2017

A KEY TO ANJELICA J. J. BUCK color *Vanity Fair* v59 no10 p180 O 2017

MORE POP, LESS POP-UP K. Sprecher and D. DeNunzio color diag *Golf Magazine* v59 no4 p54 Ap 2017

THE PATH TO GOOD POSTURE K. ROCKWOOD bw cartoon *Martha Stewart Living* no275 p52 Je 2017

Patient H69: The Story of My Second Sight *Publishers Weekly* v264 no15 p61 Ap 10 2017

Potters

BORN OF THE MUD: THE STORY OF A COLLECTION B. PAUL color *Phi Kappa Phi Forum* v97 no1 p13 Spr 2017

BOWLED OVER: Noodling around in the studio led one talented potter to a design for a hot new ramen restaurant V. FORD *Indianapolis Monthly* p38 N 2017

CERAMICS TRIAD JOHNSON *Treasures* v6 no4 p28 F/Mr 2017

This Is My Job L. Liebman color *Glamour* v115 no1 p56 Ja 2017

WINNER'S CUP: A local potter sends fans on a hunt for free mugs around the city K. FRANZMAN *Indianapolis Monthly* v12 no40 p36 Ag 2017

Potters' wheels

Ghost's Clay Foreplay S. Vilkomerson color *Entertainment Weekly* no1460/1461 p81 Ap 7-17 2017

Potters—United States

HANDS ON THE WHEEL J. ROEDEL color *Louisiana Life* v37 no3 p14 Ja/F 2017

Pottery

See also

Ceramic sculpture

Delftware

BEST NEW STORES 2017 N. MARINO color diag *GQ: Gentlemen's Quarterly* v97 no4 p92 Ap 2017

CLARE POTTER color *Architectural Digest* no6 p60 Je 1 2017

Pottery collecting

Ceramics dynamic: The only thing more remarkable than John Bullard's studio pottery collection is how quickly he became a connoisseur of the field C. Waddington color *Magazine Antiques* v184 no4 p108 Jl/Ag 2017

Nicolaus Boston H. MARTIN color *Architectural Digest* v74 no8 p18 Ag 2017

Pottery—21st century

Clay Station H. MARTIN color *Architectural Digest* no5 p40 My 2017

Pottery—Sales & prices

La Tuile à Loup M. OWENS color *Architectural Digest* no5 p46 My 2017

Potting places

TABLE MANNERS color *Sunset* v238 no4 p48 Ap 2017

Potting soils

AROUND THE GARDEN S. Bender color *Southern Living* v52 no7 p36 Jl 2017

Potts, Brian H.

The Future of Yesterday's Fuel color *Weekly Standard* v22 no29 p14 Ap 3 2017

Potts, Keagan Holt

Ethics and Cyber Warfare: The Quest for Responsible Security in the Age of Digital Warfare *Christian Century* v134 no18 p41 Ag 30 2017

POTTS, MONICA

The Social Safety Net Doesn't Exist in America bw il *Nation* v303 no18 p22 O 31 2016

Potts, Simon G.

Ten policies for pollinators bibl color *Science* v354 no6315 p975 N 25 2016

POUCH, KYLE

An Investigation of the Missing411 Conspiracy *Skeptical Inquirer* v41 no4 p54 Jl/Ag 2017

Pouches (Containers)

Hip Service color *Los Angeles Magazine* v62 no10 p26 O 2017

VICTORIAN REVIVAL color *Harper's Bazaar* no3657 p132 O 2017

WATERFIELD DESIGNS iPAD PRO GEAR CASE L. YAMSHON color *Macworld - Digital Edition* p33 Je 13 2017

WHAT WE LOVE color *Harper's Bazaar* no3655 p30 Ag 2017

Pouches (Containers)—Evaluation

BH&G throwback 1957 CLOSETS K. K. CONDON color *Better Homes & Gardens* v95 no2 p136 F 2016

Track Pants Everywhere! color *Glamour* v114 no7 p50 Jl 2016

Pouderoux, Hugo F. A.

Release of mineral-bound water prior to subduction tied to shallow seismogenic slip off Sumatra graph *Science* v356 no6340 p841 My 26 2017

Poughkeepsie (N.Y.)

Make Poughkeepsie Great Again W. BALDWIN color *Forbes* v199 no5 p40 My 16 2017

Poulos, James

Tocqueville And the Art Of Living K. CONNELL diag *National Review* v69 no5 p43 Mr 20 2017

Poulson, Charlie

My First Year K. Bonnell bw color *Glamour* v115 no1 p48 Ja 2017

Poultry

See also

Chickens

Ducks

Geese

Turkeys

All wrapped up J. Iserloh color *Yoga Journal* no289 p68 F 2017

count your chickens! S. LENZER color *Parents* v92 no3 p94 Mr 2017

Hazards of Raising Chickens *Parents* v92 no2 p32 F 2017

Learning Chinese K. SHERWOOD *Nutrition Action Health Letter* v44 no5 p12 Je 2017

Low 'n Slow K. SHERWOOD *Nutrition Action Health Letter* v44 no2 p12 Mr 2017

Mail Models A. HALPERN color *Bon Appetit* v61 no12 p69 D 2016 /Jan2017

Post-Holiday Fast Food J. Bowden and J. Bessinger color *Better Nutrition* v79 no11 p78 N 2017

RECIPE: ORANGE-SESAME CHICKEN STIR-FRY WITH BROCCOLI & PEPPERS *Tufts University Health & Nutrition Letter* p3 S 2017 Supplement

Poultry farming

See also

Turkey farming

Coop It Up E. Millard color *Log Home Living* v34 no2 p36 Mr 2017

Where Your Thanksgiving Turkey Comes From *New York Times Upfront* v149 no5 p2 N 21 2016

Poultry industry

Halal from Farm to Fork: To build trust, the halal meat certification system needs a tune-up M. ABDULLAH *Islamic Horizons* v46 no3 p32 My/Je 2017

Q AND A WITH MARYN MCKENNA S. Fennessy *Atlanta* v57 no5 p100 S 2017

A tiny country feeds the world F. Viviano color graph map *National Geographic* v232 no3 p82 S 2017

Poultry Science Association (Organization)—Congresses

Calendar of meetings *BioScience* v67 no5 p480 My 2017

Poultry—Reproduction

Role for migratory wild birds in the global spread of avian influenza H5N8 S. J. Lycett, R. Bodewes et al bibl graph map *Science* v354 no6309 p213 O 14 2016

Pound (British currency)

Hysterical History Tour color *Weekly Standard* v22 no35 p2 My 22 2017

Pound (British currency)—Economic aspects

A Serious Pounding J. Ward and L. Mnyanda color *Bloomberg Businessweek* no4497 p17 O 31 2016

Pound, Ezra, 1885-1972

The Circuitous Path of Papa and Ezra A. MENDENHALL bw *American Conservative* v16 no2 p52 Mr/Ap 2017

POUPART, LISA

The Question *O, The Oprah Magazine* p16 My 2017

Pour Some Sugar on Me (Music)

ARCADE FIRE'S WIN BUTLER L. Greenblatt color *Entertainment Weekly* no1476 p58 Ag 4 2017

Pourkheirandish, Mohammad

Wild emmer genome architecture and diversity elucidate wheat evolution and domestication color *Science* v357 no6346 p93 Jl 7 2017

Pournelle, Jerry

Writing the Future R. SIMBERG bw *Weekly Standard* v23 no4 p37 O 2 2017

Poussin, Nicolas, ca. 1594-1665

Gathering Manna in the Desert H. J. Hornik and M. C. Parsons color *Christian Century* v134 no19 p47 S 13 2017

Poutine

What a delicious mess J. RICHLER chart color *Maclean's* v130 no6 p16 Jl 2017

Poutou, Philippe

The Wild Cards of the French Election Z. Rahim color *Time* v189 no15 p9 Ap 24 2017

Pouyan, Shahpour

AWAITING ARMAGEDDON A. Wallach color *Art in America* v104 no10 p108 N 2016

Editor's Letter L. POLLOCK color *Art in America* v104 no10 p16 N 2016

Poverty

See also

Poverty reduction

Detroit's Underground Economy V. V. PANNE *In These Times* v41 no7 p8 Jl 2017

Francis for the Poor G. O'CONNELL *America* v215 no15 p26 N 14 2016

The long-run poverty and gender impacts of mobile money T. Suri and W. Jack bibl chart graph *Science* v354 no6317 p1288 D 9 2016

A New Vision for Business N. Gibbs color *Time* v188 no24 p4 D 12 2016

NOW FOR THE GOOD NEWS... *New York Times Upfront* p16 S 18 2017

'Perseverance Porn' Bolsters System by Celebrating Survivors of Its Cruelties A. Johnson *Extra!* v30 no7 p3 S 2017

Poverty and the Controversial Work of Nonprofits M. Jindra and I. Jindra *Society* v53 no6 p634 D 2016

Poverty and the Pyrite State color *Weekly Standard* v23 no5 p2 O 9 2017

REVOLUTIONARY ROAD bw *New Republic* v247 no11 p34 N 2016

THE WAR ON HILLBILLIES S. JONES color *New Republic* v248 no6 p42 Je 2017

Poverty in the Bible

The poor we have with us L. Theoharis bw *Christian Century* v134 no9 p26 Ap 26 2017

Poverty Inc. (Film)

The Philanthropist's Burden T. Sullivan color il *Harvard Business Review* v94 no12 p114 D 2016

Poverty reduction

3 Ways Businesses Are Addressing Inequality in Emerging Markets V. Govindarajan and R. Ramamurti *Harvard Business Review Digital Articles* p2 Ja 23 2015

An Approach to Ending Poverty That Works S. Davis *Harvard Business Review Digital Articles* p2 Ja 22 2015

As Schools Tackle Poverty, Attendance Goes Up, but Academic Gains Are Tepid D. R. Superville *Education Digest* v83 no2 p46 O 2017

Beyond the bubble J. Bazan color *U.S. Catholic* v82 no5 p45 My 2017

Dare to Belong color *Alternatives Journal (AJ) - Canada's Environmental Voice* v42 no3 p18 2016

How WE Is Making a Difference color *Good Housekeeping* v265 no3 p20 S 2017

Payday Predators E. J. WEISENBURGER *America* v215 no15 p24 N 14 2016

Poverty—Africa

The Contentious Politics of African Urbanization J. W. PALLER *Current History* v116 no790 p163 My 2017

Poverty—Social aspects

Brain Trust [Cover story] K. G. Noble color graph *Scientific American* v316 no3 p44 Mr 2017

Poverty—United States

Achieving Equity Amid Poverty P. D. SMITH *Education Digest* v82 no8 p45 Ap 2017

The Changing Face of Work and Poverty in Yakima D. BACON color *Progressive* v81 no6 p12 Ag/S 2017

THE Nearly Impossible DREAM C. N. MASON *Ms.* v26 no4 p30 Wint 2016

Well, No, But I Did Fly Over It Once cartoon *Weekly Standard* v22 no28 p2 Mr 27 2017

Povich, Ahriel

CHAMPERY, SWITZERLAND color *Snowboarder* v29 no5 p86 Ja 2017

Povie, Guillaume

Synthesis of a carbon nanobelt diag graph *Science* v356 no6334 p172 Ap 14 2017

Povolotskaya, Inna S.

Ancient genomic changes associated with domestication of the horse color diag *Science* v356 no6336 p442 Ap 28 2017

POWASKI, RONALD E.

CONTAINING PUTIN'S RUSSIA *USA Today Magazine* v146 no2868 p28 S 2017

Powders—Evaluation

BEAUTY NEWS bw color *Harper's Bazaar* no3648 p218 N 2016

Powdery mildew diseases—Prevention

THE GRUMPY GARDENER'S Guide to Hydrangeas S. Bender color *Southern Living* v52 no5 p106 My 2017

Powdthavee, Nattavudh (Nick)

Income Inequality Makes Whole Countries Less Happy *Harvard Business Review Digital Articles* p2 Ja 12 2016

Powell, Alison

Why Major Philanthropists Are Giving More Money to Just One Cause color *Harvard Business Review Digital Articles* p2 Ja 19 2017

POWELL, ALMA

A Plea to America's Adults color *Reader's Digest* v190 no1132 p20 Jl/Ag 2017

POWELL, ANDREA

AD SENSES: THE NEW BODY LANGUAGE cartoon *Wired* v25 no8 p22 Ag 2017

DRONE RESPONSIBLY 7 LESSONS LEARNED THE HARD WAY color graph *Wired* v25 no5 p24 My 2017

VENTURE BALL cartoon *Wired* v25 no10 p42 O 2017

Powell, Ashlea

How IDEO Designers Persuade Companies to Accept Change *Harvard Business Review Digital Articles* p2 My 17 2016

Powell, Benjamin E.

Fertile offspring from sterile sex chromosome trisomic mice chart diag *Science* v357 no6354 p932 S 1 2017

POWELL, COLIN

A Plea to America's Adults color *Reader's Digest* v190 no1132 p20 Jl/Ag 2017

Powell, Colin L., 1937—Interviews

Colin Powell C. Howorth color *Time* v189 no15 p8 Ap 24 2017

POWELL, COREY S.

Party of One color graph *Discover* v27 no10 p60 D 2016

Seeing Stars color *Discover* v38 no3 p62 Ap 2017

Powell, D. A., 1963-

Politics Was Front and Center At This Year's AWP Conference C. Teicher, C. Kirch et al color *Publishers Weekly* v264 no8 p4 F 20 2017

Powell, Dina

YOU SHOULD GET TO KNOW DINA POWELL color *Fortune* v175 no6 p10 My 1 2017

Powell, Ellen

Researchers open tomb believed to be the one where Jesus was buried *Christian Century* v133 no24 p17 N 23 2016

POWELL, ERIC A.

ANDEAN COPPER AGE color *Archaeology* v70 no5 p20 S/O 2017

Breaking Cahokia's Glass Ceiling bw color *Archaeology* v69 no6 p16 N/D 2016

The First American Revolution color *Archaeology* v70 no2 p42 Mr/Ap 2017

LATE PALEOLITHIC MASTERPIECES color *Archaeology* v70 no4 p20 Je-Ag 2017

A REMOVABLE FEAST color *Archaeology* v70 no1 p20 Ja/F 2017

RENAISSANCE MELODY color *Archaeology* v70 no4 p15 Je-Ag 2017

REVISITING MONTEZUMA CASTLE color *Archaeology* v70 no2 p12 Mr/Ap 2017

SET IN STONE color *Archaeology* v70 no4 p44 Je-Ag 2017

SQUEEZING HISTORY FROM A TURNIP color *Archaeology* v70 no3 p15 My/Je 2017

The Temple Builders of Malta color *Archaeology* v69 no6 p38 N/D 2016

THE THIRD REICH'S ARCTIC OUTPOST bw color *Archaeology* v70 no3 p22 My/Je 2017

TOP 10 DISCOVERIES OF 2016 bw cartoon color *Archaeology* v70 no1 p26 Ja/F 2017

When the Ancient Greeks Began to Write color *Archaeology* v70

POWERS, STEPHEN M.
Greenhouse Gas Emissions from Reservoir Water Surfaces: A New Global Synthesis *BioScience* v66 no11 p949 N 1 2016

Powers, Susan G.
Heterogeneous education output measures for public school students with and without disabilities bibl chart color graph *Monthly Labor Review* p1 S 2016

Powers, Thomas
The Big Thing on His Mind bw *New York Review of Books* v64 no7 p41 Ap 20 2017
The Private Heisenberg and the Absent Bomb bw *New York Review of Books* v63 no20 p65 D 22 2016

Powers-Beck, Jeffrey
Homegrown Nebraskans hit early baseball home run J. Boschen color *Nebraska Life* v21 no2 p17 Mr/Ap 2017

Powery, Luke A.
Reflections on the lectionary *Christian Century* v134 no16 p19 Ag 2 2017

Powles, Andrew
People and posts *People Management* p54 F 2017

Poyer, David—Interviews
Standing Literary Watch A. Appel color *Publishers Weekly* v263 no44 p53 O 31 2016

Poynter, Jane
Eyes on the skies L. PARKER color *Popular Science* v289 no6 p58 N/D 2017

Poynter, Phil
CONTRIBUTORS color *InStyle* v24 no9 p100 S 2017

POZEN, ROBERT C.
DECODING CEO PAY: *THE TRUTH IS BURIED IN THE FINE PRINT—AND THAT'S A PROBLEM color graph img *Harvard Business Review* v95 no4 p78 Jl/Ag 2017
A Social Security Proposal We Can All Live With *Harvard Business Review Digital Articles* p2 Je 17 2017

Pozniak, Curtis J.
Wild emmer genome architecture and diversity elucidate wheat evolution and domestication color *Science* v357 no6346 p93 Jl 7 2017

Pozzobon, Ty
RODEO'S NFL MOMENT C. GILLIS color *Maclean's* v130 no2 p52 Mr 2017

PPG Automotive Refinish (Company)
Proven Car Care color *Good Housekeeping* v265 no4 p85 O 2017

Prabhu, Jaideep
4 CEOs Who Are Making Frugal Innovation Work *Harvard Business Review Digital Articles* p2 N 28 2014
What Frugal Innovators Do *Harvard Business Review Digital Articles* p2 D 10 2014

Pracht, Katherine
Summer: The Tempest J. Rosenblum *Opera News* v81 no9 p51 Mr 2017

Practical jokes
PRANKSTERS IN CHIEF C. BOYER *National Geographic Kids* no467 p26 F 2017
PRANK YOU VERY MUCH K. Ellison color *O, The Oprah Magazine* p30 Ap 2017
WARNING: UNSAFE CONTENT color *Popular Mechanics* p30 O 2017

Practical politics
See also
Elections
Farmers—Political activity
Homosexuality & politics
Identity politics
Lobbying
Nominations for office
Political advertising
Political campaigns
Political organizations
Science & politics
Adolescent Politics H. WILHELM diag *National Review* v69 no5 p28 Mr 20 2017
THE APPROVAL MATRIX img *New York* v49 no26 p112 D 26 2016
BDS(M) Drama L. Featherstone color il *Nation* v304 no3 p5 Ja 30 2017

Divider-In-Chief S. ECKEL *Psychology Today* v50 no3 p41 My/Je 2017
FROM THE ARCHIVES V. POSTREL, T. W. HAZLETT et al cartoon *Reason* v48 no10 p66 Mr 2017
Geopolitical Shell Game: Washington and the fraudulent freedom fighters T. G. CARPENTER *American Conservative* v16 no5 p31 S/O 2017
The Hosts of Pantsuit Politics A. D. Pollard *Parents* v91 no11 p16 N 2016
THE POLARIZATION EXPRESS *Psychology Today* v50 no3 p9 My/Je 2017
President Obama's Scientific Legacy J. P. CARR *BioScience* v66 no12 p1011 D 1 2016
Should 'Ballot Box Selfies' Be Banned? W. GARDNER and G. BISSONNETTE *New York Times Upfront* v149 no4 p22 O 31 2016
The Trump-Hate Weather Vane O. Nuzzi img *New York* v50 no7 p22 Ap 3 2017

Practical politics—United States
BRICKBATS cartoon *Reason* v48 no10 p68 Mr 2017
How One Political Start-Up Is Trying to Fight Gridlock W. A. Galston *Harvard Business Review Digital Articles* p2 N 11 2014
Outposts of Rationality P. A. Harkness *Governing* v30 no6 p16 Mr 2017
Power Down *New York Times Magazine* p11 Ja 8 2017
WHITENESS UNDER THE MICROSCOPE A. CARP img *New York* v50 no6 p21 Mr 20 2017

Practical politics—United States—News briefs
NO COMMENT cartoon *Progressive* v81 no2 p10 F 2017

Practice (Sports)
THE ADVANTAGES OF YEAR-ROUND ROPING K. Santos color *Spin to Win Rodeo* v20 no11 p34 Ja 2017
TIME FOR A CHANGE M. Durland and D. DeNunzio color diag *Golf Magazine* v59 no6 p39 Je 2017

Prada, Miuccia, 1949-
MIUCCIA PRADA C. BARZINI color *Vogue* v207 no3 p406 Mr 2017
What Makes a Woman of the Year in 2016? C. Leive color *Glamour* v114 no12 p48 D 2016

Prada, Miuccia, 1949-—Interviews
Miuccia PRADA C. Leive color *Glamour* v114 no12 p208 D 2016

Prada SpA
EYE CANDY color *Harper's Bazaar* no3653 p127 My 2017
FRINGE BENEFITS color *Harper's Bazaar* no3656 p210 S 2017
ON THE CONTRARY C. ROITFELD and R. SIEGEL color *Harper's Bazaar* no3650 p118 F 2017
Red Carpet/Real Life color *InStyle* v24 no9 p230 S 2017

Pradeilles, Johan
Photoinduced decarboxylative borylation of carboxylic acids diag *Science* v357 no6348 p283 Jl 21 2017

Pradhan, Bibhudatta
India Likes Its Roads Built On Time color *Bloomberg Businessweek* no4513 p23 Mr 6 2017
Namaste Now try my herbal toothpaste color graph *Bloomberg Businessweek* no4502 p27 D 5 2016
One Tax To Rule Them All color *Bloomberg Businessweek* no4528 p28 Je 26 2017
A Slowdown in Modi's Backyard color *Bloomberg Businessweek* no4541 p36 O 9 2017

Prado, Darién
Forest conservation: Humans' handprints bibl color *Science* v355 no6324 p466 F 3 2017
Forest conservation: Remember Gran Chaco bibl color *Science* v355 no6324 p465 F 3 2017

Prado, J. L.
Decoupled ecomorphological evolution and diversification in Neogene-Quaternary horses bibl graph *Science* v355 no6325 p627 F 10 2017

Prado, Miguel A.
UBE2O remodels the proteome during terminal erythroid differentiation diag *Science* v357 no6350 p471 Ag 4 2017

Prado, R. R.
Observation of a large-scale anisotropy in the arrival directions of cosmic rays above 8×10^{18} eV *Science* v357 no6357 p1266 S 22 2017

Prado-Martinez, Javier

Chimpanzee genomic diversity reveals ancient admixture with bonobos bibl diag graph map *Science* v354 no6311 p477 O 28 2016

Praetorius, Florian
Self-assembly of genetically encoded DNA-protein hybrid nanoscale shapes *Science* v355 no6331 p1283 Mr 24 2017

Prager, Daniel
Examining Farm Sector and Farm Household Income *Amber Waves: The Economics of Food, Farming, Natural Resources, & Rural America* p23 Ag 2017
Farm Households Experience High Levels of Income Volatility *Amber Waves: The Economics of Food, Farming, Natural Resources, & Rural America* p43 F 2017

Pragmatism
The Downside of Pragmatism: It served our 'maker' cities well for a long time. Now it holds them back A. M. Renn *Governing* v30 no8 p22 My 2017

Prahalada, Srinivasa
Systemic pan-AMPK activator MK-8722 improves glucose homeostasis but induces cardiac hypertrophy graph *Science* v357 no6350 p507 Ag 4 2017

Prairie animals
PRAIRIE PORTAL L. Allen *National Parks* v91 no1 p44 Wint 2017

Prairie dogs—Behavior
CAN WE TALK? AN ARIZONA BIOLOGIST BELIEVES THAT THE SOUNDS MADE BY MANY ANIMAL SPECIES, INCLUDING THE HUMBLE PRAIRIE DOG, SHOULD BE CONSIDERED LANGUAGE—AND THAT SOMEDAY WE'LL UNDERSTAND WHAT THEY HAVE TO SAY F. Jabr *New York Times Magazine* p28 My 14 2017

Prairie restoration
Beefing Up Bird Habitat P. SAHA *Audubon* v119 no1 p16 Spr 2017

Prairies
Field Guides B. BUTLER color *Missouri Life* v44 no3 p46 My 2017

Prairies—Arizona
HART IS WHERE THE HOME IS K. MONTGOMERY *Arizona Highways* v93 no8 p46 Ag 2017

Prairie Wife, The (Short story)
The Prairie Wife C. Sittenfeld cartoon color *New Yorker* v92 no49 p76 F 13 2017

Praise
See also
Compliments
THE ULTIMATE COMPLIMENT *Women's Health* v14 no9 p8 N 2017

Prakash, Om
Evidence for bulk superconductivity in pure bismuth single crystals at ambient pressure bibl color graph *Science* v355 no6320 p1 Ja 6 2017

Prakash, Saikrishna Bangalore
Who's in Charge? T. HELFMAN *Weekly Standard* v22 no22 p33 F 13 2017

Prakash, Shailesh—Interviews
The revolution at The Washington Post K. Pope color *Columbia Journalism Review* p94 Fall/Wint 2016

Praline
Eat Praline Love *Indianapolis Monthly* v40 no5 p35 Ja 2017

Prandi, Davide
SOX2 promotes lineage plasticity and antiandrogen resistance in TP53- and RB1-deficient prostate cancer bibl graph *Science* v355 no6320 p1 Ja 6 2017

Prasad, Pankaj
Get More from Your Event Spending *Harvard Business Review Digital Articles* p2 Mr 31 2015

Prasanna, Rohit
Perovskite-perovskite tandem photovoltaics with optimized band gaps bibl chart graph *Science* v354 no6314 p861 N 18 2016

PRASHAD, VIJAY
THIS MONTH: The U.S. Is Bombing at Least Six Countries. How Can the Anti-War Movement Step Up? *In These Times* v41 no10 p14 O 2017

Prassack, Lisa—Interviews
Q&A L. Bedord *Successful Farming* v114 no12 p30 Mid-N 2016

Prat, Andrea
A Survey of How 1,000 CEOs Spend Their Day Reveals What Makes Leaders Successful *Harvard Business Review Digital Articles* p2 O 12 2017

Prater, Lisa
10 UP & COMERS: AUBREY FLETCHER *Successful Farming* v115 no8 p50 Je/Jl 2017

Prater, Lisa Foust
BECOMING A CAREGIVER *Successful Farming* v115 no2 p62 F 2017
BE OUR GUEST *Successful Farming* v115 no5 p61 Mid-Mr 2017
CAST-IRON LOVE *Successful Farming* v115 no3 p58 Mid-F 2017
CAST-IRON SKILLET CALZONE *Successful Farming* v115 no3 p59 Mid-F 2017
CHEESEBURGER SOUP: MAKE A DOUBLE BATCH AND PACK LEFTOVERS IN LUNCHES FOR SCHOOL OR TO TAKE TO THE FIELD *Successful Farming* v115 no11 p61 S 2017
CREATE AN ESTATE DIRECTORY: HAVING IMPORTANT INFORMATION IN ONE PLACE IS A GIFT TO HEIRS *Successful Farming* v115 no9 p66 Ag 2017
EASTER ANNIVERSARY: IT'S A TIME OF NEW BEGINNINGS AND A TIME TO REFLECT AND REMEMBER *Successful Farming* v115 no6 p63 Ap 2017
FARMING WITHOUT A NET: HEALTH INSURANCE CAN SAVE THE FARM, BUT BETWEEN THE COMPLICATED PROCESS AND THE EXPENSE, SOME FARMERS ARE GOING WITHOUT *Successful Farming* v115 no11 p58 S 2017
THE FARM IN THE DELL: THESE FARMS AND RANCHES GIVE ADULTS WITH DEVELOPMENTAL DISABILITIES A SENSE OF PURPOSE AND COMMUNITY *Successful Farming* v115 no12 p64 O 2017
FROM PARTS TO ART *Successful Farming* v115 no3 p56 Mid-F 2017
GET KOSELIG! *Successful Farming* v115 no2 p64 F 2017
HEALING HANDS *Successful Farming* v115 no4 p63 Mr 2017
HEART-HEALTHY CHOCOLATE CAKE *Successful Farming* v115 no2 p65 F 2017
LISTEN, LAUGH, LEARN *Successful Farming* v115 no11 p60 S 2017
MUSTANGS ON A MISSION: THESE FIVE WOMEN PLAN TO SPREAD INSPIRATION FROM MEXICO TO CANADA *Successful Farming* v115 no6 p62 Ap 2017
THE POWER OF PETS *Successful Farming* v115 no4 p64 Mr 2017
RESOLVE TO 'AGCERCISE' *Successful Farming* v115 no1 p66 Ja 2017
SOCIAL MEDIA SOUND OFF *Successful Farming* v114 no10 p63 O 2016
TAKE A FAMILY 'FIELD' TRIP: MAKE AG A PART OF YOUR VACATION PLANS - NO MATTER WHERE YOU'RE HEADED color *Successful Farming* v115 no7 p57 My 2017

Prather, Michael
Ralph J. Cicerone *Physics Today* v70 no2 p67 F 2017

Prato, Alison
Ashley GRAHAM color *Glamour* v114 no12 p222 D 2016
AYESHA CURRY "I Believe You Can Have It All" color *Health* v30 no9 p24 N 2016
CONSTANCE WU A Fresh Force color *Health* v30 no10 p24 D 2016
FIT, FUN, FABULOUS [Cover story] color *Health* v31 no2 p104 Mr 2017
Gabrielle Union IS OUR... gIrL CruSH [Cover story] color *Health* v31 no7 p116 S 2017
guts and glory [Cover story] color *Health* v30 no10 p104 D 2016
HOUGH HANGS TOUGH [Cover story] color *Health* v31 no9 p82 N 2017
KHLOÉ [Cover story] color *Health* v31 no1 p86 Ja 2017
padma heat up [Cover story] color *Health* v31 no8 p96 O 2017
UNDENIABLY EVA [Cover story] color *Health* v31 no5 p84 Je 2017

Prato, Maurizio
Nanomaterials for stimulating nerve growth color *Science* v356 no6342 p1010 Je 9 2017

Prato, Vittorio

L'Orfeo Ascending P. DEITZ color *Weekly Standard* v22 no30 p36 Ap 10 2017

Pratt, Brooke

Sweet Fun St. Louis L. A. Addington color *Missouri Life* v44 no5 p18 Ag 2017

Pratt, Cam

AGING GRACEFULLY on the Homestead *Mother Earth News* no280 p34 F/Mr 2017

Pratt, Chris, 1979-

GUARDIANS OF THE GALAXY VOL.2 C. Nashawaty color *Entertainment Weekly* no1465 p40 My 12 2017

The Guardians Return P. Travers color *Rolling Stone* no1287 p56 My 18 2017

MOM L. Rice color *Entertainment Weekly* no1446/1447 p62 D 2016/Ja 2017

SEPARATION ANXIETY D. Franich, D. Coggan et al color *Entertainment Weekly* no1478 / 1479 p14 Ag 18-25 2017

WHAT NOW? D. Coggan *Entertainment Weekly* no1478 / 1479 p16 Ag 18-25 2017

Pratt, Chris, 1979——Interviews

CALL TO STARDOM R. COHEN color *Vanity Fair* v59 no2 p62 F 2017

Pratt, Deborah

Give 'Em Shell A. HUNTER *Virginia Living* p21 2017 Smoke & Salt

Pratt, Derek A.

Synthesis of resveratrol tetramers via a stereoconvergent radical equilibrium bibl diag graph *Science* v354 no6317 p1260 D 9 2016

Pratte, André

GOOD NEWS color *Maclean's* v129 no47 p10 N 28 2016

Pratty, James

Two Ways to Better Care for Patients with Dementia *Harvard Business Review Digital Articles* p2 Ag 11 2015

Praveen, Kavita

Distribution and clinical impact of functional variants in 50,726 whole-exome sequences from the DiscovEHR study chart graph *Science* v354 no6319 paaf6814-1 D 23 2016

Prax, Elizabeth Iliff

COMING (Back) TO AMERICA color *Practical Horseman* v45 no9 p30 S 2017

HELPING GREAT HORSES STAY GREAT color *Practical Horseman* v45 no1 p30 Ja 2017

A KEY TO EVERY HORSE color *Practical Horseman* v45 no4 p28 Ap 2017

NUTRITION REPORT: AMINO ACIDS color *Practical Horseman* v45 no3 p56 Mr 2017

Prayer

See also

Invocation

Meditation

Om

Pray about it A. Scobey color *U.S. Catholic* v82 no7 p43 Jl 2017

Prayer in Christianity

MY COUNTRY, PRAYERS FOR THEE M. Reynolds color *Christianity Today* v61 no6 p21 Jl/Ag 2017

Prayer——Catholic Church

The End of Despair J. WATSON JR. il *America* v215 no19 p25 D 19 2016

Prayer——Christianity

Theology through prayer [Cover story] S. M. Brubaker color *Christian Century* v133 no24 p24 N 23 2016

Prayers

Healing With God C. Keehan color *America* v216 no13 p62 Je 12 2017

My friends are praying for me. Does God care? J. Weiss *Christian Century* v134 no8 p1 Ap 12 2017

OPEN MY HEART color *Essence* v47 no10 p108 F 2017

Prayer isn't our work, it's God's color *Christian Century* v134 no8 p1 Ap 12 2017

Prayer without answers color *Christian Century* v134 no8 p1 Ap 12 2017

Prayer——Social aspects

Denis Johnson: A Lot Like Prayer W. Blythe *New York Times Book Review* p14 Jl 30 2017

Pre-exposure prophylaxis

REAL HIV PREVENTION REQUIRES MORE THAN UNDERWEAR ADS: IF WE WANT BLACK GAY MEN TO USE PREP, WE HAVE TO CHANGE THE WAY WE'RE BRANDING IT C. STEPHENS *Advocate* no1093 p33 O/N 2017

Pre-sentence investigation reports

CANADIAN INJUSTICE K. EDWARDS color *Maclean's* v130 no10 p36 N 2017

Preacher (TV program)

The Awesome Pulp Sermon of 'Preacher' R. SHEFFIELD color *Rolling Stone* no1290 p25 Je 29 2017

Preacher A. D'Arminio *TV Guide* v65 no25 p37 Je 2017

PREACHER C. Collis color *Entertainment Weekly* no1474/1475 p74 Jl 21-28 2017

Preacher, Andy

Who I am *People Management* p45 Ag 2017

Preaching

The Best of Who We Are R. Bragg color *Southern Living* v52 no10 p136 O 2017

What Not to Do at Mass W. J. BAUSCH bw *Commonweal* v143 no20 p2 D 16 2016

Preakness Stakes

Leading Off color *Sports Illustrated* v126 no15 p6 My 29 2017

Preall, Rich

SING ABOUT SPRING *New York State Conservationist* v71 no5 p2 Ap 2017

Prebble, Stuart

The Bridge *Publishers Weekly* v264 no3 p41 Ja 16 2017

Prebiotics

The Nature of Humans *Natural History* v125 no1 p5 D 2016/Ja 2017

PREBLE, MATTHEW

CASE STUDY: FOLLOW DUBIOUS ORDERS OR SPEAK UP? AN INTERN CONTEMPLATES WHETHER SHE SHOULD COMPROMISE HER VALUES FOR A JOB il *Harvard Business Review* v95 no4 p139 Jl/Ag 2017

Precarious employment

Precarious Employment *Change* v82 no3 p31 Mr 2017

Precarity

Immigrants Prepare For Life After Obama J. Eidelson *Bloomberg Businessweek* no4501 p25 N 28 2016

Precautionary principle

Liability and Precaution I. S. Daramus bibl *Environment* v59 no5 p48 S/O 2017

Precaution and governance of emerging technologies G. E. Kaebnick, E. Heitman et al bibl color *Science* v354 no6313 p710 N 11 2016

The Precautionary Principle Under Fire R. Read and T. O'Riordan bibl *Environment* v59 no5 p4 S/O 2017

Precaution Needs to Abound, Not Wither M. Lahsen *Environment* v59 no5 p2 S/O 2017

Strengthening the Precautionary Principle in the Post-Paris Climate Regime A. Boswell bibl *Environment* v59 no5 p26 S/O 2017

PRECHT, JAY

Asserting Tribal Sovereignty through Compact Negotiations *American Indian Quarterly* v41 no1 p67 Wint 2017

Prechtel, Anton

alaskan weather *Weatherwise* v70 no5 p48 S/O 2017

Weatherwatch color map *Weatherwise* v70 no4 p38 Jl/Ag 2017

Weatherwatch *Weatherwise* v70 no1 p50 Ja/F 2017

Weatherwatch *Weatherwise* v70 no2 p38 Mr/Ap 2017

Precious metals——Economic aspects

The Loophole Under The Mountain H. Miller and S. Baker color *Bloomberg Businessweek* no4493 p48 O 3 2016

Precipitation (Meteorology)

See also

Rain & rainfall

California's Stressed Water System: A Primer J. Null *Weatherwise* v70 no1 p12 Ja/F 2017

Child growth sensitivity to rainfall variability color *Science* v355 no6325 p593 F 10 2017

PUDDLE JUMPING color *Runner's World* v52 no3 p31 Ap 2017

Volcanic Eruptions Play a Large Part *USA Today Magazine* v145 no2865 p2 Je 2017

Weatherwatch B. Rippey, J. B. Halverson et al *Weatherwise* v70 no2 p38 Mr/Ap 2017

Precision farming

BUYING USED PRECISION AG GEAR D. Mowitz *Successful Farming* v115 no1 p26 Ja 2017

POCKET PRICE GUIDE: Asking Prices for Precision Ag Displays *Successful Farming* v115 no1 p29 Ja 2017

Precision farming—Equipment & supplies

Precision Agriculture Technologies and Factors Affecting Their Adoption D. Schimmelpfennig color graph *Amber Waves: The Economics of Food, Farming, Natural Resources, & Rural America* p32 D 2016

Precision guided munitions

MASTER OF WARS K. Clarke color map *America* v216 no7 p12 Ap 3 2017

Precisioncraft Log & Timber Homes (Company)

10 Years in the Making color diag *Log Home Living* p20 2017 SpecialIssue

BEST WINDOW DESIGN color *Timber Home Living* p29 2017 SpecialIssue

Preckwinkle, Toni

WHY We LOVE CHICAGO bw cartoon color *Chicago* v66 no3 p75 Mr 2017

Preckwinkle, Toni Reed, 1947-

TONI'S SODA TAX SPIRAL C. FELSENTHAL color *Chicago* v66 no10 p21 O 2017

Precursor of the Cinema, A (Short story)

1883: New York City S. Millhauser *Lapham's Quarterly* v10 no2 p39 Spr 2017

Predation (Biology)

See also

Predation (Biology) in birds

Higher predation risk for insect prey at low latitudes and elevations S. Huang, B. Koane et al graph *Science* v356 no6339 p742 My 19 2017

Increase in predator-prey size ratios throughout the Phanerozoic history of marine ecosystems A. A. Klompmaker, M. Kowalewski et al diag *Science* v356 no6343 p1178 Je 16 2017

Killer drillers got bigger over time S. MILIUS color graph *Science News* v192 no1 p16 Ag 5 2017

A lot of life on planet Earth is awful and incredible *Science News* v192 no2 p2 Ag 19 2017

RESEARCH color *Science* v356 no6339 p712 My 19 2017

A Tangled Food Web A. Hadhazy *Natural History* v125 no2 p7 F 2017

The Truth About Frog Spit W. Lynch color *Canadian Wildlife* v23 no2 p46 My/Je 2017

Predation (Biology) in birds

Birds as Prey for Praying Mantises M. NYFFELER color *Natural History* v125 no11 p14 N 2017

The Genius of the Frigatebird W. Lynch color *Canadian Wildlife* v23 no4 p46 S/O 2017

Predator management

DAMAGE CONTROL J. R. Sullivan color *Field & Stream* v121 no8 p40 F/Mr 2017

Predatory animals

It's an Animal! It's a Plant! No, It's an Amazing Acquired Phototroph! STEALING PARTS FROM THEIR PREY, THESE HUNTERS TURN INTO FARMERS G. Schanker *Oceanus* v52 no2 p26 Spr 2017

TURBO-CHEETAH A. E. HURT cartoon color map *National Geographic Kids* no470 p16 My 2017

Predatory open access publishing

Fictive Science color *Weekly Standard* v22 no45 p3 Ag 7 2017

Medical Journals Have a Problem E. E. DEPREZ, C. CHEN et al color *Bloomberg Businessweek* no4536 p52 S 4 2017

Predatory Journals: Write, Submit, and Publish the Next Day R. HAKAMI *Skeptical Inquirer* v41 no5 p32 S/O 2017

Prediagnosis (Poem)

Prediagnosis S. Sax diag *New York Times Magazine* p17 Ag 6 2017

Prediction markets

Ask Your Customers for Predictions, Not Preferences J. W. Schlack *Harvard Business Review Digital Articles* p2 Ja 5 2015

Prediction models

Predictive Medicine Depends on Analytics J. Elton and A. Ural *Harvard Business Review Digital Articles* p2 O 23 2014

Prediction models—Software

Create a Strategy That Anticipates and Learns J. Elton and S. Arkell *Harvard Business Review Digital Articles* p2 O 6 2014

Predictions

THE GREAT UNKNOWN K. Stanley Robinson color *Scientific American* v315 no3 p80 S 2016

A MATTER OF DEGREES: America's long struggle with affirmative action M. S. Collins *Harper's Magazine* p69 S 2017

PHYSICS IN 2116 S. RICHARD *Physics Today* v69 no12 p39 D 2016

Predictive policing

CRIME FORECASTERS M. Hvistendahl color diag *Science* v353 no6307 p1484 S 30 2016

Predmore, Sheena

My Deluxe Dream Barn Will Have... color *Horse & Rider* v56 no4 p80 Ap 2017

Preece, Kathleen

ARE YOU FIREWISE? color *Cabin Living* p72 Ap 2017

FIRE-RESISTANT PLANTS color *Cabin Living* p73 Ap 2017

Preeclampsia

Circulating peptide prevents preeclampsia R. C. Wirka and T. Quertermous diag *Science* v357 no6352 p643 Ag 18 2017

ELABELA deficiency promotes preeclampsia and cardiovascular malformations in mice L. Ho, M. van Dijk et al color diag graph *Science* v357 no6352 p707 Ag 18 2017

Finding beauty in a mouse wheel of life E. S. Eaton color *Science News* v191 no7 p32 Ap 15 2017

Preexisting medical condition coverage

The War on Pre-Existing Conditions A. Adamczyk color *Money* v46 no8 p56 S 2017

Prefabricated house design & construction

Robots Will Build Your Next House P. Gopal and H. Perlberg color *Bloomberg Businessweek* no4519 p43 Ap 24 2017

Preferential ballot

Wind From Down East H. HERTZBERG *Nation* v303 no20 p4 N 14 2016

Preferred stocks

Get 5% or More From Preferreds D. FONDA color *Kiplinger's Personal Finance* v70 no12 p53 D 2016

Prefontaine, Andre

RCGS AND CPAC TEAM UP TO REACH CANADIANS A. Pope color *Canadian Geographic* v137 no2 p68 Mr/Ap 2017

Prefrontal cortex

A WEDDING bw *Women's Health* v14 no5 p78 Je 2017

Prefrontal cortex—Physiology

History of winning remodels thalamo-PFC circuit to reinforce social dominance T. Zhou, H. Zhu et al color *Science* v357 no6347 p162 Jl 14 2017

Pregenzer, Samantha

Make your closet feel twice as big! color *Redbook* p76 Ap 2017

Pregler, Art

Flying COWs and Other Drone Apps S. Berinato *Harvard Business Review Digital Articles* p2 My 17 2017

Pregnancy

See also

Pregnant women

Avoid Falling T. Reece cartoon *Parents* v92 no9 p163 S 2017

BUMP WATCH M. Gainsburg bw cartoon *Women's Health* v13 no10 p72 D 2016

Can I Keep A Baby My Boyfriend Doesn't Want? K. Anthony Appiah cartoon *New York Times Magazine* p22 Ag 6 2017

FIGHTING FOR A HEALTHY BLACK PREGNANCY D. McCLAIN bw color *Nation* v304 no7 p17 Mr 6 2017

HOW TO GET PREGNANT (AGAIN) L. Murray color *Health* v31 no1 p73 Ja 2017

"I made this decision for her" H. Kelly and S. G. Levy color *Glamour* v115 no4 p126 Ap 2017

IN UTERO POWER LIST D. Coggan color *Entertainment Weekly* no1454/1455 p21 F 24 2017

make room for dad J. MONINGER *Parents* v91 no6 p135 Je 2016

A Mighty Mess G. DOYLE color *O, The Oprah Magazine* p44 S 2017

A New Doubles Partner: Staying active during pregnancy—such as by hitting the court—can be beneficial to a woman's health color *Tennis* v53 no5 p14 S/O 2017

SERENA SERENE R. Haskell color *Vogue* v207 no9 p672 S 2017

"SOME FORM OF PUNISHMENT" N. LISS-SCHULTZ color

Mother Jones v42 no3 p48 My/Je 2017

This New Surgery Could Change Pregnancy Forever A. Sifferlin color *Time* v188 no16/17 p16 O 24 2016

WHAT IT REALLY TAKES TO GET PREGNANT AT 46 color *Redbook* p93 D 2016

WHEN I KNEW SHE WAS THE ONE color *Men's Health* v31 no10 p79 D 2016

Your True Stories IN 100 WORDS J. T. CIMICS, M. F. HEBERGER et al *Reader's Digest* v189 no1128 p36 Mr 2017

Pregnancy complications

China Needs Help Having Babies Li Hui and N. Khan bw *Bloomberg Businessweek* no4530 p15 Jl 17 2017

Pregnancy complications—Prevention

skin solutions R. GRUMMAN BENDER *Parents* v91 no9 p161 S 2016

Pregnancy—History

The Search for the Soul R. Sugg *History Today* v67 no4 p48 Ap 2017

Pregnancy—Physiological aspects

Pregnancy alters a mother's brain L. SANDERS color *Science News* v191 no2 p7 F 4 2017

Pregnancy—Psychological aspects

A prenatal sequence to Worry less and trust more A. Owens color *Yoga Journal* no294 p69 S 2017

Pregnant women

body-art q+a's T. RICE *Parents* v92 no5 p115 My 2017

BUMP WATCH M. Gainsburg bw cartoon *Women's Health* v13 no10 p72 D 2016

Data mount linking Zika, birth defects color *Science* v354 no6318 p1356 D 16 2016

DEATH BY PREGNANCY A. TODD bw color *Women's Health* v14 no9 p128 N 2017

DREAD RECKONING J. WARD color *O, The Oprah Magazine* p140 My 2017

Lest We Forget *Ms.* v27 no2 p6 Summ 2017

RIPPED FROM THE HEADLINES! cartoon color *Women's Health* v13 no10 p10 D 2016

This Just In J. Zorthian *Time* v188 no18 p21 O 31 2016

You've Come a Long Way, Baby ... Bump! M. LaScala *Parents* v91 no11 p15 N 2016

Pregnant women—Drug use

I miss my sister S. Sisco *Scholastic Choices* v32 no3 p10 N/D 2016

SHAKY START [Cover story] M. Rosen color graph map *Science News* v191 no11 p16 Je 10 2017

Pregnant women—Education

advice every new mom needs [Cover story] D. SPARROW, W. Fleisig et al color *Parents* v92 no7 p32 Jl 2017

Pregnant women—Employment

The Right and Wrong Ways to Help Pregnant Workers J. Clair, K. Jones et al *Harvard Business Review Digital Articles* p2 S 27 2016

Pregnant women—Health

Is This Pill the Future of Abortion? P. Zerwick color *Glamour* v114 no7 p134 Jl 2016

Pregnant women—Wounds & injuries

What to Extopect K. BUTLER cartoon diag graph *Mother Jones* v42 no1 p38 Ja/F 2017

Pregnant women—Legal status, laws, etc.

Pregnant Workers Have Rights, No Matter What the Supreme Court Says About UPS J. C. Williams and L. Morris *Harvard Business Review Digital Articles* p2 D 18 2014

Prehistoric antiquities

See also

Prehistoric settlements

Archaeologists find more signs of Babylonian destruction of Jerusalem M. Chabin color *Christian Century* v134 no18 p15 Ag 30 2017

Prehistoric burial

A PHARAOH'S LAST FLEET J. URBANUS color *Archaeology* v70 no1 p13 Ja/F 2017

Prehistoric peoples

'Green hell' has long been home for humans A. Curry color *Science* v354 no6310 p268 O 21 2016

Prehistoric peoples—America

Americas' first settlers debated B. BOWER color *Science News*

v191 no10 p7 My 27 2017

Prehistoric peoples—North America

STANDING STILL IN BERINGIA? N. SWAMINATHAN *Archaeology* v70 no3 p19 My/Je 2017

Prehistoric settlements

Foragers first settled Tibetan Plateau B. BOWER color *Science News* v191 no2 p8 F 4 2017

Permanent human occupation of the central Tibetan Plateau in the early Holocene M. C. Meyer, M. S. Aldenderfer et al bibl bw color diag *Science* v355 no6320 p1 Ja 6 2017

The Secrets Beneath a Suburb J. HATTAM color graph map *Discover* v38 no9 p14 N 2017

Seeing CHACO in a NEW LIGHT B. Bower color map *Science News* v191 no10 p16 My 27 2017

Prehistoric tools

See also

Banner stones

Consensual Tools C. De Robertis color *Weekly Standard* v22 no32 p2 My 1 2017

Preiser, Amy

BOTANICAL BEVERLY HILLS color *Sunset* v238 no5 p32 My 2017

Living the Country Life color *Southern Living* v52 no4 p108 Ap 2017

THE NEXT WAVE color *Sunset* v237 no5 p19 N 2016

AN OPEN INVITATION color *Southern Living* v52 no6 p84 Je 2017

untamed chic color *House Beautiful* v159 no7 p96 S 2017

Preisinger, Carol

BUILDING BLOCKS color *Golf Magazine* v59 no11 p52 N 2017

GIVE A SHORT STROKE THE FINGER color *Golf Magazine* v58 no11 p56 N 2016

WAIT FOR IT... color *Golf Magazine* v59 no8 p57 Ag 2017

Prejudices

See also

Antisemitism

Islamophobia

Racism

Sexism

43% of women have been asked to make tea in meetings *People Management* p32 My 2017

Don't Give Up on Unconscious Bias Training—Make It Better J. Emerson *Harvard Business Review Digital Articles* p2 Ap 28 2017

FIRST-TIME CALLER D. Smith cartoon *New Yorker* v92 no43 p20 Ja 2 2017

How to React to Biased Comments at Work J. Honesty, D. Maxfield et al *Harvard Business Review Digital Articles* p2 My 3 2017

Measuring and managing bias J. Berg color *Science* v357 no6354 p849 S 1 2017

Overcome Your Biases and Build a Great Team R. Gupta *Harvard Business Review Digital Articles* p2 D 25 2014

Run Meetings That Are Fair to Introverts, Women, and Remote Workers R. Cullinan *Harvard Business Review Digital Articles* p2 Ap 29 2016

Unconscious Bias in Parks and Recreation A. Holliday and A. Rajagopal-Durbin *Parks & Recreation* v52 no2 p32 F 2017

Wikipedia Is More Biased Than Britannica, but Don't Blame the Crowd W. Frick *Harvard Business Review Digital Articles* p2 D 3 2014

Prejudices—Prevention

BATTLING BIAS J. Couzin-Frankel color *Science* v356 no6339 p686 My 19 2017

Prekop, Zak, 1979-

ZAK PREKOP K. MacMillan cartoon *Art in America* v104 no11 p124 D 2016

Prell, Mark

Illuminating SNAP Performance Using the Power of Administrative Data *Amber Waves: The Economics of Food, Farming, Natural Resources, & Rural America* p14 N 2016

PRELLE, MONICA

MOUNTAIN MAN [Cover story] cartoon color *Runner's World* v52 no4 p16 My 2017

THE ROAD TO GLORY color *Runner's World* v52 no8 p18 S 2017

RUN AWAY! [Cover story] color *Runner's World* v52 no7 p54 Ag 2017

Preller, James

Better Off Undead *Publishers Weekly* v264 no38 p71 S 18 2017

Prelude Fertility (Company)

END OF THE BIOLOGICAL CLOCK [Cover story] M. HELFT color graph *Forbes* v198 no6 p84 N 8 2016

Premature infants

ARTIFICIAL WOMB FOR PREEMIES? E. Engelhaupt color *National Geographic* v232 no3 p24 S 2017

Bikers Who Deliver Breast Milk S. James color *Parents* v92 no5 p14 My 2017

bursting with goodness A. PALANJIAN color *Parents* v92 no8 p96 Ag 2017

Hope for Moms Who Need it Most S. Maglente color *Parents* v92 no7 p31 Jl 2017

Pregnancy, Interrupted N. SCHARPING color *Discover* v38 no8 p10 O 2017

Premature infants—Diseases—Prevention

Pioneering study images activity in fetal brains G. Miller bw *Science* v355 no6321 p117 Ja 13 2017

Premature infants—Medical care

Faux womb keeps preemie lambs alive T. HESMAN SAEY color *Science News* v191 no10 p6 My 27 2017

Premature infants—Prevention

A Nutrient to Avoid Early Delivery color *Parents* v92 no3 p72 Mr 2017

trendWATCH C. CROMER color *Better Nutrition* v78 no12 p10 D 2016

Premature labor

Ask the Expert R. Allen *Atlanta* v56 no7 p220 N 2016

Premature Burial, The (Short story)

DUST TO DUST E. A. Poe *Lapham's Quarterly* v10 no3 p118 Summ 2017

Premenstrual syndrome

SOS FOR PMS J. Martin color *Amazing Wellness* v8 no2 p26 Spr 2016

Premier (Company)

Premier 220 SunSation *Boating World* v38 no1 p62 Ja 2017

Preminger, Noah

NOAH PREMINGER: Distinctive Character K. Micallef color *Downbeat* v84 no8 p50 Ag 2017

Prenatal care

Crisis Pregnancy Centers in Crisis J. D. J. HAGEN color *Weekly Standard* v23 no4 p26 O 2 2017

Zika rewrites maternal immunization ethics J. Cohen color *Science* v357 no6348 p241 Jl 21 2017

Prenatal care—United States

How Mayo Clinic Is Simplifying Prenatal Care for Low-Risk Patients Y. B. Tobah and A. Famuyide *Harvard Business Review Digital Articles* p2 Je 19 2017

Prendergast, David

Femtosecond x-ray spectroscopy of an electrocyclic ring-opening reaction diag graph *Science* v356 no6333 p54 Ap 7 2017

Prentice, Jim, 1956-2016

BAD NEWS color *Maclean's* v129 no43 p9 O 31 2016

Prentice, Michelle

Big Dream, Tiny Cottage Z. Gowen color *Southern Living* v52 no3 p82 Mr 2017

PRENTIS, NICOLA

why poop changes *Parents* v92 no8 p130 Ag 2017

Prentiss, Linda

When I Was a Horse-Crazy Kid, I... color *Horse & Rider* v56 no2 p72 F 2017

Prentiss, Sean

Crossing the Plains with Bruno *Orion Magazine* v35 no4/5 p109 Jl-O 2016

Raising Wild color *Orion Magazine* v36 no2 p58 Mr/Ap 2017

Preoptic area

Thirst-associated preoptic neurons encode an aversive motivational drive W. E. Allen, L. A. Denardo et al diag *Science* v357 no6356 p1149 S 15 2017

Preparedness

See also

Civil defense readiness

Survival

Unprepared: Rookie Snowmobilers Messing Up B. JOHNSON *Idaho Magazine* v16 no8 p54 My 2017

Prepon, Laura, 1980-—Interviews

Might As Well ... Jump S. Cristobal and S. Simon color *InStyle* v24 no7 p124 Jl 2017

Preprints

How biologists pioneered preprints—with paper and postage J. Kaiser bw *Science* v357 no6358 p1348 S 29 2017

Preprint ecosystems J. Berg color *Science* v357 no6358 p1331 S 29 2017

Presbyopia

STAYING FOCUSED AFTER 40 G. Aubrey color *Maclean's* v129 no42 p34 O 24 2016

Presbyopia—Treatment

Put Down the Reading Glasses color *Prevention* v69 no4 p8 Ap 2017

Presbyterian Church

Dear potential pastor W. Collier *Christian Century* v134 no20 p28 S 27 2017

Lessons from the Keller controversy M. C. Barnes *Christian Century* v134 no17 p35 Ag 16 2017

Presbyterian Church (U.S.A.)

People color *Christian Century* v134 no4 p18 F 15 2017

Taking risks to heal hurt C. H. Merritt *Christian Century* v133 no23 p45 N 9 2016

Presbyterian Homes Inc.

Meant to Be *Atlanta* v56 no9 p143 Ja 2017

Presbyterians—Attitudes

Taking risks to heal hurt C. H. Merritt *Christian Century* v133 no23 p45 N 9 2016

Preschool children

EARLY WRITING EXPERIENCES: What every teacher and parent should know about why young children need to write D. Wells Rowe *Literacy Today (2411-7862)* v35 no2 p30 S/O 2017

Preschool children's attitudes

CHARACTER RECOGNITION: Private preschools are judging the "character" of applicants as well as their aptitude-even when children are as young as three G. Cook *Washingtonian Magazine* v53 no1 p129 O 2017

Preschool children—Education

Kids' learning curve not so smooth B. BOWER *Science News* v190 no11 p6 N 26 2016

Preschool education

Cognitive science in the field: A preschool intervention durably enhances intuitive but not formal mathematics M. R. Dillon, H. Kannan et al chart color diag graph *Science* v357 no6346 p47 Jl 7 2017

Preschool education—Evaluation

NO EASY ANSWERS J. Mervis color *Science* v355 no6325 p568 F 10 2017

Preschools

Church, State & Playgrounds R. W. Garnett color *Commonweal* v114 no14 p12 S 8 2017

Fall Fumbles color *Consumer Reports* v82 no10 p67 O 2017

Prescott (Ariz.)—Description & travel

3 Days in... Prescott, Ariz G. R. Schiavino color *American Cowboy* v23 no5 p44 F/Mr 2017

PRESCOTT LAKES LOOP K. MONTGOMERY *Arizona Highways* v93 no4 p52 Ap 2017

PRESCOTT *Los Angeles Magazine* p134 Mr 2017

Ultimate Peak-to-Desert Adventure color *Trail Rider* v29 no1 p36 Ja/F 2017

Prescott (Ariz.)—History

from our archives [April 1964] *Arizona Highways* v96 no7 p10 Jl 2017

Prescott, Brian T.

Improving Alignment between Educational Supply and Labor Market Needs *Change* v49 no1 p34 Ja/F 2017

Prescott, Dakota, 1993-

America's QB M. J. MOONEY color *GQ: Gentlemen's Quarterly* v97 no9 p168 S 2017

FAN ADVICE FROM THE TEXANIST D. COURTNEY *Texas Monthly* v45 no9 p66 S 2017

WHO DAK? [Cover story] P. Thamel color *Sports Illustrated* v125 no13 p24 O 17 2016

WHY THE 'BOYS ARE BACK D. SOLOMON *Texas Monthly*

v45 no9 p64 S 2017

Prescott, Dennis

Eat Delicious: 125 Recipes for Your Daily Dose of Awesome *Publishers Weekly* v264 no8 p79 F 20 2017

Prescription of drugs

DRUG ADVERTISING J. PEARSON, E. CRONQUIST et al color *Scientific American* v315 no3 p5 S 2016

Preseason (Sports)

Ambassadors of Defiance D. ZIRIN color *Progressive* v81 no4 p68 Ap/My 2017

Masquerade Ball M. Rosenberg color *Sports Illustrated* v127 no6 p60 Ag 28 2017

Playing Catch-up T. Keith color *Sports Illustrated* v127 no3 p14 Jl 24 2017

Preseason (Sports)—Charts, diagrams, etc.

Bracket of Brackets T. Keith color diag *Sports Illustrated* v125 no16 p18 N 14 2016

Present, The (Theatrical production)

CHEKHOV MATES A. Green bw *Vogue* v206 no12 p252 D 2016

POP STARS color *Vogue* v206 no12 p230 D 2016

Winter Preview M. Schulman cartoon *New Yorker* v92 no37 p26 N 14 2016

Preservation of airplanes

STAGGERWINGS AND SODA BOTTLES M. Lunken color *Flying* v144 no8 p67 Ag 2017

Volunteers launch Cold War icon back to life S. WOODMAN KANSTEINER color *Nebraska Life* v21 no5 p18 S/O 2017

Preservation of antiquities

Keeping history close K. INGRAM color *Maclean's* v130 no8 p13 S 2017

THE SALVATION OF MOSUL: An Iraqi archaeologist braved ISIS snipers and booby-trapped ruins to rescue cultural treasures in the city and nearby legendary Nineveh and Nimrud J. HAMMER *Smithsonian* v48 no6 p30 O 2017

Preservation of architecture

See also

Adaptive reuse of buildings

Preservation of churches

Preservation of dwellings

Preservation of historic buildings

Preservation of library buildings

Preservation of theaters

Delayed Gratification J. Berube and D. Berube color *Arts & Crafts Homes & the Revival* v12 no5 p18 Wint 2018

editor's letter color *Architectural Digest* no11 p28 N 1 2017

HOW TO PREPARE FOR A SENSITIVE RENOVATION J. Eifler color *Arts & Crafts Homes & the Revival* v12 no4 p58 Fall 2017

INSIDE TRACK K. SELZER color *Better Homes & Gardens* v95 no9 p76 S 2017

Never Too Late To Renovate D. Hochman color *AARP: The Magazine* v60 no5A p32 Ag/S 2017

Preservation of archival materials

Documented: What some of the world's most historic documents tell us about the documents of the future J. Janes color *Publishers Weekly* v264 no29 p15 Jl 17 2017

Preservation of churches

Champ Out in Church *British Heritage Travel* v38 no3 p9 My/Je 2017

Frank Lloyd Wright's Unity Temple Restored J. GAUER *Architectural Record* v205 no7 p36 Jl 2017

Preservation of dwellings

GEORGIAN BY CANDLELIGHT R. COLE color *Old House Journal* v45 no6 p24 S 2017

Restoring a Log Finish J. Cooper color *Cabin Living* p14 Ag 2017

Under the Influence P. Poore *Old House Journal* v45 no6 p8 S 2017

Preservation of food

See also

Preservation of fruit

Salting of food

Smoking (Cooking)

PRESERVING HOMEGROWN PRODUCE: Putting up the garden bounty at Polyface Farms is a family affair J. Salatin *Mother Earth News* no284 p53 O/N 2017

STRAWBERRIES PRESERVED D. Stone color *National Geographic* v232 no5 p20 N 2017

Preservation of fruit

Not Far from the Tree color *Canadian Wildlife* v23 no4 p16 S/O 2017

Preservation of gardens

Ha-has & other cool beans P. Poore cartoon *Arts & Crafts Homes & the Revival* v12 no3 p8 Summ 2017

Preservation of historic buildings

At Long Last, Labrouste: A newly restored masterwork reopens in Paris B. BERGDOLL color map *Architectural Record* v205 no8 p52 Ag 2017

McMANSIONS TO SPARE A. HOAK and L. WILLIAMSON color *Chicago* v66 no11 p22 N 2017

perspective: interiors T. METZ color map *Architectural Record* v205 no8 p33 Ag 2017

Preservation of historic buildings—United States

BOOM TOWN A. Brownlee *Cincinnati Magazine* v50 no12 p56 S 2017

Preservation of historic sites

Berlin debates restoring cross atop City Palace T. Heneghan *Christian Century* v134 no14 p16 Jl 5 2017

Preservation of kitchens

DESIGN MOTIFS FOR A KITCHEN T. Guarino color *Old House Journal* v45 no6 p32 S 2017

English Sensibility B. D. Coleman color *Old House Journal* v45 no6 p74 S 2017

MY DIY KITCHEN RENO: How I built my dream kitchen on a budget-no pricey professional designer needed K. Bennell *Washingtonian Magazine* v52 no11 p148 Ag 2017

Preservation of library buildings

How Citizen Action Saved the New York Public Library S. SHERMAN color *Nation* v305 no9 p20 O 16 2017

Preservation of monuments

Needed, A Public Monuments Plan cartoon *New Orleans Magazine* v51 no8 p22 Je 2017

What to do about the Monuments cartoon *New Orleans Magazine* v51 no7 p20 My 2017

Preservation of painting

Dusting off some faces S. PROUDFOOT color *Maclean's* p16 Je 2017

Preservation of pottery

One man's trash J. Bleem color *U.S. Catholic* v82 no7 p50 Jl 2017

Preservation of theaters

BOOM TOWN A. Brownlee *Cincinnati Magazine* v50 no12 p56 S 2017

Preservation of video tapes

The First Shock Jock K. Cook *Smithsonian* v48 no3 p16 Je 2017

Preservation of windows

Great Panes D. Mitchell color *Log Home Living* v34 no7 p26 S 2017

Preservation of wood

THE PERFECT FINISH P. MARTIN color *Popular Mechanics* p100 Jl 2017

Preservationists (Historic preservation)

A Moon Museum B. Scriber color *National Geographic* v232 no2 p62 Ag 2017

TALE OF A Charleston SINGLE HOUSE S. GROSS and S. DALEY color *Old House Journal* v45 no1 p24 F 2017

President Has Never Said the Word Black, The (Poem)

The President Has Never Said the Word Black M. Parker *New York Times Magazine* p23 O 2 2016

Presidential administrations

PRESIDENT TRUMP E. OSNOS cartoon color *New Yorker* v92 no30 p38 S 26 2016

YOU SHOULD GET TO KNOW DINA POWELL color *Fortune* v175 no6 p10 My 1 2017

Presidential administrations—History—21st century

The White House Survival Guide M. Scherer, Z. J. Miller et al color *Time* v189 no4 p30 Ja 23 2017

Why President Trump Is Struggling to Staff His Government P. Elliott and Z. J. Miller color *Time* v189 no11 p9 Mr 27 2017

Presidential candidates

ACCORDING TO THE LATEST POLL... P. SMITH and G. C. TYLER *New York Times Upfront* v149 no3 p16 O 10 2016

ALL THE PRESIDENTS' MENUS B. SCHOTT bw chart graph *Bon Appetit* v61 no11 p42 N 2016

Brazilians Look for a Trump of Their Own B. Douglas and D. Biller cartoon *Bloomberg Businessweek* no4508 p15 Ja 23 2017

Presidents—Dwellings

1800: Washington, DC A. S. Adams *Lapham's Quarterly* v10 no1 p64 Wint 2017

Unpresidential Palaces T. John color *Time* v189 no11 p14 Mr 27 2017

Presidents—Elections

See also

Presidents—United States—Election

ALL THE PRESIDENTS' MENUS B. SCHOTT bw chart graph *Bon Appetit* v61 no11 p42 N 2016

AMERICAN NIGHTMARE W. Yang *Harper's Magazine* v334 no2001 p27 F 2017

The Best of Intentions B. FEWELL *American Conservative* v16 no1 p23 Ja/F 2017

The Big Forces of History C. LAYNE il *American Conservative* v16 no1 p10 Ja/F 2017

Capitalism and Climate C. RORKE *American Conservative* v16 no1 p18 Ja/F 2017

Cover Story G. Howard *New York Times Magazine* p15 Ja 15 2017

DEMOCRACY HOW? C. Su *Harper's Magazine* v334 no2001 p35 F 2017

Down-Ballot Blues J. COST *Weekly Standard* v22 no8 p9 O 31 2016

Down-Ballot Hopefuls J. NICHOLS *Nation* v303 no18 p6 O 31 2016

THE DREAM OF THE ENEMY C. Robin *Harper's Magazine* v334 no2001 p26 F 2017

EASY CHAIR W. Kirn *Harper's Magazine* v334 no2001 p5 F 2017

Editor's Note: Why We Let Underwhelming Colleges Host the Debates *Washington Monthly* p1 S/O 2016

Florida M. Valdes *New York Times Magazine* p44 N 20 2016

HYMN TO HARM CITY L. Jackson *Harper's Magazine* v334 no2001 p31 F 2017

IN END TIME S. White *Harper's Magazine* v334 no2001 p36 F 2017

LESSONS FROM THE LAST FIGHT S. Schulman *Harper's Magazine* v334 no2001 p34 F 2017

Let's make this choice easier for you S. FESCHUK color *Maclean's* v129 no42 p65 O 24 2016

LIBIDINAL POLITICS K. Forrester *Harper's Magazine* v334 no2001 p30 F 2017

Pennsylvania E. Bazelon *New York Times Magazine* p47 N 20 2016

Predator and Strongman J. NICHOLS color *Nation* v303 no18 p3 O 31 2016

Presiding over Chaos L. SMITH color *Weekly Standard* v22 no10 p10 N 14 2016

Pundits Told Dems to Spurn Sanders for 'Electable' Clinton A. Johnson *Extra!* v29 no10 p3 D 2016

The Rules of the Game: A New Electoral System E. Maskin and A. Sen cartoon chart *New York Review of Books* v64 no1 p8 Ja 19 2017

Sound bites *Extra!* v29 no10 p2 D 2016

TERMS OF ENGAGEMENT T. Barker *Harper's Magazine* v334 no2001 p28 F 2017

A Time of Transition D. McCarthy *American Conservative* v16 no1 p5 Ja/F 2017

TROUBLE IN OHIO D. D. GUTTENPLAN color *Nation* v303 no18 p18 O 31 2016

TRUMP: A RESISTER'S GUIDE *Harper's Magazine* v334 no2001 p25 F 2017

Utah M. Friberg *New York Times Magazine* p42 N 20 2016

Virginia G. Howard *New York Times Magazine* p40 N 20 2016

Presidents—Elections—Finance

Party at the End of the World C. CALDWELL color *Weekly Standard* v22 no10 p23 N 14 2016

Presidents—Family

The Trump Effect Cuts Both Ways C. Melby color *Bloomberg Businessweek* no4523 p27 My 22 2017

Presidents—France

France's Golden Boy Loses His Luster T. John color *Time* v190 no9 p10 S 4 2017

Jacques Chirac in New Orleans E. Laborde cartoon *New Orleans*

Magazine v51 no8 p152 Je 2017

Presidents—Inauguration

Jackie Evancho *Indianapolis Monthly* p23 My 2017

Retrospect S. Potter *Weatherwise* v70 no1 p10 Ja/F 2017

This American Carnage S. MARCHE color *Walrus* v14 no3 p36 Ap 2017

Presidents—Inauguration—Social aspects

The Top Global Risks for 2017, a Year of Geopolitical Recession I. Bremmer color *Time* v189 no3 p8 Ja 16 2017

Presidents—Iran—Elections

Movers K. Stock color *Bloomberg Businessweek* no4523 p13 My 22 2017

Presidents—Mexico

MEXICO DOES NOT BELIEVE IN WALLS P. NIETO *Vital Speeches of the Day* v83 no3 p78 Mr 2017

Presidents—Mexico—Elections

Let's Make Mexico Great Again N. Cattan color *Bloomberg Businessweek* no4510 p15 F 6 2017

Presidents—Philippines—Biography

THE TOUGH GUY A. CHEN cartoon *New Yorker* v92 no38 p66 N 21 2016

Presidents—Public relations

In South Africa, more calls for Zuma to go A. Egan color *America* v216 no12 p15 My 29 2017

Presidents—Russia

The Eurasian Judo Master: Vladimir Putin uses martial-arts tactics to undergird his dangerous view of the clash of civilizations L. Aron *Commentary* v143 no1 p38 Ja 2017

Presidents—Staff

The Voice in His Ear M. WARREN color *Weekly Standard* v22 no34 p20 My 15 2017

Presidents—Term of office

The Trump Era Begins F. BARNES color *Weekly Standard* v22 no20 p9 Ja 30 2017

Presidents—Transition periods

MOVING OUT, MOVING IN D. McMillen *Prologue* v48 no4 p36 Wint 2016

NARA's Role in a Presidential Transition *Prologue* v48 no3 p2 Fall 2016

Presidents—United States

See also

African American presidents

82 MINUTES WITH...Sally Quinn B. WALLACE *New York* v49 no26 p16 D 26 2016

AMERICA FIRST D. TRUMP *Vital Speeches of the Day* v83 no3 p66 Mr 2017

Andy Jackson's Populism R. W. MERRY il *American Conservative* v16 no3 p23 My/Je 2017

Apathy in the Executive G. ALEXANDER and Y. LEVIN color *Weekly Standard* v22 no14 p24 D 12 2016

Arm's Length W. Morris *New York Times Magazine* p11 Ja 22 2017

Bare, Ruined Choirs *Commentary* v141 no10 p1 D 2016

Before Hillary F. Wiley *American History* v51 no6 p34 F 2017

The Better-than-Monroe Doctrine color *Weekly Standard* v22 no24 p2 F 27 2017

The Change We Believed In L. Lalami il *Nation* v304 no1 p8 Ja 2 2017 The Obama Years

CLIMATE AND ENERGY POLICY, AT HOME AND ABROAD *Vital Speeches of the Day* v82 no12 p365 D 2016

Comments img *New York* v49 no21 p10 O 17 2016

A disarmament of the heart B. Haile color *U.S. Catholic* v82 no2 p10 F 2017

The Education of Barack Obama D. GOLDSTEIN bw color diag *Nation* v304 no1 p64 Ja 2 2017 The Obama Years

Farewell, Obama? R. LONG color *National Review* v69 no2 p23 F 6 2017

The Folly of Wilsonism *American Conservative* v16 no3 p5 My/Je 2017

For the Record color *Time* v189 no3 p6 Ja 30 2017

Giving Madison His Due R. BURGESS color *Weekly Standard* v22 no30 p14 Ap 10 2017

The 'Global Order' Myth A. J. BACEVICH *American Conservative* v16 no3 p19 My/Je 2017

Going Off the Rails? W. S. LIND *American Conservative* v16 no3 p8 My/Je 2017

no26 p11 Mr 13 2017

Trump's 'Presidential' Moment: Turning a Massacre Into Political Gold A. Johnson *Extra!* v30 no3 p1 Ap 2017

Weapons of Mass Distraction D. D. GUTTENPLAN color *Nation* v304 no6 p8 F 27 2017

Presidents—United States—Psychology

Trump and the Pathology of Narcissism A. Morris color *Rolling Stone* no1285 p42 Ap 20 2017

Presidents—United States—Staff

NORMALIZE THIS M. Leibovich color *New York Times Magazine* p40 N 27 2016

Presidents—United States—Transition periods

Russia's Election Meddling Hampers Trump Transition M. Calabresi *Time* v188 no27-28 p16 D 26 2016

Trump Takes Over P. Elliott and Z. J. Miller color *Time* v188 no22-23 p24 N/D 2016

Presidents—United States—Charts, diagrams, etc.

Oval Office science bw *Science* v354 no6310 p276 O 21 2016

Presidents—United States—Election—2016—Charts, diagrams, etc.

JAIL BAIT cartoon *Mother Jones* v41 no6 p7 N/D 2016

The Results: President E. Barone color diag map *Time* v188 no21 p12 N 21 2016

Presidio de Nuestra Señora del Pilar de Los Adaes Site (La.)

OFF THE GRID M. GRUNBERG-BANYASZ color *Archaeology* v70 no5 p10 S/O 2017

Presley, Elvis, 1935-1977

Elvis In the Heart of America J. Meacham and A. Rumer color *Time* v190 no7 p38 Ag 21 2017

Elvis, outside of Flagstaff/Driving a camper van/Looking for meaning in a cloud mass/Sees the face of Joseph Stalin/And is disheartened N. Abebe *New York Times Magazine* p15 Jl 23 2017

FEIST L. Greenblatt color *Entertainment Weekly* no1463/1464 p104 Ap/My 2017

Is It Here to Stay? *Commentary* v142 no2 p1 S 2016

Music Lovers' Mecca M. WHITE color *AARP: The Magazine* v59 no5A p59 Ag/S 2016

WHY I OWE MY NEW JOB TO ELVIS B. RILEY *Atlanta* v57 no6 p18 O 2017

Presnell, Brian

Pot Stuff B. COOPER *Indianapolis Monthly* p27 My 2017

PreSonus Audio Electronics Inc.

PreSonus Studio 192 Mobile M. Kern color *Downbeat* v84 no2 p98 F 2017

Presque Isle (Me.)

Something New Under the Sun color diag *Log Home Living* p36 2017 SpecialIssue

Press

See also

Mass media & politics

News agencies

Presidents in the press

Press & politics

Beijing Dandelion Children's Book House color *Publishers Weekly* v264 no12 p12 Mr 20 2017

China Children's Press & Publication Group color *Publishers Weekly* v264 no12 p16 Mr 20 2017

The Danger of Governing on Social Media N. Gibbs color *Time* v189 no19 p6 My 22 2017

NOTES FROM THE VRG SCIENTIFIC DEPARTMENT *Vegetarian Journal* v35 no4 p23 2016

NOTES FROM THE VRG SCIENTIFIC DEPARTMENT *Vegetarian Journal* v36 no1 p29 2017

Press & politics

Jefferson's Warning to the White House N. Gibbs color *Time* v189 no5 p4 F 13 2017

PRESS, JESSICA

Be a hero to homeless veterans color *Redbook* p114 D 2016

Don't Get Burned! *Scholastic Choices* v32 no8 p12 My 2017

How any one of us can stop bullying color *Redbook* p109 F 2017

How Do You Say "Yum" Around the World? *Scholastic Choices* p6 O 2017

The League of Extraordinary LOSERS [Cover story] *Scholastic Choices* v32 no5 p10 F 2017

Let's celebrate AMAZING MOMS bw color *Redbook* p110 My

2017

MAKE SOME AMAZING MEMORIES color *Redbook* p88 Jl/ Ag 2017

Make this the best year for every kid color *Redbook* p110 S 2017

The most American way to help others color *Redbook* p108 N 2017

Noah Is Blind *Scholastic Choices* v32 no3 p16 N/D 2016

Sex WHILE PARENTING color *Parents* v92 no9 p106 S 2017

THEY CHANGED THEIR SCHOOL. Could You? *Scholastic Choices* v33 no1 p6 S 2017

This Cupcake Could Kill Me...But This One Won't! *Scholastic Choices* v32 no5 p20 F 2017

Turning loss into something beautiful color *Redbook* p110 Mr 2017

"We're standing up for respect" *Scholastic Choices* v32 no7 p6 Ap 2017

Press, Joy

Exile From Brooklyn: The writer Danzy Senna moved to California because New York felt like "a book party that never ended." She doesn't mean that in a good way img *New York* v50 no15 p66 Jl 24 2017

Press conferences

No Urge to Merge A. Greenblatt *Governing* v31 no1 p12 O 2017

SCOTLAND'S CHOICE: A SECOND INDEPENDENCE REFERENDUM *Vital Speeches of the Day* v83 no5 p149 My 2017

SONNY NIGHTS, NORMAN DAYS P. CARLSON *American History* v51 no6 p14 F 2017

Press criticism

Mr. President, I Demand You Do Your Duty and Insult Me. Please? J. Stein color *Time* v190 no5 p64 Jl 31 2017

Press releases

Soundbites *Extra!* v30 no4 p2 My 2017

What I Learned From 10 Years of Doing PR for Apple C. Craig *Harvard Business Review Digital Articles* p2 Jl 27 2016

Press secretaries

Staying On Message With the First Lady R. ITO *Los Angeles Magazine* p19 Ja 2017

Press secretaries—Interviews

PARODY *Weekly Standard* v22 no41 p44 Jl 3 2017

Press—Congresses

University Presses: More Relevant than Ever E. Nawotka color *Publishers Weekly* v264 no25 p12 Je 19 2017

Presser, Stanley

Contingent valuation: Flawed logic? color *Science* v357 no6349 p363 Jl 28 2017

Putting a value on injuries to natural assets: The BP oil spill chart *Science* v356 no6335 p253 Ap 21 2017

Presser Aiden, Aviva

De novo assembly of the Aedes aegypti genome using Hi-C yields chromosome-length scaffolds chart color diag *Science* v356 no6333 p92 Ap 7 2017

Pressler, Jessica

103 MINUTES WITH ... Amanda Chantal Bacon img *New York* v49 no25 p24 D 12 2016

58 MINUTES WITH...: Alec Baldwin: Swanning through the Hamptons with the presidential impersonator *New York* v50 no16 p24 Ag 7 2017

Chill lessons from Kristen Bell [Cover story] color *Redbook* p104 O 2017

CRANSTON COMES ALIVE [Cover story] bw color *Esquire* p80 N 2017

home & help img *New York* p96 Mr 6 2017

Let's See How Alive We Can Be img *New York* v49 no24 p62 N 28 2016

Lo, and Behold img *New York* v49 no22 p93 O 31 2016

LONG ON TRUMP img *New York* p26 Ja 23 2017

MaD MaN bw color *Esquire* p70 My 2017

MILEY'S SUMMER OF Love color *Harper's Bazaar* no3655 p146 Ag 2017

MODERN ROMANTIC *Smithsonian* v47 no8 p42 D 2016

On Wall Street, A Bipolar Diagnosis *New York* v49 no23 p26 N 14 2016

Ryan Lochte img *New York* v49 no21 p18 O 17 2016

SHE CAME FROM INSTAGRAM img *New York* v50 no8 p52 Ap 17 2017

THE THANKLESS TASK OF BEING MICHAEL MOORE img

New York v50 no18 p40 S 4 2017

Pressler, Tania

Emergence and spread of a human-transmissible multidrug-resistant nontuberculous mycobacterium bibl diag graph *Science* v354 no6313 p751 N 11 2016

Pressley, Ayanna

AYANNA PRESSLEY L. N. Williams color map *Essence* v47 no7 p62 N 2016

Pressley, Daron

MEET 'MR. WEALTH MANAGEMENT' JUSTIN BINION color *Black Enterprise* v47 no8 p36 Jl/Ag 2017

MEET 'MR. WINGONOMICS' MARK A. WINGO color *Black Enterprise* v47 no5 p34 Ja/F 2017

Meet "The Wine Maker" André Hueston Mack chart color *Black Enterprise* v47 no4 p33 N/D 2016

Pressman, Aaron

THE 2017 Fortune Crystal Ball color diag *Fortune* v174 no7 p11 D 1 2016

93 AT&T color *Fortune* v175 no4 p124 Mr 15 2017

THE AT&T-TIME WARNER MERGER (UNLESS ...) diag *Fortune* v174 no8 p20 D 15 2016

BETTING IT ALL, WITH BRAND-NEW CHIPS color diag *Fortune* v176 no1 p90 Jl 1 2017

CHANGE THE WORLD !!!! color diag map *Fortune* v176 no4 p74 S 15 2017

DREAM WEAVER color *Fortune* v176 no3 p74 S 1 2017

FORTY UNDER FORTY 2017 color *Fortune* v176 no3 p62 S 1 2017

THE IPHONE DECADE color diag *Fortune* v175 no7 p23 Je 1 2017

MINING COMEDY GOLD color *Fortune* v176 no3 p70 S 1 2017

THE MOBILE DATA SQUEEZE IS COMING diag *Fortune* v174 no8 p16 D 15 2016

THE NEW IPHONE HAS COMPETITION color *Fortune* v176 no5 p18 O 1 2017

THE NEW WORLD OF WATCHES color *Fortune* v175 no5 p12 Ap 1 2017

VERIZON'S STRIKE SETTLEMENT color *Fortune* v174 no8 p20 D 15 2016

WAITING ON THE WEARABLE REVOLUTION diag *Fortune* v175 no2 p14 F 1 2017

WORLD'S 50 GREATEST LEADERS [Cover story] color *Fortune* v175 no5 p46 Ap 1 2017

YOUTH REVOLT color *Fortune* v176 no3 p64 S 1 2017

PRESSNER, AMANDA

Amazing Animals color map *National Geographic Kids* no471 p12 Je/Jl 2017

Press—United States

Best press he's ever had L. Grove bw cartoon color *Columbia Journalism Review* v56 no2 p68 Fall 2017

Can the First Amendment save us? L. C. Bollinger *Columbia Journalism Review* v56 no2 p10 Fall 2017

A crisis of relevance J. Gibson color *Columbia Journalism Review* v56 no2 p23 Fall 2017

Fact: J. Tanz diag *Wired* v25 no3 p48 Mr 2017

The Fake News President W. DURST cartoon *Progressive* v81 no4 p66 Ap/My 2017

Foreign Intrigue color *Weekly Standard* v23 no5 p3 O 9 2017

JUST THE NEWS, PLEASE color *Vanity Fair* v59 no6 p46 My 2017

Reporting the facts does not make the press "the opposition." E. Markey *America* v216 no8 p10 Ap 17 2017

Stick Up for the Press B. LUEDERS *Progressive* v81 no4 p8 Ap/My 2017

Pressure cooking

Mixing Bowl color *O, The Oprah Magazine* p146 N 2017

Pressure cooking—Equipment & supplies

ONE-POT WONDERS color *Good Housekeeping* v264 no2 p121 F 2017

Pressure gages

What Is the Proper Brake System Pressure Range, and How Should it Be Checked? M. Davis color *Hot Rod* v69 no12 p86 D 2016

Pressure groups

Concerns about Cat Care *Catnip* v24 no10 p16 O 2016

Pressure washing

Last Look A. Greenblatt *Governing* v30 no9 p64 Je 2017

TIME TO RE-STAIN THE DECK color *Cabin Living* p70 Mr 2017

Pressure washing—Equipment & supplies

PRESSURE WASHERS R. ROMANSKI color *Popular Mechanics* p28 My 2017

Presti, Sam

BRICKTOWN Bricolage L. Jenkins color *Sports Illustrated* v126 no11 p76 Ap 17-24 2017

Prestige Yachts (Company)

Prestige 460 J. Y. Wood color *Power & Motoryacht* v34 no6 p32 Je 2017

Preston, Benjamin

THE FIX IS IN chart color graph *Car & Driver* v63 no1 p50 Jl 2017

INFRASTRUCTURE RUPTURE graph *Car & Driver* v63 no4 p26 O 2017

PATENTLY ABSURD? bw *Car & Driver* v62 no6 p26 D 2016

Preston, Douglas

Digging Politics J. J. MILLER *National Review* v69 no8 p42 My 2017

Fiction meets fact in science adventure tale E. Wayman color *Science News* v191 no2 p28 F 4 2017

Temples of Doom B. I. KOERNER *New York Times Book Review* p17 Ja 22 2017

Unhappy Trails: A look at the Donners and the dark side of Manifest Destiny *New York Times Book Review* p16 Jl 9 2017

PRESTON, HARRY F.

The Case for a Teacher Like Me cartoon *Education Digest* v82 no9 p4 My 2017

PRESTON, JILL

THE EVOLUTION OF PLANTS *BioScience* v67 no6 p577 Je 2017

Preston, John

NOTES ON A SCANDAL L. THOMSON *Publishers Weekly* v263 no41 p51 O 10 2016

What Rinka Wrought J. BACHRACH bw *Weekly Standard* v22 no12 p30 N 28 2016

Preston, Julia

Trump: The New Deportation Threat color *New York Review of Books* v64 no9 p8 My 25 2017

Preston, Stephanie D.

The rewarding nature of social contact color diag *Science* v357 no6358 p1353 S 29 2017

Preston Hollow (Dallas, Tex.)

HOLLOWED GROUND M. TINDERA color *Forbes* v200 no1 p15 Jl 27 2017

Prestowitz, Clyde

Don't Cry for the TPP color *Harvard Business Review Digital Articles* p2 Ja 26 2017

Prestwood, Hugh

Article So Long Love Songs *Commentary* v140 no2 p5 S 2015

Presupposition (Logic)

The Fellowship A. BECHDEL cartoon *New Yorker* v92 no32 p82 O 10 2016

Preszler, Trent

ROCKING THE BOAT J. Roth color *Esquire* p50 2017 BigBlackBook

Pret A Manger Holdings Ltd.—Officials & employees

Does work experience have to be paid? Sandwich chains woes demonstrate nuances of engaging students *People Management* p16 My 2017

Preteens—Substance use

MOM STIRS THE POT L. Rice color *Entertainment Weekly* no1435 p10 O 14 2016

Pretorius, Joelien

Ban the bomb by... banning the bomb? bibl *Bulletin of the Atomic Scientists* v73 no3 p201 My 2017

Pretrial release

Bailing OUT: Everyone agrees that America's bail system is broken. So why is it so hard to get anything done? J. Buntin *Governing* v31 no1 p30 O 2017

Pretto, Davi

RIFLE J. Cronk color *Film Comment* v53 no3 p24 My/Je 2017

Pretty Little Liars (TV program)

How Pop Culture Depicts Mental Illness J. M. Goldstein and S. G.

Levy color *Glamour* v115 no4 p120 Ap 2017

Prettyman, T. H.

Extensive water ice within Ceres' aqueously altered regolith: Evidence from nuclear spectroscopy bibl graph *Science* v355 no6320 p1 Ja 6 2017

Pretzels

BETTER BOARDWALK BITES E. Bacharach color *Women's Health* v14 no5 p141 Je 2017

Pretzsch, Hans

Positive biodiversity-productivity relationship predominant in global forests bibl chart graph map *Science* v354 no6309 paaf8957-1 O 14 2016

Preu, Eckart

MAGIC BATON K. DOANE *Cincinnati Magazine* v50 no10 p24 Jl 2017

Preusker, F.

Rosetta's comet 67P/Churyumov-Gerasimenko sheds its dusty mantle to reveal its icy nature bibl graph *Science* v354 no6319 p1566 D 23 2016

Surface changes on comet 67P/Churyumov-Gerasimenko suggest a more active past bw graph *Science* v355 no6332 p1392 Mr 31 2017

Prevas, John

Hannibal's Oath: The Life and Wars of Rome's Greatest Enemy R. A. Gabriel color *Military History* v34 no5 p72 Ja 2018

Prevenge (Film)

One Scary Mother C. Collis color *Entertainment Weekly* no1459 p50 Mr 31 2017

Prevention (Periodical)

Bright Ideas B. O'Dair *Prevention* v69 no11 p3 N 2017

Prevention of accidental falls

Avoid Falling T. Reece cartoon *Parents* v92 no9 p163 S 2017

Prevention of bites & stings

BUG OFF! V. Tweed color *Amazing Wellness* v9 no4 p26 Summ 2017

Prevention of child abuse

OUT OF THE SHADOWS L. FARMER *Governing* v30 no4 p40 Ja 2017

when a parent is about to snap [Cover story] K. LEDGER cartoon *Parents* v92 no3 p76 Mr 2017

Prevention of chronic diseases

Are You Getting Enough Vitamin E from Your Diet? *Tufts University Health & Nutrition Letter* v35 no6 p3 Ag 2017

BEAT THE HEAT C. W. KIRSHNER color *Prevention* v69 no6 p58 Je 2017

LOW-CAL SWEETENERS: Do low-calorie sweeteners like aspartame and sucralose cause cancer? Make you gain weight? Give you diabetes? Here's what the best evidence shows C. DOW *Nutrition Action Health Letter* v44 no7 p7 S 2017

Prevention of computer hacking

GOOGLE'S ELITE HACKER SWAT TEAM VS. EVERYONE R. Hackett color *Fortune* v176 no1 p60 Jl 1 2017

Prevention of discrimination in employment

Can competitive product markets reduce workplace discrimination? R. Kelley *Monthly Labor Review* p1 Ag 2017

Prevention of fraud in science

China cracks down on fraud D. Normile *Science* v357 no6350 p435 Ag 4 2017

Prevention of global warming

How to govern geoengineering? J. Pasztor, C. Scharf et al color *Science* v357 no6348 p231 Jl 21 2017

Prevention of heart diseases

Anti-inflammatory prevents heart attacks J. Couzin-Frankel color *Science* v357 no6354 p855 S 1 2017

Surprising Benefits of Aerial Yoga V. Tweed color *Amazing Wellness* v8 no2 p19 Spr 2016

Prevention of injury

Four Wise Moves P. Moore cartoon *AARP: The Magazine* v30 no6A p13 O/N 2017

Make your home truly safe [Cover story] color *Redbook* p65 Je 2017

practice safely B. Bell, A. Forrest et al color *Yoga Journal* p16 2017 SpecialIssue

SPIN THE WHEEL color *Women's Health* v14 no7 p40 S 2017

Prevention of medical errors

Be Rude at Your Own Risk K. Rockwood color *Parents* v92 no6

p28 Je 2017

Prevention of mental depression

Can You Zap Away the Blues? A. Bradley color *Health* v31 no5 p69 Je 2017

love FOR LIFE S. Sexton color *Yoga Journal* p94 2017 Special Issue

Probiotics for Less Stress color *Prevention* v69 no8 p13 Ag 2017

SCIENTIFIC UPDATE R. Mangels *Vegetarian Journal* v36 no2 p10 2017

Staying positive with age: Attitude as a route to health and happiness *Mayo Clinic Health Letter* v358 p1 2017 SpecialIssue

Prevention of obesity

BATTLING CHILDHOOD OBESITY D. WERNER *USA Today Magazine* v146 no2866 p62 Jl 2017

Prevention of school bullying

Inside out: Can social emotional learning prevent bullying in Catholic middle schools? [Cover story] C. Zulkey color *U.S. Catholic* v82 no9 p26 S 2017

Prevention of sexually transmitted diseases

News and our views *Mayo Clinic Health Letter* v35 no6 p4 Je 2017

Preventive medicine

See also

Medical self-examination

Periodic health examinations

Pre-exposure prophylaxis

Prevention of chronic diseases

Ancient Remedies for Modern Maladies R. GERACI color *Men's Health* v32 no5 p84 Je 2017

DODGE DISEASE WITH DIET [Cover story] B. LIEBMAN *Nutrition Action Health Letter* v44 no5 p3 Je 2017

Forecasting the Flu B. LUTZ color *New Orleans Magazine* v52 no1 p40 S 2017

paging mother nature S. COLINO *Parents* v91 no9 p36 S 2016

The Race to Zero A. Park and M. Fabry color diag map *Time* v188 no22-23 p38 N/D 2016

SICK SEASON SURVIVAL GUIDE J. R. MARQUEZ *Scholastic Choices* v32 no4 p16 Ja 2017

Taking Health Into Your Own Hands D. B. Agus *AARP: The Magazine* v59 no1A p24 D 2015/Ja 2016

What the U.S. Can Learn From India and Brazil About Preventive Health Care N. Sahni and M. Myers *Harvard Business Review Digital Articles* p2 N 14 2014

Prevish, Val

CALL US EARLY--CALL US FIRST DECREASES EMERGENCY ROOM VISITS *Cincinnati Magazine* v50 no12 p76 S 2017

FASTER RECOVERY FOR SHOULDER REPLACEMENT *Cincinnati Magazine* v50 no12 p86 S 2017

HEART-HEALTHY WISDOM *Cincinnati Magazine* v50 no5 p128 F 2017

THE HIGHEST STANDARDS *Cincinnati Magazine* v50 no8 p72 My 2017

IMAGING HONORS POINT TO BEST-QUALITY PRACTICES AND DIAGNOSTIC CARE *Cincinnati Magazine* v50 no12 p78 S 2017

NEW CARDIOVASCULAR PROCEDURE *Cincinnati Magazine* v50 no12 p80 S 2017

RESEARCH FOCUSES ON PREVENTING PRETERM BIRTHS *Cincinnati Magazine* v50 no12 p82 S 2017

A SURGICAL ALTERNATIVE TO PRESCRIPTION BLOOD THINNERS *Cincinnati Magazine* v50 no12 p84 S 2017

Prewitt, Alex

ALL IN color *Sports Illustrated* v125 no19 p92 D 12 2016

ALL WORK AND REPLAY color *Sports Illustrated* v126 no11 p87 Ap 17-24 2017

The Arrival color *Sports Illustrated* v126 no7 p70 Mr 6 2017

AUSTON'S POWERS color diag *Sports Illustrated* v127 no11 p38 O 9 2017

BEING NO. 2 color *Sports Illustrated* v125 no17 p98 N 21 2016 Double Issue

Bickell Brave color *Sports Illustrated* v126 no11 p21 Ap 17-24 2017

THE BIG BANG color *Sports Illustrated* v125 no12 p50 O 10 2016

The Case for ... Showing Off the Kids color *Sports Illustrated* v125 no14 p31 O 24-31 2016

Crunch Time color *Sports Illustrated* v126 no12 p44 My 1 2017

EASTERN CONFERENCE POWER RANKINGS color *Sports Illustrated* v125 no12 p56 O 10 2016

Emperor PENGUINS color *Sports Illustrated* v126 no17 p42 Je 19 2017

FRINGE BENEFICIARIES color *Sports Illustrated* v126 no14 p54 My 15-22 2017

HOCKEY AND HEALING color *Sports Illustrated* v127 no12 p15 O 16 2017

HOT ICE color *Sports Illustrated* v126 no10 p64 Ap 10 2017

I'M THE REAL SHAQUILLE color diag *Sports Illustrated* v127 no1 p60 Jl 3 2017

Pipe Dream color *Sports Illustrated* v126 no1 p14 Ja 9 2017

PRED ALERT color *Sports Illustrated* v126 no15 p46 My 29 2017

STRENGTH VS. STRENGTH color *Sports Illustrated* v126 no16 p62 Je 5 2017

Talking a BLUE STREAK color *Sports Illustrated* v126 no2 p50 Ja 16 2017

WILDEST Dreams color *Sports Illustrated* v126 no11 p84 Ap 17-24 2017

Preziosi, Dominic

Lie, Memory color *Commonweal* v144 no12 p35 Jl 7 2017

An Ordinary Sunday [Cover story] color *Commonweal* v144 no15 p11 S 22 2017

PRIBBLE, JENNIFER

Chile's Elites Face Demands for Reform *Current History* v116 no787 p49 F 2017

Pribiag, Vlad S.

A twist on the Majorana fermion graph *Science* v357 no6348 p252 Jl 21 2017

PRIBUT, STEPHEN M.

ASK RW color *Runner's World* v52 no4 p35 My 2017

Price, Bradley

1976 Ferrari Dino 208 GT4 color *Popular Mechanics* p56 S 2017

1976 Ferrari Dino 208 GT4 color *Popular Mechanics* v193 no7 p56 S 2016

Price, Cedric, 1934-2003

THE FUN PALACE AT FIFTY S. Mathews *Art in America* v104 no9 p114 O 2016

PRICE, CHRIS

BLADE RUNNERS [Cover story] color *New Orleans Magazine* v51 no10 p70 Ag 2017

Price, Daniel

The Song of the Orphans *Publishers Weekly* v264 no22 p49 My 29 2017

PRICE, DEBORAH EVANS

Miranda's RULES of friendship [Cover story] color *Redbook* p96 N 2017

Price, Feodor

Lee Rubin: Our mentor and role model *Science* v355 no6327 p806 F 24 2017

PRICE, GARETH

Can South Asia Share Its Rivers? *Current History* v116 no789 p148 Ap 2017

Price, Ken—Exhibitions

KEN PRICE G. Coxhead color *Art in America* v105 no3 p138 Mr 2017

PRICE, LEAH

JIGGERY-POKERY color *New York Times Book Review* p40 D 4 2016

PRICE, LISA

42 new ALL-STAR PRODUCTS of the year [Cover story] color *Redbook* p27 Jl/Ag 2017

PRICE, LORI

An Ecoregion-Based Approach to Protecting Half the Terrestrial Realm *BioScience* v67 no6 p534 Je 2017

Price, Michael

Tallying the tropical toll on trees from lightning color *Science* v356 no6344 p1222 Je 23 2017

Price, Neil

Viking Invasion K. B. RATTINI *National Geographic Kids* no468 p26 Mr 2017

Price, Rachel L.

BEYOND THE REVOLUTION bw color *Art in America* v105 no6 p110 Je/Jl 2017

Price, Rebecca

THE REAL WOMEN OF "MURDERESS ROW" AND THE WOMAN WHO TOLD THEIR STORY *Cincinnati Magazine* v50 no8 p16 My 2017

PRICE, RICHARD

Synthesis Centers as Critical Research Infrastructure *BioScience* v67 no8 p750 Ag 2017

Price, Roy

ROY PRICE bw color *Bloomberg Businessweek* no4511 p68 F 13 2017

Price, S. L.

CHIEF CONCERNS color *Sports Illustrated* v127 no10 p36 O 2 2017

THE FAIRY TALE AND THE NIGHTMARE color *Sports Illustrated* v127 no3 p104 Jl 24 2017

Man in the MIDDLE color *Sports Illustrated* v126 no14 p102 My 15-22 2017

Purpose Pitch color *Sports Illustrated* v125 no18 p17 D 5 2016

UNBREAKABLE color *Sports Illustrated* v127 no8 p38 S 18 2017

VENUS VENERATED color *Sports Illustrated* v127 no7 p17 S 4 2017

What We Think About When We Think About Big Ben [Cover story] color *Sports Illustrated* v126 no1 p20 Ja 9 2017

"Your Story is OUR STORY" color *Sports Illustrated* v125 no12 p38 O 10 2016

Price, Tim

A SON'S PRAYER color *America* v217 no6 p42 S 18 2017

Price, Tom, 1954-

DOCTOR'S ORDERS J. Surowiecki cartoon *New Yorker* v92 no42 p50 D 19 2016

MODERN MEDICINE MESS E. LEE VLIET and M. SINGLETON *USA Today Magazine* v145 no2862 p52 Mr 2017

NEWSMAKERS *Science* v357 no6359 p15 O 6 2017

Price Takes a Beating F. BARNES color *Weekly Standard* v22 no21 p7 F 6 2017

Upheavals continue color *Science* v355 no6326 p671 F 17 2017

Price, Vincent, 1911-1993

Sing for Your Supper S. Sifton *New York Times Magazine* p28 O 2 2016

Price cutting

See also

Discount houses (Retail trade)

Why Businesses Should Lower Prices During Natural Disasters R. Mohammed *Harvard Business Review Digital Articles* p2 S 11 2017

Price-earnings ratio

Everything You Need to Know About P/E Ratios P. J. Lim chart diag *Money* v46 no8 p36 S 2017

IS THE STOCK MARKET TOO HOT? map *Fortune* v176 no3 p15 S 1 2017

My 10 Top Stock Picks for 2017 J. K. GLASSMAN chart *Kiplinger's Personal Finance* v71 no1 p19 Ja 2017

Price fixing

The Drug Marketplace at Work: Competition already lowers the price of drugs--and it works better than price fixing ever could L. J. Chen *Hoover Digest: Research & Opinion on Public Policy* no3 p51 Summ 2017

Price increases

Fizzcal Responsibility A. Greenblatt *Governing* v30 no4 p9 Ja 2017

When Customers Will (Willingly) Pay More for Less G. Morse *Harvard Business Review Digital Articles* p2 F 24 2015

Your Next Phone Will Probably Cost $1,000 M. Gurman graph *Bloomberg Businessweek* no4538 p24 S 18 2017

Price indexes

See also

Consumer price indexes

Employment cost index

Stock price indexes

PRICES *Economic Indicators* p22 Mr 2017

Price level changes

See also

Price increases

Oil's Fall Is a Challenge for Gulf Economies, but Also an Opportunity L. El-Katiri *Harvard Business Review Digital Articles*

p2 Mr 7 2016

The Risks of Changing Your Prices Too Often U. M. Dholakia *Harvard Business Review Digital Articles* p2 Jl 6 2015

Price marks

I Don't Want a Bargain J. BOTTUM cartoon *Weekly Standard* v22 no38 p5 Je 12 2017

Price regulation

LATE-MODEL ROUND BALERS: 2014 MODEL YEAR BAL-ERS OFFER A SWEET SPOT OF POTENTIAL DEALER PRICING D. Mowitz *Successful Farming* v115 no6 p22 Ap 2017

Price regulation—United States

4 Ways to Shoot Down Skyrocketing Drug Prices H. S. Edwards color *Time* v188 no16/17 p54 O 24 2016

Price wars

BlackRock Fights A Price War, Selectively C. Stein graph *Bloomberg Businessweek* no4520 p39 My 1 2017

The Risks of Changing Your Prices Too Often U. M. Dholakia *Harvard Business Review Digital Articles* p2 Jl 6 2015

Price indexes—Charts, diagrams, etc.

PRICES *Economic Indicators* p22 F 2017

Price Is Right, The (TV program)

EYES ON THE PRIZE *Los Angeles Magazine* p140 My 2017

For the Record color *Time* v190 no14 p6 O 9 2017

LONG LIVE GAME SHOWS! I. Rudolph color *TV Guide* v64 no42 p16 O 10 2016

Priceline.com Inc.

Stock X-Ray: Priceline P. J. Lim color diag *Money* v46 no9 p52 O 2017

Prices

See also

Agricultural prices

Antiquities sales & prices

Costume—Sales & prices

Firearm sales & prices

Real property sales & prices

BUSINESSES HAVE HIKED PRICES (WAY) UP A. Vandermey diag *Fortune* v176 no4 p27 S 15 2017

INTERNATIONAL STATISTICS *Economic Indicators* p35 Ap 2017

Let Your Customers Segment Themselves by What They're Willing to Pay S. Michel *Harvard Business Review Digital Articles* p2 Mr 11 2015

A Quick Guide to Value-Based Pricing U. M. Dholakia *Harvard Business Review Digital Articles* p2 Ag 9 2016

Prices—Charts, diagrams, etc.

POCKET PRICE GUIDE: Dealer Prices On Late-Model Hopper-Bottom Trailers *Successful Farming* v115 no11 p23 S 2017

PRICES *Economic Indicators* p22 Ja 2017

PRICES *Economic Indicators* p22 My 2017

Prices—United States

YEAR-END TIMING DECISIONS S. Williamson *Successful Farming* v114 no11 p20 N 2016

Prices—United States—Charts, diagrams, etc.

PRICES *Economic Indicators* p22 N 2016

PricewaterhouseCoopers LLP

HIGH-FLYING HELP N. Strochlic color *National Geographic* v231 no6 p6 Je 2017

My brand: A "collaborative leader" fluent in two different cultures N. Granholm color *Working Mother* v40 no2 p2 Je/Jl 2017

Prichard, Skip—Interviews

Four Questions with Skip Prichard A. RICHARD ALBANESE color *Publishers Weekly* v264 no25 p58 Je 19 2017

Prichinello, Michael

Hauling Class J. CONDON color *Esquire* p62 BigBlackBook

Pricing

See also

Discount

Markup

Price cutting

Price increases

3 Big Economic Ideas in Waiting R. Litan *Harvard Business Review Digital Articles* p2 O 9 2014

Are You Really Getting a Discount, or Is It Just a Pricing Trick? R. Mohammed *Harvard Business Review Digital Articles* p2 Mr 23 2016

Erratic helium prices create research havoc D. Kramer *Physics Today* v70 no1 p26 Ja 2017

The Fine Line Between When Low Prices Work and When They Don't H. Simon *Harvard Business Review Digital Articles* p2 Mr 17 2016

Group Effort L. BARGAR SUTER *Los Angeles Magazine* v62 no6 p40 Je 2017

How Customers Perceive a Price Is as Important as the Price Itself S. Heda, S. Mewborn et al color *Harvard Business Review Digital Articles* p2 Ja 3 2017

How much will AMD's Zen cost? Here's what we think G. MAHUNG chart color *PCWorld* v35 no1 p24 Ja 2017

How Retailers Should Think About Online Versus In-Store Pricing R. Mohammed bw *Harvard Business Review Digital Articles* p2 Ja 26 2017

Of Course Disney Should Use Surge Pricing at Its Theme Parks R. Mohammed *Harvard Business Review Digital Articles* p2 Je 4 2015

POCKET PRICE GUIDE: Dealer Prices on 2014 Midsize Round Balers *Successful Farming* v115 no6 p25 Ap 2017

Price-Sensitive Customers Will Tolerate Uncertainty R. Mohammed *Harvard Business Review Digital Articles* p2 Mr 26 2015

A Quick Guide to Value-Based Pricing U. M. Dholakia *Harvard Business Review Digital Articles* p2 Ag 9 2016

The Real Cost of "High- Priced" Drugs M. Rosenblatt *Harvard Business Review Digital Articles* p2 N 17 2014

Retailers' Holiday Strategy Doesn't Have to Be "Discount Everything" R. Mohammed *Harvard Business Review Digital Articles* p2 N 29 2016

What Amazon Risks by Eliminating List Prices R. Mohammed *Harvard Business Review Digital Articles* p2 Jl 13 2016

What America's Best BBQ Joint Can Teach You About Pricing R. Mohammed *Harvard Business Review Digital Articles* p2 N 12 2015

What Economists Don't Get About Uber's Surge Pricing T. Sullivan *Harvard Business Review Digital Articles* p2 D 17 2014

When Hidden Algorithms Lead to Higher Prices M. L. Tellado *Consumer Reports* v82 no7 p4 Jl 2017

Where Predictive Analytics Is Having the Biggest Impact J. LaRiviere, P. McAfee et al *Harvard Business Review Digital Articles* p2 My 25 2016

Why Apple's New iPhone Upgrade Plan Is Driving Growth R. Mohammed *Harvard Business Review Digital Articles* p2 S 28 2015

Prick of the Litter (Music)

Good Deals HADLEY color *Downbeat* v84 no5 p58 My 2017

PRICKETT, SARAH NICOLE

Eric MACK *Interview* v46 no10 p112 D 2016/Ja 2017

Prickett, Todd D.

Landscape of immunogenic tumor antigens in successful immunotherapy of virally induced epithelial cancer graph *Science* v356 no6334 p200 Ap 14 2017

Priddle, Alisa

2017 Chrysler Pacifica Hybrid color *Motor Trend* v69 no3 p29 Mr 2017

2017 Ford Fusion Sport color *Motor Trend* v68 no12 p24 D 2016

2018 GMC Terrain color *Motor Trend* v69 no3 p21 Mr 2017

2018 Honda Accord color *Motor Trend* v69 no10 p20 O 2017

Dave Zuchowski color *Motor Trend* v68 no12 p35 D 2016

DISCO IS BACK chart color *Motor Trend* v69 no6 p98 Je 2017

EVERYDAY HEROES [Cover story] chart color *Motor Trend* v69 no5 p34 My 2017

GARAGE chart color diag *Motor Trend* v69 no9 p104 S 2017

GARRAGE cartoon chart color *Motor Trend* v69 no3 p86 Mr 2017

Genesis GV80 Concept color *Motor Trend* v69 no7 p24 Jl 2017

Håkan Samuelsson *Motor Trend* v69 no7 p30 Jl 2017

Hyundai Kona A Korea-spec taste color *Motor Trend* v69 no9 p24 S 2017

Ian Robertson color *Motor Trend* v69 no5 p24 My 2017

LUXURY START UP chart color *Motor Trend* v68 no12 p70 D 2016

Mark Fields and Raj Nair color *Motor Trend* v69 no4 p32 Ap 2017

Mark Fields out as Ford CEO color *Motor Trend* v69 no8 p24 Ag 2017

Mercedes-Benz Generation EQ Concept color *Motor Trend* v69

no1 p18 Ja 2017

New Tranny In Town color *Motor Trend* v68 no12 p66 D 2016

Peter Schreyer bw color *Motor Trend* v69 no1 p30 Ja 2017

POWER LIST cartoon *Motor Trend* v69 no1 p100 Ja 2017

Roland Krueger color *Motor Trend* v69 no8 p32 Ag 2017

Wayne Burgess color *Motor Trend* v69 no10 p26 O 2017

Pride & Joy: The Story of Alligator Records (Film)

Legends & Legacies J. EPHLAND color *Downbeat* v83 no12 p88 D 2016

Pride & vanity

The Connection Between Pride and Persistence D. DeSteno *Harvard Business Review Digital Articles* p2 Ag 22 2016

HOW VAIN ARE YOU? color *GQ: Gentlemen's Quarterly* v97 no9 p202 S 2017

Points of State Pride color *Nebraska Life* v21 no6 p21 N/D 2017

Pride & vanity—Psychological aspects

Does Pride Goeth Before...? A. ESTRADA *USA Today Magazine* v146 no2868 p27 S 2017

Pride & vanity—Social aspects

Does Pride Goeth Before...? A. ESTRADA *USA Today Magazine* v146 no2868 p27 S 2017

Pride (Music)

The Unbearable Lightness Of Being U2 D. Dark bw color *America* v217 no4 p38 Ag 21 2017

Pride Month

Editor's Note H. Goldblatt color *Entertainment Weekly* no1471 p10 Je 23 2017

Priebus, Reince, 1972-

Meanwhile... W. Kristol *Weekly Standard* v22 no46 p9 Ag 14 2017

Priest, George L.

SOMETHING SMELLS PHISHY *Claremont Review of Books* v16 no4 p57 Fall 2016

Priest holes

SECRET SPACES J. A. LOBELL bw color *Archaeology* v70 no2 p12 Mr/Ap 2017

Priesthood—Social aspects

A Brush of the Butterfly's Wing W. C. Birdsall color *Commonweal* v143 no19 p39 D 2 2016

Priestley, Joseph, 1733-1804

MONTHS PAST AUGUST J. Pollard and S. Pollard *History Today* v67 no8 p22 Ag 2017

Priests

See also

Catholic priests

Shamans

FATHER PAUL SCALIA: On his father's legacy, the Church, and why he dislikes the term "conservative" P. O'Donnell *Washingtonian Magazine* v52 no8 p45 My 2017

The God Squad E. Dias color *Time* v189 no23 p36 Je 19 2017

It takes a parish R. McCarty color *U.S. Catholic* v82 no5 p23 My 2017

An Oklahoma Martyr M. Ruiz Scaperlanda *America* v217 no6 p62 S 18 2017

Priests—Sexual behavior

CONFESSING MY PORN ADDICTION J. Smith color *America* v216 no7 p32 Ap 3 2017

Prieto, A.

Persistent effects of pre-Columbian plant domestication on Amazonian forest composition bibl chart graph map *Science* v355 no6328 p925 Mr 3 2017

Prieto, Dafnis

Dafnis Prieto's A World of Rhythmic Possibilities R. Bennett color *Downbeat* v84 no1 p106 Ja 2017

Rhythmic Independence & Musicality on the Drum Set color diag *Downbeat* v83 no11 p68 N 2016

Prieto-Samsonov, Dmitri

Vodka on the Malecon B. Dufresne color *Commonweal* v144 no1 p9 Ja 6 2017

Prim, Lynda

Genomic estimation of complex traits reveals ancient maize adaptation to temperate North America diag *Science* v357 no6350 p512 Ag 4 2017

Primack, Dan

THE NEW ESTABLISHMENT 2017 bw color *Vanity Fair* v59 no11 p87 N 2017

NEW ESTABLISHMENT bw cartoon color *Vanity Fair* v58 no11

p124 N 2016

Primaries

Hillary Clinton, Bernie Sanders, and the Tug of War Between Women J. C. Williams *Harvard Business Review Digital Articles* p2 F 22 2016

PRO CANVASSER C. Bethea cartoon *New Yorker* v93 no10 p38 Ap 24 2017

TRUMP FILLS THE VACUUM: HE EXEMPLIFIES AND ACCELERATES THE DECLINE OF AMERICA'S INSTITUTIONS [Cover story] Y. LEVIN *Commentary* v142 no5 p16 D 2016

Primary care (Medicine)

CLUB MED: At one Carmel doctor's new office, patients pay monthly dues for healthcare A. GARCEAU *Indianapolis Monthly* p79 N 2017

Expanding the Reach of Primary Care in Developing Countries K. Mossman, O. Bhattacharyya et al color *Harvard Business Review Digital Articles* p2 Je 6 2017

Get More for Your Co-Pay K. Dold color *Men's Health* v31 no10 p88 D 2016

Helping Primary Care Doctors Contain Costs M. Ferguson *Harvard Business Review Digital Articles* p2 D 30 2015

How to Choose the Right Specialist N. S. HUANG *Kiplinger's Personal Finance* v71 no4 p68 Ap 2017

Your Best Health While Traveling S. Goldberg *Cincinnati Magazine* v50 no4 p88 Ja 2017

Primary care (Medicine)—United States

Patients Get the Personal Touch S. LUTHRA cartoon *Kiplinger's Personal Finance* v71 no1 p68 Ja 2017

Primary schools

DOING GOOD S. Pulia color map *InStyle* v24 no8 p68 Ag 2017

Primate anatomy

Food for Thought L. Evans Ogden color *Natural History* v125 no7 p6 Jl/Ag 2017

Primate ecology

FINDINGS *Harper's Magazine* v334 no2004 p96 My 2017

Primate evolution

Fossil offers clues to ape evolution B. BOWER color *Science News* v192 no3 p13 S 2 2017

The road to speciation runs both ways A. R. Hoelzel bibl color map *Science* v354 no6311 p414 O 28 2016

Primate trade

Mauritius invites primate research labs to set up shop M. Wadman chart color *Science* v356 no6337 p472 My 5 2017

Primates

See also

Human beings

Monkeys

Did Lucy Fall and Not Get Up? G. TARLACH color *Discover* v38 no1 p21 Ja/F 2017

Learning from monkey "talk" C. T. Snowdon bibl chart color *Science* v355 no6330 p1120 Mr 17 2017

Primates—Genetics

Chimpanzee genomic diversity reveals ancient admixture with bonobos J. Novembre, M. Gut et al bibl diag graph map *Science* v354 no6311 p477 O 28 2016

PRIME, REBECCA

In Secrecy's Shadow: The OSS and CIA in Hollywood Cinema, 1941-1979 *Film Quarterly* v70 no3 p103 Spr 2017

Prime knots

Molecular knot is most complex yet M. ROSEN color *Science News* v191 no3 p8 F 18 2017

Prime ministers

Helmut Kohl S. Shuster color *Time* v190 no1 p13 Jl 3 2017

History Will Not Absolve Him E. ABRAMS bw color *Weekly Standard* v22 no14 p19 D 12 2016

One Europe Under Kohl L. J. O'Donovan *America* v217 no3 p54 Ag 7 2017

Our Economy Continues to Prosper: MALAYSIA IS STRONGER THAN EVER AS A RESULT OF REFORMS *Vital Speeches of the Day* v83 no9 p252 S 2017

PARODY *Weekly Standard* v22 no14 p40 D 12 2016

A Portrait of the Prime Minister As a Young Man J. Duggan color *Time* v190 no4 p36 Jl 24 2017

Recep Tayyip Erdogan J. Malsin color *Time* v188 no25-26 p106 D 19 2016 Double Issue

This One Huge Heroic Act of Togetherness: TODAY WE HAVE PUT THIS REGIME ON NOTICE *Vital Speeches of the Day* v83 no9 p263 S 2017

Victor Ponta E. Turner *Current Biography* v78 no2 p67 F 2017

Westminster, D.C.? No, the United States does not need a prime minister D. Brady *Commentary* v142 no2 p51 S 2016

Prime ministers' spouses

COLOUR, MADE IN CANADA P. Treble color *Maclean's* v129 no48/49 p68 D 5 2016

Prime ministers—Attitudes

Bibi the Strategist *Commentary* v142 no1 p1 Jl/Ag 2016

Prime ministers—Canada

THE BUMPY ROAD AHEAD [Cover story] J. GEDDES color *Maclean's* v129 no42 p14 O 24 2016

Cool while it lasted T. GLAVIN bw color *Maclean's* v129 no50 p10 D 19 2016

THE EDITORIAL *Maclean's* v129 no50 p5 D 19 2016

THE INTERVIEW P. WELLS color *Maclean's* v130 no7 p20 Ag 2017

Look at me! Look at me! Look at me now color *Maclean's* v129 no48/49 p56 D 5 2016

The North Star [Cover story] S. Rodrick bw color *Rolling Stone* no1293 p36 Ag 10 2017

Three degrees of Harper M. HEMMADI *Maclean's* p12 Je 2017

Prime ministers—Canada—History

King among PMs S. AZZI and N. HILLMER bw chart color *Maclean's* v129 no41 p19 O 17 2016

Prime ministers—France

Manuel Valls B. Lightner *Current Biography* v77 no11 p90 N 2016

Prime ministers—Great Britain

BREXIT: NO PARTIAL MEMBERSHIP IN THE EUROPEAN UNION T. MAY *Vital Speeches of the Day* v83 no3 p68 Mr 2017

SOMETHING THAT I CALL THE SHARED SOCIETY T. MAY *Vital Speeches of the Day* v83 no3 p86 Mr 2017

TOMORROW, LET THE HOUSE OF COMMONS VOTE FOR AN ELECTION *Vital Speeches of the Day* v83 no6 p186 Je 2017

Prime ministers—Israel

ISRAEL HAS A BRIGHT FUTURE AT THE UNITED NATIONS *Vital Speeches of the Day* v82 no12 p368 D 2016

Netanyahu, the AlmostAmerican *Commentary* v142 no2 p1 S 2016

There Will Be Nothing Found Because There Is Nothing There: AN UNPRECEDENTED, OBSESSIVE WITCH HUNT *Vital Speeches of the Day* v83 no9 p260 S 2017

TURNING WORDS INTO POLICIES: THE TRUMP ADMINISTRATION IS SHOWING ITS COMMITMENT TO ISRAEL *Vital Speeches of the Day* v83 no5 p146 My 2017

Prime Suspect: Tennison (TV program)

HIGHLIGHTS *TV Guide* v65 no25 p33 Je 2017

Primeau, Kristy E.

Clues in the Forest--Archaeology at Florence Hill State Forest *New York State Conservationist* v72 no1 p18 Ag 2017

Primitive warfare

This Means War! H. WATERMAN color *Discover* v38 no3 p68 Ap 2017

Primus AB

Field Notes color *Climbing* no353 p44 My/Je 2017

Prince, 1958-2016

THE 26-WORD REVIEW K. O'donnell color *Entertainment Weekly* no1465 p52 My 12 2017

After Prince's Death, His Subjects Get to Rule L. Shaw color *Bloomberg Businessweek* no4509 p21 Ja 30 2017

Autopsy: The Last Hours of Prince M. Roffman *TV Guide* v65 no21 p33 My 15 2017

The BULLSEYE M. Snetiker color *Entertainment Weekly* no1444/1445 p124 D 16 2016

THE EXTRAORDINARY ORDINARY LIFE OF THE ARTIST FORMERLY KNOWN AS PRINCE C. Heath bw color *GQ: Gentlemen's Quarterly* v86 no12 p220 D 2016

PRINCE J. SULLIVAN *New York Times Magazine* p48 D 25 2016

Prince Movie Collection M. Mettler color *Sound & Vision* v82 no2 p68 F/Mr 2017

The Prince Vault Opens D. BROWNE color *Rolling Stone* no1287

p11 My 18 2017

Screaming Karaoke M. James *New York Times Magazine* p42 O 8 2017

Prince, 1958-2016—Interviews

The Purple One color *Ebony* v72 no8 p82 Je 2017

Prince, Erik, 1969-

Should Mercenaries Take Over In Afghanistan? D. Stewart color *Time* v190 no7 p11 Ag 21 2017

Prince, Faith, 1957-

Wonderful Town S. Williams *Opera News* v81 no9 p40 Mr 2017

Prince, Harold S.

17 Shows, 1 Legend S. GOLD *Dance Magazine* v91 no8 p20 Ag 2017

The Learning Curve of Theater M. S. Eddy *Stage Directions* v30 no10 p2 O 2017

"Look What We Did!" B. Boritt, T. Yarden et al *Stage Directions* v30 no10 p19 O 2017

Prince, Josh

A Place to Play S. GOLD *Dance Magazine* v91 no1 p46 Ja 2017

PRINCE, MAX

ANTICIPAZIONE color *Road & Track* v68 no6 p66 F 2017

BACK ON THE HORSE cartoon *Road & Track* v68 no6 p88 F 2017

DIRECTOR'S CUT cartoon *Road & Track* v69 no4 p92 N 2017

FOR THE LOVE OF CARS: THE BEST RIDES OF 2017 Esquire color *Esquire* p65 O 2017

FORWARD MOMENTUM bw *Road & Track* v69 no4 p64 N 2017

A HALF CENTURY OF PENSKE color *Road & Track* v68 no5 p14 D 2016/Ja 2017

HEADSTRONG *Road & Track* v68 no8 p98 My 2017

LETTER OF INTENT color *Road & Track* v69 no1 p80 Ag 2017

OVERLAND AFFAIR color *Road & Track* v68 no9 p92 Je 2017

PURSUIT OF PERFECTION color *Road & Track* v69 no1 p74 Ag 2017

RETOOLING THE SYSTEM color *Road & Track* v69 no4 p58 N 2017

RINGERS color diag graph *Road & Track* v69 no4 p26 N 2017

RISING TIDE cartoon chart color graph *Road & Track* v68 no7 p38 Mr/Ap 2017

ROCK SOLID color *Road & Track* v68 no9 p78 Je 2017

SUPERFREAK color *Road & Track* v69 no4 p74 N 2017

THAT '70s COLOR color *Esquire* p32 O 2017

TIME FOR A MAN-CATION! color *Esquire* p114 O 2017

Prince, Richard, 1949-

How Art Can Fight Trump J. SALTZ img *New York* p70 Ja 23 2017

Prince, The (Book : Machiavelli)

YES TO FEAR, NO TO HATRED N. Machiavelli *Lapham's Quarterly* v10 no3 p153 Summ 2017

Prince, Walter

EL CARMELO GRANDE J. OBER color *Dirt Sports + Off-Road* v51 no12 p74 D 2017

Prince 4Ever (Music)

The Must List color *Entertainment Weekly* no1442 p1 D 2 2016 Rebellious Special Issue

Prince Igor (Theatrical production)

Art Meets Organization R. Minetor *Stage Directions* v30 no3 p28 Mr 2017

Prince of Broadway (Theatrical production)

Broadway's Next Bets: The stars and stories hitting stages soon S. GOLD *Dance Magazine* v91 no9 p24 S 2017

Prince William Sound (Alaska)

Northern Lights K. Laird color *Sail* v48 no1 p12 Ja 2017

Sound of Silence color *Sail* v48 no8 p8 Ag 2017

Prince Be, 1970-2016

Head Rush color *Vogue* v207 no10 p182 O 2017

Prince-Bythewood, Gina

Gina Prince-Bythewood, Filmmaker E. Dockterman color *Time* v189 no10 p54 Mr 20 2017

SHADOW PLAY bw *New York Times Magazine* p100 D 11 2016

Princecraft Boats Inc.

En Vogue A. Jones *Boating World* v37 no9 p38 N/D 2016

Pontoon For the Populous A. JONES *Boating World* v38 no3 p44 Mr 2017

Princecraft Sport 164 *Boating World* v38 no1 p68 Ja 2017

Princecraft Ventura 220 WS *Boating World* v38 no1 p50 Ja 2017

Princes

The Man Who Would Be King or Vicar: Was the new king of Sierra Leone poisoned on his return voyage from England? J. Kaifala *History Today* v67 no10 p14 O 2017

REVENGE DRAMA *Lapham's Quarterly* v10 no3 p46 Summ 2017

Princess Cruise Lines Ltd.

CRUISE LINES color *Conde Nast Traveler* v52 no10 p74 N 2017

Princess Yachts America (Company)

ASCENDING THE THRONE A. HARPER cartoon chart color *Power & Motoryacht* v32 no12 p62 D 2016

Princess Yachts International PLC

Princess 40M D. Harding color *Power & Motoryacht* v33 no4 p40 Ap 2017

Princess Diana: Her Life, Her Death, the Truth (TV program)

Princess Diana: Her Life, Her Death, the Truth B. Oates *TV Guide* v65 no21 p37 My 15 2017

Princesses

Travels Across Time and Place B. Lang *Discover* v38 no2 p7 Mr 2017

Princesses—Exhibitions

ANGLO-FILE S. Gutierrez *British Heritage Travel* v38 no2 p74 Mr/Ap 2017

Princesses—Great Britain

ENLIGHTENED PRINCESSES C. Hopley *British Heritage Travel* v38 no3 p48 My/Je 2017

Princess & the Goblin, The (Theatrical production)

ON WITH THE Encore *Atlanta* v57 no2 p130 Je 2017

Princeton Theological Seminary

PTS cancels award to Keller but not lecture C. Kennel-Shank color *Christian Century* v134 no9 p12 Ap 26 2017

Princeton University

Kiplinger's Best College Values 2017 K. PITSKER chart color *Kiplinger's Personal Finance* v71 no2 p36 F 2017

Princeton University—Curricula

Princeton University Lewis Center for the Arts *Dance Magazine* v90 p93 2016/2017 Supplement College Guide

Principal components analysis

7 WAYS TO SAVE MONEY WHEN YOU BUILD A PC B. CHACOS color *PCWorld* p131 Mr 2017

Principle (Philosophy)

Enhancing reproducibility for computational methods V. Stodden, M. McNutt et al bibl color *Science* v354 no6317 p1240 D 9 2016

Principles of Uncertainty, The (Theatrical production)

Pas de Deux L. REGENSDORF and C. SCHAMA color *Vogue* v207 no9 p612 S 2017

Prindle, Arthur

Coupling between distant biofilms and emergence of nutrient time-sharing bw color graph *Science* v356 no6338 p638 My 12 2017

Prine, John

The Legend Next Door P. Doyle bw color *Rolling Stone* no1278/1279 p38 Ja 12 2017

Pringle, Ethan

FLASH color *Climbing* no350 p8 D 2016/Ja 2017

Pringle, Heather

NEW VISIONS OF THE VIKINGS color *National Geographic* v231 no3 p30 Mr 2017

Pringle, Kirsty J.

Global atmospheric particle formation from CERN CLOUD measurements bibl graph map *Science* v354 no6316 p1119 D 2 2016

PRINGLE, ROBERT M.

Conserving the World's Megafauna and Biodiversity: The Fierce Urgency of Now *BioScience* v67 no3 p197 Mr 2017

Saving the World's Terrestrial Megafauna color *BioScience* v66 no10 p807 O 1 2016

Prinja, Anil K.

Paul Frederick Zweifel *Physics Today* v70 no8 p73 Ag 2017

Prinjha, Rab K.

Click chemistry enables preclinical evaluation of targeted epigenetic therapies diag *Science* v356 no6345 p1397 Je 30 2017

Prins, Nomi

In Need of a Fix cartoon *Progressive* p27 D 2016/Ja 2017

Prinsloo, Loni

Mobile Carriers Start Hanging Up on Africa cartoon *Bloomberg Businessweek* no4530 p18 Jl 17 2017

Printed fashion apparel

What Makes You Feel Sexy? [Cover story] color *Glamour* v115 no7 p36 Jl 2017

Printers (Persons)

40 Years IN THE Dark H. Stucker bw color *Popular Photography* v81 no2 p62 Mr/Ap 2017

Printing

See also

Fonts & typefaces

BIRD BY BIRD D. A. WOOD color *Missouri Life* v44 no3 p10 My 2017

Printing industry

Consolidation, Innovation Draw the Focus of Printers S. ODA *Publishers Weekly* v264 no24 p28 Je 12 2017

Printing plants

DESIGN AND CONQUER: OTR'S ONE-STOP BRANDING SHOP J. WILLIAMS *Cincinnati Magazine* v50 no11 p35 Ag 2017

Printing plants—Evaluation

A Font Of Hand-Crafted Artistry S. ROOT color *Los Angeles Magazine* v62 no7 p13 Jl 2017

Printing—History

THE BUDDHIST HISTORY OF MOVABLE TYPE M. S. NEWMAN color *Tricycle: The Buddhist Review* v26 no2 p46 Wint 2016

Printing—United States

LETTERS OF NOTE: The Cincinnati Type & Print Museum is looking to make the past present A. KONERMANN *Cincinnati Magazine* v50 no10 p30 Jl 2017

Printmakers

Dreamscapes of Maine: Kathleen Buchanan's handmade prints reveal a misty world of islands, seabirds, and coastal sheep A. GRAVES color *Yankee* p36 Jl 2017

Prints—Exhibitions

Depression-era prints from the Woodcut Society cartoon *Magazine Antiques* v184 no1 p44 Ja/F 2017

Restoring the lost laurels of Adolf Dehn cartoon *Magazine Antiques* v184 no1 p32 Ja/F 2017

Prinz, Fritz B.

Direct and continuous strain control of catalysts with tunable battery electrode materials bibl graph *Science* v354 no6315 p1031 N 25 2016

PRINZING, DEBRA

Dahlias! [Cover story] color *Better Homes & Gardens* v95 no8 p140 Ag 2017

DYED & TRUE color *Better Homes & Gardens* v95 no7 p140 Jl 2017

Prions

A bacterial global regulator forms a prion A. Hochschild and A. H. Yuan bibl color diag graph *Science* v355 no6321 p1 Ja 13 2017

Microbial Targets Can Help Make Parkinson's History M. STONE *BioScience* v67 no5 p484 My 2017

New blood tests make strides in detecting prion disease K. Servick color *Science* v354 no6319 p1512 D 23 2016

Prionlike protein stores memories L. SANDERS graph *Science News* v190 no12 p10 D 10 2016

Prior, David

ABSO LUTE ABRUZZO color map *Conde Nast Traveler* v52 no9 p74 O 2017

Ballymaloe House, County Cork, Ireland color *Conde Nast Traveler* v52 no2 p46 F 2017

FAR OUT color map *Conde Nast Traveler* v52 no2 p74 F 2017

Ski and The City color *Conde Nast Traveler* v51 no11 p58 D 2016

WHERE IN THE WORLD TO EAT cartoon color *Conde Nast Traveler* v52 no9 p53 O 2017

PRIOR, MICHAEL

In Cloud Country *Walrus* v14 no6 p53 Jl/Ag 2017

Priority (Philosophy)

How to Prioritize Your Work When Your Manager Doesn't A. J. Su color *Harvard Business Review Digital Articles* p2 Ja 24 2017

PRISCU, JOHN C.

The Impact of a Large-Scale Climate Event on Antarctic Ecosystem Processes chart graph *BioScience* v66 no10 p848 O 1 2016

Microbial Community Dynamics in Two Polar Extremes: The Lakes of the McMurdo Dry Valleys and the West Antarctic Peninsula Marine Ecosystem chart color graph *BioScience* v66 no10 p829 O 1 2016

Responses of Antarctic Marine and Freshwater Ecosystems to Changing Ice Conditions color graph *BioScience* v66 no10 p864 O 1 2016

Unraveling Ecosystem Responses to Climate Change on the Antarctic Continent through Long-Term Ecological Research *BioScience* v66 no10 p799 O 1 2016

Prislovsky, Lois

Valuing differences: color *Phi Delta Kappan* v98 no8 p59 My 2017

Prism Quartet (Performer)

CLASSICAL MUSIC color *New Yorker* v93 no28 p9 S 18 2017

Prison Break (TV program)

My Obsessions... *TV Guide* v65 no23 p8 My 29 2017

ONCE MORE, WITH FEELING! S. Highfill color *Entertainment Weekly* no1450 p12 Ja 27 2017

ON THE RUN AGAIN N. Abrams color *Entertainment Weekly* no1459 p54 Mr 31 2017

Prison Break M. Roffman *TV Guide* v65 no13 p28 Mr 20 2017

Prison discipline

See also

Solitary confinement

BREAKOUT! R. SOODALTER *Missouri Life* v43 no6 p42 O/N 2016

Prison industries

Closing Doors at Private Prisons A. Greenblatt *Governing* v30 no2 p9 N 2016

Prison population

See also

Prisoners

Prison reform

PRISON BREAK D. SLATER color *Mother Jones* v42 no4 p42 Jl/Ag 2017

Prison release

TIME TO BE RELEASED? M. Mccann and L. J. Wertheim color *Sports Illustrated* v126 no5 p70 F 13 2017

Prison riots—History—21st century

Why Brazil's Prisoners Are Rioting T. John color *Time* v189 no4 p11 Ja 23 2017

Prison sentences

Sleep-Deprived Judges Dole Out Harsher Punishments C. M. Barnes *Harvard Business Review Digital Articles* p2 F 15 2017

WHAT DO CRIME VICTIMS WANT FROM CRIMINAL JUSTICE REFORM? J. Keisling cartoon graph *Reason* v48 no7 p8 D 2016

Prison system

See also

Imprisonment

WRONGFUL INCARCERATION C. ROBERTSON and J. C. ROBERTSON *USA Today Magazine* v145 no2858 p26 N 2016

Prison visits

You May Hug The Screen V. Law bw *Bloomberg Businessweek* no4541 p20 O 9 2017

Prisoner (Music)

Ryan Adams Offers His Opus of Despair I. Guzmán color *Time* v189 no6 p51 F 20 2017

Ryan Adams Relives His Wonder Years J. DOLAN color *Rolling Stone* no1281/1282 p52 F 23 2017

Prisoners

See also

Ex-convicts

Prisoners of war

Breaking the Silence T. FLINT *Education Digest* v82 no6 p4 F 2017

CHEROKEE COUNTY HISTORIC COURTHOUSE CANTON 40 MILES NORTH OF ATLANTA J. GREEN *Atlanta* v56 no9 p170 Ja 2017

Crops and Robbers M. HAYES cartoon *Walrus* v13 no10 p19 D 2016

FALLEN IDOL H. BEECH bw cartoon *New Yorker* v93 no30 p22 O 2 2017

'First you survive' G. McClure color *U.S. Catholic* v82 no11 p18 N 2017

Open Book J. WILLIAMS *New York Times Book Review* p4 O 2 2016

Otto Warmbier N. Jenkins color *Time* v190 no1 p13 Jl 3 2017

Out of the tombs I. S. Villegas color *Christian Century* v134 no20 p31 S 27 2017

WRITTEN INTERACTIONS PREDICT INCARCERATION *USA Today Magazine* v145 no2860 p10 Ja 2017

Prisoners' correspondence

Love in the Time of Mass Incarceration M. Pilon color *Bloomberg Businessweek* no4531 p18 Jl 24 2017

Prisoners' families—Social conditions

INNOCENCE M. FORD *Smithsonian* v47 no9 p98 Ja/F 2017

Prisoners of war

See also

Concentration camps

Interview Paul Golz A German View of D-Day L. Bradner bw *Military History* v34 no5 p14 Ja 2018

THE SURVIVOR A. Holl *MHQ: Quarterly Journal of Military History* v29 no3 p14 Spr 2017

Prisoners of war—United States—Government policy

The Tehran Two-Step J. Lifhits color *Weekly Standard* v22 no33 p11 My 8 2017

Prisoners—Crimes against

A crisis in our prisons E. SOLOMON color *Maclean's* v130 no3 p11 Ap 2017

Prisoners—Death

CELL BLOCKS AREN'T PSYCH WARDS C. J. CIARAMELLA *Reason* v48 no10 p15 Mr 2017

Cruel and Unusual Healthcare K. R. QUANDT and J. RIDGEWAY *In These Times* v40 no12 p24 D 2016

Prisoners—Deinstitutionalization

LIFE AFTER LIFE S. Michaels color *Mother Jones* v42 no4 p10 Jl/Ag 2017

Prisoners—Education

Correction Course D. LEE *America* v215 no15 p27 N 14 2016

Prisoners—Family relationships

My incarcerated nephew, the guest of honor H. Neumark color *Christian Century* v134 no8 p1 Ap 12 2017

Prisoners—Intellectual life

REHABILITATION THROUGH HUMANISM A. S. THOMAS *Humanist* v77 no5 p42 S/O 2017

Prisoners—Recreation

Prison Ecology J. B. HICKS *Orion Magazine* v35 no4/5 p7 Jl-O 2016

Prisoners—Religious life

A church for every prisoner C. Hoke color *Christian Century* v133 no22 p24 O 26 2016

God Remembered Me in Prison G. McGuire color *Christianity Today* v61 no5 p79 Je 2017

REHABILITATION THROUGH HUMANISM A. S. THOMAS *Humanist* v77 no5 p42 S/O 2017

Prisoners—Services for

The Sister & The Lifers M. CORWIN *Los Angeles Magazine* p105 F 2017

Prisoners—Social conditions—21st century

The Social Cost of Solitary Confinement K. Reiter *Time* v188 no18 p21 O 31 2016

Prisons

See also

Prison conditions

Life on the Outside J. ROSEN color *Publishers Weekly* v264 no18 p31 My 1 2017

Out of the tombs I. S. Villegas color *Christian Century* v134 no20 p31 S 27 2017

Prisons—Brazil

Why Brazil's Prisoners Are Rioting T. John color *Time* v189 no4 p11 Ja 23 2017

Prisons—Canada

A crisis in our prisons E. SOLOMON color *Maclean's* v130 no3 p11 Ap 2017

Prisons—Design & construction

How Not to Build a Jail C. J. Ciaramella color *Reason* v48 no7 p20 D 2016

Prisons—Economic aspects

Payday for Private Prisons? *America* v216 no6 p9 Mr 20 2017

Prisons—Environmental aspects

Don't Look Away M. SCHENWAR *Earth Island Journal* v32 no2 p2 Summ 2017

Prison Ecology J. B. HICKS *Orion Magazine* v35 no4/5 p7 Jl-O 2016

Prisons—Government policy

How Not to Build a Jail C. J. Ciaramella color *Reason* v48 no7 p20 D 2016

Prisons—Louisiana

Cruel and Unusual Healthcare K. R. QUANDT and J. RIDGEWAY *In These Times* v40 no12 p24 D 2016

Prisons—Officials & employees

LIFE ON THE LINE C. G. Reid *Harper's Magazine* v334 no2002 p58 Mr 2017

Prisons—United States

AMERICA'S TOXIC PRISONS C. Bernd, Z. Loftus-Farren et al color map *Earth Island Journal* v32 no2 p17 Summ 2017

Pritchard, John

Eleanor Catton *Current Biography* v77 no10 p18 O 2016

Pritchard, Jonathan K.

Detection of human adaptation during the past 2000 years bibl graph *Science* v354 no6313 p760 N 11 2016

Pritchard, Joshua

Mario Balotelli *Current Biography* v77 no10 p7 O 2016

Pritchard, William H.

Celebration of the World bw *Commonweal* v114 no14 p33 S 8 2017

Departure Lounge *Weekly Standard* v22 no5 p32 O 10 2016

Enigma Machine color *Weekly Standard* v22 no17 p33 Ja 2 2017

Frenemies bw *Commonweal* v143 no20 p24 D 16 2016

Hardy the Londoner bw *Weekly Standard* v22 no26 p32 Mr 13 2017

The Laureate of Loneliness [Cover story] bw *Commonweal* v144 no10 p26 Je 2 2017

Magic Lantern bw *Weekly Standard* v22 no37 p33 Je 5 2017

Trails of the Jazz Age bw color *Weekly Standard* v22 no40 p30 Je 26 2017

Pritchard Patent Product Co. Ltd.

Peco charges into scenery market with static grass C. Grivno color *Model Railroader* v84 no2 p72 F 2017

Pritchett, Kelly

BEST FOODS FOR RUNNERS [Cover story] cartoon color *Runner's World* v52 no3 p54 Ap 2017

PRITCHETT, LAURA

Literary Sex *Publishers Weekly* v264 no2 p72 Ja 9 2017

Pritzker, J. B.

Battle of the Plutocrats J. MILLER *New Republic* v248 no11 p8 N 2017

CLASH OF THE TITANS J. DUGDALE color *Chicago* v66 no4 p26 Ap 2017

SPRINGFIELD OR BUST C. FELSENTHAL color *Chicago* v66 no11 p24 N 2017

Pritzker, Penny, 1959-

Commerce Secretary Pritzker on the Economy, Worker Training, and Trade with Asia W. Frick *Harvard Business Review Digital Articles* p2 Je 12 2015

Penny Pritzker J. Crelin color *Current Biography* v77 no11 p63 N 2016

Prius automobile—Design & construction

STILL UGLY, AFTER ALL THESE YEARS J. Lippert color graph *Bloomberg Businessweek* no4494 p22 O 10 2016

Prius automobile—Evaluation

10 Top Picks J. S. Bartlett color *Consumer Reports* v82 no4 p22 Ap 2017

New Car Ratings chart diag *Consumer Reports* v82 no4 p40 Ap 2017

STILL UGLY, AFTER ALL THESE YEARS J. Lippert color graph *Bloomberg Businessweek* no4494 p22 O 10 2016

Tortoise and the Hare T. QUIROGA chart color *Car & Driver* v62 no8 p48 F 2017

Toyota Prius Two Eco chart color *Motor Trend* v69 no1 p133 Ja 2017

Privacy

Passwords Are Terrible, but Will Biometrics Be Any Better? A. Rjeily and C. Jacco *Harvard Business Review Digital Articles* p1 My 11 2017

PROTECT YOUR PRIVACY color *Good Housekeeping* v265

no3 p93 S 2017

SENSORY OVERLOAD R. Greenfield color *Bloomberg Businessweek* no4512 p82 F 20 2017

Workplace Wellness Programs Could Be Putting Your Health Data at Risk I. Ajunwa color *Harvard Business Review Digital Articles* p2 Ja 19 2017

Privacy—Lawsuits & claims

Under the Law J. Underwood diag *Phi Delta Kappan* v99 no2 p76 O 2017

Privacy—United States

How to Be a Stealthy Job Seeker When You Know It's Time to Go K. Bahler color *Money* v46 no4 p17 My 2017

Private art collections

ARTISTIC TRIUMPH S. THORNTON color *Architectural Digest* v74 no8 p62 Ag 2017

Man of distinction J. Gardner cartoon *Magazine Antiques* v184 no1 p174 Ja/F 2017

Noble Spirit S. WALLIS color *Architectural Digest* no11 p62 N 1 2017

Old guard avant-garde G. Cerio color *Magazine Antiques* v184 no3 p124 My/Je 2017

Private art collections—Exhibitions

A Portrait of the Artist as a Collector S. DOUGLAS color *ARTnews* v116 no1 p42 Spr 2017

Pres. Photogenic *USA Today Magazine* v145 no2864 p32 My 2017

Private art collections—Management

THE COLLECTORS C. Neuhaus *Saturday Evening Post* v289 no3 p14 My/Je 2017

Private clubs

YOUR OWN PRIVATE MOUNTAIN R. K. Urken color *Bloomberg Businessweek* no4541 p63 O 9 2017

Private companies

Why Unicorns Are Struggling V. Govindarajan, T. Govindarajan et al *Harvard Business Review Digital Articles* p2 Ap 21 2016

Private companies—United States

Does Business Know Best? You can't run a public agency like a private company, but you can borrow ideas K. Barrett and R. Greene *Governing* v30 no10 p58 Jl 2017

Private equity

The Mistakes PE Firms Make When They Pick CEOs for Portfolio Companies M. Brubaker and M. Durrant *Harvard Business Review Digital Articles* p2 S 6 2016

Payless Flops, But the Owners Get a Payday N. Ahmed and S. Natarajan graph *Bloomberg Businessweek* no4516 p35 Mr 27 2017

PE Firms Are Creating a New Role: Leadership Capital Partner D. Ulrich and J. Allen *Harvard Business Review Digital Articles* p2 Ag 11 2017

Private Equity Is Eyeing Your Nest Egg M. Mittelman *Bloomberg Businessweek* no4519 p47 Ap 24 2017

Private Equity's New Phase D. Ulrich and J. Allen *Harvard Business Review Digital Articles* p2 Ag 9 2016

What Private Equity Investors Think They Do for the Companies They Buy P. Gompers, S. Kaplan et al *Harvard Business Review Digital Articles* p2 Je 18 2015

Private equity—Social aspects

OF VICE AND MEN E. Griffith color *Fortune* v175 no4 p71 Mr 15 2017

Private flying

FLIGHTS OF FANCY: A MIDSUMMER'S DAYDREAM S. Weigel color *Flying* v144 no10 p38 O 2017

GENERAL AVIATION IN CHINA P. BERGQVIST color map *Flying* v144 no10 p58 O 2017

Private investigators

Laughter: THE BEST MEDICINE G. BURKHART MEDEIROS color *Reader's Digest* v190 no1135 p100 N 2017

Private islands

Get Some Alone Time J. MURPHY color *Conde Nast Traveler* v51 no11 p72 D 2016

Private planes—Sales & prices

Private Jets Aren't So Private Anymore T. Black *Bloomberg Businessweek* no4498 p33 N 7 2016

Private police

See also

Bodyguards

Private investigators

Armed Guards *Lapham's Quarterly* v10 no3 p104 Summ 2017

Private residence elevators
 PERIOD ELEVATORS color *Old House Journal* v45 no7 p76 O 2017
Private schools
 Islamic Schools Face the Future: Independent schools are usually not required to adhere to education policy regulations if they receive no state or federal government funds S. BUKER *Islamic Horizons* v46 no3 p38 My/Je 2017
 SCHOOL SURVIVAL GUIDE R. Lynes *Harper's Magazine* p43 S 2017
Private schools—Administration
 GETTING IN H. M. CAULEY *Atlanta* v56 no7 p112 N 2016
Private schools—Canada
 Seize the Private School Advantage J. Southerst color *Maclean's* v130 no9 p50 O 2017
Private schools—Costs
 FINANCIAL AID C. WAYLOCK *Atlanta* v56 no7 p113 N 2016
Private schools—Finance
 CATHOLIC SCHOOLS WAIT ON TRUMP SCHOOL CHOICE PROMISES M. O'Loughlin color graph *America* v217 no4 p12 Ag 21 2017
Private schools—Law & legislation
 Little monks of Little Sands M. CAMPBELL color *Maclean's* v130 no7 p16 Ag 2017
Private schools—United States
 A Genius, If You Can Keep Him bw *Weekly Standard* v23 no4 p2 O 2 2017
Private schools—Washington (D.C.)
 GETTING SCHOOLED E. Plott *Washingtonian Magazine* v52 no1 p129 O 2016
Private secretaries
 THE DINNER PARTY J. EGAN cartoon *New Yorker* v93 no16 p50 Je 5 2017
Private sector
 The Best Health Care Money Can't Buy S. J. Keyser bw color *Washington Monthly* v49 no6-8 p55 Je-Ag 2017
 CONTRACTOR CEOS SHOULDN'T MAKE TEN TIMES MORE THAN THE POTUS J. Alvarez *Washington Monthly* v49 no6-8 p33 Je-Ag 2017
 Keeping It In-House K. Barrett and R. Greene *Governing* v30 no1 p60 O 2016
 The Power of a P3 M. Funkhouser *Governing* v30 no1 p61 O 2016
Private sector—Government policy
 Backdoor Government Decryption Hurts My Business and Yours M. Ali *Harvard Business Review Digital Articles* p2 S 15 2016
Private universities & colleges
 On Political Correctness W. DERESIEWICZ *American Scholar* v86 no2 p30 Spr 2017
Privateers
 Privateers on the Jersey Shore K. ARONOFF *In These Times* v41 no7 p10 Jl 2017
 THE TURKISH RAID E. S. ARNARSÓTTIR *Iceland Review* v55 no2 p48 Mr/Ap 2017
Private Wild, A (Short story)
 A Private Wild L. NAKANISHI *Orion Magazine* v35 no4/5 p102 Jl-O 2016
Privatization
   See also
   Privatization in education
 ATC PRIVATIZATION R. MARK bw *Flying* v144 no8 p60 Ag 2017
 NASA Has a New Way to Fly J. Kluger color *Time* v188 no27-28 p90 D 26 2016
 This Land Is Was Your Land D. Slater *Sierra* v101 no4 p24 Jl/Ag 2016
Privatization in education
 The Long Game of Betsy DeVos J. Berkshire color *Progressive* v81 no2 p28 F 2017
 Mexico's Uprising Against Education 'Reform' J. Abbott color *Progressive* v81 no2 p24 F 2017
Privatization—Israel
 HOW ISRAEL PRIVATIZED ITS OCCUPATION OF PALESTINE A. LOEWENSTEIN and M. KENNARD color il *Nation* v303 no20 p20 N 14 2016
Privatization—United States
 -A - NEW DEAL FOR WALL STREET: Trump's plan to sell off

our infrastructure, and the Democrats who paved the way R. BURNS *In These Times* v41 no8 p14 Ag 2017
 An Infrastructure Plan From Down Under M. Niquette, M. Burgess et al diag *Bloomberg Businessweek* no4534 p37 Ag 14 2017
 PRIVATIZE ATC? NO WAY! S. Pope bw *Flying* v144 no5 p8 My 2017
 Soaring Prices B. Covert *Nation* v305 no2 p5 Jl 17 2017
 Trump's Big Agenda K. PHILLIPS-FEIN color *New Republic* v248 no3 p6 Mr 2017
Privilege (Social sciences)
 HUMANISM and the CHALLENGE of PRIVILEGE A. B. PINN *Humanist* v77 no3 p22 My/Je 2017
Privitera, P.
 Observation of a large-scale anisotropy in the arrival directions of cosmic rays above 8×1018 eV *Science* v357 no6357 p1266 S 22 2017
Priya, Shashank
 Harvesting electrical energy from carbon nanotube yarn twist diag graph *Science* v357 no6353 p773 Ag 25 2017
Prizes (Contests & competitions)
 LESSONS LEARNED C. TOY bw color *Spin to Win Rodeo* v21 no1 p66 Mr 2017
 NAME THE BOAT color *Sea Magazine* v109 no7 p8 Jl 2017
 WHAT WILL YOU BE DOING THIS WINTER? color *Seventeen* v76 no12 p12 D 2016/Ja 2017
Pro-choice movement
 Letter from... IRELAND K. Cairns *Advocate* no1088 p28 D 2016/Ja 2017
 Running From Choice K. Pollitt *Nation* v305 no3 p12 Jl 31 2017
 The women who marched M. S. J. Malone *America* v216 no11 p3 My 15 2017
Pro Comp USA (Company)
 TUN OF FUN D. SCANLON color diag *Dirt Sports + Off-Road* v51 no3 p30 Mr 2017
Pro Football Hall of Fame (U.S.)
 Hall Pass T. Rohan and T. Keith color *Sports Illustrated* v127 no4 p15 Ag 7 2017
 A LEAGUE OF HER OWN C. CUNNINGHAM *Cincinnati Magazine* v50 no7 p68 Ap 2017
Pro-Ject Audio Systems (Company)
 Conversation Starter B. Ankosko color *Sound & Vision* v82 no5 p74 Je 2017
Pro-life activists
 The Courting of Pro-life Leaders F. BARNES color *Weekly Standard* v22 no16 p10 D 26 2016
Pro-life movement
 The Pro-Life Movement in Japan J. Morgan *Society* v54 no3 p238 Je 2017
Pro-life movement—United States
 Abortion & Social Justice [Cover story] G. W. Schlabach color *Commonweal* v144 no1 p11 Ja 6 2017
 The Fight for Choice K. Pollitt diag il *Nation* v304 no4 p6 F 6 2017
 Pro-Life's Reformation Ripples K. SHELLNUTT *Christianity Today* v61 no1 p21 Ja/F 2017
 A Second Chance at Choice R. Graham *New York Times Magazine* p46 Jl 23 2017
Probabilism
 A thermodynamic theory of granular material endures: Theorists have tested what seemed like an untestable conjecture: that all the possible arrangements of grains in a packing are equally probable A. G. Smart *Physics Today* v70 no9 p20 S 2017
Probability forecasts (Meteorology)
   See also
   Rainfall probabilities
 To Forecast Rain, Look to the Ocean: SCIENTISTS EXPLORE COMPELLING NEW WAY TO PREDICT SEASONAL RAINFALL L. Lippsett *Oceanus* v52 no2 p6 Spr 2017
Probert, John Llewellyn
 The Lovecraft Squad: All Hallows Horror *Publishers Weekly* v263 no51 p128 D 12 2016
Probiotics
 ASK ASKED color *Prevention* v68 no11 p11 N 2016
 ask the experts A. GILMOUR, S. HASTINGS et al cartoon color *Dressage Today* v23 no5 p64 Ja 2017
 The Dubious Science of Skin Care color *Prevention* v69 no5 p22

Aut 2017

Processions—Social aspects

Acting Out Assimilation J. R. GRAM *American Indian Quarterly* v40 no3 p251 Summ 2016

Prochazka, Zuzana

25 TRENDS ARE MAKING BOATING BETTER *Sea Magazine* v109 no4 p50 Ap 2017

7 REASONS FOR BOATING'S EXPANDING APPEAL: OWNING AND OPERATING A VESSEL HAS BECOME EASIER AND MORE ACCESSIBLE FOR A WIDER VARIETY OF PEOPLE *Sea Magazine* v109 no9 p48 S 2017

Alerion Sport 30 color *Sail* v48 no3 p26 Mr 2017

AZIMUT 50 FLYBRIDGE: A NEW ITALIAN 50-FOOTER IS MAKING WAVES ON THE WEST COAST color *Sea Magazine* v109 no8 p38 Ag 2017

AZIMUT 60 *Sea Magazine* v108 no9 p36 S 2016

Bavaria Cruiser 34 color *Sail* v48 no10 p30 O 2017

Beautiful Bequia color *Sail* v48 no10 p93 O 2017

BELT & SUSPENDERS *Sea Magazine* v108 no10 p60 O 2016

BENETEAU GRAN TURISMO 40 *Sea Magazine* v109 no1 p38 Ja 2017

Beneteau Oceanis Yacht 62 color *Sail* v48 no6 p26 Je 2017

Beneteau Sense 57 color *Sail* v48 no11 p26 N 2017

BENETEAU SWIFT TRAWLER 30 *Sea Magazine* v108 no9 p32 S 2016

Be Safer at Sea: Know what to inspect, what equipment to have and which procedures to practice color *Sea Magazine* v109 no7 p40 Jl 2017

BEST BOATS 2017 color *Sail* v47 no12 p24 D 2016

BOAT BUILDERS BUILD BETTER BOATS *Sea Magazine* v109 no2 p50 F 2017

Checkout Tips color *Sail* v48 no1 p64 Ja 2017

COBIA 277 *Sea Magazine* v108 no10 p34 O 2016

Dehler 34 cartoon color *Sail* v48 no1 p28 Ja 2017

EXPEDITION CHARTERS color *Sail* v48 no11 p32 N 2017

Five Essential Questions for Your Chart Briefing color *Sail* v47 no12 p55 D 2016

Four Things Chartering Taught Me color *Sail* v48 no7 p56 Jl 2017

GALEON 420 FLY: THE POLISH BUILDER PREMIERES A SOLID BOAT WITH A FEW NEAT TRICKS UP ITS SLEEVE *Sea Magazine* v109 no5 p40 My 2017

Hallberg-Rassy 40 Mk II color *Sail* v48 no8 p24 Ag 2017

INSIDE OUT: THE NEW BENETEAU GRAN TURISMO 46 BLENDS OUTSIDE AND INSIDE SEAMLESSLY *Sea Magazine* v109 no5 p36 My 2017

Moody DS54 cartoon color *Sail* v48 no2 p34 F 2017

Mouthy MFD *Boating World* v38 no4 p48 Ap 2017

Q+A *Boating World* v37 no9 p24 N/D 2016

Q+A *Boating World* v38 no5 p26 My 2017

Q+A *Boating World* v38 no8 p24 S/O 2017

Santa Catalina Island color *Sail* v48 no6 p42 Je 2017

A SECOND LOOK *Boating World* v38 no5 p48 My 2017

Smart Provisioning color *Sail* v48 no4 p75 Ap 2017

SOUTH for the SUMMER color map *Sail* v48 no3 p32 Mr 2017

Specialty Charters color *Sail* v48 no5 p59 My 2017

STAY SHARP! *Sea Magazine* v109 no1 p56 Ja 2017

Steady as She Goes color *Sea Magazine* v109 no8 p46 Ag 2017

St. John Sojourn color *Sail* v48 no3 p66 Mr 2017

Sublime Snorkeling Spots color *Sail* v48 no6 p59 Je 2017

TECHNOLOGY IS CHANGING HOW YACHTS ARE BUILT AND, IN TURN, HOW DECKS AND INTERIORS ARE BEING DESIGNED color *Sea Magazine* v109 no6 p46 Je 2017

THREE WORLDS, One Boat color map *Sail* v48 no10 p40 O 2017

When and Why to Use a Charter Broker color *Sail* v48 no2 p73 F 2017

Winter Charters Post Irma and Maria color *Sail* v48 no11 p64 N 2017

X-Yachts X4 color *Sail* v48 no7 p22 Jl 2017

YACHT CHARTERS for Newbies color map *Sail* v48 no10 p47 O 2017

Prochnik, George

Along for the Ride A. NEWHOUSE *New York Times Book Review* p23 My 7 2017

He Remade Kings *New York Times Book Review* p17 Ja 8 2017

Our Freudian Complex [Cover story] *New York Times Book Review* p1 Ag 20 2017

Procopio, A. John

Board Members Benefit from Becoming Mentors *Harvard Business Review Digital Articles* p2 D 16 2014

Procrastination

5 Research-Based Strategies for Overcoming Procrastination C. Bailey *Harvard Business Review Digital Articles* p2 O 4 2017

Almost All Managers Have at Least One Career-Limiting Habit J. Grenny *Harvard Business Review Digital Articles* p2 Jl 5 2016

Deadline trauma R. COUNTER color *Maclean's* v130 no2 p64 Mr 2017

How to Beat Procrastination C. Webb *Harvard Business Review Digital Articles* p2 Jl 29 2016

Keeping Anxious Thoughts at Bay W. Johnson *Harvard Business Review Digital Articles* p2 F 22 2016

News & analysis *People Management* p9 S 2017

That's Outrageous! *Reader's Digest* v189 no1128 p87 Mr 2017

Procrastination—Prevention

Prevention, Procrastination & Woe P. Reichard *New Orleans Homes & Lifestyles* v20 no2 p82 Spr 2017

Procter & Gamble Co.

Merging Two Global Company Cultures M. Bird *Harvard Business Review Digital Articles* p2 Ag 4 2015

Nelson Peltz Makes Nice A. Melin and S. Deveau bw *Bloomberg Businessweek* no4536 p30 S 4 2017

"SHAMPOOING" CONDITIONERS J. Thomas color *Good Housekeeping* v263 no5 p28 N 2016

Proctor, Coleman

CLUTCH B. Welch color *Spin to Win Rodeo* v20 no9 p50 N 2016

Weathering the Storm [Cover story] C. Toy color *Spin to Win Rodeo* v21 no4 p60 Je 2017

Proctor, Minna Zallman

Landslide: True Stories color *Publishers Weekly* v264 no22 p52 My 29 2017

Procurement of organs, tissues, etc.

THE COST OF TRANSPLANTS color diag *Fortune* v176 no4 p23 S 15 2017

Prodan, Virginia

Becoming a Christian Almost Got Me Killed bw *Christianity Today* v60 no8 p111 O 2016

Prodanovich, Todd

Can't We All Just Get Along(board)? color *Surfer* v57 no12 p14 Ja/F 2017

The Devil on My Shoulders color *Surfer* v58 no3 p94 Je 2017

Editor's Note color *Surfer* v58 no1 p10 Ap 2017

Editor's Note color *Surfer* v58 no2 p12 My 2017

Editor's Note color *Surfer* v58 no3 p10 Je 2017

For the Record color *Surfer* v58 no5 p46 S 2017

IF YOU BUILD IT, They Will Surf color *Surfer* v58 no6 p48 O 2017

IN SESSION color *Surfer* v58 no1 p48 Ap 2017

John Severson: 1933-2017 bw *Surfer* v58 no4 p132 Ag 2017

MIND CONTROL bw color *Surfer* v58 no3 p46 Je 2017

The Plastic Inevitable color *Surfer* v58 no1 p28 Ap 2017

Rise of the Machines color *Surfer* v58 no6 p28 O 2017

A Trestles Taxonomy color *Surfer* v58 no5 p32 S 2017

Welcome to the Pizote House color *Surfer* v57 no11 p12 D 2016

Pro-democracy demonstrations, Hong Kong, China, 2014-

August 2017 *Current History* v116 no792 p288 O 2017

Prodrugs

A multifunctional catalyst that stereoselectively assembles prodrugs D. A. DiRocco, Y. Ji et al diag *Science* v356 no6336 p426 Ap 28 2017

Produce trade

See also

Food prices

FARM-TO-TABLE FAVES *Indianapolis Monthly* v12 no40 p79 Ag 2017

HOW TO HUNT AND GUT YOUR OWN DINNER ... AND OTHER LIFE LESSONS FROM A HOOSIER KITCHEN RENAISSANCE WOMAN S. KROWIAK *Indianapolis Monthly* v12 no40 p72 Ag 2017

Produce trade—Export & import trade

Increased Demand for U.S. Agricultural Exports Would Likely Lead to More U.S. Jobs S. Zahniser, T. Hertz et al *Amber Waves: The Economics of Food, Farming, Natural Resources, & Rural*

America p1 Je 2017

Producers, The (Theatrical production)

Code and Coops D. Kuehler *Stage Directions* v30 no2 p28 F 2017

Product counterfeiting

Knocking It Off G. Adamson color *Magazine Antiques* v184 no4 p22 Jl/Ag 2017

Product design

5 Ways Product Design Needs to Evolve for the Internet of Things P. Daugherty, P. Banerjee et al *Harvard Business Review Digital Articles* p2 N 14 2014

The Customers Who Are Happy to Pay More for Less P. Chandon *Harvard Business Review Digital Articles* p2 O 29 2015

The Internet of Things Needs Design, Not Just Technology S. A. Nelson and P. Metaxatos *Harvard Business Review Digital Articles* p2 Ap 29 2016

Lean Doesn't Always Create the Best Products J. Kolko *Harvard Business Review Digital Articles* p2 My 14 2015

LOOK AGAIN P. ANTONELLI color *New York Times Magazine* p50 N 13 2016

Make It New J. Silverstein *New York Times Magazine* p22 N 13 2016

MAKE-OVER MANIA R. WALKER color *New York Times Magazine* p26 N 13 2016

A Process for Empathetic Product Design J. Kolko *Harvard Business Review Digital Articles* p2 Ap 23 2015

Product design—Awards

You Can Charge Women More, but Should You? R. Mohammed *Harvard Business Review Digital Articles* p2 Ja 29 2016

Product design—History

WHAT MAKES THINGS COOL D. THOMPSON color *Atlantic* v319 no1 p68 Ja/F 2017

Product differentiation

When It's Smart to Copy Your Competitor's Brand Promise Yi Zhu and A. Dukes *Harvard Business Review Digital Articles* p2 Mr 23 2017

Product instruction manuals

What Happened to User Manuals? D. Pogue color *Scientific American* v316 no4 p30 Ap 2017

Product launches

Reinventing the Wheel M. Monticello chart color *Consumer Reports* v82 no1 p52 Ja 2017

What Your Moonshot Can Learn from the Apollo Program J. Geraci *Harvard Business Review Digital Articles* p2 Ap 4 2017

When First Movers Are Rewarded, and When They're Not R. Klingebiel and J. Joseph *Harvard Business Review Digital Articles* p2 Ag 11 2015

Product liability of drugs

St. Louis Loses Favor With Plaintiffs M. C. Fisk and J. Feeley cartoon *Bloomberg Businessweek* no4532 p16 Jl 31 2017

Product liability—Lawsuits & claims

St. Louis Loses Favor With Plaintiffs M. C. Fisk and J. Feeley cartoon *Bloomberg Businessweek* no4532 p16 Jl 31 2017

Product liability—Missouri

Plaintiffs' Lawyers ? St. Louis M. C. Fisk and T. Bross *Bloomberg Businessweek* no4493 p31 O 3 2016

Product life cycle

THE LIFE CYCLE OF A CELL PHONE *New York State Conservationist* v71 no4 p6 F 2017

Product lines

THE $3,000 SOFA CHALLENGE K. O'SHEA-EVANS color *House Beautiful* v159 no2 p38 Mr 2017

emporium color *Dressage Today* v23 no7 p62 Mr 2017

Head Over Heels color *House Beautiful* v159 no2 p28 Mr 2017

"HOW MUCH TRAVEL DO I NEED?" M. Phillips and B. STRICKLAND color *Bicycling* v58 no3 p44 Ap 2017

Lush Life K. O'SHEA-EVANS color *House Beautiful* v159 no2 p31 Mr 2017

STELLAR KAYAKS color *Canoe & Kayak Magazine* v45 no1 p106 Wint 2017

Product lines—Evaluation

Legacy Audio Powerbloc2 and Powerbloc4 Amplifiers D. Kumin chart color graph *Sound & Vision* v82 no6 p58 Jl/Ag 2017

Product management

See also

New product development

Brand Management S. Rushin color *Sports Illustrated* v126 no4

p76 Ja 30 2017

Brands Are Behaving Like Organized Religions U. M. Dholakia *Harvard Business Review Digital Articles* p2 F 18 2016

Don't Overlook the Small Brands You Already Own E. Yoon *Harvard Business Review Digital Articles* p2 D 30 2016

Dysfunctional Products Come from Dysfunctional Organizations J. Kolko *Harvard Business Review Digital Articles* p2 Ja 21 2015

EXPECT THE UNEXPECTED color *Working Mother* p22 F/Mr 2017

Know the Job Your Product Was Hired for (with Help from Customer Selfies) C. M. Christensen and B. Moesta *Harvard Business Review Digital Articles* p2 Je 6 2016

The New World of Mini Consumer Packaged Goods M. Picciola and R. Wilson *Harvard Business Review Digital Articles* p2 S 26 2016

Research: Customers Notice When Products Shrink More Than When They Get Bigger P. Chandon color *Harvard Business Review Digital Articles* p2 Mr 7 2017

Product placement

James Bond, Dunder Mifflin, and the Future of Product Placement L. Muzellec *Harvard Business Review Digital Articles* p2 Je 23 2016

Product recall

See also

Automobile recall

More Robust Recalls color *Consumer Reports* v82 no11 p5 N 2017

RECALLS color *Consumer Reports* v82 no10 p26 O 2017

Samsung kills off the Galaxy Note7 to end the exploding battery debacle J. RIBEIROT color *PCWorld* v35 no11 p27 N 2016

WHY RECALLS OFTEN HURT RIVALS *Harvard Business Review* v94 no11 p26 N 2016

Product recovery

DIFFERENCE IN PARTS R. Bohacz *Successful Farming* v115 no2 p30 F 2017

Product returns

The Point of All Returns S. ADAMS color *Forbes* v200 no4 p75 O 24 2017

RETURN POLICIES THAT ROCK—AND NOT D. Rosato *Consumer Reports* v81 no12 p29 D 2016

Production (Economic theory)

See also

Agricultural productivity

Industrial efficiency

Against Big-Government Conservatism J. Krill *National Review* v69 no2 p2 F 6 2017

The Competitive Landscape for Machine Intelligence S. Zilis and J. Cham *Harvard Business Review Digital Articles* p2 N 2 2016

Economic Indicators: Prepared for the Joint Economic Committee by the Council of Economic Advisers *Economic Indicators* p1 Jl 2017

Factories 2.0 M. Mandel *MIT Technology Review* v119 no6 p10 N/D 2016

GLEANINGS A. Luety *Successful Farming* v115 no2 p8 F 2017

HOW TO MAKE HUMAN CAPITAL COUNT C. Leaf color *Fortune* v175 no2 p6 F 1 2017

The Problem with the U.S. Economy Isn't Something Politicians Can Fix M. Levinson *Harvard Business Review Digital Articles* p2 N 29 2016

THE SLO-MO ECONOMY P. Coy color *Bloomberg Businessweek* no4498 p86 N 7 2016

Production methods in oil sands

Can Oil Sands Pay Off At $50 a Barrel? K. Orland and N. O. Pearson graph *Bloomberg Businessweek* no4535 p33 Ag 28 2017

Production standards

How Labor Standards Can Be Good for Growth E. Verhoogen *Harvard Business Review Digital Articles* p2 Ap 27 2016

Production studios

THE VOICE R. O'CONNOR cartoon *Chicago* v66 no5 p40 My 2017

Production (Economic theory)—Charts, diagrams, etc.

INTERNATIONAL STATISTICS *Economic Indicators* p35 My 2017

PRODUCTION AND BUSINESS ACTIVITY *Economic Indicators* p17 My 2017

PRODUCTION AND BUSINESS ACTIVITY *Economic Indicators* p17 N 2016

TOTAL OUTPUT, INCOME, AND SPENDING *Economic Indicators* p1 My 2017

Productivity accounting

What Economists Get Wrong About Measuring Productivity R. L. Martin *Harvard Business Review Digital Articles* p2 S 14 2015

Proelite Inc.

THE $60 INTERIOR REVIVAL E. DYER color *Popular Mechanics* p42 Je 2017

Proelss, Alexander

De-extinction, nomenclature, and the law color *Science* v356 no6342 p1016 Je 9 2017

Proenneke, Richard L.

Off The Grid R. Marech *National Parks* v91 no2 p4 Spr 2017

Proenza Schouler LLC

Chloë Sevigny HER BEST EVER E. Wilson color *InStyle* v24 no5 p88 My 2017

Proestou, Dina A.

The genomic landscape of rapid repeated evolutionary adaptation to toxic pollution in wild fish bibl graph *Science* v354 no6317 p1305 D 9 2016

Professional, The (Film)

They Came to Slay E. Dockterman color *Time* v189 no9 p56 Mr 13 2017

Professional associations

To Stay Relevant, Professional Associations Must Rebrand D. L. Yohn *Harvard Business Review Digital Articles* p2 Ja 5 2016

Professional athletes

THE LIFE OF BEEF JOHNSTON I. Boudway color *Bloomberg Businessweek* no4523 p59 My 22 2017

Professional athletes—Health

The Case for ... Time Off L. J. Wertheim and T. Keith color *Sports Illustrated* v127 no1 p28 Jl 3 2017

Professional athletes—Interviews

A-RODS'S NEXT BIG SWING P. Sellers color *Fortune* v176 no2 p74 Ag 1 2017

Professional athletes—United States

As American as Refusing to Stand for the National Anthem R. Wiedeman img *New York* p34 F 20 2017

Professional baseball

Murder Analytics L. PICKER *Publishers Weekly* v264 no35 p116 Ag 28 2017

Professional corporations

See also

Group medical practice

BEST IN DALLAS *D: The Magazine of Dallas* v43 no10 p162 O 2016

Professional education

See also

Teacher education

Advancing Team Research for Science and Society R. E. GROPP *BioScience* v67 no2 p103 F 2017

EMBRACING THE UNKNOWN [Cover story] C. P. Clark color *Literacy Today (2411-7862)* v34 no5 p28 Mr/Ap 2017

Plan Your Professional Development for the Year D. Clark *Harvard Business Review Digital Articles* p2 Ja 7 2016

PROFESSIONAL DEVELOPMENT *Parks & Recreation* v51 no11 p57 N 2016

REFRAMING RESEARCH M. Ewers color *Literacy Today (2411-7862)* v34 no5 p12 Mr/Ap 2017

Score a Great Summer Internship K. Mulhere chart color *Money* v46 no1 p34 Ja/F 2017

TRAIL DAZE B. Donahue color *Backpacker* p62 O 2017

Two Ways to Clarify Your Professional Passions R. S. Kaplan *Harvard Business Review Digital Articles* p2 Mr 30 2015

When Mentorship Crosses Cultures, Both Sides Learn J. Zikic *Harvard Business Review Digital Articles* p2 Ag 5 2016

Professional employees

See also

Architects

Businesspeople

Clergy

Dentists

Economists

Editors

Educators

Engineers

Executives

Journalists

Medical personnel

Nurses

Physicians

Psychologists

Scientists

Social workers

Teachers

Veterinarians

Don't Let Inexperience Stop You from Participating in Meetings A. Molinsky and M. Hahn color *Harvard Business Review Digital Articles* p2 Ja 4 2017

Faces of the Venezuelan Exodus M. Newkirk and N. Crooks color *Bloomberg Businessweek* no4522 p15 My 15 2017

How to Say No to Things You Want to Do D. Clark *Harvard Business Review Digital Articles* p2 Ja 4 2016

How to Separate the Personal and Professional on Social Media A. Ollier-Malaterre and N. Rothbard *Harvard Business Review Digital Articles* p2 Mr 26 2015

If You're Not Outside Your Comfort Zone, You Won't Learn Anything A. Molinsky *Harvard Business Review Digital Articles* p2 Jl 29 2016

Innovation Labs: Opportunities to Share Ideas and Solutions S. ECKELBERRY *Parks & Recreation* v52 no3 p8 Mr 2017

Surgery Gone Bad A. Dike color *Sail* v48 no1 p52 Ja 2017

Taking Ownership: Finding the Right Professional for You M. Lacy *In Stride* v12 no3 p30 My 2017

A Tourist's Guide to Changing Careers J. Acuff *Harvard Business Review Digital Articles* p2 Ap 13 2015

What You Need to Stand Out in a Noisy World D. Clark color *Harvard Business Review Digital Articles* p2 Ja 6 2017

Professional employees—Congresses

Festival Preview L. N. Williams color *Essence* v48 no3 p75 Jl 2017

How to Get the Most Out of a Conference R. Knight *Harvard Business Review Digital Articles* p2 Jl 8 2015

Professional ethics

See also

Business ethics

Journalistic ethics

Medical ethics

5 Questions to Ask Before You Call Out Someone Powerful M. Reitz and J. Higgins *Harvard Business Review Digital Articles* p2 Ap 7 2017

Must I Tell My Therapist About My Other Therapist? K. A. Appiah *New York Times Magazine* p28 S 17 2017

The Newbie's Survival Guide A. Rivers color *Dance Magazine* v91 no3 p30 Mr 2017

When You Feel Pressured to Do the Wrong Thing at Work J. L. Badaracco *Harvard Business Review Digital Articles* p2 N 2 2016

Professional ethics of teachers

Should I Turn In My Tax-Cheating Relative? K. A. Appiah *New York Times Magazine* p24 Ag 27 2017

Professional Golfers' Association of America—Congresses

THE KEEPERS OF THE GAME T. CHIARELLA color *Popular Mechanics* p48 Je 2017

Professional hockey

Memorandum R. LONG *National Review* v69 no19 p50 O 16 2017

Professional identity

Professional Identity and Dishonest Behavior P. Houdek *Society* v54 no3 p253 Je 2017

Professional isolation

How to Overcome Executive Isolation R. Ashkenas color *Harvard Business Review Digital Articles* p2 F 2 2017

Professional learning communities

PLCs on steroids Moving teacher practice to the center of data teams M. J. Wasta chart il *Phi Delta Kappan* v98 no5 p67 F 2017

The right network for the right problem L. M. Gomez, J. L. Russell et al color diag *Phi Delta Kappan* v98 no3 p8 N 2016

Strategic accountability is key to making PLCs effective L. B.

Hubbard *Harvard Business Review Digital Articles* p2 Ag 12 2016

Profitability

See also

Profit margins

3 Terrible Strategies for Companies Seeking Growth U. Haque *Harvard Business Review Digital Articles* p2 O 6 2014

Boxed In G. Barkho and Jing Cao color graph *Bloomberg Businessweek* no4535 p23 Ag 28 2017

Contribution Margin: What It Is, How to Calculate It, and Why You Need It A. Gallo *Harvard Business Review Digital Articles* p2 O 13 2017

How economics can shape precision medicines A. D. Stern, B. M. Alexander et al bibl color *Science* v355 no6330 p1131 Mr 17 2017

Profit Is Less About Good Management than You Think J. A. Marco-Izquierdo *Harvard Business Review Digital Articles* p2 S 28 2015

Study: Firms with More Women in the C-Suite Are More Profitable M. Noland and T. Moran *Harvard Business Review Digital Articles* p2 F 8 2016

Study: More Frequent Sales Quotas Help Volume but Hurt Profits D. J. Chung and D. Narayandas *Harvard Business Review Digital Articles* p2 2017

Too Much Profit Can Doom Your Company B. Power and R. Merrifield *Harvard Business Review Digital Articles* p2 Je 1 2015

TYING VCs TO SHAREHOLDERS D. Lyons color *Fortune* v75 no1 p51 Ja 1 2017

When Sales Incentives Should Be Based on Profit, Not Revenue A. A. Zoltners, P. K. Sinha et al *Harvard Business Review Digital Articles* p2 Je 10 2015

Why Some Digital Companies Should Delay Profitability for as Long as They Can M. Wessel, A. Levie et al *Harvard Business Review Digital Articles* p2 My 4 2017

Profit maximization

$400 Million Richer By Pinching Pennies E. Huet *Bloomberg Businessweek* no4515 p29 Mr 20 2017

Profit—Charts, diagrams, etc.

Movers K. Stock color *Bloomberg Businessweek* no4511 p13 F 13 2017

Profit—Lawsuits & claims

News Briefs *Publishers Weekly* v264 no41 p5 O 9 2017

Profit-sharing

See also

Bonuses (Employee fringe benefits)

Profit Sharing Boosts Employee Productivity and Satisfaction A. Bryson and R. Freeman *Harvard Business Review Digital Articles* p2 D 13 2016

Profit-sharing—Case studies

Huawei: A Case Study of When Profit Sharing Works D. De Cremer and Tian Tao *Harvard Business Review Digital Articles* p2 S 24 2015

Profit-sharing—United States

Can Profit Sharing Address Income Inequality? W. Frick *Harvard Business Review Digital Articles* p2 S 7 2017

PROFITT, GARTH

Jake's John Hancock *Idaho Magazine* v16 no6 p27 Mr 2017

Progenitor cells

Lineage-dependent spatial and functional organization of the mammalian enteric nervous system R. Lasrado, W. Boesmans et al color graph *Science* v356 no6339 p722 My 19 2017

Program budgeting

12 Steps to Financial Success: Empowering At-Risk Adults B. Joergens *Bridges (Federal Reserve Bank of St. Louis)* p9 Wint 2016/2017

Program transformation (Computer programming)

Here's proof that Ryzen can benefit from optimized game code G. MAH UNG color graph *PCWorld* v35 no5 p120 My 2017

Programs of All Inclusive Care for the Elderly

Help With Home-Care Bills T. Stanger *Consumer Reports* v82 no12 p46 D 2017

Progress

New Frontiers In Medicine A. Sifferlin color *Time* v188 no27-28 p85 D 26 2016

Progressive, The (Periodical)

The Progressive N. Stockwell color *Progressive* v81 no7 p37 O/N 2017

Progressive Conservative Association of Alberta (Political party : Canada)

The right path J. MARKUSOFF color *Maclean's* v129 no48/49 p23 D 5 2016

Progressive rock music

Have Flute, Will Rock: Political reporter David Weigel outs himself as a different kind of progressive D. Marchese img *New York* v50 no11 p121 My 29 2017

THE PROG SPRING K. SANNEH bw cartoon *New Yorker* v93 no17 p67 Je 19 2017

The Whitest Music Ever J. Parker color *Atlantic* v320 no2 p32 S 2017

Progressivism

See also

Progressivism (United States politics)

The Enemy Within [Cover story] M. J. Hollerich color *Commonweal* v143 no19 p10 D 2 2016

We Must Not Be Enemies A. ETZIONI *American Scholar* v86 no1 p20 Wint 2017

Progressivism (United States politics)

Copy the Tea Party A. NABAUM *New Republic* v248 no3 p32 Mr 2017

The Crumbs of Capitalism T. Kane *Commentary* v142 no2 p11 S 2016

Free Speech on College Campuses H. W. N. THOMAS III *American Scholar* v86 no3 p4 Summ 2017

Obama's Young Garden [Cover story] H. OLSEN il *National Review* v69 no1 p24 Ja 23 2017

The Party of Liberty W. Kristol bw *Weekly Standard* v22 no16 p6 D 26 2016

Progressivism in the Boardroom [Cover story] K. D. WILLIAMSON il *National Review* v69 no4 p24 Mr 6 2017

Progressivism (United States politics)—History—21st century

How the Abortion Debate Rocked Progressivism M. Eberstadt *Time* v189 no4 p32 F 6 2017

New Friends, Common Foe C. Alter color *Time* v189 no3 p40 Ja 30 2017

RISE OF THE GRASSROOTS T. Dickinson color *Rolling Stone* no1295 p31 S 7 2017

Progressivism—Social aspects

Listening and Hearing L. Goodman *Society* v54 no2 p163 Ap 2017

Prohibition

FREE RANGE? An "old hen" found in Harrisonburg was caught before she could work her prohibited ways B. CROWDER *Virginia Living* v15 no2 p23 F 2017

Prohibition—United States—History—20th century

A Sobering Race E. Conant bw *National Geographic* v230 no4 p148 O 2016

Project Apollo (U.S.)

Moon Missions, Imperfect and Magnificent J. Kluger color *Time* v189 no13 p19 Ap 10 2017

Project finance

A Guide to Winning Support for Your New Idea or Project R. Knight *Harvard Business Review Digital Articles* p2 Je 19 2015

Project Freedom (Music)

JOEY DEFRANCESCO REJUVENATED MASTER [Cover story] D. OUELLETTE bw color *Downbeat* v84 no5 p40 My 2017

Project management

See also

Cost control

Five Critical Roles in Project Management *Harvard Business Review Digital Articles* p2 N 3 2016

The Four Phases of Project Management *Harvard Business Review Digital Articles* p2 N 3 2016

A Guide to Winning Support for Your New Idea or Project R. Knight *Harvard Business Review Digital Articles* p2 Je 19 2015

How to Be an Effective Executive Sponsor R. Ashkenas *Harvard Business Review Digital Articles* p2 My 18 2015

How to Keep Support for Your Project from Evaporating A. Rimm *Harvard Business Review Digital Articles* p2 Ag 10 2015

How to Prioritize Your Company's Projects A. Nieto-Rodriguez *Harvard Business Review Digital Articles* p2 D 13 2016

How to Stay Motivated When Everyone Else Is on Vacation D. Clark *Harvard Business Review Digital Articles* p2 Ag 8 2016

It's All in the Details G. MULLINS-COHEN *Parks & Recreation*

v52 no3 p10 Mr 2017

To Achieve a Major Goal, First Tackle a Few Small Ones A. Markman *Harvard Business Review Digital Articles* p2 F 24 2017

What Net Present Value Can't Tell You M. Wessel *Harvard Business Review Digital Articles* p2 N 20 2014

When More Is Too Much S. Sonenshein color *Time* v189 no7/8 p28 F 27 2017

You Need to Manage Digital Projects for Outcomes, Not Outputs J. Gothelf and J. Seiden color *Harvard Business Review Digital Articles* p2 F 6 2017

Your Agile Project Needs a Budget, Not an Estimate D. Madden *Harvard Business Review Digital Articles* p2 D 29 2014

Your Project Needs a Charter. Here's What That Means *Harvard Business Review Digital Articles* p2 N 3 2016

Zombie Projects: How to Find Them and Kill Them S. Anthony, D. S. Duncan et al *Harvard Business Review Digital Articles* p2 Mr 4 2015

Project managers

The 4 Types of Project Manager C. L. Pedersen and T. Ritter *Harvard Business Review Digital Articles* p2 Jl 27 2017

Big-Project Engineers Have to Deal with Too Much Red Tape S. Whitbread and N. D. Greene *Harvard Business Review Digital Articles* p2 Ja 14 2016

Five Critical Roles in Project Management *Harvard Business Review Digital Articles* p2 N 3 2016

Project method in teaching

College-level project-based learning gains popularity T. Feder *Physics Today* v70 no6 p26 Je 2017

Project Runway Junior (TV program)

FASHION'S WONDER GIRL! J. ABIDOR color *Seventeen* v76 no3 p98 My 2017

Meet Fashion's Newest Stars J. ABIDOR color *Seventeen* v76 no12 p20 D 2016/Ja 2017

We're Heading Back to Project Runway Junior! color *Seventeen* v76 no12 p10 D 2016/Ja 2017

Projectiles—Evaluation

The Drone Catcher K. ATHERTON and S. FECHT color *Popular Science* v288 no6 p64 N/D 2016

THREE NEW, AND ACCURATE, .243-CALIBER BULLETS THAT WILL DUKE IT OUT IN COMPETITION THIS YEAR J. B. SNOW color *Outdoor Life* v224 no2 p41 F/Mr 2017

Projection art

Projection *Stage Directions* v30 no7 p47 Jl 1 2017

Projection screens—Design & construction

IT'S SHOW TIME C. BOYD color *Better Homes & Gardens* v95 no8 p70 Ag 2017

Projection screens—Equipment & supplies

What can Rose Brand do for you? *Stage Directions* v30 no3 p35 Mr 2017

Projection screens—Evaluation

New Gear color *Sound & Vision* v82 no5 p28 Je 2017

Projection television

Hiding in Plain Sight J. SCIACCA color *Sound & Vision* v82 no5 p23 Je 2017

Projectors

Do You See What I See? J. V. LAST cartoon *Weekly Standard* v22 no14 p5 D 12 2016

PROJECTION'S REINVENTION R. Sabin color *Sound & Vision* v82 no4 p30 My 2017

Projectors—Evaluation

2016 TOP PICKS OF THE YEAR R. Sabin color *Sound & Vision* v82 no2 p32 F/Mr 2017

BINGE BIGGER K. Sintumuang color *Esquire* v167 no2 p60 Mr 2017

Breaking the 4K Barrier K. Deering color graph *Sound & Vision* v82 no4 p34 My 2017

Contrast and Color A. Griffin bw color graph *Sound & Vision* v82 no4 p62 My 2017

HEAD-TO-HEAD LIGHT HOUSES T. MOYNIHAN color *Wired* v25 no4 p38 Ap 2017

Laser Lightshow T. J. Norton color graph *Sound & Vision* v82 no4 p50 My 2017

Projection for All? T. J. Norton color *Sound & Vision* v82 no4 p42 My 2017

Ultra-Short-Throw Projectors color *Popular Mechanics* p28 F 2017

THE WILD, WEIRD, AND POWERFUL PC HARDWARE of CES 2017 J. PHILLIPS color *PCWorld* v35 no2 p127 F 2017

PROKESCH, STEVEN

THE EDISON OF MEDICINE color img *Harvard Business Review* v95 no2 p134 Mr/Ap 2017

EXECUTIVE SUMMARIES MARCH–APRIL 2017 color *Harvard Business Review* v95 no2 p158 Mr/Ap 2017

FIVE TRANSFORMATIONS *Harvard Business Review* v95 no5 p47 S/O 2017

REINVENTING TALENT MANAGEMENT: HOW GE USES ANALYTICS TO GUIDE A MORE DIGITAL, FAR-FLUNG WORKFORCE *Harvard Business Review* v95 no5 p54 S/O 2017

Prokurat, Alena

Higher predation risk for insect prey at low latitudes and elevations graph *Science* v356 no6339 p742 My 19 2017

Prometheus (Film)

CHOOSE YOUR OWN SPACE ADVENTURE SAVING THE GALAXY ... AGAIN M. YARM cartoon *Wired* v25 no5 p37 My 2017

Promiscuity

A LITTLE HELP FROM YOUR FRIENDS: Are friends with benefits actually benefiting you? Z. ZANE color *Advocate* no1091 p107 Je/Jl 2017

Promise, The (Film)

The Promise L. Greenblatt color *Entertainment Weekly* no1463/1464 p90 Ap/My 2017

Promises

See also

Campaign promises

God—Promises

Treat Promises to Yourself as Seriously as Promises to Others M. E. Kibler *Harvard Business Review Digital Articles* p2 S 9 2015

Promotions

Are the People Who Take Vacations the Ones Who Get Promoted? S. Achor *Harvard Business Review Digital Articles* p2 Je 12 2015

A Checklist for Someone About to Take on a Tougher Job E. Batista *Harvard Business Review Digital Articles* p2 Ja 6 2015

Convincing Your Boss to Make You a Manager A. Ranieri *Harvard Business Review Digital Articles* p2 Ap 1 2016

CORPORATE WELFARE J. Heller *Lapham's Quarterly* v10 no3 p66 Summ 2017

How to Build Expertise in a New Field D. Leonard *Harvard Business Review Digital Articles* p2 Ap 8 2015

If You Want to Get Promoted, Say So S. Nawaz color *Harvard Business Review Digital Articles* p2 Ja 5 2017

More Insiders Are Becoming CEOs, and That's a Good Thing J. L. Bower *Harvard Business Review Digital Articles* p2 Mr 18 2016

Research: Black Employees Are More Likely to Be Promoted When They Were Referred by Another Employee J. Merluzzi and A. Sterling color *Harvard Business Review Digital Articles* p2 F 28 2017

The Time-Consuming Activities That Stall Women's Careers R. Shambaugh *Harvard Business Review Digital Articles* p2 Mr 7 2016

What to Do When Your Employee Asks for a Raise Too Soon R. Knight *Harvard Business Review Digital Articles* p2 Jl 15 2016

Prompts (Psychology)

A TO Z Guide to cues [Cover story] R. PEACOCK color *Yoga Journal* no293 p71 Ag 2017

Proms

Best. Night. Ever color *Seventeen* p210 Ja 1 2017

eat your way to GORGEOUS M. MANNARINO color *Seventeen* p144 Ja 1 2017

girl meets prom J. ABIDOR color *Seventeen* p150 Ja 1 2017

Keys to Prom Style Success J. ABIDOR color *Seventeen* v76 no2 p50 Mr 2017

Prom MONEY SAVERS L. SAXTON color *Seventeen* v76 no2 p98 Mr 2017

two ways K. Foster color *Seventeen* p180 Ja 1 2017

YOUR CHEAT SHEET TO... The Perfect Prom Night M. MANNARINO color *Seventeen* p208 Ja 1 2017

Pronghorn

American Pronghorns N. Austin *Arizona Highways* v92 no11 p13 N 2016

Mammals in Motion L. Moore bw color *National Wildlife (World Edition)* v55 no4 p30 Je/Jl 2017

The Purest Type S. BUTCHER *Texas Monthly* v45 no7 p60 Jl 2017

Pronghorn hunting

PUBLIC LANDS IN PUBLIC HANDS color *Field & Stream* v122 no1 p6 My 2017

Pronghorn—Behavior

TOO TALL *South Dakota Magazine* v33 no2 p92 Jl/Ag 2017

Pronouns (Grammar)

How "you" makes meaning A. Orvell, E. Kross et al bibl diag graph *Science* v355 no6331 p1299 Mr 24 2017

Pronouns (Grammar)—Psychological aspects

Pronouns Matter when Psyching Yourself Up O. Ayduk and E. Kross *Harvard Business Review Digital Articles* p2 F 6 2015

Pronovost, Peter

How Systems Engineering Can Help Fix Health Care *Harvard Business Review Digital Articles* p2 F 9 2017

The Next Wave of Hospital Innovation to Make Patients Safer *Harvard Business Review Digital Articles* p2 Ag 8 2016

What Hospitals Can Learn from Airlines About Buying Equipment *Harvard Business Review Digital Articles* p2 Je 13 2017

Pronunciation

THE INNOCENT WHO TRAVELED ABROAD *Missouri Life* v43 no7 p10 D 2016/Ja 2017

I SAY KOCH N. Paumgarten cartoon *New Yorker* v93 no8 p19 Ap 10 2017

Proofs (Printing)

Guardians of the Galley color *Publishers Weekly* v264 no20 p(Sp)38 My 15 2017

Proopiomelanocortin

POOCHED OUT R. Khamsi color *New York Times Magazine* p44 My 21 2017

Propaganda

See also

Lobbying

A B.S. IN B.S *Esquire* p120 S 2017

Grandmasters of Fake News P. J. BUCHANAN *American Conservative* v16 no1 p26 Ja/F 2017

A Perfect Storm: American Media, Russian Propaganda S. OATES *Current History* v116 no792 p282 O 2017

TALK TO US M. O'Malley and S. Lott color graph *Chicago* v66 no8 p17 Ag 2017

Propane

Selective oxidative dehydrogenation of propane to propene using boron nitride catalysts J. T. Grant, C. A. Carrero et al bibl diag graph *Science* v354 no6319 p1570 D 23 2016

THINGS YOU NEED TO KNOW ABOUT FUEL R. BERENDSOHN and E. Dyer bw chart color *Popular Mechanics* p29 Mr 2017

Propane—Accidents

A CHRISTMAS RIFLE J. ARTERBURN cartoon *Outdoor Life* v224 no1 p114 D 2016/Ja 2017

Propane—Safety measures

Play it Safe W. Canning color *Sail* v48 no7 p50 Jl 2017

Propellers

Pontoon Propping *Boating World* v38 no5 p60 My 2017

Property

See also

Heirlooms

Home ownership

Income

Personal property

Real property

growing joy T. G. HINER color map *Cabin Living* p16 Ag 2017

MARKETPLACE EQUIPMENT, SERVICES *Sea Magazine* v108 no12 p92 D 2016

THOUGHTS ON Property J. WALLS, G. K. CHESTERTON et al *Forbes* v199 no5 p124 My 16 2017

Property Brothers (TV program)

Cabin Power D. PEAK *Log Home Living* v34 no3 p6 Ap 2017

Property Group Partners (Company)

Capitol Crossing M. M. KASHINO color *Washingtonian Magazine* v52 no7 p103 Ap 2017

Property insurance

Get Your Insurer to Pay Up K. LANKFORD color *Kiplinger's Personal Finance* v71 no8 p30 Ag 2017

Property rights

See also

Transaction costs

Squatters' 60-Year War Against Private Property: Around 1230 a.m. on August 7, 1988, a small army of police officers in riot gear covered their badges, raised their batons and charged on foot and on horseback into Tompkins Square Park on New York's... M. GARB *In These Times* v41 no7 p34 Jl 2017

Property tax

Jefferson County, U.S.A L. K. GJRLEY *In These Times* v41 no4 p60 Ap 2017

Property tax—Lawsuits & claims

How Big-Box Retailers Weaponize Old Stores S. Pettypiece color *Bloomberg Businessweek* no4503 p17 D 12 2016

Property tax—United States

How Big-Box Retailers Weaponize Old Stores S. Pettypiece color *Bloomberg Businessweek* no4503 p17 D 12 2016

Q: My property tax bill has skyrocketed. How can I reduce it? S. BLOCK color *Kiplinger's Personal Finance* v71 no5 p37 My 2017

Prophecy

Be the peace A. Camille il *U.S. Catholic* v81 no12 p47 D 2016

Prophecy—History

Predicting the Fall of Anne Boleyn A. Holroyde *History Today* v67 no5 p11 My 2017

Prophet, Tony

ON THE MOVE color *Black Enterprise* v47 no2 p26 S 2016

Proportional representation—Canada

GOOD NEWS color *Maclean's* v129 no51/52 p10 D 26 2016

Propylene oxide

Mirror-Image Molecule Far, Far Away N. SCHARPING cartoon color *Discover* v38 no1 p68 Ja/F 2017

Mirror Molecules in Space N. Collins color *Scientific American* v315 no3 p14 S 2016

Prosciutto

Easy-Peasy J. McDaniel color *AARP: The Magazine* v59 no2A p70 F/Mr 2016

NUFFIN BEATS A MUFFIN M. Kadey color *Runner's World* v52 no2 p40 Mr 2017

Peas With Prosciutto, Tomatoes and Onion color *AARP: The Magazine* v59 no2A p71 F/Mr 2016

Prose, Francine

ART IN THE EXTREME color *New York Times Book Review* p72 D 4 2016

The Cult of Saint Franz bw *New York Review of Books* v63 no16 p60 O 27 2016

DOOR TO DOOR *Harper's Magazine* p98 Ap 2017

Groping and Not Finding bw color *New York Review of Books* v64 no5 p60 Mr 23 2017

MISTER MONKEY B. JOSEF GRUBISIC color *Maclean's* v129 no45 p56 N 14 2016

Monkey In the Business [Cover story] C. Schine *New York Times Book Review* p1 O 23 2016

On the Wilder Shores of Brooklyn [Cover story] bw *New York Review of Books* v64 no15 p28 O 12 2017

The Passion and Rage of Arundhati Roy color *New York Review of Books* v64 no12 p16 Jl 13 2017

Powder Keg: Violence drives Muslims and Christians from a city of despots and collateral damage *New York Times Book Review* p10 My 21 2017

The Triumph of Foxy Grandpa color *New York Review of Books* v63 no20 p56 D 22 2016

What could 'free speech' possibly mean when a mob is bullying and beating people with whom they don't agree? *New York Times Book Review* p27 O 1 2017

What's the best book, new or old, you read this year? *New York Times Book Review* p27 D 25 2016

Prosecution

See also

Indictments

Prosecution—United States

We Have Better Things to Do Than Prosecute Insider Trading J. Fox *Harvard Business Review Digital Articles* p2 D 11 2014

Prosecutorial misconduct—Lawsuits & claims

PAYBACK TIME B. Mclean color *Fortune* v75 no1 p90 Ja 1 2017

Prosecutors
    BRICKBATS C. OLIVER cartoon *Reason* v49 no1 p72 My 2017
    The International Criminal Court on Trial color *Foreign Affairs* v96 no1 p48 Ja/F 2017
    THE WRONG MAN B. TAUB cartoon color *New Yorker* v93 no22 p46 Jl 31 2017

Proskurnikov, Anton V.
    Network science on belief system dynamics under logic constraints bibl diag graph *Science* v354 no6310 p321 O 21 2016

Prosocial behavior
    Women 'need to be confident and caring to get ahead' *People Management* p53 Ag 2017

Prospective payment systems
    How Bundled Health Care Payments Are Working in the Netherlands J. N. Struijs *Harvard Business Review Digital Articles* p2 O 12 2015

Prosser, R. Scott
    The role of dimer asymmetry and protomer dynamics in enzyme catalysis diag *Science* v355 no6322 p262 Ja 20 2017

Prostate cancer
    NEWS FROM THE World of Medicine S. RIDEOUT color *Reader's Digest* v189 no1131 p60 Je 2017
    Winning the Prostate Cancer War J. STEWART color *Men's Health* v32 no4 p75 My 2017

Prostate cancer—Diagnosis
    A Better Prostate Screening color *Prevention* v69 no5 p9 My 2017
    Overcoming prostate cancer silence A. Rohan *Successful Farming* v115 no1 p40 Ja 2017

Prostate cancer—Patients
    HOW MEDICINAL CANNABIS HELPED A CANCER SURVIVOR LIVE AGAIN A. Yu color *Maclean's* v129 no40 p61 O 10 2016

Prostate cancer—Treatment
    Overcoming prostate cancer silence A. Rohan *Successful Farming* v115 no1 p40 Ja 2017
    Rb1 and Trp53 cooperate to suppress prostate cancer lineage plasticity, metastasis, and antiandrogen resistance Sheng Yu Ku, S. Rosario et al bibl graph *Science* v355 no6320 p1 Ja 6 2017
    Reprogramming to resist K. Kelly and S. P. Balk bibl diag *Science* v355 no6320 p29 Ja 6 2017
    SOX2 promotes lineage plasticity and antiandrogen resistance in TP53- and RB1-deficient prostate cancer Ping Mu, Z. Zhang et al bibl graph *Science* v355 no6320 p1 Ja 6 2017
    Spot On *Virginia Living* v15 no1 p109 D 2016
    TALK TO US R. DePesa and J. P. Dave' color *Chicago* v66 no2 p11 F 2017

Prostate disease diagnosis
    JUST FOR MEN I. Eliaz color *Better Nutrition* v79 no6 p41 Je 2017

Prostate diseases—Prevention
    It's a Guy Thing L. TURNER color *Better Nutrition* v79 no6 p54 Je 2017
    JUST FOR MEN I. Eliaz color *Better Nutrition* v79 no6 p41 Je 2017

Prostate tumors—Risk factors
    SCIENTIFIC UPDATE R. Mangels *Vegetarian Journal* v35 no2 p26 2016

Prosthesis
    See also
    Hearing aids
    For This Issue, We're All Going a Little Bare color *Glamour* v115 no6 p20 Je 2017

Prostitution
    My Ex Is Advertising For Sugar Daddies. Can I Tell Her Mother? K. A. Appiah *New York Times Magazine* p18 O 30 2016
    REBIRTHED AFTER A LIFE IN THE SEX TRADE A. EMMANUEL color *Ebony* v72 no6 p86 Ap/My 2017

Prostitution—Law & legislation
    Why Buy Sex? E. N. Brown *Reason* v48 no7 p10 D 2016

Prostitution—Psychological aspects
    Why Buy Sex? E. N. Brown *Reason* v48 no7 p10 D 2016

Prostitution—United States
    The Right To Run Sex Ads D. Lawrence *Bloomberg Businessweek* no4493 p14 O 3 2016

Protagonist (Theatrical production)
    50 Years of Drama *Dance Magazine* v91 no4 p12 Ap 2017

Proteasomes
    Is the cell's garbage disposal sending messages? M. Leslie color *Science* v355 no6332 p1361 Mr 31 2017
    A SUMO-ubiquitin relay recruits proteasomes to chromosome axes to regulate meiotic recombination H. B. D. P. Rao, S. K. Bhatt et al bibl graph *Science* v355 no6323 p403 Ja 27 2017
    When degradation spurs segregation M. Zetka bibl diag *Science* v355 no6323 p349 Ja 27 2017

Protected areas
    See also
    Forest reserves
    National parks & reserves
    Natural areas
    Wilderness areas
    Now is the time to protect the Arctic N. E. Hussey, R. G. Harcourt et al bibl color *Science* v354 no6317 p1243 D 9 2016
    Prehistoric walrus hunting site shielded color *Science* v355 no6322 p228 Ja 20 2017
    THE Radically INTERNATIONAL History of AMERICA'S BEST IDEA T. Murphy color *Foreign Policy* no224 p66 My/Je 2017
    Scientific Evidence for Fifty Percent? Y. F. WIERSMA, D. J. H. SLEEP et al *BioScience* v67 no9 p781 S 2017
    To preserve and protect N. WALKER graph map *Canadian Geographic* v137 no1 p32 F 2017

Protected areas—Conservation & restoration
    Places Worth Preserving G. Wuerthner *Sierra* v101 no4 p48 Jl/Ag 2016

Protection for electronic appliances
    COOL IPAD CASE color *Flying* v144 no9 p13 S 2017

Protectionism
    Another Year Has Passed, but the List of Massive Global Problems Has Stayed the Same J. L. Bower *Harvard Business Review Digital Articles* p2 D 14 2015
    PULLING UP THE DRAWBRIDGE *Change* v82 no3 p30 Mr 2017

Protectionism—China
    Global Trade Is Slowing B. Einhorn, N. Brautlecht et al color *Bloomberg Businessweek* no4500 p16 N 21 2016

Protectionism—United States
    Does Foreign Steel Threaten U.S. Security? J. Deaux color *Bloomberg Businessweek* no4524 p31 My 29 2017
    The False Promise of Protectionism D. A. Irwin color *Foreign Affairs* v96 no3 p45 My/Je 2017
    Is a Bear on the Prowl? J. Bodnar *Kiplinger's Personal Finance* v71 no1 p8 Ja 2017
    Larry Summers: Business Leaders Should Stand Up to President Trump A. Ignatius bw *Harvard Business Review Digital Articles* p2 F 1 2017
    Trump and Trade I. M. STELZER color *Weekly Standard* v22 no15 p27 D 19 2016
    Trump's Reckless Threat to World Trade cartoon *Bloomberg Businessweek* no4516 p8 Mr 27 2017

Protective coatings
    See also
    Gums & resins
    Paint
    THE PERFECT FINISH P. MARTIN color *Popular Mechanics* p100 Jl 2017
    WATCHING-PAINT-DRY CAM color *Popular Mechanics* p6 O 2017

Protective coverings—Evaluation
    LIFEPROOF NÜÜD FOR THE 9.7-INCH iPAD PRO S. BELLAMY color *Macworld - Digital Edition* p37 Mr 2017

Protective equipment (Sporting goods)
    Enjoy the Silence K. D. WILLIAMSON *National Review* v69 no8 p16 My 2017

Protective eyeglasses
    See also
    Safety goggles
    Sunglasses
    The Joy of Specs color *O, The Oprah Magazine* p47 Je 2017
    Tinted Love color *GQ: Gentlemen's Quarterly* v97 no7 p72 Jl 2017

ProtectWise Inc.
    Neighborhood Watch D. Lawrence cartoon *Bloomberg Business-*

week no4514 p42 Mr 13 2017

Protein analysis

Guanine glycation repair by DJ-1/Park7 and its bacterial homologs G. Richarme, C. Liu et al chart color diag graph *Science* v357 no6347 p208 Jl 14 2017

How do miniproteins fold? D. N. Woolfson, E. G. Baker et al diag *Science* v357 no6347 p133 Jl 14 2017

Protein content of food

BENCH THE CARBS? color *Women's Health* v14 no5 p29 Je 2017

NATURAL ENERGY J. MIGALA color *Runner's World* v52 no8 p30 S 2017

Protein engineering

See also

Chemical modification of proteins

Proteins by design R. F. Service color *Science* v354 no6319 p1520 D 23 2016

Protein engineering research

Global analysis of protein folding using massively parallel design, synthesis, and testing G. J. Rocklin, T. M. Chidyausiku et al color diag *Science* v357 no6347 p168 Jl 14 2017

Protein folding

Force spectroscopy unveils hidden protein-folding states J. Miller *Physics Today* v70 no5 p16 My 2017

Global analysis of protein folding using massively parallel design, synthesis, and testing G. J. Rocklin, T. M. Chidyausiku et al color diag *Science* v357 no6347 p168 Jl 14 2017

Spread of bad proteins tied to diabetes A. CUNNINGHAM color *Science News* v192 no3 p9 S 2 2017

Protein genetics

See also

Polycomb group protein genetics

Circular RNAs hint at new realm of genetics K. Servick color *Science* v355 no6332 p1363 Mr 31 2017

Guanine glycation repair by DJ-1/Park7 and its bacterial homologs G. Richarme, C. Liu et al chart color diag graph *Science* v357 no6347 p208 Jl 14 2017

How do miniproteins fold? D. N. Woolfson, E. G. Baker et al diag *Science* v357 no6347 p133 Jl 14 2017

Of sizzling steaks and DNA repair F. A. Dingler and K. J. Patel diag *Science* v357 no6347 p130 Jl 14 2017

Protein kinase C

DNA-PKcs structure suggests an allosteric mechanism modulating DNA double-strand break repair B. L. Sibanda, D. Y. Chirgadze et al bibl graph *Science* v355 no6324 p520 F 3 2017

Protein kinase inhibitors

Systemic pan-AMPK activator MK-8722 improves glucose homeostasis but induces cardiac hypertrophy R. W. Myers, Guan et al graph *Science* v357 no6350 p507 Ag 4 2017

Protein kinases

Targeting an energy sensor to treat diabetes D. Grahame Hardie color *Science* v357 no6350 p455 Ag 4 2017

Protein metabolism

does the type of protein matter? V. Tweed color *Amazing Wellness* v9 no3 p19 EarlySumm 2017

trend WATCH V. TWEED color *Better Nutrition* v79 no4 p10 Ap 2017

Protein-protein interactions

Activity-based protein profiling reveals off-target proteins of the FAAH inhibitor BIA 10-2474 A. C. M. van Esbroeck, A. P. A. Janssen et al chart color graph *Science* v356 no6342 p1084 Je 9 2017

A conserved NAD+ binding pocket that regulates protein-protein interactions during aging J. Li, M. S. Bonkowski et al bibl graph *Science* v355 no6331 p1312 Mr 24 2017

Protein receptors

Rogue protein's partners offer hope in Parkinson's disease M. Wadman color *Science* v354 no6315 p956 N 25 2016

Protein solubility

ATP controls the crowd A. M. Rice and M. K. Rosen color *Science* v356 no6339 p701 My 19 2017

Protein stability

Quantifying protein (dis)order C. Vogel bibl diag *Science* v355 no6327 p794 F 24 2017

Protein structure

See also

Nucleoproteins—Structure

Engineering extrinsic disorder to control protein activity in living cells O. Dagliya, M. Tarnawski et al bibl color *Science* v354 no6318 p1441 D 16 2016

Principles for designing proteins with cavities formed by curved β sheets E. Marcos, B. Basanta et al bibl color graph *Science* v355 no6321 p1 Ja 13 2017

SPLIT-SECOND REACTIONS P. Fromme and J. C. H. Spence color *Scientific American* v316 no5 p62 My 2017

Protein synthesis

RNA localization feeds translation I. Gáspár and A. Ephrussi color *Science* v357 no6357 p1235 S 22 2017

Use It ... and Lose It? B. BENNETT *Climbing* no356 p39 S/O 2017

Protein synthesis—Equipment & supplies

SUPERCHARGED SUPPS color *Muscle & Performance* v9 no6 p64 Je 2017

Proteins

See also

Blood proteins

Carrier proteins

Enzymes

Microbial proteins

Milk proteins

Minichromosome maintenance proteins

Protein content of food

Transcription factors

7 NEW WAYS TO USE PROTEIN POWDERS V. Tweed color *Amazing Wellness* v9 no4 p20 Summ 2017

ATP as a biological hydrotrope A. Patel, L. Malinovska et al color graph *Science* v356 no6339 p753 My 19 2017

BEYOND CHICKEN M. KADEY cartoon color *Muscle & Performance* v9 no4 p54 Ap 2017

Beyond DNA G. TARLACH color *Discover* v38 no7 p64 S 2017

Carbon monoxide, the silent killer, may have met its match Wudan Yan *Science* v354 no6317 p1215 D 9 2016

Characterization of a dynamic metabolon producing the defense compound dhurrin in sorghum T. Laursen, J. Borch et al bibl graph *Science* v354 no6314 p890 N 18 2016

A division of labor in cells' protein factories M. Leslie color *Science* v356 no6344 p1218 Je 23 2017

Engineering extrinsic disorder to control protein activity in living cells O. Dagliya, M. Tarnawski et al bibl color *Science* v354 no6318 p1441 D 16 2016

For a Longer, Healthier Life chart color *AARP: The Magazine* v59 no3A p43 Ap/My 2016

Gene duplication can impart fragility, not robustness, in the yeast protein interaction network G. Diss, I. Gagnon-Arsenault et al bibl color graph *Science* v355 no6325 p630 F 10 2017

Genetic biomarker for cancer immunotherapy S. Goswami and P. Sharma diag *Science* v357 no6349 p358 Jl 28 2017

Mechanistic basis for a molecular triage reaction S. Shao, M. C. Rodrigo-Brenni et al bibl color graph *Science* v355 no6322 p298 Ja 20 2017

Pain promoter also acts to relieve it R. EHRENBERG *Science News* v191 no2 p6 F 4 2017

Paneth cells secrete lysozyme via secretory autophagy during bacterial infection of the intestine S. Bel, M. Pendse et al color diag *Science* v357 no6355 p1047 S 8 2017

POW(D)ER UP YOUR MEALS L. McGLASHAN color *Muscle & Performance* v9 no7 p51 Jl 2017

Prionlike protein stores memories L. SANDERS graph *Science News* v190 no12 p10 D 10 2016

Protein detects when lungs fill with air R. EHRENBERG *Science News* v191 no2 p7 F 4 2017

Protein mobs selectively kill brain cells T. H. SAEY *Science News* v190 no12 p14 D 10 2016

Protein paints chipmunks' stripes T. HESMAN SAEY color *Science News* v190 no11 p8 N 26 2016

Protein structure determination using metagenome sequence data S. Ovchinnikov, H. Park et al bibl color graph *Science* v355 no6322 p294 Ja 20 2017

RESEARCH color *Science* v355 no6330 p1169 Mr 17 2017

Rogue protein's partners offer hope in Parkinson's disease M. Wadman color *Science* v354 no6315 p956 N 25 2016

Sleep Tight with CASEIN J. WUEBBEN color *Muscle & Perfor-*

mance v9 no4 p9 Ap 2017

TZAP or not to zap telomeres G. Lossaint and J. Lingner bibl diag *Science* v355 no6325 p578 F 10 2017

Proteins in human nutrition

Ancient Super Grain color *Vegetarian Today* no2 p28 Ap 2017

FAFQ K. Patel and J. WUEBBEN *Muscle & Performance* v9 no5 p14 My 2017

Give Yourself an Energy Makeover! G. GRAVES cartoon color *Prevention* v69 no2 p44 F 2017

Power Up Your Smoothie color *Health* v31 no8 p9 O 2017

PROTEIN PROTECTION J. WUEBBEN color *Muscle & Performance* v9 no8 p11 Ag 2017

Proteins in the body

A subcellular map of the human proteome P. J. Thul, L. Åkesson et al color *Science* v356 no6340 p820 My 26 2017

Proteins—Analysis

PROTEINS SOLVE A HOMININ PUZZLE N. SWAMINA-THAN color *Archaeology* v70 no1 p11 Ja/F 2017

Proteins—Analysis—Equipment & supplies

NEW PRODUCTS: PROTEIN ANALYSIS color *Science* v354 no6310 p373 O 21 2016

Proteins—Evaluation

DYMATIZE ISO100 CLEAR color *Muscle & Performance* v9 no5 p62 My 2017

MUSCLETECH NITRO-TECH 100% WHEY GOLD color *Muscle & Performance* v9 no4 p62 Ap 2017

Proteins—Physiological effect

PROTEIN HELPER color *Muscle & Performance* v9 no1 p14 Ja 2017

Proteins—Research

Cell-wide analysis of protein thermal unfolding reveals determinants of thermostability P. Leuenberger, S. Ganscha et al color *Science* v355 no6327 p812 F 24 2017

Researchers close in on ancient dinosaur proteins R. F. Service color *Science* v355 no6324 p441 F 3 2017

Proteobacteria

Big Questions About Tiny Bacteria? J. McNichol color *Oceanus* v51 no2 p78 Wint 2016

Proteomics

Activity-based protein profiling reveals off-target proteins of the FAAH inhibitor BIA 10-2474 A. C. M. van Esbroeck, A. P. A. Janssen et al chart color graph *Science* v356 no6342 p1084 Je 9 2017

Proterra Inc.

Buses and Trucks Plug In for Power *Mother Earth News* no283 p9 Ag/S 2017

The Tesla of Buses A. OHNSMAN color *Forbes* v198 no8 p54 D 20 2016

Protest art

CAPTURE THE FLAG A. Marantz cartoon *New Yorker* v93 no7 p34 Ap 3 2017

IS POLITICAL ART THE ONLY ART THAT MATTERS NOW? THE ART WORLD IS GOING TO WAR WITH TRUMP. IF IT DOESN'T SHOOT ITSELF IN THE FOOT FIRST C. SWANSON img *New York* v50 no8 p60 Ap 17 2017

WHAT MAKES PROTEST ART GOOD? R. CORBETT img *New York* v50 no8 p66 Ap 17 2017

Protest movements

See also

Anti-globalization movement

The Acid Test of Dissent in Russia B. PARKER color *Weekly Standard* v22 no40 p15 Je 26 2017

EASY CHAIR R. Solnit *Harper's Magazine* v333 no1998 p5 N 2016

Re-enchanting the World P. GILGER color *America* v215 no10 p16 O 10 2016

The Revolution Will Be Managed G. Satell *Harvard Business Review Digital Articles* p2 My 19 2015

WHAT IS IT ASKING FOR? TO BE SOMETHING E. Zerofsky *New York Times Magazine* p50 Je 11 2017

Protest movements—United States

The Fight for Reproductive Rights A. Pettway color *Progressive* v81 no4 p16 Ap/My 2017

Hollywood Takes a Knee J. Hibberd and C. Sosenko color *Entertainment Weekly* no1485 p14 O 6 2017

Muslim Women March with the Mainstream U. ABDULLAH *Is-*

lamic Horizons v46 no2 p45 Mr/Ap 2017

Whose land, whose oil? *Christian Century* v133 no21 p7 O 12 2016

Protestant churches

See also

Lutheran Church

Presbyterian Church

Reformed Church

Churches in El Salvador help youths find life beyond gangs M. Legrain color *Christian Century* v134 no22 p16 O 25 2017

Shared space, shared vision C. H. Merritt *Christian Century* v134 no1 p45 Ja 4 2017

Protestant churches—Canada

A Protestant miracle B. BETHUNE and P. TREBLE color graph *Maclean's* v129 no47 p54 N 28 2016

Protestants

See also

Episcopalians

Puritans

After coup attempt, Turkey cracks down on Protestants D. Bonessi color *Christian Century* v134 no1 p14 Ja 4 2017

Charismatic in Chile P. Jenkins *Christian Century* v134 no12 p44 Je 7 2017

CRADLE CHRISTIANS *Christianity Today* v61 no1 p19 Ja/F 2017

Evangelizing the parish J. Byassee color *Christian Century* v134 no15 p26 Jl 19 2017

The other Eastern churches P. Jenkins *Christian Century* v134 no14 p44 Jl 5 2017

Privacy concerns prompt protests in California G. Hodgson *Physics Today* v69 no12 p46 D 2016

Protestants—Attitudes

Shall We Gather at the River? E. MUNDAHL color *Weekly Standard* v22 no14 p15 D 12 2016

Protexter, Amy

Bridging the Gap Between Marketing and IT *Harvard Business Review Digital Articles* p2 Mr 18 2016

Prothonotary warbler

WANDERING WARBLERS: These featherweight frequent fliers go the distance C. KETTLEWELL *Virginia Living* v15 no4 p19 Je 2017

Protista

Inhibitors of PEX14 disrupt protein import into glycosomes and kill Trypanosoma parasites M. Dawidowski, L. Emmanouilidis et al chart color diag graph *Science* v355 no6332 p1416 Mr 31 2017

Proto-Indo-European language

Story Time J. KEATS color *Discover* v38 no4 p16 My 2017

Proton detection

Proton structure seen in a new light S. K. Blau *Physics Today* v70 no5 p14 My 2017

Proton measurements

The Rydberg constant and proton size from atomic hydrogen A. Beyer, L. Maisenbacher et al bw chart color diag graph *Science* v357 no6359 p79 O 6 2017

Proton-proton cycle

READER GALLERY color *Astronomy* v45 no8 p88 Ag 2017

Proton pump inhibitors

Stomach Upset K. Weintraub color *Scientific American* v316 no2 p22 F 2017

Proton pumps (Biology)

A three-dimensional movie of structural changes in bacteriorhodopsin Eriko Nango, A. Royant et al bibl diag graph *Science* v354 no6319 p1552 D 23 2016

Proton spin

The Proton Puzzle E. Conover chart color diag *Science News* v191 no8 p22 Ap 29 2017

Proton synchrotrons

Proton structure seen in a new light S. K. Blau *Physics Today* v70 no5 p14 My 2017

Proton transfer reactions

Spectroscopic snapshots of the proton-transfer mechanism in water C. T. Wolke, J. A. Fournier et al bibl diag graph *Science* v354 no6316 p1131 D 2 2016

Protons

The Neutrino Puzzle [Cover story] C. Moskowitz color diag map

Scientific American v317 no4 p32 O 2017

The Proton Puzzle E. Conover chart color diag *Science News* v191 no8 p22 Ap 29 2017

The proton radius revisited W. Vassen graph *Science* v357 no6359 p39 O 6 2017

Scientists find amazement in what's most familiar *Science News* v191 no8 p2 Ap 29 2017

Protoplanetary disks

Spiral density waves in a young protoplanetary disk L. M. Pérez, J. M. Carpenter et al bibl graph *Science* v353 no6307 p1519 S 30 2016

Protostars

ALMA uncovers more ingredients for life color *Astronomy* v45 no10 p14 O 2017

Detecting structure in a protostellar disk K. Rice bibl color *Science* v353 no6307 p1492 S 30 2016

Prototype design & construction

How GE Appliances Built an Innovation Lab to Rapidly Prototype Products B. Kapoor, K. Nolan et al *Harvard Business Review Digital Articles* p2 Jl 18 2017

Prototypes

OSHKOSH OR BUST C. GREGOIRE color *Flying* v144 no11 p50 N 2017

POWER FROM THE PEOPLE E. MASTROIANNI color *Discover* v38 no10 p16 D 2017

Railway Post Office T. Burgess, R. Pugh et al color *Model Railroader* v84 no8 p16 Ag 2017

Prototypes—Design & construction

Pragmatic prototype modeling T. Koester color *Model Railroader* v84 no5 p78 My 2017

Prototyping That's Less Prone to Failure A. Richardson *Harvard Business Review Digital Articles* p2 D 7 2015

A scenic showcase S. Lamoureux color diag *Model Railroader* v84 no5 p32 My 2017

Prototypes—Evaluation

BOOM UNVEILS SUPERSONIC PROTOTYPE color *Flying* v144 no2 p18 F 2017

Protozoa

Foraminifera Invade the Mediterranean T. GUY-HAIM bw color map *Natural History* v125 no10 p12 O 2017

Proud, James

The Black Sheep B. SOLOMON and M. Drange bw color *Forbes* v199 no1 p86 Ja 24 2017

PROUDFOOT, SHANNON

The doctor who took on death color *Maclean's* v130 no8 p52 S 2017

Drinks for the House color *Maclean's* v130 no2 p12 Mr 2017

Dusting off some faces color *Maclean's* p16 Je 2017

THE HAMMER DROPS ON CARBON color *Maclean's* v129 no42 p20 O 24 2016

HARDEST WORKING color *Maclean's* v129 no47 p20 N 28 2016

THE INTERVIEW color *Maclean's* v129 no40 p14 O 10 2016

Midterm crises color *Maclean's* v129 no51/52 p30 D 26 2016

MOST KNOWLEDGEABLE color *Maclean's* v129 no47 p22 N 28 2016

A POLICE CHIEF LEGALIZES MARIJUANA color *Maclean's* v129 no40 p24 O 10 2016

THE POWER OF NO color *Maclean's* v130 no4 p30 My 2017

The puck stops here color *Maclean's* v130 no3 p16 Ap 2017

THE RISE AND RISE OF AHMED HUSSEN bw *Maclean's* v130 no3 p28 Ap 2017

Rookie in the House color *Maclean's* v130 no2 p16 Mr 2017

Some days, it just isn't #2016 color *Maclean's* v129 no45 p24 N 14 2016

The thing I wanted to say … color *Maclean's* no1 p23 F 17 2017

'THIS IS NO WAY TO LIVE' color *Maclean's* v129 no47 p14 N 28 2016

'We just can't have this' color *Maclean's* v129 no45 p26 N 14 2016

Proulx, Annie, 1935-

Barkskins D. Rothenberg color *Orion Magazine* v36 no1 p58 Ja/F 2017

A Vast and Terrifying Saga I. Frazier bw cartoon *New York Review of Books* v64 no3 p22 F 23 2017

Proulx, Gilbert

Build habitats, not fences, for caribou bibl *Science* v353 no6307 p1506 S 30 2016

Proust, Marcel, 1871-1922

CHURL NEXT DOOR *Harper's Magazine* v335 no2006 p14 Jl 2017

HOW to READ PROUST in the ORIGINAL L. Brown *New York Times Book Review* p23 Mr 5 2017

Letters to His Neighbor color *Publishers Weekly* v264 no9 p1 F 27 2017

PROUT, SARAH

The Question *O, The Oprah Magazine* p12 Mr 2017

Prouvé, Jean, 1901-1984

The French Connection E. Gaukel *Treasures* v6 no2 p4 O/N 2016

Jean Prouvé B. LIBBY *Treasures* v6 no2 p18 O/N 2016

Prouza, M.

Observation of a large-scale anisotropy in the arrival directions of cosmic rays above 8×1018 eV *Science* v357 no6357 p1266 S 22 2017

Provan, Alexander

UNKNOWN MAKERS *Art in America* v104 no9 p138 O 2016

Provence (France)

Set in Stone A. KLIMOSKI *Architectural Record* v205 no10 p74 O 2017

Providence Medical Center (Portland, Or.)

THE POLITICS OF LIFE AND DEATH M. J. O'Loughlin color *America* v217 no2 p18 Jl 24 2017

Provizer, Norman

Russell 'Dazzles' in Denver color *Downbeat* v84 no8 p17 Ag 2017

Provost, Victor

VICTOR PROVOST J. Murph color *Downbeat* v84 no3 p23 Mr 2017

Provvido, Diane

GO FORTH AND READ: How one Long Island school district started a literacy movement in its community color *Literacy Today (2411-7862)* v34 no6 p36 My/Je 2017

Prowse, Amanda

I Won't Be Home for Christmas *Publishers Weekly* v264 no18 p43 My 1 2017

Prowse, David

Punk's Blood Brothers D. FRICKE color *Rolling Stone* no1281/1282 p20 F 23 2017

Prowse, Lorraine

Sur Teddy's Magna A Great One Retires G. Dearth *Arabian Horse World* v57 no1 p94 O 2016

Proxima Centauri b (Planet)

Earth-mass vs. Earth-like D. J. Eicher color *Astronomy* v45 no1 p8 Ja 2017

The exoplanet next door D. Clery color *Science* v354 no6319 p1518 D 23 2016

EXOPLANETS t World Found Around Proxima Centauri C. M. CARLISLE *Sky & Telescope* v132 no6 p10 D 2016

The Proxima Trail P. Adams cartoon color *Popular Science* p69 Ja/F 2017

PRP Seats (Company)

SAFETY FAST S. RICHARDS color *Dirt Sports + Off-Road* v51 no6 p30 Je 2017

Prtak, Laura

Emergence and spread of a human-transmissible multidrug-resistant nontuberculous mycobacterium bibl diag graph *Science* v354 no6313 p751 N 11 2016

Prudential Insurance Co.

SCARE TACTICS *Saturday Evening Post* v289 no4 p95 Jl/Ag 2017

Prud'homme, Alex

Bon Appétit, America A. HENDER *Weekly Standard* v22 no4 p30 O 3 2016

France Is a Feast: The Photographic Journey of Paul and Julia Child *Publishers Weekly* v264 no38 p62 S 18 2017

THE FRENCH CHEF IN AMERICA J. LATIMER color *Maclean's* v129 no45 p57 N 14 2016

Prudlo, Donald S.

Infallible Saintmakers? F. Oakley color *Commonweal* v144 no10 p28 Je 2 2017

Prüfer, Kay

Neandertal and Denisovan DNA from Pleistocene sediments bw color *Science* v356 no6338 p605 My 12 2017

Pruijssers, Andrea J.
Reovirus infection triggers inflammatory responses to dietary anti-gens and development of celiac disease color diag *Science* v356 no6333 p44 Ap 7 2017

Pruitt, Robert
Wards Matter M. AGRESTA *Texas Monthly* v44 no12 p84 D 2016

Pruitt, Scott, 1968-
HORSEMEN of the TRUMPOCALYPSE J. NICHOLS color il *Nation* v305 no6 p18 S 11 2017

An Opportunity for Environmentalists I. M. Stelzer color *Weekly Standard* v22 no26 p16 Mr 13 2017

The Pruitt Backlash A. Greenblatt *Governing* v30 no5 p9 F 2017

Pruitt Faces Fire on Climate Views J. A. Dlouhy bw *Bloomberg Businessweek* no4508 p25 Ja 23 2017

SCOTT PRUITT'S CRIMES AGAINST NATURE J. GOODELL color *Rolling Stone* no1293 p44 Ag 10 2017

With Climate Denial in the White House, Will Media Echo Of-ficial Know-Nothingism? R. Richardson *Extra!* v30 no4 p4 My 2017

Will There Be Justice? *USA Today Magazine* v145 no2858 p10 N 2016

Pruitt, Scott, 1968——Political & social views
For the Record color diag *Time* v189 no11 p8 Mr 27 2017

Pruitt, Steven
A New Kind of Star Power R. Bruner, E. Berman et al color *Time* v190 no2/3 p24 Jl 10-17 2017

Prum, Richard O.
BEAUTY HAPPENS bw color *Natural History* v125 no4 p24 Ap 2017

The biology of color color *Science* v357 no6350 p470 Ag 4 2017

How Beauty Drives Evolution S. Begley color *Time* v189 no19 p18 My 22 2017

Idiosyncratic desires E. Lorraine Milam color *Science* v356 no6341 p915 Je 1 2017

Prune
POWER UP YOUR SALAD color *Good Housekeeping* v265 no2 p93 Ag 2017

Pruning
See also
Topiary work
AROUND THE GARDEN S. Bender color *Southern Living* v52 no6 p40 Je 2017

ask THE GRUMPY GARDENER S. Bender color *Southern Living* v51 no12 p60 D 2016

LIFE AND LIMB S. STALL *Indianapolis Monthly* v40 no7 p19 Mr 2017

Making the Cuts color *Southern Living* v52 no2 p44 F 2017

SHRUBS SHAPE-UP M. HUGHES color *Better Homes & Gardens* v95 no4 p82 Ap 2017

Prusak, Bernard G.
The Dean Looks Back color *Commonweal* v144 no10 p32 Je 2 2017

Holy Cities color *Commonweal* v143 no20 p20 D 16 2016

Women & Children First color *Commonweal* v143 no17 p19 O 21 2016

Prusicki, Maria Ada
RETINOBLASTOMA RELATED1 mediates germline entry in Arabidopsis color diag *Science* v356 no6336 p396 Ap 28 2017

Prussia (Germany)
ARMS RACE map *MHQ: Quarterly Journal of Military History* v29 no4 p22 Summ 2017

Pruvost, Mélanie
Ancient genomic changes associated with domestication of the horse color diag *Science* v356 no6336 p442 Ap 28 2017

PRYCE-JONES, DAVID
Dictator Erdogan color *National Review* v69 no9 p17 My 15 2017

Enfant Terrible bw color *National Review* v68 no23 p37 D 19 2016

High Treason color *National Review* v68 no21 p41 N 21 2016

The Maligning Of Israel *National Review* v69 no1 p20 Ja 23 2017

Regime Change *National Review* v69 no18 p35 O 2 2017

The Six-Day War at 50 *National Review* v69 no11 p17 Je 12 2017

Treason of The Clerks diag *National Review* v69 no4 p35 Mr 6 2017

Prychun, Debra
Dream Buddy on a Trail Ride cartoon *Horse & Rider* v56 no3

p72 Mr 2017

PRYER, KATHLEEN M.
Sex and the Single Gametophyte: Revising the Homosporous Vascular Plant Life Cycle in Light of Contemporary Research *BioScience* v66 no11 p928 N 1 2016

Pryor, Elizabeth Brown, 1951-2015
Taking Old Abe to Task D. S. Reynolds *American Scholar* v86 no2 p122 Spr 2017

Union Boss A. KESSLER-HARRIS *New York Times Book Review* p11 F 12 2017

Pryor, Frederic
Occupational choices of the elderly bibl chart color *Monthly Labor Review* p1 F 2017

Przewalski's horse
NEW LIFESTYLE FOR PRZEWALSKI'S HORSES C. Barakat and M. McCluskey color *Equus* no481 p14 O 2017

WILD WILD HORSES P. WILLIAMS *Smithsonian* v47 no8 p56 D 2016

Przybyla, Magdalena
Site-specific phosphorylation of tau inhibits amyloid-β toxicity in Alzheimer's mice bibl graph *Science* v354 no6314 p904 N 18 2016

P.S. 1 Contemporary Art Center
ART color *New Yorker* v93 no11 p6 My 1 2017

PSA Group (Company)
A Continental Retreat C. Thomas, D. Welch et al color map *Bloomberg Businessweek* no4514 p23 Mr 13 2017

PSA Peugeot Citroën SA
SACRE BLEU! A. MacKenzie color *Motor Trend* v69 no2 p102 F 2017

Psalms (Musical form)——48th Psalm
Our Two Spiritual Time Zones S. MCCRACKEN *Christianity Today* v61 no7 p30 S 2017

Psaropoulos, John
Canary in the Union color *Weekly Standard* v22 no15 p33 D 19 2016

Rocking the Cradle of Democracy *American Scholar* v86 no2 p6 Spr 2017

Shipping News color map *Weekly Standard* v22 no45 p24 Ag 7 2017

Tigers at Bay color *Weekly Standard* v22 no37 p30 Je 5 2017

PSB Speakers (Company)
PSB SubSeries 450 Subwoofer D. Vaughn color graph *Sound & Vision* v81 no10 p60 D 2016

Pseudo-Methodius
CRY HAVOC *Lapham's Quarterly* v10 no3 p147 Summ 2017

Pseudoplastic fluids
Advances in engineering hydrogels Y. Shrike Zhang and A. Khademhosseini diag *Science* v356 no6337 p500 My 5 2017

Pseudoscience
FIRE-BREATHING DINOSAURS? Physics, Fossils, and Functional Morphology vs. Pseudoscience P. J. SENTER *Skeptical Inquirer* v41 no4 p26 Jl/Ag 2017

Hassani replies S. Hassani *Physics Today* v69 no11 p12 N 2016

Humanities, Too: In New Study, History Courses in Critical Thinking Reduce Pseudoscientific Beliefs K. Frazier *Skeptical Inquirer* v41 no4 p11 Jl/Ag 2017

Pseudoscience versus science M. Beauregard, N. Trent et al *Physics Today* v69 no11 p10 N 2016

Response from Livingston and Colleagues G. LIVINGSTON *Bio-Science* v67 no2 p105 F 2017

Vaccines, Autism, and the Promotion of Irrelevant Research: A Science-Pseudoscience Analysis C. A. FOSTER and S. M. OR-TIZ *Skeptical Inquirer* v41 no3 p44 My/Je 2017

VANCE CROWE: MEET THE MAN BUILDING A VAST NET-WORK THROUGH TRIBES TO RALLY AGAINST THE PSEUDOSCIENCE ATTACKING GMOS J. Scott *Successful Farming* v115 no9 p10 Ag 2017

Psilocybin
Can You Trip Your Way Out of Anxiety? M. SHAER cartoon *Men's Health* v32 no4 p88 My 2017

Psoas muscles——Anatomy
Body of knowledge [Cover story] R. Long color *Yoga Journal* no289 p44 F 2017

Psoriasis——Treatment
Before You Take It S. KLEIN color *Prevention* p22 Mr 2017

Psych: The Movie (TV program)
PSYCH: THE MOVIE C. Agard color *Entertainment Weekly* no1474/1475 p74 Jl 21-28 2017

Psychedelic art
Peter Max: An American Artist R. Love bw color *AARP: The Magazine* v60 no5A p6 Ag/S 2017

Psychiatric diagnosis
Beyond Diagnostic Categories: Comprehensive Assessment of Psychopathology in Addiction and Mental Health Disorders V. Kumari *Psychology Today* v50 no3 p14 My/Je 2017
THE BIG DATA BULL'S-EYE P. RAEBURN *Psychology Today* v50 no5 p81 S/O 2017
Is Mental Illness the Exception or the Rule? A LONG-TERM STUDY SUGGESTS THAT MOST PEOPLE STRUGGLE AT SOME POINT D. RETTEW *Psychology Today* v50 no4 p18 Ag 2017

Psychiatric drugs
See also
Opioids
FROM THE ARCHIVES bw color *Reason* v48 no8 p62 Ja 2017

Psychiatric hospitals—New York (State)
Buffalo's Fall and Rise: An inspiring case history of an urban turnaround B. KAUFFMAN *American Conservative* v16 no5 p20 S/O 2017

Psychiatric service dogs
Hello. The Dog Will See You Now J. WILLIAMS *Cincinnati Magazine* v50 no4 p78 Ja 2017

Psychiatrists
See also
Psychoanalysts
Get more out of life M. RABBITT color *Redbook* p100 N 2017
A GLOBAL STATE OF MIND J. SILBERNER color diag *Discover* v38 no10 p30 D 2017

Psychiatrists—Humor
Laughter THE BEST MEDICINE color *Reader's Digest* v189 no1131 p96 Je 2017

Psychiatrists—United States
THE SMARTPHONE PSYCHIATRIST D. DOBBS color *Atlantic* v320 no1 p78 Jl/Ag 2017

Psychic Reader (Music)
GOINGS ON ABOUT TOWN color *New Yorker* v92 no49 p11 F 13 2017

Psychics
Frank ANDREWS F. ANDREWS *Interview* v46 no10 p46 D 2016/Ja 2017
Psychic Roundup: 'Psychics' Convicted B. RADFORD *Skeptical Inquirer* v41 no5 p9 S/O 2017
TonBenet Murder Mystery Solved? J. NICKELL *Skeptical Inquirer* v41 no4 p38 Jl/Ag 2017

Psychics—United States
MISS CLEO J. WORTHAM *New York Times Magazine* p17 D 25 2016

Psychoanalysis
Psychoanalyzing the World's Problems Won't Help Us Solve Them G. Petriglieri color *Harvard Business Review Digital Articles* p2 Ja 24 2017
THE STONE GUEST L. MENAND cartoon *New Yorker* v93 no25 p75 Ag 28 2017

Psychoanalysts
FEAR bw *Tricycle: The Buddhist Review* v27 no1 p48 Fall 2017

Psychographics
Psychographics Are Just as Important for Marketers as Demographics A. Samuel *Harvard Business Review Digital Articles* p2 Mr 11 2016

Psychological aspects of aging
CHRISTIE BRINKLEY "Feeling Good Is Looking Good" J. Andriakos color *Health* v31 no5 p19 Je 2017

Psychological factors
THE SCIENCE OF humility M. R. Mcminn *Christianity Today* v61 no6 p80 Jl/Ag 2017

Psychological ownership
How to Make Employees Feel Like They Own Their Work F. Gino *Harvard Business Review Digital Articles* p2 D 7 2015

Psychological tests
See also
Character tests

Intelligence tests
Psychometrics
Are We All Racists? M. Shermer color *Scientific American* v317 no2 p81 Ag 2017

Psychological tests—History
The wisdom of the blots B. BETHUNE bw cartoon *Maclean's* v130 no2 p66 Mr 2017

Psychologists
Dr. Phil McGraw color *AARP: The Magazine* v59 no3A p18 Ap/My 2016
Faith Healers M. Quinn, H. Delery et al *Governing* v30 no6 p6 Mr 2017
The Needle Exchanger M. Nascimento color *Foreign Policy* no222 p18 Ja/F 2017
Sleeping with the Enemy M. BECK color *O, The Oprah Magazine* p40 Ag 2017

Psychology
See also
Adaptability (Psychology)
Adjustment (Psychology)
Affect (Psychology)
Assertiveness (Psychology)
Attention
Attitude (Psychology)
Belief & doubt
Child psychology
Cognition
Consciousness
Consumer behavior
Control (Psychology)
Cynicism
Developmental psychology
Emotions (Psychology)
Experience
Failure (Psychology)
Habit
Human behavior
Ideology
Individual differences
Industrial psychology
Intellect
Introspection
Judgment (Psychology)
Memory
Mental training
Motivation (Psychology)
Pathological psychology
Perception
Personality
Political psychology
Praise
Problem solving
Religious psychology
Self-acceptance
Social interaction
Social psychology
Stimulus & response (Psychology)
Stress (Psychology)
Thought & thinking
Values (Ethics)
editor's note. On wanting more for others than they want for themselves K. Perina *Psychology Today* v49 no5 p4 S/O 2016
Employees Can't Be Summed Up by a Personality Test P. Bregman *Harvard Business Review Digital Articles* p2 Ag 19 2015
FINDINGS *Harper's Magazine* v334 no2002 p96 Mr 2017
GEORGE SAUNDERS E. Sullivan bw *Esquire* v167 no1 p58 F 2017
Mission Critical M. BECK color *O, The Oprah Magazine* p46 N 2017
The Shadow Knows B. CHELETTE *USA Today Magazine* v145 no2858 p19 N 2016

Psychology of athletes
Why There Is Crying In Baseball, and Tennis, and Golf, and Soccer ... S. Gregory color *Time* v190 no5 p25 Jl 31 2017

Psychology of dance
LEARNING Fearlessness K. Mcguire *Dance Spirit* v21 no7 p62

S 2017

Psychology of defendants

How Software Could Help Judges Reduce Crime T. Simonite il *MIT Technology Review* v120 no3 p15 My/Je 2017

Psychology of learning

See also

Behavior modification

Feedback (Psychology)

Motivation in education

Social learning

Is How You Deliver Feedback Doing More Harm than Good? T. Chamorro-Premuzic *Harvard Business Review Digital Articles* p2 Ag 10 2015

Learning to walk in another's shoes H. Gehlbach color *Phi Delta Kappan* v98 no6 p8 Mr 2017

When It's OK to Ignore Feedback D. Clark *Harvard Business Review Digital Articles* p2 Ag 4 2015

Psychology of scientists

The philosopher's view J. B. HOLBROOK *Issues in Science & Technology* v33 no3 p16 Spr 2017

Psychology of students

You Know What . . D. T. PUTERBAUGH *USA Today Magazine* v145 no2864 p80 My 2017

Psychology of women

LOUD MOUTH L. Dunham color *Vogue* v207 no6 p145 Je 2017

Psychology periodicals

Sex matters: Report experimenter gender C. D. Chapman, C. Benedict et al *Science* v356 no6341 p916 Je 1 2017

Psychology of HIV-positive people

Take a Deep Breath: Living with HIV is Like Learning to hold your breath under water T. CURRY *Advocate* no1093 p23 O/N 2017

Psychometrics

I'LL TELL YOU SOMETHING ZAHIR IRANI: The rise of psychometric testing is harming workplace diversity *People Management* p18 Jl 2017

Psychopathy

When Your Child Is a Psychopath B. B. HAGERTY color *Atlantic* v319 no5 p78 Je 2017

Why Bad Guys Win at Work T. Chamorro-Premuzic *Harvard Business Review Digital Articles* p2 N 2 2015

Psychopharmacologists

Neuropsychopharmacologist David Nutt on Alcohol, LSD, and Getting Sacked for His Findings Z. WEISSMUELLER color *Reason* v49 no4 p79 Ag/S 2017

Psychoses

DEATH OF A DYSTOPIAN A. WILKINSON bw cartoon *New Yorker* v93 no8 p22 Ap 10 2017

Psychosomatic disorders—Treatment

When the Body Speaks S. O'Sullivan *Psychology Today* v50 no1 p72 Ja/F 2017

Psychotherapists

See also

Sex therapists

Must I Tell My Therapist About My Other Therapist? K. A. Appiah *New York Times Magazine* p28 S 17 2017

Time to See A Shrink N. STAR *Publishers Weekly* v263 no41 p84 O 10 2016

Psychotherapists—Humor

Laughter *Reader's Digest* v188 no1124 p98 O 2016

Psychotherapy

See also

Behavior therapy

Cognitive therapy

Psychotherapy & religion

AMERICAN NIRVANA A. GOPNIK cartoon *New Yorker* v93 no23 p69 Ag 7 2017

Introducing a Psychotherapy for the Collective: A Paradigm Shift for College Mental Health G. D. Glass *Change* v48 no6 p16 N/D 2016

Psychotherapy & religion

I THOUGHT GOOD CATHOLICS DIDN'T NEED THERAPY. THEN I WENT S. Fisher color *America* v217 no2 p36 Jl 24 2017

Psychotherapy patients

When Television Was a Medical Device J. A. Greene *Humanities*

v38 no2 p6 Spr 2017

Ptáček, Matouž P.

Titanium isotopic evidence for felsic crust and plate tectonics 3.5 billion years ago bw color graph *Science* v357 no6357 p1271 S 22 2017

Pterosauria

Weirdest Wonders on Wings R. Conniff bw color diag *National Geographic* v232 no5 p60 N 2017

PTO Inc.

Monetizing Lost Vacation Time A. Melin and B. Steverman color *Bloomberg Businessweek* no4495 p33 O 17 2016

Ptolemy, 2nd century

Summertime clusters P. Harrington color *Astronomy* v45 no7 p68 Jl 2017

PTScientists (Company)

A New Race to the Moon color *Time* v189 no12 p12 Ap 3 2017

Pu Zhang

Response to Comments on "Reconciliation of the Devils Hole climate record with orbital forcing" bibl chart graph *Science* v354 no6310 p296-e O 21 2016

Pu Zheng

RPA binds histone H3-H4 and functions in DNA replication–coupled nucleosome assembly bibl graph *Science* v355 no6323 p415 Ja 27 2017

Puberty

Your Body Right Now! Is this weird? Is that normal? And perhaps most important—is that me I smell? Here, answers to a few of your most pressing puberty-related questions (ones you're maybe too afraid to ask!) M. Foye and M. Walker *Scholastic Choices* v32 no5 p6 F 2017

Pubic hair

THE BARE TRUTH bw *Women's Health* v14 no3 p36 Ap 2017

Does a Bare Bush Increase Your Risk for STIs? D. GUERRERO color *Advocate* no1090 p42 Ap 2017

Public administration

See also

Government accountability

Government agencies

Climate Changed M. HERTSGAARD color il *Nation* v304 no1 p70 Ja 2 2017 The Obama Years

JOE NAVARRO AGENT PROVOCATEUR H. ESTROFF MARANO *Psychology Today* v50 no2 p56 Mr/Ap 2017

Liberalism's Half-Life B. COVERT and M. KONCZAL color graph *Nation* v304 no1 p14 Ja 2 2017 The Obama Years

Making Government Reorgs Work S. Heidari-Robinson color *Harvard Business Review Digital Articles* p2 Mr 30 2017

A Proof, a Test, an Instruction M. ROBINSON color *Nation* v304 no1 p16 Ja 2 2017 The Obama Years

Public Debate, Scientific Skepticism, and Science Denial S. LEWANDOWSKY, M. E. MANN et al *Skeptical Inquirer* v41 no1 p40 Ja/F 2017

Save Our Bureaucrats! A. FERGUSON *Commentary* v144 no1 p9 Jl/Ag 2017

The Silicon President S. VAIDHYANATHAN color *Nation* v304 no1 p74 Ja 2 2017 The Obama Years

Public administration—Russia

HOW TO -NOT WHAT TO- THINK ABOUT PUTIN C. CALDWELL *USA Today Magazine* v146 no2866 p35 Jl 2017

Public administration—United States

COMMENT: FIGHTING WORDS E. Osnos bw *New Yorker* v93 no33 p35 O 23 2017

I Crunched the Numbers on the U.S. Government. Here's What I Learned S. Ballmer color *Time* v190 no5 p30 Jl 31 2017

The U.S. Cannot Be Run Like a Business H. Mintzberg *Harvard Business Review Digital Articles* p2 Mr 31 2017

Will President Trump Learn on the Job? G. Mukunda *Harvard Business Review Digital Articles* p2 My 4 2017

Public architecture—Design & construction

Go With the Flow A. MARTINS color *Architectural Record* v205 no8 p84 Ag 2017

Public art

See also

Public sculpture

Game Theory D. Daniel color *American Craft* v77 no3 p64 Je/Jl 2017

High Line Art M. Jensen *Orion Magazine* v35 no4/5 p72 Jl-O

Housekeeping v264 no6 p97 Je 2017

When Cooking Kills M. NIJHUIS color map *National Geographic* v232 no3 p76 S 2017

Public health nurses

ALL IN A Day's Work color *Reader's Digest* v189 no1130 p68 My 2017

Public health surveillance

Driving improvements in emerging disease surveillance through locally relevant capacity strengthening J. E. B. Halliday, K. Hampson et al color diag *Science* v357 no6347 p146 Jl 14 2017

Public health surveillance—International cooperation

Can we beat influenza? W. Zhang and R. G. Webster color *Science* v357 no6347 p111 Jl 14 2017

Public health—Awards

Dr. Larry Hollier F. ESKER color *Louisiana Life* v37 no3 p64 Ja/F 2017

Public health—India

Opening the Door For Future Drug Sales A. Altstedter and J. S. Hopkins color *Bloomberg Businessweek* no4533 p15 Ag 7 2017

A Place to Go E. Royte color diag map *National Geographic* v232 no2 p94 Ag 2017

Unpaid Bills J. McGowan color *Commonweal* v144 no15 p6 S 22 2017

Public health—Iraq

Black death A. R. KHAN color *Maclean's* v129 no48/49 p28 D 5 2016

Public health—Maine

Clumsy Reform A. Greenblatt *Governing* v30 no3 p10 D 2016

Public health—Maryland—Baltimore

Attacking the Roots of Violence L. S. Wen and M. C. Lloyd cartoon *Scientific American* v315 no5 p9 N 2016

Public health—Mathematical models

Forecasting the opioid epidemic D. S. Burke color *Science* v354 no6312 p529 N 4 2016

Public health—Ohio

Q+A *Cincinnati Magazine* v50 no4 p30 Ja 2017

Public health—Taiwan

ROOM FOR EVERYONE B. SU *Foreign Affairs* v96 no6 p175 N/D 2017

Public health—United States

AMERICA'S HIDDEN H.I.V. EPIDEMIC L. VILLAROSA *New York Times Magazine* p38 Je 11 2017

How to Keep America Safe B. Gates color *Time* v189 no18 p39 My 15 2017

The Walking Cure M. Quinn *Governing* v30 no4 p18 Ja 2017

Warning: The Next Global Security Threat Isn't What You Think [Cover story] B. Walsh color diag *Time* v189 no18 p32 My 15 2017

We Interviewed Health Care Leaders About Their Industry, and They're Worried M. Poku and K. A. Schulman *Harvard Business Review Digital Articles* p2 D 14 2016

Public health—United States—Government policy

Don't Pass the Weed or Say "Guns" S. Mirsky color *Scientific American* v316 no5 p78 My 2017

Public health—United States—News briefs

Public health checkup C. Martin color *Science News* v190 no13 p18 D 24 2016

Public health—Venezuela

Photostat: Going Hungry in Venezuela F. Zerpa and N. Soto color *Bloomberg Businessweek* no4540 p38 O 2 2017

Public health—Zambia

To Talk About Sex to Teens In Zambia, Play the Diva J. Scanlon and T. C. Mitimingi color *Bloomberg Businessweek* no4494 p42 O 10 2016

Public history—United States

Past Is Prologue G. Allison and N. Ferguson *Hoover Digest: Research & Opinion on Public Policy* no1 p175 Wint 2017

Public House Brewing Co.

Bourbon, Brews, BBQ & Blues D. BRESHEARS color *Missouri Life* v44 no4 p44 Je 2017

Public housing

The Demand for Responsive Architectural Planning and Production in Rapidly Urbanizing Regions: the Case of Ethiopia Z. C. Mamo *UN Chronicle* v53 no3 p15 2016

On All Floors J. Berlin color *National Geographic* v232 no4 p130 O 2017

Public housing design & construction

Last days of the Smithsons' Robin Hood Gardens H. PEARMAN *Architectural Record* v205 no9 p32 S 2017

Public housing—New York (State)

BRONX TALE J. GONNERMAN cartoon color *New Yorker* v92 no41 p36 D 12 2016

Public institutions

See also

  Correctional institutions

  Libraries

  Museums

  Prisons

  Schools

  Universities & colleges

THE GULF ART WAR N. AZIMI cartoon color *New Yorker* v92 no42 p74 D 19 2016

The Timothy Hunt Witch Hunt: A joke told, a reputation destroyed J. Foreman *Commentary* v140 no2 p41 S 2015

Public investments

An Entrepreneurial Society Needs an Entrepreneurial State M. Mazzucato *Harvard Business Review Digital Articles* p1 O 25 2016

Welcome to Festival City A. Ehrenhalt *Governing* v30 no1 p14 O 2016

Why the Keystone Pipeline Is the Wrong U.S. Energy Debate A. Winston *Harvard Business Review Digital Articles* p2 Ja 30 2015

Public lands

See also

  Forest reserves

  National parks & reserves

  Protected areas

A Free Trip D. HURTEAU and T. J. Peterson color *Field & Stream* v122 no4 p40 S 2017

From Sea to Shining Sea R. Richardson *Parks & Recreation* v52 no4 p30 Ap 2017

Hawaiian Natives Fight for Their Land A. Hannah color *Progressive* v81 no10 p32 N 2016

High Consequences J. WHEELWRIGHT color map *Discover* v38 no7 p50 S 2017

How Scientists Can Help End the Land-Use Conflict O. E. SALA *BioScience* v66 no11 p915 N 1 2016

Pubic Lands Ranching A. Rieber cartoon *American Cowboy* v23 no4 p22 D 2016/Ja 2017

PUBLIC LANDS IN PUBLIC HANDS color *Field & Stream* v122 no1 p6 My 2017

SWAMP GOBBLERS A. McKEAN color map *Outdoor Life* v224 no2 p73 F/Mr 2017

Public lands—United States

Cheers & Jeers M. James, S. Brown et al color *Field & Stream* v121 no6 p12 N 2016

Don't Mine What's Ours D. MARTINDALE *In These Times* v41 no6 p5 Je 2017

AN OPEN LETTER TO OUR NEXT PRESIDENT A. McKEAN cartoon color *Outdoor Life* v224 no1 p56 D 2016/Ja 2017

PUBLIC DOMAINS A. McKEAN color map *Outdoor Life* v224 no5 p64 Je/Jl 2017

THIS LAND WAS YOUR LAND H. HERRING, J. R. SULLIVAN et al cartoon color diag map *Field & Stream* v122 no1 p40 My 2017

Public lands—United States—Law & legislation

Federal Land Ownership and Management: Background and Current Issues *Congressional Digest* v96 no6 p3 Je 2017

LAND CLAIMS B. LONG and N. KREBS color *Outdoor Life* v224 no4 p10 My 2017

Public lands—Wyoming

PUBLIC APPEAL color *Field & Stream* v122 no4 p15 S 2017

Public libraries

CH-CH-CH-CH-CHANGES B. CROWDER *Virginia Living* v15 no3 p29 Ap 2017

Irasburg J. Johnson bw color *Old House Journal* v45 no4 p34 Je 2017

That's Outrageous! color *Reader's Digest* v189 no1129 p82 Ap 2017

Public libraries—Ohio

Q + A *Cincinnati Magazine* v50 no8 p24 My 2017

Public prosecutors
 See also
  Special prosecutors
 The Many Shades of Maíra Mutti Araújo C. DE OLIVEIRA bw color *Foreign Policy* no225 p46 Jl/Ag 2017
Public prosecutors—United States
 Is the Best Offense a Good Defense Lawyer? C. HOOKS *Texas Monthly* v44 no11 p62 N 2016
 Ken Thompson Fought to the Very End G. GRAY img *New York* v49 no25 p60 D 12 2016
Public radio
 THE COLOR OF RADIO A. Beaujon *Washingtonian Magazine* v52 no9 p53 Je 2017
Public records
 See also
  Memorandums
  Petitions
 Illuminating SNAP Performance Using the Power of Administrative Data M. Prell *Amber Waves: The Economics of Food, Farming, Natural Resources, & Rural America* p14 N 2016
Public records—United States
 The FIRST RECORDS J. Kratz *Prologue* v49 no2 p40 Summ 2017
Public relations
 See also
  Community relations
  Customer relations
  Police-community relations
  Press conferences
 Get Your Pitch Noticed by a Major Publisher K. Libert *Harvard Business Review Digital Articles* p2 O 14 2014
 How to Tell If a Company Is Good at Innovating or Just Good at PR S. Anthony *Harvard Business Review Digital Articles* p2 D 18 2014
 What I Learned From 10 Years of Doing PR for Apple C. Craig *Harvard Business Review Digital Articles* p2 Jl 27 2016
Public relations consultants
 JACK BRENNAN J. WILLIAMS *Cincinnati Magazine* v50 no5 p80 F 2017
Public relations firms
 Scared Straight A. FERGUSON cartoon *Weekly Standard* v22 no17 p5 Ja 2 2017
Public relations personnel
 See also
  Press secretaries
 Get Your Pitch Noticed by a Major Publisher K. Libert *Harvard Business Review Digital Articles* p2 O 14 2014
Public safety
 See also
  Emergency management
  Fire prevention
  Police
  Traffic safety
 Robocops (and Roboinspectors) T. Newcombe *Governing* v30 no1 p62 O 2016
Public school teachers
 Has D.C. Teacher Reform Been Successful? J. Merrow, M. Levy et al *Washington Monthly* v49 no9/10 p16 S/O 2017
Public schools
 See also
  Charter schools
 50, 100 & 150 YEARS AGO color *Scientific American* v317 no1 p75 Jl 2017
 And the Walls Came Tumbling Down J. N. LOMAX *Texas Monthly* v45 no7 p48 Jl 2017
 Boston's School for Immigrants E. Kaplan bw *Progressive* v81 no6 p38 Ag/S 2017
 The Experiment D. KUKOFF *Los Angeles Magazine* v61 no11 p144 N 2016
 Purposefully poetic D. A. Kelin II bibl chart diag *Arts Education Policy Review* v118 no4 p202 2017
 The Role of the School G. A. GOENS *USA Today Magazine* v145 no2864 p56 My 2017
 Teachable Moments: Structures don't store memories or build character--people do *Indianapolis Monthly* p168 N 2017
Public schools—Louisiana—New Orleans

Chartering the Course D. Ruth Wilson color *New Orleans Magazine* v51 no5 p32 Mr 2017
Public schools—United States
 The 49th Annual PDK Poll of the Public's Attitudes Toward the Public Schools chart color graph *Phi Delta Kappan* v99 no1 pNP1 S 2017
 Common Sense N. Hannah-Jones *New York Times Magazine* p13 F 26 2017
 The Editor's Note J. Richardson *Phi Delta Kappan* v99 no1 p4 S 2017
 Highlighted & Underlined J. Richardson color *Phi Delta Kappan* v98 no8 p6 My 2017
 Hot for Teachers T. Toch color *Washington Monthly* v49 no6-8 p47 Je-Ag 2017
 The Miseducation of Betsy DeVos D. RAVITCH *In These Times* v41 no2 p17 F 2017
 Partnerships Between Schools and Communities Promote Reading Success A. A. Arnett and S. J. Gaither *Education Digest* v83 no2 p57 O 2017
 Singled Out: Los Angeles' misguided effort to open more single-sex public schools K. SHER and G. SHERWIN *Ms.* v27 no2 p10 Summ 2017
Public schools—United States—Finance
 Lack of financial support schools' top problem graph *Phi Delta Kappan* v98 no5 p7 F 2017
Public sculpture
 Monuments to What? R. WILSON *American Scholar* v86 no4 p2 Aut 2017
 VISIONS color *National Geographic* v232 no2 p8 Ag 2017
Public sector
 The Power of a P3 M. Funkhouser *Governing* v30 no1 p61 O 2016
 What Business Can Learn from Government L. Greenspun and R. Wartzman *Harvard Business Review Digital Articles* p2 Ja 12 2015
Public sector—Great Britain
 Can the public sector survive a 1% pay rise? HR professionals are concerned about concerned about their and motivate staff - yet engagement levels have hit new highs *People Management* p8 My 2017
Public sector—Officials & employees
 Big Little Lies: Ten ways public officials fool some of the people most of the time K. Barrett and R. Greene *Governing* v30 no8 p58 My 2017
Public spaces
 See also
  Beaches
  Community centers
  Pedestrian areas
  Urban parks
 Hit the Playground! M. Anderson color *Parents* v92 no9 p104 S 2017
 HOW SHOULD CONFEDERATE STATUES IN PUBLIC SPACES BE TREATED? color *America* v217 no6 p6 S 18 2017
 Last Days Of Storyville S. ASHER bw color *New Orleans Magazine* v51 no12 p78 O 2017
 Out & About color *Martha Stewart Living* p16 O 2017
 Record Hosts 19th Innovation Conference, in San Francisco B. BROOME and J. GONCHAR *Architectural Record* v205 no7 p34 Jl 2017
 Veggie Meals in (or near!) National Parks C. Brown and H. Francis *Vegetarian Journal* v36 no1 p25 2017
 What Lurks Beneath: CONTAMINATED SOIL AND THE PUSH TO REVITALIZE PORTIONS OF THE LOS ANGELES RIVER Z. MATTHEW *Los Angeles Magazine* v62 no9 p19 S 2017
Public spaces—Design & construction
 Design of the PUBLIC REALM *Architectural Record* v205 no4 p175 Ap 2017
 On Architecture that Addresses the Street E. Plater-Zyberk *Architectural Record* v205 no4 p209 Ap 2017
Public spaces—Government policy
 A Monumental Fight K. Steinmetz color *Time* v190 no9 p30 S 4 2017
Public spaces—Law & legislation
 Public Spaces and Social Equity M. A. Currie *Parks & Recreation* v52 no3 p34 Mr 2017
Public spaces—Management

Activate Your Parks and Your People B. Tulipane *Parks & Recreation* v52 no6 p8 Je 2017

Public speaking
See also
Debates & debating
6 Ways to Look More Confident During a Presentation [Cover story] K. Wezowski *Harvard Business Review Digital Articles* p2 Ap 6 2017
The Anxious Man's Guide to Public Speaking B. Platt and C. SKIPPER color *GQ: Gentlemen's Quarterly* v97 no5 p36 My 2017
Breathing Is the Key to Persuasive Public Speaking A. Shapira *Harvard Business Review Digital Articles* p2 Je 30 2015
How Can I Survive...Public Speaking? B. Anat *Scholastic Choices* v32 no5 p24 F 2017
Laugh Lines J. FALLON color *Reader's Digest* v190 no1134 p127 O 2017
Your Presentation Needs a Punch Line A. Ferrara *Harvard Business Review Digital Articles* p2 My 21 2015

Public speaking—Humor
STRATEGIC HUMOR *Harvard Business Review* v94 no11 p32 N 2016

Public speaking—Psychological aspects
How to overcome a fear of public speaking L. Shaw *People Management* p52 O 2016

Public spending
See also
Budget
5 Simple Urban Fixes A. Marshall *Governing* v30 no5 p24 F 2017
Breakdown of Federal Spending *USA Today Magazine* v146 no2867 p7 Ag 2017
The Crumbs of Capitalism T. Kane *Commentary* v142 no2 p11 S 2016
Research: Opposition to Federal Spending Is Driven by Racial Resentment K. Krimmel and K. Rader *Harvard Business Review Digital Articles* p2 S 1 2017
Spend on Values to Feel Good J. Chatzky color *AARP: The Magazine* v60 no4A p24 Je/Jl 2017
STARVING THE SCHOOLS L. Farmer *Governing* v30 no9 p44 Je 2017
Trump budget proposal: gloomy, but just a proposal M. Hourihan and D. Parkes *Issues in Science & Technology* v33 no4 p21 Summ 2017
What to EXPECT in Your 50s S. HARRAR cartoon color *AARP: The Magazine* v60 no4A p28 Je/Jl 2017

Public spending—Law & legislation
Senate Appropriations Committee and the House Chamber Passes Respective Interior Bills *American Forests* v122 no3 p14 Fall 2016

Public spending—United States
Athwart J. LILEKS *National Review* v69 no6 p39 Ap 3 2017
HIGHER EDUCATION J. B. Wogan *Governing* v30 no4 p39 Ja 2017
The Infrastructure Myth P. R. Gregory *Hoover Digest: Research & Opinion on Public Policy* no1 p28 Wint 2017
The Next President's Financial Imperative: Fixing Social Security P. Wang color *Time* v188 no20 p20 N 14 2016
PRICEY PAYOUTS M. Maciag *Governing* v30 no2 p32 N 2016
Rebuilding Our Foundations E. Barone color diag map *Time* v188 no16/17 p46 O 24 2016
Science gets little love in Trump spending plan chart *Science* v356 no6340 p795 My 26 2017
WHERE TO SPEND ON INFRASTRUCTURE B. O'Keefe diag *Fortune* v174 no8 p192 D 15 2016

Public sphere
Back from the Brink: Truth and Trust in the Public Sphere S. JASANOFF *Issues in Science & Technology* v33 no4 p25 Summ 2017
Fictional States & Atomized Public Spheres: A Non-Western Approach to Fragility W. Reno *Daedalus* v146 no4 p139 Fall 2017

Public transit
THE CONNECTOR J. GREEN *Atlanta* v56 no12 p19 Ap 2017
THE EDITORIAL *Maclean's* v129 no47 p7 N 28 2016
KEEPING SEX ASSAULT UNDERGROUND A. KINGSTON color *Maclean's* v129 no45 p10 N 14 2016
A lesson from Pope Francis for Miami's gridlocked streets T.

Padgett color *America* v217 no6 p16 S 18 2017
Notes from Underground R. BROOKHISER il *National Review* v69 no3 p55 F 20 2017
On the Move color *Los Angeles Magazine* v62 no7 p6 Jl 2017

Public transit fare evasion
Farebox Fairness *Governing* v30 no8 p10 My 2017

Public transit—Fares
Riding Toward Equality D. R. JONES and N. RANKIN *Nation* v304 no3 p4 Ja 30 2017

Public transit—Finance
The Right to Ride *America* v216 no1 p5 Ja 2 2017

Public transit—New York (State)—New York
Riding Toward Equality D. R. JONES and N. RANKIN *Nation* v304 no3 p4 Ja 30 2017

Public transit—Ridership
BEHIND THE NUMBERS M. Maciag *Governing* v30 no5 p59 F 2017
Sick Transit D. C. Vock *Governing* v30 no2 p46 N 2016

Public transit—United States
CLOCKING THE COMMUTE *Governing* v30 no5 p58 F 2017
Growing Smart: The right kind of transit is crucial for growing cities S. Beyer *Governing* v30 no12 p23 S 2017
The Right to Ride *America* v216 no1 p5 Ja 2 2017

Public transit—United States—Finance
BIG-TICKET TRANSIT J. Surowiecki cartoon *New Yorker* v92 no46 p21 Ja 23 2017

Public universities & colleges
See also
Community colleges
IN JEFFERSON'S SHADOW N. M. Flores color *America* v216 no12 p28 My 29 2017

Public utilities
See also
Railroads
Water supply
THE BEGINNER'S GUIDE TO Making a Difference B. ROBINSON, K. SILVER et al cartoon color diag *O, The Oprah Magazine* p114 S 2017
BOAT INSURANCE INS AND OUTS B. M. KENYON *Sea Magazine* v109 no2 p44 F 2017

Public utilities—Safety measures
A Safer, Smarter Grid B. Walsh color *Time* v189 no13 p30 Ap 10 2017

Public utilities—United States
JUMP START E. HUMES *Sierra* v102 no5 p38 St/O 2017
No One Actually Knows How to Regulate the Internet J. Fox *Harvard Business Review Digital Articles* p2 N 18 2014

Public welfare
See also
Community organization
Conditional cash transfer programs
International relief
Israeli Settlements Are Illegal. Equipping Their Guards Is Tax-Deductible A. KANE *In These Times* v41 no3 p28 Mr 2017
Welfare Pasts and Futures S. King *History Today* v67 no3 p6 Mr 2017

Public welfare—United States
Deadbeat Democrats B. COVERT color *New Republic* v248 no10 p14 O 2017

Public works
See also
Infrastructure (Economics)
Too Many Infrastructure Projects Go It Alone R. M. Kanter *Harvard Business Review Digital Articles* p2 My 14 2015

Public works—Finance
The Future of Cities Depends on Innovative Financing J. D. Macomber *Harvard Business Review Digital Articles* p2 Ja 11 2016
How to Get It Right M. D. Rocca, T. Duvall et al color *Time* v189 no13 p45 Ap 10 2017
Raising Private Money For Public Projects B. Eckhouse, A. Albright et al *Bloomberg Businessweek* no4513 p46 Mr 6 2017
The U.S. Is Getting a Really Bad Deal on Infrastructure S. Smith color diag *Fortune* v175 no2 p16 F 1 2017

Public works—New York (State)
Global Ambition A. Rogers *Smithsonian* v48 no3 p11 Je 2017

Publication bias

Metaresearch for Evaluating Reproducibility in Ecology and Evolution F. FIDLER, YUNG EN CHEE et al *BioScience* v67 no3 p282 Mr 2017

Public debts—United States—Charts, diagrams, etc.

Since Obama Took Office, Debt Has Nearly Doubled V. DE RUGY graph *Reason* v48 no9 p15 F 2017

Public finance—Charts, diagrams, etc.

FEDERAL FINANCE *Economic Indicators* p32 Ja 2017

FEDERAL FINANCE *Economic Indicators* p32 Je 2017

FEDERAL FINANCE *Economic Indicators* p32 My 2017

Public finance—United States—Charts, diagrams, etc.

FEDERAL FINANCE *Economic Indicators* p32 N 2016

Public health—Charts, diagrams, etc.

A Statistical Snapshot of the World *Current History* v116 no786 p40 Ja 2017

Publicis Groupe SA

A Successful M&A Considers the Human Element R. Ashkenas *Harvard Business Review Digital Articles* p2 N 18 2014

Publicity

    See also

    Journalism

    Press

    Press conferences

    Press releases

Healthcare Debate Has Room for Critics From the Right Only M. Corcoran *Extra!* v30 no4 p3 My 2017

Public opinion polls—Charts, diagrams, etc.

MATCHUP color *Vanity Fair* v58 no11 p58 N 2016

Public opinion—United States—Charts, diagrams, etc.

Is America great? M. Schubert, V. Gaglione et al graph *America* v216 no5 p6 Mr 6 2017

Public spending—Charts, diagrams, etc.

FEDERAL FINANCE *Economic Indicators* p32 N 2016

TOTAL OUTPUT, INCOME, AND SPENDING *Economic Indicators* p1 Ja 2017

TOTAL OUTPUT, INCOME, AND SPENDING *Economic Indicators* p1 S 2016

Public Theater (New York, N.Y.)

Anticipation Index *New York* v50 no10 p92 My 15 2017

Public transit—Charts, diagrams, etc.

BEHIND THE NUMBERS M. Maciag *Governing* v30 no5 p59 F 2017

Public welfare—Societies, etc.

The New Blue S. JONES *New Republic* v248 no10 p27 O 2017

RUNNING ON HOPE [Cover story] B. AUSTEN color *New Republic* v248 no10 p18 O 2017

Publishers & publishing

    See also

    Art publishing

    Periodical publishing

    Preprints

    Publishing rights auctions

    Scholarly publishing

    Science publishing

    Serial publication of books

    Trade publications

    University presses

Ad Blocking's Unintended Consequences F. Bhat *Harvard Business Review Digital Articles* p2 Ag 12 2015

ALWAYS IN SEASON D. DILWORTH color *Publishers Weekly* v264 no16 p24 Ap 17 2017

Anhui Children's Publishing House color *Publishers Weekly* v264 no12 p10 Mr 20 2017

Around the Booths bw *Publishers Weekly* v264 no20 p(Sp)55 My 15 2017

At 25, the New Press Thrives In Politically Charged Climate C. Reid color *Publishers Weekly* v264 no12 p6 Mr 20 2017

B.C. Presses Broaden Their Reach and Band Together A. GROSS color *Publishers Weekly* v263 no47 p44 N 21 2016

Bhaskar Sunkara M. Hagan *Current Biography* v77 no11 p86 N 2016

Big Books for Big Country E. NAWOTKA *Publishers Weekly* v263 no39 p20 S 26 2016

Bookstagrammers Gain Influence in a Diffuse Marketplace J. Boog bw chart color *Publishers Weekly* v264 no38 p6 S 18 2017

Brooklyn Arts Press, Indie Publishing's NBA Champion J. Maher

color *Publishers Weekly* v263 no51 p3 D 12 2016

A Case for Multimedia Storytelling M. GREER *Publishers Weekly* v264 no26 p184 Je 26 2017

Challenges for Publishers in Uncertain Times R. Beardsley *Publishers Weekly* v263 no40 p12 O 3 2016

China Children's Press & Publication Group color *Publishers Weekly* v264 no12 p16 Mr 20 2017

Chris Jackson M. Rich *Current Biography* v77 no10 p63 O 2016

Chronicle Books at 50 J. Boog color *Publishers Weekly* v264 no24 p7 Je 12 2017

Deals D. LEFFERTS color *Publishers Weekly* v264 no1 p6 Ja 2 2017

Deals D. LEFFERTS color *Publishers Weekly* v264 no6 p8 F 6 2017

Deals R. DEAHL color *Publishers Weekly* v264 no29 p6 Jl 17 2017

Diversification Drives Gains at Abrams J. Milliot color *Publishers Weekly* v264 no35 p8 Ag 28 2017

Exploring New E-commerce Opportunities K. RAUGUST color *Publishers Weekly* v264 no29 p25 Jl 17 2017

Fall Changes L. Ahuile *Publishers Weekly* v263 no40 p19 O 3 2016

Fast, Cheap, and Good J. FRIEDMAN *Publishers Weekly* v264 no21 p50 My 22 2017

Fast-Growing Independent Publishers, 2017 J. MILLIOT and C. KIRCH chart color *Publishers Weekly* v264 no15 p36 Ap 10 2017

THE FERNDALE ENTERPRISE S. Hepworth bw *Columbia Journalism Review* v56 no1 p111 Spr 2017

Flat Sales Identified as Top Industry Problem J. Milliot graph *Publishers Weekly* v264 no40 p5 O 2 2017

Gearing Up for the Shifts and Twists in the Digital Content Industry T. TAN color *Publishers Weekly* v264 no27 p(Sp)4 Jl 3 2017

Harper Lee and Dr. Seuss Won't Save Publishing D. Clark *Harvard Business Review Digital Articles* p2 Jl 24 2015

Highlights of the Fair bw color *Publishers Weekly* v263 no44 p(Sp)3 O 31 2016

A HOT SPOT FOR COMICS AND GAMING cartoon color *Publishers Weekly* v263 no47 p38 N 21 2016

Hot Topics in Chinese Academic Publishing T. TAN *Publishers Weekly* v264 no39 p(Sp)26 S 25 2017

The Independent Spirit Flourishes in the Pacific Northwest A. GROSS color *Publishers Weekly* v263 no47 p32 N 21 2016

Indie House Rides the Pulitzer Wave J. Maher color *Publishers Weekly* v264 no22 p7 My 29 2017

Indie Spirits E. NAWOTKA *Publishers Weekly* v263 no39 p16 S 26 2016

Industry Stocks Were Mixed in 2016 J. Milliot chart *Publishers Weekly* v264 no2 p11 Ja 9 2017

IN SEARCH OF AMERICA L. Collins cartoon *New Yorker* v93 no32 p22 O 16 2017

An International Press Looks to 2017 J. Maher color *Publishers Weekly* v263 no50 p15 D 5 2016

An island moneymaker that knows everybody's secrets B. Wieners *Columbia Journalism Review* v56 no1 p80 Spr 2017

It Takes a Pillage A. SHEPHARD color *New Republic* v248 no8/9 p12 Ag/S 2017

Kay's Kind of Summer M. BLAIS color *Vanity Fair* v59 no7 p110 Summ 2017

KNOW IT ALL K. SCHULZ cartoon color *New Yorker* v93 no32 p76 O 16 2017

Leaving the Flatiron M. FLAMINI and E. BEIER bw *Publishers Weekly* v264 no35 p132 Ag 28 2017

Leftist Indies Put Politics First J. Maher color *Publishers Weekly* v264 no26 p3 Je 26 2017

Making Book: How Booksellers Are Becoming Publishers J. Rosen chart color *Publishers Weekly* v263 no47 p6 N 21 2016

MAP OF THE ARAB LITERARY WORLD map *Publishers Weekly* v263 no43 p(Sp)20 O 24 2016

Memorandum R. LONG il *National Review* v69 no5 p38 Mr 20 2017

Moppet Books Moves Forward With KinderGuides Line J. Boog color *Publishers Weekly* v264 no33 p8 Ag 14 2017

A More Inclusive Way to Publish F. NG *Los Angeles Magazine* v62 no6 p14 Je 2017

A New Literary Imprint L. Sacilotto *Publishers Weekly* v264 no3

p14 Ja 16 2017

New Publishers Give Readers More Choices L. Ahuile *Publishers Weekly* v264 no6 p18 F 6 2017

OUR STORIES TRAVEL THE WORLD T. SAID color *Publishers Weekly* v263 no43 p(Sp)9 O 24 2016

Outsourcing and the Role of Strategic Alliances R. Beardsley *Publishers Weekly* v263 no51 p6 D 12 2016

Poisoned Pen Press Celebrates 20 Years E. Nawotka color *Publishers Weekly* v264 no23 p7 Je 5 2017

The Potential of Virtual Communities in the Publishing Ecosystem R. Beardsley *Publishers Weekly* v264 no3 p12 Ja 16 2017

Predatory Journals: Write, Submit, and Publish the Next Day R. HAKAMI *Skeptical Inquirer* v41 no5 p32 S/O 2017

Print is dead. Long live print M. Rosenwald cartoon *Columbia Journalism Review* p34 Fall/Wint 2016

Print Sales Stay Hot J. Segura chart *Publishers Weekly* v264 no2 p4 Ja 9 2017

The Progressive N. Stockwell color *Progressive* v81 no4 p2 Ap/My 2017

Publishers See More Good Times Ahead for Audiobooks S. Maughan color *Publishers Weekly* v264 no3 p6 Ja 16 2017

Publishers See Third-Quarter Bounce J. Milliot chart *Publishers Weekly* v263 no46 p4 N 14 2014

Reflections on Metadata R. Beardsley *Publishers Weekly* v263 no41 p8 O 10 2016

Retooling the HONG KONG & CHINA Print Business T. TAN color *Publishers Weekly* v264 no35 p78 Ag 28 2017

The Rising Stars of the Industry L. Hartman bw color *Publishers Weekly* v264 no36 p(Sp)3 S 4 2017

Ross Richie J. Crelin color *Current Biography* v77 no11 p68 N 2016

Sales Reps: Even More Important in the Digital Age E. Nawotka color *Publishers Weekly* v264 no6 p9 F 6 2017

SHARJAH PUBLISHING CITY N. Clee color *Publishers Weekly* v263 no43 p(Sp)4 O 24 2016

Social Sciences Academic Press color *Publishers Weekly* v264 no39 p(Sp)20 S 25 2017

SPRING 2017 ADULT ANNOUNCEMENTS L. ERMELINO color *Publishers Weekly* v263 no51 p18 D 12 2016

SPRING 2017 AUDIO ANNOUNCEMENTS S. Maughan color *Publishers Weekly* v264 no6 p20 F 6 2017

Trade Publishers Focused on Strategic Deals In 2016 J. Milliot chart *Publishers Weekly* v264 no1 p7 Ja 2 2017

Tronc vs. the Right Way for Publishers to Compete in the Digital Age G. Satell *Harvard Business Review Digital Articles* p2 Je 30 2016

U.A.E.'s Kalimat Celebrates 10th Anniversary E. Nawotka color *Publishers Weekly* v264 no29 p4 Jl 17 2017

A Watermarking Update L. Dawson *Publishers Weekly* v264 no30 p20 Jl 24 2017

Weekend Closeup November 19–20 L. Hartman cartoon *Publishers Weekly* v263 no44 p(Sp)4 O 31 2016

What It Means To Live Christian A. Byle color *Publishers Weekly* v263 no43 p20 O 24 2016

What's Ahead for Bookselling in 2017 J. Rosen color *Publishers Weekly* v264 no1 p3 Ja 2 2017

Where have all the black digital publishers gone? G. H. Burkins color *Columbia Journalism Review* v56 no1 p23 Spr 2017

The World Needs More Canada E. NAWOTKA *Publishers Weekly* v263 no39 p3 S 26 2016

Publishers & publishing—Algeria

Algeria's New Imprint A. KAPLAN bw color *Nation* v304 no11 p20 Ap 3 2017

Publishers & publishing—China

Hunan Juvenile & Children's Publishing House color *Publishers Weekly* v264 no12 p18 Mr 20 2017

Juvenile & Children's Publishing House color *Publishers Weekly* v264 no12 p22 Mr 20 2017

New Titles from Chinese Academic Presses T. TAN *Publishers Weekly* v264 no39 p(Sp)28 S 25 2017

Trends in the Rights Market color *Publishers Weekly* v264 no12 p28 Mr 20 2017

Xinjiang Juvenile Publishing House color *Publishers Weekly* v264 no12 p24 Mr 20 2017

Publishers & publishing—Congresses

All Ears on APAC S. MAUGHAN color *Publishers Weekly* v264

no20 p(Sp)22 My 15 2017

Examining the Mexican-American Book Connection L. Ahuile color *Publishers Weekly* v264 no32 p16 Ag 7 2017

Finding the Right Balance J. Milliot color *Publishers Weekly* v264 no24 p5 Je 12 2017

PUB TECH CONNECT chart color *Publishers Weekly* v264 no15 p(Sp)3 Ap 10 2017

Small Stories, Big Picture A. R. Albanese color *Publishers Weekly* v263 no47 p19 N 21 2016

Storytelling, Innovation, and Digital Disruption C. Reid color *Publishers Weekly* v264 no17 p4 Ap 24 2017

Thursday, Friday BookExpo Author Highlights L. HARTMAN color *Publishers Weekly* v264 no20 p(Sp)24 My 15 2017

Publishers & publishing—Economic aspects

The Answer is... Scholastic J. Milliot *Publishers Weekly* v264 no9 p4 F 27 2017

The Year in Children's Bestsellers J. MILLIOT chart color *Publishers Weekly* v264 no6 p34 F 6 2017

Publishers & publishing—Finance

Penguin Random House Rules The Children's Book Market J. Milliot chart *Publishers Weekly* v263 no45 p4 N 7 2016

Publishers & publishing—Great Britain

Britain's Hottest Digital Publisher J. Maher *Publishers Weekly* v263 no39 p8 S 26 2016

News Briefs *Publishers Weekly* v264 no18 p6 My 1 2017

Publishers & publishing—History

HarperCollins Marks Its 200th Anniversary J. Milliot bw color *Publishers Weekly* v264 no10 p9 Mr 6 2017

Publishers & publishing—History—20th century

PEOPLE OF THE BOOK L. MENAND cartoon color *New Yorker* v92 no41 p78 D 12 2016

Publishers & publishing—History—21st century

THE KINDLE EFFECT J. Alsever chart color *Fortune* v75 no1 p32 Ja 1 2017

The Next Steps in Digitization L. Dawson *Publishers Weekly* v264 no4 p20 Ja 23 2017

Self-Publishing in 2017 A. DANIEL color *Publishers Weekly* v264 no4 p40 Ja 23 2017

Spread Your Wings and Fly, Penguin S. Nicola, R. Penty et al color graph *Bloomberg Businessweek* no4509 p17 Ja 30 2017

Publishers & publishing—Italy

When in Milan L. Ermelino color *Publishers Weekly* v264 no28 p20 Jl 10 2017

Publishers & publishing—Marketing

Speeding to Market K. Raugust color *Publishers Weekly* v263 no43 p18 O 24 2016

Publishers & publishing—Mergers

The Evolution Of RBmedia S. Maughan *Publishers Weekly* v264 no22 p11 My 29 2017

A Time to Embrace: Uncertainties and Inconsistencies T. TAN *Publishers Weekly* v264 no27 p(Sp)3 Jl 3 2017

Publishers & publishing—Moral & ethical aspects

The Slippery Slope of Free Speech R. SHUR *Publishers Weekly* v264 no3 p64 Ja 16 2017

Publishers & publishing—New York (State)

The Goddard Riverside Book Fair, 30 Years In J. Maher *Publishers Weekly* v263 no42 p10 O 17 2016

Publishers & publishing—News briefs

Deals D. LEFFERTS bw color *Publishers Weekly* v264 no3 p10 Ja 16 2017

Deals R. DEAHL color *Publishers Weekly* v264 no18 p10 My 1 2017

Deals R. DEAHL color *Publishers Weekly* v264 no33 p10 Ag 14 2017

Deals R. DEAHL *Publishers Weekly* v263 no39 p12 S 26 2016

News Briefs *Publishers Weekly* v264 no18 p6 My 1 2017

News Briefs *Publishers Weekly* v264 no36 p12 S 4 2017

NEWS ROUNDUP bw *Publishers Weekly* v264 no18 p18 My 1 2017

Readers Respond color *Publishers Weekly* v264 no8 p3 F 20 2017

Publishers & publishing—Officials & employees

Mel Shapiro Calls It a Career J. Milliot color *Publishers Weekly* v263 no43 p12 O 24 2016

Publishers & publishing—Political activity

Is Publishing's Liberal Bias a Liability? R. Deahl color *Publishers Weekly* v264 no15 p8 Ap 10 2017

Publishers & publishing—Singapore
Educational and STM Publishing in SINGAPORE T. TAN *Publishers Weekly* v263 no41 p31 O 10 2016

Publishers & publishing—Study & teaching
STRIKING THE RIGHT BALANCE L. HARTMAN bw color *Publishers Weekly* v263 no50 p26 D 5 2016

Publishers & publishing—Technological innovations
Storytelling, Innovation, and Digital Disruption C. Reid color *Publishers Weekly* v264 no17 p4 Ap 24 2017

Publishers & publishing—United States
Despite Embargo, U.S., Cuba Publishers Invoke Solidarity, Cultural Exchange C. Reid color *Publishers Weekly* v264 no8 p5 F 20 2017

Keep It Short, and Sweet C. SMYTHE color *Publishers Weekly* v264 no15 p76 Ap 10 2017

PRINTS & EDITIONS color *Art in America* v105 no1 p42 Ja 2017

Standing Up to President Trump J. Milliot *Publishers Weekly* v264 no5 p7 Ja 30 2017

Publishers & publishing—United States—History
Wayne State Benefits From Move into Trade C. Kirch color *Publishers Weekly* v263 no48 p10 N 28 2016

Publishers & publishing—United States—News briefs
News Briefs *Publishers Weekly* v264 no3 p7 Ja 16 2017

Publishers & publishing—Charts, diagrams, etc.
PEARSON RISES ABOVE J. MILLIOT chart *Publishers Weekly* v264 no35 p56 Ag 28 2017

THE WEEKLY SCORECARD Tracking Unit Print Sales (in thousands) chart *Publishers Weekly* v263 no44 p6 O 31 2016

Publishers & publishing—Finance—Charts, diagrams, etc.
THE WEEKLY SCORECARD chart *Publishers Weekly* v264 no9 p5 F 27 2017

Publishing & economics
At Quirk Books, Quirk's the Name and the Game J. Maher color *Publishers Weekly* v264 no17 p7 Ap 24 2017

Publishers Did Marginally Better in 2016 J. Milliot chart *Publishers Weekly* v264 no14 p4 Ap 3. 2017

Publishing & ethics
Brave New World M. Fermaglich color *Publishers Weekly* v264 no30 p64 Jl 24 2017

Publishing industry personnel
HEAD OF THE HOUSE A. GROSS bw color *Publishers Weekly* v264 no18 p22 My 1 2017

Publishing rights auctions
Deals R. DEAHL color *Publishers Weekly* v264 no20 p8 My 15 2017

Deals R. DEAHL color *Publishers Weekly* v264 no39 p8 S 25 2017

Puccetti, Simonetta
An accreting pulsar with extreme properties drives an ultraluminous x-ray source in NGC 5907 bibl chart graph *Science* v355 no6327 p817 F 24 2017

Pucci, Emilio, 1914-1992
Paradise FOUND color *Vogue* v206 no11 p130 N 2016

Puccinelli, Nancy M.
When Upbeat Commercials Backfire *Harvard Business Review Digital Articles* p2 O 23 2015

Puccini, Giacomo, 1858-1924
La Bohème *Opera News* v81 no7 p55 Ja 2017
Operapedia: Turandot *Opera News* v81 no9 p12 Mr 2017

Puchalski, Leigh
References Should Come from a Candidate's Coworkers, Not Just Their Boss *Harvard Business Review Digital Articles* p2 2017

Puck, Gelila Assefa
GELILA'S PICKS color *Harper's Bazaar* no3652 p174 Ap 2017

Puck, Wolfgang
A Cut Above M. MCGRATH color *Forbes* v199 no2 p104 F 28 2017

WOLFGANG GOES ROGUE S. Marikar color *Bloomberg Businessweek* no4520 p71 My 1 2017

Puckett, Andy
Is Your Firm Underperforming? Your CEO Might Be Golfing Too Much *Harvard Business Review Digital Articles* p2 N 30 2016

Puckett, Larry
ABCs of DCC power district management [Cover story] color diag *Model Railroader* v84 no10 p50 O 2017

Adding sound to a vintage Kato locomotive [Cover story] color *Model Railroader* v84 no10 p56 O 2017

Commons, grounds, and DCC color diag *Model Railroader* v84 no9 p56 S 2017

Digitrax DCS240 advanced command station provides more power and upgrades diag *Model Railroader* v83 no12 p70 D 2016

Digitrax Evolution advanced DCC starter set color *Model Railroader* v84 no5 p62 My 2017

Dual engines with a WOWSound decoder [Cover story] color *Model Railroader* v84 no7 p58 Jl 2017

Getting the most from automatic functions color *Model Railroader* v84 no5 p58 My 2017

Going Full Throttle with a LokSound decoder color *Model Railroader* v84 no4 p90 Ap 2017

Keeping short circuits at bay with DCC color *Model Railroader* v84 no6 p60 Je 2017

Making the DCC suitcase connection color diag *Model Railroader* v83 no12 p62 D 2016

New sound for an old brass steamer color *Model Railroader* v84 no1 p66 Ja 2017

Operating with Digital Command Control color *Model Railroader* v84 no2 p66 F 2017

Seven tips for better solder connections color diag *Model Railroader* v84 no8 p56 Ag 2017

Turnout control with accessory decoders color *Model Railroader* v84 no11 p60 N 2017

PUCKETT, SUSAN
ART OF THE TART color *Better Homes & Gardens* v95 no3 p124 Mr 2017

CARROTS *Atlanta* v56 no12 p62 Ap 2017

GRITS *Atlanta* v56 no7 p64 N 2016

GUACAMOLE *Atlanta* v56 no9 p58 Ja 2017

HOLIDAY COOKIES *Atlanta* v56 no8 p78 D 2016

IRON CLAD color *Better Homes & Gardens* v95 no2 p106 F 2016

MARINARA *Atlanta* v56 no10 p60 F 2017

RADISHES *Atlanta* v56 no11 p62 Mr 2017

Pucurull, Miquel
BARCELONA SPAIN color *Runner's World* v52 no8 p85 S 2017

Puddicombe, Andy
Andrew Puddicombe color *Men's Health* v32 no1 p122 Ja/F 2017

Puddings
The proof is in the Pudding P. Hise *Virginia Living* v15 no3 p54 Ap 2017

r.s.v.p L. WAHLER, H. SCHNEIDER et al bw *Bon Appetit* no11 p12 N 2017

A TASTE OF THE PAST R. Cole color *Old House Journal* v45 no6 p30 S 2017

WHAT TO PACK FOR THE ZOMBIE APOCALYPSE M. WELLS *Atlanta* v56 no10 p38 F 2017

Puddings—Evaluation
SWEETS ALL DAY *Atlanta* v56 no12 p82 Ap 2017

Pudlo, Nicholas A.
Neonatal acquisition of Clostridia species protects against colonization by bacterial pathogens diag *Science* v356 no6335 p315 Ap 21 2017

Pueblo Revolt, 1680
The First American Revolution E. A. POWELL color *Archaeology* v70 no2 p42 Mr/Ap 2017

PUENTE-MARTINEZ, RAUL
The Role of Botanical Gardens in the Conservation of Cactaceae *BioScience* v66 no12 p1057 D 1 2016

Puerto Ricans—United States
American Voices J.J. Barea S. Apstein and T. Keith color *Sports Illustrated* v126 no10 p34 Ap 10 2017

Puerto Rico—Description & travel
BRINGING ANNIE HOME E. HULL color map *Sail* v48 no4 p40 Ap 2017

Puerto Rico—Economic conditions
Can Puerto Rico Corral Its Tax Dodgers? P. Laya, J. Levin et al color graph *Bloomberg Businessweek* no4524 p17 My 29 2017

Puerto Rico—Relations—United States
Cries In the Dark M. Kaske and J. Levin color graph *Bloomberg Businessweek* no4540 p16 O 2 2017

Puerto Escondido (Oaxaca, Mexico)
puerto escondido, mexico H. MARTIN color *Architectural Digest*

no5 p86 My 2017

Puerto Rico—Politics & government—1998-

DISASTERS WILL HAPPEN A. D. Sorkin cartoon *New Yorker* v93 no32 p21 O 16 2017

Pueyo, Laurent

Relativistic deflection of background starlight measures the mass of a nearby white dwarf star chart color graph *Science* v356 no6342 p1046 Je 9 2017

Puffers (Fish)

DISH OF THE MONTH A. LIMPERT color *Washingtonian Magazine* v52 no7 p144 Ap 2017

Puget Sound (Wash.)

The Stunning Beauty of a Pacific Northwest Sea M. GRANT color *AARP: The Magazine* v60 no2A p44 F/Mr 2017

Pugh, Allison J.

What Happens at Home When People Can't Depend on Stable Work *Harvard Business Review Digital Articles* p2 Ap 4 2017

Pugh, Catrin

CATRIN'S LONG WAY BACK R. KINER *Reader's Digest* v189 no1128 p112 Mr 2017

Pugh, Florence

Hey, Lady! M. GUIDUCCI color *Vogue* v207 no7 p58 Jl 2017

Pugh, Jeremy

POWDER PLAY chart color diag *Sunset* v238 no1 p22 Ja 2017

Pugh, Mallory, 1998-

The Ten Who'll Be Next D. GORDON, S. SCHUBE et al color *GQ: Gentlemen's Quarterly* v97 no11 p114 N 2017

Pugh, Ron

Railway Post Office color *Model Railroader* v84 no8 p16 Ag 2017

PUGH, WENDY

THE WORLD'S BILLIONAIRES bw color diag graph map *Forbes* v199 no3 p84 Mr 28 2017

Puglierin, Jana

Nuclear disarmament summits: A proposal to break the international impasse bibl *Bulletin of the Atomic Scientists* v73 no4 p264 Jl 2017

Pugliese, Joe

ALL THE RIGHT MOVES *Los Angeles Magazine* p168 Mr 2017

EYES ON THE PRIZE *Los Angeles Magazine* p140 My 2017

GRIME AND PUNISHMENT *Los Angeles Magazine* p172 Ja 2017

THE TIME KEEPERS color *Los Angeles Magazine* v62 no7 p128 Jl 2017

Pugmire, John—Interviews

Bishop's Murder Case L. PICKER color *Publishers Weekly* v264 no2 p42 Ja 9 2017

Pui Lam

John Michael Julius Madey *Physics Today* v70 no1 p70 Ja 2017

Puigdemont, Carles

A Secessionist Abroad B. Soloway color *Foreign Policy* no224 p30 My/Je 2017

Pujalt Martinez, David

A Handler's Life—David Pujalt Martinez F. Aragno *Arabian Horse World* v56 no12 p226 S 2016

Pujols, Albert, 1980-

1 THE NEW TESTAMENT B. Reiter, S. Apstein et al color *Sports Illustrated* v126 no9 p40 Mr 27 2017

Pulaski (Tenn.)

Return to Milky Way Farm H. Ellis-Ashburn color *Equus* no481 p71 O 2017

Pulaski, Kazimierz, 1747-1779

THE TWO HORSEMEN OF THE REVOLUTION E. S. Rafuse bw color *MHQ: Quarterly Journal of Military History* v30 no1 p40 Aut 2017

Pulaski, Tessa

How the church can prevent climate displacement *America* v216 no6 p10 Mr 20 2017

Pulendran, Bali

mTOR regulates metabolic adaptation of APCs in the lung and controls the outcome of allergic inflammation graph *Science* v357 no6355 p1014 S 8 2017

Puleo, Stephen—Interviews

American Treasures K. Donohue *Prologue* v48 no3 p32 Fall 2016

Pulia, Shalayne

DOING GOOD color *InStyle* v24 no10 p76 O 2017

DOING GOOD color map *InStyle* v24 no8 p68 Ag 2017

Hailey Gates color *InStyle* v24 no2 p68 F 2017

Nura Afia color *InStyle* v24 no3 p174 Mr 2017

RACHEL BROSNAHAN color *InStyle* v23 no13 p128 D 2016

Sasheer Zamata color *InStyle* v24 no7 p54 Jl 2017

ZAZIE BEETZ color *InStyle* v24 no1 p44 Ja 2017

Pulido, Alfonso

3 Ways Social Entrepreneurs Can Solve Their Talent Problem *Harvard Business Review Digital Articles* p2 Je 29 2016

Pulisic, Christian

The Case for ... Christian in The Middle G. Wahl and T. Keith color *Sports Illustrated* v126 no9 p28 Mr 27 2017

The Next Great Hope G. Wahl color *Sports Illustrated* v125 no17 p92 N 21 2016 Double Issue

Pulit, Sara L.

Negative selection in humans and fruit flies involves synergistic epistasis chart graph *Science* v356 no6337 p539 My 5 2017

Pulla, Priyanka

Disease sleuths unmask deadly encephalitis culprit color *Science* v357 no6349 p344 Jl 28 2017

In India, elite institutes in shady journals *Science* v354 no6319 p1511 D 23 2016

Pullen, M. G.

Ultrafast electron diffraction imaging of bond breaking in di-ionized acetylene bibl graph *Science* v354 no6310 p308 O 21 2016

PULLEY, MICHAEL

Understanding the Victors *American Scholar* v86 no2 p3 Spr 2017

Pulley, Natasha

Adventures in Quinine: A magic realist mission in the forests of the Andes S. WHEELER *New York Times Book Review* p18 S 17 2017

Pulleys

Sliding chains keep particles together J. Ryu and S. Park diag *Science* v357 no6348 p250 Jl 21 2017

Pulliam, Becca

WILLIAM PATERSON UNIVERSITY: 'WORKING TO MAKE PLAYERS' bw color *Downbeat* v84 no10 p112 O 2017

Pullin, Jorge

METEORITE ORIGINS color *Astronomy* v45 no11 p44 N 2017

Pullman, Philip, 1946-

All at Sea: In Philip Pullman's first graphic novel, a ghostly schooner and its motley crew become unstuck in time *New York Times Book Review* p15 Je 18 2017

The Year in Reading [Cover story] *New York Times Book Review* p8 D 25 2016

Pullman, Philip, 1946-—Interviews

A NEW DARK MATERIALS TRILOGY BEGINS N. Serrao color *Entertainment Weekly* no1473 p61 Jl 7 2017

Pullovers (Sweaters)

Color Coordinated: At Paul Taylor Dance Company, its all about functional layers in colors that really pop M. DESANTIS *Dance Magazine* v91 no10 p33 O 2017

Pullovers (Sweaters)—Evaluation

Cashmere L. Indvik color *InStyle* v23 no12 p217 N 2016

The GIFT GUIDE 2016 img *New York* v49 no24 p79 N 28 2016

Outfits for Days color *Glamour* v115 no11 p60 N 2017

Stacked Lineup W. M. ROCHFORT JR. and H. ROCHFORT color *Backpacker* p41 Je 2017

Pulmonary embolism—Prevention

Pulmonary embolism: Common, life-threatening condition [Cover story] *Mayo Clinic Health Letter* v35 no11 p1 N 2017

Pulmonary hypertension—Diagnosis

Pulmonary hypertension *Mayo Clinic Health Letter* v34 no11 p4 N 2016

Pulsars

Amateur astronomer sheds light on pulsar companion's odd behavior color *Astronomy* v45 no4 p18 Ap 2017

THE BRIGHTEST, MOST DISTANT PULSAR A. Klesman color *Astronomy* v45 no6 p12 Je 2017

Pulsars at 50 still going strong [Cover story] C. R. James bw color diag graph *Astronomy* v45 no5 p22 My 2017

Pulsar timing arrays are poised to reveal gravitational waves: Radio observatories are accumulating data to detect mergers of supermassive black holes T. Feder *Physics Today* v70 no7 p26 Jl 2017

Two Pulsars Blowing in the Wind T. DIAMOND *Sky & Telescope* v133 no6 p9 Je 2017

Pulsed lasers—Evaluation

Focus on lasers, imaging, and microscopy A. Mandelis *Physics Today* v69 no11 p64 N 2016

Pumas

    See also

    Florida panther

Around the Campfire D. H. Sempter, K. B. Allen et al color *Trail Rider* v29 no1 p6 Ja/F 2017

Bigfoot on Four Paws A. TESAR cartoon *Walrus* v14 no2 p22 Mr 2017

Learning to live with mountain lions color *National Wildlife (World Edition)* v55 no3 p46 Ap/My 2017

Lion in Wait J. VAN THULL *Sierra* v101 no4 p18 Jl/Ag 2016

Scaredy-Cats J. G. Goldman color *Scientific American* v317 no4 p18 O 2017

VALLEY CATS D. GOODYEAR cartoon color *New Yorker* v92 no49 p44 F 13 2017

You Never Forget Your First Time M. Hittle, C. Lyons et al ding il *Backpacker* v45 no2 p64 Mr 2017

Pumping machinery

    See also

    Fuel pumps

    Solar pumps

ask the experts *Boating World* v38 no3 p24 Mr 2017

SILCA PISTA FLOOR PUMP M. Yozell color *Bicycling* v58 no9 p80 O 2017

Pumping machinery maintenance & repair

Directionally Challenged G. MICHAL *Boating World* v38 no6 p45 Je 2017

Pumpkin

Ask Martha *Martha Stewart Living* no268 p76 O 2016

BEAUTIFUL CREATURES J. TUNG *Martha Stewart Living* no268 p33 O 2016

IT'S GOURD SEASON E. Graves *Martha Stewart Living* no268 p8 O 2016

It's the Great Pumpkin M. Margaret Chappell color *Vegetarian Times* v43 no2 p66 N/D 2016

no-carve fun *Parents* v91 no10 p67 O 2016

Pumpkin Power! B. Lipton color *Health* v31 no8 p117 O 2017

Pumpkin growing

A Brief History of Improbably Large Produce K. Frischkorn *Smithsonian* v48 no6 p13 O 2017

In Gourd We Trust: How our most symbolic squash grew to bizarre proportions and took over the world A. Tucker *Smithsonian* v48 no6 p11 O 2017

The Origins of Pumpkin-Spice Mania O. B. Waxman *Time* v190 no13 p23 O 2 2017

Pumpkin in art

A Little Night Magic E. N. GAGE color *Martha Stewart Living* p104 O 2017

Pumpkin pies

Baker's Choice A. MASON color *Bon Appetit* v61 no11 p23 N 2016

CARAMEL PUMPKIN PIE *Washingtonian Magazine* v52 no2 p264 N 2016

Pumpkin—History

In Gourd We Trust: How our most symbolic squash grew to bizarre proportions and took over the world A. Tucker *Smithsonian* v48 no6 p11 O 2017

Pumpkinseed (Fish)

THE EVERYTHING GUIDE TO: Catching Your Lunch A. VADUKUL img *New York* v50 no13 p58 Je 26 2017

Punch-Drunk Love (Film)

PUNCH-DRUNK LOVE F. Kaplan color *Sound & Vision* v82 no3 p69 Ap 2017

Punches (Beverages)

Anniversary Punch K. O'SHEA-EVANS color *House Beautiful* v158 no9 p106 N 2016

Punches (Beverages)—Evaluation

COCKTAIL OF THE MONTH D. ALAN *Texas Monthly* v44 no11 p48 N 2016

Pund, Daniel

2016 MAZDA MX-5 MIATA CLUB color graph *Car & Driver* v63 no4 p84 O 2017

25 CARS WORTH WAITING FOR color *Car & Driver* v62 no10 p32 Ap 2017

Clowns to the Left of Me, Jokers to the Right chart color *Car & Driver* v63 no1 p104 Jl 2017

CONCEPT CARS color *Car & Driver* v62 no7 p24 Ja 2017

Cross Country Dresser color *Car & Driver* v63 no2 p92 Ag 2017

Daniel Pund color *Car & Driver* v63 no5 p30 N 2017

Fleet Files color diag *Car & Driver* v63 no1 p88 Jl 2017

Mint Jelly color diag map *Car & Driver* v62 no8 p30 F 2017

Suburban Safari color *Car & Driver* v62 no11 p98 My 2017

TWO FOR THE PRICE OF ONE color graph *Car & Driver* v62 no7 p106 Ja 2017

Punisher (Fictitious character)

NO. 44 PUNISHER A. Breznican color *Entertainment Weekly* no1436/1437 p76 O 21 2016

A Real Treasure color *Indianapolis Monthly* v42 no2 p72 O 2017

Punisher, The (TV program)

Marvel's The Punisher S. Li, A. Bacle et al color *Entertainment Weekly* no1482/1483 p106 S 22 2017

Punishment

    See also

    Capital punishment

    Discipline of children

    Future punishment

Punishment (Jewish law)

Revenge J. Rothkopf *New York Times Magazine* p26 Je 25 2017

Punk culture

WE WERE RIGHT / / WE WERE WRONG cartoon *In These Times* v40 no11 p23 N 2016

Punk rock music

    See also

    Hardcore music

Puns & punning

Your Pun-Divided Attention R. Jacobson color *Scientific American* v315 no6 p17 D 2016

Puns & punning—Competitions

Bad Puns Are How Eye Roll P. RUBIN color *Reader's Digest* v190 no1135 p108 N 2017

Laughter: THE BEST MEDICINE color *Reader's Digest* v190 no1133 p92 S 2017

Punta Cana (Dominican Republic)

DOMINICAN DREAM C. Malle color *Architectural Digest* no6 p124 Je 1 2017

Puntoni, Stefano

Consumers Don't Understand the Relationship Between Time and Speed *Harvard Business Review Digital Articles* p2 N 3 2015

Linear Thinking in a Nonlinear World bw chart diag graph img *Harvard Business Review* v95 no3 p130 My/Je 2017

Punzi, Simona

Transcriptional activation of RagD GTPase controls mTORC1 and promotes cancer growth diag *Science* v356 no6343 p1188 Je 16 2017

Pupil (Eye)

POP QUIZ: ANATOMY C. Barakat and M. Freckleton color *Equus* no473 p16 F 2017

Puppe, Birger

Lee Rubin: Our mentor and role model *Science* v355 no6327 p806 F 24 2017

Puppet making

String Beings M. W. SCHWARTZ *Missouri Life* v43 no7 p58 D 2016/Ja 2017

Puppies

THE HEART OF A TURKEY DOG G. BETHGE color *Outdoor Life* v224 no6 p52 Ag 2017

IN THE DOG HOUSE R. Bacher color *Good Housekeeping* v263 no5 p208 N 2016

A PUPPY FOR CHRISTMAS S. Evans color *Southern Living* v51 no12 p16 D 2016

Puranas. Bhagavatapurana

c . 900: India *Lapham's Quarterly* v10 no1 p91 Wint 2017

Purcell, Dominic—Interviews

Brothers in ARMS M. ROFFMAN *TV Guide* p30 Ap 17 2017

Purcell, Jim

Employers Need to Recognize That Our Wellness Starts at Work *Harvard Business Review Digital Articles* p2 N 15 2016

Meet the Wellness Programs That Save Companies Money *Harvard Business Review Digital Articles* p2 Ap 20 2016

Purcell Mountains

HIGH COUNTRY HUSTLE M. COTÉ bw color *Bike Magazine* v24 no3 p86 My 2017

You Are Not a Salt Lick M. TERRA-BERNS *Idaho Magazine* v16 no3 p6 D 2016

Purchase, Neal

A Parallel Universe M. SHAW bw color *Surfer* v58 no1 p32 Ap 2017

Purchasing

See also

Airplanes—Purchasing

Boat purchasing

Purchasing agents

Shopping

Has Google Finally Proven That Online Ads Cause Offline Purchases? N. Dawar *Harvard Business Review Digital Articles* p1 Je 1 2017

Shopper's Guide: Purchasing managers are pushing to have critical thinking lead the buying process K. Barrett and R. Greene *Governing* v30 no9 p58 Je 2017

THINGS TO CONSIDER WHEN BUYING SOMETHING NEW... *New York State Conservationist* v71 no4 p4 F 2017

The Tyranny of Tennis Rackets A. WHITING *Washingtonian Magazine* v52 no6 p54 Mr 2017

What Salespeople Need to Know About the New B2B Landscape F. V. Cespedes and T. Bova *Harvard Business Review Digital Articles* p2 Ag 5 2015

What You Can and Should Be Doing with Your Customer Journeys A. Richardson *Harvard Business Review Digital Articles* p2 Mr 25 2016

Purchasing agents

STEER CLEAR OF SCAMS *Sea Magazine* v109 no1 p61 Ja 2017

Purchasing power

About a Boycott *Commentary* v143 no3 p4 Mr 2017

Emerging Demographics Are the New Emerging Markets R. Dobbs, J. Remes et al *Harvard Business Review Digital Articles* p2 Jl 13 2016

MAD-AS-HELL MONEY MOVES A. G. SHILLING *Forbes* v198 no8 p64 D 20 2016

Purchases of Foods by Convenience Type Driven by Prices, Income, and Advertising A. Okrent *Amber Waves: The Economics of Food, Farming, Natural Resources, & Rural America* p33 N 2016

Purchasing power parity

WHO'S ON TOP? diag *Fortune* v175 no3 p11 Mr 1 2017

Purchasing—Methodology

To Persuade Others, Give Them Options S. Martin *Harvard Business Review Digital Articles* p2 D 2 2014

Purchasing—Moral & ethical aspects

Checkout charity [Cover story] S. Butler color *U.S. Catholic* v82 no7 p12 Jl 2017

PURDOM, GWENDOLYN

Widening the Whistleblower's Reach *American Scholar* v86 no1 p16 Wint 2017

Purdue University

Speed Read *Indianapolis Monthly* p16 F 2017

Purdue University—Sports

11 PURDUE BOILERMAKERS J. Fuchs chart color *Sports Illustrated* v125 no15 p70 N 7 2016

Purdum, Scott

'Stop and Drop' for Ultimate Control color *Horse & Rider* v55 no11 p36 N 2016

Purdy, G. Michael

Step up for quality research color *Science* v357 no6351 p531 Ag 11 2017

PURDY, JEDEDIAH

America's New Opposition color *New Republic* v248 no3 p26 Mr 2017

A BILLIONAIRES' REPUBLIC color *Nation* v305 no3 p27 Jl 31 2017

A RADICAL FOR ALL SEASONS il *Nation* v304 no18 p29 Je 19 2017

THE TWO POPULISMS color *Nation* v303 no18 p27 O 31 2016

Purdy, Mark

A Framework for Strategists Assessing Emerging Markets *Harvard Business Review Digital Articles* p2 Jl 2 2015

Purdy, T. P.

Quantum correlations from a room-temperature optomechanical cavity color diag graph *Science* v356 no6344 p1265 Je 23 2017

Pure Comedy (Music)

The Beautiful, Bizarre Mind of Father John Misty E. R. Brown color *Entertainment Weekly* no1462 p62 Ap 21 2017

The Gospel of Father John Misty W. HERMES cartoon *Rolling Stone* no1285 p51 Ap 20 2017

the LOONY TUNES of FATHER JOHN MISTY S. BALL color *GQ: Gentlemen's Quarterly* v97 no6 p136 Je 2017

The Playlist bw color *Rolling Stone* no1281/1282 p10 F 23 2017

Pure Fishing Inc.

ABU GARCIA REVO MGXTREME BAITCASTER color *Field & Stream* v121 no8 p93 F/Mr 2017

PENN PARALLEL PLIERS color *Field & Stream* v121 no8 p90 F/Mr 2017

Pure Land Buddhism

Techno Temple M. Scarles color *Tricycle: The Buddhist Review* v26 no4 p16 Summ 2017

PUREWAL, SARAH JACOBSSON

CASETIFY iPHONE 7 CASES AND COVERS color *Macworld - Digital Edition* v34 no4 p42 My 2017

MASTER THE SPACE-TIME CONTINUUM IN CAUSALITY, A UNIQUE PUZZLE GAME FOR iPHONE color *Macworld - Digital Edition* v34 no10 p51 O 2017

PLANTRONICS BACKBEAT PRO 2 color *Macworld - Digital Edition* p41 F 2017

Tested: 5 protective bumpers for the Apple Watch color *Macworld - Digital Edition* v34 no6 p54 Je 2017

WATERFIELD iPAD PRO SLEEVECASE *Macworld - Digital Edition* v34 no9 p37 S 2017

Purgatory (Music)

What to Stream N. Feeney color *Entertainment Weekly* no1477 p57 Ag 11 2017

Puri, Hardeep S.

Human Rights, Mass Atrocity Prevention and the United Nations Security Council: The Long Road Ahead *UN Chronicle* v53 no4 p1 2016

The Long Road Ahead *UN Chronicle* v54 no4 p28 2017

Puri, Prateek

Synthesis of mixed hypermetallic oxide BaOCa+ from laser-cooled reagents in an atom-ion hybrid trap diag graph *Science* v357 no6358 p1370 S 29 2017

Puri, Sandeep

Case Study: Which Customers Should This Restaurant Listen To? *Harvard Business Review Digital Articles* p2 Mr 29 2016

Purifoy, Noah

LOST AND FOUND L. R. Frazier and J. Lowe *New York Times Magazine* p53 O 30 2016

Puritans

Blue Laws? Blame the Puritans K. SHELDON and M. BREWER color *Yankee* v80 no6 p24 N/D 2016

Puritty, Chandler

Without inclusion, diversity initiatives may not be enough color *Science* v357 no6356 p1101 S 15 2017

Purkh Singh Khalsa, Karta

EASE ECZEMA WITH HERBS color *Amazing Wellness* v9 no3 p38 EarlySumm 2017

Purnama, Basuki Tjhaja, 1966-

1 IN 5 *Christianity Today* v61 no1 p20 Ja/F 2017

Extremists, 'X-Men,' and an Ex-Governor D. Pinault color *Commonweal* v144 no12 p12 Jl 7 2017

Indonesian Christian leader jailed under blasphemy law C. Kennel-Shank *Christian Century* v134 no12 p16 Je 7 2017

Jakarta's Christian governor P. Jenkins *Christian Century* v133 no26 p45 D 21 2016

Political Islam in Indonesia P. MARSHALL color *Weekly Standard* v22 no38 p22 Je 12 2017

Purnell, Beverly A.

GENES UNDER PRESSURE color *Science* v354 no6308 p52 O 7 2016

REPAIR AND REGENERATION [Cover story] color *Science* v356 no6342 p1020 Je 9 2017

Treecology color *Science* v354 no6317 p1227 D 9 2016

Purnell, Ella

ELLA'S A-POPPIN' D. BLASBERG color *Vanity Fair* v59 no5 p142 Ap 2017

Inactivation of porcine endogenous retrovirus in pigs using CRISPR-Cas9 diag *Science* v357 no6357 p1303 S 22 2017

Qing Hu

Protecting China's soil by law bibl *Science* v354 no6312 p562 N 4 2016

Qing Li

RPA binds histone H3-H4 and functions in DNA replication–coupled nucleosome assembly bibl graph *Science* v355 no6323 p415 Ja 27 2017

Qing Liu

Photoactivation and inactivation of Arabidopsis cryptochrome 2 bibl graph *Science* v354 no6310 p343 O 21 2016

Qing Xia

Generation of influenza A viruses as live but replication-incompetent virus vaccines bibl graph *Science* v354 no6316 p1170 D 2 2016

Qinghua Zhang

Ultrafine jagged platinum nanowires enable ultrahigh mass activity for the oxygen reduction reaction bibl chart graph *Science* v354 no6318 p1414 D 16 2016

Qing hua da xue (Beijing, China)

Tsinghua University founded *History Today* v67 no4 p8 Ap 2017

Qingjin, Meng

The Significance and Magnificence of Jehol Biota *Natural History* v124 no10 p20 N 2016

Qingjun Lu

Quality management for precision medicine clinical applications: A consensus from the China Precision Medicine Clinical Research and Application Association bibl *Science* v354 no6319 p11 D 23 2016

Qingwei Ma

Application of MALDI-TOF mass spectrometry for identifying clinical microorganisms bibl *Science* v354 no6319 p58 D 23 2016

Qingxiao Wang

MoS2 transistors with 1-nanometer gate lengths bibl color graph *Science* v354 no6308 p99 O 7 2016

Qingying Jia

Ultrafine jagged platinum nanowires enable ultrahigh mass activity for the oxygen reduction reaction bibl chart graph *Science* v354 no6318 p1414 D 16 2016

Qinhua Fang

Adapting Chinese cities to climate change bibl *Science* v354 no6311 p425 O 28 2016

Qin shi huang, Emperor of China, 259 B.C.-210 B.C.

Secrets of the Terra-Cotta Warriors A. R. Williams color *National Geographic* v230 no5 p23 N 2016

Qiu, Chenguang

Scaling carbon nanotube complementary transistors to 5-nm gate lengths bibl chart graph *Science* v355 no6322 p271 Ja 20 2017

Qiu, Cheng-Wei

Vortex generation reaches a new plateau color *Science* v357 no6352 p645 Ag 18 2017

Qiu, Jane

East Africa turmoil imperils giraffes color diag *Science* v356 no6344 p1220 Je 23 2017

Expedition probes ocean trench's deepest secrets color *Science* v355 no6321 p115 Ja 13 2017

Ice Age Tibetans color *Scientific American* v316 no3 p14 Mr 2017

Qiu, Min

A paralogous decoy protects Phytophthora sojae apoplastic effector PsXEG1 from a host inhibitor bibl graph *Science* v355 no6326 p710 F 17 2017

Qiu, Serena

Philadelphia Museum of Art color *Art in America* v105 no1 p85 Ja 2017

Qiu, Wendy

A SUMO-ubiquitin relay recruits proteasomes to chromosome axes to regulate meiotic recombination bibl graph *Science* v355 no6323 p403 Ja 27 2017

Qiu, Xiaojie

Comprehensive single-cell transcriptional profiling of a multicellular organism diag *Science* v357 no6352 p661 Ag 18 2017

Qiu Miaojin

Risk and Reward L. CORE *New York Times Book Review* p25 My 7 2017

Qu, Lan-Meng

"Perfect" designer chromosome V and behavior of a ring derivative diag *Science* v355 no6329 p1046 Mr 10 2017

Quach, Hélène

Dispersals and genetic adaptation of Bantu-speaking populations in Africa and North America diag *Science* v356 no6337 p543 My 5 2017

Quackenbos, Douglas

Does Your Company Have What It Takes to Go Global? *Harvard Business Review Digital Articles* p2 Ap 11 2016

QUADE, KIRSTIN VALDEZ

CHRISTINA THE ASTONISHING: 1150-1224 cartoon *New Yorker* v93 no22 p56 Jl 31 2017

Quade, Matthew J.

We Don't Shun Unethical Coworkers If They're High Performers *Harvard Business Review Digital Articles* p2 My 25 2016

Quadratus lumborum muscles—Anatomy

Get to know... your QL muscles N. Carollo color *Yoga Journal* p54 2017 SpecialIssue

QUADRI, HABEEB

Tackling Technology Tactfully *Islamic Horizons* v45 no6 p36 N/D 2016

Quadriplegics

Milestones color *Time* v189 no13 p12 Ap 10 2017

Quah, Nicholas

THE RISE, RISE, AND RISE OF PODCASTS color *Wired* v25 no10 p36 O 2017

Quails

FOR THE BIRDS T. KEER chart color *Outdoor Life* v224 no6 pH5 Ag 2017

Quakers—History

THE CAVE-DWELLING VEGAN WHO TOOK ON QUAKER SLAVERY AND WON: THE NATION'S FIRST RADICAL ABOLITIONIST WAS ONE OF THE MOST DRAMATIC OUTSPOKEN FIGURES OF THE 18TH CENTURY. YET FEW HISTORIANS HAVE EVEN HEARD OF THE AMAZING BENJAMIN LAY M. REDIKER *Smithsonian* v48 no5 p34 S 2017

QUALCOMM Inc.

THE BILLION-DOLLAR WAR Over an $18 Part M. Chafkin, I. King et al color graph *Bloomberg Businessweek* no4541 p52 O 9 2017

QUALCOMM Inc.—Trials, litigation, etc.

Apple Tries the Full-Court Press I. King and A. Webb color graph *Bloomberg Businessweek* no4509 p28 Ja 30 2017

Quale, Brittany

Creating a Sustainable Community Garden *Parks & Recreation* v52 no6 p26 Je 2017

QUALEY, M. LYNX

Sci-Fi Iraq *In These Times* v40 no12 p36 D 2016

Qualifying events (Sports)

PREPARING TO LAUNCH D. WILLEY color *Runner's World* v52 no3 p10 Ap 2017

Quality (Philosophy)

LESSONS AND IDEAS BY THE 100 GREATEST LIVING BUSINESS MINDS R. Lane, S. Adams et al bw color *Forbes* v200 no3 p115 S 28 2017

Whole New Ball Game S. Rushin color *Sports Illustrated* v127 no3 p116 Jl 24 2017

Quality assurance

Does It Pay to Hire Consultants? Evidence from the Bordeaux Wine Industry J. Barthelemy *Harvard Business Review Digital Articles* p2 My 19 2017

Employer-led Quality Assurance J. A. Tyszko *Change* v49 no1 p26 Ja/F 2017

Improving Natural Grass Field Quality J. Minnick *Parks & Recreation* v52 no5 p72 My 2017

Quality control

See also

Medical care—Quality control

Estimation of Relative Potency from Bioassay Data that Include Values below the Limit of Quantitation F. BURSA, K. J. FLEETWOOD et al *BioScience* v66 no11 p983 N 1 2016

Improving Natural Grass Field Quality J. Minnick *Parks & Recreation* v52 no5 p72 My 2017

Quality control of medical care

Access to quality health care has improved in most places A. Cunningham map *Science News* v191 no12 p5 Je 24 2017

Quality of life

See also

Cost & standard of living

Lifestyles

Quality of work life

Well-being

ALL THAT And More *Atlanta* v57 no2 p134 Je 2017

BRINGING IN THE BEANS: Harvest on an American family farm T. Genoways *Harper's Magazine* p53 S 2017

DO LESS, EARN MORE T. Ferriss color *Men's Health* v32 no7 p90 S 2017

HOW YOU'RE DRIVING DOWN COSTS—AND IMPROVING LIVES *Governing* v30 no1 p12 O 2016

Human health D. L. Clinciu, D. Scarf et al color *Science* v356 no6338 p590 My 12 2017

NEW NEXT NEW YORK D. VON FURSTENBERG *Interview* v46 no9 p70 N 2016

Nothing New P. GULLEY *Indianapolis Monthly* p46 F 2017

Out of the Woods? N. KIRSCHNER *American Scholar* v86 no4 p18 Aut 2017

Research: Keeping Work and Life Separate Is More Trouble than It's Worth D. Burkus *Harvard Business Review Digital Articles* p2 Ag 9 2016

THE SCRIPT OF IGNORANCE K. D. Singh color *Tricycle: The Buddhist Review* v27 no1 p18 Fall 2017

Self-Care and the Disappearance of the Adult *Commentary* v142 no1 p1 Jl/Ag 2016

Someone to Talk To D. Frolovskiy *New York Times Magazine* p23 Ja 1 2017

When the sky falls A. Camille color *U.S. Catholic* v81 no11 p47 N 2016

YOU AND IMPROVED! color *Men's Health* v32 no7 p89 S 2017

Quality of life—Measurement

Income Inequality Makes Whole Countries Less Happy De Neve and N. (. Powdthavee *Harvard Business Review Digital Articles* p2 Ja 12 2016

Quality of life—United States

Don't Poor Lives Matter? H. I. Miller *Hoover Digest: Research & Opinion on Public Policy* no1 p72 Wint 2017

Work Long and Prosper C. Blahous *Hoover Digest: Research & Opinion on Public Policy* no1 p57 Wint 2017

Quality of products

See also

Food quality

Wood quality

The Fine Line Between When Low Prices Work and When They Don't H. Simon *Harvard Business Review Digital Articles* p2 Mr 17 2016

Staying Connected E. Vohr color *Sail* v48 no10 p24 O 2017

Quality of products—Management

Is Tesla Really a Disruptor? (And Why the Answer Matters) L. Downes and P. Nunes *Harvard Business Review Digital Articles* p2 2017

Quality of work life

See also

Job satisfaction

Does Work Make You Happy? Evidence from the World Happiness Report De Neve and G. Ward *Harvard Business Review Digital Articles* p2 Mr 20 2017

An Early Warning System for Your Team's Stress Level [Cover story] T. Hellwig, C. Rook et al *Harvard Business Review Digital Articles* p2 Ap 26 2017

Hold Yourself Accountable-You'll Be Happier J. G. Miller *Time* v188 no22-23 p20 N/D 2016

How to Convince Your Boss to Let You Work from Home R. Knight *Harvard Business Review Digital Articles* p2 My 5 2017

How to Forget About Work When You're Not Working A. Markman *Harvard Business Review Digital Articles* p2 2017

Is Overwork Killing You? G. Petriglieri *Harvard Business Review Digital Articles* p2 Ag 31 2015

Surviving scientist burnout L. D. Site *Physics Today* v70 no9 p10 S 2017

What High Performers Want at Work K. Willyerd *Harvard Business Review Digital Articles* p2 N 18 2014

Why Companies Are So Bad at Treating Employees Like People H. Ibarra *Harvard Business Review Digital Articles* p2 O 29 2015

Work Mistakes to Avoid in 2017 B. Levin color *Glamour* v115 no1 p59 Ja 2017

Qualley, Margaret

Previously, on The Leftovers...: An introduction to (or reminder of) the show's sprawling cast of characters img *New York* v50 no12 p86 Je 12 2017

QUAM, CYNTHIA TODD

AN ACTION LIST FOR THE (UN) GAITHFUL *Humanist* v77 no1 p20 Ja/F 2017

Quammen, David

The Mission to Save Africa's Okavango Delta color map *National Geographic* v232 no5 p80 N 2017

Quan, Li Na

Efficient and stable solution-processed planar perovskite solar cells via contact passivation bibl graph *Science* v355 no6326 p722 F 17 2017

QUANDT, KATIE ROSE

Cruel and Unusual Healthcare *In These Times* v40 no12 p24 D 2016

Quanterix Corp.

This New Test Could Crush The NFL I. Boudway color *Bloomberg Businessweek* no4510 p48 F 6 2017

Quantico (TV program)

CHEERS & JEERS D. HOLBROOK *TV Guide* v65 no6 p88 Ja 30 2017

FRESH FACE: PEARL THUSI color *Essence* v47 no10 p38 F 2017

Quantico I. Rudolph *TV Guide* v65 no6 p36 Ja 30 2017

Quantitative research

Cancer studies fall short in redos T. H. SAEY graph *Science News* v191 no3 p10 F 18 2017

The Trump Tweetometer il *New Republic* v248 no10 p9 O 2017

Quantization (Physics)

Quantized electric multipole insulators W. A. Benalcazar, B. Andrei Bernevig et al bw color graph *Science* v357 no6346 p61 Jl 7 2017

Quantrill, William Clarke, 1837-1865

The Man Who Killed Quantrill R. J. GREEN bw cartoon *Missouri Life* v44 no3 p50 My 2017

Quantum communication

New steps toward quantum internet E. CONOVER *Science News* v190 no8 p13 O 15 2016

Quantum video chat links Asia, Europe E. CONOVER *Science News* v192 no7 p14 O 28 2017

Quantum computers

Quantum Computers GET REAL E. Conover chart color diag *Science News* v191 no13 p28 Jl 8 2017

Quantum computing

Dive deep to discover unexpected connections E. Quill *Science News* v191 no13 p2 Jl 8 2017

How to Fight Quantum Cybercrooks H. Miller and E. Chan *Bloomberg Businessweek* no4531 p43 Jl 24 2017

PRACTICAL Quantum Computers R. JUSKALIAN color *MIT Technology Review* v120 no2 p76 Mr/Ap 2017

Quantum Computers GET REAL E. Conover chart color diag *Science News* v191 no13 p28 Jl 8 2017

Quantum simulations with ultracold atoms in optical lattices C. Gross and I. Bloch cartoon color diag *Science* v357 no6355 p995 S 8 2017

QUEST FOR QUBITS G. Popkin color diag *Science* v354 no6316 p1090 D 2 2016

Quantum correlations

Quantum correlations from a room-temperature optomechanical cavity T. P. Purdy, K. E. Grutter et al color diag graph *Science* v356 no6344 p1265 Je 23 2017

Quantum dots

Maintaining a stable phase P. D. S *Science* v354 no6308 p77 O 7 2016

Majorana bound state in a coupled quantum-dot hybrid-nanowire system M. T. Deng, S. Vaitiekénas et al bibl graph *Science* v354 no6319 p1557 D 23 2016

Quantum dot-induced phase stabilization of α-CsPbI3 perovskite for high-efficiency photovoltaics A. Swarnkar, A. R. Marshall et al bibl chart graph *Science* v354 no6308 p92 O 7 2016

Quantum efficiency (Physics)

High-performance light-emitting diodes based on carbene-metal-amides D. Di, A. S. Romanov et al chart graph *Science* v356 no6334 p159 Ap 14 2017

Quantum entanglement

BLACK HOLES, WORMHO LES AND THE SECRETS OF QUANTUM SPACETIME J. Maldacena color diag *Scientific American* v315 no5 p26 N 2016

Deterministic entanglement generation from driving through quantum phase transitions Luo, Zou et al bibl color graph *Science* v355 no6325 p620 F 10 2017

Deterministic generation of a cluster state of entangled photons I. Schwartz, D. Cogan et al bibl diag graph *Science* v354 no6311 p434 O 28 2016

Entangled atoms break record E. CONOVER *Science News* v191 no8 p8 Ap 29 2017

Quantum satellite sets distance record E. CONOVER color *Science News* v192 no1 p14 Ag 5 2017

Satellite-based entanglement distribution over 1200 kilometers J. Yin, Y. Cao et al diag graph *Science* v356 no6343 p1140 Je 16 2017

Spooky action achieved at record distance [Cover story] G. Popkin color *Science* v356 no6343 p1110 Je 16 2017

Versatile cluster entangled light H. J. Briegel bibl diag *Science* v354 no6311 p416 O 28 2016

Quantum entanglement—Research

Tangled Up in Spacetime C. Moskowitz color *Scientific American* v316 no1 p32 Ja 2017

Quantum gases

Quantum gases cooled to long-range antiferromagnetic order: The observation of a checkerboard pattern in a lattice of ultracold atoms is a sign of even more exciting experiments to come J. Miller *Physics Today* v70 no8 p17 Ag 2017

Quantum gravity

The hermeneutics of bunk J. Hester color *Astronomy* v45 no7 p14 Jl 2017

NEW PARTICLE FIZZLES, LEAVING PHYSICISTS TO SOUL SEARCH N. SCHARPING color *Discover* v38 no1 p20 Ja/F 2017

Ridicule Didn't Work J. PIERESON and N. SCHAEFER RILEY color *Weekly Standard* v22 no20 p17 Ja 30 2017

Quantum Hall effect

Observation of a nematic quantum Hall liquid on the surface of bismuth B. E. Feldman, M. T. Randeria et al bibl graph *Science* v354 no6310 p316 O 21 2016

Quantum information science

See also

Quantum computing

QUEST FOR QUBITS G. Popkin color diag *Science* v354 no6316 p1090 D 2 2016

Quantum interference

Anti-coalescence of bosons on a lossy beam splitter B. Vest, Dheur et al bw chart diag graph *Science* v356 no6345 p1373 Je 30 2017

Quantum liquids

Observation of a nematic quantum Hall liquid on the surface of bismuth B. E. Feldman, M. T. Randeria et al bibl graph *Science* v354 no6310 p316 O 21 2016

Quantum measurement

Submillihertz magnetic spectroscopy performed with a nanoscale quantum sensor S. Schmitt, T. Gefen et al diag *Science* v356 no6340 p832 My 26 2017

Quantum mechanics

See also

Quantum gases

Rydberg constant

CONSTRAINING INTERPRETATIONS OF QUANTUM MECHANICS *Physics Today* v70 no2 p23 F 2017

A Dunning-Kruger universe J. HESTER color *Astronomy* v45 no6 p14 Je 2017

Quantum effect passes space test E. CONOVER *Science News* v191 no1 p12 Ja 21 2017

A Quantum Machine for All... J. KEATS color *Discover* v38 no1 p57 Ja/F 2017

THE QUANTUM MULTIVERSE [Cover story] Y. Nomura color *Scientific American* v316 no6 p28 Je 2017

Second-scale nuclear spin coherence time of ultracold 23Na40K molecules J. Woo Park, Z. Z. Yan et al diag *Science* v357 no6349 p372 Jl 28 2017

SHEDDING LIGHT (AND DARK) ON QUANTUM PROBABILITIES *Physics Today* v70 no6 p24 Je 2017

The Trouble with Quantum Mechanics S. Weinberg cartoon color *New York Review of Books* v64 no1 p51 Ja 19 2017

Quantum mechanics—Methodology

The Trouble with Quantum Mechanics S. Weinberg cartoon color *New York Review of Books* v64 no1 p51 Ja 19 2017

Quantum networks (Optics)

Entanglement distillation between solid-state quantum network nodes N. Kalb, A. A. Reiserer et al diag *Science* v356 no6341 p928 Je 1 2017

An integrated diamond nanophotonics platform for quantum-optical networks A. Sipahigil, R. E. Evans et al bibl graph *Science* v354 no6314 p847 N 18 2016

Satellite-based entanglement distribution over 1200 kilometers J. Yin, Y. Cao et al diag graph *Science* v356 no6343 p1140 Je 16 2017

Quantum optics

See also

Photon emission

Diamond defects cooperate via light R. Hanson bibl diag *Science* v354 no6314 p835 N 18 2016

Quantum optical circulator controlled by a single chirally coupled atom M. Scheucher, A. Hilico et al bibl graph *Science* v354 no6319 p1577 D 23 2016

Quantum phase transitions

Deterministic entanglement generation from driving through quantum phase transitions Luo, Zou et al bibl color graph *Science* v355 no6325 p620 F 10 2017

Universal space-time scaling symmetry in the dynamics of bosons across a quantum phase transition L. W. Clark, Lei Feng et al bibl graph *Science* v354 no6312 p606 N 4 2016

Quantum physicists

Deborah S. Jin (1968–2016) C. Regal and Jun Ye color *Science* v354 no6313 p709 N 11 2016

Quantum spin Hall effect

Bismuthene on a SiC substrate: A candidate for a high-temperature quantum spin Hall material F. Reis, G. Li et al diag graph *Science* v357 no6348 p287 Jl 21 2017

Quantum spin liquid

Neutron scattering in the proximate quantum spin liquid a-RuCl3 A. Banerjee, J. Yan et al bw diag *Science* v356 no6342 p1055 Je 9 2017

Quantum states

Second-scale nuclear spin coherence time of ultracold 23Na40K molecules J. Woo Park, Z. Z. Yan et al diag *Science* v357 no6349 p372 Jl 28 2017

Quantum systems

Solving the quantum many-body problem with artificial neural networks G. Carleo and M. Troyer bibl diag *Science* v355 no6325 p602 F 10 2017

Quantum theory

See also

Quantum computing

Quantum entanglement

Quantum gravity

Quantum mechanics

An atom-by-atom assembler of defect-free arbitrary two-dimensional atomic arrays D. Barredo, S. de Léséleuc et al bibl bw diag graph *Science* v354 no6315 p1021 N 25 2016

Atom-by-atom assembly of defect-free one-dimensional cold atom arrays M. Endres, H. Bernien et al bibl diag graph *Science* v354 no6315 p1024 N 25 2016

Einstein principle passes quantum test E. CONOVER *Science News* v191 no10 p8 My 27 2017

Probing the limits of heat flow D. Segal bibl diag *Science* v355 no6330 p1125 Mr 17 2017

Realization of two-dimensional spin-orbit coupling for Bose-Einstein condensates Zhan Wu, Long Zhang et al bibl graph *Science* v354 no6308 p83 O 7 2016

The tie that binds J. Swift bibl color *Science* v355 no6326 p701 F 17 2017

THE WAR OVER REALITY T. FOLGER color *Discover* v38 no4 p28 My 2017

Quantum theory—Bibliographies

NEW BOOKS *Physics Today* v70 no9 p62 S 2017

Quarantine (Short story)

Quarantine A. Ohlin cartoon *New Yorker* v92 no47 p56 Ja 30 2017

Quark-gluon plasma

Swirls possible in infant cosmos E. CONOVER *Science News* v190 no12 p9 D 10 2016

Quarles, Randal

A Safe Choice to Regulate Banks P. Coy color *Bloomberg Businessweek* no4519 p35 Ap 24 2017

Quarreling

See also

Reconciliation

How to Not Fight with Your Spouse When You Get Home from Work E. Batista *Harvard Business Review Digital Articles* p2 Ap 12 2016

Quarries & quarrying—Italy

WHITE GOLD S. ANDERSON *New York Times Magazine* p34 Jl 30 2017

Quarry Bank Mill

Weaving Life at Quarry Bank mill *British Heritage Travel* v37 no6 p54 N/D 2016

Quarter horse

2017 Mediterranean Championships C. Reid *Arabian Horse World* v57 no11 p124 Ag 2017

Aged Quarter Horse Geldings J. BAGKEY color *Horse & Rider* v56 no8 p51 Ag 2017

Behind the Chutes A. Bohus color *American Cowboy* v24 no1 p69 Je/Jl 2017

CONFORMATION CLINIC K. Banister color *Horse & Rider* v56 no4 p39 Ap 2017

A Gelding, a Mare, a Lesson D. Robertson color *Horse & Rider* v56 no4 p16 Ap 2017

Quarterbacking (Football)

Dominate Fake Football S. JOSEPH color diag *Men's Health* v32 no7 p38 S 2017

INSIDE THE TEXAS QUARTERBACK FACTORY E. BENSON *Texas Monthly* v45 no9 p56 S 2017

No Dumb Luck J. GUSKEY color diag *Indianapolis Monthly* v41 no2 p17 S 2017

Quarterbacks (Football)

America's QB M. J. MOONEY color *GQ: Gentlemen's Quarterly* v97 no9 p168 S 2017

Knee High M. Rosenberg and T. Keith color *Sports Illustrated* v126 no10 p21 Ap 10 2017

OUT OF OPTIONS A. Breer color *Sports Illustrated* v127 no7 p112 S 4 2017

What We Think About When We Think About Big Ben [Cover story] S. l. Price color *Sports Illustrated* v126 no1 p20 Ja 9 2017

WHO DAK? [Cover story] P. Thamel color *Sports Illustrated* v125 no13 p24 O 17 2016

Why Everyone Loves the Big Game T. AIKMAN and K. Rosen *TV Guide* v65 no6 p16 Ja 30 2017

Quarterbacks (Football)—Attitudes

GAME of THROWS J. Jones color *Sports Illustrated* v127 no5 p34 Ag 14 2017

Quarterbacks (Football)—Employment

Vince YOUNG G. Bishop color *Sports Illustrated* v127 no1 p40 Jl 3 2017

Quarterbacks (Football)—History

This is 40 B. Baskin color *Sports Illustrated* v126 no7 p79 Mr 6 2017

Quarterbacks (Football)—History—20th century

Y.A. TITTLE (1926-2017) S. Kwak color *Sports Illustrated* v127 no12 p22 O 16 2017

Quarterbacks (Football)—Universities & colleges

THROWN TO THE WOLVES A. Staples color *Sports Illustrated* v127 no8 p56 S 18 2017

TRUE GRIT A. Staples color *Sports Illustrated* v126 no11 p36 Ap 17-24 2017

Quarterbacks (Football)—Wounds & injuries

BE COOL, MAN R. Klemko chart color *Sports Illustrated* v127 no11 p34 O 9 2017

Quarterbacks (Football)—Charts, diagrams, etc.

Value Judgments J. Jones and T. Keith chart color *Sports Illustrated* v125 no19 p28 D 12 2016

Quartey, Kwei

Death by His Grace *Publishers Weekly* v264 no24 p42 Je 12 2017

Quartuch, Michael

THE PATH LESS TRAVELED color *New York State Conservationist* v71 no2 p24 O 2016

Quasars

The mystery of quasars D. J. Eicher color *Astronomy* v45 no5 p8 My 2017

New data fuel further debate on universe's expansion rate E. Conover *Science News* v191 no4 p18 Mr 4 2017

Our black hole's last known feast color *Astronomy* v45 no7 p13 Jl 2017

Quasars—Spectra

Identifying the hosts of quasar absorbers color *Science* v355 no6331 p1277 Mr 24 2017

Quasiparticles (Physics)

Faux particle commits physics faux pas E. CONOVER *Science News* v191 no13 p14 Jl 8 2017

Quaternities

Awesome Foursomes T. Keith color *Sports Illustrated* v126 no10 p28 Ap 10 2017

Quatrano, Anne

ATLANTA MAGAZINE DIGITAL *Atlanta* v57 no2 p12 Je 2017

QUATRO, JAMIE

GIFTS that UPLIFT! cartoon *O, The Oprah Magazine* p148 D 2016

Quatro Group (Company)

Marcus Leaver: CEO, Quarto Group J. Milliot color *Publishers Weekly* v263 no52 p28 D 19 2016

Quattro automobile—Evaluation

RS KICKER M. Duff color *Car & Driver* v62 no6 p21 D 2016

Quattrociocchi, Walter

INSIDE THE ECHO CHAMBER color *Scientific American* v316 no4 p60 Ap 2017

Quavo (Performer)—Interviews

Migos: The Viral MCs Are Here to Stay E. R. Brown color *Entertainment Weekly* no1451/1452 p107 F 3-10 2017

Quay (Film)

THE TEENY-TINY NOLAN MOVIE K. P. Sullivan color *Entertainment Weekly* no1474/1475 p60 Jl 21-28 2017

Quayman, R. H.—Interviews

R. H. QUAYTMAN *Interview* v46 no8 p98 O 2016

Quaytman, R. H.—Exhibitions

"R. H. Quaytman, Morning: Chapter 30" A. Doran color *ARTnews* v115 no3 p33 Fall 2016

Quazarz: Born on a Gangster Star (Music)

What to Stream color *Entertainment Weekly* no1474/1475 p115 Jl 21-28 2017

Qubits

Birth of the QUBIT T. Siegfried bw color *Science News* v191 no13 p34 Jl 8 2017

PRACTICAL Quantum Computers R. JUSKALIAN color *MIT Technology Review* v120 no2 p76 Mr/Ap 2017

Quantum sensing with arbitrary frequency resolution J. M. Boss, K. S. Cujia et al diag graph *Science* v356 no6340 p837 My 26 2017

Quantum storage device fits on a chip M. TEMMING color *Science News* v192 no5 p8 S 30 2017

Suppressing relaxation in superconducting qubits by quasiparticle pumping S. Gustavsson, Fei Yan et al bibl graph *Science* v354 no6319 p1573 D 23 2016

Québec (Province)—Economic conditions—21st century

The Habs, Poutine, Jobs: Welcome to Quebec S. Rastello and F. Tomesco graph *Bloomberg Businessweek* no4508 p16 Ja 23 2017

Quechua (South American people)

Building a Bridge Without a Plan E. Machulak *Humanities* v38 no4 p1 Fall 2017

Queen (Film : 1968)

Leading Ladies R. Brody bw *New Yorker* v93 no9 p11 Ap 17 2017

Queen (Performer)

Adam Lambert S. Lansky color *Time* v189 no4 p49 F 6 2017

QUEEN, K. H.

Less Pain, More Gain color *Forbes* v200 no4 p(Sp)1 O 24 2017

Queen Alexandra's birdwing
By the Numbers RAIN FOREST J. BEER and M. HARRIS *National Geographic Kids* no468 p8 Mr 2017

Queen Anne architecture
Saratoga Springs/New York A. M. Strauss bw color *Old House Journal* v45 no5 p34 Ag 2017

Queen Anne furniture
QUEEN ANNE CHERRY BONNET TOP HIGHBOY IN EARLY BLACK PAINT color *Magazine Antiques* v183 no6 p2 N/D 2016

Queen of the South (TV program)
ALSO COMING... A. D'Arminio and J. Russell *TV Guide* v65 no23 p25 My 29 2017
The Rise of the Telenovela S. MARSHALL color *New Republic* v248 no1/2 p64 Ja/F 2017

Queen Sugar (TV program)
THE CULTURAL CONSOLATION OF AVA DUVERNAY'S QUEEN SUGAR B. Qureshi *Film Quarterly* v70 no3 p63 Spr 2017
An Onscreen Family, Raising Cane D. D'addario color *Time* v190 no1 p52 Jl 3 2017
Queen Sugar M. Logan *TV Guide* v64 no48 p40 N 21 2016
Queen Sugar M. Logan *TV Guide* v65 no25 p39 Je 2017
Queen Sugar M. Logan *TV Guide* v65 no31 p37 Jl 24 2017
Sweet Home Louisiana M. Z. SEITZ *New York* v49 no19 p97 S 19 2016
A VIBRANT LEGACY A. Tinubu color *Ebony* v72 no9 p78 Jl/Ag 2017

Queenan, Joe
Dr. Kismet's Cure *Weekly Standard* v22 no23 p38 F 20 2017
Funny It's Not color *Weekly Standard* v22 no14 p37 D 12 2016
The Hit Parade *Weekly Standard* v22 no36 p39 My 29 2017
An Iliad Odyssey color *Weekly Standard* v22 no17 p35 Ja 2 2017
The Trump Dilemma color *Weekly Standard* v22 no19 p39 Ja 23 2017

Queens Museum
Labor Intensive A. K. Scott color *New Yorker* v92 no36 p6 N 7 2016

Queens of the Stone Age (Performer)
Josh Homme's Desert Dance Party K. GROW bw *Rolling Stone* no1291/1292 p14 Jl 13 2017
King of the Stone Age B. HIATT color *Rolling Stone* no1295 p20 S 7 2017

Queensboro Bridge (New York, N.Y.)
Queensboro Bridge color *Architectural Digest* v74 no10 p97 O 1 2017

Queen's House (London, England)
Majestic makeover [Cover story] B. Laurence Scherer color *Magazine Antiques* v184 no3 p102 My/Je 2017
The Tulip Stairs in the Queen's House color *Magazine Antiques* v184 no3 pCover My/Je 2017

Queensland
The Thermal Edge S. K. WILSON color *Natural History* v125 no3 p48 Mr 2017

Queer Eye for the Straight Guy (TV program)
QUEER EYE RETURNS! J. Hibberd color *Entertainment Weekly* no1451/1452 p20 F 3-10 2017

Quel, E. J.
Observation of a large-scale anisotropy in the arrival directions of cosmic rays above 8 × 1018 eV *Science* v357 no6357 p1266 S 22 2017

Quelch, John
To Get More Out of Social Media, Think Like an Anthropologist *Harvard Business Review Digital Articles* p2 Ag 17 2016

Quelch, John A.—Interviews
Why Sourcing Local Food Is So Hard for Restaurants N. Torres *Harvard Business Review Digital Articles* p2 Je 15 2016

Querbach, Ann Katrin
Tight Turns, Big Benefits color *Horse & Rider* v56 no7 p103 Jl 2017

Querchfeld, S.
Observation of a large-scale anisotropy in the arrival directions of cosmic rays above 8 × 1018 eV *Science* v357 no6357 p1266 S 22 2017

Queri, Jillian
TETHERED color *Skiing* p36 D 2016

Quertermous, Thomas
Circulating peptide prevents preeclampsia diag *Science* v357 no6352 p643 Ag 18 2017

Quesadillas
Carly Chaikin P. KITA cartoon color *Men's Health* v32 no9 p38 N 2017
There's an App for That D. Lewon color *Backpacker* p38 My 2017

Quesenberry, Keith A.
Conducting a Social Media Audit *Harvard Business Review Digital Articles* p2 N 18 2015
Fix Your Social Media Strategy by Taking It Back to Basics *Harvard Business Review Digital Articles* p2 Jl 25 2016
How B2B Marketers Can Get Started with Social Media *Harvard Business Review Digital Articles* p2 D 24 2015
How B2B Sales Can Benefit from Social Selling *Harvard Business Review Digital Articles* p2 N 8 2016
Social Media Is Too Important to Be Left to the Marketing Department *Harvard Business Review Digital Articles* p2 Ap 19 2016

Quesnel (B.C.)
A JOURNEYMAN'S TALE T. WILLIAMS color *Canoe & Kayak Magazine* v45 no1 p44 Wint 2017

Quest (Film)
Polarities and Pyrotechnics: True/False Festival 2017 L. Du Graf *Film Quarterly* v71 no1 p87 Fall 2017
Trails of Destruction A. TAUBIN color *Film Comment* v53 no2 p60 Mr/Ap 2017

Questell-Santiago, Ydna M.
Formaldehyde stabilization facilitates lignin monomer production during biomass depolymerization bibl diag graph *Science* v354 no6310 p329 O 21 2016

Questioning
See also
Examinations
Interviewing
How to be an American Muslim H. Moghul *Christian Century* v134 no11 p26 My 24 2017
THE LINGUISTIC ORIGINS OF THE QUESTION D. ESTES color *Christianity Today* v61 no7 p64 S 2017
Socratism as a Vocation M. Flynn *Society* v54 no1 p64 F 2017
Tactics for Asking Good Follow-Up Questions R. Davis *Harvard Business Review Digital Articles* p2 N 7 2014
The Trump Touch L. Adi color *Commonweal* v144 no9 p11 My 19 2017

Questlove (Performer)
MASTER OF CEREMONIES T. ADLER bw color *Vogue* v207 no6 p140 Je 2017

Quest University (Squamish, B.C.)
College-level project-based learning gains popularity T. Feder *Physics Today* v70 no6 p26 Je 2017

QUETTIER, NELLY
Moment to Moment bw color *Film Comment* v53 no2 p16 Mr/Ap 2017

Queuene, jenny
THE audition prep TIMELINE color *Dance Spirit* v21 no2 p42 F 2017

Queuing theory
How to Cut in Line J. Stewart color *Atlantic* v320 no2 p22 S 2017

Quezada, Veronica
FREE WEBSITE REVEALS YOUR RELATIVES AND MORE color *Money* v46 no2 p21 Mr 2017

Quick & easy cooking
Save Time IN THE KITCHEN B. GOLD color *Good Housekeeping* v264 no3 p87 Mr 2017

Quick, Tanya
Tanya Quick color *Bicycling* v58 no1 p96 Ja/F 2017

Quickenden, Stuart
Companies Shouldn't Wait to Prepare for the Post-Brexit World *Harvard Business Review Digital Articles* p2 N 3 2016

Quidditch (Game)
Quidditch for Muggles R. Kinane color *Entertainment Weekly* no1476 p20 Ag 4 2017

Quiet Man, The (Film : 1952)
THE QUIET MAN C. Chiarella color *Sound & Vision* v82 no3 p67 Ap 2017

Quiet Passion, A (Film)
ABOVE & BEYOND color *New Yorker* v93 no23 p16 Ag 7 2017

The Elusive Emily Dickinson M. ATKINSON *In These Times* v41 no5 p36 My 2017

I HEARD A FLY BUZZ S. KLAWANS color *Nation* v304 no13 p36 Ap 17 2017

POETIC LICENSE A. LANE color *New Yorker* v93 no10 p102 Ap 24 2017

Prometheus Unbound: Emily Dickinson comes confidently alive J. CHARYN *American Scholar* v86 no3 p104 Summ 2017

Raging Belle E. BLAKEMORE *Smithsonian* v48 no1 p16 Ap 2017

Spring Preview R. Brody cartoon *New Yorker* v93 no4 p6 Mr 13 2017

UNDER A BUSHEL R. Mead cartoon *New Yorker* v93 no12 p18 My 8 2017

Quietude

The Busier You Are, the More You Need Quiet Time J. Talbot-Zorn and L. Marz *Harvard Business Review Digital Articles* p2 Mr 17 2017

Quigg, Chris

John David Jackson *Physics Today* v69 no10 p68 O 2016

QUIGLEY, DAWN

Silenced *American Indian Quarterly* v40 no4 p364 Fall 2016

QUIGLEY, FRAN

Remedies Beyond Reach color *America* v215 no14 p14 N 7 2016

Quigley, Joan—Interviews

PLUCKING OUT JIM CROW N. TAPPAN *American History* v52 no1 p12 Ap 2017

Quigley, John

Latin America Drains Its Political Swamp bw *Bloomberg Businessweek* no4531 p38 Jl 24 2017

Under new management color *Bloomberg Businessweek* no4496 p18 O 24 2016

Quigley, Tom

AUXILIARY ANNOUNCEMENT *Commonweal* v144 no12 p2 Jl 7 2017

Faithless Fidel color *Commonweal* v144 no4 p10 F 24 2017

Quill, Elizabeth

2016 Year in Review [Cover story] *Science News* v190 no13 p16 D 24 2016

Conspiring with engineers helps make science great *Science News* v192 no7 p2 O 28 2017

Dive deep to discover unexpected connections *Science News* v191 no13 p2 Jl 8 2017

Expert eavesdroppers occasionally catch a break *Science News* v192 no1 p2 Ag 5 2017

If there are curious young minds, science will survive *Science News* v191 no7 p2 Ap 15 2017

Jumping genes are part of all that makes us human color *Science News* v191 no10 p2 My 27 2017

Lab tests aren't the answer for every science question *Science News* v191 no6 p2 Ap 1 2017

Learning is a ubiquitous, mysterious phenomenon *Science News* v192 no4 p2 S 16 2017

Nature offers inspiration, and occasionally courage *Science News* v192 no5 p2 S 30 2017

Science journalists don't use the science of 'nudge' *Science News* v191 no5 p2 Mr 18 2017

Science's questions rarely have clear, easy answers *Science News* v191 no4 p2 Mr 4 2017

Some topics call for science reporting from many angles *Science News* v191 no11 p2 Je 10 2017

What's Ahead in 2017 bw *Science News* v190 no13 p36 D 24 2016

Quillen, Evelyn

How My Horse De-Stresses Me color *Horse & Rider* v55 no12 p72 D 2016

Quillen, Kristi

CO-OP FARMSTANDS for Backyard Gardeners: Yard to Market Co-op has created an adaptable model for even the smallestscale growers to sell extra produce--from a bundle of herbs to dozens of eggs *Mother Earth News* no283 p36 Ag/S 2017

FARMING the Neighborhood *Mother Earth News* no279 p24 D/Ja 2017

Fresh, Homemade SALAD DRESSINGS *Mother Earth News* no281 p36 Ap/My 2017

MAKE PAPER from Grasses and Leaves: Connect with an age-old process and the life cycle of plants to make fragrant, tex-tured paper *Mother Earth News* no282 p28 Je/Jl 2017

PICKLE RECIPES for the Picking: Ferment or quick-pickle your harvest with this assortment of ideas from Mother Earth News bloggers *Mother Earth News* no282 p56 Je/Jl 2017

Quillévéré, Katell, 1980-

Heal the Living K. M. JONES color *Film Comment* v53 no2 p66 Mr/Ap 2017

Quilliam, Susan

The Fallacy of Finding Your One True Love S. Begley color *Time* v189 no4 p22 Ja 23 2017

Quillian, Lincoln

Hiring Discrimination Against Black Americans Hasn't Declined in 25 Years *Harvard Business Review Digital Articles* p2 O 11 2017

Quillico, Franco

What Big Companies Can Learn from the Success of the Unicorns *Harvard Business Review Digital Articles* p2 Mr 14 2016

Quilligan, E.

Improving global integration of crop research color *Science* v357 no6349 p359 Jl 28 2017

Quilted goods

EDITOR'S LETTER G. Cerio color *Magazine Antiques* v184 no2 p16 Mr/Ap 2017

Quilting

Outlaw Trail Byway becomes a 'Quiltway' A. J. BARTELS color *Nebraska Life* v21 no5 p88 S/O 2017

Quilts

CALENDAR OF EVENTS *Idaho Magazine* v16 no1 p58 Ap 2017

Tucson Sector Deaths 2000–2001 Quilt *Christian Century* v134 no14 p47 Jl 5 2017

Quilts—Evaluation

Modern Marriage color *House Beautiful* v159 no2 p43 Mr 2017

shopping secrets OF THE PROS K. O'SHEA-EVANS and H. BROWN color *House Beautiful* v159 no3 p46 Ap 2017

Summer Covers color *House Beautiful* v159 no5 p46 Je 2017

Quilts—Exhibitions

EVENTS S. Dalati *Magazine Antiques* v184 no2 p133 Mr/Ap 2017

A stitch in wartime: The American Folk Art Museum presents a fascinating collection of quilts made by men at arms S. C. Hollander and A. Gero bw color *Magazine Antiques* v184 no4 p92 Jl/Ag 2017

Quilts—History

LOVE YOUR HOMEMADE QUILT? THANK CAPITALISM V. POSTREL color *Reason* v48 no8 p14 Ja 2017

Quimby, R.

iPTF16geu: A multiply imaged, gravitationally lensed type Ia supernova color diag graph *Science* v356 no6335 p291 Ap 21 2017

Quimby, Roxanne

My Maine N. LUND *National Parks* v91 no2 p12 Spr 2017

Quimpo, Susan F.

Subversive Lives: A Family Memoir of the Marcos Years *Foreign Affairs* v96 no2 p188 Mr/Ap 2017

Quinault, Roland

The Double Life of the Mandarin *History Today* v67 no4 p65 Ap 2017

Who martyred the Tolpuddle Labourers? *History Today* v67 no4 p10 Ap 2017

Quinceañera (Social custom)

Rites of Passage color *Chicago* v65 no12 p104 D 2016

Quincey, James, ca. 1965

Interview Coke's James Quincey J. Kaplan color *Bloomberg Businessweek* no4522 p28 My 15 2017

Quinine

50, 100 & 150 YEARS AGO color *Scientific American* v317 no4 p93 O 2017

Quinlan, Elizabeth

IN THE DARK R. Wiedeman cartoon *New Yorker* v92 no42 p49 D 19 2016

QUINLAN, M. K.

fantasy island color *House Beautiful* v159 no7 p78 S 2017

Modern Compromise color *Southern Living* v52 no1 p15 Ja 2017

RETURN TO EDEN color *House Beautiful* v159 no3 p84 Ap 2017

STARTING FRESH color *House Beautiful* v159 no4 p108 My

2017

Quinn, Alana

Laurie Frick color *Issues in Science & Technology* v33 no1 p6 Fall 2016

Quinn, Annalisa

Fever Dreams: The 'witch hunt' once made scapegoats out of the defenseless. How did it become a complaint of the powerful? *New York Times Magazine* p13 Je 11 2017

Swipe Write: Courtney Maum's exuberant novel sends up the world of techie consumerism *New York Times Book Review* p17 Je 11 2017

Quinn, Dan

DON'T HOLD BACK G. Bishop color *Sports Illustrated* v126 no10 p60 Ap 10 2017

Quinn, Greg

A Raise for Mexican Workers? graph *Bloomberg Businessweek* no4534 p29 Ag 14 2017

Quinn, Harley (Fictitious character)

The 18th Annual Alternative Oscars color *Esquire* v167 no1 p15 F 2017

Quinn, Kevin R.

The SAILING SCENE color *Sail* v48 no11 p6 N 2017

Quinn, Matthew

Gilty Pleasure color *House Beautiful* v159 no2 p74 Mr 2017

Quinn, Mattie

Are Doctors Finally Ready for Data? 'Health informatics' focuses on delivering better medical outcomes *Governing* v31 no1 p18 O 2017

ARE WE TALKING ABOUT OPIOIDS THE WAY? Officials say they're doing everything they can to stop the epidemic. But a real solution may be a lot more complicated *Governing* v30 no10 p38 Jl 2017

A Better Rx: States are making their much-criticized drug monitoring programs easier to use *Governing* v30 no8 p18 My 2017

Community Corps *Governing* v30 no6 p44 Mr 2017

Faith Healers *Governing* v30 no4 p52 Ja 2017

Faith Healers *Governing* v30 no6 p6 Mr 2017

Free for All *Governing* v30 no1 p52 O 2016

How Safe Does a Hospital Need to Be? *Governing* v30 no6 p18 Mr 2017

In Session: School Clinics: More and more, they're seen as an important part of the social safety net *Governing* v30 no9 p18 Je 2017

A Little Learning *Governing* v30 no5 p44 F 2017

MARIJUANA *Governing* v30 no4 p34 Ja 2017

Maternity Crisis: Texas is the most dangerous place in America to have a baby. There are many reasons why *Governing* v30 no8 p50 My 2017

The Medicaid Effect *Governing* v30 no5 p20 F 2017

The Medicaid Flexibility Puzzle: How much freedom should states have to tailor the program to local conditions? *Governing* v30 no12 p18 S 2017

OBAMACARE *Governing* v30 no4 p30 Ja 2017

OPIOIDS *Governing* v30 no4 p35 Ja 2017

PUBLIC OFFICIALS OF THE YEAR *Governing* v30 no3 p26 D 2016

Right at Home: Seniors want doctors to come to them. States are still working out how to pay for it *Governing* v30 no10 p18 Jl 2017

A Shot In the Arm *Governing* v30 no3 p18 D 2016

Speeding Up Baby's First Test *Governing* v30 no2 p18 N 2016

Unhealthy Habits *Governing* v30 no1 p18 O 2016

The Walking Cure *Governing* v30 no4 p18 Ja 2017

WHAT'S LOCAL ANYWAY? *Governing* v30 no7 p50 Ap 2017

When a Health Department Fails: Is a growing focus on community factors coming at the expense of basic care? color *Governing* v30 no11 p18 Ag 2017

Where HIV and Housing Intersect *Governing* v30 no7 p18 Ap 2017

Yes, I Make House Calls: The once-antiquated practice of doctors' home visits is making a comeback--and saving states money *Governing* v30 no12 p48 S 2017

ZIKA *Governing* v30 no4 p33 Ja 2017

Quinn, Nathaniel Mary

FRACTURED MEMORIES S. WORLEY color *Chicago* v66 no9 p56 S 2017

Quinn, Nicole F.

Bugged color *Science* v356 no6342 p1007 Je 9 2017

Quinn, Peter

Out of Reach color *Commonweal* v144 no17 p11 O 20 2017

Quinn, Robert E.

Change Management and Leadership Development Have to Mesh *Harvard Business Review Digital Articles* p2 Ja 7 2016

Quinn, Ryan W.

Change Management and Leadership Development Have to Mesh *Harvard Business Review Digital Articles* p2 Ja 7 2016

Why You Shouldn't Label People "Low Performers" *Harvard Business Review Digital Articles* p2 S 14 2016

Quinn, S.

Observation of a large-scale anisotropy in the arrival directions of cosmic rays above 8×10^{18} eV *Science* v357 no6357 p1266 S 22 2017

Quinn, Sally

82 MINUTES WITH...Sally Quinn B. WALLACE *New York* v49 no26 p16 D 26 2016

SALLY QUINN'S NEXT ACT M. COTTLE *Washingtonian Magazine* v52 no12 p72 S 2017

WHEN WHO MET SALLY? A. BEAUJON *Washingtonian Magazine* v52 no2 p21 N 2016

Quinn, Sally—Interviews

Sally Quinn *New York Times Book Review* p7 S 17 2017

Quinn, Susan

'Just What You Are to Me' A. VAILL *New York Times Book Review* p11 O 16 2016

Quinn, Zoe

Crash Override: How GamerGate (Nearly) Destroyed My Life, and How We Can Win the Fight Against Online Hate color *Publishers Weekly* v264 no30 p52 Jl 24 2017

Zoë and the Trolls N. MALONE img *New York* v50 no15 p21 Jl 24 2017

Quinn Emanuel Urquhart & Sullivan LLP—Trials, litigation, etc.

A Lawyer Stalks Wall Street Banks M. Robinson color *Bloomberg Businessweek* no4528 p24 Je 26 2017

Quinoa

THE BEST FOOD FOR MEN 2017 [Cover story] P. KITA cartoon color *Men's Health* v32 no1 p106 Ja/F 2017

For a Longer, Healthier Life chart color *AARP: The Magazine* v59 no3A p43 Ap/My 2016

QUINONES, SAM

THE QUEEN OF FLORENCIA bw color *Los Angeles Magazine* v62 no10 p134 O 2017

Quintana, Catalina

Forest conservation: Humans' handprints bibl color *Science* v355 no6324 p466 F 3 2017

Forest conservation: Remember Gran Chaco bibl color *Science* v355 no6324 p465 F 3 2017

Quintana, Maclovia

Without inclusion, diversity initiatives may not be enough color *Science* v357 no6356 p1101 S 15 2017

Quintana-Murci, Lluís

Dispersals and genetic adaptation of Bantu-speaking populations in Africa and North America diag *Science* v356 no6337 p543 My 5 2017

QUINTANILLA, MARIAH

Castaway critters rafted to U.S. shores on Japan tsunami debris [Cover story] color *Science News* v192 no7 p4 O 28 2017

Debris arrivals divvied up color map *Science News* v192 no7 p32 O 28 2017

Hermit crab takes shelter in corals color *Science News* v192 no7 p14 O 28 2017

Researcher goes all in to study eel electricity color graph *Science News* v192 no6 p4 O 14 2017

Upside-down jellyfish pass sleep test color *Science News* v192 no7 p10 O 28 2017

Quintero-Bermudez, Rafael

Efficient and stable solution-processed planar perovskite solar cells via contact passivation bibl graph *Science* v355 no6326 p722 F 17 2017

Quintets

Melodic Devotion G. Himes color *Downbeat* v84 no10 p28 O 2017

zine v52 no12 p22 S 2017

Raabe, Dierk

Bone-like crack resistance in hierarchical metastable nanolaminate steels bibl color diag *Science* v355 no6329 p1055 Mr 10 2017

Rab, Lisa

CHANCES OF ACCEPTANCE: The number-one high school in America is less than 5 percent African-American and Latino. Does that make it racist? *Washingtonian Magazine* v52 no8 p48 My 2017

Rabaey, Elizabeth

In Search of Color K. Palmer color *AARP: The Magazine* v59 no4A p30 Je/Jl 2016

Rabani, Eran

Single-particle mapping of nonequilibrium nanocrystal transformations bibl bw graph *Science* v354 no6314 p874 N 18 2016

Rabanne, Paco

PACO RABANNE Fashion CRUSH E. Wilson color *InStyle* v24 no8 p140 Ag 2017

Rabarts, Dan

Hounds of the Underworld: The Path of Ra, Book 1 *Publishers Weekly* v264 no27 p58 Jl 3 2017

RABB, MARGO

Advice Needed: A teenager faces the sudden loss of her mother and her dad's new dating life *New York Times Book Review* p15 Je 18 2017

Rabbit Air (Company)

THE BEST BET img *New York* v50 no9 p59 My 1 2017

Rabbit behavior

Unleashed cartoon *National Geographic Kids* no472 p32 Ag 2017

Rabbit hunting

A LABRADOR OF LOVE J. M. TURNER cartoon *Outdoor Life* v224 no1 p16 D 2016/Ja 2017

SO, YOU WANT A RABBIT DOG? T. CARPENTER color *Outdoor Life* v224 no7 pH11 S 2017

Rabbit in the Moon (Film)

RABBIT IN AND OUT OF THE MOON: A RETROSPECTIVE OF EMIKO OMORI Ling Zhang *Film Quarterly* v71 no1 p42 Fall 2017

Rabbits

Ehh, what's up, Victoria? C. SORENSEN color *Maclean's* v129 no40 p30 O 10 2016

THE GRID: ANIMAL ANTICS *Saturday Evening Post* v289 no5 p26 S/O 2017

Guinness World Records color *National Geographic Kids* no472 p5 Ag 2017

Laugh Out Loud color *National Geographic Kids* no475 p33 N 2017

My Shot *National Geographic Kids* no469 p39 Ap 2017

UNSOLICITED BETA M. Hook, M. Bourguignon et al color *Climbing* no351 p18 F/Mr 2017

Rabbits—Behavior

Adopt a Critter S. Bower chart color *Good Housekeeping* v264 no4 p140 Ap 2017

RABBITT, MEGHAN

16 BEST YOGA ESCAPES [Cover story] color *Yoga Journal* no290 p19 Mr 2017

BLEND ambition color *Yoga Journal* no290 p77 Mr 2017

BOOST your breakfast color *Yoga Journal* no288 p73 D 2016

CHAKRA ALIGNMENT color *Yoga Journal* no288 p64 D 2016

clear THE AIR color *Yoga Journal* no290 p17 Mr 2017

EMBRACE YOUR NATURAL BEAUTY color *Yoga Journal* no294 p27 S 2017

Get more out of life color *Redbook* p100 N 2017

ghee WIZ color *Yoga Journal* no287 p63 N 2016

haute COCOA color *Yoga Journal* no289 p67 F 2017

intention INSPIRATION [Cover story] color *Yoga Journal* no290 p45 Mr 2017

Kat Fowler color *Yoga Journal* no296 p10 N 2017

meaningful MUDRAS color *Yoga Journal* no287 p31 N 2016

MEDITATE in the moment color *Yoga Journal* no291 p47 My 2017

The mindful diet color *Yoga Journal* p110 2016 Special Issue

PILGRIMAGE TO INDIA [Cover story] color *Yoga Journal* no290 p34 Mr 2017

pretty CALM color *Yoga Journal* no287 p13 N 2016

rise and RAVE color *Yoga Journal* no289 p35 F 2017

take OM HOME color *Yoga Journal* no288 p96 D 2016

take OM HOME color *Yoga Journal* no290 p96 Mr 2017

THIS IS WHAT SEVA LOOKS LIKE [Cover story] color *Yoga Journal* no295 p40 O 2017

the upside of doing NOTHING color *Yoga Journal* no289 p17 F 2017

write your mind color *Yoga Journal* no294 p53 S 2017

Rabe, Lily

American Horror Story Is Frightfully Good With Secrets D. D'Addario color *Time* v188 no19 p55 N 7 2016

Rabensteiner, Robert—Interviews

ROBERT RABENSTEINER bw color *Esquire* v167 no1 p41 F 2017

Rabesandratana, Tania

Catalan scientists ponder fate after independence vote color *Science* v357 no6359 p23 O 6 2017

Rabies

United States color *National Geographic* v232 no4 p4 O 2017

Rabies in animals

Rabies C. Barakat color *Equus* no477 p29 Je 2017

Rabies—Vaccination

TAMING RABIES E. Stokstad color graph map *Science* v355 no6322 p238 Ja 20 2017

RABIN, NINA

WOMEN ON THE RUN *Ms.* v27 no2 p18 Summ 2017

Rabinovich, Itamar

ISRAEL'S INDEPENDENT INTROVERT: The assassination of Yitzhak Rabin robbed Israel of a rare politician able to make peace with the Palestinians C. Shindler *History Today* v67 no9 p104 S 2017

The spirit of Israel K. P. Spicer *America* v216 no12 p50 My 29 2017

RABINOVITCH, LARA

FROM NAPLES TO HOLLYWOOD *Los Angeles Magazine* p44 Ja 2017

High on CottonHi *Los Angeles Magazine* v61 no11 p132 N 2016

Rabinowitz, Joshua D.

Systems-level analysis of mechanisms regulating yeast metabolic flux bibl diag graph *Science* v354 no6311 paaf2786-1 O 28 2016

Rabinyan, Dorit

Dorit Rabinyan C. Mari color *Current Biography* v78 no9 p71 S 2017

Irresistible Force D. SCHARPER *Weekly Standard* v22 no39 p39 Je 19 2017

RABITSCH, WOLFGANG

Scientific and Normative Foundations for the Valuation of Alien-Species Impacts: Thirteen Core Principles *BioScience* v67 no2 p166 F 2017

Rabkin, Jeremy

LIBERTY OR DEATH *Claremont Review of Books* v16 no4 p35 Fall 2016

Raboteau, Albert

American Prophets: Seven Religious Radicals and Their Struggle for Social and Political Justice D. Sack *Christian Century* v134 no16 p34 Ag 2 2017

What God Demands S. Haarman bw *Commonweal* v143 no18 p43 N 11 2016

Rabun, Jacqueline

Jacqueline RABUN: THE LONDON-BASED JEWELRY DESIGNER CREATES MODERN, COVETABLE WORKS OF ART MEANT TO BE WORN AND CHERISHED C. KELSEY *Interview* v47 no3 p38 Ap 2017

Raccah, Dominique

DOMINIQUE RACCAH J. MILLIOT color *Publishers Weekly* v263 no52 p20 D 19 2016

Raccoon

Cheers & Jeers R. Kidd, R. J. Hicks et al color *Field & Stream* v122 no3 p11 Ag 2017

RACCON SCALES BUILDING S. Schwartz *National Geographic Kids* no467 p12 F 2017

RACCOON S. ELDER *National Geographic Kids* no468 p20 Mr 2017

RISE of the SYNANTHROPES K. BANKS color *Canadian Geographic* v137 no3 p56 My 2017

United States color *National Geographic* v232 no4 p4 O 2017

Raccoon—Behavior

Peekaboo cartoon color *National Wildlife (World Edition)* v55 no3 p50 Ap/My 2017

Race

1970: St. Louis *Lapham's Quarterly* v10 no1 p62 Wint 2017

An Invitation C. FINNEY *Orion Magazine* v35 no4/5 p46 Jl-O 2016

MY BUS: A LOVE LETTER: What Metrobus's most popular route can tell us about our city D. Reed *Washingtonian Magazine* v52 no12 p51 S 2017

SNAPCHAT C. WARE cartoon *New Yorker* v92 no37 p44 N 14 2016

Solidarity S. BHATTI *In These Times* v41 no1 p29 Ja 2017

Race & politics

WHITE, BLACK, & RED J. A. MYERSON bw color *Nation* v304 no16 p21 My 22 2017

Race (Film)

And the Award Goes to   T. Keith color *Sports Illustrated* v126 no5 p18 F 13 2017

Race awareness

See also

Racial identity of African Americans

Racism

Q+A S. STALL *Indianapolis Monthly* v12 no40 p89 Ag 2017

Race discrimination

Basic Instinct E. Bazelon *New York Times Magazine* p13 O 23 2016

A Better Way to Fight Discrimination in the Sharing Economy Jun Li, D. Zhang et al color *Harvard Business Review Digital Articles* p2 F 27 2017

The Challenge of Being a Black Principal in Today's Racial and Political Climate L. Khan *Education Digest* v82 no4 p4 D 2016

Dealing with Unexpected Bias A. Ignatius color *Harvard Business Review* v94 no12 p12 D 2016

Don't Say Nothing J. PITTS *Education Digest* v82 no7 p50 Mr 2017

FINDINGS *Harper's Magazine* v335 no2006 p96 Jl 2017

Hair Apparent J. WEAVER *Walrus* v14 no7 p66 S 2017

On being white P. W. Marty *Christian Century* v134 no17 p3 Ag 16 2017

Segregation on the Charles K. SMITH *National Review* v69 no12 p44 Je 26 2017

The Whole World Was Watching [Cover story] C. ALLEN color *Weekly Standard* v22 no39 p26 Je 19 2017

WHY BLACK LIVES MATTER TO U.S. INTELLIGENCE *Vital Speeches of the Day* v83 no2 p55 F 2017

Race discrimination in education

Desegregation Since the Coleman Report S. RIVKIN *Education Digest* v82 no5 p26 Ja 2017

Doing science while black E. J. Smith color *Science* v353 no6307 p1586 S 30 2016

Joining Hands: Race, Social Justice, and Equal Opportunity in Your Classroom J. L. DAVIS *Education Digest* v82 no4 p42 D 2016

New Education Majority: Attitudes and Aspirations of Parents and Families of Color *Education Digest* v82 no4 p55 D 2016

Race discrimination in employment

The Talk About Racial Bias Companies Should Be Having M. Gee *Harvard Business Review Digital Articles* p2 Ag 23 2016

Race discrimination in law enforcement

The Organizational Reasons Police Departments Don't Change B. Armacost *Harvard Business Review Digital Articles* p2 Ag 19 2016

Race discrimination in medical care

The Costs of Racial Disparities in Health Care J. Z. Ayanian *Harvard Business Review Digital Articles* p2 O 1 2015

Race discrimination—South Africa

THE LAST WHITE AFRICANS E. FAIRBANKS color *Foreign Policy* no222 p48 Ja/F 2017

Race discrimination—United States

THE BE 100s FOR A NEW GENERATION E. G. Graves Jr. color *Black Enterprise* v47 no7 p8 My/Je 2017

Beyond black and white: To make conversations about race more productive, try using different metaphors for God G. Ji-Sun Kim color *U.S. Catholic* v82 no10 p25 O 2017

Desegregation Since the Coleman Report S. RIVKIN *Education*

Digest v82 no5 p26 Ja 2017

Little Coffee Shop of Horrors color *Weekly Standard* v22 no43 p2 Jl 24 2017

Off-Limits A. Greenblatt *Governing* v30 no12 p12 S 2017

SOUTHERN HARM W. Faulkner diag *Harper's Magazine* v335 no2005 p39 Je 2017

TRUMPED J. Amber color *Essence* v48 no5 p100 S 2017

"What Are You?" L. BROCK, J. Bianchi et al *Scholastic Choices* v32 no7 p20 Ap 2017

Race horses

See also

Thoroughbred horse

2017 STALLION Directory II *Arabian Horse World* v57 no6 p160 Mr 2017

BREEDERS PROFILES *Arabian Horse World* v57 no3 p120 D 2016

A CONVRSATION with Thomas Fourcy Al Shaqab Racing-Ecuric Haras Bouquetot Sas S. Andersen and D. Hearst *Arabian Horse World* v57 no6 p56 Mr 2017

DARLEY PREVIEW S. Andersen *Arabian Horse World* v57 no6 p16 Mr 2017

DREAM Team T. Layden color *Sports Illustrated* v126 no14 p50 My 15-22 2017

Horse Nonsense T. Layden and T. Keith color *Sports Illustrated* v126 no13 p18 My 8 2017

Leading Off color *Sports Illustrated* v126 no14 p8 My 15-22 2017

RANKINGS Top International Racehorses S. Andersen *Arabian Horse World* v57 no6 p60 Mr 2017

Race horses—Awards

HH Sheikh Mansoor Festival Races at Sam Houston Race Park S. Andersen color *Arabian Horse World* v57 no7 p98 Ap 2017

PERFORMANCE HORSE AWARD PROGRAM RECIPIENTS RECOGNIZED AT THE 2016 EGYPTIAN EVENT *Arabian Horse World* v57 no3 p115 D 2016

Race horses—Breeding

In Memory of Sundance Kis V. G. Dearth color *Arabian Horse World* v57 no7 p140 Ap 2017

Race horses—Health

TRAVEL TACTICS M. DEPAOLO *Arabian Horse World* v57 no6 p156 Mr 2017

Race horses—Names

In Memory of Sundance Kis V. G. Dearth color *Arabian Horse World* v57 no7 p140 Ap 2017

Race horses—Wounds & injuries

HERE YOU COME AGAIN J. Mankin color *Spin to Win Rodeo* v20 no11 p40 Ja 2017

Race identity

White like me J. RICHARDSON *Phi Delta Kappan* v98 no5 p4 F 2017

Race in literature

Beyond Genealogy: On the wealth of stories that family novels leave behind J. Lucas *New York Times Book Review* p18 S 3 2017

Race preferences (Affirmative action)—Lawsuits & claims

The Many Shades of Maíra Mutti Araújo C. DE OLIVEIRA bw color *Foreign Policy* no225 p46 Jl/Ag 2017

Race relations

See also

Postracialism

How Much Progress Has Been Made? *USA Today Magazine* v145 no2863 p3 Ap 2017

Race relations in school management

See also

School integration

Segregation in education

THE SECESSION MOVEMENT IN EDUCATION E. FELTON and N. Lewis bw color graph map *Nation* v305 no7 p12 S 25 2017

Race relations—Religious aspects—Christianity

The ministry of showing up K. Childress *Christian Century* v133 no23 p10 N 9 2016

Race—Congresses

"Teaching" Social Justice E. PEPPERS *USA Today Magazine* v145 no2864 p70 My 2017

Race—History—19th century

FABLES OF THE RECONSTRUCTION T. MURPHY bw *Moth-*

er Jones v42 no4 p55 Jl/Ag 2017

Race horses—Charts, diagrams, etc.
TOP RANKED U.S. RACEHORSES *Arabian Horse World* v57 no6 p63 Mr 2017

Race—Political aspects—History—21st century
4 Steps for the Next President O. Tometi color *Time* v188 no16/17 p63 O 24 2016

Racers (Persons)
See also
Automobile racing drivers
CHANGE IS GOOD A. Stanley bw color *Seventeen* v76 no4 p80 Jl/Ag 2017
Lewis HAMILTON S. WILLIAMS *Interview* v47 no6 p68 Ag 2017

Race—Social aspects
Blind Spots G. Marino color *Commonweal* v143 no17 p38 O 21 2016
TIM RYAN'S AWAKENING E. McGirt color diag *Fortune* v175 no2 p58 F 1 2017

Racetracks (Automobile racing)
BEST DRIVER'S LAP K. Reynolds bw color diag *Motor Trend* v69 no11 p80 N 2017
Christmas at 120 MPH bw color map *GQ: Gentlemen's Quarterly* v86 no12 p112 D 2016
A CHUNK OF BAJA J. OBER color *Dirt Sports + Off-Road* v51 no8 p74 Ag 2017
THE FAST AND THE FILTHY RICH J. DEAN color *Bloomberg Businessweek* no4510 p55 F 6 2017
I'VE GOT SOMETHING TO CONFESS... A. KELLER LAIRD color *Women's Health* v14 no2 p8 Mr 2017
LUCAS OIL OFF-ROAD RACING PUSHES EAST [Cover story] S. OCHSNER color *Dirt Sports + Off-Road* v51 no12 p24 D 2017

Racetracks (Automobile racing)—Design & construction
Walk a Line S. SMITH color *Road & Track* v69 no1 p28 Ag 2017

Racetracks (Horse racing)
SPRING RACING IN THE GULF Kahayla Classic and Qatar Gold Sword S. Andersen *Arabian Horse World* v57 no8 p117 My 2017

Rachel Maddow Show, The (TV program)
Rachel After Dark S. Smith color *Entertainment Weekly* no1435 p32 O 14 2016
THE STORYTELLER J. MALCOLM bw cartoon *New Yorker* v93 no31 p38 O 9 2017

RACHLIN, BENJAMIN
NEW HAMPSHIRE HAS THE SECOND-HIGHEST RATE OF DRUG OVERDOSES IN THE COUNTRY. A POLICE OF-FICER IN LACONIA (POPULATION 16,000) HAS BEEN ASSIGNED ONE TASK: TO STOP THEM *New York Times Magazine* p22 Jl 16 2017

RACHLOW, JANET
Tough Choices for a Pygmy Rabbit color map *Natural History* v125 no3 p9 Mr 2017

Rachman, Gideon
Can China Replace the West? [Cover story] J. T. Mathews color *New York Review of Books* v64 no8 p14 My 11 2017
Easternization: Asia's Rise and America's Decline, From Obama to Trump and Beyond A. J. Nathan *Foreign Affairs* v96 no3 p172 My/Je 2017
Hemispheric Pressures: As power shifts from West to East, what does it mean for the United States? T. J. CHRISTENSEN *New York Times Book Review* p31 My 14 2017

Racial differences
The Costs of Racial Disparities in Health Care J. Z. Ayanian *Harvard Business Review Digital Articles* p2 O 1 2015
Gun Culture in Black and White D. FRENCH *National Review* v69 no3 p36 F 20 2017
THE HIDDEN COST OF RACE J. Surowiecki cartoon *New Yorker* v92 no32 p39 O 10 2016

Racial identity of African Americans
Group Think L. Lalami *New York Times Magazine* p15 N 27 2016

Racial identity of racially mixed people
FROM THE ARCHIVES N. GILLESPIE, M. WELCH et al bw color *Reason* v49 no3 p70 Jl 2016

Racial profiling in law enforcement
The Law Is King color *Weekly Standard* v23 no1 p6 S 11 2017

Racicot, Riccardo
MUTANT VEGETARIANS? *Vegetarian Journal* v36 no1 p26 2017

Racine, Jean-François
BOOKS ON THE BIBLE color *America* v216 no9 p28 Ap 24 2017

Racing
See also
Automobile racing
Horse racing
Motorcycle racing
Off-road racing
Running races
Sailboat racing
Ski racing
Truck racing
2017 SCHEDULE chart *Dirt Sports + Off-Road* v51 no4 p73 Ap 2017
FEVERED DAZE B. Schott color *Powder* v45 no5 p102 Ja 2017

Racing automobile design & construction
RETRO FIRE S. Kwak color *Sports Illustrated* v127 no10 p20 O 2 2017

Racing automobile maintenance & repair
How Do Tuned, Equal-Length Headers Work? M. Davis color *Hot Rod* v70 no10 p86 O 2017
LOADED FOR BEARING M. Davis bw color *Hot Rod* v70 no10 p88 O 2017
Under Pressure P. Thomas color *Hot Rod* v70 no12 p26 D 2017
Why Are There 1970 1/2 Camaros? T. Taylor color *Hot Rod* v70 no10 p84 O 2017

Racing automobiles
See also
Audi R8 automobile
Dragsters
Formula One automobiles
Hot rods
McLaren automobiles
Sports cars
The Beginning of the End of the Rear-Engine Funny Car T. Taylor color *Hot Rod* v69 no12 p12 D 2016
CARS AND SAKI color *Road & Track* v69 no2 p14 S 2017
Chariot of Fire J. MacGregor *Smithsonian* v48 no3 p26 Je 2017
The Drivetrain in Kevin Maher's 1971 Dodge Challenger Has a Serious and Constant Vibration. We're Gonna Fix It M. Davis chart color diag *Hot Rod* v70 no4 p88 Ap 2017
The First HOT ROD Power Tour T. Taylor color *Hot Rod* v70 no9 p10 S 2017
The HOT ROD Archives D. Wallace color *Hot Rod* v70 no7 p14 Jl 2017
THE INSANE TURBONIQUE TALE OF MAGIC BULLET MADNESS T. Taylor bw color diag *Hot Rod* v70 no4 p52 Ap 2017
NO REGRETS B. W. SMITH color *Dirt Sports + Off-Road* v51 no5 p18 My 2017
A SHEEP IN WOLF'S CLOTHING J. BARUTH color *Road & Track* v68 no8 p30 My 2017
Take 5 With CHRIS MCGAHA color *Hot Rod* v70 no10 p18 O 2017
TRANSFORMED color *Road & Track* v69 no2 p16 S 2017
Where Should EFI Nozzles Be Located on the Intake Runner for Best Performance? M. Davis color *Hot Rod* v70 no4 p86 Ap 2017
Why the Rare Willys Was the Go-To Gasser T. Taylor color *Hot Rod* v70 no4 p84 Ap 2017

Racing automobiles—Competitions
Pomona Fairgrounds Dragstrip, May 1958 T. Taylor bw *Hot Rod* v70 no10 p10 O 2017

Racing automobiles—Conservation & restoration
Birds in the Barn—and a Charger! R. Brutt color *Hot Rod* v70 no7 p20 Jl 2017

Racing automobiles—Design & construction
CONSOLODATED POWER M. EMERY color *Dirt Sports + Off-Road* v51 no5 p34 My 2017

Racing automobiles—Equipment & supplies
CONSOLODATED POWER M. EMERY color *Dirt Sports + Off-Road* v51 no5 p34 My 2017

Naureckas *Extra!* v29 no8 p3 O 2016

Righting Words R. HILL, G. CAZARES et al color *O, The Oprah Magazine* p17 Jl 2017

"THIS IS A WAR AND WE INTEND TO WIN" W. ENZINNA bw color *Mother Jones* v42 no3 p14 My/Je 2017

A Town Violated J. Grisham color *Time* v190 no8 p44 Ag 28 2017

Unity Will Take Generations I. Omar *Time* v190 no8 p44 Ag 28 2017

WELCOME TO THE RESISTANCE Z. Exley *In These Times* v40 no12 p14 D 2016

When The Past Is Present K. JORDAN *Los Angeles Magazine* v62 no7 p15 Jl 2017

White moral infantilism and some help avoiding it color *Christian Century* v134 no8 p1 Ap 12 2017

Racism—United States—History

As Racial Tensions Lead The News, Books Follow R. FARMER color *Publishers Weekly* v263 no45 p1 N 7 2016

Racism—United States—Law & legislation

BEST of TIMES WORST of TIMES T. Heller and D. Schofield cartoon *Esquire* v166 no5 p138 D 2016/Ja 2017

Rackets (Sporting goods)

COURT ORDERS! J. Leishman and D. DeNunzio color *Golf Magazine* v59 no9 p63 S 2017

Rackets (Sporting goods)—Evaluation

BEST HEAVY HITTER color *Tennis* v53 no2 p46 Mr/Ap 2017

Raczka, Bob

Wet Cement: A Mix of Concrete Poems color *Publishers Weekly* v263 no49 p55 D 7 2016

Rada, Nicholas

Agricultural Recovery in Russia and the Rise of Its South *Amber Waves: The Economics of Food, Farming, Natural Resources, & Rural America* p10 Ap 2017

Radaelli, Enrico

De novo design of a biologically active amyloid bibl graph *Science* v354 no6313 paah4949-1 N 11 2016

Radar

HERD REPLACEMENTS: RAISE OR BUY? THAT QUESTION IS BACK ON THE RADAR WITH MUCH LOWER PRICES G. Johnston *Successful Farming* v115 no6 p59 Ap 2017

Radar indicators

Danger Zone? J. Y. WOOD color *Power & Motoryacht* v34 no11 p62 N 2017

Radar meteorology

CROWD-SOURCED WEATHER color *Flying* v144 no4 p18 Ap 2017

Radar—Equipment & supplies—Evaluation

SPOT GEN3® *Sea Magazine* v108 no12 p54 D 2016

Radar—Evaluation

NEW ELECTRONICS J. Y. WOOD color map *Power & Motoryacht* v32 no12 p26 D 2016

Radar—Software

BETTER RADAR APP color *Flying* v144 no9 p14 S 2017

Radbod, Yasmin

Being Vegan in Cairo *Vegetarian Journal* v35 no4 p24 2016

John Shields *Vegetarian Journal* v35 no4 p12 2016

A Vegan in a Refugee Camp on the Thai-Burma Border *Vegetarian Journal* v35 no2 p6 2016

Radcliffe, Daniel, 1989-

Pop Chart R. Bruner, C. Lang et al color *Time* v188 no14 p62 O 10 2016

Raddatz, Martha, 1953-

STORIES OF SERVICE AND SACRIFICE S. Goldberg color *National Geographic* v232 no5 p2 N 2017

Radel, Trey, 1976—Interviews

IN HINDSIGHT E. Plott color *Washingtonian Magazine* v52 no7 p22 Ap 2017

TREY Radel R. J. SMITH *Cincinnati Magazine* v50 no7 p58 Ap 2017

RADELOFF, CHERYL L.

SENATOR-ELECT CATHERINE CORTEZ MASTO *Ms.* v26 no3 p8 Fall 2016

Rademacher, Anne

Dramatizing Deepwater Horizon color *Science* v356 no6335 p256 Ap 21 2017

Inside Cuba bibl *Science* v355 no6320 p34 Ja 6 2017

Rader, Dana

NO MORE CHIPPING HANG-UPS color *Golf Magazine* v58 no12 p81 D 2016

Rader, Daniel J.

"Pheno"menal value for human health bibl diag *Science* v354 no6319 p1534 D 23 2016

Rader, Kelly

Research: Opposition to Federal Spending Is Driven by Racial Resentment *Harvard Business Review Digital Articles* p2 S 1 2017

Radetzky von Radetz, Johann Joseph Wenzel, Graf, 1766-1858

Radetzky's march into obscurity G. Darby *History Today* v66 no12 p28 D 2016

Radevski, Ivan

Changing climate shifts timing of European floods color graph *Science* v357 no6351 p588 Ag 11 2017

RADFORD, ANDREW N.

Shipbuilding Docks as Experimental Systems for Realistic Assessments of Anthropogenic Stressors on Marine Organisms *BioScience* v67 no9 p853 S 2017

Radford, Benjamin

Animas River Spill Spawns Conspiracy Theories *Skeptical Inquirer* v40 no6 p11 N/D 2016

Apollo Astronauts Claimed to Hear 'Space Music' *Skeptical Inquirer* v40 no6 p13 N/D 2016

Astounding Tales of Science! *Skeptical Inquirer* v41 no2 p66 Mr/Ap 2017

Can Electromagnetic Fields Create Ghosts? *Skeptical Inquirer* v41 no3 p30 My/Je 2017

Ghost Hunters in the Dark *Skeptical Inquirer* v41 no1 p32 Ja/F 2017

'Ghostly' Image at Haunted Stanley Hotel *Skeptical Inquirer* v40 no6 p9 N/D 2016

A Glimpse Backward—and Forward—at Skepticism's Big Tent *Skeptical Inquirer* v40 no6 p43 N/D 2016

A Good Analysis of Bad UFO Information *Skeptical Inquirer* v41 no4 p61 Jl/Ag 2017

Home Itch Remedies *Skeptical Inquirer* v41 no1 p66 Ja/F 2017

Kazoo Magazine Aims to Encourage Girls in Science *Skeptical Inquirer* v41 no3 p7 My/Je 2017

THE LAST LAUGH *Skeptical Inquirer* v41 no4 p66 Jl/Ag 2017

The Legacy of Fake Bomb Detectors in Iraq *Skeptical Inquirer* v41 no1 p7 Ja/F 2017

'M' Is for Mysterious Marks *Skeptical Inquirer* v40 no6 p30 N/D 2016

Mystery of the Paulding Light *Skeptical Inquirer* v41 no2 p36 Mr/Ap 2017

NEW AND NOTABLE *Skeptical Inquirer* v41 no1 p60 Ja/F 2017

NEW AND NOTABLE *Skeptical Inquirer* v41 no5 p60 S/O 2017

Odysseys in Skepticism *Skeptical Inquirer* v41 no2 p65 Mr/Ap 2017

Orbs as Plasma Life *Skeptical Inquirer* v41 no5 p28 S/O 2017

The Phoenix Driveway Ghost *Skeptical Inquirer* v41 no4 p24 Jl/Ag 2017

Psychic Arrested in Exorcism Scam *Skeptical Inquirer* v41 no1 p12 Ja/F 2017

Psychic Roundup: 'Psychics' Convicted *Skeptical Inquirer* v41 no5 p9 S/O 2017

Return of the Phantom Clowns *Skeptical Inquirer* v41 no1 p8 Ja/F 2017

SKEPTICAL ANNIVERSARIES *Skeptical Inquirer* v40 no6 p66 N/D 2016

Study Reveals How Witchcraft Harms Economies *Skeptical Inquirer* v40 no6 p8 N/D 2016

What Ghosts Mean *Skeptical Inquirer* v41 no2 p62 Mr/Ap 2017

Woman Dies Searching for Monster *Skeptical Inquirer* v40 no6 p12 N/D 2016

Radhakrishnan, Guru V.

Fatty acids in arbuscular mycorrhizal fungi are synthesized by the host plant diag graph *Science* v356 no6343 p1175 Je 16 2017

Radial (Company)

Radial Revolution L. D. JOHNSON color *Ebony* v72 no8 p73 Je 2017

Radiation

See also

Gravitational waves

Infrared radiation

Spectrum analysis

Ultraviolet radiation

Advanced Laser Promises EXCITING Applications: The extremely powerful High-Repetition-Rate Advanced Petawatt Laser System (HAPLS) is poised to be an important tool for scientific research A. Heller *Science & Technology Review* p4 Jl/Ag 2017

travel smartly J. ASHTON *Parents* v91 no12 p118 D 2016

Radiation injuries

The DNA-sensing AIM2 inflammasome controls radiation-induced cell death and tissue injury Bo Hu, Chengcheng Jin et al bibl color graph *Science* v354 no6313 p765 N 11 2016

Radiative forcing

Toward a Responsible Solar Geoengineering Research Program D. W. KEITH *Issues in Science & Technology* v33 no3 p71 Spr 2017

Radiators, The (Performer)

AULD ACQUAINTANCES M. GRIFFITH color *New Orleans Magazine* v51 no3 p46 Ja 2017

Radiators—Humor

TRANSLATING THE NOISES MY RADIATOR MAKES C. STOKES cartoon *New Yorker* v92 no47 p29 Ja 30 2017

Radic, Smiljan

Two of a Kind T. HENNIGAN *Architectural Record* v205 no6 p98 Je 2017

Radical anions

Radical-polar crossover reactions of vinylboron ate complexes M. Kischkewitz, K. Okamoto et al bibl diag *Science* v355 no6328 p936 Mr 3 2017

Radicalism

See also

Left-wing extremism

Right-wing extremism

Advice for Young Muslims O. S. Ghobash color *Foreign Affairs* v96 no1 p96 Ja/F 2017

Cyber-Extremism: Isis and the Power of Social Media I. Awan chart color *Society* v54 no2 p138 Ap 2017

Driving Lessons L. Featherstone color *Nation* v305 no3 p5 Jl 31 2017

The Dutch Give Up on Trumpism C. CALDWELL color *Weekly Standard* v22 no28 p24 Mr 27 2017

For the Record color *Time* v189 no18 p8 My 15 2017

How to Fight Back J. NICHOLS il *Nation* v304 no10 p3 Mr 27 2017

Online platforms annexed much of our public sphere, playacting as little democracies—until extremists made them reveal their true nature J. Herrman *New York Times Magazine* p18 Ag 27 2017

Wellsprings of Violence R. M. Gerecht *Hoover Digest: Research & Opinion on Public Policy* no4 p94 Fall 2016

Radicalism—Indonesia

Political Islam in Indonesia P. MARSHALL color *Weekly Standard* v22 no38 p22 Je 12 2017

Radicalism—Prevention

Preventing Radicalization A. KANJI *Islamic Horizons* v46 no2 p18 Mr/Ap 2017

Radicalism—Social aspects

The Globalization of Rage P. Mishra color *Foreign Affairs* v95 no6 p46 N/D 2016

Radicals

See also

Right-wing extremists

The New New Left C. R. Kesler *Claremont Review of Books* v17 no3 p35 Summ 2017

Radicchio

SINGULAR Sensation M. Kiesel color *O, The Oprah Magazine* p135 O 2017

Radigan, J.

Zones, spots, and planetary-scale waves beating in brown dwarf atmospheres color graph *Science* v357 no6352 p683 Ag 18 2017

Radinsky, Kira

Data Monopolists Like Google Are Threatening the Economy *Harvard Business Review Digital Articles* p2 Mr 2 2015

How to Make Better Predictions When You Don't Have Enough Data *Harvard Business Review Digital Articles* p2 D 29 2016

Using Algorithms to Predict the Next Outbreak *Harvard Business Review Digital Articles* p2 N 5 2014

You Need an Algorithm, Not a Data Scientist *Harvard Business Review Digital Articles* p2 D 15 2014

Your Algorithms Are Not Safe from Hackers *Harvard Business Review Digital Articles* p2 Ja 5 2016

Radio astronomy

See also

Solar radio bursts

Astronomers find source of fast radio burst color *Astronomy* v45 no5 p16 My 2017

Radio astronomy observatories

The Square KILOMETRE ARRAY G. Schilling *Sky & Telescope* v133 no6 p24 Je 2017

Radio audiences

Declining to Label Lies, NPR Picks Diplomacy Over Reality A. Johnson *Extra!* v30 no2 p4 Mr 2017

Radio broadcasters

See also

Disc jockeys

Radio broadcasters—Humor

Mike and ... Still Mike? T. Keith color *Sports Illustrated* v126 no3 p17 Ja 23 2017

Radio broadcasting

See also

Public radio

Radio programs

Radio stations

Radio Days K. LAUR *Cincinnati Magazine* p44 Je 2017

Radio broadcasting—Religious aspects

NO PLACE LIKE NOME P. Hovey color *America* v217 no7 p34 O 2 2017

Radio broadcasting—United States

08:01:30 G. EICHLER cartoon *New Yorker* v93 no8 p29 Ap 10 2017

Il Barbiere di Siviglia G. ROSSINI and C. STERBINI *Opera News* v81 no7 p57 Ja 2017

La Bohème G. PUCCINI, G. GIACOSA et al *Opera News* v81 no7 p55 Ja 2017

Nabucco G. VERDI and T. SOLERA *Opera News* v81 no7 p54 Ja 2017

Roméo et Juliette C. GOUNOD, J. BARBIER et al *Opera News* v81 no7 p56 Ja 2017

Trading Banjos for Balalaikas bw *Weekly Standard* v22 no42 p3 Jl 17 2017

Radio City Rockettes (Performer)

TAKING THE Radio City STAGE L. Jakowenko and C. Bowers color *Dance Spirit* v20 no10 p30 D 2016

Radio collars

Scaredy-Cats J. G. Goldman color *Scientific American* v317 no4 p18 O 2017

Radio commentaries

For those of you just tuning in color *Christian Century* v134 no8 p1 Ap 12 2017

Radio direction finders

FORGOTTEN APPROACH OPTIONS: NDB/ADF diag *Flying* v144 no6 p22 Je 2017

Radio frequency allocation

Arecibo Under the Gun J. T. Schmelz and G. L. Verschuur *Sky & Telescope* v133 no5 p84 My 2017

Radio frequency identification systems

How RFID Technology Improves Hospital Care K. S. Pasupathy and T. R. Hellmich *Harvard Business Review Digital Articles* p2 D 31 2015

Radio frequency identification systems—Equipment & supplies

Setting Standards for the Internet of Things T. H. Davenport and S. E. Sarma *Harvard Business Review Digital Articles* p2 N 21 2014

Radio in politics

Don't Call It Brexit Radio A. P. Q. Wittmeyer *Foreign Policy* no224 p29 My/Je 2017

Radio journalists

Terry Gross A. Lifson *Humanities* v37 no4 p1 Fall 2016

Radio news programs

Oy, the TRAFFIC. And it's POURING! Do I hear SIRENS? S. Van Zuylen-Wood color *Columbia Journalism Review* v56 no1 p96 Spr 2017

Radio observations of artificial satellites

Supermassive Black Holes in Close Dance M. YOUNG *Sky & Telescope* v134 no4 p13 O 2017

Radio on ships

ASK SAIL D. CASEY, G. WEST et al color *Sail* v48 no4 p68 Ap 2017

ICOM IC-M605 VHF J. Y. WOOD color *Power & Motoryacht* v34 no10 p54 O 2017

Radio One Inc.

POWER IN LONGEVITY S. FLOYD color *Black Enterprise* v47 no5 p16 Ja/F 2017

Radio operators

Thailand: The Permanent Coup R. Bernstein color *New York Review of Books* v64 no14 p69 S 28 2017

Radio personalities

BOOK IT: FAVORITE READS FROM CHARLAMAGNE THA GOD S. E. JAMISON color *Ebony* v72/73 no12/1 p85 O/N 2017

Radio programs

THE BEAUTY OF IT IS THAT A. Streep *New York Times Magazine* p31 O 2 2016

Evergreen Evasion color *Weekly Standard* v22 no39 p4 Je 19 2017

Krista Tippett E. Dias color *Time* v188 no24 p72 D 12 2016

MEET JOSHUA JOHNSON A. BEAUJON *Washingtonian Magazine* v52 no4 p22 Ja 2017

ONE CALLER HAS A TRUCK STOP NAMED AFTER HIM J. GILBERT *Cincinnati Magazine* v50 no8 p44 My 2017

The Podcast Finder E. Dockterman color *Time* v189 no13 p52 Ap 10 2017

Radio Days K. LAUR *Cincinnati Magazine* p44 Je 2017

SCREW ALGORITHMS B. Ratliff cartoon color *Esquire* v167 no2 p46 Mr 2017

Radio receiving apparatus

See also

Radio transmitter-receivers

A Short History of Radio Explains the iPhone's Success T. W. Hazlett *Harvard Business Review Digital Articles* p2 Je 29 2017

TRUTH TALKERS C. ROSE *Cincinnati Magazine* v50 no8 p23 My 2017

Radio receiving apparatus—Evaluation

Big Box Meets Little Speakers M. Fleischmann chart color graph *Sound & Vision* v82 no4 p38 My 2017

Radio receiving apparatus—History

RCA'S HOME ENTERTAINMENT CENTER *Saturday Evening Post* v289 no3 p98 My/Je 2017

Radio stations

HAPPY HOLIDAYS color *Entertainment Weekly* no1444/1445 p8 D 16 2016

How to personalize your own radio stations in Apple Music K. MCELHEARN color *Macworld - Digital Edition* v34 no6 p120 Je 2017

Local news on public airways D. Emanuel and K. Sullivan graph *Columbia Journalism Review* v56 no1 p101 Spr 2017

NO PLACE LIKE NOME P. Hovey color *America* v217 no7 p34 O 2 2017

SCREW ALGORITHMS B. Ratliff cartoon color *Esquire* v167 no2 p46 Mr 2017

The Urbanist: The Globalization of Local Radio B. ELLMAN img *New York* v49 no25 p32 D 12 2016

Radio stations—Great Britain

Don't Call It Brexit Radio A. P. Q. Wittmeyer *Foreign Policy* no224 p29 My/Je 2017

Radio stations—United States

THE COLOR OF RADIO A. Beaujon *Washingtonian Magazine* v52 no9 p53 Je 2017

Rock of Aged J. Gilbert *Cincinnati Magazine* v50 no12 p40 S 2017

Radio technology

See also

Mobile communication systems

Shortwave radio

HEAD-TO-HEAD: FINE TUNERS R. CHUN color *Wired* v25 no8 p44 Ag 2017

Radio telescopes

Fates of two big radio dishes hang in the balance T. Feder *Physics Today* v70 no2 p26 F 2017

FIRST LIGHT ı MeerKAT Online A. V. ACEVES *Sky & Tele-*

scope v132 no6 p15 D 2016

NSF says: Out with the old telescopes, in with the new D. Clery chart color *Science* v354 no6313 p693 N 11 2016

Radio telescopes—China

Chinese FAST Opens for Business D. DICKINSON *Sky & Telescope* v133 no1 p11 Ja 2017

Radio telescope gets no-fly zone color *Science* v357 no6353 p736 Ag 25 2017

Radio telescopes—Design & construction

THE BIGGEST EAR D. Normile color *Science* v353 no6307 p1488 S 30 2016

Giant radio telescope faces downsizing E. Cartlidge color *Science* v356 no6334 p124 Ap 14 2017

Mega-Eye on the Sky Renjiang Xie *Sky & Telescope* v133 no2 p26 F 2017

Reach Out & Touch G. Schilling color *Sky & Telescope* v134 no5 p84 N 2017

Radio waves

Fast Radio Burst Has Surprising Source S. HALL *Sky & Telescope* v133 no4 p10 Ap 2017

Radioactive decay

Neutron longevity remains elusive E. CONOVER *Science News* v191 no4 p13 Mr 4 2017

Radioactive substances

See also

Plutonium

Radon

HOW TO MAKE PLUTONIUM K. DUPZYK color *Popular Mechanics* p64 S 2017

Revealing the Presence of Hidden Nuclear Materials A. Chen color *Science & Technology Review* p18 Ja/F 2017

To Jupiter, Sans Nuclear S. SCOLES color diag *Discover* v27 no10 p20 D 2016

Radioactive waste disposal

Cleanup of Cold War nuclear waste drags on: Despite billions of dollars spent preparing to treat and stabilize liquid radioactive wastes, cleaning out leaking tanks at the former nuclear production site in Hanford, Washington, will take decades more D. Kramer *Physics Today* v70 no7 p28 Jl 2017

Radioactive waste disposal—United States

How to Dispose Of Nuclear Waste color *Bloomberg Businessweek* no4522 p10 My 15 2017

Radioactive waste management

Déjà vu for U.S. nuclear waste A. Macfarlane and R. Ewing color *Science* v356 no6345 p1313 Je 30 2017

Radioactive waste repositories

Death and succession among Finland's nuclear waste experts V. Ialenti *Physics Today* v70 no10 p48 O 2017

Reports raise concerns about France's nuclear waste tomb E. Pain color *Science* v357 no6354 p858 S 1 2017

WHAT LIES BENEATH A. CURRY color *Atlantic* v320 no3 p52 O 2017

Radioactive waste repositories—Design & construction

Nevada and Trump administration face off over Yucca Mountain D. Kramer *Physics Today* v70 no10 p32 O 2017

Radioactive wastes—Law & legislation

Déjà vu for U.S. nuclear waste A. Macfarlane and R. Ewing color *Science* v356 no6345 p1313 Je 30 2017

Radioactive wastes—Safety measures

Reports raise concerns about France's nuclear waste tomb E. Pain color *Science* v357 no6354 p858 S 1 2017

Radioactivity

BACK TO BIKINI: SCIENTISTS STUDY LINGERING RADIOACTIVITY AT 'GROUND ZERO' FOR NUCLEAR WEAPONS TESTING AFTER WORLD WAR II E. Lubofsky *Oceanus* v52 no2 p32 Spr 2017

Radioactivity—Research

Helium Fields Forever? J. KEATS color map *Discover* v38 no1 p87 Ja/F 2017

Radiocarbon dating

Greenland Sharks Can Live 500 Years and Counting B. ALEX color *Discover* v38 no1 p79 Ja/F 2017

Radioenzymatic assays

Direct atomic-level insight into the active sites of a high-performance PGM-free ORR catalyst H. T. Chung, D. A. Cullen et al diag graph *Science* v357 no6350 p479 Ag 4 2017

Radiographs
READING RADIOGRAPHS B. Crabbe color *Horse & Rider* v56 no2 p46 F 2017

Radiography
See also
Radiographs
A 19th versus 21st century peek inside a child mummy H. Thompson bw color *Science News* v190 no8 p32 O 15 2016

Radiohead (Performer)
RADIOHEAD'S GENIUS & PARANOIA [Cover story] A. GREENE bw color *Rolling Stone* no1289 p34 Je 15 2017

Radioisotopes
PROLONGED POWER in Remote Places L. L. Helms *Science & Technology Review* p21 Ap/My 2017

Radiologists
Business with a Cause K. F. Miller color *Practical Horseman* v45 no10 p72 O 2017

Radio transmitter-receivers
See also
Cell phones
Aziz Ansari Is From a Red State, Too: Even though he is the latest comic ambassador for New York neuroses J. Yuan img *New York* v50 no9 p79 My 1 2017
To Build A Really Loud Hailer A. MACROBERT *Sky & Telescope* v134 no3 p40 S 2017

Radishes
RADISHES S. PUCKETT *Atlanta* v56 no11 p62 Mr 2017

Radjou, Navi
4 CEOs Who Are Making Frugal Innovation Work *Harvard Business Review Digital Articles* p2 N 28 2014
Tackling Big Global Challenges with Low-Cost Innovation *Harvard Business Review Digital Articles* p2 F 17 2016
What Frugal Innovators Do *Harvard Business Review Digital Articles* p2 D 10 2014

Radke, Amanda
The Legendary Black Hills color *American Cowboy* v23 no4 p28 D 2016/Ja 2017

Radke, Michael H.
Fructose-driven glycolysis supports anoxia resistance in the naked mole-rat diag graph *Science* v356 no6335 p307 Ap 21 2017

RADLAUER, SUSAN
THE WORLD'S BILLIONAIRES bw color diag graph map *Forbes* v199 no3 p84 Mr 28 2017

Radloff, Jessica
The 3-Minute Interview color *Glamour* v114 no12 p82 D 2016
These Are Your Sexual Rights color *Glamour* v114 no7 p94 Jl 2016

Radon
THE EXCHANGE W. C. WINTER and A. Nasir cartoon chart color graph *Men's Health* v32 no9 p16 N 2017

Radosevich, Jenni
DIY Celeb Style color *Seventeen* v76 no12 p30 D 2016/Ja 2017

RADOSH, ALLIS
A Tale of Two Cubas [Cover story] color *Weekly Standard* v22 no40 p17 Je 26 2017

RADOSH, RONALD
Dark Loyalties color *National Review* v68 no20 p40 N 7 2016
Dictators' Devotees *Commentary* v143 no6 p45 Je 2017
Moral Equivalence Run Amok *Commentary* v143 no2 p39 F 2017
Soviet Spain? *Commentary* v142 no3 p10 O 2016
Stars in His Eyes *Commentary* v142 no1 p52 Jl/Ag 2016
A Tale of Two Cubas [Cover story] color *Weekly Standard* v22 no40 p17 Je 26 2017

Radtke, Kristen
The Allure of Decay C. KIRCH color *Publishers Weekly* v264 no15 p44 Ap 10 2017
IMAGINE WANTING ONLY THIS A. Ulinich *New York Times Book Review* p29 My 21 2017

Radwańska, Agnieszka, 1989-
Agnieszka Radwanska *Tennis* v53 no1 p48 Ja/F 2017

RADYK, MICHAEL
Who is pushing the craft field forward? color *American Craft* v76 no6 p26 D 2016-Ja 2017

Rae, Andy
FURNITURE BUILDING R. BERENDSOHN bw color *Popular Mechanics* p31 F 2017

Rae, Auriol
The formation of peak rings in large impact craters bibl color graph *Science* v354 no6314 p878 N 18 2016

Rae, Haniya
Designing for Change *Sierra* v102 no1 p26 Ja/F 2017

Rae, Issa, 1985-
Issa Rae B. SPANOS bw color *Rolling Stone* no1295 p47 S 7 2017
Issa Rae J. Crelin color *Current Biography* v78 no4 p68 Ap 2017
Issa Rae's Insecure Is the Sharpest Comedy of the Year D. D'addario color *Time* v190 no4 p50 Jl 24 2017
L.A. Bohème K. SMITH color *Vanity Fair* v59 no9 p198 S 2017
Meet the Awkward Black Supergirl R. SHEFFIELD color *Rolling Stone* no1275 p28 D 1 2016
my style color *InStyle* v24 no7 p70 Jl 2017
Rap Sesh M. WAKIM color *Los Angeles Magazine* v62 no7 p44 Jl 2017

Rae, Issa, 1985——Interviews
3 ROUNDS WITH INSECURE D. Franich color *Entertainment Weekly* no1468/1469 p44 Je 2-9 2017
Insecure A. D'Arminio *TV Guide* v64 no40 p58 O 3 2016
Issa Rae J. ZAMBRANO color *O, The Oprah Magazine* p28 Ag 2017
THE Work Wives E. Mahaney color *Glamour* v115 no10 p162 O 2017

RAE, PEPPER
Your True Stories IN 100 WORDS color *Reader's Digest* v189 no1131 p32 Je 2017

Rae Sremmurd (Performer)
Meet the Black Beatles B. SPANOS color *Rolling Stone* no1278/1279 p15 Ja 12 2017

RAEBEL, EVA M.
Some Animals Are More Equal than Others: Wild Animal Welfare in the Media *BioScience* v67 no1 p62 Ja 2017

RAEBURN, PAUL
THE BIG DATA BULL'S-EYE *Psychology Today* v50 no5 p81 S/O 2017

Rael, Ronald
The Great Divide J. Gauer *Architectural Record* v205 no4 p77 Ap 2017

Rafaelian, Carolyn
Bangle Billionaire [Cover story] C. O'CONNOR bw color *Forbes* v199 no6 p70 Je 13 2017
The Jewelry Queen's Castle color *Forbes* v199 no6 p16 Je 13 2017

Rafaelian, Carolyn——Interviews
Alex and Ani E. Wilson color *InStyle* v23 no12 p102 N 2016

Rafelski, Marc
[C II] 158-μm emission from the host galaxies of damped Lyman-alpha systems bibl color graph *Science* v355 no6331 p1285 Mr 24 2017

Raff, Martin
Lee Rubin: Our mentor and role model *Science* v355 no6327 p806 F 24 2017

Raffaele Caruso SpA
Our Hyper-Evolutionary Moment J. Fielden color *Esquire* p18 2017 BigBlackBook

Rafferty, Penny
LIZ MAGOR color *Art in America* v105 no5 p137 My 2017

Rafferty, Sara Greenberger
The Artist's Artist A Rauschenberg Symposium color *Art in America* v105 no1 p44 Ja 2017

Rafferty, Terrence
The Heat Made Them Do It color *New York Times Book Review* p12 S 25 2016
HORROR *New York Times Book Review* p20 O 30 2016
Horror *New York Times Book Review* p42 Je 4 2017
Inspector In the Labyrinth [Cover story] *New York Times Book Review* p1 F 26 2017
The Master of Highbrow Horror cartoon *Atlantic* v318 no4 p48 N 2016

Raffice, Joe
Research: Are Clients Loyal to Your Firm, or the People in It? color *Harvard Business Review Digital Articles* p2 Ja 31 2017

Raffoni, Melissa
How to Respond When You're Left Out of Important Meetings *Harvard Business Review Digital Articles* p2 N 17 2016

p97 Mr 17 2017

The Girlfriend Experience color *Entertainment Weekly* no1482/1483 p38 S 22 2017

Good Behavior *Entertainment Weekly* no1482/1483 p39 S 22 2017

The Good Place color *Entertainment Weekly* no1482/1483 p86 S 22 2017

Gotham *Entertainment Weekly* no1482/1483 p84 S 22 2017

Great News color *Entertainment Weekly* no1482/1483 p88 S 22 2017

Grey's Anatomy color diag *Entertainment Weekly* no1482/1483 p89 S 22 2017

Hit the Road *Entertainment Weekly* no1482/1483 p60 S 22 2017

How to Get Away With Murder *Entertainment Weekly* no1482/1483 p91 S 22 2017

Is This Guy Making the Next Girls? color *Entertainment Weekly* no1454/1455 p86 F 24 2017

JASON RITTER OF Kevin (Probably) Saves the World color *Entertainment Weekly* no1482/1483 p61 S 22 2017

John Oliver color *Entertainment Weekly* no1453 p18 F 17 2017

Keepin' It 1600 With Jon Favreau & Dan Pfeiffer color *Entertainment Weekly* no1435 p12 O 14 2016

LATE-NIGHT POLIT-O-METER color diag *Entertainment Weekly* no1457/1458 p15 Mr 17 2017

Law & Order True Crime: The Menendez Murders color *Entertainment Weekly* no1482/1483 p62 S 22 2017

Lethal Weapon color *Entertainment Weekly* no1482/1483 p60 S 22 2017

Life in Pieces *Entertainment Weekly* no1482/1483 p88 S 22 2017

Madam Secretary color *Entertainment Weekly* no1482/1483 p39 S 22 2017

Major Crimes *Entertainment Weekly* no1482/1483 p66 S 22 2017

Marvel's The Punisher color *Entertainment Weekly* no1482/1483 p106 S 22 2017

Me, Myself & I color *Entertainment Weekly* no1482/1483 p48 S 22 2017

Michael Bolton's Funny Valentine color *Entertainment Weekly* no1453 p52 F 17 2017

The Mick *Entertainment Weekly* no1482/1483 p67 S 22 2017

The Middle color *Entertainment Weekly* no1482/1483 p60 S 22 2017

Mindhunter color *Entertainment Weekly* no1482/1483 p107 S 22 2017

The Mindy Project *Entertainment Weekly* no1482/1483 p107 S 22 2017

MOLLY'S GAME color *Entertainment Weekly* no1478 / 1479 p67 Ag 18-25 2017

Mom color *Entertainment Weekly* no1482/1483 p85 S 22 2017

MUSIC color *Entertainment Weekly* no1444/1445 p88 D 16 2016

NCIS *Entertainment Weekly* no1482/1483 p60 S 22 2017

NCIS: Los Angeles *Entertainment Weekly* no1482/1483 p38 S 22 2017

NCIS: New Orleans *Entertainment Weekly* no1482/1483 p67 S 22 2017

The Orville *Entertainment Weekly* no1482/1483 p85 S 22 2017

Outlander color *Entertainment Weekly* no1482/1483 p26 S 22 2017

Poldark *Entertainment Weekly* no1482/1483 p38 S 22 2017

Poll Watchers: A Late-Night Guide color *Entertainment Weekly* no1438 p18 N 4 2017

RIHANNA CHECKS INTO BATES MOTEL color *Entertainment Weekly* no1453 p51 F 17 2017

Riviera color *Entertainment Weekly* no1482/1483 p106 S 22 2017

RIZ AHMED: THE NEW BOY ON GIRLS color *Entertainment Weekly* no1453 p52 F 17 2017

Ryan Hansen Solves Crimes on Television* *Entertainment Weekly* no1482/1483 p109 S 22 2017

SAMANTHA BEE color *Entertainment Weekly* no1444/1445 p18 D 16 2016

SARAH SILVERMAN I Love You, America color *Entertainment Weekly* no1482/1483 p108 S 22 2017

Scandal *Entertainment Weekly* no1482/1483 p88 S 22 2017

Shameless color *Entertainment Weekly* no1482/1483 p30 S 22 2017

Showbiz's Multiple-Personality Meter color *Entertainment Weekly* no1472 p49 Je 30 2017

The Simpsons color *Entertainment Weekly* no1482/1483 p34 S 22 2017

SMILF *Entertainment Weekly* no1482/1483 p43 S 22 2017

Star Trek Discovery color *Entertainment Weekly* no1482/1483 p104 S 22 2017

StartUp *Entertainment Weekly* no1482/1483 p109 S 22 2017

Stranger Things 2 color *Entertainment Weekly* no1482/1483 p100 S 22 2017

Supernatural color *Entertainment Weekly* no1482/1483 p84 S 22 2017

Superstore color *Entertainment Weekly* no1482/1483 p84 S 22 2017

S.W.A.T color *Entertainment Weekly* no1482/1483 p90 S 22 2017

Taboo's Biggest Taboo color *Entertainment Weekly* no1450 p53 Ja 27 2017

Ten Days in the Valley color *Entertainment Weekly* no1482/1483 p43 S 22 2017

This Is Us color *Entertainment Weekly* no1482/1483 p56 S 22 2017

Tin Star *Entertainment Weekly* no1482/1483 p109 S 22 2017

Transparent color *Entertainment Weekly* no1482/1483 p109 S 22 2017

TV chart color *Entertainment Weekly* no1444/1445 p66 D 16 2016

The Walking Dead color *Entertainment Weekly* no1482/1483 p38 S 22 2017

What to Watch color *Entertainment Weekly* no1448 p56 Ja 13 2017

What to Watch color *Entertainment Weekly* no1459 p56 Mr 31 2017

What to Watch color *Entertainment Weekly* no1471 p58 Je 23 2017

What to Watch color *Entertainment Weekly* no1486 p54 O 13 2017

White Famous color *Entertainment Weekly* no1482/1483 p36 S 22 2017

Will & Grace color *Entertainment Weekly* no1482/1483 p80 S 22 2017

Wisdom of the Crowd color *Entertainment Weekly* no1482/1483 p34 S 22 2017

Rahn, David

ENEMY color *Christian Century* v134 no5 p20 Mr 1 2017

Rai, Saritha

Cash Comes Back in India color *Bloomberg Businessweek* no4529 p25 Jl 3 2017

Finally, a Cheap(ish) iPhone color *Bloomberg Businessweek* no4527 p30 Je 19 2017

Indians Reconsider Life in America graph *Bloomberg Businessweek* no4516 p13 Mr 27 2017

Laid-Off Indian IT Workers Blame Trump graph *Bloomberg Businessweek* no4525 p14 Je 5 2017

A Startup That Dare Not Speak Its Name *Bloomberg Businessweek* no4504 p21 D 19 2016

TFW Your Country's Shredding Money And You Own a Payment App bw *Bloomberg Businessweek* no4507 p30 Ja 16 2017

The Trump-Valley Fight Starts to Take Shape *Bloomberg Businessweek* no4510 p26 F 6 2017

Raichlen, Steven

SEASON OF SMOKE: Bring exceptional flavor to backyard cookouts this season by trying these hot-smoking and hay-smoking methods *Mother Earth News* no282 p34 Je/Jl 2017

RAID (Computer science)

How to configure a software RAID in macOS Sierra's Disk Utility R. LOYOLA color *Macworld - Digital Edition* v33 no11 p130 N 2016

Raids (Military science)

A STORM IN EVERY PORT D. Stadtler cartoon color map *Military History* v34 no1 p62 My 2017

TURNING POINT IN KARGIL P. Shukla color map *Military History* v34 no2 p38 Jl 2017

Railroad accidents

Derailments of the curious kind J. Kelly color *Model Railroader* v84 no7 p22 Jl 2017

Railroad bridges—Design & construction

ASK MR S. Otte color *Model Railroader* v83 no12 p20 D 2016

A scenic showcase S. Lamoureux color diag *Model Railroader* v84 no5 p32 My 2017

Railroad cars—Evaluation

Rivarossi HO scale 50-foot boxcar C. Grivno color *Model Railroader* v84 no1 p74 Ja 2017

WalthersMainline HO scale Plymouth ML-8 D. Kawala color *Model Railroader* v84 no6 p62 Je 2017

Railroad cars—Models

See also

Models of railroad passenger cars

BUILD A SINGLE-POINT TURNOUT [Cover story] J. F. Cordaro color *Model Railroader* v84 no7 p48 Jl 2017

Fox Valley Models N scale 7-post boxcar C. Grivno *Model Railroader* v84 no7 p66 Jl 2017

HO scale freight cars C. Grivno *Model Railroader* v84 no7 p11 Jl 2017

Rapido HO New Haven cars E. White *Model Railroader* v84 no7 p63 Jl 2017

Trackside Photos color *Model Railroader* v84 no8 p66 Ag 2017

Upgrade a Varney gondola kit [Cover story] C. Grivno color *Model Railroader* v84 no7 p24 Jl 2017

WalthersMainline HO covered hopper C. Grivno color *Model Railroader* v84 no7 p64 Jl 2017

Railroad cars—Models—Evaluation

Accurail HO scale 36-foot double-sheathed boxcar kit D. Kawala color *Model Railroader* v84 no8 p62 Ag 2017

Athearn HO scale class Z-8 Challenger D. Kawala chart color *Model Railroader* v84 no8 p58 Ag 2017

Bachmann Sound Value HO scale PCC trolley E. White chart color diag *Model Railroader* v84 no8 p60 Ag 2017

Micro-Trains N scale 70-foot TTX Husky-Stack car S. Otte color *Model Railroader* v84 no8 p63 Ag 2017

Railroad commuter service

Getting Mumbai On Track S. Sundria and D. Pandya *Bloomberg Businessweek* no4536 p35 S 4 2017

Railroad companies—Management

THE LAST RAILROAD TYCOON S. Tully color diag map *Fortune* v176 no3 p84 S 1 2017

Railroad conductors

Fulfilling the role of conductor J. Dziedzic bw *Model Railroader* v84 no3 p71 Mr 2017

Railroad construction & design

Getting Mumbai On Track S. Sundria and D. Pandya *Bloomberg Businessweek* no4536 p35 S 4 2017

The Legend Comes to Town: And I Will Get That Ride A. SCHENK *Idaho Magazine* v16 no10 p42 Jl 2017

Railroad mergers

Variety from a second-hand Rose T. Koester *Model Railroader* v84 no10 p78 O 2017

Railroad museums

ALL ABOARD! N. HAWKINS bw color *Missouri Life* v44 no6 p30 S 2017

GWR ON DISPLAY D. Huntley color *British Heritage Travel* v38 no5 p38 S/O 2017

SIMPLY THE WORLD'S GREATEST RAILWAY MUSEUM D. Huntley *British Heritage Travel* v38 no2 p54 Mr/Ap 2017

Railroad passenger cars—Evaluation

Upgrading streamlined passenger cars V. S. Roseman color diag *Model Railroader* v84 no5 p26 My 2017

Railroad passenger cars—Models—Evaluation

Bachmann introduces new N scale lighted streamlined passenger cars E. White color *Model Railroader* v84 no1 p72 Ja 2017

Railroad periodicals

From the Editor H. Miller *Model Railroader* v84 no10 p8 O 2017

Railroad routing

Train Orders and Form D's J. Dziedzic chart color *Model Railroader* v84 no5 p57 My 2017

Railroad signal manufacturing

Build a signal system with Arduino microcontrollers D. Kurpanek color diag *Model Railroader* v83 no12 p42 D 2016

Railroad sounds

Sounds In the Night E. Laborde bw *New Orleans Magazine* v51 no5 p152 Mr 2017

Railroad stations

Flagstaff Train Station N. AUSTIN *Arizona Highways* v93 no1 p6 Ja 2017

Railroad stations—California

Transbay Transit Center *Architectural Record* v205 no4 p202 Ap 2017

Railroad stations—Design & construction

Brightline B. Schreiner *Architectural Record* v205 no4 p205 Ap 2017

Railroad stations—Remodeling

Belmont Blue Line Station A. Schneider *Architectural Record* v205 no4 p204 Ap 2017

Railroad switching

BUILD A LAYOUT IN A WEEKEND P. Boehlert color *Model Railroader* v84 no9 p26 S 2017

Railroad terminals

See also

Railroad yards

TRACKSIDE PHOTOS color *Model Railroader* v84 no2 p78 F 2017

Railroad terminals—Design & construction

Modeling a COMPACT DIESEL SERVICE TERMINAL T. Klimoski color *Model Railroader* v84 no1 p40 Ja 2017

Railroad tickets

JOKES *Saturday Evening Post* v288 no6 p34 N/D 2016

Railroad tracks

ASK MR S. Otte color *Model Railroader* v84 no2 p26 F 2017

BALLASTING main lines & sidings [Cover story] L. Sassi color *Model Railroader* v84 no7 p36 Jl 2017

Dispatching with track warrants J. Dziedzic chart *Model Railroader* v84 no8 p65 Ag 2017

The Inside Track A. J. BARTELS color *Nebraska Life* v21 no2 p20 Mr/Ap 2017

Model tracks in dirt and cinders K. Nipkow color *Model Railroader* v84 no7 p40 Jl 2017

Multiple deck design, or 'rinse and repeat' T. Koester color *Model Railroader* v84 no8 p78 Ag 2017

Track 101 S. Otte color diag *Model Railroader* v84 no7 p28 Jl 2017

TRACKS: How many lives intersect our own, just out of view? G. LEGLER color *Orion Magazine* v36 no1 p54 Ja/F 2017

TRACKSIDE PHOTOS color *Model Railroader* v83 no12 p76 D 2016

Trackside Photos color *Model Railroader* v84 no11 p68 N 2017

Railroad tracks—Design & construction

Two railroads in one bedroom B. Sprague color diag *Model Railroader* v84 no1 p62 Ja 2017

Railroad trains

See also

Passenger trains

HIGH-ALTITUDE TRAINING P. DIBNER color *Conde Nast Traveler* v52 no9 p14 O 2017

Intel bw chart *Conde Nast Traveler* v52 no5 p129 My 2017

Leaving On That Late- Night Train A. KONERMANN *Cincinnati Magazine* p59 Je 2017

No Cars Allowed A. Marshall *Governing* v30 no3 p22 D 2016

Strangers on a Train R. Ebrahim *New York Times Magazine* p25 Mr 5 2017

SURVIVAL TRAINING ENTER THE CHAMBER A. MARSHALL color *Wired* v25 no5 p38 My 2017

Trackside Photos color *Model Railroader* v84 no6 p70 Je 2017

Railroad trains—Speed

Identifying which train just went by J. Dziedzic color *Model Railroader* v84 no6 p69 Je 2017

Railroad travel

Excursions and passenger specials J. Dziedzic color *Model Railroader* v84 no2 p76 F 2017

HIGH-ALTITUDE TRAINING P. DIBNER color *Conde Nast Traveler* v52 no9 p14 O 2017

Strangers on a Train R. Ebrahim *New York Times Magazine* p25 Mr 5 2017

Subway Napping A. Deutsch *New York Times Magazine* p18 F 26 2017

Railroad travel—Government policy

Kiev and the Kremlin Face Narrowing Options In Ukraine I. Bremmer *Time* v189 no12 p16 Ap 3 2017

Railroad tunnels—Maintenance & repair

Tunnel Out of Danger S. Gregory color *Time* v189 no13 p37 Ap 10 2017

Railroad yards

Automotive Archaeology Train Station in the Junkyard?! R. Brutt color *Hot Rod* v69 no12 p16 D 2016

Railroad yards—Design & construction
BUILDING A PORTABLE STAGING FIDDLE YARD R. De
   Candido color diag *Model Railroader* v84 no3 p38 Mr 2017
But how did he build that? N. Besougloff *Model Railroader* v84
   no2 p8 F 2017
Scratchbuild a lumber yard from styrene S. Otte color diag *Model*
   Railroader v84 no3 p52 Mr 2017
Railroads
     See also
      Railroad trains
Automotive Archaeology Train Station in the Junkyard?! R. Brutt
   color *Hot Rod* v69 no12 p16 D 2016
Brain Bogglers S. W. DRIMMMER color *National Geographic*
   Kids no470 p34 My 2017
Fall Foliage Trains: All aboard for autumn thrills on New Eng-
   land's historic rails K. K. BECKIUS *Yankee* v81 no5 p76 S/O
   2017
Union Pacific's Spine Line in HO and N B. Sprague color diag
   map *Model Railroader* v84 no4 p72 Ap 2017
What's special about instructions? J. Dziedzic color *Model Rail-*
   roader v84 no9 p68 S 2017
Railroads—Buildings & structures
     See also
      Engine houses (Railroads)
      Railroad stations
      Railroad terminals
UPSTATE NEW YORK IN 1948 J. Heidt color map *Model Rail-*
   roader v84 no2 p46 F 2017
Railroads—California
FORWARD MOTION D. L. ULIN *Los Angeles Magazine* p90
   My 2017
Railroads—Commuting traffic—Florida
Brightline B. Schreiner *Architectural Record* v205 no4 p205 Ap
   2017
Railroads—Curves & turnouts
5 ways to interchange freight cars T. Koester color *Model Rail-*
   roader v83 no12 p38 D 2016
Ask MR S. Otte color *Model Railroader* v84 no4 p30 Ap 2017
Railroads—Design & construction
     See also
      Railroad tracks—Design & construction
Connecticut Tells Amtrak to Slow Down E. Young color *Bloom-*
   berg Businessweek no4493 p37 O 3 2016
Railroads—Dieselization
News & Products color *Model Railroader* v84 no6 p10 Je 2017
Railroads—Economic aspects
Clearing the Line: In the Railroad's Heyday T. WAITE *Idaho*
   Magazine v16 no10 p27 Jl 2017
Connecticut Tells Amtrak to Slow Down E. Young color *Bloom-*
   berg Businessweek no4493 p37 O 3 2016
Railroads—Germany
Hardware Krupp 28 cm K5(E) Railway Gun J. Guttman color
   Military History v34 no2 p20 Jl 2017
Railroads—Great Britain
GOD'S WONDERFUL RAILWAY S. Lawrence *British Heritage*
   Travel v38 no2 p38 Mr/Ap 2017
Railroads—Maintenance & repair
     See also
      Locomotives—Maintenance & repair
High-Speed Waste E. Boehm *Reason* v48 no7 p8 D 2016
Railroads—Signaling
A signal system to FIT ANY RAILROAD B. Carpenter color diag
   Model Railroader v84 no4 p66 Ap 2017
Railroads—Timetables
Identifying which train just went by J. Dziedzic color *Model Rail-*
   roader v84 no6 p69 Je 2017
Train Orders and Form D's J. Dziedzic chart color *Model Rail-*
   roader v84 no5 p57 My 2017
Railroads—United States
     See also
      Cumbres & Toltec Scenic Railroad
Small Wins Go a Long Way in Improving U.S. Rail Transporta-
   tion R. M. Kanter *Harvard Business Review Digital Articles* p2
   My 12 2015
Time traveling via model railroads J. Dziedzic color *Model Rail-*
   roader v83 no12 p74 D 2016

Where the 21st century meets the 19th J. Dziedzic *Model Rail-*
   roader v84 no10 p68 O 2017
Railway artillery
Hardware Krupp 28 cm K5(E) Railway Gun J. Guttman color
   Military History v34 no2 p20 Jl 2017
Raimondi, Andrea
Reticulon 3–dependent ER-PM contact sites control EGFR non-
   clathrin endocytosis color diag graph *Science* v356 no6338
   p617 My 12 2017
RAIMONDI, PETER T.
Long-Term Studies Contribute Disproportionately to Ecology and
   Policy *BioScience* v67 no3 p271 Mr 2017
Rain & rainfall
     See also
      Rain-making
      Rainstorms
LAST PAGE P. STEFÁNSSON *Iceland Review* v55 no1 p112
   Ja/F 2017
Misty Weather color *House Beautiful* v159 no2 p26 Mr 2017
Rain G. TARLACH color *Discover* v38 no3 p74 Ap 2017
weather gets weird M. D. Kaufman diag *Popular Science* v289
   no4 p10 Jl/Ag 2017
weather watch B. RIPPEY *Weatherwise* v70 no5 p42 S/O 2017
Rain & rainfall periodicity
ABBEY WICK: SOIL HEALTH SPECIALIST KNOWS HOW
   TO CONNECT WITH FARMERS G. Gullickson bw *Successful*
   Farming v115 no7 p5 My 2017
Rain & rainfall India
Asia K. Stock color map *Bloomberg Businessweek* no4536 p10
   S 4 2017
Rain & rainfall—United States
Weatherwatch B. Rippey, J. B. Halverson et al map *Weatherwise*
   v69 no6 p46 N-D 2016
Rain forest animals
From The Pages Of Quiz Whiz: Stump Your Parents color *Na-*
   tional Geographic Kids no473 p38 S 2017
Funny Fill-In A. SHAW cartoon *National Geographic Kids* no473
   p34 S 2017
Rain forest ecology
30 Cool Things About Rain Forest Cultures J. BEER color *Na-*
   tional Geographic Kids no473 p24 S 2017
Rain forest plants
What In The World? color *National Geographic Kids* no473 p35
   S 2017
Rain forests
30 Cool Things About Rain Forest Cultures J. BEER color *Na-*
   tional Geographic Kids no473 p24 S 2017
CRISIS AMONG The Palms J. Conant color *Earth Island Journal*
   v32 no2 p33 Summ 2017
Funny Fill-In A. SHAW cartoon *National Geographic Kids* no473
   p34 S 2017
'Green hell' has long been home for humans A. Curry color *Sci-*
   ence v354 no6310 p268 O 21 2016
LIFE IS THIRSTY J. Brown *Popular Science* v289 no2 p6 Mr/
   Ap 2017
What In The World? color *National Geographic Kids* no473 p35
   S 2017
Rain forests—Amazon River Valley
Ancient peoples reshaped Amazon B. BOWER *Science News*
   v191 no6 p13 Ap 1 2017
Rain forests—Colombia
Colombia peace deal blow dismays ecologists L. Wade color *Sci-*
   ence v354 no6310 p271 O 21 2016
Rain forests—Peru
Bet You Didn't Know E. WHITMER color *National Geographic*
   Kids no473 p11 S 2017
Rain forests—South America
Bet You Didn't Know E. WHITMER color *National Geographic*
   Kids no473 p11 S 2017
Rain gauges
Weather Queries J. M. Brown color graph *Weatherwise* v70 no4
   p35 Jl/Ag 2017
Rain-making
HARNESSING MOTHER NATURE: The Storied History of
   Hurricane Control and Cloud Seeding J. Williams *Weatherwise*
   v70 no5 p25 S/O 2017

How Cloud Seeding Works *Weatherwise* v70 no5 p30 S/O 2017

RAINA, PAMPOSH
  Out of India color *Foreign Policy* no225 p62 Jl/Ag 2017

Raina, Sahil
  Research: The Gender Gap in Startup Success Disappears When Women Fund Women *Harvard Business Review Digital Articles* p2 Jl 19 2016

Rainbow (Music)
  Kesha E. R. Brown color *Entertainment Weekly* no1478 / 1479 p103 Ag 18-25 2017
  Kesha's Battle Cry of Many Colors B. SPANOS color *Rolling Stone* no1294 p53 Ag 24 2017
  KESHA'S LUCKY CHARMS color *Entertainment Weekly* no1478 / 1479 p102 Ag 18-25 2017
  The Must List color *Entertainment Weekly* no1478 / 1479 p1 Ag 18-25 2017

Rainbow flags (LGBT symbol)
  Gilbert Baker M. Vella color *Time* v189 no14 p15 Ap 17 2017

Rainbow trout
  SOUTH COAST HABITAT RESTORATION: If You Build It, They Will Come: Bringing Steelhead Back to the Central Coast M. GOMEZ color *Earth Island Journal* v32 no4 p16 Wint 2017

Rainbows
  DOUBLE THE FUN *South Dakota Magazine* v33 no3 p92 S/O 2017
  From the Editor M. Benner Smidt *Weatherwise* v70 no2 p4 Mr/Ap 2017
  Rainbow Detectives: When Art Gets Meteorology Wrong R. C. Balling, R. Cerveny et al *Weatherwise* v70 no2 p24 Mr/Ap 2017
  United States color *National Geographic* v230 no5 p9 N 2016

Raincoats
  Raingear T. J. BROWN color *Backpacker* p46 My 2017

Raindrop size
  Weather Queries J. M. Brown color graph *Weatherwise* v70 no4 p35 Jl/Ag 2017

Rainer, Yvonne, 1934-
  MOVING BEYOND V. Lucca bw *Film Comment* v53 no4 p42 Jl/Ag 2017

Rainey, Candice
  A Good Run bw color *Conde Nast Traveler* v52 no1 p94 Ja 2017
  Los Angeles color map *Conde Nast Traveler* v51 no10 p64 N 2016
  Second Coming color *Conde Nast Traveler* v52 no5 p56 My 2017
  TIME FOR A MAN-CATION! color *Esquire* p114 O 2017

Rainey, Clint
  THE MAD CHEESE SCIENTISTS color graph *Bloomberg Businessweek* no4531 p56 Jl 24 2017
  OBAMA'S AMERICA img *New York* v49 no20 p12 O 3 2016

Rainfall probabilities
  To Forecast Rain, Look to the Ocean: SCIENTISTS EXPLORE COMPELLING NEW WAY TO PREDICT SEASONAL RAINFALL L. Lippsett *Oceanus* v52 no2 p6 Spr 2017

Rainforth, W. M.
  Direct observation of individual hydrogen atoms at trapping sites in a ferritic steel bibl diag *Science* v355 no6330 p1196 Mr 17 2017

RAINS, PAT
  BACK FROM THE DEAD *Sea Magazine* v108 no10 p18 O 2016
  Deep INTO THE Delta *Sea Magazine* v108 no9 p40 S 2016
  FOREIGN FISHING color map *Sea Magazine* v109 no6 p18 Je 2017
  HECK OF A COMMUTE *Sea Magazine* v109 no2 p14 F 2017
  HIDDEN GEMS *Sea Magazine* v108 no8 p14 Ag 2016
  HOST FOR THE HOLIDAYS *Sea Magazine* v108 no12 p16 D 2016
  HOT TIME IN MEXICO *Sea Magazine* v108 no9 p18 S 2016
  HOW TO HOP DOWN BAJA IN NOVEMBER *Sea Magazine* v108 no10 p18 O 2016
  IT'S THE LITTLE THINGS: MANY OF THE DIFFERENCES BETWEEN CRUISING IN THE U.S AND CRUISING IN MEXICO ARE SUBTLE color *Sea Magazine* v109 no8 p14 Ag 2017
  MEXICO MADE EASIER *Sea Magazine* v109 no1 p18 Ja 2017
  NEW & IMPROVED MARINA PUERTO ESCONDIDO: THE MARINA NEAR LORETO BENEFITS FROM AN OWNER-SHIP GROUP THAT LOVES TO GO BOATING *Sea Magazine* v109 no9 p18 S 2017

SAFE & SECURE BY SUNSET *Sea Magazine* v109 no4 p18 Ap 2017
  SUMMER GETAWAYS: IT'S POSSIBLE TO ENJOY MINI-CRUISES IN THE SEA OF CORTEZ WHILE STAYING CLOSE TO A HURRICANE HOLE color map *Sea Magazine* v109 no7 p12 Jl 2017

Rains, Valerie
  YOU CAN GO HOME AGAIN color *Southern Living* v52 no9 p92 S 2017

Rainsberry, Gracie—Political & social views
  Pop Chart R. Bruner, C. Lang et al color *Time* v189 no3 p58 Ja 30 2017

Rainstorms
  FROM A DISTANCE K. Vaughn *Arizona Highways* v93 no8 p28 Ag 2017

Rainwater, Brooks
  WHY *FREE MONEY COULD BE THE FUTURE OF WORK color diag *Fortune* v176 no1 p68 Jl 1 2017

RAINWATER, THOMAS
  Gator Growth and Reproduction color graph map *Natural History* v125 no7 p10 Jl/Ag 2017

Raised field agriculture
  AGING GRACEFULLY on the Homestead H. Will, S. Heggestad et al *Mother Earth News* no280 p34 F/Mr 2017

Raisfeld, Robin
  16 Ways to Hack Your Hoagie img *New York* v49 no20 p102 O 3 2016
  the absolute best *New York* p74 Mr 6 2017
  Chè Sundae img *New York* v50 no6 p67 Mr 20 2017
  Cold Fish: After declaring independence from Brushstroke, Ichimura raises its prices and loses some of its charm img *New York* v50 no10 p76 My 15 2017
  Congee: The Original Grain Bowl img *New York* v50 no6 p68 Mr 20 2017
  Eggs on a Roll img *New York* v50 no8 p112 Ap 17 2017
  home & help img *New York* p96 Mr 6 2017
  Ikinari Steak img *New York* v50 no7 p68 Ap 3 2017
  It's a Wonderful Time to Be a DUMPLING img *New York* v49 no25 p98 D 12 2016
  Øllebrød img *New York* v49 no25 p112 D 12 2016
  Modern Mexican: Atla is designed for how New Yorkers eat now img *New York* v50 no15 p50 Jl 24 2017
  Novel Noodles: Two new shops shine a light on the seldom-seen Yunnanese rice variety img *New York* v50 no9 p74 My 1 2017
  The Other Drinkable Rye: Old-world kvass gets a fresh Brooklyn spin img *New York* v50 no18 p62 S 4 2017
  Prix Fixe Banchan, New Nordic à la Carte img *New York* v49 no25 p110 D 12 2016
  Progressive Chinese img *New York* v49 no15 p66 Jl 25 2016
  Spaghetti and Meatballs for the Masses img *New York* v50 no17 p72 Ag 21 2017
  Spring Has Sprung img *New York* v49 no19 p72 S 19 2016
  Strawberries img *New York* v50 no18 p60 S 4 2017
  The Underground Gourmet Digest img *New York* v50 no18 p62 S 4 2017
  Wet Hot American Sandwich *New York* p52 Ja 23 2017
  Where (And What) You'll Be Eating Next img *New York* p60 F 20 2017

Raising Arizona (Film)
  HOLLY HUNTER MY LIFE IN PICTURES J. McGovern color *Entertainment Weekly* no1473 p32 Jl 7 2017

Raissig, Michael T.
  Mobile MUTE specifies subsidiary cells to build physiologically improved grass stomata bibl diag *Science* v355 no6330 p1215 Mr 17 2017

Raitt, Bonnie, 1949-
  SING IT STRONG N. Paumgarten cartoon *New Yorker* v92 no33 p26 O 17 2016

Raitt, Bonnie, 1949-—Interviews
  Bonnie Raitt P. DOYLE bw *Rolling Stone* no1287 p58 My 18 2017

Raitt, Neil
  NEIL RAITT J. S. Li color *Art in America* v104 no10 p159 N 2016

Raj, Arjun
  Mitotic transcription and waves of gene reactivation during mi-

totic exit color graph *Science* v357 no6359 p119 O 6 2017

Raj, Ritu
Posttranslational mutagenesis: A chemical strategy for exploring protein side-chain diversity diag *Science* v354 no6312 p597 N 4 2016

Raja, Tasneem
IT HAPPENS HERE color *Mother Jones* v42 no4 p13 Jl/Ag 2017
UNIVERSAL REMOTE cartoon *Mother Jones* v42 no2 p62 Mr/Ap 2017

Rajagopalan, Rajesh
China's proper role in the global nuclear order *Bulletin of the Atomic Scientists* v73 no2 p133 Mr 2017

Rajagopal-Durbin, Aparna
Unconscious Bias in Parks and Recreation *Parks & Recreation* v52 no2 p32 F 2017

Rajantie, Arttu
The search for MAGNETIC MONOPOLES *Physics Today* v69 no10 p40 O 2016

Rajapaksa, Roshini
Our Doc Will See You Now color *Health* v31 no1 p80 Ja 2017
Our Doc Will See You Now color *Health* v31 no2 p86 Mr 2017
Our Doc Will See You Now color *Health* v31 no6 p71 Jl 2017
Our Doc Will See You Now color *Health* v31 no7 p92 S 2017
Our doc will see you now color *Health* v31 no9 p66 N 2017

Rajewsky, Nikolaus
Loss of a mammalian circular RNA locus causes miRNA deregulation and affects brain function color *Science* v357 no6357 p1254 S 22 2017

Rajgopal, Shivaram
Managers Aren't Doing Enough to Encourage Whistleblowing bw *Harvard Business Review Digital Articles* p2 F 7 2017
Research: Firms Give More Stock Options When They're Committing Fraud color *Harvard Business Review Digital Articles* p2 Ja 26 2017

Rajman, Luis A.
A conserved NAD+ binding pocket that regulates protein-protein interactions during aging bibl graph *Science* v355 no6331 p1312 Mr 24 2017

Rajoy, Mariano, 1955-
Don't Call It the "End of the Siesta": What Spain's New Work Hours Really Mean M. Mayo *Harvard Business Review Digital Articles* p2 Ap 13 2016

Rakes
THE SANTA CATALINAS: TUCSON'S NEARBY WILDERNESS C. BOWDEN *Arizona Highways* v93 no6 p46 Je 2017

Rakoff, Jed S.
Why You Won't Get Your Day in Court bw cartoon *New York Review of Books* v63 no18 p4 N 24 2016
Will the Death Penalty Ever Die? color *New York Review of Books* v64 no10 p46 Je 8 2017

Rakover, Jeffrey
4 Steps to Sustaining Improvement in Health Care *Harvard Business Review Digital Articles* p2 N 9 2016
A Simple Way to Involve Frontline Clinicians in Managing Costs *Harvard Business Review Digital Articles* p2 O 11 2017

Rakowitz, Michael
IDENTITY ARTIST J. FOUMBERG color *Chicago* v66 no10 p72 O 2017

Rakuten Kobo Inc.
SHARJAH INTERNATIONAL BOOK FAIR Q&A WITH MICHAEL TAMBLYN *Publishers Weekly* v263 no43 p(Sp)22 O 24 2016

Raleigh Bicycle Co.
"I LOVE OLD-SCHOOL STEEL BIKES." J. Sherry and B. STRICKLAND color *Bicycling* v58 no3 p78 Ap 2017

Ralph, John
Formaldehyde stabilization facilitates lignin monomer production during biomass depolymerization bibl diag graph *Science* v354 no6310 p329 O 21 2016

RALPH, MICHAEL
The Slave Insurance Market map *Foreign Policy* no222 p22 Ja/F 2017

Ralph Lauren Corp.
Clothes Make the Man C. Edwards cartoon *O, The Oprah Magazine* p122 Mr 2017
COUNTER INTELLIGENCE M. M. GOLDSTEIN *Martha Stew-*

art Living no269 p50 N 2016
IN THE DETAILS color *Harper's Bazaar* no3650 p101 F 2017
TOUGH LOVE color *O, The Oprah Magazine* p61 O 2017
THE WINNING LOOK R. Lauren and J. Marksbury color *Golf Magazine* v59 no9 p40 S 2017

Ralph Pucci International (Company)
Hot Zone M. RUS color *Architectural Digest* v74 no4 p52 Ap 2017

Ralph M. Captain Elementary School (Clayton, Mo.)
Sam Altman J. Crelin color *Current Biography* v78 no4 p7 Ap 2017

Ralston, Katherine
School Districts in the Northeast Are Most Likely To Serve Local Foods on a Daily Basis *Amber Waves: The Economics of Food, Farming, Natural Resources, & Rural America* p1 My 2017
USDA's National School Lunch Program Reduces Food Insecurity *Amber Waves: The Economics of Food, Farming, Natural Resources, & Rural America* p38 Ag 2017

RALSTON, PETER
'Wyeth World': On the centennial of the birth of Andrew Wyeth, a fellow artist and lifelong friend offers this one-of-a-kind remembrance bw color *Yankee* p18 Jl 2017

Ram, Rajeev
Hometown Hero J. SCOTT *Tennis* v52 no6 p38 N/D 2016
TENNIS, ANYONE? J. WERTHEIM *Indianapolis Monthly* v40 no4 p96 D 2016

Ram, Sangeeth
The World's Housing Crisis Doesn't Need a Revolutionary Solution *Harvard Business Review Digital Articles* p2 D 25 2014

Ram truck
RAM RUNNER [Cover story] M. EMERY color *Dirt Sports + Off-Road* v51 no1 p24 Ja 2017

Ram truck—Evaluation
Ram 2500/3500 HD chart color *Motor Trend* v69 no1 p88 Ja 2017
Ram Rebel TRX Concept S. Ogbac color *Motor Trend* v69 no1 p16 Ja 2017

Ramadan
Ramadan in Scandinavia: Muslims face the choice between "excessive" and "moderate" fasting E. POLJAREVIC *Islamic Horizons* v46 no3 p48 My/Je 2017
When Less Means More: Conservation and protecting the environment adds to the blessings of Ramadan and one's year-round worship M. A. SHAH *Islamic Horizons* v46 no3 p46 My/Je 2017

Ramakers, Meine
De novo design of a biologically active amyloid bibl graph *Science* v354 no6313 paah4949-1 N 11 2016

Ramakrishnan, Charu
Thirst-associated preoptic neurons encode an aversive motivational drive diag *Science* v357 no6356 p1149 S 15 2017

Ramakrishnan, Naren
Growing pains for global monitoring of societal events bibl graph *Science* v353 no6307 p1502 S 30 2016

Ramakrishnan, S.
Evidence for bulk superconductivity in pure bismuth single crystals at ambient pressure bibl color graph *Science* v355 no6320 p1 Ja 6 2017

Ramakrishnan, Uma
Merging paleobiology with conservation biology to guide the future of terrestrial ecosystems color *Science* v355 no6325 p594 F 10 2017

Ramakrishnan, V.
The structure of the yeast mitochondrial ribosome bibl color *Science* v355 no6324 p528 F 3 2017
Translational termination without a stop codon bibl color *Science* v354 no6318 p1437 D 16 2016

Ramalingam, Suresh S.
Rescue of exhausted CD8 T cells by PD-1-targeted therapies is CD28-dependent bw diag graph *Science* v355 no6332 p1423 Mr 31 2017

Ramamurti, Ravi
3 Ways Businesses Are Addressing Inequality in Emerging Markets *Harvard Business Review Digital Articles* p2 Ja 23 2015

Raman, Ananth
Shutting Down Stores Doesn't Have to Be Bad for Business *Harvard Business Review Digital Articles* p2 Je 26 2015

Raman, T. R. Shankar
Elephant Crossing T. R. SHANKAR RAMAN *Orion Magazine* v35 no3 p6 My/Je 2016

Ramanantsoa, Sylvie
Working with Strong Service Providers to Address the Urban Water and Sanitation Challenge *UN Chronicle* v53 no3 p28 2016

Ramanathan, V.
A climate policy pathway for near- and long-term benefits color *Science* v356 no6337 p493 My 5 2017

Ramani, Vijay
Comprehensive single-cell transcriptional profiling of a multicellular organism diag *Science* v357 no6352 p661 Ag 18 2017

Ramanuja, 1017-1137
A toast to Ramanuja C. Zaleski *Christian Century* v134 no6 p37 Mr 15 2017

Ramanujam, Madhavan
In Product Development, Let Your Customers Define Perfection *Harvard Business Review Digital Articles* p2 My 9 2016
Your New Hit Product Might Be Underpriced *Harvard Business Review Digital Articles* p2 My 24 2016

Ramaswamy, Aparna
whyidance A. Ramaswamy *Dance Magazine* v90 no12 p128 D 2016

Ramaswamy, Satya
How Companies Are Already Using AI *Harvard Business Review Digital Articles* p2 Ap 14 2017
Using IoT Data to Understand How Your Products Perform *Harvard Business Review Digital Articles* p2 Je 16 2016

Ramaswamy, Sree
The Most Digital Companies Are Leaving All the Rest Behind *Harvard Business Review Digital Articles* p2 Ja 21 2016
We Can't Undo Globalization, but We Can Improve It color *Harvard Business Review Digital Articles* p2 Ja 10 2017
Which Industries Are the Most Digital (and Why)? *Harvard Business Review Digital Articles* p2 Ap 1 2016

Ramaswamy, Vasant Kumar
Bridging Health Care's Innovation-Education Gap *Harvard Business Review Digital Articles* p2 N 11 2014

Ramaswamy, Vivek
This Pharma Company Stays Innovative by Doing Two Things *Harvard Business Review Digital Articles* p2 Mr 14 2017

Rambaut, Andrew
Role for migratory wild birds in the global spread of avian influenza H5N8 bibl graph map *Science* v354 no6309 p213 O 14 2016

Rambharose, Amber
THE Fresh Faces color *Glamour* v115 no10 p178 O 2017
These Fall Perfumes Gave Us All the Feels bw color *Glamour* v115 no10 p98 O 2017

Rambla, Jose Luis
A chemical genetic roadmap to improved tomato flavor bibl graph *Science* v355 no6323 p391 Ja 27 2017

Rambo, Cat
Neither Here Nor There color *Publishers Weekly* v263 no45 p44 N 7 2016

Ramdas, Kamalini
Build a Company Where Everyone's Looking for New Ideas *Harvard Business Review Digital Articles* p2 D 11 2014

Ramen
15-Minute All-Organic Meal under $15 color *Prevention* v68 no11 p14 N 2016
RAMEN EMPIRE color *Women's Health* v14 no1 p44 Ja/F 2017
Ramen Gone Wild B. HALLOCK *Los Angeles Magazine* p48 F 2017
SUPER BOWLS *Los Angeles Magazine* v62 no9 p108 S 2017
(THE JAPANESE FOOD LOVERS GUIDE) RAMEN! TEMPURA! SUSHI! YAKITORI! MOCHI! *Los Angeles Magazine* v62 no9 p104 S 2017

Ramer, Rosalee
Taking Flight in Vegas color *O, The Oprah Magazine* p100 Je 2017

Ramey, Andrew M.
A genetic signature of the evolution of loss of flight in the Galapagos cormorant color diag *Science* v356 no6341 p921 Je 1 2017

RAMEY, TONYA L.
Terrestrial Invertebrates in the Riparian Zone: Mechanisms Underlying Their Unique Diversity *BioScience* v67 no9 p808 S

2017

Rami, Trupti
4 Could This Be in Your Living Rooms Future? img *New York* v49 no21 p92 O 17 2016
Beyond the Brita img *New York* p61 F 9 2017
PARTY LINES img *New York* v50 no16 p110 Ag 7 2017

Ramirez, Amanda
Regeneration of fat cells from myofibroblasts during wound healing bibl color graph *Science* v355 no6326 p748 F 17 2017

Ramirez, Arcelia
A brilliant nun with no time for short-sighted men N. Ripatrazone color *America* v216 no7 p49 Ap 3 2017

RAMIREZ, CAIN
THANKS FOR THE RIDE color *Bicycling* v58 no10 p15 N/D 2017

RAMIREZ, ELAINE
Asia's Rising Stars color *Forbes* v199 no5 p20 My 16 2017

Ramirez, Jordan
WILDTHINGS J. ROEDEL bw color *Louisiana Life* v37 no4 p16 Mr/Ap 2017

Ramirez, Martin, 1895-1963
Current and coming N. Anderson, S. Dalati et al bw color *Magazine Antiques* v184 no5 p26 S/O 2017

Ramirez, Pedro J.
Active sites for CO2 hydrogenation to methanol on Cu/ZnO catalysts bibl graph *Science* v355 no6331 p1296 Mr 24 2017
TECHNICAL COMMENT ABSTRACTS *Science* v357 no6354 p881 S 1 2017

Ramirez, Ricardo N.
Regeneration of fat cells from myofibroblasts during wound healing bibl color graph *Science* v355 no6326 p748 F 17 2017

Ramirez-Angulo, H.
Persistent effects of pre-Columbian plant domestication on Amazonian forest composition bibl chart graph map *Science* v355 no6328 p925 Mr 3 2017

Ramirez-Llodra, E.
An ecosystem-based deep-ocean strategy bibl color map *Science* v355 no6324 p452 F 3 2017

Ramirez-Martinez, Andres
Control of muscle formation by the fusogenic micropeptide myomixer diag *Science* v356 no6335 p323 Ap 21 2017

Ramirez Molina, Cesar
Click chemistry enables preclinical evaluation of targeted epigenetic therapies diag *Science* v356 no6345 p1397 Je 30 2017

Ramirez-Rosa, Carlos
Carlos Ramirez-Rosa E. KANG color *Chicago* v66 no6 p95 Je 2017
Meet Chicago's Movement Politician D. D. GUTTENPLAN color *Nation* v305 no3 p22 Jl 31 2017

Ramli, David
Airbnb Finds China Is A Crowded House color *Bloomberg Businessweek* no4527 p23 Je 19 2017
AI With Chinese Characteristics color diag *Bloomberg Businessweek* no4515 p38 Mr 20 2017
China's Twitter Returns From the Dead color graph *Bloomberg Businessweek* no4526 p28 Je 12 2017
THE TALKING CAT AND THE PEROXIDE CORPORATION color *Bloomberg Businessweek* no4523 p54 My 22 2017
When the Teacher Is An Ocean Away color graph *Bloomberg Businessweek* no4505 p22 D 26 2016

RAMMEL, KEEGAN
SOCCER FANS AT CHATHAM TAP *Indianapolis Monthly* v40 no5 p14 Ja 2017

Ramos, Alejandra
Priming HIV-1 broadly neutralizing antibody precursors in human Ig loci transgenic mice bibl graph *Science* v353 no6307 p1557 S 30 2016

Ramos, Clint
The Activist ARTIST L. Mulcahy *Stage Directions* v30 no3 p56 Mr 2017

Ramos, J. F.
Persistent effects of pre-Columbian plant domestication on Amazonian forest composition bibl chart graph map *Science* v355 no6328 p925 Mr 3 2017

Ramos, Jorge—Interviews
30 Years of Jorge Ramos L. Ahuile bw *Publishers Weekly* v263

no44 p(Sp)20 O 31 2016

Ramos, Mireya

They're with the Banda M. GOLDBERG color *O, The Oprah Magazine* p23 Jl 2017

Ramos, Raul

Regeneration of fat cells from myofibroblasts during wound healing bibl color graph *Science* v355 no6326 p748 F 17 2017

Ramos, Sean

U.S. Agricultural Trade in 2016: Major Commodities and Trends *Amber Waves: The Economics of Food, Farming, Natural Resources, & Rural America* p1 My 2017

Ramos-Pollan, R.

Observation of a large-scale anisotropy in the arrival directions of cosmic rays above 8 × 1018 eV *Science* v357 no6357 p1266 S 22 2017

Rampage truck

Roadster Shop's Widebody 1970 Camaro Track Weapoon RAMPAGE B. Gillogly color *Hot Rod* v69 no12 p18 D 2016

RAMPE, AMELIA

Waffle On color *Bon Appetit* p76 S 2017

Rampe, E. B.

Redox stratification of an ancient lake in Gale crater, Mars color *Science* v356 no6341 p922 Je 1 2017

Rampell, Ed

FOLLOW THE FUNNY: SPEAKING JOKES TO POWER color *Progressive* v81 no6 p48 Ag/S 2017

The Making of Donald Trump/The Politics of Murder: Organized Crime in Barry Goldwater's Arizona/Spooked: How the CIA Manipulates the Media and Hoodwinks Hollywood... color *Progressive* p60 D 2016/Ja 2017

Must-See TV *Sierra* v101 no6 p9 N/D 2016

Ramphastos

TOUCAN GETS NEW BEAK! R. Davidson *National Geographic Kids* no466 p12 D 2016/Ja 2017

Rampling, Charlotte, 1946-

IMPRESSIONS OF A LIFE L. THOMSON bw color *Publishers Weekly* v264 no21 p43 My 22 2017

Rampone & Cazzani (Company)

Rampone & Cazzani 'Two Voices' J. Bowes color *Downbeat* v84 no5 p84 My 2017

Ramqvist, Karolina

The White City *Publishers Weekly* v263 no52 p92 D 19 2016

Rams

TESTING THE AIR *South Dakota Magazine* v32 no4 p108 N/D 2016

Ramsay, Bertram H.

MASTERMIND OF DUNKIRK [Cover story] P. J. Kiger bw color map *MHQ: Quarterly Journal of Military History* v30 no1 p30 Aut 2017

Ramsay, Gordon, 1966-

Hell's Kitchen N. Abrams, S. Highfill et al *Entertainment Weekly* no1482/1483 p99 S 22 2017

MasterChef Junior M. Logan *TV Guide* v65 no6 p41 Ja 30 2017

Out & About *TV Guide* v65 no25 p2 Je 2017

Ramsay, Gordon, 1966—Interviews

Fired Up M. LOGAN *TV Guide* v65 no23 p16 My 29 2017

Ramsay, Kay A.

Emergence and spread of a human-transmissible multidrug-resistant nontuberculous mycobacterium bibl diag graph *Science* v354 no6313 p751 N 11 2016

Ramsay-Levi, Natacha

La Femme Natacha M. HOLGATE color *Vogue* v207 no7 p94 Jl 2017

Ramsey, Aaron

FUN & GAMES color *Backpacker* p71 Je 2017

Ramsey, Drew

Eat these to stress less cartoon *Redbook* p92 F 2017

Ramsey, James

The Lowline D. A. Ciampaglia *Architectural Record* v205 no4 p213 Ap 2017

Ramsey, JonBenet, d. 1996

TonBenet Murder Mystery Solved? J. NICKELL *Skeptical Inquirer* v41 no4 p38 Jl/Ag 2017

RAMSEY, REBECCA

Nine Cool Girls img *New York* v50 no10 p60 My 15 2017

THE VERY RED CARPET: And other trends that most caught

our eye on the runways img *New York* v50 no16 p58 Ag 7 2017

Ramy El-Maarry, M.

Surface changes on comet 67P/Churyumov-Gerasimenko suggest a more active past bw graph *Science* v355 no6332 p1392 Mr 31 2017

RAMZI, LILAH

Comme les COLOMBIENS color *Vogue* v207 no7 p42 Jl 2017

IN Season color *Vogue* v206 no12 p212 D 2016

MIAMI Rhapsody color *Vogue* v206 no11 p180 N 2016

Paper Trail color *Vogue* v207 no9 p614 S 2017

SOFIA Boutella color *Vogue* v207 no7 p48 Jl 2017

THE WORLD'S HIS STAGE bw *Vogue* v207 no6 p109 Je 2017

Zoë Kravitz and Karl Glusman color *Vogue* v207 no6 p58 Je 2017

Ran An

A nuclease that mediates cell death induced by DNA damage and poly(ADP-ribose) polymerase-1 bw graph *Science* v354 no6308 paad6872-1 O 7 2016

Rana, Mohammed Waheed-uz-Zaman

IN MEMORIAM *Islamic Horizons* v46 no1 p41 Ja/F 2017

Ranallo, Andrew

Ali Sandifer color *American Craft* v77 no3 p45 Je/Jl 2017

Amara Hark-Weber color *American Craft* v77 no3 p40 Je/Jl 2017

Emily Nachison color *American Craft* v77 no3 p47 Je/Jl 2017

Greycork color *American Craft* v77 no2 p12 Ap/My 2017

Janice Arnold color *American Craft* v77 no3 p44 Je/Jl 2017

Maria Molteni color *American Craft* v77 no3 p12 Je/Jl 2017

Martinez Studio color *American Craft* v77 no3 p46 Je/Jl 2017

Rana Plaza factory collapse, 2013

The Toll of Cheap Clothing V. Vara color *Bloomberg Businessweek* no4497 p10 O 31 2016

Ranch, The (TV program)

URBAN Cowboy D. HOLBROOK *TV Guide* v65 no25 p16 Je 2017

Ranch houses

Home on the Ranch H. WILHELM *National Review* v69 no17 p44 S 11 2017

Proud To Be a Rancher K. Owen color *Southern Living* v52 no2 p26 F 2017

Shooting Life BELOW ZERO color *Nebraska Life* v21 no1 p36 Ja/F 2017

Ranch houses—Interior decoration

BACK AT THE RANCH L. CUTRONE color *Louisiana Life* v37 no4 p28 Mr/Ap 2017

Ranch life—West (U.S.)

ELEANOR'S ARABIAN FARM G. Dearth *Arabian Horse World* v57 no10 p1 Jl 2017

Ranch roping

50 Reasons to Love Being 50+ color *AARP: The Magazine* v59 no1A p49 D 2015/Ja 2016

BACK-TO-BACK color *Spin to Win Rodeo* v20 no10 p17 D 2016

NEW PRODUCTS color *Spin to Win Rodeo* v21 no5 p18 Jl 2017

Rancher, Farmer, Fisherman (Film)

Rancher, Farmer, Fisherman C. Wolner color *Science* v356 no6337 p483 My 5 2017

Ranchero automobile

Who Needs TV? E. Perkins color *Hot Rod* v70 no8 p8 Ag 2017

Ranchers

See also

Women ranchers

ACCESS AGENTS A. McKEAN color *Outdoor Life* v224 no1 p32 D 2016/Ja 2017

The Long Rope C. Hutchison color *American Cowboy* v23 no4 p42 D 2016/Ja 2017

THE MAVERICK: "Doc "Doc; Luce" "The Maverick Doctor"... these are just some of the names people use when referring to Sam Luce. The names vary, but the regal'd is the same: Sam Luce is a legend down in the Blue K. VAUGHN *Arizona Highways* v96 no7 p34 Jl 2017

MORE LEGUMES *Successful Farming* v114 no13 p64 D 2016

Thoughts on previous issues R. Trotman, C. S. Underwood et al color *American Cowboy* v23 no4 p26 D 2016/Ja 2017

Ranches

Crescent Moon Ranch A. McGIVNEY color *Arizona Highways* v93 no5 p14 My 2017

FAB FIRST IMPRESSIONS M. M. Kashino *Washingtonian Magazine* v52 no9 p156 Je 2017

Falling in love with New Mexico B. Jo Lieberman color *Equus* no477 p46 Je 2017

Guest-Ranch Guide color *Trail Rider* v29 no3 p84 Ap 2017

Pretty farmhouse in Keya Paha color *Nebraska Life* v21 no4 p16 Jl/Ag 2017

Southwest Solitude K. KRONE and C. KRONE color *Horse & Rider* v56 no9 p94 S 2017

The Spirit of the West B. Welch *American Cowboy* v24 no1 p8 Je/Jl 2017

Ranches—Arizona

Arizona Paradise J. DROWN color *Trail Rider* v29 no3 p54 Ap 2017

BABACOMARI: 50 Years Later B. Cossavella *Arizona Highways* v93 no4 p43 Ap 2017

El Rancho Robles A. McGIVNEY *Arizona Highways* v93 no1 p14 Ja 2017

IT'S GOOD TO BE Home K. VAUGHN *Arizona Highways* v93 no4 p44 Ap 2017

Rancho de la Osa K. MONTGOMERY *Arizona Highways* v92 no7 p8 Jl 2016

SAN IGNACIO DEL BABACOMARI F. C. BROPHY *Arizona Highways* v93 no4 p36 Ap 2017

TAKING THE TOUR 2017 K. MONTGOMERY *Arizona Highways* v93 no11 p40 N 2017

Ranches—California

Ride California's Wine Country A. PAVIA color *Trail Rider* v29 no3 p42 Ap 2017

Ranches—Colorado

Working Vacation K. KRONE and C. KRONE color *Trail Rider* v29 no3 p46 Ap 2017

Ranches—Conservation & restoration

Buildings Like Bones S. J. Dahlstrom color *American Cowboy* p62 LEGENDS OF TEXAS Special Issue 2017

RANCH REDEMPTION P. POORE color *Arts & Crafts Homes & the Revival* v11 no5 p48 Wint 2017

Ranches—Evaluation

El Rancho Robles A. McGIVNEY *Arizona Highways* v93 no1 p14 Ja 2017

In Search of Serenity C. Hall color *AARP: The Magazine* v60 no3A p40B Ap/My 2017

Ranches—Florida

Splash in the Sunshine State C. MCFARLAND color *Trail Rider* v29 no3 p50 Ap 2017

Ranches—Management

Reaching the Next Level B. Welch color *American Cowboy* v24 no1 p20 Je/Jl 2017

Ranches—Montana

Working Vacation K. KRONE and C. KRONE color *Trail Rider* v29 no3 p46 Ap 2017

Ranches—New Mexico

Decision time B. Jo Lieberman color *Equus* no480 p60 S 2017

Ranches—Texas

Buildings Like Bones S. J. Dahlstrom color *American Cowboy* p62 LEGENDS OF TEXAS Special Issue 2017

Cast Out OF EDEN L. REIGSTAD *Texas Monthly* v45 no3 p51 Mr 2017

THE FAMOUS BRANDS OF TEXAS color *American Cowboy* p85 LEGENDS OF TEXAS Special Issue 2017

Great Texas Ranches color *American Cowboy* p71 LEGENDS OF TEXAS Special Issue 2017

Guest Ranch Redefined: EVERYTHING OLD IS NEW AGAIN AT THIS HILL COUNTRY HIDEAWAY L. SMITH FORD *Texas Monthly* v45 no9 p13 S 2017

High Sierras, Low Stress E. D. Klepper color map *American Cowboy* p78 LEGENDS OF TEXAS Special Issue 2017

HOTELS and B&B's *Texas Monthly* v45 no3 p102 Mr 2017

Ranching

Family T-i-e-s K. Santos color *Team Roping Journal* p94 O 2017

Pubic Lands Ranching A. Rieber cartoon *American Cowboy* v23 no4 p22 D 2016/Ja 2017

Ranching—Economic aspects

The Heart of Cowboy Camp J. Young bw color *American Cowboy* v23 no6 p48 Ap/My 2017

Ranching—Equipment & supplies

NEW PRODUCTS color *Spin to Win Rodeo* v21 no5 p18 Jl 2017

Rancho de la Osa (Sasabe, Ariz.)

Rancho de la Osa K. MONTGOMERY *Arizona Highways* v92 no7 p8 Jl 2016

RANCO, DARREN

Invasive Species, Indigenous Stewards, and Vulnerability Discourse chart diag map *American Indian Quarterly* v41 no3 p201 Summ 2017

Rand, Ayn, 1905-1982

Objectively Speaking, Rand Is History: The recent presidential race made it obvious: conservatives have shrugged off Ayn Rand J. Burns *Hoover Digest: Research & Opinion on Public Policy* no3 p170 Summ 2017

THOUGHTS ON Conflict *Forbes* v199 no4 p112 Ap 25 2017

Randall, Brianna

I Tried Going Diaper-Free. It Stunk cartoon *Working Mother* p58 F/Mr 2017

Randall, Caitlin

Trump Finds Support in Britain's Brexit Capital *Wilson Quarterly* p5 Spr 2017

Randall, Chris

How Consumer Brands Can Connect with Customers in a Changing Retail Landscape *Harvard Business Review Digital Articles* p2 Ag 4 2017

How Subscriptions Are Creating Winners and Losers in Retail *Harvard Business Review Digital Articles* p2 Ja 8 2016

How to Know Which Digital Trends Are Worth Chasing *Harvard Business Review Digital Articles* p2 Jl 7 2016

Randall, Kayla

THE CHESAPEAKE'S FEMINIST LIGHTHOUSE *Washingtonian Magazine* v52 no7 p157 Ap 2017

FACEBOOK FOR GRANDMA *Washingtonian Magazine* v52 no9 p21 Je 2017

GARDEN VARIETY *Washingtonian Magazine* v52 no9 p28 Je 2017

HOUSES WITH HISTORY *Washingtonian Magazine* v52 no9 p172 Je 2017

IN BLOOM *Washingtonian Magazine* v52 no11 p24 Ag 2017

SAIGON SUPERSTORE *Washingtonian Magazine* v52 no8 p28 My 2017

SPACE CONSERVATION *Washingtonian Magazine* v52 no12 p24 S 2017

TIGER TOMBSTONE *Washingtonian Magazine* v52 no9 p24 Je 2017

WHERE & WHEN: 17 THINGS YOU REALLY OUGHT TO DO THIS MONTH *Washingtonian Magazine* v53 no1 p31 O 2017

WHERE & WHEN: 18 THINGS YOU REALLY OUGHT TO DO THIS MONTH *Washingtonian Magazine* v52 no12 p29 S 2017

WHERE & WHEN color *Washingtonian Magazine* v52 no7 p31 Ap 2017

WHERE & WHEN *Washingtonian Magazine* v52 no8 p35 My 2017

THE WHOLE HILL *Washingtonian Magazine* v52 no9 p162 Je 2017

RANDALL, LISA

A COSMIC CONTROVERSY color *Scientific American* v317 no1 p5 Jl 2017

Unpeeling the Universe: A physicist offers a brief tour of reality and considers the quantum nature of space and time *New York Times Book Review* p15 Mr 5 2017

Randall, Tom

FLASH color *Climbing* no351 p8 F/Mr 2017

THE FUTURE ACCORDING TO MUSK bw color *Bloomberg Businessweek* no4529 p48 Jl 3 2017

Randall, Trish

Odysseys in Skepticism *Skeptical Inquirer* v41 no2 p65 Mr/Ap 2017

Randall, Willard Sterne

Unshackling America: How the War of 1812 Truly Ended the American Revolution color *Publishers Weekly* v264 no18 p51 My 1 2017

Randeria, Mallika T.

Observation of a nematic quantum Hall liquid on the surface of bismuth bibl graph *Science* v354 no6310 p316 O 21 2016

Randeria, Mohit

Introduction to Many-Body Physics *Physics Today* v70 no5 p59 My 2017

Randerson, J. T.

How to remove ransomware: Use this battle plan to fight back M. HACHMAN color *PCWorld* v35 no4 p129 Ap 2017

Old Windows PCs can stop WannaCry ransomware with new Microsoft patch M. KAN color map *PCWorld* v35 no6 p22 Je 2017

Wanawiki is the WannaCry fix that might save affected PCs M. HACHMAN color *PCWorld* v35 no6 p25 Je 2017

Ranunculus

PAPER POSIES L. HEDRICK color *Better Homes & Gardens* v95 no5 p39 My 2017

RAO, ANJULIE

GET BEACHED color *Chicago* v66 no7 p50 Jl 2017

KIDS THESE DAYS cartoon *Chicago* v66 no4 p40 Ap 2017

Range Design color *Chicago* v66 no6 p82 Je 2017

ROCK THE BLOCK color *Chicago* v66 no7 p52 Jl 2017

WHY We LOVE CHICAGO bw cartoon color *Chicago* v66 no3 p75 Mr 2017

Rao, Ercole

Trispecific broadly neutralizing HIV antibodies mediate potent SHIV protection in macaques color graph *Science* v357 no6359 p85 O 6 2017

Rao, H. B. D. Prasada

A SUMO-ubiquitin relay recruits proteasomes to chromosome axes to regulate meiotic recombination bibl graph *Science* v355 no6323 p403 Ja 27 2017

RAO, JOE

The 2017 Total Solar Eclipse *Weatherwise* v70 no2 p12 Mr/Ap 2017

Cluster Shots [Cover story] color *Natural History* v125 no11 p44 N 2017

The Crow and the Cup color *Natural History* v125 no4 p44 Ap 2017

Early Spring color *Natural History* v125 no3 p45 Mr 2017

Flu Season color *Natural History* v125 no9 p46 S 2017

Getting in Step *Natural History* v125 no1 p38 D 2016/Ja 2017

The Kneeler color *Natural History* v125 no6 p45 Je 2017

A Moment of Darkness color *Natural History* v125 no7 p43 Jl/Ag 2017

The Month of Venus *Natural History* v125 no2 p44 F 2017

Moonlighting in May color *Natural History* v125 no5 p45 My 2017

Occulting the Little King color *Natural History* v125 no10 p45 O 2017

OCTOBER NIGHTS OUT *Natural History* v125 no10 p45 O 2017

Spring Tide *Natural History* v124 no10 p45 N 2016

Rao, Justin

Where Predictive Analytics Is Having the Biggest Impact *Harvard Business Review Digital Articles* p2 My 25 2016

Rao, Leena

2 JEFF BEZOS color *Fortune* v174 no7 p74 D 1 2016

4 LARRY PAGE color *Fortune* v174 no7 p75 D 1 2016

BREAKTHROUGH BRANDS 2017 color diag *Fortune* v75 no1 p64 Ja 1 2017

A FORERUNNER IN VENTURE CAPITAL color *Fortune* v176 no1 p36 Jl 1 2017

OUT OF THE BOX color *Fortune* v174 no7 p22 D 1 2016

PERSON OF INTEREST color *Fortune* v174 no6 p23 N 1 2016

THE REVOLUTION STARTS HERE color *Fortune* v174 no7 p26 D 1 2016

THE VALLEY'S FAVORITE BRITISH IMPORT color *Fortune* v174 no6 p46 N 1 2016

Rao, Michael

MAKE THE WORLD MORE BEAUTIFUL M. RAO *Vital Speeches of the Day* v83 no8 p246 Ag 2017

Rao, Priya

LOSING IT color *Women's Health* v14 no2 p43 Mr 2017

Rao, Sameer R.

Water harvesting from air with metal-organic frameworks powered by natural sunlight diag *Science* v356 no6336 p430 Ap 28 2017

Rao, Shalini

If CEOs Care About the Long Term, Why Don't They Talk About It? *Harvard Business Review Digital Articles* p2 N 13 2015

Rao, Srikumar

To Build Your Resilience, Ask Yourself Two Simple Questions *Harvard Business Review Digital Articles* p2 Je 13 2017

Rao, Stephen

Alzheimer's and the 15-Year Window M. Cohen color *Prevention* v69 no8 p80 Ag 2017

Rao, Swarna Subba

Vertically Challenged? color *Earth Island Journal* v32 no1 p6 Spr 2017

Rao, Tejal

Buttered Up: Sweet and supple, kubaneh is shot through with fat to create a melting, airy bread *New York Times Magazine* p30 Je 25 2017

Comfort Food *New York Times Book Review* p13 Jl 2 2017

Good Vibration *New York Times Magazine* p30 O 16 2016

A Grandmother's Secret Prescription *New York Times Magazine* p24 Ja 22 2017

Hot-Weather Comfort Food: Cold pork noodles dressed in vinegar, from the East Village by way of Yunnan *New York Times Magazine* p28 Jl 23 2017

India in an Instant: The secret to an amazing mango kulfi comes in a can *New York Times Magazine* p34 S 17 2017

In Praise of the Prune *New York Times Magazine* p24 F 19 2017

Oysters: A Love Story *New York Times Magazine* p24 Ag 20 2017

Provence in a Bowl: Jessica B. Harris's soupe au pistou will take you from spring through summer, with your pot reflecting the bounty of the seasons *New York Times Magazine* p30 Ap 30 2017

The Ultimate Comfort Food *New York Times Magazine* p32 N 20 2016

Rao, Valluri R. M.

Community network for deaf scientists color *Science* v356 no6336 p386 Ap 28 2017

Raonic, Milos, 1990-

LEARNING FROM... MILOS RAONIC S. Tignor *Tennis* v53 no1 p17 Ja/F 2017

Milos Raonic *Tennis* v53 no1 p16 Ja/F 2017

Ready to Launch S. TIGNOR *Tennis* v53 no4 p52 Jl/Ag 2017

Rao's Restaurant Group LLC

No Place Like Rao's A. WITCHEL bw color *Vanity Fair* v58 no11 p170 N 2016

Rap, Alexandru

Global atmospheric particle formation from CERN CLOUD measurements bibl graph map *Science* v354 no6316 p1119 D 2 2016

Rap music

'90s TILL INFINITY: LEADERS OF THE NEW SCHOOL M. A. GONZALES bw color *Ebony* v72 no8 p90 Je 2017

CHICER THAN RAP: HIP-HOP'S MOST FORMIDABLE FASHION VENTURES N. SANTOS and B. GARWOOD color map *Ebony* v72 no11 p80 S 2017

CLIVE DAVIS N. Maslow color *Entertainment Weekly* no1486 p59 O 13 2017

DONALD GLOVER M. A. GREEN color *GQ: Gentlemen's Quarterly* v86 no12 p188 D 2016

HIP-HOP AND HYPERMASCULINITY A. EMMANUEL color *Ebony* v72 no8 p67 Je 2017

HIP-HOP'S FAB THREE J. WEINER color *Rolling Stone* no1281/1282 p38 F 23 2017

TALK TO US color *Chicago* v65 no11 p16 N 2016

THE WOUNDED HEART OF MACHINE GUN KELLY B. HIATT color *Rolling Stone* no1290 p40 Je 29 2017

Rap musicians

5 JUICY QUESTIONS with... Riz Ahmed C. Keller color *Women's Health* v13 no10 p108 D 2016

FRESH C. Battan cartoon *New Yorker* v93 no18 p18 Je 26 2017

GOINGS ON ABOUT TOWN color *New Yorker* v93 no27 p7 S 11 2017

HOOKED ON HER M. Nance color *Essence* v47 no7 p48 N 2016

Hot Rebel MC Lil Yachty J. WEINER bw color *Rolling Stone* no1274 p38 N 17 2016

Hot Tracks D. DIGGS color *Vanity Fair* v59 no1 p96 Holiday 2017

Mike WiLL Made-It J. Black color *Esquire* p46 Ag 2017

Salomon FAYE D. HYMAN *Interview* v47 no3 p24 My 2017

A TALE OF TUPAC M. LOSGAR color *Vanity Fair* v59 no7 p115 Summ 2017

TALK TO US color *Chicago* v65 no11 p16 N 2016

Viva los Migos Z. BARON color *GQ: Gentlemen's Quarterly* v97 no5 p104 My 2017

2017

O, Pioneer bw *Film Comment* v53 no2 p10 Mr/Ap 2017

Parting the Clouds bw *Film Comment* v53 no4 p10 Jl/Ag 2017

Rich and Strange color *Film Comment* v52 no6 p10 N/D 2016

Ship of Fools bw color *Film Comment* v53 no5 p8 S/O 2017

Raponi, A.

Localized aliphatic organic material on the surface of Ceres bibl graph *Science* v355 no6326 p719 F 17 2017

Seasonal exposure of carbon dioxide ice on the nucleus of comet 67P/Churyumov-Gerasimenko bibl bw graph *Science* v354 no6319 p1563 D 23 2016

RAPOPORT, ADAM

12 Questions for Kumail Nanjiani bw *Bon Appetit* v62 no7 p24 Jl 2017

THE ART of SIMPLICITY color *Bon Appetit* no8 p56 Ag 2017

A BLOODY GOOD TIME color *Bon Appetit* no11 p10 N 2017

Cheesesteaks for All color *Bon Appetit* no1 p36 F 2017

CHEF'S SALAD *Bon Appetit* v62 no7 p10 Jl 2017

COMING TO AMERICA bw *Bon Appetit* v62 no2 p12 Mr 2017

Dinner Tonight color *Bon Appetit* no11 p43 N 2017

editor's letter bw *Bon Appetit* p14 S 2017

Katsu Son color *Bon Appetit* v62 no6 p38 Je 2017

LET'S GET HEALTHY-ISH color *Bon Appetit* no1 p8 F 2017

The No-Frills NEGRONI color *Glamour* v115 no1 p96 Ja 2017

PURE AND SIMPLE color *Bon Appetit* no8 p12 Ag 2017

r.s.v.p.: BEST NEW RESTAURANTS EDITION bw color *Bon Appetit* p16 S 2017

starters color *Bon Appetit* p25 S 2017

TENDER IS THE NIGHT color *Bon Appetit* v61 no12 p18 D 2016 /Jan2017

Thanksgiving LESSONS [Cover story] color *Bon Appetit* no11 p82 N 2017

THAT SWEET CHAR color *Bon Appetit* no11 p128 N 2017

UNCHARTED WATERS color *Bon Appetit* v61 no11 p12 N 2016

WHERE IT ALL BEGINS color *Bon Appetit* v62 no4 p8 Ap 2017

Rapoport, Ron

The Savvy Rube cartoon *Weekly Standard* v22 no43 p30 Jl 24 2017

RAPOZA, KENNETH

Build the Wall! Por Favor color *Forbes* v199 no6 p66 Je 13 2017

Rappaport, Alfred

Reclaiming the Idea of Shareholder Value *Harvard Business Review Digital Articles* p2 Jl 1 2016

What Should U.S. Companies Do If Congress Ever Passes a Tax Holiday? *Harvard Business Review Digital Articles* p1 Je 21 2017

RAPPAPORT, EMILY

"MADE IN L.A. 2016" bw color *ARTnews* v115 no4 p128 Wint 2016/2017

Rappaport, Erika

A Thirst for Empire: How Tea Shaped the Modern World color *Publishers Weekly* v264 no23 p45 Je 5 2017

Rappaport, Helen

Caught in the Revolution: Petrograd, Russia, 1917— A World on the Edge *Publishers Weekly* v263 no52 p108 D 19 2016

Front Row to Revolution O. MATTHEWS *New York Times Book Review* p8 F 26 2017

RAPP BLACK, EMILY

My Professor, My Mentor, My Rock *Reader's Digest* v189 no1129 p44 Ap 2017

Rappelling

Rap Smart A. FLOWER and M. OAKLEY color *Climbing* no356 p40 S/O 2017

Tag-Line Rappels J. LUCAS color *Climbing* no351 p50 F/Mr 2017

RAPP LEARN, JOSHUA

Blame Canada map *Canadian Geographic* v135 no6 p34 D 2015

Rapport, Mike

Europe Transformed *New York Times Book Review* p13 D 18 2016

Up in Arms: The lessons of three very different 18th-century revolutions R. Shorto *New York Times Book Review* p26 My 21 2017

RAPSON, RIP

THE GIFT OF LENI SINCLAIR: INTERTWINED ART, ACTIVISIM AND LOVE FOR COMMUNITY *Vital Speeches of the Day* v83 no1 p21 Ja 2017

Rapture (Christian eschatology)

Stay Awake! M. R. SIMONE il *America* v215 no16 p38 N 21 2016

Raqib, Jamila

Nonviolence, Power, and Possibility J. L. VanHise bw *Progressive* v81 no4 p51 Ap/My 2017

Raqs Media Collective (Organization)

Raqs Media Collective R. Simonini color *Art in America* v104 no11 p37 D 2016

Raquel Allegra (Company)

Maternity Clothes N. ALCALA *Los Angeles Magazine* p38 Ap 2017

Rare birds

A Flight for Their Lives D. Cubie color *National Wildlife (World Edition)* v54 no6 p30 O/N 2016

Home on the Sage [Cover story] T. Williams color map *National Wildlife (World Edition)* v54 no6 p22 O/N 2016

Rare book libraries

The Cloistered Books of Peru H. HAZEN *American Scholar* v86 no2 p64 Spr 2017

Rare diseases

The Cost of Drugs for Rare Diseases Is Threatening the U.S. Health Care System A. G. Smith *Harvard Business Review Digital Articles* p2 Ap 7 2017

Rare earth ions

Storing light in a tiny box E. Waks and E. A. Goldschmidt diag *Science* v357 no6358 p1354 S 29 2017

Ras oncogenes

Drugging RAS: Know the enemy B. Papke and C. J. Der bibl diag *Science* v355 no6330 p1158 Mr 17 2017

RASCHKE, ERIK

Immigrants and the Jinn color *America* v216 no1 p24 Ja 2 2017

Rascouet, Angelina

The Tables Have Turned cartoon graph *Bloomberg Businessweek* no4493 p47 O 3 2016

Rasenberger, Mary

Free the Copyright Office *Publishers Weekly* v264 no19 p64 My 8 2017

A Way to Make the National Digital Library Work: An Exchange bw *New York Review of Books* v63 no20 p101 D 22 2016

Rash, Ron

Mine the Past C. J. SCALIA color *Weekly Standard* v22 no10 p32 N 14 2016

Rashad, Condola—Interviews

CLOSE UP WITH CONDOLA RASHAD L. Cross color *Ebony* v72 no6 p22 Ap/My 2017

Rashdan, Mahmoud Ayed

Mahmoud Ayed Rashdan An Empowering Leader 1939 - 2017 *Islamic Horizons* v46 no3 p8 My/Je 2017

Rashid, Ahmed

Seeing the Despair of Jihad cartoon color *New York Review of Books* v63 no18 p51 N 24 2016

Rashid, Qasim

Now What? color *Time* v188 no21 p42 N 21 2016

Rashid, Ripa

Diversity Doesn't Stick Without Inclusion color *Harvard Business Review Digital Articles* p2 F 1 2017

Leading Across Cultures Is More Complicated for Women *Harvard Business Review Digital Articles* p2 D 2 2015

When Employees Think the Boss Is Unfair, They're More Likely to Disengage and Leave *Harvard Business Review Digital Articles* p2 Ag 1 2017

Rasin, Mladen-Roko

Control of species-dependent cortico-motoneuronal connections underlying manual dexterity diag graph *Science* v357 no6349 p400 Jl 28 2017

Raška, Jiří, 1941-2012

Reindeer games R. Stuart color map *Canadian Geographic* v135 no6 p28 D 2015

Raskin, Erika

Best Intentions *Publishers Weekly* v264 no25 p88 Je 19 2017

Who Needs An Outline? color *Publishers Weekly* v264 no25 p116 Je 19 2017

Raskin, Jamie—Interviews

JAMIE RASKIN P. O'Donnell *Washingtonian Magazine* v52 no7 p41 Ap 2017

Raskin, Laura

Arts and Crafts *Architectural Record* v204 no10 p37 O 2016

sky and M. Hahn *Harvard Business Review Digital Articles* p2 Mr 16 2016

The Basic Principles of Strategy Haven't Changed in 30 Years A. Campbell *Harvard Business Review Digital Articles* p2 Ap 23 2015

A Better Way to Calculate the ROI of Your Marketing Investment W. Reinartz and R. Venkatesan *Harvard Business Review Digital Articles* p2 N 10 2015

Comparing the ROI of Content Marketing and Native Advertising K. Libert *Harvard Business Review Digital Articles* p2 Jl 6 2015

Integrate Analytics Across Your Entire Business B. McCarthy *Harvard Business Review Digital Articles* p2 O 3 2014

Merging Their Money and Their Goals J. BENNETT CLARK color *Kiplinger's Personal Finance* v71 no5 p72 My 2017

The Most Common Mistake People Make In Calculating ROI J. Knight *Harvard Business Review Digital Articles* p2 Ap 9 2015

A Refresher on Internal Rate of Return A. Gallo *Harvard Business Review Digital Articles* p2 Mr 17 2016

A Refresher on Payback Method A. Gallo *Harvard Business Review Digital Articles* p2 Ap 18 2016

A Refresher on Return on Assets and Return on Equity A. Gallo *Harvard Business Review Digital Articles* p2 Ap 4 2016

SURVIVORS' GILT A. GARA bw chart *Forbes* v200 no3 p48 S 28 2017

Why Trump Is Making Bond Markets Nervous S. Barton, Y. Li et al *Bloomberg Businessweek* no4500 p39 N 21 2016

Rate of return on stocks—Charts, diagrams, etc.

Funds Thrive on Slow Growth T. Tepper chart *Money* v46 no7 p80 Ag 2017

Rates

See also

Airline industry—Rates

Better Rates for Savers, Finally J. R. KOSNETT color *Kiplinger's Personal Finance* v71 no6 p53 Je 2017

Rath, Meaghan

Hawaii Five-O N. Abrams, S. Highfill et al *Entertainment Weekly* no1482/1483 p99 S 22 2017

RATHBONE, EMMA

Almost Ready to Do My Taxes! *Reader's Digest* v189 no1129 p15 Ap 2017

BEFORE THE INTERNET cartoon *New Yorker* v93 no18 p29 Je 26 2017

Rather, Dan, 1931—Interviews

CENTRAL INTELLIGENCE P. COLLOFF *Texas Monthly* v45 no2 p106 F 2017

Rathi, Anil

To Encourage Innovation, Make It a Competition *Harvard Business Review Digital Articles* p2 N 19 2014

Rathod, Sara

PATRIOT GAMES bw cartoon color *Mother Jones* v41 no6 p21 N/D 2016

RATHOD, SARASWATI

THE BIRTH OF A NOTION *Mother Jones* v42 no1 p28 Ja/F 2017

RATHVON, HENRY

IT PAYS TO INCREASE YOUR Word Power *Reader's Digest* v188 no1125 p145 N 2016

IT PAYS TO INCREASE YOUR Word Power *Reader's Digest* v189 no1128 p131 Mr 2017

IT PAYS TO INCREASE YOUR Word Power *Reader's Digest* v190 no1132 p135 Jl/Ag 2017

IT PAYS TO INCREASE YOUR Word Power *Reader's Digest* v190 no1135 p133 N 2017

Word Power *Reader's Digest* v188 no1124 p139 O 2016

Rating of chief executive officers

The Best-Performing CEOs in the World [Cover story] img *Harvard Business Review* v94 no11 p41 N 2016

How Do You Rank the World's Best CEOs? C. Fombrun *Harvard Business Review Digital Articles* p2 F 6 2015

Resisting the Lure of Short-Termism [Cover story] D. McGinn *Harvard Business Review* v94 no11 p42 N 2016

Where Are the Women? A. Ignatius *Harvard Business Review* v94 no11 p12 N 2016

Would You Let This Man Run Your Company? [Cover story] J. Micklethwait bw *Bloomberg Businessweek* no4523 p8 My 22 2017

Rating of physicians

BEST DOCTORS *Louisiana Life* v37 no2 p59 N/D 2016

Health Care Providers Should Publish Physician Ratings A. K. Jha *Harvard Business Review Digital Articles* p2 O 23 2015

What Makes Doctors Value Patient Feedback D. E. Mylod and T. H. Lee *Harvard Business Review Digital Articles* p2 N 30 2015

Rating of public officers

The Liberal lowlights J. GEDDES color *Maclean's* p29 Je 2017

Rating of women executives

MOST POWERFUL WOMEN INTERNATIONAL C. Austin, L. Entis et al color *Fortune* v176 no5 p111 O 1 2017

Research: Vague Feedback Is Holding Women Back S. Correll and C. Simard *Harvard Business Review Digital Articles* p2 Ap 29 2016

Ratings & rankings of business enterprises

See also

Architectural firms—Ratings & rankings

Corporate ratings

The 10 Best Workplaces for Millennials C. Austin color *Fortune* v176 no2 p20 Ag 1 2017

LARGEST U.S. CORPORATIONS [Cover story] chart color *Fortune* v175 no8 pF1 Je 15 2017

NOTES *Fortune* v175 no8 pF28 Je 15 2017

RANKED WITHIN INDUSTRIES chart diag *Fortune* v175 no8 pF33 Je 15 2017

RANKED WITHIN STATES chart map *Fortune* v175 no8 pF41 Je 15 2017

REBEL TERRITORY C. Leaf color *Fortune* v175 no8 p24 Je 15 2017

Top 300 Firms: Gensler Maintains Leading Revenue for Six Years Straight M. SITZ color *Architectural Record* v205 no8 p19 Ag 2017

TURNOVER chart *Fortune* v175 no8 pF27 Je 15 2017

Ratings & rankings of public debts

Illinois Budget Woes Head From Bad to Junk E. Campbell and J. McCormick graph map *Bloomberg Businessweek* no4529 p36 Jl 3 2017

Ratings & rankings of universities & colleges

2018 UNIVERSITY RANKINGS color *Maclean's* v130 no10 p51 N 2017

AMERICA'S BEST COLLEGES FOR ADULT LEARNERS P. Glastris *Washington Monthly* v49 no9/10 p25 S/O 2017

America's Top Architecture Schools 2018 A. Fixsen chart *Architectural Record* v205 no9 p72 S 2017

THE BEST COLLEGES FOR YOUR MONEY 2017 K. Clark and K. Mulhere chart color *Money* v46 no7 p52 Ag 2017

INTRODUCTION: A DIFFERENT KIND OF COLLEGE RANKING K. Carey chart *Washington Monthly* v49 no9/10 p21 S/O 2017

Rewarding Rigor N. S. RILEY color *Weekly Standard* v23 no4 p18 O 2 2017

THE YEAR'S BEST chart color *Maclean's* v130 no10 p83 N 2017

Ratings of cities & towns

THE BEST PLACES TO LIVE IN AMERICA [Cover story] K. A. Renzulli, I. S. Mangla et al chart color map *Money* v46 no9 p54 O 2017

EDITOR'S NOTE color *Money* v46 no9 p7 O 2017

SUSTAINING OUR CITIES K. Nowakowski graph *National Geographic* v231 no5 p10 My 2017

Rational expectations (Economic theory)

How Rational Are Rational Expectations? A. Mayeda and C. Torres *Bloomberg Businessweek* no4501 p13 N 28 2016

Rationalization (Psychology)

When to Stay Inside Your Comfort Zone A. Molinsky *Harvard Business Review Digital Articles* p2 S 7 2016

Ratledge, Ingela

ALSO COMING... *TV Guide* v65 no37 p44 S 4 2017

America's Next Top Model *TV Guide* p44 D 5 2016

Arnold Takes the Boardroom: Schwarzenegger inherits Donald Trump's role as chairman of NBC's rebooted Celebrity Apprentice *TV Guide* v65 no2 p20 Ja 2 2017

The Bachelorette Breaks Barriers *TV Guide* v65 no21 p12 My 15 2017

black-ish color *TV Guide* v65 no7 p36 F 13 2017

black-ish *TV Guide* v65 no19 p28 My 1 2017

BLACK-ISH *TV Guide* v65 no43 p26 O 16 2017

Boy Band *TV Guide* v65 no25 p38 Je 2017

Call Of DUTY [Cover story] *TV Guide* v64 no46 p14 N 7 2016

DESIGNATED SURVIVOR *TV Guide* p26 Ap 17 2017

Designated Survivor *TV Guide* v64 no46 p30 N 7 2016

DESIGNATED SURVIVOR *TV Guide* v65 no39 p42 S 18 2017

Downward Dog *TV Guide* v65 no21 p35 My 15 2017

FAMILY ALBUM *TV Guide* v64 no46 p24 N 7 2016

FAMILY TIES *TV Guide* v65 no11 p32 Mr 6 2017

Friends From College *TV Guide* v65 no25 p24 Je 2017

George Michael: Freedom *TV Guide* v65 no43 p34 O 16 2017

Get Shorty *TV Guide* v65 no35 p37 Ag 21 2017

Gilmore Girls: A Year in the Life *TV Guide* v64 no40 p30 O 3 2016

Girls *TV Guide* v65 no14 p36 Ap 3 2017

HAPPY CAMPERS: The funny franchise's new sequel heads into the 1990s--Big Chill style--with a bevy of fresh Camp Firewood faces worth a hearty salute *TV Guide* v65 no31 p24 Jl 24 2017

have a safe summer! color *Parents* v92 no6 p32 Je 2017

HOST STORIES *TV Guide* v65 no14 p28 Ap 3 2017

Hunted *TV Guide* v65 no4 p36 Ja 16 2017

Imaginary Mary *TV Guide* v65 no13 p26 Mr 20 2017

Jerrod Carmichael: 8 *TV Guide* v65 no11 p38 Mr 6 2017

KEVIN CAN WAIT *TV Guide* v65 no39 p32 S 18 2017

Lone Star LADIES *TV Guide* v64 no15 p44 Ap 4 2016

MR. PENN GOES TO WASHINGTON *TV Guide* v64 no40 p44 O 3 2016

Mr. Robot *TV Guide* v65 no41 p37 O 2 2017

New Year's Eve Roundup *TV Guide* p41 D 19 2016

The Odd Couple color *TV Guide* v64 no42 p38 O 10 2016

POWER GRAB: Starz's No. 1-rated original series--sorry, Outlander!--is back for its juiciest (and most intense) season yet *TV Guide* v65 no25 p28 Je 2017

Power *TV Guide* v65 no27 p30 Je 26 2017

The Real Housewives of New Jersey *TV Guide* v65 no41 p32 O 2 2017

The Real Housewives of Orange County *TV Guide* v65 no31 p32 Jl 24 2017

RETURN TO STARS HOLLOW *TV Guide* v64 no48 p30 N 21 2016

Shooter *TV Guide* p43 D 5 2016

Shorty and Sweet *TV Guide* v65 no23 p9 My 29 2017

Steve Guttenberg Joins Ballers *TV Guide* v65 no25 p8 Je 2017

THIS IS US *TV Guide* p28 D 5 2016

THIS IS US *TV Guide* v65 no39 p36 S 18 2017

Top Chef *TV Guide* v64 no48 p41 N 21 2016

TRUE GRIT: WWE phenom John Cena transforms average Joes into G.I. Joes on Season 2 of Fox's reality competition American Grit *TV Guide* v65 no27 p22 Jc 26 2017

TV's HOTTEST COUPLES *TV Guide* v64 no15 p28 Ap 4 2016

White Famous *TV Guide* v65 no41 p34 O 2 2017

Whitney: Can I Be Me *TV Guide* v65 no35 p32 Ag 21 2017

Ratliff, Ben

At Home in Her Range *New York Times Book Review* p17 Ja 15 2017

BEYOND COACHAPALOOZAROO cartoon color *Esquire* p32 My 2017

Chaos Reigns cartoon *Esquire* v166 no5 p40 D 2016/Ja 2017

Enter Sampha color *Esquire* v167 no1 p18 F 2017

Play All color *Esquire* v166 no4 p28 N 2016

SCREW ALGORITHMS cartoon color *Esquire* v167 no2 p46 Mr 2017

SEX, DRUGS, AND DISCO bw color *Esquire* p44 S 2017

TRUE NOTE bw cartoon *Esquire* p33 Ap 2017

Ratmansky, Alexei, 1968-

ABOVE & BEYOND cartoon *New Yorker* v93 no12 p12 My 8 2017

BONBON VOYAGE A. FINE COLLINS color *Vanity Fair* v59 no6 p88 My 2017

GOINGS ON ABOUT TOWN color *New Yorker* v93 no14 p5 My 22 2017

Kiss and Tell J. Acocella cartoon *New Yorker* v92 no47 p6 Ja 30 2017

SPUN SUGAR J. ACOCELLA color *New Yorker* v93 no17 p72 Je 19 2017

Ratmansky, Alexei, 1968---Interviews

Master Reinventor H. Rubin color *Dance Magazine* v91 no3 p35 Mr 2017

Ratnayake, Daya

Fragile Peace R. Draper color map *National Geographic* v230 no5 p108 N 2016

Ratner, Brett

SUN VALLEY FILM FEST J. Hibberd color *Entertainment Weekly* no1459 p48 Mr 31 2017

Ratner, Ely

Course Correction color *Foreign Affairs* v96 no4 p64 Jl/Ag 2017

RATNER, LIZZY

THE LAST TIME WE CLOSED THE GATES bw color *Nation* v304 no5 p20 F 20 2017

Speech Lessons *Nation* v303 no19 p4 N 7 2016

Ratner, Megan

TONI ERDMANN, FAUX PA: INTERVIEW WITH MAREN ADE *Film Quarterly* v70 no3 p43 Spr 2017

Ratner, Vaddey

Instruments of Memory G. BAHADUR *New York Times Book Review* p10 My 28 2017

Ratnesar, Romesh

After the Bombs Have Fallen color *Bloomberg Businessweek* no4531 p34 Jl 24 2017

The Boy Scout Leading State color *Bloomberg Businessweek* no4513 p14 Mr 6 2017

Olathe, Kansas, became a global magnet for tech talent, thanks to plentiful jobs, cheap housing, and good schools. Then someone opened fire on a pair of Indian-born engineers [Cover story] color *Bloomberg Businessweek* no4522 p60 My 15 2017

Ratni, Mohamed

'Wanted,' one more time M. FRISCOLANTI color *Maclean's* no1 p13 F 17 2017

Rats

STUMP YOUR PARENTS color *National Geographic Kids* no470 p32 My 2017

Rattenborg, Niels

Birds Sleep During Flights, Too B. ALEX color *Discover* v38 no1 p49 Ja/F 2017

Winks on the Wing A. Braun *Natural History* v124 no10 p6 N 2016

Ratti, Carlo

FROM PARKING LOT TO PARADISE color diag *Scientific American* v317 no1 p54 Jl 2017

If Work Is Digital, Why Do We Still Go to the Office? *Harvard Business Review Digital Articles* p2 Ap 13 2016

Rattini, Kristin Baird

ALL About MONEY! color *National Geographic Kids* no465 p8 N 2016

All About Money! color *National Geographic Kids* no473 p9 S 2017

Amazing Animals color *National Geographic Kids* no475 p10 N 2017

Animal Killers Busted color *National Geographic Kids* no471 p24 Je/Jl 2017

Haunted White House color *National Geographic Kids* no474 p24 O 2017

The Lost City Of Pompeii cartoon color map *National Geographic Kids* no471 p20 Je/Jl 2017

Stone Forest color map *National Geographic Kids* no473 p20 S 2017

Viking Invasion *National Geographic Kids* no468 p26 Mr 2017

Rattlesnake National Recreation Area (Mont.)

The Great Wide Open E. KWAK-HEFFERAN color map *Backpacker* p12 Je 2017

Rattlesnakes

Bet You Didn't Know S. YOUNGSON and A. SILEN color *National Geographic Kids* no474 p6 O 2017

Black-Tailed Rattlesnakes N. Austin *Arizona Highways* v93 no1 p13 Ja 2017

Can't Hurry Love N. WILSON color *Natural History* v125 no4 p48 Ap 2017

CRITTER CHAT A. SHAW color *National Geographic Kids* no470 p31 My 2017

Guinness Guinness Records K. BOATNER color *National Geographic Kids* no474 p5 O 2017

Ratushinskaya, Irina, 1954-2017

Milestones *Time* v190 no5 p17 Jl 31 2017

Ratzinger, Jospeh

'Music Is Life and Life Is Poetry' J. Hoover il *America* v216 no13 p48 Je 12 2017

Rauber, Paul
100% Clean National Park *Sierra* v101 no4 p30 Jl/Ag 2016
Backpacking With Benefits *Sierra* v102 no1 p16 Ja/F 2017
HIGH-SEAS POWER *Sierra* v102 no1 p46 Ja/F 2017
Itty-Bitty Reindeer *Sierra* v101 no6 p21 N/D 2016
The Power of a Good Example *Sierra* v102 no5 p22 St/O 2017
Solar-Ready Vet *Sierra* v102 no2 p26 Mr/Ap 2017
Up to Speed: Two Months, One Page *Sierra* v101 no4 p26 Jl/Ag 2016
Up to Speed: Two Months, One Page *Sierra* v102 no2 p22 Mr/Ap 2017
Up to Speed: Two Months, One Page *Sierra* v102 no3 p22 My/Je 2017
Up to Speed: Two Months, One Page *Sierra* v102 no5 p20 St/O 2017
Where the Wild Things Are *Sierra* v101 no5 p18 S/O 2016

Rauch, Jonathan
The Conservative Case for Unions color graph *Atlantic* v320 no1 p15 Jl/Ag 2017
CONTAINING TRUMP cartoon color *Atlantic* v319 no2 p60 Mr 2017
FROM THE ARCHIVES color *Reason* v49 no4 p78 Ag/S 2017
Is free speech under threat IN THE UNITED STATES? WE RE-CEIVED TWENTY-SEVEN RESPONSES. WE PUBLISH THEM HERE, IN ALPHABETICAL ORDER *Commentary* v144 no1 p13 Jl/Ag 2017
Leaving a Clean Desk color *Atlantic* v318 no5 p15 D 2016
A Less Perfect Union color *New York Times Book Review* p14 Ja 29 2017
Speaking as a... bw color *New York Review of Books* v64 no17 p10 N 9 2017

Rauch, Melissa
My Obsessions... *TV Guide* v65 no19 p8 My 1 2017

Rauch, Ursula
A pathogenic role for T cell–derived IL-22BP in inflammatory bowel disease bibl graph *Science* v354 no6310 p358 O 21 2016

Raugust, Karen
Celebrating the Holidays With Favorite Friends color *Publishers Weekly* v263 no50 p21 D 5 2016
Consolidation in Book Plus And the Evolution of Coloring color *Publishers Weekly* v264 no9 p7 F 27 2017
Exploring New E-commerce Opportunities color *Publishers Weekly* v264 no29 p25 Jl 17 2017
Licensing Expo 2017 Highlights Synergies Between Books and Tie-in Products color *Publishers Weekly* v264 no24 p20 Je 12 2017
Speeding to Market color *Publishers Weekly* v263 no43 p18 O 24 2016
Tracking Tie-in Trends color *Publishers Weekly* v264 no16 p19 Ap 17 2017

Rauner, Bruce, 1957-
CHICAGO'S POPULATION PROBLEM D. MENDELL color *Chicago* v66 no6 p19 Je 2017
LAST MADIGAN STANDING E. McCLELLAND color *Chicago* v66 no11 p19 N 2017

Raunser, Stefan
The molecular basis of Alzheimer's plaques color *Science* v357 no6359 p45 O 6 2017

Rausch, David
TOWN COUNTRY K. FRANZMAN color *Indianapolis Monthly* v42 no2 p78 O 2017

Rausch, Lesley
READY, SET—PLACES! J. Ouellette color *Dance Spirit* v20 no10 p46 D 2016

Rausch, Thomas P.
LANDING IN DULLES T. W. TILLEY *America* v215 p34 N 28 2016
A Muslim journalist sets out to investigate Jesus Christ color *America* v216 no6 p42 Mr 20 2017

Rauschenberg, Robert, 1925-2008
The Artist's Artist A Rauschenberg Symposium M. Reid Kelley, J. Stockholder et al color *Art in America* v105 no1 p44 Ja 2017
The Collected Works of ROBERT RAUSCHENBERG J. H. RICHARDSON color *Esquire* p74 S 2017

Going the Distance D. White and L. A. Miller bw *Art in America* v104 no11 p59 D 2016
RAZZLE DOWN (SALVAGE) color *Art in America* v104 no10 p11 N 2016
Rebel's Reward J. GARDNER bw color *Weekly Standard* v22 no46 p38 Ag 14 2017
THE WAVE OF HISTORY P. SCHJELDAHL bw *New Yorker* v93 no15 p60 My 29 2017
ZERO GRAVITY B. SCHWABSKY color *Nation* v305 no6 p32 S 11 2017

Rauschenberg, Robert, 1925-2008—Exhibitions
ART color *New Yorker* v93 no16 p14 Je 5 2017
The Confidence Man of American Art [Cover story] J. Perl bw color *New York Review of Books* v64 no8 p18 My 11 2017

Rauschenbeutel, Arno
Quantum optical circulator controlled by a single chirally coupled atom bibl graph *Science* v354 no6319 p1577 D 23 2016

Rauser, Randal
An Atheist and a Christian Walk into a Bar: Talking about God, the Universe, and Everything *Publishers Weekly* v263 no41 p74 O 10 2016

Raushenbush, Bret
Left Out *Harper's Magazine* v334 no2000 p2 Ja 2017

Raustiala, Kal
An Internet Whole and Free color *Foreign Affairs* v96 no2 p140 Mr/Ap 2017

Rautenberg, J.
Observation of a large-scale anisotropy in the arrival directions of cosmic rays above 8×10^{18} eV *Science* v357 no6357 p1266 S 22 2017

Rauwald, Christoph
The Chinese Rediscover Luxury color *Bloomberg Businessweek* no4509 p15 Ja 30 2017
Engineering the Sound Of Silence at Porsche color graph *Bloomberg Businessweek* no4499 p44 N 14 2016
Reinventing These Wheels color graph *Bloomberg Businessweek* no4504 p19 D 19 2016
VW's Latest Woe: A Reliance on Mexico *Bloomberg Businessweek* no4512 p20 F 20 2017
Will Bosch Choke on VW's Exhaust? bw color *Bloomberg Businessweek* no4534 p12 Ag 14 2017

Rava, Enrico, 1939-
Vocal Dynamos Add Spark to Umbria Jazz Fest D. Ouellette color *Downbeat* v84 no10 p22 O 2017

Ravalli County (Mont.)
RAVALLI COUNTY, MONTANA C. T. Tobin *Harper's Magazine* p27 O 2017

Ravassard, Pascal M.
Dynamics of cortical dendritic membrane potential and spikes in freely behaving rats diag *Science* v355 no6331 p1281 Mr 24 2017

Ravech, Karl
MAJOR LEAGUE BASEBALL K. Rosen *TV Guide* v64 no15 p47 Ap 4 2016

RAVELLA, SHILPA
Head in Hand color *Discover* v38 no3 p22 Ap 2017

Ravelli, Raimond B. G.
Fibril structure of amyloid-β(1–42) by cryo–electron microscopy color diag *Science* v357 no6359 p116 O 6 2017

Raven, Emma L.
Locked and loaded for apoptosis diag *Science* v356 no6344 p1236 Je 23 2017

Raven, Peter
MAKING OUR PLANET SUSTAINABLE AGAIN *Vital Speeches of the Day* v83 no6 p174 Je 2017

Raven behavior
A raven's memories are for the future M. Boeckle and N. S. Clayton color *Science* v357 no6347 p126 Jl 14 2017

RAVENAL, EARL C.
FROM THE ARCHIVES bw color *Reason* v49 no3 p70 Jl 2017

Ravens
WHERE IS THIS? *Arizona Highways* v93 no1 p56 Ja 2017

Ravenscroft, Janet
Royal Renegades *History Today* v67 no4 p57 Ap 2017

Raverat, Anna
Lover *Publishers Weekly* v264 no4 p51 Ja 23 2017

RAVET, STEVE

ROAR OF THE CROWD *Texas Monthly* v45 no7 p12 Jl 2017

Ravetch, Jeffrey V.

IgG antibodies to dengue enhanced for FcγRIIIA binding determine disease severity bibl graph *Science* v355 no6323 p395 Ja 27 2017

Ravi, V.

iPTF16geu: A multiply imaged, gravitationally lensed type Ia supernova color diag graph *Science* v356 no6335 p291 Ap 21 2017

The magnetic field and turbulence of the cosmic web measured using a brilliant fast radio burst bibl chart graph *Science* v354 no6317 p1249 D 9 2016

Ravichandran, Hiranmayi

Decoupling genetics, lineages, and microenvironment in IDH-mutant gliomas by single-cell RNA-seq diag *Science* v355 no6332 p1391 Mr 31 2017

Ravichandran, Rashmi

Global analysis of protein folding using massively parallel design, synthesis, and testing color diag *Science* v357 no6347 p168 Jl 14 2017

Ravignani, D.

Observation of a large-scale anisotropy in the arrival directions of cosmic rays above 8 × 1018 eV *Science* v357 no6357 p1266 S 22 2017

RAVILIOUS, KATE

THE FIRST AUSTRALIANS [Cover story] color *Archaeology* v70 no4 p49 Je-Ag 2017

Ravindran, Rajesh

mTOR regulates metabolic adaptation of APCs in the lung and controls the outcome of allergic inflammation graph *Science* v357 no6355 p1014 S 8 2017

Ravine, M.

Jupiter's interior and deep atmosphere: The initial pole-to-pole passes with the Juno spacecraft [Cover story] color graph *Science* v356 no6340 p821 My 26 2017

Ravioli

WEEKNIGHT COOKING color *Sunset* v239 no1 p94 Jl 2017

Ravishankara, A.

A climate policy pathway for near- and long-term benefits color *Science* v356 no6337 p493 My 5 2017

Ravitch, Diane

The Miseducation of Betsy DeVos *In These Times* v41 no2 p17 F 2017

The Miseducation of Liberals il *New Republic* v248 no6 p16 Je 2017

When Public Goes Private, as Trump Wants: What Happens? color *New York Review of Books* v63 no19 p58 D 8 2016

RAVITS, SARAH

BEST DOCS: 559 PHYSICIANS IN 77 SPECIALTIES [Cover story] color *New Orleans Magazine* v51 no10 p84 Ag 2017

HUMILITY & EMPOWERMENT color *New Orleans Magazine* v51 no3 p167 Ja 2017

Kelly Stomps color *Louisiana Life* v37 no3 p58 Ja/F 2017

THE STATE OF WOMEN'S HEALTH IN THE STATE bw *Louisiana Life* v37 no2 p54 N/D 2016

Ravitz, Alan

How Systems Engineering Can Help Fix Health Care *Harvard Business Review Digital Articles* p2 F 9 2017

What Hospitals Can Learn from Airlines About Buying Equipment *Harvard Business Review Digital Articles* p2 Je 13 2017

Raviv, Shaun

Mr. Rigolizzo and the amazing miracle weed that will save Sparta! (Or not.) *Atlanta* v57 no2 p84 Je 2017

RAVpower Inc.

RAVPOWER 26800MAH PORTABLE CHARGER: COMPACT, AFFORDABLE BATTERY DELIVERS USB-C LAPTOP CHARGING G. FLEISHMAN color *Macworld - Digital Edition* v34 no10 p25 O 2017

Raw (Film)

ANIMAL KINGDOMS A. LANE color *New Yorker* v93 no4 p84 Mr 13 2017

Girl, You'll Be a Cannibal Soon M. ATKINSON *In These Times* v41 no4 p52 Ap 2017

Healthy Appetite N. Rapold color *Film Comment* v52 no6 p8 N/D 2016

PLEASURES OF THE FLESH M. BARTON-FUMO color *Film Comment* v53 no2 p42 Mr/Ap 2017

Raw C. Nashawaty color *Entertainment Weekly* no1457/1458 p74 Mr 17 2017

Raw *New Yorker* v93 no8 p10 Ap 10 2017

Raw file formats (Digital photography)

How to split a raw+JPEG photo file into its separate parts G. FLEISHMAN bw color *Macworld - Digital Edition* v34 no10 p107 O 2017

Raw foods

In The Raw A. Roman color *Bon Appetit* v62 no7 p78 Jl 2017

Raw materials

See also

Forest products

TAPPING THE TRASH M. E. Webber color diag *Scientific American* v317 no1 p48 Jl 2017

Rawabi (West Bank)

If You Build It, Will Peace Come? J. Ferziger and D. Rocks color *Bloomberg Businessweek* no4519 p19 Ap 24 2017

Rawat, Shivani

THE SUNDANCE KID D. Walters color *Bloomberg Businessweek* no4507 p59 Ja 16 2017

Rawlence, Ben

CITY OF THORNS B. COLVIN *Phi Kappa Phi Forum* v96 no4 p30 Wint 2016

The First Rule of Book Club Is . . color *New York Times Book Review* p25 Ja 29 2017

RAWLINGS, TIMOTHY

Worm-snail Ships Out! bw color *Natural History* v125 no6 p10 Je 2017

RAWSON, CASEY H.

Synthesis Centers as Critical Research Infrastructure *BioScience* v67 no8 p750 Ag 2017

Rawson, Kristin

LIVING LAID-BACK & DOWN UNDER K. K. CONDON color *Better Homes & Gardens* v95 no8 p142 Ag 2017

Ray, Anuradha

mTOR regulates metabolic adaptation of APCs in the lung and controls the outcome of allergic inflammation graph *Science* v357 no6355 p1014 S 8 2017

Ray, Carl—Interviews

Meet Michelle Obama's Secret Weapon T. Williams and Ying Chu color *Glamour* v115 no2 p54 F 2017

This Issue Was Brought to You by... Women C. Leive color *Glamour* v115 no2 p18 F 2017

Ray, H.

Observation of coherent elastic neutrino-nucleus scattering diag *Science* v357 no6356 p1123 S 15 2017

Ray, James

SIX TRUMP ADVISERS WITH TIES TO THE WORLD'S BIGGEST PRIVATIZERS *In These Times* v41 no8 p19 Ag 2017

RAY, JOE

KNEAD TO KNOW bw color *Wired* v25 no10 p26 O 2017

Ray, L. Bryan

ON THE CLOCK color *Science* v354 no6315 p986 N 25 2016

Ray, Leigh Belz

John Legend color *InStyle* v24 no2 p64 F 2017

Making Myself Heard color *InStyle* v24 no7 p52 Jl 2017

My Blond color *InStyle* v24 no5 p216 My 2017

When There's Another You color *InStyle* v24 no10 p116 O 2017

Wild Women Do color *InStyle* v24 no9 p208 S 2017

The Woman of Many Faces [Cover story] color *InStyle* v24 no10 p206 O 2017

Ray, Satyajit, 1921-1992

1961: Calcutta *Lapham's Quarterly* v10 no2 p109 Spr 2017

Ray, Shaunak

Emission of volatile organic compounds from petunia flowers is facilitated by an ABC transporter diag *Science* v356 no6345 p1386 Je 30 2017

Ray, Stephen

'Old Gray Ancients' A. GRAVES and M. FLEMING color *Yankee* p41 My/Je 2017

Ray, Vanessa

Blue Bloods *TV Guide* v65 no6 p37 Ja 30 2017

Ray BLK (Performer)

NIGHT LIFE *New Yorker* v93 no17 p15 Je 19 2017

Ray BLK H. WEISS *Interview* v47 no1 p18 F 2017

Ray Donovan (TV program)
DAWN OF A NEW RAY M. LOGAN *TV Guide* v65 no35 p24 Ag 21 2017
Ray Donovan M. Logan *TV Guide* v65 no41 p36 O 2 2017

RAYA, AGGA B.
CHERRY PICKED color *Chicago* v65 no11 p48 N 2016
PARTY IN PINK color *Chicago* v65 no12 p54 D 2016

Raya, Marcos
NIGHTMARES REVISITED J. FOUMBERG color *Chicago* v66 no7 p28 Jl 2017

Rayamajhi, Arpana
Outfits for Days color *Glamour* v115 no5 p50 My 2017

Raybern, J.
Observation of coherent elastic neutrino-nucleus scattering diag *Science* v357 no6356 p1123 S 15 2017

Raychem Corp.
Topped Out: Utilize any of these basic solutions for a well-protected, beautiful, and long-lasting roof R. C. Orrell color *Architectural Record* v205 no5 p77 My 2017

Raycroft, Jim
Operation Vacation! color *Power & Motoryacht* v34 no10 p94 O 2017

Rayess, Randy
5 Basic Needs of Virtual Workforces *Harvard Business Review Digital Articles* p2 Mr 17 2015

Rayfield, Bronwyn
Effects of network modularity on the spread of perturbation impact in experimental metapopulations diag graph *Science* v357 no6347 p199 Jl 14 2017

Raygorodetsky, Gleb
Life on the Edge bw color graph map *National Geographic* v232 no4 p108 O 2017
PACHAMAMA'S BLOOD color *Earth Island Journal* v32 no3 p34 Aut 2017

Raykovicz, Mike
A SPY IN THE WOODS color *New York State Conservationist* v71 no2 p6 O 2016

Rayman, Marc D.
Dawn of Discovery at Ceres *Sky & Telescope* v132 no6 p16 D 2016
Extensive water ice within Ceres' aqueously altered regolith: Evidence from nuclear spectroscopy bibl graph *Science* v355 no6320 p1 Ja 6 2017

Raymarine PLC
Mission Ready J. Y. WOOD color *Power & Motoryacht* v34 no9 p36 S 2017
Raymarine EV-100 Wheelpilot P. Nielsen color *Sail* v48 no4 p70 Ap 2017

RAYMER, MILES
Joe FreshGoods color *Chicago* v66 no6 p87 Je 2017

RAYMOND, ADAM K.
THE 67 GREATEST, CRAZIEST, AND MOST PERSISTENT POP-CULTURE CONSPIRACY THEORIES OF ALL TIME img *New York* v49 no23 p72 N 14 2016

Raymond, C. A.
Extensive water ice within Ceres' aqueously altered regolith: Evidence from nuclear spectroscopy bibl graph *Science* v355 no6320 p1 Ja 6 2017
Localized aliphatic organic material on the surface of Ceres bibl graph *Science* v355 no6326 p719 F 17 2017

RAYMOND, CHRISTOPHER M.
Incorporating Sociocultural Phenomena into Ecosystem-Service Valuation: The Importance of Critical Pluralism *BioScience* v67 no3 p233 Mr 2017

Raymond, John A.
CHURCHILL'S IMPROBABLE ARMY *MHQ: Quarterly Journal of Military History* v29 no3 p78 Spr 2017

RAYMOND, ONEIKA
5 Reasons to Visit the First Free Black Republic color *Ebony* v72 no4 p68 F 2017
Mom and Me: 4 Destinations to Explore with Your Mother color *Ebony* v72 no6 p58 Ap/My 2017
Starcation: Atlanta color *Ebony* v72 no5 p59 Mr 2017

Raymond Herbert, Cathy
The Real-Deal DIYer [Cover story] color *Horse & Rider* v55 no11

p60 N 2016

Raymund, Monica
Chicago Fire I. Rudolph *TV Guide* v65 no43 p34 O 16 2017

Raymundo, Oscar
10.5-INCH iPAD PRO: IF ANY iPAD REPLACES THE MACBOOK, IT'S THIS ONE color *Macworld - Digital Edition* v34 no8 p69 Ag 2017
Apple investigates iPhone 7 Plus that 'blew up' color *Macworld - Digital Edition* p15 Ap 2017
How the iPhone 8 can live up to all the crazy hype color *Macworld - Digital Edition* v34 no9 p42 S 2017
How to take best advantage of iCloud Desktop and Documents across Macs color *Macworld - Digital Edition* v34 no4 p96 My 2017
How to use Messages in iOS 10, from special effects to iMessage apps cartoon color *Macworld - Digital Edition* v33 no11 p67 N 2016
iOS 11 FAQ: EVERYTHING WE KNOW ABOUT NEW SIRI, PHOTOS, APPLE PAY, & MESSAGES [Cover story] color *Macworld - Digital Edition* p65 Je 13 2017
IT professionals think Apple devices are easier to manage, according to new survey color *Macworld - Digital Edition* v34 no4 p94 My 2017
JAYBIRD FREEDOM WIRELESS HEADPHONES color *Macworld - Digital Edition* v33 no11 p52 N 2016
News: Corrupt video link causes iPhones to crash color *Macworld - Digital Edition* p8 Ja 2017
Office for Mac gets Touch Bar support color *Macworld - Digital Edition* p10 Ap 2017
Siri vs. Google Assistant: Which is better for iPhone users? color *Macworld - Digital Edition* p37 Je 13 2017
TIMBUK2 AUTHORITY PACK color *Macworld - Digital Edition* v34 no9 p36 S 2017
Tim Cook: Augmented reality will be an essential part of your daily life, like the iPhone color *Macworld - Digital Edition* p61 D 2016

Raynaud's disease
Defending My Mother S. Nevins bw color *AARP: The Magazine* v60 no5A p61 Ag/S 2017

Rayner, Timothy F.
Aging increases cell-to-cell transcriptional variability upon immune stimulation color diag graph *Science* v355 no6332 p1433 Mr 31 2017

Raynor, Madeline
What to Watch color *Entertainment Weekly* no1441 p50 N 25 2016
What to Watch color *Entertainment Weekly* no1450 p54 Ja 27 2017

Raynor, Michael E.
Performance Can't Be Measured by Company Growth Alone *Harvard Business Review Digital Articles* p2 Je 5 2015
A Way to Gauge How Well Your Company Is Really Performing *Harvard Business Review Digital Articles* p2 My 8 2015
A Way to Know If Your Corporate Goals Are Too Aggressive *Harvard Business Review Digital Articles* p2 Jl 13 2015

RAYO, MANDO
starters color *Bon Appetit* v62 no6 p17 Je 2017

Rayport, Jeffrey F.
Is Programmatic Advertising the Future of Marketing? *Harvard Business Review Digital Articles* p2 Je 22 2015

Raz, Guy
REALITY BREAK C. Everett color *Entertainment Weekly* no1454/1455 p98 F 24 2017

Raz, Lior
OCCUPATIONAL HAZARDS D. REMNICK cartoon *New Yorker* v93 no26 p32 S 4 2017

Razor blades—Evaluation
A Razor Built for Assisted Shaving A. Fitzpatrick color *Time* v190 no1 p19 Jl 3 2017

Razors
Extraordinary Reuses For Ordinary Things J. LABIANCA color *Reader's Digest* v189 no1129 p35 Ap 2017
FACE-SAVING CROP OF WINNERS O. J. WILLIAMS color *Ebony* v72 no11 p52 S 2017

Razors—Evaluation
Shaving Razors: A Reckoning R. BERENDSOHN chart color *Popular Mechanics* p20 Mr 2017

Razzouk, Nayla

The Tables Have Turned cartoon graph *Bloomberg Businessweek* no4493 p47 O 3 2016

RCA & Arista Album Collection, The (Music)

THE RCA & ARISTA ALBUM COLLECTION LOU REED M. Mettler bw color *Sound & Vision* v82 no4 p72 My 2017

Rea, Peter

Corporate Ethics Can't Be Reduced to Compliance *Harvard Business Review Digital Articles* p2 Ap 29 2016

Reach (Music)

Christian Sands D. Ouellette color *Downbeat* v84 no7 p42 Jl 2017

Reaching for Indigo (Music)

A FRINGE FANTASIA D. HYMAN color *Chicago* v66 no10 p77 O 2017

Reaction forces

Mechanochemical unzipping of insulating polyladderene to semi-conducting polyacetylene [Cover story] Z. Chen, J. A. M. Mercer et al diag *Science* v357 no6350 p475 Ag 4 2017

Read, Daniel

Research: Missing Product Information Doesn't Bother Consumers as Much as It Should *Harvard Business Review Digital Articles* p2 S 28 2017

READ, MAX

The Internet Is Under This Manhole img *New York* v49 no25 p75 D 12 2016

Maybe the Internet Is Just Terrible After All *New York* v49 no24 p38 N 28 2016

THE MOVEMENT'S NEW VANGUARD IS TEENAGE "SHIT-LORDS." THE WORLD IS THEIR MESSAGE BOARD NOW img *New York* v50 no9 p34 My 1 2017

OBAMA'S AMERICA img *New York* v49 no20 p12 O 3 2016

TO UNDERSTAND THIS NEW RIGHT, IT HELPS TO SEE IT NOT AS A FRINGE MOVEMENT, BUT A POWERFUL COUNTERCULTURE img *New York* v50 no9 p24 My 1 2017

WHICH MEANS THE NEW RIGHT IS NOT GOING ANY-WHERE img *New York* v50 no9 p50 My 1 2017

THE YEAR IN MEMES img *New York* v49 no26 p38 D 26 2016

READ, MIMI

#5: In a classic Southern home, Melissa Rufty keeps the best of the past while injecting chic colors and patterns—from cantaloupe walls to animal prints—that say, "This isn't your grandmother's house" color *House Beautiful* v159 no2 p116 Mr 2017

A House Full of Memories color *Southern Living* v52 no2 p98 F 2017

PALETTE CLEANSER color *House Beautiful* v158 no10 p76 D 2016/Ja 2017

TURNING BACK TIME color *House Beautiful* v159 no1 p58 F 2017

WATER COLORS color *House Beautiful* v158 no9 p138 N 2016

Read, Rupert

The Precautionary Principle Under Fire bibl *Environment* v59 no5 p4 S/O 2017

ReaderLink Distribution Services LLC

Readerlink Rules J. Milliot *Publishers Weekly* v263 no40 p5 O 3 2016

Reader's Digest (Periodical)

"I've Come to Clean Your Shoes" M. HARRAH color *Reader's Digest* v189 no1130 p52 My 2017

Kids Think The Craziest Things! color *Reader's Digest* v189 no1130 p96 My 2017

Nicest Place IN America 2017 color *Reader's Digest* v189 no1130 p12 My 2017

This Is What Friends Are For color *Reader's Digest* v189 no1130 p108 My 2017

THE Wackiest Law IN EVERY STATE B. SPECKTOR color *Reader's Digest* v190 no1132 p68 Jl/Ag 2017

Your True Stories IN 100 WORDS K. GEMMELL, D. DEATON et al color *Reader's Digest* v189 no1130 p32 My 2017

Readership

See also

Reading interests

ALL IN A Day's Work S. SHORT, K. SKOPHAMMER et al *Reader's Digest* v189 no1128 p60 Mr 2017

Readiness for school

Highlighted & Underlined color graph *Phi Delta Kappan* v98 no3 p6 N 2016

Reading

See also

Books & reading

Content area reading

Reading (Elementary)

Backtalk L. Porosoff *Phi Delta Kappan* v99 no2 p80 O 2017

BOOK BREAK S. Jacobson color *Literacy Today (2411-7862)* v34 no5 p46 Mr/Ap 2017

FROM REALITY TO THE PAGE— AND BACK AGAIN M. Lu bw color *Literacy Today (2411-7862)* v34 no5 p16 Mr/Ap 2017

Is Kindergarten the New First Grade? *USA Today Magazine* v146 no2867 p5 Ag 2017

The Literacy of Long-form Thinking J. Patterson color *Time* v188 no16/17 p77 O 24 2016

MY HOMETOWN PAPER: Lauren Williams L. Williams color *Columbia Journalism Review* v56 no1 p46 Spr 2017

Reading her novels on the bicentennial of her death A. VALI-UNAS color *Weekly Standard* v22 no42 p28 Jl 17 2017

Reading in a digital age N. S. Baron graph il *Phi Delta Kappan* v99 no2 p15 O 2017

SKIRTING QUESTIONS D. L. Wolter color *Literacy Today (2411-7862)* v34 no3 p10 N/D 2016

spread the word! K. CICERO *Parents* p29 2015

This Year's Winning Reads K. CICERO color *Parents* v92 no11 p64 N 2017

THREE COMPONENTS TO READING SUCCESS: Guide readers from striving to thriving through reading volume A. Ward color *Literacy Today (2411 7862)* v34 no6 p10 My/Je 2017

VALUING THEIR CHOICES: Fuel students' love for literature with their own reading picks C. Maloney map *Literacy Today (2411-7862)* v34 no6 p12 My/Je 2017

Visual Literacy S. SHAFER *Publishers Weekly* v264 no24 p68 Je 12 2017

Why it pays to increase your WORD POWER [Cover story] B. SPECKTOR color *Reader's Digest* v190 no1133 p66 S 2017

YA Stories You Should Snatch Up K. Kemp color *Parents* v92 no7 p16 Jl 2017

Reading (Elementary)

See also

Reading games

Reading readiness

Moving readers from struggling to proficient D. Wolter color *Phi Delta Kappan* v99 no1 p37 S 2017

Reading associations

RECOGNIZING WHAT STUDENTS WANT TO READ: The Florida Reading Association-Children's Book Award K. Fontaine diag *Literacy Today (2411-7862)* v34 no6 p44 My/Je 2017

Reading comprehension

EXECUTIVE-LEVEL THINKING: Teaching 21st-century skills for effective reading comprehension K. B. Cartwright color *Literacy Today (2411-7862)* v34 no6 p38 My/Je 2017

RIGOR VS. EASE Sarah Lupo color *Literacy Today (2411-7862)* v34 no4 p30 Ja/F 2017

Reading games

Stay Sharp M. DANESI color *Prevention* v69 no11 p96 N 2017

Reading interests

See also

Newspaper reading

IGNITING A Love of Literature: How ILA's Choices project inspires the next generation of lifelong readers C. McCall *Literacy Today (2411-7862)* v35 no2 p44 S/O 2017

The one thing I'd save in a fire is... *Reader's Digest* v189 no1128 p34 Mr 2017

So Many Books H. STERNBERG *Publishers Weekly* v264 no7 p80 F 13 2017

Reading interests of children

See also

Reading interests of school children

BOOKS FOR EVERY CHILD: How the Greenbrier Bookcase Project ensures young readers have access to quality books at home A. Betancourt *Literacy Today (2411-7862)* v35 no2 p36 S/O 2017

CHILDREN'S BESTSELLERS chart *Publishers Weekly* v264 no17 p16 Ap 24 2017

The Garden of Learning E. K. Cahill color *America* v216 no9 p62 Ap 24 2017

Reading interests of school children
Addressing Low Reading Scores N. Derringer *Education Digest* v83 no1 p59 S 2017

Reading interests—Social aspects
'Mason & Dixon' and Me: A personal foray into the long-lost Pynchon tapes A. Nazaryan *New York Times Book Review* p18 My 21 2017

Reading materials
See also
Nonfiction reading materials
Forever Frankfurt D. H. SMYK color *Publishers Weekly* v264 no41 p72 O 9 2017

Reading mobile apps
Serial Fiction on Tap J. D. BIERSDORFER *New York Times Book Review* p12 My 14 2017

Reading motivation
IGNITING A Love of Literature: How ILA's Choices project inspires the next generation of lifelong readers C. McCall *Literacy Today (2411-7862)* v35 no2 p44 S/O 2017

Reading promotion
See also
Summer reading programs
Use the News to Teach Reading Comprehension M. Zalaznick bw *Education Digest* v83 no3 p12 N 2017

Reading readiness
Publisher Spotlights and Highlights E. NAWOTKA bw color *Publishers Weekly* v264 no41 p22 O 9 2017

Reading software
See also
Reading mobile apps
Keeping the Spark Alive D. DILWORTH color *Publishers Weekly* v264 no23 p18 Je 5 2017

Reading teachers
EMBRACING A LEADING ROLE: A look at the schoolwide impact of reading specialists A. Swan Dagen *Literacy Today (2411-7862)* v35 no2 p22 S/O 2017

Reading—Ability testing
THE PARADOX OF THE WHOLE-CLASS NOVEL K. Roberts color *Literacy Today (2411-7862)* v34 no5 p42 Mr/Ap 2017
RIGOR VS. EASE Sarah Lupo color *Literacy Today (2411-7862)* v34 no4 p30 Ja/F 2017

Reading—Congresses
EVENTS *Literacy Today (2411-7862)* v34 no3 p38 N/D 2016
EVENTS *Literacy Today (2411-7862)* v34 no6 p48 My/Je 2017
EVENTS *Literacy Today (2411-7862)* v35 no2 p40 S/O 2017
A MARATHON RECORD color *Literacy Today (2411-7862)* v34 no3 p36 N/D 2016

Reading—Exhibitions
Oscar Wilde's 'Living Death' I. Buruma bw *New York Review of Books* v63 no18 p66 N 24 2016

Reading interests—Charts, diagrams, etc.
CONVERSATION A. WILSON color graph *Forbes* v198 no8 p36 D 20 2016

Reading—Law & legislation
Addressing Low Reading Scores N. Derringer *Education Digest* v83 no1 p59 S 2017

Reading—New York (State)
GO FORTH AND READ: How one Long Island school district started a literacy movement in its community J. Keegan, D. Provvido et al color *Literacy Today (2411-7862)* v34 no6 p36 My/Je 2017

Reading—Psychological aspects
How Making Time for Books Made Me Feel Less Busy H. McGuire *Harvard Business Review Digital Articles* p2 S 1 2015
Read a Novel: It's Just What the Doctor Ordered S. Begley color *Time* v188 no19 p58 N 7 2016

Reading—Social aspects
CONVERSATIONS WITH KEYNOTERS C. Kirch color *Publishers Weekly* v264 no3 p4 Ja 16 2017

Reading—Societies, etc.
GOT IT! T. Erdos Brocious color *Literacy Today (2411-7862)* v34 no3 p34 N/D 2016
A MARATHON RECORD color *Literacy Today (2411-7862)* v34 no3 p36 N/D 2016

Reading—Societies, etc.—Congresses
EVENTS *Literacy Today (2411-7862)* v34 no4 p40 Ja/F 2017

Reading—United States
THE PATH TO EXEMPLARY E. Center, K. Bailey et al color *Literacy Today (2411-7862)* v34 no4 p34 Ja/F 2017

Ready, Douglas A.
4 Things Successful Change Leaders Do Well *Harvard Business Review Digital Articles* p2 Ja 28 2016
Getting Employees Excited About a New Direction *Harvard Business Review Digital Articles* p2 N 20 2015

Ready meals
Meal Kits Won't Start a Cooking Revolution-Yet A. Sifferlin color *Time* v190 no5 p18 Jl 31 2017

Ready Player One (Film)
READY PLAYER ONE A. Breznican color *Entertainment Weekly* no1474/1475 p44 Jl 21-28 2017

Ready Take One (Music)
Studio Cuts: Tales of the Tape J. EPHLAND bw *Downbeat* v83 no11 p61 N 2016

Ready to drink beverages—Evaluation
DYMATIZE ISO100 CLEAR color *Muscle & Performance* v9 no5 p62 My 2017

Reagan, Ron, 1958-
ENVY IS THE NEW GREED M. KINSLEY color *Vanity Fair* v58 no12 p102 D 2016

Reagan, Ronald, 1911-2004
50 STATES, 50 HEROES *Tennis* v52 no6 p8 N/D 2016
Best Excuses for Sleeping on the Job T. John color *Time* v189 no20 p11 My 29 2017
Bold Enough to Compromise I. Morgan *History Today* v66 no12 p72 D 2016
INQUIETUDE J. Lepore cartoon *New Yorker* v93 no31 p17 O 9 2017
John Hinckley Left the Mental Hospital Seven Months Ago L. MILLER img *New York* v50 no6 p42 Mr 20 2017
A Non-transformational President R. PONNURU il *National Review* v69 no1 p16 Ja 23 2017

REAGIN, MISTY
FLIGHT OF FANCY color *Louisiana Life* v37 no5 p28 My/Je 2017

Real Enemies (Music)
Chords & Discords T. HUDAK, S. ROWE et al bw *Downbeat* v83 no12 p10 D 2016

Real estate agents
2017 WASHINGTONIAN TOP AGENTS, PRESENTED BY MVB MORTGAGE *Washingtonian Magazine* v52 no12 p136 S 2017
EVENTS *D: The Magazine of Dallas* v43 no10 p297 O 2016
MOVING HOUSES J. Gatehouse color *Maclean's* v129 no48/49 p58 D 5 2016
Upcoming in 2017 *Washingtonian Magazine* v52 no7 p134 Ap 2017
WAR STORIES, THE SEQUEL color *Los Angeles Magazine* v62 no10 p132 O 2017

Real estate agents—Awards
HOW TO SELL YOUR HOUSE—FAST *Los Angeles Magazine* pFS1 Mr 2017

Real estate agents—Malpractice
Realtors gone wild J. CASTALDO color *Maclean's* p14 Je 2017

Real estate agents—United States
'I can help you transform a fixer-upper, but how do I go from architect to real estate agent?' K. Palmer color *AARP: The Magazine* v59 no5A p36 Ag/S 2016

Real estate appraisers
Mamas, Don't Let Your Babies Grow Up to Be Appraisers J. Light color *Bloomberg Businessweek* no4530 p29 Jl 17 2017

Real estate bubbles
Hands off my bubble [Cover story] C. SORENSEN color graph *Maclean's* v129 no41 p36 O 17 2016

Real estate business
See also
Home ownership
House buying
House selling
Lease & rental services
Real property sales & prices
Rental housing
EVENTS *D: The Magazine of Dallas* v43 no10 p297 O 2016

THE HOUSING MARKET & BLACK AMERICA M. HOBSON color *Black Enterprise* v47 no8 p22 Jl/Ag 2017

Putting Home Sales Ahead of Paperwork S. Soper *Bloomberg Businessweek* no4526 p38 Je 12 2017

There Goes The Neighborhood S. ROOT color map *Los Angeles Magazine* v62 no10 p126 O 2017

THERE'S A SECRET STASH OF HOUSES FOR SALE M. M. KASHINO color *Washingtonian Magazine* v52 no7 p107 Ap 2017

Real estate business—Illinois—Chicago
CHICAGO'S POPULATION PROBLEM D. MENDELL color *Chicago* v66 no6 p19 Je 2017

Real estate business—Ohio
HOME IS WHERE YOU MAKE IT L. MURTHA *Cincinnati Magazine* v50 no6 p23 Mr 2017

Real estate business—Ontario—Toronto
Buy Today. Take a Close Look Tomorrow K. Chipman color *Bloomberg Businessweek* no4518 p39 Ap 10 2017

Real estate business—United States
HOME SHOPPING NETWORKERS A. FELDMAN cartoon color *Forbes* v198 no8 p94 D 20 2016

THE MAKING OF WASHINGTON J. KNAPP color *Washingtonian Magazine* v52 no7 p10 Ap 2017

Real estate developers
Squatters' 60-Year War Against Private Property: Around 1230 a.m. on August 7, 1988, a small army of police officers in riot gear covered their badges, raised their batons and charged on foot and on horseback into Tompkins Square Park on New York's... M. GARB *In These Times* v41 no7 p34 Jl 2017

Real estate development
See also
Mixed-use developments
Barrens to Blueberries J. D. SHORTHOUSE color map *Natural History* v125 no6 p34 Je 2017

No Place Like Home L. MURTHA *Cincinnati Magazine* v50 no2 p40 N 2016

Our Colleges Are Finally Neighborhood shapers D. REED color *Washingtonian Magazine* v52 no7 p110 Ap 2017

Self-Driving Cars will change local real estate M. J. GAYNOR color *Washingtonian Magazine* v52 no7 p96 Ap 2017

Win Community Approval for New Business Construction P. M. Saint *Harvard Business Review Digital Articles* p2 My 29 2015

Real estate development—California—Los Angeles
An AIDS Charity Fights Builders in L.A N. Piper *Bloomberg Businessweek* no4513 p42 Mr 6 2017

Banking On the Arts District M. SEGAL *Los Angeles Magazine* p38 D 2016

Real estate development—Canada
Affordability Is the Hardest Shade of Green Y. Afshar color *Alternatives Journal (AJ) - Canada's Environmental Voice* v42 no2 p40 2016

Real estate development—China
Welcome to The Neighborhood L. Hui and E. Dong color *Bloomberg Businessweek* no4525 p19 Je 5 2017

Real estate development—England—London
Chinese Investors Hear London Calling color *Bloomberg Businessweek* no4501 p34 N 28 2016

Real estate development—Florida—Miami
The X Factor D. KAZANJIAN color *Vogue* v206 no12 p126 D 2016

Real estate development—Georgia—Atlanta
THE EMPEROR OF EMPTY LOTS C. Pomorski bw color *Bloomberg Businessweek* no4538 p42 S 18 2017

Real estate development—India
SALESMEN OF THE SUBCONTINENT N. KARMALI color *Forbes* v199 no3 p80 Mr 28 2017

Real estate development—New York (State)—New York
MAN OF PROPERTIES D. Eng color *Fortune* v175 no2 p30 F 1 2017

Real estate development—United States
HOW TO AVOID A BIDDING WAR: "CLOSE DOWN THE OPEN HOUSE" B. FREED color *Washingtonian Magazine* v52 no7 p98 Ap 2017

THE MAKING OF WASHINGTON J. KNAPP color *Washingtonian Magazine* v52 no7 p10 Ap 2017

Real estate investment

DREAM LAND W. BRANTLEY color *Field & Stream* v122 no2 p92 Je/Jl 2017

Get the Lay of the Land cartoon *Timber Home Living* p30 2017 Annual Buyers

Reality check B. J. Lieberman color *Equus* no481 p54 O 2017

Real estate investment trusts—Economic aspects
Low on REITs, High on Returns D. FONDA chart *Kiplinger's Personal Finance* v71 no11 p63 N 2017

Real estate investment—Eastern Europe
Investment in Real Estate on the Rise color *Foreign Affairs* v96 no3 p86j My/Je 2017

Real estate listings
THERE'S A SECRET STASH OF HOUSES FOR SALE M. M. KASHINO color *Washingtonian Magazine* v52 no7 p107 Ap 2017

This Mansion Just Took a $66 Million Price Cut R. Wile color diag map *Money* v46 no5 p18 Je 2017

Real estate management
See also
Housing management

Real estate sales
See also
Home sales
PILLAR OF WISDOM T. BRAND *Indianapolis Monthly* v40 no5 p22 Ja 2017

Real estate sales tax
Chinese Buyers Move On From Vancouver K. Dmitrieva chart *Bloomberg Businessweek* no4504 p37 D 19 2016

Real property
See also
Betterments
Commercial real estate
Farms
Inheritance & succession
Residential real estate
Blessings in Disguise M. Bodgas color *Working Mother* v40 no4 p6 O/N 2017

DYING TO KNOW S. STALL color *Indianapolis Monthly* p17 Ap 2017

HOME IS WHERE YOU MAKE IT L. MURTHA *Cincinnati Magazine* v50 no6 p23 Mr 2017

New in New Orleans Real Estate K. FINN color *New Orleans Magazine* v52 no1 p34 S 2017

Real property acquisition
Move Over D. Paul *Indianapolis Monthly* v40 no3 p160 N 2016

Real property auctions
New House on the Block S. SHARF color *Forbes* v199 no1 p40 Ja 24 2017

Real property sales & prices
See also
Dwellings leasing & renting
CAN THEIR PROBLEM BE SOLVED? M. Friesen *Successful Farming* v114 no10 p69 O 2016

Home In the Range M. SEGAL color *Los Angeles Magazine* v62 no10 p10 O 2017

Homes Under $950K M. GLUCK color *Los Angeles Magazine* v62 no10 p122 O 2017

It's About the Porch color *Old House Journal* v45 no4 p36 Je 2017

LAND HO! HERE ARE THE TOP 10 THINGS YOU NEED TO KNOW ABOUT FARMLAND B. Freese *Successful Farming* v115 no8 p56 Je/Jl 2017

PERMANENT COLLECTION G. MONTES color *Architectural Digest* v73 no12 p66 D 2016

South Florida color *New York Times Magazine* p51 F 12 2017

SQUARE FEET: THE WAITING GAME M. LAWLER color *Chicago* v66 no9 p36 S 2017

THERE GOES THE NEIGHBORHOOD F. SCHRUERS *Los Angeles Magazine* p102 F 2017

THROUGH THE ROOF [Cover story] J. CASTALDO color *Maclean's* v130 no4 p48 My 2017

Town for sale: needs work M. CAMPBELL *Maclean's* v130 no2 p13 Mr 2017

Real property—California
An AIDS Charity Fights Builders in L.A N. Piper *Bloomberg Businessweek* no4513 p42 Mr 6 2017

Real property—Canada

THROUGH THE ROOF [Cover story] J. CASTALDO color *Maclean's* v130 no4 p48 My 2017

Real property—China

China's Housing Bubble Wobble B. EINHORN *Bloomberg Businessweek* no4496 p52 O 24 2016

Real property—Finance

Low on REITs, High on Returns D. FONDA chart *Kiplinger's Personal Finance* v71 no11 p63 N 2017

STOCKS WITH A SHAKY FOUNDATION R. Derousseau color diag *Fortune* v174 no6 p39 N 1 2016

Real property—Florida

South Florida J. Forsythe color *New York Times Magazine* p53 D 4 2016

Real property—Japan

Japan's Priests Turn to Property Development J. Clenfield, K. Kuwako et al color *Bloomberg Businessweek* no4521 p38 My 8 2017

Real property—Maps

WHERE TO LIVE IN AMERICA, 2100 A.D P. HESS cartoon *Popular Science* p32 Ja/F 2017

Real property—Texas

AUSTIN POWERED N. VARDI color *Forbes* v200 no1 p98 Jl 27 2017

Real property—United States

The Case for Density M. Funkhouser *Governing* v30 no12 p4 S 2017

GONE BABY GONE R. MONROE color *New Republic* v248 no10 p34 O 2017

Memphis Fights Blight: Collaborating to Win the Battle Against Vacant and Abandoned Property S. Barlow *Bridges (Federal Reserve Bank of St. Louis)* p8 Fall 2016

POWER HOUSES *Washingtonian Magazine* v52 no1 p72 O 2016

South Florida color *New York Times Magazine* p51 F 12 2017

Real property—Valuation

POWER HOUSES *Washingtonian Magazine* v52 no1 p72 O 2016

THERE GOES THE NEIGHBORHOOD F. SCHRUERS *Los Angeles Magazine* p102 F 2017

Real-time computing

See also

Online chat

Your Data Should Be Faster, Not Just Bigger R. Bean *Harvard Business Review Digital Articles* p2 F 4 2015

Real Women Have Curves (Film)

America ferrera Will Not Just Stick to Acting img *New York* v50 no7 p81 Ap 3 2017

Real World (TV program)

My Love Affair With Reality TV A. COHEN *TV Guide* v65 no21 p14 My 15 2017

Reale, Dan

The SAILING SCENE color *Sail* v48 no7 p6 Jl 2017

Real estate agents—Salaries, etc.

Realty Check cartoon *Men's Health* v32 no5 p42 Je 2017

Real Housewives of Atlanta, The (TV program)

WHEN REAL HOUSEWIVES OF ATLANTA DEBUTED IN FALL 2008 *Atlanta* v57 no1 p80 My 2017

Real Housewives of Dallas, The (TV program)

Lone Star LADIES I. RATLEDGE *TV Guide* v64 no15 p44 Ap 4 2016

Real Housewives of New Jersey, The (TV program)

The Real Housewives of New Jersey I. Ratledge *TV Guide* v65 no41 p32 O 2 2017

Real Housewives of New York City, The (TV program)

CHEERS & JEERS D. HOLBROOK *TV Guide* v65 no35 p76 Ag 21 2017

Realism

Realism? Use white paint N. Besougloff *Model Railroader* v84 no3 p8 Mr 2017

Realism—Moral & ethical aspects

Saving Realism from the So-Called Realists: A foreign-policy approach based in security and pragmatism is now characterized by retrenchment and radicalism H. Brands and P. Feaver *Commentary* v144 no2 p15 S 2017

Reality

See also

Experience

Virtual reality

Don't Be a Hypocrite About Failure J. Brady *Harvard Business Review Digital Articles* p2 Ag 4 2016

Two Routes to the Truth C. M. Carlisle *Sky & Telescope* v133 no6 p84 Je 2017

THE WAR OVER REALITY T. FOLGER color *Discover* v38 no4 p28 My 2017

Reality Bites (Film)

Reality Bites B. L. Heldman color *Entertainment Weekly* no1460/1461 p82 Ap 7-17 2017

Reality television program participants

The Challenge Hall of Fame B. L. Heldman color *Entertainment Weekly* no1474/1475 p107 Jl 21-28 2017

NeNe Leakes for President! M. Snetiker color *Entertainment Weekly* no1436/1437 p16 O 21 2016

Suitors to Watch S. Highfill color *Entertainment Weekly* no1468/1469 p19 Je 2-9 2017

Survivor: an Outing and an Ousting N. Serrao, P. Gomez et al color *Entertainment Weekly* no1463/1464 p21 Ap/My 2017

Will These Five Survive? D. Ross color *Entertainment Weekly* no1454/1455 p19 F 24 2017

Reality television programs

BEHIND THE SCENES C. BETHEA *Atlanta* v57 no1 p86 My 2017

DRAFTING THE BACHELOR FANTASY LEAGUE R. Desantis color *Entertainment Weekly* no1446/1447 p26 D 2016/Ja 2017

GAME ON! The classic Battle of the Network Stars is back, and your TV favorites are ready to wage war--on each other! J. HALTERMAN *TV Guide* v65 no27 p24 Je 26 2017

Meet Fashion's Newest Stars J. ABIDOR color *Seventeen* v76 no12 p20 D 2016/Ja 2017

My Love Affair With Reality TV A. COHEN *TV Guide* v65 no21 p14 My 15 2017

REAL APPEAL J. R. MARQUEZ *Atlanta* v57 no1 p82 My 2017

The Trouble With the Bachelorette (This Time) D. D'addario color *Time* v189 no24 p47 Je 26 2017

The Voice Soars M. ROFFMAN *TV Guide* v65 no19 p20 My 1 2017

You the Jury *TV Guide* p36 Ap 17 2017

Reality television programs—Reviews

THE 8-SECOND REVIEW N. Maslow color *Entertainment Weekly* no1466 p46 My 19 2017

First Dates D. Holbrook *TV Guide* v65 no14 p34 Ap 3 2017

Undercover Grief J. J. CONLEY *America* v215 no15 p29 N 14 2016

Realmac Software Ltd.

RAPIDWEAVER 7: GREAT NEW FEATURES BUT NEGLECTS EXISTING GAPS N. ALDERMAN color *Macworld - Digital Edition* v33 no11 p38 N 2016

Real O'Neals, The (TV program)

THE REAL O'NEALS M. Roffman *TV Guide* p30 D 5 2016

Real property—Charts, diagrams, etc.

So You Want an Outdoor Shower... img *New York* v50 no15 p48 Jl 24 2017

Realuyo, Celina B.

Can Bankers Fight Terrorism? *Foreign Affairs* v96 no6 p144 N/D 2017

REAM, TODD C.

BRINGING BACK BAYLOR color *Christianity Today* v61 no7 p54 S 2017

REAMER, ANDREW

Better Jobs Information Benefits Everyone *Issues in Science & Technology* v33 no1 p58 Fall 2016

Rear-end collisions

SAFE AND SLOW THEN DANGEROUS N. Ienatsch color *Cycle World* v56 no5 p26 Je 2017

Reardon, Dan

Do You Have SKINNY GENES? A. Synnott color *InStyle* v24 no1 p64 Ja 2017

REARDON, JOHN

YEA BOXY BRONCOS, NAY BEATNIK BOLSHEVIKS bw color *Forbes* v200 no2 p31 S 5 2017

Reardon, Kathleen Kelley

7 Things to Say When a Conversation Turns Negative *Harvard Business Review Digital Articles* p2 My 11 2016

Office Politics Isn't Something You Can Sit Out *Harvard Business*

Review Digital Articles p2 Ja 12 2015

Reason

Anxious about anxiety C. Zaleski *Christian Century* v134 no14 p35 Jl 5 2017

Civil Society and a Public Argument M. Malone *America* v217 no7 p3 O 2 2017

The Sympathetic Formation of Reason and the Limits of Science E. Matson *Society* v54 no3 p246 Je 2017

Reasoning (Logic)

See also

Uncertainty

IT'S CRITICAL L. ELDER *USA Today Magazine* v145 no2860 p42 Ja 2017

Rebala, Pratheek

Can Trump Handle the Truth? [Cover story] color *Time* v189 no12 p32 Ap 3 2017

Hacking Democracy Inside Russia's Social Media War on America color *Time* v189 no20 p30 My 29 2017

Russia and the Trump Campaign color *Time* v189 no12 p36 Ap 3 2017

Silent Partners color diag *Time* v188 no14 p40 O 10 2016

Trump Country Worries About Replacing Obamacare color *Time* v189 no10 p14 Mr 20 2017

Rebates

See also

Tax rebates

$1,388 Average spending for the holidays A. Cao color *Money* v45 no11 p13 D 2016

Ombudsman: A Mega-Pricey Missed Flight R. Marnell color *Conde Nast Traveler* v52 no2 p109 F 2017

Save on Airline Costs E. AMBROSE color *AARP: The Magazine* v60 no3A p21 Ap/My 2017

Rebec, S.

Femtosecond electron-phonon lock-in by photoemission and x-ray free-electron laser chart diag *Science* v357 no6346 p71 Jl 7 2017

Rebecca (Film)

Suspenseful Silence C. Fleming *Weekly Standard* v22 no47 p41 Ag 21 2017

Rebecca Minkoff LLC—Awards

Next: The Backpack color *Glamour* v114 no7 p48 Jl 2016

Rebecca Taylor (Company)

How Did I Get Here? R. TAYLOR bw color *Bloomberg Businessweek* no4523 p68 My 22 2017

Rebeka, Marina

Luminous A. WASSERMAN *Opera News* v81 no9 p28 Mr 2017

REBELE, REB

BEAT GENEROSITY BURNOUT color *Harvard Business Review Digital Articles* p3 Ja 1 2017

GENEROSITY BURNOUT color *Harvard Business Review* v95 no2 p162 Mr/Ap 2017

MORE ON BEING GENEROUS WITHOUT BEING A DOORMAT color *Harvard Business Review Digital Articles* p18 Ja 1 2017

More on Being Generous Without Being a Doormat *Harvard Business Review Digital Articles* p2 F 22 2017

Rebell, Bobbi

The Bank of Mom and Dad S. PERRINE color *AARP: The Magazine* v60 no1A p20 D 2016/Ja 2017

Rebelo, Sergio

Recessions Push People to Buy Cheap Things, Which Just Makes Everything Worse *Harvard Business Review Digital Articles* p2 My 12 2017

Rebensburg, Stephanie V.

Cryo-EM structures and atomic model of the HIV-1 strand transfer complex intasome bibl color *Science* v355 no6320 p1 Ja 6 2017

Rebolledo-Vieyra, Mario

The formation of peak rings in large impact craters bibl color graph *Science* v354 no6314 p878 N 18 2016

Rebounding (Exercise)

On the Rebound E. Batuman bw *Vogue* v207 no11 p154 N 2017

Rebranding (Marketing)

What's In a (Brand) Name? K. Samuelson color *Time* v190 no7 p12 Ag 21 2017

WHAT'S IN A NAME? J. Surowiecki cartoon *New Yorker* v92 no37 p35 N 14 2016

"Your employees are your best ambassadors": An HR-marketing marriage was the secret to changing perceptions of a 100-year-old accountancy firm *People Management* p22 Jl 2017

Rebus, Inspector (Fictitious character)

A Mortal Detective J. FOSTER color *Publishers Weekly* v263 no48 p46 N 28 2016

Rec Boat Holdings LLC

Wake Up A. JONES *Boating World* v38 no4 p34 Ap 2017

Receipt Bank (Company)

We get our coaching expertise through an app G. GYTON *People Management* p25 F 2017

Receipts (Acknowledgments)

Organize your way richer N. Lapin color *Redbook* p25 Jl/Ag 2017

Receipts (Acknowledgments)—Charts, diagrams, etc.

FEDERAL FINANCE *Economic Indicators* p32 F 2017

Receiving antennas

Connection Conundrums A. L. GRIFFIN color *Sound & Vision* v82 no2 p26 F/Mr 2017

Fascia of the Future M. Fleischmann color *Sound & Vision* v82 no8 p54 O 2017

HDMI Anxiety A. GRIFFIN color *Sound & Vision* v82 no7 p24 S 2017

Receiving antennas—Evaluation

RECEIVER REBOOT A. McConnell and L. Bedord *Successful Farming* v115 no1 p32 Ja 2017

UAVIONIX ADS-B PRODUCTS color *Flying* v144 no2 p16 F 2017

Reception, The (Theatrical production)

DANCE *New Yorker* v93 no17 p13 Je 19 2017

Recessions

See also

Recessions—2008-2013

Brexit Could Deepen Europe's Digital Recession B. Chakravorti *Harvard Business Review Digital Articles* p2 Jl 5 2016

Growth and Inequality *Commentary* v141 no10 p1 D 2016

Growth and Inequality *Commentary* v142 no5 p1 D 2016

A Recession Doesn't Mean Your Startup Can't Grow M. Roberge *Harvard Business Review Digital Articles* p2 F 24 2016

You Can't Understand China's Slowdown Without Understanding Supply Chains D. Simchi-Levi *Harvard Business Review Digital Articles* p2 S 4 2015

Recessions—2008-2013

Food Insecurity Among Children Declined to Pre-Recession Levels in 2015 A. Coleman-Jensen and M. Smith *Amber Waves: The Economics of Food, Farming, Natural Resources, & Rural America* p41 N 2016

Non-explanation for Non-recovery R. J. Barro *Hoover Digest: Research & Opinion on Public Policy* no1 p53 Wint 2017

Recessions—Economic aspects

Recessions Push People to Buy Cheap Things, Which Just Makes Everything Worse S. Rebelo *Harvard Business Review Digital Articles* p2 My 12 2017

Recessions—United States

Pockets of Growth: Suburban counties are once again gaining population at the expense of the cities around them M. Maciag *Governing* v30 no9 p56 Je 2017

Recessions—United States—History—21st century

ECONOMIC REPORT OF THE PRESIDENT *Economic Indicators* p3 S 2016

Recht, Hannah

Obamacare's Problems Still Need Solving map *Bloomberg Businessweek* no4531 p37 Jl 24 2017

Rechtin, Mark

Bona Fides Does a car company need a car guy for a CEO? color *Motor Trend* v69 no9 p26 S 2017

Dieselgate and Dollars cartoon *Motor Trend* v68 no12 p28 D 2016

Dodging monsoons and haboobs color *Motor Trend* v69 no1 p84 Ja 2017

Dumb and Dumber America's driver education is failing us all color *Motor Trend* v69 no8 p28 Ag 2017

GARAGE chart color diag *Motor Trend* v69 no11 p106 N 2017

GARAGE chart color diag *Motor Trend* v69 no8 p96 Ag 2017

Genesis Reveals: Product Plan Through 2021 color *Motor Trend* v69 no11 p22 N 2017

the leftovers... [Cover story] chart color *Motor Trend* v69 no4 p36 Ap 2017

Recreation v51 no11 p32 N 2016

great weekend getaways *Washingtonian Magazine* v52 no11 p80 Ag 2017

a movable feast *Parents* v91 no9 p27 S 2016

National 'Meet Me at the Park' Grant Recipients Selected *Parks & Recreation* v52 no9 p100 S 2017

New Orleans: Notable Local Places *Parks & Recreation* v52 no9 p84 S 2017

New Orleans Overachievers: The 2017 Conference Program Committee *Parks & Recreation* v52 no9 p87 S 2017

NRPA Live: Your Virtual Conference Experience *Parks & Recreation* v52 no9 p90 S 2017

Overcoming the Flaws of Needs Assessments: The new realm of big data A. Mitra *Parks & Recreation* v52 no9 p24 S 2017

The Playborhood M. Thernstrom *New York Times Magazine* p42 O 23 2016

Portable Picnic Feasts N. Berkoff *Vegetarian Journal* v36 no2 p6 2017

Public Park Usage: Motives and Challenges K. Roth *Parks & Recreation* v51 no10 p16 O 2016

Special Events *Parks & Recreation* v52 no9 p88 S 2017

Steal Their Weekends: Sick of your same old summer routine? Then take someone else's. We found dozens of opinionated locals to pick from K. SCHNEIDER img *New York* v50 no12 p63 Je 12 2017

weekend getaways: just do it A. BEAUJON *Washingtonian Magazine* v52 no11 p82 Ag 2017

Recreation & Park Commission for the Parish of East Baton Rouge

Member Spotlight: Diane Drake C. Jones *Parks & Recreation* v52 no10 p47 O 2017

Recreation agencies

2017 Agency Performance Survey Now Open *Parks & Recreation* v52 no10 p49 O 2017

Arts and Parks: A Natural Fit G. MULLINS-COHEN *Parks & Recreation* v52 no8 p10 Ag 2017

Email Marketing Best Practices *Parks & Recreation* v52 no5 p19 My 2017

Email Marketing: Still the killer app to beat for park and recreation agencies J. Dysart *Parks & Recreation* v52 no5 p18 My 2017

Five Reasons to Post Your Open Position on the NRPA Career Center *Parks & Recreation* v52 no8 p65 Ag 2017

Laying the Groundwork for Park Metrics K. Roth and M. May *Parks & Recreation* v52 no1 p12 Ja 2017

NRPA Update: More Health and Wellness Sessions Offered at Conference This Year T. Crosley *Parks & Recreation* v52 no6 p40 Je 2017

Wild and Wonderful M. May and S. Ozbenian *Parks & Recreation* v52 no3 p14 Mr 2017

Recreation area parking facilities

Bentonville Gets the Country's First-Ever Bike Playground D. Wright *Parks & Recreation* v52 no5 p24 My 2017

From Young Professional to Respected Leader: Navigating the park and recreation career ladder R. Fink II *Parks & Recreation* v52 no5 p34 My 2017

Recreation areas

See also

Camp sites, facilities, etc.

Parks

Picnic grounds

Resorts

Aquatics Trends G. Deines *Parks & Recreation* v51 no12 p50 D 2016

From the Director's Chair S. Bartram *Parks & Recreation* v51 no10 p30 O 2016

Introducing NRPA Park Metrics K. Roth *Parks & Recreation* v51 no11 p12 N 2016

Peace Amid Chaos *Parks & Recreation* v52 no4 p64 Ap 2017

Staying Ahead of the Curve K. Hobson and K. Stokke *Parks & Recreation* v52 no3 p18 Mr 2017

Transportation Planning Must Mitigate Park Impacts J. C. Kozlowski *Parks & Recreation* v52 no5 p28 My 2017

Recreation areas—Access

'Hold Harmless' Incentive in Recreational Use Statute J. C. Kozlowski *Parks & Recreation* v51 no10 p44 O 2016

Turning the Tide on a Generation Left Inside J. Ostfeld *Parks &*

Recreation v52 no4 p18 Ap 2017

Recreation areas—Colorado

on the rocks: GRANITE GAINS IN COLORADO'S HIGH DESERT t. weaver strokes color *Bike Magazine* v24 no8 p30 N 2017

Recreation areas—Design & construction

See also

Golf courses—Design & construction

The Green line E. Moreno *Parks & Recreation* v51 no11 p44 N 2016

Recreation areas—Equipment & supplies

Products *Parks & Recreation* v52 no4 p58 Ap 2017

Recreation areas—Law & legislation

Park Permit for Commercial Wedding Photos J. C. Kozlowski *Parks & Recreation* v52 no4 p22 Ap 2017

Recreation areas—Management

See also

Park management

Movable Chairs S. Myriok *Parks & Recreation* v51 no11 p64 N 2016

Recreation areas—South Dakota

EAST RIVER EVENTS *South Dakota Magazine* v33 no3 p82 S/O 2017

Recreation centers

See also

Equestrian centers

Physical fitness centers

Promoting LGBT Inclusion and Awareness in Programs and Facilities J. Martin *Parks & Recreation* v52 no6 p28 Je 2017

Social Equity: Plays Key Role in New Braunfels' New Recreation Center S. L. Dicke and S. Springs *Parks & Recreation* v52 no10 p40 O 2017

Recreation for LGBT people

Promoting LGBT Inclusion and Awareness in Programs and Facilities J. Martin *Parks & Recreation* v52 no6 p28 Je 2017

Recreation industry

See also

Outdoor recreation industry

The Future of Community Recreation B. TULIPANE *Parks & Recreation* v52 no9 p8 S 2017

Hate Has No Place Here G. MULLINS-COHEN *Parks & Recreation* v52 no9 p10 S 2017

NRPA Park Pulse *Parks & Recreation* v52 no10 p14 O 2017

Overcoming the Flaws of Needs Assessments: The new realm of big data A. Mitra *Parks & Recreation* v52 no9 p24 S 2017

Park Champion of the Year: Portland's Som Subedi: Promoting equity and inclusion while ensuring congressional support for parks and recreation J. Rasmussen and C. Hodgkins *Parks & Recreation* v52 no10 p16 O 2017

Recreation industry—Employees

Green Workers Certification May Create New Training Opportunities R. J. Dolesh *Parks & Recreation* v51 no10 p54 O 2016

A Guiding Hand G. MULLINS-COHEN *Parks & Recreation* v52 no2 p10 F 2017

NRPA Park and Recreation Salary Survey Says... K. Roth *Parks & Recreation* v52 no9 p12 S 2017

Recreation rooms—Interior decoration

The cheap, joyful HOME MAKEOVER [Cover story] color *Redbook* p108 Jl/Ag 2017

Recreational clubs

SOUTH color *Downbeat* v84 no2 p52 F 2017

Recreational Equipment Inc.

A RETAILER FINDS ITS VOICE C. Zillman color *Fortune* v176 no4 p46 S 15 2017

Will You Go Out With Us? *Parks & Recreation* v51 no11 p56 N 2016

Recreational vehicle camping

The Lady In the Camper D. KUIPERS color *Los Angeles Magazine* v62 no7 p50 Jl 2017

Recreational vehicle parks—Evaluation

NEW MANAGEMENT, POSITIVE CHANGES AHEAD FOR AREA BFE color *Dirt Sports + Off-Road* v51 no4 p8 Ap 2017

Recreational vehicles

See also

Camping trailers

TOW TAPPERS J. Chamberlain color *Sunset* v239 no1 p32 Jl 2017

Je 26 2017

Red Wheel/Weiser LLC

NEW VOICES ON TIMELESS SUBJECTS L. GARRETT color *Publishers Weekly* v264 no32 p24 Ag 7 2017

Red wines

See also

Beaujolais (Wine)

ASK CAROLYN C. FORTÉ color *Good Housekeeping* v264 no3 p53 Mr 2017

The Cocktail Justification Matrix S. Dreisbach and S. G. Levy cartoon chart color *Glamour* v114 no12 p153 D 2016

GAME PLAN M. Zimmerman color graph *Men's Health* v32 no9 p8 N 2017

r.s.v.p cartoon *Bon Appetit* v62 no6 p10 Je 2017

What's My Age Again? E. Freud color *InStyle* v24 no9 p206 S 2017

The wise woman's guide to booze D. VILIBERT color *Redbook* p89 D 2016

Red wines—Evaluation

Uncharted Terroir J. Clarke color *Bloomberg Businessweek* no4517 p72 Ap 3 2017

Redbord, Michael

Scaling Customer Service as Your Startup Grows *Harvard Business Review Digital Articles* p2 S 11 2017

Red.com Inc.

FETISH MATINEE IDOL T. MOYNIHAN color *Wired* v25 no5 p43 My 2017

Redd, Miles

Miles Redd M. RUS color *Architectural Digest* v74 no8 p28 Ag 2017

Rhymes with Smiles K. O'Shea-Evans color *House Beautiful* p26 Jl 2017

Redd, Nola Taylor

Impostors in the asteroid belt bw color diag *Astronomy* v45 no4 p28 Ap 2017

Preteen Astronomer Shines at AAS Meeting *Sky & Telescope* v133 no4 p12 Ap 2017

Separated at Birth chart color diag *Discover* v38 no10 p38 D 2017

The solar system's violent past [Cover story] bw color diag *Astronomy* v45 no2 p22 F 2017

REDDING, ANN

FANCY THAT! color *Bon Appetit* v61 no11 p104 N 2016

REDDING, CHARLES

LIVES OVER LANDFILLS *USA Today Magazine* v145 no2858 p34 N 2016

Redding, Kevin E.

Structure of a symmetric photosynthetic reaction center–photosystem color *Science* v357 no6355 p1021 S 8 2017

Redding, Otis, 1941-1967

Next Stop: Otis in 1966 J. Johnson color *Downbeat* v83 no12 p90 D 2016

Reddington, Carly L. S.

Global atmospheric particle formation from CERN CLOUD measurements bibl graph map *Science* v354 no6316 p1119 D 2 2016

Reddit Inc.

How Reddit the Business Lost Touch With Reddit the Culture A. Debigare and D. Weinberger *Harvard Business Review Digital Articles* p2 Jl 14 2015

A KINDER, GENTLER REDDIT J. STEIN cartoon color *Bloomberg Businessweek* no4503 p65 D 12 2016

Reddy, Chris

Scientists and the Navy Join Forces: NATO SEEKS ADVICE TO AVOID COLLATERAL ENVIRONMENTAL DAMAGE L. Lippsett *Oceanus* v52 no2 p6 Spr 2017

Reddy, Francis

Cornelis A. Gehrels *Physics Today* v70 no10 p75 O 2017

UNVEILING A GIANT [Cover story] bw chart color diag *Astronomy* v45 no10 p20 O 2017

Why we need dark matter color *Astronomy* v45 no11 p30 N 2017

REDDY, FRANK

ROOM TO GROW: A private school with a noble mission gets a new lease on life--and a new building *Atlanta* v57 no3 p24 Jl 2017

Reddy, Pramod

Quantized thermal transport in single-atom junctions bibl diag graph *Science* v355 no6330 p1192 Mr 17 2017

REDEL, VICTORIA

Let it go! [Cover story] color *O, The Oprah Magazine* p92 Ag 2017

Redemption—Christianity

The Cry of Abel's Blood J. A. Miller cartoon *Commonweal* v144 no7 p16 Ap 14 2017

The redemption of ex-prisoners is a duty of the church J. Mc-Greevey *America* v217 no7 p10 O 2 2017

Redfin Corp.

How Did I Get Here? GLENN KELMAN bw color *Bloomberg Businessweek* no4515 p68 Mr 20 2017

Redflex Traffic Systems Inc.

WHERE RADAR CAMERAS FEAR TO TREAD J. D. TUCILLE bw *Reason* v49 no1 p10 My 2017

REDFORD, GABRIELLE deGROOT

Get Smart About Stroke cartoon *AARP: The Magazine* v60 no1A p18 D 2016/Ja 2017

Save Your Eyesight color *AARP: The Magazine* v60 no2A p26 F/Mr 2017

Your Brain Behaving Badly color *AARP: The Magazine* v60 no5A p22 Ag/S 2017

Redford, Robert, 1936-

Climate Change Affects Every Issue Voters Face color *Time* v188 no16/17 p79 O 24 2016

OUR SOULS AT NIGHT J. McGovern color *Entertainment Weekly* no1446/1447 p54 D 2016/Ja 2017

Redford, Robert, 1936—Interviews

THE NATURAL [Cover story] M. Hainey bw color *Esquire* p92 O 2017

WONDERLAND J. FIELDEN color *Esquire* p22 O 2017

Redhead, J.

Country-specific effects of neonicotinoid pesticides on honey bees and wild bees diag map *Science* v356 no6345 p1393 Je 30 2017

Redheads

RIDE OR DYE L. DUNHAM color *Vogue* v207 no9 p728 S 2017

Red Horse, Chief

The Face of Battle without the Rules of War: Lessons from Red Horse & the Battle of the Little Bighorn S. D. Sagan *Daedalus* v146 no1 p25 Wint 2017

Red-Horse, Valerie

Choctaw Code Talkers M. K. Bowannie *American Indian Quarterly* v40 no4 p385 Fall 2016

Rediker, Marcus

THE CAVE-DWELLING VEGAN WHO TOOK ON QUAKER SLAVERY AND WON: THE NATION'S FIRST RADICAL ABOLITIONIST WAS ONE OF THE MOST DRAMATIC OUTSPOKEN FIGURES OF THE 18TH CENTURY. YET FEW HISTORIANS HAVE EVEN HEARD OF THE AMAZING BENJAMIN LAY *Smithsonian* v48 no5 p34 S 2017

The Fearless Benjamin Lay: The Quaker Dwarf Who Became the First Revolutionary Abolitionist *Publishers Weekly* v264 no26 p167 Je 26 2017

REDix, ERIK M.

"Our Hope and Our Protection": Misko-biiwaabik (Copper) and Tribal Sovereignty in Michigan bw map *American Indian Quarterly* v41 no3 p224 Summ 2017

Red Letter Plays, The (Theatrical production)

Theater img *New York* v50 no17 p126 Ag 21 2017

THE THEATRE *New Yorker* v93 no27 p14 S 11 2017

Redlin, Josephine

Dad's Journey Home—for Antone Pressler 1916-1990 *South Dakota Magazine* v33 no2 p90 Jl/Ag 2017

Redlon, Matt

A Guide to Selecting an Analytics Vendor *Harvard Business Review Digital Articles* p2 O 23 2015

Redman, Joshua

FLOATING & FLYING J. WOODARD color *Downbeat* v83 no11 p36 N 2016

Redman, Rich

Amelia's Big Fish *New York State Conservationist* v71 no5 p40 Ap 2017

Redman, Thomas C.

4 Business Models for the Data Age *Harvard Business Review Digital Articles* p2 My 20 2015

4 Steps for Thinking Critically About Data Measurements *Harvard Business Review Digital Articles* p2 Mr 17 2016

Assess Whether You Have a Data Quality Problem *Harvard Business Review Digital Articles* p2 Jl 28 2016

The Best Data Scientists Get Out and Talk to People color *Harvard Business Review Digital Articles* p2 Ja 26 2017

Can Your Data Be Trusted? *Harvard Business Review Digital Articles* p2 O 29 2015

Data Quality Should Be Everyone's Job *Harvard Business Review Digital Articles* p2 My 20 2016

Dispel Your Team's Fear of Data *Harvard Business Review Digital Articles* p2 Jl 16 2015

Does Your Company Know What to Do with All Its Data? *Harvard Business Review Digital Articles* p2 Je 15 2017

Only 3% of Companies' Data Meets Basic Quality Standards *Harvard Business Review Digital Articles* p2 S 11 2017

Overcome Your Company's Resistance to Data *Harvard Business Review Digital Articles* p2 Mr 30 2015

Root Out Bias from Your Decision-Making Process color *Harvard Business Review Digital Articles* p2 Mr 10 2017

Stop Making Excuses for Your Flawed Data *Harvard Business Review Digital Articles* p2 F 12 2015

When It Comes to Data, Skepticism Matters *Harvard Business Review Digital Articles* p2 O 22 2014

Redman, Tom—Interviews

A Refresher on Randomized Controlled Experiments A. Gallo *Harvard Business Review Digital Articles* p2 Mr 30 2016

Redmayne, Eddie, 1982-

Eddie Redmayne Wants to Make You Believe In Magic Again M. McCluskey color *Time* v188 no22-23 p106 N/D 2016

Eddie Redmayne Works His Magic D. Coggan color *Entertainment Weekly* no1441 p13 N 25 2016

Fantastic Beasts and Where to Find Them C. Nashawaty color *Entertainment Weekly* no1441 p36 N 25 2016

A FIELD GUIDE TO FANTASTIC BEASTS J. Hibberd color *Entertainment Weekly* no1442 p8 D 2 2016 Rebellious Special Issue

Redmercedes (Music)

The Playlist color *Rolling Stone* no1284 p10 Ap 6 2017

Redmond, Ashley

THE FUTURE IS HERE N. Farrell, C. Lamers et al color diag *Sunset* v238 no4 p54 Ap 2017

Redmond, Brandi

Lone Star LADIES I. RATLEDGE *TV Guide* v64 no15 p44 Ap 4 2016

REDMOND, JENNIFER HOGAN

2017 CANCER REPORT *Cincinnati Magazine* p78 Je 2017

DOES YOUR CHOICE MEASURE UP? Check out the numbers surrounding popular degree choices and careers *Cincinnati Magazine* v50 no11 pCG8 Ag 2017

FIGHTING BACK: HOW LOCAL TEAMS ARE TREATING A CHALLENGING DISEASE color *Cincinnati Magazine* v51 no1 p91 O 2017

LIVING BETTER WITH ARTHRITIS *Cincinnati Magazine* v50 no7 p90 Ap 2017

Redondo, Dolores

Latino Authors Celebrated At Annual Book Awards A. Bardales *Publishers Weekly* v264 no40 p18 O 2 2017

Redondo, Roger L.

Engrams and circuits crucial for systems consolidation of a memory diag *Science* v356 no6333 p73 Ap 7 2017

REDPATH, STEPHEN

International Wildlife Law: Understanding and Enhancing Its Role in Conservation *BioScience* v67 no9 p784 S 2017

Red Shoes, The (Theatrical production)

From Screen to Stage *Dance Magazine* v90 no12 p25 D 2016

Redstone, Suzanne Blank

SUZANNE BLANK REDSTONE G. Allen color *Art in America* v104 no11 p126 D 2016

Red Turtle, The (Film)

NOW PLAYING color *Entertainment Weekly* no1454/1455 p83 F 24 2017

The Red Turtle J. McGovern color *Entertainment Weekly* no1450 p44 Ja 27 2017

Reduced gravity environments

Wickless heat pipes in microgravity J. L. Plawsky and Thao Nguyen *Physics Today* v70 no9 p82 S 2017

Reducing diets

See also

Low-carbohydrate diet

5 LESSONS FROM THE NEW PALEO L. SCHULER and L. TEDESCO color *Men's Health* v32 no7 p104 S 2017

Buy 5, Drop 5 K. Glassman color *Women's Health* v14 no1 p138 Ja/F 2017

Change Is Good B. O'Dair color *Prevention* v69 no1 p3 Ja 2017

CUT IT OUT K. Ansel color *Women's Health* v14 no3 p108 Ap 2017

How This Dad Lost 100 Pounds P. Kita color *Men's Health* v32 no2 p26 Mr 2017

I Tried Dieting Like My Mom B. Hauser color *Health* v30 no10 p55 D 2016

LOSING IT T. Brodesser-Akner bw color *New York Times Magazine* p34 Ag 6 2017

"WHY I LOVE not dieting" K. Miller color *Good Housekeeping* v263 no5 p159 N 2016

World-Class Fat-Blasting Secrets B. GREGORY color map *Men's Health* v32 no5 p89 Je 2017

YES, THIS IS HEALTHY J. Gordinier cartoon color *Esquire* p23 Ap 2017

Reducing exercises

SCULL YOUR WAY SLIM K. LOREN chart color *Muscle & Performance* v9 no4 p18 Ap 2017

Reductases

Methanogenic heterodisulfide reductase (HdrABC-MvhAGD) uses two noncubane [4Fe-4S] clusters for reduction T. Wagner, J. Koch et al color *Science* v357 no6352 p699 Ag 18 2017

Reduction mammaplasty

Let's Talk About... BODY IMAGE A. STANLEY cartoon color *Seventeen* v75 no11 p76 N 2016

Reductive coupling reactions (Chemistry)

Metal-catalyzed reductive coupling of olefin-derived nucleophiles: Reinventing carbonyl addition K. D. Nguyen, B. Y. Park et al diag *Science* v354 no6310 paah5133-1 O 21 2016

Redway, Lacy

When Do You Feel Most Beautiful? color *Glamour* v115 no4 p32 Ap 2017

Redwine, Robert P.

Virginia Ruth Brown *Physics Today* v69 no10 p67 O 2016

Redwood (Wood)

How to Make a... RAISED FLOWER BED [Cover story] bw chart *Popular Mechanics* v193 no7 p70 S 2016

Redwood National Park (Calif.)

Tall Trees Grove: Redwood National Park, CA diag *Backpacker* p104 N 2017

Redwoods

last look M. FORSTER *American Forests* v122 no3 p48 Fall 2016

Redzepi, Nadine Levy

Off the Menu L. REGENSDORF, M. HOLGATE et al color *Vogue* v207 no9 p380 S 2017

Redzepi, René, 1977-

Off the Menu L. REGENSDORF, M. HOLGATE et al color *Vogue* v207 no9 p380 S 2017

REEB, RICHARD H., JR.

Free Speech and Its Enemies *Commentary* v144 no3 p4 O 2017

Those '60s Flashbacks *Commentary* v142 no4 p10 N 2016

Reece, Erik

Utopia Drive M. P. Branch color *Orion Magazine* v36 no1 p59 Ja/F 2017

REECE, TAMEKIA

Avoid Falling cartoon *Parents* v92 no9 p163 S 2017

brushing up *Parents* v91 no12 p120 D 2016

easily embarrassed *Parents* v92 no6 p138 Je 2017

fighting frustration *Parents* v91 no10 p136 O 2016

getting physical *Parents* v91 no11 p140 N 2016

HOW TO Avoid Losing Things *Parents* v92 no11 p120 N 2017

HOW TO Decode Your Discharge color *Parents* v92 no11 p117 N 2017

imitation game *Parents* v92 no3 p108 Mr 2017

making sense *Parents* v91 no9 p165 S 2016

new power struggles *Parents* v92 no6 p136 Je 2017

social influence *Parents* v92 no5 p119 My 2017

uphill battle *Parents* v91 no6 p140 Je 2016

Reed, B. Cameron

REVISITING THE LOS ALAMOS PRIMER: A concise packet of

Blackouts cast Australia's green energy in dim light color *Science* v355 no6329 p1001 Mr 10 2017

Island extinctions weren't inevitable color *Science* v356 no6339 p674 My 19 2017

Swell or High Water color graph *Scientific American* v316 no6 p21 Je 2017

Reese, Curtis W.

What's In The Name? ALL OF US: CELEBRATING A CENTURY OF HUMANISM L. L. SIMPSON *Humanist* v77 no5 p25 S/O 2017

REESE, JOEL

CAN NAVY PIER EVER BE COOL? color *Chicago* v66 no8 p21 Ag 2017

FIELD GUIDE: ELMHURST color map *Chicago* v66 no9 p41 S 2017

HIGHWOOD color *Chicago* v66 no10 p32 O 2017

HINSDALE color map *Chicago* v66 no7 p20 Jl 2017

HUMBOLDT PARK cartoon color *Chicago* v66 no4 p31 Ap 2017

IRVING PARK cartoon color *Chicago* v66 no2 p20 F 2017

KENWOOD color map *Chicago* v66 no1 p32 Ja 2017

LAKE VIEW color map *Chicago* v66 no8 p30 Ag 2017

NORTH CENTER color map *Chicago* v66 no11 p29 N 2017

SKOKIE cartoon color *Chicago* v66 no3 p37 Mr 2017

SOUTH SHORE color map *Chicago* v66 no6 p28 Je 2017

TINLEY PARK color *Chicago* v65 no12 p37 D 2016

TOP CANCER DOCTORS color *Chicago* v66 no1 p84 Ja 2017

UPTOWN cartoon color *Chicago* v66 no5 p37 My 2017

WILMETTE color map *Chicago* v65 no11 p29 N 2016

Reese, Linda W.

Trail Sisters: Freedwomen in Indian Territory, 1850-1890 A. L. Coleman *American Indian Quarterly* v40 no3 p274 Summ 2016

Reese, Sammy

GOING LONG color *Outdoor Life* v223 no9 p40 N 2016

Reese, Tracy

Forever Tracy J. Wilson color *Essence* v48 no5 p96 S 2017

Reesman, Bryan

Art of the SOUND INSTALL *Stage Directions* v29 no11 p14 N 2016

Audio Alternatives *Stage Directions* v30 no1 p8 Ja 2017

A Cappella Adventures *Stage Directions* v30 no2 p12 F 2017

Closing TIME *Stage Directions* v30 no5 p12 My 2017

Elevating the Pit *Stage Directions* v30 no4 p8 Ap 2017

FAST AND FURIOUS *Stage Directions* v30 no9 p14 S 2017

It's All in the Details *Stage Directions* v30 no3 p42 Mr 2017

Mixing Without Leading *Stage Directions* v29 no10 p18 O 2016

(Re)Creating The Encounter [Cover story] *Stage Directions* v29 no12 p12 D 2016

THE SOUND OF IMAGINATION: Andrew Keister's Sound Design for Charlie and the Chocolate Factory *Stage Directions* v30 no6 p12 Je 2017

Reess, J. M.

Seasonal exposure of carbon dioxide ice on the nucleus of comet 67P/Churyumov-Gerasimenko bibl bw graph *Science* v354 no6319 p1563 D 23 2016

Reeve, John N.

Structure of histone-based chromatin in Archaea diag *Science* v357 no6351 p609 Ag 11 2017

Reeve, Philip, 1966-

Railhead color *Publishers Weekly* v263 no49 p112 D 7 2016

Reeves, Jay

Firebrand Moore wins GOP primary runoff color *Christian Century* v134 no22 p15 O 25 2017

REEVES, JOSHUA

RECOGNIZE, RESIST, REPORT cartoon *Reason* v49 no1 p38 My 2017

Reeves, Keanu, 1964-

5 JUICY CONFESSIONS with... Keanu Reeves C. Keller color *Women's Health* v14 no2 p126 Mr 2017

The Hit Parade J. QUEENAN *Weekly Standard* v22 no36 p39 My 29 2017

JOHN WICK: CHAPTER 2 C. Collis color *Entertainment Weekly* no1446/1447 p51 D 2016/Ja 2017

Keanu Reeves' Contract Killer With Feelings Returns S. Lansky color *Time* v189 no5 p49 F 13 2017

Vengeance, the Slow Way S. Zacharek color *Time* v189 no6 p50 F 20 2017

Reeves, Martin

A CEO's Guide to Navigating Brexit *Harvard Business Review Digital Articles* p2 Je 29 2016

Companies Shouldn't Wait to Prepare for the Post-Brexit World *Harvard Business Review Digital Articles* p2 N 3 2016

Designing the Machines That Will Design Strategy *Harvard Business Review Digital Articles* p2 Ap 18 2016

Don't Let Your Company Get Trapped by Success *Harvard Business Review Digital Articles* p2 N 19 2015

Games Can Make You a Better Strategist *Harvard Business Review Digital Articles* p2 S 7 2015

Google Couldn't Survive with One Strategy *Harvard Business Review Digital Articles* p2 Ag 18 2015

How to Regain the Lost Art of Reflection *Harvard Business Review Digital Articles* p2 S 25 2017

Navigating the Dozens of Different Strategy Options *Harvard Business Review Digital Articles* p2 Je 24 2015

Rethinking Your Supply Chain in an Era of Protectionism *Harvard Business Review Digital Articles* p2 Mr 22 2017

Using M&A to Increase Your Capacity for Growth *Harvard Business Review Digital Articles* p2 Jl 13 2016

What China's 13th Five-Year Plan Means for Business *Harvard Business Review Digital Articles* p2 D 7 2015

The World Just Got More Uncertain and Your Strategy Needs to Adjust *Harvard Business Review Digital Articles* p2 N 11 2016

Reeves, Matt

THE APES ARE COMING T. GRIERSON color *Popular Mechanics* p12 Jl 2017

Do Humans Even Deserve War for the Planet of the Apes? S. Zacharek color *Time* v190 no4 p47 Jl 24 2017

Don of the Planet of the Apes K. P. Sullivan color *Entertainment Weekly* no1474/1475 p94 Jl 21-28 2017

War for the Planet of the Apes C. Nashawaty color *Entertainment Weekly* no1474/1475 p95 Jl 21-28 2017

WAR FOR THE PLANET OF THE APES D. Franich color *Entertainment Weekly* no1463/1464 p70 Ap/My 2017

WAR FOR THE PLANET OF THE APES K. P. Sullivan color *Entertainment Weekly* no1446/1447 p54 D 2016/Ja 2017

Reeves, Randall R.

Dams threaten rare Mekong dolphins bibl color *Science* v355 no6327 p805 F 24 2017

U.S. seafood import restriction presents opportunity and risk bibl color map *Science* v354 no6318 p1372 D 16 2016

Reeves, Richard V.

The Great Ladder R. VERBRUGGEN *National Review* v69 no16 p42 Ag 28 2017

Reeves, Sam

The Tao of Sam M. Bamberger color *Golf Magazine* v59 no5 p120 My 2017

Reeves, Scott

Living History at Open Air Museums *British Heritage Travel* v38 no1 p48 Ja/F 2017

Our Exotic Architecture: An Imperial Legacy *British Heritage Travel* v38 no4 p32 Jl/Ag 2017

THOSE MAGNIFICENT BRITISH FLYING MACHINES *British Heritage Travel* v38 no2 p48 Mr/Ap 2017

Reeves-Rush, Jessica

Country Lore *Mother Earth News* no281 p84 Ap/My 2017

Reference sources

THE ARCHIVES Bookshelf *Prologue* v48 no4 p59 Wint 2016

Referendum

California Split B. KAUFFMAN *American Conservative* v16 no2 p39 Mr/Ap 2017

Dictator Erdogan D. PRYCE-JONES color *National Review* v69 no9 p17 My 15 2017

The Referendum Vote That Could Fracture Iraq J. Malsin map *Time* v190 no12 p13 S 25 2017

THE SEARCH FOR A PLACE TO TOKE UP J. SULLUM color *Reason* v49 no3 p6 Jl 2017

Referendum—California

The Golden State's Big Green Bet K. Steinmetz color *Time* v188 no20 p38 N 14 2016

No, California [Cover story] K. D. WILLIAMSON color *National Review* v69 no7 p27 Ap 17 2017

Where the Rubber Meets the Road A. FERGUSON color *Weekly Standard* v22 no9 p10 N 7 2016

Referendum—Colombia

Colombians Yank The Welcome Mat M. Bristow color *Bloomberg Businessweek* no4537 p30 S 11 2017

Why Referendums Have Been Backfiring I. Bremmer *Time* v188 no15 p8 O 17 2016

Referendum—Great Britain

See also

Brexit Referendum, 2016

UK science mired in uncertainty about Brexit T. Feder *Physics Today* v70 no3 p24 Mr 2017

Referendum—Iraq

Lightbox color *Time* v190 no14 p18 O 9 2017

Referendum—Italy

Banks? E. Robinson and S. Sirletti cartoon *Bloomberg Businessweek* no4503 p32 D 12 2016

A Petri Dish of Populist Dissent A. Migliaccio and J. Follain cartoon *Bloomberg Businessweek* no4501 p14 N 28 2016

Referendum—Puerto Rico

Can statehood save Puerto Rico? T. Padget color *America* v216 no13 p15 Je 12 2017

Referendum—Scotland

Untied Kingdom D. GREEN color map *Weekly Standard* v22 no30 p26 Ap 10 2017

Referendum—Turkey

In Turkey, New Powers Won't Fix Old Problems I. Finkel and S. Hacaoglu color *Bloomberg Businessweek* no4519 p17 Ap 24 2017

Turkey's Controversial Referendum J. Malsin color *Time* v189 no11 p11 Mr 27 2017

Will Turkey Vote to Give Erdogan Even More Power? J. Malsin color *Time* v189 no4 p11 F 6 2017

Referendum—United States

Measuring Up L. YOUNG *Ms.* v26 no4 p12 Wint 2016

Repeal and Replace C. CHANG il *New Republic* v248 no11 p12 N 2017

States Lean Left on Local Votes J. Sanburn color *Time* v188 no21 p16 N 21 2016

Refinancing

MORTGAGE HELP FOR DEBT-SADDLED GRADS P. MERTZ ESSWEIN color graph *Kiplinger's Personal Finance* v71 no8 p15 Ag 2017

Reflecting telescopes

See also

Cassegrainian telescopes

FROM OUR READERS M. Lewicki, T. Sales et al *Sky & Telescope* v133 no1 p6 Ja 2017

M33 in a 10-inch Scope S. French *Sky & Telescope* v132 no6 p54 D 2016

Reflecting telescopes—Evaluation

Meade's LightBridge Mini Series T. Flanders *Sky & Telescope* v132 no6 p58 D 2016

The Zhumell Z130: This remarkably inexpensive tabletop Dob is an outstanding performer T. Flanders color *Sky & Telescope* v134 no2 p58 Ag 2017

Reflection (Music)

BEGIN ANYWHERE A. PETRUSICH color *Nation* v304 no10 p36 Mr 27 2017

Reflection (Optics)

the straw that appears broken color *Popular Science* v289 no2 p88 Mr/Ap 2017

Reflexotherapy

refresh your soul retreat E. MARGLIN color *Yoga Journal* no287 p14 N 2016

Reforestation

How Panamanians and Trees Are Saving Each Other Suah Cheong *American Forests* v123 no2 p6 Summ 2017

Justin Hynicka, Manager of Forest Conservation *American Forests* v123 no3 p8 Fall 2017

Modern Amazonia Y. Gross color map *National Geographic* v231 no2 p120 F 2017

Planting Hope J. DALEY *American Forests* v123 no3 p2 Fall 2017

Rising from the Ashes: Restoring Kentucky's Appalachian Forests A. Wisniewski *American Forests* v123 no3 p6 Fall 2017

Reform Judaism—History

An Inconvenient Maverick P. Schröder *History Today* v67 no2 p4

F 2017

Reform Zionism

Wouldn't It Be Nice? W. Kristol *Weekly Standard* v22 no48 p8 S 4 2017

Reformation

Can Catholics celebrate the Reformation? J. Kohlhaas color *U.S. Catholic* v82 no2 p49 F 2017

Can the Churches Be Reunited? [Cover story] G. Hunsinger color *Commonweal* v144 no17 p14 O 20 2017

Mothers imprisoned under El Salvador's abortion ban spark debate about reform C. F. Martins color *Christian Century* v134 no19 p14 S 13 2017

On Luther and his lies N. E. Marans *Christian Century* v134 no22 p10 O 25 2017

The Quiz T. BALAZO color *Maclean's* v129 no51/52 p72 D 26 2016

Reformation 2.0 [Cover story] E. Simon color *Commonweal* v144 no17 p31 O 20 2017

Reformation (Company)

Bricks and Clicks K. CHAYKOWSKI and G. PUTNAM color *Forbes* v200 no4 p40 O 24 2017

Reformation—Germany

MARTIN LUTHER AND THE GERMAN REFORMATION B. Heal *History Today* v67 no3 p28 Mr 2017

Reformatories for women

The Women of Baylor K. DONNELLY il *America* v215 no14 p25 N 7 2016

Reformed Church

Reformed churches affirm Catholic-Lutheran accord T. Heneghan *Christian Century* v134 no16 p12 Ag 2 2017

Reformers

Refugees and the Reformation J. WILLIS color *Christianity Today* v61 no7 p68 S 2017

Reforms—Social aspects

Royal Visionary Meets Popular Pushback D. Abu-Nasr *Bloomberg Businessweek* no4528 p35 Je 26 2017

Refracting telescopes

The 102-mm FCD100 Triplet APO Refractor A. Dyer *Sky & Telescope* v133 no6 p58 Je 2017

Heavenly Host L. VACCARIELLO *Cincinnati Magazine* v50 no7 p168 Ap 2017

Three Centuries, One Scope J. Church and W. Murray *Sky & Telescope* v132 no6 p84 D 2016

Refraction (Optics)

through the looking glass C. Maldarelli bw *Popular Science* v289 no2 p86 Mr/Ap 2017

Refractors

See also

Refracting telescopes

HOW TO choose a telescope for the eclipse M. E. Bakich color *Astronomy* v45 no7 p64 Jl 2017

The Lesson of the Great Paris Telescope J. Hecht *Sky & Telescope* v134 no1 p28 Jl 2017

Summer Highlights: Warm nights and dark skies are ideal for enjoying these classic beauties S. French *Sky & Telescope* v134 no1 p54 Jl 2017

Refractors—Evaluation

Grab Explore Scientific's 80mm APO, and go! G. Chaple color *Astronomy* v45 no4 p64 Ap 2017

NEW PRODUCTS color map *Astronomy* v45 no5 p68 My 2017

Reframing (Business)

ARE YOU SOLVING THE RIGHT PROBLEMS? T. WEDELL-WEDELLSBORG color diag *Harvard Business Review* v95 no1 p76 Ja/F 2017

Refrigerated foods

KEEP YOUR SALAD SAFE color *Prevention* p6 Mr 2017

WHAT'S IN THEIR FRIDGE? [Cover story] C. schedler color *Chicago* v66 no7 p72 Jl 2017

Refrigerated storage

This Teen Invented a Lifesaving Vehicle: More than a million children worldwide die every year from preventable diseases. One teen's invention could change that B. ROSS img *New York Times Upfront* v149 no12 p12 Ap 24 2017

Refrigeration & refrigerating machinery

See also

Vapor compression cycle

THE FRIDGE S. Bower color *Good Housekeeping* v265 no3 p104 S 2017

THE ORIGIN OF ICE-IES J. Brown color *Popular Science* v289 no2 p29 Mr/Ap 2017

S'mores Icebox Cake color *Good Housekeeping* v265 no3 p113 S 2017

Winning Kitchen Combos P. Hope chart color *Consumer Reports* v82 no10 p20 O 2017

Refrigeration & refrigerating machinery—Evaluation

Keep Your Cool M. SMITH color *Power & Motoryacht* v34 no6 p72 Je 2017

Refrigerators

Can Your Refrigerator Help? B. Pike color *Power & Motoryacht* v33 no3 p120 Mr 2017

Ice S. PERKOWITZ bw color diag *Discover* v38 no6 p66 Jl/Ag 2017

YOUR GUIDE TO A Fridge Makeover (for easy party hosting!) J. Phillip cartoon color *Good Housekeeping* v263 no5 p62 N 2016

Refrigerators—Evaluation

DO I NEED A SMART... S. Franke, C. Forté et al color *Popular Mechanics* p76 My 2017

It's Getting Bot In the Kitchen L. Eadicicco color *Time* v189 no22 p18 Je 12 2017

Keep Your Cool M. SMITH color *Power & Motoryacht* v34 no6 p72 Je 2017

Winning Kitchen Combos P. Hope chart color *Consumer Reports* v82 no10 p20 O 2017

Refrigerators—Sales & prices

When to Get the Best Deals color graph *Consumer Reports* v82 no9 p40 S 2017

Refugee camps

The church's peacekeepers K. Clarke color *U.S. Catholic* v82 no2 p42 F 2017

CRISIS OF THE HEART C. AMANPOUR color *Vanity Fair* v59 no9 p217 S 2017

DID WE ADOPT A JIHADIST? S. Sayare color *GQ: Gentlemen's Quarterly* v97 no11 p126 N 2017

A PLACE OF REFUGE: A small Idaho city has endured many months of anti-immigrant hostility--and emerged stronger as a result D. C. Vock *Governing* v30 no9 p36 Je 2017

Tiny Ruins J. Berlin color *National Geographic* v231 no4 p124 Ap 2017

Waiting for Maryan A. Hussein *New York Times Magazine* p29 N 20 2016

Refugee camps—Greece

The "Laundromat" bw *Nation* v33 no21 p13 N 21 2016

My time at a refugee camp in Greece: Waiting in Malakasa A. Zwartjes color *Christian Century* v134 no2 p30 Ja 18 2017

Our Journey Begins N. Gibbs color *Time* v188 no27-28 p6 D 26 2016

Refugee camps—Kenya

LETTER FROM KAKUMA J. KUSHNER color *Nation* v304 no6 p12 F 27 2017

Refugee camps—Lebanon

How to Fund a Refugee Camp School D. Kenner color *Foreign Policy* no224 p28 My/Je 2017

Refugee camps—Social conditions—21st century

'WE ARE ORPHANS HERE' LIFE AND DEATH IN EAST JE-RUSALEM'S PALESTINIAN REFUGEE CAMP R. KUSH-NER color *New York Times Magazine* p44 D 4 2016

Refugee children

See also

Unaccompanied refugee children

Our Journey Begins N. Gibbs color *Time* v188 no27-28 p6 D 26 2016

Unaccompanied Minors Neglected As Calais Camp Is Demolished D. STEWART color *America* v215 no16 p8 N 21 2016

'WE ARE ORPHANS HERE' LIFE AND DEATH IN EAST JE-RUSALEM'S PALESTINIAN REFUGEE CAMP R. KUSH-NER color *New York Times Magazine* p44 D 4 2016

Refugee children—Health

THE APATHETIC R. AVIV cartoon color *New Yorker* v93 no7 p68 Ap 3 2017

Refugee children—Services for

THE CHILDREN'S ODYSSEY L. COLLINS bw cartoon *New Yorker* v93 no2 p52 F 27 2017

Refugee families

No Way Home A. Baker and M. Fareej color *Time* v189 no14 p34 Ap 17 2017

Refugee resettlement

The church's peacekeepers K. Clarke color *U.S. Catholic* v82 no2 p42 F 2017

THE FIRST FLIGHT M. FRISCOLANTI and A. HUTCHINS color *Maclean's* v129 no48/49 p14 D 5 2016

I'm Not Broken, Just Bent B. E. Hategekimana *UN Chronicle* v53 no4 p1 2016

KEY L.A. WOMAN MOMENTS OF 2017 *Los Angeles Magazine* v62 no9 p94 S 2017

Refugee plan divides religious leaders H. Bruinius, H. Lafranchi et al color *Christian Century* v134 no5 p12 Mr 1 2017

Refugee resettlement works *Christian Century* v133 no23 p7 N 9 2016

Right Aid D. MANN *Texas Monthly* v44 no11 p26 N 2016

Welcome to Missoula A. Frykholm color *Christian Century* v133 no26 p22 D 21 2016

Refugee resettlement services

Christian aid group cuts staff members in wake of Trump's order on refugees E. M. Miller *Christian Century* v134 no6 p13 Mr 15 2017

Paying It Forward S. Pathberyia cartoon color *Alternatives Journal (AJ) - Canada's Environmental Voice* v42 no3 p62 2016

Refugee screening

Refugee Security Screening Process *Congressional Digest* v96 no3 p8 Mr 2017

Travel ban confusion continues even after Supreme Court weighs in K. Clarke color *America* v217 no2 p16 Jl 24 2017

Refugee services

Feeding the Spirit D. SACHS bw *Rodale's Organic Life* v2 no7 p36 D 2016/Ja 2017

The Global Refugee Crisis: Regional Destabilization & Humanitarian Protection S. K. Lischer *Daedalus* v146 no4 p85 Fall 2017

The most American way to help others J. PRESS color *Redbook* p108 N 2017

The Refugee Puppeteer Hamzeh al-Hussein A. SU color *Foreign Policy* no223 p18 Mr/Ap 2017

Refugee services—International cooperation

U.N. Summit Seeks New Strategy On Global Migration Crisis color *America* v215 no10 p9 O 10 2016

Refugees

See also

Refugee resettlement

Refugees in the Syrian Civil War, 2011-

THE CROSSING color *New Republic* v248 no8/9 p50 Ag/S 2017

CROTONE, ITALY *In These Times* v41 no7 p7 Jl 2017

DID WE ADOPT A JIHADIST? S. Sayare color *GQ: Gentlemen's Quarterly* v97 no11 p126 N 2017

I'm Not Broken Just Bent B. E. HATEGEKIMANA *UN Chronicle* v54 no4 p32 2017

In Middle East conflicts, families struggle to care for elderly members S. Peterson *Christian Century* v134 no3 p16 F 2017

Island Escape A. WARDAK *Ms.* v27 no2 p24 Summ 2017

Lifeline for refugee scholars A. Goodman color *Science* v354 no6317 p1207 D 9 2016

Lightbox color *Time* v189 no22 p12 Je 12 2017

Lightbox F. Solomon color *Time* v190 no10/11 p22 S 18 2017

LOST & FOUND *Texas Monthly* v44 no12 p112 D 2016

Moments A. Katz color *Time* v188 no25-26 p18 D 19 2016 Double Issue

Muslim refugees to U.S. have decreased in 2017 M. Buckley *Christian Century* v134 no17 p17 Ag 16 2017

OUT of the RUBBLE A. AVUTU *Atlanta* v57 no1 p100 My 2017

Realizing the Dream of Citizenship *Saturday Evening Post* v289 no2 p104 Mr/Ap 2017

Refugees. Immigrants. Abortion. Did you hear about current events at Mass? graph *America* v216 no4 p6 F 20 2017

Refugees risk lives to flee the U.S. for Canada D. Dettloff color *America* v217 no5 p17 S 4 2017

Saving Syria M. Boot *Commentary* v143 no1 p8 Ja 2017

SELF-WILLED DELUSION E. J. ERLER *USA Today Magazine* v145 no2860 p50 Ja 2017

Tech Companies Should Speak Up for Refugees, Not Only High-

Skilled Immigrants M. Latonero *Harvard Business Review Digital Articles* p2 My 16 2017

Was Jesus a refugee? A. Camille color *U.S. Catholic* v82 no8 p49 Ag 2017

Where Decency Resides M. Funkhouser *Governing* v30 no9 p4 Je 2017

Where Is My Brother? E. Reidy color map *Wired* v25 no4 p84 Ap 2017

THE YEAR IN PICTURES [Cover story] color *Maclean's* v129 no50 p21 D 19 2016

Refugees—Canada

Borderline chaos J. MARKUSOFF color *Maclean's* v130 no3 p30 Ap 2017

Escape to Canada A. R. KHAN color *Maclean's* v130 no8 p42 S 2017

A NEW UNDERGROUND RAILROAD J. HALPERN cartoon color *New Yorker* v93 no4 p32 Mr 13 2017

PREPARING FOR 'MONTH 13' [Cover story] M. FRISCOLANTI color *Maclean's* v129 no51/52 p34 D 26 2016

THE PROBLEM WITH REFUGEES T. GLAVIN color *Maclean's* v130 no3 p34 Ap 2017

Refugees—Canada—Government policy

A pivot to the pragmatic J. GEDDES color *Maclean's* v129 no42 p26 O 24 2016

The time for brave things T. GLAVIN color *Maclean's* v130 no2 p9 Mr 2017

Refugees—Congresses

U.N. Summit Seeks New Strategy On Global Migration Crisis color *America* v215 no10 p9 O 10 2016

Refugees—Economic aspects

Research: Refugees Can Bolster a Region's Economy J. E. Taylor *Harvard Business Review Digital Articles* p2 O 5 2016

Refugees—Economic conditions

Refugees, immigrants, expatriates. For some politicians, they're scapegoats. For Western Union, they're customers D. Bennett and L. Etter color *Bloomberg Businessweek* no4527 p74 Je 19 2017

Refugees—Education

Learning on the Margins W. Massey color *America* v216 no3 p17 F 6 2017

Refugees—Employment

Alexander Betts A. Cohen color *Bloomberg Businessweek* no4532 p68 Jl 31 2017

Europe Can Find Better Ways to Get Refugees into Workforces L. N. Van Wassenhove and O. Boufaied *Harvard Business Review Digital Articles* p2 O 5 2015

Refugees Need Jobs. Entrepreneurship Can Help S. R. Koltai *Harvard Business Review Digital Articles* p2 D 29 2016

Refugees—Europe

See also

European Migrant Crisis, 2015-

Africa img *New York Times Upfront* v149 no6 p20 D 12 2016

Brave New World M. EDDY *New York Times Upfront* v149 no5 p12 N 21 2016

Europe's far right attempts to harass refugees on Mediterranean D. Stewart color *America* v217 no5 p16 S 4 2017

Gimme Shelter A. ALTMAN color *New Republic* v247 no11 p12 N 2016

THE NEW EUROPEANS R. Kunzig color graph map *National Geographic* v230 no4 p82 O 2016

SHELTERING L. Collins cartoon *New Yorker* v92 no36 p18 N 7 2016

What's Europe's Long- Term Plan for Integrating Refugees? L. N. Van Wassenhove *Harvard Business Review Digital Articles* p2 S 22 2015

When Home Isn't Where the Heart Is A. Baker, H. Roonemaa et al color map *Time* v189 no21 p40 Je 5 2017

Refugees—Europe—Social conditions—21st century

Reversing previous trend, worldwide restrictions on religion are up E. M. Miller *Christian Century* v134 no10 p15 My 10 2017

Refugees—France

The First of Many L. Hannant *History Today* v67 no1 p17 Ja 2017

Refugees—Germany

ECHT DEUTSCH Y. Mounk *Harper's Magazine* p66 Ap 2017

WHISTLING IN THE DARK R. Adler *Lapham's Quarterly* v10 no1 p191 Wint 2017

Refugees—Government policy

Making Sense of the New Refugee Policy: The drive to stop the flow of history, which has been tried repeatedly throughout history, is ill founded L. SAFI *Islamic Horizons* v46 no3 p50 My/Je 2017

Refugee resettlement works *Christian Century* v133 no23 p7 N 9 2016

Refugees—Government policy—United States

The time for brave things T. GLAVIN color *Maclean's* v130 no2 p9 Mr 2017

Which Refugees? N. RUSH *National Review* v69 no4 p16 Mr 6 2017

Refugees in the Syrian Civil War, 2011-

THE DISCOMFORTS OF HOME T. W. O'Brien color *America* v217 no3 p26 Ag 7 2017

Refugees—Mental health

How Refugee Diasporas Respond to Trauma M. KOINOVA *Current History* v115 no784 p322 N 2016

Refugees—Poland

The Triumph of Mrs. L A. Zagajewski bw *New York Review of Books* v64 no5 p26 Mr 23 2017

Refugees—Rwanda

Research: Refugees Can Bolster a Region's Economy J. E. Taylor *Harvard Business Review Digital Articles* p2 O 5 2016

Refugees—Social conditions

At Home in a Strange Land J. McDermott color *America* v216 no4 p28 F 20 2017

A FOUR-STAR RESPONSE TO THE REFUGEE CRISIS P. STRICKLAND *In These Times* v41 no7 p44 Jl 2017

I'm Not Broken, Just Bent B. E. Hategekimana *UN Chronicle* v53 no4 p1 2016

A PLACE OF REFUGE: A small Idaho city has endured many months of anti-immigrant hostility--and emerged stronger as a result D. C. Vock *Governing* v30 no9 p36 Je 2017

Refugees—Somalia

CITY OF HOPE C. ANDERSON and A. TOENSING color *Yankee* p118 Mr 2017

Refugees—Study & teaching

NEW LIFE LESSONS J. GEDDES color *Maclean's* v130 no4 p35 My 2017

Refugees—Travel

Lightbox color *Time* v189 no4 p14 F 6 2017

Refugees—United States

HOME ECONOMICS FOR REFUGEES M. R. WHITEHEAD color map *Reason* v49 no2 p48 Je 2017

The most American way to help others J. PRESS color *Redbook* p108 N 2017

Muslims in America R. MARC GERECHT color *Weekly Standard* v22 no9 p23 N 7 2016

PHOTO color *Reason* v48 no8 p9 Ja 2017

Refugee work H. Simon, P. Blackwell et al *Christian Century* v134 no2 p6 Ja 18 2017

"We welcomed them" J. Molyneux *U.S. Catholic* v81 no12 p17 D 2016

You invited me in [Cover story] P. Feuerherd color *U.S. Catholic* v81 no12 p12 D 2016

Refugees—United States—Government policy

Forsaken at the Border? J. McDERMOTT *America* v215 no11 p11 O 17 2016

The Treason of the Bureaucrats *Commentary* v143 no4 p33 Ap 2017

Refugees—United States—Legal status, laws, etc.

Big Meat Braces for A Labor Shortage L. Etter and S. Singh color *Bloomberg Businessweek* no4511 p19 F 13 2017

Trump's Immigration Order Is Legal-for Now M. Calabresi color diag *Time* v189 no5 p7 F 13 2017

Regal, Cindy

Bringing order to neutral atom arrays bibl diag *Science* v354 no6315 p972 N 25 2016

Deborah S. Jin (1968–2016) color *Science* v354 no6313 p709 N 11 2016

Regal Yachts (Company)

REGAL 42 FLY: WHO KNEW A GREAT PACIFIC NORTHWEST BOAT WOULD BE DESIGNED AND BUILT IN FLORIDA? R. McAFEE color *Sea Magazine* v109 no7 p32 Jl 2017

Regalado, Antonio

Baby Genome Sequencing for Sale in China il *MIT Technology Review* v120 no5 p13 S/O 2017

Can CRISPR Save Ben Dupree? color *MIT Technology Review* v119 no6 p80 N/D 2016

ENTREPRENEURS color il *MIT Technology Review* v120 no5 p48 S/O 2017

Gene-Therapy Cure Has Money-Back Guarantee il *MIT Technology Review* v119 no6 p24 N/D 2016

Google's Long Strange Life Span Trip color *MIT Technology Review* v120 no1 p52 Ja/F 2017

A NEW WAY TO REPRODUCE color *MIT Technology Review* v120 no5 p32 S/O 2017

One Man's Quest to Hack His Own Genes color il *MIT Technology Review* v120 no2 p13 Mr/Ap 2017

On Patrol with America's Top Bioterror Cop color diag *MIT Technology Review* v120 no1 p15 Ja/F 2017

Oxford Nanopore color il *MIT Technology Review* v120 no4 p66 Jl/Ag 2017

REVERSING Paralysis color *MIT Technology Review* v120 no2 p82 Mr/Ap 2017

VISIONARIES color il *MIT Technology Review* v120 no5 p42 S/O 2017

Regalia (Insignia)

See also

Orbs

Regan, Christopher

Save Time and Add Convenience il *Consumer Reports* v82 no3 p24 Mr 2017

Regan, Katy

Deals R. DEAHL color *Publishers Weekly* v264 no18 p10 My 1 2017

Regan, Priscilla

Opening Windows on Surveillance: the Scholarship of Gary Marx *Society* v54 no4 p363 Ag 2017

REGAN, SHAWN

How Capitalism Saved the Bees [Cover story] color graph *Reason* v49 no4 p62 Ag/S 2017

Regattas

The 12s are Better than Ever! color *Sail* v48 no6 p18 Je 2017

All Hands on Deck color *Sail* v48 no6 p8 Je 2017

DON'T MISS LIST: JUNE 2017 *Sea Magazine* v109 no6 pPNW-14 Je 2017

Maine Event color *Sail* v48 no1 p10 Ja 2017

RACING THE STORM M. TEAGUE *Smithsonian* v48 no4 p64 Jl/Ag 2017

A Season for the Record Books A. Cort color *Sail* v48 no7 p16 Jl 2017

SUN, SURF AND SWANS A. CORT color *Sail* v48 no7 p30 Jl 2017

When the Oyster is Your World... color *Sail* v47 no12 p10 D 2016

REGE, LAURA

BIRD IS THE WORD color *Martha Stewart Living* p60 My 2017

BRING ON BRINNER color *Martha Stewart Living* p64 Mr 2017

Chicken Noodle Soup color *Martha Stewart Living* no271 p61 Ja/F 2017

Power Pods color *Martha Stewart Living* no275 p74 Je 2017

Start With Beans color *Martha Stewart Living* p66 Mr 2017

Sugar & Spice color *Martha Stewart Living* p66 My 2017

SUPER BOWLS color *Martha Stewart Living* no271 p70 Ja/F 2017

TEA TIME color *Martha Stewart Living* p78 Jl/Ag 2017

Regeneration (Biology)

Regenerating optic pathways from the eye to the brain B. Laha, B. K. Stafford et al diag *Science* v356 no6342 p1031 Je 9 2017

REPAIR AND REGENERATION [Cover story] B. A. Purnell and P. J. Hines color *Science* v356 no6342 p1020 Je 9 2017

Self-repairing cells: How single cells heal membrane ruptures and restore lost structures S. K. Y. Tang and W. F. Marshall diag *Science* v356 no6342 p1022 Je 9 2017

Regeneration (Biology)—Research

Regeneration of fat cells from myofibroblasts during wound healing M. V. Plikus, C. F. Guerrero-Juarez et al bibl color graph *Science* v355 no6326 p748 F 17 2017

Regenerative medicine

MIRACLE MAKER M. SHAER *Smithsonian* v47 no8 p40 D

2016

Regeni, Giulio

A DEATH IN CAIRO D. Walsh *New York Times Magazine* p26 Ag 20 2017

REGENSDORF, LAURA

The ETSY Effect color *Vogue* v207 no3 p374 Mr 2017

GOING Blondie color *Vogue* v206 no12 p200 D 2016

Going Hollywood color *Vogue* v207 no9 p444 S 2017

Heads Up color *Vogue* v207 no11 p146 N 2017

Into the Mild color *Vogue* v207 no10 p220 O 2017

Making Moves color *Vogue* v207 no9 p452 S 2017

Off the Menu color *Vogue* v207 no9 p380 S 2017

Pas de Deux color *Vogue* v207 no9 p612 S 2017

Real Talk color *Vogue* v207 no4 p167 Ap 2017

SEE Change cartoon *Vogue* v206 no11 p162 N 2016

Slick Days color *Vogue* v207 no7 p54 Jl 2017

Taste MAKERS color *Vogue* v207 no3 p334 Mr 2017

Regent's Park (London, England)

It's Eccentric Glamor in Regents Park S. Lawrence color *British Heritage Travel* v38 no5 p24 S/O 2017

Regev, Aviv

Decoupling genetics, lineages, and microenvironment in IDH-mutant gliomas by single-cell RNA-seq diag *Science* v355 no6332 p1391 Mr 31 2017

High-resolution interrogation of functional elements in the noncoding genome bibl graph *Science* v353 no6307 p1545 S 30 2016

Nucleic acid detection with CRISPR-Cas13a/C2c2 color diag *Science* v356 no6336 p438 Ap 28 2017

Single-cell RNA-seq reveals new types of human blood dendritic cells, monocytes, and progenitors color *Science* v356 no6335 p283 Ap 21 2017

Single-cell transcriptomics to explore the immune system in health and disease diag *Science* v357 no6359 p58 O 6 2017

Writ large: Genomic dissection of the effect of cellular environment on immune response bibl diag *Science* v354 no6308 p64 O 7 2016

Regev, Miri

SETTLING SCORES R. MARGALIT *New York Times Magazine* p36 O 23 2016

Regev, Oded

Modern Fluid Dynamics for Physics and Astrophysics G. Lodato *Physics Today* v70 no5 p60 My 2017

Reggiani, Maurizio

Maurizio Reggiani H. Elliott color *Bloomberg Businessweek* no4541 p68 O 9 2017

Regina (Music)

Singer-Songwriters Follow Their Muses A. MORRISON color *Downbeat* v84 no5 p60 My 2017

REGINATO, JAMES

La Vita Brandolini bw color *Vanity Fair* v59 no7 p128 Summ 2017

Under Mica's Spell color *Vanity Fair* v59 no6 p116 My 2017

Regional economics—Latin America

How Marketing Is Evolving in Latin America N. Kelly *Harvard Business Review Digital Articles* p2 Je 1 2015

Regionalism—United States

Analyzing OMB classification of regions: three case studies E. S. Baker *Monthly Labor Review* p1 N 2016

Regnerus, Mark

Market Penetration N. S. RILEY *Commentary* v144 no2 p46 S 2017

Regnery Publishing Inc.

Regnery Publishing: More Than Just Politics J. Milliot color *Publishers Weekly* v264 no12 p10 Mr 20 2017

Regnier, Pat

Thank You For Calling Equifax, Your Business Is Not Important to Us *Bloomberg Businessweek* no4538 p38 S 18 2017

Regolith

See also

Soils

A measure of mantle melting P. D. Asimow bibl graph *Science* v355 no6328 p908 Mr 3 2017

Regression analysis

A Refresher on Regression Analysis A. Gallo *Harvard Business Review Digital Articles* p2 N 4 2015

Regulated industries

Companies in Regulated Industries Can Also Do Digital Marketing M. W. Schaefer *Harvard Business Review Digital Articles* p2 Ja 15 2016

Regulation of blood pressure

Simple Ways To Cut the Top Blood Pressure Number A. A. LEVITT and A. JUNG color *Reader's Digest* v190 no1134 p56 O 2017

Regulation of body weight

cheat, drink, & still shrink A. Rios color *Yoga Journal* p19 2017 Special Issue

Eat these to hit your perfect weight M. TAYLOR color *Redbook* p82 N 2017

NEWSBITES [Cover story] *Tufts University Health & Nutrition Letter* v35 no5 p1 Jl 2017

NEWS BITES [Cover story] *Tufts University Health & Nutrition Letter* v35 no8 p1 O 2017

NEWtrition Facts|Labels L. MOYER and B. LIEBMAN *Nutrition Action Health Letter* v44 no7 p10 S 2017

Regulator Marine Inc.

OFFSHORE AND MORE S. SHIBATA *Boating World* v38 no2 p8 F 2017

Regulatory reform

Fighting Government's Fourth Branch T. J. DONOHUE *Weekly Standard* v22 no15 p9 D 19 2016

A Lasting Solution to the Regulatory Nightmare T. J. Donohue *Weekly Standard* v22 no33 p35 My 8 2017

Regulatory Reform [Cover story] C. S. DEMUTH color *Weekly Standard* v22 no20 p26 Ja 30 2017

Regulatory Rollback A. J. WHITE color *Weekly Standard* v23 no1 p27 S 11 2017

SEDENTARY SENATE T. MCCLINTOCK *USA Today Magazine* v145 no2864 p22 My 2017

Rehabilitation

ALL IN A Day's Work color *Reader's Digest* v190 no1133 p64 S 2017

Nothing Solid B. Glassman *Tricycle: The Buddhist Review* v26 no4 p71 Summ 2017

Rehabilitation Basics L. Simons color *Dressage Today* v23 no5 p36 Ja 2017

Rehabilitation centers

A Community for Growth... Sear Gisler *Psychology Today* v50 no3 p36 My/Je 2017

RICH KIDS ANONYMOUS R. KOLKER color *Bloomberg Businessweek* no4500 p48 N 21 2016

REHAGEN, TONY

ALBERT SCHWEITZER ORGAN VS. THE MIGHTY MO *Atlanta* v57 no1 p30 My 2017

ALMOST FAMOUS *Atlanta* v56 no10 p36 F 2017

PAY INSIDE CASH color *Popular Mechanics* p18 Jl 2017

A Turtle's Pace? bw color *Indianapolis Monthly* v42 no2 p15 O 2017

UNCHARTED WATERS *Indianapolis Monthly* p84 N 2017

WHITE SPACE bw *Indianapolis Monthly* p74 Ap 2017

WORTH OF MOUTH: One doctor uses a DNA swab to put the chill on opioid pills *Indianapolis Monthly* p73 N 2017

Rehearsal, The (Film)

Class Act N. Rapold color *Film Comment* v53 no1 p8 Ja/F 2017

Rehkamp, Sarah

A Look at Calorie Sources in the American Diet color graph *Amber Waves: The Economics of Food, Farming, Natural Resources, & Rural America* p23 D 2016

The Relationship Between Energy Prices and Food-Related Energy Use in the United States *Amber Waves: The Economics of Food, Farming, Natural Resources, & Rural America* p17 Je 2017

Since 2009, Restaurant Prices Have Generally Risen Faster Than Grocery Store Prices *Amber Waves: The Economics of Food, Farming, Natural Resources, & Rural America* p53 Ag 2017

REHMEYER, JULIE

LOST AND FOUND color *O, The Oprah Magazine* p102 Je 2017

Mathematicians Find the Answers diag *Discover* v38 no1 p41 Ja/F 2017

Rehoboam, King of Judah

Cowboy Chicken L. J. Green *Successful Farming* v115 no1 p44 Ja 2017

Reibarkh, Mikhail

A multifunctional catalyst that stereoselectively assembles prodrugs diag *Science* v356 no6336 p426 Ap 28 2017

Reich, Cindy

2016 U.S. NATIONALS HALTER DIVISION *Arabian Horse World* v57 no4 p130 Ja 2017

African Horse Sickness—Could It Be Our Next West Nile? *Arabian Horse World* v57 no8 p155 My 2017

BEAUTY IN WILD PLACES—NAMBIA, AFRICA: AT CHARLOTTENBERG ARABIANS *Arabian Horse World* v57 no8 p102 My 2017

Cal Poly Pomona Auction Grosses $126,950 *Arabian Horse World* v57 no11 p162 Ag 2017

A Conversation with Michael Byatt *Arabian Horse World* v57 no3 p265 D 2016

December Duties *Arabian Horse World* v57 no3 p212 D 2016

February Madness *Arabian Horse World* v57 no5 p232 F 2017

FITTING TACK, PART 1: HALTER AND WESTERN *Arabian Horse World* v57 no1 p89 O 2016

FOR THE HORSE *Arabian Horse World* v57 no6 p150 Mr 2017

FOR THE HORSE In the stable *Arabian Horse World* v56 no12 p82 S 2016

FOR THE HORSE In the training barn: LONG LINING, PART 2 WITH JOHN LAMBERT *Arabian Horse World* v57 no12 p64 S 2017

FOR THE HORSE: LONG LINING PART 1 *Arabian Horse World* v57 no10 p66 Jl 2017

Getting Ready for the Coming Season *Arabian Horse World* v57 no4 p186 Ja 2017

GUEST EDITORIAL: MAKE HALTER GREAT AGAIN? *Arabian Horse World* v57 no4 p142 Ja 2017

Hariry Al Shaqab color *Arabian Horse World* v57 no7 p113 Ap 2017

The Mysterious Case of the Heavy Rain and the Television Show *Arabian Horse World* v57 no6 p152 Mr 2017

Parting is Bittersweet, But Essential *Arabian Horse World* v57 no12 p186 S 2017

Pint-sized Dynamos: Tyler Hardin and "Zipy" *Arabian Horse World* v57 no4 p110 Ja 2017

Stella Bella Arabians color *Arabian Horse World* v57 no7 p118 Ap 2017

STUD FARM DIARIES *Arabian Horse World* v56 no12 p246 S 2016

STUD FARM DIARIES *Arabian Horse World* v57 no2 p134 N 2016

STUD FARM DIARIES: A Very Curious Case, Plus Answers to Common Foaling Questions *Arabian Horse World* v57 no9 p161 Je 2017

STUD FARM DIARIES color *Arabian Horse World* v57 no7 p134 Ap 2017

STUD FARM DIARIES: Less is More: Methods of Restraint *Arabian Horse World* v57 no11 p166 Ag 2017

STUD FARM DIARIES: "On the Bottle"—Feeding the Orphan or Rejected Foal *Arabian Horse World* v57 no10 p98 Jl 2017

Up to the Challenge - Changes Coming for U.S. Nationals Halter Classes *Arabian Horse World* v57 no5 p235 F 2017

USEF Pegasus Award Banquet *Arabian Horse World* v57 no5 p235 F 2017

THE USEF RULING ON SHANKING *Arabian Horse World* v56 no12 p71 S 2016

WARRIOR HORSE *Arabian Horse World* v57 no9 p38 Je 2017

WHAT IN THE WORLD: Conformation Clinic at Om El Arab *Arabian Horse World* v57 no11 p10 Ag 2017

Reich, Justin

Closing global achievement gaps in MOOCs graph *Science* v355 no6322 p251 Ja 20 2017

Reich, Lee

GRAFTING FRUIT TREES: Fuse stems with rootstocks to form fast-growing, fruit-bearing plants *Mother Earth News* no282 p39 Je/Jl 2017

Reich, Peter B.

Forest value: More than commercial *Science* v354 no6319 p1541 D 23 2016

Global climatic drivers of leaf size [Cover story] graph *Science* v357 no6354 p917 S 1 2017

Positive biodiversity-productivity relationship predominant

in global forests bibl chart graph map *Science* v354 no6309 paaf8957-1 O 14 2016

REICH, REBECCA

Women on the Battlefield: Conversations with female combatants in Russia's war against Hitler *New York Times Book Review* p11 Ag 20 2017

REICH, ROBERT B.

What's Happened to Us? *New York Times Book Review* p16 Jl 23 2017

Reich, Robert—Interviews

Robert Reich on Redefining Full-Time Work, Obamacare, and Employer Benefits W. Frick *Harvard Business Review Digital Articles* p2 Ja 21 2015

Robert Reich's Plan To Save the Democrats J. BLEIFUSS *In These Times* v41 no1 p30 Ja 2017

Reich, Sarah, 1989-

The Bandleader: Sarah Reich is bringing tap to new audiences with innovative collaborations and daring creativity R. P. CASEY *Dance Magazine* v91 no9 p58 S 2017

Reich, Steve, 1936-

Less Is More R. Platt cartoon *New Yorker* v93 no7 p20 Ap 3 2017

Reich, Taly

Research: Consumers Prefer Products Created by Mistake *Harvard Business Review Digital Articles* p2 S 20 2017

Reich, Wade

The South's Best Butts M. Moore color *Southern Living* v52 no4 p134 Ap 2017

Reichard, Peter

Making Room for Hobbies *New Orleans Homes & Lifestyles* v20 no1 p90 Wint 2016

Outliers: Is opportunity knocking in the suburbs? *New Orleans Homes & Lifestyles* v20 no3 p94 Summ 2017

Prevention, Procrastination & Woe *New Orleans Homes & Lifestyles* v20 no2 p82 Spr 2017

Reichardt, Kelly

Certain Women Burns Slow but True S. Zacharek color *Time* v188 no16/17 p88 O 24 2016

Certain Women color *New Yorker* v92 no35 p22 O 31 2016

Just Enough D. CHEW-BOSE color *Film Comment* v52 no6 p16 N/D 2016

PASSING TIME WITH CERTAIN WOMEN A. Hastie *Film Quarterly* v70 no3 p74 Spr 2017

THE PRECISIONIST *New York Times Magazine* p36 O 16 2016

Reichert, Jeff

BIG PLANS SMALL MINDS color *Film Comment* v53 no1 p78 Ja/F 2017

Lost Highway color *Film Comment* v53 no4 p20 Jl/Ag 2017

Reichl, Ruth, 1948-

My Delicious Summer M. True color *Sunset* v238 no6 p64 Je 2017

Reicks, Dale

10 SUCCESSFUL FARMERS: DALE REICKS B. Freese *Successful Farming* v115 no8 p16 Je/Jl 2017

Reid, Barbara E.

In her shoes *U.S. Catholic* v82 no1 p20 Ja 2017

Reid, Barbara—Interviews

In her shoes B. E. Reid *U.S. Catholic* v82 no1 p20 Ja 2017

Reid, Calvin

50 Years of Black Literature and Politics at Third World Press bw chart *Publishers Weekly* v264 no40 p8 O 2 2017

At 25, the New Press Thrives In Politically Charged Climate color *Publishers Weekly* v264 no12 p6 Mr 20 2017

Covering The World of Children's Publishing color *Publishers Weekly* v263 no51 p1 D 12 2016

DC Goes All-Out Marketing Rebirth Book Collections color *Publishers Weekly* v264 no13 p11 Mr 27 2017

Despite Embargo, U.S., Cuba Publishers Invoke Solidarity, Cultural Exchange color *Publishers Weekly* v264 no8 p5 F 20 2017

Goodreads Marks 10 Years of Supporting Books, Reading color *Publishers Weekly* v264 no39 p12 S 25 2017

Humble Bundle Reports $11 Million From E-book Bundles in 2016 *Publishers Weekly* v264 no27 p11 Jl 3 2017

Insight Editions Launches Comics Imprint color *Publishers Weekly* v263 no43 p10 O 24 2016

It Was the Year of March at Diamond Book Distributors color *Publishers Weekly* v264 no7 p6 F 13 2017

Kickstarter Publishing in 2016 *Publishers Weekly* v264 no6 p7 F 6 2017

Like His Publisher, Crime Novelist Alex Segura Wears Many Hats color *Publishers Weekly* v264 no16 p8 Ap 17 2017

Lisa Lucas: Executive Director, National Book Foundation *Publishers Weekly* v263 no52 p29 D 19 2016

Louise Erdrich, Matthew Desmond Win 2017 NBCC Awards color *Publishers Weekly* v264 no12 p14 Mr 20 2017

SAN DIEGO COMIC-CON 2017: Comics in Libraries and Schools color *Publishers Weekly* v264 no28 p54 Jl 10 2017

Selling Graphic Novels to a Diverse Audience color *Publishers Weekly* v264 no31 p4 Jl 31 2017

Skybound's Walking Dead Graphic Novel Sales Won't Die chart color *Publishers Weekly* v263 no45 p5 N 7 2016

Storytelling, Innovation, and Digital Disruption color *Publishers Weekly* v264 no17 p4 Ap 24 2017

Taking a Look at Apple's and Amazon's E-book Bestsellers chart *Publishers Weekly* v264 no29 p8 Jl 17 2017

To Sell or Not to Sell: Censorship Or Free Speech for Bookstores? color *Publishers Weekly* v264 no26 p9 Je 26 2017

Twenty Years of Books on Social Justice color *Publishers Weekly* v263 no52 p11 D 19 2016

Using Graphic Novels, Bill Jemas Resurrects 'Night of the Living Dead' *Publishers Weekly* v263 no40 p6 O 3 2016

Wattpad Grows from Reading Site to Multiplatform Entertainment Venue color *Publishers Weekly* v263 no50 p10 D 5 2016

The Year that Created Modernism color *Publishers Weekly* v264 no29 p210 Jl 17 2017

Reid, Calvin G.

LIFE ON THE LINE *Harper's Magazine* v334 no2002 p58 Mr 2017

reid, carlton

room with a pew color *Bike Magazine* v24 no7 p36 S 2017

Reid, Caroline

2017 Mediterranean Championships *Arabian Horse World* v57 no11 p124 Ag 2017

26th Qatar International Arabian Horse Show *Arabian Horse World* v57 no9 p86 Je 2017

the 27th ukiahs a-show *Arabian Horse World* v57 no2 p122 N 2016

Bahrain and the ARABIAN FARM TOURS hosted under the patronage of His Majesty King Hamad bin Isa Al Khalifa and the Royal Arabian Studs of Bahrain, February 15, 2017 *Arabian Horse World* v57 no8 p128 My 2017

Paris *Arabian Horse World* v57 no5 p216 F 2017

Salon Du Cheval d'El Jadida *Arabian Horse World* v57 no3 p276 D 2016

Reid, Craig D.

Old Legends, Neo-Heroes and Modern Dragons color *Black Belt* v55 no5 p28 Ag/S 2017

Wall and Polo and Wick - Oh, My! color *Black Belt* v55 no4 p28 Je/Jl 2017

Woman of Wonder, God of War, Shortcomings of Yoga and Hero of India color *Black Belt* v55 no6 p28 O/N 2017

Reid, Dereesa

Getting Bundled Payments Right in Health Care *Harvard Business Review Digital Articles* p2 O 19 2015

Reid, Eric Todd, 1991-

CENTURY marks *Christian Century* v134 no22 p8 O 25 2017

Reid, Erin

Why Some Men Pretend to Work 80-Hour Weeks *Harvard Business Review Digital Articles* p2 Ap 28 2015

Reid, Gregor

Seasonal cycling in the gut microbiome of the Hadza hunter-gatherers of Tanzania diag *Science* v357 no6353 p802 Ag 25 2017

Reid, Harry, 1939-

Comments img *New York* p8 Ja 9 2017

Filibusted J. Cost color *Weekly Standard* v22 no31 p6 Ap 17 2017

Leaders color *Time* v189 no16/17 p64 My 1-8 2017

TO DONALD TRUMP: TAKE RESPONSIBILITY H. REID *Vital Speeches of the Day* v83 no1 p6 Ja 2017

Who Will Do What Harry Reid Did Now That Harry Reid Is Gone? J. Zengerle img *New York* v49 no26 p32 D 26 2016

Reid, Hilary

home & help img *New York* p96 Mr 6 2017

REID, J. C.

LINK TO THE PAST *Texas Monthly* v45 no6 p117 Je 2017

Reid, Jeffrey G.

Distribution and clinical impact of functional variants in 50,726 whole-exome sequences from the DiscovEHR study chart graph *Science* v354 no6319 paaf6814-1 D 23 2016

Genetic identification of familial hypercholesterolemia within a single U.S. health care system chart graph *Science* v354 no6319 paaf7000-1 D 23 2016

REID, JOY-ANN

Black Deaths Matter *New York Times Book Review* p9 N 20 2016

Reid, Joy—Interviews

Joy Reid Has Never Heard a Good Argument For Trump A. M. Cox color *New York Times Magazine* p54 Ja 29 2017

Reid, Kate—Interviews

WATER COLORS M. READ color *House Beautiful* v158 no9 p138 N 2016

Reid, Liza—Interviews

THE INTERVIEW B. D. JOHNSON color *Maclean's* v129 no42 p12 O 24 2016

Reid, Michelle D.

Sustained virologic control in SIV+ macaques after antiretroviral and α4β7 antibody therapy bibl graph *Science* v354 no6309 p197 O 14 2016

Reid, Neal

True Champion color *American Cowboy* v23 no4 p80 D 2016/Ja 2017

YOUTH MOVEMENT bw cartoon *American Cowboy* v23 no4 p72 D 2016/Ja 2017

Reid, Noah M.

The genomic landscape of rapid repeated evolutionary adaptation to toxic pollution in wild fish bibl graph *Science* v354 no6317 p1305 D 9 2016

Reid, Robert Leonard

A Western Love Story G. WINGENBACH color *Earth Island Journal* v32 no3 p55 Aut 2017

Reid, T. R.

Simplify, Simplify, Simplify D. C. JOHNSTON *New York Times Book Review* p10 Je 25 2017

Reid, Toni

PERSON OF INTEREST L. Rao color *Fortune* v174 no6 p23 N 1 2016

Reid Smith Architects (Company)

BIG SKY LIVING M. MYLCHREEST color diag *Cabin Living* p38 Ag 2017

Reidelbach, M.

A nontoxic pain killer designed by modeling of pathological receptor conformations bibl diag graph *Science* v355 no6328 p966 Mr 3 2017

Reid Kelley, Mary

The Artist's Artist A Rauschenberg Symposium color *Art in America* v105 no1 p44 Ja 2017

Reid's Heritage Homes (Company)

Reid's Heritage Homes on Constructing Residential to the Net-Zero Standard C. Metler color *Maclean's* v129 no50 p43 D 19 2016

REIDY, ERIC

The General and the Refugee color *New Republic* v248 no4 p38 Ap 2017

Where Is My Brother? color map *Wired* v25 no4 p84 Ap 2017

Reidy, Gearoid

Changes On Tap for Japan's Beer Tax color *Bloomberg Businessweek* no4513 p29 Mr 6 2017

Reif, John H.

DNA robots sort as they walk diag *Science* v357 no6356 p1095 S 15 2017

Reif, L. Rafael

How to Maintain America's Edge color *Foreign Affairs* v96 no3 p95 My/Je 2017

REIGH, CINDY

FOR THE HORSE In the stable *Arabian Horse World* v57 no2 p104 N 2016

Reign, April

We Have So Much Power! color *Essence* v47 no9 p94 Ja 2017

Reign of Henry VIII, England, 1509-1547

Predicting the Fall of Anne Boleyn A. Holroyde *History Today* v67 no5 p11 My 2017

REIGSTAD, LEIF

Cast Out OF EDEN *Texas Monthly* v45 no3 p51 Mr 2017

CROSSING THE LINE IN EL CENIZO *Texas Monthly* v45 no9 p76 S 2017

Reik, Nicole Anne

Pinball Wizard J. DeMELO color *O, The Oprah Magazine* p28 D 2016

Reik, Wolf

Single-cell epigenomics: Recording the past and predicting the future diag *Science* v357 no6359 p69 O 6 2017

Reiko Okubo-Suzuki

Overlapping memory trace indispensable for linking, but not recalling, individual memories bibl graph *Science* v355 no6323 p398 Ja 27 2017

Reiley, Carol

COMPUTER ON WHEELS color *Popular Science* p17 Ja/F 2017

Deep Driving *MIT Technology Review* v119 no6 p10 N/D 2016

Reilich, Rachel

THE MAN DEV PATEL color *InStyle* v23 no13 p118 D 2016

Reilly, Brendan

SECRETS OF THE DEAD *Saturday Evening Post* v289 no3 p56 My/Je 2017

REILLY, DAN

For Mel Gibson, War Is (Very Bloody) Hell img *New York* v49 no22 p96 O 31 2016

Hitting the High(ish) Ones img *New York* v49 no20 p117 O 3 2016

Reilly, Edward

What Companies Have Learned from Losing Billions in Emerging Markets *Harvard Business Review Digital Articles* p2 S 16 2015

Reilly, Kathleen A.

bless the mess *Parents* v92 no5 p118 My 2017

Observing peers develops practice, changes culture il *Phi Delta Kappan* v98 no6 p13 Mr 2017

Reilly, Katie

The Campus Culture Wars color *Time* v190 no16/17 p48 O 23 2017

A Deadly Campus Tradition color *Time* v190 no16/17 p56 O 23 2017

Lightbox color *Time* v190 no1 p14 Jl 3 2017

Other Big Issues on the Ballot color *Time* v188 no20 p39 N 14 2016

The United Patients of America color *Time* v190 no4 p28 Jl 24 2017

Why the U.S. Is Cracking Down on Gadgets In Airplane Cabins color *Time* v189 no12 p11 Ap 3 2017

Reilly, Michael

Uber's Ad-Toting Drones Are Heckling Drivers Stuck in Traffic color *MIT Technology Review* v120 no1 p24 Ja/F 2017

Reilly, Phoebe

Freedom Rock: Halsey lost a boyfriend, a producer, and, for a time, her sense of self. What she gained was a new sound and her first No. 1 album img *New York* v50 no13 p69 Je 26 2017

Reilly, Rick

ACE IN THE CROWD color *Golf Magazine* v58 no12 p52 D 2016

It's a One-derful Life color *Golf Magazine* v59 no1 p28 Ja 2017

Reilly, Robert R.

Cogs in the Machine *Claremont Review of Books* v17 no3 p48 Summ 2017

FOR GOD AND COUNTRY *Claremont Review of Books* v17 no3 p44 Summ 2017

Harmonizing Sentiments *Claremont Review of Books* v17 no3 p47 Summ 2017

Misquoting Madison *Claremont Review of Books* v17 no3 p45 Summ 2017

Not My Philosopher *Claremont Review of Books* v17 no3 p47 Summ 2017

Scorning America *Claremont Review of Books* v17 no3 p44 Summ 2017

Reimel, Erin

THE 2017 GLAMOUR BEAUTY AWARD color *Glamour* v115 no4 p81 Ap 2017

Burning, Man! cartoon color *Glamour* v114 no12 p124 D 2016

Double-Tap This color *Glamour* v115 no3 p102 Mr 2017

Fashion Does Fragrance color *Glamour* v114 no11 p106 N 2016

Fiery Ombré Lips color *Glamour* v115 no1 p39 Ja 2017

Glow Up color *Glamour* v115 no10 p94 O 2017

Good Lighting color *Glamour* v115 no6 p70 Je 2017

Mermaid Eyes color *Glamour* v115 no9 p84 S 2017

Need a Makeup Refresh? cartoon *Glamour* v115 no2 p52 F 2017

Not Your Average Lipstick color *Glamour* no8 p86 Ag 2017

Self-Care Sunday color *Glamour* v115 no11 p72 N 2017

Self-Tanners, Decoded color *Glamour* v115 no6 p78 Je 2017

Split Ends, Begone! color *Glamour* v115 no5 p78 My 2017

Sunny Side Up! color *Glamour* v115 no7 p52 Jl 2017

Your Cat Eye, Customized color *Glamour* v115 no3 p108 Mr 2017

You Smell Amazing color *Glamour* v115 no5 p76 My 2017

REIMER, JESSICA

Long-Term Studies Contribute Disproportionately to Ecology and Policy *BioScience* v67 no3 p271 Mr 2017

REIMERS, MARK

WHAT THE REVOLUTION IN NEUROSCIENCE WILL MEAN FOR *Humanist* v77 no2 p27 Mr/Ap 2017

REINA, PETER

Grenfell Tower Fire Tragedy Sparks Safety Dispute color *Architectural Record* v205 no8 p17 Ag 2017

Reinacher, Chris

MAKE A POWER PLAY D. HOCHMAN *Los Angeles Magazine* p114 Ap 2017

Reinartz, Elke

Fibril structure of amyloid-β(1–42) by cryo–electron microscopy color diag *Science* v357 no6359 p116 O 6 2017

Reinartz, Werner

A Better Way to Calculate the ROI of Your Marketing Investment *Harvard Business Review Digital Articles* p2 N 10 2015

In the Future of Retail, We're Never Not Shopping *Harvard Business Review Digital Articles* p2 Mr 10 2016

Reincarnation—Buddhism

A MORE ENLIGHTENED WAY OF BEING S. ZUIHO SEGALL color *Tricycle: The Buddhist Review* v26 no2 p54 Wint 2016

Reindeer

Itty-Bitty Reindeer P. Rauber *Sierra* v101 no6 p21 N/D 2016

Reindeer games R. Stuart color map *Canadian Geographic* v135 no6 p28 D 2015

THE WAGER A. McKEAN color *Outdoor Life* v224 no8 p57 O 2017

REINECKE, DAVID

Infrastructure and Democracy *Issues in Science & Technology* v33 no2 p24 Wint 2017

Reinecker, Hans-Christian

Reovirus infection triggers inflammatory responses to dietary antigens and development of celiac disease color diag *Science* v356 no6333 p44 Ap 7 2017

Reinforcement (Psychology)

The limits of Negative Reinforcement [Cover story] J. L. Jones bw color *Equus* no480 p40 S 2017

TRAINING TECHNIQUE HELPS HORSES "TALK" C. Barakat and M. McCluskey color *Equus* no472 p10 Ja 2017

Reinforcement learning

Playtime's Over E. Brunskill *MIT Technology Review* v120 no2 p10 Mr/Ap 2017

Reinforcement LEARNING W. KNIGHT color il *MIT Technology Review* v120 no2 p32 Mr/Ap 2017

Reingold, Jennifer

Kent Is Leaving, but Coke's Problems Remain color *Fortune* v75 no1 p16 Ja 1 2017

Reinhard, Marco Eli

Metalloprotein entatic control of ligand-metal bonds quantified by ultrafast x-ray spectroscopy diag *Science* v356 no6344 p1276 Je 23 2017

Reinhardt, Deborah M.

VISIONS OF SUGARPLUMS M. W. SCHWARTZ *Missouri Life* v43 no7 p16 D 2016/Ja 2017

Reinhardt, Forest L.

Case Study: How Would You Save This Farm? il *Harvard Business Review* v94 no11 p105 N 2016

MANAGING CLIMATE CHANGE: LESSONS FROM THE U.S. NAVY chart color il img *Harvard Business Review* v95 no4 p102 Jl/Ag 2017

Reinhardt, Forest—Interviews

What Climate Change Means for Business Before and After Paris S. Cliffe *Harvard Business Review Digital Articles* p2 D 15 2015

Reinhardt, Liz

Rebels Like Us cartoon color *Seventeen* v76 no2 p130 Mr 2017

Reinhart, Kurt O.

Plant-soil feedbacks and mycorrhizal type influence temperate forest population dynamics bibl graph map *Science* v355 no6321 p1 Ja 13 2017

Reining (Horsemanship)

Half Halts and Sliding Stops L. Mulvany color *Dressage Today* v23 no12 p62 S 2017

The Real-Deal DIYer [Cover story] C. Raymond Herbert color *Horse & Rider* v55 no11 p60 N 2016

Reining by the Bay color map *Horse & Rider* v56 no7 p28 Jl 2017

Reinisch, Karin M.

Lipid transport by TMEM24 at ER-plasma membrane contacts regulates pulsatile insulin secretion diag *Science* v355 no6326 p709 F 17 2017

Reinke, Tony

Do Smartphones Give Your Soul Cancer? A balanced, biblical take on the devices we can't seem to live without J. HAANEN color *Christianity Today* v61 no4 p64 My 2017

Reinold, Mike

MORE PRESSURE, LESS PAIN color *Men's Health* v32 no5 p56 Je 2017

Reinstetle, Matt

STEM CELL THERAPY AND WILLIE NELSON: Rebels by Their Own Rules *Saturday Evening Post* v289 no2 p92 Mr/Ap 2017

Reinsurance companies

The Fading Financial Magic Of Reinsurance S. BASAK and N. BUHAYAR cartoon *Bloomberg Businessweek* no4496 p52 O 24 2016

Reintegration of veterans

Troops for Fitness Engages Military Veterans in Community Health and Wellness Programming M. Collum *Parks & Recreation* v51 no11 p34 N 2016

Reinvestment

See also

Dividend reinvestment

Make Stock Investing Affordable C. M. Brown color *Black Enterprise* v47 no4 p16 N/D 2016

When Dividends Don't Pay J. Waggoner diag *Money* v46 no7 p34 Ag 2017

Your Guide to Recycling Black Dollars G. JEFFERS cartoon color *Ebony* v72 no3 p100 D 2016/Ja 2017

Reis, F.

Bismuthene on a SiC substrate: A candidate for a high-temperature quantum spin Hall material diag graph *Science* v357 no6348 p287 Jl 21 2017

Reis, N. F. Costa

Persistent effects of pre-Columbian plant domestication on Amazonian forest composition bibl chart graph map *Science* v355 no6328 p925 Mr 3 2017

REIS, VANESSA

A Global Assessment of Inland Wetland Conservation Status *BioScience* v67 no6 p523 Je 2017

Reis-Nichols Inc.

2016 Legacy *Indianapolis Monthly* v40 no4 p129 D 2016

Reischl, Catherine H.

Cultivating a school-university partnership for teacher learning color *Phi Delta Kappan* v98 no8 p48 My 2017

Reiser, P.

Spectral narrowing of x-ray pulses for precision spectroscopy with nuclear resonances diag *Science* v357 no6349 p375 Jl 28 2017

Reiser, Paul

My Obsessions... *TV Guide* v64 no46 p10 N 7 2016

Reiserer, A. A.

Entanglement distillation between solid-state quantum network nodes diag *Science* v356 no6341 p928 Je 1 2017

Reisman, Heather

Canada's Most Influential Reader E. NAWOTKA *Publishers Weekly* v264 no41 p16 O 9 2017

Reisman, Richard

The Elements of Value: Interaction *Harvard Business Review* v94 no11 p18 N 2016

Reisner, Bob

Bob Reisner's "Invader" Twin-Everything Roadster T. Taylor bw *Hot Rod* v70 no8 p10 Ag 2017

REISNER, ROSALIND
Women Rule *Publishers Weekly* v264 no23 p56 Je 5 2017

Reiss, Benjamin
Call It Sleep K. GULLIVER *Weekly Standard* v22 no35 p35 My 22 2017
The Evolution of Sleep S. Begley color *Time* v189 no9 p20 Mr 13 2017

Reiss, Bob
STALKING AN ELUSIVE PRIZE IN ALASKA color diag map *Fortune* v176 no4 p144 S 15 2017

REISS, DAWN
BOOM IN THE BURBS color *Chicago* v66 no1 p26 Ja 2017

Reiss, Jason
Greg Zoetmulder's Supercharged Small-Block Jeep Runs 8s With Ease color *Hot Rod* v70 no1 p50 Ja 2017

Reiss, Lina A. J.
Community network for deaf scientists color *Science* v356 no6336 p386 Ap 28 2017

Reiss, Valerie
You have too much stuff color *Yoga Journal* p49 2016 Special Issue

Reiter, Ben
1 THE NEW TESTAMENT color *Sports Illustrated* v126 no9 p40 Mr 27 2017
5 BOLD PREDICTIONS FOR MLB'S SECOND HALF color *Sports Illustrated* v127 no2 p39 Jl 17 2017
6 THE LONG GAME color *Sports Illustrated* v126 no9 p48 Mr 27 2017
The Class Of 2016 *Sports Illustrated* v125 no15 p36 N 7 2016
Ghostbusters [Cover story] color *Sports Illustrated* v125 no12 p24 O 10 2016
IT'S ALIVE! THE SLASHER COULD BE MAKING A Comeback color *Sports Illustrated* v126 no12 p29 My 1 2017
Leading Off color *Sports Illustrated* v125 no13 p6 O 17 2016
Leading Off color *Sports Illustrated* v126 no10 p10 Ap 10 2017
Leading Off color *Sports Illustrated* v127 no12 p6 O 16 2017
Made for TV color *Sports Illustrated* v125 no15 p35 N 7 2016
OVER UNDER color *Sports Illustrated* v126 no7 p66 Mr 6 2017
PER ASPERA AD ASTRO color *Sports Illustrated* v127 no9 p20 S 25 2017
Pieces of a Dream color *Sports Illustrated* v125 no16 p33 N 14 2016
Players Of the Year color *Sports Illustrated* v125 no20 p92 D 19 2016
PLAYING IT SAFER color *Sports Illustrated* v127 no10 p60 O 2 2017
THE SEEKER color *Sports Illustrated* v127 no4 p60 Ag 7 2017
Seven for The Road color *Sports Illustrated* v125 no20 p122 D 19 2016
THE SLUGGER THE SCOUT color *Sports Illustrated* v126 no13 p58 My 8 2017
SYNDERELLA color *Sports Illustrated* v126 no5 p64 F 13 2017

Reiter, Chris
Reinventing These Wheels color graph *Bloomberg Businessweek* no4504 p19 D 19 2016

Reiter, Johannes G.
Origins of lymphatic and distant metastases in human colorectal cancer diag graph *Science* v357 no6346 p55 Jl 7 2017

Reiter, Keramet
The Social Cost of Solitary Confinement *Time* v188 no18 p21 O 31 2016

Reitman, Janet
BETSY DEVOS' HOLY WAR bw color *Rolling Stone* no1283 p26 Mr 23 2017
THE MAKING—AND BREAKING—OF MARINES: THE DEATH OF A MUSLIM RECRUIT LAST YEAR HAS DRAWN SCRUTINY TO THE U.S. MARINES' TRAINING BASE AT PARRIS ISLAND, WHERE BRUTAL HAZING HAS FLOURISHED. IS THIS REALLY THE ONLY WAY TO CREATE A WARRIOR? *New York Times Magazine* p32 Jl 9 2017
THE ROLLING STONE INTERVIEW: Rachel Maddow [Cover story] bw color *Rolling Stone* no1290 p34 Je 29 2017
TRUMP'S RADICAL ATTORNEY GENERAL color *Rolling Stone* no1294 p28 Ag 24 2017

REITMEYER, JOHN

Supermall, Superstalled color *Bloomberg Businessweek* no4504 p44 D 19 2016

REITZ, ERICA YOUNG
5 Ways to Make the Most of College *Christianity Today* p68 Mr 2017
From College to Career: The Struggle Is Real color *Christianity Today* p63 Mr 2017

Reitz, Erin
FULL CIRCLE M. OZAWA color *Martha Stewart Living* p60 O 2017

Reitz, Megan
5 Questions to Ask Before You Call Out Someone Powerful *Harvard Business Review Digital Articles* p2 Ap 7 2017
How to Bring Mindfulness to Your Company's Leadership *Harvard Business Review Digital Articles* p2 D 1 2016
How to introduce mindfulness at work *People Management* p48 D 2016/Ja 2017
Mindfulness Works but Only If You Work at It *Harvard Business Review Digital Articles* p2 N 4 2016
The Problem with Saying "My Door Is Always Open" color *Harvard Business Review Digital Articles* p2 Mr 9 2017

Rejection (Psychology)
Quenching Your Thirst R. Gay color *InStyle* v24 no9 p214 S 2017
To Recover Faster from Rejection, Shift Your Mindset N. Torres *Harvard Business Review Digital Articles* p2 Ap 6 2016

Rekdal, Vayu Maini
Chemical transformation of xenobiotics by the human gut microbiota diag *Science* v356 no6344 p1246 Je 23 2017

Reklis, Kathryn
The lords of no mercy *Christian Century* v134 no17 p44 Ag 16 2017
The myth of white innocence color *Christian Century* v134 no19 p44 S 13 2017
Outside the frame color *Christian Century* v133 no21 p58 O 12 2016
Resistance on the inside *Christian Century* v134 no13 p42 Je 21 2017
Robots of the West color *Christian Century* v134 no1 p43 Ja 4 2017
Total (and equal) depravity color *Christian Century* v134 no11 p44 My 24 2017
Two visions of creativity color *Christian Century* v134 no4 p59 F 15 2017
The visions of Nat Turner *Christian Century* v133 no24 p43 N 23 2016
A wild ride with The Leftovers color *Christian Century* v134 no15 p44 Jl 19 2017

Relational databases
The Promise of Blockchain Is a World Without Middlemen V. Gupta color *Harvard Business Review Digital Articles* p2 Mr 6 2017

Relationship abuse
Bad Romance S. DOLGOFF *Scholastic Choices* v32 no5 p16 F 2017

Relationship breakup
DON'T LET HER HAUNT YOU [Cover story] J. VRABEL cartoon color *Men's Health* v32 no1 p114 Ja/F 2017
How to DUMP SOMEONE S. Goddard color *Seventeen* v76 no12 p74 D 2016/Ja 2017
Hurts So Good G. D. MELTON cartoon *O, The Oprah Magazine* p48 F 2017

Relationship quality
We are one J. Bleem color *U.S. Catholic* v82 no5 p50 My 2017

Relatives
ALMOST A Calamity C. WHITE *Idaho Magazine* v16 no5 p48 F 2017

Relativity
A Taste of Relativity P. Tyson *Sky & Telescope* v134 no1 p4 Jl 2017

Relativity (Physics)
Albert Einstein M. DARNA color *Discover* v38 no4 p36 My 2017
Anatomy of a Black Hole C. M. Carlisle *Sky & Telescope* v133 no2 p16 F 2017

Relaxation (Health)
AFTER THE SHOW C. Bowers *Dance Spirit* v21 no4 p42 Ap 2017

get ready to relax E. Seidman color *Health* v31 no6 p116 Jl 2017

HIDING IN PLAIN SIGHT P. C. Dodson cartoon *O, The Oprah Magazine* p125 Mr 2017

Meet your next teacher Colleen Saidman Yee [Cover story] color *Yoga Journal* no295 p85 O 2017

nourish yourself J. RODRIGUE color *Yoga Journal* p102 2017 Special Issue

Q: What adventure would you love to share with your best friend? D. LEMOINE, J. POWELL et al color *O, The Oprah Magazine* p12 Ja 2017

REST DAY color *Health* v31 no8 p10 O 2017

sitting pretty color *Yoga Journal* p106 2017 Special Issue

sneaky practice plan cartoon color *Yoga Journal* p120 2017 Special Issue

take OM HOME E. Marglin color *Yoga Journal* no293 p104 Ag 2017

Relaxation (Health)—Psychological aspects

the upside of doing NOTHING M. RABBITT color *Yoga Journal* no289 p17 F 2017

Relaxation (Nuclear physics)

Suppressing relaxation in superconducting qubits by quasiparticle pumping S. Gustavsson, Fei Yan et al bibl graph *Science* v354 no6319 p1573 D 23 2016

Relaxation techniques

pretty CALM M. RABBITT color *Yoga Journal* no287 p13 N 2016

You just woke up and already feel behind P. Moffitt color *Yoga Journal* p38 2016 Special Issue

Relaxation therapy

Sweet Dreams Are Made of This M. Labash color *Weekly Standard* v22 no33 p5 My 8 2017

Relaxer (Music)

Alt-J color *Rolling Stone* no1289 p58 Je 15 2017

Reliability (Personality trait)

See also
> Integrity
> Truthfulness & falsehood

CHILDREN AND CHORES: Give kids responsibilities that will help them thrive while learning self-reliance J. Salatin *Mother Earth News* no283 p59 Ag/S 2017

Relics

Relics of the first Americans? L. Wade color map *Science* v356 no6333 p13 Ap 7 2017

Reliford, Alexis

awesome women Awards 2017 [Cover story] bw color *Good Housekeeping* v265 no3 p67 S 2017

EVERYDAY HEROES Raising Grateful Kids color *Good Housekeeping* v265 no5 p82 N 2017

Give Your Body a Break color *Essence* v47 no9 p86 Ja 2017

GO FOR A "HELPER'S HIGH" color *Good Housekeeping* v264 no6 p84 Je 2017

JUST 3 MOVES color *Good Housekeeping* v265 no4 p100 O 2017

KNOW YOUR MIGRAINE TRIGGERS color *Good Housekeeping* v265 no4 p88 O 2017

Saving the Family Business color *Good Housekeeping* v265 no1 p63 Jl 2017

TAKE A VACAY color *Good Housekeeping* v265 no1 p90 Jl 2017

TONE YOUR TUSH color *Good Housekeeping* v265 no1 p92 Jl 2017

Religion

See also
> Autobiography—Religious aspects
> Belief & doubt
> Cosmology
> Faith
> Psychotherapy & religion
> Religion & law
> Religion & science
> Religion & the press
> Religious life
> Religious psychology
> Superstition
> Women & religion

CAN BACTERIA Help Us Understand RELIGION? V. TARICO *Humanist* v77 no3 p16 My/Je 2017

Christian Zionism G. R. McDermott color *Christian Century* v134 no20 p6 S 27 2017

The god of Science D. RUTH and A. MCCAIG *USA Today Magazine* v145 no2860 p70 Ja 2017

Hallowing the Gaps R. M. Pennoyer II color *Commonweal* v144 no11 p26 Je 16 2017

The Martyr Complex J. Marley color *Commonweal* v144 no6 p19 Mr 24 2017

NOT GETTING 'GETTING RELIGION' K. L. WOODWARD and N. DALLAVALLE *Commonweal* v144 no6 p4 Mr 24 2017

THE POLITICIZATION of Scientific Issues: Looking through Galileo's Lens or through the Imaginary Looking Glass J. GOLDBERG *Skeptical Inquirer* v41 no5 p34 S/O 2017

SCIENTIFIC UPDATE. Long-Term Studies of Vegetarians in the Past 35 Years R. Mangels *Vegetarian Journal* v36 no3 p28 2017

Spiritual but not Religious L. WEBSTER color *Tricycle: The Buddhist Review* v26 no3 p46 Spr 2017

Religion & culture

See also
> Christianity & culture

Religion vs. Culture R. ASLAN and B. Allen-Ebrahimian color *Foreign Policy* no225 p112 Jl/Ag 2017

Religion & education

BETSY DEVOS' HOLY WAR J. Reitman bw color *Rolling Stone* no1283 p26 Mr 23 2017

Christians among higher educated, though not in U.S L. Markoe color *Christian Century* v134 no2 p14 Ja 18 2017

More education doesn't mean less religious commitment among Christians, Pew says E. M. Miller *Christian Century* v134 no11 p17 My 24 2017

Religion & justice

God Is Not Out to Get You J. TREAT color *Christianity Today* v60 no9 p64 N 2016

Religion & law

See also
> Christianity & law

A Letter from a Person of Quality *Lapham's Quarterly* v10 no3 p211 Summ 2017

Religion & literature

Faith Matters S. Paulsell color *Christian Century* v133 no25 p44 D 7 2016

Religion & marriage

Vows of Friendship E. Tushnet bw color *America* v216 no3 p24 F 6 2017

Religion & politics

See also
> Islam & politics

New York Stands with Muslims *Islamic Horizons* v46 no3 p15 My/Je 2017

Religion & politics—Mexico

IN SOUTHERN MEXICO, TRACKING THE LEGACY OF BISHOP SAMUEL RUIZ Hootsen color *America* v217 no4 p18 Ag 21 2017

Religion & politics—United States

Breaking Faith P. BEINART color *Atlantic* v319 no3 p15 Ap 2017

The hard blue glow K. Childress *Christian Century* v134 no13 p10 Je 21 2017

Politics As Usual *Commonweal* v143 no18 p5 N 11 2016

Religion & science

AAAS reaches out to theology students M. Jarvis color *Science* v354 no6319 p1544 D 23 2016

Committee for Skeptical Inquiry Timeline, 2001-2016 K. Frazier *Skeptical Inquirer* v40 no6 p51 N/D 2016

Diamond's Space A. K. Ladas, C. Coon et al *Humanist* v77 no1 p5 Ja/F 2017

Evolution in the College Classroom Facilitating Conversations about Science and Religion M. NISBET *Skeptical Inquirer* v41 no5 p22 S/O 2017

Faith and Science at a Crossroad G. Imm, D. Waters et al *Sky & Telescope* v134 no3 p6 S 2017

SCIENCE & RELIGION in the Rough J. Diamond *Humanist* v76 no6 p12 N/D 2016

Two Routes to the Truth C. M. Carlisle *Sky & Telescope* v133 no6 p84 Je 2017

Who Would You Believe? *USA Today Magazine* v145 no2860 p71 Ja 2017

Religion & the press

A Pope for the (Media) Masses R. A. Schroth color *America* v217 no4 p58 Ag 21 2017

Religion historians

Editor's Note D. Skinner *Humanities* v37 no4 p1 Fall 2016

Religion in the workplace

What Companies Can Do When Work and Religion Conflict K. K. Chang *Harvard Business Review Digital Articles* p2 Mr 15 2016

Religion on television

Are You There God? It's Me Television J. Jensen color *Entertainment Weekly* no1463/1464 p92 Ap/My 2017

Religion—Economic aspects

U.S. religion worth $1.2 trillion L. Markoe graph *Christian Century* v133 no21 p14 O 12 2016

Religion—Exhibitions

Smithsonian exhibit shows religious diversity in early American life A. M. Banks *Christian Century* v134 no18 p16 Ag 30 2017

Religion—Government policy

Smithsonian exhibit shows religious diversity in early American life A. M. Banks *Christian Century* v134 no18 p16 Ag 30 2017

Religion—Humor

THE CHURCH OF THE FLYING SPAGHETTI MONSTER K. Gilsinan cartoon *Atlantic* v318 no4 p23 N 2016

Laughter THE BEST MEDICINE J. GAFFIGAN *Reader's Digest* v189 no1128 p78 Mr 2017

Religion—News briefs

CENTURY marks cartoon graph *Christian Century* v134 no5 p8 Mr 1 2017

CENTURY marks graph *Christian Century* v134 no10 p8 My 10 2017

marks bw graph *Christian Century* v133 no21 p8 O 12 2016

Religions

See also

Buddhism
Christianity
Confucianism
Islam

Calm After the Storm D. POLISH color *America* v215 no14 p19 N 7 2016

Here are the "America Jeopardy!" questions, er, answers M. Malone *America* v217 no2 p3 Jl 24 2017

Losing Their Religion L. Garrett bw color *Publishers Weekly* v264 no13 p19 Mr 27 2017

Religions—Relations

See also

Interfaith dialogue

Christians, Muslims stump together in Jordan T. Luck color *Christian Century* v133 no22 p14 O 26 2016

Religions—Study & teaching

Identity as a calling C. Zaleski *Christian Century* v133 no24 p35 N 23 2016

Religion—Terminology

SBNR PAST & PRESENT W. B. PARSONS cartoon *Tricycle: The Buddhist Review* v26 no3 p48 Spr 2017

Religion—United States

AS HISPANIC CATHOLIC NUMBERS GROW, CENTER OF GRAVITY FOR U.S. CHURCH SHIFTS TO SOUTH AND WEST M. J. O'Loughlin bw color graph *America* v217 no7 p12 O 2 2017

LAND OF CONFUSION: THE RELIGIOUS RIGHT, TRUMP, AND 'POST-TRUTH' AMERICA R. BOSTON *Humanist* v77 no2 p32 Mr/Ap 2017

Most of the unaffiliated just "stopped believing," according to new study K. Winston graph *Christian Century* v133 no22 p16 O 26 2016

Religious adherents

See also

Buddhists
Christians
Jews
Muslims

Contentious Christians J. Kinlaw color *Commonweal* v144 no16 p14 O 6 2017

MEET THE "BUDDHISH" NONES K. OAKES cartoon *Tricycle: The Buddhist Review* v26 no3 p50 Spr 2017

Religious art

The Buddha and the Pantocrator C. Zaleski *Christian Century* v134 no2 p33 Ja 18 2017

Religious art—Exhibitions

See also

Islamic art & symbolism—Exhibitions

Jerusalem 1000 - 1400: Every People Under Heaven M. MIRZA *Islamic Horizons* v45 no6 p52 N/D 2016

Museum exhibit reveals many sides of Jerusalem in Middle Ages and today D. Van Biema color *Christian Century* v133 no22 p17 O 26 2016

Religious awakening

China's Great Awakening I. Johnson color *Foreign Affairs* v96 no2 p83 Mr/Ap 2017

Religious communities

How were your children received by your parish? graph il *America* v216 no13 p6 Je 12 2017

Of Saints and Kings W. L. Belcher *History Today* v66 no11 p52 N 2016

Partial depravity S. Wells *Christian Century* v133 no21 p57 O 12 2016

Where and who you are N. Flores, J. Essmann et al color *U.S. Catholic* v82 no1 p12 Ja 2017

Religious discrimination

Bigger and Better R. CONNIFF *Progressive* v81 no4 p5 Ap/My 2017

Expelling Islamophobia S. McCOLLUM *Education Digest* v82 no8 p14 Ap 2017

What Companies Can Do When Work and Religion Conflict K. K. Chang *Harvard Business Review Digital Articles* p2 Mr 15 2016

Religious discrimination—Lawsuits & claims

Recycling Religiously? T. Eastland color *Weekly Standard* v22 no10 p7 N 14 2016

Religious doctrines

Reflections on the lectionary L. Barlow *Christian Century* v134 no12 p21 Je 7 2017

Sola Scriptura M. GALLI bw *Christianity Today* v61 no5 p50 Je 2017

Religious education

See also

Discussion in religious education

Just friends: Is friendship the key to strengthening global relationships? J. Mahallati color *U.S. Catholic* v82 no8 p34 Ag 2017

South Carolina Dharma Group W. J. Biddlecombe color *Tricycle: The Buddhist Review* v27 no1 p24 Fall 2017

Religious films

quick takes color *U.S. Catholic* v82 no8 p39 Ag 2017

Religious Freedom Restoration Act of 1993 (U.S.)

Off-Court Issues C. FEHRMAN *Indianapolis Monthly* v40 no7 p51 Mr 2017

Religious fundamentalism

Fundamentalism ON TRIAL B. BOLTON *Humanist* v77 no2 p18 Mr/Ap 2017

Religious fundamentalism & politics

The Religious Right & Wrong *Commonweal* v144 no13 p5 Ag 11 2017

Religious gatherings

Faith that grows W. Massey color *U.S. Catholic* v82 no6 p22 Je 2017

Religious gatherings—Congresses

The 'no cross talk' rule A. B. Robinson *Christian Century* v134 no10 p10 My 10 2017

Religious groups

See also

Buddhists
Christians
Jews
Muslims

THE CLASH OF POPULATIONS? K. Clarke color graph *America* v216 no10 p12 My 1 2017

Reunion! C. Sinyai bw cartoon *Commonweal* v144 no16 p10 O 6 2017

Second Coming [Cover story] J. BARDE color *Walrus* v14 no9 p22 N 2017

Studies reveal how faith counts in placing spiritual before material goods D. Briggs *Christian Century* v134 no1 p17 Ja 4 2017

Religious institutions

See also
> Buddhist sanghas
> Catholic institutions
> Convents
> Monasteries
> Temples

A Bell for the Queen: In a High-Desert Haven M. N. O'MALLEY *Idaho Magazine* v16 no10 p24 Jl 2017

Did you receive support from your faith community while you were experiencing depression and/or anxiety? B. Collier, T. Trinko et al graph *America* v216 no12 p6 My 29 2017

DUNGEONS AND DRAGONS D. Goodyear cartoon *New Yorker* v93 no15 p18 My 29 2017

Faith-based groups, others put pressure on UN for its role in Haiti cholera deaths C. Kennel-Shank *Christian Century* v133 no24 p15 N 23 2016

GLEANINGS graph *Christianity Today* v61 no7 p18 S 2017

Reunion! C. Sinyai bw cartoon *Commonweal* v144 no16 p10 O 6 2017

The Teacher Racket D. CLARKSON FISHER bw *Tricycle: The Buddhist Review* v26 no2 p26 Wint 2016

The Web of Shared Support J. Shaheen color *Tricycle: The Buddhist Review* v27 no1 p10 Fall 2017

Religious institutions—Finance
Methodist agency leaves NYC as other institutions face rising property costs L. Bloom color *Christian Century* v133 no23 p17 N 9 2016

Religious institutions—Social aspects
FAMILY L. Foust Prater *Successful Farming* v114 no11 p62 N 2016

Religious leaders
See also
> Clergy

CLERGY MARCH ON WASHINGTON A. M. Banks color *Christian Century* v134 no20 p18 S 27 2017

Faith Healers M. Quinn *Governing* v30 no4 p52 Ja 2017

Studies show help, hurt that can come from how clergy talk about end-of-life care D. Briggs *Christian Century* v134 no15 p16 Jl 19 2017

Religious leaders—Congresses
IS IT A SPIRITUAL OR A MENTAL HEALTH CRISIS? W. Massey bw *America* v216 no6 p12 Mr 20 2017

Religious leadership
See also
> Christian leadership
> Islamic leadership

LIVING BY The Word S. D. Anderson *Christian Century* v133 no22 p23 O 26 2016

Religious leaders—United States
When hatred rises *Christian Century* v134 no7 p7 Mr 29 2017

Religious life
See also
> Christian life
> Spiritual life

AS HISPANIC CATHOLIC NUMBERS GROW, CENTER OF GRAVITY FOR U.S. CHURCH SHIFTS TO SOUTH AND WEST M. J. O'Loughlin bw color graph *America* v217 no7 p12 O 2 2017

Spiritual Costs of Debt S. SALAI color *America* v215 no15 p21 N 14 2016

Religious life of clergy
Truth-shaped living P. W. Marty *Christian Century* v134 no10 p3 My 10 2017

Religious life of college students
How did your faith change in college? graph *America* v217 no4 p6 Ag 21 2017

Religious life of LGBT people
See also
> Transgender people—Religious life

Religious orthodoxy
A DECADE OF CHANGE H. B. SMITH color *Christianity Today* v60 no8 p11 O 2016

THE OTHER CHRISTIANITY TODAY T. OLSEN *Christianity Today* v60 no8 p7 O 2016

Religious psychology
THE ART THAT OPENS D. PENICK color *Tricycle: The Buddhist Review* v27 no1 p82 Fall 2017

Religious right—United States
Religious Right, Resurgent K. Pollitt diag il *Nation* v304 no6 p6 F 27 2017

The Religious Right's Demise I. TUTTLE color *National Review* v68 no20 p20 N 7 2016

Religious tolerance
Interfaith support rises along with attacks K. Winston, L. Markoe et al color *Christian Century* v134 no7 p12 Mr 29 2017

Religious tourism
Five-Star Pilgrimage J. Casper *Christianity Today* v61 no6 p18 Jl/Ag 2017

Religious work with prisoners
A church for every prisoner C. Hoke color *Christian Century* v133 no22 p24 O 26 2016

God Remembered Me in Prison G. McGuire color *Christianity Today* v61 no5 p79 Je 2017

Religiousness
MEIR SOLOVEICHIK M. SOLOVEICHIK *Commentary* v142 no1 p37 Jl/Ag 2016

Relman, David A.
Rethinking biosecurity bw *Issues in Science & Technology* v33 no2 p13 Wint 2017

Relocation
See also
> Employee relocation
> Household moving
> Involuntary relocation

Best Places to Retire S. Max color *Money* v45 no10 p64 N 2016

HOME FOR THE HOLIDAYS L. McCarthy color *Harper's Bazaar* no3649 p245 D 2016/Ja 2017

Sketchbook Liniers *New York Times Book Review* p30 Ag 27 2017

Vying for medicines agency *Science* v355 no6323 p330 Ja 27 2017

Relocation—History
JUST RELOCATE, BABY! J. Feldman color map *Sports Illustrated* v126 no11 p66 Ap 17-24 2017

Relton, Jane
Lee Rubin: Our mentor and role model *Science* v355 no6327 p806 F 24 2017

Rem-Fit (Company)
Sleeping with Apps M. ANTONOFF color *Sound & Vision* v82 no8 p22 O 2017

Remainers (Poem)
REMAINERS G. Foust *Harper's Magazine* v334 no2001 p68 F 2017

Remanufacturing
DIFFERENCE IN PARTS R. Bohacz *Successful Farming* v115 no2 p30 F 2017

Remarriage—Charts, diagrams, etc.
Getting Over My Divorce? Studying the Numbers Helped C. Wilson color diag *Time* v189 no7/8 p115 F 27 2017

Remarriage—Religious aspects—Christianity
'Amoris' opens the door to Communion for Catholics in irregular unions G. O'Connell color *America* v216 no6 p17 Mr 20 2017

Rember, Robert
Greater role for Atlantic inflows on sea-ice loss in the Eurasian Basin of the Arctic Ocean chart diag graph *Science* v356 no6335 p285 Ap 21 2017

Rembert, Jason
24 HOURS with JASON REMBERT O. J. WILLIAMS color *Ebony* v72 no11 p94 S 2017

Rème, H.
Xenon isotopes in 67P/Churyumov-Gerasimenko show that comets contributed to Earth's atmosphere diag *Science* v356 no6342 p1069 Je 9 2017

Remember Pearl Harbor (TV program)
Programming Highlights color *New Orleans Magazine* v51 no3 pD2 Ja 2017

WYES-TV/CHANNEL 12 PROGRAM GUIDE bw color *New Orleans Magazine* v51 no3 pD11 Ja 2017

Remembering Pearl Harbor (Film)
Virtually There T. Burr bw *MIT Technology Review* v120 no2 p96 Mr/Ap 2017

Remembering the Masters (Music)
Singing on Solid Ground HADLEY color *Downbeat* v83 no11 p56 N 2016

Cryo-EM structures and atomic model of the HIV-1 strand transfer complex intasome bibl color *Science* v355 no6320 p1 Ja 6 2017

Renck, Lauren

THE Dance Spirit 2016 COSTUME GUIDE *Dance Spirit* v20 no9 p76 N 2016

RENDA, KATHLEEN

#1: For a dapper New Yorker, Nick Olsen crafts a kaleidoscopic fantasia of freewheeling color, one-of a-kind auction finds, and yin-yang contrasts—plus a bedroom as handsomely tailored as a bespoke suit color *House Beautiful* v159 no2 p82 Mr 2017

2017 KITCHEN OF THE YEAR color *House Beautiful* v159 no8 p76 O 2017

Above and Beyond color *House Beautiful* p17 Jl 2017

A Battle Royal color *House Beautiful* v159 no7 p34 S 2017

BETTER WITH AGE color *House Beautiful* v159 no3 p76 Ap 2017

Bridle Party color *House Beautiful* v159 no5 p78 Je 2017

BRITISH ACCENT [Cover story] color *House Beautiful* v158 no10 p82 D 2016/Ja 2017

COLOR FULL color *House Beautiful* v158 no9 p41 N 2016

Dune color *House Beautiful* v159 no4 p25 My 2017

Farm, Fresher color *House Beautiful* p41 Jl 2017

Fig Purple color *House Beautiful* v159 no7 p29 S 2017

for 2018 [Cover story] color *House Beautiful* v159 no9 p29 N 2017

Full of Grace color *House Beautiful* v159 no3 p65 Ap 2017

Going the Distance color *House Beautiful* p18 Jl 2017

Have It Both Ways color *House Beautiful* v159 no4 p30 My 2017

In This Luxe Kitchen, Purple Reigns color *House Beautiful* v159 no7 p38 S 2017

JUST ADD WATER color *House Beautiful* v159 no1 p47 F 2017

A LABOR OF LOVE color *House Beautiful* v159 no1 p66 F 2017

LADY OF THE LAKE color *House Beautiful* v159 no4 p116 My 2017

Less Is More color *House Beautiful* v159 no4 p28 My 2017

luxe be a lady color *House Beautiful* v159 no7 p88 S 2017

Matcha Green color *House Beautiful* v159 no5 p29 Je 2017

Meet in the Middle color *House Beautiful* v158 no10 p39 D 2016/Ja 2017

Pink Grapefruit color *House Beautiful* v159 no2 p23 Mr 2017

Pitch Perfect color *House Beautiful* p60 Jl 2017

Rolling in the Deep color *House Beautiful* v159 no4 p32 My 2017

Rolling the Dice color *House Beautiful* v159 no9 p84 N 2017

Set the Stage color *House Beautiful* v159 no7 p33 S 2017

A STUDY IN CONTRAST color *House Beautiful* v159 no2 p16 Mr 2017

Sunset Orange color *House Beautiful* p15 Jl 2017

Tuscan Olive color *House Beautiful* v159 no8 p21 O 2017

ZINGING THE BLUES [Cover story] color *House Beautiful* v158 no9 p120 N 2016

Rendell, Jim

On a Question of the Day color *Black Belt* v55 no6 p16 O/N 2017

Rendleman, Emily J.

PAF1 regulation of promoter-proximal pause release via enhancer activation color *Science* v357 no6357 p1294 S 22 2017

RENDON, JIM

Even a Shark Attack Can't Stop This Surfer color *Popular Science* v288 no6 p90 N/D 2016

Renewable energy industry

Better Batteries J. Worland color *Time* v189 no13 p29 Ap 10 2017

The complicated geopolitics of renewable energy S. Paltsev bibl *Bulletin of the Atomic Scientists* v72 no6 p390 N 2016

A Fight Over the Electric Grid Could Reshape America's Green Power Boom J. Worland color *Time* v190 no2/3 p26 Jl 10-17 2017

Greening Business, One Project at a Time C. Martin bw color *Bloomberg Businessweek* no4505 p34 D 26 2016

Hey Mr. Green! Is liquid soap worse than bar soap? B. Schildgen *Sierra* v102 no4 p12 Jl/Ag 2017

Kerry Emanuel: A climate scientist for nuclear energy D. Stover bibl *Bulletin of the Atomic Scientists* v73 no1 p7 Ja 2017

Negative Energy K. Wong *Sierra* v101 no6 p26 N/D 2016

Warren Buffett's All-In Clean-Energy Bet S. Gandel and K. Fehrenbacher color diag map *Fortune* v174 no8 p158 D 15 2016

Renewable energy industry—Government policy

Blackouts cast Australia's green energy in dim light A. Reese

color *Science* v355 no6329 p1001 Mr 10 2017

Renewable energy sources

See also

Solar energy

Water power

Wind power

THE BRIGHT STUFF G. Barber color *Wired* v24 no11 p90 N 2016

Electric Renaissance A. Sneed color *Scientific American* v316 no6 p20 Je 2017

Going Clean map *Earth Island Journal* v32 no1 p8 Spr 2017

GREEN LEADERSHIP GROWING AMONG CANADIAN BUSINESSES D. F. McCourt color *Maclean's* v129 no50 p40 D 19 2016

HARVESTING THE SUN C. Huttes *Successful Farming* v115 no2 p32 F 2017

How Industrial Firms Invest in Renewable Energy, Affordably A. Winston *Harvard Business Review Digital Articles* p2 Ag 5 2016

The Internet Shouldn't Run on Dirty Energy N. Springer and K. Gallo *Harvard Business Review Digital Articles* p2 D 17 2015

Kenya's Energy Quandary R. C. Thornett color map *Earth Island Journal* v32 no2 p39 Summ 2017

POWERING THE FUTURE J. Thompson color *Essence* v47 no9 p56 Ja 2017

A SUSTAINABLE SOLUTION J. BHATIA *Ms.* v27 no1 p38 Spr 2017

Terawatt-scale photovoltaics: Trajectories and challenges N. M. Haegel, R. Margolis et al chart graph *Science* v356 no6334 p141 Ap 14 2017

Renewable energy sources—Economic aspects

The 3 Stages of a Country Embracing Renewable Energy C. Burger and J. Weinmann *Harvard Business Review Digital Articles* p2 Ap 17 2017

Why Your Power Company Wants to Sell You More Than Electricity J. Worland color *Time* v189 no20 p20 My 29 2017

Renewable energy sources—Finance

The Drop in Oil Prices Might Be Bad for Business A. Winston *Harvard Business Review Digital Articles* p2 D 3 2014

Renewable energy sources—Germany

THE BEST ENERGY REVOLUTION MONEY CAN BUY J. Ball color diag map *Fortune* v175 no4 p172 Mr 15 2017

Renewable energy sources—United States

Crossing the Red-Blue Divide: One Tennessee group has taken the politics out of renewable energy E. Daigneau *Governing* v30 no12 p20 S 2017

NATIONS RISING R. Johnson, M. N. Mitra et al color *Earth Island Journal* v32 no4 p18 Wint 2017

The Power of a Good Example P. Rauber *Sierra* v102 no5 p22 S/O 2017

Requesting Backup L. SCHLEY color map *Discover* v38 no8 p15 O 2017

Renewable energy transition (Government policy)

Inside the Energiewende C. STURM color *Issues in Science & Technology* v33 no2 p41 Wint 2017

Renewable energy sources—Charts, diagrams, etc.

Renewable Energy Hits a Milestone diag *Fortune* v176 no2 p15 Ag 1 2017

Renewable energy sources—United States—Charts, diagrams, etc.

SOLAR POWER BOOMS diag *Fortune* v175 no8 p36 Je 15 2017

Renfrew, Gregg

second nature L. HEDRICK color *Better Homes & Gardens* v95 no9 p54 S 2017

Renfro, Charles

On Private Projects for the Public *Architectural Record* v205 no4 p203 Ap 2017

Rénia, Laurent

Mapping the human DC lineage through the integration of high-dimensional techniques diag *Science* v356 no6342 p1044 Je 9 2017

Renick, Patricia

MOTHER ART C. ROSE *Cincinnati Magazine* v50 no6 p90 Mr 2017

Renick, Tim

The Sixteen Most Innovative People in Higher Education G. Edel-

The Ultimate Guide to Retirement: Couples Edition [Cover story] color diag *Money* v45 no10 p48 N 2016

When One Spouse Reaches Retirement First color diag *Money* v46 no8 p25 S 2017

Renzullo, Remy

Sitting Pretty J. K. DE VALLE color *Architectural Digest* v74 no9 p41 S 2017

REO, NICHOLAS J.

Invasive Species, Indigenous Stewards, and Vulnerability Discourse chart diag map *American Indian Quarterly* v41 no3 p201 Summ 2017

Reolink (Company)

REOLINK KEEN: BATTERY-POWERED CAMERA OFFERS WIRELESS SECURITY FOR CHEAP J. R. BOOKWALTER color *Macworld - Digital Edition* p23 Je 13 2017

Reovirus diseases

Reovirus infection triggers inflammatory responses to dietary antigens and development of celiac disease R. Bouziat, R. Hinterleitner et al color diag *Science* v356 no6333 p44 Ap 7 2017

Reoviruses

IN SCIENCE JOURNALS color *Science* v356 no6333 p37 Ap 7 2017

Repair & maintenance service personnel

Home Wrecker J. LEVIN and S. TRELEAVEN cartoon *Walrus* v14 no6 p28 Jl/Ag 2017

Repair & maintenance services

TECH TAKES THE FIELD H. Clancy color *Fortune* v175 no3 p32 Mr 1 2017

Repairing

See also

Automobile repair

Buildings—Repair & reconstruction

Bedroom Basics L. Elliott cartoon *Old House Journal* v44 no8 p52 D 2016

REPAIR MAKE-DOs D. Mowitz *Successful Farming* v115 no2 p24 F 2017

Reparation (Criminal justice)

The Forgotten Victims D. DAYEN il *New Republic* v247 no12 p10 D 2016

Repatriated foreign earnings—Taxation

A PATH THROUGH THE GRIDLOCK A. Murray color *Fortune* v75 no1 p6 Ja 1 2017

Repatriation of cultural property

"Our Hope and Our Protection": Misko-biiwaabik (Copper) and Tribal Sovereignty in Michigan E. M. REDix bw map *American Indian Quarterly* v41 no3 p224 Summ 2017

Seminary returns rare manuscript to Greek Orthodox C. Kennel-Shank color *Christian Century* v133 no26 p14 D 21 2016

Repayments

Climb Out of Student Debt K. Mulhere chart color *Money* v45 no10 p29 N 2016

Repeal of legislation

DELISLE, MISSISSIPPI J. Ward *Harper's Magazine* p32 O 2017

A Disappointing Start *National Review* v69 no6 p9 Ap 3 2017

Everybody's Fault J. COST color *Weekly Standard* v22 no30 p10 Ap 10 2017

Free speech in the pulpit D. Laycock *Christian Century* v134 no6 p10 Mr 15 2017

The Health-Care Crack-Up R. PONNURU il *National Review* v69 no7 p16 Ap 17 2017

Keeping an Eye on Obamacare L. Zamosky diag *Money* v46 no3 p23 Ap 2017

The National Interest: Jonathan Chait img *New York* p10 Ja 23 2017

Obamacare's Problems Still Need Solving Z. Tracer and H. Recht map *Bloomberg Businessweek* no4531 p37 Jl 24 2017

Out of Luck M. Wilson O'reilly color *Commonweal* v144 no4 p6 F 24 2017

Repeal Is Easy. Replace? Not So Much T. Newmyer color *Fortune* v175 no2 p9 F 1 2017

Repeal, Replace, Reboot *National Review* v69 no7 p13 Ap 17 2017

Repeal, Replace, Resist F. BARNES color *Weekly Standard* v22 no12 p13 N 28 2016

Revolt and Rebuild P. Ryan color *Nation* v304 no4 p4 F 6 2017

Suffer the Children *In These Times* v41 no6 p32 Je 2017

Trump Country Worries About Replacing Obamacare S. Frizell, P. Rebala color *Time* v189 no10 p14 Mr 20 2017

Where Trump Voters and Socialists Agree: Single-payer healthcare is picking up unexpected steam T. ANDERSON *In These Times* v41 no6 p24 Je 2017

Repentance

HOW TO BE FAULTLESS M. SHENG YEN color *Tricycle: The Buddhist Review* v26 no2 p34 Wint 2016

Let's Try This Again M. R. SIMONE *America* v215 p39 N 28 2016

Repentance in Judaism

A Useful David J. HELBERG and D. J. FRIEDMAN *Commentary* v144 no3 p5 O 2017

Repercussions & Reverberations (Theatrical production)

Weaving Conductive Threads R. Dionne *Stage Directions* v30 no1 p28 Ja 2017

Repetition Works for the Moon (Poem)

Repetition Works for the Moon S. Firer *New York Times Magazine* p15 F 19 2017

Repino, Robert

D'Arc *Publishers Weekly* v264 no10 p44 Mr 6 2017

Replacements (Performer)

BILLIE JOE ARMSTRONG E. R. Brown color *Entertainment Weekly* no1435 p54 O 14 2016

Replacements, The (Performer)

Tim Kaine's Top Five A. GREENE color *Rolling Stone* no1273 p15 N 3 2016

Replication protein A

RPA binds histone H3-H4 and functions in DNA replication–coupled nucleosome assembly Shaofeng Liu, Zhiyun Xu et al bibl graph *Science* v355 no6323 p415 Ja 27 2017

Repo Man (Film)

CHARACTER FLAWLESS D. Franich color *Entertainment Weekly* no1484 p17 S 29 2017

Report writing—Software

Capture Your Creativity with a Digital Notebook A. Samuel *Harvard Business Review Digital Articles* p2 My 29 2015

Reporters & reporting

See also

Investigative reporting

War correspondents

AND BARD GRADS, TOO *New York* v50 no9 p45 My 1 2017

Covering a country where race is everywhere C. Meyerson bw *Columbia Journalism Review* v56 no2 p31 Fall 2017

Gnawing Anonymice M. Hemingway *Weekly Standard* v22 no24 p14 F 27 2017

Hiding DAPL Violence Behind 'Nothing to See Here' Headlines J. Naureckas *Extra!* v30 no1 p4 Ja/F 2017

OF MANY THINGS A. McKINLESS *America* v215 no15 p2 N 14 2016

Rebranding Trump's White Supremacist Strategist J. Jackson *Extra!* v30 no1 p1 Ja/F 2017

THE SUPERFAN C. ZULKEY color *Chicago* v65 no11 p24 N 2016

Trump and the Watergate effect M. Sullivan bw *Columbia Journalism Review* v56 no2 p27 Fall 2017

Reporters & reporting—History

THOSE Magnificent Women AND THEIR TYPING MACHINES K. TODD *Smithsonian* v47 no7 p60 N 2016

Reporters & reporting—United States

MEDIA CIRCUS MAXIMUS J. WOLCOTT color *Vanity Fair* v59 no2 p50 F 2017

They Didn't Always Meet the Press bw *Weekly Standard* v22 no43 p14 Jl 24 2017

The Trump Conundrum R. G. Lawrence, A. E. Boydstun et al color graph *Columbia Journalism Review* v56 no2 p42 Fall 2017

Repp, Jo

The WestStar Open color *Spin to Win Rodeo* v20 no9 p20 N 2016

REPPENHAGEN, GARETT

Mission Critical *Sierra* v101 no4 p42 Jl/Ag 2016

REPPY, JUDITH

Rethinking biosecurity diag *Issues in Science & Technology* v33 no2 p11 Wint 2017

Representative government

See also

Apportionment (Election law)

When Corporate Philanthropy Makes the Recipient Look Bad Y. Shymko and T. Roulet *Harvard Business Review Digital Articles* p2 Ag 24 2016

Requests for proposals (Public contracts)

Mission Compromised: Trump backers are in for a rude awakening should his current proposals succeed D. F. Kettl *Governing* v30 no9 p16 Je 2017

Required courses (Education)

REFLECTING READERS AND THE REAL WORLD J. Stallworth color *Literacy Today (2411-7862)* v34 no4 p32 Ja/F 2017

Resale

FASHION FORWARD M. Berlinger color *Bloomberg Businessweek* no4510 p60 F 6 2017

Resale value

9 Upgrades That Pay You Back J. F. WASIK color *AARP: The Magazine* v59 no3A p21 Ap/My 2016

The Beckers Make Their Move P. M. ESSWEIN color *Kiplinger's Personal Finance* v70 no12 p72 D 2016

BUYING A NEW CAR? CHECK THE RESALE VALUE M. CROSS color *Kiplinger's Personal Finance* v71 no10 p13 O 2017

Resch, Brandon

OLD FLAMES color *Field & Stream* v122 no1 p10 My 2017

Rescue dogs

Amazing Animals S. Schwartz and K. Baird Rattini color *National Geographic Kids* no475 p10 N 2017

Rescue dogs—Training of

Ask Martha *Martha Stewart Living* no268 p76 O 2016

Rescue work

See also

   Ambulance service

   Animal rescue

   Rescue work-fire integration

LUCKY AND GOOD J. MACDONALD and S. MACDONALD *Sea Magazine* v109 no4 p12 Ap 2017

UPDATE: Syria's Civil War P. Smith *New York Times Upfront* v149 no5 p16 N 21 2016

Rescue work-fire integration

The Baby Catchers E. RINEHART color *Reader's Digest* v190 no1133 p12 S 2017

Research

See also

   Animal experimentation

   Archaeological research

   Biological research

   Cooperative research

   Discoveries in science

   Education research

   Field work (Research)

   Human experimentation

   Intelligence service

   Internet research

   Medical research

   Observatories

   Postdoctoral researchers

   Quantitative research

   Reproducible research

   Research & development

   Scientific development

50, 100 & 150 YEARS AGO color *Scientific American* v317 no1 p75 Jl 2017

The dual frontier: Patented inventions and prior scientific advance M. Ahmadpoor and B. F. Jones graph *Science* v357 no6351 p583 Ag 11 2017

Knowledge Is Infrastructure R. Dijkgraaf color *Scientific American* v316 no6 p8 Je 2017

March for science J. Berg color *Science* v356 no6333 p7 Ap 7 2017

Precaution: Open gene drive research K. M. Esvelt bibl *Science* v355 no6325 p589 F 10 2017

RENOVATION MADE EASIER E. Mann color *Cabin Living* p64 S 2017

RESEARCH color *Science* v355 no6324 p490 F 3 2017

Science Communication J. M. VERDIER and S. L. COLLINS *BioScience* v67 no6 p487 Je 2017

Science without Walls color *Scientific American* v316 no6 p7 Je 2017

Theory and Truth M. DiChristina color *Scientific American* v315 no5 p4 N 2016

Research & development

See also

   Drug development

   Research & development projects

4 Things Your Innovation Efforts Shouldn't Focus On A. Ruelas-Gossi *Harvard Business Review Digital Articles* p2 Ap 4 2017

CAPITOL IDEA: SCIENTISTS, PLEASE RUN FOR OFFICE C. THOMPSON color *Wired* v25 no8 p34 Ag 2017

Charging the Future S. Gaidos bw color diag *Science News* v191 no1 p22 Ja 21 2017

Do Most Companies Even Try to Innovate Anymore? P. Hünermund *Harvard Business Review Digital Articles* p2 Ap 14 2017

Local R&D Won't Help You Go Global T. J. Hannigan and R. Mudambi *Harvard Business Review Digital Articles* p2 Je 25 2015

Managing Multiparty Innovation N. Furr, K. O'Keeffe et al color img *Harvard Business Review* v94 no11 p76 N 2016

R&D: Apple's Global Web A. Webb map *Bloomberg Businessweek* no4541 p23 O 9 2017

Research: Innovation Suffers When Drug Companies Merge J. Haucap and J. Stiebale *Harvard Business Review Digital Articles* p2 Ag 3 2016

Want to Do Corporate Innovation Right? Go Inside Google Brain G. Satell *Harvard Business Review Digital Articles* p2 Je 1 2016

What the Two Most Innovation-Friendly States Have in Common A. M. Knott *Harvard Business Review Digital Articles* p2 D 4 2014

Which U.S. Companies Are Doing the Most R&D in China and India? V. Govindarajan, G. Bagla et al *Harvard Business Review Digital Articles* p2 Mr 26 2015

Research & development projects

Is R&D Getting Harder, or Are Companies Just Getting Worse At It? A. M. Knott *Harvard Business Review Digital Articles* p2 Mr 21 2017

It's the Partnership, Stupid B. SHNEIDERMAN and J. HENDLER *Issues in Science & Technology* v33 no4 p37 Summ 2017

The Man in the Mirror D. C. Paris *Change* v48 no6 p4 N/D 2016

Measuring research benefits C. T. HILL *Issues in Science & Technology* v33 no4 p14 Summ 2017

Using Longitudinal Data on Career Outcomes to Promote Improvements and Diversity in Graduate Education A. Mathur, A. L. Feig et al *Change* v48 no6 p42 N/D 2016

Research & development—Economic aspects

Make America Great Again *MIT Technology Review* v120 no3 p2 My/Je 2017

Research & development—Finance

Are Moonshots Giant Leaps of Faith? W. D. VALDIVIA *Issues in Science & Technology* v33 no3 p51 Spr 2017

The Innovator Gap I. Gur *MIT Technology Review* v120 no4 p10 Jl/Ag 2017

Sometimes Cutting R&D Spending Can Yield More Innovation R. Mudambi, T. Swift et al *Harvard Business Review Digital Articles* p2 Ja 8 2015

Stealing industrial secrets pays off—at first C. Matacic bw graph *Science* v357 no6350 p434 Ag 4 2017

Stock Buybacks Aren't Hurting Innovation G. Satell *Harvard Business Review Digital Articles* p2 Mr 31 2015

Research ethics

Academies Report Urges Bolstered Efforts to Protect Integrity of Science K. Frazier *Skeptical Inquirer* v41 no4 p5 Jl/Ag 2017

U.S. report calls for research integrity board J. Mervis diag *Science* v356 no6334 p123 Ap 14 2017

Research grants

AIA Pleased to Announce New Research and Fieldwork Grants color *Archaeology* v70 no2 p65 Mr/Ap 2017

The Arabian Horse Foundation Continues Funding of Research Projects to Protect the Arabian Horse *Arabian Horse World* v57 no5 p237 F 2017

Research grants—United States

Measuring research benefits B. GODIN *Issues in Science & Technology* v33 no4 p14 Summ 2017

NIH abandons grant cap, offers new help to younger scientists J. Kaiser *Science* v356 no6343 p1108 Je 16 2017

Teachers receive $100,000 in STEM Research Grants color *Sci-*

ence News v192 no1 p28 Ag 5 2017

Research institutes

See also

Botanical gardens

Despite financial squeeze, Japan continues drive to globalize its science enterprise T. Feder *Physics Today* v70 no1 p24 Ja 2017

Haymarket Books: Publishing Books in the Current Moment C. Kirch color *Publishers Weekly* v263 no42 p11 O 17 2016

INSIDE GOOGLE'S MOONSHOT FACTORY D. Thompson cartoon color *Atlantic* v320 no4 p60 N 2017

Is OpenAI Solving the Wrong Problem? J. Allworth *Harvard Business Review Digital Articles* p2 D 15 2015

NYT Exposes a Favorite Source as War Industry Flack A. Johnson *Extra!* v29 no8 p4 O 2016

Step up for quality research N. J. Schrag and G. M. Purdy color *Science* v357 no6351 p531 Ag 11 2017

Synthesis Centers as Critical Research Infrastructure J. S. BARON, A. SPECHT et al *BioScience* v67 no8 p750 Ag 2017

TREE ENTERPRISE *Arizona Highways* v92 no7 p48 Jl 2016

Why Today's Corporate Research Centers Need to Be in Cities B. J. Katz and S. Andes *Harvard Business Review Digital Articles* p2 Mr 1 2016

Research institutes—Canada

Behind the Big Red Machine A. KINGSTON color *Maclean's* v130 no10 p24 N 2017

Research institutes—Security measures

What life scientists should know about security threats K. M. Berger bibl color diag *Science* v354 no6317 p1237 D 9 2016

Research management

Why There Is a Need to Discuss the Gap Between Research and Practice J. Stamborski *Parks & Recreation* v52 no5 p12 My 2017

Research methodology

See also

Case study (Research)

Internet research

The scientific swerve: Changing your research focus C. Tachibana color *Science* v357 no6359 p126 O 6 2017

What to Do When Someone Angrily Challenges Your Data J. M. Jachimowicz color *Harvard Business Review Digital Articles* p2 Ap 5 2017

Why the Future of Social Science Is with Private Companies M. Schrage *Harvard Business Review Digital Articles* p2 S 1 2015

Research personnel

See also

Scholars

Panel urges steps to boost evidence-based policy J. Mervis color *Science* v357 no6355 p959 S 8 2017

Research night owls Y. N. Majchrzak, M. Soták et al color *Science* v354 no6315 p964 N 25 2016

THE SCIENTIFIC NIGHT SHIFT S. Kean color *Science* v354 no6315 p988 N 25 2016

Research stations

Traces of the Future color map *National Geographic* v230 no6 p122 D 2016

Research teams

Let's talk about language barriers A. Deczkowska color *Science* v356 no6341 p978 Je 1 2017

Research vessels

Our Ship Comes In K. Kostel *Oceanus* v52 no1 p36 Summ 2016

Research—Abstracts

Advances in thermoelectric materials research: Looking back and moving forward J. He and T. M. Tritt diag *Science* v357 no6358 p1369 S 29 2017

Research—Canada

Research frozen in Canada budget *Science* v355 no6332 p1354 Mr 31 2017

Research—Equipment & supplies

See also

Scientific apparatus & instruments

new products color *Science* v357 no6347 p217 Jl 14 2017

Research—Evaluation

Nutrition Then and Now: The science of nutrition is ever-evolving, resulting in small changes and larger shifts in dietary advice over time *Tufts University Health & Nutrition Letter* v35 no7 p4 S 2017

Research—Finance

See also

Endowment of research

Federal aid to research

Ambitious web fundraising startup fails to meet big goals M. Harris *Science* v354 no6312 p534 N 4 2016

At 10, Europe's 'excellence' fund ponders changes K. Kupferschmidt and E. Pain color graph *Science* v355 no6329 p1002 Mr 10 2017

The boldness of philanthropists D. Baltimore color *Science* v353 no6307 p1473 S 30 2016

Brazil's 'doomsday' scenario H. Escobar color *Science* v355 no6323 p334 Ja 27 2017

California rules U.S. corporate research J. Mervis graph *Science* v354 no6312 p537 N 4 2016

ERC—the next 10 years H. Nowotny color *Science* v355 no6329 p997 Mr 10 2017

Foreign-born scientists find a home in China S. Williams color *Science* v354 no6312 p644 N 4 2016

A lifeline for Greek science—or living on borrowed time? E. Stokstad color *Science* v353 no6307 p1481 S 30 2016

Trump's 2018 budget proposal 'devalues' science J. Mervis color graph *Science* v355 no6331 p1246 Mr 24 2017

Trump targets environmental science for cuts D. Malakoff and W. Cornwall color graph *Science* v355 no6329 p1000 Mr 10 2017

Research—Finance—Government policy

Research frozen in Canada budget *Science* v355 no6332 p1354 Mr 31 2017

Research—Government policy

Philosopher's Corner: The End of Puzzle Solving R. FRODEMAN *Issues in Science & Technology* v33 no2 p19 Wint 2017

Research—Moral & ethical aspects

Human tissues in a dish: The research and ethical implications of organoid technology A. L. Bredenoord, H. Clevers et al diag *Science* v355 no6322 p260 Ja 20 2017

Research—News briefs

RESEARCH color *Science* v356 no6343 p1134 Je 16 2017

RESEARCH color *Science* v357 no6348 p263 Jl 21 2017

Research Digest *Alternatives Journal (AJ) - Canada's Environmental Voice* v42 no3 p11 2016

This Just In J. Zorthian *Time* v188 no15 p15 O 17 2016

This Just In J. Zorthian *Time* v189 no9 p23 Mr 13 2017

This Just In J. Zorthian *Time* v190 no6 p25 Ag 7 2017

Research—Safety measures—Moral & ethical aspects

Rethinking biosecurity D. A. Relman bw *Issues in Science & Technology* v33 no2 p13 Wint 2017

Research—Social aspects

Big studies clash over fetal growth rates J. de Vrieze graph *Science* v355 no6323 p336 Ja 27 2017

Research—Societies, etc.

A better research-practice partnership E. Henrick, M. A. Munoz et al color *Phi Delta Kappan* v98 no3 p23 N 2016

Help Create a Veggie World *Vegetarian Journal* v36 no1 p32 2017

Research—United States

Philosopher's Corner: The End of Puzzle Solving R. FRODEMAN *Issues in Science & Technology* v33 no2 p19 Wint 2017

Research—United States—Finance

Cutting Off Your Base To Spite Your Foes S. J. DOUGLAS *In These Times* v41 no5 p16 My 2017

Research—United States—Government policy

A March for Science Is Not Enough color *Scientific American* v316 no5 p9 My 2017

Research—Universities & colleges

High-energy-density science blooms at NIF D. Kramer *Physics Today* v70 no2 p33 F 2017

Innovative Companies Get Their Best Ideas from Academic Research—Here's How They Do It G. Satell *Harvard Business Review Digital Articles* p2 Ap 19 2016

RULES OF EVIDENCE W. Cornwall color *Science* v355 no6325 p564 F 10 2017

Resende, Marcio F. R., Jr.

A chemical genetic roadmap to improved tomato flavor bibl graph *Science* v355 no6323 p391 Ja 27 2017

Resentment

Let it go! [Cover story] R. ROMM, K. ARNOLD-RATLIFF et al color *O, The Oprah Magazine* p92 Ag 2017

The Real Big Lie E. Alterman il *Nation* v305 no7 p6 S 25 2017

Take Lord, Receive M. Simone *America* v217 no4 p56 Ag 21 2017

What I Know for Sure Oprah color *O, The Oprah Magazine* p124 Ag 2017

Reservation systems

See also

Restaurants—Reservation systems

Preserving Our Parks color *Earth Island Journal* v32 no3 p6 Aut 2017

Reservoir-triggered seismicity

Understanding induced seismicity D. Elsworth, C. J. Spiers et al bibl color graph *Science* v354 no6318 p1380 D 16 2016

Reservoirs

GET TO THE POINT M. VINCENT and G. BETHGE cartoon *Outdoor Life* v224 no2 p32 F/Mr 2017

South Florida's Toxic Summer M. SHAW color *Surfer* v58 no4 p42 Ag 2017

Reservoirs—Environmental aspects

HOW TO WEATHERPROOF YOUR FARM (SORT OF) [Cover story] G. GULUCKSON *Successful Farming* v114 no11 p30 N 2016

Reseska, David

The SAILING SCENE color *Sail* v48 no6 p6 Je 2017

Resident Evil: The Final Chapter (Film)

KATE BECKINSALE & MILLA JOVOVICH RESIDENT QueenS of the UNDERWORLD D. Franich color *Entertainment Weekly* no1450 p38 Ja 27 2017

Resident Evil: The Final Chapter J. HOGAN *TV Guide* v65 no39 p61 S 18 2017

Residential areas

See also

Residential real estate

THE FORGOTTEN HISTORY OF U STREET B. THOMAS *Washingtonian Magazine* v52 no5 p60 F 2017

HAUTE HOUSES: The 2017 Washingtonian Residential Design Awards' 12 winning projects M. M. Kashino *Washingtonian Magazine* v52 no11 p70 Ag 2017

Residential care—Evaluation

ETC M. Cameran color *New Orleans Magazine* v51 no4 p143 F 2017

Residential real estate

See also

Housing

GONE BABY GONE R. MONROE color *New Republic* v248 no10 p34 O 2017

JULIA STREET color *New Orleans Magazine* v51 no12 p24 O 2017

OFF THE MARKET! color *Washingtonian Magazine* v52 no7 p169 Ap 2017

OFF THE MARKET!: The nuts and bolts of some of Washington's most expensive residential transactions *Washingtonian Magazine* v53 no1 p197 O 2017

Think You Can Flip a House? J. BARGER color *Washingtonian Magazine* v52 no7 p95 Ap 2017

Residential real estate—Economic aspects

South Florida J. Forsythe color *New York Times Magazine* p53 D 4 2016

Residential real estate—Marketing

OFF THE MARKET! *Washingtonian Magazine* v52 no1 p187 O 2016

Residential real estate—Sales & price

OFF THE MARKET! The nuts and bolts of some of Washington's most expensive residential transactions *Washingtonian Magazine* v52 no11 p157 Ag 2017

OFF THE MARKET! *Washingtonian Magazine* v52 no1 p187 O 2016

Residents

See also

Seasonal residents

Who's on First? D. Sanford *Parks & Recreation* v52 no3 p64 Mr 2017

Residents (Medicine)

Knocking on opportunity's door D. Shao cartoon *Science* v354 no6310 p382 O 21 2016

Residents—Attitudes

Starting a Difficult Conversation V. Paynich *Parks & Recreation*

v52 no1 p30 Ja 2017

Residents—United States

The Death of a Hero E. J. Dionne Jr. color *Commonweal* v144 no5 p8 Mr 10 2017

Resignation

How to Quit Your Job Without Burning Bridges R. Knight *Harvard Business Review Digital Articles* p2 D 4 2014

Resignation from public office

The Art of the Squeal cartoon *Weekly Standard* v22 no48 p14 S 4 2017

Head of France's main funding body resigns amid acrimony E. Pain *Science* v357 no6349 p341 Jl 28 2017

Home from the Capitol A. Greenblatt *Governing* v30 no5 p12 F 2017

Mayor Meltdown *Texas Monthly* v45 no3 p66 Mr 2017

Resignation of employees

See also

Resignation of executives

7 Ways People Quit Their Jobs A. C. Klotz and M. C. Bolino *Harvard Business Review Digital Articles* p2 S 15 2016

BrexIt 'triggers resignations' *People Management* p14 O 2016

Editor's Letter bw *Advocate* no1089 p8 F/Mr 2017

Employees Leave Good Bosses Nearly as Often as Bad Ones R. S. Gajendran and D. Somaya *Harvard Business Review Digital Articles* p2 Mr 8 2017

Milestones *Time* v189 no18 p15 My 15 2017

People C. Kennel-Shank *Christian Century* v134 no13 p17 Je 21 2017

The Right Way to Off-Board a Departing Employee R. Knight *Harvard Business Review Digital Articles* p2 Ja 15 2016

Staff are holding us to ransom S. Sales *People Management* p53 Mr 2017

What to Do After You Tell Your Boss You're Leaving C. O'Hara *Harvard Business Review Digital Articles* p2 Ag 11 2016

When an Employee Quits and You Didn't See It Coming R. Knight *Harvard Business Review Digital Articles* p2 Mr 12 2015

Why People Quit Their Jobs: Interaction L. Viar, D. Eikenberg et al *Harvard Business Review* v94 no11 p18 N 2016

Resignation of executives

THE BIG QUESTION P. Keoghan, B. Wolly et al cartoon *Atlantic* v319 no5 p96 Je 2017

Boardrooms of the Living Dead J. Green and A. Ritcey *Bloomberg Businessweek* no4534 p27 Ag 14 2017

Marissa Mayer's Departure from Yahoo and the Challenge of Drawing Lessons from an N of 1 T. Chamorro-Premuzic *Harvard Business Review Digital Articles* p2 Je 15 2017

Resilience (Personality trait)

5 Ways to Boost Your Resilience at Work R. Fernandez *Harvard Business Review Digital Articles* p2 Je 27 2016

The Better You Know Yourself, the More Resilient You'll Be R. Carucci *Harvard Business Review Digital Articles* p2 S 4 2017

Healing Advice A. Nash color *AARP: The Magazine* v60 no4A p55 Je/Jl 2017

Hurricane Sandy's Lesson: Resilience Isn't Enough A. Winston *Harvard Business Review Digital Articles* p2 O 29 2014

Localism Means Security W. S. LIND *American Conservative* v15 no6 p10 N/D 2016

Parks, Recreation and Resilience R. Richardson and J. Cox *Parks & Recreation* v51 no12 p26 D 2016

Resilience Is About How You Recharge, Not How You Endure S. Achor and M. Gielan *Harvard Business Review Digital Articles* p2 Je 24 2016

Rest, reflect, and refresh color *Yoga Journal* p64 2016 Special Issue

To Build Your Resilience, Ask Yourself Two Simple Questions S. Rao *Harvard Business Review Digital Articles* p2 Je 13 2017

What We Can Learn About Resilience from Female Leaders of the UN M. Valcour *Harvard Business Review Digital Articles* p2 S 28 2017

You're More Resilient Than You Give Yourself Credit For A. Molinsky bw *Harvard Business Review Digital Articles* p2 Ja 25 2017

Resilience (Personality trait)—Study & teaching

When the Worst Happens S. SANDBERG and A. GRANT color *AARP: The Magazine* v60 no4A p52 Je/Jl 2017

Resistance (Philosophy)

The Before and After Picture N. RAPOLD color *Film Comment* v53 no1 p48 Ja/F 2017

DARING TO DREAM IN THE AGE OF TRUMP [Cover story] N. Klein color *Nation* v305 no1 p14 Jl 3 2017

VOICES OF The RESISTANCE color *Progressive* v81 no4 p15 Ap/My 2017

Resistance (Psychoanalysis)

WELCOME TO THE RESISTANCE Z. Exley *In These Times* v40 no12 p14 D 2016

Resistance bands (Exercise equipment)

JUST 3 MOVES A. Reliford color *Good Housekeeping* v265 no3 p109 S 2017

The RBG Workout B. Johnson color *Glamour* v115 no10 p120 O 2017

The Resistance (Band) Rises! M. GAINSBURG color *Women's Health* v14 no9 p61 N 2017

TIGHTER TUSH S. Walter color *Good Housekeeping* v264 no4 p103 Ap 2017

Resistance to change

The Elusive Easy-Peasy D. T. PUTERBAUGH *USA Today Magazine* v146 no2868 p80 S 2017

Overcome Your Company's Resistance to Data T. C. Redman *Harvard Business Review Digital Articles* p2 Mr 30 2015

What FDR Knew About Managing Fear in Times of Change V. Govindarajan and H. Faber *Harvard Business Review Digital Articles* p2 My 4 2016

Resistance to government

See also

Civil disobedience

Civil war

Cuba Profile *Congressional Digest* v95 no10 p3 D 2016

GOP HEALTHCARE FAILURE: RESISTANCE IS STILL NOT FUTILE G. CHRISTINA *Humanist* v77 no3 p36 My/Je 2017

WHAT CAN WE DO? G. CHRISTINA *Humanist* v77 no2 p34 Mr/Ap 2017

Resistance to government—Economic aspects

CHECKS AND BALANCES A. KROLL color *Mother Jones* v42 no4 p36 Jl/Ag 2017

Resistance to government—United States

Negative Energy B. Gage *New York Times Magazine* p11 F 5 2017

Organize a Moral Resistance A. NABAUM *New Republic* v248 no3 p36 Mr 2017

THE PATH OF MOST RESISTANCE J. HEER diag il *New Republic* v248 no6 p22 Je 2017

The Prospects for Resistance F. F. PIVEN il *Nation* v304 no4 p13 F 6 2017

A Roar of Resistance M. HERTSGAARD color *Nation* v304 no5 p4 F 20 2017

Think Globally, Resist Locally B. BARBER color *Nation* v304 no4 p17 F 6 2017

Resistive force—Research

Once-baffling success of granular resistive force theory explained Sung Chang *Physics Today* v69 no11 p22 N 2016

Resolute Forest Products (Company)

Publishers Find Themselves Enmeshed in Greenpeace–Paper Company Fight J. Milliot *Publishers Weekly* v264 no25 p6 Je 19 2017

Resolution (Optics)

See also

Deconvolution of digital images

WAYPOINT N. KREBS color *Outdoor Life* v224 no5 p7 Je/Jl 2017

Resonance Records (Company)

Record Store Day's Spring Awakening P. MARGASAK color *Downbeat* v84 no6 p22 Je 2017

Resonant states

Exceptional points make for exceptional sensors J. Miller *Physics Today* v70 no10 p23 O 2017

Resorts

See also

Health resorts

50 Things Every Georgian Must Do *Atlanta* v57 no2 p64 Je 2017

593" M. Hansen bw color *Powder* p64 S 2017

Give-Back Getaways C. Kopaczewski color *Good Housekeeping* v264 no5 p69 My 2017

Golden Rules P. Guzmán bw *Conde Nast Traveler* v52 no1 p20

Ja 2017

RESORTS color *Conde Nast Traveler* v52 no10 p80 N 2017

RULE THE WATER *Saturday Evening Post* v289 no4 p23 Jl/Ag 2017

'TIS THE SEASON! cartoon *Powder* v45 no4 p54 D 2016

UP ALL NIGHT E. Ehmsen color *Sunset* v237 no5 p25 N 2016

weekend getaways: spirit *Washingtonian Magazine* v52 no11 p97 Ag 2017

Resorts—Austria

JET — SET SPAE SCAPES S. GRINNELL color map *Vanity Fair* v58 no12 p81 D 2016

Resorts—British Columbia

SKIING, BRITISH COLUMBIA—STYLE C. Ciarmello and D. Hanson chart color *Sunset* v237 no6 p38 D 2016

Resorts—Evaluation

cabins For Snow play K. BASTONE color *Cabin Living* p52 D 2016

CAPITAL COMMENT *Washingtonian Magazine* v52 no3 p16 D 2016

A CENTURY OLD & NEW AGAIN: ROSARIO RESORT GOT A FACELIFT, A NEW MARINA CONFIGURATION AND MUCH MORE D. HISLOP color map *Sea Magazine* v109 no7 pPNW-1 Jl 2017

Coeur d'Alene Resort, Idaho S. Citron *Saturday Evening Post* v289 no3 p27 My/Je 2017

THE COSMOPOLITAN OF LAS VEGAS *Los Angeles Magazine* p78 Mr 2017

Discover Saddlebrook *Tennis* v53 no1 p74 Ja/F 2017

FIT FOR A WHALE C. R. JOYNT *Washingtonian Magazine* v52 no5 p26 F 2017

Gal-Pal Getaway M. Santos color *Working Mother* v40 no3 p48 Ag/S 2017

Get Some Alone Time J. MURPHY color *Conde Nast Traveler* v51 no11 p72 D 2016

HOME SWEET HOMESTEAD A. COCHRAN *Washingtonian Magazine* v52 no3 p16 D 2016

Into the WILD color *Vogue* v207 no6 p84 Je 2017

Island Time A. SESSA color *Architectural Digest* v74 no4 p80 Ap 2017

MORONGO CASINO, RESORT & SPA *Los Angeles Magazine* p82 F 2017

Out & About color *Martha Stewart Living* p10 Mr 2017

SLEEP EASY: FIVE OF OUR FAVORITE PLACES TO STAY IN THE VALLEY A. C. POE *Washingtonian Magazine* v53 no1 p100 O 2017

SOUTH'S BEST RESORT A. Nash color *Southern Living* v52 no4 p86 Ap 2017

STRESS-BUSTING VACATIONS S. BLOCK color *Kiplinger's Personal Finance* v71 no7 p62 Jl 2017

TEE TIME IN TEXAS *Texas Monthly* v45 no3 p124 Mr 2017

They're SORT OF OUT OF THE WAY BUT WORTH THE TRIP color *Conde Nast Traveler* v52 no1 p80 Ja 2017

WELL TRAVELED C. Coen cartoon *Louisiana Life* v37 no2 p80 N/D 2016

WHERE Winter is Grand B. SGHELLER *Yankee* v81 no1 p84 Ja/F 2017

Wild Vacation J. KIFFEL-ALCHEH color *National Geographic Kids* no471 p6 Je/Jl 2017

Resorts—Hawaii

HAWAII FOR FAMILY B. VAN GORDER color *Advocate* no1089 p54 F/Mr 2017

Resorts—Idaho

Coeur d'Alene Resort, Idaho S. Citron *Saturday Evening Post* v289 no3 p27 My/Je 2017

Resorts—India

Wild Vacation J. KIFFEL-ALCHEH color *National Geographic Kids* no471 p6 Je/Jl 2017

Resorts—Mexico

PICK YOUR MEXICO PARADISE C. Ciarmello, E. Ehmsen et al color *Sunset* v237 no5 p29 N 2016

Resorts—Montana

A Day in the Life at Lone Mountain Ranch [Cover story] H. Long color *Log Home Living* v34 no3 p24 Ap 2017

Resorts—Reviews

COLD COMFORT K. SCHNEIDER *Indianapolis Monthly* v40 no4 p46 D 2016

Resorts—Seychelles

WORD OF MOUTH color *Conde Nast Traveler* v51 no11 p53 D 2016

Resorts—Texas

THE SOUNDS OF VACATION L. MYERS cartoon *Missouri Life* v44 no5 p66 Ag 2017

Resorts—Virginia

EASTERN VIRGINIA *Virginia Living* p58 2017 Best 20of Virginia

Resorts—Washington (State)

Be Starstruck: Remote Primland Resort is off the grid yet finely attuned to creature comforts, outdoor fun, and the human fascination with stars in the night sky D. LEATHERMAN *Washingtonian Magazine* v52 no11 p92 Ag 2017

Resource exploitation

The Complex Business of Sustainable Exploitation of Wildlife: Researchers grapple with the many unknowns L. E. OGDEN *BioScience* v67 no8 p691 Ag 2017

My Tribe's Stand Against Corporate Mining M. A. ROLO *Progressive* v81 no10 p22 N 2016

Respect

The Leadership Behavior That's Most Important to Employees C. Porath *Harvard Business Review Digital Articles* p2 My 11 2015

The New Rules of Engaging with Women S. BEE color *GQ: Gentlemen's Quarterly* v87 no1 p22 Ja 2017

Slam Bunk D. Greene, T. Keith et al color *Sports Illustrated* v127 no5 p19 Ag 14 2017

Son, Here Is How You Save M. HOUSEL color *Reader's Digest* v189 no1129 p38 Ap 2017

Respect (Music)

Paying R-E-S-P-E-C-T to "Respect" J. Goodman color *Entertainment Weekly* no1453 p59 F 17 2017

Respect for persons

See also

Self-esteem

Half of Employees Don't Feel Respected by Their Bosses C. Porath *Harvard Business Review Digital Articles* p2 N 19 2014

A Time to Fight B. LUEDERS *Progressive* p8 D 2016/Ja 2017

Respiration

Breathing Is the Key to Persuasive Public Speaking A. Shapira *Harvard Business Review Digital Articles* p2 Je 30 2015

THE EXCHANGE J. ELEFTERIADES and K. Cockerham cartoon color graph *Men's Health* v32 no8 p16 O 2017

Locked and loaded for apoptosis K. L. Bren and E. L. Raven diag *Science* v356 no6344 p1236 Je 23 2017

Poses of the month C. Owerko color *Yoga Journal* no290 p47 Mr 2017

SLY SLEEP TIPS *Saturday Evening Post* v289 no4 p76 Jl/Ag 2017

STRESSED OUT? *Scholastic Choices* v32 no6 p20 Mr 2017

TESTING THE AIR *South Dakota Magazine* v32 no4 p108 N/D 2016

To help stabilize your upper body... cartoon *Dressage Today* v23 no7 p72 Mr 2017

Yoga G. TARLACH color *Discover* v38 no6 p98 Jl/Ag 2017

Respiration—Physiological aspects

Breathing to inspire and arouse S. Sheikhbahaei and J. C. Smith bw *Science* v355 no6332 p1370 Mr 31 2017

Respiration—Psychological aspects

Breathing control center neurons that promote arousal in mice K. Yackle, L. A. Schwarz et al diag graph *Science* v355 no6332 p1411 Mr 31 2017

Respirators (Medical equipment)

Innovation M. Belfiore bw color *Bloomberg Businessweek* no4524 p37 My 29 2017

Respiratory diseases

See also

Legionnaires' disease

Respiratory infections

FINDINGS *Harper's Magazine* p96 S 2017

HYDRATION VITAL FOR SHIPPING FEVER RECOVERY C. Barakat and M. McCluskey color *Equus* no477 p18 Je 2017

Universal Appeal S. Oliynyk *Practical Horseman* v45 no8 p8 Ag 2017

Respiratory infections

See also

Cold (Disease)

Influenza

Legionnaires' disease

SARS (Disease)

NEWS FROM THE World of Medicine color *Reader's Digest* v190 no1134 p60 O 2017

Respiratory obstructions

See also

Obstructive lung diseases

Excess Gas in a Horse With Heaves M. ESSER *Horse & Rider* v55 no1 p14 N 2016

Respiratory organs

See also

Trachea

FESTIVE HOLIDAY SCENTS C. Cromer color *Amazing Wellness* v9 no6 p80 EarlyWint 2017

Respiratory therapy—Equipment & supplies

Our Doc Will See You Now R. Rajapaksa color *Health* v31 no1 p80 Ja 2017

Response rates

Longitudinal data from the Occupational Employment Statistics survey M. Dey and E. W. Handwerker bibl chart color graph *Monthly Labor Review* p1 O 2016

Responsibility

See also

Educational accountability

Social responsibility of business

3 Ways to Make Less Biased Decisions H. J. Ross *Harvard Business Review Digital Articles* p2 Ap 16 2015

Class Act S. TIGNOR *Tennis* v52 no6 p57 N/D 2016

Despite What Zappos Says, Middle Managers Still Matter J. Whitehurst *Harvard Business Review Digital Articles* p2 My 28 2015

DRIVERLESS DELAY P. HEANEY *Scientific American* v315 no3 p6 S 2016

Most Resolutions Fail Because They're Not Important Enough S. Friedman *Harvard Business Review Digital Articles* p2 Ja 14 2016

The Right Way to Hold People Accountable *Harvard Business Review Digital Articles* p2 Ja 11 2016

What It Really Means to Be a Chief Innovation Officer T. Wedell-Wedellsborg *Harvard Business Review Digital Articles* p2 D 5 2014

Responsibility—Moral & ethical aspects

Should I Out My Friend's 'Service Dog' Scam? K. A. Appiah *New York Times Magazine* p22 D 4 2016

Responsibility—Research

How Family Ties Keep You Going, In Sickness and In Health A. Sifferlin color *Time* v189 no5 p20 F 13 2017

Ress, Chad

OJAI VALLEY, CALIFORNIA *Harper's Magazine* p38 O 2017

Ressler, Steve

How Local Governments Are Using Technology to Serve Citizens Better *Harvard Business Review Digital Articles* p2 Ja 12 2016

Rest

See also

Relaxation (Health)

Sleep

BED REST W. CANNING color *Sail* v48 no9 p58 S 2017

The Pause THAT REFRESHES F. TORABI cartoon *O, The Oprah Magazine* p40 Ap 2017

SPRINTS J. WUEBBEN color *Muscle & Performance* v9 no9 p18 S 2017

REST, KATHLEEN

Chemical safety *Issues in Science & Technology* v33 no1 p17 Fall 2016

Rest periods

See also

Lunch breaks (Business)

School recess breaks

The Case for ... Time Off L. J. Wertheim and T. Keith color *Sports Illustrated* v127 no1 p28 Jl 3 2017

STILL GOING STRONG [Cover story] J. GALLOWAY cartoon *Runner's World* v51 no10 p42 N 2016

Restaurant advertising

The Sales of Summertime color *Consumer Reports* v82 no7 p67 Jl 2017

Restaurant costs

5 Cheap Things Restaurants Love to Overcharge You For J. Calfas color *Money* v46 no6 p15 Jl 2017

Restaurant design & construction

Cloud Nine D. COHN *Architectural Record* v205 no9 p92 S 2017

Hush Hush *Atlanta* v57 no5 p64 S 2017

KENGO KUMA INFUSES A MODEST RESTAURANT IN PORTLAND, OREGON, WITH THE CRAFT AND AURA OF JAPAN N. R. POLLOCK *Architectural Record* v205 no7 p43 Jl 2017

A Landmark Restaurant Redux W. MOONAN *Architectural Record* v205 no9 p52 S 2017

On a Clear Day N. R. POLLOCK color *Architectural Record* v205 no8 p102 Ag 2017

snapshot A. Klimoski *Architectural Record* v205 no9 p188 S 2017

Restaurant directories

DINING LISTINGS color *New Orleans Magazine* v51 no12 p118 O 2017

Restaurant employees

See also

Dishwashers (Persons)

THE TIME KEEPERS color *Los Angeles Magazine* v62 no7 p128 Jl 2017

Restaurant employees—United States

TABLE TALK J. Sidman *Washingtonian Magazine* v52 no9 p146 Je 2017

Restaurant kitchens

QUICK TAKES: First impressions of three restaurants A. Limpert and A. Spiegel *Washingtonian Magazine* v52 no11 p132 Ag 2017

Restaurant management

Cooking in My Own Voice: Chowder-soaked toast is a dish any chef would want to claim G. Hamilton *New York Times Magazine* p36 My 21 2017

FEAST IN NYC G. HAMILTON color *New York Times Magazine* p54 N 27 2016

Fine Dining for the Masses J. SUROWIECKI color *Bon Appetit* no11 p28 N 2017

Noah Sandoval C. SCHEDLER color *Chicago* v66 no6 p88 Je 2017

Restaurant menus

Augie's K. MONTGOMERY *Arizona Highways* v93 no9 p14 S 2017

Babylonstoren, South Africa S. KHAN color *Conde Nast Traveler* v51 no10 p60 N 2016

A Berry Good Idea A. MASON color *Bon Appetit* no8 p28 Ag 2017

BUDGET PICK: AUNTY JOY'S JAMAICAN KITCHEN C. SCHEDLER color *Chicago* v66 no9 p66 S 2017

Case Study: Which Customers Should This Restaurant Listen To? S. Puri, K. Khanzode et al *Harvard Business Review Digital Articles* p2 Mr 29 2016

Culinary Power Plants P. KUH *Los Angeles Magazine* p62 D 2016

THE FULL LEADED JACKET AT LEADBELLY A. Staples color *Sports Illustrated* v127 no5 p74 Ag 14 2017

Guilin Mi Fen Noodles M. J. WEEDMAN img *New York* v50 no16 p95 Ag 7 2017

Meat J. Forman color *New Orleans Magazine* v51 no4 p84 F 2017

News From the Kitchens R. Peyton color *New Orleans Magazine* v51 no4 p86 F 2017

Rebel Yell S. KROWIAK color *Indianapolis Monthly* p42 Ap 2017

REVIEWS: FIRST IMPRESSIONS J. RUBY color *Chicago* v66 no9 p70 S 2017

Strawberries R. Patronite and R. Raisfeld img *New York* v50 no18 p60 S 4 2017

TREND: NO LONGER JUST A SANDWICH N. SCHNITZLER color *Chicago* v66 no9 p64 S 2017

Restaurant Opportunities Centers United (Organization)

Saru Jayaraman J. Eidelson color *Bloomberg Businessweek* no4528 p76 Je 26 2017

Restaurant reviews

See also

Diners (Restaurants)—Evaluation

49th & Penn A. LYNCH color *Indianapolis Monthly* v42 no2 p38 O 2017

8 Arm *Atlanta* v57 no5 p85 S 2017

abcV C. Kormann color *New Yorker* v93 no15 p13 My 29 2017

ABSO LUTE ABRUZZO D. Prior color map *Conde Nast Traveler* v52 no9 p74 O 2017

ALL ABOARD: AT DTLA ARTS DISTRICT'S WESTBOUND, NEW FLAVORS MIX WITH SENTIMENTAL HISTORY B. WRIGHT color *Los Angeles Magazine* v62 no7 p53 Jl 2017

ALL ABOUT ANNIE J. BAINBRIDGE *Atlanta* v57 no2 p78 Je 2017

AMERICAN *Cincinnati Magazine* v50 no10 p127 Jl 2017

AMERICAN *Cincinnati Magazine* v50 p145 Ag 2017 Supplement

Atla S. Lyon color *New Yorker* v93 no16 p32 Je 5 2017

The Beatrice Inn S. Lyon color *New Yorker* v93 no22 p15 Jl 31 2017

Belgian Bites M. MCLAUGHLIN color *Indianapolis Monthly* v41 no2 p39 S 2017

The Best New RESTAURANTS IN AMERICA, 2017 J. GORDINIER bw color *Esquire* p62 N 2017

BEST NEW RESTAURANTS J. Bainbridge, C. Lauterbach et al *Atlanta* v57 no5 p78 S 2017

Big Earl's Greasy Eats: Although its building is listed on the National Register of Historic Places, the food at Big Earl's is anything but dated. The burgers are made with Harris Ranch or Kobe beef, and the delicious home made buns are baked daily N. B. TRULSSON *Arizona Highways* v93 no11 p12 N 2017

BLOCK PARTY: Everything you need to know about Annandale's hot new food hall J. Sidman and A. Spiegel *Washingtonian Magazine* v52 no8 p128 My 2017

Bobby D's BBQ K. VAUGHN color *Arizona Highways* v93 no5 p12 My 2017

Brasa Bound J. FORMAN and E. CARO color *New Orleans Magazine* v51 no12 p110 O 2017

Brunches by the Bunches J. BENSON color *New Orleans Magazine* v51 no7 p60 My 2017

Brunch, Lunch, Lanche, and Dinner: Four Lisboan chefs on where to eat four Lisboan meals img *New York* v50 no9 p65 My 1 2017

Bucktown Nouveau [Cover story] J. FORMAN color *New Orleans Magazine* v52 no1 p102 S 2017

BUDGET PICK: AUNTY JOY'S JAMAICAN KITCHEN C. SCHEDLER color *Chicago* v66 no9 p66 S 2017

CAFÉ DE FLOREA: Chef Mike Florea whips up phenomenal farm-to-table fare at MARIBELLE'S *Cincinnati Magazine* v50 p138 Ag 2017 Supplement

CAJUN/CARIBBEAN *Cincinnati Magazine* v50 no8 p116 My 2017

CALCULATED RISK J. RUBY color *Chicago* v66 no10 p56 O 2017

Cannes Do!: French burgers that rival the fries A. BRANDT *Cincinnati Magazine* v50 no10 p120 Jl 2017

Carbon Beach P. GUZMÁN color *Conde Nast Traveler* v52 no7 p32 Ag 2017

CHAIN REACTION: At the Smith, the menu aims to please all tastes A. Limpert *Washingtonian Magazine* v52 no8 p125 My 2017

Cheers for Speer P. SHARPE *Texas Monthly* v45 no6 p30 Je 2017

Cheeseboat D. Kortava color *New Yorker* v93 no28 p15 S 18 2017

CHINESE *Cincinnati Magazine* v50 p146 Ag 2017 Supplement

Chouchou Jiayang Fan color *New Yorker* v93 no20 p21 Jl 10 2017

Chucktown Fresh M. ROTHSTEIN and N. Richardson color *Bon Appetit* no8 p48 Ag 2017

Clean Eats: A new wave transforms health food from bland to bold [Cover story] J. Forman color *New Orleans Magazine* v51 no10 p172 Ag 2017

CLUB MED A. AHUJA *Cincinnati Magazine* p108 Je 2017

THE COMFORTS OF PASTA G. Kurz color *Los Angeles Magazine* v62 no10 p14 O 2017

Crudité at Bar One Fourteen *Indianapolis Monthly* v40 no11 p44 Jl 2017

CUBA FEASTS M. Ruhlman color *Conde Nast Traveler* v52 no9 p100 O 2017

'CUES AND Brews A. SELBY *Atlanta* v57 no2 p126 Je 2017

CULINARY SURPRISES S. Katzman and L. A. Addington color *Missouri Life* v44 no2 p92 Ap 2017

Delightful fusion of worldly food in Omaha S. W. KANSTEINER color *Nebraska Life* v21 no4 p50 Jl/Ag 2017

DIM SUM AT BEST BBQ J. ZYMAN *Atlanta* v57 no3 p54 Jl 2017

DINING GUIDE *Atlanta* v57 no3 p163 Jl 2017

DINING GUIDE *Cincinnati Magazine* v50 no12 p107 S 2017

Dinner and a Show B. PHILLIPS *Texas Monthly* v45 no8 p20 Ag 2017

DOWNTOWN *Indianapolis Monthly* v40 no11 p112 Jl 2017

DOWNTOWN *Indianapolis Monthly* v42 no2 p114 O 2017

EAST *Indianapolis Monthly* v42 no2 p120 O 2017

EAT IT ON A STICK C. SCHEDLER color *Chicago* v66 no7 p58 Jl 2017

ECLECTIC *Cincinnati Magazine* v50 no10 p128 Jl 2017

ECLECTIC *Cincinnati Magazine* v50 p147 Ag 2017 Supplement

EL FLORIDITA #2 AT 8ARM J. BAINBRIDGE *Atlanta* v57 no4 p38 Ag 2017

THE EMBARGO DIET N. Sneider color *Atlantic* v319 no5 p18 Je 2017

An Empire Built on Tacos: With his posh new midtown Empellón, Alex Stupak means business A. PLATT img *New York* v50 no11 p102 My 29 2017

Extremely Fine And Incredibly Close G. FERGUSON *Los Angeles Magazine* v62 no9 p52 S 2017

Family Dinner: A follow-up to the Fortville original, FoxGardin Family Kitchen delivers more top-nosh grub J. Spalding *Indianapolis Monthly* v40 no10 p44 Je 2017

FEASTING AND FROLICKING J. Benson color *Louisiana Life* v37 no5 p50 My/Je 2017

Flora Bar D. Wenger color *New Yorker* v93 no11 p15 My 1 2017

FOOD *Cincinnati Magazine* v50 no8 p48 My 2017

Food & Drink *Virginia Living* p145 2017 Best 20of Virginia

Food Terminal J. ZYMAN *Atlanta* v57 no2 p60 Je 2017

Four-Leaf Dining and Drinking J. Passov color *Golf Magazine* v59 no7 p94 Jl 2017

FRENCH *Cincinnati Magazine* v50 p147 Ag 2017 Supplement

FRESH ON THE SCENE A. Spiegel *Washingtonian Magazine* v52 no9 p148 Je 2017

FRESH ON THE SCENE: The new and exciting in the food world-ranked! A. Spiegel *Washingtonian Magazine* v52 no8 p136 My 2017

Fry Away S. Krowiak *Indianapolis Monthly* v40 no10 p39 Je 2017

GENIE IN A BOTTLE J. Gordinier cartoon color *Esquire* p42 S 2017

Going Up P. SHARPE *Texas Monthly* v45 no9 p18 S 2017

GREAT NEW RESTAURANTS *Washingtonian Magazine* v52 no12 p89 S 2017

The Grill img *New York* v50 no9 p76 My 1 2017

HEAR THEM ROAR J. RUBY color *Chicago* v66 no6 p52 Je 2017

Hello, Darkness J. STEIN *Los Angeles Magazine* v62 no9 p49 S 2017

Helpful High Street Shops *British Heritage Travel* v38 no4 p17 Jl/Ag 2017

HERO WORSHIP G. SNYDER color *Los Angeles Magazine* v62 no10 p48 O 2017

Hotel de Russie, Rome A. WHITTLE color *Conde Nast Traveler* v52 no7 p36 Ag 2017

The Hot List P. POLLACK color *Chicago* v66 no6 p51 Je 2017

The Hot List P. POLLACK color *Chicago* v66 no8 p53 Ag 2017

HOT SPOT T. P. Bowles color *Conde Nast Traveler* v52 no9 p88 O 2017

How the Shishito Conquered New York img *New York* v50 no10 p79 My 15 2017

I'll Get the Next One: If someone else is paying, by all means try the new version of the Four Seasons Grill Room A. PLATT img *New York* v50 no16 p94 Ag 7 2017

INDIAN *Cincinnati Magazine* v50 no8 p121 My 2017

INDIAN *Cincinnati Magazine* v50 p148 Ag 2017 Supplement

Into the Fold A downtown remake as simple and straightforward as its name. The Taco Shop does one thing and does it well J. SPALDING *Indianapolis Monthly* v40 no11 p42 Jl 2017

ITALIAN *Cincinnati Magazine* v50 p149 Ag 2017 Supplement

JAI HO *Atlanta* v57 no2 p58 Je 2017

Jamaica Style J. Forman color *New Orleans Magazine* v51 no9 p80 Jl 2017

Jean-Georges's Double Life: Opening two restaurants at once yields mixed results A. PLATT img *New York* v50 no18 p58 S 4 2017

KNOTTY BUT NICE T. KIRTS color *Indianapolis Monthly* v42 no2 p43 O 2017

LA GUNS J. Benson color *Louisiana Life* v37 no6 p50 Jl/Ag 2017

La Morada N. Niarchos color *New Yorker* v93 no30 p15 O 2 2017

The Last Bento-Ya In Boyle Heights P. KUH *Los Angeles Magazine* v62 no9 p116 S 2017

LATE-NIGHT Bites K. SMITH *Atlanta* v57 no2 p128 Je 2017

Lighten Up, New York M. YOUNG color *Bon Appetit* v62 no7 p46 Jl 2017

THE LIST HOT *Los Angeles Magazine* v62 no9 p118 S 2017

Magnolia Room Cafeteria C. LAUTERBACH *Atlanta* v57 no3 p58 Jl 2017

Malta Made Me Do It M. Peters color *Conde Nast Traveler* v52 no9 p45 O 2017

A Mano C. LAUTERBACH *Atlanta* v57 no6 p60 O 2017

MEATY MATTERS: Red Apron Burger Bar is doing wonders with Virginia beef a. Limpert *Washingtonian Magazine* v52 no8 p132 My 2017

MEDITERRANEAN *Cincinnati Magazine* v50 no8 p123 My 2017

Mettä J. Fan color *New Yorker* v93 no27 p18 S 11 2017

MGM RESORT EXPERIENCES B. Wright color *Los Angeles Magazine* v62 no10 p109 O 2017

Miami Heat E. S. BENN color *Bon Appetit* v62 no10 p56 O 2017

MINOR SENSATIONS: Find tender smoked brisket, craft beer kiosks and deep bistory at Virginia's 9 minor league ballparks G. MARTIN *Virginia Living* v15 no4 p21 Je 2017

MIRABELLE A. Limpert *Washingtonian Magazine* v52 no9 p139 Je 2017

Modern Mexican: Atla is designed for how New Yorkers eat now R. RAISFELD and R. PATRONITE img *New York* v50 no15 p50 Jl 24 2017

Monroe B. Cooper color *New Yorker* v93 no13 p28 My 15 2017

MR. MOMO: A former Blue Duck Tavern server brings a taste of Nepal to Del Ray A. Limpert *Washingtonian Magazine* v53 no1 p146 O 2017

New Flame: With Stella, Neal Brown gets his groove back, quietly serving rustic Southern European food cooked by open fire. That's hot J. SPALDING color *Indianapolis Monthly* v41 no2 p44 S 2017

News From the Kitchen R. PEYTON color *New Orleans Magazine* v51 no12 p112 O 2017

News From the Kitchens: Public Service, Piece of Meat Butcher & Restaurant, Sprout and Press R. Peyton color *New Orleans Magazine* v51 no10 p174 Ag 2017

News From the Kitchens R. Peyton color *New Orleans Magazine* v51 no8 p102 Je 2017

Noble Parentage D. Breshears color *Missouri Life* v44 no2 p98 Ap 2017

NORTHEAST *Indianapolis Monthly* v40 no11 p121 Jl 2017

NORTHEAST *Indianapolis Monthly* v42 no2 p123 O 2017

NORTH SUBURBAN *Indianapolis Monthly* v40 no11 p119 Jl 2017

NORTH SUBURBAN *Indianapolis Monthly* v42 no2 p120 O 2017

Novel Noodles: Two new shops shine a light on the seldom-seen Yunnanese rice variety R. RAISFELD and R. PATRONITE img *New York* v50 no9 p74 My 1 2017

OFF the BEATEN PATH N. MARINO, J. NELSON et al color *GQ: Gentlemen's Quarterly* v97 no9 p154 S 2017

The Other Drinkable Rye: Old-world kvass gets a fresh Brooklyn spin R. Patronite and R. Raisfeld img *New York* v50 no18 p62 S 4 2017

THE OTTOLENGHI GUIDE TO EATING AND DRINKING YOUR WAY AROUND GEORGIA color *Conde Nast Traveler* v52 no9 p40 O 2017

Otway S. Lyon color *New Yorker* v93 no18 p15 Je 26 2017

THE OUT OF TOWNERS P. GIANOPULOS color *Chicago* v66 no11 p54 N 2017

PARTY CITY J. DRILLING color *Cincinnati Magazine* v51 no1 p153 O 2017

PENNY'S NEW FAVE color *Chicago* v66 no8 p58 Ag 2017

THE PERFECT NIGHT OUT: GQ'S BEST NEW RESTAU-

RANTS 2017 B. Martin color *GQ: Gentlemen's Quarterly* v97 no5 p88 My 2017

Pinoy Power: AT LASA, TWO BROTHERS DELIVER FILIPINO COMFORT WITH CALIFORNIA STYLE G. SNYDER *Los Angeles Magazine* v62 no9 p54 S 2017

Pith E. Allen color *New Yorker* v93 no14 p23 My 22 2017

PLEASE ADVISE A. AHUJA *Cincinnati Magazine* v50 no8 p99 My 2017

Pure Bar J. DRILLING *Cincinnati Magazine* p114 Je 2017

Purple Reign B. Smith color *Chicago* v66 no11 p74 N 2017

Q BY PETER CHANG: The famed Chinese chef puts down roots in Bethesda A. Limpert *Washingtonian Magazine* v53 no1 p143 O 2017

QUICK TAKES: First impressions of three new seafood-focused restaurants A. Limpert *Washingtonian Magazine* v53 no1 p148 O 2017

QUICK TAKES: First impressions of three restaurants A. Limpert and A. Spiegel *Washingtonian Magazine* v52 no11 p132 Ag 2017

Red Meat, Brown Liquor, Tight Squeeze A. PLATT img *New York* v50 no8 p109 Ap 17 2017

Restaurant GUIDE color map *Indianapolis Monthly* v41 no2 p154 S 2017

REVIEWS: FIRST IMPRESSIONS J. RUBY color *Chicago* v66 no9 p70 S 2017

Riviera Revival A. LOBRANO color *Conde Nast Traveler* v52 no7 p34 Ag 2017

ROOM SERVICE: COPPIN'S built a regional menu. Will locavores come? A. AHUJA *Cincinnati Magazine* v50 no10 p118 Jl 2017

THE ROOM TO BOOK A. SESSA color *Conde Nast Traveler* v52 no10 p36 N 2017

Safari N. Niarchos color *New Yorker* v93 no26 p17 S 4 2017

Sauce Boss J. K. WOLFE *Cincinnati Magazine* v50 p141 Ag 2017 Supplement

Secret Sauce: WHAT MAKES THE BOLOGNESE AT STEVE SAMSON'S ROSSOBLU SO GOOD? P. KUH *Los Angeles Magazine* v62 no9 p53 S 2017

Sen Sakana C. Kormann color *New Yorker* v93 no32 p18 O 16 2017

Setting the Mood O. Strand color *Vogue* v207 no7 p112 Jl 2017

Simple Pleasures E. WARTZMAN color *Bon Appetit* no8 p22 Ag 2017

south park & historic core color *Los Angeles Magazine* v62 no7 p72 Jl 2017

SOUTH SUBURBAN *Indianapolis Monthly* v40 no11 p126 Jl 2017

SOUTH SUBURBAN *Indianapolis Monthly* v42 no2 p126 O 2017

Space Oddity G. SNYDER color *Los Angeles Magazine* v62 no10 p40 O 2017

Spice Trade J. Forman color *New Orleans Magazine* v51 no7 p84 My 2017

Spice World A. KONERMANN color *Cincinnati Magazine* v51 no1 p156 O 2017

SPLIT DECISION J. RUBY color *Chicago* v66 no7 p46 Jl 2017

Sprouted Corn Cavatelli S. BAHR color *Indianapolis Monthly* v41 no2 p46 S 2017

SQUARE MEALS T. Kirts *Indianapolis Monthly* v40 no10 p40 Je 2017

STOMP TOWN T. KIRTS *Indianapolis Monthly* v12 no40 p44 Ag 2017

Sunchoke, Kumquat, Black Cardamom img *New York* v50 no11 p104 My 29 2017

TABLE TALK color *New Orleans Magazine* v51 no12 p109 O 2017

Take a Left At the Fork A. WHITTLE bw color map *Conde Nast Traveler* v52 no9 p50 O 2017

TEXAS WELCOME H. Anders bw color *Louisiana Life* v38 no1 p48 S/O 2017

THAI *Cincinnati Magazine* v50 p150 Ag 2017 Supplement

There Goes the Neighborhood Restaurant: A regular's lament M. SHERATON img *New York* v50 no9 p76 My 1 2017

The Toasted Owl A. McGIVNEY *Arizona Highways* v93 no8 p12 Ag 2017

Toast of the Town S. KROWIAK color *Indianapolis Monthly* v42 no2 p41 O 2017

Top Shelf: Celeb chef Ed Lee has a new burgers-and-bourbon spot. Let's go eat in Louisville M. C. Austin *Indianapolis Monthly* v40 no10 p36 Je 2017

Tree House J. Drilling *Cincinnati Magazine* v50 no12 p103 S 2017

Turkish Delight J. DRILLING color *Cincinnati Magazine* v51 no1 p157 O 2017

The Underground Gourmet Digest img *New York* v50 no10 p78 My 15 2017

The Underground Gourmet Digest R. Patronite and R. Raisfeld img *New York* v50 no18 p62 S 4 2017

Upbeat C. Lauterbach *Atlanta* v57 no5 p60 S 2017

URBAN COUNTRY CLUB P. POLLACK color *Chicago* v66 no11 p49 N 2017

V8 Vegan Burger T. KIRTS color *Indianapolis Monthly* v42 no2 p48 O 2017

Variety on Piety J. Forman color *New Orleans Magazine* v51 no8 p100 Je 2017

Varuni Napoli C. LAUTERBACH *Atlanta* v57 no4 p44 Ag 2017

VENKMAN'S PATTY MELT J. ZYMAN *Atlanta* v57 no2 p52 Je 2017

WAYDOWN C. SCHEDLER color *Chicago* v66 no11 p56 N 2017

What a Catch! S. KROWIAK *Indianapolis Monthly* v40 no11 p37 Jl 2017

WHERE IN THE WORLD TO EAT A. Helou, P. Guzmán et al cartoon color *Conde Nast Traveler* v52 no9 p53 O 2017

Where the Plate Is the Canvas M. BUSICO color *Los Angeles Magazine* v62 no7 p65 Jl 2017

Where to Eat Now: OUR CAREFULLY CURATED GUIDE TO THE BEST RESTAURANTS IN TEXAS AND SOME NOTEWORTHY NEW ARRIVALS *Texas Monthly* v45 no7 p102 Jl 2017

Where to Eat Now *Texas Monthly* v45 no6 p132 Je 2017

Where to Eat Now *Texas Monthly* v45 no9 p24 S 2017

WURST BEHAVIOR A. Ahuja *Cincinnati Magazine* v50 no12 p100 S 2017

Young Lettuces img *New York* v50 no13 p57 Je 26 2017

Zero Forks Given: Forget what your mother taught you and roll up your sleeves; these dishesare meant to be eaten with nothing but your hands M. VEGA *Atlanta* v57 no4 p35 Ag 2017

Restaurants

        See also

    Barbecue restaurants

    Chain restaurants

    Delicatessens

    Diners (Restaurants)

    Ice cream parlors

    Seafood restaurants

    Steak houses

48 hours in VANCOUVER S. Walter color *Good Housekeeping* v264 no2 p35 F 2017

ARE YOU Worthy OF THIS MAN'S Coffee? C. SCHEDLER cartoon color *Chicago* v66 no5 p104 My 2017

Ayesha's Falafel img *New York* v50 no7 p66 Ap 3 2017

Backyard Billfish J. BROWNLEE color *Power & Motoryacht* v34 no10 p46 O 2017

Beef, Buns & Brews Perryville J. B. Patton color *Missouri Life* v44 no3 p78 My 2017

BEST BETS img *New York* v49 no22 p72 O 31 2016

Best Of Los Angeles *Los Angeles Magazine* p25 Ag 2017

Better Fish in the Sea A. STANEK color *Bon Appetit* no8 p20 Ag 2017

Bon Appétit M. Rubino *Indianapolis Monthly* p10 My 2017

Branching Out S. KROWIAK *Indianapolis Monthly* v40 no3 p54 N 2016

THE CALL OF THE NORTH R. O'CONNOR color *Chicago* v66 no7 p13 Jl 2017

The Cheesecake Factory P. Kita color *Men's Health* v32 no3 p70 Ap 2017

COMING TO AMERICA A. RAPOPORT bw *Bon Appetit* v62 no2 p12 Mr 2017

THE COUNTER JOINT AS COMMUNITY BOOSTER R. WILLIAMS bw *Bon Appetit* v62 no2 p70 Mr 2017

CUBA FEASTS M. Ruhlman color *Conde Nast Traveler* v52 no9 p100 O 2017

CURD APPEAL T. KIRTS *Indianapolis Monthly* p39 F 2017

DAFT ABOUT DILL M. Allan, Á. Snorradóttir et al *Iceland Review* v55 no3 p46 My/Je 2017

DINING GUIDE *Cincinnati Magazine* p117 Je 2017

DINING GUIDE M. Cameran color *New Orleans Magazine* v51 no4 p92 F 2017

DOWN SHIFTING A. Postman color map *Conde Nast Traveler* v52 no10 p122 N 2017

EAT OUT WITH ZERO REGRET *Health* v30 no10 p23 D 2016

Fish Tacos Were Just the Beginning K. SOLLER color map *Bon Appetit* v62 no6 p52 Je 2017

FIVE REASONS TO LOVE... MARIETTA L. MOWRY *Atlanta* v56 no8 p66 D 2016

FOODSTUFFS J. ZYMAN, C. VAN DUSEN et al *Atlanta* v56 no9 p54 Ja 2017

Future World: Food K. DE SEVE color *National Geographic Kids* no472 p24 Ag 2017

Granny Ambition: 22nd Street Diner gives comfort food a good, old-fashioned schooling J. SPALDING *Indianapolis Monthly* p50 N 2017

The Gratitude Meter Z. Donaldson color *O, The Oprah Magazine* p24 My 2017

Greencastle: Reasons to cheer the charming college town this month K. F. WELLS *Indianapolis Monthly* p40 N 2017

How One Chef Created THE WORLD'S BEST BOWL OF RAMEN E. Lin color *Los Angeles Magazine* v62 no10 p4 O 2017

HOW TO SOUND LIKE A SERIOUS GASTRONOME J. Gordinier cartoon *Esquire* p121 S 2017

I Got the Powder C. KWAK color *Bon Appetit* v62 no4 p22 Ap 2017

AN INDONESIAN FEAST J. R. FULLER color *Chicago* v66 no7 p44 Jl 2017

Instagram Feeding Frenzies J. SCHERER *Los Angeles Magazine* p42 My 2017

Jim Stacy, 2.0 3.0 4.0 C. BETHEA *Atlanta* v56 no10 p53 F 2017

The Limits of Café Urbanism A. Ehrenhalt *Governing* v30 no6 p14 Mr 2017

Living Out Loud: On good food, great reads, and strong women G. DUNCAN, M. E. ZIEGLER et al color *O, The Oprah Magazine* p20 S 2017

LOG HOME ROAD TRIP New England bw color map *Log Home Living* v34 no6 p56 Ag 2017

THE LOOK BOOK A. SWERDLOFF img *New York* p51 F 20 2017

Man On Fire P. KUH color *Los Angeles Magazine* v62 no10 p44 O 2017

Meeting Place J. ANDREWS *South Dakota Magazine* v32 no6 p36 Mr/Ap 2017

My Place color *Vanity Fair* v59 no7 p46 Summ 2017

Near Southside J. BREAL *Texas Monthly* v45 no1 p28 Ja 2017

NEW COURSE: A fresh start awaits pastry chef Pete Schmutte after five years spent preparing finales at Cerulean S. KROWIAK *Indianapolis Monthly* p48 N 2017

New Orleans Picks *Opera News* v81 no6 p17 D 2016

NORTHERN MOROCCO Y. EDWARDS and A. WHITTLE color map *Conde Nast Traveler* v52 no4 p64 Ap 2017

Paowalla S. Lyon color *New Yorker* v93 no29 p33 S 25 2017

PENNY'S NEW FAVE color *Chicago* v66 no7 p40 Jl 2017

Prime Rib img *New York* v50 no7 p69 Ap 3 2017

Q + A J. Gilbert *Cincinnati Magazine* v50 no10 p32 Jl 2017

Research: When a Retail Store Closes, Crime Increases Around It T. Y. Chang and M. Jacobson *Harvard Business Review Digital Articles* p2 Je 29 2017

reviews. CROSSROADS D. Wasserman *Vegetarian Journal* v35 no4 p30 2016

Route 66 J. BREAL *Texas Monthly* v45 no3 p38 Mr 2017

Salem, Massachusetts: Maritime history and witchy lore exist side by side in one of the most idiosyncratic towns in the country A. GRAVES *Yankee* v81 no5 p70 S/O 2017

THE SALT LINE: Chef Kyle Bailey makes a splash right next door to Nats Park A. Limpert *Washingtonian Magazine* v52 no11 p130 Ag 2017

September F. ESKER color *New Orleans Magazine* v52 no1 p26 S 2017

SPENT D. Garner color *Esquire* p72 S 2017

STRESS-BUSTING VACATIONS S. BLOCK color *Kiplinger's Personal Finance* v71 no7 p62 Jl 2017

THE SYMMETRY OF 50 S. FENNESSY *Atlanta* v57 no2 p18 Je 2017

THE TEXANIST J. THOMAS *Texas Monthly* v45 no8 p148 Ag 2017

THAI SOCIETY T. KIRTS *Indianapolis Monthly* p46 N 2017

That Sublime Slice of American Cheese J. SCHERER *Los Angeles Magazine* p46 Ja 2017

Tiki Torch P. LISTON *Indianapolis Monthly* v40 no4 p49 D 2016

The truth about your takeout color *Health* v31 no8 p49 O 2017

Turkish "Disco" Pistachios img *New York* v49 no21 p77 O 17 2016

Turning the Tables *Conde Nast Traveler* v52 no9 p12 O 2017

Unleashed cartoon *National Geographic Kids* no475 p34 N 2017

UPDATES: VEGAN FOOD IN CHAIN RESTAURANTS *Vegetarian Journal* v36 no3 p7 2017

You've Never Seen a Pork Chop Like This A. GOMEZ color *Bon Appetit* v62 no2 p71 Mr 2017

Restaurants maintenance & repair

Catalytic Converters: Emily Wolff and Paul Weckman aim to stabilize Covington's MainStrasse one property at time A. BRANDT *Cincinnati Magazine* v50 no11 p80 Ag 2017

Restaurants sanitation

City Governments Are Using Yelp to Tell You Where Not to Eat M. Luca and L. Lowe *Harvard Business Review Digital Articles* p2 F 12 2015

OF MICE AND MEAT R. O'CONNOR color *Chicago* v66 no10 p34 O 2017

Restaurants—Arizona

Gourmet Girls K. MONTGOMERY *Arizona Highways* v93 no3 p12 Mr 2017

Simpson Hotel K. MONTGOMERY *Arizona Highways* v93 no10 p14 O 2017

Table 10 K. MONTGOMERY *Arizona Highways* v93 no1 p12 Ja 2017

The Toasted Owl A. McGIVNEY *Arizona Highways* v93 no8 p12 Ag 2017

Restaurants—Arkansas

Ozark Magic J. Jennings color *Southern Living* v52 no9 p63 S 2017

Restaurants—Awards

FRESH ON THE SCENE A. Spiegel *Washingtonian Magazine* v52 no1 p150 O 2016

Restaurants—California

THE BEST LITTLE BIKE TOUR IN DTLA *Los Angeles Magazine* v61 no11 p62 N 2016

Cambria M. JAFFE *Los Angeles Magazine* p90 Ap 2017

CHANGING COURSE T. Adler color *Vogue* v207 no9 p724 S 2017

THE COMFORTS OF PASTA G. Kurz color *Los Angeles Magazine* v62 no10 p14 O 2017

FIESTA TIME I. Edwards color *Sunset* v238 no3 p4 Mr 2017

From Dawn Till Dusk A. WANG color *Los Angeles Magazine* v62 no10 p46 O 2017

HERO WORSHIP G. SNYDER color *Los Angeles Magazine* v62 no10 p48 O 2017

High Flying J. SCHERER *Los Angeles Magazine* v61 no11 p60 N 2016

THE HOT LIST color *Los Angeles Magazine* v62 no10 p160 O 2017

THE HOT LIST *Los Angeles Magazine* p116 Ag 2017

LAND OF THE LEAF EATERS L. BANS color *Bon Appetit* no1 p80 F 2017

Mapping It Out: Downtown L.A B. HENNEMUTH cartoon *Vanity Fair* p98 Hollywood 2017 Supplement

Mesa Verde Restaurant J. Lewis color *Vegetarian Times* v43 no2 p20 N/D 2016

My Place color *Vanity Fair* p91 Hollywood 2017 Supplement

THE PERFECT BITE: PORK BELLY WITH FAVA LEAF MOLE color *Los Angeles Magazine* v62 no7 p94 Jl 2017

The Pita Rising P. KUH *Los Angeles Magazine* v62 no6 p42 Je 2017

Space Oddity G. SNYDER color *Los Angeles Magazine* v62 no10 p40 O 2017

Stirring The Pot L. BALLA *Los Angeles Magazine* p62 Mr 2017

Where the Plate Is the Canvas M. BUSICO color *Los Angeles*

Magazine v62 no7 p65 Jl 2017

Restaurants—California—Los Angeles

ALL ABOARD: AT DTLA ARTS DISTRICT'S WESTBOUND, NEW FLAVORS MIX WITH SENTIMENTAL HISTORY B. WRIGHT color *Los Angeles Magazine* v62 no7 p53 Jl 2017

THE BEST NEW RESTAURANTS P. KUH, J. SCHERER et al *Los Angeles Magazine* p86 Ja 2017

Change Thy Ways: A LITTLE FRIENDLY ADVICE FOR NEW YORK CHEFS OPENING OUTPOSTS HERE J. STEIN color *Los Angeles Magazine* v62 no7 p33 Jl 2017

A coffee shop for Christ color *U.S. Catholic* v82 no6 p8 Je 2017

Eat *Los Angeles Magazine* p39 Ag 2017

Group Effort L. BARGAR SUTER *Los Angeles Magazine* v62 no6 p40 Je 2017

THE HOT LIST color *Los Angeles Magazine* v62 no7 p86 Jl 2017

THE HOT LIST *Los Angeles Magazine* p120 My 2017

Majestic Baja P. KUH *Los Angeles Magazine* v62 no6 p36 Je 2017

Taste The New Hope L. B. SUTER *Los Angeles Magazine* p48 My 2017

This Food Podcast Turns It Up to 11 H. EATON *Los Angeles Magazine* p66 D 2016

Wait in Line? I Can't Even J. STEIN *Los Angeles Magazine* p60 D 2016

WATER GRILL J. Lurie *Los Angeles Magazine* p4 Ap 2017

WOLFGANG GOES ROGUE S. Marikar color *Bloomberg Businessweek* no4520 p71 My 1 2017

Restaurants—California—Napa Valley

Simple Pleasures E. WARTZMAN color *Bon Appetit* no8 p22 Ag 2017

Restaurants—California—San Francisco

COAST TO COAST J. Steingarten color *Vogue* v207 no11 p208 N 2017

Fine Dining for the Masses J. SUROWIECKI color *Bon Appetit* no11 p28 N 2017

Restaurants—Canada

Fine dining at the Legion J. MARKUSOFF color *Maclean's* v130 no9 p14 O 2017

THE FRASERHOOD SHORT LIST color *Conde Nast Traveler* v52 no5 p60 My 2017

Stuck in the craw J. RICHLER color *Maclean's* v130 no3 p70 Ap 2017

There Goes The Neighborhood H. WALLACE color *Conde Nast Traveler* v52 no5 p60 My 2017

Restaurants—Connecticut

happy place P. GUGLIELMETTI color *Better Homes & Gardens* v95 no11 p18 N 2017

Old Wethersfield, Connecticut A. GRAVES color map *Yankee* p68 Mr 2017

Restaurants—Customer services

THE CHRISTIANE CHRONICLES C. LAUTERBACH *Atlanta* v56 no8 p76 D 2016

EAT, DRINK & BE FRIENDLY S. DANLER cartoon *O, The Oprah Magazine* p100 Ap 2017

FEAST IN NYC G. HAMILTON color *New York Times Magazine* p54 N 27 2016

Restaurants—Design & construction

Second Course W. MOONAN *Architectural Record* v205 no4 p166 Ap 2017

Set the Stage S. AMELAR *Architectural Record* v205 no4 p158 Ap 2017

Restaurants—Economic aspects

DINING GUIDE M. Cameran color *New Orleans Magazine* v51 no2 p92 D 2016

Restaurants—Economic conditions

WHAT'S EATING CLEVELAND PARK? Explaining an upscale neighborhood's restaurant die-off J. SIDMAN *Washingtonian Magazine* v52 no11 p20 Ag 2017

Restaurants—England

WHITBY *British Heritage Travel* v38 no1 p24 Ja/F 2017

Restaurants—Evaluation

See also
Diners (Restaurants)—Evaluation

100 VERY BEST RESTAURANTS [Cover story] *Washingtonian Magazine* v52 no5 p70 F 2017

1633 N. Niarchos color *New Yorker* v92 no33 p20 O 17 2016

2017 DINING GUIDE WHERE TO EAT P. POLLACK bw color

Chicago v65 no12 p(Sp)1 D 2016

50 Best, Refreshed C. KUMMER, C. LAUTERBACH et al *Atlanta* v56 no11 p2 Mr 2017

ABOVE AND BEYOND M. FERNANDEZ *Indianapolis Monthly* v40 no7 p72 Mr 2017

THE AFTER-AFTER-PARTY *Indianapolis Monthly* p67 F 2017

AFTER HOURS J. Sidman *Washingtonian Magazine* v52 no2 p261 N 2016

an after noon in JERSEY CITY color *Good Housekeeping* v263 no5 p44 N 2016

Agern C. Kormann color *New Yorker* v92 no45 p19 Ja 16 2017

ALL RISE T. KIRTS *Indianapolis Monthly* v40 no3 p56 N 2016

Antichuco de Pulpo *Indianapolis Monthly* v40 no3 p61 N 2016

ATLANTA MAGAZINE DIGITAL *Atlanta* v56 no12 p8 Ap 2017

Audubon Road K. FRANZMAN color *Indianapolis Monthly* p32 Ap 2017

Augustine B. Cooper color *New Yorker* v93 no7 p27 Ap 3 2017

Austin *Texas Monthly* v45 no3 p129 Mr 2017

BAO, WOW! J. ZYMAN *Atlanta* v56 no12 p78 Ap 2017

Barbecue Italian Style D. VAUGHN *Texas Monthly* v45 no4 p34 Ap 2017

THE Beaches WE RETURN TO AGAIN AND AGAIN... bw color *Conde Nast Traveler* v52 no1 p70 Ja 2017

Bean Counter J. K. WOLFE *Cincinnati Magazine* v50 no6 p145 Mr 2017

Beginnings: A Restaurant with A Literary Bent J. Maher color *Publishers Weekly* v263 no43 p6 O 24 2016

Behemoth 'Coffee Burger' Rides Again in Sioux County N. Buck color *Nebraska Life* v21 no1 p15 Ja/F 2017

BEST IN BIRD P. GIANOPULOS color *Chicago* v65 no11 p58 N 2016

THE BEST LITTLE BIKE TOUR IN DTLA *Los Angeles Magazine* v61 no11 p62 N 2016

Best New Restaurants L. Bailey, K. Kendall et al *Indianapolis Monthly* p58 My 2017

THE BEST NEW RESTAURANTS P. KUH, J. SCHERER et al *Los Angeles Magazine* p86 Ja 2017

BEST OF THE WEST C. Dash, S. Granada et al color *Sunset* v238 no5 p11 My 2017

BEST OF WASHINGTON HALL OF FAME *Washingtonian Magazine* v52 no2 p302 N 2016

BEST POOR BOY E. Laborde *New Orleans Magazine* v51 no2 p16 D 2016

THE BIG CELEBRATION *Indianapolis Monthly* p63 F 2017

BITE THEIR TONGUES P. GIANOPULOS color *Chicago* v66 no3 p66 Mr 2017

BLUE PLATE SPECIALS *Cincinnati Magazine* v50 no2 p65 N 2016

Boho Bistro J. DRILLING *Cincinnati Magazine* v50 no6 p142 Mr 2017

Brazilian for Breakfast B. Doherty img *New York* v49 no19 p77 S 19 2016

BREAKFAST BOMBS *Washingtonian Magazine* v52 no1 p88 O 2016

Breakfast Town M. RIGBY color *Bon Appetit* v62 no2 p46 Mr 2017

Brennan's R. Peyton color *New Orleans Magazine* v51 no2 p66 D 2016

Brooklyn Pastoral A. PLATT img *New York* v49 no23 p58 N 14 2016

BRUNCH OF CHAMPIONS *Indianapolis Monthly* v40 no7 p58 Mr 2017

BRUNCH, YOUR WAY C. SCHEDLER cartoon color *Chicago* v66 no5 p65 My 2017

Brush Sushi Izakaya J. ZYMAN *Atlanta* v56 no11 p66 Mr 2017

Café Giovanni T. McNally color *New Orleans Magazine* v51 no2 p80 D 2016

CAKES, PASTRIES, PIES, COOKIES, HOT FUDGE, GALATO, BROWNIES & MORE! C. Boers, P. Pollack et al chart color *Chicago* v65 no11 p70 N 2016

Caribbean Room J. Forman color *New Orleans Magazine* v51 no2 p72 D 2016

Casino Cuisine C. NUTTALL-SMITH color *Walrus* v14 no4 p22 My 2017

CASOLARE A. Limpert *Washingtonian Magazine* v52 no1 p145 O 2016

Fall Creek Place: A neighborhood once known as "Dodge City" thrives anew K. F. Wells *Indianapolis Monthly* v40 no10 p32 Je 2017

KNOTTY BUT NICE T. KIRTS color *Indianapolis Monthly* v42 no2 p43 O 2017

THE MERINGUE GANG L. BAILEY *Indianapolis Monthly* v40 no7 p41 Mr 2017

Mucho Gusto J. SPALDING *Indianapolis Monthly* v40 no7 p44 Mr 2017

Raising the Bar: Cocktails and small plates create a stir at Bar One Fourteen, the Patachou family's sexy black sheep J. SPALDING color *Indianapolis Monthly* v42 no2 p46 O 2017

Restaurant GUIDE *Indianapolis Monthly* p149 N 2017

Restaurant GUIDE *Indianapolis Monthly* v40 no7 p125 Mr 2017

Shrimp and Grits M. Stum *Indianapolis Monthly* v40 no7 p46 Mr 2017

Toast of the Town S. KROWIAK color *Indianapolis Monthly* v42 no2 p41 O 2017

V8 Vegan Burger T. KIRTS color *Indianapolis Monthly* v42 no2 p48 O 2017

Restaurants—Indiana—Indianapolis
CITIZEN CANE: Chris Coy gets a little tiki behind the bar at The Inferno Room, opening this fall S. KROWIAK *Indianapolis Monthly* v12 no40 p46 Ag 2017

Hola Again J. SPALDING color *Indianapolis Monthly* p44 Ap 2017

LOCAL FLAVOR: Kimbal Musk considers Indy fertile ground for continuing his food fight S. Krowiak *Indianapolis Monthly* v40 no10 p42 Je 2017

Restaurant GUIDE color map *Indianapolis Monthly* p99 Ap 2017

RISING STARS: The humble biscuit goes big-time S. KROWIAK color *Indianapolis Monthly* v41 no2 p41 S 2017

Selling the Sizzle J. SPALDING *Indianapolis Monthly* p40 F 2017

STOMP TOWN T. KIRTS *Indianapolis Monthly* v12 no40 p44 Ag 2017

Zern's Hoagie *Indianapolis Monthly* v12 no40 p47 Ag 2017

Restaurants—Italy
ABSO LUTE ABRUZZO D. Prior color map *Conde Nast Traveler* v52 no9 p74 O 2017

With GUSTO H. BLOOMINGDALE color *Vogue* v206 no12 p170 D 2016

Restaurants—Italy—Evaluation
Take a Left At the Fork A. WHITTLE bw color map *Conde Nast Traveler* v52 no9 p50 O 2017

Restaurants—Kentucky
Euro Zone A. BROWNLEE *Cincinnati Magazine* v50 no8 p102 My 2017

LOCAL WONDER A. AHUJA *Cincinnati Magazine* v50 no7 p150 Ap 2017

ROOM SERVICE: COPPIN'S built a regional menu. Will locavores come? A. AHUJA *Cincinnati Magazine* v50 no10 p118 Jl 2017

Restaurants—Louisiana
Brasa Bound J. FORMAN and E. CARO color *New Orleans Magazine* v51 no12 p110 O 2017

Brunches by the Bunches J. BENSON color *New Orleans Magazine* v51 no7 p60 My 2017

CENTRAL J. FROIS color *Louisiana Life* v37 no3 p98 Ja/F 2017

DINING GUIDE color *New Orleans Magazine* v51 no10 p180 Ag 2017

FEASTING AND FROLICKING J. Benson color *Louisiana Life* v37 no5 p50 My/Je 2017

FROM THE SOUL A. McLellan color *Louisiana Life* v37 no6 p52 Jl/Ag 2017

LA GUNS J. Benson color *Louisiana Life* v37 no6 p50 Jl/Ag 2017

MARKET FRESH J. BENSON color *Louisiana Life* v37 no3 p20 Ja/F 2017

May Showers Bring... T. McNally color *New Orleans Magazine* v51 no7 p88 My 2017

News From the Kitchens R. Peyton color *New Orleans Magazine* v51 no8 p102 Je 2017

NORTH J. FROIS color *Louisiana Life* v37 no3 p97 Ja/F 2017

PLANTATION COUNTRY J. FROIS color map *Louisiana Life* v37 no4 p96 Mr/Ap 2017

Southern Cooking D. Curry color *New Orleans Magazine* v51 no7 p70 My 2017

SOUTH'S BEST RESTAURANT H. Hayes color *Southern Living* v52 no4 p88 Ap 2017

Spice Trade J. Forman color *New Orleans Magazine* v51 no7 p84 My 2017

TABLE TALK color *New Orleans Magazine* v51 no12 p109 O 2017

Restaurants—Louisiana—New Orleans
Brennan's R. Peyton color *New Orleans Magazine* v51 no2 p66 D 2016

Café Giovanni T. McNally color *New Orleans Magazine* v51 no2 p80 D 2016

Caribbean Room J. Forman color *New Orleans Magazine* v51 no2 p72 D 2016

The Company Burger J. Forman color *New Orleans Magazine* v51 no2 p78 D 2016

Counter Culture J. Forman color *New Orleans Magazine* v51 no6 p84 Ap 2017

DINING GUIDE A. McLellan and M. Cameran color *New Orleans Magazine* v51 no6 p92 Ap 2017

DINING GUIDE color *New Orleans Magazine* v51 no3 p120 Ja 2017

DINING LISTINGS color *New Orleans Magazine* v51 no12 p118 O 2017

Little Korea BBQ R. Peyton color *New Orleans Magazine* v51 no2 p74 D 2016

McClure's Barbecue T. McNally color *New Orleans Magazine* v51 no2 p80 D 2016

My Favorite Block E. Laborde *New Orleans Magazine* v51 no6 p14 Ap 2017

Neighborhoods color *New Orleans Magazine* v51 no6 p105 Ap 2017

News From the Kitchen R. PEYTON color *New Orleans Magazine* v51 no12 p112 O 2017

NEWS FROM THE KITCHENS R. PEYTON color *New Orleans Magazine* v51 no2 p86 D 2016

News From the Kitchens R. Peyton color *New Orleans Magazine* v51 no6 p86 Ap 2017

Seaworthy T. McNally color *New Orleans Magazine* v51 no2 p79 D 2016

State of the Market J. FORMAN, T. MCNALLY et al *New Orleans Magazine* v51 no2 p69 D 2016

tops OF THE TOWN bw color *New Orleans Magazine* v51 no3 p68 Ja 2017

Tujague's J. Forman color *New Orleans Magazine* v51 no2 p70 D 2016

WITH POYDRAS THE PARROT J. Street bw *New Orleans Magazine* v51 no9 p22 Jl 2017

Restaurants—Louisiana—New Orleans—Evaluation
FOCUSING ON THE FUNDAMENTALS J. FORMAN color *New Orleans Magazine* v51 no3 p112 Ja 2017

NEWS FROM THE KITCHENS R. PEYTON color *New Orleans Magazine* v51 no3 p114 Ja 2017

Restaurants—Marketing
Neal Brown Restaurateur *Indianapolis Monthly* v40 no11 p46 Jl 2017

Restaurants—Maryland
DOUGHNUTS *Washingtonian Magazine* v52 no1 p98 O 2016

QUICK TAKES A. Spiegel *Washingtonian Magazine* v52 no6 p146 Mr 2017

Restaurants—Maryland—Baltimore
TASTE Baltimore's TRANSFORMATION *Washingtonian Magazine* v53 no1 p12 O 2017

Restaurants—Mexico
La Paloma Restaurant K. MONTGOMERY *Arizona Highways* v93 no10 p12 O 2017

MADE IN MÉRIDA P. Brady color *Conde Nast Traveler* v52 no5 p118 My 2017

San Miguel Modern S. Deseran color *Sunset* v237 no6 p52 D 2016

Thompson Playa del Carmen, Mexico color *Conde Nast Traveler* v52 no5 p54 My 2017

Restaurants—Michigan
Only in DETROIT color *Popular Mechanics* p69 D 2016/Ja 2017

Restaurants—Missouri
ALL AROUND Missouri color *Missouri Life* v44 no4 p81 Je 2017

As the Windmill Turns St. Louis J. B. Patton color *Missouri Life* v44 no5 p74 Ag 2017

AMERICAN *Cincinnati Magazine* v50 no8 p114 My 2017

AS GOOD AS IT GETS A. AHUJA *Cincinnati Magazine* v50 no4 p144 Ja 2017

BLUE PLATE SPECIALS *Cincinnati Magazine* v50 no2 p65 N 2016

CAJUN/CARIBBEAN *Cincinnati Magazine* v50 no8 p116 My 2017

COW PALACE A. AHUJA *Cincinnati Magazine* v50 no2 p118 N 2016

Cuban Missile J. K. WOLFE *Cincinnati Magazine* v50 no2 p120 N 2016

DINING GUIDE *Cincinnati Magazine* v51 no1 p158 O 2017

ENDLESS LOVE A. BRANDT *Cincinnati Magazine* v50 no2 p56 N 2016

HAVE IT YOUR WAY A. B. WALTERS *Cincinnati Magazine* v50 no2 p58 N 2016

ITALIAN *Cincinnati Magazine* v50 no10 p130 Jl 2017

JAPANESE *Cincinnati Magazine* v50 no8 p122 My 2017

Moving Day J. K. WOLFE *Cincinnati Magazine* v50 no7 p153 Ap 2017

PARTY CITY J. DRILLING color *Cincinnati Magazine* v51 no1 p153 O 2017

PREMIER CRU CREW J. DRILLING *Cincinnati Magazine* v50 no6 p72 Mr 2017

Spice World A. KONERMANN color *Cincinnati Magazine* v51 no1 p156 O 2017

STEAKS *Cincinnati Magazine* v50 no8 p125 My 2017

Stir It Up *Cincinnati Magazine* v50 no2 p64 N 2016

THAI *Cincinnati Magazine* v50 no8 p126 My 2017

Turkish Delight J. DRILLING color *Cincinnati Magazine* v51 no1 p157 O 2017

Restaurants—Oregon—Portland

BEST OF THE WEST C. Dash, S. Granada et al color *Sunset* v238 no5 p11 My 2017

Restaurants—Pennsylvania

PRESQUE ISLE STATE PARK A. BROWNLEE color *Cincinnati Magazine* v51 no1 p34 O 2017

Restaurants—Pennsylvania—Philadelphia

Philadelphia M. Rosano color *Canadian Geographic* v135 no6 p18 D 2015

Restaurants—Québec (Province)

Casino Cuisine C. NUTTALL-SMITH color *Walrus* v14 no4 p22 My 2017

Restaurants—Remodeling

interiors C. A. PEARSON color diag *Architectural Record* v205 no2 p33 F 2017

Restaurants—Reservation systems

FINE DINING, FINE PRINT A. Spiegel *Washingtonian Magazine* v52 no2 p362 N 2016

TABLE TALK A. Hankinson cartoon *New Yorker* v93 no25 p33 Ag 28 2017

Restaurants—Social aspects

Early Check-In color *Conde Nast Traveler* v51 no10 p24 N 2016

Vodka on the Malecon B. Dufresne color *Commonweal* v144 no1 p9 Ja 6 2017

Restaurants—South Carolina

THE SOUTH'S BEST Biscuits J. V. Cole color *Southern Living* v52 no1 p63 Ja 2017

Restaurants—Southern States

The South's Best color *Southern Living* v52 no4 p67 Ap 2017

Restaurants—Tennessee

STAR TREK: Prime viewing of a rare celestial phenomenon puts a different kind of spotlight on Nashville R. ANNIS *Indianapolis Monthly* v12 no40 p40 Ag 2017

Restaurants—Texas

THE GOLDEN AGE OF BBQ D. VAUGHN *Texas Monthly* v45 no6 p94 Je 2017

The Guide *D: The Magazine of Dallas* v43 no10 p270 O 2016

A Guide to Our New Dining Guide T. TALIAFERRO *Texas Monthly* v45 no9 p6 S 2017

LINK TO THE PAST J. C. REID *Texas Monthly* v45 no6 p117 Je 2017

The Next Global Food Mecca Is in...Texas?! color *GQ: Gentlemen's Quarterly* v86 no12 p114 D 2016

On Tapa His Game P. SHARPE *Texas Monthly* v45 no1 p34 Ja 2017

Our Ramen Changed Texas... ...and Texas Changed Our Ramen T. AIKAWA and T. MATSUMOTO color *Bon Appetit* v62 no2 p66 Mr 2017

PARLEZ-VOUS BBQ? J. SALAMON *Texas Monthly* v45 no6 p111 Je 2017

THE REST *Texas Monthly* v45 no6 p104 Je 2017

THE TEXANIST *Texas Monthly* v45 no9 p152 S 2017

TYLER TWO-STEP M. HALL *Texas Monthly* v45 no6 p118 Je 2017

Use Your Noodle: SAN ANTONIO'S BATTALION SERVES PRIMO ITALIAN, INCLUDING SOME OF THE BEST PASTA IN THE STATE P. SHARPE *Texas Monthly* v45 no7 p34 Jl 2017

Where to Eat Now: OUR CAREFULLY CURATED GUIDE TO THE BEST RESTAURANTS IN TEXAS AND SOME NOTEWORTHY NEW ARRIVALS *Texas Monthly* v45 no7 p102 Jl 2017

Where to Eat Now *Texas Monthly* v44 no12 p128 D 2016

Where to Eat Now *Texas Monthly* v45 no2 p112 F 2017

Where to Eat Now *Texas Monthly* v45 no6 p132 Je 2017

Where to Eat Now *Texas Monthly* v45 no9 p24 S 2017

Restaurants—Texas—Dallas

The Dark Prince D. SEARCY *Texas Monthly* v45 no3 p86 Mr 2017

Going Up P. SHARPE *Texas Monthly* v45 no9 p18 S 2017

WHERE TO EAT TO EAT NOW 2017 P. Sharpe *Texas Monthly* v45 no2 p98 F 2017

Restaurants—Texas—Houston

EDITOR'S LETTER T. TALIAFERRO *Texas Monthly* v45 no5 p14 My 2017

Feel the Burn P. SHARPE *Texas Monthly* v44 no12 p50 D 2016

Fish on the Half Shell E. Laborde *New Orleans Magazine* v51 no9 p14 Jl 2017

Here's the Beef P. SHARPE *Texas Monthly* v45 no2 p38 F 2017

High Five P. SHARPE *Texas Monthly* v45 no5 p36 My 2017

Restaurants—Thailand

THAI *Cincinnati Magazine* v50 p150 Ag 2017 Supplement

Restaurants—United States

Best New Restaurants L. Bailey, K. Kendall et al *Indianapolis Monthly* p58 My 2017

By Any Measurement T. McNally color *New Orleans Magazine* v51 no4 p90 F 2017

CRAZY FOR CAULIFLOWER C. Suddath color *Bloomberg Businessweek* no4521 p66 My 8 2017

Crudité at Bar One Fourteen *Indianapolis Monthly* v40 no11 p44 Jl 2017

DINING GUIDE *Cincinnati Magazine* v50 no2 p124 N 2016

DOWNTOWN *Indianapolis Monthly* v40 no11 p112 Jl 2017

ECLECTIC *Cincinnati Magazine* v50 no10 p128 Jl 2017

Englewood: This up-and-coming stretch of East Washington Street is sprouting some quirky gems JUSSI KENT-DOOLAN *Indianapolis Monthly* v40 no11 p30 Jl 2017

FERMENTATION NATION A. MASON color *Bon Appetit* no1 p66 F 2017

Field to Vase B. MCKIBBEN *Atlanta* v57 no1 p55 My 2017

FRENCH *Cincinnati Magazine* v50 no8 p120 My 2017

FRESH ON THE SCENE C. LAUTERBACH *Atlanta* v57 no1 p66 My 2017

GOOD CHEMISTRY J. DRILLING *Cincinnati Magazine* v50 no2 p60 N 2016

Hush Hush *Atlanta* v57 no5 p64 S 2017

If These Walls Could Talk color *Bon Appetit* v62 no7 p21 Jl 2017

INDIAN *Cincinnati Magazine* v50 no8 p121 My 2017

Into the Fold A downtown remake as simple and straightforward as its name, The Taco Shop does one thing and does it well J. SPALDING *Indianapolis Monthly* v40 no11 p42 Jl 2017

ITALIAN *Cincinnati Magazine* v50 no8 p121 My 2017

JOCKS AND TOQUES A. SPIEGEL color *Washingtonian Magazine* v52 no7 p18 Ap 2017

KEY *Indianapolis Monthly* v40 no11 p112 Jl 2017

LETTER FROM THE EDITOR J. STOWE *Cincinnati Magazine* v50 no2 p12 N 2016

Meat J. Forman color *New Orleans Magazine* v51 no4 p84 F 2017

MEDITERRANEAN *Cincinnati Magazine* v50 no8 p123 My 2017

MEXICAN *Cincinnati Magazine* v50 no8 p123 My 2017

NEW JAM S. KROWIAK *Indianapolis Monthly* p42 My 2017

THE NEW QUEUE: Washington's strange new affinity for waiting in line M. Schaffer *Washingtonian Magazine* v52 no9 p17 Je 2017

News From the Kitchens R. Peyton color *New Orleans Magazine* v51 no4 p86 F 2017

THE NEXT MEAT MAESTROS J. Gordinier color *Esquire* p20 Je/Jl 2017

NORTHEAST *Indianapolis Monthly* v40 no11 p121 Jl 2017

NORTH SUBURBAN *Indianapolis Monthly* v40 no11 p119 Jl 2017

THE PERFECT NIGHT OUT: GQ'S BEST NEW RESTAURANTS 2017 B. Martin color *GQ: Gentlemen's Quarterly* v97 no5 p88 My 2017

Poke Go, Go, Go K. Krader color *Bloomberg Businessweek* no4529 p77 Jl 3 2017

Restaurant GUIDE *Indianapolis Monthly* v40 no10 p144 Je 2017

RESTAURANTS' DIGITAL DILEMMA J. Kell color *Fortune* v175 no8 p57 Je 15 2017

Southern Living CAST YOUR VOTE FOR THE SOUTH'S BEST! *Southern Living* v52 no9 p14 S 2017

SOUTH SUBURBAN *Indianapolis Monthly* v40 no11 p126 Jl 2017

A Town Every 10 Miles: Trains don't stop in most Corson County towns today, but that doesn't mean you shouldn't B. HUNHOFF *South Dakota Magazine* v33 no2 p20 Jl/Ag 2017

Unhappy Meal M. LABASH color *Weekly Standard* v22 no11 p5 N 21 2016

WE'RE IN THE MIDST OF A DINER BOOM *Washingtonian Magazine* v52 no1 p100 O 2016

What a Catch! S. KROWIAK *Indianapolis Monthly* v40 no11 p37 Jl 2017

WHAT'S LOCAL ANYWAY? M. Quinn *Governing* v30 no7 p50 Ap 2017

Restaurants—United States—Evaluation

The U.S. of yum color *O, The Oprah Magazine* p92 Jl 2017

Restaurants—Virginia

ALEXANDRIA: Where to eat, shop, and explore K. Olsen *Washingtonian Magazine* v53 no1 p176 O 2017

The Best BBQ Awards 2017 *Virginia Living* p31 2017 Smoke & Salt

Deep Cuts L. WARD *Virginia Living* v15 no1 p54 D 2016

FIELD & MAIN J. Haddad *Virginia Living* v15 no1 p25 D 2016

Food & Drink *Virginia Living* p121 2017 Best 20of Virginia

Heaven on the Half Shell *Virginia Living* p23 2017 Smoke & Salt

THE ITINERARY: LOUDOUN COUNTY K. Giglio *Washingtonian Magazine* v52 no1 p113 O 2016

MINOR SENSATIONS: Find tender smoked brisket, craft beer kiosks and deep bistory at Virginia's 9 minor league ballparks G. MARTIN *Virginia Living* v15 no4 p21 Je 2017

MR. MOMO: A former Blue Duck Tavern server brings a taste of Nepal to Del Ray A. Limpert *Washingtonian Magazine* v53 no1 p146 O 2017

Restaurants—Washington (D.C.)

100 VERY BEST RESTAURANTS [Cover story] *Washingtonian Magazine* v52 no5 p70 F 2017

BEST OF WASHINGTON HALL OF FAME *Washingtonian Magazine* v52 no1 p206 O 2016

BLOCK PARTY: Everything you need to know about Annandale's hot new food hall J. Sidman and A. Spiegel *Washingtonian Magazine* v52 no8 p128 My 2017

CASOLARE A. Limpert *Washingtonian Magazine* v52 no1 p145 O 2016

CHAIN REACTION: At the Smith, the menu aims to please all tastes A. Limpert *Washingtonian Magazine* v52 no8 p125 My 2017

DISH OF THE MONTH A. LIMPERT *Washingtonian Magazine* v52 no9 p142 Je 2017

DISH OF THE MONTH A. SPIEGEL *Washingtonian Magazine* v53 no1 p152 O 2017

DISH OF THE MONTH J. SIDMAN *Washingtonian Magazine* v52 no6 p149 Mr 2017

FRESH ON THE SCENE A. Spiegel *Washingtonian Magazine* v52 no9 p148 Je 2017

GREAT NEW RESTAURANTS *Washingtonian Magazine* v52 no12 p89 S 2017

HOT OPENINGS J. Sidman *Washingtonian Magazine* v52 no4 p181 Ja 2017

JEWEL IN THE ROUGH C. Kummer *Washingtonian Magazine* v52 no4 p175 Ja 2017

MEATY MATTERS: Red Apron Burger Bar is doing wonders with Virginia beef a. Limpert *Washingtonian Magazine* v52 no8 p132 My 2017

MIRABELLE A. Limpert *Washingtonian Magazine* v52 no9 p139 Je 2017

NO-STAR REVIEW *Washingtonian Magazine* v52 no1 p22 O 2016

PANCAKES *Washingtonian Magazine* v52 no1 p89 O 2016

PEAK RESTAURANT? J. Sidman *Washingtonian Magazine* v52 no4 p15 Ja 2017

THE PURSGLOVES' TOP ONE PERCENT J. KNAPP *Washingtonian Magazine* v52 no5 p12 F 2017

SUPERSIZE MENU A. Spiegel *Washingtonian Magazine* v52 no6 p144 Mr 2017

TACO TIME A. Spiegel *Washingtonian Magazine* v52 no4 p179 Ja 2017

Too Cool to Fail: Why Trump Can't Kill D.C.'s Mojo M. BYRNE color *GQ: Gentlemen's Quarterly* v97 no4 p52 Ap 2017

WHARF TOUR: What's coming to DC's new restaurant hub A. Spiegel *Washingtonian Magazine* v53 no1 p150 O 2017

WINNER'S CIRCLE A. Spiegel *Washingtonian Magazine* v52 no3 p150 D 2016

Restaurants—Washington (State)

AND NOW FOR THE NEXT COURSE A. WHITING *Washingtonian Magazine* v52 no1 p10 O 2016

Seattle J. McCULLUM color *Martha Stewart Living* p140 O 2017

Restaurateurs

> *See also*
> Women restaurateurs

CLAUS MEYER bw color *Bloomberg Businessweek* no4510 p64 F 6 2017

Danny MEYER M. Hainey color *Esquire* p74 Je/Jl 2017

Feather in His Cap S. KROWIAK *Indianapolis Monthly* v40 no5 p37 Ja 2017

THE GENEALOGY OF WASHINGTON RESTAURANTS A. LIMPERT *Washingtonian Magazine* v52 no1 p64 O 2016

NEXT GENERATION color *Bon Appetit* v62 no2 p58 Mr 2017

STEPHEN STARR L. M. M. BLUME bw *Vanity Fair* v59 no2 p48 F 2017

UPSIDE DOWN, ON THE CEILING J. FIELDEN color *Esquire* v167 no2 p36 Mr 2017

Restaurateurs—Interviews

HOW I GOT MY STYLE: LARRY McGUIRE P. L. Underwood color *Esquire* p55 N 2017

Restaurateurs—United States

The Staff Of Life R. BROOKHISER *National Review* v69 no9 p43 My 15 2017

Reston, James

The Art of War: A history of how a bitter controversy over the Vietnam Veterans Memorial ended in national reconciliation M. J. LEWIS *New York Times Book Review* p21 S 17 2017

Reston, James, 1909-1995

The Trump Disruption A. FERGUSON *Commentary* v143 no1 p10 Ja 2017

RESTON, LAURA

Blocking the Detectives color *New Republic* v248 no7 p6 Jl 2017

How Russia Weaponizes Fake News il *New Republic* v248 no6 p6 Je 2017

The NRA's New Scare Tactics il *New Republic* v248 no11 p6 N 2017

Trump's Fuzzy Border Math color *New Republic* v248 no4 p6 Ap 2017

Restoration ecology

> *See also*
> Stream restoration

Optimal Tree Canopy Cover during Ecological Restoration: A Case Study of Possible Ecological Thresholds in Changting, China SHIXIONG CAO, CHENXI LU et al *BioScience* v67 no3 p221 Mr 2017

Restoration monitoring (Ecology)

HAWAII & AMERICAN CARIBBEAN *Sierra* v102 no1 p55 Ja/F 2017

Restorative justice
New Orleans High School Turbocharges Restorative Justice J. SHAW cartoon *Education Digest* v82 no7 p4 Mr 2017
Restrepo, Brandon
Blood Levels of Trans Fats Among American Adults Fell from 1999 to 2010 *Amber Waves: The Economics of Food, Farming, Natural Resources, & Rural America* p39 Je 2017
Body Weight Fell Following Mandatory Calorie-Labeling Laws for New York Restaurant Menus *Amber Waves: The Economics of Food, Farming, Natural Resources, & Rural America* p11 F 2017
Restroom design & construction
Powder Rooms & Half Baths B. D. Coleman color diag *Old House Journal* v45 no6 p64 S 2017
Restrooms—Law & legislation
Bathroom wars 2.0 E. ALINI color *Maclean's* v129 no43 p48 O 31 2016
Résumés (Employment)
How to Write a Résumé That Stands Out A. Gallo *Harvard Business Review Digital Articles* p2 D 19 2014
Improve Your Résumé by Turning Bullet Points into Stories J. Heifetz *Harvard Business Review Digital Articles* p2 My 4 2016
JOB HUNTING? ERASE YOUR PAST D. Lyons color *Fortune* v175 no2 p46 F 1 2017
Research: How Subtle Class Cues Can Backfire on Your Resume L. Rivera and A. Tilcsik *Harvard Business Review Digital Articles* p2 D 21 2016
Writing Your Résumé When Your Job Title Doesn't Reflect Your Responsibilities J. Heifetz *Harvard Business Review Digital Articles* p2 My 16 2017
Yes, Your Résumé Needs a Summary J. Heifetz *Harvard Business Review Digital Articles* p2 Jl 28 2015
Resuscitation
See also
CPR (First aid)
COLD REMEDY N. TWILLEY cartoon color *New Yorker* v92 no39 p36 N 28 2016
Family Presence During Resuscitation *USA Today Magazine* v145 no2861 p7 F 2017
Resveratrol
Face OFF color *O, The Oprah Magazine* p72 S 2017
A WAY TO GET MORE FROM HOCK INJECTIONS C. Barakat and M. McCluskey color *Equus* no472 p12 Ja 2017
Resveratrol—Research
Resveratrol Boosts Blood-Brain Barrier *USA Today Magazine* v145 no2861 p14 F 2017
Retail bakeries
HOLEY ROLLERS: A GUIDE TO L.A.'S NEW-WAVE BAGEL MAKERS G. SNYDER *Los Angeles Magazine* v62 no9 p56 S 2017
Retail bakeries—Evaluation
Crust Belt S. KROWIAK *Indianapolis Monthly* p37 F 2017
TEATIME P. POLLACK color *Chicago* v66 no5 p72 My 2017
Retail industry
See also
Advertising
Display of merchandise
Franchises (Retail trade)
Markup
Retail stores
Retail stores—Management
Selling
Shopping
4 Reasons Retail Jobs Are About to Get Better Z. Ton *Harvard Business Review Digital Articles* p2 S 4 2015
Are You Really Getting a Discount, or Is It Just a Pricing Trick? R. Mohammed *Harvard Business Review Digital Articles* p2 Mr 23 2016
The Best Retailers Combine Bricks and Clicks D. S. Evans and R. Schmalensee *Harvard Business Review Digital Articles* p2 My 30 2016
Buy Retail Stocks at Wholesale Prices J. K. GLASSMAN chart *Kiplinger's Personal Finance* v71 no5 p18 My 2017
BYE-BYE, DISCOUNTS. HELLO, MARGINS P. Wahba color *Fortune* v176 no4 p30 S 15 2017
CURING THE ADDICTION TO GROWTH M. FISHER, V.

GAUR et al color graph il img *Harvard Business Review* v95 no1 p66 Ja/F 2017
E-COMMERCE: BETTER LATE THAN NEVER P. Wahba color diag *Fortune* v176 no3 p18 S 1 2017
E-tailers Widen Bookselling Edge J. Milliot and E. Nawotka chart graph *Publishers Weekly* v264 no18 p4 My 1 2017
How 4 Retailers Became "Best Places to Work" Z. Ton and S. Kalloch color *Harvard Business Review Digital Articles* p2 Ja 2 2017
How Predictive AI Will Change Shopping A. Sharma *Harvard Business Review Digital Articles* p2 N 18 2016
How Retail Can Thrive in a World Without Stores A. Sharma *Harvard Business Review Digital Articles* p2 Jl 21 2017
How Retailers Should Think About Online Versus In-Store Pricing R. Mohammed bw *Harvard Business Review Digital Articles* p2 Ja 26 2017
In the Future of Retail, We're Never Not Shopping W. Reinartz *Harvard Business Review Digital Articles* p2 Mr 10 2016
Material World H. MARTIN color *Architectural Digest* v74 no9 p56 S 2017
THE QUEEN OF HEELS TALKS SHOP(S) color *Fortune* v175 no7 p12 Je 1 2017
Resources color *House Beautiful* v159 no3 p122 Ap 2017
Retailers Can't Rely on Holiday-Season Gimmicks Like They Used To D. L. Yohn *Harvard Business Review Digital Articles* p2 N 3 2015
THE SLOW- MOTION RETAIL TRAIN WRECK *Fortune* v175 no6 p9 My 1 2017
Toys 'R' Us Might Be Dying, but Physical Retail Isn't G. Satell *Harvard Business Review Digital Articles* p2 S 20 2017
Why Online Retailers Are Starting to Care About Your Feelings R. Bolton *Harvard Business Review Digital Articles* p2 Ja 12 2015
Why the Print Catalog Is Back in Style D. L. Yohn *Harvard Business Review Digital Articles* p2 F 25 2015
Retail industry research
LESSONS FROM THE SUSHI CONVEYOR BELT il *Harvard Business Review* v95 no4 p28 Jl/Ag 2017
Retail industry statistics
Back-to-School Shopping Still Exists J. Porter color diag *Fortune* v176 no4 p30 S 15 2017
Retail industry—California
A Changing Grand Central Market *Los Angeles Magazine* p18 D 2016
Retail industry—Finance
PLAYED OUT S. Kolhatkar color *New Yorker* v93 no31 p23 O 9 2017
Shopping the Retail Apocalypse D. Carey and L. Coleman-Lochner color *Bloomberg Businessweek* no4523 p37 My 22 2017
Retail industry—Florida
INSTYLE [Loves] MIAMI E. N. Gage color *InStyle* v23 no13 p217 D 2016
Retail industry—Japan
Japan's Furniture King Caters to the Plebes J. Clenfield, M. Horie et al color *Bloomberg Businessweek* no4526 p19 Je 12 2017
Retail industry—New York (State)—New York—Finance
THIS MAY BE PEAK FIFTH AVENUE P. Wahba diag *Fortune* v174 no8 p17 D 15 2016
Retail industry—Russia
Buying Syrian Shoes To Bolster Putin's Pride I. Khrennikov color *Bloomberg Businessweek* no4524 p24 My 29 2017
Retail industry—United States
Disputing Credit Card Charges Gets Easy J. Surane color *Bloomberg Businessweek* no4529 p28 Jl 3 2017
ERS's Updated Food Access Research Atlas Shows an Increase in Low-Income and Low-Supermarket Access Areas in 2015 A. Rhone and M. Ver Ploeg *Amber Waves: The Economics of Food, Farming, Natural Resources, & Rural America* p1 F 2017
EVERYTHING MUST GO P. Wahba color diag *Fortune* v175 no3 p94 Mr 1 2017
HOW E-COMMERCE IS MAKING STORES RELEVANT AGAIN P. Wahba color *Fortune* v175 no5 p24 Ap 1 2017
RETAILERS HAVE THEIR EYE ON YOU L. GERSTNER color *Kiplinger's Personal Finance* v71 no5 p12 My 2017
STORES' BLEAK BLACK FRIDAY P. Wahba *Fortune* v174 no6 p11 N 1 2016
Survival of the Fitted S. McBride graph *Bloomberg Businessweek*

Retail industry—Charts, diagrams, etc.

Movers K. Stock cartoon color *Bloomberg Businessweek* no4514 p13 Mr 13 2017

Retail industry—Employees—Salaries, wages, etc.

THE LOOMING RETAIL BAILOUT G. ANDERS color graph map *Forbes* v199 no6 p94 Je 13 2017

Retail industry—United States—Charts, diagrams, etc.

THE LOOMING RETAIL BAILOUT G. ANDERS color graph map *Forbes* v199 no6 p94 Je 13 2017

Retail stores—Charts, diagrams, etc.

Top Shops for Tech chart *Consumer Reports* v81 no12 p33 D 2016

Retaining walls—Design & construction

ASK ROY R. BERENDSOHN color *Popular Mechanics* p34 Ap 2017

Retallick, Beau

Cashing In on The Fear Factor J. Clenfield and P. Alpeyev color *Bloomberg Businessweek* no4495 p35 O 17 2016

RETICA, AARON

Silk on a Stick: The world's flags and what they mean *New York Times Book Review* p16 Jl 2 2017

Reticulocytes

UBE2O remodels the proteome during terminal erythroid differentiation A. T. Nguyen, M. A. Prado et al diag *Science* v357 no6350 p471 Ag 4 2017

Retinal degeneration

iPS cell therapy reported safe D. Normile color *Science* v355 no6330 p1109 Mr 17 2017

Retinal ganglion cells

Regenerating optic pathways from the eye to the brain B. Laha, B. K. Stafford et al diag *Science* v356 no6342 p1031 Je 9 2017

Retired athletes

The AFTER-PARTY L. J. Wertheim color *Sports Illustrated* v127 no1 p48 Jl 3 2017

Justin LEONARD J. Garrity color *Sports Illustrated* v127 no1 p74 Jl 3 2017

Usain Bolt S. Gregory color *Time* v190 no7 p13 Ag 21 2017

Retired military personnel—Interviews

A Veteran's Odyssey G. GURLEY *Publishers Weekly* v264 no23 p42 Je 5 2017

Retired military personnel—United States

Six's technical adviser, Mitch Hall D. Holbrook *TV Guide* v65 no8 p15 F 27 2017

Retirees

Moving in Retirement? How to Time It Right E. O'Brien color diag *Money* v46 no5 p27 Je 2017

RETIREES FLOCK SOUTH AND WEST D. Kadlec color *Money* v46 no2 p20 Mr 2017

A Social Security Perk for Some Older Parents L. Asinof diag *Money* v46 no5 p29 Je 2017

Retirees—Employment

Grab a Spot in the Sharing Economy I. Case diag *Money* v46 no2 p44 Mr 2017

Living on 4 Percent—Or Less B. Steverman cartoon *Bloomberg Businessweek* no4493 p56 O 3 2016

A retirement 'hobby' J. H. Borden color *Science* v355 no6324 p542 F 3 2017

Retirees—Finance

The Challenge: Agreeing on the Perfect Retirement Locale K. A. Renzulli color diag *Money* v45 no11 p40 D 2016

Four Tips for Going Solo E. O'brien chart color *Money* v46 no2 p41 Mr 2017

Janet Yellen Can't Help Retirees C. Condon color *Bloomberg Businessweek* no4540 p50 O 2 2017

Living on 4 Percent—Or Less B. Steverman cartoon *Bloomberg Businessweek* no4493 p56 O 3 2016

Retirees—Psychology

How to Become a Happy Retiree N. K. Schlossberg color *Money* v46 no4 p28 My 2017

Retirees—Research

The Grayest Professions In America C. Wilson color diag map *Time* v189 no15 p20 Ap 24 2017

Retirees—Services for

MAKING TIME FOR FUN: Retirement is a great time to take up new interests and activities C. Barker *Washingtonian Magazine* v52 no8 p145 My 2017

Use Your Home to Get More Income [Cover story] P. M. ESS-

WEIN color graph *Kiplinger's Personal Finance* v71 no10 p38 O 2017

Retirees—Taxation

Blue State Blues A. EBELING map *Forbes* v199 no2 p102 F 28 2017

Retirees—Travel

Best Places to Retire S. Max color *Money* v45 no10 p64 N 2016

Enjoy a Senior Term Abroad I. Case color *Money* v46 no2 p43 Mr 2017

Retirement

See also

Early retirement

Teacher retirement

A Bird in the Hand D. WESTON, P. SCHMIDT et al color graph *Kiplinger's Personal Finance* v71 no2 p6 F 2017

Chief Concerns P. A. Harkness *Governing* v30 no2 p16 N 2016

Chords & Discords H. STARK, D. HENDLEY et al color *Downbeat* v84 no8 p10 Ag 2017

Dale Earnhardt Jr S. Gregory color *Time* v189 no18 p15 My 15 2017

DAYTIME M. LOGAN *TV Guide* v65 no19 p42 My 1 2017

ENOUGH? D. TREMAYNE bw color *Road & Track* v68 no7 p68 Mr/Ap 2017

GAME PLAN S. BLOCK cartoon *Kiplinger's Personal Finance* v71 no3 p31 Mr 2017

Great Places to Retire J. Bodnar *Kiplinger's Personal Finance* v71 no8 p6 Ag 2017

How to Become a Coach or Consultant After You Retire D. Clark *Harvard Business Review Digital Articles* p2 My 12 2017

Ming Cho Lee to step down from teaching postion at Yale *Stage Directions* v30 no3 p4 Mr 2017

THE NEW RETIREMENT AGE S. Sataline *Washingtonian Magazine* v52 no3 p109 D 2016

Prince Philip Retires--at 95 *British Heritage Travel* v38 no4 p8 Jl/Ag 2017

Senior LIVING R. Bird *Cincinnati Magazine* v50 no4 p87 Ja 2017

THE SPLENDID END D. Karl color *Flying* v144 no2 p70 F 2017

Terry Gibbs Returns with Homemade Recording K. Silsbee color *Downbeat* v84 no7 p18 Jl 2017

Thriving After an Early Retirement K. LANKFORD color *Kiplinger's Personal Finance* v71 no7 p72 Jl 2017

WHAT YOU REALLY NEED FOR A HAPPY LIFE A. Traister color *Redbook* p100 F 2017

Why Retirement Is a Flawed Concept N. Pasricha *Harvard Business Review Digital Articles* p2 Ap 13 2016

The Year That Was . . *Texas Monthly* v45 no1 p6 Ja 2017

Retirement age

How Work Will Change When Most of Us Live to 100 L. Gratton and A. Scott *Harvard Business Review Digital Articles* p2 Je 27 2016

When Is a Judge Too Old? A. Greenblatt *Governing* v30 no1 p10 O 2016

Retirement age—Law & legislation

Get Ready for the New Math K. Damato color diag *Money* v46 no1 p37 Ja/F 2017

Retirement communities

Aging Parents color *New Orleans Magazine* v51 no6 p135 Ap 2017

A Family Affair *Atlanta* v56 no9 p140 Ja 2017

LOOK FORWARD TO RETIREMENT *Washingtonian Magazine* v52 no1 p173 O 2016

Meant to Be *Atlanta* v56 no9 p143 Ja 2017

More Bang for Your Vacation Buck *Cincinnati Magazine* v50 no4 p88 Ja 2017

The Right Decision A. MEADOWS *Atlanta* v56 no9 p139 Ja 2017

Retirement communities—Evaluation

LIVING WELL F. Esker color *Louisiana Life* v37 no2 p76 N/D 2016

Retirement income

See also

Retirement income—Planning

Help Make America Compassionate Again E. J. Schneidewind *AARP: The Magazine* v60 no5A p67 Ag/S 2017

Retirement income—Management

TAKE STEPS TO SECURE YOUR RETIREMENT NOW! D. T. Dingle graph *Black Enterprise* v47 no3 p48 O 2016

Retirement income—Planning

3 Tips From Millionaires That Can Improve Your Retirement W. Updegrave color diag *Money* v46 no9 p35 O 2017

The End of 4%? Smarter Ways to Generate Income for Life E. O'brien chart color *Money* v46 no9 p38 O 2017

Planning for a Low-Tax, High-Deficit World L. Braham *Bloomberg Businessweek* no4516 p42 Mr 27 2017

RETIRE WHEN YOU WANT J. B. CLARK color *Kiplinger's Personal Finance* v71 no3 p22 Mr 2017

Retirement planning

5 Ways Retirement Savers Put Their Dreams at Risk W. Updegrave color *Money* v46 no7 p28 Ag 2017

5 WAYS YOUR 401(K) IS HELPING YOU SAVE BETTER P. Wang color diag *Money* v46 no1 p78 Ja/F 2017

Blueprint for Retirement *Forbes* v199 no2 p89 F 28 2017

The Challenge: Making a Job Change on the Road to Retirement K. A. Renzulli color diag *Money* v46 no1 p40 Ja/F 2017

Controlling Your Future Savings B. TULIPANE *Parks & Recreation* v52 no2 p8 F 2017

Design a Retirement That Excites You J. Giesea *Harvard Business Review Digital Articles* p2 N 17 2015

FINANCIAL FUTURE: Planning for retirement? Here's why your family and a professional should be involved M. K. Farr *Washingtonian Magazine* v52 no8 p140 My 2017

GET INCOME FOR LIFE [Cover story] E. AMBROSE and S. BLOCK chart color *Kiplinger's Personal Finance* v71 no10 p26 O 2017

HAVEN'T PLANNED FOR RETIREMENT? HERE ARE THREE PITFALLS TO AVOID G. Thill *Washingtonian Magazine* v52 no8 p144 My 2017

Hello, Reader. Let's Talk *Kiplinger's Personal Finance* v71 no10 p4 O 2017

It's Great to Hear From You! color *Money* v46 no5 p8 Je 2017

Lessons From the Rich N. Wertheimer chart color *AARP: The Magazine* v60 no2A p38 F/Mr 2017

Long-Term Saving Strategies for the Self-Employed R. T. Beckwith color *Time* v189 no3 p12 Ja 30 2017

MID-YEAR FINANCIAL CHECKUP J. McKinney diag graph *Black Enterprise* v47 no8 p52 Jl/Ag 2017

The New Retirement [Cover story] T. Stanger color *Consumer Reports* v82 no1 p22 Ja 2017

Planning Your Post-Retirement Career D. Clark *Harvard Business Review Digital Articles* p2 Ap 28 2016

RETIRE EARLY: HOW THEY CAN DO IT C. Weisser chart color diag *Money* v46 no3 p44 Ap 2017

RETIRE EARLY? YES YOU CAN [Cover story] E. O'brien color diag *Money* v46 no3 p34 Ap 2017

Retirement Planning Needs a Better UX S. Benartzi *Harvard Business Review Digital Articles* p2 My 1 2015

Retirement Plans for Going It Alone L. Asinof color *Money* v46 no8 p28 S 2017

Retirement's Scariest Question: How Long? B. Steverman bw *Bloomberg Businessweek* no4498 p51 N 7 2016

Secrets to being smart with money N. Lapin color *Redbook* p30 N 2017

A Simple Habit With a Big Payoff W. Updegrave diag *Money* v46 no9 p41 O 2017

Sleazy Image, Smart Play L. GENSLER color *Forbes* v199 no7 p126 Je 29 2017

Start Your Retirement With a Tax Break! K. A. Renzulli color *Money* v46 no8 p30 S 2017

Stock-Market Highs Pose Vexing Questions for the Soon-to-Be Retired L. Shen color *Time* v190 no12 p28 S 25 2017

The Ultimate Guide to Retirement: Couples Edition [Cover story] P. Wang, E. O'Brien et al color diag *Money* v45 no10 p48 N 2016

What's Lost When Experts Retire D. Leonard, W. Swap et al *Harvard Business Review Digital Articles* p2 D 2 2014

When One Spouse Reaches Retirement First K. A. Renzulli color diag *Money* v46 no8 p25 S 2017

Your Partner for Every Stage of Life M. L. Tellado *Consumer Reports* v82 no1 p5 Ja 2017

Your Retirement: A Team Effort color *Money* v45 no10 p12 N 2016

Retirement planning—Law & legislation

States Try to Save Retirement While Washington Waits P. Wang

color diag *Time* v188 no14 p14 O 10 2016

Retirement—Finance

What You Should NEVER Put in Your Will! F. K. Wood *Saturday Evening Post* v289 no4 p85 Jl/Ag 2017

Retirement—Government policy

The Costs We Will Bear M. Funkhouser *Governing* v30 no11 p4 Ag 2017

NO 401(K)? SOME STATES HAVE YOU COVERED L. Farmer color *Governing* v30 no11 p50 Ag 2017

Retirement—Law & legislation

NO 401(K)? SOME STATES HAVE YOU COVERED L. Farmer color *Governing* v30 no11 p50 Ag 2017

Retirement planning—Charts, diagrams, etc.

401(k) Nation: Who's Left Out B. Steverman color *Bloomberg Businessweek* no4540 p49 O 2 2017

Retirement—United States

The Costs We Will Bear M. Funkhouser *Governing* v30 no11 p4 Ag 2017

FINANCIAL FUTURE: Planning for retirement? Here's why your family and a professional should be involved M. K. Farr *Washingtonian Magazine* v52 no8 p140 My 2017

GET INCOME FOR LIFE [Cover story] E. AMBROSE and S. BLOCK chart color *Kiplinger's Personal Finance* v71 no10 p26 O 2017

Me, Retire? C. Hymowitz color *Bloomberg Businessweek* no4540 p47 O 2 2017

The Same Gold Watch, It Just Arrives Later C. Hymowitz chart color *Bloomberg Businessweek* no4504 p20 D 19 2016

Retirement—United States—Planning

The Challenge: Agreeing on the Perfect Retirement Locale K. A. Renzulli color diag *Money* v45 no11 p40 D 2016

Moving to Be Near the Grandkids J. BENNETT CLARK *Kiplinger's Personal Finance* v71 no5 p46 My 2017

Revising Retirement S. Woolley color *Bloomberg Businessweek* no4522 p43 My 15 2017

Retreats

A Traveler's Best Friend M. ALLEN color *Yankee* p12 My/Je 2017

Retreats—Evaluation

CLOSE ENCOUNTERS C. Colin color *Sunset* v238 no3 p20 Mr 2017

In Search of Serenity C. Hall color *AARP: The Magazine* v60 no3A p40B Ap/My 2017

Retreats—Social aspects

Legacy of Nature C. Kolb color *New Orleans Magazine* v51 no9 p38 Jl 2017

Retribution

The Best Remedy -. Clements color *Tricycle: The Buddhist Review* v26 no2 p42 Wint 2016

Retribution (Music)

A Little Bit of Everything J. POET color *Downbeat* v84 no2 p78 F 2017

Retrievers

See also

Labrador retriever

FIVE WAYS TO KILL YOUR DOG color *Outdoor Life* v224 no6 p39 Ag 2017

Retrospective exhibitions

MIGHTY MURAKAMI J. FOUMBERG color *Chicago* v66 no6 p38 Je 2017

A WOMAN'S VIEW P. SCHJELDAHL color *New Yorker* v92 no47 p72 Ja 30 2017

Retrospective studies

Looking backward to move regulations forward M. Cropper, A. Fraas et al color *Science* v355 no6332 p1375 Mr 31 2017

Retroviruses

See also

Simian immunodeficiency virus

Inactivation of porcine endogenous retrovirus in pigs using CRISPR-Cas9 D. Niu, Wei et al diag *Science* v357 no6357 p1303 S 22 2017

Retro Virus A. Braun color *Natural History* v125 no5 p6 My 2017

RETTEW, DAVID

Is Mental Illness the Exception or the Rule? A LONG-TERM STUDY SUGGESTS THAT MOST PEOPLE STRUGGLE AT SOME POINT *Psychology Today* v50 no4 p18 Ag 2017

RETTIE, JOHN

2017 SONORA RALLY color *Dirt Sports + Off-Road* v51 no8 p18 Ag 2017

SWEEPING UP AT THE NORRA MEXICAN 1000 color *Dirt Sports + Off-Road* v51 no10 p14 O 2017

Return (Poem)

Return R. ARMANTROUT *Nation* v303 no25/26 p30 D 19 2016

Return migration

Importing Business Lessons From El Norte C. Elton diag *Bloomberg Businessweek* no4495 p38 O 17 2016

Return of Ulysses (Theatrical production)

The Long Road J. Acocella cartoon *New Yorker* v92 no36 p11 N 7 2016

Return on assets

A Refresher on Return on Assets and Return on Equity A. Gallo *Harvard Business Review Digital Articles* p2 Ap 4 2016

Return to Love (Music)

Hot Band Lvl Up J. DOLAN color *Rolling Stone* no1274 p36 N 17 2016

Return to work programs

If You Offer Mid-Career Internships, Flaunt It C. F. Cohen *Harvard Business Review Digital Articles* p2 Jl 4 2016

Retzker, Alex

Observing chemical shifts from nanosamples diag graph *Science* v357 no6346 p38 Jl 7 2017

Submillihertz magnetic spectroscopy performed with a nanoscale quantum sensor diag *Science* v356 no6340 p832 My 26 2017

Reuben, Alexandre

Potential role of intratumor bacteria in mediating tumor resistance to the chemotherapeutic drug gemcitabine diag *Science* v357 no6356 p1156 S 15 2017

Reuck, Reesa

Thoughts on previous issues color *American Cowboy* v24 no1 p24 Je/Jl 2017

REUEL, MARC GERECHT

Muslims in America color *Weekly Standard* v22 no9 p23 N 7 2016

Reuel, Reuben

BREAKING ALL THE REUELS *Virginia Living* p60 2017 Best 20of Virginia

Reunion Project, The (Performer)

The Beautiful Sound A. MORRISON bw *Downbeat* v84 no7 p59 Jl 2017

Reunions

Q + A *Cincinnati Magazine* v50 no7 p26 Ap 2017

Reus, Magali, 1981——Interviews

MAGALI REUS IN THE STUDIO A. Hickey color *Art in America* v104 no10 p136 N 2016

REUSING, ANDREA

r.s.v.p bw color *Bon Appetit* v62 no7 p12 Jl 2017

Reuter, Rolf

Nanoscale nuclear magnetic resonance with chemical resolution diag *Science* v357 no6346 p67 Jl 7 2017

Reva, Maria

NOVOSTROÏKA color *Atlantic* v318 no5 p80 D 2016

Reve, Gerard

The Age of Anxiety B. Bawer *Weekly Standard* v22 no33 p42 My 8 2017

Revelation——Christianity

Seek Out and Save J. W. MARTENS il *America* v215 no12 p39 O 24 2016

Revelle, Roger, 1909-1991

SEA CHANGE S. RICHARDSON bw color *American History* v52 no2 p28 Je 2017

Revenant, The (Film)

Wrong From Right B. HUNHOFF *South Dakota Magazine* v32 no4 p87 N/D 2016

REVENGA, ANA L.

WOMEN'S WORK color graph *Scientific American* v317 no3 p72 S 2017

Revenge

Home Wrecker J. LEVIN and S. TRELEAVEN cartoon *Walrus* v14 no6 p28 Jl/Ag 2017

Liberals Plot Revenge M. Scherer color *Time* v189 no3 p38 Ja 30 2017

Psst! Wanna Hear a Secret? J. Nilsson *Saturday Evening Post* v289 no1 p106 Ja/F 2017

Revenge Drama (Short story)

REVENGE DRAMA *Lapham's Quarterly* v10 no3 p46 Summ 2017

Revenge porn

The New Scarlet Letter C. Alter color *Time* v190 no2/3 p60 Jl 10-17 2017

TAKING TROLLS TO COURT M. TALBOT cartoon color *New Yorker* v92 no40 p56 D 5 2016

Revenu, B.

Observation of a large-scale anisotropy in the arrival directions of cosmic rays above 8×1018 eV *Science* v357 no6357 p1266 S 22 2017

Revenue

YOUR LIFE *USA Today Magazine* v145 no2858 p6 N 2016

Revenue——Accounting

STRUGGLE IN THE PARK M. Maciag *Governing* v30 no3 p56 D 2016

Revenue——Charts, diagrams, etc.

X-Ray: Walmart C. Bigda diag *Money* v45 no10 p43 N 2016

Revere, Evans

North Korea: How to Stop Kim Jong Un color *Time* v189 no12 p40 Ap 3 2017

Reveriego, Miguel

What Little Act of Courage Inspired You This Year? bw color *Glamour* v114 no12 p52 D 2016

Reversade, Bruno

ELABELA deficiency promotes preeclampsia and cardiovascular malformations in mice color diag graph *Science* v357 no6352 p707 Ag 18 2017

Reverse mortgage loans

Sleazy Image, Smart Play L. GENSLER color *Forbes* v199 no7 p126 Je 29 2017

Use Your Home to Get More Income [Cover story] P. M. ESSWEIN color graph *Kiplinger's Personal Finance* v71 no10 p38 O 2017

Reverse outsourcing

When robots steal your job S. GILMORE color *Maclean's* no1 p8 F 17 2017

Revesz, Richard

Best cost estimate of greenhouse gases *Science* v357 no6352 p655 Ag 18 2017

Estimating the health benefits of environmental regulations color *Science* v357 no6350 p457 Ag 4 2017

Revilla, J. D. Cardenas

Persistent effects of pre-Columbian plant domestication on Amazonian forest composition bibl chart graph map *Science* v355 no6328 p925 Mr 3 2017

Revis, Eric

ERIC REVIS: Endless Possibilities J. WOODARD color *Downbeat* v84 no10 p50 O 2017

Revivals (Religion)

China's Great Awakening I. Johnson color *Foreign Affairs* v96 no2 p83 Mr/Ap 2017

Revlon Inc.

Dayle Haddon E. PERETZ color *Vanity Fair* v58 no11 p183 N 2016

Revolution Radio (Music)

Green Day K. O'donnell color *Entertainment Weekly* no1435 p55 O 14 2016

Revolutionaries

How Castro Will Be Trump's First Foreign Policy Test K. Vick, D. Mascareñas et al color *Time* v188 no24 p46 D 12 2016

Style Over Substance: Why Fidel Castro's Revolutionary Chic Was a Fraud J. Klein color *Time* v188 no24 p38 D 12 2016

Revolutionaries——United States

Race to Remember L. C. Kerpelman bw color *American History* v52 no2 p48 Je 2017

Revolution for What? *Commentary* v142 no1 p1 Jl/Ag 2016

(R)evolution of Steve Jobs, The (Theatrical production)

THE GRAND iOPERA: STEVE JOBS, ULTIMATE DIVA L. MURROW color *Wired* v25 no7 p22 Jl 2017

Revolutions

See also

Civil war

Counterrevolutions

Coups d'état

Insurgency

AMID THE RUINS OF A REVOLUTION, THE CHURCH ENDURES [Cover story] J. D. Hirst color il *America* v216 no11 p26 My 15 2017

Mexico's Uprising Against Education 'Reform' J. Abbott color *Progressive* v81 no2 p24 F 2017

Rebellion, War Aims & the Laws of War T. M. Fazal *Daedalus* v146 no1 p71 Wint 2017

Revolution: Removing its Halo E. Goodheart *Society* v54 no2 p100 Ap 2017

Still waiting D. D. Collum color *U.S. Catholic* v82 no11 p38 N 2017

Revolutions—History

HORROR STORIES H. Tuma *Lapham's Quarterly* v10 no3 p151 Summ 2017

PEOPLE OF THE FUTURE: The October Revolution of 1917 inspired a generation of young Russians to embrace new ideals of socialist living A. Willimott *History Today* v67 no10 p24 O 2017

Talkin' 'bout a revolution D. Armitage *History Today* v67 no2 p72 F 2017

Revolutions—Russia

PEOPLE OF THE FUTURE: The October Revolution of 1917 inspired a generation of young Russians to embrace new ideals of socialist living A. Willimott *History Today* v67 no10 p24 O 2017

The Prospects for a Color Revolution in Russia V. Bunce *Daedalus* v146 no2 p19 Spr 2017

THE ROAD TO REVOLUTION J. HAMMER bw color map *Smithsonian* v47 no10 p66 Mr 2017

Revolvers

CHOOSING SIDES color *Military History* v34 no5 p48 Ja 2018

Revzin, Alexander

Microbiota-activated PPAR-γ signaling inhibits dysbiotic Enterobacteriaceae expansion graph *Science* v357 no6351 p570 Ag 11 2017

Reward (Psychology)

How to Treat Phobias T. John color *Time* v189 no6 p12 F 20 2017

How to Trick Yourself into Doing Tasks You Dread A. Samuel *Harvard Business Review Digital Articles* p2 Ja 19 2015

In Search of Answers M. Huston *Psychology Today* v50 no3 p10 My/Je 2017

Teamwork Works Best When Top Performers Are Rewarded B. Kirkman, Ning Li et al *Harvard Business Review Digital Articles* p2 Mr 14 2016

Rewards programs (Criminal investigation)

Case NOT closed A. J. BARTELS color *Nebraska Life* v21 no5 p41 S/O 2017

Rewind (Music)

'REWIND' J. WORTHAM color *New York Times Magazine* p29 Mr 12 2017

Rex, Adam

XO, OX: A Love Story color *Publishers Weekly* v263 no42 p66 O 17 2016

Rexnord Inc.

The Jobs That Weren't Saved S. Gregory color *Time* v189 no20 p36 My 29 2017

Rey, Ana Maria

Cold molecules: Progress in quantum engineering of chemistry and quantum matter bw color *Science* v357 no6355 p1002 S 8 2017

Rey, Stan

HIGHWAY RUN S. Mait bw color *Skiing* p30 Wint 2017

Reyburn, Hugh

Resistance to malaria through structural variation of red blood cell invasion receptors diag *Science* v356 no6343 p1139 Je 16 2017

Reyersbach, Hans

Escape Artist J. MacGregor *Smithsonian* v47 no7 p13 N 2016

Reyes, Amy

The Thread *New York Times Magazine* p10 O 23 2016

Reyes, Emma

DEVIL'S ADVOCATE *Lapham's Quarterly* v10 no3 p167 Summ 2017

THE GENERAL *Harper's Magazine* v335 no2005 p19 Je 2017

Reyes, José, 1983-

Sports Funnies K. MILLER color *National Geographic Kids* no475 p6 N 2017

Reyes, Karen Westerberg

DON'T PATRONIZE ME! *Saturday Evening Post* v288 no6 p30 N/D 2016

THE TROUBLE WITH MIA: At what point do our adult children cease to be the adoring babies we once knew? *Saturday Evening Post* v289 no5 p18 S/O 2017

Reyes, Maridel

HIT ME WITH YOUR BEST SHOTS color *Bloomberg Businessweek* no4506 p63 Ja 9 2017

This Vacation Could Save Your Life! color *Bloomberg Businessweek* no4522 p81 My 15 2017

Reyes, Patrick B.

Nobody Cries When We Die: God, Community, and Surviving to Adulthood R. Saler *Christian Century* v134 no13 p39 Je 21 2017

Reyes Beverage Group (Company)

Making a multimedia HIGHWAY OVERPASS D. Kawala color diag *Model Railroader* v84 no5 p50 My 2017

Reygondeau, Gabriel

Large benefits to marine fisheries of meeting the 1.5°C global warming target bibl graph *Science* v354 no6319 p1591 D 23 2016

Reykjavík (Iceland)

THE COLORS OF PRIDE P. STEFÁNSSON color *Iceland Review* v54 no5 p3 S-O 2016

THE DUDE ABIDES *Iceland Review* v54 no6 p132 N/D 2016

PUNK FINDS A HOME A. M. I. GRÍMSSON *Iceland Review* v55 no1 p8 Ja/F 2017

TO MARKET Z. Robert color *Iceland Review* v54 no5 p46 S-O 2016

Reykjavík (Iceland)—Description & travel

The Jet-Setters' Guide to Weekends N. K. HAHN color *Chicago* v66 no10 p92 O 2017

Reykjavík Letterpress (Company)

PRESSING IDEAS R. Mercer *Iceland Review* v54 no6 p24 N/D 2016

Reyna, D.

Observation of coherent elastic neutrino-nucleus scattering diag *Science* v357 no6356 p1123 S 15 2017

REYNAERT, BENJAMIN

Above and Beyond color *House Beautiful* p17 Jl 2017

A Battle Royal color *House Beautiful* v159 no7 p34 S 2017

Fig Purple color *House Beautiful* v159 no7 p29 S 2017

Going the Distance color *House Beautiful* p18 Jl 2017

In This Luxe Kitchen, Purple Reigns color *House Beautiful* v159 no7 p38 S 2017

Set the Stage color *House Beautiful* v159 no7 p33 S 2017

Sunset Orange color *House Beautiful* p15 Jl 2017

Tuscan Olive color *House Beautiful* v159 no8 p21 O 2017

Reynaud-Dewar, Lili—Exhibitions

LILI REYNAUD-DEWAR M. Heddaya color *Art in America* v105 no4 p123 Ap 2017

Reynold, Dan

HOW TO REMAKE A CITY J. WILLIAMS *Cincinnati Magazine* v50 no7 p46 Ap 2017

Reynolds, Aaron

Sea Monkey & Bob *Publishers Weekly* v264 no7 p73 F 13 2017

REYNOLDS, ALAN

FROM THE ARCHIVES cartoon *Reason* v48 no10 p66 Mr 2017

Reynolds, Alison

Teams Solve Problems Faster When They're More Cognitively Diverse color graph *Harvard Business Review Digital Articles* p2 Mr 30 2017

Reynolds, Alison M.

Early childhood arts education in the United States: A special issue of Arts Education Policy Review bibl *Arts Education Policy Review* v118 no3 p133 2017

Serve and return: Communication foundations for early childhood music policy stakeholders bibl *Arts Education Policy Review* v118 no3 p140 2017

Reynolds, Anita

we asked you answered color *Cabin Living* p8 D 2016

REYNOLDS, BRANDON R.

A DAMN FINE REBOOT DAVID LYNCH RETURNS TO TWIN PEAKS color *Wired* v25 no5 p20 My 2017

Inching Ahead With Hyperloop *Los Angeles Magazine* p18 Ja

GQ: Gentlemen's Quarterly v86 no12 p172 D 2016
RYAN REYNOLDS T. Stack color *Entertainment Weekly*
no1444/1445 p14 D 16 2016

Reynolds, Simon
THIS IS GLAM ROCK J. WILLIAMS color *New York Times Book Review* p48 D 4 2016

Reynolds-Kaye, Jennifer
When the Bauhaus came to Monte Albán cartoon *Magazine Antiques* v184 no1 p166 Ja/F 2017

Reynoso, Patricia
2017 Best Beauty BUYS color *InStyle* v24 no5 p169 My 2017

Rezac, Lance
10 SUCCESSFUL FARMERS: PEOPLE TO WATCH IN AGRICULTURE D. Mawita *Successful Farming* v115 no8 p12 Je/Jl 2017

Rezaee-Zavareh, Mohammad Saeid
Creating a culture of ethics in Iran bibl *Science* v354 no6310 p296 O 21 2016

Rezakhani, Khodadad
ARAB CONQUESTS and SASANIAN IRAN *History Today* v67 no4 p28 Ap 2017

Rezende, Marcelo
The extent of forest in dryland biomes [Cover story] chart map *Science* v356 no6338 p635 My 12 2017

Reznick, Jane
Fructose-driven glycolysis supports anoxia resistance in the naked mole-rat diag graph *Science* v356 no6335 p307 Ap 21 2017

Reznik, Irina
Does Putin Still Favor His Sidekick? color graph *Bloomberg Businessweek* no4520 p28 My 1 2017
FROM RUSSIA WITH LATTES color *Bloomberg Businessweek* no4534 p42 Ag 14 2017
Moscow Confidential: Private Jets for Dogs bw color *Bloomberg Businessweek* no4498 p24 N 7 2016
Putin Isn't So Sure Trump's a Pal color *Bloomberg Businessweek* no4509 p13 Ja 30 2017

RGM Watch Co.
AMERICAN RENAISSANCE J. BROWN color *Popular Science* v289 no5 p66 S/O 2017

RH factor
Everything You Know about Being Rh-Negative Is Wrong D. E. K. TARR *Skeptical Inquirer* v41 no3 p53 My/Je 2017

Rha, J. Y. -E.
An artificial metalloenzyme with the kinetics of native enzymes bibl diag graph *Science* v354 no6308 p102 O 7 2016

Rhabdomyolysis—Prevention
When Pain Surpasses Gain J. Lisanti and T. Keith color *Sports Illustrated* v126 no4 p20 Ja 30 2017

Rhebok
The Intersection color *Runner's World* v52 no9 p58 O 2017

Rhee, James
How I Brought Ashley Stewart Back from Bankruptcy *Harvard Business Review Digital Articles* p2 Jl 31 2015

Rhee, Michelle A., 1969-
Has D.C. Teacher Reform Been Successful? J. Merrow, M. Levy et al *Washington Monthly* v49 no9/10 p16 S/O 2017

Rhee, Mooweon
K-Pop's Global Success Didn't Happen by Accident *Harvard Business Review Digital Articles* p2 N 10 2016

RHEE, NISSA
HOW TO Reboot a Holiday Classic color *Chicago* v65 no12 p92 D 2016
INDIA'S LOST WONDERS color *Chicago* v66 no4 p94 Ap 2017
PICK YOUR PODCAST color diag *Chicago* v65 no11 p42 N 2016
Teri Arvesu color *Chicago* v66 no6 p81 Je 2017
WHY We LOVE CHICAGO bw cartoon color *Chicago* v66 no3 p75 Mr 2017

Rhee, Robert
MARIA ANTELMAN color *Art in America* v105 no4 p119 Ap 2017

Rhemann, Gerald
READER GALLERY color *Astronomy* v44 no12 p70 D 2016

Rhesus monkey
30 Cool Things About Cities S. McCOLLUM color *National Geographic Kids* no472 p28 Ag 2017

IN SEARCH OF A RED-HOT LOVER P. Edmonds color *National Geographic* v231 no6 p29 Je 2017

Rhesus monkey—Reproduction
IN SEARCH OF A RED-HOT LOVER P. Edmonds color *National Geographic* v231 no6 p29 Je 2017

Rhetorical questions
Relearning the Art of Asking Questions T. Pohlmann and N. M. Thomas *Harvard Business Review Digital Articles* p2 Mr 27 2015

Rhett, Thomas, 1990-
On the Road With Thomas Rhett M. Vain color *Entertainment Weekly* no1484 p58 S 29 2017
Thomas Rhett B. Muteba color *Current Biography* v78 no2 p70 F 2017

Rheumatoid arthritis—Diagnosis
Could that joint pain be rheumatoid arthritis? *Harvard Health Letter* v42 no6 p3 Ap 2017

Rhimes, Shonda, 1970-
10 YEARS TEN STORIES C. Murray color *Essence* v47 no11 p96 Mr 2017
13 POWER PLAYERS R. R. Robertson color *Essence* v47 no11 p104 Mr 2017
Grey's Anatomy: The Body Bomb L. Rice color *Entertainment Weekly* no1460/1461 p98 Ap 7-17 2017
"My beauty standard is me" A. Gardner color *Glamour* v115 no10 p92 O 2017
SCOOP DREAMS color *New Yorker* v92 no32 p64 O 10 2016
State of Her Union L. Rice color *Entertainment Weekly* no1467 p11 My 26 2017

Rhimes, Shonda, 1970——Interviews
Shonda RHIMES color *Vanity Fair* v59 no11 p178 N 2017

RHINEHART, CHARLENE
4 CAREER GEMS FROM BLACK BUSINESS MASTERMINDS color *Black Enterprise* v47 no7 p25 My/Je 2017

Rhinehart, Rob
Ready For the Next Phase A. ROSENBLUM *Los Angeles Magazine* v62 no9 p17 S 2017

Rhinitis—Prevention
Good News for Thumb-Suckers *Parents* v91 no12 p28 D 2016

Rhinoceroses
DEHORNING dilemma K. JOHNSTON *Earth Island Journal* v32 no4 p33 Wint 2017
LAST CHANCE TO BE R. JUSKALIAN color map *Discover* v38 no9 p50 N 2017
LAST CHANCE TO SEE S. Liew *New York Times Book Review* p27 O 15 2017
Poachers Target Zoo color *Earth Island Journal* v32 no2 p9 Summ 2017

Rhinoceroses—Conservation
at the SHARP END A. Toon and S. Toon color diag *Earth Island Journal* v32 no4 p30 Wint 2017
A Rise In Rhino Poaching? K. Samuelson color *Time* v189 no12 p16 Ap 3 2017

Rhoads, Loren
Open Book J. WILLIAMS *New York Times Book Review* p6 O 1 2017

RHOADS, STEVEN E.
Sense and License color *Weekly Standard* v23 no6 p23 O 16 2017

Rhodan, Maya
After Life color diag *Time* v188 no19 p38 N 7 2016
After the Massacre [Cover story] color diag *Time* v190 no15 p22 O 16 2017
The Campus Culture Wars color *Time* v190 no16/17 p48 O 23 2017
Cops May Get Freer Hand Under Trump color *Time* v189 no14 p10 Ap 17 2017
Country First [Cover story] color *Time* v190 no7 p26 Ag 21 2017
A Dream Derailed: Trump Revokes Young Immigrants' Protections color *Time* v190 no10/11 p36 S 18 2017
Emotional Divide color diag *Time* v189 no7/8 p38 F 27 2017
The End of an Era color *Time* v188 no21 p62 N 21 2016
Federal Workers Who Made a Difference color *Time* v190 no13 p26 O 2 2017
Going After the 'Really Bad Dudes' color *Time* v190 no2/3 p12 Jl 10-17 2017
Hacking the Voter [Cover story] color *Time* v188 no14 p30 O 10

2016

A New Hard Line Would Affect Millions color *Time* v188 no22-23 p33 N/D 2016

Obamacare Sticker Shock *Time* v188 no19 p10 N 7 2016

The Other Side [Cover story] color diag *Time* v189 no4 p24 F 6 2017

Sentencing Reversal Angers Both Sides color *Time* v189 no20 p11 My 29 2017

Sheriffs May Join President Trump's Deportation Force color *Time* v189 no12 p18 Ap 3 2017

Trump Questions a Rule Obliging Financial Advisers to Put Clients' Interests First color *Time* v189 no6 p14 F 20 2017

Trump's Immigration Crackdown Seems Designed to Spread Fear color *Time* v189 no7/8 p15 F 27 2017

The U.S. Continues to Come Apart In the Wake of a Divisive Election color diag *Time* v188 no22-23 p9 N/D 2016

Why D.C.'s Missing Children Became a Political Rallying Cry color *Time* v189 no13 p17 Ap 10 2017

Why the U.S. Is Cracking Down on Gadgets In Airplane Cabins color *Time* v189 no12 p11 Ap 3 2017

Will Women Ever Break the Bronze Ceiling? color *Time* v190 no9 p28 S 4 2017

Rhode, Deborah L.

How Unusual Is the Roger Ailes Sexual Harassment Case? *Harvard Business Review Digital Articles* p2 Ag 10 2016

Understanding Your Legal Options If You've Been Sexually Harassed *Harvard Business Review Digital Articles* p1 Je 22 2017

Rhode Island

Paradise Island M. Bamberger color *Golf Magazine* v59 no11 p112 N 2017

Rhode Island—Description & travel

RHODE ISLAND *Yankee* p166 My/Je 2017

RHODEEN, PENN

THE WAR COMES HOME TO WISCONSIN: In an indelible picture 50 years ago, one family faces a loss in Vietnam *Smithsonian* v48 no5 p26 S 2017

Rhodehamel, John

First in Hearts E. ACHORN color *Weekly Standard* v22 no34 p44 My 15 2017

Rhoden, Stuart

TALK TO US color graph *Chicago* v65 no12 p24 D 2016

Rhodes, Dwight E.

Show what you know color *Phi Delta Kappan* v98 no8 p38 My 2017

Rhodes, Ken

Lee Rubin: Our mentor and role model *Science* v355 no6327 p806 F 24 2017

Rhodes, Margaret

GRAPHIC SCIENCE color *Wired* v25 no3 p30 Mr 2017

WISH LIST 2016 color *Wired* v24 no12 p45 D 2016

Rhodes, Terrel L.

The VALUE of Assessment: Transforming the Culture of Learning *Change* v48 no5 p36 S/O 2016

Rhodes, Trevante

Trevante RHODES R. JUZWIAK *Interview* v46 no9 p22 N 2016

Rhodes, Zandra, 1940—Interviews

10 Remarkable People on Having a Career That Matters *Harvard Business Review Digital Articles* p2 D 24 2014

Rhodes scholarships

Great Expectations M. MARSHALL *Texas Monthly* v45 no2 p78 F 2017

Rhodopsin

The form and function of channelrhodopsin K. Deisseroth and P. Hegemann diag *Science* v357 no6356 p1111 S 15 2017

Rhone, Alana

ERS's Updated Food Access Research Atlas Shows an Increase in Low-Income and Low-Supermarket Access Areas in 2015 *Amber Waves: The Economics of Food, Farming, Natural Resources, & Rural America* p1 F 2017

Low-Income Areas With Low Supermarket Access Increased in Urban Areas, But Not in Rural Areas, Between 2010 and 2015 *Amber Waves: The Economics of Food, Farming, Natural Resources, & Rural America* p22 Ap 2017

Rhubarb

HOMESTEAD HACKS: Our readers share clever projects that will help you live a self-sufficient life in the country, the sub-urbs, or the city S. Verberg *Mother Earth News* no283 p54 Ag/S 2017

INVIGORATING INVENTIONS Z. ROBERT *Iceland Review* v55 no1 p22 Ja/F 2017

RHYMES, SHAMEIKA

Global Decor color *Ebony* v72 no6 p56 Ap/My 2017

Rhyner, Jakob

Making SDGs Work for Climate Change Hotspots bibl *Environment* v58 no6 p24 N/D 2016

Rhys, Matthew

'The Americans': From Russia With Love R. SHEFFIELD color *Rolling Stone* no1283 p19 Mr 23 2017

Rhys, Matthew—Interviews

Girls I. Ratledge color *TV Guide* v65 no7 p43 F 13 2017

Rhythm

Rhythmic Independence & Musicality on the Drum Set D. PRIETO color diag *Downbeat* v83 no11 p68 N 2016

Rhythm & blues music

How Khalid Makes Music R. Bruner color *Time* v189 no14 p51 Ap 17 2017

Rhythm & blues musicians

WE ARE ONE R. Davis color *Essence* v48 no3 p58 Jl 2017

Rhythm & blues music—Reviews

Good to Us C. FLEMING bw *Weekly Standard* v22 no21 p33 F 6 2017

Rialmo, Robert

S.O.B. STORY *Harper's Magazine* v334 no2000 p21 Ja 2017

RIAZ, NIMRAH

The Deen Chasers *Islamic Horizons* v45 no6 p23 N/D 2016

Ribas, Moon

She's got the shakes in her elbow N. SAYEJ color *Maclean's* v129 no45 p55 N 14 2016

Ribbons

Hair Ribbons color *InStyle* v23 no13 p180 D 2016

Ribcraft USA LLC

TOP 10 TENDERS C. CASWELL color *Power & Motoryacht* v33 no4 p84 Ap 2017

Ribeiro, Fabio H.

Dynamic multinuclear sites formed by mobilized copper ions in NOx selective catalytic reduction bw color diag graph *Science* v357 no6354 p898 S 1 2017

Ribeiro, Flavio

Handcrafted Creations color *Horse & Rider* v56 no7 p36 Jl 2017

RIBEIRO, JOHN

News: Apple may produce wearable AR glasses color *Macworld - Digital Edition* p12 Ja 2017

News: Apple to replace faulty iPhone 6s batteries color *Macworld - Digital Edition* p4 Ja 2017

Privacy legislation reintroduced for mail older than 180 days color *PCWorld* v35 no2 p43 F 2017

Samsung kills off the Galaxy Note7 to end the exploding battery debacle color *PCWorld* v35 no11 p27 N 2016

RIBONS, HILARY

THE BIG GAMERS cartoon color *Field & Stream* v121 no7 p82 D 2016/Ja 2017

FOR THE RECORD color *Field & Stream* v121 no7 p17 D 2016/Ja 2017

Ribosomal DNA

Engineering the ribosomal DNA in a megabase synthetic chromosome W. Zhang, G. Zhao et al diag *Science* v355 no6329 p1049 Mr 10 2017

Ribosomal RNA

Architecture of the yeast small subunit processome M. Chaker-Margot, J. Barandun et al bibl color *Science* v355 no6321 p1 Ja 13 2017

Ribosomes

CAT-tailing as a fail-safe mechanism for efficient degradation of stalled nascent polypeptides K. K. Kostova, K. L. Hickey et al diag *Science* v355 no6349 p414 Jl 28 2017

A division of labor in cells' protein factories M. Leslie color *Science* v356 no6344 p1218 Je 23 2017

Ribosomes—Structure

The cryo-EM structure of a ribosome–Ski2-Ski3-Ski8 helicase complex C. Schmidt, E. Kowalinski et al bibl color graph *Science* v354 no6318 p1431 D 16 2016

Ribs (Anatomy)

Some woolly rhinos grew odd neck ribs S. MILIUS color *Science News* v192 no5 p10 S 30 2017

Ribs (Cooking)

Bad to the Bone *Atlanta* v57 no4 p42 Ag 2017

BRAISED AND SMOKED BOAR RIBS J. Miles color *Field & Stream* v122 no6 p24 N 2017

A CUT AbOVə ThE RƎST [Cover story] M. Sheraton color *Bon Appetit* p142 S 2017

THE KITCHEN COOKBOOK color *Better Homes & Gardens* v95 no5 p142 My 2017

KNIVES OUT C. Bond, A. Johnston et al *Texas Monthly* v44 no12 p90 D 2016

License to GRILL A. Sánchez color *O, The Oprah Magazine* p109 Je 2017

SHUCK AND Sizzle *Virginia Living* p50 2017 Smoke & Salt

STICK TO THE RIBS M. Driskill color *Southern Living* v52 no6 p98 Je 2017

Ricadela, Aaron

Artifact: General Electric Lightbulb color *Bloomberg Businessweek* no4527 p25 Je 19 2017

Europe's Startup Factory Sputters color *Bloomberg Businessweek* no4495 p31 O 17 2016

How Adidas Got Back In the Game color graph *Bloomberg Businessweek* no4493 p32 O 3 2016

Is Amazon Europe's Next Top Model? color *Bloomberg Businessweek* no4505 p21 D 26 2016

A Mouse (Maker) Roars At the Industry's Giants color *Bloomberg Businessweek* no4515 p30 Mr 20 2017

RICAPITO, MARIA

Room to Improve color *Women's Health* v14 no9 p98 N 2017

Ricard, Matthieu

A Plea for the Animals: The Moral, Philosophical, and Evolutionary Imperative to Treat All Beings with Compassion M. SCARLES *Tricycle: The Buddhist Review* v26 no2 p90 Wint 2016

Ricard, R. Tony—Interviews

REV. R. TONY RICARD F. DAWSON color *New Orleans Magazine* v51 no2 p30 D 2016

Ricardo, Trey

#trailchat color *Backpacker* v45 no2 p10 Mr 2017

Ricca, Brad—Interviews

PW TALKS WITH BRAD RICCA L. PICKER bw *Publishers Weekly* v263 no46 p42 N 14 2016

Riccardi, Pierfrancesco

The beauty of outreach cartoon *Science* v354 no6312 p674 N 4 2016

Ricci, Christina, 1980-

MY BEAUTY MARK ... Christina Ricci color *InStyle* v24 no7 p97 Jl 2017

Z: The Beginning of Everything A. D'ARMINIO *TV Guide* v65 no4 p43 Ja 16 2017

Ricci, Connie

Exposing Unfair Pricing in Auto Insurance Rates color *Consumer Reports* v82 no5 p6 My 2017

Ricci, Luca

Spiral density waves in a young protoplanetary disk bibl graph *Science* v353 no6307 p1519 S 30 2016

Ricci, Stefano

The extent of forest in dryland biomes [Cover story] chart map *Science* v356 no6338 p635 My 12 2017

Ricciardi, Jillian

Our Love Story, in One Picture A. L. Greco bw *Glamour* v115 no1 p54 Ja 2017

Riccobono, Francesco

Global atmospheric particle formation from CERN CLOUD measurements bibl graph map *Science* v354 no6316 p1119 D 2 2016

Rice

COOKING INDIAN WITH A MASTER M. JAFFREY and C. HONG color *Martha Stewart Living* p96 Mr 2017

GOLDEN CHILD N. RICHARDSON color *Bon Appetit* v62 no2 p100 Mr 2017

Golden Risotto color *Vegetarian Today* no1 p24 F 2017

Spice is Nice color *Vegetarian Today* no2 p8 Ap 2017

Start With Beans L. REGE color *Martha Stewart Living* p66 Mr 2017

Rice, Allyson M.

ATP controls the crowd color *Science* v356 no6339 p701 My 19 2017

Rice, Andrew

73 MINUTES WITH ... Eric Schneiderman img *New York* v50 no10 p22 My 15 2017

The ACLU Is Ready to Rumble img *New York* v49 no25 p59 D 12 2016

Is Trump Inc. the President's Greatest Vulnerability? A group of enterprising lawyers thinks it might be, whether all roads lead to Russia or not img *New York* v50 no12 p40 Jé 12 2017

Most Likely to Destroy a Governor img *New York* v49 no19 p48 S 19 2016

The Russians Are Coming! img *New York* p110 Mr 6 2017

THE YOUNG TRUMP [Cover story] img *New York* p22 Ja 9 2017

Rice, Anne, 1941-

Prince Lestat and the Realms of Atlantis *Publishers Weekly* v263 no44 p57 O 31 2016

Rice, Charles M.

Mouse models of acute and chronic hepacivirus infection *Science* v357 no6347 p204 Jl 14 2017

Rice, Condoleezza, 1954-

Keeper of the Flame W. R. MEAD *New York Times Book Review* p14 My 7 2017

The Uncomfortable Truth Z. R. WOOD *Weekly Standard* v22 no8 p13 O 31 2016

Rice, Condoleezza, 1954-—Interviews

The Core of a Just Society C. Phenicie *Hoover Digest: Research & Opinion on Public Policy* no2 p146 Spr 2017

Rice, Donald Tunnicliff

Cast in Deathless Bronze: Andrew Rowan, the Spanish-American War, and the Origins of American Empire color *Publishers Weekly* v263 no44 p66 O 31 2016

RICE, JACK

The Professor's Dilemma *Commentary* v144 no3 p6 O 2017

Rice, Jake

Achieving and Maintaining Sustainable Fisheries *UN Chronicle* v54 no1/2 p1 2017

Rice, Jenn

CREATE A capsule cabinet chart color *Amazing Wellness* v9 no2 p54 Spr 2017

QUICK FIXES color *Amazing Wellness* v8 no2 p40 Spr 2016

STAGES OF COLDS & FLU color *Amazing Wellness* v8 no6 p52 Early Winter2016

Rice, John

Looking for Answers to the World's Biggest Challenges In the Eternal City color *Time* v188 no24 p31 D 12 2016

Rice, Jordan

IO'S ATMOSPHERE PERIODICALLY COLLAPSES color *Astronomy* v44 no12 p8 D 2016

Lost Body *New York Times Magazine* p17 F 12 2017

Rice, Ken

Detecting structure in a protostellar disk bibl color *Science* v353 no6307 p1492 S 30 2016

Rice, Lynette

1921-2017 REMEMBERING MONTY HALL color *Entertainment Weekly* no1486 p50 O 13 2017

(1922-2016) Agnes Nixon color *Entertainment Weekly* no1435 p50 O 14 2016

1932-2016 William Christopher color *Entertainment Weekly* no1448 p53 Ja 13 2017

5 MORE SHOWS YOU NEED TO SEE color *Entertainment Weekly* no1435 p24 O 14 2016

7 Things You Didn't See color *Entertainment Weekly* no1449 p14 Ja 20 2017

9JKL color *Entertainment Weekly* no1482/1483 p49 S 22 2017

ADAM SCOTT AND CRAIG ROBINSON color *Entertainment Weekly* no1482/1483 p42 S 22 2017

After the Verdict color *Entertainment Weekly* no1482/1483 p62 S 22 2017

American Housewife *Entertainment Weekly* no1482/1483 p79 S 22 2017

Arrow *Entertainment Weekly* no1482/1483 p84 S 22 2017

Bachelor in Paradise Halts Production color *Entertainment Weekly* no1471 p16 Je 23 2017

BAYWATCH color *Entertainment Weekly* no1446/1447 p56 D 2016/Ja 2017

Better Things color *Entertainment Weekly* no1482/1483 p91 S 22

2017

black-ish *Entertainment Weekly* no1482/1483 p63 S 22 2017

The Blacklist color *Entertainment Weekly* no1482/1483 p74 S 22 2017

Bob's Burgers *Entertainment Weekly* no1482/1483 p34 S 22 2017

The Brave color *Entertainment Weekly* no1482/1483 p55 S 22 2017

Breaking Big BRANDON MICHEAL HALL color *Entertainment Weekly* no1482/1483 p65 S 22 2017

Breaking Big EMMA DUMONT color *Entertainment Weekly* no1482/1483 p51 S 22 2017

Broad City color *Entertainment Weekly* no1482/1483 p79 S 22 2017

Bull color *Entertainment Weekly* no1482/1483 p66 S 22 2017

CAN ALLIED SURVIVE THE BREAKUP? color *Entertainment Weekly* no1434 p13 O 7 2016

The Cast of Grey's Anatomy color *Entertainment Weekly* no1439 p23 N 11 2016

CHARO CHA-CHAS ONTO DWTS color *Entertainment Weekly* no1456 p18 Mr 10 2017

Chicago Fire *Entertainment Weekly* no1482/1483 p91 S 22 2017

Chicago P.D *Entertainment Weekly* no1482/1483 p79 S 22 2017

CHIPS color *Entertainment Weekly* no1446/1447 p49 D 2016/Ja 2017

CLASH OF THE TARTANS [Cover story] color *Entertainment Weekly* no1434 p20 O 7 2016

Confessions of a Reality TV FELON color *Entertainment Weekly* no1463/1464 p80 Ap/My 2017

Criminal Minds color *Entertainment Weekly* no1482/1483 p79 S 22 2017

Curb Your Enthusiasm color *Entertainment Weekly* no1482/1483 p40 S 22 2017

Dancing With the Stars *Entertainment Weekly* no1482/1483 p48 S 22 2017

DC's Legends of Tomorrow color *Entertainment Weekly* no1482/1483 p66 S 22 2017

DEMI MOORE OF Empire color *Entertainment Weekly* no1482/1483 p78 S 22 2017

Designated Survivor color *Entertainment Weekly* no1482/1483 p74 S 22 2017

The Deuce color *Entertainment Weekly* no1482/1483 p29 S 22 2017

DIVE INTO Brooklyn Nine-Nine color *Entertainment Weekly* no1482/1483 p67 S 22 2017

DORIS ROBERTS color *Entertainment Weekly* no1446/1447 p86 D 2016/Ja 2017

Dynasty color *Entertainment Weekly* no1482/1483 p76 S 22 2017

Editor's Note color *Entertainment Weekly* no1439 p23 N 11 2016

EXAMINING THE GRAMMYS' RACE ISSUE color *Entertainment Weekly* no1454/1455 p13 F 24 2017

Family Guy *Entertainment Weekly* no1482/1483 p34 S 22 2017

Fantastic Beasts and Where to Find Them color *Entertainment Weekly* no1439 p18 N 11 2016

The Flash color *Entertainment Weekly* no1482/1483 p66 S 22 2017

Flip or Flop's Marital Flap color *Entertainment Weekly* no1446/1447 p28 D 2016/Ja 2017

FLORENCE HENDERSON color *Entertainment Weekly* no1446/1447 p94 D 2016/Ja 2017

FREDDIE HIGHMORE OF The Good Doctor color *Entertainment Weekly* no1482/1483 p54 S 22 2017

Fresh Off the Boat color *Entertainment Weekly* no1482/1483 p63 S 22 2017

From CLAIRE To ETERNITY [Cover story] color *Entertainment Weekly* no1480 p22 S 1 2017

The Gifted color *Entertainment Weekly* no1482/1483 p50 S 22 2017

Gilmore Girls: A Year in the Life color *Entertainment Weekly* no1439 p18 N 11 2016

The Girlfriend Experience color *Entertainment Weekly* no1482/1483 p38 S 22 2017

GOING OUT WITH A BANG color *Entertainment Weekly* no1463/1464 p10 Ap/My 2017

The Goldbergs color *Entertainment Weekly* no1482/1483 p74 S 22 2017

Good Behavior *Entertainment Weekly* no1482/1483 p39 S 22

2017

THE GOOD FIGHT color *Entertainment Weekly* no1446/1447 p68 D 2016/Ja 2017

GOOD NEWS color *Entertainment Weekly* no1453 p28 F 17 2017

The Good Place color *Entertainment Weekly* no1482/1483 p86 S 22 2017

Gotham *Entertainment Weekly* no1482/1483 p84 S 22 2017

GRANT TINKER color *Entertainment Weekly* no1446/1447 p89 D 2016/Ja 2017

Great News color *Entertainment Weekly* no1482/1483 p88 S 22 2017

Grey's Anatomy color diag *Entertainment Weekly* no1482/1483 p89 S 22 2017

Grey's Anatomy: The Body Bomb color *Entertainment Weekly* no1460/1461 p98 Ap 7-17 2017

HAPPY ENDINGS color *Entertainment Weekly* no1439 p20 N 11 2016

Hit the Road *Entertainment Weekly* no1482/1483 p60 S 22 2017

Hot Date *Entertainment Weekly* no1482/1483 p74 S 22 2017

How to Get Away With Murder *Entertainment Weekly* no1482/1483 p91 S 22 2017

IT'S GO TIME [Cover story] color *Entertainment Weekly* no1477 p20 Ag 11 2017

JASON RITTER OF Kevin (Probably) Saves the World color *Entertainment Weekly* no1482/1483 p61 S 22 2017

KATHY BATES color *Entertainment Weekly* no1478 / 1479 p92 Ag 18-25 2017

Kevin Can Wait color *Entertainment Weekly* no1482/1483 p52 S 22 2017

THE KIDS OF STRANGER THINGS color *Entertainment Weekly* no1444/1445 p32 D 16 2016

Law & Order: Special Victims Unit *Entertainment Weekly* no1482/1483 p75 S 22 2017

Law & Order True Crime: The Menendez Murders color *Entertainment Weekly* no1482/1483 p62 S 22 2017

Lethal Weapon color *Entertainment Weekly* no1482/1483 p60 S 22 2017

Life in Pieces *Entertainment Weekly* no1482/1483 p88 S 22 2017

A Lighter Touch color *Entertainment Weekly* no1456 p30 Mr 10 2017

LITTLE BIG TOWN color *Entertainment Weekly* no1456 p34 Mr 10 2017

Lucifer *Entertainment Weekly* no1482/1483 p48 S 22 2017

Madam Secretary color *Entertainment Weekly* no1482/1483 p39 S 22 2017

Major Crimes *Entertainment Weekly* no1482/1483 p66 S 22 2017

Me, Myself & I color *Entertainment Weekly* no1482/1483 p48 S 22 2017

The Mick *Entertainment Weekly* no1482/1483 p67 S 22 2017

The Middle color *Entertainment Weekly* no1482/1483 p60 S 22 2017

Miguel Ferrer color *Entertainment Weekly* no1451/1452 p20 F 3-10 2017

Modern Family *Entertainment Weekly* no1482/1483 p75 S 22 2017

MOM color *Entertainment Weekly* no1446/1447 p62 D 2016/Ja 2017

Mom color *Entertainment Weekly* no1482/1483 p85 S 22 2017

MOM STIRS THE POT color *Entertainment Weekly* no1435 p10 O 14 2016

MORE POWER TO YOU color *Entertainment Weekly* no1473 p38 Jl 7 2017

Mr. Robot color *Entertainment Weekly* no1482/1483 p77 S 22 2017

MUSIC MADE THE PEOPLE COME TOGETHER color *Entertainment Weekly* no1439 p22 N 11 2016

NCIS *Entertainment Weekly* no1482/1483 p60 S 22 2017

NCIS: Los Angeles *Entertainment Weekly* no1482/1483 p38 S 22 2017

NCIS: New Orleans *Entertainment Weekly* no1482/1483 p67 S 22 2017

A NIGHT of FIRSTS color *Entertainment Weekly* no1484 p18 S 29 2017

The Opposition With Jordan Klepper *Entertainment Weekly* no1482/1483 p55 S 22 2017

The Orville *Entertainment Weekly* no1482/1483 p85 S 22 2017

OUTLANDER color *Entertainment Weekly* no1446/1447 p60 D 2016/Ja 2017

OUTLANDER color *Entertainment Weekly* no1474/1475 p72 Jl 21-28 2017

OUTLANDER'S NEW LADS color *Entertainment Weekly* no1434 p23 O 7 2016

Packing Even More Punch Into The Good Fight color *Entertainment Weekly* no1463/1464 p14 Ap/My 2017

PATTY DUKE color *Entertainment Weekly* no1446/1447 p92 D 2016/Ja 2017

Poldark *Entertainment Weekly* no1482/1483 p38 S 22 2017

POWER color *Entertainment Weekly* no1468/1469 p54 Je 2-9 2017

THE PROS OF CON color *Entertainment Weekly* no1476 p32 Ag 4 2017

Riverdale color *Entertainment Weekly* no1482/1483 p68 S 22 2017

SCANDAL color *Entertainment Weekly* no1448 p40 Ja 13 2017

Scandal *Entertainment Weekly* no1482/1483 p88 S 22 2017

SCANDAL WITH CARE color *Entertainment Weekly* no1451/1452 p30 F 3-10 2017

THE SCOOP, STARS & SONGS color *Entertainment Weekly* no1439 p16 N 11 2016

Scorpion color *Entertainment Weekly* no1482/1483 p55 S 22 2017

SEAL Team color *Entertainment Weekly* no1482/1483 p76 S 22 2017

Shameless color *Entertainment Weekly* no1482/1483 p30 S 22 2017

The Shannara Chronicles *Entertainment Weekly* no1482/1483 p79 S 22 2017

SHARK TANK'S WACKIEST MONEYMAKERS color *Entertainment Weekly* no1439 p51 N 11 2016

SHOCK of MOONLIGHT color *Entertainment Weekly* no1456 p42 Mr 10 2017

The Simpsons color *Entertainment Weekly* no1482/1483 p34 S 22 2017

SMILF *Entertainment Weekly* no1482/1483 p43 S 22 2017

Speechless color *Entertainment Weekly* no1482/1483 p75 S 22 2017

Star color *Entertainment Weekly* no1482/1483 p76 S 22 2017

State of Her Union color *Entertainment Weekly* no1467 p11 My 26 2017

STAY TUNED color *Entertainment Weekly* no1440 p13 N 18 2016

ST. ELMO'S FIRE color *Entertainment Weekly* no1460/1461 p34 Ap 7-17 2017

STILL STAR-CROSSED color *Entertainment Weekly* no1468/1469 p60 Je 2-9 2017

Straight Outta Kong color *Entertainment Weekly* no1457/1458 p26 Mr 17 2017

Supergirl *Entertainment Weekly* no1482/1483 p49 S 22 2017

Superior Donuts color *Entertainment Weekly* no1482/1483 p52 S 22 2017

Supernatural color *Entertainment Weekly* no1482/1483 p84 S 22 2017

Superstore color *Entertainment Weekly* no1482/1483 p84 S 22 2017

Survivor: Heroes vs. Healers vs. Hustlers *Entertainment Weekly* no1482/1483 p75 S 22 2017

S.W.A.T color *Entertainment Weekly* no1482/1483 p90 S 22 2017

A Tale of Two Sheldons color *Entertainment Weekly* no1482/1483 p44 S 22 2017

Ten Days in the Valley color *Entertainment Weekly* no1482/1483 p43 S 22 2017

This Is Us color *Entertainment Weekly* no1482/1483 p56 S 22 2017

A True Texas Gentleman color *Entertainment Weekly* no1456 p12 Mr 10 2017

TV IN THE TRUMP AGE color *Entertainment Weekly* no1441 p9 N 25 2016

TV YOU'LL FALL FOR color *Entertainment Weekly* no1467 p10 My 26 2017

Valor color *Entertainment Weekly* no1482/1483 p52 S 22 2017

The Voice color *Entertainment Weekly* no1482/1483 p49 S 22 2017

The Walking Dead color *Entertainment Weekly* no1482/1483 p38

S 22 2017

WATCH THIS/SORRY ABOUT THAT color *Entertainment Weekly* no1450 p51 Ja 27 2017

What's the Most Bingeworthy Show? color *Entertainment Weekly* no1443 p21 D 9 2016

What's Up With the Game Show Boom? color *Entertainment Weekly* no1472 p16 Je 30 2017

What to Watch color *Entertainment Weekly* no1441 p50 N 25 2016

What to Watch color *Entertainment Weekly* no1450 p54 Ja 27 2017

What to Watch color *Entertainment Weekly* no1473 p52 Jl 7 2017

What to Watch color *Entertainment Weekly* no1485 p52 O 6 2017

White Famous color *Entertainment Weekly* no1482/1483 p36 S 22 2017

Will & Grace color *Entertainment Weekly* no1471 p44 Je 23 2017

Will & Grace color *Entertainment Weekly* no1482/1483 p80 S 22 2017

WINNERS AND LOSERS color *Entertainment Weekly* no1440 p12 N 18 2016

Wisdom of the Crowd color *Entertainment Weekly* no1482/1483 p34 S 22 2017

Wrong TURN color *Entertainment Weekly* no1474/1475 p86 Jl 21-28 2017

RICE, ROBERT A.

Using Plant-Animal Interactions to Inform Tree Selection in Tree-Based Agroecosystems for Enhanced Biodiversity *BioScience* v66 no12 p1046 D 1 2016

Rice, Susan E., 1964-

Susan Rice: Talking Trump and tennis with the former national-security adviser M. TOMASKY *New York* v50 no13 p16 Je 26 2017

Unmasking and Leaks: Trump's Russia Retort M. Calabresi color *Time* v189 no14 p15 Ap 17 2017

RICE, TAMEKIA

body-art q+a's *Parents* v92 no5 p115 My 2017

Rice, Theresa

Without limits color *Equus* no472 p63 Ja 2017

Rice, Travis

THE POWDER AND THE GLORY B. BRADLEY color *Vanity Fair* v58 no11 p184 N 2016

Rice, Travis—Interviews

FOURTHCOMING P. Bridges bw color *Snowboarder* v29 no4 p68 D 2016

Rice blast disease

Evolution of the wheat blast fungus through functional losses in a host specificity determinant Y. Inoue, T. T. P. Vy et al diag map *Science* v357 no6346 p80 Jl 7 2017

Rice products—Evaluation

Thank You Very Mochi G. SNYDER *Los Angeles Magazine* v62 no9 p116 S 2017

Rice University

Hot Rockets P. Patel bw color *Scientific American* v317 no1 p20 Jl 2017

Rice wines

DRINK UP *Los Angeles Magazine* v62 no9 p115 S 2017

Rice—Environmental aspects

Reinventing Rice for a World Transformed by Climate Change J. Temple color *MIT Technology Review* v120 no4 p15 Jl/Ag 2017

Rice—Varieties

SL cooking school K. Hammonds color *Southern Living* v52 no2 p142 F 2017

Rice—Yields

Durable resistance to rice blast Wang and B. Valent bibl color *Science* v355 no6328 p906 Mr 3 2017

Rich, Adrienne, 1929-2012

Finding the Catholic Voices In Social Justice Poetry L. Ampleman color *America* v216 no10 p42 My 1 2017

Rich, B. Ruby

The Seen and The Unseen *Film Quarterly* v71 no1 p5 Fall 2017

Sundance 2017: Of Snow and Anguish *Film Quarterly* v70 no4 p99 Summ 2017

Under Duress *Film Quarterly* v70 no4 p5 Summ 2017

When History Makes the Cut *Film Quarterly* v70 no3 p6 Spr 2017

RICH, BERND HEIN

Conversing with a Sapsucker *Natural History* v124 no10 p13 N 2016

Rich, Buddy, 1917-1987

Buddy Rich J. McDonough bw *Downbeat* v84 no1 p42 Ja 2017

Rich, Doug

(At home with) G. R. SCHIAVINO color *Team Roping Journal* p44 O 2017

Rich, Frank

A Call to (Emotional) Arms *New York* v49 no15 p20 Jl 25 2016

The Establishment Never Had a Chance img *New York* v49 no23 p24 N 14 2016

OBAMA'S AMERICA img *New York* v49 no20 p12 O 3 2016

Rich, G. C.

Observation of coherent elastic neutrino-nucleus scattering diag *Science* v357 no6356 p1123 S 15 2017

Rich, Jessica—Interviews

Empowering Consumers in a Digital World color *Consumer Reports* v82 no9 p5 S 2017

Rich, Larry

ASK THE EXPERTS color *Runner's World* v51 no11 p42 D 2016

Rich, Mari

Adam Grant color *Current Biography* v78 no9 p27 S 2017

Andrew Bacevich color *Current Biography* v77 no11 p12 N 2016

Angel Olsen [Cover story] color *Current Biography* v78 no6 p83 Je 2017

Anne Case color *Current Biography* v78 no3 p8 Mr 2017

Avery Amereau color *Current Biography* v78 no8 p3 Ag 2017

Barry Jenkins bw *Current Biography* v78 no5 p39 My 2017

Braden Holtby color *Current Biography* v78 no1 p27 Ja 2017

Bryson Tiller color *Current Biography* v78 no3 p78 Mr 2017

Carol Anderson color *Current Biography* v78 no2 p3 F 2017

Chris Jackson *Current Biography* v77 no10 p63 O 2016

Christopher Kimball color *Current Biography* v78 no6 p59 Je 2017

Deborah Levy color *Current Biography* v78 no5 p49 My 2017

Emma Cline color *Current Biography* v78 no8 p17 Ag 2017

Helen Marten color *Current Biography* v78 no4 p52 Ap 2017

Iliza Shlesinger color *Current Biography* v78 no4 p72 Ap 2017

James Corden color *Current Biography* v78 no2 p21 F 2017

Julia Garner color *Current Biography* v78 no6 p43 Je 2017

Julien Baker color *Current Biography* v77 no11 p17 N 2016

Margot Robbie color *Current Biography* v78 no1 p69 Ja 2017

Massimo Bottura color *Current Biography* v78 no4 p12 Ap 2017

Melissa Villaseñor bw *Current Biography* v78 no2 p79 F 2017

Neil Gorsuch color *Current Biography* v78 no9 p23 S 2017

Ruth Negga color *Current Biography* v78 no5 p63 My 2017

Von Miller color *Current Biography* v78 no3 p68 Mr 2017

Yuja Wang color *Current Biography* v78 no1 p86 Ja 2017

Rich, Nathaniel

Inside the Sacrifice Zone color *New York Review of Books* v63 no17 p15 N 10 2016

Joan Didion in the Deep South bw *New York Review of Books* v64 no4 p8 Mr 9 2017

Lessons of the Hermit color *Atlantic* v319 no3 p41 Ap 2017

Mixed-Up Kids bw color *New York Review of Books* v64 no6 p14 Ap 6 2017

Moscow Believes in Tears color *New York Times Book Review* p11 Ja 29 2017

THE PREACHER AND THE SHERIFF color *New York Times Magazine* p28 F 12 2017

THE Prophecies of Jane Jacobs cartoon color *Atlantic* v318 no4 p98 N 2016

Robert B. Silvers (1929–2017) [Cover story] bw color *New York Review of Books* v64 no8 p31 My 11 2017

Rushdie's New York Bubble bw *New York Review of Books* v64 no16 p33 O 26 2017

Rich, Rob

BETTER WITH BEAVERS color *Earth Island Journal* v32 no1 p30 Spr 2017

Rich, Ruby

Film Criticism in the Era of Algorithms *Film Quarterly* v70 no2 p5 Wint 2016

Reporting the Start of a Season: Toronto International Film Festival *Film Quarterly* v70 no2 p81 Wint 2016

Rich, Seth

Prime-Time Conspiracy Theory [Cover story] J. Mccormack color *Weekly Standard* v22 no37 p11 Je 5 2017

RICH, SIMON

THE BOOK OF SIMON cartoon *New Yorker* v92 no30 p31 S 26 2016

Rich people

See also

Billionaires

Children of the rich

Ultra high net worth individuals

The $150 BILLION MOMENT A. BROWN color *Forbes* v200 no5 p21 N 14 2017

America's Richest Celebrities Z. O. GREENBURG, N. ROBEHMED et al color *Forbes* v198 no9 p18 D 30 2016

America's Richest Self-Made Women color *Forbes* v199 no6 p86 Je 13 2017

THE APPLE CORPS A. AU-YEUNG color *Forbes* v200 no1 p26 Jl 27 2017

Are the Super-Rich Really Ruining the World's Great Cities? R. Florida *Harvard Business Review Digital Articles* p2 Je 9 2017

CONVERSATION A. WILSON color graph *Forbes* v200 no1 p32 Jl 27 2017

DECEASED, DECLINED OR LEFT BEHIND M. TINDERA color *Forbes* v200 no5 p28 N 14 2017

Down And Out M. TINDERA color *Forbes* v199 no3 p34 Mr 28 2017

Forbes 400 index *Forbes* v200 no5 p166 N 14 2017

FROM THE EDITOR P. Laif *History Today* v67 no3 p2 Mr 2017

HOLLOWED GROUND M. TINDERA color *Forbes* v200 no1 p15 Jl 27 2017

THE INTEREST GRAPH A. WILSON graph *Forbes* v199 no4 p30 Ap 25 2017

Microaggression and Macrononsense A. FERGUSON color *Weekly Standard* v22 no25 p26 Mr 6 2017

NINE ZEROS: OCTOBER 9, 2006 A. BROWN color *Forbes* v200 no5 p36 N 14 2017

One Winner, One Loser After a Fortune's Split D. Pendleton and Y. Benmeleh color *Bloomberg Businessweek* no4506 p33 Ja 9 2017

THE ORIGINAL RICH LIST C. PETERSON-WITHORN bw chart color *Forbes* v200 no3 p34 S 28 2017

OTHER LESSONS FROM THE RICH P. J. Lim *Money* v46 no9 p37 O 2017

THE PRICE OF THE GOOD LIFE A. MURPHY color graph *Forbes* v200 no5 p32 N 14 2017

Rethinking the Way L. D'VORKIN *Forbes* v198 no5 p26 O 25 2016

A SNACK BEFORE THE BANQUET T. CLARKSON *Commonweal* v144 no11 p2 Je 16 2017

SUPPORT FROM THE RICH FRINGE SHOWS NO SIGNS OF DRYING UP img *New York* v50 no9 p48 My 1 2017

SURVIVAL OF THE RICHEST E. OSNOS cartoon color *New Yorker* v92 no47 p36 Ja 30 2017

Why Rich People Aren't as Happy as They Could Be R. Raghunathan *Harvard Business Review Digital Articles* p2 Je 8 2016

THE WORLD'S BILLIONAIRES L. KROLL, K. A. DOLAN et al bw color diag graph map *Forbes* v199 no3 p84 Mr 28 2017

Rich people—China

China's Richest K. A. DOLAN color map *Forbes* v198 no7 p28 N 29 2016

Rich people—Finance

The Expense of Exclusive Living A. BROWN and A. MURPHY color graph *Forbes* v198 no5 p46 O 25 2016

Rich people—History—20th century

Sept. 13, 1982: The First Forbes 400 A. BROWN bw color *Forbes* v198 no5 p54 O 25 2016

Rich people—India

India's Richest People color *Forbes* v198 no6 p34 N 8 2016

Rich people—Investments

How America's Wealthiest Black Families Invest Money S. G. Carmichael *Harvard Business Review Digital Articles* p2 F 10 2015

Rich people—New York (State)—New York

LEASHED J. Torres color *New Yorker* v92 no32 p60 O 10 2016

Rich people—Political activity

WEST BLING D. Gilson *Mother Jones* v42 no2 p4 Mr/Ap 2017

Rich people—Psychology

MONEY THERAPISTS A. GARA, A. EBELING et al color *Forbes* v200 no4 p104 O 24 2017

Rich people—Russia

RUSSIA HAS EVEN MORE OFFSHORE WEALTH THAN WE THOUGHT color *Fortune* v176 no4 p30 S 15 2017

Rich people—Taxation

Planning for a Low-Tax, High-Deficit World L. Braham *Bloomberg Businessweek* no4516 p42 Mr 27 2017

Untaxing the Rich R. PONNURU color *National Review* v69 no19 p21 O 16 2017

Richard & Lucille Durrell Edge of Appalachia Preserve System (Ohio)

AU NATUREL: Eighty miles east of downtown, Edge of Appalachia Nature Preserve is expanding, and late summer is peak time to visit its prairie lands A. KONERMANN *Cincinnati Magazine* v50 no11 p26 Ag 2017

Richard, Cliff

Chuck Berry color *Time* v189 no12 p19 Ap 3 2017

Richard, Dawn

Dawn Richard: Out of This World M. Vain color *Entertainment Weekly* no1441 p54 N 25 2016

Richard, Rhen

Richard Recovering from Thumb-Reattachment color *Spin to Win Rodeo* v21 no2 p20 Ap 2017

RICHARD, SCOTT

PHYSICS IN 2116 *Physics Today* v69 no12 p39 D 2016

Richard Meier & Partners Architects LLP

sources *Architectural Digest* v74 no1 p230 Ja 2017

Richard Nixon Library & Birthplace

New Looks for Museums At Presidential Libraries *Prologue* v49 no1 p69 Spr 2017

Renovated Nixon Library Reopening *Prologue* v48 no3 p68 Fall 2016

Richard III, King of England, 1452-1485

Richard III—Resting in Peace D. Huntley *British Heritage Travel* v38 no1 p8 Ja/F 2017

RICHARDS, ALECIA

A DOWN PAYMENT ON ENDING MASS INCARCERATION *In These Times* v41 no1 p11 Ja 2017

RICHARDS, ANDREA

Rats? In My House? Say It Ain't So *Los Angeles Magazine* p70 F 2017

Richards, Byron

ACCESS AGENTS A. McKEAN color *Outdoor Life* v224 no1 p32 D 2016/Ja 2017

Richards, Cecile

Due CARE A. Wintour color *Vogue* v207 no7 p30 Jl 2017

My Desk: CECILE RICHARDS color *Vanity Fair* v59 no11 p62 N 2017

ON the FRONT LINES J. Van Meter bw color *Vogue* v207 no7 p84 Jl 2017

Richards, Cory—Interviews

Cory Richards T. FOSTER color *Men's Health* v32 no6 p136 Ag 2017

Richards, Daniel

Benefits of trees in tropical cities color *Science* v356 no6344 p1241 Je 23 2017

RICHARDS, DOUGLAS E.

10 FREAKY FORCES OF NATURE color *National Geographic Kids* no465 p26 N 2016

Richards, E. Randolph

The Bossy Apostle color *Christianity Today* v60 no9 p74 N 2016

Richards, Keith, 1943-

'The Granddaddy of Us All' bw *Rolling Stone* no1285 p34 Ap 20 2017

Random Notes color *Rolling Stone* no1274 p20 N 17 2016

Richards, Keith, 1943-—Interviews

The Rolling Stones, Recharged C. Collis color *Entertainment Weekly* no1440 p58 N 18 2016

RICHARDS, LAURA

When Small Changes Can Earn You Big Bucks color *Reader's Digest* v190 no1134 p52 O 2017

Richards, Matt

Dutch election highlights divisions about religion and immigration *Christian Century* v134 no8 p1 Ap 12 2017

Somebody to Love D. ANDERSON-MINSHALL bw color *Advocate* no1089 p60 F/Mr 2017

Richards, Nigel A. D.

Global atmospheric particle formation from CERN CLOUD measurements bibl graph map *Science* v354 no6316 p1119 D 2 2016

Richards, Renée, 1934-

The SUMMER of 1977 S. TIGNOR bw color *Tennis* v53 no5 p68 S/O 2017

Richards, Sian

100 Surprising Innovations TO MAKE THIS YEAR YOUR Happiest AND Healthiest, MOST Organic YEAR EVER cartoon color *Rodale's Organic Life* v3 no1 p49 Ja 2017

RICHARDS, SIMON

FAST CORNERS AND FLYING HIGH color *Dirt Sports + Off-Road* v51 no11 p36 N 2017

GIVING BACK color *Dirt Sports + Off-Road* v51 no9 p58 S 2017

AN INTERESTING TWIST color diag *Dirt Sports + Off-Road* v51 no11 p62 N 2017

LEGACY LEGITIMIZATION color *Dirt Sports + Off-Road* v51 no11 p10 N 2017

MINOR INFRACTION color *Dirt Sports + Off-Road* v51 no4 p18 Ap 2017

ONE-HOUR WONDER color *Dirt Sports + Off-Road* v51 no7 p58 Jl 2017

REAREND REDUX color *Dirt Sports + Off-Road* v51 no11 p26 N 2017

SAFETY FAST color *Dirt Sports + Off-Road* v51 no6 p30 Je 2017

SMOKE AND MIRRORS color *Dirt Sports + Off-Road* v51 no9 p26 S 2017

TWO HOUR WONDER: PUTTING THE FOX IN THE PENTHOUSE color *Dirt Sports + Off-Road* v51 no8 p62 Ag 2017

RICHARDS, TODD

THANKS FOR THE RIDE color *Bicycling* v58 no10 p15 N/D 2017

Richards, Tom

BUCKLE UP with Tom Richards C. Toy color *Spin to Win Rodeo* v21 no1 p21 Mr 2017

Richards-Kortum, Rebecca

SMILE AND SAY, "MALAWI!" *Texas Monthly* v44 no12 p14 D 2016

Richards-Kortum, Rebecca—Interviews

OUT OF Africa M. SWARTZ *Texas Monthly* v44 no12 p74 D 2016

Richardson, Adam

Great UX Doesn't Guarantee a Great Customer Experience *Harvard Business Review Digital Articles* p2 Ag 12 2015

Prototyping That's Less Prone to Failure *Harvard Business Review Digital Articles* p2 D 7 2015

What You Can and Should Be Doing with Your Customer Journeys *Harvard Business Review Digital Articles* p2 Mr 25 2016

Richardson, Brenda

Conservation Begins With Your Boots On The Ground D. IRVIN *American Forests* v123 no2 p46 Summ 2017

RICHARDSON, BURTON

7 SILAT SOLUTIONS color *Black Belt* v55 no3 p46 Ap/My 2017

Richardson, Carmen

Teachers are designers color il *Phi Delta Kappan* v99 no2 p60 O 2017

Richardson, Carol M.

WARFARE, TERROR, MURDER AND BLOODSHED: A compelling narrative on the machinations of a Borgia pope and his offspring, with the added spice of Machiavelli's cool observations *History Today* v67 no7 p96 Jl 2017

Richardson, Chris

Statin Denialism? *Skeptical Inquirer* v41 no5 p63 S/O 2017

RICHARDSON, DAVID M.

Scientific and Normative Foundations for the Valuation of Alien-Species Impacts: Thirteen Core Principles *BioScience* v67 no2 p166 F 2017

Richardson, H. H. (Henry Hobson), 1838-1886

Richardson Revival B. BROOME *Architectural Record* v205 no9 p78 S 2017

Richardson, Haley Lu, 1995-

Building Blocks R. Brody color *New Yorker* v93 no17 p6 Je 19 2017

Columbus *New Yorker* v93 no23 p10 Ag 7 2017

HALEY LU RICHARDSON D. Coggan color *Entertainment Weekly* no1478 / 1479 p86 Ag 18-25 2017

SCENE STEALERS S. BAHR bw color *Indianapolis Monthly*

v41 no2 p78 S 2017

Richardson, Henry

Love and Justice for Each: Martha C. Nussbaum Through the Eyes of a Friend and Colleague *Humanities* v38 no2 p3 Spr 2017

Richardson, Joan

Charter schools don't serve black children well color *Phi Delta Kappan* v98 no5 p41 F 2017

The Editor's Note *Phi Delta Kappan* v98 no4 p4 D 2016/Ja 2017

The Editor's Note *Phi Delta Kappan* v98 no7 p4 Ap 2017

The Editor's Note *Phi Delta Kappan* v98 no8 p4 My 2017

The Editor's Note *Phi Delta Kappan* v99 no1 p4 S 2017

Highlighted & Underlined color diag *Phi Delta Kappan* v99 no1 p6 S 2017

Highlighted & Underlined color *Phi Delta Kappan* v98 no8 p6 My 2017

White like me *Phi Delta Kappan* v98 no5 p4 F 2017

RICHARDSON, JOHN

TRACKING MYTHS color *Scientific American* v316 no4 p6 Ap 2017

Richardson, John H.

THE BALLAD OF KELCY WARREN cartoon *Mother Jones* v42 no2 p12 Mr/Ap 2017

The Collected Works of ROBERT RAUSCHENBERG color *Esquire* p74 S 2017

The CONVERSATION of Art bw color *Esquire* p76 Je/Jl 2017

RICHARDSON, JOHN S.

Terrestrial Invertebrates in the Riparian Zone: Mechanisms Underlying Their Unique Diversity *BioScience* v67 no9 p808 S 2017

Richardson, Kaylin

SADDLE UP D. Pogge bw color *Skiing* p48 Wint 2017

Richardson, Kim Michele

The Sisters of Glass Ferry *Publishers Weekly* v264 no41 p42 O 9 2017

RICHARDSON, NICK

THEY'VE CREATED HEIR OWN MEDIA ECOSYSTEM img *New York* v50 no9 p46 My 1 2017

Richardson, Nikita

BRIGHT SPOTS color *Bon Appetit* v62 no2 p86 Mr 2017

Chucktown Fresh color *Bon Appetit* no8 p48 Ag 2017

Cook Like a Pro: Summer Edition [Cover story] bw color diag *Bon Appetit* v62 no7 p56 Jl 2017

A Day at the Beach color *Bon Appetit* v62 no7 p18 Jl 2017

EATING LUNCH AT YOUR DESK color *Bloomberg Businessweek* no4493 p86 O 3 2016

The French Are Coming! bw color *Bon Appetit* v62 no4 p15 Ap 2017

GOd bLeSS ReD SAUCe AMeRiCA color *Bon Appetit* p126 S 2017

GOLDEN CHILD color *Bon Appetit* v62 no2 p100 Mr 2017

Home Shucked color *Bon Appetit* no11 p36 N 2017

Meet Me in Vegas color *Bon Appetit* v62 no4 p24 Ap 2017

prep school bw color *Bon Appetit* v62 no10 p105 O 2017

prep school bw color *Bon Appetit* v62 no4 p112 Ap 2017

prep school bw color *Bon Appetit* v62 no7 p97 Jl 2017

Punch Up Your Summer color *Bon Appetit* no8 p42 Ag 2017

Spring Pasta color *Bon Appetit* v62 no4 p76 Ap 2017

starters bw color diag *Bon Appetit* v62 no2 p19 Mr 2017

starters color *Bon Appetit* p25 S 2017

starters color *Bon Appetit* v62 no6 p17 Je 2017

This Month in Beer color *Bon Appetit* no8 p24 Ag 2017

THE WRINGER color *Bon Appetit* no8 p102 Ag 2017

Richardson, Rachel

Rachel Richardson G. KOURLAS *Dance Magazine* v90 no11 p22 N 2016

Richardson, Reed

With Climate Denial in the White House, Will Media Echo Official Know-Nothingism? *Extra!* v30 no4 p4 My 2017

Richardson, Roland

From Sea to Shining Sea *Parks & Recreation* v52 no4 p30 Ap 2017

Parks, Recreation and Resilience *Parks & Recreation* v51 no12 p26 D 2016

Richardson, Sally

That Was the Week That Was color *Publishers Weekly* v264 no24 p26 Je 12 2017

Richardson, Sam

CRAFTING SUCCESS T. Foster color *Men's Health* v32 no2 p36 Mr 2017

Richardson, Sam—Interviews

Sam Richardson E. Berman color *Time* v189 no6 p48 F 20 2017

VEEP'S SAM RICHARDSON GETS OUR VOTE N. Maslow color *Entertainment Weekly* no1467 p52 My 26 2017

Richardson, Sarah

Before Bernie *American History* v52 no1 p34 Ap 2017

The Circus is Not in Town color *American History* v52 no2 p7 Je 2017

Decalifornication bw *American History* v52 no4 p6 O 2017

Early Algonquian Tomes Displayed color *American History* v52 no2 p8 Je 2017

FISTS OF CLAY *American History* v52 no1 p24 Ap 2017

From Revolution to Rhythm & Blues bw color *American History* v52 no3 p6 Ag 2017

Hard Times at Mid-Continent color *American History* v52 no2 p10 Je 2017

Hemp Harvest in Virginia *American History* v52 no1 p8 Ap 2017

I See Your Cahokia and Raise You My Quivira color *American History* v52 no4 p8 O 2017

Lynchings Remembered color *American History* v52 no3 p10 Ag 2017

Made-in-America—The Colony color *American History* v52 no2 p8 Je 2017

PATRON OF THE PILL *American History* v51 no6 p24 F 2017

Remembering Reconstruction color *American History* v52 no2 p9 Je 2017

RESISTERHOOD IS POWERFUL bw color *American History* v52 no3 p24 Ag 2017

RESTLESS ROAMER color *American History* v52 no4 p26 O 2017

SEA CHANGE bw color *American History* v52 no2 p28 Je 2017

Synthesis, debugging, and effects of synthetic chromosome consolidation: synVI and beyond color *Science* v355 no6329 p1045 Mr 10 2017

Tubman Time bw *American History* v52 no2 p6 Je 2017

White Supremacist Monument Ditched *American History* v51 no6 p6 F 2017

Whose Representative Government, Again? *American History* v52 no1 p6 Ap 2017

Richardson, Sarah M.

Bug mapping and fitness testing of chemically synthesized chromosome X diag *Science* v355 no6329 p1048 Mr 10 2017

Deep functional analysis of synII, a 770-kilobase synthetic yeast chromosome diag *Science* v355 no6329 p1047 Mr 10 2017

Design of a synthetic yeast genome bibl chart color graph *Science* v355 no6329 p1040 Mr 10 2017

Engineering the ribosomal DNA in a megabase synthetic chromosome diag *Science* v355 no6329 p1049 Mr 10 2017

Richardson, Stephen H.

Large gem diamonds from metallic liquid in Earth's deep mantle bibl color *Science* v354 no6318 p1403 D 16 2016

Richardson, W. D.

The sacral autonomic outflow is sympathetic bibl color diag *Science* v354 no6314 p893 N 18 2016

Richardson-Price, Alex

The Soil Depletion Crisis *History Today* v66 no12 p4 D 2016

Richarme, Gilbert

Guanine glycation repair by DJ-1/Park7 and its bacterial homologs chart color diag graph *Science* v357 no6347 p208 Jl 14 2017

Richaud, Pierre

An algal photoenzyme converts fatty acids to hydrocarbons color graph *Science* v357 no6354 p903 S 1 2017

Richdale, Andrew

THE IMPOSSIBLE LIST bw cartoon color *Esquire* v167 no1 p70 F 2017

Rich Eisen Show, The (TV program)

Rich Eisen J. Marksbury and J. Marksbury color *Golf Magazine* v59 no10 p32 O 2017

Richer, Jean-François

The Gibson Quandary J. PODHORETZ *Weekly Standard* v22 no4 p38 O 3 2016

Richer, Mark—Interviews

ATSC 3.0: TV's Next Generation B. Ankosko color *Sound & Vision* v82 no7 p18 S 2017

Richers, Sami

SADDLE CHAT bw color graph *Horse & Rider* v56 no11 p21 N 2017

Richey, Roberta

Designing Woman color *Log Home Living* v34 no1 p16 F 2017

Richie, Christopher T.

Chemogenetics revealed: DREADD occupancy and activation via converted clozapine graph *Science* v357 no6350 p503 Ag 4 2017

Richie, Lionel, 1949-

A NEW GROOVE L. IMMEDIATO *Los Angeles Magazine* p34 Ja 2017

Richie, Nicole

My Skin color *InStyle* v24 no5 p240 My 2017

Richie, Ross, 1970-

Ross Richie J. Crelin color *Current Biography* v77 no11 p68 N 2016

Richler, Emma

Emma's Version L. MCLAREN *Walrus* v14 no2 p55 Mr 2017

RICHLER, JACOB

The best meat you don't eat color *Maclean's* v130 no2 p70 Mr 2017

Beware of cookery 'science' color *Maclean's* p59 Je 2017

Calling for kelp color *Maclean's* no1 p63 F 17 2017

Have it your whey color *Maclean's* v129 no51/52 p68 D 26 2016

Kill What You Eat color *Walrus* v14 no4 p15 My 2017

Last call at Le Mas color *Maclean's* v129 no40 p75 O 10 2016

Now you seafood, now you don't color *Maclean's* v130 no4 p66 My 2017

Stuck in the craw color *Maclean's* v130 no3 p70 Ap 2017

Welcome, quinoa tartare color *Maclean's* v129 no46 p58 N 21 2016

What a delicious mess chart color *Maclean's* v130 no6 p16 Jl 2017

Richler, Noah

Noah and the Liberal flood B. BETHUNE color *Maclean's* v129 no41 p24 O 17 2016

Road to Everywhere cartoon map *Walrus* v14 no6 p19 Jl/Ag 2017

RICHMA, ALAN

SCENE STEALER color *Esquire* v166 no4 p124 N 2016

Richman, Barak

How to Make Health Care Accountable When We Don't Know What Works *Harvard Business Review Digital Articles* p2 N 25 2014

Richmond (Va.)—Description & travel

Out & About *Martha Stewart Living* no269 p6 N 2016

TAKE A DRIVE: RICHMOND S. Breijo color *Washingtonian Magazine* v52 no7 p123 Ap 2017

Richmond, Brian

Curator resigns after sexual misconduct investigations A. Gibbons color *Science* v354 no6317 p1216 D 9 2016

Richmond, Laurel P.

Providing Equal Access to Aquatic Facility Locker Rooms for People Who are Transgender *Parks & Recreation* v51 no10 p88 O 2016

Richmond, Michelle

The Marriage Pact *Publishers Weekly* v264 no20 p37 My 15 2017

Richmond Park (London, England)

England color *National Geographic* v231 no3 p10 Mr 2017

Rich people—Charts, diagrams, etc.

DOCTORATE, DEGREE OR DROPOUT? D. CAM and A. AU-YEUNG diag graph *Forbes* v200 no5 p24 N 14 2017

THE FORBES 400 bw color *Forbes* v200 no5 p86 N 14 2017

THE PLANET'S RICHEST PERSON K. VINTON bw color graph *Forbes* v200 no2 p30 S 5 2017

Three Decades of Ten-Figure Fortunes K. BLANKFELD and M. TINDERA graph *Forbes* v199 no3 p30 Mr 28 2017

Richtel, Matt

DRIVEN TO DISTRACTION *New York Times Upfront* v149 no10 p10 Mr 13 2017

Richter, Daniel

DANIEL RICHTER K. Bellmann color *Art in America* v105 no5 p139 My 2017

Richter, David H.

OCEAN SPRAY: AN OUTSIZED INFLUENCE ON WEATHER

AND CLIMATE *Physics Today* v69 no11 p34 N 2016

Richter, Dominik—Interviews

DOMINIK RICHTER color *Harvard Business Review* v95 no2 p156 Mr/Ap 2017

Richter, Gerhard, 1932-

A B color *Art in America* v104 no10 p46 N 2016

Richter, Johannes M.

High-performance light-emitting diodes based on carbene-metal-amides chart graph *Science* v356 no6334 p159 Ap 14 2017

RICHTER, KAT

the case for ballet in college *Dance Magazine* p14 2016/2017

the case for ballet in college: How a ballet degree can lead to a performance career *Dance Magazine* v90 p14 2016/2017 Supplement College Guide

Richter, Nathan

Is Rooftop Solar Finally Good Enough to Disrupt the Grid? *Harvard Business Review Digital Articles* p2 My 21 2015

RICHTER, TARA

Alpha Male vs. Alpha Female *USA Today Magazine* v145 no2862 p66 Mr 2017

Richter Goods (Company)

Richter Goods *Texas Monthly* v45 no3 p33 Mr 2017

Rich & the Ruthless, The (TV program)

STREAMING A. D'ARMINIO *TV Guide* v65 no31 p38 Jl 24 2017

Ricin

Researchers close in on ricin antidote M. ROSEN color *Science News* v191 no4 p14 Mr 4 2017

Rick & Morty (TV program)

Extradimensional: Rick and Morty is as affecting as it is loopy M. Z. SEITZ img *New York* v50 no16 p107 Ag 7 2017

Why Is Rick and Morty So Fun? It's All About the References L. Eadicicco color *Time* v190 no6 p53 Ag 7 2017

Rick, Christian

Transient compartmentalization of RNA replicators prevents extinction due to parasites bibl chart graph *Science* v354 no6317 p1293 D 9 2016

Rickaby, Dave

Rio Grande through the West color map *Model Railroader* v84 no2 p58 F 2017

Rickards, Tuck

The Board Directors You Need for a Digital Transformation *Harvard Business Review Digital Articles* p2 Jl 13 2017

RICKART, ERIC

Transformational Principles for NEON Sampling of Mammalian Parasites and Pathogens: A Response to Springer and Colleagues *BioScience* v66 no11 p917 N 1 2016

Ricketts, Lowell R.

Does College Level the Playing Field? *Bridges (Federal Reserve Bank of St. Louis)* p7 Spr 2017

RICKETTS, TAYLOR H.

When, Where, and How Nature Matters for Ecosystem Services: Challenges for the Next Generation of Ecosystem Service Models *BioScience* v67 no9 p820 S 2017

RICKEY, CARRIE

Director: Her Art and Resilience in Times of Transition *Film Quarterly* v70 no4 p124 Summ 2017

Haunted: On Ghosts, Witches, Vampires, Zombies, and Other Monsters of the Natural and Supernatural *Film Quarterly* v71 no1 p111 Fall 2017

Steven Spielberg: A Life in Films *Film Quarterly* v70 no3 p92 Spr 2017

When Broadway Went to Hollywood *Film Quarterly* v70 no2 p101 Wint 2016

Ricklefs,, M.C.

A Flawed Portrait *History Today* v67 no7 p6 Jl 2017

Rickles, Don, 1926-2017

Dinner With Don—and AARP R. Love color *AARP: The Magazine* v30 no6A p4 O/N 2017

Don Rickles 1926-2017 M. Roush *TV Guide* p12 Ap 17 2017

Don Rickles P. Oswalt color *Time* v189 no15 p13 Ap 24 2017

Longevity bw color *Forbes* v199 no2 p110 F 28 2017

Rickman, Alan, 1946-2016

ALAN RICKMAN K. Winslet and C. Nashawaty color *Entertainment Weekly* no1446/1447 p92 D 2016/Ja 2017

Rickman, H.

Rosetta's comet 67P/Churyumov-Gerasimenko sheds its dusty mantle to reveal its icy nature bibl graph *Science* v354 no6319 p1566 D 23 2016

Surface changes on comet 67P/Churyumov-Gerasimenko suggest a more active past bw graph *Science* v355 no6332 p1392 Mr 31 2017

Ricks, Thomas E.

Churchill & Orwell: The Fight for Freedom *Publishers Weekly* v264 no11 p68 Mr 13 2017

The Two Winstons: A dual biography of two independent thinkers R. ALDOUS *New York Times Book Review* p9 Je 11 2017

War Stories: Military History *New York Times Book Review* p20 My 28 2017

War Stories / Military History *New York Times Book Review* p40 N 13 2016

We Are (Still) Living in an Orwellian World color *Foreign Policy* no225 p80 Jl/Ag 2017

Writers and truth tellers, defined by war T. Maier bw *America* v217 no7 p46 O 2 2017

Rickshaws

How Mobile Apps Are Improving India's Rickshaws A. Dasgupta *Harvard Business Review Digital Articles* p1 Ja 13 2016

Ricoh camera—Evaluation

THEATER IN THE ROUND A. Ryder color *Popular Photography* v81 no1 p20 Ja/F 2017

RICZO, STEVE

REPEAL AND REPLACE? *USA Today Magazine* v145 no2860 p24 Ja 2017

RID, THOMAS

THE PLOT AGAINST AMERICA cartoon color *Esquire* v166 no5 p130 D 2016/Ja 2017

Ridder, Katie

small wonders color *Architectural Digest* v74 no4 p93 Ap 2017

RIDDERBUSCH, KATJA

The Body's Repair Kit at Work *Atlanta* v56 no7 p212 N 2016

A Bridge Back to Life *Atlanta* v56 no7 p214 N 2016

Knowledge that Empowers *Atlanta* v56 no7 p218 N 2016

When Time is Brain *Atlanta* v56 no7 p215 N 2016

Riddihough, Guy

BUILDING ON NATURE'S DESIGN [Cover story] color *Science* v355 no6329 p1038 Mr 10 2017

Ridding, L.

Country-specific effects of neonicotinoid pesticides on honey bees and wild bees diag map *Science* v356 no6345 p1393 Je 30 2017

Riddle, Dean

BEYOND THE GARDEN GATE M. OZAWA *Martha Stewart Living* no267 p94 S 2016

Ride Along 2 (Film)

NEW AVAILABLE MOVIES M. FELL *TV Guide* v64 no40 p60 O 3 2016

Ride or Die (Music)

SON'S RISE A. BURGER color *Missouri Life* v44 no2 p24 Ap 2017

RIDEOUT, SAMANTHA

NEWS FROM THE World of Medicine color *Reader's Digest* v189 no1129 p56 Ap 2017

NEWS FROM THE World of Medicine color *Reader's Digest* v190 no1133 p61 S 2017

NEWS FROM THE World of Medicine *Reader's Digest* v188 no1124 p66 O 2016

NEWS FROM THE World of Medicine *Reader's Digest* v189 no1128 p57 Mr 2017

World of Medicine *Reader's Digest* v188 no1126 p61 D 2016/Ja 2017

Ridesharing

How to Think About the Future of Cars M. Wessel *Harvard Business Review Digital Articles* p2 Jl 27 2015

No Car, No Problem W. P. BARRETT and L. GENSLER color *Forbes* v199 no2 p99 F 28 2017

The Real Reason Uber Is Giving Up in China W. C. Kirby *Harvard Business Review Digital Articles* p2 Ag 2 2016

UBER, BUT FOR SCHOOL BUSES T. KOTESKEY color *Reason* v49 no3 p10 Jl 2017

What Uber Drivers Really Make R. Wile color *Money* v46 no9 p20 O 2017

Ridesharing services

A Better Way to Fight Discrimination in the Sharing Economy Jun Li, D. Zhang et al color *Harvard Business Review Digital Articles* p2 F 27 2017

Dial-a-Caravan P. OLSON color *Forbes* v199 no7 p41 Je 29 2017

Juno Got Sold, and Its Drivers Got Stiffed J. Brustein *Bloomberg Businessweek* no4521 p33 My 8 2017

Keep Austin ... Tough To Get Around? J. Brustein *Bloomberg Businessweek* no4515 p31 Mr 20 2017

MAKING ENDS MEET IN THE SHARING ECONOMY diag *Fortune* v176 no1 p9 Jl 1 2017

The Truth About How Uber's App Manages Drivers A. Rosenblat *Harvard Business Review Digital Articles* p2 Ap 6 2016

An Uber-Tinder Mashup Hits the Spanish Steps C. Albanese and A. Migliaccio color *Bloomberg Businessweek* no4502 p42 D 5 2016

Wait up, not so fast E. Loh color *Motor Trend* v69 no3 p14 Mr 2017

Waze Wants to Help You Hitch a Ride A. Satariano and M. Bergen *Bloomberg Businessweek* no4523 p34 My 22 2017

Ridesharing services—Software

Calling All Cars K. LUNDERS *D: The Magazine of Dallas* v43 no10 p50 O 2016

Ridesharing—Software

Calling All Cars K. LUNDERS *D: The Magazine of Dallas* v43 no10 p50 O 2016

Ridge, Jason W.

10 Years of Data on Baseball Teams Shows When Pay Transparency Backfires *Harvard Business Review Digital Articles* p2 My 9 2017

Ridgeline truck—Evaluation

Honda Ridgeline chart color *Motor Trend* v69 no1 p85 Ja 2017

The Truck YOU Really WANT vs. the Truck You NEED color *Esquire* v166 no4 p80 N 2016

Ridgely, Tom

BLUEPRINT Specials: SOLDIER MUSICALS *Stage Directions* v30 no6 p24 Je 2017

G.I. Jive M. Schulman cartoon *New Yorker* v92 no44 p9 Ja 9 2017

Ridgeway, Dale

Appalachian scenes along the B&O color diag map *Model Railroader* v84 no3 p44 Mr 2017

RIDGEWAY, JAMES

Cruel and Unusual Healthcare *In These Times* v40 no12 p24 D 2016

Ridgway, Brett

Are Three School Chiefs Better Than One? A. PASCOPELLA *Education Digest* v82 no5 p21 Ja 2017

RIDING, ALAN

A Writer of Lost Loves: The life of a poet who evoked a timeless countryside when England was becoming increasingly urban *New York Times Book Review* p19 Jl 30 2017

Riding clubs

Mare and Foals In September *Arabian Horse World* v57 no9 p145 Je 2017

Riding crops

Get your horse moving forward J. Field bw color *Equus* no472 p29 Ja 2017

Riding lawn mowers

The Diesel Weasel Mow-Kart! P. Thomas chart color *Hot Rod* v70 no6 p12 Je 2017

Riding schools

SCHOOL SMOOTH N. Ienatsch color *Cycle World* v56 no10 p20 N 2017

Riding whips

To develop the ability to use your whip with accuracy and finesse... B. Baumert color *Dressage Today* v24 no2 p72 N 2017

Ridky, J.

Observation of a large-scale anisotropy in the arrival directions of cosmic rays above 8 × 1018 eV *Science* v357 no6357 p1266 S 22 2017

Ridland, John

Ever Green J. M. WILSON color *Weekly Standard* v22 no45 p36 Ag 7 2017

Ridley, Daisy, 1992-

Daisy Ridley J. Crelin color *Current Biography* v77 no11 p73 N 2016

THE FORCE WAS WITH HER D. KAMP color *Vanity Fair* v59

no7 p36 Summ 2017

Miss Universe [Cover story] G. Wood color *Vogue* v207 no11 p190 N 2017

On the Verge A. WINTOUR color *Vogue* v207 no11 p74 N 2017

Ridley, John, 1965-

Get Serious D. Marchese img *New York* v50 no8 p120 Ap 17 2017

Ridley, John, 1965—Interviews

JOHN RIDLEY J. HALTERMAN *TV Guide* v65 no19 p9 My 1 2017

Ridley, Robyn E.

Without inclusion, diversity initiatives may not be enough color *Science* v357 no6356 p1101 S 15 2017

Ridley Bikes (Company)

"I WANT A BIKE THAT GIVES ME EVERY SPEED ADVANTAGE." J. Lindsey and B. STRICKLAND color *Bicycling* v58 no3 p104 Ap 2017

RIDNER, ADRIAN

The Affordability Factor *USA Today Magazine* v145 no2864 p64 My 2017

Ridolfo, Frank

FROM OUR READERS *Sky & Telescope* v133 no1 p6 Ja 2017

RIDSDALE, CAROLYN

HOW TO FIGHT FAIR *Scholastic Choices* v32 no4 p12 Ja 2017

Rie Tanaka

A three-dimensional movie of structural changes in bacteriorhodopsin bibl diag graph *Science* v354 no6319 p1552 D 23 2016

RIEB, JESSE T.

When, Where, and How Nature Matters for Ecosystem Services: Challenges for the Next Generation of Ecosystem Service Models *BioScience* v67 no9 p820 S 2017

Rieber, Andy

Pubic Lands Ranching cartoon *American Cowboy* v23 no4 p22 D 2016/Ja 2017

Riebling, Mark

Humanity's Conscience? J. Connelly color *Commonweal* v144 no4 p16 F 24 2017

RIEBLING, RENEÉ SAGIV

build bigger skills *Parents* v92 no4 p128 Ap 2017

raise happy siblings *Parents* v91 no6 p56 Je 2016

Ried, Kimberlee N.

A GATEWAY to the West *Prologue* v48 no3 p20 Fall 2016

Rieder, Dylan, 1988-2016

Long May You Ride A. Fenwick and T. Keith color *Sports Illustrated* v125 no14 p26 O 24-31 2016

Rieder, Stefan

Ancient genomic changes associated with domestication of the horse color diag *Science* v356 no6336 p442 Ap 28 2017

RIEDERER, RACHEL

Floatopia color diag *New Republic* v248 no6 p58 Je 2017

RIEDL, HANNAH L.

Addressing the Gender Gap in Distinguished Speakers at Professional Ecology Conferences *BioScience* v67 no5 p464 My 2017

Riefberg, Vivian

How Reducing Gender Inequality Could Boost U.S. GDP by $2.1 Trillion *Harvard Business Review Digital Articles* p2 Ap 12 2016

Rieff, David

In Praise of Forgetting D. Lowenthal *History Today* v67 no3 p64 Mr 2017

Riegel, Deborah Grayson

When to Skip a Difficult Conversation *Harvard Business Review Digital Articles* p2 Mr 1 2016

When Your Employee Doesn't Take Feedback *Harvard Business Review Digital Articles* p2 N 6 2015

Riegel, Katherine

Snow White *Orion Magazine* v36 no1 p23 Ja/F 2017

Riegel, Matthew Lynn

Sin Boldly! Justifying Faith for Fragile and Broken Souls color *Christian Century* v134 no11 p36 My 24 2017

Rieger, Michael A.

Pcdhac2 is required for axonal tiling and assembly of serotonergic circuitries in mice diag *Science* v356 no6336 p406 Ap 28 2017

Rieger, Susan

Are You My Father? C. LEAVITT *New York Times Book Review* p18 Je 25 2017

Riegle, Greg

Around here, developers don't just build buildings—they build entire neighborhoods M. M. KASHINO color *Washingtonian Magazine* v52 no7 p102 Ap 2017

RIEGLER, AMY

The Way Forward color *O, The Oprah Magazine* p18 My 2017

RIEGLER, SHAX

AD visits: Change Agent color *Architectural Digest* no11 p46 N 1 2017

Riehn, F.

Observation of a large-scale anisotropy in the arrival directions of cosmic rays above 8×1018 eV *Science* v357 no6357 p1266 S 22 2017

Rieko Setsuie

Causal neural network of metamemory for retrospection in primates bibl diag graph *Science* v355 no6321 p1 Ja 13 2017

Riel, Louis, 1844-1885

A Rebel Returns *Opera News* v81 no9 p16 Mr 2017

Riemelt, Max

STREAMING A. D'ARMINIO *TV Guide* v65 no19 p40 My 1 2017

Riepenhoff, Meghann

Super Soaker color *O, The Oprah Magazine* p28 F 2017

RIEPPEL, OLIVIER

All Boxed Up bw color *Natural History* v125 no10 p22 O 2017

Riesch, Rüdiger

EVOLUTION AT THE LIMITS color diag map *Scientific American* v316 no4 p54 Ap 2017

Species IN THE Making color diag *Scientific American* v315 no5 p54 N 2016

Riese & Müller GmbH

LOAD TOURING C. Giddings color *Bicycling* v58 no8 p(Sp)8 S 2017

Riese, Martin—Interviews

Ask a Water Sommelier S. TISHGART *New York* p60 F 9 2017

Riesling (Wine)—Evaluation

SUMMER WHITES S. Schneider color *Sunset* v238 no6 p100 Je 2017

Riesman, Abraham

Archie and Betty and Veronica and Zombies img *New York* p62 Ja 23 2017

Future Shock img *New York* v49 no26 p73 D 26 2016

Kevin Smith's Celebrity Reboot: After years in critical exile, the onetime poster boy for slacker filmmaking reinvents himself for an era of narrowcast fame img *New York* v50 no18 p78 S 4 2017

Sight Unseen img *New York* v50 no17 p102 Ag 21 2017

Riess, Jana

Kenneth A. Briggs color *Publishers Weekly* v263 no45 p20 N 7 2016

Rietveld, Bob

To Get More Out of Social Media, Think Like an Anthropologist *Harvard Business Review Digital Articles* p2 Ag 17 2016

Rifai, Taleb

Tourism: Committed to Preserving Life below Water *UN Chronicle* v54 no1/2 p1 2017

Rifkin, Mark

Settler Common Sense: Queerness and Everyday Colonialism in the American Renaissance G. D. Smithers *American Indian Quarterly* v41 no2 p180 Spr 2017

Rifkin, Rachael

How to Flip Your Money Script C. de León color *Glamour* v115 no5 p124 My 2017

Rifle (Film)

RIFLE J. Cronk color *Film Comment* v53 no3 p24 My/Je 2017

Rifle-ranges

BULL'S-EYE E. Allen cartoon *New Yorker* v92 no47 p19 Ja 30 2017

Humor in Uniform color *Reader's Digest* v190 no1133 p139 S 2017

Rifles

See also

Hunting rifles

Remington rifles

BEAT THE WIND B. FITZPATRICK color *Outdoor Life* v224 no8 p28 O 2017

Custom-Shop Shooter M. R. Shea color *Field & Stream* v122 no5 pF6 O 2017

Cutting Edges A. MCKEAN and N. KREBS *Outdoor Life* v224 no2 p11 F/Mr 2017

NO SMALL MATTER T. E. Nickens color *Field & Stream* v122 no6 p20 N 2017

OPENING ROUND color *MHQ: Quarterly Journal of Military History* v30 no1 p3 Aut 2017

Q & A D. E. Petzal cartoon *Field & Stream* v121 no8 p24 F/Mr 2017

Q & A D. E. Petzal color *Field & Stream* v122 no6 p19 N 2017

The Response: THE LIGHTWEIGHT PERSONAL BAZOOKA color *Popular Mechanics* p75 Mr 2017

SHOOT 2X2X2 B. M. TOWSLEY color *Outdoor Life* v224 no4 pP13 My 2017

STATE OF THE DEER RIFLE J. B. Snow color *Outdoor Life* v223 no9 p71 N 2016

Rifles—Design & construction
RIGHT ON TARGET C. Kearns *Field & Stream* v122 no3 p6 Ag 2017

Rifles—Equipment & supplies
ELITE IRON REVOLUTION J. B. SNOW color *Outdoor Life* v224 no5 pR6 Je/Jl 2017

FIRST-PLANE REVOLUTION A. McKEAN chart color *Outdoor Life* v224 no5 p15 Je/Jl 2017

HIGH-SPEED RELOADING C. GITTINGS and J. B. SNOW color *Outdoor Life* v224 no1 pR1 D 2016/Ja 2017

Rifles—Equipment & supplies—Evaluation
INLINE OPTICS A. Mckean color *Outdoor Life* v223 no9 p28 N 2016

SADDLE UP J. B. SNOW color *Outdoor Life* v224 no1 p90 D 2016/Ja 2017

Rifles—Evaluation
6.5 CREEDMOOR J. B. SNOW color *Outdoor Life* v224 no5 p57 Je/Jl 2017

BARRETT FIELDCRAFT J. B. SNOW color *Outdoor Life* v224 no6 p72 Ag 2017

FIXED FOCUS A. McKEAN color *Outdoor Life* v224 no9 p34 N 2017

GUNS FOR WOMEN L. HOLDING color *Outdoor Life* v224 no6 p67 Ag 2017

KIMBER M84 HUNTER J. B. SNOW chart color *Outdoor Life* v224 no2 p88 F/Mr 2017

LONG-RANGE/TACTICAL RIFLES D. E. Petzal and R. Mann color *Field & Stream* v122 no5 p80 O 2017

THE RETURN OF RIGBY W. van Zwoll bw *Outdoor Life* v224 no2 p63 F/Mr 2017

RIFLES ON HORSEBACK D. AADLAND color *Outdoor Life* v224 no6 p70 Ag 2017

SAUER 100 CLASSIC XT J. B. Snow chart color *Outdoor Life* v223 no9 p74 N 2016

Rifles—History
THE BIG 1-5-0 D. E. PETZAL and P. BOURJAILY color *Field & Stream* v121 no6 p64 N 2016

Rifles—Maintenance & repair
HIGH-SPEED RELOADING C. GITTINGS and J. B. SNOW color *Outdoor Life* v224 no1 pR1 D 2016/Ja 2017

Rift in Decorum: Live at the Village Vanguard, A (Music)
AMBROSE AKINMUSIRE: THE THINKER [Cover story] Y. Kato color *Downbeat* v84 no9 p28 S 2017

Riga (Latvia)
RIGA, LATVIA S. Kerrick Sullivan color *Snowboarder* v29 no2 p104 O 2016

RIGBY, CLAIRE
AROUND RIO DE JANEIRO cartoon color *ARTnews* v115 no3 p150 Fall 2016

Rigby, Darrell K.
The Amazon-Whole Foods Deal Means Every Other Retailer's Three-Year Plan Is Obsolete *Harvard Business Review Digital Articles* p1 Je 21 2017

The Secret History of Agile Innovation *Harvard Business Review Digital Articles* p2 Ap 20 2016

Two Digital Myths That Trip Up the C-Suite *Harvard Business Review Digital Articles* p2 F 24 2016

Rigby, Jim
PHOTO color *Reason* v49 no3 p7 Jl 2017

RIGBY, MYFFY
Breakfast Town color *Bon Appetit* v62 no2 p46 Mr 2017

Riggall, Adam C.
Reactivation of latent working memories with transcranial magnetic stimulation bibl graph *Science* v354 no6316 p1136 D 2 2016

Riggio, Ronald
16 LIFE LESSONS *Psychology Today* v49 no5 p62 S/O 2016

Riggs, Bobby, 1918-1995
LOVE ALL M. Schulman cartoon *New Yorker* v93 no27 p26 S 11 2017

Riggs, Brady
ALTERNATE ROUTES color *Golf Magazine* v59 no6 p54 Je 2017

Fringe Benefit color *Golf Magazine* v59 no2 p50 F 2017

Split the Middle color *Golf Magazine* v58 no12 p84 D 2016

TOWER OF POWER color *Golf Magazine* v59 no11 p48 N 2017

Watch + Learn color *Golf Magazine* v59 no10 p28 O 2017

Watch + Learn color *Golf Magazine* v59 no3 p32 Mr 2017

Riggs, Cynthia
Trumpet of Death: A Martha's Vineyard Mystery *Publishers Weekly* v264 no8 p67 F 20 2017

Riggs, Marlon, 1957-1994
Black Is... Black Ain't G. SHAMBU color *Film Comment* v53 no1 p62 Ja/F 2017

Why Black Gay Filmmaker Marlon Riggs Matters Now C. STEPHENS bw *Advocate* no1090 p63 Ap 2017

RIGGS, MIKE
HOW WASHINGTON LOST THE WAR ON MUSCLE color *Reason* v49 no2 p54 Je 2017

WHEN PRISONS BECOME NURSING HOMES bw *Reason* v49 no6 p8 N 2017

Riggs, Ransom
DOUBLE VISION A. Breznican color *Entertainment Weekly* no1434 p60 O 7 2016

Right & left (Political science)
See also
New left (Politics)
America's New Opposition J. PURDY color *New Republic* v248 no3 p26 Mr 2017

Asymmetric Rhetorical Warfare D. FOSTER *National Review* v68 no20 p48 N 7 2016

Centrist Pundits Prepared Way for Trump Smear of 'Alt-Left' A. Johnson *Extra!* v30 no8 p1 O 2017

How Good We Had It K. Pollitt diag il *Nation* v304 no1 p12 Ja 2 2017 The Obama Years

The Luxury of Indecision J. THINDWA *In These Times* v40 no11 p7 N 2016

Monumentally Naïve K. SMITH *National Review* v69 no17 p30 S 11 2017

THE NEW PARANOIA C. DICKEY color *New Republic* v248 no7 p22 Jl 2017

Off Center N. Saval *New York Times Magazine* p11 Jl 9 2017

Thoughts from an Ocean Crossing J. LILEKS *National Review* v69 no18 p33 O 2 2017

WHEN VIOLENCE COMES S. ABRAMSKY color *Nation* v305 no10 p16 O 23 2017

Right & left (Political science)—History—21st century
Can the Left Find Its Voice in the 21st Century? J. HARRIS color il *Nation* v303 no22 p16 N 28 2016

Right of asylum
No Safe Haven A. L. CORREA *Publishers Weekly* v263 no40 p128 O 3 2016

Right of asylum—Canada
THE NEW UNDERGROUND RAILROAD [Cover story] J. Markusoff color *Maclean's* v130 no2 p20 Mr 2017

Right of asylum—Europe
How economic, humanitarian, and religious concerns shape European attitudes toward asylum seekers K. Bansak, J. Hainmueller et al bibl graph map *Science* v354 no6309 p217 O 14 2016

Right of privacy
Flat Organizations Like Zappos Need Pockets of Privacy E. Bernstein *Harvard Business Review Digital Articles* p2 N 28 2014

HOW TO HIDE YOUR ONLINE FOOTPRINT S. BLOCK cartoon *Kiplinger's Personal Finance* v71 no7 p13 Jl 2017

Smile, you're in the database! *Maclean's* v130 no4 p4 My 2017

Under the Law J. Underwood diag *Phi Delta Kappan* v99 no2 p76 O 2017

Will Alexa Take the Witness Stand? Our electronic gadgets are collecting data about us that police are using to solve When does that violate our constitutional right to privacy? [Cover story] P. SMITH *New York Times Upfront* v150 no1 p6 S 4 2017

Your In-Store Customers Want More Privacy C. Esmark *Harvard Business Review Digital Articles* p2 D 28 2016

Right of privacy—United States

Broadband Industry Self-Regulation: Federal Trade Commission Consumer Privacy Principles *Congressional Digest* v96 no5 p7 My 2017

FCC Proposed Privacy Rules: Choice, Transparency, and Security of Personal Broadband Data *Congressional Digest* v96 no5 p4 My 2017

Legislative Background on Broadband Privacy: Recent Action by Congress on the FCC Rulemaking *Congressional Digest* v96 no5 p9 My 2017

The Pros and Cons of the FCC's Broadband Consumer Privacy Rules *Congressional Digest* v96 no5 p10 My 2017

What Customer Data Collection Could Mean for Workers S. Barocas and K. Levy *Harvard Business Review Digital Articles* p2 Ag 31 2016

Right of privacy—United States—Government policy

Would You Pay for Your Online Privacy? bw *Bloomberg Businessweek* no4519 p12 Ap 24 2017

Right of privacy—United States—History

U.S. Privacy Laws: A Timeline of Statutes Protecting the Privacy Rights of Citizens *Congressional Digest* v96 no5 p3 My 2017

Right of privacy—United States—Lawsuits & claims

A MATTER OF PRIVACY D. B. MOSKOWITZ bw *American History* v52 no3 p22 Ag 2017

Right to die

The Charlie Gard case reveals a persistent bias against disability J. Bennett *America* v217 no3 p10 Ag 7 2017

Right to education

CHANGING attitudes F. Majdalawi color *Literacy Today (2411-7862)* v34 no4 p44 Ja/F 2017

Getting More Students to College, Without Breaking School Budgets L. Page *Harvard Business Review Digital Articles* p2 F 15 2016

NATIONAL ARCHIVES FOUNDATION A: Bundles *Prologue* v49 no1 p70 Spr 2017

Right to Internet access

Digitally Unequal J. Hovis *MIT Technology Review* v120 no1 p11 Ja/F 2017

From the Editor *MIT Technology Review* v120 no1 p2 Ja/F 2017

Right to water

WATER WORKS: Can this 29-year-old gay man end the global water crisis? *Advocate* no1093 p48 O/N 2017

Right whales

Research *Oceanus* v52 no2 p1 Spr 2017

Right-wing extremism

See also

Alt-Right (Political science)

Europe's far right attempts to harass refugees on Mediterranean D. Stewart color *America* v217 no5 p16 S 4 2017

MAKE AMERICA HATE AGAIN J. HARKINSON, S. Posner et al bw cartoon *Mother Jones* v42 no1 p24 Ja/F 2017

A moment of painful truth M. CAMPBELL, A. HUTCHINS et al color *Maclean's* v130 no2 p18 Mr 2017

TROLLS FOR TRUMP A. MARANTZ cartoon *New Yorker* v92 no35 p42 O 31 2016

Right Stuff, The (Film)

ED HARRIS J. Hibberd color *Entertainment Weekly* no1438 p52 N 4 2016

Sam Shepard: America's cowboy Jeremiah R. Weinert-Kendt color *America* v217 no5 p51 S 4 2017

Rignot, Eric

Death watch for climate probe P. Voosen color *Science* v357 no6357 p1225 S 22 2017

Rigol, Natalia

A Friend's Support Can Make Women Better Entrepreneurs *Harvard Business Review Digital Articles* p2 Je 19 2015

Rigolleto (Theatrical production)

Patience Rewarded: Quinn Kelsey waited to sing the great Verdi baritone roles until the time was right. This month, he's San Francisco Opera's Rigoletto F. P. Driscoll *Opera News* v81 no12

p45 Je 2017

Rigoni, Brandon

Developing Employees' Strengths Boosts Sales, Profit, and Engagement *Harvard Business Review Digital Articles* p2 S 1 2016

What Millennials Want from a New Job *Harvard Business Review Digital Articles* p2 My 11 2016

Rihanna, 1988-

BEST DRESS E. Wilson color *InStyle* v24 no9 p177 S 2017

Damson IDRIS *Interview* v47 no5 p69 Je/Jl 2017

the FENTY FACE J. Wilson color *Essence* v48 no6 p54 O 2017

Mogul Matchup R. Nussbaum color *Glamour* v115 no11 p88 N 2017

On Technology J. Wortham *New York Times Magazine* p16 Je 11 2017

Pop Chart R. Bruner, C. Lang et al color *Time* v190 no7 p54 Ag 21 2017

RIHANNA CHECKS INTO BATES MOTEL N. Abrams and R. Rahman color *Entertainment Weekly* no1453 p51 F 17 2017

Rihanna HER BEST EVER E. Wilson color *InStyle* v24 no7 p50 Jl 2017

Rihanna's Midnight Magic F. Kane color *Glamour* v114 no11 p40 N 2016

Rihanna's Out-of-This-World Role J. McGovern color *Entertainment Weekly* no1440 p17 N 18 2016

RIHANNA TAKES FLIGHT bw color *Harper's Bazaar* no3651 p380 Mr 2017

Rihanna, 1988-—Political & social views

Pop Chart R. Bruner, C. Lang et al color *Time* v188 no15 p62 O 17 2016

Riina, Ricarda

Forest conservation: Humans' handprints bibl color *Science* v355 no6324 p466 F 3 2017

Forest conservation: Remember Gran Chaco bibl color *Science* v355 no6324 p465 F 3 2017

Riis, Jacob A. (Jacob August), 1849-1914

1890: New York City J. Riis *Lapham's Quarterly* v10 no1 p87 Wint 2017

Riise, Trond

β2-Adrenoreceptor is a regulator of the a-synuclein gene driving risk of Parkinson's disease cartoon chart graph *Science* v357 no6354 p891 S 1 2017

Rijli, Filippo M.

Gene bivalency at Polycomb domains regulates cranial neural crest positional identity diag *Science* v355 no6332 p1390 Mr 31 2017

Rikers Island Correctional Facility (New York, N.Y.)

FIELD TRIP TO RIKERS E. W. SCHMIDT *America* v215 no18 p32 D 5 2016

Rikleen, Lauren Stiller

Older Women Are Being Forced Out of the Workforce *Harvard Business Review Digital Articles* p2 Mr 10 2016

Riklin, Frank

snapshot A. Klimoski *Architectural Record* v204 no10 p184 O 2016

Riklin, Patrick

snapshot A. Klimoski *Architectural Record* v204 no10 p184 O 2016

RILEY, BETSY

ATLANTA *Atlanta* v56 no10 p70 F 2017

BEST OF ATLANTA *Atlanta* v56 no8 p106 D 2016

BLUES CLUES *Atlanta* v57 no6 p50 O 2017

THE DEWBERRY *Atlanta* v57 no1 p99 My 2017

GREEN HOUSES *Atlanta* v56 no10 p28 F 2017

PICNIC PERFECT *Atlanta* v57 no3 p46 Jl 2017

South MEETS Southwest: Atlantans discover Texas's mammoth Round Top Antiques Week *Atlanta* v57 no3 p87 Jl 2017

Splendid Setting *Atlanta* v56 no9 p44 Ja 2017

WHY I OWE MY NEW JOB TO ELVIS *Atlanta* v57 no6 p18 O 2017

Riley, Caroline M.

THE PULPIT AND THE PAINTBRUSH bw color *Magazine Antiques* v183 no6 p84 N/D 2016

RILEY, DANIEL

Confidence color *GQ: Gentlemen's Quarterly* v86 no11 p114 N 2016

The Fifty Greatest Living Athletes bw color *GQ: Gentlemen's*

Quarterly v97 no11 p96 N 2017

The Ten Who'll Be Next color *GQ: Gentlemen's Quarterly* v97 no11 p114 N 2017

WELCOME TO HAWLEYWOOD color *GQ: Gentlemen's Quarterly* v86 no12 p140 D 2016

Riley, Donna

Building the future bibl color *Science* v355 no6326 p702 F 17 2017

Riley, Eleanor

Resistance to malaria through structural variation of red blood cell invasion receptors diag *Science* v356 no6343 p1139 Je 16 2017

Riley, Gwendoline

Odd Coupling: Why does a young writer fall in love with a misogynist bully? J. Lasdun *New York Times Book Review* p11 My 21 2017

Riley, Margaret F.

Revisit NIH biosafety guidelines color *Science* v357 no6352 p627 Ag 18 2017

Riley, Michael

Crappy, Buggy, Obsolete Voting Technology We Trust color *Bloomberg Businessweek* no4493 p60 O 3 2016

The Equifax Job bw graph *Bloomberg Businessweek* no4541 p26 O 9 2017

The Mauritania Exploit bw *Bloomberg Businessweek* no4508 p48 Ja 23 2017

Stand By...Scanning for Viruses and Secrets cartoon *Bloomberg Businessweek* no4530 p21 Jl 17 2017

Training Companies To Handle a Hack *Bloomberg Businessweek* no4501 p29 N 28 2016

Riley, Naomi Schaefer

An Alarming Admission color *Weekly Standard* v22 no48 p19 S 4 2017

Bury Their Future at Standing Rock: The truth about the shutdown of the Dakota Pipeline *Commentary* v143 no1 p29 Ja 2017

Closing Options for Adoptions color *Weekly Standard* v22 no40 p12 Je 26 2017

Harvard Finds a Scapegoat color *Weekly Standard* v22 no44 p16 Jl 31 2017

He's No Mitt *Weekly Standard* v22 no5 p11 O 10 2016

LOSING GROUND T. Sandefur *Claremont Review of Books* v17 no1 p63 Wint 2016/2017

Market Penetration *Commentary* v144 no2 p46 S 2017

Married, Bored, and Confused bw *Weekly Standard* v23 no3 p37 S 25 2017

No-Collateral Damage color *Weekly Standard* v22 no36 p15 My 29 2017

One Man's Pontiff *Weekly Standard* v22 no18 p38 Ja 16 2017

Parent Trap *Commentary* v142 no2 p56 S 2016

Progressives, Inc color *Weekly Standard* v22 no31 p24 Ap 17 2017

Put the Kids First color *Weekly Standard* v22 no41 p18 Jl 3 2017

Rewarding Rigor color *Weekly Standard* v23 no4 p18 O 2 2017

Ridicule Didn't Work color *Weekly Standard* v22 no20 p17 Ja 30 2017

Shiny Unhappy People *Commentary* v144 no1 p54 Jl/Ag 2017

Techie Largesse *Weekly Standard* v22 no24 p18 F 27 2017

We See You *Commentary* v143 no2 p44 F 2017

When East Meets East *Commentary* v142 no4 p40 N 2016

Zoo U *Commentary* v143 no3 p56 Mr 2017

Riley, René E.

Blazing a New Trail *Trail Rider* v29 no4 p6 My 2017

Riley, Russell L.

The 1990s Are Back L. Rothman color *Time* v188 no14 p60 O 10 2016

Riley, Sheri

BREAK THE MOLD IN 2017! color *Essence* v47 no9 p76 Ja 2017

THE PATH TO PEACE C. V. CLARKE color *Black Enterprise* v47 no5 p36 Ja/F 2017

Rilinger, Holly

GET LIFTED L. MCGLASHAN color *Muscle & Performance* v9 no6 p16 Je 2017

Rilke, Rainer Maria, 1875-1926

1908: Paris R. M. Rilke *Lapham's Quarterly* v10 no2 p148 Spr 2017

Riller, Ulrich

The formation of peak rings in large impact craters bibl color

graph *Science* v354 no6314 p878 N 18 2016

Rim, Sujean

Chee-Kee: A Panda in Bearland *Publishers Weekly* v263 no47 p105 N 21 2016

Rimac, Mate

ELECTRIC YOUTH M. DE PAULA color *Road & Track* v69 no4 p60 N 2017

Rimac Automobili (Company)

ELECTRIC YOUTH M. DE PAULA color *Road & Track* v69 no4 p60 N 2017

Rimal, D.

Observation of coherent elastic neutrino-nucleus scattering diag *Science* v357 no6356 p1123 S 15 2017

RIMBAWANTO, ANTO

Opportunities for Improved Transparency in the Timber Trade through Scientific Verification *BioScience* v66 no11 p990 N 1 2016

Rimini, Laura Sartori

MASTER CLASS bw color *Architectural Digest* v74 no1 p176 Ja 2017

Rimini Protokoll (Performer)

Drama In the Streets S. FITZ-GERALD *Los Angeles Magazine* p68 Mr 2017

Rimm, Allison

How to Keep Support for Your Project from Evaporating *Harvard Business Review Digital Articles* p2 Ag 10 2015

Knowing When to Fire Someone *Harvard Business Review Digital Articles* p2 Ja 7 2015

A One-Page Exercise to Get Stress Under Control *Harvard Business Review Digital Articles* p2 S 15 2015

What I Learned About Helpfulness When I Used a Cane Instead of Crutches *Harvard Business Review Digital Articles* p2 D 30 2016

Rimmel London (Company)

cheap THRILLS E. STOVALL color *Seventeen* v76 no5 p62 S 2017

Rimmer, Maureen

Increased Demand for U.S. Agricultural Exports Would Likely Lead to More U.S. Jobs *Amber Waves: The Economics of Food, Farming, Natural Resources, & Rural America* p1 Je 2017

Rimowa GmbH

Die Hard E. FLORIO color *Conde Nast Traveler* v52 no1 p116 Ja 2017

High Rollers H. ROLLERS color *Forbes* v198 no8 p22 D 20 2016

My Place bw color map *Vanity Fair* v58 no11 p84 N 2016

Rimowa Topas Suitcase color *Bloomberg Businessweek* no4536 p71 S 4 2017

Rinaldi, G.

Seasonal exposure of carbon dioxide ice on the nucleus of comet 67P/Churyumov-Gerasimenko bibl bw graph *Science* v354 no6319 p1563 D 23 2016

Rinaldi, Giavanna—Awards

Summer Champions Crowned *In Stride* v11 no6 p14 N 2016

Rinaldi, Luca

Rescuing my time from science color *Science* v354 no6319 p1666 D 23 2016

Rinaldi, Ray Mark

Dream of the Red Chamber *Opera News* v81 no6 p40 D 2016

Rinaldi, Robin

soul FOOD color *Yoga Journal* no288 p75 D 2016

RINALDI, TOM

Running for Their Lives *New York Times Book Review* p26 Ag 27 2017

Rince, Celestian

Freedom Thirty-Five T. Henley color *Walrus* v14 no5 p16 Je 2017

Rincon Mountains (Ariz.)

The Long Way Home: Returns C. C. CHOJNACKY *Backpacker* p13 S 2017

Rindfleisch, Bryan

First Manhattans: A History of the Indians of Greater New York *American Indian Quarterly* v40 no4 p382 Fall 2016

Rindone, Ron

SHOW HIM THE MONEY R. O'CONNOR color *Chicago* v65 no11 p32 N 2016

Rine, Jasper

Aggregation of the Whi3 protein, not loss of heterochromatin, causes sterility in old yeast cells bibl diag *Science* v355 no6330 p1184 Mr 17 2017

RINEHART, EARL

The Baby Catchers color *Reader's Digest* v190 no1133 p12 S 2017

RINELLA, STEVEN

The Outdoorsman's Essentials color *Men's Health* v32 no6 p32 Ag 2017

Rines, Lawrence

Ballet's Backbone A. RIVERS *Dance Magazine* v90 no12 p54 D 2016

Ring, Michael

BUSHWHACKERS M. Healy-Rae color *Harper's Magazine* v335 no2005 p18 Je 2017

RING, TRUDY

THE BIGGEST HOMOPHOBES: THE LGBT RIGHTS MOVEMENT HAS HAD ITS SHARE OF VILLAINS color *Advocate* no1091 p102 Je/Jl 2017

MERCHANT'S IVORY: James Ivory sails on without his partner Ismail Merchant, lovingly restoring the films that were their lives's work, like the newly re-released Maurice color *Advocate* no1091 p28 Je/Jl 2017

Ring lasers

LORD OF THE RINGS E. Hand color diag *Science* v356 no6335 p236 Ap 21 2017

Ring Nebula

Summer Highlights: Warm nights and dark skies are ideal for enjoying these classic beauties S. French *Sky & Telescope* v134 no1 p54 Jl 2017

Who Discovered the Ring Nebula? [Cover story] D. Olson and G. M. Caglieris *Sky & Telescope* v133 no6 p32 Je 2017

Ring-necked duck

HUNT THE PUDDLE DIVER T. CARPENTER color *Outdoor Life* v224 no8 pW6 O 2017

Ring-opening reactions

Femtosecond x-ray spectroscopy of an electrocyclic ring-opening reaction A. R. Attar, A. Bhattacherjee et al diag graph *Science* v356 no6333 p54 Ap 7 2017

Following photoexcited electrons in reactions R. Sension color *Science* v356 no6333 p31 Ap 7 2017

Ringbrothers (Company)

The Ringbrothers' G-Code Camaro BLUEPRINTED B. Gillogly color *Hot Rod* v70 no6 p50 Je 2017

RingCentral Inc.

The Next Frontier of Collaborative Communications D. Gould color *Bloomberg Businessweek* no4500 pC1 N 21 2016

Ringling Brothers Barnum & Bailey Combined Shows

Circus at Sunset C. ALLEN color *Weekly Standard* v22 no35 p36 My 22 2017

The Circus is Not in Town S. Richardson color *American History* v52 no2 p7 Je 2017

Circus Maximus T. Keith color *Sports Illustrated* v126 no15 p19 My 29 2017

The Last Act D. Von Drehle color *Time* v189 no18 p44 My 15 2017

Ringling Bros. Strikes Its Tent color *Time* v189 no3 p11 Ja 30 2017

Ringmaster of the Universe K. VINTON color *Forbes* v198 no8 p50 D 20 2016

Sky Driver color *Reader's Digest* v189 no1130 p20 My 2017

Rings (Gymnastics)

5 WAYS... TO USE THE RINGS J. CONNOR color *Muscle & Performance* v9 no4 p66 Ap 2017

Rings (Jewelry)

See also

Wedding & engagement rings

Style As Substance color *InStyle* v24 no3 p360 Mr 2017

WHAT WE LOVE color *Harper's Bazaar* no3657 p58 O 2017

Work the LOOK: FALL'S MUST-HAVES color *Harper's Bazaar* no3656 p293 S 2017

Rings (Jewelry)—Evaluation

$25 & Under Statement Jewelry color *Seventeen* v76 no12 p32 D 2016/Ja 2017

THE A-LIST color *O, The Oprah Magazine* p59 Mr 2017

ASHLEY GRAHAM'S PARTY PICKS color *InStyle* v23 no13 p146 D 2016

The BEST OF SUMMER O List color *O, The Oprah Magazine* p43 Je 2017

THE BEST OF WHAT'S NEW color *Harper's Bazaar* no3655 p107 Ag 2017

Bling It On L. IMMEDIATO color *Los Angeles Magazine* v62 no10 p25 O 2017

CAFÉ SOCIETY color *Conde Nast Traveler* v52 no9 p19 O 2017

CAT'S MEOW J. MOAZAMI color *Chicago* v66 no6 p42 Je 2017

CHERRY BOMB color *Harper's Bazaar* no3649 p191 D 2016/Ja 2017

FABULOUS at Every Age color *Harper's Bazaar* no3651 p299 Mr 2017

FASHION UNDER $100 color *Redbook* p55 Mr 2017

FROM RUNWAY TO O-WAY color *O, The Oprah Magazine* p60 Mr 2017

GLAM BY TONIGHT Guarnieri color *Harper's Bazaar* no3649 p251 D 2016/Ja 2017

Hold, PLEASE *Interview* v47 no6 p32 Ag 2017

Hot Rocks R. WALDMAN color *Vogue* v207 no4 p162 Ap 2017

If You Like It... color *Glamour* v115 no7 p30 Jl 2017

IRON MAN L. IMMEDIATO *Los Angeles Magazine* p27 My 2017

the life C. Dash color *InStyle* v24 no4 p215 Ap 2017

LINES IN THE SAND color *Harper's Bazaar* no3652 p234 Ap 2017

ON THE LINE color *Harper's Bazaar* no3657 p131 O 2017

Out on the Town B. TURVETT color *Working Mother* p10 F/Mr 2017

PATTERN PLAY color *Harper's Bazaar* no3651 p246 Mr 2017

POP OF COLOR color *Harper's Bazaar* no3653 p274 My 2017

SEEING RED color *Harper's Bazaar* no3648 p252 N 2016

SHOW YOUR METAL color *Esquire* p41 Ag 2017

SO BAZAAR color *Harper's Bazaar* no3648 p280 N 2016

SO BAZAAR color *Harper's Bazaar* no3652 p250 Ap 2017

STONE COLD FOXES color *Conde Nast Traveler* v52 no5 p40 My 2017

The Style REPORT color *Harper's Bazaar* no3653 p119 My 2017

STYLISH SOIRÉE bw color *Vanity Fair* v58 no12 p74 D 2016

To Give And To Get color *Conde Nast Traveler* v51 no11 p29 D 2016

Totally NUDE color *O, The Oprah Magazine* p154 My 2017

WHAT WE LOVE color *Harper's Bazaar* no3649 p44 D 2016/Ja 2017

WHERE FASHION GETS PERSONAL color *Harper's Bazaar* no3649 p181 D 2016/Ja 2017

THE WOMAN Jessica Alba E. Wilson color *InStyle* v23 no13 p110 D 2016

Rings of Saturn

Cassini Finds Empty Space on First Finale Pass D. Dickinson color *Sky & Telescope* v134 no2 p12 Ag 2017

Cassini weaves through Saturn's rings color *Astronomy* v45 no8 p18 Ag 2017

Close encounters with the RINGED PLANET L. Kruesi bw color diag *Astronomy* v45 no10 p28 O 2017

Rink, Floor

The Biases That Punish Racially Diverse Teams *Harvard Business Review Digital Articles* p2 F 22 2016

Rinker, Sherri Duskey

Lives to Learn From M. RUSSO *New York Times Book Review* p29 Ag 27 2017

Rinker Boat Co.

Rinker QX 29 Bow Rider *Boating World* v38 no1 p44 Ja 2017

Rinne, Jennifer

Activity-dependent spatially localized miRNA maturation in neuronal dendrites bibl graph *Science* v355 no6325 p634 F 10 2017

Rinqvist, Emma

Local amplifiers of IL-4Rα-mediated macrophage activation promote repair in lung and liver diag *Science* v356 no6342 p1076 Je 9 2017

Rinzler, Lodro—Interviews

Befriending Heartbreak S. SATTERLEE color *Publishers Weekly* v263 no51 p141 D 12 2016

Rio Tinto Co.

Mining Without Miners T. Simonite color *MIT Technology Review* v120 no1 p94 Ja/F 2017

Rio Tinto and the Mines A. LEDERER bw color *Natural History* v125 no5 p36 My 2017

Rio Yachts (Company)

The Art of Refreshment A. HARPER cartoon chart color *Power & Motoryacht* v32 no12 p50 D 2016

Rio Yachts 58 GTS D. Harding color *Power & Motoryacht* v33 no2 p46 F 2017

RIOFRIO, MELISSA

Hands-on: Running Android apps on a Chromebook could be the best of both worlds color *PCWorld* p112 Mr 2017

Lenovo Yoga Book: Unique touch features let you be hands-on creative color *PCWorld* v35 no11 p82 N 2016

Windows 10 Creators Update could ship March 31, and we're already worried about bugs color *PCWorld* p14 Mr 2017

Rio Grande (South), The (Poem)

The Rio Grande (South) J. Poch *America* v216 no13 p49 Je 12 2017

Riordan, Michael

A BRIDGE TOO FAR The demise of the Superconducting Super Collider *Physics Today* v69 no10 p48 O 2016

The Rise and Fall of the Fifth Force: Discovery, Pursuit, and Justification in Modern Physics *Physics Today* v70 no4 p56 Ap 2017

Riordan, Rick

CHILDREN'S BEST SELLERS *New York Times Book Review* p79 D 4 2016

Rios, Amber

CHEAT, DRINK & STILL SHRINK color *Runner's World* v52 no6 p45 Jl 2017

cheat, drink, & still shrink color *Yoga Journal* no291 p29 My 2017

cheat, drink, & still shrink color *Yoga Journal* no294 p11 S 2017

cheat, drink, & still shrink color *Yoga Journal* p19 2017 Special Issue

cheat, drink, & stil shrink color *Yoga Journal* no293 p9 Ag 2017

CHEAT YOUR WAY TO LEAN color *Yoga Journal* no290 p7 Mr 2017

Cheat Your Way to Lean! *Runner's World* v52 no3 p41 Ap 2017

RIOS, CARMEN

The Condom Campaign *Ms.* v26 no4 p10 Wint 2016

A Museum of Our Own: Congress takes steps to turn the longtime dream of a national women's history museum into reality *Ms.* v27 no3 p10 Fall 2017

RIOS, EDWIN

REUNION color *Mother Jones* v42 no6 p6 N/D 2017

RIOS, JAIME

I Survived! [Cover story] *Reader's Digest* v189 no1128 p62 Mr 2017

Ríos, Luis

The growth pattern of Neandertals, reconstructed from a juvenile skeleton from El Sidrón (Spain) color graph *Science* v357 no6357 p1282 S 22 2017

Ríos, Miguel Angel

THE LOOK BOOK A. SWERDLOFF img *New York* v50 no8 p83 Ap 17 2017

Ríos-Muñoz, César A.

Mexico's ambiguous invasive species plan bibl *Science* v355 no6329 p1033 Mr 10 2017

Riots

The Truth About Sweden P. Neuding color *Weekly Standard* v22 no26 p27 Mr 13 2017

Riots—England—History

EVIL MAY DAY 1517: Foreign traders were attracted to the City of London by England's prosperous trade in wool and cloth. They were not always made welcome D. Wilson *History Today* v67 no6 p66 Je 2016

Riots—United States

The Language of the Unheard: Fifty years on, the flames of the 1967 Detroit uprising still burn *In These Times* v41 no8 p25 Ag 2017

Rip currents

The Riddle of Rip Currents M. Moulton color *Oceanus* v51 no2 p44 Wint 2016

Ripa, Kelly, 1970-

SEACREST IN! M. LOGAN *TV Guide* v65 no21 p13 My 15 2017

Sound Bites color *Entertainment Weekly* no1472 p8 Je 30 2017

THE WORLD ACCORDING TO Gayle color *O, The Oprah Magazine* p36 D 2016

Riparian areas

Salty & Satisfying D. J. Harding color *Power & Motoryacht* v34 no10 p32 O 2017

Terrestrial Invertebrates in the Riparian Zone: Mechanisms Underlying Their Unique Diversity T. L. RAMEY and J. S. RICHARDSON *BioScience* v67 no9 p808 S 2017

Riparian areas—Management

TREES FOR TRIBS TURNS 10 S. Walsh *New York State Conservationist* v71 no4 p20 F 2017

Riparian ecology

Applying Functional Traits to Ecogeomorphic Processes in Riparian Ecosystems R. M. DIEHL, D. M. MERRITT et al *BioScience* v67 no8 p729 Ag 2017

Ripatrazone, Nick

Binding Wounds color *National Review* v69 no19 p55 O 16 2017

A brilliant nun with no time for short-sighted men color *America* v216 no7 p49 Ap 3 2017

In 'The Keepers,' the Hopes of Vatican II Crumble Amid Sexual Abuse and Murder bw color *America* v216 no13 p42 Je 12 2017

A RADICAL FAITH color *U.S. Catholic* v82 no3 p41 Mr 2017

Survival is sacred *Christian Century* v134 no16 p24 Ag 2 2017

'The Young Pope' The Catholic art that Catholics need—but might not want color *America* v216 no3 p38 F 6 2017

Ripert, Éric, 1965-

Food for the Soul E. Ripert color *AARP: The Magazine* v59 no5A p66 Ag/S 2016

RIPKEN, NIK

UNDER DISCUSSION *Christianity Today* p17 Ap 2017

RIPLEY, AMANDA

How America Outlawed Adolescence bw color *Atlantic* v318 no4 p86 N 2016

Ripley, Becky

How Your Company Can Better Retain Employees Who Are Veterans *Harvard Business Review Digital Articles* p2 Jl 11 2017

Ripley, Mike

Mr. Campion's Abdication *Publishers Weekly* v264 no36 p67 S 4 2017

Ripon College

BEST BANG FOR THE BUCK MIDWEST COLLEGES chart *Washington Monthly* v49 no9/10 p48 S/O 2017

Town and Gown Goes Downscale A. M. Renn *Governing* v30 no6 p22 Mr 2017

Ripp, Victor

Hell's Traces: One Murder, Two Families, Thirty-Five Holocaust Memorials *Publishers Weekly* v263 no51 p135 D 12 2016

Rippe, James

nitric oxide V. Tweed color *Amazing Wellness* v9 no6 p13 EarlyWint 2017

Ripper, Kris

As La Vista Turns: Queers of La Vista color *Publishers Weekly* v264 no4 p63 Ja 23 2017

The Queer and the Restless *Publishers Weekly* v263 no40 p106 O 3 2016

Rippey, Brad

Weatherwatch color map *Weatherwise* v70 no4 p38 Jl/Ag 2017

Weatherwatch map *Weatherwise* v69 no6 p46 N-D 2016

Weatherwatch *Weatherwise* v70 no2 p38 Mr/Ap 2017

weather watch *Weatherwise* v70 no5 p42 S/O 2017

Ripple (Company)

DISH OF THE MONTH A. SPIEGEL *Washingtonian Magazine* v52 no1 p148 O 2017

RIPPLE, MARTHA

Silence Like a Symphony: Canoeing Silver Creek *Idaho Magazine* v16 no11 p10 Ag 2017

Ripple, William J.

Conserving the World's Megafauna and Biodiversity: The Fierce Urgency of Now *BioScience* v67 no3 p197 Mr 2017

Making a New Dog? *BioScience* v67 no4 p374 Ap 2017

Modernization, Risk, and Conservation of the World's Largest Carnivores *BioScience* v67 no7 p646 Jl 2017

Saving the World's Terrestrial Megafauna color *BioScience* v66 no10 p807 O 1 2016

We Need a Biologically Sound North American Conservation Plan *BioScience* v67 no8 p685 Ag 2017

Wildlife-snaring crisis in Asian forests color *Science* v355 no6322 p255 Ja 20 2017

Ripsman, Norrin M.

p27 Ag 14 2017

Ritchey-Chrétien telescopes
Seeing Through the Dust: Turning to technology can improve your resolution of globular clusters E. Mihelich *Sky & Telescope* v134 no1 p57 Jl 2017

Ritchey Design Inc.
"I WANT TO GET AWAY." M. Phillips and B. STRICKLAND color *Bicycling* v58 no3 p82 Ap 2017

RITCHIE, CARRIE
A Lot on the Line *Indianapolis Monthly* v40 no3 p68 N 2016

Ritchie, Cinthia
The Confrontation color *New York Times Magazine* p38 N 27 2016

RITCHIE, EUAN G.
Making a New Dog? *BioScience* v67 no4 p374 Ap 2017

Ritchie, Gordon
FASTEST ON THE FLIPSIDE color *Cycle World* v56 no3 p64 Ap 2017

Ritchie, Guy, 1968-
King Arthur as a Knockabout Guy S. Zacharek color *Time* v189 no19 p54 My 22 2017
King Arthur: Legend of the Sword C. Nashawaty color *Entertainment Weekly* no1466 p40 My 19 2017

Ritchie, Marilyn D.
Distribution and clinical impact of functional variants in 50,726 whole-exome sequences from the DiscovEHR study chart graph *Science* v354 no6319 paaf6814-1 D 23 2016
Genetic identification of familial hypercholesterolemia within a single U.S. health care system chart graph *Science* v354 no6319 paaf7000-1 D 23 2016

Ritchie, Michael
L.A. LUMINARIES *Los Angeles Magazine* p116 F 2017

RITCHIE, WILL
SHASTA TO THE SEA bw color *Bike Magazine* v24 no2 p66 Mr 2017

Rite of Spring, The (Theatrical production)
Fall Preview M. Harss color *New Yorker* v93 no25 p20 Ag 28 2017

Rites & ceremonies
See also
　Christian rites & ceremonies
　Exorcism
　Fasts & feasts
　Funerals
　Liturgies
　Weddings
Can I Get an Amen? R. Bragg color *Southern Living* v51 no11 p172 N 2016
A family holiday A. Scobey color *U.S. Catholic* v81 no12 p43 D 2016
HOLIDAYS IN THE LITTLE HILLS N. PLEGGE *Missouri Life* v43 no7 p50 D 2016/Ja 2017
The Importance of Family Connections *Natural History* v125 no3 p5 Mr 2017
Research: Performing a Ritual Before a Stressful Task Improves Performance A. W. Brooks color *Harvard Business Review Digital Articles* p2 Ja 10 2017
Singing for shelter P. Hovey color *U.S. Catholic* v81 no12 p19 D 2016
Why Your Company Needs More Ceremonies P. Sanchez *Harvard Business Review Digital Articles* p2 Jl 27 2016

Rites & ceremonies—United States
Shared Rituals Are the Tie That Binds S. Schrobsdorff color *Time* v189 no3 p59 Ja 30 2017

RITHMIRE, MEG
China Gambles on Modernizing Through Urbanization *Current History* v116 no791 p203 S 2017

Rithy Panh, 1964-
EXILE, WITHIN AND WITHOUT: NEWWORK IN TWO MODES FROM RITHY PANH D. Boyle *Film Quarterly* v71 no1 p10 Fall 2017

RITLAND, LAURA
Fortress of Care *Walrus* v14 no9 p76 N 2017

Ritort, Felix
Experimental measurement of binding energy, selectivity, and allostery using fluctuation theorems bibl graph *Science* v355 no6323 p412 Ja 27 2017

Ritter, Jason, 1980-

JASON RITTER OF Kevin (Probably) Saves the World S. Highfill, N. Abrams et al color *Entertainment Weekly* no1482/1483 p61 S 22 2017
KEVIN (PROBABLY) SAVES THE WORLD M. Roffman *TV Guide* v65 no37 p30 S 4 2017

Ritter, Jörg
Why Family Firms in East Asia Struggle with Succession *Harvard Business Review Digital Articles* p2 Mr 24 2015

Ritter, Krysten, 1981-
Badass with a Heart M. STACEY color *Women's Health* v14 no9 p93 N 2017

Ritter, Scott
THE TROUBLE WITH DEFECTORS *Harper's Magazine* v334 no2000 p30 Ja 2017

Ritter, Thomas
The 4 Types of Project Manager *Harvard Business Review Digital Articles* p2 Jl 27 2017

Ritterhouse, Jennifer
Southern Man E. M. J. YODER color *Weekly Standard* v23 no3 p36 S 25 2017

Rituals Cosmetics eCommerce BV
"I Traveled 19 Hours to Chill Out" color *Glamour* v115 no11 p80 N 2017

Ritz, Aspen
Glitter Galore color *Dance Spirit* v20 no9 p26 N 2016

RITZ, DAVID
The Fighting Side of Sturgill Simpson color *Rolling Stone* no1272 p22 O 20 2016

Ritz, Jessica
BEST OF THE WEST color *Sunset* v238 no4 p17 Ap 2017
Pastries Galore *Los Angeles Magazine* v61 no11 p126 N 2016

Ritz, Wendy
Corporate Ethics Can't Be Reduced to Compliance *Harvard Business Review Digital Articles* p2 Ap 29 2016

RITZEL, REBECCA f.
SLEEPING BEAUTY *Virginia Living* v15 no1 p33 D 2016

Ritzel, Rebecca J.
Bibliophile bw color *American Craft* v76 no6 p42 D 2016-Ja 2017

Ritzenthaler, Mary Lynn
The Declaration of Independence and the Hand of Time *Prologue* v48 no3 p46 Fall 2016
Preserving Family Recipes *Prologue* v48 no3 p31 Fall 2016

Rius, Cristina
Clonal hematopoiesis associated with TET2 deficiency accelerates atherosclerosis development in mice bibl diag *Science* v355 no6327 p842 F 24 2017

RIVA, PETER
Those Amazon Numbers color *Publishers Weekly* v263 no44 p80 O 31 2016

Rivalus (Company)
NATIVE PRO 100 color *Muscle & Performance* v9 no1 p62 Ja 2017

Rivas, G.
Persistent effects of pre-Columbian plant domestication on Amazonian forest composition bibl chart graph map *Science* v355 no6328 p925 Mr 3 2017

Rivas, Luz
Luz Rivas A. HEROLD *Los Angeles Magazine* v62 no9 p92 S 2017

River boats
See also
　Ferries
Love Boat A. S. Greer color *Sunset* v238 no6 p78 Je 2017

River channels
See also
　Arroyos
Arroyos N. G. Shannon *New York Times Magazine* p18 Mr 5 2017
How to model a river channel T. Oxnard color diag *Model Railroader* v84 no3 p41 Mr 2017

River ecology
Envisioning, Quantifying, and Managing Thermal Regimes on River Networks E. A. STEEL, T. J. BEECHIE et al *BioScience* v67 no6 p506 Je 2017

River pollution
FISH FOR THOUGHT C. Zuckerman color *National Geographic* v231 no4 p16 Ap 2017

Mexico City's Last Living River color *Foreign Policy* no224 p16 My/Je 2017

River sediments

SEDIMENT SUPPLY PREDICTS RIVER GEOMETRY *Physics Today* v70 no6 p26 Je 2017

River travel

CANOE & KAYAK *Sierra* v102 no1 p73 Ja/F 2017

Confluence T. Valtin *Sierra* v101 no4 p52 Jl/Ag 2016

The Crown Jewel: A Rare Float on the Best Wilderness River in America L. JACKSON *Idaho Magazine* v16 no12 p6 S 2017

Rivera, Alicia

ALICIA RIVERA: THE COMMUNITY ORGANIZER DETAILS HER QUEST FOR ENVIRONMENTAL JUSTICE IN WILMINGTON, WHERE RESIDENTS LIVE IN THE SHADOW OF AN OIL FACILITY J. HERBST *Los Angeles Magazine* v62 no9 p97 S 2017

Rivera, Carlos

What Is Art Really Worth? M. GLUCK *Los Angeles Magazine* p36 D 2016

Rivera, Coryn

JOIN THE RIDE L. FLICKINGER color *Bicycling* v58 no10 p10 N/D 2017

Rivera, Coryn—Interviews

CORYN RIVERA IS NOT LIKE THE REST OF US G. LIU color *Bicycling* v58 no10 p32 N/D 2017

Rivera, Eléna

Scaffolding *Publishers Weekly* v263 no42 p48 O 17 2016

Rivera, Gabby—Interviews

God Bless America S. ABADSIDIS color *Advocate* no1090 p59 Ap 2017

Rivera, Gerald Maxwell

STYLED to the MAX(WELL) bw *Ebony* v72/73 no12/1 p32 O/N 2017

Rivera, José

SOMEBODY TO LOVE D. ARTAVIA color *Advocate* no1091 p34 Je/Jl 2017

Rivera, Kristin

CEOs Are Getting Fired for Ethical Lapses More Than They Used To *Harvard Business Review Digital Articles* p2 Je 6 2017

Rivera, Lanie L.

Peering into the FUTURE of LICK OBSERVATORY *Science & Technology Review* p16 S 2016

Rivera, Lauren

Firms Are Wasting Millions Recruiting on Only a Few Campuses *Harvard Business Review Digital Articles* p2 O 23 2015

Research: How Subtle Class Cues Can Backfire on Your Resume *Harvard Business Review Digital Articles* p2 D 21 2016

Rivera, Miguel N.

Decoupling genetics, lineages, and microenvironment in IDH-mutant gliomas by single-cell RNA-seq diag *Science* v355 no6332 p1391 Mr 31 2017

Rivera, Nilza

Bound for the Heavens color *National Wildlife (World Edition)* v55 no1 p50 D/Ja 2016

Rivera, Rachel

LIFE ON THE EDGE *Sierra* v102 no4 p42 Jl/Ag 2017

Rivera, Suzanne M.

What do revised U.S. rules mean for human research? color *Science* v357 no6352 p650 Ag 18 2017

Rivera-Chávez, Fabian

Microbiota-activated PPAR-γ signaling inhibits dysbiotic Enterobacteriaceae expansion graph *Science* v357 no6351 p570 Ag 11 2017

River Below, A (Film)

Give and Take E. Hynes color *Film Comment* v53 no4 p14 Jl/Ag 2017

Riverdale (TV program)

Archie and Betty and Veronica and Zombies A. Riesman img *New York* p62 Ja 23 2017

Archie and the Gang Come Back to a Much Darker World D. D'Addario color *Time* v189 no4 p47 F 6 2017

FAKE I.D.'S E. NUSSBAUM cartoon *New Yorker* v93 no7 p100 Ap 3 2017

Riverdale D. Holbrook *TV Guide* v65 no2 p26 Ja 2 2017

Riverdale J. Jensen color *Entertainment Weekly* no1450 p50 Ja 27 2017

Riverdale T. Stack color *Entertainment Weekly* no1448 p42 Ja 13 2017

Riverdale T. Stack, N. Abrams et al color *Entertainment Weekly* no1482/1483 p68 S 22 2017

What to Watch R. Rahman, D. Schwartz et al color *Entertainment Weekly* no1486 p54 O 13 2017

Riverkeeper Inc.

A River Runs Through It S. MORFORD *USA Today Magazine* v146 no2866 p66 Jl 2017

Rivero, y Mendez, Isel

Fighting for Their Lives: In their first U.S. interview, Spain's hunger strikers against gender violence tell Ms. what motivates them *Ms.* v27 no3 p14 Fall 2017

Rivers

See also

Estuaries

River channels

Waterfalls

BORDER BUNNIES A. McKEAN color *Outdoor Life* v224 no1 p34 D 2016/Ja 2017

Defining the topography of a planetary body D. Burr map *Science* v356 no6339 p708 My 19 2017

The Meandering Poultney River R. H. MOHLENBROCK *Natural History* v125 no11 p36 D 2016/Ja 2017

A new angle on streams color *Science* v355 no6331 p1278 Mr 24 2017

Rivers, Ashley

7 common questions about applying for college: Advice from parents, dancers, and directors *Dance Magazine* p12 2016/2017

7 common questions about applying for college: Advice from parents, dancers, and directors *Dance Magazine* v90 p12 2016/2017 Supplement College Guide

back to school (again) *Dance Magazine* p24 2016/2017

back to school (again): Professional dancer Ida Saki on why she chose to return to college *Dance Magazine* v90 p24 2016/2017 Supplement College Guide

Ballet's Backbone *Dance Magazine* v90 no12 p54 D 2016

Happy Feet: What are your foot-care must-haves? *Dance Magazine* v91 no10 p36 O 2017

The Newbie's Survival Guide color *Dance Magazine* v91 no3 p30 Mr 2017

Raising Revenues: Ballet companies today are proving that building new audiences for dance is possible *Dance Magazine* v91 no9 p54 S 2017

Unstoppable *Dance Magazine* v90 no11 p26 N 2016

YOUR QUESTIONS ANSWERED *Dance Magazine* p10 2016/2017

YOUR QUESTIONS ANSWERED: What to ask to find the right college dance program *Dance Magazine* v90 p10 2016/2017 Supplement College Guide

Rivers, Joan, 1933-2014

THE RIVERS EDGE J. WOLCOTT bw *Vanity Fair* v58 no11 p153 N 2016

Rivers—Arizona

See also

Burro Creek (Mohave County, Ariz.)

THE ONE DESN'T EVEN NEED A HEADLINE M. DO-BROWNER *Arizona Highways* v92 no11 p32 N 2016

Rivers—Asia

Can South Asia Share Its Rivers? G. PRICE and S. MITTRA *Current History* v116 no789 p148 Ap 2017

Rivers—Charts, diagrams, etc.

THE PRINCIPAL MOUNTAINS AND RIVERS OF THE WORLD, 1829 K. Wiles *History Today* v67 no5 p4 My 2017

Rivers—Colorado

See also

Yampa River (Colo.)

Q&A: Amy S. Martin A. S. Martin *Arizona Highways* v93 no11 p9 N 2017

Running Water *Arizona Highways* v92 no11 p5 N 2016

Standing Alone *Arizona Highways* v93 no11 p5 N 2017

Rivers—Environmental conditions

OVER THE RIVER R. Manning *Harper's Magazine* v334 no2000 p36 Ja 2017

Rivers—Georgia

See also

Chattahoochee River
THE FUTURE OF THE CHATTAHOOCHEE: Long overlooked, the river s segment along Atlanta's west side has endless opportunity T. WHEATLEY *Atlanta* v57 no4 p57 Ag 2017
HOW CLEAN IS THE WATER REALLY? Well, it depends. But seriously, don't swallow the water C. PANDLEY *Atlanta* v57 no4 p54 Ag 2017
LAND: ATLANTA'S OUTDOOR RECREATION PLAYGROUND J. GREEN *Atlanta* v57 no4 p56 Ag 2017
OUR RIVER K. EDELSTEIN *Atlanta* v57 no4 p58 Ag 2017

Rivers—Iceland
FOOTSTEPS *Iceland Review* v55 no4 p36 Jl/Ag 2017
LOW LIGHT P. STEFÁNSSON *Iceland Review* v55 no1 p66 Ja/F 2017

Rivers—Idaho
AHSAHKA: WHERE RIVERS MEET AND LINES ARE CAST C. BONK *Idaho Magazine* v16 no8 p32 My 2017
All the Demons of Hell: Turned Loose in 1974 J. LEONARD *Idaho Magazine* v16 no8 p18 My 2017
THE RAVAGES OF MARCH: A FAR-FLUNG FAMILY STRUCK BY FLOODS K. WRIGHT *Idaho Magazine* v16 no8 p48 My 2017

Riverside Health System (Company)
Gathering Around *Virginia Living* v15 no1 p103 D 2016

Rivers—India
HOW TO STEAL A RIVER R. Romig *New York Times Magazine* p42 Mr 5 2017

Rivers—Indiana
See also
Tippecanoe River (Ind.)
TROUBLED WATERS M. WRIGHT *Indianapolis Monthly* v40 no3 p90 N 2016

Rivers—Laos
THE LAST DAYS OF THE NAM OU RIVER A. BARON *Orion Magazine* v35 no3 p36 My/Je 2016
River of Change *Orion Magazine* v35 no3 p66 My/Je 2016

Rivers—Law & legislation
Free Flow R. WICHELNS *Backpacker* p21 O 2017

Rivers—Management
MAKING A SPLASH R. Annis, S. Bahr et al color *Indianapolis Monthly* v41 no2 p76 S 2017
RIVER: SIGNS OF CIVILIZATIONS PAST T. WHEATLEY *Atlanta* v57 no4 p55 Ag 2017

Rivers—Mexico
Mexico City's Last Living River color *Foreign Policy* no224 p16 My/Je 2017

Rivers—Missouri
FAR FROM THE MADDING CROWD C. TOMLIN cartoon color *Missouri Life* v44 no4 p30 Je 2017
RIVER TALES D. A. WOOD color *Missouri Life* v44 no4 p10 Je 2017

Rivers—Montana
THE FIRE ISSUE color *Field & Stream* v121 no8 p42 F/Mr 2017

Rivers—Nebraska
SUMMERTIME color *Nebraska Life* v21 no4 p18 Jl/Ag 2017

Rivers—New York (State)
A PLACE IN THE SUN C. Kearns color *Field & Stream* v122 no2 p10 Je/Jl 2017

Rivett, Jasmine P. H.
High-performance light-emitting diodes based on carbene-metal-amides chart graph *Science* v356 no6334 p159 Ap 14 2017

Rivette, Jacques, 1928-2016
The Greatest Enigma of French Film L. Sante bw color *New York Review of Books* v63 no16 p54 O 27 2016
JACQUES RIVETTE & ABBAS KIAROSTAM A. O. SCOTT *New York Times Magazine* p57 D 25 2016

Riviera (Company)
RIVIERA 575 SUV *Sea Magazine* v109 no2 p42 F 2017

Riviera (France)
Riviera Revival A. LOBRANO color *Conde Nast Traveler* v52 no7 p34 Ag 2017

Riviera (TV program)
Riviera A. Bacle, K. Connolly et al color *Entertainment Weekly* no1482/1483 p106 S 22 2017

Riviera Australia Pty. Ltd.
Riviera 4800 Sport Yacht D. Harding color *Power & Motoryacht*

v33 no2 p40 F 2017

Riviera automobile—Evaluation
RIVIERA 575 SUV *Sea Magazine* v109 no2 p42 F 2017

Riviera Boats (Company)
Sea Ray SLX 400 B. Pike color *Power & Motoryacht* v34 no10 p64 O 2017

Riviera Yachts (Company)
RIVIERA 4800 SPORT YACHT: THE LATEST IN TECHNOLOGY AND PROPULSION COMBINE WITH STYLE AND STRENGTH M. WERLING color *Sea Magazine* v109 no7 p28 Jl 2017
RIVIERA 6000 SPORT YACHT R. MCAFEE *Sea Magazine* v108 no10 p44 O 2016
Riviera 68 Sports Motor Yacht D. J. Harding color *Power & Motoryacht* v34 no10 p62 O 2017

Rivkin, Jan W.
The U.S. Economy Is Doing Only Half Its Job *Harvard Business Review Digital Articles* p2 D 17 2015

RIVKIN, STEVEN
Desegregation Since the Coleman Report *Education Digest* v82 no5 p26 Ja 2017

Rivlin, Gary
How long can a progressive federal agency, the Consumer Financial Protection Bureau, stand firm against the deregulatory pressures of the Trump administration? *New York Times Magazine* p18 Ap 23 2017
On Money color *New York Times Magazine* p18 My 21 2017

RIVLIN-NADLER, MAX
Trump the Union Buster color *New Republic* v248 no7 p8 Jl 2017

RIX, ERIKA
Astronomy Tools Actions Set color *Astronomy* v44 no12 p66 D 2016
Distorted galaxies color *Astronomy* v45 no3 p66 Mr 2017
Hickson groups diag *Astronomy* v45 no6 p66 Je 2017
Kepler near the terminator bw color *Astronomy* v45 no11 p64 N 2017
Memory hooks bw *Astronomy* v45 no2 p68 F 2017
Sandpaper blocks color *Astronomy* v45 no5 p64 My 2017
Sketching totality bw color *Astronomy* v45 no9 p66 S 2017

Rizal Bin Sumatoh, Hermi
Mapping the human DC lineage through the integration of high-dimensional techniques diag *Science* v356 no6342 p1044 Je 9 2017

RIZER, ARTHUR
'Demilitarize' the Police? color *Weekly Standard* v22 no7 p17 O 24 2016

RIZGA, KRISTINA
Bully Pulpit cartoon *Mother Jones* v42 no1 p13 Ja/F 2017
Heavens to Betsy cartoon chart map *Mother Jones* v42 no2 p30 Mr/Ap 2017

Rizi, V.
Observation of a large-scale anisotropy in the arrival directions of cosmic rays above 8×10^{18} eV *Science* v357 no6357 p1266 S 22 2017

Rizk, Levi
DESTINATION WASHINGTON C. CUNNINGHAM *Washingtonian Magazine* v52 no5 p22 F 2017

Rizo, Alexandrea N.
Ratchet-like polypeptide translocation mechanism of the AAA+ disaggregase Hsp104 diag *Science* v357 no6348 p273 Jl 21 2017

Rizopoulos, Natasha
Embodying the sutra color *Yoga Journal* no296 p51 N 2017
Get Hip color *Yoga Journal* p70 2017 Special Issue
Master class color *Yoga Journal* p46 2017 SpecialIssue
Q: What do you consistently do to boost happiness? color *Yoga Journal* no296 p12 N 2017
A smart start to vinyasa color *Yoga Journal* no296 p89 N 2017
Teacher's Pet color *Yoga Journal* p14 2017 Special Issue

Rizvanovic, Mirnesa
An Anthropocene map of genetic diversity bibl graph map *Science* v353 no6307 p1532 S 30 2016

Rizvi, Ali
Rizvi's Reformation *Commentary* v141 no9 p1 N 2016
Rizvi's Reformation *Commentary* v142 no4 p1 N 2016
Rizvi's Reformation O. KESSLER *Commentary* v142 no4 p38 N

2016

RIZZA, CINDY

Painting the Fence color *Yankee* p114 Mr 2017

Rizzo, Carita

TV's HOTTEST COUPLES *TV Guide* v64 no15 p28 Ap 4 2016

RIZZO, JOHNNA

The Truth Behind 3 AWESOME MOVIES *National Geographic Kids* no466 p22 D 2016/Ja 2017

Rizzu, Patrizia

β2-Adrenoreceptor is a regulator of the a-synuclein gene driving risk of Parkinson's disease cartoon chart graph *Science* v357 no6354 p891 S 1 2017

Rjd2 (Performer)

New Routes M. Trammell cartoon *New Yorker* v92 no44 p15 Ja 9 2017

Rjeily, Anthony

Passwords Are Terrible, but Will Biometrics Be Any Better? *Harvard Business Review Digital Articles* p1 My 11 2017

RLJ Cos.

Blazing New Trails [Cover story] K. Meeks color *Black Enterprise* v47 no4 p12 N/D 2016

RNA

See also

Messenger RNA

CRISPRi-based genome-scale identification of functional long noncoding RNA loci in human cells M. A. Horlbeck, S. J. Liu et al bibl graph *Science* v355 no6320 p1 Ja 6 2017

Kinetics of dCas9 target search in Escherichia coli D. Lawson Jones, P. Leroy et al diag *Science* v357 no6358 p1420 S 29 2017

RNA localization feeds translation I. Gáspár and A. Ephrussi color *Science* v357 no6357 p1235 S 22 2017

WORD EXCHANGE A. Ward, E. Cummings et al *Natural History* v125 no2 p9 F 2017

Zika virus produces noncoding RNAs using a multi-pseudoknot structure that confounds a cellular exonuclease B. M. Akiyama, H. M. Laurence et al bibl color graph *Science* v354 no6316 p1148 D 2 2016

RNA-binding proteins

Cyclin A2 is an RNA binding protein that controls Mre11 mRNA translation A. Kanakkanthara, K. B. Jeganathan et al bibl graph *Science* v353 no6307 p1549 S 30 2016

Key Discoveries on Cellular Regeneration *USA Today Magazine* v145 no2865 p14 Je 2017

RNA editing

Cephalopod smarts tied to RNA edits T. H. SAEY color *Science News* v191 no8 p6 Ap 29 2017

RNA interference

Host cell attachment elicits posttranscriptional regulation in infecting enteropathogenic bacteria N. Katsowich, N. Elbaz et al bibl graph *Science* v355 no6326 p735 F 17 2017

RNA interference is essential for cellular quiescence B. Roche, B. Arcangioli et al bibl diag graph *Science* v354 no6313 paah5651-1 N 11 2016

RNA polymerases

RNA polymerase motions during promoter melting A. Feklistov, B. Bae et al color diag graph *Science* v356 no6340 p863 My 26 2017

RNA replicase

Transient compartmentalization of RNA replicators prevents extinction due to parasites Shigeyoshi Matsumura, A. Kun et al bibl chart graph *Science* v354 no6317 p1293 D 9 2016

RNA-seq

Comprehensive single-cell transcriptional profiling of a multicellular organism J. Cao, J. S. Packer et al diag *Science* v357 no6352 p661 Ag 18 2017

Decoupling genetics, lineages, and microenvironment in IDH-mutant gliomas by single-cell RNA-seq A. S. Venteicher, I. Tirosh et al diag *Science* v355 no6332 p1391 Mr 31 2017

Single-cell RNA-seq reveals new types of human blood dendritic cells, monocytes, and progenitors Villani, R. Satija et al color *Science* v356 no6335 p283 Ap 21 2017

RNA viruses

See also

Encephalitis viruses

Flaviviruses

Reoviruses

Why are neurons susceptible to Zika virus? D. E. Griffin diag *Science* v357 no6346 p33 Jl 7 2017

RNA—Analysis—Equipment & supplies

NEW PRODUCTS: DNA/RNA ANALYSIS color *Science* v354 no6317 p1309 D 9 2016

new products: dna/rna analysis color *Science* v355 no6326 p761 F 17 2017

RNA—Therapeutic use

How a Boy's Lazarus-like Revival Points to a New Generation of Drugs K. Weintraub color *MIT Technology Review* v120 no4 p24 Jl/Ag 2017

Rønning, Joachim

PIRATES OF THE CARIBBEAN: DEAD MEN TELL NO TALES M. Snetiker color *Entertainment Weekly* no1463/1464 p36 Ap/My 2017

WHEN ZOMBIE SHARKS ATTACK D. Coggan color *Entertainment Weekly* no1468/1469 p84 Je 2-9 2017

RO, CHRISTINE

Flights of Fancy color *Earth Island Journal* v32 no2 p54 Summ 2017

Roach, Clare Deckelman

Speak up color *U.S. Catholic* v82 no4 p5 Ap 2017

Roach, John C.

The "marriage premium" and the economic impact it can have on children *Monthly Labor Review* p1 My 2017

Roach, Levi

Henry IV of Germany: a 'Bad King'? *History Today* v67 no3 p4 Mr 2017

READY TO RULE *History Today* v67 no5 p24 My 2017

ROACH, MARY

GO WITH THE FLOW *Smithsonian* v48 no1 p48 Ap 2017

Grunt R. Soodalter *MHQ: Quarterly Journal of Military History* v29 no2 p93 Wint 2017 The Rest Stop Road Trip color *Reader's Digest* v189 no1131 p72 Je 2017

Road bicycles

"SHOULD I GET A ROAD BIKE WITH DISC BRAKES? L. Flickinger and B. STRICKLAND color diag *Bicycling* v58 no3 p30 Ap 2017

Road bicycles—Evaluation

"HOW MUCH TRAVEL DO I NEED?" M. Phillips and B. STRICKLAND color *Bicycling* v58 no3 p44 Ap 2017

"I WANT A BIKE THAT WILL LAST ME 15 YEARS." M. Yozell and B. STRICKLAND color *Bicycling* v58 no3 p52 Ap 2017

"I WANT TO GO ON DIRT-ROAD ADVENTURES." L. Tanner and B. STRICKLAND color *Bicycling* v58 no3 p42 Ap 2017

"WHAT'S A GOOD BIKE FOR RIDING HOME FROM THE BAR?" G. Liu and B. STRICKLAND color *Bicycling* v58 no3 p54 Ap 2017

"WHERE DO I WANT TO RIDE? DUH, EVERYWHERE." J. Lindsey and B. STRICKLAND color *Bicycling* v58 no3 p48 Ap 2017

"WHY SHOULD I SPEND $5,000 ON A BIKE?" R. Koch and B. STRICKLAND color *Bicycling* v58 no3 p46 Ap 2017

Road design & construction

See also

Street design & construction

Over the Edge S. F. HAYWARD bw color *Weekly Standard* v22 no44 p27 Jl 31 2017

Road interchanges & intersections

A Night at the Crossroads of America G. WOOD color *Missouri Life* v44 no4 p98 Je 2017

Road maps

Map Out a Plan D. PEAK *Log Home Living* v34 no6 p6 Ag 2017

Start your engines map *Backpacker* p13 My 2017

Road markings

THE BRITISH HERITAGE TRAVEL PUZZLER *British Heritage Travel* v38 no1 p78 Ja/F 2017

Road rage

People L. Markoe color *Christian Century* v134 no15 p19 Jl 19 2017

Road Runner automobile

The Dream Car D. Freiburger color *Hot Rod* v70 no3 p106 Mr 2017

Road running

The HOT ROD Archives D. Wallace color *Hot Rod* v70 no4 p14 Ap 2017

It's Not the Same as Running Around the Block K. DUPZYK color *Popular Mechanics* v193 no7 p41 S 2016

STREAKER KING S. Douglas bw color *Runner's World* v51 no10 p46 N 2016

Roadkill

The Car and Driver Guide to Automotive Bullsh!t J. Gall color *Car & Driver* v63 no1 p76 Jl 2017

Roadrunner

Greater Roadrunners E. Balli *Arizona Highways* v93 no9 p15 S 2017

Roads

> See also
> Dirt roads
> Driveways
> Express highways
> Racetracks (Automobile racing)
> Streets
> Trails

Global roadless areas: Hidden roads A. C. Hughes color *Science* v355 no6332 p1381 Mr 31 2017

Overseas Highway V. SACKETT color map *AARP: The Magazine* v60 no3A p51 Ap/My 2017

Pacific Coast Highway B. NEWCOTT color map *AARP: The Magazine* v60 no3A p48 Ap/My 2017

Route 66 A. SACHS color map *AARP: The Magazine* v60 no3A p53 Ap/My 2017

Roads—Arizona

BLUE RANGE LOOP N. AUSTIN *Arizona Highways* v92 no7 p52 Jl 2016

CONTROL ROAD K. MONTGOMERY color map *Arizona Highways* v93 no5 p52 My 2017

OH, HOW I HAVE ENJOYED J. Lee, C. Singleton et al *Arizona Highways* v93 no10 p4 O 2017

Roads—Canada

The great Canadian road trip map *Maclean's* no1 p15 F 17 2017

Road to Everywhere N. RICHLER cartoon map *Walrus* v14 no6 p19 Jl/Ag 2017

Roads—China

Border Trouble: China and India Face Off D. TWEED bw map *Bloomberg Businessweek* no4534 p32 Ag 14 2017

Contemplating Decline: China's challenge to America percolates on many fronts C. LAYNE *American Conservative* v16 no4 p29 Jl/Ag 2017

Roads—Design & construction

> See also
> Streets—Design & construction

Boulevard Dreams A. Ehrenhalt *Governing* v30 no3 p14 D 2016

Roads—Design & construction—Finance

Last Look D. Kidd *Governing* v30 no6 p64 Mr 2017

Roads—England—London—Maps—History—17th century

'The Road from London to Dover', 1675 K. Wiles *History Today* v67 no2 p18 F 2017

Roads—Environmental aspects

Global roadless areas: Consider terrain R. Wu, W. Wang et al color *Science* v355 no6332 p1381 Mr 31 2017

Roads—India—Design & construction

India Likes Its Roads Built On Time I. Marlow and B. Pradhan color *Bloomberg Businessweek* no4513 p23 Mr 6 2017

Roads—Interchanges & intersections

> See also
> Crossovers (Highway engineering)

The Perfect Crossing T. De Chant cartoon *Wired* v24 no11 p66 N 2016

Roads—Louisiana

A Rose is A Rose: Bayou Road Renaissance C. Kolb color *New Orleans Magazine* v51 no10 p50 Ag 2017

Roads—Maintenance & repair

BRIDGING THE JAMES B. HUNHOFF *South Dakota Magazine* v32 no6 p20 Mr/Ap 2017

Roads—New York (State)

DRIVE TIME I. FRAZIER cartoon color *New Yorker* v93 no25 p34 Ag 28 2017

Roadster Shop (Company)

INFERNO [Cover story] B. Gillogly color *Hot Rod* v70 no8 p24 Ag 2017

Roads—Texas

DOWN ON HIGHWAY 59 A. LOCKE *Texas Monthly* v45 no9 p34 S 2017

Roads—United States

> See also
> United States Highway 66

BEST OF BRICKBATS: THE OBAMA YEARS, 2009-2016 C. OLIVER cartoon *Reason* v48 no9 p72 F 2017

EDITOR'S LETTER K. WOLFKILL *Road & Track* v68 no9 p186 Je 2017

Go color *Road & Track* v68 no9 p6 Je 2017

SIGNS and WONDERS J. D. DANIELS color *Esquire* p107 My 2017

Roads—United States—Finance

INFRASTRUCTURE UNDER DURESS diag *Fortune* v175 no5 p11 Ap 1 2017

Roads—United States—Maintenance & repair

INFRASTRUCTURE UNDER DURESS diag *Fortune* v175 no5 p11 Ap 1 2017

Roasted nuts

Stocking Your Pantry Like a Pro K. O'SHEA-EVANS color *House Beautiful* v159 no2 p72 Mr 2017

Roasting (Cooking)

THE ART OF THE ROAST M. True color *Sunset* v237 no6 p70 D 2016

Flipping the Bird *Martha Stewart Living* no269 p82 N 2016

THE HANDBOOK *Martha Stewart Living* no268 p137 O 2016

HOLIDAY SPIRIT I. Edwards color *Sunset* v237 no6 p8 D 2016

it's going to be a / ROAST D. BOWEN *Martha Stewart Living* no268 p106 O 2016

PERFECTING THE... ROAST CHICKEN *Martha Stewart Living* no267 p71 S 2016

Screw the Turkey! P. KITA cartoon color *Men's Health* v32 no9 p57 N 2017

Side Hustle C. SAFFITZ color *Bon Appetit* p68 S 2017

A Simple Roast Chicken C. MOROCCO and A. STANEK color *Bon Appetit* v62 no10 p64 O 2017

Tom Kitchin's Traditional Pot-Roasted Chicken S. Gutierrez color *British Heritage Travel* v38 no5 p74 S/O 2017

Roasting (Cooking)—Equipment & supplies

The Home Coffee Revolution color diag *Popular Mechanics* p21 F 2017

ROASTING PANS M. XERAKIA color *Better Homes & Gardens* v95 no11 p142 N 2017

Roback, Diane

A Big Week for Children's Books color *Publishers Weekly* v264 no16 p4 Ap 17 2017

ROBARE, MATTHEW M.

From Chapels to Condos bw *American Conservative* v16 no1 p6 Ja/F 2017

Robb, Ali

Emergence and spread of a human-transmissible multidrug-resistant nontuberculous mycobacterium bibl diag graph *Science* v354 no6313 p751 N 11 2016

Robb, Amanda

Christine LAGARDE color *Glamour* v114 no12 p220 D 2016

The Making of an American Terrorist chart color il *New Republic* v248 no1/2 p34 Ja/F 2017

Surviving the '80s color *AARP: The Magazine* v59 no5A p47 Ag/S 2016

Robb, Candace

A Twisted Vengeance: A Kate Clifford Mystery *Publishers Weekly* v264 no13 p79 Mr 27 2017

Robb, Steve

STOCKING FISH + SAVING A LIFE *New York State Conservationist* v71 no5 p18 Ap 2017

Röbbel, Nathalie

Green Spaces: An Invaluable Resource for Delivering Sustainable Urban Health *UN Chronicle* v53 no3 p6 2016

Robbers

The merry dance of the HIGHWAYMAN J. Sugden *History Today* v67 no3 p48 Mr 2017

Strangers in the House J. Maynard color *AARP: The Magazine* v30 no6A p68 O/N 2017

Wild West Josie N. BRULLIARD *National Parks* v91 no1 p58 Wint 2017

Robbie, Margot, 1990-

Best-Dressed LIST L. McCarthy color *Harper's Bazaar* no3649 p140 D 2016/Ja 2017

THE BIG SHORT color *Alternatives Journal (AJ) - Canada's Environmental Voice* v42 no2 p18 2016

Margot Robbie M. Rich color *Current Biography* v78 no1 p69 Ja 2017

Margot Robbie's Gold-Medal Makeover C. M. Smith color *Entertainment Weekly* no1450 p16 Ja 27 2017

ROBBINS, BRUCE

THE RED EMIGRANT color *Nation* v304 no13 p27 Ap 17 2017

A STARTING POINT FOR POLITICS bw *Nation* v303 no20 p27 N 14 2016

Robbins, Jerome

DANCE *New Yorker* v93 no33 p28 O 23 2017

Robbins, Kathleen R.

Around the Campfire color *Trail Rider* v29 no1 p6 Ja/F 2017

Robbins, Liz

Should They Stay or Should They Go? The debate over President Trump's crackdown on undocumented immigrants *New York Times Upfront* v149 no13 p6 My 15 2017

TRUMP'S TRAVEL BAN *New York Times Upfront* v149 no10 p6 Mr 13 2017

Robbins, Michael W.

Scars of Independence *MHQ: Quarterly Journal of Military History* v29 no3 p93 Spr 2017

Waging War: Conflict, Culture, and Innovation in World History *MHQ: Quarterly Journal of Military History* v29 no4 p94 Summ 2017

Robbins, Paul F.

Landscape of immunogenic tumor antigens in successful immunotherapy of virally induced epithelial cancer graph *Science* v356 no6334 p200 Ap 14 2017

ROBBINS, PETE

10! cartoon color *Field & Stream* v122 no1 p30 My 2017

Robbins, Peter

Classic Cowpunchers bw color *American Cowboy* v24 no1 p10 Je/Jl 2017

Robbins, Royal, 1935-2017

Hello, Again M. SAMET color *Climbing* no353 p17 My/Je 2017

ROBBINS, SARAH J.

STRATEGY SESSION color diag *Publishers Weekly* v264 no21 p35 My 22 2017

WHERE DO WE GO FROM HERE? color map *Publishers Weekly* v264 no4 p22 Ja 23 2017

YA Authors Turn Advocates *Publishers Weekly* v263 no41 p40 O 10 2016

Robbins, Tony, 1960-

It Used to Be So Easy *Money* v46 no4 p5 My 2017

Robbins, Tony, 1960——Interviews

THE OUTSIDER [Cover story] T. Robbins and J. Bogle color *Money* v46 no4 p38 My 2017

ROBEHMED, NATALIE

America's Richest Celebrities color *Forbes* v198 no9 p18 D 30 2016

Bestselling Business Books color *Forbes* v198 no6 p36 N 8 2016

BOOKING IT color *Forbes* v200 no2 p22 S 5 2017

GONZO GOLD RUSH color *Forbes* v200 no1 p24 Jl 27 2017

LESSONS AND IDEAS BY THE 100 GREATEST LIVING BUSINESS MINDS bw color *Forbes* v200 no3 p115 S 28 2017

Netflix Zombies bw *Forbes* v199 no7 p98 Je 29 2017

Old World, Young Promise color *Forbes* v199 no1 p20 Ja 24 2017

We Knew Them When color *Forbes* v199 no1 p22 Ja 24 2017

THE WORLD'S BILLIONAIRES bw color diag graph map *Forbes* v199 no3 p84 Mr 28 2017

Roben, Scott

Buchholz color *Art in America* v105 no6 p134 Je/Jl 2017

Roberge, Mark

How Morale Changes as a Startup Grows *Harvard Business Review Digital Articles* p2 Mr 24 2017

A Recession Doesn't Mean Your Startup Can't Grow *Harvard Business Review Digital Articles* p2 F 24 2016

ROBERSON, BLYTHE

FUTURE AUSTEN ADAPTATIONS cartoon *New Yorker* v93 no23 p29 Ag 7 2017

ROBERT, ARNAUD

The Side Effect color *National Geographic* v231 no6 p128 Je 2017

Robert, Caroline

pretty IS AS PRETTY does: A FLOOD DAMAGED OLD METAIRIE HOUSE IS GIVEN A SECOND CHANCE V. HART *New Orleans Homes & Lifestyles* v20 no4 p56 Aut 2017

Robert, Katee

The Devil's Daughter *Publishers Weekly* v263 no46 p38 N 14 2016

Robert, Kevin

The Saatchi Ouster Shows Leaders Need to Be Gender Smart, Not Gender Blind A. Wittenberg-Cox *Harvard Business Review Digital Articles* p2 Ag 3 2016

Robert, Zoë

THE CASE OF BIRNA *Iceland Review* v55 no2 p42 Mr/Ap 2017

CELEBRATING SOCCER SUCCESS color *Iceland Review* v54 no5 p32 S-O 2016

FROSTY WELCOME color *Iceland Review* v54 no5 p72 S-O 2016

GOING PLACES? color *Iceland Review* v54 no5 p76 S-O 2016

HEALTH AND HEALING IN HVERAGERÐI *Iceland Review* v54 no6 p40 N/D 2016

INVIGORATING INVENTIONS *Iceland Review* v55 no1 p22 Ja/F 2017

ON FIRE *Iceland Review* v54 no6 p14 N/D 2016

SOLDIER FOR SUSTAINABILITY *Iceland Review* v55 no1 p62 Ja/F 2017

STATE OF THE FOURTH ESTATE *Iceland Review* v54 no6 p72 N/D 2016

TO MARKET color *Iceland Review* v54 no5 p46 S-O 2016

TOWARDS A CLEANER CONSCIENCE *Iceland Review* v55 no4 p50 Jl/Ag 2017

THE WOMEN AT BESSASTAÐIR: A look at how the role of the first lady of Iceland has evolved over the years *Iceland Review* v55 no3 p21 My/Je 2017

Robert Bosch Tool Corp.

THE Right TOOL R. BERENDSOHN and R. ROMANSKI color *Popular Mechanics* p80 N 2017

Robert W. Woodruff Arts Center

One for All: The Woodruff Arts Center's new CEO aims to boost arts groups citywide S. HENRY *Atlanta* v57 no6 p75 O 2017

Robert Wood Johnson Foundation

Health Equity: Leading Through Programs, Environmental Changes and Policies K. Soohoo *Parks & Recreation* v52 no10 p28 O 2017

STATES OF EMERGENCY cartoon chart color *Muscle & Performance* v9 no1 p15 Ja 2017

Robert Bosch GmbH—Trials, litigation, etc.

Will Bosch Choke on VW's Exhaust? D. Lawrence, K. Mehrotra et al bw color *Bloomberg Businessweek* no4534 p12 Ag 14 2017

Roberts, Adam

COULD THE ANSWER TO OUR MOST URGENT HEALTH CRISIS BE FOUND ON A TOILET SEAT? M. McKENNA color *Atlantic* v320 no1 p88 Jl/Ag 2017

Roberts, Andrew

THE BIG QUESTION cartoon *Atlantic* v318 no4 p112 N 2016

Churchill Challenged *Commentary* v143 no4 p47 Ap 2017

Dunkirk Undone *Commentary* v144 no2 p51 S 2017

The Identitarians *Commentary* v142 no4 p51 N 2016

Mr. Attlee's Hour bw color *Weekly Standard* v22 no27 p34 Mr 20 2017

Sacrifice on the Western Front J. S. GORDON *Commentary* v142 no1 p50 Jl/Ag 2016

Winston's Folly bw *Weekly Standard* v22 no41 p27 Jl 3 2017

Win-Winston *Commentary* v144 no3 p52 O 2017

Roberts, Aryeh

COMO UN SOLO HOMBRE *Hoover Digest: Research & Opinion on Public Policy* no1 p219 Wint 2017

ROBERTS, BRADLEY H. JR.

BEEN THERE, DONE THAT *Foreign Affairs* v95 no6 p196 N/D 2016

Roberts, Brian

Putting your liberal arts degree to work *Career Outlook* p1 Ag 2017

Roberts, Bryan

Why So Many New Tech Companies Are Getting into Health Care *Harvard Business Review Digital Articles* p2 D 8 2014

Roberts, Catherine

Eat Smarter, Eat Healthier [Cover story] color *Consumer Reports* v82 no11 p18 N 2017

The New War on Obesity chart color diag *Consumer Reports* v82 no10 p48 O 2017

Stay Safer il *Consumer Reports* v82 no3 p27 Mr 2017

Roberts, Craig

Welcome to the Club J. PODHORETZ *Weekly Standard* v22 no18 p43 Ja 16 2017

Roberts, D. Allan

Guns on campus: Is that physics? *Physics Today* v70 no6 p15 Je 2017

Roberts, Dave

Bad to the Bone *Atlanta* v57 no4 p42 Ag 2017

"I'm sold on Harlequin Floors *Dance Magazine* v91 no10 p5 O 2017

Roberts, Debbie

THE MOST POWERFUL WOMEN IN BUSINESS [Cover story] S. Floyd, K. Wilder et al color *Black Enterprise* v47 no5 p56 Ja/F 2017

ROBERTS, DEBRA

Planning for the Future of Urban Biodiversity: A Global Review of City-Scale Initiatives *BioScience* v67 no4 p332 Ap 2017

Roberts, Dexter

The Asian Jobs Ladder Is Broken *Bloomberg Businessweek* no4528 p58 Je 26 2017

Beijing Moves to Curb Overseas Investments *Bloomberg Businessweek* no4504 p17 D 19 2016

Beijing Wants One Union To Rule Them All bw graph *Bloomberg Businessweek* no4499 p38 N 14 2016

China's Numbers Man color *Bloomberg Businessweek* no4516 p12 Mr 27 2017

China's Real Economic Problem *Bloomberg Businessweek* no4530 p33 Jl 17 2017

CHINA'S ROBOT REVOLUTION color graph *Bloomberg Businessweek* no4520 p32 My 1 2017

China's Shift to Services Hits a Snag color *Bloomberg Businessweek* no4521 p16 My 8 2017

China Unleashes Its Farmers color *Bloomberg Businessweek* no4540 p36 O 2 2017

Global Trade Is Slowing color *Bloomberg Businessweek* no4500 p16 N 21 2016

No Golden Years for China's Villagers color *Bloomberg Businessweek* no4506 p13 Ja 9 2017

The riddle of Xi color *Bloomberg Businessweek* no4496 p17 O 24 2016

School Choice, Beijing Edition color *Bloomberg Businessweek* no4526 p15 Je 12 2017

Roberts, Doris, 1925-2016

DORIS ROBERTS R. Romano and L. Rice color *Entertainment Weekly* no1446/1447 p86 D 2016/Ja 2017

Roberts, Elizabeth

THE BEST-LAID (KITCHEN) PLANS J. TUNG *Martha Stewart Living* no268 p98 O 2016

Roberts, Heather Hogan

IF THESE WALLS COULD TALK... K. HACKETT *Better Homes & Gardens* v95 no1 p94 Ja 2017

Roberts, Jason

Mmm, Poke! color *Bicycling* v58 no6 p32 Jl 2017

Roberts, Jeff John

100 FASTEST-GROWING COMPANIES chart color diag map *Fortune* v176 no4 p157 S 15 2017

THE 2017 Fortune Crystal Ball color diag *Fortune* v174 no7 p11 D 1 2016

63 DELTA color *Fortune* v175 no4 p106 Mr 15 2017

BEARDED MEN DISCOVER BEAUTY PRODUCTS diag *Fortune* v75 no1 p24 Ja 1 2017

BLINK OF AN EYE color *Fortune* v175 no4 p36 Mr 15 2017

BLOCKCHAIN IN REAL LIFE *Fortune* v176 no3 p49 S 1 2017

BREAKING THE BITCOIN BANK color *Fortune* v176 no5 p26 O 1 2017

COUNTING COINS *Fortune* v175 no5 p15 Ap 1 2017

CRYSTAL CLEAR PROVENANCE color *Fortune* v176 no4 p44 S 15 2017

DIGITAL DOINGS IN DELAWARE *Fortune* v176 no3 p50 S 1 2017

DREAM WEAVER color *Fortune* v176 no3 p74 S 1 2017

FORTY UNDER FORTY 2017 color *Fortune* v176 no3 p62 S 1 2017

GADGETRY color *Fortune* v174 no8 p22 D 15 2016

GLOBALIZATION BITES BACK color diag *Fortune* v176 no2 p82 Ag 1 2017

HACKED [Cover story] color diag *Fortune* v176 no1 p52 Jl 1 2017

HOW MUCH IS SECURITY WORTH? *Fortune* v175 no2 p14 F 1 2017

INSIDER-TRADING LAW: A SUPREME COURT RULING GIVES PROSECUTORS A BOOST *Fortune* v75 no1 p94 Ja 1 2017

INVESTORS SEEK SWEET COIN diag *Fortune* v176 no1 p88 Jl 1 2017

MINING COMEDY GOLD color *Fortune* v176 no3 p70 S 1 2017

NOW TRENDING: #ethicalproblems color *Fortune* v174 no8 p42 D 15 2016

TECH FIGHT ON THE FARM color *Fortune* v176 no1 p24 Jl 1 2017

Time for a (Virtual) Reality Check color *Fortune* v175 no3 p14 Mr 1 2017

TROLL HUNTERS color *Fortune* v175 no2 p22 F 1 2017

WANTED: FRESH SOLUTIONS FOR AGE-OLD PROBLEMS color diag *Fortune* v175 no6 p68 My 1 2017

WHEN YOUR STUFF SPIES ON YOU color *Fortune* v175 no7 p26 Je 1 2017

Why Executives Don't Go to Prison Anymore color *Fortune* v176 no1 p16 Jl 1 2017

WORLD'S 50 GREATEST LEADERS [Cover story] color *Fortune* v175 no5 p46 Ap 1 2017

YOUTH REVOLT color *Fortune* v176 no3 p64 S 1 2017

Roberts, Jennifer

SECRETS of People with HIGHLY STRESSFUL JOBS M. CROUCH cartoon *Prevention* v69 no2 p64 F 2017

Roberts, Joanne

How to Pay for Health Care/The Case for Capitation: Interaction *Harvard Business Review* v94 no11 p20 N 2016

ROBERTS, JODY A.

New toxic chemical regulations *Issues in Science & Technology* v33 no2 p9 Wint 2017

Roberts, Johannes

47 METERS DOWN C. Holub color *Entertainment Weekly* no1463/1464 p57 Ap/My 2017

Roberts, John

A Working from Home Experiment Shows High Performers Like It Better *Harvard Business Review Digital Articles* p2 Ja 23 2015

Roberts, John D., 1918-2016

John D. Roberts (1918–2016) G. M. Whitesides color *Science* v354 no6318 p1382 D 16 2016

Roberts, John G., 1955-

THE MESSAGE IN YOUR MISFORTUNES *Vital Speeches of the Day* v83 no9 p265 S 2017

Roberts, Jonathan

Don't Let Frustration Make You Say the Wrong Thing *Harvard Business Review Digital Articles* p2 D 24 2015

Roberts, Julia, 1967-

Big5-Oh C. Ianzito color *AARP: The Magazine* v30 no6A p76 O/N 2017

Points to Ponder D. CHAPPELLE, M. KURLANSKY et al color *Reader's Digest* v190 no1134 p35 O 2017

WONDER I. Biedenharn color *Entertainment Weekly* no1478 / 1479 p65 Ag 18-25 2017

Roberts, Kale

Creating Custom Furniture from SALVAGED WOOD: Bootstrap business Baldwin Custom Woodworking transforms diseased trees into nandmade heirloom woodworks *Mother Earth News* no282 p66 Je/Jl 2017

Roberts, Kate

THE PARADOX OF THE WHOLE-CLASS NOVEL color *Literacy Today (2411-7862)* v34 no5 p42 Mr/Ap 2017

Roberts, Leonard

Major Crimes N. Abrams, A. Bacle et al *Entertainment Weekly* no1482/1483 p66 S 22 2017

Roberts, Leslie

BITING BACK color *Science* v354 no6309 p162 O 14 2016

THE FUTURE OF PAIN RESEARCH color *Science* v354 no6312 p565 N 4 2016

NIGERIA'S INVISIBLE CRISIS [Cover story] color map *Science* v356 no6333 p18 Ap 7 2017

Revolutionary malaria tests have unexpected downsides color *Science* v357 no6351 p536 Ag 11 2017

Roberts, Lindsey M.

GROWN AT HOME color *National Geographic* v232 no5 p18 N 2017

Roberts, Lori

BEST OF THE FESTS color *Indianapolis Monthly* v41 no2 p92 S 2017

BONE-A FIDE ADVICE color *Indianapolis Monthly* v42 no2 p99 O 2017

DIVE IN THE DEEP END *Indianapolis Monthly* v40 no7 p88 Mr 2017

Expert OPINION: FIVE WEDDING VETERANS GIVE US THEIR TIPS AND TRICKS FOR GETTING THE MOST OUT OF VENDORS *Indianapolis Monthly* v12 no40 p18 Ag 2017

SAVED BY THE DELL *Indianapolis Monthly* p79 F 2017

SOMETHING TO SMILE ABOUT *Indianapolis Monthly* v40 no11 p100 Jl 2017

Sweet Dreams *Indianapolis Monthly* p24 My 2017

Welcome to the Monkey House *Indianapolis Monthly* p134 My 2017

Roberts, Michael

Queen of the Jungle L. YAEGER, M. HOLGATE et al color *Vogue* v207 no9 p396 S 2017

ROBERTS, NADIM

Peace Be upon You color *Walrus* p24 Ja\F 2017

Roberts, Nicholas W.

The biology of color color *Science* v357 no6350 p470 Ag 4 2017

ROBERTS, PAUL

Hedge City Blues color graph *Mother Jones* v42 no3 p40 My/ Je 2017

Roberts, Peter

Glycomics and its application potential in precision medicine bibl diag *Science* v354 no6319 p36 D 23 2016

Startup Accelerators Have Become More Popular in Emerging Markets—and They're Working *Harvard Business Review Digital Articles* p2 O 2 2017

Roberts, Richard G.

Neandertal and Denisovan DNA from Pleistocene sediments bw color *Science* v356 no6338 p605 My 12 2017

Roberts, Rob

Custom-Shop Shooter M. R. Shea color *Field & Stream* v122 no5 pF6 O 2017

ROBERTS, ROBIN

ADVENTURES IN ALASKA *Sea Magazine* v109 no2 p18 F 2017

Roberts, Rodney

WHY DID THIS INNOCENT MAN PLEAD GUILTY? A. GOLDET color *Reader's Digest* v189 no1131 p118 Je 2017

Roberts, Russell

The Human Side of Trade: In a dynamic economy, short-term pain is real. But over the longer term? Free trade leads to better, richer lives *Hoover Digest: Research & Opinion on Public Policy* no2 p13 Spr 2017

When Eugenics Was Progressive: Improve society by improving human stock? A century ago, the Progressive movement cheered that disturbing idea. Historian Thomas Leonard, author of Illiberal Reformers, explains *Hoover Digest: Research & Opinion on Public Policy* no3 p175 Summ 2017

ROBERTS, SAM

The Little Rock Nine: Sixty years ago this month, President Eisenhower sent federal troops into Arkansas to enforce the desegregation of Little Rock's Central High School *New York Times Upfront* v150 no1 p18 S 4 2017

Roberts, Sarah Jakes

My Soul Looks Back in Wonder color *Essence* v47 no11 p124 Mr 2017

Roberts, Sophy

at home in ROME color *Conde Nast Traveler* v52 no8 p108 S 2017

BEAUTY AND THE BEASTS bw color *Conde Nast Traveler* v51

no10 p158 N 2016

CENTRAL KENYA bw color *Conde Nast Traveler* v52 no4 p88 Ap 2017

Cold Comfort color *Conde Nast Traveler* v51 no11 p74 D 2016

MADAGASCAR bw color *Conde Nast Traveler* v52 no4 p74 Ap 2017

WE'RE TURNING 30 bw chart color *Conde Nast Traveler* v52 no8 p55 S 2017

Roberts, Susan B.

THE MESSY TRUTH ABOUT WEIGHT LOSS color graph *Scientific American* v316 no6 p36 Je 2017

Roberts, Tara

Love at First Touch color *Parents* v92 no6 p20 Je 2017

Roberts-grey, Gina

Fall Back in Love With Your Job color *Essence* v47 no10 p71 F 2017

Forgive: Your Life Could Depend on It color *Essence* v48 no2 p111 Je 2017

HOW I'M THRIVING WITH HIV color *Essence* v47 no8 p144 D 2016

OUR FATHERS IN THEIR OWN WORDS color *Essence* v48 no2 p94 Je 2017

OVER 50 AND FABULOUS color *Essence* v47 no8 p140 D 2016

STAND UP FOR HIS HEALTH color *Essence* v47 no10 p101 F 2017

STAY WELL AND SAVE MONEY color *Essence* v47 no12 p117 Ap 2017

THERAPY SAVED ME color *Essence* v47 no7 p107 N 2016

Robertson, Avril A. B.

Clonal hematopoiesis associated with TET2 deficiency accelerates atherosclerosis development in mice bibl diag *Science* v355 no6327 p842 F 24 2017

Robertson, Benjamin

Targeting the Nest Eggs Of U.K. Expats *Bloomberg Businessweek* no4524 p39 My 29 2017

ROBERTSON, CHRISTOPHER

WRONGFUL INCARCERATION *USA Today Magazine* v145 no2858 p26 N 2016

Robertson, Claire

Decoding hormones for a stem cell niche color *Science* v356 no6335 p250 Ap 21 2017

Robertson, Colin—Interviews

'THE ONLY ONE SMILING WILL BE PUTIN' J. GEDDES color *Maclean's* v129 no46 p40 N 21 2016

Robertson, Dana A.

TEACHER TALK AS AN INSTRUCTIONAL TOOL: Tips for making use of the "third turn" *Literacy Today (2411-7862)* v35 no1 p34 Jl/Ag 2017

Robertson, David

How Gatorade Invented New Products by Revisiting Old Ones *Harvard Business Review Digital Articles* p2 2017

Robertson, David—Interviews

Q&A: The Interview color *Maclean's* v130 no9 p53 O 2017

Robertson, Denise

A Gelding, a Mare, a Lesson color *Horse & Rider* v56 no4 p16 Ap 2017

Robertson, G. Philip

Cellulosic biofuel contributions to a sustainable energy future: Choices and outcomes color *Science* v356 no6345 p1349 Je 30 2017

Robertson, Homer

All the Fixin's color *American Cowboy* p68 LEGENDS OF TEXAS Special Issue 2017

Robertson, Ian

How Stressing Out Can Help You Succeed *Time* v189 no4 p23 Ja 23 2017

Robertson, Ian—Interviews

Ian Robertson A. Priddle color *Motor Trend* v69 no5 p24 My 2017

ROBERTSON, JAMIE COX

WRONGFUL INCARCERATION *USA Today Magazine* v145 no2858 p26 N 2016

Robertson, Jordan

Crappy, Buggy, Obsolete Voting Technology We Trust color *Bloomberg Businessweek* no4493 p60 O 3 2016

The Equifax Job bw graph *Bloomberg Businessweek* no4541 p26 O 9 2017

The Mauritania Exploit bw *Bloomberg Businessweek* no4508 p48 Ja 23 2017

Stand By...Scanning for Viruses and Secrets cartoon *Bloomberg Businessweek* no4530 p21 Jl 17 2017

The Yahoo! Hack Goes From Bad to Worse *Bloomberg Businessweek* no4505 p36 D 26 2016

Your Money Or Your Data! color *Bloomberg Businessweek* no4523 p15 My 22 2017

Robertson, L. F.
Two Lost Boys color *Publishers Weekly* v264 no11 p61 Mr 13 2017

Robertson, Lori
Collaborating with Communities Strengthens Green Infrastructure Outcomes *Parks & Recreation* v52 no8 p32 Ag 2017

Empowering Volunteers to Take the Lead *Parks & Recreation* v51 no11 p32 N 2016

Southwest Airlines and NRPA: Helping to Restore Monarch Habitat *Parks & Recreation* v52 no1 p40 Ja 2017

Robertson, Matt
NORTHERN EXPOSURE color *Spin to Win Rodeo* v20 no11 p12 Ja 2017

Robertson, Owen Druce
POWER [Cover story] color *Christian Century* v134 no1 p22 Ja 4 2017

Robertson, Regina R.
13 POWER PLAYERS color *Essence* v47 no11 p104 Mr 2017

BLACK WOMEN IN HOLLYWOOD color *Essence* v47 no11 p87 Mr 2017

THE CHANGE AGENT color *Essence* v47 no8 p88 D 2016

GIRL TRIPPING color *Essence* v48 no3 p82 Jl 2017

Lalah Hathaway color *Essence* v48 no2 p36 Je 2017

LOVE & MARRIAGE color *Essence* v47 no7 p47 N 2016

ME...SLOW DOWN? HELL, NO! color *Essence* v47 no11 p59 Mr 2017

NO LONGER SILENT color *Essence* v47 no7 p82 N 2016

ROCKIN' ROBIN color *Essence* v48 no5 p61 S 2017

THE TIES THAT BIND [Cover story] color *Essence* v47 no8 p94 D 2016

Robertson, Robbie
THE BIRTH OF THE BAND R. ROBERTSON bw *Rolling Stone* no1274 p48 N 17 2016

The Brotherhood of Rock G. Marcus bw color *New York Review of Books* v64 no5 p45 Mr 23 2017

STRIKE UP THE BAND P. ELIE *New York Times Book Review* p66 D 4 2016

We Were the Band bw color *Vanity Fair* v58 no11 p176 N 2016

Robertson, Robbie—Interviews
THE INTERVIEW M. BARCLAY color *Maclean's* v129 no46 p10 N 21 2016

Robertson, Robin
Cooking with Chia Seeds [Cover story] color *Amazing Wellness* v9 no6 p90 EarlyWint 2017

Veganize It! Easy DIY Recipes for a Plant-Based Kitchen *Publishers Weekly* v263 no52 p118 D 19 2016

Robertson, Ross
6 Simple Steps to a Custom Track System *Boating World* v37 no9 p22 N/D 2016

BURNING RUBBER cartoon color *Field & Stream* v121 no8 p72 F/Mr 2017

Drop It Like It's Hot color *Field & Stream* v121 no9 pF1 Ap 2017

SPEED KILLS color *Outdoor Life* v224 no4 p68 My 2017

Robertson, Selina
"WE CAN MAKE SOMETHING OUT OF ANYTHING": SALLY POTTER'S THRILLER AND LONDON'S HISTORY OF QUEER FEMINIST FILM SPACES *Film Quarterly* v70 no4 p39 Summ 2017

Robes
WAKE-UP Call *Interview* v46 no10 p61 D 2016/Ja 2017

ROBESON, BILL
READERS' THOUGHTS ON PAST ISSUES color *Motor Trend* v69 no2 p26 F 2017

Robeson, Lloyd M.
Maximizing the right stuff: The trade-off between membrane permeability and selectivity color *Science* v356 no6343 p1137 Je 16 2017

Robespierre, Gillian

Landline Is a Message from a Lost World: the 1990s S. Zacharek color *Time* v190 no5 p58 Jl 31 2017

Landline L. Greenblatt color *Entertainment Weekly* no1474/1475 p99 Jl 21-28 2017

Robespierre, Maximilien
HOMELAND SECURITY *Lapham's Quarterly* v10 no3 p159 Summ 2017

Robichaud, Chloe
BOUNDARIES (PAYS) J. Teodoro color *Film Comment* v53 no2 p22 Mr/Ap 2017

Robichaud, Jon—Interviews
GET IN THE VAN! D. NORD color *Bicycling* v58 no8 p18 S 2017

Robichaud, Pam—Interviews
GET IN THE VAN! D. NORD color *Bicycling* v58 no8 p18 S 2017

Robichaud, William
Saving the saola from extinction color *Science* v357 no6357 p1248 S 22 2017

Robie, Chet
References Should Come from a Candidate's Coworkers, Not Just Their Boss *Harvard Business Review Digital Articles* p2 2017

Robillard, Stephane
Gala: Each year, an Event highlight is always the Gala dinner and Fundraiser Auction, held this year at Fasig Tipton. Great toed, camaraderie, spirited bidding, and dancing put everyone in good spirits *Arabian Horse World* v57 no11 p44 Ag 2017

Robin, Corey
THE DREAM OF THE ENEMY *Harper's Magazine* v334 no2001 p26 F 2017

Robin, Craig
MIAMI HEAT H. SILVA color *Architectural Digest* v74 no9 p149 S 2017

Robin, Marci
THE HANGOVER IS ... OVER color *InStyle* v23 no13 p186 D 2016

TORY BURCH'S Icons color *InStyle* v24 no3 p264 Mr 2017

Robin, Raizel
Maxed Out [Cover story] color *Walrus* v14 no5 p28 Je 2017

Robin, Ron
The Cold War They Made: The Strategic Legacy of Roberta and Albert Wohlstetter L. D. Freedman *Foreign Affairs* v96 no1 p160 Ja/F 2017

Mr. and Mrs. Nuclear War P. TAUBMAN *New York Times Book Review* p17 O 23 2016

Robin Hood Farms Inc.
2015 NATIONAL CHAMPION MARES *Arabian Horse World* v56 no12 p160 S 2016

Robin the Boy Wonder (Fictitious character)
NO: 20 Robin J. Hibberd color *Entertainment Weekly* no1436/1437 p60 O 21 2016

Robins
My Shot color *National Geographic Kids* no465 p37 N 2016

Robins, Harlan S.
Landscape of immunogenic tumor antigens in successful immunotherapy of virally induced epithelial cancer graph *Science* v356 no6334 p200 Ap 14 2017

Robins, Natalie
GETTING EVEN V. GORNICK bw *Nation* v304 no18 p18 Je 19 2017

The Untold Journey: The Life of Diana Trilling *Publishers Weekly* v264 no11 p76 Mr 13 2017

A WOMAN UNDER THE INFLUENCE T. HASLETT bw cartoon *New Yorker* v93 no15 p63 My 29 2017

Robinson, Aaron
25 CARS WORTH WAITING FOR color *Car & Driver* v62 no10 p32 Ap 2017

Aaron Robinson *Car & Driver* v62 no8 p26 F 2017

Aaron Robinson color *Car & Driver* v62 no11 p30 My 2017

Aaron Robinson color *Car & Driver* v63 no1 p32 Jl 2017

ATOMIC PROSPECTOR chart color diag *Car & Driver* v63 no2 p42 Ag 2017

Feel Lucky, Punk? [Cover story] color *Car & Driver* v63 no1 p36 Jl 2017

Ford's fabulous GT takes its lucky, if cramped, pilot right back to Le Mans color *Car & Driver* v63 no1 p46 Jl 2017

LIGHTNING LAP [Cover story] color graph map *Car & Driver* v63 no4 p45 O 2017

ONE-CAR WONDERS chart color *Car & Driver* v62 no10 p62 Ap 2017

PENNY WISER color diag *Car & Driver* v62 no11 p84 My 2017

Redemption Songs color graph *Car & Driver* v62 no7 p110 Ja 2017

Ringing the Bull color diag *Car & Driver* v62 no6 p52 D 2016

Trailer Queen color *Car & Driver* v62 no6 p102 D 2016

Wear Your Flare color *Car & Driver* v62 no8 p86 F 2017

WINNERS AND LOSERS color *Car & Driver* v62 no7 p18 Ja 2017

ROBINSON, ALEX

BEAST MODE color *Outdoor Life* v224 no8 pW5 O 2017

COLD CASE color *Outdoor Life* v224 no6 p47 Ag 2017

COMMON GROUND color *Outdoor Life* v224 no5 p70 Je/Jl 2017

DIY TURKEY GUN color *Outdoor Life* v224 no2 p86 F/Mr 2017

HARDSHIP HONKERS color *Outdoor Life* v224 no8 p43 O 2017

THE JUMP-SHOOTER'S PLAYBOOK color *Outdoor Life* v224 no8 pW8 O 2017

MEAT EATERS color *Outdoor Life* v224 no1 p21 D 2016/Ja 2017

PARADISE FOUND color *Outdoor Life* v224 no1 p60 D 2016/ Ja 2017

START WITH A BANG color *Outdoor Life* v224 no7 pW1 S 2017

ROBINSON, ANDREA

YEA BOXY BRONCOS, NAY BEATNIK BOLSHEVIKS bw color *Forbes* v200 no2 p31 S 5 2017

Robinson, Andrew

THE ANCIENTS HAD STARS IN THEIR EYES: Since its surprising discovery on the Aegean seabed over a century ago, the Antikythera Mechanism has intrigued astrologers, classicists and historians of science *History Today* v67 no9 p97 S 2017

Asylums and after bibl bw *Science* v354 no6309 p188 O 14 2016

Divining science color *Science* v354 no6319 p1539 D 23 2016

Einstein's magnum opus color *Science* v357 no6353 p763 Ag 25 2017

Little More than Tea and Cricket *History Today* v67 no4 p63 Ap 2017

The Tale of the Axe *History Today* v66 no10 p57 O 2016

Robinson, Angela

NOW STREAMING! A. TINUBU color *Ebony* v72 no11 p86 S 2017

Professor Marston and the Wonder Women *New Yorker* v93 no32 p12 O 16 2017

PROFESSOR MARSTON & THE WONDER WOMEN C. Agard color *Entertainment Weekly* no1478/1479 p51 Ag 18-25 2017

Robinson, Angela—Interviews

REVEALING THE "THROUPLE" BEHIND WONDER WOMAN: Did you know the world's hottest superhero was inspired by a polyamorous relationship? D. ANDERSON-MINSHALL and T. GILCHRIST *Advocate* no1093 p27 O/N 2017

Robinson, Anthony B.

Caring for Joy: Narrative, Theology and Practice *Christian Century* v134 no14 p39 Jl 5 2017

Getting past the past color *Christian Century* v133 no22 p36 O 26 2016

Listening to Louisiana color *Christian Century* v133 no26 p36 D 21 2016

The 'no cross talk' rule *Christian Century* v134 no10 p10 My 10 2017

ROBINSON, BRIAN E.

When, Where, and How Nature Matters for Ecosystem Services: Challenges for the Next Generation of Ecosystem Service Models *BioScience* v67 no9 p820 S 2017

Robinson, Britany

THE BEGINNER'S GUIDE TO Making a Difference cartoon color diag *O, The Oprah Magazine* p114 S 2017

Oregon's Trail of Tears *Sierra* v102 no5 p14 St/O 2017

Robinson, Carla

HOW DO YOU HOLD TOGETHER YOUR TRANS IDENTITY AND YOUR LIFE OF FAITH? color *Christian Century* v134 no2 p22 Ja 18 2017

Robinson, Charles Samuel

Trail Broke B. Welch bw color *American Cowboy* v23 no6 p62 Ap/My 2017

Robinson, Corey

Big Man on Campus P. Thamel and T. Keith color *Sports Illustrated* v125 no13 p16 O 17 2016

Robinson, Craig, 1971-

3 THINGS TO KNOW ABOUT GHOSTED M. Roffman *TV Guide* v65 no37 p42 S 4 2017

The Duke of Diversion M. BAZER *Chicago* v66 no10 p72 O 2017

GHOSTED D. Snierson color *Entertainment Weekly* no1474/1475 p74 Jl 21-28 2017

Poets, Prophets, Ghosts color *Chicago* v66 no10 p70 O 2017

Robinson, Craig, 1971—Interviews

ADAM SCOTT AND CRAIG ROBINSON D. Snierson, A. Bacle et al color *Entertainment Weekly* no1482/1483 p42 S 22 2017

Robinson, David A.

The 2015-2016 U.S. Snow Report: A Slim Year with A Few Surprises chart color map *Weatherwise* v69 no6 p21 N-D 2016

Robinson, Edward

Banks? cartoon *Bloomberg Businessweek* no4503 p32 D 12 2016

Changing the Way Cash Is Sent Home color graph *Bloomberg Businessweek* no4522 p44 My 15 2017

Some Things Not Doing So Well at the Moment color *Bloomberg Businessweek* no4494 p38 O 10 2016

Robinson, Frances—Interviews

THE LOOK OF LOVE M. BOBO color *Ebony* v72 no4 p55 F 2017

Robinson, Gene E.

Epigenetics and the evolution of instincts color diag *Science* v356 no6333 p26 Ap 7 2017

Robinson, J. M.

A Fermi-degenerate three-dimensional optical lattice clock color diag graph *Science* v357 no6359 p90 O 6 2017

Robinson, Jack

BEST TUBE RIDER color *Surfing Magazine* v53 no1 p44 Ja 2017

FAT JACK'S "TOO LOW TOO FAST" 1951 F1 FORD T. Taylor color *Hot Rod* v70 no1 p68 Ja 2017

MOST FEARLESS color *Surfing Magazine* v53 no1 p50 Ja 2017

Robinson, Jackie, 1919-1972

History's Greatest Hits K. BOATNER *National Geographic Kids* no469 p11 Ap 2017

ROBINSON, JAMES

Dinner Is Served *Opera News* v81 no9 p20 Mr 2017

Robinson, James E.

Structural basis for antibody-mediated neutralization of Lassa virus [Cover story] color diag *Science* v356 no6341 p923 Je 1 2017

Robinson, Jill K.

SEARCHING FOR TIA: In modern Vietnam, memories of the war still linger *Saturday Evening Post* v289 no4 p56 Jl/Ag 2017

The Swing of Things *Sierra* v102 no4 p16 Jl/Ag 2017

Robinson, Jim

Building His Audience J. Hyatt color *Money* v45 no11 p27 D 2016

Robinson, Joanna

THE NEW ESTABLISHMENT 2017 bw color *Vanity Fair* v59 no11 p87 N 2017

NEW ESTABLISHMENT bw cartoon color *Vanity Fair* v58 no11 p124 N 2016

ROBINSON, JONATHAN

Long-Term Studies Contribute Disproportionately to Ecology and Policy *BioScience* v67 no3 p271 Mr 2017

Robinson, Joseph

Joe FreshGoods M. RAYMER color *Chicago* v66 no6 p87 Je 2017

Robinson, Kelsey

What It Will Take to Make the Tech Industry More Diverse *Harvard Business Review Digital Articles* p2 Mr 15 2016

Robinson, Kerry Alys

The Magnanimity of the Gospel color *America* v217 no5 p54 S 4 2017

Robinson, Kim Stanley

The next New York C. Abbott bibl color *Science* v355 no6330 p1135 Mr 17 2017

Welcome To New York! A. Rutkoff cartoon *Bloomberg Businessweek* no4514 p67 Mr 13 2017

Robinson, Laura F.

Ocean mixing and ice-sheet control of seawater 234U/238U during the last deglaciation bibl graph *Science* v354 no6312 p626 N 4 2016

Robinson, Leah
Using Longitudinal Data on Career Outcomes to Promote Improvements and Diversity in Graduate Education *Change* v48 no6 p42 N/D 2016

ROBINSON, LISA
FKA twigs color *Vanity Fair* v58 no12 p88 D 2016
Hot Tracks color *Vanity Fair* v59 no2 p38 F 2017
Hot Tracks color *Vanity Fair* v59 no5 p54 Ap 2017
Hot Tracks: JASON ISBELL color *Vanity Fair* v59 no11 p76 N 2017
Hot Tracks: RYAN ADAMS color *Vanity Fair* v59 no9 p140 S 2017
Queen of Hearts bw color *Vanity Fair* v58 no12 p122 D 2016

Robinson, Lisa A.
Consumer Warning Labels Aren't Working *Harvard Business Review Digital Articles* p2 N 30 2016

Robinson, Loren
10 THINGS WE'RE TALKING ABOUT T. A. Christian color *Essence* v47 no9 p46 Ja 2017

Robinson, Marilynne
Acts of Faith *Harper's Magazine* v333 no1998 p2 N 2016
IOWA CITY, IOWA *Harper's Magazine* p37 O 2017
A Proof, a Test, an Instruction color *Nation* v304 no1 p16 Ja 2 2017 The Obama Years
Toward Essentials *New York Times Book Review* p13 S 24 2017
What Are We Doing Here? bw color *New York Review of Books* v64 no17 p28 N 9 2017

Robinson, Marilynne, 1943——Interviews
Saving Calvin from Clichés [Cover story] M. Sitman bw *Commonweal* v144 no17 p18 O 20 2017

Robinson, Mark D.
Male sex in houseflies is determined by Mdmd, a paralog of the generic splice factor gene CWC22 bw color *Science* v356 no6338 p642 My 12 2017

Robinson, Matt
A Lawyer Stalks Wall Street Banks color *Bloomberg Businessweek* no4528 p24 Je 26 2017
Targeting the Nest Eggs Of U.K. Expats *Bloomberg Businessweek* no4524 p39 My 29 2017

ROBINSON, MICHAEL
Hunting for credit color *Maclean's* v129 no44 p70 N 7 2016
STUDENT DOWNLOADERS BEWARE color *Maclean's* v129 no44 p56 N 7 2016

Robinson, Peter
"Growth Is the Problem": Lower tax rates, broaden the base. Such simple changes are all that we need, says Hoover fellow John H. Cochrane *Hoover Digest: Research & Opinion on Public Policy* no3 p143 Summ 2017
John Hennessy: The Exit Interview *Hoover Digest: Research & Opinion on Public Policy* no4 p170 Fall 2016
A Miracle or a Relic *Hoover Digest: Research & Opinion on Public Policy* no1 p165 Wint 2017
Rhapsody in Blue and Red: "We don't need less partisanship. We need better partisanship." Russell Muirhead shows how political parties get things done *Hoover Digest: Research & Opinion on Public Policy* no3 p153 Summ 2017
Rust Belt Prophet *Hoover Digest: Research & Opinion on Public Policy* no1 p154 Wint 2017
Wealth, Poverty; and Politics *Hoover Digest: Research & Opinion on Public Policy* no2 p166 Spr 2017

Robinson, Peter——Interviews
John Hennessy: The Exit Interview P. Robinson *Hoover Digest: Research & Opinion on Public Policy* no4 p170 Fall 2016

Robinson, Phoebe
The Girly Show cartoon *O, The Oprah Magazine* p120 Mr 2017
THE Good Guy color *Glamour* v115 no10 p168 O 2017
OBAMA'S AMERICA img *New York* v49 no20 p12 O 3 2016

Robinson, Phoebe——Interviews
Two Peas in a Podcast color *O, The Oprah Magazine* p26 Ap 2017

ROBINSON, ROXANA
Bound by War color *New York Times Book Review* p17 Ja 29 2017

Robinson, Sandra L.
When You're the Person Your Colleagues Always Vent To *Harvard Business Review Digital Articles* p2 N 30 2016

Robinson, Sharon A.
Biodiversity redistribution under climate change: Impacts on ecosystems and human well-being color *Science* v355 no6332 p1389 Mr 31 2017

Robinson, Smokey, 1940——Interviews
THE LOOK OF LOVE M. BOBO color *Ebony* v72 no4 p55 F 2017

ROBINSON, STEPHANIE
Righting Words color *O, The Oprah Magazine* p17 Jl 2017

Robinson, Timothy P.
Reducing antimicrobial use in food animals color graph *Science* v357 no6358 p1350 S 29 2017
Role for migratory wild birds in the global spread of avian influenza H5N8 bibl graph map *Science* v354 no6309 p213 O 14 2016

Robinson, Walter
The Spin Zone color *Art in America* v104 no10 p65 N 2016
WALTER ROBINSON D. Ebony cartoon *Art in America* v104 no11 p122 D 2016

ROBINSON, WALTER M.
This Will Sting & Burn *Reader's Digest* v189 no1127 p96 F 2017

Robinson, Walter——Exhibitions
Reality Principle P. Schjeldahl cartoon *New Yorker* v92 no30 p8 S 26 2016

ROBINSON, WHITNEY
Sacred Spaces color *Esquire* p126 BigBlackBook

Robinson, Will
OFFICE CHRISTMAS PARTY color *Entertainment Weekly* no1438 p39 N 4 2016

Robinson, William A.
Skepticism Should Be Nonpartisan *Skeptical Inquirer* v41 no3 p63 My/Je 2017

Robison, Peter
Cessna Flights For the Masses *Bloomberg Businessweek* no4524 p35 My 29 2017
DONNY AND ERIC MIND THE STORE color *Bloomberg Businessweek* no4535 p54 Ag 28 2017
In Case of Low Revenue cartoon *Bloomberg Businessweek* no4497 p50 O 31 2016
A Is for Arbitrage [Cover story] color *Bloomberg Businessweek* no4502 p52 D 5 2016
RED STATE VENTURE CAPITAL color *Bloomberg Businessweek* no4508 p42 Ja 23 2017
So you want to move to the U.S color diag graph *Bloomberg Businessweek* no4538 p48 S 18 2017
Trump Plays Six Degrees of the KGB color *Bloomberg Businessweek* no4506 p22 Ja 9 2017

Robitzski, Dan
A Spare Hand color *Scientific American* v316 no5 p17 My 2017

ROBLEDO, S. JHOANNA
The Urbanist: The Rise of the Frankenmansion img *New York* v49 no24 p41 N 28 2016

Robles, Hansel
Leading Off color *Sports Illustrated* v126 no8 p6 Mr 20 2017

Robo-advisors (Financial planning)
Robot Advisers Can Be Conflicted, Too H. Son cartoon *Bloomberg Businessweek* no4532 p28 Jl 31 2017

ROBOCK, ALAN
Climate engineering *Issues in Science & Technology* v33 no4 p8 Summ 2017

Robot control systems
Apple's new Swift Playgrounds 1.5 includes controls for robots R. LOYOLA color *Macworld - Digital Edition* p16 Je 13 2017

Robot design & construction
High Robot E. Biba graph *Scientific American* v316 no5 p21 My 2017
Robo Pizzaiolo J. Beebe color *Scientific American* v316 no6 p22 Je 2017

Robotham, Michael, 1960-
The Secrets She Keeps *Publishers Weekly* v264 no22 p47 My 29 2017

Robotic exoskeletons
Better Typing Through Mind Control J. Wise color *Bloomberg Businessweek* no4537 p74 S 11 2017
Fast exoskeleton optimization P. Malcolm, S. Galle et al color graph *Science* v356 no6344 p1230 Je 23 2017
Human-in-the-loop optimization of exoskeleton assistance during walking J. Zhang, P. Fiers et al diag *Science* v356 no6344 p1280 Je 23 2017

Robotic exoskeletons—Design & construction

Innovation M. Belfiore color *Bloomberg Businessweek* no4505 p37 D 26 2016

Robotics

See also
Animatronics
Robotics in education
Robots

AI Apparently Is for Real J. M. LAING and T. ATWOOD *USA Today Magazine* v145 no2862 p35 Mr 2017

The Foregone Alternative C. HOCHART *USA Today Magazine* v145 no2862 p61 Mr 2017

Grandma's Robot Helper C. Caruso color *Scientific American* v317 no1 p24 Jl 2017

New lightweight bot leaps with zip M. ROSEN color *Science News* v191 no1 p12 Ja 21 2017

The Pros and Cons of Robot Managers T. Chamorro-Premuzic and G. Ahmetoglu *Harvard Business Review Digital Articles* p2 D 12 2016

A Real Life Transformer *New York Times Upfront* v149 no13 p2 My 15 2017

REWIRING THE SENSE OF TOUCH E. Conant color *National Geographic* v232 no3 p19 S 2017

Robots Are Learning Complex Tasks Just by Watching Humans Do Them J. Shah *Harvard Business Review Digital Articles* p2 Je 21 2016

WILL A ROBOT TAKE YOUR JOB? E. SHERMAN and R. ZISSOU *New York Times Upfront* v149 no3 p10 O 10 2016

Robotics in education

CODING: The New 21st-Century Literacy? S. Lafee *Education Digest* v83 no2 p25 O 2017

Robotics in medicine

A cargo-sorting DNA robot A. J. Thubagere, W. Li et al color *Science* v357 no6356 p1112 S 15 2017

DNA robots sort as they walk J. H. Reif diag *Science* v357 no6356 p1095 S 15 2017

Robotics software

Autopilot E. J. Wallace color *Virginia Living* v15 no5 p37 Ag 2017

Robotics—China

CHINA'S ROBOT REVOLUTION D. Roberts, R. Chang et al color graph *Bloomberg Businessweek* no4520 p32 My 1 2017

Robotics—Competitions

Education Robot Fight Club M. Belfiore color *Bloomberg Businessweek* no4505 p35 D 26 2016

Robotics—Economic aspects

Are ROBOTS Going to Steal Our Jobs? [Cover story] R. BAILEY bw color *Reason* v49 no3 p24 Jl 2017

Robotics—Evaluation

LEGO BOOST C. HUEY-YOU and C. HUEY-YOU color *Popular Mechanics* p96 S 2017

Robotics—Exhibitions

Mechanized creatures P. Sareh and M. Kovac color *Science* v355 no6332 p1379 Mr 31 2017

Robotics—Law & legislation

The 2017 Fear Index N. Hopper color diag *Time* v188 no27-28 p68 D 26 2016

Robotics—News briefs

Real-Life Robocops J. Zorthian color *Time* v189 no21 p10 Je 5 2017

Robotics—Study & teaching

Education Robot Fight Club M. Belfiore color *Bloomberg Businessweek* no4505 p35 D 26 2016

Robots

See also
Industrial robots

5 SMART Toys C. BOYER *National Geographic Kids* no466 p18 D 2016/Ja 2017

Artificial Intelligence Invades the Home ... In Toys L. Eadicicco color *Time* v188 no24 p20 D 12 2016

Ayanna Howard *Atlanta* v57 no2 p104 Je 2017

Caring Computers [Cover story] J. KEATS color *Discover* v38 no4 p10 My 2017

THE Chef of the Future MARES ONLY ONE DISH CRAB BISQUE à la robot D. MARCHESE img *New York* p40 F 9 2017

Future World: Homes K. DE SEVE color *National Geographic Kids* no475 p20 N 2017

Grandma's Robot Helper C. Caruso color *Scientific American* v317 no1 p24 Jl 2017

Guinness World Records *National Geographic Kids* no469 p6 Ap 2017

High-Tech Camel Races *New York Times Upfront* v149 no9 p2 F 20 2017

How AI Is Getting More Human L. Eadicicco color *Time* v188 no27-28 p96 D 26 2016

Innovation Yardbot M. Belfiore color *Bloomberg Businessweek* no4504 p33 D 19 2016

IRON GIANT: GET READY TO ROBO-RUMBLE! D. FERRY color diag *Wired* v25 no8 p24 Ag 2017

IS YOUR JOB ROBOT-PROOF? D. BRANCACCIO color *Popular Mechanics* p78 Jl 2017

New lightweight bot leaps with zip M. ROSEN color *Science News* v191 no1 p12 Ja 21 2017

Origami outfits help bots retool M. TEMMING color *Science News* v192 no7 p13 O 28 2017

REAL OR FAKE? E. KRIEGER *National Geographic Kids* no469 p18 Ap 2017

Research: Technology Is Only Making Social Skills More Important N. Torres *Harvard Business Review Digital Articles* p2 Ag 26 2015

ROBOT AWAKENING M. Rosen chart color *Science News* v190 no10 p18 N 12 2016

The Robotic Grocery Store of the Future Is Here J. Condliffe color *MIT Technology Review* v120 no2 p22 Mr/Ap 2017

Stop Worrying About Whether Machines Are "Intelligent" J. C. Spender *Harvard Business Review Digital Articles* p2 Ag 4 2015

THINKING OUTSIDE THE BOTS G. SHTEYNGART *Smithsonian* v48 no3 p66 Je 2017

Uncovering the secrets of the USS Arizona in Pearl Harbor color *PCWorld* p192 D 2016

Very Light Jockeys color *MIT Technology Review* v120 no2 p18 Mr/Ap 2017

What Is a Robot, Anyway? H. J. Wilson *Harvard Business Review Digital Articles* p2 Ap 15 2015

When to Trust Robots with Decisions, and When Not To V. Dhar *Harvard Business Review Digital Articles* p2 My 17 2016

Which Virtual Assistant Tells the Best Jokes? B. SPECKTOR color *Reader's Digest* v189 no1129 p126 Ap 2017

WHY *FREE MONEY COULD BE THE FUTURE OF WORK C. Dillow and B. Rainwater color diag *Fortune* v176 no1 p68 Jl 1 2017

WHY ROBOTS WON'T FARM R. Holtzmann *South Dakota Magazine* v33 no2 p44 Jl/Ag 2017

The World's First RoboCop *New York Times Upfront* v150 no1 p2 S 4 2017

Robots in literature—History

A POCKET GUIDE TO THE ROBOT REVOLUTION I. BOGOST color *Atlantic* v318 no4 p84 N 2016

Robots—Control systems

Should a Robot Manage Your Money? J. GARSKOF cartoon *AARP: The Magazine* v60 no3A p22 Ap/My 2017

Robots—Design & construction

Bots in Your Bloodstream P. Patel diag *Scientific American* v316 no2 p15 F 2017

Laundroid Y. Nakamura and H. Nakagawa color *Bloomberg Businessweek* no4510 p28 F 6 2017

Meet the Octobot J. Sklar color *MIT Technology Review* v120 no1 p108 Ja/F 2017

THE MOST IMPORTANT FRONTIER FOR ROBOTS IS NOT THE WORK THEY TAKE FROM HUMANS BUT THE WORK THEY DO WITH HUMANS—WHICH REQUIRES A LOT OF LEARNING ON BOTH SIDES K. Tingley *New York Times Magazine* p30 F 26 2017

Robots—Evaluation

A Real Life Transformer *New York Times Upfront* v149 no13 p2 My 15 2017

The Rise of the Room-Service Robots C. Morris color *Fortune* v175 no7 p16 Je 1 2017

SPHERO R2-D2 APP-ENABLED DROID A. HAYWARD color *Macworld - Digital Edition* v34 no11 p35 N 2017

Robots—Exhibitions

Holiday in The Desert D. ROTHBART *Los Angeles Magazine* p76 D 2016

tal Articles p2 N 4 2016

Why More and More Companies Are Ditching Performance Ratings Harvard Business Review Digital Articles p2 S 8 2015

Rock, Mick

Mick Rock C. Collis color Entertainment Weekly no1460/1461 p27 Ap 7-17 2017

Rock analysis

How Dry the Moon H. Leifert bw color Natural History v125 no11 p7 N 2017

ROCKS THAT TALK color Popular Science v289 no5 p43 S/O 2017

Rock art (Archaeology)

Desert Dream A. JURRIES color Backpacker v45 no2 p26 Mr 2017

For the Good of the People M. Jacobs color Black Belt v55 no6 p74 O/N 2017

INSIDE OUT K. VAUGHN Arizona Highways v93 no10 p32 O 2017

Rock Band (Game)

Rock Band VR: Rock Band's roaring PC debut showcases Oculus Touch's potential H. DINGMAN color PCWorld v35 no5 p125 My 2017

Rock climbing

All 50 Classics, for Your Pleasure Z. GATES Climbing no355 p66 Ag 2017

Approach the altar color Backpacker p20 My 2017

Arabian Nights K. Corrigan and J. Lucas color Climbing no357 p48 N 2017

Breakfast (and Dinner) of Champions P. CLAASSEN color Climbing no353 p29 My/Je 2017

Chamonix J. Ellison color Climbing no355 p34 Ag 2017

Chess with Death color Climbing no355 p13 Ag 2017

CLIMBING AT THE NEW cartoon Climbing no356 p18 S/O 2017

Climbing for Mental Health H. MOORE color Climbing no352 p10 Ap 2017

CLIMBING TO A BETTER FUTURE B. Broudy color Climbing no351 p64 F/Mr 2017

COMMITTED C. Kassar color Climbing no355 p62 Ag 2017

THE DESCENT A. BURR color Climbing no357 p72 N 2017

THE DESCENT J. ELLISON color Climbing no352 p88 Ap 2017

THE DESCENT M. EARLE color Climbing no355 p80 Ag 2017

Double Vision K. CORDES color Climbing no355 p26 Ag 2017

Field Notes color Climbing no355 p44 Ag 2017

FLASH color Climbing no355 p6 Ag 2017

Forlorn Pinnacle M. JENKINS bw color Climbing no355 p72 Ag 2017

THE GERMAN WAY [Cover story] S. TROTTER color Climbing no349 p26 N 2016

Getting a Grip in NYC A. SHIRAISHI color O, The Oprah Magazine p114 Mr 2017

The Givers J. Abegg color Climbing no355 p52 Ag 2017

Harness Your Inner "Gym Beast" M. SAMET Climbing no355 p47 Ag 2017

Head, Fingers, Knees, and Toes K. LAMBERT Climbing no355 p30 Ag 2017

Hello, Again M. SAMET color Climbing no353 p17 My/Je 2017

Highball Tactics N. WILLIAMS color Climbing no350 p50 D 2016/Ja 2017

ISRAEL UPRISING S. DAVIS color Climbing no349 p38 N 2016

Jessie Graff P. KITA cartoon color Men's Health v32 no8 p35 O 2017

Let's Get Ready to Rambla! [Cover story] Z. GATES color Climbing no353 p31 My/Je 2017

Lift Off M. Brown cartoon Vogue v206 no11 p170 N 2016

LOST IN TOKYO C. MCINERNEY color Climbing no349 p48 N 2016

Middle of Somewhere O. Summerscales color Climbing no357 p36 N 2017

Moose's Tooth J. LUCAS color Climbing no355 p28 Ag 2017

A New Joe's C. WEBBER color Climbing no353 p22 My/Je 2017

Old Dominion Granite S. Derr color Climbing no353 p32 My/Je 2017

Opening Season B. HOINESS color Climbing no355 p32 Ag 2017

Rock the Gym L. Jhung color Men's Health v31 no10 p32 D 2016

Scary (and true) tales from a crag near you Mark and T. Jenkin

Climbing no352 p11 Ap 2017

Scary (and true) tales from a crag near you M. Parker and J. Lucas Climbing no350 p19 D 2016/Ja 2017

Southern Super Nova E. Elliott color Climbing no350 p22 D 2016/Ja 2017

THANKS, VOLCANOES K. CORRIGAN color Climbing no349 p69 N 2016

TOWERS OF POWER J. EVANS color Climbing no353 p58 My/Je 2017

TRAIN SMART B. BLANCHARD color Climbing no351 p54 F/Mr 2017

Traverse of the Clods L. HAAS color Climbing no353 p36 My/Je 2017

TWO TOWERS B. R. AND and M. SMITH-GOBAT color Climbing no349 p58 N 2016

UNSOLICITED BETA P. Sodano, S. Scarpa et al color Climbing no349 p8 N 2016

YOU SHOULD KNOW color Bicycling v58 no10 p88 N/D 2017

Rock climbing techniques

Cross a Talus Field C. BUHAY color Backpacker p33 Ag 2017

Ride the Wave J. Sjong color Climbing no357 p44 N 2017

Rock climbing training

How to Not Train K. CORRIGAN color Climbing no353 p38 My/Je 2017

Ride the Wave J. Sjong color Climbing no357 p44 N 2017

Rock climbing—Equipment & supplies

Climber's Little Helper J. LUCAS color Climbing no351 p44 F/Mr 2017

Rock climbing—Psychological aspects

UPWARDLY MOBILE E. Williamson Virginia Living v15 no3 p24 Ap 2017

Rock climbing—Safety measures

Inflating Grades and Egos J. LUCAS color Climbing no351 p22 F/Mr 2017

Rock concerts

The Biggest Tours of 2017, From GNR to Bieber S. KNOPPER color Rolling Stone no1278/1279 p14 Ja 12 2017

Green Day's New Fire A. GREENE color Rolling Stone no1284 p13 Ap 6 2017

MISSOURI TO TEXAS BY WAY OF OKLAHOMA M. W. SCHWARTZ Missouri Life v43 no6 p22 O/N 2016

Rock concerts—Reviews

54 GREAT THINGS TO DO THIS MONTH J. FOUMBERG, J. HARDBERGER et al color Chicago v66 no1 p117 Ja 2017

U2 Reinvent 'The Joshua Tree' [Cover story] A. GREENE bw color Rolling Stone no1289 p16 Je 15 2017

Rock Dog (Film)

NEWLY AVAILABLE MOVIES J. HOGAN TV Guide v65 no43 p40 O 16 2017

Rock groups

FAMILY TRADITION: Roanoke's Rutledge is a little bit country, a little bit rock 'n' roll D. HARRISON Virginia Living v15 no4 p31 Je 2017

THE LAST HAIR METAL BAND E. Hedegaard color Rolling Stone no1288 p44 Je 1 2017

The Last Moment of the Last Great Rock Band L. Goodman img New York v50 no10 p86 My 15 2017

The ORWELLS D. HYMAN Interview v47 no1 p16 F 2017

THIS IS HOW YOU MAKE A MISIC M. Rapkin color Popular Mechanics p74 O 2017

Rock groups—Interviews

FAMILY Style J. Abidor color Seventeen v76 no4 p68 Jl/Ag 2017

Rock in the Red Zone (Film)

Wide range of offerings at region's Jewish film festivals Successful Farming v115 no1 p23 Ja 2017

Rock music

See also

Progressive rock music

Founding Rocker A. CLINE bw National Review v69 no7 p24 Ap 17 2017

Hail! Hail! rock 'n' roll! A. G. ARONOWITZ Saturday Evening Post v289 no4 p40 Jl/Ag 2017

NIGHT LIFE New Yorker v93 no30 p5 O 2 2017

Q: What is the most significant fad of all time? D. Sim, H. George-Warren et al color Atlantic v319 no3 p96 Ap 2017

So...Rock Is Dead? F. Guan img New York v50 no10 p91 My 15

2017

We're With the Band color *Glamour* v115 no2 p128 F 2017

YOUTH CULTURE S. Slon *Saturday Evening Post* v289 no4 p6 Jl/Ag 2017

Rock music festivals

THE MUSIC FEST THAT TIME FORGOT E. HIMMELSBACH-WEINSTEIN color *Los Angeles Magazine* v62 no7 p80 Jl 2017

Rock music—Awards

Rock Hall's Epic Night A. GREENE color *Rolling Stone* no1286 p9 My 4 2017

Rock music—History & criticism

Is It Here to Stay? Rock'n'roll considered T. TEACHOUT *Commentary* v142 no2 p66 S 2016

Rock music—History—20th century

The Whitest Music Ever J. Parker color *Atlantic* v320 no2 p32 S 2017

Rock musicians

Chester Bennington E. Berman color *Time* v190 no6 p17 Ag 7 2017

Chuck Berry 1926-2017 M. GILMORE bw color *Rolling Stone* no1285 p22 Ap 20 2017

LE TEMPS PERDU J. Seabrook cartoon *New Yorker* v92 no44 p21 Ja 9 2017

Madame Butterfly C. Battan color *Vogue* v207 no10 p290 O 2017

Rock musicians—Interviews

DEREK TRUCKS J. R. MARQUEZ *Atlanta* v57 no3 p32 Jl 2017

Marilyn Manson A. GREENE bw *Rolling Stone* no1298 p55 O 19 2017

Rock musicians—Substance use

Chester's Last Days K. GROW and S. Appleford color *Rolling Stone* no1294 p13 Ag 24 2017

Rock musicians—United States

Riding With Chuck M. JACOBSON color *Rolling Stone* no1285 p35 Ap 20 2017

'The Granddaddy of Us All' K. RICHARDS bw *Rolling Stone* no1285 p34 Ap 20 2017

Rock music—Reviews

NIGHT LIFE *New Yorker* v93 no20 p6 Jl 10 2017

Rock music—Social aspects

Is It Here to Stay? Rock'n'roll considered T. TEACHOUT *Commentary* v142 no2 p66 S 2016

Rock music—To 1961

Essential Chuck D. Browne, J. Dolan et al color *Rolling Stone* no1285 p36 Ap 20 2017

Rock music—United States

Is It Here to Stay? *Commentary* v142 no2 p1 S 2016

Rock Hall's Epic Night A. GREENE color *Rolling Stone* no1286 p9 My 4 2017

Rock music—Writing & publishing

Jack Antonoff's Therapy Rock P. DOYLE color *Rolling Stone* no1290 p22 Je 29 2017

Rock-paper-scissors (Game)

WHO KNEW? Win at Rock, Paper, Scissors (And Other Sly Gimmicks) A. SIMMONS *Reader's Digest* v189 no1127 p124 F 2017

Rockberg, Johan

A subcellular map of the human proteome color *Science* v356 no6340 p820 My 26 2017

Rock Creek Park (Washington, D.C.)

Soaking It All In: The woods are lovely, dark and deep—perfect for forest bathers searching for a little peace of mind N. BRULLIARD *National Parks* v91 no3 p12 Summ 2017

Rockefeller, David, 1915-2017

LIVE LIKE A ROCKEFELLER S. SHARF color *Forbes* v200 no4 p28 O 24 2017

Rockefeller, John D. (John Davison), 1839-1937

THE ORIGINAL RICH LIST C. PETERSON-WITHORN bw chart color *Forbes* v200 no3 p34 S 28 2017

Rockefeller Center

A PIECE OF THE ROCK A. GARA color *Forbes* v200 no1 p28 Jl 27 2017

Rocket Internet AG

Europe's Startup Factory Sputters J. Kahn, S. Nicola et al color *Bloomberg Businessweek* no4495 p31 O 17 2016

Rocket mass heaters

How to Make a... ROCKET STOVE color *Popular Mechanics*

p74 S 2017

Rocketry

See also

Rockets (Aeronautics)

Space vehicles

Sky's the Limit Festus Z. Glasgow color *Missouri Life* v44 no5 p14 Ag 2017

Rockets (Aeronautics)

See also

Ballistic missiles

Reusable rockets' red glare E. DeMarco color *Science News* v190 no13 p44 D 24 2016

The Young Rocketeers J. PAPPALARDO color *Popular Mechanics* p26 N 2017

Rockets (Aeronautics)—Accidents

2014: Los Angeles *Lapham's Quarterly* v10 no2 p23 Spr 2017

Rockets (Aeronautics)—Design & construction

A New Leader in the Suborbital Space Race M. Belfiore color *Bloomberg Businessweek* no4497 p35 O 31 2016

Rockets (Ordnance)—Design & construction

July 1, 1958: Rocket Men A. BROWN bw color *Forbes* v199 no1 p30 Ja 24 2017

Rockett, Kirk A.

Resistance to malaria through structural variation of red blood cell invasion receptors diag *Science* v356 no6343 p1139 Je 16 2017

Rockfall

Yosemite Rockfall U. CHROBAK color *Climbing* no357 p24 N 2017

Rocking chairs

Chesterton's Throne M. W. Jones bw *Commonweal* v144 no13 p39 Ag 11 2017

DR. KNOW *Cincinnati Magazine* v50 no11 p28 Ag 2017

Fun For the Kids *Treasures* v6 no3 p6 D 2016/Ja 2017

My Live-Work Loft B. COOPER color *Indianapolis Monthly* p33 Ap 2017

Rockis, John

FROM OUR READERS *Sky & Telescope* v133 no4 p6 Ap 2017

Rockliff, Mara

Anything But Ordinary Addie: The True Story of Adelaide Herrmann, Queen of Magic *Publishers Weekly* v263 no49 p44 D 7 2016

Rocklin, Gabriel J.

Global analysis of protein folding using massively parallel design, synthesis, and testing color diag *Science* v357 no6347 p168 Jl 14 2017

Rock music, 1961-1970

THE 50 GREATEST CONCERTS OF THE LAST 50 YEARS J. DOLAN, D. BROWNE et al bw color *Rolling Stone* no1286 p30 My 4 2017

Rock music—1971-1980

THE 50 GREATEST CONCERTS OF THE LAST 50 YEARS J. DOLAN, D. BROWNE et al bw color *Rolling Stone* no1286 p30 My 4 2017

Rock music—2011-2020

Neil Young: Restless as Ever B. HIATT color *Rolling Stone* no1278/1279 p19 Ja 12 2017

Rock music—2011-2020—Reviews

THE SHINS M. Vain color *Entertainment Weekly* no1446/1447 p75 D 2016/Ja 2017

SPOON K. O'Donnell *Entertainment Weekly* no1446/1447 p75 D 2016/Ja 2017

Rocks

See also

Crystals

The formation of peak rings in large impact craters J. V. Morgan, S. P. S. Gulick et al bibl color graph *Science* v354 no6314 p878 N 18 2016

NEWFOUND ROCKS MAY BE PROGENY OF PRIMORDIAL CRUST *Physics Today* v70 no5 p22 My 2017

Revealing the dynamics of a large impact P. Barton bibl color *Science* v354 no6314 p836 N 18 2016

Rock of Ages color *Log Home Living* v34 no6 p16 Ag 2017

Rocks, David

A Continental Retreat color map *Bloomberg Businessweek* no4514 p23 Mr 13 2017

Engineering the Sound Of Silence at Porsche color graph *Bloom-*

berg *Businessweek* no4499 p44 N 14 2016

Gaining From the EU But Hating It Anyway bw *Bloomberg Businessweek* no4537 p38 S 11 2017

How to Lose $6 Billion color graph *Bloomberg Businessweek* no4512 p19 F 20 2017

If You Build It, Will Peace Come? color *Bloomberg Businessweek* no4519 p19 Ap 24 2017

The Lawsuits Keep Coming for J&J bw *Bloomberg Businessweek* no4514 p21 Mr 13 2017

Music Festivals Have A Volume Problem color diag *Bloomberg Businessweek* no4512 p21 F 20 2017

Telemundo's Ratings Are Made in the USA *Bloomberg Businessweek* no4514 p22 Mr 13 2017

VW's Latest Woe: A Reliance on Mexico *Bloomberg Businessweek* no4512 p20 F 20 2017

RockShox Inc.

ROCKSHOX REVERB 1X REMOTE M. Yozell color *Bicycling* v58 no8 p66 S 2017

Rockström, Johan

A roadmap for rapid decarbonization bibl color graph *Science* v355 no6331 p1269 Mr 24 2017

ROCKWELL, JOHN

Berlin Stories *New York Times Book Review* p49 Je 4 2017

Rockwell, Norman, 1894-1978

Crowd-Sourced J. Nilsson *Saturday Evening Post* v288 no6 p114 N/D 2016

Sweet Memories J. Nilsson *Saturday Evening Post* v289 no5 p99 S/O 2017

WAR STORIES B. Hogan *MHQ: Quarterly Journal of Military History* v29 no2 p25 Wint 2017

Willie Gillis Comes Home J. Nilsson *Saturday Evening Post* v289 no3 p102 My/Je 2017

Rockwell Automation Inc.

White Men Can Change At Rockwell Automation C. Hymowitz cartoon *Bloomberg Businessweek* no4520 p24 My 1 2017

Rockwell Collins Inc.

Rockwell Collins Inc E. Hammond, R. Clough et al *Bloomberg Businessweek* no4537 p29 S 11 2017

Rockwood, Kate

2017 BACK-TO-SCHOOL GUIDE color *Good Housekeeping* v265 no3 p139 S 2017

Acupuncture for Colicky Babies?! Yes, It's a Thing! color *Parents* v92 no7 p26 Jl 2017

Are You Smarter Than a HEART ATTACK? cartoon *O, The Oprah Magazine* p90 F 2017

awesome ideas for your little one's summer color *Parents* v92 no8 p68 Ag 2017

Be Rude at Your Own Risk color *Parents* v92 no6 p28 Je 2017

"HOW I LOST 90 LBS AFTER 2 SETS OF TWINS!" color *Good Housekeeping* v265 no5 p77 N 2017

Live large for less color *Redbook* p109 S 2017

MAKE YOUR HOME HEALTHIER color *Health* v31 no4 p59 My 2017

the night shift *Parents* v92 no1 p20 Ja 2017

THE PATH TO GOOD POSTURE bw cartoon *Martha Stewart Living* no275 p52 Je 2017

Prevent Medication Mix-Ups *Parents* v91 no12 p30 D 2016

A TRUE SOAP STAR color *Good Housekeeping* v265 no2 p134 Ag 2017

tummy troubles *Parents* v92 no2 p98 F 2017

What's Your Headache IQ? color *O, The Oprah Magazine* p102 N 2017

Your Ultimate Guide to OTC Medicine color diag *Health* v31 no6 p79 Jl 2017

YOU'VE GOT TO TRY Turmeric color diag *O, The Oprah Magazine* p98 Mr 2017

Rocky (Film)

1977: A LOOK BACK L. Bonner bw color *Equus* no482 p39 N 2017

Rocky, A$ap

Icons color *Time* v189 no16/17 p122 My 1-8 2017

Rocky Horror Picture Show: Let's Do the Time Warp Again (TV program)

Laverne Cox's Horror Story T. Stack color *Entertainment Weekly* no1435 p48 O 14 2016

THE WILD BUNC D. HOLBROOK color *TV Guide* v64 no42

p24 O 10 2016

Rocky Mountain Bicycles (Company)

Rocky Mountain R. Palmer color *Bike Magazine* v24 no7 p100 S 2017

Rocky Mountain National Park (Colo.)—Travel

Lonely at the Top C. LYONS color *Backpacker* p16 O 2017

Rocky Mountain News (Newspaper)

America's growing news deserts Y. Bucay, V. Elliott et al map *Columbia Journalism Review* v56 no1 p34 Spr 2017

Rocky Mountains—Description & travel

Alberta's Hidden Gem color *Horse & Rider* v56 no8 p28 Ag 2017

Rocky Horror Picture Show, The (Theatrical production)

NORTHLAKE MALL 1993 T. WHEATLEY *Atlanta* v57 no6 p144 O 2017

Roczen, Ken

ROCZEN ROLL B. Smith color *Cycle World* v55 no10 p60 N 2016

Rodan + Fields (Company)

Beauty Boss M. Santos color *Working Mother* v40 no2 p16 Je/Jl 2017

Rodarte (Company)

COAST to Coach E. ELWICK-BATES color *Vogue* v207 no4 p134 Ap 2017

my style color *InStyle* v24 no2 p88 F 2017

Roday, James, 1976-

PSYCH: THE MOVIE C. Agard color *Entertainment Weekly* no1474/1475 p74 Jl 21-28 2017

Rodden, John

Donald and Winston at the Ministry of Alternative Facts *Society* v54 no3 p215 Je 2017

Erratum to: Donald and Winston at the Ministry of Alternative Facts *Society* v54 no3 p312 Je 2017

The Intellectual Species: Evolution or Extinction? *Society* v54 no4 p352 Ag 2017

Rodden, John—Interviews

The Strange Happy Life of a Scholar Gipsy H. Vynkier *Society* v53 no6 p581 D 2016

Roddick, Andy, 1982-

I'll be in the Room S. TIGNOR color *Tennis* v53 no5 p64 S/O 2017

The Torch Bearer C. SHMERLER *Tennis* v52 no6 p56 N/D 2016

Rodell, Besha

AVOCADO TOAST J. Birdsall color *Bon Appetit* no8 p92 Ag 2017

Rodell, Susanna

From Pony Club Mom to Horsemaster color *Practical Horseman* v44 no12 p72 D 2016

Rodemann, Katharyn

KNIVES OUT *Texas Monthly* v44 no12 p90 D 2016

Roden, Raymond P.

How do I respond when ICE comes for my flock? color *America* v216 no10 p38 My 1 2017

Roden Crater (Ariz.)

INCIDENTS E. Kolbert bw cartoon *New Yorker* v93 no17 p23 Je 19 2017

Rodenbeck, Eric

Eric Rodenbeck A. Popescu color *Bloomberg Businessweek* no4539 p76 S 25 2017

Rodent genomes

Protein paints chipmunks' stripes T. HESMAN SAEY color *Science News* v190 no11 p8 N 26 2016

Rodent physiology

Northern pocket gopher color *Canadian Wildlife* v23 no4 p9 S/O 2017

Rodents

See also

Beavers

In the Presence of Greatness E. KANZE color *Natural History* v125 no5 p48 My 2017

Rats? In My House? Say It Ain't So A. RICHARDS *Los Angeles Magazine* p70 F 2017

Rodeo announcers

Hadley Barrett: Sept. 18, 1929-March 2, 2017 color *Spin to Win Rodeo* v21 no3 p18 My 2017

Rodeo equipment

new products color *Team Roping Journal* p38 O 2017

Rodeo performers

    See also
      Bull riders
      Women rodeo performers

2016 PRORODEO WORLD CHAMPS B. Welch color *Spin to Win Rodeo* v20 no11 p54 Ja 2017

ALL HEART color *Spin to Win Rodeo* v20 no9 p14 N 2016

BILL HUBER WINS '02 NATIONAL TITLE WITH ARENA RECORD J. Mankin color *Spin to Win Rodeo* v21 no3 p88 My 2017

Bits for Head Horses: Tips from Professional Headers color *Team Roping Journal* p72 O 2017

CANADIAN PRCA WORLD CHAMPIONS bw *Spin to Win Rodeo* v20 no12 p96 F 2017

COUNTING THE BIG BUCKS: Yes or No? C. O. Cooper and K. Santos color *Team Roping Journal* p50 O 2017

Crawford Dominates WPRA Finals color *Spin to Win Rodeo* v20 no11 p16 Ja 2017

DEAR ROPER B. Welch color *Spin to Win Rodeo* v20 no11 p8 Ja 2017

FIVE FLAT [Cover story] C. Toy color *Spin to Win Rodeo* v21 no4 p31 Je 2017

FIVE FLAT with Dakota Kirchenschlager C. Toy color *Spin to Win Rodeo* v20 no12 p33 F 2017

FREEZE FRAME C. Toy color *Spin to Win Rodeo* v20 no10 p52 D 2016

FREEZE FRAME WITH LEVI SIMPSON C. Toy color *Spin to Win Rodeo* v20 no12 p44 F 2017

Hitting the Road J. Bailey and C. Shaffer color *Team Roping Journal* p75 O 2017

LIVIN' IT UP IN THE CITY A. WILSON color *Spin to Win Rodeo* v20 no10 p86 D 2016

NFR NUMBERS color *Horse & Rider* v56 no11 p85 N 2017

PACING PRACTICE: FAST OR SLOW? K. Santos color *Spin to Win Rodeo* v20 no12 p46 F 2017

PDT IS PDQ IN ABQ color *Spin to Win Rodeo* v20 no9 p16 N 2016

Raising a Phenom J. Mankin color *Spin to Win Rodeo* v20 no10 p34 D 2016

Resistol Hosts Second Annual Rookie of the Year Luncheon color *Spin to Win Rodeo* v20 no12 p20 F 2017

RYAN JARRETT IS TOP '05 ALL-AROUND COWBOY J. Mankin color *Spin to Win Rodeo* v20 no10 p120 D 2016

SOUTH BY SOUTHEAST color *Spin to Win Rodeo* v20 no9 p13 N 2016

Tierney Trifecta at the Timed Event K. Santos color *Spin to Win Rodeo* v21 no3 p64 My 2017

TOP MOUNTS color *Spin to Win Rodeo* v20 no10 p26 D 2016

TRIPPED UP color *Spin to Win Rodeo* v20 no11 p11 Ja 2017

Why do I rope? G. Miller color *Team Roping Journal* p152 O 2017

The World of TEAM ROPING G. R. Schiavino chart color map *Team Roping Journal* p96 O 2017

Rodeo performers—Awards

PRCA Resistol Rookies of the Year color *Spin to Win Rodeo* v20 no10 p29 D 2016

Rodeo performers—Interviews

Lovell Kisses Full-Time Rodeo Trail Goodbye K. Santos color *Spin to Win Rodeo* v20 no12 p24 F 2017

Rodeo performers—United States

HARRY VOLD color *Horse & Rider* v56 no11 p86 N 2017

STAGE SHOW SLATE color *Horse & Rider* v56 no11 p75 N 2017

WRANGLER NFR AFTER PARTIES color *Horse & Rider* v56 no11 p84 N 2017

Rodeo performers—Wounds & injuries

Richard Recovering from Thumb-Reattachment color *Spin to Win Rodeo* v21 no2 p20 Ap 2017

RODEO'S NFL MOMENT C. GILLIS color *Maclean's* v130 no2 p52 Mr 2017

Rodeo stock contractors

Harry Vold: Jan. 29, 1924-March 13, 2017 color *Spin to Win Rodeo* v21 no3 p20 My 2017

Rodeo techniques

FREEZE FRAME C. Toy color *Spin to Win Rodeo* v21 no2 p44 Ap 2017

Freeze Frame Junior Nogueira color *Team Roping Journal* p70

O 2017

FREEZE FRAME WITH PAUL EAVES C. Toy color *Spin to Win Rodeo* v21 no1 p44 Mr 2017

GETTING INTO THE SWING OF THINGS K. Santos color *Spin to Win Rodeo* v21 no1 p46 Mr 2017

GETTING STARTED ON THE RIGHT (ROPING) FOOT J. BARNES color *Spin to Win Rodeo* v21 no2 p38 Ap 2017

Knowing How to Win K. Driggers color *Team Roping Journal* p74 O 2017

Swing Consistency T. Graves and C. Shaffer color *Team Roping Journal* p58 O 2017

WHAT MAKES A HEEL LOOP WORK? K. Santos color *Spin to Win Rodeo* v20 no9 p42 N 2016

Rodeo training & conditioning

DON'T FORGET TO BARRIER BREAK YOUR HORSE [Cover story] K. Santos color *Spin to Win Rodeo* v21 no4 p36 Je 2017

Rodeo Drive (Beverly Hills, Calif.)

Left Hooked *Los Angeles Magazine* p20 F 2017

Rodeos

    See also
      Calf roping
      Steer roping
      Team roping
      Women in rodeos

2016 PRORODEO WORLD CHAMPS B. Welch color *Spin to Win Rodeo* v20 no11 p54 Ja 2017

2016 WRANGLER NATIONAL FINALS RODEO PREVIEW B. Welch color *Spin to Win Rodeo* v20 no10 p78 D 2016

$50K A MAN CHANGES EVERYTHING color *Team Roping Journal* p24 S 2017

AMERICAN DREAM color *Spin to Win Rodeo* v20 no10 p20 D 2016

Bigger Picture B. Welch color *American Cowboy* v23 no4 p8 D 2016/Ja 2017

Bird and Cardoza Keep Rolling in Grand Island color *Spin to Win Rodeo* v21 no3 p20 My 2017

BUCKLE UP C. Toy color *Spin to Win Rodeo* v21 no3 p17 My 2017

BUCKLE UP with Dustin Egusquiza C. Toy color *Spin to Win Rodeo* v21 no6 p19 Ag 2017

BUCKLE UP with Jeremy Buhler C. Toy color *Spin to Win Rodeo* v20 no10 p25 D 2016

BUCKLE UP with Tom Richards C. Toy color *Spin to Win Rodeo* v21 no1 p21 Mr 2017

Class of 2016 color *Spin to Win Rodeo* v20 no10 p70 D 2016

FIVE FLAT with Jake Long B. Welch color *Spin to Win Rodeo* v20 no10 p41 D 2016

FIVE FLAT with Paul David Tierney C. Toy color *Spin to Win Rodeo* v21 no1 p33 Mr 2017

FREEZE FRAME WITH JUSTIN DAVIS C. Toy color *Spin to Win Rodeo* v21 no4 p42 Je 2017

GOING LEFT color *Spin to Win Rodeo* v21 no3 p14 My 2017

The Greatest L. FELDMAN bw color *American Cowboy* v24 no1 p67 Je/Jl 2017

HAPPY BIRTHDAY [Cover story] K. Santos color *Spin to Win Rodeo* v21 no1 p54 Mr 2017

HOMETOWN ADVANTAGE color *Spin to Win Rodeo* v21 no3 p11 My 2017

JUNIOR NATIONAL FINALS RODEO color *Horse & Rider* v56 no11 p72 N 2017

KING OF QUEENS color *Spin to Win Rodeo* v21 no4 p11 Je 2017

LESSONS LEARNED C. TOY bw color *Spin to Win Rodeo* v21 no1 p66 Mr 2017

Mastering the Entering Game C. Toy color *Spin to Win Rodeo* v21 no3 p22 My 2017

Merrill and Salgado Take #12 Heartland color *Team Roping Journal* p34 S 2017

MONTANA MAYHEM color *Spin to Win Rodeo* v21 no1 p18 Mr 2017

Nastri Sets Records at First Frontier Circuit Finals color *Spin to Win Rodeo* v21 no1 p22 Mr 2017

NEW LIVING ARRANGEMENTS B. Welch color *Spin to Win Rodeo* v20 no11 p88 Ja 2017

NFR by the Numbers bw color *American Cowboy* v23 no4 p88 D 2016/Ja 2017

NO BIGGIE color *Spin to Win Rodeo* v21 no4 p12 Je 2017

THE DEVIL'S ADVOCATE bw color *Esquire* p58 Ag 2017

Inside Tom Petty's Last Big Tour color *Rolling Stone* no1291/1292 p22 Jl 13 2017

The North Star [Cover story] bw color *Rolling Stone* no1293 p36 Ag 10 2017

THE RADICAL CRUSADE OF MIKE PENCE cartoon color *Rolling Stone* no1280 p44 F 9 2017

ROCK IN A HARD PLACE [Cover story] bw color *Rolling Stone* no1287 p28 My 18 2017

Sting's Rock & Roll Salvation bw color *Rolling Stone* no1276 p48 D 15 2016

TUCKER CARLSON IS SORRY FOR BEING MEAN color graph *GQ: Gentlemen's Quarterly* v97 no10 p84 O 2017

RODRIGO, ALLEN

Synthesis Centers as Critical Research Infrastructure *BioScience* v67 no8 p750 Ag 2017

Rodrigo, R.

Rosetta's comet 67P/Churyumov-Gerasimenko sheds its dusty mantle to reveal its icy nature bibl graph *Science* v354 no6319 p1566 D 23 2016

Surface changes on comet 67P/Churyumov-Gerasimenko suggest a more active past bw graph *Science* v355 no6332 p1392 Mr 31 2017

Rodrigo-Brenni, Monica C.

Mechanistic basis for a molecular triage reaction color graph *Science* v355 no6322 p298 Ja 20 2017

RODRIGUE, JENNIFER

heart wide open color *Yoga Journal* p40 2017 Special Issue

nourish yourself color *Yoga Journal* p102 2017 Special Issue

opening ceremony color *Yoga Journal* p32 2017 Special Issue

Rodrigues, Alan R.

Emergent cellular self-organization and mechanosensation initiate follicle pattern in the avian skin color *Science* v357 no6353 p811 Ag 25 2017

RODRIGUES, CAROLINE

PLAN TO PERFECTION color *House Beautiful* p92 Ag 2017

ULTIMATE GUIDE TO REVAMP BUYS color *House Beautiful* p102 Ag 2017

WASH AND GO color *House Beautiful* p133 Ag 2017

Rodrigues, Jeanette

The ABCs of India's GST color graph *Bloomberg Businessweek* no4496 p19 O 24 2016

Rodrigues, João Pedro

Get Lost color *Film Comment* v53 no2 p6 Mr/Ap 2017

The Ornithologist A. CHAN color *Film Comment* v53 no3 p66 My/Je 2017

Rodriguez, A.

Inhibitors of PEX14 disrupt protein import into glycosomes and kill Trypanosoma parasites chart color diag graph *Science* v355 no6332 p1416 Mr 31 2017

Rodriguez, Alex, 1975-

Ask the Host T. Keith color *Sports Illustrated* v126 no4 p19 Ja 30 2017

Rodriguez, Alex, 1975—Interviews

A-RODS'S NEXT BIG SWING P. Sellers color *Fortune* v176 no2 p74 Ag 1 2017

Rodriguez, Alex, 1975—Substance use

Made for TV B. Reiter color *Sports Illustrated* v125 no15 p35 N 7 2016

WHAT IF? ... THE PLAYERS' UNION HADN'T REJECTED A-ROD'S 2003 TRADE TO THE RED SOX? C. P. Pierce and J. Feldman color *Sports Illustrated* v126 no11 p55 Ap 17-24 2017

Rodriguez, Ashley

THE LIST B. APPÉTIT color *Bon Appetit* v61 no12 p172 D 2016 /Jan2017

Rodriguez, Dana

SHOW TIME I. Edwards color *Sunset* v238 no6 p6 Je 2017

RODRIGUEZ, GEORGE

What do you collect and why? color *American Craft* v77 no2 p20 Ap/My 2017

Rodríguez, Gerardo

Build the Wall! Por Favor K. RAPOZA and M. CHAIKIN color *Forbes* v199 no6 p66 Je 13 2017

Rodriguez, Gina, 1984-

"Jane the Virgin" offers a refreshing look at Christian sexuality C. Addington color *America* v216 no6 p38 Mr 20 2017

Jane the Virgin S. Highfill, N. Abrams et al color *Entertainment Weekly* no1482/1483 p95 S 22 2017

Rodriguez, Guillermo—Interviews

JIMMY KIMMEL LIVE! L. ACKEN color *TV Guide* v64 no42 p47 O 10 2016

RODRIGUEZ, JAVY

The Question *O, The Oprah Magazine* p16 My 2017

Rodriguez, José A.

Active sites for CO2 hydrogenation to methanol on Cu/ZnO catalysts bibl graph *Science* v355 no6331 p1296 Mr 24 2017

Atomic-layered Au clusters on α-MoC as catalysts for the low-temperature water-gas shift reaction chart diag graph *Science* v357 no6349 p389 Jl 28 2017

TECHNICAL COMMENT ABSTRACTS *Science* v357 no6354 p881 S 1 2017

Rodriguez, Karina F.

Elimination of the male reproductive tract in the female embryo is promoted by COUP-TFII in mice color graph *Science* v357 no6352 p717 Ag 18 2017

Rodriguez, Lilia

ALL ABOUT EVE color *Los Angeles Magazine* v62 no10 p156 O 2017

Rodríguez, Lionel A.

Chemogenetics revealed: DREADD occupancy and activation via converted clozapine graph *Science* v357 no6350 p503 Ag 4 2017

Rodriguez, Maria I.

Protecting unauthorized immigrant mothers improves their children's mental health diag *Science* v357 no6355 p1041 S 8 2017

Rodriguez, Melissa

Is It Better to Burn Carbs or Burn Fat? color *Black Belt* v55 no1 p18 D 2016/Ja 2017

Rodriguez, Raphaël

Click chemistry enables preclinical evaluation of targeted epigenetic therapies diag *Science* v356 no6345 p1397 Je 30 2017

Rodríguez Castillo, Guillermo A.

An accreting pulsar with extreme properties drives an ultraluminous x-ray source in NGC 5907 bibl chart graph *Science* v355 no6327 p817 F 24 2017

Rodriguez-Diaz, Teo—Interviews

Q&A *Los Angeles Magazine* p92 Ja 2017

Rodriguez Esteban, Concepcion

Integration of CpG-free DNA induces de novo methylation of CpG islands in pluripotent stem cells diag *Science* v356 no6337 p503 My 5 2017

Rodriguez Fernandez, G.

Observation of a large-scale anisotropy in the arrival directions of cosmic rays above 8 × 1018 eV *Science* v357 no6357 p1266 S 22 2017

Rodriguez-Gaztelumendi, A.

A nontoxic pain killer designed by modeling of pathological receptor conformations bibl diag graph *Science* v355 no6328 p966 Mr 3 2017

Rodriguez Mega, Emiliano

Turmoil imperils research university in Andes color *Science* v357 no6349 p340 Jl 28 2017

Rodriguez-Mias, Ricard A.

Evolution of protein phosphorylation across 18 fungal species bibl graph *Science* v354 no6309 p229 O 14 2016

Rodriguez-Nieva, Joaquin F.

An on/off Berry phase switch in circular graphene resonators diag graph *Science* v356 no6340 p845 My 26 2017

Rodriguez Plate, S. Brent

Currents of Race and Religion Flowing Along the Waters Of the Erie Canal color graph *America* v217 no6 p46 S 18 2017

Rodriguez-Rincon, Daniela

Emergence and spread of a human-transmissible multidrug-resistant nontuberculous mycobacterium bibl diag graph *Science* v354 no6313 p751 N 11 2016

Rodriguez Rojo, J.

Observation of a large-scale anisotropy in the arrival directions of cosmic rays above 8 × 1018 eV *Science* v357 no6357 p1266 S 22 2017

Rodríguez-Sánchez, Francisco

Academia's failure to retain data scientists bibl *Science* v355 no6323 p357 Ja 27 2017

Rodríguez Vilá, Omar
COMPETING ON SOCIAL PURPOSE: BRANDS THAT WIN BY TYING MISSION TO GROWTH chart diag il img *Harvard Business Review* v95 no5 p94 S/O 2017

Roe, Dan
SLEEP WITH ANY WOMAN cartoon color *Men's Health* v32 no1 p94 Ja/F 2017

Roe v. Wade (Supreme Court case)
LIFE BEFORE ROE R. B. GOLD and M. K. DONOVAN color *Scientific American* v317 no3 p58 S 2017

Roebling, John A.
VIEW FROM THE BRIDGE J. STOWELL *Cincinnati Magazine* v50 no2 p70 N 2016

Roedel, Jeffrey
BEYOND THE SURFACE color *Louisiana Life* v38 no1 p18 S/O 2017
FOG MACHINE bw color *Louisiana Life* v37 no5 p16 My/Je 2017
HANDS ON THE WHEEL color *Louisiana Life* v37 no3 p14 Ja/F 2017
IN STITCHES color *Louisiana Life* v37 no2 p16 N/D 2016
SAVOIR 'FAIR' color *Louisiana Life* v37 no6 p14 Jl/Ag 2017
WILDTHINGS bw color *Louisiana Life* v37 no4 p16 Mr/Ap 2017

Roederer, Mario
Rapid development of a DNA vaccine for Zika virus bibl graph *Science* v354 no6309 p237 O 14 2016
Trispecific broadly neutralizing HIV antibodies mediate potent SHIV protection in macaques color graph *Science* v357 no6359 p85 O 6 2017

Roehrig, Caleb
Last Seen Leaving color *Publishers Weekly* v263 no49 p115 D 7 2016

Roein-Peikar, Mehdi
Notch-Jagged complex structure implicates a catch bond in tuning ligand sensitivity bibl diag graph *Science* v355 no6331 p1320 Mr 24 2017

Roelofsen, Erik
CASE STUDY: IS HOLACRACY FOR US? color il *Harvard Business Review* v95 no2 p151 Mr/Ap 2017
Case Study: Is Holacracy for Us? *Harvard Business Review Digital Articles* p2 D 8 2016

Roemer, Lizabeth
Food Coloring S. KLEIN bw color *Prevention* v68 no12 p96 D 2016

Roemers, Martin
METROPOLIS color *National Geographic* v231 no3 p120 Mr 2017

Roese, Neal J.
Being Too Busy for Friends Won't Help Your Career *Harvard Business Review Digital Articles* p1 Jl 28 2017

ROEST, KARIN
MEDITATION AND MARGARITAS *USA Today Magazine* v146 no2868 p64 S 2017

Roethlisberger, Ben, 1982-
What We Think About When We Think About Big Ben [Cover story] S. l. Price color *Sports Illustrated* v126 no1 p20 Ja 9 2017

Roffman, Karin
His True Vocation: The biography of a shy boy who overcame a hostile culture to become one of the great poets of his age A. EPSTEIN bw *New York Times Book Review* p12 Ag 6 2017
IT WANTS TO GO TO BED WITH US: John Ashbery's well-spent youth M. Bevis color *Harper's Magazine* v335 no2005 p88 Je 2017
Tuning In & Out [Cover story] F. B. Farrell color *Commonweal* v144 no17 p24 O 20 2017

Roffman, Marisa
24: Legacy *TV Guide* v65 no11 p41 Mr 6 2017
24: LEGACY *TV Guide* v65 no14 p26 Ap 3 2017
24: Legacy *TV Guide* v65 no2 p38 Ja 2 2017
3 THINGS TO KNOW ABOUT GHOSTED *TV Guide* v65 no37 p42 S 4 2017
The 59th Annual Grammy Awards *TV Guide* v65 no6 p40 Ja 30 2017
9JKL *TV Guide* v65 no37 p26 S 4 2017
Autopsy: The Last Hours of Prince *TV Guide* v65 no21 p33 My 15 2017

Beat Shazam *TV Guide* v65 no21 p38 My 15 2017
BONES BIDS ADIEU *TV Guide* v65 no13 p16 Mr 20 2017
Bones' Big Send-Off *TV Guide* v65 no8 p10 F 27 2017
BONES *TV Guide* v64 no15 p54 Ap 4 2016
Bones *TV Guide* v65 no2 p26 Ja 2 2017
Booth Searches for Brennan on Bones *TV Guide* p12 D 19 2016
Brothers in ARMS *TV Guide* p30 Ap 17 2017
Candy Crush *TV Guide* v65 no23 p26 My 29 2017
Chris Pratt on Mom! *TV Guide* v65 no4 p10 Ja 16 2017
The Dance of Being a Judge *TV Guide* v65 no25 p12 Je 2017
DAVID BOREANAZ *TV Guide* v65 no37 p32 S 4 2017
THE DUFFER BROTHERS *TV Guide* p16 D 19 2016
Goliath *TV Guide* v64 no40 p38 O 3 2016
Hamilton Comes to TV! *TV Guide* v64 no40 p15 O 3 2016
HOLLYWOOD DISPATCH *TV Guide* v65 no35 p5 Ag 21 2017
Inside Scorpion's Nest *TV Guide* v64 no40 p48 O 3 2016
Is Your Favorite Show Safe? *TV Guide* v65 no21 p6 My 15 2017
iZombie *TV Guide* v65 no14 p33 Ap 3 2017
Kennedy Center Honors *TV Guide* p39 D 19 2016
KEVIN (PROBABLY) SAVES THE WORLD *TV Guide* v65 no37 p30 S 4 2017
THE LATE LATE SHOW WITH JAMES CORDEN *TV Guide* p45 Ap 17 2017
Legion *TV Guide* v65 no6 p38 Ja 30 2017
Lou Diamond Phillips: Worst Dad Ever? *TV Guide* v65 no43 p7 O 16 2017
The Lowe Files *TV Guide* v65 no31 p36 Jl 24 2017
MARVEL'S AGENTS OF S.H.I.E.L.D *TV Guide* v64 no15 p46 Ap 4 2016
Marvel's The Defenders *TV Guide* v65 no25 p23 Je 2017
Meet the crew... *TV Guide* v65 no11 p13 Mr 6 2017
My 20 Years on Television *TV Guide* v65 no41 p12 O 2 2017
Prison Break *TV Guide* v65 no14 p35 Ap 3 2017
PUT ON YOUR GAME FACE! *TV Guide* v65 no31 p8 Jl 24 2017
THE REAL O'NEALS *TV Guide* p30 D 5 2016
Rob Thomas Belts It Out on iZombie *TV Guide* v64 no15 p15 Ap 4 2016
Scorpion color *TV Guide* v64 no42 p39 O 10 2016
Scorpion's Deep Freeze *TV Guide* v65 no2 p13 Ja 2 2017
Scorpion *TV Guide* v65 no19 p24 My 1 2017
SCORPION *TV Guide* v65 no35 p20 Ag 21 2017
Shots Fired *TV Guide* v65 no13 p27 Mr 20 2017
Sleepy Hollow's New Team *TV Guide* v64 no48 p10 N 21 2016
Superstore *TV Guide* v64 no40 p59 O 3 2016
Superstore *TV Guide* v65 no19 p39 My 1 2017
THINGS THAT GO BUMP IN THE NIGHT: They ain't afraid of no ghosts! Netflix's monster hit Stranger Things returns *TV Guide* v65 no43 p22 O 16 2017
Tick... Tick... BOOM! [Cover story] *TV Guide* v65 no6 p20 Ja 30 2017
Toby and Happy's Scorpion Wedding! *TV Guide* p9 Ap 17 2017
T.R. Knight Is J. Edgar Hoover *TV Guide* v65 no14 p8 Ap 3 2017
The Voice Soars *TV Guide* v65 no19 p20 My 1 2017
Why I Push the Social Envelope: Actor-writer Jerrod Carmichael takes on tough subjects--like gun control, euthanasia and using the N-word--all while getting major laughs *TV Guide* v65 no27 p10 Je 26 2017

ROGACHEVSKY, NEIL
After Netanyahu color *Weekly Standard* v23 no6 p32 O 16 2017

Rogatchevskaia, Katya
RUSSIA'S GRASSROOTS REVOLUTION: Underneath the sweeping history of the Russian Revolution is another story, one told through the lesser-known people, moments and objects of a world in transformation *History Today* v67 no6 p42 Je 2016

Rogelj, Joeri
A roadmap for rapid decarbonization bibl color graph *Science* v355 no6331 p1269 Mr 24 2017

Roger & Me (Film)
THE THANKLESS TASK OF BEING MICHAEL MOORE J. PRESSLER img *New York* v50 no18 p40 S 4 2017

Roger, Derek
Pressure Doesn't Have to Turn into Stress N. Petrie *Harvard Business Review Digital Articles* p2 Mr 16 2017

Roger Vivier (Company)
Don't get your feet wet! color *InStyle* v24 no9 p392 S 2017

Rogers (Ark.)

Beacon of Health J. MINUTILLO *Architectural Record* v205 no7 p94 Jl 2017

Rogers, Adam
For the Love of Jimi B. Milkowski color *Downbeat* v84 no9 p24 S 2017
Global Ambition *Smithsonian* v48 no3 p11 Je 2017
How GPS Learns to Speak Your Language *Smithsonian* v48 no4 p20 Jl/Ag 2017
LUC BESSON'S OUTER LIMITS cartoon color *Wired* v25 no7 p64 Jl 2017

Rogers, Al
The Last Wing Car bw color *Hot Rod* v70 no6 p40 Je 2017

Rogers, Caroline
A Highlands Garden Paradise color *Southern Living* v52 no6 p92 Je 2017
rooms IN BLOOM color *Southern Living* v52 no3 p88 Mr 2017
A WALK IN THE GARDEN color *Southern Living* v52 no7 p78 Jl 2017

Rogers, Claudia
CHRISTOPHER WHO? *History Today* v67 no8 p38 Ag 2017

Rogers, Dale
The Rise of FinTech in Supply Chains *Harvard Business Review Digital Articles* p2 Je 22 2016

ROGERS, DAVID A.
Combining Biodiversity Resurveys across Regions to Advance Global Change Research *BioScience* v67 no1 p73 Ja 2017

ROGERS, DUKE S.
Transformational Principles for NEON Sampling of Mammalian Parasites and Pathogens: A Response to Springer and Colleagues *BioScience* v66 no11 p917 N 1 2016

Rogers, Erich
BACK-TO-BACK color *Spin to Win Rodeo* v20 no10 p17 D 2016
FIVE FLAT C. Toy color *Spin to Win Rodeo* v21 no5 p25 Jl 2017
FREEZE FRAME B. Welch color *Spin to Win Rodeo* v20 no9 p40 N 2016
HOMETOWN ADVANTAGE color *Spin to Win Rodeo* v21 no3 p11 My 2017
OUT OF TOWNERS color *Spin to Win Rodeo* v21 no2 p14 Ap 2017
Short Memories with Erich Rogers color *Team Roping Journal* p78 S 2017
Webb and VonAhn Tie Rogers and Petska for Cheyenne Frontier Days Title color *Team Roping Journal* p38 S 2017
WYO CHAMPS color *Team Roping Journal* p18 S 2017

Rogers, Garrett
BUCKLE UP *Spin to Win Rodeo* v21 no2 p19 Ap 2017

Rogers, Garrett—Interviews
Rogers Riding into Vegas with Herd of Finals Freshmen color *Spin to Win Rodeo* v20 no9 p24 N 2016

Rogers, Gerald Adam
Transforming Ethnohistories: Narrative, Meaning, and Community *American Indian Quarterly* v40 no3 p285 Summ 2016

Rogers, J. T.
A False Theatrical Peace J. S. TOBIN *Commentary* v143 no2 p52 F 2017
OSLO CONFIDENTIAL M. BRENNER color *Vanity Fair* v59 no5 p133 Ap 2017

Rogers, Jennifer
Further Notes of a Recycled Housewife img *New York* v50 no11 p12 My 29 2017

ROGERS, JOHN
FIRST cartoon *Wired* v25 no1 p30 Ja 2017

Rogers, John A.
Double-heterojunction nanorod light-responsive LEDs for display applications bibl color graph *Science* v355 no6325 p616 F 10 2017

Rogers, John H.
Jupiter – From Earth to Juno color *Sky & Telescope* v134 no5 p52 N 2017

Rogers, Jordan
A Global Survey Explains Why Your Employees Don't Innovate *Harvard Business Review Digital Articles* p2 F 24 2016

Rogers, Joseph
Ponce de León Dept cartoon *Weekly Standard* v22 no27 p3 Mr 20 2017

Rogers, Kenny, 1938-
EASY CHAIR R. Solnit *Harper's Magazine* v334 no2004 p4 My 2017
Kenny Rogers Is Walkin' Away A. Nash color *AARP: The Magazine* v59 no4A p14 Je/Jl 2016

Rogers, Maggie
ALL IN A. PETRUSICH color *New Yorker* v93 no4 p80 Mr 13 2017
Maggie Rogers' Folk Fairy Tale D. BROWNE color *Rolling Stone* no1285 p15 Ap 20 2017
MAGGIE ROGERS N. Feeney color *Entertainment Weekly* no1454/1455 p95 F 24 2017

Rogers, Mark
Koreatown Blues *Publishers Weekly* v263 no47 p90 N 21 2016

Rogers, Rebecca
PRESIDENT'S PERSPECTIVE *Arabian Horse World* v57 no3 p10 D 2016

ROGERS, SEAN
This Scribbly Stuff cartoon *Walrus* v14 no6 p70 Jl/Ag 2017

Rogers, Shelagh
Q&A C. Fisher Tully color *Walrus* v14 no9 p40 N 2017

Rogers, Steven P.
Double-heterojunction nanorod light-responsive LEDs for display applications bibl color graph *Science* v355 no6325 p616 F 10 2017

Rogers, Thomas
Pump Up the Geopolitical Volume color *Bloomberg Businessweek* no4526 p52 Je 12 2017

ROGERS, TIM
My Pokémon Addiction *D: The Magazine of Dallas* v43 no10 p94 O 2016

Rogers Island (Washington County, N.Y.)
OFF THE GRID M. G. BANYASZ color *Archaeology* v70 no1 p12 Ja/F 2017

Rogge, Mike
The Best Boots of 2018 color *Powder* p95 S 2017
First bw color *Powder* v45 no3 p74 N 2016
STATE OF THE ART color *Powder* v45 no3 p146 N 2016

Rogger, Magdalena
Changing climate shifts timing of European floods color graph *Science* v357 no6351 p588 Ag 11 2017

Rogoff, Kenneth S., 1953-
THE CURSE OF CASH B. BETHUNE color *Maclean's* v129 no40 p77 O 10 2016
The Curse of Cash R. N. Cooper *Foreign Affairs* v96 no3 p156 My/Je 2017
Paper Problem *MIT Technology Review* v120 no2 p11 Mr/Ap 2017

Rogozin, D.
Observation of a large-scale anisotropy in the arrival directions of cosmic rays above 8 × 1018 eV *Science* v357 no6357 p1266 S 22 2017

Rogue One: A Star Wars Story (Film)
THE EMPIRE WILL RISE [Cover story] A. Breznican color *Entertainment Weekly* no1442 p14 D 2 2016 Rebellious Special Issue
Forward to the Past J. PODHORETZ color *Weekly Standard* v22 no17 p39 Ja 2 2017
How Rogue One: A Star Wars Story is connected to the Mac J. SNELL color *Macworld - Digital Edition* p16 F 2017
Knoll R. Capps color *Wired* v24 no12 p124 D 2016
May the Force Be With Us K. ARONOFF *In These Times* v41 no2 p36 F 2017
Rebel With a Cause A. Breznican color *Entertainment Weekly* no1443 p22 D 9 2016
ROGUE ONE: A STAR WARS STORY A. Breznican color *Entertainment Weekly* no1438 p43 N 4 2016
ROGUE ONE: A STAR WARS STORY A. Greengart color *Sound & Vision* v82 no7 p70 S 2017
A ROGUE RETURNS A. Breznican color *Entertainment Weekly* no1443 p18 D 9 2016
ROGUE'S SECRET REBELS ROOTS A. Breznican color *Entertainment Weekly* no1446/1447 p32 D 2016/Ja 2017

Rogue planets
Giant solo planets are in limited supply A. YEAGER *Science News* v192 no2 p10 Ag 19 2017

Rogue River (Klamath County-Curry County, Or.)
FREE AT LAST D. ARNOLD *Sierra* v102 no3 p52 My/Je 2017

Rohan, Alicia
   Overcoming prostate cancer silence *Successful Farming* v115 no1 p40 Ja 2017
Rohan, Tim
   Hall Pass color *Sports Illustrated* v127 no4 p15 Ag 7 2017
   How to Win At the SLOTS color diag *Sports Illustrated* v125 no12 p32 O 10 2016
   LONDON CALLING color *Sports Illustrated* v127 no11 p14 O 9 2017
   TIM TEBOW BELIEVES. DO YOU? color *Sports Illustrated* v126 no14 p40 My 15-22 2017
Rohatyn, Jeanne Greenberg—Interviews
   UNITED FRONT S. COCHRAN color *Architectural Digest* no5 p138 My 2017
Rohde, Katja
   De-extinction, nomenclature, and the law color *Science* v356 no6342 p1016 Je 9 2017
Rohingya (Burmese people)
   Burma's Oppressed Muslims at Crisis Point F. Solomon *Time* v188 no24 p15 D 12 2016
   Lightbox F. Solomon color *Time* v190 no10/11 p22 S 18 2017
Rohingya (Burmese people)—Crimes against
   Lightbox color *Time* v189 no3 p14 Ja 30 2017
   What She Did Not Tell Me Was the Story A. M. MUJAHID *Islamic Horizons* v46 no2 p50 Mr/Ap 2017
   Without a Home, and Without Hope B. LARMER bw color map *National Geographic* v232 no4 p100 O 2017
Rohingya (Burmese people)—Social conditions
   backstory color *New Republic* v248 no11 p68 N 2017
   Myanmar's Shame E. Dias and F. Solomon color *Time* v190 no13 p42 O 2 2017
   Slaves Are Catching Our Shrimp S. Ruden color *Commonweal* v144 no13 p8 Ag 11 2017
ROHIT, PARIMAL M.
   A LIFELONG LOVE OF YACHTS *Sea Magazine* v108 no10 pCA-6 O 2016
   SB 1 ENSURES A GAS HIKE IS COMING color *Sea Magazine* v109 no8 pCA-9 Ag 2017
Röhlsberger, R.
   Spectral narrowing of x-ray pulses for precision spectroscopy with nuclear resonances diag *Science* v357 no6349 p375 Jl 28 2017
Rohm, Rory J.
   Systemic pan-AMPK activator MK-8722 improves glucose homeostasis but induces cardiac hypertrophy graph *Science* v357 no6350 p507 Ag 4 2017
Rohr, Jason R.
   Chemical safety must extend to ecosystems *Science* v356 no6341 p917 Je 1 2017
Rohrbach, Kelly
   ICONS UNPLUGGED BRIGITTE LACOMBE [Cover story] C. ROITFELD bw color *Harper's Bazaar* no3656 p397 S 2017
   KELLY ROHRBACH K. SMITH color *Vanity Fair* v59 no6 p49 My 2017
   STOP RIGHT THERE, MISTER E. Sullivan color *Esquire* p108 Je/Jl 2017
Rohrer, Gregory S.
   Segregation-induced ordered superstructures at general grain boundaries in a nickel-bismuth alloy color *Science* v357 no6359 p97 O 6 2017
ROHRER, TULLY
   Long-Term Studies Contribute Disproportionately to Ecology and Policy *BioScience* v67 no3 p271 Mr 2017
Röhrl, Walter—Interviews
   What I'd Do Differently: Walter Röhrl, 70 M. DUFF *Car & Driver* v63 no2 p104 Ag 2017
Rohter, Larry
   Viva Tropicália! color *New York Review of Books* v64 no14 p28 S 28 2017
Roit, Jennifer
   DANCE SPIRIT Auditions Guide 2017 *Dance Spirit* v21 no2 p60 F 2017
ROITFELD, CARINE
   CARINE ON THE COLLECTIONS. A NEW PERSPECTIVE color *Harper's Bazaar* no3651 p349 Mr 2017
   COLOR AND CONTRAST color *Harper's Bazaar* no3653 p195 My 2017

ICONS UNPLUGGED BRIGITTE LACOMBE [Cover story] bw color *Harper's Bazaar* no3656 p397 S 2017
   IN TO THE WILD color *Harper's Bazaar* no3649 p273 D 2016/Ja 2017
   ON THE CONTRARY color *Harper's Bazaar* no3650 p118 F 2017
Roivant Sciences Ltd.
   This Pharma Company Stays Innovative by Doing Two Things V. Ramaswamy and K. Banta *Harvard Business Review Digital Articles* p2 Mr 14 2017
Rojas, Nubia
   People color *Christian Century* v134 no1 p18 Ja 4 2017
Rojas, Pamela—Interviews
   The Muralist color *Alternatives Journal (AJ) - Canada's Environmental Voice* v42 no3 p14 2016
Rojas, Rafael
   Rafael Rojas: Fighting Over Fidel: the New York Intellectuals and the Cuban Revolution P. Hollander *Society* v54 no2 p210 Ap 2017
Rojas Rojas, Cecilia Costigliolo
   Phytochrome B integrates light and temperature signals in Arabidopsis bibl graph *Science* v354 no6314 p897 N 18 2016
Rojek, Taylor
   #BIKECRUSH color *Bicycling* v58 no7 p65 Ag 2017
   CHAMOIS UP color *Bicycling* v58 no8 p60 S 2017
   HOW CYCLING WORKS cartoon diag *Bicycling* v58 no9 p21 O 2017
   "I NEED A YETI." color *Bicycling* v58 no3 p64 Ap 2017
   "I WANT A GOOD ROAD BIKE, BUT I DON'T WANT TO SPEND MORE THAN $1,000." color *Bicycling* v58 no3 p50 Ap 2017
   NO LIMITS color *Bicycling* v58 no9 p34 O 2017
   Oooh... Cozy! color *Bicycling* v58 no1 p64 Ja/F 2017
   Ornot Bar Bag color *Bicycling* v58 no4 p79 My 2017
   TAYLOR ROJEK color *Bicycling* v58 no3 p116 Ap 2017
Roke, Sylvie
   Optical imaging of surface chemistry and dynamics in confinement color *Science* v357 no6353 p784 Ag 25 2017
Roker, Al, 1954-
   Christmas in Rockefeller Center J. Russell *TV Guide* v64 no48 p39 N 21 2016
Rokeya, Begama, 1880-1932
   1928: Bengal B. Rokeya *Lapham's Quarterly* v10 no1 p113 Wint 2017
Rokita, Andy
   FROM OUR READERS color *Sky & Telescope* v134 no5 p6 N 2017
Rokita, Todd
   The Pros and Cons of Federally Funded School Choice Programs *Congressional Digest* v96 no7 p12 S 2017
Rokke, Kjell Inge
   Permission Granted M. PETERS color *Power & Motoryacht* v34 no8 p22 Ag 2017
Roku Inc.
   Roku Ultra Streaming Player B. Gonzalez color *Sound & Vision* v82 no2 p48 F/Mr 2017
Roland Corp.
   Detroit Techno S. Haider *New York Times Magazine* p18 Jl 16 2017
   Roland Aerophone AE-10 E. Enright color *Downbeat* v84 no6 p88 Je 2017
   Roland FP-90 R. Gehrenbeck color *Downbeat* v84 no1 p107 Ja 2017
   Roland RD-2000 C. Neville color *Downbeat* v84 no9 p98 S 2017
Rolander, Niclas
   Hello, Ericsson. 'The Butcher' Is on the Line color *Bloomberg Businessweek* no4526 p35 Je 12 2017
Role models
   Date with DIANE color *InStyle* v24 no3 p184 Mr 2017
   How to Rediscover Your Inspiration at Work K. Hedges *Harvard Business Review Digital Articles* p1 S 5 2017
   How Women (and Men) Can Find Role Models When None Are Obvious W. Murphy *Harvard Business Review Digital Articles* p2 Je 1 2016
   September Was Huge color *Glamour* v114 no11 p42 N 2016
Roleplaying games

LIGHTSEEKERS SMART FIGURES A. HAYWARD color *Macworld - Digital Edition* v34 no8 p47 Ag 2017

TORMENT: TIDES OF NUMENERA: ONE OF THE BEST BOOKS YOU'LL EVER PLAY S. BELLAMY color *Macworld - Digital Edition* p26 Je 13 2017

Roles (Social aspects)

    See also

        Children's conduct of life

        Communities—Social aspects

Life is Complex. God Is Not D. Rishmawy *Christianity Today* v61 no6 p24 Jl/Ag 2017

Rolex 24 (Race)

HIDDEN FIGURES P. LERNER color *Road & Track* v68 no8 p56 My 2017

THE NEOPHYTE D. CURCURITO color *Road & Track* v68 no8 p64 My 2017

A NEW GOLDEN AGE color *Road & Track* v68 no8 p28 My 2017

Rolex SA

AQUA Fresh color *InStyle* v24 no10 p137 O 2017

The Imperial Rolex M. SOLOMON color *Forbes* v199 no5 p34 My 16 2017

THE IMPOSSIBLE LIST N. Sullivan, F. Arbona et al bw cartoon color *Esquire* v167 no1 p70 F 2017

A Rolex Hat Trick For Michael Jung [Cover story] J. Wofford chart color *Practical Horseman* v45 no7 p10 Jl 2017

ROLEX PARTNERS WITH NATIONAL GEOGRAPHIC ON A VITAL MISSION G. E. Knell color *National Geographic* v232 no1 p9 Jl 2017

Up to the Minute H. MARTIN color *Architectural Digest* v74 no9 p62 S 2017

Rolex SA—History

The Rolex President M. SOLOMON color *Forbes* v198 no5 p52 O 25 2016

Rolfe, Helen

25 DAYS of Gift-mas *Dance Spirit* v20 no10 p48 D 2016

ALEXANDER MARYIANOWSKI *Dance Spirit* v21 no3 p40 Mr 2017

ALL THAT GLITTERS... color *Dance Spirit* v20 no9 p59 N 2016

Amy SEIWERT *Dance Spirit* v21 no7 p50 S 2017

AnD WHat a MasqUeRaDe *Dance Spirit* v21 no1 p48 Ja 2017

BACK TO BLACK (AND WHITE) bw *Dance Spirit* v21 no8 p76 O 2017

BATTLE OF THE Bars *Dance Spirit* v21 no7 p54 S 2017

Cross-Disciplinary Heaven *Dance Spirit* v21 no7 p104 S 2017

Don't THINK PINK *Dance Spirit* v21 no3 p56 Mr 2017

DRESS THE PART *Dance Spirit* v21 no3 p50 Mr 2017

Easton PAYNE bw *Dance Spirit* v21 no8 p119 O 2017

THE FINALS COUNTDOWN color *Dance Spirit* v21 no8 p60 O 2017

GET Her Look color *Dance Spirit* v21 no1 p54 Ja 2017

GET HER LOOK: Ella Titus *Dance Spirit* v21 no7 p96 S 2017

Kennadi BOESE *Dance Spirit* v21 no7 p119 S 2017

MINIMALIST MAGIC *Dance Spirit* v21 no7 p90 S 2017

Pain POINTERS color *Dance Spirit* v21 no8 p48 O 2017

Pumped-Up KICKS *Dance Spirit* v21 no4 p50 Ap 2017

STRAP - Happy color *Dance Spirit* v21 no8 p86 O 2017

STRIKE a Pose *Dance Spirit* v21 no7 p56 S 2017

#STYLESQUARED *Dance Spirit* v21 no4 p45 Ap 2017

Sweater WEATHER *Dance Spirit* v20 no10 p54 D 2016

ROLI Ltd.

ROLI Seaboard Rise C. Neville color *Downbeat* v83 no12 p107 D 2016

Rolison, Debra R.

Rechargeable nickel–3D zinc batteries: An energy-dense, safer alternative to lithium-ion bw chart diag *Science* v356 no6336 p415 Ap 28 2017

Roll Over Beethoven (Music)

THE ESSENTIAL CHUCK BERRY J. Farber *Entertainment Weekly* no1459 p15 Mr 31 2017

ROLLENHAGEN, LUISA

Manual cartoon color *GQ: Gentlemen's Quarterly* v97 no7 p11 Jl 2017

Roller, Scott

From Steel to Green: Revitalizing Pittsburgh Through Its Park System: The Pittsburgh Parks Conservancy shares lessons learned as it celebrates 20 years *Parks & Recreation* v52 no8 p18 Ag 2017

Innovative Community Celebrations in an Urban Green Space [Cover story] *Parks & Recreation* v51 no12 p32 D 2016

Roller bearings

Bearings, blocks, and more D. Everitt color *Sail* v48 no8 p62 Ag 2017

Roller bearings—Evaluation

Old Tech, New Tech color *Old House Journal* v45 no2 p50 Ap 2017

Roller coasters

Roller coaster knocks out stones in kidney model L. Beil color *Science News* v190 no10 p4 N 12 2016

Splashdown! cartoon *National Geographic Kids* no471 p28 Je/Jl 2017

What In The World? color *National Geographic Kids* no471 p29 Je/Jl 2017

ROLLEY, LYNNE

Belinda Bencic's Running Backhand bw chart color *Tennis* v53 no2 p64 Mr/Ap 2017

Rolling friction

Are You Rolling Wrong? N. Wozny color *Dance Magazine* v91 no3 p40 Mr 2017

Rolling pins—Evaluation

the aspiring pastry chef color *House Beautiful* v159 no8 p72 O 2017

Southern Comfort color *Log Home Living* v34 no2 p38 Mr 2017

Rolling Stone (Periodical)

Covering the Climate J. GOODELL color *Rolling Stone* no1297 p22 O 5 2017

Dr. Hunter S. Thompson P. DOYLE bw color *Rolling Stone* no1284 p24 Ap 6 2017

The Drug Chronicles D. BROWNE bw color *Rolling Stone* no1293 p28 Ag 10 2017

Eagles vs. the Editors A. GREENE bw *Rolling Stone* no1287 p21 My 18 2017

The Early Scoops A. GREENE bw color *Rolling Stone* no1283 p20 Mr 23 2017

For the Record J. LEVY bw color *Rolling Stone* no1285 p18 Ap 20 2017

Interviewing Dylan A. GREENE bw color *Rolling Stone* no1281/1282 p24 F 23 2017

Jann Wenner color *AARP: The Magazine* v30 no6A p16 O/N 2017

Lennon Revealed A. GREENE bw color *Rolling Stone* no1291/1292 p32 Jl 13 2017

Making the First Issue A. GREENE bw color *Rolling Stone* no1278/1279 p24 Ja 12 2017

The Man in White D. BROWNE bw color *Rolling Stone* no1289 p24 Je 15 2017

Peace, Love, Death D. BROWNE bw color *Rolling Stone* no1280 p22 F 9 2017

Shining a Light D. BROWNE color *Rolling Stone* no1295 p24 S 7 2017

Taking On Guns T. DICKINSON color *Rolling Stone* no1294 p25 Ag 24 2017

Talking to Power A. GREENE bw color *Rolling Stone* no1288 p20 Je 1 2017

The Ties That Bind A. GREENE bw color *Rolling Stone* no1298 p20 O 19 2017

Rolling Stones (Performer)

Back to the Blues [Cover story] B. HIATT bw color *Rolling Stone* no1275 p40 D 1 2016

MICK TALKS S. Mooallem bw color *Harper's Bazaar* no3649 p336 D 2016/Ja 2017

The Playlist color *Rolling Stone* no1273 p10 N 3 2016

Shining a Light D. BROWNE color *Rolling Stone* no1295 p24 S 7 2017

The Sun & the Moon & the Rolling Stones R. Cohen color *AARP: The Magazine* v59 no4A p52 Je/Jl 2016

WELCOME TO THE ISSUE color *Harper's Bazaar* no3649 p40 D 2016/Ja 2017

Rolling Stones (Performer)—Exhibitions

MEMORY MOTEL J. Seabrook cartoon *New Yorker* v92 no41 p29 D 12 2016

The Rolling Stones, Recharged C. Collis color *Entertainment Weekly* no1440 p58 N 18 2016

ROLLINS, HENRY
  What I Learned AT MY Summer Job cartoon *Popular Mechanics*
    p64 Je 2017
Rollins, Meredith
  Finding a fresh start *Redbook* p21 F 2017
  Happily out of reach *Redbook* p12 D 2016
  How to choose a happy life, by Sheryl Crow color *Redbook* p103
    Je 2017
  Let's talk about bullies *Redbook* p12 O 2017
  Let yourself be astonished *Redbook* p8 Mr 2017
  Making the right memories color *Redbook* p6 Je 2017
  My favorite star color *Redbook* p12 S 2017
  THE NO-FLY, ALL-FUN VACATION [Cover story] color diag
    Redbook p97 Jl/Ag 2017
  What keeps me feeling cozy *Redbook* p14 N 2017
  What's your superpower? color *Redbook* p10 My 2017
  Why respect matters color *Redbook* p18 Ap 2017
Rollo, Holly
  Your Company Needs a Communications Plan for Data Breaches
    Harvard Business Review Digital Articles p2 O 7 2016
Rollover protective structures (Machinery)
  PUTTING FARM SAFETY INTO PRACTICE: THAT'S THE
    THEME OF THIS YEAR'S NATIONAL FARM SAFETY
    AND HEALTH WEEK J. Scott *Successful Farming* v115 no11
    p54 S 2017
Rolls, Anthony
  Scarweather *Publishers Weekly* v264 no7 p52 F 13 2017
Rolls-Royce automobile
    See also
      Phantom automobile
  Rolls-Royce: Phantom K. Pleskot color *Motor Trend* v69 no11
    p20 N 2017
Rolls-Royce Motor Cars Ltd.
  KING CUSH M. Duff color *Car & Driver* v63 no4 p21 O 2017
Rollwagen, Carrie
  SOUTH'S BEST SHOP color *Southern Living* v52 no4 p92 Ap
    2017
Rolo, Mark Anthony
  The Indian Wars Have Never Ended bw *Progressive* v81 no2 p35
    F 2017
  My Tribe's Stand Against Corporate Mining *Progressive* v81 no10
    p22 N 2016
Rolte, Helen
  QUICK CHANGE color *Dance Spirit* v21 no2 p48 F 2017
Roman, Alison
  In The Raw color *Bon Appetit* v62 no7 p78 Jl 2017
  it's not Entertaining it's "having people over" color *Bon Appetit*
    v62 no10 p78 O 2017
  starters bw color diag *Bon Appetit* v62 no2 p19 Mr 2017
Roman, Amanda
  What My Horse Wears on His Feet cartoon *Horse & Rider* v56
    no5 p80 My 2017
Roman, Kaia
  The Joy Plan: How I Took 30 Days to Stop Worrying, Quit Com-
    plaining, and Find Ridiculous Happiness *Publishers Weekly*
    v264 no19 p50 My 8 2017
Roman, Nancy Grace
  Following my lucky star color *Science* v354 no6317 p1346 D 9
    2016
Roman amphitheaters
  TAKE ME OUT TO THE BALL GAME [Cover story] J. URBA-
    NUS color *Archaeology* v70 no4 p16 Je-Ag 2017
Roman antiquities in Great Britain
  THE COAST OF KENT P. Huntley *British Heritage Travel* v38
    no4 p50 Jl/Ag 2017
Roman baths
  BATHING, ANCIENT ROMAN STYLE J. A. LOBELL color *Ar-
    chaeology* v70 no2 p20 Mr/Ap 2017
Roman painting
  Echoes of Pompeii Found in France A. R. Williams color *National
    Geographic* v230 no4 p20 O 2016
Romance fiction
  HOMETOWN IS WHERE THE HEART IS N. A. SPECTOR
    color *Publishers Weekly* v263 no46 p24 N 14 2016
  Leakage color *Publishers Weekly* v263 no43 p50b O 24 2016
Romance in motion pictures

  Hermia & Helena color *New Yorker* v93 no15 p6 My 29 2017
  Remember These Forgotten Men T. TEACHOUT *Commentary*
    v143 no1 p58 Ja 2017
Romance on television
  HONORABLE MENTIONS D. Holbrook *TV Guide* p27 D 19
    2016
Roman history, 53-44 B.C.
  POMPEY THE GREAT: BORN 29 SEPTEMBER 106 BC Justin
    and S. Pollard *History Today* v67 no9 p22 S 2017
Romani, Sandro
  Behavioral time scale synaptic plasticity underlies CA1 place
    fields diag *Science* v357 no6355 p1033 S 8 2017
Romania—Politics & government—1989-
  Romanian researchers decry sudden power grab A. Nistoroiu
    color *Science* v356 no6342 p994 Je 9 2017
Romaniuk, Joseph A. H.
  Mechanochemical unzipping of insulating polyladderene to semi-
    conducting polyacetylene [Cover story] diag *Science* v357
    no6350 p475 Ag 4 2017
Romano, Ray
  DORIS ROBERTS color *Entertainment Weekly* no1446/1447 p86
    D 2016/Ja 2017
Romano, Richard M.
  The Community College and the Business Cycle *Change* v48 no5
    p52 S/O 2016
Romanov, Alexander S.
  High-performance light-emitting diodes based on carbene-metal-
    amides chart graph *Science* v356 no6334 p159 Ap 14 2017
Romanowicz, Barbara
  Seismic evidence for partial melting at the root of major hot spot
    plumes diag graph *Science* v357 no6349 p393 Jl 28 2017
Romans
  Romans, Huns sometimes got along B. BOWER color *Science
    News* v191 no8 p18 Ap 29 2017
Romans, Ben
  YOUR Wildest DREAMS color *Field & Stream* v122 no5 p38
    O 2017
Romans—Germany
  The Road Almost Taken A. CURRY color *Archaeology* v70 no2
    p32 Mr/Ap 2017
ROMANSKI, RICHARD
  Circular Saws color *Popular Mechanics* p26 F 2017
  CORDLESS ELECTRIC CHAINSAWS color *Popular Mechan-
    ics* p94 N 2017
  Entry-Level Planers color *Popular Mechanics* p40 D 2016/Ja
    2017
  Impact Drivers bw color *Popular Mechanics* p34 Mr 2017
  PORTABLE TABLE SAWS color *Popular Mechanics* p94 S 2017
  PRESSURE WASHERS color *Popular Mechanics* p28 My 2017
  THE Right TOOL color *Popular Mechanics* p80 N 2017
Romantic comedy films
  Rise of the Neo Rom-Com J. Chaney img *New York* p70 F 20 2017
  Runaway Starlets K. Buchanan img *New York* p71 F 20 2017
Romantic comedy television programs
  Rise of the Neo Rom-Com J. Chaney img *New York* p70 F 20 2017
Romantic love
  "Don't Make My Love Mistake!" J. DeMelo color *Women's
    Health* v14 no3 p119 Ap 2017
  Fired Up A. PATUREL color *Discover* v38 no3 p26 Ap 2017
  A Grand Passion A. Pasternak bw color *Vogue* v206 no12 p120
    D 2016
  My husband's been totally focused on our baby L. Chrisler, J.
    Breakwell et al color *Glamour* v115 no1 p52 Ja 2017
  Searching for a Soul Mate Is Futile. The Ideal Partner Is the One
    You Create A. Calhoun color *Time* v189 no20 p22 My 29 2017
  You and Your Date Night B. GADDIS cartoon *Working Mother*
    p50 F/Mr 2017
  YOU'RE YOUNGER. HE'S OLDER. WHY DO PEOPLE STILL
    CARE? R. Oltuski color *Women's Health* v14 no5 p108 Je 2017
Romantic love—Psychological aspects
  Which Would You Rather: a Million Dollars or True Love? A.
    McNearney color diag *Money* v46 no4 p18 My 2017
Romanticism
  weekend getaways: romance *Washingtonian Magazine* v52 no11
    p94 Ag 2017
Rome

The Anti-Axial Age S. Balch *Society* v54 no4 p346 Ag 2017

at home in ROME S. ROBERTS color *Conde Nast Traveler* v52 no8 p108 S 2017

Echoes of Pompeii Found in France A. R. Williams color *National Geographic* v230 no4 p20 O 2016

THE MAP ROME, 1942 K. Wiles *History Today* v67 no9 p4 S 2017

Rome (Italy)—Description & travel

The Riches of the Church J. MARTIN *America* v216 no1 p12 Ja 2 2017

Rome O. COHANE, M. ELLWOOD et al bw chart color map *Conde Nast Traveler* v52 no3 p52 Mr 2017

ROME, DAVID

FOCUSING: A PRACTICE TO COMPLEMENT MEDITATION color *Tricycle: The Buddhist Review* v27 no1 p40 Fall 2017

Rome, Howard

FOR WHOM THE BELL TOLLS *Harper's Magazine* v334 no2002 p19 Mr 2017

FOR WHOM THE BELL TOLLS H. Rome *Harper's Magazine* v334 no2002 p19 Mr 2017

Rome—Army—Religious life

THE RITUAL LANDSCAPE color *Archaeology* v70 no3 p35 My/Je 2017

Rome—Civilization

Writing on the Walls V. D. Hanson *Hoover Digest: Research & Opinion on Public Policy* no4 p163 Fall 2016

Romeo & Juliet (Theatrical production)

Romeo & Juliet *Cincinnati Magazine* v50 no12 p63 S 2017

Romeo et Juliette (Theatrical production)

Berlioz: Roméo et Juliette J. Malafronte *Opera News* v81 no9 p52 Mr 2017

CLASSICAL MUSIC *New Yorker* v92 no44 p12 Ja 9 2017

Roméo et Juliette C. GOUNOD, J. BARBIER et al *Opera News* v81 no7 p56 Ja 2017

Roméo et Juliette F. P. Driscoll *Opera News* v81 no9 p33 Mr 2017

Romer, Megan

HOUSE MUSIC color *Louisiana Life* v37 no4 p110 Mr/Ap 2017

ON THE RUN color *Louisiana Life* v37 no3 p38 Ja/F 2017

Romer, Paul

How Rational Are Rational Expectations? A. Mayeda and C. Torres *Bloomberg Businessweek* no4501 p13 N 28 2016

Romero, Carissa

How to Signal That Your Company Cares About Diversity *Harvard Business Review Digital Articles* p2 D 3 2015

Romero, George A., 1940-2017

The Beauty of Chaos N. PINKERTON bw color *Film Comment* v53 no5 p66 S/O 2017

George Romero M. Brooks color *Time* v190 no5 p17 Jl 31 2017

Romero, M. Ross

DEATH OF A PHILOSOPHER C. DICKINSON color *America* v215 no16 p35 N 21 2016

Romero, Michele

1951-2017 GEORGE PITTS color *Entertainment Weekly* no1457/1458 p17 Mr 17 2017

RICK GRIMES' WATCH color *Entertainment Weekly* no1460/1461 p94 Ap 7-17 2017

Romero, Oscar A. (Oscar Arnulfo), 1917-1980

New cardinal wants to revive legacy of Óscar Romero in El Salvador M. Vida color *America* v217 no5 p15 S 4 2017

Opposition to Óscar Romero's canonization was political J. Dueño color *America* v216 no8 p17 Ap 17 2017

Romero, Tony

Street matriculation: Chicago student finds a way out of homelessness J. Valente color *America* v216 no5 p15 Mr 6 2017

ROMERO-HARO, ANA ÁNGELA

The Oxidative Cost of Reproduction: Theoretical Questions and Alternative Mechanisms *BioScience* v67 no3 p258 Mr 2017

Romero-Muñoz, Alfredo

Forest conservation: Remember Gran Chaco bibl color *Science* v355 no6324 p465 F 3 2017

Rome—Social life & customs

Hotel de Russie, Rome A. WHITTLE color *Conde Nast Traveler* v52 no7 p36 Ag 2017

Rometty, Ginni, 1957-

Looking for Answers to the World's Biggest Challenges In the Eternal City color *Time* v188 no24 p31 D 12 2016

WHY I'M HERE V. M. ". ROMETTY *Vital Speeches of the Day* v83 no1 p19 Ja 2017

Rometty, Ginni, 1957——Interviews

Ginni Rometty: CEO, IBM M. Murphy color *Bloomberg Businessweek* no4539 p62 S 25 2017

Romig, Rollo

HOW TO STEAL A RIVER *New York Times Magazine* p42 Mr 5 2017

Romito, Dan

4 Types of Activist Investors and How to Spot Them *Harvard Business Review Digital Articles* p2 O 7 2015

ROMITO, LEAH WYAR

INDEPENDENT SPIRIT color *O, The Oprah Magazine* p113 My 2017

Romm, Aviva

ASK THE EXPERT *Prevention* v69 no1 p10 Ja 2017

Romm, Eliza Sydnor

5 Tips to Improve MENTAL FOCUS color *Dressage Today* v24 no1 p36 O 2017

Romm, Robin

Double Bind: Women on Ambition *Publishers Weekly* v264 no2 p52 Ja 9 2017

Let it go! [Cover story] color *O, The Oprah Magazine* p92 Ag 2017

Romme, Georges

The Big Misconceptions Holding Holacracy Back *Harvard Business Review Digital Articles* p2 S 10 2015

Rommetty, Virginia

"DON'T TRY TO PROTECT THE PAST": A CONVERSATION WITH IBM CEO GINNI ROMETTY A. IGNATIUS color graph img *Harvard Business Review* v95 no4 p126 Jl/Ag 2017

Romney, Jonathan

Gatekeeping Without Tears color *Film Comment* v53 no4 p78 Jl/Ag 2017

THE MATERIAL WORLD color *Film Comment* v53 no2 p36 Mr/Ap 2017

OCCIDENTAL color *Film Comment* v53 no2 p22 Mr/Ap 2017

ROMNEY, LYNTHIA

IN GOOD Company color *Forbes* v198 no9 p67 D 30 2016

In Good COMPANY color *Forbes* v200 no3 p85 S 28 2017

Romo, Tony, 1980-

The Case for ... Fewer Cowboys J. Gorant and T. Keith color *Sports Illustrated* v126 no11 p29 Ap 17-24 2017

Romolini, Jennifer

The Perks of Being Weird In the Workplace S. Begley color *Time* v189 no23 p20 Je 19 2017

Rompers (Clothing)—Evaluation

BEAST MODE *Indianapolis Monthly* v40 no7 p28 Mr 2017

Romualdez, Daniel

editor's letter color *Architectural Digest* no6 p28 Je 1 2017

Made in Montauk B. COLACELLO color *Vanity Fair* v59 no8 p96 Ag 2017

sea for days D. BLASBERG color *Architectural Digest* no6 p98 Je 1 2017

Romy: Anatomy of a Face (Film)

First Person Singular R. Brody bw *New Yorker* v92 no36 p9 N 7 2016

Rona, Jess

How to Primp Your Pooch J. Harman color *Glamour* v114 no12 p88 D 2016

Ronald, Pamela C., 1961-

Reinventing Rice for a World Transformed by Climate Change J. Temple color *MIT Technology Review* v120 no4 p15 Jl/Ag 2017

Ronaldo, Cristiano, 1985-

Cristiano Ronaldo and the 'Volatile' Investments D. Griffin cartoon *Bloomberg Businessweek* no4539 p27 S 25 2017

Ronalds-Hannon, Eliza

Why Suppliers Will Still Play With Toys 'R' Us color *Bloomberg Businessweek* no4539 p17 S 25 2017

RONAN, ALEX

Fashion Cares For Its Own img *New York* v49 no25 p84 D 12 2016

Ronan, Mark

THE GREAT EXPEDITION: A Danish-German survey sought to unearth the roots of the Hebrew Bible in Arabia. It became the first to comprehend a new Islamic ideology, which now threatens the West *History Today* v67 no6 p72 Je 2016

1830 HOUSE IN ROSLYN R. COLE color *Old House Journal* v45 no4 p22 Je 2017

Roofs—Design & construction

ASK ROY R. BERENDSOHN color diag *Popular Mechanics* p48 Mr 2017

Rooftop architecture

See also

Roof terraces

Making a SPLASH in the CITY D. Garner color *Esquire* p44 Ag 2017

Rooftop construction

See also

Penthouses

PENTHOUSE PEOPLE C. KOLB color *New Orleans Magazine* v51 no3 p36 Ja 2017

Rook, Caroline

An Early Warning System for Your Team's Stress Level [Cover story] *Harvard Business Review Digital Articles* p2 Ap 26 2017

Rookey, Kolleen M.

Still worried *U.S. Catholic* v82 no10 p5 O 2017

Rookie basketball players

RAGING BULL J. WUEBBEN chart color *Muscle & Performance* v9 no10 p38 O 2017

Why Your Team Needs Rookies L. Wiseman *Harvard Business Review Digital Articles* p2 O 2 2014

Rookie football players

HOT | NOT S. Kwak color *Sports Illustrated* v127 no11 p20 O 9 2017

Rookie hockey players

WHO IS THE NEXT BREAKOUT STAR? J. Fuchs color *Sports Illustrated* v127 no11 p43 O 9 2017

ROOKWOOD, DAN

MAVERICKS OF STYLE color *Esquire* v166 no5 p98 D 2016/Ja 2017

Rookwood Pottery Co.

Rookwood Pottery M. E. Polson color *Arts & Crafts Homes & the Revival* v12 no2 p48 Spr 2017

Room 104 (TV program)

Room 104 J. Russell *TV Guide* v65 no31 p33 Jl 24 2017

Room design & construction

BEST BEDROOM color *Timber Home Living* p22 2017 Special-Issue

BEST GREAT ROOM color *Timber Home Living* p18 2017 SpecialIssue

Stack 'Em Up color *Log Home Living* v34 no6 p8 Ag 2017

Room layout (Dwellings)

RENOVATION DIARY: Behind the scenes of my $140,000, six-month remodel in Arlington J. Sergent *Washingtonian Magazine* v52 no11 p142 Ag 2017

Room service

The Rise of the Room-Service Robots C. Morris color *Fortune* v175 no7 p16 Je 1 2017

Roomba vacuum cleaner

How I Learned to Stop Worrying and Love the Roomba K. Van Ogtrop color *Time* v189 no13 p55 Ap 10 2017

Roomba vacuum cleaner—Evaluation

For the Gadget Geek bw color *Consumer Reports* v81 no12 p26 D 2016

Roommates

WORST POTENTIAL ROOM MATES D. Franich color *Entertainment Weekly* no1436/1437 p50 O 21 2016

Rooms

See also

Artists' studios

Bedrooms

Fitting rooms

Living rooms

Motion picture studios

Offices

THE COLOR ISSUE color *House Beautiful* v159 no2 p81 Mr 2017

From Our Editor S. Donelson color *House Beautiful* p2 Jl 2017

Going the Distance K. RENDA and B. REYNAERT color *House Beautiful* p18 Jl 2017

Rooms—Design & construction

HIT REFRESH E. Graves *Martha Stewart Living* no267 p8 S

2016

SLEEP TIGHT E. STEIN cartoon *Wired* v24 no12 p90 D 2016

Rooms—Maintenance & repair

ROOM WITH A VIEW P. STEFÁNSSON *Iceland Review* v55 no3 p88 My/Je 2017

Roonemaa, Holger

When Home Isn't Where the Heart Is color map *Time* v189 no21 p40 Je 5 2017

Rooney, Andy, 1919-2011

Laugh Lines *Reader's Digest* v188 no1126 p91 D 2016/Ja 2017

Rooney, Kathleen

IN PRAISE OF WALKING C. ZULKEY color *Chicago* v66 no1 p44 Ja 2017

LESSONS ON EXPULSION color *New York Times Book Review* p26 Ag 6 2017

One Hand Slapping *New York Times Book Review* p18 Ap 9 2017

Rooney, Sally

Love and Marriage color *Publishers Weekly* v264 no20 p2 My 15 2017

The Passive Voice: In this smart novel, the narrator strives to matter C. LORENTZEN img *New York* v50 no15 p71 Jl 24 2017

TALK TO ME A. SCHWARTZ cartoon color *New Yorker* v93 no22 p74 Jl 31 2017

Roos, Christian

Sustained virologic control in SIV+ macaques after antiretroviral and α4β7 antibody therapy bibl graph *Science* v354 no6309 p197 O 14 2016

Roos, Johan

Build STEM Skills, but Don't Neglect the Humanities *Harvard Business Review Digital Articles* p2 Je 24 2015

Roose, Kevin

THE NEW ESTABLISHMENT 2017 bw color *Vanity Fair* v59 no11 p87 N 2017

NEW ESTABLISHMENT bw cartoon color *Vanity Fair* v58 no11 p124 N 2016

Next Waves *New York Times Book Review* p15 Ja 1 2017

Roosevelt, Eleanor, 1884-1962

Trailblazing Trip C. ZEIGLER bw *Indianapolis Monthly* p20 Ap 2017

Roosevelt, Franklin D. (Franklin Delano), 1882-1945

THE DAY WASHINGTON WOKE UP J. Lacey *MHQ: Quarterly Journal of Military History* v29 no3 p46 Spr 2017

FIRST IN WAR B. Hogan *MHQ: Quarterly Journal of Military History* v29 no3 p26 Spr 2017

Initiating a New Social Contract G. E. MARSH *USA Today Magazine* v145 no2860 p22 Ja 2017

The Liberal Ideological Complex J. BERGNER color *Weekly Standard* v22 no16 p26 D 26 2016

Roosevelt's War Against the Press D. BEITO bw color *Reason* v49 no1 p54 My 2017

Should Congress Have Term Limits? *New York Times Upfront* p22 S 18 2017

They Didn't Always Meet the Press bw *Weekly Standard* v22 no43 p14 Jl 24 2017

Roosevelt, Franklin D. (Franklin Delano), 1882-1945—Hundred Days, 1933

THE HUNDRED DAYS HUSTLE C. R. Kesler *Claremont Review of Books* v17 no2 p5 Spr 2017

Roosevelt, Kermit III

My Kind of Landscape color *AARP: The Magazine* v59 no3A p76 Ap/My 2016

Roosevelt, Theodore, 1858-1919

CLASS ACT T. Roosevelt *Lapham's Quarterly* v10 no3 p120 Summ 2017

Establishment of National Monuments: Controversies Surrounding the Antiquities Act *Congressional Digest* v96 no6 p6 Je 2017

ONLY ON OUR WEBSITE *South Dakota Magazine* v33 no3 p19 S/O 2017

PARTING SHOT *Arizona Highways* v92 no8 p56 Ag 2016

Prosperity bw color *Forbes* v199 no3 p152 Mr 28 2017

WHEN TITANS TANGLED S. Kinzer bw cartoon color *American History* v52 no4 p40 O 2017

Roosevelt, Theodore, 1887-1944

WHAT IF? ... ONE PRESIDENT'S PROGENY HADN'T ALTERED FOOTBALL FOREVER? J. Fuchs and J. Feldman color *Sports Illustrated* v126 no11 p64 Ap 17-24 2017

Roosevelt University (Chicago, Ill.)
Carla Hayden J. Johnson color *Current Biography* v78 no3 p28 Mr 2017

Roosth, Sophia
Our synthetic moment L. Campos color *Science* v355 no6330 p1136 Mr 17 2017

Root, Andrew
God's Canine Counselors A. Root color *Christianity Today* v61 no6 p91 Jl/Ag 2017
NEVER LET THEM SEE YOU CRY cartoon color *Christianity Today* p57 Mr 2017

Root, Damon
FREDERICK DOUGLASS HATED SOCIALISM bw *Reason* v48 no11 p8 Ap 2017
A FREE MARKET FRIEND AT THE FTC *Reason* v48 no8 p16 Ja 2017
ONE CHEER FOR JUSTICE SOTOMAYOR color *Reason* v48 no9 p11 F 2017
USE A CELLPHONE, VOID THE FOURTH AMENDMENT? color *Reason* v49 no4 p6 Ag/S 2017
WHEN COURTS KILL EXECUTIVE ORDERS bw *Reason* v49 no1 p12 My 2017
WHEN THE GOVERNMENT DECLARED WAR ON THE FIRST AMENDMENT color *Reason* v49 no5 p18 O 2017
WHY DID A CONSERVATIVE JUDGE UPHOLD AN AS-SAULT WEAPONS BAN? color *Reason* v49 no3 p6 Jl 2017
WILL LIBERALS LEARN TO LOVE THE 10TH AMEND-MENT? color *Reason* v48 no10 p6 Mr 2017

Root, R.
Exposing Unfair Pricing in Auto Insurance Rates color *Consumer Reports* v82 no5 p6 My 2017

ROOT, STEVE
A Font Of Hand-Crafted Artistry color *Los Angeles Magazine* v62 no7 p13 Jl 2017
There Goes The Neighborhood color map *Los Angeles Magazine* v62 no10 p126 O 2017

Root beer
How to Make a... ROOT BEER B. KAUFMAN color *Popular Mechanics* p76 S 2017
How to Make a... ROOT BEER B. KAUFMAN color *Popular Mechanics* v193 no7 p76 S 2016

Root crops
See also
Potatoes

Roots (Botany)
Root diffusion barrier control by a vasculature-derived peptide binding to the SGN3 receptor V. G. Doblas, E. Smakowska-Luzan et al bibl color *Science* v355 no6322 p280 Ja 20 2017

ROOTS, FRED
THE NORTH POLE map *Canadian Geographic* v137 no2 p46 Mr/Ap 2017

Roots, Humble
Why God Won't Answer Right Away color *Christianity Today* v60 no8 p81 O 2016

Rootstocks
GRAFTING FRUIT TREES: Fuse stems with rootstocks to form fast-growing, fruit-bearing plants L. Reich *Mother Earth News* no282 p39 Je/Jl 2017

Rope
See also
Cables
Cordage
A Theoretical Climbing Rope B. BLANCHARD *Climbing* no349 p10 N 2016

Rope bridges
Building a Bridge Without a Plan E. Machulak *Humanities* v38 no4 p1 Fall 2017

Rope Partners (Company)
Scaling New Heights K. Wong *Sierra* v102 no3 p26 My/Je 2017

Ropeadope Records (Company)
FOSTERING WIDESPREAD COLLABORATION K. Micallef bw color *Downbeat* v84 no9 p48 S 2017

Rope—Evaluation
Riding for the Brand color *American Cowboy* v23 no5 p48 F/Mr 2017

Tools of the Trade *Stage Directions* v29 no10 p6 O 2016

Rope—History
NYLON RIOT color *Spin to Win Rodeo* v20 no9 p96 N 2016

ROPEIK, DAVID
Clean Energy Mind Games: If policy makers want to accelerate the transition to a low-carbon economy, they should heed the lessons of the decision sciences and take another look at nuclear energy *Issues in Science & Technology* v33 no4 p59 Summ 2017

ROPER, CAITLIN
KATHERINE DUNN *New York Times Magazine* p51 D 25 2016

Roper, Ingrid
Spring 2017 Flying Starts color *Publishers Weekly* v264 no27 p36 Jl 3 2017

Roper, Lyndal
Luther's World J. R. PAYTON JR. color *Weekly Standard* v22 no34 p42 My 15 2017

Ropers, C.
Real-time spectral interferometry probes the internal dynamics of femtosecond soliton molecules diag *Science* v356 no6333 p50 Ap 7 2017

Ropers, Claus
Tailored semiconductors for high-harmonic optoelectronics graph *Science* v357 no6348 p303 Jl 21 2017

Ropes courses
THE TOP 10 BEST FUNCTIONAL EXERCISES M. Berg bw color *Muscle & Performance* v8 no12 p46 D 2016

Roquefort cheese
A THANKSGIVING TURKEY TWIST FROM BOB'S BURG-ERS color *Entertainment Weekly* no1441 p16 N 25 2016

Rorai, Alberto
Measurement of the small-scale structure of the intergalactic me-dium using close quasar pairs diag graph *Science* v356 no6336 p418 Ap 28 2017

RORK, PETER
Rescue from the Meat Farm: Flying Dogs to Safety *Idaho Maga-zine* v16 no11 p6 Ag 2017

RORKE, CATRINA
Capitalism and Climate *American Conservative* v16 no1 p18 Ja/F 2017

Rorschach, Hermann
PICTURES OF MENTAL HEALTH N. Strochlic color *National Geographic* v232 no3 p16 S 2017

Rorschach Test
Hope I Die Before I Get Young J. Epstein *Commentary* v143 no2 p34 F 2017
The wisdom of the blots B. BETHUNE bw cartoon *Maclean's* v130 no2 p66 Mr 2017

Rosa, Christopher
Everything Is 25 This Summer color *Glamour* no8 p38 Ag 2017

Rosado, Michelle Brittan
ODE TO THE DOUBLE "L" *New Yorker* v93 no5 p60 Mr 20 2017

Rosado, Rafael
'THE BRIEF WONDROUS LIFE OF OSCAR WAO' *New York Times Book Review* p30 Ja 8 2017

Rosano, Michela
Dome sweet dome color *Canadian Geographic* v137 no2 p26 Mr/Ap 2017
FEATURED FELLOW: BRANDON PARDY color *Canadian Geographic* v137 no2 p70 Mr/Ap 2017
FEATURED FELLOW: GEORGE JACOB color *Canadian Geo-graphic* v136 no6 p78 D 2016
FEATURED FELLOW: GORDON HARRIS color *Canadian Geographic* v137 no3 p78 My 2017
FEATURED FELLOW: MILBRY POLK color *Canadian Geo-graphic* v135 no6 p82 D 2015
FLORIDA color map *Canadian Geographic* v135 no6 p24 D 2015
Ice-free in the Arctic color map *Canadian Geographic* v135 no6 p30 D 2015
The land is the classroom color *Canadian Geographic* v137 no2 p58 Mr/Ap 2017
On our radar color *Canadian Geographic* v135 no6 p12 D 2015
Philadelphia color *Canadian Geographic* v135 no6 p18 D 2015
RIVER OF THE ICE GRIZZLIES color *Canadian Geographic* v137 no5 p42 S/O 2017
Southern sippin' color *Canadian Geographic* v137 p16 2017

Travel

Washington, D.C color *Canadian Geographic* v137 p20 2017

Rosario, Spencer

Rb1 and Trp53 cooperate to suppress prostate cancer lineage plasticity, metastasis, and antiandrogen resistance bibl graph *Science* v355 no6320 p1 Ja 6 2017

Rosas, Antonio

The growth pattern of Neandertals, reconstructed from a juvenile skeleton from El Sidrón (Spain) color graph *Science* v357 no6357 p1282 S 22 2017

Neandertal and Denisovan DNA from Pleistocene sediments bw color *Science* v356 no6338 p605 My 12 2017

Rosati, Andrew

A Development Bank Stops Lending Abroad color *Bloomberg Businessweek* no4503 p13 D 12 2016

Leading a Double Life In Caracas color *Bloomberg Businessweek* no4531 p30 Jl 24 2017

Meet Venezuela's New Iron-Fisted No. 2 color *Bloomberg Businessweek* no4511 p16 F 13 2017

Rosato, Donna

GIFTS THAT GO THE DISTANCE color *Consumer Reports* v81 no12 p45 D 2016

HOW SENIORS SUPPORT EACH OTHER color *Consumer Reports* v82 no12 p48 D 2017

How to Hire In-Home Help *Consumer Reports* v82 no12 p50 D 2017

How to Survive a High-Deductible Health Plan color *Consumer Reports* v82 no1 p16 Ja 2017

RETURN POLICIES THAT ROCK—AND NOT *Consumer Reports* v81 no12 p29 D 2016

Taking Patients for a Ride color graph *Consumer Reports* v82 no5 p52 My 2017

Rosato, Steve—Interviews

OverDrive Pushes into Spanish *Publishers Weekly* v264 no1 p16 Ja 2 2017

Rosberg, Nico, 1985-

A WINNING FORMULA color *Road & Track* v68 no6 p14 F 2017

Rösch, Thomas

A pathogenic role for T cell–derived IL-22BP in inflammatory bowel disease bibl graph *Science* v354 no6310 p358 O 21 2016

Roscigno, Vincent J.

Music for the people: the role of music in the southern textile strikes of 1929-34 R. Weir *Monthly Labor Review* p1 My 2017

Rose, Alexander, 1971-

Men of War: The American Soldier in Combat at Bunker Hill, Gettysburg and Iwo Jima S. L. Hoffman *Military History* v33 no6 p70 Mr 2017

Rose, Amber, 1983-

Amber Rose Isn't Here for Your Opinions color *Glamour* v114 no11 p102 N 2016

Everybody Loves Stripes color *Glamour* v115 no6 p148 Je 2017

ROSE, BRAD

Insights into Student Gains from Undergraduate Research Using Pre- and Post-Assessments *BioScience* v66 no12 p1070 D 1 2016

ROSE, BRENT

TOP THREE: TRICK SHOTS color *Wired* v25 no7 p44 Jl 2017

ROSE, CEDRIC

BIG WOOF *Cincinnati Magazine* v50 no5 p19 F 2017

DOG DAZE *Cincinnati Magazine* v50 no10 p52 Jl 2017

Lunch Ladies *Cincinnati Magazine* v50 no7 p156 Ap 2017

MOTHER ART *Cincinnati Magazine* v50 no6 p90 Mr 2017

RIDE ALONG *Cincinnati Magazine* v50 no4 p22 Ja 2017

TRUTH TALKERS *Cincinnati Magazine* v50 no8 p23 My 2017

Rose, Charlie

Charlie Rose talks about... Cybersecurity bw *Bloomberg Businessweek* no4504 p31 D 19 2016

Rose, Chris

CALL OF THE WILD color *New Orleans Magazine* v51 no3 p40 Ja 2017

Closing the door: And opening another one [Cover story] color *New Orleans Magazine* v51 no10 p54 Ag 2017

Dancing in the Field color *New Orleans Magazine* v51 no6 p42 Ap 2017

If Elected [Cover story] color *New Orleans Magazine* v52 no1 p50 S 2017

I REDISCOVERED ARMSTRONG PARK color *New Orleans Magazine* v51 no2 p46 D 2016

Krewesin' for a Brewsin' color *New Orleans Magazine* v51 no4 p42 F 2017

Mayor Trump color *New Orleans Magazine* v51 no7 p44 My 2017

Mr. Rose's wild ride color *New Orleans Magazine* v51 no9 p74 Jl 2017

Purge the Surge color *New Orleans Magazine* v51 no12 p52 O 2017

Summer Living cartoon *New Orleans Magazine* v51 no8 p44 Je 2017

Understanding New Orleans color *New Orleans Magazine* v51 no5 p44 Mr 2017

WIZARD WATCH cartoon *New Orleans Magazine* v51 no1 p46 N 2016

Rose, Daniel

INFRASTRUCTURE NOW! *Vital Speeches of the Day* v83 no10 p306 O 2017

SEAFOOD STEW FOR TWO img *New York* v49 no22 p88 O 31 2016

TA-NEHISI COATES--LOOKING BACKWARD OR FORWARD? *Vital Speeches of the Day* v83 no6 p182 Je 2017

Rose, Daniel Asa

SEPARATED AT BIRTH *Harper's Magazine* v333 no1999 p33 D 2016

Rose, David—Interviews

The House That Actually Makes the Internet of Things Easy S. G. Carmichael *Harvard Business Review Digital Articles* p2 N 12 2014

Rose, Derek C.

Restoring auditory cortex plasticity in adult mice by restricting thalamic adenosine signaling graph *Science* v356 no6345 p1352 Je 30 2017

Rose, E. M.

The First Blood Libel Against the Jews E. Duffy cartoon *New York Review of Books* v63 no16 p51 O 27 2016

Rose, Flemming

I Told Steve Bannon: 'We Are Not At War With Islam.' He Disagreed *NPQ: New Perspectives Quarterly* v34 no2 p17 My 2017

Rose, Gideon

THE POWER OF POPULISM *Foreign Affairs* v95 no6 p1g N/D 2016

PRESENT AT THE DESTRUCTION? color *Foreign Affairs* v96 no3 pviii My/Je 2017

WHAT NOW? *Foreign Affairs* v96 no4 p1h Jl/Ag 2017

ROSE, JEREMY M.

Long-Term Studies Contribute Disproportionately to Ecology and Policy *BioScience* v67 no3 p271 Mr 2017

Rose, Jonathan F. P.

In Harmony J. Gauer *Architectural Record* v204 no11 p49 N 2016

Striking the right chord S. D. Campbell bibl bw color *Science* v354 no6311 p423 O 28 2016

Rose, Justin

Rethinking Your Supply Chain in an Era of Protectionism *Harvard Business Review Digital Articles* p2 Mr 22 2017

Rose, Justin, 1980-

BE Clutch HAVE Fun GO Low [Cover story] J. Rose and D. Denunzio chart color *Golf Magazine* v58 no11 p61 N 2016

MAKE YOUR GAME PRESSURE-PROOF D. M. Clarke color *Golf Magazine* v58 no11 p10 N 2016

Rose, Kathleen M.

Mapping the Landscape of Public Attitudes on Synthetic Biology *BioScience* v67 no3 p290 Mr 2017

U.S. attitudes on human genome editing color graph *Science* v357 no6351 p553 Ag 11 2017

Rose, Kevin C.

A river runs through it color *Science* v356 no6334 p146 Ap 14 2017

Rose, Martine

Martine Rose color *Vogue* v207 no11 p118 N 2017

ROSE, MEGAN

Kafka in Vegas bw color *Vanity Fair* v59 no7 p116 Summ 2017

Rose, Molly Jo

Cake pops and communion wafers color *U.S. Catholic* v82 no3

p22 Mr 2017

THE HAMILTON MIXTAPE color *U.S. Catholic* v82 no3 p40 Mr 2017

A SERIES OF UNFORTUNATE EVENTS bw *U.S. Catholic* v82 no6 p40 Je 2017

Start with a cup of coffee color *U.S. Catholic* v81 no11 p25 N 2016

TV guide color *U.S. Catholic* v82 no4 p22 Ap 2017

Verso l'alto bw *U.S. Catholic* v82 no11 p45 N 2017

Rose, Nathan S.

Reactivation of latent working memories with transcranial magnetic stimulation bibl graph *Science* v354 no6316 p1136 D 2 2016

Rose, Pete, 1941-

The Man Who Spewed Too Much B. WOODIWISS cartoon *Cincinnati Magazine* v51 no1 p70 O 2017

Rose, Sviatlana

Fabrication of fillable microparticles and other complex 3D microstructures color diag *Science* v357 no6356 p1138 S 15 2017

Rose Associates Inc.—Officials & employees

INFRASTRUCTURE NOW! *Vital Speeches of the Day* v83 no10 p306 O 2017

TA-NEHISI COATES--LOOKING BACKWARD OR FORWARD? *Vital Speeches of the Day* v83 no6 p182 Je 2017

Rose Brand (Company)

What can Rose Brand do for you? *Stage Directions* v30 no3 p35 Mr 2017

Rose breeding

first BLUSH color *Vogue* v207 no6 p112 Je 2017

Rose gardens—Design & construction

WHEN JACKIE MET BUNNY M. GORDON color *Vanity Fair* v59 no10 p144 O 2017

Rose gardens—Evaluation

A ROSE FOR ROMANCE N. STOCKEN color diag *House Beautiful* p148 Ag 2017

Rosé wines

A HOUSE UNITED BY ROSÉ J. Kell color *Fortune* v176 no2 p44 Ag 1 2017

Rosefeldt, Julian

Manifesto C. Nashawaty color *Entertainment Weekly* no1466 p43 My 19 2017

Rosegrant, M. W.

Improving global integration of crop research color *Science* v357 no6349 p359 Jl 28 2017

Rosei, Federico

A low-loss origami plasmonic waveguide diag *Science* v357 no6350 p452 Ag 4 2017

Roseman, V. S.

Upgrading streamlined passenger cars color diag *Model Railroader* v84 no5 p26 My 2017

ROSEN, ALISON

Andrew Rannells color *Bon Appetit* v61 no11 p28 N 2016

Rosen, Allen

Caring for Aging Loved Ones color *Consumer Reports* v82 no12 p6 D 2017

Rosen, Anna Levin

Reading Genesis: Beginnings color *Christian Century* v134 no10 p47 My 10 2017

Rosen, Annabeth

ANNABETH ROSEN G. Adamson color *Art in America* v105 no5 p122 My 2017

Rosen, Barbara A.

A selective insecticidal protein from Pseudomonas for controlling corn rootworms bibl chart graph *Science* v354 no6312 p634 N 4 2016

Rosen, Christine

The Do-Not-Think Tank color *Weekly Standard* v23 no2 p24 S 18 2017

The Dystopian Style in American Politics *Commentary* v143 no6 p9 Je 2017

Harassment Is Not the Same Thing as Assault *Commentary* v142 no3 p4 O 2016

The Harm of Smarm *Commentary* v142 no1 p4 Jl/Ag 2016

An Inquiry Into the Nature and Causes of the Wealth of Rich People *Commentary* v144 no3 p7 O 2017

In the Future, Everyone Will Be Dead for 15 Minutes color *Commentary* v143 no2 p1 F 2017

In the Future, Everyone Will Be Dead for 15 Minutes *Commentary* v143 no2 p4 F 2017

The Lifestyle of Protest *Commentary* v144 no1 p7 Jl/Ag 2017

Retreating Inside the Bubble *Commentary* v143 no4 p7 Ap 2017

Self-Care and the Disappearance of the Adult *Commentary* v142 no2 p4 S 2016

They Weren't with Her *Commentary* v142 no5 p4 D 2016

To the Bitchhouse: The Way We Live Now *Commentary* v142 no4 p6 N 2016

You Can't Handle the Post-Truth *Commentary* v143 no1 p4 Ja 2017

You Will Not Think Outside the Box *Commentary* v144 no2 p7 S 2017

ROSEN, JAMES

At Sea in The Sixties color *National Review* v69 no6 p43 Ap 3 2017

Books for Children: A Symposium *National Review* v69 no19 p48 O 16 2017

The Ghost in Our Midst *Psychology Today* v49 no5 p44 S/O 2016

That Magic Feeling bw *National Review* v69 no17 p19 S 11 2017

ROSEN, JODY

'MOURN AT NIGHT' color *New York Times Magazine* p40 Mr 12 2017

Rosen, Jonathan W.

ACCURACY IS EXTREMELY IMPORTANT color *MIT Technology Review* v120 no4 p46 Jl/Ag 2017

Ghana's Last Mile color map *MIT Technology Review* v120 no1 p74 Ja/F 2017

ZIP LINE: Help from Above color *MIT Technology Review* v120 no4 p36 Jl/Ag 2017

ROSEN, JOSEPH

Among the Hasidim cartoon *Walrus* v14 no2 p32 Mr 2017

Rosen, Judith

Anne DeCourcey: PW's Rep of the Year color *Publishers Weekly* v264 no20 p(Sp)12 My 15 2017

Bargain Books in the Digital Age color *Publishers Weekly* v264 no39 p4 S 25 2017

A Big Week for Children's Books color *Publishers Weekly* v264 no16 p4 Ap 17 2017

Bookselling in a Time of Political Upheaval color *Publishers Weekly* v264 no6 p5 F 6 2017

CHILDREN'S INSTITUTE HEADS TO PORTLAND cartoon *Publishers Weekly* v264 no11 p21 Mr 13 2017

Chilling Out in Minneapolis color *Publishers Weekly* v264 no3 p3 Ja 16 2017

College Stores—and the Businesses That Serve Them—in a Time of Change color *Publishers Weekly* v263 no48 p5 N 28 2016

An Energetic Season of Regional Shows Wraps Up color *Publishers Weekly* v263 no45 p10 N 7 2016

FALL REGIONALS NAVIGATE TURBULENT TIMES color *Publishers Weekly* v264 no36 p28 S 4 2017

Gayatri Patnaik color *Publishers Weekly* v263 no42 p5 O 17 2016

Gottwals Books Turns 10, Adds 15th Store color *Publishers Weekly* v264 no10 p5 Mr 6 2017

Happy Holidays for Indies in 2016 color *Publishers Weekly* v264 no2 p6 Ja 9 2017

Indie Booksellers See Early Holiday Boost color *Publishers Weekly* v263 no50 p4 D 5 2016

Kimball Returns to Cookbook Publishing color *Publishers Weekly* v264 no5 p3 Ja 30 2017

Lessons from Some of the Country's Oldest Children's Bookstores color *Publishers Weekly* v264 no29 p22 Jl 17 2017

Life on the Outside color *Publishers Weekly* v264 no18 p31 My 1 2017

Making Book: How Booksellers Are Becoming Publishers chart color *Publishers Weekly* v263 no47 p6 N 21 2016

National Association of College Stores Gears Up to Fight for Indies color *Publishers Weekly* v264 no11 p4 Mr 13 2017

Niche Stores Find Their Way *Publishers Weekly* v263 no40 p10 O 3 2016

Reservoir 13 color *Publishers Weekly* v264 no35 p47 Ag 28 2017

SEPARATING FACT FROM FICTION color *Publishers Weekly* v264 no5 p16 Ja 30 2017

Surviving color *Publishers Weekly* v263 no42 p42 O 17 2016

TIME FOR A GOOD BOOK color *Publishers Weekly* v263 no46

p12 N 14 2016

What's Ahead for Bookselling in 2017 color *Publishers Weekly* v264 no1 p3 Ja 2 2017

Why Backlist Matters color *Publishers Weekly* v264 no7 p4 F 13 2017

Rosen, Julia

Built by Birds *Orion Magazine* v35 no3 p9 My/Je 2016

California rains put spotlight on atmospheric rivers color *Science* v355 no6327 p787 F 24 2017

CRYSTAL CLOCKS color diag *Science* v354 no6314 p822 N 18 2016

Gas changes signal eruptions color graph *Science* v354 no6315 p952 N 25 2016

How an ocean climate cycle favored Harvey color graph *Science* v357 no6354 p853 S 1 2017

Hurricane Harvey provides lab for U.S. forecast experiments *Science* v357 no6354 p854 S 1 2017

Seismic array shifts to Alaska color *Science* v357 no6359 p22 O 6 2017

ROSEN, KAREN

CATHOLICS VS. CONVICTS *TV Guide* p52 D 5 2016

COLLEGE HOOPS TIP-OFF MARATHON *TV Guide* v64 no46 p46 N 7 2016

FIGURE SKATING *TV Guide* v65 no4 p48 Ja 16 2017

GOING GAGA AT HALFTIME! *TV Guide* v65 no6 p48 Ja 30 2017

MAJOR LEAGUE BASEBALL *TV Guide* v64 no15 p47 Ap 4 2016

MLB PLAYOFFS *TV Guide* v64 no40 p66 O 3 2016

NFL PLAYOFFS *TV Guide* v65 no2 p48 Ja 2 2017

SPORTS *TV Guide* v64 no48 p48 N 21 2016

Why Everyone Loves the Big Game *TV Guide* v65 no6 p16 Ja 30 2017

Rosen, Larry

Relax, Turn Off Your Phone, and Go to Sleep *Harvard Business Review Digital Articles* p2 Ag 31 2015

YOUR PAL HARRY C. MCINTYRE color *Maclean's* v130 no2 p46 Mr 2017

Rosen, Larry D.

The distracted student mind — enhancing its focus and attention chart color diag graph il *Phi Delta Kappan* v99 no2 p8 O 2017

Rosen, Mark

What I Learned About Coaching After Losing the Ability to Speak *Harvard Business Review Digital Articles* p2 S 20 2017

Rosen, Meghan

Ancient avian voice box unearthed color *Science News* v190 no10 p7 N 12 2016

Ancient birds could achieve liftoff *Science News* v190 no11 p9 N 26 2016

Brain protein's grip on LSD imaged *Science News* v191 no4 p16 Mr 4 2017

Budget proposal would slash science *Science News* v191 no7 p15 Ap 15 2017

Cells gobble up strands of silicon *Science News* v191 no1 p9 Ja 21 2017

Color Me Dino bw color diag *Science News* v190 no11 p24 N 26 2016

Concern grows over Zika birth defects color diag *Science News* v190 no9 p14 O 29 2016

DNA vaccines for Zika show promise color diag *Science News* v191 no5 p12 Mr 18 2017

Dragon dinosaur met a muddy end cartoon *Science News* v190 no12 p5 D 10 2016

Fossil find revises history of jaws color *Science News* v190 no11 p12 N 26 2016

Genetic stability found in Russia map *Science News* v191 no4 p10 Mr 4 2017

Microcephaly rises in Colombia graph *Science News* v191 no1 p17 Ja 21 2017

Molecular knot is most complex yet color *Science News* v191 no3 p8 F 18 2017

New lightweight bot leaps with zip color *Science News* v191 no1 p12 Ja 21 2017

Nobels honor the small and exotic cartoon color *Science News* v190 no9 p6 O 29 2016

Researchers close in on ricin antidote color *Science News* v191

no4 p14 Mr 4 2017

ROBOT AWAKENING chart color *Science News* v190 no10 p18 N 12 2016

SHAKY START [Cover story] color graph map *Science News* v191 no11 p16 Je 10 2017

Shocking stories tell tale of zoo's founding cartoon color *Science News* v191 no6 p28 Ap 1 2017

The Survivors cartoon *Science News* v191 no2 p22 F 4 2017

Testosterone therapy is a mixed bag graph *Science News* v191 no6 p8 Ap 1 2017

Tiny fossils could be oldest signs of life color *Science News* v191 no6 p6 Ap 1 2017

XPRIZE launched new kind of space race color *Science News* v190 no8 p28 O 15 2016

Zika's baby photo snapped color *Science News* v191 no4 p32 Mr 4 2017

Zika virus devastates Brazil, spreads fear across Americas color *Science News* v190 no13 p19 D 24 2016

Rosen, Michael K.

ATP controls the crowd color *Science* v356 no6339 p701 My 19 2017

Rosen, Michael M.

Coming Apart color *Weekly Standard* v22 no35 p34 My 22 2017

Every Picture Tells color *Weekly Standard* v22 no23 p34 F 20 2017

Feeling Your Pain color *Weekly Standard* v22 no28 p38 Mr 27 2017

In the Long Run *Weekly Standard* v22 no11 p36 N 21 2016

Rosen, Mordecai D.

Abraham Szöke *Physics Today* v70 no10 p76 O 2017

Rosen, Peg

STAY WELL, Raise Hell color *O, The Oprah Magazine* p65 Jl 2017

Rosen, Peter

The Saarinens: Father and Son D. A. CIAMPAGLIA *Architectural Record* v205 no1 p38 Ja 2017

Rosen, Richard

Fab Abs color *Yoga Journal* p56 2017 Special Issue

LOWER-BACK LOVE color *Yoga Journal* p80 2017 Special Issue

Stand Strong color *Yoga Journal* p46 2017 Special Issue

Rosen, Scott

READER GALLERY color *Astronomy* v45 no1 p72 Ja 2017

ROSEN, SIOBHAN

YOU'RE OVER-DOING IT color *GQ: Gentlemen's Quarterly* v97 no3 p138 Mr 2017

Rosen, Steven

Early Days M. S. Eddy *Stage Directions* v29 no10 p12 O 2016

Rosenbaum, Jonathan

A Pen Is a Tool color *Film Comment* v53 no4 p79 Jl/Ag 2017

ROSENBAUM, LARA

Forge Real Fitness with Top E-Trainers color *Men's Health* v32 no7 p45 S 2017

THE WORLD IS YOUR GYM bw color *Men's Health* v32 no6 p114 Ag 2017

Rosenbaum, Mark

Why Two Financial Targets Can Be Better than One *Harvard Business Review Digital Articles* p2 D 20 2016

Rosenbaum, S. I.

Love in the Time of YouTube: De'arra and Ken 4 Life are just your typical couple trying to live their lives. Except they're doing it in public, for millions of fans img *New York* v50 no16 p100 Ag 7 2017

When Every Day Is Groundhog Day img *New York* v50 no7 p71 Ap 3 2017

Rosenberg, Andrew A.

Ensuring scientific integrity in the Age of Trump bibl cartoon *Science* v355 no6326 p696 F 17 2017

Watch what you write *Issues in Science & Technology* v33 no3 p16 Spr 2017

Rosenberg, Anna

7 Myths About Doing Business in Sub-Saharan Africa *Harvard Business Review Digital Articles* p2 Jl 3 2015

The Dos and Don'ts of Working with Emerging-Market Data *Harvard Business Review Digital Articles* p2 Jl 8 2016

Sub-Saharan Africa's Most and Least Resilient Economies *Har-*

ROSENKRANZ, NICHOLAS QUINN

Is free speech under threat IN THE UNITED STATES? WE RECEIVED TWENTY-SEVEN RESPONSES. WE PUBLISH THEM HERE, IN ALPHABETICAL ORDER *Commentary* v144 no1 p13 Jl/Ag 2017

Rosenmeyer, Aoife

"ACTION!" color *Art in America* p132 O 2017

DOUGLAS GORDON color *Art in America* v105 no4 p125 Ap 2017

GUILLAUME PILET color *Art in America* v104 no10 p162 N 2016

HERNAN BAS color *Art in America* v105 no8 p132 S 2017

Kunsthalle Zurich color *Art in America* v105 no1 p91 Ja 2017

Kunstmuseum Bern color *Art in America* v105 no6 p148 Je/Jl 2017

LIN MAY SAEED cartoon *Art in America* v104 no11 p132 D 2016

MARK DION color *Art in America* v105 no5 p138 My 2017

Rosenmund, Christian

Loss of a mammalian circular RNA locus causes miRNA deregulation and affects brain function color *Science* v357 no6357 p1254 S 22 2017

Rosenshine, Ilan

Host cell attachment elicits posttranscriptional regulation in infecting enteropathogenic bacteria bibl graph *Science* v355 no6326 p735 F 17 2017

Rosenstein, Bob

FROM OUR READERS *Sky & Telescope* v134 no4 p6 O 2017

Rosenstein, Eddie

The Freedom to Marry L. Greenblatt color *Entertainment Weekly* no1456 p56 Mr 10 2017

Rosenstein, Rod, 1965-

The Fall Guy T. Schoenberg and C. Strohm bw *Bloomberg Businessweek* no4523 p24 My 22 2017

Special Counsel Named In Russia Probe M. Duffy color *Time* v189 no20 p29 My 29 2017

Rosenstiel, Tom

Shining City *Publishers Weekly* v263 no46 p31 N 14 2016

Rosenstiel, Tom—Interviews

Empathizing with the Villain M. BARSON color *Publishers Weekly* v263 no50 p50 D 5 2016

ROSENSTRACH, JENNY

Cooking *New York Times Book Review* p38 Je 4 2017

The Holly, the Ivy and the Sherry Trifle *New York Times Book Review* p7 D 25 2016

starters bw color diag *Bon Appetit* v62 no2 p19 Mr 2017

A Very Organized Thanksgiving color *Bon Appetit* no11 p19 N 2017

Rosental, Benyamin

Hydraulic control of tuna fins: A role for the lymphatic system in vertebrate locomotion color *Science* v357 no6348 p310 Jl 21 2017

Rosenthal, Amy Krouse, 1965-2017

Milestones *Time* v189 no11 p15 Mr 27 2017

That's Me Loving You *Publishers Weekly* v263 no44 p74 O 31 2016

Rosenthal, Elisabeth

THE CODE RUSH *New York Times Magazine* p42 Ap 2 2017

Is affordable health care possible? K. Sue Smith color *America* v217 no5 p44 S 4 2017

Rosenthal, Gil G.

Pairing off L. Sun color *Science* v357 no6356 p1103 S 15 2017

Rosenthal, Jane—Interviews

You Talkin; to us? M. MURPHY color *Bloomberg Businessweek* no4519 p68 Ap 24 2017

Rosenthal, Laura

What nurses tell their friends color *Redbook* p82 My 2017

Rosenthal, Peggy

The Turning Aside: The Kingdom Poets Book of Contemporary Christian Poetry/The Paraclete Poetry Anthology: Selected and New Poems color *Christian Century* v134 no22 p42 O 25 2017

Rosenthal, Tracy Jeanne

Jasmine Nyende color *Art in America* v104 no11 p27 D 2016

RITUAL WORK bw color *Art in America* v105 no3 p82 Mr 2017

Rosenwald, Lawrence

Barbara Cassin, ed; Emily Apter, Jacques Lezra, and Michael Wood, English trans. eds; translated by Christian Hubert, Jeffrey Mehlman, Steven Rendall, Nathaniel Stein, and Michael Syrotinsky. Dictionary of Untranslatables: A Philosophical Lexicon *Society* v53 no6 p662 D 2016

Rosenwald, Michael

Is the quest for profits and clicks killing local news? color *Columbia Journalism Review* v56 no1 p36 Spr 2017

Making media literacy great again color *Columbia Journalism Review* v56 no2 p94 Fall 2017

Print is dead. Long live print cartoon *Columbia Journalism Review* p34 Fall/Wint 2016

ROSENWASSER, TAMZIN

A Hill Too Steeped in Lies *USA Today Magazine* v145 no2862 p25 Mr 2017

Rosenwinkel, Kurt

Kurt Rosenwinkel Goes DIY, Forms New Label B. Milkowski color *Downbeat* v83 no12 p15 D 2016

Roser, Anne

CHARACTER *Christian Century* v134 no17 p22 Ag 16 2017

Roses

EVERYDAY ROSÉ S. Schneider color *Sunset* v238 no5 p98 My 2017

Old Rose for a New Garden V. F. Luesse color *Southern Living* v52 no4 p15 Ap 2017

Welcome J. Goodwin *House Beautiful* p3 Ag 2017

Roses—Pictorial works

MOONLIGHT & ROSES color *Vogue* v207 no6 p102 Je 2017

Rosetta (Spacecraft)

Anatomy of a COMET J. Parker *Sky & Telescope* v133 no5 p14 My 2017

Rosetta ends 2-year comet mission with final descent D. Clery bw *Science* v353 no6307 p1482 S 30 2016

Rosetta's comet 67P/Churyumov-Gerasimenko sheds its dusty mantle to reveal its icy nature S. Fornasier, S. Mottola et al bibl graph *Science* v354 no6319 p1566 D 23 2016

Rosetta's Grand Finale D. DICKINSON *Sky & Telescope* v133 no1 p12 Ja 2017

Rosetta's last moments, in pictures bw *Science* v354 no6308 p16 O 7 2016

Roshbom, Menahem

A WINDOW TO THE WORLD I. B. Singer *Harper's Magazine* v334 no2000 p85 Ja 2017

ROSHI, ROBERT AITKEN

Zen Master Raven Stories bw *Tricycle: The Buddhist Review* v27 no1 p120 Fall 2017

Rosin, Hanna

But Am I Happy Enough? *New York Times Book Review* p8 O 30 2016

National Delusions *New York Times Book Review* p1 S 10 2017

Poppy's Secret *New York Times Book Review* p20 F 12 2017

Roslin, Tomas

Higher predation risk for insect prey at low latitudes and elevations graph *Science* v356 no6339 p742 My 19 2017

Rosling, Hans, 1948-2017

Hans Rosling (1948–2017) B. Gates and M. Gates color *Science* v355 no6331 p1268 Mr 24 2017

Hans Rosling Brought Data to Life, Showed Our Misconceptions about the World A. Sarma *Skeptical Inquirer* v41 no4 p9 Jl/Ag 2017

Rosner, Helge

Strong peak in Tc of Sr2RuO4 under uniaxial pressure bibl color graph *Science* v355 no6321 p1 Ja 13 2017

Rosner, Hillary

ALL TOO HUMAN color *Scientific American* v315 no3 p70 S 2016

THE BLAME CHANGER color *Popular Science* v289 no4 p24 Jl/Ag 2017

A RECIPE FOR TOMORROW color *Wired* v24 no11 p104 N 2016

Rosner, Robert

What role could nuclear power play in limiting climate change? bibl *Bulletin of the Atomic Scientists* v73 no1 p2 Ja 2017

ROSNER, STU

CHRISTMAS in Boston color *Yankee* v80 no6 p108 N/D 2016

Rosow, Bernard

ALL TIME color *Powder* v45 no5 p8 Ja 2017

Ross, Alec

The Industries of the Future R. N. Cooper *Foreign Affairs* v96 no1 p159 Ja/F 2017

ROSS, ALEX

CATACLYSM color *New Yorker* v93 no13 p92 My 15 2017

CATHER PEOPLE bw cartoon *New Yorker* v93 no30 p32 O 2 2017

DEPARTURES AND ARRIVALS cartoon *New Yorker* v93 no19 p72 Jl 3 2017

DESERT BLOOM cartoon color *New Yorker* v92 no37 p62 N 14 2016

GUERRILLA MINIMALISM bw *New Yorker* v92 no46 p78 Ja 23 2017

HOLY DREAD cartoon *New Yorker* v92 no43 p66 Ja 2 2017

In Extremis cartoon *New Yorker* v92 no44 p11 Ja 9 2017

Inner Landscape color *New Yorker* v93 no20 p8 Jl 10 2017

L.A. Rhapsody cartoon *New Yorker* v93 no5 p18 Mr 20 2017

THE MAGUS OF PARIS bw cartoon *New Yorker* v93 no18 p67 Je 26 2017

NORDIC FIRE color *New Yorker* v93 no11 p78 My 1 2017

On the Town cartoon *New Yorker* v93 no31 p12 O 9 2017

POWER PLAY color *New Yorker* v93 no24 p80 Ag 21 2017

PYRAMIDS AND WIKILEAKS cartoon *New Yorker* v92 no41 p86 D 12 2016

RITE OF SPRING cartoon *New Yorker* v93 no9 p76 Ap 17 2017

SHOWS OF FORCE cartoon *New Yorker* v93 no32 p94 O 16 2017

SINGING PHILOSOPHY cartoon *New Yorker* v93 no2 p74 F 27 2017

SLEIGHT OF HAND cartoon *New Yorker* v92 no44 p74 Ja 9 2017

SOUND WAVES cartoon *New Yorker* v92 no35 p96 O 31 2016

A SUDDEN SHADOW cartoon *New Yorker* v92 no36 p76 N 7 2016

TEMPLES OF SOUND cartoon *New Yorker* v93 no14 p90 My 22 2017

To Lou, with Love color *New Yorker* v93 no10 p18 Ap 24 2017

Voice of the Viola cartoon *New Yorker* v92 no38 p20 N 21 2016

WAGNER WEEKEND cartoon *New Yorker* v92 no33 p104 O 17 2016

ROSS, ANDREW

FINDING THAT SILVER LINING color *Flying* v144 no1 p20 Ja 2017

Ross, Andrew, 1956-

1999: Celebration, FL A. Ross *Lapham's Quarterly* v10 no1 p45 Wint 2017

Ross, Ari

Do You Speak Emoji? color *Sports Illustrated* v126 no7 p23 Mr 6 2017

Triple Double Bubble color diag *Sports Illustrated* v126 no3 p16 Ja 23 2017

UCONN WOMEN'S WINNING STREAK 11/23/14 color diag *Sports Illustrated* v126 no2 p15 Ja 16 2017

ROSS, ASHLEY

MOTHERS DAUGHTERS STRANGERS color *Women's Health* v14 no2 p152 Mr 2017

Ross, Bobby, Jr.

In rural Canada, churches find a new connection in welcoming Syrian refugees color *Christian Century* v134 no10 p16 My 10 2017

ROSS, BROOKE

Should They Stay or Should They Go? The debate over President Trump's crackdown on undocumented immigrants *New York Times Upfront* v149 no13 p6 My 15 2017

This Teen Invented a Lifesaving Vehicle: More than a million children worldwide die every year from preventable diseases. One teen's invention could change that img *New York Times Upfront* v149 no12 p12 Ap 24 2017

ROSS, CARNE

Africa's Last Colony bw color *New Republic* v248 no5 p46 My 2017

Ross, Caroline A.

Control and local measurement of the spin chemical potential in a magnetic insulator bw diag *Science* v357 no6347 p195 Jl 14 2017

Ross, Cindy

#trailchat color *Backpacker* v45 no2 p10 Mr 2017

Ross, Dalton

ADAM SCOTT AND CRAIG ROBINSON color *Entertainment Weekly* no1482/1483 p42 S 22 2017

American Housewife *Entertainment Weekly* no1482/1483 p79 S 22 2017

ANDREW LINCOLN color *Entertainment Weekly* no1438 p26 N 4 2016

BACK FROM THE DEAD color *Entertainment Weekly* no1450 p30 Ja 27 2017

The Best Sci-Fi Show You Aren't Watching color *Entertainment Weekly* no1453 p53 F 17 2017

The Blacklist color *Entertainment Weekly* no1482/1483 p74 S 22 2017

Bob's Burgers *Entertainment Weekly* no1482/1483 p34 S 22 2017

Broad City color *Entertainment Weekly* no1482/1483 p79 S 22 2017

Chicago P.D *Entertainment Weekly* no1482/1483 p79 S 22 2017

Criminal Minds color *Entertainment Weekly* no1482/1483 p79 S 22 2017

Curb Your Enthusiasm color *Entertainment Weekly* no1482/1483 p40 S 22 2017

DEMI MOORE OF Empire color *Entertainment Weekly* no1482/1483 p78 S 22 2017

Designated Survivor color *Entertainment Weekly* no1482/1483 p74 S 22 2017

The Deuce color *Entertainment Weekly* no1482/1483 p29 S 22 2017

Dynasty color *Entertainment Weekly* no1482/1483 p76 S 22 2017

Family Guy *Entertainment Weekly* no1482/1483 p34 S 22 2017

Fear the Walking Dead's Next Steps color *Entertainment Weekly* no1468/1469 p93 Je 2-9 2017

The Girlfriend Experience color *Entertainment Weekly* no1482/1483 p38 S 22 2017

The Goldbergs color *Entertainment Weekly* no1482/1483 p74 S 22 2017

Gone Glenn [Cover story] color *Entertainment Weekly* no1438 p22 N 4 2016

Good Behavior *Entertainment Weekly* no1482/1483 p39 S 22 2017

GUESS WHO'S COMING TO DINNER... [Cover story] color *Entertainment Weekly* no1484 p24 S 29 2017

Hot Date *Entertainment Weekly* no1482/1483 p74 S 22 2017

LAUREN COHAN color *Entertainment Weekly* no1438 p25 N 4 2016

Law & Order: Special Victims Unit *Entertainment Weekly* no1482/1483 p75 S 22 2017

Madam Secretary color *Entertainment Weekly* no1482/1483 p39 S 22 2017

Modern Family *Entertainment Weekly* no1482/1483 p75 S 22 2017

Mr. Robot color *Entertainment Weekly* no1482/1483 p77 S 22 2017

NCIS: Los Angeles *Entertainment Weekly* no1482/1483 p38 S 22 2017

NORMAN REEDUS color *Entertainment Weekly* no1438 p26 N 4 2016

Outlander color *Entertainment Weekly* no1482/1483 p26 S 22 2017

Poldark *Entertainment Weekly* no1482/1483 p38 S 22 2017

Riverdale color *Entertainment Weekly* no1482/1483 p68 S 22 2017

SEAL Team color *Entertainment Weekly* no1482/1483 p76 S 22 2017

Shameless color *Entertainment Weekly* no1482/1483 p30 S 22 2017

The Shannara Chronicles *Entertainment Weekly* no1482/1483 p79 S 22 2017

The Simpsons color *Entertainment Weekly* no1482/1483 p34 S 22 2017

SMILE *Entertainment Weekly* no1482/1483 p43 S 22 2017

A Song for Abraham color *Entertainment Weekly* no1438 p26 N 4 2016

Speechless color *Entertainment Weekly* no1482/1483 p75 S 22 2017

Star color *Entertainment Weekly* no1482/1483 p76 S 22 2017

Survivor: an Outing and an Ousting color *Entertainment Weekly* no1463/1464 p21 Ap/My 2017

Survivor: Heroes vs. Healers vs. Hustlers *Entertainment Weekly* no1482/1483 p75 S 22 2017

Ten Days in the Valley color *Entertainment Weekly* no1482/1483 p43 S 22 2017

Tony Turns 90 color *Entertainment Weekly* no1443 p21 D 9 2016

The Walking Dead color *Entertainment Weekly* no1482/1483 p38 S 22 2017

We Say Goodbye to One of Our Own color *Entertainment Weekly* no1480 p3 S 1 2017

What's Next for the Survivors color *Entertainment Weekly* no1438 p27 N 4 2016

What to Watch color *Entertainment Weekly* no1436/1437 p94 O 21 2016

What to Watch color *Entertainment Weekly* no1451/1452 p100 F 3-10 2017

What to Watch color *Entertainment Weekly* no1477 p50 Ag 11 2017

White Famous color *Entertainment Weekly* no1482/1483 p36 S 22 2017

Will These Five Survive? color *Entertainment Weekly* no1454/1455 p19 F 24 2017

Wisdom of the Crowd color *Entertainment Weekly* no1482/1483 p34 S 22 2017

Ross, Diana, 1944-

ANYTHING WENT bw *Vanity Fair* v59 no9 p131 S 2017

July Jammin' M. Griffith color *New Orleans Magazine* v51 no9 p46 Jl 2017

WOKE WONDERLAND V. K. De Luca color *Essence* v48 no6 p14 O 2017

Ross, Eddie

WORK IN PROGRESS color *House Beautiful* v159 no1 p42 F 2017

ROSS, FOBYN

The Stars at Night *Texas Monthly* v45 no4 p56 Ap 2017

Ross, Harold Wallace, 1892-1951

You DIDN'T HEAR IT from Me... D. Garner color *Esquire* p62 My 2017

Ross, Howard J.

3 Ways to Make Less Biased Decisions *Harvard Business Review Digital Articles* p2 Ap 16 2015

Ross, Jeanne W.

The Problem with Product Proliferation color *Harvard Business Review* v95 no3 p104 My/Je 2017

THE PROBLEM WITH PRODUCT PROLIFERATION: INTERACTION color graph *Harvard Business Review* v95 no5 p16 S/O 2017

Why Nordstrom's Digital Strategy Works (and Yours Probably Doesn't) *Harvard Business Review Digital Articles* p2 Ja 14 2015

Ross, Jon

Atlanta Jazz Fest Mixes Global Icons, Local Talent color *Downbeat* v84 no5 p105 My 2017

Hampton Fest Spotlights Stars, Students color *Downbeat* v84 no5 p15 My 2017

Thriving in Idaho color *Downbeat* v84 no1 p92 Ja 2017

Ross, Kirk

What the Nation Can Learn from North Carolina color *Progressive* v81 no4 p34 Ap/My 2017

Ross, Lillian, 1918-2017

LILLIAN ROSS R. Mead cartoon *New Yorker* v93 no30 p21 O 2 2017

Ross, Marisa

Marisa Ross B. GOLDEN color *Chicago* v66 no6 p86 Je 2017

ROSS, MARISSA A.

The Case for Cases color *Bon Appetit* no11 p34 N 2017

From Noon to Noir color *Bon Appetit* v61 no11 p36 N 2016

Large and in Charge color *Bon Appetit* v61 no12 p58 D 2016 / Jan2017

IIIƎ'LL HAVə WiNE, ИATURALLY color *Bon Appetit* p118 S 2017

A Real-Life Guide to Buying Wine color *Bon Appetit* v62 no7 p22 Jl 2017

starters color *Bon Appetit* v62 no6 p17 Je 2017

ROSS, MARTY

BEARDED IRIS color *Better Homes & Gardens* v95 no6 p72 Je

2017

CALADIUMS color *Better Homes & Gardens* v95 no7 p86 Jl 2017

GEUMS color *Better Homes & Gardens* v95 no4 p74 Ap 2017

HARDY HIBISCUS color *Better Homes & Gardens* v95 no8 p100 Ag 2017

jewel box garden color *Better Homes & Gardens* v95 no7 p80 Jl 2017

Ross, Matt

Captain Fantastic A. D'ARMINIO *TV Guide* v65 no8 p36 F 27 2017

THE POPULAR MECHANICS GUIDE TO SELF-SUFFICIENCY [Cover story] color *Popular Mechanics* p55 F 2017

Ross, Olivia A.

Why GE, Boeing, Lowe's, and Walmart Are Directly Buying Health Care for Employees *Harvard Business Review Digital Articles* p2 Je 9 2017

Ross, Rob

2017 WASHINGTONIAN TOP AGENTS, PRESENTED BY MVB MORTGAGE *Washingtonian Magazine* v52 no12 p136 S 2017

Ross, Robert

Retrospect: August 24–25, 1814: Burning of Washington, D.C S. Potter il *Weatherwise* v70 no4 p10 Jl/Ag 2017

ROSS, ROBYN

Critical Mass *Texas Monthly* v45 no6 p70 Je 2017

Next on Bachelor in Paradise color *Entertainment Weekly* no1473 p14 Jl 7 2017

Takin' It To the STREETS *Texas Monthly* v44 no11 p53 N 2016

Ross, Ryan

THAT TIME RYAN ROSS DANCED WITH WINONA RYDER J. DEFORE *Texas Monthly* v45 no2 p46 F 2017

Ross, Scot

DeVos, Trump Make the Student Loan Crisis Worse color *Progressive* v81 no6 p44 Ag/S 2017

Ross, Shane

high–flying microbes color *Scientific American* v316 no2 p40 F 2017

Ross, Tim

May Spells Out Her Ambitious Wish List *Bloomberg Businessweek* no4508 p14 Ja 23 2017

No Way Out bw *Bloomberg Businessweek* no4539 p41 S 25 2017

Preparing for Brexit Just Got Harder color *Bloomberg Businessweek* no4507 p15 Ja 16 2017

Theresa May and the EU Square Off Over Brexit color *Bloomberg Businessweek* no4515 p16 Mr 20 2017

Ross, Tracee Ellis, 1972-

black-ish I. Ratledge color *TV Guide* v65 no7 p36 F 13 2017

black-ish N. Abrams, A. Bacle et al *Entertainment Weekly* no1482/1483 p63 S 22 2017

HAPPY SUMMER! [Cover story] color *Redbook* p85 Jl/Ag 2017

IT'S GOOD TO BE QUEEN color *InStyle* v24 no3 p350 Mr 2017

MAKING THE COVER: September color *Ebony* v72 no11 p14 S 2017

Tracee Ellis Ross J. Crelin color *Current Biography* v78 no1 p74 Ja 2017

true beauties inside & out L. MAJEWSKI color *Good Housekeeping* v264 no5 p44 My 2017

Ross, Tracee Ellis, 1972——Interviews

BLACK-ISH STARS ACT LIKE REAL-LIFE HUSBAND & WIFE [Cover story] B. VIERA color *Ebony* v72 no11 p68 S 2017

SHE'S A JOY [Cover story] M. C. HAREL color *Redbook* p86 Jl/Ag 2017

Ross, Tracy

5 REASONS TO GO PLAY color *Rodale's Organic Life* v2 no7 p95 D 2016/Ja 2017

Ethical Evergreens color *Rodale's Organic Life* v2 no7 p94 D 2016/Ja 2017

Hikes Gone Wrong: We all love the trail. Sometimes love hurts color il *Backpacker* p69 S 2017

LIFTING THE DARKNESS color *Rodale's Organic Life* v2 no7 p80 D 2016/Ja 2017

Ross, Turner

Contemporary Color V. LUCCA color *Film Comment* v53 no2 p69 Mr/Ap 2017

Ross, Wilbur L., 1937-
THE APPROVAL MATRIX img *New York* p148 Mr 6 2017
Leader Board color *Forbes* v198 no9 p20 D 30 2016
WHAT'S ROSS WORTH? D. Alexander color *Forbes* v200 no5 p42 N 14 2017

Ross, Wilbur L., 1937——Finance
MAN OF THE (VERY RICH) PEOPLE [Cover story] M. Abelson and D. Carey color *Bloomberg Businessweek* no4509 p38 Ja 30 2017

Ross Barney Architects Inc.
Belmont Blue Line Station A. Schneider *Architectural Record* v205 no4 p204 Ap 2017

Ross Chapin Architects (Company)
Saratoga Cabin [Cover story] color diag *Cabin Living* p67 Ag 2017

Ross Sea (Antarctica)
A Happy Feat for Antarctica G. TARLACH color *Discover* v38 no1 p75 Ja/F 2017
Scientists hope risky winter voyage yields icy rewards W. Cornwall color graph *Science* v356 no6335 p234 Ap 21 2017

Ross Stores Inc.
17 BARBARA RENTLER P. Wahba *Fortune* v174 no7 p89 D 1 2016

Rossby, Carl-Gustaf, 1898-1957
Carl-Gustaf Rossby J. R. Fleming *Physics Today* v70 no1 p50 Ja 2017

Rossdale, Gavin, 1965-
GAVIN ROSSDALE R. Rahman color *Entertainment Weekly* no1457/1458 p97 Mr 17 2017

Rossellini, Isabella, 1952-
ISABELLA ROSSELLINI D. KAMP bw *Vanity Fair* v59 no1 p106 Holiday 2017

Rossello, Ricardo
Can statehood save Puerto Rico? T. Padget color *America* v216 no13 p15 Je 12 2017
A Political Scion Tries To Right Puerto Rico R. Spalding and J. Levin color *Bloomberg Businessweek* no4519 p18 Ap 24 2017

Rosset, Barney
Bohemian Grove B. YAGODA *New York Times Book Review* p14 O 16 2016

Rossetto, Maurizio
Publish openly but responsibly color *Science* v357 no6347 p141 Jl 14 2017

Rossi, Alexander
AMERICAN PRIDE color *Road & Track* v68 no6 p12 F 2017
YOUTH BE KNOWN S. Kwak color *Sports Illustrated* v127 no10 p20 O 2 2017

Rossi, Anthony M.
Glia relay differentiation cues to coordinate neuronal development in Drosophila color *Science* v357 no6354 p886 S 1 2017

Rossi, Anthony T.
Nov. 15, 1971: High Tech, High Anxiety bw color *Forbes* v198 no6 p38 N 8 2016

ROSSI, CAREY
Why Your Hammies Are Tight chart color *Muscle & Performance* v9 no8 p28 Ag 2017

Rossi, F.
The sacral autonomic outflow is sympathetic bibl color diag *Science* v354 no6314 p893 N 18 2016

Rossi, John
Ronan Fanning, Eamon de Valera: A Will to Power *Society* v54 no3 p310 Je 2017

Rossi, Marcello
The Winter Maestro bw color *Climbing* no350 p52 D 2016/Ja 2017

Rossi, Mario
The Last Wing Car A. Rogers bw color *Hot Rod* v70 no6 p40 Je 2017

Ross-Ibarra, Jeffrey
Genomic estimation of complex traits reveals ancient maize adaptation to temperate North America diag *Science* v357 no6350 p512 Ag 4 2017

Rossin, Ross
LARGER THAN LIFE S. HENRY *Atlanta* v56 no7 p23 N 2016

ROSSINGTON, KATE
Shipbuilding Docks as Experimental Systems for Realistic As-

sessments of Anthropogenic Stressors on Marine Organisms *BioScience* v67 no9 p853 S 2017

Rossini, Gioachino, 1792-1868
Guillaume Tell *Opera News* v81 no9 p59 Mr 2017
Il Barbiere di Siviglia *Opera News* v81 no7 p57 Ja 2017
Rossini: L'Inganno Felice P. Dillon *Opera News* v81 no9 p53 Mr 2017
Signor Tambourossini [Cover story] L. Wolff color *New York Review of Books* v64 no15 p17 O 12 2017

Rossiter, Alison
The Darkroom *Art in America* v104 no9 p50 O 2016

Rossiter, Kel
Green Ice color *Climbing* no350 p32 D 2016/Ja 2017

Rossiter, Nan
Summer Dance color *Publishers Weekly* v264 no16 p38 Ap 17 2017

Rossler, David
OBAMA'S AMERICA img *New York* v49 no20 p12 O 3 2016

Rossmeisl, Jan
Toward sustainable fuel cells bibl graph *Science* v354 no6318 p1378 D 16 2016

Rosso, Kevin M.
Direction-specific van der Waals attraction between rutile TiO_2 nanocrystals diag *Science* v356 no6336 p434 Ap 28 2017

Ross Romero, M.
A man of many commitments color *America* v216 no13 p54 Je 12 2017

Rossum, Emmy, 1986——Interviews
GRITTY WOMAN M. LOGAN *TV Guide* v64 no40 p46 O 3 2016

Rost, Andrea
Brahms: Lieder and Liebeslieder Waltzes J. Rosenblum *Opera News* v81 no5 p58 N 2016

Roston, Eric
Time for Going-Away Gifts? color *Bloomberg Businessweek* no4525 p6 Je 5 2017

Roswell Park Cancer Institute (Buffalo, N.Y.)
20 Best Medical Breakthroughs of 2016 B. HOWARD bw color *Prevention* v68 no12 p48 D 2016

Rotaliana (Company)
FETISH B. BARRETT color *Wired* v25 no3 p33 Mr 2017

Rotary combustion engines
ROTARY RISING P. Garrison diag *Flying* v144 no8 p80 Ag 2017

Rotation of galaxies
75, 50 & 25 YEARS AGO R. W. Sinnott *Sky & Telescope* v133 no6 p7 Je 2017
Explaining a few discoveries S. Tremaine, A. Garscadden et al *Physics Today* v70 no9 p12 S 2017

Rotational grazing
Small-Scale MOB GRAZING J. Salatin *Mother Earth News* no279 p72 D/Ja 2017
WATERING SYSTEMS FOR ROTATIONAL GRAZING: KEEP ANIMALS HYDRATED WHILE MOVING THEM AROUND J. Henke *Successful Farming* v115 no12 p54 O 2017

Rotational motion
hip to it J. Crandell color *Yoga Journal* p48 2017 Special Issue

Rotator cuff
FASTER RECOVERY FOR SHOULDER REPLACEMENT V. Prevish *Cincinnati Magazine* v50 no12 p86 S 2017

Rotbart, Harley A.
advice every new mom needs [Cover story] color *Parents* v92 no7 p32 Jl 2017
good sports *Parents* v92 no3 p114 Mr 2017

Rotchford, Lesley
THE BEST WEIGHT-LOSS ADVICE EVER! color *Women's Health* v14 no1 p126 Ja/F 2017

Rotel Co. Ltd.
Rotel A12 Integrated Amplifier M. Fleischmann chart color graph *Sound & Vision* v82 no3 p42 Ap 2017

Rotella, Carlo
KIMBO SLICE *New York Times Magazine* p30 D 25 2016
The Pipe Fitter *New York Times Magazine* p47 F 26 2017

Rotella, Mark
Cooking & Food color *Publishers Weekly* v263 no51 p38 D 12 2016
Cooking & Food color *Publishers Weekly* v264 no26 p42 Je 26 2017

Memoirs & Biographies bw color *Publishers Weekly* v264 no26 p81 Je 26 2017

Rotenberg, Marc

Equifax, the Credit Reporting Industry, and What Congress Should Do Next *Harvard Business Review Digital Articles* p2 S 20 2017

ROTH, ALLAN

The 7 Deadly Sins of Personal Finance color *AARP: The Magazine* v59 no1A p16 D 2015/Ja 2016

True Confessions of a Money Man color graph *AARP: The Magazine* v59 no5A p28 Ag/S 2016

Roth, Anna M.

Health Care Needs Less Innovation and More Imitation *Harvard Business Review Digital Articles* p2 N 19 2014

Roth, Chloe

KAUAI'S NEXT WAVE [Cover story] color *Sunset* v238 no3 p44 Mr 2017

Roth, Frederick P.

Exploring genetic suppression interactions on a global scale diag *Science* v354 no6312 p599 N 4 2016

Roth, John

From Pain to Gain for This Fidelity Fund N. S. HUANG chart *Kiplinger's Personal Finance* v70 no12 p60 D 2016

Roth, Jon

2017 MaVeRicks OF Style bw color *Esquire* p81 S 2017

the best way to DROP ACID color *Esquire* p60 2017 BigBlackBook

A BRUTAL EFFORT bw color *Esquire* p34 My 2017

Bulletproof! color *Esquire* p66 Ag 2017

A Century of Style bw color *Esquire* p77 O 2017

DAVID CASAVANT color *Esquire* p54 Ap 2017

DON'T CALL IT ATHLEISURE color *Esquire* p30 Ag 2017

the FAB five color *Esquire* p64 2017 BigBlackBook

A FANTASTIC BEAST... ...And where to FIND it color *Esquire* p40 O 2017

Frozen Assets color *Esquire* p72 BigBlackBook

Guglielmo Miani color *Esquire* p134 2017 BigBlackBook

HANG LOOSE bw color *Esquire* v167 no2 p128 Mr 2017

THE HARD STUFF color *Esquire* p47 Ap 2017

HIGH TREK color *Esquire* v167 no2 p65 Mr 2017

HOW I DISCOVERED MY STYLE cartoon color *Esquire* p48 My 2017

HOW I GOT MY STYLE color *Esquire* p40 Je/Jl 2017

HOW I GOT MY STYLE color *Esquire* p44 O 2017

HOW I GOT MY STYLE: JAMES FRANCO bw color *Esquire* p58 S 2017

HOW I GOT MY STYLE: MARK CHO color *Esquire* p32 Ag 2017

HOW TO SUMMER IN STYLE color *Esquire* p54 2017 BigBlackBook

LUST FOR LIFE cartoon color *Esquire* p110 2017 BigBlackBook

POSTCARDS FROM HELL color *Esquire* p51 BigBlackBook

Q: What's the right way to cover DWYANE WADE? color *Esquire* p110 Ap 2017

ROCKING THE BOAT color *Esquire* p50 2017 BigBlackBook

SCIENCE OF SMOOTH cartoon color *Men's Health* v32 no2 p71 Mr 2017

STAND OUT IN CAMO bw color *Esquire* v167 no2 p114 Mr 2017

THE SWEET SCENT OF SUCCESS color *Bloomberg Businessweek* no4504 p66 D 19 2016

THE TAO OF LAIRD HAMILTON color *Esquire* p54 O 2017

THIS COAT'S A CINCH FOR FALL color *Esquire* p55 S 2017

THREE WISE MEN bw color *Esquire* p88 2017 BigBlackBook

TURN A CORNER color *Esquire* p37 N 2017

WHEN OPPOSITES ATTRACT color *Esquire* p35 Je/Jl 2017

THE WHITE STUFF bw color *Esquire* p39 My 2017

Roth, Kenneth

Must It Always Be Wartime? color *New York Review of Books* v64 no4 p19 Mr 9 2017

Pioneers [Cover story] color *Time* v189 no16/17 p14 My 1-8 2017

What Trump Should Do in Syria color *New York Review of Books* v63 no20 p50 D 22 2016

Roth, Kevin

The Gathering Pension Storm *Parks & Recreation* v52 no2 p34 F 2017

Introducing NRPA Park Metrics *Parks & Recreation* v51 no11 p12 N 2016

Laying the Groundwork for Park Metrics *Parks & Recreation* v52 no1 p12 Ja 2017

NRPA Park and Recreation Salary Survey Says... *Parks & Recreation* v52 no9 p12 S 2017

NRPA Research Year in Review *Parks & Recreation* v51 no12 p12 D 2016

Park Agencies: Contributors to Sustainability in Their Communities *Parks & Recreation* v52 no4 p12 Ap 2017

Public Park Usage: Motives and Challenges *Parks & Recreation* v51 no10 p16 O 2016

Research. Parks and Recreation: Meeting Community Fitness Needs at All Levels *Parks & Recreation* v52 no6 p12 Je 2017

Rising Pension Liabilities *Parks & Recreation* v52 no2 p12 F 2017

The Story Is in the Data *Parks & Recreation* v52 no5 p14 My 2017

What Drives Public Officials' Budget Priorities? *Parks & Recreation* v52 no10 p12 O 2017

Roth, M.

Observation of a large-scale anisotropy in the arrival directions of cosmic rays above 8×10^{18} eV *Science* v357 no6357 p1266 S 22 2017

Roth, Martin S.

Does Your Company Have What It Takes to Go Global? *Harvard Business Review Digital Articles* p2 Ap 11 2016

Roth, Nickolas

The future of US–Russian nuclear deterrence and arms control bibl *Bulletin of the Atomic Scientists* v73 no4 p271 Jl 2017

Roth, Philip, 1933-

Adapting the unadaptable J. J. WEINMAN color *Maclean's* v129 no42 p56 O 24 2016

I HAVE FALLEN IN LOVE WITH AMERICAN NAMES bw *New Yorker* v93 no16 p46 Je 5 2017

ROTH ON TRUMP J. Thurman cartoon *New Yorker* v92 no47 p18 Ja 30 2017

Roth, Richard H.

Homer1a drives homeostatic scaling-down of excitatory synapses during sleep bibl graph *Science* v355 no6324 p511 F 3 2017

Roth, Tim, 1961-

Tin Star A. Bacle, K. Connolly et al *Entertainment Weekly* no1482/1483 p109 S 22 2017

Roth, Veronica, 1988-

VERONICA ROTH color *Entertainment Weekly* no1450 p61 Ja 27 2017

Roth, Zachary

The Real Voter Fraud color *New Republic* v248 no8/9 p10 Ag/S 2017

Voting Wrongs A. WOLFE il *New Republic* v247 no11 p53 N 2016

Rothbard, Nancy

How to Separate the Personal and Professional on Social Media *Harvard Business Review Digital Articles* p2 Mr 26 2015

How Your Morning Mood Affects Your Whole Workday *Harvard Business Review Digital Articles* p2 Jl 21 2016

ROTHBART, DAVY

Glow, Baby, Glow color *Los Angeles Magazine* v62 no7 p45 Jl 2017

Holiday in The Desert *Los Angeles Magazine* p76 D 2016

A Little Slice Of Havana *Los Angeles Magazine* p55 F 2017

Secret Circus *Los Angeles Magazine* p86 Ap 2017

Rothbaum, Barbara

Barbara Rothbaum *Atlanta* v57 no2 p106 Je 2017

Rothberg, Amy

What doctors tell their friends about weight loss [Cover story] L. MULCAHY color *Redbook* p72 Mr 2017

Rothberg, Helen

Bartending Is Better Than Business School S. Begley color *Time* v190 no2/3 p20 Jl 10-17 2017

A Tip Worth Remembering color *Money* v46 no8 p80 S 2017

Rothenberg, Ben

Equal Pay for Equal Play? *New York Times Upfront* v149 no7 p16 Ja 9 2017

Rothenberg, David

Barkskins color *Orion Magazine* v36 no1 p58 Ja/F 2017

Rothenberg, Mike

nology v33 no1 p47 Fall 2016

Rothy's (Company)

These Shoes Used to Be Water Bottles [Cover story] E. Velluto color *Glamour* v114 no11 p50 N 2016

Rotibi, Sammi

WELCOME TO MARS L. HILL color *Wired* v24 no11 p134 N 2016

Rotman, David

Capitalism Behaving Badly il *MIT Technology Review* v119 no6 p96 N/D 2016

DESKTOP METAL THINKS ITS MACHINES WILL GIVE DESIGNERS AND MANUFACTURERS A PRACTICAL AND AFFORDABLE WAY TO PRINT METAL PARTS [Cover story] chart color *MIT Technology Review* v120 no3 p42 My/Je 2017

HOTTER DAYS WILL DRIVE GLOBAL INEQUALITY graph map *MIT Technology Review* v120 no1 p60 Ja/F 2017

It Pays to Be Smart [Cover story] graph *MIT Technology Review* v120 no4 p54 Jl/Ag 2017

"The Relentless Pace of Automation" color graph *MIT Technology Review* v120 no2 p92 Mr/Ap 2017

Rotner, Shelley

Grow! Raise! Catch! C. Ash color *Science* v354 no6317 p1222 D 9 2016

Rotors—Evaluation

Products *Parks & Recreation* v52 no10 p56 O 2017

Rotskoff, Grant M.

Single-particle mapping of nonequilibrium nanocrystal transformations bibl bw graph *Science* v354 no6314 p874 N 18 2016

Rotter, Ron

MONEYGAMI G. WEBER *Washingtonian Magazine* v52 no4 p23 Ja 2017

Rottermann, Silke

Train for Your Horse's Pleasure [Cover story] color *Dressage Today* v23 no9 p30 Je 2017

Rottet Studio (Company)

Rottet Studio One Lux Studio D. Sokol color diag *Architectural Record* v205 no2 p112 F 2017

Röttger, Max

High-performance vitrimers from commodity thermoplastics through dioxaborolane metathesis color diag *Science* v356 no6333 p62 Ap 7 2017

Röttgering, H. J. A.

Molecular gas in the halo fuels the growth of a massive cluster galaxy at high redshift bibl graph *Science* v354 no6316 p1128 D 2 2016

Rottman, Carol J.

POWER [Cover story] color *Christian Century* v134 no1 p22 Ja 4 2017

Rottman, Christina—Interviews

ALL DRESSED UP D. A. Keeps color *House Beautiful* v159 no8 p104 O 2017

Rottweiler dog

Amazing Animals A. PRESSNER color map *National Geographic Kids* no471 p12 Je/Jl 2017

Rouault, Georges, 1871-1958—Exhibitions

A Rebel's Faith L. D. ALSPAUGH bw *Weekly Standard* v22 no34 p45 My 15 2017

Rouault, Hervé

Ring attractor dynamics in the Drosophila central brain diag graph *Science* v356 no6340 p849 My 26 2017

Self-organized Notch dynamics generate stereotyped sensory organ patterns in Drosophila color *Science* v356 no6337 p501 My 5 2017

ROUCO, CARLOS

New Zealand Shouldn't Ignore Feral Cats *BioScience* v67 no8 p686 Ag 2017

Roudinesco, Élisabeth

The Doctor Is In G. A. HORNSTEIN bw color *Weekly Standard* v22 no19 p30 Ja 23 2017

FREUD B. BETHUNE bw *Maclean's* v129 no50 p60 D 19 2016

Freud: What's Left? F. Crews bw *New York Review of Books* v64 no3 p6 F 23 2017

A WHOLE CLIMATE S. MOYN bw *Nation* v33 no21 p25 N 21 2016

Rough Night (Film)

Rough Night L. Greenblatt color *Entertainment Weekly* no1471 p51 Je 23 2017

SLAY, GIRL, SLAY J. Black color *Esquire* p29 Je/Jl 2017

Roughead, Gary

How to Sustain Our Military *Hoover Digest: Research & Opinion on Public Policy* no4 p90 Fall 2016

Roughgarden, Joan

HOW DO YOU HOLD TOGETHER YOUR TRANS IDENTITY AND YOUR LIFE OF FAITH? color *Christian Century* v134 no2 p22 Ja 18 2017

Roulet, E.

Observation of a large-scale anisotropy in the arrival directions of cosmic rays above 8×1018 eV *Science* v357 no6357 p1266 S 22 2017

Roulet, Thomas

What a Study of French Auditors Shows About Homophobia at Work *Harvard Business Review Digital Articles* p2 Mr 29 2017

When Corporate Philanthropy Makes the Recipient Look Bad *Harvard Business Review Digital Articles* p2 Ag 24 2016

Roulin, Alexandre

The biology of color color *Science* v357 no6350 p470 Ag 4 2017

Round, Ekaterina

Mechanism of transmembrane signaling by sensor histidine kinases color *Science* v356 no6342 p1043 Je 9 2017

Round Trip (Music)

Round Trip/Ternion Quartet Y. Kato color *Downbeat* v84 no9 p65 S 2017

Roundabout, The (Theatrical production)

GOINGS ON ABOUT TOWN bw *New Yorker* v93 no28 p4 S 18 2017

Roundell, Lara

Fashion HOUSE H. Bowles bw color *Vogue* v207 no4 p212 Ap 2017

Rountree, Alicia

A FASHIONABLE ESCAPE L. Christensen color *Harper's Bazaar* no3653 p280 My 2017

ROUNTREE, SAGE

JIFFY MOVES color *Runner's World* v52 no8 p22 S 2017

Rouse, Doug

UNSOLICITED BETA color *Climbing* no349 p8 N 2016

Rousey, Ronda, 1987-

Fading Fast L. J. Wertheim and T. Keith color *Sports Illustrated* v127 no1 p14 Jl 3 2017

ROUSH, ANDREW

Forecast *Texas Monthly* v45 no3 p190 Mr 2017

THE UNDERDOG'S ON TOP *Texas Monthly* v45 no3 p112 Mr 2017

ROUSH, MATT

Adam West (1928-2017) *TV Guide* v65 no27 p3 Je 26 2017

Alan Thicke: 1947-2016 *TV Guide* v65 no2 p10 Ja 2 2017

American Gods *TV Guide* v65 no19 p18 My 1 2017

The Americans *TV Guide* v65 no23 p13 My 29 2017

America's top TV critic Matt Roush answers your burning questions color *TV Guide* v64 no42 p6 O 10 2016

America's top TV critic Matt Roush answers your burning questions color *TV Guide* v65 no7 p5 F 13 2017

America's top TV critic Matt Roush answers your burning questions *TV Guide* p6 D 19 2016

America's top TV critic Matt Roush answers your burning questions *TV Guide* v65 no13 p4 Mr 20 2017

America's top TV critic Matt Roush answers your burning questions *TV Guide* v65 no21 p5 My 15 2017

America's top TV critic Matt Roush answers your burning questions *TV Guide* v65 no27 p2 Je 26 2017

America's top TV critic Matt Roush answers your burning questions *TV Guide* v65 no31 p2 Jl 24 2017

Ask Matt *TV Guide* v64 no46 p5 N 7 2016

Ask Matt *TV Guide* v65 no11 p4 Mr 6 2017

THE BEST ON THE BEAT *TV Guide* v65 no8 p21 F 27 2017

THE BEST TV OF 2016 [Cover story] *TV Guide* p20 D 19 2016

Broadchurch: The detective drama goes out on an emotional high *TV Guide* v65 no27 p12 Je 26 2017

CARRIE FISHER *TV Guide* v65 no4 p14 Ja 16 2017

Chuck Barris 1929-2017 *TV Guide* v65 no14 p13 Ap 3 2017

Confirmation *TV Guide* v64 no15 p20 Ap 4 2016

The Crown *TV Guide* v64 no46 p12 N 7 2016

DALL *New York Times Book Review* p15 Mr 5 2017

Rovenich, Hanna

The receptor kinase FER is a RALF-regulated scaffold controlling plant immune signaling graph *Science* v355 no6322 p287 Ja 20 2017

Rovenstine, Dalene

THE 22-WORD REVIEW color *Entertainment Weekly* no1476 p50 Ag 4 2017

5 — KEVIN'S INTERVIEW *Entertainment Weekly* no1444/1445 p60 D 16 2016

American Housewife *Entertainment Weekly* no1482/1483 p79 S 22 2017

The Blacklist color *Entertainment Weekly* no1482/1483 p74 S 22 2017

Broad City color *Entertainment Weekly* no1482/1483 p79 S 22 2017

Chicago P.D *Entertainment Weekly* no1482/1483 p79 S 22 2017

Criminal Minds color *Entertainment Weekly* no1482/1483 p79 S 22 2017

DEMI MOORE OF Empire color *Entertainment Weekly* no1482/1483 p78 S 22 2017

Designated Survivor color *Entertainment Weekly* no1482/1483 p74 S 22 2017

Dynasty color *Entertainment Weekly* no1482/1483 p76 S 22 2017

FIXER UPPER FILL-INS TO FLIP OVER color *Entertainment Weekly* no1486 p51 O 13 2017

The Goldbergs color *Entertainment Weekly* no1482/1483 p74 S 22 2017

Hot Date *Entertainment Weekly* no1482/1483 p74 S 22 2017

Law & Order: Special Victims Unit *Entertainment Weekly* no1482/1483 p75 S 22 2017

Modern Family *Entertainment Weekly* no1482/1483 p75 S 22 2017

Mr. Robot color *Entertainment Weekly* no1482/1483 p77 S 22 2017

Riverdale color *Entertainment Weekly* no1482/1483 p68 S 22 2017

SEAL Team color *Entertainment Weekly* no1482/1483 p76 S 22 2017

The Shannara Chronicles *Entertainment Weekly* no1482/1483 p79 S 22 2017

Speechless color *Entertainment Weekly* no1482/1483 p75 S 22 2017

Star color *Entertainment Weekly* no1482/1483 p76 S 22 2017

Survivor: Heroes vs. Healers vs. Hustlers *Entertainment Weekly* no1482/1483 p75 S 22 2017

What to Watch color *Entertainment Weekly* no1440 p52 N 18 2016

What to Watch color *Entertainment Weekly* no1472 p54 Je 30 2017

Rover, Kristin

Catching Up With Olympian Lucy Davis *In Stride* v12 no1 p46 Ja 2017

CORE Clinics *In Stride* v11 no6 p43 N 2016

The EAP Regionals Open Eyes--and Doors--Throughout the Country *In Stride* v12 no5 p27 S 2017

Getting to Know Your Zone Committee Chairs *In Stride* v12 no2 p39 Mr 2017

Hunter Championships Conclude in the North *In Stride* v11 no6 p47 N 2016

Karen Golding Is a Steward for the Horse: This horse show icon believes that safeguarding equine welfare is her No. 1 priority as a steward *In Stride* v12 no3 p37 My 2017

Rover automobile—Evaluation

Suburban Safari D. Pund color *Car & Driver* v62 no11 p98 My 2017

Rovero, A. C.

Observation of a large-scale anisotropy in the arrival directions of cosmic rays above 8 × 1018 eV *Science* v357 no6357 p1266 S 22 2017

Rovero, Francesco

Positive biodiversity-productivity relationship predominant in global forests bibl chart graph map *Science* v354 no6309 paaf8957-1 O 14 2016

Roving vehicles (Astronautics)

Scientists, visionaries, evangelists, dreamers color *National Geographic* v232 no2 p30 Ag 2017

Shoot for the moon. Again S. Howe Verhovek color diag *National Geographic* v232 no2 p32 Ag 2017

Rovira, Miguel

Tissue damage and senescence provide critical signals for cellular reprogramming in vivo bibl chart graph *Science* v354 no6315 paaf4445-1 N 25 2016

Rovzar, Chris

Tegan Passalacqua color *Bloomberg Businessweek* no4533 p64 Ag 7 2017

Row house remodeling

THE FORMAL FAÇADE IMPROVED R. Olsen color *Old House Journal* v45 no5 p32 Ag 2017

Row houses

STRATEGIST img *New York* v49 no21 p73 O 17 2016

The Urbanist: The Rise of the Frankenmansion S. J. ROBLEDO img *New York* v49 no24 p41 N 28 2016

Row houses—Design & construction

Wish Fulfillment S. COCHRAN color *Architectural Digest* v74 no1 p84 Ja 2017

Row houses—Interior decoration

A VERY CHARLOTTE CHRISTMAS K. O'SHEA-EVANS color *House Beautiful* v158 no10 p54 D 2016/Ja 2017

Rowan, Andrew

Origins of lymphatic and distant metastases in human colorectal cancer diag graph *Science* v357 no6346 p55 Jl 7 2017

Rowan & Martin's Laugh-In (TV program)

GOLDIE Hawn L. Bans color *GQ: Gentlemen's Quarterly* v97 no6 p124 Je 2017

Rowbotham, Ian

Hydraulic control of tuna fins: A role for the lymphatic system in vertebrate locomotion color *Science* v357 no6348 p310 Jl 21 2017

Rowbotham, Sheila

The First Hippies J. MILLER *In These Times* v41 no1 p41 Ja 2017

MORE THAN FREE LOVE AND SANDALS: The lives of six Victorian radicals shed light on the struggle to establish feminism, social reform and the Labour movement P. Thane *History Today* v67 no7 p102 Jl 2017

Rowden, John

CALL OF THE WILD M. OZAWA color *Martha Stewart Living* p40 Mr 2017

Rowe, Barbara Kieffer

PAINTING AN ANCIENT WORLD *South Dakota Magazine* v32 no6 p43 Mr/Ap 2017

Rowe, Christopher

Telling the Map *Publishers Weekly* v264 no22 p38 My 29 2017

Rowe, Claudia

The Spider and the Fly: A Reporter, a Serial Killer, and the Meaning of Murder *Publishers Weekly* v263 no47 p100 N 21 2016

Rowe, Josephine

Wrinkles in Time: In small-town Australia, a Vietnam veteran disappears as his family struggles with intergenerational trauma S. HUNT *New York Times Book Review* p20 O 8 2017

Rowe, Maggie

Sin Bravely: A Memoir of Spiritual Disobedience T. Peters *Christian Century* v134 no9 p34 Ap 26 2017

ROWE, MIKE

What I Learned AT MY Summer Job cartoon *Popular Mechanics* p64 Je 2017

ROWE, SIMON

Chords & Discords bw *Downbeat* v83 no12 p10 D 2016

Rowe, Wendy

Mixing Bowl color *O, The Oprah Magazine* p110 Ja 2017

ROWEN, BEN

The End of Forgetting color *Atlantic* v319 no5 p24 Je 2017

Losers, Weepers cartoon *Atlantic* v318 no4 p33 N 2016

A Resort for the Apocalypse bw cartoon color diag map *Atlantic* v319 no2 p30 Mr 2017

What's Normal? cartoon *Atlantic* v320 no4 p28 N 2017

Rowen, John

Owls *New York State Conservationist* v71 no4 p32 F 2017

Rower, Alexander S. C.

Family Circus bw *Art in America* v104 no10 p79 N 2016

Rowin, Michael Joshua

Color Box bw *Film Comment* v53 no2 p77 Mr/Ap 2017

EVERYTHING ALL AT ONCE bw color *Film Comment* v53 no3

p48 My/Je 2017

Head On bw *Film Comment* v53 no1 p92 Ja/F 2017

Land of Mine color *Film Comment* v53 no1 p86 Ja/F 2017

Memory Bank color *Film Comment* v53 no4 p34 Jl/Ag 2017

Metaphors on Vision bw *Film Comment* v53 no5 p78 S/O 2017

Slacker color *Film Comment* v53 no1 p63 Ja/F 2017

Rowing—Physiological aspects

Row bots Boucher, R. Labbé et al *Physics Today* v70 no6 p82 Je 2017

Rowitch, David H.

Extensive migration of young neurons into the infant human frontal lobe color diag graph *Science* v354 no6308 paaf7073-1 O 7 2016

Rowland, Deborah

Leading Across Cultures Requires Flexibility and Curiosity *Harvard Business Review Digital Articles* p2 My 30 2016

What's Worse than a Difficult Conversation? Avoiding One *Harvard Business Review Digital Articles* p2 Ap 8 2016

Rowland, Hannah M.

The biology of color color *Science* v357 no6350 p470 Ag 4 2017

Rowland, Ingrid D.

The Long Reach of Rome cartoon *New York Review of Books* v64 no7 p16 Ap 20 2017

Martin Luther's Burning Questions [Cover story] color *New York Review of Books* v64 no10 p10 Je 8 2017

Robert B. Silvers (1929–2017) [Cover story] bw color *New York Review of Books* v64 no8 p31 My 11 2017

The Virtuoso of Compassion [Cover story] bw color *New York Review of Books* v64 no8 p8 My 11 2017

Rowland, Julie

Complex multifault rupture during the 2016 Mw 7.8 Kaikōura earthquake, New Zealand color map *Science* v356 no6334 p154 Ap 14 2017

ROWLAND, KATHERINE

QUEST FOR FIRE: FEMALE DESIRE IS ONE OF THE MOST ELUSIVE FACETS OF HUMAN BEHAVIOR--AND ITS ABSENCE IS WOMEN'S MOST COMMON SEXUAL COMPLAINT. CAN SCIENCE FIGURE OUT HOW TO IGNITE IT? *Psychology Today* v50 no5 p62 S/O 2017

Rowland, Kelly, 1981-

No Child's Play N. HEMPHILL REEDER color *Ebony* v72 no8 p62 Je 2017

Rowland, Laura Joh

The Ripper's Shadow: A Victorian Mystery *Publishers Weekly* v263 no43 p58 O 24 2016

Rowland, Megan M.

Structural basis for antibody-mediated neutralization of Lassa virus [Cover story] color diag *Science* v356 no6341 p923 Je 1 2017

Rowland, Robin

Unfinished Business *MHQ: Quarterly Journal of Military History* v30 no1 p12 Aut 2017

Rowlands, Kate

Resistance to malaria through structural variation of red blood cell invasion receptors diag *Science* v356 no6343 p1139 Je 16 2017

Rowling, J. K., 1965-

CONVERSATION A. WILSON color *Forbes* v200 no4 p32 O 24 2017

Hogwarts in America A. H. Sturgis color *Reason* v48 no7 p48 D 2016

J.K. ROWLING M. Snetiker color *Entertainment Weekly* no1444/1445 p23 D 16 2016

Preserving The Magic D. P. DEAVEL and C. J. DEAVEL color *National Review* v69 no4 p45 Mr 6 2017

Sales Recover from Potter Curse, Hold Even in the Week chart *Publishers Weekly* v264 no34 p8 Ag 21 2017

Wizards in New York B. F. Jones color *Christian Century* v133 no26 p44 D 21 2016

Rowling, J. K., 1965—Finance

BOOKING IT H. CUCCINELLO, N. ROBEHMED et al color *Forbes* v200 no2 p22 S 5 2017

ROY, ADAM

ESSENTIALS bw color *Backpacker* p93 N 2017

Roy, Anuradha

An Illicit Past M. SURI color *New York Times Book Review* p9 S 25 2016

Roy, Arundhati, 1946-

Arundhati Roy's Fascinating Mess P. SEHGAL color *Atlantic* v320 no1 p36 Jl/Ag 2017

CIVIL WARS J. ACOCELLA bw cartoon color *New Yorker* v93 no16 p98 Je 5 2017

Come Together K. Mahajan *New York Times Book Review* p1 Je 11 2017

INDIAN SUMMER D. Beal color *Vogue* v207 no6 p130 Je 2017

The Passion and Rage of Arundhati Roy F. Prose color *New York Review of Books* v64 no12 p16 Jl 13 2017

Roy's Return to Form S. Begley color *Time* v189 no22 p50 Je 12 2017

Worth the Wait R. Boyagoda color *Commonweal* v114 no14 p35 S 8 2017

Roy, Avik

The Doomsayer M. BALL cartoon *Atlantic* v318 no4 p24 N 2016

Roy, Brett A.—Trials, litigation, etc.

Fateful Dive into 'Closed' Park Pond J. C. Kozlowski *Parks & Recreation* v51 no12 p20 D 2016

Roy, Dheeraj S.

Engrams and circuits crucial for systems consolidation of a memory diag *Science* v356 no6333 p73 Ap 7 2017

Ventral CA1 neurons store social memory bibl graph *Science* v353 no6307 p1536 S 30 2016

ROY, HELEN E.

Scientific and Normative Foundations for the Valuation of Alien-Species Impacts: Thirteen Core Principles *BioScience* v67 no2 p166 F 2017

Roy, Mark

CANADIAN PRCA WORLD CHAMPIONS bw *Spin to Win Rodeo* v20 no12 p96 F 2017

Roy, Noah C.

Restoring auditory cortex plasticity in adult mice by restricting thalamic adenosine signaling graph *Science* v356 no6345 p1352 Je 30 2017

Roy, Olivier

Political Islam After the Arab Spring color *Foreign Affairs* v96 no6 p127 N/D 2017

ROY, SANHITHA SINHA

BEHIND THE SCENES bw color *In These Times* v40 no11 p48 N 2016

Roy, Stéphanie

The DNA methyltransferase DNMT3C protects male germ cells from transposon activity bibl diag graph *Science* v354 no6314 p909 N 18 2016

Royal, Cindy

SCHOOL OF JOURNALISM AND MASS COMMUNICATION TAKES DIGITAL MEDIA TO NEW HEIGHTS *Texas Monthly* v44 no11 p46 N 2016

Royal, Leslie E.

LOVE LIKE A WOMAN color *Essence* v47 no7 p101 N 2016

ROCK YOUR ROAD TRIP color *Essence* v47 no12 p123 Ap 2017

ROYAL, MARIAN

The Question *O, The Oprah Magazine* p18 S 2017

Royal Blues (Music)

DRAGONETTE DANCE THE PAIN AWAY N. Feeney color *Entertainment Weekly* no1440 p59 N 18 2016

Royal Canadian Geographical Society

THE 2015 RCGS HONOUREES color *Canadian Geographic* v135 no6 p79 D 2015

2016 RCGS MEDALLISTS H. Wilson color *Canadian Geographic* v136 no6 p76 D 2016

ATTENBOROUGH AWARDED RCGS GOLD A. Pope color *Canadian Geographic* v137 no3 p73 My 2017

BEST OF THE 2016 RCGS AWARDS AND FELLOWS DINNER A. Pope color *Canadian Geographic* v137 no1 p75 F 2017

Bird of a Nation D. Bird color *Canadian Wildlife* v23 no1 p40 Mr/Ap 2017

Confluence of history A. Pope color map *Canadian Geographic* v137 no4 p26 Jl/Ag 2017

THE EXPEDITIONS J. Heinerth, N. Martinez et al color map *Canadian Geographic* v137 no4 p49 Jl/Ag 2017

FEATURED FELLOW: JESSICA LINDSAY PHILLIPS J. Pearce color *Canadian Geographic* v137 no4 p78 Jl/Ag 2017

A NEW HOME FOR THE RCGS: 50 SUSSEX N. Walker color

Rubin, Mark A.
SOX2 promotes lineage plasticity and antiandrogen resistance in TP53- and RB1-deficient prostate cancer bibl graph *Science* v355 no6320 p1 Ja 6 2017

RUBIN, MICHAEL
Turkey's Coming Chaos color *National Review* v69 no11 p27 Je 12 2017
Turkey's Reichstag Fire: Explaining Erdogan's long game *Commentary* v142 no2 p46 S 2016

RUBIN, NEAL S.
Sport Promoting Human Development and Well-Being: Psychological Components of Sustainability *UN Chronicle* v53 no2 p30 2016

RUBIN, PETER
Bad Puns Are How Eye Roll color *Reader's Digest* v190 no1135 p108 N 2017

Rubin, Robert Melvin
What About Bob? M. Bamberger color *Golf Magazine* v59 no2 p104 F 2017

Rubin, Robert S.
Research: We're Not Very Self-Aware, Especially at Work *Harvard Business Review Digital Articles* p2 Mr 12 2015

Rubin, Tibor, 1929-2015
Valor The Selfless Survivor J. Guttman bw color *Military History* v34 no1 p16 My 2017

Rubin, Vera C., 1928-2016
1986: Washington, DC V. Rubin *Lapham's Quarterly* v10 no2 p51 Spr 2017
HOMO FABER L. H. Lapham *Lapham's Quarterly* v10 no2 p13 Spr 2017
SOCIETY UPDATE A. Yeager bw color *Science News* v191 no3 p30 F 18 2017
Vera Cooper Rubin (1928—2016) C. M. Urry bw *Science* v355 no6324 p462 F 3 2017
Vera Cooper Rubin N. A. Bahcall *Physics Today* v70 no3 p73 Mr 2017
Vera Rubin's Universe A. Yeager bw color graph *Sky & Telescope* v134 no2 p36 Ag 2017
Vera Rubin was a pioneer in dark matter research bw *Astronomy* v45 no4 p19 Ap 2017

Rubini, Julie
How "Claire's Day" Began L. VACCARIELLO *Reader's Digest* v188 no1125 p35 N 2016

Rubin Museum of Art (New York, N.Y.)
SONIC HEALING A. Russell cartoon *New Yorker* v93 no20 p26 Jl 10 2017

Rubino, Francesco
OPERATION: DIABETES color *Scientific American* v317 no1 p60 Jl 2017

Rubino, Michael
Ad Nauseam *Indianapolis Monthly* p12 F 2017
Ben Higgins Reality Star *Indianapolis Monthly* v40 no3 p62 N 2016
The Best Medicine *Indianapolis Monthly* p12 N 2017
BEST NEW Breweries *Indianapolis Monthly* v40 no11 p57 Jl 2017
Better With Age *Indianapolis Monthly* v40 no11 p10 Jl 2017
Bon Appétit *Indianapolis Monthly* p10 My 2017
Change of Pace *Indianapolis Monthly* p12 Ap 2017
First Things First *Indianapolis Monthly* v40 no7 p14 Mr 2017
Flexing His Muscle: Can Ah-nold create buzz around one of Indiana's most neglected issues come November 22? *Indianapolis Monthly* p20 N 2017
The HOOSIER KITCHEN *Indianapolis Monthly* v12 no40 p60 Ag 2017
Old Favorites *Indianapolis Monthly* v42 no2 p10 O 2017
ON A FIRST DATE *Indianapolis Monthly* p65 F 2017
Parental Guidance *Indianapolis Monthly* v40 no4 p12 D 2016
Rachael Heger Do-gooder *Indianapolis Monthly* v40 no4 p60 D 2016
Reel Talk *Indianapolis Monthly* v41 no2 p14 S 2017
ROLL CALL: Reporting for duty: I tracked down a long-lost IM recipe *Indianapolis Monthly* v12 no40 p73 Ag 2017
Room for Debate *Indianapolis Monthly* v40 no5 p8 Ja 2017
Sorry Not Sorry *Indianapolis Monthly* v12 no40 p10 Ag 2017
TOP PICKS *Indianapolis Monthly* v12 no40 p62 Ag 2017

Worried Sick *Indianapolis Monthly* v40 no3 p12 N 2016

Rubins, Daniel
Systemic pan-AMPK activator MK-8722 improves glucose homeostasis but induces cardiac hypertrophy graph *Science* v357 no6350 p507 Ag 4 2017

Rubinstein, Helena
BEAUTY QUEEN BEES J. Thurman cartoon *New Yorker* v93 no8 p21 Ap 10 2017

Rubinstein, Raphael
BERRY HORTON color *Art in America* v104 no10 p156 N 2016
Bertha and Karl Leubsdorf Art Gallery color *Art in America* v105 no1 p84 Ja 2017
POEMS WITHOUT WORDS cartoon color *Art in America* v105 no4 p94 Ap 2017

RUBIO, MARCO
IF THIS BODY LOSES THE ABILITY TO DEBATE, THEN WHERE IS THAT GOING TO HAPPEN? *Vital Speeches of the Day* v83 no4 p134 Ap 2017
Proverbial Politics color *Weekly Standard* v22 no43 p3 Jl 24 2017

Rubio, Ricky—Interviews
WORDS WITH... Ricky Rubio A. Sharp and T. Keith color *Sports Illustrated* v126 no3 p20 Ja 23 2017

Ruby, Jeff
BEST NEW RESTAURANTS color *Chicago* v66 no5 p80 My 2017
CAKES, PASTRIES, PIES, COOKIES, HOT FUDGE, GALATO, BROWNIES & MORE! chart color *Chicago* v65 no11 p70 N 2016
CALCULATED RISK color *Chicago* v66 no10 p56 O 2017
DIM SUM STAR color *Chicago* v66 no4 p60 Ap 2017
GEM IN THE ROUGH color *Chicago* v66 no2 p54 F 2017
HEAR THEM ROAR color *Chicago* v66 no6 p52 Je 2017
#King Of The Mitzvahs bw color *Chicago* v66 no8 p80 Ag 2017
MEAT OR VEG color *Chicago* v66 no3 p70 Mr 2017
REVIEWS: FIRST IMPRESSIONS color *Chicago* v66 no9 p70 S 2017
SHARPEN YOUR KNIVES [Cover story] color *Chicago* v66 no11 p60 N 2017
SMALLVILLE color *Chicago* v65 no11 p62 N 2016
SPLIT DECISION color *Chicago* v66 no7 p46 Jl 2017
SUSHI FOR ADULTS color *Chicago* v66 no8 p60 Ag 2017
UPSTAIRS, DOWNSTAIRS color *Chicago* v65 no12 p68 D 2016
WHY We LOVE CHICAGO bw cartoon color *Chicago* v66 no3 p75 Mr 2017
WINGS OF DESIRE color *Chicago* v66 no1 p64 Ja 2017

Ruby, Laura
Secrets of the Metropolis: Set in a steampunk version of New York, this novel sends precocious twins back in time to solve a puzzle and save the city J. STEPHENS *New York Times Book Review* p21 My 14 2017

Ruby Princess Runs Away, The (Film)
CLIMB ABOARD, YE WHO SEEK THE TRUTH! B. DICKEY color *Popular Mechanics* p84 S 2017

Rucc, March
The Mayo Clinic Model for Running a Value-Improvement Program *Harvard Business Review Digital Articles* p2 O 22 2015

Ruchon, T.
Attosecond dynamics through a Fano resonance: Monitoring the birth of a photoelectron bibl graph *Science* v354 no6313 p734 N 11 2016

Ruchti, Cynthia
As My Parents Age: Reflections on Life, Love, and Change *Publishers Weekly* v264 no15 p67 Ap 10 2017

Ruck, James
Love in an Age of Alzheimer's color *America* v216 no6 p32 Mr 20 2017

Ruck, Rebecca T.
A multifunctional catalyst that stereoselectively assembles prodrugs diag *Science* v356 no6336 p426 Ap 28 2017

Ruckelshaus, Mary
Toward a national, sustained U.S. ecosystem assessment bibl color *Science* v354 no6314 p838 N 18 2016

Rucki, Agnieszka A.
Mismatch repair deficiency predicts response of solid tumors to PD-1 blockade chart graph *Science* v357 no6349 p409 Jl 28 2017

Rudan, Pavao

Neandertal and Denisovan DNA from Pleistocene sediments bw color *Science* v356 no6338 p605 My 12 2017

Rudas, A.

Persistent effects of pre-Columbian plant domestication on Amazonian forest composition bibl chart graph map *Science* v355 no6328 p925 Mr 3 2017

RUDD, ETHAN

DOG DAZE *Cincinnati Magazine* v50 no10 p52 Jl 2017

RUDD, MURRAY A.

Ocean Research Priorities: Similarities and Differences among Scientists, Policymakers, and Fishermen in the United States *BioScience* v67 no5 p418 My 2017

Rudd, Paul, 1969-

Jake Tapper: So, how'd you get so fit? D. WALTERS color *Bon Appetit* no8 p106 Ag 2017

Paul Rudd Was a Nightmare in Bridesmaids N. Sperling color *Entertainment Weekly* no1460/1461 p94 Ap 7-17 2017

Ruddy, Erin Zammett

75 ways to be a grown-up *Parents* v91 no11 p95 N 2016

avoid the homework trap *Parents* v91 no9 p96 S 2016

believe *Parents* v91 no12 p82 D 2016

pants on fire color graph *Parents* v92 no8 p56 Ag 2017

Solve My Screen-Time Skirmishes color graph *Parents* v92 no9 p56 S 2017

Ruddy, Michael

Emergence and spread of a human-transmissible multidrug-resistant nontuberculous mycobacterium bibl diag graph *Science* v354 no6313 p751 N 11 2016

Rude, Janice

JANICE RUDE and PRENTISS WILLSON color *AARP: The Magazine* v59 no2A p48 F/Mr 2016

RUDEBUSCH, FAITH

The Vole's Fate: Eat and Be Eaten *Idaho Magazine* v16 no11 p20 Ag 2017

Ruden, Sarah

Ancient Identities color *Commonweal* v144 no16 p31 O 6 2017

Books for Children: A Symposium *National Review* v69 no19 p48 O 16 2017

The Face of Water: A Translator on Beauty and Meaning in the Bible J. C. Howell color *Christian Century* v134 no15 p36 Jl 19 2017

Feast of Eden: A look at humanity's most famous star-crossed couple *American Scholar* v86 no4 p122 Aut 2017

Shop Talk J. Miles bw *Commonweal* v144 no12 p31 Jl 7 2017

Slaves Are Catching Our Shrimp color *Commonweal* v144 no13 p8 Ag 11 2017

Unreal Fictions color *National Review* v68 no24 p41 D 31 2016

Voice of Anger color *National Review* v68 no23 p39 D 19 2016

The Word And Its Words N. FRANKOVICH color *National Review* v69 no8 p38 My 2017

Ruder, Chris—Interviews

An Old Game Gets a Do-Over P. MERTZ ESSWEIN color *Kiplinger's Personal Finance* v71 no8 p20 Ag 2017

RUDICK, JENNIFER ASH

SEASIDE BOHEMIA color *Architectural Digest* v74 no7 p36 Jl 2017

Rudik, D.

Observation of coherent elastic neutrino-nucleus scattering diag *Science* v357 no6356 p1123 S 15 2017

Rudisill, Shelley

Cooking Up New Ideas S. M. Mullins *Cincinnati Magazine* v50 no8 p83 My 2017

Rudner, David Z.

Bacillus subtilis SMC complexes juxtapose chromosome arms as they travel from origin to terminus bibl graph *Science* v355 no6324 p524 F 3 2017

RUDNICK, PAUL

JARED & IVANKA'S GUIDE TO MINDFUL MARRIAGE cartoon *New Yorker* v93 no17 p29 Je 19 2017

MELANIA'S DIARY 1/21/2017 cartoon *New Yorker* v92 no48 p27 F 6 2017

Rudnicki, Chris

How Companies Can Help Rebuild America's Common Resources *Harvard Business Review Digital Articles* p2 S 21 2015

Rudolph, Amelia

WHERE ARE YOU GOING? color *O, The Oprah Magazine* p116 O 2017

Rudolph, Ileane

18 YEARS... 400 EPISODES... ONE UNSTOPPABLE FRANCHISE! [Cover story] *TV Guide* v65 no4 p18 Ja 16 2017

60 Minutes Turns 50 *TV Guide* v65 no41 p4 O 2 2017

ALL GEARED UP *TV Guide* p36 D 5 2016

Bates Motel color *TV Guide* v65 no7 p40 F 13 2017

Billions *TV Guide* v65 no2 p38 Ja 2 2017

The Blacklist *TV Guide* p37 Ap 17 2017

The Blacklist *TV Guide* v65 no19 p31 My 1 2017

Black Sails *TV Guide* v65 no4 p40 Ja 16 2017

Blue Bloods *TV Guide* v65 no19 p26 My 1 2017

Broadchurch *TV Guide* v65 no27 p29 Je 26 2017

Chicago Fire's Severide in Custody! *TV Guide* p13 D 19 2016

Chicago Fire *TV Guide* v65 no43 p34 O 16 2017

Chicago P.D.'s New Detective *TV Guide* v65 no19 p10 My 1 2017

CHICAGO P.D *TV Guide* v65 no39 p44 S 18 2017

Colony Is Back in Action *TV Guide* p12 D 5 2016

Colony *TV Guide* v65 no2 p27 Ja 2 2017

Diana and the Paparazzi/Diana: The Day We Said Goodbye *TV Guide* v65 no35 p30 Ag 21 2017

DOLLY'S TRUE COLORS *TV Guide* v64 no48 p28 N 21 2016

EDIE FALCO *TV Guide* v65 no37 p28 S 4 2017

Election 2016: Winners & Losers *TV Guide* v64 no46 p6 N 7 2016

Elementary color *TV Guide* v64 no42 p40 O 10 2016

ERIC KRIPKE AND SHAWN RYAN *TV Guide* v65 no6 p10 Ja 30 2017

FIRST LOOKS: Cranston in Charge *TV Guide* v65 no2 p12 Ja 2 2017

Flint *TV Guide* v65 no43 p38 O 16 2017

FROM THE PAGE TO THE SCREEN: True Blood and Midnight, Texas author Charlaine Harris shares what it's like to see her beloved characters on TV *TV Guide* v65 no31 p12 Jl 24 2017

The Future of Fox News *TV Guide* v65 no19 p16 My 1 2017

Genius *TV Guide* v65 no13 p32 Mr 20 2017

THE GOOD DOCTOR *TV Guide* v65 no37 p24 S 4 2017

GOOD GIRL GONE BAD *TV Guide* v64 no46 p22 N 7 2016

The GOOD LIFE color *TV Guide* v65 no7 p30 F 13 2017

The Heat Is On *TV Guide* p20 Ap 17 2017

High Times: Kathy Bates lights up talking about her new comedy, Disjointed *TV Guide* v65 no35 p3 Ag 21 2017

Homeland *TV Guide* v65 no11 p42 Mr 6 2017

Homeland *TV Guide* v65 no2 p24 Ja 2 2017

HOUSE OF LIES *TV Guide* v64 no15 p50 Ap 4 2016

"I Have Zero Doubt I Can Do This Job": Former Fox News anchor Megyn Kelly faces off against 60 Minutes and Kelly Ripa in her quest to take over both primetime and daytime with two new NBC shows *TV Guide* v65 no27 p14 Je 26 2017

IS TV NEWS TOO VIOLENT? *TV Guide* v65 no25 p6 Je 2017

JULIE PLEC *TV Guide* v65 no13 p11 Mr 20 2017

JUSTICE LEAGUE *TV Guide* v65 no8 p24 F 27 2017

KYRA SEDGWICK *TV Guide* v65 no37 p39 S 4 2017

The Last Ship's Captain Takes a Break *TV Guide* v65 no21 p11 My 15 2017

Law & Order: SVU *TV Guide* v65 no21 p39 My 15 2017

LAW & ORDER: SVU *TV Guide* v65 no39 p46 S 18 2017

LONG LIVE GAME SHOWS! color *TV Guide* v64 no42 p16 O 10 2016

Mac Attack! color *TV Guide* v64 no42 p11 O 10 2016

MACGYVER'S DYNAMIC DUO *TV Guide* v64 no46 p26 N 7 2016

MACGYVER *TV Guide* v65 no39 p52 S 18 2017

Meet the crew... *TV Guide* v64 no48 p12 N 21 2016

Megyn in the Morning: The former Fox News golden girl turned NBC multitasker hopes to rise--and shine--as her new a.m. talk show debuts *TV Guide* v65 no39 p10 S 18 2017

Midnight, Texas *TV Guide* v65 no23 p30 My 29 2017

Morning Glory *TV Guide* v65 no7 p20 F 13 2017

My Days in Morning *TV Guide* v65 no2 p16 Ja 2 2017

The Originals *TV Guide* v65 no25 p38 Je 2017

PIERCE BROSNAN GOES WEST *TV Guide* v65 no14 p20 Ap 3 2017

Politics = Big Ratings *TV Guide* v65 no11 p7 Mr 6 2017

Quantico *TV Guide* v65 no6 p36 Ja 30 2017

REAGAN REVISITED color *TV Guide* v64 no42 p26 O 10 2016

THE RIGHT PATH *TV Guide* v65 no6 p28 Ja 30 2017

Salvation *TV Guide* v65 no23 p23 My 29 2017

Season Finale Shockers! *TV Guide* v65 no25 p4 Je 2017

Snowfall *TV Guide* v65 no27 p33 Je 26 2017

Super Bowl Sunday Presidential Sit-Down *TV Guide* v65 no6 p11 Ja 30 2017

Taken *TV Guide* v65 no2 p36 Ja 2 2017

Timeless *TV Guide* p40 D 5 2016

Timeless *TV Guide* v65 no4 p34 Ja 16 2017

TONY BENNETT He's Still Got That SWING! *TV Guide* p32 D 19 2016

TRIBUTES *TV Guide* v65 no23 p11 My 29 2017

TV's HOTTEST COUPLES *TV Guide* v64 no15 p28 Ap 4 2016

The Vampire Diaries *TV Guide* v65 no11 p38 Mr 6 2017

Why Viewers Love True-Crime Shows *TV Guide* v64 no40 p10 O 3 2016

Rudolph, Jennifer

The China Questions: Critical Insights into a Rising Power *Publishers Weekly* v264 no41 p53 O 9 2017

Rudolph the Red Nosed Reindeer (TV program)

Athwart J. LILEKS il *National Review* v68 no24 p33 D 31 2016

Rudy, Bernardo

Layer-specific modulation of neocortical dendritic inhibition during active wakefulness bibl diag *Science* v355 no6328 p954 Mr 3 2017

Rue, George

DRAWN OUT K. Krichko il *Backpacker* v45 no1 p87 Ja 2017

RUECK, BEN

TWO TOWERS color *Climbing* no349 p58 N 2016

Ruefle, Mary

At Home in Her Range B. RATLIFF *New York Times Book Review* p17 Ja 15 2017

Ruehl, Mercedes

EDWARD ALBEE color *Entertainment Weekly* no1446/1447 p96 D 2016/Ja 2017

Ruehl, P.

Observation of a large-scale anisotropy in the arrival directions of cosmic rays above 8×1018 eV *Science* v357 no6357 p1266 S 22 2017

Ruelas-Gossi, Alejandro

4 Things Your Innovation Efforts Shouldn't Focus On *Harvard Business Review Digital Articles* p2 Ap 4 2017

Why Mexico's Economy Doesn't Depend on the Next U.S. President *Harvard Business Review Digital Articles* p2 N 9 2016

Ruf, Alois

ANGRY BIRD S. SMITH color *Road & Track* v68 no10 p72 Jl 2017

Ruf Automobile GmbH

ANGRY BIRD S. SMITH color *Road & Track* v68 no10 p72 Jl 2017

Rüffer, R.

Spectral narrowing of x-ray pulses for precision spectroscopy with nuclear resonances diag *Science* v357 no6349 p375 Jl 28 2017

Ruffin, Chad V.

Community network for deaf scientists color *Science* v356 no6336 p386 Ap 28 2017

Ruffin, Nicolas

Mapping the human DC lineage through the integration of high-dimensional techniques diag *Science* v356 no6342 p1044 Je 9 2017

Ruffin, Phil

THE PRESIDENT'S GAMBLING BUDDY D. ALEXANDER color *Forbes* v199 no3 p66 Mr 28 2017

Ruffini, Remo

REMO RUFFINI color *Esquire* v167 no1 p112 F 2017

Ruffino, Matthew

Ruffino Custom Closets P. Marquis *New Orleans Homes & Lifestyles* v20 no1 p95 Wint 2016

Ruffle, Libby

VESSELS OF THE GODS [Cover story] *History Today* v67 no5 p50 My 2017

RUFFNER, ZOE

Big SPLASH color *Vogue* v207 no6 p74 Je 2017

Model G color *Vogue* v207 no11 p159 N 2017

Rufty, Melissa

#5: In a classic Southern home, Melissa Rufty keeps the best of the

past while injecting chic colors and patterns—from cantaloupe walls to animal prints—that say, "This isn't your grandmother's house" M. READ color *House Beautiful* v159 no2 p116 Mr 2017

Rug design

Magic Carpets H. MARTIN color *Architectural Digest* v74 no10 p40 O 1 2017

Rugby football

GEORGIAN RUGBY UNiTES TO END VIOLENCE AGAINST WOMEN AND GIRLS I. JAPHARIDZE *UN Chronicle* v53 no2 p33 2016

Rugby football players

50 Reasons to Love Being 50+ G. Greenberg color *AARP: The Magazine* v60 no5A p57 Ag/S 2017

Rugby football players—Attitudes

RUGBY UNION J. Fuchs and T. Keith color *Sports Illustrated* v127 no8 p24 S 18 2017

Rugby football players—Physiology

Full-Body Fat Loss J. WUEBBEN color *Muscle & Performance* v9 no11 p20 N 2017

Rugby football teams

50 Reasons to Love Being 50+ G. Greenberg color *AARP: The Magazine* v60 no5A p57 Ag/S 2017

Rugby football teams—History

RUGBY UNION J. Fuchs and T. Keith color *Sports Illustrated* v127 no8 p24 S 18 2017

Ruger & Co. Inc.

RUGER LCP II Y. SUED and J. B. SNOW color *Outdoor Life* v224 no4 pP1 My 2017

Rüger, Jan

BLOW THE BLOODY PLACE UP! *History Today* v67 no8 p24 Ag 2017

Heligoland: Britain, Germany and the Struggle for the North Sea J. Callo *Military History* v34 no2 p73 Jl 2017

RUGGIERO, ANTHONY

Pyongyang's Playbook color *Weekly Standard* v23 no1 p14 S 11 2017

Ruggiero, Tony

POWER CORD color *Golf Magazine* v59 no7 p44 Jl 2017

Ruggles, Bonnie—Interviews

THE WAITING GAME J. WILLIAMS *Cincinnati Magazine* v50 no2 p59 N 2016

Rugs

COLOR REGAL PURPLES N. DAYTON *Better Homes & Gardens* v94 no11 p33 N 2016

curtains to carpets *Design Center Sourcebook* p68 2017

A Great Fall Makeover... in 5 Easy Steps V. DRORBAUGH *Better Homes & Gardens* v94 no11 p2 N 2016

How Can I Add Excitement to a Boxy, Bland Room? T. BROOKS and H. HUNT cartoon color *Chicago* v66 no4 p72 Ap 2017

WE ASKED THE PROS *Washingtonian Magazine* v52 no6 p160 Mr 2017

Rugs—Design & construction

Magic Carpets H. MARTIN color *Architectural Digest* no5 p37 My 2017

Rugs—Evaluation

2017'S HOTTEST COLOR COMBOS color *Good Housekeeping* v265 no5 p60A N 2017

Age of Opulence color *Architectural Digest* v74 no4 p46 Ap 2017

Do Look Down D. Selig color *Bloomberg Businessweek* no4495 p72 O 17 2016

Dreamy Headboard color *Good Housekeeping* v265 no5 p39 N 2017

Get in Line J. J. CONDON color *House Beautiful* v159 no4 p40 My 2017

GLOBAL DESIGNS color *Better Homes & Gardens* v95 no4 p8 Ap 2017

Lime Light color *Timber Home Living* v27 no5 p16 O 2017

Magic Carpets H. MARTIN color *Architectural Digest* no5 p37 My 2017

MUSEUM–WORTHY K. GIVEN color *Architectural Digest* v73 no12 p41 D 2016

OBSESSED WITH TRIM & TASSELS P. GUGLIELMETTI color *Better Homes & Gardens* v95 no10 p16 O 2017

shopping: Moody Blooms color *Architectural Digest* no11 p52 N 1 2017

TEXTILES cartoon color *Arts & Crafts Homes & the Revival* v12
no1 p14 2017 Resouce Guide
TROPICAL PUNCH color *Better Homes & Gardens* v95 no2 p24
F 2016

RUGY, VERONIQUE DE
CAN'T AFFORD A VACATION? BLAME THE STATE! color
Reason v49 no4 p10 Ag/S 2017

Rūhānī, Hasan, 1948-
Iran: Still Waiting for Democracy C. de Bellaigue color *New York
Review of Books* v64 no12 p25 Jl 13 2017
Misreporting Iran K. J. Torrance color *Weekly Standard* v22 no37
p16 Je 5 2017
Who's Who In Iran's Elections K. A. Serjoie color *Time* v189
no19 p11 My 22 2017

RUHE, PIERRE
A POWERFUL VOICE *Atlanta* v56 no7 p42 N 2016

Ruhl, J. B.
Harnessing legal complexity diag graph *Science* v355 no6332
p1377 Mr 31 2017

Ruhl, Sarah
First Star to the Right H. Als cartoon *New Yorker* v93 no27 p14
S 11 2017

Ruhle, Stephanie
LIFE IS NOT FAIR S. RUHLE *Vital Speeches of the Day* v83 no8
p248 Ag 2017

Ruhlman, Michael
CUBA FEASTS color *Conde Nast Traveler* v52 no9 p100 O 2017
How to Grill Every Meal bw color *Men's Health* v32 no5 p72
Je 2017
José Andrés *Humanities* v37 no4 p1 Fall 2016
Paper, Plastic—or prime? V. MATUS color *Weekly Standard* v23
no1 p38 S 11 2017

Ruhn, Kelly A.
The intestinal microbiota regulates body composition through
NFIL3 and the circadian clock diag *Science* v357 no6354 p912
S 1 2017
Paneth cells secrete lysozyme via secretory autophagy during bac-
terial infection of the intestine color diag *Science* v357 no6355
p1047 S 8 2017

Ruhtenberg, Vess
DO THE WRIGHT THING color *Indianapolis Monthly* p36 Ap
2017
My Living Room *Indianapolis Monthly* v40 no5 p33 Ja 2017

Rui Bai
Structure of a yeast step II catalytically activated spliceosome bibl
diag *Science* v355 no6321 p1 Ja 13 2017

Rui Zhang
China's policies regarding next-generation sequencing diagnostic
tests *Science* v354 no6319 p9 D 23 2016

Ruidong Chen
Dopamine neurons encode performance error in singing birds bibl
graph *Science* v354 no6317 p1278 D 9 2016

Ruifu Yang
Expert consensus on point-of-care testing *Science* v354 no6319
p15 D 23 2016
Recommendations on the management and use of POCT in medical institutions (nosocomial) *Science* v354 no6319 p13 D 23
2016

Ruigrok, Elmer
Elastic-wave propagation and the Coriolis force *Physics Today*
v69 no12 p90 D 2016

Ruijter, Jan M.
An interactive three-dimensional digital atlas and quantitative
database of human development bibl color graph *Science* v354
no6315 paag0053-1 N 25 2016

RUIJUN LONG
Bridging the Gaps between Science and Policy for the Sustainable
Management of Rangeland Resources in the Developing World
BioScience v67 no7 p656 Jl 2017

Ruitenberg, Rudy
Bacchus Takes an Ice Bath in Bordeaux color *Bloomberg Businessweek* no4522 p24 My 15 2017

Ruiwu Wang
Structural basis for the gating mechanism of the type 2 ryanodine
receptor RyR2 bibl color graph *Science* v354 no6310 paah5324-
1 O 21 2016

Ruixue Wan
Structure of a yeast step II catalytically activated spliceosome bibl
diag *Science* v355 no6321 p1 Ja 13 2017

Ruiz, Gregory M.
Tsunami-driven rafting: Transoceanic species dispersal and implications for marine biogeography color graph *Science* v357
no6358 p1402 S 29 2017

Ruiz, Leti—Interviews
THE LOOK BOOK L. RUIZ img *New York* v49 no25 p97 D 12
2016

Ruiz, Marcel
One Day at a Time M. Logan *TV Guide* v65 no2 p28 Ja 2 2017

Ruiz, Michelle
Sorry Not Sorry *Women's Health* v14 no2 p128 Mr 2017
A WOMAN'S WORK color *Women's Health* v14 no8 p113 O
2017

Ruiz, Oscar—Awards
How to make a (zebra)fish face E. DeMarco color *Science News*
v190 no10 p32 N 12 2016

Ruiz, Pedro
WARNING: UNSAFE CONTENT color *Popular Mechanics* p30
O 2017

Ruiz, Raúl, 1941-2011
The Memory Card R. Brody color *New Yorker* v92 no42 p30 D
19 2016

RUIZ-CAMACHO, ANTONIO
Papa Don't Preach: Two sons watch as their post-divorce father
drifts into addiction color *New York Times Book Review* p10 Ap
23 2017

Rukeyser, Muriel, 1913-1980
c. 1900: New Haven M. Rukeyser *Lapham's Quarterly* v10 no2
p69 Spr 2017

Ruktanonchai, Corrine Warren
Making SDGs Work for Climate Change Hotspots bibl *Environment* v58 no6 p24 N/D 2016

Rule of law
Obama's Civil-Rights Legacy—and Ours D. COLE color *Nation*
v304 no1 p34 Ja 2 2017 The Obama Years

Rule of law—United States
Restoring Order to the Rule of Law J. Sanburn color *Time* v188
no16/17 p61 O 24 2016

Rules
    See also
    Employee rules
AUCTION PURCHASER TERMS AND CONDITIONS *Arabian
Horse World* v57 no4 p15 Ja 2017
GENERAL RULES *Arabian Horse World* v57 no4 p18 Ja 2017

Rules Don't Apply (Film)
THE CHECKLIST *Texas Monthly* v44 no12 p72 D 2016
COME-BACK KID A. Wallace bw color *GQ: Gentlemen's Quar-
terly* v86 no12 p194 D 2016
Hollywood Can Wait S. KASHNER bw color *Vanity Fair* v58
no11 p186 N 2016
NEWLY AVAILABLE MOVIES J. HOGAN *TV Guide* v65 no35
p40 Ag 21 2017
Rules Don't Apply L. Greenblatt color *Entertainment Weekly*
no1442 p42 D 2 2016 Rebellious Special Issue
Warren and Howard J. PODHORETZ *Weekly Standard* v22 no14
p39 D 12 2016
WarReN BEAtty An ORAL HISTORY C. Nashawaty, A. Breznican et al color *Entertainment Weekly* no1440 p30 N 18 2016
Winter Preview R. Brody cartoon *New Yorker* v92 no37 p18 N
14 2016

Rules of engagement (Armed forces)
The Changing Rules of War S. D. Sagan *Daedalus* v146 no1 p6
Wint 2017
Strategy & Entailments: The Enduring Role of Law in the U.S.
Armed Forces L. F. Savarese and J. F. Witt *Daedalus* v146 no1
p11 Wint 2017

Ruling class
A Hatred for Hindus M. Bose *History Today* v66 no12 p3 D 2016

Rum
BAR EXAM [Cover story] T. McNally color *New Orleans Magazine* v51 no3 p56 Ja 2017
Have Your Fruitcake R. MARTINEZ color *Bon Appetit* v61 no12
p94 D 2016 /Jan2017

p84 Je 2017

Western States Master M. HAMILTON bw color *Runner's World* v52 no5 p58 Je 2017

THE ZEN OF HUFFING AND PUFFING D. AYERS *USA Today Magazine* v146 no2868 p66 S 2017

Runners (Sports) physiology

MARATHON MAN (AND WOMAN) V. Tweed chart color *Amazing Wellness* v8 no2 p80 Spr 2016

Runners (Sports)—Equipment & supplies

STYLE FOR MILES J. DENGATE bw color *Runner's World* v52 no6 p36 Jl 2017

VISION QUEST [Cover story] J. DENGATE color *Runner's World* v52 no6 p34 Jl 2017

Runners (Sports)—Health

FEAST FIRST L. APPLEGATE color *Runner's World* v52 no1 p56 Ja/F 2017

Runners (Sports)—Nutrition

BEST BITES L. APPLEGATE color *Runner's World* v51 no10 p50 N 2016

HERE YOU ARE [Cover story] cartoon color graph *Runner's World* v51 no10 p91 N 2016

Runnin' (Music)

The MUST LIST color *Entertainment Weekly* no1444/1445 p1 D 16 2016

Running

See also

Jogging

Long-distance running

Running for women

Sprinting

Trail running

ASK MILES cartoon *Runner's World* v52 no3 p23 Ap 2017

ASK THE EXPERTS L. Johnson, S. Sellitto et al color *Runner's World* v51 no11 p42 D 2016

BARCELONA SPAIN M. Pucurull and S. Gearhart color *Runner's World* v52 no8 p85 S 2017

BE SELFIE-AWARE C. Kuzma cartoon *Runner's World* v52 no3 p32 Ap 2017

BUILD YOUR OWN CREW J. MIGALA color *Runner's World* v52 no8 p20 S 2017

CASE STUDY: YOU M. Hamilton cartoon *Runner's World* v52 no1 p44 Ja/F 2017

Catching Fire J. BEVERLY color *Runner's World* v52 no7 p52 Ag 2017

COME TOGETHER A. NOLAN color *Runner's World* v52 no2 p15 Mr 2017

DERBY DAY R. A. BERENZ *TV Guide* v65 no19 p46 My 1 2017

Embrace the Tough Stuff C. KUZMA color *Runner's World* v52 no8 p56 S 2017

Emotions Per Mile P. SAGAL cartoon *Runner's World* v52 no4 p42 My 2017

END ON A HIGH NOTE K. DOLD color *Runner's World* v52 no9 p80 O 2017

Finding Grace C. MICHEL cartoon color *Runner's World* v52 no6 p52 Jl 2017

FIND YOUR SPARK [Cover story] K. Bastone color *Runner's World* v51 no11 p34 D 2016

FIND YOUR WAY BACK J. GALLOWAY color *Runner's World* v52 no1 p42 Ja/F 2017

FIT AND JOLLY! J. GALLOWAY cartoon *Runner's World* v51 no11 p36 D 2016

GREAT INSPIRATIONS D. KASTOR color *Runner's World* v51 no10 p28 N 2016

THE GUIDE / 02.17 *Los Angeles Magazine* p58 F 2017

Hanging It Up K. ARNOLD color *Runner's World* v52 no5 p56 Je 2017

HEAR ME OUT J. GALLOWAY cartoon *Runner's World* v52 no6 p26 Jl 2017

HOW TO RUN MORE LIKE THIS GUY [Cover story] A. HUTCHINSON cartoon color *Runner's World* v51 no11 p38 D 2016

JENNIFER WEINER D. Meltzer Zepeda color *Runner's World* v52 no7 p92 Ag 2017

JUST FIVE MINUTES [Cover story] J. GALLOWAY cartoon *Runner's World* v52 no4 p24 My 2017

THE LIGHT AT THE END OF THE RUN J. DUCHARME color

Women's Health v14 no9 p118 N 2017

Long Trails to Recovery E. STROUT color *Runner's World* v52 no8 p46 S 2017

LOST AND FOUND A. NOLAN color *Runner's World* v52 no8 p80 S 2017

MOUNTAIN MAN [Cover story] M. PRELLE cartoon color *Runner's World* v52 no4 p16 My 2017

NEW YORK, NEW YORK color *Runner's World* v51 no10 p10 N 2016

POLITICAL RACE N. WELDON color *Runner's World* v51 no10 p26 N 2016

ROBYN O'BRIEN D. M. Zepeda color *Runner's World* v52 no3 p96 Ap 2017

Running for Her Life [Cover story] J. Brant bw color *Runner's World* v52 no6 p82 Jl 2017

Running Skirts Rock! color *Health* v31 no4 p12 My 2017

RUN YOUR BEST 5K J. B. Polloreno color *Men's Health* v32 no3 p30 Ap 2017

#RWDOGRUN color *Runner's World* v52 no4 p12 My 2017

SHOULD YOU KEEP GOING? A. HUTCHINSON color *Runner's World* v52 no3 p36 Ap 2017

Start Where You Are [Cover story] K. Bastone color *Runner's World* v52 no1 p66 Ja/F 2017

STERLING K. BROWN D. Zepeda color *Runner's World* v52 no8 p96 S 2017

SWEAT TO SUCCEED A. C. Shilton cartoon *Runner's World* v51 no11 p40 D 2016

THIRST IS FIRST A. HUTCHINSON color *Runner's World* v52 no7 p20 Ag 2017

Three Ways to Walk Off the Weight K. Canning color *Health* v31 no4 p53 My 2017

Today I Get to Run J. BEVERLY color *Runner's World* v52 no5 p52 Je 2017

Ultra days L. JHUNG color *Runner's World* v52 no6 p50 Jl 2017

Want My Advice? M. REMY color *Runner's World* v52 no7 p49 Ag 2017

YOU DON'T KNOW PHEIDIPPIDES! [Cover story] D. KARNAZES bw cartoon color map *Runner's World* v51 no11 p72 D 2016

Running backs (Football)

Clinton PORTIS B. Burnsed color *Sports Illustrated* v127 no1 p98 Jl 3 2017

ENCORE PERFORMANCE J. Vrentas color *Sports Illustrated* v127 no7 p104 S 4 2017

Rush More [Cover story] J. Feldman color *Sports Illustrated* v127 no8 p30 S 18 2017

WHO'S GOT NEXT? [Cover story] M. BAZER color *Chicago* v66 no6 p78 Je 2017

Running equipment

BOTTOMS UP J. DENGATE color *Runner's World* v52 no5 p38 Je 2017

KICKING ASPHALT J. Ator color *Women's Health* v14 no6 p(Sp)16 Jl 2017

What You Need K. DUPZYK color *Popular Mechanics* p42 S 2017

Running for His Life (Film)

Waiting on the Docs R. Deitsch and T. Keith color *Sports Illustrated* v125 no20 p29 D 19 2016

Running for women

HOW FAST COULD YOU RUN... HOW FAR COULD YOU GO... IF YOU TOOK OFF YOUR TRACKER AND RAN FREE? M. Easter color *Women's Health* v14 no7 p168 S 2017

Running injuries

JOINT ACTION [Cover story] A. C. Shilton color *Runner's World* v51 no10 p54 N 2016

Running injuries—Treatment

FAST FIXES J. Migala cartoon *Runner's World* v52 no1 p60 Ja/F 2017

Running on Empty (Music)

QUEENS OF THE STONE AGE'S JOSHUA HOMME E. R. Brown color *Entertainment Weekly* no1480 p48 S 1 2017

Running races

See also

Marathon running

CALENDAR OF EVENTS *Idaho Magazine* v16 no12 p61 S 2017

DON'T MISS LIST BOAT SHOWS :EVENTS *Sea Magazine*

v109 no1 pCA-7 Ja 2017

FORMULA FOR SUCCESS A. HUTCHINSON color diag *Runner's World* v52 no1 p46 Ja/F 2017

HERE YOU ARE [Cover story] cartoon color graph *Runner's World* v51 no10 p91 N 2016

MAKOROBONDO "DEE" SALUKOMBO N. WELDON color *Runner's World* v52 no1 p84 Ja/F 2017

MATTHEW CENTROWITZ E. STROUT color *Runner's World* v52 no1 p82 Ja/F 2017

RUN THE RIVERFRONT M. Marker color map *Runner's World* v52 no1 p80 Ja/F 2017

UNITED WE RUN D. WILLEY color *Runner's World* v52 no1 p14 Ja/F 2017

Running Room Canada Inc.

A place to run C. MCINTYRE color *Maclean's* v130 no8 p50 S 2017

Running shoes

Go The Distance M. BERG chart color *Muscle & Performance* v9 no8 p20 Ag 2017

SPEED RACERS J. DENGATE color *Runner's World* v52 no5 p36 Je 2017

Running shoes—Design & construction

BEST in SHOE [Cover story] J. BEVERLY bw color *Runner's World* v51 no10 p96 N 2016

Put Your Best Foot Forward L. BOYCE color *Muscle & Performance* v9 no8 p18 Ag 2017

Running shoes—Evaluation

The 2017 Performance Gear Awards bw color *Men's Health* v32 no4 p39 My 2017

FALL SHOE GUIDE [Cover story] J. DENGATE and M. SHORTEN color graph *Runner's World* v52 no8 p59 S 2017

FOR YOUR FEET ONLY T. Newcomb color *Runner's World* v52 no4 p16 My 2017

RUNNING LIST J. WUEBBEN color *Muscle & Performance* v9 no4 p12 Ap 2017

Shoes made for running M. SHIEH graph *Popular Science* v289 no6 p36 N/D 2017

A Sneaker for Every State J. Zorthian color *Time* v190 no5 p27 Jl 31 2017

SOLID FOOTING J. DENGATE and M. SHORTEN cartoon color graph *Runner's World* v52 no3 p83 Ap 2017

STYLE FOR MILES J. DENGATE bw color *Runner's World* v52 no6 p36 Jl 2017

These skis fold in half! B. Broudy and R. Verger color diag *Popular Science* v289 no6 p30 N/D 2017

Running shoes—History

BEST in SHOE [Cover story] J. BEVERLY bw color *Runner's World* v51 no10 p96 N 2016

Running shoes—Sales & prices

IT'S MARATHON TIME. HERE'S WHO'S WINNING P. Wahba color diag *Fortune* v174 no6 p12 N 1 2016

Running techniques

BREAK THE TRANSCONTINENTAL RECORD! K. FOX color *Runner's World* v52 no2 p22 Mr 2017

CRUSH IT. THEN COOL IT [Cover story] C. Kuzma color *Runner's World* v52 no2 p28 Mr 2017

DOUBLE DIGITS? SWEET! J. GALLOWAY color *Runner's World* v52 no8 p14 S 2017

THE FAST BREAK S. Douglas cartoon *Runner's World* v52 no2 p33 Mr 2017

RAPID DESCENT A. HUTCHINSON color *Runner's World* v52 no2 p32 Mr 2017

THE ROAD TO GLORY M. PRELLE color *Runner's World* v52 no8 p18 S 2017

THE RUN TO THE RACE J. BEVERLY cartoon *Runner's World* v52 no2 p24 Mr 2017

Running training

See also

Marathon running training

CRUSH ANY GOAL B. PIERCE and S. MURR color *Runner's World* v52 no8 p74 S 2017

THE ROAD TO GLORY M. PRELLE color *Runner's World* v52 no8 p18 S 2017

Running—Equipment & supplies

BEWARE WARDROBE FAT M. REMY cartoon *Runner's World* v52 no1 p24 Ja/F 2017

A RUN TO FORGET K. ARNOLD cartoon *Runner's World* v51 no11 p24 D 2016

STORM STOPPERS J. Dengate color *Runner's World* v52 no3 p51 Ap 2017

VEST IN CLASS color *Runner's World* v52 no3 p53 Ap 2017

Running—Equipment & supplies—Evaluation

RISE OF THE MACHINES [Cover story] J. Dengate color *Runner's World* v51 no10 p60 N 2016

Running—News briefs

THE INTERSECTION color *Runner's World* v51 no10 p29 N 2016

The Intersection color *Runner's World* v52 no5 p60 Je 2017

Running—Physiological aspects

IF THEY CAN'T SAY SOMETHING NICE... J. GALLOWAY color *Runner's World* v52 no7 p29 Ag 2017

A RUN TO FORGET K. ARNOLD cartoon *Runner's World* v51 no11 p24 D 2016

Trail Mix I. McMahan and T. Keith color *Sports Illustrated* v126 no17 p22 Je 19 2017

THE UNSTOPPABLES N. Weldon color *Runner's World* v51 no10 p112 N 2016

Running—Psychological aspects

RUNNING ERRANDS M. REMY cartoon *Runner's World* v52 no3 p28 Ap 2017

Running—Safety measures

LIGHT THE WAY color *Runner's World* v52 no1 p37 Ja/F 2017

Running—Social aspects

For the Love of Fighting Bob J. HIGHTOWER cartoon *Progressive* v81 no10 p46 N 2016

Running—Software

THE RUNNING DEAD K. ARNOLD cartoon *Runner's World* v52 no1 p30 Ja/F 2017

Runs (Baseball)

See also

Home runs (Baseball)

Runway localizing beacons

CHART WISE R. MARK and J. BLAIR map *Flying* v144 no11 p25 N 2017

Runways (Aeronautics)

Unfinished Business R. Rowland *MHQ: Quarterly Journal of Military History* v30 no1 p12 Aut 2017

Runways (Aeronautics)—Equipment & supplies

RUNWAY STATUS LIGHTS R. Lengel color *Flying* v144 no4 p34 Ap 2017

Runways (Aeronautics)—Safety measures

A COMPLICATED SIMPLE REQUEST L. Abend *Flying* v144 no7 p72 Jl 2017

Runyon, Blaise

I Wish My Horse's Mentor Could Be... color *Horse & Rider* v56 no6 p88 Je 2017

Runyon, Damon, 1880-1946

THE BALLAD OF OLD JOE D. Runyon *MHQ: Quarterly Journal of Military History* v29 no2 p90 Wint 2017

Ruomeng Cui

A Better Way to Fight Discrimination in the Sharing Economy color *Harvard Business Review Digital Articles* p2 F 27 2017

RUOPPO, ALTHEA

The Light Inside *Texas Monthly* v44 no11 p105 N 2016

RuPaul, 1960-

Power Tools: Titans C. Alter color *Time* v189 no16/17 p118 My 1-8 2017

RuPaul Gets Political S. KORNHABER bw *Atlantic* v319 no5 p20 Je 2017

TV's Real Mother of Draggin' D. D'addario color *Time* v190 no1 p53 Jl 3 2017

World of Wonder Life's a Drag A. Sakoui color *Bloomberg Businessweek* no4521 p22 My 8 2017

RuPaul, 1960—Interviews

From Drag to Riches [Cover story] M. Snetiker color *Entertainment Weekly* no1471 p23 Je 23 2017

RuPaul's Drag Race (TV program)

The Must List color *Entertainment Weekly* no1459 p2 Mr 31 2017

TV's Real Mother of Draggin' D. D'addario color *Time* v190 no1 p53 Jl 3 2017

Rupayana, Disha

References Should Come from a Candidate's Coworkers, Not Just

Their Boss *Harvard Business Review Digital Articles* p2 2017

Rupee (Indian currency)

Cash Comes Back in India A. Antony and S. Rai color *Bloomberg Businessweek* no4529 p25 Jl 3 2017

Many economists would like to abolish cash, which enables tax avoidance and crime. But would a cashless world be a fairer one? J. Lanchester *New York Times Magazine* p18 Ja 15 2017

Rupee (Indian currency)—Government policy

India's Cash-Canceling Experiment B. Einhorn, V. Beniwal et al color *Bloomberg Businessweek* no4501 p12 N 28 2016

Rupp, Joyce

Choose children A. Scobey color *U.S. Catholic* v82 no4 p43 Ap 2017

Rupp, Lindsey

China's Elusive Goal: A Global Apparel Brand color *Bloomberg Businessweek* no4532 p12 Jl 31 2017

Selling Experience color *Bloomberg Businessweek* no4496 p60 O 24 2016

What Hudson's Bay Likes About Macy's graph *Bloomberg Businessweek* no4511 p21 F 13 2017

Ruppert, Sean

THE BARN BY THE BEACH M. M. Kashino *Washingtonian Magazine* v52 no9 p151 Je 2017

Rural crimes

MURDER VILLAGES AND SCAM TOWNS R. Foyle Hunwick color *Atlantic* v319 no3 p21 Ap 2017

Rural development

Near Southside J. BREAL *Texas Monthly* v45 no1 p28 Ja 2017

Rural development—Africa

Will Africa's Growth Help Africa's People? K. F. Nwanze *Harvard Business Review Digital Articles* p2 Jl 16 2015

Rural elderly—Economic conditions

No Golden Years for China's Villagers D. Roberts color *Bloomberg Businessweek* no4506 p13 Ja 9 2017

Rural elderly—Health

No Golden Years for China's Villagers D. Roberts color *Bloomberg Businessweek* no4506 p13 Ja 9 2017

Rural geography

The great divide K. Clarke color *U.S. Catholic* v82 no9 p42 S 2017

PARODY color *Weekly Standard* v22 no21 p40 F 6 2017

Rural health services—United States

The Decline of the Rural American Hospital and How to Reverse It N. T. Washburn and K. A. Brown *Harvard Business Review Digital Articles* p2 Ja 30 2015

Rural health—United States

THE DENTAL DIVIDE M. OTTO cartoon *Mother Jones* v42 no5 p68 S/O 2017

Rural land use

See also

Farms

Feudalism

Land settlement

Good Neighbors T. DEAN *American Scholar* v86 no1 p60 Wint 2017

Rural poor

Jefferson County, U.S.A L. K. GJRLEY *In These Times* v41 no4 p60 Ap 2017

Rural population—Canada

In rural Canada, churches find a new connection in welcoming Syrian refugees B. Ross Jr. color *Christian Century* v134 no10 p16 My 10 2017

Rural population—United States

"WE JUST FEEL LIKE WE DON'T BELONG HERE ANY-MORE" B. Andrews color *Mother Jones* v42 no6 p14 N/D 2017

Rural roads

Hard Drive E. CLARK *Yankee* v81 no1 p14 Ja/F 2017

Rural schools

Learning from our elders R. Moore bw *Phi Delta Kappan* v98 no5 p15 F 2017

Strategies for Implementing Personalized Learning in Rural Schools *Education Digest* v83 no3 p40 N 2017

Rural tourism

See also

Agritourism

Bay Watch E. J. CURRAN *Virginia Living* p11 2017 Smoke &

Salt

Rural-urban differences

Red State, Blue City D. A. GRAHAM cartoon *Atlantic* v319 no2 p24 Mr 2017

Rurality

PEARL R. CUNNINGHAM *Idaho Magazine* v16 no5 p32 F 2017

RUS, MAYER

The Archers color *Architectural Digest* v74 no10 p106 O 1 2017

BACK TO CALI color *Architectural Digest* v74 no10 p140 O 1 2017

debut: Popular Demand color *Architectural Digest* no11 p44 N 1 2017

Executive Order [Cover story] color *Architectural Digest* v73 no12 p78 D 2016

Flip the Script color *Architectural Digest* no11 p104 N 1 2017

Get into the Groove color *Architectural Digest* v74 no4 p72 Ap 2017

THE GOOP LIFE color *Architectural Digest* no6 p120 Jc 1 2017

Hot Zone color *Architectural Digest* v74 no4 p52 Ap 2017

keep it classic color *Architectural Digest* v74 no10 p134 O 1 2017

Miles Redd color *Architectural Digest* v74 no8 p28 Ag 2017

PHOTO FINISH color *Architectural Digest* v74 no2 p96 F 2017

Quiet Riot color *Architectural Digest* v74 no2 p40 F 2017

sand castle color *Architectural Digest* v74 no4 p158 Ap 2017

SLEEPING BEAUTY color *Architectural Digest* v74 no10 p160 O 1 2017

Rusalka (Theatrical production)

CLASSICAL MUSIC *New Yorker* v93 no2 p14 F 27 2017

GOINGS ON ABOUT TOWN color *New Yorker* v92 no48 p4 F 6 2017

Rusbridger, Alan

The Big Stash of the Big Rich: What Can We Know? color *New York Review of Books* v63 no17 p47 N 10 2016

Kenya: The Devious Art of Censorship bw color *New York Review of Books* v63 no19 p47 D 8 2016

Panama: The Hidden Trillions bw color *New York Review of Books* v63 no16 p33 O 27 2016

RUSBY, ERIN BANKS

Life on Ice color *Earth Island Journal* v32 no2 p27 Summ 2017

Sharing Our Spaces color *Earth Island Journal* v32 no3 p27 Aut 2017

RUSCHA, ED

The Year in Reading [Cover story] *New York Times Book Review* p8 D 25 2016

Ruschel, A. R.

Persistent effects of pre-Columbian plant domestication on Amazonian forest composition bibl chart graph map *Science* v355 no6328 p925 Mr 3 2017

Rüschlikon (Switzerland)

Hip to be Square M. PEPCHINSKI *Architectural Record* v205 no1 p106 Ja 2017

Rush, Adrian

Speak up color *U.S. Catholic* v82 no4 p5 Ap 2017

Rush, Elizabeth

Memorial for the Future color *Orion Magazine* v36 no1 p9 Ja/F 2017

STORMY WATERS: The fight over New York City's flood lines map *Harper's Magazine* v335 no2005 p46 Je 2017

Rush, Geoffrey, 1951-

Drama of Einstein's life unfolds in new series E. Conover color *Science News* v191 no8 p34 Ap 29 2017

GAME PLAN M. Zimmerman color graph *Men's Health* v32 no5 p10 Je 2017

Genius I. Rudolph *TV Guide* v65 no13 p32 Mr 20 2017

Rush, Geoffrey, 1951-—Interviews

PLAYING THE PART OF GENIUS color *National Geographic* v231 no4 p6 Ap 2017

RUSH, NAYLA

Which Refugees? *National Review* v69 no4 p16 Mr 6 2017

Rush, Norman

A Burning Collection color *New York Review of Books* v64 no6 p23 Ap 6 2017

A Masterpiece from the Muck bw color *New York Review of Books* v63 no16 p18 O 27 2016

Rush, Stockton

Now Boarding For the Titanic Tour J. Dean color *Bloomberg Busi-*

nessweek no4537 p54 S 11 2017

Rushdie, Salman, 1947-

2017 Fall Books Preview S. Begley color *Time* v190 no12 p54 S 25 2017

Leadership Lessons from 10 Wildly Successful People A. Beard *Harvard Business Review Digital Articles* p2 D 29 2015

The Midas Touch: Salman Rushdie's new novel, set in New York, follows the story of an enigmatic family from abroad during the Obama years M. ALI *New York Times Book Review* p14 S 17 2017

Rushdie's New York Bubble N. Rich bw *New York Review of Books* v64 no16 p33 O 26 2017

The Year in Reading [Cover story] *New York Times Book Review* p8 D 25 2016

Rushin, Steve

AT HOME IN THE HALL color *Sports Illustrated* v127 no8 p68 S 18 2017

Brand Management color *Sports Illustrated* v126 no4 p76 Ja 30 2017

Cheer and Trebling color *Sports Illustrated* v127 no5 p116 Ag 14 2017

Cole Mining color *Sports Illustrated* v126 no8 p88 Mr 20 2017

Embrace The Crazy color *Sports Illustrated* v126 no15 p60 My 29 2017

Finally, All Is Revealed color *Sports Illustrated* v126 no2 p64 Ja 16 2017

From Eternity To Here color *Sports Illustrated* v126 no10 p80 Ap 10 2017

THE GOOD BOOK color *Sports Illustrated* v125 no17 p76 N 21 2016 Double Issue

Look Who's Talking color *Sports Illustrated* v126 no12 p60 My 1 2017

AN ODE TO THE HOT DOG color *Sports Illustrated* v127 no1 p104 Jl 3 2017

PICK 'N' ROLL HIGH SCHOOL color *Sports Illustrated* v127 no12 p50 O 16 2017

PLASTIC MOLDING color *Sports Illustrated* v126 no18 p46 Je 26 2017

Stan on Two Feet color *Sports Illustrated* v125 no20 p138 D 19 2016

STILL A SERIES TO SAVOR color *Sports Illustrated* v125 no14 p44 O 24-31 2016

Sting-Ray Afternoons: A Memoir *Publishers Weekly* v264 no19 p51 My 8 2017

Whole New Ball Game color *Sports Illustrated* v127 no3 p116 Jl 24 2017

Rushkoff, Douglas

Corporations Weren't Designed to Run on Code *Harvard Business Review Digital Articles* p2 Mr 2 2016

RUSHTON, CHRISTINE

GO ON STRIKE bw *Runner's World* v52 no7 p36 Ag 2017

Rushworth, Katie

Welcome J. Goodwin *House Beautiful* p3 Ag 2017

Ruskin, John, 1819-1900

John Ruskin Taught Victorian Readers and Travelers the Art of Cultivation D. Heitman *Humanities* v38 no1 p1 Wint 2017

Ruskovich, Emily

MEMENTO K. LUCE cartoon color *O, The Oprah Magazine* p100 F 2017

Pieces of Truth S. HENDERSON *New York Times Book Review* p20 Ja 8 2017

Rusnak, Sonja

You Never Forget Your First Time diag il *Backpacker* v45 no2 p64 Mr 2017

Russ, Brendan E.

Can T cells be too exhausted to fight back? bibl diag *Science* v354 no6316 p1104 D 2 2016

Russ Wernimont Designs (Company)

MCKILLER M. EMERY color *Dirt Sports + Off-Road* v51 no4 p38 Ap 2017

Russakoff, Dale

'The Only Way We Can Fight Back Is to Excel' color *New York Times Magazine* p36 Ja 29 2017

Russakovsky, Olga

INVENTORS E. Beras, C. Garling et al color il *MIT Technology Review* v120 no5 p56 S/O 2017

Russell, A. G.

Trusty Bargains A. McKEAN and N. KREBS color *Outdoor Life* v224 no4 p8 My 2017

Russell, Alyce

Glycomics and its application potential in precision medicine bibl diag *Science* v354 no6319 p36 D 23 2016

Russell, Ann E.

Forestry for a Low-Carbon Future: Integrating Forests and Wood Products Into Climate Change Strategies bibl color *Environment* v59 no2 p16 Mr/Ap 2017

Russell, Anna

DIALOGUE bw *New Yorker* v93 no24 p18 Ag 21 2017

FINNISH LINE cartoon *New Yorker* v93 no30 p18 O 2 2017

HAT TIP cartoon *New Yorker* v93 no10 p36 Ap 24 2017

SONIC HEALING cartoon *New Yorker* v93 no20 p26 Jl 10 2017

UNICORN ROOM cartoon *New Yorker* v93 no19 p19 Jl 3 2017

Russell, April

DRONES ON MARS color *Astronomy* v45 no7 p34 Jl 2017

Russell, Brandon

Solar-Ready Vet P. Rauber *Sierra* v102 no2 p26 Mr/Ap 2017

Russell, Brian

OLD WEST DAYS *New Yorker* v92 no39 p68 N 28 2016

Russell, C. T.

Extensive water ice within Ceres' aqueously altered regolith: Evidence from nuclear spectroscopy bibl graph *Science* v355 no6320 p1 Ja 6 2017

Localized aliphatic organic material on the surface of Ceres bibl graph *Science* v355 no6326 p719 F 17 2017

Structure, force balance, and topology of Earth's magnetopause diag graph *Science* v356 no6341 p960 Je 1 2017

Russell, Catherine

Catherine Russell T. Panken color *Downbeat* v84 no4 p98 Ap 2017

Harlem On My Mind J. McDonough color *Downbeat* v83 no11 p49 N 2016

The Hot Box chart *Downbeat* v83 no11 p51 N 2016

Russell 'Dazzles' in Denver N. Provizer color *Downbeat* v84 no8 p17 Ag 2017

Russell, Christian

Ruffino Custom Closets P. Marquis *New Orleans Homes & Lifestyles* v20 no1 p95 Wint 2016

Russell, Colin A.

Sick birds don't fly...or do they? bibl color map *Science* v354 no6309 p174 O 14 2016

Russell, Danica

A Little Radical: The ABCs of Activism *Publishers Weekly* v264 no35 p77e Ag 28 2017

Russell, David W.

Healthy, Sustainable Growth on the Menu color *Forbes* v199 no1 p(Sp)5 Ja 24 2017

NEW OPPORTUNITY UNDER THE ABE ADMINISTRATION color *Forbes* v199 no1 p(Sp)1 Ja 24 2017

A Sharper Focus on Constant Transformation color *Forbes* v199 no1 p(Sp)6 Ja 24 2017

THK: Embarking on a New Era color *Forbes* v199 no1 p(Sp)9 Ja 24 2017

Traditional Values Bring Tectonic Shift to Trading Sector color *Forbes* v199 no1 p(Sp)3 Ja 24 2017

Russell, Gerard

What Chance for Democracy in the Middle East? color *New York Review of Books* v63 no16 p44 O 27 2016

Russell, Harold W.

PLANS FOR A DISTINCTIVE TRACKSIDE SHED bw diag *Model Railroader* v84 no1 p60 Ja 2017

Russell, Heidi—Interviews

The mystery of faith and science color *U.S. Catholic* v81 no11 p18 N 2016

Russell, James S.

Too Much of a Good Thing *Architectural Record* v205 no6 p49 Je 2017

Russell, Jason

HEALTHY BROTHERHOOD M. WORTHINGTON color *Runner's World* v52 no1 p22 Ja/F 2017

Russell, Jennifer L.

The right network for the right problem color diag *Phi Delta Kappan* v98 no3 p8 N 2016

Russell, John

5 THINGS TO KNOW ABOUT... THE GUEST BOOK *TV Guide* v65 no31 p20 Jl 24 2017

ALSO COMING... *TV Guide* v65 no23 p19 My 29 2017

ALSO COMING... *TV Guide* v65 no2 p39 Ja 2 2017

And Don't Miss... *TV Guide* v65 no13 p37 Mr 20 2017

Angie Tribeca *TV Guide* v65 no14 p37 Ap 3 2017

Anne of Green Gables *TV Guide* v64 no48 p36 N 21 2016

BEING JOHN LITHGOW *TV Guide* v65 no11 p26 Mr 6 2017

Blindspot *TV Guide* v65 no43 p38 O 16 2017

Christmas in Rockefeller Center *TV Guide* v64 no48 p39 N 21 2016

Crashing color *TV Guide* v65 no7 p38 F 13 2017

Dancing King *TV Guide* v64 no40 p40 O 3 2016

Dark Angel *TV Guide* v65 no21 p34 My 15 2017

The Detour *TV Guide* v65 no8 p35 F 27 2017

Eyewitness color *TV Guide* v64 no42 p36 O 10 2016

A Fourth of July Fireworks Roundup! *TV Guide* v65 no27 p32 Je 26 2017

FULL FRONTAL WITH SAMANTHA BEE *TV Guide* v64 no40 p63 O 3 2016

THE GOOD PLACE *TV Guide* v65 no39 p47 S 18 2017

Great News *TV Guide* p40 Ap 17 2017

Halt and Catch Fire *TV Guide* v65 no35 p37 Ag 21 2017

The Hollow Crown: The Wars of the Roses *TV Guide* p42 D 5 2016

Into the Badlands *TV Guide* v65 no11 p43 Mr 6 2017

JOKERS WILD *TV Guide* v65 no6 p30 Ja 30 2017

The Kids Are Alright: Why networks are betting on junior versions of top competition series *TV Guide* v65 no35 p4 Ag 21 2017

The Leftovers *TV Guide* v65 no13 p30 Mr 20 2017

The Leftovers *TV Guide* v65 no14 p38 Ap 3 2017

MARVEL'S INHUMANS *TV Guide* v65 no37 p40 S 4 2017

THE MAYOR *TV Guide* v65 no37 p29 S 4 2017

Meet The Gong Show's New Host *TV Guide* v65 no27 p4 Je 26 2017

The Missing *TV Guide* v65 no6 p40 Ja 30 2017

Mozart in the Jungle *TV Guide* v64 no40 p37 O 3 2016

MY LIFE ON TV *TV Guide* p28 Ap 17 2017

Nobodies *TV Guide* p38 Ap 17 2017

PBS: WHAT'S AT STAKE *TV Guide* p6 Ap 17 2017

Red Oaks *TV Guide* v64 no40 p34 O 3 2016

Room 104 *TV Guide* v65 no31 p33 Jl 24 2017

SPY GAME color *TV Guide* v65 no7 p28 F 13 2017

STATE OF THE AFFAIR *TV Guide* v64 no48 p26 N 21 2016

Trial & Erro's stunt double Arthur Davis *TV Guide* p15 Ap 17 2017

Undercover *TV Guide* v64 no46 p36 N 7 2016

Victoria *TV Guide* v65 no2 p34 Ja 2 2017

Why I Still Love The Walking Dead *TV Guide* v65 no11 p18 Mr 6 2017

Will TV Go Dark This Summer? What a possible writers' strike means for viewers *TV Guide* v65 no19 p6 My 1 2017

Wrecked *TV Guide* v65 no27 p28 Je 26 2017

Wrecked *TV Guide* v65 no35 p31 Ag 21 2017

Writers' Strike Averted! *TV Guide* v65 no21 p11 My 15 2017

THE X FACTOR *TV Guide* v65 no35 p14 Ag 21 2017

Russell, John Scott

CLIPPERS, YACHTS, and the false promise of the wave line: John Scott Russell's 19th-century theory of ship design promised speed and delivered elegance. But, ultimately, it didn't hold water L. D. Ferreiro and A. Pollara *Physics Today* v70 no7 p52 Jl 2017

Russell, Kailub

VICTORY! color *Cycle World* v56 no1 p66 Ja/F 2017

RUSSELL, KAREN

OBJECT PERMANENCE cartoon *New Yorker* v93 no26 p54 S 4 2017

Russell, Katie

Hunters and Scavengers J. POCOCK color *Orion Magazine* v36 no2 p11 Mr/Ap 2017

Russell, Keri, 1976-

THE AMERICANS J. Hibberd color *Entertainment Weekly* no1446/1447 p61 D 2016/Ja 2017

The Americans M. ROUSH *TV Guide* v65 no23 p13 My 29 2017

The Russians Are Coming! A. Rice img *New York* p110 Mr 6 2017

Russell, Kurt, 1951-——Interviews

KURT RUSSELL E. SPITZNAGEL bw *Men's Health* v32 no3 p128 Ap 2017

Russell, Leigh

Deadly Alibi: A DI Geraldine Steel Mystery *Publishers Weekly* v264 no31 p65 Jl 31 2017

Russell, Leon, 1942-2016

Leon Russell I. Guzmán color *Time* v188 no22-23 p13 N/D 2016

Russell, Matthew

Economic productivity in the air transportation industry: multifactor and labor productivity trends, 1990-2014 bibl chart color diag graph *Monthly Labor Review* p1 Mr 2017

Russell, Michelle Stohlmeyer

How We Closed the Gap Between Men's and Women's Retention Rates *Harvard Business Review Digital Articles* p2 My 19 2017

Russell, Patrick J.

Nuclear Power and Risk Psychology *Skeptical Inquirer* v41 no2 p64 Mr/Ap 2017

RUSSELL, RHIANNON

Industrialist vs. Indigenous color *Walrus* v14 no3 p24 Ap 2017

Russell, Richard

TRACK RECORD M. TRAMMELL cartoon *New Yorker* v93 no13 p44 My 15 2017

RUSSELL, SHARMAN APT

ORDINARY MIRACLES On hope, howling, and weeds *Orion Magazine* v35 no3 p12 My/Je 2016

Russell, Susan Garnett

Global Refugee Study Highlights a Gap Between Policy and Practices C. M. Rubin *Education Digest* v83 no3 p51 N 2017

RUSSELL, THADDEUS

NO WAY OUT bw *Reason* v48 no9 p58 F 2017

Russell 2000 Index

The Mystery of the 4,555 Percent Return L. Katz and Z. Faux graph *Bloomberg Businessweek* no4517 p40 Ap 3 2017

Sized Right for Ample Returns R. ERMEY chart *Kiplinger's Personal Finance* v71 no12 p57 D 2017

RUSSELL-KRAFT, STEPHANIE

Rise of the Zombie Hospitals il *New Republic* v247 no12 p12 D 2016

RUSSETH, ANDREW

AROUND NEW YORK bw cartoon color *ARTnews* v116 no1 p106 Spr 2017

AROUND NEW YORK bw color *ARTnews* v115 no4 p124 Wint 2016/2017

AROUND SAN FRANCISCO bw cartoon color *ARTnews* v115 no3 p142 Fall 2016

Clean, Well-Lighted Places bw *ARTnews* v115 no3 p46 Fall 2016

EDITORS' PICKS color *ARTnews* v115 no4 p26 Wint 2016/2017

INSIDE JOB color *ARTnews* v115 no4 p102 Wint 2016/2017

To All Tomorrow's Parties bw cartoon *ARTnews* v116 no1 p26 Spr 2017

Wait-What Was That?! bw color *ARTnews* v116 no1 p96 Spr 2017

Russia

Those Hacking Charges color *Nation* v304 no2 p3 Ja 16 2017

Russia. Supreme Court

Russia's top court bans Jehovah's Witnesses D. Stanglin *Christian Century* v134 no11 p14 My 24 2017

Russia——Armed Forces——1991-

Russia's Rehearsal for World War S. Shuster color *Time* v190 no10/11 p12 S 18 2017

Russia——Armed Forces——1991——History

What Drives Moscow's Military Adventurism? P. K. BAEV *Current History* v115 no783 p251 O 2016

Russia——Economic conditions

World Affairs 2017 *New York Times Upfront* v149 no6 p14 D 12 2016

Russia——Economic conditions——21st century

For Manufacturers, Russia Is Now a Bargain O. Tanas, I. Khrennikov et al graph *Bloomberg Businessweek* no4501 p15 N 28 2016

Russia——Economic conditions——1991-

PUMP IT LIKE THE RUSSIANS S. Bierman color *Bloomberg Businessweek* no4496 p78 O 24 2016

Russia——Foreign relations

backstory color *New Republic* v248 no4 p64 Ap 2017

EVERYMAN'S WAR: The paramilitary fighters training to keep Russia out of the Baltics E. Zerofsky *Harper's Magazine* p69 O 2017

Russia—Foreign relations—Turkey

A Putin Fixer Claims Success With Turkey H. Meyer and O. Ant color *Bloomberg Businessweek* no4512 p15 F 20 2017

Turkey's Tenuous Pivot Toward Russia A. PAUL *Current History* v115 no783 p277 O 2016

Russia—Foreign relations—Ukraine—History—21st century

Kiev and the Kremlin Face Narrowing Options In Ukraine I. Bremmer *Time* v189 no12 p16 Ap 3 2017

Russia—Foreign relations—United States

Are We Heading Toward a New COLD WAR? C. STOFFERS and M. Wines *New York Times Upfront* v149 no3 p18 O 10 2016

Break Up the Bromance: Just getting along with Russia isn't going to be good enough. If the new administration wants a "reset" of its own, it will need to demonstrate clarity and strength M. A. McFaul *Hoover Digest: Research & Opinion on Public Policy* no2 p86 Spr 2017

Can Trump Handle Putin? P. R. Gregory *Hoover Digest: Research & Opinion on Public Policy* no1 p103 Wint 2017

Chicken Soup for the Russian Soul: A strongman with a messianic streak, Vladimir Putin might almost have stepped from the pages of Russian history R. Peters *Hoover Digest: Research & Opinion on Public Policy* no2 p101 Spr 2017

A Different "Special Relationship" K. Drozdova *Hoover Digest: Research & Opinion on Public Policy* no1 p108 Wint 2017

THE DISRUPTION: How the Kremlin built a vast network of TV stations, online media outlets and social-media accounts to wage a new kind of information war J. RUTENBERG *New York Times Magazine* p44 S 17 2017

Europe Fumes Over Russian Gas G. Smith color *Fortune* v176 no3 p16 S 1 2017

Fair Is Foul and Foul Is Fair A. Greenwald color *Commentary* v143 no2 p1 F 2017

HACKER, BANKER, SOLDIER, SPY A. Dejean, H. Levintova et al bw color *Mother Jones* v42 no4 p19 Jl/Ag 2017

How Russia Weaponizes Fake News L. RESTON il *New Republic* v248 no6 p6 Je 2017

How to Ease Europe's Fears About the New U.S.-Russia Relationship A. J. Stavridis color *Time* v190 no6 p28 Ag 7 2017

"It's Best Not to Mess with Us": The nuclear poker game with Moscow has already begun--or, rather, resumed P. R. Gregory *Hoover Digest: Research & Opinion on Public Policy* no2 p97 Spr 2017

It's Not McCarthyism K. Pollitt diag il *Nation* v304 no15 p6 My 8 2017

Legitimate Differences P. GRENIER *American Conservative* v16 no1 p33 Ja/F 2017

THE PLOT AGAINST AMERICA T. RID and V. WARD cartoon color *Esquire* v166 no5 p130 D 2016/Ja 2017

Realism on Russia K. V. HEUVEL *Nation* v305 no4 p4 Ag 14 2017

The Real Story in U.S.-Russia Relations Can Be Seen In the Skies Above Syria I. Bremmer *Time* v190 no1 p12 Jl 3 2017

Red Dawn E. Cawthorne *Hoover Digest: Research & Opinion on Public Policy* no2 p108 Spr 2017

Responding to Russia's Resurgence I. H. Daalder color *Foreign Affairs* v96 no6 p30 N/D 2017

Russia: Friend, Enemy, or Frenemy? With relations between the U.S. and Russia at their lowest point in decades, President Trump has called for improving ties. But can Russian President Vladimir Putin be trusted? M. WINES *New York Times Upfront* v149 no12 p8 Ap 24 2017

THE RUSSIAN CONNECTION D. Corn, A. Dejean et al color *Mother Jones* v42 no4 p16 Jl/Ag 2017

The Russia Question: American relations with Moscow have become a geopolitical mess--a mess, very largely, of our own making N. Ferguson *Hoover Digest: Research & Opinion on Public Policy* no2 p76 Spr 2017

RUSSIA'S GLOBAL ANTI-LIBERTARIAN CRUSADE [Cover story] C. YOUNG color *Reason* v49 no4 p18 Ag/S 2017

Sanctions: Russia & Iran color *Bloomberg Businessweek* no4531 p39 Jl 24 2017

The Spy Who Loved Me T. HORWITZ color *New Republic* v248 no5 p6 My 2017

Trump's Russian Laundromat C. UNGER color *New Republic* v248 no8/9 p26 Ag/S 2017

U.S.-Russian Tensions Thwart Cooperation K. CLARKE color *America* v215 no12 p9 O 24 2016

Russia—Foreign economic relations—1991-

Russia's Deadly Mideast Game C. Matlack, M. Champion et al *Bloomberg Businessweek* no4505 p16 D 26 2016

Russia—Foreign relations—1991-

Contagious Tales of Russian Origin and Putin's Evolution V. Gatov *Society* v53 no6 p619 D 2016

THE EDITORIAL *Maclean's* v129 no45 p5 N 14 2016

Gaining Followers: The Internet and Cold War-Style Propaganda in the Former Soviet Republic A. VanderMey *Wilson Quarterly* v40 no4 p2 Fall 2016

Hybrid war: Russian contemporary political warfare C. S. Chivvis bibl *Bulletin of the Atomic Scientists* v73 no5 p316 2017

THE KREMLIN'S GREMLINS A. Dejean, H. Levintova et al color *Mother Jones* v42 no4 p20 Jl/Ag 2017

Moscow's Wounded Pride S. Kotkin *Hoover Digest: Research & Opinion on Public Policy* no4 p99 Fall 2016

Tensions With Russia Rise In the Baltics map *Time* v189 no10 p8 Mr 20 2017

Russia—Foreign relations—United States—1991-

ACTIVE MEASURES E. OSNOS, D. REMNICK et al cartoon color *New Yorker* v93 no3 p40 Mr 6 2017

After Comey, Keeping a Sense of Balance *America* v216 no12 p8 My 29 2017

The Entitled: Why the Kremlin Had Such Big Expectations for a Trump Presidency M. Trudolyubov *Wilson Quarterly* p2 Spr 2017

Even President Trump Couldn't Turn Russia Into a Friend of the U.S M. Gessen color *Time* v188 no16/17 p35 O 24 2016

The Game Putin Plays P. Coy and H. Meyer color *Bloomberg Businessweek* no4506 p6 Ja 9 2017

Hacking the Voter [Cover story] M. Calabresi, S. Shuster et al color *Time* v188 no14 p30 O 10 2016

How Putin Plays Trump Like a Piano: The Republican nominee and his team of paid Moscow apologists J. Kirchick *Commentary* v142 no2 p25 S 2016

Moscow Cozies Up to the Right A. Altman, E. Dias et al color *Time* v189 no10 p32 Mr 20 2017

The National Interest: Jonathan Chait img *New York* p17 Mr 6 2017

The National Interest: Jonathan Chait: The Republican Party's Obstruction of Justice: A devastating series of events is shrugged off as business as usual img *New York* v50 no12 p17 Je 12 2017

THE NEW RED SCARE A. Cockburn *Harper's Magazine* v333 no1999 p25 D 2016

An Oily Reset in U.S.-Russia Relations M. Philips graph *Bloomberg Businessweek* no4507 p38 Ja 16 2017

Peace as Cold as Siberia M. A. McFaul *Hoover Digest: Research & Opinion on Public Policy* no4 p110 Fall 2016

Putin Isn't So Sure Trump's a Pal H. Meyer, I. Arkhipov et al color *Bloomberg Businessweek* no4509 p13 Ja 30 2017

Russia and the Trump Campaign M. Scherer, S. Frizell et al color *Time* v189 no12 p36 Ap 3 2017

Russia's Election Meddling Hampers Trump Transition M. Calabresi *Time* v188 no27-28 p16 D 26 2016

Trump and Russia E. Rumer, R. Sokolsky et al color *Foreign Affairs* v96 no2 p12 Mr/Ap 2017

The Trump-Putin Reset Is Dead-but Don't Rule Out an Amicable Settlement S. Shuster color *Time* v189 no15 p7 Ap 24 2017

U.S.-Russia Tensions Reach Dangerous New Level M. Calabresi, S. Shuster et al color *Time* v188 no16/17 p5 O 24 2016

Vladimir Putin's PR Victory G. KASPAROV color *Weekly Standard* v22 no43 p13 Jl 24 2017

What Happened in Hamburg E. EDELMAN cartoon *Weekly Standard* v22 no43 p10 Jl 24 2017

What You Said About ... color *Time* v189 no11 p7 Mr 27 2017

Why the Russian Hacks of Hillary Clinton's Campaign Should Reassure Us All J. Klein color *Time* v188 no16/17 p18 O 24 2016

Wrapped in an Enigma color *Weekly Standard* v22 no43 p6 Jl 24 2017

Russia—History

THE BATTLE FOR BAIKAL [Cover story] K. J. McNamara bw

Acting Up *New York Times Book Review* p27 My 14 2017

Bookshelf *New York Times Book Review* p15 F 12 2017

Bookshelf / Oh, Baby! *New York Times Book Review* p22 N 13 2016

Bookshelf: Philosophical *New York Times Book Review* p17 Jl 16 2017

Bookshelf / Wild Life *New York Times Book Review* p33 N 13 2016

Bookshelf/Yikes! *New York Times Book Review* p25 S 10 2017

Feel the Power of the Dark Side *New York Times Book Review* p23 N 6 2016

Home for the Holidays *New York Times Book Review* p19 D 18 2016

Lives to Learn From *New York Times Book Review* p29 Ag 27 2017

School Days *New York Times Book Review* p27 Ag 27 2017

So Long, Summer *New York Times Book Review* p19 O 9 2016

Wings and Feathers *New York Times Book Review* p25 My 14 2017

Russo, Monica

Treecology B. A. Purnell color *Science* v354 no6317 p1227 D 9 2016

Russo, N. Dello

More than a day in the life of a comet bibl bw diag *Science* v354 no6319 p1536 D 23 2016

Russo, Richard, 1949-

Pride and Principle: Richard Russo's collection turns from his familiar blue-collar types to cast a sympathetic eye on upper-middle-class professionals A. WALDMAN *New York Times Book Review* p13 Je 11 2017

RUSSO, ROMAN

F. Ronstadt Hardware Co.: Although Linda Ronstadt is the most famous Ronstadt, it was her grandfather, Federico Jose Maria Ronstadt, w ho made the family name synonymous w ith Tucson, Arizona *Arizona Highways* v96 no7 p8 Jl 2017

RUSSO, TIFFANY

good to the CORE [Cover story] color *Yoga Journal* no291 p66 My 2017

RUSSO-CRAIG, LISA

The Question *O, The Oprah Magazine* p16 Ap 2017

Russound/fmp Inc.

Russound MCA-88X Streaming Housewide Audio Controller J. Sciacca color *Sound & Vision* v82 no2 p60 F/Mr 2017

Russo-Young, Ry

CRITICS' CHOICE N. Davis, R. Horton et al bw chart color *Film Comment* v53 no2 p12 Mr/Ap 2017

Russworm, TreaAndrea M.

Blackness Is Burning: Civil Rights, Popular Culture, and the Problem of Recognition M. J. PETTY *Film Quarterly* v70 no4 p133 Summ 2017

Rust, Marina

Stem Sell color *Vogue* v207 no7 p114 Jl 2017

RUSTAD, HARLEY

Bitcoin for Bohemians cartoon *Walrus* v13 no10 p24 D 2016

Rustication (Architecture)

RUSTIC STYLE F. Sigurdsson color *Cabin Living* p10 S 2017

Rustomji, Cyrus S.

Liquefied gas electrolytes for electrochemical energy storage devices graph *Science* v356 no6345 p1351 Je 30 2017

RUST-TIERNEY, DIANN

Should the Death Penalty Be Abolished? *New York Times Upfront* v149 no9 p22 F 20 2017

RUTA, DOMENICA

Return of the Native: A woman finds sobriety in the rural rituals of her Orkney home *New York Times Magazine* p10 Ap 30 2017

Ruta, Frank

DAN ABOUT TOWN: Party photographer Dan Swartz's monthly roundup of bashes, balls, and benefits *Washingtonian Magazine* v52 no8 p30 My 2017

Rutai Hui

Cardiovascular precision medicine in China bibl *Science* v354 no6319 p66 D 23 2016

RUTBERG, ELON

Eli Russell LINNETZ: ONE OF KANYE'S CLOSEST CREATIVE COLLABORATORS HAS ALREADY ANNOUNCED HIMSELF AS SOMETHING OF A WUNDERKIND WITH HIS VIDEO WORK FOR THE RAPPER *Interview* v47 no3 p28 Ap 2017

RUTENBERG, JIM

THE DISRUPTION: How the Kremlin built a vast network of TV stations, online media outlets and social-media accounts to wage a new kind of information war *New York Times Magazine* p44 S 17 2017

Rutgers University (Camden, N.J.)

Train to Teach: Fit dance pedagogy into your higher ed experience L. WINGENROTH *Dance Magazine* v91 no9 p52 S 2017

Rutgers University (New Brunswick, N.J.). Mason Gross School of the Arts

Mason Gross School of the Arts at Rutgers University *Dance Magazine* v90 p117 2016/2017 Supplement College Guide

Ruth, Babe, 1895-1948

WHAT IF? ... BABE RUTH HAD BEEN DEALT TO THE WHITE SOX—GASP!—INSTEAD OF TO THE YANKEES? D. Greene and J. Feldman color *Sports Illustrated* v126 no11 p57 Ap 17-24 2017

RUTH, DAVID

The god of Science *USA Today Magazine* v145 no2860 p70 Ja 2017

Ruth, Dawn

The Deeper Side of Mardi Gras color *New Orleans Magazine* v51 no4 p32 F 2017

Ruth, Mike

Watch Legendary Pro Stocks From the 1970s and 1980s Run Again T. Taylor color *Hot Rod* v70 no7 p70 Jl 2017

Ruthenium

Ruthenium-catalyzed insertion of adjacent diol carbon atoms into C-C bonds: Entry to type II polyketides M. Bender, B. W. H. Turnbull et al diag *Science* v357 no6353 p779 Ag 25 2017

Rutherford, Craig

Next-Gen Par *Stage Directions* v29 no12 p24 D 2016

Profile of a Profile *Stage Directions* v30 no3 p76 Mr 2017

Simply Powerful *Stage Directions* v29 no10 p33 O 2016

Rutherford, Scott

"We Have Bigotry All Right-- but No Alabamas" *American Indian Quarterly* v41 no2 p159 Spr 2017

Ruthven, Malise

The Caliphate: From Grand to Sordid bw cartoon color *New York Review of Books* v64 no1 p36 Ja 19 2017

The Islamic Road to the Modern World bw color *New York Review of Books* v64 no11 p22 Je 22 2017

On Today's Refugee Road color map *New York Review of Books* v63 no18 p27 N 24 2016

Rutkoff, Aaron

Welcome To New York! cartoon *Bloomberg Businessweek* no4514 p67 Mr 13 2017

Rutkowska, Anna

Click chemistry enables preclinical evaluation of targeted epigenetic therapies diag *Science* v356 no6345 p1397 Je 30 2017

Rutland (England)

RUTLAND AND HIDDEN ENGLAND *British Heritage Travel* v38 no3 p40 My/Je 2017

Rutledge, Colleen

DEVELOP A STRONG GALLOPING POSITION color *Practical Horseman* v45 no5 p38 My 2017

A Sport of Leaders E. Daily color *Practical Horseman* v45 no5 p8 My 2017

Rutledge, Derrick

Behind the Scenes color *O, The Oprah Magazine* p16 O 2017

Rutledge, Fleming

THE 2017 BOOK of the YEAR A. Crouch color *Christianity Today* v61 no1 p57 Ja/F 2017

Rutledge, Matthew S.

The labor supply of veterans with disabilities, 1995-2014 bibl chart color graph *Monthly Labor Review* p1 O 2016

Ruttan, Rachel

It's Harder to Empathize with People If You've Been in Their Shoes *Harvard Business Review Digital Articles* p2 O 20 2015

Rutte, Mark, 1967-

Movers K. Stock cartoon color *Bloomberg Businessweek* no4515 p13 Mr 20 2017

Ruttenberg, Kathy—Interviews

Creature Comforts B. K. Mahoney color *American Craft* v76 no6

Ja/F 2017

HAPPY MEDIUM color *Popular Photography* v80 no11 p14 D 2016

NEW BOSS color graph *Popular Photography* v81 no2 p78 Mr/ Ap 2017

ONE OF A KIND color diag *Popular Photography* v80 no11 p72 D 2016

SLOW AND FAST color graph *Popular Photography* v81 no1 p98 Ja/F 2017

TOUGH LOVE color graph *Popular Photography* v81 no2 p82 Mr/Ap 2017

Ryan, Randall

WHAT IT TAKES TO... RUN RELAYS ALL YEAR N. WEL- DON color *Runner's World* v52 no1 p34 Ja/F 2017

Ryan, Randy

WHAT IT TAKES TO... RUN RELAYS ALL YEAR N. WEL- DON color *Runner's World* v52 no1 p34 Ja/F 2017

Ryan, Rebecca

Leading in a 20-Year Winter M. Funkhouser *Governing* v30 no2 p59 N 2016

Ryan, Sam

SAM RYAN N. Weldon color *Runner's World* v52 no4 p78 My 2017

Ryan, Sean

How Loss Aversion and Conformity Threaten Organizational Change *Harvard Business Review Digital Articles* p2 N 15 2016

Ryan, Shawn—Interviews

ERIC KRIPKE AND SHAWN RYAN I. RUDOLPH *TV Guide* v65 no6 p10 Ja 30 2017

RYAN, STEVE

BASS OF A DIFFERENT STRIPE color *Outdoor Life* v224 no4 p64 My 2017

BRUISER BROWNS color *Outdoor Life* v224 no7 p55 S 2017

RUNNING OF THE BULLS color *Outdoor Life* v224 no3 p59 Ap 2017

RYAN, THOMAS

How to update your PC's BIOS color *PCWorld* v35 no4 p144 Ap 2017

Ryan, Tim

The Democrats' Dilemmas [Cover story] P. Elliott color diag map *Time* v190 no13 p36 O 2 2017

TIM RYAN'S AWAKENING E. McGirt color diag *Fortune* v175 no2 p58 F 1 2017

RYAN, WILL

FALL IN LINE color *Field & Stream* v122 no4 p16 S 2017

RYAN, WILLIAM

COMPLICATED CARE *Commonweal* v114 no14 p2 S 8 2017

Ryan Hansen Solves Crimes on Television (TV program)

Ryan Hansen Solves Crimes on Television* A. Bacle, K. Connolly et al *Entertainment Weekly* no1482/1483 p109 S 22 2017

Ryanodine receptors

Structural basis for the gating mechanism of the type 2 ryanodine receptor RyR2 Wei Peng, Huaizong Shen et al bibl color graph *Science* v354 no6310 paah5324-1 O 21 2016

Rybak-Wolf, Agnieszka

Loss of a mammalian circular RNA locus causes miRNA deregu- lation and affects brain function color *Science* v357 no6357 p1254 S 22 2017

Rybczynski, Witold

c. 1300: France *Lapham's Quarterly* v10 no1 p115 Wint 2017

Rybolovlev, Dmitry, 1966——Trials, litigation, etc.

Paint, by Numbers cartoon *Forbes* v199 no4 p24 Ap 25 2017

Rychert, Catherine

A unified continental thickness from seismology and diamonds suggests a melt-defined plate graph map *Science* v357 no6351 p580 Ag 11 2017

Ryckelynck, Michael

Transient compartmentalization of RNA replicators prevents ex- tinction due to parasites bibl chart graph *Science* v354 no6317 p1293 D 9 2016

Ryckman, Thomas

The Strange Physics of Nothing *Physics Today* v70 no9 p59 S 2017

Rydberg constant

The Rydberg constant and proton size from atomic hydrogen A. Beyer, L. Maisenbacher et al bw chart color diag graph *Science*

v357 no6359 p79 O 6 2017

Ryden, Hope, 1929-2017

Milestones *Time* v190 no2/3 p11 Jl 10-17 2017

Ryder, Adam

GLASS APPEAL color *Popular Photography* v81 no2 p18 Mr/ Ap 2017

MAN OF STEEL color *Popular Photography* v81 no2 p90 Mr/ Ap 2017

PINE SENSE color *Popular Photography* v81 no2 p26 Mr/Ap 2017

SKY EYE color *Popular Photography* v81 no1 p18 Ja/F 2017

SWEET 17 color *Popular Photography* v81 no2 p16 Mr/Ap 2017

THEATER IN THE ROUND color *Popular Photography* v81 no1 p20 Ja/F 2017

RYDER, ROBERT RANDALL

A (Frightening) Bird's Eye View *USA Today Magazine* v145 no2858 p41 N 2016

Ryder, Winona, 1971-

The Society PAGE *Interview* v47 no2 p62 Mr 2017

Ryder Cup (Golf tournament)

Happy Warrior H. WILHELM *National Review* v68 no19 p52 O 24 2016

Ryder Cup (Golf tournament)—History—21st century

Leading Off A. Shipnuck color *Sports Illustrated* v125 no12 p8 O 10 2016

Rye

The Last Straw *Los Angeles Magazine* p62 Mr 2017

Rye bread

DAILY BREADS W. Akin *Mother Earth News* no279 p30 D/Ja 2017

Rye whiskey

Halloween Spirits T. MCNALLY color *New Orleans Magazine* v51 no12 p116 O 2017

Rye Revival W. BROCK *Atlanta* v56 no11 p55 Mr 2017

Ryerson, James

How does a tolerant society work? Do we need to operate un- der less romantic notions of civility? Three books look beyond agreeing to disagree *New York Times Book Review* p27 Ja 15 2017

Ivory Tower color *New York Times Book Review* p31 S 25 2016

Ivory Tower *New York Times Book Review* p27 Jl 2 2017

Ivory Tower *New York Times Book Review* p31 Mr 12 2017

Three books examine the human propensity for sharing num- bers—in more ways than you might think *New York Times Book Review* p31 My 7 2017

Ryerson, Richard Alan

Finding the Founder J. M. J. BANNER color *Weekly Standard* v22 no32 p37 My 1 2017

Rykiel, Sonia, 1930-2016

SONIA RYKIEL color *Harper's Bazaar* no3648 p98 N 2016

Rylaarsdam, Katharine W.

WE HEAR YOU *Progressive* v81 no6 p9 Ag/S 2017

RYLAN, ELIZABETH

THE SECRET LIFE OF ANIMALS cartoon *Reader's Digest* v190 no1134 p38 O 2017

Rylant, Cynthia, 1954-

Henny, Penny, Lenny, Denny, and Mike *Publishers Weekly* v264 no28 p86 Jl 10 2017

RYN, CLAES G.

Conservatives in Denial *American Conservative* v15 no6 p32 N/D 2016

Rynerson, Steve

A Cottage All Grown Up B. D. Coleman color *Old House Journal* v44 no8 p16 D 2016

Ryrie, Alec

Protestants: The Faith That Made the Modern World color *Pub- lishers Weekly* v264 no7 p70 F 13 2017

Ryu, Annie—Interviews

A FEW WORDS WITH JACKFRUIT ANNIE R. Jacobsen color *Rodale's Organic Life* v3 no1 p57 Ja 2017

Ryu, Jaegeon

Sliding chains keep particles together diag *Science* v357 no6348 p250 Jl 21 2017

Ryu, Jaewon

Why GE, Boeing, Lowe's, and Walmart Are Directly Buying Health Care for Employees *Harvard Business Review Digital*

Articles p2 Je 9 2017

Ryu, Jekwan

Mutations in the promoter of the telomerase gene TERT contribute to tumorigenesis by a two-step mechanism diag *Science* v357 no6358 p1416 S 29 2017

Ryugo Hayano

Buffer-gas cooling of antiprotonic helium to 1.5 to 1.7 K, and antiproton-to-electron mass ratio bibl chart diag graph *Science* v354 no6312 p610 N 4 2016

Ryu So-Yeon, 1990-

The New Queen Bee M. Washchyshyn and J. Marksbury color *Golf Magazine* v59 no10 p21 O 2017

S

S., Kelly

Climbr: Climbing Partner Reviews *Climbing* no356 p32 S/O 2017

S-Town (TV program)

Total (and equal) depravity K. Reklis color *Christian Century* v134 no11 p44 My 24 2017

Saab, Michelle

More time for learning color *Phi Delta Kappan* v98 no4 p26 D 2016/Ja 2017

Saadawi, Ahmed

Frankenstein in Baghdad bw *Publishers Weekly* v264 no41 p40 O 9 2017

Saadiyat Island (United Arab Emirates)

Louvre of Arabia R. COUNTER color *Maclean's* v129 no51/52 p71 D 26 2016

Saalman, Dustin Ray

Promoting human rights through science color *Science* v357 no6359 p34 O 6 2017

Saar, Betye

Collage As an Act of Defiance SU WU *Los Angeles Magazine* p56 My 2017

Saar, Betye—Exhibitions

Acquisitions & mergers: A new exhibition at the Craft and Folk Art Museum in Los Angeles is the latest showcase for the powerful work of assemblage artist Betye Saar M. Slenske bw color *Magazine Antiques* v184 no4 p84 Jl/Ag 2017

Saarela, Jeffery

Flora finders J. BENNETT color *Canadian Geographic* v136 no6 p31 D 2016

Saari, John

Sculptural Arts Coating, Inc *Stage Directions* v30 no3 p41 Mr 2017

Saariaho, Kaija, 1952-

L'Amour de Loin *New York* v49 no24 p158 N 28 2016

The Sound of Love R. Platt cartoon *New Yorker* v92 no40 p11 D 5 2016

Saatchi & Saatchi (Company)—Officials & employees

The Saatchi Ouster Shows Leaders Need to Be Gender Smart, Not Gender Blind A. Wittenberg-Cox *Harvard Business Review Digital Articles* p2 Ag 3 2016

Saatchi Gallery (London, England)

ABOVE & BEYOND cartoon *New Yorker* v93 no6 p12 Mr 27 2017

Saatva (Company)

SOFT LANDINGS IN MATTRESSES L. Entis color *Fortune* v75 no1 p26 Ja 1 2017

SABA, GRACE

The Impact of a Large-Scale Climate Event on Antarctic Ecosystem Processes chart graph *BioScience* v66 no10 p848 O 1 2016

Sabahattin Ali, ca. 1906-1948

Madonna in a Fur Coat *Publishers Weekly* v264 no39 p82 S 25 2017

SABAL, MEGAN

Long-Term Studies Contribute Disproportionately to Ecology and Policy *BioScience* v67 no3 p271 Mr 2017

Saban, Haim, 1944-

$10,000,000 Says Hillary Wins [Cover story] D. LEONARD color *Bloomberg Businessweek* no4495 p44 O 17 2016

MIGHTY MORPHIN POWER PLAYER A. KROLL cartoon *Mother Jones* v41 no6 p46 N/D 2016

Sabatier, D.

Persistent effects of pre-Columbian plant domestication on Amazonian forest composition bibl chart graph map *Science* v355 no6328 p925 Mr 3 2017

Sabatine, Teresa

Leading Lady D. S. COMISKEY *Indianapolis Monthly* v40 no4 p66 D 2016

Sabatini, Jeff

2017 JAGUAR XE 35T AWD R-SPORT color *Car & Driver* v62 no10 p78 Ap 2017

25 CARS WORTH WAITING FOR color *Car & Driver* v62 no10 p32 Ap 2017

auto no mo' us bw color diag graph *Car & Driver* v63 no5 p58 N 2017

Enemy of the Estate bw chart color diag *Car & Driver* v63 no4 p74 O 2017

THE FIX IS IN chart color graph *Car & Driver* v63 no1 p50 Jl 2017

Fleet Files color diag *Car & Driver* v63 no1 p88 Jl 2017

Neither Snow nor Rain nor Heat nor Gloom of Night color *Car & Driver* v62 no6 p100 D 2016

Nonstandardized Testing chart color *Car & Driver* v62 no8 p66 F 2017

On our summer vacation, we took a bunch of new three-row SUVs to camp. You guys want to see the slideshow? chart color *Car & Driver* v63 no2 p54 Ag 2017

The Red Pill color *Car & Driver* v62 no10 p84 Ap 2017

THE RETREADS color *Car & Driver* v62 no7 p50 Ja 2017

Smashing NAFTA Apart Is Harder Than It Seems, Especially When You're Blindfolded color graph *Car & Driver* v62 no11 p90 My 2017

Sub-Suburban color *Car & Driver* v63 no5 p116 N 2017

What Do We Mean by Best? color *Car & Driver* v62 no7 p104 Ja 2017

What Do We Mean by "Wagon"? bw color *Car & Driver* v63 no4 p72 O 2017

SABBAGE, SOPHIE

Grief Is a Genesis. Not a Finale *Psychology Today* v50 no3 p44 My/Je 2017

SABBAT, LUKA

WHEN WE GO LOW. ALSO GO HIGH color *GQ: Gentlemen's Quarterly* v97 no4 p120 Ap 2017

Sabeco (Company)

Movers K. Stock color *Bloomberg Businessweek* no4519 p15 Ap 24 2017

Sabella, Jeremy

Realism without despair *Christian Century* v134 no18 p10 Ag 30 2017

A theologian of unmatched influence M. E. Marty color *America* v216 no10 p49 My 1 2017

Saber-toothed tigers

A modern diagnosis of an ancient cat L. E. Ogden color *Science News* v192 no7 p5 O 28 2017

Sabesan, Ramkumar

Color vision strategy defies textbooks T. H. SAEY color *Science News* v190 no8 p10 O 15 2016

Sabeti, Pardis C.

Nucleic acid detection with CRISPR-Cas13a/C2c2 color diag *Science* v356 no6336 p438 Ap 28 2017

Sabian Ltd.

Crescent by Sabian Stanton Moore Collection M. Kern color *Downbeat* v83 no12 p108 D 2016

Sabian Artisan Elites M. Kern color *Downbeat* v84 no6 p86 Je 2017

SABIN, BRIAN

HAMSTRING HELPERS color *Runner's World* v51 no11 p54 D 2016

POSITION STATEMENT [Cover story] color *Runner's World* v51 no11 p52 D 2016

Sabin, Rob

2016 TOP PICKS OF THE YEAR color *Sound & Vision* v82 no2 p32 F/Mr 2017

THE ADVENTURES OF K'SCAPE *Sound & Vision* v81 no10 p8 D 2016

Bars on a Budget color graph *Sound & Vision* v81 no10 p40 D 2016

DAILY DOUBLE [Cover story] bw color *Sound & Vision* v82 no3

p34 Ap 2017

THE END OF THE EARLY ADOPTER color *Sound & Vision* v82 no4 p8 My 2017

FEAR AND LOATHING BEYOND VEGAS *Sound & Vision* v82 no3 p6 Ap 2017

HOW TO BUY AN A/V RECEIVER color *Sound & Vision* v81 no9 p32 N 2016

IT 'S STILL THE SOFTWARE, STUPID color *Sound & Vision* v82 no7 p8 S 2017

IT'S THE SOFTWARE, STUPID *Sound & Vision* v82 no5 p8 Je 2017

LG 65UH8500 LCD Ultra HDTV color graph *Sound & Vision* v82 no1 p46 Ja 2017

McIntosh RS100 Wireless Speaker color graph *Sound & Vision* v82 no5 p48 Je 2017

PROJECTION'S REINVENTION color *Sound & Vision* v82 no4 p30 My 2017

Soundcast VG7 Outdoor Wireless Speaker color *Sound & Vision* v82 no6 p54 Jl/Ag 2017

STILL BAKING color *Sound & Vision* v82 no8 p8 O 2017

Thanks for the MEMORIES color *Sound & Vision* v82 no5 p30 Je 2017

TOP PICKS OF THE TOP PICKS *Sound & Vision* v82 no2 p8 F/Mr 2017

TURNIN' THE INSIDE OUT *Sound & Vision* v82 no6 p8 Jl/Ag 2017

ULTRA HD SETTLES IN *Sound & Vision* v82 no1 p8 Ja 2017

YOU CAN'T BURY IT IF IT 'S NOT DEAD *Sound & Vision* v81 no9 p8 N 2016

Sabina, María

c. 1880: Río Santiago *Lapham's Quarterly* v10 no2 p161 Spr 2017

SABMiller PLC

Better, Bigger, Beerier color *Weekly Standard* v22 no45 p2 Ag 7 2017

Saboia, Fernanda

The Rise of WhatsApp in Brazil Is About More than Just Messaging *Harvard Business Review Digital Articles* p2 Ap 15 2016

Sabraw, John

Remediation Art M. N. MITRA cartoon color *Earth Island Journal* v32 no4 p27 Wint 2017

Sabre Defence Industries (Company)

WHAT'S NEW? *USA Today Magazine* v146 no2868 p74 S 2017

Sabre Yachts Corp.

Break From Tradition D. CAPRIO chart color *Power & Motoryacht* v34 no11 p118 N 2017

Sabri, P.

A nontoxic pain killer designed by modeling of pathological receptor conformations bibl diag graph *Science* v355 no6328 p966 Mr 3 2017

SAC Capital Advisors LP

TOTAL RETURN S. KOLHATKAR cartoon *New Yorker* v92 no45 p34 Ja 16 2017

Sacarny, Adam

Research: Perhaps Market Forces Do Work in Health Care After All *Harvard Business Review Digital Articles* p2 D 5 2016

Saccharomyces

See also

Saccharomyces cerevisiae

Young phosphorylation is functionally silent O. Matalon, B. Dubreuil et al bibl diag *Science* v354 no6309 p176 O 14 2016

Saccharomyces cerevisiae

Aggregation of the Whi3 protein, not loss of heterochromatin, causes sterility in old yeast cells G. Schlissel, M. K. Krzyzanowski et al bibl diag *Science* v355 no6330 p1184 Mr 17 2017

Exploring genetic suppression interactions on a global scale J. van Leeuwen, C. Pons et al diag *Science* v354 no6312 p599 N 4 2016

Saccharomyces cerevisiae—Research

Bug mapping and fitness testing of chemically synthesized chromosome X Y. Wu, Li et al diag *Science* v355 no6329 p1048 Mr 10 2017

Sachar, Alon

Jerusalem Revisited D. EPHRON *New York Times Book Review* p29 D 11 2016

Sachdev, Sharad

Business Processes Are Learning to Hack Themselves *Harvard*

Business Review Digital Articles p2 Je 27 2016

How Companies Are Using Machine Learning to Get Faster and More Efficient *Harvard Business Review Digital Articles* p2 My 3 2016

Sachdev, Shiv

Most On-Demand Businesses Aren't Actually Disruptive *Harvard Business Review Digital Articles* p2 S 29 2015

Sachgau, Oliver

Germany's Maternity Wards Are Booked color graph *Bloomberg Businessweek* no4504 p16 D 19 2016

Sachid, Angada B.

MoS2 transistors with 1-nanometer gate lengths bibl color graph *Science* v354 no6308 p99 O 7 2016

SACHS, ANDREA

Route 66 color map *AARP: The Magazine* v60 no3A p53 Ap/My 2017

Sachs, Anne—Interviews

Profile M. S. Eddy *Stage Directions* v30 no3 p20 Mr 2017

SACHS, DANA

Feeding the Spirit bw *Rodale's Organic Life* v2 no7 p36 D 2016/ Ja 2017

Sachs, Harvey

Allegro Con Brio R. Gottlieb *New York Times Book Review* p1 Jl 2 2017

Maestrissimo J. NORDLINGER bw *National Review* v69 no15 p39 Ag 14 2017

The Perfectionist T. Page bw *New York Review of Books* v64 no17 p14 N 9 2017

Toscanini: Musician of Conscience bw color *Publishers Weekly* v264 no4 p69 Ja 23 2017

Sachs, Jeffrey D.

The Democratization of US Foreign Policy color *Nation* v304 no2 p19 Ja 16 2017

Global Fund lessons for Sustainable Development Goals color *Science* v356 no6333 p32 Ap 7 2017

Toward a New Foreign Policy [Cover story] bw *Nation* v304 no2 p12 Ja 16 2017

SACHS, LEXIE

15 WAYS TO SLEEP BETTER TONIGHT color *Good Housekeeping* v265 no4 p77 O 2017

Silky Pillowcases color *Good Housekeeping* v263 no5 p133 N 2016

Sachs, Roya

ROYA SACHS: Independent Curator J. ORTVED color *Vogue* v207 no10 p196 O 2017

Sachs, Stephen—Interviews

We Can't Remain Silent K. M. Mitchell *Stage Directions* v30 no4 p4 Ap 2017

Sachs, Wiebke

Interacting amino acid replacements allow poison frogs to evolve epibatidine resistance chart diag graph *Science* v357 no6357 p1261 S 22 2017

Sacilotto, Loriana

A New Literary Imprint *Publishers Weekly* v264 no3 p14 Ja 16 2017

Sack, Daniel

American Prophets: Seven Religious Radicals and Their Struggle for Social and Political Justice *Christian Century* v134 no16 p34 Ag 2 2017

Sack, Graham

In 'Lincoln in the Bardo,' Saunders's Fiction Becomes Virtual Reality J. Maher color *Publishers Weekly* v264 no9 p8 F 27 2017

Sack, Lawren

Global climatic drivers of leaf size [Cover story] graph *Science* v357 no6354 p917 S 1 2017

Plant diversity increases with the strength of negative density dependence at the global scale diag *Science* v356 no6345 p1389 Je 30 2017

SACKETT, VICTORIA

Overseas Highway color map *AARP: The Magazine* v60 no3A p51 Ap/My 2017

Sackler, Mortimer

House of Pain C. Glazek bw color *Esquire* p100 N 2017

Sackler, Raymond

House of Pain C. Glazek bw color *Esquire* p100 N 2017

SACK-MIN, JOETTA

Social Media Helps Educators Build Professional Learning Communities *Education Digest* v82 no6 p25 F 2017

Sacks, Lee

How Every Hospital Should Start the Day *Harvard Business Review Digital Articles* p2 D 5 2014

Sacks, Oliver, 1933-2015

Essays offer peek into the mind of Oliver Sacks L. Sanders color *Science News* v192 no6 p28 O 14 2017

Sacks, Rodney

9 RODNEY SACKS L. Entis color *Fortune* v174 no7 p85 D 1 2016

Sacks, Sam

LIFE CHOICES *Harper's Magazine* v334 no2001 p88 F 2017

They Could Be Heroes bw color *New Republic* v248 no4 p44 Ap 2017

Sacramento Kings (Basketball team)

14 Kings B. Golliver, R. Mahoney et al color *Sports Illustrated* v125 no14 p114 O 24-31 2016

14 KINGS color *Sports Illustrated* v127 no12 p96 O 16 2017

Sacramento Kings (Basketball team)—History

Misery Index T. Keith color *Sports Illustrated* v125 no16 p18 N 14 2016

Sacramento Bee, The (Newspaper)

MY HOMETOWN PAPER: Erin Ailworth E. Ailworth color *Columbia Journalism Review* v56 no1 p81 Spr 2017

Sacraments

See also

Marriage

and the survey says *U.S. Catholic* v82 no3 p23 Mr 2017

Sacred (Film)

Common faith: Documentary film Sacred explores ritual and prayer as primary human experiences D. Duncan Collum color *U.S. Catholic* v82 no8 p38 Ag 2017

Sacred books

See also

Bible

Qur'an

Harry Potter, holy writ S. Paulsell *Christian Century* v133 no22 p35 O 26 2016

Is the Bible infallible? A. Camille color *U.S. Catholic* v81 no11 p49 N 2016

Sacred Cantatas (Music)

Philippe Jaroussky: Sacred Cantatas W. R. Braun *Opera News* v81 no9 p55 Mr 2017

Sacred groves

Can the Spiritual Values of Forests Inspire Effective Conservation? M. D. LOWMAN and P. A. SINU *BioScience* v67 no8 p688 Ag 2017

Sacred Hearts Club (Music)

What to Stream color *Entertainment Weekly* no1474/1475 p115 Jl 21-28 2017

Sacred meals

See also

Lord's Supper

Holy crumbs M. Florer-Bixler color *Christian Century* v134 no1 p10 Ja 4 2017

THE INVENTION OF THANKSGIVING S. Evans *Saturday Evening Post* v288 no6 p86 N/D 2016

Sacred music

See also

Church music

Music and the Aesthetic in Worship and Collective Singing: England since 1840 D. Martin *Society* v53 no6 p647 D 2016

THE MUSIC OF TIME NO 2: ANGELIC CHOIRS AND DEVILISH VOICES A. Lee *History Today* v67 no8 p86 Ag 2017

Sacred Water: Standing Rock (Film)

Sacred Water: Standing Rock K. Servick *Science* v356 no6337 p480 My 5 2017

Sacroiliac joint

Get to know... your SI joint J. H. Lasater color *Yoga Journal* p60 2017 SpecialIssue

Sad Clowns & Hillbillies (Music)

John Mellencamp Continues to Explore His American Roots With Sad Clowns & Hillbillies M. METTLER bw color *Sound & Vision* v82 no7 p30 S 2017

Sadan, Josie G.

Ready for Anything color *Dance Magazine* v91 no3 p46 Mr 2017

What It Takes to Create a Choreographer *Dance Magazine* v90 no12 p65 D 2016

Sadat, Kosh

Staying the Course in Afghanistan color *Foreign Affairs* v96 no6 p2 N/D 2017

Saddle blankets

Which Saddle is for You? [Cover story] J. Jahiel color *Trail Rider* v29 no2 p36 Mr 2017

Saddlery

FOR THE HORSE In the stable C. REIGH *Arabian Horse World* v57 no2 p104 N 2016

HOW MUCH DOES DENTAL WORK HELP? C. Barakat and M. McCluskey color *Equus* no481 p17 O 2017

Saddle Savvy L. Feldman color *American Cowboy* v23 no6 p44 Ap/My 2017

SUBURBAN COWBOY E. O'NEILL color *Missouri Life* v44 no5 p26 Ag 2017

Tack Room color *Practical Horseman* v45 no9 p77 S 2017

Textiles to Ride: The Saddle Blanket Weaver G. WIER *Idaho Magazine* v16 no9 p7 Je 2017

THREE SQUARED G. R. Schiavino color *Team Roping Journal* p58 S 2017

Yes—You Can Develop Feel [Cover story] L. Walker and J. F. Meyer color *Horse & Rider* v56 no1 p34 Ja 2017

Saddlery—Evaluation

emporium color *Dressage Today* v24 no1 p64 O 2017

STYLE color *Horse & Rider* v56 no6 p32 Je 2017

TRAIL & CAMPING GEAR L. BERGER O'CONNOR color *Trail Rider* v29 no4 p48 My 2017

Turn and Burn color *American Cowboy* v24 no1 p44 Je/Jl 2017

Sad Fact, The (Short story)

THE SAD FACT R. Cusk *Harper's Magazine* v334 no2000 p25 Ja 2017

Sadler, E. M.

Molecular gas in the halo fuels the growth of a massive cluster galaxy at high redshift bibl graph *Science* v354 no6316 p1128 D 2 2016

Sadler, John

Caesar's Greatest Victory: The Battle of Alesia, Gaul, 52 BC D. Saunders *Military History* v34 no2 p71 Jl 2017

Operation Agreement: Jewish Commandos and the Raid on Tobruk R. Guttman *Military History* v33 no5 p72 Ja 2017

Sadlier, Allison

4 — IN THE DARK *Entertainment Weekly* no1444/1445 p114 D 16 2016

5 — BI2TCH SESH: A REAL HOUSEWIVES BREAKDOWN color *Entertainment Weekly* no1444/1445 p114 D 16 2016

What to Watch color *Entertainment Weekly* no1435 p51 O 14 2016

Sadness

Hurts So Good G. D. MELTON cartoon *O, The Oprah Magazine* p48 F 2017

Sadoski, Thomas

Life in Pieces' Game Day J. Halterman *TV Guide* p13 D 19 2016

Sadovskii, Michael V.

Leonid Keldysh *Physics Today* v70 no6 p75 Je 2017

Sadr, Moqtada, 1973-

In Iraq, mercurial cleric redefines himself as a nationalist patriot J. Arraf *Christian Century* v134 no13 p14 Je 21 2017

Sadreyev, Ruslan I.

Mutation of a nucleosome compaction region disrupts Polycomb-mediated axial patterning bibl chart diag *Science* v355 no6329 p1081 Mr 10 2017

SADUN, RAFFAELLA

Google's Secret Formula for Management? Doing the Basics Well *Harvard Business Review Digital Articles* p2 2017

A Survey of How 1,000 CEOs Spend Their Day Reveals What Makes Leaders Successful *Harvard Business Review Digital Articles* p2 O 12 2017

WHY DO WE UNDERVALUE COMPETENT MANAGEMENT? NEITHER GREAT LEADERSHIP NOR BRILLIANT STRATEGY MATTERS WITHOUT OPERATIONAL EXCELLENCE graph il img *Harvard Business Review* v95 no5 p120 S/O 2017

Sadza, Roel

Controlled growth and form of precipitating microsculptures bw color diag graph *Science* v355 no6332 p1395 Mr 31 2017

Saebens, Billie Jack

FREEZE FRAME WITH BILLIE JACK SAEBENS C. Toy color *Spin to Win Rodeo* v20 no11 p32 Ja 2017

Weathering the Storm [Cover story] C. Toy color *Spin to Win Rodeo* v21 no4 p60 Je 2017

Saebjornsson, Egill

From the Editor P. Stefánsson color *Iceland Review* v54 no5 p4 S-O 2016

MASTER OF ILLUSION V. HAFSTAÐ color *Iceland Review* v54 no5 p12 S-O 2016

Saeed, Lin May

LIN MAY SAEED A. Rosenmeyer cartoon *Art in America* v104 no11 p132 D 2016

SÁENZ, BENJAMIN ALIRE

Give Ghosts a Chance: Banishing the spirits of the dead has put a town on the path to destruction *New York Times Book Review* p17 O 8 2017

SAEY, TINA HESMAN

Alzheimer's-linked gene is triple threat color *Science News* v192 no6 p13 O 14 2017

Antibody combats variety of cancers color *Science News* v191 no13 p7 Jl 8 2017

Bacteria's physical playbook color *Science News* v192 no6 p17 O 14 2017

Biochemist brews a wild beer color *Science News* v192 no5 p4 S 30 2017

Birth of 'three-parent baby' prompts hope and concern color *Science News* v190 no13 p22 D 24 2016

Budget proposal would slash science *Science News* v191 no7 p15 Ap 15 2017

Cancer studies fall short in redos graph *Science News* v191 no3 p10 F 18 2017

Cephalopod smarts tied to RNA edits color *Science News* v191 no8 p6 Ap 29 2017

Chimps, bonobos interbred long ago color *Science News* v190 no11 p19 N 26 2016

Color vision strategy defies textbooks color *Science News* v190 no8 p10 O 15 2016

The Difference Makers [Cover story] color diag *Science News* v191 no10 p22 My 27 2017

DNA bucks tale of horse taming color *Science News* v191 no10 p10 My 27 2017

DNA data point to unknown hominid *Science News* v190 no10 p13 N 12 2016

DNA errors play big role in cancer color *Science News* v191 no7 p6 Ap 15 2017

DNA tests inflate species counts color *Science News* v191 no4 p6 Mr 4 2017

DNA variants tied to dog sociability color *Science News* v190 no9 p12 O 29 2016

Edited embryos reveal gene's function bw *Science News* v192 no6 p8 O 14 2017

Eggs grown from mouse skin cells color *Science News* v190 no10 p6 N 12 2016

Faux womb keeps preemie lambs alive color *Science News* v191 no10 p6 My 27 2017

Female embryos dismantle male tissue color *Science News* v192 no4 p10 S 16 2017

Heart mutation fixed in embryos bw *Science News* v192 no3 p6 S 2 2017

HIV's U.S. arrival gets pushed back diag map *Science News* v190 no11 p7 N 26 2016

Human-animal chimeras created color *Science News* v191 no3 p6 F 18 2017

Human embryo editing yields results color *Science News* v191 no7 p16 Ap 15 2017

Human knockouts provide drug clues graph *Science News* v191 no9 p10 My 13 2017

Microbes reveal their inner selves color *Science News* v192 no1 p12 Ag 5 2017

New views snag science Nobels bw *Science News* v192 no7 p6 O 28 2017

Nobels honor the small and exotic cartoon color *Science News* v190 no9 p6 O 29 2016

Nose's flu fighters have long memories color *Science News* v191 no13 p16 Jl 8 2017

One Africa exodus populated globe color *Science News* v190 no8 p6 O 15 2016

On Titan, possible life ingredient seen color *Science News* v192 no3 p12 S 2 2017

Photosynthesis treats ailing hearts *Science News* v192 no1 p8 Ag 5 2017

Protein mobs selectively kill brain cells *Science News* v190 no12 p14 D 10 2016

Protein paints chipmunks' stripes color *Science News* v190 no11 p8 N 26 2016

Proteins turn back aging clock color graph *Science News* v191 no1 p6 Ja 21 2017

THE ROAD TO TAMENESS color diag map *Science News* v191 no13 p20 Jl 8 2017

Scientists try to replay domestication color *Science News* v191 no9 p29 My 13 2017

Some cells survive attempted suicide color *Science News* v191 no1 p10 Ja 21 2017

Species resurrection raises ethical questions color *Science News* v192 no7 p28 O 28 2017

Tardigrades aren't genetic mash-ups color *Science News* v192 no2 p13 Ag 19 2017

Toxicologists look to epigenetics color graph *Science News* v190 no13 p12 D 24 2016

U.S. panel backs human gene editing *Science News* v191 no5 p7 Mr 18 2017

Variations on a cell color *Science News* v191 no8 p40 Ap 29 2017

Zika mutation linked to microcephaly color *Science News* v192 no7 p9 O 28 2017

Zika virus 'spillback' into monkeys raises risk of future outbreaks color *Science News* v191 no4 p15 Mr 4 2017

Saez, Emmanuel

Your Neighbor's Fancy Car Should Make You Feel Better About Income Inequality J. V. C. NYE color graph *Reason* v49 no3 p42 Jl 2017

Safar, Erez

West Adams J. HERBST *Los Angeles Magazine* p62 My 2017

Safari (Computer software)

MacOS High Sierra: The new Safari takes steps to reduce persistent user tracking, but is it enough? J. BATTERSBY color *Macworld - Digital Edition* v34 no9 p82 S 2017

Troubleshooting some nasty Safari malware J. Snell color diag *Macworld - Digital Edition* p51 Ap 2017

Safaris

MADAGASCAR S. ROBERTS bw color *Conde Nast Traveler* v52 no4 p74 Ap 2017

NON-JEEPS INVADE EASTER JEEP SAFARI J. HEADLEE color *Dirt Sports + Off-Road* v51 no9 p40 S 2017

Sri Lanka A. Solomon color *Conde Nast Traveler* v51 no11 p92 D 2016

Safaris—Africa

Time for africa color *Conde Nast Traveler* v52 no4 p28 Ap 2017

SAFAVI, CHARLOTTE

PARTY DOWN *Better Homes & Gardens* v95 no1 p33 Ja 2017

Safdie, Benny, 1986-

Caught in the Act R. Brody cartoon *New Yorker* v93 no23 p10 Ag 7 2017

Safdie, Josh, 1984- —Interviews

Seducing Robert Pattinson: How directors Josh and Benny Safdie landed the star for their heist thriller Good Time C. Swanson img *New York* v50 no16 p97 Ag 7 2017

Safecraft (Company)

ONE-HOUR WONDER BURN OUT M. EMERY color *Dirt Sports + Off-Road* v51 no4 p46 Ap 2017

Safes—Design & construction

How to Make a... BOOK SAFE color *Popular Mechanics* v193 no7 p81 S 2016

Safes—Security measures

How to Make a... BOOK SAFE color *Popular Mechanics* v193 no7 p81 S 2016

Safety

See also

Fire prevention

Industrial safety

School safety

O 2017

Sage, Lisette
Driving Home the Safety Discussion il *Consumer Reports* v82 no9 p6 S 2017

Sage grouse
Spirit of the West A. Opar color *Audubon* v119 no3 p3 Fall 2017

Sage Marine (Company)
Sage 15 A. Cort color *Sail* v48 no3 p27 Mr 2017

Sageer, Julie Ann
Julie Taboulie's Lebanese Kitchen *Publishers Weekly* v264 no10 p55 Mr 6 2017

Sager, Gene
Captive Royals & Meat MACHINES ANIMALS in AMERICA TODAY *Vegetarian Journal* v35 no2 p18 2016

SAGER, JEANNE
"OUR BIG SISTER is our guardian angel" bw color *Good Housekeeping* v265 no2 p71 Ag 2017

SAGER, Mike
Beauty and the Beast Mode cartoon color *Men's Health* v32 no3 p19 Ap 2017
DINOSAUR COWBOY *Smithsonian* v48 no4 p52 Jl/Ag 2017
THE LONELY HEDONIST bw color *Esquire* v166 no4 p116 N 2016
My Son, the Man of Tomorrow color *Men's Health* v32 no5 p119 Je 2017
THE ULTIMATE MEN'S HEALTH GUY bw cartoon color *Men's Health* v32 no9 p96 N 2017
UNCONDITIONAL color *Men's Health* v32 no5 p112 Je 2017

Saginaw, Paul
What Price Growth? B. BURLINGHAM color *Forbes* v198 no6 p56 N 8 2016

Sagittarius A* (Astronomy)
Coming soon: Our first picture of a black hole A. Klesman color *Astronomy* v45 no8 p13 Ag 2017

Sagittarius (Constellation)
Our galaxy's center creates planet-sized swarms of gas color *Astronomy* v45 no5 p21 My 2017
Rogue globular clusters P. HARRINGTON color *Astronomy* v45 no9 p68 S 2017

Sagittarius dwarf irregular galaxy
When galaxies become CANNIBALS [Cover story] M. West color *Astronomy* v44 no12 p20 D 2016

Sagner, Karin
Women Walking: Freedom, Adventure, Independence *Publishers Weekly* v264 no32 p65 Ag 7 2017

SAGOFF, MARK
Medical crises color *Issues in Science & Technology* v33 no1 p8 Fall 2016
Pricing an ecosystem *Issues in Science & Technology* v33 no1 p11 Fall 2016

SAGON, CANDY
Feast. Fast. Repeat color *AARP: The Magazine* v60 no1A p14 D 2016/Ja 2017
Mysteries of the Human Body EXPLAINED! cartoon color *AARP: The Magazine* v60 no3A p26 Ap/My 2017

Saguaro
The Bones of a Saguaro K. VAUGEN *Arizona Highways* v93 no3 p34 Mr 2017
BORN SURVIVOR L. W. CHEEK *Arizona Highways* v93 no3 p44 Mr 2017
GRAVE SITUATION N. AUSTIN *Arizona Highways* v93 no3 p50 Mr 2017
A Saguaro's universe J. HESTER color *Astronomy* v45 no4 p20 Ap 2017
WE KNOW IT'S COMING R. STIEVE *Arizona Highways* v93 no3 p2 Mr 2017
WITH A 10-FEET POLE K. MONTGOMERY *Arizona Highways* v93 no3 p38 Mr 2017

Saguaro National Park (Ariz.)
The Big Pictures: SAGUARO NATIONAL PARK *Arizona Highways* v93 no3 p16 Mr 2017
The Bones of a Saguaro K. VAUGEN *Arizona Highways* v93 no3 p34 Mr 2017
GRAVE SITUATION N. AUSTIN *Arizona Highways* v93 no3 p50 Mr 2017
HOPE CAMP TRAIL R. STIEVE *Arizona Highways* v93 no2 p54

F 2017
WE KNOW IT'S COMING R. STIEVE *Arizona Highways* v93 no3 p2 Mr 2017
THE WILDERNESS OF unreality N. N. DODGE *Arizona Highways* v93 no3 p28 Mr 2017
WITH A 10-FEET POLE K. MONTGOMERY *Arizona Highways* v93 no3 p38 Mr 2017

Sah, Sunita
Forensic Science Must Be Scientific color *Scientific American* v317 no4 p12 O 2017
Research: Missing Product Information Doesn't Bother Consumers as Much as It Should *Harvard Business Review Digital Articles* p2 S 28 2017

Saha, Ambarneil
Metal-catalyzed electrochemical diazidation of alkenes diag *Science* v357 no6351 p575 Ag 11 2017

Saha, O.
The sacral autonomic outflow is sympathetic bibl color diag *Science* v354 no6314 p893 N 18 2016

SAHA, PURBITA
Beefing Up Bird Habitat *Audubon* v119 no1 p16 Spr 2017
Birds for the Battle-worn color *Audubon* v119 no3 p26 Fall 2017
An Environmental (Dirty) Laundry List *Audubon* v119 no1 p18 Spr 2017
EYES IN THE SKIES color *Audubon* v119 no3 p46 Fall 2017
Let It Grow *Audubon* v119 no3 p13 Fall 2017
Sweet Deal *Audubon* v119 no1 p17 Spr 2017

Saha, Shambaditya
ATP as a biological hydrotrope color graph *Science* v356 no6339 p753 My 19 2017

Sahara desert ant
Sahara's Coolest Ants N. Strochlic color *National Geographic* v230 no5 p19 N 2016

Sahara—Social conditions
HIGHWAY THROUGH HELL T. MCCORMICK color *Foreign Policy* no226 p34 S/O 2017

Sahni, Nidhi
What the U.S. Can Learn From India and Brazil About Preventive Health Care *Harvard Business Review Digital Articles* p2 N 14 2014

Sahni, Nikhil
How the U.S. Can Reduce Waste in Health Care Spending by $1 Trillion *Harvard Business Review Digital Articles* p2 O 13 2015

Sahrawi (African people)—Political activity
Africa's Last Colony C. ROSS bw color *New Republic* v248 no5 p46 My 2017

Sahu, Biswajyoti
Impact of cytosine methylation on DNA binding specificities of human transcription factors diag *Science* v356 no6337 p502 My 5 2017

Sahu, Kailash
HUBBLE WEIGHS A WHITE DWARF A. Klesman color *Astronomy* v45 no10 p12 O 2017
Relativistic deflection of background starlight measures the mass of a nearby white dwarf star chart color graph *Science* v356 no6342 p1046 Je 9 2017

Sahún Logroño, Rosa
RETINOBLASTOMA RELATED1 mediates germline entry in Arabidopsis color diag *Science* v356 no6336 p396 Ap 28 2017

Said, Boris
EDITOR'S LETTER K. WOLFKILL *Road & Track* v69 no3 p24 O 2017

Said, Edward W., 1935-2003
The Case of the Missing Stylist L. Smith color *Weekly Standard* v22 no37 p5 Je 5 2017

SAID, TAMER
OUR STORIES TRAVEL THE WORLD color *Publishers Weekly* v263 no43 p(Sp)9 O 24 2016

Saiga—Diseases
Fatal virus felling rare antelope color *Science* v355 no6324 p436 F 3 2017

Saik, Rob—Interviews
THE SUCCESSFUL INTERVIEW A. McConnell *Successful Farming* v115 no4 p12 Mr 2017

SAIKIN, ANNA
Pay Your Respects color map *Backpacker* p28 My 2017

Je 2017

Volvo Race Renews its U.S. Roots color *Sail* v48 no6 p17 Je 2017

Sailing equipment

See also

    Sailboats

Lockers D. Everitt color *Sail* v48 no9 p64 S 2017

SAILING INSTRUMENTS [Cover story] P. Gutowski color *Sail* v48 no8 p38 Ag 2017

Sailing equipment—Evaluation

COASTAL CRUISING Gear P. Nielsen color *Sail* v48 no5 p26 My 2017

HOLIDAY GIFT GUIDE A. Wisch color *Sail* v47 no12 p22 D 2016

Sailing instruction

No Man's Land: SHARPENING SAILING SKILLS ON A WOMEN-ONLY COURSE A. Wisch color map *Sail* v48 no8 p41 Ag 2017

Sailing ships

In Svalbard L. OSOFSKY *Orion Magazine* v35 no4/5 p12 Jl-O 2016

SCHOONERMEN in the CARIBBEAN 600 T. CUNLIFFE color map *Sail* v48 no6 p32 Je 2017

Sailing ships—Design & construction

A Lighter Mainsail S. Parry color *Sail* v48 no9 p54 S 2017

Sailing techniques

ASK SAIL D. CASEY, B. HANCOCK et al color *Sail* v48 no2 p70 F 2017

CRUISING TIPS T. Cunliffe color *Sail* v48 no6 p48 Je 2017

Weather Cloths D. Everitt cartoon *Sail* v48 no2 p68 F 2017

Sailing—Awards

U.S. Sonar Crew Scores Paralympic Silver A. Cort color *Sail* v47 no12 p18 D 2016

Sailing—Equipment & supplies

Gear P. NIELSEN color *Sail* v48 no10 p32 O 2017

Sailing—History

Longue Route 2018 C. J. Doane color *Sail* v48 no8 p88 Ag 2017

Sailing—Safety measures

STAYING ALIVE P. Nielsen color *Sail* v48 no7 p42 Jl 2017

Sailliot, Franck

THE FRENCH DEFECTION J. ANGELOS bw color *New York Times Magazine* p44 Ja 29 2017

Sailors

CHANGE OF VENUE, CHANGE OF NAME M. Werling *Sea Magazine* v108 no9 p6 S 2016

Crazy Times at Sea P. Nielsen *Sail* v48 no3 p4 Mr 2017

Discussion C. H. Schwefel, P. Ensley et al *Smithsonian* v48 no5 p4 S 2017

Fools Afloat! color *Sail* v48 no11 p8 N 2017

MEET STEPHEN JACKSON *Sea Magazine* v109 no2 pCA-5 F 2017

Understanding Set and Drift C. McBride graph *Sail* v47 no12 p44 D 2016

UNFINISHED BUSINESS color map *Sail* v47 no12 p40 D 2016

Sailors—Competitions

Bigger Than the Cup C. J. Doane color *Sail* v48 no1 p18 Ja 2017

Sailors—History

RACING THE STORM M. TEAGUE *Smithsonian* v48 no4 p64 Jl/Ag 2017

Sailors—Interviews

John Rousmaniere A. Schell color *Sail* v48 no4 p16 Ap 2017

Sailors—United States

Valor He Built, He Fought J. W. Brown bw color *Military History* v34 no2 p16 Jl 2017

Sailors—United States—History

Searching for Captain Blye A. J. Begley *Prologue* v49 no1 p58 Spr 2017

Sails—Evaluation

Higher Tech P. Nielsen color *Sail* v48 no7 p48 Jl 2017

Sails—Maintenance & repair

Sail Care P. Nielsen color *Sail* v48 no1 p44 Ja 2017

Saini, Angela

How science has fed female stereotypes E. Engelhaupt color *Science News* v192 no3 p27 S 2 2017

Saint, P. Michael

Win Community Approval for New Business Construction *Harvard Business Review Digital Articles* p2 My 29 2015

Saint, Sanjay

6 Things Every Mentor Should Do *Harvard Business Review Digital Articles* p2 Mr 29 2017

Saint, The (TV program)

MOORE THAN BOND C. Nashawaty color *Entertainment Weekly* no1468/1469 p81 Je 2-9 2017

Saint Augustine (Fla.)—Description & travel

BEST IN TRAVEL 2017 K. A. Renzulli, M. Leonhardt et al color *Money* v46 no3 p58 Ap 2017

Saint-Barthélemy—Description & travel

Yes, You Can Do Low-Key St. Barts A. Brooks color *Conde Nast Traveler* v52 no1 p60 Ja 2017

Saint Croix (Me.)

The Caribbean With a Twang B. NEWCOTT color *AARP: The Magazine* v59 no2A p44 F/Mr 2016

Saint George's Day

ABOVE & BEYOND bw *New Yorker* v93 no10 p32 Ap 24 2017

Saint Helena

Freedom in Exile [Cover story] E. CALLAWAY color graph map *Natural History* v125 no3 p18 Mr 2017

Saint John (United States Virgin Islands)—Description & travel

St. John Sojourn Z. Prochazka color *Sail* v48 no3 p66 Mr 2017

Saint Johns River (Fla.)

A World Apart S. MURRAY bw color *Power & Motoryacht* v33 no4 p56 Ap 2017

Saint Louis (Mo.)

2016 NRPA Annual Conference Special Events [Cover story] *Parks & Recreation* v51 no10 p70 O 2016

CORRECTION *House Beautiful* p94 Jl 2017

St. Louis Bound *Parks & Recreation* v51 no10 p24 O 2016

Saint Lucian poets

Derek Walcott S. Begley color *Time* v189 no12 p19 Ap 3 2017

Saint Martin (West Indies)

JUST ANOTHER DAY ON INDIGO E. SANFORD cartoon color *Sail* v48 no11 p48 N 2017

THREE WORLDS, One Boat Z. PROCHAZKA color map *Sail* v48 no10 p40 O 2017

Saint Martinville (La.)—Description & travel

MEMORY LANE P. F. STAHLS JR. color *Louisiana Life* v37 no3 p34 Ja/F 2017

Saint Patrick's Day

EVENTS OF THE YEAR *Advocate* no1088 p38 D 2016/Ja 2017

THE INVENTION OF ST. PATRICK'S DAY M. Cronin *Saturday Evening Post* v289 no2 p78 Mr/Ap 2017

MARCH/APRIL K. MASSICOT color *Louisiana Life* v37 no4 p108 Mr/Ap 2017

My Shot *National Geographic Kids* no468 p35 Mr 2017

Saint Patrick's Day—History

The Political History of St. Patrick's Day Green O. B. Waxman *Time* v189 no11 p27 Mr 27 2017

Saint Paul (Minn.)—Description & travel

A Maker's Guide to... MINNEAPOLIS-ST. PAUL F. MAROUKIAN color map *Popular Mechanics* p26 D 2016/Ja 2017

Saint Peter's Day

In a Cape Cod fishing town, Catholic culture is a blessing M. J. O'Loughlin color *America* v217 no2 p17 Jl 24 2017

Saint Simons Island (Ga.)

SOUTH'S BEST BARBECUE R. Moss color *Southern Living* v52 no4 p70 Ap 2017

Saint Anthony High School (Jersey City, N.J.)

School Ties D. Hurley color *Sports Illustrated* v126 no11 p116 Ap 17-24 2017

Saintcrow, Lilith

Cormorant Run *Publishers Weekly* v264 no17 p72 Ap 24 2017

Saint-Exupéry, Antoine de, 1900-1944

c. 1930: Patagonia A. de Saint-Exupéry *Lapham's Quarterly* v10 no2 p156 Spr 2017

Saint John, Bozoma

Total Boz Moves A. TILLERY and S. T. BROWN color *Ebony* v72 no5 p72 Mr 2017

Saint John, Bozoma, 1976-—Interviews

"Be your whole self" A. D. Barnett color *Glamour* v115 no9 p130 S 2017

Bozoma Saint John Wants To Humanize Uber A. M. Cox *New York Times Magazine* p58 S 3 2017

Saint Laurent, Yves, 1936-2008

SO SAINT LAURENT bw *Harper's Bazaar* no3656 p184 S 2017

Yves, Please! J. Lance cartoon *Glamour* v114 no12 p56 D 2016

Saint Mary's College of California (Moraga, Calif.)

Saint Mary's College of California *Dance Magazine* v90 p120 2016/2017 Supplement College Guide

Saint Petersburg (Russia)—Buildings, structures, etc.

Blooming Genius M. OWENS color *Architectural Digest* v74 no10 p180 O 1 2017

Saints

See also

Christian saints

The Fastest Nun in the West H. NORDHAUS *Smithsonian* v47 no7 p35 N 2016

Saints—History

Learning to love Thérèse S. Guthrie *Christian Century* v133 no25 p10 D 7 2016

Saints—Legends

SAINTS NOT SUPERHEROES [Cover story] R. Ellsberg color *America* v216 no6 p28 Mr 20 2017

Saint Xavier High School (Cincinnati, Ohio)

Q + A *Cincinnati Magazine* v50 no7 p26 Ap 2017

Saito, Riichiro

Mildred S. Dresselhaus *Physics Today* v70 no6 p73 Je 2017

Saitou, Mitinori

Fertile offspring from sterile sex chromosome trisomic mice chart diag *Science* v357 no6354 p932 S 1 2017

Saizarbitoria, Ramón, 1944-

A Game of Love and Chance T. Parks bw color *New York Review of Books* v64 no10 p44 Je 8 2017

Sajad Esmaeily, Amir

All-printed thin-film transistors from networks of liquid-exfoliated nanosheets diag *Science* v356 no6333 p69 Ap 7 2017

Sajti, Eniko

An environment-dependent transcriptional network specifies human microglia identity color *Science* v356 no6344 p1248 Je 23 2017

Sajwani, Hussain

THE DONALD OF THE DESERT A. BROWN color *Forbes* v199 no3 p62 Mr 28 2017

Sakai, Sonoko

The Next Generation: MEET THE CHEFS BROADENING L.A.'S DEFINITION OF JAPANESE FOOD G. SNYDER *Los Angeles Magazine* v62 no9 p110 S 2017

Sakamoto, Kei

Neonatal acquisition of Clostridia species protects against colonization by bacterial pathogens diag *Science* v356 no6335 p315 Ap 21 2017

Sakavic, Nora

The Game Changer J. McCARTNEY color *Publishers Weekly* v263 no43 p41 O 24 2016

Sake cups

HIGHBROW GIFT GUIDE E. FISHMAN bw color *Chicago* v65 no12 p52 D 2016

Sakey, Marcus

Afterlife C. Collis color *Entertainment Weekly* no1473 p62 Jl 7 2017

The Sticky Dark color *Publishers Weekly* v264 no26 p157 Je 26 2017

Saki, Ida

back to school (again) A. RIVERS *Dance Magazine* p24 2016/2017

Saklani, Praful

Sometimes "Small Data" Is Enough to Create Smart Products *Harvard Business Review Digital Articles* p2 Jl 19 2017

Sakoui, Anousha

And Then There Was Hannity bw color *Bloomberg Businessweek* no4520 p54 My 1 2017

Can VR Find a Seat In the Parlor? color *Bloomberg Businessweek* no4524 p22 My 29 2017

"HOLLYWOOD" color *Bloomberg Businessweek* no4511 p18 F 13 2017

Hollywood Hunts for Its Next Pot of Gold bw *Bloomberg Businessweek* no4540 p24 O 2 2017

World of Wonder Life's a Drag color *Bloomberg Businessweek* no4521 p22 My 8 2017

Saks Fifth Avenue Inc.

Downtown Style L. C. LENTZ *Architectural Record* v204 no11 p37 N 2016

THE GRAND GARDEN PARTY color *Harper's Bazaar* no3653 p144 My 2017

Sakuja, Jugnu

A 4-Step Process to Help Senior Teams Prioritize Decisions color *Harvard Business Review Digital Articles* p2 Mr 27 2017

Sakurai, Keiichiro

Terawatt-scale photovoltaics: Trajectories and challenges chart graph *Science* v356 no6334 p141 Ap 14 2017

SALA, OSVALDO E.

How Scientists Can Help End the Land-Use Conflict *BioScience* v66 no11 p915 N 1 2016

SALABERT, SHAWNTÉ

THE SHARPEST TOOL IN THE SHED color *Backpacker* p71 Ag 2017

Salad dressing

BLOOD ORANGES M. XERAKIA *Better Homes & Gardens* v95 no1 p63 Ja 2017

Dress Appropriately C. SAFFITZ color *Bon Appetit* v62 no10 p42 O 2017

Fresh, Homemade SALAD DRESSINGS K. Quillen, M. Wick et al *Mother Earth News* no281 p36 Ap/My 2017

Saladino, Kristen

HOW TO WEAR IT... anywhere! color *Good Housekeeping* v264 no5 p20 My 2017

HOW TO WEAR IT... anywhere! color *Good Housekeeping* v265 no5 p16 N 2017

HOW TO WEAR IT color *Good Housekeeping* v264 no2 p16 F 2017

HOW TO WEAR IT... color *Good Housekeeping* v265 no2 p14 Ag 2017

Salads

See also

Potato salads

15-Minute Meal under $15 color *Prevention* v69 no1 p14 Ja 2017

20-MINUTE MEALS color *Good Housekeeping* v264 no6 p111 Je 2017

THE 5-INGREDIENT Farmers' Market Cookbook L. Cericola, K. Hammonds et al color *Southern Living* v52 no7 p61 Jl 2017

THE ART of SIMPLICITY C. Saffitz, A. Knowlton et al color *Bon Appetit* no8 p56 Ag 2017

BUY 5, DROP 5 K. Glassman color *Women's Health* v14 no6 p104 Jl 2017

CAESAR SALAD *Martha Stewart Living* no268 p81 O 2016

California Dreaming B. Ng color *Bon Appetit* v62 no7 p36 Jl 2017

CHEF'S SALAD A. RAPOPORT *Bon Appetit* v62 no7 p10 Jl 2017

Dinner Tonight A. RAPOPORT color *Bon Appetit* no11 p43 N 2017

Easy Backyard BBQ [Cover story] K. Hymore color *Prevention* v69 no6 p82 Je 2017

End-of-Summer Crostini color *Good Housekeeping* v265 no2 p109 Ag 2017

Healthyish C. SAFFITZ color *Bon Appetit* v62 no6 p35 Je 2017

INTO THE SPOTLIGHT S. BOCAR color *Martha Stewart Living* p62 My 2017

Little Big Time A. STANEK color *Bon Appetit* v62 no4 p28 Ap 2017

LUNCH BOXES [Cover story] J. Waldbieser color *Women's Health* v14 no6 p87 Jl 2017

MEAL OF THE MONTH color *Prevention* v69 no4 p17 Ap 2017

Meet your new favorite vegetable C. Hall color *Redbook* p22 Je 2017

Mixing Bowl color *O, The Oprah Magazine* p108 Je 2017

A New Spin on Succotash J. Levy color *Southern Living* v52 no6 p136 Je 2017

POWER UP YOUR SALAD color *Good Housekeeping* v265 no2 p93 Ag 2017

PUT SOME FETA AT THE BOTTOM M. J. WEEDMAN img *New York* v49 no20 p106 O 3 2016

Rainbow Rolls color *Good Housekeeping* v264 no6 p101 Je 2017

Rainbow Salad img *New York* v49 no23 p60 N 14 2016

RETURN TO GLAMOUR M. True color *Sunset* v239 no3 p80 S 2017

r.s.v.p.: BEST NEW RESTAURANTS EDITION E. WARTZ-

MAN, A. RAPOPORT et al bw color *Bon Appetit* p16 S 2017

SALAD DAYS M. HENNESSY color *Chicago* v66 no10 p50 O 2017

SALAD DAYS N. Olsson color *House Beautiful* p164 Ag 2017

The Salad Pizza *Saturday Evening Post* v289 no2 p23 Mr/Ap 2017

Seasonal Salads color *Amazing Wellness* v9 no2 p82 Spr 2017

Simple, slimming sides L. Lillien color *Redbook* p98 O 2017

SIMPLY FRESH S. Dry bw color *Louisiana Life* v37 no5 p54 My/Je 2017

SINGULAR Sensation M. Kiesel color *O, The Oprah Magazine* p106 Je 2017

SINGULAR Sensation M. Kiesel color *O, The Oprah Magazine* p143 N 2017

SUMMER B. HOSTETTER *Indianapolis Monthly* v12 no40 p64 Ag 2017

SUMMER on a PLATE R. Martinez color *Bon Appetit* no8 p82 Ag 2017

summer on the side Y. Ottolenghi color *Bon Appetit* v62 no7 p50 Jl 2017

SUPER-SATISFYING SALADS color *Redbook* p118 Je 2017

THAI SOCIETY T. KIRTS *Indianapolis Monthly* p46 N 2017

The Thrifty Girl's Guide to Brunch S. Sampson and S. G. Levy color *Glamour* v115 no3 p127 Mr 2017

TURN OVƏR A NƏIII LЄAf A. STANEK color *Bon Appetit* p110 S 2017

WEEKNIGHT COOKING C. March color *Sunset* v238 no3 p80 Mr 2017

WEEKNIGHT COOKING color *Sunset* v239 no1 p94 Jl 2017

Where the Wild Things Are In the Suburbs E. BASTOS color *Reader's Digest* v189 no1130 p56 My 2017

Whole-Grain Goodness P. Grandjean color *Southern Living* v52 no5 p144 My 2017

THE WORKBOOK color *Martha Stewart Living* p124 Ap 2017

Yellow Lentil Salad color *Prevention* v69 no5 p17 My 2017

SALAHUDDIN, PATRICIA

Deepening Students' Understanding of the Qur'anic Text [Cover story] *Islamic Horizons* v46 no2 p34 Mr/Ap 2017

SALAI, SEAN

Spiritual Costs of Debt color *America* v215 no15 p21 N 14 2016

SALAM, REIHAN

The Case for Skills-Based Immigration [Cover story] color *National Review* v69 no16 p24 Ag 28 2017

Democrats And Plutocrats *National Review* v69 no18 p14 O 2 2017

Trump the Triangulator? color *National Review* v68 no22 p33 D 5 2016

Who Needs Advisory Boards? *National Review* v69 no17 p13 S 11 2017

Salam, Reihan—Interviews

What I Wear to Work: REIHAN SALAM J. Chen color *Bloomberg Businessweek* no4495 p75 O 17 2016

Salamanders as pets

Save our salamanders P. CHRISTIE color *Maclean's* v130 no7 p11 Ag 2017

Salamanders—Diseases

SAVING EUROPE'S SALAMANDERS E. Stokstad color map *Science* v357 no6348 p242 Jl 21 2017

WILDLIFE color *Canadian Geographic* v137 no5 p20 S/O 2017

Salamati, Payman

Creating a culture of ethics in Iran bibl *Science* v354 no6310 p296 O 21 2016

Salami, Jemilat

Waste disposal–An attractive strategy for cancer therapy bibl chart diag *Science* v355 no6330 p1163 Mr 17 2017

Salamida, F.

Observation of a large-scale anisotropy in the arrival directions of cosmic rays above 8 × 1018 eV *Science* v357 no6357 p1266 S 22 2017

Salamis Island (Greece)

FLASHBACK bw color *MHQ: Quarterly Journal of Military History* v30 no1 p6 Aut 2017

SALAMON, JEFF

A CITY SLICKER in the PANHANDLE *Texas Monthly* v45 no8 p6 Ag 2017

ENEMIES, A Love Story *Texas Monthly* v45 no2 p56 F 2017

HOW TRUMP DID IT *Texas Monthly* v45 no1 p52 Ja 2017

THE ONE QUESTION INTERVIEW: ADAM STERNBERGH *Texas Monthly* v45 no8 p42 Ag 2017

PARLEZ-VOUS BBQ? *Texas Monthly* v45 no6 p111 Je 2017

REVENGE OF THE FILM NERDS *Texas Monthly* v45 no7 p70 Jl 2017

SALAS, ABEL

Real Estate and The Art Of War *Los Angeles Magazine* p15 My 2017

Salas, Christian

Positive biodiversity-productivity relationship predominant in global forests bibl chart graph map *Science* v354 no6309 paaf8957-1 O 14 2016

Salatin, Joel

CHILDREN AND CHORES: Give kids responsibilities that will help them thrive while learning self-reliance *Mother Earth News* no283 p59 Ag/S 2017

COMPOSTING MANURE The Scoop on Poop *Mother Earth News* no280 p72 F/Mr 2017

PRESERVING HOMEGROWN PRODUCE: Putting up the garden bounty at Polyface Farms is a family affair *Mother Earth News* no284 p53 O/N 2017

Profitable PERMACULTURE PRINCIPLES: The application of permaculture design at Polyface has helped increase the farm's efficiency and functionality *Mother Earth News* no282 p75 Je/Jl 2017

Small-Scale MOB GRAZING *Mother Earth News* no279 p72 D/Ja 2017

Turn Food Scraps Into POULTRY FEASTS *Mother Earth News* no281 p99 Ap/My 2017

Salay, Lauren E.

The [4Fe4S] cluster of human DNA primase functions as a redox switch using DNA charge transport color *Science* v355 no6327 p813 F 24 2017

Salazar, Angela

HOORAY FOR Hollywood color *InStyle* v23 no12 p252 N 2016

KIERNAN SHIPKA color *InStyle* v24 no5 p57 My 2017

LUCY HALE color *InStyle* v24 no4 p57 Ap 2017

TOVE LOVE color *InStyle* v24 no1 p22 Ja 2017

SALAZAR, CARLOS

GRILLED SWEET POTATOES *Indianapolis Monthly* v12 no40 p69 Ag 2017

Salazar, H.

Observation of a large-scale anisotropy in the arrival directions of cosmic rays above 8 × 1018 eV *Science* v357 no6357 p1266 S 22 2017

Salcedo, Doris—Exhibitions

SEEING WAR THROUGH ROSE PETALS A. WILLIS *In These Times* v41 no2 p41 F 2017

Salcedo, Ignacio

The extent of forest in dryland biomes [Cover story] chart map *Science* v356 no6338 p635 My 12 2017

Salcido, Marie

POWDER PLAY chart color diag *Sunset* v238 no1 p22 Ja 2017

THE Trip color *Sunset* v238 no1 p48 Ja 2017

SALCITO, JORDAN

Why You Should Become a Wine Snob color *GQ: Gentlemen's Quarterly* v97 no10 p80 O 2017

Saldana, Zoë, 1978-

Double Take E. Wilson color *InStyle* v24 no5 p68 My 2017

Gamora the Merrier C. Collis color *Entertainment Weekly* no1465 p20 My 12 2017

Sound Bites color *Entertainment Weekly* no1466 p10 My 19 2017

Zoe Saldana, Actor E. Dockterman color *Time* v189 no3 p60 Ja 16 2017

Saldanha, Carlos, 1965-

FERDINAND D. Heching color *Entertainment Weekly* no1478 / 1479 p75 Ag 18-25 2017

Sale, Kirkpatrick, 1937-

The Decentralist J. MCCLAUGHRY color *Reason* v49 no1 p66 My 2017

Sale of business enterprises

See also

Liquidation

Dealing with the Emotional Fallout of Selling Your Business J. Giesea *Harvard Business Review Digital Articles* p2 S 1 2015

How Talent Pulls One Over on the Capitalists R. L. Martin *Har-*

vard Business Review Digital Articles p2 Ag 4 2015

Saleem, Basharat

The Stage Sets for Convention 2017: In selecting the theme, the ISNA leadership considered the situation as challenges facing Muslims intensify *Islamic Horizons* v46 no3 p18 My/Je 2017

SALEEM, MUHAMMAD

An Ecoregion-Based Approach to Protecting Half the Terrestrial Realm *BioScience* v67 no6 p534 Je 2017

Saleh, A.

Observation of a large-scale anisotropy in the arrival directions of cosmic rays above 8 × 1018 eV *Science* v357 no6357 p1266 S 22 2017

Saleh, Tamjeed

Enzymes at work are enzymes in motion bibl diag *Science* v355 no6322 p247 Ja 20 2017

Saleh, Tarik

A Dirty Business N. Rapold color *Film Comment* v53 no2 p8 Mr/Ap 2017

Salehi, M.

Quantized Faraday and Kerr rotation and axion electrodynamics of a 3D topological insulator bibl graph *Science* v354 no6316 p1124 D 2 2016

Salem (Mass.)—Description & travel

Salem, Massachusetts: Maritime history and witchy lore exist side by side in one of the most idiosyncratic towns in the country A. GRAVES *Yankee* v81 no5 p70 S/O 2017

Salem, Yasir

Runner's Digest K. FOX color *Runner's World* v52 no8 p48 S 2017

Salem Witch Trials, 1692-1693

A BRIEF HISTORY OF WITCH HUNTS K. Harloe color *Mother Jones* v42 no6 p60 N/D 2017

Salén, Bjarne

Fated J. Stifter bw cartoon color *Powder* v45 no5 p52 Ja 2017

Saler, Robert

Nobody Cries When We Die: God, Community, and Surviving to Adulthood *Christian Century* v134 no13 p39 Je 21 2017

Reflections on the lectionary *Christian Century* v133 no26 p21 D 21 2016

SALERNO, JONATHAN

The Consequences of Internal Migration in Sub-Saharan Africa: A Case Study *BioScience* v67 no7 p664 Jl 2017

Sales

See also

Antiquities sales & prices

Costume—Sales & prices

Delivery of goods (Law)

Firearm sales & prices

6 Reasons Salespeople Win or Lose a Sale S. W. Martin *Harvard Business Review Digital Articles* p2 Je 23 2017

AMAZON BECOMES A PUBLISHING FORCE *Publishers Weekly* v263 no47 p34 N 21 2016

B&N Still Searching For "Magic Bullet" to Stop Sales Slide J. Milliot chart *Publishers Weekly* v264 no10 p4 Mr 6 2017

DC Goes All-Out Marketing Rebirth Book Collections C. Reid color *Publishers Weekly* v264 no13 p11 Mr 27 2017

Developing Employees' Strengths Boosts Sales, Profit, and Engagement B. Rigoni and J. Asplund *Harvard Business Review Digital Articles* p2 S 1 2016

Driving Sales Success This Quarter, This Year, and Beyond A. A. Zoltners, P. K. Sinha et al *Harvard Business Review Digital Articles* p2 D 1 2016

The End-of-Quarter Sales Rush Costs Companies Money K. Krogue *Harvard Business Review Digital Articles* p2 2017

The Harry Potter Effect color *Earth Island Journal* v32 no3 p4 Aut 2017

How AI Is Streamlining Marketing and Sales B. Power *Harvard Business Review Digital Articles* p2 Je 12 2017

How to Improve Your Sales Skills, Even If You're Not a Salesperson R. Knight *Harvard Business Review Digital Articles* p2 My 22 2017

In the Best Sales Teams, About Half of the People Are in Support Roles M. Viertler, D. Sprengel et al *Harvard Business Review Digital Articles* p2 My 25 2016

Parneros Charged with Reversing B&N Sales Slide J. Milliot chart *Publishers Weekly* v264 no18 p5 My 1 2017

Reinvent Your Sales Process While Still Hitting Your Numbers F. V. Cespedes and T. Bova *Harvard Business Review Digital Articles* p2 F 18 2015

The Technology Trends That Matter to Sales Teams A. A. Zoltners, P. K. Sinha et al *Harvard Business Review Digital Articles* p2 My 7 2015

To Improve Sales, Pay More Attention to Presales H. Hatami, C. L. Plotkin et al *Harvard Business Review Digital Articles* p2 F 17 2015

Why Sex and Violence Don't Sell N. Torres *Harvard Business Review Digital Articles* p2 S 4 2015

You Can Make Your Sales Data a Lot Better with a Little Discipline J. Fowler *Harvard Business Review Digital Articles* p2 Je 13 2017

Sales & prices of government securities—Economic aspects

Mnuchin Ponders Locking in Low Rates L. Capo McCormick and S. Mohsin *Bloomberg Businessweek* no4521 p39 My 8 2017

Sales, Samantha

Employee's time off is adding up *People Management* p53 F 2017

Is 'cosy' deal with ex-staff fair? PM's Fixer Samantha Sales tackles readers' big issues *People Management* p52 Jl 2017

No one will challenge this bully *People Management* p53 S 2017

Staff are holding us to ransom *People Management* p53 Mr 2017

Sales, Tom

Celebrating S&T's 75th Anniversary *Sky & Telescope* v133 no2 p6 F 2017

FROM OUR READERS *Sky & Telescope* v133 no1 p6 Ja 2017

Sales culture

4 Ways to Build a Productive Sales Culture F. V. Cespedes and S. Maughan *Harvard Business Review Digital Articles* p2 Je 16 2015

Sales executives

The 7 Attributes of the Most Effective Sales Leaders S. W. Martin *Harvard Business Review Digital Articles* p2 S 11 2015

Muy Maravilloso color *Weekly Standard* v22 no31 p4 Ap 17 2017

When You Need Sales Specialists, Not Sales Generalists M. Kovac *Harvard Business Review Digital Articles* p2 F 18 2016

Sales executives—Attitudes

A Portrait of the Overperforming Salesperson S. W. Martin *Harvard Business Review Digital Articles* p2 Je 20 2016

Sales force management

Great Salespeople Are Born, but Great Sales Forces Are Made A. A. Zoltners, P. K. Sinha et al *Harvard Business Review Digital Articles* p2 My 20 2016

Ineffective Sales Leaders Can Cause Lasting Damage A. A. Zoltners, P. K. Sinha et al color *Harvard Business Review Digital Articles* p2 Ja 30 2017

Why Sales Teams Should Reexamine Territory Design A. A. Zoltners, P. K. Sinha et al *Harvard Business Review Digital Articles* p2 Ag 7 2015

Sales forecasting

Intel demotes PCs, giving datacenter chips first crack at new technologies M. HACHMAN color *PCWorld* p22 Mr 2017

Setting Big Hairy Goals—and Missing P. Wahba color *Fortune* v176 no2 p16 Ag 1 2017

Want Growth? Focus on Sales J. K. GLASSMAN color *Kiplinger's Personal Finance* v70 no12 p18 D 2016

Why the future is bright for Apple's iPad J. Snell color diag *Macworld - Digital Edition* p103 Ap 2017

Sales incentive programs

There's No One System for Paying Your Global Sales Force A. A. Zoltners, P. K. Sinha et al *Harvard Business Review Digital Articles* p2 N 13 2015

Sales management

See also

Sales reporting

4 Ways to Build a Productive Sales Culture F. V. Cespedes and S. Maughan *Harvard Business Review Digital Articles* p2 Je 16 2015

The 7 Attributes of the Most Effective Sales Leaders S. W. Martin *Harvard Business Review Digital Articles* p2 S 11 2015

Companies with a Formal Sales Process Generate More Revenue J. Jordan and R. Kelly *Harvard Business Review Digital Articles* p2 Ja 21 2015

Help Your Salespeople Spend Time on the Right Things A. A. Zoltners, P. K. Sinha et al *Harvard Business Review Digital Ar-*

NOW PLAYING color *Entertainment Weekly* no1457/1458 p79 Mr 17 2017

The Salesman J. McGovern color *Entertainment Weekly* no1451/1452 p91 F 3-10 2017

UNSEEN AND UNHEARD S. KLAWANS color *Nation* v304 no7 p36 Mr 6 2017

Sales—Methodology

How to Actually Put Your Marketing Data to Use B. Gilad *Harvard Business Review Digital Articles* p2 O 27 2015

Sales-Pardo, Marta

The importance of being modular diag *Science* v357 no6347 p128 Jl 14 2017

Sales personnel—Salaries, etc.

When Sales Incentives Should Be Based on Profit, Not Revenue A. A. Zoltners, P. K. Sinha et al *Harvard Business Review Digital Articles* p2 Je 10 2015

Sales reporting—Charts, diagrams, etc.

PRODUCTION AND BUSINESS ACTIVITY *Economic Indicators* p17 N 2016

Sales—Social aspects

THE MAGIC OF "CROWDSOURCING" il *Harvard Business Review* v95 no1 p28 Ja/F 2017

Sales—Statistics

Print Sales Stay Hot J. Segura chart *Publishers Weekly* v264 no2 p4 Ja 9 2017

Sales—United States

B&N Looking for a Sales Rebound I. Milliot chart color *Publishers Weekly* v263 no48 p4 N 28 2016

SALETAN, WILLIAM

The Conversation Google Killed *Weekly Standard* v22 no48 p31 S 4 2017

Salgado, Gabriela

Merrill and Salgado Take #12 Heartland color *Team Roping Journal* p34 S 2017

Saliba, Michael

Incorporation of rubidium cations into perovskite solar cells improves photovoltaic performance bibl graph *Science* v354 no6309 p206 O 14 2016

Salice, Christopher J.

Chemical safety must extend to ecosystems *Science* v356 no6341 p917 Je 1 2017

Salières, P.

Attosecond dynamics through a Fano resonance: Monitoring the birth of a photoelectron bibl graph *Science* v354 no6313 p734 N 11 2016

Salina, G.

Observation of a large-scale anisotropy in the arrival directions of cosmic rays above 8×10^{18} eV *Science* v357 no6357 p1266 S 22 2017

Salinas, José L.

Changing climate shifts timing of European floods color graph *Science* v357 no6351 p588 Ag 11 2017

Saline water conversion plants

WHERE THEY TAME THE UNDRINKABLE OCEAN K. ATHERTON color *Popular Science* v289 no2 p66 Mr/Ap 2017

Saline waters

See also

Seawater

THE GREAT LAKES: Present and Future Perils D. EGAN color graph map *Natural History* v125 no3 p24 Mr 2017

Salinger, J. D. (Jerome David), 1919-2010

Being Salinger K. ANG cartoon color *Esquire* v167 no1 p21 F 2017

Salis, Steve

GUEST LIST *Washingtonian Magazine* v52 no4 p24 Ja 2017

Salisbury, Ian

THE 2017 WASHINGTON WISH LIST color diag *Money* v46 no1 p96 Ja/F 2017

36 APPS THAT WILL SAVE YOU MONEY color *Money* v46 no4 p46 My 2017

5 Signals to Look For If You're Worried About the Market *Money* v46 no8 p35 S 2017

Foreign Stocks Emerge chart *Money* v46 no8 p77 S 2017

THE FUND REPORT diag *Money* v46 no1 p108 Ja/F 2017

THE HIGH STAKES ELECTION color diag *Money* v45 no10 p78 N 2016

HOW WASHINGTON TAX CUTS WILL AFFECT YOUR WALLET color diag *Money* v46 no2 p60 Mr 2017

THE MONEY CHAMPIONS [Cover story] color *Money* v45 no11 p52 D 2016

THE SMARTEST, MOST INTERESTING THING EVERY U.S. PRESIDENT EVER SAID ABOUT MONEY color diag *Money* v46 no6 p51 Jl 2017

Stocks Hit a Small Glitch chart *Money* v46 no9 p89 O 2017

Stock X-Ray: H&R Block diag *Money* v46 no4 p36 My 2017

Salit, Cathy

To Ace Your Job Interview, Get into Character and Rehearse *Harvard Business Review Digital Articles* p2 Ap 21 2017

Saliva

Oral precision medicine: Identification of microbes from saliva by mass spectrometry Yifei Zhang, Chong Ding et al bibl *Science* v354 no6319 p60 D 23 2016

What gives frogs the gift of grab S. MILIUS color *Science News* v191 no4 p11 Mr 4 2017

Saliva examination

NEW TEST FOR TAPEWORMS C. Barakat and M. McCluskey color *Equus* no481 p14 O 2017

Salje, Henrik

Dengue diversity across spatial and temporal scales: Local structure and the effect of host population size bibl graph *Science* v355 no6331 p1302 Mr 24 2017

Salk Institute for Biological Studies

Not just Salk C. Greider, N. Hopkins et al color *Science* v357 no6356 p1105 S 15 2017

SALKIN, ALLEN

THE RUNAWAY VEGAN bw color *Vanity Fair* v58 no12 p106 D 2016

SALKOWITZ, ROB

DIY Self-Help color *Publishers Weekly* v264 no31 p38 Jl 31 2017

Salle, David, 1952-

ART APPRECIATION R. WHITE *New York Times Book Review* p57 D 4 2016

Clothes That Don't Need You [Cover story] bw color *New York Review of Books* v64 no14 p10 S 28 2017

The CONVERSATION of Art J. H. Richardson and D. Salle bw color *Esquire* p76 Je/Jl 2017

School of Presentation D. SALLE color *ARTnews* v115 no4 p82 Wint 2016/2017

'The Sheer Excitement of Being an Artist' S. Schwartz color *New York Review of Books* v64 no5 p20 Mr 23 2017

Salle, David, 1952——Interviews

David SALLE E. CLINE *Interview* v46 no9 p110 N 2016

SALLEE, MARK RYAN

Your Getaway Vehicle bw cartoon color *Men's Health* v32 no5 p32 Je 2017

Sally Hansen (Company)

VIP TREATMENT color *O, The Oprah Magazine* p47 Ja 2017

Salm, Ryan

GLASS J. FOERSTERLING color *Powder* p12 S 2017

Salman, David

HIGH and DRY K. BARNES color *Better Homes & Gardens* v95 no3 p71 Mr 2017

Salmon

See also

Atlantic salmon

4 small health tweaks with huge rewards color *Redbook* p89 Mr 2017

EAT TO BEAT MIGRAINES color *Good Housekeeping* v264 no4 p97 Ap 2017

THREE, TWO, ONE... APPS! E. N. GAGE color *Martha Stewart Living* no275 p19 Je 2017

SALMON, FELIX

Material World: A French essayist and intellectual looks at financial considerations philosophically *New York Times Book Review* p15 My 14 2017

OBAMA'S AMERICA img *New York* v49 no20 p12 O 3 2016

Salmon Arms (Company)

GARAGE BRANDS C. Liska color *Snowboarder* v29 no4 p32 D 2016

Salmon fishing

Brother Act H. Smith *Sierra* v102 no5 p62 St/O 2017

LOCKJAW LESSONS T. E. Nickens color *Field & Stream* v122

no4 p32 S 2017

Salmonella diseases

FREE BIRD *Atlanta* v57 no5 p96 S 2017

Salmonella diseases—Risk factors

Hazards of Raising Chickens *Parents* v92 no2 p32 F 2017

KEEP YOUR SALAD SAFE color *Prevention* p6 Mr 2017

Quick Hits A. Marks map *Scientific American* v316 no6 p18 Je 2017

Salmon—Environmental aspects

OF THE RIVER AND TIME B. Voss color *Oceanus* v51 no2 p4 Wint 2016

Salna, Karlis

Justice Served With a Dash of Chili color *Bloomberg Businessweek* no4524 p18 My 29 2017

Salo, Tom

Non-lead Ammunition--a safer alternative *New York State Conservationist* v72 no2 p8 O 2017

Salomão, R. P.

Persistent effects of pre-Columbian plant domestication on Amazonian forest composition bibl chart graph map *Science* v355 no6328 p925 Mr 3 2017

Salome (Play)

DIVINE SALOMÉ: Wild yet chaste, impudent and ageless, Sarah Bernhardt was inescapably Oscar Wilde's Salomé, 'the most splendid creation' E. Fitzsimons *History Today* v67 no7 p66 Jl 2017

Salomon, Guillaume

Revealing hidden antiferromagnetic correlations in doped Hubbard chains via string correlators bw diag graph *Science* v357 no6350 p484 Ag 4 2017

Salomon SAS

SALMON SNOWBOARDS cartoon *Snowboarder* v29 no4 p8 D 2016

Salomone, Joseph

Control of species-dependent cortico-motoneuronal connections underlying manual dexterity diag graph *Science* v357 no6349 p400 Jl 28 2017

Salonen, Esa-Pekka, 1958-

L.A. Rhapsody A. Ross cartoon *New Yorker* v93 no5 p18 Mr 20 2017

Salsa (Dance)—Competitions

WORLD SALSA CHAMPIONSHIP J. BAINBRIDGE *Atlanta* v56 no10 p26 F 2017

Salsa Cycles (Company)

Salsa Deadwood J. Weber color *Bike Magazine* v24 no5 p84 Jl 2017

SALSA REDPOINT color *Bike Magazine* v23 no9 p84 D 2016

Salsas (Cooking)

Horror D'Oeuvres color *Martha Stewart Living* p36 O 2017

Stellar, surprising salsas C. Hall color *Redbook* p30 My 2017

Salt

Salt. a love/hate story K. W. LAWLESS color *Women's Health* v13 no10 p132 D 2016

Salt for the Earth C. Leu *Sierra* v101 no6 p11 N/D 2016

To Control Blood Pressure chart color *AARP: The Magazine* v59 no3A p34 Ap/My 2016

Salt content of food

GO AHEAD, PUT SALT ON YOUR FOOD R. BAILEY color *Reason* v49 no4 p6 Ag/S 2017

Salt deposits

See also

Salt domes

Salt flats

FAKE LAKE S. ELDER *National Geographic Kids* no469 p20 Ap 2017

Salt domes

Cold Comfort L. VACCARIELLO *Cincinnati Magazine* v50 no5 p176 F 2017

Salt flats

FAKE LAKE S. ELDER *National Geographic Kids* no469 p20 Ap 2017

Salt industry

Salt. a love/hate story K. W. LAWLESS color *Women's Health* v13 no10 p132 D 2016

SALT OF THE EARTH N. Paumgarten color *Bon Appetit* v62 no4 p84 Ap 2017

Salt licks—Evaluation

PRACTICAL PRODUCTS L. BACK color *Trail Rider* v29 no1 p53 Ja/F 2017

Salt—Analysis

An easy way to soup up your diet chart *Harvard Health Letter* v41 no12 p5 O 2016

Saltarelli, Andrew J.

Closing global achievement gaps in MOOCs graph *Science* v355 no6322 p251 Ja 20 2017

Salter, Ammon

The Biases That Keep Good R&D Projects from Getting Funded *Harvard Business Review Digital Articles* p2 Mr 17 2017

Salter, Mary Jo

Aloe *American Scholar* v86 no3 p59 Summ 2017

The Fortune Cookie *American Scholar* v86 no3 p55 Summ 2017

Fruitcake *American Scholar* v86 no3 p60 Summ 2017

Last Words *American Scholar* v86 no3 p57 Summ 2017

So Far *American Scholar* v86 no3 p58 Summ 2017

Salting of food

editor's letter A. RAPOPORT bw *Bon Appetit* p14 S 2017

Salts

Why I Love LAVENDER BATH SALTS I. Glazer color *InStyle* v24 no7 p142 Jl 2017

Saltsman, Amelia

a new (old) TRADITION *Better Homes & Gardens* v94 no12 p88 D 2016

Saltwater fishing

WINDS OF CHANGE J. McMURRAY and G. BETHGE color map *Outdoor Life* v224 no5 p33 Je/Jl 2017

Saltz, Gail

Find Your Peace of Mind color *Health* v30 no10 p77 D 2016

The Stress Problems No One Talks About color *Health* v31 no3 p72 Ap 2017

Stressproof Your Work Life color *Health* v31 no4 p68 My 2017

Your Top Stresses, Handled color *Health* v30 no9 p82 N 2016

SALTZ, JERRY

The American Artist img *New York* v50 no18 p82 S 4 2017

The Art-History Straitjacket img *New York* v49 no19 p96 S 19 2016

The Drawing I Can't Stop Thinking About img *New York* v50 no11 p112 My 29 2017

How Art Can Fight Trump img *New York* p70 Ja 23 2017

Left Behind img *New York* v49 no23 p76 N 14 2016

MY LIFE AS A FAILED ARTIST img *New York* v50 no8 p28 Ap 17 2017

The One and Only Hillary Clinton Whitney Biennial img *New York* v50 no6 p82 Mr 20 2017

Pain Is Good img *New York* v49 no23 p22 N 14 2016

Painting Late America img *New York* v49 no26 p89 D 26 2016

The Painting Our Art Critic Can't Stop Thinking About img *New York* v49 no22 p102 O 31 2016

The Photographs I Can't Stop Thinking About img *New York* v50 no6 p74 Mr 20 2017

The Ten Best Art Shows of the Year img *New York* v49 no25 p128 D 12 2016

To Do img *New York* p78 F 20 2017

To Do: Twenty-five things to see, hear, watch, and read img *New York* v50 no10 p106 My 15 2017

Saltzman, Daniela

How Laws and Culture Hold Back Socially Minded Companies *Harvard Business Review Digital Articles* p2 My 18 2017

If CEOs Care About the Long Term, Why Don't They Talk About It? *Harvard Business Review Digital Articles* p2 N 13 2015

Salukombo, Makorobondo

MAKOROBONDO "DEE" SALUKOMBO N. WELDON color *Runner's World* v52 no1 p84 Ja/F 2017

Salutations

Good Tidings, Fellow Male: A Modern Guide to Man-to-Man Greetings C. SKIPPER bw color diag graph *GQ: Gentlemen's Quarterly* v97 no10 p154 O 2017

Salutations (Music)

Indie Rock May Be Dislocated, but It's Far from Dead M. Johnston color *Time* v189 no11 p63 Mr 27 2017

Salvacruz, Joseph

Case Study: Competing Against Bling il *Harvard Business Review* v95 no3 p155 My/Je 2017

Case Study: How Should an Understated Luxury Brand Compete Against Bling? color *Harvard Business Review Digital Articles* p2 F 28 2017

Salvador, Karen
Intersections between music education and music therapy: Education reform, arts education, exceptionality, and policy at the local level bibl *Arts Education Policy Review* v118 no2 p93 2017

Salvant, Cécile McLorin, 1989-
And All That Jazz *Los Angeles Magazine* p67 Mr 2017
KIND OF NEW F. KAPLAN bw cartoon *New Yorker* v93 no14 p34 My 22 2017
'THE TROLLEY SONG' M. JEFFERSON color *New York Times Magazine* p53 Mr 12 2017

Salvaterra, Ruben
An accreting pulsar with extreme properties drives an ultraluminous x-ray source in NGC 5907 bibl chart graph *Science* v355 no6327 p817 F 24 2017

SALVATI, MADI
Conquer Slot Canyons il *Backpacker* p26 O 2017

Salvatierra, Alexia—Interviews
Seeking refuge A. Frykholm color *Christian Century* v134 no5 p32 Mr 1 2017

Salvation
See also
Faith

Salvation (TV program)
Salvation I. Rudolph *TV Guide* v65 no23 p23 My 29 2017

Salvatore Ferragamo Italia SpA
The BUY Fashion color *Harper's Bazaar* no3648 p86 N 2016
FILLING THE SHOES J. FERRAGAMO color *Esquire* p62 2017 BigBlackBook
Ground Control N. SULLIVAN color *Esquire* v166 no4 p66 N 2016
The In/Out LIST color *Harper's Bazaar* no3649 p134 D 2016/ Ja 2017
Wait LIST color *Harper's Bazaar* no3653 p96 My 2017

Salvetti, David
An accreting pulsar with extreme properties drives an ultraluminous x-ray source in NGC 5907 bibl chart graph *Science* v355 no6327 p817 F 24 2017

Salvinia
CREATURE FROM THE GREEN LAGOON L. BEIL *Texas Monthly* v45 no9 p72 S 2017

Salwitz, Christina
Your CHECKLIST color *Sunset* v237 no6 p50 D 2016

Salyer, Kirsten
It's a Mean, Sometimes Sad World-but Reading Can Help color *Time* v188 no24 p66 D 12 2016

Salz, Peggy Anne
The Changing Economics of App Development *Harvard Business Review Digital Articles* p2 N 4 2015

Salzberg, Andrew
GUEST LIST *Washingtonian Magazine* v52 no6 p22 Mr 2017

Salzberg, Sharon
Real Love color *Tricycle: The Buddhist Review* v26 no4 p26 Summ 2017

Salzburger Festspiele
POWER PLAY A. ROSS color *New Yorker* v93 no24 p80 Ag 21 2017
A Salzburg Trio J. NORDLINGER color *National Review* v69 no17 p40 S 11 2017

SALZMAN, JAMES
Biology and the Law *BioScience* v66 no11 p999 N 1 2016

SALZMAN, JIM
Green accounting *Issues in Science & Technology* v33 no2 p16 Wint 2017

Salzman, Rachel S.
Will climate-change efforts affect EU–Russian relations? (Probably not.) bibl *Bulletin of the Atomic Scientists* v72 no6 p384 N 2016

Sam, James
A Bomb to Remember *Hoover Digest: Research & Opinion on Public Policy* no1 p184 Wint 2017

Sam, Katerina
Higher predation risk for insect prey at low latitudes and elevations graph *Science* v356 no6339 p742 My 19 2017

Sam, Kim
North Korea Is Hacking Bitcoin *Bloomberg Businessweek* no4538 p29 S 18 2017

Sam, Saji
What Low Oil Prices Really Mean *Harvard Business Review Digital Articles* p2 Mr 28 2016

Sam Houston State University
Sam Houston State University *Dance Magazine* v90 p120 2016/2017 Supplement College Guide

Samach, Gabriel
Suppressing relaxation in superconducting qubits by quasiparticle pumping bibl graph *Science* v354 no6319 p1573 D 23 2016

Samani, Milan
Your Leadership Development Program Needs an Overhaul *Harvard Business Review Digital Articles* p2 D 5 2016

Samanta, Dipak
Clathrates grow up bibl color *Science* v355 no6328 p912 Mr 3 2017

Samara, Patrice
10 THINGS WE'RE TALKING ABOUT T. A. Christian color map *Essence* v48 no5 p71 S 2017

Samaritan woman (Biblical figure)
Christ and the Woman of Samaria at the Well by Guercino (Giovanni Francesco Barbieri) H. J. Hornik and M. C. Parsons color *Christian Century* v134 no5 p47 Mr 1 2017
The Light of New Life M. R. Simone *America* v216 no5 p69 Mr 6 2017
LIVING BY The Word *Christian Century* v134 no5 p18 Mr 1 2017

Samashev, Zainolla
Ancient genomic changes associated with domestication of the horse color diag *Science* v356 no6336 p442 Ap 28 2017

Samauov, Zhastalap
KARATEPRO AWARDS BIG BUCKS IN LAS VEGAS color *Black Belt* v55 no1 p10 D 2016/Ja 2017

Sambandan, Sivakumar
Activity-dependent spatially localized miRNA maturation in neuronal dendrites bibl graph *Science* v355 no6325 p634 F 10 2017

Samberg, Andy, 1978-
BROOKLYN NINE-NINE D. Holbrook *TV Guide* p30 D 5 2016
Tour de Pharmacy A. D'Arminio *TV Guide* v65 no27 p34 Je 26 2017

Samberg, Andy, 1978-—Interviews
Boy-Band Heaven K. Branch color *Glamour* v114 no7 p38 Jl 2016
Brooklyn Nine-Nine D. Holbrook *TV Guide* v65 no19 p38 My 1 2017

Sambo, Paula
The Lady Teaching Brazilians How to Shop Online *Bloomberg Businessweek* no4536 p21 S 4 2017

Samburu (African people)
Warriors to the Rescue A. VITALE color map *National Geographic* v232 no2 p76 Ag 2017

Same-sex marriage
Benjamin Moser *New York Times Book Review* p27 F 19 2017

Same-sex marriage—Law & legislation
Australia Has Its Say on Same-Sex Marriage T. John color *Time* v190 no15 p11 O 16 2017
Milestones color *Time* v189 no21 p14 Je 5 2017

Same-sex marriage—News briefs
Americas K. Stock bw color *Bloomberg Businessweek* no4538 p10 S 18 2017

Same-sex marriage—Religious aspects—Christianity
The Methodists after unity G. J. MacDonald color *Christian Century* v133 no24 p28 N 23 2016

Same-sex marriage—United States
MODERN LOVE: Once a die-hard bachelor, this former supermodel's marriage is a reminder of why marriage equality is so important for our collective self-esteem DAM color *Advocate* no1091 p82 Je/Jl 2017

Same-sex marriage—United States—Lawsuits & claims
MARRIAGE EQUALITY WAS WON BY WIDOWERS: THE LOVE STORIES BEHIND THE LANDMARK COURT CASES BOTH ENDED TRAGICALLY J. ANDERSON-MINSHALL bw color *Advocate* no1091 p80 Je/Jl 2017

Same-sex relationships
NO COMMENT cartoon *Progressive* p9 D 2016/Ja 2017

To Arms Over LGBT? C. MOORE *USA Today Magazine* v145 no2860 p54 Ja 2017

SAMET, ELIZABETH D.
Dishonorable Behavior: THE SCOURGE OF MILITARY SEXUAL ASSAULT AND THE WARRIOR'S MASCULINE CODE *American Scholar* v86 no3 p30 Summ 2017

Samet, Kenneth A.—Awards
TRADE SECRETS L. Milk *Washingtonian Magazine* v52 no2 p63 N 2016

SAMET, MATT
FROM PORTUGAL WITH LOVE bw color *Climbing* no353 p66 My/Je 2017
Harness Your Inner "Gym Beast" *Climbing* no355 p47 Ag 2017
Hello, Again color *Climbing* no353 p17 My/Je 2017
Hero Shot color *Climbing* no354 p13 Jl 2017

Samit, Jay
OTT Video Is Creating Cord-Extenders, Not Cord-Cutters *Harvard Business Review Digital Articles* p2 Jl 17 2015

Sammet, Jean E., 1928-2017
Milestones *Time* v189 no23 p15 Je 19 2017

Sammet, Jean E.—Interviews
The Tech Visionary You've Never Heard Of G. Jacobs color *Glamour* v115 no5 p186 My 2017

Sammon, Alexander
A BRIEF HISTORY OF GPS cartoon color *Mother Jones* v41 no6 p54 N/D 2016

Sammon, David
Only 3% of Companies' Data Meets Basic Quality Standards *Harvard Business Review Digital Articles* p2 S 11 2017

Sammons, Morgan A.
Epigenetic stability of exhausted T cells limits durability of reinvigoration by PD-1 blockade bibl graph *Science* v354 no6316 p1160 D 2 2016

Sampaio, A. F.
Persistent effects of pre-Columbian plant domestication on Amazonian forest composition bibl chart graph map *Science* v355 no6328 p925 Mr 3 2017

Sampaio, Emiliano
The Forbidden Dance/Óbvio B. Zimmerman color *Downbeat* v84 no1 p76 Ja 2017

Sampat, Bhaven N.
The applied value of public investments in biomedical research diag graph *Science* v356 no6333 p78 Ap 7 2017

Sampedro, Laura
Extreme Makeover: Breakfast Edition [Cover story] color *Women's Health* v14 no1 p111 Ja/F 2017

Sampere, Juan Pablo Vazquez
Apple Pay Is Just a Big Giveaway to Credit Card Companies *Harvard Business Review Digital Articles* p2 Ap 14 2015
Apple's Shrinking Impact in the Smartphone Industry *Harvard Business Review Digital Articles* p2 F 2 2016
Selling GE Capital Was Both a Brave and a Good Idea *Harvard Business Review Digital Articles* p2 Ap 28 2015
Uber's Food Delivery Experiment in Barcelona *Harvard Business Review Digital Articles* p2 F 25 2015
When Old Technologies Create New Industries *Harvard Business Review Digital Articles* p2 Jl 18 2016
Why Social Networks Still Haven't Cracked the Job Search Puzzle *Harvard Business Review Digital Articles* p2 Ja 13 2015

Samperton, Schuyler—Interviews
Living the Lush Life D. A. KEEPS color *House Beautiful* v159 no5 p84 Je 2017

Sampha (Performer)
Enter Sampha B. RATLIFF color *Esquire* v167 no1 p18 F 2017
Hip-Hop's Secret Weapon Steps Into the Spotlight J. Cox color *Time* v189 no5 p51 F 13 2017
ON THE BACK OF A BREEZE C. BATTAN cartoon *New Yorker* v92 no48 p70 F 6 2017

Sample, Hilary, 1972-
The Perplexities of Keeping Fit A. Bierig *Architectural Record* v205 no4 p81 Ap 2017

SAMPLE, HOLBROOK
MARKET VALUE *Cincinnati Magazine* p112 Je 2017

Sample, K. Jake
Restoring auditory cortex plasticity in adult mice by restricting thalamic adenosine signaling graph *Science* v356 no6345 p1352 Je 30 2017

Samplers
Outstanding New Hampshire Sampler by Harriet F. Hayden of Fitzwilliam color *Magazine Antiques* v183 no6 p20 N/D 2016

Sampling (Sound)
Secrets of the Funky Drummer C. R. WEINGARTEN bw color *Rolling Stone* no1283 p12 Mr 23 2017

Sampling error (Statistics)
A Refresher on Statistical Significance A. Gallo *Harvard Business Review Digital Articles* p2 F 16 2016

Sampson, Sally
The Thrifty Girl's Guide to Brunch color *Glamour* v115 no3 p127 Mr 2017

Sampson, Scott
Rewilding the Kids W. Becktold *Sierra* v101 no5 p10 S/O 2016
Urban Rewilding *Parks & Recreation* v51 no11 p40 N 2016

SAMS, AARON
Three Ways the Flipped Classroom Leads to Better Subject Mastery *Education Digest* v82 no5 p52 Ja 2017

Sam's West Inc.
China's High – End Retail Emporium color *Bloomberg Businessweek* no4498 p29 N 7 2016

Samsom, Janneke N.
Reovirus infection triggers inflammatory responses to dietary antigens and development of celiac disease color diag *Science* v356 no6333 p44 Ap 7 2017

SAMSON, ALAIN
CHEATING TO KEEP *Psychology Today* v50 no2 p19 Mr/Ap 2017

Samson et Dalila (Theatrical production)
Samson et Dalila S. J. Mudge *Opera News* v81 no7 p45 Ja 2017

Samson-Robert, O.
Chronic exposure to neonicotinoids reduces honey bee health near corn crops diag *Science* v356 no6345 p1395 Je 30 2017

Samsung Electronics Co. Ltd.
AMD's FreeSync 2 tech debuts in a wild 49-inch Samsung HDR monitor B. CHACOS color *PCWorld* v35 no7 p25 Jl 2017
Hands-on: Samsung DeX for Galaxy S8 J. NOREM color *PCWorld* v35 no5 p210 My 2017
iPhones outsell Samsung smartphones P. Sayer color *Macworld - Digital Edition* p12 Ap 2017
Playing Dumb Didn't Help Samsung's Heir Apparent S. Kim color *Bloomberg Businessweek* no4536 p22 S 4 2017
Q and Me T. J. Norton bw color graph *Sound & Vision* v82 no8 p48 O 2017
Samsung DeX: 7 days using the DeX dock and a Galaxy S8+ as a desktop PC J. PHILLIPS color *PCWorld* v35 no6 p117 Je 2017
Samsung Galaxy Book: An excellent 2-in-1 for a good price M. HACHMAN color graph *PCWorld* v35 no7 p71 Jl 2017
Samsung HW-K950 Soundbar System M. Trei color graph *Sound & Vision* v81 no9 p48 N 2016
Samsung KS9800 4K UHD, 65-inch smart TV: Quantum dots + HDR = Wow! J. L. JACOBI color *PCWorld* p141 D 2016
Samsung launches the Galaxy S8 with a stunning design and Bixby AI assistant M. SIMON color *PCWorld* v35 no5 p23 My 2017
Samsung, Lee Jae-yong's Conviction, and How Business in South Korea Is Changing Hansoo Choi *Harvard Business Review Digital Articles* p2 S 29 2017
Samsung Pay's Older Technology Could Be an Advantage Dae Ryun Chang *Harvard Business Review Digital Articles* p2 Jl 27 2015
Samsung's ArtPC Pulse is a cylindrical desktop PC with 360-degree sound J. PHILLIPS color *PCWorld* v35 no11 p11 N 2016
Samsung's Bixby won't support voice commands when it debuts on the Galaxy S8 M. SIMON color *PCWorld* v35 no5 p29 My 2017
Samsung, Shame, and Corporate Atonement R. Chun *Harvard Business Review Digital Articles* p2 My 17 2017
Samsung's New Board Gets Back to Business B. Einhorn, S. Kim et al color *Bloomberg Businessweek* no4513 p21 Mr 6 2017
Samsung to brick Galaxy Note7s through software M. SIMON color *PCWorld* v35 no1 p27 Ja 2017
Samsung Would Love to Talk About This Phone M. Gurman and S. Kim color *Bloomberg Businessweek* no4517 p36 Ap 3 2017
TRENDING color *Forbes* v198 no8 p49 D 20 2016

Ultra Style B. Ankosko color *Sound & Vision* v81 no9 p74 N 2016

Samsung Galaxy Note (Smartphone)

THE APPROVAL MATRIX img *New York* v49 no21 p140 O 17 2016

THE NEW IPHONE HAS COMPETITION A. Pressman color *Fortune* v176 no5 p18 O 1 2017

Samsung Galaxy Note 8: Don't call it a comeback, call it the phone of the year M. SIMON color *PCWorld* v35 no10 p57 O 2017

Samsung kills off the Galaxy Note7 to end the exploding battery debacle J. RIBEIROT color *PCWorld* v35 no11 p27 N 2016

TESTED: GALAXY NOTE 8 LIVE FOCUS VS. iPHONE 7 PLUS PORTRAIT MODE A. P. Murray color *Macworld - Digital Edition* v34 no10 p75 O 2017

You won't have to hear about the Galaxy Note7 on flights anymore M. SIMON color *PCWorld* v35 no2 p33 F 2017

Samsung Galaxy S (Smartphone)

Galaxy S8 battery life tips: How to control battery drain F. ION color *PCWorld* v35 no10 p116 O 2017

Samsung's Bixby won't support voice commands when it debuts on the Galaxy S8 M. SIMON color *PCWorld* v35 no5 p29 My 2017

Samsung Galaxy S (Smartphone)—Evaluation

8 WAYS THE iPHONE 8 CAN BEAT THE GALAXY S8 [Cover story] M. Simon color graph *Macworld - Digital Edition* v34 no6 p91 Je 2017

Galaxy S8+ review: The future of Android is now M. SIMON color graph *PCWorld* v35 no6 p94 Je 2017

Hands-on: Samsung DeX for Galaxy S8 J. NOREM color *PCWorld* v35 no5 p210 My 2017

Have More Fun With Your Phone M. Gikas chart color il *Consumer Reports* v82 no3 p48 Mr 2017

Samsung launches the Galaxy S8 with a stunning design and Bixby AI assistant M. SIMON color *PCWorld* v35 no5 p23 My 2017

your PERSONAL GADGETS N. SAPORITA, G. GRAJEK et al color diag *Good Housekeeping* v263 no6 p105 D 2016

Samsung Group (Company)

Are Drugs Samsung's Next Big Thing? N. Khan and S. Kim color graph *Bloomberg Businessweek* no4523 p23 My 22 2017

Samsung televisions—Evaluation

Samsung KS9800 4K UHD, 65-inch smart TV: Quantum dots + HDR = Wow! J. L. JACOBI color *PCWorld* p141 D 2016

TVS THAT HANG LIKE PAINTINGS color *Popular Mechanics* p16 S 2017

Samsung Group (Company)—Trials, litigation, etc.

Summer of Samsung B. Stone, S. Kim et al bw color diag graph *Bloomberg Businessweek* no4532 p42 Jl 31 2017

Samuel, Alexandra

5 Work Stresses You Can Alleviate with Tech *Harvard Business Review Digital Articles* p2 Ag 25 2015

6 Ways to Tell Stories with Data Throughout the Customer Lifecycle *Harvard Business Review Digital Articles* p2 O 2 2015

7 Email Problems, Solved *Harvard Business Review Digital Articles* p2 D 29 2016

The 8 Digital Productivity Tools Everyone Should Adopt *Harvard Business Review Digital Articles* p2 Je 20 2016

Being Professionally Personable on Facebook *Harvard Business Review Digital Articles* p2 Ag 14 2015

The Best Data Storytellers Aren't Always the Numbers People *Harvard Business Review Digital Articles* p2 O 28 2015

Capture Your Creativity with a Digital Notebook *Harvard Business Review Digital Articles* p2 My 29 2015

Collaborating Online Is Sometimes Better than Face-to-Face *Harvard Business Review Digital Articles* p2 Ap 1 2015

Conquer Your To-Do List with Your Phone *Harvard Business Review Digital Articles* p2 D 1 2014

Data Is the Next Big Thing in Content Marketing *Harvard Business Review Digital Articles* p2 S 14 2015

Digital Tools to Make Your Next Meeting More Productive *Harvard Business Review Digital Articles* p2 Jl 3 2015

Ease the Pain of Returning to Work After Time Off *Harvard Business Review Digital Articles* p2 Je 8 2015

Have LinkedIn and Medium Killed the Old-Fashioned Blog? *Harvard Business Review Digital Articles* p2 Je 30 2015

How America Lost Its Mind color *Atlantic* v320 no4 p12 N 2017

How Bots Took Over Twitter *Harvard Business Review Digital Articles* p2 Je 19 2015

How Content Marketers Can Tell Better Stories with Data *Harvard Business Review Digital Articles* p2 D 15 2015

How Pinterest's Buy Buttons Can Change e- Commerce *Harvard Business Review Digital Articles* p2 Je 9 2015

How the Sharing Economy Can Improve Your Next Business Trip *Harvard Business Review Digital Articles* p2 N 2 2015

How to Give a Data-Heavy Presentation *Harvard Business Review Digital Articles* p2 O 16 2015

How to Trick Yourself into Doing Tasks You Dread *Harvard Business Review Digital Articles* p2 Ja 19 2015

The More People We Connect with on LinkedIn, the Less Valuable It Becomes *Harvard Business Review Digital Articles* p2 My 5 2016

Psychographics Are Just as Important for Marketers as Demographics *Harvard Business Review Digital Articles* p2 Mr 11 2016

The Social Cost of Bad Online Marketing *Harvard Business Review Digital Articles* p2 Ap 20 2016

The Soft Skills of Great Digital Organizations *Harvard Business Review Digital Articles* p2 F 5 2016

Strategies for Every Type of Email Pain *Harvard Business Review Digital Articles* p2 My 20 2015

Things to Buy, Download, or Do When Working Remotely *Harvard Business Review Digital Articles* p2 F 4 2015

The Tools You Need to Make Every Meeting More Productive *Harvard Business Review Digital Articles* p2 Mr 12 2015

Turn Digital Overload to Your Advantage *Harvard Business Review Digital Articles* p2 My 12 2015

Using Social Media to Build Professional Skills *Harvard Business Review Digital Articles* p2 Ag 4 2016

Using Social Media Without Jeopardizing Your Career *Harvard Business Review Digital Articles* p2 Jl 20 2015

What Customers Want from the Collaborative Economy *Harvard Business Review Digital Articles* p2 O 8 2015

What Technology Companies Can Learn from Toy Makers *Harvard Business Review Digital Articles* p2 Mr 30 2016

What the Death of Topsy Tells Us About Today's Social Web *Harvard Business Review Digital Articles* p2 D 23 2015

What to Do with All the Business Cards from Your Last Conference *Harvard Business Review Digital Articles* p2 N 13 2015

Your Biggest Social Media Fans Might Not Be Your Best Customers *Harvard Business Review Digital Articles* p2 D 24 2014

Your Digital Year in Review *Harvard Business Review Digital Articles* p2 D 31 2015

Samuel, Curtis

Leading Off color *Sports Illustrated* v125 no18 p10 D 5 2016

NEW YORK JET P. Thamel color *Sports Illustrated* v125 no21 p38 D 26 2016

Samuel, Ebenezer

18-MINUTE MIRACLE WORKOUT bw color *Men's Health* v32 no7 p96 S 2017

Best Bets for Cord Cutting color *Entertainment Weekly* no1442 p33 D 2 2016 Rebellious Special Issue

Jumpstart Your Abs color *Men's Health* v32 no6 p58 Ag 2017

Move the Chains color *Men's Health* v32 no8 p10 O 2017

No-Gear Total-Body Blast color *Men's Health* v32 no8 p46 O 2017

THE WORLD IS YOUR GYM bw color *Men's Health* v32 no6 p114 Ag 2017

SAMUEL, PETER

FROM THE ARCHIVES bw *Reason* v49 no1 p70 My 2017

Samuelson, Kate

7 Ideas from Other Countries That Could Improve U.S. Elections color *Time* v188 no20 p11 N 14 2016

Back to the Wild color *Time* v190 no12 p12 S 25 2017

The Best 25 Inventions of 2016 color *Time* v188 no22-23 p43 N/D 2016

Britain's 'Rock' In Spain Gets Caught In a Hard Place color *Time* v189 no14 p11 Ap 17 2017

Cameos on the Catwalk color *Time* v190 no15 p12 O 16 2017

Domhnall Gleeson Proves (Once More) He Can Do Almost Anything color *Time* v190 no16/17 p104 O 23 2017

It Could Be You ... Twice color *Time* v190 no4 p13 Jl 24 2017

The Ivory Trade Loses Its Biggest Player color *Time* v189 no3

p6 Ja 16 2017

Manuel Antonio Noriega color *Time* v189 no22 p11 Je 12 2017

Monumental Offenses color *Time* v188 no18 p13 O 31 2016

New Words for a New World *Time* v190 no13 p16 O 2 2017

Next Generation Leaders color *Time* v188 no15 p41 O 17 2016

Next Generation Leaders color *Time* v189 no9 p38 Mr 13 2017

Off-Color Ads by Beauty Brands color *Time* v190 no16/17 p16 O 23 2017

'Plus Size' Goes Out of Fashion color *Time* v190 no12 p14 S 25 2017

Queen Elizabeth II, for 65 Years color *Time* v189 no6 p13 F 20 2017

A Rise In Rhino Poaching? color *Time* v189 no12 p16 Ap 3 2017

Roads? Where We're Going ... color *Time* v189 no23 p14 Je 19 2017

Taking on the Animal Kingdom color *Time* v190 no1 p12 Jl 3 2017

Weird Things from the Blue color *Time* v190 no6 p16 Ag 7 2017

What's In a (Brand) Name? color *Time* v190 no7 p12 Ag 21 2017

Winnie the Pooh and Homer Too color *Time* v190 no5 p16 Jl 31 2017

World Wonders Under Wraps color *Time* v190 no9 p14 S 4 2017

Samuelson, Katie Lou

Taking HER SHOT S. Apstein color *Sports Illustrated* v126 no8 p62 Mr 20 2017

Samuelson, Robert J.

WHAT HATH GREENSPAN WROUGHT *Claremont Review of Books* v17 no1 p70 Wint 2016/2017

Samuelsson, Hakan—Interviews

Håkan Samuelsson A. Priddle *Motor Trend* v69 no7 p30 Jl 2017

Samuelsson, Marcus, 1970-

HARLEM ON HIS MIND P. H. Bass color *Essence* v47 no7 p55 N 2016

Samurai

See also
Bushido

PASCAL FAULIOT cartoon *Tricycle: The Buddhist Review* v26 no3 p19 Spr 2017

PTSD and the Samurai D. Lowry color *Black Belt* v55 no1 p20 D 2016/Ja 2017

Samurai—Social aspects

A Toothpick When You're Hungry D. Lowry color *Black Belt* v55 no6 p26 O/N 2017

Samway, Patrick S. J.

The Letters of Robert Giroux and Thomas Merton L. T. Johnson bw *Commonweal* v144 no3 p35 F 10 2017

Samyn, Philippe, 1948-

The E.U.'s New Digs J. Zorthian color *Time* v189 no3 p19 Ja 16 2017

San (African people)

An ethics code for studying the San color *Science* v355 no6331 p1244 Mr 24 2017

San, Elia

LOST & FOUND *Texas Monthly* v44 no12 p112 D 2016

San Angelo (Tex.)

3 Days in... San Angelo, Texas G. R. SCHIAVINO color *American Cowboy* v23 no6 p34 Ap/My 2017

San Antonio (Tex.)

TIME TO BE A TEXAN A. R. ALBANESE *Publishers Weekly* v264 no14 p22 Ap 3. 2017

San Antonio (Tex.)—Description & travel

Deep in the Heart T. Ethington color *American Cowboy* v23 no6 p24 Ap/My 2017

San Antonio (Tex.)—History—Social aspects

A Mission to Grow S. C. P. WILLIAMS *National Parks* v91 no2 p16 Spr 2017

San Antonio Spurs (Basketball team)

2 Spurs R. Nadkarni, B. Golliver et al color *Sports Illustrated* v125 no14 p98 O 24-31 2016

3 SPURS color *Sports Illustrated* v127 no12 p81 O 16 2017

San Blas Islands (Panama)—Description & travel

THE DREAM ISLANDS M. STOUT and R. STOUT color map *Sail* v48 no1 p30 Ja 2017

San Diego (Calif.)

Better Batteries J. Worland color *Time* v189 no13 p29 Ap 10 2017

San Diego (Calif.). Tourism Authority

WIN THIS COASTAL ESCAPE! color *Sunset* v238 no1 p98 Ja 2017

San Diego (Calif.)—Description & travel

CABRILLO ISLE MARINA SAN DIEGO *Sea Magazine* v109 no2 p99 F 2017

San Diego (Calif.)—Officials & employees

IT NOW FALLS TO CALIFORNIA REPUBLICANS *Vital Speeches of the Day* v83 no10 p297 O 2017

San Diego Bay (Calif.)

CABRILLO ISLE MARINA SAN DIEGO *Sea Magazine* v109 no2 p99 F 2017

San Diego Chargers (Football team)

City of Angles W. Leitch and T. Keith color *Sports Illustrated* v126 no3 p14 Ja 23 2017

HOT | NOT T. Keith color *Sports Illustrated* v126 no3 p17 Ja 23 2017

PEYTON'S (OTHER) PLACE L. Jenkins and J. Feldman color *Sports Illustrated* v126 no11 p48 Ap 17-24 2017

San Diego Convention Center Corp.

STAYING SAFE AT SAN DIEGO COMIC-CON 2017 H. MAC-DONALD color *Publishers Weekly* v264 no28 p48 Jl 10 2017

San Diego Padres (Baseball team : National League of Professional Baseball Clubs)

5 PADRES color *Sports Illustrated* v126 no9 p114 Mr 27 2017

THAT '70s COLOR M. Prince color *Esquire* p32 O 2017

San Fernando Brewing Co.

HOPS OVER THE HILL J. M. VERIVE *Los Angeles Magazine* p46 My 2017

San Francisco (Calif.)

The Best New RESTAURANTS IN AMERICA, 2017 J. GORDINIER bw color *Esquire* p62 N 2017

NEIGHBOR TO ALL K. Oakes color *America* v216 no7 p18 Ap 3 2017

San Francisco (Calif.)—Description & travel

San Francisco A. WHITTLE color map *Conde Nast Traveler* v52 no6 p50 Je/Jl 2017

San Francisco (Calif.)—History—20th century

THE POSTER CRAZE: Freaky, funny, and fashionable, in the '60s, these were the signs of our times H. Gold *Saturday Evening Post* v289 no4 p41 Jl/Ag 2017

SLOUCHING TOWARDS BETHLEHEM J. DIDION *Saturday Evening Post* v289 no4 p38 Jl/Ag 2017

San Francisco 49ers (Football team)

4 San Francisco 49ers color *Sports Illustrated* v127 no7 p103 S 4 2017

San Francisco Ballet (Company)

Gravitas, Russian-Style *Dance Magazine* v91 no1 p38 Ja 2017

Natasha Sheehan D. KELLY *Dance Magazine* v91 no4 p22 Ap 2017

Prima, Puppies, Premieres J. Stahl *Dance Magazine* v91 no9 p10 S 2017

Sofiane Sylve: San Francisco Ballet's enigmatic ballerina opens up C. BAUER *Dance Magazine* v91 no9 p30 S 2017

San Francisco Giants (Baseball team)

2 GIANTS color *Sports Illustrated* v126 no9 p110 Mr 27 2017

San Francisco Opera

Mark Cavagnero Associates L. Lee *Architectural Record* v205 no4 p130 Ap 2017

What Design Thinking Is Doing for the San Francisco Opera D. Hoyt and R. I. Sutton *Harvard Business Review Digital Articles* p2 Je 3 2016

San Francisco Peaks (Ariz.)

Arizona's TIP TOP W. HEALD *Arizona Highways* v93 no8 p32 Ag 2017

FROM A DISTANCE K. Vaughn *Arizona Highways* v93 no8 p28 Ag 2017

HART IS WHERE THE HOME IS K. MONTGOMERY *Arizona Highways* v93 no8 p46 Ag 2017

San Jose (Calif.)

WWDC17 heading to San Jose C. McGarry color *Macworld - Digital Edition* p6 Ap 2017

San Jose del Cabo (Mexico)

snapshot A. Klimoski *Architectural Record* v205 no7 p176 Jl 2017

San Jose State University—Sports

Week 1 color *Sports Illustrated* v127 no5 p52 Ag 14 2017

San Juan (P.R.)—Description & travel

Stubborn in the Sun M. TAHL *Sierra* v102 no4 p18 Jl/Ag 2017

San Juan Island (Wash.)—Description & travel
UNPLUGGING IN PREVOST HARBOR D. HISLOP *Sea Magazine* v108 no8 pPNW-1 Ag 2016

San Juan Islands (Wash.)—Description & travel
Go West, Young Men S. Murray color *Power & Motoryacht* v34 no11 p72 N 2017

San Juan Mountains (Colo.)
shelter from the storm t. weaver strokes color *Bike Magazine* v24 no3 p40 My 2017

San Juan National Forest (Colo.)
See in color color *Backpacker* p8 Je 2017

San Salvador (El Salvador)
THE LOCALS' GUIDE TO FAR-FLUNG PLACES N. K. Hahn bw color *Chicago* v66 no1 p98 Ja 2017

San Xia Dam (China)—Design & construction
UP AND OVER D. Stone diag *National Geographic* v231 no3 p22 Mr 2017

Sanacore, Joseph
THE ROOT OF CONNECTION color *Literacy Today (2411-7862)* v34 no4 p8 Ja/F 2017

Sanatoriums
St. Luke's Sanatorium N. AUSTIN *Arizona Highways* v93 no11 p8 N 2017

Sanborn, Mark
The Potential Principle: A Proven System for Closing the Gap Between How Good You Are and How Good You Could Be *Publishers Weekly* v264 no27 p67 Jl 3 2017

Sanburn, Josh
25th JFK Assassination Secrets Scheduled for 2017 Release color *Time* v188 no27-28 p119 D 26 2016
The Case for Community College color *Time* v189 no22 p44 Je 12 2017
A Confederate Monument Solution, With Context color *Time* v190 no1 p17 Jl 3 2017
The Death and Life of the Shopping Mall color *Time* v190 no5 p40 Jl 31 2017
Emotional Divide color diag *Time* v189 no7/8 p38 F 27 2017
Hate Incidents Sow Fear Across U.S color *Time* v189 no9 p13 Mr 13 2017
Inside Donald Trump's War Against the State [Cover story] color *Time* v189 no10 p26 Mr 20 2017
Lightbox color *Time* v189 no7/8 p20 F 27 2017
Making Trains Run on Time color diag *Time* v189 no13 p38 Ap 10 2017
New Orleans Confronts Its Confederate History color *Time* v189 no19 p12 My 22 2017
The Other Side [Cover story] color diag *Time* v189 no4 p24 F 6 2017
Pick a Lock color *Time* v189 no13 p33 Ap 10 2017
Restoring Order to the Rule of Law color *Time* v188 no16/17 p61 O 24 2016
Shots Fired color *Time* v190 no13 p48 O 2 2017
States Lean Left on Local Votes color *Time* v188 no21 p16 N 21 2016
Trump Overseas color *Time* v189 no23 p28 Je 19 2017
Trump's American Vision [Cover story] color *Time* v189 no3 p24 Ja 30 2017
The Waterworks color *Time* v189 no13 p36 Ap 10 2017
What It Will Take to Rebuild America [Cover story] color *Time* v189 no13 p22 Ap 10 2017
A Year Later, Flint Still Can't Drink the Water *Time* v189 no4 p12 Ja 23 2017

Sancar, Aziz
Bifurcating electron-transfer pathways in DNA photolyases determine the repair quantum yield bibl graph *Science* v354 no6309 p209 O 14 2016
Oliver Smithies (1925-2017) color *Science* v355 no6326 p695 F 17 2017

Sánchez, Aaron
AARÓN SÁNCHEZ M. LOGAN *TV Guide* v65 no31 p11 Jl 24 2017
License to GRILL color *O, The Oprah Magazine* p109 Je 2017

Sanchez, Anita L.
The Four Sacred Gifts: Indigenous Wisdom for Modern Times *Publishers Weekly* v264 no28 p82 Jl 10 2017

Sanchez, August

Get It, Girls! color *Glamour* v115 no4 p30 Ap 2017

Sánchez, Cecilia
Creating our own community color *Science* v355 no6332 p1446 Mr 31 2017

Sanchez, Desiree
A Warrior Chorus: Aquila Theatre, Veterans, and Our Trojan War H. Sherman *Stage Directions* v30 no6 p18 Je 2017

Sanchez, Erika L.
I Am Not Your Perfect Mexican Daughter *Publishers Weekly* v264 no32 p74 Ag 7 2017
AN IMMIGRANT DAUGHTER'S SONG A. S. GIBBS bw *Chicago* v66 no7 p30 Jl 2017
LESSONS ON EXPULSION K. Rooney color *New York Times Book Review* p26 Ag 6 2017
Lessons on Expulsion: Poems *Publishers Weekly* v264 no20 p33 My 15 2017

Sanchez, F.
Observation of a large-scale anisotropy in the arrival directions of cosmic rays above 8 × 1018 eV *Science* v357 no6357 p1266 S 22 2017

Sánchez, Gary, 1992-
6 THE LONG GAME B. Reiter color *Sports Illustrated* v126 no9 p48 Mr 27 2017
Gary Sánchez M. Hagan color *Current Biography* v78 no5 p77 My 2017

SANCHEZ, KARINA M.
Deforestation and Coca Cultivation Rooted in Twentieth-Century Development Projects *BioScience* v66 no11 p974 N 1 2016

Sanchez, Kelly
Where WORK is PLAY color *Dressage Today* v24 no2 p46 N 2017

Sánchez, Maria
NEW FOOTING E. Laase and T. Keith color *Sports Illustrated* v127 no9 p18 S 25 2017

Sanchez, Michelle
Dethroning the idols *Christian Century* v134 no18 p30 Ag 30 2017

Sanchez, Nicole—Interviews
THE POWER OF THE PIVOT J. Thompson color *Essence* v47 no7 p74 N 2016

Sanchez, Patti
Leaders Who Get Change Right Know How to Listen *Harvard Business Review Digital Articles* p2 O 17 2016
Why Your Company Needs More Ceremonies *Harvard Business Review Digital Articles* p2 Jl 27 2016

Sánchez, Sergio García
'Moby-Dick,' Part 1 *New York Times Book Review* p54 Je 4 2017
'Moby-Dick,' Part 3 *New York Times Book Review* p22 Je 18 2017

Sanchez, Sofia
WORLDLY ADVICE E. FLORIO and C. TATTOLI color *Conde Nast Traveler* v52 no6 p22 Je/Jl 2017

Sanchez, Susi—Interviews
By Design color *Working Mother* p8 F/Mr 2017

SÁNCHEZ, YOLANDA
What's your favorite work of public art? color *American Craft* v77 no3 p16 Je/Jl 2017

Sanchez-Lucas, P.
Observation of a large-scale anisotropy in the arrival directions of cosmic rays above 8 × 1018 eV *Science* v357 no6357 p1266 S 22 2017

Sánchez-Ortiz, Efrain
Control of muscle formation by the fusogenic micropeptide myomixer diag *Science* v356 no6335 p323 Ap 21 2017

Sanchez-Paus Diaz, Alfonso
The extent of forest in dryland biomes [Cover story] chart map *Science* v356 no6338 p635 My 12 2017

Sanchez-Yamagishi, J. D.
Magnetic resonance spectroscopy of an atomically thin material using a single-spin qubit bibl color diag graph *Science* v355 no6324 p503 F 3 2017

Sancho-Martinez, Ignacio
Integration of CpG-free DNA induces de novo methylation of CpG islands in pluripotent stem cells diag *Science* v356 no6337 p503 My 5 2017

Sancta Susanna (Theatrical production)
Cavalleria Rusticana/Sancta Susanna S. J. Mudge *Opera News*

v81 no9 p47 Mr 2017

Sanctions (International law)

See also

Economic sanctions

Asia K. Stock color *Bloomberg Businessweek* no4538 p11 S 18 2017

The Long View R. LONG il *National Review* v68 no24 p34 D 31 2016

Navigating the Complexities of Doing Business in Russia M. McNamee *Harvard Business Review Digital Articles* p2 My 29 2017

The Nuclear Deal Is Only Half of It L. SMITH *Weekly Standard* v23 no3 p16 S 25 2017

Russia Sanctions *Congressional Digest* v96 no3 p31 Mr 2017

Sanctions: Russia & Iran color *Bloomberg Businessweek* no4531 p39 Jl 24 2017

The Week color *National Review* v69 no11 p4 Je 12 2017

Sanctions (International law)—Economic aspects

A FRAGILE BORDER P. Martin and S. Chen color *Bloomberg Businessweek* no4539 p33 S 25 2017

SANCTON, JULIAN

SILICON VALLEY'S SEXUAL REVOLUTION cartoon graph *Wired* v25 no4 p22 Ap 2017

Sancton, Tom

Magic in Miniature bw color *Vanity Fair* v59 no9 p98 S 2017

Tom Sancton J. Berry color *New Orleans Magazine* v51 no9 p28 Jl 2017

Sanctuary cities

Reckless sanctuary *Maclean's* v130 no3 p5 Ap 2017

Sanctuary Cities for the Disabled *USA Today Magazine* v145 no2861 p14 F 2017

Sanctuary Cities in an Age of Resistance J. K. Leon color *Progressive* v81 no3 p13 Mr 2017

WILL LIBERALS LEARN TO LOVE THE 10TH AMENDMENT? D. ROOT color *Reason* v48 no10 p6 Mr 2017

Sanctuary cities—Law & legislation

The point of sanctuary cities *Christian Century* v134 no11 p7 My 24 2017

Sanctuary movement

MONARCHS J. Jelly-Schapiro cartoon *New Yorker* v93 no31 p20 O 9 2017

More congregations become sanctuaries for immigrants under threat of deportation E. Evans, Y. Shimron et al *Christian Century* v133 no26 p18 D 21 2016

Sanctuary churches, cities may face consequences from federal authorities K. Winston and A. Hoover color *Christian Century* v134 no9 p13 Ap 26 2017

Seeking refuge A. Frykholm color *Christian Century* v134 no5 p32 Mr 1 2017

Sand

See also

Particles

A looming tragedy of the sand commons A. Torres, J. Brandt et al color *Science* v357 no6355 p970 S 8 2017

Sand & gravel dredging

HOW TO STEAL A RIVER R. Romig *New York Times Magazine* p42 Mr 5 2017

Sand & gravel industry—California

BRICKBATS C. OLIVER color *Reason* v49 no3 p72 Jl 2017

SAND, LARRY

The Unionista il *National Review* v68 no19 p33 O 24 2016

Sand Castle (Film)

Sand Castle *TV Guide* p43 Ap 17 2017

Sand Creek Post & Beam (Company)

HOME ON THE RANGE [Cover story] color *Timber Home Living* v27 no5 p88 O 2017

Sand dune plants

Kelso Dunes R. H. MOHLENBROCK *Natural History* v125 no2 p40 F 2017

Sand dunes

SANDBOX IN THE SKY M. D. G. KAPLAN and M. HEIM *National Parks* v91 no2 p40 Spr 2017

Sand dunes—California

Kelso Dunes R. H. MOHLENBROCK *Natural History* v125 no2 p40 F 2017

Sandage, Allan

HUBBLE TROUBLE J. Sokol bw color *Science* v355 no6329 p1010 Mr 10 2017

Sandahl, Gary A.

A selective insecticidal protein from Pseudomonas for controlling corn rootworms bibl chart graph *Science* v354 no6312 p634 N 4 2016

Sandals

Berry Pretty color *Good Housekeeping* v264 no5 p19 My 2017

CRYSTAL CLEAR color *Harper's Bazaar* no3656 p312 S 2017

FANCY FREE J. Attenberg color *O, The Oprah Magazine* p118 Mr 2017

Trendspotting M. L. BIKOFF *Atlanta* v56 no11 p44 Mr 2017

Would You Rather... color *Seventeen* v76 no4 p96 Jl/Ag 2017

Sandals—Evaluation

2016 Holiday GIFT GUIDE A. Vorrasi, M. Gleeson et al color *InStyle* v23 no13 p249 D 2016

BETH'S PICKS color *Harper's Bazaar* no3649 p248 D 2016/Ja 2017

Check LIST color *Harper's Bazaar* no3648 p114 N 2016

Coco Served HOT *Interview* v47 no6 p33 Ag 2017

the cover color *InStyle* v24 no4 p32 Ap 2017

CULTURE CLUB color *Harper's Bazaar* no3648 p134 N 2016

Denim updates to wear everywhere B. Goreski color *Redbook* p19 My 2017

DINERS, DRESSES & DIVES color *Chicago* v66 no3 p116 Mr 2017

Dolce & Gabbana slides, $995 color *Vogue* v207 no6 p162 Je 2017

The Dress REPORT color *Harper's Bazaar* no3648 p175 N 2016

DYNAMIC DUO color *Essence* v48 no2 p15 Je 2017

Electric Slides color *O, The Oprah Magazine* p51 Ap 2017

FLAT-OUT FABULOUS color *Essence* v48 no3 p17 Jl 2017

FLATS vs. HEELS color *Harper's Bazaar* no3648 p205 N 2016

Fresh SQUEEZED: THE SEASON'S RUBBERY SLIDE SANDAL FROM MIU MIU IS A JUICED-UP REFRESH OF A SUMMER STAPLE *Interview* v47 no3 p45 Ap 2017

GET THESE looks for less color *Good Housekeeping* v265 no3 p42 S 2017

Give 'Em The Slip *Los Angeles Magazine* v62 no6 p26 Je 2017

GREAT BUYS UNDER $100 color *O, The Oprah Magazine* p60 My 2017

GREAT BUYS UNDER $100: GRAPHIC CONTENT color *O, The Oprah Magazine* p48 Jl 2017

Heart and Sole L. Yaeger, M. HOLGATE et al color *Vogue* v207 no9 p388 S 2017

HIDE-AND-SEEK color *Harper's Bazaar* no3648 p130 N 2016

HOW TO WEAR IT... anywhere! color *Good Housekeeping* v265 no1 p14 Jl 2017

HVN color *Harper's Bazaar* no3648 p174 N 2016

IF THE SHOE FITS color *Vogue* v207 no1 p100 Ja 2017

In a Stitch color *Seventeen* v76 no3 p36 My 2017

The In/Out LIST color *Harper's Bazaar* no3652 p96 Ap 2017

IN THE BUFF M. BOBO color *Ebony* v72 no4 p50 F 2017

Kindred SOLES R. WALDMAN color *Vogue* v206 no12 p158 D 2016

Kyma Sandals color *Bloomberg Businessweek* no4531 p71 Jl 24 2017

LET IT SLIDE color *Women's Health* v14 no5 p52 Je 2017

the life C. Dash color *InStyle* v24 no4 p215 Ap 2017

The LIST color *Harper's Bazaar* no3648 p107 N 2016

The LIST color *Harper's Bazaar* no3653 p85 My 2017

The LIST color *Harper's Bazaar* no3654 p57 Je/Jl 2017

Market color *Vanity Fair* v59 no7 p44 Summ 2017

on demand color *InStyle* v24 no5 p51 My 2017

on demand color *InStyle* v24 no7 p33 Jl 2017

On Point! color *Glamour* no8 p64 Ag 2017

ON THE DOT color *Essence* v48 no6 p27 O 2017

PARTY IN PINK A. B. RAYA color *Chicago* v65 no12 p54 D 2016

pastels color *Good Housekeeping* v264 no5 p54 My 2017

Pom-Tastic! color *Seventeen* v76 no2 p44 Mr 2017

SHOP THE ISSUE bw color *Harper's Bazaar* no3648 p70 N 2016

Silver and Gold for the Win E. Velluto color *Glamour* v114 no12 p100 D 2016

Silver Belles color *Good Housekeeping* v265 no4 p17 O 2017

SILVER LINING color *Harper's Bazaar* no3655 p118 Ag 2017

SO BAZAAR color *Harper's Bazaar* no3653 p296 My 2017

SO BAZAAR color *Harper's Bazaar* no3657 p250 O 2017
the start color *InStyle* v24 no6 p25 Je 2017
Totally NUDE color *O, The Oprah Magazine* p154 My 2017
TROPICAL THUNDER color *Harper's Bazaar* no3648 p132 N 2016
Twice? Nice! color *Glamour* v115 no5 p52 My 2017
Wait LIST color *Harper's Bazaar* no3653 p96 My 2017
WARM FRONT color *Harper's Bazaar* no3648 p155 N 2016
a week of AWESOME OUTFITS color *Good Housekeeping* v265 no1 p26 Jl 2017
WHAT WE LOVE color *Harper's Bazaar* no3648 p44 N 2016
WHAT WE LOVE color *Harper's Bazaar* no3652 p42 Ap 2017
WHERE TO BUY color *Essence* v48 no6 p128 O 2017
Wish LIST N. Fritton color *Harper's Bazaar* no3648 p110 N 2016
THE WOMAN Naomie Harris E. Wilson color *InStyle* v24 no6 p54 Je 2017
THE WOMAN Solange Knowles E. Wilson color *InStyle* v24 no4 p90 Ap 2017

Sandback, Peter
Nailed It M. OZAWA *Martha Stewart Living* no268 p44 O 2016

Sandbags
5 WAYS: ...to Use a Sandbag S. MAIN color *Muscle & Performance* v9 no8 p66 Ag 2017

Sandbank, Judith
Potential role of intratumor bacteria in mediating tumor resistance to the chemotherapeutic drug gemcitabine diag *Science* v357 no6356 p1156 S 15 2017

Sandberg, David F.
ANNABELLE: CREATION D. Coggan color *Entertainment Weekly* no1474/1475 p48 Jl 21-28 2017

Sandberg, Sheryl, 1969-
Back to Life cartoon color *O, The Oprah Magazine* p46 My 2017
FINDING STRENGTH IN GREAT LOSS [Cover story] cartoon color *Redbook* p122 My 2017
Healing Advice A. Nash color *AARP: The Magazine* v60 no4A p55 Je/Jl 2017
How to Talk to a Loved One Who Is Suffering color *Time* v189 no15 p43 Ap 24 2017
Leaders color *Time* v189 no16/17 p64 My 1-8 2017
Life After Death [Cover story] B. Luscombe color *Time* v189 no15 p38 Ap 24 2017
SURVIVAL of the SHARINGEST S. Frier bw *Bloomberg Businessweek* no4520 p60 My 1 2017
Warm Comfort: Four years after 'Lean In,' Sheryl Sandberg shares new perspectives gained from grief C. FLANAGAN *New York Times Book Review* p14 My 14 2017
What Successful Work and Life Integration Looks Like S. Friedman *Harvard Business Review Digital Articles* p2 O 7 2014
What You Said About ... color *Time* v189 no18 p6 My 15 2017
When the Worst Happens S. SANDBERG and A. GRANT color *AARP: The Magazine* v60 no4A p52 Je/Jl 2017

Sandberg, Sheryl, 1969—Interviews
"Above All, Acknowledge the Pain" A. IGNATIUS color *Harvard Business Review* v95 no3 p142 My/Je 2017
"My self-confidence was shattered overnight" T. Dufu and E. Mahaney bw color *Glamour* v115 no6 p108 Je 2017
THE POWER OF PEERS S. Sandberg *National Geographic* v231 no1 p10 Ja 2017

Sandefur, Timothy
LOSING GROUND *Claremont Review of Books* v17 no1 p63 Wint 2016/2017
Mother, May I? D. GOLDMAN color *Weekly Standard* v22 no27 p40 Mr 20 2017
ZERO SHADES OF GRAY J. Tartakovsky *Claremont Review of Books* v17 no2 p90 Spr 2017

Sandell, Laurie
The many shades of AMBER color *InStyle* p88 Home & Design 2016

Sanders, Aric W.
Hidden dynamics in the unfolding of individual bacteriorhodopsin proteins bibl diag *Science* v355 no6328 p945 Mr 3 2017

Sanders, Ashton
SUPPORTING ACTOR CONTENDER ASHTON SANDERS N. Sperling color *Entertainment Weekly* no1438 p48 N 4 2016

Sanders, Bernard, 1941-
Bernie's Bad Medicine C. POPE color *National Review* v69 no19 p26 O 16 2017
Bernie's Brilliant Bill *Nation* v305 no8 p3 O 9 2017
A Budget for the Rest of Us J. BLEIFUSS *In These Times* v41 no7 p5 Jl 2017
Corporate Media Threatens Our Democracy *In These Times* v41 no2 p28 F 2017
THE DREAM DEFERRED B. WALLACE-WELLS cartoon *New Yorker* v93 no23 p30 Ag 7 2017
The False Promise of "Free College" I. Palmer *Washington Monthly* p1 S/O 2016
Left Out B. Raushenbush *Harper's Magazine* v334 no2000 p2 Ja 2017
A Party for the People D. D. GUTTENPLAN color *Nation* v305 no1 p4 Jl 3 2017
PAY DAYS A. Davidson cartoon *New Yorker* v93 no13 p31 My 15 2017
Rising to the Occasion color *Weekly Standard* v22 no40 p6 Je 26 2017
VOICES of 2016 cartoon *Christian Century* v133 no26 p8 D 21 2016

Sanders, Bernard, 1941—Interviews
Bernie Looks Ahead E. BATES bw color *New Republic* v247 no11 p24 N 2016
BETTER TO BERN OUT J. Zengerle *GQ: Gentlemen's Quarterly* v86 no12 p207 D 2016
Where We Go From Here M. TAIBBI color *Rolling Stone* no1276 p42 D 15 2016

SANDERS, FRED
DOES PROTESTANTISM NEED TO DIE? cartoon color *Christianity Today* v60 no9 p69 N 2016

Sanders, Jane
The Little College That Couldn't A. B. LLOYD color *Weekly Standard* v22 no45 p17 Ag 7 2017

SANDERS, JOEL
Blurring the Boundaries *Architectural Record* v205 no1 p34 Ja 2017

Sanders, Kashay
How the Social Sector Can Attract More Young Talent *Harvard Business Review Digital Articles* p2 D 7 2016

SANDERS, LAURA
40 more genes linked to intelligence *Science News* v191 no12 p14 Je 24 2017
Body's perception of time still a puzzle bw *Science News* v191 no3 p28 F 18 2017
Brain's physical structure aids wiring color *Science News* v190 no8 p12 O 15 2016
Brain waves fight Alzheimer's protein color *Science News* v191 no1 p13 Ja 21 2017
Digital Minds bw color graph *Science News* v191 no6 p18 Ap 1 2017
Early body layout depends on brain *Science News* v192 no7 p12 O 28 2017
Essays offer peek into the mind of Oliver Sacks color *Science News* v192 no6 p28 O 14 2017
Flex Time [Cover story] color diag graph *Science News* v192 no4 p22 S 16 2017
Frequent lying alters brain activity *Science News* v190 no11 p12 N 26 2016
Improvisation helps reveal our inner lives color *Science News* v192 no6 p21 O 14 2017
Memory training rejiggers the brain diag *Science News* v191 no6 p7 Ap 1 2017
A newborn's pain registers in the brain color *Science News* v191 no11 p8 Je 10 2017
New citizen science project turns Alzheimer's research into a game *Science News* v190 no11 p28 N 26 2016
Parkinson's may begin in the gut color *Science News* v190 no12 p12 D 10 2016
Pregnancy alters a mother's brain color *Science News* v191 no2 p7 F 4 2017
Prionlike protein stores memories graph *Science News* v190 no12 p10 D 10 2016
Promising Alzheimer's drug will test amyloid hypothesis color *Science News* v190 no13 p27 D 24 2016
Rogue dopamine linked to Parkinson's bw *Science News* v192 no5 p7 S 30 2017

Scientists seek early signs of autism color graph *Science News* v191 no8 p10 Ap 29 2017

Sensory overload hurts young brains *Science News* v190 no12 p12 D 10 2016

Young human plasma renews old mice color *Science News* v191 no9 p7 My 13 2017

Sanders, Lisa

A college student experienced stomach pain and vomiting that quickly devolved into something much worse. No one could fi gure out the problem—until it was too late *New York Times Magazine* p24 Ap 30 2017

Diagnosis color *New York Times Magazine* p30 My 21 2017

Diagnosis *New York Times Magazine* p18 S 3 2017

Diagnosis *New York Times Magazine* p32 O 16 2016

Doctors in the hospital thought the 93-year-old woman was getting better. But her children thought she was dying. What was going on? *New York Times Magazine* p18 Je 25 2017

For years, her arthritis was under control, and she could work in her garden. But then a rash appeared and crippled her hand. Why? *New York Times Magazine* p22 Mr 5 2017

He thought he was getting the same stomach bug that his co-worker had. But his symptoms wound up being completely different color *New York Times Magazine* p18 Ag 6 2017

It started as a normal bout of hiccups—but then it wouldn't stop. What was causing these relentless spasms? *New York Times Magazine* p22 Jl 23 2017

The man had suffered two strokes and was on medication to prevent more. Was this another stroke? Or something else? *New York Times Magazine* p20 My 14 2017

The rash formed rings around the young boy's ankles, and his joints hurt. Was it an allergy? *New York Times Magazine* p18 Jl 9 2017

She had plenty of headaches in the past, but this pain felt different. Could it be something more dangerous than a migraine? *New York Times Magazine* p24 S 17 2017

She was 94, and all signs pointed to a stroke. But when tests came back negative, the doctors had to explore more unusual possibilities *New York Times Magazine* p20 O 1 2017

The sudden blackouts were distressing, but the woman felt mostly fine. Then her doctors called with an urgent request *New York Times Magazine* p16 Ag 20 2017

A vigorous 81-year-old had struggled with high blood pressure for years—but suddenly it was dangerously low. Why? *New York Times Magazine* p22 Ja 15 2017

Why was the 3-year-old so irritable, and what was wrong with her eye? *New York Times Magazine* p20 F 19 2017

Sanders, Marilyn

Must-Haves color *American Cowboy* v23 no4 p87 D 2016/Ja 2017

Sanders, Rob

Rodzilla *Publishers Weekly* v264 no11 p82 Mr 13 2017

Sanders, Rogier W.

HIV's ACHILLES' HEEL color diag *Scientific American* v315 no6 p50 D 2016

Sanders, Rupert, 1971-

Ghost in the Shell *New Yorker* v93 no10 p24 Ap 24 2017

Sanders, Scott Loring

APPALACHIAN SLY: Unfortunate characters suffer multiple miseries before attempting to turn calamity into good fortune B. GLOSE *Virginia Living* v15 no6 p27 O 2017

SANDERS, SCOTT RUSSELL

Kinship and Kindness *Orion Magazine* v35 no3 p26 My/Je 2016

Sanders, Sean

Precision medicine in the 21st century *Science* v354 no6319 p3 D 23 2016

Sandford, Christopher

Bridge Across the Atlantic R. D. LURIE *National Review* v69 no15 p44 Ag 14 2017

That man Robert Mitchum: remembering an enigmatic American original bw *America* v217 no5 p38 S 4 2017

SANDGREN, GILBERT R.

As the Free World Turns *Commentary* v144 no2 p4 S 2017

Sandhu, Manjinder S.

A Neolithic expansion, but strong genetic structure, in the independent history of New Guinea diag *Science* v357 no6356 p1160 S 15 2017

Sandhu, Rima

Control of meiotic pairing and recombination by chromosomally tethered 26S proteasome bibl graph *Science* v355 no6323 p408 Ja 27 2017

Sandhu, Sukhdev

MARK LECKEY color *Art in America* v104 no11 p88 D 2016

San Diego Comic-Con

ENTERTAINMENT WEEKLY PRESENTS COMIC-CON 2017 color *Entertainment Weekly* no1474/1475 p27 Jl 21-28 2017

EW AT COMIC-CON color *Entertainment Weekly* no1474/1475 p28 Jl 21-28 2017

EW IS COMIC-CONNECTED! H. Goldblatt color *Entertainment Weekly* no1476 p10 Ag 4 2017

Pop Chart E. Dockterman color *Time* v190 no6 p58 Ag 7 2017

THE PROS OF CON D. Franich, S. Li et al color *Entertainment Weekly* no1476 p32 Ag 4 2017

San Diego Public Library (San Diego, Calif.)

SAN DIEGO COMIC-CON 2017: Comics in Libraries and Schools C. REID color *Publishers Weekly* v264 no28 p54 Jl 10 2017

Sandifer, Andre

Ali Sandifer A. Ranallo color *American Craft* v77 no3 p45 Je/Jl 2017

Sanding machines

How to Make a... SPINDLE SANDER FROM A BLENDER J. SCHADEWALD color *Popular Mechanics* p71 S 2017

How to Make a... SPINDLE SANDER J. SCHADEWALD cartoon color *Popular Mechanics* v193 no7 p71 S 2016

Sanding machines—Evaluation

THE COMPLETE CORDLESS ARSENAL color *Popular Mechanics* p32 My 2017

Great Outdoors color *Old House Journal* v45 no5 p52 Ag 2017

Sandisk Corp.

Best USB-C memory card readers J. CARLSON color graph *Macworld - Digital Edition* v34 no9 p71 S 2017

Sandkühler, J.

Gliogenic LTP spreads widely in nociceptive pathways bibl graph *Science* v354 no6316 p1144 D 2 2016

Sandler, Richard

Scenes from a Lost World R. CAMPBELL *American Scholar* v86 no2 p102 Spr 2017

SANDLIN, AMANDA

Extreme Weirdness color *National Geographic Kids* no472 p8 Ag 2017

Guinness World Records *National Geographic Kids* no467 p6 F 2017

Sandman (Fictitious character : Gaiman)

NO. 48 MORPHEUS J. Jensen color *Entertainment Weekly* no1436/1437 p78 O 21 2016

Sandman, Kathleen

Structure of histone-based chromatin in Archaea diag *Science* v357 no6351 p609 Ag 11 2017

Sandman, The (Short story)

NIGHT VISION E. T. A. Hoffmann *Lapham's Quarterly* v10 no3 p136 Summ 2017

SANDOM, CHRISTOPHER J.

Conserving the World's Megafauna and Biodiversity: The Fierce Urgency of Now *BioScience* v67 no3 p197 Mr 2017

Saving the World's Terrestrial Megafauna color *BioScience* v66 no10 p807 O 1 2016

Sandor, Marjorie

A Winter's Journey *Opera News* v81 no5 p32 N 2016

Sandoval, Alba Alvarado

The Condom Campaign C. RIOS *Ms.* v26 no4 p10 Wint 2016

Sandoval, Aristoteles

Give Us Your Coders Yearning to Be Free A. Navarro color graph *Bloomberg Businessweek* no4518 p16 Ap 10 2017

Sandoval, Arturo

Java Jazz Provides Sonic Travelogue J. Ephland color *Downbeat* v84 no6 p14 Je 2017

Sandoval, Brian, 1963-

SCHOOL CHOICE A. Greenblatt *Governing* v30 no4 p38 Ja 2017

Sandoval, E. H. Valderrama

Persistent effects of pre-Columbian plant domestication on Amazonian forest composition bibl chart graph map *Science* v355 no6328 p925 Mr 3 2017

Sandoval, Justin P.

How Trump Could Change America *New York Times Upfront* v149 no7 p8 Ja 9 2017

Nation-Building's Siren Song *New York Times Book Review* p8 Ja 1 2017

Sanger, Jonathan

Magical Kingdom J. PODHORETZ *Weekly Standard* v22 no25 p43 Mr 6 2017

Sanger, Margaret, 1879-1966

America's first birth control clinic R. Cavendish *History Today* v66 no10 p9 O 2016

Sanger, Michael

What Leadership Looks Like in Different Cultures *Harvard Business Review Digital Articles* p2 My 6 2016

Sanghani, Rupa

HEART HEALTH M. COHEN color *Good Housekeeping* v264 no2 p101 F 2017

Sanghavi, Darshak

advice every new mom needs [Cover story] color *Parents* v92 no7 p32 Jl 2017

Sangiovanni, Giorgio

Robust spin-polarized midgap states at step edges of topological crystalline insulators bibl graph *Science* v354 no6317 p1269 D 9 2016

Sangkijporn, Somchai

Dengue diversity across spatial and temporal scales: Local structure and the effect of host population size bibl graph *Science* v355 no6331 p1302 Mr 24 2017

Sangria

THE KITCHEN COOKBOOK color *Better Homes & Gardens* v95 no7 p146 Jl 2017

Sangster, Caitlin

Last Star Burning *Publishers Weekly* v264 no36 p101 S 4 2017

Sangwook Lee

Anomalously low electronic thermal conductivity in metallic vanadium dioxide bibl graph *Science* v355 no6323 p371 Ja 27 2017

Sanitary napkins

10 THINGS WE'RE TALKING ABOUT T. A. Christian color *Essence* v47 no11 p67 Mr 2017

PAD LAUNCH Y. BHATTACHARJEE color *New York Times Magazine* p78 N 13 2016

Sanitation

See also

Waste management

100% Clean National Park P. Rauber *Sierra* v101 no4 p30 Jl/Ag 2016

Archive Dive: The Last Time the Cubs Won the World Series... bw *Publishers Weekly* v263 no45 p3 N 7 2016

Can Tidying Up Change Your Life? P. M. ESSWEIN cartoon *Kiplinger's Personal Finance* v71 no7 p39 Jl 2017

WHAT'S THAT ODOR? D. HISLOP *Sea Magazine* v108 no9 p28 S 2016

Sanitation workers

13 Things Garbage Collectors Want You to Know M. CROUCH color *Reader's Digest* v190 no1134 p128 O 2017

Sanjai, P. R.

India's War Over Water—and Soft Drinks map *Bloomberg Businessweek* no4515 p15 Mr 20 2017

Namaste Now try my herbal toothpaste color graph *Bloomberg Businessweek* no4502 p27 D 5 2016

Sanjana, Neville E.

High-resolution interrogation of functional elements in the non-coding genome bibl graph *Science* v353 no6307 p1545 S 30 2016

Sankaram, Kamala

Kamala Sankaram H. STEWART *Opera News* v81 no7 p10 Ja 2017

Sankaran, Banumathi

Principles for designing proteins with cavities formed by curved β sheets bibl color graph *Science* v355 no6321 p1 Ja 13 2017

Sankaranarayanan, Subramanian K. R. S.

Quantitative 3D evolution of colloidal nanoparticle oxidation in solution diag graph *Science* v356 no6335 p303 Ap 21 2017

Sanli, Kemal

A pathology atlas of the human cancer transcriptome diag *Science* v357 no6352 p660 Ag 18 2017

Sanlikol, Mehmet Ali

MEHMET ALI SANLIKOL F. Bouchard color *Downbeat* v84 no1 p22 Ja 2017

Sanlorenzo Americas (Company)

Sanlorenzo SL78 J. Y. Wood color *Power & Motoryacht* v33 no1 p48 Ja 2017

San Luis, Bryan-Joseph

Exploring genetic suppression interactions on a global scale diag *Science* v354 no6312 p599 N 4 2016

Sanna, Alessandro

Pinocchio: The Origin Story color *Publishers Weekly* v263 no49 p28 D 7 2016

Sanna, Emily

Does the Bible condone violence? *U.S. Catholic* v82 no10 p49 O 2017

THE FAR AWAY BROTHERS *U.S. Catholic* v82 no10 p41 O 2017

Identity in ink bw il *U.S. Catholic* v81 no12 p26 D 2016

A liturgy for families suffering a miscarriage *U.S. Catholic* v81 no11 p35 N 2016

Radical hospitality *U.S. Catholic* v82 no6 p4 Je 2017

Sing a new song *U.S. Catholic* v82 no3 p4 Mr 2017

The ties that bind *U.S. Catholic* v82 no9 p4 S 2017

Sanneh, Kelefa

As Is cartoon *New Yorker* v93 no5 p24 Mr 20 2017

COLOR CORRECTED cartoon color *New Yorker* v93 no31 p71 O 9 2017

COMING TO AMERICA cartoon *New Yorker* v92 no35 p84 O 31 2016

THE MORAL MINORITY cartoon *New Yorker* v92 no36 p34 N 7 2016

ON THE CONTRARY cartoon color *New Yorker* v93 no8 p50 Ap 10 2017

PINK LEMONADE cartoon *New Yorker* v92 no37 p89 N 14 2016

THE PROG SPRING bw cartoon *New Yorker* v93 no17 p67 Je 19 2017

SECRET ADMIRERS cartoon *New Yorker* v92 no44 p24 Ja 9 2017

SANO, EMILY

STANDARDS AND EMBLEMS OF THE BATTLE OF SEKIGAHARA *Texas Monthly* v44 no11 p102 N 2016

Sano, Soichi

Clonal hematopoiesis associated with TET2 deficiency accelerates atherosclerosis development in mice bibl diag *Science* v355 no6327 p842 F 24 2017

Sanok Kim—Interviews

In Conversation: A Jewish Grandma and a Korean Grandma on Their Dumplings C. CROWLEY img *New York* v49 no25 p102 D 12 2016

SANS Institute

Tech threats that scare the experts M. Hachman color *Macworld - Digital Edition* p41 Ap 2017

Sanssouci Park Potsdam (Germany)

ROYAL FLUSH G. Pines color *Conde Nast Traveler* v52 no2 p96 F 2017

Santa Barbara (Calif.)

Theory institute opens residence hall for visitors T. Feder *Physics Today* v70 no4 p32 Ap 2017

Santa Barbara (TV program)

Santa Barbara Forevah! M. IOSSEL color *Foreign Policy* no225 p54 Jl/Ag 2017

Santa Catalina Island (Calif.)

Catalina TO PORT G. Rosenkrans color *Sail* v48 no8 p44 Ag 2017

GUESS THE LOCATION *Sea Magazine* v109 no4 p11 Ap 2017

Santa Catalina Island (Calif.)—Description & travel

ESCAPE TO AVALON S. SHIBATA and M. WERLING *Sea Magazine* v108 no10 pCA-1 O 2016

Mini-Cruise M. Werling and S. Shibata *Sea Magazine* v109 no5 p20 My 2017

Santa Catalina Mountains (Ariz.)

IDENTIFYING FLYING OBJECTS M. JAFFE *Arizona Highways* v93 no6 p32 Je 2017

Santa Catalina Mountains (Ariz.)—Description & travel

PITCH A TENT & HIT THE TRAIL: Lewis and Clark, Simon and Garfunkel, peanut butter and chocolate... there's a long list of great combinations. In the summer in the Santa Catalina Mountains, the best combo might be hiking and camping. Here's a little... R. STIEVE and K. VAUGHN *Arizona Highways* v93 no6 p38 Je 2017

THE SANTA CATALINAS: TUCSON'S NEARBY WILDERNESS C. BOWDEN *Arizona Highways* v93 no6 p46 Je 2017

Santa Clarita Diet (TV program)

Drew Barrymore's Brilliant Zombie Return R. SHEFFIELD color *Rolling Stone* no1281/1282 p22 F 23 2017

Santa Clarita Diet M. ROUSH *TV Guide* v65 no6 p18 Ja 30 2017

Television Manages to Put a New Twist on the California State of Mind D. D'Addario color *Time* v189 no6 p47 F 20 2017

UNDEAD AND LOVING IT A. D'ARMINIO *TV Guide* v65 no6 p24 Ja 30 2017

Santa Claus

Athwart J. LILEKS il *National Review* v68 no24 p33 D 31 2016

Customers Who Like Santa Also Like...Nicotine Gum? A. Choudhary *Harvard Business Review Digital Articles* p2 O 22 2015

IT TAKES A VILLAGE R. O'CONNOR color *Chicago* v66 no8 p32 Ag 2017

JOLLY GOOD FELLAS J. Sugarman *Washingtonian Magazine* v52 no3 p94 D 2016

SKETCHBOOK G. BOOTH cartoon *New Yorker* v92 no41 p59 D 12 2016

A SLEIGHFUL OF SANTAS, SURVEYED P. Edmonds color *National Geographic* v230 no6 p12 D 2016

Socks, Underwear, and a Camaro R. Bragg color *Southern Living* v51 no12 p234 D 2016

Santa Claus—Interviews

Terry Hilderbrand S. STALL *Indianapolis Monthly* v40 no4 p29 D 2016

Santa Cruz (Calif.)—Description & travel

SEASIDE AMUSEMENT AND MORE!: SANTA CRUZ IS A SLEEPY BEACH TOWN WITH A RICH AND UNIQUE HISTORY *Sea Magazine* v109 no5 pCA-1 My 2017

Santa Cruz Bicycles LLC

Reinventing the Wheels color *Men's Health* v32 no6 p57 Ag 2017

santa cruz tallboy c B. Minnigh color *Bike Magazine* v24 no3 p108 My 2017

Santa Cruz Guitar Co.

Santa Cruz Guitar Co. FS Model C. Morrison color *Downbeat* v84 no7 p80 Jl 2017

Santa Fe automobile—Evaluation

Ratings chart *Consumer Reports* v82 no1 p60 Ja 2017

Santa Fe Natural Tobacco Co. Inc.

Nature's Cancer Sticks P. Brownfield cartoon color *Bloomberg Businessweek* no4499 p64 N 14 2016

Santa Fe Opera

Rediscovering a Neglected Treasure S. Williams *Opera News* v81 no5 p40 N 2016

Santa Monica (Calif.)

A Font Of Hand-Crafted Artistry S. ROOT color *Los Angeles Magazine* v62 no7 p13 Jl 2017

Pass the Mike P. KUH *Los Angeles Magazine* p58 Mr 2017

Santa Monica to Adopt Ambitious Zero Net Energy Requirements D. S. GLENN color *Architectural Record* v204 no12 p18 D 2016

THE UNNECESSARY EXPRESS [Cover story] Z. Bowman, S. Smith et al color *Cycle World* v56 no5 p32 Je 2017

Santa Monica Municipal Airport

THE SANTA MONICA PRECEDENT S. Pope color *Flying* v144 no4 p10 Ap 2017

Santa Anna, Antonio Lopez de, ca. 1794-1876

The Alamo Remembered G. R. Schiavino bw *American Cowboy* p38 LEGENDS OF TEXAS Special Issue 2017

Santa Clara Valley (Santa Clara County, Calif.)—Economic conditions

A TO-DO LIST FOR THE TECH INDUSTRY J. Tanz cartoon *Wired* v24 no11 p92 N 2016

Santa-Cruz, Nestor

Frame of Reference J. MISCHNER color *House Beautiful* v159 no9 p76 N 2017

Santagata, Marco, 1947-

Dante: He Went Mad in His Hell R. P. Harrison cartoon *New York Review of Books* v63 no16 p30 O 27 2016

The Divine Mr. D J. MATTHEW WILSON color *Weekly Standard* v22 no20 p30 Ja 30 2017

Santagata, Sandro

Susan Lindquist (1949–2016) color *Science* v354 no6315 p974 N 25 2016

SantaMaria, Anna M.

Restored iron transport by a small molecule promotes absorption and hemoglobinization in animals color graph *Science* v356 no6338 p608 My 12 2017

Santana, Amar

TOP CHEFS A. M. Panoringan color *Los Angeles Magazine* v62 no10 p8 O 2017

Santana, Carlos, 1947—Interviews

Carlos Santana D. BROWNE bw *Rolling Stone* no1291/1292 p70 Jl 13 2017

Santangelo, Philip J.

Sustained virologic control in SIV+ macaques after antiretroviral and α4β7 antibody therapy bibl graph *Science* v354 no6309 p197 O 14 2016

Santangelo, Thomas J.

Structure of histone-based chromatin in Archaea diag *Science* v357 no6351 p609 Ag 11 2017

Santantonio, Alex

How Transom Windows Work color *Old House Journal* v45 no7 p50 O 2017

SANTE, LUC

The Greatest Enigma of French Film bw color *New York Review of Books* v63 no16 p54 O 27 2016

His Lofty Ascent: Gaspard-Félix Tournachon, the great French photographer, had an antic personality and a gift for self-promotion *New York Times Book Review* p23 Jl 23 2017

John Ashbery (1927–2017) [Cover story] bw *New York Review of Books* v64 no15 p4 O 12 2017

PHOTOGRAPHY color *New York Times Book Review* p62 D 4 2016

Santee, Endia J.

Human health color *Science* v356 no6338 p590 My 12 2017

SANTELISES, SONJA BROOKINS

Are High Schools Preparing Students to Be College- and Career-Ready? cartoon *Education Digest* v82 no8 p60 Ap 2017

Santiago, Jose

MASTERS OF TECH color *Literacy Today (2411-7862)* v34 no3 p12 N/D 2016

Santiago, Sofia

LAUGHING ALL THE WAY TO SUCCESS M. W. SCHWARTZ *Missouri Life* v43 no6 p18 O/N 2016

Santiago-Hudson, Ruben

GOINGS ON ABOUT TOWN color *New Yorker* v92 no43 p6 Ja 2 2017

Santiago Muñoz, Beatriz, 1972-

BEATRIZ SANTIAGO MUÑOZ E. Lyle *Art in America* v104 no9 p156 O 2016

Santillan, Noel

WHERE THE @#$% AM I? D. KUSHNER color map *Reader's Digest* v189 no1130 p88 My 2017

SANTISTEVAN, RYAN

Dwight B. Heard: Although his legacy lives on in a world-renowned museum that bears his name, Dwight Bancroft Heard made a name for himself as a newspaper publisher, cattle baron and political ally of Teddy Roosevelt *Arizona Highways* v93 no10 p8 O 2017

Santo Domingo (Dominican Republic)

Festive Activism T. Panken color *Downbeat* v83 no11 p99 N 2016

Santo Domingo, Lauren, 1976-

Waist Not, Want Not E. ELWICK-BATES bw color *Vogue* v206 no12 p156 D 2016

Santoro, Gene

Companion Pieces bw color *AARP: The Magazine* v60 no3A p64 Ap/My 2017

Santos, Alejandro

Peru: Staying the Course of Economic Success R. Feinberg *Foreign Affairs* v96 no1 p169 Ja/F 2017

Santos, David P.

Dopamine oxidation mediates mitochondrial and lysosomal dysfunction in Parkinson's disease graph *Science* v357 no6357 p1255 S 22 2017

Santos, E.

Observation of a large-scale anisotropy in the arrival directions

of cosmic rays above 8 × 1018 eV *Science* v357 no6357 p1266 S 22 2017

Santos, E. M.

Observation of a large-scale anisotropy in the arrival directions of cosmic rays above 8 × 1018 eV *Science* v357 no6357 p1266 S 22 2017

Santos, Fernanda

Should They Stay or Should They Go? The debate over President Trump's crackdown on undocumented immigrants *New York Times Upfront* v149 no13 p6 My 15 2017

Santos, Juan C.

Interacting amino acid replacements allow poison frogs to evolve epibatidine resistance chart diag graph *Science* v357 no6357 p1261 S 22 2017

Santos, Kendra

THE ADVANTAGES OF YEAR-ROUND ROPING color *Spin to Win Rodeo* v20 no11 p34 Ja 2017

The ALL-NEW RACE for the ULTIMATE CROWN in Cowboy Town [Cover story] color *Spin to Win Rodeo* v20 no10 p62 D 2016

THE BAR JUST KEEPS BEING RAISED color *Spin to Win Rodeo* v20 no11 p26 Ja 2017

Broc Cresta color *Spin to Win Rodeo* v21 no5 p60 Jl 2017

COMMUNICATION IS KEY TO ALL SUCCESSFUL PARTNERSHIPS color *Spin to Win Rodeo* v21 no5 p40 Jl 2017

COUNTING THE BIG BUCKS: Yes or No? color *Team Roping Journal* p50 O 2017

DON'T FORGET TO BARRIER BREAK YOUR HORSE [Cover story] color *Spin to Win Rodeo* v21 no4 p36 Je 2017

DON'T OVERTHINK THINGS color *Spin to Win Rodeo* v21 no3 p46 My 2017

Driggers Doesn't Let Roping Define Him *Spin to Win Rodeo* v21 no1 p26 Mr 2017

FALL FIGHT to the finish color *Team Roping Journal* p48 O 2017

Family T-i-e-s color *Team Roping Journal* p94 O 2017

GAME PLAN for Gaining Success color *Team Roping Journal* p54 S 2017

GETTING INTO THE SWING OF THINGS color *Spin to Win Rodeo* v21 no1 p46 Mr 2017

Going, Going, Gone color *Team Roping Journal* p84 O 2017

GOLD RUSH [Cover story] color *Spin to Win Rodeo* v21 no4 p56 Je 2017

HANDLES ARE SPEEDING UP WITH THE TIMES color *Spin to Win Rodeo* v20 no12 p38 F 2017

HAPPY BIRTHDAY [Cover story] color *Spin to Win Rodeo* v21 no1 p54 Mr 2017

Hass Takes Aim in Two Events color *Spin to Win Rodeo* v21 no5 p22 Jl 2017

HORSEPOWER IS NEVER TO BE TAKEN FOR GRANTED color *Spin to Win Rodeo* v21 no6 p44 Ag 2017

HUSBAND AND WIFE HIT $200K JACKPOT at the Reno Million color *Team Roping Journal* p91 S 2017

IN IT FOR THE LONG HAUL color *Spin to Win Rodeo* v21 no1 p38 Mr 2017

LEARNING BY WATCHING AND LISTENING TO OTHERS [Cover story] color *Spin to Win Rodeo* v21 no4 p44 Je 2017

Lovell Kisses Full-Time Rodeo Trail Goodbye color *Spin to Win Rodeo* v20 no12 p24 F 2017

Luke Brown & Jake Long Master the BFI Mountain [Cover story] color *Spin to Win Rodeo* v21 no6 p56 Ag 2017

MAXIMIZING THE BENEFITS of Minimal Practice color *Team Roping Journal* p56 S 2017

PACING PRACTICE: FAST OR SLOW? color *Spin to Win Rodeo* v20 no12 p46 F 2017

Patience and Perseverance Pay for Long color *Spin to Win Rodeo* v21 no4 p28 Je 2017

PRIME PRACTICE PAYS PREMIUMS color *Spin to Win Rodeo* v20 no9 p34 N 2016

REED AND PEARCE CAP ROP ING ROLL WITH PENDLETON WIN color *Spin to Win Rodeo* v20 no9 p54 N 2016

ROPING IN THE THOMAS & MACK ...ANYTHING BUT AVERAGE bw color *Spin to Win Rodeo* v20 no12 p66 F 2017

SIMPSON AND BUHLER REWRITE TEAM ROPING HISTORY [Cover story] color *Spin to Win Rodeo* v20 no11 p48 Ja 2017

SLACK SOMETIMES GETS A BAD RAP color *Spin to Win Rodeo* v20 no10 p46 D 2016

Small Shifts Gears from Steers to School *Spin to Win Rodeo* v21 no2 p30 Ap 2017

Snow Rides Into First NFR Hot color *Spin to Win Rodeo* v20 no11 p18 Ja 2017

TALK IT OVER, MAKE A PLAN AND EXECUTE color *Spin to Win Rodeo* v21 no5 p30 Jl 2017

Team Roping Spices Up World All-Around Race *Spin to Win Rodeo* v21 no6 p28 Ag 2017

Thorp Thrives on Team Roping *Spin to Win Rodeo* v21 no3 p30 My 2017

Thumbs Up on Dakota K's Recovery *Spin to Win Rodeo* v20 no10 p32 D 2016

Tierney Trifecta at the Timed Event color *Spin to Win Rodeo* v21 no3 p64 My 2017

TIMING THAT FIRST AVAILABLE SHOT color *Spin to Win Rodeo* v20 no10 p54 D 2016

TODAY'S TEAM-ROPING TALENT POOL RUNS DEEP color *Spin to Win Rodeo* v21 no6 p36 Ag 2017

WHAT MAKES A HEEL LOOP WORK? color *Spin to Win Rodeo* v20 no9 p42 N 2016

WHERE DOES IT GO FROM HERE? color *Spin to Win Rodeo* v21 no3 p38 My 2017

Santos, Luisa

This Is My Job J. Militare color *Glamour* v115 no5 p122 My 2017

Santos, Maricar

Beauty Boss color *Working Mother* v40 no2 p16 Je/Jl 2017

From Dinner Failure to Mealtime Maven color *Working Mother* v40 no4 p10 O/N 2017

Gal-Pal Getaway color *Working Mother* v40 no3 p48 Ag/S 2017

Got a Cold? Do This color *Working Mother* p57 F/Mr 2017

Hassle-Free Family Getaways [Cover story] color *Working Mother* v40 no2 p56 Je/Jl 2017

"I Can't Unplug from Work, and It' Affecting My Colleague's Job" cartoon color *Working Mother* v40 no3 p8 Ag/S 2017

"I Feel Guilty When I Can't Help My Colleague Because of My Kids" [Cover story] color *Working Mother* v40 no2 p14 Je/Jl 2017

must-buys color *Working Mother* v40 no3 p16 Ag/S 2017

Must-Buys color *Working Mother* v40 no4 p16 O/N 2017

Style Star color *Working Mother* v40 no3 p10 Ag/S 2017

WORKS FOR US! color *Working Mother* p19 F/Mr 2017

Santos, Nate

CHICER THAN RAP: HIP-HOP'S MOST FORMIDABLE FASHION VENTURES color map *Ebony* v72 no11 p80 S 2017

GRIDIRON GRIDLOCK color *Ebony* v72/73 no12/1 p90 O/N 2017

LOOKING FOR REVENGE color *Ebony* v72 no11 p88 S 2017

THE MUSIC MAN bw *Ebony* v72 no9 p98 Jl/Ag 2017

She Got Game color *Ebony* v72 no9 p31 Jl/Ag 2017

SOUND OFF color *Ebony* v72 no11 p90 S 2017

VR GOALS color *Ebony* v72/73 no12/1 p93 O/N 2017

WHAT STREAMS ARE MADE OF color *Ebony* v72/73 no12/1 p86 O/N 2017

Santos, Neymar da Silva, 1992-

OUT OF THE SHADOWS [Cover story] B. Straus color *Sports Illustrated* v127 no4 p28 Ag 7 2017

Santos, Noa

What I Wear to Work: NOA SANTOS J. Chen color *Bloomberg Businessweek* no4520 p75 My 1 2017

Santos, Romeo, 1981-

The Love Doctor Is In P. Mejia img *New York* v50 no18 p71 S 4 2017

The New Bronx Cheer color *GQ: Gentlemen's Quarterly* v97 no7 p80 Jl 2017

Sanu, Mohamed

Leading Off color *Sports Illustrated* v126 no3 p6 Ja 23 2017

Sanwen Huang

A chemical genetic roadmap to improved tomato flavor bibl graph *Science* v355 no6323 p391 Ja 27 2017

Sanz, Joaquín

Social status alters immune regulation and response to infection in macaques bibl graph *Science* v354 no6315 p1041 N 25 2016

Sanz-Briz, Ángel

THE ANGEL OF BUDAPEST R. Philpot *History Today* v67 no1 p21 Ja 2017

Sanzenbacher, Geoffrey T.

The labor supply of veterans with disabilities, 1995-2014 bibl chart color graph *Monthly Labor Review* p1 O 2016

Saola

Saving the saola from extinction A. Tilker, B. Long et al color *Science* v357 no6357 p1248 S 22 2017

Sap (Plant)

See also

Maple sap

MAKE SYRUP from Birch, Walnut, and Sycamore Trees B. McLeod *Mother Earth News* no280 p60 F/Mr 2017

TAP IT YOURSELF J. Nick cartoon *Rodale's Organic Life* v3 no1 p92 Ja 2017

What's On Tap? S. FORBES color *Rodale's Organic Life* v3 no1 p46 Ja 2017

SAP SE

"Authenticity makes us stand out from our competitors": Why the software company had to revamp its employer brand to secure top talent *People Management* p25 Ap 2017

SAP's CEO on Being the American Head of a German Multinational B. McDermott bw graph img *Harvard Business Review* v94 no11 p35 N 2016

Saphier, Jon

Getting students to believe in themselves color diag il *Phi Delta Kappan* v98 no5 p48 F 2017

Saphire, Erica Ollmann

A "Trojan horse" bispecific-antibody strategy for broad protection against ebolaviruses bibl graph *Science* v354 no6310 p350 O 21 2016

Saphos, Nicole

THE RIGHT MOVE M. J. West color *Downbeat* v84 no3 p48 Mr 2017

Sapir, Nir

From Agricultural Benefits to Aviation Safety: Realizing the Potential of Continent-Wide Radar Networks *BioScience* v67 no10 p912 O 2017

Mass seasonal bioflows of high-flying insect migrants bibl graph *Science* v354 no6319 p1584 D 23 2016

Sapolsky, Robert M.

Brain Teasers: A neurobiologist serves up his science with a big dose of hipster humor R. WRANGHAM *New York Times Book Review* p15 Jl 9 2017

Human nature F. de Waal color *Science* v356 no6344 p1239 Je 23 2017

It's Complicated: Unraveling the mystery of why people act as they do *American Scholar* v86 no3 p109 Summ 2017

Proinflammatory primates bibl color *Science* v354 no6315 p967 N 25 2016

Sapolsky, Robert—Interviews

Your Brain Behaving Badly G. deGROOT REDFORD color *AARP: The Magazine* v60 no5A p22 Ag/S 2017

Saporita, Nicole

10 GENIUS WAYS TO make money in your $pare time [Cover story] color *Good Housekeeping* v265 no2 p79 Ag 2017

BEST TOY AWARDS 2017 color *Good Housekeeping* v265 no5 p85 N 2017

GOOD HOUSEKEEPING REGISTRY WISH LIST color *Good Housekeeping* v264 no6 p49 Je 2017

MONEY SAVING GUIDE [Cover story] cartoon color *Good Housekeeping* v264 no2 p79 F 2017

smart ENTERTAINMENT diag *Good Housekeeping* v263 no5 p143 N 2016

Summer SURVIVAL GUIDE color *Good Housekeeping* v264 no6 p69 Je 2017

TRIP OF A LIFETIME [Cover story] color *Good Housekeeping* v265 no3 p146 S 2017

your PERSONAL GADGETS color diag *Good Housekeeping* v263 no6 p105 D 2016

Saporito, Bill

Why a Rate Hike Is an Indicator of a Healthy Economy color *Time* v189 no11 p30 Mr 27 2017

Sapphires

Quick Hits L. Nemo map *Scientific American* v317 no4 p22 O 2017

Sappho, ca. 630 B.C.-570 B.C.

SAPPHO and her brothers D. Gribble *History Today* v66 no10 p46 O 2016

Saracco, Guido

Improving efficiency and stability of perovskite solar cells with photocurable fluoropolymers bibl chart graph *Science* v354 no6309 p203 O 14 2016

Saraceno, Jon

Bob Costas color *AARP: The Magazine* v59 no5A p13 Ag/S 2016

Surviving the '80s color *AARP: The Magazine* v59 no5A p47 Ag/S 2016

Saracho, Tanya

Theater of the Real *Chicago* v66 no10 p81 O 2017

Sarafian, Adam R.

Experimental constraints on the damp peridotite solidus and oceanic mantle potential temperature bibl diag *Science* v355 no6328 p942 Mr 3 2017

How Did Earth Gets Its Ocean? color *Oceanus* v51 no2 p100 Wint 2016

Sarafian, Emily

Experimental constraints on the damp peridotite solidus and oceanic mantle potential temperature bibl diag *Science* v355 no6328 p942 Mr 3 2017

Sarah, Robert, 1945-

The Catholic surge in Africa P. Jenkins *Christian Century* v134 no6 p45 Mr 15 2017

Sarah, Robyn, 1949-

In the Palm of Her Hand A. LAHEY *Walrus* v14 no9 p72 N 2017

Saraiva, Catarina

Outlook Where the Growth Is map *Bloomberg Businessweek* no4517 p17 Ap 3 2017

Sarandon, Susan, 1946-

ARCH NEMESES E. NUSSBAUM cartoon *New Yorker* v93 no5 p98 Mr 20 2017

Feud: Bette and Joan J. Jensen color *Entertainment Weekly* no1454/1455 p84 F 24 2017

Killing Richard Glossip J. Halterman *TV Guide* p35 Ap 17 2017

Season of the Bitch: Bette vs. Joan R. SHEFFIELD color *Rolling Stone* no1284 p22 Ap 6 2017

Sarandon, Susan, 1946-—Interviews

Ray Donovan M. Logan *TV Guide* v65 no41 p36 O 2 2017

Susan Sarandon Is Ready to Rumble img *New York* p112 Mr 6 2017

Sarao, Navinder Singh, 1980-

A STOCK TRADER LOSES IN COURT. IT'S NO REASON TO CELEBRATE S. Gandel color *Fortune* v174 no6 p14 N 1 2016

Sarasota Ballet (Performer)

Danielle Brown C. Seidman color *Dance Magazine* v91 no3 p44 Mr 2017

Sarasota County (Fla.)

Nathan Benderson Park: A Classic Reclamation Project R. Sullivan *Parks & Recreation* v51 no10 p28 O 2016

Sarazin, F.

Observation of a large-scale anisotropy in the arrival directions of cosmic rays above 8×1018 eV *Science* v357 no6357 p1266 S 22 2017

Sarcasm

The Reader Page G. Jones, J. Berkley color *Popular Mechanics* v193 no7 p4 S 2016

Sarcoidosis

SOME SMALL SARCOIDS GO AWAY ON THEIR OWN C. Barakat and M. McCluskey color *Equus* no473 p11 F 2017

SARCONI, PAUL

FETISH: DIVER DOWN color *Wired* v25 no7 p37 Jl 2017

GEARHEAD: TRAIL MIX color *Wired* v25 no7 p40 Jl 2017

HOW TO SHOOT IN 360 color *Wired* v25 no5 p50 My 2017

OK, HOUSE. GET SMART chart color *Wired* v25 no6 p39 Je 2017

THE SETUP UNREAL ESTATE cartoon *Wired* v25 no4 p40 Ap 2017

Sarcopenia—Prevention

trendWATCH C. CROMER color *Better Nutrition* v78 no12 p10 D 2016

Sarcophagi

Fit for a King S. Jenkins bw *Smithsonian* v47 no10 p40 Mr 2017

Sareer, Ahmed

Protecting Small Island Developing States from Pollution and the Effects of Climate Change *UN Chronicle* v54 no1/2 p1 2017

Sareh, Pooya

Mechanized creatures color *Science* v355 no6332 p1379 Mr 31 2017

Sarel, Ayelet
Vectorial representation of spatial goals in the hippocampus of bats bibl graph *Science* v355 no6321 p1 Ja 13 2017

Sargeant, Alexi
History Is for Making Great Citizens *National Review* v69 no19 p42 O 16 2017
A Touch of Woody Allen bw *Commonweal* v143 no20 p26 D 16 2016
Warlike Thrust color *Weekly Standard* v22 no48 p39 S 4 2017

Sargent, Anneila I.
Kwok-Yung Lo *Physics Today* v70 no8 p71 Ag 2017
Spiral density waves in a young protoplanetary disk bibl graph *Science* v353 no6307 p1519 S 30 2016

SARGENT, BETTY KELLY
Ask the Editor *Publishers Weekly* v264 no13 p52 Mr 27 2017
Ask the Editor *Publishers Weekly* v264 no9 p51 F 27 2017

Sargent, Don
DO A HEAD CHECK color diag *Golf Magazine* v59 no11 p47 N 2017
TRY THIS! CURVE BALLS color *Golf Magazine* v59 no10 p44 O 2017

Sargent, Edward H.
Efficient and stable solution-processed planar perovskite solar cells via contact passivation bibl graph *Science* v355 no6326 p722 F 17 2017

Sargent, John Singer, 1856-1925
Arts and letters: A new exhibition explores the affinities between the work of Henry James and the American painting of his time E. Pochoda color *Magazine Antiques* v184 no4 p68 Jl/Ag 2017
WOMEN AND WATER COLOR K. A. Foster cartoon color *Magazine Antiques* v184 no2 p84 Mr/Ap 2017

Sargent, John Singer, 1856-1925—Exhibitions
Water and Light D. GREEN color *Weekly Standard* v23 no5 p44 O 9 2017

Sargent, Ron
Here's How color *Practical Horseman* v45 no2 p58 F 2017

Sargent, Sarah
ESSENTIAL TRUTH *Virginia Living* v15 no1 p31 D 2016
IN THE GROOVE: Sheep Jones' striking textured surfaces imbue simple subjects with soulful wonder *Virginia Living* v15 no4 p33 Je 2017
IN THE OEUVR *Virginia Living* v15 no3 p17 Ap 2017

Sargent, Vern
Z SCALE IN A CLOSET color *Model Railroader* v84 no11 p50 N 2017

Sargsyan, Ashot
How NASA Uses Telemedicine to Care for Astronauts in Space *Harvard Business Review Digital Articles* p2 Jl 6 2017

Sargsyan, Tigran
SAVE THE DATE color *Dance Spirit* v21 no8 p35 O 2017

Saris Cycling Group Inc.
EASY ON, EASY OFF! G. Liu, R. Koch et al color *Bicycling* v58 no7 p82 Ag 2017

Saritoprak, Zeki
Who is Jesus for Muslims? A. Frykholm *Christian Century* v134 no12 p32 Je 7 2017

SARKADI, LAURIE
'Listen to what the land wants, listen to what the lake wants, listen to what the animals want' color map *Canadian Geographic* v137 no1 p34 F 2017

Sarkar, Jayita
Managing nuclear risk in South Asia bibl *Bulletin of the Atomic Scientists* v73 no1 p59 Ja 2017

SARKAR, SAHOTRA
THE ZIKA CRISIS: A RESULT OF NEGLECT diag *Phi Kappa Phi Forum* v96 no4 p22 Wint 2016

Särkinen, Tiina
Forest conservation: Remember Gran Chaco bibl color *Science* v355 no6324 p465 F 3 2017

Sarkizova, Siranush
Single-cell RNA-seq reveals new types of human blood dendritic cells, monocytes, and progenitors color *Science* v356 no6335 p283 Ap 21 2017

Sarli-Freeman, Elise

SADDLE CHAT bw color graph *Horse & Rider* v56 no7 p21 Jl 2017

Sarma, Amardeo
Hans Rosling Brought Data to Life, Showed Our Misconceptions about the World *Skeptical Inquirer* v41 no4 p9 Jl/Ag 2017

Sarma, Sanjay E.
Setting Standards for the Internet of Things *Harvard Business Review Digital Articles* p2 N 21 2014

Sarmento, R.
Observation of a large-scale anisotropy in the arrival directions of cosmic rays above 8 × 1018 eV *Science* v357 no6357 p1266 S 22 2017

Sarmiento, C. A.
Observation of a large-scale anisotropy in the arrival directions of cosmic rays above 8 × 1018 eV *Science* v357 no6357 p1266 S 22 2017

Sarnela, Nina
Global atmospheric particle formation from CERN CLOUD measurements bibl graph map *Science* v354 no6316 p1119 D 2 2016

SAROS, JASMINE E.
The Arctic in the Twenty-First Century: Changing Biogeochemical Linkages across a Paraglacial Landscape of Greenland *BioScience* v67 no2 p118 F 2017

Saros cycle
Love affair with a saros B. BERMAN color *Astronomy* v45 no11 p10 N 2017

Sárospataki, M.
Country-specific effects of neonicotinoid pesticides on honey bees and wild bees diag map *Science* v356 no6345 p1393 Je 30 2017

Sarrazin, Hugo
Your Company Should Be Helping Customers on Social *Harvard Business Review Digital Articles* p2 Jl 15 2015

Sarrou, Iosifina
Structure of a symmetric photosynthetic reaction center–photosystem color *Science* v357 no6355 p1021 S 8 2017

SARS (Disease)
In Sickness and in Health D. L. HEYMANN color *Natural History* v125 no9 p43 S 2017

Sarstedt Inc.
new products color *Science* v357 no6358 p1425 S 29 2017

SARTAIN, J. D.
7 Excel tips for huge spreadsheets: Split Screen, Freeze Panes, Format Painter and more color *PCWorld* v35 no8 p154 Ag 2017
Excel tips: 6 slick shortcuts, handy functions, and random-number generators diag *PCWorld* v35 no11 p148 N 2016

SARTOGO, MARTINA MONDADORI
A Lasting Memory color *Architectural Digest* v74 no10 p168 O 1 2017

Sartore, Joel
The Gratitude Meter Z. Donaldson color *O, The Oprah Magazine* p22 Jl 2017
The Photo Ark: One Man's Quest to Document the World's Animals color *Publishers Weekly* v264 no3 p48 Ja 16 2017

SAS Ocean Phoenix (Company)
Taking In the Trash E. Strickland *Sierra* v102 no1 p24 Ja/F 2017

SASAKI, MISAO
A COSMIC CONTROVERSY color *Scientific American* v317 no1 p5 Jl 2017

SASAKI, NOPHEA
Opportunities for Improved Transparency in the Timber Trade through Scientific Verification *BioScience* v66 no11 p990 N 1 2016

Sasaki, S.
Crystallization and vitrification of electrons in a glass-forming charge liquid bw *Science* v357 no6358 p1381 S 29 2017

Sasaki, T.
Crystallization and vitrification of electrons in a glass-forming charge liquid bw *Science* v357 no6358 p1381 S 29 2017

Sashco Sealants Inc.
Sashco Turns 80! bw color *Log Home Living* v33 no7 p17 S 2016

Sashes (Clothing)
Finishing Touches FOR WINDOWS & WALLS L. Elliott cartoon *Old House Journal* v45 no1 p48 F 2017

Sasikumar, Karthika
After nuclear midnight: The impact of a nuclear war on India and Pakistan bibl *Bulletin of the Atomic Scientists* v73 no4 p226 Jl

Why No One Is Reading Your Marketing Content *Harvard Business Review Digital Articles* p2 D 9 2015

You Don't Need to Adopt Holacracy to Get Some of Its Benefits *Harvard Business Review Digital Articles* p2 Ag 28 2015

Your Company's Networks Might Matter More than Its Strategy *Harvard Business Review Digital Articles* p2 Je 10 2015

Satellite radio services

Forecasting Weather the Old-Fashioned Way F. Larson bw color diag il *Weatherwise* v70 no4 p28 Jl/Ag 2017

Satellite radio services—Evaluation

Why I Didn't Buy the Benz K. C. POHLMANN color *Sound & Vision* v82 no6 p21 Jl/Ag 2017

Satellites of Pluto

Spacecraft finds no rings around Pluto [Cover story] L. GROSSMAN color *Science News* v192 no7 p15 O 28 2017

SATENSTEIN, LIANA

NAOMIE Harris color *Vogue* v207 no3 p322 Mr 2017

Sater, Felix

Intrigue: Andrew Rice: Who Is Felix Sater? Donald Trump's original Russia-connected business partner is quite a talker img *New York* v50 no16 p19 Ag 7 2017

Satija, Rahul

Single-cell RNA-seq reveals new types of human blood dendritic cells, monocytes, and progenitors color *Science* v356 no6335 p283 Ap 21 2017

Satire

See also
> Irony
> Political satire
> Satire in journalism

ARE YOU LAUGHIN' AT ME? O. ELLICKSON cartoon color *Wired* v25 no4 p64 Ap 2017

Boiling it down G. Gundersen color *Bloomberg Businessweek* no4526 p76 Je 12 2017

DRAWN & QUARTERED color *MHQ: Quarterly Journal of Military History* v29 no4 p96 Summ 2017

Satire in journalism

The Duck That Clipped Fillon's Wings A. Boksenbaum-Granier and G. Amiel color *Bloomberg Businessweek* no4518 p17 Ap 10 2017

Satirists

MAN IN THE MIRROR M. Mechanic color *Mother Jones* v41 no6 p57 N/D 2016

Satisfaction

See also
> Customer satisfaction
> Housing—Resident satisfaction
> Job satisfaction

It's What You Do That Counts A. K. SMITH color *Kiplinger's Personal Finance* v70 no12 p42 D 2016

LET IT GO [Cover story] J. K. LINDLEY color *Redbook* p91 Je 2017

SUTTON FOSTER "Youthfulness Comes from Within" L. Desantis color *Health* v31 no4 p21 My 2017

Sato, R.

Observation of a large-scale anisotropy in the arrival directions of cosmic rays above 8 × 1018 eV *Science* v357 no6357 p1266 S 22 2017

Sato, T.

Electronic crystal growth bw diag graph *Science* v357 no6358 p1378 S 29 2017

Sato, Takuma—Interviews

Road to Joy J. Feldman and T. Keith color *Sports Illustrated* v126 no17 p26 Je 19 2017

Satoshi Hirata

Great apes anticipate that other individuals will act according to false beliefs bibl chart diag graph *Science* v354 no6308 p110 O 7 2016

Satoshi Kawatake

A three-dimensional movie of structural changes in bacteriorhodopsin bibl diag graph *Science* v354 no6319 p1552 D 23 2016

Satoshi Yamazaki

Depleting dietary valine permits nonmyeloablative mouse hematopoietic stem cell transplantation bibl graph *Science* v354 no6316 p1152 D 2 2016

Satow, Elizabeth

Revolutionary Empowerment for Girls in Nepal color *Maclean's* v130 no3 p65 Ap 2017

Satran, Pamela Redmond

10-Year-Old-Girl Powers We Should All Reclaim color *Glamour* v115 no5 p195 My 2017

12 Sex Things We Still Don't Understand color *Glamour* v115 no7 p109 Jl 2017

13 Accomplishments That Are Bigger Than They Seem color *Glamour* v115 no6 p147 Je 2017

13 Resolutions Other People Really Need to Make This Year color *Glamour* v115 no1 p99 Ja 2017

13 Things That Should Be A Thing color *Glamour* v114 no11 p183 N 2016

14 Totally Legit Expectations in Love color *Glamour* v115 no2 p127 F 2017

32 Weirdly Random Thoughts We've Had During Yoga color *Glamour* v115 no9 p215 S 2017

Satsukawa, T.

Coseismic rupturing stopped by Aso volcano during the 2016 Mw 7.1 Kumamoto earthquake, Japan bibl color graph *Science* v354 no6314 p869 N 18 2016

Satter, David, 1947-

Russia needs a truth commission now R. A. Schroth color *America* v216 no6 p44 Mr 20 2017

Satterlee, Seth

Befriending Heartbreak color *Publishers Weekly* v263 no51 p141 D 12 2016

FALL 2017 RELIGION & SPIRITUALITY ANNOUNCEMENTS color *Publishers Weekly* v264 no28 p22 Jl 10 2017

Home and Away: Writing the Beautiful Game color *Publishers Weekly* v263 no50 p60 D 5 2016

Locus Solus color *Publishers Weekly* v263 no43 p54 O 24 2016

SPRING 2017 RELIGION & SPIRITUALITY ANNOUNCEMENTS color graph *Publishers Weekly* v264 no8 p24 F 20 2017

SATTLER, ANDREA

A Messy World *Commentary* v143 no1 p6 Ja 2017

Sattler, M.

Inhibitors of PEX14 disrupt protein import into glycosomes and kill Trypanosoma parasites chart color diag graph *Science* v355 no6332 p1416 Mr 31 2017

SATTLER, MARTIN

A Messy World *Commentary* v143 no1 p6 Ja 2017

Saturday Night Fever (Film)

SATURDAY NIGHT FEVER DIRECTOR'S CUT M. Mettler color *Sound & Vision* v82 no8 p70 O 2017

Saturday Night Live (TV program)

Happy Warrior H. WILHELM *National Review* v68 no24 p44 D 31 2016

Kate McKinnon Didn't Make a Joke R. TRAISTER img *New York* v49 no25 p50 D 12 2016

LIVE FROM DC *Washingtonian Magazine* v53 no1 p70 O 2017

Prince of the City A. BALDWIN color *Vanity Fair* v59 no5 p104 Ap 2017

The Quiz T. BALAZO color *Maclean's* v129 no43 p64 O 31 2016

Saturday Night Live's Weirdo in Chief A. MORRIS color *Rolling Stone* no1272 p26 O 20 2016

The Uncanny Catharsis of Saturday Night Live D. D'Addario color *Time* v189 no7/8 p23 F 27 2017

WHO'S LAUGHING NOW? The tragicomedy of Donald Trump on Saturday Night Live T. Bissell *Harper's Magazine* p61 O 2017

Saturday Evening Post, The (Periodical)

Cover Page *Saturday Evening Post* v289 no3 p2 My/Je 2017

Saturn (Planet)

35 Cool Things About Space S. ORNES color *National Geographic Kids* no471 p22 Je/Jl 2017

CASSINI AT SATURN C. Porco and E. Bell color *Scientific American* v317 no4 p78 O 2017

CASSINI'S Curtain Call L. Lisa Grossman bw color *Science News* v192 no3 p16 S 2 2017

Close encounters with the RINGED PLANET L. Kruesi bw color diag *Astronomy* v45 no10 p28 O 2017

THE FINAL DAYS OF CASSINI K. N. Smith bw color diag *Astronomy* v45 no1 p26 Ja 2017

A legacy of discovery P. Voosen color *Science* v357 no6357 p1220 S 22 2017

OBSERVING August 2017 color *Sky & Telescope* v134 no2 p41 Ag 2017

October 2017: Uranus glows brightly M. RATCLIFFE and A. LING bw chart color *Astronomy* v45 no10 p36 O 2017

Saturn (Planet)—Ring system

Saturn Has a Southern Apparition A. MacRobert *Sky & Telescope* v133 no5 p48 My 2017

Saturn (Planet)—Ring system—Research

Age of Saturn's rings debated C. CROCKETT bw *Science News* v190 no10 p10 N 12 2016

Saturn (Planet)—Satellites

See also

Dione (Satellite)

75, 50 & 25 YEARS AGO R. W. Sinnott *Sky & Telescope* v133 no2 p8 F 2017

Saturn exploration

Mission Extraordinaire *Sky & Telescope* v134 no3 p4 S 2017

Worlds of Wonder L. Dones *Sky & Telescope* v134 no3 p16 S 2017

Satyal, Rakesh

Breaking the Mold: A tale of Indian-Americans balancing community and selves J. SHARMA *New York Times Book Review* p30 My 14 2017

No One Can Pronounce My Name *Publishers Weekly* v264 no13 p69 Mr 27 2017

Sauces

See also

Applesauce

Cranberry sauce

Pestos

Salad dressing

Salsas (Cooking)

38 Easy Ways to CLEAN HOUSE C. Forte and S. Walter color *Good Housekeeping* v265 no3 p60A S 2017

ALL THE THINGS S. KROWIAK *Indianapolis Monthly* v40 no4 p54 D 2016

The Gratitude Meter Z. Donaldson color *O, The Oprah Magazine* p20 Ja 2017

THE HANDBOOK *Martha Stewart Living* no270 p145 D 2016

MARINARA S. PUCKETT *Atlanta* v56 no10 p60 F 2017

Meatball Makeovers B. P. KATZ and C. SULLIVAN color *Martha Stewart Living* p83 O 2017

One Fine Piece of Meat: Braised tongue with sauce gribiche can make you appreciate a cut you might otherwise avoid G. Hamilton *New York Times Magazine* p20 Jl 16 2017

PERFECT SPROUTS M. HENNESSY color *Chicago* v65 no12 p64 D 2016

THAT'S BEERLICIOUS! [Cover story] Y. LEE color *Runner's World* v52 no4 p31 My 2017

To-Die-For Pie color *Southern Living* v52 no1 p128 Ja 2017

Where Sugar Bombs Hide cartoon chart color *Men's Health* v32 no1 p64 Ja/F 2017

Sauces—Evaluation

THE BEST UNSUNG SAUCES color *Men's Health* v32 no4 p114 My 2017

Kitted Out color *Martha Stewart Living* p25 My 2017

SUMMER HEAT color *Nebraska Life* v21 no4 p69 Jl/Ag 2017

Saucier, Frank—Interviews

Project Manage Your Life D. Rousmaniere *Harvard Business Review Digital Articles* p2 F 10 2015

Saudi Arabia—Economic conditions

Can the Saudi Economy Be Reformed? K. E. YOUNG *Current History* v115 no785 p355 D 2016

Saudi Arabia's New Economic Reforms: A Concise Explainer L. El-Katiri *Harvard Business Review Digital Articles* p2 My 17 2016

Saudi Arabia—Economic conditions—21st century

Saudi Arabia's Labor Market Challenge L. El-Katiri *Harvard Business Review Digital Articles* p2 Jl 6 2016

Saudi Arabia—Economic policy

Can the Saudi Economy Be Reformed? K. E. YOUNG *Current History* v115 no785 p355 D 2016

Help Wanted in Saudi Arabia: Savvy Investors M. Martin, G. Carey et al color graph *Bloomberg Businessweek* no4513 p41 Mr 6 2017

Saudi Arabia—Foreign relations

A Mideast Rivalry Leads to a Split D. Abu-Nasr, Z. Fattah et al color map *Bloomberg Businessweek* no4526 p23 Je 12 2017

Saudi Arabia—Foreign relations—21st century

The War in Yemen Tests Saudi Arabia's Clout G. Carey and N. Syeed color *Bloomberg Businessweek* no4508 p12 Ja 23 2017

Saudi Arabia—Foreign relations—United States

Current U.S.-Saudi Arabia Relationship *Congressional Digest* v95 no9 p3 N 2016

Lightbox K. Vick color *Time* v189 no21 p22 Je 5 2017

U.S.-Saudi Arabia Relations Timeline *Congressional Digest* v95 no9 p2 N 2016

Saudi Arabia—Politics & government

Rapprochement with Putin—and Olga *American Conservative* v16 no1 p58 Ja/F 2017

Saudi Arabia—Social conditions

Saudi Arabia Profile *Congressional Digest* v95 no9 p4 N 2016

Saudi Arabia—Social conditions—21st century

Royal Visionary Meets Popular Pushback D. Abu-Nasr *Bloomberg Businessweek* no4528 p35 Je 26 2017

Saudi Oger Ltd.

A Building Collapse in the Desert V. Nereim, S. Algethami et al color *Bloomberg Businessweek* no4538 p32 S 18 2017

Saudi Arabia—Politics & government—1982-

Saudi Arabia Profile *Congressional Digest* v95 no9 p4 N 2016

Sauer, Eric

Creating Safe Routes to Parks *Parks & Recreation* v52 no9 p46 S 2017

Sauer, Gregory S.

Metal-catalyzed electrochemical diazidation of alkenes diag *Science* v357 no6351 p575 Ag 11 2017

SAUER, MARY

Protein Surprises in The Produce Section color *Reader's Digest* v190 no1133 p38 S 2017

Sauer, Sarah—Interviews

Q&A *Texas Monthly* v45 no8 p18 Ag 2017

Sauer, Tom

How will NATO's non-nuclear members handle the UN's ban on nuclear weapons? bibl *Bulletin of the Atomic Scientists* v73 no3 p177 My 2017

Sauerhaft, Rob

The 43% Solution chart color *Golf Magazine* v59 no6 p32 Je 2017

BETTER PLAYER DRIVERS color diag *Golf Magazine* v59 no3 p82 Mr 2017

BETTER PLAYER FAIRWAY WOODS color *Golf Magazine* v59 no5 p86 My 2017

BETTER PLAYER HYBRIDS color *Golf Magazine* v59 no5 p94 My 2017

BETTER PLAYER IRONS color *Golf Magazine* v59 no4 p112 Ap 2017

BLADE PUTTERS color *Golf Magazine* v59 no6 p84 Je 2017

BOOM SERVICE color *Golf Magazine* v58 no11 p84 N 2016

Boom Times chart color *Golf Magazine* v59 no3 p55 Mr 2017

COR Strength color *Golf Magazine* v59 no7 p82 Jl 2017

First Look STEALTH BOMBERS color *Golf Magazine* v58 no11 p78 N 2016

FIT BITS color *Golf Magazine* v59 no8 p90 Ag 2017

GAME IMPROVEMENT DRIVERS color diag *Golf Magazine* v59 no3 p74 Mr 2017

GAME IMPROVEMENT FAIRWAY WOODS color *Golf Magazine* v59 no5 p82 My 2017

GAME IMPROVEMENT HYBRIDS color *Golf Magazine* v59 no5 p90 My 2017

GAME IMPROVEMENT IRONS color *Golf Magazine* v59 no4 p104 Ap 2017

GET SMART color *Golf Magazine* v59 no7 p85 Jl 2017

GO BIG OR GO HOME color *Golf Magazine* v58 no11 p80 N 2016

GOOD WOOD color *Golf Magazine* v59 no8 p86 Ag 2017

GREAT LENGTHS color *Golf Magazine* v59 no1 p86 Ja 2017

HELPING HANDS color *Golf Magazine* v58 no11 p82 N 2016

HIGH-END HAMMERS color *Golf Magazine* v59 no7 p80 Jl 2017

HIGH FIVE color *Golf Magazine* v59 no2 p80 F 2017

LARGE MALLET PUTTERS color *Golf Magazine* v59 no6 p92 Je 2017

LONG-GAME CHANGERS color *Golf Magazine* v59 no8 p89 Ag 2017

LONG SHOTS color *Golf Magazine* v59 no1 p84 Ja 2017

MATERIAL WORLD color *Golf Magazine* v59 no2 p78 F 2017

MAX GAME IMPROVEMENT DRIVERS color diag *Golf Magazine* v59 no3 p92 Mr 2017

MAX GAME IMPROVEMENT IRONS color *Golf Magazine* v59 no4 p117 Ap 2017

MIDSIZE MALLET PUTTERS color *Golf Magazine* v59 no6 p88 Je 2017

ONE LENGTH ONLY? color *Golf Magazine* v58 no11 p86 N 2016

PLAYING FAVORITES color *Golf Magazine* v59 no7 p86 Jl 2017

ROCK IT & ROLL IT color *Golf Magazine* v59 no3 p99 Mr 2017

SMART MISSILES color *Golf Magazine* v59 no1 p82 Ja 2017

SOLE PROV IDERS color *Golf Magazine* v59 no8 p84 Ag 2017

SWING SET color *Golf Magazine* v59 no3 p96 Mr 2017

THESE DRIVERS ARE EPIC color *Golf Magazine* v59 no2 p82 F 2017

THIS MONTH: DRIVERS color *Golf Magazine* v59 no3 p72 Mr 2017

THIS MONTH: Fairway Woods + Hybrids color *Golf Magazine* v59 no5 p81 My 2017

THIS MONTH: Irons! color *Golf Magazine* v59 no4 p103 Ap 2017

THIS MONTH: Putters + Wedges color *Golf Magazine* v59 no6 p83 Je 2017

TIP THE SCALES chart color *Golf Magazine* v59 no4 p58 Ap 2017

WEDGES color *Golf Magazine* v59 no6 p98 Je 2017

Sauers, Eleanor

Beyond Brick & Mortar color *Commonweal* v144 no3 p30 F 10 2017

Sauers, Gene

The Other Player of the Year M. Bamberger color *Golf Magazine* v59 no1 p108 Ja 2017

SAUJANI, RESHMA

GIRL CODE color *Scientific American* v317 no3 p66 S 2017

Saul, Stephanie

TRUMP'S TRAVEL BAN *New York Times Upfront* v149 no10 p6 Mr 13 2017

SAUL, WOLF-CHRISTIAN

Scientific and Normative Foundations for the Valuation of Alien-Species Impacts: Thirteen Core Principles *BioScience* v67 no2 p166 F 2017

Sauls, Scott—Interviews

We Need More Odd Couples R. Clark color *Christianity Today* v60 no8 p83 O 2016

Saum, Bradley

THE STORY OF BLACK ELK PEAK: Characters and tales behind South Dakota's highest point *South Dakota Magazine* v33 no3 p59 S/O 2017

Saum, Steven Boyd

Chasing Honey *Orion Magazine* v35 no3 p10 My/Je 2016

Chasing Honey S. B. SAUM *Orion Magazine* v35 no3 p10 My/Je 2016

Sauna

FINNISH LINE A. Russell cartoon *New Yorker* v93 no30 p18 O 2 2017

See the Light L. Bolt color graph *Bloomberg Businessweek* no4509 p60 Ja 30 2017

Sauna—Design & construction

Sweden's Solar Egg Sauna J. Zorthian color *Time* v189 no20 p19 My 29 2017

Saunder, George

Coming Out Buddhist A. Barrodale color *Tricycle: The Buddhist Review* v26 no4 p88 Summ 2017

Saunders, Brent

Great Strategy Begins with a CEO on the Frontlines *Harvard Business Review Digital Articles* p2 O 7 2014

Saunders, Chasity

CHADWICK BOSEMAN UPS HIS GAME [Cover story] color *Ebony* v72/73 no12/1 p70 O/N 2017

Saunders, David

Betrayal of an Army: Mesopotamia, 1914-1916 *Military History* v33 no5 p75 Ja 2017

The Boy in the Mask: The Hidden World of Lawrence of Arabia *Military History* v33 no5 p69 Ja 2017

Caesar's Greatest Victory: The Battle of Alesia, Gaul, 52 BC *Military History* v34 no2 p71 Jl 2017

God's Wolf: The Life of the Most Notorious of All Crusaders, Scourge of Saladin *Military History* v34 no1 p71 My 2017

Hero of the Empire: The Boer War, a Daring Escape and the Making of Winston Churchill *Military History* v33 no6 p72 Mr 2017

The Second Anglo-Sikh War color *Military History* v34 no4 p74 N 2017

Saunders, Elizabeth Grace

4 Ways to Manage Deadlines on Cross-Cultural Teams *Harvard Business Review Digital Articles* p2 Je 10 2016

Accomplish More by Committing to Less *Harvard Business Review Digital Articles* p2 Ja 30 2015

Are You Proud of How You're Spending Your Time? *Harvard Business Review Digital Articles* p2 F 13 2015

Cancelling One-on-One Meetings Destroys Your Productivity *Harvard Business Review Digital Articles* p2 Mr 9 2015

Commit to Under-Scheduling in 2016 *Harvard Business Review Digital Articles* p2 D 21 2015

Do You Really Need to Hold That Meeting? *Harvard Business Review Digital Articles* p2 Mr 20 2015

A Formula to Stop You from Overcommitting Your Time *Harvard Business Review Digital Articles* p2 F 19 2015

Give Yourself Permission to Work Fewer Hours *Harvard Business Review Digital Articles* p2 Jl 13 2016

Going on Vacation Doesn't Have to Stress You Out at Work *Harvard Business Review Digital Articles* p2 Je 2 2015

How to Establish a Meeting-Free Day Each Week color *Harvard Business Review Digital Articles* p2 F 28 2017

How to Get into a Rhythm at Work If You Can't Stick to a Schedule *Harvard Business Review Digital Articles* p2 Ap 14 2016

How to Plan Your Week to Keep Your Weekend Free *Harvard Business Review Digital Articles* p2 Ap 27 2015

How to Stay Focused When You're Working from Home *Harvard Business Review Digital Articles* p2 S 28 2017

How to Stop Overplanning (Even If You're a Perfectionist) *Harvard Business Review Digital Articles* p2 Ag 24 2015

If You Dread Deadlines, You're Thinking About Them All Wrong *Harvard Business Review Digital Articles* p2 Mr 18 2016

The Perils of Overmonitoring Your Behavior and Goals *Harvard Business Review Digital Articles* p2 F 19 2016

Stop Playing the Victim with Your Time *Harvard Business Review Digital Articles* p2 Ja 21 2015

A Way to Plan If You're Bad at Planning *Harvard Business Review Digital Articles* p2 Jl 4 2017

You May Hate Planning, But You Should Do It Anyway color *Harvard Business Review Digital Articles* p2 S 19 2016

Saunders, George

THE ANTICIPATION INDEX img *New York* p80 Ja 9 2017

Between heaven and hell, a half-lit existence J. Anderson color *America* v216 no9 p58 Ap 24 2017

Chattering Spirits C. Baxter bw *New York Review of Books* v64 no7 p30 Ap 20 2017

GEORGE SAUNDERS E. Sullivan bw *Esquire* v167 no1 p58 F 2017

GO TO HIS GRAVE T. MALLON cartoon *New Yorker* v92 no49 p89 F 13 2017

GRAVEYARD GOINGS-ON E. DONALDSON color *Maclean's* v130 no2 p68 Mr 2017

THE GREATEST AUDIOBOOK CAST IN HISTORY I. Biedenharn color *Entertainment Weekly* no1453 p61 F 17 2017

IN THE SICK-BOX J. BASKIN color *Nation* v304 no16 p35 My 22 2017

Limbo of the Patriarch N. Hopper color *Time* v189 no7/8 p101 F 27 2017

Lincoln in the Bardo: A Novel D. Crowe color *Christian Century* v134 no10 p37 My 10 2017

Lincoln in the Bardo L. Greenblatt color *Entertainment Weekly* no1453 p60 F 17 2017

Lincoln's Grief, and Ours C. Lehmann *In These Times* v41 no3 p40 Mr 2017

Moonlight Sonata H. CAIN cartoon color *O, The Oprah Magazine* p103 Mr 2017

Points to Ponder color *Reader's Digest* v189 no1131 p22 Je 2017

The Sentimental Sadist C. CRAIN cartoon color *Atlantic* v319

no2 p36 Mr 2017

When Spirits Linger C. Whitehead *New York Times Book Review* p1 F 12 2017

Saunders, George W.

The Long Drive R. Soodalter bw *American Cowboy* v23 no6 p20 Ap/My 2017

Saunders, George, 1762-1839

The first and last Christian? G. L. Buckley color *America* v216 no9 p54 Ap 24 2017

THOUGHTS ON Conflict G. SAUNDERS, F. NIETZSCHE et al *Forbes* v199 no4 p112 Ap 25 2017

Saunders, George—Interviews

'A Kindly Presence of Mind' A. Domestico color *Commonweal* v144 no12 p14 Jl 7 2017

ENEMIES, A Love Story J. SALAMON *Texas Monthly* v45 no2 p56 F 2017

George Saunders *New York Times Book Review* p8 F 19 2017

THE GHOSTS OF GEORGE SAUNDERS T. Murphy bw *Mother Jones* v42 no2 p53 Mr/Ap 2017

In George Saunders' Debut Novel, Moving Tales from the Crypt S. Begley color *Time* v189 no7/8 p99 F 27 2017

Saunders, Jasper

Meet 'The Technology Specialist' Jasper Saunders T. Townsend color *Black Enterprise* v47 no2 p33 S 2016

Saunders, Jonathan, 1977-

Jonathan SAUNDERS C. KELSEY *Interview* v47 no2 p112 Mr 2017

Prints Charming E. Wilson color *InStyle* v24 no3 p132 Mr 2017

Saunders, Jonathan, 1977—Interviews

The Man Who Loves Women N. Silverstein, F. Kane et al color *Glamour* v115 no3 p94 Mr 2017

Saunders, Matt

The Artist's Artist A Rauschenberg Symposium color *Art in America* v105 no1 p44 Ja 2017

SAUNDERS, NICOLE

The Question *O, The Oprah Magazine* p18 S 2017

SAUNDERS, RICHARD

The Day the World Changed ... for Me *Skeptical Inquirer* v40 no6 p47 N/D 2016

Saunders, Wade

NOT VITAL bw *Art in America* v105 no4 p124 Ap 2017

Saupe, Karen

Reading and Writing Cancer: How Words Heal *Christian Century* v133 no26 p42 D 21 2016

Sauquet, Eric

Changing climate shifts timing of European floods color graph *Science* v357 no6351 p588 Ag 11 2017

Saure, C.

Country-specific effects of neonicotinoid pesticides on honey bees and wild bees diag map *Science* v356 no6345 p1393 Je 30 2017

Saurí, Josep

Unequivocal determination of complex molecular structures using anisotropic NMR measurements color *Science* v356 no6333 p43 Ap 7 2017

Sausage Party (Film)

No. 1 THE FOOD ORGY L. Greenblatt color *Entertainment Weekly* no1444/1445 p58 D 16 2016

Sausages

FIRE UP THE GRILL! [Cover story] color *Good Housekeeping* v265 no2 p58 Ag 2017

Full of Flavor L. Cericola and A. Hickman color *Southern Living* v52 no6 p123 Je 2017

Light Pasta with a Kick L. Cericola color *Southern Living* v52 no1 p124 Ja 2017

starters A. MASON, A. STANEK et al color *Bon Appetit* v62 no6 p17 Je 2017

SAUTNER, STEPHEN

FALSE TRUTHS color *Outdoor Life* v224 no7 p60 S 2017

Sauvage, Pierre

TRUE BLUE I. LEVINE bw color *Architectural Digest* v74 no8 p48 Ag 2017

Sauvage, X.

Grain boundary stability governs hardening and softening in extremely fine nanograined metals bibl color graph *Science* v355 no6331 p1292 Mr 24 2017

Savaadra, Rachel

To help with the timing of your half halt in trot... cartoon *Dressage Today* v23 no8 p72 Ap 2017

Savage, Andy

BOOK SMARTS B. FITZPATRICK and A. McKEAN color *Outdoor Life* v224 no2 p76 F/Mr 2017

SAVAGE, BILL

CONFESSIONS OF A BI-SIDER color *Chicago* v66 no8 p86 Ag 2017

Savage, Brian

A seismic shift in continental tectonic plates color *Science* v357 no6351 p549 Ag 11 2017

Savage, Charlie

The Terror Hydra: An original terror warrior returns to take stock of our progress *New York Times Book Review* p19 Je 11 2017

Was Snowden a Russian Agent? cartoon color *New York Review of Books* v64 no2 p16 F 9 2017

Savage, Dan

WHY We LOVE CHICAGO bw cartoon color *Chicago* v66 no3 p75 Mr 2017

Savage, Fred

FRIENDS FROM COLLEGE S. Li color *Entertainment Weekly* no1468/1469 p40 Je 2-9 2017

Savage, John F.

SOMETHING TO rely on: Through changing times, ILA, and its dedicated network of educators, remains the constant *Literacy Today (2411-7862)* v35 no1 p44 Jl/Ag 2017

SAVAGE, LORRAINE

Girl Higher Power color *Publishers Weekly* v264 no33 p72 Ag 14 2017

Savage, Stephen

The Mixed-Up Truck color *Publishers Weekly* v263 no49 p14 D 7 2016

Savage, Susan

Dream Buddy on a Trail Ride cartoon *Horse & Rider* v56 no3 p72 Mr 2017

Savage, Tiwa

Tiwa Savage Is Roc Steady V. L. HARRISON color *Ebony* v72 no8 p30 Je 2017

Savage Kingdom (TV program)

WILD GAME OF THRONES K. HAHN *TV Guide* v64 no48 p24 N 21 2016

Saval, Nikil

Off Center *New York Times Magazine* p11 Jl 9 2017

POLANYI IN OUR TIMES bw *Nation* v304 no2 p27 Ja 16 2017

UNCOMMON GROUND *New York Times Magazine* p72 N 13 2016

SAVALI, KIRSTEN WEST

THE WAY FORWARD bw color *Ebony* v72 no4 p84 F 2017

Savani, Krishna

To Make Better Choices, Look at All Your Options Together *Harvard Business Review Digital Articles* p2 Je 28 2017

Savannah (Ga.)

SAVANNAH, GEORGIA A. BROWNLEE *Cincinnati Magazine* v50 no5 p40 F 2017

SOUTH'S BEST INN R. F. Hayes color *Southern Living* v52 no4 p80 Ap 2017

SOUTH'S BEST SHOP C. Rollwagen color *Southern Living* v52 no4 p92 Ap 2017

Savannah (Ga.)—Description & Travel

Meet Me in Savannah A. R. Williams color *Southern Living* v52 no2 p79 F 2017

Reboot Your Romance M. SHAPIRO color *AARP: The Magazine* v59 no5A p62 Ag/S 2016

Savannah, Georgia A. BROWNLEE *Cincinnati Magazine* p52 Je 2017

Savarese, Laura Ford

Strategy & Entailments: The Enduring Role of Law in the U.S. Armed Forces *Daedalus* v146 no1 p11 Wint 2017

Savas, Jeffrey N.

Dopamine oxidation mediates mitochondrial and lysosomal dysfunction in Parkinson's disease graph *Science* v357 no6357 p1255 S 22 2017

Savazzi, Caryn

WHAT MAKES A WINNER? *People Management* p35 N 2016

SAVCHUK, KATIA

America's Top Philanthropists color graph *Forbes* v198 no5 p44

O 25 2016

Save the Children (U.S.)

DOING GOOD S. Simon color *InStyle* v24 no5 p62 My 2017

Savery, Nancy

Just North of Alliance color *Nebraska Life* v20 no6 p38 N/D 2016

Saviano, Nunzio

your good-hair GAME PLAN G. MONSMA color *Better Homes & Gardens* v95 no10 p24 O 2017

Savile Row Co.

THE BIG TEN J. FIELDEN color *Esquire* p32 BigBlackBook

SAVIN, JENNIFER

Sweat Out Your Blahs color *Seventeen* v76 no12 p65 D 2016/Ja 2017

Saving & investment

5 SMART SAVING TIPS FOR SINGLE WOMEN J. Hazelwood color *Black Enterprise* v47 no7 p17 My/Je 2017

Bad Ideas Gone Good [Cover story] color *Forbes* v199 no7 p123 Je 29 2017

Get a Boost From a Floating-Rate Fund J. R. KOSNETT color *Kiplinger's Personal Finance* v70 no12 p58 D 2016

Got Cheap Genes? M. P. Dunleavey bw *AARP: The Magazine* v60 no2A p34 F/Mr 2017

How Can I ... Save More $$$? *Scholastic Choices* v32 no7 p24 Ap 2017

INVEST IN YOURSELF IN 2017 A. M. Fox, G. Jimmere et al color *Black Enterprise* v47 no5 p46 Ja/F 2017

Lessons From the Rich N. Wertheimer chart color *AARP: The Magazine* v60 no2A p38 F/Mr 2017

MONEY SAVING GUIDE [Cover story] N. SAPORITA, C. FORTÉ et al cartoon color *Good Housekeeping* v264 no2 p79 F 2017

Mother and Daughter Score With Micro Caps R. ERMEY chart *Kiplinger's Personal Finance* v70 no12 p61 D 2016

SAVING FOR YOUR LONG-TERM GOAL: Q&A WITH A FINANCIAL EXPERT *Scholastic Choices* p4 O 2017 Supplement

Sharing Is (Kind of) Saving J. Marlowe *Governing* v30 no5 p64 F 2017

SNAP UP THESE DEALS color *Kiplinger's Personal Finance* v71 no6 p33 Je 2017

Spendthrift or Skinflint? color *AARP: The Magazine* v60 no2A p30 F/Mr 2017

Stage APPROPRIATE F. TORABI color *O, The Oprah Magazine* p46 F 2017

WANT A CAR? MAKE A PLAN... img *Scholastic Choices* p3 O 2017 Supplement

Saving & investment—Psychological aspects

10 WAYS TO BECOME A MONEY BADASS J. Sincero color *Money* v46 no5 p62 Je 2017

How Mindfulness Can Save You Money C. Hammond *Time* v188 no15 p15 O 17 2016

Saving & investment—United States

8 Money Moves Before the Ball Drops K. A. Renzulli color *Money* v45 no11 p26 D 2016

Time for a Portfolio Pit Stop C. Fried color diag *Money* v46 no6 p33 Jl 2017

Saving Private Ryan (Film)

THE 25 MOST PATRIOTIC MOVIES OF ALL TIME A. Breznican, S. Li et al color *Entertainment Weekly* no1472 p30 Je 30 2017

Savings accounts

See also

    Education savings accounts

    Emergency savings accounts

    Medical savings accounts

Better Rates for Savers, Finally J. R. KOSNETT color *Kiplinger's Personal Finance* v71 no6 p53 Je 2017

Savings accounts—Computer network resources

Digit review: Online account service needs better controls J. BATTERSBY color *Macworld - Digital Edition* p88 Je 13 2017

Savings bonds

When You Need Cash Quick E. AMBROSE color *AARP: The Magazine* v60 no4A p21 Je/Jl 2017

SAVKA, NATALYA

POWER HUNGRY *Sierra* v102 no5 p44 St/O 2017

Savol, Andrej J.

Mutation of a nucleosome compaction region disrupts Polycomb-mediated axial patterning bibl chart diag *Science* v355 no6329

p1081 Mr 10 2017

Savory, Allan

THE SACRED COW C. Ketcham *Sierra* v102 no2 p34 Mr/Ap 2017

Savory Collection: Body & Soul: Coleman Hawkins & Friends, The (Music)

Treasures Abound in 'Savory Collection' T. Panken bw *Downbeat* v84 no1 p19 Ja 2017

Savoy, Lauret

Trace M. Landrigan *Orion Magazine* v35 no3 p55 My/Je 2016

Savtchouk, Iaroslav

Three-dimensional Ca2+ imaging advances understanding of astrocyte biology diag *Science* v356 no6339 p715 My 19 2017

Sawaya, Michael R.

The cytotoxic Staphylococcus aureus PSMα3 reveals a cross-α amyloid-like fibril bibl color diag graph *Science* v355 no6327 p831 F 24 2017

SAWHNEY, ALISHA

The three faces of id color *Maclean's* v129 no44 p58 N 7 2016

Sawlogs

my miracle log home L. W. MACAULAY color map *Cabin Living* p13 O 2017

SIBERIAN WOOD P. STEFÁNSSON *Iceland Review* v55 no3 p92 My/Je 2017

Sawmills

Benefits of a Local Lumber Mill J. Irwin *Mother Earth News* no282 p83 Je/Jl 2017

Saws—Evaluation

Circular Saws R. ROMANSKI color *Popular Mechanics* p26 F 2017

PORTABLE TABLE SAWS R. ROMANSKI color *Popular Mechanics* p94 S 2017

Sawtooth Mountains (Idaho)

LATITUDES FAT TIMES [Cover story] M. Hansen color *Powder* v45 no6 p54 F 2017

Sawyer, Donald

Civil Society and Environmental Change in Brazil's Cerrado bibl *Environment* v58 no6 p16 N/D 2016

Sawyer, Katina

The Men Who Mentor Women *Harvard Business Review Digital Articles* p2 D 7 2016

Research: Why Employer Support Is So Important for Transgender Employees *Harvard Business Review Digital Articles* p2 O 3 2017

Sawyer, Keegan

Precaution and governance of emerging technologies bibl color *Science* v354 no6313 p710 N 11 2016

Sawyer, Sam

Physics matters in "The Expanse." Sin does, too color *America* v216 no3 p48 F 6 2017

Short attention spans, short news cycles and short form Gospels *America* v216 no7 p3 Ap 3 2017

Sawyer, Teresa

Modern Aquatic Therapy and a New Clientele *Parks & Recreation* v51 no11 p58 N 2016

Sawyers, Charles L.

Rb1 and Trp53 cooperate to suppress prostate cancer lineage plasticity, metastasis, and antiandrogen resistance bibl graph *Science* v355 no6320 p1 Ja 6 2017

SOX2 promotes lineage plasticity and antiandrogen resistance in TP53- and RB1-deficient prostate cancer bibl graph *Science* v355 no6320 p1 Ja 6 2017

Sax, David

Game On! color *Bloomberg Businessweek* no4509 p55 Ja 30 2017

Pause! We Can Go Back! B. McKibben bw *New York Review of Books* v64 no2 p4 F 9 2017

POD HELP ME cartoon *Bloomberg Businessweek* no4512 p78 F 20 2017

TALE OF THE TAPE color *Bloomberg Businessweek* no4517 p70 Ap 3 2017

TIME FOR A MAN-CATION! color *Esquire* p114 O 2017

Sax, Sam

Prediagnosis diag *New York Times Magazine* p17 Ag 6 2017

Saxby, Sheila

And The Winning Photo Is.... *British Heritage Travel* v37 no6 p88 N/D 2016

color *AARP: The Magazine* v59 no1A p50 D 2015/Ja 2016

Scaling (Social sciences)
See also
Psychometrics
THE WARP-SPEED ENTREPRENEUR R. KARLGAARD color
Forbes v200 no5 p34 N 14 2017

Scalise, Steve, 1965-
It Was a Dark and Stormy Night … color *Weekly Standard* v22
no40 p2 Je 26 2017
Loyal Opposition J. COST color *Weekly Standard* v22 no41 p10
Jl 3 2017

Scalley, Christopher
ATLANTA'S BLUE-RIBBON TROUT STREAM *Atlanta* v57
no4 p50 Ag 2017

Scallops
SINGING PINK SCALLOPS color *Sea Magazine* v109 no6
pPNW-5 Je 2017
Sunken Treasure J. KERR *Yankee* v81 no1 p54 Ja/F 2017

Scally, Aylwyn
Chimpanzee genomic diversity reveals ancient admixture with
bonobos bibl diag graph map *Science* v354 no6311 p477 O 28
2016

Scalp massage
Priyanka Chopra S. Zuckerman color *InStyle* v24 no2 p112 F 2017
Scalp Care 101 A. Jordan color *Essence* v48 no5 p50 S 2017

Scaltriti, Maurizio
PI3K pathway regulates ER-dependent transcription in breast cancer through the epigenetic regulator KMT2D bibl graph *Science*
v355 no6331 p1324 Mr 24 2017

Scaltsas, Theodore
A Cognitive Trick for Solving Problems Creatively *Harvard Business Review Digital Articles* p2 My 4 2016

Scandal (TV program)
BACK IN THE WHITE HOUSE M. LOGAN *TV Guide* v65 no4
p26 Ja 16 2017
Election Night on Scandal M. Logan *TV Guide* p12 D 19 2016
The Must List color *Entertainment Weekly* no1450 p1 Ja 27 2017
Returning TV That Deserves a Second Chance E. Dockterman
color *Time* v190 no14 p49 O 9 2017
SCANDAL L. Rice color *Entertainment Weekly* no1448 p40 Ja
13 2017
Scandal M. Logan *TV Guide* v65 no14 p39 Ap 3 2017
Scandal N. Abrams, B. L. Heldman et al *Entertainment Weekly*
no1482/1483 p88 S 22 2017
SCANDAL WITH CARE L. Rice color *Entertainment Weekly*
no1451/1452 p30 F 3-10 2017
State of Her Union L. Rice color *Entertainment Weekly* no1467
p11 My 26 2017
VIBRANT, RAW & IN LIVING COLOR: EBONY'S 2017 FALL
TV PREVIEW A. TINUBU color *Ebony* v72 no11 p78 S 2017
What to Watch R. Rahman, L. Rice et al color *Entertainment
Weekly* no1450 p54 Ja 27 2017

Scandals
The Case of the Christmas Stockings J. Borden color *Southern
Living* v51 no12 p136 D 2016
Scandal? What Scandal? M. HEMINGWAY *Weekly Standard* v22
no8 p28 O 31 2016
Uber Can't Be Fixed—It's Time for Regulators to Shut It Down
B. Edelman *Harvard Business Review Digital Articles* p1 Je 21
2017
Why a Corporate Scandal Will Follow You Even If You Weren't
Involved V. Molinaro *Harvard Business Review Digital Articles*
p2 D 4 2014

Scandals—Social aspects
Deactivated E. Newcomer color *Bloomberg Businessweek* no4527
p27 Je 19 2017

Scandinavian arts
Modernity H. MARTIN color *Architectural Digest* no6 p34 Je 1
2017

Scandinavians
See also
Icelanders
Drink Like a Scandinavian F. MAROUKIAN color map *Popular
Mechanics* p16 F 2017

SCANLON, DEANNA
AFFORDABLE OFF-ROADING color *Dirt Sports + Off-Road*

v51 no5 p58 My 2017
FORCING THE ISSUE color graph *Dirt Sports + Off-Road* v51
no7 p38 Jl 2017
LOW DOWN AND DIRTY color *Dirt Sports + Off-Road* v51 no2
p34 F 2017
RUNNING WILD [Cover story] color *Dirt Sports + Off-Road*
v51 no12 p40 D 2017
TUN OF FUN color diag *Dirt Sports + Off-Road* v51 no3 p30
Mr 2017

Scanlon, Jessie
To Talk About Sex to Teens In Zambia, Play the Diva color
Bloomberg Businessweek no4494 p42 O 10 2016

Scanners (Music)
Greg Osby T. PANKEN color *Downbeat* v84 no3 p122 Mr 2017

Scanning probe microscopy—Equipment & supplies
Focus on microscopy, imaging, and nanotechnology A. Mandelis
Physics Today v70 no9 p64 S 2017

Scanning systems—Evaluation
new products color *Science* v356 no6344 p1298 Je 23 2017

Scanning tunneling microscopy
Nanocrystalline copper films are never flat X. Zhang, J. Han et al
diag graph *Science* v357 no6349 p397 Jl 28 2017

Scapellato, Joseph
Big Lonesome *Publishers Weekly* v263 no51 p120 D 12 2016

Scaperlanda, María Ruiz
An Oklahoma Martyr *America* v217 no6 p62 S 18 2017

Scarab Boats (Company)
Grand Opening A. JONES *Boating World* v38 no3 p32 Mr 2017

Scaramucci, Anthony
LONG ON TRUMP J. Pressler img *New York* p26 Ja 23 2017
Mystery Deal Z. Mider, K. Burton et al *Bloomberg Businessweek*
no4510 p33 F 6 2017

SCARBOROUGH, DOROTHY
A Little Bit Braver Now color *O, The Oprah Magazine* p18 D
2016

Scarborough, Joe, 1963-
Donald Trump Is Not Invited to the Wedding: Joe, Mika and their
star-crossed relationship with the president O. Nuzzi img *New
York* v50 no15 p16 Jl 24 2017
Scarborough Fare color *Weekly Standard* v22 no41 p4 Jl 3 2017

SCARBOROUGH, SHEILA
Righting Words color *O, The Oprah Magazine* p17 Jl 2017

Scarcity
See also
Energy shortages
Water shortages

Scarcity—Social aspects
Life-saving diphtheria drug is running out K. Kupferschmidt bw
Science v355 no6321 p118 Ja 13 2017

SCARDELLI, LARELL
ONE TO GROW ON color *Rodale's Organic Life* v2 no7 p34 D
2016/Ja 2017

Scarf, Damian
Human health color *Science* v356 no6338 p590 My 12 2017

Scarles, Marie
AFGHANISTAN'S FEMALE KUNG FU FIGHTERS color *Tri-
cycle: The Buddhist Review* v27 no1 p16 Fall 2017
BOOKS IN BRIEF color *Tricycle: The Buddhist Review* v26 no3
p92 Spr 2017
BOOKS IN BRIEF color *Tricycle: The Buddhist Review* v26 no4
p94 Summ 2017
BOOKS IN BRIEF color *Tricycle: The Buddhist Review* v27 no1
p100 Fall 2017
The Buddha Before Buddhism: Wisdom from the Early Teachings
color *Tricycle: The Buddhist Review* v26 no2 p90 Wint 2016
Buddhist Bad Boys color *Tricycle: The Buddhist Review* v26 no4
p17 Summ 2017
CAMP DHARMA bw color *Tricycle: The Buddhist Review* v26
no4 p54 Summ 2017
THE CASE OF THE DISEMBODIED MONK color *Tricycle:
The Buddhist Review* v26 no2 p18 Wint 2016
IF SUPER MARIO WENT TO THE BARDO color *Tricycle: The
Buddhist Review* v26 no2 p19 Wint 2016
IN MEMORIAM bw color *Tricycle: The Buddhist Review* v26
no3 p16 Spr 2017
Kodo Nishimura color *Tricycle: The Buddhist Review* v27 no1

p22 Fall 2017

Mapping Your Mind: The Original Buddhist Psychology color diag *Tricycle: The Buddhist Review* v27 no1 p90 Fall 2017

Michelin Monastic color *Tricycle: The Buddhist Review* v26 no4 p17 Summ 2017

A Plea for the Animals: The Moral, Philosophical, and Evolutionary Imperative to Treat All Beings with Compassion *Tricycle: The Buddhist Review* v26 no2 p90 Wint 2016

Techno Temple color *Tricycle: The Buddhist Review* v26 no4 p16 Summ 2017

Thai Temple Soundtrack Tangle color *Tricycle: The Buddhist Review* v27 no1 p17 Fall 2017

Tibetan Faith Meets Gaelic Culture color *Tricycle: The Buddhist Review* v27 no1 p17 Fall 2017

Scarlet macaw

CAMP MACAW M. Harbison *Audubon* v119 no1 p26 Spr 2017

Scarlet Letter, The (Theatrical production)

MOTHER! H. ALS cartoon *New Yorker* v93 no30 p76 O 2 2017

Scarnecchia, Dante

SCAR'S TO PROVE IT G. A. Bedard color *Sports Illustrated* v126 no4 p36 Ja 30 2017

Scarpa (Company)

CLIMBING J. ELLISON color *Backpacker* v45 no3 p120 Ap 2017

Scarpa, Sunnie

UNSOLICITED BETA color *Climbing* no349 p8 N 2016

Scarpino, Betty J.

To The Editor color *American Craft* v77 no3 p10 Je/Jl 2017

Scarred Hearts (Film)

Scarred Hearts color *New Yorker* v92 no46 p11 Ja 23 2017

Scarry, Elaine

Too Much Poetic License A. Motion *American Scholar* v86 no1 p118 Wint 2017

Scars—Prevention

Fibroblasts become fat to reduce scarring C. K. F. Chan and M. T. Longaker bibl diag *Science* v355 no6326 p693 F 17 2017

Scarton, Cheryl G.

Committing to socially responsible seafood color *Science* v356 no6341 p912 Je 1 2017

SCARVELIS, NICHOLAS

Bringing Better Hip-Hop To Asia *Los Angeles Magazine* p22 F 2017

Scarves

FALL FORWARD *Martha Stewart Living* no268 p56 O 2016

INSTANT ART *Martha Stewart Living* no267 p21 S 2016

SCARVES AS HAIR ACCESSORIES O. Watson cartoon *Women's Health* v14 no9 p34 N 2017

STOCK THE PANTRY J. Goodman color *Bloomberg Businessweek* no4500 p70 N 21 2016

WILD & WOOLLY color *Harper's Bazaar* no3656 p260 S 2017

Scarves—Evaluation

Call It the Neck Tie of Winter color *GQ: Gentlemen's Quarterly* v86 no12 p88 D 2016

Cover Story E. ELWICK-BATES color *Vogue* v207 no9 p738 S 2017

Craft Culture color *Vogue* v207 no4 p242 Ap 2017

Flashback Fashion color *American Cowboy* v23 no5 p53 F/Mr 2017

In the Loop *Indianapolis Monthly* v40 no7 p27 Mr 2017

My Beauty Passport to Paris J. Mulrow color *Glamour* v115 no9 p100 S 2017

THE PERFECT NEW YORK BLOCK color *Esquire* v166 no5 p65 D 2016/Ja 2017

RESORT REPORT bw color *Harper's Bazaar* no3657 p179 O 2017

SEW CUTE L. BAILEY *Indianapolis Monthly* p28 My 2017

STYLE color *Horse & Rider* v56 no1 p22 Ja 2017

Scatena, Jenna

BEST OF THE WEST color *Sunset* v238 no1 p11 Ja 2017

DESERT COOL chart color *Sunset* v238 no5 p26 My 2017

LOCAL MOTION color *Sunset* v238 no4 p23 Ap 2017

PICK YOUR MEXICO PARADISE color *Sunset* v237 no5 p29 N 2016

Scattering (Physics)

Observing the ultrafast buildup of a Fano resonance in the time domain A. Kaldun, A. Blättermann et al bibl graph *Science* v354

no6313 p738 N 11 2016

SCATTON, LINDA

The Question *O, The Oprah Magazine* p16 Ap 2017

Scaturro, Michael

Elsie Will Text You When She's in Heat color *Bloomberg Businessweek* no4498 p52 N 7 2016

Innovation Fill-Air Flow diag *Bloomberg Businessweek* no4495 p28 O 17 2016

Will Not-Quite-Fiber Make the Grade? diag *Bloomberg Businessweek* no4495 p27 O 17 2016

Scavenger Fly (Company)

TREASURE CHEST J. Cermele color *Field & Stream* v122 no1 p24 My 2017

SCAVIA, DONALD

Ecological Forecasting and the Science of Hypoxia in Chesapeake Bay *BioScience* v67 no7 p614 Jl 2017

Scelfo, Julie

CITY DAMES M. O'CONNOR color *New York Times Book Review* p44 D 4 2016

Scellato, Giuseppe

Crossing borders along an endless frontier color *Science* v356 no6339 p694 My 19 2017

Scemama, Steve

Prepare Your Workforce for the Automation Age *Harvard Business Review Digital Articles* p2 N 23 2016

Scenes (Motion pictures)

See also

Chase scenes in motion pictures

10 — THE NYC CHASE K. P. Sullivan *Entertainment Weekly* no1444/1445 p61 D 16 2016

7 — THE ACTING CLASS J. McGovern *Entertainment Weekly* no1444/1445 p60 D 16 2016

8 — THE DMV M. Snetiker color *Entertainment Weekly* no1444/1445 p60 D 16 2016

THE BLAIR WITCH PROJECT R. Kinane color *Entertainment Weekly* no1460/1461 p75 Ap 7-17 2017

A FERRY TALE S. Vilkomerson color *Entertainment Weekly* no1473 p22 Jl 7 2017

Trainspotting's Toilet Dive S. Vilkomerson color *Entertainment Weekly* no1460/1461 p71 Ap 7-17 2017

What Really Happened After This Kiss in E.T.? A. Breznican and D. Coggan color *Entertainment Weekly* no1460/1461 p46 Ap 7-17 2017

Scenic transportation

CHOP, CHOP! color *Iceland Review* v54 no5 p102 S-O 2016

Scenic views

arizona is GORGES N. AUSTIN *Arizona Highways* v92 no12 p2 D 2016

It seemed like such a simple R. STIEVE *Arizona Highways* v92 no12 p1 D 2016

Scented candles—Evaluation

coming up ROSES S. BRICKELL color *Better Homes & Gardens* v95 no2 p16 F 2016

Off the Wall L. BAILEY *Indianapolis Monthly* v40 no7 p29 Mr 2017

Scented geraniums

PLUGGED IN I. Edwards color *Sunset* v238 no4 p14 Ap 2017

SMELL-GOOD GREENERY J. Silver color *Sunset* v238 no4 p46 Ap 2017

schaaf, Fred

Aim High *Sky & Telescope* v133 no6 p46 Je 2017

At the Edge of the Day color *Sky & Telescope* v134 no5 p46 N 2017

Between the Dogs *Sky & Telescope* v133 no2 p45 F 2017

Brilliant Venus Owns the Evening Sky *Sky & Telescope* v133 no2 p46 F 2017

A Cornucopia of Celestial Curiosities: The year's end prompts reminiscences of stellar things past *Sky & Telescope* v134 no6 p45 D 2017

December Delights: The Moon occults Aldebaran, and Mars and Jupiter dance with a star *Sky & Telescope* v134 no6 p46 D 2017

Diamond of Three Rings: A total solar eclipse offers the most spectacular of jewels *Sky & Telescope* v134 no3 p45 S 2017

Eclipse, At Last: The "Great American" total solar eclipse is this month's star attraction color *Sky & Telescope* v134 no2 p46 Ag 2017

Enter the Summer Citadel: The sights and scents of the season encourage a visit to an old friend *Sky & Telescope* v134 no1 p45 Jl 2017

The Evening Star Reigns Supreme *Sky & Telescope* v133 no1 p46 Ja 2017

Four Out of Five: Whether you're a night owl or an early riser, you can observe a bright planet this month *Sky & Telescope* v134 no1 p46 Jl 2017

Jove Owns the Night *Sky & Telescope* v133 no5 p46 My 2017

Mercury Maxes Out *Sky & Telescope* v133 no4 p46 Ap 2017

Morning Marvels: Look to the pre-dawn sky for a series of close planetary pairings this month *Sky & Telescope* v134 no3 p46 S 2017

Night Train *Sky & Telescope* v133 no6 p45 Je 2017

A Pretty Pair: Venus and Mars dance at dawn. Saturn sets early in the evening *Sky & Telescope* v134 no4 p46 O 2017

Shadow From Beyond Our World: How can we describe the wonder and awe we experience during a total solar eclipse? color *Sky & Telescope* v134 no2 p45 Ag 2017

Stellar Splendor: A deepest, darkest sky offers an extraordinary encounter with the stars *Sky & Telescope* v134 no4 p45 O 2017

A Thrilling Trio *Sky & Telescope* v134 no5 p45 N 2017

Through a High Window *Sky & Telescope* v132 no6 p45 D 2016

Virgo's Flames *Sky & Telescope* v133 no5 p45 My 2017

Winter Departs *Sky & Telescope* v133 no4 p45 Ap 2017

Wonders of the Year-Start Sky *Sky & Telescope* v133 no1 p45 Ja 2017

Schaal, Barbara

Informing policy with science color *Science* v355 no6324 p435 F 3 2017

Schaal, Kristen

KRISTEN SCHAAL N. Weldon color *Runner's World* v52 no5 p96 Je 2017

Schaap, Rosie

Amaro for Everyone color *New York Times Magazine* p37 N 27 2016

Good Blood *New York Times Magazine* p32 O 30 2016

Hold the Liquor *New York Times Magazine* p22 Ja 1 2017

Take It Slow *New York Times Magazine* p23 F 26 2017

A Victorian Toast color *New York Times Magazine* p42 D 11 2016

SCHABAUER, ROSALIA

Inspired by Athena and Aided by Facebook *USA Today Magazine* v145 no2862 p74 Mr 2017

SCHABLITSKY, JULIE M.

Belvoir's Legacy color *Archaeology* v69 no6 p55 N/D 2016

Schabram, Kira

When You're the Person Your Colleagues Always Vent To *Harvard Business Review Digital Articles* p2 N 30 2016

SCHACHTER, ABBY W.

Food Fight *Commentary* v143 no1 p50 Ja 2017

Help Isn't on the Way *Commentary* v142 no5 p43 D 2016

The King's Man color *National Review* v68 no21 p44 N 21 2016

No Help for the Weary B. MANDEL *Commentary* v142 no3 p46 O 2016

The Regulators' Bad Day in Court color *Weekly Standard* v22 no14 p17 D 12 2016

Schade, Leah D.

Eco-Reformation: Grace and Hope for a Planet in Peril *Christian Century* v134 no16 p33 Ag 2 2017

Schade, U.

Seasonal exposure of carbon dioxide ice on the nucleus of comet 67P/Churyumov-Gerasimenko bibl bw graph *Science* v354 no6319 p1563 D 23 2016

SCHADEWALD, JAMES

AIR HOCKEY TABLE! color diag *Popular Mechanics* p114 Ap 2017

BEDROOM DOORBELL! bw chart color *Popular Mechanics* p102 S 2017

BEDROOM DOORBELL! bw chart color *Popular Mechanics* v193 no7 p102 S 2016

BOOK LIGHT! color diag *Popular Mechanics* p96 N 2017

Candy Dispenser! chart color *Popular Mechanics* p108 D 2016/ Ja 2017

ELECTRIC MOWERS color *Popular Mechanics* p22 Je 2017

How to Make a... SPINDLE SANDER cartoon color *Popular Mechanics* v193 no7 p71 S 2016

How to Make a... SPINDLE SANDER FROM A BLENDER color *Popular Mechanics* p71 S 2017

How to Make a... SPINDLE SANDER FROM A BLENDER color *Popular Mechanics* v193 no7 p71 S 2016

HOW TO MAKE ICE CREAM bw color diag *Popular Mechanics* p80 S 2017

Matchbox Car Belt! chart color diag *Popular Mechanics* p104 Mr 2017

PAPER AIRPLANE LAUNCHER! cartoon color *Popular Mechanics* p104 Je 2017

THE ULTIMATE BACKYARD MOVIE SETUP color diag *Popular Mechanics* p97 Jl 2017

Schadlow, Nadia

The Morning After M. T. OWENS *Weekly Standard* v22 no34 p40 My 15 2017

Schaedel, Laura

Microtubules acquire resistance from mechanical breakage through intraluminal acetylation diag graph *Science* v356 no6335 p328 Ap 21 2017

Schaedelin, Pierre

Martha's Month *Martha Stewart Living* no269 p4 N 2016

Schaefer, Bradley E.

The strange star discovered by Planet Hunters *Physics Today* v70 no3 p82 Mr 2017

Schaefer, Brian

Dance in the Age of Black Lives Matter *Dance Magazine* v90 no12 p38 D 2016

Dancing Transgender *Dance Magazine* v91 no4 p38 Ap 2017

THE HOLLYWOOD HEALER: Choreographer Ryan Heffington has emerged as the most unlikely in-demand dancemaker working in the commercial world today *Dance Magazine* v91 no10 p26 O 2017

The MOST INFLUENTIAL PEOPLE IN DANCE TODAY: THE MOVERS, SHAKERS AND CHANGEMAKERS HAVING THE BIGGEST IMPACT ON DANCE RIGHT NOW *Dance Magazine* v91 no7 p27 Jl 2017

Schaefer, Estelle

The preprophase band of microtubules controls the robustness of division orientation in plants graph *Science* v356 no6334 p186 Ap 14 2017

Schaefer, Kayleen

BROW WOW WOW color *Bloomberg Businessweek* no4525 p59 Je 5 2017

Don't let the Smondays* ruin your life color *Bloomberg Businessweek* no4495 p67 O 17 2016

FEEL THE BURNOUT cartoon *Bloomberg Businessweek* no4516 p68 Mr 27 2017

Get Some Rest! color *Bloomberg Businessweek* no4506 p64 Ja 9 2017

Go From Sucking to 60 img *New York* v49 no23 p68 N 14 2016

HARDER, BETTER, FASTER, STRONGER color *Bloomberg Businessweek* no4511 p66 F 13 2017

Smoothies at Your Service color *Bloomberg Businessweek* no4520 p70 My 1 2017

SCHAEFER, MARGRET

STEM CELL RESEARCH *Skeptical Inquirer* v41 no1 p34 Ja/F 2017

Schaefer, Mark W.

6 Reasons Marketing Is Moving In-House *Harvard Business Review Digital Articles* p2 Jl 30 2015

Companies in Regulated Industries Can Also Do Digital Marketing *Harvard Business Review Digital Articles* p2 Ja 15 2016

Get More Value from "Gray Social" *Harvard Business Review Digital Articles* p2 Ap 29 2015

What Marketers Need to Know About Chat Apps *Harvard Business Review Digital Articles* p2 Je 14 2016

Why (and How) HR Needs to Act More Like Marketing *Harvard Business Review Digital Articles* p2 N 24 2016

SCHAEFER, STEVE

THE JUST 100: AMERICA'S BEST CORPORATE CITIZENS color *Forbes* v198 no8 p82 D 20 2016

Nature's Bounty color *Forbes* v199 no2 p34 F 28 2017

Paper Chase cartoon *Forbes* v198 no5 p42 O 25 2016

The Trump Discount color *Forbes* v199 no1 p60 Ja 24 2017

Schaefer Yachts (Company)

THE OTHER AMERICA C. CASWELL chart color *Power &*

Motoryacht v34 no11 p92 N 2017

Schaefer Yachts 560 A. Parkinson color *Power & Motoryacht* v33 no3 p54 Mr 2017

Schaeffer, John

The All-New 6-Move Quad Crusher bw color *Men's Health* v31 no10 p126 D 2016

Schaeffer, Rebecca

THE SCHAEFFER EFFECT J. McGovern color *Entertainment Weekly* no1457/1458 p70 Mr 17 2017

When DEVOTION Turns DEADLY J. McGovern color *Entertainment Weekly* no1457/1458 p64 Mr 17 2017

Schaeffer, Zoe

Can't. Look. Away color *Women's Health* v14 no2 p78 Mr 2017

Ethical Evergreens color *Rodale's Organic Life* v2 no7 p94 D 2016/Ja 2017

The Itchy and Scratchy Show color *Rodale's Organic Life* v2 no7 p90 D 2016/Ja 2017

Organic for Everyone color *Rodale's Organic Life* v3 no1 p33 Ja 2017

WHERE THE WILD THINGS ARE color *Sunset* v238 no4 p32 Ap 2017

SCHAEFFER-DUFFY, CLAIRE

OUR NUCLEAR COMPLEX color *America* v215 no19 p35 D 19 2016

Schaeppi, Joe

A Data-Driven Approach to Group Creativity *Harvard Business Review Digital Articles* p? Jl 12 2016

Schaerer, Michael

Having Too Many Options Can Make You a Worse Negotiator *Harvard Business Review Digital Articles* p2 My 24 2017

Schafel, Garrett

Where the Heart Is color *AARP: The Magazine* v59 no3A p86 Ap/ My 2016

Schäfer, Eberhard

Phytochrome B integrates light and temperature signals in Arabidopsis bibl graph *Science* v354 no6314 p897 N 18 2016

Phytochromes function as thermosensors in Arabidopsis bibl graph *Science* v354 no6314 p886 N 18 2016

Schafer, Gil

7 rules for a great room color *Redbook* p132 O 2017

Schäfer, J.

Bismuthene on a SiC substrate: A candidate for a high-temperature quantum spin Hall material diag graph *Science* v357 no6348 p287 Jl 21 2017

SCHAFER, JONATHAN

Bet you didn't know color *National Geographic Kids* no465 p10 N 2016

Schafer, Tim

ROCK this WAY color *Cabin Living* p49 D 2016

SCHAFFEL, GARRETT

25 People Who Bust the Myths color *AARP: The Magazine* v59 no4A p42 Je/Jl 2016

Schaffer, Akiva—Interviews

Boy-Band Heaven K. Branch color *Glamour* v114 no7 p38 Jl 2016

Schaffer, Kirsten

Emergence and spread of a human-transmissible multidrug-resistant nontuberculous mycobacterium bibl diag graph *Science* v354 no6313 p751 N 11 2016

Schaffer, Michael

19 THINGS YOU REALLY OUGHT TO DO THIS MONTH *Washingtonian Magazine* v52 no1 p33 O 2016

EDITOR'S LETTER *Washingtonian Magazine* v52 no9 p14 Je 2017

THE NEW QUEUE: Washington's strange new affinity for waiting in line *Washingtonian Magazine* v52 no9 p17 Je 2017

WHERE & WHEN: 17 THINGS YOU REALLY OUGHT TO DO THIS MONTH *Washingtonian Magazine* v53 no1 p31 O 2017

Schaffer, Robert H.

To Get Better at Your Job, Work Practice into Your Routine *Harvard Business Review Digital Articles* p2 Ja 29 2016

Schaffner, Liana

NEW SKIN NO DOWNTIME color *Harper's Bazaar* no3649 p330 D 2016/Ja 2017

Schaible, Glenn

Understanding Irrigated Agriculture *Amber Waves: The Economics of Food, Farming, Natural Resources, & Rural America* p9

Je 2017

Schain, Martin

Why Do Some Countries Get Away With Taking Fewer Refugees? K. SURANA bw *Foreign Policy* no226 p14 S/O 2017

Schake, Kori

Trump and the "New Nationalism": It's not new at all. Andrew Jackson, almost two centuries ago, also championed a populist style--and, in the end, strengthened American democracy *Hoover Digest: Research & Opinion on Public Policy* no3 p23 Summ 2017

Will Washington Abandon the Order? color *Foreign Affairs* v96 no1 p41 Ja/F 2017

Schall, Peter

Positive biodiversity-productivity relationship predominant in global forests bibl chart graph map *Science* v354 no6309 paaf8957-1 O 14 2016

Schaller, Andreas

Precursor processing for plant peptide hormone maturation by subtilisin-like serine proteinases bibl color graph *Science* v354 no6319 p1594 D 23 2016

Schaller, Morgan F.

Impact ejecta at the Paleocene-Eocene boundary bibl bw graph *Science* v354 no6309 p225 O 14 2016

Schallon, Lindsay

Jessica Chastain vs. the Machine color *Glamour* v115 no11 p74 N 2017

Seeing Red color *Glamour* v114 no11 p34 N 2016

SCHAMA, CHLOE

Borderlands color *Vogue* v207 no9 p620 S 2017

Holding Court bw color *Vogue* v207 no9 p618 S 2017

The Long View color *Vogue* v207 no9 p616 S 2017

Looking Sharp color *Vogue* v207 no9 p611 S 2017

New Wave color *Vogue* v207 no9 p614 S 2017

Paper Trail color *Vogue* v207 no9 p614 S 2017

Pas de Deux color *Vogue* v207 no9 p612 S 2017

The Stallion in the Room *New York Times Book Review* p22 O 9 2016

Triple Bull's-Eye color *Vogue* v207 no9 p624 S 2017

Schama, Simon, 1945-

Cheek to Jowl *Commentary* v141 no10 p1 D 2016

Cheek to Jowl W. WHELDON *Commentary* v142 no5 p53 D 2016

The Face of Britain: The History of the Nation Through Its Portraits A. Moravcsik *Foreign Affairs* v96 no2 p178 Mr/Ap 2017

Picture Imperfect E. Short bw color *Weekly Standard* v22 no26 p37 Mr 13 2017

Portraits Put to Use—and Misuse A. Spawls color *New York Review of Books* v64 no3 p51 F 23 2017

When British Eyes Were Smiling C. BENFEY color *New York Times Book Review* p13 S 25 2016

Schanelec, Angela

THE DREAMED PATH J. Cronk color *Film Comment* v53 no1 p24 Ja/F 2017

Schanker, Gwendolyn

It's an Animal! It's a Plant! No, It's an Amazing Acquired Phototroph! STEALING PARTS FROM THEIR PREY, THESE HUNTERS TURN INTO FARMERS *Oceanus* v52 no2 p26 Spr 2017

Let There Be Laser Light *Oceanus* v52 no1 p26 Summ 2016

Life Dwells Deep Within Earth's Crust *Oceanus* v52 no1 p48 Summ 2016

The Quest for the Moho *Oceanus* v52 no1 p44 Summ 2016

Shark Tales *Oceanus* v52 no1 p32 Summ 2016

A Slithery Ocean Mystery *Oceanus* v52 no1 p16 Summ 2016

Schar, Daniel

Invest in insects color *Science* v356 no6343 p1131 Je 16 2017

Unlikely allies color *Science* v356 no6343 p1130 Je 16 2017

Schardon, Katharina

Precursor processing for plant peptide hormone maturation by subtilisin-like serine proteinases bibl color graph *Science* v354 no6319 p1594 D 23 2016

SCHARDT, DAVID

Caffeine *Nutrition Action Health Letter* v44 no1 p7 Ja/F 2017

It takes a village *Nutrition Action Health Letter* v43 no10 p9 D 2016

MULTI-TASKING [Cover story] *Nutrition Action Health Letter* v43 no9 p3 N 2016

Probiotics: What's in a name? *Nutrition Action Health Letter* v44 no6 p8 Jl/Ag 2017

Spice of Life: Take 2 cups of ginger tea and call me in the morning *Nutrition Action Health Letter* v44 no5 p6 Je 2017

Tracking Telomeres: Short telomeres are bad. Can you lengthen yours? *Nutrition Action Health Letter* v44 no4 p7 My 2017

Scharen, Christian

Decline and rise color *Christian Century* v134 no4 p46 F 15 2017

Reimaging Seminary cartoon color *Christianity Today* v61 no1 p75 Ja/F 2017

Scharf, Alan

"Dirty Dancing" brings Borscht Belt veteran full circle L. J. Green *Successful Farming* v115 no1 p43 Ja 2017

Scharf, Cynthia

How to govern geoengineering? color *Science* v357 no6348 p231 Jl 21 2017

SCHARPER, DIANE

GOD TALK WITH IRONY *America* v215 no15 p34 N 14 2016

Irresistible Force *Weekly Standard* v22 no39 p39 Je 19 2017

SCHARPER, JULIE

Nature Fix *National Parks* v91 no4 p14 Fall 2017

A People's Historian: Talking about the past and the future with the Park Service's new chief historian *National Parks* v91 no3 p10 Summ 2017

SCHARPING, NATHANIEL

Asteroids diag graph map *Discover* v38 no6 p50 Jl/Ag 2017

CAN AMERICA AVOID ANOTHER FLINT? color *Discover* v38 no1 p18 Ja/F 2017

Charles Darwin color *Discover* v38 no4 p42 My 2017

Degas' Other Woman cartoon *Discover* v38 no1 p91 Ja/F 2017

Easter Island's Last Endemics Flirt With Extinction [Cover story] color *Discover* v38 no4 p24 My 2017

The Eternal Princesses cartoon color diag map *Discover* v38 no2 p38 Mr 2017

A Mightier Mouse color *Discover* v38 no5 p10 Je 2017

Mirror-Image Molecule Far, Far Away cartoon color *Discover* v38 no1 p68 Ja/F 2017

NEW PARTICLE FIZZLES, LEAVING PHYSICISTS TO SOUL SEARCH color *Discover* v38 no1 p20 Ja/F 2017

Oldest Book in the Americas Authenticated cartoon *Discover* v38 no1 p66 Ja/F 2017

THE OZONE HOLE IS FINALLY HEALING color *Discover* v38 no1 p24 Ja/F 2017

Pregnancy, Interrupted color *Discover* v38 no8 p10 O 2017

WELCOME TO THE ANTHROPOCENE color *Discover* v38 no1 p89 Ja/F 2017

Schatz, Ben

LATE BLOOMER J. Toobin cartoon *New Yorker* v93 no32 p23 O 16 2017

Schatz, Bryan

DOUBLE CROSSED color *Mother Jones* v42 no5 p6 S/O 2017

HACKER, BANKER, SOLDIER, SPY bw color *Mother Jones* v42 no4 p19 Jl/Ag 2017

HACKS, LEAKS, AND TWEETS color *Mother Jones* v42 no4 p22 Jl/Ag 2017

KILLER INSTINCTS *Mother Jones* v42 no2 p28 Mr/Ap 2017

THE KREMLIN'S GREMLINS color *Mother Jones* v42 no4 p20 Jl/Ag 2017

ON KOMPROMAT bw *Mother Jones* v42 no4 p24 Jl/Ag 2017

PUTIN'S LONG GAME color *Mother Jones* v42 no4 p26 Jl/Ag 2017

THE RUSSIAN CONNECTION color *Mother Jones* v42 no4 p16 Jl/Ag 2017

WIKILEAKS' ROLE *Mother Jones* v42 no4 p30 Jl/Ag 2017

Schauß, Peter

Spin-imbalance in a 2D Fermi-Hubbard system diag graph *Science* v357 no6358 p1385 S 29 2017

Schaub, Diana

Allen C. Guelzo, Redeeming the Great Emancipator *Society* v54 no2 p196 Ap 2017

BAD COMPANY *Claremont Review of Books* v16 no4 p81 Fall 2016

SCHAUB, MICHAEL

Rich Is Rabbit: Matthew Klam's debut novel tells the tale of a conflicted adulterer *New York Times Book Review* p11 Jl 30 2017

Schauch, Marita

CERVICAL DYSPLASIA & CERVICAL CANCER: NATURAL THERAPIES FOR TREATMENT & PREVENTION color *Better Nutrition* p41 My 2017

Schauer, Andy

GRAND CANYON EXPEDITION J. KOPYCINSKI color *Dirt Sports + Off-Road* v51 no5 p46 My 2017

Schauer, M.

Observation of a large-scale anisotropy in the arrival directions of cosmic rays above 8×1018 eV *Science* v357 no6357 p1266 S 22 2017

Schaufenbuel, Kimberly

Why Google, Target, and General Mills Are Investing in Mindfulness *Harvard Business Review Digital Articles* p2 D 28 2015

Schaumleffel, Nathan A.

Forget About Grants! *Parks & Recreation* v52 no2 p38 F 2017

Schauss, Alexander

MOVE OVER, MILLENNIAL PINK color *Women's Health* v14 no7 p36 S 2017

Schawinski, Kevin

Machines that make sense of the sky J. Sokol color *Science* v357 no6346 p26 Jl 7 2017

Scheben, Armin

Genome editors take on crops bibl diag *Science* v355 no6330 p1122 Mr 17 2017

SCHECHTER, DAVE

THE TEMPLE BOMBING *Atlanta* v56 no10 p41 F 2017

Scheckel, Paul

Country Lore *Mother Earth News* no281 p84 Ap/My 2017

Schecter, Jerrold

Bonnie Angelo color *Time* v190 no13 p17 O 2 2017

Schedler, Carrie

ARE YOU Worthy OF THIS MAN'S Coffee? cartoon color *Chicago* v66 no5 p104 My 2017

BRUNCH, YOUR WAY cartoon color *Chicago* v66 no5 p65 My 2017

BUDGET PICK: AUNTY JOY'S JAMAICAN KITCHEN color *Chicago* v66 no9 p66 S 2017

BUDGET PICK color *Chicago* v66 no6 p48 Je 2017

CAKES, PASTRIES, PIES, COOKIES, HOT FUDGE, GALATO, BROWNIES & MORE! chart color *Chicago* v65 no11 p70 N 2016

Charlie Trotter Is Alive And Well bw color *Chicago* v66 no8 p98 Ag 2017

EAST MEETS MIDWEST color *Chicago* v66 no1 p55 Ja 2017

EAT IT ON A STICK color *Chicago* v66 no7 p58 Jl 2017

FILIPINO BOUNTY color *Chicago* v65 no12 p59 D 2016

HAVE A BALL WITH BOCCE color *Chicago* v66 no7 p51 Jl 2017

The Insider's Guide to FARMERS' MARKETS [Cover story] color *Chicago* v66 no6 p72 Je 2017

Matt Eisler and Kevin Heisner color *Chicago* v66 no6 p80 Je 2017

My Dinner Party with GRANT color *Chicago* v66 no10 p98 O 2017

Noah Sandoval color *Chicago* v66 no6 p88 Je 2017

NORTHERN TASTE color *Chicago* v66 no10 p54 O 2017

PAST PERFECTED color *Chicago* v65 no11 p56 N 2016

PEAK FRUIT color *Chicago* v66 no9 p61 S 2017

SHARPEN YOUR KNIVES [Cover story] color *Chicago* v66 no11 p60 N 2017

SPILT MILK PASTRY color *Chicago* v66 no2 p50 F 2017

Thirsty? color diag *Chicago* v66 no2 p57 F 2017

TURN UP THE HEAT color *Chicago* v66 no3 p64 Mr 2017

WAYDOWN color *Chicago* v66 no11 p56 N 2017

WHAT'S IN THEIR FRIDGE? [Cover story] color *Chicago* v66 no7 p72 Jl 2017

WHY We LOVE CHICAGO bw cartoon color *Chicago* v66 no3 p75 Mr 2017

Schedler, Johannes

Amateur Astrophotographers Wanted D. Martinez-Delgado *Sky & Telescope* v133 no4 p29 Ap 2017

Scheduling

See also

Employees—Workload

3 Ways to Make Time for the Little Tasks You Never Make Time For D. Clark *Harvard Business Review Digital Articles* p2 F 14 2017

Scheel, Troels K. H.
Mouse models of acute and chronic hepacivirus infection *Science* v357 no6347 p204 Jl 14 2017

Scheele, Ben
Do not publish color diag *Science* v356 no6340 p800 My 26 2017
Publish openly but responsibly color *Science* v357 no6347 p141 Jl 14 2017

SCHEELER, CECELIA
"HERE'S WHAT IT REALLY FEELS LIKE to have OCD ... welcome to my brain" color *Good Housekeeping* v265 no1 p96 Jl 2017

Scheeler, Martin W.
Complete measurement of helicity and its dynamics in vortex tubes color diag graph *Science* v357 no6350 p487 Ag 4 2017

Scheer, Andrew, 1979-
AW SHUCKS. ME? LEADER? J. GEDDES color *Maclean's* v130 no7 p32 Ag 2017

Scheerer, Tom—Interviews
PALETTE CLEANSER M. READ color *House Beautiful* v158 no10 p76 D 2016/Ja 2017

SCHEERES, JULIA
Whither Thou Goest: A mother and daughter become enmeshed in a cult *New York Times Book Review* p23 S 10 2017

Schefer, Jean Louis, 1938-
Monstrous Wonder P. FILERI bw *Film Comment* v52 no6 p95 N/D 2016
WIKTOR GÓRKA A A Curry cartoon *Film Comment* v52 no6 p96 N/D 2016

Scheffer, Marten
Social norms as solutions bibl color *Science* v354 no6308 p42 O 7 2016

Scheffers, Brett R.
Biodiversity redistribution under climate change: Impacts on ecosystems and human well-being color *Science* v355 no6332 p1389 Mr 31 2017
The broad footprint of climate change from genes to biomes to people bibl chart color *Science* v354 no6313 paaf7671-1 N 11 2016

Schefferville (Québec)
Riding the Tshiuetin C. ELLINGSON bw color *Walrus* v14 no9 p54 N 2017

Schefler, Jared
The Hill Workout cartoon color *Field & Stream* v121 no7 p46 D 2016/Ja 2017

SCHEI, FRIDE HØISTAD
Combining Biodiversity Resurveys across Regions to Advance Global Change Research *BioScience* v67 no1 p73 Ja 2017

SCHEINER, DAVID
MY LAST PATIENT color *Chicago* v66 no1 p80 Ja 2017

Scheinfeld, John
Chasing Trane: The John Coltrane Documentary *New Yorker* v93 no13 p16 My 15 2017

Schelhaas, Mart-Jan
Positive biodiversity-productivity relationship predominant in global forests bibl chart graph map *Science* v354 no6309 paaf8957-1 O 14 2016

Schell, Andy
After 15,000 Miles: LESSONS LEARNED FROM HARDCORE OCEAN SAILING [Cover story] color *Sail* v48 no8 p46 Ag 2017
Gary Jobson color *Sail* v48 no1 p14 Ja 2017
Jeremy Davis color *Sail* v48 no6 p12 Je 2017
John Kretschmer color *Sail* v48 no2 p14 F 2017
John Rousmaniere color *Sail* v48 no4 p16 Ap 2017
Magnus Rassy color *Sail* v48 no3 p14 Mr 2017
Pam Wall color *Sail* v48 no5 p14 My 2017
Rick Tomlinson color *Sail* v48 no7 p12 Jl 2017
Sara Hastreiter color *Sail* v48 no8 p16 Ag 2017
Susie Goodall color *Sail* v48 no10 p18 O 2017
SV Delos color *Sail* v48 no11 p12 N 2017

SCHELL, ORVILLE
The Quarrels of '49: A history of the pivotal year that set the course of Chinese-American relations *New York Times Book Review* p12 O 8 2017

Schellenbaum, Amy
Ia's far-ranging roots map *Popular Science* v289 no2 p17 Mr/Ap 2017

Schellenberg, Matthew J.
ZATT (ZNF451)–mediated resolution of topoisomerase 2 DNA-protein cross-links diag *Science* v357 no6358 p1412 S 29 2017

Schellenberger, Ute
A selective insecticidal protein from Pseudomonas for controlling corn rootworms bibl chart graph *Science* v354 no6312 p634 N 4 2016

SCHELLER, BILL
HIDDEN GOLD: A VERMONT INSIDERS GUIDE to finding UNDERTHERADAR, OVERTHETOP COLOR *Yankee* v81 no5 p96 S/O 2017

Schelling, Andrew
Locking Brows with BHARTRIHARI cartoon *Tricycle: The Buddhist Review* v26 no3 p72 Spr 2017

Schelling, Thomas C., 1921-2016
Thomas Crombie Schelling (1921–2016) R. Zeckhauser color *Science* v355 no6327 p800 F 24 2017

Schellnhuber, Hans Joachim
A roadmap for rapid decarbonization bibl color graph *Science* v355 no6331 p1269 Mr 24 2017

Schemmel, Eve
Committing to socially responsible seafood color *Science* v356 no6341 p912 Je 1 2017

Schenck, Bradley W.
Slaves of the Switchboard of Doom: A Novel of Retropolis *Publishers Weekly* v264 no17 p73 Ap 24 2017

Schenck, Landon
Community Center. How to Keep Citizens Informed About the Threat of Zika in Your Community *Parks & Recreation* v52 no6 p16 Je 2017

SCHENCK, SARAH
Gut Check cartoon *Rodale's Organic Life* v3 no1 p34 Ja 2017

Schendler, Auden
Corporations Will Never Solve Climate Change *Harvard Business Review Digital Articles* p2 D 4 2015

Schengber, Klaus
Let's Welcome Children to U.S. Dressage Shows color *Dressage Today* v23 no12 p22 S 2017

SCHENK, ALICE
Hooked on Rafting: A Lochsa River Adventure *Idaho Magazine* v16 no12 p40 S 2017
The Legend Comes to Town: And I Will Get That Ride *Idaho Magazine* v16 no10 p42 Jl 2017

Schenk, Carla
Fibril structure of amyloid-$\beta(1$–$42)$ by cryo–electron microscopy color diag *Science* v357 no6359 p116 O 6 2017

Schenkel, Jason M.
Epigenetic stability of exhausted T cells limits durability of reinvigoration by PD-1 blockade bibl graph *Science* v354 no6316 p1160 D 2 2016

Schenkman, Lauren
A Disobedient Woman *New York Times Magazine* p34 Mr 26 2017

SCHENWAR, MAYA
Don't Look Away *Earth Island Journal* v32 no2 p2 Summ 2017

Scher, Abby
Bolder Is Better color *Progressive* v81 no3 p30 Mr 2017

Scher, Robin
EDITORS' PICKS color *ARTnews* v115 no4 p26 Wint 2016/2017

Scherer, And Michael
Will Bob Mueller Separate Fact from Fiction? [Cover story] color *Time* v190 no1 p24 Jl 3 2017

Scherer, Barrymore Laurence
Majestic makeover [Cover story] color *Magazine Antiques* v184 no3 p102 My/Je 2017
Metal of honor color *Magazine Antiques* v184 no3 p42 My/Je 2017
Pocket-size punch color *Magazine Antiques* v184 no2 p52 Mr/Ap 2017

SCHERER, JOSH
THE BEST NEW RESTAURANTS *Los Angeles Magazine* p86 Ja 2017
High Flying *Los Angeles Magazine* v61 no11 p60 N 2016
Instagram Feeding Frenzies *Los Angeles Magazine* p42 My 2017
That Sublime Slice of American Cheese *Los Angeles Magazine* p46 Ja 2017

Scherer, Michael

As the White House Turns: A Guide to the Shifting Power Centers Among Trump's Top Advisers color *Time* v189 no15 p10 Ap 24 2017

Bigots, Boosted by the Bully Pulpit color *Time* v190 no8 p30 Ag 28 2017

Can He Be Tamed? color *Time* v189 no24 p36 Je 26 2017

Can Trump Handle the Truth? [Cover story] color *Time* v189 no12 p32 Ap 3 2017

Family First [Cover story] color *Time* v189 no22 p24 Je 12 2017

How Donald Trump Jr.'s Emails Have Cranked Up the Heat on His Family [Cover story] color *Time* v190 no4 p22 Jl 24 2017

How Senator Ben Sasse Became the Anti-Trump color *Time* v189 no19 p16 My 22 2017

The Incredible Shrinking Power of the President's Threats color *Time* v189 no14 p9 Ap 17 2017

Liberals Plot Revenge color *Time* v189 no3 p38 Ja 30 2017

Moscow Cozies Up to the Right color *Time* v189 no10 p32 Mr 20 2017

No Good Options on North Korea color *Time* v190 no4 p10 Jl 24 2017

The Person of the Year [Cover story] color diag map *Time* v188 no25-26 p46 D 19 2016 Double Issue

Russia and the Trump Campaign color *Time* v189 no12 p36 Ap 3 2017

The Second Most Powerful Man In the World? [Cover story] color *Time* v189 no5 p24 F 13 2017

A Shooting and the Risks of Political Outrage color *Time* v189 no24 p12 Je 26 2017

Trump After Hours [Cover story] color *Time* v189 no19 p28 My 22 2017

Trump and His Allies Stumble As Russia Probe Moves Closer to the White House color *Time* v189 no21 p9 Je 5 2017

Trump's Loyalty Test [Cover story] color *Time* v189 no20 p24 My 29 2017

The Truth Is Out There color *Time* v188 no15 p28 O 17 2016

The White House Survival Guide color *Time* v189 no4 p30 Ja 23 2017

Scherer, Nora

Contingent valuation: Flawed logic? color *Science* v357 no6349 p363 Jl 28 2017

Putting a value on injuries to natural assets: The BP oil spill chart *Science* v356 no6335 p253 Ap 21 2017

Scherer, Philipp E.

An adipo-biliary-uridine axis that regulates energy homeostasis diag *Science* v355 no6330 p1173 Mr 17 2017

Scherer-Lorenzen, Michael

Positive biodiversity-productivity relationship predominant in global forests bibl chart graph map *Science* v354 no6309 paaf8957-1 O 14 2016

Scherini, V.

Observation of a large-scale anisotropy in the arrival directions of cosmic rays above 8 × 1018 eV *Science* v357 no6357 p1266 S 22 2017

Schermelleh, Lothar

PCGF3/5–PRC1 initiates Polycomb recruitment in X chromosome inactivation color *Science* v356 no6342 p1081 Je 9 2017

Scherpf, Stephani E

Sonia Destri Lie color *Dance Magazine* v91 no3 p18 Mr 2017

Scherr, Elana

ROADKILL DAYS LEAD TO ROADKILL NIGHTS color *Hot Rod* v70 no1 p84 Ja 2017

Scherrer, Robert

Gary Steigman *Physics Today* v70 no8 p72 Ag 2017

Scherry, Stephen

On Patrol *New York State Conservationist* v71 no3 p25 D 2016

On Patrol *New York State Conservationist* v71 no5 p20 Ap 2017

On Patrol *New York State Conservationist* v71 no6 p25 Je 2017

On Patrol: Real stories from Conservation Officers and Forest Rangers in the field *New York State Conservationist* v72 no1 p33 Ag 2017

Schertler, Gebhard

A three-dimensional movie of structural changes in bacteriorhodopsin bibl diag graph *Science* v354 no6319 p1552 D 23 2016

Scherzer, Clemens R.

β2-Adrenoreceptor is a regulator of the a-synuclein gene driving risk of Parkinson's disease cartoon chart graph *Science* v357 no6354 p891 S 1 2017

Scherzer, Max, 1984-

PAIR OF ACES S. Apstein color *Sports Illustrated* v127 no11 p28 O 9 2017

Scheucher, Michael

Quantum optical circulator controlled by a single chirally coupled atom bibl graph *Science* v354 no6319 p1577 D 23 2016

Scheuer, Jochen

Submillihertz magnetic spectroscopy performed with a nanoscale quantum sensor diag *Science* v356 no6340 p832 My 26 2017

Scheuer, Mary Ann

POWERFUL PARTNERSHIPS: Literacy, your librarian, and you *Literacy Today (2411-7862)* v35 no1 p14 Jl/Ag 2017

Scheufele, Dietram A.

Mapping the Landscape of Public Attitudes on Synthetic Biology *BioScience* v67 no3 p290 Mr 2017

U.S. attitudes on human genome editing color graph *Science* v357 no6351 p553 Ag 11 2017

Scheutz, Matthias

THE CASE FOR Robot Disobedience [Cover story] color *Scientific American* v316 no1 p44 Ja 2017

Scheve, Kenneth

Taxing the Rich: A History of Fiscal Fairness in the United States and Europe R. N. Cooper *Foreign Affairs* v95 no6 p175 N/D 2016

SCHEVE, NEVA KITTRELL

The Open Road color *Trail Rider* v29 no1 p56 Ja/F 2017

PREPARE FOR A TRAILERING EMERGENCY *Trail Rider* v29 no3 p65 Ap 2017

The Ride Inside color *Trail Rider* v29 no4 p54 My 2017

Trailer-Buying Guide color *Trail Rider* v29 no2 p58 Mr 2017

SCHEVE, TOM

The Open Road color *Trail Rider* v29 no1 p56 Ja/F 2017

The Ride Inside color *Trail Rider* v29 no4 p54 My 2017

Trailer-Buying Guide color *Trail Rider* v29 no2 p58 Mr 2017

Schiaparelli, Elsa, 1890-1973

"PANTSUIT" /PANT SOOT/ B. PETERSON *Washingtonian Magazine* v52 no3 p18 D 2016

Schiaparelli, G. V. (Giovanni Virginio), 1835-1910

ExoMars Lander Fails, Orbiter Succeeds D. DICKINSON *Sky & Telescope* v133 no2 p10 F 2017

Schiavino, G. R.

175 WAYS TO GET WESTERN cartoon color *American Cowboy* v23 no5 p26 F/Mr 2017

3 Days in... Cheyenne, Wyo color *American Cowboy* v24 no1 p38 Je/Jl 2017

3 Days in... Prescott, Ariz color *American Cowboy* v23 no5 p44 F/Mr 2017

3 Days in... San Angelo, Texas color *American Cowboy* v23 no6 p34 Ap/My 2017

The Alamo Remembered bw *American Cowboy* p38 LEGENDS OF TEXAS Special Issue 2017

(At home with) color *Team Roping Journal* p44 O 2017

Back to the Future color *Spin to Win Rodeo* v21 no6 p104 Ag 2017

Closing the Loop color *Team Roping Journal* p94 S 2017

Cowgirl Flair bw color *American Cowboy* v23 no6 p40 Ap/My 2017

It Happened Here: Nacogdoches, Texas color *American Cowboy* v23 no6 p36 Ap/My 2017

It Happened Here: Pinos Altos, N.M color *American Cowboy* v23 no5 p43 F/Mr 2017

It Happened Here: The Great Plains, 1867 bw *American Cowboy* v24 no1 p41 Je/Jl 2017

Northern Nevada's Cowboy Culture map *American Cowboy* v23 no5 p45 F/Mr 2017

The North Texas Loop map *American Cowboy* v23 no6 p35 Ap/My 2017

ROAD TRIP color *American Cowboy* v24 no1 p39 Je/Jl 2017

THREE SQUARED color *Team Roping Journal* p58 S 2017

The Warrior Rides Again color *American Cowboy* v24 no1 p58 Je/Jl 2017

The World of TEAM ROPING chart color map *Team Roping Journal* p96 O 2017

Schiavo, Rosaria

Germ line–inherited H3K27me3 restricts enhancer function during maternal-to-zygotic transition diag *Science* v357 no6347 p212 Jl 14 2017

Schiavone, Aldo

Pilate as an agent of salvation J. S. J. von Arx *America* v216 no10 p48 My 1 2017

Pilate Error H. ANDREWS cartoon *Weekly Standard* v22 no28 p35 Mr 27 2017

SCHIAVONE, GENE

CHRISTMAS in Boston color *Yankee* v80 no6 p108 N/D 2016

Schick, Philip

A TOWN RECYCLED AND ITS MASTERFUL MOVER K. CAMPBELL WIDNER *Idaho Magazine* v17 no1 p42 Ja 2017

Schick, Vicky

DANCE *New Yorker* v92 no44 p10 Ja 9 2017

Schickel, Richard, 1933-2017

EDITOR'S LETTER N. Rapold color *Film Comment* v53 no2 p4 Mr/Ap 2017

Milestones color *Time* v189 no9 p14 Mr 13 2017

Schief, William R.

Priming HIV-1 broadly neutralizing antibody precursors in human Ig loci transgenic mice bibl graph *Science* v353 no6307 p1557 S 30 2016

Schieffer, Bob, 1937——Interviews

Bob SCHIEFFER color *Vanity Fair* v59 no10 p216 O 2017

Schieler, H.

Observation of a large-scale anisotropy in the arrival directions of cosmic rays above 8 × 1018 eV *Science* v357 no6357 p1266 S 22 2017

Schierhorn, Florian

Global Demand for Food Is Rising. Can We Meet It? *Harvard Business Review Digital Articles* p2 Ap 7 2016

Schietgat, Leander

Predicting human olfactory perception from chemical features of odor molecules bibl diag graph *Science* v355 no6327 p820 F 24 2017

Schietti, J.

Persistent effects of pre-Columbian plant domestication on Amazonian forest composition bibl chart graph map *Science* v355 no6328 p925 Mr 3 2017

Schifeling, Todd

Why Companies Are Becoming B Corporations *Harvard Business Review Digital Articles* p2 Je 17 2016

Schiff, Adam

A Local Pol with A Global Profile G. KAHN color *Los Angeles Magazine* v62 no7 p58 Jl 2017

Schiff, Gordon

Get Advice From a Pharmacist color *Kiplinger's Personal Finance* v71 no4 p70 Ap 2017

Schiff, Stacy

Affable, He Convicted Salem Innocents color *New York Review of Books* v64 no4 p22 Mr 9 2017

History's FIRST DRAFT color *Vanity Fair* v59 no10 p158 O 2017

OBAMA'S AMERICA img *New York* v49 no20 p12 O 3 2016

Schiffer, Claudia, 1970-

LIVING THE DREAM [Cover story] J. K. DE VALLE color *Architectural Digest* v74 no9 p114 S 2017

Schiffer, Pete—Interviews

The Big Picture J. K. HANUS color il *American Craft* v76 no6 p22 D 2016-Ja 2017

Schiffer Publishing Ltd.

The Big Picture J. K. HANUS color il *American Craft* v76 no6 p22 D 2016-Ja 2017

Schiffman, Richard

Professor Caveman color *Atlantic* v319 no3 p18 Ap 2017

WILDLIFE WARRIOR color *Scientific American* v316 no1 p64 Ja 2017

SCHIFFRES, MANUEL

U.S. Stocks Win Again chart *Kiplinger's Personal Finance* v71 no3 p52 Mr 2017

SCHIFFRIN, ANYA

BUT WHO WILL COVER THE SWILL MILK? color *Nation* v304 no5 p35 F 20 2017

Schifrin, Matt

100 YEARS OF HITS AND FLOPS color *Forbes* v200 no3 p54 S 28 2017

BOND OF BROTHERS bw *Forbes* v200 no3 p78 S 28 2017

A BOUNTIFUL MIND bw color *Forbes* v199 no1 p94 Ja 24 2017

LESSONS AND IDEAS BY THE 100 GREATEST LIVING BUSINESS MINDS bw color *Forbes* v200 no3 p115 S 28 2017

Rowing Upstream color graph *Forbes* v199 no7 p50 Je 29 2017

School of Quant color *Forbes* v200 no2 p54 S 5 2017

THE WORLD'S BILLIONAIRES bw color diag graph map *Forbes* v199 no3 p84 Mr 28 2017

Schildgen, Bob

Hey Mr. Green! Do alien bees threaten native species? *Sierra* v101 no5 p14 S/O 2016

Hey Mr. Green! Is it better to scoop or to bury dog poop? *Sierra* v102 no3 p12 My/Je 2017

Hey Mr. Green! Should receipts be recycled? *Sierra* v102 no2 p12 Mr/Ap 2017

Hey Mr. Green! What's a good ecofriendly tile cleaner? *Sierra* v102 no1 p14 Ja/F 2017

Hey Mr. Green! What's the greenest way to weatherize? *Sierra* v102 no5 p12 S/O 2017

Hey Mr. Green! Why are organics plastic-wrapped? *Sierra* v101 no4 p12 Jl/Ag 2016

SCHILDHAUER, MARK P.

Skills and Knowledge for Data-Intensive Environmental Research *BioScience* v67 no6 p546 Je 2017

SCHILDHOUSE, JILL

12 Smart Food Choices cartoon color *Muscle & Performance* v9 no5 p55 My 2017

6 FOOD MYTHS YOU CAN FORGET color *Muscle & Performance* v9 no5 p26 My 2017

7 TIPS FOR INDULGING THIS HOLIDAY SEASON color *Muscle & Performance* v8 no12 p28 D 2016

GET TO KNOW: BEAST SPORTS NUTRITION color *Muscle & Performance* v9 no6 p32 Je 2017

Get to Know: Carlson Laboratories color *Muscle & Performance* v9 no11 p42 N 2017

Get to Know: Designer Protein color *Muscle & Performance* v9 no8 p32 Ag 2017

GET TO KNOW: FINAFLEX color *Muscle & Performance* v9 no4 p32 Ap 2017

Get to Know: GAT SPORT color *Muscle & Performance* v9 no7 p30 Jl 2017

GET TO KNOW: IFORCE NUTRITION color *Muscle & Performance* v8 no12 p34 D 2016

GET TO KNOW: INNER ARMOUR color *Muscle & Performance* v9 no1 p34 Ja 2017

Get to Know: MuscleTech color *Muscle & Performance* v9 no10 p34 O 2017

Get to Know: Nordic Naturals color *Muscle & Performance* v9 no9 p34 S 2017

GET TO KNOW: NUBREED NUTRITION color *Muscle & Performance* v9 no5 p32 My 2017

The Guru of Abs color *Muscle & Performance* v9 no11 p40 N 2017

Jojo's Got the Mojo color *Muscle & Performance* v9 no9 p32 S 2017

NO EXCUSES color *Muscle & Performance* v9 no1 p28 Ja 2017

Schildmeijer, Reggie

An interactive three-dimensional digital atlas and quantitative database of human development bibl color graph *Science* v354 no6315 paag0053-1 N 25 2016

Schill, Caroline

Social norms as solutions bibl color *Science* v354 no6308 p42 O 7 2016

Schillace, Brandy

Clockwork Futures D. M. Kahler color *Science* v357 no6355 p967 S 8 2017

Schilling, Govert

Hubble Spies Faint Galaxies in Early Universe *Sky & Telescope* v133 no6 p8 Je 2017

Lofty telescope will survey the cool universe color *Science* v356 no6340 p789 My 26 2017

Reach Out & Touch color *Sky & Telescope* v134 no5 p84 N 2017

The Square KILOMETRE ARRAY *Sky & Telescope* v133 no6 p24 Je 2017

Schilling, Mary Kaye

Bring "Your Ugly Stuff" img *New York* v50 no13 p74 Je 26 2017

Tragedy Foretold img *New York* v60 p60 Ja 23 2017

SCHILLING, MELISSA

WHAT'S YOUR BEST INNOVATION BET? BY MAPPING A TECHNOLOGY'S PAST, YOU CAN PREDICT WHAT FUTURE CUSTOMERS WILL WANT bw chart color graph img *Harvard Business Review* v95 no4 p86 Jl/Ag 2017

Schilling, Taylor, 1984-

No Break for Orange's Prisoners D. D'Addario color *Time* v189 no23 p53 Je 19 2017

Schillinger, Liesl

Bookends *New York Times Book Review* p27 S 3 2017

Do the Right Thing *New York Times Book Review* p10 Ag 27 2017

My Millennial Friend color *Vogue* v206 no11 p74 N 2016

Somewhere, MY LOVE cartoon color *O, The Oprah Magazine* p99 F 2017

SPIRITED AWAY color *Vogue* v207 no3 p476 Mr 2017

TRAVEL color *New York Times Book Review* p18 D 4 2016

Travel *New York Times Book Review* p16 Je 4 2017

WHAT A BOOK CAN DO [Cover story] color *O, The Oprah Magazine* p76 Jl 2017

What's the best book, new or old, you read this year? *New York Times Book Review* p27 D 25 2016

WOULDN'T IT BE NICE? cartoon *O, The Oprah Magazine* p98 Ap 2017

Schilp, John F.

The 2018 revision of the Consumer Price Index geographic sample bibl chart color diag map *Monthly Labor Review* p1 O 2016

Schimmelpfennig, David

Precision Agriculture Technologies and Factors Affecting Their Adoption color graph *Amber Waves: The Economics of Food, Farming, Natural Resources, & Rural America* p32 D 2016

SCHIMMERLING, WALTER

Moses and DeMille *Commentary* v143 no6 p7 Je 2017

Schimp, M.

Observation of a large-scale anisotropy in the arrival directions of cosmic rays above 8 × 1018 eV *Science* v357 no6357 p1266 S 22 2017

Schindel, John

Posthole color *Powder* v45 no5 p108 Ja 2017

Schinder, Alejandro F.

A disynaptic feedback network activated by experience promotes the integration of new granule cells bibl graph *Science* v354 no6311 p459 O 28 2016

Schindler, Bill

Professor Caveman R. SCHIFFMAN color *Atlantic* v319 no3 p18 Ap 2017

Schindler, Kevin

PERCIVAL LOWELL A life in astronomy bw color map *Astronomy* v45 no4 p44 Ap 2017

Schindler, Roland A.

Terawatt-scale photovoltaics: Trajectories and challenges chart graph *Science* v356 no6334 p141 Ap 14 2017

Schine, Cathleen

Monkey In the Business [Cover story] *New York Times Book Review* p1 O 23 2016

No Love Without Delusion bw *New York Review of Books* v64 no2 p8 F 9 2017

The Wisdom of the Yard color *New York Review of Books* v64 no6 p33 Ap 6 2017

Schine, Eric

On the Stump for Macron—in Florida color *Bloomberg Businessweek* no4525 p12 Je 5 2017

Schinko, Thomas

Identifying the policy space for climate loss and damage bibl color diag *Science* v354 no6310 p290 O 21 2016

Schiöth, H. B.

Sex matters: Report experimenter gender *Science* v356 no6341 p916 Je 1 2017

SCHIPANI, VANESSA

The Virtual Forest *American Scholar* v86 no2 p16 Spr 2017

SCHIPANSKI, MEAGAN E.

Agriculture in 2050: Recalibrating Targets for Sustainable Intensification *BioScience* v67 no4 p386 Ap 2017

Schipper, A. M.

The impact of hunting on tropical mammal and bird populations graph map *Science* v356 no6334 p180 Ap 14 2017

SCHIRMER, MARK

THE SPECIALISTS color *Road & Track* v68 no6 p48 F 2017

Schirmer, Teresa Engle

40 Years IN THE Dark H. Stucker bw color *Popular Photography* v81 no2 p62 Mr/Ap 2017

Schist sculpture

RENAISSANCE MELODY E. A. POWELL color *Archaeology* v70 no4 p15 Je-Ag 2017

Schitt's Creek (TV program)

GRAND MOTEL D. KAMP color *Vanity Fair* v59 no1 p166 Holiday 2017

Schizoaffective disorders

Life's Work: An Interview with Brian Wilson A. Beard bw *Harvard Business Review* v94 no12 p120 D 2016

Schizophrenia

See also

Schizoaffective disorders

The Domesticated Human C. BADCOCK *Psychology Today* v50 no1 p41 Ja/F 2017

Schizophrenia treatment

SCHIZOPHRENIA'S UNYIELDING MYSTERIES M. BALTER color diag *Scientific American* v316 no5 p54 My 2017

Understanding Health Care's Short-Termism Problem A. Chandra and D. Goldman *Harvard Business Review Digital Articles* p2 S 28 2015

Schizophrenia—Diagnosis

LISTEN TO THE VOICES IN YOUR HEAD S. M. SHAPIRO color map *Foreign Policy* no222 p56 Ja/F 2017

Schizophrenia—Research

Schizophrenia's Genetic Spark P. SMAGLIK cartoon *Discover* v38 no1 p60 Ja/F 2017

Schjeldahl, Peter

THE BETTER LIFE cartoon *New Yorker* v92 no36 p78 N 7 2016

BEYOND BEAUTY color *New Yorker* v93 no30 p74 O 2 2017

Down and In cartoon *New Yorker* v92 no49 p17 F 13 2017

DRAWING LINES cartoon *New Yorker* v92 no33 p106 O 17 2016

FRESH PAINT cartoon *New Yorker* v92 no48 p76 F 6 2017

FULL IMMERSION color *New Yorker* v93 no22 p78 Jl 31 2017

HOME AND AWAY color *New Yorker* v93 no18 p72 Je 26 2017

KNOCK ON WOOD cartoon *New Yorker* v92 no37 p92 N 14 2016

LOOKING AND SEEING color *New Yorker* v93 no12 p72 My 8 2017

MAN OF MANY WORDS cartoon *New Yorker* v92 no49 p96 F 13 2017

NEW LIVES cartoon *New Yorker* v93 no2 p72 F 27 2017

Of Late cartoon *New Yorker* v92 no42 p27 D 19 2016

Plus Ça Change cartoon *New Yorker* v92 no35 p14 O 31 2016

Reality Principle cartoon *New Yorker* v92 no30 p8 S 26 2016

THE ROARING STETTIES color *New Yorker* v93 no13 p90 My 15 2017

SAFE SPACE color *New Yorker* v93 no31 p78 O 9 2017

SECOND IMPRESSIONS cartoon *New Yorker* v93 no9 p74 Ap 17 2017

TROUBLE MAKER cartoon *New Yorker* v92 no39 p92 N 28 2016

THE WAVE OF HISTORY bw *New Yorker* v93 no15 p60 My 29 2017

WHAT'S NEW? cartoon *New Yorker* v93 no6 p76 Mr 27 2017

A WOMAN'S VIEW color *New Yorker* v92 no47 p72 Ja 30 2017

THE XX FACTOR color *New Yorker* v93 no10 p100 Ap 24 2017

SCHLABACH, GERALD

BEYOND "JUST CAUSE" color *Commonweal* v144 no16 p4 O 6 2017

Schlabach, Gerald W.

Abortion & Social Justice [Cover story] color *Commonweal* v144 no1 p11 Ja 6 2017

Just War? bw *Commonweal* v144 no11 p11 Je 16 2017

Schlabach, Gerald—Interviews

Pacifism in action color *U.S. Catholic* v82 no2 p28 F 2017

Schlachetzki, Johannes C. M.

An environment-dependent transcriptional network specifies human microglia identity color *Science* v356 no6344 p1248 Je 23 2017

Schlack, Julie Wittes

Ask Your Customers for Predictions, Not Preferences *Harvard Business Review Digital Articles* p2 Ja 5 2015

The Brands That Make Customers Feel Respected *Harvard Business Review Digital Articles* p2 N 1 2016

Use Your Customers as Ethnographers *Harvard Business Review Digital Articles* p2 Ag 17 2015

Schlafly, Phyllis, 1924-2016

THE BIGGEST HOMOPHOBES: THE LGBT RIGHTS MOVEMENT HAS HAD ITS SHARE OF VILLAINS L. GRINDLEY, T. RING et al color *Advocate* no1091 p102 Je/Jl 2017

Schlager, Noah

Feeding the Soul *Sierra* v102 no5 p10 St/O 2017

Schlangenstein, Mary

China Challenges the Giants With Low Fares color graph *Bloomberg Businessweek* no4504 p22 D 19 2016

A Fast-Track Promotion—With a Catch diag *Bloomberg Businessweek* no4536 p19 S 4 2017

The Short Flight From Clerk to Cockpit *Bloomberg Businessweek* no4494 p25 O 10 2016

Trump's Real Jobs Crisis chart *Bloomberg Businessweek* no4528 p32 Je 26 2017

Schlapman, Kimberly—Interviews

LITTLE BIG TOWN L. Rice color *Entertainment Weekly* no1456 p34 Mr 10 2017

Schlatter, Thomas W.

A Tribute to Thomas W. Schlatter M. Benner Smidt *Weatherwise* v70 no2 p5 Mr/Ap 2017

Weather Queries *Weatherwise* v70 no1 p44 Ja/F 2017

Weather Queries *Weatherwise* v70 no2 p32 Mr/Ap 2017

Schlaudecker, Jeffrey D.—Interviews

Senior LIVING R. Bird *Cincinnati Magazine* v50 no7 p73 Ap 2017

Schlechter, Annie

Halloween All Year img *New York* v49 no15 p69 Jl 25 2016

Schlegel, Cori

THE BIG QUESTION cartoon *Atlantic* v318 no4 p112 N 2016

Schlemmer, Oskar, 1888-1943

ROYA SACHS: Independent Curator J. ORTVED color *Vogue* v207 no10 p196 O 2017

Schlemmer, Ross H.

Community arts: (Re)contextualizing the narrative of teaching and learning bibl *Arts Education Policy Review* v118 no1 p27 2017

Schlenzka, Jenny

JENNY SCHLENZKA: Performance Space 122 M. GUIDUCCI color *Vogue* v207 no10 p192 O 2017

SCHLESINGER, ARTHUR M. (Arthur Meier), 1917-2007

Joe College Is Dead: In an essay directed at bewildered '60s-era parents, a noted historian attempts to explain the roots of student unrest *Saturday Evening Post* v289 no4 p44 Jl/Ag 2017

Schlesinger, Arthur, Jr.

The Great Carter Mystery *New Republic* v248 no6 p4 Je 2017

Schlesinger, Len

Giving Patients an Active Role in Their Health Care *Harvard Business Review Digital Articles* p2 N 21 2016

When Your Boss Gives You Conflicting Messages *Harvard Business Review Digital Articles* p2 N 27 2014

SCHLEY, LACY

Adipocytes color *Discover* v38 no9 p20 N 2017

Building Blocks color *Discover* v38 no7 p18 S 2017

Building Blocks color *Discover* v38 no9 p18 N 2017

Charting the Unseen Sky color *Discover* v38 no9 p19 N 2017

Cognitive Offloading cartoon *Discover* v27 no10 p14 D 2016

Deep Dive color *Discover* v38 no4 p14 My 2017

Degrees of Separation *Discover* v38 no10 p14 D 2017

How Accurate Is Your Fitness Tracker? color graph *Discover* v38 no7 p18 S 2017

In the Bag color *Discover* v38 no2 p14 Mr 2017

Marie Curie color *Discover* v38 no4 p38 My 2017

Marijuana color diag *Discover* v38 no6 p56 Jl/Ag 2017

Mini Measure color *Discover* v38 no9 p22 N 2017

Nobel by the Numbers color graph *Discover* v38 no9 p16 N 2017

The Original Brexit color *Discover* v38 no7 p19 S 2017

Pingo *Discover* v38 no7 p12 S 2017

The Problem With E-Cigarettes *Discover* v38 no10 p14 D 2017

PUSHING THE LIMITS OF LIFE IN THE LAB color *Discover* v38 no1 p38 Ja/F 2017

Requesting Backup color map *Discover* v38 no8 p15 O 2017

The River Overfloweth map *Discover* v38 no10 p15 D 2017

Spidey Senses color *Discover* v38 no2 p10 Mr 2017

Suicide Rates of U.S. Farmers and Agriculture Workers, 1992-2010 graph *Discover* v38 no8 p14 O 2017

Superhydrophobic cartoon *Discover* v38 no3 p14 Ap 2017

Syzygy color *Discover* v38 no5 p20 Je 2017

Tag, They're It color *Discover* v38 no4 p18 My 2017

TRENDING color diag graph *Discover* v38 no6 p12 Jl/Ag 2017

TRENDING graph map *Discover* v38 no5 p16 Je 2017

The Truth About Our Trash color graph *Discover* v38 no9 p18 N 2017

What Makes a Creep? cartoon *Discover* v27 no10 p8 D 2016

When Brain Imaging Goes Awry color *Discover* v38 no1 p72 Ja/F 2017

Schlichting, Ilme

Engineering extrinsic disorder to control protein activity in living cells bibl color *Science* v354 no6318 p1441 D 16 2016

Schliebs, W.

Inhibitors of PEX14 disrupt protein import into glycosomes and kill Trypanosoma parasites chart color diag graph *Science* v355 no6332 p1416 Mr 31 2017

Schliemann, Heinrich, 1822-1890

One-Off S. Moyer *Humanities* v37 no4 p1 Fall 2016

Schlinger, Amy

5 Signs You're Working Out Too Much color *Health* v30 no9 p65 N 2016

Schlipf, Rich

Precision: PAIN POINTS L. Bedord *Successful Farming* v115 no9 p43 Ag 2017

Schlissel, Gavin

Aggregation of the Whi3 protein, not loss of heterochromatin, causes sterility in old yeast cells bibl diag *Science* v355 no6330 p1184 Mr 17 2017

Schlitzer, Andreas

Mapping the human DC lineage through the integration of high-dimensional techniques diag *Science* v356 no6342 p1044 Je 9 2017

Schloesser, Stephen

Without Walls bw *Commonweal* v144 no11 p35 Je 16 2017

Schloss, Andrew

Amazing (Mostly) Edible Science K. Servick color *Science* v354 no6317 p1226 D 9 2016

Schlossberg, Nancy K.

How to Become a Happy Retiree color *Money* v46 no4 p28 My 2017

SCHLOSSBERG, TATIANA

Idle Power Hogs *Reader's Digest* v189 no1128 p41 Mr 2017

SCHLOZMAN, DANIEL

IN EQUILIBRIO color *Nation* v305 no7 p35 S 25 2017

Schlueter, Nathan W.

CON-FUSION D. Azerrad *Claremont Review of Books* v17 no3 p28 Summ 2017

Schlueter, Paul III

Skepticism Should Be Nonpartisan *Skeptical Inquirer* v41 no3 p63 My/Je 2017

Schlumberger, Jean—Exhibitions

INSPIRED BY NATURE *Virginia Living* v15 no2 p69 F 2017

Schlüter, Maja

Social norms as solutions bibl color *Science* v354 no6308 p42 O 7 2016

Schlütz, F.

Permanent human occupation of the central Tibetan Plateau in the early Holocene bibl bw color diag *Science* v355 no6320 p1 Ja 6 2017

Schmale, David

high–flying microbes color *Scientific American* v316 no2 p40 F 2017

Schmalensee, Richard

The Best Retailers Combine Bricks and Clicks *Harvard Business Review Digital Articles* p2 My 30 2016

A Deep Look Inside Apple Pay's Matchmaker Economics *Harvard Business Review Digital Articles* p2 Je 17 2016

Reforming the U.S. coal leasing program color graph *Science* v354 no6316 p1096 D 2 2016

Some of the Most Successful Platforms Are Ones You've Never Heard Of *Harvard Business Review Digital Articles* p2 Mr 28 2016

What Platforms Do Differently than Traditional Businesses *Harvard Business Review Digital Articles* p2 My 11 2016

Why Winner-Takes-All Thinking Doesn't Apply to the Platform Economy *Harvard Business Review Digital Articles* p2 My 4 2016

Schmalz, Martin

One Big Reason There's So Little Competition Among U.S. Banks *Harvard Business Review Digital Articles* p2 Je 13 2016

Warren Buffett Is Betting the Airline Oligopoly Is Here to Stay *Harvard Business Review Digital Articles* p2 N 17 2016

SCHMECKPEPER, SHERYL

Murder in the Sandhills bw color *Nebraska Life* v21 no5 p36 S/O 2017

Schmelling, Nicolas

Structures of the cyanobacterial circadian oscillator frozen in a fully assembled state bibl diag *Science* v355 no6330 p1181 Mr 17 2017

Schmelz, Joan T.

Arecibo Under the Gun *Sky & Telescope* v133 no5 p84 My 2017

SCHMELZER, J.P.

How to Get Squirrels Out of Your Attic color *Yankee* p28 Mr 2017

Schmid, Ann

POWER [Cover story] color *Christian Century* v134 no1 p22 Ja 4 2017

Schmid, Bernhard

Positive biodiversity-productivity relationship predominant in global forests bibl chart graph map *Science* v354 no6309 paaf8957-1 O 14 2016

Schmid, Edward T.

Macrophage function in tissue repair and remodeling requires IL-4 or IL-13 with apoptotic cells diag *Science* v356 no6342 p1072 Je 9 2017

Schmid, Helen

Should You Compete with Amazon or Sell on Amazon? *Harvard Business Review Digital Articles* p2 My 23 2016

SCHMID, JAMIE

Protein Surprises in The Produce Section color *Reader's Digest* v190 no1133 p38 S 2017

Schmid, John

HOW STRONG IS YOUR BANK? EVEN WITH LOW COMMODITY PRICES, BANKS THAT LEND TO AGRICULTURE CONTIUNE TO STRENGTHEN D. LOOKER *Successful Farming* v115 no12 p24 O 2017

STAYING AFLOAT: MANAGING FINANCIAL UNCERTAINTY IS KEY D. Looker *Successful Farming* v115 no12 p14 O 2017

Schmid, Martin

DeepStack: Expert-level artificial intelligence in heads-up no-limit poker [Cover story] chart diag *Science* v356 no6337 p508 My 5 2017

Schmid, Megan E.

Promoting Student Academic Achievement Through Faculty Development about Inclusive Teaching *Change* v48 no5 p16 S/O 2016

Schmid, Sandra

Not just Salk color *Science* v357 no6356 p1105 S 15 2017

Schmidgall, E. R.

Deterministic generation of a cluster state of entangled photons bibl diag graph *Science* v354 no6311 p434 O 28 2016

Schmidle, Nicholas

BAD GUYS cartoon *New Yorker* v92 no37 p32 N 14 2016

CAN FOOTBALL BE SAVED? cartoon color *New Yorker* v92 no44 p38 Ja 9 2017

GENERAL CHAOS cartoon *New Yorker* v93 no2 p40 F 27 2017

HIGH STAKES cartoon *New Yorker* v93 no23 p22 Ag 7 2017

Schmidt, Anja

RETINOBLASTOMA RELATED1 mediates germline entry in Arabidopsis color diag *Science* v356 no6336 p396 Ap 28 2017

Schmidt, Anna

Neandertal and Denisovan DNA from Pleistocene sediments bw color *Science* v356 no6338 p605 My 12 2017

SCHMIDT, BENJAMIN

CHADWICK BOSEMAN UPS HIS GAME [Cover story] color *Ebony* v72/73 no12/1 p70 O/N 2017

SCHMIDT, BLAKE

DEPT. OF SHELL COMPANIES CLANDESTINE ACCOUNTS,

& BRIBERY cartoon color *Bloomberg Businessweek* no4526 p46 Je 12 2017

Schmidt, Cédric

Time-resolved x-ray absorption spectroscopy with a water window high-harmonic source bibl graph *Science* v355 no6322 p264 Ja 20 2017

Schmidt, Charles

Children with cancer get more access to experimental drugs color *Science* v357 no6351 p540 Ag 11 2017

DON'T DRINK THE WATER color map *Scientific American* v316 no4 p64 Ap 2017

Pediatric Predicament color *Scientific American* v317 no3 p24 S 2017

When Medical Tests Mislead color *Scientific American* v315 no6 p28 D 2016

Schmidt, Chris

Genomic estimation of complex traits reveals ancient maize adaptation to temperate North America diag *Science* v357 no6350 p512 Ag 4 2017

Schmidt, Christian

The cryo-EM structure of a ribosome–Ski2-Ski3-Ski8 helicase complex bibl color graph *Science* v354 no6318 p1431 D 16 2016

Schmidt, D.

Observation of a large-scale anisotropy in the arrival directions of cosmic rays above 8×10^{18} eV *Science* v357 no6357 p1266 S 22 2017

Schmidt, Detlef

State of the Art – Today: Here's a look at the cutting edge of telescope technology now J. Oltion color *Sky & Telescope* v134 no5 p72 N 2017

SCHMIDT, EDMUND W.

FIELD TRIP TO RIKERS *America* v215 no18 p32 D 5 2016

OF MANY THINGS *America* v215 no13 p2 O 31 2016

Schmidt, Edward W.

Florence's gift to the people, believers and nonbelievers alike color *America* v217 no4 p52 Ag 21 2017

Schmidt, Eric

Cyberwars: We Must Prepare Ourselves for the Wars of the Future *Time* v188 no27-28 p25 D 26 2016

Schmidt, Gavin A.

Scientific advocacy: A tool for assessing the risks of engagement bibl *Bulletin of the Atomic Scientists* v73 no5 p344 2017

Schmidt, Henrik

Robust spin-polarized midgap states at step edges of topological crystalline insulators bibl graph *Science* v354 no6317 p1269 D 9 2016

SCHMIDT, INGRID

That Magic Formula: GLAMGLOW FOUNDERS GLENN AND SHANNON DELLIMORE BUILT A FAST FORTUNE WITH A QUICK ACTING FACIAL MUD. AS THEY RAMP UP FOR THEIR NEXT MOVE, THE BEAUTY WORLD IS WATCHING *Los Angeles Magazine* p64 Ag 2017

Schmidt, Jens

A general, modular method for the catalytic asymmetric synthesis of alkylboronate esters bibl color *Science* v354 no6317 p1265 D 9 2016

Schmidt, Johannes

The Vanishing Eels E. BETZ bw color map *Discover* v38 no8 p22 O 2017

Schmidt, Joshua M.

Chimpanzee genomic diversity reveals ancient admixture with bonobos bibl diag graph map *Science* v354 no6311 p477 O 28 2016

Schmidt, Judy

STELLAR NURSERY E. MASTROIANNI color *Discover* v38 no3 p18 Ap 2017

Schmidt, Kai-Uwe

How to govern geoengineering? color *Science* v357 no6348 p231 Jl 21 2017

Schmidt, Karl

Why Self Image Matters in B2B Sales *Harvard Business Review Digital Articles* p2 Ap 2 2015

Schmidt, Kimberly Biehl

Old Hollywood Haunt A. HEROLD *Los Angeles Magazine* p38 Ja 2017

Schmidt, Kolton
TOP MOUNTS color *Spin to Win Rodeo* v20 no10 p26 D 2016

Schmidt, Lanny D.
Robert Gomer *Physics Today* v70 no5 p67 My 2017

Schmidt, Leigh Eric
Village Atheists: How America's Unbelievers Made Their Way in a Godly Nation K. PLOETZ *Humanist* v77 no2 p40 Mr/Ap 2017

SCHMIDT, LUCINDA
THE WORLD'S BILLIONAIRES bw color diag graph map *Forbes* v199 no3 p84 Mr 28 2017

Schmidt, M. E.
Redox stratification of an ancient lake in Gale crater, Mars color *Science* v356 no6341 p922 Je 1 2017

Schmidt, Maarten
The mystery of quasars D. J. Eicher color *Astronomy* v45 no5 p8 My 2017

Schmidt, Markus
FRIGHT NIGHT *Virginia Living* v15 no6 p19 O 2017
ROCKET WOMAN: Zena Cardman of Williamsburg joins NASA's 2017 class of astronauts *Virginia Living* v15 no6 p23 O 2017

Schmidt, Mikolaj K.
Single-molecule optomechanics in "picocavities" bibl graph *Science* v354 no6313 p726 N 11 2016

SCHMIDT, NICOLE
Melts in Your Mouth cartoon *Walrus* p22 Ja\F 2017

Schmidt, Niels M.
Higher predation risk for insect prey at low latitudes and elevations graph *Science* v356 no6339 p742 My 19 2017

Schmidt, Oliver
Speedy Delivery C. Zuckerman color *National Geographic* v230 no4 p18 O 2016

SCHMIDT, PAUL
A Bird in the Hand color graph *Kiplinger's Personal Finance* v71 no2 p6 F 2017

Schmidt, Paul J.
UBE2O remodels the proteome during terminal erythroid differentiation diag *Science* v357 no6350 p471 Ag 4 2017

Schmidt, Philip
Do-It-Yourself OFF-GRID SOLAR: Explore the components and considerations for creating your own off-grid photovoltaic system *Mother Earth News* no282 p16 Je/Jl 2017

Schmidt, Richard
Ultrafast many-body interferometry of impurities coupled to a Fermi sea bibl diag graph *Science* v354 no6308 p96 O 7 2016

Schmidt, Robert
Greece's Least Wanted Man Lives in Maryland color *Bloomberg Businessweek* no4493 p25 O 3 2016
Hellllp! color *Bloomberg Businessweek* no4526 p22 Je 12 2017
A Hillary Fan Inside Trump's Treasury color *Bloomberg Businessweek* no4517 p30 Ap 3 2017
SEC's Acting Chair Acts Like He Runs the Place bw *Bloomberg Businessweek* no4512 p29 F 20 2017

Schmidt, Sarah
Forty Whacks? P. McGRATH *New York Times Book Review* p12 Ag 27 2017
The Unkillable Lizzie Borden L. Greenblatt color *Entertainment Weekly* no1477 p60 Ag 11 2017

Schmidt, Stephen D.
Trispecific broadly neutralizing HIV antibodies mediate potent SHIV protection in macaques color graph *Science* v357 no6359 p85 O 6 2017

Schmidt, Thomas M.
Neonatal acquisition of Clostridia species protects against colonization by bacterial pathogens diag *Science* v356 no6335 p315 Ap 21 2017

SCHMIDT, WOLFGANG
Combining Biodiversity Resurveys across Regions to Advance Global Change Research *BioScience* v67 no1 p73 Ja 2017

Schmidt-Traub, Guido
Global Fund lessons for Sustainable Development Goals color *Science* v356 no6333 p32 Ap 7 2017

Schmieder, Daniela
Acoustic mirrors as sensory traps for bats diag *Science* v357 no6355 p1045 S 8 2017

Schmitt, B.
Seasonal exposure of carbon dioxide ice on the nucleus of comet 67P/Churyumov-Gerasimenko bibl bw graph *Science* v354 no6319 p1563 D 23 2016

Schmitt, Douglas R.
The formation of peak rings in large impact craters bibl color graph *Science* v354 no6314 p878 N 18 2016

Schmitt, Gary
French Adoption color *Weekly Standard* v22 no44 p19 Jl 31 2017
Imperial Branches *Weekly Standard* v22 no24 p7 F 27 2017
A Military in Need color *Weekly Standard* v22 no32 p9 My 1 2017
Presidential Power color *Weekly Standard* v22 no21 p18 F 6 2017
Safe for Democracy color *Weekly Standard* v22 no33 p43 My 8 2017
Trump's Fake Defense Buildup color *Weekly Standard* v22 no26 p9 Mr 13 2017
An Uncertain Trumpet *Weekly Standard* v22 no17 p8 Ja 2 2017

Schmitt, Ian
Kona Honzo color *Bike Magazine* v24 no6 p118 Ag 2017

Schmitt, Kristen
This Is My Job color *Glamour* v115 no10 p132 O 2017

Schmitt, Mark
The Myth of the Powell Memo *Washington Monthly* p1 S/O 2016

Schmitt, Simon
Submillihertz magnetic spectroscopy performed with a nanoscale quantum sensor diag *Science* v356 no6340 p832 My 26 2017

Schmitt-Kopplin, Philippe
Dissolved organic sulfur in the ocean: Biogeochemistry of a petagram inventory bibl chart diag graph *Science* v354 no6311 p456 O 28 2016
Genomic databases: A WHO affair *Science* v356 no6340 p812 My 26 2017

Schmitz, Christoph
The Dirty Little Secret About Digitally Transforming Operations *Harvard Business Review Digital Articles* p2 My 31 2016

Schmitz, Sabrina
"My goal is to find the easiest way to look effortless and unique." bw color *Women's Health* v14 no3 p52 Ap 2017

Schnabel, Julian, 1951—Interviews
Q&A: Julian Schnabel B. POWERS bw color *ARTnews* v115 no4 p18 Wint 2016/2017

Schnabel, Landon
Jane Crow: The Life of Pauli Murray *Christian Century* v134 no22 p40 O 25 2017

Schnaidt, Mike
A Letter Opener bw *Men's Health* v32 no5 p140 Je 2017

Schnaithman, Tyler
10 UP & COMERS: TYLER SCHNAITHMAN J. Davey *Successful Farming* v115 no8 p34 Je/Jl 2017

Schnapp, Noah, 2004-
THINGS THAT GO BUMP IN THE NIGHT: They ain't afraid of no ghosts! Netflix's monster hit Stranger Things returns M. ROFFMAN *TV Guide* v65 no43 p22 O 16 2017

Schnapper, Dominique
Dominique Schnapper: The Democratic Spirit of Law W. Morrisey *Society* v53 no6 p672 D 2016

Schnatter, John
JOHN SCHNATTER color *Bloomberg Businessweek* no4525 p64 Je 5 2017

Schnebly, Sedona
A WOMAN BY THE NAME OF Sedona L. S. HEIDINGER *Arizona Highways* v93 no11 p48 N 2017

Schneeweiss, Zoe
France's Industrial Past Haunts Macron color *Bloomberg Businessweek* no4536 p44 S 4 2017

Schneider, Andrew
Belmont Blue Line Station *Architectural Record* v205 no4 p204 Ap 2017

Schneider, Christian
Synthesis of mixed hypermetallic oxide BaOCa+ from laser-cooled reagents in an atom-ion hybrid trap diag graph *Science* v357 no6358 p1370 S 29 2017

Schneider, David J.
Volcanic tremor and plume height hysteresis from Pavlof Volcano, Alaska bibl graph *Science* v355 no6320 p1 Ja 6 2017

Schneider, Diane L.

Strong BONES, Flat BELLY K. ASP color *Prevention* v69 no8 p70 Ag 2017

Schneider, Friedrich

Navigating the shadow economy: only the shadow knows A. M. Koehn *Monthly Labor Review* p1 Ap 2017

SCHNEIDER, HAYLEY

r.s.v.p bw *Bon Appetit* no11 p12 N 2017

SCHNEIDER, HOWARD

Nutshell *Humanist* v77 no1 p40 Ja/F 2017

Willoughbyland: England's Lost Colony *Humanist* v77 no3 p44 My/Je 2017

Schneider, Jack

The best of both worlds color *Phi Delta Kappan* v98 no3 p60 N 2016

Building a better measure of school quality color il *Phi Delta Kappan* v98 no7 p43 Ap 2017

Schneider, Jane

Farewell to the World's Smallest Tarantula? color *National Wildlife (World Edition)* v55 no6 p10 O/N 2017

SCHNEIDER, JARON

Get the Shot color *Backpacker* p61 Je 2017

Schneider, Joan

10 Tactics for Launching a Product Using Social Media *Harvard Business Review Digital Articles* p2 Ap 16 2015

How to Market to the iGeneration *Harvard Business Review Digital Articles* p2 My 6 2015

Schneider, Katy

Citi Bike HQ Has a Wall of Fame, With Many Leos img *New York* v49 no25 p52 D 12 2016

OBAMA'S AMERICA img *New York* v49 no20 p12 O 3 2016

Steal Their Weekends: Sick of your same old summer routine? Then take someone else's. We found dozens of opinionated locals to pick from img *New York* v50 no12 p63 Je 12 2017

Stores img *New York* v50 no17 p80 Ag 21 2017

SCHNEIDER, KIM

COLD COMFORT *Indianapolis Monthly* v40 no4 p46 D 2016

OUT OF THIS WORLD *Indianapolis Monthly* v40 no7 p36 Mr 2017

SCHNEIDER, LINDSAY

SHOOTING STARS bw *Vanity Fair* v59 no11 p69 N 2017

Schneider, Maria, 1960-

Chords & Discords V. SNIECKUS, H. DWYER et al color *Downbeat* v84 no7 p10 Jl 2017

MARIA SCHNEIDER ATTACKING THE 'DATA LORDS' [Cover story] A. MORRISON color *Downbeat* v83 no12 p26 D 2016

Schneider, Michael

Brothers in Comedy *TV Guide* v64 no15 p16 Ap 4 2016

Harvey Lands His Big Shot *TV Guide* v64 no15 p6 Ap 4 2016

Schneider, Nathan

THE $164 BILLION CO-OPS YOU DON'T KNOW ABOUT color *Nation* v304 no16 p26 My 22 2017

Adoration Economy color *America* v216 no7 p37 Ap 3 2017

Find Your Tribe *America* v215 p14 N 28 2016

HOW COMMUNISTS AND CATHOLICS BUILT A COMMONWEALTH color *America* v217 no6 p18 S 18 2017

An Internet of Our Own *Nation* v303 no18 p4 O 31 2016

A Neglected Order *America* v215 no11 p12 O 17 2016

Schneider, Paul

The SAILING SCENE color *Sail* v48 no7 p6 Jl 2017

Schneider, Rachel

We Tracked Every Dollar 235 U.S. Households Spent for a Year, and Found Widespread Financial Vulnerability *Harvard Business Review Digital Articles* p2 Ap 12 2017

Schneider, Romy, 1938-1982

TORY BURCH'S Icons M. Robin color *InStyle* v24 no3 p264 Mr 2017

Schneider, Sara

BAJA ON FIRE color *Sunset* v239 no4 p70 O 2017

THE BEST WINES OF THE YEAR color *Sunset* v239 no4 p94 O 2017

BROWN LIQUOR FRIDAYS color *Sunset* v237 no5 p93 N 2016

CALIFORNIA'S BEST-KEPT SECRETS color *Sunset* v238 no3 p86 Mr 2017

EVERYDAY ROSÉ color *Sunset* v238 no5 p98 My 2017

LODI LEADS color *Sunset* v239 no3 p102 S 2017

THE NEW APERITIF color *Sunset* v238 no2 p90 F 2017

RETURN OF THE KING color *Sunset* v239 no1 p102 Jl 2017

A SHOP OF YOUR OWN color *Sunset* v238 no4 p98 Ap 2017

SO YOU WANT TO BE A WINEMAKER? color *Sunset* v238 no1 p92 Ja 2017

SUMMER WHITES color *Sunset* v238 no6 p100 Je 2017

SUPER BOTTLES color *Sunset* v237 no6 p100 D 2016

Schneider, Simon

4 Mistakes That Kill Crowdsourcing Efforts *Harvard Business Review Digital Articles* p2 Jl 21 2017

Stop Treating B2B Customers Like Digital Novices *Harvard Business Review Digital Articles* p2 My 10 2016

Schneider, Stephen

Imaginary Mary I. Ratledge *TV Guide* v65 no13 p26 Mr 20 2017

Schneider, William F.

Dynamic multinuclear sites formed by mobilized copper ions in NOx selective catalytic reduction bw color diag graph *Science* v357 no6354 p898 S 1 2017

Schneiderinan, Jill S.

Against all odds bibl color *Science* v354 no6312 p559 N 4 2016

Schneiderman, Eric T., 1954-

73 MINUTES WITH ... Eric Schneiderman A. RICE img *New York* v50 no10 p22 My 15 2017

Schneidewind, Eric J.

AARP Is Good for Your Brain Health *AARP: The Magazine* v59 no5A p75 Ag/S 2016

Fight Isolation With Kindness and Tech color *AARP: The Magazine* v60 no1A p61 D 2016/Ja 2017

Harvey Response: 'That's What We're All About' *AARP: The Magazine* v30 no6A p73 O/N 2017

Help AARP Help Family Caregivers *AARP: The Magazine* v59 no6A p76 O/N 2016

Help Make America Compassionate Again *AARP: The Magazine* v60 no5A p67 Ag/S 2017

I Leave You With These Challenges for Society color *AARP: The Magazine* v59 no4A p69 Je/Jl 2016

Planning to Live to 100? Volunteer! *AARP: The Magazine* v60 no4A p65 Je/Jl 2017

Tell Congress: Don't Mess With Medicare *AARP: The Magazine* v60 no3A p71 Ap/My 2017

We Can Improve Our Long-Term Care *AARP: The Magazine* v60 no2A p79 F/Mr 2017

SCHNEIER, BRUCE

BOTNETS of Things chart color map *MIT Technology Review* v120 no2 p88 Mr/Ap 2017

SCHNEIER, MATTHEW

VANITY FAIR color *New York Times Book Review* p61 D 4 2016

Schnell, Lindsay

9 GONZAGA BULLDOGS chart color *Sports Illustrated* v125 no15 p68 N 7 2016

BLOWING UP THE BCS color *Sports Illustrated* v125 no19 p52 D 12 2016

Budda's DELIGHT color *Sports Illustrated* v125 no18 p50 D 5 2016

The Case for ... Athletes In Office color *Sports Illustrated* v125 no15 p28 N 7 2016

CASE FOR ... WASHINGTON color *Sports Illustrated* v125 no19 p39 D 12 2016

OFF TO THE RACES color *Sports Illustrated* v125 no15 p48 N 7 2016

OUTSIDE JOB color *Sports Illustrated* v126 no8 p46 Mr 20 2017

Schnell, Mattheas

The XIT Ranch B. Welch bw color *American Cowboy* p88 LEGENDS OF TEXAS Special Issue 2017

SCHNELLER, J. JAKOB

Sex and the Single Gametophyte: Revising the Homosporous Vascular Plant Life Cycle in Light of Contemporary Research *BioScience* v66 no11 p928 N 1 2016

Schnetzer, Ben, 1990-

Ben SCHNETZER M. MARTIN *Interview* v46 no8 p30 O 2016

Schniederjans, Ollie

Watch + Learn S. Foley and C. Barrett color *Golf Magazine* v59 no6 p26 Je 2017

Schniederjans, Ollie—Interviews

Hats Off to Ollie P. Madden and C. Barrett color *Golf Magazine* v59 no5 p27 My 2017

Schnittger, Arp
RETINOBLASTOMA RELATED1 mediates germline entry in Arabidopsis color diag *Science* v356 no6336 p396 Ap 28 2017

Schnitzler, Jan
Merging paleobiology with conservation biology to guide the future of terrestrial ecosystems color *Science* v355 no6325 p594 F 10 2017

Schnitzler, Nicole
CAKES, PASTRIES, PIES, COOKIES, HOT FUDGE, GALATO, BROWNIES & MORE! chart color *Chicago* v65 no11 p70 N 2016
TREND: NO LONGER JUST A SANDWICH color *Chicago* v66 no9 p64 S 2017

Schnitzspahn, Doug
In Deep color *Backpacker* p10 Je 2017
Winterize Your Workouts color *Men's Health* v31 no10 p45 D 2016

Schnoor, Craig
THE FARM *Successful Farming* v115 no11 p75 S 2017

Schnorr, Kirsten
Femtosecond x-ray spectroscopy of an electrocyclic ring-opening reaction diag graph *Science* v356 no6333 p54 Ap 7 2017

Schnuer, Jenna
BECAUSE DOGS LOVE WINTER, TOO color *Rodale's Organic Life* v2 no7 p16 D 2016/Ja 2017

Schobesberger, Siegfried
Global atmospheric particle formation from CERN CLOUD measurements bibl graph map *Science* v354 no6316 p1119 D 2 2016

Schock Boats (Company)
PRETTY IN PLATINUM C. D. MIRANDA *Sea Magazine* v108 no10 pCA-4 O 2016

Schoemer, Nate
This New Animal Planet Show Will Make You Weep C. Collis color *Entertainment Weekly* no1478 / 1479 p90 Ag 18-25 2017

Schoen, Douglas E.
AMERICA'S RELENTLESS SUITOR J. J. Pitney Jr. *Claremont Review of Books* v16 no4 p22 Fall 2016
Cold War Redux J. FUND color *National Review* v68 no20 p44 N 7 2016

Schoenberg, Arnold, 1874-1951
Applying 12-Tone Rows to Bass, Guitar J. DURSO color diag *Downbeat* v84 no7 p76 Jl 2017

Schoenberg, Tom
The Fall Guy bw *Bloomberg Businessweek* no4523 p24 My 22 2017
LEGAL JEOPARDY bw color *Bloomberg Businessweek* no4541 p35 O 9 2017
Mueller's Dream Team Gears Up bw *Bloomberg Businessweek* no4527 p46 Je 19 2017
The Other Wall Trump Hasn't Built color *Bloomberg Businessweek* no4534 p34 Ag 14 2017
What's Jeff Sessions Up To? color *Bloomberg Businessweek* no4529 p34 Jl 3 2017

SCHOENBERGER, LEONARD
Old World, Young Promise color *Forbes* v199 no1 p20 Ja 24 2017
THE WORLD'S BILLIONAIRES bw color diag graph map *Forbes* v199 no3 p84 Mr 28 2017

Schoenbrod, David
Cover Your Acts S. BANGALORE PRAKASH bw *Weekly Standard* v22 no40 p32 Je 26 2017

Schoenenberger, P.
Superficial layers of the medial entorhinal cortex replay independently of the hippocampus bibl graph *Science* v355 no6321 p1 Ja 13 2017

Schoenfeld, Bruce
Beyond Relief: Managers rarely use their closers—often the most dominant pitchers in baseball—for more than a few outs at the end of the game. Is that beginning to change? *New York Times Magazine* p42 O 1 2017
CAN THE EMERGENCE OF A HIGH-TECH TOOL BRING BASE BALL'S STATISTICAL REVOLUTION TO FIELDING? *New York Times Magazine* p48 O 2 2016
THE JUSTICE LEAGUE bw color *Esquire* p90 N 2017

SCHOENFELD, GABRIEL
The Enigma Machine *Weekly Standard* v22 no22 p30 F 13 2017
Remember Malmedy bw *Weekly Standard* v22 no39 p36 Je 19

2017

Schoenfeld, Heather
How Do You Get Ideologues to Change Their Minds? *Washington Monthly* p1 S/O 2016

Schoenfeld, Nook
See Clearly *Stage Directions* v29 no12 p20 D 2016
Show Offs *Stage Directions* v29 no12 p6 D 2016

Schoenfelder, Pat
SHOWCASE SHOTS color *Nebraska Life* v21 no2 p80 Mr/Ap 2017

Schoening, Janne
Red squirrels in the British Isles are infected with leprosy bacilli bibl color diag map *Science* v354 no6313 p744 N 11 2016

Schoenlein-Henoch purpura—Case studies
The rash formed rings around the young boy's ankles, and his joints hurt. Was it an allergy? L. Sanders *New York Times Magazine* p18 Jl 9 2017

Schoeppner, Michael
Nuclear safety regulation in the post-Fukushima era color *Science* v356 no6340 p808 My 26 2017

Schofield, Daniel
BEST of TIMES WORST of TIMES cartoon *Esquire* v166 no5 p138 D 2016/Ja 2017

SCHOFIELD, OSCAR
Responses of Antarctic Marine and Freshwater Ecosystems to Changing Ice Conditions color graph *BioScience* v66 no10 p864 O 1 2016

Schofler, Patti
Hail to the MARES color *Dressage Today* v23 no11 p28 Ag 2017
Producing The FINEST color *Dressage Today* v23 no8 p58 Ap 2017

Scholarly periodical corrections
Rethinking the dreaded r-word M. Enserink *Science* v356 no6342 p998 Je 9 2017

Scholarly periodicals
IN REFEREES WE TRUST? M. Baldwin *Physics Today* v70 no2 p44 F 2017

Scholarly publishing
See also
University presses
Can Apple Attract Top Researchers If It Keeps Their Research Secret? W. Frick *Harvard Business Review Digital Articles* p2 N 2 2015
New Titles from Chinese Academic Presses T. TAN *Publishers Weekly* v264 no39 p(Sp)28 S 25 2017

Scholarly publishing—China
The Academic Book Market in China T. TAN color *Publishers Weekly* v264 no39 p(Sp)3 S 25 2017
Beijing Jiaotong University Press color *Publishers Weekly* v264 no39 p(Sp)8 S 25 2017
Beijing Normal University Press Group color *Publishers Weekly* v264 no39 p(Sp)10 S 25 2017
Chongqing University Press color *Publishers Weekly* v264 no39 p(Sp)12 S 25 2017
East China Normal University Press color *Publishers Weekly* v264 no39 p(Sp)14 S 25 2017
Guangxi Normal University Press Group color *Publishers Weekly* v264 no39 p(Sp)16 S 25 2017
Hot Topics in Chinese Academic Publishing T. TAN *Publishers Weekly* v264 no39 p(Sp)26 S 25 2017
Shaanxi Normal University General Publishing House color *Publishers Weekly* v264 no39 p(Sp)18 S 25 2017
Social Sciences Academic Press color *Publishers Weekly* v264 no39 p(Sp)20 S 25 2017
Xi'an Jiaotong University Press color *Publishers Weekly* v264 no39 p(Sp)22 S 25 2017

Scholars
See also
Historians
History's FIRST DRAFT J. MEACHAM, S. SCHIFF et al color *Vanity Fair* v59 no10 p158 O 2017
What Are Libraries For? T. MARKATOS bw color *Weekly Standard* v23 no6 p36 O 16 2017

Scholarships
See also
Athletic scholarships

ALL THE PLACES YOU CAN GO TO COLLEGE FOR FREE K. Mulhere color *Money* v46 no9 p82 O 2017

Architectural Record Traveling Fellowships Awarded to Lea Oxenhandler and Benjamin Halpern D. COHEN color *Architectural Record* v205 no8 p20 Ag 2017

BENEFITS AND AWARDS *Phi Kappa Phi Forum* v97 no1 p35 Spr 2017

BENEFITS AND AWARDS *Phi Kappa Phi Forum* v97 no2 p35 Summ 2017

Chile unprepared for Ph.D. influx N. S. Morales and I. C. Fernández *Science* v356 no6343 p1131 Je 16 2017

HANGING ONTO HOPE H. M. CAULEY *Atlanta* v56 no11 p124 Mr 2017

INSPIRATION, REWARDED M. CAMPBELL color *Maclean's* v130 no10 p74 N 2017

noted graph *Architectural Record* v204 no12 p20 D 2016

PDK Connection color *Phi Delta Kappan* v98 no7 p79 Ap 2017

Research on a razor's edge E. Dexter *Science* v356 no6342 p1094 Je 9 2017

TALK color graph *Horse & Rider* v56 no2 p16 F 2017

Traband Receives Hamel Scholarship *In Stride* v12 no5 p10 S 2017

Scholarships—Government policy

Suing Choice Away J. BEDRICK *National Review* v68 no19 p35 O 24 2016

Scholarships—United States

D.C. Opportunity Scholarship Program: Impacts of a Federally Funded School Voucher Program *Congressional Digest* v96 no7 p7 S 2017

Scholarships—Universities & colleges

Not just for super geniuses V. GALT color *Maclean's* v130 no10 p68 N 2017

Scholastic Inc.

Scholastic Aims to Improve Profits J. Milliot chart color *Publishers Weekly* v264 no30 p5 Jl 24 2017

Scholberg, K.

Observation of coherent elastic neutrino-nucleus scattering diag *Science* v357 no6356 p1123 S 15 2017

SCHOLES, LUCY

Missed Connections: Four troubled characters face London's summer of bombs *New York Times Magazine* p10 Ap 30 2017

Scholten, F.

Rosetta's comet 67P/Churyumov-Gerasimenko sheds its dusty mantle to reveal its icy nature bibl graph *Science* v354 no6319 p1566 D 23 2016

Surface changes on comet 67P/Churyumov-Gerasimenko suggest a more active past bw graph *Science* v355 no6332 p1392 Mr 31 2017

Scholten, O.

Observation of a large-scale anisotropy in the arrival directions of cosmic rays above 8×1018 eV *Science* v357 no6357 p1266 S 22 2017

Scholz, B. J.

Observation of coherent elastic neutrino-nucleus scattering diag *Science* v357 no6356 p1123 S 15 2017

SCHOLZ, LAURA

Come on in... *Atlanta* v57 no2 p37 Je 2017

FIGHT CLUB *Atlanta* v57 no6 p46 O 2017

FIT FOR FREE *Atlanta* v57 no1 p40 My 2017

SCOUT ABOUT TOWN *Atlanta* v56 no12 p44 Ap 2017

Schölzel, Daniel

Fibril structure of amyloid-β(1–42) by cryo–electron microscopy color diag *Science* v357 no6359 p116 O 6 2017

Schombs, Matthew W.

Posttranslational mutagenesis: A chemical strategy for exploring protein side-chain diversity diag *Science* v354 no6312 p597 N 4 2016

Schonbek, Amelia

...AND NINE THEY NEED TO PROTECT *New York* v50 no7 p31 Ap 3 2017

TO UNDERSTAND THIS NEW RIGHT, IT HELPS TO SEE IT NOT AS A FRINGE MOVEMENT, BUT A POWERFUL COUNTERCULTURE img *New York* v50 no9 p24 My 1 2017

What'll it be FOR THE NEW YORK DINER? img *New York* v50 no13 p30 Je 26 2017

Schöngart, J.

Persistent effects of pre-Columbian plant domestication on Amazonian forest composition bibl chart graph map *Science* v355 no6328 p925 Mr 3 2017

School administration

See also

Medical school administration

Race relations in school management

School discipline

Sci High Flies High D. R. WILSON color *New Orleans Magazine* v51 no12 p40 O 2017

SUMMER BRAIN DRAIN: FIND A FUN WAY TO HELP YOUR KIDS KEEP THEIR MINDS ENGAGED ONCE SCHOOL IS OUT color *Successful Farming* v115 no7 p60 My 2017

School administration—Colorado

DeVos vs. Denver A. Greenblatt *Governing* v30 no9 p10 Je 2017

School administration—Finance

Spending dollars to make a difference J. P. STARR color *Phi Delta Kappan* v98 no5 p72 F 2017

School administration—United States

Improve governance for charters C. E. Finn, B. V. Manno et al *Phi Delta Kappan* v98 no6 p63 Mr 2017

School administrators

See also

School principals

School superintendents

This Is My Job J. Militare color *Glamour* no8 p114 Ag 2017

School administrators—Great Britain

The One Type of Leader Who Can Turn Around a Failing School A. Hill, L. Mellon et al bw color *Harvard Business Review Digital Articles* p2 O 20 2016

School admission

7 common questions about applying for college: Advice from parents, dancers, and directors A. RIVERS *Dance Magazine* v90 p12 2016/2017 Supplement College Guide

INQUIRING MINDS: CFI schools, open-air conventions, and Holliday Park ruins. Ask the Hoosierist S. STALL *Indianapolis Monthly* v12 no40 p18 Ag 2017

NEW LIFE LESSONS J. GEDDES color *Maclean's* v130 no4 p35 My 2017

School Choice, Beijing Edition D. Roberts color *Bloomberg Businessweek* no4526 p15 Je 12 2017

School autonomy

Self-governing schools, parental choice, and the need to protect the public interest E. B. Fiske and H. F. Ladd *Phi Delta Kappan* v99 no1 p31 S 2017

School boards—Congresses

Speak freely to the school board J. UNDERWOOD color *Phi Delta Kappan* v98 no5 p76 F 2017

School boards—United States

Leadership J. P. Starr *Phi Delta Kappan* v99 no1 p40 S 2017

School building design & construction

Is Design to Blame When a School Underperforms? A. FIXSEN color *Architectural Record* v205 no5 p30 My 2017

Southern Revival B. BROOME *Architectural Record* v205 no7 p80 Jl 2017

School buildings

See also

Classrooms

Class Dismissed *Arizona Highways* v93 no6 p56 Je 2017

History lessonend E. H. Gustafson color *Magazine Antiques* v184 no4 p128 Jl/Ag 2017

School buildings—Design & construction

The Big Idea M. COCKRAM *Architectural Record* v205 no1 p70 Ja 2017

A Bright Future C. FOGES *Architectural Record* v205 no1 p78 Ja 2017

Building Confidence L. RASKIN *Architectural Record* v205 no1 p90 Ja 2017

Hip to be Square M. PEPCHINSKI *Architectural Record* v205 no1 p106 Ja 2017

A Measure of Harmony M. PEPCHINSKI color diag *Architectural Record* v205 no3 p72 Mr 2017

Out of the Woods A. FIXSEN *Architectural Record* v205 no1 p84 Ja 2017

Raising the Grade J. M. MCKNIGHT *Architectural Record* v205 no1 p96 Ja 2017

Safe Havens K. Logan *Architectural Record* v205 no1 p112 Ja 2017

SCHOOLS OF THE 21ST CENTURY *Architectural Record* v205 no1 p69 Ja 2017

Springs Forward: Major transformation continues *Successful Farming* v115 no1 p38 Ja 2017

School buildings—Remodeling

CAUSE & EFFECT C. Shanahan color *InStyle* v24 no3 p138 Mr 2017

LESSON PLAN F. A. BERNSTEIN color *Architectural Digest* v73 no11 p84 N 2016

School buildings—Remodeling for other use

The Residences at P.S. 186 *Architectural Record* v205 no4 p196 Ap 2017

School buildings—United States

Holt County's Christmas Lesson P. B. KARO cartoon *Nebraska Life* v20 no6 p48 N/D 2016

School bullying

Anti-Bullying Buddies J. Chen color *Good Housekeeping* v265 no2 p67 Ag 2017

School Bullying Linked to Lower Academic Achievement cartoon *Education Digest* v82 no8 p53 Ap 2017

School bullying—Social aspects

Bully, Bully cartoon *Weekly Standard* v22 no29 p3 Ap 3 2017

School buses

STUCK IN THE ORANGE WHALE W. DUFFIELD *South Dakota Magazine* v32 no6 p96 Mr/Ap 2017

School camps

CAMP AND SCHOOL PROFILES 2017 *Washingtonian Magazine* v52 no5 p121 F 2017

CAMP AVID S. MaHan *Washingtonian Magazine* v52 no5 p117 F 2017

School children

See also
Kindergarten children

10 THINGS WE'RE TALKING ABOUT T. A. Christian color *Essence* v48 no6 p79 O 2017

2017 BACK-TO-SCHOOL GUIDE K. ROCKWOOD color *Good Housekeeping* v265 no3 p139 S 2017

GET SMART: WHEN DECIDING WHICH SCHOOL IS THE BEST FIT FOR YOUR FAMILY, THESE ARE JUST A FEW VARIABLES TO CONSIDER N. CROWE *Indianapolis Monthly* p102 N 2017

Get Your Kid Moving *Parents* p46 2015

Movement and learning in elementary school S. F. Lindt and S. C. Miller color *Phi Delta Kappan* v98 no7 p34 Ap 2017

This Week in Trumpoplexy color *Weekly Standard* v22 no20 p3 Ja 30 2017

School children—China

I-Spy in China: a revival of Mao-era paranoia? V. Yu color *America* v216 no12 p16 My 29 2017

School children—Food—United States

Good Food Rising A. Lappé color *Earth Island Journal* v32 no4 p13 Wint 2017

School children—United States

Islamic Schools for a Changing World: Are Islamic schools preparing their students to function effectively in a rapidly changing world? F. M. KHATRI *Islamic Horizons* v46 no4 p24 Jl/Ag 2017

School choice

FROM THE ARCHIVES cartoon *Reason* v48 no9 p70 F 2017

THE PLEASE *Texas Monthly* v45 no2 p88 F 2017

THE RIGHT SCHOOL H. M. CAULEY *Atlanta* v56 no7 p110 N 2016

Self-governing schools, parental choice, and the need to protect the public interest E. B. Fiske and H. F. Ladd *Phi Delta Kappan* v99 no1 p31 S 2017

Where School Choice Is a Way of Life G. NORMAN color *Weekly Standard* v22 no21 p20 F 6 2017

School choice—Law & legislation

Legislative Background on School Choice: Recent Action by Congress on Funding for Private Education *Congressional Digest* v96 no7 p11 S 2017

School Choice *Congressional Digest* v96 no1 p16 Ja 2017

School choice—Lawsuits & claims

Suing Choice Away J. BEDRICK *National Review* v68 no19 p35

O 24 2016

School choice—United States

Betsy DeVos and the Segregation of School Choice M. Wilkerson *Education Digest* v82 no8 p19 Ap 2017

FREE EXERCISE S. E. ZYLSTRA color *Christianity Today* v61 no7 p15 S 2017

The Pros and Cons of Federally Funded School Choice Programs B. DeVos, P. Murray et al *Congressional Digest* v96 no7 p12 S 2017

School Choice 2017-2018 Policy Debate Topic *Congressional Digest* v96 no7 p2 S 2017

School Choice *Congressional Digest* v96 no1 p16 Ja 2017

Teachers Union Head Casts School Choice as Racism S. Shackford color *Reason* v49 no5 p14 O 2017

The Unionista L. SAND il *National Review* v68 no19 p33 O 24 2016

School choice—United States—Law & legislation

School choice and the common good *America* v216 no4 p8 F 20 2017

School closings

Michigan Shuts Down Bad Schools. Leading States Build Them Up C. P. DAWSEY *Education Digest* v82 no9 p34 My 2017

School directors

THE ROLE OF THE FAMILY L. Deloza color *Literacy Today (2411-7862)* v34 no5 p24 Mr/Ap 2017

School discipline

The shame of shaming J. F. Goodman color *Phi Delta Kappan* v99 no2 p26 O 2017

School discipline—United States

How America Outlawed Adolescence A. RIPLEY bw color *Atlantic* v318 no4 p86 N 2016

LEFT BEHIND R. Clarren color *Nation* v305 no4 p12 Ag 14 2017

School discipline—United States—Law & legislation

School Discipline Reform and Disorder M. Eden *Education Digest* v83 no1 p22 S 2017

School districts

Black History, Black Future K. Kyles *Ebony* v72 no4 p16 F 2017

Few Women Run the Nation's School Districts. Why? D. R. SUPERVILLE *Education Digest* v82 no6 p14 F 2017

Leadership J. P. Starr *Phi Delta Kappan* v98 no4 p72 D 2016/Ja 2017

School Districts in the Northeast Are Most Likely To Serve Local Foods on a Daily Basis J. Hyman and K. Ralston *Amber Waves: The Economics of Food, Farming, Natural Resources, & Rural America* p1 My 2017

School districts—California

Change for a Dollar? B. Whalen *Hoover Digest: Research & Opinion on Public Policy* no1 p180 Wint 2017

A Southern California District Resists Bad Education Policy J. Bryant color *Progressive* v81 no6 p40 Ag/S 2017

School districts—Colorado

DeVos vs. Denver A. Greenblatt *Governing* v30 no9 p10 Je 2017

School districts—Management

FAMILY L. Foust Prater *Successful Farming* v114 no11 p62 N 2016

School districts—New York (State)

GO FORTH AND READ: How one Long Island school district started a literacy movement in its community J. Keegan, D. Provvido et al color *Literacy Today (2411-7862)* v34 no6 p36 My/Je 2017

School districts—United States

Aligned Transitions T. J. PACE and J. J. GARCIA *Education Digest* v82 no5 p12 Ja 2017

School elections

Chartering the Course D. Ruth Wilson color *New Orleans Magazine* v51 no5 p32 Mr 2017

The Little School District That Could E. Gunn bw color *Progressive* v81 no3 p20 Mr 2017

School environment

See also
School bullying

NOTE FROM THE SENIOR EDITOR. THE VRG INTERN EXPERIENCE S. Gendler *Vegetarian Journal* v35 no1 p4 2016

Student Success Built on a Positive School Climate L. WARNER and P. HEINDEL *Education Digest* v82 no7 p10 Mr 2017

School environment—United States

Highlighted & Underlined bw chart color graph il *Phi Delta Kappan* v98 no6 p6 Mr 2017

Taking care of ourselves and others L. Nazareno and A. Krafel color *Phi Delta Kappan* v98 no6 p25 Mr 2017

School failure

Will Eliminating the 'F' Eliminate Bad School Design? J. F. FISHER *Education Digest* v82 no4 p47 D 2016

School field trips—Finance

Money for Class Trips *New York State Conservationist* v71 no4 p28 F 2017

School field trips—Social aspects

FIELD TRIP TO RIKERS E. W. SCHMIDT *America* v215 no18 p32 D 5 2016

School gardens

WEST COUNTY DIGS: Sowing Stewardship K. MONTANA color *Earth Island Journal* v32 no1 p15 Spr 2017

School gardens—Social aspects

GROWING LEADERS S. HENRY *Sierra* v101 no5 p44 S/O 2016

School improvement programs—United States

Using data wisely at the system level M. Lockwood, M. Dillman et al chart color *Phi Delta Kappan* v99 no1 p25 S 2017

School integration—Mississippi

OVERDUE ASSIGNMENTS color *Mother Jones* v42 no5 p16 S/O 2017

REUNION E. RIOS color *Mother Jones* v42 no6 p6 N/D 2017

School integration—United States

GUESS WHO'S COMING TO KINDERGARTEN P. Wall *Mother Jones* v42 no5 p17 S/O 2017

How School Desegregation Unraveled L. HANCOCK bw color *Nation* v303 no19 p16 N 7 2016

School involvement

Highlighted & Underlined color graph *Phi Delta Kappan* v98 no4 p6 D 2016/Ja 2017

School librarians

POWERFUL PARTNERSHIPS: Literacy, your librarian, and you J. K. Valenza and M. A. Scheuer *Literacy Today (2411-7862)* v35 no1 p14 Jl/Ag 2017

School libraries—Illinois

EveryLibrary, Follett Partner to Save School Librarians S. MAUGHAN color *Publishers Weekly* v264 no34 p56 Ag 21 2017

School libraries—Louisiana

A WAVE OF GENEROSITY: Just one example of how the ILA network and book lovers everywhere helped restore libraries--and hope T. Veazey color *Literacy Today (2411-7862)* v34 no6 p42 My/Je 2017

School music

Why Johnny Can't Sing, Dance, Saw, or Bake J. BERCKEMEYER *Education Digest* v82 no4 p25 D 2016

School music—Instruction & study (Early childhood)

Serve and return: Communication foundations for early childhood music policy stakeholders A. M. Reynolds and S. L. Burton bibl *Arts Education Policy Review* v118 no3 p140 2017

School name changes

Change for a Dollar? B. Whalen *Hoover Digest: Research & Opinion on Public Policy* no1 p180 Wint 2017

School of Rock (Theatrical production)

SCHOOL OF ROCK TEACHES US TO BREAK THE MOLD G. Holt *Cincinnati Magazine* v50 no8 p14 My 2017

School plant management

Q+A J. Gilbert *Cincinnati Magazine* v50 no3 p38 D 2016

School police

Atlanta Schools Start Over with Police E. BLAD *Education Digest* v82 no8 p38 Ap 2017

WHY ARE COPS PUTTING KIDS IN CUFFS? R. SOAVE and T. KOTESKEY color *Reason* v48 no10 p46 Mr 2017

School prayer—Law & legislation

PRAYING FOR CLARITY D. B. MOSKOWITZ bw *American History* v52 no2 p26 Je 2017

School principals

This Is My Job J. Militare color *Glamour* no8 p114 Ag 2017

School principals—Interviews

Q&A: The Interview color *Maclean's* v130 no9 p53 O 2017

School principals—United States

The Challenge of Being a Black Principal in Today's Racial and

Political Climate L. Khan *Education Digest* v82 no4 p4 D 2016

School recess breaks

5 Fantastic Ideas *Scholastic Choices* pT1 S 2017 Supplement

Debate: Do Teens Need Recess? *Scholastic Choices* pT3 S 2017 Supplement

Do Teens Need Recess? *Scholastic Choices* v33 no1 p2 S 2017

Why Kids Need Recess A. WONG color *Atlantic* v318 no5 p22 D 2016

School safety

ARGYLE, TEXAS S. Johnson *Harper's Magazine* p29 O 2017

School shootings

A Prayer For Our Daily Murder B. Doyle color *U.S. Catholic* v82 no2 p22 F 2017

School shootings—Virginia

See also

Virginia Tech shootings, Blacksburg, Va., 2007

VIRGINIA TECH, TEN YEARS LATER B. PETERSON color *Washingtonian Magazine* v52 no7 p69 Ap 2017

School sports

See also

College sports

FACES IN THE CROWD T. Keith color *Sports Illustrated* v125 no13 p20 O 17 2016

Win GAME DAY C. CHASE color *Seventeen* v75 no11 p65 N 2016

School superintendents

Leadership J. P. Starr *Phi Delta Kappan* v98 no7 p72 Ap 2017

One State's School Duel *Governing* v30 no8 p12 My 2017

the Unifier d. ruth wilson color *New Orleans Magazine* v51 no3 p84 Ja 2017

School-to-work transition

5 Ways to Make the Most of College E. Y. REITZ *Christianity Today* p68 Mr 2017

From College to Career: The Struggle Is Real E. Y. Reitz color *Christianity Today* p63 Mr 2017

School uniforms

Should Schools Have Dress Codes? *New York Times Upfront* v149 no8 p22 Ja 30 2017

School vacations

See also

Summer vacations (Schools)

THE REAL SUMMER EXPERIENCE: Going beyond the vacation essay to foster deeper school-community relationships M. P. Ghiso and G. Campano *Literacy Today (2411-7862)* v35 no1 p8 Jl/Ag 2017

School's Out for... the Masters?! M. Bamberger color *Golf Magazine* v59 no4 p140 Ap 2017

School violence

See also

School shootings

A Prayer For Our Daily Murder B. Doyle color *U.S. Catholic* v82 no2 p22 F 2017

School volunteers

Orchestrating a new approach to learning M. Kaplan color *Phi Delta Kappan* v98 no7 p23 Ap 2017

School year

Washington View M. Ferguson diag *Phi Delta Kappan* v98 no4 p74 D 2016/Ja 2017

Schoolbags—Evaluation

Best in Class color *Martha Stewart Living* p26 S 2017

Schoolhouse Electric & Supply Co.

BRIGHT IDEAS: The perfect pendant lights are like jewelry for your kitchen. Here are a few of our favorites F. Stephanie *Washingtonian Magazine* v53 no1 p157 O 2017

School lunchrooms, cafeterias, etc.—Environmental aspects

THE CLIQUE THAT'S CHANGING HOW SCHOOLKIDS EAT C. LEU *Sierra* v101 no5 p46 S/O 2016

Schools

See also

Charter schools

Cooking schools

Dance schools

Disadvantaged schools

Elementary schools

Flight schools

Music conservatories

Preschools
Private schools
Public schools
Riding schools
Rural schools
Schools of architecture
Theater schools
Universities & colleges

ALWAYS A STUDENT E. Graves color *Martha Stewart Living* p8 S 2017

bus behavior R. DELANEY *Parents* v91 no9 p170 S 2016

THE FOUNDATION of It All *Literacy Today (2411-7862)* v35 no1 p43 Jl/Ag 2017

History lessonend E. H. Gustafson color *Magazine Antiques* v184 no4 p128 Jl/Ag 2017

let's get real *Parents* v91 no9 p79 S 2016

No Janitor, No Lunch K. WRIGHT *Idaho Magazine* v16 no3 p12 D 2016

play school *Parents* v91 no9 p74 S 2016

SCHOOLS Around the world cartoon color map *Seventeen* v75 no11 p98 N 2016

SCHOOL'S OUT P. STEFÁNSSON *Iceland Review* v55 no3 p76 My/Je 2017

SCHOOL UNIFORMS WE WISH EXISTED *Parents* v91 no9 p104 S 2016

TEAMWORK CITY OF HOPE C. MURPHY color *Vanity Fair* v59 no8 p83 Ag 2017

Understanding Academic Language and its Connection to School Success C. FRIEDBERG, A. MITCHELL et al *Education Digest* v82 no6 p58 F 2017

Schools & the environment

COOL SCHOOLS 2017 K. O'Reilly *Sierra* v102 no5 p41 St/O 2017

TOP OF THEIR CLASS *Sierra* v102 no5 p42 St/O 2017

Schools of architecture

ARCHITECTURE EDUCATION NOW *Architectural Record* v205 no9 p71 S 2017

Schools—Admission

See also

Early admission (School)
Universities & colleges—Admission

CAMP AND SCHOOL PROFILES 2017 *Washingtonian Magazine* v52 no5 p121 F 2017

GETTING IN H. M. CAULEY *Atlanta* v56 no7 p112 N 2016

THE RIGHT SCHOOL H. M. CAULEY *Atlanta* v56 no7 p110 N 2016

Schools—Communication systems—Research

Learn to Ad: Madison Avenue Strategies to Strengthen School Communication B. CASTLEMAN and J. SKILLMAN *Education Digest* v82 no6 p34 F 2017

Schools—Environmental aspects

THE 10 COOLEST SCHOOL 10 YEARS ON A. Andrews *Sierra* v101 no5 p39 S/O 2016

Schools—Furniture, equipment, etc.

Work Wonders *Martha Stewart Living* no267 p22 S 2016

Schools—Illinois

Classes of Kindergarteners F. M. HESS and G. ADDISON il *National Review* v69 no19 p36 O 16 2017

Schools—Indiana

THE BRIDGE TO COLLEGE N. CROWE color *Indianapolis Monthly* v41 no2 p144 S 2017

GET SMART: WHEN DECIDING WHICH SCHOOL IS THE BEST FIT FOR YOUR FAMILY, THESE ARE JUST A FEW VARIABLES TO CONSIDER N. CROWE *Indianapolis Monthly* p102 N 2017

LET'S START AT THE VERY BEGINNING S. HELD color *Indianapolis Monthly* v41 no2 p138 S 2017

Schools—Psychological aspects

class wars J. MANN *Parents* v92 no1 p78 Ja 2017

Schools—Ratings & rankings

Alexina Medley D. R. WILSON *New Orleans Magazine* v52 no1 p38 S 2017

ARCHITECTURE EDUCATION NOW *Architectural Record* v205 no9 p71 S 2017

Schools—Safety measures

Safe Havens K. Logan *Architectural Record* v205 no1 p112 Ja

2017

Schools—Social aspects

The Role of the School G. A. GOENS *USA Today Magazine* v145 no2864 p56 My 2017

Schools—Trials, litigation, etc.

Code School's Out S. McBride color *Bloomberg Businessweek* no4504 p29 D 19 2016

Schools—United States

American Muslim Students Need Understanding and Support F. N. Shah *Education Digest* v83 no2 p33 O 2017

Archbishop McNicholas High School S. Kapp color *Cincinnati Magazine* v51 no1 p104 O 2017

Bethany School S. Snavely *Cincinnati Magazine* v51 no1 p105 O 2017

Cincinnati Waldorf School K. Crick *Cincinnati Magazine* v51 no1 p108 O 2017

Experimenting on the Young K. KERSTEN color *Weekly Standard* v22 no43 p19 Jl 24 2017

Guardian Angels School T. Strah *Cincinnati Magazine* v51 no1 p109 O 2017

How States Can Promote Local Innovation, Options, and Problem-Solving in Public Education J. Posamentier, R. Lake et al bw *Education Digest* v83 no3 p30 N 2017

OPEN HOUSE GUIDE color *Cincinnati Magazine* v51 no1 p001 O 2017

Prodigy Education Center S. Shirley *Cincinnati Magazine* v51 no1 p112 O 2017

Should Schools Have Dress Codes? *New York Times Upfront* v149 no8 p22 Ja 30 2017

St. Ursula Academy J. Cahill *Cincinnati Magazine* v51 no1 p113 O 2017

St. Ursula Villa M. Runnels *Cincinnati Magazine* v51 no1 p114 O 2017

Sub Shortage Leaves Schools Scrambling T. García Mathewson *Education Digest* v83 no3 p24 N 2017

Schools—United States—Government policy

Use Your Words--And Your Ideas: Arguments over education have divided America. Here's how reformers can swap acrimony for action M. J. Petrilli *Hoover Digest: Research & Opinion on Public Policy* no2 p155 Spr 2017

Schools—United States—Safety measures

Atlanta Schools Start Over with Police E. BLAD *Education Digest* v82 no8 p38 Ap 2017

Schoonebeek, Danniel

Trébuchet *Publishers Weekly* v263 no42 p49 O 17 2016

Schooners

SCHOONERMEN in the CARIBBEAN 600 T. CUNLIFFE color map *Sail* v48 no6 p32 Je 2017

Schoonover, Karl—Interviews

Queering the Globe: A conversation with Rosalind Galt and Karl Schoonover on Queer Cinema in the World R. Longo *Film Quarterly* v70 no2 p94 Wint 2016

Schoop, Allison

Stop Designing for Millennials *Harvard Business Review Digital Articles* p2 Je 10 2015

Schootstra, Emma

Can 10 Minutes of Meditation Make You More Creative? *Harvard Business Review Digital Articles* p2 Ag 29 2017

Schor, Esther

RETURN TO BABEL J. ACOCELLA cartoon *New Yorker* v92 no35 p90 O 31 2016

Yiddish for Everyone M. WEX *New York Times Book Review* p37 N 13 2016

Schorcht, Steffan

Sharp and Shelley Bank $37,700 in Stephenville color *Team Roping Journal* p32 S 2017

Schorderet, Patrick

Mutation of a nucleosome compaction region disrupts Polycomb-mediated axial patterning bibl chart diag *Science* v355 no6329 p1081 Mr 10 2017

Schörghofer, N.

Extensive water ice within Ceres' aqueously altered regolith: Evidence from nuclear spectroscopy bibl graph *Science* v355 no6320 p1 Ja 6 2017

Schorpp, K.

Inhibitors of PEX14 disrupt protein import into glycosomes and kill Trypanosoma parasites chart color diag graph *Science* v355 no6332 p1416 Mr 31 2017

SCHOTT, BEN

ALL THE PRESIDENTS' MENUS bw chart graph *Bon Appetit* v61 no11 p42 N 2016

Schott, Brian

FEVERED DAZE color *Powder* v45 no5 p102 Ja 2017

Schottky-barrier diodes

Subthreshold Schottky-barrier thin-film transistors with ultralow power and high intrinsic gain Sungsik Lee and A. Nathan bibl graph *Science* v354 no6310 p302 O 21 2016

Schouten, R. N.

Demonstration of an ac Josephson junction laser bibl diag *Science* v355 no6328 p939 Mr 3 2017

Schovanek, P.

Observation of a large-scale anisotropy in the arrival directions of cosmic rays above 8×1018 eV *Science* v357 no6357 p1266 S 22 2017

Schrader, Krysta

ST. MICHAEL, MINNESOTA color *Washington Monthly* v49 no3-5 p30 Mr-My 2017

Schrader, Matt

Score: A Film Music Documentary D. Coggan color *Entertainment Weekly* no1471 p53 Je 23 2017

Schrag, Daniel P.

Unmask temporal trade-offs in climate policy debates color *Science* v356 no6337 p492 My 5 2017

Schrag, Naomi J.

Step up for quality research color *Science* v357 no6351 p531 Ag 11 2017

Schrage, Michael

4 Models for Using AI to Make Decisions color *Harvard Business Review Digital Articles* p2 Ja 27 2017

5 Questions That Will Help You Stay Ahead of Your Disruptors *Harvard Business Review Digital Articles* p2 My 5 2016

AI Is Going to Change the 80/20 Rule color *Harvard Business Review Digital Articles* p2 F 28 2017

AI's Real Risk *Harvard Business Review Digital Articles* p2 D 16 2015

The Best Entrepreneurs Think Globally, Not Just Digitally *Harvard Business Review Digital Articles* p2 Mr 10 2016

The Best Platforms Are More than Matchmakers *Harvard Business Review Digital Articles* p2 Ag 2 2016

Board Members Should Have to Take a Personality Test *Harvard Business Review Digital Articles* p2 N 10 2014

Collaboration, from the Wright Brothers to Robots *Harvard Business Review Digital Articles* p2 Mr 23 2015

Companies Are Now Making Innovation Everyone's Job *Harvard Business Review Digital Articles* p2 Ja 21 2016

Customers Like Self- Service, Unless It Undermines Customer Support *Harvard Business Review Digital Articles* p2 Jl 28 2015

Data-Driven Management Can Also Be Compassionate *Harvard Business Review Digital Articles* p2 Ag 24 2015

Engagement Is a Means, Not an End *Harvard Business Review Digital Articles* p2 F 22 2016

Feedback Without Measurement Won't Do Any Good *Harvard Business Review Digital Articles* p2 Ag 5 2015

Get More Innovative by Rethinking the Way You Think *Harvard Business Review Digital Articles* p2 N 5 2015

Great CEOs See the Importance of Being Understood *Harvard Business Review Digital Articles* p2 D 16 2016

Great Digital Companies Build Great Recommendation Engines *Harvard Business Review Digital Articles* p2 Ag 1 2017

How the Big Data Explosion Has Changed Decision Making *Harvard Business Review Digital Articles* p2 Ag 25 2016

How the Navy SEALs Train for Leadership Excellence *Harvard Business Review Digital Articles* p2 My 28 2015

How to Give a Robot a Job Review *Harvard Business Review Digital Articles* p2 Mr 30 2016

If You're Not Collecting Productivity Data, You'll Never Succeed at Work *Harvard Business Review Digital Articles* p2 F 4 2016

Instead of Optimizing Processes, Reimagine Them as Platforms *Harvard Business Review Digital Articles* p2 D 30 2016

Is VW's Fraud the End of Large-Scale Corporate Deception? *Harvard Business Review Digital Articles* p2 S 29 2015

Let Data Ask Questions, Not Just Answer Them *Harvard Business*

Review *Digital Articles* p2 O 8 2014

Love Your Ex-Employees and They'll Love You Back *Harvard Business Review Digital Articles* p2 N 18 2015

Pokémon Go, Amazon Dash, and the Future of User Interaction *Harvard Business Review Digital Articles* p2 Jl 14 2016

PRODUCTIVITY Bots Won't Just Help Us Buy Stuff. They'll Help Us Become Better Versions of Ourselves *Harvard Business Review Digital Articles* p2 Je 1 2017

Reward Your Best Teams, Not Just Star Players *Harvard Business Review Digital Articles* p2 Je 30 2015

Sentiment Analysis Can Do More than Prevent Fraud and Turnover *Harvard Business Review Digital Articles* p2 Ja 5 2016

The Sony Hack Shows How Lawless the Internet Really Is *Harvard Business Review Digital Articles* p2 D 17 2014

Tesco's Downfall Is a Warning to Data-Driven Retailers *Harvard Business Review Digital Articles* p2 O 28 2014

A Testable Idea Is Better than a Good Idea *Harvard Business Review Digital Articles* p2 D 24 2014

VW's Problem Is Bad Management, Not Rogue Engineers *Harvard Business Review Digital Articles* p2 O 15 2015

What Happens If Apple Starts Making Cars *Harvard Business Review Digital Articles* p2 F 19 2015

What Most Companies Miss About Customer Lifetime Value *Harvard Business Review Digital Articles* p2 Ap 18 2017

When Authenticity Does More Harm than Good *Harvard Business Review Digital Articles* p2 O 26 2015

When Do Regulators Become More Important than Customers? *Harvard Business Review Digital Articles* p2 Ja 26 2015

Whether You're Qualified Depends on How You're Quantified *Harvard Business Review Digital Articles* p2 O 12 2015

Why the Future of Social Science Is with Private Companies *Harvard Business Review Digital Articles* p2 S 1 2015

Why User Experience Always Has to Come First *Harvard Business Review Digital Articles* p2 S 8 2016

Why Your Customer Loyalty Program Isn't Working *Harvard Business Review Digital Articles* p2 Mr 10 2015

Your Calendar Needs an Upgrade *Harvard Business Review Digital Articles* p2 Jl 9 2015

Your Customers' Behavior Is a Competitive Advantage *Harvard Business Review Digital Articles* p2 Ja 16 2015

Schrager, Ian

Life of the Party M. ROZZO bw color *Architectural Digest* v74 no9 p98 S 2017

REDUX I. Parker cartoon *New Yorker* v93 no26 p20 S 4 2017

SEX, DRUGS, AND DISCO B. Ratliff bw color *Esquire* p44 S 2017

Studio Fever B. COLACELLO bw color *Vanity Fair* v59 no9 p134 S 2017

Schrager, Ian—Interviews

THE ORIGINAL HOSPITALITY DISRUPTER L. Gallagher color *Fortune* v175 no8 p87 Je 15 2017

Schramm, Gloria

A role model color *Equus* no482 p72 N 2017

Schramm, J. D.

A Refresher on Storytelling 101 *Harvard Business Review Digital Articles* p2 O 8 2014

Schrefer, Eliot

Rescued color *Publishers Weekly* v263 no49 p101 D 7 2016

SCHREIBER, ABBY

OR BE THE FIRST TO PARTY AT ... img *New York* v50 no12 p66 Je 12 2017

SCHREIBER, KATHERINE

POISON PEOPLE CAUTION [Cover story] *Psychology Today* v50 no3 p50 My/Je 2017

Schreiber, Liev, 1967-

BROADWAY'S GAME CHANGERS M. Snetiker color *Entertainment Weekly* no1434 p63 O 7 2016

DAWN OF A NEW RAY M. LOGAN *TV Guide* v65 no35 p24 Ag 21 2017

OUT-GUTTING T. Friend cartoon *New Yorker* v93 no14 p30 My 22 2017

SCHREIBER, RONNEE

She Runs WE WIN *Ms.* v27 no1 p28 Spr 2017

Schreiber, Ryan

PiTCHFORK GROWS UP D. Leonard color *Bloomberg Businessweek* no4521 p59 My 8 2017

Schreier, Martin

Crowdsourced Products Sell Better When They're Marketed That Way *Harvard Business Review Digital Articles* p2 N 8 2016

Sometimes the Best Ideas Come from Outside Your Industry *Harvard Business Review Digital Articles* p2 N 21 2014

Schreiner, Bonnie

Brightline *Architectural Record* v205 no4 p205 Ap 2017

Schreyer, Luisa

Loss of a mammalian circular RNA locus causes miRNA deregulation and affects brain function color *Science* v357 no6357 p1254 S 22 2017

Schreyer, Peter—Interviews

Peter Schreyer, 63 M. DUFF cartoon *Car & Driver* v62 no10 p92 Ap 2017

Peter Schreyer A. Priddle bw color *Motor Trend* v69 no1 p30 Ja 2017

Schriber, Abbe

LESLIE HEWITT color *Art in America* v104 no10 p152 N 2016

Schrier, Karen

WORK OUT LIKE A PRO C. VAN DUSEN *Atlanta* v56 no9 p112 Ja 2017

Schrobsdorff, Susanna

Amazing Race color *Sports Illustrated* v126 no11 p106 Ap 17-24 2017

Anytime but Now: The Perils of Fighting Last Year's Wars and Pining for Yesterday's Heroes color *Time* v190 no7 p55 Ag 21 2017

As Congress Fights, Thousands Camp Out for Free Health Care color *Time* v190 no6 p14 Ag 7 2017

Dear Evan Hansen, Thanks for Finding Us. We've Been Waiting for a Musical Like You color *Time* v189 no10 p59 Mr 20 2017

Double Standards: Available In His and Hers color *Time* v188 no14 p63 O 10 2016

Hillary Clinton Writes the First Draft of Her History color *Time* v190 no12 p67 S 25 2017

Icons color *Time* v189 no16/17 p122 My 1-8 2017

It's Time for Our Real-Life Female Leaders to Act Like Selina Meyer color *Time* v190 no4 p55 Jl 24 2017

It Takes a Disaster to Remind Us of Our Common Humanity. Let's Not Forget That Too Soon color *Time* v190 no10/11 p115 S 18 2017

The Kids Are Not All Right [Cover story] color diag *Time* v188 no19 p44 N 7 2016

The Other Side [Cover story] color diag *Time* v189 no4 p24 F 6 2017

Red Vs. Pink: The Politics of Fashion and Why a Hat Is No Longer Just a Hat color *Time* v189 no6 p55 F 20 2017

Shared Rituals Are the Tie That Binds color *Time* v189 no3 p59 Ja 30 2017

There Is No Right Way to Unplug from Work color *Time* v189 no3 p19 Ja 30 2017

The Tipping Point: When Do Female Leaders Become the Norm? color *Time* v190 no16/17 p38 O 23 2017

The Tragedies of 2017 Will Test the Bonds That Connect Us, Now and for Years to Come color *Time* v190 no15 p59 O 16 2017

The Unexpected Benefits of Ending Up at the Back of the Pack color *Time* v189 no3 p63 Ja 16 2017

Viral Anger Spreads Like a Disease—and It's Making the Country Sick color *Time* v190 no2/3 p19 Jl 10-17 2017

What It Feels Like When All Your Parental Nightmares Are Rolled Into One TV Series color *Time* v189 no19 p56 My 22 2017

Whose Privilege Is Showing? Probably Mine. But Don't Ask Me to Check Anyone Else color *Time* v189 no18 p59 My 15 2017

Wonder Woman: A Perfect Paradox for the Generation That Expects to Have It All color *Time* v189 no22 p58 Je 12 2017

Schrock, Madeline

The Best of 2016 *Dance Magazine* v90 no12 p84 D 2016

Funny Girl *Dance Magazine* v91 no4 p58 Ap 2017

LAR LUBOVITCH *Dance Magazine* v90 no12 p48 D 2016

The MOST INFLUENTIAL PEOPLE IN DANCE TODAY: THE MOVERS, SHAKERS AND CHANGEMAKERS HAVING THE BIGGEST IMPACT ON DANCE RIGHT NOW *Dance Magazine* v91 no7 p27 Jl 2017

What's Not Okay to Ask a Dancer to Do? *Dance Magazine* v91 no4 p31 Ap 2017

Schroder, F. G.

Observation of a large-scale anisotropy in the arrival directions of cosmic rays above 8×10^{18} eV *Science* v357 no6357 p1266 S 22 2017

Schröder, Gunnar F.

Fibril structure of amyloid-β(1–42) by cryo–electron microscopy color diag *Science* v357 no6359 p116 O 6 2017

Schröder, Peter

An Inconvenient Maverick *History Today* v67 no2 p4 F 2017

PENN'S PLAN for a united Europe *History Today* v66 no10 p32 O 2016

SCHROEDEL, JEAN REITH

A Case Study of Descriptive Representation: The Experience of Native American Elected Officials in South Dakota *American Indian Quarterly* v41 no3 p250 Summ 2017

Schroeder, Allison

THE BIG QUESTION cartoon *Atlantic* v319 no2 p100 Mr 2017

Schroeder, Bob C.

Highly stretchable polymer semiconductor films through the nanoconfinement effect bibl graph *Science* v355 no6320 p1 Ja 6 2017

SCHROEDER, CHRISTINA

ROAR OF THE CROWD *Texas Monthly* v45 no7 p12 Jl 2017

Schroeder, Christopher M.

A Different Story from the Middle East: Entrepreneurs Building an Arab Tech Economy bw *MIT Technology Review* v120 no5 p64 S/O 2017

Schroeder, Grant G.

Emergent cellular self-organization and mechanosensation initiate follicle pattern in the avian skin color *Science* v357 no6353 p811 Ag 25 2017

Schroeder, Juliana

Match Your Motivational Tactic to the Situation *Harvard Business Review Digital Articles* p2 Ja 8 2016

The Science of Sounding Smart *Harvard Business Review Digital Articles* p2 O 7 2015

Schröter, C. D.

Ultrafast electron diffraction imaging of bond breaking in di-ionized acetylene bibl graph *Science* v354 no6310 p308 O 21 2016

SCHRÖTER, MATTHIAS

National Ecosystem Assessments in Europe: A Review chart *BioScience* v66 no10 p813 O 1 2016

When, Where, and How Nature Matters for Ecosystem Services: Challenges for the Next Generation of Ecosystem Service Models *BioScience* v67 no9 p820 S 2017

Schroth, Raymond A.

THE ENEMIES OF EMPATHY *America* v215 no14 p36 N 7 2016

The Faces of Courage color *America* v215 no18 p20 D 5 2016

Ken Burns revisits the division and bloodshed wrought by 'a barbaric war' bw *America* v217 no7 p50 O 2 2017

The moral blindness of war color *America* v217 no2 p49 Jl 24 2017

More things to read and watch and learn color *America* v216 no9 p6 Ap 24 2017

A Pope for the (Media) Masses color *America* v217 no4 p58 Ag 21 2017

Rethinking Russia color *America* v215 no12 p17 O 24 2016

THE RETURN OF JAMES BALDWIN bw color *America* v216 no9 p8 Ap 24 2017

Russia needs a truth commission now color *America* v216 no6 p44 Mr 20 2017

The virtue of a Catholic journalist M. Malone *America* v217 no3 p3 Ag 7 2017

Welcome to America's biannual literary review *America* v216 no9 p3 Ap 24 2017

SCHRUERS, FRED

THERE GOES THE NEIGHBORHOOD *Los Angeles Magazine* p102 F 2017

Schruf, Eva

Mutations in the promoter of the telomerase gene TERT contribute to tumorigenesis by a two-step mechanism diag *Science* v357 no6358 p1416 S 29 2017

SCHUBE, SAM

How Koreatown Became the Cool Center of L.A color *GQ: Gentlemen's Quarterly* v97 no11 p54 N 2017

The Ten Who'll Be Next color *GQ: Gentlemen's Quarterly* v97 no11 p114 N 2017

Schübeler, Dirk

Impact of cytosine methylation on DNA binding specificities of human transcription factors diag *Science* v356 no6337 p502 My 5 2017

Schubert, Michael

Is America great? graph *America* v216 no5 p6 Mr 6 2017

Schubert, Mikkel

Ancient genomic changes associated with domestication of the horse color diag *Science* v356 no6336 p442 Ap 28 2017

Schubert Corp.

FETISH: SKULL CADDY A. MARSHALL color *Wired* v25 no10 p47 O 2017

SCHUCHARDT, READ MERCER

ANALOG CHURCH bw color *Christianity Today* v60 no8 p40 O 2016

Schueller, Jake

Life's work: Building the church takes everyone [Cover story] color *U.S. Catholic* v82 no8 p22 Ag 2017

Schuenemann, Susan Kendrick

TRACE OF HOPE M. COHEN MARILL *Atlanta* v56 no8 p144 D 2016

Schuenemann, Verena J.

Genomic estimation of complex traits reveals ancient maize adaptation to temperate North America diag *Science* v357 no6350 p512 Ag 4 2017

Schuessler, Jennifer

Have You Met Miss Jane?: Test your Austen I.Q.—from family scandals to a wet-shirted Colin Firth *New York Times Book Review* p15 Jl 16 2017

SCHUETTPELZ, ERIC

Sex and the Single Gametophyte: Revising the Homosporous Vascular Plant Life Cycle in Light of Contemporary Research *BioScience* v66 no11 p928 N 1 2016

SCHUG, KATHERINE

This Cupcake Could Kill Me...But This One Won't! *Scholastic Choices* v32 no5 p20 F 2017

Schuh, Melina

Actin protects mammalian eggs against chromosome segregation errors color *Science* v357 no6353 p772 Ag 25 2017

SCHUHRKE, JEFF

We Could Still Win Free College *In These Times* v40 no12 p8 D 2016

SCHUKAR, ALYSSA

Industrial Evolution *American Scholar* v86 no3 p10 Summ 2017

Schuknecht, Catherine

Lady Gaga-ntuan *Sierra* v101 no4 p23 Jl/Ag 2016

Richmond's "Resident Rosie" *Sierra* v101 no4 p66 Jl/Ag 2016

Schüle, Birgitt

β2-Adrenoreceptor is a regulator of the a-synuclein gene driving risk of Parkinson's disease cartoon chart graph *Science* v357 no6354 p891 S 1 2017

SCHULER, LOU

4 Steps to REVERSE DIABETES Naturally [Cover story] color *Prevention* p78 Mr 2017

5 LESSONS FROM THE NEW PALEO color *Men's Health* v32 no7 p104 S 2017

THE BIG DIABETES IS AMERICA'S STEALTHY KILLER cartoon color *Men's Health* v32 no2 p96 Mr 2017

FIX IT WITH THE BACK MECHANIC cartoon color *Men's Health* v32 no1 p43 Ja/F 2017

A New Take on Classic Lifts cartoon *Men's Health* v32 no4 p48 My 2017

A New Way to Attack Your Six-Pack cartoon color *Men's Health* v32 no5 p47 Je 2017

Schuller, Ivan

Arthur J. Freeman *Physics Today* v69 no11 p69 N 2016

Schuller, Jan M.

Structures of the cyanobacterial circadian oscillator frozen in a fully assembled state bibl diag *Science* v355 no6330 p1181 Mr 17 2017

SCHULLER, MARK

Haiti's 'Republic of NGOs' *Current History* v116 no787 p68 F 2017

Schulman, Ari N.

The Plague and the Judgment: When Ebola became something other than a contagious disease *Commentary* v143 no6 p31 Je 2017

Schulman, Dan

PAYPAL'S CEO ON CREATING PRODUCTS FOR UNDER-SERVED MARKETS color diag graph img *Harvard Business Review* v94 no12 p35 D 2016

SCHULMAN, DANIEL

Banking on America *American Scholar* v86 no4 p18 Aut 2017

SCHULMAN, HELEN

Winging Single *New York Times Book Review* p18 Mr 19 2017

Schulman, Joshua

In the Bag M. OWENS color *Architectural Digest* v74 no9 p52 S 2017

Schulman, Kevin A.

Bridging Health Care's Innovation-Education Gap *Harvard Business Review Digital Articles* p2 N 11 2014

We Interviewed Health Care Leaders About Their Industry, and They're Worried *Harvard Business Review Digital Articles* p2 D 14 2016

Schulman, Loren DeJonge

Secret Wars *Harper's Magazine* no2007 p2 Ag 2017

Schulman, Michael

American Carnage color *New Yorker* v93 no20 p12 Jl 10 2017

DEARLY DEPARTED cartoon *New Yorker* v93 no18 p20 Je 26 2017

DIAL-A-FEMINIST cartoon *New Yorker* v93 no14 p32 My 22 2017

DISOBEDIENT cartoon *New Yorker* v93 no25 p30 Ag 28 2017

DOUBLE-SIDED cartoon *New Yorker* v93 no9 p22 Ap 17 2017

Fall Preview color *New Yorker* v93 no25 p6 Ag 28 2017

G.I. Jive cartoon *New Yorker* v92 no44 p9 Ja 9 2017

Happenings color *New Yorker* v93 no11 p8 My 1 2017

Honest Iago cartoon *New Yorker* v92 no39 p22 N 28 2016

Lend Me Your Ears color *New Yorker* v93 no15 p10 My 29 2017

THE LISTENER cartoon color *New Yorker* v93 no6 p30 Mr 27 2017

LOVE ALL cartoon *New Yorker* v93 no27 p26 S 11 2017

LUCKY cartoon *New Yorker* v93 no2 p25 F 27 2017

The Mind-Bending Mr. Cumberbatch bw color *Vanity Fair* v58 no11 p146 N 2016

MODEL CITIZEN cartoon color *New Yorker* v92 no30 p26 S 26 2016

The Old Normal cartoon *New Yorker* v92 no32 p18 O 10 2016

OSCAR DEAREST cartoon *New Yorker* v93 no2 p26 F 27 2017

OVER THE RAINBOW color *New Yorker* v93 no29 p78 S 25 2017

PLANE PEOPLE cartoon *New Yorker* v93 no6 p19 Mr 27 2017

Post-Ingénue color *New Yorker* v93 no29 p12 S 25 2017

QUOTE MACHINE cartoon *New Yorker* v92 no40 p24 D 5 2016

RETURN ENGAGEMENT cartoon *New Yorker* v92 no30 p24 S 26 2016

Russian Unorthodox cartoon *New Yorker* v92 no34 p9 O 24 2016

Serenity Now! color *New Yorker* v93 no33 p22 O 23 2017

Spring Preview cartoon *New Yorker* v93 no4 p15 Mr 13 2017

Sugar, Butter, Flour cartoon *New Yorker* v93 no7 p14 Ap 3 2017

Summer Preview cartoon *New Yorker* v93 no14 p8 My 22 2017

Wigstock cartoon *New Yorker* v93 no28 p10 S 18 2017

Winter Preview cartoon *New Yorker* v92 no37 p26 N 14 2016

Schulman, Rebecca

DNA sequence–directed shape change of photopatterned hydrogels via high-degree swelling color diag *Science* v357 no6356 p1126 S 15 2017

SCHULMAN, SAM

The Not-Talking Cure color *Weekly Standard* v22 no15 p11 D 19 2016

Schulman, Sarah

LESSONS FROM THE LAST FIGHT *Harper's Magazine* v334 no2001 p34 F 2017

The Thread *New York Times Magazine* p8 Je 25 2017

SCHULTE, LISA A.

When, Where, and How Nature Matters for Ecosystem Services: Challenges for the Next Generation of Ecosystem Service Models *BioScience* v67 no9 p820 S 2017

Schultz, Carsten

mTORC1 activity repression by late endosomal phosphatidylinositol 3,4-bisphosphate diag *Science* v356 no6341 p968 Je 1 2017

Schultz, Charles Marshall

SIMON STARLING color *Art in America* v105 no3 p125 Mr 2017

Schultz, Dana

Inappropriation Dept color *Weekly Standard* v22 no30 p3 Ap 10 2017

SCHULTZ, FRANCES

A REFINED AFFAIR color *House Beautiful* v159 no3 p112 Ap 2017

Schultz, Howard D., 1953-

HOWARD SCHULTZ HAS SOMETHING LEFT TO PROVE B. Kowitt chart color *Fortune* v175 no8 p114 Je 15 2017

Schultz, Jacqueline

MOST OUTSTANDING WOMEN *Washingtonian Magazine* v53 no1 p64 O 2017

Schultz, Nate

WHY FACEBOOK IS KEEPING PERFORMANCE REVIEWS: INTERACTION color *Harvard Business Review* v95 no1 p18 Ja/F 2017

Schultz, Neal

the secret to GLOWY SKIN K. S. BOX color *Better Homes & Gardens* v95 no3 p16 Mr 2017

Schultz, Philip

GOOGLING OURSELVES *New Yorker* v93 no33 p76 O 23 2017

Schultz, Philip, 1945-

At 30, the Writers Studio Gets an Anthology J. Maher chart *Publishers Weekly* v264 no19 p7 My 8 2017

Schultz, Valerie

Sunday Crybaby *America* v216 no4 p58 F 20 2017

Schultze, Joachim L.

Mapping the human DC lineage through the integration of high-dimensional techniques diag *Science* v356 no6342 p1044 Je 9 2017

Schulz, A.

Observation of a large-scale anisotropy in the arrival directions of cosmic rays above 8 × 1018 eV *Science* v357 no6357 p1266 S 22 2017

Schulz, Eric

EVERYDAY BEAUTY J. Silver color diag *Sunset* v239 no3 p41 S 2017

Schulz, Frederik

Giant viruses with an expanded complement of translation system components diag *Science* v356 no6333 p82 Ap 7 2017

Schulz, Kathryn

CALL AND RESPONSE cartoon color *New Yorker* v93 no3 p26 Mr 6 2017

Kathryn Schulz D. Kiper *Current Biography* v78 no6 p92 Je 2017

KNOW IT ALL cartoon color *New Yorker* v93 no32 p76 O 16 2017

LOSING STREAK cartoon *New Yorker* v92 no49 p66 F 13 2017

POLAR EXPRESSED cartoon color *New Yorker* v93 no10 p88 Ap 24 2017

SAINT PAULI bw cartoon *New Yorker* v93 no9 p67 Ap 17 2017

Schulz, Laura E.

Infants make more attempts to achieve a goal when they see adults persist chart color *Science* v357 no6357 p1290 S 22 2017

Schulz, Martin, 1955-

An Establishment Firebrand in Germany B. Jennen, R. Buergin et al color *Bloomberg Businessweek* no4514 p28 Mr 13 2017

It's Merkel 3, Schulz 0 In German Campaign A. Delfs, P. Donahue et al color *Bloomberg Businessweek* no4523 p16 My 22 2017

Martin Schulz, Germany's Bernie Sanders T. John color diag *Time* v189 no12 p14 Ap 3 2017

Schulz, S. A.

Breaking Lorentz reciprocity to overcome the time-bandwidth limit in physics and engineering bw diag graph *Science* v356 no6344 p1260 Je 23 2017

Schulze, Ernst-Detlef

Positive biodiversity-productivity relationship predominant in global forests bibl chart graph map *Science* v354 no6309 paaf8957-1 O 14 2016

Schulze, Morgan W.

Thermal processing of diblock copolymer melts mimics metallurgy diag graph *Science* v356 no6337 p520 My 5 2017

Schulze, Waltraud

Precursor processing for plant peptide hormone maturation by subtilisin-like serine proteinases bibl color graph *Science* v354 no6319 p1594 D 23 2016

Schulze-Lefert, Paul

Caught in the jump color *Science* v357 no6346 p31 Jl 7 2017

Schumacher, J.

Observation of a large-scale anisotropy in the arrival directions of cosmic rays above 8 × 1018 eV *Science* v357 no6357 p1266 S 22 2017

Schumacher, Joel

ST. ELMO'S FIRE L. Rice color *Entertainment Weekly* no1460/1461 p34 Ap 7-17 2017

Schumacher, John

Poses of the month [Cover story] color *Yoga Journal* no289 p37 F 2017

Schumacher, Patrik

LEGACY BUILDING S. COCHRAN color *Architectural Digest* v74 no1 p232 Ja 2017

Schumacher, Troy

DANCE *New Yorker* v93 no32 p16 O 16 2017

Schumacher, Troy—Interviews

Troy Schumacher: The choreographer is premiering three ballets in a span of four weeks M. HARSS *Dance Magazine* v91 no10 p18 O 2017

Schuman, Erin M.

Activity-dependent spatially localized miRNA maturation in neuronal dendrites bibl graph *Science* v355 no6325 p634 F 10 2017

Schuman, Michael

The Great Mall of China chart color *Forbes* v198 no8 p48 D 20 2016

History of child labor in the United States--part 1: little children working bibl bw color *Monthly Labor Review* p1 Ja 2017

History of child labor in the United States--part 2: the reform movement bibl bw color *Monthly Labor Review* p1 Ja 2017

How Do You Say Déjà Vu in Chinese? bw color *Bloomberg Businessweek* no4498 p14 N 7 2016

How the Kims Came to Love The Bomb color *Bloomberg Businessweek* no4537 p12 S 11 2017

How to Win a Trade War With China bw *Bloomberg Businessweek* no4512 p6 F 20 2017

The Once and Future Financial Crisis color *Bloomberg Businessweek* no4529 p10 Jl 3 2017

Smiles Aren't Factory-Made color *Bloomberg Businessweek* no4526 p8 Je 12 2017

The South Korean Mirage cartoon *Bloomberg Businessweek* no4515 p8 Mr 20 2017

Why Wages Aren't Growing *Bloomberg Businessweek* no4539 p12 S 25 2017

You don't have to lose your job if you lose your sight *Bloomberg Businessweek* no4508 p6 Ja 23 2017

SCHUMAN, NICOLE

The Most Wonderful Time of the Year *USA Today Magazine* v145 no2858 p64 N 2016

Schuman, Philip

LIFELONG PASSION J. Mankin color *Team Roping Journal* p52 O 2017

Schumann-Heink, Ernestine, 1861-1936

National Treasure P. G. DAVIS *Opera News* v81 no5 p24 N 2016

Schumer, Amy, 1981-

THE APPROVAL MATRIX img *New York* v49 no20 p160 O 3 2016

digital directory color *InStyle* v24 no5 p16 My 2017

A GIRL LIKE I H. ALS cartoon *New Yorker* v92 no32 p106 O 10 2016

Hello! L. Brown color *InStyle* v24 no5 p18 My 2017

her style color *InStyle* v24 no5 p32 My 2017

Sound Bites color *Entertainment Weekly* no1457/1458 p12 Mr 17 2017

Trainwreck M. FELL *TV Guide* p51 D 5 2016

Schumer, Amy, 1981—Interviews

amy [Cover story] color *InStyle* v24 no5 p210 My 2017

Who's A PRETTY Girl? [Cover story] S. Vilkomerson color *Entertainment Weekly* no1462 p20 Ap 21 2017

Schumer, Charles E., 1950-

Democrats Look for an Upside In Obamacare's Repeal H. S. Edwards and S. Frizell color diag *Time* v189 no3 p5 Ja 16 2017

The Face of the Opposition [Cover story] S. Frizell and Z. J. Miller color *Time* v189 no6 p26 F 20 2017

Make 50 the New 60 W. Kristol color *Weekly Standard* v22 no22

p6 F 13 2017

MINORITY REPORT E. KOLBERT cartoon *New Yorker* v93 no6
p20 Mr 27 2017

The Pros and Cons of the President's Immigrant Travel Ban *Congressional Digest* v96 no3 p17 Mr 2017

What You Said About ... color *Time* v189 no7/8 p2 F 27 2017

Schumer, Charles E., 1950—Political & social views

Power Tools: Artists C. Alter color *Time* v189 no16/17 p62 My
1-8 2017

Schumer or Later P. Beinart color *New Republic* v248 no11 p5
N 2017

SCHUMPETER, JOSEPH

THOUGHTS ON Conflict *Forbes* v199 no4 p112 Ap 25 2017

Schupbach, John

A Simple Way to Measure Health Care Outcomes *Harvard Business Review Digital Articles* p2 D 8 2016

Schupp, Karen

Merging movements: Diverse dance practices in postsecondary
education bibl *Arts Education Policy Review* v118 no2 p104
2017

Schur, Michael

I LOVE LUCIFER E. NUSSBAUM cartoon *New Yorker* v92
no48 p78 F 6 2017

Schuster, Jack H.

Whither the Faculty? *Change* v49 no4 p43 Jl/Ag 2017

Schustertaken, Harland

SHOWCASE SHOTS color *Nebraska Life* v21 no1 p80 Ja/F 2017

Schuth, Katarina, 1941-

The Perils of Apartness T. Baker color *Commonweal* v144 no3
p23 F 10 2017

SCHUTT, BILL

The Case for Cannibalism cartoon *Discover* v38 no3 p56 Ap 2017

Grisly dining habit not taboo among animals S. Perkins color *Science News* v191 no3 p29 F 18 2017

Pass the Fava Beans S. MONTGOMERY *New York Times Book Review* p20 F 26 2017

Schutten, Rutger

A subcellular map of the human proteome color *Science* v356
no6340 p820 My 26 2017

Schutz, Dana

TROUBLING PICTURES C. TOMKINS cartoon color *New Yorker* v93 no8 p30 Ap 10 2017

Schuur, Ted

THE PERMAFROST PREDICTION color map *Scientific American* v315 no6 p56 D 2016

Schuurink, Robert C.

Emission of volatile organic compounds from petunia flowers is
facilitated by an ABC transporter diag *Science* v356 no6345
p1386 Je 30 2017

SCHUYLER, DEVON

A Scary New Hip Trend color diag *Men's Health* v32 no6 p89
Ag 2017

Schuyler, George S. (George Samuel), 1895-1977

1934: Harlem G. S. Schuyler *Lapham's Quarterly* v10 no2 p33
Spr 2017

Schuyler, Samantha

Nation Voices 2016 *Nation* v304 no2 p8 Ja 16 2017

Schwab, Keri

Stay on Your Smartphone! *Parks & Recreation* v51 no11 p14 N
2016

Schwab, Klaus, 1938—Interviews

Klaus Schwab M. Duffy color *Time* v189 no4 p56 Ja 23 2017

SCHWAB, KRISTIN

A COMPANY IN MOTION *Dance Magazine* v91 no8 p26 Ag
2017

Dancers as Activists *Dance Magazine* v90 no11 p14 N 2016

Dancing with Asthma *Dance Magazine* v90 no12 p90 D 2016

David Dorfman *Dance Magazine* v91 no4 p18 Ap 2017

The Gallim Dream color *Dance Spirit* v21 no2 p34 F 2017

It's the Little Things *Dance Magazine* v91 no1 p120 Ja 2017

Lonely at the Top *Dance Magazine* v90 no11 p50 N 2016

On the Circuit *Dance Magazine* v90 no11 p54 N 2016

Stretch Yourself *Dance Magazine* v91 no1 p138 Ja 2017

Stuck in the Middle *Dance Magazine* v91 no1 p126 Ja 2017

SCHWABSKY, BARRY

THE BRILLIANCE OF LINES *Nation* v303 no20 p33 N 14 2016

COLOR AS CODE *Nation* v304 no4 p31 F 6 2017

DO SOMETHING WITH IT color *Nation* v305 no2 p35 Jl 17
2017

FACE TO FACE color *Nation* v305 no9 p35 O 16 2017

IS TRAGEDY A CHOICE? bw *Nation* v304 no2 p32 Ja 16 2017

PICABIA'S MONSTERS color il *Nation* v304 no8 p35 Mr 13
2017

PLAYING WITH MIRRORS color *Nation* v304 no16 p41 My 22
2017

WHEN DOWNTOWN WAS UP *Nation* v304 no11 p35 Ap 3 2017

ZERO GRAVITY color *Nation* v305 no6 p32 S 11 2017

Schwalbe, Will

Book Learning A. J. JACOBS *New York Times Book Review* p17
D 25 2016

Schwalje, Adam T.

Community network for deaf scientists color *Science* v356
no6336 p386 Ap 28 2017

Schwall, David

The Sales Director Who Turned Work into a Fantasy Sports Competition E. Bernstein and H. Blunden *Harvard Business Review
Digital Articles* p2 Mr 27 2015

Schwander, Thomas

A synthetic pathway for the fixation of carbon dioxide in vitro bibl
graph *Science* v354 no6314 p900 N 18 2016

Schwandt, Hannes

Why So Many of Us Experience a Midlife Crisis *Harvard Business Review Digital Articles* p2 Ap 20 2015

Schwanen, Tim

Sociotechnical transitions for deep decarbonization color diag *Science* v357 no6357 p1242 S 22 2017

SCHWARB, JOHN

Best Pit Stop Ever *Indianapolis Monthly* p15 My 2017

Schwarber, Kyle, 1993-

THE SLUGGER THE SCOUT B. Reiter color *Sports Illustrated*
v126 no13 p58 My 8 2017

TALK TO US R. Ferry-Rooney color *Chicago* v66 no4 p19 Ap
2017

Schwarting, Michael—Interviews

Michael Schwarting and Frances Campani S. STEPHENS color
Architectural Record v205 no3 p26 Mr 2017

SCHWARTZ, ALEXANDRA

BELIEVE YOU ME bw cartoon *New Yorker* v93 no12 p66 My
8 2017

COLD HEART color *New Yorker* v92 no48 p73 F 6 2017

TALK TO ME cartoon color *New Yorker* v93 no22 p74 Jl 31 2017

TWO STEP cartoon *New Yorker* v92 no37 p81 N 14 2016

WATCH CLOSELY cartoon color map *New Yorker* v93 no32 p56
O 16 2017

WHAT SHE'S HAVING cartoon *New Yorker* v92 no33 p80 O 17
2016

Schwartz, Brad

5 SMALLER NETWORKS YOU NEED TO KNOW ABOUT D.
HOLBROOK *TV Guide* v65 no31 p6 Jl 24 2017

SCHWARTZ, CASEY

ADDERALL *New York Times Magazine* p54 O 16 2016

Your Inner Voices *New York Times Book Review* p25 O 23 2016

Schwartz, Dana

THE GOOD PLACE'S (VERY GOOD) BAD SEED color *Entertainment Weekly* no1485 p46 O 6 2017

What to Watch color *Entertainment Weekly* no1484 p53 S 29 2017

Why You Should Never Date Anyone You Meet IRL color *Glamour* v115 no9 p126 S 2017

Schwartz, Deb

NOBLE PURPLES color *Better Homes & Gardens* v95 no9 p34
S 2017

PROVING GROUND color *Better Homes & Gardens* v95 no6
p126 Je 2017

SOFAS DECONSTRUCTED color *Southern Living* v52 no1 p96
Ja 2017

table talk color *Better Homes & Gardens* v95 no5 p14 My 2017

"YOU CAN GET AWAY WITH MORE IN A SMALL SPACE,"
color *Better Homes & Gardens* v95 no9 p36 S 2017

Schwartz, Erika

Lewellen artist takes 'most unlikely' journey home color *Nebraska Life* v21 no4 p72 Jl/Ag 2017

On the trail of the Nance County bear cartoon *Nebraska Life* v20 no6 p16 N/D 2016

Photographer was eyewitness to Nebraska's birth bw *Nebraska Life* v20 no6 p60 N/D 2016

Schwartz, Evan I.

What the Best Transformational Leaders Do *Harvard Business Review Digital Articles* p2 My 8 2017

Schwartz, Gary

Pseudoscience versus science *Physics Today* v69 no11 p10 N 2016

SCHWARTZ, HERMAN

HOW TRUMP'S ASSAULT ON IMMIGRANTS WILL DAMAGE THE ECONOMY color *Nation* v304 no11 p16 Ap 3 2017

Schwartz, I.

Deterministic generation of a cluster state of entangled photons bibl diag graph *Science* v354 no6311 p434 O 28 2016

Schwartz, J.

Best cost estimate of greenhouse gases *Science* v357 no6352 p655 Ag 18 2017

SCHWARTZ, JANET

WHAT'S THE VALUE OF A LIKE? color *Harvard Business Review* v95 no2 p108 Mr/Ap 2017

Schwartz, Jen

Do Not Fear Gene-Edited Food color *Popular Science* v288 no6 p82 N/D 2016

I WISH SOMEONE WOULD INVENT… color *Popular Science* v288 no6 p114 N/D 2016

The Roots of Science Denial color *Scientific American* v317 no4 p66 O 2017

THIS COULD HAPPEN IN YOUR HOMETOWN bw color *Women's Health* v14 no7 p88 S 2017

Tunnel Through the Alps color *Popular Science* v288 no6 p78 N/D 2016

Schwartz, John

10 SUCCESSFUL FARMERS: JOHN SCHWARTZ B. Freese *Successful Farming* v115 no8 p23 Je/Jl 2017

SCHWARTZ, JON

ROAR OF THE CROWD *Texas Monthly* v45 no6 p10 Je 2017

SCHWARTZ, JOSEPH

Countering Capitalism bw cartoon *In These Times* v40 no11 p44 N 2016

Schwartz, Lillian

LILLIAN SCHWARTZ W. Vogel cartoon *Art in America* v104 no11 p119 D 2016

Schwartz, Linda

HAMBURGER HILL *AARP: The Magazine* v59 no3A p67 Ap/My 2016

Q: What was the greatest summer read of your life? color *O, The Oprah Magazine* p16 Jl 2017

Schwartz, Madeleine

READINGS *Harper's Magazine* p11 Ap 2017

Schwartz, Marie Jenkins

Slaves in the White House S. Dunn color *New York Review of Books* v64 no8 p55 My 11 2017

Schwartz, Martin W.

Afternoons and Popeye Cartoons *Missouri Life* v43 no7 p38 D 2016/Ja 2017

COMMON SCENTS color *Missouri Life* v44 no3 p18 My 2017

DELI DELIGHTS color *Missouri Life* v44 no3 p72 My 2017

A Helping Paw color *Missouri Life* v44 no2 p16 Ap 2017

IT'S ALL RELATIVE *Missouri Life* v43 no7 p26 D 2016/Ja 2017

LAUGHING ALL THE WAY TO SUCCESS *Missouri Life* v43 no6 p18 O/N 2016

Mighty Peculiar bw color *Missouri Life* v44 no3 p62 My 2017

Missouriana *Missouri Life* v43 no7 p98 D 2016/Ja 2017

MISSOURI TO TEXAS BY WAY OF OKLAHOMA *Missouri Life* v43 no6 p22 O/N 2016

OVER HERE bw color *Missouri Life* v44 no2 p32 Ap 2017

Prepping for the Really Big Show chart color diag *Missouri Life* v44 no2 p28 Ap 2017

SERVICE & SACRIFICE color *Missouri Life* v44 no3 p56 My 2017

Speaking of Springfield Music… color *Missouri Life* v44 no3 p22 My 2017

String Beings *Missouri Life* v43 no7 p58 D 2016/Ja 2017

VISIONS OF SUGARPLUMS *Missouri Life* v43 no7 p16 D 2016/Ja 2017

Schwartz, Mattathias

THE @-BOMB *New York Times Magazine* p30 Ja 8 2017

Schwartz, Matthew G.

Mutation of a nucleosome compaction region disrupts Polycomb-mediated axial patterning bibl chart diag *Science* v355 no6329 p1081 Mr 10 2017

Schwartz, Michal

Can immunotherapy treat neurodegeneration? color *Science* v357 no6348 p254 Jl 21 2017

SCHWARTZ, PEGGY COOPER

Q: What was the greatest summer read of your life? color *O, The Oprah Magazine* p16 Jl 2017

Schwartz, Sanford

The Genius of Making It Small color *New York Review of Books* v63 no17 p12 N 10 2016

The Master of Eglfing-Haar color *New York Review of Books* v64 no16 p20 O 26 2017

Picabia's Big Moment color *New York Review of Books* v64 no3 p12 F 23 2017

A Swedish Collector in Paris [Cover story] color *New York Review of Books* v64 no8 p24 My 11 2017

Taking Her Place in American Art color *New York Review of Books* v64 no12 p11 Jl 13 2017

'The Sheer Excitement of Being an Artist' color *New York Review of Books* v64 no5 p20 Mr 23 2017

Schwartz, Sara

Amazing Animals color map *National Geographic Kids* no472 p10 Ag 2017

Amazing Animals color *National Geographic Kids* no475 p10 N 2017

KITTEN ON BOARD *National Geographic Kids* no469 p13 Ap 2017

KOALAS SNAP "SELFIES" *National Geographic Kids* no468 p12 Mr 2017

Penguin and Human BFFs color *National Geographic Kids* no465 p12 N 2016

RACCON SCALES BUILDING *National Geographic Kids* no467 p12 F 2017

Schwartz, Sol

A Legacy Lives On *Tennis* v52 no6 p46 N/D 2016

Schwartz, Suze Yalof

We Should All Be Meditating S. Y. Schwartz and S. G. Levy color *Glamour* v115 no3 p130 Mr 2017

Schwartz, Tony

How to Become a More Well-Rounded Leader *Harvard Business Review Digital Articles* p2 Jl 21 2017

SCHWARTZ, ZANE

NOSTALGIA color *Maclean's* v129 no40 p76 O 10 2016

Why bombs won't stop terrorism color *Maclean's* v129 no42 p60 O 24 2016

SCHWARTZBERG, LAUREN

AMERICAN HUSTLERS color *Wired* v25 no6 p86 Je 2017

BEST BETS img *New York* v49 no19 p61 S 19 2016

Desus and Mero img *New York* v50 no6 p14 Mr 20 2017

Do You Want to Try One Out in Person? Here's how you can, following the bring-your-own-pillow-and-rest-for-at-least-seven-minutes advice of clinical psychologist and sleep expert Dr. Michael Breus *New York* v50 no9 p69 My 1 2017

Eleven Things You're Likely to Do Poorly (But Love Anyway) img *New York* v49 no23 p66 N 14 2016

Go From Sucking to 60 img *New York* v49 no23 p68 N 14 2016

home & help img *New York* p96 Mr 6 2017

Jordan Barrett img *New York* v49 no19 p18 S 19 2016

The Return of the Squiggle img *New York* v50 no11 p96 My 29 2017

Why Hasn't Millennial Pink Faded Away? img *New York* v50 no6 p58 Mr 20 2017

SCHWARZ, BENJAMIN

The Self-Indulgence of Today's New Elite *American Conservative* v16 no5 p52 S/O 2017

Schwarz, Ilai

Submillihertz magnetic spectroscopy performed with a nanoscale quantum sensor diag *Science* v356 no6340 p832 My 26 2017

SCHWARZ, KIRSTEN

Ecology for the Shrinking City *BioScience* v66 no11 p965 N 1 2016

Schwarz, Lindsay A.

Breathing control center neurons that promote arousal in mice diag graph *Science* v355 no6332 p1411 Mr 31 2017

Schwarz, Roger

5 Ways Meetings Get Off Track, and How to Prevent Each One *Harvard Business Review Digital Articles* p2 My 3 2016

8 Ground Rules for Great Meetings *Harvard Business Review Digital Articles* p2 Je 15 2016

Getting Teams with Different Subcultures to Collaborate *Harvard Business Review Digital Articles* p2 Jl 22 2016

How Leaders Can Help Others Influence Them *Harvard Business Review Digital Articles* p2 Ag 24 2016

How to Break Through Deadlock on Your Team *Harvard Business Review Digital Articles* p2 Jl 7 2015

How to Design an Agenda for an Effective Meeting *Harvard Business Review Digital Articles* p2 Mr 19 2015

Is Your Team Coordinating Too Much, or Not Enough? *Harvard Business Review Digital Articles* p2 Mr 23 2017

What the Research Tells Us About Team Creativity and Innovation *Harvard Business Review Digital Articles* p2 D 15 2015

When to Give Feedback in a Group and When to Do It One-on-One *Harvard Business Review Digital Articles* p2 Ag 19 2015

SCHWARZBAUM, LISA

Affairs to Remember: An entertainment journalist argues that Nora Ephron took a Hollywood genre and made it her own *New York Times Book Review* p13 S 3 2017

Different Lenses *New York Times Book Review* p10 Ja 8 2017

Film Studies *New York Times Book Review* p47 Je 4 2017

Schwarzenegger, Arnold, 1947-

Arnold Takes the Boardroom: Schwarzenegger inherits Donald Trump's role as chairman of NBC's rebooted Celebrity Apprentice I. RATLEDGE *TV Guide* v65 no2 p20 Ja 2 2017

Flexing His Muscle: Can Ah-nold create buzz around one of Indiana's most neglected issues come November 22? M. RUBINO *Indianapolis Monthly* p20 N 2017

Get to Know: GAT SPORT J. SCHILDHOUSE color *Muscle & Performance* v9 no7 p30 Jl 2017

Pioneers [Cover story] color *Time* v189 no16/17 p14 My 1-8 2017

Sound Bites color *Entertainment Weekly* no1448 p6 Ja 13 2017

Trump Learned Lessons About Reality TV That The Apprentice Hasn't D. D'Addario color *Time* v189 no4 p47 Ja 23 2017

TRUMP'S SCHWARZENEGGER PROBLEM M. WELCH color *Reason* v48 no11 p14 Ap 2017

Turn Fear into Fuel T. FERRISS bw color *Men's Health* v32 no6 p38 Ag 2017

Who's Hired? Schwarzenegger shares his performance reviews of this season's standouts *TV Guide* v65 no2 p23 Ja 2 2017

Schwarzkopf, Lin

Amphibians on the brink color map *Science* v357 no6350 p454 Ag 4 2017

Schweblin, Samanta

IRMAN *Harper's Magazine* p18 O 2017

THE SIZE OF THINGS cartoon *New Yorker* v93 no15 p56 My 29 2017

Schwehn, Kaethe

The Art of Waiting color *Orion Magazine* v35 no6 p61 N/D 2016

Schweisguth, François

Self-organized Notch dynamics generate stereotyped sensory organ patterns in Drosophila color *Science* v356 no6337 p501 My 5 2017

SCHWEITZER, ALBERT

LAST LOOK color *Yoga Journal* p112 2017 SpecialIssue

Schweitzer, Glenn

U.S.-Iran science exchange color *Science* v357 no6359 p11 O 6 2017

Schweitzer, Mary

KEEPING THE FAITH R. F. Service color *Science* v357 no6356 p1088 S 15 2017

Schweitzer, Maurice E.

When Trust Is Easily Broken, and When It's Not *Harvard Business Review Digital Articles* p2 F 17 2016

Schweitzer, Sharon

The Fine Art of Changing the Subject color *Weekly Standard* v22 no20 p2 Ja 30 2017

Schweizerische Bundesbahnen AG

WAIT A SECOND (AND A HALF) R. Verger color *Popular Science* v289 no5 p24 S/O 2017

SCHWENDENER, MARTHA

There at the Creation *New York Times Book Review* p18 F 26 2017

Schwenk, Jochen M.

A pathology atlas of the human cancer transcriptome diag *Science* v357 no6352 p660 Ag 18 2017

A subcellular map of the human proteome color *Science* v356 no6340 p820 My 26 2017

Schwenkler, John

An Ordinary Sunday [Cover story] color *Commonweal* v144 no15 p11 S 22 2017

Schwentke, Robert

ALLEGIANT D. Vaughn color *Sound & Vision* v81 no9 p67 N 2016

Schwimmer, David, 1966-

David Schwimmer C. Ianzito color *AARP: The Magazine* v59 no6A p80 O/N 2016

SCHWINDT, BEV

Creighton creates magic in holiday SantaLand color *Nebraska Life* v21 no6 p69 N/D 2017

Schwitters, Kurt, 1887-1948

The Growing Charm of Dada A. Brendel bw cartoon color *New York Review of Books* v63 no16 p22 O 27 2016

KURT SCHWITTERS T. Jeppesen *Art in America* v104 no9 p163 O 2016

PARISER FRÜHLING (PARISIAN SPRING) color *Art in America* v104 no10 p17 N 2016

Schwob, James

Lee Rubin: Our mentor and role model *Science* v355 no6327 p806 F 24 2017

Schwulst, Laurel

PERSONAL VOICE *Art in America* v104 no9 p108 O 2016

Schybergson, Olof

Gestures Will Be the Interface for the Internet of Things *Harvard Business Review Digital Articles* p2 Jl 8 2015

Schymkowitz, Joost

De novo design of a biologically active amyloid bibl graph *Science* v354 no6313 paah4949-1 N 11 2016

SCIACCA, JOHN

The 5.1 Basics of Surround Audio diag *Sound & Vision* v82 no2 p19 F/Mr 2017

Decorator-Friendly Bass color *Sound & Vision* v82 no6 p23 Jl/Ag 2017

Did Streaming Finally Kill Serving? color *Sound & Vision* v81 no10 p26 D 2016

Hiding in Plain Sight color *Sound & Vision* v82 no5 p23 Je 2017

How to Win at Wi-Fi color *Sound & Vision* v82 no4 p23 My 2017

Maximizing Your Network Performance color *Sound & Vision* v82 no3 p21 Ap 2017

Outfitting a Custom Toolkit color *Sound & Vision* v82 no8 p28 O 2017

Poolside Video color *Sound & Vision* v81 no9 p19 N 2016

Russound MCA-88X Streaming Housewide Audio Controller color *Sound & Vision* v82 no2 p60 F/Mr 2017

Top CI Trends from CEDIA 2016 color *Sound & Vision* v82 no1 p19 Ja 2017

Top Four System Install Mistakes color *Sound & Vision* v82 no7 p28 S 2017

Scialabba, George

Five Who Shook the World: A group biography of young Americans who embraced reform, socialism and woman suffrage *New York Times Book Review* p21 Jl 23 2017

The Free Banquet color *Commonweal* v144 no8 p19 My 5 2017

Sciamma, Céline, 1980-

SCENES OF HURT AND RAPTURE: CÉLINE SCIAMMA'S GIRLHOOD E. Wilson *Film Quarterly* v70 no3 p10 Spr 2017

Science

See also

Forensic sciences

Metrology

Religion & science

Science & state

Sports sciences

5 THINGS WE KNOW TO BE TRUE M. SHERMER, H. HALL et al cartoon *Scientific American* v315 no5 p46 N 2016

Advocacy in brief J. Sills color *Science* v356 no6333 p24 Ap 7 2017

Areas to watch in 2017 color *Science* v354 no6319 p1524 D 23 2016

Astounding Tales of Science! B. RADFORD *Skeptical Inquirer* v41 no2 p66 Mr/Ap 2017

THE ATLANTA SCIENCE FESTIVAL IS BACK K. VIMAL *Atlanta* v56 no11 p148 Mr 2017

Breakdowns of the year color *Science* v354 no6319 p1525 D 23 2016

Conspiring with engineers helps make science great E. Quill *Science News* v192 no7 p2 O 28 2017

Cover *Time* v189 no18 pC1 My 15 2017

A Forum for Integrating the Life Sciences J. M. VERDIER and S. L. COLLINS *BioScience* v67 no10 p871 O 2017

From the Front Lines of Science K. VINAL *Atlanta* v56 no11 p154 Mr 2017

GENIUS C. KALB bw color diag *National Geographic* v231 no5 p30 My 2017

GIVEN the EVIDENCE *Humanist* v77 no4 p8 Jl/Ag 2017

Idol Minds P. GULLEY *Indianapolis Monthly* v40 no7 p48 Mr 2017

In Colombia, peace dividend for science proves elusive L. Wade color graph *Science* v357 no6355 p958 S 8 2017

In defense of Crazy Ideas D. Stevenson *Physics Today* v70 no4 p10 Ap 2017

The journey of a scientist mother P. de Tezanos Pinto color *Science* v356 no6339 p774 My 19 2017

MEETING NOTES B. Bower color *Science News* v190 no13 p9 D 24 2016

Moonwalkers and women scientists highlighted at STARMUS IV D. J. Eicher color *Astronomy* v45 no6 p50 Je 2017

Moving forward after the march R. D. Holt *Science* v356 no6337 p467 My 5 2017

NSF: Time for Big Ideas R. E. GROPP *BioScience* v66 no11 p920 N 1 2016

PEOPLE ON THE MOVE [Cover story] E. Culotta color *Science* v356 no6339 p676 My 19 2017

RESEARCH color *Science* v356 no6337 p497 My 5 2017

Science Communication J. M. VERDIER and S. L. COLLINS *BioScience* v67 no6 p487 Je 2017

Science is indeed special J. Winkler *Physics Today* v70 no4 p12 Ap 2017

Science's rightful place J. Berg color *Science* v354 no6318 p1355 D 16 2016

SCIENTIFIC SPIRITUALITY M. HEDSTROM cartoon *Tricycle: The Buddhist Review* v26 no3 p56 Spr 2017

Shared history E. D. Maier and F. R. Beardsley *Science* v356 no6338 p591 My 12 2017

Teaching Skepticism: How Early Can We Begin? S. O. LILIENFELD *Skeptical Inquirer* v41 no5 p30 S/O 2017

Tear Down This Wall M. Huston *Psychology Today* v49 no6 p9 N/D 2016

Telling the Story of Science R. E. GROPP *BioScience* v67 no4 p319 Ap 2017

Thank God for the stars M. Murphy-Gill *U.S. Catholic* v81 no11 p4 N 2016

TRENDING NOW M. Mertyl, K. Hawlk et al color *Wired* v25 no4 p12 Ap 2017

An unprecedented march for science T. Appenzeller color *Science* v356 no6336 p356 Ap 28 2017

What's Ahead in 2017 E. Quill bw *Science News* v190 no13 p36 D 24 2016

What's That Buzzing Noise? Public Opinion on the Use of Drones for Conservation Science E. M. MARKOWITZ, M. C. NISBET et al *BioScience* v67 no4 p382 Ap 2017

What Would Happen? C. BOYER *National Geographic Kids* no469 p5 Ap 2017

Why science? Scientists share their stories color *Science* v356 no6338 p590 My 12 2017

Science & ethics

Academies Report Urges Bolstered Efforts to Protect Integrity of Science K. Frazier *Skeptical Inquirer* v41 no4 p5 Jl/Ag 2017

Science & history

50, 100 & 150 YEARS AGO bw color *Scientific American* v315 no5 p79 N 2016

Science and History Get Personal M. BOOTH *Skeptical Inquirer* v41 no3 p32 My/Je 2017

Science & law

Harnessing legal complexity J. B. Ruhl, D. Martin Katz et al diag graph *Science* v355 no6332 p1377 Mr 31 2017

Science & mythology

Mind Games S. KLEIN cartoon *Prevention* v68 no11 p30 N 2016

Science vs. Silliness for Parents: Debunking the Myths of Child Psychology S. HUPP, A. STARY et al *Skeptical Inquirer* v41 no1 p44 Ja/F 2017

Science & politics

See also

Climate change & politics

Cassandra smiling J. HESTER color *Astronomy* v45 no9 p16 S 2017

The Inquisitor's Heirs K. D. WILLIAMSON color *National Review* v69 no9 p14 My 15 2017

Reason on the Ropes color *Scientific American* v317 no4 p64 O 2017

'We Have Science!' J. LILEKS *National Review* v69 no9 p33 My 15 2017

Science & spiritualism

WHY OUR BODY DESTROY ITSELF L. STOKES bw color *Christianity Today* v61 no1 p60 Ja/F 2017

Science & state

See also

Technology & state

A MATTER OF FACT D. Malakoff color *Science* v355 no6325 p562 F 10 2017

No Time for Certainty A. J. SCOTT *Skeptical Inquirer* v41 no1 p56 Ja/F 2017

Prepare to March for Science and the Climate C. F. Naff *Humanist* v77 no3 p9 My/Je 2017

Putting technology to work A. N. LINK and E. D. O'SULLIVAN *Issues in Science & Technology* v33 no3 p14 Spr 2017

Republicans ready a regulatory rollback D. Malakoff color *Science* v354 no6315 p951 N 25 2016

The War on Facts Undermines Democracy J. Foley color *Scientific American* v316 no5 p10 My 2017

Science & state—Brazil

Brazil's 'doomsday' scenario H. Escobar color *Science* v355 no6323 p334 Ja 27 2017

Science & state—Congresses

Conference navigates gap between science and government M. Jarvis color *Science* v354 no6311 p427 O 28 2016

Science & state—Great Britain

A plan for U.K. science after the European Union referendum M. Galsworthy and M. McKee bibl color *Science* v355 no6320 p31 Ja 6 2017

Science & state—United States

AAAS seeks to uphold science's role in policy-making B. Ham color *Science* v355 no6332 p1383 Mr 31 2017

AAAS urges Trump team to value science and its benefits M. Jarvis color *Science* v355 no6323 p359 Ja 27 2017

Back from the Brink: Truth and Trust in the Public Sphere S. JASANOFF *Issues in Science & Technology* v33 no4 p25 Summ 2017

The Fires of Creationists, and Rallying for Science K. FRAZIER *Skeptical Inquirer* v41 no4 p4 Jl/Ag 2017

How a War on Science Could Hurt the U.S.-and Its Citizens J. Kluger and J. Worland color *Time* v189 no5 p17 F 13 2017

Informing policy with science B. Schaal color *Science* v355 no6324 p435 F 3 2017

Making big science decisions N. LANE *Issues in Science & Technology* v33 no4 p13 Summ 2017

The March for Science: Partisan Protests Put Public Trust in Scientists at Risk M. NISBET *Skeptical Inquirer* v41 no4 p18 Jl/Ag 2017

Regulators drop controversial biospecimen consent proposal J. Kaiser color *Science* v355 no6323 p335 Ja 27 2017

SCIENCE LESSONS FOR THE NEXT PRESIDENT D. Malakoff and J. Mervis color *Science* v354 no6310 p274 O 21 2016

The Trump era: 10 questions J. Mervis color *Science* v355 no6323 p333 Ja 27 2017

Trump's science shop is small and waiting for leadership J. Mervis color *Science* v357 no6347 p117 Jl 14 2017

U.S. Policies Informed by Science J. Worland color *Time* v189 no5 p19 F 13 2017

What's Next for Science? M. DiChristina color *Scientific American* v316 no1 p3 Ja 2017

White House science adviser talks space, climate change, and budgets D. Kramer *Physics Today* v69 no10 p27 O 2016

With Trump in charge, uncharted waters lie ahead for science D. Kramer *Physics Today* v70 no1 p29 Ja 2017

Science & state—United States—History

How to Maintain America's Edge L. R. Reif color *Foreign Affairs* v96 no3 p95 My/Je 2017

Science (Periodical)

The Origins of Dogs G. TARLACH bw cartoon color graph map *Discover* v27 no10 p32 D 2016

Science awards

Elizabeth Loftus Wins 2016 John Maddox Prize for Standing Up for Science *Skeptical Inquirer* v41 no2 p7 Mr/Ap 2017

New views snag science Nobels B. Bower, E. Conover et al bw *Science News* v192 no7 p6 O 28 2017

Science competitions

Congratulations to Regeneron Science Talent Search Top 40 Finalists color *Science News* v191 no4 p29 Mr 4 2017

GENERATION EXCELLENT E. Craig bw *Wired* v24 no11 p58 N 2016

Science consultants

Time to codify scientific integrity P. D. Tonko *Science* v356 no6344 p1241 Je 23 2017

Science databases

No Denying It D. HURLEY color *Discover* v38 no8 p78 O 2017

Science education

See also
  Computer science education
  Science education (Higher)

Addressing the Gender Gap in Distinguished Speakers at Professional Ecology Conferences C. M. FARR, S. P. BOMBACI et al *BioScience* v67 no5 p464 My 2017

A Case for Wonder: In science education, nothing is more important than developing the capacity for amazement C. NORMENT bw color *Orion Magazine* v35 no6 p13 N/D 2016

Evolution Education and State Politics J. P. CARR *BioScience* v67 no8 p687 Ag 2017

How I found my outreach niche M. Wheeler-Dubas color *Science* v357 no6353 p837 Ag 25 2017

Inspire your students with the Society's Science News in High Schools program color *Science News* v191 no11 p30 Je 10 2017

Intelligent design endangers education H. Machado-Silva color *Science* v357 no6354 p880 S 1 2017

Origins of Science Faculty with Education Specialties: Hiring Motivations and Prior Connections Explain Institutional Differences in the SFES Phenomenon S. D. BUSH, M. T. STEVENS et al *BioScience* v67 no5 p452 My 2017

What the Science Actually Says About Gender Gaps in the Workplace S. K. Johnson *Harvard Business Review Digital Articles* p2 2017

Science education (Higher)

TODAY'S BEST COLLEGES FOR TOMORROW'S WORLD 2017 color *Popular Mechanics* p66 N 2017

Science education—Methodology

SIDE-BY-SIDE LEARNING: A summer program focused on science disciplinary literacy C. Condie and J. Ippolito *Literacy Today (2411-7862)* v35 no1 p30 Jl/Ag 2017

Science education—United States

What does it take to sustain a productive partnership in education? K. Hammerness, A. MacPherson et al color *Phi Delta Kappan* v99 no1 p15 S 2017

Science exhibitions

See also
  Science fairs

ABOVE & BEYOND cartoon *New Yorker* v92 no33 p19 O 17 2016

A big, bug science party C. M. Gibson color *Science* v355 no6321 p141 Ja 13 2017

Museums Lighting Up A. Popescu color *Bloomberg Businessweek* no4522 p39 My 15 2017

'Specimens' goes behind the scenes H. Wolinsky color *Science News* v191 no7 p28 Ap 15 2017

Science fairs

Students seek scientific solutions at Broadcom MASTERS International color *Science News* v191 no13 p40 Jl 8 2017

Science fiction

3 Questions: William shatner J. Wolf *Saturday Evening Post* v289 no5 p27 S/O 2017

AI, people, and society E. Horvitz *Science* v357 no6346 p7 Jl 7 2017

THE GREAT UNKNOWN K. Stanley Robinson color *Scientific American* v315 no3 p80 S 2016

The Journeys of Ursula K. Le Guin Z. CARPENTER bw color *Nation* v303 no17 p22 O 24 2016

Land of the Lost img *New York* p108 Mr 6 2017

THE POWER OF SCIENCE FICTION S. DADICH *Wired* v25 no1 p3 Ja 2017

READ, WHITE AND BLUE: Which books do Americans take on vacation? Our analysis uncovered some surprises A. Clemens *Smithsonian* v48 no4 p14 Jl/Ag 2017

THE Real Worlds A. DANIEL color *Publishers Weekly* v263 no43 p26 O 24 2016

Stardom & Sci-Fi N. D. TYSON bw color *National Geographic* v231 no2 p24 F 2017

Why Business Leaders Need to Read More Science Fiction E. Peper *Harvard Business Review Digital Articles* p2 Jl 14 2017

Science fiction films

See also
  Planet of the Apes films
  Star Wars films
  Superhero films

America's top TV critic Matt Roush answers your burning questions Caryle and Dave *TV Guide* v65 no14 p4 Ap 3 2017

Blade Runner J. HOGAN *TV Guide* v65 no41 p39 O 2 2017

Do Androids Dream of Electric Sequels? N. Jenkins color *Time* v190 no15 p53 O 16 2017

Logan C. Chiarella color *Sound & Vision* v82 no8 p66 O 2017

TOMORROWLANDS color *Wired* v24 no11 p144 N 2016

Science fiction films—History & criticism

GIRL POWER: BACK TO THE FUTURE OF FEMINIST SCIENCE FICTION WITH INTO THE FOREST AND ARRIVAL S. Mayer *Film Quarterly* v70 no3 p32 Spr 2017

Science fiction films—Reviews

MASTER OF STRANGE E. Poenisch bw color *Esquire* p13 Ag 2017

Science fiction television programs

GEEK IDOLS R. KEEGAN color *Vanity Fair* v59 no9 p147a S 2017

Physics matters in "The Expanse." Sin does, too S. Sawyer and E. Sundrup color *America* v216 no3 p48 F 6 2017

WESTWORLD R. SOAVE color *Reason* v48 no8 p60 Ja 2017

Science journalism

SCIENCE JOURNALISM D. CORDELL, T. J. MARTIN et al color *Scientific American* v316 no2 p5 F 2017

This Is, and No Mistake P. Tyson *Sky & Telescope* v133 no5 p4 My 2017

Watch what you write A. A. ROSENBERG *Issues in Science & Technology* v33 no3 p16 Spr 2017

Science journalism—Awards

AAAS Kavli Science Journalism Award winners named E. Lane color *Science* v355 no6323 p362 Ja 27 2017

Science Museum (Great Britain)

Mechanized creatures P. Sareh and M. Kovac color *Science* v355 no6332 p1379 Mr 31 2017

Science museums—United States

RENO'S CAL AVE S. Spellman color map *Sunset* v238 no6 p24 Je 2017

Science news briefs

AROUND THE WORLD color *Science* v357 no6346 p8 Jl 7 2017

AROUND THE WORLD color *Science* v357 no6347 p112 Jl 14 2017

EYE ON 45 color *Science* v357 no6348 p233 Jl 21 2017

IN SCIENCE JOURNALS color *Science* v355 no6327 p808 F 24 2017

IN THE NEWS map *Scientific American* v315 no5 p18 N 2016

NEWSMAKERS *Science* v357 no6359 p15 O 6 2017

Quick Hits map *Scientific American* v316 no2 p16 F 2017

Quick Hits map *Scientific American* v316 no3 p22 Mr 2017

RESEARCH color *Science* v356 no6344 p1243 Je 23 2017

Science News for Students K. Hulick, B. Brookshire et al color

Science News v192 no4 p33 S 16 2017

Science periodical publishing

Watch what you write A. A. ROSENBERG *Issues in Science & Technology* v33 no3 p16 Spr 2017

Science publishing

See also

Science periodical publishing

The call of the wild J. R. I. Mendelson color *Science* v357 no6348 p326 Jl 21 2017

In India, elite institutes in shady journals P. Pulla *Science* v354 no6319 p1511 D 23 2016

Publication ban upends NIH lab, collaborators J. Couzin-Frankel color *Science* v355 no6327 p783 F 24 2017

Science funders plunge into publishing M. Enserink color *Science* v355 no6332 p1357 Mr 31 2017

Steady, strong growth is expected for open-access journals D. Kramer *Physics Today* v70 no5 p24 My 2017

The thing I wanted to say … S. PROUDFOOT color *Maclean's* no1 p23 F 17 2017

Science publishing—Government policy

Publish openly but responsibly A. J. Lowe, A. K. Smyth et al color *Science* v357 no6347 p141 Jl 14 2017

Science skepticism

See also

Climate change skepticism

Library Catalogs Deny Science Denial S. HERMAN *Skeptical Inquirer* v41 no3 p8 My/Je 2017

Reason on the Ropes color *Scientific American* v317 no4 p64 O 2017

SAVING SCIENCE K. Burdette color *Fortune* v175 no5 p18 Ap 1 2017

Science, Public Trust, and CSICon 2016 K. FRAZIER *Skeptical Inquirer* v41 no1 p4 Ja/F 2017

The Spectrum of Skepticism K. FRAZIER *Skeptical Inquirer* v41 no5 p4 S/O 2017

Science students

A Case for Wonder: In science education, nothing is more important than developing the capacity for amazement C. NORMENT bw color *Orion Magazine* v35 no6 p13 N/D 2016

No, the Best Science Students Aren't Becoming Financiers N. Torres *Harvard Business Review Digital Articles* p2 D 22 2015

Science teachers—Congresses

Building a 'community of geeks' color *Science News* v190 no10 p29 N 12 2016

Science—China

It's whom you know that counts Y. Xie bibl color *Science* v355 no6329 p1022 Mr 10 2017

Science—Congresses

AAAS 2017 ANNUAL MEETING PROGRAM chart color *Science* v354 no6310 p363 O 21 2016

CSICon 2016 Lights Up Las Vegas P. Fidalgo *Skeptical Inquirer* v41 no2 p8 Mr/Ap 2017

Designing nutritional games and brains for space color *Science News* v190 no11 p27 N 26 2016

Haze may explain Pluto's red spots A. YEAGER color *Science News* v191 no7 p14 Ap 15 2017

Science—Equipment & supplies

new products color *Science* v355 no6320 p96 Ja 6 2017

new products color *Science* v357 no6355 p1053 S 8 2017

raise a science lover M. CROUCH *Parents* v92 no2 p56 F 2017

Science fiction—Charts, diagrams, etc.

CATEGORY BESTSELLERS AUG. 29-SEPT. 25, 2016 *Publishers Weekly* v263 no41 p18 O 10 2016

CATEGORY BESTSELLERS C. JURIS chart *Publishers Weekly* v264 no41 p15 O 9 2017

CATEGORY BESTSELLERS C. JURIS chart *Publishers Weekly* v264 no7 p16 F 13 2017

iBooks Bestsellers chart color *Publishers Weekly* v264 no2 p19 Ja 9 2017

iBooks Bestsellers C. JURIS chart color *Publishers Weekly* v264 no41 p17 O 9 2017

Science—History—Study & teaching

MAKERS S. Kean cartoon *New Yorker* v92 no30 p25 S 26 2016

Science—Periodicals

THE POWER OF SCIENCE FICTION S. DADICH *Wired* v25 no1 p3 Ja 2017

RESEARCH color *Science* v355 no6325 p591 F 10 2017

This Is, and No Mistake P. Tyson *Sky & Telescope* v133 no5 p4 My 2017

Science—Political aspects

See also

Climatic changes—Political aspects

Corporate Scientists Go to Washington E. Fry color *Fortune* v175 no5 p13 Ap 1 2017

Donald Trump's Campaign for Science Illiteracy cartoon *Scientific American* v315 no5 p8 N 2016

EVEN IF PEOPLE CAN'T MOVE FREELY IDEAS MUST J. PAYNE *Vital Speeches of the Day* v83 no4 p118 Ap 2017

From Politics to Science: The Way Forward R. E. GROPP *BioScience* v66 no12 p1007 D 1 2016

How I'm standing up for science S. J. Cheng color *Science* v355 no6327 p878 F 24 2017

President Obama's Scientific Legacy J. P. CARR *BioScience* v66 no12 p1011 D 1 2016

The Tweets We Hold to Be Self-Evident color *Scientific American* v315 no3 p7 S 2016

Science—Public opinion

Mapping the Landscape of Public Attitudes on Synthetic Biology H. AKIN, K. M. ROSE et al *BioScience* v67 no3 p290 Mr 2017

Science—Social aspects

Celebrity science J. GREENBERG color *Issues in Science & Technology* v33 no1 p19 Fall 2016

CITIZEN SCIENCE PROGRAMS S. Doyle color *Canadian Geographic* v135 no6 p80 D 2015

The Enlightenment Wrapped Up in an Organizational Package *Skeptical Inquirer* v41 no2 p9 Mr/Ap 2017

Journalism under Attack K. KLOOR *Issues in Science & Technology* v33 no2 p60 Wint 2017

Prepare to March for Science and the Climate C. F. Naff *Humanist* v77 no3 p9 My/Je 2017

A short presidential reading list J. Berg color *Science* v354 no6310 p265 O 21 2016

Science—Social aspects—United States

Science's Role in Reducing US Racial Tensions T. S. WOODSON *Issues in Science & Technology* v33 no2 p21 Wint 2017

Science—Societies, etc.

CENTER FOR INQUIRY *Skeptical Inquirer* v41 no2 p5 Mr/Ap 2017

Why Skepticism? R. A. LINDSAY *Skeptical Inquirer* v41 no2 p46 Mr/Ap 2017

Science & state—United States—Charts, diagrams, etc.

Oval Office science bw *Science* v354 no6310 p276 O 21 2016

Science—Study & teaching

CITIZEN SCIENCE PROGRAMS S. Doyle color *Canadian Geographic* v135 no6 p80 D 2015

Young science officers lead by example D. Iyer bibl color *Science* v355 no6322 p256 Ja 20 2017

Science—Study & teaching—United States

Building a 'community of geeks' color *Science News* v190 no10 p29 N 12 2016

Science—United States

The Gathering Storms till looms D. Kramer *Physics Today* v69 no11 p29 N 2016

Science gets little love in Trump spending plan chart *Science* v356 no6340 p795 My 26 2017

A short presidential reading list J. Berg color *Science* v354 no6310 p265 O 21 2016

What now for science? R. D. Holt cartoon *Science* v354 no6315 p947 N 25 2016

Science—United States—Social aspects

Science for life B. Alberts color *Science* v355 no6332 p1353 Mr 31 2017

What's Next for Science? M. DiChristina color *Scientific American* v316 no1 p3 Ja 2017

Scientific apparatus & instruments

See also

Astronomical instruments

Electronic apparatus & appliances

Measuring instruments

A CLASSROOM IN THE AGE OF ENLIGHTENMENT E. W. Lasser bw color *Magazine Antiques* v184 no3 p90 My/Je 2017

Scientific apparatus & instruments—Evaluation

new products color *Science* v357 no6347 p217 Jl 14 2017

new products: genomics color *Science* v355 no6321 p210 Ja 13 2017

Scientific community

Academics can help shape Wikipedia T. Shafee, D. Mietchen et al *Science* v357 no6351 p557 Ag 11 2017

Are Moonshots Giant Leaps of Faith? W. D. VALDIVIA *Issues in Science & Technology* v33 no3 p51 Spr 2017

Catalan scientists ponder fate after independence vote T. Rabesandratana color *Science* v357 no6359 p23 O 6 2017

A COSMIC CONTROVERSY A. H. GUTH, D. I. KAISER et al color *Scientific American* v317 no1 p5 Jl 2017

EYE ON 45 color *Science* v357 no6353 p739 Ag 25 2017

A New World of Applications at ELI Beamlines *Science & Technology Review* p11 Jl/Ag 2017

Northeast Asia trip bolsters ongoing scientific cooperation M. Jarvis color *Science* v354 no6315 p979 N 25 2016

Step up for quality research N. J. Schrag and G. M. Purdy color *Science* v357 no6351 p531 Ag 11 2017

Too much democracy? N. STEHR and T. TAMURA *Issues in Science & Technology* v33 no1 p5 Fall 2016

U.S.-Iran science exchange G. Schweitzer color *Science* v357 no6359 p11 O 6 2017

Scientific development

c. 2500: United States T. Chiang *Lapham's Quarterly* v10 no2 p133 Spr 2017

Challenges of S&T system reform in China C. Cao and R. P. Suttmeier bibl color *Science* v355 no6329 p1019 Mr 10 2017

Eureka in the Arctic M. CAMPBELL color *Maclean's* v130 no3 p18 Ap 2017

Improving global integration of crop research M. P. Reynolds, H. J. Braun et al color *Science* v357 no6349 p359 Jl 28 2017

Scientific Edge LLC

New electronic lure may catch too many fish; one state bans it M. Butler and N. KREBS color *Outdoor Life* v224 no3 p6 Ap 2017

New electronic lure may catch too many fish; one state bans it M. Butler color *Field & Stream* v122 no2 p35 Je/Jl 2017

Scientific expeditions

EXPLORATORY WORKS: DRAWINGS FROM THE DEPARTMENT OF TROPICAL RESEARCH FIELD EXPEDITIONS *Issues in Science & Technology* v33 no4 p71 Summ 2017

The New Age of Discovery R. CONNIFF color *Smithsonian* v47 no10 p21 Mr 2017

Scientific experimentation

Art Zone color *National Geographic Kids* no472 p35 Ag 2017

Scientific knowledge

Applying Science R. E. GROPP *BioScience* v67 no9 p779 S 2017

At the Boundary of Knowledge M. Shermer color *Scientific American* v315 no3 p88 S 2016

Science is indeed special J. Winkler *Physics Today* v70 no4 p12 Ap 2017

Theory and Truth M. DiChristina color *Scientific American* v315 no5 p4 N 2016

Scientific literature

A family analysis J. Berg color *Science* v355 no6320 p9 Ja 6 2017

The Pace of Scientific Research Is Picking Up I. Madisch *Harvard Business Review Digital Articles* p2 Ag 3 2015

Scientific method

See also

Forecasting

Observation (Scientific method)

Making my own home F. Kaplan color *Science* v354 no6309 p254 O 14 2016

March for science J. Berg color *Science* v356 no6333 p7 Ap 7 2017

PREDICTION AND ITS LIMITS [Cover story] B. R. Jasny and R. Stone color *Science* v355 no6324 p468 F 3 2017

Scientific software

new products: software/data analysis color *Science* v357 no6348 p319 Jl 21 2017

Scientists

See also

Anthropologists

Cartographers

Ecologists

Environmentalists

Mathematicians

Ornithologists

Physicists

Social scientists

Women scientists

Advocacy in brief J. Sills color *Science* v356 no6333 p24 Ap 7 2017

Ahmed Hassan Zewail M. Chergui *Physics Today* v69 no12 p69 D 2016

BIOLOGY OF THE BOOK A. Gibbons color diag *Science* v357 no6349 p346 Jl 28 2017

Cash incentives for papers go global A. Abritis and A. McCook graph *Science* v357 no6351 p541 Ag 11 2017

Catalan scientists ponder fate after independence vote T. Rabesandratana color *Science* v357 no6359 p23 O 6 2017

Drawing connections J. McDermott color *Science* v356 no6343 p1202 Je 16 2017

THE ELEGANT TRANSLATOR *Psychology Today* v49 no6 p14 N/D 2016

Ensuring scientific integrity in the Age of Trump G. T. Goldman, E. Berman et al bibl cartoon *Science* v355 no6326 p696 F 17 2017

Family-friendly science A. Zellmer cartoon *Science* v354 no6315 p1070 N 25 2016

Gathering the human stories of science G. A. Good *Physics Today* v70 no5 p74 My 2017

The god of Science D. RUTH and A. MCCAIG *USA Today Magazine* v145 no2860 p70 Ja 2017

Hans Rosling Brought Data to Life, Showed Our Misconceptions about the World A. Sarma *Skeptical Inquirer* v41 no4 p9 Jl/Ag 2017

Heroes of Science cartoon *Discover* v38 no4 p34 My 2017

In Canada, case spurs concern over misconduct secrecy A. Komnenic color *Science* v354 no6318 p1361 D 16 2016

It's whom you know that counts Y. Xie bibl color *Science* v355 no6329 p1022 Mr 10 2017

LAUNCH color *Wired* v25 no8 p5 Ag 2017

THE LIFE EXPANDERS N. Barzilai chart color *Men's Health* v32 no7 p116 S 2017

A Man Among Bees color *Canadian Wildlife* v23 no1 p44 Mr/Ap 2017

Migration today: Displaced scientists R. Mustafa color *Science* v356 no6339 p698 My 19 2017

NIH tests blind reviews *Science* v356 no6342 p990 Je 9 2017

Promoting human rights through science J. Sills, L. Segal et al color *Science* v357 no6359 p34 O 6 2017

Quantifying the evolution of individual scientific impact R. Sinatra, Dashun Wang et al graph *Science* v354 no6312 p596 N 4 2016

Ralph J. Cicerone (1943–2016) J. P. Holdren and M. K. McNutt color *Science* v354 no6316 p1107 D 2 2016

RESTLESS MINDS J. Bohannon color graph *Science* v356 no6339 p690 My 19 2017

Roger Y. Tsien (1952–2016) S. J. Lippard color *Science* v354 no6308 p41 O 7 2016

Romanian researchers decry sudden power grab A. Nistoroiu color *Science* v356 no6342 p994 Je 9 2017

THE SACRED COW C. Ketcham *Sierra* v102 no2 p34 Mr/Ap 2017

Scientific advocacy: A tool for assessing the risks of engagement G. A. Schmidt and S. D. Donner bibl *Bulletin of the Atomic Scientists* v73 no5 p344 2017

The scientific swerve: Changing your research focus C. Tachibana color *Science* v357 no6359 p126 O 6 2017

Scientists need social media influencers M. Galetti and R. Costa-Pereira *Science* v357 no6354 p880 S 1 2017

Scientists start to parse a Trump presidency J. Mervis color *Science* v354 no6314 p811 N 18 2016

Social media: More scientists needed S. Mojarad *Science* v357 no6358 p1362 S 29 2017

Scientists' attitudes

The sustainable scientist J. J. Mcdonnell color *Science* v357 no6356 p1202 S 15 2017

Scientists in government

Empowering science advice V. Turekian color *Science* v357 no6353 p735 Ag 25 2017

The Explorer A. SHEPHARD color *New Republic* v247 no12 p9 D 2016

Science advice in the Trump White House [Cover story] K. R. W. Matthews, K. M. Evans et al bibl color *Science* v355 no6325 p574 F 10 2017

Scientists on television

The image of scientists in The Big Bang Theory M. A. Weitekamp *Physics Today* v70 no1 p40 Ja 2017

Scientists with disabilities

See also

Deaf scientists

Community network for deaf scientists H. J. Adler, K. L. Anbuhl et al color *Science* v356 no6336 p386 Ap 28 2017

Scientists—Awards

Teen scientists already changing the world color *Science News* v191 no7 p29 Ap 15 2017

Scientists—China

Foreign-born scientists find a home in China S. Williams color *Science* v354 no6312 p644 N 4 2016

Scientists—Congresses

Calendar of meetings *BioScience* v67 no2 p183 F 2017

Scientists—Education

Coping with class in science C. D. Holder color *Science* v355 no6325 p658 F 10 2017

Scientists—Finance

U.K. scientists gird for future break with EU E. Stokstad color graph *Science* v355 no6330 p1107 Mr 17 2017

Scientists—Iran

Iran's science landscape in context R. Mansouri *Science* v354 no6319 p1542 D 23 2016

Scientists—Mexico

Mexican scientists feel the Trump effect L. Wade and J. Mervis color *Science* v355 no6324 p440 F 3 2017

Scientists—Political activity

HOW TO BE HEARD E. Stokstad *Science* v355 no6325 p572 F 10 2017

Scientists—Salaries, wages, etc.

Can Apple Attract Top Researchers If It Keeps Their Research Secret? W. Frick *Harvard Business Review Digital Articles* p2 N 2 2015

NSF requests salary cost-sharing *Science* v354 no6311 p394 O 28 2016

Scientists—Services for

Building community for deaf scientists G. Buckley, S. Smith et al bibl color *Science* v355 no6322 p255 Ja 20 2017

Scientists—Social aspects

Take a Deep Breath K. FINNERAN *Issues in Science & Technology* v33 no2 p17 Wint 2017

Scientists—Social conditions

It's the Weekend! Why Are You Working? F. Gino and B. Staats *Harvard Business Review Digital Articles* p2 Ap 10 2015

Scientists—United States

How I'm standing up for science S. J. Cheng color *Science* v355 no6327 p878 F 24 2017

MAD SCIENTISTS GET EVEN N. BAJWA *In These Times* v41 no3 p11 Mr 2017

POLITICAL SCIENCE D. JOHNS color *Scientific American* v317 no3 p7 S 2017

Ralph J. Cicerone M. Prather and R. Stolarski *Physics Today* v70 no2 p67 F 2017

Scientists can't be silent C. Coons color *Science* v357 no6350 p431 Ag 4 2017

Scientists—United States—Attitudes

Scientific Controversies as Proxy Politics D. J. HICKS *Issues in Science & Technology* v33 no2 p67 Wint 2017

Scientists—United States—Political activity

Act for science R. Holt color *Science* v355 no6325 p551 F 10 2017

From a tweet, a March for Science is born L. Wessel color *Science* v355 no6325 p556 F 10 2017

Scientology

"WE NEED TO CONTINUE TO TELL THESE STORIES" J. Nolfi color *Entertainment Weekly* no1459 p44 Mr 31 2017

Scillian, Devin

Missile Toe: A Very Confused Christmas *Publishers Weekly* v264 no36 p98 S 4 2017

Scintillators

Novel Scintillator Improves X-Ray Imaging A. Chen color *Science & Technology Review* p12 Ja/F 2017

Sciortino, Karley

THE BIG QUESTION cartoon *Atlantic* v320 no4 p124 N 2017

"People should be less scared of sex." [Cover story] A. Lauren Greco color *Glamour* v115 no7 p88 Jl 2017

Scirghi, Thomas J.

How to build a better preacher S. Callahan *America* v217 no3 p46 Ag 7 2017

Inside the Cenacle *America* v216 no12 p50 My 29 2017

Scissors & shears

Getting Snippy With It *Atlanta* v56 no11 p60 Mr 2017

Handy Hints color *American Cowboy* v24 no1 p50 Je/Jl 2017

Scissors & shears—Design & construction

A GOOD CLIP F. VIGNA *Martha Stewart Living* no270 p166 D 2016

SCISSORS, DEREK

Trade Reciprocity With China [Cover story] color *National Review* v69 no2 p25 F 6 2017

Sciutto, S. J.

Observation of a large-scale anisotropy in the arrival directions of cosmic rays above 8×10^{18} eV *Science* v357 no6357 p1266 S 22 2017

SCL Group Ltd.

Cambridge Analytica's Low-Tech Fisticuffs S. Baker, D. Kocieniewski et al color *Bloomberg Businessweek* no4516 p23 Mr 27 2017

SCLATER, J. A.

COSMOS CONSENSUS? *Scientific American* v317 no4 p8 O 2017

Scleractinia

Biological control of aragonite formation in stony corals S. Von Euw, Q. Zhang et al bw color graph *Science* v356 no6341 p933 Je 1 2017

Scobey, Annemarie

Baby love: Forget the stages--be present to parenting color *U.S. Catholic* v82 no10 p43 O 2017

Become more prayerful this year color *U.S. Catholic* v82 no1 p43 Ja 2017

Be not afraid color *U.S. Catholic* v82 no11 p25 N 2017

Choose children color *U.S. Catholic* v82 no4 p43 Ap 2017

A chronic issue color *U.S. Catholic* v82 no7 p29 Jl 2017

Face to face color *U.S. Catholic* v82 no2 p43 F 2017

Faith away from home: Early faith formation prepares young adults for college--years before the admission letters arrive color *U.S. Catholic* v82 no9 p23 S 2017

A family holiday color *U.S. Catholic* v81 no12 p43 D 2016

Grow in gratitude color *U.S. Catholic* v81 no11 p43 N 2016

Let's talk color *U.S. Catholic* v82 no3 p43 Mr 2017

Life unexpected: When plans go awry, consider the possibilities color *U.S. Catholic* v82 no8 p43 Ag 2017

A love that heals color *U.S. Catholic* v82 no5 p36 My 2017

Out of the ordinary color *U.S. Catholic* v82 no11 p43 N 2017

Pray about it color *U.S. Catholic* v82 no7 p43 Jl 2017

Summer service color *U.S. Catholic* v82 no6 p43 Je 2017

Take a break color *U.S. Catholic* v82 no5 p43 My 2017

Terms and conditions: Parents can make smartphone use for kids safer by writing their own fine print color *U.S. Catholic* v82 no9 p43 S 2017

We always do that color *U.S. Catholic* v81 no11 p36 N 2016

We need to talk color *U.S. Catholic* v82 no1 p36 Ja 2017

Winter together color *U.S. Catholic* v82 no3 p36 Mr 2017

Scoblic, J. Peter

Bringing probability judgments into policy debates via forecasting tournaments bibl color *Science* v355 no6324 p481 F 3 2017

Scocca, Tom

The Harm of Smarm C. ROSEN *Commentary* v142 no1 p4 Jl/Ag 2016

Scofield, Merry Ellen—Interviews

The origins of caller ID? E. H. Gustafson color *Magazine Antiques* v184 no1 p216 Ja/F 2017

Scolari, Vittore F.

3D organization of synthetic and scrambled chromosomes diag *Science* v355 no6329 p1050 Mr 10 2017

Scolds

THE SHAMING OF THE SHREW D. Ugrešić *Harper's Magazine* v334 no2000 p23 Ja 2017

Scoles, Sarah

Alien Contact bw color diag graph *Discover* v38 no6 p58 Jl/Ag 2017

Astronomer hustles to find E.T E. Conover color *Science News* v192 no1 p26 Ag 5 2017

Mind Melt bw color *Discover* v38 no7 p30 S 2017

Mod squad cartoon *Popular Science* v289 no4 p42 Jl/Ag 2017

NEXT LIST 2017 bw graph *Wired* v25 no5 p63 My 2017

PARCHED color *Popular Science* v289 no2 p58 Mr/Ap 2017

To Jupiter, Sans Nuclear color diag *Discover* v27 no10 p20 D 2016

World Weary? The Best Is Yet to Come color *Discover* v38 no3 p40 Ap 2017

Sconces

Big Ideas for Tight Spots C. SWANSON color *House Beautiful* v159 no5 p59 Je 2017

Sconces—Evaluation

LIGHTING & ART GLASS color *Arts & Crafts Homes & the Revival* v12 no1 p46 2017 Resouce Guide

Scones

Fruity Teatime Sweets S. Gutierrez *British Heritage Travel* v38 no4 p74 Jl/Ag 2017

Scoops

SCOOPED! M. GLISAN color *Better Homes & Gardens* v95 no5 p134 My 2017

Scooterino (Company)

An Uber-Tinder Mashup Hits the Spanish Steps C. Albanese and A. Migliaccio color *Bloomberg Businessweek* no4502 p42 D 5 2016

Scooters

BOOT SCOOT BOOGIE J. PEARLEY HUFFMAN chart color *Car & Driver* v63 no1 p64 Jl 2017

Scopelliti, Demetrio

Consumer spending: past and present *Monthly Labor Review* p1 N 2016

Score: A Film Music Documentary (Film)

Score: A Film Music Documentary D. Coggan color *Entertainment Weekly* no1471 p53 Je 23 2017

Score Baja (All terrain vehicle race)

LARRY RAGLAND FIVE BAJA WINS [Cover story] J. OBER color *Dirt Sports + Off-Road* v51 no1 p74 Ja 2017

ROB MAC RIPS TO THREE-PEAT BAJA 1000 OVERALL M. EMERY color *Dirt Sports + Off-Road* v51 no4 p10 Ap 2017

Score International (Company)

A NATION'S DATEBOOK *Dirt Sports + Off-Road* v51 no6 p72 Je 2017

Scoring rubrics

A Rubric to Evaluate Citizen-Science Programs for Long-Term Ecological Monitoring C. A. TREDICK, R. L. LEWISON et al *BioScience* v67 no9 p834 S 2017

Scorpion (TV program)

Inside Scorpion's Nest M. ROFMAN *TV Guide* v64 no40 p48 O 3 2016

Scorpion M. Roffman color *TV Guide* v64 no42 p39 O 10 2016

Scorpion M. Roffman *TV Guide* v65 no19 p24 My 1 2017

Scorpion N. Abrams, C. Holub et al color *Entertainment Weekly* no1482/1483 p55 S 22 2017

Scorpion's Deep Freeze M. Roffman *TV Guide* v65 no2 p13 Ja 2 2017

Toby and Happy's Scorpion Wedding! M. Roffman *TV Guide* p9 Ap 17 2017

What to Watch R. Rahman, J. Jensen et al color *Entertainment Weekly* no1466 p53 My 19 2017

What to Watch R. Rahman, L. Greenblatt et al color *Entertainment Weekly* no1434 p50 O 7 2016

Scorpions

Behind the scenes What ha' happen was... color *Motor Trend* v69 no1 p42 Ja 2017

Scorpius (Constellation)

Cosmic cats and crustaceans color *Astronomy* v45 no6 p74 Je 2017

Scorsese, Martin, 1942-

ALONE WITH YOU N. PINKERTON color *Film Comment* v53 no3 p33 My/Je 2017

Artists color *Time* v189 no16/17 p40 My 1-8 2017

"Every Man Has to Go Through Hell to Reach Paradise" A. STERNBERGH img *New York* p114 Mr 6 2017

A Faith for Failures J. Ryan color *Commonweal* v144 no1 p39 Ja 6 2017

Fear and Trembling R. DOUTHAT color *National Review* v69 no3 p54 F 20 2017

Japan: Beautiful, Savage, Mute I. Buruma color *New York Review of Books* v64 no2 p27 F 9 2017

The Light Touch S. Zacharek color *Time* v189 no6 p38 F 20 2017

REDEMPTION [Cover story] P. ELIE color *New York Times Magazine* p44 N 27 2016

Silence *New Yorker* v92 no42 p36 D 19 2016

When God is silent P. Jenkins color *Christian Century* v134 no5 p44 Mr 1 2017

Why He Deserves It M. Ford bw *New York Review of Books* v63 no19 p16 D 8 2016

Scorsese, Martin, 1942-—Interviews

Creating 'Silence' J. MARTIN *America* v215 no19 p16 D 19 2016

EDITOR'S LETTER N. Rapold color *Film Comment* v53 no1 p4 Ja/F 2017

Trials of Faith R. R. Cooper color *Commonweal* v144 no2 p8 Ja 27 2017

YOU TALKIN' TO ME? N. PINKERTON color *Film Comment* v53 no1 p26 Ja/F 2017

Scotland—Biography

The Good Duchess J. Dismore *History Today* v66 no10 p4 O 2016

Scotland—Description & travel

Aberdeenshire *British Heritage Travel* v37 no6 p64 N/D 2016

Aberdeenshire: Scotland's Enchanted Northeast Kingdom color *British Heritage Travel* v38 no5 p50 S/O 2017

Bonnie Scotland by Train *British Heritage Travel* v38 no2 p16 Mr/Ap 2017

ST. ANDREWS color *British Heritage Travel* v38 no5 p22 S/O 2017

Take a Few Days in the Scottish Borders color *British Heritage Travel* v38 no5 p20 S/O 2017

While You're In the Neighborhood... A Top 100 Trip Planner J. Passov color *Golf Magazine* v59 no10 p92 O 2017

Scotland—History—Exhibitions

ANGLO-FILE S. Gutierrez *British Heritage Travel* v38 no3 p12 My/Je 2017

Scots pine

WHICH BEDDING HARBORS MORE BACTERIA? C. Barakat and M. McCluskey color *Equus* no471 p11 D 2016

Scotson, Lorraine

Wildlife-snaring crisis in Asian forests bibl color *Science* v355 no6322 p255 Ja 20 2017

SCOTT, A. O.

16 ACTORS color *New York Times Magazine* p52 D 11 2016

A CRASH COURSE IN FOREIGN CINEMA color *Esquire* p122 S 2017

DEALING bw color *Esquire* p94 My 2017

In the Driver's Seat color *Esquire* v167 no2 p100 Mr 2017

JACQUES RIVETTE & ABBAS KIAROSTAM *New York Times Magazine* p57 D 25 2016

L. A. NOIR bw *New York Times Magazine* p64 D 11 2016

Story After Story [Cover story] *New York Times Book Review* p1 N 20 2016

SCOTT, AARON

The Cure for Everything (Seriously) cartoon map *Men's Health* v32 no9 p67 N 2017

Scott, Adam, 1973-

Wet Hot's Face-off D. Snierson color *Entertainment Weekly* no1476 p52 Ag 4 2017

What You Should Know About ADAM SCOTT D. KAMP bw *Vanity Fair* p108 Hollywood 2017 Supplement

Scott, Adam, 1973-—Interviews

5 Loaded Questions for Adam Scott J. Harman color *Glamour* v115 no11 p44 N 2017

ADAM SCOTT AND CRAIG ROBINSON D. Snierson, A. Bacle et al color *Entertainment Weekly* no1482/1483 p42 S 22 2017

Droll Model M. WAKIM color *Los Angeles Magazine* v62 no10 p84 O 2017

Scott, Adam, 1980-

Watch + Learn B. Riggs and J. Marksbury color *Golf Magazine*

v59 no10 p28 O 2017

SCOTT, ALAN J.

No Time for Certainty *Skeptical Inquirer* v41 no1 p56 Ja/F 2017

Scott, Alec

BACK TO THE LAND color *Sunset* v239 no4 p60 O 2017

SHELTER AT THE EDGE OF THE WORLD color *Sunset* v239 no3 p62 S 2017

Scott, Amanda

The Reluctant Highlander: Highland Romance, Book 1 color *Publishers Weekly* v264 no17 p74 Ap 24 2017

Scott, Andrea K.

Arc of Joan color *New Yorker* v93 no15 p7 My 29 2017

Fall Preview color *New Yorker* v93 no25 p10 Ag 28 2017

Labor Intensive color *New Yorker* v92 no36 p6 N 7 2016

Live Wire cartoon *New Yorker* v93 no19 p10 Jl 3 2017

Never-Ending Story cartoon *New Yorker* v93 no13 p10 My 15 2017

On Message color *New Yorker* v92 no46 p13 Ja 23 2017

On the Ball color *New Yorker* v93 no8 p12 Ap 10 2017

Spring Preview cartoon *New Yorker* v93 no4 p18 Mr 13 2017

Summer Preview cartoon *New Yorker* v93 no14 p14 My 22 2017

Winter Preview cartoon *New Yorker* v92 no37 p24 N 14 2016

Woman on Wire color *New Yorker* v93 no31 p8 O 9 2017

Scott, Andrew

How Work Will Change When Most of Us Live to 100 *Harvard Business Review Digital Articles* p2 Je 27 2016

Our Assumptions About Old and Young Workers Are Wrong *Harvard Business Review Digital Articles* p2 N 14 2016

What Younger Workers Can Learn from Older Workers, and Vice Versa *Harvard Business Review Digital Articles* p2 N 18 2016

Scott, Bobby

The Pros and Cons of Federally Funded School Choice Programs *Congressional Digest* v96 no7 p12 S 2017

Scott, Brian

A WINDOW INTO FARMING *Successful Farming* v115 no3 p16 Mid-F 2017

Scott, Britain

Beyond the roots of human inaction: Fostering collective effort toward ecosystem conservation color diag *Science* v356 no6335 p275 Ap 21 2017

Scott, Donna

Oral Health for Healthy Aging color *Maclean's* v129 no40 p59 O 10 2016

Scott, Dread

BANNER YEAR A. CAMPBELL bw color *ARTnews* v115 no4 p110 Wint 2016/2017

Scott, Drew

Small Talk with HGTV's Property Brothers D. Peak color *Log Home Living* v34 no3 p18 Ap 2017

Scott, Ellen Warner

Profiles in Courage *Sierra* v102 no4 p4 Jl/Ag 2017

SCOTT, EUGENIE

Bigfoot and I: Reflections on Forty Years of Skepticism *Skeptical Inquirer* v40 no6 p35 N/D 2016

Scott, Gary G.

Polymeric peptide pigments with sequence-encoded properties color graph *Science* v356 no6342 p1064 Je 9 2017

Scott, Georgia—Interviews

Beauty Unwrapped P. GABBARA and M. BOBO color *Ebony* v72 no5 p43 Mr 2017

Scott, Gwendolyn

The Politics of Late-Night Comedy color *Atlantic* v320 no1 p10 Jl/Ag 2017

Scott, Harry

Quite a Catch J. Hilliard color diag *Log Home Living* v34 no5 p36 Jl 2017

Things to Do Today: Make My Dreams Come True D. PEAK *Log Home Living* v34 no5 p6 Jl 2017

Scott, Hugh, 1900-1994

THE SILENT MAJORITY J. Toobin cartoon *New Yorker* v93 no14 p27 My 22 2017

Scott, Jacqueline

ordinary PEOPLE LIKE US D. J. Gladstone bw color *Missouri Life* v44 no6 p58 S 2017

SCOTT, JAKE

DOG DAZE *Cincinnati Magazine* v50 no10 p52 Jl 2017

Scott, James C.

BARBARIAN VIRTUES S. MOYN color *Nation* v305 no10 p27 O 23 2017

The perils of permanence S. Shablovsky color *Science* v357 no6350 p459 Ag 4 2017

Rise of civilization came at a big cost, book claims B. Bower color *Science News* v192 no6 p28 O 14 2017

Scott, Jane

LET THE GOOD TIMES ROLL H. Brown color *House Beautiful* v159 no8 p112 O 2017

Scott, Jared P.

The Age of Consequences D. Chevlen *Science* v356 no6337 p481 My 5 2017

Scott, Jason

Australia Battles Its Gambling Addiction cartoon *Bloomberg Businessweek* no4493 p24 O 3 2016

China's Troubles Down on the Farm color *Bloomberg Businessweek* no4525 p16 Je 5 2017

A Rogue State Could Swing Australia Left *Bloomberg Businessweek* no4532 p33 Jl 31 2017

Scott, Jeremy, 1975-

the buzz color *InStyle* v24 no8 p122 Ag 2017

Scott, Jessie

10 UP & COMERS: NATHAN KATZER *Successful Farming* v115 no8 p42 Je/Jl 2017

6 WAYS TO BUILD TRUST WITH A CONCERNED CONSUMER *Successful Farming* v115 no2 p18 F 2017

BUILDING YOUR FARM'S BRAND: YOUR BRAND IS A TOOL THAT CAN HELP YOU ACHIEVE YOUR FARM'S GOALS *Successful Farming* v115 no12 p18 O 2017

FARM-TOUGH UTVS: OUR 2017 UTV TEST RESULTS ARE IN! color *Successful Farming* v115 no7 p24 My 2017

FEEDING THE BEAST *Successful Farming* v114 no11 p20 N 2016

FIGHTER TO FARMER: NOMINATE FARMER VETERANS YOU KNOW FOR THE 2017 CONTEST *Successful Farming* v115 no6 p54 Ap 2017

FIGHTER TO FARMER *Successful Farming* v115 no4 p62 Mr 2017

FROM FIGHTER TO FARMER *Successful Farming* v114 no11 p50 N 2016

GET BEYOND THE SCIENCE *Successful Farming* v115 no1 p17 Ja 2017

GOING ELECTRIC *Successful Farming* v115 no4 p46 Mr 2017

GROW YOUR TRIBE *Successful Farming* v115 no5 p16 Mid-Mr 2017

HANDLING A CRISIS color *Successful Farming* v115 no7 p13 My 2017

JOE BASSETT *Successful Farming* v115 no5 p8 Mid-Mr 2017

MEET THE FIGHTER TO FARMER RECIPIENTS *Successful Farming* v114 no10 p58 O 2016

PASSION FOR FARM AND COUNTRY: VIETNAM WAR VETERAN STEVE CONRAD HAS A DEEP LOVE FOR HIS EIGHTH-GENERATION FARM AND THE COUNTRY HE FOUGHT FOR *Successful Farming* v115 no12 p60 O 2017

PUTTING FARM SAFETY INTO PRACTICE: THAT'S THE THEME OF THIS YEAR'S NATIONAL FARM SAFETY AND HEALTH WEEK *Successful Farming* v115 no11 p54 S 2017

SHARE WHAT YOU KNOW *Successful Farming* v114 no13 p20 D 2016

SNAPS OF REALITY *Successful Farming* v115 no4 p20 Mr 2017

STARTING A PODCAST *Successful Farming* v115 no6 p16 Ap 2017

VANCE CROWE: MEET THE MAN BUILDING A VAST NETWORK THROUGH TRIBES TO RALLY AGAINST THE PSEUDOSCIENCE ATTACKING GMOS *Successful Farming* v115 no9 p10 Ag 2017

What's Your Land Worth? *Successful Farming* v114 no12 p66 Mid-N 2016

WINTER WORK GLOVES *Successful Farming* v114 no11 p58 N 2016

Scott, Jim

Senior LIVING R. Bird *Cincinnati Magazine* v50 no4 p87 Ja 2017

SCOTT, JOAN W.

THE CULTURE VEIL color *Nation* v305 no8 p25 O 9 2017

Scott, Joanna

Good Press: A tale of plot twists and publicists in midcentury New York A. GREGORY *New York Times Book Review* p15 S 10 2017

Scott, John D.

Local protein kinase A action proceeds through intact holoenzymes color diag graph *Science* v356 no6344 p1288 Je 23 2017

Scott, Jonathan

Hometown Hero *Tennis* v52 no6 p38 N/D 2016

Small Talk with HGTV's Property Brothers D. Peak color *Log Home Living* v34 no3 p18 Ap 2017

Scott, Kendra

Rock Solid color *Forbes* v199 no6 p77 Je 13 2017

Scott, Kim

How to Be a Kickass Boss, with Kim Scott A. Gross color *Publishers Weekly* v264 no3 p8 Ja 16 2017

Small Talk Is an Overrated Way to Build Relationships with Your Employees *Harvard Business Review Digital Articles* p1 Jl 25 2017

Scott, Kim—Interviews

"Bad bosses are the cause of so much misery": Author Kim Scott on how honesty at work can make us happier and more productive C. NEWBERRY *People Management* p13 Mr 2017

Scott, Laurence

Multimediated Lives J. SILVERMAN *New York Times Book Review* p14 Ja 1 2017

Scott, Margaret

Indonesia: The Saudis Are Coming color *New York Review of Books* v63 no16 p56 O 27 2016

SCOTT, MARK

DOUBLE TROUBLE bw color *Outdoor Life* v224 no1 p44 D 2016/Ja 2017

SCOTT, MICHAEL L.

Applying Functional Traits to Ecogeomorphic Processes in Riparian Ecosystems *BioScience* v67 no8 p729 Ag 2017

Scott, Patrick

FREE FALLING PURSUITS color *Bloomberg Businessweek* no4527 p83 Je 19 2017

Scott, Paul, 1920-1978

THE ORIGINAL BREXIT: REDISCOVERING THE JEWEL IN THE CROWN B. Qureshi *Film Quarterly* v71 no1 p59 Fall 2017

Revisiting the Raj I. CHOTINER *New York Times Book Review* p13 S 10 2017

Scott, Phil

The Virtue of Holdovers *Governing* v30 no6 p11 Mr 2017

Scott, Rick, 1952-—-Political & social views

The Governor's Superstorm J. GOODELL color *Rolling Stone* no1297 p31 O 5 2017

Scott, Ridley, 1937-

ALIEN AWAKENS K. P. Sullivan color *Entertainment Weekly* no1467 p44 My 26 2017

ALIEN: COVENANT S. Vilkomerson color *Entertainment Weekly* no1446/1447 p53 D 2016/Ja 2017

ALIEN: COVENANT S. Vilkomerson color *Entertainment Weekly* no1463/1464 p42 Ap/My 2017

ALIEN S. Vilkomerson color *Entertainment Weekly* no1460/1461 p28 Ap 7-17 2017

ALL THE MONEY IN THE WORLD S. Li color *Entertainment Weekly* no1478 / 1479 p75 Ag 18-25 2017

Monster Mash R. DOUTHAT color *National Review* v69 no11 p42 Je 12 2017

MONSTERS' BALL A. LANE cartoon *New Yorker* v93 no15 p74 My 29 2017

RIDLEY SCOTT A LIFE IN PICTURES S. Vilkomerson color *Entertainment Weekly* no1465 p34 My 12 2017

Scott, Robert W.

FOUR ERAS OVER WP'S FEATHER RIVER ROUTE color diag *Model Railroader* v83 no12 p46 D 2016

Scott, Sophfronia

LOVE AND LUST P. H. Bass color *Essence* v48 no6 p76 O 2017

Scott, Sydney

THE NEW FACE OF R&B color *Essence* v48 no6 p68 O 2017

Scott, Travis, 1992-

Hip-Hop's King of Chaos J. Weiner color *Rolling Stone* no1297 p40 O 5 2017

Scott, Walter K.

Walter K. Scott B. Droitcour color *Art in America* v105 no1 p23 Ja 2017

SCOTT, WILLARD

BECOMING WILLARD *Washingtonian Magazine* v52 no1 p224 O 2016

SCOTT Sports SA

Scott T. Engel color *Bike Magazine* v24 no4 p90 Je 2017

Scott Diamond, Jeremy

Brexit Could Hurt the Most Here graph map *Bloomberg Businessweek* no4527 p20 Je 19 2017

SCOTT-DUPREE, CYNTHIA D.

Bee Ecotoxicology and Data Veracity: Appreciating the GLP Process *BioScience* v66 no12 p1066 D 1 2016

Scottish Nationalist Party (Political party : Scotland)

A Fiery Scotswoman: The youngest MP in 350 years, Mhairi Black is making a name for herself as a leader on the left B. HEING *Ms.* v27 no2 p16 Summ 2017

Scottish Opera Chorus & Orchestra (Performer)

A SPY IN THE WOODS M. Raykovicz color *New York State Conservationist* v71 no2 p6 O 2016

Sullivan: H.M.S. Pinafore R. Pines *Opera News* v81 no5 p57 N 2016

Scottish poets—18th century—Biography

Robert Burns of the Ages F. Inglis color *British Heritage Travel* v38 no5 p33 S/O 2017

Scottoline, Lisa

BESTSELLERS chart *Publishers Weekly* v264 no17 p14 Ap 24 2017

Scott Williams, R.

ZATT (ZNF451)–mediated resolution of topoisomerase 2 DNA-protein cross-links diag *Science* v357 no6358 p1412 S 29 2017

Scout automobile

Restoring the Beauty in the Beast D. TOHT *Treasures* v6 no5 p22 Ap/My 2017

Scouting cameras

REMOTE SCOUTING T. FAULKNER color *Outdoor Life* v224 no6 pH6 Ag 2017

Scouts (Youth organization members)

See also

Girl Scouts

MEET CAPT. AL BRUCE *Sea Magazine* v108 no12 pPNW-12 D 2016

Scrap metals

THE WAR TRUNK J. DETWILER chart color *Popular Mechanics* v193 no7 p97 S 2016

Scrapbooks

iSCRAPBOOK 7: COLOR TOOLS KEEP MAC DESIGN SOFTWARE ATOP SCRAP HEAP J. R. BOOKWALTER color *Macworld - Digital Edition* v34 no4 p37 My 2017

Screen Actors Guild Awards

ENTERTAINMENT WEEKLY'S SAG-ADELIC PARTY color *Entertainment Weekly* no1453 p4 F 17 2017

THE STATE OF THE OSCAR RACE N. Sperling color *Entertainment Weekly* no1446/1447 p23 D 2016/Ja 2017

Screenplays

GOOD WILL HUNTING J. Shipley *Yankee* p27 Mr 2017

The view from Hollywood V. M. Gezari color *Columbia Journalism Review* p42 Fall/Wint 2016

Screens (Furniture)

Rock Star H. MARTIN color *Architectural Digest* v74 no9 p36 S 2017

Screens (Furniture)—Design & construction

ILLUMINATED PRIVACY SCREEN D. KUCZYNSKI color *Cabin Living* p58 Mr 2017

Screenwriters

See also

Women screenwriters

Julian Fellowes M. Hagan color *Current Biography* v77 no11 p44 N 2016

O, Pioneer N. Rapold bw *Film Comment* v53 no2 p10 Mr/Ap 2017

A SENSE OF PLACE: PAZ ENCINA'S RADICAL POETICS N. Brizuela *Film Quarterly* v70 no4 p49 Summ 2017

STEVE CONRAD N. PARSI bw color *Chicago* v66 no2 p30 F 2017

Screenwriters—United States

Get Serious D. Marchese img *New York* v50 no8 p120 Ap 17 2017

RISING TIDES LIFT ALL BOATS D. ANDERSON-MINSHALL color *Advocate* no1090 p22 Ap 2017

Screwdrivers

ALL AROUND THE FARM® J. Glanzer, B. Broering et al *Successful Farming* v115 no6 p77 Ap 2017

Hose Clamp Smarts B. PIKE color *Power & Motoryacht* v34 no6 p79 Je 2017

Screwdrivers—Evaluation

RATCHETING SCREWDRIVERS color *Popular Mechanics* p26 Jl 2017

Screws

Candy Dispenser! J. SCHADEWALD chart color *Popular Mechanics* p108 D 2016/Ja 2017

HANDLE WITH CARE color *Cabin Living* p67 Je 2017

MECHANIC MAKE-DOs D. Mowitz *Successful Farming* v114 no13 p40 D 2016

THE NUTS AND BOLTS D. HISLOP *Sea Magazine* v109 no2 p30 F 2017

WHAT SHE DID color *Better Homes & Gardens* v95 no2 p56 F 2016

When Nobody Else Is Around B. PIKE color *Power & Motoryacht* v34 no8 p90 Ag 2017

Scriber, Brad

A Moon Museum color *National Geographic* v232 no2 p62 Ag 2017

Scrimgeour, Andrew

SURPRISE *Christian Century* v134 no12 p22 Je 7 2017

Scripts

FROM PAGE TO SCREEN color *Entertainment Weekly* no1468/1469 p66 Je 2-9 2017

Scritchfield, Rebecca

The "Body Kindness" Workout color *Amazing Wellness* v9 no1 p78 Wint 2017

Scrolls (Decorative arts)

What lies ahead J. Bleem color *U.S. Catholic* v82 no11 p50 N 2017

Scrotal Recall (TV program)

MORE TITLES TO MAKE YOU BLUSH D. Snierson color *Entertainment Weekly* no1465 p48 My 12 2017

Scrottron, Samuel R.

Hanging Curtains & Drapery: 1900–1939 B. D. Coleman color *Arts & Crafts Homes & the Revival* v12 no4 p22 Fall 2017

Scruton, Roger, 1944-

More than Animals G. Gutting color *Commonweal* v144 no9 p28 My 19 2017

ON HUMAN NATURE B. BETHUNE color *Maclean's* v130 no2 p68 Mr 2017

SONG OF MYSELF *Claremont Review of Books* v17 no1 p38 Wint 2016/2017

True and Beautiful M. D. AESCHLIMAN color *National Review* v69 no12 p42 Je 26 2017

Scrutton, Nigel S.

Enzymes make light work of hydrocarbon production diag *Science* v357 no6354 p872 S 1 2017

Scuba divers

Murky WATERS P. BEACH *Texas Monthly* v44 no12 p55 D 2016

Swimming with Sharks color *O, The Oprah Magazine* p104 Ag 2017

Scuba diving

GET ON THE WATER J. DUGDALE color *Chicago* v66 no7 p60 Jl 2017

In a shark's eye J. HESTER color *Astronomy* v44 no12 p14 D 2016

SAILING AND SCUBA DIVING D. DODGEN color *Sail* v48 no5 p36 My 2017

Take Me Away! E. O'NEILL color *Missouri Life* v44 no3 p32 My 2017

Scudder, Brad

FIND YOUR COURSE TO SUCCESS T. Daswick cartoon color *Men's Health* v32 no3 p24 Ap 2017

Scully, Matt

HOW TO MAKE A €367 MILLION LOSS DISAPPEAR *Bloomberg Businessweek* no4508 p36 Ja 23 2017

Short the Food Court color *Bloomberg Businessweek* no4515 p34 Mr 20 2017

SCULLY, MATTHEW

A Case of Compassion color *National Review* v68 no20 p22 N 7 2016

Father of Trumpism color *National Review* v69 no11 p35 Je 12 2017

SCULLY, PAMELA

Iron Lady *Ms.* v27 no1 p45 Spr 2017

SCULLY, ROBERT E.

LIVES AND DEATHS OF THE TSARS *America* v216 no1 p40 Ja 2 2017

Sculptors

See also

    Women sculptors

ADVENTURES WITH ZIOLKOWSKI *South Dakota Magazine* v32 no6 p53 Mr/Ap 2017

BEYOND BEAUTY P. SCHJELDAHL color *New Yorker* v93 no30 p74 O 2 2017

FROM PARTS TO ART L. F. Prater *Successful Farming* v115 no3 p56 Mid-F 2017

WHOLLY MOSELEY D. BLASBERG color *Vanity Fair* v58 no12 p160 D 2016

Sculptors—Interviews

THE LOOK BOOK A. SWERDLOFF img *New York* v50 no16 p89 Ag 7 2017

Martin Kuntz Sculptor S. BAHR color *Indianapolis Monthly* v42 no2 p49 O 2017

Sculpture

See also

    Buddhist sculpture

    Carving (Decorative arts)

    Ceramic sculpture

    Monuments

    Photography of sculpture

    Public sculpture

    Statues

The Artist's Artist A Rauschenberg Symposium M. Reid Kelley, J. Stockholder et al color *Art in America* v105 no1 p44 Ja 2017

Before the Fight: Sculpture captures Fitzmaurice's last night in Khe Sanh *South Dakota Magazine* v33 no3 p56 S/O 2017

BIRTH OF THE PICASSO H. NYHART bw *Chicago* v66 no5 p30 My 2017

Character Study A. Tambellini and L. A. Miller bw *Art in America* v105 no3 p57 Mr 2017

Culture Shocks D. Bishop bw color *American Craft* v76 no6 p74 D 2016-Ja 2017

Dignity of Earth and Sky *South Dakota Magazine* v32 no4 p13 N/D 2016

Glow Sticks S. STEVENSON color *Indianapolis Monthly* v41 no2 p29 S 2017

HEAVY P. Williams cartoon *New Yorker* v93 no16 p42 Je 5 2017

Heraldic Bourgogne color *Art in America* v104 no10 p15 N 2016

LOOK AGAIN S. COCHRAN color *Architectural Digest* v73 no12 p64 D 2016

MAGALI REUS IN THE STUDIO A. Hickey color *Art in America* v104 no10 p136 N 2016

MASTER OF THE ARTS K. VAUGHN *Arizona Highways* v92 no11 p22 N 2016

A Montréal Gem E. GAUKEL *Treasures* v6 no5 p48 Ap/My 2017

Monumental Offenses K. Samuelson color *Time* v188 no18 p13 O 31 2016

On the trail of Peru's enigmatic cliff artist D. LEFEVERS color *Nebraska Life* v21 no5 p82 S/O 2017

PAINT THE TOWN J. L. BELCOVE color *Architectural Digest* v74 no2 p68 F 2017

Place Markers G. Moreno bw color *Art in America* v105 no3 p33 Mr 2017

Studio Bedfellows L. Lou color *Art in America* v105 no1 p35 Ja 2017

Tape Player color *O, The Oprah Magazine* p26 Ag 2017

the thrill of the [ART] HUNT K. K. CONDON color *Better Homes & Gardens* v95 no10 p86 O 2017

Turkish Hairlines color *Art in America* v105 no1 pC1 Ja 2017

Water works M. HEMMADI color *Maclean's* v130 no9 p20 O 2017

Sculpture exhibitions

See also

Architectural sculpture—Exhibitions

ANTHONY CARO D. Ebony color *Art in America* v105 no4 p111 Ap 2017

AROUND BASEL S. DOUGLAS cartoon color *ARTnews* v115 no3 p138 Fall 2016

THE CITY'S NEW ART HUB J. FOUMBERG color *Chicago* v66 no1 p42 Ja 2017

DIANE SIMPSON R. Wetzler color *Art in America* v105 no3 p129 Mr 2017

DO SOMETHING WITH IT B. SCHWABSKY color *Nation* v305 no2 p35 Jl 17 2017

DUANE LINKLATER E. Buhe color *Art in America* v105 no3 p128 Mr 2017

"ENCODED" G. Kroeber color *Art in America* v105 no4 p117 Ap 2017

The Genius of Making It Small S. Schwartz color *New York Review of Books* v63 no17 p12 N 10 2016

Getting Things Moving J. GARDNER color *Weekly Standard* v23 no6 p43 O 16 2017

THE GUIDE/05.17 M. WAKIM *Los Angeles Magazine* p60 My 2017

Homage to Rodin at the Legion of Honor color *Magazine Antiques* v184 no1 p46 Ja/F 2017

Horse Nation *South Dakota Magazine* v32 no6 p41 Mr/Ap 2017

JIRO TAKAMATSU R. Holmberg color *Art in America* v105 no3 p131 Mr 2017

KATHLEEN RYAN J. S. Li color *Art in America* v105 no4 p118 Ap 2017

The Last Stand *South Dakota Magazine* v33 no2 p46 Jl/Ag 2017

MARIA ANTELMAN R. Rhee color *Art in America* v105 no4 p119 Ap 2017

MICHELLE GRABNER G. Adamson color *Art in America* v105 no3 p127 Mr 2017

MUSEUM PREVIEWS bw color *Art in America* v105 no7 p21 Ag 2017

Pocket-size punch B. L. Scherer color *Magazine Antiques* v184 no2 p52 Mr/Ap 2017

SAM PULITZER AND PETER WÄCHTLER C. Moloney color *Art in America* v105 no3 p136 Mr 2017

Saving the Kokomo Inn *South Dakota Magazine* v33 no2 p72 Jl/Ag 2017

Skylights and Shadows: Philip Johnson's Sculpture Gallery at the Glass House shines once again M. SITZ bw color *Architectural Record* v205 no5 p49 My 2017

THE TASK OF ART C. P. Heuer cartoon color *Art in America* v105 no4 p82 Ap 2017

Sculpture parks—New York (State)

VISIONS color *National Geographic* v232 no2 p8 Ag 2017

Sculpture—20th century

Victor Vasarely Sculpture from Leah Gordaon color *Magazine Antiques* v183 no6 p33 N/D 2016

Sculpture—21st century

Girl, Misplaced J. NORDLINGER color *National Review* v69 no8 p18 My 2017

Sculpture—California

Stand to Reason E. MERCADO *Los Angeles Magazine* p156 D 2016

Sculpture—Conservation & restoration

See also

Monuments—Conservation & restoration

Statues—Conservation & restoration

OUTSIDER ART H. MARTIN color *Architectural Digest* v73 no12 p52 D 2016

Sculpture—Mutilation, defacement, etc.

THE APPROVAL MATRIX img *New York* v50 no16 p128 Ag 7 2017

Sculpture—Themes, motives

Mergers M. Guerber color *American Craft* v76 no6 p38 D 2016-Ja 2017

Scurr, Ruth

The Dreams and the Demons of Fasting color *New York Review of Books* v64 no5 p53 Mr 23 2017

Passions for the Past: The Aubrey Story N. Malcolm color *New York Review of Books* v63 no19 p36 D 8 2016

Sort of Life M. FORBES *Weekly Standard* v22 no6 p34 O 17 2017

Their Faithful Servant color *New York Review of Books* v64 no14

p4 S 28 2017

SDN Communications (Company)

TOP 7 *South Dakota Magazine* v32 no6 p17 Mr/Ap 2017

Sdoia, Roseann

WHAT POSTRACE FOOD IS YOUR BIGGEST GUILTY PLEASURE? cartoon color *Runner's World* v52 no3 p14 Ap 2017

Se7en (Film)

SE7EN J. Hibberd color *Entertainment Weekly* no1460/1461 p62 Ap 7-17 2017

Sea birds

Birds of a (Faux) Feather L. FOPPICK color *Audubon* v119 no3 p14 Fall 2017

Sea control

Terrorists Have Been All Too Effective by Air and Land. What If They Hit by Sea? J. Stavridis color *Time* v190 no2/3 p29 Jl 10-17 2017

Sea-Doo Sport Boats (Company)

TRIXX Aren't Just For Kids: The Spark TRIXX makes everyone a PWC trick artist hero in a matter of minutes A. JONES *Boating World* v38 no5 p36 My 2017

Sea horses

The genes that make seahorses so weird color *Science* v354 no6318 p1357 D 16 2016

Sea ice

Shrinking sea ice threatens mobility S. MILIUS bw color *Science News* v190 no9 p8 O 29 2016

Sky Cycle: Aerial images of water in all of its forms color *Orion Magazine* v36 no2 p28 Mr/Ap 2017

Sea ice thawing

Observed Arctic sea-ice loss directly follows anthropogenic CO_2 emission D. Notz and J. Stroeve bibl graph *Science* v354 no6313 p747 N 11 2016

Yeah, THE WEATHER Has Been WEIRD K. Hayhoe color *Foreign Policy* no224 p40 My/Je 2017

Sea ice—Antarctica

Scientists hope risky winter voyage yields icy rewards W. Cornwall color graph *Science* v356 no6335 p234 Ap 21 2017

Sea ice shrinks in step with carbon emissions W. Cornwall color map *Science* v354 no6312 p533 N 4 2016

Sea ice—Arctic regions

Citizen observers chart Arctic change A. G. Smart *Physics Today* v70 no2 p29 F 2017

Darkness Falls in the Arctic J. T. Mathis color *Wilson Quarterly* p1 Summ 2017

Radical idea could restore Arctic Ocean's sea ice S. Perkins color graph *Science News* v191 no9 p4 My 13 2017

Sea Island (Ga.)

Get Away to Sea Island *New York* v50 no17 p146 Ag 21 2017

Sea level

THE CRISIS ON THE ICE D. FOX bw color map *National Geographic* v232 no1 p30 Jl 2017

THE DELUGE J. Mooallem *New York Times Magazine* p36 Ap 23 2017

Election Fever A. H. McGowan *Environment* v59 no1 p2 2017

How high will the seas rise? M. Oppenheimer and R. B. Alley bibl color graph *Science* v354 no6318 p1375 D 16 2016

More Floods and Faster-Rising Sea Levels: GEOLOGICAL RECORDS HELP FORECAST ESCALATING COASTAL HAZARDS L. Lippsett *Oceanus* v52 no2 p8 Spr 2017

OMG NASA! C. Armstrong color *Alternatives Journal (AJ) - Canada's Environmental Voice* v42 no2 p11 2016

Rising Sea Levels Won't Doom U.S. Coastal Cities M. E. Kahn *Harvard Business Review Digital Articles* p2 Ja 20 2016

UP & OUT S. Subramanian *New York Times Magazine* p46 Ap 23 2017

Sea level & the environment

Antarctic Snowfall May Offset Sea-Level Rise *USA Today Magazine* v145 no2865 p5 Je 2017

Sea level—Environmental aspects

Seas are rising sooner than you think P. Voosen color *Science* v354 no6310 p276 O 21 2016

Sea level—Research

A Mooring in Iceberg Alley R. Jackson color *Oceanus* v51 no2 p16 Wint 2016

Scientists Find Trigger That Cracks lakes L. Stevens color *Ocea-*

nus v51 no2 p20 Wint 2016

Sea Lion Caves (Or.)
ROLLING WITH IT J. Berger color *Sunset* v239 no1 p19 Jl 2017

Sea lions
Ensuring a Moveable Feast K. Olsen color *National Wildlife (World Edition)* v55 no2 p14 F/Mr 2017

Sea Magazine (Periodical)
NAMETHEBOAT *Sea Magazine* v109 no2 p96 F 2017

Sea monsters
What the Heck Is That Thing? S. Mirsky color *Scientific American* v317 no4 p90 O 2017

Sea monsters in art
Art Zone cartoon *National Geographic Kids* no474 p34 O 2017

Sea otter
OTTER THIS WORLD K. MASSICOT color *New Orleans Magazine* v51 no2 p151 D 2016

Sea Ray (Company)
THE GOOD LIFE J. WOOLDRIDGE color *Power & Motoryacht* v34 no11 p136 N 2017
Seas the Day [Cover story] D. HARDING color *Power & Motoryacht* v33 no4 p50 Ap 2017

Sea Rescue (TV program)
ANIMALS ON DEMAND S. Weldon color *Entertainment Weekly* no1478 / 1479 p90 Ag 18-25 2017

Sea salt
Altered State: Taking to the sky to show how industry shapes the earth A. CRAWFORD *Smithsonian* v48 no2 p12 My 2017

Sea turtles
8 totally wild facts about animals E. WHITMER *National Geographic Kids* no469 p10 Ap 2017
Hot nests a major sea turtle threat S. MILIUS color *Science News* v191 no4 p16 Mr 4 2017
Notes FROM THE COAST *Texas Monthly* v45 no5 p22 My 2017

Sea turtles—Behavior
To Track a Sea Turtle: UNDERWATER VEHICLES FOLLOW TAGGED TURTLES IN THE WILD K. Kostel *Oceanus* v52 no2 p18 Spr 2017

Sea urchins
The Two Sides of Sea Otters Sea otters I. Groc color *Canadian Wildlife* v22 no5 p24 N/D 2016

Sea-walls
Q+A *Cincinnati Magazine* v50 no4 p30 Ja 2017

Seabaugh, Christian
5 THINGS TO KNOW ABOUT THE 2017 JEEP GRAND CHEROKEE SUMMIT color *Motor Trend* v69 no2 p57 F 2017
BOUGIE BUICK chart color *Motor Trend* v69 no2 p48 F 2017
Changing Times chart color *Motor Trend* v68 no12 p82 D 2016
DIVINE DRIVES [Cover story] color diag graph map *Motor Trend* v69 no11 p34 N 2017
EVERYDAY HEROES [Cover story] chart color *Motor Trend* v69 no5 p34 My 2017
GARAGE chart color diag *Motor Trend* v69 no11 p106 N 2017
GARAGE chart color diag *Motor Trend* v69 no9 p104 S 2017
GET USED TO THIS MUG chart color *Motor Trend* v69 no6 p82 Je 2017
High Voltage [Cover story] chart color graph *Motor Trend* v69 no2 p30 F 2017
KING IN THE NORTH chart color map *Motor Trend* v69 no10 p68 O 2017
the leftovers... [Cover story] chart color *Motor Trend* v69 no4 p36 Ap 2017
THE LEGEND RETURNS chart color *Motor Trend* v69 no2 p42 F 2017
LITTLE GUY LEADING THE CHARGE color *Motor Trend* v69 no2 p52 F 2017
OVER LANDER'S DREAM chart color *Motor Trend* v69 no2 p54 F 2017
SIZE MATTERS chart color *Motor Trend* v69 no2 p72 F 2017
WINTER is here chart color *Motor Trend* v69 no2 p84 F 2017
YOUNG LOVE chart color *Motor Trend* v69 no8 p72 Ag 2017

Seabourn Cruise Line Ltd.
Rising Tides J. von Sothen color *Bon Appetit* no1 p46 F 2017

Seabrook, John
FLAMES cartoon *New Yorker* v93 no29 p38 S 25 2017
HIGH CEILINGS cartoon *New Yorker* v93 no24 p17 Ag 21 2017
THE IMMACULATE LINEUP cartoon *New Yorker* v93 no9 p30

Ap 17 2017
LE TEMPS PERDU cartoon *New Yorker* v92 no44 p21 Ja 9 2017
MEMORY MOTEL cartoon *New Yorker* v92 no41 p29 D 12 2016
MY FATHER'S CELLAR cartoon color *New Yorker* v92 no46 p22 Ja 23 2017

Seacrest, Ryan, 1974-
RYAN SEACREST D. WALTERS color *Bon Appetit* v61 no12 p174 D 2016 /Jan2017
Seacrest IN! D. Coggan and E. Strohm color *Entertainment Weekly* no1465 p17 My 12 2017

Seafaring life
Great American Cruises color *AARP: The Magazine* v60 no2A p40 F/Mr 2017

Seafood
See also
Fish as food
Aloha, Poke A. Mason color *Bon Appetit* p89 S 2017
Americans' Seafood Consumption Below Recommendations L. Kantor *Amber Waves: The Economics of Food, Farming, Natural Resources, & Rural America* p1 O 2016
Better Fish in the Sea A. STANEK color *Bon Appetit* no8 p20 Ag 2017
BOUNTY OF THE SEA: THE OCEAN PROVIDES SUSTENANCE THAT IS FRESH, NUTRITIOUS AND FUN TO HARVEST D. HISLOP color *Sea Magazine* v109 no7 pPNW-14 Jl 2017
Cheers for Tiers A. MASON color *Bon Appetit* v62 no7 p20 Jl 2017
NEW WAY TO EAT E. N. GAGE and S. BOCAR color *Martha Stewart Living* p92 Ap 2017
RISING TIDE J. FORMAN color *New Orleans Magazine* v51 no1 p112 N 2016
This Just In J. Zorthian *Time* v188 no20 p19 N 14 2016
TIERS OF JOY *Chicago* v65 no12 p66 D 2016

Seafood industry—Law & legislation
The Codfather B. GOLDFARB color *Mother Jones* v42 no2 p38 Mr/Ap 2017

Seafood industry—United States
The Codfather B. GOLDFARB color *Mother Jones* v42 no2 p38 Mr/Ap 2017

Seafood markets
WIN THIS COASTAL ESCAPE! color *Sunset* v238 no1 p98 Ja 2017

Seafood restaurants
FLORIDA M. Rosano color map *Canadian Geographic* v135 no6 p24 D 2015
Heaven on the Half Shell *Virginia Living* p23 2017 Smoke & Salt
Island Life in Galveston R. Walsh color *Southern Living* v52 no3 p69 Mr 2017
Seattle J. McCULLUM color *Martha Stewart Living* p140 O 2017
SOUTHERN COMFORT S. Evans color *Southern Living* v52 no1 p12 Ja 2017

Seafood restaurants—Evaluation
FOCUSING ON THE FUNDAMENTALS J. FORMAN color *New Orleans Magazine* v51 no3 p112 Ja 2017
Noble Fin C. KUMMER *Atlanta* v56 no7 p68 N 2016
QUICK TAKES: First impressions of three new seafood-focused restaurants A. Limpert *Washingtonian Magazine* v53 no1 p148 O 2017
WATER GRILL J. Lurie *Los Angeles Magazine* p4 Ap 2017
Where to Eat Now *Texas Monthly* v45 no1 p110 Ja 2017

Seafood sauces
"WEEKENDS" WARRIOR A. Traverso, M. FLEMING et al color *Yankee* p50 Mr 2017

Seafood—Congresses
PILLAR OF THE ECONOMY *Iceland Review* v54 no6 p118 N/D 2016

Seafood—Evaluation
Mixing Bowl color *O, The Oprah Magazine* p138 O 2017

Seafood—Sales & prices
Now you seafood, now you don't J. RICHLER color *Maclean's* v130 no4 p66 My 2017

Seagate Technology LLC
Seagate Barracuda Pro 10TB hard drive: Vast and amazingly fast (for a hard drive) J. L. JACOBI color graph *PCWorld* p99 O 2016

Seager, Sara, 1971-
BODIES IN TRANSIT C. Jones bw color *New York Times Magazine* p90 D 11 2016

Seagrasses
Accelerating Tropicalization and the Transformation of Temperate Seagrass Meadows G. A. HYNDES, K. L. HECK, Jr. et al *BioScience* v66 no11 p938 N 1 2016
Seagrass ecosystems reduce exposure to bacterial pathogens of humans, fishes, and invertebrates J. B. Lamb, J. A. J. M. van de Water et al bibl graph *Science* v355 no6326 p731 F 17 2017

Seagrasses—Environmental aspects
Seagrasses combat harmful bacteria L. HAMERS *Science News* v191 no5 p14 Mr 18 2017

Seakeeper Inc.
At Sea With Seakeeper M. SMITH color *Power & Motoryacht* v34 no11 p141 N 2017
A NEW CLASS OF STABILITY-INTRODUCING THE SEAKEEPER 3 *Sea Magazine* v108 no12 p10 D 2016
Stabilizing the Market J. Y. WOOD color *Power & Motoryacht* v32 no11 p146 N 2016

SEAL, MARK
DEPP FINANCING color *Vanity Fair* v59 no8 p110 Ag 2017
HIS KIND OF TOWN color *Vanity Fair* v59 no2 p82 F 2017
L'Affaire Kardashian color *Vanity Fair* v59 no1 p150 Holiday 2017

Seal, Moorea
north by northwest C. FISHMAN cartoon color *Better Homes & Gardens* v95 no2 p14 F 2016

Seal, Rebecca
Lisbon: Recipes from the Heart of Portugal color *Publishers Weekly* v264 no23 p47 Je 5 2017

Seal, Rebecca P.
Neural circuits for pain: Recent advances and current views bibl diag *Science* v354 no6312 p578 N 4 2016

SEAL Team (TV program)
DAVID BOREANAZ M. Roffman *TV Guide* v65 no37 p32 S 4 2017
Network TV's Calorie-Free Take on American Patriotism D. D'addario color *Time* v190 no13 p63 O 2 2017
SEAL Team N. Abrams, B. L. Heldman et al color *Entertainment Weekly* no1482/1483 p76 S 22 2017

Seale, Bobby, 1936-—Interviews
Bobby Seale L. Rothman color *Time* v188 no15 p64 O 17 2016

Seale, Patrick
Regeneration of fat cells from myofibroblasts during wound healing bibl color graph *Science* v355 no6326 p748 F 17 2017

Seale, Yasmine
UNSEEN WORLDS *Harper's Magazine* v334 no2004 p82 My 2017

Sealed Air Corp.
Innovation Fill-Air Flow E. Pfanner and M. Scaturro diag *Bloomberg Businessweek* no4495 p28 O 17 2016

SEALES, AMANDA
These Are Your Sexual Rights color *Glamour* v114 no7 p94 Jl 2016

Seales, Brent
History Unwrapped M. BARNA color *Discover* v38 no5 p12 Je 2017

Sealey, Nicole
Even the Gods *New York Times Magazine* p20 S 10 2017

Sealing compounds industry
Sashco Turns 80! bw color *Log Home Living* v33 no7 p17 S 2016

Sealing compounds—Evaluation
Effetto Mariposa Zot! Nano and Caffélatex color *Bicycling* v58 no4 p80 My 2017

Seals (Animals)
Itty-Bitty Reindeer P. Rauber *Sierra* v101 no6 p21 N/D 2016

Seals (Animals)—Behavior
Seal Whiskers Inspire Marine Technology H. Beem color *Oceanus* v51 no4 p82 Wint 2016

Seals (Animals)—Export & import trade
Deal the seal C. SORENSEN color *Maclean's* v130 no2 p11 Mr 2017

Seals (Animals)—Psychology
The Remarkable Timing of Seals J. G. Goldman color *Scientific American* v316 no1 p17 Ja 2017

Seaman, Donna
There at the Creation M. SCHWENDENER *New York Times Book Review* p18 F 26 2017

SEAMANS, MICHAEL
A 'Very Impressive Rock' bw color *Yankee* p20 My/Je 2017
We Remember color *Yankee* v80 no6 p96 N/D 2016

Seamanship
See also
Heavy weather seamanship
Offshore sailing
STAYING ALIVE P. Nielsen color *Sail* v48 no7 p42 Jl 2017

Seamounts—Research
Beneath the Sea, the Galápagos Reveal More Marvels E. Koenig *Oceanus* v52 no1 p8 Summ 2016

Séamus Davis, J. C.
Discovery of orbital-selective Cooper pairing in FeSe diag *Science* v357 no6346 p75 Jl 7 2017

Seaplanes
In the Name of Love R. Cusk color *Conde Nast Traveler* v52 no2 p60 F 2017

Search & rescue operations
See also
Mountaineering—Search & rescue operations
DISASTER DOGS M. D. G. Kaplan *Washingtonian Magazine* v52 no6 p185 Mr 2017

Search advertising (World Wide Web)
DO SEARCH ADS REALLY WORK? bw *Harvard Business Review* v95 no2 p26 Mr/Ap 2017
DO SEARCH ADS REALLY WORK?: INTERACTION S. Panjwani, M. Luca et al color *Harvard Business Review* v95 no3 p20 My/Je 2017

Search committees (Personnel)
See also
Employee selection

Search dogs
Amazing Animals S. Schwartz and K. Baird Rattini color *National Geographic Kids* no475 p10 N 2017

Search engines
6 Money-Saving Travel Hacks K. A. Renzulli color *Money* v46 no8 p16 S 2017
Do Tech Companies Really Need All That User Data? W. Frick *Harvard Business Review Digital Articles* p2 S 21 2017
SEO Beyond Google C. SIM *Publishers Weekly* v264 no28 p92 Jl 10 2017

Search for Extraterrestrial Intelligence (Study group : U.S.)
16 TIMES WE DIDN'T FIND E.T J. Wenz cartoon *Astronomy* v45 no9 p34 S 2017
Alien Contact S. SCOLES bw color diag graph *Discover* v38 no6 p58 Jl/Ag 2017
Much media ado about a SETI nothing color *Astronomy* v44 no12 p9 D 2016
Searching a Trillion Stars for ET R. H. Gray *Sky & Telescope* v134 no3 p38 S 2017

Search Party (TV program)
ALL ABOUT ALIA D. Franich color *Entertainment Weekly* no1441 p30 N 25 2016
Search Party J. Jensen color *Entertainment Weekly* no1441 p46 N 25 2016
The Ten Best TV Shows of the Year M. Z. Seitz img *New York* v49 no25 p120 D 12 2016
WIKIPEDIA BROWN E. NUSSBAUM cartoon *New Yorker* v92 no42 p126 D 19 2016

Searches & seizures of cell phones
USE A CELLPHONE, VOID THE FOURTH AMENDMENT? D. ROOT color *Reason* v49 no4 p6 Ag/S 2017

Search for Everything, The (Music)
Mayer's Heartbreak Diary J. ELISCU bw *Rolling Stone* no1281/1282 p18 F 23 2017

SEARCY, DAVID
The Dark Prince *Texas Monthly* v45 no3 p86 Mr 2017

Searle, Eric B.
Positive biodiversity-productivity relationship predominant in global forests bibl chart graph map *Science* v354 no6309 paaf8957-1 O 14 2016

Searle, Ronald
HELL ON THE RIVER KWAI P. D. Toler *MHQ: Quarterly Jour-*

nal of Military History v29 no3 p89 Spr 2017

Searls, Damion

The Eye of the Beholder M. EMRE *New Republic* v248 no3 p63 Mr 2017

Revealing Rorschach E. McKay color *Science* v355 no6325 p588 F 10 2017

This Is Only a Test R. WHIPPMAN *New York Times Book Review* p21 Mr 19 2017

Searls, Doc

Ad Blockers and the Next Chapter of the Internet *Harvard Business Review Digital Articles* p2 N 6 2015

Sears, Adam P.

Suppressing relaxation in superconducting qubits by quasiparticle pumping bibl graph *Science* v354 no6319 p1573 D 23 2016

Sears, David

Cheating Death *American History* v51 no6 p60 F 2017

Sears Brands LLC

Sears Has Come Back from the Brink Before A. Ovans *Harvard Business Review Digital Articles* p2 O 28 2014

Sears Holdings Corp.

Is It Too Late for Sears to Save Itself? D. Lee Yohn color *Harvard Business Review Digital Articles* p2 Mr 30 2017

THE SINKING OF SEARS T. C. FISHMAN color *Chicago* v66 no4 p28 Ap 2017

Seascape (Company)

Seascape 18 C. J. Doane color *Sail* v48 no5 p23 My 2017

Seaside resorts

THE BEACH RESET K. Sintumuang color *Esquire* p18 Ag 2017

Stopover of a Lifetime: Nemberala Beach Resort J. Honscheid bw color *Surfer* v57 no11 p35 D 2016

Seasonal affective disorder

DON'T BE SAD [Cover story] J. Martin color *Amazing Wellness* v9 no6 p28 EarlyWint 2017

WHEN LIGHT color *Women's Health* v14 no6 p38 Jl 2017

Seasonal affective disorder—Prevention

Find Your Peace of Mind G. Saltz color *Health* v30 no10 p77 D 2016

Seasonal affective disorder—Treatment

Happy News for SAD People cartoon *Prevention* v69 no2 p8 F 2017

My Energy Makeover B. O'Dair *Prevention* v69 no2 p3 F 2017

Seasonal distribution of insects

Like birds, insects may travel in sync with the seasons E. Pennisi color *Science* v354 no6319 p1515 D 23 2016

Overlooked mass migration spotted S. MILIUS cartoon color *Science News* v191 no2 p12 F 4 2017

Trillions of Insects Migrate M. Fischetti color graph *Scientific American* v316 no4 p84 Ap 2017

Seasonal effects on wildlife

The life and times of dodos revealed S. MILIUS color *Science News* v192 no4 p6 S 16 2017

Seasonal influenza

Ah-CHOO! color *Missouri Life* v44 no2 p66 Ap 2017

Seasonal residents

CHARLESTON, SOUTH CAROLINA color *Washington Monthly* v49 no3-5 p26 Mr-My 2017

Seasonal sales promotion

Retailers Can't Rely on Holiday-Season Gimmicks Like They Used To D. L. Yohn *Harvard Business Review Digital Articles* p2 N 3 2015

Seasonal variations of diseases

Started School and Sick Already color *Parents* v92 no9 p26 S 2017

Seasons

See also
　Autumn
　Summer
　Winter

Downright Cool K. Shapiro color *Health* v30 no9 p37 N 2016

grapefruit color *Vegetarian Today* no1 p14 F 2017

transition WITH STYLE color *Yoga Journal* no294 p18 S 2017

Seasons—Charts, diagrams, etc.

See the Light R. ZURER color *Backpacker* v45 no2 p21 Mr 2017

Seasons—Psychological aspects

How to Eat Healthy—and Love It C. McHugh color *Health* v31 no5 p4 Je 2017

Season With, A (TV program)

FIELD OF VISION J. MALESIC color *America* v215 no11 p29 O 17 2016

SeaStar Solutions (Company)

Joy(sticks) to the World M. SMITH color diag *Power & Motoryacht* v33 no2 p126 F 2017

Seat belts

Do worry, be happy color *Redbook* p103 O 2017

Seat at the Table, A (Music)

The 10 Best Albums J. Cox color *Time* v188 no25-26 p152 D 19 2016 Double Issue

Solange Takes a Seat but Stands on Her Own S. Lansky color *Time* v188 no15 p55 O 17 2016

Seating (Furniture)

See also
　Airplane seats
　Automobile seats
　Chairs

John Anson Ford Amphitheatre Sparkles in LA *Stage Directions* v30 no9 p4 S 2017

VERN YIP ON PERFECT MEASUREMENTS K. O'SHEA-EVANS color *House Beautiful* v159 no5 p57 Je 2017

Seating (Furniture)—Equipment & supplies

Take Make a Seat J. Oltion *Sky & Telescope* v132 no6 p70 D 2016

Seating (Furniture)—Evaluation

My Dog Reviews the Furniture He Has Eaten A. SIMMONS *Reader's Digest* v188 no1124 p15 O 2016

Seating design & construction

Blurred Lines K. L. Beamon *Architectural Record* v205 no9 p65 S 2017

SEATON, JAIMIE

THE BEGINNER'S GUIDE TO Making a Difference cartoon color diag *O, The Oprah Magazine* p114 S 2017

GREENER PASTURES color *O, The Oprah Magazine* p28 O 2017

Seattle (Wash.)

AMAZON BOOKS LOCATIONS, MARCH 2017 map *Publishers Weekly* v264 no13 p4 Mr 27 2017

IN THE "FIGHT FOR 15," LABOR MAY LAND A PYRRHIC VICTORY A. Vandermey color *Fortune* v176 no2 p17 Ag 1 2017

Seattle (Wash.)—Description & travel

Be More Pacific J. VOELKER *Indianapolis Monthly* p38 My 2017

Seattle (Wash.)—Politics & government

Mayoral Roller Coaster: Why can't Seattle find leaders it wants to keep? A. Greenblatt *Governing* v31 no1 p17 O 2017

Seattle Mariners (Baseball team)

3 MARINERS color *Sports Illustrated* v126 no9 p91 Mr 27 2017

Seattle Seahawks (Football team)

1 Seattle Seahawks color *Sports Illustrated* v127 no7 p100 S 4 2017

INTERNAL DEBATE R. Klemko color *Sports Illustrated* v127 no10 p33 O 2 2017

Seavees (Company)

GET FRESH color *Martha Stewart Living* p57 Ap 2017

SEAVEY, TODD

FROM THE ARCHIVES bw color *Reason* v49 no3 p70 Jl 2017

Seaward, Paul

Order from chaos *History Today* v67 no4 p38 Ap 2017

SEAWARD, STEPHEN M.

THE VIRTUE OF DOING LESS: BERTRAND RUSSELL'S IDLENESS *Humanist* v77 no1 p38 Ja/F 2017

Seawater

DEEP-SEA VINO N. Strochlic color *National Geographic* v231 no4 p22 Ap 2017

The OCEAN IS SALTY m. Diffee bw cartoon color *Esquire* p106 O 2017

Ocean mixing and ice-sheet control of seawater 234U/238U during the last deglaciation Tianyu Chen, L. F. Robinson et al bibl graph *Science* v354 no6312 p626 N 4 2016

Seawater corrosion

Keeping Your Cool P. Gutowski color diag *Sail* v48 no4 p64 Ap 2017

Seawater—Environmental aspects

The geologic history of seawater pH I. Halevy and A. Bachan bibl

Secret societies
THE LONELY HEDONIST M. SAGER bw color *Esquire* v166 no4 p116 N 2016
Secretaries of State (State governments)
Ballot Blockers P. Levy *Mother Jones* v42 no6 p27 N/D 2017
Secret Life of Pets, The (Film)
THE SECRET LIFE OF PETS T. J. Norton color *Sound & Vision* v82 no4 p68 My 2017
Secret Lives of Edward Gorey, The (Theatrical production)
The Secret Lives of Edward Gorey J. GREEN *New York* v49 no25 p142 D 12 2016
Secrets of the Six Wives (TV program)
WYES-TV/CHANNEL 12 PROGRAM GUIDE bw color *New Orleans Magazine* v51 no3 pD11 Ja 2017
Secularism
Art for Secularism's Sake J. Spofforth *Humanist* v77 no3 p5 My/Je 2017
Fundamentalism ON TRIAL B. BOLTON *Humanist* v77 no2 p18 Mr/Ap 2017
IN SEARCH OF THE SACRED D. LOY cartoon *Tricycle: The Buddhist Review* v26 no3 p82 Spr 2017
THE NEW SECULAR MOMENT T. KRATTENMAKER *Humanist* v77 no2 p16 Mr/Ap 2017
Secularism—Societies, etc.
CENTER FOR INQUIRY *Skeptical Inquirer* v41 no2 p5 Mr/Ap 2017
Securities industry—United States
FRIENDS IN HIGH PLACES A. MACGILLIS cartoon *New Yorker* v92 no37 p36 N 14 2016
What It Will Take to Change the Culture of Wall Street S. G. Mandis *Harvard Business Review Digital Articles* p2 O 24 2014
Securities markets
See also
    Stock exchanges
The Business Guide to Europe's Wild Year V. Walt and G. Smith chart color diag *Fortune* v175 no5 p9 Ap 1 2017
Liability and Precaution I. S. Daramus bibl *Environment* v59 no5 p48 S/O 2017
MONEY, CREDIT, AND SECURITY MARKETS *Economic Indicators* p26 Ap 2017
MONEY, CREDIT, AND SECURITY MARKETS *Economic Indicators* p26 D 2016
THE TRUMP EFFECT ON FINANCIAL MARKETS A. K. SMITH graph *Kiplinger's Personal Finance* v71 no2 p13 F 2017
WHEN THE MARKETS SCREW UP color *Fortune* v75 no1 p18 Ja 1 2017
Securities—Hungary
Friendship Is a Bountiful Thing Z. Simon bw *Bloomberg Businessweek* no4532 p27 Jl 31 2017
Securities industry—Charts, diagrams, etc.
MONEY, CREDIT, AND SECURITY MARKETS *Economic Indicators* p26 My 2017
Securities markets—Charts, diagrams, etc.
MONEY, CREDIT, AND SECURITY MARKETS *Economic Indicators* p26 My 2017
MONEY, CREDIT, AND SECURITY MARKETS *Economic Indicators* p26 S 2016
Securities—Prices—Charts, diagrams, etc.
Foreign Funds Bounce Back T. Tepper chart *Money* v46 no2 p86 Mr 2017
Tech Stocks Join Market Rally chart diag *Money* v46 no2 p84 Mr 2017
Securities—Rate of return
Tech Stocks Are Back chart diag *Money* v46 no8 p76 S 2017
Securities—United States
Tech Stocks Are Back chart diag *Money* v46 no8 p76 S 2017
Security (Psychology)
Failure to Launch S. Tia Brown color *Ebony* v72 no8 p66 Je 2017
How and Why We Lie at Work T. Chamorro-Premuzic *Harvard Business Review Digital Articles* p2 Ja 2 2015
What to Do If Your Boss Is a Control Freak K. Dillon *Harvard Business Review Digital Articles* p2 D 23 2014
Security classification (Government documents)—United States
Hidden Agenda *New York Times Magazine* p15 Ag 27 2017
Trump's Loyalty Test [Cover story] M. Scherer, A. Altman et al

color *Time* v189 no20 p24 My 29 2017
Yes, 'It's a Scandal' M. Hemingway color *Weekly Standard* v22 no9 p8 N 7 2016
Security management
See also
    Cities & towns—Security measures
    Data security
The Drone Catcher K. ATHERTON and S. FECHT color *Popular Science* v288 no6 p64 N/D 2016
Security management—Equipment & supplies
Apricorn Aegis Secure Key 3z: This USB thumbdrive is small, secure, and device-agnostic J. L. JACOBI color graph *PCWorld* p79 Mr 2017
Security management—Finance
Who'll Pay to Protect Trump's Towers? S. Baker, B. Harvey et al *Bloomberg Businessweek* no4503 p35 D 12 2016
Security systems
See also
    Computer security
    Electronic surveillance
    Locks & keys
    Police
How People Are Actually Using the Internet of Things H. J. Wilson, B. Shah et al *Harvard Business Review Digital Articles* p2 O 28 2015
Security systems—Design & construction
To Fix Your Terrible Passwords, Kill Them N. Lanxon color *Bloomberg Businessweek* no4524 p36 My 29 2017
Security systems—Equipment & supplies
Always Watching G. DELL'ABATE and B. BOOEY color *Popular Mechanics* p38 Mr 2017
Security systems—Evaluation
Hardware, Software & Control Systems color *Architectural Record* v204 no12 p122 D 2016
NEW ELECTRONICS J. Y. WOOD color *Power & Motoryacht* v34 no9 p42 S 2017
PEACE OF MIND [Cover story] J. Cooper color *Cabin Living* p68 O 2017
Sedacca, Matthew
Better Batteries color *Scientific American* v317 no4 p23 O 2017
Plastic-Eating Worms color *Scientific American* v317 no2 p21 Ag 2017
Skinlike Sunscreen color *Scientific American* v317 no3 p15 S 2017
Sedaris, Amy, 1961-
Every Home Needs a Wig Wall A. Sternbergh img *New York* v50 no18 p74 S 4 2017
My Legs color *InStyle* v24 no10 p224 O 2017
NOW AND JEN color *Harper's Bazaar* no3657 p205 O 2017
Sedaris, Amy, 1961—Interviews
At Home With Amy Sedaris D. Holbrook *TV Guide* v65 no43 p37 O 16 2017
Sedaris, David, 1956-
David Sedaris Wants You to Read His Diary A. M. Cox *New York Times Magazine* p54 Jl 2 2017
David Sedaris What's your cooking philosophy? D. WALTERS bw color *Bon Appetit* v62 no6 p114 Je 2017
DEAR ME F. MAAZEL color *O, The Oprah Magazine* p80 Je 2017
Dentists Without Borders: A unique encounter with socialized medicine *Saturday Evening Post* v289 no5 p40 S/O 2017
Him Write Pretty One Day P. OSWALT *New York Times Book Review* p18 Je 4 2017
WHY AREN'T YOU LAUGHING? bw cartoon *New Yorker* v93 no17 p30 Je 19 2017
The Year in Reading [Cover story] *New York Times Book Review* p8 D 25 2016
Sedaris, David, 1956—Interviews
Oh, golly! J. SEMLEY color *Maclean's* p56 Je 2017
Quick Talk: David Sedaris L. Feldman color *Time* v189 no22 p52 Je 12 2017
What Makes Me Laugh: An interview with david sedaris P. Perry *Saturday Evening Post* v289 no5 p36 S/O 2017
Sedatives
STUD FARM DIARIES: Less is More: Methods of Restraint C. Reich *Arabian Horse World* v57 no11 p166 Ag 2017

SEDGWICK, JOHN
Harvard's Club Brawl color *Vanity Fair* v59 no9 p224 S 2017
Sedgwick, Kyra, 1965-
Sedgwick As a Tormented Hard-Ass D. D'addario *Time* v190 no15 p57 O 16 2017
Ten Days in the Valley A. Bacle, D. Coggan et al color *Entertainment Weekly* no1482/1483 p43 S 22 2017
Ten Days in the Valley: Getting hooked on a nail-biter that would feel at home on cable M. ROUSH *TV Guide* v65 no43 p14 O 16 2017
Sedgwick, Kyra, 1965----Interviews
KYRA SEDGWICK I. Rudolph *TV Guide* v65 no37 p39 S 4 2017
Sedgwick, Marcus
Mister Memory color *Publishers Weekly* v264 no2 p42 Ja 9 2017
Sedgwick, Marcus---Interviews
Total Recall L. PICKER color *Publishers Weekly* v264 no4 p56 Ja 23 2017
Sediments (Geology)
See also
Detritus
Mud
Blue Hotes Hurricanes: GEOLOGICAL MARVELS ARE GOLD MINES FOR CLIMATE HISTORY D. Levin *Oceanus* v52 no2 p44 Spr 2017
Features *Oceanus* v52 no2 p31 Spr 2017
Finding China's Great Flood B. ALEX color map *Discover* v38 no1 p31 Ja/F 2017
The International Seabed Authority and Deep Seabed Mining M. Lodge *UN Chronicle* v54 no1/2 p1 2017
Neandertal and Denisovan DNA from Pleistocene sediments V. Slon, C. Hopfe et al bw color *Science* v356 no6338 p605 My 12 2017
SEDIMENT SUPPLY PREDICTS RIVER GEOMETRY *Physics Today* v70 no6 p26 Je 2017
Sedmak, Clemens
A theology that weeps J. A. Coleman color *America* v216 no6 p44 Mr 20 2017
Sedona (Ariz.)---Description & travel
COMFORT ZONES S. Renner chart color *Sunset* v239 no4 p21 O 2017
DEVIL'S BRIDGE TRAIL R. STIEVE color map *Arizona Highways* v93 no5 p54 My 2017
See, Jen
38 REASONS TO GO GA-GA FOR THE TOUR DE FRANCE color *Bicycling* v58 no7 p24 Ag 2017
HOW CYCLING WORKS cartoon diag *Bicycling* v58 no9 p21 O 2017
THIS GRANDMOTHER CLIMBED ALPE D'HUEZ EIGHT TIMES IN ONE DAY! color *Bicycling* v58 no6 p22 Jl 2017
WHAT IT TAKES TO RIDE... MONT VENTOUX color *Bicycling* v58 no9 p36 O 2017
SEE, KELLY E.
The Stretch Goal Paradox color diag il img *Harvard Business Review* v95 no1 p92 Ja/F 2017
SEE, LISA
Join Together: Two lonely kids form a lifesaving friendship in a tale from one of China's most popular authors *New York Times Book Review* p21 My 14 2017
See, Peter
Mapping the human DC lineage through the integration of high-dimensional techniques diag *Science* v356 no6342 p1044 Je 9 2017
SEEBENS, HANNO
Scientific and Normative Foundations for the Valuation of Alien-Species Impacts: Thirteen Core Principles *BioScience* v67 no2 p166 F 2017
Seed + Mill (Company)
OPEN SESAME *Martha Stewart Living* no268 p90 O 2016
Seed catalogs
Seed Catalogs W. Blackmore *New York Times Magazine* p20 F 5 2017
Seed crops
See also
Coffee
Grain
Nuts

Go With the Grain L. J. Solmonson *Sierra* v102 no4 p8 Jl/Ag 2017
MATTRACKS SAVE SEED CROPS: WRESTLING WITH DOING FIELD OPERATIONS ON SOGGY SOILS? THESE RUBBER TRACKS CAN HELP D. Goerge *Successful Farming* v115 no12 p54 O 2017
Seed industry
BIG FOOD bw *Nation* v305 no11 p39 O 30 2017
A Gathering of Seed Savers *Mother Earth News* no284 p3 O/N 2017
Seed industry---Mergers
Mergers and Competition in Seed and Agricultural Chemical Markets J. M. MacDonald *Amber Waves: The Economics of Food, Farming, Natural Resources, & Rural America* p1 Ap 2017
Seed pods
Sow kindness J. Bleem color *U.S. Catholic* v82 no9 p50 S 2017
Summer's Confetti K. Owen color *Southern Living* v52 no6 p32 Je 2017
Seed Savers Exchange (Organization)
Apple Eaters A. WELDON *Orion Magazine* v35 no6 p12 N/D 2016
Seed Savers Exchange (Organization)---Congresses
A Gathering of Seed Savers *Mother Earth News* no284 p3 O/N 2017
Seedlings
Your CHECKLIST M. Irvine and E. Jardina color *Sunset* v239 no4 p50 O 2017
Seeds
See also
Seed crops
Cultivating a Seed Community L. Noyes *Mother Earth News* no282 p9 Je/Jl 2017
EDIBLE HEIRLOOMS *Successful Farming* v115 no5 p62 Mid-Mr 2017
Organic Seed Cultivars to Try This Year S. Stonebrook *Mother Earth News* no281 p8 Ap/My 2017
Pod Cast color *National Wildlife (World Edition)* v54 no6 p50 O/N 2016
SOMETHING BORROWED, SOMETHING BLUE: A GREAT-AUNT'S LEGACY LIVES ON THROUGH A PACKET OF DELPHINIUM SEEDS J. SHIPLEY *Yankee* v81 no5 p126 S/O 2017
Super seeds A. Gorin color *Yoga Journal* no287 p66 N 2016
UGANDA'S BAD SEEDS F. TORO color *Reason* v48 no10 p24 Mr 2017
a whole lot of wholesome B. P. KATZ color *Martha Stewart Living* p82 Mr 2017
Seeds (Poem)
Seeds J. M. Pitas color *U.S. Catholic* v82 no1 p11 Ja 2017
Seeds---Storage
TABLE MANNERS color *Sunset* v238 no4 p48 Ap 2017
Seeds---Therapeutic use
Spotting whole grains at the grocery store *Harvard Health Letter* v42 no5 p5 Mr 2017
Seegal, Frederic M.
WHAT'S NEXT *Dance Magazine* v91 no1 p36 Ja 2017
Seeger, Pete, 1919-2014
Quotable Quotes *Reader's Digest* v189 no1128 p136 Mr 2017
Seeger, Ruth Crawford, 1901-1953
Woman, Interrupted R. Platt color *New Yorker* v93 no33 p26 O 23 2017
Seeing You (Theatrical production)
Happenings M. Schulman color *New Yorker* v93 no11 p8 My 1 2017
Seekell, David
Passing the point of no return bibl graph *Science* v354 no6316 p1109-C D 2 2016
Seeley, Thomas D.
A BEELINE INTO BEE-LINING U. ERNST color *BioScience* v66 no10 p908 O 1 2016
Seeley, Wes
Soaring with Eagles color *Log Home Living* v34 no4 p18 My 2017
Seen (Poem)
SEEN M. Glazer *New Yorker* v93 no6 p63 Mr 27 2017
Seesaw (Theatrical production)
35 Years Ago This Month *Dance Magazine* v91 no9 p67 S 2017
Seestrom, Susan J.

Virginia Ruth Brown *Physics Today* v69 no10 p67 O 2016

Seewald, Jeffrey S.

Detecting molecular hydrogen on Enceladus color *Science* v356 no6334 p132 Ap 14 2017

Sefolosha, Bertille

Bertille Sefolosha F. SUN *Atlanta* v56 no11 p46 Mr 2017

Segal, Dvira

Probing the limits of heat flow bibl diag *Science* v355 no6330 p1125 Mr 17 2017

Segal, Francesca

The Youngs H. HOBY *New York Times Book Review* p36 Je 4 2017

Segal, Lauren

Promoting human rights through science color *Science* v357 no6359 p34 O 6 2017

SEGAL, LORE

Ladies' Lunch cartoon *New Yorker* v93 no2 p62 F 27 2017

Segal, Lucas

"What Would You Think If I Walked Into the Girls' Bathroom?" A. STANLEY color *Seventeen* v76 no3 p20 My 2017

SEGAL, MATTHEW

An Abundance Of Bones color *Los Angeles Magazine* v62 no7 p18 Jl 2017

Banking On the Arts District *Los Angeles Magazine* p38 D 2016

A City On the Move *Los Angeles Magazine* v62 no7 p10 Jl 2017

Drawing On Its Past *Los Angeles Magazine* p26 Ap 2017

Form Versus Function: L.A.'S DIRECTOR OF PLANNING, VINCE BERTONI, OFFERS INSIGHTS ON THE CITY TAKING SHAPE BEFORE OUR EYES *Los Angeles Magazine* p18 Ag 2017

Home In the Range color *Los Angeles Magazine* v62 no10 p10 O 2017

More Reasons To Roam *Los Angeles Magazine* p10 Ag 2017

Ramen Is My Copilot *Los Angeles Magazine* v62 no9 p14 S 2017

A Thirst For Blood bw *Los Angeles Magazine* v62 no10 p14 O 2017

Where the Rubber Meets the Road *Los Angeles Magazine* p14 F 2017

Segal, Miriam

THE BIG QUESTION cartoon *Atlantic* v319 no2 p100 Mr 2017

Segale, Blandina, 1850-1941

The Fastest Nun in the West H. NORDHAUS *Smithsonian* v47 no7 p35 N 2016

Segall, Avner

Teaching with evidence diag *Phi Delta Kappan* v98 no7 p67 Ap 2017

SEGALL, SETH ZUIHO

A MORE ENLIGHTENED WAY OF BEING color *Tricycle: The Buddhist Review* v26 no2 p54 Wint 2016

Segawa, Yasutomo

Synthesis of a carbon nanobelt diag graph *Science* v356 no6334 p172 Ap 14 2017

Segedunum Roman Fort Site (Wallsend, England)

WHERE WERE THE STABLES? color *Archaeology* v70 no3 p31 My/Je 2017

Segel, Kenneth T.

Bureaucracy Is Keeping Health Care from Getting Better *Harvard Business Review Digital Articles* p2 O 13 2017

Seger, Bob

GLENN FREY color *Entertainment Weekly* no1446/1447 p91 D 2016/Ja 2017

Seger, Jiri

A Compass/Level color *Men's Health* v32 no5 p138 Je 2017

Segev, Mordechai

Observation of Anderson localization in disordered nanophotonic structures diag graph *Science* v356 no6341 p953 Je 1 2017

Seghers, Hercules, 17th century—Exhibitions

A hallucinatory Old Master at the Met color *Magazine Antiques* v184 no2 p34 Mr/Ap 2017

Segment (Music)

Christian McBride D. OUELLETTE color *Downbeat* v84 no1 p114 Ja 2017

Segnit, Nat

GOOD PLAIN ENGLISH *Harper's Magazine* v334 no2002 p86 Mr 2017

NECESSARY DRIVING SKILLS *Harper's Magazine* p79 Ap

2017

Segovia, Oliver

How the Philippines Became Tech Startups' New Source for Talent *Harvard Business Review Digital Articles* p2 Ag 5 2015

Segrè, Gino

He's the Bomb G. HERKEN *New York Times Book Review* p23 N 20 2016

The Little Match's Momentous Legacy: The Pope of Physics: Enrico Fermi and the Birth of the Atomic Age W. Lanouette *Issues in Science & Technology* v33 no3 p93 Spr 2017

The Pope of Physics C. Westfall *Physics Today* v69 no12 p57 D 2016

Segregation in education

'Conversations Aren't Enough' M. LINDBERG *Education Digest* v82 no9 p9 My 2017

THE SECESSION MOVEMENT IN EDUCATION E. FELTON and N. Lewis bw color graph map *Nation* v305 no7 p12 S 25 2017

Segregation in education—United States

Betsy DeVos and the Segregation of School Choice M. Wilkerson *Education Digest* v82 no8 p19 Ap 2017

The Little Rock Nine: Sixty years ago this month, President Eisenhower sent federal troops into Arkansas to enforce the desegregation of Little Rock's Central High School S. ROBERTS and C. Staffers *New York Times Upfront* v150 no1 p18 S 4 2017

Segregation Now and Forever: Betsy DeVos and the Looting of Public Education S. Hutchinson *Humanist* v77 no1 p9 Ja/F 2017

Segregation in transportation—United States—Lawsuits & claims

No, I Will Not Move to the Back of the Bus D. B. Moskowitz bw color *American History* v52 no3 p40 Ag 2017

Segregation—United States

Koched-Up Economics C. LEHMANN *In These Times* v41 no8 p37 Ag 2017

Segreto, A.

Observation of a large-scale anisotropy in the arrival directions of cosmic rays above 8×10^{18} eV *Science* v357 no6357 p1266 S 22 2017

SEGUI, LEAH M.

Long-Term Studies Contribute Disproportionately to Ecology and Policy *BioScience* v67 no3 p271 Mr 2017

SEGUÍN, BÉCQUER

The Catalonia Question [Cover story] *Nation* v305 no10 p4 O 23 2017

Seguin-Orlando, Andaine

Ancient genomic changes associated with domestication of the horse color diag *Science* v356 no6336 p442 Ap 28 2017

Segura, Alex

Like His Publisher, Crime Novelist Alex Segura Wears Many Hats C. Reid color *Publishers Weekly* v264 no16 p8 Ap 17 2017

Segura, Jonathan

HERE IT IS: OUR BIG FALL BOOKS PREVIEW *Publishers Weekly* v264 no26 p20 Je 26 2017

Print Sales Stay Hot chart *Publishers Weekly* v264 no2 p4 Ja 9 2017

Segura, Olga

El Sueño Americano de Junot Díaz bw color *America* v216 no12 p42 My 29 2017

WELCOME TO THE BOOGIE DOWN *America* v215 no10 p42 O 10 2016

What can Beyoncé and Pope Francis teach us about love? color *America* v216 no11 p56 My 15 2017

Segway Inc.

The Segway PT H. Tourgee color *Yankee* p24 Mr 2017

Segway Personal Transporter (Electric transportation device)—Evaluation

The Segway PT H. Tourgee color *Yankee* p24 Mr 2017

Sehested, Jens

TECHNICAL COMMENT ABSTRACTS *Science* v357 no6354 p881 S 1 2017

Sehgal, Kabir

3 Ways to Get More Done Right Now *Harvard Business Review Digital Articles* p2 F 23 2017

How to Write Email with Military Precision *Harvard Business Review Digital Articles* p2 N 22 2016

What Happens to Your Brain When You Negotiate About Money

Harvard Business Review Digital Articles p2 O 26 2015

Sehgal, Parul

Arundhati Roy's Fascinating Mess color *Atlantic* v320 no1 p36 Jl/Ag 2017

International Literature: Writers have found freedom and restriction working in other languages. For Leonora Carrington, alternatives to English offered her access to secret selves *New York Times Book Review* p59 Je 4 2017

The Reading Lesson *New York Times Book Review* p12 Ap 2 2017

Remains of Day: What can writers' diaries tell us about our vexed relationship with time? *New York Times Book Review* p27 Jl 30 2017

Roving Eye *New York Times Book Review* p27 Ap 9 2017

Sehgal, Tino, 1976-—Exhibitions

TINO SEHGAL K. Green cartoon *Art in America* v105 no3 p139 Mr 2017

Seidel, Frederick, 1936-

ATHENA *New York Review of Books* v64 no11 p55 Je 22 2017

Start Your Engines! color *New York Review of Books* v64 no1 p16 Ja 19 2017

Seidel, James

The Bottom Line color *Sail* v48 no4 p60 Ap 2017

SEIDEL, MATT

The Day the Dead Come Back color *Publishers Weekly* v264 no31 p32 Jl 31 2017

A View of South Africa bw *Publishers Weekly* v264 no12 p45 Mr 20 2017

Seidelmann, Sarah Bamford

Swimming with Elephants: My Unexpected Pilgrimage from Physician to Healer *Publishers Weekly* v264 no33 p75 Ag 14 2017

Seiden, Josh

You Need to Manage Digital Projects for Outcomes, Not Outputs color *Harvard Business Review Digital Articles* p2 F 6 2017

Seider, Scott

Critical consciousness A key to student achievement bw il *Phi Delta Kappan* v98 no5 p18 F 2017

SEIDLER, REINMAR

Communicating the Science and Human Significance of Climate Change *BioScience* v67 no3 p306 Mr 2017

Seidman, Carrie

Danielle Brown color *Dance Magazine* v91 no3 p44 Mr 2017

Seidman, Dov

THE FOUR PILLARS OF MORAL LEADERSHIP color *Fortune* v176 no4 p90 S 15 2017

From the Knowledge Economy to the Human Economy *Harvard Business Review Digital Articles* p2 N 12 2014

We've Forgotten What "Greatness" Really Means *Harvard Business Review Digital Articles* p2 Mr 4 2016

Seidman, Ellen

Drugstore shopping is my therapy color *Health* v31 no9 p65 N 2017

get ready to relax color *Health* v31 no6 p116 Jl 2017

What's That Rash?! color *Health* v31 no1 p77 Ja 2017

Seife, Charles

SCIENCE JOURNALISM color *Scientific American* v316 no2 p5 F 2017

Seifert, Chris

What's Your Land Worth? J. SCOTT and B. SPIEGEL *Successful Farming* v114 no12 p66 Mid-N 2016

SEIFF, ABBY

The Minesweeper Sok Chenda color *Foreign Policy* no221 p24 N/D 2016

Seiffert, Rachel

Do the Right Thing L. SCHILLINGER *New York Times Book Review* p10 Ag 27 2017

Seigal, Joshua

Morris Wants More... for Christmas *Publishers Weekly* v264 no36 p91 S 4 2017

Seigfried (Music)

'Seigfried' J. PARHAM *New York Times Magazine* p61 Mr 12 2017

Seigo Shima

The methanogenic CO2 reducing-and-fixing enzyme is bifunctional and contains 46 [4Fe-4S] clusters bibl diag *Science* v354 no6308 p114 O 7 2016

Seiko Epson Corp.

EPSON DS-320 REVIEW: PORTABLE PRODUCTIVITY SCANNER, SANS WIRELESS J. R. BOOKWALTER color *Macworld - Digital Edition* v34 no6 p42 Je 2017

EPSON FASTFOTO FF-640: QUICK, CONVENIENT PHOTO SCANS DON'T COME CHEAP J. R. BOOKWALTER color *Macworld - Digital Edition* p31 Mr 2017

Laser Lightshow T. J. Norton color graph *Sound & Vision* v82 no4 p50 My 2017

You Can Find Just Your Type! chart color *Consumer Reports* v82 no3 p9 Mr 2017

Seinfeld (TV program)

Life's Work: An Interview with JERRY SEINFELD D. McGinn bw *Harvard Business Review* v95 no1 p172 Ja/F 2017

Seinfeld's Lost Story Lines D. Snierson color *Entertainment Weekly* no1460/1461 p64 Ap 7-17 2017

Tony's Dead, Walt's Not, and Phoebe's Hooked on Meth A. STERNBERGH img *New York* v50 no12 p102 Je 12 2017

Seinfeld, Jerry, 1954-

Jerry Seinfeld C. WEAVER color *GQ: Gentlemen's Quarterly* v97 no6 p126 Je 2017

Seinfeld, Jerry, 1954-—Interviews

Life's Work: An Interview with JERRY SEINFELD D. McGinn bw *Harvard Business Review* v95 no1 p172 Ja/F 2017

Seinfeld, Jessica

FRESH FOR DINNER [Cover story] color *Redbook* p144 My 2017

the life C. Stern color *InStyle* v24 no7 p131 Jl 2017

My LIST B. Mazurek bw color *Harper's Bazaar* no3654 p66 Je/Jl 2017

Sei Shonagon, b. ca. 967

c. 1000: Heian-kyo Sei Shonagon *Lapham's Quarterly* v10 no1 p99 Wint 2017

Seismic event location

Walking With Venus' Wind J. KEATS color diag *Discover* v38 no3 p10 Ap 2017

Seismic prospecting equipment

Seismic array shifts to Alaska J. Rosen color *Science* v357 no6359 p22 O 6 2017

Seismic waves

Continents' bottoms found M. TEMMING diag *Science News* v192 no4 p11 S 16 2017

A seismic shift in continental tectonic plates B. Savage color *Science* v357 no6351 p549 Ag 11 2017

SPYING ON NUCLEAR BLASTS [Cover story] A. Witze color graph *Science News* v192 no1 p18 Ag 5 2017

Seismologists

Big quake hopscotched across faults T. SUMNER *Science News* v191 no8 p14 Ap 29 2017

New Zealand earthquake rattles experts color *Science* v354 no6314 p808 N 18 2016

Seismology

See also

Earthquake zones

Seismic waves

Apple seismology K. van Wijk and S. Hitchman *Physics Today* v70 no10 p94 O 2017

Recurring and triggered slow-slip events near the trench at the Nankai Trough subduction megathrust E. Araki, D. M. Saffer et al diag graph *Science* v356 no6343 p1157 Je 16 2017

Seismic evidence for partial melting at the root of major hot spot plumes K. Yuan and B. Romanowicz diag graph *Science* v357 no6349 p393 Jl 28 2017

A unified continental thickness from seismology and diamonds suggests a melt-defined plate S. Tharimena, C. Rychert et al graph map *Science* v357 no6351 p580 Ag 11 2017

Seismology—International cooperation

Expedition probes ocean trench's deepest secrets J. Qiu color *Science* v355 no6321 p115 Ja 13 2017

Seismology—Observations

Seasonal water storage, stress modulation, and California seismicity C. W. Johnson, Y. Fu et al diag graph *Science* v356 no6343 p1161 Je 16 2017

Seismometers

Expanding the Scientific Arsenal L. Lippsett *Oceanus* v52 no2 p60 Spr 2017

SEITZ, BLAKE

Atlanta Blues color *National Review* v69 no12 p29 Je 26 2017

Glimpses of Will *Weekly Standard* v22 no22 p31 F 13 2017

Lennart Nilsson's Unborn Beauties color *National Review* v69 no5 p36 Mr 20 2017

Seitz, Mark J.

El Paso bishop urges deportation halt until immigration is fixed M. J. O'Loughlin color *America* v217 no3 p16 Ag 7 2017

Seitz, Matt Zoller

American Horse Story img *New York* v49 no15 p87 Jl 25 2016

Artificial Grit img *New York* v49 no20 p128 O 3 2016

Difficult Pontiff img *New York* p82 Ja 9 2017

Do Endings Matter Anymore? Yes, but not nearly as much as they used to. TV is moving away from finale fever—which is making for better TV *New York* v50 no12 p92 Je 12 2017

Extradimensional: Rick and Morty is as affecting as it is loopy img *New York* v50 no16 p107 Ag 7 2017

The Next Chapter: Television's best shows are taking their cues from literature img *New York* v50 no10 p98 My 15 2017

Nice Hat img *New York* v49 no23 p84 N 14 2016

No Rest for the Wicked img *New York* p76 F 9 2017

Sweet Home Louisiana *New York* v49 no19 p97 S 19 2016

The Ten Best TV Shows of the Year img *New York* v49 no25 p120 D 12 2016

That '70s Show img *New York* v50 no18 p83 S 4 2017

To Do img *New York* p86 Ja 9 2017

To Do img *New York* v49 no20 p136 O 3 2016

To Do: Twenty-five things to see, hear, watch, and read img *New York* v50 no10 p106 My 15 2017

Who Is the Best TV Couple? img *New York* v49 no22 p100 O 31 2016

Wrath of the Showrunners img *New York* v50 no8 p130 Ap 17 2017

You Were Expecting Pie? In his scalding Twin Peaks revisit, David Lynch doubles down on being David Lynch img *New York* v50 no11 p124 My 29 2017

SEITZ, SUZANNE LAURY

STORIES WE TELL OURSELVES color *Vanity Fair* v58 no11 p88 N 2016

Seitzinger, Sybil P.

Nitrogen stewardship in the Anthropocene color *Science* v357 no6349 p350 Jl 28 2017

Seiwert, Amy

Amy SEIWERT H. Rolfe *Dance Spirit* v21 no7 p50 S 2017

AXIS Dance Company Turns 30! color *Dance Spirit* v21 no8 p36 O 2017

Sejnowski, Terrence J.

Single-cell methylomes identify neuronal subtypes and regulatory elements in mammalian cortex diag *Science* v357 no6351 p600 Ag 11 2017

Sekaran, Shanthi

An Immigrant Experience A. GROSS color *Publishers Weekly* v263 no50 p41 D 5 2016

Sekeris, Evan

Can You Put a Dollar Amount on Your Company's Cyber Risk? *Harvard Business Review Digital Articles* p2 O 5 2016

Sekine, Shun-ichi

Structure of the complete elongation complex of RNA polymerase II with basal factors map *Science* v357 no6354 p921 S 1 2017

Sela, Hanan

Wild emmer genome architecture and diversity elucidate wheat evolution and domestication color *Science* v357 no6346 p93 Jl 7 2017

SELBY, AMY

'CUES AND Brews *Atlanta* v57 no2 p126 Je 2017

Selcer, Richard

NOR PRAYERS FOR MERCY *Military History* v33 no5 p23 Ja 2017

Seldon, Anthony

The Double Life of the Mandarin R. Quinault *History Today* v67 no4 p65 Ap 2017

Seldon, Willa

Connecting Unemployed Youth with Organizations That Need Talent *Harvard Business Review Digital Articles* p2 N 3 2016

Why - and How - to Hire Young People Without Diplomas *Harvard Business Review Digital Articles* p2 Ap 28 2015

Selection & appointment of corporate directors

Boardrooms of the Living Dead J. Green and A. Ritcey *Bloomberg Businessweek* no4534 p27 Ag 14 2017

Selection & appointment of U.S. Supreme Court justices

The Court Moves Right D. COLE *Nation* v305 no2 p4 Jl 17 2017

Selection rules (Nuclear physics)

MANIPULATING ULTRACOLD MATTER [Cover story] J. Stajic, E. Hand et al color *Science* v357 no6355 p984 S 8 2017

Selee, Andrew

A New Migration Agenda between the United States and Mexico *Wilson Quarterly* p1 Wint 2017

Selene, Belinda

"I take my makeup off on QVC 100 times a year." color *Glamour* v115 no4 p112 Ap 2017

Selenium isotopes

Rocks hint at early oxygen oases T. SUMNER *Science News* v191 no3 p16 F 18 2017

Selenko, Philipp

Opposing effects of Elk-1 multisite phosphorylation shape its response to ERK activation bibl graph *Science* v354 no6309 p233 O 14 2016

Seles, Monica—Health

WHAT IF? ... THESE FIVE CAREERS HADN'T BEEN ALTERED BY INJURY? J. Feldman color *Sports Illustrated* v126 no11 p53 Ap 17-24 2017

Self

    See also

    Human body

    Identity (Psychology)

    Satisfaction

    Self-interest

Going Bare... A. GRAHAM, P. LOCKWOOD et al color *Glamour* v115 no6 p138 Je 2017

Make Peace with Your Unlived Life M. F. R. K. de Vries *Harvard Business Review Digital Articles* p2 D 21 2016

My Soul Looks Back in Wonder S. J. Roberts color *Essence* v47 no11 p124 Mr 2017

Self-acceptance

KIERSEY'S GUIDE TO Feeling Good color *InStyle* v24 no9 p232 S 2017

Self-actualization (Psychology)

Get More Done by Focusing Less on Work S. Friedman *Harvard Business Review Digital Articles* p2 F 5 2015

How Gratitude Can Help Your Career P. Bregman *Harvard Business Review Digital Articles* p2 O 1 2015

Let's Be Less Stupid P. MARX *Reader's Digest* v189 no1128 p108 Mr 2017

Self-confidence

50 States of Women S. Dreisbach bw chart color map *Glamour* v115 no9 p146 S 2017

Canter with Confidence J. GOODNIGHT and H. MELOCCO color *Trail Rider* v29 no4 p44 My 2017

Create a Confident Mindset [Cover story] V. Hargis and J. F. Meyer color *Horse & Rider* v56 no3 p32 Mr 2017

Finding the Healthy Tension Between Being Confident and Collaborative L. Levy bw *Harvard Business Review Digital Articles* p2 Ja 10 2017

The Hidden Benefits of Short-Term Business Travel A. Molinsky and M. Hahn *Harvard Business Review Digital Articles* p2 Je 13 2016

How Well Do You Know... You? Are you an assertive "eagle"? A social "parrot"? This fun--and surprisingly accurate!--quiz will help you identify the personality traits that make you special *Scholastic Choices* p12 O 2017

The Man Who Would Be Kempton A. FERGUSON color *Weekly Standard* v23 no6 p21 O 16 2017

The Mindset That Leads People to Be Dangerously Overconfident H. G. Halvorson *Harvard Business Review Digital Articles* p2 Ap 19 2016

SHE'S A JOY [Cover story] M. C. HAREL color *Redbook* p86 Jl/Ag 2017

You + your Body M. Jesser color diag graph *Seventeen* v76 no5 p86 S 2017

Self-consciousness (Awareness)

50 States of Women S. Dreisbach bw chart color map *Glamour* v115 no9 p146 S 2017

5 Ways to Become More Self-Aware A. K. Tjan *Harvard Business*

Review Digital Articles p2 F 11 2015

Getting Out of One's Own Way A. Braun color *Natural History* v125 no7 p6 Jl/Ag 2017

Research: We're Not Very Self-Aware, Especially at Work E. C. Dierdorff and R. S. Rubin *Harvard Business Review Digital Articles* p2 Mr 12 2015

Signs That You Lack Emotional Intelligence M. M. Wilkins *Harvard Business Review Digital Articles* p2 D 31 2014

Stop Trying to Find Your True Self at Work G. Petriglieri *Harvard Business Review Digital Articles* p2 Ap 3 2015

Successful Leaders Know What Made Them Who They Are B. Swain *Harvard Business Review Digital Articles* p2 S 5 2016

Two Ways to Clarify Your Professional Passions R. S. Kaplan *Harvard Business Review Digital Articles* p2 Mr 30 2015

Two Words to Help You Gut Check Your Career M. Chussil *Harvard Business Review Digital Articles* p2 N 5 2015

"YOU DON'T HAVE TO PRETEND TO KNOW EVERY-THING": Organisational psychologist Dr Tasha Eurich on the power of self-awareness—and why Uber is getting it badly wrong C. NEWBERY *People Management* p40 Jl 2017

Self-control

See also

Anger management

3 Ways Managers Start Off On the Wrong Foot H. G. Halvorson *Harvard Business Review Digital Articles* p2 O 6 2015

CAN YOU CONTROL YOURSELF? [Cover story] B. WRIGHT and D. CARREON color graph *Christianity Today* v61 no4 p34 My 2017

Have We Been Thinking About Willpower the Wrong Way for 30 Years? N. Eyal *Harvard Business Review Digital Articles* p2 N 23 2016

Leadership Takes Self-Control. Here's What We Know About It Kai Chi (Sam) Yam, Huiwen Lian et al color *Harvard Business Review Digital Articles* p2 Je 5 2017

WHAT GREEN TARA CAN TEACH US ABOUT FEAR: A CALMING EXERCISE M. CLAVIJO bw *Tricycle: The Buddhist Review* v27 no1 p60 Fall 2017

What to Do Before You Lose Your Cool at Work N. M. Williams color *Black Enterprise* v47 no3 p38 O 2016

WHITHER WILLPOWER? When entering disputed territory, you need a good guide T. OLSEN color *Christianity Today* v61 no4 p7 My 2017

Self-control in children

African farmers' kids ace willpower test B. BOWER *Science News* v192 no1 p13 Ag 5 2017

Self-culture

See also

Mnemonics

To Grow as a Person, Selectively Forget the Past V. Govindarajan *Harvard Business Review Digital Articles* p2 My 12 2016

Why Self-Improvement Should Be a Group Activity R. Carucci *Harvard Business Review Digital Articles* p2 F 22 2017

Self-deception—Religious aspects

The Word *Christian Century* v133 no21 p20 O 12 2016

Self-defense

See also

Boxing

Mixed martial arts

The Ascendancy of Tracy Kenpo B. Mornar color *Black Belt* v55 no4 p74 Je/Jl 2017

Boost Your Immunity K. ASP color *Martha Stewart Living* p68 O 2017

LET THE EXPERIMENTS BEGIN! A. TAYLOR and C. THOMAS color *Black Belt* v55 no4 p66 Je/Jl 2017

The Light at the End of the Tunnel K. McCann color *Black Belt* v55 no4 p18 Je/Jl 2017

RAZOR'S EDGE B. CAMPBELL color *Black Belt* v55 no5 p60 Ag/S 2017

SECRETS OF SYSTEMA K. SECOURS color *Black Belt* v55 no5 p66 Ag/S 2017

Self-Defense or Self-Offense? K. McCann color *Black Belt* v55 no5 p18 Ag/S 2017

SELF-TAUGHT MMA THUGS, PART 1 P. BAMBURAK bw *Black Belt* v55 no3 p40 Ap/My 2017

Singapore, Part 2: Caught Up in Catch Wrestling A. Graceffo color *Black Belt* v55 no5 p22 Ag/S 2017

Self-defense for women

FIGHTING WORDS C. Cunningham *Washingtonian Magazine* v52 no2 p230 N 2016

HOW TO STAY SAFE ... *Washingtonian Magazine* v52 no2 p233 N 2016

I Am a Weapon: Her Martial Art of Choice A. SERRA *Idaho Magazine* v16 no8 p23 My 2017

Self-defense instruction

Avoid Rather Than Fight K. McCann color *Black Belt* v55 no6 p18 O/N 2017

A Down-and-Dirty Guide to Striking [Cover story] K. McCann color *Black Belt* v55 no2 p16 F/Mr 2017

FIGHTING WORDS C. Cunningham *Washingtonian Magazine* v52 no2 p230 N 2016

Self-defense—Equipment & supplies

See also

Pepper spray

The Light at the End of the Tunnel K. McCann color *Black Belt* v55 no4 p18 Je/Jl 2017

SELF-DEFENSE FLASH-LIGHTS R. MANN color *Outdoor Life* v224 no8 pP1 O 2017

Training, Not Trinkets K. McCann color *Black Belt* v55 no3 p16 Ap/My 2017

Self-destructive behavior

ART IS LIFE: AND LACK OF IT ALMOST KILLED ME J. TOOKEY *Idaho Magazine* v16 no9 p12 Je 2017

Don't Let Shame Become a Self-Destructive Spiral M. F. R. Kets de Vries *Harvard Business Review Digital Articles* p1 Je 1 2017

Self-determination theory

Grant-Writing Bootcamp: An Intervention to Enhance the Research Capacity of Academic Women in STEM J. L. SMITH, C. STOOP et al *BioScience* v67 no7 p638 Jl 2017

Self-directed work teams

How Self-Managed Teams Can Resolve Conflict A. Maimon *Harvard Business Review Digital Articles* p2 Ap 17 2017

The Problem with Saying "Don't Bring Me Problems, Bring Me Solutions" S. Nawaz *Harvard Business Review Digital Articles* p2 S 1 2017

Self-directed work teams—Case studies

Case Study: Is Holacracy for Us? E. Roelofsen and Tao Yue *Harvard Business Review Digital Articles* p2 D 8 2016

Self-disclosure

THE FRAUD WHO ISN'T C. FLORA *Psychology Today* v49 no6 p70 N/D 2016

Self-doubt

Stop Second-Guessing Your Decisions at Work C. O'Hara *Harvard Business Review Digital Articles* p2 N 6 2015

Self-efficacy

The Jock Whisperer color *O, The Oprah Magazine* v25 Ap 2017

A Quiet Revolution A. SMARICK color *Weekly Standard* v22 no7 p20 O 24 2016

Tap your willpower color *Yoga Journal* p52 2016 Special Issue

A Tip Worth Remembering H. Rothberg color *Money* v46 no8 p80 S 2017

Self-efficacy in teachers

The power of reflective action to build teacher efficacy T. Awkard color *Phi Delta Kappan* v98 no6 p53 Mr 2017

Self-employed

7 Questions to Ask Yourself Before Going Freelance A. Gallo *Harvard Business Review Digital Articles* p2 Jl 14 2015

7 Tips for Managing Freelancers and Independent Contractors A. Gallo *Harvard Business Review Digital Articles* p2 Ag 17 2015

9 Tips for Freelancers Negotiating New Assignments J. Younger *Harvard Business Review Digital Articles* p2 Je 7 2016

The Big Factors That Attract the Best Freelancers J. Younger, S. Patterson et al *Harvard Business Review Digital Articles* p2 D 10 2015

How Freelancers Can Make Sure They Get Paid on Time R. Knight *Harvard Business Review Digital Articles* p2 2017

How to Become a Successful Freelancer A. Gallo *Harvard Business Review Digital Articles* p2 Jl 20 2016

Learning How to Collaborate When You're Self-Employed D. Clark *Harvard Business Review Digital Articles* p2 D 28 2016

Stake Your Claim H. VILLA *Publishers Weekly* v264 no12 p76 Mr 20 2017

Who Benefits from the Peer-to-Peer Economy? R. Chase *Harvard*

Magazine p17 Mr 5 2017

Self-promotion

Get Your Message Across to a Skeptical Audience S. Martin *Harvard Business Review Digital Articles* p2 My 28 2015

How to Promote Yourself Without Looking Like a Jerk D. Clark *Harvard Business Review Digital Articles* p2 D 22 2014

Lifestyles of the Rich and Not-Quite Internet Famous M. Chafkin color *Bloomberg Businessweek* no4524 p63 My 29 2017

Managing Your Professional Identity During a Gender Change D. Clark *Harvard Business Review Digital Articles* p2 F 3 2015

Marketing Mistakes Z. WHITTENBURG *Dance Magazine* v91 no6 p52 Je 2017

Self-publishing

Design Options for Self-Publishers J. FRIEDLANDER *Publishers Weekly* v263 no43 p42 O 24 2016

Horror Authors Take a Stab at Self-Publishing N. A. SPECTOR bw color *Publishers Weekly* v263 no43 p38 O 24 2016

How to Market Self-Published E-books to Libraries M. COKER *Publishers Weekly* v264 no13 p45 Mr 27 2017

The Indie E-Books Evolution A. DANIEL *Publishers Weekly* v263 no39 p48 S 26 2016

THE KINDLE EFFECT J. Alsever chart color *Fortune* v75 no1 p32 Ja 1 2017

A New Concept for Indie Bookstores P. GOODMAN *Publishers Weekly* v264 no20 p60 My 15 2017

SMASHWORDS SELF-PUBLISHED BESTSELLERS LIST, MAY 2017 C. JURIS chart color *Publishers Weekly* v264 no28 p19 Jl 10 2017

Self-publishing—Methodology

Self-Publishing in 2017 A. DANIEL color *Publishers Weekly* v264 no4 p40 Ja 23 2017

Self-reliance

CHILDREN AND CHORES: Give kids responsibilities that will help them thrive while learning self-reliance J. Salatin *Mother Earth News* no283 p59 Ag/S 2017

NOT OFF THE GRID, BUT WE CAN SEE THE EDGE FROM HERE J. D. TUCCILLE color *Reason* v48 no10 p16 Mr 2017

Self-reliant living

AGING GRACEFULLY on the Homestead H. Will, S. Heggestad et al *Mother Earth News* no280 p34 F/Mr 2017

THE NEW SELF-SUFFICIENCY R. D'AGOSTINO *Popular Mechanics* p4 F 2017

THE POPULAR MECHANICS GUIDE TO SELF-SUFFICIENCY [Cover story] T. Chiarella, W. Dufresne et al color *Popular Mechanics* p55 F 2017

Rewilders S. PIKE *Orion Magazine* v35 no4/5 p10 Jl-O 2016

Self-righteousness

The Righteous Ones J. W. MARTENS *America* v215 no11 p38 O 17 2016

Self-service (Economics)

Customers Like Self- Service, Unless It Undermines Customer Support M. Schrage *Harvard Business Review Digital Articles* p2 Jl 28 2015

GREAT UNKNOWNS cartoon *Popular Mechanics* v193 no7 p26 S 2016

Self-service laundries

Where We Vote *Governing* v30 no1 p40 O 2016

Self-service storage facilities

Hoarder Control K. CHAYKOWSKI, S. SHARF et al color *Forbes* v200 no2 p42 S 5 2017

STORAGE WARS N. KÖHLER color *Maclean's* v130 no7 p52 Ag 2017

Self-talk

TALKING TO OURSELVES C. Fernyhough color diag *Scientific American* v317 no2 p74 Ag 2017

Talking to Yourself (Out Loud) Can Help You Learn U. Boser *Harvard Business Review Digital Articles* p2 My 5 2017

Talk It Out color *Dance Spirit* v21 no8 p48 O 2017

Selfie sticks

LAST PAGE P. STEFÁNSSON *Iceland Review* v55 no2 p128 Mr/Ap 2017

Selfies

ADIR ABERGEL The Mane Man S. Zuckerman color *InStyle* v24 no11 p132 N 2017

KOALAS SNAP "SELFIES" S. Schwartz *National Geographic Kids* no468 p12 Mr 2017

selfie indulgence m. ferrentino color *Bike Magazine* v24 no7 p52 S 2017

The Selfie Samurai A. CARTER bw *Vanity Fair* v59 no10 p182 O 2017

Taking the Perfect Selfie A. Graham color *InStyle* v24 no3 p186 Mr 2017

The Ultimate Surf Selfie color *Surfer* v57 no13 p96 Mr 2017

What Your SELFIE Says ABOUT YOU A. STANLEY color *Seventeen* v76 no12 p68 D 2016/Ja 2017

The White House Selfie: The Visual Web's Latest Victory P. Hewitt *Harvard Business Review Digital Articles* p2 Jl 2 2015

Selfish genetic elements

A maternal-effect selfish genetic element in Caenorhabditis elegans E. Ben-David, A. Burga et al diag *Science* v356 no6342 p1051 Je 9 2017

Poisons, antidotes, and selfish genes N. Phadnis diag *Science* v356 no6342 p1013 Je 9 2017

Selfish DNA fooled scientists for years S. MILIUS bw *Science News* v191 no12 p10 Je 24 2017

Selfishness

Signs You Might Be a Toxic Colleague H. G. Halvorson *Harvard Business Review Digital Articles* p2 Mr 2 2016

SUICIDE NOTES D. Merkin *Harper's Magazine* v334 no2000 p17 Ja 2017

Selflessness (Psychology)

HOW AND WHEN SELFLESSNESS AT WORK BACKFIRES graph *Harvard Business Review Digital Articles* p16 Ja 1 2017

Self-publishing—Charts, diagrams, etc.

SMASHWORDS SELF-PUBLISHED BESTSELLERS LIST, DECEMBER 2016 chart color *Publishers Weekly* v264 no6 p17 F 6 2017

Selfridges & Co.

Introducing the Man You've Been Listening to All Year D. FRIEDMAN color *GQ: Gentlemen's Quarterly* v86 no12 p104 D 2016

Selgas, José

Extraterrestrial Encounter: Spanish firm SelgasCano pays respect to nature by jolting it with the surreal A. COHN color *Architectural Record* v205 no8 p64 Ag 2017

Selig, Danielle

Do Look Down color *Bloomberg Businessweek* no4495 p72 O 17 2016

Seligson, Hannah

The queen of spin color *Columbia Journalism Review* v56 no2 p100 Fall 2017

Selina Wang

The Future Of Farming Is Looking Up color *Bloomberg Businessweek* no4537 p62 S 11 2017

Selinger, Jonathan V.

Introduction to the Theory of Soft Matter From Ideal Gases to Liquid Crystals G. Grason *Physics Today* v69 no11 p60 N 2016

Selingo, Jeffrey J.

FROM GOWN TO TOWN J. MALESIC color *America* v215 no13 p34 O 31 2016

THERE IS LIFE AFTER COLLEGE D. J. SILVA color *Phi Kappa Phi Forum* v97 no2 p28 Summ 2017

Two-Thirds of College Grads Struggle to Launch Their Careers *Harvard Business Review Digital Articles* p2 My 31 2016

Selkoe, Dennis J.

β2-Adrenoreceptor is a regulator of the a-synuclein gene driving risk of Parkinson's disease cartoon chart graph *Science* v357 no6354 p891 S 1 2017

Sellafield (England)

It's a Dirty Job, But Something's Gotta Do It A. Satariano color *Bloomberg Businessweek* no4512 p31 F 20 2017

Sellars, Kim

Attitudes of Influential Leadership *Parks & Recreation* v52 no5 p65 My 2017

Selldorf Architects LLC

Back on Track C. ROUX color diag *Architectural Record* v205 no2 p80 F 2017

Selle Royal SpA

FI'ZI:K R1B UOMO L. Flickinger color *Bicycling* v58 no4 p88 My 2017

Selleck, Tom, 1945-—Interviews

Tom Selleck J. STOWE color *Men's Health* v32 no9 p124 N 2017

SELLERS, HEATHER
"I had no recipe for normal" bw color *Good Housekeeping* v264 no5 p77 My 2017

Sellers, John A.
A Big Week for Children's Books color *Publishers Weekly* v264 no16 p4 Ap 17 2017

Sellers, Patricia
A-RODS'S NEXT BIG SWING color *Fortune* v176 no2 p74 Ag 1 2017

Sellers, Robert
A MERCURIAL CHARACTER R. A. BLAKE *America* v215 no18 p38 D 5 2016

Sellier, Anne-Laure
WE LOOK LIKE OUR NAMES S. Berinato color img *Harvard Business Review* v95 no5 p32 S/O 2017

Sellin, Mikael E.
Inflammation boosts bacteriophage transfer between Salmonella spp bibl diag *Science* v355 no6330 p1211 Mr 17 2017

Selling
See also
Closing the sale
Sales management

7 Reasons Salespeople Don't Close the Deal S. W. Martin *Harvard Business Review Digital Articles* p2 Ag 2 2017

How to Improve Your Sales Skills, Even If You're Not a Salesperson R. Knight *Harvard Business Review Digital Articles* p2 My 22 2017

Ode to a Couch I. Brannon color *Weekly Standard* v22 no47 p5 Ag 21 2017

THE QUEEN WHO BECAME A WENCH D. A. WOOD color *Missouri Life* v44 no5 p10 Ag 2017

Sales Reps, Stop Asking Leading Questions S. Edinger *Harvard Business Review Digital Articles* p2 Mr 17 2017

SECRET PASSAGE L. MURTHA *Cincinnati Magazine* v50 no3 p46 D 2016

Selling to Customers Who Do Their Homework Online F. V. Cespedes and J. Hamilton *Harvard Business Review Digital Articles* p2 Mr 16 2016

Why the Best Salespeople Get So Lucky J. Le Bon *Harvard Business Review Digital Articles* p2 Ap 13 2015

Your Elevator Pitch Needs an Elevator Pitch T. David *Harvard Business Review Digital Articles* p2 D 30 2014

Selling—Life insurance
How Life Insurers Can Bring Their Business into the 21st Century P. Lyons and B. Demaster *Harvard Business Review Digital Articles* p2 Mr 25 2015

YOUR MONEY OR YOUR LIFE V. POSTREL color *Reason* v49 no3 p8 Jl 2017

Selling—Methodology
B2B Salespeople Can Survive If They Reimagine Their Roles J. A. Narus *Harvard Business Review Digital Articles* p2 Ap 17 2015

How One Startup Developed a Sales Model That Works in Emerging Markets J. Cedar *Harvard Business Review Digital Articles* p2 S 7 2016

How to Actually Put Your Marketing Data to Use B. Gilad *Harvard Business Review Digital Articles* p2 O 27 2015

Selling—Psychological aspects
When to Sell with Facts and Figures, and When to Appeal to Emotions M. D. Harris *Harvard Business Review Digital Articles* p2 Ja 26 2015

Selling—Study & teaching (Higher)
More Universities Need to Teach Sales F. V. Cespedes and D. Weinfurter *Harvard Business Review Digital Articles* p2 Ap 26 2016

SELLMAN, LIN
ROAR OF THE CROWD *Texas Monthly* v45 no1 p8 Ja 2017

Sellschop, Richard
The Age of Smart, Safe, Cheap Robots Is Already Here *Harvard Business Review Digital Articles* p2 Je 15 2015

The Dirty Little Secret About Digitally Transforming Operations *Harvard Business Review Digital Articles* p2 My 31 2016

Selma (Film)
THE MOVEMENT IN MOTION: 4 ESSENTIAL CIVIL RIGHTS FILMS J. BENNETT bw color *Ebony* v72/73 no12/1 p84 O/N 2017

Sels, Luc
What to Do Before You Fire a Pivotal Employee *Harvard Business Review Digital Articles* p2 Ja 29 2016

Selters water
Carry-On Health B. HOWARD color *AARP: The Magazine* v60 no5A p19 Ag/S 2017

Selva, Nuria
A global map of roadless areas and their conservation status bibl color graph map *Science* v354 no6318 p1423 D 16 2016

Global roadless areas: Consider terrain color *Science* v355 no6332 p1381 Mr 31 2017

Selway River (Idaho)
The Crown Jewel: A Rare Float on the Best Wilderness River in America L. JACKSON *Idaho Magazine* v16 no12 p6 S 2017

SELZER, KIT
DISHWASHERS bw color *Better Homes & Gardens* v95 no11 p52 N 2017

i did it! *Better Homes & Gardens* v94 no11 p58 N 2016

i did it! color *Better Homes & Gardens* v95 no8 p58 Ag 2017

i did it! color *Better Homes & Gardens* v95 no9 p64 S 2017

INSIDE TRACK color *Better Homes & Gardens* v95 no9 p76 S 2017

PUNCH LIST color *Better Homes & Gardens* v95 no10 p62 O 2017

PUNCH LIST color *Better Homes & Gardens* v95 no2 p58 F 2016

PUNCH LIST color *Better Homes & Gardens* v95 no3 p56 Mr 2017

PUNCH LIST color *Better Homes & Gardens* v95 no8 p66 Ag 2017

PUT IT in NEUTRAL color *Better Homes & Gardens* v95 no4 p26 Ap 2017

thanks, bro color diag *Better Homes & Gardens* v95 no10 p54 O 2017

WHAT THEY DID color *Better Homes & Gardens* v95 no9 p66 S 2017

Semantics
See also
Idioms
Plays on words

Semantics derived automatically from language corpora contain human-like biases A. Caliskan, J. J. Bryson et al chart graph *Science* v356 no6334 p183 Ap 14 2017

Semento, Larry
Tears in the Wind: Triumph and Tragedy on America's Highest Peak *Publishers Weekly* v264 no12 p67 Mr 20 2017

Semiconductor devices
Dual-comb spectroscopy of water vapor with a free-running semiconductor disk laser S. M. Link, D. J. H. C. Maas et al diag *Science* v356 no6343 p1164 Je 16 2017

Semiconductor doping
See also
Doping profiles (Semiconductors)

Photonic doping of epsilon-near-zero media I. Liberal, A. M. Mahmoud et al bibl diag *Science* v355 no6329 p1058 Mr 10 2017

Semiconductor industry—China
China's Big Play for Small Chips R. Hackett color *Fortune* v175 no3 p16 Mr 1 2017

Semiconductor materials
THE PRICE OF A DIGITAL WORLD C. Simpson, B. Elgin et al color *Bloomberg Businessweek* no4527 p58 Je 19 2017

Semiconductors
See also
Thermoelectric materials

EXOTIC FORMS of SILICON P. C. Taylor *Physics Today* v69 no12 p34 D 2016

Tailored semiconductors for high-harmonic optoelectronics M. Sivis, M. Taucer et al graph *Science* v357 no6348 p303 Jl 21 2017

Seminarians
See also
Gay seminarians

At-Home Seminary A. C. EASTEP color *Christianity Today* v61 no4 p67 My 2017

The God Squad E. Dias color *Time* v189 no23 p36 Je 19 2017

Seminars
Peter's Choice R. PERLSTEIN cartoon *Mother Jones* v42 no1 p9

Ja/F 2017

Seminole War, 2nd, 1835-1842

Whose War Was It? C. S. MONACO *American Indian Quarterly* v41 no1 p31 Wint 2017

Semiochemicals—Research

NEW FLY REPELLENT IN THE WORKS C. Barakat and M. McCluskey color *Equus* no471 p10 D 2016

Semiskilled labor

Better Jobs Information Benefits Everyone A. REAMER *Issues in Science & Technology* v33 no1 p58 Fall 2016

Defining Skilled Technical Work J. ROTHWELL chart *Issues in Science & Technology* v33 no1 p47 Fall 2016

What are middle skills? M. F. HANDEL bw *Issues in Science & Technology* v33 no2 p6 Wint 2017

SEMKIW, SANDRA

STORIES WE TELL OURSELVES color *Vanity Fair* v58 no11 p88 N 2016

SEMLEY, JOHN

Black and blue color *Maclean's* v129 no43 p56 O 31 2016

Oh, golly! color *Maclean's* p56 Je 2017

Rape comedy? Really? color *Maclean's* v129 no47 p63 N 28 2016

Seriously funny and funnily serious color *Maclean's* v129 no42 p63 O 24 2016

SEMLITSCH, RAYMOND D.

Overcoming Challenges to the Recovery of Declining Amphibian Populations in the United States *BioScience* v67 no2 p156 F 2017

SEMMENS, JACK

FROM THE ARCHIVES color *Reason* v49 no4 p78 Ag/S 2017

SEMMES, ANNE W.

Lessons from the Osprey Garden color *Natural History* v125 no7 p28 Jl/Ag 2017

Semolina

EAT YOUR MEAT (AND FEEL BETTER ABOUT IT) A. STANEK and C. SAFFITZ cartoon color diag *Bon Appetit* no1 p88 F 2017

Sémon, T.

Xenon isotopes in 67P/Churyumov-Gerasimenko show that comets contributed to Earth's atmosphere diag *Science* v356 no6342 p1069 Je 9 2017

Semper-Pascual, Asunción

Forest conservation: Remember Gran Chaco bibl color *Science* v355 no6324 p465 F 3 2017

Semple, Maria

Today Will Be Different L. Greenblatt color *Entertainment Weekly* no1434 p59 O 7 2016

Women on the Verge [Cover story] *New York Times Book Review* p1 O 9 2016

Semple, Maria—Interviews

MARIA SEMPLE color *Entertainment Weekly* no1434 p59 O 7 2016

Sempra Energy (Company)

Americas K. Stock color *Bloomberg Businessweek* no4535 p9 Ag 28 2017

Sempter, Debbie Hoover

Around the Campfire color *Trail Rider* v29 no1 p6 Ja/F 2017

Semrad, Carol E.

Reovirus infection triggers inflammatory responses to dietary antigens and development of celiac disease color diag *Science* v356 no6333 p44 Ap 7 2017

Sem-Sandberg, Steve

Selected for Death S. R. SULEIMAN *New York Times Book Review* p20 O 23 2016

Sen, Aarohi

How Manufacturers Can Get Faster, More Flexible, and Cheaper bw *Harvard Business Review Digital Articles* p2 F 27 2017

Sen, Amartya

A Better Way to Choose Presidents color *New York Review of Books* v64 no10 p61 Je 8 2017

The Rules of the Game: A New Electoral System cartoon chart *New York Review of Books* v64 no1 p8 Ja 19 2017

Sen, Debattama R.

The epigenetic landscape of T cell exhaustion bibl graph *Science* v354 no6316 p1165 D 2 2016

Epigenetic stability of exhausted T cells limits durability of reinvigoration by PD-1 blockade bibl graph *Science* v354 no6316

p1160 D 2 2016

Sen Li

An Anthropocene map of genetic diversity bibl graph map *Science* v353 no6307 p1532 S 30 2016

SENATORE, LEONARDO

A COSMIC CONTROVERSY color *Scientific American* v317 no1 p5 Jl 2017

Senators (U.S.)

See also

Women senators (U.S.)

Al FRANKEN color *Vanity Fair* v59 no7 p144 Summ 2017

DANCE OUTLAWS E. Witt cartoon *New Yorker* v93 no20 p24 Jl 10 2017

DEMOCRACY ON THE LINE B. YEOMAN color map *Nation* v305 no9 p16 O 16 2017

The Gentleman From Arizona M. Coppins color *Atlantic* v320 no2 p18 S 2017

The Happy Warrior [Cover story] M. Binelli bw color *Rolling Stone* no1289 p46 Je 15 2017

HOW MANY CHANGES DO YOU GET TO BE AN AMERICAN HERO? [Cover story] G. SHERMAN img *New York* p22 F 20 2017

IF THIS BODY LOSES THE ABILITY TO DEBATE, THEN WHERE IS THAT GOING TO HAPPEN? M. RUBIO *Vital Speeches of the Day* v83 no4 p134 Ap 2017

THE LIONESS IN WINTER G. SHEEHY and M. Tinoco bw color *Mother Jones* v42 no3 p34 My/Je 2017

MONTANANS ARE BEST AT RUNNING MONTANA S. DAINES *Vital Speeches of the Day* v83 no4 p111 Ap 2017

Schumer or Later P. Beinart color *New Republic* v248 no11 p5 N 2017

Search Party J. Mahler *New York Times Magazine* p9 Ja 1 2017

SENATOR-ELECT CATHERINE CORTEZ MASTO C. L. RADELOFF *Ms.* v26 no3 p8 Fall 2016

SENATOR-ELECT KAMALA HARRIS D. BARTLOW *Ms.* v26 no3 p6 Fall 2016

SENATOR-ELECT MAGGIE HASSAN D. DECKER *Ms.* v26 no3 p5 Fall 2016

SENATOR-ELECT TAMMY DUCKWORTH J. R. ENSZER *Ms.* v26 no3 p7 Fall 2016

Senators (U.S.)—Attitudes

Supreme Extremism *America* v216 no6 p8 Mr 20 2017

Where We Go From Here M. TAIBBI color *Rolling Stone* no1276 p42 D 15 2016

Senators (U.S.)—Elections

Firebrand Moore wins GOP primary runoff K. Chandler, B. Barrow et al color *Christian Century* v134 no22 p15 O 25 2017

Senators (U.S.)—Interviews

Bernie Looks Ahead E. BATES bw color *New Republic* v247 no11 p24 N 2016

Elizabeth Warren S. Frizell color *Time* v189 no21 p68 Je 5 2017

LIVE FROM D.C.! C. P. Pierce color *Esquire* p30 Je/Jl 2017

Send My Love (To Your New Lover) (Music)

'Send My Love (to Your New Lover)' W. MORRIS color *New York Times Magazine* p18 Mr 12 2017

Sendai Earthquake, Japan, 2011

Castaway critters rafted to U.S. shores on Japan tsunami debris [Cover story] M. Quintanilla color *Science News* v192 no7 p4 O 28 2017

Sendak, Rebecca

Trispecific broadly neutralizing HIV antibodies mediate potent SHIV protection in macaques color graph *Science* v357 no6359 p85 O 6 2017

Sendamarai, Anoop K.

UBE2O remodels the proteome during terminal erythroid differentiation diag *Science* v357 no6350 p471 Ag 4 2017

Seneca, Lucius Annaeus, ca. 4 B.C.-65 A.D.

AT HOME WITH THE STOICS: Do Stoic philosophy and the family mix? The writings of Seneca show how the model Stoic, relying on nothing but his own mind, can still be a loving family man L. Gloyn *History Today* v67 no9 p48 S 2017

Senegal—Description & travel

Yes, You Can Travel on a Dime! T. E. Holmes color map *Essence* v48 no2 p71 Je 2017

Senftleben, A.

Ultrafast electron diffraction imaging of bond breaking in di-ionized acetylene bibl graph *Science* v354 no6310 p308 O 21 2016

Seng, Teak

Wildlife-snaring crisis in Asian forests bibl color *Science* v355 no6322 p255 Ja 20 2017

SENGENBERGER, JIMMY

The Higher and Higher Cost of Higher Ed color *Weekly Standard* v22 no35 p19 My 22 2017

SENGER, EMILY

1983-2016 Jonathan Robert Sobol color *Maclean's* v129 no41 p62 O 17 2016

Mary Elizabeth Lynch: 1933 — 2016 color *Maclean's* v129 no46 p66 N 21 2016

Sengupta, Kamalika

Global atmospheric particle formation from CERN CLOUD measurements bibl graph map *Science* v354 no6316 p1119 D 2 2016

Senior, John

5 Ways to Increase Your Cross-Selling *Harvard Business Review Digital Articles* p2 N 22 2016

Senior centers

Senior Living J. YOUNG cartoon color *Indianapolis Monthly* v42 no2 p95 O 2017

Senior housing—United States

See also

Congregate housing

Back Home Again J. YOUNG *Indianapolis Monthly* p94 F 2017

Bowman Senior Residences *Architectural Record* v205 no4 p198 Ap 2017

The Home of the Future K. Vick color *Time* v189 no12 p46 Ap 3 2017

Peripheral vision J. Bouchard color *U.S. Catholic* v82 no5 p12 My 2017

SENIOR LIVING COMMUNITY DIRECTORY *Cincinnati Magazine* v50 no4 p92 Ja 2017

Who Will Care for You? [Cover story] P. Wang, E. Stark et al chart color map *Consumer Reports* v82 no10 p28 O 2017

Senior leadership teams

See also

Chief executive officers

Chief information officers

Chief operating officers

Companies Should Be Required to Disclose Their Gender Stats A. Wittenberg-Cox *Harvard Business Review Digital Articles* p2 D 23 2014

Content Marketers Should Find Spokespeople Outside the C-Suite J. Hall *Harvard Business Review Digital Articles* p2 Ja 7 2016

The C-Suite and IT Need to Get on the Same Page on Cybersecurity C. McKinty *Harvard Business Review Digital Articles* p2 Ap 26 2017

How Senior Executives Find Time to Be Creative E. Seppala *Harvard Business Review Digital Articles* p2 S 14 2016

How to Get on the Shortlist for the C-Suite C. Frangos color *Harvard Business Review Digital Articles* p2 Mr 2 2017

Leading in a World of Resource Constraints and Extreme Weather A. Winston *Harvard Business Review Digital Articles* p2 Je 16 2015

The Secrets of Great CEO Selection R. CHARAN color *Harvard Business Review* v94 no12 p52 D 2016

To Grow as a Leader, Seek More Complex Assignments C. Fernández-Aráoz *Harvard Business Review Digital Articles* p2 Jl 20 2017

What to Do and Say After a Tough Reorganization R. Knight *Harvard Business Review Digital Articles* p2 O 23 2015

When Was the Last Time You Asked, "Why Are We Doing It This Way?" H. Gregersen *Harvard Business Review Digital Articles* p2 Ap 1 2016

Senko, Crystal

Atom-by-atom assembly of defect-free one-dimensional cold atom arrays bibl diag graph *Science* v354 no6315 p1024 N 25 2016

Senna, Ayrton, 1960-1994

Live at Birdland S. SMITH color *Road & Track* v68 no10 p24 Jl 2017

Senna, Danzy

Blackish R. ALAM color *O, The Oprah Magazine* p91 S 2017

Exile From Brooklyn: The writer Danzy Senna moved to California because New York felt like "a book party that never ended."

She doesn't mean that in a good way J. Press img *New York* v50 no15 p66 Jl 24 2017

Love STORY bw color *Vogue* v206 no11 p189 N 2016

Passing: A novel grapples with the impossibility of transcending race A. KLEEMAN *New York Times Book Review* p10 O 8 2017

PLAYING IN THE DARK P. H. Bass color *Essence* v48 no5 p68 S 2017

Sennett, Richard

Smart Cities, Smarter Citizens S. Begley color *Time* v189 no13 p18 Ap 10 2017

Sennheiser Electronic Corp.

TAKE IT WITH YOU M. DURAN color *Wired* v24 no12 p84 D 2016

SENO, ALEXANDRA A.

Diamond Standard: A high-rise for a Chinese conglomerate showcases its distinctive structural system color diag map *Architectural Record* v205 no5 p110 My 2017

Factory Finish *Architectural Record* v205 no9 p110 S 2017

perspective interiors: AN INNOVATIVE MOVIE THEATER DESIGNED BY ONE PLUS PARTNERSHIP LIMITED BECOMES PART OF THE SHOW color *Architectural Record* v205 no5 p41 My 2017

Senot, Claire

What Has the Biggest Impact on Hospital Readmission Rates *Harvard Business Review Digital Articles* p2 S 23 2015

Sens, Jean-Mark

VIC'S AUTO GLASS, for Rachel *Commonweal* v144 no16 p26 O 6 2017

Sens, Josh

COLLISION COURSE color *Sports Illustrated* v126 no17 p62 Je 19 2017

Dream On color *Golf Magazine* v59 no6 p62 Je 2017

Drink color *Sunset* v237 no5 p62 N 2016

GOLF'S KING OF COOL color *Golf Magazine* v58 no12 p42 D 2016

How to be British color *Golf Magazine* v59 no7 p73 Jl 2017

Pebble Beach The Golfer's Ultimate Guide color *Golf Magazine* v59 no2 p84 F 2017

Soothe Moves color *Golf Magazine* v59 no5 p103 My 2017

TEEING OFF color *Golf Magazine* v59 no5 p18 My 2017

TEEING OFF color *Golf Magazine* v59 no8 p16 Ag 2017

The Tick List color *Golf Magazine* v59 no3 p108 Mr 2017

United Steaks color *Golf Magazine* v58 no11 p96 N 2016

Water Whirl color *Golf Magazine* v58 no11 p90 N 2016

Sensabaugh, Brittani

SNAP JUDGMENTS color *O, The Oprah Magazine* p22 Je 2017

Spotlight on Brittani "Brittsense" Sensabaugh L. CROSS color *Ebony* v72 no3 p43 D 2016/Ja 2017

Sense organs

See also

Nose

Photoreceptors

SCENTS & SENSIBILITY [Cover story] M. ZARASKA bw color diag graph *Discover* v38 no9 p42 N 2017

Self-organized Notch dynamics generate stereotyped sensory organ patterns in Drosophila F. Corson, L. Couturier et al color *Science* v356 no6337 p501 My 5 2017

A Sense of Our Own B. Lang *Discover* v38 no9 p6 N 2017

Sense8 (TV program)

STREAMING A. D'ARMINIO *TV Guide* v65 no19 p40 My 1 2017

Sense of an Ending, The (Film)

ANGLO-FILE S. Gutierrez *British Heritage Travel* v38 no2 p74 Mr/Ap 2017

Senser, Kelly

Tips for Gardening with Kids color *National Wildlife (World Edition)* v55 no3 p16 Ap/My 2017

Senses & sensation

See also

Control (Psychology)

Drinking behavior

Hearing

Pain

Sexual excitement

Vision

Caught by surprise P. W. Marty *Christian Century* v134 no12 p3

Je 7 2017

DYNAMIC RELIEF E. CALDERONE color *Muscle & Performance* v9 no6 p24 Je 2017

From Man to Machine *New York Times Magazine* p12 O 16 2016

ROBOT AWAKENING M. Rosen chart color *Science News* v190 no10 p18 N 12 2016

SIGHT UNSEEN N. TWILLEY cartoon diag *New Yorker* v93 no13 p38 My 15 2017

Spidey Senses L. SCHLEY color *Discover* v38 no2 p10 Mr 2017

Sension, Roseanne

Following photoexcited electrons in reactions color *Science* v356 no6333 p31 Ap 7 2017

Sensory deprivation

The New Quiet Time K. Massicot color *New Orleans Magazine* v51 no5 p36 Mr 2017

Sensory stimulation

clock-stoppers C. Maldarelli color *Popular Science* v289 no5 p88 S/O 2017

Sensory stimulation—Psychological aspects

Sweet Dreams Are Made of This M. Labash color *Weekly Standard* v22 no33 p5 My 8 2017

Sens-Schönfelder, Christoph

Elastic-wave propagation and the Coriolis force *Physics Today* v69 no12 p90 D 2016

Sentences (Criminal procedure)

See also

Pre-sentence investigation reports

Code of Silence R. Wexler color *Washington Monthly* v49 no6-8 p18 Je-Ag 2017

Sentences (Criminal procedure)—Florida

FLORIDA CHANGES HARSH SENTENCING LAW, TOO LATE FOR MANY INMATES L. KRISAI and C. J. CIARAMELLA color *Reason* v49 no3 p48 Jl 2017

SENTER, PHILIP J.

DID AUSTRALIA'S ABORIGINES SEE PLESIOSAURS? YES-IN A CHILDREN'S BOOK *Skeptical Inquirer* v41 no4 p34 Jl/Ag 2017

FIRE-BREATHING DINOSAURS? Physics, Fossils, and Functional Morphology vs. Pseudoscience *Skeptical Inquirer* v41 no4 p26 Jl/Ag 2017

Sentilles, Sarah

Broken Bodies, Broken Forms: What relation does art bear to suffering? *American Scholar* v86 no3 p121 Summ 2017

THOU SHALT NOT KILL S. D'ERASMO color *O, The Oprah Magazine* p83 Ag 2017

Sentiment analysis

Sentiment Analysis Can Do More than Prevent Fraud and Turnover M. Schrage *Harvard Business Review Digital Articles* p2 Ja 5 2016

SentinelOne (Company)

YOUR TV MIGHT BE SPYING ON YOU L. GERSTNER color *Kiplinger's Personal Finance* v71 no6 p14 Je 2017

Sentra automobile

DATA CENTRAL K. C. Colwell cartoon diag graph *Car & Driver* v62 no7 p20 Ja 2017

Sentra automobile—Evaluation

On the Shoulders of Giants J. Gall color *Car & Driver* v62 no11 p118 My 2017

Seo, B. R.

Tough adhesives for diverse wet surfaces diag *Science* v357 no6349 p378 Jl 28 2017

Seo, Jangwon

Colloidally prepared La-doped BaSnO3 electrodes for efficient, photostable perovskite solar cells graph *Science* v356 no6334 p167 Ap 14 2017

Iodide management in formamidinium-lead-halide–based perovskite layers for efficient solar cells bw diag *Science* v356 no6345 p1376 Je 30 2017

Seo, Sang-Uk

Neonatal acquisition of Clostridia species protects against colonization by bacterial pathogens diag *Science* v356 no6335 p315 Ap 21 2017

Seo, Young Ah

Restored iron transport by a small molecule promotes absorption and hemoglobinization in animals color graph *Science* v356 no6338 p608 My 12 2017

Seog-Jin Jeon

Dynamic creation and evolution of gradient nanostructure in single-crystal metallic microcubes bibl bw *Science* v354 no6310 p312 O 21 2016

Seok, Sang Il

Colloidally prepared La-doped BaSnO3 electrodes for efficient, photostable perovskite solar cells graph *Science* v356 no6334 p167 Ap 14 2017

Seong, S.D.

Martial Ops Ups the Ante color *Black Belt* v55 no1 p60 D 2016/Ja 2017

Seoul (Korea)

A Facial Worth the Flight E. FLORIO color map *Conde Nast Traveler* v52 no8 p50 S 2017

Seoul (Korea)—Description & travel

THE URBANIST: Seoul: Soy-brined fried pickhs, abandoned amusement parks, sneaker bars A. HALPERN img *New York* v50 no16 p90 Ag 7 2017

SEPANSKI, ASHLEY

GIFTS that UPLIFT! cartoon *O, The Oprah Magazine* p148 D 2016

Separation (Psychology)

GOODBYE MY BROTHER E. ACKERMAN color map *Esquire* p84 Ap 2017

How to DUMP SOMEONE S. Goddard color *Seventeen* v76 no12 p74 D 2016/Ja 2017

Separation, A (Film)

A CRASH COURSE IN FOREIGN CINEMA A. O. Scott color *Esquire* p122 S 2017

Separation anxiety

OBJECT PERMANENCE J. MOYER color *Orion Magazine* v36 no2 p64 Mr/Ap 2017

Separatists—Political activity

BLUEXIT K. BAKER il *New Republic* v248 no4 p18 Ap 2017

SEPETYS, RUTA

Long Road Home: A memoir about a boy who survived Auschwitz summons a family's traditions as well as its tragedies *New York Times Book Review* p27 My 14 2017

Sephora USA Inc.

Cheepers BY THE DOZEN color *O, The Oprah Magazine* p61 Ap 2017

DOES IT REALLY WORK? A. Jordan color *Essence* v48 no2 p43 Je 2017

FALL IS IN THE AIR color *Good Housekeeping* v263 no5 p24 N 2016

Sepik River (Indonesia & Papua New Guinea)

Papua New Guinea's genetic diversity withstood farming A. Gibbons color *Science* v357 no6356 p1086 S 15 2017

Seppala, Emma

Burnout at Work Isn't Just About Exhaustion. It's Also About Loneliness *Harvard Business Review Digital Articles* p2 Je 29 2017

Good Bosses Create More Wellness than Wellness Plans Do *Harvard Business Review Digital Articles* p2 Ap 8 2016

Happy Workplaces Can Also Be Candid Workplaces *Harvard Business Review Digital Articles* p2 My 31 2016

The Hard Data on Being a Nice Boss *Harvard Business Review Digital Articles* p2 N 24 2014

Having Work Friends Can Be Tricky, but It's Worth It *Harvard Business Review Digital Articles* p2 Ag 8 2017

How Meditation Benefits CEOs *Harvard Business Review Digital Articles* p2 D 14 2015

How Senior Executives Find Time to Be Creative *Harvard Business Review Digital Articles* p2 S 14 2016

If You Can't Take a Vacation, Get the Most Out of Minibreaks *Harvard Business Review Digital Articles* p2 Jl 14 2015

Positive Teams Are More Productive *Harvard Business Review Digital Articles* p2 Mr 18 2015

Proof That Positive Work Cultures Are More Productive *Harvard Business Review Digital Articles* p2 D 1 2015

To Motivate Employees, Do 3 Things Well *Harvard Business Review Digital Articles* p2 Ja 4 2016

What Bosses Gain by Being Vulnerable *Harvard Business Review Digital Articles* p2 D 11 2014

What to Do When You're the Target of a Hurtful Office Rumor *Harvard Business Review Digital Articles* p2 D 2 2016

Sergunin, Alexander

Is Russia Going Hard or Soft in the Arctic? color map *Wilson Quarterly* p1 Summ 2017

Serial murder investigation

MURDER, HE CALCULATED R. Kolker color diag graph *Bloomberg Businessweek* no4511 p48 F 13 2017

Serial murderers

CIVICS 101 S. FENNESSY *Atlanta* v56 no10 p16 F 2017

The Monster of Florence: Case Closed? The Terrifying Story of the Most Infamous Ritual Murders in Italian History, Part 1 M. POLIDORO *Skeptical Inquirer* v41 no4 p16 Jl/Ag 2017

My Father Was the BTK Killer R. WENZL *Reader's Digest* v188 no1126 p112 D 2016/Ja 2017

Serial murderers—History—20th century

INTERSTATE 5 KILLER L. J. Wertheim, M. Cohen et al color *Sports Illustrated* v125 no17 p108 N 21 2016 Double Issue

Serial publication of books

INTRODUCING A WORLD of ENDLESS MISADVENTURES M. Wild *Publishers Weekly* v264 no9 pC1 F 27 2017

Moppet Books Moves Forward With KinderGuides Line J. Boog color *Publishers Weekly* v264 no33 p8 Ag 14 2017

Serial publications

See also

Newspapers

Periodicals

FANTASTIC FINDS *Psychology Today* v50 no3 p94 My/Je 2017

the funny factor D. Points *Parents* p12 2015

future focus D. Points *Parents* v91 no10 p12 O 2016

Series of Unfortunate Events book series

ABOVE & BEYOND bw *New Yorker* v93 no28 p14 S 18 2017

Series of Sneaks, A (Music)

A Fanboy's Notes J. SPONG *Texas Monthly* v45 no3 p94 Mr 2017

Series of Unfortunate Events, A (TV program)

The Must List color *Entertainment Weekly* no1449 p3 Ja 20 2017

Neil Patrick Harris E. Dockterman color *Time* v189 no3 p50 Ja 30 2017

A SERIES OF UNFORTUNATE EVENTS M. J. Rose bw *U.S. Catholic* v82 no6 p40 Je 2017

A Series of Unfortunate Events M. Snetiker color *Entertainment Weekly* no1448 p38 Ja 13 2017

To Do M. Z. SEITZ, C. JENKINS et al img *New York* p86 Ja 9 2017

What to Watch R. Rahman, J. Jensen et al color *Entertainment Weekly* no1448 p56 Ja 13 2017

Serine, Kate

Concealed: A Dark Alliance Novel *Publishers Weekly* v264 no10 p46 Mr 6 2017

Serio, Louise

Mistakes: The Big Picture T. Johnston color *Practical Horseman* v45 no1 p22 Ja 2017

Serio, Tom

Attitude Adjustment *Boating World* v37 no9 p50 N/D 2016

BET YOU DON'T KNOW SPORTFISHING BOATS *Sea Magazine* v109 no9 p54 S 2017

CARVER 52 COMMAND BRIDGE *Sea Magazine* v109 no1 p34 Ja 2017

Find YOUR Center *Boating World* v37 no9 p54 N/D 2016

HORIZON E75 *Sea Magazine* v109 no4 p42 Ap 2017

THE HULL STORY: WHEN'S THE LAST TIME YOU THOUGHT ABOUT HULL INNOVATION? NOW'S THE TIME *Boating World* v38 no8 p54 S/O 2017

NO LIMIT SHIPS 1550: THIS UNUSUAL BOAT FROM THE NETHERLANDS IS A GLOBAL TROTTER AND A LOCAL CRUISER color *Sea Magazine* v109 no6 p42 Je 2017

Seriola

POKE 1-2-3 A. BARAGHANI color *Bon Appetit* no1 p56 F 2017

Seriously Funny (TV program)

UNSTOPPABLE [Cover story] M. M. Lewis color *Essence* v48 no2 p88 Je 2017

Serjeant, Emma

KINETIC CLUTTER L. WARNECKE color *Chicago* v66 no3 p52 Mr 2017

Serjoie, Kay Armin

The Death of Iran's Ultimate Political Insider Gives Hard-Liners an Edge color *Time* v189 no4 p13 Ja 23 2017

Who's Who In Iran's Elections color *Time* v189 no19 p11 My 22

2017

Serkin, Rachel

LET THEM EAT MEAT *History Today* v67 no8 p50 Ag 2017

Serling, Rod, 1924-1975

WE CROSSED OVER INTO THE TWILIGHT ZONE. . .AND NEVER LOOKED BACK D. Bianculli *TV Guide* v65 no41 p8 O 2 2017

Sermon (Literary form)

Word Power E. COX and H. RATHVON *Reader's Digest* v188 no1124 p139 O 2016

Sermon on the mount

I Tell You: Do Not Worry! M. R. Simone *America* v216 no4 p52 F 20 2017

Serna, Gwen

oops *Parents* v92 no7 p132 Jl 2017

Serna, Rodrigo de la, 1976-

A political life of Pope Francis, from Argentina to the Vatican J. Anderson color *America* v216 no8 p48 Ap 17 2017

Serota, Nicholas

ARTWORLD color *Art in America* v104 no10 p168 N 2016

Serotonin

Nerve cell miswiring tied to depression E. S. EATON color *Science News* v191 no10 p12 My 27 2017

Serotonin receptors

Brain protein's grip on LSD imaged M. ROSEN *Science News* v191 no4 p16 Mr 4 2017

Serotoninergic mechanisms

Pcdhαc2 is required for axonal tiling and assembly of serotonergic circuitries in mice W. V. Chen, C. L. Nwakeze et al diag *Science* v356 no6336 p406 Ap 28 2017

Serov, P.

Massive blow-out craters formed by hydrate-controlled methane expulsion from the Arctic seafloor graph map *Science* v356 no6341 p948 Je 1 2017

Serpa, Sara

All The Dreams/Dream In The Blue A. Morrison color *Downbeat* v83 no11 p60 N 2016

Serpell, Louise

De novo design of a biologically active amyloid bibl graph *Science* v354 no6313 paah4949-1 N 11 2016

Serra, Albert

The Inner Sanctum bw color *Film Comment* v53 no1 p6 Ja/F 2017

THE SETTING SUN Y. TALU color *Film Comment* v53 no2 p24 Mr/Ap 2017

SERRA, ASHLEE

I Am a Weapon: Her Martial Art of Choice *Idaho Magazine* v16 no8 p23 My 2017

Serra, Carolyn

HOME OF THE Braves: A beginner's guide to Cobb County's new game-day headquarters K. SMITH *Atlanta* v57 no2 p122 Je 2017

Serrano, Angelique

Best Face Forward color *InStyle* v24 no11 p125 N 2017

The Bob SQUAD color *InStyle* v24 no6 p81 Je 2017

Can You Bare It? color *InStyle* v24 no8 p99 Ag 2017

CHARLOTTE TILBURY'S Magic Touch color *InStyle* v24 no10 p171 O 2017

A Classic Reimagined color *InStyle* v24 no9 p325 S 2017

David Colbert color *InStyle* v24 no7 p94 Jl 2017

MICHAEL KORS'S Icons color *InStyle* v24 no8 p108 Ag 2017

The Party Starts Here color *InStyle* v23 no13 p165 D 2016

Scent of Attraction color *InStyle* v23 no12 p175 N 2016

SPRING PREVIEW color *InStyle* v24 no1 p55 Ja 2017

Serrano, Manuel

Tissue damage and senescence provide critical signals for cellular reprogramming in vivo bibl chart graph *Science* v354 no6315 paaf4445-1 N 25 2016

Serrao, Erik

A supramolecular assembly mediates lentiviral DNA integration bibl color *Science* v355 no6320 p1 Ja 6 2017

SERRAO, JOHN

THE NATURAL EXPLANATION color *Natural History* v125 no10 p2 O 2017

Significant Other *Natural History* v125 no1 p48 D 2016/Ja 2017

Serrao, Nivea

6 — LORE *Entertainment Weekly* no1444/1445 p114 D 16 2016

THE 8-SECOND REVIEW color *Entertainment Weekly* no1470 p46 Je 16 2017

BEST COMIC BOOKS color *Entertainment Weekly* no1444/1445 p110 D 16 2016

Chris Colfer color *Entertainment Weekly* no1457/1458 p102 Mr 17 2017

COULD THAT REALLY HAPPEN ON GAME OF THRONES? color *Entertainment Weekly* no1441 p62 N 25 2016

DEGRASSI DOES IT AGAIN color *Entertainment Weekly* no1474/1475 p22 Jl 21-28 2017

The Fate of the Tearling color *Entertainment Weekly* no1442 p62 D 2 2016 Rebellious Special Issue

JAGGER THE DOG color *Entertainment Weekly* no1466 p50 My 19 2017

Kindred color *Entertainment Weekly* no1450 p63 Ja 27 2017

NEIL GAIMAN color *Entertainment Weekly* no1454/1455 p101 F 24 2017

A NEW DARK MATERIALS TRILOGY BEGINS color *Entertainment Weekly* no1473 p61 Jl 7 2017

No. 8 THE SUN IS ALSO A STAR color *Entertainment Weekly* no1444/1445 p106 D 16 2016

Spring's Best Graphic Novels color *Entertainment Weekly* no1465 p62 My 12 2017

Summer's 20 MUST-READ BOOKS color *Entertainment Weekly* no1467 p58 My 26 2017

The Sun Is Also a Star color *Entertainment Weekly* no1440 p62 N 18 2016

Survivor: an Outing and an Ousting color *Entertainment Weekly* no1463/1464 p21 Ap/My 2017

A Very Sordid Return color *Entertainment Weekly* no1462 p47 Ap 21 2017

Watchmen: Behind the Smiley Face color *Entertainment Weekly* no1470 p62 Je 16 2017

What to Watch color *Entertainment Weekly* no1457/1458 p88 Mr 17 2017

What to Watch color *Entertainment Weekly* no1468/1469 p94 Je 2-9 2017

What to Watch color *Entertainment Weekly* no1474/1475 p108 Jl 21-28 2017

Your Sunshiny, Stupendous, Seriously Spectacular SUMMER BUCKET LIST color *Entertainment Weekly* no1470 p32 Je 16 2017

Serratia

Driving mosquito refractoriness to Plasmodium falciparum with engineered symbiotic bacteria S. Wang, A. L. A. Dos-Santos et al color graph *Science* v357 no6358 p1399 S 29 2017

Serres-Armero, Aitor

Ancient genomic changes associated with domestication of the horse color diag *Science* v356 no6336 p442 Ap 28 2017

SerVaas, Cory

BRAIN-ZAP WEIGHT LOSS PROGRAM *Saturday Evening Post* v289 no5 p69 S/O 2017

SerVaas, Joan

Finders Keepers, Losers Weepers *Saturday Evening Post* v289 no2 p23 Mr/Ap 2017

For Want of a Comma *Saturday Evening Post* v289 no3 p23 My/Je 2017

Money in the Bag *Saturday Evening Post* v289 no4 p25 Jl/Ag 2017

A Real Grass Act *Saturday Evening Post* v289 no5 p25 S/O 2017

Root of the Problem *Saturday Evening Post* v288 no6 p27 N/D 2016

Who Owns the Air? *Saturday Evening Post* v289 no1 p27 Ja/F 2017

Servant leadership

How the U.S. Marines Encourage Service-Based Leadership A. Morgan and C. Lynch color *Harvard Business Review Digital Articles* p2 F 2 2017

New Managers Need a Philosophy About How They'll Lead C. A. Walker *Harvard Business Review Digital Articles* p2 S 15 2015

Server farms (Computer network management)

DATA CENTERS GO EXOTIC J. Vanian color *Fortune* v175 no5 p20 Ap 1 2017

Service, Robert F.

Chemistry Nobel heralds age of molecular machines color *Science* v354 no6309 p158 O 14 2016

Cleaning up coal—cost-effectively color *Science* v356 no6340 p798 My 26 2017

Cost of carbon capture drops, but does anyone want it? color graph *Science* v354 no6318 p1362 D 16 2016

FOSSIL POWER, GUILT FREE color diag *Science* v356 no6340 p796 My 26 2017

KEEPING THE FAITH color *Science* v357 no6356 p1088 S 15 2017

Metalenses, megapromise color *Science* v354 no6319 p1523 D 23 2016

Metallic hydrogen created in diamond vise color graph *Science* v355 no6323 p332 Ja 27 2017

A moonshot for chemistry color *Science* v356 no6335 p231 Ap 21 2017

Neural networks learn the art of chemical synthesis *Science* v357 no6346 p27 Jl 7 2017

Perovskite solar cells gear up to go commercial color *Science* v354 no6317 p1214 D 9 2016

Proteins by design color *Science* v354 no6319 p1520 D 23 2016

A push for low-carbon fuels pays off in California color graph *Science* v357 no6347 p120 Jl 14 2017

RESCUING THE GUARDIAN OF THE GENOME color diag *Science* v354 no6308 p26 O 7 2016

Researchers close in on ancient dinosaur proteins color *Science* v355 no6324 p441 F 3 2017

Trump team targets key climate metric color *Science* v354 no6318 p1364 D 16 2016

Service, Robert W. (Robert William), 1874-1958

POETRY: TO FIGHT ANOTHER DAY bw color *MHQ: Quarterly Journal of Military History* v30 no1 p90 Aut 2017

Service, Robert, 1947-

How Did the Huge War Really End? A. Brown bw color *New York Review of Books* v64 no5 p55 Mr 23 2017

Service dogs

Should I Out My Friend's 'Service Dog' Scam? K. A. Appiah *New York Times Magazine* p22 D 4 2016

Service Employees International Union

Mary Kay Henry I. Boudway color *Bloomberg Businessweek* no4496 p24 O 24 2016

Service industries

See also
  Barbershops
  Collection agencies
  Dating services
  Financial services industry
  Food service
  Lease & rental services
  Tourism

At Work With Rent-a-Dad P. Alpeyev color *Bloomberg Businessweek* no4535 p41 Ag 28 2017

The End of Expertise B. Fischer *Harvard Business Review Digital Articles* p2 O 19 2015

TOP WEDDING VENDORS *Virginia Living* v15 no2 p99 F 2017

Service industries—China

China's Shift to Services Hits a Snag D. Roberts color *Bloomberg Businessweek* no4521 p16 My 8 2017

Service industries—Customer services

How Service Companies Can Earn Customer Trust and Keep It L. L. Berry *Harvard Business Review Digital Articles* p2 Ap 19 2017

Service industries—United States

Automation Makes Things Cheaper, So Why Doesn't It Feel That Way? W. H. Davidow color *Harvard Business Review Digital Articles* p2 Ap 3 2017

Companies Need an Option Between Contractor and Employee A. Hagiu and R. Biederman *Harvard Business Review Digital Articles* p2 Ag 21 2015

Service learning

Place-Based Desing and Civic Health: New findings from the Center for Active Design's Assembly Civic Engagement Survey S. Nienaber *Parks & Recreation* v52 no9 p62 S 2017

Service stations

Blakely Glassware bw *Arizona Highways* v93 no5 p8 My 2017

GREAT UNKNOWNS color *Popular Mechanics* p26 S 2017

GREAT UNKNOWNS color *Popular Mechanics* v193 no7 p26 S 2016

OF WAVES AND WHITE ELEPHANTS K. TAYLOR color *Surfer* v58 no4 p86 Ag 2017

PAY INSIDE CASH T. REHAGEN color *Popular Mechanics* p18 Jl 2017

Service stations & the environment

Recipe for Disaster B. Lutz color *New Orleans Magazine* v51 no9 p34 Jl 2017

Service stations—Evaluation

Services *Virginia Living* p79 2017 Best 20of Virginia

Service industries workers—Salaries, wages, etc.

POPULAR IDEAS ABOUT THE WORKING CLASS ARE WOEFULLY OUT OF DATE. HERE ARE NINE PEOPLE WHO TELL A TRUER STORY OF WHAT THE AMERICAN WORK FORCE DOES TODAY—AND WILL DO TOMORROW B. Appelbaum *New York Times Magazine* p36 F 26 2017

Services for children with disabilities

Hitting the Sweet Spot N. Lopez color *AARP: The Magazine* v30 no6A p64 O/N 2017

Services for older people

See also

Programs of All Inclusive Care for the Elderly

The Octogenarians Who Love Amazon's Alexa E. Woyke il *MIT Technology Review* v120 no5 p17 S/O 2017

Uber Without the Smartphone J. Green and E. Newcomer color *Bloomberg Businessweek* no4530 p22 Jl 17 2017

Services for older people—United States

FACEBOOK FOR GRANDMA K. RANDALL *Washingtonian Magazine* v52 no9 p21 Je 2017

Services for people with disabilities

Essential Framework for Adaptive Aquatics R. Barley, I. Hausknecht et al *Parks & Recreation* v52 no10 p54 O 2017

Services for people with visual disabilities

The Gratitude Meter Z. Donaldson color *O, The Oprah Magazine* p24 Ag 2017

Services for students

A Look at the Educational Structure in Cuba D. Domenech *Education Digest* v83 no3 p57 N 2017

Services for the aged

The Art of Aging K. Donohue color *Maclean's* v129 no40 p60 O 10 2016

Your AARP color *AARP: The Magazine* v59 no2A p80 F/Mr 2016

Servick, Kelly

Amazing (Mostly) Edible Science color *Science* v354 no6317 p1226 D 9 2016

Circular RNAs hint at new realm of genetics color *Science* v355 no6332 p1363 Mr 31 2017

Congress votes on sweeping biomedical bill color *Science* v354 no6316 p1085 D 2 2016

Embryo editing takes another step to clinic bw *Science* v357 no6350 p436 Ag 4 2017

Failed spinal cord trial offers cautionary tale color *Science* v355 no6326 p679 F 17 2017

Genome writing project confronts technology hurdles color *Science* v356 no6339 p673 My 19 2017

New blood tests make strides in detecting prion disease color *Science* v354 no6319 p1512 D 23 2016

ON MESSAGE color diag graph *Science* v355 no6324 p446 F 3 2017

PRIMED FOR PAIN color *Science* v354 no6312 p569 N 4 2016

Sacred Water: Standing Rock *Science* v356 no6337 p480 My 5 2017

Stem cell approach for cataracts challenged color *Science* v356 no6345 p1318 Je 30 2017

THE STEM CELL SKEPTIC color graph *Science* v357 no6350 p441 Ag 4 2017

The strange case of the orange petunias color *Science* v356 no6340 p792 My 26 2017

Texas signals support for unproven stem cell therapies *Science* v356 no6344 p1219 Je 23 2017

WINGED WARRIORS color diag *Science* v354 no6309 p164 O 14 2016

Xenotransplant advances may prompt human trials *Science* v357 no6358 p1338 S 29 2017

Servilio, Lisa

Ecological speciation of bacteriophage lambda in allopatry and sympatry bibl graph *Science* v354 no6317 p1301 D 9 2016

Servon, Lisa

Living Without Banks J. D. TUCCILLE color *Reason* v48 no10 p62 Mr 2017

Making Nice With the Loan Sharks L. Colarusso color *Washington Monthly* v49 no3-5 p63 Mr-My 2017

Sesame Street (TV program)

PBS: WHAT'SAT STAKE J. RUSSELL *TV Guide* p6 Ap 17 2017

The Quiz T. BALAZO color *Maclean's* v129 no48/49 p37 D 5 2016

Street Cred B. Luscombe color *Time* v189 no14 p44 Ap 17 2017

What Sesame Street's Move to HBO Says About the Media Business J. Balis *Harvard Business Review Digital Articles* p2 Ag 20 2015

Sesardic, Neven

Excellently Foolish J. POSTELL color *National Review* v69 no3 p52 F 20 2017

Seshadri, Mukund

Rb1 and Trp53 cooperate to suppress prostate cancer lineage plasticity, metastasis, and antiandrogen resistance bibl graph *Science* v355 no6320 p1 Ja 6 2017

SESSA, ANDREW

Home in On color *Conde Nast Traveler* v51 no11 p54 D 2016

Island Time color *Architectural Digest* v74 no4 p80 Ap 2017

london, england color *Architectural Digest* no5 p88 My 2017

THE ROOM TO BOOK color *Conde Nast Traveler* v52 no10 p36 N 2017

Start with a Clean Slate color *Conde Nast Traveler* v52 no1 p22 Ja 2017

SESSA, EMILY B.

Sex and the Single Gametophyte: Revising the Homosporous Vascular Plant Life Cycle in Light of Contemporary Research *BioScience* v66 no11 p928 N 1 2016

Sessi, Paolo

Robust spin-polarized midgap states at step edges of topological crystalline insulators bibl graph *Science* v354 no6317 p1269 D 9 2016

SESSIONS, DAVID

The Rise of the Thought Leader bw *New Republic* v248 no7 p48 Jl 2017

Sessions, Jeff, 1946-

Attorney General Sessions A. C. MCCARTHY il *National Review* v68 no23 p20 D 19 2016

For the Record color *Time* v189 no24 p4 Je 26 2017

THE HARSH, PETTY, AND HIGHLY POLITICAL LAW OF JEFF SESSIONS P. LEVY bw color *Mother Jones* v42 no3 p30 My/Je 2017

In Defense of Jeff Sessions H. MAC DONALD *National Review* v69 no16 p27 Ag 28 2017

'Law and Order' Should Not Mean Wiping Out Civil Rights Protections *America* v216 no11 p8 My 15 2017

Let the Police Police H. M. DONALD *National Review* v69 no9 p28 My 15 2017

Mucking Out the Justice Department F. BARNES cartoon *Weekly Standard* v22 no17 p9 Ja 2 2017

A NATIVIST IS IN CHARGE OF THE POLICE STATE E. LEVITZ img *New York* v50 no9 p48 My 1 2017

On Infighting and Real Fighting D. FOSTER *National Review* v69 no15 p48 Ag 14 2017

OUR CONCEPTS OF RELIGIOUS FREEDOM *Vital Speeches of the Day* v83 no9 p263 S 2017

Trump's Constitutional Crisis [Cover story] D. Cole color *New York Review of Books* v64 no10 p51 Je 8 2017

Trump's Dangerous Kill Box P. J. BUCHANAN *American Conservative* v16 no5 p12 S/O 2017

TRUMP'S RADICAL ATTORNEY GENERAL J. Reitman color *Rolling Stone* no1294 p28 Ag 24 2017

Trump's Troubling Attorney General Pick J. SULLUM color *Reason* v48 no10 p6 Mr 2017

WaPo Spun Scoop to Shelter Sessions J. Naureckas *Extra!* v30 no3 p4 Ap 2017

We Firmly Believe This Is the Responsible Path *Vital Speeches of the Day* v83 no10 p288 O 2017

What's Jeff Sessions Up To? T. Schoenberg color *Bloomberg Businessweek* no4529 p34 Jl 3 2017

Sessions, Jeff, 1946——Political & social views

JEFF SESSIONS, GLUTTON FOR PUNISHMENT J. Sullum

Reason v49 no5 p6 O 2017

Judging Jeff Sessions A. BERMAN *Nation* v304 no4 p5 F 6 2017

Sessoms, Allen

Helping less-prepared students excel color *Science* v357 no6352 p654 Ag 18 2017

Sessoms, William E.

EYE on the PRIZE E. J. WALLACE *Virginia Living* v15 no3 p90 Ap 2017

SEA CHANGE E. PARKHURST *Virginia Living* v15 no3 p13 Ap 2017

Sestan, Nenad

Control of species-dependent cortico-motoneuronal connections underlying manual dexterity diag graph *Science* v357 no6349 p400 Jl 28 2017

Intersection of diverse neuronal genomes and neuropsychiatric disease: The Brain Somatic Mosaicism Network color *Science* v356 no6336 p395 Ap 28 2017

Set design

The 411 On Curtain Clean-Up L. Mulcahy *Stage Directions* v30 no4 p16 Ap 2017

Closing TIME B. Reesman *Stage Directions* v30 no5 p12 My 2017

Color and Light L. Mulcahy *Stage Directions* v30 no2 p20 F 2017

Shall We Dance? C. Collis color *Entertainment Weekly* no1454/1455 p32 F 24 2017

Teaching Aesthetics R. Minetor *Stage Directions* v30 no4 p10 Ap 2017

Set design—Equipment & supplies

The skills of scenic artists can take a design to the next level J. Coakley *Stage Directions* v30 no2 p16 F 2017

Set designers

SETTING THE SCENE M. Feldman color *House Beautiful* v159 no8 p86 O 2017

Set designers—Interviews

Projecting the Reflected Soul: San Francisco Opera's Mirror Solution for Don Giovanni M. S. Eddy *Stage Directions* v30 no9 p16 S 2017

Set It Off (Film)

IT'S GOOD TO BE QUEEN T. E. Ross color *InStyle* v24 no3 p350 Mr 2017

Sethi, Amit

A selective insecticidal protein from Pseudomonas for controlling corn rootworms bibl chart graph *Science* v354 no6312 p634 N 4 2016

Sethi, Ramit

75 ways to be a grown-up *Parents* v91 no11 p95 N 2016

SETHI, SIMRAN

As American as Apple Pie? color *Reader's Digest* v190 no1132 p40 Jl/Ag 2017

Sethian, John

Big and busy on the Pennsy [Cover story] color diag *Model Railroader* v84 no11 p32 N 2017

Setsuie, Rieko

Conversion of object identity to object-general semantic value in the primate temporal cortex color graph *Science* v357 no6352 p687 Ag 18 2017

Sette, Alessandro

A large fraction of HLA class I ligands are proteasome-generated spliced peptides bibl graph *Science* v354 no6310 p354 O 21 2016

SETTE, LISA

Google Haul Out: Earth Observation Imagery and Digital Aerial Surveys in Coastal Wildlife Management and Abundance Estimation *BioScience* v67 no8 p760 Ag 2017

Settembre, Carmine

Transcriptional activation of RagD GTPase controls mTORC1 and promotes cancer growth diag *Science* v356 no6343 p1188 Je 16 2017

SETTIMI, CHRISTINA

INSIDE THE HUDDLE color *Forbes* v200 no4 p15 O 24 2017

The Most Valuable Baseball Teams chart color *Forbes* v199 no5 p28 My 16 2017

The Most Valuable NBA Teams chart color *Forbes* v199 no2 p30 F 28 2017

The Most Valuable NFL Teams color graph *Forbes* v198 no5 p32 O 25 2016

THE WORLD'S MOST VALUABLE SOCCER TEAMS chart color *Forbes* v199 no7 p32 Je 29 2017

Settimo, M.

Observation of a large-scale anisotropy in the arrival directions of cosmic rays above 8×1018 eV *Science* v357 no6357 p1266 S 22 2017

Setting & scenery for motion pictures

See also

Stage props

SHIP HAPPENS: 25,000 square feet covering two sound-stages, with tons of high-tech touches--the spaceship on Fox's out-of-this world hit The Orville is a stunner D. HOLBROOK *TV Guide* v65 no41 p22 O 2 2017

Settis, Salvatore

Blind Venetians C. W. Westfall color *Weekly Standard* v22 no29 p34 Ap 3 2017

That Sinking Feeling P. Nobel *Architectural Record* v204 no10 p51 O 2016

Setton, Dolly

Gifts for Budding Scientists *Natural History* v125 no1 p44 D 2016/Ja 2017

Seung Pil Yun

Pathological α-synuclein transmission initiated by binding lymphocyte-activation gene 3 bibl graph *Science* v353 no6307 paah3374-1 S 30 2016

Seung Woo Cho

CRISPRi-based genome-scale identification of functional long noncoding RNA loci in human cells bibl graph *Science* v355 no6320 p1 Ja 6 2017

Seutter, Matthäus

HEART ATTACK! *MHQ: Quarterly Journal of Military History* v29 no3 p20 Spr 2017

Sevak, Mihir

The Elements of Value: Interaction *Harvard Business Review* v94 no11 p18 N 2016

Sevareid, Eric, 1912-1992

BECOMING WILLARD W. SCOTT *Washingtonian Magazine* v52 no1 p224 O 2016

Sevdaliza (Performer)

SEVDALIZA: FOR THE IRANIAN DITCH SINGER-SONGWRITER, BOUNDARIES IN HER LIFE AND ART ARE MEANT TO BE BROKEN H. WEISS *Interview* v47 no3 p32 My 2017

Seven Cycles Inc.

"I WANT A BIKE THAT WILL LAST ME 15 YEARS." M. Yozell and B. STRICKLAND color *Bicycling* v58 no3 p52 Ap 2017

Seven Devils Mountains (Idaho)

ACROSS THE DEVILS BACK IN 1973 L. ADDINGTON *Idaho Magazine* v16 no10 p12 Jl 2017

Seven Secrets of Snow (Music)

Seven Secrets Of Snow B. Zimmerman color *Downbeat* v84 no2 p85 F 2017

Seven Stories Press (Company)

Twenty Years of Books on Social Justice C. Reid color *Publishers Weekly* v263 no52 p11 D 19 2016

Seventh Generation Inc.

IT ISN'T EASY BEING GREEN B. Kowitt color *Fortune* v174 no7 p100 D 1 2016

Seventko, Lindsay

Rebuilding the Home of the "People of the Forest" *American Forests* v122 no3 p7 Fall 2016

Severance pay

Letting Good People Go When It's Time P. Wadors *Harvard Business Review Digital Articles* p2 O 2 2015

Severin, Thomas

READER COMMENTS *America* v216 no7 p7 Ap 3 2017

Severson, John

John Severson: 1933-2017 T. PRODANOVICH bw *Surfer* v58 no4 p132 Ag 2017

Lessons From John D. KAMPION bw color *Surfer* v58 no6 p56 O 2017

Sevigny, Chloë, 1974-

Chloë Sevigny HER BEST EVER E. Wilson color *InStyle* v24 no5 p88 My 2017

DUA LIPA C. Stern color *InStyle* v24 no6 p33 Je 2017

Sevigny, Melissa L.

Mythical River A. C. Gottlieb *Orion Magazine* v35 no4/5 p107 Jl-O 2016

Seville, Emma—Trials, litigation, etc.

New mother wins flexhwork case *People Management* p19 O 2016

Sevush, Ralph

Spira Mirabilis: Fantastic Tales from the Marvelous Spiral color *Publishers Weekly* v263 no43 p50c O 24 2016

Sewage

Have it your whey J. RICHLER color *Maclean's* v129 no51/52 p68 D 26 2016

Sewage & the environment

Fringe on the brink: Intertidal reefs at risk R. Andrades, Joyeux et al color *Science* v357 no6348 p261 Jl 21 2017

Sewage purification

TURNING WASTE INTO GOLD (OR COPPER) J. Alsever color *Fortune* v175 no8 p66 Je 15 2017

Sewage—Environmental aspects

Animas River Spill Spawns Conspiracy Theories B. RADFORD *Skeptical Inquirer* v40 no6 p11 N/D 2016

SEWALL, GILBERT T.

Pitirim Sorokin Revisited: He predicted the West's societal deterioration *American Conservative* v16 no5 p42 S/O 2017

Seward, Caroline

Media Engagement *Parks & Recreation* p12 Aquatics Guide 2017

Seward, Desmond

Defender of civilisation *History Today* v67 no1 p61 Ja 2017

SEWARD, INGRID

REMEMBERING DIANA color *AARP: The Magazine* v60 no5A p50 Ag/S 2017

Sewatanon, Jaturong

IgG antibodies to dengue enhanced for FcγRIIIA binding determine disease severity bibl graph *Science* v355 no6323 p395 Ja 27 2017

Sewell, Rufus, 1967-—Interviews

VICTORIA STARS JENNA COLEMAN AND RUFUS SEWELL D. CLEHANE *British Heritage Travel* v38 no1 p32 Ja/F 2017

Sewerage

CAN YOU DIG IT? R. Annis, S. Bahr et al diag *Indianapolis Monthly* v41 no2 p72 S 2017

Climate Change is a Waste Management Problem K. S. LACKNER and C. JOSPE *Issues in Science & Technology* v33 no3 p83 Spr 2017

Lessons from Venice A. Marshall *Governing* v30 no7 p22 Ap 2017

Sewing

See also

Quilting

The Best of The Information bw color *Esquire* p132 BigBlackBook

Getting Started In... SEWING L. SOROKANICH color diag *Popular Mechanics* p46 N 2017

MY MOTHER, SEWING V. HARTMAN *Washingtonian Magazine* v52 no3 p192 D 2016

ONENESS WITH EVERY STITCH B. CONNELLY color *Tricycle: The Buddhist Review* v26 no2 p74 Wint 2016

Sex & the City (TV program)

GIRL TALK C. MALLE color *Vogue* v207 no1 p76 Ja 2017

The Sex and the City Opening Credits C. Brody color *Entertainment Weekly* no1460/1461 p72 Ap 7-17 2017

Sex (Biology)

EVERYTHING YOU KNOW ABOUT SEX IS WRONG: PART 1: THE GENDER BINARY A. HAFER *Humanist* v77 no4 p24 Jl/Ag 2017

Hotter Sex in Just Minutes! A. BRESLAW *Men's Health* v32 no6 p97 Ag 2017

Regarding People Who Don't Have Period Sex A. L. Grecoq color *Glamour* no8 p110 Ag 2017

Sex addiction

Why Didn't Anyone Teach Us the Good Stuff? L. King-Miller color *Glamour* v115 no7 p64 Jl 2017

Sex Box (TV program)

MORE TITLES TO MAKE YOU BLUSH D. Snierson color *Entertainment Weekly* no1465 p48 My 12 2017

Sex chromosomes

Fertile offspring from sterile sex chromosome trisomic mice T. Hirota, H. Ohta et al chart diag *Science* v357 no6354 p932 S

1 2017

Lurid Confusion Over "X" and "Y" *USA Today Magazine* v145 no2858 p32 N 2016

Sex crime investigation

Next on Bachelor in Paradise S. Highfill and R. Ross color *Entertainment Weekly* no1473 p14 Jl 7 2017

Sex crimes

See also

Adultery

Human trafficking

Sexual assault

Breach of Faith R. WILSON *American Scholar* v86 no3 p2 Summ 2017

LETTER FROM THE EDITOR J. STOWE *Cincinnati Magazine* p14 Je 2017

Sex offenders anonymous M. FRISCOLANTI *Maclean's* v130 no3 p15 Ap 2017

Sex crimes—Great Britain

The Road to Equality: The Sexual Offences Act of 1967 was not the great step forward it is sometimes purported to be Joyce *History Today* v67 no7 p11 Jl 2017

Sex crimes—Prevention

See also

Sexual assault—Prevention

See No Evil P. NEUDING color *Weekly Standard* v22 no20 p18 Ja 30 2017

Sex crimes—United States

Dishonorable Behavior: THE SCOURGE OF MILITARY SEXUAL ASSAULT AND THE WARRIOR'S MASCULINE CODE E. D. SAMET *American Scholar* v86 no3 p30 Summ 2017

My Country: Liz Meriweather img *New York* v49 no22 p15 O 31 2016

Sex differences (Biology)

American Girl T. Rosenberg cartoon color *National Geographic* v231 no1 p110 Ja 2017

The Dangerous Lives of Girls A. Okeowo color *National Geographic* v231 no1 p130 Ja 2017

It's Hard to Be Female: the Statistics cartoon *National Geographic* v231 no1 p128 Ja 2017

Making a Man C. Brown cartoon color *National Geographic* v231 no1 p74 Ja 2017

Our Evolving Sense of Self SLAUGHTER cartoon *National Geographic* v231 no1 p152 Ja 2017

Parental Leave On Dads' Terms P. EDMONDS color *National Geographic* v231 no1 p104 Ja 2017

Sex differentiation disorders

See also

Gynandromorphism

Gynandromorphism [Cover story] C. A. BUTLER color *Natural History* v125 no5 p20 My 2017

Sex discrimination

See also

Sex discrimination against women

Sex discrimination in employment

BRICKBATS cartoon *Reason* v48 no8 p64 Ja 2017

Documents detail gender-related tensions at Salk M. Wadman *Science* v357 no6353 p741 Ag 25 2017

Hillary Clinton, Bernie Sanders, and the Tug of War Between Women J. C. Williams *Harvard Business Review Digital Articles* p2 F 22 2016

Uber and Other Tech Companies Could Make Simple Changes to Avoid Driving Away Their Female Engineers M. Multhaup and J. C. Williams color *Harvard Business Review Digital Articles* p2 F 28 2017

Sex discrimination against men

Why More American Men Feel Discriminated Against D. Cassino *Harvard Business Review Digital Articles* p2 S 29 2016

Sex discrimination against women

A Case of Double Standards S. Lipscomb *History Today* v66 no10 p53 O 2016

Not just Salk C. Greider, N. Hopkins et al color *Science* v357 no6356 p1105 S 15 2017

Science Has a Gender Problem H. A. Valantine color *Scientific American* v315 no6 p12 D 2016

Why Gender Balance Can't Wait M. Landel *Harvard Business Review Digital Articles* p2 Mr 8 2016

17 2017

When Bobby Met Billie Jean C. Bonanos img *New York* v50 no17 p28 Ag 21 2017

Why Beauty Matters C. Leive color *Glamour* v115 no4 p28 Ap 2017

Sexism in mass media

Women's work P. H. Nettleton color *U.S. Catholic* v82 no3 p38 Mr 2017

Sexism—United States

Academia needs to confront sexism color *Science* v357 no6347 p222 Jl 14 2017

Sexology

See also

　　Sex research

EROTIC INTELLIGENCE color *Men's Health* v32 no7 p112 S 2017

"I like to fashion myself as the Walmart greeter of sex ed." color *Glamour* v115 no7 p93 Jl 2017

Sexsmith, Trevor Donald

Trevor Donald Sexsmith A. A. DAVIS color *Maclean's* v129 no44 p118 N 7 2016

Sextants—Design & construction

Make a Sextant from Junk S. BUSHWICK color *Popular Science* p84 Ja/F 2017

Sexton, Jared

Black Like Me *Harper's Magazine* p2 S 2017

Sexton, Jared Yates

The Best Words: A Hoosier author writes what may be the definitive account of the 2016 election C. FEHRMAN color *Indianapolis Monthly* v41 no2 p25 S 2017

The People Are Going to Rise Like the Waters upon Your Shore: A Story of American Rage *Publishers Weekly* v264 no20 p47 My 15 2017

Sexton, Joe

GARAGE BRANDS C. Liska color *Snowboarder* v29 no2 p32 O 2016

Sexton, Josie

BEST OF THE WEST color *Sunset* v238 no2 p7 F 2017

Sexton, Margaret Wilkerson

Disenchanting Optimism: Three generations of a New Orleans family struggle and endure J. McCARTHY *New York Times Book Review* p15 S 10 2017

A Kind of Freedom color *Publishers Weekly* v264 no23 p27 Je 5 2017

Sexton, Shannon

The best medicine color *Yoga Journal* p108 2017 Special Issue

gather ROUND chart color *Yoga Journal* no287 p68 N 2016

love FOR LIFE color *Yoga Journal* p94 2017 Special Issue

Sextus, Empiricus, 160-210

c. 200: Rome S. Empiricus *Lapham's Quarterly* v10 no2 p123 Spr 2017

Sexual abuse victims

See also

　　Adult child sexual abuse victims

Heeding Marie Collins's Voice *America* v216 no7 p8 Ap 3 2017

Sexual aggression

The Antidote to Toxic Masculinity S. J. DOUGLAS *In These Times* v41 no8 p13 Ag 2017

Sexual assault

The algebra of sexual violence A. KINGSTON *Maclean's* v130 no9 p10 O 2017

Don't Stop Believin' M. DEAN il *New Republic* v247 no12 p14 D 2016

Emily Doe C. Leive color *Glamour* v114 no12 p214 D 2016

From the beginning, I was told I was a best case scenario E. Doe *Glamour* v114 no12 p215 D 2016

Harassment Is Not the Same Thing as Assault C. ROSEN *Commentary* v142 no3 p4 O 2016

The Injustice of the 'Rape-Culture' Theory: For those in the grips of hysteria, proof is the enemy C. Young *Commentary* v144 no3 p26 O 2017

KEEPING SEX ASSAULT UNDERGROUND A. KINGSTON color *Maclean's* v129 no45 p10 N 14 2016

L'Affaire Galloway K. GOLD cartoon *Walrus* v13 no9 p40 N 2016

LETTER FROM THE EDITOR J. STOWE *Cincinnati Magazine*

p14 Je 2017

Not OK H. ALEJANDRO and D. S. KATZ *Ms.* v26 no4 p38 Wint 2016

RAPE CULTURE LIVES HERE S. STANKORB *Cincinnati Magazine* p68 Je 2017

Rape on Campus V. Grigoriadis color *Glamour* v115 no9 p139 S 2017

Redemption Time L. BARCA *Ms.* v26 no4 p37 Wint 2016

See No Evil P. NEUDING color *Weekly Standard* v22 no20 p18 Ja 30 2017

Sexual assault— it's on us *Christian Century* v133 no24 p7 N 23 2016

Shackled and abandoned A. KINGSTON *Maclean's* v130 no8 p10 S 2017

WE ALL SCREAM FOR THE ICE CREAM MAN'S HEAD L. SKENAZY cartoon *Reason* v49 no2 p6 Je 2017

When sexual assault goes viral J. Valente *America* v216 no10 p16 My 1 2017

Sexual assault—Law & legislation

SHORT TAKES *Ms.* v26 no4 p13 Wint 2016

Where Catcalling Is Criminalized T. John color *Time* v188 no27-28 p12 D 26 2016

Sexual assault—Lawsuits & claims

Protect and Serve L. Green, T. Keith et al color *Sports Illustrated* v126 no7 p17 Mr 6 2017

Sexual assault—Prevention

Female-Only Transport T. John color *Time* v189 no3 p10 Ja 30 2017

STRONGER TOGETHER A. GLASER *Wired* v24 no12 p23 D 2016

Sexual assault—Universities & colleges

See also

　　Rape in universities & colleges

BEWARE THE RED ZONE S. KARDIAN *USA Today Magazine* v146 no2868 p42 S 2017

Fair hearings on campus cartoon color *Christian Century* v134 no22 p7 O 25 2017

Sentence First... cartoon *Weekly Standard* v22 no7 p3 O 24 2016

Who Is Betsy DeVos? And how did she get to be head of our schools? L. Miller img *New York* v50 no15 p28 Jl 24 2017

Sexual assault—Universities & colleges—Law & legislation

CIVIL RIGHTS WRONGED C. N. BAKER *Ms.* v27 no3 p20 Fall 2017

NOT BACKING DOWN: We at Ms. promise to never let up with our reporting, rebelling and truth-telling K. SPILLAR *Ms.* v27 no3 p39 Fall 2017

Sexual behavior in animals

Animal Valentines *National Geographic Kids* no467 p28 F 2017

Fighting Fit D. STARIN color *Natural History* v125 no10 p28 O 2017

FINDINGS *Harper's Magazine* p96 O 2017

Made for Each Other P. Edmonds color *National Geographic* v230 no4 p31 O 2016

SEX THAT WORKS UP A LATHER P. Edmonds color *National Geographic* v231 no3 p29 Mr 2017

Sexual behavior in birds

SHE MATES, HE INCUBATES P. Edmonds color *National Geographic* v231 no5 p29 My 2017

Sexual dimorphism (Biology)

ONE PART HE, ONE PART SHE P. Edmonds color *National Geographic* v231 no1 p26 Ja 2017

Sexual dimorphism in plants

Flower hosts its own war of the sexes S. MILIUS color *Science News* v192 no1 p10 Ag 5 2017

Sexual dominance & submission

BDS(M) Drama L. Featherstone color il *Nation* v304 no3 p5 Ja 30 2017

Sexual dysfunction

See also

　　Impotence

Understanding ED I. Kerner color *Prevention* v69 no2 p28 F 2017

Sexual dysfunction—Psychological aspects

QUEST FOR FIRE: FEMALE DESIRE IS ONE OF THE MOST ELUSIVE FACETS OF HUMAN BEHAVIOR--AND ITS ABSENCE IS WOMEN'S MOST COMMON SEXUAL COMPLAINT. CAN SCIENCE FIGURE OUT HOW TO IGNITE

IT? K. ROWLAND *Psychology Today* v50 no5 p62 S/O 2017

Sexual ethics

    See also

      Adultery

      Birth control

      Sexual harassment

Is It O.K. to Have Another Man Satisfy Me Sexually, Since My Husband Can't? K. A. Appiah *New York Times Magazine* p26 O 9 2016

The Itsy-Bitsy, Teensy-Weensy, Tiny Fine Print That Can Allow Sexual Harassment to Go Unheard E. Dias and E. Dockterman color *Time* v188 no18 p32 O 31 2016

Sexual excitement

    See also

      Lust

Getting Comfortable I. Kerner color *Prevention* v69 no9 p26 O 2017

SEXPECTATIONS *Health* v31 no2 p16 Mr 2017

Sometimes when I get incredibly horny A. Gesselman, A. A. Hasinoff et al color *Glamour* v114 no12 p172 D 2016

Sexual freedom

To Arms Over LGBT? C. MOORE *USA Today Magazine* v145 no2860 p54 Ja 2017

Sexual freedom—Social aspects

Sex, Power, and Posting L. Dunham color *Glamour* v115 no7 p89 Jl 2017

Sexual harassment

Gretchen Carlson's Next Fight [Cover story] B. Luscombe color *Time* v188 no18 p26 O 31 2016

Harassment Is Not the Same Thing as Assault C. ROSEN *Commentary* v142 no3 p4 O 2016

How Unusual Is the Roger Ailes Sexual Harassment Case? D. L. Rhode *Harvard Business Review Digital Articles* p2 Ag 10 2016

LESSONS IN UBER'S ROUGH RIDE E. Griffith color *Fortune* v175 no6 p32 My 1 2017

The Omissions That Make So Many Sexual Harassment Policies Ineffective D. S. Dougherty *Harvard Business Review Digital Articles* p2 My 31 2017

Running While Female [Cover story] M. HAMILTON bw cartoon *Runner's World* v51 no11 p78 D 2016

The Silent Battle: Surviving Sexual Trauma D. POINTDUJOUR color *Ebony* v72 no4 p72 F 2017

SPEAK OUT J. OWENS bw *Working Mother* p16 F/Mr 2017

Too Many Men Are Silent Bystanders to Sexual Harassment W. B. Johnson and D. G. Smith *Harvard Business Review Digital Articles* p2 Mr 13 2017

Uber, But for Melt downs: Sexual harassment, corporate-espionage charges, taking advantage of drivers: The company that practically courts bad PR has an even greater, more existential dilemma R. Wiedeman img *New York* v50 no11 p34 My 29 2017

When Male Unemployment Rates Rise, So Do Sexual Harassment Claims D. Cassino *Harvard Business Review Digital Articles* p2 2017

Why I Decided to Make My Future About Fighting Back G. Carlson *Time* v190 no16/17 p33 O 23 2017

Why respect matters M. Rollins color *Redbook* p18 Ap 2017

Why Sexual Harassment Is More of a Problem in Venture Capital J. C. Williams *Harvard Business Review Digital Articles* p2 Jl 12 2017

Sexual harassment in mass media

The Real-Life Rebellion Behind Amazon's Good Girls Revolt E. Dockterman color *Time* v188 no20 p56 N 14 2016

Sexual harassment of women—Prevention

'I mean, is there anti-murder training?' C. Suddath *Bloomberg Businessweek* no4501 p42 N 28 2016

Sexual harassment of women—United States

'I mean, is there anti-murder training?' C. Suddath *Bloomberg Businessweek* no4501 p42 N 28 2016

Sexual harassment—Investigation

Bachelor in Paradise Halts Production L. Rice color *Entertainment Weekly* no1471 p16 Je 23 2017

Sexual harassment—Law & legislation—United States

Understanding Your Legal Options If You've Been Sexually Harassed J. L. Grossman and D. L. Rhode *Harvard Business Review Digital Articles* p1 Je 22 2017

Sexual harassment—Lawsuits & claims

GROWING INTO Feminism G. Carlson color *InStyle* v24 no11 p208 N 2017

OUT–FOXED D. Bacher color *Esquire* v166 no4 p86 N 2016

Power: Gabriel Sherman img *New York* v50 no10 p26 My 15 2017

ROGER, OVER AND OUT! S. ELLISON cartoon *Vanity Fair* v58 no11 p104 N 2016

Sexual harassment—Lawsuits & claims—News briefs

Understanding Your Legal Options If You've Been Sexually Harassed J. L. Grossman and D. L. Rhode *Harvard Business Review Digital Articles* p1 Je 22 2017

Sexual harassment—United States

Cracking the Bro Code S. McBride, L. Chapman et al cartoon *Bloomberg Businessweek* no4533 p18 Ag 7 2017

The Itsy-Bitsy, Teensy-Weensy, Tiny Fine Print That Can Allow Sexual Harassment to Go Unheard E. Dias and E. Dockterman color *Time* v188 no18 p32 O 31 2016

Sexual harassment—United States—Lawsuits & claims

This Is How Sexism Works in Silicon Valley My lawsuit failed. Others won't E. Pao img *New York* v50 no17 p56 Ag 21 2017

Sexual health

    See also

      Condoms

His & Hers M. Burklund color *Amazing Wellness* v9 no1 p32 Wint 2017

A home practice to awaken your sexual vitality [Cover story] L. Catone color *Yoga Journal* no289 p51 F 2017

HOW I REBOOTED MY SEX LIFE J. Dunn color *Health* v31 no3 p98 Ap 2017

MAINTAINING BISEXUAL SEXUAL HEALTH AND WELL-NESS D. GUERRERO and J. ANDERSON-MINSHALL bw *Advocate* no1090 p46 Ap 2017

Our Doc Will See You Now R. Rajapaksa color *Health* v31 no3 p65 Ap 2017

SISTERS ARE DOING IT FOR THEMSELVES: BLACK QUEER WOMEN TAKE SEXUAL HEALTH INTO THIER OWN HANDS R. NEIRENE color *Advocate* no1091 p112 Je/Jl 2017

Sexual health—Equipment & supplies

A Startup That Dare Not Speak Its Name S. Rai *Bloomberg Businessweek* no4504 p21 D 19 2016

Sexual intercourse

    See also

      Sexual aggression

ALL MY ORGASMS [Cover story] E. Sole color *Women's Health* v14 no3 p124 Ap 2017

THE BEST (SEX) IS YET TO COME color *Health* v31 no1 p18 Ja 2017

Feel Great After a Bad Night of Sleep J. COVERT cartoon *Men's Health* v32 no4 p80 My 2017

For Better Sex, Ask Her This color *Men's Health* v31 no10 p38 D 2016

Love Is Messy, and I'm Good With That A. de Cadenet color *Glamour* v115 no10 p128 O 2017

PARTY LINES T. Ferber and K. V. Syckle img *New York* v50 no15 p73 Jl 24 2017

SEX TONIGHT J. BENJAMIN color *Good Housekeeping* v264 no5 p107 My 2017

YOUR SENSUAL SUMMER IS HERE C. K. Jackson color *Essence* v48 no3 p103 Jl 2017

Sexual intercourse in literature

Literary Sex L. PRITCHETT *Publishers Weekly* v264 no2 p72 Ja 9 2017

Sexual intercourse—Moral & ethical aspects

Is It Ethical to Have Sex With a Robot? E. Dockterman *Time* v189 no7/8 p104 F 27 2017

Sexual intercourse—Psychological aspects

Getting Close [Cover story] L. A. PHILLIPS *Psychology Today* v50 no1 p44 Ja/F 2017

This Is You on Sex A. Levi color *Health* v31 no6 p86 Jl 2017

Who Are You Sexually? L. Brody color *Glamour* v115 no7 p68 Jl 2017

Sexual intercourse—Social aspects

THE LUST LOCKDOWN L. L. Joiner color *Essence* v47 no11 p107 Mr 2017

Sexual minority men

    See also

Female-to-male transsexuals

HIV TESTING DOESN'T HAVE TO SUCK Z. ZANE color *Advocate* no1091 p52 Je/Jl 2017

A LITTLE HELP FROM YOUR FRIENDS: Are friends with benefits actually benefiting you? Z. ZANE color *Advocate* no1091 p107 Je/Jl 2017

Sexual misconduct by clergy

The church must build 'spiritual ramps' for abuse survivors L. Karen Kivi *America* v216 no12 p10 My 29 2017

Partial depravity S. Wells *Christian Century* v133 no21 p57 O 12 2016

Sexual objectification

Sexual Racism and Reckoning with Robert Mapplethorpe C. STEPHENS bw *Advocate* no1091 p44 Je/Jl 2017

Sexual orientation

HELPING FAMILIES TALK ABOUT GENDER cartoon *National Geographic* v231 no1 p16 Ja 2017

Lurid Confusion Over "X" and "Y" *USA Today Magazine* v145 no2858 p32 N 2016

Sexual orientation identity

Who Are You Sexually? L. Brody color *Glamour* v115 no7 p68 Jl 2017

Sexual orientation—Social aspects

Come Out, Come Out, Whoever You Are G. Doyle color *O, The Oprah Magazine* p41 O 2017

Sexual partners

THE BEST (SEX) IS YET TO COME color *Health* v31 no1 p18 Ja 2017

Sexual positions

HAVE SEX IN TREES! color *Men's Health* v32 no6 p103 Ag 2017

WHEN I KNEW SHE WAS THE ONE color *Men's Health* v31 no10 p79 D 2016

YOU'RE OVER-DOING IT S. ROSEN color *GQ: Gentlemen's Quarterly* v97 no3 p138 Mr 2017

Sexually transmitted disease diagnosis

HIV TESTING DOESN'T HAVE TO SUCK Z. ZANE color *Advocate* no1091 p52 Je/Jl 2017

Sexually transmitted diseases

THE BARE TRUTH bw *Women's Health* v14 no3 p36 Ap 2017

STD Results in Minutes E. Biba color *Scientific American* v316 no3 p18 Mr 2017

What's Your STI-Q? K. MICKLE color *Seventeen* v76 no4 p52 Jl/Ag 2017

Sexy Getting Ready Song, The (Music)

Why TV. Musicals Matter R. BLOOM and A. D'Arminio *TV Guide* v64 no48 p16 N 21 2016

Seychelles—Description & travel

The Esquire Travel Dossier 2017 S. CLEMENCE color *Esquire* v166 no5 p42 D 2016/Ja 2017

Seydoux, Geraldine

Not just Salk color *Science* v357 no6356 p1105 S 15 2017

Seyedkazemi, V.

An artificial metalloenzyme with the kinetics of native enzymes bibl diag graph *Science* v354 no6308 p102 O 7 2016

Seymour, Daniel

Winning Streaks: The Power of Virtuous Cycles in Higher Education *Change* v49 no3 p28 My/Je 2017

Seymour, Gerald

No Mortal Thing *Publishers Weekly* v264 no24 p40 Je 12 2017

SEYMOUR, MIRANDA

HUSTLE BUSTLE color *New York Times Book Review* p40 D 4 2016

Under Germany's Thumb: An Englishwoman's journals shed new light on the occupation of Belgium during World War I *New York Times Book Review* p20 Jl 2 2017

Seymour, N.

Molecular gas in the halo fuels the growth of a massive cluster galaxy at high redshift bibl graph *Science* v354 no6316 p1128 D 2 2016

SEYMOUR, ROGER S.

Anesthesia and Euthanasia of Amphibians and Reptiles Used in Scientific Research: Should Hypothermia and Freezing Be Prohibited? *BioScience* v67 no1 p53 Ja 2017

Sezak-Blatt, Aiyanna

Country Lore *Mother Earth News* no280 p85 F/Mr 2017

Seznec, Jean-Francois

Saudi Arabia's sell-off of Aramco: Risk or opportunity? bibl *Bulletin of the Atomic Scientists* v72 no6 p378 N 2016

Sfeir, M. Y.

Extremely efficient internal exciton dissociation through edge states in layered 2D perovskites bibl graph *Science* v355 no6331 p1288 Mr 24 2017

Sfjazz Collective (Performer)

Music Of Miles Davis & Original Compositions Y. Kato color *Downbeat* v84 no7 p58 Jl 2017

Sfraga, Michael

The Arctic, from Romance to Reality bw color *Wilson Quarterly* p1 Summ 2017

SGHELLER, BILL

WHERE Winter is Grand *Yankee* v81 no1 p84 Ja/F 2017

Sgt. Pepper's Lonely Hearts Club Band (Music)

Beatles Open 'Sgt. Pepper' Vault R. SHEFFIELD bw color *Rolling Stone* no1286 p16 My 4 2017

A New Trip Through Pepper-Land M. GILMORE color *Rolling Stone* no1288 p49 Je 1 2017

THE REAL SGT. PEPPER color *MHQ: Quarterly Journal of Military History* v30 no1 p15 Aut 2017

SGT. PEPPER'S LONELY HEARTS CLUB BAND TURNS 50 E. R. Brown color *Entertainment Weekly* no1467 p56 My 26 2017

SH Group Operations LLC

OUR Favorite HOTELS IN FIVE OF THE WORLD'S GREATEST CITIES color *Conde Nast Traveler* v52 no1 p76 Ja 2017

SH Productions (Company)

Producing The FINEST P. Schofler color *Dressage Today* v23 no8 p58 Ap 2017

Sha, G.

Grain boundary stability governs hardening and softening in extremely fine nanograined metals bibl color graph *Science* v355 no6331 p1292 Mr 24 2017

Shaber, Sarah R.

Louise's Lies *Publishers Weekly* v263 no41 p58 O 10 2016

Shablovsky, Suzanne

The legacy of the Spanish flu bw color *Science* v357 no6357 p1245 S 22 2017

The perils of permanence color *Science* v357 no6350 p459 Ag 4 2017

SHACKELFORD, BRUCE

KEYS TO THE ALAMO *Texas Monthly* v44 no11 p98 N 2016

Shackford, Scott

BIG BROTHER IN THE U.K *Reason* v48 no10 p9 Mr 2017

Death from Above *Reason* v48 no7 p60 D 2016

FLORISTS LOSE ON FREE EXPRESSION color *Reason* v49 no2 p6 Je 2017

Teachers Union Head Casts School Choice as Racism color *Reason* v49 no5 p14 O 2017

Shadbolt, Jess

King S. Lyon color *New Yorker* v93 no10 p33 Ap 24 2017

Shadel, Doug

7 Ways to Block Computer Viruses color *AARP: The Magazine* v60 no5A p26 Ag/S 2017

All That Glitters ... color *AARP: The Magazine* v59 no5A p38 Ag/S 2016

Build a Better Password cartoon *AARP: The Magazine* v60 no3A p24 Ap/My 2017

Time-Share Bandits color *AARP: The Magazine* v60 no4A p48 Je/Jl 2017

When a Con Man Calls cartoon *AARP: The Magazine* v30 no6A p24 O/N 2017

Shades & shadows

Add shadows to structures with paint T. Koester color *Model Railroader* v84 no9 p50 S 2017

Coronal shadows S. JAMES O'MEARA color *Astronomy* v45 no8 p80 Ag 2017

Made in the Shade P. GULLEY cartoon *Indianapolis Monthly* v42 no2 p51 O 2017

Shades & shadows in architecture

Northern Exposure color *House Beautiful* v158 no10 p17 D 2016/ Ja 2017

Shades of Blue (TV program)

ALSO COMING . . J. Russell *TV Guide* v65 no2 p40 Ja 2 2017

Feeling Blue M. Logan *TV Guide* v65 no6 p9 Ja 30 2017

IN THE LINE OF FIRE M. LOGAN *TV Guide* v65 no8 p18 F 27 2017

Shades of Blue M. Logan *TV Guide* v65 no14 p34 Ap 3 2017

Shadkam, A.

Observation of a large-scale anisotropy in the arrival directions of cosmic rays above 8 × 1018 eV *Science* v357 no6357 p1266 S 22 2017

Shadley, Stephen

ELEMENTAL VISION W. James color *Old House Journal* v45 no3 p32 My 2017

Shadow Tech LLC

SADDLE UP J. B. SNOW color *Outdoor Life* v224 no1 p90 D 2016/Ja 2017

Shaefer, H. Luke

How should we define "low-wage" work? An analysis using the Current Population Survey bibl chart color graph *Monthly Labor Review* p1 O 2016

Shaer, Matthew

Can You Trip Your Way Out of Anxiety? cartoon *Men's Health* v32 no4 p88 My 2017

EXONERATION *Smithsonian* v47 no9 p80 Ja/F 2017

Fighting the Nazis With Fake News *Smithsonian* v48 no1 p22 Ap 2017

THE HOLOCAUST'S GREAT ESCAPE bw color map *Smithsonian* v47 no10 p42 Mr 2017

MIRACLE MAKER *Smithsonian* v47 no8 p40 D 2016

Stampede: How the symbol of the frontier became a nuisance *Smithsonian* v48 no2 p11 My 2017

States of Denial color map *New Republic* v248 no11 p16 N 2017

STILL SO DEF *Atlanta* v57 no1 p84 My 2017

Shaeri, Fatemeh

Exploring genetic suppression interactions on a global scale diag *Science* v354 no6312 p599 N 4 2016

Shafaieh, Charles

THE WALL cartoon *New Yorker* v93 no26 p21 S 4 2017

Shafak, Elif

The Builder's Art A. BAKSHIAN JR. *Weekly Standard* v22 no6 p36 O 17 2016

Shafee, Thomas

Academics can help shape Wikipedia *Science* v357 no6351 p557 Ag 11 2017

SHAFER, JACK

Where Did All the Investigative Journalism Go? bw cartoon *Reason* v48 no11 p64 Ap 2017

Shafer, Mike

SHE'S GONE: A 17-YEAR LOVE AFFAIR COMES TO AN ABRUPT END D. Karl color *Flying* v144 no10 p70 O 2017

SHAFER, SUSAN

Visual Literacy *Publishers Weekly* v264 no24 p68 Je 12 2017

Shaffer, Alyssa

BEAT the HEAT color *Better Homes & Gardens* v95 no7 p161 Jl 2017

The Everything Guide to Running chart color *Health* v31 no3 p35 Ap 2017

FAMILY-STYLE BOOT CAMP color *Better Homes & Gardens* v95 no9 p154 S 2017

Fight Gravity with Yoga color *Health* v31 no1 p98 Ja 2017

FIT IN 15 core values *Better Homes & Gardens* v94 no11 p164 N 2016

STRONGER & FASTER cartoon color *Better Homes & Gardens* v95 no2 p132 F 2016

UNDER PRESSURE cartoon color *Better Homes & Gardens* v95 no4 p158 Ap 2017

WE'VE GOT YOURBACK color *Better Homes & Gardens* v95 no10 p174 O 2017

YOUR BODY ON TECH color *Better Homes & Gardens* v95 no4 p152 Ap 2017

Shaffer, Ashley

LIQUID ASSETS color *Wired* v24 no12 p78 D 2016

WISH LIST 2016 color *Wired* v24 no12 p45 D 2016

Shaffer, Chelsea

(At home with) color *Team Roping Journal* p50 S 2017

Hitting the Road color *Team Roping Journal* p75 O 2017

Iconic Moments in US Finals History color *Team Roping Journal* p90 O 2017

No-Nonsense Soundness color *Team Roping Journal* p80 S 2017

Raising the Bar [Cover story] color *Team Roping Journal* p82 S 2017

Riding Out of the Box color *Team Roping Journal* p66 S 2017

Swing Consistency color *Team Roping Journal* p58 O 2017

Shaffer, Earl

Trails and Tribulations: In 1948, a haunted Army veteran became the first to hike the entire Appalachian Trail A. Tucker *Smithsonian* v48 no4 p26 Jl/Ag 2017

Shaffer, Jody Jensen

Prudence the Part-Time Cow *Publishers Weekly* v264 no18 p56 My 1 2017

Shafi, Nadia

Emergence and spread of a human-transmissible multidrug-resistant nontuberculous mycobacterium bibl diag graph *Science* v354 no6313 p751 N 11 2016

Shafie, Hadieh

Bibliophile R. J. Ritzel bw color *American Craft* v76 no6 p42 D 2016-Ja 2017

Shafrir, Doree

Click Bait: A debut novel about the pitfalls of startup culture L. VAPNYAR *New York Times Book Review* p11 My 14 2017

Just Out of Reach: This novel's heroine has turned 30, but she still doesn't have her life figured out *New York Times Book Review* p18 Jl 30 2017

Startup *Publishers Weekly* v264 no8 p59 F 20 2017

Shafroth, Frank

Back in Black: Cities that once faced bankruptcy have made remarkable recoveries *Governing* v30 no10 p62 Jl 2017

Self-Driving the Economy *Governing* v30 no4 p62 Ja 2017

Shelter and the Storm *Governing* v30 no6 p62 Mr 2017

Shop 'Til You Drop: An empty shopping mall can mean lost jobs and lower revenues--but not always *Governing* v30 no8 p62 My 2017

Stadium Shutout: Localities are no longer so willing to take on the risky business of building a ballpark *Governing* v30 no12 p63 S 2017

Tax Targets *Governing* v30 no2 p62 N 2016

Shafting

See also

Cranks & crankshafts

TIP THE SCALES R. Sauerhaft and D. DeNunzio chart color *Golf Magazine* v59 no4 p58 Ap 2017

Shafting—Evaluation

Justin Thomas C. Barrett color *Golf Magazine* v59 no4 p33 Ap 2017

SHAH, AGAM

Apple Mac shipments take a beating in the third quarter as PC shipments decline color *PCWorld* v35 no11 p19 N 2016

How Alienware's 20-year history with PC gaming can help drive the future of VR color *PCWorld* v35 no11 p21 N 2016

More high-end GPUs are now compatible with Dell's 8K monitor color *PCWorld* v35 no5 p43 My 2017

Shah, Baiju

How People Are Actually Using the Internet of Things *Harvard Business Review Digital Articles* p2 O 28 2015

SHAH, BEEJOLI

REVENGE OF THE FILM NERDS *Texas Monthly* v45 no7 p70 Jl 2017

Shah, Farhana N.

American Muslim Students Need Understanding and Support *Education Digest* v83 no2 p33 O 2017

Shah, Julie

Robots Are Learning Complex Tasks Just by Watching Humans Do Them *Harvard Business Review Digital Articles* p2 Je 21 2016

Shah, Kushal K.

Methods for teaching traditional physics *Physics Today* v69 no12 p12 D 2016

SHAH, MASROOR A.

When Less Means More: Conservation and protecting the environment adds to the blessings of Ramadan and one's year-round worship *Islamic Horizons* v46 no3 p46 My/Je 2017

Shah, Neel

Crowdsource This color *Glamour* v115 no9 p124 S 2017

SOX2 promotes lineage plasticity and antiandrogen resistance in TP53- and RB1-deficient prostate cancer bibl graph *Science* v355 no6320 p1 Ja 6 2017

Shah, Nilay D.

Why Health Care May Finally Be Ready for Big Data *Harvard Business Review Digital Articles* p2 D 3 2014

Shah, Nirav R.

Health Care Providers Must Stop Wasting Patients' Time *Harvard Business Review Digital Articles* p2 My 24 2017

Shah, Rishi

FEVER HIGH M. HERPER and A. KONRAD color *Forbes* v199 no7 p26 Je 29 2017

Shah, Sagar

NRPA Update. Introducing the Health and Wellness Advisory Panel's Newest Members *Parks & Recreation* v52 no6 p38 Je 2017

Shah, Sonia

Contagions Make a Comeback [Cover story] color *Science News* v190 no13 p32 D 24 2016

Shahan, Shirley—Interviews

Take 5 With SHIRLEY SHAHAN T. Taylor bw color *Hot Rod* v70 no4 p16 Ap 2017

Shaheen, Jack G.

WE HEAR YOU *Progressive* v81 no6 p9 Ag/S 2017

Shaheen, James

10,000 Dharma Doors *Tricycle: The Buddhist Review* v26 no2 p12 Wint 2017

The Buddha's Politics *Tricycle: The Buddhist Review* v26 no3 p10 Spr 2017

Dissolving the Boundary Lines *Tricycle: The Buddhist Review* v26 no4 p10 Summ 2017

The Web of Shared Support color *Tricycle: The Buddhist Review* v27 no1 p10 Fall 2017

Shahghasemi, Ehsan

Human Rights against Human Rights: Sexism in Human Rights Discourse for Sakineh Mohammadi *Society* v53 no6 p614 D 2016

Shahidi, Yara

Best Face Forward A. Serrano and D. Mazzone color *InStyle* v24 no11 p125 N 2017

BLACK-ISH I. Ratledge *TV Guide* v65 no39 p41 S 18 2017

Generation bw color *Glamour* v115 no11 p124 N 2017

We Are Family A. Teran color *Glamour* v115 no5 p180 My 2017

Yara Shahidi color *Seventeen* v76 no5 p30 S 2017

SHAHIN, JIM

The Healing Hoagie *Reader's Digest* v189 no1128 p48 Mr 2017

Shahrokhabadi, Shahriar

Lessons from the Oroville dam bibl *Science* v355 no6330 p1139 Mr 17 2017

Shaich, Ron

How Did I Get Here?: RON SHAICH bw color *Bloomberg Businessweek* no4493 p92 O 3 2016

Shaikh, Nadeem

The Financial Industry Needs to Start Planning for the Next 50 Years, Not the Next Five *Harvard Business Review Digital Articles* p2 Jl 17 2017

Shaiman, Marc

GOINGS ON ABOUT TOWN color *New Yorker* v93 no10 p13 Ap 24 2017

Shain, Susan

OUTSIDER'S PASSAGE color *Sunset* v239 no3 p19 S 2017

Shaker, Mariela

This Is Our Time A. Behm and E. Krapcha color *Glamour* v115 no7 p14 Jl 2017

Shaker Workshops (Company)

THE SHAKER CHAIR color *Old House Journal* v45 no2 p78 Ap 2017

Shakers

SIMPLY SHAKER D. DICKINSON color *Better Homes & Gardens* v95 no11 p112 N 2017

Shakespeare, Lain

Going Ape for Local Art: Thanks to a key hire, MailChimp has quietly become one of the city's biggest corporate supporters of local art S. DAZEY *Atlanta* v57 no6 p77 O 2017

SHAKESPEARE, MARGARET

EMPIRE OF GLASS bw color *Archaeology* v70 no2 p55 Mr/Ap 2017

Shakespeare, William, 1564-1616

Demoting Shakespeare *Weekly Standard* v22 no16 p2 D 26 2016

GHOST STORY W. Shakespeare *Lapham's Quarterly* v10 no3 p126 Summ 2017

Glenda Jackson's Great Lear F. O'Toole color *New York Review of Books* v63 no20 p16 D 22 2016

IF YOU PRICK US S. GREENBLATT cartoon color *New Yorker* v93 no20 p34 Jl 10 2017

PARODY color *Weekly Standard* v22 no24 p44 F 27 2017

Roméo et Juliette *Opera News* v81 no7 p56 Ja 2017

Shakespeare's Characters Show Us How Personal Growth Should Happen D. Fitzsimons color *Harvard Business Review Digital Articles* p2 Ja 30 2017

Shakespeare in Love (Theatrical production)

DOUBLET TROUBLE L. Vaccariello *Cincinnati Magazine* v50 no12 p59 S 2017

Shakespeare in the Park (Theatrical production)

But Will It Wash Off... J. Duckworth *Stage Directions* v30 no8 p28 Ag 2017

Shakir, Imran

Three-dimensional holey-graphene/niobia composite architectures for ultrahigh-rate energy storage color diag graph *Science* v356 no6338 p599 My 12 2017

Shakirov, A.

Observation of coherent elastic neutrino-nucleus scattering diag *Science* v357 no6356 p1123 S 15 2017

SHAKLEE, RON

ROUTE RECALCULATION: NAVIGATING WHERE WE ARE, WHERE WE'RE GOING, AND WHAT WE'VE MISSED ALONG THE WAY diag *Phi Kappa Phi Forum* v97 no1 p23 Spr 2017

Shakoor, Nadia

10 UP & COMERS: NADIA SHAKOOR B. Freese *Successful Farming* v115 no8 p44 Je/Jl 2017

Shakur, Afeni, 1947-2016

AFENI SHAKUR J. HUGHES *New York Times Magazine* p50 D 25 2016

Shakur, Sáde—Interviews

THE LOOK BOOK A. SWERDLOFF img *New York* p55 Ja 9 2017

Shakur, Tupac, 1971-1996

CALIFORNIA LOVE B. WESTHOFF *Los Angeles Magazine* v61 no11 p78 N 2016

A TALE OF TUPAC M. LOSGAR color *Vanity Fair* v59 no7 p115 Summ 2017

Shalaev, Vladimir M.

Applying plasmonics to a sustainable future color *Science* v356 no6341 p908 Je 1 2017

Shalapyonok, Alexi

Physiological and ecological drivers of early spring blooms of a coastal phytoplankter bibl graph *Science* v354 no6310 p326 O 21 2016

Shale

See also
Oil shales

The Cartel That Failed I. M. Stelzer color *Weekly Standard* v22 no29 p11 Ap 3 2017

Shale gas industry—Economic aspects

Why the Oil Glut Isn't Gone Yet J. Blas graph *Bloomberg Businessweek* no4514 p39 Mr 13 2017

Shale oils

New Genus of Bacteria Found in Fracking Wells *USA Today Magazine* v146 no2867 p8 Ag 2017

Shalem, Ophir

High-resolution interrogation of functional elements in the noncoding genome bibl graph *Science* v353 no6307 p1545 S 30 2016

Shalev, Kuty

How I Hired an Entirely Remote Workforce *Harvard Business Review Digital Articles* p2 Ap 14 2016

Shalin, Dmitri

Extended Mind and Embodied Social Psychology: Contemporary Perspectives *Society* v54 no3 p279 Je 2017

Extended Mind and Embodied Social Psychology: Historical Perspectives *Society* v54 no2 p171 Ap 2017

Shallot

EASY WEEKNIGHTS color *Good Housekeeping* v264 no2 p125 F 2017

how to cook HERB SALSA M. GLISAN color *Better Homes & Gardens* v95 no4 p88 Ap 2017

SWEET POTATOES & SHALLOTS to Savor in Winter *Mother Earth News* no279 p10 D/Ja 2017

Shallows, The (Film)

THE SHALLOWS D. Vaughn color *Sound & Vision* v82 no2 p69 F/Mr 2017

Shamans

Desperate for a Cure M. KOHUT color *National Geographic* v232 no1 p74 Jl 2017

The Shaman Masters of Hohhot Have Returned color *Foreign Policy* no225 p5 Jl/Ag 2017

Shamary, Ammar Al

Displaced Iraqi Christians await return to Mosul color *Christian Century* v133 no24 p14 N 23 2016

Shambaugh, Rebecca

Are Chore Wars at Home Holding You Back at Work? color *Harvard Business Review Digital Articles* p2 Ja 19 2017

The Fine Line Between a Collaborative Employee and One Who Doesn't Get Enough Done *Harvard Business Review Digital Articles* p2 Je 30 2016

Getting More Women into Senior Management *Harvard Business Review Digital Articles* p2 My 25 2015

Having the Here's-What-IWant Conversation With Your Boss *Harvard Business Review Digital Articles* p2 N 20 2015

The Time-Consuming Activities That Stall Women's Careers *Harvard Business Review Digital Articles* p2 Mr 7 2016

SHAMBU, GIRISH

Black Is... Black Ain't color *Film Comment* v53 no1 p62 Ja/F 2017

Broadcast Messiahs color *Film Comment* v53 no3 p79 My/Je 2017

A DOUBLE LIFE bw color *Film Comment* v53 no5 p56 S/O 2017

Shame

Don't Let Shame Become a Self-Destructive Spiral M. F. R. Kets de Vries *Harvard Business Review Digital Articles* p1 Je 1 2017

Pepsi, United, and the Speed of Corporate Shame A. Winston *Harvard Business Review Digital Articles* p2 Ap 12 2017

The shame of shaming J. F. Goodman color *Phi Delta Kappan* v99 no2 p26 O 2017

Shameless (TV program)

Shameless M. Snetiker, A. Bacle et al color *Entertainment Weekly* no1482/1483 p30 S 22 2017

Shameless *TV Guide* p45 D 5 2016

Shames, Shauna L.

Will Millennials Start Running for Office? S. Begley color *Time* v189 no6 p20 F 20 2017

Shamim, Amna

Generation Nomad [Cover story] color *Glamour* no8 p148 Ag 2017

Shamim, Amna—Interviews

Generation Nomad [Cover story] A. Shamim color *Glamour* no8 p148 Ag 2017

Shamim, Muhammad S.

De novo assembly of the Aedes aegypti genome using Hi-C yields chromosome-length scaffolds chart color diag *Science* v356 no6333 p92 Ap 7 2017

SHAMMA, FREDA

Why Can't They All be Doctors? [Cover story] *Islamic Horizons* v46 no2 p22 Mr/Ap 2017

SHAMOON, EVAN

Hot Digital Psychedelia Rez Infinite and Thumper color *Rolling Stone* no1274 p47 N 17 2016

SHAMOUN-BARANES, JUDY

From Agricultural Benefits to Aviation Safety: Realizing the Potential of Continent-Wide Radar Networks *BioScience* v67 no10 p912 O 2017

Shampoos

ASK APRIL A. FRANZINO color *Good Housekeeping* v265 no2 p16 Ag 2017

ask REDBOOK color *Redbook* p16 My 2017

The Bare ESSENTIALS E. MUSIWA color *Ebony* v72 no11 p54 S 2017

DID YOU KNOW? O. Manno color *Dance Spirit* v20 no9 p32 N 2016

digital directory color *InStyle* v24 no5 p16 My 2017

The Dry Shampoo Mania Continues K. Erickson color *Glamour* v115 no10 p106 O 2017

GREAT HAIR STARTS IN THE SHOWER [Cover story] A. FRANZINO bw chart color *Good Housekeeping* v265 no5 p43 N 2017

Holidays GIFTS in Every Price Range V. Green-Gott color *Practical Horseman* v45 no11 p56 N 2017

HOW WELL DO YOU KNOW YOUR Hair? M. Goldberg color *O, The Oprah Magazine* p59 Ag 2017

MANE MATTERS J. AMAY color *Ebony* v72/73 no12/1 p52 O/N 2017

THE OTHER STUFF color *Backpacker* v45 no3 p128 Ap 2017

Our Most-Loved Hair & Makeup Looks for Fall J. Mulrow color *Glamour* no8 p73 Ag 2017

your BEAUTY PROBLEMS solved! A. FRANZINO cartoon color *Good Housekeeping* v264 no4 p33 Ap 2017

Shampoos—Evaluation

2017 Best Beauty BUYS K. D. Hodes and P. Reynoso color *InStyle* v24 no5 p169 My 2017

Bath & Beyond C. ELLENBERG color *Vogue* v207 no11 p162 N 2017

BEAUTY BUYS from $4 color *Good Housekeeping* v264 no4 p30 Ap 2017

beauty NEWSFEED K. CASTAÑON color *Seventeen* v75 no11 p54 N 2016

CHARCOAL cleansers color *Better Homes & Gardens* v95 no8 p20 Ag 2017

The Dirt on Clean Skin S. Nygaard color *Men's Health* v32 no1 p83 Ja/F 2017

Fast Beauty FIXES color *InStyle* v23 no13 p175 D 2016

HEALTHY SHINY HAIR color *Harper's Bazaar* no3652 p249 Ap 2017

Hydrating Shampoos & Conditioners color *Good Housekeeping* v265 no5 p49 N 2017

Made for Me K. Erickson and Ying Chu color *Glamour* v115 no3 p104 Mr 2017

Market color *Vanity Fair* v59 no7 p44 Summ 2017

"No, I won't color my hair" J. M. Hickman color *Glamour* no8 p82 Ag 2017

PAMPER YOUR CURLS *Better Homes & Gardens* v94 no11 p27 N 2016

PRACTICAL MAGIC A. Finney color *Women's Health* v14 no3 p(Sp)18 Ap 2017

Steal Her Stuff S. NYGAARD color *Men's Health* v32 no4 p62 My 2017

STOCK & TRADE color *Equus* no476 p92 My 2017

STRIKING GOLD color *Essence* v47 no10 p52 F 2017

Val's Guide to GORGEOUS V. Monroe color *O, The Oprah Magazine* p64 Ap 2017

Val's Guide to GORGEOUS V. Monroe color *O, The Oprah Magazine* p83 Mr 2017

ZEN AND THE ART OF HAIR [Cover story] C. K. Kaye color *Women's Health* v14 no3 p(Sp)24 Ap 2017

Shamrock Cycles (Company)

Off the Chain R. ANNIS *Indianapolis Monthly* p30 My 2017

Shamsie, Kamila

Divided Loyalties: Two families, separated by class as much as piety, in a retelling of 'Antigone.' P. HO DAVIES *New York Times Book Review* p19 O 1 2017

Shan, Yehua

Release of mineral-bound water prior to subduction tied to shallow seismogenic slip off Sumatra graph *Science* v356 no6340 p841 My 26 2017

Shan, Yue

Why tolerance invites resistance bibl diag *Science* v355 no6327 p796 F 24 2017

Shanahan, Cate

Old School Food J. Lisanti and T. Keith color *Sports Illustrated* v126 no2 p18 Ja 16 2017

Shanahan, Christina

Cause & Effect color *InStyle* v23 no13 p72 D 2016

CAUSE & EFFECT color *InStyle* v24 no3 p138 Mr 2017

DOING GOOD color *InStyle* v24 no4 p70 Ap 2017

NAOMIE'S MOMENT color *InStyle* v23 no13 p232 D 2016

Tapped IN color *InStyle* v23 no12 p155 N 2016

SHANAHAN, DANIELLE F.

Doses of Neighborhood Nature: The Benefits for Mental Health of Living with Nature *BioScience* v67 no2 p147 F 2017

Shanbhag, Vivek

Roving Eye P. Sehgal *New York Times Book Review* p27 Ap 9 2017

Shandling, Garry, 1949-2016

GARRY SHANDLING B. Maher and D. Franich color *Entertainment Weekly* no1446/1447 p98 D 2016/Ja 2017

Stars We Loved and Lost A. D'Arminio *TV Guide* p28 D 19 2016

SHANE, CHARLOTTE

A QUIET DISCONTENT color *Nation* v304 no18 p42 Je 19 2017

A Woman's March bw color il *New Republic* v248 no6 p61 Je 2017

SHANE, JANELLE

US AND HIS KINGDOM OF THE FLUBBINGS OF SHADOWS cartoon color *Wired* v25 no10 p22 O 2017

SHANE, SCOTT

The Not-So-Secret War *New York Times Book Review* p12 F 5 2017

Shanghai (China)

11th SHANGHAI BIENNALE Y. FUCA color *ARTnews* v116 no1 p122 Spr 2017

Shanghai (China)—Description & travel

LOOK OVER HERE Z. BROCKETT bw color *Conde Nast Traveler* v52 no3 p88 Mr 2017

Shanghai Biennale

Raqs Media Collective R. Simonini color *Art in America* v104 no11 p37 D 2016

THE SHANGHAI SHOW Jiayang Fan bw color *Conde Nast Traveler* v52 no3 p82 Mr 2017

Shanghai Century Publishing Co.

Juvenile & Children's Publishing House color *Publishers Weekly* v264 no12 p22 Mr 20 2017

Shanghai Quartet (Performer)

CLASSICAL MUSIC *New Yorker* v93 no18 p9 Je 26 2017

Shanghai zheng quan jiao yi suo

China's Slowdown: The First Stage of the Bullwhip Effect Y. Sheffi *Harvard Business Review Digital Articles* p2 S 9 2015

Shangri La (Honolulu, Hawaii)

THE GATHERING PLACE A. Erace color *Fortune* v176 no4 p64 S 15 2017

Shank, Jenny

In the old neighborhoods of Brooklyn, Sister knows best graph *America* v217 no6 p52 S 18 2017

Shankar, Maya

GOOD BEHAVIOR S. STILLMAN cartoon *New Yorker* v92 no46 p46 Ja 23 2017

SHANKAR RAMAN, T. R.

Elephant Crossing *Orion Magazine* v35 no3 p6 My/Je 2016

Shankle, Mike

Posthole color *Powder* v45 no4 p146 D 2016

Shankleman, Jess

We're Going To Need More Lithium diag graph map *Bloomberg Businessweek* no4537 p60 S 11 2017

SHANKLIN, MITCHELL

DOUBLE JEOPARDY cartoon color *Outdoor Life* v224 no3 p12 Ap 2017

Shanley, Betsy

The Reader Page color *Popular Mechanics* p5 F 2017

Shanmuganathan, Vivekanandan

The cryo-EM structure of a ribosome–Ski2-Ski3-Ski8 helicase complex bibl color graph *Science* v354 no6318 p1431 D 16 2016

Shannara Chronicles, The (TV program)

The Shannara Chronicles N. Abrams, B. L. Heldman et al *Entertainment Weekly* no1482/1483 p79 S 22 2017

Shannon, Erika

just 3 moves TOWEL TONE-UP color *Good Housekeeping* v264 no1 p102 Ja 1 2017

Shannon, Michael

That Certain LOOK P. DEMARCHELIER bw color *Vanity Fair* v59 no4 p174 Mr 2017

TURN IT UP TO 11 J. YUAN img *New York* v49 no24 p114 N 28 2016

Shannon, Molly, 1964-

Divorce *TV Guide* v64 no46 p33 N 7 2016

Shannon, Noah Gallagher

Arroyos *New York Times Magazine* p18 Mr 5 2017

Shannon, R. M.

The magnetic field and turbulence of the cosmic web measured using a brilliant fast radio burst bibl chart graph *Science* v354 no6317 p1249 D 9 2016

Shannon, Riley Fullton, 1996-2017

Riley Fullton Shannon A. A. DAVIS color *Maclean's* p66 Je 2017

Shantz, Jacob Y.

Building Community bw *Alternatives Journal (AJ) - Canada's Environmental Voice* v42 no3 p17 2016

Shao, Benjamin B. M.

Hidden Suppliers Can Make or Break Your Operations *Harvard Business Review Digital Articles* p2 My 29 2015

Shao, Brian

Arylation of hydrocarbons enabled by organosilicon reagents and weakly coordinating anions diag *Science* v355 no6332 p1403 Mr 31 2017

Shao, Diane

Knocking on opportunity's door cartoon *Science* v354 no6310 p382 O 21 2016

Shao, Mengle

Regeneration of fat cells from myofibroblasts during wound healing bibl color graph *Science* v355 no6326 p748 F 17 2017

Shao, Qian

Formation of α-chiral centers by asymmetric β-C(sp3)–H arylation, alkenylation, and alkynylation bibl diag *Science* v355 no6324 p499 F 3 2017

Shao, Qiming

Chiral Majorana fermion modes in a quantum anomalous Hall insulator–superconductor structure diag *Science* v357 no6348 p294 Jl 21 2017

Shao, Sichen

Mechanistic basis for a molecular triage reaction bibl color graph *Science* v355 no6322 p298 Ja 20 2017

Shao De Bu

Quality management for precision medicine clinical applications: A consensus from the China Precision Medicine Clinical Research and Application Association bibl *Science* v354 no6319 p11 D 23 2016

Shaochuan Luo

Highly stretchable polymer semiconductor films through the nanoconfinement effect bibl graph *Science* v355 no6320 p1 Ja 6 2017

Shaofeng Liu

RPA binds histone H3-H4 and functions in DNA replication–coupled nucleosome assembly bibl graph *Science* v355 no6323 p415 Ja 27 2017

Shaohua Fan

Going global by adapting local: A review of recent human adaptation bibl diag graph *Science* v354 no6308 p54 O 7 2016

Shaojun Guo

Biaxially strained PtPb/Pt core/shell nanoplate boosts oxygen reduction catalysis bibl color graph *Science* v354 no6318 p1410 D 16 2016

SHAOLIANG YI

Bridging the Gaps between Science and Policy for the Sustainable Management of Rangeland Resources in the Developing World *BioScience* v67 no7 p656 Jl 2017

Shaowen Chen

Electron optics with p-n junctions in ballistic graphene bibl graph *Science* v353 no6307 p1522 S 30 2016

Shape of the earth

Synestia \sin-ES-ti-ə\ n A. Yeager color *Science News* v192 no1 p5 Ag 5 2017

Shape of You (Music)

R&B's New Wave Is Embracing Creative Destruction J. Cox color *Time* v189 no14 p49 Ap 17 2017

Shape of Water, The (Film)

ALSO PLAYING color *Entertainment Weekly* no1478 / 1479 p73 Ag 18-25 2017

Shapes

What in the World? *National Geographic Kids* no467 p31 F 2017

Shapira, Allison

Breathing Is the Key to Persuasive Public Speaking *Harvard Business Review Digital Articles* p2 Je 30 2015

Kitchen in the Craftsman Spirit P. Poore color diag *Arts & Crafts Homes & the Revival* v11 no5 p23 Wint 2017

Sharf, Samantha

THE AMERICAN DREAM IS ALIVE AND WELL...ON THE FORBES 400 color graph map *Forbes* v198 no5 p58 O 25 2016

American Riviera color *Forbes* v198 no8 p20 D 20 2016

Divide Your Home color *Forbes* v199 no7 p136 Je 29 2017

The Fintech 50 color *Forbes* v198 no7 p90 N 29 2016

Hoarder Control color *Forbes* v200 no2 p42 S 5 2017

LIVE LIKE A ROCKEFELLER color *Forbes* v200 no4 p28 O 24 2017

New House on the Block color *Forbes* v199 no1 p40 Ja 24 2017

TRUMP AMERICA bw *Forbes* v199 no3 p72 Mr 28 2017

The XX Factor color *Forbes* v199 no4 p58 Ap 25 2017

Sharfstein, Daniel J.—Interviews

THUNDER in the MOUNTAINS K. Donohue *Prologue* v49 no1 p28 Spr 2017

Shariat, Hormoz

God in Iran (Still) K. A. Ellis *Christianity Today* v61 no6 p26 Jl/Ag 2017

Sharing

THE OVERCOMMITTED ORGANIZATION: WHY IT'S HARD TO SHARE PEOPLE ACROSS MULTIPLE TEAMS—AND WHAT TO DO ABOUT IT [Cover story] M. MORTENSEN and H. K. GARDNER chart graph il img *Harvard Business Review* v95 no5 p58 S/O 2017

Sharing economy

THE GIG IS UP N. HELLER cartoon *New Yorker* v93 no13 p52 My 15 2017

Grab a Spot in the Sharing Economy I. Case diag *Money* v46 no2 p44 Mr 2017

How the Sharing Economy Can Improve Your Next Business Trip A. Samuel *Harvard Business Review Digital Articles* p2 N 2 2015

How Uber and the Sharing Economy Can Win Over Regulators S. Cannon and L. H. Summers *Harvard Business Review Digital Articles* p2 O 13 2014

Limit Your Exposure M. C. White color map *Money* v46 no2 p29 Mr 2017

MAKING ENDS MEET IN THE SHARING ECONOMY diag *Fortune* v176 no1 p9 Jl 1 2017

The Sharing Economy Isn't About Sharing at All G. M. Eckhardt and F. Bardhi *Harvard Business Review Digital Articles* p2 Ja 28 2015

Sharing Is (Kind of) Saving J. Marlowe *Governing* v30 no5 p64 F 2017

What Customers Want from the Collaborative Economy A. Samuel *Harvard Business Review Digital Articles* p2 O 8 2015

Sharing economy—Law & legislation

REGULATORS ARE SQUEEZING THE VALLEY'S DARLINGS M. Ingram color *Fortune* v175 no3 p16 Mr 1 2017

Sharing economy—Social aspects

Dealing with Unexpected Bias A. Ignatius color *Harvard Business Review* v94 no12 p12 D 2016

FIXING DISCRIMINATION IN ONLINE MARKETPLACES R. FISMAN and M. LUCA color *Harvard Business Review* v94 no12 p88 D 2016

Sharjah (United Arab Emirates)

DATING IN SHARJAH M. MOUSHABECK *Publishers Weekly* v263 no43 p(Sp)16 O 24 2016

HOW TO MAKE THE SHARJAH INTERNATIONAL BOOK FAIR PROFESSIONAL PROGRAM & TRANSLATION GRANT REWARDING G. ISHMAEL color *Publishers Weekly* v263 no43 p(Sp)14 O 24 2016

INTRODUCTION R. TAGHOLM *Publishers Weekly* v263 no43 p(Sp)4 O 24 2016

PROFESSIONAL PROGRAM PROFILE D. WALLACE *Publishers Weekly* v263 no43 p(Sp)17 O 24 2016

SHARJAH INTERNATIONAL BOOK FAIR/AMERICAN LIBRARY ASSOCIATION LIBRARY CONFERENCE NOW IN ITS THIRD YEAR M. MACKAY and M. DOWLING color *Publishers Weekly* v263 no43 p(Sp)6 O 24 2016

SHARJAH PUBLISHING CITY N. Clee color *Publishers Weekly* v263 no43 p(Sp)4 O 24 2016

WELCOME A. A. AMERI *Publishers Weekly* v263 no43 p(Sp)2 O 24 2016

Sharjah Arts Biennial

Sharjah Biennial W. S. Smith bw color *Art in America* v105 no5 p140 My 2017

Shark attacks

Editor's Note T. PRODANOVICH color *Surfer* v58 no1 p10 Ap 2017

How Sharks Became So Scary O. B. Waxman *Time* v189 no22 p17 Je 12 2017

SAFETY NOT GUARANTEED J. HOUSMAN color *Surfer* v58 no1 p68 Ap 2017

Shark Helmet (Company)

Devinci: SPARTAN CARBON | X01EAGLE R. Palmer color *Bike Magazine* v24 no8 p70 N 2017

Shark Tank (TV program)

I Love My Rope Swing color *House Beautiful* v159 no7 p124 S 2017

JUST MY TYPE D. Patrick and T. Keith color *Sports Illustrated* v125 no12 p23 O 10 2016

Shark Tank J. Caman color *New York Times Magazine* p24 O 1 2017

Shark Tank's Toothless Deals E. CANAL, J. KAUFLIN et al color graph *Forbes* v198 no7 p24 N 29 2016

SHARK TANK'S WACKIEST MONEYMAKERS L. Rice color *Entertainment Weekly* no1439 p51 N 11 2016

Sharkasi, Nahil—Interviews

This Is My Job J. Militare bw cartoon color *Glamour* v115 no4 p146 Ap 2017

Sharks

Catching Memories D. J. Harding color *Power & Motoryacht* v34 no7 p12 Jl 2017

In a shark's eye J. HESTER color *Astronomy* v44 no12 p14 D 2016

Meet Your Shark Bestle A. SHAW color *National Geographic Kids* no472 p20 Ag 2017

Safe to Swim color *Earth Island Journal* v32 no2 p7 Summ 2017

Shark Tales G. Schanker *Oceanus* v52 no1 p32 Summ 2016

SNORKEL WITH SHARKS A. HALPERN color *Wired* v25 no10 p38 O 2017

Swimming with Sharks color *O, The Oprah Magazine* p104 Ag 2017

Technology *Oceanus* v52 no1 p19 Summ 2016

When the Hunter Became the Hunted V. LaCapra *Oceanus* v52 no1 p21 Summ 2016

Sharks—Charts, diagrams, etc.

SWIMMING WITH SHARKS C. Sosenko color *Entertainment Weekly* no1476 p19 Ag 4 2017

Sharks—Social aspects

WORLD ROUNDUP J. URBANUS color map *Archaeology* v70 no3 p24 My/Je 2017

SHARLET, JEFF

Pew Research bw color il *New Republic* v248 no6 p50 Je 2017

Sharlot Hall Museum (Prescott, Ariz.)

3 Days in... Prescott, Ariz G. R. Schiavino color *American Cowboy* v23 no5 p44 F/Mr 2017

Sharma, Ajay N.

A SUMO-ubiquitin relay recruits proteasomes to chromosome axes to regulate meiotic recombination bibl graph *Science* v355 no6323 p403 Ja 27 2017

Sharma, Akash

Male sex in houseflies is determined by Mdmd, a paralog of the generic splice factor gene CWC22 bw color *Science* v356 no6338 p642 My 12 2017

Sharma, Akhil

Bad Boys: Akhil Sharma's story collection is a cultural exposé and a lacerating critique of a certain type of male ego A. TOMINE *New York Times Book Review* p15 Ag 20 2017

THE NIGHT SHIFT cartoon *New Yorker* v93 no16 p80 Je 5 2017

You Are Happy? cartoon color *New Yorker* v93 no9 p58 Ap 17 2017

Sharma, Amit

How Predictive AI Will Change Shopping *Harvard Business Review Digital Articles* p2 N 18 2016

How Retail Can Thrive in a World Without Stores *Harvard Business Review Digital Articles* p2 Jl 21 2017

Online Retailers Should Care More About the Post-Purchase Experience *Harvard Business Review Digital Articles* p2 My 24 2016

Prediction and explanation in social systems bibl diag graph *Science* v355 no6324 p486 F 3 2017

Sharma, Charu

Why Leadership Training Fails—and What to Do About It: Interaction *Harvard Business Review* v94 no12 p19 D 2016

Sharma, Chris, 1981-

Find Calm amid the Chaos cartoon *Men's Health* v32 no1 p125 Ja/F 2017

UNSOLICITED BETA P. Sodano, S. Scarpa et al color *Climbing* no349 p8 N 2016

SHARMA, JADE

Breaking the Mold: A tale of Indian-Americans balancing community and selves *New York Times Book Review* p30 My 14 2017

Sharma, Kunal

Prison Break M. Roffman *TV Guide* v65 no13 p28 Mr 20 2017

Sharma, Mahesh Chandra

CONFESSIONS OF A BEEF EATER A. KUMAR color *Nation* v305 no11 p32 O 30 2017

Sharma, Padmanee

Genetic biomarker for cancer immunotherapy diag *Science* v357 no6349 p358 Jl 28 2017

Sharma, Patrick

Robert McNamara's Other War: The World Bank and International Development R. N. Cooper *Foreign Affairs* v96 no6 p153 N/D 2017

Sharma, Ruchir

The Boom Was a Blip color *Foreign Affairs* v96 no3 p104 My/Je 2017

Sharma, Shubhendu

MEET THE MASTER OF THE LUSH (PLANT) LIFE M. McKinnon color *Rodale's Organic Life* v3 no1 p71 Ja 2017

Sharma, Vijay Shekhar

The Young and the Restless K. VINTON color *Forbes* v199 no3 p32 Mr 28 2017

Sharon, Amir

Sterilizing immunity in the lung relies on targeting fungal apoptosis-like programmed cell death color diag *Science* v357 no6355 p1037 S 8 2017

Wild emmer genome architecture and diversity elucidate wheat evolution and domestication color *Science* v357 no6346 p93 Jl 7 2017

Sharon, Keren

BLACK AND BLUE MOON color *Astronomy* v44 no12 p44 D 2016

Sharot, Tali

Emotion, the Great Manipulator S. Begley color *Time* v190 no13 p22 O 2 2017

Junk cognition N. J. Enfield color *Science* v357 no6358 p1361 S 29 2017

What Motivates Employees More: Rewards or Punishments? *Harvard Business Review Digital Articles* p2 S 26 2017

Sharp, Adrienne

The Magnificent Adrienne Sharp L. Ermelino color *Publishers Weekly* v264 no32 p22 Ag 7 2017

Sharp, Alex, 1989-

Alex Sharp D. Kiper color *Current Biography* v78 no2 p74 F 2017

Sharp, Andrew

10 Bucks color *Sports Illustrated* v125 no14 p84 O 24-31 2016

10 Mavericks color *Sports Illustrated* v125 no14 p110 O 24-31 2016

11 Bulls color *Sports Illustrated* v125 no14 p86 O 24-31 2016

11 Pelicans color *Sports Illustrated* v125 no14 p111 O 24-31 2016

12 Heat color *Sports Illustrated* v125 no14 p88 O 24-31 2016

12 Suns color *Sports Illustrated* v125 no14 p112 O 24-31 2016

13 Magic color *Sports Illustrated* v125 no14 p89 O 24-31 2016

13 Nuggets color *Sports Illustrated* v125 no14 p113 O 24-31 2016

14 76ers color *Sports Illustrated* v125 no14 p90 O 24-31 2016

14 Kings color *Sports Illustrated* v125 no14 p114 O 24-31 2016

15 Lakers color *Sports Illustrated* v125 no14 p116 O 24-31 2016

15 Nets color *Sports Illustrated* v125 no14 p92 O 24-31 2016

1 Cavaliers color *Sports Illustrated* v125 no14 p72 O 24-31 2016

1 Warriors color *Sports Illustrated* v125 no14 p96 O 24-31 2016

2 Celtics *Sports Illustrated* v125 no14 p74 O 24-31 2016

2 Spurs color *Sports Illustrated* v125 no14 p98 O 24-31 2016

3 Clippers color *Sports Illustrated* v125 no14 p99 O 24-31 2016

3 Raptors color *Sports Illustrated* v125 no14 p75 O 24-31 2016

4 Pistons color *Sports Illustrated* v125 no14 p76 O 24-31 2016

4 Trail Blazers color *Sports Illustrated* v125 no14 p100 O 24-31 2016

5 Hornets color *Sports Illustrated* v125 no14 p78 O 24-31 2016

5 Thunder color *Sports Illustrated* v125 no14 p102 O 24-31 2016

6 Hawks color *Sports Illustrated* v125 no14 p80 O 24-31 2016

6 Jazz color *Sports Illustrated* v125 no14 p103 O 24-31 2016

7 Grizzlies color *Sports Illustrated* v125 no14 p104 O 24-31 2016

7 Pacers color *Sports Illustrated* v125 no14 p81 O 24-31 2016

8 Rockets color *Sports Illustrated* v125 no14 p106 O 24-31 2016

8 Wizards color *Sports Illustrated* v125 no14 p82 O 24-31 2016

9 Knicks color *Sports Illustrated* v125 no14 p83 O 24-31 2016

9 Timberwolves color *Sports Illustrated* v125 no14 p108 O 24-31 2016

FOX ON THE RUN color *Sports Illustrated* v126 no18 p30 Je 26 2017

Scouting Reports color *Sports Illustrated* v125 no14 p70 O 24-31 2016

SCOUTING REPORTS color *Sports Illustrated* v127 no12 p54 O 16 2017

SI's Top 100 color *Sports Illustrated* v125 no14 p94 O 24-31 2016

WORDS WITH... Ricky Rubio color *Sports Illustrated* v126 no3 p20 Ja 23 2017

Sharp, Andy

Is Japan Ready To Abandon Pacifism? color *Bloomberg Businessweek* no4536 p37 S 4 2017

Where a Bad World Means Good Business color *Bloomberg Businessweek* no4533 p16 Ag 7 2017

Sharp, Buchanan

CRISIS MANAGEMENT FOR FEEDING THE POOR: England's population boomed between the 11th and 16th centuries. It became increasingly difficult to feed a hungry nation P. J. Murray *History Today* v67 no7 p92 Jl 2017

Sharp, Christine

AMERICAN PLACES *American Scholar* v86 no2 p128 Spr 2017

Sharp, Gene

How Nonviolent Resistance Can Change the World color *Progressive* v81 no4 p54 Ap/My 2017

Nonviolence, Power, and Possibility J. L. VanHise bw *Progressive* v81 no4 p51 Ap/My 2017

Sharp, Joanne P.

Driving improvements in emerging disease surveillance through locally relevant capacity strengthening color diag *Science* v357 no6347 p146 Jl 14 2017

Sharp, Nathan Y.

Research: Board Directors Are More Likely to Leave When a Firm Is Getting Criticized *Harvard Business Review Digital Articles* p2 Ag 9 2017

Sharp, Phil

Convergence: The future of health bibl color *Science* v355 no6325 p589 F 10 2017

SHARP, W. BRIAN

Google Haul Out: Earth Observation Imagery and Digital Aerial Surveys in Coastal Wildlife Management and Abundance Estimation *BioScience* v67 no8 p760 Ag 2017

Sharp Objects (TV program)

"GET ME ANOTHER HANDMAID'S TALE!" I. Biedenharn color *Entertainment Weekly* no1472 p60 Je 30 2017

Sharp-tailed grouse

wild things color *Canadian Geographic* v135 no6 p66 D 2015

Sharpe, Andrew G.

Wild emmer genome architecture and diversity elucidate wheat evolution and domestication color *Science* v357 no6346 p93 Jl 7 2017

Sharpe, Anita

The Equifax Job bw graph *Bloomberg Businessweek* no4541 p26 O 9 2017

Sharpe, Arlene H.

Rescue of exhausted CD8 T cells by PD-1–targeted therapies is CD28-dependent bw diag graph *Science* v355 no6332 p1423 Mr 31 2017

Sharpe, Cassandra

Looking Sharpe B. Warren color *New Orleans Magazine* v51 no4 p54 F 2017

Sharpe, James

MAKING AN IMPACT ON VIOLENCE C. Emsley *History To-*

v67 no5 p102 My 2017

E, PATRICIA

Apprentice *Texas Monthly* v45 no4 p40 Ap 2017

ers for Speer *Texas Monthly* v45 no6 p30 Je 2017

the Burn *Texas Monthly* v44 no12 p50 D 2016

m Far and Wide *Texas Monthly* v45 no8 p22 Ag 2017

ing Up *Texas Monthly* v45 no9 p18 S 2017

lden Age *Texas Monthly* v44 no11 p44 N 2016

ere's the Beef *Texas Monthly* v45 no2 p38 F 2017

igh Five *Texas Monthly* v45 no5 p36 My 2017

NIVES OUT *Texas Monthly* v44 no12 p90 D 2016

On Tapa His Game *Texas Monthly* v45 no1 p34 Ja 2017

Rabbit at Rest *Texas Monthly* v45 no3 p46 Mr 2017

Use Your Noodle: SAN ANTONIO'S BATTALION SERVES PRIMO ITALIAN, INCLUDING SOME OF THE BEST PASTA IN THE STATE *Texas Monthly* v45 no7 p34 Jl 2017

WHERE TO EAT TO EAT NOW 2017 *Texas Monthly* v45 no2 p98 F 2017

SHARPE, ROCHELLE

Wrong! cartoon *Prevention* v69 no7 p48 Jl 2017

Sharton, Brenda R.

Equifax and Why It's So Hard to Sue a Company for Losing Your Personal Information *Harvard Business Review Digital Articles* p2 S 22 2017

Shary, Timothy

Fade to Gray: Aging in American Cinema S. BAKERMAN *Film Quarterly* v70 no3 p96 Spr 2017

Shasta, Mount (Calif. : Mountain)

Land of Lakes D. Hanson color *Sunset* v239 no1 p66 Jl 2017

SHASTA TO THE SEA W. RITCHIE bw color *Bike Magazine* v24 no2 p66 Mr 2017

Shatner, William, 1931-

Star Trek: Discovery A. D'ARMINIO *TV Guide* v65 no41 p41 O 2 2017

Shatner, William, 1931- —Interviews

3 Questions: William shatner J. Wolf *Saturday Evening Post* v289 no5 p27 S/O 2017

William Shatner: Still Beaming After All These Years B. Newcott color *AARP: The Magazine* v59 no5A p14 Ag/S 2017

SHATWELL, JUSTIN

Curious About George *Yankee* v81 no1 p111 Ja/F 2017

TWILIGHT IN DINOSAUR LAND: In Western Massachusetts, a family business unlike any other is in the hands of its last heir—a man who dutifully digs for dinosaur tracks as he ponders the end of an era color map *Yankee* p100 Jl 2017

Shatz, Adam

FREE AT LAST color graph *Nation* v305 no4 p32 Ag 14 2017

Ghost Notes: Craig Taborn has become one of the best jazz pianists alive—by disappearing almost completely into his music *New York Times Magazine* p54 Je 25 2017

Shaub, Suzy

The Pride of Union, Maine J. Ianello color *Yankee* v80 no6 p44 N/D 2016

SHAUERS, RYAN

HOW TO MAKE ANYTHING [Cover story] color diag *Popular Mechanics* p56 S 2017

Shaughnessy, Dawn—Interviews

THE END OF THE PERIODIC TABLE? E. BETZ color *Discover* v38 no1 p32 Ja/F 2017

Shaughnessy, Maura

Not Your Average Utility Fund R. ERMEY chart *Kiplinger's Personal Finance* v71 no5 p63 My 2017

SHAUKAT, KHALID

A Shared Lunar Calendar for Muslims *Islamic Horizons* v45 no6 p59 N/D 2016

Shaun T (Author)

SHAUN T LETS NOTHING STOP HIM D. BACKSTROM color *Ebony* v72 no11 p65 S 2017

Shaver, Amanda O.

Social status alters immune regulation and response to infection in macaques bibl graph *Science* v354 no6315 p1041 N 25 2016

Shaver, Nat

WONDERFUL FLYING MACHINES C. Museler color *Sail* v48 no5 p32 My 2017

SHAVIN, NAOMI

In Search of MLK's Atlanta *Smithsonian* v47 no9 p18 Ja/F 2017

Shaving

Does a Bare Bush Increase Your Risk for STIs? D. GUERRERO color *Advocate* no1090 p42 Ap 2017

Shaving cream

BEAUTY BUYS from $6 color *Good Housekeeping* v265 no1 p16 Jl 2017

The Perfect Dopp Kit… color *Esquire* p138 BigBlackBook

Shaving cream—Evaluation

Date Ready! M. BOBO color *Ebony* v72 no4 p58 F 2017

DREAM CREAM color *Esquire* v166 no4 p68 N 2016

GQ'S 2016 Grooming Awards A. GOBLE color *GQ: Gentlemen's Quarterly* v86 no11 p130 N 2016

Shaving—Equipment & supplies

See also

Aftershave

Razors

Shaving cream

A Razor Built for Assisted Shaving A. Fitzpatrick color *Time* v190 no1 p19 Jl 3 2017

Shaving—Equipment & supplies—Evaluation

Beard Be Gone M. STEFANOV bw color *Esquire* v167 no1 p46 F 2017

SCIENCE OF SMOOTH J. Roth cartoon color *Men's Health* v32 no2 p71 Mr 2017

Shaving Razors: A Reckoning R. BERENDSOHN chart color *Popular Mechanics* p20 Mr 2017

Shaw, Allyson

CRITTER CHAT color *National Geographic Kids* no470 p31 My 2017

Critter Chat color *National Geographic Kids* no473 p37 S 2017

CRiTTER CHAT *National Geographic Kids* no467 p29 F 2017

DOG WEARS BRACES *National Geographic Kids* no468 p13 Mr 2017

Extreme Weirdness color *National Geographic Kids* no473 p7 S 2017

EXTREME WEIRDNESS *National Geographic Kids* no469 p9 Ap 2017

from AROUND the WORLD *National Geographic Kids* no467 p5 F 2017

Funny Fill-In cartoon *National Geographic Kids* no473 p34 S 2017

Funny FiLL-IN *National Geographic Kids* no469 p31 Ap 2017

Keep Earth Wild *National Geographic Kids* no468 p14 Mr 2017

Meet Your Shark Bestie color *National Geographic Kids* no472 p20 Ag 2017

Sloth Bear Rescue color *National Geographic Kids* no473 p22 S 2017

Tricks For Treats color *National Geographic Kids* no474 p12 O 2017

TURTLES GROOM WARTHOG color *National Geographic Kids* no465 p13 N 2016

UNICORNS OF THE SEA *National Geographic Kids* no467 p24 F 2017

Shaw, Bernard, 1856-1950

Humor in Uniform *Reader's Digest* v188 no1126 p134 D 2016/Ja 2017

On Great Ideas bw color *Forbes* v198 no6 p112 N 8 2016

Shaw, Cameron

Narrative Patterning *Art in America* v104 no9 p42 O 2016

Shaw, Christopher

Anchor Management O. Geden color *Issues in Science & Technology* v33 no2 p91 Wint 2017

SHAW, DAN

Perfect Harmony color *Architectural Digest* v73 no12 p112 D 2016

Shaw, Darren J.

Red squirrels in the British Isles are infected with leprosy bacilli bibl color diag map *Science* v354 no6313 p744 N 11 2016

SHAW, ELIZABETH

QUESTION: Can I be vegetarian and still gain muscle? color *Muscle & Performance* v9 no11 p38 N 2017

SHAW, ETHAN

The Griz is Good for Ya il *Backpacker* p18 S 2017

Shaw, Frankie

Singled Out K. HALE color *Vogue* v207 no11 p166 N 2017

Shaw, George

THE CHECK LIST *Texas Monthly* v45 no1 p58 Ja 2017

Shaw, Hank
Savory, Satisfying VENISON RECIPES: Learn the quirks of cooking with venison and use it in these flavorful preparations *Mother Earth News* no284 p28 O/N 2017

Shaw, Irwin
Commonplace Book *American Scholar* v86 no4 p126 Aut 2017

Shaw, Jason D.
What China's Shift to a Service Economy Means for Its Managers *Harvard Business Review Digital Articles* p2 Jl 26 2016

SHAW, JENNIFER
New Orleans High School Turbocharges Restorative Justice cartoon *Education Digest* v82 no7 p4 Mr 2017

Shaw, Jim
GENTLEMEN, AMERICA IS IN TROUBLE bw color *Art in America* v104 no10 p66 N 2016

Shaw, Jonathan—Interviews
Ink Stains K. TONNIGES bw *Publishers Weekly* v264 no5 p171 Ja 30 2017

Shaw, Joseph R.
The genomic landscape of rapid repeated evolutionary adaptation to toxic pollution in wild fish bibl graph *Science* v354 no6317 p1305 D 9 2016

Shaw, Justine D.
Biodiversity redistribution under climate change: Impacts on ecosystems and human well-being color *Science* v355 no6332 p1389 Mr 31 2017

Shaw, Lucas
After Prince's Death, His Subjects Get to Rule color *Bloomberg Businessweek* no4509 p21 Ja 30 2017
Hulu Reboots for A Post-Cable Age graph *Bloomberg Businessweek* no4502 p30 D 5 2016
THE MILLENNIAL CORD CUTTING SINGULARITY IS NIGH color *Bloomberg Businessweek* no4513 p56 Mr 6 2017
Music Festivals Have A Volume Problem color diag *Bloomberg Businessweek* no4512 p21 F 20 2017
NETFLIX PRESENTS BUILDING A WORLD OF BINGE-WATCHERS color *Bloomberg Businessweek* no4507 p40 Ja 16 2017
No One Wants to Pay $9.99 for Your Remixes color *Bloomberg Businessweek* no4506 p25 Ja 9 2017
Politics [Cover story] color graph *Bloomberg Businessweek* no4498 p60 N 7 2016
A Standalone Podcast Network, Just Maybe cartoon *Bloomberg Businessweek* no4499 p50 N 14 2016
A Star Is Born color graph *Bloomberg Businessweek* no4520 p22 My 1 2017
Two Latin Singers—and Justin Bieber—Hit No. 1 bw color *Bloomberg Businessweek* no4525 p21 Je 5 2017
Where YouTube Meets The Boob Tube graph *Bloomberg Businessweek* no4512 p44 F 20 2017

Shaw, Lynda
How to overcome a fear of public speaking *People Management* p52 O 2016

Shaw, Mary Lou
Grow Your Own Miniature Fruit Trees *Mother Earth News* no282 p89 Je/Jl 2017

Shaw, Matthew
Javanese Blend color *Surfer* v58 no5 p48 S 2017
A Parallel Universe bw color *Surfer* v58 no1 p32 Ap 2017
South Florida's Toxic Summer color *Surfer* v58 no4 p42 Ag 2017
THOMAS CAMPBELL 47, FILMMAKER/PHOTOGRAPHER/ARTIST color *Surfer* v57 no13 p34 Mr 2017

Shaw, Matthew D.
Nanophotonic rare-earth quantum memory with optically controlled retrieval diag graph *Science* v357 no6358 p1392 S 29 2017

Shaw, McKenzie L.
Decoupling genetics, lineages, and microenvironment in IDH-mutant gliomas by single-cell RNA-seq diag *Science* v355 no6332 p1391 Mr 31 2017

Shaw, Michael
End note color *Columbia Journalism Review* p112 Fall/Wint 2016

Shaw, Nina
Nina Shaw M. WAKIM *Los Angeles Magazine* v62 no9 p99 S 2017

Shaw, Robert
A Man for All Seasons At 50 P. TONGUETTE bw *National Review* v68 no21 p45 N 21 2016

Shaw, Tamsin
Invisible Manipulators of Your Mind color *New York Review of Books* v64 no7 p62 Ap 20 2017

Shaw, William
The Birdwatcher bw *Publishers Weekly* v264 no14 p52 Ap 3, 2017

Shawcross, Conrad
Conrad Shawcross J. Tarmy *Bloomberg Businessweek* no4530 p68 Jl 17 2017

Shawcross, Teresa
Q: Who Is the Worst Leader of All Time? color *Atlantic* v319 no1 p100 Ja/F 2017

Shawkat, Alia
ALL ABOUT ALIA D. Franich color *Entertainment Weekly* no1441 p30 N 25 2016
Freckles, Lace, and Curls C. CHOCANO img *New York* v50 no6 p49 Mr 20 2017
That GIRL J. POWERS color *Vogue* v206 no11 p178 N 2016

SHAWL, NISI
Feminism Cranked Up *Ms.* v27 no1 p44 Spr 2017

Shawshank Redemption, The (Film)
A Pictorial Toast TO The Celebrated Life AND Stellar Career OF THE ACTOR Morgan Freeman D. HOCHMAN bw color *AARP: The Magazine* v60 no2A p46 F/Mr 2017

Shaw (Washington, D.C.)
HAIKAN C. Kummer *Washingtonian Magazine* v52 no3 p148 D 2016

Shay, Jerry W.
New insights into melanoma development diag *Science* v357 no6358 p1358 S 29 2017

Shaya, Alon
SIMMER ALL DAY, PARTY ALL NIGHT color *Southern Living* v52 no2 p110 F 2017

SHAYKETT, JESSICA
The Box Project: Works from the Lloyd Cotsen Collection color *American Craft* v77 no2 p16 Ap/My 2017

Shchedrin (Music)
Shchedrin: The Left-Hander W. R. Braun *Opera News* v81 no6 p50 D 2016

She Loves Me (Theatrical production)
5 — SHE LOVES ME M. Snetiker *Entertainment Weekly* no1444/1445 p118 D 16 2016

Shea, Michael R.
ADVENTURES IN SQUIRREL COUNTRY cartoon *Field & Stream* v122 no5 p59 O 2017
Custom-Shop Shooter color *Field & Stream* v122 no5 pF6 O 2017
THE SPORT OF KINGS cartoon *Field & Stream* v122 no1 p22 My 2017
YOUR Wildest DREAMS color *Field & Stream* v122 no5 p38 O 2017

Shea, Patricia
The Interstate Passport: A New Framework for Seamless Student Transfer *Change* v48 no5 p44 S/O 2016

Shea, Rachel Hartigan
ANIMAL HACKS color *National Geographic* v231 no3 p18 Mr 2017
DIGITIZED MENAGERIE color *National Geographic* v231 no5 p8 My 2017
MISSION INTO THE HEAT OF THE SUN color *National Geographic* v232 no2 p29 Ag 2017

Sheaffer, Robert
A Good Analysis of Bad UFO Information B. RADFORD *Skeptical Inquirer* v41 no4 p61 Jl/Ag 2017
'Mirage Men'-Disinformation Agents or Just a Mirage? *Skeptical Inquirer* v41 no1 p23 Ja/F 2017
MUFON Gets into the Bigfoot Business *Skeptical Inquirer* v40 no6 p25 N/D 2016
'UFO Disclosure' Fizzles Again in 2016 *Skeptical Inquirer* v41 no2 p32 Mr/Ap 2017

Shear, Michael D.
How Trump Could Change America *New York Times Upfront* v149 no7 p8 Ja 9 2017
Should They Stay or Should They Go? The debate over President Trump's crackdown on undocumented immigrants *New York*

Times Upfront v149 no13 p6 My 15 2017

Sheard, Catherine

Avian egg shape: Form, function, and evolution color diag *Science* v356 no6344 p1249 Je 23 2017

Shearer, Andrew

Thinking clearly about China's layered Indo-Pacific strategy bibl *Bulletin of the Atomic Scientists* v73 no5 p305 2017

Shearer, Christine

Chemtrails? In First Peer-Reviewed Published Survey, Atmospheric Scientists Say No K. FRAZIER *Skeptical Inquirer* v40 no6 p6 N/D 2016

Shearer, Harry, 1943-

Spinal Tap vs. Hollywood A. WALLACE bw color *GQ: Gentlemen's Quarterly* v97 no6 p72 Je 2017

Shearer, Steven—Exhibitions

Steven SHEARER M. MULLEN *Interview* v46 no9 p38 N 2016

SHEBEST, ANNIE

Q: What adventure would you love to share with your best friend? color *O, The Oprah Magazine* p12 Ja 2017

SHEBLE, LAURA A.

Synthesis Centers as Critical Research Infrastructure *BioScience* v67 no8 p750 Ag 2017

Sheboygan (Wis.)

The Good Life on $40,000 a year S. MAHONEY color map *AARP: The Magazine* v59 no6A p58 O/N 2016

Shedden, Flora

Gatherings: Recipes for Feasts Great and Small *Publishers Weekly* v264 no10 p54 Mr 6 2017

Sheds—Design & construction

Build a Backyard Retreat B. COCHRAN color *Timber Home Living* v27 no2 p8 Ap 2017

BUILDING small J. BREWSTER color *Cabin Living* p42 Mr 2017

IDEA OF THE MONTH: CATTLE HANDLING CAN BE A ONE-PERSON JOB P. Barbour color *Successful Farming* v115 no7 p68 My 2017

NOT BY THE HAIR ON MY CHINNY, CHIN, CHIN P. JONES bw color *Cycle World* v56 no10 p21 N 2017

Sheds—Interior decoration

a SHED of one's own K. WHOULEY color *Yankee* p32 My/Je 2017

Shee, Kevin

Potential role of intratumor bacteria in mediating tumor resistance to the chemotherapeutic drug gemcitabine diag *Science* v357 no6356 p1156 S 15 2017

SHEEHAN, DAVID

ROAR OF THE CROWD *Texas Monthly* v45 no7 p12 Jl 2017

Sheehan, James J.

Destined to Lead? color *Commonweal* v144 no8 p42 My 5 2017

Election 2016 [Cover story] color *Commonweal* v144 no1 p14 Ja 6 2017

Our Prisons Are a Crime bw *Commonweal* v144 no2 p25 Ja 27 2017

When Was It Better? [Cover story] bw *Commonweal* v144 no17 p22 O 20 2017

Sheehan, Joe

TREND SPOTTING chart color *Sports Illustrated* v126 no16 p44 Je 5 2017

Sheehan, Natasha

Natasha Sheehan D. KELLY *Dance Magazine* v91 no4 p22 Ap 2017

Sheehan, Paul

Kilogram-scale prexasertib monolactate monohydrate synthesis under continuous-flow CGMP conditions chart diag *Science* v356 no6343 p1144 Je 16 2017

Sheehan, William

The Schröter Effect: A Retrospective *Sky & Telescope* v133 no1 p52 Ja 2017

SHEEHY, GAIL

AGE BEFORE BEAUTY color *Harper's Bazaar* no3652 p155 Ap 2017

EDITOR'S LETTER G. Bailey color *Harper's Bazaar* no3652 p88 Ap 2017

THE LIONESS IN WINTER bw color *Mother Jones* v42 no3 p34 My/Je 2017

Sheen, Martin, 1940-

Martin Sheen color *Entertainment Weekly* no1438 p34 N 4 2016

Sheen, Ray

Why I Challenged My Kids to Start Companies Before College *Harvard Business Review Digital Articles* p2 Ja 22 2016

Sheep

See also

Lambs

COMING AROUND THE MOUNTAIN E. S. ARNARSDÓTTIR color *Iceland Review* v54 no5 p82 S-O 2016

The First Flock *Reader's Digest* v189 no1127 p22 F 2017

Sheep in art

Herd Mentality H. MARTIN bw color *Architectural Digest* v74 no3 p26 Mr 2017

Sheep ranches

BUILDING A DREAM P. SYKES color *Vogue* v206 no11 p228 N 2016

Sheep ranches—Management

GREENER PASTURES J. Seaton color *O, The Oprah Magazine* p28 O 2017

Sheep reproduction

Bighorn Sheep color *Nebraska Life* v21 no4 p66 Jl/Ag 2017

Sheep-shearing

Weird but true! J. BEER and M. HARRIS *National Geographic Kids* no468 p4 Mr 2017

Sheepfolds

COMING AROUND THE MOUNTAIN E. S. ARNARSDÓTTIR color *Iceland Review* v54 no5 p82 S-O 2016

Sheeran, Ed, 1991-

Ed Sheeran J. ZAMBRANO color *O, The Oprah Magazine* p25 Jl 2017

A Global Hit Machine Scores Again S. Lansky color *Time* v189 no10 p53 Mr 20 2017

Hard~core Trou~bad~our color *Rolling Stone* no1283 p34 Mr 23 2017

Name Game O. B. Waxman *Time* v189 no16/17 p152 My 1-8 2017

Titans color *Time* v189 no16/17 p94 My 1-8 2017

Sheeran, Ed, 1991-—Interviews

ED SHEERAN M. Vain color *Entertainment Weekly* no1473 p54 Jl 7 2017

Sheet-metal

SHEETMETAL WITH A FLARE [Cover story] J. KOPYCINSKI color *Dirt Sports + Off-Road* v51 no1 p64 Ja 2017

Sheet music

Choir S. Manguso *New York Times Magazine* p22 O 23 2016

Sheets

MAKE YOUR BED... AMAZING S. JEAN SHELTON color *Redbook* p136 O 2017

Sheets, Hilarie M.

HIDDEN LIGHTS bw color *ARTnews* v116 no1 p60 Spr 2017

ROBERT LONGO bw *Art in America* v105 no8 p122 S 2017

Sheets, Taylor

Meet Yr Match! R. Nelson color *Glamour* v115 no5 p116 My 2017

Sheets, Tommy

Horse & Rider BEST QUOTES color *Horse & Rider* v55 no12 p39 D 2016

Sheets—Evaluation

15 WAYS TO SLEEP BETTER TONIGHT C. FORTÉ and L. SACHS color

v265 no4 p77 O 2017

Sheffi, Yossi

China's Slowdown: The First Stage of the Bullwhip Effect *Harvard Business Review Digital Articles* p2 S 9 2015

Sheffield, Cory—Interviews

A Man Among Bees color *Canadian Wildlife* v23 no1 p44 Mr/Ap 2017

SHEFFIELD, ROB

THE 50 FUNNIEST PEOPLE RIGHT NOW! color *Rolling Stone* no1287 p35 My 18 2017

THE 50 GREATEST CONCERTS OF THE LAST 50 YEARS bw color *Rolling Stone* no1286 p30 My 4 2017

The Awesome Pulp Sermon of 'Preacher' color *Rolling Stone* no1290 p25 Je 29 2017

Beatles Open 'Sgt. Pepper' Vault bw color *Rolling Stone* no1286 p16 My 4 2017

A Disco-Punk Epic for the Age of Trump color *Rolling Stone* no1295 p53 S 7 2017

Drake's Playful World Tour color *Rolling Stone* no1285 p52 Ap 20 2017

Drew Barrymore's Brilliant Zombie Return color *Rolling Stone* no1281/1282 p22 F 23 2017

Essential Elton John bw color *Rolling Stone* no1283 p52 Mr 23 2017

The First Black Lives Matter Superhero color *Rolling Stone* no1272 p29 O 20 2016

Gaga's Totally Nineties Cowgirl Blues color *Rolling Stone* no1274 p57 N 17 2016

The Genius of George Michael bw *Rolling Stone* no1280 p16 F 9 2017

How the 'Game' Changed Everything bw color *Rolling Stone* no1291/1292 p50 Jl 13 2017

Julia Louis-Dreyfus color *Rolling Stone* no1287 p20 My 18 2017

Lost Souls at the Dawn of the Crack Crisis color *Rolling Stone* no1293 p25 Ag 10 2017

Meet the Awkward Black Supergirl color *Rolling Stone* no1275 p28 D 1 2016

Nashville Rebels Try a Little Sincerity color *Rolling Stone* no1297 p53 O 5 2017

The New Rebel Queen of Pop's Badlands [Cover story] color *Rolling Stone* no1289 p55 Je 15 2017

The Nineties Rise Again color *Rolling Stone* no1293 p23 Ag 10 2017

Season of the Bitch: Bette vs. Joan color *Rolling Stone* no1284 p22 Ap 6 2017

Season of the Weird color *Rolling Stone* no1297 p21 O 5 2017

The Season's Peak [Cover story] color *Rolling Stone* no1289 p29 Je 15 2017

SINGLES OF THE YEAR color *Rolling Stone* no1276 p18 D 15 2016

Sleaze and the City color *Rolling Stone* no1297 p20 O 5 2017

TELEVISION OF THE YEAR color *Rolling Stone* no1276 p22 D 15 2016

'The Americans': From Russia With Love color *Rolling Stone* no1283 p19 Mr 23 2017

'The Defenders': Three and a Half Superheroes color *Rolling Stone* no1294 p24 Ag 24 2017

The Triumph of Aziz Ansari color *Rolling Stone* no1288 p19 Je 1 2017

A 'Twilight Zone' for the iPhone Era color *Rolling Stone* no1274 p19 N 17 2016

'Veep' in the Age of Trump color *Rolling Stone* no1285 p17 Ap 20 2017

When 'Blade Runner' Meets 'Deadwood' color *Rolling Stone* no1273 p23 N 3 2016

Sheffield, Sharon
Odysseys in Skepticism *Skeptical Inquirer* v41 no2 p65 Mr/Ap 2017

SHEFFIELD, STEPHEN
Caring for Books You Value color *Yankee* v80 no6 p28 N/D 2016
THE WAY BACK color *Yankee* v80 no6 p124 N/D 2016

SHEIFFER, BARBARA
Learning How to Live color *Powder* v46 no2 p94 O 2017

Sheikh, Knvul
COLIN DEVEY cartoon *Popular Science* p53 Ja/F 2017
The Kilogram Makeover color graph *Scientific American* v315 no3 p18 S 2016
LOOKING GLASS cartoon *Popular Science* p14 Ja/F 2017
Saving Face bw color *Scientific American* v317 no2 p12 Ag 2017

Sheikhbahaei, Shahriar
Breathing to inspire and arouse bw *Science* v355 no6332 p1370 Mr 31 2017

Sheinfux, Hanan Herzig
Observation of Anderson localization in disordered nanophotonic structures diag graph *Science* v356 no6341 p953 Je 1 2017

Sheinkin, Steve
Field Goals C. WALLACE *New York Times Book Review* p19 Ja 15 2017

Shekhar, Karthik
Single-cell RNA-seq reveals new types of human blood dendritic cells, monocytes, and progenitors color *Science* v356 no6335 p283 Ap 21 2017

Shelby, Ashley
Freezer Burn: The atmosphere at a polar research station heats up when a climate-change denier arrives A. Becker *New York Times Book Review* p15 Ag 13 2017

SHELBY, GRAHAM
A Veteran's Son Goes to VIETNAM *Reader's Digest* v188 no1125 p114 N 2016

Shelby automobile—Evaluation
RETURN OF THE KING [Cover story] P. G. Nichols color *Hot Rod* v70 no6 p26 Je 2017

Sheldon, Ben C.
Precipitation drives global variation in natural selection bibl chart diag map *Science* v355 no6328 p959 Mr 3 2017

Sheldon, Janet
SADDLE CHAT bw color graph *Horse & Rider* v56 no9 p21 S 2017

SHELDON, KEN
Blue Laws? Blame the Puritans color *Yankee* v80 no6 p24 N/D 2016

Sheldon, Myrna Perez
Darwin's American ascendancy color *Science* v355 no6323 p356 Ja 27 2017

Sheldon, Oliver
The Biases That Punish Racially Diverse Teams *Harvard Business Review Digital Articles* p2 F 22 2016

Shelf-life dating of food
Mashed Potatoes & Minced Words *Consumer Reports* v82 no11 p67 N 2017

Shelke, Kantha
Up from Macaroni P. CATTON bw *Weekly Standard* v22 no20 p33 Ja 30 2017

Shell, Karen
Q&A: Karen Shell J. KIDA *Arizona Highways* v93 no8 p9 Ag 2017

Shell, Maria
To The Editor color *American Craft* v76 no6 p10 D 2016-Ja 2017

Shell Oil Co.
What's That, Deep in the Gulf of Mexico? K. DUPZYK cartoon color *Popular Mechanics* p8 Ap 2017

SHELLABARGER, RUTHANNE
DANCE REVOLUTION *Indianapolis Monthly* p32 F 2017
MEET Rock 'n' Roll Hair Stylists *Indianapolis Monthly* v40 no4 p24 D 2016

Shellard, R. C.
Observation of a large-scale anisotropy in the arrival directions of cosmic rays above 8 × 1018 eV *Science* v357 no6357 p1266 S 22 2017

Shelley, Sandra
GO NUTS *Virginia Living* v15 no3 p9 Ap 2017
GRIN & BEAR IT color *Virginia Living* v15 no5 p76 Ag 2017
Smart Cookie *Virginia Living* v15 no3 p49 Ap 2017

Shelley, Thomas J.
THE COLONIAL BEGINNINGS OF NORTH AMERICAN CATHOLICISM: color diag *America* v216 no9 p38 Ap 24 2017
FORDHAM: A NEW YORK STORY J. T. McGreevy color *America* v216 no9 p41 Ap 24 2017

Shelley, Troy
DROP IT LIKE IT'S HOT J. Mankin color *Team Roping Journal* p76 O 2017

Shellnutt, Kate
Bearing Burdens After Obamacare *Christianity Today* v61 no4 p18 My 2017
BRINGING LIGHT TO THE TRAFFICKING FIGHT [Cover story] color graph *Christianity Today* v61 no5 p26 Je 2017
CALVARY CHAPEL GOES GLOBAL cartoon *Christianity Today* p15 Mr 2017
Defending the Faith (of Others) *Christianity Today* v61 no5 p17 Je 2017
HOW CHRISTIANS SEE MUSLIMS color *Christianity Today* v61 no5 p13 Je 2017
THE MAINLINE'S SAVING GRACE? Even in secular Canada's declining denominations, conservative theology correlates with church growth color *Christianity Today* v61 no4 p13 My 2017
Overhead Overhaul color *Christianity Today* v60 no8 p25 O 2016
Pro-Life's Reformation Ripples *Christianity Today* v61 no1 p21 Ja/F 2017

UNLOCKING CAMBODIAN CHRISTIANITY color *Christianity Today* v61 no5 p34 Je 2017

Shelton, Chris

ONE STEP BEYOND color *Hot Rod* v70 no3 p68 Mr 2017

THEN, NOW, AND FOREVER color *Hot Rod* v70 no3 p16 Mr 2017

THINKING OUTSIDE THE (Shoe) BOX bw color *Hot Rod* v70 no7 p60 Jl 2017

Shelton, Joanna Reed

Finding Jesus in Japan color *Christianity Today* v60 no10 p79 D 2016

Shelton, John M.

Control of muscle formation by the fusogenic micropeptide myomixer diag *Science* v356 no6335 p323 Ap 21 2017

SHELTON, JUDY

Hello, Central color *Weekly Standard* v22 no9 p34 N 7 2016

Shelton, Paige

Of Books and Bagpipes *Publishers Weekly* v264 no7 p51 F 13 2017

SHELTON, SARAH JEAN

The cure for a bland sofa color *Redbook* p136 Ap 2017

Early Bird Gift Guide color *Redbook* p112 N 2017

Keys to a tidy, pretty entryway color *Redbook* p132 N 2017

LITTLE TRICKS FOR A LOVELY BEDROOM color *Redbook* p130 F 2017

MAKE YOUR BED... AMAZING color *Redbook* p136 O 2017

Shelving (Furniture)

Make your closet feel twice as big! color *Redbook* p76 Ap 2017

Shelf Brackets Rehab B. D. Coleman color *Old House Journal* v45 no2 p56 Ap 2017

SUPPLY & DEMAND A. PANOS color *Better Homes & Gardens* v95 no8 p62 Ag 2017

top design QUESTIONS ANSWERED! A. LONGOBUCCO chart color *Good Housekeeping* v264 no2 p41 F 2017

Shelving (Furniture)—Evaluation

Fit for a Bath M. E. Polson color *Old House Journal* v45 no1 p76 F 2017

ULTIMATE GUIDE TO REVAMP BUYS C. RODRIGUES color *House Beautiful* p102 Ag 2017

Shelving for books

deck your walks color *Good Housekeeping* v263 no6 p35 D 2016

PEDRO ALMODÓVAR color *Vanity Fair* v58 no12 p80 D 2016

SHEN, CHENCHEN

Long-Term Studies Contribute Disproportionately to Ecology and Policy *BioScience* v67 no3 p271 Mr 2017

Shen, Huaizong

Structure of a eukaryotic voltage-gated sodium channel at near-atomic resolution diag graph *Science* v355 no6328 p924 Mr 3 2017

Shen, Kang

Optical control of cell signaling by single-chain photoswitchable kinases bibl diag *Science* v355 no6327 p836 F 24 2017

Shen, Kyle M.

Putting the squeeze on superconductivity bibl diag *Science* v355 no6321 p133 Ja 13 2017

Shen, L.

Breaking Lorentz reciprocity to overcome the time-bandwidth limit in physics and engineering bw diag graph *Science* v356 no6344 p1260 Je 23 2017

Shen, Li

Early life stress confers lifelong stress susceptibility in mice via ventral tegmental area OTX2 diag *Science* v356 no6343 p1185 Je 16 2017

Shen, Lucinda

BANKING *Fortune* v175 no7 p64 Je 1 2017

CHANGE THE WORLD !!!! color diag map *Fortune* v176 no4 p74 S 15 2017

Stock-Market Highs Pose Vexing Questions for the Soon-to-Be Retired color *Time* v190 no12 p28 S 25 2017

STOCKS THAT ARE BETTER-OFF SINGLE color *Fortune* v175 no4 p48 Mr 15 2017

WHERE BULLS ARE CHINA-SHOPPING color diag *Fortune* v176 no2 p23 Ag 1 2017

Shen, Michael

3D organization of synthetic and scrambled chromosomes diag *Science* v355 no6329 p1050 Mr 10 2017

Bug mapping and fitness testing of chemically synthesized chromosome X diag *Science* v355 no6329 p1048 Mr 10 2017

Shen, Ming-Hua

"Perfect" designer chromosome V and behavior of a ring derivative diag *Science* v355 no6329 p1046 Mr 10 2017

Shen, Patrick

Code of Silence K. O'Reilly *Sierra* v102 no3 p10 My/Je 2017

Shen, Peng-Xiang

Formation of α-chiral centers by asymmetric β-C(sp3)–H arylation, alkenylation, and alkynylation bibl diag *Science* v355 no6324 p499 F 3 2017

Shen, Rong

The complex effects of ocean acidification on the prominent N2-fixing cyanobacterium Trichodesmium graph *Science* v356 no6337 p527 My 5 2017

Shen, Yue

3D organization of synthetic and scrambled chromosomes diag *Science* v355 no6329 p1050 Mr 10 2017

Deep functional analysis of synII, a 770-kilobase synthetic yeast chromosome diag *Science* v355 no6329 p1047 Mr 10 2017

Engineering the ribosomal DNA in a megabase synthetic chromosome diag *Science* v355 no6329 p1049 Mr 10 2017

"Perfect" designer chromosome V and behavior of a ring derivative diag *Science* v355 no6329 p1046 Mr 10 2017

Shen, Z.-X.

Femtosecond electron-phonon lock-in by photoemission and x-ray free-electron laser chart diag *Science* v357 no6346 p71 Jl 7 2017

Shenandoah National Park (Va.)

6 WEIRD WINTER SITES AROUND WASHINGTON M. Blitz *Washingtonian Magazine* v52 no4 p18 Ja 2017

Walk This Way: FIVE OF SHENANDOAH NATIONAL PARK'S BEST DAY HIKES E. V. Clark *Washingtonian Magazine* v53 no1 p96 O 2017

weekend getaways: just do it A. BEAUJON *Washingtonian Magazine* v52 no11 p82 Ag 2017

Shenandoah River Valley (Va. & W. Va.)

Explore the Shenandoah *Washingtonian Magazine* v53 no1 p88 O 2017

ROAD SHOWS: FOUR SCENIC DRIVES WHERE YOU CAN TAKE IN FALL LEAVES, SAMPLE WINES, EXPLORE HISTORY, AND GET A TASTE OF THE VALLEY L. Ward *Washingtonian Magazine* v53 no1 p94 O 2017

Shenandoah River Valley (Va. & W. Va.)—History

National Treasure L. Ward *Washingtonian Magazine* v53 no1 p91 O 2017

Shendure, Jay

Comprehensive single-cell transcriptional profiling of a multicellular organism diag *Science* v357 no6352 p661 Ag 18 2017

Sheng, Ellen

The Artificial Pancreas Gets Real bw *Scientific American* v315 no5 p14 N 2016

Sheng Guo

Coordination-induced weakening of ammonia,water, and hydrazine X–H bonds in a molybdenum complex bibl diag *Science* v354 no6313 p730 N 11 2016

Sheng Yu Ku

Rb1 and Trp53 cooperate to suppress prostate cancer lineage plasticity, metastasis, and antiandrogen resistance bibl graph *Science* v355 no6320 p1 Ja 6 2017

SOX2 promotes lineage plasticity and antiandrogen resistance in TP53- and RB1-deficient prostate cancer bibl graph *Science* v355 no6320 p1 Ja 6 2017

Sheng Lau, Mei

Mutation of a nucleosome compaction region disrupts Polycomb-mediated axial patterning bibl chart diag *Science* v355 no6329 p1081 Mr 10 2017

Shengold, David

Breaking the Waves *Opera News* v81 no6 p42 D 2016

Frederica von Stade: The Complete Columbia Recital Albums *Opera News* v81 no6 p55 D 2016

Hitting the Mark *Opera News* v81 no7 p32 Ja 2017

In War and Peace *Opera News* v81 no9 p34 Mr 2017

Lebanon, NH *Opera News* v81 no5 p44 N 2016

Shengqun You

Application of MALDI-TOF mass spectrometry for identifying

clinical microorganisms bibl *Science* v354 no6319 p58 D 23 2016

SHENG YEN, MASTER

HOW TO BE FAULTLESS color *Tricycle: The Buddhist Review* v26 no2 p34 Wint 2016

Shenhav, Rom

Global mRNA polarization regulates translation efficiency in the intestinal epithelium diag *Science* v357 no6357 p1299 S 22 2017

Shenk, Jon

An Inconvenient Sequel: Truth to Power C. Nashawaty color *Entertainment Weekly* no1476 p47 Ag 4 2017

Shenk, Taylor

What My Horse Wears on His Feet cartoon *Horse & Rider* v56 no5 p80 My 2017

SHENK, TIMOTHY

Dead Center color il *New Republic* v248 no1/2 p61 Ja/F 2017

DEMOCRACY'S REVENGE color *Nation* v303 no19 p27 N 7 2016

SHENNAN-FARPÓN, YARA

An Ecoregion-Based Approach to Protecting Half the Terrestrial Realm *BioScience* v67 no6 p534 Je 2017

Shental, Noam

Potential role of intratumor bacteria in mediating tumor resistance to the chemotherapeutic drug gemcitabine diag *Science* v357 no6356 p1156 S 15 2017

Shenzhen (Guangdong Sheng, China : East)

A SINGLE MOMENT OF LIGHT J. Brown *Popular Science* p8 Ja/F 2017

Shenzhen (Guangdong Sheng, China : East)—Description & travel

LIFE MADE IN CHINA J. BROWN color *Popular Science* p36 Ja/F 2017

Shenzhen (Guangdong Sheng, China : East)—Economic conditions

LIFE MADE IN CHINA J. BROWN color *Popular Science* p36 Ja/F 2017

Shepard, Dax, 1975-

CHIPS L. Rice color *Entertainment Weekly* no1446/1447 p49 D 2016/Ja 2017

Shepard, Dax, 1975-—Interviews

HIT AND RUN J. ANDERSON-MINSHALL color *Advocate* no1090 p38 Ap 2017

Shepard, Jim

Steeled to the Storm: Jim Shepard's stories course toward crisis points, amid whipping winds and rising water C. TAYLOR *New York Times Book Review* p8 Mr 5 2017

Shepard, Karen

Kiss Me Someone *Publishers Weekly* v264 no28 p60 Jl 10 2017

Shepard, Lorrie A.

Design principles for new systems of assessment color *Phi Delta Kappan* v98 no6 p47 Mr 2017

Shepard, Matthew, 1976-1998

Johnson: Considering Matthew Shepard J. Rosenblum *Opera News* v81 no6 p51 D 2016

Shepard, Sam, 1943-2017

A MAN IN FULL J. Nolfi color *Entertainment Weekly* no1477 p14 Ag 11 2017

Masculinity and Its Perils M. HASKELL *New York Times Book Review* p9 F 26 2017

Sam Shepard: America's cowboy Jeremiah R. Weinert-Kendt color *America* v217 no5 p51 S 4 2017

Sam Shepard S. Vilkomerson color *Entertainment Weekly* no1477 p14 Ag 11 2017

TINY MAN cartoon *New Yorker* v92 no40 p66 D 5 2016

Shepard, Sara

The Amateurs color *Publishers Weekly* v263 no49 p113 D 7 2016

SHEPARD, SUSAN ELIZABETH

Beast of Burden color *Cincinnati Magazine* v50 no2 p46 N 2016

ENCYCLOPEDIA CINCINNATI bw cartoon color *Cincinnati Magazine* v51 no1 p42 O 2017

SHEPHARD, ALEX

Art of the Steal il *New Republic* v248 no10 p12 O 2017

Cage Match il *New Republic* v247 no11 p11 N 2016

The Democrats' Biggest Disaster color *New Republic* v248 no1/2 p8 Ja/F 2017

The Explorer color *New Republic* v247 no12 p9 D 2016

It Takes a Pillage color *New Republic* v248 no8/9 p12 Ag/S 2017

THE RUMBLE IN RICHMOND: THE BIGGEST DEMOCRATIC TITLE BOUT SINCE HILLARY VS. BERNIE color *New Republic* v248 no6 p18 Je 2017

Trump's Think Tank color *New Republic* v248 no3 p10 Mr 2017

Shephard, Nelson

Special Delivery F. Lidz *Smithsonian* v47 no7 p46 N 2016

Shepherd, Jean

CLASH OF THE TITANS W. T. GULLETTE, F. K. PLOUS et al cartoon *Vanity Fair* p84 Hollywood 2017 Supplement

Shepherd, Jennifer

Find Your Fit color *Dressage Today* v23 no5 p28 Ja 2017

SHEPHERD, JULIANNE ESCOBEDO

'I'm Better' *New York Times Magazine* p21 Mr 12 2017

Shepherd, Marshall—Interviews

On The Job: Marshall Shepherd K. Cutlip *Weatherwise* v70 no2 p29 Mr/Ap 2017

Shepherd, William John

Hallowed Ground Bushy Run Battlefield, Pennsylvania color *Military History* v34 no2 p76 Jl 2017

Hallowed Ground Fort Necessity National Battlefield *Military History* v33 no5 p76 Ja 2017

Hallowed Ground Monocacy Junction, Maryland color *Military History* v34 no5 p76 Ja 2018

Hallowed Ground Moores Creek National Battlefield *Military History* v33 no6 p75 Mr 2017

The Templars: The Rise and Spectacular Fall of God's Holy Warriors color *Military History* v34 no5 p74 Ja 2018

Waging War: The Clash Between Presidents and Congress, 1776 to ISIS *Military History* v33 no6 p72 Mr 2017

Shepherds

Turkey color *National Geographic* v230 no5 p7 N 2016

Shepley, Nick

DOINGS AND UNDOINGS L. ROBSON bw cartoon *New Yorker* v92 no33 p94 O 17 2016

Shepp, Archie—Interviews

ARCHIE SHEPP PROUD PIONEER [Cover story] J. EPHLAND bw color *Downbeat* v84 no5 p36 My 2017

Shepp, Jonah

Why They Hate Us color *Commonweal* v143 no18 p40 N 11 2016

Sheppard, John

THE air THAT WE BREATHE *New York State Conservationist* v72 no1 p26 Ag 2017

John Sheppard: Supporting the "TEAM" Improving our Air Quality *New York State Conservationist* v72 no1 p29 Ag 2017

Sheppard, Sam, 1923-1970—Trials, litigation, etc.

A CITY ON FIRE M. Bechtel color *Sports Illustrated* v126 no14 p86 My 15-22 2017

Sheppard, Scott S.

The Hunt for Planet X: Evidence is building that a large world lurks far beyond Pluto and the Kuiper Belt. The race to find it is on *Sky & Telescope* v134 no4 p16 O 2017

SHEPPARD, SI

Obama Wasn't No FDR *USA Today Magazine* v145 no2862 p22 Mr 2017

Sheppard, Whit

BLACK GOLD *Virginia Living* v15 no3 p27 Ap 2017

Bubbling Up: Afton's Thibaut-Janisson Winery brings sparkling wine to the forefront *Virginia Living* v15 no6 p45 O 2017

HISTORIC SPACES, MODERN FACES: New uses for rooms from bygone eras *Virginia Living* v15 no4 p83 Je 2017

SEARCH AND RESCUE: At first, it seemed clear who needed whom the most *Virginia Living* v15 no6 p25 O 2017

Why We Ride: Great bikes and the people who love them bw color *Virginia Living* v15 no5 p90 Ag 2017

SHEPPARD, WILSON

Make it Final with Vinyl *Boating World* v38 no1 p28 Ja 2017

Sher, Abby

All the Ways the World Can End *Publishers Weekly* v264 no20 p56 My 15 2017

Sher, Bartlett

THE QUINTESSENTIAL DIRECTOR FOR THE QUINTESSENTIAL PRODUCTION G. Holt *Cincinnati Magazine* v50 no8 p18 My 2017

Roméo et Juliette F. P. Driscoll *Opera News* v81 no9 p33 Mr 2017

SHER, KATHY

Singled Out: Los Angeles' misguided effort to open more single-sex public schools *Ms.* v27 no2 p10 Summ 2017

Sheraton, Mimi

A CUT AbOVə ThE RƎST [Cover story] color *Bon Appetit* p142 S 2017

There Goes the Neighborhood Restaurant: A regular's lament img *New York* v50 no9 p76 My 1 2017

Sherbin, Laura

Diversity Doesn't Stick Without Inclusion color *Harvard Business Review Digital Articles* p2 F 1 2017

When Employees Think the Boss Is Unfair, They're More Likely to Disengage and Leave *Harvard Business Review Digital Articles* p2 Ag 1 2017

Sherer, Edward C.

A multifunctional catalyst that stereoselectively assembles pro-drugs diag *Science* v356 no6336 p426 Ap 28 2017

Sherer, Lori

5 Ways to Increase Your Cross-Selling *Harvard Business Review Digital Articles* p2 N 22 2016

Gamification Can Help People Actually Use Analytics Tools *Harvard Business Review Digital Articles* p2 F 25 2015

Help Reluctant Employees Put Analytic Tools to Work *Harvard Business Review Digital Articles* p2 O 7 2014

Sherf, Elad N.

How to Get Men Involved with Gender Parity Initiatives *Harvard Business Review Digital Articles* p2 S 13 2017

Sheridan, C. F.

Demons of the Hallowed Dome: Acheron, Book 1 *Publishers Weekly* v264 no9 p66b F 27 2017

Sheridan, Nyssa

My Most Amazing 24 Hours color *Horse & Rider* v55 no12 p10 D 2016

Sheridan, Taylor, ca. 1969-

Corpse in the Snow T. MARKATOS color *Weekly Standard* v22 no48 p42 S 4 2017

The Self-Made Screenwriter: Taylor Sheridan has a two-step approach to becoming an Oscar-nominated writer. One: Read lots of bad scripts. Two: Do better D. Marchese img *New York* v50 no15 p62 Jl 24 2017

Wind River L. Greenblatt color *Entertainment Weekly* no1477 p38 Ag 11 2017

Sheridan, Wayne

Who Saved Whom? bw *Commonweal* v144 no4 p31 F 24 2017

SHERIFF, ASHUNTA

42 new ALL-STAR PRODUCTS of the year [Cover story] color *Redbook* p27 Jl/Ag 2017

Sheriffs

Sheriffs May Join President Trump's Deportation Force M. Rhodan color *Time* v189 no12 p18 Ap 3 2017

Sheriffs—Elections

She's the SHERIFF M. HARDY *Texas Monthly* v45 no1 p60 Ja 2017

Sherin, Miriam Gamoran

Teacher self-captured video color il *Phi Delta Kappan* v98 no7 p49 Ap 2017

Sherkow, Jacob S.

CRISPR, surrogate licensing, and scientific discovery bibl diag *Science* v355 no6326 p698 F 17 2017

Patent pools for CRISPR technology bibl color *Science* v355 no6331 p1274 Mr 24 2017

Sherlock (TV program)

The Must List color *Entertainment Weekly* no1446/1447 p7 D 2016/Ja 2017

Programming Highlights color *New Orleans Magazine* v51 no3 pD2 Ja 2017

Sherlock A. D'Arminio *TV Guide* p40 D 19 2016

Sherlock Shocker: Her Last Bow J. Hibberd color *Entertainment Weekly* no1448 p13 Ja 13 2017

What to Watch R. Rahman, J. Hibberd et al color *Entertainment Weekly* no1446/1447 p112 D 2016/Ja 2017

Sherman, Alex

AMATEUR HOUR T. Bird bw color *Snowboarder* v29 no2 p90 O 2016

Jack Dorsey Is Losing Control of Twitter cartoon graph *Bloomberg Businessweek* no4495 p26 O 17 2016

YOUNG MONEY color *Bloomberg Businessweek* no4511 p54 F 13 2017

Sherman, Alex—Interviews

ALEX SHERMAN B. Merrill color *Snowboarder* v29 no3 p48 N 2016

Sherman, Cindy, 1954-

Cindy Sherman *Cincinnati Magazine* v50 no12 p64 S 2017

Sherman, Don

25 CARS WORTH WAITING FOR color *Car & Driver* v62 no10 p32 Ap 2017

Evolutionary Success color *Car & Driver* v63 no1 p100 Jl 2017

THE FIX IS IN chart color graph *Car & Driver* v63 no1 p50 Jl 2017

Return Engagement color diag *Car & Driver* v62 no8 p72 F 2017

SKINNY LEGS AND ALL chart color graph *Car & Driver* v62 no6 p72 D 2016

Sherman, Elisabeth

WELCOME TO THE GOLDEN AGE OF SEX cartoon chart color *Men's Health* v32 no2 p102 Mr 2017

SHERMAN, ERIK

WILL A ROBOT TAKE YOUR JOB? *New York Times Upfront* v149 no3 p10 O 10 2016

SHERMAN, GABRIEL

34 MINUTES WITH...Jeff Zucker img *New York* p12 Ja 23 2017

FINAL DAYS img *New York* v49 no22 p28 O 31 2016

HOW MANY CHANGES DO YOU GET TO BE AN AMERICAN HERO? [Cover story] img *New York* p22 F 20 2017

OBAMA'S AMERICA img *New York* v49 no20 p12 O 3 2016

Sherman, Howard

Elusive Illusions *Stage Directions* v30 no8 p16 Ag 2017

Lighting the Story *Stage Directions* v30 no5 p20 My 2017

A Maple Leaf in the Big Apple *Stage Directions* v30 no9 p24 S 2017

A Veteran's Voice: John Meyer's Odyssey in service and on stage *Stage Directions* v30 no6 p32 Je 2017

A Warrior Chorus: Aquila Theatre, Veterans, and Our Trojan War *Stage Directions* v30 no6 p18 Je 2017

Sherman, Jane

The Interstate Passport: A New Framework for Seamless Student Transfer *Change* v48 no5 p44 S/O 2016

SHERMAN, JEREMY

Freeing Up *Psychology Today* v50 no1 p36 Ja/F 2017

Sherman, John—Interviews

Q&A: John Sherman *Arizona Highways* v93 no4 p9 Ap 2017

Sherman, Julia

Taste MAKERS L. REGENSDORF, M. HOLGATE et al color *Vogue* v207 no3 p334 Mr 2017

SHERMAN, LEONIE

Abysmal Belay *Sierra* v102 no5 p16 St/O 2017

Sherman, Maria

A Prom for My Mom color *Money* v46 no5 p80 Je 2017

Sherman, Maxwell A.

Intersection of diverse neuronal genomes and neuropsychiatric disease: The Brain Somatic Mosaicism Network color *Science* v356 no6336 p395 Ap 28 2017

Sherman, Rachel

Poor Little Rich Folks D. Bennett cartoon *Bloomberg Businessweek* no4539 p74 S 25 2017

SHERMAN, SCOTT

How Citizen Action Saved the New York Public Library color *Nation* v305 no9 p20 O 16 2017

Sherman, Wendy

North Korea: How to Stop Kim Jong Un color *Time* v189 no12 p40 Ap 3 2017

Sherman, William T. (William Tecumseh), 1820-1891

THE TRIAL OF THOMAS KNOX J. A. Haymond color *MHQ: Quarterly Journal of Military History* v29 no4 p14 Summ 2017

SHERMAN, ZANDER

Cottage Country Murder color *Walrus* v14 no9 p32 N 2017

Sherman-Palladino, Amy

Table for two P. H. Nettleton color *U.S. Catholic* v81 no12 p38 D 2016

Sherman-Palladino, Amy—Interviews

GILMORE GIRLS: ANOTHER YEAR IN THE LIFE?! S. Highfill color *Entertainment Weekly* no1457/1458 p18 Mr 17 2017

STARS HOLLOW HOMECOMING [Cover story] S. Highfill

color *Entertainment Weekly* no1441 p18 N 25 2016

Shermer, Michael

5 THINGS WE KNOW TO BE TRUE cartoon *Scientific American* v315 no5 p46 N 2016

ALTERNATIVE ARCHAEOLOGY *Scientific American* v317 no4 p9 O 2017

Apocalypse AI color *Scientific American* v316 no3 p77 Mr 2017

Are We All Racists? color *Scientific American* v317 no2 p81 Ag 2017

At the Boundary of Knowledge color *Scientific American* v315 no3 p88 S 2016

Born This Way color *Scientific American* v315 no6 p84 D 2016

Imagine No Universe color *Scientific American* v316 no2 p73 F 2017

More Than Human *American Scholar* v86 no2 p113 Spr 2017

On Witches and Terrorists color *Scientific American* v316 no5 p77 My 2017

Postmodernism vs. Science color *Scientific American* v317 no3 p90 S 2017

Romance of the Vanished Past color *Scientific American* v316 no6 p75 Je 2017

Sky Gods for Skeptics color *Scientific American* v317 no4 p88 O 2017

What Is Truth, Anyway? color *Scientific American* v316 no4 p78 Ap 2017

When Facts Backfire color *Scientific American* v316 no1 p69 Ja 2017

Who Are You? color *Scientific American* v317 no1 p73 Jl 2017

Why Gloom Trumps Glad cartoon *Scientific American* v315 no5 p77 N 2016

Sherpa Foods SPC

BREAKFAST/DRINKS/DINNER... A. JURRIES color *Backpacker* v45 no3 p106 Ap 2017

Sherraden, Margaret S.

Back to the Future: Financial Capability in Social Work Practice *Bridges (Federal Reserve Bank of St. Louis)* p10 Spr 2017

Sherrard, Laura J.

Emergence and spread of a human-transmissible multidrug-resistant nontuberculous mycobacterium bibl diag graph *Science* v354 no6313 p751 N 11 2016

Sherratt, David J.

Chromosome stitch-up? bibl color *Science* v355 no6324 p460 F 3 2017

Sherratt, Thomas N.

The biology of color color *Science* v357 no6350 p470 Ag 4 2017

SHERRILL, STEPHEN

How American Are You, Really? The Citizenship Test for Citizens color graph *GQ: Gentlemen's Quarterly* v97 no6 p62 Je 2017

Sherrill, Steven

Trading Mazes A. GURGANUS *New York Times Book Review* p18 O 2 2016

SHERRIN, DAVID

A Day in Court *Education Digest* v82 no8 p28 Ap 2017

Sherrod, Blackie, 1919-2016

The Write Stuff T. EASTLAND *Weekly Standard* v22 no6 p5 O 17 2016

Sherry, Jennifer

#BIKECRUSH color *Bicycling* v58 no7 p65 Ag 2017

GIORDANA NX-G JACKET color *Bicycling* v58 no9 p88 O 2017

"I LOVE OLD-SCHOOL STEEL BIKES." color *Bicycling* v58 no3 p78 Ap 2017

SUPER COMMUTER+ 8S color *Bicycling* v58 no8 p(Sp)16 S 2017

SHERWIN, GALEN

Singled Out: Los Angeles' misguided effort to open more single-sex public schools *Ms.* v27 no2 p10 Summ 2017

Sherwin-Williams Co.

Living Large color *House Beautiful* v159 no3 p28 Ap 2017

Sherwood, Bill

Parting Glances M. CONNOLLY color *Film Comment* v53 no1 p64 Ja/F 2017

SHERWOOD, KATE

Beans & Rice! *Nutrition Action Health Letter* v43 no10 p12 D 2016

Can't-Say-No Risotto *Nutrition Action Health Letter* v44 no3 p13

Ap 2017

Go Fish: Ripe, juicy tomatoes and fresh fish--could it get any better? Don't have heirlooms? Use cherry or campari tomatoes *Nutrition Action Health Letter* v44 no7 p13 S 2017

Learning Chinese *Nutrition Action Health Letter* v44 no5 p12 Je 2017

Low 'n Slow *Nutrition Action Health Letter* v44 no2 p12 Mr 2017

Must-Have Salads *Nutrition Action Health Letter* v44 no4 p12 My 2017

Super Supper Salads *Nutrition Action Health Letter* v44 no6 p12 Jl/Ag 2017

Veggie Nice! *Nutrition Action Health Letter* v43 no9 p11 N 2016

Veg In! *Nutrition Action Health Letter* v44 no1 p12 Ja/F 2017

Sherwood, Mark

7 TIPS FOR INDULGING THIS HOLIDAY SEASON J. SCHILDHOUSE color *Muscle & Performance* v8 no12 p28 D 2016

Sherwood, Matt, 1969-

BIG SKY BONUS color *Team Roping Journal* p14 O 2017

Sherwood, Trevor C.

Catalytic intermolecular hydroaminations of unactivated olefins with secondary alkyl amines bibl diag *Science* v355 no6326 p727 F 17 2017

SHESS, THOMAS

Staying True color *Old House Journal* v45 no7 p24 O 2017

Shetland (Scotland)

NEW VISIONS OF THE VIKINGS H. Pringle color *National Geographic* v231 no3 p30 Mr 2017

Shetterly, Margot Lee

IN THE SPOTLIGHT B. GLOSE *Virginia Living* v15 no3 p31 Ap 2017

Shetty, Reshma

Actress Reshma Shetty is busy being a mom at the moment. The baby monitor in her Manhattan *Virginia Living* v15 no4 p17 Je 2017

Shetty, Shatabhisha

Europe's nuclear woes: Mitigating the challenges of the next years bibl *Bulletin of the Atomic Scientists* v73 no4 p245 Jl 2017

Shevchenko, Christine

Unflappable M. HARSS *Dance Magazine* v91 no10 p30 O 2017

SHEVEL, OXANA

The Battle for Historical Memory in Postrevolutionary Ukraine *Current History* v115 no783 p258 O 2016

SHEVITZ, MATT

Embracing Your Current Improv Vocabulary bw color *Downbeat* v84 no5 p80 My 2017

Sheyenne National Grassland (N.D.)

Pioneer Days K. PETERSON diag *Backpacker* p22 Je 2017

Shi, Chuan

Atomic-layered Au clusters on α-MoC as catalysts for the low-temperature water-gas shift reaction chart diag graph *Science* v357 no6349 p389 Jl 28 2017

Shi, Dalin

The complex effects of ocean acidification on the prominent N2-fixing cyanobacterium Trichodesmium graph *Science* v356 no6337 p527 My 5 2017

Shi, Ting

Will Beijing Also Have A Friend at State? bw *Bloomberg Businessweek* no4504 p26 D 19 2016

Shi, X.

Rosetta's comet 67P/Churyumov-Gerasimenko sheds its dusty mantle to reveal its icy nature bibl graph *Science* v354 no6319 p1566 D 23 2016

Surface changes on comet 67P/Churyumov-Gerasimenko suggest a more active past bw graph *Science* v355 no6332 p1392 Mr 31 2017

Shi, Y. N.

Grain boundary stability governs hardening and softening in extremely fine nanograined metals bibl color graph *Science* v355 no6331 p1292 Mr 24 2017

Shi, Yuan

UBE2O remodels the proteome during terminal erythroid differentiation diag *Science* v357 no6350 p471 Ag 4 2017

Shi, Yu-Feng

A central neural circuit for itch sensation color graph *Science* v357 no6352 p695 Ag 18 2017

Shi, Zhan Michael

Hidden Suppliers Can Make or Break Your Operations *Harvard Business Review Digital Articles* p2 My 29 2015

Shi-Bing Li

Precision medicine for nasopharyngeal carcinoma bibl diag *Science* v354 no6319 p24 D 23 2016

Shi-Kuo Li

Synthetic nacre by predesigned matrix-directed mineralization bibl bw diag graph *Science* v354 no6308 p107 O 7 2016

Shi Shu

Bifurcating electron-transfer pathways in DNA photolyases determine the repair quantum yield bibl graph *Science* v354 no6309 p209 O 14 2016

Shi'ah—Relations—Sunnites

Why 'Artificiality' Fails to Explain Iraq's Woes F. HADDAD *Current History* v115 no785 p343 D 2016

Shian-Jiann Lin

THE WEATHER MASTER P. Voosen color *Science* v356 no6334 p128 Ap 14 2017

Shibata, Stephanie

ANYTIME GETAWAY *Sea Magazine* v109 no2 pPNW-1 F 2017

Big on Innovation *Sea Magazine* v108 no10 p10 O 2016

CROSSOVER CAT *Boating World* v38 no3 p8 Mr 2017

Danish Treat color *Boating World* v38 no7 p6 Jl 2017

ESCAPE TO AVALON *Sea Magazine* v108 no10 pCA-1 O 2016

Expansionism *Sea Magazine* v109 no4 p10 Ap 2017

FAMILY FISHER *Boating World* v38 no5 p8 My 2017

Fishing Platform *Boating World* v38 no6 p6 Je 2017

Frankenboat *Boating World* v38 no4 p6 Ap 2017

GATEWAY TO THE ISLANDS: CHANNEL ISLANDS HARBOR IS FAMILY AND FOODIE FRIENDLY, AND ITS LOCATION IS IDEAL FOR A TRIP TO THE OFFSHORE PARK AND SANCTUARY color map *Sea Magazine* v109 no7 pCA-1 Jl 2017

Going Dutch *Sea Magazine* v108 no10 p11 O 2016

ITALIAN COOKING *Sea Magazine* v108 no9 p10 S 2016

ITALIAN OASIS *Sea Magazine* v108 no12 pCA-1 D 2016

It's a Gusher *Sea Magazine* v108 no9 p14 S 2016

Luxury Class: The smallest entry in the yacht line provides plenty of space, performance and luxury color *Sea Magazine* v109 no6 p10 Je 2017

MEET BETSY DAVIS AND CHRISTINA COGAN *Sea Magazine* v108 no10 pPNW-1 O 2016

Middle-of-Nowhere Regatta *Sea Magazine* v108 no10 p14 O 2016

Mini-Cruise *Sea Magazine* v109 no5 p20 My 2017

MODERN THROWBACK *Sea Magazine* v108 no12 p8 D 2016

MORE THAN MEETS THE EYE *Sea Magazine* v109 no1 p10 Ja 2017

NAME THE BOAT color *Sea Magazine* v109 no8 p10 Ag 2017

NAME THE BOAT *Sea Magazine* v108 no10 p12 O 2016

NEW FROM THE ETERNAL CITY: AN ITALIAN BUILDER RECALLS GLORIES PAST FOR ITS LATEST MODEL NAME, AND GLORIES PRESENT FOR ITS DESIGN AND BUILD color *Sea Magazine* v109 no7 p6 Jl 2017

OFFSHORE AND MORE *Boating World* v38 no2 p8 F 2017

Open for Anything *Boating World* v37 no9 p8 N/D 2016

SCANDINAVIAN STYLE *Boating World* v38 no1 p6 Ja 2017

...SINCEREST FORM OF FLATTERY color *Sea Magazine* v109 no8 p8 Ag 2017

SUMMER SHOWTIME: THE PREMIER BOATING SHOW FOR THE SAN DIEGO AREA IS BACK ON FATHER'S DAY WEEKEND color *Sea Magazine* v109 no6 pCA-1 Je 2017

Sunreef Power Day Cat: Sunreef 's latest is a 60-knot, 41-foot catamaran with a penchant for dayboating *Sea Magazine* v109 no9 p10 S 2017

Superyacht Features *Sea Magazine* v108 no10 p12 O 2016

A TENDER THAT'S 'MO *Sea Magazine* v108 no8 p8 Ag 2016

THESE DIVES HAVE RAISED THE BAR *Sea Magazine* v108 no10 pCA-1 O 2016

TUBE CARE color *Boating World* v38 no7 p54 Jl 2017

WAKE UP: MONTEREY UTILIZES FORWARD DRIVE TO LAUNCH A SURFING BOAT WITH PIZZAZZ *Boating World* v38 no8 p6 S/O 2017

WAY UP THE COAST *Sea Magazine* v109 no2 pCA-1 F 2017

WEST COAST FOCUS *Sea Magazine* v108 no10 p10 O 2016

WEST COAST FOCUS *Sea Magazine* v108 no12 p12 D 2016

What's in a Name? color *Sea Magazine* v109 no8 p12 Ag 2017

WHERE IN THE WORLD? *Boating World* v38 no2 p9 F 2017

Who Named It? *Sea Magazine* v108 no8 p12 Ag 2016

YOU GOT A LOTTA VERVE *Sea Magazine* v109 no2 p6 F 2017

Shibazaki, Bunichiro

Imaging the distribution of transient viscosity after the 2016 Mw 7.1 Kumamoto earthquake map *Science* v356 no6334 p163 Ap 14 2017

Shicheng Xu

Direct and continuous strain control of catalysts with tunable battery electrode materials bibl graph *Science* v354 no6315 p1031 N 25 2016

SHIEH, MARISSA

the 10-second marathon color *Popular Science* v289 no5 p16 S/O 2017

Shoes made for running graph *Popular Science* v289 no6 p36 N/D 2017

snakes on a plane color *Popular Science* v289 no5 p84 S/O 2017

Shiekhattar, Ramin

PAF1 regulation of promoter-proximal pause release via enhancer activation color *Science* v357 no6357 p1294 S 22 2017

Shield, Andrew

FOCAL POINTS color *Surfer* v57 no13 p74 Mr 2017

Shields, Annie

How I Survived The Election color *Nation* v33 no21 p10 N 21 2016

Shields, Brenda C.

Deconstructing behavioral neuropharmacology with cellular specificity color *Science* v356 no6333 p42 Ap 7 2017

Shields, Brooke, 1965-

contributors color *InStyle* v24 no5 p26 My 2017

My Brows color *InStyle* v24 no5 p226 My 2017

Shields, David

Minding the Gaps C. MARTIN *New York Times Book Review* p25 Mr 12 2017

Shields, John

SLIPPERY SLOPE? DURKIN *Commonweal* v114 no14 p4 S 8 2017

Shields, Jon A.

Jon A. Shields and Joshua M. Dunn, Sr., Passing on the Right: Conservative Professors in the Progressive University P. Wood *Society* v54 no1 p89 F 2017

SECOND-CLASS CITIZENS B. C. S. Watson *Claremont Review of Books* v16 no4 p44 Fall 2016

Shields, Nancy

Her Healing Garden G. GRAVES color *Prevention* v69 no4 p30 Ap 2017

Shields, Patrick M.

Solving the teacher shortage color *Phi Delta Kappan* v98 no8 p8 My 2017

SHIELDS, TRISHA

Get Moving! color *Horse & Rider* v56 no11 p48 N 2017

SHIFLETT, DAVE

Lost in the Stars *Weekly Standard* v22 no4 p36 O 3 2016

Shifty Jelly Pty. Ltd.

POCKET CASTS 6.5: iOS PODCAST APP EMPHASIZES GRAPHICS AND SIMPLICITY G. FLEISHMAN color *Macworld - Digital Edition* v34 no4 p53 My 2017

Shigeki Owada

A three-dimensional movie of structural changes in bacteriorhodopsin bibl diag graph *Science* v354 no6319 p1552 D 23 2016

Shigematsu, Hideki

Structure of the complete elongation complex of RNA polymerase II with basal factors map *Science* v357 no6354 p921 S 1 2017

Shigeru Matsuoka

A three-dimensional movie of structural changes in bacteriorhodopsin bibl diag graph *Science* v354 no6319 p1552 D 23 2016

Shigeyoshi Itohara

Ventral CA1 neurons store social memory bibl graph *Science* v353 no6307 p1536 S 30 2016

Shigeyoshi Matsumura

Transient compartmentalization of RNA replicators prevents extinction due to parasites bibl chart graph *Science* v354 no6317 p1293 D 9 2016

Shih, Arthur J.

Dynamic multinuclear sites formed by mobilized copper ions in NOx selective catalytic reduction bw color diag graph *Science*

v357 no6354 p898 S 1 2017

Shih, Changming

Ephrin B1–mediated repulsion and signaling control germinal center T cell territoriality and function color *Science* v356 no6339 p716 My 19 2017

Shih, Michelle

ALL RISE color *Martha Stewart Living* p110 O 2017

FULL OF SURPRISES color *Martha Stewart Living* p86 S 2017

HOLIDAY MEAL *Martha Stewart Living* no270 p104 D 2016

HOW TO GET RID OF ANYTHING cartoon color *Martha Stewart Living* p118 Ap 2017

LIFE'S A PICNIC color *Martha Stewart Living* no275 p78 Je 2017

SHIH, VICTOR

Chinese Politics in the Xi Jinping Era: Reassessing Collective Leadership *Foreign Affairs* v96 no1 p177 Ja/F 2017

Shih, Willy C.

Breaking the Death Grip of Legacy Technologies *Harvard Business Review Digital Articles* p2 My 28 2015

Does Hardware Even Matter Anymore? *Harvard Business Review Digital Articles* p2 Je 9 2015

What You Won't Hear About Trade and Manufacturing on the Campaign Trail *Harvard Business Review Digital Articles* p2 My 2 2016

Shiitake

Fungi Fever color *Prevention* v69 no5 p12 My 2017

Grow Your Own SHIITAKE MUSHROOMS S. Tipton-Fox *Mother Earth News* no281 p24 Ap/My 2017

Shikaloff, Nina

Being Engaged at Work Is Not the Same as Being Productive *Harvard Business Review Digital Articles* p2 F 16 2017

What Great Managers Do Daily *Harvard Business Review Digital Articles* p2 D 14 2016

Shikanai, Toshiharu

Holliday junction resolvases mediate chloroplast nucleoid segregation diag *Science* v356 no6338 p631 My 12 2017

SHIKUI DONG

Bridging the Gaps between Science and Policy for the Sustainable Management of Rangeland Resources in the Developing World *BioScience* v67 no7 p656 Jl 2017

Shilatifard, Ali

PAF1 regulation of promoter-proximal pause release via enhancer activation color *Science* v357 no6357 p1294 S 22 2017

SHILIANG LIU

Bridging the Gaps between Science and Policy for the Sustainable Management of Rangeland Resources in the Developing World *BioScience* v67 no7 p656 Jl 2017

Shiller, Robert J., 1946-

THOUGHTS ON BUBBLES bw color *Forbes* v200 no1 p112 Jl 27 2017

Shiller, Robert J., 1946—Interviews

A STOCK-MARKET SKEPTIC EYES THE TRUMP BUMP color *Fortune* v175 no8 p40 Je 15 2017

SHILLING, A. GARY

MAD-AS-HELL MONEY MOVES *Forbes* v198 no8 p64 D 20 2016

Shilton, A. C.

Decode the Fish Counter color *Men's Health* v32 no2 p58 Mr 2017

HEAT color *Men's Health* v32 no4 p112 My 2017

HOW CYCLING WORKS cartoon diag *Bicycling* v58 no9 p21 O 2017

JOINT ACTION [Cover story] color *Runner's World* v51 no10 p54 N 2016

A RACE FOR EVERY PACE [Cover story] cartoon color *Runner's World* v52 no1 p97 Ja/F 2017

RACE TO THE AFTER-PARTY [Cover story] color *Runner's World* v52 no2 p86 Mr 2017

STEPHANIE CASE color *Runner's World* v52 no1 p85 Ja/F 2017

STRONG MUSCLES, HEALTHY JOINTS color *Runner's World* v51 no10 p58 N 2016

Sugar High! color *Bicycling* v58 no6 p36 Jl 2017

SWEAT TO SUCCEED cartoon *Runner's World* v51 no11 p40 D 2016

THIS IS YOUR BODY ON CYCLING cartoon color *Bicycling* v58 no1 p17 Ja/F 2017

Shiltsev, Vladimir

John Michael Julius Madey *Physics Today* v70 no1 p70 Ja 2017

Shim, Mike

What I Wear to Work J. Chen color *Bloomberg Businessweek* no4498 p91 N 7 2016

Shim, Moonsub

Double-heterojunction nanorod light-responsive LEDs for display applications bibl color graph *Science* v355 no6325 p616 F 10 2017

Shima, Seigo

Methanogenic heterodisulfide reductase (HdrABC-MvhAGD) uses two noncubane [4Fe-4S] clusters for reduction color *Science* v357 no6352 p699 Ag 18 2017

Shimamura, Shigeharu

FOOD R. GIBSON *Alternatives Journal (AJ) - Canada's Environmental Voice* v42 no2 p80 2016

Shimano Inc.

clutch move b. minnigh color *Bike Magazine* v24 no3 p54 My 2017

STEADY PULL: SHIMANO'S SLX BRAKES ARE SO GOOD, IT'S ALMOST BORING J. Weber color *Bike Magazine* v24 no7 p120 S 2017

Shimizu, Jenny

MODERN LOVE: Once a die-hard bachelor, this former supermodel's marriage is a reminder of why marriage equality is so important for our collective self-esteem DAM color *Advocate* no1091 p82 Je/Jl 2017

SHIMLAVI, HILAL

Why Muslim Governments Have Abandoned Xinjiang *Islamic Horizons* v46 no1 p56 Ja/F 2017

Shimoni, Baruch

Mega Donors' Perspectives on Philanthropy and Government Relations in Israel *Society* v54 no3 p261 Je 2017

Shimron, Yonat

More congregations become sanctuaries for immigrants under threat of deportation *Christian Century* v133 no26 p18 D 21 2016

Muslim agency joins disaster relief in the American South color *Christian Century* v134 no20 p17 S 27 2017

Religious groups rally around issues after election color *Christian Century* v133 no25 p12 D 7 2016

Shin, Kunyoo

Stromal Gli2 activity coordinates a niche signaling program for mammary epithelial stem cells color *Science* v356 no6335 p284 Ap 21 2017

SHIN, LAURA

BITCOIN'S BLUE CHIP color graph *Forbes* v198 no8 p88 D 20 2016

THE EMPEROR'S NEW COINS [Cover story] chart color diag *Forbes* v200 no1 p62 Jl 27 2017

The Fintech 50 color *Forbes* v198 no7 p90 N 29 2016

SHIN, MELISSA

CAKES, PASTRIES, PIES, COOKIES, HOT FUDGE, GALATO, BROWNIES & MORE! chart color *Chicago* v65 no11 p70 N 2016

TOP CANCER DOCTORS color *Chicago* v66 no1 p84 Ja 2017

Shin, Seong Sik

Colloidally prepared La-doped BaSnO3 electrodes for efficient, photostable perovskite solar cells graph *Science* v356 no6334 p167 Ap 14 2017

Iodide management in formamidinium-lead-halide–based perovskite layers for efficient solar cells bw diag *Science* v356 no6345 p1376 Je 30 2017

Shin, Yongdae

Liquid phase condensation in cell physiology and disease *Science* v357 no6357 p1253 S 22 2017

Shinas, Valerie Harlow

IT'S NOT THE TOOLS ...IT'S THE TEACHING color *Literacy Today (2411-7862)* v34 no3 p22 N/D 2016

Shinbrot, Troy

Interplanetary sand traps *Physics Today* v70 no8 p78 Ag 2017

Peer review as collaboration *Physics Today* v70 no10 p15 O 2017

Shindell, D.

A climate policy pathway for near- and long-term benefits color *Science* v356 no6337 p493 My 5 2017

Shindell, Matthew

Placing Outer Space An Earthly Ethnography of Other Worlds

Physics Today v70 no3 p59 Mr 2017

Shindler, Colin

ISRAEL'S INDEPENDENT INTROVERT: The assassination of Yitzhak Rabin robbed Israel of a rare politician able to make peace with the Palestinians *History Today* v67 no9 p104 S 2017

The Road Not Taken: History With a Sigh *History Today* v67 no3 p60 Mr 2017

Shine, Jacqui

The Rothko Chapel *New York Times Magazine* p26 Ag 27 2017

SHINE, RICHARD

Anesthesia and Euthanasia of Amphibians and Reptiles Used in Scientific Research: Should Hypothermia and Freezing Be Prohibited? *BioScience* v67 no1 p53 Ja 2017

SHINER, LINDA

The Lost Cadet *Smithsonian* v47 no7 p20 N 2016

Shingles (Building materials)

ASK ROY R. BERENDSOHN cartoon *Popular Mechanics* p44 My 2017

Shingles (Disease)

Shingles A Pain That Lasts I. Nath color *Maclean's* v129 no40 p64 O 10 2016

Shining, The (Film)

THE SHINING J. Hibberd color *Entertainment Weekly* no1460/1461 p44 Ap 7-17 2017

Your Ultimate Halloween Watch Guide C. Collis color *Entertainment Weekly* no1436/1437 p86 O 21 2016

Shinitzky, Meir

One Simple Trick to Reversing Memory Loss S. Wuzubia *Saturday Evening Post* v288 no6 p93 N/D 2016

One Simple Trick to Reversing Memory Loss S. Wuzubia *Saturday Evening Post* v289 no2 p99 Mr/Ap 2017

One Simple Trick to Reversing Memory Loss: World's Leading Brain Expert and Winner of the Prestigious Kennedy Award, Unveils Exciting News For the Scattered, Unfocused and Forgetful S. Wuzubia *Saturday Evening Post* v289 no4 p70 Jl/Ag 2017

Shinohara, Gabriel

Brazil's Great Leap Backward diag *Bloomberg Businessweek* no4535 p30 Ag 28 2017

Shinohara, Hidefumi

A peptide hormone required for Casparian strip diffusion barrier formation in Arabidopsis roots bibl color graph *Science* v355 no6322 p284 Ja 20 2017

Shinohara, Yoshiko

Ceiling Crasher C. SORVINO color *Forbes* v199 no2 p24 F 28 2017

She Became a Billionaire at Age 82 R. Wile color diag *Money* v46 no4 p14 My 2017

Shinola/Detroit LLC

FEEL THE SOUND S. NYGAARD color *Men's Health* v32 no2 p(Sp)13 Mr 2017

The O List color *O, The Oprah Magazine* p41 Jl 2017

Welcome to My Doghouse color *InStyle* v23 no12 p290 N 2016

WRIST WATCH K. Dupzyk color *Popular Mechanics* p76 Jl 2017

Shins, The (Performer)

JAMES MERCER'S NEW FRONTIER M. Vain color *Entertainment Weekly* no1457/1458 p92 Mr 17 2017

THE SHINS M. Vain color *Entertainment Weekly* no1446/1447 p75 D 2016/Ja 2017

The Shins' New Adventures in Alt-Pop Romance J. DOLAN color *Rolling Stone* no1283 p50 Mr 23 2017

Shintaro Yamada

A global view of meiotic double-strand break end resection bibl graph *Science* v355 no6320 p1 Ja 6 2017

Shinto shrines

mothers of pearl A. H. Graham bw color map *Conde Nast Traveler* v52 no6 p78 Je/Jl 2017

Shintomi, Keishi

Mitotic chromosome assembly despite nucleosome depletion in Xenopus egg extracts diag *Science* v356 no6344 p1284 Je 23 2017

Ship brokers

ASKABROKER color *Sea Magazine* v109 no8 p69 Ag 2017

Ship burials—Scotland

THE VIKINGS' WIDE REACH J. URBANUS color *Archaeology* v70 no3 p20 My/Je 2017

Ship captains

Crazy Times at Sea P. Nielsen *Sail* v48 no3 p4 Mr 2017

Ship handling

See also

Boats & boating

CRUISING TIPS T. Cunliffe bw color *Sail* v48 no8 p55 Ag 2017

HOW TO HOP DOWN BAJA IN NOVEMBER P. RAINS *Sea Magazine* v108 no10 p18 O 2016

THIS TOO SHALL PASS . N. GOLDBERG *Sea Magazine* v108 no10 p20 O 2016

Ship propulsion

BOAT BUILDERS BUILD BETTER BOATS Z. PROCHAZKA *Sea Magazine* v109 no2 p50 F 2017

Ship trials

Guardian Angels B. PIKE cartoon *Power & Motoryacht* v33 no1 p168 Ja 2017

Shipbuilding

Shipshape and Well-Equipped K. Kostel *Oceanus* v52 no1 p38 Summ 2016

Shipbuilding industry

Who's Driving? J. MOSER color *Power & Motoryacht* v34 no8 p24 Ag 2017

Shipbuilding industry—Economic aspects

Finally, Some Good News for Shipyards K. Park and D. Murtaugh *Bloomberg Businessweek* no4518 p23 Ap 10 2017

Shipilov, Andrew

A Better Way to Manage Corporate Alliances *Harvard Business Review Digital Articles* p2 D 2 2014

How One Company Reduced Email by 64% *Harvard Business Review Digital Articles* p2 Je 18 2015

Shiping Yao

Expert consensus on point-of-care testing *Science* v354 no6319 p15 D 23 2016

Recommendations on the management and use of POCT in medical institutions (nosocomial) *Science* v354 no6319 p13 D 23 2016

Shipka, Kiernan

digital directory color *InStyle* v24 no8 p22 Ag 2017

KIERNAN SHIPKA A. Salazar color *InStyle* v24 no5 p57 My 2017

Shipley, Jordan

Wrecked J. Russell *TV Guide* v65 no27 p28 Je 26 2017

Shipley, Julia

EMILY DICKINSON *Yankee* p27 My/Je 2017

Far Enough *Orion Magazine* v35 no3 p59 My/Je 2016

GOOD WILL HUNTING *Yankee* p27 Mr 2017

Last Call *Yankee* v81 no1 p124 Ja/F 2017

Riverine color *Orion Magazine* v36 no1 p60 Ja/F 2017

SOMETHING BORROWED, SOMETHING BLUE: A GREAT-AUNT'S LEGACY LIVES ON THROUGH A PACKET OF DELPHINIUM SEEDS *Yankee* v81 no5 p126 S/O 2017

A 'Very Impressive Rock' bw color *Yankee* p20 My/Je 2017

SHIPLEY, LISA

Tough Choices for a Pygmy Rabbit color map *Natural History* v125 no3 p9 Mr 2017

Shipman, Todd

Nothing in Moderation B. Court color *Men's Health* v32 no7 p10 S 2017

Shipment of goods

Alexa: Is There a Safer Way to Bet on the Amazon Economy? J. Waggoner diag *Money* v46 no8 p38 S 2017

Georgetown Group Celebrates 50 Years E. NAWOTKA *Publishers Weekly* v263 no39 p22 S 26 2016

SHIP SHAPE diag *Fortune* v75 no1 p15 Ja 1 2017

Shipment of goods—Charts, diagrams, etc.

PRICES *Economic Indicators* p22 O 2016

Shipnuck, Alan

A "Dear Jay" Letter color *Golf Magazine* v59 no1 p24 Ja 2017

Designated Drivers color *Golf Magazine* v59 no3 p28 Mr 2017

Dwayne Johnson ALMIGHTY BALLER [Cover story] color *Sports Illustrated* v125 no18 p28 D 5 2016

EXECUTIVE ORDERS color *Sports Illustrated* v127 no11 p18 O 9 2017

A Few of My Favorite Things color *Golf Magazine* v58 no11 p26 N 2016

Finishing Rush color *Sports Illustrated* v127 no5 p26 Ag 14 2017

SHIVELY, DAVE
  The Battle Within J. Moag color *Canoe & Kayak Magazine* v45 no1 p4 Wint 2017
  HEALING WATERS color *Canoe & Kayak Magazine* v45 no1 p46 Wint 2017
SHIVENER, RICH
  New York Comic Con 2017 Adds Library Programming color *Publishers Weekly* v264 no38 p25 S 18 2017
ShivHans Pictures (Company)
  THE SUNDANCE KID D. Walters color *Bloomberg Businessweek* no4507 p59 Ja 16 2017
Shivni, Rashmi
  Nest Quest color *Audubon* v119 no3 p46 Fall 2017
SHIXIONG CAO
  Optimal Tree Canopy Cover during Ecological Restoration: A Case Study of Possible Ecological Thresholds in Changting, China *BioScience* v67 no3 p221 Mr 2017
Shklar, Judith N., 1928-1992—Political & social views
  "The Liberalism of Fear" *Lapham's Quarterly* v10 no3 p211 Summ 2017
Shkreli, Martin, 1983-
  The Big Case: 'Pharma Bro' on Trial P. M. Barrett color *Bloomberg Businessweek* no4527 p29 Je 19 2017
  MARTIN SHKRELI IS STILL TALKING S. Kolhatkar cartoon *New Yorker* v93 no9 p23 Ap 17 2017
  PUBLIC ENEMY *Harper's Magazine* p15 S 2017
Shkriabai, Nikoloz
  Cryo-EM structures and atomic model of the HIV-1 strand transfer complex intasome bibl color *Science* v355 no6320 p1 Ja 6 2017
Shkurenko, Aleksander
  Hydrolytically stable fluorinated metal-organic frameworks for energy-efficient dehydration diag *Science* v356 no6339 p731 My 19 2017
SHLAES, AMITY
  FRANK IMMIGRATION TALK *Forbes* v198 no8 p38 D 20 2016
  HAIL THE (ED) WORK-AROUND *Forbes* v199 no4 p32 Ap 25 2017
  METLIFE TAKES THE LEAD color *Forbes* v198 no6 p42 N 8 2016
  MILLENNIALS NEED THIS (GOP) BREAK *Forbes* v199 no2 p40 F 28 2017
  REVOLUTION AT LABOR *Forbes* v199 no1 p32 Ja 24 2017
Shlesinger, Iliza, 1983-
  CHEERS & JEERS D. HOLBROOK *TV Guide* v65 no25 p80 Je 2017
  Iliza Shlesinger M. Rich color *Current Biography* v78 no4 p72 Ap 2017
Shlezinger, Neta
  Sterilizing immunity in the lung relies on targeting fungal apoptosis-like programmed cell death color diag *Science* v357 no6355 p1037 S 8 2017
Shlian, Matthew
  CHIRLITY color *Issues in Science & Technology* v33 no1 p64 Fall 2016
SHMERLER, CINDY
  The Future of Tennis *Tennis* v53 no3 p62 My/Je 2017
  Nirvana with NETS color *Tennis* v53 no2 p56 Mr/Ap 2017
  Stronger Than EVER *Tennis* v52 no6 p48 N/D 2016
  The Torch Bearer *Tennis* v52 no6 p56 N/D 2016
  Winning Pair *Tennis* v52 no6 p40 N/D 2016
SHNAYERSON, MICHAEL
  Growing Up Kennedy *New York Times Book Review* p11 N 20 2016
SHNEIDERMAN, BEN
  It's the Partnership, Stupid *Issues in Science & Technology* v33 no4 p37 Summ 2017
Shoaib, Fakhruddin
  'Afghanistan Is the Front Line' color *Time* v189 no22 p38 Je 12 2017
Shoalts, Adam
  Alone Across the Arctic S. DOYLE map *Canadian Geographic* v137 no2 p30 Mr/Ap 2017
  THE GEAR *Canadian Geographic* v136 no6 p35 D 2016
  INTO THE ROCKY MOUNTAIN WILD color *Canadian Geographic* v136 no6 p34 D 2016
Shochet, Melvyn J.
  James Watson Cronin *Physics Today* v70 no3 p72 Mr 2017

Shock absorbers
  Clovis spearpoints absorbed shock B. BOWER color *Science News* v191 no9 p8 My 13 2017
  SHOCK TREATMENT J. NEEVES color graph *Sail* v48 no9 p46 S 2017
  TRAILING-LINK LANDING GEAR R. Mark color *Flying* v144 no3 p20 Mr 2017
Shock waves
  Shock waves rocked baby universe E. CONOVER *Science News* v190 no9 p7 O 29 2016
SHOCKERS, SHELL
  TALES & TRIVIA: WHEREIN WE CONSIDER THE LOBSTER, A CREATURE AS FASCINATING AS IT IS DELICIOUS color *Yankee* p96 Jl 2017
Shockey, Kirsten K.
  FIERY FERMENTS to Preserve Your Peppers: Unlike storebought condiments, these spicy concoctions are rich with nutrients and flavor developed through the process of lacto-fermentation *Mother Earth News* no283 p22 Ag/S 2017
  Fresh, Homemade SALAD DRESSINGS *Mother Earth News* no281 p36 Ap/My 2017
  PICKLE RECIPES for the Picking: Ferment or quick-pickle your harvest with this assortment of ideas from Mother Earth News bloggers *Mother Earth News* no282 p56 Je/Jl 2017
Shockley, Evie
  Semiautomatic *Publishers Weekly* v264 no34 p86 Ag 21 2017
Shockley, James E.
  THE CONVERSATION color *Atlantic* v320 no2 p8 S 2017
Shoe design
  The Essential: Loafer M. MILRAD GOLDSTEIN color *Martha Stewart Living* p50 S 2017
  HAPPY FEET L. GOLDMAN color *Better Homes & Gardens* v95 no6 p152 Je 2017
  Outfits for Days M. Giudicelli color *Glamour* v115 no10 p70 O 2017
Shoe industry—United States
  Can Sneaker Makers Come Home Again? M. Townsend cartoon *Bloomberg Businessweek* no4510 p17 F 6 2017
  Where Buffett Failed N. Buhayar color *Bloomberg Businessweek* no4527 p41 Je 19 2017
Shoe soles—Evaluation
  A Shoe Sole That Won't Slip on Ice B. BROUDY and G. MILLIKEN color *Popular Science* v288 no6 p58 N/D 2016
Shoe stores
  Do You Know These Labels? N. Silverstein, E. Velluto et al bw color *Glamour* v115 no3 p86 Mr 2017
  THE DTLA LOOP J. HERBST *Los Angeles Magazine* v62 no6 p72 Je 2017
Shoe stores—Evaluation
  OLD TOWN, NEW VIBE: One of the area's most interesting fashion hubs these days? Try Alexandria, with its delightful mix of independent boutiques J. Barger *Washingtonian Magazine* v52 no8 p115 My 2017
  THE UPTOWN EXPERIENCE [Cover story] R. STEPHANIE BRUNO color *New Orleans Magazine* v51 no6 p58 Ap 2017
Shoelaces
  A 10-Second Shoe Hack A. L. Greco color *Glamour* v115 no7 p19 Jl 2017
Shoemaker, Camelia Lopez
  FABULOUS AT EVERY AGE CELEBRATION color *Harper's Bazaar* no3648 p206 N 2016
Shoemaker, Joe
  SPINNING WOOLLEN T. BRAND *Indianapolis Monthly* p33 F 2017
Shoemaker, John
  CLEAN LIVING: A minimalist home for a design sophisticate has maximum impact in its downtown neighborhood J. PAYTON *Indianapolis Monthly* p92 N 2017
Shoemaker, Sarah
  Mr. Rochester *Publishers Weekly* v264 no12 p51 Mr 20 2017
Shoemakers
  Swiss Precision Instrument B. BLANCHARD color *Climbing* no353 p40 My/Je 2017
Shoes
  See also

A fully programmable 100-spin coherent Ising machine with all-to-all connections bibl diag graph *Science* v354 no6312 p614 N 4 2016

Shomura, Y.

Structural basis of the redox switches in the NAD+-reducing soluble [NiFe]-hydrogenase diag *Science* v357 no6354 p928 S 1 2017

SHONE, TOM

HOLLYWOOD color *New York Times Book Review* p38 D 4 2016

The Producers: The film critic David Thomson takes on the Warner brothers, especially one irresistible showman and show-off *New York Times Book Review* p12 S 3 2017

A Shivering, Shuddering Human Being *New York Times Book Review* p18 O 30 2016

Shonin

The Great Divide color *Tricycle: The Buddhist Review* v26 no4 p80 Summ 2017

Shook, Jon

Table for Two, No Waiting S. Sifton color *New York Times Magazine* p24 F 12 2017

Shook, Teresa

Muslim Women March with the Mainstream U. ABDULLAH *Islamic Horizons* v46 no2 p45 Mr/Ap 2017

Seeing Pink C. ALLEN color *Weekly Standard* v22 no21 p8 F 6 2017

Shooter (TV program)

Call Of DUTY [Cover story] I. RATLEDGE *TV Guide* v64 no46 p14 N 7 2016

SHOOTER COVER PARTY, LOS ANGELES *TV Guide* v64 no48 p3 N 21 2016

Shooter I. Ratledge *TV Guide* p43 D 5 2016

Shooters of firearms

It's Always Men J. Filipovic *Time* v190 no15 p29 O 16 2017

Shooting (Sports)

See also

Fowling

Pistol shooting

Rifle-ranges

Target practice

BEAT THE WIND B. FITZPATRICK color *Outdoor Life* v224 no8 p28 O 2017

CENTERFIRE SHOOTOUT 2017 R. Mann and D. E. Petzal color *Field & Stream* v122 no5 p74 O 2017

CONCENTRICITY R. MANN and J. B. SNOW color *Outdoor Life* v224 no5 pR4 Je/Jl 2017

THE Perfect SHOOTER C. KEARNS color *Field & Stream* v121 no6 p67 N 2016

SHOT TIMERS R. MANN and J. B. SNOW color *Outdoor Life* v224 no5 pR10 Je/Jl 2017

SPEED & PRECISION DRILL B. M. TOWSLEY and J. B. SNOW color *Outdoor Life* v224 no5 pR1 Je/Jl 2017

Shooting (Sports)—Equipment & supplies

RANGE MASTERS A. McKEAN chart color *Outdoor Life* v224 no8 p11 O 2017

Shooting equipment

See also

Firearms

SQUEEZE PLAY J. Johnston color *Field & Stream* v121 no8 p33 F/Mr 2017

Shooting equipment—Evaluation

3-GUN KICKS J. B. SNOW color *Outdoor Life* v224 no1 pR6 D 2016/Ja 2017

BALLISTIC BELLY FLOPS B. M. TOWSLEY color *Outdoor Life* v224 no1 p87 D 2016/Ja 2017

PATROL BELT J. B. SNOW color *Outdoor Life* v224 no1 pR5 D 2016/Ja 2017

Shooting guards (Basketball)—Universities & colleges

Big SHOTS B. Hamilton, L. Winn et al color *Sports Illustrated* v126 no8 p32 Mr 20 2017

Shooting techniques

The Jump Shot P. Bourjaily color *Field & Stream* v122 no4 pF10 S 2017

The Morning After R. Jeremy color *Field & Stream* v122 no4 pF12 S 2017

POINT SHOOTING B. M. TOWSLEY color *Outdoor Life* v224 no8 pP7 O 2017

TARGET TRANSITIONS J. B. SNOW color *Outdoor Life* v224 no1 pR9 D 2016/Ja 2017

TERMINAL BALLISTICS PRIMER R. MANN color *Outdoor Life* v224 no4 pP6 My 2017

Shootings (Crime)

See also

Mass shootings

THE CHIEF C. PENDLEY *Atlanta* v57 no2 p23 Je 2017

A FORCE FOR GOOD D. Kennedy *O, The Oprah Magazine* p142 My 2017

IN CHICAGO, LET'S GET TO WORK R. EMANUEL *Vital Speeches of the Day* v82 no11 p335 N 2016

Murderous Manila: On the Night Shift J. Fenton color *New York Review of Books* v64 no2 p22 F 9 2017

MY KID PACKS HEAT J. D. TUCCILLE color *Reason* v48 no8 p10 Ja 2017

Quotes *Time* v188 no25-26 p17 D 19 2016 Double Issue

The SAINT V. THE 'THUG' R. O'brien color *Sports Illustrated* v125 no13 p48 O 17 2016

A Shooting in the Neighborhood D. SKINNER color *Weekly Standard* v22 no41 p5 Jl 3 2017

Stories color *Time* v188 no25-26 p14 D 19 2016 Double Issue

When DEVOTION Turns DEADLY J. McGovern color *Entertainment Weekly* no1457/1458 p64 Mr 17 2017

Shootings (Crime)—History—21st century

Teen Tragedy A. Fenwick and T. Keith color *Sports Illustrated* v125 no15 p26 N 7 2016

Shootings (Crime)—Prevention

BULLETS ON BOURBON A. J. JOHNSON color *New Orleans Magazine* v51 no3 p34 Ja 2017

St. Louis Episcopalians act against gun violence as homicide rate spikes D. Paulsen color *Christian Century* v134 no9 p14 Ap 26 2017

Shootings (Crime)—Social aspects

Gun Culture in Black and White D. FRENCH *National Review* v69 no3 p36 F 20 2017

Shopify (Company)

THE INVISIBLE SELLING MACHINE S. M. Baldwin color *Fortune* v175 no4 p162 Mr 15 2017

Shopkeepers (Retail)

OBSESSED WITH HUNTER-GATHERERS M. B. EYERS color *Better Homes & Gardens* v95 no9 p16 S 2017

Shoplifting—Prevention

Why Didn't I Think of That?! A. SIMMONS *Reader's Digest* v189 no1128 p88 Mr 2017

Shopping

See also

Grocery shopping

Online shopping

Product returns

$1,388 Average spending for the holidays A. Cao color *Money* v45 no11 p13 D 2016

15 MINUTES *Cincinnati Magazine* v50 no4 p45 Ja 2017

The 7 Rules of Smarter Shopping D. Hochman color *AARP: The Magazine* v60 no2A p28 F/Mr 2017

the buzz color *InStyle* v24 no9 p358 S 2017

DAVID YURMAN'S PURE FORM COLLECTION LAUNCH *Washingtonian Magazine* v52 no2 p238 N 2016

EASY CHAIR: Shopping-Mall Time Machine W. Kirn *Harper's Magazine* v335 no2005 p5 Je 2017

Good buys E. Marglin color *Yoga Journal* no295 p22 O 2017

HAPPY HOLIDAY SHOPPING C. W. DINEEN *Better Homes & Gardens* v94 no12 p154 D 2016

How More Accessible Information Is Forcing B2B Sales to Adapt A. A. Zoltners, P. K. Sinha et al *Harvard Business Review Digital Articles* p2 Ja 6 2016

Mikey MADISON *Interview* v47 no5 p70 Je/Jl 2017

NOTE FROM THE COORDINATORS. NATURAL FOODS: UPSCALE OR DOWNSCALE? MANY ROLES FOR PROMOTING VEGANISM D. Wasserman and C. Stabler *Vegetarian Journal* v35 no2 p4 2016

On the PLUS SIDE color *InStyle* v24 no9 p404 S 2017

Peak Lunching J. MURPHY color *Conde Nast Traveler* v52 no2 p42 F 2017

The Right Mix: Portland's Eastside neighborhoods offer easy living and shopping S. Beyer *Governing* v30 no10 p23 Jl 2017

Shop 'til you Drop color *American Cowboy* v23 no4 p53 D 2016/
Ja 2017

Spendthrift or Skinflint? color *AARP: The Magazine* v60 no2A
p30 F/Mr 2017

STYLE CRUSH Elizabeth Olsen S. Simon color *InStyle* v24 no11
p86 N 2017

SWEEPSTAKES *Nebraska Life* v20 no6 p13 N/D 2016

TAKE A DRIVE: FELLS POINT: Even if you love our town, it's
nice to get away. This month-new reasons to visit a historic waterfront neighborhood in Baltimore J. Sugarman *Washingtonian
Magazine* v52 no12 p106 S 2017

thrift like a pro P. PORTER color *Better Homes & Gardens* v95
no3 p38 Mr 2017

your 2015 gift list M. LILES *Parents* p107 2015

Your Foolproof Holiday Budget T. E. Holmes color *Essence* v47
no7 p69 N 2016

Shopping bags

Hey Mr. Green! Should I cut down trees for solar panels? *Sierra*
v101 no6 p12 N/D 2016

Shopping centers

See also

Shopping malls

Intel bw chart *Conde Nast Traveler* v52 no8 p119 S 2017

Shopping centers—California

FIFTY Favorites G. Kurz, B. Epstein et al *Los Angeles Magazine*
p8 Ap 2017

Shopping centers—California—Los Angeles

FAR OUT H. EATON *Los Angeles Magazine* p52 Ap 2017

Shopping centers—Evaluation

THE FORUM SHOPS AT CAESARS PALACE MARKS ITS
25TH ANNIVERSARY *Los Angeles Magazine* p80 Mr 2017

SAIGON SUPERSTORE K. RANDALL *Washingtonian Magazine* v52 no8 p28 My 2017

Shopping centers—Washington (D.C.)

TOWN CENTERS EVERYWHERE! D. Reed *Washingtonian
Magazine* v52 no2 p57 N 2016

Shopping malls

BEST BETS L. Schwartzberg and B. Doherty *New York* v49 no15
p63 Jl 25 2016

Click and Spend K. Finn color *New Orleans Magazine* v51 no8
p32 Je 2017

The Death and Life of the Shopping Mall J. Sanburn color *Time*
v190 no5 p40 Jl 31 2017

Malls A New Use For Empty Spaces H. Perlberg color *Bloomberg
Businessweek* no4521 p40 My 8 2017

No Street Cred *Atlanta* v56 no7 p62 N 2016

Q+A J. Gilbert *Cincinnati Magazine* v50 no5 p28 F 2017

Reinventing the American Mall P. Wahba color diag *Fortune* v174
no8 p148 D 15 2016

Shop 'Til You Drop: An empty shopping mall can mean lost jobs
and lower revenues--but not always F. Shafroth *Governing* v30
no8 p62 My 2017

There's More to Haya Than the Hijab: To understand hijab as an
act of worship, it is first crucial to consider other common acts
of worship and see the correlation between them S. MEHDI *Islamic Horizons* v46 no4 p38 Jl/Ag 2017

THERE'S MORE TO THE MALL THAN SHOPPING K. PITSK-
ER color *Kiplinger's Personal Finance* v70 no12 p13 D 2016

Shopping malls—Design & construction

Supermall, Superstalled S. BERFIELD, I. MARRITZ et al color
Bloomberg Businessweek no4504 p44 D 19 2016

Shopping malls—England

Something Else To Blame on Brexit J. Sidders *Bloomberg Businessweek* no4537 p28 S 11 2017

Shopping malls—Evaluation

FAR OUT H. EATON *Los Angeles Magazine* p52 Ap 2017

Play Hard at ROW DTLA L. IMMEDIATO color *Los Angeles
Magazine* v62 no7 p66 Jl 2017

Smooth Operators: From New York's East Village to The Fashion
Mall: brand-new digs for Kiehl's J. Kent-Doolan *Indianapolis
Monthly* v40 no10 p29 Je 2017

WESTSIDE STORY M. L. BIKOFF *Atlanta* v56 no7 p50 N 2016

Shopping malls—Finance

Short the Food Court R. Evans and M. Scully color *Bloomberg
Businessweek* no4515 p34 Mr 20 2017

Shopping malls—Sales & prices

Something Else To Blame on Brexit J. Sidders *Bloomberg Businessweek* no4537 p28 S 11 2017

Shopping—Computer network resources

Le Click! E. ELWICK-BATES color *Vogue* v207 no6 p62 Je 2017

Shopping—Evaluation

Rigged! Supermarket shelves for sale *Nutrition Action Health Letter* v43 no9 p8 N 2016

Shopping—Moral & ethical aspects

Going Cold Turkey J. Chatzky color *AARP: The Magazine* v59
no5A p30 Ag/S 2016

Shopping—Social aspects

Why Online Retailers Are Starting to Care About Your Feelings R.
Bolton *Harvard Business Review Digital Articles* p2 Ja 12 2015

Shopping—Software

Shopping with Apps M. ANTONOFF color *Sound & Vision* v82
no2 p24 F/Mr 2017

Shore, Amy

SLIPSTREAM color *Cycle World* v55 no11 p70 D 2016

Shore, Debby

WASHINGTONIANS OF THE YEAR L. MILK *Washingtonian
Magazine* v52 no4 p54 Ja 2017

SHORE, MARCI

The Unbreakable Broken: The tale of a Soviet housing complex
and the Bolshevik elite that suffered there *New York Times Book
Review* p10 Ag 20 2017

Shore, R. F.

Country-specific effects of neonicotinoid pesticides on honey bees
and wild bees diag map *Science* v356 no6345 p1393 Je 30 2017

Shore birds

Silent Seashores? C. Berger color *National Wildlife (World Edition)* v55 no5 p28 Ag/S 2017

Shores, Del—Interviews

A Very Sordid Return N. Serrao color *Entertainment Weekly*
no1462 p47 Ap 21 2017

Shoresh, Noam

Antibiotic tolerance facilitates the evolution of resistance bibl bw
chart diag graph *Science* v355 no6327 p826 F 24 2017

SHORROCK, TIM

Dual Freeze on Korea? *Nation* v305 no6 p4 S 11 2017

SHORT, CHRISTOPHER

Nebraska raises the steaks on ag bw color *Nebraska Life* v21 no5
p20 S/O 2017

Short, Edward

Picture Imperfect bw color *Weekly Standard* v22 no26 p37 Mr 13
2017

Short, Mark

Kenmark - Exceptional scenic images, on time shipping, and outstanding customer service *Stage Directions* v30 no3 p30 Mr
2017

SHORT, SIBYL

ALL IN A Day's Work *Reader's Digest* v189 no1128 p60 Mr 2017

Short-beaked echidna—Behavior

Mixed-up mammal mixes soil Down Under S. Milius color *Science News* v190 no11 p4 N 26 2016

Short circuits

ARKS OF THE APOCALYPSE M. WOLLAN *New York Times
Magazine* p34 Jl 16 2017

Keeping short circuits at bay with DCC L. Puckett color *Model
Railroader* v84 no6 p60 Je 2017

Short circuits—Prevention

COMBINE TLC: HOW TO SCRUTINIZE YOUR COMBINE
TO SHORT-CIRCUIT BREAKDOWNS D. MOWITZ *Successful Farming* v115 no11 p28 S 2017

Short-eared owl

SNOWBIRDS C. Hoh *New York State Conservationist* v71 no3
p2 D 2016

You're getting sleepy... color *National Wildlife (World Edition)*
v55 no6 p50 O/N 2017

Short films

Influencing the Influential color *Time* v189 no16/17 p8 My 1 8
2017

Short game (Golf)

WIN WITH YOUR WEDGES D. Denunzio color *Golf Magazine*
v58 no11 p41 N 2016

Short stature

HELP! I'm Too Short! K. Holmes color *Dance Spirit* v21 no4 p38

Ap 2017

Short story (Literary form)

F.A.Q.s A. GOODMAN cartoon *New Yorker* v93 no27 p62 S 11 2017

Funny Fill-In S. YOUNGSON cartoon *National Geographic Kids* no472 p34 Ag 2017

Short-term memory

Energy pulses reveal possible new state of memory J. Boddy *Science* v354 no6316 p1089 D 2 2016

Let's Be Less Stupid P. MARX *Reader's Digest* v189 no1128 p108 Mr 2017

The Reason Smart People Sometimes Struggle with "Aha" Moments S. G. Carmichael *Harvard Business Review Digital Articles* p2 Ag 26 2015

The Ways Your Brain Manages Overload, and How to Improve Them S. Pillay color *Harvard Business Review Digital Articles* p2 Je 7 2017

Short term planning

Aligning Your Organization with an Agile Workforce J. Younger and N. Smallwood *Harvard Business Review Digital Articles* p2 F 11 2016

Shortbread

BIG-BATCH GIFTS E. Johnson color *Sunset* v237 no6 p81 D 2016

PIPE DOWN C. SAFFITZ color *Bon Appetit* v61 no12 p165 D 2016 /Jan2017

SHORTEN, MARTYN

FALL SHOE GUIDE [Cover story] color graph *Runner's World* v52 no8 p59 S 2017

GROUND BREAKERS color *Runner's World* v52 no9 p71 O 2017

SOLID FOOTING cartoon color graph *Runner's World* v52 no3 p83 Ap 2017

Spring SHOE GUIDE cartoon chart color diag *Runner's World* v52 no2 p71 Mr 2017

TEST OF TIME color *Runner's World* v52 no4 p14 My 2017

winter SHOE GUIDE cartoon chart color diag graph *Runner's World* v51 no11 p87 D 2016

Shorter, James

Ratchet-like polypeptide translocation mechanism of the AAA+ disaggregase Hsp104 diag *Science* v357 no6348 p273 Jl 21 2017

Shorter, Wayne, 1933-

Shorter, Metheny Play it Cool at Monterey Jazz Fest D. Ouellette color *Downbeat* v83 no12 p14 D 2016

Shorter, Wayne, 1933—Interviews

The Science of Jazz N. deGrasse Tyson color *National Geographic* v231 no3 p26 Mr 2017

Shortfin mako

BOLT FROM THE BLUE G. Hodges color map *National Geographic* v232 no2 p120 Ag 2017

Short History of Zaka the Zulu, A (Short story)

A Short History of Zaka the Zulu P. Gappah cartoon color *New Yorker* v92 no30 p58 S 26 2016

SHORTHOUSE, JOSEPH D.

Barrens to Blueberries color map *Natural History* v125 no6 p34 Je 2017

Shorto, Russell

Revolution Song: A Story of American Freedom *Publishers Weekly* v264 no36 p80 S 4 2017

Up in Arms: The lessons of three very different 18th-century revolutions *New York Times Book Review* p26 My 21 2017

Shorts (Clothing)

BOTTOMS UP J. DENGATE color *Runner's World* v52 no5 p38 Je 2017

WEATHER THE WEATHER J. GALLOWAY cartoon *Runner's World* v52 no3 p40 Ap 2017

Shorts (Clothing)—Evaluation

10 new denim picks color *Seventeen* v76 no2 p42 Mr 2017

The Blueprint J. LOVE and M. BOBO color *Ebony* v72 no5 p50 Mr 2017

Fall into Festival Fashion M. CAMERAN color *New Orleans Magazine* v52 no1 p44 S 2017

Getting Started In... TRAIL RUNNING K. DUPZYK cartoon color *Popular Mechanics* v193 no7 p41 S 2016

HOW TO WEAR IT... anywhere! color *Good Housekeeping*

v265 no1 p14 Jl 2017

KHAKI, CLASS OF '17 color *Women's Health* v14 no3 p47 Ap 2017

Look Good Half Naked D. MICHEL color *Men's Health* v32 no6 p80 Ag 2017

LUCY HALE A. Salazar color *InStyle* v24 no4 p57 Ap 2017

THE MAN IN THE TIGHT GLOWING SHORTS P. MARTIN color *Popular Mechanics* p74 My 2017

MIX IT UP color *Seventeen* v76 no3 p84 My 2017

PEARL IZUMI PI DRY APPAREL M. Phillips color *Bicycling* v58 no9 p81 O 2017

a week of AWESOME OUTFITS color *Good Housekeeping* v265 no1 p26 Jl 2017

Shortsleeve, Cassie

This Woman Was So Mortified... color *Women's Health* v14 no2 p90 Mr 2017

Shortwave radio

See also

Microwaves

ICOM IC-M605 VHF J. Y. WOOD color *Power & Motoryacht* v34 no10 p54 O 2017

Shosenberg, James W.

NAPOLÉON'S EGYPTIAN RIDDLE cartoon color map *Military History* v34 no1 p22 My 2017

SHOSTAK, SETH

5 THINGS WE KNOW TO BE TRUE cartoon *Scientific American* v315 no5 p46 N 2016

Shot (Pellets)

See also

Non-toxic shot (Pellets)

LIGHT UPLAND LOADS J. HAVILAND color *Outdoor Life* v224 no7 p68 S 2017

Shotguns

See also

Beretta shotguns

THE AMERICAN SIDE-BY-SIDE T. WIELAND and J. M. TAYLOR color *Outdoor Life* v224 no5 p72 Je/Jl 2017

DOUBLE VISION P. Bourjaily color *Field & Stream* v121 no8 p34 F/Mr 2017

FIRE DRILLS J. JOHNSTON and P. BOURJAILY bw color *Field & Stream* v121 no8 p64 F/Mr 2017

Full Circles A. McKEAN and N. KREBS *Outdoor Life* v224 no5 p10 Je/Jl 2017

Mossberg Memories R. Kellogg *New York State Conservationist* v72 no2 p32 O 2017

ONE, TWO PUNCH T. KEER chart color *Outdoor Life* v224 no6 p40 Ag 2017

SHOOT FASTER, SHOOT BETTER B. FITZPATRICK color *Outdoor Life* v224 no9 p66 N 2017

TOP SHOTS J. Taylor chart color *Outdoor Life* v223 no9 p77 N 2016

Shotguns—Design & construction

BARREL LENGTH WISDOM B. FITZPATRICK color *Outdoor Life* v224 no1 p92 D 2016/Ja 2017

Shotguns—Evaluation

BERETTA 690 FIELD I J. B. SNOW chart color *Outdoor Life* v224 no7 p66 S 2017

DREAM GUNS P. Bourjaily cartoon color *Field & Stream* v122 no1 p28 My 2017

GREAT DUCK GUNS J. SPILGER color *Outdoor Life* v224 no8 p32 O 2017

HENRY .410 LEVER ACTION chart color *Outdoor Life* v224 no8 p30 O 2017

OVER, UNDER, AND IN-BETWEEN A. McKEAN color *Outdoor Life* v224 no5 p90 Je/Jl 2017

SHOTGUN SHOOTOUT 2017 [Cover story] P. Bourjaily color *Field & Stream* v122 no6 p72 N 2017

Shots Fired (TV program)

Bad Boys (and Girls) Return to Fox In Shots Fired D. D'Addario color *Time* v189 no12 p53 Ap 3 2017

Calling the Shots, Making an Impact C. Agard color *Entertainment Weekly* no1457/1458 p80 Mr 17 2017

FIRST LOOK: SHOTS FIRED L. CROSS color *Ebony* v72 no5 p26 Mr 2017

Gina Prince-Bythewood, Filmmaker E. Dockterman color *Time* v189 no10 p54 Mr 20 2017

Shots Fired M. ROUSH *TV Guide* v65 no13 p18 Mr 20 2017

ShotSpotter Inc.

Shots Fired J. Sanburn color *Time* v190 no13 p48 O 2 2017

Shotz, Jennifer

Could His Hip-Hop Save the Earth? *Scholastic Choices* v32 no6 p22 Mr 2017

Shoulda Known Better (Music)

Personal Strains of the Blues HADLEY color *Downbeat* v84 no3 p60 Mr 2017

Shoulder

See also

Shoulder joint

Get to know... Shoulderstand R. Long color *Yoga Journal* p28 2017 SpecialIssue

IN THIS SECTION color *Yoga Journal* p24 2017 Special Issue

Master class N. Rizopoulos color *Yoga Journal* p46 2017 SpecialIssue

Save your shoulders J. Crandell color *Yoga Journal* p40 2017 SpecialIssue

Shoulder exercises

BEST. EXERCISE. EVER cartoon chart color *Men's Health* v32 no5 p130 Je 2017

just 3 moves TOWEL TONE-UP E. Shannon color *Good Housekeeping* v264 no1 p102 Ja 1 2017

REAR-DELT MACHINE FLYE (AKA REVERSE PEC DECK) J. WUEBBEN cartoon *Muscle & Performance* v8 no12 p16 D 2016

Shore Up Your Shoulders J. Covert cartoon color *Men's Health* v32 no1 p26 Ja/F 2017

Work That Body L. Leicht color *Glamour* v114 no7 p138 Jl 2016

Shoulder injuries—Diagnosis

Shoulder strength *Mayo Clinic Health Letter* v35 no7 p6 Jl 2017

Shoulder injuries—Prevention

Get to know... the shoulder girdle J. Miller color *Yoga Journal* p36 2017 SpecialIssue

Shoulder strength *Mayo Clinic Health Letter* v35 no7 p6 Jl 2017

Shoulder joint

SHOULDER SAVERS J. Crandell color *Yoga Journal* p34 2017 Special Issue

Shoulder joint—Rotator cuff—Anatomy

Rotator cuff injury [Cover story] *Mayo Clinic Health Letter* v35 no3 p1 Mr 2017

Shoulder pain treatment

Don't shrug off shoulder pain *Harvard Health Letter* v42 no10 p6 Ag 2017

A healing sequence to ease neck & shoulder pain G. Kraftsow color *Yoga Journal* p25 2017 SpecialIssue

Shoulder & wrist pain color *Yoga Journal* p35 2017 SpecialIssue

Shoulder straps

FOR THE HORSE: LONG LINING PART 1 C. Reich *Arabian Horse World* v57 no10 p66 Jl 2017

Shoulder surgery

Loud And Clear A. Shipnuck color *Sports Illustrated* v126 no4 p68 Ja 30 2017

Shoulder—Anatomy

Get to know... the shoulder girdle J. Miller color *Yoga Journal* p36 2017 SpecialIssue

The shoulder girdle [Cover story] J. Miller color *Yoga Journal* no291 p56 My 2017

Shoulder—Wounds & injuries—Prevention

Lighten Their Load *Parents* v91 no9 p27 S 2016

The shoulder girdle [Cover story] J. Miller color *Yoga Journal* no291 p56 My 2017

Shoulder—Wounds & injuries—Treatment

Shore Up Your Shoulders J. Covert cartoon color *Men's Health* v32 no1 p26 Ja/F 2017

SHOUMATOFF, ALEX

MYSTERY ON THE SAVANNA [Cover story] color map *Smithsonian* v47 no10 p53 Mr 2017

Shouval, Dror S.

Anti-inflammatory effect of IL-10 mediated by metabolic reprogramming of macrophages diag *Science* v356 no6337 p513 My 5 2017

Shovels—Evaluation

HARVEST OF HEALTH T. G. HOPE cartoon color *Better Homes & Gardens* v95 no3 p136 Mr 2017

Show, Grant, 1962-

DYNASTY D. Holbrook *TV Guide* v65 no37 p34 S 4 2017

Show Don't Tell (Short story)

SHOW DON'T TELL C. SITTENFELD bw cartoon *New Yorker* v93 no16 p62 Je 5 2017

Show horses

See also

Arabian English pleasure horses

Captive Style N. Chirico color *Horse & Rider* v55 no11 p17 N 2016

The Perfect Horse at the Perfect Time A. Spiler color *Practical Horseman* v45 no7 p72 Jl 2017

Show jumpers (Horses)

Choose the Best Warmblood Jumper J. Winkel color *Practical Horseman* v44 no12 p13 D 2016

DITCH YOUR DITCH TROUBLES K. Carter color diag *Practical Horseman* v45 no11 p32 N 2017

Four Riders with Good Legs G. H. Morris color *Practical Horseman* v45 no7 p8 Jl 2017

HUNTING FOR PERFECTION [Cover story] T. Conahan color diag *Practical Horseman* v45 no11 p22 N 2017

Pony Derby Established *In Stride* v11 no6 p14 N 2016

Show jumping

7 Things to Do in JULY *Practical Horseman* v45 no7 p64 Jl 2017

CLASSIC MEETS CUTTING-EDGE [Cover story] K. F. Miller color *Practical Horseman* v45 no7 p26 Jl 2017

Emerging Jumper Rider Program Launched *In Stride* v12 no4 p8 Jl 2017

Harnessing the Power Of Observation [Cover story] T. Johnston color *Practical Horseman* v45 no7 p20 Jl 2017

OMAHA RAISES THE BAR [Cover story] N. Jaffer color *Practical Horseman* v45 no6 p22 Je 2017

RIDE YOUR HUNTER ROUND LIKE A PRO [Cover story] T. Brennan color *Practical Horseman* v45 no2 p28 F 2017

SHOW-JUMPING WARM-UP STRATEGIES THAT WORK S. Taylor color *Practical Horseman* v45 no2 p50 F 2017

Taking on the Big-Sister Role K. F. Miller color *Practical Horseman* v45 no6 p80 Je 2017

Trainers Will Have 2 Tracks & 4 Levels for Certification L. Taylor *In Stride* v12 no3 p24 My 2017

Two Good Legs; Two That Have Slipped Back G. H. Morris color *Practical Horseman* v45 no2 p10 F 2017

Winner's CIRCLE color *Practical Horseman* v45 no6 p72 Je 2017

Worth the Effort S. Oliynyk *Practical Horseman* v45 no2 p8 F 2017

Show jumping—Competitions

Longines FEI World Cup North American League News color *Practical Horseman* v45 no2 p63 F 2017

Longines FEI World Cup North American League News color *Practical Horseman* v45 no8 p66 Ag 2017

Show Me the Body (Performer)

NIGHT LIFE *New Yorker* v93 no25 p14 Ag 28 2017

Show riders

THE LAUNCH 2016 T. Bird bw color *Snowboarder* v29 no2 p74 O 2016

Show riding

See also

Show riders

Hymns of the Western Peaks: Loose Change in India D. Crosilla bw color *Snowboarder* v29 no2 p82 O 2016

John French Wins Wire-To-Wire in the WCHR Professional Finals T. Booker *In Stride* v11 no6 p22 N 2016

THE LAUNCH 2016 T. Bird bw color *Snowboarder* v29 no2 p74 O 2016

SHOWALTER, ELAINE

The Austenista *New Republic* v248 no8/9 p72 Ag/S 2017

Claims to Fame *New York Times Book Review* p16 My 28 2017

Showalter, Elaine, 1941-

The Battles Over Julia Ward Howe W. Lesser bw cartoon *New York Review of Books* v63 no18 p54 N 24 2016

Fighting Words bw color il *New Republic* v247 no11 p42 N 2016

First Lady to the World *New York Times Book Review* p12 N 20 2016

Showalter, Michael

The Big Sick C. Nashawaty color *Entertainment Weekly* no1472 p42 Je 30 2017

HAPPY CAMPERS: The funny franchise's new sequel heads into the 1990s--Big Chill style--with a bevy of fresh Camp Firewood faces worth a hearty salute I. RATLEDGE *TV Guide* v65 no31 p24 Jl 24 2017

KUMAIL NANJIANI S. Vilkomerson color *Entertainment Weekly* no1463/1464 p54 Ap/My 2017

The Little Sick J. PODHORETZ color *Weekly Standard* v22 no44 p39 Jl 31 2017

Showalter, Shirley Hershey
Somewhere near the end color *Christian Century* v133 no21 p32 O 12 2016

Shower curtains—Evaluation
CANVAS SHOWER CURTAINS E. MOODY color *Martha Stewart Living* p38 Ap 2017

Showers (Plumbing fixtures)
SLEEP TIGHT E. STEIN cartoon *Wired* v24 no12 p90 D 2016
So You Want an Outdoor Shower... img *New York* v50 no15 p48 Jl 24 2017
Take a Very Cool Shower color *Log Home Living* v34 no4 p20 My 2017

Showers (Plumbing fixtures)—Design & construction
chance OF SHOWERS J. BREWSTER color *Cabin Living* p51 S 2017

Showers (Plumbing fixtures)—Equipment & supplies
CANVAS SHOWER CURTAINS E. MOODY color *Martha Stewart Living* p38 Ap 2017

Showers (Plumbing fixtures)—Evaluation
Aging in Place M. E. Polson color *Old House Journal* v45 no7 p74 O 2017
PUNCH LIST K. SELZER *Better Homes & Gardens* v94 no11 p65 N 2016
SUPERB SOAKER color *Esquire* p27 Ag 2017
UNDER PRESSURE C. Iozzio color *Popular Science* v289 no2 p32 Mr/Ap 2017

Showers Pass (Company)
BAMBOO-MERINO HENLEY color *Bike Magazine* v24 no4 p106 Je 2017

Showroom design & construction
TNT E. Von Thurn Und Taxis, M. HOLGATE et al color *Vogue* v207 no9 p392 S 2017

Showrooms
Quiet Riot M. RUS color *Architectural Digest* v74 no2 p40 F 2017
YOU'LL LAUGH! CRY! (MAYBE BUY.) E. Griffith color *Fortune* v175 no8 p94 Je 15 2017

Showrooms—Decoration
world of Vincent Darré M. OWENS color *Architectural Digest* no11 p40 N 1 2017

Showrooms—Lighting
Rottet Studio One Lux Studio D. Sokol color diag *Architectural Record* v205 no2 p112 F 2017

Shpak, Guy
Activity-based protein profiling reveals off-target proteins of the FAAH inhibitor BIA 10-2474 chart color graph *Science* v356 no6342 p1084 Je 9 2017

Shpak, Josh
VARIED SKILLS YIELD REWARDS P. Lutz color *Downbeat* v84 no6 p100 Je 2017

Shrack, Kimberly
Words to Live By G. PALMIERI *Indianapolis Monthly* p28 F 2017

Shrank, William H.
A Case for Why Health Systems Should Partner with Pharmacies *Harvard Business Review Digital Articles* p2 O 14 2015

Shrem, Charlie, 1989-
CAN BITCOIN'S FIRST FELON HELP MAKE CRYPTOCURRENCY A TRILLION-DOLLAR MARKET? B. P. Eha color diag *Fortune* v176 no1 p78 Jl 1 2017

SHRESTHA, ANUJ
TRANSFORMATIONS cartoon *Wired* v25 no1 p3 Ja 2017

Shreve, Anita, 1946-
Out of the Ashes M. POLS *New York Times Book Review* p17 My 7 2017

Shriber, Justin
How B2B Sellers Are Offering Personalization at Scale *Harvard Business Review Digital Articles* p2 Jl 12 2017

Shrike Zhang, Yu

Advances in engineering hydrogels diag *Science* v356 no6337 p500 My 5 2017

Shrimps
Cheers for Tiers A. MASON color *Bon Appetit* v62 no7 p20 Jl 2017
EASTER FEAST C. HONG and F. BOSWELL color *Martha Stewart Living* p100 Ap 2017
SINGULAR Sensation M. Kiesel cartoon color *O, The Oprah Magazine* p131 Ap 2017

Shriner, Kin—Interviews
GENERAL HOSPITAL M. LOGAN *TV Guide* v65 no31 p42 Jl 24 2017

Shrivastava, Bhuma
Rich Returns From Poor Women Collecting Debts color *Bloomberg Businessweek* no4541 p18 O 9 2017

Shriver, Lionel
Lionel Shriver Is Out of Line: And thank God J. Foreman *Commentary* v142 no5 p31 D 2016
Lionel Shriver Is Out of Line *Commentary* v141 no10 p1 D 2016
Lionel Shriver Is Out of Line *Commentary* v142 no5 p1 D 2016
So You Want to Write a Novel D. GREEN *Weekly Standard* v22 no4 p15 O 3 2016

Shriver, Lionel—Interviews
DID THE LIBERTARIAN PARTY BLOW IT IN 2016? B. DOHERTY and M. WELCH color *Reason* v48 no9 p44 F 2017
LIONEL SHRIVER DOESN'T CARE IF YOU HATE HER SOMBRERO K. MANGU-WARD cartoon color *Reason* v48 no9 p36 F 2017

SHRIVER, MARIA
Ladies, Check Your BRAINS color *O, The Oprah Magazine* p68 Je 2017

Shriver, Maria, 1955—Interviews
The Fight for Women's Minds color *Prevention* v69 no6 p20 Je 2017
Ladies, Check Your BRAINS M. SHRIVER color *O, The Oprah Magazine* p68 Je 2017

Shriver, Mark K.
Catholic Mission A. L. GOLDMAN *New York Times Book Review* p19 N 27 2016
One Man's Pontiff N. S. RILEY *Weekly Standard* v22 no18 p38 Ja 16 2017

Shriver, Mark K. (Mark Kennedy), 1964-
On the trail of Jorge Bergoglio B. Jones *America* v216 no4 p48 F 20 2017

Shrock, Ellen
Inactivation of porcine endogenous retrovirus in pigs using CRISPR-Cas9 diag *Science* v357 no6357 p1303 S 22 2017

Shroder, Tom
Fame Is Fickle R. K. Landers color *Commonweal* v144 no13 p31 Ag 11 2017

Shrove Tuesday
The Deeper Side of Mardi Gras D. Ruth color *New Orleans Magazine* v51 no4 p32 F 2017
Libation Situation K. Massicot color *New Orleans Magazine* v51 no4 p34 F 2017
Lundi Gras E. Laborde *New Orleans Magazine* v51 no4 p14 F 2017
Mardi Gras bw *New Orleans Magazine* v51 no4 p20 F 2017
Old Men Behaving Badly R. Bragg color *Southern Living* v52 no2 p146 F 2017

Shrublands
Plant-soil feedback and the maintenance of diversity in Mediterranean-climate shrublands F. P. Teste, P. Kardol et al bibl graph *Science* v355 no6321 p1 Ja 13 2017

Shrubs
THE GRUMPY GARDENER S. Bender color *Southern Living* v52 no11 p48 N 2017

Shrum, Trisha—Interviews
Parent Power W. Becktold *Sierra* v102 no2 p59 Mr/Ap 2017

Shteamer, Hank
Essential Chuck color *Rolling Stone* no1285 p36 Ap 20 2017
The Road Heats Up bw color *Rolling Stone* no1288 p11 Je 1 2017
THINKING OUTSIDE THE BOTS *Smithsonian* v48 no3 p66 Je 2017

Shteyngart, Gary
AFTERMATH bw cartoon *New Yorker* v92 no38 p48 N 21 2016

TIME OUT cartoon *New Yorker* v93 no5 p36 Mr 20 2017

Shtulman, Andrew

Scienceblind J. B. Grace *Christian Century* v134 no19 p42 S 13 2017

Shu, Rong

Satellite-based entanglement distribution over 1200 kilometers diag graph *Science* v356 no6343 p1140 Je 16 2017

Shu-Hong Yu

Synthetic nacre by predesigned matrix-directed mineralization bibl bw diag graph *Science* v354 no6308 p107 O 7 2016

Shu Qin Jia

Quality management for precision medicine clinical applications: A consensus from the China Precision Medicine Clinical Research and Application Association bibl *Science* v354 no6319 p11 D 23 2016

Urgent need for implementation of precision medicine in gastric cancer in China bibl chart *Science* v354 no6319 p39 D 23 2016

Shu Zhang

Pathological α-synuclein transmission initiated by binding lymphocyte-activation gene 3 bibl graph *Science* v353 no6307 paah3374-1 S 30 2016

Shu Zhu

The DNA-sensing AIM2 inflammasome controls radiation-induced cell death and tissue injury bibl color graph *Science* v354 no6313 p765 N 11 2016

Shuai Chen

Realization of two-dimensional spin-orbit coupling for Bose-Einstein condensates bibl graph *Science* v354 no6308 p83 O 7 2016

Shub, Isaac

...AND NINE THEY NEED TO PROTECT *New York* v50 no7 p31 Ap 3 2017

Shubinski, Raymond

ASK ASTR0 color diag *Astronomy* v45 no3 p34 Mr 2017

Memories from a BACKYARD OBSERVER color *Astronomy* v45 no10 p62 O 2017

PLANETARY WEIGHT LOSS color *Astronomy* v45 no4 p34 Ap 2017

POINT-SIZED UNIVERSE? color *Astronomy* v45 no2 p34 F 2017

A short history of ECLIPSES bw color *Astronomy* v45 no5 p49 My 2017

STILL IN THE FAMILY color *Astronomy* v45 no1 p34 Ja 2017

Stormy skies and starry nights color graph *Astronomy* v45 no4 p52 Ap 2017

SHUCART, BRENDEN

THE EMPTY "CHOICE" ARGUMENT *Advocate* no1088 p18 D 2016/Ja 2017

ONE IN FIVE STRAIGHT MEN WATCHES GAY SEX color *Advocate* no1089 p17 F/Mr 2017

Shucheng Chen

Highly stretchable polymer semiconductor films through the nanoconfinement effect bibl graph *Science* v355 no6320 p1 Ja 6 2017

Shue, Elisabeth, 1963-

Your Serve, Elisabeth color *AARP: The Magazine* v60 no5A p11 Ag/S 2017

Shuey, Mark

HOW A SENIOR SALVAGED HIS MARTIAL ARTS CAREER — TWICE! F. Burk color *Black Belt* v55 no3 p14 Ap/My 2017

Shuffle Along (Theatrical production)

The 10 Best Shows R. Zoglin color *Time* v188 no25-26 p156 D 19 2016 Double Issue

Shuffleboard

IN STITCHES J. ROEDEL color *Louisiana Life* v37 no2 p16 N/D 2016

Shugar, Aaron

Where science meets art bibl bw color *Science* v354 no6314 p826 N 18 2016

Shuhei Tamate

A coherent Ising machine for 2000-node optimization problems bibl diag graph *Science* v354 no6312 p603 N 4 2016

A fully programmable 100-spin coherent Ising machine with all-to-all connections bibl diag graph *Science* v354 no6312 p614 N 4 2016

Shuhei Tsujimura

Overlapping memory trace indispensable for linking, but not re-

calling, individual memories bibl graph *Science* v355 no6323 p398 Ja 27 2017

Shukla, Paraag

TURNING POINT IN KARGIL color map *Military History* v34 no2 p38 Jl 2017

Shukla, Prashant

Companies Are Reimagining Business Processes with Algorithms *Harvard Business Review Digital Articles* p2 F 8 2016

How One Clothing Company Blends AI and Human Expertise *Harvard Business Review Digital Articles* p2 N 21 2016

SHUKMAN, HENRY

THE MEETING cartoon *Tricycle: The Buddhist Review* v26 no3 p78 Spr 2017

Shukui Dong

Expert consensus on point-of-care testing *Science* v354 no6319 p15 D 23 2016

Recommendations on the management and use of POCT in medical institutions (nosocomial) *Science* v354 no6319 p13 D 23 2016

Shukun Yao

Quality management for precision medicine clinical applications: A consensus from the China Precision Medicine Clinical Research and Application Association bibl *Science* v354 no6319 p11 D 23 2016

Shuldiner, Alan R.

Distribution and clinical impact of functional variants in 50,726 whole-exome sequences from the DiscovEHR study chart graph *Science* v354 no6319 paaf6814-1 D 23 2016

Genetic identification of familial hypercholesterolemia within a single U.S. health care system chart graph *Science* v354 no6319 paaf7000-1 D 23 2016

Shulenin, Sergey

A "Trojan horse" bispecific-antibody strategy for broad protection against ebolaviruses bibl graph *Science* v354 no6310 p350 O 21 2016

Shuler, Ashley

CIRCLE CITY AERODROME *Indianapolis Monthly* p21 My 2017

Time MACHINES *Indianapolis Monthly* v40 no10 p78 Je 2017

SHULEVITZ, JUDITH

Dating, Disrupted cartoon color *Atlantic* v318 no4 p52 N 2016

Is free speech under threat IN THE UNITED STATES? WE RECEIVED TWENTY-SEVEN RESPONSES. WE PUBLISH THEM HERE, IN ALPHABETICAL ORDER *Commentary* v144 no1 p13 Jl/Ag 2017

Shulman, David

Israel's Irrational Rationality bw color *New York Review of Books* v64 no11 p44 Je 22 2017

The Wonderful Allure of Tamil W. Cox color *New York Review of Books* v64 no5 p51 Mr 23 2017

SHULMAN, RICHARD H.

Presidents and Parliaments *Commentary* v142 no4 p13 N 2016

Shulman, Robin

The Syrians Next Door color *Time* v188 no20 p40 N 14 2016

Shults, Trey Edward

Ellar COLTRANE *Interview* v47 no1 p102 F 2017

IT COMES AT NIGHT C. Collis color *Entertainment Weekly* no1463/1464 p58 Ap/My 2017

Shultz, George P.

America the Fixer-Upper *Hoover Digest: Research & Opinion on Public Policy* no4 p14 Fall 2016

Book on Sakharov raises issues *Physics Today* v70 no2 p14 F 2017

Learning From Experience W. R. Mead *Foreign Affairs* v96 no2 p176 Mr/Ap 2017

A Tax with a Twist: A novel idea to distribute carbon dividends that's both fair and workable *Hoover Digest: Research & Opinion on Public Policy* no3 p73 Summ 2017

Shumpert, Iman

BACKSTORY color *GQ: Gentlemen's Quarterly* v97 no3 p168 Mr 2017

the sexiest couple on the planet C. SKIPPER bw color *GQ: Gentlemen's Quarterly* v97 no3 p130 Mr 2017

Shumway, Jeff

Bridging the Gap Between Marketing and IT *Harvard Business Review Digital Articles* p2 Mr 18 2016

Shumway, Nicole

Australia needs a wake-up call bibl color *Science* v355 no6328 p918 Mr 3 2017

Shunkov, Michael V.

Neandertal and Denisovan DNA from Pleistocene sediments bw color *Science* v356 no6338 p605 My 12 2017

Shupe, Joanna

Baron *Publishers Weekly* v263 no40 p107 O 3 2016

SHUR, RUDY

The Slippery Slope of Free Speech *Publishers Weekly* v264 no3 p64 Ja 16 2017

Shurter, Stephen

Saving the saola from extinction color *Science* v357 no6357 p1248 S 22 2017

Shurtleff, Robert

My Deluxe Dream Barn Will Have... color *Horse & Rider* v56 no4 p80 Ap 2017

Shuster, Jay

THE CREATIVE GENIUSES BEHIND "CARS" D. Hakim color *Hot Rod* v70 no8 p42 Ag 2017

Shuster, Simon

The Biggest Absence at This Year's G-20? Moral Authority color *Time* v190 no4 p12 Jl 24 2017

Dark Secrets, Dirty Bombs [Cover story] color map *Time* v189 no14 p28 Ap 17 2017

Denied Clemency, Snowden Remains Trapped In Putin's Game color *Time* v189 no3 p7 Ja 30 2017

Hacking the Voter [Cover story] color *Time* v188 no14 p30 O 10 2016

Helmut Kohl color *Time* v190 no1 p13 Jl 3 2017

How Donald Trump Jr.'s Emails Have Cranked Up the Heat on His Family [Cover story] color *Time* v190 no4 p22 Jl 24 2017

How People Power Is Splitting Europe color diag *Time* v188 no25-26 p80 D 19 2016 Double Issue

A New Kind of Star Power color *Time* v190 no2/3 p24 Jl 10-17 2017

The Next Fake-News War color *Time* v190 no10/11 p48 S 18 2017

Next Generation Leaders color *Time* v189 no9 p38 Mr 13 2017

Promised Land color *Time* v190 no14 p40 O 9 2017

Putin's Children color *Time* v189 no23 p30 Je 19 2017

Russia's Rehearsal for World War color *Time* v190 no10/11 p12 S 18 2017

Savagery In the U.K. Britain Comes Under Attack at a Turning Point color *Time* v189 no21 p34 Je 5 2017

Stanislav Petrov color *Time* v190 no13 p17 O 2 2017

TIME's Foreign Correspondents on How the World Sees the U.S. Election *Time* v188 no16/17 p34 O 24 2016

The Trouble With Russia color map *Time* v189 no7/8 p44 F 27 2017

Trump Gives the U.N. His Vision of a World Governed by Self-Interest color *Time* v190 no13 p13 O 2 2017

The Trump-Putin Reset Is Dead-but Don't Rule Out an Amicable Settlement color *Time* v189 no15 p7 Ap 24 2017

U.S.-Russia Tensions Reach Dangerous New Level color *Time* v188 no16/17 p5 O 24 2016

SHUSTER, WILLIAM D.

Ecology for the Shrinking City *BioScience* v66 no11 p965 N 1 2016

Shut Eye (TV program)

Shut Eye J. Halterman *TV Guide* v64 no40 p32 O 3 2016

SHUTE, LINDSEY

THE NEW FACE OF FAMILY FARMS *Nation* v305 no11 p16 O 30 2017

Shuteriqi, Ermira

Exploring genetic suppression interactions on a global scale diag *Science* v354 no6312 p599 N 4 2016

Shutian Zhang

Quality management for precision medicine clinical applications: A consensus from the China Precision Medicine Clinical Research and Application Association bibl *Science* v354 no6319 p11 D 23 2016

Shutter Craft (Company)

A Happy Cottage Home color *Old House Journal* v45 no4 p72 Je 2017

Shvarts, Andrew

Royal Bastards *Publishers Weekly* v264 no16 p70 Ap 17 2017

Shy, Yael

Why NYU's B-School Teaches Mindfulness *Harvard Business Review Digital Articles* p2 D 31 2015

Shyamalan, M. Night, 1970-

M. Night Shyamalan, Filmmaker E. Berman color *Time* v189 no3 p54 Ja 30 2017

A Night's Tale J. McGovern color *Entertainment Weekly* no1449 p24 Ja 20 2017

NIGHT TIME J. McGovern color *Entertainment Weekly* no1451/1452 p16 F 3-10 2017

Scared Straight J. Podhoretz color *Weekly Standard* v22 no23 p39 F 20 2017

Split L. Greenblatt color *Entertainment Weekly* no1450 p42 Ja 27 2017

Shyer, Amy E.

Emergent cellular self-organization and mechanosensation initiate follicle pattern in the avian skin color *Science* v357 no6353 p811 Ag 25 2017

Shymko, Yuliya

When Corporate Philanthropy Makes the Recipient Look Bad *Harvard Business Review Digital Articles* p2 Ag 24 2016

Shyu, Esther

Sex, Games, and the Evolution of Gender Gaps color *Oceanus* v51 no2 p110 Wint 2016

Shyu, Jen

JEN SHYU: Perpetually Compelling K. Micallef color *Downbeat* v84 no8 p53 Ag 2017

Si-Cong Ji

Realization of two-dimensional spin-orbit coupling for Bose-Einstein condensates bibl graph *Science* v354 no6308 p83 O 7 2016

Si-Ming Chen

Synthetic nacre by predesigned matrix-directed mineralization bibl bw diag graph *Science* v354 no6308 p107 O 7 2016

Siana, Mohamed Amine

Mohamed Amine Siana J. Hruska bw color *Architectural Record* v204 no12 p38 D 2016

Siba, Peter

A Neolithic expansion, but strong genetic structure, in the independent history of New Guinea diag *Science* v357 no6356 p1160 S 15 2017

Sibanda, Bancinyane L.

DNA-PKcs structure suggests an allosteric mechanism modulating DNA double-strand break repair bibl graph *Science* v355 no6324 p520 F 3 2017

Siber, Kate

Fuel your WILLPOWER [Cover story] color *Yoga Journal* no289 p56 F 2017

The Great Escape: Bill Sycalik walked away from an unfulfilling corporate job. Now he is on a quest to complete marathons in all 59 national parks *National Parks* v91 no3 p16 Summ 2017

let it GO color *Yoga Journal* p88 2017 Special Issue

The Long Way Home *National Parks* v91 no2 p32 Spr 2017

LOST BEARS: WILL GRIZZLY BEARS RETURN TO THE NORTH CASCADES? *National Parks* v91 no3 p36 Summ 2017

A Rare Tuft *National Parks* v91 no1 p26 Wint 2017

REAPPEARING ACT *National Parks* v91 no2 p20 Spr 2017

AN UNCERTAIN FUTURE *National Parks* v91 no4 p36 Fall 2017

WHERE THE WILD THINGS WERE: Denali paleontologists brave blizzards and bears to find fossils that could challenge what we know about dinosaurs *National Parks* v91 no3 p46 Summ 2017

Your greatest asset color *Yoga Journal* p80 2017 Special Issue

Siberia (Russia)

FROM RUSSIA, WITH LIES *Harper's Magazine* v334 no2002 p14 Mr 2017

Siberia (Russia)—Antiquities

SQUEEZING HISTORY FROM A TURNIP E. A. POWELL color *Archaeology* v70 no3 p15 My/Je 2017

Siberia (Russia)—Description & travel

Cold Comfort S. Roberts color *Conde Nast Traveler* v51 no11 p74 D 2016

Siberia (Russia)—Environmental conditions

Pleistocene Park R. ANDERSEN color *Atlantic* v319 no3 p74 Ap 2017

Sibert, Olin

ENVIRONMENT *New York State Conservationist* v71 no6 p27 Je 2017

Get Out There M. BRUNE *Sierra* v101 no4 p4 Jl/Ag 2016

THE PEOPLE'S POWER LIST *Sierra* v102 no3 p48 My/Je 2017

Tear Down These Walls J. Mark *Sierra* v102 no3 p4 My/Je 2017

To Change Everything, It Takes Everyone: The Sierra Club is part of a larger ecosystem of progressive change-makers M. BRUNE *Sierra* v102 no4 p6 Jl/Ag 2017

Sierra Club—History

History Lessons and Future Dreams M. BRUNE *Sierra* v102 no3 p6 My/Je 2017

SIERWALD, PETRA

Worm-snail Ships Out! bw color *Natural History* v125 no6 p10 Je 2017

Sies Marjan (Company)

Sies Marjan Shoes C. NNADI, M. HOLGATE et al color *Vogue* v207 no9 p362 S 2017

Siewert, Charles E.

Paul Frederick Zweifel *Physics Today* v70 no8 p73 Ag 2017

Siewny, Matthew G. W.

Hidden dynamics in the unfolding of individual bacteriorhodopsin proteins bibl diag *Science* v355 no6328 p945 Mr 3 2017

Siff, Ira

Marian Anderson: Let Freedom Ring *Opera News* v81 no9 p55 Mr 2017

ROBERTA PETERS *Opera News* v81 no10 p64 Ap 2017

Sifferlin, Alexandra

6 More Reasons to Get Up and Move color *Time* v190 no4 p40 Jl 24 2017

6 Surprising Things That May Improve Breast-Cancer Treatment color *Time* v190 no15 p45 O 16 2017

Are These 'Healthy' Foods Really Good for You? color *Time* v190 no10/11 p32 S 18 2017

The Best 25 Inventions of 2016 color *Time* v188 no22-23 p43 N/D 2016

Death, Disrupted color *Time* v189 no7/8 p80 F 27 2017

Dr. Cristin Kearns color *Time* v188 no27-28 p97 D 26 2016

The Drug That's Treating Everything [Cover story] color diag *Time* v189 no3 p38 Ja 16 2017

Emotional Divide color diag *Time* v189 no7/8 p38 F 27 2017

How Family Ties Keep You Going, In Sickness and In Health color *Time* v189 no5 p20 F 13 2017

How to Become a Morning Person color *Time* v189 no10 p24 Mr 20 2017

How to Eat Well-and Still Feel Full color *Time* v189 no12 p26 Ap 3 2017

The Latest Word on Fake Sugar color *Time* v190 no5 p18 Jl 31 2017

Meal Kits Won't Start a Cooking Revolution-Yet color *Time* v190 no5 p18 Jl 31 2017

Meet the Class of 2016 color *Time* v188 no18 p22 O 31 2016

New Frontiers In Medicine color *Time* v188 no27-28 p85 D 26 2016

New Ways to Become Happier—and Healthier color *Time* v190 no13 p30 O 2 2017

This Diet May Help You Lose Weight./ This Diet May Help You Lose Weight [Cover story] color *Time* v189 no21 p48 Je 5 2017

This New Surgery Could Change Pregnancy Forever color *Time* v188 no16/17 p16 O 24 2016

What the World Health Organization's New Leader Must Tackle color *Time* v189 no21 p11 Je 5 2017

Why More Women Are Getting a Double Mastectomy diag *Time* v190 no15 p41 O 16 2017

SIFRY, MICAH L.

Antitrust Facebook *Nation* v305 no11 p4 O 30 2017

OBAMA'S LOST ARMY [Cover story] color *New Republic* v248 no3 p18 Mr 2017

Sifton, Sam

American Pie *New York Times Magazine* p32 Ja 15 2017

The Art of Uncooking *New York Times Magazine* p32 Ap 23 2017

Burn Your Vegetables: For this Mexican-style slaw, employ the power of fire and smoke color *New York Times Magazine* p26 Ag 6 2017

Firehouse Food: For first responders, a shared meal is more than simply fuel *New York Times Magazine* p20 O 8 2017

A French-Canadian Christmas Carol color *New York Times Maga-* *zine* p44 D 11 2016

From the Wild: You don't need much more than butter to pan-roast Alaskan king salmon. But a little jalapeño is nice *New York Times Magazine* p26 Jl 9 2017

A Gyro From Down Under *New York Times Magazine* p28 Je 11 2017

The Harder They Come: The hard-shell tacos of childhood still bring joy to the dinner table *New York Times Magazine* p26 My 14 2017

Larger Than Life *New York Times Magazine* p22 Ap 2 2017

Not All Ragùs Are Italian *New York Times Magazine* p28 N 6 2016

Sing for Your Supper *New York Times Magazine* p28 O 2 2016

The Swedish Season *New York Times Magazine* p26 Mr 5 2017

Table for Two, No Waiting color *New York Times Magazine* p24 F 12 2017

When Too Much Is Just Enough *New York Times Magazine* p26 S 3 2017

SIGAL, CLANCY

The Meaning of Zelda *Commentary* v144 no1 p6 Jl/Ag 2017

Sigalet, Jordan

Unstoppable S. DEZIEL color *Maclean's* v130 no6 p60 Jl 2017

Sigismund, Sara

Reticulon 3–dependent ER-PM contact sites control EGFR non-clathrin endocytosis color diag graph *Science* v356 no6338 p617 My 12 2017

Sigl, G.

Observation of a large-scale anisotropy in the arrival directions of cosmic rays above 8×1018 eV *Science* v357 no6357 p1266 S 22 2017

Sigma Corp. of America

OPTICS ACE J. Silber color graph *Popular Photography* v81 no2 p85 Mr/Ap 2017

Sigma Global Corp.

ONE OF A KIND P. Ryan color diag *Popular Photography* v80 no11 p72 D 2016

Sigman, Daniel M.

21st-century rise in anthropogenic nitrogen deposition on a remote coral reef diag graph *Science* v356 no6339 p749 My 19 2017

Sigman, Mariano

The Secret Life of the Mind S. Kelly *Science* v356 no6342 p1006 Je 9 2017

Sigman, Matthew

Safe Haven: The U.S. premiere of Donizetti's Assedio di Calais at Glimmerglass fits the festival's "home and homeland" theme *Opera News* v81 no12 p54 Je 2017

Sign, The (Music)

1994 L. Greenblatt color *Entertainment Weekly* no1466 p58 My 19 2017

Sign of the Times (Music)

THE 16-WORD REVIEW H. Goldblatt color *Entertainment Weekly* no1462 p60 Ap 21 2017

Signal (Short story)

SIGNAL J. LANCHESTER cartoon *New Yorker* v93 no7 p78 Ap 3 2017

Signal lights

Living technologies color *Natural History* v125 no5 p5 My 2017

Signals & signaling

See also

Aids to navigation

Flares

Scary (and true) tales from a crag near you Alan and Matt *Climbing* no349 p11 N 2016

Signals & signaling—Equipment & supplies

PIXIE SMART TAGS J. R. BOOKWALTER color *Macworld - Digital Edition* v34 no4 p43 My 2017

Signature Move (Film)

A STUDY ON MODERN LOVE color *Chicago* v66 no10 p82 O 2017

Signature Theatre Co.

A Maple Leaf in the Big Apple H. Sherman *Stage Directions* v30 no9 p24 S 2017

Signer, Mike

THESE MONUMENTS WERE TRANSFORMED INTO LIGHTNING RODS *Vital Speeches of the Day* v83 no10 p285 O 2017

Significant Other (Theatrical production)

The Light Touch S. Zacharek color *Time* v189 no6 p38 F 20 2017

NEWLY AVAILABLE MOVIES J. HOGAN *TV Guide* v65 no35 p40 Ag 21 2017

Not Without My Mother D. EDELSTEIN img *New York* v49 no25 p132 D 12 2016

REDEMPTION [Cover story] P. ELIE color *New York Times Magazine* p44 N 27 2016

Scorsese's Passion P. Travers color *Rolling Stone* no1278/1279 p52 Ja 12 2017

Silence *New Yorker* v92 no42 p36 D 19 2016

Song and Solitude R. R. Cooper *Commonweal* v144 no2 p22 Ja 27 2017

When God is silent P. Jenkins color *Christian Century* v134 no5 p44 Mr 1 2017

YOU TALKIN' TO ME? N. PINKERTON color *Film Comment* v53 no1 p26 Ja/F 2017

Silence (Philosophy)

Don't Say Nothing J. PITTS *Education Digest* v82 no7 p50 Mr 2017

Silencers (Firearms)

The Case for Suppressor Technology R. J. Duncan *Time* v190 no15 p30 O 16 2017

Don't Silence the Sound of Gunfire *Bloomberg Businessweek* no4539 p14 S 25 2017

SILENCE, PLEASE J. Johnston color *Field & Stream* v122 no2 p34 Je/Jl 2017

Silent films—Exhibitions

GOINGS ON ABOUT TOWN bw *New Yorker* v92 no45 p5 Ja 16 2017

Silent Light (Music)

6-String Sidestream B. MILKOWSKI color *Downbeat* v84 no8 p73 Ag 2017

DOMINIC MILLER B. Milkowski color *Downbeat* v84 no7 p25 Jl 2017

Silhouettes

Git Along *Arizona Highways* v93 no2 p56 F 2017

Silica

LASER EXPERIMENTS ILLUMINATE THE COSMOS *Science & Technology Review* p4 D 2016

Silicon

BLACK MARKET B. I. KOERNER cartoon color *Wired* v25 no10 p106 O 2017

Epitaxial lift-off of electrodeposited single-crystal gold foils for flexible electronics N. K. Mahenderkar, Q. Chen et al bibl bw diag *Science* v355 no6330 p1203 Mr 17 2017

EXOTIC FORMS of SILICON P. C. Taylor *Physics Today* v69 no12 p34 D 2016

MoS2 transistors with 1-nanometer gate lengths S. B. Desai, S. R. Madhvapathy et al bibl color graph *Science* v354 no6308 p99 O 7 2016

Silicon carbide

Circuitry made robust enough for Venus M. Wilson *Physics Today* v70 no3 p19 Mr 2017

Silicon isotopes

Physicists discover 'bubble nucleus' E. CONOVER color *Science News* v190 no11 p11 N 26 2016

Silicon nanowires

Cells gobble up strands of silicon M. ROSEN *Science News* v191 no1 p9 Ja 21 2017

Silicon Valley (TV program)

DISRUPTION BY DESIGN S. NYGAARD color *Men's Health* v32 no7 p(Sp)28 S 2017

Silicondust (Company)

How to turn your Mac into a digital video recorder for over-the-air TV G. FLEISHMAN color *Macworld - Digital Edition* v34 no6 p113 Je 2017

Silicones

Easy Squeezy color *O, The Oprah Magazine* p146 N 2017

new products color *Science* v356 no6337 p547 My 5 2017

THE ORIGIN OF ICE-IES J. Brown color *Popular Science* v289 no2 p29 Mr/Ap 2017

Silicones in surgery

Bigger Breasts Without Implants? *USA Today Magazine* v146 no2869 p5 O 2017

Silicon—Therapeutic use

Imaginary futures C. Day *Physics Today* v69 no12 p8 D 2016

Silicon Valley (Santa Clara County, Calif.)

A BLIND EYE TO THE TRUTH E. Griffith color *Fortune* v176 no2 p46 Ag 1 2017

Does Silicon Valley Still Care About Climate Change? W. Frick *Harvard Business Review Digital Articles* p2 My 30 2017

So You Want to Be Like Silicon Valley? D. Gambrell and P. Coy *Bloomberg Businessweek* no4537 p48 S 11 2017

What's in a Valley Valuation? A. Vandermey diag *Fortune* v176 no3 p19 S 1 2017

When Silicon Valley Took Over Journalism F. Foer color *Atlantic* v320 no2 p28 S 2017

WORKERS OF SILICON VALLEY UNITE! J. Eidelson *Bloomberg Businessweek* no4538 p22 S 18 2017

Silk

THE BEST BET img *New York* v50 no6 p55 Mr 20 2017

Silky Pillowcases L. SACHS color *Good Housekeeping* v263 no5 p133 N 2016

Silk, Anna, 1974-

Anna Silk A. Pope color *Canadian Geographic* v137 no3 p82 My 2017

Silk, Joseph

Where are they? *Physics Today* v70 no3 p50 Mr 2017

SILK, MARK

Before the Scandal Broke *Smithsonian* v47 no7 p25 N 2016

SILK, MATTHEW J.

Using Social Network Measures in Wildlife Disease Ecology, Epidemiology, and Management *BioScience* v67 no3 p245 Mr 2017

Silk Road

Road to Greener Pastures A. Hadhazy color *Natural History* v125 no5 p8 My 2017

SAND TRICKS N. Strochlic color *National Geographic* v232 no5 p144 N 2017

Silkin, Vyacheslav M.

Angular momentum–induced delays in solid-state photoemission enhanced by intra-atomic interactions chart color graph *Science* v357 no6357 p1274 S 22 2017

Silky shark

Populations Smaller than Previously Thought *USA Today Magazine* v145 no2865 p8 Je 2017

Silla (Kingdom)

DOLL STORY KIM bw *Archaeology* v70 no5 p12 S/O 2017

GUIDE TO THE AFTERLIFE KIM color *Archaeology* v70 no1 p16 Ja/F 2017

Silli, G.

Observation of a large-scale anisotropy in the arrival directions of cosmic rays above 8 × 1018 eV *Science* v357 no6357 p1266 S 22 2017

Sills, David

Back at the Starting Line J. Fuchs and T. Keith color *Sports Illustrated* v126 no1 p18 Ja 9 2017

'TIS BETTER TO RECEIVE A. Staples color *Sports Illustrated* v127 no6 p46 Ag 28 2017

Sills, Jennifer

Advocacy in brief color *Science* v356 no6333 p24 Ap 7 2017

Artificial intelligence in research color *Science* v357 no6346 p28 Jl 7 2017

Promoting human rights through science color *Science* v357 no6359 p34 O 6 2017

Silman, M. R.

Persistent effects of pre-Columbian plant domestication on Amazonian forest composition bibl chart graph map *Science* v355 no6328 p925 Mr 3 2017

Silsbee, Kirk

Blue Whale Nurtures Creativity color *Downbeat* v84 no2 p51 F 2017

Gentlemen Prefer Song color *Downbeat* v83 no11 p54 N 2016

Horn of Plenty bw *Downbeat* v83 no12 p13 D 2016

Magic on the Bandstand bw *Downbeat* v84 no4 p65 Ap 2017

Seventh Inning Stretch color *Downbeat* v84 no6 p76 Je 2017

Terry Gibbs Returns with Homemade Recording color *Downbeat* v84 no7 p18 Jl 2017

Silva, Alcino J.

MEMORY'S INTRICATE WEB color diag *Scientific American* v317 no1 p30 Jl 2017

Silva, Ana P. G.

Site-specific phosphorylation of tau inhibits amyloid-β toxicity in

Alzheimer's mice bibl graph *Science* v354 no6314 p904 N 18 2016

Silva, Arnaldo
OUR FATHERS IN THEIR OWN WORDS G. Roberts-Grey, R. Carroll et al color *Essence* v48 no2 p94 Je 2017

Silva, Daniel-Adriano
Principles for designing proteins with cavities formed by curved β sheets bibl color graph *Science* v355 no6321 p1 Ja 13 2017

SILVA, DAVID J.
THERE IS LIFE AFTER COLLEGE color *Phi Kappa Phi Forum* v97 no2 p28 Summ 2017

Silva, David L.
On a Question of the Day color *Black Belt* v55 no6 p16 O/N 2017

Silva, Horacio
BACK TO Barbados color diag *Conde Nast Traveler* v52 no1 p82 Ja 2017
MIAMI HEAT color *Architectural Digest* v74 no9 p149 S 2017
SINGAPORE color *Conde Nast Traveler* v52 no3 p24 Mr 2017

Silva, José Graziano da
Making the Ocean a Partner in Our Quest for a Sustainable Future *UN Chronicle* v54 no1/2 p1 2017

Silva, LAURA De
FROM Comps To Campus color *Dance Spirit* v21 no8 p96 O 2017

Silva, Lucas C. R.
Carbon sequestration beyond tree longevity bibl *Science* v355 no6330 p1141 Mr 17 2017

Silva, Miranda
dream scape color *Martha Stewart Living* p116 O 2017
PUSHING the LIMITS color map *Better Homes & Gardens* v95 no4 p66 Ap 2017

Silva-Jelly, Natasha
AMAZING GRACE color *Harper's Bazaar* no3657 p244 O 2017
Bazaar's Best-Dressed LIST color *Harper's Bazaar* no3656 p230 S 2017
GWYNETH PALTROW'S SHOE SECRETS color *Harper's Bazaar* no3657 p242 O 2017
My LIST: 24 hours with Cindy Crawford color *Harper's Bazaar* no3657 p126 O 2017
PLATINUM REWARDS color *Harper's Bazaar* no3657 p163 O 2017
RAF SIMONS'S BRAVE NEW WORLD color *Harper's Bazaar* no3654 p96 Je/Jl 2017
TRUE WEST bw color *Harper's Bazaar* no3656 p430 S 2017

Silveira, Geri
WHAT HAPPENS AFTER A CRASH? color *Flying* v144 no5 p60 My 2017

Silveira, M.
Persistent effects of pre-Columbian plant domestication on Amazonian forest composition bibl chart graph map *Science* v355 no6328 p925 Mr 3 2017

Silver, Anya Krugovoy
From Nothing: Poems S. Cairns *Christian Century* v134 no5 p39 Mr 1 2017
The Virginia State Colony for Epileptics and Feebleminded: Poems color *Christian Century* v134 no10 p55 My 10 2017

Silver, Horace, 1928-2014
Louis Hayes T. PANKEN color *Downbeat* v84 no9 p106 S 2017

Silver, Johanna
BEST OF THE WEST color *Sunset* v238 no3 p7 Mr 2017
EVERYDAY BEAUTY color diag *Sunset* v239 no3 p41 S 2017
A FLORAL AFFAIR color *Sunset* v238 no6 p39 Je 2017
THE FRONT-YARD FIX color *Sunset* v238 no4 p42 Ap 2017
HERBS FOR THE WIN color *Sunset* v238 no6 p52 Je 2017
Living laboratory color *Sunset* v238 no5 p52 My 2017
PLANT KINGDOM color *Sunset* v238 no2 p60 F 2017
THE PLANT PIONEER color *Sunset* v237 no5 p64 N 2016
ROCKY MOUNTAIN HIGH color *Sunset* v239 no1 p50 Jl 2017
SMELL-GOOD GREENERY color *Sunset* v238 no4 p46 Ap 2017
THE SWEETEST PEAS color *Sunset* v238 no2 p33 F 2017
Your CHECKLIST color *Sunset* v239 no3 p60 S 2017

SILVER, KATE
THE BEGINNER'S GUIDE TO Making a Difference cartoon color diag *O, The Oprah Magazine* p114 S 2017

Silver, Larry
Silver Prints *American History* v51 no6 p52 F 2017

Silver, Margarita Gokun

Lady in Red cartoon *O, The Oprah Magazine* p124 Mr 2017

Silver, Marisa
The Shape She's Shifting M. BELL *New York Times Book Review* p11 O 2 2016
What Happens Next (or Doesn't) *New York Times Book Review* p15 F 26 2017

Silver, Mitchell J.
Parks Without Borders *Parks & Recreation* v52 no3 p40 Mr 2017

Silver, Nicky
The Next Stage for Rejected Scripts B. R. REYNOLDS *Los Angeles Magazine* v61 no11 p102 N 2016

Silver, Vernon
Can a lonely man in a tiny bedroom deliver a real October surprise? color *Bloomberg Businessweek* no4495 p62 O 17 2016
COME FOR THE GOULASH, STAY FOR THE DEMOCRACY color *Bloomberg Businessweek* no4529 p60 Jl 3 2017
The German Far Right Gets American Aid color *Bloomberg Businessweek* no4540 p42 O 2 2017
Hostile Takeover High color *Bloomberg Businessweek* no4541 p46 O 9
How to Launder A Russian graph *Bloomberg Businessweek* no4522 p17 My 15 2017
HOW TO MAKE A €367 MILLION LOSS DISAPPEAR *Bloomberg Businessweek* no4508 p36 Ja 23 2017
In Case of Low Revenue cartoon *Bloomberg Businessweek* no4497 p50 O 31 2016
To the Tipsy Guy on the Lido Deck! color *Bloomberg Businessweek* no4504 p50 D 19 2016

Silver coins
OLD MONEY C. R. JOYNT *Washingtonian Magazine* v52 no4 p26 Ja 2017

Silver crystals
Dynamic creation and evolution of gradient nanostructure in single-crystal metallic microcubes R. Thevamaran, O. Lawal et al bibl bw *Science* v354 no6310 p312 O 21 2016

Silver mines & mining
MIGRANTS J. Mark *Sierra* v102 no5 p30 St/O 2017

Silver Spoon Ode (Poem)
Silver Spoon Ode S. OLDS *Nation* v304 no4 p36 F 6 2017

Silver Surfer (Fictitious character)
NO. 28 SILVER SURFER K. P. Sullivan color *Entertainment Weekly* no1436/1437 p64 O 21 2016

Silvera, Isaac F.
Observation of the Wigner-Huntington transition to metallic hydrogen bibl chart color graph *Science* v355 no6326 p715 F 17 2017

Silverado truck
THE GALLOPING GHOST M. EMERY color *Dirt Sports + Off-Road* v51 no6 p42 Je 2017

Silverado truck—Evaluation
HEAVY-DUTY PICKUP REVIEW D. Mowitz *Successful Farming* v115 no2 p38 F 2017
RUNNING WITH THE DEVIL M. EMERY color *Dirt Sports + Off-Road* v51 no3 p18 Mr 2017

Silverberg, Robert
The Emperor and the Maula *Publishers Weekly* v264 no28 p69 Jl 10 2017
First-Person Singularities *Publishers Weekly* v264 no34 p94 Ag 21 2017

Silver Creek (Blaine County, Idaho)
Silence Like a Symphony: Canoeing Silver Creek M. RIPPLE *Idaho Magazine* v16 no11 p10 Ag 2017

Silvered Water, Syria Self-Portrait (Film)
EDITOR'S LETTER N. Rapold color *Film Comment* v53 no2 p4 Mr/Ap 2017

SILVERGLATE, HARVEY
Is free speech under threat IN THE UNITED STATES? WE RECEIVED TWENTY-SEVEN RESPONSES. WE PUBLISH THEM HERE, IN ALPHABETICAL ORDER *Commentary* v144 no1 p13 Jl/Ag 2017

Silverlake Life: The View From Here (Film)
Through the Darkness R. Campillo color *Film Comment* v53 no4 p6 Jl/Ag 2017

Silverman, David J.
Thundersticks: Firearms and the Violent Transformation of Native America J. Black *History Today* v67 no1 p58 Ja 2017

Silverman, Elissa
 GUEST LIST *Washingtonian Magazine* v52 no5 p20 F 2017
SILVERMAN, HERB
 His Porn, Her Pain: Confronting Americas PornPanic With Honest Talk About Sex *Humanist* v77 no1 p42 Ja/F 2017
Silverman, Jacob
 Multimediated Lives *New York Times Book Review* p14 Ja 1 2017
 The Night Shift *New Republic* v248 no4 p61 Ap 2017
 Spin Cycle *New York Times Magazine* p11 S 3 2017
Silverman, Laura—Interviews
 TORUK: The First Flight F. Esker color *New Orleans Magazine* v51 no4 p27 F 2017
Silverman, Sarah, 1970-
 A Mother in Arms J. Ferrise color *InStyle* v24 no6 p148 Je 2017
Silverman, Sarah, 1970-—Interviews
 SARAH SILVERMAN I Love You, America R. Rahman, A. Bacle et al color *Entertainment Weekly* no1482/1483 p108 S 22 2017
Silverman, Susan
 Casting Lots: Creating a Family in a Beautiful, Broken World A. B. Lehn *Christian Century* v134 no3 p34 F 2017
 'Who's My Tummy Mommy?' color *Reader's Digest* v190 no1135 p102 N 2017
Silvers, Robert B., 1929-2017
 Remembering Bob Silvers: The legendary New York Review of Books editor knew everybody, had read everything, and oversaw every stage of what he published G. WILLS *American Scholar* v86 no3 p106 Summ 2017
 Robert B. Silvers (1929-2017) [Cover story] R. Hederman, E. BLAIR et al bw color *New York Review of Books* v64 no8 p31 My 11 2017
 Robert B. Silvers (1929-2017) D. Mendelsohn bw *New York Review of Books* v64 no7 p8 Ap 20 2017
Silver—Sales & prices
 SILVER IS THE NEW OIL D. M. Engstrom graph *Kiplinger's Personal Finance* v71 no4 p43 Ap 2017
Silversmiths
 Act of Faith C. STOCKS color *Architectural Digest* v74 no4 p76 Ap 2017
SILVERSTEIN, EVA
 A COSMIC CONTROVERSY color *Scientific American* v317 no1 p5 Jl 2017
Silverstein, Jake
 Make It New *New York Times Magazine* p22 N 13 2016
Silverstein, Jonathan
 Venturing for a Cure color *Forbes* v199 no4 p90 Ap 25 2017
Silverstein, Michael J.
 What It Takes to Build a Startup into a Brand *Harvard Business Review Digital Articles* p2 Mr 9 2016
Silverstein, Noah
 Bathleisure: It's a Thing color *Glamour* v115 no1 p16 Ja 2017
 Do You Know These Labels? bw color *Glamour* v115 no3 p86 Mr 2017
 Hoodie, Yes. Pants, No color *Glamour* v114 no12 p78 D 2016
 Katy's Got Sole color *Glamour* v115 no2 p25 F 2017
 The Man Who Loves Women color *Glamour* v115 no3 p94 Mr 2017
 Not Your Basic Bag, Man color *Glamour* v115 no4 p48 Ap 2017
 Perfect Match bw color *Glamour* v115 no5 p54 My 2017
 Renting Just Got Better color *Glamour* v114 no12 p112 D 2016
 Royal Anniversary [Cover story] color *Glamour* v114 no11 p50 N 2016
 What to Know NOW color *Glamour* v114 no11 p72 N 2016
 The White-Sneaker Revolution color *Glamour* v114 no7 p60 Jl 2016
Silverstone, Alicia
 Garden of Life color *Amazing Wellness* v9 no4 p1 Summ 2017
 Graden of Life: mykind ORGANICS color *Better Nutrition* v79 no9 p1 S 2017
 mykind ORGANICS color *Amazing Wellness* p1 Fall 2017
 mykind ORGANICS GUMMIES color *Amazing Wellness* v9 no6 pC1 EarlyWint 2017
Silverstone, Yaarit
 How Smart CEOs Use Social Tools to Their Advantage *Harvard Business Review Digital Articles* p2 Mr 9 2015
Silverswords (Plants)
 Silversword Fight E. MOUNT *National Parks* v91 no2 p28 Spr

2017
Silverton, Nancy—Interviews
 NANCY SILVERTON MAKES LOS ANGELES THAT MUCH SWEETER *Los Angeles Magazine* v61 no11 p131 N 2016
Silvertown, Jonathan
 Dinner with Darwin V. Johnson color *Science* v357 no6355 p968 S 8 2017
Silverware—Exhibitions
 Polished Performances: Classic and contemporary silver in dialogue at the Museum of the City of New York M. Bartolucci color *Magazine Antiques* v184 no5 p78 S/O 2017
Silverware—Maintenance & repair
 A lot of holiday recipes call for candied citron. What exactly is it? *Martha Stewart Living* no270 p86 D 2016
Silverwork
 Custom Silverwork color *Horse & Rider* v56 no8 p36 Ag 2017
 Mario Buccellati Large Seafood Basket color *Magazine Antiques* v184 no3 p36 My/Je 2017
Silvester, Victor
 The War Before the Waltz R. Hughes *History Today* v66 no12 p40 D 2016
Silvestre, Fran
 Blurring the Clean Lines of MODERNISM J. Tarmy color *Bloomberg Businessweek* no4533 p55 Ag 7 2017
Silvestri, Lucia
 To Rome with Love J. K. DE VALLE color *Architectural Digest* v74 no1 p66 Ja 2017
Silvestri, Luciana
 What Makes FC Barcelona Such a Successful Business *Harvard Business Review Digital Articles* p2 Je 16 2015
SILVESTRI, SARA
 Misperceptions of the 'Muslim Diaspora' *Current History* v115 no784 p319 N 2016
Silvestro, Daniele
 Characterization of a dynamic metabolon producing the defense compound dhurrin in sorghum bibl graph *Science* v354 no6314 p890 N 18 2016
Silvicultural systems
 GIFTS OF A FOREST Devereux, Catherine et al *New York State Conservationist* v71 no5 p24 Ap 2017
SIM, CHRIS
 SEO Beyond Google *Publishers Weekly* v264 no28 p92 Jl 10 2017
Sim, David
 Q: What is the most significant fad of all time? color *Atlantic* v319 no3 p96 Ap 2017
Sim Trava (Company)
 We used to know all our colleagues - and their dogs *People Management* p24 D 2016/Ja 2017
Sima, Jessie
 Not Quite Narwhal *Publishers Weekly* v263 no50 p71 D 5 2016
Sima, O.
 Observation of a large-scale anisotropy in the arrival directions of cosmic rays above 8×1018 eV *Science* v357 no6357 p1266 S 22 2017
Simard, Caroline
 Research: Vague Feedback Is Holding Women Back *Harvard Business Review Digital Articles* p2 Ap 29 2016
Simard, Claude—Exhibitions
 A Portrait of the Artist as a Collector S. DOUGLAS color *ARTnews* v116 no1 p42 Spr 2017
Simard, Luc
 Star struck N. Walker color *Canadian Geographic* v137 no4 p28 Jl/Ag 2017
Simavorian, Tatevik
 TZAP: A telomere-associated protein involved in telomere length control bibl diag graph *Science* v355 no6325 p638 F 10 2017
SIMBERG, RAND
 The Surprisingly Long History of Private Space Exploration color *Reason* v49 no4 p70 Ag/S 2017
 Writing the Future bw *Weekly Standard* v23 no4 p37 O 2 2017
SIMBERLOFF, DANIEL
 Nonnative Fish to Control Aedes Mosquitoes: A Controversial, Harmful Tool *BioScience* v67 no1 p84 Ja 2017
Simbotin, Ionel
 Synthesis of mixed hypermetallic oxide BaOCa+ from laser-cooled reagents in an atom-ion hybrid trap diag graph *Science*

v357 no6358 p1370 S 29 2017

Simchi-Levi, David

Find the Weak Link in Your Supply Chain *Harvard Business Review Digital Articles* p2 Je 9 2015

You Can't Understand China's Slowdown Without Understanding Supply Chains *Harvard Business Review Digital Articles* p2 S 4 2015

Simcoe, John Graves, 1752-1806

John vs. George E. Dale Santos color *MHQ: Quarterly Journal of Military History* v30 no1 p12 Aut 2017

Simcoe, Mike—Interviews

Mike Simcoe M. Rechtin color *Motor Trend* v69 no3 p34 Mr 2017

SIMEK, PETER

Flat Broke *D: The Magazine of Dallas* v43 no10 p88 O 2016

HOW TO BUILD A MEGA-CITY *D: The Magazine of Dallas* v43 no10 p156 O 2016

Simen, Patrick

Why does time seem to fly when we're having fun? bibl color *Science* v354 no6317 p1231 D 9 2016

Simerson, Keith

A Story from Google Shows You Don't Need Power to Drive Strategy *Harvard Business Review Digital Articles* p2 Ap 29 2015

Simester, Duncan

Run Field Experiments to Make Sense of Your Big Data *Harvard Business Review Digital Articles* p2 N 12 2015

Simhat Torah

Love and the Law M. Y. SOLOVEICHIK *Commentary* v143 no6 p13 Je 2017

Simian immunodeficiency virus

Trispecific broadly neutralizing HIV antibodies mediate potent SHIV protection in macaques L. Xu, A. Pegu et al color graph *Science* v357 no6359 p85 O 6 2017

Simic, Charles

Inexhaustible & Brilliant bw color *New York Review of Books* v64 no3 p26 F 23 2017

Magnetic Point: Selected Poems bw *Publishers Weekly* v264 no38 p51 S 18 2017

Must Lerner Connect? bw *New York Review of Books* v64 no6 p31 Ap 6 2017

A Voice for the Voiceless bw *New York Review of Books* v64 no11 p42 Je 22 2017

Simien, Justin—Interviews

DEAR IN THE SPOTLIGHT C. Agard color *Entertainment Weekly* no1472 p52 Je 30 2017

SIMINGTON, MAIRE O.

AT THE FOREFRONT OF INNOVATION il *Phi Kappa Phi Forum* v97 no2 p9 Summ 2017

CHASING A DREAM color *Phi Kappa Phi Forum* v96 no4 p11 Wint 2016

DUST IN THE WIND color *Phi Kappa Phi Forum* v97 no1 p11 Spr 2017

SIMIS-WILKINSON, MOLLY

Mapping the Landscape of Public Attitudes on Synthetic Biology *BioScience* v67 no3 p290 Mr 2017

Simkin, Daniil

Between the Idea and the Reality: Inside a rehearsal of Daniil Simkin's Rotunda Project C. ESCOYNE *Dance Magazine* v91 no9 p37 S 2017

Simmens, Samuel J.

Science in litigation, the third branch of U.S. climate policy graph *Science* v357 no6355 p979 S 8 2017

SIMMONS, ANDY

Animal House color *Reader's Digest* v189 no1130 p8 My 2017

Bald Is Beautiful! color *Reader's Digest* v190 no1133 p11 S 2017

Cliff-Hanger *Reader's Digest* v189 no1128 p12 Mr 2017

The Cover-Up color *Reader's Digest* v189 no1131 p11 Je 2017

My Dog Reviews the Furniture He Has Eaten *Reader's Digest* v188 no1124 p15 O 2016

The Online Troll Patrol *Reader's Digest* v189 no1127 p12 F 2017

Sergeant Turner's Ride Home color *Reader's Digest* v190 no1132 p12 Jl/Ag 2017

The Storybook Barber *Reader's Digest* v188 no1126 p8 D 2016/Ja 2017

They Did the Right Thing cartoon *Reader's Digest* v190 no1134 p88 O 2017

WHO KNEW? Win at Rock, Paper, Scissors (And Other Sly Gimmicks) *Reader's Digest* v189 no1127 p124 F 2017

Why Didn't I Think of That?! *Reader's Digest* v189 no1128 p88 Mr 2017

Simmons, Ben, 1996-

LOOKING FOR REVENGE N. SANTOS color *Ebony* v72 no11 p88 S 2017

Simmons, Brandyn

ENEMY color *Christian Century* v134 no5 p20 Mr 1 2017

Simmons, Edward G.

Talking Back to the Bible: A Historian's Approach to Bible Study *Publishers Weekly* v264 no26 p146e Je 26 2017

Simmons, Elizabeth H.

Updating the Two Cultures: How Structures Can Promote Interdisciplinary Cultures *Change* v48 no6 p28 N/D 2016

Simmons, Gene, 1949—Interviews

Gene Simmons A. GREENE bw *Rolling Stone* no1297 p58 O 5 2017

Simmons, Justin

Leading Off color *Sports Illustrated* v125 no17 p10 N 21 2016 Double Issue

Simmons, Lee

A Foretaste of 2018: Hoover fellow David Brady, surveying the political landscape, sees "knife-edge electoral instability" *Hoover Digest: Research & Opinion on Public Policy* no3 p28 Summ 2017

Simmons, Ralph O.

Edwin Leo Goldwasser *Physics Today* v70 no9 p70 S 2017

Simmons, Richard, 1948-

The Leave-Taking of Jesus Christ (and Richard Simmons) J. McDermott color *America* v216 no8 p49 Ap 17 2017

AN ODE TO RICHARD SIMMONS cartoon *Women's Health* v14 no6 p36 Jl 2017

RICHARD, CAN YOU HEAR US? C. Everett color *Entertainment Weekly* no1456 p71 Mr 10 2017

Still Missing Richard Simmons C. Everett color *Entertainment Weekly* no1459 p12 Mr 31 2017

Simmons, Russell, 1957-

Russell SIMMONS color *Esquire* p128 Ap 2017

SIMMONS, THOMAS

Primal Wounds: A poetry collection rooted in the grotesque weaves the religious with the obscene bw *New York Times Book Review* p10 Ag 6 2017

SIMMONS, TRACY LEE

A Family Riven by Revolution *National Review* v69 no16 p44 Ag 28 2017

Of Arts and the Man color *Weekly Standard* v22 no21 p30 F 6 2017

Simmons Bedding Co. LLC

Do You Want to Try One Out in Person? Here's how you can, following the bring-your-own-pillow-and-rest-for-at-least-seven-minutes advice of clinical psychologist and sleep expert Dr. Michael Breus L. SCHWARTZBERG *New York* v50 no9 p69 My 1 2017

Simms, James

Asia's Rising Stars color *Forbes* v199 no5 p20 My 16 2017

OVER BY CHRISTMAS? *Military History* v33 no5 p54 Ja 2017

THE WORLD'S BILLIONAIRES bw color diag graph map *Forbes* v199 no3 p84 Mr 28 2017

SIMMS, JANE

Bank transfer... 2 seconds Movie download... 2 minutes Grocery delivery... 1 hour Appraisal... 12 months? *People Management* p44 Je 2017

But all I said was 'nice buns, ladies' *People Management* p40 O 2016

"People don't seem so keen to move to our US offices all of a sudden...": The tricky logistics of global mobility - and HR's crucial role in getting it right *People Management* p46 Mr 2017

There's more than one way to solve a dispute: Resolving workplace differences is a fine art - and many businesses have been getting it dramatically wrong *People Management* p32 Ag 2017

We wanted to understand the state of HR outsourcing...so we asked you to do the work for us *People Management* p44 D 2016/Ja 2017

Simms, Molly

THE BEGINNER'S GUIDE TO Making a Difference cartoon

color diag *O, The Oprah Magazine* p114 S 2017

Look at Us NOW! color *O, The Oprah Magazine* p67 Ap 2017

Lost and Found color *O, The Oprah Magazine* p21 Ja 2017

A PLACE IN THE SUN color *O, The Oprah Magazine* p130 S 2017

YOUR ONE WILD AND PRECIOUS SUMMER color *O, The Oprah Magazine* p86 Je 2017

Simms Fishing Products LLC

Protect and Serve D. HARDING JR. color *Power & Motoryacht* v32 no12 p28 D 2016

Simon & Schuster Inc.

Deals R. DEAHL bw *Publishers Weekly* v264 no19 p10 My 8 2017

News Briefs *Publishers Weekly* v264 no16 p6 Ap 17 2017

The Slippery Slope of Free Speech R. SHUR *Publishers Weekly* v264 no3 p64 Ja 16 2017

Simon, B.

Fostering reproducibility in industry-academia research color *Science* v357 no6353 p759 Ag 25 2017

Simon, Clulow

Amphibians on the brink color map *Science* v357 no6350 p454 Ag 4 2017

Simon, Dan

Twenty Years of Books on Social Justice C. Reid color *Publishers Weekly* v263 no52 p11 D 19 2016

Simon, David, 1960-

Mean Streets R. SYME *New Republic* v248 no10 p54 O 2017

Simon, David—Interviews

PROJECT RED LIGHT A. Carter bw color *Esquire* p37 S 2017

Simon, Denis

How Chinese Companies Disrupt Through Business Model Innovation *Harvard Business Review Digital Articles* p2 Jl 8 2016

Simon, Ed

Reformation 2.0 [Cover story] color *Commonweal* v144 no17 p31 O 20 2017

Simon, Frank

Leading Ladies R. Brody bw *New Yorker* v93 no9 p11 Ap 17 2017

Simon, Hank

Refugee work *Christian Century* v134 no2 p6 Ja 18 2017

Simon, Hermann

The Fine Line Between When Low Prices Work and When They Don't *Harvard Business Review Digital Articles* p2 Mr 17 2016

Whole Foods Is Becoming Amazon's Brick-and-Mortar Pricing Lab *Harvard Business Review Digital Articles* p2 S 12 2017

Why Germany Still Has So Many Middle-Class Manufacturing Jobs *Harvard Business Review Digital Articles* p2 My 2 2017

Simon, John

Dressed for Success bw *Weekly Standard* v22 no23 p35 F 20 2017

French Lessons *New York Times Book Review* p22 D 11 2016

Simon, Linda

The original "It" Girl: Flappers took the country by storm in the roaring '20s and then suddenly vanished. Or did they? *Smithsonian* v48 no5 p9 S 2017

Simon, Mario

Global atmospheric particle formation from CERN CLOUD measurements bibl graph map *Science* v354 no6316 p1119 D 2 2016

SIMON, MASHAUN D.

In Our Cities color *Ebony* v72 no8 p32 Je 2017

Simon, Matt

Meet Earth's most fanciful creatures C. Martin color *Science News* v190 no8 p28 O 15 2016

SIMON, MICHAEL

8 WAYS THE iPHONE 8 CAN BEAT THE GALAXY S8 [Cover story] color graph *Macworld - Digital Edition* v34 no6 p91 Je 2017

AI TEST DRIVE: IS ALEXA ON YOUR PHONE AS GOOD AS IT IS IN YOUR HOME? color *PCWorld* v35 no5 p149 My 2017

ANDROID 8 OREO color *PCWorld* v35 no10 p95 O 2017

Apple's updated Android 'Switch' campaign explains why people move to iPhone color *Macworld - Digital Edition* p44 Je 13 2017

Apple Watch can detect an early sign of heart disease color *Macworld - Digital Edition* p48 Je 13 2017

THE ESSENTIAL PHONE IS A BEAUTIFUL EXAMPLE OF EVERYTHING THAT'S WRONG WITH ANDROID [Cover story] color *PCWorld* v35 no7 p161 Jl 2017

Galaxy S8+ review: The future of Android is now color graph *PCWorld* v35 no6 p94 Je 2017

Google makes the best Android apps easier to find with Android Excellence color *PCWorld* v35 no7 p47 Jl 2017

Google's next wearable is a $350 Levi's jacket that controls music by brushing your sleeve color *PCWorld* v35 no4 p29 Ap 2017

HTC U11 : A powerful Android phone that knows how to have fun color graph *PCWorld* v35 no7 p116 Jl 2017

iPhone 8 has the best smartphone camera, DxOMark says, but iPhone X will probably beat it color *Macworld - Digital Edition* v34 no11 p54 N 2017

The iPhone switcher's guide: Move from iOS to Android and keep all your stuff color *PCWorld* v35 no1 p173 Ja 2017

LG V30 hands-on: A 6-inch beast with more power and fewer gimmicks color *PCWorld* v35 no10 p74 O 2017

macOS HIGH SIERRA: FEATURES, SYSTEM REQUIREMENTS, RELEASE DATE, AND MORE color *Macworld - Digital Edition* p72 Je 13 2017

Meet the new Wunderlist: Microsoft's To-Do task manager takes over color *Macworld - Digital Edition* v34 no6 p103 Je 2017

Samsung Galaxy Note 8: Don't call it a comeback, call it the phone of the year color *PCWorld* v35 no10 p57 O 2017

Samsung launches the Galaxy S8 with a stunning design and Bixby AI assistant color *PCWorld* v35 no5 p23 My 2017

Samsung's Bixby won't support voice commands when it debuts on the Galaxy S8 color *PCWorld* v35 no5 p29 My 2017

Samsung to brick Galaxy Note7s through software color *PCWorld* v35 no1 p27 Ja 2017

Siri vs. Google Assistant: Which is better for iPhone users? color *Macworld - Digital Edition* p37 Je 13 2017

The timing is perfect for a new Chromebook Pixel color *PCWorld* v35 no10 p16 O 2017

Today at Apple could make Apple's growth troubles a thing of the past color *Macworld - Digital Edition* p7 Je 13 2017

Transfer everything from your old Android phone to your new one bw color *PCWorld* v35 no8 p134 Ag 2017

You can now send and receive money right in the Android Gmail app color *PCWorld* v35 no4 p44 Ap 2017

You won't have to hear about the Galaxy Note7 on flights anymore color *PCWorld* v35 no2 p33 F 2017

Simon, Michael Anthony

SPIDERWEB-MAN N. Paumgarten cartoon *New Yorker* v93 no6 p18 Mr 27 2017

Simon, Nissa

20 Quirky Summer Health Tips (That Actually Work) color *AARP: The Magazine* v59 no4A p19 Je/Jl 2016

SIMON, PAUL

The Year in Reading [Cover story] *New York Times Book Review* p8 D 25 2016

Simon, Raphael

All-of-a-Kind Family *New York Times Book Review* p15 Ap 9 2017

Simon, Samantha

DOING GOOD color *InStyle* v24 no5 p62 My 2017

The GREAT Debate color *InStyle* v24 no11 p92 N 2017

Might As Well ... Jump color *InStyle* v24 no7 p124 Jl 2017

STYLE CRUSH Alanna Arrington color *InStyle* v24 no8 p80 Ag 2017

STYLE CRUSH Anya Taylor-Joy color *InStyle* v24 no4 p94 Ap 2017

STYLE CRUSH Barbara Palvin color *InStyle* v24 no1 p34 Ja 2017

STYLE CRUSH Bella Heathcote color *InStyle* v24 no5 p96 My 2017

STYLE CRUSH Elizabeth Olsen color *InStyle* v24 no11 p86 N 2017

STYLE CRUSHES Chloe & Halle color *InStyle* v23 no12 p76 N 2016

STYLE CRUSH Haley Bennett color *InStyle* v24 no9 p192 S 2017

STYLE CRUSH Jenna Coleman color *InStyle* v24 no6 p56 Je 2017

STYLE CRUSH Kenya Kinski-Jones color *InStyle* v24 no3 p170 Mr 2017

STYLE CRUSH Nicola Peltz color *InStyle* v24 no2 p62 F 2017

STYLE CRUSH Olivia Culpo color *InStyle* v23 no13 p116 D 2016

Simon, Steven H.

Strong peak in Tc of Sr2RuO4 under uniaxial pressure bibl color graph *Science* v355 no6321 p1 Ja 13 2017

Simon, Steven N.

Trump and the Holy Land color *Foreign Affairs* v96 no2 p37 Mr/Ap 2017

Simon, Taryn, 1975——Exhibitions

Taryn Simon's photographs — canny, unsentimental and meticulously made — attend to the details of how power works T. Cole color *New York Times Magazine* p18 D 4 2016

Simon, William E.

Beyond Brick & Mortar E. Sauers color *Commonweal* v144 no3 p30 F 10 2017

Simon, Zoltan

Friendship Is a Bountiful Thing bw *Bloomberg Businessweek* no4532 p27 Jl 31 2017

In Europe, Brain Drain Flows the Other Way *Bloomberg Businessweek* no4517 p16 Ap 3 2017

Simon Fraser University

The walking man walks A. A. DAVIS color *Maclean's* v129 no44 p62 N 7 2016

Simon Property Group Inc.

Reinventing the American Mall P. Wahba color diag *Fortune* v174 no8 p148 D 15 2016

Simonds, Sandra

8. I Love Wine! *New York Times Magazine* p17 Ap 2 2017

Simone, Michael

The Audacious Seeker *America* v217 no2 p50 Jl 24 2017

Becoming the Body of Christ *America* v216 no13 p58 Je 12 2017

Clothing Ourselves in Love *America* v217 no7 p53 O 2 2017

Encounters With Angels *America* v215 no18 p42 D 5 2016

Ever Deeper Faith *America* v217 no2 p52 Jl 24 2017

Forgive and Be Forgiven *America* v217 no5 p53 S 4 2017

Formed in Their Likeness *America* v216 no12 p56 My 29 2017

The Freedom of the Father's Children *America* v216 no3 p52 F 6 2017

From Ashes to Fire *America* v216 no12 p54 My 29 2017

Go Out to All Nations *America* v216 no11 p60 My 15 2017

God's Perfect Instructions *America* v216 no3 p50 F 6 2017

Great Is Your Faith! *America* v217 no3 p52 Ag 7 2017

I Make All Things New *America* v216 no8 p50 Ap 17 2017

"Incredible Things Today" *America* v216 no8 p52 Ap 17 2017

I Tell You: Do Not Worry! *America* v216 no4 p52 F 20 2017

I Will Raise You Up *America* v216 no6 p52 Mr 20 2017

The Jesus Who Cannot Be *America* v216 no6 p50 Mr 20 2017

Keep and Ponder *America* v215 no19 p39 D 19 2016

Let's Try This Again *America* v215 p39 N 28 2016

A Life of Boldness *America* v216 no13 p60 Je 12 2017

The Light of New Life *America* v216 no5 p69 Mr 6 2017

Not My Will, But Yours *America* v216 no7 p50 Ap 3 2017

On Earth as It Is in Heaven *America* v216 no5 p66 Mr 6 2017

Pour Out Light Unshadowed *America* v216 no7 p52 Ap 3 2017

The Presence *America* v216 no11 p58 My 15 2017

The Power of the Church at Work *America* v217 no5 p52 S 4 2017

The Right Word il *America* v215 no19 p38 D 19 2016

Show Us the Father *America* v216 no10 p53 My 1 2017

Stay Awake! il *America* v215 no16 p38 N 21 2016

Submerged in the Spirit *America* v216 no1 p43 Ja 2 2017

Take Lord, Receive *America* v217 no4 p56 Ag 21 2017

Tell Me Who You Are *America* v215 no18 p41 D 5 2016

To Show the Way *America* v216 no1 p42 Ja 2 2017

Tune Out the Noise *America* v217 no3 p50 Ag 7 2017

Turning Over Our Will *America* v216 no4 p55 F 20 2017

Where Is God at Work? *America* v217 no6 p60 S 18 2017

'You Are the One!' *America* v217 no4 p54 Ag 21 2017

Simone, Nina, 1933-2003

THE HIGH PRIESTESS OF SOUL G. BLACK bw *Ebony* v72 no5 p98 Mr 2017

SIMONEAUX, MARIE

LOUISIANA PROUD color *Louisiana Life* v37 no2 p20 N/D 2016

NEW CLASSIC color *Louisiana Life* v37 no4 p20 Mr/Ap 2017

Simonet, Pascal

Microbial mass movements color *Science* v357 no6356 p1099 S 15 2017

Simonini, Ross

Alejandro Jodorowsky bw color *Art in America* p31 O 2017

ANICKA YI IN THE STUDIO color *Art in America* v105 no4 p100 Ap 2017

Estrellita Brodsky color *Art in America* v104 no10 p37 N 2016

Jamillah James color *Art in America* v105 no8 p37 S 2017

Kasper König color *Art in America* v105 no6 p49 Je/Jl 2017

Lynne Cooke color *Art in America* v105 no1 p25 Ja 2017

Raqs Media Collective color *Art in America* v104 no11 p37 D 2016

SIGHTLINES color *Art in America* v105 no3 p41 Mr 2017

Simonite, Tom

AI Software Learns to Make AI Software *MIT Technology Review* v120 no3 p16 My/Je 2017

AI That Dreams Up Drugs il *MIT Technology Review* v120 no1 p18 Ja/F 2017

Alphabet color il *MIT Technology Review* v120 no4 p58 Jl/Ag 2017

Betting on the Blockchain il *MIT Technology Review* v120 no1 p29 Ja/F 2017

Google's Quantum Leap color *MIT Technology Review* v120 no4 p22 Jl/Ag 2017

How a College Kid Made His Honda Civic Self-Driving for $700 il *MIT Technology Review* v120 no3 p13 My/Je 2017

How Software Could Help Judges Reduce Crime il *MIT Technology Review* v120 no3 p15 My/Je 2017

A Job Plan for Robots and Humans color *MIT Technology Review* v120 no4 p34 Jl/Ag 2017

Microsoft's Civil Rights Crusader bw diag *MIT Technology Review* v119 no6 p13 N/D 2016

Mining Without Miners color *MIT Technology Review* v120 no1 p94 Ja/F 2017

One Startup's Vision to Reinvent the Web for Better Privacy il *MIT Technology Review* v120 no2 p20 Mr/Ap 2017

The President of Search Giant Baidu Has Global Plans color *MIT Technology Review* v120 no4 p52 Jl/Ag 2017

Reinventing Intel color *MIT Technology Review* v119 no6 p20 N/D 2016

Self-Driving Cars' Spinning-Laser Problem color *MIT Technology Review* v120 no4 p27 Jl/Ag 2017

Simonovic, Ivan

The Responsibility to Protect *UN Chronicle* v53 no4 p1 2016

THE RESPONSIBILITY TO PROTECT *UN Chronicle* v54 no4 p18 2017

Simons, Christina

GLOBAL PROFESSIONAL, PERSONAL PASSION A. ELLIOTT *Iceland Review* v55 no3 p58 My/Je 2017

Simons, Jared

AMERICA'S FITTEST CHEFS J. DEAN cartoon color *Men's Health* v32 no3 p104 Ap 2017

Simons, Lilly

Rehabilitation Basics color *Dressage Today* v23 no5 p36 Ja 2017

Simons, Raf, 1968-

CAPTURING CALVIN KLEIN B. COLACELLO color *Vanity Fair* v59 no9 p218 S 2017

Simons, Ron

MASTER'S PROGRAM J. BARUTH color *Road & Track* v69 no3 p68 O 2017

Simons, Timothy——Interviews

Are Arrogant Men Still Funny? J. M. Goldstein color *Glamour* v115 no5 p152 My 2017

SIMONSEN, LONE

Death March of 1918 bw color *Natural History* v125 no9 p11 S 2017

Simoudis, Evangelos

The 5 Things IBM Needs to Do to Win at AI *Harvard Business Review Digital Articles* p2 F 3 2016

Simplicity

BREATHE color *Prevention* v69 no9 p18 O 2017

Simplified I.T. Products LLC

PICTURE KEEPER CONNECT: SIMPLE PHOTO BACKUP FOR THE ENTIRE FAMILY J. R. BOOKWALTER color *Macworld - Digital Edition* v33 no11 p92 N 2016

Simpson, Cam

After the Bombs Have Fallen color *Bloomberg Businessweek* no4531 p34 Jl 24 2017

THE PRICE OF A DIGITAL WORLD color *Bloomberg Businessweek* no4527 p58 Je 19 2017

Simpson, Clyde

FROM OUR READERS *Sky & Telescope* v133 no6 p6 Je 2017

Simpson, Cody

The Puberty Problem S. Knopper img *New York* v49 no20 p118 O 3 2016

Simpson, David

Green accounting J. SALZMAN *Issues in Science & Technology* v33 no2 p16 Wint 2017

Simpson, Diane—Exhibitions

DIANE SIMPSON R. Wetzler color *Art in America* v105 no3 p129 Mr 2017

SIMPSON, DOUG

Underwater Barrens *Natural History* v125 no2 p24 F 2017

Simpson, Helen, 1959-

Cockfosters color *Publishers Weekly* v264 no17 p64 Ap 24 2017

Tick-Tock E. LIPMAN *New York Times Book Review* p25 Je 4 2017

Simpson, Jeff

The Perfect-Plot Ambush bw cartoon *Field & Stream* v121 no7 p49 D 2016/Ja 2017

Simpson, John

Stuff of Language D. SKINNER color *Weekly Standard* v22 no13 p40 D 5 2016

Simpson, Levi

SIMPSON AND BUHLER REWRITE TEAM ROPING HISTORY [Cover story] K. SANTOS color *Spin to Win Rodeo* v20 no11 p48 Ja 2017

YOUNG GUNS C. Toy color *Spin to Win Rodeo* v21 no2 p24 Ap 2017

Simpson, Lori

Dad's Happy Place L. Simpson color *New York State Conservationist* v71 no2 p32 O 2016

SIMPSON, LYLE L.

What's In The Name? ALL OF US: CELEBRATING A CENTURY OF HUMANISM *Humanist* v77 no5 p25 S/O 2017

Simpson, O. J., 1947-—Trials, litigation, etc.

TIME TO BE RELEASED? M. Mccann and L. J. Wertheim color *Sports Illustrated* v126 no5 p70 F 13 2017

Simpson, Rose B.—Exhibitions

Shows to See color *American Craft* v76 no6 p20 D 2016-Ja 2017

SIMPSON, STEPHEN D.

Shipbuilding Docks as Experimental Systems for Realistic Assessments of Anthropogenic Stressors on Marine Organisms *BioScience* v67 no9 p853 S 2017

Simpson, Steve

Is Insulting Your Rival's Supporters Ever a Good Idea? *Harvard Business Review Digital Articles* p2 O 7 2016

Simpson, Sturgill, 1978-

Sturgill Simpson D. Kiper color *Current Biography* v78 no4 p77 Ap 2017

Simpson, Sturgill—Interviews

The Fighting Side of Sturgill Simpson D. RITZ color *Rolling Stone* no1272 p22 O 20 2016

Simpson, Victor R.

Red squirrels in the British Isles are infected with leprosy bacilli bibl color diag map *Science* v354 no6313 p744 N 11 2016

Simpson, Yvette

House Mother: MAUREEN WOOD SPENT A LIFETIME CREATING A SENSE OF HOME FOR OTHERS L. PIKE *Cincinnati Magazine* v50 no11 p44 Ag 2017

SEE YVETTE YRUN L. MURTHA *Cincinnati Magazine* v50 no4 p82 Ja 2017

THE YEAR OF THE BLACK WOMAN MAYOR D. M. Owens color *Essence* v47 no12 p78 Ap 2017

Simpson Desert

Australia to ax support for long-term ecology sites J. Pickrell color *Science* v357 no6352 p632 Ag 18 2017

Simpsons, The (TV program)

600 AND COUNTING... M. LOGAN cartoon *TV Guide* v64 no42 p30 O 10 2016

My Obsessions... *TV Guide* v64 no46 p10 N 7 2016

The Rise of Homer Sapiens J. Ortved *Smithsonian* v48 no1 p13 Ap 2017

SALUTE THE OLD GUARD D. Bianculli *TV Guide* v65 no31 p10 Jl 24 2017

The Simpsons A. Bacle, D. Coggan et al color *Entertainment*

Weekly no1482/1483 p34 S 22 2017

TV'S WINNERS AND LOSERS BY THE NUMBERS *TV Guide* v64 no48 p13 N 21 2016

Simrad Yachting (Company)

NEW ELECTRONICS J. Y. WOOD color *Power & Motoryacht* v33 no2 p54 F 2017

Sims, Angela D.

Angela D. Sims: The Legacy of Lynching R. Farmer bw color *Publishers Weekly* v263 no45 p24 N 7 2016

Sims, George

The End of the Web *Publishers Weekly* v264 no36 p68 S 4 2017

SIMS, JARED

Closing the Book, Opening the Ears bw *Downbeat* v84 no8 p84 Ag 2017

Sims, Kate

Career and Technical Education for Youth at Park & Rec Agencies *Parks & Recreation* v52 no8 p22 Ag 2017

Educating the New Administration and Congress About Park & Rec Programs *Parks & Recreation* v52 no9 p28 S 2017

Federal Budget Cuts Threaten Educational Funding *Parks & Recreation* v52 no6 p18 Je 2017

Sims, Michael

The Fabulous Baker Street Boys G. MOORE color *New York Times Book Review* p8 Ja 29 2017

Sims, Molly

family FIRST color *Good Housekeeping* v265 no5 p48 N 2017

Sims, Shari

Spring Clean Your Life [Cover story] color *Prevention* v69 no4 p40 Ap 2017

Simsion, Graeme

The Best of Adam Sharp *Publishers Weekly* v264 no10 p38 Mr 6 2017

Inaugural Season color *Publishers Weekly* v264 no3 p15 Ja 16 2017

Simulation methods & models

See also

Computer simulation

Mathematical models

Baking a Universe B. Skuse *Sky & Telescope* v133 no5 p34 My 2017

DRONE RESPONSIBLY 7 LESSONS LEARNED THE HARD WAY A. POWELL color graph *Wired* v25 no5 p24 My 2017

Simuliidae

Buffalo Gnats J. R. Erickson cartoon *American Cowboy* v23 no5 p22 F/Mr 2017

Sinaloa (Mexico : State)

Savouring SINALOA T. BURKE color map *Canadian Geographic* v135 no6 p34 D 2015

Sinan, Moaz

Community network for deaf scientists color *Science* v356 no6336 p386 Ap 28 2017

Sinatra, Frank, 1915-1998

Revisiting Sinatra's Bossa Gems A. Morrison color *Downbeat* v84 no9 p13 S 2017

Sinatra Keeps on Ticking J. MCDONOUGH color *Downbeat* v84 no8 p79 Ag 2017

Sinatra, Frank, Jr., 1944-2016

FRANK SINATRA JR. & RICCI MARTIN E. McCRACKEN *New York Times Magazine* p26 D 25 2016

Jason SUDEIKIS J. SUDEIKIS *Vanity Fair* v59 no2 p128 F 2017

Sinatra, Roberta

Data-driven predictions in the science of science bibl color diag *Science* v355 no6324 p477 F 3 2017

Quantifying the evolution of individual scientific impact graph *Science* v354 no6312 p596 N 4 2016

Sinca, F.

Airborne laser-guided imaging spectroscopy to map forest trait diversity and guide conservation bibl chart graph *Science* v355 no6323 p385 Ja 27 2017

Sincero, Jen

10 WAYS TO BECOME A MONEY BADASS color *Money* v46 no5 p62 Je 2017

CA$HING IN C. WAXLER color *Publishers Weekly* v263 no50 p34 D 5 2016

Sinclair, Charles

mTOR regulates metabolic adaptation of APCs in the lung and

controls the outcome of allergic inflammation graph *Science* v357 no6355 p1014 S 8 2017

Sinclair, David A.

A conserved NAD+ binding pocket that regulates protein-protein interactions during aging bibl graph *Science* v355 no6331 p1312 Mr 24 2017

Sinclair, Iain

The Last London: True Fictions from an Unreal City *Publishers Weekly* v264 no40 p125 O 2 2017

Sinclair, Mima

A BRIGHT IDEA color *O, The Oprah Magazine* p122 Ag 2017

Sinclair, Robert

Highly stretchable polymer semiconductor films through the nanoconfinement effect bibl graph *Science* v355 no6320 p1 Ja 6 2017

Sinclair Broadcast Group Inc.

REMOTE CONTROLLED A. KROLL and R. Choma color graph *Mother Jones* v42 no6 p48 N/D 2017

THE REVOLUTION WILL BE TELEVISED (IT'LL JUST HAVE LOW PRODUCTION VALUES) [Cover story] F. GIL-LETTE bw color map *Bloomberg Businessweek* no4531 p44 Jl 24 2017

Sindbaek, Sören Michael

Three Qs color *Science* v357 no6353 p737 Ag 25 2017

Sindelar, Allan

The Basics of BATTERY POWER *Mother Earth News* no279 p61 D/Ja 2017

Sindelar, Robert

New ABA President Outlines Priorities E. Nawotka chart color *Publishers Weekly* v264 no36 p12 S 4 2017

SINE, RICHARD

Hearts On Demand: Mass General Surgeon Makes Critical Strides in Regenerating Organs color *Forbes* v200 no3 p56 S 28 2017

Sinev, G.

Observation of coherent elastic neutrino-nucleus scattering diag *Science* v357 no6356 p1123 S 15 2017

Sinfield, Joe

How CFOs Can Take the Long-Term View in a Short-Term Economy *Harvard Business Review Digital Articles* p2 Mr 15 2016

How Industrial Systems Are Turning into Digital Services *Harvard Business Review Digital Articles* p2 Je 23 2015

Sing (Film)

McConaughey Goes Carly Rae In Animated Sing E. Berman color *Time* v188 no22-23 p109 N/D 2016

Sing D. Coggan color *Entertainment Weekly* no1446/1447 p103 D 2016/Ja 2017

SING T. J. Norton color *Sound & Vision* v82 no7 p70 S 2017

The Story of Reese [Cover story] color *InStyle* v23 no13 p226 D 2016

Sing, David K.

HAT-P-26b: A Neptune-mass exoplanet with a well-constrained heavy element abundance chart diag graph *Science* v356 no6338 p628 My 12 2017

Sing Street (Film)

No. 9 SING STREET L. Greenblatt color *Entertainment Weekly* no1444/1445 p56 D 16 2016

SING STREET D. Vaughn color *Sound & Vision* v81 no10 p71 D 2016

Singal, Jesse

50 Things Black Mirror Is Made Of img *New York* v49 no21 p106 O 17 2016

THE CONVERSATION color *Atlantic* v320 no2 p8 S 2017

Singapore

Getting (Ka)Popped in Singapore A. Graceffo color *Black Belt* v55 no2 p20 F/Mr 2017

Literary Publishing in SINGAPORE T. TAN *Publishers Weekly* v263 no41 p23 O 10 2016

Weatherscapes: Singapore – The Diamond Island City-State E. Darack *Weatherwise* v70 no1 p8 Ja/F 2017

Singapore (Poem)

An invitation to wonder D. D. Murphy bw *Christian Century* v134 no9 p20 Ap 26 2017

Singapore—Description & travel

SINGAPORE H. SILVA color *Conde Nast Traveler* v52 no3 p24 Mr 2017

State of the City R. WHITCOMB color *Weekly Standard* v22 no39 p38 Je 19 2017

Singapore—Economic conditions—21st century

How Singapore Sees Asia-and America I. Bremmer *Time* v188 no19 p10 N 7 2016

Singapore—History—1819-1867

For the Love of Welsh Rarebit C. TAN color *Foreign Policy* no225 p84 Jl/Ag 2017

Singapore—History—1867-1942

THE TRAGEDY OF FORCE Z: The sinking by Japanese aircraft of HMS Prince of Wales and HMS Repulse in December 1941 and the subsequent loss of Singapore was a grievous blow to British morale. But have historians misunderstood what really happened? A. Boyd *History Today* v67 no9 p64 S 2017

Singapore—History—Japanese occupation, 1942-1945

What We Learned From... The Fall of Singapore, 1942 J. Byrne *Military History* v33 no6 p14 Mr 2017

Singapore—Officials & employees

Multiracialism, Meritocracy and Stewardship *Vital Speeches of the Day* v83 no10 p290 O 2017

Singel, Mark S.

I PARDONED A CONVICT WHO KILLED AGAIN color *America* v217 no3 p34 Ag 7 2017

Singer, Bryan, 1965-

X-MEN: APOCALYPSE C. Chiarella color *Sound & Vision* v82 no2 p71 F/Mr 2017

Singer, Burton H.

Fund global health: Save lives and money color *Science* v356 no6342 p1018 Je 9 2017

SINGER, DAN

He Shoots! He Scores! *Texas Monthly* v45 no8 p36 Ag 2017

Singer, Drew

Secondary Offerings Take Center Stage graph *Bloomberg Businessweek* no4520 p43 My 1 2017

SINGER, GAIL

Summa Cum Lettuce color *Walrus* v14 no9 p82 N 2017

Singer, Isaac Bashevis

A WINDOW TO THE WORLD *Harper's Magazine* v334 no2000 p85 Ja 2017

Singer, Jo

Adopting the Right Cat for You *Catnip* v24 no10 p10 O 2016

Singer, Len

You Never Forget Your First Time diag il *Backpacker* v45 no2 p64 Mr 2017

SINGER, LENA

Queen of Cool *Chicago* v66 no10 p74 O 2017

Singer, Marc

Your Company Should Be Helping Customers on Social *Harvard Business Review Digital Articles* p2 Jl 15 2015

Singer, Margot

Missed Connections: Four troubled characters face London's summer of bombs L. SCHOLES *New York Times Book Review* p10 Ap 30 2017

Singer, Mark

AFTERMATH bw cartoon *New Yorker* v92 no38 p48 N 21 2016

BANK SHOT cartoon *New Yorker* v92 no30 p22 S 26 2016

FIRED UP cartoon *New Yorker* v92 no48 p18 F 6 2017

NEW YORK STRIP cartoon *New Yorker* v92 no45 p22 Ja 16 2017

Singer, Marty

"Get Me Marty Singer!" D. MARGOLICK color *Vanity Fair* p154 Hollywood 2017 Supplement

The Great Beauty Shake-Up bw color *Vogue* v207 no3 p436 Mr 2017

Singer, Maya

Personal Best color *Vogue* v207 no11 p160 N 2017

Singer, P. W.

WAR GOES VIRAL HOW SOCIAL MEDIA IS BEING WEAP-ONIZED color *Atlantic* v318 no4 p70 N 2016

SINGER, SALLY

DONATELLA VERSACE bw color *Vogue* v207 no3 p424 Mr 2017

Singer, Thea

THE EVOLUTION OF DANCE color *Scientific American* v317 no1 p66 Jl 2017

Singer-songwriters

1950-2017 Tom Petty E. R. Brown color *Entertainment Weekly* no1486 p18 O 13 2017

1963 - 2016 GEORGE MICHAEL N. Feeney color *Entertainment Weekly* no1448 p28 Ja 13 2017

Alessia Cara B. HIATT color *Rolling Stone* no1283 p18 Mr 23 2017

Better Than Ever M. Walker color *Wired* v24 no11 p48 N 2016

Beyoncé M. Harris-perry color *Time* v188 no25-26 p124 D 19 2016 Double Issue

Billy Joel [Cover story] P. DOYLE bw *Rolling Stone* no1289 p62 Je 15 2017

Bonnie Raitt P. DOYLE bw *Rolling Stone* no1287 p58 My 18 2017

Chester Bennington E. R. Brown color *Entertainment Weekly* no1476 p62 Ag 4 2017

Chris Cornell N. Feeney color *Entertainment Weekly* no1468/1469 p20 Je 2-9 2017

Cole Offers Exquisite Take on Standards B. Doerschuk color *Downbeat* v84 no10 p23 O 2017

Dua LIPA: THE BRITISH SINGER SONGWRITER FUSES SOUL AND POP BY MAKING IT PERSONAL C. KELSEY *Interview* v47 no3 p22 Ap 2017

Goodnight, grocer of despair M. BARCLAY color *Maclean's* v129 no47 p52 N 28 2016

THE GOOD SEED C. HEATH bw color *GQ: Gentlemen's Quarterly* v97 no5 p124 My 2017

Hard~core Trou~bad~our color *Rolling Stone* no1283 p34 Mr 23 2017

Hot Tracks: RYAN ADAMS L. ROBINSON color *Vanity Fair* v59 no9 p140 S 2017

HOW THE LIGHT GETS IN D. REMNICK bw cartoon *New Yorker* v92 no33 p46 O 17 2016

In Control R. Haskell *Vogue* v207 no6 p144 Je 2017

LEONARD COHEN S. Vega and L. Greenblatt color *Entertainment Weekly* no1446/1447 p98 D 2016/Ja 2017

Letter from Mexico City: The Life and Death of Juan Gabriel P. J. Smith *Film Quarterly* v70 no3 p69 Spr 2017

LORDE'S GROWING PAINS A. MORRIS bw color *Rolling Stone* no1288 p32 Je 1 2017

Maggie Rogers' Folk Fairy Tale D. BROWNE color *Rolling Stone* no1285 p15 Ap 20 2017

Neil Young color *AARP: The Magazine* v59 no2A p12 F/Mr 2016

The New Norah J. WEINER bw color *Rolling Stone* no1273 p18 N 3 2016

PRINCE J. SULLIVAN *New York Times Magazine* p48 D 25 2016

Q&A: John Mayer P. DOYLE color *Rolling Stone* no1291/1292 p30 Jl 13 2017

RAMBLING MAN N. PAUMGARTEN cartoon color *New Yorker* v93 no18 p36 Je 26 2017

Sam Smith's Raw Return P. DOYLE bw color *Rolling Stone* no1298 p13 O 19 2017

SO LONG, LEONARD color *Maclean's* v129 no47 p50 N 28 2016

SPARC OF GENIUS J. TUPPONCE *Virginia Living* v15 no3 p33 Ap 2017

Tom Petty: 1950-2017 D. Fricke bw *Rolling Stone* no1299 p12 N 2 2017

Singer-songwriters—Interviews

Iggy Pop Traded In His Sports Car D. Itzkoff color *New York Times Magazine* p70 D 4 2016

Q&A: Jason Isbell P. DOYLE color *Rolling Stone* no1293 p26 Ag 10 2017

Singerman, Brian

Power Player A. KONRAD color diag *Forbes* v199 no4 p84 Ap 25 2017

SINGER MORAN, LISA

second-trimester surprises *Parents* v92 no8 p128 Ag 2017

Singers

See also

Mezzo-sopranos

Opera singers

Singer-songwriters

Sopranos (Singers)

Tenors (Singers)

Women singers

Alessia Cara B. Muteba color *Current Biography* v77 no11 p26 N 2016

ALMOST FAMOUS T. REHAGEN *Atlanta* v56 no10 p36 F 2017

BIBI BOURELLY L. N. Williams color map *Essence* v47 no8 p80 D 2016

Bono C. Amanpour color *Glamour* v114 no12 p212 D 2016

COAL AND STEEL FOR Rod Stewart's masterpiece [Cover story] C. Swanson color *Model Railroader* v84 no6 p42 Je 2017

Conor Oberst Goes Home L. Goodman img *New York* v49 no19 p88 S 19 2016

Debbie Harry What's your backstage essential? D. WALTERS color *Bon Appetit* v62 no4 p118 Ap 2017

GÉORI BOUÉ *Opera News* v81 no10 p66 Ap 2017

GIRL ON FIRE A. Green color *Vogue* v207 no3 p464 Mr 2017

GOING SOLO J. Weiner *New York Times Magazine* p26 F 19 2017

Greg Lake and ELP Welcome Us Back to the Hi-Fi Show That Never Ends M. METTLER and C. Crowley bw color *Sound & Vision* v81 no10 p24 D 2016

THE HIGH PRIESTESS OF SOUL G. BLACK bw *Ebony* v72 no5 p98 Mr 2017

Katy's Got Sole N. Silverstein, F. Kane et al color *Glamour* v115 no2 p25 F 2017

The Legend Next Door P. Doyle bw color *Rolling Stone* no1278/1279 p38 Ja 12 2017

LEONARD COHEN 1934-2016 M. Gilmore bw color *Rolling Stone* no1276 p52 D 15 2016

LP: HAVING CRAFTED HITS FOR SOME OF THE BIGGEST NAMES IN MUSIC, THE CAPTIVATING SINGER-SONG-WRITER IS NOW TAKING HER OWN STARDOM FOR A SPIN S. RONSON *Interview* v47 no3 p22 My 2017

MALAIKA CHANEY A. Jordan color *Essence* v48 no6 p46 O 2017

Meet the Celebrity Judge J. LABIANCA color *Reader's Digest* v190 no1135 p80 N 2017

MILEY'S SUMMER OF Love J. Pressler color *Harper's Bazaar* no3655 p146 Ag 2017

The New Bronx Cheer color *GQ: Gentlemen's Quarterly* v97 no7 p80 Jl 2017

Rachel Platten M. Hagan color *Current Biography* v77 no11 p59 N 2016

Ray BLK H. WEISS *Interview* v47 no1 p18 F 2017

Remembering James Cotton J. Johnson bw *Downbeat* v84 no6 p25 Je 2017

RETURN ENGAGEMENT M. Schulman cartoon *New Yorker* v92 no30 p24 S 26 2016

THE RISE OF CAROLYN MALACHI *Washingtonian Magazine* v52 no5 p18 F 2017

Ryan Adams L. BROWN img *New York* p20 Mr 6 2017

SEVDALIZA: FOR THE IRANIAN DITCH SINGER-SONG-WRITER, BOUNDARIES IN HER LIFE AND ART ARE MEANT TO BE BROKEN H. WEISS *Interview* v47 no3 p32 My 2017

Sharon Jones J. NEWMAN color *Rolling Stone* no1276 p30 D 15 2016

SIGRID H. WEISS *Interview* v47 no6 p12 Ag 2017

SINGING IN THE DARK S. BURT color *Nation* v305 no6 p35 S 11 2017

Singing seldom-told Sandhills stories A. J. Bartels color *Nebraska Life* v21 no1 p63 Ja/F 2017

SOLANGE by BEYONCÉ *Interview* v47 no1 p40 F 2017

Solange Knowles HER BEST EVER E. Wilson color *InStyle* v24 no9 p184 S 2017

A Still-Dangerous Don J. NORDLINGER color *National Review* v69 no11 p40 Je 12 2017

THOMAS J. HUBBARD: SHARON, CT, NOVEMBER 20, 1924--DELRAY BEACH, FL, MARCH 20, 2017 *Opera News* v81 no12 p11 Je 2017

TONY BENNETT He's Still Got That SWING! I. RUDOLPH *TV Guide* p32 D 19 2016

WE DON'T CHANGE *Vital Speeches of the Day* v83 no10 p307 O 2017

WEEKND UPDATE B. Mazurek bw *Harper's Bazaar* no3656 p398 S 2017

Singers—Attitudes

Free Jazzmeia N. CHINEN *Texas Monthly* v45 no6 p88 Je 2017

Harry Styles' New Direction [Cover story] C. Crowe color *Rolling Stone* no1286 p20 My 4 2017

JUST camila M. TOPRAN color *Seventeen* v76 no2 p102 Mr 2017

Singers—Biography

Charlie Puth B. Muteba color *Current Biography* v78 no1 p64 Ja 2017

DAYMÉ AROCENA J. Murph color *Downbeat* v84 no4 p26 Ap 2017

Zara Larsson C. Mari color *Current Biography* v78 no2 p39 F 2017

Singers—Canada

THE NEW FACE OF R&B S. Scott color *Essence* v48 no6 p68 O 2017

Riley Fullton Shannon A. A. DAVIS color *Maclean's* p66 Je 2017

Singers—Interviews

Eric Church P. DOYLE bw *Rolling Stone* no1272 p58 O 20 2016

Hot Tracks: CHARLOTTE GAINSBOURG bw *Vanity Fair* v59 no10 p132 O 2017

Hot Tracks color *Vanity Fair* v59 no7 p52 Summ 2017

Idina Menzel S. STALL *Indianapolis Monthly* v12 no40 p25 Ag 2017

John Legend B. HIATT color *Rolling Stone* no1278/1279 p23 Ja 12 2017

John Mellencamp B. HIATT bw *Rolling Stone* no1286 p18 My 4 2017

The Neal Morse Band Progresses Into the Realization of a Fine Sonic Dream M. METTLER and C. Crowley color *Sound & Vision* v82 no5 p24 Je 2017

Phil Collins A. GREENE bw *Rolling Stone* no1275 p70 D 1 2016

Sheryl Crow B. HIATT cartoon *Rolling Stone* no1286 p82 My 4 2017

True Bruce [Cover story] B. HIATT bw color *Rolling Stone* no1272 p32 O 20 2016

Singers—United States

BAD GIRLS GET OLD J. STANFORD *Texas Monthly* v45 no7 p92 Jl 2017

BEHIND THE SCENES WITH Sabrina Carpenter color *Seventeen* p28 Ja 1 2017

BOOK AND BANJO J. BERRY color *New Orleans Magazine* v51 no3 p50 Ja 2017

THE EXTRAORDINARY ORDINARY LIFE OF THE ARTIST FORMERLY KNOWN AS PRINCE C. Heath bw color *GQ: Gentlemen's Quarterly* v86 no12 p220 D 2016

Lady Gaga color *InStyle* v24 no3 p274 Mr 2017

Lalah Hathaway B. Muteba color *Current Biography* v77 no10 p53 O 2016

Life on Planet Mars J. EELLS bw color *Rolling Stone* no1274 p28 N 17 2016

MAKE AMERICA HAPPY AGAIN J. GORDINIER color *Esquire* v167 no1 p60 F 2017

MAVIS STAPLES B. Zehme cartoon *Chicago* v65 no11 p168 N 2016

MY TOWN A. Whiting *Washingtonian Magazine* v52 no9 p174 Je 2017

A Pop Prodigy on the Edge of 13 B. SPANOS color *Rolling Stone* no1278/1279 p18 Ja 12 2017

Singers and Songwriters bw cartoon color *American Cowboy* p22 LEGENDS OF TEXAS Special Issue 2017

Still Shining On [Cover story] C. Penn color *Essence* v48 no6 p94 O 2017

Singers—United States—Biography

Thomas Rhett B. Muteba color *Current Biography* v78 no2 p70 F 2017

Singh, Aditya

Deep Learning Will Radically Change the Ways We Interact with Technology bw color diag *Harvard Business Review Digital Articles* p2 Ja 30 2017

Singh, Amarpal

The Second Anglo-Sikh War D. Saunders color *Military History* v34 no4 p74 N 2017

Singh, Jagmeet

The newest new NDP P. WELLS color *Maclean's* v130 no10 p8 N 2017

THE NEW ORANGE CRUSH N. KÖHLER color *Maclean's* v130 no8 p26 S 2017

SINGH, KARTIKEYA

Of Sun Gods and Solar Energy color *Issues in Science & Technology* v33 no2 p48 Wint 2017

Singh, Kathleen Dowling

THE SCRIPT OF IGNORANCE color *Tricycle: The Buddhist Review* v27 no1 p18 Fall 2017

Singh, Lilly—Interviews

3 QUESTIONS FOR LILLY SINGH I. Biedenharn color *Entertainment Weekly* no1462 p65 Ap 21 2017

SINGH, MICHAEL

Strength in a Tougher World color *National Review* v68 no22 p43 D 5 2016

Singh, Raghubir—Exhibitions

GOINGS ON ABOUT TOWN color *New Yorker* v93 no32 p5 O 16 2017

Singh, Rajat

Self-renewal of a purified Tie2+ hematopoietic stem cell population relies on mitochondrial clearance bibl graph *Science* v354 no6316 p1156 D 2 2016

Singh, Rajesh Kumar

India's Nuclear Industry Needs a Jolt color diag *Bloomberg Businessweek* no4526 p17 Je 12 2017

Rich Returns From Poor Women Collecting Debts color *Bloomberg Businessweek* no4541 p18 O 9 2017

Singh, Ravi P.

Improving global integration of crop research color *Science* v357 no6349 p359 Jl 28 2017

Singh, Ronnie

FACE OF THE FRANCHISE S. Kwak color *Sports Illustrated* v127 no11 p20 O 9 2017

Singh, Shruti

Big Meat Braces for A Labor Shortage color *Bloomberg Businessweek* no4511 p19 F 13 2017

Singh, Sushant K.

Global Arsenic Contamination: Living With the Poison Nectar bibl color map *Environment* v59 no2 p24 Mr/Ap 2017

Singh, Vishal

Even a 14-Cent Food Tax Could Lead to Healthier Choices *Harvard Business Review Digital Articles* p2 S 29 2016

SINGH KHALSA, KARTA PURKH

Mineral-Rich Herbs color *Better Nutrition* v78 no12 p20 D 2016

Singin' in the Rain (Film)

Working It M. KORESKY color *Film Comment* v53 no3 p42 My/ Je 2017

Singing

Confessions of a Total Poseur D. SKINNER color *Weekly Standard* v23 no5 p5 O 9 2017

Eliane Elias Returns to Samba A. Morrison color *Downbeat* v84 no6 p18 Je 2017

Pleasurable Health Hacks That Actually Work T. DUMAIN *Reader's Digest* v188 no1124 p60 O 2016

Single & Satisfied (TV program)

PARTY OF ONE color *Essence* v48 no2 p101 Je 2017

Single cell proteins

Single-cell transcriptomics to explore the immune system in health and disease M. J. T. Stubbington, O. Rozenblatt-Rosen et al diag *Science* v357 no6359 p58 O 6 2017

Single electron devices

Strong coupling of a single electron in silicon to a microwave photon J. V. Cady, D. M. Zajac et al bibl graph *Science* v355 no6321 p1 Ja 13 2017

Single fathers

Father's Day: The Real Stories of Black Single Dads G. JEFFERS color *Ebony* v72 no8 p58 Je 2017

THE YEAR OF MAGICAL PARENTING P. OSWALT color *GQ: Gentlemen's Quarterly* v86 no12 p158 D 2016

Single men

See also

Divorced men

The Guys Next Door D. Stattmann, P. Kita et al *Women's Health* v14 no2 p20 Mr 2017

Single mothers

Couponing for Charity C. NOWAK color *Reader's Digest* v190 no1132 p8 Jl/Ag 2017

The Helsinki Formula J. KAY *Walrus* v13 no9 p74 N 2016

"I AM ENOUGH" [Cover story] A. SPENCER cartoon color *Redbook* p100 Ap 2017

IF CLASSIC BOOKS BECAME CLICKBAIT *Reader's Digest* v190 no1133 p65 S 2017

MY BADASS MOM M. EASTER bw *Men's Health* v32 no4 p122

My 2017

They Did the Right Thing A. LEWIS, A. SIMMONS et al cartoon *Reader's Digest* v190 no1134 p88 O 2017

Single mothers—Social conditions

THE MOTHERS K. Hayeri *Harper's Magazine* v334 no2004 p63 My 2017

Single mothers—Taxation

How Trump's Tax Proposals Will Affect Single Working Mothers S. Damaske *Harvard Business Review Digital Articles* p2 D 22 2016

Single nucleotide polymorphisms

Single-cell whole-genome analyses by Linear Amplification via Transposon Insertion (LIANTI) C. Chen, D. Xing et al graph *Science* v356 no6334 p189 Ap 14 2017

Single parents

See also

Single fathers

Single mothers

Rock On, Single Moms S. S. GOLD *Parents* v92 no1 p16 Ja 2017

Single parents—Social conditions

THE MOTHERS K. Hayeri *Harper's Magazine* v334 no2004 p63 My 2017

Single-payer health care

THE BIG IDEA *In These Times* v41 no10 p39 O 2017

AN EXPENSIVE EXPERIMENT WITH SINGLE-PAYER HEALTH CARE E. Boehm color *Reason* v49 no5 p15 O 2017

Is the U.S. Ready for a Single-Payer Health Care System? S. Galea *Harvard Business Review Digital Articles* p2 Jl 18 2017

Single Payer Here We Come J. BLEIFUSS *In These Times* v41 no5 p5 My 2017

Single people

See also

Single men

Four Tips for Going Solo E. O'brien chart color *Money* v46 no2 p41 Mr 2017

Single people—Religious life

New rituals for new realities C. H. Merritt *Christian Century* v133 no21 p61 O 12 2016

Single sex schools

Singled Out: Los Angeles' misguided effort to open more single-sex public schools K. SHER and G. SHERWIN *Ms.* v27 no2 p10 Summ 2017

Single tracks (Railroads)

the missing link r. stuart color *Bike Magazine* v24 no2 p34 Mr 2017

one more climb b. minnigh color *Bike Magazine* v24 no2 p21 Mr 2017

AN UNCERTAIN ROAD S. STOREY bw color *Bike Magazine* v24 no2 p56 Mr 2017

Single women

See also

Single mothers

5 SMART SAVING TIPS FOR SINGLE WOMEN J. Hazelwood color *Black Enterprise* v47 no7 p17 My/Je 2017

The Ambition-Marriage Trade-Off Too Many Single Women Face L. Bursztyn, T. Fujiwara et al *Harvard Business Review Digital Articles* p2 My 8 2017

Everyone Calm Down About My Being Single, Please C. Fisher color *Glamour* v114 no11 p132 N 2016

Single women—United States

What Single Women Need to Know J. BODNAR color *Kiplinger's Personal Finance* v71 no11 p25 N 2017

Singleleaf pinyon

Singleleaf Pinyon Pine *American Forests* v123 no1 p11 Wint/Spr 2017

Singles: The Definitive 45s Collection 1952-1991 (Music)

Magic on the Bandstand M. LONGLEY bw *Downbeat* v84 no5 p64 My 2017

SINGLETARY, KIMBERLY

Andrea Norman color *Louisiana Life* v37 no3 p56 Ja/F 2017

People TO WATCH [Cover story] color *New Orleans Magazine* v52 no1 p76 S 2017

Singleton, Charlotte

OH, HOW I HAVE ENJOYED *Arizona Highways* v93 no10 p4 O 2017

Singleton, John

BOYZ N THE HOOD S. Li color *Entertainment Weekly* no1460/1461 p76 Ap 7-17 2017

SINGLETON, MARILYN

Goodbye to You—and You *USA Today Magazine* v145 no2860 p11 Ja 2017

Are the Liberal Democrats Serious?—Is Everyone (read, Republicans) Really Racist? *USA Today Magazine* v145 no2863 p4 Ap 2017

MODERN MEDICINE MESS *USA Today Magazine* v145 no2862 p52 Mr 2017

A Very Expensive Free lunch *USA Today Magazine* v146 no2868 p16 S 2017

Sinha, E.

Eutrophication will increase during the 21st century as a result of precipitation changes map *Science* v357 no6349 p405 Jl 28 2017

Sinha, Gunjan

THE ORGANOID ARCHITECT color *Science* v357 no6353 p746 Ag 25 2017

Sinha, Janmejaya

Navigating the Dozens of Different Strategy Options *Harvard Business Review Digital Articles* p2 Je 24 2015

Sinha, Kalyan K.

Distortion of histone octamer core promotes nucleosome mobilization by a chromatin remodeler diag *Science* v355 no6322 p263 Ja 20 2017

Sinha, Manisha

America's Greatest Movement J. M. McPherson cartoon *New York Review of Books* v63 no16 p63 O 27 2016

Sinha, P. K.

Are Sales Incentives Becoming Obsolete? *Harvard Business Review Digital Articles* p2 Ag 3 2017

Can Your Sales Team Actually Achieve Their Stretch Goals? *Harvard Business Review Digital Articles* p2 Jl 11 2016

Despite Dire Predictions, Salespeople Aren't Going Away *Harvard Business Review Digital Articles* p2 Mr 31 2016

Driving Sales Success This Quarter, This Year, and Beyond *Harvard Business Review Digital Articles* p2 D 1 2016

Great Salespeople Are Born, but Great Sales Forces Are Made *Harvard Business Review Digital Articles* p2 My 20 2016

Help Your Salespeople Spend Time on the Right Things *Harvard Business Review Digital Articles* p2 F 15 2016

How More Accessible Information Is Forcing B2B Sales to Adapt *Harvard Business Review Digital Articles* p2 Ja 6 2016

How to Spot Hidden Opportunities for Sales Growth *Harvard Business Review Digital Articles* p2 S 17 2015

Ineffective Sales Leaders Can Cause Lasting Damage color *Harvard Business Review Digital Articles* p2 Ja 30 2017

Sales Bonuses Are Supposed to Motivate, So Don't Waste Them on Easy Targets *Harvard Business Review Digital Articles* p2 S 14 2017

The Technology Trends That Matter to Sales Teams *Harvard Business Review Digital Articles* p2 My 7 2015

There's No One System for Paying Your Global Sales Force *Harvard Business Review Digital Articles* p2 N 13 2015

When Sales Incentives Should Be Based on Profit, Not Revenue *Harvard Business Review Digital Articles* p2 Je 10 2015

Why Sales Ops Is So Hard to Get Right *Harvard Business Review Digital Articles* p2 D 29 2014

Why Sales Teams Should Reexamine Territory Design *Harvard Business Review Digital Articles* p2 Ag 7 2015

Sinha, Rachel

Bringing an Entrepreneurial Mindset to the World's Failing Systems *Harvard Business Review Digital Articles* p2 F 2 2015

Sink, Justin

The Wall Needs the Consent of Many map *Bloomberg Businessweek* no4510 p13 F 6 2017

Sinkholes

Some Queensland Mysteries J. NICKELL *Skeptical Inquirer* v41 no3 p14 My/Je 2017

Sinks (Plumbing fixtures)

SINK SMARTS color *Good Housekeeping* v265 no4 p64d O 2017

Sinks (Plumbing fixtures)—Evaluation

A Housewife's Kitchen, 1931 color *Old House Journal* v45 no7 p70 O 2017

Sinks (Plumbing fixtures)—Maintenance & repair

THE FIX E. Johnson cartoon *Old House Journal* v45 no6 p56
S 2017

Sinner, The (TV program)
Darkness Under the Sun on USA's Gripping Drama the Sinner D.
D'addario color *Time* v190 no6 p51 Ag 7 2017
The Sinner J. Jensen color *Entertainment Weekly* no1476 p50 Ag
4 2017
THE SINNER T. Stack color *Entertainment Weekly* no1468/1469
p62 Je 2-9 2017

Sinnott, Roger W.
75, 50 & 25 YEARS AGO color *Sky & Telescope* v134 no2 p8
Ag 2017
75, 50 & 25 YEARS AGO *Sky & Telescope* v133 no1 p7 Ja 2017
75, 50 & 25 YEARS AGO *Sky & Telescope* v133 no4 p8 Ap 2017
75, 50 & 25 YEARS AGO *Sky & Telescope* v134 no6 p8 D 2017

Sinogeikin, Stanislav
Quantum and isotope effects in lithium metal color diag graph *Science* v356 no6344 p1254 Je 23 2017

Sinovets, Polina
Ban the bomb by... banning the bomb? bibl *Bulletin of the Atomic
Scientists* v73 no3 p197 My 2017
Europe's nuclear woes: Mitigating the challenges of the next years
bibl *Bulletin of the Atomic Scientists* v73 no4 p245 Jl 2017

SINRICH, JENN
No More Flu Shot Excuses! color *Reader's Digest* v190 no1135
p46 N 2017

Sin—Social aspects
What is sin? K. Considine *U.S. Catholic* v82 no7 p49 Jl 2017

SINTUMUANG, Kevin
BACK TO THE FUTURE color *Esquire* p16 Ag 2017
THE BEACH RESET color *Esquire* p18 Ag 2017
Best FAST CAR for Around $50K color *Esquire* v166 no4 p74
N 2016
BINGE BIGGER color *Esquire* v167 no2 p60 Mr 2017
DITCH THE LAPTOP? cartoon color *Esquire* p52 S 2017
FOR THE LOVE OF CARS: THE BEST RIDES OF 2017 Esquire color *Esquire* p65 O 2017
Hardware Update Is Available color *Esquire* p74 BigBlackBook
THE IMPOSSIBLE LIST bw cartoon color *Esquire* v167 no1 p70
F 2017
Is This How You Use the Poo Emoji? color *Esquire* v166 no4 p30
N 2016
THE MAVERICKS OF HOLLYWOOD 2017 bw color *Esquire*
v167 no2 p89 Mr 2017
ON THE WAGON color *Esquire* p18 Je/Jl 2017
PLEASURE CRUISE color *Esquire* p35 N 2017
RELEASE THE BEAST color *Esquire* p24 My 2017
A Sedan with Sprezzatura color *Esquire* v167 no1 p22 F 2017
TOO FUN TO FAIL cartoon color *Esquire* p32 Ap 2017
Tuned to THRILL bw *Esquire* p52 2017 BigBlackBook

SINU, PALATTY ALLESH
Can the Spiritual Values of Forests Inspire Effective Conservation? *BioScience* v67 no8 p688 Ag 2017

Sinusitis—Treatment
Sinus Solutions E. A. KANE color *Better Nutrition* v78 no11 p28
N 2016

Sinyai, Clayton
Reunion! bw cartoon *Commonweal* v144 no16 p10 O 6 2017

SINZER, CHASE
Why You Should Become a Wine Snob color *GQ: Gentlemen's
Quarterly* v97 no10 p80 O 2017

Siomi, Haruhiko
Mobile elements control stem cell potency bibl diag *Science* v355
no6325 p581 F 10 2017

Sipahigil, A.
An integrated diamond nanophotonics platform for quantum-optical networks bibl graph *Science* v354 no6314 p847 N 18 2016

Sipiagin, Alex
Sipiagin Assembles Elite Sextet for New Album of Original Music
T. Panken color *Downbeat* v84 no6 p16 Je 2017

Sipilä, Mikko
Global atmospheric particle formation from CERN CLOUD measurements bibl graph map *Science* v354 no6316 p1119 D 2 2016

Siqi Ge
Glycomics and its application potential in precision medicine bibl
diag *Science* v354 no6319 p36 D 23 2016

Siqueira, Carla C.
Brazil's public universities in crisis color *Science* v356 no6340
p812 My 26 2017

Sirbasku, Judy
OUR 2016 SPONSORS *Arabian Horse World* v57 no3 p28 D
2016

Sircar, Tiya
THE GOOD PLACE'S (VERY GOOD) BAD SEED D. Schwartz
color *Entertainment Weekly* no1485 p46 O 6 2017

Siren, Pontus M. A.
The 6 Most Common Innovation Mistakes Companies Make *Harvard Business Review Digital Articles* p2 Je 23 2015
Calculate How Much Your Company Should Invest in Innovation
Harvard Business Review Digital Articles p2 D 17 2014
Innovation Isn't the Answer to All Your Problems *Harvard Business Review Digital Articles* p2 Je 2 2015
Zombie Projects: How to Find Them and Kill Them *Harvard
Business Review Digital Articles* p2 Mr 4 2015

Siren Marine LLC
Siren Marine MTC Boat-Monitoring System J. Y. WOOD color
Power & Motoryacht v34 no7 p28 Jl 2017

Sirena Marine Maritime Industry & Trade Inc.
Sirena 64 J. Y. Wood color *Power & Motoryacht* v33 no4 p38
Ap 2017

Sirenia
See also
Manatees
Watch: The Bachelorette A. WUNDERMAN color *Backpacker*
p22 S 2017

Siri
Now Is the Greatest Time To Shed Your Pathetic Flesh cartoon
Bloomberg Businessweek no4496 p28 O 24 2016

Siriano, Christian
The Power of an Outsider E. Mahaney and K. Branch color *Glamour* v115 no1 p62 Ja 2017

Siriboe, Kofi
Queen Sugar M. Logan *TV Guide* v65 no31 p37 Jl 24 2017
STYLE YOUR GUY A. Dorsey color *Essence* v48 no6 p36 O
2017
Sweet Home Louisiana M. Z. SEITZ *New York* v49 no19 p97 S
19 2016

Siriboe, Kofi—Interviews
MAN OF STYLE Kofi Siriboe F. Penn color *InStyle* v23 no12
p92 N 2016

Sirima, Sodiomon B.
Resistance to malaria through structural variation of red blood cell
invasion receptors diag *Science* v356 no6343 p1139 Je 16 2017

Sirin Labs (Company)
HOW VULNERABLE IS YOUR PHONE? D. PIERCE diag
Wired v25 no6 p37 Je 2017

Sirius (Star)
Wonders of the Year-Start Sky F. Schaaf *Sky & Telescope* v133
no1 p45 Ja 2017

Sirius XM Radio Inc.
Why I Didn't Buy the Benz K. C. POHLMANN color *Sound &
Vision* v82 no6 p21 Jl/Ag 2017

SIRIWARDENA, GAVIN M.
Doses of Neighborhood Nature: The Benefits for Mental Health of
Living with Nature *BioScience* v67 no2 p147 F 2017

Sirkin, Harold
A Way to Assess and Prioritize Your Change Efforts *Harvard
Business Review Digital Articles* p2 Jl 9 2015

Sirletti, Sonia
Banks? cartoon *Bloomberg Businessweek* no4503 p32 D 12 2016

Sirota, Nadia
String Theory: Classical music needs new superfans. Nadia Sirota
is doing her best to create them J. Davidson img *New York* v50
no15 p60 Jl 24 2017

Sirotnak, Joe
A Rare Tuft K. SIBER *National Parks* v91 no1 p26 Wint 2017

SIRTORI-CORTINA, DANIELA
The $4.5 Billion Cabinet color *Forbes* v199 no1 p26 Ja 24 2017
Billionaire Ballot Boxes color *Forbes* v198 no5 p50 O 25 2016
HOW MUCH IS PRESIDENT TRUMP WORTH NOW? color
Forbes v199 no3 p82 Mr 28 2017
Rocky Road color *Forbes* v199 no1 p28 Ja 24 2017

SOUTH OF THE WALL bw *Forbes* v199 no3 p74 Mr 28 2017

THE TRUMP CLONE [Cover story] bw color *Forbes* v199 no3 p50 Mr 28 2017

Sisay-Joof, Fatoumatta

Resistance to malaria through structural variation of red blood cell invasion receptors diag *Science* v356 no6343 p1139 Je 16 2017

Sisco, Samantha

I miss my sister *Scholastic Choices* v32 no3 p10 N/D 2016

Siscoe, George

Book Review: Where Meteorology Meets Art *Weatherwise* v70 no2 p37 Mr/Ap 2017

Sisk, Sidney Vaneyck

The Thread *New York Times Magazine* p10 Ap 30 2017

SISKIND, TAYLOR

Circles in the Sand color *Natural History* v125 no10 p48 O 2017

Sisson, Carly

Alen 45 color *Power & Motoryacht* v34 no11 p78 N 2017

BETTER WITH AGE bw color *Power & Motoryacht* v34 no10 p106 O 2017

Green Machine color *Power & Motoryacht* v34 no10 p38 O 2017

Sisterhoods

THIS IS US color map *Glamour* v115 no9 p163 S 2017

Sisters

See also
  Twin sisters

Back Talk *National Geographic Kids* no469 p38 Ap 2017

Face OF Bass R. SULLIVAN color *Vogue* v207 no7 p44 Jl 2017

HER SISTER'S KEEPER? A. Day color *O, The Oprah Magazine* p76 Je 2017

Hope for all R. Miska color *U.S. Catholic* v82 no2 p45 F 2017

Learning CURVE C. Kitchener color *Vogue* v207 no4 p116 Ap 2017

Waiting for Maryan A. Hussein *New York Times Magazine* p29 N 20 2016

Sisters' Boy (Short story)

Sisters' Boy J. EPSTEIN *Commentary* v143 no6 p35 Je 2017

Sisters-in-law

Snow Me Something M. Gunch color *New Orleans Magazine* v51 no5 p46 Mr 2017

Sisters of Mercy

BLESS IS MORE E. Dwyer *Saturday Evening Post* v289 no4 p28 Jl/Ag 2017

Sital, Krystal A.

At the Threshold color *New York Times Magazine* p28 D 4 2016

Sitaraman, Ganesh

A BILLIONAIRES' REPUBLIC J. PURDY color *Nation* v305 no3 p27 Jl 31 2017

The Constitutional Case for Equality K. Carty color *Washington Monthly* v49 no9/10 p133 S/O 2017

Created Equal W. McCORMACK color *New Republic* v248 no8/9 p74 Ag/S 2017

DIVIDED WE FALL color *New Republic* v248 no5 p42 My 2017

Site, Luigi Delle

Surviving scientist burnout *Physics Today* v70 no9 p10 S 2017

Site Report: Syracuse (Poem)

Site Report: Syracuse B. SMITH *Progressive* v81 no7 p69 O/N 2017

Sitka Gear (Company)

NEW HIDES color *Outdoor Life* v224 no6 p42 Ag 2017

SITKIN, SIM B.

The Stretch Goal Paradox color diag il img *Harvard Business Review* v95 no1 p92 Ja/F 2017

Sitko, Matthew

Cliff-Hanger A. SIMMONS *Reader's Digest* v189 no1128 p12 Mr 2017

Sitman, Matthew

Saving Calvin from Clichés [Cover story] bw *Commonweal* v144 no17 p18 O 20 2017

Sittenfeld, Curtis

The Prairie Wife cartoon color *New Yorker* v92 no49 p76 F 13 2017

SHOW DON'T TELL bw cartoon *New Yorker* v93 no16 p62 Je 5 2017

Sitting position

LOWER-BACK LOVE R. Rosen color *Yoga Journal* p80 2017 Special Issue

MANSPREADERS OF THE YEAR L. FINCK cartoon chart *New Yorker* v93 no17 p40 Je 19 2017

TAKE A SEAT C. Krucoff color *Yoga Journal* p62 2017 Special Issue

WE'VE GOT YOURBACK A. SHAFFER color *Better Homes & Gardens* v95 no10 p174 O 2017

Situation comedies (Television programs)

Powerless J. Pfeiffer *TV Guide* v65 no6 p36 Ja 30 2017

Will & GRace: (KAREN, JACK, AND ROSARIO, TOO): THE NBC SITCOM'S MUCH-ANTICIPATED REVIVAL IS JUST WHAT AMERICA NEEDS NOW D. REYNOLDS *Advocate* no1093 p34 O/N 2017

Situational awareness

A STICKY SITUATION B. HEAVEY cartoon *Field & Stream* v121 no9 p86 Ap 2017

Sitz, Miriam

2017 Women in Architecture Awards Honor Pioneering Professionals *Architectural Record* v205 no9 p34 S 2017

The Art of the Deal *Architectural Record* v204 no10 p78 O 2016

Confluence Park *Architectural Record* v205 no4 p208 Ap 2017

CUAC Arquitectura bw color *Architectural Record* v204 no12 p56 D 2016

Design Community Reacts to Paris Agreement Withdrawal *Architectural Record* v205 no7 p32 Jl 2017

Design Unveiled for Heatherwick's Vessel at Hudson Yards *Architectural Record* v204 no10 p24 O 2016

Diane L. Max Health Center *Architectural Record* v205 no4 p187 Ap 2017

Diébédo Francis Kéré *Architectural Record* v205 no6 p28 Je 2017

Eric Cesal *Architectural Record* v205 no1 p23 Ja 2017

house of the month *Architectural Record* v205 no1 p27 Ja 2017

house of the month color diag *Architectural Record* v205 no3 p33 Mr 2017

New Arc Platform Aims to Streamline and Integrate Green Certification for Existing Buildings *Architectural Record* v204 no11 p27 N 2016

Northwest Passage *Architectural Record* v205 no7 p104 Jl 2017

perspective house of the month: A FIRM REVISITS THE SITE OF ITS FIRST RESIDENCE TO CREATE A RELAXING BACKYARD RETREAT FOR A LONGTIME CLIENT AND FRIEND color map *Architectural Record* v205 no5 p37 My 2017

Reeling from Hurricanes, U.S. Architects Get to Work *Architectural Record* v205 no10 p21 O 2017

Skylights and Shadows: Philip Johnson's Sculpture Gallery at the Glass House shines once again bw color *Architectural Record* v205 no5 p49 My 2017

The Sum of Its Parts *Architectural Record* v205 no6 p86 Je 2017

Top 300 Firms: Gensler Maintains Leading Revenue for Six Years Straight color *Architectural Record* v205 no8 p19 Ag 2017

To the Rescue color diag *Architectural Record* v205 no3 p118 Mr 2017

Up and Coming: These eight towers around the world, some in planning and others approaching completion, project ambition in scale and form color *Architectural Record* v205 no5 p122 My 2017

U.S. Pavilion to Explore Citizenship at 2018 Venice Architecture Biennale *Architectural Record* v205 no10 p28 O 2017

Siu, Alice

Applying Deliberative Democracy in Africa: Uganda's First Deliberative Polls *Daedalus* v146 no3 p140 Summ 2017

Deliberation & the Challenge of Inequality *Daedalus* v146 no3 p119 Summ 2017

Siu, Michelle

backstory color *New Republic* v248 no6 p72 Je 2017

Siva (Hindu deity)

Locking Brows with BHARTRIHARI A. Schelling cartoon *Tricycle: The Buddhist Review* v26 no3 p72 Spr 2017

Sivaram, Varun

THE GLOBAL WARMING WILD CARD bw color *Scientific American* v316 no5 p48 My 2017

Unlocking Clean Energy bw color *Issues in Science & Technology* v33 no2 p31 Wint 2017

Siver, David

The SAILING SCENE color *Sail* v48 no9 p6 S 2017

Sivertsson, Åsa

A subcellular map of the human proteome color *Science* v356 no6340 p820 My 26 2017

Sivis, Murat

Tailored semiconductors for high-harmonic optoelectronics graph *Science* v357 no6348 p303 Jl 21 2017

Siwy, Zuzanna

Improving on aquaporins diag *Science* v357 no6353 p753 Ag 25 2017

Six (TV program)

MEN OF HONOR D. HOLBROOK *TV Guide* v65 no4 p28 Ja 16 2017

Six J. Jensen color *Entertainment Weekly* no1449 p50 Ja 20 2017

Six Flags Over Georgia (Ga.)

50 YEARS OF SIX FLAGS J. GREEN *Atlanta* v57 no2 p32 Je 2017

EASY Rider *Atlanta* v57 no2 p132 Je 2017

Six Senses Hotels Resorts Spas (Company)

WORD OF MOUTH color *Conde Nast Traveler* v51 no11 p53 D 2016

Sixteenth Street Baptist Church (Birmingham, Ala.)

THE STEPS WE TOOK J. Lewis color *Southern Living* v52 no2 p106 F 2017

Sixth Sense, The (Film)

M. NIGHT SHYAMALAN'S SCORECARD color *Entertainment Weekly* no1450 p43 Ja 27 2017

SIYUE LI

Greenhouse Gas Emissions from Reservoir Water Surfaces: A New Global Synthesis *BioScience* v66 no11 p949 N 1 2016

Size of brain

7 Bite-size Facts About Dinosaurs color *National Geographic Kids* no475 p9 N 2017

Food for Thought L. Evans Ogden color *Natural History* v125 no7 p6 Jl/Ag 2017

Size of business enterprises

It Pays to Be Smart [Cover story] D. Rotman graph *MIT Technology Review* v120 no4 p54 Jl/Ag 2017

THE SIZE OF THINGS S. SCHWEBLIN cartoon *New Yorker* v93 no15 p56 My 29 2017

Sizemore, H. G.

Extensive water ice within Ceres' aqueously altered regolith: Evidence from nuclear spectroscopy bibl graph *Science* v355 no6320 p1 Ja 6 2017

SIZEMORE, NICKI

SUMMERTIME + THE COOKING IS SLOW color *Parents* v92 no6 p122 Je 2017

SIZER, NIGEL

An Ecoregion-Based Approach to Protecting Half the Terrestrial Realm *BioScience* v67 no6 p534 Je 2017

Sjalfstaeoisflokkurinn (Iceland)

TAKING COMMAND E. S. ARNARSÓTTIR *Iceland Review* v55 no2 p52 Mr/Ap 2017

Sjöblom, Tobias

A pathology atlas of the human cancer transcriptome diag *Science* v357 no6352 p660 Ag 18 2017

Sjong, Justen

Ride the Wave color *Climbing* no357 p44 N 2017

Van Mouse K. CORRIGAN color *Climbing* no351 p24 F/Mr 2017

Sjöstedt, Evelina

A pathology atlas of the human cancer transcriptome diag *Science* v357 no6352 p660 Ag 18 2017

A subcellular map of the human proteome color *Science* v356 no6340 p820 My 26 2017

Skagen Denmark Ltd.

Côte d'Azur color *House Beautiful* v159 no3 p23 Ap 2017

SKAGGS, RANDI

Home of the Brave cartoon *Reader's Digest* v190 no1132 p99 Jl/Ag 2017

Skagit River Valley (B.C. & Wash.)

AMERICAN PLACES *American Scholar* v86 no2 p128 Spr 2017

Skakel, Sallie

My President Was Black *Atlantic* v319 no2 p8 Mr 2017

Skal, David J.

Father of Dracula J. ZINOMAN *New York Times Book Review* p19 O 30 2016

Skalak, Matt

Potential role of intratumor bacteria in mediating tumor resistance

to the chemotherapeutic drug gemcitabine diag *Science* v357 no6356 p1156 S 15 2017

Skariton, Jonathan

Séance Infernale *Publishers Weekly* v264 no26 p155 Je 26 2017

Skaros, Damianos

RIVER REBORN *New York State Conservationist* v71 no4 p10 F 2017

Skarsgård, Alexander, 1976-

Alexander Skarsgård R. Means color *Current Biography* v78 no1 p78 Ja 2017

Bill SKARSGÅRD *Interview* v47 no5 p58 Je/Jl 2017

The Legend of Tarzan M. Fell color *TV Guide* v65 no7 p49 F 13 2017

Skarsgard, Bill

Bill SKARSGÅRD A. Skarsgard *Interview* v47 no5 p58 Je/Jl 2017

Skateboarders

Gang's All Here J. Harman color *Glamour* v115 no5 p178 My 2017

Long May You Ride A. Fenwick and T. Keith color *Sports Illustrated* v125 no14 p26 O 24-31 2016

Skateboarding

AMATEUR HOUR T. Bird bw color *Snowboarder* v29 no2 p90 O 2016

MOUNTAIN DEW SUPERSNAKE SIERRA-AT-TAHOE, CA T. Bird color *Snowboarder* v29 no2 p108 O 2016

Skateboarding parks

Lords of Newport L. MURTHA *Cincinnati Magazine* v50 no8 p56 My 2017

Skateboards

Performance with purpose K. C. Horning color *U.S. Catholic* v81 no11 p12 N 2016

Skateboards—Evaluation

Get-Around Work-Arounds M. Kotack *Sierra* v101 no6 p19 N/D 2016

Skaters

Lords of Newport L. MURTHA *Cincinnati Magazine* v50 no8 p56 My 2017

Skaters—Societies, etc.

Bewitched L. GÖKSENIN color *Vogue* v207 no4 p160 Ap 2017

Skating

FIGURE SKATING SHOWDOWN! K. Rosen *TV Guide* v65 no13 p49 Mr 20 2017

Holidays on the Square *South Dakota Magazine* v32 no4 p99 N/D 2016

THE ITINERARY: TYSONS C. Hacinli *Washingtonian Magazine* v52 no3 p101 D 2016

Memories on Ice R. Marshall color *Money* v46 no2 p88 Mr 2017

Skelding, Kimberly A.

Distribution and clinical impact of functional variants in 50,726 whole-exome sequences from the DiscovEHR study chart graph *Science* v354 no6319 paaf6814-1 D 23 2016

Skeletal muscle

See also

Abdominal muscles

Leg muscles

Control of muscle formation by the fusogenic micropeptide myomixer P. Bi, A. Ramirez-Martinez et al diag *Science* v356 no6335 p323 Ap 21 2017

I HEART TAURINE D. N. JACKSON color *Muscle & Performance* v9 no10 p18 O 2017

Skeletal muscle physiology

CLOSING THE (THIGH) GAP N. TUMMINELLO cartoon *Muscle & Performance* v9 no5 p22 My 2017

Muscle health: Strong for life *Mayo Clinic Health Letter* v35 p1 2017 SepcialReport

Skeleton

See also

Ribs (Anatomy)

Ask the Biologist D. Kreinheder *New York State Conservationist* v72 no2 p31 O 2017

THE GREAT TAKEOVER D. EGAN color map *Discover* v38 no8 p56 O 2017

The growth pattern of Neandertals, reconstructed from a juvenile skeleton from El Sidrón (Spain) A. Rosas, L. Rios et al color graph *Science* v357 no6357 p1282 S 22 2017

Kennewick Man buried, along with conflict color *Science* v355 no6328 p892 Mr 3 2017

Skeleton Coast (Namibia)

In the Wind W. Bendix and A. Van Gysen bw color *Surfing Magazine* v53 no3 p50 Mr 2017

Skeleton—Exhibitions

The Politics of Rotting Blubber S. LEWSEN color *Walrus* v14 no3 p59 Ap 2017

Skelhorn, John

The biology of color color *Science* v357 no6350 p470 Ag 4 2017

Skelly, Julia

A Peaceable Kingdom color *Orion Magazine* v35 no6 p32 N/D 2016

SKENAZY, LENORE

ODE TO THE OFFICE FRIDGE *Reader's Digest* v188 no1126 p65 D 2016/Ja 2017

PREDATORS AND POPCORN bw color *Reason* v48 no9 p16 F 2017

THE SCHOOL PROJECT THAT SETS PARENTS FREE color *Reason* v48 no10 p10 Mr 2017

WANT TO TREAT YOUR KID LIKE A FELON ON PAROLE? THERE'S AN APP FOR THAT color *Reason* v49 no4 p12 Ag/S 2017

WE ALL SCREAM FOR THE ICE CREAM MAN'S HEAD cartoon *Reason* v49 no2 p6 Je 2017

WHEN PLAYBOY MADE IT BIG *Reason* v48 no11 p6 Ap 2017

YE OLDE IKEA SEX TRAFFICKERS color *Reason* v49 no6 p15 N 2017

Skeptical Inquirer (Periodical)

A Glimpse Backward—and Forward—at Skepticism's Big Tent B. RADFORD *Skeptical Inquirer* v40 no6 p43 N/D 2016

How I Got Hooked on the Skeptical World S. GERBIC *Skeptical Inquirer* v40 no6 p45 N/D 2016

Notable Articles about the Creation of CSICOP and SKEPTICAL INQUIRER T. BINGA *Skeptical Inquirer* v41 no1 p19 Ja/F 2017

Skepticism

See also

Cynicism

The Age of Misinformation B. j. Gould, D. W. Briggs et al *Skeptical Inquirer* v41 no5 p63 S/O 2017

All the Skeptic Ladies C. Ward *Skeptical Inquirer* v41 no3 p66 My/Je 2017

CSICon in Limelight, The Selfish Gene Revisited K. FRAZIER *Skeptical Inquirer* v41 no2 p4 Mr/Ap 2017

THE FALLACY FORK: Why It's time to Get Rid of Fallacy Theory M. BOUDRY *Skeptical Inquirer* v41 no5 p46 S/O 2017

A Glimpse Backward—and Forward—at Skepticism's Big Tent B. RADFORD *Skeptical Inquirer* v40 no6 p43 N/D 2016

The Great Unplugging H. WILHELM color *National Review* v69 no11 p22 Je 12 2017

an introduction to JERRY ANDRUS R. Worth, J. Collver et al *Skeptical Inquirer* v41 no1 p65 Ja/F 2017

Jagged Little Pills P. PEARSON color *Walrus* v14 no8 p42 O 2017

The More Climate Skeptics There Are, the Fewer Climate Entrepreneurs M. E. Kahn and D. Zhao *Harvard Business Review Digital Articles* p2 Mr 16 2017

More on 'WhySkepticism?' J. Clinger and W. Hodgins *Skeptical Inquirer* v41 no4 p63 Jl/Ag 2017

My Personal Odyssey in Skepticism H. HALL *Skeptical Inquirer* v40 no6 p37 N/D 2016

Nicely Subversive R. Ward *Skeptical Inquirer* v41 no5 p65 S/O 2017

Odysseys in Skepticism T. Randall, J. Cooper et al *Skeptical Inquirer* v41 no2 p65 Mr/Ap 2017

The Roots of Science Denial K. Hayhoe and J. Schwartz color *Scientific American* v317 no4 p66 O 2017

Skeptical about Skeptics? R. Rood *Skeptical Inquirer* v41 no3 p65 My/Je 2017

Skeptical Activism from the Bottom Up M. MARSHALL *Skeptical Inquirer* v40 no6 p49 N/D 2016

Skepticism, at Heart, Is Not Partisan C. A. FOSTER *Skeptical Inquirer* v41 no1 p14 Ja/F 2017

Skepticism Should Be Nonpartisan R. A. Billinghurst, W. A. Robinson et al *Skeptical Inquirer* v41 no3 p63 My/Je 2017

Skeptics' Odysseys and Star Trek's Voyages K. FRAZIER *Skepti-*

cal Inquirer v40 no6 p4 N/D 2016

Spreading Skepticism W. GROSSMAN *Skeptical Inquirer* v40 no6 p41 N/D 2016

Statin Denialism? D. Dusa, J. Behn et al *Skeptical Inquirer* v41 no5 p63 S/O 2017

Still 'Amazing': A Conversation with James Randi *Skeptical Inquirer* v41 no2 p16 Mr/Ap 2017

Teaching Skepticism: How Early Can We Begin? S. O. LILIENFELD *Skeptical Inquirer* v41 no5 p30 S/O 2017

The Virtuous Skeptic M. PIGLIUCCI *Skeptical Inquirer* v41 no2 p54 Mr/Ap 2017

Skepticism—Congresses

CSICon 2016 Lights Up Las Vegas P. Fidalgo *Skeptical Inquirer* v41 no2 p8 Mr/Ap 2017

Skepticism—Social aspects

Why Skepticism? R. A. LINDSAY *Skeptical Inquirer* v41 no2 p46 Mr/Ap 2017

Skeptics (Greek philosophy)

How I Got Hooked on the Skeptical World S. GERBIC *Skeptical Inquirer* v40 no6 p45 N/D 2016

Skerry, Brian

DARE to EXPLORE C. M. TOMLIN *National Geographic Kids* no468 p6 Mr 2017

EXPLORER HONOR TO BRIAN SKERRY P. Edmonds color *National Geographic* v232 no1 p24 Jl 2017

Meet Your Shark Bestie A. SHAW color *National Geographic Kids* no472 p20 Ag 2017

SKERRY, PETER

Mexican Americans color *Weekly Standard* v22 no22 p16 F 13 2017

Skewer cooking

See also

Kebabs

15-Minute All-Organic Meal Under $15 color *Prevention* v69 no8 p14 Ag 2017

SUMMER QUICKIES K. Donnelly color *Women's Health* v14 no5 p92 Je 2017

Ski bindings

Come on in... L. SCHOLZ *Atlanta* v57 no2 p37 Je 2017

Ski boots

The 2018 Buyer's Guide M. Hansen color *Powder* p80 S 2017

Boot Up, Shred Down color *Powder* p96 S 2017

Hillbangin' color *Powder* p98 S 2017

Skin To Win color *Powder* p100 S 2017

Ski boots—Design & construction

COMFY CARVING M. BEHAR color *Bloomberg Businessweek* no4506 p59 Ja 9 2017

Ski boots—Evaluation

THE GEAR TO GET OUT color *Skiing* p76 D 2016

VANS cartoon color *Snowboarder* v29 no4 p124 D 2016

Ski coaches

The Heartbeat M. Hansen color *Powder* v45 no6 p36 F 2017

Ski lifts

I WAS A MIDDLE-AGED LIFTIE R. CONERY color *Powder* p28 S 2017

A Winter Lift *South Dakota Magazine* v32 no4 p18 N/D 2016

Ski mountaineering

CANADA'S GRANDEST TRAVERSE A. Findlay color map *Skiing* p88 D 2016

There's Something in the Snow at Mount Baker H. Hansman color *Powder* v46 no2 p33 O 2017

THE TITUS MIRACLE C. KELLY color *Powder* v46 no2 p30 O 2017

Ski patrollers

Skiing Is Politics M. Peruzzi color *Powder* p38 S 2017

Ski poles—Evaluation

Accessorize D. Pogge color *Skiing* p86 D 2016

Ski racing

THE FAMILY J. Stifter bw *Powder* v45 no6 p34 F 2017

Lessons In Ego Checking S. Jane cartoon *Powder* p44 S 2017

SEE YOU IN JUNE H. LUDWIG color *Powder* p48 S 2017

Siri: Alta, Utah J. C. DAVIES color *Powder* p9 S 2017

Ski resorts

125 DECLARATIONS OF INTERDEPENDENCE R. SOLNIT *Sierra* v102 no3 p37 My/Je 2017

How to Tell Someone to Shut Up About Alta, Already S. Jane

color *Powder* v46 no2 p38 O 2017

THE JADED LOCAL color *Powder* p30 S 2017

LATITUDES E. Catino bw color *Powder* v45 no5 p46 Ja 2017

SEE YOU IN JUNE H. LUDWIG color *Powder* p48 S 2017

Skiing Is Politics M. Peruzzi color *Powder* p38 S 2017

THE TOWER OF SUN J. CLARY DAVIES color map *Powder* v46 no2 p52 O 2017

Yes, You Can Ski and Ride in October B. E. CLARK bw *Conde Nast Traveler* v51 no10 p172 N 2016

YOUR OWN PRIVATE MOUNTAIN R. K. Urken color *Bloomberg Businessweek* no4541 p63 O 9 2017

Ski resorts—Chile

A Good Run C. Rainey bw color *Conde Nast Traveler* v52 no1 p94 Ja 2017

Ski resorts—Evaluation

A Good Run C. Rainey bw color *Conde Nast Traveler* v52 no1 p94 Ja 2017

The SKI LODGES THAT always DELIVER bw chart *Conde Nast Traveler* v52 no1 p75 Ja 2017

WINTER WONDERLANDS N. Ekstein color *Bloomberg Businessweek* no4541 p59 O 9 2017

Ski resorts—France

Ski and The City D. PRIOR color *Conde Nast Traveler* v51 no11 p58 D 2016

WINTER WONDERLANDS N. Ekstein color *Bloomberg Businessweek* no4541 p59 O 9 2017

Ski resorts—Law & legislation

The Case of The Deadly Avalanche V. GLEMBOCKI *Reader's Digest* v188 no1126 p21 D 2016/Ja 2017

Ski resorts—United States

Cozy Slopeside Cabin In Heart of Scenic Ski Town color *Powder* v46 no2 p28 O 2017

Ski resorts—Utah—Evaluation

The SKI LODGES THAT always DELIVER bw chart *Conde Nast Traveler* v52 no1 p75 Ja 2017

Ski training

Kids Will Ruin Your Life S. Metcalf color *Powder* v46 no2 p36 O 2017

Skidmore Owings & Merrill LLP

Diamond Standard: A high-rise for a Chinese conglomerate showcases its distinctive structural system A. A. SENO color diag map *Architectural Record* v205 no5 p110 My 2017

Drawing On Its Past M. SEGAL *Los Angeles Magazine* p26 Ap 2017

Skiers

See also
    Ski patrollers
    Women skiers

16" color *Powder* v45 no4 p10 D 2016

ALL OR NOTHING S. Davis color *Powder* v45 no5 p106 Ja 2017

ALL TIME color *Powder* v45 no3 p10 N 2016

THE ART OF FUN K. KRICHKO bw color *Powder* v45 no5 p92 Ja 2017

AWAKENING K. Krichko bw color *Powder* v45 no4 p80 D 2016

THE BOYS' CLUB A. Barronian cartoon *Powder* v45 no4 p50 D 2016

CHICKEN WINGS M. Michelson color *Skiing* p38 D 2016

COMEBACK KID? T. Neville color *Skiing* p15 Wint 2017

COMMANDER IN CHAIN K. Krichko color *Powder* v45 no5 p38 Ja 2017

Downhill dynamo R. VERGER color *Popular Science* v289 no6 p34 N/D 2017

EDITORS' 100 D. Pogge, K. Beekman et al bw color *Skiing* p36 Wint 2017

THE FAMILY J. Stifter bw *Powder* v45 no6 p34 F 2017

FAREWELL FACIAL L. COHEN color *Skiing* p80 Wint 2017

First M. Rogge bw color *Powder* v45 no3 p74 N 2016

Forward M. Hansen cartoon color *Powder* v45 no4 p68 D 2016

Fun Things to Do on the Chairlift color *Powder* v45 no4 p152 D 2016

The Gear Hacking Legends of Skiing M. Coté color *Powder* p35 S 2017

GLASS J. FOERSTERLING color *Powder* p12 S 2017

THE GREAT ESCAPE K. Beekman color *Skiing* p62 D 2016

HERE'S TO No. 83 R. Story color *Skiing* p18 Wint 2017

INSTAGRAM FOR SKIERS, 101 *Powder* v45 no5 p40 Ja 2017

IV: In Deep J. C. Davies color *Powder* v45 no4 p13 D 2016

LATITUES J. Brown color *Powder* v45 no4 p60 D 2016

LUCAS STÅL-MADISON S. Davis color *Powder* v46 no2 p92 O 2017

MY MUSTACHE AND ME M. Hansen color *Powder* v45 no6 p48 F 2017

No Pro Go color *Powder* v45 no5 p104 Ja 2017

The Peaks of PERFECTION J. Murphy color *Esquire* p54 Big-BlackBook

THE right PWC J. HEMMEL color *Cabin Living* p76 Ja/F 2017

SHINY, TASTY THINGS K. Luby color *Skiing* p32 Wint 2017

SHOOTING GALLERY color *Powder* v45 no3 p30 N 2016

STATE OF THE ART M. Rogge color *Powder* v45 no3 p146 N 2016

WHAT REALLY MATTERS M. Hansen color *Powder* v45 no5 p34 Ja 2017

WHY WE SKI K. BEEKMAN color *Skiing* p12 Wint 2017

Skiers—Accidents

Trevor Donald Sexsmith A. A. DAVIS color *Maclean's* v129 no44 p118 N 7 2016

Skiers—Attitudes

Find Your Spirit Animal color *Powder* v46 no2 p96 O 2017

Signs You're Doing It Right color *Powder* v45 no6 p98 F 2017

Skiers—Diseases

Common Ailments of the Common Skier M. Hansen color *Powder* v46 no2 p40 O 2017

Skiers—Interviews

JUST MY TYPE D. Patrick and T. Keith color *Sports Illustrated* v125 no13 p22 O 17 2016

MAGIC CARPET RIDE K. Krichko color *Powder* v45 no4 p52 D 2016

Skiers—Social conditions

HIGHCOUNTRY EXODUS M. Davis bw *Skiing* p21 D 2016

Skiers—Travel

VI: The Good Life J. C. Davies bw *Powder* v45 no6 p11 F 2017

Skiffs

Boat of all Trades color *Power & Motoryacht* v34 no6 p18 Je 2017

Skiff's Notes: A skiff provides an inexpensive alternative to the big boat and delivers a different sort of boating experience A. JONES *Boating World* v38 no8 p48 S/O 2017

Skiing accidents

Confidence Lessons [Cover story] T. BLACKSTONE color *Redbook* p70 Je 2017

SIX HUNDRED MILES WITH SKIS, KITES, AND WIND K. Long color *National Geographic* v231 no3 p14 Mr 2017

Skiing competitions

TURNED SCREWS GONE LOOSE D. Bertsch color *Powder* v45 no6 p90 F 2017

Voyageur [Cover story] H. Ludwig color *Powder* v45 no6 p60 F 2017

Skiing equipment industry

The Skis of the Year E. GERRMANN, H. VICTORY et al color *Powder* p82 S 2017

Skiing for children

Kids Will Ruin Your Life S. Metcalf color *Powder* v46 no2 p36 O 2017

Skiing for women

TATUM MONOD T. W. Strokes color *Skiing* p34 D 2016

Skiing instruction

THE GREAT ESCAPE K. Beekman color *Skiing* p62 D 2016

Skijoring

Slide into Ski Joring S. HAMILTON color *Trail Rider* v29 no1 p26 Ja/F 2017

Skilled labor

Defining Skilled Technical Work J. ROTHWELL chart *Issues in Science & Technology* v33 no1 p47 Fall 2016

How to Successfully Work Across Countries, Languages, and Cultures T. Neeley *Harvard Business Review Digital Articles* p2 Ag 29 2017

Identifying the Skills That Can Help You Change Careers C. Bowe *Harvard Business Review Digital Articles* p2 Ag 6 2015

MADE IN LA *Los Angeles Magazine* p100 Mr 2017

Your Company Needs Independent Workers S. King and G. Zaino *Harvard Business Review Digital Articles* p2 N 23 2015

Skilled labor recruitment

The Myth of the Skills Gap A. Weaver color *MIT Technology Re-*

view v120 no5 p76 S/O 2017

Skilled labor supply & demand

The Myth of the Skills Gap A. Weaver color *MIT Technology Review* v120 no5 p76 S/O 2017

Paying Skilled Workers More Would Create More Skilled Workers T. van Rens *Harvard Business Review Digital Articles* p2 My 19 2016

Skillet cooking

Skillet Wings P. Kita cartoon color *Men's Health* v32 no2 p31 Mr 2017

TAPPED POTENTIAL S. Collins and S. Bocar color *Martha Stewart Living* p82 My 2017

Skillets

CAST-IRON LOVE L. F. Prater *Successful Farming* v115 no3 p58 Mid-F 2017

THE NONSTICK PAN cartoon color *Men's Health* v32 no8 p82 O 2017

Top-Tested Cooking Tips color *Good Housekeeping* v263 no5 p140 N 2016

Skillets in art

American Skillet Co D. DANIEL color map *American Craft* v77 no3 p14 Je/Jl 2017

Skillets—Evaluation

SKILLETS color *Good Housekeeping* v264 no3 p128 Mr 2017

SKILLMAN, JO

Learn to Ad: Madison Avenue Strategies to Strengthen School Communication *Education Digest* v82 no6 p34 F 2017

SKILLMAN, SUSAN M.

Pathways to Middle-Skill Allied Health Care Occupations chart *Issues in Science & Technology* v33 no1 p52 Fall 2016

Skin

See also

Human skin color

The Best Laser for Your Skin chart color *Health* v30 no10 p16 D 2016

The mechanics of positioning skin follicles S. W. Grill color *Science* v357 no6353 p750 Ag 25 2017

the secret to FOUNDATION E. METZGER color *Better Homes & Gardens* v95 no9 p26 S 2017

The "tao" of integuments Yung Chih Lai and Cheng-Ming Chuong bibl color diag *Science* v354 no6319 p1533 D 23 2016

Your New Beauty Meal Plan A. C. Bacon and Y. Chu color *Glamour* v114 no11 p108 N 2016

Skin aging—Prevention

STOP THE SIGNS OF AGING V. Tweed color *Amazing Wellness* v8 no2 p48 Spr 2016

Skin cancer

See also

Melanoma

Neural Network Model Can Predict Melanoma *USA Today Magazine* v146 no2869 p12 O 2017

Shade Is Good A. JONES color *Boating World* v38 no7 p4 Jl 2017

Skin cancer—Diagnosis

Man vs. Machine: Dermatology M. Bergen color *Bloomberg Businessweek* no4529 p23 Jl 3 2017

Skin care

THE 2017 GLAMOUR BEAUTY AWARD A. Grooms, K. Erickson et al color *Glamour* v115 no4 p81 Ap 2017

22 ways to get SUMMERLICIOUS A. FRANZINO color *Good Housekeeping* v265 no1 p21 Jl 2017

3 experts on... AGE SPOTS color *Good Housekeeping* v265 no2 p22 Ag 2017

5 beauty tricks I just learned V. Kirby color *Redbook* p65 D 2016

6 Annoying Winter Skin Issues, Solved C. Mueller color *Glamour* v114 no12 p144 D 2016

AFTER-SUN CARE for Skin and Hair: After spending time in the sun, try these recipes for cooling masks, mists, bath soaks, gels, and more J. Cox *Mother Earth News* no283 p32 Ag/S 2017

Anti-aging by the numbers M. ABERMAN *Redbook* p50 O 2017

The Bare ESSENTIALS E. MUSIWA color *Ebony* v72 no11 p54 S 2017

BEACH, PLEASE help me calm down... STRENGTHEN MY LEGS... BRING ME CLOSER TO THE PEOPLE I LOVE. BUT BEACH, PLEASE DON'T burn my skin. OR WRECK MY ANKLES. OR CRUSH MY CONFIDENCE OKAY? [Cover story] color *Women's Health* v14 no5 p132 Je 2017

Beauty Adventures in Japan color *Glamour* no8 p90 Ag 2017

BEAUTY LESSONS FROM AMAZING-LOOKING WOMEN [Cover story] G. Way color *Redbook* p38 Mr 2017

the best way to DROP ACID J. Roth color *Esquire* p60 2017 Big-BlackBook

Better Skin, Distilled M. MILRAD GOLDSTEIN *Martha Stewart Living* no267 p44 S 2016

Body WISE color *O, The Oprah Magazine* p72 F 2017

Bright On! color *O, The Oprah Magazine* p52 Ja 2017

Clear, Glowy SKIN—Now Z. NTLOKO and P. Stables color *Seventeen* v76 no5 p38 S 2017

Concealer game changer L. Desantis color diag *Health* v31 no8 p30 O 2017

THE DAY & NIGHT GUIDE TO GORGEOUS SKIN G. WAY color *Redbook* p1c O 2017

DITCH THAT ITCH D. D. Engelman color *Good Housekeeping* v264 no3 p32 Mr 2017

DIY Fall Skin Treats K. FOSTER color *Seventeen* v75 no11 p44 N 2016

DOING GOOD S. Pulia color *InStyle* v24 no9 p168 S 2017

Dry & flaky? Put down that moisturizer! [Cover story] A. PATZ color *Prevention* v69 no2 p56 F 2017

EASE ECZEMA WITH HERBS K. Purkh Singh Khalsa color *Amazing Wellness* v9 no3 p38 EarlySumm 2017

the exact SKIN-CARE ROUTINE for you C. MUELLER color *Redbook* p24 My 2017

EXOTIC OILS [Cover story] L. Turner color *Amazing Wellness* v9 no6 p82 EarlyWint 2017

Face Off K. MASSICOT color *New Orleans Magazine* v52 no1 p166 S 2017

Forever Young J. Amay color *Ebony* v72 no9 p92 Jl/Ag 2017

Fresh Face D. Mazzone color *InStyle* v24 no3 p259 Mr 2017

get a fresh start *Parents* v91 no10 p85 O 2016

The Get-Glowing WORKOUT C. Innes cartoon color *Seventeen* p142 Ja 1 2017

Getting OUTSIDE J. Francisco color *Good Housekeeping* v264 no6 p8 Je 2017

The Girl with the Magic Hands K. Diamond color *InStyle* v24 no3 p262 Mr 2017

GLOW ALL OUT I. VAN LOTRINGEN and M. ABERMAN color diag *Seventeen* v76 no5 p100 S 2017

How School MESSES WITH YOUR SKIN K. CASTAÑON color *Seventeen* v75 no11 p52 N 2016

HOW TO winterize your skin A. FRANZINO color *Good Housekeeping* v264 no1 p25 Ja 1 2017

If You Gild It K. D. HODES color *Women's Health* v14 no9 p45 N 2017

"I'm complicated, but my beauty routine is simple" F. Valdesolo color *Glamour* v115 no9 p94 S 2017

Into the Mild L. REGENSDORF color *Vogue* v207 no10 p220 O 2017

The Itchy and Scratchy Show Z. SCHAEFFER color *Rodale's Organic Life* v2 no7 p90 D 2016/Ja 2017

LOOK YOUNGER WITHOUT TRYING K. D. HODES color *Redbook* p30 My 2017

Magic weapons for great skin P. STABLES cartoon *Redbook* p52 Ap 2017

My LIST L. McCarthy color *Harper's Bazaar* no3651 p224 Mr 2017

My Obsessions J. Larkworthy color *InStyle* v24 no10 p226 O 2017

My Skin N. Richie and C. Whitney color *InStyle* v24 no5 p240 My 2017

new rules for cleansing color *Parents* v92 no6 p83 Je 2017

no more excuses color *Parents* v92 no5 p67 My 2017

Orange you pretty Y. M. Alpert color *Yoga Journal* no292 p26 Je 2017

Our fave superfoods for your face L. Desantis color *Health* v31 no8 p33 O 2017

passport to pretty H. C. CORBETT *Parents* v92 no2 p66 F 2017

RADIANT SKIN Guarnieri color *Harper's Bazaar* no3651 p314 Mr 2017

Refresh Your Chest color *Health* v30 no10 p12 D 2016

SKIN DEEP color *Vogue* v207 no9 p438 S 2017

Skin Deep K. Massicot color *New Orleans Magazine* v51 no6 p36 Ap 2017

SKIN IN THE GAME L. WELLS color *Harper's Bazaar* no3651

The trick that makes you glow M. Roncal color *Redbook* p20b S 2017

Skin color lighteners—Evaluation

6 ways to revolutionize your beauty routine *Redbook* pC1 Mr 2017

The Pick color *InStyle* v24 no1 p68 Ja 2017

Skin disease diagnosis

Should I see a doctor for a mole that bleeds on occasion? *Mayo Clinic Health Letter* v35 no7 p8 Jl 2017

Skin disease prevention

Is your skin freaking out? M. Chadwick color *Health* v31 no8 p25 O 2017

Skin disease treatment

Good for What Ails You B. Lutz color *New Orleans Magazine* v51 no7 p34 My 2017

Skin diseases

See also

Skin cancer

Skin inflammation

8 Ways to Ruin Your Summer A. SWARTZ cartoon color *Men's Health* v32 no6 p94 Ag 2017

Is "Sensitive Skin" B.S.? F. Valdesolo color *Glamour* v115 no9 p86 S 2017

Skin diseases—Prevention

Learn from a Beauty Boss color *Health* v30 no9 p18 N 2016

mask your problem T. PEREZ color *Parents* v92 no4 p86 Ap 2017

Nothing to Sneeze At J. SZABO color *Better Nutrition* v79 no4 p32 Ap 2017

Skin divers

Sublime Snorkeling Spots Z. Prochazka color *Sail* v48 no6 p59 Je 2017

Skin diving

Not Breathing R. Bradley *New York Times Magazine* p16 Ja 1 2017

Snorkeling With the President C. Welch color *National Geographic* v231 no2 p76 F 2017

SOUTH for the SUMMER Z. Prochazka color map *Sail* v48 no3 p32 Mr 2017

Sublime Snorkeling Spots Z. Prochazka color *Sail* v48 no6 p59 Je 2017

Skin diving equipment

Breathe Easy S. MURRAY color *Power & Motoryacht* v34 no7 p39 Jl 2017

Skin diving—Physiological aspects

FREE FALLING PURSUITS P. Scott color *Bloomberg Businessweek* no4527 p83 Je 19 2017

Skin inflammation

Is "Sensitive Skin" B.S.? F. Valdesolo color *Glamour* v115 no9 p86 S 2017

Scratches L. Bonner color *Equus* no474 p18 Mr 2017

Skin inflammation—Treatment

What's that rash? A quick guide to itchy skin *Mayo Clinic Health Letter* v35 no10 p6 O 2017

Skin—Aging

BE HAPPIER IN YOUR SKIN G. WAY color *Redbook* p93 My 2017

FIGHT LINES AT EVERY AGE L. Whitmore color *Health* v31 no4 p94 My 2017

no more excuses color *Parents* v92 no5 p67 My 2017

THE SURPRISING WAYS AGING AFFECTS YOUR SKIN E. A. LIOTTA color *Redbook* p26 Mr 2017

Skin—Cancer—Patients

"I never thought I'd get skin cancer" G. Field color *Glamour* v115 no5 p105 My 2017

SkinCeuticals Inc.

ANTI-AGING SERUMS color *Good Housekeeping* v264 no1 p30 Ja 1 2017

FACE SAVERS M. M. GOLDSTEIN *Martha Stewart Living* no269 p46 N 2016

SKINFESSIONS color *Women's Health* v13 no10 p55 D 2016

Skinner, B. F. (Burrhus Frederic), 1904-1990

Education & Success bw color *Forbes* v200 no5 p172 N 14 2017

Skinner, David

Confessions of a Total Poseur color *Weekly Standard* v23 no5 p5 O 9 2017

Editor's Note *Humanities* v37 no4 p1 Fall 2016

Egged On color *Weekly Standard* v22 no32 p5 My 1 2017

James McBride *Humanities* v37 no4 p1 Fall 2016

A Shooting in the Neighborhood color *Weekly Standard* v22 no41 p5 Jl 3 2017

Stuff of Language color *Weekly Standard* v22 no13 p40 D 5 2016

Writing on Deadline color *Weekly Standard* v22 no24 p5 F 27 2017

Skinner, Ginger

Can You Get Hooked on OTC Sleep Aids? color *Consumer Reports* v82 no2 p24 F 2017

'Natural' Sleep Supplements Carry Serious Safety Concerns *Consumer Reports* v82 no2 p25 F 2017

Too Many Meds? [Cover story] color *Consumer Reports* v82 no9 p24 S 2017

SKINNER, TOBY

BACK TO BASICS ICELAND AS IT'S MEANT TO BE SEEN color map *Conde Nast Traveler* v52 no10 p40 N 2017

Skins (Film)

Spirituality and the Reclamation of Lakota Masculinity in Chris Eyre's Skins (2002) P. L. BAYERS *American Indian Quarterly* v40 no3 p191 Summ 2016

Skin—Tumors—Prevention

Dramatic rise of deadly skin cancer in older adults *Mayo Clinic Health Letter* v35 no4 p4 Ap 2017

Skipper, Clay

The 27-Year-Old Cologne Virgin bw *GQ: Gentlemen's Quarterly* v97 no5 p43 My 2017

The Anxious Man's Guide to Public Speaking color *GQ: Gentlemen's Quarterly* v97 no5 p36 My 2017

CHECK YOUR COAT color *GQ: Gentlemen's Quarterly* v97 no9 p172 S 2017

The Fifty Greatest Living Athletes bw color *GQ: Gentlemen's Quarterly* v97 no11 p96 N 2017

Good Tidings, Fellow Male: A Modern Guide to Man-to-Man Greetings bw color diag graph *GQ: Gentlemen's Quarterly* v97 no10 p154 O 2017

I GOT YOU, BABE bw color *GQ: Gentlemen's Quarterly* v97 no6 p96 Je 2017

The Resurrection Zoo bw color *GQ: Gentlemen's Quarterly* v86 no11 p96 N 2016

the sexiest couple on the planet bw color *GQ: Gentlemen's Quarterly* v97 no3 p130 Mr 2017

Stop Paying for the Gym! color *GQ: Gentlemen's Quarterly* v87 no1 p15 Ja 2017

The Ten Who'll Be Next color *GQ: Gentlemen's Quarterly* v97 no11 p114 N 2017

Skirble, Rosanne

Sacred and secular unite on Basque church's walls color *Christian Century* v134 no2 p17 Ja 18 2017

Skirts

Adam's STYLE SHEET color *O, The Oprah Magazine* p54 Ap 2017

BACK TO BLACK (AND WHITE) H. Rolfe bw *Dance Spirit* v21 no8 p76 O 2017

THE CIRCLE GAME color *Vogue* v207 no3 p490 Mr 2017

Country Club E. ELWICK-BATES color *Vogue* v207 no11 p234 N 2017

Dressing the Part P. Guzmán bw *Conde Nast Traveler* v52 no3 p16 Mr 2017

RETHINK YOUR ... SNEAKERS color *InStyle* v23 no12 p127 N 2016

Skirts vs. Skins E. Wilson color *InStyle* v23 no12 p64 N 2016

A skirt that goes anywhere K. Smith color *Redbook* p76 My 2017

Tuck IN color *Vogue* v206 no12 p150 D 2016

Skirts—Evaluation

15 WAYS TO DO tinsell color *Good Housekeeping* v263 no6 p74A D 2016

Anatomy of a Do color *Glamour* v114 no7 p36 Jl 2016

COLOR AND CONTRAST C. ROITFELD color *Harper's Bazaar* no3653 p195 My 2017

DANCING ON AIR color *Harper's Bazaar* no3648 p238 N 2016

Extra SPECIAL color *InStyle* v24 no3 p250 Mr 2017

FASHION UNDER $100 color *Redbook* p60 Ap 2017

FASHION UNDER $100 color *Redbook* p69 S 2017

Fold 'Em E. Wilson color *InStyle* v24 no1 p33 Ja 2017

For the Win F. Kane color *Glamour* v115 no4 p62 Ap 2017

From Catlike to Classical S. Friscia color *Dance Magazine* v91

no3 p38 Mr 2017

FROM RUNWAY TO O-WAY color *O, The Oprah Magazine* p60 Mr 2017

THE GIRL Willow Smith E. Wilson color *InStyle* v24 no5 p91 My 2017

GREAT BUYS UNDER $100 color *O, The Oprah Magazine* p42 Ja 2017

Holidays Two Ways color *Seventeen* v76 no12 p28 D 2016/Ja 2017

HOW TO WEAR IT... anywhere! K. SALADINO and L. BER-GAMOTTO color *Good Housekeeping* v264 no5 p20 My 2017

If You Love a Good Throwback S. P. Nadella and A. Hou color *Glamour* v115 no9 p58 S 2017

If You're Living for the Weekend S. P. Nadella and A. Hou color *Glamour* v115 no9 p56 S 2017

instant style color *InStyle* v24 no4 p105 Ap 2017

instant style color *InStyle* v24 no6 p63 Je 2017

It's a Cinch color *Los Angeles Magazine* v62 no10 p28 O 2017

Jersey GIRL *Interview* v47 no5 p80 Je/Jl 2017

THE LADY Helen Mirren E. Wilson color *InStyle* v24 no5 p94 My 2017

THE LADY Isabelle Huppert E. Wilson color *InStyle* v24 no6 p55 Je 2017

MAKING waves color *Harper's Bazaar* no3648 p226 N 2016

Millennial Pink: At New York City Ballet, the dancers add a bright twist to classic ballet pink M. DESANTIS *Dance Magazine* v91 no9 p40 S 2017

Next WAVE *Interview* v46 no8 p56 O 2016

NOW TRENDING color *Seventeen* v76 no4 p20 Jl/Ag 2017

Out fits for Days color *Glamour* no8 p60 Ag 2017

PARKER POSEY J. LURIE *Interview* v46 no8 p88 O 2016

THE SEASON'S MOST DARING LOOKS color *Harper's Bazaar* no3648 p60 N 2016

The season's most flattering trend B. Goreski color *Redbook* p15 Je 2017

SHINING MOMENT N. McGOVERN color *O, The Oprah Magazine* p16 S 2017

Stripe Hype S. P. Nadella color *Glamour* v115 no2 p28 F 2017

Sun's Out Buns Out L. Balsamo color *Seventeen* v76 no3 p92 My 2017

TOP THAT! color *O, The Oprah Magazine* p63 Mr 2017

Wear All Your Shoes With This Skirt color *Glamour* v115 no10 p76 O 2017

THE WELL-SPENT $ DOLLAR color *Harper's Bazaar* no3648 p136 N 2016

WHERE FASHION GETS PERSONAL color *Harper's Bazaar* no3652 p129 Ap 2017

Wish LIST N. Fritton color *Harper's Bazaar* no3649 p130 D 2016/Ja 2017

Skis & skiing

See also

    Backcountry skiing

    Photography of skiing

    Ski lifts

    Ski mountaineering

    Ski racing

    Skiing for children

    Water skiing

18 DAYS ON DENALI D. Pogge color *Skiing* p52 D 2016

362" N. Paumgarten color graph *Powder* p68 S 2017

515" L. Anthony color *Powder* p66 S 2017

597" A. Barronian bw *Powder* p62 S 2017

618" H. Ludwig color *Powder* p70 S 2017

ALL TIME color *Powder* v45 no5 p8 Ja 2017

Aspen K. BASTONE *Los Angeles Magazine* v61 no11 p86 N 2016

THE BEST DEAL IN SKIING S. Davis color *Powder* v45 no3 p54 N 2016

BETTER FOR IT P. Fox bw *Powder* v45 no4 p36 D 2016

BRING BEER, TOILET PAPER, SOAP S. Jane cartoon *Powder* v45 no3 p58 N 2016

Cascadia H. Hansman color *Powder* v45 no3 p108 N 2016

Claire Smallwood is a Champion for Women M. MICHELSON color *Powder* v46 no2 p26 O 2017

COWBOY DOWNHILL color *Spin to Win Rodeo* v21 no1 p16 Mr 2017

decay [Cover story] J. C. Davies color *Powder* v45 no6 p66 F 2017

A Dream Shared [Cover story] J. LEONARD *Idaho Magazine* v16 no6 p11 Mr 2017

EATING CAKE L. Hittmeier color *Skiing* p64 D 2016

EDITORS' 100 D. Pogge, K. Beekman et al bw color *Skiing* p36 Wint 2017

Ex-Racer color *Powder* p88 S 2017

FINDING YOUR PERSONAL SUMMIT color *Powder* v45 no6 p92 F 2017

FLY-IN FORT M. Coté bw color *Skiing* p24 Wint 2017

FOR GENERATIONS D. Taylor color *Powder* v45 no3 p40 N 2016

Forward M. Hansen cartoon color *Powder* v45 no4 p68 D 2016

The Free Spirit A. Barronian color *Powder* v45 no3 p42 N 2016

Fun Things to Do on the Chairlift color *Powder* v45 no4 p152 D 2016

GLASS bw *Powder* v45 no5 p20 Ja 2017

GLASS J. FOERSTERLING color *Powder* v46 no2 p18 O 2017

HERE'S TO No. 83 R. Story color *Skiing* p18 Wint 2017

High-Wire Act J. LABIANCA color *Reader's Digest* v189 no1129 p8 Ap 2017

How Much Do You Love Your Skis? color *Powder* p136 S 2017

HOW TO OWN A SKI AREA J. Brown color *Powder* v45 no4 p46 D 2016

How to Tell Someone to Shut Up About Alta, Already S. Jane color *Powder* v46 no2 p38 O 2017

IF YOU BUILD IT K. Krichko color *Powder* v45 no3 p56 N 2016

III: Just Go J. C. Davies bw *Powder* v45 no3 p13 N 2016

IV: In Deep J. C. Davies color *Powder* v45 no4 p13 D 2016

I WAS A MIDDLE-AGED LIFTIE R. CONERY color *Powder* p28 S 2017

THE JADED LOCAL color *Powder* p30 S 2017

LATITUDES FAT TIMES [Cover story] M. Hansen color *Powder* v45 no6 p54 F 2017

LATITUES J. Brown color *Powder* v45 no4 p60 D 2016

Learning How to Live B. SHEIFFER color *Powder* v46 no2 p94 O 2017

Lessons In Ego Checking S. Jane cartoon *Powder* p44 S 2017

Letter of the Month R. Carpenter, S. Doran et al color *Powder* v45 no6 p96 F 2017

MASHED M. Hansen color *Powder* v45 no3 p140 N 2016

NAKED & AFRAID K. Beekman color *Skiing* p44 D 2016

One-Ski Wonder color *Powder* p90 S 2017

Pacific Coast Highway B. NEWCOTT color map *AARP: The Magazine* v60 no3A p48 Ap/My 2017

Playful color *Powder* p86 S 2017

Posthole B. Finley, L. Joseph et al color *Powder* v45 no5 p108 Ja 2017

POSTHOLE C. CAPELLI, S. CUNHA et al color *Powder* v46 no2 p94 O 2017

POWDER PLAY J. Pugh, M. Mccrea et al chart color diag *Sunset* v238 no1 p22 Ja 2017

Pow Sticks color *Powder* p92 S 2017

Resilience M. MICHELSON bw color *Powder* p54 S 2017

SHINY, TASTY THINGS K. Luby color *Skiing* p32 Wint 2017

SHOOTING GALLERY bw color *Powder* v45 no4 p24 D 2016

SHOOTING GALLERY color *Powder* p20 S 2017

Signs You're Doing It Right color *Powder* v45 no6 p98 F 2017

SKIING IS THE BESTEST R. Story color *Powder* v45 no5 p22 Ja 2017

SKI, SNOWSHOE & DOGSLED *Sierra* v102 no1 p75 Ja/F 2017

SKI TOWN TINDER J. Brown cartoon *Powder* v45 no3 p60 N 2016

Snow Me Something M. Gunch color *New Orleans Magazine* v51 no5 p46 Mr 2017

STACY BARE J. Foersterling color *Skiing* p28 Wint 2017

Stiff AF color *Powder* p87 S 2017

TAKE A DRIVE: SNOWSHOE D. A. Leatherman *Washingtonian Magazine* v52 no4 p116 Ja 2017

Taking on Tahoe N. Walker color map *Canadian Geographic* v137 p14 2017 Travel

THIS COULD BE YOU D. Wolman color *Bloomberg Businessweek* no4499 p83 N 14 2016

'TIS THE SEASON! cartoon *Powder* v45 no4 p54 D 2016

THE TITUS MIRACLE C. KELLY color *Powder* v46 no2 p30

O 2017

#trailchat color *Backpacker* p4 N 2017

TURN THIS MOTHER OUT K. Krichko color *Powder* v45 no4 p140 D 2016

Uphill Oriented color *Powder* p89 S 2017

VI: The Good Life J. C. Davies bw *Powder* v45 no6 p11 F 2017

V: Our Own Sense of Time J. C. Davies bw *Powder* v45 no5 p11 Ja 2017

What in the World? *National Geographic Kids* no466 p35 D 2016/ Ja 2017

What loss taught me about life M. Celeste Beall color *Redbook* p115 O 2017

When It's Time To Go Home R. Stevenson color *Powder* v45 no3 p152 N 2016

WHY WE SKI K. BEEKMAN color *Skiing* p12 Wint 2017

Winterize Your Workouts D. Schnitzspahn color *Men's Health* v31 no10 p45 D 2016

WISH YOU WEREN'T HERE! color *Powder* v45 no3 p142 N 2016

You Might be a Photographer If... color *Powder* v45 no5 p112 Ja 2017

YOU SHOULD KNOW color *Bicycling* v58 no10 p88 N/D 2017

Skis & skiing equipment
See also
Ski boots

The 2018 Apparel Guide bw color *Powder* v46 no2 p70 O 2017

The 2018 Buyer's Guide M. Hansen color *Powder* p80 S 2017

Ex-Racer color *Powder* p88 S 2017

The Gear Hacking Legends of Skiing M. Coté color *Powder* p35 S 2017

One-Ski Wonder color *Powder* p90 S 2017

Playful color *Powder* p86 S 2017

Pow Sticks color *Powder* p92 S 2017

A Skier's Must-Have: THE BIG DUMPS TI 5000 2 J. C. Davies diag *Powder* p46 S 2017

The Skis of the Year E. GERRMANN, H. VICTORY et al color *Powder* p82 S 2017

Uphill Oriented color *Powder* p89 S 2017

Skis & skiing—Alaska

LIFTING THE DARKNESS T. ROSS color *Rodale's Organic Life* v2 no7 p80 D 2016/Ja 2017

Skis & skiing—China

AWAKENING K. Krichko bw color *Powder* v45 no4 p80 D 2016

Skis & skiing—Environmental aspects

THE NEXT ERA P. Fox color *Powder* v45 no6 p44 F 2017

Skis & skiing—Equipment & supplies

Natural Selection B. Rassler *Sierra* v102 no2 p18 Mr/Ap 2017

Skis & skiing—Equipment & supplies—Evaluation

Accessorize D. Pogge color *Skiing* p86 D 2016

THE GEAR TO GET OUT color *Skiing* p76 D 2016

I Can See Clearly Now J. Brown color *Powder* v45 no4 p40 D 2016

PACKS D. Pogge and K. Beekman color *Skiing* p82 D 2016

SHE SHREDS, SHE SCORES! color *Women's Health* v13 no10 p118 D 2016

SLOPE STYLE J. MOAZAMI color *Chicago* v66 no1 p48 Ja 2017

Skis & skiing—Evaluation

These skis fold in half! B. Broudy and R. Verger color diag *Popular Science* v289 no6 p30 N/D 2017

Skis & skiing—New York (State)

NEW YORK STATE OF MIND A. BARRONIAN color *Powder* v46 no2 p42 O 2017

Skis & skiing—Vermont

The Best Time color *Yankee* p26 Mr 2017

Sklar, Julia

Injectable Wires for Fixing the Brain bw color *MIT Technology Review* v119 no6 p104 N/D 2016

Meet the Octobot color *MIT Technology Review* v120 no1 p108 Ja/F 2017

VISIONARIES color il *MIT Technology Review* v120 no5 p42 S/O 2017

Sklarew, Renee

Before CAMP DAVID *Washingtonian Magazine* v53 no1 p101 O 2017

TAKE A DRIVE: INTO THE HIGHLANDS *Washingtonian Mag-*

azine v52 no6 p100 Mr 2017

Skloot, Rebecca—Interviews

Rebecca Skloot Feels Indebted To Henrietta Lacks A. M. Cox *New York Times Magazine* p74 Ap 23 2017

Sklute, Ken

Choosing Equipment for Eclipse Photography color *Astronomy* v45 no7 p7 Jl 2017

Skoda automobile

ON THE ROAD C. BLOOR and M. MCCARTHY color *House Beautiful* p162 Ag 2017

Tested for you G. Buckley color *House Beautiful* p160 Ag 2017

Skogmo, Jonathan

click doctors J. L. Keiles *New York Times Magazine* p24 Ja 1 2017

Skogs, Marie

A subcellular map of the human proteome color *Science* v356 no6340 p820 My 26 2017

Skokie (Ill.)—Description & travel

SKOKIE J. REESE cartoon color *Chicago* v66 no3 p37 Mr 2017

Skola, Dylan

An environment-dependent transcriptional network specifies human microglia identity color *Science* v356 no6344 p1248 Je 23 2017

Skolnick, Adam

HOG HELL *Sierra* v102 no2 p28 Mr/Ap 2017

Purging Plastic *Sierra* v102 no3 p24 My/Je 2017

Skolnick, Alex

Metal Guitarist Skolnick Gets Jazzy on Trio Project B. Milkowski color *Downbeat* v84 no1 p15 Ja 2017

SKOLNIK, DEBORAH

a modest proposal [Cover story] color *Parents* v92 no3 p52 Mr 2017

Skolnik, Heidi

THE TRUTH ABOUT Sugar N. Lceffler-Gladstone *Dance Spirit* v21 no3 p30 Mr 2017

SKOMAL, GREGORY B.

Gray Seals and White Sharks Meet Anew color *Natural History* v125 no7 p22 Jl/Ag 2017

SKOPHAMMER, KAREN

ALL IN A Day's Work *Reader's Digest* v189 no1128 p60 Mr 2017

Skorka, Abraham, 1950-

The Dialogue of Fraternity J. L. Fredericks color *Commonweal* v144 no6 p10 Mr 24 2017

SKOUSEN, MARK

FROM THE ARCHIVES color *Reason* v49 no4 p78 Ag/S 2017

Skovron, Jon

Bane and Sorrow: Empire of Storms, Book 2 *Publishers Weekly* v264 no1 p41 Ja 2 2017

Skow, John

MARIO IS FEELING FINE *Saturday Evening Post* v289 no3 p52 My/Je 2017

SKOWRONSKI, TOMASZ

Our Vegan Polish Spot Is So Polish, Polish-Americans Don't Think It's Polish color *Bon Appetit* v62 no2 p69 Mr 2017

Skrebneski, Victor

VICTOR SKREBNESKI B. Zehme color *Chicago* v66 no8 p132 Ag 2017

Skrein, Ed

In a Handbasket Dept color *Weekly Standard* v23 no1 p2 S 11 2017

Skrypuch, Marsha Forchuk, 1954-

Making Bombs for Hitler *Publishers Weekly* v263 no48 p67 N 28 2016

Skudin, Will

Lining Up color *Surfer* v58 no2 p18 My 2017

Skull—Anatomy

Fossil offers clues to ape evolution B. BOWER color *Science News* v192 no3 p13 S 2 2017

Skunks

City Creatures G. VAN HORN *Orion Magazine* v35 no4/5 p9 Jl-O 2016

Sea Otters. Supercute, Supertough R. A. MUSGRAVE color *National Geographic Kids* no475 p24 N 2017

Skunks—Behavior

Notorious—or Not? Reeking reputation aside, skunks are full of surprises, as science is showing L. Warren color *National Wildlife (World Edition)* v55 no3 p40 Ap/My 2017

Skunks—Diseases

Notorious—or Not? Reeking reputation aside, skunks are full of surprises, as science is showing L. Warren color *National Wildlife (World Edition)* v55 no3 p40 Ap/My 2017

Skurnick, Lizzie

In sequels, prequels and spinoffs, Joan Aiken took up some of the stories Austen never intended to tell *New York Times Book Review* p12 Jl 16 2017

Skuse, Benjamin

Baking a Universe *Sky & Telescope* v133 no5 p34 My 2017

THE RACE TO MARS: Timing is everything in space exploration, and in 2020 the time will be right to launch an armada of explorers to the Red Planet in search of signs of life [Cover story] color *Sky & Telescope* v134 no5 p14 N 2017

Skvarla, Diane K.

The Kindergarten Years color *Dressage Today* v23 no5 p42 Ja 2017

SKWIRE, SARAH

Getting the State Out of Marriage color *Reason* v49 no6 p56 N 2017

Sky

See also

Constellations

FINDING PATTERNS IN THE SKY P. Harrington chart color *Astronomy* v45 no1 p60 Ja 2017

STAR DOME chart map *Astronomy* v45 no4 p38 Ap 2017

STAR DOME M. RATCLIFFE and A. LING chart color *Astronomy* v44 no12 p38 D 2016

Stellar rhythm B. BERMAN color *Astronomy* v45 no2 p10 F 2017

WORKING EVERY DAY AT 35,000 FEET M. VANHOENACKER color *Reader's Digest* v189 no1130 p114 My 2017

Sky & Telescope (Periodical)

75, 50 & 25 YEARS AGO R. W. Sinnott *Sky & Telescope* v133 no4 p8 Ap 2017

75, 50 & 25 YEARS AGO R. W. Sinnott *Sky & Telescope* v134 no6 p8 D 2017

Sky, Emma

Mission Still Not Accomplished in Iraq color *Foreign Affairs* v96 no6 p9 N/D 2017

Sky brightness

Bright-Sky Imaging R. Brecher color *Sky & Telescope* v134 no5 p68 N 2017

Brilliant Venus Owns the Evening Sky F. Schaaf *Sky & Telescope* v133 no2 p46 F 2017

Cloudshine S. James O'meara color *Astronomy* v45 no7 p20 Jl 2017

GALLERY *Sky & Telescope* v133 no2 p72 F 2017

Getting in Step J. RAO *Natural History* v125 no1 p38 D 2016/Ja 2017

How FLAGSTAFF is preserving DARK SKIES C. Luginbuhl and J. Hall color graph *Astronomy* v45 no9 p54 S 2017

IDENTIFYING FLYING OBJECTS M. JAFFE *Arizona Highways* v93 no6 p32 Je 2017

It's All About the Ears S. French *Sky & Telescope* v133 no2 p54 F 2017

OBSERVING *Sky & Telescope* v133 no2 p41 F 2017

A Rainbow in the Velvet of the Night L. E. Jasinski *Sky & Telescope* v133 no2 p84 F 2017

September 2017: An ice giant pinnacle M. RATCLIFFE and A. LING chart color *Astronomy* v45 no9 p36 S 2017

The Stars at Night F. ROSS *Texas Monthly* v45 no4 p56 Ap 2017

Through a High Window F. Schaaf *Sky & Telescope* v132 no6 p45 D 2016

Sky-Watcher USA (Company)

Sky-Watcher USA's new COMPOUND SCOPE P. Harrington color *Astronomy* v45 no3 p62 Mr 2017

Sky Zone Franchise Group LLC

Learning On the Fly N. KIRSCH color *Forbes* v199 no7 p60 Je 29 2017

SKYBETTER, SYDNEY

Gone Viral *Dance Magazine* v90 no12 p59 D 2016

SkyBridge Capital LLC

Mystery Deal Z. Mider, K. Burton et al *Bloomberg Businessweek* no4510 p33 F 6 2017

Skydiving

big dog M. POTTER bw color *Esquire* p72 Ap 2017

THE MAN WHO FELL TO EARTH N. PENN color *GQ: Gentlemen's Quarterly* v86 no12 p148 D 2016

Skydiving for people with disabilities

50 SECONDS FROM DEATH R. KIENER color *Reader's Digest* v189 no1131 p88 Je 2017

Skydiving study & teaching

We Have Lift Off! C. Winter color diag *Bloomberg Businessweek* no4520 p67 My 1 2017

Skye, Emily

Emily Skye P. KITA bw color *Men's Health* v32 no6 p40 Ag 2017

THE POWER OF "WHY" A. K. LAIRD color *Women's Health* v14 no6 p10 Jl 2017

SKYE HIGH CONFIDENCE [Cover story] L. Goldman color *Women's Health* v14 no6 p63 Jl 2017

Skye, June

ENEMY color *Christian Century* v134 no5 p20 Mr 1 2017

Skye, Obert

Mutant Bunny Island *Publishers Weekly* v264 no38 p69 S 18 2017

Skyfall (Film)

NAOMIE'S MOMENT C. Shanahan color *InStyle* v23 no13 p232 D 2016

Skyhawk (Jet attack plane)

DIESEL SKYHAWK JT-A ENTERS THE MARKET color *Flying* v144 no8 p18 Ag 2017

Skylis, Mary Beth

out alive: stranded bw *Backpacker* p37 O 2017

Skylis, Mary Beth "Mouse"

HIKER LOOK BOOK color *Backpacker* v45 no1 p78 Ja 2017

Skype (Electronic resource)

How to use Skype without an account I. PAUL color *PCWorld* v35 no1 p198 Ja 2017

Skype like a boss with these hidden chat commands I. PAUL color *PCWorld* v35 no4 p149 Ap 2017

What's worth saving C. Zaleski *Christian Century* v134 no22 p37 O 25 2017

Skyscraper design & construction

High Times: Skyscrapers continue to capture the imagination of architects, who are finding more freedom to innovate and enliven the skylines of our cities bw color *Architectural Record* v205 no5 p20 My 2017

Up and Coming: These eight towers around the world, some in planning and others approaching completion, project ambition in scale and form M. SITZ color *Architectural Record* v205 no5 p122 My 2017

Skyscraper safety measures

THE VISTA TOWER T. C. FISHMAN color *Chicago* v66 no10 p24 O 2017

Skyscrapers—China—Design & construction

China's 'Mountain' Skyscrapers J. Zorthian color *Time* v190 no13 p23 O 2 2017

Skyscrapers—Illinois

Found in Chicago T. CHIARELLA color *Chicago* v66 no10 p86 O 2017

THE VISTA TOWER T. C. FISHMAN color *Chicago* v66 no10 p24 O 2017

Skyscrapers—New York (State)

The Most Expensive Building in NYC D. Kocieniewski and C. Melby color *Bloomberg Businessweek* no4515 p27 Mr 20 2017

Skyscrapers—New York (State)—Design & construction

River Dance: A chiseled skyscraper anchors Manhattan's new west-side neighborhood color diag map *Architectural Record* v205 no5 p116 My 2017

Skywalks

Denmark's Treetop Walkway J. Zorthian color *Time* v190 no2/3 p23 Jl 10-17 2017

Slabs (Structural geology)

Perfect Day, New England color *Surfer* v58 no1 p104 Ap 2017

Slack, Emma

Inflammation boosts bacteriophage transfer between Salmonella spp bibl diag *Science* v355 no6330 p1211 Mr 17 2017

Slack Bay (Film)

Slack Bay *New Yorker* v93 no11 p11 My 1 2017

Slack Technologies Inc.

Slack Technologies E. Huet chart color *Bloomberg Businessweek* no4503 p42 D 12 2016

Slack Technologies Inc.—Officials & employees

SLACK'S QUEST TO MAKE WORK EASIER M. Lev-ram color *Fortune* v176 no1 p21 Jl 1 2017

Slackers (Film)

Slacker M. J. ROWIN color *Film Comment* v53 no1 p63 Ja/F 2017

Slade, Alison

Higher predation risk for insect prey at low latitudes and elevations graph *Science* v356 no6339 p742 My 19 2017

Slade, Eleanor M.

Higher predation risk for insect prey at low latitudes and elevations graph *Science* v356 no6339 p742 My 19 2017

Slade, Rachel

A Fatal Mistake color map *Yankee* v80 no6 p136 N/D 2016

Slade, Seven

Coming Out color *Publishers Weekly* v264 no3 p46 Ja 16 2017

Slade, Stephanie

ACLU V CATHOLIC HEALTH CARE [Cover story] color il *America* v216 no13 p18 Je 12 2017

Christians Started the Wedding Wars cartoon *Reason* v48 no11 p56 Ap 2017

HACKSAW RIDGE color *Reason* v48 no10 p64 Mr 2017

THE Never-Ending Pursuit of Religious Liberty bw color *America* v216 no6 p18 Mr 20 2017

OBAMA'S BETRAYAL OF BELIEVERS bw cartoon *Reason* v48 no9 p12 F 2017

WHIPLASH AND BACKLASH IN THE REPUBLIC OF CUBA color *Reason* v49 no5 p28 O 2017

Slade, Victor

Higher predation risk for insect prey at low latitudes and elevations graph *Science* v356 no6339 p742 My 19 2017

Sladen, Anthony

Mega-earthquakes rupture flat megathrusts bibl graph *Science* v354 no6315 p1027 N 25 2016

Slag

Slag for dry lot rehab? E. Fabian-Wheeler *Equus* no473 p67 F 2017

Slagle, Ali

GET WITH THE (MEAL) PLAN cartoon *Bloomberg Businessweek* no4493 p90 O 3 2016

Slalom skiing

Get Yer Slalom On Z. BILAS *Boating World* v38 no6 p16 Je 2017

Slang

Latest Language Abuse S. BEAUCHAMP *American Conservative* v16 no3 p9 My/Je 2017

Slants, The (Performer)

Battle of the Banned J. Alvarez color *Washington Monthly* v49 no6-8 p7 Je-Ag 2017

Slap, The (TV program)

MAKENZIE LEIGH K. SMITH color *Vanity Fair* v58 no11 p77 N 2016

Slape-Hoysagk, Susan

Organic Slug Control *Mother Earth News* no282 p83 Je/Jl 2017

SLATE, JEFF

Sound and Vision bw color *Esquire* v166 no4 p27 N 2016

Slate, Jenny, 1982-

THE CULTURAL SATURATION CHART C. WEAVER and J. WILLIS bw cartoon color *GQ: Gentlemen's Quarterly* v97 no4 p59 Ap 2017

The Year of Living Publicly J. Yuan img *New York* v50 no6 p71 Mr 20 2017

Slate, Jenny, 1982—Interviews

Jenny Slate Hates Being Oversimplified A. M. Cox *New York Times Magazine* p54 Jl 16 2017

Jenny Slate I. Biedenharn color *Entertainment Weekly* no1442 p62 D 2 2016 Rebellious Special Issue

Stupid QUESTIONS WITH... Jenny Slate D. Snierson color *Entertainment Weekly* no1474/1475 p22 Jl 21-28 2017

Slater, Christian, 1969-

Christian Slater: How do you navigate a dinner party? D. WALTERS bw color *Bon Appetit* v62 no10 p112 O 2017

MR. ROBOT K. P. Sullivan color *Entertainment Weekly* no1474/1475 p66 Jl 21-28 2017

Slater, Dan

Streets of Laredo N. BLAKESLEE *New York Times Book Review* p9 O 16 2016

Slater, Dashka

CAN WE TALK? color *Mother Jones* v42 no6 p59 N/D 2017

DIRTY POWER PLAN *Sierra* v101 no5 p36 S/O 2016

Footing the Bill *Sierra* v101 no6 p22 N/D 2016

Here Comes the "Green Rush" *Sierra* v102 no2 p20 Mr/Ap 2017

PRISON BREAK color *Mother Jones* v42 no4 p42 Jl/Ag 2017

THE PROMISED LAND color *Sunset* v238 no4 p68 Ap 2017

Shake, Rattle, and Sue: Oklahoma's oil industry ducks and covers to avoid taking responsibility for the state's earthquake boom *Sierra* v102 no4 p20 Jl/Ag 2017

This Land Is Was Your Land *Sierra* v101 no4 p24 Jl/Ag 2016

Why-o-fuel? *Sierra* v102 no1 p20 Ja/F 2017

Slater, Louise J.

Measuring the changing pulse of rivers color *Science* v357 no6351 p552 Ag 11 2017

Slatin MotoGear (Company)

SLATIN MOTOGEAR EZ-1 SUPERFABRIC MESH JACKET P. Dean color *Cycle World* v55 no10 p18 N 2016

SLATIN, PETER

Light Touch *Architectural Record* v204 no10 p41 O 2016

Slaughter, Anne-Marie, 1958-

The Chessboard and the Web: Strategies of Connection in a Networked World G. J. Ikenberry *Foreign Affairs* v96 no3 p154 My/Je 2017

The Do-Not-Think Tank C. ROSEN color *Weekly Standard* v23 no2 p24 S 18 2017

How to Succeed in the Networked World color *Foreign Affairs* v95 no6 p76 N/D 2016

Making Caregiving Compatible with Work N. Fondas *Harvard Business Review Digital Articles* p2 O 12 2015

The Only Way Forward color *Foreign Policy* no221 p64 N/D 2016

Our Evolving Sense of Self cartoon *National Geographic* v231 no1 p152 Ja 2017

Slaughter, Anne-Marie, 1958—Interviews

Anne-Marie Slaughter D. Von Drehle color *Time* v189 no11 p64 Mr 27 2017

Slaughtering & slaughterhouses

FOOTPRINT IN MOUTH LIND cartoon *Alternatives Journal (AJ) - Canada's Environmental Voice* v42 no3 p10 2016

The Hunt: In Native Alaska, whaling ties people to history, culture, and one another M. M. LANE color *Orion Magazine* v36 no1 p24 Ja/F 2017

PLEASE PASS THE DZ R. Wiltz *South Dakota Magazine* v33 no3 p96 S/O 2017

THROWBACK: FARMING 100 YEARS AGO *Successful Farming* v115 no1 p8 Ja 2017

Slave trade

The Door of No Return R. Brown color *Commonweal* v144 no9 p39 My 19 2017

THE LILA OF THE GNAWA K. GREENSPAN bw color *Natural History* v125 no3 p34 Mr 2017

The Slave Insurance Market M. RALPH and W. RANKIN map *Foreign Policy* no222 p22 Ja/F 2017

Slave trade—Atlantic Ocean Region

Freedom in Exile [Cover story] E. CALLAWAY color graph map *Natural History* v125 no3 p18 Mr 2017

Slave trade—Atlantic Ocean Region—History—18th century

The Importance of Family Connections *Natural History* v125 no3 p5 Mr 2017

Slavens, Mike

UNSOLICITED BETA color *Climbing* no351 p18 F/Mr 2017

Slavery

CARTOONS *In These Times* v41 no7 p32 Jl 2017

Currents of Race and Religion Flowing Along the Waters Of the Erie Canal S. Brent Rodriguez Plate color graph *America* v217 no6 p46 S 18 2017

South Carolina J. Woodson *New York Times Magazine* p58 N 20 2016

Watch what you eat K. Clarke color *U.S. Catholic* v82 no6 p42 Je 2017

Slavery—History

Justifying Slavery J. MacKechnie *History Today* v67 no5 p18 My 2017

Slavery—Reparations

Georgetown Steps Up J. CARR color *America* v215 no10 p14 O 10 2016

Reparations' Best Chance Since 1865 S. MUWAKKIL *In These Times* v41 no5 p17 My 2017

N 21 2016

WHaT'S WORTH WaTCHING *TV Guide* v64 no15 p47 Ap 4 2016

Sleeves

Is Your Suit Too Tight? N. SULLIVAN color *Esquire* v167 no1 p34 F 2017

Sleight (Film)

FIRST LOOK: SLEIGHT D. PHILYAW and L. CROSS color *Ebony* v72 no6 p24 Ap/My 2017

Sleight of Hand (Music)

The Long Run J. Potter color *Downbeat* v84 no9 p26 S 2017

Sleire, Sveinung

Norway Ditches The 'Fossil Car' color *Bloomberg Businessweek* no4525 p31 Je 5 2017

Slenske, Michael

Acquisitions & mergers: A new exhibition at the Craft and Folk Art Museum in Los Angeles is the latest showcase for the powerful work of assemblage artist Betye Saar bw color *Magazine Antiques* v184 no4 p84 Jl/Ag 2017

Artful Living color *Architectural Digest* v74 no7 p88 Jl 2017

Dancing in the Streets bw color *Architectural Digest* v74 no3 p62 Mr 2017

PRIDE OF PLACE color *Architectural Digest* v73 no11 p64 N 2016

Slepian, Michael

Secrets and Lies M. Hutson graph *Scientific American* v317 no1 p18 Jl 2017

Sletten, Deanna Lynn

Walking Sam *Publishers Weekly* v263 no43 p63 O 24 2016

Slettento, Amy

From FEEDLOT to FINALS J. M. Keeler color *Dressage Today* p56 My 2017

Sletvold, Nina

Precipitation drives global variation in natural selection bibl chart diag map *Science* v355 no6328 p959 Mr 3 2017

Slezkine, Yuri

The House of Government: A Saga of the Russian Revolution R. Legvold *Foreign Affairs* v96 no6 p166 N/D 2017

The Insatiable Utopia M. HARWOOD color *Reason* v49 no6 p74 N 2017

The Unbreakable Broken: The tale of a Soviet housing complex and the Bolshevik elite that suffered there M. SHORE *New York Times Book Review* p10 Ag 20 2017

Slice, Kimbo, 1974-2016

KIMBO SLICE C. ROTELLA *New York Times Magazine* p30 D 25 2016

Slick, Grace

CLUCK OFF JAM bw *Advocate* no1091 p26 Je/Jl 2017

Slide (Music)

THE BEST SONGS OF 2017 (SO FAR) color *Entertainment Weekly* no1468/1469 p100 Je 2-9 2017

The Playlist color *Rolling Stone* no1283 p8 Mr 23 2017

YOUR "SPRING IS COMING!" PLAYLIST color *Entertainment Weekly* no1456 p64 Mr 10 2017

Slide projection

SLIDE PROJECTION (19 SLIDES) color *Art in America* v105 no1 p15 Ja 2017

Slides (Photography)

SLIDE PROJECTION (19 SLIDES) color *Art in America* v105 no1 p15 Ja 2017

Sliding doors

BARN DOORS D. Howland color *Cabin Living* p9 Je 2017

Horizontal Sliding Fire Doors: Architectural Design Freedom K. Tetlow color diag *Architectural Record* v204 no12 p188 D 2016

Slide On Over color *Log Home Living* v33 no7 p16 S 2016

Slimane, Hedi, 1968-

Hedi Slimane: The Steve Jobs of Fashion U. Haque *Harvard Business Review Digital Articles* p2 Ap 1 2016

Slinky (Toy)

BENCHMARK: SPRING FLING J. KEATS color *Wired* v25 no9 p50 S 2017

Slippers (Footwear)

And Now for Your Toes color *Glamour* v115 no5 p46 My 2017

Fashion Month Throwback! color *Glamour* v115 no9 p64 S 2017

THE OTHER STUFF color *Backpacker* v45 no3 p128 Ap 2017

Slippers (Footwear)—Evaluation

THE BEST BET img *New York* p39 Ja 23 2017

Glass Slipper (But Hipper) [Cover story] J. Palermo color *Glamour* v115 no4 p45 Ap 2017

Let It SLIDE color *Seventeen* p58 Ja 1 2017

MAGIC SLIPPERS color *Conde Nast Traveler* v52 no1 p38 Ja 2017

MUST-BUYS M. Santos color *Working Mother* v40 no2 p20 Je/Jl 2017

Slip into Something More Colorful color *GQ: Gentlemen's Quarterly* v97 no11 p44 N 2017

the start color *InStyle* v24 no8 p43 Ag 2017

Slipski, M.

Mars' atmospheric history derived from upper-atmosphere measurements of 38 Ar/36Ar diag *Science* v355 no6332 p1408 Mr 31 2017

Sliwa, J.

A dedicated network for social interaction processing in the primate brain color diag *Science* v356 no6339 p745 My 19 2017

Sljoka, Adnan

The role of dimer asymmetry and protomer dynamics in enzyme catalysis diag *Science* v355 no6322 p262 Ja 20 2017

SLOAN, ALLISON

Beyond Words color *O, The Oprah Magazine* p17 Ap 2017

SLOAN, ERICA

WATER GATE: Could Trump once again make the Washington Aqueduct a center of political intrigue? *Washingtonian Magazine* v52 no12 p20 S 2017

WHERE & WHEN: 17 THINGS YOU REALLY OUGHT TO DO THIS MONTH *Washingtonian Magazine* v53 no1 p31 O 2017

WHERE & WHEN: 18 THINGS YOU REALLY OUGHT TO DO THIS MONTH *Washingtonian Magazine* v52 no11 p31 Ag 2017

Sloan, Holly Goldberg

Big Dreams A. BENJAMIN *New York Times Book Review* p19 Ja 15 2017

Jailbirds *New York Times Book Review* p15 F 12 2017

SLOAN, LEA

The Making of a Leader in Forestry *American Forests* v122 no3 p46 Fall 2016

Pioneer in American Forests' Boardroom *American Forests* v123 no1 p46 Wint/Spr 2017

Sloan School of Management

How a Flex-Time Program at MIT Improved Productivity, Resilience, and Trust P. Hirst *Harvard Business Review Digital Articles* p2 Je 30 2016

What MIT Is Learning About Online Courses and Working from Home S. G. Carmichael *Harvard Business Review Digital Articles* p2 Mr 30 2015

Sloane, William Milligan, 1850-1928

BEHIND THE DOOR W. Sloane *Lapham's Quarterly* v10 no3 p51 Summ 2017

SLOBIG, ZACHARY

HIGHER GROUND *Orion Magazine* v35 no4/5 p20 Jl-O 2016

Slocum, Dale L.

CORONADO TRAIL *Arizona Highways* v93 no4 p10 Ap 2017

Slogans

Last Look D. Kidd *Governing* v31 no1 p64 O 2017

Sloman, Steven

The Essential Power of the Hive Mind S. Begley color *Time* v189 no10 p20 Mr 20 2017

Received Ideas We know less than we think we do. Groupthink fills in the gaps Y. HARARI color *New York Times Book Review* p15 Ap 23 2017

Slon, Steven

THE ACTING COACH *Saturday Evening Post* v289 no3 p18 My/Je 2017

AMERICA'S MAGAZINE *Saturday Evening Post* v289 no2 p4 Mr/Ap 2017

DRIVING LESSON *Saturday Evening Post* v289 no3 p4 My/Je 2017

FRESH BEGINNINGS *Saturday Evening Post* v289 no1 p5 Ja/F 2017

FUNNY STUFF! *Saturday Evening Post* v289 no5 p6 S/O 2017

THE MAGIC OF GALÁPAGOS: to visit these unspoiled islands is to be transported back through the eons *Saturday Evening Post* v289 no5 p54 S/O 2017

MARIO ANDRETTI *Saturday Evening Post* v289 no3 p48 My/Je 2017

Painting the American Adventure *Saturday Evening Post* v289 no1 p40 Ja/F 2017

Wild Alaska *Saturday Evening Post* v289 no2 p54 Mr/Ap 2017

YOUTH CULTURE *Saturday Evening Post* v289 no4 p6 Jl/Ag 2017

Slon, Viviane

Neandertal and Denisovan DNA from Pleistocene sediments bw color *Science* v356 no6338 p605 My 12 2017

Slopes (Physical geography)

PATRICK READS K. Kirk and D. DeNunzio color *Golf Magazine* v59 no1 p44 Ja 2017

SLOSBERG, STEVEN

Stepping into Another World color *Yankee* p95 Mr 2017

Slot cars

140-MPH, Slot-Car Drag Racing P. Thomas color *Hot Rod* v70 no7 p12 Jl 2017

Slota, Will W.

DO SEARCH ADS REALLY WORK?: INTERACTION color *Harvard Business Review* v95 no3 p20 My/Je 2017

Slotcavage, Daniel J.

Perovskite-perovskite tandem photovoltaics with optimized band gaps bibl chart graph *Science* v354 no6314 p861 N 18 2016

Sloths

HANG IN THERE color *Natural History* v125 no7 p2 Jl/Ag 2017

Sloths, The (Performer)

Last Band Standing D. Dudley color *AARP: The Magazine* v59 no4A p55 Je/Jl 2016

Sloths—Behavior

THE NATURAL EXPLANATION K. MOORE color *Natural History* v125 no7 p4 Jl/Ag 2017

Slotkin, Jonathan R.

How an Early Adopter of Electronic Health Records Uses Big Data *Harvard Business Review Digital Articles* p2 D 15 2016

Why GE, Boeing, Lowe's, and Walmart Are Directly Buying Health Care for Employees *Harvard Business Review Digital Articles* p2 Je 9 2017

Why This Health System Offers Refunds to Dissatisfied Patients *Harvard Business Review Digital Articles* p2 N 16 2016

SLOTTERBACK, CARISSA

Society Is Ready for a New Kind of Science--Is Academia? *BioScience* v67 no7 p591 Jl 2017

Slouka, Mark

His Dark Material A. LEVE *New York Times Book Review* p43 N 13 2016

Slow cookers

NICE AND SLOW N. H. Reeder color *Ebony* v72 no9 p48 Jl/Ag 2017

Slow cooking

NICE AND SLOW N. H. Reeder color *Ebony* v72 no9 p48 Jl/Ag 2017

SLOW, STEADY... READY! *Martha Stewart Living* no268 p84 O 2016

Slugs (Mollusks)

Designing a better glue from slug goo L. HAMERS color *Science News* v192 no5 p14 S 30 2017

Heavy metals? No problem for this snail color *Science* v356 no6334 p150 Ap 14 2017

Organic Slug Control S. Slape-Hoysagk *Mother Earth News* no282 p83 Je/Jl 2017

TARNISHED TROPHIES J. ARTERBURN *Outdoor Life* v224 no5 p102 Je/Jl 2017

Sluis, Katrina

THE DIGITAL NON-VISITOR *Art in America* v104 no9 p98 O 2016

Sluman, Jeff—Interviews

Jeff Sluman J. Marksbury and C. Barrett color *Golf Magazine* v59 no8 p39 Ag 2017

Slums—India

Rich Returns From Poor Women Collecting Debts B. Shrivastava and R. K. Singh color *Bloomberg Businessweek* no4541 p18 O 9 2017

Slusarczyk, Martin

A general, modular method for the catalytic asymmetric synthesis of alkylboronate esters bibl color *Science* v354 no6317 p1265

D 9 2016

Slusher, Scott

Frontiers color *American Cowboy* p12 LEGENDS OF TEXAS Special Issue 2017

Sly, Peter D.

Emergence and spread of a human-transmissible multidrug-resistant nontuberculous mycobacterium bibl diag graph *Science* v354 no6313 p751 N 11 2016

SMAGLIK, PAUL

First Glance Into the Gut cartoon color *Discover* v38 no1 p63 Ja/F 2017

Regulating the Brave New World of Human Gene Editing color diag *Discover* v38 no1 p30 Ja/F 2017

Schizophrenia's Genetic Spark cartoon *Discover* v38 no1 p60 Ja/F 2017

Smail, Kate

UNSOLICITED BETA color *Climbing* no349 p8 N 2016

Smakowska-Luzan, Elwira

The receptor kinase FER is a RALF-regulated scaffold controlling plant immune signaling graph *Science* v355 no6322 p287 Ja 20 2017

Root diffusion barrier control by a vasculature-derived peptide binding to the SGN3 receptor bibl color *Science* v355 no6322 p280 Ja 20 2017

Smales, Caroline

Lee Rubin: Our mentor and role model *Science* v355 no6327 p806 F 24 2017

Small, Carla E.

How a Startup Accelerator at Boston Children's Hospital Helps Launch Companies color *Harvard Business Review Digital Articles* p2 Je 5 2017

SMALL, JONATHAN

"ALL I WANNA DO IS STAND UP and DANCE! " color *Good Housekeeping* v265 no4 p69 O 2017

bath bombs color *Parents* v92 no3 p48 Mr 2017

"I HAD TO WALK THROUGH FIRE for my kids" color *Good Housekeeping* v265 no1 p69 Jl 2017

Small, Zac

Match Made in Houston C. Toy color *Spin to Win Rodeo* v21 no3 p54 My 2017

Small, Zac—Interviews

Small Shifts Gears from Steers to School K. Santos *Spin to Win Rodeo* v21 no2 p30 Ap 2017

Small art works

BLAST from the PAST K. Kendall *Indianapolis Monthly* v40 no10 p86 Je 2017

MARCH 2017 color *Art in America* v105 no3 p73 Mr 2017

Small business

The 4 Types of Small Businesses, and Why Each One Matters K. Mills *Harvard Business Review Digital Articles* p2 Ap 30 2015

THE ETHICISTS *Los Angeles Magazine* p106 Mr 2017

How Small Businesses Can Increase Their Digital Capabilities J. Beatty *Harvard Business Review Digital Articles* p1 Jl 25 2017

If America's Economy Is Winner-Take-All, Why Are Some Smaller Businesses Thriving? K. Smith *Harvard Business Review Digital Articles* p2 S 1 2017

Meet Small Business Owners Who Depend on Trade T. J. DONOHUE *Weekly Standard* v22 no39 p31 Je 19 2017

Moving to the Middle G. JEFFERS and S. T. BROWN color *Ebony* v72 no6 p70 Ap/My 2017

THE NOSTALGISTS *Los Angeles Magazine* p102 Mr 2017

THE OUTLIERS *Los Angeles Magazine* p108 Mr 2017

THE PURISTS *Los Angeles Magazine* p104 Mr 2017

Small and Young Businesses Are Especially Vulnerable to Extreme Weather B. Collier *Harvard Business Review Digital Articles* p2 N 23 2016

The Soft Edge That's Landing Solid Sales K. Angel color *Bloomberg Businessweek* no4535 p39 Ag 28 2017

Start-ups Should Sell to Small Businesses, Not Big Enterprises T. Bartman *Harvard Business Review Digital Articles* p2 Ja 27 2015

Supports Women and Their Small Businesses Through Education and Networking M. Sponagle color *Maclean's* v130 no3 p60 Ap 2017

Sweet Fun St. Louis L. A. Addington color *Missouri Life* v44 no5 p18 Ag 2017

They won't hire an HR director - but I deserve the job *People Management* p49 Ag 2017

WANTED: FRESH SOLUTIONS FOR AGE-OLD PROBLEMS J. Alsever, V. Zarya et al color diag *Fortune* v175 no6 p68 My 1 2017

You Should Consider Buying a Small Business, But When? R. S. Ruback and R. Yudkoff *Harvard Business Review Digital Articles* p2 F 15 2017

Small business management

"We can't let size get in the way of culture": HR is helping a growing SME make an impact on the global stage *People Management* p20 S 2017

Small business—Awards

2017 SMALL BUSINESS ACHIEVEMENT AWARDS bw color *Maclean's* v130 no2 p39 Mr 2017

Small business—California

California's Big IRA Push P. Wang color *Money* v45 no10 p21 N 2016

Small business—Canada

2017 SMALL BUSINESS ACHIEVEMENT AWARDS bw color *Maclean's* v130 no2 p39 Mr 2017

Bill Morneau is wrong *Maclean's* v130 no10 p4 N 2017

Small business—China

A Bodega Once Stood Here J. Palmer color *Foreign Policy* no224 p32 My/Je 2017

Small business—Economic aspects

Optimism Soars for Midsize Businesses T. J. Donohue *Weekly Standard* v22 no29 p9 Ap 3 2017

Small business—Great Britain

"We can't let size get in the way of culture": HR is helping a growing SME make an impact on the global stage *People Management* p20 S 2017

Small business—Officials & employees

Daring To Be Different K. Meeks and C. M. BROWN color *Black Enterprise* v47 no3 p19 O 2016

Small business—Spain

A Recovery That's Not Micro Enough N. Leiber graph *Bloomberg Businessweek* no4517 p46 Ap 3 2017

Small business—Taxation

Taxing issues R. SPENCE color *Maclean's* no1 p50 F 17 2017

Small business—Taxation—United States

The MONEY Do List color *Money* v46 no2 p19 Mr 2017

A Playbook for Making America More Entrepreneurial K. Mills *Harvard Business Review Digital Articles* p2 My 27 2015

Small business—United States

Are Americans Enamored with the Wrong Kinds of Entrepreneurs? R. L. Martin *Harvard Business Review Digital Articles* p2 N 11 2016

Optimism Soars for Midsize Businesses T. J. Donohue *Weekly Standard* v22 no29 p9 Ap 3 2017

Small capitalization stocks

Funds That Let Their Brood Grow J. Waggoner color *Money* v45 no10 p42 N 2016

Small capitalization stocks—Rate of return

SMALL CAPS WITH BIG YIELDS J. DOBOSZ chart color *Forbes* v198 no9 p98 D 30 2016

Small churches

The Waiting Room D. Bonessi and M. Abunnassr color *Commonweal* v144 no5 p39 Mr. 10 2017

Small cities

May's Small-Town Brexit Strategy T. Penny color *Bloomberg Businessweek* no4522 p18 My 15 2017

Southern Living IS LOOKING FOR THE SOUTH'S BEST *Southern Living* v51 no12 p20 D 2016

Small cities in literature

HOMETOWN IS WHERE THE HEART IS N. A. SPECTOR color *Publishers Weekly* v263 no46 p24 N 14 2016

Small colleges—Finance

Little Good News For the Little Ivies M. McDonald and K. Smith graph *Bloomberg Businessweek* no4505 p41 D 26 2016

Small farms

See also

Hobby farms

Small game hunting

See also

Rabbit hunting

Squirrel hunting

SO, YOU WANT A RABBIT DOG? T. CARPENTER color *Outdoor Life* v224 no7 pH11 S 2017

SQUIRREL TALK J. SPILGER color *Outdoor Life* v224 no7 p23 S 2017

Small gardens

Succulent Savvy *Atlanta* v56 no12 p43 Ap 2017

Small house design & construction

What a tiny house can teach you color *Redbook* p148 S 2017

Small houses

See also

Cottages

outside in J. GARLOCK color *Better Homes & Gardens* v95 no8 p44 Ag 2017

Plane-Spotting at Edgar's E. CLARK color *Yankee* p14 Mr 2017

Small houses—Design & construction

LESS IS MORE M. COHEN MARILL *Atlanta* v56 no8 p32 D 2016

Small houses—Evaluation

A House by the Lake T. CHIARELLA bw color *Popular Mechanics* p88 D 2016/Ja 2017

Small houses—Maintenance & repair

outside in J. GARLOCK color *Better Homes & Gardens* v95 no8 p44 Ag 2017

Small intestinal bacterial overgrowth

SIBO SOLUTIONS J. Teitelbaum color *Amazing Wellness* v9 no4 p32 Summ 2017

Small intestine

Diagnosis L. Sanders *New York Times Magazine* p32 O 16 2016

Small intestine diseases

See also

Small intestinal bacterial overgrowth

SIBO SOLUTIONS J. Teitelbaum color *Amazing Wellness* v9 no4 p32 Summ 2017

Small magellanic cloud

Superstars of the SMC color *Astronomy* v45 no9 p74 S 2017

Two for the price of one color *Astronomy* v45 no5 p74 My 2017

Small Mouth Sounds (Theatrical production)

The Ten Best Theater Events of the Year J. Green img *New York* v49 no25 p126 D 12 2016

Small talk

Should You Chat Informally Before an Interview? B. Swider, B. Harris et al *Harvard Business Review Digital Articles* p2 S 14 2016

Small Town (Music)

BILL FRISELL [Cover story] B. MILKOWSKI color *Downbeat* v84 no7 p28 Jl 2017

Smalley, Adam P.

A general catalytic β-C–H carbonylation of aliphatic amines to β-lactams bibl diag *Science* v354 no6314 p851 N 18 2016

Small Flame, A (Short story)

A SMALL FLAME YIYUN LI cartoon *New Yorker* v93 no12 p54 My 8 2017

Smallmouth bass

The Big Unit A. WHITCOMB *Boating World* v38 no2 p18 F 2017

PITCH-BLACK BRONZEBACKS J. Cermele color *Field & Stream* v122 no4 p36 S 2017

Smallmouth bass fishing

The Circle of Life: Spawning Behaviors of Smallmouth Bass R. Michelson *New York State Conservationist* v71 no6 p22 Je 2017

HOT BRONZE S. CULTON color *Field & Stream* v122 no3 p51 Ag 2017

Mining for Bronze J. Cermele color *Field & Stream* v121 no9 pF7 Ap 2017

SEASON'S EATINGS M. Modoski bw color *Field & Stream* v122 no5 p20 O 2017

Smallmouth bass—Behavior

The Circle of Life: Spawning Behaviors of Smallmouth Bass R. Michelson *New York State Conservationist* v71 no6 p22 Je 2017

Smallpox diagnosis

A PLAGUE TAMED: AMALLPOX WAS RECURRING MENACE AROUND THE WORLD--UNTIL A BRTITISH DOCTOR FIGURED OUT HOW TO PITONE VIRUS AGAINST ANOTHER M. M. SOLLY *Smithsonian* v48 no5 p72 S 2017

Smallpox vaccination

Stamping Out Smallpox W. H. FOEGE bw *Natural History* v125

no9 p24 S 2017

Smallpox—Genetic aspects

Labmade smallpox is possible, study shows K. Kupferschmidt color *Science* v357 no6347 p115 Jl 14 2017

Smallpox—History

A PLAGUE TAMED: AMALLPOX WAS RECURRING MENACE AROUND THE WORLD--UNTIL A BRTITISH DOCTOR FIGURED OUT HOW TO PITONE VIRUS AGAINST ANOTHER M. M. SOLLY *Smithsonian* v48 no5 p72 S 2017

A POX On History L. WADE color *Smithsonian* v47 no10 p16 Mr 2017

Stamping Out Smallpox W. H. FOEGE bw *Natural History* v125 no9 p24 S 2017

Smalls, Joan, 1988——Interviews

Joan Smalls K. B. Brown color *InStyle* v24 no3 p290 Mr 2017

Small ubiquitin-related modifier proteins

A SUMO-ubiquitin relay recruits proteasomes to chromosome axes to regulate meiotic recombination H. B. D. P. Rao, S. K. Bhatt et al bibl graph *Science* v355 no6323 p403 Ja 27 2017

UBE2O is a quality control factor for orphans of multiprotein complexes K. Yanagitani, S. Juszkiewicz et al diag *Science* v357 no6350 p472 Ag 4 2017

ZATT (ZNF451)–mediated resolution of topoisomerase 2 DNA-protein cross-links M. J. Schellenberg, J. Ariel Lieberman et al diag *Science* v357 no6358 p1412 S 29 2017

Smallwood, Christine

ALIENS: THE WORLD'S LEADING SCIENTISTS ON THE SEARCH FOR EXTRATERRESTRIAL LIFE *Harper's Magazine* v334 no2004 p81 My 2017

FACE VALUE: THE IRRESISTIBLE INFLUENCE OF FIRST IMPRESSION *Harper's Magazine* v334 no2004 p80 My 2017

NEW BOOKS bw color *Harper's Magazine* v335 no2005 p85 Je 2017

NEW BOOKS *Harper's Magazine* p83 O 2017

NEW BOOKS *Harper's Magazine* p91 Ap 2017

NEW BOOKS *Harper's Magazine* v333 no1999 p81 D 2016

THERE'S A MYSTERY THERE: THE PRIMAL VISION OF MAURICE SENDAK *Harper's Magazine* v334 no2004 p79 My 2017

Smallwood, Claire

Claire Smallwood is a Champion for Women M. MICHELSON color *Powder* v46 no2 p26 O 2017

Smallwood, Norm

Aligning Your Organization with an Agile Workforce *Harvard Business Review Digital Articles* p2 F 11 2016

How to Select the Right Freelancer for the Work *Harvard Business Review Digital Articles* p2 F 23 2016

Managing On-Demand Talent *Harvard Business Review Digital Articles* p2 Ja 28 2016

Performance Management in the Gig Economy *Harvard Business Review Digital Articles* p2 Ja 11 2016

SMARICK, ANDY

The Jobs Problem bw color *Weekly Standard* v23 no4 p22 O 2 2017

A Quiet Revolution color *Weekly Standard* v22 no7 p20 O 24 2016

A Trump in a China Shop? [Cover story] color *Weekly Standard* v22 no31 p30 Ap 17 2017

With Smugness Toward None... bw cartoon color *Weekly Standard* v22 no12 p26 N 28 2016

Smart, Andrew J.

How Overfocusing on Goals Can Hold Us Back *Harvard Business Review Digital Articles* p2 Mr 17 2016

Smart, Ashley G.

Citizen observers chart Arctic change *Physics Today* v70 no2 p29 F 2017

A droplet that won't freeze harbors a crystal that won't melt *Physics Today* v69 no10 p18 O 2016

Magnetic trap snares methyl radicals *Physics Today* v70 no4 p18 Ap 2017

Polymer-based transistors bring fully stretchable devices within reach *Physics Today* v70 no3 p14 Mr 2017

Quantum entanglement reaches new heights: The satellite-based distribution of entangled photons to cities 1200 km apart bolsters prospects for a global quantum communication network *Physics Today* v70 no8 p14 Ag 2017

Spiral arms detected around an infant star *Physics Today* v69 no12

p22 D 2016

Supercooled water survives in no-man's-land *Physics Today* v70 no2 p18 F 2017

Taking the measure of water's whirl *Physics Today* v70 no10 p20 O 2017

A thermodynamic theory of granular material endures: Theorists have tested what seemed like an untestable conjecture: that all the possible arrangements of grains in a packing are equally probable *Physics Today* v70 no9 p20 S 2017

Smart, Jean

ROLE CALL JEAN SMART S. Vilkomerson color *Entertainment Weekly* no1449 p34 Ja 20 2017

SMART, VICTOR

People like me don't normally speak up *People Management* p32 F 2017

Smart cards—Design & construction

SD memory cards: The features and specifications to look for J. CARLSON color *Macworld - Digital Edition* v34 no9 p76 S 2017

Smart cards—Equipment & supplies

SD memory cards: The features and specifications to look for J. CARLSON color *Macworld - Digital Edition* v34 no9 p76 S 2017

VERBATIM USB-C POCKET CARD READER: A GREAT COMBINATION OF PRICE AND PERFORMANCE J. CARLSON color *Macworld - Digital Edition* v34 no11 p32 N 2017

Smart cities

Smart Cities Are Going to Be a Security Nightmare T. Thibodeaux *Harvard Business Review Digital Articles* p2 Ap 28 2017

Smart Fortwo automobile

John Phillips J. Phillips color *Car & Driver* v63 no5 p28 N 2017

Smart locks

The Internet of "Meh" D. GERSHGORN color *Popular Science* v288 no6 p72 N/D 2016

Smart locks—Evaluation

Pick Your Lock color *Log Home Living* v34 no3 p16 Ap 2017

THE WELL-MONITORED HOME T. CHIARELLA color *Popular Mechanics* p78 My 2017

Smart speakers (Wireless technology)

See also

Amazon Echo (Smart speaker)

Google Home (Smart speaker)

18 New Climbing Slang Terms color *Climbing* no357 p22 N 2017

Alexa Takes the Stand: Listening Devices Raise Privacy Issues H. S. Edwards color *Time* v189 no18 p28 My 15 2017

Decorator-Friendly Bass J. SCIACCA color *Sound & Vision* v82 no6 p23 Jl/Ag 2017

HomePod first impressions: Lots of unknowns, but its sound is impressive J. SNELL color *Macworld - Digital Edition* v34 no8 p115 Ag 2017

How to stop Google Home or Amazon Echo from making unwanted online purchases F. ION color *PCWorld* v35 no9 p107 S 2017

Soundcast VG7 Outdoor Wireless Speaker R. Sabincolor *Sound & Vision* v82 no6 p54 Jl/Ag 2017

Smart speakers (Wireless technology)—Evaluation

Talk to Your Home D. Pogue cartoon *AARP: The Magazine* v60 no2A p16 F/Mr 2017

Smart structure design & construction

Bold, Beautiful, Brutal T. CHIARELLA color *Chicago* v66 no11 p82 N 2017

Smart television devices

smart ENTERTAINMENT N. SAPORITA diag *Good Housekeeping* v263 no5 p143 N 2016

Smart television devices—Evaluation

For When You Have The Urge to Splurge color *Consumer Reports* v81 no12 p62 D 2016

GEARHEAD SCREEN PLAY T. MOYNIHAN color *Wired* v25 no4 p36 Ap 2017

Ultra Style B. Ankosko color *Sound & Vision* v81 no9 p74 N 2016

Smartphone industry

Apple's Shrinking Impact in the Smartphone Industry J. P. V. Sampere *Harvard Business Review Digital Articles* p2 F 2 2016

Xiaomi, Not Apple, Is Changing the Smartphone Industry J. P. Vazquez Sampere *Harvard Business Review Digital Articles* p2 O 14 2014

Smartphone sales & prices

THE IPHONE DECADE A. Pressman color diag *Fortune* v175 no7 p23 Je 1 2017

Your Next Phone Will Probably Cost $1,000 M. Gurman graph *Bloomberg Businessweek* no4538 p24 S 18 2017

Smartphones

See also

iPhone (Smartphone)

Samsung Galaxy Note (Smartphone)

Samsung Galaxy S (Smartphone)

15 Minutes to a Simpler Day L. Fenton color *Parents* v92 no9 p158 S 2017

4 ways to keep from sleeping through your Android alarm B. PATTERSON color *PCWorld* v35 no2 p193 F 2017

6 settings to make your Android phone anticipate your needs B. PATTERSON color *PCWorld* p168 D 2016

Ask Our Experts color *Consumer Reports* v82 no1 p21 Ja 2017

Building the Third Offset A. FRANK *Commentary* v142 no3 p8 O 2016

Conquer Your To-Do List with Your Phone A. Samuel *Harvard Business Review Digital Articles* p2 D 1 2014

Do You Still Need a 'Real' Camera? M. Leuchter color *Popular Photography* v81 no2 p60 Mr/Ap 2017

End note M. Shaw color *Columbia Journalism Review* p112 Fall/Wint 2016

THE ENEMIES OF EMPATHY R. A. SCHROTH *America* v215 no14 p36 N 7 2016

Frontiers of Citizen Science B. BAKER *BioScience* v66 no11 p921 N 1 2016

Help, hope, and hype: Ethical dimensions of neuroprosthetics J. Clausen, E. Fetz et al color *Science* v356 no6345 p1338 Je 30 2017

Instagram Explore M. Young *New York Times Magazine* p18 Ja 8 2017

The iPhone switcher's guide: Move from iOS to Android and keep all your stuff M. SIMON color *PCWorld* v35 no1 p173 Ja 2017

The Least Distracting Distraction D. CURCURITO and E. DYER color *Popular Mechanics* p62 Mr 2017

Mac 911 G. FLEISHMAN color *Macworld - Digital Edition* p111 Je 13 2017

News: Corrupt video link causes iPhones to crash O. Raymundo color *Macworld - Digital Edition* p8 Ja 2017

PUT YOUR YEAR IN GEAR L. GOLDMAN color *Better Homes & Gardens* v95 no9 p158 S 2017

Safeguard Your Smartphone *Parents* v91 no12 p46 D 2016

SMARTPHONE DENIERS C. Neuhaus *Saturday Evening Post* v289 no1 p14 Ja/F 2017

Snap the Night Sky on a Phone S. BUSHWICK cartoon *Popular Science* p78 Ja/F 2017

Terms and conditions: Parents can make smartphone use for kids safer by writing their own fine print A. Scobey color *U.S. Catholic* v82 no9 p43 S 2017

There Is No Right Way to Unplug from Work S. Schrobsdorff color *Time* v189 no3 p19 Ja 30 2017

Transfer everything from your old Android phone to your new one M. SIMON and D. WALTER bw color *PCWorld* v35 no8 p134 Ag 2017

What You're Hiding from When You Constantly Check Your Phone C. Lieberman *Harvard Business Review Digital Articles* p2 Ja 19 2016

Your Body on a Cell Phone color *Prevention* p11 Mr 2017

Smartphones—Design & construction

Feature: 2017 could see just one OLED iPhone C. McGarry color *Macworld - Digital Edition* p100 Ja 2017

Samsung Would Love to Talk About This Phone M. Gurman and S. Kim color *Bloomberg Businessweek* no4517 p36 Ap 3 2017

Smartphones—Equipment & supplies

iOS Accessories J. Mathis color *Macworld - Digital Edition* v34 no10 p60 O 2017

Logitech ZeroTouch: This Android smartphone holder puts Amazon's Alexa in your car M. BROWN color map *PCWorld* v35 no5 p132 My 2017

Samsung DeX: 7 days using the DeX dock and a Galaxy S8+ as a desktop PC J. PHILLIPS color *PCWorld* v35 no6 p117 Je 2017

Somebody Solved the Ugly-Cord-and-Charger Thing G. MUNCE color *GQ: Gentlemen's Quarterly* v97 no10 p76 O 2017

Smartphones—Equipment & supplies—Evaluation

Wireless for Less R. Broida color *Money* v45 no10 p23 N 2016

Smartphones—Evaluation

8 times Google savagely burned Apple during the Pixel announcement L. YAMSHON cartoon color diag *PCWorld* v35 no11 p127 N 2016

THE ESSENTIAL PHONE IS A BEAUTIFUL EXAMPLE OF EVERYTHING THAT'S WRONG WITH ANDROID [Cover story] M. SIMON color *PCWorld* v35 no7 p161 Jl 2017

Galaxy S8+ review: The future of Android is now M. SIMON color graph *PCWorld* v35 no6 p94 Je 2017

HP Elite x3: This could be the last great Windows phone M. HACHMAN color graph *PCWorld* v35 no11 p68 N 2016

HTC U11 : A powerful Android phone that knows how to have fun M. SIMON color graph *PCWorld* v35 no7 p116 Jl 2017

LG V20 hands-on: A 5.7-inch phablet for smartphone content creators J. PHILLIPS color *PCWorld* p104 O 2016

LG V20 Smartphone M. Fleischmann color *Sound & Vision* v82 no3 p52 Ap 2017

LG V20: The Android phone for hard-core enthusiasts J. PHILLIPS color *PCWorld* v35 no1 p108 Ja 2017

LG V30 hands-on: A 6-inch beast with more power and fewer gimmicks M. SIMON color *PCWorld* v35 no10 p74 O 2017

Look familiar? M. Gurman color *Bloomberg Businessweek* no4494 p33 O 10 2016

Moto Z Play: Long-lasting, affordable, and modular too J. CROSS color graph *PCWorld* p114 O 2016

THE NEW IPHONE HAS COMPETITION A. Pressman color *Fortune* v176 no5 p18 O 1 2017

Pixel XL review : Google's new phone isn't a Nexus—it's better J. CROSS color graph *PCWorld* v35 no11 p46 N 2016

Samsung Galaxy Note 8: Don't call it a comeback, call it the phone of the year M. SIMON color *PCWorld* v35 no10 p57 O 2017

The United Nations of Mobile Networks X. HARDING and A. SMITH color *Popular Science* v288 no6 p74 N/D 2016

Ups K. Stock color *Bloomberg Businessweek* no4494 p15 O 10 2016

With the Galaxy Note7 dead, here are 7 other Android phablets to consider I. PAUL color *PCWorld* v35 no11 p31 N 2016

Smartphones—Psychological aspects

Digital Minds L. Sanders bw color graph *Science News* v191 no6 p18 Ap 1 2017

The distracted student mind — enhancing its focus and attention L. D. Rosen chart color diag graph il *Phi Delta Kappan* v99 no2 p8 O 2017

YOUR BODY ON TECH A. SHAFFER color *Better Homes & Gardens* v95 no4 p152 Ap 2017

Smartphones—Sales & prices

The Cheap Phone Is Dead In China B. Einhorn cartoon color *Bloomberg Businessweek* no4496 p36 O 24 2016

Smartphones—Security measures

5 alternative (and easier) ways to unlock your Android phone B. PATTERSON color *PCWorld* v35 no4 p136 Ap 2017

HOW VULNERABLE IS YOUR PHONE? D. PIERCE diag *Wired* v25 no6 p37 Je 2017

SMARTPHONE SECURITY L. Bedord *Successful Farming* v114 no11 p18 N 2016

Smartphones—Social aspects

HAS THE SMARTPHONE DESTROYED A GENERATION? J. M. Twenge color graph *Atlantic* v320 no2 p58 S 2017

The Ripple Effects of Parents Not Using Their Vacation Time S. G. Carmichael *Harvard Business Review Digital Articles* p2 O 12 2015

VERTICAL REALITY: PHONES HAVE TILTED OUR WORLDVIEW C. THOMPSON cartoon *Wired* v25 no9 p40 S 2017

Smartwatches

Apple Watch can detect an early sign of heart disease M. SIMON color *Macworld - Digital Edition* p48 Je 13 2017

THE FRIGHT BEFORE CHRISTMAS M. GUNCH color *New Orleans Magazine* v51 no2 p48 D 2016

THE NEW WORLD OF WATCHES A. Pressman color *Fortune* v175 no5 p12 Ap 1 2017

A Personality of Its Own A. C. Clarke color *MIT Technology Review* v120 no5 p20 S/O 2017

Smartwatches—Equipment & supplies

KANEX GOPOWER WATCH AND ZENS POWERBANK FOR APPLE WATCH: CONVENIENT CHARGING SUSIE OCHS color *Macworld - Digital Edition* p55 F 2017

Tested: 5 protective bumpers for the Apple Watch S. J. PUREWAL color *Macworld - Digital Edition* v34 no6 p54 Je 2017

Smartwatches—Evaluation

APPLE WATCH SERIES 2 REVIEW: A FASTER, BRIGHTER FITNESS MACHINE C. McGARRY color map *Macworld - Digital Edition* v33 no11 p113 N 2016

Face off r. palmer color *Bike Magazine* v24 no7 p112 S 2017

For When You Have The Urge to Splurge color *Consumer Reports* v81 no12 p62 D 2016

Garmin Quatix 5 Marine GPS Smartwatch J. Y. WOOD color *Power & Motoryacht* v34 no7 p28 Jl 2017

GOING GRAPHIC color *Harper's Bazaar* no3649 p166 D 2016/Ja 2017

Holiday Gift Guide D. HOLBROOK *TV Guide* p20 D 5 2016

iOS Accessories J. Mathis color *Macworld - Digital Edition* p62 Mr 2017

iOS Accessories J. Mathis color *Macworld - Digital Edition* v34 no9 p56 S 2017

The iPod's successor is the Apple Watch J. SNELL color *Macworld - Digital Edition* v34 no10 p39 O 2017

Nixon Mission: A hardcore Android Wear watch for surf and snow J. PHILLIPS color *PCWorld* v35 no11 p104 N 2016

Pokémon Go on Apple Watch vs. Pokémon Go Plus: Which should you wear? A. HAYWARD color *Macworld - Digital Edition* p43 Mr 2017

RECODE YOUR HEALTH B. COURT color *Men's Health* v32 no7 p118 S 2017

ROAD TESTING THE HUAWEI FIT color *Black Enterprise* v47 no5 p26 Ja/F 2017

SMART WATCHES, DISSECTED D. GERSHGORN and A. GOLDBERG color *Popular Science* v288 no6 p20 N/D 2016

SOMETHING COOL FOR EVERYONE color *Popular Mechanics* p94 D 2016/Ja 2017

TAG Heuer Connected Modular 45: Hands on with the swankiest Wear watch of all J. PHILLIPS color *PCWorld* v35 no5 p140 My 2017

Tapped IN C. Shanahan color *InStyle* v23 no12 p155 N 2016

Watch and Learn J. Y. WOOD color *Power & Motoryacht* v34 no11 p68 N 2017

WatchOS 3 guide: 15 essential tips to transform your Apple Watch C. McGARRY color *Macworld - Digital Edition* v33 no11 p75 N 2016

your PERSONAL GADGETS N. SAPORITA, G. GRAJEK et al color diag *Good Housekeeping* v263 no6 p105 D 2016

SmaXtec Animal Care Sales GmbH

Elsie Will Text You When She's in Heat M. Scaturro color *Bloomberg Businessweek* no4498 p52 N 7 2016

SMEAL, ELEANOR

BEYOND THE GENDER GAP *Ms.* v26 no4 p26 Wint 2016

last word *Ms.* v26 no3 p16 Fall 2016

Ms. letter *Ms.* v26 no3 p2 Fall 2016

Smeenk, Jenna

Barrel Arc and Counter-Arc [Cover story] color *Horse & Rider* v55 no12 p25 D 2016

Smeets, Job

THE FAST & THE FURIOUS H. MARTIN color *Architectural Digest* v74 no7 p84 Jl 2017

Smell

Poor human olfaction is a 19th-century myth J. P. McGann color *Science* v356 no6338 p597 My 12 2017

Smell disorders

Poor human olfaction is a 19th-century myth J. P. McGann color *Science* v356 no6338 p597 My 12 2017

Smell like Sheep (Poem)

Smell like Sheep P. C. Kolin bw *U.S. Catholic* v82 no7 p11 Jl 2017

SMELT, JORDAN

Summer... Reds?! *Atlanta* v57 no4 p40 Ag 2017

Smeltz, Kevin

STAND AND DELIVER color *Golf Magazine* v59 no1 p48 Ja 2017

Smetannikova, Nataly

READING THAT UNITES US: Discovering the science of literature through our favorite books color *Literacy Today (2411-*

7862) v34 no6 p46 My/Je 2017

Smeyne, Richard J.

Restoring auditory cortex plasticity in adult mice by restricting thalamic adenosine signaling graph *Science* v356 no6345 p1352 Je 30 2017

Smialek, Jeanna

'Chairman Cohn' Has a Nice Ring to It color graph *Bloomberg Businessweek* no4533 p32 Ag 7 2017

Federal Agencies Play 'Not It' With Flood Insurance *Bloomberg Businessweek* no4538 p28 S 18 2017

The Heroin Business Is Booming in America color *Bloomberg Businessweek* no4522 p32 My 15 2017

Neel Kashkari color *Bloomberg Businessweek* no4527 p92 Je 19 2017

Possibly color *Bloomberg Businessweek* no4507 p14 Ja 16 2017

Why the Fed Cares About America's Opioid Crisis graph *Bloomberg Businessweek* no4532 p34 Jl 31 2017

Smick, David M.

An Economic Primer for Stagnant Times C. WHALEN *American Conservative* v16 no2 p47 Mr/Ap 2017

Smidt, Caleb

PICKING THE FAVORITES B. Welch color *American Cowboy* v23 no4 p64 D 2016/Ja 2017

Team Roping Spices Up World All-Around Race K. Santos *Spin to Win Rodeo* v21 no6 p28 Ag 2017

Smidt, Margaret Benner

From the Editor *Weatherwise* v70 no2 p4 Mr/Ap 2017

from the editor *Weatherwise* v70 no5 p4 S/O 2017

A Tribute to Thomas W. Schlatter *Weatherwise* v70 no2 p5 Mr/Ap 2017

SMIETANA, BOB

GOD, GUNS, AND OIL color *Christianity Today* v61 no7 p46 S 2017

Smigel, Robert—Interviews

LOOKWELL D. Snierson color *Entertainment Weekly* no1460/1461 p70 Ap 7-17 2017

Smil, Vaclav, 1943-

Why manufacturing matters E. H. Landuyt diag *Monthly Labor Review* p1 O 2016

Smilan, Cathy

Visual immersion for cultural understanding and multimodal literacy bibl color *Arts Education Policy Review* v118 no4 p220 2017

SmileOnMyMac LLC

PDFPEN 9 AND PDFPENPRO 9: EDITING APPS GET SOLID ENHANCEMENTS OVER PREVIOUS VERSIONS G. FLEISHMAN color *Macworld - Digital Edition* v34 no6 p21 Je 2017

Smiley, Jane

Portraits of a Lady: Three books about Jane Austen explore her fans, her cultural influence and what she learned from theater *New York Times Book Review* p10 Jl 16 2017

SMILEY, LAUREN

Machine Error il *New Republic* v247 no11 p8 N 2016

MURDER IN THE HEARTLAND bw color map *Wired* v25 no7 p72 Jl 2017

Smiley, Mark

COMMITTED C. Kassar color *Climbing* no355 p62 Ag 2017

Smiley, Patricia

Outside the Wire: A Pacific Homicide Novel color *Publishers Weekly* v264 no39 p88 S 25 2017

Smiley, Tavis

Dick Gregory color *Time* v190 no9 p17 S 4 2017

From Selma to Charlottesville, the Ghosts of Our Past *Time* v190 no8 p45 Ag 28 2017

Smiley, Tavis, 1964—Interviews

Tavis Smiley Smiles on the KING of POP B. Levine bw *Publishers Weekly* v263 no44 p(Sp)28 O 31 2016

Smilf (TV program)

Singled Out K. HALE color *Vogue* v207 no11 p166 N 2017

SMILF A. Bacle, D. Coggan et al *Entertainment Weekly* no1482/1483 p43 S 22 2017

Smiling

5 new ways to DEFY YOUR AGE A. FRANZINO color *Good Housekeeping* v264 no3 p27 Mr 2017

How to feel beautiful *Redbook* p160 My 2017

How to Handle an Annoying Cubs Fan chart color *Men's Health* v32 no3 p12 Ap 2017

I would tell my teenage self ... *Reader's Digest* v188 no1125 p48 N 2016

Smile, and the Sun Will Come Shining Through R. CASTELLANO *USA Today Magazine* v145 no2862 p62 Mr 2017

Taking the Perfect Selfie A. Graham color *InStyle* v24 no3 p186 Mr 2017

Smilovic, Amy

my style color *InStyle* v24 no5 p122 My 2017

Smirnoff, Yakov

WHAT A COUNTRY! (AGAIN!): WHO'D HAVE THOUGHT THERE'D COME A TIME WHEN THE KING OF COLD WAR COMEDY, YAKOV SIMIRNOFF, JUST MIGHT MAKE A COMEBACK? AN ONLY-IN-AMERICA-RIGHT-NOW STORY L. MULLINS *Washingtonian Magazine* v52 no12 p64 S 2017

Smit, Jan

The formation of peak rings in large impact craters bibl color graph *Science* v354 no6314 p878 N 18 2016

Smite, Klinta

AnD WHat a MasqUeRaDe H. Rolfe *Dance Spirit* v21 no1 p48 Ja 2017

Smith, A. Gordon

The Cost of Drugs for Rare Diseases Is Threatening the U.S. Health Care System *Harvard Business Review Digital Articles* p2 Ap 7 2017

Price Gouging and the Dangerous New Breed of Pharma Companies *Harvard Business Review Digital Articles* p2 Jl 6 2016

Smith, A. J.

The Red Prince: The Long War, Book 3 *Publishers Weekly* v264 no8 p70 F 20 2017

Smith, Abby Hadassah

RESISTERHOOD IS POWERFUL S. RICHARDSON bw color *American History* v52 no3 p24 Ag 2017

Smith, Adam

Trespass Against Us C. Collis color *Entertainment Weekly* no1450 p46 Ja 27 2017

Smith, Adam, 1723-1790

ADAM SMITH NEEDS A PAPER CLIP V. POSTREL cartoon *Reason* v49 no1 p14 My 2017

OLD and RIGHT *American Conservative* v16 no2 p29 Mr/Ap 2017

Smith, Airy

THE Flip SIDE color *Dance Spirit* v21 no4 p52 Ap 2017

Smith, Alex

A Highlands Garden Paradise C. Rogers color *Southern Living* v52 no6 p92 Je 2017

rooms IN BLOOM C. Rogers color *Southern Living* v52 no3 p88 Mr 2017

Smith, Ali, 1962-

Ali Smith *New York Times Book Review* p8 F 12 2017

LIBRARY AS MUSE E. WHITE color *New York Times Book Review* p12 D 4 2016

OMENS OF DISASTER N. SMITH color *Nation* v304 no13 p32 Ap 17 2017

Rogue Britannia S. LYALL *New York Times Book Review* p16 F 19 2017

Smith, Amy

consider COMMUNITY COLLEGE *Dance Magazine* p16 2016/2017

consider COMMUNITY COLLEGE: There are perks to starting small *Dance Magazine* v90 p16 2016/2017 Supplement College Guide

EMBRACING YOUR "Type" color *Dance Spirit* v21 no2 p52 F 2017

SOLO Solutions color *Dance Spirit* v20 no9 p70 N 2016

tacking two: Should you double-major? *Dance Magazine* v90 p22 2016/2017 Supplement College Guide

tackling two *Dance Magazine* p22 2016/2017

"WHAT I WISH I'D KNOWN" *Dance Spirit* v21 no7 p72 S 2017

Smith, Amy M.

Retrieval practice protects memory against acute stress bibl chart graph *Science* v354 no6315 p1046 N 25 2016

Smith, Andrea

The Mechanic You Want in Your Corner C. GIDDINGS bw color

Bicycling v58 no1 p26 Ja/F 2017

A real console, really mobile color *Popular Science* v289 no6 p18 N/D 2017

The Sweet Sound of Virtual Reality color *Popular Science* v288 no6 p48 N/D 2016

Toy story color *Popular Science* v289 no6 p44 N/D 2017

The United Nations of Mobile Networks color *Popular Science* v288 no6 p74 N/D 2016

Smith, Anna Deavere, 1950-

GOINGS ON ABOUT TOWN color *New Yorker* v92 no33 p5 O 17 2016

Scholars Behind Bars J. Zimmerman color *New York Review of Books* v64 no3 p43 F 23 2017

Smith, Anna Deavere, 1950-—Interviews

Anna Deavere Smith E. Berman color *Time* v188 no19 p64 N 7 2016

SMITH, ANNE KATES

THE FALLOUT FROM RISING RATES cartoon *Kiplinger's Personal Finance* v71 no3 p11 Mr 2017

How Much Risk Can You Stand? color *Kiplinger's Personal Finance* v71 no2 p24 F 2017

Inflation-Proof Your Assets cartoon chart *Kiplinger's Personal Finance* v71 no4 p59 Ap 2017

Investing With a Conscience chart color *Kiplinger's Personal Finance* v71 no7 p54 Jl 2017

It's What You Do That Counts color *Kiplinger's Personal Finance* v70 no12 p42 D 2016

PAPA GRONK'S SECRETS FOR MONEY SMART KIDS color *Kiplinger's Personal Finance* v70 no12 p14 D 2016

The Psychology of a Market Bubble *Kiplinger's Personal Finance* v71 no11 p16 N 2017

THE TRUMP EFFECT ON FINANCIAL MARKETS graph *Kiplinger's Personal Finance* v71 no2 p13 F 2017

What Kind of Investor Are You? *Kiplinger's Personal Finance* v71 no6 p25 Je 2017

When Will the Bull Market End? color *Kiplinger's Personal Finance* v71 no10 p59 O 2017

Where to Invest in 2017 cartoon graph *Kiplinger's Personal Finance* v71 no1 p42 Ja 2017

Where to Invest Now cartoon graph *Kiplinger's Personal Finance* v71 no7 p46 Jl 2017

WILL WHITE HOUSE WORRIES HIT STOCKS? color *Kiplinger's Personal Finance* v71 no8 p11 Ag 2017

Smith, Annick

Crossing the Plains with Bruno S. Prentiss *Orion Magazine* v35 no4/5 p109 Jl-O 2016

Smith, Anthony

AGNOSTIC AGGRESSION color *Bike Magazine* v24 no1 p106 Ja/F 2017

BEATDOWN color *Bike Magazine* v24 no4 p112 Je 2017

flat out color *Bike Magazine* v24 no3 p112 My 2017

GET IN GEAR bw color *Bike Magazine* v24 no1 p122 Ja/F 2017

slow down bw *Bike Magazine* v24 no6 p23 Ag 2017

TRANSITION PATROL CARBON color *Bike Magazine* v23 no9 p86 D 2016

Smith, April

Home Sweet Home: A Novel *Publishers Weekly* v264 no17 p88 Ap 24 2017

Smith, Austin

THE LORDS OF LAMBEAU *Harper's Magazine* v334 no2000 p50 Ja 2017

Smith, Barney

Circling the Drain W. FERGUSON *Texas Monthly* v45 no9 p38 S 2017

Smith, Becca

mom wins... ...and fails color *Working Mother* v40 no2 p8 Je/Jl 2017

Smith, Ben

Your tax dollars at work color *Columbia Journalism Review* v56 no1 p30 Spr 2017

Smith, Bessie, 1894-1937

EVENT CALENDAR *Washingtonian Magazine* v52 no12 p165 S 2017

Smith, Bob—Interviews

Quarter-Crack Q&A color *Horse & Rider* v55 no11 p21 N 2016

Smith, Brad D.

6 BRAD SMITH G. Colvin color *Fortune* v174 no7 p84 D 1 2016

Smith, Bradford L., 1959-

Microsoft's Civil Rights Crusader T. Simonite bw diag *MIT Technology Review* v119 no6 p13 N/D 2016

Smith, Brad—Interviews

Tech's Resilient Force color *Forbes* v199 no5 p30 My 16 2017

Smith, Brendan L.

SOUTH BEACH IN SOUTHWEST *Washingtonian Magazine* v52 no1 p47 O 2016

Smith, Brett

ROCZEN ROLL color *Cycle World* v55 no10 p60 N 2016

Smith, Brian D.

Dams threaten rare Mekong dolphins bibl color *Science* v355 no6327 p805 F 24 2017

Drawn Away *Indianapolis Monthly* p49 F 2017

SMITH, BRUCE

COOL MOVE [Cover story] color *Dirt Sports + Off-Road* v51 no12 p62 D 2017

FSB REBIRTH PART 2: E40D OVERHAUL color *Dirt Sports + Off-Road* v51 no5 p52 My 2017

FSB REBIRTH PART I: ENGINE REBUILD color *Dirt Sports + Off-Road* v51 no4 p28 Ap 2017

IN THE COMFORT ZONE color *Dirt Sports + Off-Road* v51 no9 p46 S 2017

MOSSY OAK DEFENDER color *Dirt Sports + Off-Road* v51 no5 p24 My 2017

NO REGRETS color *Dirt Sports + Off-Road* v51 no5 p18 My 2017

RED BALL EXPRES color *Dirt Sports + Off-Road* v51 no2 p14 F 2017

Site Report: Syracuse *Progressive* v81 no7 p69 O/N 2017

SWITCH IT UP [Cover story] color *Dirt Sports + Off-Road* v51 no10 p48 O 2017

TAILGATE PARTY color *Dirt Sports + Off-Road* v51 no3 p52 Mr 2017

X-FACTOR TURBO RS color *Dirt Sports + Off-Road* v51 no2 p48 F 2017

Smith, Bryan

THE BALLAD OF ED "BAD BOY" BROWN bw color *Chicago* v66 no4 p106 Ap 2017

THE DOOMSDAY SQUAD color *Chicago* v66 no2 p84 F 2017

THE DOUBLE LIFE OF AHMAD OBALI bw color map *Chicago* v65 no11 p104 N 2016

"I'M A POET." color *Chicago* v65 no12 p98 D 2016

Purple Reign color *Chicago* v66 no11 p74 N 2017

WHY We LOVE CHICAGO bw cartoon color *Chicago* v66 no3 p75 Mr 2017

SMITH, BYRON

The Battle for Mosul: A Humanitarian Disaster color *Progressive* v81 no7 p12 O/N 2017

Smith, C. Molly

BEYOND BLACK AND WHITE *Entertainment Weekly* no1451/1452 p43 F 3-10 2017

DAVID BOREANAZ ON BUFFY, BONES, AND BEYOND color *Entertainment Weekly* no1457/1458 p86 Mr 17 2017

JERMAINE FOWLER color *Entertainment Weekly* no1451/1452 p97 F 3-10 2017

Julie Bowen color *Entertainment Weekly* no1454/1455 p20 F 24 2017

KATHERINE HEIGL GUARDS DOGS (AND CATS) color *Entertainment Weekly* no1462 p16 Ap 21 2017

The Kong Show color *Entertainment Weekly* no1440 p16 N 18 2016

LOWRIDERS color *Entertainment Weekly* no1463/1464 p38 Ap/My 2017

Margot Robbie's Gold-Medal Makeover color *Entertainment Weekly* no1450 p16 Ja 27 2017

Megan Mullally: How to Meet Your In-Laws color *Entertainment Weekly* no1446/1447 p102 D 2016/Ja 2017

WarReN BEatty An ORAL HISTORY color *Entertainment Weekly* no1440 p30 N 18 2016

What to Watch color *Entertainment Weekly* no1436/1437 p94 O 21 2016

WHICH FICTIONAL CHARACTER'S WARDROBE DO YOU COVET THE MOST? color *Entertainment Weekly* no1449 p18 Ja 20 2017

WORLD OF DANCE color *Entertainment Weekly* no1468/1469 p64 Je 2-9 2017

Smith, C. R.

An ecosystem-based deep-ocean strategy bibl color map *Science* v355 no6324 p452 F 3 2017

Smith, Caitlin

Mouse with a milkshake: Behavioral windows into brain function color *Science* v354 no6312 p638 N 4 2016

SMITH, CAMERON

Getting Juiced by the Roadside *Weekly Standard* v22 no6 p14 O 17 2016

Smith, Carey

Do Your Customers Actually Want a "Smart" Version of Your Product? *Harvard Business Review Digital Articles* p2 Ag 8 2017

Smith, Carol

Intercellular communication and conjugation are mediated by ESX secretion systems in mycobacteria bibl diag graph *Science* v354 no6310 p347 O 21 2016

Smith, Chad

A BRACE IN THE SUN P. BOURJAILY color *Field & Stream* v121 no8 p16 F/Mr 2017

Smith, Chandler Klang

The Sky Is Yours *Publishers Weekly* v264 no41 p40 O 9 2017

Smith, Che—Interviews

THE STATE OF BLUES M. POLLOCK color *Chicago* v66 no6 p33 Je 2017

SMITH, CHRIS

IN CONVERSATION Bill de Blasio img *New York* v50 no18 p24 S 4 2017

Smith, Chris, 1979-

THE DAILY SHOW'S DARKEST DAY color *Entertainment Weekly* no1442 p26 D 2 2016 Rebellious Special Issue

JON STEWART'S DAILY REVOLUTION C. SMITH bw color *Vanity Fair* v58 no12 p162 D 2016

WHEN FAKE NEWS WAS FUNNY J. KOBLIN color *New York Times Book Review* p41 D 4 2016

Smith, Christie

Help Your Employees Be Themselves at Work *Harvard Business Review Digital Articles* p2 N 3 2014

Smith, Chuck

CALVARY CHAPEL GOES GLOBAL K. SHELLNUTT cartoon *Christianity Today* p15 Mr 2017

Smith, Claire

I TYPED AND DREAMED *Vital Speeches of the Day* v83 no9 p276 S 2017

Smith, Clay

FIVE FLAT C. Toy color *Spin to Win Rodeo* v21 no3 p33 My 2017

HEELIN' FEELIN' color *Team Roping Journal* p16 S 2017

Smith, Corey

HOME OF THE Braves: A beginner's guide to Cobb County's new game-day headquarters K. SMITH *Atlanta* v57 no2 p122 Je 2017

Smith, Dale

BEST ORATOR color *Maclean's* v129 no47 p22 N 28 2016

THE RIGHT COLLEGE CAN GET YOUR AVIATION CAREER OFF TO A FLYING START color *Flying* v144 no11 p64 N 2017

SMITH, DAN

THE LOOP bw color *Runner's World* v51 no11 p18 D 2016

Smith, Dana

OUR 11TH ANNUAL APPRECIATION OF Angels AMONG US color *Yankee* v80 no6 p130 N/D 2016

Smith, Danez

& even the black guy's profile reads sorry, no black guys D. Smith *New York Times Magazine* p21 Ag 27 2017

SPOKEN FOR D. CHIASSON cartoon *New Yorker* v93 no30 p72 O 2 2017

Smith, Daniel

FIRST-TIME CALLER cartoon *New Yorker* v92 no43 p20 Ja 2 2017

Solange Knowles B. Muteba color *Current Biography* v78 no4 p47 Ap 2017

TO THE BRIDGE cartoon *New Yorker* v93 no24 p16 Ag 21 2017

WAR GAMES cartoon *New Yorker* v92 no40 p22 D 5 2016

Smith, David

Declines in Pollinator Forage Suitability Were Concentrated in the

Midwest, the Over-Summering Grounds for Many Honeybees *Amber Waves: The Economics of Food, Farming, Natural Resources, & Rural America* p1 Jl 2017

Smith, David A.
Potential role of intratumor bacteria in mediating tumor resistance to the chemotherapeutic drug gemcitabine diag *Science* v357 no6356 p1156 S 15 2017

Smith, David E.
Gravity field of the Orientale basin from the Gravity Recovery and Interior Laboratory Mission bibl graph *Science* v354 no6311 p438 O 28 2016

Smith, David G.
How to Mentor a Narcissist *Harvard Business Review Digital Articles* p2 S 19 2017
How to Mentor a Perfectionist *Harvard Business Review Digital Articles* p2 F 21 2017
Male Mentors Shouldn't Hesitate to Challenge Their Female Mentees *Harvard Business Review Digital Articles* p2 My 29 2017
Men Can Improve How They Mentor Women. Here's How *Harvard Business Review Digital Articles* p2 D 5 2016
Men Shouldn't Refuse to Be Alone with Female Colleagues *Harvard Business Review Digital Articles* p2 My 5 2017
Too Many Men Are Silent Bystanders to Sexual Harassment *Harvard Business Review Digital Articles* p2 Mr 13 2017

Smith, David Harris
What a Hitchhiking Robot Can Teach Us About Automated Coworkers *Harvard Business Review Digital Articles* p2 D 18 2014

SMITH, DAVID L.
Malaria Dollars and Sense bw color *Natural History* v125 no9 p28 S 2017

Smith, David T.
Inviting and Efficient T. Tanner color *Old House Journal* v44 no8 p70 D 2016

Smith, Deb—Awards
In Recognition of Excellence *Parks & Recreation* v51 no11 p42 N 2016

Smith, Dominic
THE CRIMINAL'S MASK J. LEVASSEUR color *America* v215 no13 p37 O 31 2016
Storm Front: Life can be threatening for the characters in Richard Bausch's stories *New York Times Magazine* p21 Ap 30 2017

Smith, Don
Why People Quit Their Jobs: Interaction *Harvard Business Review* v94 no11 p18 N 2016

Smith, Donovan
A TRUE SOAP STAR K. ROCKWOOD color *Good Housekeeping* v265 no2 p134 Ag 2017

Smith, Douglas
Rasputin: Faith, Power, and the Twilight of the Romanovs R. Legvold *Foreign Affairs* v95 no6 p187 N/D 2016
RASPUTIN P. TREBLE color *Maclean's* v129 no47 p60 N 28 2016
A Very Close Friend of the Family O. Figes bw *New York Review of Books* v63 no19 p40 D 8 2016

SMITH, DREW
THE DESCENT color *Climbing* no349 p80 N 2016

Smith, E. J.
Jupiter's interior and deep atmosphere: The initial pole-to-pole passes with the Juno spacecraft [Cover story] color graph *Science* v356 no6340 p821 My 26 2017
Jupiter's magnetosphere and aurorae observed by the Juno spacecraft during its first polar orbits diag graph *Science* v356 no6340 p826 My 26 2017

Smith, Ebony
CHANGING GEARS: Cycling for Social Change B. LUCK color *Earth Island Journal* v32 no3 p15 Aut 2017

Smith, Edward J.
Doing science while black color *Science* v353 no6307 p1586 S 30 2016

Smith, Edwin R.
PAF1 regulation of promoter-proximal pause release via enhancer activation color *Science* v357 no6357 p1294 S 22 2017

SMITH, ELISE
ACCEPTING AND EVALUATING VALUES IN SCIENCE FUNDING, RESEARCH, COMMUNICATION, AND POLICY *BioScience* v67 no10 p938 O 2017

Smith, Emily Esfahani
How to Find Meaning in a Job That Isn't Your "True Calling" *Harvard Business Review Digital Articles* p2 Ag 3 2017

SMITH, EMMA
Of Debt and Detriment *Weekly Standard* v22 no22 p22 F 13 2017

Smith, Eric
The Emergence of the Fourth Geosphere S. I. Walker *Physics Today* v70 no9 p58 S 2017
r.s.v.p bw color *Bon Appetit* v62 no7 p12 Jl 2017

Smith, Erin A.
The Late Great Planet Earth Made the Apocalypse a Popular Concern *Humanities* v38 no1 p1 Wint 2017

Smith, Evan J.
Dream Test color *Hot Rod* v70 no10 p54 O 2017

Smith, Evan M.
Large gem diamonds from metallic liquid in Earth's deep mantle bibl color *Science* v354 no6318 p1403 D 16 2016

Smith, Ewan St. J.
Fructose-driven glycolysis supports anoxia resistance in the naked mole-rat diag graph *Science* v356 no6335 p307 Ap 21 2017

Smith, Fran
THE ADDICTED BRAIN [Cover story] color *National Geographic* v232 no3 p30 S 2017

Smith, Frederick W., 1945-
Free Trade Can't Get a Break A. Murray color *Fortune* v175 no4 p16 Mr 15 2017

SMITH, GARY L.
Your True Stories *Reader's Digest* v188 no1124 p22 O 2016

Smith, Genevieve
Lego Is the Perfect Toy img *New York* v49 no24 p54 N 28 2016

Smith, Geoffrey
THE 2017 Fortune Crystal Ball color diag *Fortune* v174 no7 p11 D 1 2016
The Business Guide to Europe's Wild Year chart color diag *Fortune* v175 no5 p9 Ap 1 2017
Europe Fumes Over Russian Gas color *Fortune* v176 no3 p16 S 1 2017
It's Time to Worry About Italian Debt diag *Fortune* v176 no2 p17 Ag 1 2017
Macron Economics color *Fortune* v175 no7 p13 Je 1 2017
So Much for That Brexit Mandate color *Fortune* v176 no1 p11 Jl 1 2017
TRUMP, BREXIT, AND THE CHINA SLOWDOWN color *Fortune* v174 no8 p24 D 15 2016
Why Deutsche Bank Is Spooking the Markets color *Time* v188 no15 p7 O 17 2016

Smith, Gerry
29 Reasons Why BuzzFeed Is Getting Into the TV Game color *Bloomberg Businessweek* no4526 p60 Je 12 2017
Breitbart Advertisers Take Political Fire, Too color *Bloomberg Businessweek* no4502 p31 D 5 2016
CNN Has Had Enough color graph *Bloomberg Businessweek* no4528 p20 Je 26 2017
THE DEATH OF Syndicated Reruns cartoon color *Bloomberg Businessweek* no4496 p68 O 24 2016
Home Is Where The Heart (of Cable) Is color diag *Bloomberg Businessweek* no4506 p18 Ja 9 2017
Politics [Cover story] color graph *Bloomberg Businessweek* no4498 p60 N 7 2016
Telemundo's Ratings Are Made in the USA *Bloomberg Businessweek* no4514 p22 Mr 13 2017
TRONC IF YOU WANT TO SAVE JOURNALISM [Cover story] color *Bloomberg Businessweek* no4498 p74 N 7 2016
Where the Future's AT(&T) cartoon *Bloomberg Businessweek* no4497 p22 O 31 2016

Smith, Glenn—Interviews
Expert OPINION: FIVE WEDDING VETERANS GIVE US THEIR TIPS AND TRICKS FOR GETTING THE MOST OUT OF VENDORS L. Roberts *Indianapolis Monthly* v12 no40 p18 Ag 2017

Smith, Gordon T.
SCRIPTURE, SACRAMENT, AND SPIRIT M. BIRD cartoon color *Christianity Today* p67 Ap 2017

Smith, Grant
The Tables Have Turned cartoon graph *Bloomberg Businessweek* no4493 p47 O 3 2016

SMITH, HAROLD B.
A DECADE OF CHANGE color *Christianity Today* v60 no8 p11 O 2016

Smith, Harrison, 1989-
DEEP PURPLE B. Baskin color *Sports Illustrated* v125 no13 p30 O 17 2016

Smith, Hayes
Smith and Davis Surge color *Team Roping Journal* p34 O 2017

Smith, Heather
Brother Act *Sierra* v102 no5 p62 St/O 2017

Smith, Hilary
Four Wise Moves P. Moore cartoon *AARP: The Magazine* v30 no6A p13 O/N 2017

Smith, Imogen Sara
Army of One bw *Film Comment* v53 no1 p16 Ja/F 2017
RUNNING DEEP bw *Film Comment* v53 no5 p38 S/O 2017
SHEET MUSIC color *Film Comment* v53 no4 p36 Jl/Ag 2017

Smith, J. J.
Lean, Green, Business Machine C. V. Clarke color *Black Enterprise* v47 no4 p31 N/D 2016

SMITH, JACQUELINE
The Question *O, The Oprah Magazine* p14 F 2017

Smith, Jada Pinkett, 1971——Interviews
DEEP DISH WITH THE STARS OF GIRLS TRIP T. Stack color *Entertainment Weekly* no1474/1475 p100 Jl 21-28 2017
Q&A: QUEEN LATIFAH & JADA PINKETT SMITH T. Stack color *Entertainment Weekly* no1463/1464 p68 Ap/My 2017

Smith, James N.
Global atmospheric particle formation from CERN CLOUD measurements bibl graph map *Science* v354 no6316 p1119 D 2 2016

SMITH, JAMIL
Voice of America *New York Times Book Review* p19 Ja 22 2017

Smith, Jane
It's Halloween, Chloe Zoe! *Publishers Weekly* v264 no26 p177 Je 26 2017

SMITH, JAY
Buzz Feud cartoon *Walrus* v13 no9 p19 N 2016

Smith, Jean Kennedy
Growing Up Kennedy M. SHNAYERSON *New York Times Book Review* p11 N 20 2016

Smith, Jeff
ALL IN THE TIMING chart color graph *Hot Rod* v70 no9 p70 S 2017
COLD-AIR CARBS color graph *Hot Rod* v70 no11 p86 N 2017
The Future of Fueling color *Hot Rod* v70 no2 p78 F 2017
I've Taken the Silver D. Freiburger color *Hot Rod* v70 no2 p106 F 2017

Smith, Jeffrey C.
Breathing to inspire and arouse bw *Science* v355 no6332 p1370 Mr 31 2017

Smith, Jennifer Chappell
The Great Guadalupe color *Southern Living* v52 no7 p45 Jl 2017

Smith, Jesse W.
Saddle Savvy L. Feldman color *American Cowboy* v23 no6 p44 Ap/My 2017

SMITH, JESSI L.
Grant-Writing Bootcamp: An Intervention to Enhance the Research Capacity of Academic Women in STEM *BioScience* v67 no7 p638 Jl 2017

Smith, Jim
Living the Lake Life C. Wood color diag *Log Home Living* v33 no9 p56 D 2016
PROWLER (SLED) PUSHES J. WUEBBEN color *Muscle & Performance* v9 no6 p14 Je 2017

Smith, Joanne
After the Vote was Won *History Today* v67 no1 p47 Ja 2017

Smith, Joel Larue
Recalling Generations K. Micallef color *Downbeat* v84 no6 p31 Je 2017

Smith, John
CONFESSING MY PORN ADDICTION color *America* v216 no7 p32 Ap 3 2017

Smith, John, 1580-1631
MAYFLOWER IN LONDON: Where the famous voyage really began in Rotherhithe J. Wade *British Heritage Travel* v38 no2 p44 Mr/Ap 2017

Unearthing a Lost City N. BRULLIARD *National Parks* v91 no2 p66 Spr 2017

Smith, Jordan
Suit Up for Less color *Health* v31 no1 p53 Ja 2017
Tech for Your Fittest Year Yet color *Health* v31 no1 p23 Ja 2017
Who to Follow on Snapchat Now color *Health* v31 no2 p66 Mr 2017

SMITH, JORDAN MICHAEL
How to Die color *Atlantic* v320 no3 p20 O 2017
Why We Like Ike bw *American Conservative* v15 no6 p46 N/D 2016

Smith, Jordy——Interviews
extra hours A. Van Gysen color *Surfing Magazine* v53 no2 p52 F 2017

SMITH, JOY BETH
FLYING SOLO IN A FAMILY-CENTERED CHURCH color *Christianity Today* v61 no5 p65 Je 2017

Smith, Judy
HOUR GLASS J. OBER color *Dirt Sports + Off-Road* v51 no2 p74 F 2017

Smith, Julia Evelina, 1792-1886
RESISTERHOOD IS POWERFUL S. RICHARDSON bw color *American History* v52 no3 p24 Ag 2017

SMITH, JULIANNE
What Would America Do? color *Foreign Policy* no225 p82 Jl/Ag 2017

Smith, Justin E. H.
BLOOD AND SOIL *Harper's Magazine* v334 no2001 p84 F 2017
Lovers of Wisdom L. KLEPP cartoon *Weekly Standard* v22 no7 p33 O 24 2016

SMITH, K. N.
THE FINAL DAYS OF CASSINI bw color diag *Astronomy* v45 no1 p26 Ja 2017
They're Taking Our Tires! color *Discover* v38 no9 p12 N 2017

Smith, Kaitlyn Aurelia
MY SPACE: SYNTH CITY R. CHUN color *Wired* v25 no8 p46 Ag 2017

SMITH, KAREN E.
The European Union in an Illiberal World *Current History* v116 no788 p83 Mr 2017

Smith, Karen Sue
From the Monstrous To the Ordinary color il *America* v216 no9 p22 Ap 24 2017
Is affordable health care possible? color *America* v217 no5 p44 S 4 2017
NO ORDINARY LIFE color *America* v215 p30 N 28 2016

Smith, Karl
If America's Economy Is Winner-Take-All, Why Are Some Smaller Businesses Thriving? *Harvard Business Review Digital Articles* p2 S 1 2017

Smith, Karl J. P.
Lunar Landscaping diag *Scientific American* v315 no5 p16 N 2016
Surge Protector color *Scientific American* v315 no6 p21 D 2016

Smith, Kate
The College Endowment Gap *Bloomberg Businessweek* no4531 p25 Jl 24 2017
Little Good News For the Little Ivies graph *Bloomberg Businessweek* no4505 p41 D 26 2016

SMITH, KATHLEEN
Life cartoon *Reader's Digest* v190 no1132 p30 Jl/Ag 2017

Smith, Kathryn
Celebrating Firsts S. Cooney color *Time* v190 no12 p6 S 25 2017
Greatest Showman on Earth A. Paletta *Architectural Record* v205 no7 p59 Jl 2017

SMITH, KATY SIMPSON
A Lover and a Fighter *New York Times Book Review* p18 F 5 2017

Smith, Kellie N.
Mismatch repair deficiency predicts response of solid tumors to PD-1 blockade chart graph *Science* v357 no6349 p409 Jl 28 2017

SMITH, KELUNDRA
HOME OF THE Braves: A beginner's guide to Cobb County's new game-day headquarters *Atlanta* v57 no2 p122 Je 2017
LATE-NIGHT Bites *Atlanta* v57 no2 p128 Je 2017

Smith, Ken
SHOWCASE SHOTS color *Nebraska Life* v20 no6 p80 N/D 2016

Smith, Kevin
    Kevin Smith's Celebrity Reboot: After years in critical exile, the onetime poster boy for slacker filmmaking reinvents himself for an era of narrowcast fame A. Riesman img *New York* v50 no18 p78 S 4 2017
    The Quiz T. BALAZO color *Maclean's* v129 no40 p80 O 10 2016

Smith, Kiki, 1954-—Interviews
    KIKI SMITH H. JULAVITS *Interview* v47 no6 p86 Ag 2017

Smith, Kimberly
    A skirt that goes anywhere color *Redbook* p76 My 2017

SMITH, KRISTA
    ALISON SUDOL color *Vanity Fair* v58 no12 p73 D 2016
    Brie Spirit [Cover story] color *Vanity Fair* v59 no6 p76 My 2017
    CARSON MEYER color *Vanity Fair* v59 no4 p101 Mr 2017
    FANTASY LEAGUE color *Vanity Fair* p77 Hollywood 2017 Supplement
    GRACE VAN PATTEN color *Vanity Fair* v59 no10 p89 O 2017
    HIS MARSHALL PLAN color *Vanity Fair* v59 no11 p122 N 2017
    A HOT TIME IN THE OLD TOWN color *Vanity Fair* v59 no9 p78 S 2017
    JUDE DEMOREST color *Vanity Fair* v59 no1 p65 Holiday 2017
    KELLY ROHRBACH color *Vanity Fair* v59 no6 p49 My 2017
    KIERSEY CLEMONS color *Vanity Fair* v59 no8 p41 Ag 2017
    L.A. Bohème color *Vanity Fair* v59 no9 p198 S 2017
    LUCY BOYNTON color *Vanity Fair* v59 no11 p59 N 2017
    MAKENZIE LEIGH color *Vanity Fair* v58 no11 p77 N 2016
    MATILDA LUTZ color *Vanity Fair* v59 no2 p29 F 2017
    SOFIA BOUTELLA color *Vanity Fair* v59 no7 p41 Summ 2017
    STYLE with SUBSTANCE color *Vanity Fair* v59 no4 p96 Mr 2017
    SUKI WATERHOUSE color *Vanity Fair* v59 no5 p45 Ap 2017
    SYLVIA HOEKS color *Vanity Fair* v59 no9 p113 S 2017
    ZENDAYA color *Vanity Fair* p87 Hollywood 2017 Supplement

Smith, Kristie
    SEX AND THE SUBURBS J. PAYTON *Indianapolis Monthly* p36 My 2017

SMITH, KYLE
    The Fred & Karl Show *National Review* v69 no16 p48 Ag 28 2017
    Her Chelseaness il *National Review* v69 no9 p30 My 15 2017
    The Minimal Mayor [Cover story] color *National Review* v69 no18 p22 O 2 2017
    Monumentally Naïve *National Review* v69 no17 p30 S 11 2017
    Obama's Book of Balderdash color *National Review* v69 no11 p15 Je 12 2017
    Segregation on the Charles *National Review* v69 no12 p44 Je 26 2017
    The Senator Who Was Not Funny *National Review* v69 no15 p30 Ag 14 2017

Smith, Larry
    Don't Talk Yourself Out of Trying a Second Career *Harvard Business Review Digital Articles* p2 Ap 27 2016

Smith, Laura
    BATTLE OF ALL MOTHERS color *Mother Jones* v42 no3 p12 My/Je 2017
    A BRIEF HISTORY OF LEISURE bw color *Mother Jones* v42 no4 p59 Jl/Ag 2017

Smith, Lee
    The Art of Undoing the Iran Deal color *Weekly Standard* v22 no11 p25 N 21 2016
    The Case of the Missing Stylist color *Weekly Standard* v22 no37 p5 Je 5 2017
    A Disaster He's Proud Of *Weekly Standard* v22 no18 p8 Ja 16 2017
    Doomed Deal color *Weekly Standard* v22 no12 p7 N 28 2016
    Gone but Not Forgotten color *Weekly Standard* v23 no2 p5 S 18 2017
    How to Defeat ISIS *Weekly Standard* v22 no29 p8 Ap 3 2017
    Impossible Dream color *Weekly Standard* v22 no23 p17 F 20 2017
    Iran on Notice color *Weekly Standard* v22 no32 p8 My 1 2017
    Love and Rage color *Weekly Standard* v22 no19 p13 Ja 23 2017
    The Nuclear Deal Is Only Half of It *Weekly Standard* v23 no3 p16 S 25 2017
    Of Tribes and Terrorism color *Weekly Standard* v22 no39 p24 Je 19 2017
    The Old Brawl Game color *Weekly Standard* v22 no40 p5 Je 26 2017

    Phone Home cartoon *Weekly Standard* v22 no13 p5 D 5 2016
    Play Ball color *Weekly Standard* v22 no31 p5 Ap 17 2017
    Presiding over Chaos color *Weekly Standard* v22 no10 p10 N 14 2016
    Reflections on the Scandal at Choate color *Weekly Standard* v22 no35 p17 My 22 2017
    The Verdict on Castro bw *Weekly Standard* v22 no14 p12 D 12 2016

Smith, Leon Polk
    Leon Polk Smith Works *Treasures* v5 no5 p12 Ap/My 2016

Smith, Lillian M.
    Engrams and circuits crucial for systems consolidation of a memory diag *Science* v356 no6333 p73 Ap 7 2017

Smith, Lindell
    The blackest man on council A. DOMISE color *Maclean's* v129 no44 p20 N 7 2016

Smith, Lois
    Columbus artist paints farm-fresh art A. J. BARTELS color *Nebraska Life* v21 no5 p74 S/O 2017
    Disrupting Widowhood: Dead loved ones come back as holograms in Marjorie Prime D. EDELSTEIN img *New York* v50 no16 p108 Ag 7 2017

Smith, Lynette M.
    The "Write" Way to Show Gratitude *USA Today Magazine* v145 no2862 p64 Mr 2017

Smith, Maggie, 1934-
    A HISTORIC NIGHT AT THE EMMYS M. Roush *TV Guide* v64 no40 p12 O 3 2016

Smith, Mariah
    THE BREAK-OUTS 2016 color *GQ: Gentlemen's Quarterly* v86 no12 p198 D 2016

Smith, Mark A.
    What Drives Social Justice? S. Buntz *Washington Monthly* p13 N/D 2016

Smith, Matt
    Alabama's "Chemical Katrina" *Sierra* v102 no3 p20 My/Je 2017
    How Companies Are Using Simulations, Competitions, and Analytics to Hire *Harvard Business Review Digital Articles* p2 Ap 22 2017

Smith, Matt, 1982-
    ANOTHER SIDE OF MATT SMITH S. Vilkomerson color *Entertainment Weekly* no1439 p24 N 11 2016
    The CROWN SEASON 2 S. Perry color *Entertainment Weekly* no1478 / 1479 p24 Ag 18-25 2017
    Fit to be KING P. SYKES color *Vogue* v206 no11 p174 N 2016

Smith, Maurice
    MAURICE SMITH bw *Black Belt* v55 no5 p12 Ag/S 2017

SMITH, MEGAN
    TQ TECH QUOTIENT *Foreign Policy* no221 p104 N/D 2016

SMITH, MELISSA DIANE
    10 Hidden Sources of Gluten During the Holidays [Cover story] color *Better Nutrition* v79 no11 p72 N 2017
    Against-the-Grain Holidays color *Better Nutrition* v78 no11 p88 N 2016
    A Cut Above [Cover story] color *Amazing Wellness* v9 no6 p92 EarlyWint 2017
    Dietary Solutions for Menstrual Cramps color *Better Nutrition* p58 My 2017
    Get a Collagen Boost color *Better Nutrition* v79 no9 p62 S 2017
    The Happiness Effect color *Better Nutrition* v79 no1 p62 Ja 2017
    How to Avoid Glyphosate color *Better Nutrition* v79 no7 p54 Jl 2017
    Organic and Non-GMO, Simplified! color *Better Nutrition* v79 no10 p72 O 2017
    PUMP IT UP! color *Amazing Wellness* v9 no6 p32 EarlyWint 2017
    Snacks for Your Summer Travels color *Better Nutrition* v79 no6 p58 Je 2017
    Sneaky Forms of Sugar color *Better Nutrition* v79 no3 p60 Mr 2017
    Talking to Kids about GMOs color *Better Nutrition* v79 no4 p66 Ap 2017

Smith, Michael
    The Arranger color *Bloomberg Businessweek* no4503 p60 D 12 2016
    Cambridge Analytica's Low-Tech Fisticuffs color *Bloomberg*

Physics Today v70 no3 p59 Mr 2017

Smith, Peter Andrey

LUCKY BREAK *Smithsonian* v48 no3 p30 Je 2017

THE SQUISHY SCIENCE OF NEUROFEEDBACK color *Bloomberg Businessweek* no4523 p30 My 22 2017

Smith, Phillip K. III

DESERT X: Reimagining the Landscape *Issues in Science & Technology* v33 no3 p63 Spr 2017

Smith, Phillippe

A story in STONE G. E. CLARKE bw color *Canadian Geographic* v137 no4 p42 Jl/Ag 2017

SMITH, R. J.

BEAT MASTER *Cincinnati Magazine* v50 no8 p45 My 2017

CASH CROP *Cincinnati Magazine* v50 no12 p70 S 2017

CHATTANOOGA, TENNESSEE *Cincinnati Magazine* v50 no12 p38 S 2017

DOG DAZE *Cincinnati Magazine* v50 no10 p52 Jl 2017

FABLES OF THE RECONSTRUCTION *Cincinnati Magazine* v50 no11 p86 Ag 2017

IS DAYTON THE WORLD CAPITAL OF FUNK? *Cincinnati Magazine* p72 Je 2017

A Man in Need *Cincinnati Magazine* v50 no3 p92 D 2016

NIGHT MOVES *Cincinnati Magazine* v50 no8 p40 My 2017

NO FILTER A. Belth bw color *Esquire* p26 N 2017

Overdue Notice *Cincinnati Magazine* v50 no5 p68 F 2017

SCREAM QUEENS *Cincinnati Magazine* v50 no8 p104 My 2017

They vs. Them *Cincinnati Magazine* v50 no7 p42 Ap 2017

TREY Radel *Cincinnati Magazine* v50 no7 p58 Ap 2017

Smith, Randall D.

VULTURE CAPITALISTS DEVOUR THE NEWS J. REYNOLDS color map *Nation* v305 no9 p12 O 16 2017

Smith, Rasheeda

AN AMERICAN PLACE bw color *American History* v52 no3 p72 Ag 2017

CIRCUS DAYS bw *American History* v52 no3 p56 Ag 2017

SMITH, RICHARD G.

Agriculture in 2050: Recalibrating Targets for Sustainable Intensification *BioScience* v67 no4 p386 Ap 2017

Smith, Rick

YOUR PUP'S FIRST YEAR S. LINDEN color *Outdoor Life* v224 no3 p28 Ap 2017

Smith, Robert

Targeted Ads Don't Just Make You More Likely to Buy—They Can Change How You Think About Yourself *Harvard Business Review Digital Articles* p2 Ap 4 2016

Smith, Robert F.

Philanthropy Paves Road to Riches M. S. Hopkins color *Ebony* v72 no9 p76 Jl/Ag 2017

Smith, Robert P.

Two- and three-body contacts in the unitary Bose gas bibl diag graph *Science* v355 no6323 p377 Ja 27 2017

Smith, Robin E.

ON-TRAIL FIRST-AID KIT color *Trail Rider* v29 no3 p64 Ap 2017

Smith, Rosanna K.

Research: Consumers Prefer Products Created by Mistake *Harvard Business Review Digital Articles* p2 S 20 2017

Smith, Roy—Interviews

THE SUCCESSFUL INTERVIEW M. McGinnis *Successful Farming* v114 no11 p12 N 2016

Smith, Ryan

Join Our Click bw color *Ebony* v72 no8 p12 Je 2017

The Most Common Reasons Customer Experience Programs Fail *Harvard Business Review Digital Articles* p2 D 28 2016

Why Every Startup Should Bootstrap *Harvard Business Review Digital Articles* p2 Mr 2 2016

SMITH, S. E.

Making College Free Again *In These Times* v41 no4 p8 Ap 2017

SMITH, SALLY BEDELL

THE Lonely Heir bw color *Vanity Fair* v59 no5 p144 Ap 2017

Pity the Prince: Sally Bedell Smith's biography offers a sympathetic view of the English heir W. BOYD *New York Times Book Review* p18 My 14 2017

REMEMBERING DIANA color *AARP: The Magazine* v60 no5A p50 Ag/S 2017

SMITH, SAM

ANGRY BIRD color *Road & Track* v68 no10 p72 Jl 2017

BABBITT BEARINGS color *Road & Track* v69 no1 p94 Ag 2017

Borrowed Time bw color *Road & Track* v69 no2 p24 S 2017

Color Schemes cartoon *Road & Track* v68 no6 p20 F 2017

CROSSING OVER color diag *Road & Track* v68 no10 p54 Jl 2017

DAY OF THUNDER color *Road & Track* v69 no3 p52 O 2017

EDITOR'S LETTER K. WOLFKILL *Road & Track* v68 no10 p18 Jl 2017

EDITOR'S LETTER K. WOLFKILL *Road & Track* v69 no3 p24 O 2017

Exit Strategery bw color *Road & Track* v68 no8 p24 My 2017

JURASSIC WORLD color *Road & Track* v68 no6 p34 F 2017

Live at Birdland color *Road & Track* v68 no10 p24 Jl 2017

THE LONELIEST FERRARI color *Road & Track* v68 no9 p46 Je 2017

THE MAGIC OF KARTS color *Road & Track* v68 no5 p111 D 2016/Ja 2017

Miata, People cartoon *Road & Track* v68 no7 p26 Mr/Ap 2017

THE ONE color *Road & Track* v68 no10 p30 Jl 2017

Purple Kart color *Road & Track* v68 no5 p38 D 2016/Ja 2017

Race to the Bottom color *Road & Track* v68 no9 p22 Je 2017

ROTARY INTERNATIONAL bw color *Road & Track* v69 no2 p44 S 2017

Shock and awe [Cover story] color diag *Popular Science* v289 no6 p38 N/D 2017

Unfamiliar Familiar color *Road & Track* v69 no3 p26 O 2017

THE UNNECESSARY EXPRESS [Cover story] color *Cycle World* v56 no5 p32 Je 2017

Walk a Line color *Road & Track* v69 no1 p28 Ag 2017

Smith, Sam, 1992-

Sam Smith's Raw Return P. DOYLE bw color *Rolling Stone* no1298 p13 O 19 2017

Smith, Sarah

THE SECRETS TO Floor Plan Perfection diag *Log Home Living* v34 no1 p44 F 2017

Smith, Scott

Building community for deaf scientists color *Science* v355 no6322 p255 Ja 20 2017

Smith, Sean

A GAY Old Timeline color diag *Entertainment Weekly* no1471 p32 Je 23 2017

Rachel After Dark color *Entertainment Weekly* no1435 p32 O 14 2016

We Say Goodbye to One of Our Own color *Entertainment Weekly* no1480 p3 S 1 2017

Smith, Sean M.

How safe are the workers who process our food? bibl *Monthly Labor Review* p1 Jl 2017

Smith, Shane

GONZO GOLD RUSH N. ROBEHMED color *Forbes* v200 no1 p24 Jl 27 2017

Smith, Shannon

Executive Function with Shannon Smith T. Linse *Humanities* v37 no4 p1 Fall 2016

Smith, Shaun

Classic Country J. Borden color *Southern Living* v52 no11 p36 N 2017

Smith, Shawn

How America Lost Its Mind color *Atlantic* v320 no4 p12 N 2017

SMITH, SONIA

A HOME OF LAST RESORT *Texas Monthly* v45 no5 p81 My 2017

'HOW WOULD AN ETHICAL OFFICER REACT?' *New York Times Magazine* p36 Ag 20 2017

Social Graces *Education Digest* v82 no6 p49 F 2017

WORKING WITH The Donald *Texas Monthly* v45 no3 p82 Mr 2017

Smith, Stacey

ASK THE EXPERTS color *Runner's World* v52 no3 p42 Ap 2017

Smith, Stacy

Decide Whether That Board Seat Is Right for You *Harvard Business Review Digital Articles* p2 My 20 2015

Smith, Stacy Jenel

Back in the Picture bw color *AARP: The Magazine* v60 no5A p59 Ag/S 2017

and Divides R. Jones color *Time* v188 no21 p70 N 21 2016

On Optimism and Despair color *New York Review of Books* v63 no20 p36 D 22 2016

PLAYING DOUBLES A. KIRSCH il *Nation* v33 no21 p17 N 21 2016

Robert B. Silvers (1929–2017) [Cover story] bw color *New York Review of Books* v64 no8 p31 My 11 2017

Swing Time L. Greenblatt color *Entertainment Weekly* no1440 p60 N 18 2016

Tomorrow bw color *Forbes* v199 no1 p112 Ja 24 2017

Tribal Dress *Commentary* v143 no4 p43 Ap 2017

TWO STEP A. SCHWARTZ cartoon *New Yorker* v92 no37 p81 N 14 2016

TWO to Tango M. O'GRADY bw color *Vogue* v206 no11 p186 N 2016

Unreal Fictions S. RUDEN color *National Review* v68 no24 p41 D 31 2016

What Is Fame For? C. LORENTZEN *New York* v49 no22 p107 O 31 2016

WHO OWNS BLACK PAIN? ON RACE AND RISK IN AMERICAN CULTURE *Harper's Magazine* v335 no2006 p83 Jl 2017

Zadie Smith's Dance of Ambivalence D. TORTORICI color *Atlantic* v318 no5 p32 D 2016

Smith, Zadie, 1975—Interviews

By the Book Z. Smith *New York Times Book Review* p8 N 20 2016

Zadie SMITH cartoon *Vanity Fair* v58 no12 p184 D 2016

Smith, Zakiya

WOMEN TO WATCH L. Milk *Washingtonian Magazine* v53 no1 p62 O 2017

Smith College

FCDD Smith College *Dance Magazine* v90 p62 2016/2017 Supplement College Guide

Smith-Anoa'i, Tiffany—Interviews

THE CHANGE AGENT R. R. Robertson color *Essence* v47 no8 p88 D 2016

SMITH-BRUNETEAU, QIANNA

THE STRUGGLE OF THE BLACK DESIGNER bw color *Ebony* v72 no11 p44 S 2017

Smithers, Christopher B.

AMERICA IN PERIL *Weekly Standard* v22 no38 p41 Je 12 2017

Smithers, Gregory D.

Settler Common Sense: Queerness and Everyday Colonialism in the American Renaissance *American Indian Quarterly* v41 no2 p180 Spr 2017

Smithfield Foods Inc.

TOP 35 U.S. PORK POWERHOUSES 2016 *Successful Farming* v114 no13 p58 D 2016

Smithfield (London, England)

Peel Back the Centuries in Smithfield and Clerkenwell *British Heritage Travel* v38 no4 p26 Jl/Ag 2017

SMITH-GOBAT, MAYAN

TWO TOWERS color *Climbing* no349 p58 N 2016

Smithies, Oliver, 1925-2017

Oliver Smithies (1925-2017) A. Sancar color *Science* v355 no6326 p695 F 17 2017

Vitamin B3 modulates mitochondrial vulnerability and prevents glaucoma in aged mice bibl graph *Science* v355 no6326 p756 F 17 2017

Smithies, Wayne

There's still a lot of fear and prejudice around hiring disabled people: Employers urgently need a mindset shift, says disability recruitment specialist Wayne Smithies *People Management* p13 Ap 2017

Smithson, Robert, 1938-1973

THE ART AT THE END OF THE WORLD H. Julavits *New York Times Magazine* p44 Jl 9 2017

Where Time Wears Thin I. TUTTLE color *National Review* v68 no21 p24 N 21 2016

Smithsonian Institution (Washington, D.C.)

Admission is free. Exit is not A. ABEL bw color *Maclean's* v129 no40 p36 O 10 2016

THE CRUCIBLE OF A CULTURE L. J. O'DONOVAN bw color *America* v216 no1 p32 Ja 2 2017

FULL ATTIC? B. Freed *Washingtonian Magazine* v52 no2 p17 N 2016

RINGING THE FREEDOM BELL E. A. DUNBAR color *Nation*

v303 no25/26 p22 D 19 2016

Smith & the Devil, The (Fairy tale)

Story Time J. KEATS color *Discover* v38 no4 p16 My 2017

Smits, Jennifer

Publish openly but responsibly color *Science* v357 no6347 p141 Jl 14 2017

Smits, Jimmy

Sufficient unto the Day J. LILEKS *National Review* v69 no4 p33 Mr 6 2017

Smits, Samuel A.

Seasonal cycling in the gut microbiome of the Hadza hunter-gatherers of Tanzania diag *Science* v357 no6353 p802 Ag 25 2017

Smoke, Paul

U.S. Racing at Delaware Park S. Andersen *Arabian Horse World* v56 no12 p194 S 2016

Smokejumpers

Baptism by Fire T. HANEY color *Backpacker* p84 Ag 2017

Smokejumping

The Baby Catchers E. RINEHART color *Reader's Digest* v190 no1133 p12 S 2017

SMOKER, JOE

Chatter *Indianapolis Monthly* v40 no7 p15 Mr 2017

Smokers (Outdoor cooking)

STAFF PICK: A-MAZE-N SMOKER bw color *Bon Appetit* v62 no6 p110 Je 2017

Smokers (Outdoor cooking)—Design & construction

Build an OUTDOOR OVEN W. Rubel *Mother Earth News* no281 p50 Ap/My 2017

Smoking

See also

Passive smoking

Smoking policy

Rock 'n' Roll, Medicare and Me R. Love cartoon color *AARP; The Magazine* v60 no1A p2 D 2016/Ja 2017

Smoking (Cooking)

WHERE THERE'S SMOKE ... C. MOROCCO color *Bon Appetit* no11 p127 N 2017

Smoking cessation

CURBING THE HABIT Your Own Way D. Keating color *Maclean's* v129 no47 p47 N 28 2016

Customers Who Like Santa Also Like...Nicotine Gum? A. Choudhary *Harvard Business Review Digital Articles* p2 O 22 2015

Smoking Quit Rates Rise After Nurse Talk *USA Today Magazine* v146 no2869 p6 O 2017

Smoking cessation products

CURBING THE HABIT Your Own Way D. Keating color *Maclean's* v129 no47 p47 N 28 2016

Smoking cessation—Computer network resources

Simple Digital Technologies Can Reduce Health Care Costs A. L. Fogel and J. C. Kvedar *Harvard Business Review Digital Articles* p2 N 14 2016

Smoking policy

Smoke-Free Parks: Why Park and Recreation Departments Should Lead the Effort J. Hurdle *Parks & Recreation* v51 no10 p42 O 2016

Smoking—Genetic aspects

Cigarettes cause telltale DNA damage R. EHRENBERG diag *Science News* v190 no11 p14 N 26 2016

Smoking—Health aspects

How tobacco smoke changes the (epi)genome G. P. Pfeifer bibl color diag *Science* v354 no6312 p549 N 4 2016

Smoking—Risk factors

DNA errors play big role in cancer T. HESMAN SAEY color *Science News* v191 no7 p6 Ap 15 2017

Smollett-Bell, Jurnee

Jurnee toward justice M. CHARLES color *Ebony* v72 no5 p76 Mr 2017

MAKING THE COVER color *Ebony* v72 no5 p18 Mr 2017

My Sister's Keeper K. Kyles *Ebony* v72 no5 p14 Mr 2017

SMOOT, GEORGE F. III

A COSMIC CONTROVERSY color *Scientific American* v317 no1 p5 Jl 2017

Smoot, Kendra

O CHRISTMAS TREE [Cover story] color *Sunset* v237 no6 p62 D 2016

Smooth green snake

MEET THE ANIMALS OF THE YOUNG FOREST color *New York State Conservationist* v71 no2 p4 O 2016

Smooth Shake (Music)

Mightier Than the Sword C. Wolff color *Downbeat* v84 no4 p55 Ap 2017

Smoothies (Beverages)

4-BERRY BELLY BLAST [Cover story] color *Prevention* p14 Mr 2017

ACHE BREAKER [Cover story] color *Prevention* v69 no1 p15 Ja 2017

ALLERGY BUSTER [Cover story] color *Prevention* v69 no6 p13 Je 2017

Better, slimmer smoothies L. Lillien color *Redbook* p74 Jl/Ag 2017

BLOOD SUGAR BOOST color *Prevention* v68 no12 p14 D 2016

BUY 5, DROP 5 K. Glassman color *Women's Health* v14 no6 p104 Jl 2017

THE COLD CRUSHER color *Prevention* v69 no2 p14 F 2017

Drink Up! color *Amazing Wellness* v9 no4 p82 Summ 2017

GO ON A BLENDER E. Rothman and D. DeNunzio chart color *Golf Magazine* v59 no8 p55 Ag 2017

THE HEART HELPER *Prevention* v69 no4 p15 Ap 2017

power up with BREAKFAST M. GLISAN color *Better Homes & Gardens* v95 no8 p116 Ag 2017

SKIN SAVER color *Prevention* v69 no9 p13 O 2017

SMARTEN UP TO SHRINK YOUR GUT C. HANSEN color *Men's Health* v32 no4 p52 My 2017

SMOOTHIE MOVE D. DeNunzio color *Golf Magazine* v59 no4 p64 Ap 2017

Smoothies at Your Service K. Schaefer color *Bloomberg Businessweek* no4520 p70 My 1 2017

SMOOTH MOVE M. KADEY color *Runner's World* v52 no7 p22 Ag 2017

WEIGHT LOSS WINNER color *Prevention* v69 no5 p14 My 2017

YOU'VE GOT TO TRY Turmeric K. Rockwood color diag *O, The Oprah Magazine* p98 Mr 2017

Smoothies (Beverages)—Evaluation

Warming Trends color *Amazing Wellness* v9 no2 p88 Spr 2017

Smothers, Jack

How to Do Walking Meetings Right *Harvard Business Review Digital Articles* p2 Ag 5 2015

Smoyer, Lawrence

Case NOT closed A. J. BARTELS color *Nebraska Life* v21 no5 p41 S/O 2017

Murder in the Sandhills S. SCHMECKPEPER bw color *Nebraska Life* v21 no5 p36 S/O 2017

Politics and murder C. Amundson *Nebraska Life* v21 no5 p11 S/O 2017

Sandhills murders solved after 80 years A. J. BARTELS bw color *Nebraska Life* v21 no6 p18 N/D 2017

Smucker, Jonathan Matthew

A PRIMER FOR SMARTER ORGANIZING *In These Times* v41 no2 p40 F 2017

THE TROUBLE WITH "ACTIVIST": A case for dropping the A-word *In These Times* v41 no6 p28 Je 2017

Smugglers

The King of Rum Row C. J. Doane bw *Sail* v48 no1 p88 Ja 2017

Smuggling

See also

Human smuggling

Between Two Worlds K. Vick color *Time* v188 no18 p36 O 31 2016

Ghana Pays the Price Of Cheap Cocoa E. Dontoh color *Bloomberg Businessweek* no4539 p28 S 25 2017

Smulders, Cobie, 1982-

Cobie Smulders' Guide to Getting Action D. Franich color *Entertainment Weekly* no1436/1437 p84 O 21 2016

Smulders, Cobie, 1982—Interviews

3 Rounds WITH TARAN Killam & COUBIE Smulders S. Vilkomerson color *Entertainment Weekly* no1457/1458 p50 Mr 17 2017

Smullyan, Raymond M., 1919-2017

Milestones *Time* v189 no7/8 p19 F 27 2017

Smulyan, Gary

Gary Smulyan's Baritone Sax Solo on 'Sassy Missy' J. DURSO bw color *Downbeat* v84 no10 p192 O 2017

Smy, Pam

Girls, Interrupted: An abandoned orphanage fascinates a lonely daughter in this eerie illustrated novel with echoes of "Jane Eyre" L. BROWN *New York Times Book Review* p17 O 8 2017

SMYK, DOROTHY HALL

Forever Frankfurt color *Publishers Weekly* v264 no41 p72 O 9 2017

Smylie, Mark

Positive school leadership color *Phi Delta Kappan* v99 no1 p21 S 2017

Smyth, Anita K.

Publish openly but responsibly color *Science* v357 no6347 p141 Jl 14 2017

Smyth, Joshua

SOUND EFFECTS F. Williams cartoon *Mother Jones* v42 no1 p53 Ja/F 2017

Smyth, Joshua M.

The Two Main Sources of Stress for High-Status Workers *Harvard Business Review Digital Articles* p2 Ap 25 2016

Smyth, Kathleen

100 FASTEST-GROWING COMPANIES chart color diag map *Fortune* v176 no4 p157 S 15 2017

SMYTHE, CHRISTIAN

Keep It Short, and Sweet color *Publishers Weekly* v264 no15 p76 Ap 10 2017

Snack food industry

Pot's Nerdy Cousin D. R. REYNOLDS *Los Angeles Magazine* v62 no9 p22 S 2017

Snack food industry—Equipment & supplies

REDBOOK snack AWARDS [Cover story] color *Redbook* p127 Mr 2017

Snack foods

Build the perfect snack L. Lillien color *Redbook* p86 D 2016

COFFEE PERKS A. MACMILLAN color *Runner's World* v52 no5 p29 Je 2017

creative cookies *Parents* v91 no12 p98 D 2016

Crunch It Out B. Lipton color *Health* v31 no3 p114 Ap 2017

DIY Delicious [Cover story] S. Morrow and M. M. Chappell color *Vegetarian Times* v43 no2 p45 N/D 2016

Eat these for better sleep M. TAYLOR color *Redbook* p84 D 2016

Fresh & slimming snacks [Cover story] I. Lillien color *Redbook* p74 Je 2017

Get the Party Started A. BARAGHANI color *Bon Appetit* v61 no12 p60 D 2016 /Jan2017

Gluten-Free Desserts color *Health* v30 no9 p16 N 2016

GRAB & GO! [Cover story] color *Yoga Journal* no293 p18 Ag 2017

HAND to MOUTH J. Steingarten cartoon *Vogue* v207 no3 p474 Mr 2017

An Interstellar Party color *Martha Stewart Living* p15 Mr 2017

Is This the Perfect POWER SNACK! S. KUZEMCHAK *Scholastic Choices* v33 no1 p16 S 2017

The New Pop Stars color *Health* v31 no4 p109 My 2017

Next-Level SNACK HACKS L. SAXTON color *Seventeen* v76 no2 p90 Mr 2017

ON-THE-GO SNACKDOWN! color *Good Housekeeping* v264 no4 p100 Ap 2017

OUTSMART THE VENDING MACHINE color *Prevention* v69 no7 p14 Jl 2017

Pack & Play D. DeNunzio color *Golf Magazine* v59 no5 p60 My 2017

Pot's Nerdy Cousin B. R. REYNOLDS *Los Angeles Magazine* v62 no9 p22 S 2017

Power Pods L. REGE color *Martha Stewart Living* no275 p74 Je 2017

Product Spotlights color *Better Nutrition* v79 no9 p71 S 2017

Snacking Before Exercise color *Kiplinger's Personal Finance* v71 no7 p71 Jl 2017

spooky snacks F. LARGEMAN-ROTH *Parents* v91 no10 p74 O 2016

Time for Breakfast! C. THORP color *Seventeen* v76 no5 p68 S 2017

Vegan Snacks for Runners S. Lawrence *Vegetarian Journal* v36 no2 p24 2017

veggie bits *Vegetarian Journal* v36 no2 p28 2017

Ag 2017

The iPod's successor is the Apple Watch color *Macworld - Digital Edition* v34 no10 p39 O 2017

Troubleshooting some nasty Safari malware color diag *Macworld - Digital Edition* p51 Ap 2017

What the Mac needs in 2017 color *Macworld - Digital Edition* p10 F 2017

Why the future is bright for Apple's iPad color diag *Macworld - Digital Edition* p103 Ap 2017

A wish list for the iPhone in 2017 color *Macworld - Digital Edition* p43 F 2017

Snell, Laurie

Health Care Meets High Tech color *Alternatives Journal (AJ) - Canada's Environmental Voice* v42 no3 p32 2016

Snell, M. R.

How to model REPAIRED HOPPERS color *Model Railroader* v84 no9 p32 S 2017

Model a MOW BOXCAR color diag *Model Railroader* v84 no8 p53 Ag 2017

Model an aluminum billet load color diag *Model Railroader* v84 no3 p35 Mr 2017

Snetiker, Marc

10 — THE CRUCIBLE *Entertainment Weekly* no1444/1445 p118 D 16 2016

17 Things That Will Definitely Maybe Happen in 2017, According to Real Science color *Entertainment Weekly* no1448 p11 Ja 13 2017

2004 color *Entertainment Weekly* no1435 p49 O 14 2016

THE 25 MOST PATRIOTIC MOVIES OF ALL TIME color *Entertainment Weekly* no1472 p30 Je 30 2017

3 — BRIGHT STAR *Entertainment Weekly* no1444/1445 p118 D 16 2016

3 ROUNDS WITH DNCE color *Entertainment Weekly* no1441 p26 N 25 2016

5 — SHE LOVES ME *Entertainment Weekly* no1444/1445 p118 D 16 2016

7 Things You Didn't See color *Entertainment Weekly* no1449 p14 Ja 20 2017

8 — THE DMV color *Entertainment Weekly* no1444/1445 p60 D 16 2016

8 — WAITRESS *Entertainment Weekly* no1444/1445 p118 D 16 2016

9 — ECLIPSED color *Entertainment Weekly* no1444/1445 p118 D 16 2016

ALL ABOUT LEGO BATMAN'S ROGUES' GALLERY color *Entertainment Weekly* no1454/1455 p19 F 24 2017

AMERICAN GODS color *Entertainment Weekly* no1446/1447 p62 D 2016/Ja 2017

Becoming Gaston color *Entertainment Weekly* no1457/1458 p78 Mr 17 2017

BEN PLATT color *Entertainment Weekly* no1438 p69 N 4 2016

BROADWAY'S GAME CHANGERS color *Entertainment Weekly* no1434 p63 O 7 2016

The Bullseye color *Entertainment Weekly* no1449 p64 Ja 20 2017

The Bullseye color *Entertainment Weekly* no1456 p72 Mr 10 2017

The / Bullseye color *Entertainment Weekly* no1460/1461 p102 Ap 7-17 2017

The Bullseye color *Entertainment Weekly* no1463/1464 p114 Ap/My 2017

The Bullseye color *Entertainment Weekly* no1477 p64 Ag 11 2017

But Seriously, Folks color *Entertainment Weekly* no1434 p62 O 7 2016

CAN YOU SPOT THE FAKES? color *Entertainment Weekly* no1444/1445 p104 D 16 2016

CARS 3 ADDS TO ITS FLEET color *Entertainment Weekly* no1448 p13 Ja 13 2017

CARS 3 color *Entertainment Weekly* no1463/1464 p50 Ap/My 2017

COCO color *Entertainment Weekly* no1446/1447 p46 D 2016/Ja 2017

COCO color *Entertainment Weekly* no1478 / 1479 p58 Ag 18-25 2017

DESPICABLE ME 3 color *Entertainment Weekly* no1463/1464 p44 Ap/My 2017

Disney's Next Teen Queen color *Entertainment Weekly* no1474/1475 p106 Jl 21-28 2017

DuckTales for a New Generation color *Entertainment Weekly* no1470 p10 Je 16 2017

EYES ON THE RISE color *Entertainment Weekly* no1454/1455 p87 F 24 2017

Fantastic Beasts and Where to Find Them color *Entertainment Weekly* no1439 p18 N 11 2016

Fifth Harmony color *Entertainment Weekly* no1480 p50 S 1 2017

From Drag to Riches [Cover story] color *Entertainment Weekly* no1471 p23 Je 23 2017

A Frozen Treat color *Entertainment Weekly* no1471 p18 Je 23 2017

Getting Med-ucated color *Entertainment Weekly* no1462 p53 Ap 21 2017

GODS GONE WILD color *Entertainment Weekly* no1462 p26 Ap 21 2017

THE GREATEST DISNEY SONGS OF ALL TIME color *Entertainment Weekly* no1454/1455 p36 F 24 2017

THE HAMILTON SATISFACTION SCALE color *Entertainment Weekly* no1444/1445 p119 D 16 2016

Hot Takes and Cold Shoulders color *Entertainment Weekly* no1465 p10 My 12 2017

HOW CARLY RAE JEPSEN AND LEAP! GAVE US SUMMER'S BEST POP ANTHEM color *Entertainment Weekly* no1480 p50 S 1 2017

HOW COMEDY'S SECRET WEAPON GOT SCHOOLED color *Entertainment Weekly* no1463/1464 p96 Ap/My 2017

Is American Gods the Most Outrageous Show on TV? color *Entertainment Weekly* no1467 p53 My 26 2017

J.K. ROWLING color *Entertainment Weekly* no1444/1445 p23 D 16 2016

KATY MIXON color *Entertainment Weekly* no1434 p47 O 7 2016

THE LEGO BATMAN MOVIE color *Entertainment Weekly* no1446/1447 p55 D 2016/Ja 2017

Lin-Manuel Miranda color *Entertainment Weekly* no1444/1445 p18 D 16 2016

MADDIE BAILLIO color *Entertainment Weekly* no1442 p51 D 2 2016 Rebellious Special Issue

MAKING WAVES WITH MOANA color *Entertainment Weekly* no1442 p12 D 2 2016 Rebellious Special Issue

Mary Poppins Returns color *Entertainment Weekly* no1457/1458 p22 Mr 17 2017

Meet Broadway's Frozen Foursome color *Entertainment Weekly* no1480 p59 S 1 2017

MEET THE NEW MINION color *Entertainment Weekly* no1467 p13 My 26 2017

MOANA color *Entertainment Weekly* no1438 p44 N 4 2016

NeNe Leakes for President! color *Entertainment Weekly* no1436/1437 p16 O 21 2016

NEXT UP IN THE RING! color *Entertainment Weekly* no1473 p27 Jl 7 2017

No. 1 THE HUMANS color *Entertainment Weekly* no1444/1445 p116 D 16 2016

Our Ridiculously Early Tony Preview color *Entertainment Weekly* no1462 p14 Ap 21 2017

PIRATES OF THE CARIBBEAN: DEAD MEN TELL NO TALES color *Entertainment Weekly* no1463/1464 p36 Ap/My 2017

THE POSTHUMOUS RETURN OF PAUL NEWMAN color *Entertainment Weekly* no1471 p49 Je 23 2017

THE PROS OF CON color *Entertainment Weekly* no1476 p32 Ag 4 2017

RISKY BUSINESS color *Entertainment Weekly* no1449 p38 Ja 20 2017

Salvation Song color *Entertainment Weekly* no1486 p23 O 13 2017

A Series of Unfortunate Events color *Entertainment Weekly* no1448 p38 Ja 13 2017

Shameless color *Entertainment Weekly* no1482/1483 p30 S 22 2017

SHOCK of MOONLIGHT color *Entertainment Weekly* no1456 p42 Mr 10 2017

SING color *Entertainment Weekly* no1438 p38 N 4 2016

TREY PARKER'S DESPICABLE DEBUT color *Entertainment Weekly* no1473 p14 Jl 7 2017

TV chart color *Entertainment Weekly* no1444/1445 p66 D 16 2016

UP TO THE Highest HEIGHT [Cover story] color *Entertainment Weekly* no1470 p18 Je 16 2017

WHAT DOES JULIE THINK? color *Entertainment Weekly* no1470 p23 Je 16 2017

What's Next for Hamilton's Breakout Stars? color *Entertainment Weekly* no1454/1455 p104 F 24 2017

What to Watch color *Entertainment Weekly* no1449 p54 Ja 20 2017

What to Watch color *Entertainment Weekly* no1468/1469 p94 Je 2-9 2017

WHO WILL YOU SPEND NEW YEAR'S EVE WITH? color *Entertainment Weekly* no1446/1447 p109 D 2016/Ja 2017

A Wrinkle in Time color *Entertainment Weekly* no1474/1475 p96 Jl 21-28 2017

You Can't Stop the Chic color *Entertainment Weekly* no1442 p51 D 2 2016 Rebellious Special Issue

Your Sunshiny, Stupendous, Seriously Spectacular SUMMER BUCKET LIST color *Entertainment Weekly* no1470 p32 Je 16 2017

Sng, Oliver—Interviews

CROWDED PLACES MAKE PEOPLE THINK MORE ABOUT THE FUTURE A. Beard graph img *Harvard Business Review* v95 no4 p34 Jl/Ag 2017

Snøhetta AS

Times Square Reconstruction New York J. Minutillo *Architectural Record* v205 no4 p210 Ap 2017

Snider, Grant

Sketchbook *New York Times Book Review* p27 N 20 2016

SNIDER, LESA

4 secrets for editing images in Apple Photos color *Macworld - Digital Edition* p117 F 2017

How to use Levels adjustments in Photos and how to use Copy Adjustments to tweak other images diag *Macworld - Digital Edition* p122 F 2017

How to use Photoshop Elements to combine images like a pro color *Macworld - Digital Edition* p122 D 2016

How to use Siri in macOS Sierra to find pictures in Photos on the fly color *Macworld - Digital Edition* p125 F 2017

How to watermark multiple photos in Lightroom color *Macworld - Digital Edition* p128 D 2016

SNIECKUS, VICTOR

Chords & Discords color *Downbeat* v84 no7 p10 Jl 2017

Snieder, Roel

Elastic-wave propagation and the Coriolis force *Physics Today* v69 no12 p90 D 2016

Snierson, Dan

ADAM SCOTT AND CRAIG ROBINSON color *Entertainment Weekly* no1482/1483 p42 S 22 2017

ALAN THICKE color *Entertainment Weekly* no1446/1447 p84 D 2016/Ja 2017

Blast from the Past color *Entertainment Weekly* no1456 p38 Mr 10 2017

Bob's Burgers *Entertainment Weekly* no1482/1483 p34 S 22 2017

COZY UP! IT'S YOUR HOLIDAY TV-MOVIE CHEAT SHEET color *Entertainment Weekly* no1443 p51 D 9 2016

Curb Your Enthusiasm color *Entertainment Weekly* no1482/1483 p40 S 22 2017

The Deuce color *Entertainment Weekly* no1482/1483 p29 S 22 2017

DIVE INTO Brooklyn Nine-Nine color *Entertainment Weekly* no1482/1483 p67 S 22 2017

THE EMOJI MOVIE color *Entertainment Weekly* no1463/1464 p70 Ap/My 2017

EMOJIS THAT CONFUSE ANNA FARIS color *Entertainment Weekly* no1476 p46 Ag 4 2017

Family Guy *Entertainment Weekly* no1482/1483 p34 S 22 2017

GARRY MARSHALL color *Entertainment Weekly* no1446/1447 p86 D 2016/Ja 2017

GHOSTED color *Entertainment Weekly* no1474/1475 p74 Jl 21-28 2017

The Girlfriend Experience color *Entertainment Weekly* no1482/1483 p38 S 22 2017

GOING OUT WITH A BANG color *Entertainment Weekly* no1463/1464 p10 Ap/My 2017

Good Behavior *Entertainment Weekly* no1482/1483 p39 S 22 2017

A GOOD MAN EMERGES color *Entertainment Weekly* no1471 p56 Je 23 2017

THE GOOD PLACE BREAKS BAD color *Entertainment Weekly* no1472 p14 Je 30 2017

THE GOOD PLACE color *Entertainment Weekly* no1477 p29 Ag 11 2017

HAPPY ENDINGS color *Entertainment Weekly* no1439 p20 N 11 2016

HAVE YOURESELF A FILTHY LITTLE CHRISTMAS [Cover story] color diag *Entertainment Weekly* no1443 p28 D 9 2016

INSIDE ELLEN'S COMING-OUT color *Entertainment Weekly* no1465 p49 My 12 2017

James Blunt color *Entertainment Weekly* no1459 p60 Mr 31 2017

KAITLIN OLSON color *Entertainment Weekly* no1446/1447 p110 D 2016/Ja 2017

Laura Linney's Ozark Adventure color *Entertainment Weekly* no1476 p51 Ag 4 2017

LOOKWELL color *Entertainment Weekly* no1460/1461 p70 Ap 7-17 2017

Madam Secretary color *Entertainment Weekly* no1482/1483 p39 S 22 2017

The MARY MARY MARY MARY MARY MARY MARY I Knew color *Entertainment Weekly* no1453 p34 F 17 2017

METALLICA'S LARS ULRICH color *Entertainment Weekly* no1442 p58 D 2 2016 Rebellious Special Issue

MORE TITLES TO MAKE YOU BLUSH color *Entertainment Weekly* no1465 p48 My 12 2017

NCIS: Los Angeles *Entertainment Weekly* no1482/1483 p38 S 22 2017

A NIGHT of FIRSTS color *Entertainment Weekly* no1484 p18 S 29 2017

OFFICE CHRISTMAS PARTY color *Entertainment Weekly* no1438 p39 N 4 2016

Outlander color *Entertainment Weekly* no1482/1483 p26 S 22 2017

OZARK color *Entertainment Weekly* no1468/1469 p66 Je 2-9 2017

Paul Bettany Is the Unabomber color *Entertainment Weekly* no1467 p13 My 26 2017

Poldark *Entertainment Weekly* no1482/1483 p38 S 22 2017

Portlandia's "Put a Bird on It!" color *Entertainment Weekly* no1454/1455 p89 F 24 2017

THE PROS OF CON color *Entertainment Weekly* no1476 p32 Ag 4 2017

REBOOTS, REVIVALS & ROCKY BALBOA! color *Entertainment Weekly* no1478 / 1479 p20 Ag 18-25 2017

RETURN OF THE KINGPIN color *Entertainment Weekly* no1462 p54 Ap 21 2017

Seinfeld's Lost Story Lines color *Entertainment Weekly* no1460/1461 p64 Ap 7-17 2017

Shameless color *Entertainment Weekly* no1482/1483 p30 S 22 2017

The Simpsons color *Entertainment Weekly* no1482/1483 p34 S 22 2017

SMILF *Entertainment Weekly* no1482/1483 p43 S 22 2017

The Story of Us [Cover story] color *Entertainment Weekly* no1435 p18 O 14 2016

Stupid QUESTIONS WITH... Jenny Slate color *Entertainment Weekly* no1474/1475 p22 Jl 21-28 2017

Ten Days in the Valley color *Entertainment Weekly* no1482/1483 p43 S 22 2017

This Is Us: Before They Met color *Entertainment Weekly* no1457/1458 p83 Mr 17 2017

This Is Us Can't Quit Ron Cephas Jones color *Entertainment Weekly* no1484 p52 S 29 2017

THIS IS US color *Entertainment Weekly* no1477 p28 Ag 11 2017

T.J. MILLER color *Entertainment Weekly* no1442 p50 D 2 2016 Rebellious Special Issue

A TV Casting Titan Tells All color *Entertainment Weekly* no1462 p55 Ap 21 2017

TV chart color *Entertainment Weekly* no1444/1445 p66 D 16 2016

The Walking Dead color *Entertainment Weekly* no1482/1483 p38 S 22 2017

WATCH THIS/SORRY ABOUT THAT color *Entertainment Weekly* no1438 p51 N 4 2016

We Say Goodbye to One of Our Own color *Entertainment Weekly* no1480 p3 S 1 2017

Wet Hot's Face-off color *Entertainment Weekly* no1476 p52 Ag 4 2017

What to Watch color *Entertainment Weekly* no1449 p54 Ja 20 2017

What to Watch color *Entertainment Weekly* no1462 p57 Ap 21 2017

What to Watch color *Entertainment Weekly* no1471 p58 Je 23 2017

What to Watch color *Entertainment Weekly* no1480 p46 S 1 2017

White Famous color *Entertainment Weekly* no1482/1483 p36 S 22 2017

Will Parks and Recreation Predict 2017? color *Entertainment Weekly* no1449 p50 Ja 20 2017

Wisdom of the Crowd color *Entertainment Weekly* no1482/1483 p34 S 22 2017

Snijder, Joost
Structures of the cyanobacterial circadian oscillator frozen in a fully assembled state bibl diag *Science* v355 no6330 p1181 Mr 17 2017

Snipers
Kill Shot B. POPPLEWELL cartoon *Walrus* v14 no2 p42 Mr 2017

Snipes, Wesley, 1962-
Just How Important Is Wesley Snipes? K. Lincoln img *New York* v50 no6 p78 Mr 20 2017

Talon of God *Publishers Weekly* v264 no19 p42 My 8 2017

Snitow, Ann—Interviews
Q&A A. SNITOW il *Nation* v303 no16 p5 O 17 2016

Snoke, David W.
The new era of POLARITON CONDENSATES *Physics Today* v70 no10 p54 O 2017

Snook, Graham
Rigging Adjustable Sheet Leads color *Sail* v48 no5 p44 My 2017

Snook, Raven
home & help img *New York* p96 Mr 6 2017

Snoring—Prevention
Does It Work? Antisnoring Devices S. ANDERSON WITMER color *Prevention* v69 no11 p18 N 2017

Snoring—Treatment
Problem Solved! [Cover story] R. LALIBERTE cartoon *Prevention* v69 no2 p18 F 2017

Snorradóttir, Áslaug
DAFT ABOUT DILL *Iceland Review* v55 no3 p46 My/Je 2017

INVIGORATING INVENTIONS Z. ROBERT *Iceland Review* v55 no1 p22 Ja/F 2017

PICTURESQUE PICNIC *Iceland Review* v55 no4 p42 Jl/Ag 2017

Snow
See also
Snowmelt

593" M. Hansen bw color *Powder* p64 S 2017

618" H. Ludwig color *Powder* p70 S 2017

THE DESCENT A. BURR color *Climbing* no350 p80 D 2016/Ja 2017

DIG IN, DIG OUT P. STEFÁNSSON *Iceland Review* v55 no3 p82 My/Je 2017

ENVIRONMENTALLY SUSTAINABLE ADVENTURE *Iceland Review* v55 no3 p104 My/Je 2017

FACE TO FACE WITH THE GLACIERS OF ICELAND *Iceland Review* v55 no3 p104 My/Je 2017

From the Editor M. Benner Smidt *Weatherwise* v69 no6 p4 N-D 2016

our swiftly dimming planet K. Pierre-Louis color *Popular Science* v289 no4 p23 Jl/Ag 2017

PEAK EXPERIENCE *Iceland Review* v55 no3 p98 My/Je 2017

PICTURE PERFECT *Saturday Evening Post* v288 no6 p116 N/D 2016

Six Idiotic Idioms—and What's Wrong with Them B. SPECKTOR color *Reader's Digest* v189 no1130 p134 My 2017

Snow Days S. KLEIN bw color *Prevention* v69 no1 p96 Ja 2017

The Ultimate Winter Adventure Guide color *Wired* v24 no12 p93 D 2016

Walk on Snow M. ATTEBERRY il *Backpacker* p28 N 2017

WHEN IT SNOWS E. Laborde *Louisiana Life* v37 no2 p6 N/D 2016

Winter Wonderland WEEKEND M. FREITAG bw color *Cabin Living* p88 D 2016

Snow & ice climbing techniques
Scary (and true) tales from a crag near you Brandon and Spencer *Climbing* no353 p21 My/Je 2017

YES, YOU CAN! CLIMB A MOUNTAIN J. Ator color *Women's Health* v14 no8 p69 O 2017

Snow, Carmel
ASTONISH ME S. Mooallem bw color *Harper's Bazaar* no3651 p436 Mr 2017

DIOR'S REVOLUTION color *Harper's Bazaar* no3651 p182 Mr 2017

Snow, Cody—Interviews
Snow Rides Into First NFR Hot K. Santos color *Spin to Win Rodeo* v20 no11 p18 Ja 2017

Snow, G. R.
Observation of a large-scale anisotropy in the arrival directions of cosmic rays above 8×1018 eV *Science* v357 no6357 p1266 S 22 2017

SNOW, JOHN B.
22 NOSLER chart color *Outdoor Life* v224 no4 p28 My 2017

.38 SPECIALS color *Outdoor Life* v224 no8 pP8 O 2017

3-GUN KICKS color *Outdoor Life* v224 no1 pR6 D 2016/Ja 2017

6.5 CREEDMOOR color *Outdoor Life* v224 no5 p57 Je/Jl 2017

BARRETT FIELDCRAFT color *Outdoor Life* v224 no6 p72 Ag 2017

BENELLI SBE 3 chart color *Outdoor Life* v224 no4 p24 My 2017

BERETTA 690 FIELD I chart color *Outdoor Life* v224 no7 p66 S 2017

BIRD SEASON COUNTDOWN color *Outdoor Life* v224 no4 p26 My 2017

COLD BAY ALASKA color *Outdoor Life* v224 no9 p46 N 2017

CONCENTRICITY color *Outdoor Life* v224 no5 pR4 Je/Jl 2017

DIY TURKEY GUN color *Outdoor Life* v224 no2 p86 F/Mr 2017

ELITE IRON REVOLUTION color *Outdoor Life* v224 no5 pR6 Je/Jl 2017

THE ENDURING .45/70 color *Outdoor Life* v224 no7 p62 S 2017

GOING LIGHT color *Outdoor Life* v224 no2 p83 F/Mr 2017

GRAND OPENING color *Outdoor Life* v224 no1 p95 D 2016/Ja 2017

GUN TEST 2017 [Cover story] bw chart color *Outdoor Life* v224 no5 p42 Je/Jl 2017

HIGH-SPEED RELOADING color *Outdoor Life* v224 no1 pR1 D 2016/Ja 2017

HOW OL'S WILDCAT CAME TO DOMINATE LONG-RANGE PRECISION-RIFLE SHOOTING color graph *Outdoor Life* v224 no2 p36 F/Mr 2017

KIMBER M84 HUNTER chart color *Outdoor Life* v224 no2 p88 F/Mr 2017

KIMBER SUPER JAGARE chart color *Outdoor Life* v224 no9 p68 N 2017

MEET THE TECH THAT MAKES BALLISTIC COEFFICIENTS OBSOLETE color diag *Outdoor Life* v224 no2 p40 F/Mr 2017

NIGHTFORCE 4-16X42 F1 ATACR color *Outdoor Life* v224 no1 pR16 D 2016/Ja 2017

PATROL BELT color *Outdoor Life* v224 no1 pR5 D 2016/Ja 2017

REALITY CHECK color *Outdoor Life* v223 no9 p21 N 2016

RUGER LCP II color *Outdoor Life* v224 no4 pP1 My 2017

RUGER MK IV chart color *Outdoor Life* v224 no1 p84 D 2016/Ja 2017

SADDLE UP color *Outdoor Life* v224 no1 p90 D 2016/Ja 2017

SAUER 100 CLASSIC XT chart color *Outdoor Life* v223 no9 p74 N 2016

SHOT TIMERS color *Outdoor Life* v224 no5 pR10 Je/Jl 2017

SPEED & PRECISION DRILL color *Outdoor Life* v224 no5 pR1 Je/Jl 2017

STATE OF THE DEER RIFLE color *Outdoor Life* v223 no9 p71 N 2016

STI 211 HEX TACTICAL chart color *Outdoor Life* v224 no1 pR13 D 2016/Ja 2017

TARGET TRANSITIONS color *Outdoor Life* v224 no1 pR9 D 2016/Ja 2017

THERMAL IMAGERS HAVE BECOME BETTER AND

CHEAPER. HERE'S WHY color diag *Outdoor Life* v224 no2 p42 F/Mr 2017

THREE NEW, AND ACCURATE, .243-CALIBER BULLETS THAT WILL DUKE IT OUT IN COMPETITION THIS YEAR color *Outdoor Life* v224 no2 p41 F/Mr 2017

TOP 5 SHOOTING MISTAKES color *Outdoor Life* v224 no4 p22 My 2017

ULTIMATE DRIFT BOAT diag *Outdoor Life* v224 no1 p104 D 2016/Ja 2017

WAYPOINT: COLD BAY, AK color *Outdoor Life* v224 no9 p9 N 2017

SNOW, OLIVIA

Junkies get their fix at Junkstock festival color *Nebraska Life* v21 no5 p84 S/O 2017

Snow, W. M.

Observation of coherent elastic neutrino-nucleus scattering diag *Science* v357 no6356 p1123 S 15 2017

Snow accumulation

HOW TO CROSS A FIELD OF SNOW R. Moor *Lapham's Quarterly* v10 no2 p181 Spr 2017

Snow camping

TENTPOLERS B. PLUMB color *Snowboarder* v29 no4 p62 D 2016

Snow cover

HOW TO CROSS A FIELD OF SNOW R. Moor *Lapham's Quarterly* v10 no2 p181 Spr 2017

Snow goose

Search for the blue goose J. Pearce bw color *Canadian Geographic* v137 no5 p22 S/O 2017

Snow Kreilich Architects (Company)

Newport Transit Station *Architectural Record* v205 no4 p206 Ap 2017

Snow protection

Snowball Solutions F. Jurga color *Trail Rider* v29 no1 p30 Ja/F 2017

Snow removal—Equipment & supplies

See also
  Snowblowers

LET IT BLOW D. DiClerico chart *Consumer Reports* v81 no12 p10 D 2016

Snow White (Poem)

Snow White K. Riegel *Orion Magazine* v36 no1 p23 Ja/F 2017

Snow White (Tale)

PARODY C. Heller *Weekly Standard* v22 no37 p40 Je 5 2017

SNOWBARGER, JEFF

Buffaloed color *Orion Magazine* v36 no1 p12 Ja/F 2017

Snowblowers

Ask Our Experts il *Consumer Reports* v82 no3 p21 Mr 2017

Snowblowers—Evaluation

LET IT BLOW D. DiClerico chart *Consumer Reports* v81 no12 p10 D 2016

Snowboarders

2017 RESORT GUIDE T. Monterosso color map *Snowboarder* v29 no5 p90 Ja 2017

ALEX SHERMAN B. Merrill color *Snowboarder* v29 no3 p48 N 2016

BLAKE PAUL color *Snowboarder* v29 no5 p122 Ja 2017

Chloe Kim J. Crelin color *Current Biography* v78 no1 p32 Ja 2017

CHRISTIAN HOBUSH B. Merrill color *Snowboarder* v29 no3 p50 N 2016

COLDFRONT B. Merrill color *Snowboarder* v29 no3 p14 N 2016

DARRELL MATHES bw color *Snowboarder* v29 no2 p144 O 2016

DOUBLE VISION J. Paul color *Snowboarder* v29 no3 p74 N 2016

ELEMENTS color *Snowboarder* v29 no2 p98 O 2016

ELEMENTS color *Snowboarder* v29 no5 p70 Ja 2017

ENDER ENDER color *Snowboarder* v29 no2 p145 O 2016

ENDER ENDER color *Snowboarder* v29 no5 p123 Ja 2017

GABE TAYLOR T. Bird color *Snowboarder* v29 no2 p36 O 2016

GORDON HARRISON B. Merrill and N. Müller color *Snowboarder* v29 no3 p42 N 2016

IN FOCUS O. Gagnon color *Snowboarder* v29 no3 p66 N 2016

KING OF THE MOUNTAIN J. Dean color *Sunset* v238 no2 p25 F 2017

NILS MINDNICH color *Snowboarder* v29 no3 p134 N 2016

SALT LAKE CITY, UT B. Merrill bw color *Snowboarder* v29 no3 p98 N 2016

SCOTT BLUM T. Monterosso color *Snowboarder* v29 no5 p34 Ja 2017

SICK DAYS B. Merrill color *Snowboarder* v29 no3 p92 N 2016

Snowboarders—Interviews

GARAGE BRANDS B. Merrill color *Snowboarder* v29 no3 p32 N 2016

JUDD HENKES P. Strout color *Snowboarder* v29 no5 p40 Ja 2017

Snowboarders—Substance use

THE EIGHTH PHASE C. LISKA bw cartoon color *Snowboarder* v29 no4 p54 D 2016

Snowboarding

AV CLUB C. Liska color *Snowboarder* v29 no2 p33 O 2016

BEN FERGUSON T. Monterosso cartoon color *Snowboarder* v29 no4 p40 D 2016

BENNY MILAM P. G. Strout color *Snowboarder* v29 no2 p46 O 2016

BROCK CROUCH P. Harrington color *Snowboarder* v29 no2 p44 O 2016

THE CASCADES, WASHINGTON M. Yoshida bw color *Snowboarder* v29 no4 p100 D 2016

CHAMPERY, SWITZERLAND A. Povich color *Snowboarder* v29 no5 p86 Ja 2017

CHRIS BRADSHAW T. Monterosso color *Snowboarder* v29 no2 p39 O 2016

ENDER ENDER color *Snowboarder* v29 no2 p145 O 2016

GARAGE BRANDS C. Liska color *Snowboarder* v29 no2 p32 O 2016

HARMONIC CONVERGENCE O. Gagnon bw *Snowboarder* v29 no4 p14 D 2016

"HOLY SHIT." B. Birk color *Snowboarder* v29 no5 p14 Ja 2017

JP WALKER T. Monterosso color *Snowboarder* v29 no5 p33 Ja 2017

MOUNTAIN DEW SUPERSNAKE SIERRA-AT-TAHOE, CA T. Bird color *Snowboarder* v29 no2 p108 O 2016

NEW YORK CITY, NY O. Gagnon bw cartoon color *Snowboarder* v29 no5 p82 Ja 2017

OLI GAGNON SHOT C. Navin bw *Snowboarder* v29 no4 p12 D 2016

PATRICK MCCARTHY T. Bird cartoon color *Snowboarder* v29 no5 p32 Ja 2017

SEQUENCE & DESTROY color *Snowboarder* v29 no5 p36 Ja 2017

SOUTH OF THE BOARDERS M. Georges cartoon color *Snowboarder* v29 no5 p64 Ja 2017

SUPER FRIENDS P. Bridges color *Snowboarder* v29 no5 p24 Ja 2017

SUPER PARK 20 P. Bridges bw cartoon color *Snowboarder* v29 no5 p42 Ja 2017

TENTPOLERS B. PLUMB color *Snowboarder* v29 no4 p62 D 2016

UNION STRIKE MISSION E-STONE cartoon color *Snowboarder* v29 no5 p58 Ja 2017

USUALLY J. Baker color *Snowboarder* v29 no5 p12 Ja 2017

Snowboarding for women

Amusement Mountain color *Snowboarder* v29 no4 p77 D 2016

Snowboarding techniques

ENDER/ENDER color *Snowboarder* v29 no4 p136 D 2016

JONI MALMI T. Bird bw cartoon color *Snowboarder* v29 no4 p38 D 2016

METHOD OF THE MONTH cartoon color *Snowboarder* v29 no4 p134 D 2016

SEQUENCE DESTROY color *Snowboarder* v29 no4 p46 D 2016

Snowboarding—Congresses

SUPER FRIENDS P. Bridges color *Snowboarder* v29 no5 p24 Ja 2017

Snowboarding—Equipment & supplies

2017 HOLIDAY GIFT GUIDE T. Monterosso bw *Snowboarder* v29 no4 p108 D 2016

GARAGE BRANDS T. Bird color *Snowboarder* v29 no5 p28 Ja 2017

Snowboarding—Equipment & supplies—Evaluation
2017 ACCESSORIES GUIDE T. Monterosso color *Snowboarder* v29 no3 p104 N 2016
anon cartoon color *Snowboarder* v29 no4 p110 D 2016
bollé cartoon color *Snowboarder* v29 no4 p112 D 2016
BURTON cartoon color *Snowboarder* v29 no4 p114 D 2016
GEAR TO TIE DYE FOR P. Bridges color *Snowboarder* v29 no3 p128 N 2016
K2 cartoon color *Snowboarder* v29 no4 p116 D 2016
THE NORTH .FACE cartoon color *Snowboarder* v29 no4 p122 D 2016
QUICKSILVER cartoon color *Snowboarder* v29 no4 p120 D 2016
SHORTIES — LESS IS MORE P. Bridges cartoon color *Snowboarder* v29 no4 p132 D 2016
SNOW BALLERS P. Bridges color *Snowboarder* v29 no4 p128 D 2016
SQUAD GOALS P. Bridges cartoon color *Snowboarder* v29 no5 p118 Ja 2017
TOP OF THE FALL LINE P. Bridges color *Snowboarder* v29 no3 p132 N 2016
VANS cartoon color *Snowboarder* v29 no4 p124 D 2016

Snowboards
MIKKEL BANG BURTON color *Snowboarder* v29 no4 p2 D 2016
The Soft Edge That's Landing Solid Sales K. Angel color *Bloomberg Businessweek* no4535 p39 Ag 28 2017
Your True Stories L. ELSNER, J. L. DAVIS et al *Reader's Digest* v188 no1124 p22 O 2016

Snowboards—Evaluation
ANGLE GRINDERS P. Bridges bw color *Snowboarder* v29 no2 p142 O 2016
THE BLACK BOARD EXPERIMENT [Cover story] T. Bird bw color *Snowboarder* v29 no2 p52 O 2016
BURTON cartoon color *Snowboarder* v29 no4 p114 D 2016
K2 cartoon color *Snowboarder* v29 no4 p116 D 2016
NEVER SUMMER cartoon color *Snowboarder* v29 no4 p118 D 2016
SHORTIES — LESS IS MORE P. Bridges cartoon color *Snowboarder* v29 no4 p132 D 2016
SQUAD GOALS P. Bridges cartoon color *Snowboarder* v29 no5 p118 Ja 2017
TOP OF THE FALL LINE P. Bridges color *Snowboarder* v29 no3 p132 N 2016

Snowboy Productions (Company)
HOLY BOWLY MAMMOTH MTN, CA M. Walsh color *Snowboarder* v29 no4 p104 D 2016

Snowden (Film)
Full Pardon D. EDELSTEIN img *New York* v49 no19 p94 S 19 2016
LEAK, PAY, LOVE J. ANDERSON color *America* v215 no10 p43 O 10 2016
Snowden *New Yorker* v92 no30 p17 S 26 2016

Snowden, Edward Joseph, 1983-
Denied Clemency, Snowden Remains Trapped In Putin's Game S. Shuster color *Time* v189 no3 p7 Ja 30 2017
Don't Pardon Edward Snowden bw *Bloomberg Businessweek* no4493 p16 O 3 2016
Reporters Need Edward Snowden A. Greenberg cartoon *Wired* v25 no3 p66 Mr 2017
The Snowden Cure J. Goldsmith *Hoover Digest: Research & Opinion on Public Policy* no4 p133 Fall 2016
SNOWDEN'S BOX J. Bruder and D. Maharidge *Harper's Magazine* v334 no2004 p25 My 2017
Unpardonable *Weekly Standard* v22 no4 p2 O 3 2016
Was Snowden a Soviet Agent? C. Savage cartoon color *New York Review of Books* v64 no2 p16 F 9 2017

SNOWDEN, SUSAN
Q: What did you let go of that changed your life? color *O, The Oprah Magazine* p16 Ag 2017

Snowdon (Wales)
And the Winning Photo Is... D. Tura *British Heritage Travel* v38 no4 p80 Jl/Ag 2017

Snowdon, Antony Armstrong-Jones, Earl of, 1930-2017
A LIFE IN FOCUS G. CARTER and D. JONES bw *Vanity Fair* v59 no6 p100 My 2017
Milestones *Time* v189 no3 p11 Ja 30 2017

Snowdon, Charles T.
Learning from monkey "talk" bibl chart color *Science* v355 no6330 p1120 Mr 17 2017

Snowfall (TV program)
FX's Exploration of the Crack Epidemic Falters D. D'addario color *Time* v190 no2/3 p92 Jl 10-17 2017
Lost Souls at the Dawn of the Crack Crisis R. SHEFFIELD color *Rolling Stone* no1293 p25 Ag 10 2017
Snowfall J. Jensen color *Entertainment Weekly* no1473 p50 Jl 7 2017

Snowflakes
Freeze Frame color *National Wildlife (World Edition)* v55 no2 p20 F/Mr 2017
The Most Wonderful Time of the Year N. SCHUMAN *USA Today Magazine* v145 no2858 p64 N 2016

Snow Maiden, The (Theatrical production)
The Snow Maiden G. Hall *Opera News* v81 no10 p46 Ap 2017

Snowmaking—Equipment & supplies
It is a dark and stormy night... *Stage Directions* v30 no5 p24 My 2017

Snowman, Daniel
CULTURAL AND INTELLECTUAL ENRICHMENT EN-MASSE: One of our foremost cultural historians examines the impact of immigration on the transfer of knowledge *History Today* v67 no10 p91 O 2017
Secret History and Historical Consciousness *History Today* v67 no2 p57 F 2017

Snowman, The (Film)
THE SNOWMAN S. Vilkomerson color *Entertainment Weekly* no1478 / 1479 p55 Ag 18-25 2017

Snow—Measurement
The 2015–2016 U.S. Snow Report: A Slim Year with A Few Surprises D. A. Robinson chart color map *Weatherwise* v69 no6 p21 N-D 2016

Snowmelt
See also
Ice jams (Geology)
Algae speed up melting of glacial snow L. HAMERS color *Science News* v192 no6 p10 O 14 2017
How Antarctica Is Being Invaded T. John color *Time* v190 no1 p10 Jl 3 2017
The River Overfloweth L. SCHLEY map *Discover* v38 no10 p15 D 2017
When It Rains *Arizona Highways* v93 no11 p56 N 2017

Snowmelt—Research
Joint research push targets fast-melting Antarctic ice P. Voosen color *Science* v354 no6309 p159 O 14 2016

Snowmen
Bet you didn't know E. WHITMER *National Geographic Kids* no466 p10 D 2016/Ja 2017

Snowmobiles
COOL inventions C. M. TOMLIN *National Geographic Kids* no467 p11 F 2017

Snowmobiles—Sales & prices
BUYING A USED SNOWMOBILE M. Boncher color *Cabin Living* p10 D 2016

Snowmobiling
Discover the Wonder of Winter in Montana *Texas Monthly* v44 no11 p40 N 2016
Unprepared: Rookie Snowmobilers Messing Up B. JOHNSON *Idaho Magazine* v16 no8 p54 My 2017

Snowpack augmentation
How Cloud Seeding Works *Weatherwise* v70 no5 p30 S/O 2017

Snowshoes & snowshoeing
ARTIFACT J. A. LOBELL color *Archaeology* v70 no1 p68 Ja/F 2017
Hut to Hut G. Vercesi *Sierra* v101 no6 p17 N/D 2016
Skishoe L. JHUNG il *Backpacker* p30 N 2017
SKI, SNOWSHOE & DOGSLED *Sierra* v102 no1 p75 Ja/F 2017
SNOWSHOEING J. LYNCH color *Popular Mechanics* p49 D 2016/Ja 2017

Snowshoes & snowshoeing—Equipment & supplies
Snowshoes T. J. BROWN color *Backpacker* v45 no2 p42 Mr 2017

Snowstorms (Weather)
inside a smog dome E. Cummins color *Popular Science* v289 no4 p20 Jl/Ag 2017

Snowy owl
Fossil Record C. Cox *Orion Magazine* v35 no4/5 p32 Jl-O 2016
In the Presence of Greatness E. KANZE color *Natural History* v125 no5 p48 My 2017
Weird but true! J. BEER and M. HARRIS *National Geographic Kids* no466 p4 D 2016/Ja 2017

Snowy Range (Wyo.)
Weatherscapes: The Snowy Range – Hidden Alpine Gem E. Darack *Weatherwise* v69 no6 p8 N-D 2016

Snubbers (Electrical engineering)
SHOCK TREATMENT J. NEEVES color graph *Sail* v48 no9 p46 S 2017

Snuka, Jimmy, 1943-2017
Jimmy Snuka (1943-2017) J. Fuchs and T. Keith color *Sports Illustrated* v126 no4 p22 Ja 30 2017

Snyder, Ceci
FOOD TRENDS G. Johnston *Successful Farming* v114 no10 p60 O 2016

Snyder, Christina
Great Crossings: Indians, Settlers, and Slaves in the Age of Jackson *Publishers Weekly* v263 no50 p59 D 5 2016

Snyder, Elliott
How Facebook Could Stop bw color *Bloomberg Businessweek* no4524 p56 My 29 2017

Snyder, Evan Y.
Finding a new purpose for old drugs color *Science* v357 no6354 p869 S 1 2017

Snyder, Gabriel
Keeping Up with the Times bw cartoon color graph *Wired* v25 no3 p50 Mr 2017

SNYDER, GARRETT
GRAB A BISCUIT *Los Angeles Magazine* p116 Ap 2017
HERO WORSHIP color *Los Angeles Magazine* v62 no10 p48 O 2017
HOLEY ROLLERS: A GUIDE TO L.A.'S NEW-WAVE BAGEL MAKERS *Los Angeles Magazine* v62 no9 p56 S 2017
More than Meets the Izakaya *Los Angeles Magazine* v62 no9 p114 S 2017
The Next Generation: MEET THE CHEFS BROADENING L.A.'S DEFINITION OF JAPANESE FOOD *Los Angeles Magazine* v62 no9 p110 S 2017
Niki Nakayama *Los Angeles Magazine* v62 no9 p98 S 2017
Pinoy Power: AT LASA, TWO BROTHERS DELIVER FILIPINO COMFORT WITH CALIFORNIA STYLE *Los Angeles Magazine* v62 no9 p54 S 2017
Space Oddity color *Los Angeles Magazine* v62 no10 p40 O 2017
Square Meal *Los Angeles Magazine* v62 no9 p107 S 2017
Thank You Very Mochi *Los Angeles Magazine* v62 no9 p116 S 2017

Snyder, Jack
JUSTICE LEAGUE D. Franich color *Entertainment Weekly* p18 Jl 24 2017

Snyder, Jon
BRUSH YOUR TEETH WITH GASOLINE color *Esquire* v167 no2 p28 Mr 2017

Snyder, Kim A.
Newtown: A Vivid Portrait of a Grieving Community S. Zacharek *Time* v188 no15 p52 O 17 2016

Snyder, Laura J.
The Reinvention of Seeing H. Grootenboer *History Today* v67 no2 p60 F 2017

SNYDER, LAUREL
Hard Times in Paradise *New York Times Book Review* p25 N 13 2016

Snyder, Lynsi
Burger Queen C. SORVINO color *Forbes* v199 no6 p22 Je 13 2017

SNYDER, MELISSA
MEN BEHAVING BADLY color *Vanity Fair* v59 no11 p54 N 2017

Snyder, Stephanie
DO THE TWIST color *Yoga Journal* p68 2017 Special Issue

SNYDER, TIMOTHY
Especially Those at Home *New York Times Book Review* p14 N 27 2016

Snyder, Timothy D., 1969-

Horrible Histories [Cover story] J. HEER color *New Republic* v248 no4 p52 Ap 2017
On Tyranny: Twenty Lessons from the Twentieth Century *Christian Century* v134 no13 p21 Je 21 2017

Snyder, Todd
MODERN CLASSIC M. BERLINGER color *Bloomberg Businessweek* no4494 p67 O 10 2016

Snyder, Zack, 1966-
BATMAN V SUPERMAN: DAWN OF JUSTICE C. Chiarella color *Sound & Vision* v81 no9 p70 N 2016
Family Tragedy Rocks Justice League N. Sperling color *Entertainment Weekly* no1468/1469 p24 Je 2-9 2017
JUSTICE LEAGUE D. Franich color *Entertainment Weekly* no1474/1475 p49 Jl 21-28 2017
JUSTICE LEAGUE N. Sperling color *Entertainment Weekly* no1446/1447 p48 D 2016/Ja 2017

Snyder-Mackler, Noah
Social status alters immune regulation and response to infection in macaques bibl graph *Science* v354 no6315 p1041 N 25 2016

So, Wesley
Meeting the God of Chess color *Christianity Today* v61 no7 p88 S 2017

So Far (Poem)
So Far M. J. Salter *American Scholar* v86 no3 p58 Summ 2017

So Iwata
A three-dimensional movie of structural changes in bacteriorhodopsin bibl diag graph *Science* v354 no6319 p1552 D 23 2016

So Many Things (Music)
Anne Sofie von Otter: So Many Things J. Cadagin *Opera News* v81 no9 p54 Mr 2017

So You Think You Can Dance (TV program)
Quiz: How Well Do You Know Dance Spirit? *Dance Spirit* v21 no7 p38 S 2017
The "So You Think You Can Dance" Effect S. FRISCIA *Dance Magazine* v91 no6 p34 Je 2017
So You Think You Can Dance M. Logan *TV Guide* v65 no25 p34 Je 2017
What to Watch R. Rahman, B. L. Heldman et al color *Entertainment Weekly* no1472 p54 Je 30 2017

Soalt, Melissa
What Brought You to the Martial Path? color *Black Belt* v55 no5 p76 Ag/S 2017

Soap
Hey Mr. Green! Is liquid soap worse than bar soap? B. Schildgen *Sierra* v102 no4 p12 Jl/Ag 2017
Raising the Bar (Soap) color *Health* v30 no10 p23 D 2016
A TRUE SOAP STAR K. ROCKWOOD color *Good Housekeeping* v265 no2 p134 Ag 2017

Soap bubbles
Arresting soap-bubble flows *Physics Today* v69 no11 p88 N 2016
Soap bubbles show their dark side E. Conover color *Science News* v191 no1 p32 Ja 21 2017

Soap manufacturing
MAKE SOAP the Old-Fashioned Way S. Verberg *Mother Earth News* no279 p40 D/Ja 2017

Soap—Equipment & supplies
Grooming Gems color *Essence* v48 no2 p40 Je 2017

Soap—Evaluation
THE DIGITAL AGE M. M. GOLDSTEIN color *Martha Stewart Living* p44 Jl/Ag 2017
GOAT MILK SOAP *South Dakota Magazine* v33 no3 p39 S/O 2017
GOOD-FOR-YOU GIFT GUIDE color *Prevention* v68 no12 p68 D 2016
JUST ADD WATER T. BRAND *Indianapolis Monthly* v40 no5 p26 Ja 2017
O's 2016 BEAUTY GIFT GUIDE color *O, The Oprah Magazine* p112 D 2016
Soap Opera M. STEFANOV color *Esquire* v166 no4 p70 N 2016
Super Naturals M. M. GOLDSTEIN color *Martha Stewart Living* p60 Ap 2017
Val's Guide to GORGEOUS V. Monroe color *O, The Oprah Magazine* p116 D 2016
Val's Guide to GORGEOUS V. Monroe color *O, The Oprah Magazine* p83 Mr 2017

Soapstone

Why European Soccer Is Coming To America E. Novy-Williams color *Bloomberg Businessweek* no4534 p15 Ag 14 2017

Sociability

'Friendliness' genes identified in dogs A. YEAGER *Science News* v192 no2 p8 Ag 19 2017

Market to Millennials by Getting Out of the Way R. Faris *Harvard Business Review Digital Articles* p2 D 9 2015

Social action

See also

Activism

Collective action

Standing Rock Says No to the Dakota Access Pipeline E. CASSIDY color *Progressive* v81 no10 p10 N 2016

To Vegas, With Love from Orlando R. J. Negron-almodovar *Time* v190 no15 p26 O 16 2017

Social advocacy

See also

Human rights advocacy

Corrections & Clarifications *Bloomberg Businessweek* no4506 p4 Ja 9 2017

Scientific advocacy: A tool for assessing the risks of engagement G. A. Schmidt and S. D. Donner bibl *Bulletin of the Atomic Scientists* v73 no5 p344 2017

Social advocacy—History—21st century

... And Now What? G. Bishop and B. Baskin color *Sports Illustrated* v125 no20 p64 D 19 2016

Social attitudes

See also

Equality

Social network B. Haile color *U.S. Catholic* v82 no8 p10 Ag 2017

Social background

Research: How Subtle Class Cues Can Backfire on Your Resume L. Rivera and A. Tilcsik *Harvard Business Review Digital Articles* p2 D 21 2016

Social behavior in animals

Tale from the Land of Oz A. Mitchell color *Canadian Wildlife* v23 no4 p14 S/O 2017

Social behavior in animals—Research

One's True Nature J. G. Goldman color *Scientific American* v315 no6 p24 D 2016

Social behavior in chimpanzees—Research

Low-status chimps are trendsetters B. BOWER *Science News* v191 no6 p8 Ap 1 2017

Social behavior in dogs

DNA variants tied to dog sociability T. H. SAEY color *Science News* v190 no9 p12 O 29 2016

Dog Behavior G. Paul *Skeptical Inquirer* v41 no1 p63 Ja/F 2017

THE VINE LIFE M. D. G. Kaplan *Washingtonian Magazine* v52 no1 p205 O 2016

Social bonds

THE EVOLUTION OF DANCE T. Singer color *Scientific American* v317 no1 p66 Jl 2017

The rewarding nature of social contact S. D. Preston color diag *Science* v357 no6358 p1353 S 29 2017

Social capital (Sociology)

The dual components of mental health—Response J. Cilliers, O. Dube et al bibl color *Science* v354 no6314 p840 N 18 2016

How to Decide Which Conferences Are Worth Your Time D. Clark color *Harvard Business Review Digital Articles* p2 Ja 10 2017

Social capital (Sociology)—Economic aspects

Are We Still Bowling Alone? In broken communities, the focus should be on social capital, not just the economy A. M. Renn *Governing* v30 no12 p22 S 2017

Social change

See also

Agricultural sociology

Communitarian Antidotes to Populism A. Etzioni *Society* v54 no2 p95 Ap 2017

Corrections & Clarifications *Bloomberg Businessweek* no4506 p4 Ja 9 2017

Fading Humor J. EPSTEIN color *Weekly Standard* v22 no39 p5 Je 19 2017

Look to Government—Yes, Government—for New Social Innovations C. Bason and P. Colligan *Harvard Business Review Digital Articles* p2 N 20 2014

Love and Haight: In the brief span of a summer, an effervescent cultural revolution based on sex, drugs, rock 'n' roll, and, you know, pure love, was taking place in the tiny pocket of San Francisco known as Haight-Ashbury. By October of '67, the... C. NeuHAuS *Saturday Evening Post* v289 no4 p32 Jl/Ag 2017

More Reasons To Roam M. SEGAL *Los Angeles Magazine* p10 Ag 2017

The Opening of the North Korean Mind J. Baek cartoon *Foreign Affairs* v96 no1 p104 Ja/F 2017

What Successful Movements Have in Common G. Satell *Harvard Business Review Digital Articles* p2 N 30 2016

Social change—Exhibitions

GOINGS ON ABOUT TOWN cartoon *New Yorker* v92 no47 p4 Ja 30 2017

Social change—International cooperation

AUDACIOUS PHILANTHROPY: LESSONS FROM 15 WORLD-CHANGING INITIATIVES S. W. DITKOFF and A. GRINDLE chart img *Harvard Business Review* v95 no5 p110 S/O 2017

Social change—United States

The New Normal A. J. Bacevich color *Commonweal* v144 no12 p8 Jl 7 2017

THE POWER OF POP CULTURE: ELLEN DEGENERES CHANGED EVERYTHING, BUT SHE DIDN'T DO IT ALONE D. ANDERSON-MINSHALL color *Advocate* no1091 p83 Je/Jl 2017

Social classes

See also

Intellectuals

Middle class

Poor people

Rich people

Working class

Clashes over security at Jerusalem Temple Mount M. Chabin, L. Markoe et al *Christian Century* v134 no17 p14 Ag 16 2017

Coping with class in science C. D. Holder color *Science* v355 no6325 p658 F 10 2017

Research: How You Feel About Individualism Is Influenced by Your Social Class N. Stephens and S. Townsend *Harvard Business Review Digital Articles* p2 My 22 2017

THE ROAD TAKEN D. Garner color *Esquire* v167 no1 p52 F 2017

Solidarity S. BHATTI *In These Times* v41 no1 p29 Ja 2017

Social classes—United States

What So Many People Don't Get About the U.S. Working Class J. C. Williams *Harvard Business Review Digital Articles* p2 N 10 2016

WHITE, BLACK, & RED J. A. MYERSON bw color *Nation* v304 no16 p21 My 22 2017

Social clubs

No Boys Allowed D. EVANS img *New York* v49 no21 p67 O 17 2016

TRENDING SOCIAL E. J. Wallace *Virginia Living* v15 no6 p13 O 2017

Social cohesion

3 Ways Leaders Undermine Cohesion by Trying to Create It R. Carucci *Harvard Business Review Digital Articles* p2 D 23 2015

Caution Ahead W. Voegeli *Claremont Review of Books* v17 no3 p13 Summ 2017

High-Performing Teams Need Psychological Safety. Here's How to Create It L. Delizonna *Harvard Business Review Digital Articles* p2 2017

Social conditions in Denmark

THE WORLD'S HAPPIEST PLACES [Cover story] D. BUETTNER color diag graph *National Geographic* v232 no5 p30 N 2017

Social conditions of African American women

PICK UP HER CROWN L. J. S. Porter color *Essence* v48 no3 p122 Jl 2017

Social conditions of Jews

Grave Matter *Commentary* v143 no4 p15 Ap 2017

The Secret Jews of The Hobbit *Commentary* v142 no1 p1 Jl/Ag 2016

Social conditions of LGBT people

THERE GOES THE GAYBORHOOD: As DC's LGBTQ community has evolved, traditional gay areas have grown less vital. It's a welcome sign of progress--and also a bit sad D. Reed *Wash-*

ingtonian Magazine v53 no1 p47 O 2017

Social conditions of women
    See also
      Legal status of women
  Afghanistan's Romeo & Juliet: The true story of two young Afghans who risked death by defying their families and their culture to be together R. NORDLAND *New York Times Upfront* v150 no1 p14 S 4 2017
  Equal Opportunity C. McGuigan *Architectural Record* v205 no9 p24 S 2017
  A Steppe Forward: Women for Change advances women's rights in Mongolia A. MENARNDT *Ms.* v27 no2 p15 Summ 2017
  WOMEN'S WORK A. L. REVENGA and A. M. M. BOUDET color graph *Scientific American* v317 no3 p72 S 2017

Social conflict
    See also
      Conflict management
      Culture conflict
      Ethnic conflict
      Generation gap
  After weeks of terrorism and tragedy, divisions emerge in Britain D. Stewart color *America* v217 no2 p15 Jl 24 2017
  The dual components of mental health—Response J. Cilliers, O. Dube et al bibl color *Science* v354 no6314 p840 N 18 2016

Social conflict—United States
  Divided We Stand L. Lalami il *Nation* v303 no22 p10 N 28 2016

Social contract
  From Boom to Bust: Hardship, Mobilization & Russia's Social Contract S. A. Greene chart graph *Daedalus* v146 no2 p113 Spr 2017
  Harmonizing Sentiments R. R. Reilly *Claremont Review of Books* v17 no3 p47 Summ 2017
  Initiating a New Social Contract G. E. MARSH *USA Today Magazine* v145 no2860 p22 Ja 2017

Social Darwinism
  The National Interest: Jonathan Chait: Deluded Social Darwinist Fred Trump taught his son that the rich are better people. Who in the GOP disagrees? img *New York* v50 no13 p13 Je 26 2017

Social desirability
  Get more out of life M. RABBITT color *Redbook* p100 N 2017

Social development
  The '60s C. R. Kesler *Claremont Review of Books* v17 no3 p31 Summ 2017
  CLOSE ENCOUNTERS C. Siebert and H. Bateman color *New York Times Magazine* p48 My 21 2017
  THE OLD NEW LEFT AND THE NEW NEW LEFT C. R. Kesler *Claremont Review of Books* v17 no3 p31 Summ 2017
  What China's 13th Five-Year Plan Means for Business M. Reeves and D. He *Harvard Business Review Digital Articles* p2 D 7 2015

Social enterprises
  Air pollution, in real time color *Science* v354 no6315 p949 N 25 2016
  All of Africa Will Be Bright S. Butler *Sierra* v101 no5 p24 S/O 2016
  Saving the planet starts here color *Redbook* p100 Je 2017

Social entrepreneurship
  3 Ways Social Entrepreneurs Can Solve Their Talent Problem R. Doherty and A. Pulido *Harvard Business Review Digital Articles* p2 Je 29 2016
  Bringing an Entrepreneurial Mindset to the World's Failing Systems C. Love and R. Sinha *Harvard Business Review Digital Articles* p2 F 2 2015
  How Social Entrepreneurs Make Change Happen R. L. Martin and S. R. Osberg *Harvard Business Review Digital Articles* p2 O 14 2015
  The Traits of Socially Innovative Companies G. F. Davis and C. White *Harvard Business Review Digital Articles* p2 Ap 17 2015
  Why Social Ventures Need Systems Thinking V. Kirsch, J. Bildner et al *Harvard Business Review Digital Articles* p2 Jl 25 2016

Social factors
  SUSTAINING OUR CITIES K. Nowakowski graph *National Geographic* v231 no5 p10 My 2017

Social finance
    See also
      Ethical investments

Spend on Values to Feel Good J. Chatzky color *AARP: The Magazine* v60 no4A p24 Je/Jl 2017

Social groups
    See also
      Coalitions
      Communities
      Dominance (Psychology)
      Elite (Social sciences)
      LGBT organizations
      Polarization (Social sciences)
      Secret societies
      Social networks
      Social psychology
      Teams
      Teams in the workplace
  Network science on belief system dynamics under logic constraints N. E. Friedkin, A. V. Proskurnikov et al bibl diag graph *Science* v354 no6310 p321 O 21 2016
  Why It's Hard to Measure Improved Population Health S. Galea *Harvard Business Review Digital Articles* p2 S 16 2015

Social hierarchies—History
  The Dark Origins of Dog Breeding O. B. Waxman *Time* v189 no7/8 p27 F 27 2017

Social history
    See also
      Social change
      Social movements
      Social problems
      Urbanization
  Populist goes the world S. GILMORE color *Maclean's* v130 no3 p25 Ap 2017

Social impact
  Mitchell-Innes & Nash R. Aima color *Art in America* v105 no1 p83 Ja 2017

Social influence
    See also
      Attitude change (Psychology)
      Imitation
      Peer pressure
      Propaganda
      Social bonds
  20 ESSENTIAL FIT-FLUENCERS B. COURT bw color *Men's Health* v32 no9 p108 N 2017
  Sharing the limelight P. TREBLE color *Maclean's* v129 no40 p48 O 10 2016
  Who has the most influential moral voice in the United States? graph *America* v216 no10 p6 My 1 2017
  Winning Isn't Everything G. Younge *Nation* v305 no8 p10 O 9 2017

Social influence—Computer network resources
  Insta-fluencer M. Chafkin color *Bloomberg Businessweek* no4502 p66 D 5 2016

Social injustice
  Fighting the Bosses D. MOBERG color *In These Times* v40 no11 p24 N 2016
  Her Louisiana Love A. R. HARRISON bw *New Orleans Magazine* v52 no1 p28 S 2017
  Our Bail-Bond System Is Predatory and Destroys Families S. Carter color *Time* v190 no2/3 p28 Jl 10-17 2017

Social innovation
  Look to Government—Yes, Government—for New Social Innovations C. Bason and P. Colligan *Harvard Business Review Digital Articles* p2 N 20 2014

Social institutions
    See also
      Families
  The Road to Liberty W. Kristol *Weekly Standard* v22 no17 p7 Ja 2 2017

Social integration
  Onboarding Isn't Enough M. BYFORD, M. D. WATKINS et al color diag graph il img *Harvard Business Review* v95 no3 p78 My/Je 2017
  Parks for Inclusion Launches During Annual Conference M. Acquino *Parks & Recreation* v52 no10 p48 O 2017

Social integration—History—21st century
  Feminism for All K. Pollitt bw diag *Nation* v304 no8 p6 Mr 13

2017

Social intelligence

Great Teams Need Social Intelligence, Equal Participation, and More Women C. R. Sunstein and R. Hastie *Harvard Business Review Digital Articles* p2 D 16 2014

What to Do When Your Boss Is Socially Awkward R. Knight *Harvard Business Review Digital Articles* p2 D 7 2016

Social intelligence—Research

The Brainy Big Cats J. G. Goldman color *Scientific American* v315 no6 p18 D 2016

Social interaction

See also

Gift giving

Personality & situation

Visiting (Social interaction)

A dedicated network for social interaction processing in the primate brain J. Sliwa and W. A. Freiwald color diag *Science* v356 no6339 p745 My 19 2017

Designing Parks for Health J. Lombard *Parks & Recreation* v51 no10 p77 O 2016

Eliminating the Human D. Byrne il *MIT Technology Review* v120 no5 p8 S/O 2017

A Friend's Support Can Make Women Better Entrepreneurs E. Field, S. Jayachandran et al *Harvard Business Review Digital Articles* p2 Je 19 2015

It's OK If Going to a Conference Doesn't Feel Like Real Work K. Dillon *Harvard Business Review Digital Articles* p2 O 7 2015

REALLY I'M SORRY cartoon *Seventeen* v76 no2 p96 Mr 2017

Save the DATE! bw color *Seventeen* v76 no2 p14 Mr 2017

Stand-Up Meetings Don't Work for Everybody B. Frisch *Harvard Business Review Digital Articles* p2 My 27 2016

Start with a cup of coffee M. J. Rose color *U.S. Catholic* v81 no11 p25 N 2016

What I Know for Sure color *O, The Oprah Magazine* p182 D 2016

Social interaction research

Technology to the Rescue? A. AUMEN *USA Today Magazine* v146 no2868 p34 S 2017

Social interaction—History

Goodbye to Westbrook Acres: AS A WRITER WALKS AND MUSES, THE WORLD'S SORROWS INTRUDE UPON THE PEACEFUL STREETS HE WILL BE LEAVING A. HUDGINS *American Scholar* v86 no3 p80 Summ 2017

Social interaction—Psychological aspects

THE EMOTIONAL WAKE A. Calhoun color *Women's Health* v14 no7 p122 S 2017

Social isolation

See also

Loneliness

ARTIFICIAL INTELLIGENCE, FOR REAL: YOU'VE BEEN TOLD IT WILL TRANSFORM EVERYTHING. YOU'VE BEEN TOLD YOU NEED TO INVEST IN IT. BUT YOU HAVEN'T BEEN TOLD HOW. START HERE E. BRYNJOLFSSON and A. MCAFEE *Harvard Business Review Digital Articles* p1 Jl 1 2017

THE POWER OF ONE A. Davies color *Women's Health* v14 no5 p101 Je 2017

The Social Muscle J. T. Cacioppo and S. Cacioppo *Harvard Business Review Digital Articles* p2 O 2 2017

Social justice

See also

Anti-racism

Free Speech and Its Enemies S. KARETZKY, R. H. REEB JR. et al *Commentary* v144 no3 p4 O 2017

Joining Hands: Race, Social Justice, and Equal Opportunity in Your Classroom J. L. DAVIS *Education Digest* v82 no4 p42 D 2016

PDK Connection color *Phi Delta Kappan* v99 no2 p79 O 2017

PROMOTING EMPATHY C. Patrice Clark *Literacy Today (2411-7862)* v34 no3 p2 N/D 2016

SOCIAL JUSTICE IN A DIGITAL AGE [Cover story] M. Hernandez color *Literacy Today (2411-7862)* v34 no3 p18 N/D 2016

Social justice conferences

"Teaching" Social Justice E. PEPPERS *USA Today Magazine* v145 no2864 p70 My 2017

Social justice—International cooperation

THE ACTIVIST SOUL J. Medefind color *Christianity Today* v61 no6 p70 Jl/Ag 2017

Social justice—Psychological aspects

The Long Road to "Politically Correct" J. MCWHORTER *Psychology Today* v49 no6 p48 N/D 2016

Social justice—Study & teaching

Teaching Social Justice at Islamic Schools [Cover story] A. YILDIZ-ODEH and S. AZMAT *Islamic Horizons* v46 no2 p30 Mr/Ap 2017

Social justice—United States

Counter Offensive: The American far right has become remarkably adept at commandeering ideas from its enemies. Now it's pulling off its trickiest switch yet: billing itself as the new 'alternative' culture J. Herrman *New York Times Magazine* p11 Jl 2 2017

Social learning

Abuse hinders children's social learning B. BOWER *Science News* v191 no5 p10 Mr 18 2017

Madam Secretary, help us improve social-emotional learning M. J. Elias, S. J. Nayman et al color *Phi Delta Kappan* v98 no8 p64 My 2017

Social marginality

GOING TO THE MARGINS K. Clarke color *America* v216 no13 p32 Je 12 2017

SNAP JUDGMENTS color *O, The Oprah Magazine* p22 Je 2017

Social marketing

Building Better Cause-Marketing Relationships T. L. Kuntz and R. B. Dieser *Parks & Recreation* v52 no5 p60 My 2017

The Elements of an Effective Cause Marketing Campaign J. Panepinto *Harvard Business Review Digital Articles* p2 F 19 2016

Social media

See also

Blogs

False news (Social media)

Online social networks

Podcasts

Social media in business

The 20 People You Hate on Social Media bw color *GQ: Gentlemen's Quarterly* v97 no3 p92 Mr 2017

2 + 2 Can Equal 5 D. Mills color *Commonweal* v144 no3 p8 F 10 2017

5 small steps to better health color *Redbook* p96 D 2016

The 7 Attributes of CEOs Who Get Social Media T. Coiné and M. Babbitt *Harvard Business Review Digital Articles* p2 D 3 2014

#Always Trump J. HEER color *New Republic* v248 no10 p28 O 2017

AND THIS WAS BEFORE INSTAGRAM J. DUBOFF color *Vanity Fair* v59 no10 p197 O 2017

Antitrust Facebook M. L. SIFRY *Nation* v305 no11 p4 O 30 2017

Are Emojis Making Us Lazy? *Scholastic Choices* v32 no6 p2 Mr 2017

Are We Too Wired? *New York Times Upfront* v149 no12 p22 Ap 24 2017

ASK THE EXPERTS L. Johnson, S. Sellitto et al color *Runner's World* v51 no11 p42 D 2016

ATLANTA MAGAZINE DIGITAL *Atlanta* v56 no9 p8 Ja 2017

Attention Deficit C. Chocano *New York Times Magazine* p11 O 1 2017

Beast of Burden S. E. SHEPARD *Cincinnati Magazine* v50 no2 p46 N 2016

The Benefits of Giving Away What Your Company Knows C. V. Harquail *Harvard Business Review Digital Articles* p2 O 14 2014

Caisson Communism color *Weekly Standard* v23 no6 p4 O 16 2017

Cartoons *New York Times Upfront* v149 no12 p24 Ap 24 2017

CELEBRITIES AREN'T REQUIRED TO BE ACTIVISTS B. VIERA color *Ebony* v72 no11 p26 S 2017

Change Management Meets Social Media S. Clayton *Harvard Business Review Digital Articles* p2 N 10 2015

CRITTER CHAT A. SHAW color *National Geographic Kids* no470 p31 My 2017

Critter Chat A. SHAW color *National Geographic Kids* no473 p37 S 2017

CRITTER CHAT A. SHAW *National Geographic Kids* no467 p29 F 2017

The Danger of Governing on Social Media N. Gibbs color *Time* v189 no19 p6 My 22 2017

Date with DIANE D. V. Furstenberg color *InStyle* v24 no9 p202 S 2017

Does Engaging with Customers on Facebook Lead to Better Product Ideas? I. Bertschek and R. Kesler *Harvard Business Review Digital Articles* p2 O 12 2017

Emilia Clarke K. B. Brown color *InStyle* v24 no9 p349 S 2017

Family Matters L. Lavelle color *Working Mother* v40 no4 p96 O/N 2017

Fix Your Social Media Strategy by Taking It Back to Basics K. A. Quesenberry *Harvard Business Review Digital Articles* p2 Jl 25 2016

The Great Unplugging H. WILHELM color *National Review* v69 no11 p22 Je 12 2017

Hashtags A. Hoffman color *Time* v188 no25-26 p28 D 19 2016 Double Issue

Hashtags, memes and viral hits P. Treble cartoon color *Maclean's* v129 no48/49 p68 D 5 2016

Hate.Net J. MARTIN *America* v215 no13 p14 O 31 2016

HAVEN IN A HASHTAG D. BLASBERG color *Vanity Fair* v58 no11 p174 N 2016

Hidden AD-gendas? C. STOFFERS *New York Times Upfront* v149 no11 p14 Ap 3 2017

How Academics and Researchers Can Get More Out of Social Media L. Duque *Harvard Business Review Digital Articles* p2 Je 8 2016

How algorithms can analyze the mood of the masses M. Hutson *Science* v357 no6346 p23 Jl 7 2017

How B2B Marketers Can Get Started with Social Media L. Minsky and K. A. Quesenberry *Harvard Business Review Digital Articles* p2 D 24 2015

How I Survived The Election A. Shields color *Nation* v33 no21 p10 N 21 2016

How should you deal with social media's constantly increasing demands? Be more like Beyoncé J. Wortham *New York Times Magazine* p20 O 2 2016

How to Separate the Personal and Professional on Social Media A. Ollier-Malaterre and N. Rothbard *Harvard Business Review Digital Articles* p2 Mr 26 2015

If You Build It, They Will Come M. BERG bw *Forbes* v199 no7 p102 Je 29 2017

If You Want a Pop of Color E. Velluto color *Glamour* v115 no9 p52 S 2017

I'm With Him S. GREEN *Washingtonian Magazine* v52 no4 p102 Ja 2017

INSIDE THE KEN PAGAN WITCHHUNT A. LEE color *Maclean's* v129 no42 p11 O 24 2016

Is This How You Use the Poo Emoji? K. SINTUMUANG color *Esquire* v166 no4 p30 N 2016

Karaoke at Home J. Zhang *New York Times Magazine* p24 Jl 9 2017

KEEPING QUIET color *Seventeen* v75 no11 p70 N 2016

Keeping Up With the Jones C. J. Doane color *Sail* v48 no9 p96 S 2017

Lifestyles of the Rich and Not-Quite Internet Famous M. Chafkin color *Bloomberg Businessweek* no4524 p63 My 29 2017

The List color *Men's Health* v31 no10 p130 D 2016

Meet the New Money Experts L. B. West-Rosenthal color *Glamour* v115 no9 p134 S 2017

mom wins & fails color *Working Mother* v40 no3 p46 Ag/S 2017

The More People We Connect with on LinkedIn, the Less Valuable It Becomes A. Samuel *Harvard Business Review Digital Articles* p2 My 5 2016

MUSCLE IN THE AGE OF INSTAGRAM D. KUNITZ color *Men's Health* v32 no9 p90 N 2017

MY PAL WON'T TEXT ME BECAUSE I DON'T USE SIGNAL. BUT HE'LL SAY ANYTHING ON SOCIAL MEDIA. HE'S BEING ANNOYING, RIGHT? J. MOOALLEM cartoon *Wired* v25 no5 p30 My 2017

NEW ONLINE *American Forests* v123 no1 p12 Wint/Spr 2017

New Ways to Become Happier—and Healthier M. Heid, A. MacMillan et al color *Time* v190 no13 p30 O 2 2017

THE NEW WAY TO TRAVEL color *Wired* v24 no12 p81 D 2016

NO FILTER A. B. WALTERS *Cincinnati Magazine* p24 Je 2017

No-Filter Fams *Parents* v91 no10 p15 O 2016

Online platforms annexed much of our public sphere, playacting as little democracies—until extremists made them reveal their true nature J. Herrman *New York Times Magazine* p18 Ag 27 2017

OUR FIRST COMMUNITY R. CLARK cartoon *Christianity Today* p23 Mr 2017

OUR SOCIAL MEDIA MISSION S. Goldberg color *National Geographic* v231 no4 p4 Ap 2017

Parents Need to Be Clued in on Teens *USA Today Magazine* v145 no2863 p11 Ap 2017

PARIS IN APRIL D. BLASBERG color *Vanity Fair* v59 no6 p90 My 2017

'Perseverance Porn' Bolsters System by Celebrating Survivors of Its Cruelties A. Johnson *Extra!* v30 no7 p3 S 2017

POLARIZED R. M. HOGARTH and E. SOYER *USA Today Magazine* v145 no2860 p44 Ja 2017

Pretty Little Likes color *InStyle* v24 no6 p60 Je 2017

Putting the Right Information on Twitter in a Crisis S. G. Carmichael *Harvard Business Review Digital Articles* p2 N 20 2015

real style color *InStyle* v24 no11 p40 N 2017

Room for Debate M. Rubino *Indianapolis Monthly* v40 no5 p8 Ja 2017

RULES OF ENGAGEMENT L. BAYER *O, The Oprah Magazine* p100 Ap 2017

Scientists need social media influencers M. Galetti and R. Costa-Pereira *Science* v357 no6354 p880 S 1 2017

Select All: Maureen O'Connor: Social Media Ruined Social Climbing Popularity didn't used to be quantifiable img *New York* v50 no9 p20 My 1 2017

The Skin We're In F. Valdesolo color *Glamour* v115 no11 p95 N 2017

Social Animals C. O'CONNOR color *Forbes* v199 no4 p26 Ap 25 2017

THE SOCIAL ISSUE color *Men's Health* v32 no9 p89 N 2017

Social Media color *Architectural Digest* v73 no11 p50 N 2016

Social media: More scientists needed S. Mojarad *Science* v357 no6358 p1362 S 29 2017

Social Networking for Kids *USA Today Magazine* v145 no2860 p34 Ja 2017

SOCIAL SET S. ORR *Better Homes & Gardens* v95 no9 p10 S 2017

Standing Out from the Pack A. DANIEL color *Publishers Weekly* v263 no47 p60 N 21 2016

street style: FITNESS EDITION color *Women's Health* v14 no8 p16 O 2017

Super Fine A. Syrett color *InStyle* v24 no10 p236 O 2017

TECH COMPANIES NEED WOMEN V. Zarya color *Fortune* v174 no6 p14 N 1 2016

To Get More Out of Social Media, Think Like an Anthropologist S. Fournier, J. Quelch et al *Harvard Business Review Digital Articles* p2 Ag 17 2016

TREASURE CHEST J. Cermele color *Field & Stream* v122 no1 p24 My 2017

TWEETING TERROR A. NICODEMO *USA Today Magazine* v145 no2860 p46 Ja 2017

Tweet Your Way to Better Service D. Bortz chart *Money* v46 no2 p32 Mr 2017

Using Social Media to Build Professional Skills A. Samuel *Harvard Business Review Digital Articles* p2 Ag 4 2016

WHAT IS IT ASKING FOR? TO BE SOMETHING E. Zerofsky *New York Times Magazine* p50 Je 11 2017

When sexual assault goes viral J. Valente *America* v216 no10 p16 My 1 2017

Where's My Story? C. GRISE *Scholastic Choices* v32 no4 p22 Ja 2017

Why Startups Shouldn't Chase Media Buzz A. Zacharakis and A. Jno-Charles color *Harvard Business Review Digital Articles* p2 Je 5 2017

Why You Need Your Feed color *Seventeen* v76 no3 p71 My 2017

You Don't Have to Go to a Conference to Enjoy It S. Kaplan *Harvard Business Review Digital Articles* p2 O 6 2015

Your Biggest Social Media Fans Might Not Be Your Best Customers A. Samuel *Harvard Business Review Digital Articles* p2 D 24 2014

Social media & politics

Bot-hunters eye mischief in German election K. Kupferschmidt

See also
  Anthropologists
  Economists
Crossing borders along an endless frontier G. Scellato, C. Franzoni et al color *Science* v356 no6339 p694 My 19 2017
Is Nationhood Obsolete? W. Voegeli *Claremont Review of Books* v17 no3 p9 Summ 2017

Social security
  See also
    Disability insurance
  Estimate Your Social Security Benefit K. LANKFORD *Kiplinger's Personal Finance* v71 no2 p50 F 2017
  SOCIAL SECURITY: The Real Crisis K. McCORMALLY cartoon graph *Kiplinger's Personal Finance* v71 no6 p26 Je 2017

Social security beneficiaries
  A Social Security Perk for Some Older Parents L. Asinof diag *Money* v46 no5 p29 Je 2017

Social security records
  When You Crash a Rental Car K. LANKFORD *Kiplinger's Personal Finance* v71 no7 p43 Jl 2017

Social security reform
  The High Middle Ground on Social Security F. Luntz color *Time* v188 no16/17 p55 O 24 2017

Social security—Finance—Law & legislation
  Spring budget was a damp squib *People Management* p6 Ap 2017

Social security—Government policy
  Arise, Ye Boomers of the Nation S. J. DOUGLAS *In These Times* v41 no2 p16 F 2017

Social security—Law & legislation—United States
  Get Ready for the New Math K. Damato color diag *Money* v46 no1 p37 Ja/F 2017

Social security—United States
  An analysis of private long-term disability insurance access, cost, and trends P. Anand and D. Wittenburg bibl chart color *Monthly Labor Review* p1 Mr 2017
  The Disabled American Worker B. Greeley graph map *Bloomberg Businessweek* no4504 p24 D 19 2016
  The Myth of the Virtuous Poor D. FRENCH *National Review* v69 no2 p30 F 6 2017
  The Next President's Financial Imperative: Fixing Social Security P. Wang color *Time* v188 no20 p20 N 14 2016
  Social Security Cuts Target Trump Voters J. Green color map *Bloomberg Businessweek* no4525 p27 Je 5 2017

Social security—United States—Government policy
  Let's Strengthen Social Security R. Love color *AARP: The Magazine* v59 no5A p2 Ag/S 2016

Social segmentation
  COMIX NATION J. Sorensen *Nation* v305 no1 p8 Jl 3 2017

Social services
  See also
    Charities
    Family planning services
    Service learning
    Social advocacy
  Back to the Future: Financial Capability in Social Work Practice M. S. Sherraden *Bridges (Federal Reserve Bank of St. Louis)* p10 Spr 2017
  MAKING GOOD: HUMANIST PHILANTHROPY & THE DUTY TO GIVE M. TRAFAS *Humanist* v77 no5 p12 S/O 2017
  Out of the Margins E. Parker *History Today* v66 no11 p25 N 2016
  Proactive Intervention T. Barton diag graph *Alternatives Journal (AJ) - Canada's Environmental Voice* v42 no3 p40 2016
  RUNNING ON HOPE B. AUSTEN color *New Republic* v248 no10 p18 O 2017
  Walk with Me K. Storring color *Alternatives Journal (AJ) - Canada's Environmental Voice* v42 no3 p26 2016

Social services—Canada
  Is Canadian Philanthropy Ready for the Future? A. Chunilall color *Walrus* v14 no5 p36 Je 2017

Social services—Finance
  Budget Fight Bruises the Needy J. VALENTE *America* v215 no10 p12 O 10 2016

Social services—United States
  Workforce growth in community-based care: meeting the needs of an aging population K. Sullivan *Monthly Labor Review* p1 D 2016

Social skills
  I COULD BE WORSE: IN ADMITTING OUR FAULTS, WE STILL FIND WAYS TO CAST OURSELVES IN A POSITIVE LIGHT M. HUSTON *Psychology Today* v50 no4 p19 Ag 2017
  SOBER SATURDAY NIGHTS *Health* v31 no1 p14 Ja 2017
  You're More Resilient Than You Give Yourself Credit For A. Molinsky bw *Harvard Business Review Digital Articles* p2 Ja 25 2017

Social skills education
  Humanlike helpers teach social skills B. Bower color *Science News* v192 no6 p19 O 14 2017

Social status
  See also
    Social classes
  "CRAZY BUSY": THE NEW STATUS SYMBOL *Harvard Business Review* v95 no2 p28 Mr/Ap 2017
  Money Talks L. LAPIN *USA Today Magazine* v145 no2862 p77 Mr 2017
  Research: Why Americans Are So Impressed by Busyness S. Bellezza, N. Paharia et al *Harvard Business Review Digital Articles* p2 D 15 2016
  Social status alters immune regulation and response to infection in macaques N. Snyder-Mackler, J. Sanz et al bibl graph *Science* v354 no6315 p1041 N 25 2016
  Social status alters immune system R. EHRENBERG color *Science News* v190 no13 p7 D 24 2016

Social structure
  Networking was key to human success B. BOWER color *Science News* v192 no7 p7 O 28 2017

Social surveys
  See also
    Demographic surveys
    Public opinion polls
  and the survey says *U.S. Catholic* v82 no3 p23 Mr 2017
  What Millennials Want from Work, Charted Across the World H. Bresman *Harvard Business Review Digital Articles* p2 F 23 2015

Social sustainability
  THE HUNGRY TIDE J. N. LOMAX *Texas Monthly* v45 no5 p80 My 2017

Social systems
  SOUTHERN HARM W. Faulkner diag *Harper's Magazine* v335 no2005 p39 Je 2017

Social theory
  See also
    Normalization (Sociology)
  In Praise of Thomas Sowell M. Helprin *Claremont Review of Books* v17 no3 p90 Summ 2017
  PATRICK J. MCGINNIS WEIGHS THE RISKS *Lapham's Quarterly* v10 no3 p78 Summ 2017

Social unrest
  The Burning Heart of Africa P. Gwin color map *National Geographic* v231 no5 p56 My 2017
  Can Pope Francis help Venezuela step back from the edge? T. Padgett color *America* v217 no3 p15 Ag 7 2017
  An Elegy for Venezuela's Revolution M. GONZALEZ *In These Times* v41 no7 p15 Jl 2017

Social workers
  See also
    Women social workers
  Ahmad Kathrada 1929 - 2017 M. Haron *Islamic Horizons* v46 no4 p60 Jl/Ag 2017
  Corporate America Ready for Social Workers *USA Today Magazine* v145 no2863 p11 Ap 2017

Social change—United States—Charts, diagrams, etc.
  The Changing United States img *New York Times Upfront* v149 no5 p8 N 21 2016

Socialism
  See also
    Democratic socialism
    Technocracy
  FREDERICK DOUGLASS HATED SOCIALISM D. ROOT bw *Reason* v48 no11 p8 Ap 2017
  Socialism Is Back I. WELLS color *Walrus* v14 no7 p14 S 2017

Socialism—United States
  Countering Capitalism J. SCHWARTZ bw cartoon *In These Times*

v40 no11 p44 N 2016

Socialism's Trump Bump K. ARONOFF *In These Times* v41 no2 p10 F 2017

THREE BIG IDEAS: TWO BAD, ONE GOOD D. N. MCCLOS-KEY cartoon *Reason* v48 no9 p8 F 2017

Socialists

SIBLING RIVALRY J. HEER bw color il *New Republic* v248 no11 p26 N 2017

Socialists—United States—Biography

Before Bernie S. Richardson *American History* v52 no1 p34 Ap 2017

Socialization

See also

Social skills

Research: Millennials Think About Work Too Much R. Zilca *Harvard Business Review Digital Articles* p2 Jl 15 2016

Social network B. Haile color *U.S. Catholic* v82 no8 p10 Ag 2017

SWING TIME L. MCCAFFREY *Psychology Today* v50 no4 p20 Ag 2017

Social media in business—Charts, diagrams, etc.

ASK A FLOWCHART R. CAPPS diag *Wired* v25 no6 p96 Je 2017

Societies

See also

Book clubs (Bookselling)

Music—Societies, etc.

Women—Societies & clubs

Retreating Inside the Bubble *Commentary* v143 no4 p22 Ap 2017

Society (Periodical)

Social Science and the Public Interest *Society* v54 no1 p1 F 2017

Society for Economic Botany (U.S.)

Calendar of meetings *BioScience* v67 no5 p480 My 2017

Society for Integrative & Comparative Biology—Congresses

Calendar of meetings *BioScience* v67 no1 p95 Ja 2017

Society for the Prevention of Cruelty to Animals (Organization)

ANA ZORRILLA F. Dawson color *New Orleans Magazine* v51 no1 p30 N 2016

Society of Vertebrate Paleontology (Organization)—Congresses

Calendar of meetings *BioScience* v66 no10 p910 O 1 2016

Sociobiology

Unfamiliar Terms R. Brandshaft *Skeptical Inquirer* v41 no3 p64 My/Je 2017

Sociocultural factors

UNHOLY DREAD *Lapham's Quarterly* v10 no3 p116 Summ 2017

Socioeconomic factors

Money Talks L. LAPIN *USA Today Magazine* v145 no2862 p77 Mr 2017

Socioeconomics

See also

Families—Economic aspects

Portrait of the Author as a Historian A. Lee *History Today* v66 no11 p54 N 2016

Research: The Rise of Superstar Firms Has Been Better for Investors than for Employees J. Van Reenen and C. Patterson *Harvard Business Review Digital Articles* p1 My 11 2017

TOWERS OF POWER D. C. Weinczok *History Today* v66 no11 p34 N 2016

Sociolinguistics

See also

Racism in language

Voice—Social aspects

On Money J. Lanchester *New York Times Magazine* p18 N 6 2016

Sociologists—Interviews

Cresting a gravitational wave A. Cho color *Science* v355 no6332 p1380 Mr 31 2017

Sociologists—United States

Eve Ewing H. NYHART color *Chicago* v66 no6 p82 Je 2017

Sociology

See also

Archaeology & sociology

Communication

Conservatism

Equality

Family systems theory

Human settlements

Individualism

Liberalism

Motion pictures—Social aspects

Organizational sociology

Population

Power (Social sciences)

Science—Social aspects

Secret societies

Social capital (Sociology)

Social conflict

Social contract

Social groups

Social institutions

Social psychology

Socialization

Sociolinguistics

Sports—Sociological aspects

Urban ecology (Sociology)

Work—Sociological aspects

Four-to-the-Floor: The Techno Discourse and Aesthetic Work in Berlin B. Biehl and D. Lehn color *Society* v53 no6 p608 D 2016

Sociology of emotions

Social Emotional Learning in Elementary School: Preparation for Success L. Dusenbury and R. P. Weissberg *Education Digest* v83 no1 p36 S 2017

Sociology of work

See also

Coworker relationships

Calling Dr. Chilton: GETTING TO THE BOTTOM OF THE BAFFLING BACKSTORY OF LUBBOCK'S LEGENDARY LEMONY LIBATION-ONE REFRESHING SIP AT A TIME D. COURTNEY *Texas Monthly* v45 no7 p168 Jl 2017

Having Work Friends Can Be Tricky, but It's Worth It E. Seppala and M. King *Harvard Business Review Digital Articles* p2 Ag 8 2017

How to Work with a Bad Listener R. Knight *Harvard Business Review Digital Articles* p2 2017

The truth about competition *Redbook* p152 O 2017

What Happens When Work Becomes a Nonstop Chat Room M. FISCHER *New York* v50 no10 p40 My 15 2017

Sociology teachers—Interviews

Bad Education R. M. COHEN color *New Republic* v248 no1/2 p11 Ja/F 2017

Sociology—United States

Make today great again P. W. Marty *Christian Century* v133 no22 p3 O 26 2016

Sociometry

Select All: Maureen O'Connor: Social Media Ruined Social Climbing Popularity didn't used to be quantifiable img *New York* v50 no9 p20 My 1 2017

Sociotechnical systems

Sociotechnical transitions for deep decarbonization F. W. Geels, B. K. Sovacool et al color diag *Science* v357 no6357 p1242 S 22 2017

Sock, Birame

Sock it to 'Em! C. V. Clarke color *Black Enterprise* v47 no2 p30 S 2016

Sock manufacturing

Skeptical Speculators Swoon for Socks S. McBride color *Bloomberg Businessweek* no4541 p21 O 9 2017

Sockeye salmon

From the Wild: You don't need much more than butter to pan-roast Alaskan king salmon. But a little jalapeño is nice S. Sifton *New York Times Magazine* p26 Jl 9 2017

Socks

DOG EATS SOCKS K. Jazynka *National Geographic Kids* no466 p13 D 2016/Ja 2017

"MY PACKING ADVICE? ROLL EVERYTHING AND BRING A DRY SHAMPOO" A. WHITTLE color *Conde Nast Traveler* v52 no4 p26 Ap 2017

SLIP ON A PAIR OF WHITE SOCKS S. Kennedy color *Bloomberg Businessweek* no4518 p74 Ap 10 2017

The Style Guy M. Anthony Green color *GQ: Gentlemen's Quarterly* v97 no10 p70 O 2017

THE WHITE STUFF J. Roth bw color *Esquire* p39 My 2017

Socks—Evaluation

ANDY'S Candy E. BROWN *Interview* v47 no3 p37 Ap 2017

COLD COMFORT S. L. White color *Field & Stream* v121 no6 p80 N 2016

HOME TOWN HERO B. Blais-Billie color *Glamour* v115 no9 p174 S 2017

Let's Talk About Socks S. YEAGER, J. LINDSEY et al color *Bicycling* v58 no4 p74 My 2017

Oooh... Cozy! L. FLICKINGER, T. ROJEK et al color *Bicycling* v58 no1 p64 Ja/F 2017

SHOP ON SI's GIFT GUIDE color *Sports Illustrated* v125 no18 p48 D 5 2016

SOCK IT TO ME L. BAILEY *Indianapolis Monthly* v40 no3 p34 N 2016

TREKKING POLES/SOCKS P. CHISHOLM color *Backpacker* v45 no3 p126 Ap 2017

WHEN WE GO LOW. ALSO GO HIGH L. SABBAT color *GQ: Gentlemen's Quarterly* v97 no4 p120 Ap 2017

WOWZA! color *Bicycling* v58 no9 p46 O 2017

Socorro Cortina, Niña

A synthetic pathway for the fixation of carbon dioxide in vitro bibl graph *Science* v354 no6314 p900 N 18 2016

Socratic method (Education)

Socratism as a Vocation M. Flynn *Society* v54 no1 p64 F 2017

Soda bread

ASK SUSAN S. WESTMORELAND color *Good Housekeeping* v264 no3 p116 Mr 2017

Soda industry—Taxation

Fizzy Math color *Weekly Standard* v22 no26 p2 Mr 13 2017

Sodano, Paul

UNSOLICITED BETA color *Climbing* no349 p8 N 2016

Soderbergh, Steven, 1963-

Logan Lucky C. Nashawaty color *Entertainment Weekly* no1478 / 1479 p82 Ag 18-25 2017

Striking It Logan Lucky S. Zacharek color *Time* v190 no8 p48 Ag 28 2017

Soderbergh, Steven, 1963- — Interviews

The Man Who Escaped Hollywood Z. BARON color *GQ: Gentlemen's Quarterly* v97 no9 p104 S 2017

Soderblom, Jason M.

Formation of the Orientale lunar multiring basin bibl graph *Science* v354 no6311 p441 O 28 2016

Gravity field of the Orientale basin from the Gravity Recovery and Interior Laboratory Mission bibl graph *Science* v354 no6311 p438 O 28 2016

Soderland, Sukanya

What the Insurance Industry Can Do to Fix Health Care *Harvard Business Review Digital Articles* p2 D 23 2014

SODERSTROM, ROBERT

r.s.v.p bw *Bon Appetit* v61 no12 p20 D 2016 /Jan2017

Sodhi, Virender

Ayurvedic HERB GUIDE V. Tweed color *Amazing Wellness* v9 no2 p38 Spr 2017

Söding, Johannes

Big-data approaches to protein structure prediction color diag graph *Science* v355 no6322 p248 Ja 20 2017

Sodium

Elemental haiku *Science* v357 no6350 p461 Ag 4 2017

Sodium channels

Structure of a eukaryotic voltage-gated sodium channel at near-atomic resolution H. Shen, Q. Zhou et al diag graph *Science* v355 no6328 p924 Mr 3 2017

Sodium compounds

Compound defies helium's inertness E. CONOVER color *Science News* v191 no5 p8 Mr 18 2017

Sodium content of food

GO AHEAD, PUT SALT ON YOUR FOOD R. BAILEY color *Reason* v49 no4 p6 Ag/S 2017

Sodium salts

See also
   Salt

Should I be eating less salt? A. Weil color graph *Prevention* v68 no12 p26 D 2016

Soe, C. M. M.

Extremely efficient internal exciton dissociation through edge states in layered 2D perovskites bibl graph *Science* v355 no6331 p1288 Mr 24 2017

Soe Zeya Tun

Myanmar color *National Geographic* v230 no5 p5 N 2016

Soeiro, Liz Phipps

For the Record color *Time* v190 no15 p6 O 16 2017

Soekadar, Surjo R.

Help, hope, and hype: Ethical dimensions of neuroprosthetics color *Science* v356 no6345 p1338 Je 30 2017

Soetaert, Karine

Reversion of antibiotic resistance in Mycobacterium tuberculosis by spiroisoxazoline SMARt-420 bibl diag *Science* v355 no6330 p1206 Mr 17 2017

Soethoudt, Marjolein

Activity-based protein profiling reveals off-target proteins of the FAAH inhibitor BIA 10-2474 chart color graph *Science* v356 no6342 p1084 Je 9 2017

Sofacy (Group)

THE WORLD'S MOST DANGEROUS HACKER GROUPS R. Hackett *Fortune* v176 no1 p55 Jl 1 2017

Sofas

Do Right with White Z. Gowen color *Southern Living* v52 no1 p24 Ja 2017

Ode to a Couch I. Brannon color *Weekly Standard* v22 no47 p5 Ag 21 2017

SOFAS DECONSTRUCTED D. Schwartz color *Southern Living* v52 no1 p96 Ja 2017

Sofas—Design & construction

Ahead of the Curve H. MARTIN bw color *Architectural Digest* v74 no4 p32 Ap 2017

the DUNDAS SOFA C. GERVAIS *Texas Monthly* v44 no11 p111 N 2016

Sofas—Evaluation

THE $3,000 SOFA CHALLENGE K. O'SHEA-EVANS color *House Beautiful* v159 no2 p38 Mr 2017

Adam's Home STYLE SHEET color *O, The Oprah Magazine* p67 My 2017

Ahead of the Curve H. MARTIN bw color *Architectural Digest* v74 no4 p32 Ap 2017

Eucalyptus color *House Beautiful* v159 no1 p17 F 2017

HIGH or LOW? color *Good Housekeeping* v264 no5 p60 My 2017

LA BREA *Los Angeles Magazine* v62 no6 p70 Je 2017

A SERENE DRAWING ROOM H. BROWN and K. O'SHEA-EVANS color *House Beautiful* v159 no7 p65 S 2017

The Wellness Factor R. C. Orrell *Architectural Record* v205 no7 p69 Jl 2017

WHAT WILL YOU CREATE? color *House Beautiful* v159 no7 p1 S 2017

Sofas—Exhibitions

Window-Shopping Milan J. Zorthian color *Time* v189 no15 p19 Ap 24 2017

Soft drink containers

WITH POYDRAS THE PARROT J. STREET color *New Orleans Magazine* v51 no1 p24 N 2016

Soft drink industry

Should soft-drink makers be held liable for the health risks of sugar? K. KIPLINGER *Kiplinger's Personal Finance* v71 no10 p14 O 2017

Soft drink industry—India

India's War Over Water—and Soft Drinks P. R. Sanjai and A. Chaudhary map *Bloomberg Businessweek* no4515 p15 Mr 20 2017

Soft drinks

See also
   Root beer

THE EXCHANGE M. Wolff color graph *Men's Health* v32 no7 p16 S 2017

Fizzcal Responsibility A. Greenblatt *Governing* v30 no4 p9 Ja 2017

Soft drinks & health

Sugarcoating THE TRUTH: As the battle over soda and obesity heats up, researchers say the sugar and beverage industries paid for dozens of studies that conclude their products don't pose health risks P. SMITH *New York Times Upfront* v149 no13 p10 My 15 2017

Soft drinks—Evaluation

POP REVIVAL E. JACKSON *Atlanta* v56 no7 p83 N 2016

Soft drinks—Health aspects

Should Soda Have a Warning Label? *Scholastic Choices* v32 no7 p2 Ap 2017

Soft drinks—Taxation

THE NEW SODA TAX H. CONICK color *Chicago* v66 no7 p18 Jl 2017

Soft power (Social sciences)

A Unanimous Vote For Soft Power *Bloomberg Businessweek* no4538 p14 S 18 2017

Soft skills

Practice for Tough Situations as You'd Practice a Sport A. Molinsky *Harvard Business Review Digital Articles* p2 F 18 2016

The Soft Skills of Great Digital Organizations A. Samuel *Harvard Business Review Digital Articles* p2 F 5 2016

Two-Thirds of College Grads Struggle to Launch Their Careers J. J. Selingo *Harvard Business Review Digital Articles* p2 My 31 2016

Soft tissue tumors

FINDINGS *Harper's Magazine* v334 no2001 p96 F 2017

Soft X rays

Soft x-ray excitonics A. Moulet, J. B. Bertrand et al bw diag *Science* v357 no6356 p1134 S 15 2017

Softball players

FACES IN THE CROWD T. Keith color *Sports Illustrated* v126 no16 p32 Je 5 2017

Softbank Corp.

SCOREBOARD color *Forbes* v199 no1 p28 Ja 24 2017

SOFTBANK IS HANDING OUT FUNDING. TECH GIANTS DON'T MIND IF THEY DO A. Lashinsky color *Fortune* v176 no3 p19 S 1 2017

Software analytics

The 4 Mistakes Most Managers Make with Analytics A. Lambrecht and C. Tucker *Harvard Business Review Digital Articles* p2 Jl 12 2016

Analytics Training Isn't Enough to Create a Data-Driven Workforce A. Sweetwood *Harvard Business Review Digital Articles* p2 Ag 3 2017

Better Questions to Ask Your Data Scientists M. Li, M. Kassengaliyeva et al *Harvard Business Review Digital Articles* p2 N 15 2016

Clinton's Towering Fiasco C. De Robertis color *Weekly Standard* v22 no32 p2 My 1 2017

Create a Strategy That Anticipates and Learns J. Elton and S. Arkell *Harvard Business Review Digital Articles* p2 O 6 2014

Gamification Can Help People Actually Use Analytics Tools L. Sherer *Harvard Business Review Digital Articles* p2 F 25 2015

Help Reluctant Employees Put Analytic Tools to Work M. C. Mankins and L. Sherer *Harvard Business Review Digital Articles* p2 O 7 2014

Here's the Pitch: Analytics for Managing School Buildings D. T. BROWN *Education Digest* v82 no6 p20 F 2017

How Chief Data Officers Can Get Their Companies to Collect Clean Data G. Berkooz *Harvard Business Review Digital Articles* p2 F 16 2017

How to Integrate Data and Analytics into Every Part of Your Organization C. Carande, P. Lipinski et al *Harvard Business Review Digital Articles* p2 Je 23 2017

If Your Company Isn't Good at Analytics, It's Not Ready for AI N. Harrison and D. O'Neill color *Harvard Business Review Digital Articles* p2 Je 7 2017

Nudged Out T. Newcombe *Governing* v30 no5 p62 F 2017

Predictive Medicine Depends on Analytics J. Elton and A. Ural *Harvard Business Review Digital Articles* p2 O 23 2014

Quantifying the Impact of Marketing Analytics M. Ariker, D. Diaz et al *Harvard Business Review Digital Articles* p2 N 5 2015

The Reason So Many Analytics Efforts Fall Short C. McShea, D. Oakley et al *Harvard Business Review Digital Articles* p2 Ag 29 2016

The Rise of Data-Driven Decision Making Is Real but Uneven K. McElheran and E. Brynjolfsson *Harvard Business Review Digital Articles* p2 F 3 2016

Tesco's Downfall Is a Warning to Data-Driven Retailers M. Schrage *Harvard Business Review Digital Articles* p2 O 28 2014

Software as a service

How Investors React When Companies Announce They're Moving to a SaaS Business Model J. Nurkka, J. Waltl et al color *Harvard Business Review Digital Articles* p2 Ja 12 2017

Software engineers

The Conversation Google Killed W. SALETAN *Weekly Standard* v22 no48 p31 S 4 2017

Kayvon Beykpour J. Crelin color *Current Biography* v78 no2 p12 F 2017

The Killer Wrote Code B. Crair bw color *Bloomberg Businessweek* no4512 p68 F 20 2017

Software maintenance

See also

Software analytics

Mac 911 G. FLEISHMAN color *Macworld - Digital Edition* p135 D 2016

Softwood

Low Key Floors M. Ellen Polson color *Arts & Crafts Homes & the Revival* v12 no5 p34 Wint 2018

Soghoian, Sal

News: Apple to support automation in Sierra R. Loyola color *Macworld - Digital Edition* p16 Ja 2017

Sohai, Mashaal

Negative selection in humans and fruit flies involves synergistic epistasis chart graph *Science* v356 no6337 p539 My 5 2017

Sohee Kim

Beijing Is Mad About Thaad color *Bloomberg Businessweek* no4514 p16 Mr 13 2017

Sohm, Aldo

Magnum Force M. BYRNE color *Esquire* p58 BigBlackBook

SoHo (New York, N.Y.)

Floyd's New Bread Bar A. PLATT img *New York* v49 no21 p76 O 17 2016

Sohr, Gen

SUMMER MAGIC color *House Beautiful* v159 no5 p56 Je 2017

Soifer, H.

Femtosecond electron-phonon lock-in by photoemission and x-ray free-electron laser chart diag *Science* v357 no6346 p71 Jl 7 2017

Soil-binding plants

See also

Cover crops

COVER CROPS CREATE SAVINGS: UTILIZING COVER CROPS CAN BOOST SOIL HEALTH, REDUCE PESTS, AND CYCLE NUTRIENTS D. Goerge *Successful Farming* v115 no6 p41 Ap 2017

Soil erosion

BEAUTY AND THE BEAST: Tame erosion with solutions that work: no-till and cover crops K. Birchmier color *Successful Farming* v115 no7 p30 My 2017

DOWN TO BUSINESS: WE COVER THE BUSINESS, PRODUCTION, AND FUN ASPECTS OF FARMING D. Kurns color *Successful Farming* v115 no7 p4 My 2017

Lessons from the Oroville dam F. Vahedifard, A. AghaKouchak et al bibl *Science* v355 no6330 p1139 Mr 17 2017

NO-TILL OR NEVER-TILL? STORY ON THE EFFECT OF TILLAGE GETS READER REACTIONS D. KURNS *Successful Farming* v115 no11 p4 S 2017

Soil fertility

HOW TO SORT SOIL FERTILITY CLAIMS G. Gullickson *Successful Farming* v114 no10 p14 O 2016

Soil management

See also

Soil productivity

10 SUCCESSFUL FARMERS: DAVE LEGVOLD K. Birchmier *Successful Farming* v115 no8 p26 Je/Jl 2017

An Economic Perspective on Soil Health M. Bowman, S. Wallander et al *Amber Waves: The Economics of Food, Farming, Natural Resources, & Rural America* p18 S 2016

Soil maps

Modern Maps G. Gullickson *Successful Farming* v114 no12 p16 Mid-N 2016

Soil pollution—Prevention—Government policy

Protecting China's soil by law Jinnan Wang, Qing Hu et al bibl *Science* v354 no6312 p562 N 4 2016

Soil productivity

HOW TO SORT SOIL FERTILITY CLAIMS G. Gullickson *Successful Farming* v114 no10 p14 O 2016

Soil quality

Colloidally prepared La-doped $BaSnO_3$ electrodes for efficient, photostable perovskite solar cells S. S. Shin, E. J. Yeom et al graph *Science* v356 no6334 p167 Ap 14 2017

Hot SOLAR Cells J. TEMPLE color *MIT Technology Review* v120 no2 p52 Mr/Ap 2017

Iodide management in formamidinium–lead–halide–based perovskite layers for efficient solar cells W. S. Yang, Park et al bw diag *Science* v356 no6345 p1376 Je 30 2017

POWER UP L. Hamers color diag graph *Science News* v192 no1 p22 Ag 5 2017

Solar cells

Ask Our Experts *Mother Earth News* no279 p77 D/Ja 2017

Charge of the Light Brigade E. STRICKLAND color *Foreign Policy* no222 p24 Ja/F 2017

DIY Solar: Build Your Own System V. Aggarwal *Mother Earth News* no282 p91 Je/Jl 2017

Do-It-Yourself OFF-GRID SOLAR: Explore the components and considerations for creating your own off-grid photovoltaic system J. Burdick and P. Schmidt *Mother Earth News* no282 p16 Je/Jl 2017

Efficient and stable solution-processed planar perovskite solar cells via contact passivation H. Tan, A. Jain et al bibl graph *Science* v355 no6326 p722 F 17 2017

How to Cut the Costs of Going Solar V. Aggarwal *Mother Earth News* no280 p77 F/Mr 2017

How to Install a Solar Panel K. HARRIS color *Boating World* v38 no7 p26 Jl 2017

Incorporation of rubidium cations into perovskite solar cells improves photovoltaic performance M. Saliba, Taisuke Matsui et al bibl graph *Science* v354 no6309 p206 O 14 2016

Is Rooftop Solar Finally Good Enough to Disrupt the Grid? N. Richter *Harvard Business Review Digital Articles* p2 My 21 2015

A Moment of Reckoning for a Soaring Solar Industry J. Worland color *Time* v190 no12 p30 S 25 2017

Perovskite-perovskite tandem photovoltaics with optimized band gaps G. E. Eperon, T. Leijtens et al bibl chart graph *Science* v354 no6314 p861 N 18 2016

Powering up perovskite photoresponse O. M. Bakr and O. F. Mohammed bibl color *Science* v355 no6331 p1260 Mr 24 2017

RAY OF HOPE S. STALL *Indianapolis Monthly* p17 My 2017

Solar cells—Design & construction

Hot SOLAR Cells J. TEMPLE color *MIT Technology Review* v120 no2 p52 Mr/Ap 2017

Solar cells—Export & import trade

A Solar Trade Case Tailor-Made for Trump J. Ryan and J. A. Dlouhy color graph *Bloomberg Businessweek* no4527 p49 Je 19 2017

Solar collectors—Evaluation

Find Your Power *Log Home Living* v33 no9 p18 D 2016

Solar cooking

A Flair for Solar Cooking: And Distrust of the "Hippy" Method K. WRIGHT *Idaho Magazine* v16 no11 p48 Ag 2017

Solar corona

Day of darkness color *Science* v357 no6353 p736 Ag 25 2017

Diamond of Three Rings: A total solar eclipse offers the most spectacular of jewels F. Schaaf *Sky & Telescope* v134 no3 p45 S 2017

WHY IS THE SUN'S CORONA SO HOT? WHY ARE PROMINENCES SO COOL? J. B. Zirker and O. Engvold *Physics Today* v70 no8 p35 Ag 2017

Solar cycle

See also

Maunder minimum (Solar cycle)

Another Maunder Minimum? M. YOUNG *Sky & Telescope* v133 no6 p9 Je 2017

Solar eclipses

See also

Total solar eclipses

1,000 YEARS OF SOLAR ECLIPSES M. Fischetti diag graph map *Scientific American* v317 no2 p62 Ag 2017

19 big eclipse surprises M. E. Bakich color map *Astronomy* v45 no7 p60 Jl 2017

The 2017 Total Solar Eclipse J. Rao *Weatherwise* v70 no2 p12 Mr/Ap 2017

The Agony of 'Old Probabilities' D. BARON bw color *Natural History* v125 no5 p30 My 2017

Cooling Effect of an Eclipse H. Leifert *Natural History* v125 no1 p7 D 2016/Ja 2017

Coronal shadows S. JAMES O'MEARA color *Astronomy* v45 no8 p80 Ag 2017

Dark Skies Over Nebraska A. J. BARTELS cartoon color *Nebraska Life* v21 no4 p80 Jl/Ag 2017

Day of darkness color *Science* v357 no6353 p736 Ag 25 2017

The Deeper Meaning of the Great American Eclipse J. Kluger color map *Time* v190 no7 p19 Ag 21 2017

Diamond of Three Rings: A total solar eclipse offers the most spectacular of jewels F. Schaaf *Sky & Telescope* v134 no3 p45 S 2017

Eclipse chasing B. BERMAN color *Astronomy* v45 no8 p10 Ag 2017

Eclipse Day's Big Unknown P. Tyson color *Sky & Telescope* v134 no2 p4 Ag 2017

Eclipse, Epidemic, Evolution, Ecology *Natural History* v125 no7 p5 Jl/Ag 2017

The Eclipse Megamovie Project H. Hudson and M. Bender bw color *Sky & Telescope* v134 no2 p20 Ag 2017

Eclipse time! P. HARRINGTON color *Astronomy* v45 no8 p78 Ag 2017

FROM OUR READERS A. Rokita, E. Zanders et al color *Sky & Telescope* v134 no5 p6 N 2017

The Great American Eclipse E. Barone color diag map *Time* v190 no2/3 p14 Jl 10-17 2017

THE GREAT AMERICAN ECLIPSE OF 2017 E. STEED cartoon *New Yorker* v93 no27 p65 S 11 2017

THE GREAT SOLAR ECLIPSE of 2017 J. M. Pasachoff color *Scientific American* v317 no2 p54 Ag 2017

HERE COMES THE SUN R. MARR cartoon *Missouri Life* v44 no5 p64 Ag 2017

How to choose the right camera for the eclipse M. E. Bakich color *Astronomy* v45 no4 p50 Ap 2017

How To Shoot a Solar Eclipse chart color *Sky & Telescope* v134 no2 p14 Ag 2017

In the Beginning M. DiChristina color *Scientific American* v317 no2 p4 Ag 2017

Join us for a new solar eclipse trip! D. J. EICHER color *Astronomy* v45 no2 p6 F 2017

Low-Tech Eclipse Viewing: What to do if you're caught without optics on eclipse day J. Oltion color *Sky & Telescope* v134 no2 p66 Ag 2017

Make a Solar Filter J. Oltion *Sky & Telescope* v133 no6 p38 Je 2017

Mind Melt S. SCOLES bw color *Discover* v38 no7 p30 S 2017

Perfect totality B. BERMAN color *Astronomy* v45 no6 p10 Je 2017

Relativistic deflection of background starlight measures the mass of a nearby white dwarf star K. C. Sahu, J. Anderson et al chart color graph *Science* v356 no6342 p1046 Je 9 2017

Shadow Play E. MASTROIANNI color *Discover* v38 no1 p96 Ja/F 2017

Shadow transit double header G. CHAPLE color *Astronomy* v45 no5 p18 My 2017

A short history of ECLIPSES R. Shubinski bw color *Astronomy* v45 no5 p49 My 2017

Show Time M. JOHNSON-GROH color diag *Backpacker* p30 Ag 2017

Sketching totality E. RIX bw color *Astronomy* v45 no9 p66 S 2017

The Solar Eclipse for the Rest of Us A. Macrobert bw color *Sky & Telescope* v134 no2 p48 Ag 2017

Solar eclipse geometry M. E. Bakich color map *Astronomy* v45 no5 p34 My 2017

Solar Eclipse Geometry M. E. BAKICH diag *Discover* v38 no7 p34 S 2017

A step-by-step guide to the Great American Eclipse R. Talcott bw color *Astronomy* v45 no8 p26 Ag 2017

Talking totality B. BERMAN *Astronomy* v45 no1 p9 Ja 2017

TARGETING THE "Tutulemma" T. Tezel *Sky & Telescope* v132 no6 p66 D 2016

Total Eclipse of the Park T. Keith and S. Kwak color map *Sports Illustrated* v127 no5 p24 Ag 14 2017

TOTALLY J. Kersten cartoon *New Yorker* v93 no25 p28 Ag 28 2017

LING bw chart color *Astronomy* v45 no3 p36 Mr 2017

May 2017: Venus dazzles before dawn M. RATCLIFFE and A. LING color *Astronomy* v45 no5 p36 My 2017

Meet the primordial asteroid family F. DeMeo color diag *Science* v357 no6355 p972 S 8 2017

NASA pushes for diversity in planetary science P. Voosen diag *Science* v356 no6337 p475 My 5 2017

Our Rocks, Ourselves D. FOX color *Discover* v38 no5 p60 Je 2017

PATH OF THE PLANETS chart diag graph map *Astronomy* v45 no10 p40 O 2017

PATH OF THE PLANETS chart diag graph map *Astronomy* v45 no4 p40 Ap 2017

Persistence Counts B. Lang *Discover* v38 no10 p6 D 2017

The solar system's violent past [Cover story] N. T. Redd bw color diag *Astronomy* v45 no2 p22 F 2017

STAR DOME chart color *Astronomy* v45 no5 p38 My 2017

The Stone Tree P. Tyson *Sky & Telescope* v134 no4 p4 O 2017

Syzygy L. SCHLEY color *Discover* v38 no5 p20 Je 2017

TRAPPIST-1 and the Seven Exoplanets color *Discover* v38 no5 p17 Je 2017

UNVEILING A GIANT [Cover story] F. Reddy bw chart color diag *Astronomy* v45 no10 p20 O 2017

Voyager's great legacy D. J. EICHER color *Astronomy* v45 no10 p6 O 2017

Written in the Star P. Tyson *Sky & Telescope* v134 no4 p22 O 2017

Your guide to the oceans of our solar system M. Carroll color *Astronomy* v45 no11 p24 N 2017

Solar system—History

Meteorite magnetism in the early solar system *Science* v355 no6325 p591 F 10 2017

Solar system—Origin

See also

Protoplanetary disks

SPACE ODDITY P. FARSON and B. COLE *Scientific American* v315 no3 p5 S 2016

Solar system—Origin—Research

SOLAR SYSTEM SMASHUP L. T. Elkins-Tanton color diag *Scientific American* v315 no6 p42 D 2016

Solar system—Research

Top 10 space stories of 2016 [Cover story] L. Kruesi color *Astronomy* v45 no1 p18 Ja 2017

Solar technology

See also

Artificial photosynthesis

Solar pumps

ENERGIERICH: Sowing Seeds of Solar D. MONTAGUE color *Earth Island Journal* v32 no3 p16 Aut 2017

Solar technology—Equipment & supplies

Sun Blocks R. C. Orrell *Architectural Record* v205 no7 p73 Jl 2017

Solar technology—Government policy

Solar Is Being Held Back by Regulations, Not Technology J. M. Pearce *Harvard Business Review Digital Articles* p2 D 15 2016

Solar telescopes

NEW PRODUCTS color *Astronomy* v45 no7 p69 Jl 2017

Solar Finders: How to point out the obvious J. Oltion *Sky & Telescope* v134 no1 p72 Jl 2017

Solar telescopes—Evaluation

25 HOT ECLIPSE PRODUCTS P. Harrington color *Astronomy* v45 no6 p54 Je 2017

Solar wind

Aurora in a bottle *Physics Today* v69 no10 p88 O 2016

Structure, force balance, and topology of Earth's magnetopause C. T. Russell, R. J. Strangeway et al diag graph *Science* v356 no6341 p960 Je 1 2017

SolarCity Corp.

Tesla Is Betting on Solar, Not Just Batteries G. Battisti and M. Giulietti *Harvard Business Review Digital Articles* p2 Jl 2 2015

The Unstoppable Green Power Revolution H. Wasserman cartoon color *Progressive* v81 no5 p40 Je/Jl 2017

Solar energy—Charts, diagrams, etc.

SOLAR POWER BOOMS diag *Fortune* v175 no8 p36 Je 15 2017

Solari, Katherine

Merging paleobiology with conservation biology to guide the future of terrestrial ecosystems color *Science* v355 no6325 p594

F 10 2017

Solaris Yachts Srl

Solaris 50 C. J. Doane color *Sail* v48 no5 p20 My 2017

Solar system—Charts, diagrams, etc.

History Of MARKS MISSIONS C. M. Carlisle *Sky & Telescope* v134 no5 p16 N 2017

Soldani, Neto—Interviews

A Conversation with Neto Soldani L. Gaston *Arabian Horse World* v56 no12 p104 S 2016

Soldatov, Andrei

WIKILEAKS' ROLE A. Dejean, H. Levintova et al *Mother Jones* v42 no4 p30 Jl/Ag 2017

Solder & soldering

BOOK LIGHT! J. SCHADEWALD color diag *Popular Mechanics* p96 N 2017

Seven tips for better solder connections L. Puckett color diag *Model Railroader* v84 no8 p56 Ag 2017

Soldier, Layli Long

From "Whereas Statements" L. L. Soldier *New York Times Magazine* p21 D 4 2016

Soldiers' letters—History—20th century

Letter from the Front B. Finlay *American History* v52 no1 p51 Ap 2017

Soldiers' monuments

The Monument MEN J. N. LOMAX *Texas Monthly* v45 no8 p31 Ag 2017

Soldiers' monuments—Southern States

In Trump they trust P. WELLS color *Maclean's* v130 no9 p39 O 2017

Notes on an Imagined Plaque to Be Added to the Statue of General Nathan Bedford Forrest N. DIMEO bw *Mother Jones* v42 no6 p62 N/D 2017

Solé, Carme

Evolution of protein phosphorylation across 18 fungal species bibl graph *Science* v354 no6309 p229 O 14 2016

Sole, Elise

ALL MY ORGASMS [Cover story] color *Women's Health* v14 no3 p124 Ap 2017

Soleil O (Film)

First-World Problems M. Nelson bw *Film Comment* v53 no5 p11 S/O 2017

Solem, Callan

ALLOW YOUR HORSE TO 'HEAR' YOU A. Carter color diag *Practical Horseman* v45 no10 p42 O 2017

SOLERA, TEMISTOCLE

Nabucco *Opera News* v81 no7 p54 Ja 2017

Soleri, Paolo, 1919-2013

Last Look D. Kidd *Governing* v30 no4 p64 Ja 2017

Sole-Smith, Virginia

COULD YOU BE ADDICTED—AND NOT KNOW IT? color *Redbook* p88 N 2017

a game changer for ADHD color *Parents* v92 no5 p30 My 2017

get through your child's hospital stay color *Parents* v92 no4 p34 Ap 2017

a lawn that loves you back bw color *Parents* v92 no4 p114 Ap 2017

neck on the line bw color *Women's Health* v14 no8 p144 O 2017

STOP BEATING YOURSELF UP ABOUT FOOD color *Health* v31 no8 p112 O 2017

the truth about selling from home *Parents* v91 no6 p96 Je 2016

Solheim, Anders

Giant undersea craters were blown out by decomposing methane hydrates: Although the craters likely formed about 12 000 years ago, methane is still leaking profusely around and between them M. Wilson *Physics Today* v70 no8 p21 Ag 2017

SOLHEIM, MARK

The Best Bank for You cartoon *Kiplinger's Personal Finance* v71 no7 p26 Jl 2017

Paying It Forward *Kiplinger's Personal Finance* v71 no11 p4 N 2017

Solheim, Nathan

THE GUN THAT WON THE WEST bw cartoon color *American Cowboy* p46 LEGENDS OF TEXAS Special Issue 2017

Solid & Striped LLC

Away You Go! color *Glamour* v115 no7 p38 Jl 2017

Solid hydrogen

Metallic hydrogen created in diamond vise R. F. Service color graph *Science* v355 no6323 p332 Ja 27 2017

Solid state disks

How to know when your SSD could die J. NOREM color diag *PCWorld* v35 no11 p159 N 2016

Solid state disks—Evaluation

OCZ VX500: A featherlight SATA SSD that's ideal for laptop upgrades J. L. JACOBI color graph *PCWorld* v35 no11 p100 N 2016

Toshiba OCZ's TL100: A budget SSD that's not a bargain J. L. JACOBI color graph *PCWorld* p95 D 2016

Solid state physics

Entanglement distillation between solid-state quantum network nodes N. Kalb, A. A. Reiserer et al diag *Science* v356 no6341 p928 Je 1 2017

Solids

See also

Crystals

Supersolids made from exotic matter E. CONOVER *Science News* v190 no12 p8 D 10 2016

Solis, Hilda L., 1957-

L.A. Women LEAD THE WAY N. L. COHEN and J. M. ... PISCOPO *Ms.* v27 no1 p32 Spr 2017

Solis-Rivera, Vivienne

Committing to socially responsible seafood color *Science* v356 no6341 p912 Je 1 2017

Solitary confinement

1,560 DAYS [Cover story] M. Patriquin and N. Macdonald color *Maclean's* v129 no45 p16 N 14 2016

52 months of torture and zero answers S. GILMORE color *Maclean's* v129 no45 p20 N 14 2016

Buried Alive: Stories from Inside Solitary Confinement N. PENN color map *GQ: Gentlemen's Quarterly* v97 no3 p154 Mr 2017

The Social Cost of Solitary Confinement K. Reiter *Time* v188 no18 p21 O 31 2016

Solitary confinement—Psychological aspects

SURVIVING SOLITARY R. AVIV cartoon color *New Yorker* v92 no45 p54 Ja 16 2017

Solitons

Formation of matter-wave soliton trains by modulational instability J. H. V. Nguyen, D. Luo et al diag *Science* v356 no6336 p422 Ap 28 2017

Probing the interaction of solitons color *Science* v356 no6333 p37 Ap 7 2017

Real-time spectral interferometry probes the internal dynamics of femtosecond soliton molecules G. Herink, F. Kurtz et al diag *Science* v356 no6333 p50 Ap 7 2017

Solitude

solo mission k. butcher bw *Bike Magazine* v24 no4 p50 Je 2017

Solitude Square (Film)

Of Stars and Solitude: Two Mexican Documentaries P. J. Smith *Film Quarterly* v71 no1 p73 Fall 2017

Söll, Dieter

A chemical biology route to site-specific authentic protein modifications bibl diag graph *Science* v354 no6312 p623 N 4 2016

Soller, Kurt

BLACK IS THE NEW BLACK color *Bloomberg Businessweek* no4521 p63 My 8 2017

EAT LIKE a GREEK color *Bon Appetit* no8 p84 Ag 2017

Fish Tacos Were Just the Beginning color map *Bon Appetit* v62 no6 p52 Je 2017

FLAVOR EXPLOSION color *Bon Appetit* v62 no6 p88 Je 2017

home & help img *New York* p96 Mr 6 2017

starters color *Bon Appetit* v62 no6 p17 Je 2017

Thanksgiving LESSONS [Cover story] color *Bon Appetit* no11 p82 N 2017

Sollerman, J.

iPTF16geu: A multiply imaged, gravitationally lensed type Ia supernova color diag graph *Science* v356 no6335 p291 Ap 21 2017

Solli, D. R.

Real-time spectral interferometry probes the internal dynamics of femtosecond soliton molecules diag *Science* v356 no6333 p50 Ap 7 2017

SOLLINGER, MARC

A cocreator of horror podcasts finds inspiration in fiction color

Publishers Weekly v263 no46 p60 N 14 2016

Sollosi, Mary

What to Watch color *Entertainment Weekly* no1466 p53 My 19 2017

SOLLY, MEILAN M.

A PLAGUE TAMED: AMALLPOX WAS RECURRING MENACE AROUND THE WORLD--UNTIL A BRTITISH DOCTOR FIGURED OUT HOW TO PITONE VIRUS AGAINST ANOTHER *Smithsonian* v48 no5 p72 S 2017

The Sultry Spy and the Coverup *Smithsonian* v48 no5 p19 S 2017

Solmonson, Lesley Jacobs

Go With the Grain *Sierra* v102 no4 p8 Jl/Ag 2017

That's the Spirit *Sierra* v102 no3 p8 My/Je 2017

Solnit, Rebecca

125 DECLARATIONS OF INTERDEPENDENCE *Sierra* v102 no3 p37 My/Je 2017

EASY CHAIR *Harper's Magazine* v334 no2000 p10 Ja 2017

EASY CHAIR *Harper's Magazine* v334 no2002 p5 Mr 2017

EASY CHAIR *Harper's Magazine* v334 no2004 p4 My 2017

EASY CHAIR: Now and Then *Harper's Magazine* p5 S 2017

EASY CHAIR: Occupied Territory *Harper's Magazine* v335 no2006 p5 Jl 2017

Hope's Edge A. Lappé color *Earth Island Journal* v32 no1 p13 Spr 2017

The Mother of All Questions *Publishers Weekly* v263 no52 p110 D 19 2016

A Woman's March C. SHANE bw color il *New Republic* v248 no6 p61 Je 2017

Solntseva, Yulia

Family Business R. Brody color *New Yorker* v93 no24 p6 Ag 21 2017

Solo (Musical form)

Creating a Convincing Solo Piano Performance R. PIKET and R. Piket bw color *Downbeat* v83 no12 p102 D 2016

Solo, Han (Fictitious character)

THE LONG SOLO FLIGHT OF HARRISON FORD [Cover story] J. MOORE bw color *GQ: Gentlemen's Quarterly* v97 no10 p116 O 2017

Solo albums (Sound recordings)

Dan Auerbach's Nashville Love Letter J. HUDAK color *Rolling Stone* no1278/1279 p22 Ja 12 2017

Soloists (Dancers)

CATCHING THE Ballet Bug M. McNamara *Dance Spirit* v21 no3 p42 Mr 2017

THE DIRT color *Dance Spirit* v20 no9 p24 N 2016

Stuck in the Middle K. SCHWAB *Dance Magazine* v91 no1 p126 Ja 2017

Solomon, Akiba

SOLO STAR color *Essence* v47 no12 p67 Ap 2017

SOLOMON, ALISA

PLENTY'S DISCONTENT bw *Nation* v304 no4 p27 F 6 2017

Solomon, Andrew

Descent Into Darkness *New York Times Book Review* p1 F 5 2017

Fatal Genes color *New York Review of Books* v64 no17 p25 N 9 2017

HISTORICAL REVISION color *Architectural Digest* v74 no3 p136 Mr 2017

OBAMA'S AMERICA img *New York* v49 no20 p12 O 3 2016

Sri Lanka color *Conde Nast Traveler* v51 no11 p92 D 2016

WE'RE TURNING 30 bw chart color *Conde Nast Traveler* v52 no8 p55 S 2017

SOLOMON, ANNA

Writer, Writer, Pants on Fire *New York Times Book Review* p33 O 23 2016

SOLOMON, BRIAN

The Black Sheep bw color *Forbes* v199 no1 p86 Ja 24 2017

LOCKED IN bw color *Forbes* v199 no3 p76 Mr 28 2017

UBER'S BOLD MOVE [Cover story] color *Forbes* v198 no9 p58 D 30 2016

THE WORLD'S BILLIONAIRES bw color diag graph map *Forbes* v199 no3 p84 Mr 28 2017

Solomon, Caroline

Meet Us at the Beach color *Glamour* v114 no7 p74 Jl 2016

Solomon, Christopher

Life in the Balance chart color map *National Geographic* v231 no6 p52 Je 2017

WHAT SEA RISE? color *National Geographic* v231 no5 p158 My 2017

SOLOMON, DAN

REVENGE OF THE FILM NERDS *Texas Monthly* v45 no7 p70 Jl 2017

WHY THE 'BOYS ARE BACK *Texas Monthly* v45 no9 p64 S 2017

Worst. Listening. Party. Ever *Texas Monthly* v44 no12 p70 D 2016

SOLOMON, DEBORAH

CLAUDE MONET *New York Times Book Review* p68 D 4 2016

Solomon, Edward I.

Metalloprotein entatic control of ligand-metal bonds quantified by ultrafast x-ray spectroscopy diag *Science* v356 no6344 p1276 Je 23 2017

SOLOMON, EVAN

Canada's rocky path ahead *Maclean's* no1 p10 F 17 2017

CHILLY TIMES AHEAD FOR THE LIBERALS color *Maclean's* v129 no40 p12 O 10 2016

A crisis in our prisons color *Maclean's* v130 no3 p11 Ap 2017

THE DAWN OF THE STRONGMAN ERA IS HERE color *Maclean's* v129 no48/49 p12 D 5 2016

A LOSER-TAKE-ALL ELECTION color *Maclean's* v129 no46 p37 N 21 2016

THE MOMENT CYNICISM JUST BURNED AWAY color *Maclean's* v129 no44 p10 N 7 2016

TAMPERING WITH THE HEART OF DEMOCRACY color *Maclean's* v129 no43 p11 O 31 2016

THE TORIES ARE STUCK IN THE PAST ON CARBON *Maclean's* v129 no42 p10 O 24 2016

TRUMP IS A CHANGED MAN? DON'T BET ON IT *Maclean's* v129 no47 p12 N 28 2016

THE UNEVEN JOURNEY TO THE NEW NORMAL color *Maclean's* v129 no45 p23 N 14 2016

Solomon, Feliz

Burma's Oppressed Muslims at Crisis Point *Time* v188 no24 p15 D 12 2016

Hong Kong Jails Its First Prisoners of Conscience color *Time* v190 no9 p13 S 4 2017

Lightbox color *Time* v190 no10/11 p22 S 18 2017

Myanmar's Shame color *Time* v190 no13 p42 O 2 2017

Next Generation Leaders color *Time* v189 no9 p38 Mr 13 2017

Solomon, Jay

Bomb Scares S. MALONEY *New York Times Book Review* p10 O 2 2016

Dangerous Gamble A. HERMAN color *National Review* v68 no24 p35 D 31 2016

The Iran Wars: Spy Games, Bank Battles, and the Secret Deals That Reshaped the Middle East J. Waterbury *Foreign Affairs* v96 no1 p174 Ja/F 2017

Let's Make a Bad Deal O. CEREN *Commentary* v142 no3 p48 O 2016

Solomon, King of Israel, ca. 1011 B.C.-931 B.C.

"Fear Itself," Itself *Lapham's Quarterly* v10 no3 p62 Summ 2017

Solomon, Lou

Becoming Powerful Makes You Less Empathetic *Harvard Business Review Digital Articles* p2 Ap 21 2015

The Top Complaints from Employees About Their Leaders *Harvard Business Review Digital Articles* p2 Je 24 2015

Two-Thirds of Managers Are Uncomfortable Communicating with Employees *Harvard Business Review Digital Articles* p2 Mr 9 2016

SOLOMON, MATTHEW

Supernatural Entertainments: Victorian Spiritualism and the Rise of Modern Media Culture *Film Quarterly* v71 no1 p121 Fall 2017

SOLOMON, MICHAEL

THE CARTIER TANK AT 100 bw color *Forbes* v200 no4 p20 O 24 2017

THE CLASS OF 1917 color *Forbes* v200 no3 p32 S 28 2017

The Corvette at 65 bw color *Forbes* v199 no6 p26 Je 13 2017

FAKE NEWSSTAND! color *Forbes* v200 no3 p92 S 28 2017

Flight Time color *Forbes* v199 no1 p24 Ja 24 2017

Hello, Dalí color *Forbes* v198 no8 p30 D 20 2016

The Imperial Rolex color *Forbes* v199 no5 p34 My 16 2017

JIMMY CHOO'S OWN ADVENTURE color *Forbes* v200 no2 p28 S 5 2017

LESSONS AND IDEAS BY THE 100 GREATEST LIVING BUSINESS MINDS bw color *Forbes* v200 no3 p115 S 28 2017

Regal Rides color *Forbes* v198 no7 p30 N 29 2016

The Rolex President color *Forbes* v198 no5 p52 O 25 2016

THE SUN NEVER SETS ON FORBES color *Forbes* v200 no3 p104 S 28 2017

SWINDLERS LIST color *Forbes* v200 no3 p62 S 28 2017

Turbocharge Your Business in 2017 color diag *Forbes* v198 no8 p24 D 20 2016

Solomon, Norman

NewsHour Distracted by Distraction *Extra!* v30 no1 p3 Ja/F 2017

Solomon, Rivers

An Unkindness of Ghosts color *Publishers Weekly* v264 no33 p53 Ag 14 2017

Solomon, Scott

Oh the Places We'll Go P. Lauritzen color *Commonweal* v144 no6 p30 Mr 24 2017

Solomon, Sean C.

Gravity field of the Orientale basin from the Gravity Recovery and Interior Laboratory Mission bibl graph *Science* v354 no6311 p438 O 28 2016

Solomon, Susan—Interviews

THE OZONE HOLE IS FINALLY HEALING N. SCHARPING color *Discover* v38 no1 p24 Ja/F 2017

Solomon Islands

THE DROWNING ISLES A. DOUGLAS color *Surfer* v58 no4 p76 Ag 2017

Editor's Note color *Surfer* v58 no4 p12 Ag 2017

Solomon R. Guggenheim Museum

Charmed circle: A new exhibition at the Guggenheim examines the supernatural symbolist artists of late nineteenth-century France J. Gardner color *Magazine Antiques* v184 no4 p102 Jl/Ag 2017

DRAWING LINES P. SCHJELDAHL cartoon *New Yorker* v92 no33 p106 O 17 2016

Guggenheim Helsinki Scrapped A. KLIMOSKI *Architectural Record* v205 no1 p20 Ja 2017

SOLON, OLIVIA

THE GOD COMPLEX color *Wired* v25 no3 p18 Mr 2017

Solotaroff, Paul

The Dog Factory color *Rolling Stone* no1278/1279 p42 Ja 12 2017

THE HUNT FOR EL CHAPO color *Rolling Stone* no1294 p44 Ag 24 2017

The Liberation of Kevin Durant [Cover story] color *Rolling Stone* no1273 p34 N 3 2016

Solotki, Raygan—Interviews

Northern Bounty C. Armstrong color *Alternatives Journal (AJ) - Canada's Environmental Voice* v42 no2 p14 2016

Soloveichik, Meir

David Frum on Yuval Levin's 'The Fractured Republic' *Commentary* v142 no1 p1 Jl/Ag 2016

Kevin D. Williamson on Yuval Levin's 'The Fractured Republic' *Commentary* v142 no1 p1 Jl/Ag 2016

Matthew Continetti on Yuval Levin's 'The Fractured Republic' *Commentary* v142 no1 p1 Jl/Ag 2016

MEIR SOLOVEICHIK *Commentary* v142 no1 p37 Jl/Ag 2016

The Secret Jews of The Hobbit *Commentary* v142 no2 p62 S 2016

SOLOVEICHIK, MEIR Y.

Cecil B. DeMille Was Right *Commentary* v143 no4 p11 Ap 2017

David, We Hardly Knew Ye *Commentary* v144 no1 p11 Jl/Ag 2017

Love and the Law *Commentary* v143 no6 p13 Je 2017

May You Be Inscribed for a Good Laugh *Commentary* v144 no2 p11 S 2017

One Brief Kaddish, Summer 2017 *Commentary* v144 no3 p11 O 2017

Solovyev, Paul

ON ART color *Christian Century* v133 no26 p47 D 21 2016

Solow, Andrew R.

Physiological and ecological drivers of early spring blooms of a coastal phytoplankter bibl graph *Science* v354 no6310 p326 O 21 2016

Soloway, Benjamin

A Secessionist Abroad color *Foreign Policy* no224 p30 My/Je 2017

Soloway, Jill, 1965-

Dick Comes to Marfa J. McBride img *New York* v49 no15 p80
Jl 25 2016

Eyes on the Guys R. SYME color *New Republic* v248 no5 p60
My 2017

INSPIRATION T. Friend cartoon *New Yorker* v93 no15 p17 My
29 2017

Prime Opportunity R. MONROE *Texas Monthly* v45 no5 p56 My
2017

PUBLIC DISPLAY *Harper's Magazine* v334 no2001 p15 F 2017

The Year in Reading [Cover story] *New York Times Book Review*
p8 D 25 2016

Soloway, Jill, 1965——Interviews

THE Disruptor A. Friedman color *Glamour* v115 no10 p166 O
2017

Solstice (Music)

The Hot Box chart *Downbeat* v84 no3 p55 Mr 2017

Solstice (Short story)

Solstice A. Enright color *New Yorker* v93 no4 p68 Mr 13 2017

Solt, Steve

#BIKECRUSH color *Bicycling* v58 no8 p53 S 2017

Solter, Davor

ELABELA deficiency promotes preeclampsia and cardiovascular
malformations in mice color diag graph *Science* v357 no6352
p707 Ag 18 2017

Soltes, Eugene

Why It's So Hard to Train Someone to Make an Ethical Decision
color *Harvard Business Review Digital Articles* p2 Ja 11 2017

Soluble glass

the straw that appears broken color *Popular Science* v289 no2 p88
Mr/Ap 2017

Solus (Company)

Solus Audio Entré II Loudspeaker M. Fleischmanncolor graph
Sound & Vision v82 no6 p62 Jl/Ag 2017

Solwitz, Sharon

Once, In Lourdes color *Publishers Weekly* v264 no11 p54 Mr 13
2017

Somalia—Social conditions

OUT OF BOUNDS A. OKEOWO cartoon *New Yorker* v93 no27
p34 S 11 2017

Somalis

Lightbox color *Time* v189 no13 p14 Ap 10 2017

Somalis—Canada

Enemies of the state A. R. KHAN color *Maclean's* p42 Je 2017

Somalis—Social conditions

snapshot *In These Times* v41 no5 p7 My 2017

Somalis—United States

'Minnesota Men' Go To Prison S. W. JOHNSON color *Weekly
Standard* v22 no12 p20 N 28 2016

Somatic mutation

Mismatch repair deficiency predicts response of solid tumors to
PD-1 blockade D. T. Le, J. N. Durham et al chart graph *Science*
v357 no6349 p409 Jl 28 2017

Stem cell divisions, somatic mutations, cancer etiology, and cancer prevention C. Tomasetti, L. Li et al bibl chart diag graph
Science v355 no6331 p1330 Mr 24 2017

Somatosensory cortex

Neural correlates of ticklishness in the rat somatosensory cortex S.
Ishiyama and M. Brecht bibl graph *Science* v354 no6313 p757
N 11 2016

Somatostatin

Layer-specific modulation of neocortical dendritic inhibition during active wakefulness W. Muñoz, R. Tremblay et al bibl diag
Science v355 no6328 p954 Mr 3 2017

Somatotropin

See also

Porcine somatotropin

FACTORS FOR GROWTH A. GONZALEZ color *Muscle & Performance* v9 no9 p50 S 2017

Somaya, Deepak

Employees Leave Good Bosses Nearly as Often as Bad Ones *Harvard Business Review Digital Articles* p2 Mr 8 2016

Some Other Time (Music)

HISTORICAL ALBUM OF THE YEAR bw color *Downbeat* v84
no8 p40 Ag 2017

Somebody to Love (Music)

SOMEBODY TO LOVE D. ARTAVIA color *Advocate* no1091

p34 Je/Jl 2017

Somerhalder, Ian, 1978-

The Vampire Diaries I. Rudolph *TV Guide* v65 no11 p38 Mr 6
2017

Somers, Ken

The Dirty Little Secret About Digitally Transforming Operations
Harvard Business Review Digital Articles p2 My 31 2016

Somerville, Keith

Ivory: Power and Poaching in Africa *Publishers Weekly* v263
no41 p67 O 10 2016

Something to Tell Her (Music)

Something to Tell You (Music)

Haim Doesn't Want to Be "Cool" J. Harman color *Glamour* no8
p38 Ag 2017

Haim J. Bernstein color *Entertainment Weekly* no1473 p57 Jl 7
2017

Haim's Bright Retro-Pop Future J. DOLAN color *Rolling Stone*
no1291/1292 p63 Jl 13 2017

Sisters in Arms J. Weiner bw color *Rolling Stone* no1287 p40 My
18 2017

Something Gold, Something Blue (Music)

The Hot Box chart *Downbeat* v83 no12 p65 D 2016

Something Gold, Something Blue P. de Barros color *Downbeat*
v83 no12 p63 D 2016

Somm (Film)

SHAKING IT UP bw cartoon color *GQ: Gentlemen's Quarterly*
v87 no1 p58 Ja 2017

Somme, 1st Battle of the, France, 1916

Sacrifice on the Western Front *Commentary* v142 no1 p1 Jl/Ag
2016

Sommeliers

Ask a Water Sommelier S. TISHGART img *New York* p60 Ja 9
2017

The Valentine's Day Wine Survival Guide T. CONFOY, J. Mason
bw *Esquire* v167 no1 p17 F 2017

Sommer, Claudia

Exploring pain pathophysiology in patients bibl diag *Science* v354
no6312 p588 N 4 2016

Sommer, David

The Social Network *Tennis* v52 no6 p52 N/D 2016

SOMMER, REINHARD

Chords & Discords bw *Downbeat* v84 no1 p10 Ja 2017

Sommerkamp, Pia

Metabolic cues for hematopoietic stem cells bibl diag *Science*
v354 no6316 p1103 D 2 2016

Sommers, P.

Observation of a large-scale anisotropy in the arrival directions
of cosmic rays above 8×1018 eV *Science* v357 no6357 p1266
S 22 2017

Sommers, Steve

ONE CALLER HAS A TRUCK STOP NAMED AFTER HIM J.
GILBERT *Cincinnati Magazine* v50 no8 p44 My 2017

SOMMERVILLE, DIANE MILLER

Play Ball-Everywhere! *USA Today Magazine* v145 no2858 p48
N 2016

Somnology

For the Record color *Time* v190 no9 p6 S 4 2017

WEIGHT FOR IT... M. Easter color *Women's Health* v14 no5 p57
Je 2017

Son, Hugh

JPMorgan Traders Get Into Property Deals *Bloomberg Businessweek* no4504 p35 D 19 2016

Robot Advisers Can Be Conflicted, Too cartoon *Bloomberg Businessweek* no4532 p28 Jl 31 2017

Where a Graying Herd Still Thunders cartoon *Bloomberg Businessweek* no4503 p34 D 12 2016

Son, Masayoshi, 1957-

SOFTBANK IS HANDING OUT FUNDING. TECH GIANTS
DON'T MIND IF THEY DO A. Lashinsky color *Fortune* v176
no3 p19 S 1 2017

Son, Masayoshi, 1957-—Finance

SCOREBOARD color *Forbes* v199 no1 p28 Ja 24 2017

Son, The (TV program)

Oilmen and Indians In a Saga of American West D. D'Addario
color *Time* v189 no14 p52 Ap 17 2017

PIERCE BROSNAN GOES WEST I. RUDOLPH *TV Guide* v65

no14 p20 Ap 3 2017

The Son M. ROUSH *TV Guide* v65 no14 p19 Ap 3 2017

Son Volt (Performer)

March Forth M. Griffith color *New Orleans Magazine* v51 no5 p50 Mr 2017

Sonar

THE LEADING EDGE OF SHOOTING, FISHING AND WILD-LIFE MANAGEMENT color *Outdoor Life* v224 no2 p34 F/Mr 2017

Sonar equipment

See also

Ultrasonic equipment

NEW ELECTRONICS J. Y. WOOD color *Power & Motoryacht* v34 no6 p26 Je 2017

NEW ELECTRONICS J. Y. WOOD color *Power & Motoryacht* v34 no9 p42 S 2017

Sonar in fishing

SUMMER CRUSH J. CERMELE color *Field & Stream* v122 no2 p18 Je/Jl 2017

Sonder, K.

Improving global integration of crop research color *Science* v357 no6349 p359 Jl 28 2017

Sonderhouse, L.

A Fermi-degenerate three-dimensional optical lattice clock color diag graph *Science* v357 no6359 p90 O 6 2017

Sonders, Liz Ann—Interviews

KEEPING AN EYE ON THE ANIMALS M. Heimer color *Fortune* v75 no1 p40 Ja 1 2017

Sondheim, Stephen, 1930-

WHALES AND DINOSAURS D. T. Max cartoon *New Yorker* v93 no13 p32 My 15 2017

Sonenshein, Scott

How to Create More from What You Already Have *Time* v189 no7/8 p28 F 27 2017

What to Do When Your Boss Says No color *Harvard Business Review Digital Articles* p2 F 6 2017

When More Is Too Much color *Time* v189 no7/8 p28 F 27 2017

Sones, Todd

Watch + Learn color *Golf Magazine* v59 no1 p30 Ja 2017

Song, Insun

Release of mineral-bound water prior to subduction tied to shallow seismogenic slip off Sumatra graph *Science* v356 no6340 p841 My 26 2017

Song, Jie

Reconfiguration of DNA molecular arrays driven by information relay diag *Science* v357 no6349 p371 Jl 28 2017

Song, Li-Xiang

"Perfect" designer chromosome V and behavior of a ring derivative diag *Science* v355 no6329 p1046 Mr 10 2017

Song, Pingping

Dopamine oxidation mediates mitochondrial and lysosomal dysfunction in Parkinson's disease graph *Science* v357 no6357 p1255 S 22 2017

Song, S.

BOLD-SOUNDING THINGS D. HAJDU *Nation* v304 no17 p42 Je 5 2017

Femtosecond electron-phonon lock-in by photoemission and x-ray free-electron laser chart diag *Science* v357 no6346 p71 Jl 2017

Song, Saera

Intersection of diverse neuronal genomes and neuropsychiatric disease: The Brain Somatic Mosaicism Network color *Science* v356 no6336 p395 Ap 28 2017

Song, Tianqiao

A paralogous decoy protects Phytophthora sojae apoplastic effector PsXEG1 from a host inhibitor bibl graph *Science* v355 no6326 p710 F 17 2017

Song, Tian-Qing

Bug mapping and fitness testing of chemically synthesized chromosome X diag *Science* v355 no6329 p1048 Mr 10 2017

"Perfect" designer chromosome V and behavior of a ring derivative diag *Science* v355 no6329 p1046 Mr 10 2017

Song lyrics

Elvis, outside of Flagstaff/Driving a camper van/Looking for meaning in a cloud mass/Sees the face of Joseph Stalin/And is disheartened N. Abebe *New York Times Magazine* p15 Jl 23

2017

The Hot Box J. Corbett, J. Macnie et al chart *Downbeat* v84 no2 p71 F 2017

PARODY color *Weekly Standard* v22 no10 p40 N 14 2016

Play Ball-Everywhere! D. M. SOMMERVILLE *USA Today Magazine* v145 no2858 p48 N 2016

RHYMES WITH "FORBES" B. Z. O. GREENBURG color *Forbes* v200 no3 p100 S 28 2017

Song lyrics—Study & teaching

TRAGICALLY HIP ADDED TO THE SYLLABUS M. BARCLAY color *Maclean's* v129 no44 p50 N 7 2016

Song of Ice & Fire book series

KILL THE BoY.......LET THE MaN BE BORN! [Cover story] L. Hill bw color *Esquire* p78 Je/Jl 2017

Song Sun

Exploring genetic suppression interactions on a global scale diag *Science* v354 no6312 p599 N 4 2016

Song to Song (Film)

THE NOT-SO-SECRET LIFE OF TERRENCE MALICK E. BENSON *Texas Monthly* v45 no4 p114 Ap 2017

Tiny Dancers Abound In Song to Song S. Zacharek color *Time* v189 no12 p57 Ap 3 2017

Song Yu

c . 270 BC: Chen *Lapham's Quarterly* v10 no1 p61 Wint 2017

Songbiao Yan

Quality management for precision medicine clinical applications: A consensus from the China Precision Medicine Clinical Research and Application Association bibl *Science* v354 no6319 p11 D 23 2016

Songbirds

See also

Sparrows

Mind the gap: Neural coding of species identity in birdsong prosody Makoto Araki, M. M. Bandi et al bibl graph *Science* v354 no6317 p1282 D 9 2016

Songkick.com Inc.

THE SHOW MUST GO ON D. LEONARD color *Bloomberg Businessweek* no4504 p57 D 19 2016

Songs of Experience (Music)

U2's New Fire [Cover story] A. GREENE color *Rolling Stone* no1297 p11 O 5 2017

Songs—Charts, diagrams, etc.

Songs That Won the Summer R. Bruner color *Time* v190 no9 p54 S 4 2017

Songs—Psychological aspects

Can't Get That Song Out of Your Head? color *Prevention* v69 no2 p12 F 2017

Soni, Jimmy

THE FATHER OF THE INFORMATION AGE (FINALLY) GETS HIS OWN BOOK R. Hackett color *Fortune* v176 no2 p17 Ag 1 2017

SONI, NEHA

THE WORLD'S BILLIONAIRES bw color diag graph map *Forbes* v199 no3 p84 Mr 28 2017

Sonia Kashuk Inc.

The Shining color *Women's Health* v13 no10 p52 D 2016

Sonic Boom (Performer)

THINGS THAT GO BOOM R. GRANT *Smithsonian* v47 no9 p54 Ja/F 2017

Sonké, Bonaventure

Positive biodiversity-productivity relationship predominant in global forests bibl chart graph map *Science* v354 no6309 paaf8957-1 O 14 2016

Sonneman, Robert

DISCO FEVER S. COCHRAN bw color *Architectural Digest* v73 no11 p82 N 2016

SONNENBURG, ERICA

feed your child's gut *Parents* v91 no10 p42 O 2016

Sonnenburg, Erica D.

Seasonal cycling in the gut microbiome of the Hadza hunter-gatherers of Tanzania diag *Science* v357 no6353 p802 Ag 25 2017

Sonnenburg, Justin L.

Seasonal cycling in the gut microbiome of the Hadza hunter-gatherers of Tanzania diag *Science* v357 no6353 p802 Ag 25 2017

Sonner, William

Saving Grace L. Cutrone color *New Orleans Magazine* v51 no7

p56 My 2017

Sonntag, S.

Observation of a large-scale anisotropy in the arrival directions of cosmic rays above 8 × 1018 eV *Science* v357 no6357 p1266 S 22 2017

Son of Joseph, The (Film)

The Son of Joseph Y. TALU color *Film Comment* v53 no1 p85 Ja/F 2017

Sonoita (Ariz.)

RUNE with a VIEW N. AUSTIN *Arizona Highways* v93 no4 p50 Ap 2017

Sonoma County (Calif.)—Description & travel

Going Back to Cali Wine Country P. BRADY color *Conde Nast Traveler* v52 no3 p50 Mr 2017

Wine, Dine and Wine Some More C. HALL color *AARP: The Magazine* v59 no5A p59 Ag/S 2016

Sonoran Desert

BORN SURVIVOR L. W. CHEEK *Arizona Highways* v93 no3 p44 Mr 2017

Gambel's Quail K. Vaughn *Arizona Highways* v93 no3 p13 Mr 2017

Living Lab for Sustainable Cities E. BARTON *USA Today Magazine* v146 no2868 p69 S 2017

Q&A: Don Lawrence *Arizona Highways* v93 no10 p9 O 2017

United States color *National Geographic* v230 no5 p9 N 2016

Sonos Inc.

Sonos Playbase D. Wilkinson color *Sound & Vision* v82 no5 p40 Je 2017

Your Buyer's Guide to the New 4K TVs A. H. BIBLE cartoon color *Men's Health* v32 no8 p28 O 2017

Sons

See also

Fathers & sons

Accounting for TASTE T. Adler color *Vogue* v207 no7 p32 Jl 2017

MY KID PACKS HEAT J. D. TUCCILLE color *Reason* v48 no8 p10 Ja 2017

RETURN OF THE MISSING DAUGHTERS M. D. GUPTA color graph *Scientific American* v317 no3 p80 S 2017

Sonus Faber (Company)

Come Fly With Me B. Ankosko color *Sound & Vision* v82 no2 p74 F/Mr 2017

Sony audio equipment

Solidly Serious D. Kumin chart color graph *Sound & Vision* v82 no7 p58 S 2017

Sony audio equipment—Evaluation

Holiday Tech Guide B. Ankosko color *Sound & Vision* v81 no10 p34 D 2016

Sony Walkman NW-ZX100HN Hi-Res Music Player Bundle M. Fleischmann color *Sound & Vision* v81 no10 p54 D 2016

Sony cameras—Evaluation

SLOW AND FAST P. Ryan color graph *Popular Photography* v81 no1 p98 Ja/F 2017

Sony Corp.

The Big Short [Cover story] A. Griffin color graph *Sound & Vision* v82 no8 p36 O 2017

Bring on the Joy T. Bufete and J. Willcox chart il *Consumer Reports* v82 no3 p31 Mr 2017

How to Create an Exponential Mindset M. Bonchek *Harvard Business Review Digital Articles* p2 Jl 27 2016

Movers K. Stock color graph *Bloomberg Businessweek* no4513 p19 Mr 6 2017

NEW BOSS P. Ryan color graph *Popular Photography* v81 no2 p78 Mr/Ap 2017

Noise Cancellation Goes Blue L. Dragan and C. Crowley color *Sound & Vision* v82 no2 p18 F/Mr 2017

Projection for All? T. J. Norton color *Sound & Vision* v82 no4 p42 My 2017

SLOW AND FAST P. Ryan color graph *Popular Photography* v81 no1 p98 Ja/F 2017

SLOW DOWN THE WORLD S. Horaczek color *Popular Science* v289 no5 p30 S/O 2017

Sony CAS-1 Compact Audio System M. Fleischmann color *Sound & Vision* v82 no2 p58 F/Mr 2017

Sony MDR-Z1R Headphones S. Guttenberg color *Sound & Vision* v82 no3 p62 Ap 2017

Sony's Bet on Gamers Can't Get Much Bigger B. Einhorn bw

Bloomberg Businessweek no4499 p48 N 14 2016

Sony's Bravia OLED: the first flat-screen TV with sound that doesn't suck M. BROWN color *PCWorld* v35 no2 p21 F 2017

Sony UBP-X800 Ultra HD Blu-ray Player A. Griffin color *Sound & Vision* v82 no6 p38 Jl/Ag 2017

Sony Walkman NW-ZX100HN Hi-Res Music Player Bundle M. Fleischmann color *Sound & Vision* v81 no10 p54 D 2016

TOP PICKS OF THE TOP PICKS R. SABIN *Sound & Vision* v82 no2 p8 F/Mr 2017

Your Buyer's Guide to the New 4K TVs A. H. BIBLE cartoon color *Men's Health* v32 no8 p28 O 2017

Sony video games—Evaluation

The Sweet Sound of Virtual Reality X. HARDING and A. SMITH color *Popular Science* v288 no6 p48 N/D 2016

Soo, Phillipa, 1990-

On the Bright Side A. GREEN and V. STEIKER color *Vogue* v207 no3 p384 Mr 2017

Phillipa Soo M. Hagan color *Current Biography* v77 no11 p77 N 2016

Soo, Phillipa, 1990—Interviews

Phillipa Soo Doesn't Leave It All Onstage D. Itzkoff *New York Times Magazine* p54 Ap 2 2017

Soo, Rochelle M.

On the origins of oxygenic photosynthesis and aerobic respiration in Cyanobacteria chart diag *Science* v355 no6332 p1436 Mr 31 2017

Sood, K.

Chronic exposure to neonicotinoids reduces honey bee health near corn crops diag *Science* v356 no6345 p1395 Je 30 2017

Soodalter, Ron

444 DAYS IN HELL *Military History* v33 no6 p18 Mr 2017

BREAKOUT! *Missouri Life* v43 no6 p42 O/N 2016

Building a Legacy: The King Ranch bw *American Cowboy* p64 LEGENDS OF TEXAS Special Issue 2017

Code of the West, History vs. Hollywood cartoon *American Cowboy* v24 no1 p22 Je/Jl 2017

FORLORN VICTORY [Cover story] bw color map *Military History* v34 no4 p38 N 2017

Grunt *MHQ: Quarterly Journal of Military History* v29 no2 p93 Wint 2017

Lincoln's Greatest Journey *MHQ: Quarterly Journal of Military History* v29 no3 p94 Spr 2017

The Long Drive bw *American Cowboy* v23 no6 p20 Ap/My 2017

MCCLELLAN'S BIG MISS *MHQ: Quarterly Journal of Military History* v29 no2 p76 Wint 2017

ON THE INSIDE UNDER FIRE bw color *Military History* v34 no2 p62 Jl 2017

A Quest for the Best Man: Missouri's First Governors color map *Missouri Life* v44 no4 p52 Je 2017

THAT BAD MAN STAGGER LEE bw *Missouri Life* v44 no2 p52 Ap 2017

A YANK IN THE SS *Military History* v33 no5 p40 Ja 2017

Soohoo, Karen

Health Equity: Leading Through Programs, Environmental Changes and Policies *Parks & Recreation* v52 no10 p28 O 2017

Soojung-Kim Pang, Alex

The Rest of Your Life A. HUFFINGTON *New York Times Book Review* p10 D 18 2016

Sookocheff, Carey, 1972-

Wet *Publishers Weekly* v264 no15 p72 Ap 10 2017

Soong, Wendy

Who's Afraid of Low Volatility? cartoon graph *Bloomberg Businessweek* no4533 p23 Ag 7 2017

Soon Im, Doo

β2-Adrenoreceptor is a regulator of the a-synuclein gene driving risk of Parkinson's disease cartoon chart graph *Science* v357 no6354 p891 S 1 2017

Soothe (Company)

The most intimate of ubers R. COUNTER color *Maclean's* v129 no41 p53 O 17 2016

Sopadjieva, Emma

A Study of 46,000 Shoppers Shows That Omnichannel Retailing Works color *Harvard Business Review Digital Articles* p2 Ja 3 2017

Soper, Kate

SINGING PHILOSOPHY A. ROSS cartoon *New Yorker* v93 no2

p74 F 27 2017

Soper, Spencer

The Airbnb Of Warehousing *Bloomberg Businessweek* no4523 p32 My 22 2017

Amazon Goes After The Walmart Shopper *Bloomberg Businessweek* no4508 p19 Ja 23 2017

Cracking the Bro Code cartoon *Bloomberg Businessweek* no4533 p18 Ag 7 2017

EBay Tries to Push Past Its Tag-Sale Roots bw graph *Bloomberg Businessweek* no4493 p42 O 3 2016

Jeff Bezos Goes Grocery Shopping color *Bloomberg Businessweek* no4517 p21 Ap 3 2017

Now on EBay: Russian Micro-Multinationals *Bloomberg Businessweek* no4515 p19 Mr 20 2017

Putting Home Sales Ahead of Paperwork *Bloomberg Businessweek* no4526 p38 Je 12 2017

Soponyai, György

MERGING TIME E. MASTROIANNI color *Discover* v38 no2 p9 Mr 2017

Sopranos (Singers)

ANNE PASHLEY *Opera News* v81 no7 p58 Ja 2017

BACKSTORY: Susan Graham F. COHN *Opera News* v81 no5 p64 N 2016

Born to Sing J. ALLISON *Opera News* v81 no6 p18 D 2016

CHRISTINE GOERKE H. Stewart *Opera News* v81 no10 p28 Ap 2017

DANIELA DESSÌ. GENOA, ITALY, MAY 14,1957-BRESCIA, ITALY, AUGUST 20, 2016 F. P. Driscoll *Opera News* v81 no5 p62 N 2016

Dateline *Opera News* v81 no6 p8 D 2016

Dazzling *Opera News* v81 no5 p20 N 2016

Luminous A. WASSERMAN *Opera News* v81 no9 p28 Mr 2017

Lyric Tradition S. HASTINGS *Opera News* v81 no7 p16 Ja 2017

Modifiers and the Met *Weekly Standard* v23 no6 p5 O 16 2017

PATRICE MUNSEL. SPOKANE, WA, MAY 14, 1925-SCHROON LAKE, NY, AUGUST 4, 2016 B. Kellow *Opera News* v81 no5 p62 N 2016

ROBERTA PETERS I. Siff *Opera News* v81 no10 p64 Ap 2017

Sopranos (Singers)—Interviews

Sarah Jane McMahon A. McLellan color *New Orleans Magazine* v51 no7 p28 My 2017

Sopranos, The (TV program)

Funny Girl color *InStyle* v24 no6 p58 Je 2017

The Sopranos Kiss Adriana Goodbye J. Hibberd color *Entertainment Weekly* no1470 p46 Je 16 2017

SOPRANZETTI, CLAUDIO

The Tightening Authoritarian Grip on Thailand *Current History* v116 no791 p230 S 2017

SORANNO, PATRICIA A.

Conceptions of Good Science in Our Data-Rich World chart *BioScience* v66 no10 p1 O 1 2016

Sorek, Rotem

Intracellular signaling in CRISPR-Cas defense color *Science* v357 no6351 p550 Ag 11 2017

Sorel, Edward

Babylon Illustrated D. THOMSON bw *Film Comment* v52 no6 p94 N/D 2016

Her Little Black Book [Cover story] W. Allen *New York Times Book Review* p1 Ja 1 2017

WHACK JOBS cartoon *New Yorker* v93 no27 p56 S 11 2017

SORELL, GINA

How I really met my mother color *Good Housekeeping* v264 no5 p73 My 2017

Soren, David

CAPTAIN UNDERPANTS D. Coggan color *Entertainment Weekly* no1446/1447 p51 D 2016/Ja 2017

CAPTAIN UNDERPANTS: THE FIRST EPIC MOVIE D. Coggan color *Entertainment Weekly* no1463/1464 p53 Ap/My 2017

Sorensen, Amelia

I Wish My Horse's Mentor Could Be... color *Horse & Rider* v56 no6 p88 Je 2017

Sorensen, Brett

Brave Hearts color *O, The Oprah Magazine* p14 Mr 2017

SORENSEN, CHRIS

Deal the seal color *Maclean's* v130 no2 p11 Mr 2017

Ehh, what's up, Victoria? color *Maclean's* v129 no40 p30 O 10

2016

Hands off my bubble [Cover story] color graph *Maclean's* v129 no41 p36 O 17 2016

THE INTERVIEW color *Maclean's* v129 no44 p12 N 7 2016

Let the market freak-out begin color *Maclean's* v129 no46 p35 N 21 2016

Rocket plan cartoon color *Maclean's* v129 no48/49 p64 D 5 2016

Rough seas ahead for trade color *Maclean's* v129 no45 p40 N 14 2016

WAITING FOR THE PAYOFF FROM BIGGER DEFICITS color *Maclean's* v129 no42 p16 O 24 2016

What happens when the walls go up color *Maclean's* v129 no47 p34 N 28 2016

Sorensen, Jen

COMIX NATION *Nation* v305 no1 p8 Jl 3 2017

Sorensen, Lars R., 1954-—Interviews

What CEOs Really Worry About [Cover story] A. Ignatius bw color img *Harvard Business Review* v94 no11 p52 N 2016

Sorensen, Stacie

GO-TO GIRL chart color *Team Roping Journal* p64 S 2017

Sorensen, Sue

SURPRISE *Christian Century* v134 no12 p22 Je 7 2017

Sorenson, Arne

MARRIOTT GOES ALL IN S. Tully chart color diag *Fortune* v175 no8 p200 Je 15 2017

Sorenson, Marlene

pontoon mania color *Cabin Living* p60 Je 2017

Sorenson, Olav

Expand innovation finance via crowdfunding bibl color graph map *Science* v354 no6319 p1526 D 23 2016

Research: Junior Female Scientists Aren't Getting the Credit They Deserve *Harvard Business Review Digital Articles* p2 Mr 22 2017

Soressi, Marie

Neandertal and Denisovan DNA from Pleistocene sediments bw color *Science* v356 no6338 p605 My 12 2017

Sorey, Tyshawn

Inner Landscape A. Ross color *New Yorker* v93 no20 p8 Jl 10 2017

Sorghum irrigation

GIVE-AND-TAKE IRRIGATION: TEXAS FARMER USES MULTIPLE PRACTICES TO EARN STRONG YIELDS ON MINIMAL ACRE-INCHES OF WATER T. Gaines *Successful Farming* v115 no11 p46 S 2017

Sorghum—Yields

WATER-SAVING SORGHUM D. Mowitz *Successful Farming* v114 no10 p47 O 2016

SORIA, SANDRA S.

Christmas in the country *Better Homes & Gardens* v94 no12 p39 D 2016

Sorigué, Damien

An algal photoenzyme converts fatty acids to hydrocarbons color graph *Science* v357 no6354 p903 S 1 2017

Sorkin, Aaron, 1961-

MOLLY'S GAME R. Rahman color *Entertainment Weekly* no1478 / 1479 p67 Ag 18-25 2017

Sorkin's West Wing Swan Song C. Agard color *Entertainment Weekly* no1460/1461 p95 Ap 7-17 2017

Sorkin, Amy Davidson

ARE THEY WITH HIM? cartoon *New Yorker* v93 no22 p17 Jl 31 2017

DISASTERS WILL HAPPEN cartoon *New Yorker* v93 no32 p21 O 16 2017

IN THE DARK bw *New Yorker* v93 no29 p37 S 25 2017

MISDIAGNOSING A CRISIS cartoon *New Yorker* v93 no24 p15 Ag 21 2017

Sorkin, Andrew Ross

Andrew Ross SORKIN M. Hainey color *Esquire* p68 My 2017

Inside Additions *New York Times Book Review* p12 F 19 2017

SORKIN, MADALEINE

Build Mental Muscle color *Climbing* no354 p44 Jl 2017

SORKIN, MICHAEL

The Autonomobile and the City *Architectural Record* v205 no4 p64 Ap 2017

Sorofman, Jake

The Best CMOs Combine 4 Leadership Styles *Harvard Business Review Digital Articles* p2 My 12 2015

Sorokanich, Bob

APOCALYPSE NOW color *Road & Track* v68 no9 p38 Je 2017

FOR THE LOVE OF CARS: THE BEST RIDES OF 2017 Esquire color *Esquire* p65 O 2017

SHOCK DOCTRINE color *Road & Track* v69 no1 p84 Ag 2017

Sorokanich, Lara

3D PRINTED FOOD color *Popular Mechanics* p78 D 2016/Ja 2017

3D Printing Reaches the Ocean Floor color *Popular Mechanics* p18 Mr 2017

Baldness: The Final Frontier color *Popular Mechanics* p26 Ap 2017

BORN THIS WAY color *Popular Mechanics* p88 My 2017

BREAK THROUGH AWARDS 2017 [Cover story] bw color *Popular Mechanics* p56 N 2017

Getting Started In… SEWING color diag *Popular Mechanics* p46 N 2017

GREAT MOMENTS IN VIDEO TUTORIALS color *Popular Mechanics* p94 O 2017

Meet the NFL's Newest Stadium color *Popular Mechanics* p20 S 2017

Meet the NFL's Newest Stadium color *Popular Mechanics* v193 no7 p20 S 2016

Why We Should Be Excited About the Future color *Popular Mechanics* p95 My 2017

SOROKANICH, ROBERT

Reviving an OLD-SCHOOL American Legend color *Esquire* v166 no4 p76 N 2016

Sorokin, J.

Observation of a large-scale anisotropy in the arrival directions of cosmic rays above 8×1018 eV *Science* v357 no6357 p1266 S 22 2017

Sorokin, Jordan M.

Breathing control center neurons that promote arousal in mice diag graph *Science* v355 no6332 p1411 Mr 31 2017

Sorokin, Pitirim Aleksandrovich, 1889-1968

Pitirim Sorokin Revisited: He predicted the West's societal deterioration G. T. SEWALL *American Conservative* v16 no5 p42 S/O 2017

Sorrell, Michael

Labor of Love M. Connolly *Washington Monthly* p1 S/O 2016

Sorrell, Steve

Sociotechnical transitions for deep decarbonization color diag *Science* v357 no6357 p1242 S 22 2017

Sorrentino, Paolo, 1970-

Difficult Pontiff M. Z. SEITZ img *New York* p82 Ja 9 2017

POPE IN A SOAP T. Friend cartoon *New Yorker* v92 no46 p19 Ja 23 2017

'The Young Pope' The Catholic art that Catholics need—but might not want N. Ripatrazone color *America* v216 no3 p38 F 6 2017

Sorte, Cascade J. B.

Biodiversity redistribution under climate change: Impacts on ecosystems and human well-being color *Science* v355 no6332 p1389 Mr 31 2017

SORVINO, CHLOE

The $4.5 Billion Cabinet color *Forbes* v199 no1 p26 Ja 24 2017

THE BIG CHEESE color *Forbes* v199 no6 p100 Je 13 2017

Bowled Over color *Forbes* v199 no5 p26 My 16 2017

Burger Queen color *Forbes* v199 no6 p22 Je 13 2017

Ceiling Crasher color *Forbes* v199 no2 p24 F 28 2017

A Cut Above color diag *Forbes* v200 no4 p92 O 24 2017

The IT Girl color *Forbes* v199 no6 p80 Je 13 2017

The Kushner Kingdom color *Forbes* v199 no2 p32 F 28 2017

SOUTH OF THE WALL bw *Forbes* v199 no3 p74 Mr 28 2017

TRUMP AMERICA bw *Forbes* v199 no3 p72 Mr 28 2017

Sorvino, Mira

The Power of Speaking Out color *Time* v190 no16/17 p33 O 23 2017

Sosa, Arturo

Jesuits: Models of Reconciliation For a World in Need of Mercy color *America* v215 no19 p9 D 19 2016

Sosebee, Rick

FARM-TOUGH UTVS: OUR 2017 UTV TEST RESULTS ARE IN! J. Scott color *Successful Farming* v115 no7 p24 My 2017

Sosenko, Carla

Hollywood Takes a Knee color *Entertainment Weekly* no1485 p14

O 6 2017

RED-CARPET INTELLIGENCE Emmys Edition color *Entertainment Weekly* no1484 p22 S 29 2017

STARTED FROM THE BOTTOM NOW SHE'S HERE color *Entertainment Weekly* no1480 p18 S 1 2017

SWIMMING WITH SHARKS color *Entertainment Weekly* no1476 p19 Ag 4 2017

Sosik, Heidi M.

Physiological and ecological drivers of early spring blooms of a coastal phytoplankter bibl graph *Science* v354 no6310 p326 O 21 2016

SOSINSKI, ANTHONY

A Speck In the Sea bw color *Power & Motoryacht* v34 no7 p48 Jl 2017

Soskin, Betty Reid

Richmond's "Resident Rosie" C. Schuknecht *Sierra* v101 no4 p66 Jl/Ag 2016

Sosnovtsev, V.

Observation of coherent elastic neutrino-nucleus scattering diag *Science* v357 no6356 p1123 S 15 2017

Sostrin, Jesse

To Be a Great Leader, You Have to Learn How to Delegate Well *Harvard Business Review Digital Articles* p2 O 10 2017

Soták, Matúš

Research night owls color *Science* v354 no6315 p964 N 25 2016

Sótér, Anna

Buffer-gas cooling of antiprotonic helium to 1.5 to 1.7 K, and antiproton-to-electron mass ratio bibl chart diag graph *Science* v354 no6312 p610 N 4 2016

Sotheby's (Company)

HOUSE ARREST N. FREEMAN bw cartoon *ARTnews* v115 no3 p92 Fall 2016

SOTO, EUGENIA SANTIESTEBAN

BOTANY color *Better Homes & Gardens* v95 no5 p10 My 2017

OBSESSED WITH CATS color *Better Homes & Gardens* v95 no2 p10 F 2016

OBSESSED WITH RUSHES, REEDS & GRASSES color *Better Homes & Gardens* v95 no3 p10 Mr 2017

OBSESSED WITH TILE MOTIFS color *Better Homes & Gardens* v95 no4 p6 Ap 2017

OBSESSED WITH WOODSY DECOR *Better Homes & Gardens* v94 no11 p11 N 2016

Soto, Noris

Meet Venezuela's New Iron-Fisted No. 2 color *Bloomberg Businessweek* no4511 p16 F 13 2017

Photostat: Going Hungry in Venezuela color *Bloomberg Businessweek* no4540 p38 O 2 2017

Sotomayor, Sonia

Leaders color *Time* v189 no16/17 p64 My 1-8 2017

ONE CHEER FOR JUSTICE SOTOMAYOR D. ROOT color *Reason* v48 no9 p11 F 2017

Sotsass, Ettore

Glass Vases by Ettore Sotsass: The late Italian architect and designer, known as much for his product designs as his buildings, was a master of color and shape E. GAUKEL *Treasures* v6 no6 p40 Je/Jl 2017

Sottile, Stephen

A life with loss color *U.S. Catholic* v82 no1 p5 Ja 2017

Sottsass, Ettore—Exhibitions

ART color *New Yorker* v93 no24 p8 Ag 21 2017

beyond MEMPHIS H. MARTIN color *Architectural Digest* no6 p138 Je 1 2017

Technicolor Dreams J. Tarmy color *Bloomberg Businessweek* no4532 p66 Jl 31 2017

Soufan, Ali

The Terror Hydra: An original terror warrior returns to take stock of our progress C. SAVAGE *New York Times Book Review* p19 Je 11 2017

Soufani, Khaled

Companies Are Working with Consumers to Reduce Waste *Harvard Business Review Digital Articles* p2 Je 7 2016

How Businesses Can Support a Circular Economy *Harvard Business Review Digital Articles* p2 F 1 2016

Soufflés

OATMEAL SOUFFLÉ: How to make the Hay-Adams hotel's genius breakfast confection *Washingtonian Magazine* v53 no1

p151 O 2017

Soul

See also

Personality

Psychology

7 heart-pumping facts E. WHITMER *National Geographic Kids* no467 p10 F 2017

Soul mates

Searching for a Soul Mate Is Futile. The Ideal Partner Is the One You Create A. Calhoun color *Time* v189 no20 p22 My 29 2017

Soul musicians

GOINGS ON ABOUT TOWN bw *New Yorker* v92 no44 p7 Ja 9 2017

Soul—Christianity

Reflections on the lectionary M. M. White *Christian Century* v134 no15 p21 Jl 19 2017

SoulCycle LLC

SOULCYCLE'S CEO ON SUSTAINING GROWTH IN A FADDISH INDUSTRY: It's all about friendship and community M. Whelan color img *Harvard Business Review* v95 no4 p37 Jl/Ag 2017

Soule, Maris

Echoes of Terror *Publishers Weekly* v264 no4 p59 Ja 23 2017

SOULÉ, MICHAEL

We Need a Biologically Sound North American Conservation Plan *BioScience* v67 no8 p685 Ag 2017

Soule, Sarah A.

Changing Company Culture Requires a Movement, Not a Mandate *Harvard Business Review Digital Articles* p2 Je 20 2017

Souleiman, Eugene

Friendship Ponies color *Glamour* v115 no7 p17 Jl 2017

Soules, Gerard

Kafka in Vegas M. ROSE bw color *Vanity Fair* v59 no7 p116 Summ 2017

Souleyman, Omar, 1966-

The Wedding Singer M. Trammell cartoon *New Yorker* v93 no26 p15 S 4 2017

Soulfire (Music)

Little Steven Is His Own Boss Again B. HIATT bw color *Rolling Stone* no1288 p16 Je 1 2017

Soul—History of doctrines

The Search for the Soul R. Sugg *History Today* v67 no4 p48 Ap 2017

Soulpepper Theatre Co.

A Maple Leaf in the Big Apple H. Sherman *Stage Directions* v30 no9 p24 S 2017

Soul's Soundtrack, The (Poem)

THE SOUL'S SOUNDTRACK Y. Komunyakaa *New Yorker* v93 no13 p70 My 15 2017

Sound

See also

Sounds

THE SPEED OF SOUND R. Lengel chart color *Flying* v144 no1 p24 Ja 2017

Sound & Fury (Short story)

SOUND AND FURY P. Handke *Harper's Magazine* v333 no1999 p19 D 2016

Sound, The (Music)

The 10 Best Songs J. Cox color *Time* v188 no25-26 p154 D 19 2016 Double Issue

Sound bites

Short attention spans, short news cycles and short form Gospels M. Malone and S. Sawyer *America* v216 no7 p3 Ap 3 2017

Sound design

Audio Alternatives B. Reesman *Stage Directions* v30 no1 p8 Ja 2017

Balancing Audio and Life V. Olivieri *Stage Directions* v30 no3 p10 Mr 2017

Elevating the Pit B. Reesman *Stage Directions* v30 no4 p8 Ap 2017

High Fidelity T. PAUL color *Film Comment* v52 no6 p22 N/D 2016

Sound designers & design

High Fidelity T. PAUL color *Film Comment* v52 no6 p22 N/D 2016

THE SOUND OF IMAGINATION: Andrew Keister's Sound De-

sign for Charlie and the Chocolate Factory B. Reesman *Stage Directions* v30 no6 p12 Je 2017

Sound editing—Software

ADOBE AUDITION CC (2015.2): AUDIO EDITING BECOMES MORE USER-FRIENDLY J. R. BOOKWALTER color *Macworld - Digital Edition* p37 D 2016

Sound engineers

Class D-Mystified C. Crowley bw color *Sound & Vision* v82 no5 p16 Je 2017

Sound mixers & mixing—Software

WHAT'S NEW AT THE APP STORE color *Macworld - Digital Edition* p65 F 2017

Sound production by animals

CAN WE TALK? AN ARIZONA BIOLOGIST BELIEVES THAT THE SOUNDS MADE BY MANY ANIMAL SPECIES, INCLUDING THE HUMBLE PRAIRIE DOG, SHOULD BE CONSIDERED LANGUAGE—AND THAT SOMEDAY WE'LL UNDERSTAND WHAT THEY HAVE TO SAY F. Jabr *New York Times Magazine* p28 My 14 2017

Vocalizations channeled by developmental affordances color *Science* v355 no6326 p708 F 17 2017

Sound production by birds

SPECIALIZED VOCAL ORGANS GIVE SOME BIRDS THEIR UNIQUE SONGS *Physics Today* v70 no10 p29 O 2017

Sound recording & reproducing

AND THEN SHE APPEARED M. SUMELL color *Popular Mechanics* p32 O 2017

An Engineer's Approach to Modern Big Band Recording F. BREITBERG color *Downbeat* v84 no2 p92 F 2017

St. Beauty T. MALONE *Atlanta* v57 no4 p30 Ag 2017

Sound recording & reproducing—Equipment & supplies

See also

Audio equipment in automobiles

Onkyo audio equipment

Sony audio equipment

Sound systems

GEAR BOX color *Downbeat* v84 no6 p90 Je 2017

LAST CHANCE TO SEE S. Liew *New York Times Book Review* p27 O 15 2017

RECORDS OF REBELLION N. Daly bw color *National Geographic* v231 no5 p16 My 2017

Sound recording & reproducing—Equipment & supplies—Evaluation

GEAR BOX color *Downbeat* v84 no2 p100 F 2017

Sound recording & reproducing—Sales & prices

Print, Audio Keep Publishers Moving Ahead J. Milliot chart *Publishers Weekly* v264 no36 p4 S 4 2017

Sound recording awards

TRUE BLUES D. BLASBERG color *Vanity Fair* v59 no10 p125 O 2017

Sound recording executives & producers

David Guetta M. Hagan color *Current Biography* v78 no1 p18 Ja 2017

DIANA KRALL For Tommy [Cover story] P. LUTZ color *Downbeat* v84 no6 p34 Je 2017

GEORGE MARTIN P. McCartney and K. O'Donnell color *Entertainment Weekly* no1446/1447 p88 D 2016/Ja 2017

Hot Secret Weapon Rostam Batmanglij P. DOYLE color *Rolling Stone* no1274 p37 N 17 2016

In Memoriam: Tommy LiPuma color *Downbeat* v84 no6 p26 Je 2017

Sound recording executives & producers—United States

DJ KHALED cartoon *Vanity Fair* v59 no1 p192 Holiday 2017

Peter Cottontale M. POLLOCK color *Chicago* v66 no6 p94 Je 2017

Sound recording industry

See also

Audiobook industry

Recording studios

Danger Mouse's 30th Century Vision E. R. Brown color *Entertainment Weekly* no1438 p60 N 4 2016

AN ECLECTIC SONIC SQUAD E. R. Brown color *Entertainment Weekly* no1438 p60 N 4 2016

Odradek's Juried Art T. Staudter bw *Downbeat* v84 no3 p18 Mr 2017

SAYING 'YES' TO THE AVANT-GARDE P. Lutz color *Down-*

beat v84 no3 p50 Mr 2017

Sound recording industry—News briefs

HDR Is Getting Support From M. Fleischmann and C. Crowley color *Sound & Vision* v82 no2 p17 F/Mr 2017

Sound recording industry—Officials & employees

Label Owner Joe Fields Dies at 88 color *Downbeat* v84 no10 p26 O 2017

Sound recording industry—United States

THE RECORD INDUSTRY SEES A SAVIOR IN STREAMING diag *Fortune* v174 no6 p11 N 1 2016

Stax Celebrateds 60 Years A. Cohen color *Downbeat* v84 no9 p18 S 2017

Sound recordings

See also

Audiobooks

Podcasts

The 2017 Album Watch List R. Bruner color *Time* v188 no27-28 p106 D 26 2016

DEEP LISTENING D. Fox *National Parks* v91 no1 p36 Wint 2017

How Streaming Is Changing Music (Again) M. Luca and C. McFadden *Harvard Business Review Digital Articles* p2 D 12 2016

HOW TO BUY RECORDS R. D'AGOSTINO color *Popular Mechanics* p38 My 2017

Jamie Crewe P. Epps color *Art in America* v105 no3 p29 Mr 2017

Remembering Rudy Van Gelder, Who Defined the Sound of Jazz bw *Downbeat* v83 no11 p23 N 2016

TAKE IT FROM THE TOP J. R. MARQUEZ *Atlanta* v56 no8 p52 D 2016

To Do img *New York* v50 no18 p140 Ap 17 2017

Voices of America M. DEAN *New Republic* v248 no4 p56 Ap 2017

Sound recordings—Awards—United States

See also

Grammy Awards

Sound recordings—Conservation & restoration

New Smithsonian museum aids Baylor's preservation of black gospel recordings T. L. Goodrich *Christian Century* v133 no21 p18 O 12 2016

Sound recordings—Equipment & supplies—Evaluation

MUSICIANS' GEAR GUIDE BEST OF THE 2017 NAMM SHOW Ž. Čuntova, E. Enright et al color *Downbeat* v84 no4 p70 Ap 2017

Sound recordings—Evaluation

Manuel Valera T. PANKEN color *Downbeat* v84 no10 p202 O 2017

Sound recordings—Production & direction

Jack Johnson's New Wave K. GROW bw color *Rolling Stone* no1291/1292 p20 Jl 13 2017

Josh Homme's Desert Dance Party K. GROW bw *Rolling Stone* no1291/1292 p14 Jl 13 2017

Sound recordings—Reviews

Long & Short Commentary B. REED color *Downbeat* v84 no10 p8 O 2017

Sound systems

See also

Wireless sound systems

Bluesound Pulse Soundbar and Pulse Sub D. Kumin color graph *Sound & Vision* v82 no5 p52 Je 2017

Fishman SA Performance Audio Systems K. Baumann *Downbeat* v84 no8 p90 Ag 2017

Legacy Audio Powerbloc2 and Powerbloc4 Amplifiers D. Kumin chart color graph *Sound & Vision* v82 no6 p58 Jl/Ag 2017

New Gear color *Sound & Vision* v82 no8 p32 O 2017

Petite and Discreet B. Ankosko color *Sound & Vision* v82 no8 p74 O 2017

Products *Parks & Recreation* v52 no8 p74 Ag 2017

TOP THREE: SOUND WAVES M. CALORE color *Wired* v25 no8 p40 Ag 2017

Sound systems—Equipment & supplies

Bars on a Budget R. Sabin color graph *Sound & Vision* v81 no10 p40 D 2016

Holiday Tech Guide B. Ankosko color *Sound & Vision* v81 no10 p34 D 2016

New Gear color *Sound & Vision* v81 no10 p32 D 2016

Sound systems—Evaluation

Bars on a Budget R. Sabin color graph *Sound & Vision* v81 no10 p40 D 2016

Come Fly With Me B. Ankosko color *Sound & Vision* v82 no2 p74 F/Mr 2017

Gallons of Sound, Pint-Sized Speaker M. Trei color *Sound & Vision* v82 no4 p46 My 2017

NEW ELECTRONICS J. Y. WOOD bw color *Power & Motoryacht* v33 no4 p36 Ap 2017

Sony CAS-1 Compact Audio System M. Fleischmann color *Sound & Vision* v82 no2 p58 F/Mr 2017

Sounds Terrific J. Y. WOOD color *Power & Motoryacht* v33 no3 p42 Mr 2017

X Marks the Spot A. Griffin color graph *Sound & Vision* v82 no4 p58 My 2017

Sound systems—Installation

Art of the SOUND INSTALL B. Reesman *Stage Directions* v29 no11 p14 N 2016

New sound for an old brass steamer L. Puckett color *Model Railroader* v84 no1 p66 Ja 2017

Sound waves

Solar Waves Reveal Core's Spin C. M. CARLISLE color *Sky & Telescope* v134 no5 p10 N 2017

Soundararajan, Thenmozhi—Interviews

THENMOZHI SOUNDARARAJAN il *Nation* v304 no11 p5 Ap 3 2017

Soundcast (Company)

Soundcast VG7 Outdoor Wireless Speaker R. Sabincolor *Sound & Vision* v82 no6 p54 Jl/Ag 2017

SoundCloud Ltd.

The disappearance of SoundCloud has become a real possibility. What would that mean for the music culture that thrives on the site? J. Wortham color *New York Times Magazine* p14 Ag 6 2017

No One Wants to Pay $9.99 for Your Remixes A. Satariano and L. Shaw color *Bloomberg Businessweek* no4506 p25 Ja 9 2017

Sound—Equipment & supplies

See also

Loudspeakers

Go Ahead... Ask Us Anything M. Klein color *Popular Science* v288 no6 p102 N/D 2016

Home Audio Comes Roaring Back K. C. POHLMANN color *Sound & Vision* v82 no4 p21 My 2017

Sound—Equipment & supplies—Evaluation

AirPods: They sound great, but Siri holds them back S. OCHS color *PCWorld* v35 no2 p116 F 2017

Making Wafes M. Fleischmann color graph *Sound & Vision* v82 no7 p54 S 2017

New Gear color *Sound & Vision* v82 no4 p28 My 2017

smart SPEAKERS D. DICKINSON color *Better Homes & Gardens* v95 no6 p65 Je 2017

Sound recording industry—Societies, etc.

Wireless Hi-Res C. Crowley color *Sound & Vision* v82 no2 p16 F/Mr 2017

Sound—Religious aspects

Scholars re-create the sounds of worship at an ancient Greek church Z. Abrams color *Christian Century* v134 no10 p20 My 10 2017

Sounds

See also

Airplane sounds

Household sounds

Railroad sounds

Theaters—Sound effects

30 Cool THINGS ABOUT SOUND A. SILEN *National Geographic Kids* no468 p22 Mr 2017

SOUND EFFECTS F. Williams cartoon *Mother Jones* v42 no1 p53 Ja/F 2017

Sounds From the Deep Field (Music)

Copeland Taps Cosmic Vibes for Aardvarks' Disc K. Micallef color *Downbeat* v84 no8 p16 Ag 2017

Soundscapes (Auditory environment)

Beyond the Five Senses M. HUTSON bw color *Atlantic* v320 no1 p28 Jl/Ag 2017

Soup mixes

Winter WARMER-UPPERS N. BUCK color *Nebraska Life* v21 no6 p64 N/D 2017

Soups

See also
Soup mixes
Vegetable soup
15-Minute All-Organic Meal under $15 color *Prevention* v68 no12 p16 D 2016
The Autumnal Table Throw a dinner party Featuring the hearty bounty of the season M. HERMANSON *Virginia Living* v15 no6 p68 O 2017
BEST OF WHAT'S LEFT L. Cericola color *Southern Living* v51 no11 p156 N 2016
CELERIAC S. SPUNGEN color *Rodale's Organic Life* v3 no1 p21 Ja 2017
CHEESEBURGER SOUP: MAKE A DOUBLE BATCH AND PACK LEFTOVERS IN LUNCHES FOR SCHOOL OR TO TAKE TO THE FIELD L. F. Prater *Successful Farming* v115 no11 p61 S 2017
Chill Out Cool Summer soups P. Hise *Virginia Living* v15 no4 p72 Je 2017
COLD SUMMER SOUPS A. Sussman color *Sunset* v239 no1 p89 Jl 2017
Comforting dinners for cold, wintry nights color *Redbook* p136 D 2016
Dinner Tonight C. L. MUSIC color *Bon Appetit* no1 p29 F 2017
EAT YOUR WAY TO PROSPERITY C. K. Jackson and N. Jordan color *Essence* v47 no9 p83 Ja 2017
Give Peas a Chance color *House Beautiful* v159 no1 p44 F 2017
Holiday Escape color *Bon Appetit* v61 no12 p80 D 2016 /Jan2017
Love Your Leftovers K. HYMORE color *Prevention* v69 no11 p86 N 2017
Mixing Bowl color *O, The Oprah Magazine* p148 F 2017
O CHRISTMAS TREE [Cover story] C. Lamers and K. Smoot color *Sunset* v237 no6 p62 D 2016
POT LUCK J. YONAN color *Better Homes & Gardens* v95 no10 p146 O 2017
SHOW-ME Flavor color *Missouri Life* v44 no5 p72 Ag 2017
SL COOKING SCHOOL color *Southern Living* v52 no10 p132 O 2017
Slim and satisfying soups L. Lillien color *Redbook* p94 F 2017
Soup Is the New Juice S. Dreisbach color *Glamour* v114 no7 p89 Jl 2016
The Soup of Summer P. Grandjean color *Southern Living* v52 no7 p120 Jl 2017
Soup's On! K. Rankin color *Southern Living* v52 no10 p109 O 2017
Soup's On S. BRILLS, J. WINBERG et al color *Backpacker* v45 no2 p36 Mr 2017
VISUALIZE WHIRLED PEAS *Cincinnati Magazine* v50 no10 p117 Jl 2017
WINTER SOUPS TAKE ROOT C. Stone *Saturday Evening Post* v289 no1 p78 Ja/F 2017
Soups—Evaluation
The Best Soups for Men cartoon color *Men's Health* v32 no9 p62 N 2017
Souq.com FZ-LLC
SOUQ.COM'S CEO ON BUILDING AN E-COMMERCE POWERHOUSE IN THE MIDDLE EAST: Winning trust in regions where payments are made in cash R. Mouchawar color *Harvard Business Review* v95 no5 p35 S/O 2017
Source, The (Theatrical production)
PYRAMIDS AND WIKILEAKS A. ROSS cartoon *New Yorker* v92 no41 p86 D 12 2016
Sourcebooks Inc.
Keeping the Spark Alive D. DILWORTH color *Publishers Weekly* v264 no23 p18 Je 5 2017
Sourdough bread
WONDER BREADS J. DRILLING *Cincinnati Magazine* v50 no10 p124 Jl 2017
Sousa, Vitor C.
Chimpanzee genomic diversity reveals ancient admixture with bonobos bibl diag graph map *Science* v354 no6311 p477 O 28 2016
South Africa—Description & travel
TRIPS THAT TRANSPORT AND TRANSFORM J. BROUGHTON, J. FELDMAR et al color *Martha Stewart Living* p102 Mr 2017
South Africa—Social conditions—21st century

South Africa Tries to End a Leadership Crisis M. Cohen color *Bloomberg Businessweek* no4499 p40 N 14 2016
South America—News briefs
Americas K. Stock bw color *Bloomberg Businessweek* no4529 p8 Jl 3 2017
South America *New York Times Upfront* v149 no7 p26 Ja 9 2017
South Australia
Blackouts cast Australia's green energy in dim light A. Reese color *Science* v355 no6329 p1001 Mr 10 2017
South Australia—Economic conditions
A Rogue State Could Swing Australia Left J. Scott *Bloomberg Businessweek* no4532 p33 Jl 31 2017
South by Southwest Music & Media Conference
SXSW'S GREATEST HITS color *Entertainment Weekly* no1459 p16 Mr 31 2017
South Carolina
Too Much Tolerance *Governing* v30 no6 p12 Mr 2017
South Carolina—Description & travel
Do the Charleston B. PORTER KATZ color *Martha Stewart Living* p110 My 2017
HIGHS AND LOW COUNTRY T. E. Nickens color *Field & Stream* v121 no9 p58 Ap 2017
South China Sea
Asia & Oceania *New York Times Upfront* v149 no7 p28 Ja 9 2017
A SEA'S FADING BOUNTY R. BALE color map *National Geographic* v231 no3 p74 Mr 2017
TOP SECRET: CONFIDENTIAL B. FEIRSTEIN color *Vanity Fair* v59 no9 p136 S 2017
South Dakota
FARMERS MARKER DISCOVERIS: Plus other joyful life lessons learned at the farmers markets B. Hunhoff and K. Hunhoff *South Dakota Magazine* v33 no3 p27 S/O 2017
HOT SPRINGS *South Dakota Magazine* v33 no3 p37 S/O 2017
ONLY ON OUR WEBSITE *South Dakota Magazine* v32 no4 p19 N/D 2016
THE RIVER AT SPRINGFIELD B. Hunhoff *South Dakota Magazine* v32 no4 p28 N/D 2016
SOUTH DAKOTA TRIVIA *South Dakota Magazine* v32 no4 p16 N/D 2016
South Dakota Magazine (Periodical)
OUR 'COUSIN' MERLE K. Hunlioff *South Dakota Magazine* v32 no6 p8 Mr/Ap 2017
South Dakota—Description & travel
THE DUSTY TRAIL: The Fort Meade National Backcountry Byway might be our most historic gravel road J. Andrews *South Dakota Magazine* v33 no3 p74 S/O 2017
EAST RIVER EVENTS *South Dakota Magazine* v33 no3 p82 S/O 2017
TOP 7 Things Christine Erickson Loves About South Dakota *South Dakota Magazine* v32 no4 p17 N/D 2016
TOP 7: Things Darla Drew Lerdal Loves About South Dakota *South Dakota Magazine* v33 no3 p17 S/O 2017
South Florida Trail Riders Inc.
TRAIL ASSOCIATIONS color *Trail Rider* v29 no3 p66 Ap 2017
South Island (N.Z.)—Description & Travel
What I Know for Sure Oprah color *O, The Oprah Magazine* p112 Je 2017
South Korean conglomerate corporations
See also
Samsung Group (Company)
South Lake Tahoe (Calif.)—Description & travel
IF YOU BUILD IT, WILL THEY COME? D. Duane color *Bloomberg Businessweek* no4509 p59 Ja 30 2017
South Pacific (Theatrical production)
Scene, Not Heard L. KO *O, The Oprah Magazine* p149 My 2017
South Park (TV program)
BIGGER, RISKIER & STILL 100% UN COUTH D. Franich color *Entertainment Weekly* no1435 p30 O 14 2016
South Pole
Where is the South Pole? E. LEANE *Natural History* v124 no10 p48 N 2016
South Sudan—Social conditions—21st century
Pope Francis calls for action as famine declared in South Sudan K. Clarke color *America* v216 no6 p15 Mr 20 2017
South Texas Trail Riders Inc.
TRAIL ASSOCIATIONS color *Trail Rider* v29 no3 p66 Ap 2017

South Africa—Economic conditions—1991-

South Africa Needs a New Direction *Bloomberg Businessweek* no4531 p10 Jl 24 2017

South Africa—Politics & government—1994-

The Race to Lead South Africa Is On M. Cohen, D. Malingha Doya et al color *Bloomberg Businessweek* no4524 p15 My 29 2017

South Africa Needs a New Direction *Bloomberg Businessweek* no4531 p10 Jl 24 2017

South Africa Tries to End a Leadership Crisis M. Cohen color *Bloomberg Businessweek* no4499 p40 N 14 2016

Southampton (England)

SOUTHAMPTON: Take the QEII Mile Through the Sea City *British Heritage Travel* v38 no4 p24 Jl/Ag 2017

Southeast Asia—Foreign relations—United States

The U.S. Dimension *Foreign Affairs* v95 no6 p(Sp)2 N/D 2016

Southeast Asian cooking

See also

Indonesian cooking

Vietnamese cooking

EAT. DRINK. ENJOY J. Forman, T. Mcnally et al color *New Orleans Magazine* v51 no9 p56 Jl 2017

Southeastern Conference

The Voice V. Lundquist color *Sports Illustrated* v125 no18 p64 D 5 2016

Southerland, Elizabeth

You're Retired! cartoon color *Weekly Standard* v22 no46 p3 Ag 14 2017

Southerland, Jenna Bergen

10 Minutes a Day [Cover story] bw color *Prevention* v69 no1 p46 Ja 2017

Simply Toned color *Prevention* v69 no9 p74 O 2017

YOUR BEST BODY [Cover story] color *Prevention* v69 no6 p40 Je 2017

Southerland, Jesse

Fast and Happy cartoon color *Bicycling* v58 no8 p24 S 2017

JAEGHER TS-38 INTERCEPTOR S-STIFF color *Bicycling* v58 no10 p52 N/D 2017

Southern Alps/Kā Tiritiri o te Moana (N.Z.)

GRAVITY IN MIDDLE EARTH B. Fredlund color *Skiing* p66 D 2016

Southern Baptist Convention—Political activity

Russell Moore Can't Support Either Candidate A. M. Cox *New York Times Magazine* p66 O 16 2016

Southern Blood (Music)

Gregg Allman's Last Ride D. BROWNE color *Rolling Stone* no1294 p18 Ag 24 2017

Southern California Timing Association (Organization)

A RECORD 48 YEARS IN THE MAKING B. Gillogly color *Hot Rod* v70 no1 p34 Ja 2017

Salt-Flat Racing Happens at a Different Pace E. Perkins color *Hot Rod* v69 no12 p10 D 2016

Southern Poverty Law Center

Hate Groups in America: Organizations that spread hate have grown in the past two decades *New York Times Upfront* p9 S 18 2017

Southerners (U.S.)

Stories for the Memory Books *Southern Living* v51 no12 p130 D 2016

Southerst, John

College All Stars: Galaxy of Success color *Maclean's* v129 no46 p44 N 21 2016

Continuing Education: Achieving the Dream color *Maclean's* v129 no51/52 p58 D 26 2016

Seize the Private School Advantage color *Maclean's* v130 no9 p50 O 2017

Western Colleges: Career Take-off color *Maclean's* v130 no10 p111 N 2017

Southland (N.Z.)

1642: Batavia *Lapham's Quarterly* v10 no2 p55 Spr 2017

Southland (Theatrical production)

Before #BlackLivesMatter: A Timeline E. M. THEYS *Dance Magazine* v90 no12 p43 D 2016

Southon, Emma

Tacitus' Perfect Man *History Today* v67 no8 p18 Ag 2017

Southward, David

How America Lost Its Mind color *Atlantic* v320 no4 p12 N 2017

Southward, Pat

Q: What is the most significant fad of all time? color *Atlantic* v319 no3 p96 Ap 2017

Southwell (Nottinghamshire, England)

SOUTHWELL *British Heritage Travel* v38 no3 p24 My/Je 2017

Southwest Airlines Co.

How Southwest Airlines Hires Such Dedicated People J. Weber *Harvard Business Review Digital Articles* p2 D 2 2015

Southwest Airlines and NRPA: Helping to Restore Monarch Habitat L. Robertson *Parks & Recreation* v52 no1 p40 Ja 2017

Southwestern States—Environmental conditions

THE DESCENT A. BURR color *Climbing* no350 p80 D 2016/Ja 2017

Southwood, Kate

Evensong *Publishers Weekly* v264 no13 p72 Mr 27 2017

Southworth, Daniel R.

Ratchet-like polypeptide translocation mechanism of the AAA+ disaggregase Hsp104 diag *Science* v357 no6348 p273 Jl 21 2017

Soutter, Madora

Critical consciousness A key to student achievement bw il *Phi Delta Kappan* v98 no5 p18 F 2017

Souvenirs (Keepsakes)

Global Decor S. RHYMES and D. POINTDUJOUR color *Ebony* v72 no6 p56 Ap/My 2017

Yes!!! C. O'CONNELL *Texas Monthly* v45 no8 p48 Ag 2017

Souza, P.

Persistent effects of pre-Columbian plant domestication on Amazonian forest composition bibl chart graph map *Science* v355 no6328 p925 Mr 3 2017

Souza, Pete

All the President's Pictures M. GOLDBERG color *O, The Oprah Magazine* p30 N 2017

Souza, Sandra C.

Systemic pan-AMPK activator MK-8722 improves glucose homeostasis but induces cardiac hypertrophy graph *Science* v357 no6350 p507 Ag 4 2017

Souza Filho, Antonio G.

Mildred S. Dresselhaus *Physics Today* v70 no6 p73 Je 2017

SOVACOOL, BENJAMIN

Advancing clean energy *Issues in Science & Technology* v33 no3 p5 Spr 2017

Nuclear power: Serious risks *Science* v354 no6316 p1112 D 2 2016

Sociotechnical transitions for deep decarbonization color diag *Science* v357 no6357 p1242 S 22 2017

Sovereign wealth funds—Norway

Europe K. Stock color graph *Bloomberg Businessweek* no4535 p8 Ag 28 2017

Sovereignty (Political science)

See also

Legitimacy of governments

Social contract

States' rights (American politics)

An Empire for Liberty T. Donnelly and W. Kristol *Weekly Standard* v23 no4 p7 O 2 2017

For a Concert of Powers S. H. BALCH *American Conservative* v15 no6 p23 N/D 2016

Happy Texas Week, Y'all! D. COURTNEY *Texas Monthly* v45 no3 p212 Mr 2017

Soviet espionage—United States

HOUSE OF SPIES [Cover story] M. Friscolanti color *Maclean's* v130 no8 p30 S 2017

The Two Worlds of a Soviet Spy H. Klehr, J. E. Haynes et al bw *Commentary* v143 no3 p27 Mr 2017

Soviet Union. Komitet gosudarstvennoi bezopasnosti

THE PLOT AGAINST AMERICA T. RID and V. WARD cartoon color *Esquire* v166 no5 p130 D 2016/Ja 2017

Vaporized D. MARGOLIN bw color *Weekly Standard* v22 no17 p24 Ja 2 2017

Soviet Union—Economic conditions

PORTRAIT OF THE AUTHOR AS A HISTORIAN NO. 12: SVETLANA ALEXIEVICH: Attempting to recover the human experience of Communism in the post-Soviet era, a Belarusian investigative journalist found pessimistic nostalgia in place of hope for the future A. Lee *History Today* v67 no6 p86 Je 2016

Soviet Union—History

Bone Records K. C. POHLMANN and C. Crowley color *Sound & Vision* v81 no9 p26 N 2016

Vaporized D. MARGOLIN bw color *Weekly Standard* v22 no17 p24 Ja 2 2017

Soviet Union—Military history

THE KORSUN NOOSE R. M. Citino *MHQ: Quarterly Journal of Military History* v29 no2 p26 Wint 2017

Soviet Union—Politics & government

PORTRAIT OF THE AUTHOR AS A HISTORIAN NO. 12: SVETLANA ALEXIEVICH: Attempting to recover the human experience of Communism in the post-Soviet era, a Belarusian investigative journalist found pessimistic nostalgia in place of hope for the future A. Lee *History Today* v67 no6 p86 Je 2016

Soviet Union—Economic conditions—1985-1991

The Hesitant U.S. Rescue of the Soviet Economy D. V. Negroponte *Wilson Quarterly* v40 no4 p4 Fall 2016

Soviet Union—Politics & government—1953-1985

THE IRON CURTAIN TORN BY ISRAEL G. Laron *History Today* v67 no5 p36 My 2017

Sowder, Amy

Karen refugees revitalize two mainline churches, inspire film All Saints color *Christian Century* v134 no20 p15 S 27 2017

Sowell, Thomas, 1930-

In Praise of Thomas Sowell M. Helprin *Claremont Review of Books* v17 no3 p90 Summ 2017

Thomas Sowell's Legacy: Invaluable insights into wealth, poverty, and politics A. ARCHIE *American Conservative* v16 no4 p45 Jl/Ag 2017

Visions of Entitlement *Hoover Digest: Research & Opinion on Public Policy* no4 p192 Fall 2016

Sowell, Thomas, 1930—Interviews

Wealth, Poverty; and Politics P. Robinson *Hoover Digest: Research & Opinion on Public Policy* no2 p166 Spr 2017

SOWERS, STEPHANIE

Tips for Getting the New School Year Rolling *Education Digest* v82 no9 p49 My 2017

Sows

SOW PROLAPSE SYNDROME: AN INCREASE IN THIS MYSTERIOUS PROBLEM HAS THE INDUSTRY SEARCHING FOR ANSWERS B. Freese *Successful Farming* v115 no6 p40 Ap 2017

Soyars, Maureen

Firms' productivity rises as women become executives *Monthly Labor Review* p1 Ja 2017

Soybean

GET BEYOND THE SCIENCE J. Scott *Successful Farming* v115 no1 p17 Ja 2017

WHEAT BEATS ANOTHER RETREAT *Successful Farming* v115 no5 p11 Mid-Mr 2017

WHERE DICAMBA STANDS FOR 2017 G. Gullickson *Successful Farming* v115 no1 p16 Ja 2017

Soybean farming

FARMING IN SPACE: CAN WE GROW CROPS ON MARS? RESEARCHERS ARE TRYING TO FEED ASTRONAUTS D. KURNS *Successful Farming* v115 no12 p6 O 2017

SPACE FARMING: HUMANS MUST MASS-PRODUCE FOOD ON THE RED PLANET IF THE JOURNEY IS TO BE SUSTAINABLE L. Bedord *Successful Farming* v115 no12 p32 O 2017

Soybean industry—Economic aspects

SOYBEAN-TO-CORN PRICE RATIO FAVORS BEANS A. Kluis *Successful Farming* v115 no3 p17 Mid-F 2017

Soybean—Sales & prices

GET READY TO MAKE MORE SALES: HERE ARE THE KEY WEEKS YOU'LL WANT TO WATCH IN 2017 A. Kluis graph *Successful Farming* v115 no7 p14 My 2017

ODDS FAVOR HIGHER PRICES FOR 2017 M. McGinnis *Successful Farming* v115 no4 p18 Mr 2017

SOYBEAN-TO-CORN PRICE RATIO FAVORS BEANS A. Kluis *Successful Farming* v115 no3 p17 Mid-F 2017

Soyer, Emre

POLARIZED *USA Today Magazine* v145 no2860 p44 Ja 2017

Stop Reading Lists of Things Successful People Do *Harvard Business Review Digital Articles* p2 Mr 13 2017

Soyfoods

Cooking with Tempeh N. Berkoff *Vegetarian Journal* v35 no1 p9 2016

Eat Like a Champ color *Health* v31 no7 p146 S 2017

This Just In J. Zorthian *Time* v189 no10 p21 Mr 20 2017

VEGGIE BURGERS ROCK! From B.C.E to OMG! Z. Allen *Vegetarian Journal* v35 no2 p10 2016

Zoodle Ramen Bowl J. BOWDEN and J. BESSINGER color *Better Nutrition* v79 no3 p70 Mr 2017

Sozen, Berna

Assembly of embryonic and extraembryonic stem cells to mimic embryogenesis in vitro diag *Science* v356 no6334 p153 Ap 14 2017

Sozialdemokratische Partei Deutschlands (Political party : Germany)

An Establishment Firebrand in Germany B. Jennen, R. Buergin et al color *Bloomberg Businessweek* no4514 p28 Mr 13 2017

Merkel May Be Struggling, but Don't Count Her Out I. Brenner *Time* v189 no6 p12 F 20 2017

Sozzani, Franca, 1950-2016

My Fearless Friend A. Wintour bw *Vogue* v207 no3 p198 Mr 2017

Spa pools

HOT SPOT J. Wignall color *Popular Photography* v81 no2 p34 Mr/Ap 2017

Spaar, Lisa Russ

Orexia *Publishers Weekly* v264 no3 p37 Ja 16 2017

Space

See also

Outer space

Space & time

Vacuum

No. 1 FOUND: Einstein's Ripples in Space-Time E. BETZ bw color diag graph *Discover* v38 no1 p7 Ja/F 2017

Surviving Space K. HAYNES color *Discover* v38 no6 p70 Jl/Ag 2017

UP IN THE AIR C. FISHMAN *Smithsonian* v48 no3 p32 Je 2017

Space & time

See also

Wormholes (Physics)

African Arrow sees hints of structure in the fabric of space P. Kornilovich *Physics Today* v69 no12 p49 D 2016

Tangled Up in Spacetime C. Moskowitz color *Scientific American* v316 no1 p32 Ja 2017

Space archaeology

ANCIENT SITES AS SEEN FROM SPACE A. R. Williams color *National Geographic* v232 no2 p138 Ag 2017

Space biology

See also

Space medicine

If Life Can Make It Here, It Can Make It Anywhere *USA Today Magazine* v145 no2865 p11 Je 2017

X-RAY VISIONARY L. PARKER color *Wired* v25 no10 p20 O 2017

Space colonies

OUR LIVING SPHERE D. HEITMAN *Phi Kappa Phi Forum* v97 no1 p36 Spr 2017

Space cooling

See also

Air conditioning

Space debris

Here Comes the Space Cleanup Crew J. Bachman bw color diag *Bloomberg Businessweek* no4525 p32 Je 5 2017

If there are curious young minds, science will survive E. Quill *Science News* v191 no7 p2 Ap 15 2017

Space elevators

FUTURE WORLD: Transportation K. DE SEVE color *National Geographic Kids* no470 p20 My 2017

Space environment

See also

Cosmic rays

Interstellar matter

Space debris

Space Weather Forecast H. Leifert color *Natural History* v125 no6 p7 Je 2017

Surviving Space K. HAYNES color *Discover* v38 no6 p70 Jl/Ag 2017

Space environment—Research

DEEP-SPACE DEAL BREAKER C. L. Limoli color diag *Scientific American* v316 no2 p54 F 2017

Space exploration

See also

Lunar exploration

Planetary exploration

Space probes

The Enduring Mystery of Luna 2: Amateur observers claimed to see its impact—but no trace of the crash site has ever been found T. A. Dobbins and T. DOBBINS *Sky & Telescope* v134 no3 p52 S 2017

Exoplanet probe has focus problem color *Science* v357 no6350 p432 Ag 4 2017

Help Verify a Giant Ringed Exoplanet: For about 25 days in September, its ring system should cross an easily watched star A. MacRobert *Sky & Telescope* v134 no3 p48 S 2017

Kepler Team Releases Final Catalog S. HALL *Sky & Telescope* v134 no4 p10 O 2017

Morning Marvels: Look to the pre-dawn sky for a series of close planetary pairings this month F. schaaf *Sky & Telescope* v134 no3 p46 S 2017

A Mystery for the Age P. Tyson *Sky & Telescope* v133 no6 p4 Je 2017

OBSERVING September 2017 *Sky & Telescope* v134 no3 p41 S 2017

Picturing the Universe P. MURDIN color *Natural History* v125 no11 p24 N 2017

Showpiece Doubles: Point your telescope toward these gems of the late-summer sky S. French *Sky & Telescope* v134 no3 p54 S 2017

Understanding Surface Brightness J. Oltion *Sky & Telescope* v134 no6 p28 D 2017

Space Exploration Technologies Corp.

The Falcon Has Landed. Now SpaceX Is Eyeing Mars E. BETZ color *Discover* v38 no1 p27 Ja/F 2017

Inching Ahead With Hyperloop B. R. REYNOLDS *Los Angeles Magazine* p18 Ja 2017

Reusable rockets' red glare E. DeMarco color *Science News* v190 no13 p44 D 24 2016

TRIAL BALLOONS A. Mann color diag *Science* v356 no6344 p1227 Je 23 2017

TUNNEL VISION M. CHAFKIN color *Bloomberg Businessweek* no4512 p52 F 20 2017

Space exploration—Equipment & supplies

NEW PRODUCT SHOWCASE *Sky & Telescope* v134 no3 p64 S 2017

Space exploration—International cooperation

Treaty tested by space miners D. Clery color *Science* v357 no6359 p19 O 6 2017

Space flight

See also

Manned space flight

NASA Has a New Way to Fly J. Kluger color *Time* v188 no27-28 p90 D 26 2016

White House science adviser talks space, climate change, and budgets D. Kramer *Physics Today* v69 no10 p27 O 2016

Space flight to Mars

See also

Curiosity (Spacecraft)

nap your way to Mars J. Lederman cartoon *Popular Science* v289 no5 p18 S/O 2017

Space flight to the moon—Competitions

AROUND THE WORLD *Science* v357 no6358 p1332 S 29 2017

A New Race to the Moon color *Time* v189 no12 p12 Ap 3 2017

XPrize finalists mull payloads to the moon D. Clery color diag *Science* v354 no6319 p1510 D 23 2016

Space launch industry—United States

Commercial Space Flight *Congressional Digest* v96 no7 p30 S 2017

ROCKET BOOM IN THE DESERT J. Alsever color *Fortune* v175 no3 p20 Mr 1 2017

Space medicine

Man vs. Machine: Space Medicine color *Bloomberg Businessweek* no4534 p23 Ag 14 2017

Space photography

See also

Lunar photography

Ethics in Astrophotography: Seeing isn't always believing in the digital age J. Lodriguss *Sky & Telescope* v134 no3 p66 S 2017

GALLERY *Sky & Telescope* v134 no3 p72 S 2017

Moon Missions, Imperfect and Magnificent J. Kluger color *Time* v189 no13 p19 Ap 10 2017

Space probes

See also

Juno (Space probe)

New Horizons (Spacecraft)

NASA Hopes to Make History With Its Latest Mission—to the Sun J. Kluger color *Time* v189 no22 p7 Je 12 2017

Reflections on Voyager D. J. Eicher color *Astronomy* v45 no10 p8 O 2017

Space race

The Developing Space Race T. John color *Time* v188 no14 p8 O 10 2016

Space sciences

See also

Outer space

Funny FILL-IN J. FANSLAU *National Geographic Kids* no466 p34 D 2016/Ja 2017

Space security

The New Star Wars S. STIRONE color *New Republic* v248 no6 p10 Je 2017

Space stations

Spooky action achieved at record distance [Cover story] G. Popkin color *Science* v356 no6343 p1110 Je 16 2017

Space suit design & construction

WELL SUITED FOR SPACE WORK J. Berlin color *National Geographic* v232 no2 p18 Ag 2017

Space suits

going for boeing S. Chodosh color *Popular Science* v289 no6 p80 N/D 2017

Space suits—Evaluation

Rocket to the Red Planet K. D. Atherton and S. Chodosh color diag *Popular Science* v289 no6 p54 N/D 2017

Space telescopes

See also

Hubble Space Telescope (Spacecraft)

AROUND THE WORLD color *Science* v357 no6359 p14 O 6 2017

WEBB DESIGN E. MASTROIANNI color *Discover* v38 no6 p83 Jl/Ag 2017

Space telescopes—Design & construction

Telescopic Tag Team J. Hsu color *Scientific American* v316 no1 p16 Ja 2017

Space tourism

A Humongous Rocket That Just Might Work B. FERDOWSI color diag *Popular Mechanics* p12 S 2017

Space vehicle accidents

Mars lander crash adds to 2020 rover worries D. Clery color *Science* v354 no6311 p397 O 28 2016

Space vehicle launching

The Cassini-Huygens space probe [Cover story] A. ABEL color *Maclean's* v129 no51/52 p74 D 26 2016

LAUNCHED INTO MEMORY A. Crawford *Smithsonian* v48 no3 p14 Je 2017

Space vehicle maintenance & repair

SPACE CONSERVATION K. RANDALL *Washingtonian Magazine* v52 no12 p24 S 2017

Space vehicles

See also

Artificial satellites

Space probes

Space telescopes

75, 50 & 25 YEARS AGO R. W. Sinnott *Sky & Telescope* v134 no6 p8 D 2017

AERO-SPACE K. D. ATHERTON and S. BUSHWICK color *Popular Science* v288 no6 p52 N/D 2016

APOLLO TO CELEBRATE ITS 50TH AT AIRVENTURE bw color *Flying* v144 no4 p20 Ap 2017

Cassini's Grand Finale: 20 years in the making M. Carroll bw color diag *Astronomy* v45 no9 p28 S 2017

HOW AN INTERPLANETARY MISSION CHANGED THE

WORLD S. Stirone cartoon *Astronomy* v45 no10 p56 O 2017

How to... DESTROY ANYTHING cartoon color *Popular Mechanics* v193 no7 p83 S 2016

A JunoCam close-up *Physics Today* v70 no8 p80 Ag 2017

Memories from a BACKYARD OBSERVER R. Shubinski color *Astronomy* v45 no10 p62 O 2017

Sailing on Sunshine J. Hsu color *Scientific American* v317 no4 p24 O 2017

Saturn spacecraft's swan song color *Science* v357 no6355 p952 S 8 2017

VOYAGER REVEALED! J. Wenz color diag graph *Astronomy* v45 no10 p34 O 2017

Space vehicles—Evaluation

50 Years of Martian Invasions color *National Geographic* v230 no5 p17 N 2016

Rocket to the Red Planet K. D. Atherton and S. Chodosh color diag *Popular Science* v289 no6 p54 N/D 2017

Space vehicles—Landing—Mars (Planet)

Mars lander crash adds to 2020 rover worries D. Clery color *Science* v354 no6311 p397 O 28 2016

Space warfare

Spooks in Space J. BAMFORD color *Foreign Policy* no221 p96 N/D 2016

Space Between Us, The (Film)

BIRTH OF A MARTIAN K. M. MCFARLAND cartoon *Wired* v24 no12 p34 D 2016

Boys Are from Mars, Girls Are from Earth S. Zacharek color *Time* v189 no5 p50 F 13 2017

Spacey, Kevin, 1959-

Cards Returns With a Thud D. D'Addario color *Time* v189 no21 p63 Je 5 2017

HOUSE OF CARDS ROCKS THE VOTE T. Stack color *Entertainment Weekly* no1463/1464 p20 Ap/My 2017

SPADACCINI, STEPHANIE

Just for the Halibut *AARP: The Magazine* v59 no4A p71 Je/Jl 2016

Spadaro, Antonio

2 + 2 Can Equal 5 D. Mills color *Commonweal* v144 no3 p8 F 10 2017

SPADE, KATE VALENTINE

SHE'S GOT THE LOOK *O, The Oprah Magazine* p121 Mr 2017

Spader, James, 1960-

The Blacklist I. Rudolph *TV Guide* v65 no19 p31 My 1 2017

The Blacklist N. Abrams, B. L. Heldman et al color *Entertainment Weekly* no1482/1483 p74 S 22 2017

The Blacklist's Big Reveal N. Abrams color *Entertainment Weekly* no1467 p14 My 26 2017

Spadoni, Cesare

Lee Rubin: Our mentor and role model *Science* v355 no6327 p806 F 24 2017

Spaghetti

ballers C. MOROCCO color *Bon Appetit* v62 no10 p90 O 2017

MMM... MORNING color *Good Housekeeping* v264 no3 p143 Mr 2017

Noodling Around C. Henry color *O, The Oprah Magazine* p135 Ap 2017

super skillets color *Good Housekeeping* v264 no3 p118 Mr 2017

Spahn, V.

A nontoxic pain killer designed by modeling of pathological receptor conformations bibl diag graph *Science* v355 no6328 p966 Mr 3 2017

Spain, Sarah

TALK TO US M. O'Connor, D. McGill et al color graph *Chicago* v65 no12 p24 D 2016

Spain, Sarah—Interviews

THE SUPERFAN C. ZULKEY color *Chicago* v65 no11 p24 N 2016

Spain—Antiquities

Landscape of Secrets S. S. PATEL bw color *Archaeology* v70 no5 p48 S/O 2017

Spain—Foreign relations

Soviet Spain? A. HOCHSCHILD *Commentary* v142 no3 p9 O 2016

Spain—History—Civil War, 1936-1939

The First of Many L. Hannant *History Today* v67 no1 p17 Ja 2017

Retrieving Bones, Reviving Memories N. Stockwell color *Progressive* v81 no2 p32 F 2017

Spaldin, Nicola A.

Sounding out optical phonons diag *Science* v357 no6354 p873 S 1 2017

Spalding, Esperanza, 1984-

NIGHT LIFE *New Yorker* v92 no47 p5 Ja 30 2017

Thriving in Idaho J. Ross color *Downbeat* v84 no1 p92 Ja 2017

The Unexpected Beauty of Tearing Things Apart: Grammy Award-winning musician Esperanza Spalding puts her spin on the history of design at Smithsonian's Cooper Hewitt museum in a show about transformation, the motif of her latest Interview by Katie... K. Nodjimbadem *Smithsonian* v48 no5 p22 S 2017

Spalding, Esperanza, 1984—Interviews

Esperanza Spalding As a Real-Time Innovator R. Bruner color *Time* v190 no10/11 p106 S 18 2017

SPALDING, GORDON

Chatter *Indianapolis Monthly* v40 no7 p15 Mr 2017

Spalding, Julia

best of Indy *Indianapolis Monthly* v40 no4 p73 D 2016

Conic Boom *Indianapolis Monthly* p45 N 2017

Family Dinner: A follow-up to the Fortville original, FoxGardin Family Kitchen delivers more top-nosh grub *Indianapolis Monthly* v40 no10 p44 Je 2017

First Things First M. Rubino *Indianapolis Monthly* v40 no7 p14 Mr 2017

Granny Ambition: 22nd Street Diner gives comfort food a good, old-fashioned schooling *Indianapolis Monthly* p50 N 2017

High on the Hog *Indianapolis Monthly* v40 no5 p38 Ja 2017

Hola Again color *Indianapolis Monthly* p44 Ap 2017

Into the Fold A downtown remake as simple and straightforward as its name, The Taco Shop does one thing and does it well *Indianapolis Monthly* v40 no11 p42 Jl 2017

Mucho Gusto *Indianapolis Monthly* v40 no7 p44 Mr 2017

New Flame: With Stella, Neal Brown gets his groove back, quietly serving rustic Southern European food cooked by open fire. That's hot color *Indianapolis Monthly* v41 no2 p44 S 2017

New Wave *Indianapolis Monthly* v40 no4 p56 D 2016

PINOT FREEZIO *Indianapolis Monthly* v40 no10 p41 Je 2017

Raising the Bar: Cocktails and small plates create a stir at Bar One Fourteen, the Patachou family's sexy black sheep color *Indianapolis Monthly* v42 no2 p46 O 2017

Selling the Sizzle *Indianapolis Monthly* p40 F 2017

Small But Meaty *Indianapolis Monthly* v40 no3 p58 N 2016

SMOKE RING: The litmus test for good barbecue, tender, nononsense beef brisket represents low, slow food at its best *Indianapolis Monthly* v12 no40 p45 Ag 2017

Tony Baloney *Indianapolis Monthly* p43 My 2017

Spalding, Rebecca

A Political Scion Tries To Right Puerto Rico color *Bloomberg Businessweek* no4519 p18 Ap 24 2017

Spam (Email)

How to stop spam emails from reaching your inbox G. FLEISHMAN color *Macworld - Digital Edition* v34 no11 p111 N 2017

Spampinato, Francesco

31 DAYS in the LIFE of the CULTURE bw cartoon color *Vanity Fair* v59 no4 p113 Mr 2017

Spang, Anja

Genomic exploration of the diversity, ecology, and evolution of the archaeal domain of life color *Science* v357 no6351 p563 Ag 11 2017

Spaniola, Shay—Interviews

SHAY spaniola A. MAZE color *Better Homes & Gardens* v95 no4 p34 Ap 2017

Spanish American literature

Olé! Spanish Language Programs at the Fair L. Ahuile bw color *Publishers Weekly* v263 no44 p(Sp)21 O 31 2016

Spanish architecture

Spain: Looking Back 25 Years D. COHN color *Architectural Record* v205 no8 p43 Ag 2017

Spanish architecture—20th century

Staying True T. SHESS color *Old House Journal* v45 no7 p24 O 2017

Spanish art—Exhibitions

"A JOSEPH BEUYS" S. ADAMS color *ARTnews* v115 no4 p138 Wint 2016/2017

Spanish cooking

WHARF TOUR: What's coming to DC's new restaurant hub A.

Spiegel *Washingtonian Magazine* v53 no1 p150 O 2017

Spanish films

Letter from Madrid: Spanish Screenings and Julieta P. J. Smith *Film Quarterly* v70 no2 p63 Wint 2016

Spanish language

Distributors and Wholesalers Meet the Growing Demand For Books in Spanish L. AHUILE color *Publishers Weekly* v263 no46 p6 N 14 2016

Spanish literature

See also

Spanish American literature

Fall Changes L. Ahuile *Publishers Weekly* v263 no40 p19 O 3 2016

Olé! Spanish Language Programs at the Fair L. Ahuile bw color *Publishers Weekly* v263 no44 p(Sp)21 O 31 2016

Spanish literature—Foreign countries

Distributors and Wholesalers Meet the Growing Demand For Books in Spanish L. AHUILE color *Publishers Weekly* v263 no46 p6 N 14 2016

Spanish mural painting & decoration

Sacred and secular unite on Basque church's walls R. Skirble color *Christian Century* v134 no2 p17 Ja 18 2017

Spanish television broadcasting

Telemundo's Ratings Are Made in the USA G. Smith and D. Rocks *Bloomberg Businessweek* no4514 p22 Mr 13 2017

Spanish-American War, 1898—Campaigns

LIFE ON A TORPEDO BOAT M. McDowell *MHQ: Quarterly Journal of Military History* v29 no2 p84 Wint 2017

Spanish Civil War, 1936-1939

Landscape of Secrets S. S. PATEL bw color *Archaeology* v70 no5 p48 S/O 2017

Soviet Spain? R. Radosh *Commentary* v142 no3 p10 O 2016

Spann, Susan

Betrayal at Iga: A Hiro Hattori Novel *Publishers Weekly* v264 no19 p39 My 8 2017

Spannagl, Manuel

Wild emmer genome architecture and diversity elucidate wheat evolution and domestication color *Science* v357 no6346 p93 Jl 7 2017

Spanos, Brittany

THE 50 GREATEST CONCERTS OF THE LAST 50 YEARS bw color *Rolling Stone* no1286 p30 My 4 2017

FALL ALBUM PREVIEW *Rolling Stone* no1297 p12 O 5 2017

Hot Pop Tinashe color *Rolling Stone* no1274 p35 N 17 2016

Issa Rae bw *Rolling Stone* no1295 p47 S 7 2017

Kesha's Battle Cry of Many Colors color *Rolling Stone* no1294 p53 Ag 24 2017

Meet the Black Beatles color *Rolling Stone* no1278/1279 p15 Ja 12 2017

The Photo Issue [Cover story] bw *Rolling Stone* no1299 p24 N 2 2017

A Pop Prodigy on the Edge of 13 color *Rolling Stone* no1278/1279 p18 Ja 12 2017

The Road Heats Up bw color *Rolling Stone* no1288 p11 Je 1 2017

Tove Lo's High Life color *Rolling Stone* no1275 p18 D 1 2016

Spanos, Dean

DEAN OF IMPUDENCE M. Rosenberg color *Sports Illustrated* v127 no12 p108 O 16 2017

Spare parts

CLEVER STORAGE J. KOPYCINSKI color *Dirt Sports + Off-Road* v51 no7 p64 Jl 2017

SPARE CHANGE J. Jacquot chart color *Car & Driver* v62 no8 p22 F 2017

Spark Business Academy (Company)

A Is for Arbitrage [Cover story] P. Robison color *Bloomberg Businessweek* no4502 p52 D 5 2016

Spark ignition engines

Think First G. MICHAL *Boating World* v38 no6 p22 Je 2017

Spark ignition engines—Evaluation

The Future of Fueling J. Smith color *Hot Rod* v70 no2 p78 F 2017

Sparkling wines

Bubbling Up: Afton's Thibaut-Janisson Winery brings sparkling wine to the forefront W. SHEPPARD *Virginia Living* v15 no6 p45 O 2017

For Chandon in China, a Kick From Champagne? B. Einhorn graph *Bloomberg Businessweek* no4501 p21 N 28 2016

Sparks, Nicholas

Q: What was the most important letter in history? color *Atlantic* v320 no2 p104 S 2017

Sparks, R. Stephen J.

Vertically extensive and unstable magmatic systems: A unified view of igneous processes color *Science* v355 no6331 p1280 Mr 24 2017

SPARKS, ROSE ANN

ROAR OF THE CROWD *Texas Monthly* v45 no6 p10 Je 2017

SPARKS, SARAH D.

One Key to Reducing School Suspension: A Little Respect *Education Digest* v82 no4 p8 D 2016

Sparktacular Inc.

Sparktacular's Sparkular *Stage Directions* v30 no5 p26 My 2017

Sparkular (Company)

Sparktacular A Piece of Technological History in the Making *Stage Directions* v30 no3 p48 Mr 2017

SPARRGROVE, ERIC

ROAR OF THE CROWD *Texas Monthly* v44 no11 p14 N 2016

Sparrow, Ben

The extent of forest in dryland biomes [Cover story] chart map *Science* v356 no6338 p635 My 12 2017

Publish openly but responsibly color *Science* v357 no6347 p141 Jl 14 2017

SPARROW, DAVID

advice every new mom needs [Cover story] color *Parents* v92 no7 p32 Jl 2017

Sparrows

Bird's-Eye View R. BROOKHISER il *National Review* v69 no1 p43 Ja 23 2017

Sparta (Extinct city)—History

The Quiz *History Today* v67 no4 p71 Ap 2017

Spartina 449 (Company)

GREAT BUYS UNDER $100: WOMAN OF THE WORLD color *O, The Oprah Magazine* p46 Jl 2017

Spathiflorae

See also

Duckweeds

Mr. Rigolizzo and the amazing miracle weed that will save Sparta! (Or not.) S. Raviv *Atlanta* v57 no2 p84 Je 2017

Spatial distribution (Quantum optics)

Bringing order to neutral atom arrays C. Regal bibl diag *Science* v354 no6315 p972 N 25 2016

Spaulding, Elizabeth

Hackathons Aren't Just for Coders *Harvard Business Review Digital Articles* p2 Ap 1 2016

Spaun, B.

Direct frequency comb measurement of OD + CO→DOCO kinetics bibl graph *Science* v354 no6311 p444 O 28 2016

Spauwen, Lorraine

BLUE DEW color *Popular Photography* v80 no11 p36 D 2016

Spavronskaya, Alisa

Rainbow Detectives: When Art Gets Meteorology Wrong *Weatherwise* v70 no2 p24 Mr/Ap 2017

Spawls, Alice

Portraits Put to Use—and Misuse color *New York Review of Books* v64 no3 p51 F 23 2017

SPBI SA

POCKETS GET POPULAR M. WERLING color *Sea Magazine* v109 no8 p4 Ag 2017

Speak Low (Music)

Speak Low/Speak Low Renditions B. Bambarger bw *Downbeat* v84 no6 p71 Je 2017

Speaker, Kristin J.

Ask anything [Cover story] color *Women's Health* v14 no1 p24 Ja/F 2017

Spear, Andrew

The Polls Are Open color *Bloomberg Businessweek* no4498 p34 N 7 2016

Spear, Sarah

Sarah Spear *Atlanta* v56 no7 p52 N 2016

Spearfish (S.D.)

Community Caves: Short and Steep A. Boe *South Dakota Magazine* v33 no2 p93 Jl/Ag 2017

SPEARFISH: HIPPIE HAVEN? P. Higbee *South Dakota Magazine* v32 no4 p54 N/D 2016

Spearman, Joah—Interviews

KEEPING IT LOCAL S. Blodgett and S. Lynn color *Black Enterprise* v47 no8 p13 Jl/Ag 2017

Spearman, Mitchell

AID FOR WHAT AILS YOU color *Golf Magazine* v59 no1 p39 Ja 2017

SPECHT, ALISON

Synthesis Centers as Critical Research Infrastructure *BioScience* v67 no8 p750 Ag 2017

Specht, S. E.

Selective oxidative dehydrogenation of propane to propene using boron nitride catalysts bibl diag graph *Science* v354 no6319 p1570 D 23 2016

Special advertising sections

A NOTE FROM OUR PUBLISHER S. Katz *Mother Jones* v42 no6 p16 N/D 2017

Special days

See also

　　Gay Pride Day

　　Women's Equality Day

ABOVE & BEYOND cartoon *New Yorker* v92 no43 p14 Ja 2 2017

Changing the World One Pose at a Time T. A. POWER *USA Today Magazine* v145 no2862 p40 Mr 2017

How Families Throw Birthday Parties R. Straetker color graph *Parents* v92 no4 p18 Ap 2017

if you ask me… S. JAMES color *Parents* v92 no4 p100 Ap 2017

It's Gavin's Builder Party color *Parents* v92 no9 p136 S 2017

Price Out the Party Places *Parents* v91 no9 p146 S 2016

Vonnegut Fest M. D. ALLAN *Indianapolis Monthly* v40 no5 p12 Ja 2017

Special economic zones

Time for Investment *Foreign Affairs* v95 no6 p(Sp)4 N/D 2016

Special education

On the Trail Of a Fairy Queen L. VACCARIELLO *Reader's Digest* v189 no1127 p32 F 2017

Special Ed Teacher Puts His Background to Work in the Classroom C. Veiga bw *Education Digest* v83 no2 p21 O 2017

Special education—Finance

AS IF ANY FURTHER *Texas Monthly* v45 no4 p8 Ap 2017

Special education—Study & teaching

THE LOOK BOOK A. SWERDLOFF img *New York* v50 no13 p55 Je 26 2017

Special effects (Motion pictures)

THE INCREDIBLY SPECIAL EFFECTS AWARDS T. GRIERSON bw color *Popular Mechanics* p75 F 2017

Special effects (Theater)

See also

　　Stage flying

Affecting Effects M. S. Eddy *Stage Directions* v30 no5 p2 My 2017

Making Christmas Magic R. Minetor *Stage Directions* v29 no10 p8 O 2016

Special Effects *Stage Directions* v30 no7 p53 Jl 1 2017

Special elections

Atlanta Blues B. SEITZ color *National Review* v69 no12 p29 Je 26 2017

THE BATTLE FOR MONTANA T. Dickinson color *Rolling Stone* no1288 p26 Je 1 2017

No need to apply, Dutch science academy tells men M. Enserink color *Science* v354 no6314 p815 N 18 2016

Special events

See also

　　Memorials

　　Parades

　　Special days

　　Special months

　　Special weeks

2016 WASHINGTONIAN BUD & BURGER BATTLE *Washingtonian Magazine* v52 no1 p42 O 2016

63 GREAT THINGS TO DO THIS MONTH J. FOUMBERG, J. HARDBERGER et al color *Chicago* v66 no8 p105 Ag 2017

ABOVE & BEYOND cartoon *New Yorker* v92 no39 p28 N 28 2016

Almost Too Much Music M. Griffith color *New Orleans Magazine* v51 no7 p50 My 2017

APOLLO TO CELEBRATE ITS 50TH AT AIRVENTURE bw

color *Flying* v144 no4 p20 Ap 2017

Arts, Culture & Entertainment *Virginia Living* p140 2017 Best 20of Virginia

August Events F. Esker color *New Orleans Magazine* v51 no10 p38 Ag 2017

BACK TO THE SALT B. Gillogly chart color *Hot Rod* v70 no1 p28 Ja 2017

CELEBRATING 28 YEARS OF REAL MEN COOK A. V. WATSON color *Ebony* v72 no8 p48 Je 2017

DAN ABOUT TOWN: Party photographer Dan Swartz's monthly roundup of bashes, balls, and benefits *Washingtonian Magazine* v53 no1 p28 O 2017

EVENTS + EXHIBITS color *Arts & Crafts Homes & the Revival* v12 no4 p20 Fall 2017

For the Love of Fighting Bob J. HIGHTOWER cartoon *Progressive* v81 no10 p46 N 2016

FOTOWEEKDC M. J. Gaynor, R. Cartagena et al *Washingtonian Magazine* v52 no2 p35 N 2016

GOINGS ON ABOUT TOWN color *New Yorker* v93 no25 p5 Ag 28 2017

THE GUIDE / 10.17 M. WAKIM color *Los Angeles Magazine* v62 no10 p92 O 2017

Inter Continental Los Angeles Downtown *Los Angeles Magazine* v62 no9 p86 S 2017

INTERNATIONAL color *Downbeat* v83 no11 p96 N 2016

Jazzahead! Draws Record Number of Attendees B. Zimmerman color *Downbeat* v84 no7 p16 Jl 2017

LA SOCIAL bw color *Los Angeles Magazine* v62 no10 p93 O 2017

Lucky Break *National Geographic Kids* no468 p28 Mr 2017

MARK YOUR CALENDAR *Cincinnati Magazine* v50 no12 p96 S 2017

Mass Transit, Mass Art: MARTA finds new ways to use its vast spaces as a canvas for local artists J. HOWARD *Atlanta* v57 no6 p80 O 2017

Outlaw Trail Byway becomes a 'Quiltway' A. J. BARTELS color *Nebraska Life* v21 no5 p88 S/O 2017

Paleo-Tech L. A. HENION *Sierra* v102 no1 p104 Ja/F 2017

PARTY LINES img *New York* p67 Ja 23 2017

Rebranding Canada 150 N. MACDONALD *Maclean's* v130 no3 p14 Ap 2017

Schedule of Events *South Dakota Magazine* p24 S/O 2017 Supplement

Solar Eclipse City Event Guide *Missouri Life* v44 no4 p27 Je 2017

The Stars Are Out R. Love color *AARP: The Magazine* v59 no3A p4 Ap/My 2016

Stars Salute Ella at Lincoln Center R. Musto color *Downbeat* v84 no7 p13 Jl 2017

TEARING IT UP IN TEXAS [Cover story] M. KAUSCH color *Dirt Sports + Off-Road* v51 no12 p10 D 2017

TOP PICKS F. Esker color *New Orleans Magazine* v51 no7 p26 My 2017

TWISTED TERRIBLE TAKES! *Atlanta* v57 no6 p52 O 2017

UNITED STATES color *Downbeat* v83 no11 p90 N 2016

WHERE & WHEN M. J. G. nor, R. Cartagena et al *Washingtonian Magazine* v52 no5 p31 F 2017

WINNING A DAY WITH WOFFORD AND WHITE J. Pierce color *Practical Horseman* v44 no12 p38 D 2016

Special events—Management

Get More from Your Event Spending F. V. Cespedes and P. Prasad *Harvard Business Review Digital Articles* p2 Mr 31 2015

Special forces (Military science)

'I came to fight for all Iraqis' C. MACDIARMID color *Maclean's* v129 no44 p32 N 7 2016

Special forces (Military science)—United States

Make Your Team Less Hierarchical C. Fussell *Harvard Business Review Digital Articles* p2 Jl 15 2015

Special issues of periodicals

EDITOR'S LETTER D. ANDERSON-MINSHALL bw color *Advocate* no1091 p8 Je/Jl 2017

Special months

A Shared Passion for Reading D. A. WOOD color *Missouri Life* v44 no6 p10 S 2017

The Sisters of Prayer Town *Texas Monthly* v44 no12 p40 D 2016

Special needs students

Valuing differences: B. Rentenbach, L. Prislovsky et al color *Phi*

Delta Kappan v98 no8 p59 My 2017

Special Olympics

DOING HER BEST: HOW GROWING UP ON A FARM HELPED MY SISTER-IN-LAW LEARN TO LIVE INDEPENDENTLY *Successful Farming* v115 no12 p66 O 2017

TAKING THE PLUNGE J. R. MARQUEZ *Atlanta* v56 no10 p35 F 2017

Special operations (Military science)

See also

Special forces (Military science)

BLINDING SADDAM B. Underwood *Military History* v33 no6 p38 Mr 2017

Why Special Ops Stopped Relying So Much on Top-Down Leadership C. Fussell *Harvard Business Review Digital Articles* p2 My 27 2015

Special prosecutors

Trump Gets Himself in Hot Water—Again F. BARNES color *Weekly Standard* v22 no35 p12 My 22 2017

Special Victims Unit (TV program)

18 YEARS... 400 EPISODES... ONE UNSTOPPABLE FRANCHISE! [Cover story] I. RUDOLPH *TV Guide* v65 no4 p18 Ja 16 2017

SECRET FILES *TV Guide* v65 no4 p22 Ja 16 2017

SVU STAR POWER E. Aslanian *TV Guide* v65 no4 p21 Ja 16 2017

Special weeks

The Importance of Scholarship N. MITCHELL and P. BERKERY *Publishers Weekly* v264 no38 p76 S 18 2017

Specialists

See also

Consultants

Medicine—Specialties & specialists

2017 TECH TITANS M. J. GAYNOR *Washingtonian Magazine* v52 no8 p59 My 2017

The Danger of Having Too Many Experts N. Lovegrove *Time* v188 no19 p17 N 7 2016

The Expertocracy B. SWAIM color *Weekly Standard* v22 no35 p26 My 22 2017

Fast Times At Forbes Media L. D'VORKIN *Forbes* v199 no6 p8 Je 13 2017

IoT IS NOT A TREND: IT IS TRANSFORMATIVE AND HERE TO STAY color *Maclean's* v129 no40 p23 O 10 2016

When Having Too Many Experts on the Board Backfires A. Tilcsik and J. Almandoz *Harvard Business Review Digital Articles* p2 Ag 29 2016

Specialized Bicycle Components Inc.

HEAD-TO-HEAD: WATTS HAPPENING S. PEARSON color *Wired* v25 no7 p38 Jl 2017

SPECIALIZED S-WORKS ENDURO 29 B. Minnigh color *Bike Magazine* v23 no9 p88 D 2016

SPECIALIZED WOMEN'S DIVERGE COMP L. Flickinger color *Bicycling* v58 no9 p66 O 2017

THAT FRESH TIRE FEEL J. Lindsey, R. Koch et al color *Bicycling* v58 no7 p84 Ag 2017

Turbo Levo color *Bike Magazine* v24 no5 p6 Jl 2017

Special Supplemental Food Program for Women, Infants & Children (U.S.)

Revised WIC Food Packages Increase Purchases of Whole Grains I. Rahkovsky *Amber Waves: The Economics of Food, Farming, Natural Resources, & Rural America* p37 Ap 2017

Special Supplemental Nutrition Program for Women, Infants, & Children (U.S.)

WIC Participation Continues To Decline V. Oliveira *Amber Waves: The Economics of Food, Farming, Natural Resources, & Rural America* p53 Je 2017

Specialty Equipment Market Association (Organization)

SMOKE AND MIRRORS S. RICHARDS color *Dirt Sports + Off-Road* v51 no9 p26 S 2017

Specialty Equipment Market Association (Organization)—Congresses

THE 50TH ANNUAL SEMA SHOW M. EMERY color *Dirt Sports + Off-Road* v51 no3 p24 Mr 2017

Specialty Equipment Market Association (Organization)—Exhibitions

SEMA NEW PRODUCTS 2016 M. EMERY color *Dirt Sports + Off-Road* v51 no4 p52 Ap 2017

Specialty license plates

VEHICULAR VANITY RUN AMUCK R. NELSON *Virginia Living* v15 no1 p112 D 2016

Specialty Store Services (Company)

A PLACE IN TIME C. HONG *Martha Stewart Living* no268 p130 O 2016

Specialty stores

See also

Bicycle stores

Bookstores

Cheese shops

Clothing stores

Cosmetics stores

Pet shops

Toy stores

Dance SPIRIT 2017 Survival GUIDE *Dance Spirit* v21 no4 p58 Ap 2017

DEARLY DEPARTED M. Schulman cartoon *New Yorker* v93 no18 p20 Je 26 2017

Niche Stores Find Their Way J. Rosen *Publishers Weekly* v263 no40 p10 O 3 2016

Wings on His Feet J. HOUSMAN color *Surfer* v58 no5 p30 S 2017

Specialty stores—Evaluation

BE OUR GUEST A. BRANDT *Cincinnati Magazine* v50 no6 p44 Mr 2017

Candy Land J. ZYMAN *Atlanta* v56 no8 p69 D 2016

NAUTI-CAL BY NATURE *Sea Magazine* v109 no1 pCA-1 Ja 2017

SUGAR BUZZ C. JAY color *Louisiana Life* v37 no2 p102 N/D 2016

Speciation (Biology)

Ecological speciation of bacteriophage lambda in allopatry and sympatry J. R. Meyer, D. T. Dobias et al bibl graph *Science* v354 no6317 p1301 D 9 2016

Sosebee Cove, Georgia R. H. MOHLENBROCK *Natural History* v124 no10 p42 N 2016

Watching speciation in action B. R. Grant and P. R. Grant bibl color *Science* v355 no6328 p910 Mr 3 2017

Species

See also

Animal species

Endangered species

Numbers of species

Plant species

Ask the Biologist D. Kreinheder *New York State Conservationist* v72 no2 p31 O 2017

Canada's 150th Nature Celebration color *Canadian Wildlife* v23 no1 p42 Mr/Ap 2017

Mexico's ambiguous invasive species plan L. M. Ochoa-Ochoa, O. A. Flores-Villela et al bibl *Science* v355 no6329 p1033 Mr 10 2017

Mind the gap: Neural coding of species identity in birdsong prosody Makoto Araki, M. M. Bandi et al bibl graph *Science* v354 no6317 p1282 D 9 2016

Opening Arctic passageways will shake up ecosystems S. Milius color *Science News* v190 no13 p23 D 24 2016

Science's questions rarely have clear, easy answers E. Quill *Science News* v191 no4 p2 Mr 4 2017

A shortcut to a species E. Pennisi color *Science* v354 no6314 p818 N 18 2016

Species distribution

Every Tree, an Island K. Moore *Natural History* v125 no2 p8 F 2017

Modernization, Risk, and Conservation of the World's Largest Carnivores J. T. BRUSKOTTER, J. A. VUCETICH et al *BioScience* v67 no7 p646 Jl 2017

Species diversity

Crossing Scales: The Complexity of Barrier-Island Processes for Predicting Future Change J. C. ZINNERT, J. A. STALLINS et al *BioScience* v67 no1 p39 Ja 2017

Every Tree, an Island K. Moore *Natural History* v125 no2 p8 F 2017

Species specificity

Tension in Taxonomy K. Long cartoon *Scientific American* v315 no5 p13 N 2016

Specifications

See also

Building—Estimates

HOW TO BUY AN A/V RECEIVER R. Sabin color *Sound & Vision* v81 no9 p32 N 2016

Speck, Angela

The eclipse of a generation *Physics Today* v70 no8 p10 Ag 2017

Speck, Will

OFFICE CHRISTMAS PARTY D. Snierson and W. Robinson color *Entertainment Weekly* no1438 p39 N 4 2016

SPECKTOR, BRANDON

13 Things You Didn't Know About the Macy's Thanksgiving Parade bw color *Reader's Digest* v190 no1135 p124 N 2017

50 Everyday Mistakes And How to Fix Them [Cover story] color *Reader's Digest* v189 no1129 p62 Ap 2017

5 Great Songs Almost Ruined by Their Original Titles *Reader's Digest* v188 no1124 p134 O 2016

Brilliant Uses for Pennies *Reader's Digest* v188 no1125 p68 N 2016

First Drafts of History bw *Reader's Digest* v190 no1132 p130 Jl/Ag 2017

Hail to the Chief Doodles *Reader's Digest* v189 no1127 p126 F 2017

Here's Why Seven Is Most Likely Your Favorite Number color *Reader's Digest* v190 no1133 p134 S 2017

Logophile Heaven! color *Reader's Digest* v190 no1133 p78 S 2017

Mind-Blowing Facts About The Statue Of Liberty *Reader's Digest* v188 no1124 p122 O 2016

Mind-Blowing Facts About Your Money *Reader's Digest* v189 no1128 p128 Mr 2017

Never Fear! There's History Behind These Superstitions color *Reader's Digest* v190 no1134 p130 O 2017

Six Idiotic Idioms—and What's Wrong with Them color *Reader's Digest* v189 no1130 p134 My 2017

The Truth About That White Dress (and 7 Other Wedding Traditions) color *Reader's Digest* v189 no1131 p130 Je 2017

THE Wackiest Law IN EVERY STATE color *Reader's Digest* v190 no1132 p68 Jl/Ag 2017

When Pizza Saved a Life *Reader's Digest* v188 no1124 p12 O 2016

Which Virtual Assistant Tells the Best Jokes? color *Reader's Digest* v189 no1129 p126 Ap 2017

Why it pays to increase your WORD POWER [Cover story] color *Reader's Digest* v190 no1133 p66 S 2017

Why There's No Clean Way to Peel An Orange color *Reader's Digest* v189 no1130 p132 My 2017

Spectacular, The

Sideshow Effect C. P. Pierce and T. Keith color *Sports Illustrated* v127 no3 p16 Jl 24 2017

Spectators

Fast on a Different Track C. BETHEA color *Runner's World* v52 no9 p56 O 2017

SPECTER, MICHAEL

REWRITING THE CODE OF LIFE cartoon *New Yorker* v92 no43 p34 Ja 2 2017

SPECTOR, LINCOLN

How to stream media from your PC to your HDTV over Wi-Fi color *PCWorld* v35 no10 p112 O 2017

If we show you how to back up your PC for free, will you finally do it? color *PCWorld* p155 Mr 2017

SPECTOR, NICOLE AUDREY

Bending Genres And Giving Back color *Publishers Weekly* v264 no4 p38 Ja 23 2017

HOMETOWN IS WHERE THE HEART IS color *Publishers Weekly* v263 no46 p24 N 14 2016

Horror Authors Take a Stab at Self-Publishing bw color *Publishers Weekly* v263 no43 p38 O 24 2016

Meet the Finalists for the booklife Prize in Fiction color *Publishers Weekly* v263 no52 p78 D 19 2016

Meet the Judges color *Publishers Weekly* v263 no47 p62 N 21 2016

Spectral imaging

Airborne laser-guided imaging spectroscopy to map forest trait diversity and guide conservation G. P. Asner, R. E. Martin et al bibl chart graph *Science* v355 no6323 p385 Ja 27 2017

THE POWER OF IMAGING WITH PHASE, NOT POWER G. Popescu *Physics Today* v70 no5 p34 My 2017

Submillihertz magnetic spectroscopy performed with a nanoscale quantum sensor S. Schmitt, T. Gefen et al diag *Science* v356 no6340 p832 My 26 2017

Spectrographs

HALO HUNTER E. MASTROIANNI color *Discover* v38 no8 p9 O 2017

Spectrometers

NEW PRODUCTS bw *Science* v354 no6314 p913 N 18 2016

new products color *Science* v357 no6351 p613 Ag 11 2017

Specks in the Spectrometer S. Rosengard color *Oceanus* v51 no2 p86 Wint 2016

Spectrometry

Microresonator soliton dual-comb spectroscopy Myoung-Gyun Suh, Qi-Fan Yang et al bibl diag graph *Science* v354 no6312 p600 N 4 2016

Observing chemical shifts from nanosamples N. Bar-Gill and A. Retzker diag graph *Science* v357 no6346 p38 Jl 7 2017

Spectral narrowing of x-ray pulses for precision spectroscopy with nuclear resonances K. P. Heeg, A. Kaldun et al diag *Science* v357 no6349 p375 Jl 28 2017

Spectrophotometers—Evaluation

NEW PRODUCTS *Physics Today* v70 no1 p64 Ja 2017

Spectroscope

Dual-comb spectroscopy of water vapor with a free-running semiconductor disk laser S. M. Link, D. J. H. C. Maas et al diag *Science* v356 no6343 p1164 Je 16 2017

Spectrum analysis

See also

Magnetic circular dichroism

Four Planets for Tau Ceti M. YOUNG *Sky & Telescope* v134 no6 p11 D 2017

The many dimensions of Earth's landscapes Sung Chang *Physics Today* v70 no6 p21 Je 2017

Microresonator soliton dual-comb spectroscopy Myoung-Gyun Suh, Qi-Fan Yang et al bibl diag graph *Science* v354 no6312 p600 N 4 2016

Nanoscale nuclear magnetic resonance with chemical resolution N. Aslam, M. Pfender et al diag *Science* v357 no6346 p67 Jl 7 2017

An on/off Berry phase switch in circular graphene resonators F. Ghahari, D. Walkup et al diag graph *Science* v356 no6340 p845 My 26 2017

The proton radius revisited W. Vassen graph *Science* v357 no6359 p39 O 6 2017

An unusual white dwarf star may be a surviving remnant of a subluminous Type Ia supernova S. Vennes, P. Nemeth et al chart diag *Science* v357 no6352 p680 Ag 18 2017

Spectrum Brands Inc.

Secrets of a Weekend Lock Picker D. DUBNO cartoon color *Popular Mechanics* v193 no7 p29 S 2016

Speculative fiction

THE Real Worlds A. DANIEL color *Publishers Weekly* v263 no43 p26 O 24 2016

Speculators

Short the Food Court R. Evans and M. Scully color *Bloomberg Businessweek* no4515 p34 Mr 20 2017

Speech

See also

Verbal ability

THE DEREGULATOR? M. WELCH color *Reason* v49 no2 p18 Je 2017

From the Mouths of (Celebs') Babes J. Hartshorn color *Parents* v92 no8 p20 Ag 2017

Speech anxiety

The Anxious Man's Guide to Public Speaking B. Platt and C. SKIPPER color *GQ: Gentlemen's Quarterly* v97 no5 p36 My 2017

Speech anxiety—Prevention

How to overcome a fear of public speaking L. Shaw *People Management* p52 O 2016

Speeches, addresses, etc.

See also

Award presentations

Public speaking

Good Writer's Disease? B. SWAIM color *Weekly Standard* v23 no5 p42 O 9 2017

Hillary Clinton's Acceptance Speech *Congressional Digest* v95 no8 p4 O 2016

How Can I Survive...Public Speaking? B. Anat *Scholastic Choices* v32 no5 p24 F 2017

JESSE WILLIAMS C. Glazek color *Esquire* v166 no5 p94 D 2016/Ja 2017

Speeches, addresses, etc.—Humor

Cue the Walking Music bw *Weekly Standard* v22 no19 p2 Ja 23 2017

...The best concession speech ever S. FESCHUK color *Maclean's* v129 no43 p65 O 31 2016

Speech—Law & legislation

See also

Freedom of speech

Speechless (TV program)

Comedies Get Serious J. HALTERMAN *TV Guide* v64 no48 p7 N 21 2016

So Long, June Cleaver M. DRIVER *TV Guide* p16 Ap 17 2017

Speechless Gets Real About Families Affected by Disability D. D'addario color *Time* v188 no15 p56 O 17 2016

Speechless N. Abrams, B. L. Heldman et al color *Entertainment Weekly* no1482/1483 p75 S 22 2017

Speechwriters

PARODY color *Weekly Standard* v22 no34 p48 My 15 2017

'THE AMERICAN DREAM MOVED TO CANADA' J. GEDDES color *Maclean's* v129 no47 p28 N 28 2016

Speed

See also

Speed of light

Velocity

Effective Transitions L. LaPLANTE and J. PAULSON color *Horse & Rider* v56 no9 p43 S 2017

The Finer Points of Fencing B. Avila and J. Paulson *Horse & Rider* v56 no6 p40 Je 2017

ICE FLOW J. Fuchs and T. Keith color *Sports Illustrated* v127 no9 p16 S 25 2017

Speed, Michael P.

The biology of color color *Science* v357 no6350 p470 Ag 4 2017

Speed, Terence P.

Deficiency of microRNA miR-34a expands cell fate potential in pluripotent stem cells diag *Science* v355 no6325 p596 F 10 2017

Speed 2: Cruise Control (Film)

The Quiz T. BALAZO color *Maclean's* v130 no7 p65 Ag 2017

Speed of airplanes

EVERYTHING ABOUT V SPEEDS EXPLAINED: PART ONE R. Lengel color *Flying* v144 no8 p28 Ag 2017

HIGH, HEAVY AND SLOW P. Garrison *Flying* v144 no8 p34 Ag 2017

Speed of light

the 10-second marathon M. Shieh color *Popular Science* v289 no5 p16 S/O 2017

Speed reducers

Variable Frequency Drives in the Aquatics Industry B. Babcock *Parks & Recreation* p2 Aquatics Guide 2017

Speedman, Scott

Animal Kingdom J. Halterman *TV Guide* v65 no35 p35 Ag 21 2017

Speedman, Scott—Interviews

5 JUICY QUESTIONS with... SCOTT SPEEDMAN C. Keller color *Women's Health* v14 no4 p128 My 2017

Speedometers

Nonstandardized Testing J. Sabatini chart color *Car & Driver* v62 no8 p66 F 2017

Speedometers—Evaluation

GEARBOX color *Dirt Sports + Off-Road* v51 no4 p68 Ap 2017

Speer, Andy

The Stretch-and-Shred Home Workout color *Men's Health* v32 no7 p14 S 2017

Speers, Steven

"THIS IS A WAR AND WE INTEND TO WIN" W. ENZINNA bw color *Mother Jones* v42 no3 p14 My/Je 2017

SPEIER, JACKIE

Should Women Have to Register for the Draft? *New York Times Upfront* v149 no11 p22 Ap 3 2017

Spektor, G.

Revealing the subfemtosecond dynamics of orbital angular momentum in nanoplasmonic vortices bibl diag *Science* v355 no6330 p1187 Mr 17 2017

Spelke, Elizabeth S.

Cognitive science in the field: A preschool intervention durably enhances intuitive but not formal mathematics chart color diag graph *Science* v357 no6346 p47 Jl 7 2017

Spelling bees

Take a Small Knee J. LILEKS *National Review* v69 no19 p51 O 16 2017

Spelling competitions

BEE--BRAINED V. Vara *Harper's Magazine* v334 no2004 p54 My 2017

Spelling errors

Errata *American Indian Quarterly* v40 no3 p292 Summ 2016

Spellings, Matthew

Clathrate colloidal crystals bibl color *Science* v355 no6328 p931 Mr 3 2017

Spellman, Brandon

The Sun Stove T. LEAVY color *Popular Science* p88 Ja/F 2017

SPELLMAN, KATIE V.

Validating Herbarium-Based Phenology Models Using Citizen-Science Data chart graph *BioScience* v66 no10 p897 O 1 2016

Spellman, Spencer

RENO'S CAL AVE color map *Sunset* v238 no6 p24 Je 2017

SPELLMEYER, KURT

Is the Dharma Democratic? bw *Tricycle: The Buddhist Review* v26 no3 p62 Spr 2017

Spellmeyer, Kurt—Interviews

Dialogue Across Difference A. Cooper color *Tricycle: The Buddhist Review* v26 no4 p48 Summ 2017

Spelunkers

Into the Deep M. Synnott color map *National Geographic* v231 no3 p104 Mr 2017

SPENADEL, SUSAN

Q: What adventure would you love to share with your best friend? color *O, The Oprah Magazine* p12 Ja 2017

Spence, Charles

Not by Taste Alone: The flavor of food is produced by all of the senses *American Scholar* v86 no3 p114 Summ 2017

The Shape and Sound of a Perfect Meal L. Feldman color *Time* v190 no4 p54 Jl 24 2017

SHRINK YOUR GUT WITH GASTROPHYSICS S. Subramanian color *Men's Health* v32 no2 p63 Mr 2017

There's more to a meal J. Ubbink color *Science* v356 no6343 p1129 Je 16 2017

SPENCE, EVELYN

FIVE PLACES YOU HAVE TO RIDE BEFORE THEY CHANGE FOREVER color *Bicycling* v58 no7 p36 Ag 2017

Lose Weight Your Way [Cover story] color *Prevention* v69 no9 p32 O 2017

Spence, Jo-Anne

COMMENT color *Canadian Geographic* v137 no1 p72 F 2017

Spence, John C. H.

SPLIT-SECOND REACTIONS color *Scientific American* v316 no5 p62 My 2017

Spence, Katy

Natural Hydrologists *Natural History* v125 no1 p22 D 2016/Ja 2017

Spence, Michael

Globalism and Its Discontents *Hoover Digest: Research & Opinion on Public Policy* no1 p40 Wint 2017

Why Globalization Stalled color *Foreign Affairs* v96 no4 p54 Jl/Ag 2017

Spence, Patrick—Interviews

Winning Wireless C. Crowley color *Sound & Vision* v81 no10 p16 D 2016

SPENCE, RICK

Taxing issues color *Maclean's* no1 p50 F 17 2017

Spence, Steve

STEVE SPENCE N. WELDON color *Runner's World* v51 no10 p36 N 2016

Spencer

Scary (and true) tales from a crag near you *Climbing* no353 p21 My/Je 2017

Spencer, Abigail

Grey's Anatomy M. Logan *TV Guide* v65 no43 p39 O 16 2017

Timeless I. Rudolph *TV Guide* v65 no4 p34 Ja 16 2017

Spencer, Amy

AMERICA [Cover story] color *Redbook* p94 Mr 2017

HOW TO BE HAPPY color *Good Housekeeping* v264 no1 p75 Ja 1 2017

"I AM ENOUGH" [Cover story] cartoon color *Redbook* p100 Ap 2017

"I'M REALLY LUCKY" [Cover story] color *Health* v31 no6 p100 Jl 2017

Jillian Gets You Strong [Cover story] color *Health* v30 no9 p116 N 2016

Love on the Run color *Good Housekeeping* v264 no3 p151 Mr 2017

SLY'S ANGELS color *Harper's Bazaar* no3653 p167 My 2017

Tracee Ellis Ross: "I DIDN'T WAKE UP LIKE THIS" [Cover story] color *Health* v31 no3 p82 Ap 2017

Spencer, Chris C. A.

Resistance to malaria through structural variation of red blood cell invasion receptors diag *Science* v356 no6343 p1139 Je 16 2017

Spencer, Daniel

THE SIGNED DANIEL SPENCER (1741-1801) CHIPPEN-DALE DESK AND BOOKCASE color *Magazine Antiques* v183 no6 p1 N/D 2016

SPENCER, DARRONN

COPS SHOULD NOT PLAY JEOPARDY *USA Today Magazine* v146 no2868 p32 S 2017

Spencer, Jesse, 1979-

The Heat Is On I. RUDOLPH *TV Guide* p20 Ap 17 2017

Spencer, Larry

The Tipping Point of Oliver Bass *Publishers Weekly* v264 no24 p44 Je 12 2017

SPENCER, LINDA

Digital Piracy color *Publishers Weekly* v263 no45 p64 N 7 2016

Spencer, Lisa

Ranch with a View J. Brewster color diag *Log Home Living* v34 no4 p40 My 2017

SPENCER, MARK PATRICK

HOPPY TRAILS bw color *Louisiana Life* v37 no5 p32 My/Je 2017

SUMMERING color *Louisiana Life* v37 no5 p48 My/Je 2017

Spencer, Melanie Warner

ARDENT SPRITS color *Louisiana Life* v37 no6 p8 Jl/Ag 2017

CRAWFISH MIRAGE color *Louisiana Life* v37 no5 p8 My/Je 2017

Flower Power *New Orleans Homes & Lifestyles* v20 no2 p104 Spr 2017

Fruits of Summer: The season's bounty in flavor-packed parcels *New Orleans Homes & Lifestyles* v20 no3 p112 Summ 2017

Louisianians of the Year *Louisiana Life* v37 no3 p50 Ja/F 2017

Mastering Design *New Orleans Homes & Lifestyles* v20 no4 p16 Aut 2017

Naked Lunch: Oysters on the half shell are on the menu this fall *New Orleans Homes & Lifestyles* v20 no4 p112 Aut 2017

Notable Addiction *New Orleans Homes & Lifestyles* v20 no1 p104 Wint 2016

Spring Fling *New Orleans Homes & Lifestyles* v20 no2 p14 Spr 2017

Summer Lovin' *New Orleans Homes & Lifestyles* v20 no3 p14 Summ 2017

THE TREE FUNERAL color *Louisiana Life* v38 no1 p10 S/O 2017

Winterizing *New Orleans Homes & Lifestyles* v20 no1 p14 Wint 2016

Spencer, Nancy

from you, the reader color graph *Horse & Rider* v56 no8 p22 Ag 2017

Spencer, O'Shea

snapshot *In These Times* v41 no4 p7 Ap 2017

Spencer, Octavia, 1970-

Hidden Figures *New Yorker* v92 no43 p11 Ja 2 2017

No Longer 'Hidden Figures' M. CHARLES and L. CROSS color *Ebony* v72 no3 p30 D 2016/Ja 2017

Spencer, Richard B., 1978-

HIS KAMPF G. WOOD bw *Atlantic* v319 no5 p40 Je 2017

THE SUPREMACIST NEXT DOOR: What to do about a notorious new neighbor? K. OLSEN *Washingtonian Magazine* v52 no11 p21 Ag 2017

Spencer, Richard D.

Kilogram-scale prexasertib monolactate monohydrate synthesis under continuous-flow CGMP conditions chart diag *Science* v356 no6343 p1144 Je 16 2017

Spencer, Scott

Sold Out: A writer and his artist wife come to regret their choices R. R. COOPER *New York Times Book Review* p21 Ag 20 2017

Spencer, Stephanie

In the SUNSET KITCHEN color *Sunset* v238 no5 p94 My 2017

Spencer-Brown, Lesha

Empowering Older Adults to Age Out Loud! *Parks & Recreation* v52 no5 p38 My 2017

Spencer-Dene, Bradley

The linker histone H1.0 generates epigenetic and functional intra-tumor heterogeneity bibl graph *Science* v353 no6307 paaf1644-1 S 30 2016

Spender, J. C.

Stop Worrying About Whether Machines Are "Intelligent" *Harvard Business Review Digital Articles* p2 Ag 4 2015

Spengler, Oswald, 1880-1936

Oswald Spengler: Pessimism's Prophet B. R. MYERS *American Conservative* v15 no6 p51 N/D 2016

Spenner, Patrick

Avoid These Common B2B Content Marketing Mistakes *Harvard Business Review Digital Articles* p2 F 10 2016

Spent reactor fuels

Forty years of impasse: The United States, Japan, and the plutonium problem Masafumi Takubo and F. von Hippel bibl *Bulletin of the Atomic Scientists* v73 no5 p337 2017

Sperling, Nicole

THE 25 MOST PATRIOTIC MOVIES OF ALL TIME color *Entertainment Weekly* no1472 p30 Je 30 2017

7 Things You Didn't See color *Entertainment Weekly* no1449 p14 Ja 20 2017

ACTION HERO color *Entertainment Weekly* no1454/1455 p74 F 24 2017

ATOMIC BLONDE color *Entertainment Weekly* no1463/1464 p60 Ap/My 2017

BEN AFFLECK'S LIVE BY NIGHT color *Entertainment Weekly* no1439 p42 N 11 2016

BEST ACTOR color diag *Entertainment Weekly* no1451/1452 p54 F 3-10 2017

BEST ACTRESS color diag *Entertainment Weekly* no1451/1452 p44 F 3-10 2017

BEST ACTRESS CONTENDER ANNETTE BENING color *Entertainment Weekly* no1446/1447 p104 D 2016/Ja 2017

BEST ACTRESS CONTENDER ISABELLE HUPPERT color *Entertainment Weekly* no1440 p46 N 18 2016

BEST DIRECTOR color diag *Entertainment Weekly* no1451/1452 p66 F 3-10 2017

BEST DIRECTOR CONTENDER KENNETH LONERGAN color *Entertainment Weekly* no1441 p40 N 25 2016

BEST PICTURE CONTENDER LA LA LAND color *Entertainment Weekly* no1442 p44 D 2 2016 Rebellious Special Issue

BEST SUPPORTING ACTRESS color diag *Entertainment Weekly* no1451/1452 p62 F 3-10 2017

The Birth of a Star color *Entertainment Weekly* no1435 p14 O 14 2016

CAN ALLIED SURVIVE THE BREAKUP? color *Entertainment Weekly* no1434 p13 O 7 2016

CAN ANYTHING STOP LA LA LAND? color *Entertainment Weekly* no1449 p12 Ja 20 2017

Charlize Theron in Atomic Blonde color *Entertainment Weekly* no1457/1458 p76 Mr 17 2017

Could Deadpool Get a Best Picture Nod? color *Entertainment Weekly* no1450 p16 Ja 27 2017

Could Trump's Trade Policy Hurt the Movie Biz? color *Entertainment Weekly* no1441 p10 N 25 2016

Family Tragedy Rocks Justice League color *Entertainment Weekly* no1468/1469 p24 Je 2-9 2017

FENCES color *Entertainment Weekly* no1438 p42 N 4 2016

FINALLY [Cover story] color *Entertainment Weekly* no1467 p20 My 26 2017

Gal Gadot color *Entertainment Weekly* no1444/1445 p52 D 16 2016

THE HOUSE color *Entertainment Weekly* no1463/1464 p49 Ap/ My 2017

JUSTICE LEAGUE color *Entertainment Weekly* no1446/1447 p48 D 2016/Ja 2017

KATE McKINNON color *Entertainment Weekly* no1444/1445 p24 D 16 2016

LEAD ACTOR CONTENDER ANDREW GARFIELD color *Entertainment Weekly* no1439 p46 N 11 2016

A MONSTER CALLS color *Entertainment Weekly* no1438 p39 N 4 2016

The MORNING AFTER color *Entertainment Weekly* no1456 p52 Mr 10 2017

NO. 22 Black Widow color *Entertainment Weekly* no1436/1437 p61 O 21 2016

NO. 38 Vision color *Entertainment Weekly* no1436/1437 p72 O 21 2016

NO. 4 SUPERMAN color *Entertainment Weekly* no1436/1437 p47 O 21 2016

NORMAN LEAR & KENYA BARRIS color *Entertainment Weekly* no1460/1461 p22 Ap 7-17 2017

Ooh La La! color *Entertainment Weekly* no1468/1469 p22 Je 2-9 2017

The Oscar Race Is On! color *Entertainment Weekly* no1436/1437 p24 O 21 2016

OSCAR SECRET BALLOT color *Entertainment Weekly* no1454/1455 p52 F 24 2017

OSCARS SO RIGHT? [Cover story] color *Entertainment Weekly* no1451/1452 p40 F 3-10 2017

OSCARS TURNED UPSIDE DOWN color *Entertainment Weekly* no1453 p13 F 17 2017

The OTHER RACES color *Entertainment Weekly* no1454/1455 p50 F 24 2017

Paul Rudd Was a Nightmare in Bridesmaids color *Entertainment Weekly* no1460/1461 p94 Ap 7-17 2017

PICTURE color diag *Entertainment Weekly* no1451/1452 p70 F 3-10 2017

Sasha Lane color *Entertainment Weekly* no1434 p44 O 7 2016

SHOCK of MOONLIGHT color *Entertainment Weekly* no1456 p42 Mr 10 2017

Should Awards Shows Be Gender-Neutral? color *Entertainment Weekly* no1466 p16 My 19 2017

THE STATE OF THE OSCAR RACE color *Entertainment Weekly* no1446/1447 p23 D 2016/Ja 2017

SUPPORTING ACTOR CONTENDER ASHTON SANDERS color *Entertainment Weekly* no1438 p48 N 4 2016

SUPPORTING ACTRESS CONTENDER VIOLA DAVIS color *Entertainment Weekly* no1443 p46 D 9 2016

Tatum O'Neal color *Entertainment Weekly* no1460/1461 p30 Ap 7-17 2017

TOP of HER Class color *Entertainment Weekly* no1440 p38 N 18 2016

VIOLA DAVIS color *Entertainment Weekly* no1444/1445 p36 D 16 2016

WarReN BEAtty An ORAL HISTORY color *Entertainment Weekly* no1440 p30 N 18 2016

What to Watch color *Entertainment Weekly* no1459 p56 Mr 31 2017

What to Watch color *Entertainment Weekly* no1465 p50 My 12 2017

WHO WILL WIN color *Entertainment Weekly* no1454/1455 p44 F 24 2017

Will Ferrell and Amy Poehler Bet on The House color *Entertainment Weekly* no1453 p12 F 17 2017

WONDER WOMAN color *Entertainment Weekly* no1446/1447 p56 D 2016/Ja 2017

WONDER WOMAN color *Entertainment Weekly* no1463/1464 p50 Ap/My 2017

WONDER WOMAN WINS color *Entertainment Weekly* no1470 p8 Je 16 2017

The WRONG ENVELOPE: HOW IT HAPPENED color *Entertainment Weekly* no1456 p46 Mr 10 2017

Your Sunshiny, Stupendous, Seriously Spectacular SUMMER BUCKET LIST color *Entertainment Weekly* no1470 p32 Je 16 2017

Sperm count

How Strong Is Your Sperm? D. CRANE bw cartoon graph *Men's Health* v32 no5 p81 Je 2017

Spermatozoa

Building Blocks L. SCHLEY color *Discover* v38 no7 p18 S 2017

Spark of Life K. KORNEI bw color *Discover* v38 no1 p53 Ja/F 2017

SPERRY, JINELLE H.

Reproductive Decisions in Anurans: A Review of How Predation and Competition Affects the Deposition of Eggs And Tadpoles *BioScience* v67 no1 p26 Ja 2017

Sperti, Carmel Ann

What My Horse Wears on His Feet cartoon *Horse & Rider* v56 no5 p80 My 2017

Spettacolo (Film)

Acting Out E. HYNES color *Film Comment* v53 no5 p18 S/O 2017

All the World's Their Stage M. ATKINSON *In These Times* v41 no10 p44 O 2017

Spetzler, Carl

An Organization-Wide Approach to Good Decision Making *Harvard Business Review Digital Articles* p2 My 27 2015

You Can't Make Good Predictions Without Embracing Uncertainty *Harvard Business Review Digital Articles* p2 My 18 2016

Spetzler, David

Mismatch repair deficiency predicts response of solid tumors to PD-1 blockade chart graph *Science* v357 no6349 p409 Jl 28 2017

Spey casting

Whip It Good H. FRINT color *Field & Stream* v122 no5 p10 O 2017

Spheres in art

A Sphere for Spearfish *South Dakota Magazine* v33 no3 p13 S/O 2017

Spherical astronomy

See also

Celestial sphere

Eclipses

Nautical astronomy

Let the Stones Stand Again R. Erganbright *Sky & Telescope* v133 no4 p84 Ap 2017

Planetary Almanac *Sky & Telescope* v134 no4 p44 O 2017

Sphero (Company)

SPHERO R2-D2 APP-ENABLED DROID A. HAYWARD color *Macworld - Digital Edition* v34 no11 p35 N 2017

Sphingidae

Hawkmoths use nectar sugar to reduce oxidative damage from flight E. Levin, G. Lopez-Martinez et al bibl graph *Science* v355 no6326 p733 F 17 2017

Sphinxes (Mythology)

See also

Great Sphinx (Egypt)

Buried Secrets S. W. DRIMMER bw color map *National Geographic Kids* no470 p26 My 2017

Spic-O-Rama (Theatrical production)

John LEGUIZAMO MIRANDA color *Vanity Fair* p144 Hollywood 2017 Supplement

Spice Girls (Performer)

DEMI LOVATO M. Vain color *Entertainment Weekly* no1485 p56 O 6 2017

Ginger Spice J. Goodman color *Entertainment Weekly* no1460/1461 p71 Ap 7-17 2017

Spicer, André

The Research We've Ignored About Happiness at Work *Harvard Business Review Digital Articles* p2 Jl 21 2015

What Companies Should Ask Before Embracing Wearables *Harvard Business Review Digital Articles* p2 My 20 2015

Spicer, Kevin P.

The spirit of Israel *America* v216 no12 p50 My 29 2017

Spicer, Matt

Ingrid Goes West L. Greenblatt color *Entertainment Weekly* no1478 / 1479 p83 Ag 18-25 2017

Spicer, Sean, 1971-

This Town Melts Down: At large in Trump's Washington M. Leibovich *New York Times Magazine* p30 Jl 16 2017

The Week *National Review* v69 no15 p4 Ag 14 2017

Sketchbook / Graphic Review *New York Times Book Review* p51 N 13 2016

Spiegelman, Nadja
I'm Supposed to Protect You from All This *Publishers Weekly* v263 no44 p71 O 31 2016
'Moby-Dick,' Part 1 S. G. Sánchez *New York Times Book Review* p54 Je 4 2017

Spiegelman, Wülard
Eugene Onegin *Opera News* v81 no7 p34 Ja 2017

Spielberg (Film)
Spielberg A. D'Arminio *TV Guide* v65 no41 p32 O 2 2017
Spielberg: Celebrating a life making movies that defined many moviegoers' lives M. ROUSH *TV Guide* v65 no41 p14 O 2 2017

Spielberg, Steven, 1946-
READY PLAYER ONE A. Breznican color *Entertainment Weekly* p16 Jl 24 2017
SPIELBERG AT SEVENTY D. DENBY cartoon *New Yorker* v92 no45 p76 Ja 16 2017

Spielgel, Bill
CROP DIVERSITY PAYDAY *Successful Farming* v114 no11 p44 N 2016

Spielkamp, Matthias
Inspecting Algorithms for Bias diag *MIT Technology Review* v120 no4 p96 Jl/Ag 2017

Spierig, Michael
JIGSAW C. Collis color *Entertainment Weekly* p19 Jl 24 2017

Spiers, Christopher J.
Understanding induced seismicity bibl color graph *Science* v354 no6318 p1380 D 16 2016

Spies
The Fake Russian D. WISE *Smithsonian* v47 no7 p38 N 2016
GREAT UNKNOWNS color *Popular Mechanics* p112 Je 2017
Mad, Democrats? Blame the Iran Deal *Commentary* p1 Ja 2017
Mad, Democrats? Blame the Iran Deal *Commentary* v143 no1 p1 Ja 2017
Spies Like Us *American Scholar* v86 no1 p14 Wint 2017
THE SPY WHO CAME TO DINNER J. KNAPP *Washingtonian Magazine* v52 no6 p10 Mr 2017
The Sultry Spy and the Coverup M. Solly *Smithsonian* v48 no5 p19 S 2017

Spies—Government policy
Trump Versus the Spies: All presidents clash with their intelligence experts, but the hostility the new administration has displayed is unusual--and risky A. B. Zegart *Hoover Digest: Research & Opinion on Public Policy* no2 p117 Spr 2017

Spies—History
SPY VS. SPY VS. SPY R. BROOKHISER bw color *American History* v52 no2 p22 Je 2017

Spieth, Jordan, 1993-
The Case for ... The Career Slam M. Bamberger and T. Keith color *Sports Illustrated* v127 no4 p24 Ag 7 2017
Jordan Spieth B. Muteba color *Current Biography* v78 no5 p82 My 2017
Jordan Spieth S. Gregory color *Time* v190 no6 p17 Ag 7 2017
THE MASTERS R. A. BERENZ *TV Guide* v65 no14 p46 Ap 3 2017
PAR EXCELLENCE T. Keith chart color *Sports Illustrated* v127 no8 p18 S 18 2017

SPIGA, ILARIA
Shipbuilding Docks as Experimental Systems for Realistic Assessments of Anthropogenic Stressors on Marine Organisms *BioScience* v67 no9 p853 S 2017

Spike, Carlett
Hey, big funder color *Columbia Journalism Review* v56 no1 p60 Spr 2017
HOOKER COUNTY TRIBUNE bw *Columbia Journalism Review* v56 no1 p95 Spr 2017
THE NOME NUGGET color *Columbia Journalism Review* v56 no1 p63 Spr 2017
Where the digital dollars have gone graph *Columbia Journalism Review* p58 Fall/Wint 2016

Spikeball Inc.
An Old Game Gets a Do-Over P. MERTZ ESSWEIN color *Kiplinger's Personal Finance* v71 no8 p20 Ag 2017

SPIKER, TED
5 Surprising Reasons Your Back Is Killing You color *AARP: The Magazine* v59 no2A p16 F/Mr 2016
For a Fabulous 2016, One Tip: Take It Slow color *AARP: The Magazine* v59 no1A p22 D 2015/Ja 2016
HIRED! cartoon color graph *Men's Health* v32 no3 p96 Ap 2017

Spiler, Amber
The Perfect Horse at the Perfect Time color *Practical Horseman* v45 no7 p72 Jl 2017

SPILGER, JARROD
GREAT DUCK GUNS color *Outdoor Life* v224 no8 p32 O 2017
SQUIRREL TALK color *Outdoor Life* v224 no7 p23 S 2017

Spill (Play)
Dramatizing Deepwater Horizon A. Rademacher color *Science* v356 no6335 p256 Ap 21 2017

SPILLAR, KATHERINE
NOT BACKING DOWN: We at Ms. promise to never let up with our reporting, rebelling and truth-telling *Ms.* v27 no3 p39 Fall 2017

Spillar, Kathy
Ms. letter *Ms.* v26 no3 p2 Fall 2016

Spilsbury, E. A.
CAPTURING THE CAT: The arrival of big cats to 19th-century London forced a change in the image left by mythology and the Old Masters C. Good *History Today* v67 no10 p36 O 2017

Spin-off television programs
Does HBO's Future Include a Game of Thrones Spin-off? J. Hibberd color *Entertainment Weekly* no1435 p9 O 14 2016
THE GOOD FIGHT L. Rice color *Entertainment Weekly* no1446/1447 p68 D 2016/Ja 2017
The Never-Ending Story? J. Hibberd color *Entertainment Weekly* no1466 p14 My 19 2017
Supernatural's Sister Act S. Highfill color *Entertainment Weekly* no1472 p16 Je 30 2017

Spin-orbit coupling
Cold atoms twisting spin and momentum M. Aidelsburger bibl diag *Science* v354 no6308 p35 O 7 2016
A parity-breaking electronic nematic phase transition in the spin-orbit coupled metal Cd2Re2O7 J. W. Harter, Z. Y. Zhao et al diag *Science* v356 no6335 p295 Ap 21 2017

Spin-orbit interactions (Physics)
Realization of two-dimensional spin-orbit coupling for Bose-Einstein condensates Zhan Wu, Long Zhang et al bibl graph *Science* v354 no6308 p83 O 7 2016

Spin waves
Control and local measurement of the spin chemical potential in a magnetic insulator C. Du, T. van der Sar et al bw diag *Science* v357 no6347 p195 Jl 14 2017

Spina bifida
Wheelchair Parkour S. Trumper color *Walrus* v14 no5 p21 Je 2017

Spinach
THE COLD CRUSHER color *Prevention* v69 no2 p14 F 2017
Dirty Secrets color *Prevention* v69 no7 p12 Jl 2017
A Fine Meze color *Vegetarian Today* no1 p34 F 2017
Warm Winter Menus For Two color *Vegetarian Today* no1 p16 F 2017

Spinal cord—Regeneration
Injury-induced ctgfa directs glial bridging and spinal cord regeneration in zebrafish M. H. Mokalled, C. Patra et al bibl graph *Science* v354 no6312 p630 N 4 2016

Spinal cord—Surgery
RESURRECTION R. Story bw color *Skiing* p66 Wint 2017

Spinal muscular atrophy—Treatment
Antisense rescues babies from killer disease M. Wadman color diag *Science* v354 no6318 p1359 D 16 2016

Spinal nerve root diseases
PAIN E. Hayasaki color *Wired* v25 no5 p84 My 2017

Spinal Tap (Performer)
Spinal Tap vs. Hollywood A. WALLACE bw color *GQ: Gentlemen's Quarterly* v97 no6 p72 Je 2017

Spinale, Wendy
Everland color *Publishers Weekly* v263 no49 p107 D 7 2016

Spine
REINVENT YOUR WHEEL A. Ferretti and J. Crandell color *Yoga Journal* p72 2017 Special Issue

Spine—Anatomy
Get to know... Shoulderstand R. Long color *Yoga Journal* p28 2017 SpecialIssue

Get to know... your QL muscles N. Carollo color *Yoga Journal* p54 2017 SpecialIssue

Get to know ... Your thoracic spine J. Miller color *Yoga Journal* no296 p64 N 2017

A home practice to re-energize and find greater joy A. Kaivalya color *Yoga Journal* no288 p55 D 2016

Spinelli, Jerry

Jailbirds H. G. SLOAN *New York Times Book Review* p15 F 12 2017

The Warden's Daughter *Publishers Weekly* v263 no46 p56 N 14 2016

Spinellis, Diomidis

Simple Online Tools to Make Hiring Easier *Harvard Business Review Digital Articles* p2 My 4 2015

Spiner, Wade

UNSOLICITED BETA color *Climbing* no351 p18 F/Mr 2017

Spinks, Rosie

Two Words: No. Plastic *Sierra* v101 no5 p12 S/O 2016

Spinnakers

Looking after Halyards D. Everitt color *Sail* v48 no5 p52 My 2017

SPINNER, ESTHER

Tokens of Our Affection cartoon *O, The Oprah Magazine* p17 F 2017

Spinney, Laura

The legacy of the Spanish flu S. Shablovsky bw color *Science* v357 no6357 p1245 S 22 2017

Monuments to Catastrophe *History Today* v67 no4 p72 Ap 2017

Science seeks to explain racism color *Science News* v191 no10 p28 My 27 2017

Spinning reels—Evaluation

HELL ON REELS 2017 M. Modoski and J. Cermele color *Field & Stream* v121 no9 p67 Ap 2017

Spinoza, Baruch

SUPERSTITIOUS MINDS *Lapham's Quarterly* v10 no3 p163 Summ 2017

Spinoza, Benedictus de, 1632-1677

Assessing Spinoza *Commentary* v142 no1 p1 Jl/Ag 2016

SUPERSTITIOUS MINDS B. Spinoza *Lapham's Quarterly* v10 no3 p163 Summ 2017

Spinx, Jeronimo—Interviews

Interview with a ... Character actor D. Angeles *Career Outlook* p1 F 2017

SPIOTTA, DANA

D.I.Y cartoon *New Yorker* v93 no26 p42 S 4 2017

Spiral galaxies

EYES IN THE SKY J. Berlin color *National Geographic* v231 no2 p132 F 2017

A Galaxy in the Giraffe M. Wedel *Sky & Telescope* v132 no6 p42 D 2016

READER GALLERY color *Astronomy* v45 no4 p72 Ap 2017

Spiral arms detected around an infant star A. G. Smart *Physics Today* v69 no12 p22 D 2016

Why do spiral galaxies spiral? D. J. Eicher color *Astronomy* v44 no12 p7 D 2016

Spiral Jetty (Earthwork)

THE ART AT THE END OF THE WORLD H. Julavits *New York Times Magazine* p44 Jl 9 2017

Where Time Wears Thin I. TUTTLE color *National Review* v68 no21 p24 N 21 2016

Spiral staircases

RISE AND SHINE J. BREWSTER color *Cabin Living* p46 O 2017

Spirals

Detecting structure in a protostellar disk K. Rice bibl color *Science* v353 no6307 p1492 S 30 2016

Spire Global Inc.

CubeSat networks hasten shift to commercial weather data E. Hand color *Science* v357 no6347 p118 Jl 14 2017

Spirit

See also

Consciousness

Ismael Cala: CNN Host Turned Life Strategist L. Ahuile color *Publishers Weekly* v264 no18 p18 My 1 2017

Spirit (Music)

DEPECHE MODE L. Greenblatt *Entertainment Weekly* no1446/1447 p75 D 2016/Ja 2017

Spirit photography

Spirits of Our Galaxy's Past M. Young *Sky & Telescope* v133 no4 p22 Ap 2017

Spirits

See also

Ghosts

Respect for the ancients F. Beardsley color *Science* v354 no6317 p1242 D 9 2016

Spirits (Music)

Exploring Musical Branches K. Micallef color *Downbeat* v84 no10 p31 O 2017

Spiritual care (Medical care)

Rise of the Wellness Coach G. Graves color *Women's Health* v14 no2 p121 Mr 2017

Spiritual formation

tricycle / ONLINE bw color *Tricycle: The Buddhist Review* v26 no4 p6 Summ 2017

Spiritual gifts

See also

Spiritual healing

Our Spiritual Gifts Have an Expiration Date A. WILSON *Christianity Today* v61 no5 p22 Je 2017

Spiritual healing

Desperate for a Cure M. KOHUT color *National Geographic* v232 no1 p74 Jl 2017

Healing With God C. Keehan color *America* v216 no13 p62 Je 12 2017

Spiritual life

See also

Meditation

Spiritual retreats

Become more prayerful this year A. Scobey color *U.S. Catholic* v82 no1 p43 Ja 2017

Bowie brought us together S. Johnson *U.S. Catholic* v82 no1 p4 Ja 2017

Brave new world A. Camille color *U.S. Catholic* v82 no4 p47 Ap 2017

A chance to retreat: Spiritual retreats help those who struggle with homelessness and addiction move forward J. Parrott color *U.S. Catholic* v82 no10 p32 O 2017

Food of THE GODS M. BECK color *O, The Oprah Magazine* p36 Jl 2017

The Heart Beat [Cover story] E. DIAS color *America* v215 no15 p15 N 14 2016

Northern Warning J. T. KEANE *America* v215 no16 p12 N 21 2016

Popular piety R. Throm, P. Cronin et al color *U.S. Catholic* v82 no2 p5 F 2017

Spiritual Costs of Debt S. SALAI color *America* v215 no15 p21 N 14 2016

Spiritual retreat centers

AMERICA'S GUIDE TO RETREATS *America* v217 no6 p31 S 18 2017

Community practice: Founding a community for lay members to live lives of peace and justice took years of commitment M. O'Brien color *U.S. Catholic* v82 no9 p45 S 2017

Find Some Peace: A spiritual retreat can let you not only achieve some calm but also contemplate the important things in life A. COCHRAN *Washingtonian Magazine* v52 no11 p96 Ag 2017

Life amid Loss K. Kilby *Commonweal* v144 no4 p13 F 24 2017

Spiritual retreats

Find Some Peace: A spiritual retreat can let you not only achieve some calm but also contemplate the important things in life A. COCHRAN *Washingtonian Magazine* v52 no11 p96 Ag 2017

Spiritual retreats—Catholic Church

A chance to retreat: Spiritual retreats help those who struggle with homelessness and addiction move forward J. Parrott color *U.S. Catholic* v82 no10 p32 O 2017

Spiritualism

See also

Spirit photography

The Selfie, Medieval Style E. Goodwin *History Today* v67 no2 p6 F 2017

Spiritualism—History

THE MAGIC MOUNTAIN F. LIDZ *Smithsonian* v48 no2 p48 My 2017

Spirituality

Awesomeness Is Everything M. HUTSON color *Atlantic* v319 no1 p15 Ja/F 2017

Brave new world A. Camille color *U.S. Catholic* v82 no4 p47 Ap 2017

CENTURY marks *Christian Century* v134 no17 p8 Ag 16 2017

Kat Fowler M. RABBITT color *Yoga Journal* no296 p10 N 2017

Losing Their Religion L. Garrett bw color *Publishers Weekly* v264 no13 p19 Mr 27 2017

THE MEETING H. SHUKMAN cartoon *Tricycle: The Buddhist Review* v26 no3 p78 Spr 2017

OPEN YOUR EYES color *Essence* v47 no9 p88 Ja 2017

A PLACE FOR WHOLE-PERSON RECOVERY *Psychology Today* v49 no6 p20 N/D 2016

SBNR PAST & PRESENT W. B. PARSONS cartoon *Tricycle: The Buddhist Review* v26 no3 p48 Spr 2017

SCIENTIFIC SPIRITUALITY M. HEDSTROM cartoon *Tricycle: The Buddhist Review* v26 no3 p56 Spr 2017

Spiritual but not Religious L. WEBSTER color *Tricycle: The Buddhist Review* v26 no3 p46 Spr 2017

The ties that bind E. Sanna *U.S. Catholic* v82 no9 p4 S 2017

Trying to Lose My Religion S. DIMITROPOULOS bw *Discover* v38 no7 p26 S 2017

WAITING FOR WATER K. VAUGHN *Arizona Highways* v93 no11 p28 N 2017

Spirituality in art

REACHING FOR THE STARS bw cartoon *ARTnews* v116 no1 p127 Spr 2017

Spirituality—Christianity

Exploring God's Call A. M. BRENNAN color *America* v215 no18 p27 D 5 2016

Faith Matters S. Paulsell *Christian Century* v134 no19 p40 S 13 2017

How spiritual practices can foster creativity R. Muthiah *Christian Century* v134 no8 p1 Ap 12 2017

A LESSON IN LISTENING C. HERMAN bw *Christianity Today* v61 no5 p40 Je 2017

Life together as an empire collapses color *Christian Century* v134 no8 p1 Ap 12 2017

A WALKING DISASTER J. ATEN color *Christianity Today* v61 no5 p44 Je 2017

THE WORK OF LOVE R. Mawhood Lee color *America* v216 no3 p32 F 6 2017

Wrestling with Eternity F. A. JAMES III *Christianity Today* v60 no10 p58 D 2016

YOU DON'T DO GOD ALONE B. McGARVEY bw *America* v215 no12 p32 O 24 2017

Spirituality—History

You Are What You Eat E. Fudge *History Today* v67 no2 p41 F 2017

Spirituality—Study & teaching

TWO SIDES OF THE SAME COIN D. WINSTON color *Tricycle: The Buddhist Review* v26 no3 p60 Spr 2017

Spitfire (Company)

Primary Cool color *Glamour* v115 no7 p28 Jl 2017

Spitsbergen Island (Norway)

In Svalbard L. OSOFSKY *Orion Magazine* v35 no4/5 p12 Jl-O 2016

Spitz, David

Marketers Don't Need to Be Data Scientists *Harvard Business Review Digital Articles* p2 O 6 2014

SPITZER, SUZANNE E.

Ecological Forecasting and the Science of Hypoxia in Chesapeake Bay *BioScience* v67 no7 p614 Jl 2017

Spitzer Space Telescope (Spacecraft)

Seven planets packed in like Jupiter's moons color *Astronomy* v45 no6 p13 Je 2017

STELLAR NURSERY E. MASTROIANNI color *Discover* v38 no3 p18 Ap 2017

Spitznagel, Eric

Battle of the Brains color *Men's Health* v31 no10 p110 D 2016

KURT RUSSELL bw *Men's Health* v32 no3 p128 Ap 2017

Life Advice from Kids bw cartoon color *Men's Health* v32 no1 p140 Ja/F 2017

Michigan *New York Times Magazine* p24 Ap 23 2017

PHIL JACKSON color *Men's Health* v32 no2 p120 Mr 2017

A Pirate's Life for Me color *Money* v46 no7 p84 Ag 2017

Ron Howard bw *Men's Health* v32 no1 p38 Ja/F 2017

Stupid Stuff Guys Do to Lose Weight cartoon *Men's Health* v32 no2 p66 Mr 2017

TONY BENNETT bw *Men's Health* v31 no10 p120 D 2016

WHAT YOUR TV CRUSH SAYS ABOUT YOU color *Men's Health* v32 no3 p83 Ap 2017

Why Ladies Pick Guitar Players bw *Men's Health* v31 no10 p42 D 2016

Spitz-Oener, Alexandra

The Real Reason the German Labor Market Is Booming *Harvard Business Review Digital Articles* p2 Mr 13 2017

SPIVA, HOWARD

Headlong into Danger *USA Today Magazine* v146 no2866 p64 Jl 2017

Spivack, Matthew

What to Know About Doing Business in Iran *Harvard Business Review Digital Articles* p2 My 5 2016

Splash & Bubbles (TV program)

DAY TIME M. LOGAN *TV Guide* v64 no48 p44 N 21 2016

Splendor Boats (Company)

Splendor 239 SunStar *Boating World* v38 no1 p52 Ja 2017

Splendor in the Grass (Film)

Where the #@$%! Have You Been, Warren Beatty? J. NEWMAN color *AARP: The Magazine* v59 no6A p42 O/N 2016

Spliceosomes

Structure of a yeast step II catalytically activated spliceosome Chuangye Yan, Ruixue Wan et al bibl diag *Science* v355 no6321 p1 Ja 13 2017

Split (Film)

DEPTHS OF FEAR A. LANE cartoon *New Yorker* v92 no47 p76 Ja 30 2017

M. Night Shyamalan, Filmmaker E. Berman color *Time* v189 no3 p54 Ja 30 2017

A Night's Tale J. McGovern color *Entertainment Weekly* no1449 p24 Ja 20 2017

NIGHT TIME J. McGovern color *Entertainment Weekly* no1451/1452 p16 F 3-10 2017

Scared Straight J. Podhoretz color *Weekly Standard* v22 no23 p39 F 20 2017

Split L. Greenblatt color *Entertainment Weekly* no1450 p42 Ja 27 2017

Split Rock Lighthouse (Minn.)

The Best of Both Worlds: Gooseberry Falls and Split Rock Lighthouse State Parks, Minnesota K. PETERSON color *Backpacker* p24 S 2017

Spofforth, John

Art for Secularism's Sake *Humanist* v77 no3 p5 My/Je 2017

Spohr, Kristina

The Global Chancellor: Helmut Schmidt and the Reshaping of the International Order A. Moravcsik *Foreign Affairs* v96 no1 p165 Ja/F 2017

SPOMER, RON

GET YOUR GOBBLER color *Outdoor Life* v224 no4 p43 My 2017

THE KNOCKDOWN MYTH color *Outdoor Life* v224 no8 p26 O 2017

TOP 5 SHOOTING MISTAKES color *Outdoor Life* v224 no4 p22 My 2017

WALK SOFTLY color *Outdoor Life* v224 no3 p30 Ap 2017

Sponagle, Michele

Insulin Pump Technology Gives Greater Freedom and Flexibility cartoon *Maclean's* v129 no48/49 p42 D 5 2016

Living Life to the Fullest with a Rare Blood Disorder, Thanks to Innovative Therapies *Maclean's* v130 no9 p37 O 2017

Say Goodbye to Contact Lenses and Glasses with PiXLTM — the New Non-Invasive Vision Improvement Procedure color *Maclean's* v129 no42 p36 O 24 2016

The Social and etalk's Lainey Lui Turns Caregiver for Her Mother color *Maclean's* v130 no9 p36 O 2017

Supports Women and Their Small Businesses Through Education and Networking color *Maclean's* v130 no3 p60 Ap 2017

VISION LOOS DUE TO DIABETES ON THE RISE cartoon *Maclean's* v129 no48/49 p43 D 5 2016

Sponberg, Simon

The emergent physics of animal locomotion: Many physiological systems must work together to enable movement in animals and other organisms. Neuromechanics explores how those systems interact with each other and the environment *Physics Today* v70 no9 p34 S 2017

Sponenberg, D. Phillip
GENETICS Going gray color *Equus* no470 p68 N 2016

SPONG, JOHN
A Fanboy's Notes *Texas Monthly* v45 no3 p94 Mr 2017
The Writer's Life *Texas Monthly* v45 no4 p18 Ap 2017

Spong, John Shelby
A BRIDGE SUPREME: Connecting Humanism to a Liberal, Loving Christianity J. Shelby Spong *Humanist* v76 no6 p21 N/D 2016

Sponge (Material)
TEXTURE-CHANGING SPONGES color *Popular Mechanics* p84 D 2016/Ja 2017

Sponges (Invertebrates)
Can We Save Coral Reefs? C. Manfrino *UN Chronicle* v54 no1/2 p1 2017

Sponsler, Erika
Discussion *Smithsonian* v48 no1 p10 Ap 2017

Spoon (Performer)
A Fanboy's Notes J. SPONG *Texas Monthly* v45 no3 p94 Mr 2017
SPOON K. O'Donnell *Entertainment Weekly* no1446/1447 p75 D 2016/Ja 2017
Spoon's Secret Influences K. GROW bw color *Rolling Stone* no1284 p18 Ap 6 2017

Spooner, Nigel
STATE OF PRESERVATION *Archaeology* v70 no5 p8 S/O 2017

Spoons
coffee mug mixers color *Good Housekeeping* v263 no6 p30 D 2016

Spoons—Evaluation
BOWL—ED OVER color *Bon Appetit* v62 no10 p74 O 2017
TOAST THE HOST color *Martha Stewart Living* p68 Jl/Ag 2017

Spores
FROM PLEBE WEED TO FAMOUS FLORA E. MASTROIANNI color *Discover* v38 no2 p11 Mr 2017

Spörhase, Ulrike
Help, hope, and hype: Ethical dimensions of neuroprosthetics color *Science* v356 no6345 p1338 Je 30 2017

Sport clothes
AT YOUR LEISURE color *Women's Health* v14 no9 p134 N 2017
The Dos & Don'ts of Athleisure color *Glamour* v114 no7 p52 Jl 2016
DRESSING DOWN D. Clemente *Saturday Evening Post* v289 no3 p80 My/Je 2017
Is Your Locker MAKING YOU SICK? A. STANLEY color *Seventeen* v76 no2 p92 Mr 2017
LOONEY FUMES M. Zeitler color *Women's Health* v14 no4 p40 My 2017
Men in tights M. CAMPBELL color *Maclean's* v129 no43 p63 O 31 2016
Our Favorite Sports Bras Now R. S. Frazier color *Health* v31 no3 p54 Ap 2017
The perfect LBB R. S. Frazier color *Health* v31 no8 p52 O 2017
THE RISE OF ACTIVE STYLE J. V. AMODIO color *Men's Health* v32 no7 p(Sp)4 S 2017
Sporty Vibes color *Glamour* v115 no5 p44 My 2017
STUFF WE LOVE color *Golf Magazine* v59 no11 p64 N 2017
WEATHER THE WEATHER J. GALLOWAY cartoon *Runner's World* v52 no3 p40 Ap 2017
Workout Gear for All Women color *Health* v31 no6 p18 Jl 2017

Sport clothes for women—Evaluation
PICK OF THE LAYERS [Cover story] L. Jhung color *Runner's World* v52 no1 p62 Ja/F 2017

Sport clothes stores—Evaluation
Flex Appeal: The city's newest athleisure shop pushes style to the edge S. BAHR *Indianapolis Monthly* v12 no40 p34 Ag 2017

Sport clothes—Design & construction
FROM THE GYM TO THE RUNWAY J. Kell color diag *Fortune* v174 no6 p67 N 1 2016
GAME TIME DECISIONS E. NOVY-WILLIAMS color *Bloomberg Businessweek* no4515 p59 Mr 20 2017

Sport clothes—Economic aspects
FROM THE GYM TO THE RUNWAY J. Kell color diag *Fortune*

v174 no6 p67 N 1 2016

Sport clothes—Evaluation
The 2018 Apparel Guide bw color *Powder* v46 no2 p70 O 2017
$50 & Under Team Spirit color *Seventeen* v75 no11 p32 N 2016
ASHLEY GRAHAM'S GYM PICKS color *InStyle* v24 no1 p52 Ja 2017
COOL RUNNERS L. JHUNG color *Runner's World* v52 no7 p26 Ag 2017
Fitness Clothes That Actually Fit [Cover story] color *Prevention* v69 no9 p50 O 2017
IT'S IN THE BAG J. Dengate color *Runner's World* v52 no2 p48 Mr 2017
PEARL IZUMI PI DRY APPAREL M. Phillips color *Bicycling* v58 no9 p81 O 2017
Retro Sport color *O, The Oprah Magazine* p61 Mr 2017
Sweatshirt + Dress = Yes! color *Glamour* v114 no7 p54 Jl 2016
Swimsuits for Every Sport R. S. Frazier color *Health* v31 no6 p54 Jl 2017
WANNA PLAY? color *Seventeen* v75 no11 p92 N 2016
What You Need K. DUPZYK color *Popular Mechanics* v193 no7 p42 S 2016
THE WINNING LOOK R. Lauren and J. Marksbury color *Golf Magazine* v59 no9 p40 S 2017
WORKOUT LEGGINGS chart color *Good Housekeeping* v264 no1 p106 Ja 1 2017

Sport utility vehicle sales
The People's Choice M. Monticello color diag graph *Consumer Reports* v82 no4 p7 Ap 2017
The Real Cause of the U.S. Car Slide: SUVs D. Welch, J. Butters et al diag *Bloomberg Businessweek* no4518 p24 Ap 10 2017
Why the SUV boom is great news for sedan drivers M. Rechtin color *Motor Trend* v69 no10 p22 O 2017

Sport utility vehicle testing
FARM-TOUGH UTVS: OUR 2017 UTV TEST RESULTS ARE IN! J. Scott color *Successful Farming* v115 no7 p24 My 2017

Sport utility vehicles
See also
Acura MDX sport utility vehicle
Cayenne automobile
Escalade sport utility vehicle
Toyota 4Runner sport utility vehicle
Cruising on a Sunday Afternoon: In a country hamlet, everyone notices when the police chief is driving around color *Yankee* p12 Jl 2017
Ratings chart *Consumer Reports* v82 no10 p64 O 2017
Road Test color *Consumer Reports* v82 no9 p62 S 2017
Route 66 A. SACHS color map *AARP: The Magazine* v60 no3A p53 Ap/My 2017
SUVOCABULARY M. Cantu bw *Motor Trend* v69 no10 p65 O 2017
Volkswagen B-SUV F. Markus color *Motor Trend* v68 no12 p22 D 2016

Sport utility vehicles—Awards
EVERYBODY'S EVERYTHING C. Walton color *Motor Trend* v69 no1 p38 Ja 2017
The finalist round J. Cammisa color *Motor Trend* v69 no1 p64 Ja 2017
The Finalists... color *Motor Trend* v69 no1 p62 Ja 2017

Sport utility vehicles—Evaluation
2017 Land Rover Discovery E. DYER color *Popular Mechanics* p43 S 2017
2018 GMC Terrain A. Priddle color *Motor Trend* v69 no3 p21 Mr 2017
THE BEST NEVER REST C. Walton chart color *Motor Trend* v69 no6 p76 Je 2017
Canyonero? No B. Halvorson cartoon color *Car & Driver* v62 no10 p86 Ap 2017
The Complete Package H. Elliott chart color *Bloomberg Businessweek* no4538 p60 S 18 2017
FJORD EXPLORER E. Loh chart color *Motor Trend* v69 no11 p100 N 2017
GARRAGE bw chart color *Motor Trend* v69 no6 p104 Je 2017
Genesis GV80 Concept A. Priddle color *Motor Trend* v69 no7 p24 Jl 2017
GET USED TO THIS MUG C. Seabaugh and E. Ayapana chart color *Motor Trend* v69 no6 p82 Je 2017

HEAD VS. HEART [Cover story] S. Evans chart color *Motor Trend* v69 no8 p38 Ag 2017

IDENTITY CRISIS S. Evans chart color *Motor Trend* v69 no6 p66 Je 2017

It's a Hellcat Thing J. GALL color *Car & Driver* v63 no5 p100 N 2017

JAMBOREE B. S. ANICH color *Road & Track* v69 no4 p80 N 2017

Leading from the Front C. Walton chart color *Motor Trend* v69 no3 p52 Mr 2017

A New Heading G. Fink cartoon color *Car & Driver* v62 no10 p88 Ap 2017

The New Luxury Trucks E. DYER color *Popular Mechanics* v193 no7 p50 S 2016

NEW SUVS & TRUCKS 2018-2019 [Cover story] M. Cantu, Z. Gale et al color *Motor Trend* v69 no10 p32 O 2017

On our summer vacation, we took a bunch of new three-row SUVs to camp. You guys want to see the slideshow? J. Sabatini chart color *Car & Driver* v63 no2 p54 Ag 2017

Range Rover Velar A. MacKenzie color *Motor Trend* v69 no5 p14 My 2017

Ratings chart *Consumer Reports* v81 no12 p76 D 2016

Ratings chart *Consumer Reports* v82 no7 p64 Jl 2017

Road Report color *Consumer Reports* v81 no12 p74 D 2016

ROCK SOLID M. PRINCE color *Road & Track* v68 no9 p78 Je 2017

SIZE MATTERS J. H. HARPER color *Road & Track* v69 no1 p86 Ag 2017

The SUV Just Went Topless D. DEMURO color *GQ: Gentlemen's Quarterly* v86 no11 p54 N 2016

Tesla Model X chart color *Motor Trend* v69 no1 p68 Ja 2017

Velar–Oh! D. G. Johnson color *Car & Driver* v63 no5 p112 N 2017

VELOCEE BELLA M. Rechtin chart color *Motor Trend* v69 no10 p82 O 2017

WHICH Luxury SUV Are YOU? color *Esquire* v166 no4 p78 N 2016

Sport utility vehicles—Testing

Behind the scenes What ha' happen was... color *Motor Trend* v69 no1 p42 Ja 2017

The finalist round J. Cammisa color *Motor Trend* v69 no1 p64 Ja 2017

Sportage automobile—Evaluation

Kia Sportage chart color *Motor Trend* v69 no1 p50 Ja 2017

Sportcoats

AN AIRPLANE HANGER-ON D. Karl color *Flying* v144 no7 p68 Jl 2017

Sportcoats—Evaluation

BEATDOWN A. Smith color *Bike Magazine* v24 no4 p112 Je 2017

Puff, Puff, Puff C. Sagan color *Powder* v45 no6 p50 F 2017

SPORTELLI, NATALIE

GREEN THUMBS color *Forbes* v199 no7 p28 Je 29 2017

Warning Signs color *Forbes* v200 no4 p46 O 24 2017

WELL BEINGS color *Forbes* v200 no1 p18 Jl 27 2017

Sporting events tickets—Computer network resources

'Sold Out' Is for Suckers E. Novy-Williams cartoon *Bloomberg Businessweek* no4495 p70 O 17 2016

Sporting goods

See also

Golf clubs (Sporting goods)

Hiking equipment

Mountaineering equipment

Surfboards

Swimming equipment

BETTER PLAYER DRIVERS M. Chwasky, M. Dee et al color diag *Golf Magazine* v59 no3 p82 Mr 2017

GAME IMPROVEMENT DRIVERS M. Chwasky, M. Dee et al color diag *Golf Magazine* v59 no3 p74 Mr 2017

MAX GAME IMPROVEMENT DRIVERS M. Chwasky, M. Dee et al color diag *Golf Magazine* v59 no3 p92 Mr 2017

Sporting goods—Evaluation

ANGLE GRINDERS P. Bridges bw color *Snowboarder* v29 no2 p142 O 2016

THE BLACK BOARD EXPERIMENT [Cover story] T. Bird bw color *Snowboarder* v29 no2 p52 O 2016

ESSENTIAL GEAR color *Black Belt* v55 no4 p72 Je/Jl 2017

GRAND STANDS A. Johnson color *Golf Magazine* v59 no9 p88 S 2017

HAPPY TRAILS J. Dengate color *Runner's World* v52 no9 p78 O 2017

KICKING ASPHALT J. Ator color *Women's Health* v14 no6 p(Sp)16 Jl 2017

LONG-GAME CHANGERS M. Chwasky and R. Sauerhaft color *Golf Magazine* v59 no8 p89 Ag 2017

LOOK SHARP M. Chwasky color *Golf Magazine* v59 no9 p86 S 2017

NEVER SUMMER cartoon color *Snowboarder* v29 no4 p118 D 2016

Sports

See also

Aeronautical sports

Age & sports

Aquatic sports

Ball games

Endurance sports

Extreme sports

Gymnastics

Motorsports

Music & sports

Photography of sports

Rodeos

Shooting (Sports)

Sports competitions

Sports for children

Sports for women

Sports forecasting

Sports penalties

Sports teams

Targets (Sports)

Winter sports

THE APPROVAL MATRIX img *New York* v49 no26 p112 D 26 2016

Family Valued color *Sports Illustrated* v125 no21 p10 D 26 2016

GAME ON! H. STEINBERGER *Boating World* v38 no2 p54 F 2017

GAME PLAN M. Zimmerman bw color graph *Men's Health* v32 no7 p8 S 2017

How to Handle an Annoying Cubs Fan chart color *Men's Health* v32 no3 p12 Ap 2017

'I Love Watching You Play' S. ECKELBERRY *Parks & Recreation* v52 no5 p8 My 2017

Jason Day J. Crelin color *Current Biography* v78 no3 p20 Mr 2017

LET'S MAKE FOOTBALL A COLLEGE MAJOR D. V. Johnson *Saturday Evening Post* v288 no6 p12 N/D 2017

A Note to Our Readers *Current Biography* v77 no10 p2 O 2016

PLAY IT FORWARD M. BOBENRIETH *UN Chronicle* v53 no2 p17 2016

Rearview Sharer C. P. Pierce and T. Keith color *Sports Illustrated* v125 no21 p20 D 26 2016

The Soccer Mom's Lament C. VAN DUSEN *Atlanta* v56 no11 p93 Mr 2017

Sports Funnies color *National Geographic Kids* no471 p8 Je/Jl 2017

STEVE SPENCE N. WELDON color *Runner's World* v51 no10 p36 N 2016

Why Sports Are a Terrible Metaphor for Business B. Taylor bw *Harvard Business Review Digital Articles* p2 F 3 2017

The World Nomad Games J. Wendle color *Atlantic* v318 no5 p18 D 2016

Sports & state

WAS THAT THE MOST POLITICAL SUPER BOWL EVER? D. Coggan color *Entertainment Weekly* no1453 p17 F 17 2017

Sports & state—United States

CHIEF CONCERNS S. I. Price color *Sports Illustrated* v127 no10 p36 O 2 2017

THE JUSTICE LEAGUE B. SCHOENFELD bw color *Esquire* p90 N 2017

Should professional athletes be allowed to use their status to talk about things more important than the games they play? J. C. Kang *New York Times Magazine* p12 F 19 2017

A TIME TO TAKE A STAND [Cover story] color *Sports Illustrated* v127 no10 p26 O 2 2017

Sports & technology

Hot Spot L. J. Wertheim and T. Keith color *Sports Illustrated* v126 no13 p16 My 8 2017

Sports, Asap

Still Going Strong color *Golf Magazine* v59 no9 p25 S 2017

Sports bars

The Sports Bar B. Gregory and P. Kita cartoon *Men's Health* v32 no2 p30 Mr 2017

Sports bars—Evaluation

HAVE A BALL WITH BOCCE C. SCHEDLER color *Chicago* v66 no7 p51 Jl 2017

Sports betting

Betting on Ice In the Desert P. Brownfield color *Bloomberg Businessweek* no4540 p64 O 2 2017

If sports betting is legalized, could its hunger for analytics restore an older, purer version of fandom? J. C. Kang *New York Times Magazine* p16 Ap 30 2017

A Wall Street Legend Flops in Sports Betting B. Louis and C. Palmeri *Bloomberg Businessweek* no4515 p35 Mr 20 2017

Sports bras

DON'T BELIEVE HER SPORTS BRA [Cover story] C. Connors color *Women's Health* v14 no4 p61 My 2017

PORT DE Bras O. Manno *Dance Spirit* v21 no1 p32 Ja 2017

THE QUESTION cartoon color *Runner's World* v51 no11 p19 D 2016

Sports Bras That Don't Suck color *Glamour* v115 no6 p85 Je 2017

Sports Support L. McGLASHAN color *Muscle & Performance* v9 no7 p26 Jl 2017

Women SUPPORTING Women K. BASTONE bw color *Runner's World* v52 no7 p86 Ag 2017

Sports bras—Evaluation

2017 Women's Gear Guide color *Climbing* no356 p34 S/O 2017

Athleisure Remix! color *Glamour* v115 no7 p24 Jl 2017

Fitness Clothes That Actually Fit [Cover story] color *Prevention* v69 no9 p50 O 2017

SHOW of SUPPORT K. BASTONE color *Runner's World* v52 no7 p78 Ag 2017

Sporty Cool cartoon color *Seventeen* v76 no12 p41 D 2016/Ja 2017

Tack Room color *Practical Horseman* v45 no6 p77 Je 2017

WANNA PLAY? color *Seventeen* v75 no11 p92 N 2016

Sports business

See also

   Baseball attendance

   Football attendance

The future of basketball as both sport and marketing enterprise can be glimpsed in the moves of seven-foot wonder athletes who handle the ball like point guards J. C. Kang *New York Times Magazine* p17 Ja 22 2017

RACING TO BUILD AN ENDURANCE SPORTS EMPIRE P. Wahba color diag *Fortune* v176 no5 p116 O 1 2017

Sports car design & construction

THINKING OUTSIDE THE (Shoe) BOX C. Shelton bw color *Hot Rod* v70 no7 p60 Jl 2017

Sports car events

LOORRS TO ADD SXSs TO NATIONAL SCHEDULE color *Dirt Sports + Off-Road* v51 no4 p8 Ap 2017

Sports car racing

EDITOR'S LETTER K. WOLFKILL color *Road & Track* v68 no8 p20 My 2017

A NEW GOLDEN AGE color *Road & Track* v68 no8 p28 My 2017

Sports cars

See also

   Corvette automobile

   Ford GT automobile

   Jaguar E-type automobile

   Porsche 911 automobile

   Viper automobile

Chariot of Fire J. MacGregor *Smithsonian* v48 no3 p26 Je 2017

Friends for Life P. EGAN color diag *Road & Track* v68 no10 p26 Jl 2017

Live at Birdland S. SMITH color *Road & Track* v68 no10 p24 Jl 2017

THE NEOPHYTE D. CURCURITO color *Road & Track* v68 no8 p64 My 2017

NOTES ON BDC 2017 E. Loh color *Motor Trend* v69 no11 p14 N 2017

What's On Demand This Month? E. Loh *Motor Trend* v69 no11 p14 N 2017

Sports cars—Congresses

THE 18TH ANNUAL SAND SPORTS SUPER SHOW M. EMERY color *Dirt Sports + Off-Road* v51 no2 p8 F 2017

Sports cars—Evaluation

2017 JAGUAR XE 35T AWD R-SPORT J. Sabatini color *Car & Driver* v62 no10 p78 Ap 2017

APOCALYPSE NOW B. SOROKANICH color *Road & Track* v68 no9 p38 Je 2017

Don't Call It a Wagon E. Tingwall color *Car & Driver* v63 no4 p80 O 2017

THE FOREVER WAR [Cover story] J. Lieberman chart color diag graph *Motor Trend* v69 no8 p48 Ag 2017

LETTER OF INTENT M. PRINCE color *Road & Track* v69 no1 p80 Ag 2017

LIGHTNING LAP [Cover story] K. C. COLWELL, J. JACQUOT et al color graph map *Car & Driver* v63 no4 p45 O 2017

Luck of the half Irish E. Loh *Motor Trend* v69 no6 p8 Je 2017

Poster Boy J. Gall color *Car & Driver* v63 no1 p98 Jl 2017

The Real Cars of Geneva color *Motor Trend* v69 no6 p16 Je 2017

RETRO, ACTIVE R. PINTO color *Road & Track* v69 no1 p64 Ag 2017

SPORTS-CAR RACING 101 P. LERNER color *Road & Track* v68 no8 p50 My 2017

Three for the Road H. Elliott color *Bloomberg Businessweek* no4528 p70 Je 26 2017

Sports collectibles

Major League Memorabilia J. Paskin color *Bloomberg Businessweek* no4524 p68 My 29 2017

Sports competitions

See also

   Cycling competitions

ARAB YEAR color *Arabian Horse World* v57 no7 p144 Ap 2017

FIGHT CLUB S. Stankorb *Cincinnati Magazine* v50 no12 p28 S 2017

Get It Right, Keep It Right [Cover story] J. Gibbs and A. Boatwright color *Horse & Rider* v56 no6 p48 Je 2017

Sports Direct International PLC—Finance

Spare any change, Mike? *People Management* p6 O 2016

Sports drinks—Evaluation

GREEN ENERGY color *Runner's World* v51 no10 p39 N 2016

Sports events

See also

   Championships

   Cycling competitions

   Marathons (Sports)

Duel of the Duals T. Taylor color *Hot Rod* v70 no4 p10 Ap 2017

snapshots 2017 img *New York Times Upfront* v149 no6 p38 D 12 2016

USA HALF MARATHON INVITATIONAL B. McANENY, W. O'DWYER et al color *Runner's World* v51 no11 p98 D 2016

Sports facilities

See also

   Arenas

   Basketball courts

   Golf courses

   Racetracks (Automobile racing)

   Recreation areas

   Stadiums

   Swimming pools

Island Fever J. Passov color *Golf Magazine* v59 no5 p100 My 2017

Left Hooked *Los Angeles Magazine* p20 F 2017

Welcome to Festival City A. Ehrenhalt *Governing* v30 no1 p14 O 2016

"We're standing up for respect" J. PRESS *Scholastic Choices* v32 no7 p6 Ap 2017

WHOLE NEW BALL GAME T. Wendel *Washingtonian Magazine* v52 no5 p125 F 2017

Sports facilities—Design & construction

Another Transformation in Queens E. McGrogan *Tennis* v52 no6 p64 N/D 2016

Sports facilities—France

Paris' Technicolor Basketball Court J. Zorthian color *Time* v190 no4 p19 Jl 24 2017

Sports facilities—Washington (State)

YOUNG GLOVE M. M. KASHINO *Washingtonian Magazine* v53 no1 p26 O 2017

Sports facility design & construction

Crowd Festivities Can Shake Richter Scale *USA Today Magazine* v145 no2865 p12 Je 2017

Sports facility management

Another Transformation in Queens E. McGrogan *Tennis* v52 no6 p64 N/D 2016

Sports films

AV CLUB Davidaisy bw *Snowboarder* v29 no5 p29 Ja 2017

BIG BEAR, CALIFORNIA J. Miller bw color *Snowboarder* v29 no4 p96 D 2016

DUELING ROLES S. Kwak color *Sports Illustrated* v127 no10 p17 O 2 2017

HOLY BOWLY MAMMOTH MTN, CA M. Walsh color *Snowboarder* v29 no4 p104 D 2016

SEB PICARD P. Harrington bw cartoon color *Snowboarder* v29 no4 p50 D 2016

Sports films—Awards

And the Award Goes to ... T. Keith color *Sports Illustrated* v126 no5 p18 F 13 2017

Sports for children

See also

Skiing for children

Cover *Time* v190 no9 pC1 S 4 2017

JUNIOR NATIONAL FINALS RODEO color *Horse & Rider* v56 no11 p72 N 2017

Kid Sports Inc [Cover story] S. Gregory, A. Abrams et al color diag *Time* v190 no9 p42 S 4 2017

Sports for older people

A BOY OF 62 B. Heavey *Field & Stream* v122 no1 p78 My 2017

Sports for people with disabilities

See also

Paralympics

Sports and Autism L. J. Wertheim and S. Apstein color *Sports Illustrated* v125 no16 p52 N 14 2016

Sports for women

See also

Running for women

Tennis for women

Counternarrative color *Climbing* no356 p16 S/O 2017

Sports for youth

Embrace The Crazy S. Rushin color *Sports Illustrated* v126 no15 p60 My 29 2017

GOOD LUCK, COACH *USA Today Magazine* v145 no2864 p74 My 2017

Sports forecasting

10 GRIZZLIES color *Sports Illustrated* v127 no12 p90 O 16 2017

10 KNICKS color *Sports Illustrated* v127 no12 p68 O 16 2017

11 PACERS color *Sports Illustrated* v127 no12 p70 O 16 2017

11 PELICANS color *Sports Illustrated* v127 no12 p92 O 16 2017

12 HAWKS color *Sports Illustrated* v127 no12 p71 O 16 2017

12 MAVERICKS color *Sports Illustrated* v127 no12 p94 O 16 2017

13 LAKERS color *Sports Illustrated* v127 no12 p95 O 16 2017

13 MAGIC color *Sports Illustrated* v127 no12 p72 O 16 2017

14 KINGS color *Sports Illustrated* v127 no12 p96 O 16 2017

14 NETS color *Sports Illustrated* v127 no12 p73 O 16 2017

15 BULLS color *Sports Illustrated* v127 no12 p74 O 16 2017

15 SUNS color *Sports Illustrated* v127 no12 p97 O 16 2017

1 Atlanta Falcons color *Sports Illustrated* v127 no7 p96 S 4 2017

1 CAVALIERS color *Sports Illustrated* v127 no12 p56 O 16 2017

1 Minnesota Vikings color *Sports Illustrated* v127 no7 p92 S 4 2017

1 New England Patriots color *Sports Illustrated* v127 no7 p64 S 4 2017

1 New York Giants color *Sports Illustrated* v127 no7 p86 S 4 2017

1 Oakland Raiders color *Sports Illustrated* v127 no7 p80 S 4 2017

1 Pittsburgh Steelers color *Sports Illustrated* v127 no7 p70 S 4 2017

1 Seattle Seahawks color *Sports Illustrated* v127 no7 p100 S 4 2017

1 Tennessee Titans color *Sports Illustrated* v127 no7 p74 S 4 2017

1 WARRIORS color *Sports Illustrated* v127 no12 p78 O 16 2017

2017 SI'S (WAY TOO EARLY) TOP 10 A. Staples color *Sports Illustrated* v126 no2 p33 Ja 16 2017

2 Arizona Cardinals color *Sports Illustrated* v127 no7 p101 S 4 2017

2 Baltimore Ravens color *Sports Illustrated* v127 no7 p71 S 4 2017

2 CELTICS color *Sports Illustrated* v127 no12 p58 O 16 2017

2 Dallas Cowboys color *Sports Illustrated* v127 no7 p88 S 4 2017

2 Green Bay Packers color *Sports Illustrated* v127 no7 p93 S 4 2017

2 Houston Texans color *Sports Illustrated* v127 no7 p76 S 4 2017

2 Kansas City Chiefs color *Sports Illustrated* v127 no7 p81 S 4 2017

2 Miami Dolphins color *Sports Illustrated* v127 no7 p66 S 4 2017

2 ROCKETS color *Sports Illustrated* v127 no12 p80 O 16 2017

2 Tampa Bay Buccaneers color *Sports Illustrated* v127 no7 p97 S 4 2017

3 Buffalo Bills color *Sports Illustrated* v127 no7 p67 S 4 2017

3 Carolina Panthers color *Sports Illustrated* v127 no7 p98 S 4 2017

3 Chicago Bears color *Sports Illustrated* v127 no7 p94 S 4 2017

3 Cincinnati Bengals color *Sports Illustrated* v127 no7 p72 S 4 2017

3 Indianapolis Colts color *Sports Illustrated* v127 no7 p78 S 4 2017

3 Los Angeles Chargers color *Sports Illustrated* v127 no7 p82 S 4 2017

3 Los Angeles Rams color *Sports Illustrated* v127 no7 p102 S 4 2017

3 Philadelphia Eagles color *Sports Illustrated* v127 no7 p89 S 4 2017

3 SPURS color *Sports Illustrated* v127 no12 p81 O 16 2017

3 WIZARDS color *Sports Illustrated* v127 no12 p59 O 16 2017

4 Cleveland Browns color *Sports Illustrated* v127 no7 p73 S 4 2017

4 Denver Broncos color *Sports Illustrated* v127 no7 p84 S 4 2017

4 Detroit Lions color *Sports Illustrated* v127 no7 p95 S 4 2017

4 Jacksonville Jaguars color *Sports Illustrated* v127 no7 p79 S 4 2017

4 New Orleans Saints color *Sports Illustrated* v127 no7 p99 S 4 2017

4 New York Jets color *Sports Illustrated* v127 no7 p68 S 4 2017

4 RAPTORS color *Sports Illustrated* v127 no12 p60 O 16 2017

4 San Francisco 49ers color *Sports Illustrated* v127 no7 p103 S 4 2017

4 THUNDER color *Sports Illustrated* v127 no12 p82 O 16 2017

4 Washington Redskins color *Sports Illustrated* v127 no7 p90 S 4 2017

5 BOLD PREDICTIONS FOR MLB'S SECOND HALF B. Reiter color *Sports Illustrated* v127 no2 p39 Jl 17 2017

5 BUCKS color *Sports Illustrated* v127 no12 p61 O 16 2017

5 TIMBERWOLVES color *Sports Illustrated* v127 no12 p84 O 16 2017

6 HORNETS color *Sports Illustrated* v127 no12 p62 O 16 2017

6 TRAIL BLAZERS color *Sports Illustrated* v127 no12 p86 O 16 2017

7 CLIPPERS color *Sports Illustrated* v127 no12 p87 O 16 2017

7 HEAT color *Sports Illustrated* v127 no12 p64 O 16 2017

8 JAZZ color *Sports Illustrated* v127 no12 p88 O 16 2017

8 PISTONS color *Sports Illustrated* v127 no12 p65 O 16 2017

9 76ERS color *Sports Illustrated* v127 no12 p66 O 16 2017

9 NUGGETS color *Sports Illustrated* v127 no12 p89 O 16 2017

COLLEGE FOOTBALL SCOUTING REPORTS color *Sports Illustrated* v127 no5 p87 Ag 14 2017

Fighting Words T. Keith color *Sports Illustrated* v127 no6 p22 Ag 28 2017

THE FOUR TOPS color *Sports Illustrated* v125 no19 p30 D 12 2016

INSIDE THE RANKINGS L. Winn and D. Hanner color *Sports Illustrated* v125 no15 p56 N 7 2016

LOTTERY TICKETS color *Sports Illustrated* v126 no18 p33 Je 26 2017

OVER UNDER B. Reiter color *Sports Illustrated* v126 no7 p66

Mr 6 2017

Scouting Reports B. Golliver, R. Mahoney et al color *Sports Illustrated* v125 no14 p70 O 24-31 2016

SCOUTING REPORTS chart color *Sports Illustrated* v126 no9 p74 Mr 27 2017

SCOUTING REPORTS R. Nadkarni and A. Sharp color *Sports Illustrated* v127 no12 p54 O 16 2017

Sports forecasting—Humor

What Will Be T. Keith color *Sports Illustrated* v126 no1 p15 Ja 9 2017

Sports goggles

ICY STARE A. Westenfeld color *Esquire* p38 N 2017

Sports goggles—Evaluation

2017 ACCESSORIES GUIDE T. Monterosso color *Snowboarder* v29 no3 p104 N 2016

anon cartoon color *Snowboarder* v29 no4 p110 D 2016

Give Good Gift S. P. Nadella and E. Velluto color *Glamour* v114 no12 p183 D 2016

I Can See Clearly Now J. Brown color *Powder* v45 no4 p40 D 2016

Sports halls of fame

OFF-ROAD MOTORSPORTS HALL OF FAME 2017 INDUCTEES ANNOUNCED *Dirt Sports + Off-Road* v51 no12 p8 D 2017

Sports helmets—Evaluation

ESSENTIAL GEAR color *Black Belt* v55 no1 p58 D 2016/Ja 2017

Sports Illustrated (Periodical)

Family Valued color *Sports Illustrated* v125 no21 p10 D 26 2016

So What Do You Do, CHRISTIE BRINKLEY? color *InStyle* v24 no7 p84 Jl 2017

Sports in art—Exhibitions

On the Ball A. K. Scott color *New Yorker* v93 no8 p12 Ap 10 2017

Sports in popular culture

The Case for ... Peak NBA L. J. Wertheim and T. Keith color *Sports Illustrated* v127 no2 p27 Jl 17 2017

Sports injuries

See also

Football injuries

Sports injury prevention

Body of knowledge [Cover story] R. Long color *Yoga Journal* no290 p54 Mr 2017

Sports instruction

See also

Dance education

Golf instruction

Horsemanship instruction

Motorsports instruction

LEARNING BY WATCHING AND LISTENING TO OTHERS [Cover story] K. Santos color *Spin to Win Rodeo* v21 no4 p44 Je 2017

Sports journalism

See also

Sportscasters

Television broadcasting of sports

Wolff Whistles color *Sports Illustrated* v125 no13 p14 O 17 2016

Sports journalism—Computer network resources

A New Sports Authority J. Brustein *Bloomberg Businessweek* no4532 p20 Jl 31 2017

Sports journalism—History

CONFESSIONS OF A SPORTSWRITER F. Deford color *Sports Illustrated* v126 no16 p68 Je 5 2017

Sports journalism—Humor

From Eternity To Here S. Rushin color *Sports Illustrated* v126 no10 p80 Ap 10 2017

Sports literature

The Game Changer J. McCARTNEY color *Publishers Weekly* v263 no43 p41 O 24 2016

Sports medicine

See also

Equine sports medicine

Nutrition of athletes

THE END OF PAIN? [Cover story] B. STULBERG cartoon color *Runner's World* v52 no2 p50 Mr 2017

Sports medicine education

Belhaven University *Dance Magazine* v90 p46 2016/2017 Supplement College Guide

Sports participation—Social aspects

BIG RESULTS M. Moore *Arabian Horse World* v57 no6 p146 Mr 2017

Sports penalties

ASK THE RULES GUY R. Guy and C. Barrett color *Golf Magazine* v59 no2 p30 F 2017

ASK THE RULES GUY R. Guy and C. Barrett color *Golf Magazine* v59 no3 p34 Mr 2017

FLAG FOOTBALL J. Dickey chart color *Sports Illustrated* v125 no21 p46 D 26 2016

Sports periodicals

See also

Golf periodicals

Sports personnel—Health

Performance Climbing Nutrition J. DELVES bw color graph *Climbing* no353 p48 My/Je 2017

Sports psychology

The Clinic PHOTO CRITIQUES S. von Dietze chart color *Dressage Today* v24 no1 p22 O 2017

Rediscover the Joy of Riding J. Susser *Dressage Today* v24 no1 p18 O 2017

Sports records

See also

Cycling records

Sports sciences

See also

Physical fitness

Sports psychology

Pitch Ahead T. Taylor and T. Keith color *Sports Illustrated* v127 no4 p18 Ag 7 2017

Sports spectators

See also

Automobile racing fans

Basketball fans

Football fans

HOW TO BE A BLEACHER-STOMPING, BEER-TOSSING D.C. UNITED FAN R. CARTAGENA, G. WEBER et al *Washingtonian Magazine* v52 no6 p70 Mr 2017

USHJA Focuses on Growth and Sport Integrity K. F. Miller color *Practical Horseman* v45 no3 p66 Mr 2017

Would major professional sports be better if the star athletes made more money and ran the leagues? J. C. Kang *New York Times Magazine* p14 Jl 30 2017

Sports spectators—Attitudes

Entitled Behavior W. Leitch and T. Keith color *Sports Illustrated* v125 no20 p20 D 19 2016

Sports sponsorship

See also

Horse sports sponsorship

No Pro Go color *Powder* v45 no5 p104 Ja 2017

What I'd Do Differently: Walter Röhrl, 70 M. DUFF *Car & Driver* v63 no2 p104 Ag 2017

Sports team mascots

MASCOT MATH T. Keith color *Sports Illustrated* v127 no8 p20 S 18 2017

Mr. Met S. Stein color *New York Times Magazine* p34 My 21 2017

Sports team mascots—History

DAWG DAYS J. Gorant, T. Keith et al color *Sports Illustrated* v127 no5 p28 Ag 14 2017

Sports team mascots—Humor

Green Day T. Keith color *Sports Illustrated* v125 no12 p19 O 10 2016

Sports teams

See also

Baseball teams

Football teams

Rugby football teams

Soccer teams

ANOTHER LAP R. KOTHE color map *Sail* v48 no10 p50 O 2017

In Defense of Larry Ellison C. J. DOANE color *Sail* v48 no10 p120 O 2017

Pride and Joy E. PARKHURST *Virginia Living* v15 no2 p36 F 2017

Sports teams—Sales & prices

Who's the Boss? M. Rosenberg color *Sports Illustrated* v126 no13 p68 My 8 2017

Sports television programs
    See also
    Golf on television
Sports tournaments
    See also
        Football—Tournaments
        Golf tournaments
        Skiing competitions
        Tennis—Tournaments
    2017 Tennis Calendar chart *Tennis* v53 no1 p80 Ja/F 2017
    lines in the sand b. minnigh color *Bike Magazine* v24 no4 p48
        Je 2017
Sports upsets
    Keys to a Canelo upset ... B. Baskin color *Sports Illustrated* v127
        no6 p56 Ag 28 2017
    Keys to a McGregor upset ... B. Baskin color *Sports Illustrated*
        v127 no6 p54 Ag 28 2017
Sports upsets—Universities & colleges
    CHAOS THEORIES A. Staples color *Sports Illustrated* v125
        no17 p82 N 21 2016 Double Issue
    'Tis the Season M. Rosenberg color *Sports Illustrated* v125 no19
        p80 D 12 2016
Sports watches
    DIVE IN color *Conde Nast Traveler* v52 no9 p30 O 2017
Sports watches—Evaluation
    Accent the BOATER *Sea Magazine* v108 no12 p42 D 2016
    AQUA Fresh color *InStyle* v24 no10 p137 O 2017
    Track Action for Less L. Eadicicco color *Money* v46 no2 p23 Mr
        2017
Sportscasters
    HOT | NOT T. Keith color *Sports Illustrated* v125 no12 p19 O
        10 2016
    Joe Buck Knows Why You Hate Him A. M. Cox *New York Times
        Magazine* p50 F 5 2017
    LOUD & CLEAR C. FEHRMAN bw color *Cincinnati Magazine*
        v51 no1 p74 O 2017
Sportscasters—Attitudes
    Bob Costas J. Saraceno color *AARP: The Magazine* v59 no5A p13
        Ag/S 2016
    The Voice V. Lundquist color *Sports Illustrated* v125 no18 p64
        D 5 2016
Sportscenter (TV program)
    GOT ANY IDEAS? [Cover story] I. BOUDWAY and M.
        CHAFKIN color graph *Bloomberg Businessweek* no4517 p48
        Ap 3 2017
    Shifting Center R. Deitsch and T. Keith color *Sports Illustrated*
        v126 no5 p25 F 13 2017
Sports—Charts, diagrams, etc.
    Pop Chart R. Bruner, C. Lang et al color *Time* v189 no18 p58
        My 15 2017
Sports—Collectibles—Sales & prices
    Money for Something S. Apstein and T. Keith color *Sports Illus-
        trated* v126 no9 p24 Mr 27 2017
Sports—Corrupt practices
    See also
        Corrupt practices in college sports
Sports—Economic aspects
    The Most Valuable Sports Brands M. K. OZANIAN chart color
        Forbes v198 no8 p34 D 20 2016
Sports—Exhibitions
    AMERICAN ARTISTS TACKLE THE GRIDIRON *USA Today
        Magazine* v146 no2868 p50 S 2017
Sports—History
    Awesome Foursomes T. Keith color *Sports Illustrated* v126 no10
        p28 Ap 10 2017
    Lost to History T. Keith color *Sports Illustrated* v126 no17 p18
        Je 19 2017
Sports—History—20th century
    Past Blast color *Sports Illustrated* v127 no1 p112 Jl 3 2017
Sportsmanship
    We Deserve Fair Play T. Brennan *In Stride* v12 no2 p25 Mr 2017
Sportsmanship—Awards
    Nancy Crary Jones: An Amateur with a Professional Mindset T.
        Booker *In Stride* v12 no4 p39 Jl 2017
Sports—New Zealand
    A Heroic Win C. Museler color *Sail* v48 no9 p16 S 2017

A New Kiwi Magic color *Sail* v48 no9 p8 S 2017
Sports—News briefs
    GO FIGURE T. Keith color *Sports Illustrated* v125 no17 p24 N
        21 2016 Double Issue
    The Intersection color *Runner's World* v52 no7 p48 Ag 2017
    Longines FEI World Cup North American League News color
        Practical Horseman v45 no2 p63 F 2017
    News BITS color *Practical Horseman* v45 no2 p64 F 2017
Sports—Rules
    Play Ball L. SMITH color *Weekly Standard* v22 no31 p5 Ap 17
        2017
Sports—Safety measures
    See also
        Aquatic sports safety measures
        Hunting safety
    Take Up the Slack C. CARTER color graph *Men's Health* v32
        no9 p84 N 2017
Sports—Societies, etc.
    AMERICAN DREAM S. TIGNOR *Tennis* v52 no6 p26 N/D 2016
Sports—Sociological aspects
    To the Rescue M. Rosenberg color *Sports Illustrated* v125 no13
        p60 O 17 2016
Sports teams—Names—Charts, diagrams, etc.
    How Lo Can They Go T. Keith chart color *Sports Illustrated* v125
        no18 p20 D 5 2016
Sports—Texas
    VITAL SIGNS A. AHMED and S. TRAVIS *Texas Monthly* v45
        no9 p62 S 2017
Sports—United States
    The Year's at the Spring W. Kristol *Weekly Standard* v22 no30
        p8 Ap 10 2017
Sports—United States—History
    AN ODE TO THE HOT DOG S. Rushin color *Sports Illustrated*
        v127 no1 p104 Jl 3 2017
    PATRIOT GAMES A. Lawrence color *Sports Illustrated* v126 no3
        p52 Ja 23 2017
Sports—United States—History—21st century
    Shock Jocks J. Dickey and T. Keith color *Sports Illustrated* v126
        no5 p14 F 13 2017
Sportswriters
    Frank Deford 1938-2017 A. Wolff and T. Keith color *Sports Il-
        lustrated* v126 no16 p19 Je 5 2017
    Robert H. Boyle (1928-2017) J. Fuchs and T. Keith color *Sports
        Illustrated* v126 no16 p32 Je 5 2017
Sportswriters—United States
    Bambi Wulf 1954-2017 T. Keith color *Sports Illustrated* v126
        no17 p18 Je 19 2017
Sport utility vehicles—Evaluation—Charts, diagrams, etc.
    Ratings chart *Consumer Reports* v82 no8 p60 Ag 2017
Spot Brand Bicycles (Company)
    Spot: MAYHEM 27.5+ 4-STAR BUILD T. Engel and A. Emanuel
        color *Bike Magazine* v24 no8 p74 N 2017
Spot LLC
    SPOT GEN3® *Sea Magazine* v108 no12 p54 D 2016
Spot shrimp
    DEEP DIVE M. BUSICO *Los Angeles Magazine* v62 no6 p38 Je
        2017
Spotify AB
    How Spotify Balances Employee Autonomy and Accountability
        M. Mankins and E. Garton color *Harvard Business Review Dig-
        ital Articles* p2 F 9 2017
    How Spotify Creates Hits S. KNOPPER color *Rolling Stone*
        no1294 p17 Ag 24 2017
Spötl, Christoph
    Response to Comments on "Reconciliation of the Devils Hole cli-
        mate record with orbital forcing" bibl chart graph *Science* v354
        no6310 p296-e O 21 2016
Spotlight (Film)—Awards
    Movies for Grownups B. NEWCOTT color *AARP: The Magazine*
        v59 no2A p61 F/Mr 2016
Spotnitz, Frank
    The Man in the High Castle J. Halterman *TV Guide* v64 no40 p36
        O 3 2016
Spotting (Cleaning)
    ASK CAROLYN C. FORTÉ color diag *Good Housekeeping* v264
        no1 p48 Ja 1 2017

GET ANYTHING OUT C. FORTÉ chart color *Good Housekeeping* v263 no6 p90 D 2016

Spotting (Cleaning)—Equipment & supplies

K2R SPOT-LIFTER: NO PAIN, NO STAIN C. LEU color *Wired* v25 no9 p36 S 2017

Spottiswoode, Claire N.

The most perfect thing, explained diag *Science* v356 no6344 p1234 Je 23 2017

Spouses

See also

Husbands

Prime ministers' spouses

Increase the Odds of Achieving Your Goals by Setting Them with Your Spouse J. Coleman and J. Coleman *Harvard Business Review Digital Articles* p2 F 3 2015

make room for dad J. MONINGER *Parents* v91 no6 p135 Je 2016

You Snooze, You Spoon C. Pikul color *Good Housekeeping* v263 no5 p149 N 2016

Spouses of clergy

Life in a fishbowl: Survey reveals stresses and joys of pastors' spouses A. M. Banks color *Christian Century* v134 no22 p18 O 25 2017

Spouses—Health

A WOMAN'S WORK M. Ruiz color *Women's Health* v14 no8 p113 O 2017

Spradley, Nykia

the COMPACT color *Essence* v47 no12 p46 Ap 2017

the COMPACT color *Essence* v47 no9 p30 Ja 2017

Curly Cues color *Essence* v47 no11 p47 Mr 2017

The Eye of the Beholder color *Essence* v47 no9 p23 Ja 2017

for the Win color *Essence* v47 no12 p57 Ap 2017

Hat Hair color *Essence* v47 no10 p45 F 2017

Hit Refresh color *Essence* v47 no12 p29 Ap 2017

Insider Tips color *Essence* v47 no7 p23 N 2016

Merry Manes color *Essence* v47 no8 p61 D 2016

THE NEW CONTOUR color *Essence* v47 no7 p30 N 2016

the RUN-DOWN color *Essence* v47 no11 p33 Mr 2017

She's Bangin' color *Essence* v47 no7 p39 N 2016

Strokes of Genius color *Essence* v47 no8 p45 D 2016

THERMAL BRUSH color *Essence* v47 no11 p55 Mr 2017

TONAL VISION color *Essence* v47 no12 p51 Ap 2017

Spradling, Allan

Not just Salk color *Science* v357 no6356 p1105 S 15 2017

Sprague, Bob

CSX up on Rocky Top color diag map *Model Railroader* v84 no8 p34 Ag 2017

Two railroads in one bedroom color diag *Model Railroader* v84 no1 p62 Ja 2017

Union Pacific's Spine Line in HO and N color diag map *Model Railroader* v84 no4 p72 Ap 2017

SPRAGUE, COLE

ANZA ADVENTURES color *Dirt Sports + Off-Road* v51 no6 p8 Je 2017

SPRAGUE, ERIC

WILDLANDS FOR WILDLIFE: Working to protect and restore forest habitat for at-risk wildlife across the United States *American Forests* v123 no2 p20 Summ 2017

Sprague, Shawn A.

Estimating the U.S. labor share bibl chart color graph *Monthly Labor Review* p1 F 2017

Sprain prevention

Get to know... your hamstrings J. Gudmestad color *Yoga Journal* p90 2017 SpecialIssue

Spratly Islands

SAVING THE SOUTH CHINA SEA D. LAWRENCE and W. FAN color map *Bloomberg Businessweek* no4505 p78 D 26 2016

Sprau, P. O.

Discovery of orbital-selective Cooper pairing in FeSe diag *Science* v357 no6346 p75 Jl 7 2017

Spray nozzles

KNOW NOZZLES G. Guilickson *Successful Farming* v115 no2 p41 F 2017

Spray painting

DOING THE DISHES *Saturday Evening Post* v289 no1 p28 Ja/F 2017

Spray skirts (Kayaks)

LEVEL SIX color *Canoe & Kayak Magazine* v45 no1 p91 Wint 2017

Spraying

Innovation: Spray-On Touchpad M. Belfiore color *Bloomberg Businessweek* no4532 p23 Jl 31 2017

Spraying & dusting in agriculture

See also

Pesticides

IDEA OF THE MONTH P. Barbour *Successful Farming* v115 no11 p76 S 2017

IDEA OF THE MONTH: SHOP-BUILT SIDEDRESSER CONVERTED FROM SPRAYER ALLOWS SPLIT APPLICATIONS P. Barbour *Successful Farming* v115 no6 p78 Ap 2017

Spraying & dusting in agriculture—Equipment & supplies

LONG WINTER LAYOFF L. Bedord *Successful Farming* v114 no13 p46 D 2016

Sprecher, Kevin

MORE POP, LESS POP-UP color diag *Golf Magazine* v59 no4 p54 Ap 2017

Run It or Fly It color *Golf Magazine* v59 no3 p48 Mr 2017

TURN STYLE color *Golf Magazine* v59 no6 p42 Je 2017

Why Do I Hit My Irons Thin? *Golf Magazine* v59 no8 p48 Ag 2017

Sprecher, Mary Helen

Tennis, Everyone Adaptive tennis programs in the parks can bring future players off the sidelines and into the game: *Parks & Recreation* v52 no9 p74 S 2017

Sprengel, David

In the Best Sales Teams, About Half of the People Are in Support Roles *Harvard Business Review Digital Articles* p2 My 25 2016

Sprenger, C.

Interactions between brain and spinal cord mediate value effects in nocebo hyperalgesia color *Science* v357 no6359 p105 O 6 2017

Spribille, Toby

Triple Symbiosis N. Wilson *Natural History* v124 no10 p7 N 2016

Spring

See also

Vernal equinox

Back Again: Our Migrating Contributors C. Amundson *Nebraska Life* v21 no2 p9 Mr/Ap 2017

The Best Time color *Yankee* p26 Mr 2017

Drop It Like It's Hot R. Robertson color *Field & Stream* v121 no9 pF1 Ap 2017

Early Spring J. RAO color *Natural History* v125 no3 p45 Mr 2017

Spring, Joe

Climate Steward *Sierra* v101 no6 p63 N/D 2016

Water Wizard *Sierra* v102 no1 p103 Ja/F 2017

Spring, Justin

The Gourmands' Way: Six Americans in Paris and the Birth of a New Gastronomy *Publishers Weekly* v264 no33 p65 Ag 14 2017

Spring festivals

SPRING FESTIVALS C. JAY *Louisiana Life* v37 no4 p62 Mr/Ap 2017

Spring Mills Inc.

Spring Mills Depot HO wagontop hopper E. White color *Model Railroader* v84 no6 p66 Je 2017

Springer, Anna-Sophie

The New Hillary Library? R. Darnton color *New York Review of Books* v63 no16 p4 O 27 2016

SPRINGER, BILL

THE FINAL FRONTIER color *Power & Motoryacht* v34 no9 p82 S 2017

Springer, George

Leading Off B. Reiter color *Sports Illustrated* v127 no12 p6 O 16 2017

LOVE SPRINGS ETERNAL T. Verducci color *Sports Illustrated* v127 no4 p38 Ag 7 2017

Springer, Jerry, 1944-

LETTER FROM THE EDITOR J. FOX cartoon *Cincinnati Magazine* v51 no1 p14 O 2017

Springer, Nate

The Internet Shouldn't Run on Dirty Energy *Harvard Business Review Digital Articles* p2 D 17 2015

Springer, Tom

5 Ways to Increase Your Cross-Selling *Harvard Business Review*

Digital Articles p2 N 22 2016

Springfield (Ohio)—Economic conditions
A THOUSAND CUTS M. Maciag and J. B. Wogan *Governing* v30 no5 p32 F 2017

Springfield, Rick—Interviews
Supernatural color *TV Guide* v64 no42 p41 O 10 2016

Springs, Stephen
Social Equity: Plays Key Role in New Braunfels' New Recreation Center *Parks & Recreation* v52 no10 p40 O 2017

Springsteen, Bruce, 1949-
Born to Run C. Collis color *Entertainment Weekly* no1434 p58 O 7 2016
Bruce Springsteen, Artful Leadership, and What Rock Star Bosses Do G. Petriglieri *Harvard Business Review Digital Articles* p2 S 27 2017
Bruce Springsteen E. Gundersen bw *AARP: The Magazine* v60 no1A p13 D 2016/Ja 2017
A GREAT AND HARSH BEAUTY A. A. O'DONNELL *America* v215 no13 p33 O 31 2016
A Human Hero E. Blondiau color *America* v216 no1 p21 Ja 2 2017
No Surrender D. BROOKS bw *Atlantic* v318 no4 p44 N 2016
Random Notes color *Rolling Stone* no1276 p32 D 15 2016
Random Notes color *Rolling Stone* no1298 p22 O 19 2017
REDEMPTION SONG D. HAJDU color *Nation* v303 no25/26 p36 D 19 2016
Runaway American Dream R. Ford color *New York Times Book Review* p1 S 25 2016
Swept Away by Springsteen J. Pareles bw *New York Review of Books* v63 no20 p44 D 22 2016
The Ties That Bind A. GREENE bw color *Rolling Stone* no1298 p20 O 19 2017
A Troubadour in the Age of Trump *Commentary* v141 no10 p1 D 2016
A Troubadour in the Age of Trump *Commentary* v142 no5 p1 D 2016
Working Man's Bard R. D. LURIE bw *National Review* v68 no24 p40 D 31 2016

Springsteen, Bruce, 1949-—Interviews
True Bruce [Cover story] B. HIATT bw color *Rolling Stone* no1272 p32 O 20 2016

Sprinklers—Evaluation
MOTHER'S Product Picks *Mother Earth News* no283 p14 Ag/S 2017

Sprint Corp.
WHAT PRESIDENT TRUMP'S ELECTION CAN TEACH US ABOUT MANAGING OUR HUMAN RESOURCES *Vital Speeches of the Day* v83 no5 p141 My 2017
Why Sprint and Radio Shack Are Shacking Up D. Dahlhoff *Harvard Business Review Digital Articles* p2 F 10 2015

Sprinting
ASK MILES cartoon *Runner's World* v52 no3 p23 Ap 2017
Short Runs, Big Gains E. ABBATE cartoon chart color *Men's Health* v32 no8 p58 O 2017
SPRINTS J. WUEBBEN color *Muscle & Performance* v9 no9 p18 S 2017

Sprites (Atmospheric lightning)
Telescopic sprites S. J. O'MEARA color *Astronomy* v45 no4 p66 Ap 2017

Sprouse, Cole
Riverdale D. Holbrook *TV Guide* v65 no2 p26 Ja 2 2017
Riverdale T. Stack, N. Abrams et al color *Entertainment Weekly* no1482/1483 p68 S 22 2017
Sound Bites color *Entertainment Weekly* no1478 / 1479 p6 Ag 18-25 2017

Sprout a Revolution Inc.—Awards
THE 2017 GLAMOUR BEAUTY AWARD A. Grooms, K. Erickson et al color *Glamour* v115 no4 p81 Ap 2017

Sprouts
Battle of the Breads color *Prevention* v69 no8 p15 Ag 2017

Spruce
TIMBER TUMBLE cartoon color *Outdoor Life* v224 no9 p16 N 2017

Spruce, Lanae—Interviews
You're a what? Social media specialist E. Torpey color *Career Outlook* p1 N 2016

Spruill, Marjorie J.
Divided We Stand: The Battle Over Women's Rights and Family Values That Polarized American Politics color *Publishers Weekly* v263 no52 p114 D 19 2016
Turning Point G. THOMAS *New York Times Book Review* p12 Mr 12 2017
THE TWO WOMEN'S MOVEMENTS K. PHILLIPS-FEIN bw *Nation* v304 no18 p33 Je 19 2017
Who Killed the ERA? [Cover story] L. Greenhouse bw color *New York Review of Books* v64 no15 p6 O 12 2017

Spruyt, Hendrik
Civil Wars as Challenges to the Modern International System *Daedalus* v146 no4 p112 Fall 2017

Spry, Maxine
Actes and Angels: Early Protestants were suspicious of the supernatural. Despite this, John Foxe's martyrology was replete with angels *History Today* v67 no9 p18 S 2017

Spry-Marqués, Pía
Pig/Pork: Archaeology, Zoology, and Edibility L. A. MARSCHALL color *Natural History* v125 no7 p46 Jl/Ag 2017

Spufford, Francis, 1964-
MANHATTAN TRANSFER L. MILLER cartoon *New Yorker* v93 no19 p67 Jl 3 2017

Spufford, Francis, 1964-—Interviews
'Contrary by Temperament' A. Domestico bw *Commonweal* v144 no13 p10 Ag 11 2017

SPUNGEN, SUSAN
CELERIAC color *Rodale's Organic Life* v3 no1 p21 Ja 2017

Spurgeon, Oliver III
Elements of a Blueprint for ACA Replacement *Parks & Recreation* v52 no3 p22 Mr 2017
The New Markets Tax Credit *Parks & Recreation* v51 no11 p24 N 2016
Replacing the Affordable Care Act *Parks & Recreation* v52 no2 p20 F 2017

Spurling, Hilary
High-Wire Act color *New York Review of Books* v64 no17 p20 N 9 2017

Spurlock, Michael
Inspiration Is Everywhere L. Garrett color *Publishers Weekly* v264 no17 p20 Ap 24 2017

Spurs
Education vs. Strength H. Hugo-Vidal color *Practical Horseman* v45 no4 p22 Ap 2017

Spurs (Horse)
My Collection B. Welch color *Horse & Rider* v56 no7 p112 Jl 2017

Sputtering (Physics)
Atmosphere Lost to Space C. M. CARLISLE *Sky & Telescope* v134 no1 p11 Jl 2017

SPYRA, JEN
FAMILY-VACATION BREAKDOWN cartoon *New Yorker* v93 no25 p41 Ag 28 2017
WHEN I KNEW I FOUND THE ONE cartoon *New Yorker* v92 no38 p41 N 21 2016

SPYREAS, GREG
Long-Term Trends in Midwestern Milkweed Abundances and Their Relevance to Monarch Butterfly Declines *BioScience* v67 no4 p343 Ap 2017

SPYROU, MARIA A.
Tracking Ancient Plagues bw color *Natural History* v125 no9 p18 S 2017

Squamata
See also
Chameleons
Lizards
Snakes
THE OCELLATED LIZARD IS A COMPUTER GAME COME TO LIFE *Physics Today* v70 no6 p25 Je 2017

Squamous cell carcinoma
Genetic Test: Squamous Cell Carcinoma S. Dulai Wenholz color *Practical Horseman* v45 no10 p68 O 2017

Squance, Joe
WAIT FOR IT color *Rodale's Organic Life* v3 no1 p96 Ja 2017

Square, The (Film)
Art Brute C. LORENTZEN il *New Republic* v248 no11 p50 N

2017

The Danish Boy J. POWERS color *Vogue* v207 no10 p228 O 2017

Square Enix Holdings Co. Ltd.

DISNEY MEETS FINAL FANTASY (AND TEDIUM) IN KINGDOM HEARTS UNION X[CROSS] A. HAYWARD color *Macworld - Digital Edition* v34 no10 p55 O 2017

Squartini, R.

Observation of a large-scale anisotropy in the arrival directions of cosmic rays above 8 × 1018 eV *Science* v357 no6357 p1266 S 22 2017

Squassoni, Sharon

The incredible shrinking nuclear offset to climate change bibl *Bulletin of the Atomic Scientists* v73 no1 p17 Ja 2017

Squat (Weight lifting)

15 MINUTE WORKOUT color *Women's Health* v14 no7 p80 S 2017

15 MINUTE WORKOUT M. Gainsburg color *Women's Health* v14 no5 p64 Je 2017

30 MUST-DO MOVES for 2017 L. McGLASHAN color *Muscle & Performance* v9 no1 p44 Ja 2017

5 WAYS ...TO BUILD ON THE CLASSIC SQUAT J. CONNOR cartoon *Muscle & Performance* v9 no1 p66 Ja 2017

5 WAYS: ...to Use a Sandbag S. MAIN color *Muscle & Performance* v9 no8 p66 Ag 2017

5 WAYS... TO USE A SMITH MACHINE J. WUEBBEN color *Muscle & Performance* v9 no6 p66 Je 2017

Abs Made Easy A. COSGROVE color *Men's Health* v32 no5 p50 Je 2017

AROUND THE HOUSE color *AARP: The Magazine* v59 no3A p44 Ap/My 2016

THE BAYWATCH BODY BURN cartoon *Women's Health* v14 no5 p143 Je 2017

BULGARIAN SPLIT SQUAT J. WUEBBEN color *Muscle & Performance* v9 no8 p14 Ag 2017

Catching Fire J. BEVERLY color *Runner's World* v52 no7 p52 Ag 2017

The Couch Crusher B. J. Gaddour cartoon color *Men's Health* v32 no3 p14 Ap 2017

Easy exercises that keep you young H. Powell color *Redbook* p77 Mr 2017

FLEX TIME M. Gainsburg chart color *Women's Health* v14 no8 p78 O 2017

FRONT SQUAT color *Muscle & Performance* v9 no1 p17 Ja 2017

FULL FRONTAL J. CISSIK chart color *Muscle & Performance* v9 no5 p18 My 2017

Get Ripped on These 6 Trips T. GRAHAM color *Men's Health* v32 no6 p29 Ag 2017

HEIGHT TRAINING HACKS L. BOYCE color *Muscle & Performance* v9 no1 p24 Ja 2017

THE LEG PRESS, PERFECTED L. McGLASHAN chart color *Muscle & Performance* v8 no12 p18 D 2016

NEVER SKIP LEG DAY [Cover story] M. Gainsburg color *Women's Health* v14 no6 p(Sp)20 Jl 2017

One speedy move for a toned core E. Ziel color *Redbook* p90 D 2016

Performance Yoga S. MAIN color *Muscle & Performance* v9 no8 p24 Ag 2017

Put Your Best Foot Forward L. BOYCE color *Muscle & Performance* v9 no8 p18 Ag 2017

Six Simple Moves for Total-Body Strength I. Creighton color *Men's Health* v32 no6 p16 Ag 2017

SQUAT TO GET LEAN? YEP L. MCGLASHAN cartoon chart *Muscle & Performance* v8 no12 p22 D 2016

Tailor-Made SQUATS E. CALDERONE color *Muscle & Performance* v9 no4 p40 Ap 2017

The Three-B Workout L. McGLASHAN chart color *Muscle & Performance* v9 no8 p16 Ag 2017

The Triathlon Training Trifecta bw color *Men's Health* v32 no2 p114 Mr 2017

TRX, REDEFINED L. MCGLASHAN chart color *Muscle & Performance* v9 no1 p22 Ja 2017

Unassailable Ankles L. Boyce color *Muscle & Performance* v9 no8 p53 Ag 2017

Welcome to the Jungle Gym M. ARAGONCILLO color *Men's Health* v32 no6 p50 Ag 2017

Your Back Pain Prescription B. J. Gaddour bw color *Men's Health*

v32 no1 p137 Ja/F 2017

Squaw Valley (Calif.)

Taking on Tahoe N. Walker color map *Canadian Geographic* v137 p14 2017 Travel

Squids

Eye patches: Protein assembly of index-gradient squid lenses J. Cai, J. P. Townsend et al bw color graph *Science* v357 no6351 p564 Ag 11 2017

How squid build their graded-index spherical lenses Sung Chang *Physics Today* v70 no10 p26 O 2017

Patchy proteins form a perfect lens T. Madl color *Science* v357 no6351 p546 Ag 11 2017

Tagging a Squishy Squid E. Koenig *Oceanus* v52 no1 p24 Summ 2016

Squire (Company)

THE 5 HOTTEST BLACK-OWNED BEAUTY TECH START-UPS S. Blodgett color *Black Enterprise* v47 no8 p28 Jl/Ag 2017

Squires, David A.

White Americans' Mortality Rates Are Rising. Something Similar Happened in Russia from 1965 to 2005 *Harvard Business Review Digital Articles* p2 Je 26 2017

Squires, Kathleen

Prime Time color *Bloomberg Businessweek* no4510 p61 F 6 2017

Squirrel hunting

ADVENTURES IN SQUIRREL COUNTRY W. BRANTLEY, T. E. NICKENS et al cartoon *Field & Stream* v122 no5 p59 O 2017

NO SMALL MATTER T. E. Nickens color *Field & Stream* v122 no6 p20 N 2017

THE SQUIRREL RUT W. Brantley color *Field & Stream* v121 no7 p24 D 2016/Ja 2017

SQUIRREL TALK J. SPILGER color *Outdoor Life* v224 no7 p23 S 2017

Squirrels

Art Zone cartoon *National Geographic Kids* no471 p34 Je/Jl 2017

The Big Pictures: SANTA CATALINA MOUNTAINS J. KIDA *Arizona Highways* v93 no6 p16 Je 2017

The Gratitude Meter Z. Donaldson color *O, The Oprah Magazine* p20 Je 2017

weird but true! M. HARRIS and J. BEER *National Geographic Kids* no467 p4 F 2017

Squirrels—Behavior

How to Get Squirrels Out of Your Attic J. BILLS and J. P. SCHMELZER color *Yankee* p28 Mr 2017

Squyres, Georgia R.

Treadmilling by FtsZ filaments drives peptidoglycan synthesis and bacterial cell division bibl graph *Science* v355 no6326 p739 F 17 2017

SRAGOW, MICHAEL

Adventure Time color *Film Comment* v53 no5 p74 S/O 2017

Šraj, Mojca

Changing climate shifts timing of European floods color graph *Science* v357 no6351 p588 Ag 11 2017

SRAM Corp.

THE ANSWER IS ETAP M. Phillips color *Bicycling* v58 no10 p58 N/D 2017

BEATDOWN r. cleek *Bike Magazine* v24 no3 p120 My 2017

BEATDOWN t. engel color *Bike Magazine* v24 no5 p102 Jl 2017

Sørensen, Erik Ø.

Research: Moral Appeals Can Help Reduce Tax Evasion *Harvard Business Review Digital Articles* p2 Jl 20 2017

Sørensen, Lars Rebien

Fighting Diabetes in the 21st Century *Harvard Business Review Digital Articles* p2 D 29 2015

Sri Lanka—Description & travel

Colombo, Sri Lanka A. PERERA color *Foreign Policy* no222 p74 Ja/F 2017

Srikrishna, Devabhaktuni

The Fight Against Zika Can't Wait for a Vaccine *Harvard Business Review Digital Articles* p2 Ag 18 2016

To Fight the Zika Pandemic, Learn from Ebola *Harvard Business Review Digital Articles* p2 F 4 2016

What We've Learned About Fighting Ebola *Harvard Business Review Digital Articles* p2 Jl 16 2015

The World Is Completely Unprepared for a Global Pandemic *Harvard Business Review Digital Articles* p2 Mr 15 2017

Sri Lanka—History—Civil War, 1983-2009
The Tangled Politics of Postwar Justice in Sri Lanka J. GOOD-HAND and O. WALTON *Current History* v116 no789 p130 Ap 2017

Srinivas, Niranjan
A cargo-sorting DNA robot color *Science* v357 no6356 p1112 S 15 2017

SRINIVASAN, AMIA
A RIGHTEOUS FURY il *Nation* v303 no25/26 p33 D 19 2016

Srinivasan, Bhu
Americana: A 400-Year History of American Capitalism *Publishers Weekly* v264 no34 p101 Ag 21 2017

Srinivasan, Jayakanth
How the U.S. Army Personalized Its Mental Health Care *Harvard Business Review Digital Articles* p2 D 7 2016

Srinivasan, K.
Quantum correlations from a room-temperature optomechanical cavity color diag graph *Science* v356 no6344 p1265 Je 23 2017

Srinivasan, Shrividhya
Blocking promiscuous activation at cryptic promoters directs cell type–specific gene expression diag *Science* v356 no6339 p717 My 19 2017

Srinivasarao, Mohan
Bioinspired Hierarchical-Structured Surfaces for Green Science and Technology *Physics Today* v70 no9 p60 S 2017

SRIRAM, ADITI
Underground Affair *New York Times Book Review* p9 D 18 2016

Srivastava, L.
A climate policy pathway for near- and long-term benefits color *Science* v356 no6337 p493 My 5 2017

Sroka, Denise
KITCHEN-TESTED TIPS color *Vegetarian Today* no2 p4 Ap 2017

Srolovitz, David J.
Nanocrystalline copper films are never flat diag graph *Science* v357 no6349 p397 Jl 28 2017

Ssentongo, Julius
Applying Deliberative Democracy in Africa: Uganda's First Deliberative Polls *Daedalus* v146 no3 p140 Summ 2017

St. Andrews (Scotland)
Leaders in the Clubhouse J. Passov color *Golf Magazine* v58 no11 p94 N 2016

St. Andrews (Scotland)—Description & travel
ST. ANDREWS color *British Heritage Travel* v38 no5 p22 S/O 2017

St. Bonaventure University
Mentoring from the first semester on in St. Bonaventure University's Theater Program *Stage Directions* v30 no3 p73 Mr 2017

St. Elizabeth Healthcare (Company)
IMAGING HONORS POINT TO BEST-QUALITY PRACTICES AND DIAGNOSTIC CARE V. Prevish *Cincinnati Magazine* v50 no12 p78 S 2017

St. Elmo's Fire (Film)
ST. ELMO'S FIRE L. Rice color *Entertainment Weekly* no1460/1461 p34 Ap 7-17 2017

St. Louis Cardinals (Baseball team)
2 CARDINALS color *Sports Illustrated* v126 no9 p104 Mr 27 2017
St. Louis S. CHWAST *Audubon* v119 no1 p52 Spr 2017

St. Louis Cardinals (Baseball team)—History—21st century
Bader Up T. Keith and S. Kwak color *Sports Illustrated* v127 no5 p30 Ag 14 2017

St. Paul & the Broken Bones (Performer)
St. Paul's Southern Soul Revival D. PEISNER color *Rolling Stone* no1275 p16 D 1 2016

St. Vincent's Healthcare Group Ltd.
MISSION POSSIBLE J. YOUNG color *Indianapolis Monthly* v41 no2 p33 S 2017

Staaf, Danna
Survival of the spineless S. J. McAnulty color *Science* v357 no6359 p53 O 6 2017

Staats, Bradley
Developing Employees Who Think for Themselves *Harvard Business Review Digital Articles* p2 Je 3 2015
Does Doing the Same Work Over and Over Again Make You Less Ethical? *Harvard Business Review Digital Articles* p2 Mr 28 2017

It's OK to Move Down (Yes, Down) the Value Chain *Harvard Business Review Digital Articles* p2 Je 2 2015
It's the Weekend! Why Are You Working? *Harvard Business Review Digital Articles* p2 Ap 10 2015
The Powerful Way Onboarding Can Encourage Authenticity *Harvard Business Review Digital Articles* p2 N 26 2015
Reclaim Your Commute color *Harvard Business Review* v95 no3 p149 My/Je 2017
The Remedy for Unproductive Busyness *Harvard Business Review Digital Articles* p2 Ap 24 2015
Your Desire to Get Things Done Can Undermine Your Effectiveness *Harvard Business Review Digital Articles* p2 Mr 22 2016

Stabbings (Crime)
A Glimpse Inside a Violent Gang T. MECIA color *Weekly Standard* v22 no46 p19 Ag 14 2017

Stability (Mechanics)—Equipment & supplies
new products color *Science* v356 no6344 p1298 Je 23 2017

Stabler, Charles
THE FUTURE OF VEGANISM *Vegetarian Journal* v36 no1 p4 2017
NOTE FROM THE COORDINATORS. NATURAL FOODS: UPSCALE OR DOWNSCALE? MANY ROLES FOR PROMOTING VEGANISM *Vegetarian Journal* v35 no2 p4 2016
VEGETARIAN DIETS AND WATER *Vegetarian Journal* v36 no2 p4 2017

Stables
EDUCATING THE NEXT GENERATION T. Booker color *Practical Horseman* v45 no8 p40 Ag 2017
STALL vs. PASTURE E. Pascoe color *Practical Horseman* v45 no10 p48 O 2017
Time to Ride Challenge Winners color *Trail Rider* v29 no1 p10 Ja/F 2017

STABLES, PAIGE
BEAUTY UNDER $25 bw color *Redbook* p34 N 2017
Clear, Glowy SKIN—Now color *Seventeen* v76 no5 p38 S 2017
Dressed-up hair that's so simple color *Redbook* p60 D 2016
Give yourself better brows cartoon color *Redbook* p18 My 2017
Lash miracles! color *Redbook* p46 N 2017
Magic weapons for great skin cartoon *Redbook* p52 Ap 2017
Make your brushes work harder color *Redbook* p10 My 2017
PLAY UP YOUR natural beauty [Cover story] bw color *Redbook* p50 F 2017

Stables—Design & construction
My Deluxe Dream Barn Will Have... R. Shurtleff, F. A. Nole Hall et al color *Horse & Rider* v56 no4 p80 Ap 2017
Region 7: ARIZONA, NEVADA, AND UTAH W. Tinker color *Arabian Horse World* v57 no7 p28 Ap 2017

Stables—Equipment & supplies
Barn Life, Made Easy H. S. Thomas color *Horse & Rider* v56 no4 p43 Ap 2017

Stables—Maintenance & repair
Keep a Fresh, Clean Barn color *Horse & Rider* v56 no4 p26 Ap 2017

Stacey, Michelle
Badass with a Heart color *Women's Health* v14 no9 p93 N 2017
THE BUSINESS OF FRIENDSHIP color *Redbook* p108 D 2016
CAN YOU BUILD A BETTER SUGAR? color *Women's Health* v14 no4 p112 My 2017
THE JOY OF YOGA [Cover story] cartoon color *Women's Health* v14 no1 p77 Ja/F 2017
THIS IS FASTING? color *Women's Health* v14 no8 p106 O 2017
The World Is Her Playground [Cover story] color *Women's Health* v14 no8 p130 O 2017

Stach, Reiner
The Cult of Saint Franz F. Prose bw *New York Review of Books* v63 no16 p60 O 27 2016
Hurt into Literature J. Meyers bw *Commonweal* v144 no6 p27 Mr 24 2017

Stack, Balaram
Perfect Day, New England color *Surfer* v58 no1 p104 Ap 2017

Stack, Jack
GAMING THE SYSTEM P. CARBONARA color *Forbes* v199 no4 p98 Ap 25 2017

Stack, Mike
Behaving Badly *Governing* v30 no10 p12 Jl 2017

Stack, Tim

ADAM SCOTT AND CRAIG ROBINSON color *Entertainment Weekly* no1482/1483 p42 S 22 2017

After the Verdict color *Entertainment Weekly* no1482/1483 p62 S 22 2017

AMAZON BETS ON THE LAST TYCOON color *Entertainment Weekly* no1476 p53 Ag 4 2017

AMERICAN CRIME color *Entertainment Weekly* no1446/1447 p61 D 2016/Ja 2017

American Housewife *Entertainment Weekly* no1482/1483 p79 S 22 2017

America's Next Top Model Struts Again color *Entertainment Weekly* no1443 p52 D 9 2016

BEHIND THE LENS color *Entertainment Weekly* no1462 p34 Ap 21 2017

Being Mary Jane color *Entertainment Weekly* no1448 p37 Ja 13 2017

BEST SUPPORTING ACTRESS color diag *Entertainment Weekly* no1451/1452 p62 F 3-10 2017

black-ish *Entertainment Weekly* no1482/1483 p63 S 22 2017

The Blacklist color *Entertainment Weekly* no1482/1483 p74 S 22 2017

Bob's Burgers *Entertainment Weekly* no1482/1483 p34 S 22 2017

Breaking Big BRANDON MICHEAL HALL color *Entertainment Weekly* no1482/1483 p65 S 22 2017

The BRIGHT Stuff color *Entertainment Weekly* no1446/1447 p34 D 2016/Ja 2017

Broad City color *Entertainment Weekly* no1482/1483 p79 S 22 2017

Bull color *Entertainment Weekly* no1482/1483 p66 S 22 2017

The Cast of Grey's Anatomy color *Entertainment Weekly* no1439 p23 N 11 2016

Chicago P.D *Entertainment Weekly* no1482/1483 p79 S 22 2017

CRIME OF Fashion [Cover story] color *Entertainment Weekly* no1472 p22 Je 30 2017

Criminal Minds color *Entertainment Weekly* no1482/1483 p79 S 22 2017

Curb Your Enthusiasm color *Entertainment Weekly* no1482/1483 p40 S 22 2017

DC's Legends of Tomorrow color *Entertainment Weekly* no1482/1483 p66 S 22 2017

DEEP DISH WITH THE STARS OF GIRLS TRIP color *Entertainment Weekly* no1474/1475 p100 Jl 21-28 2017

DEMI MOORE OF Empire color *Entertainment Weekly* no1482/1483 p78 S 22 2017

Designated Survivor color *Entertainment Weekly* no1482/1483 p74 S 22 2017

The Deuce color *Entertainment Weekly* no1482/1483 p29 S 22 2017

DIVE INTO Brooklyn Nine-Nine color *Entertainment Weekly* no1482/1483 p67 S 22 2017

Dynasty color *Entertainment Weekly* no1482/1483 p76 S 22 2017

Editor's Note color *Entertainment Weekly* no1439 p23 N 11 2016

The Enduring Legacy of Diana color *Entertainment Weekly* no1476 p13 Ag 4 2017

Family Guy *Entertainment Weekly* no1482/1483 p34 S 22 2017

Fantastic Beasts and Where to Find Them color *Entertainment Weekly* no1439 p18 N 11 2016

The Flash color *Entertainment Weekly* no1482/1483 p66 S 22 2017

Fresh Off the Boat color *Entertainment Weekly* no1482/1483 p63 S 22 2017

A GAY Old Timeline color diag *Entertainment Weekly* no1471 p32 Je 23 2017

Gilmore Girls: A Year in the Life color *Entertainment Weekly* no1439 p18 N 11 2016

The Girlfriend Experience color *Entertainment Weekly* no1482/1483 p38 S 22 2017

GOING OUT WITH A BANG color *Entertainment Weekly* no1463/1464 p10 Ap/My 2017

The Goldbergs color *Entertainment Weekly* no1482/1483 p74 S 22 2017

Good Behavior *Entertainment Weekly* no1482/1483 p39 S 22 2017

THE GREATEST SHOWMAN color *Entertainment Weekly* no1478 / 1479 p70 Ag 18-25 2017

HAPPY ENDINGS color *Entertainment Weekly* no1439 p20 N 11 2016

Hit the Road *Entertainment Weekly* no1482/1483 p60 S 22 2017

Hot Date *Entertainment Weekly* no1482/1483 p74 S 22 2017

HOUSE OF CARDS ROCKS THE VOTE color *Entertainment Weekly* no1463/1464 p20 Ap/My 2017

Hugh Jackman in The Greatest Showman color *Entertainment Weekly* no1467 p46 My 26 2017

IF HE HAD A HAMMER... [Cover story] color *Entertainment Weekly* no1457/1458 p28 Mr 17 2017

JASON RITTER OF Kevin (Probably) Saves the World color *Entertainment Weekly* no1482/1483 p61 S 22 2017

THE KIDS OF STRANGER THINGS color *Entertainment Weekly* no1444/1445 p32 D 16 2016

Laverne Cox's Horror Story color *Entertainment Weekly* no1435 p48 O 14 2016

Law & Order: Special Victims Unit *Entertainment Weekly* no1482/1483 p75 S 22 2017

Law & Order True Crime: The Menendez Murders color *Entertainment Weekly* no1482/1483 p62 S 22 2017

Lethal Weapon color *Entertainment Weekly* no1482/1483 p60 S 22 2017

LOVE CONNECTION color *Entertainment Weekly* no1468/1469 p49 Je 2-9 2017

The L Word Returns! color *Entertainment Weekly* no1474/1475 p18 Jl 21-28 2017

Madam Secretary color *Entertainment Weekly* no1482/1483 p39 S 22 2017

Major Crimes *Entertainment Weekly* no1482/1483 p66 S 22 2017

The Mick *Entertainment Weekly* no1482/1483 p67 S 22 2017

The Middle color *Entertainment Weekly* no1482/1483 p60 S 22 2017

Mindhunter color *Entertainment Weekly* no1482/1483 p107 S 22 2017

Modern Family *Entertainment Weekly* no1482/1483 p75 S 22 2017

Mr. Robot color *Entertainment Weekly* no1482/1483 p77 S 22 2017

MUSIC MADE THE PEOPLE COME TOGETHER color *Entertainment Weekly* no1439 p22 N 11 2016

NCIS *Entertainment Weekly* no1482/1483 p60 S 22 2017

NCIS: Los Angeles *Entertainment Weekly* no1482/1483 p38 S 22 2017

NCIS: New Orleans *Entertainment Weekly* no1482/1483 p67 S 22 2017

Nelsan Ellis color *Entertainment Weekly* no1474/1475 p20 Jl 21-28 2017

A NIGHT of FIRSTS color *Entertainment Weekly* no1484 p18 S 29 2017

NO. 14 JEAN GREY color *Entertainment Weekly* no1436/1437 p56 O 21 2016

NO. 19 PROFESSOR X color *Entertainment Weekly* no1436/1437 p59 O 21 2016

NO. 5 Wolverine color *Entertainment Weekly* no1436/1437 p48 O 21 2016

Outlander color *Entertainment Weekly* no1482/1483 p26 S 22 2017

PICTURE color diag *Entertainment Weekly* no1451/1452 p70 F 3-10 2017

Poldark *Entertainment Weekly* no1482/1483 p38 S 22 2017

THE PROS OF CON color *Entertainment Weekly* no1476 p32 Ag 4 2017

Q&A: QUEEN LATIFAH & JADA PINKETT SMITH color *Entertainment Weekly* no1463/1464 p68 Ap/My 2017

Reality By Her Rules color *Entertainment Weekly* no1438 p53 N 4 2016

THE REDEMPTION OF SPIKE color *Entertainment Weekly* no1460/1461 p60 Ap 7-17 2017

REunIons The L Word color *Entertainment Weekly* no1471 p38 Je 23 2017

Riverdale color *Entertainment Weekly* no1448 p42 Ja 13 2017

Riverdale color *Entertainment Weekly* no1482/1483 p68 S 22 2017

RYAN REYNOLDS color *Entertainment Weekly* no1444/1445 p14 D 16 2016

Sarah Paulson color *Entertainment Weekly* no1444/1445 p34 D

16 2016

THE SCOOP, STARS & SONGS color *Entertainment Weekly* no1439 p16 N 11 2016

SEAL Team color *Entertainment Weekly* no1482/1483 p76 S 22 2017

SEPARATION ANXIETY color *Entertainment Weekly* no1478 / 1479 p14 Ag 18-25 2017

Shameless color *Entertainment Weekly* no1482/1483 p30 S 22 2017

The Shannara Chronicles *Entertainment Weekly* no1482/1483 p79 S 22 2017

The Simpsons color *Entertainment Weekly* no1482/1483 p34 S 22 2017

THE SINNER color *Entertainment Weekly* no1468/1469 p62 Je 2-9 2017

SMILF *Entertainment Weekly* no1482/1483 p43 S 22 2017

Speechless color *Entertainment Weekly* no1482/1483 p75 S 22 2017

Star color *Entertainment Weekly* no1482/1483 p76 S 22 2017

STRANGER DANGER [Cover story] color *Entertainment Weekly* no1453 p22 F 17 2017

Stranger Things 2 color *Entertainment Weekly* no1482/1483 p100 S 22 2017

Survivor: Heroes vs. Healers vs. Hustlers *Entertainment Weekly* no1482/1483 p75 S 22 2017

Ten Days in the Valley color *Entertainment Weekly* no1482/1483 p43 S 22 2017

THINGS ARE LOOKING UP... SIDE DOWN [Cover story] color *Entertainment Weekly* no1485 p16 O 6 2017

Things Get Stranger color *Entertainment Weekly* no1440 p13 N 18 2016

This Is Us color *Entertainment Weekly* no1482/1483 p56 S 22 2017

THOR: RAGNAROK color *Entertainment Weekly* no1478 / 1479 p62 Ag 18-25 2017

THE TRANSFORMATION OF KATY PERRY color *Entertainment Weekly* no1467 p28 My 26 2017

TV chart color *Entertainment Weekly* no1444/1445 p66 D 16 2016

UNDEAD AGAIN [Cover story] color *Entertainment Weekly* no1460/1461 p50 Ap 7-17 2017

The Walking Dead color *Entertainment Weekly* no1482/1483 p38 S 22 2017

WAR MACHINE color *Entertainment Weekly* no1463/1464 p34 Ap/My 2017

What's the Most Bingeworthy Show? color *Entertainment Weekly* no1443 p21 D 9 2016

What to Watch color *Entertainment Weekly* no1442 p53 D 2 2016 Rebellious Special Issue

What to Watch color *Entertainment Weekly* no1486 p54 O 13 2017

White Famous color *Entertainment Weekly* no1482/1483 p36 S 22 2017

WHO WOULD WIN? WOLVERINE VS. IRON MAN *Entertainment Weekly* no1436/1437 p49 O 21 2016

Wisdom of the Crowd color *Entertainment Weekly* no1482/1483 p34 S 22 2017

Stack-Morgan, K.

Redox stratification of an ancient lake in Gale crater, Mars color *Science* v356 no6341 p922 Je 1 2017

Štacko, Peter

Locked synchronous rotor motion in a molecular motor diag *Science* v356 no6341 p964 Je 1 2017

STACKPOLE, THOMAS

The Glitterati *Smithsonian* v47 no7 p22 N 2016

Stacy, Jim

Jim Stacy, 2.0 3.0 4.0 C. BETHEA *Atlanta* v56 no10 p53 F 2017

Stacy, Michelle

The Billion-Dollar Opportunity in Single-Serve Food *Harvard Business Review Digital Articles* p2 O 23 2015

Stadium seats

The Case of The Lousy Super Bowl Seats V. GLEMBOCKI *Reader's Digest* v189 no1127 p35 F 2017

Stadiums

See also

Football stadiums

THE END OF SAND D. OWEN cartoon color *New Yorker* v93 no15 p28 My 29 2017

The Name Game P. Bodo color *Tennis* v53 no5 p6 S/O 2017

The Ol' Ballgame J. Williams *Cincinnati Magazine* v50 no5 p63 F 2017

Stadiums—Design & construction—Economic aspects

The Case for ... A Stadium-Funding Stiff-Arm J. Dickey and T. Keith color *Sports Illustrated* v126 no2 p20 Ja 16 2017

Stadiums—Evaluation

Diamond in the Rough B. PHILLIPS *Texas Monthly* v45 no6 p26 Je 2017

Meet the NFL's Newest Stadium L. SOROKANICH color *Popular Mechanics* v193 no7 p20 S 2016

Stadiums—Food service

Biter Beware J. Tayler and T. Keith color *Sports Illustrated* v127 no1 p22 Jl 3 2017

OVER-THE-TOP DOGS B. Baskin color *Sports Illustrated* v127 no1 p108 Jl 3 2017

Stadiums—Georgia—Atlanta

AMERICAN CATHEDRAL S. Fennessy *Atlanta* v57 no5 p88 S 2017

Stadiums—Texas

Diamond in the Rough B. PHILLIPS *Texas Monthly* v45 no6 p26 Je 2017

Stadler, Charlotte

A subcellular map of the human proteome color *Science* v356 no6340 p820 My 26 2017

Stadler, Christian

3 Things Driving Entrepreneurial Growth in Africa color *Harvard Business Review Digital Articles* p2 F 1 2017

What Western Investors Want from African Entrepreneurs *Harvard Business Review Digital Articles* p2 N 11 2014

Stadler, Michael B.

Gene bivalency at Polycomb domains regulates cranial neural crest positional identity diag *Science* v355 no6332 p1390 Mr 31 2017

Stadtler, Deborah

FRONTLINE FOCUS *Military History* v33 no6 p56 Mr 2017

THE HARVEST OF BATTLE cartoon *Military History* v34 no1 p56 My 2017

A STORM IN EVERY PORT cartoon color map *Military History* v34 no1 p62 My 2017

WAR IN STILL LIFE bw *Military History* v34 no2 p48 Jl 2017

Staes, An

De novo design of a biologically active amyloid bibl graph *Science* v354 no6313 paah4949-1 N 11 2016

Staff, Jeremy

How Unemployment Affects Twentysomethings' Self-Worth *Harvard Business Review Digital Articles* p2 D 22 2016

Staff meetings

Debriefing: A Simple Tool to Help Your Team Tackle Tough Problems D. Sundheim *Harvard Business Review Digital Articles* p2 Jl 2 2015

Don't Wait Until After the Meeting to Start Your Action Items K. S. Milway *Harvard Business Review Digital Articles* p2 Ap 28 2016

Use Your Staff Meeting for Peer-to-Peer Coaching K. Ferrazzi *Harvard Business Review Digital Articles* p2 F 24 2015

When Your Boss Is Terrible at Leading Meetings P. Axtell *Harvard Business Review Digital Articles* p2 My 16 2016

Staffanson, Robert

Witness to Spirit D. Kuipers *Orion Magazine* v35 no4/5 p108 Jl-O 2016

Staffers, Carl

The Little Rock Nine: Sixty years ago this month, President Eisenhower sent federal troops into Arkansas to enforce the desegregation of Little Rock's Central High School *New York Times Upfront* v150 no1 p18 S 4 2017

Stafford, Abi

Ache, Throb, Hurt *Dance Magazine* v91 no1 p83 Ja 2017

What's on Your Mind? color *Dance Magazine* v91 no3 p6 Mr 2017

Stafford, Ben K.

Regenerating optic pathways from the eye to the brain diag *Science* v356 no6342 p1031 Je 9 2017

Stafford, Fiona

What the Trees Say T. Pakenham bw color *New York Review of Books* v63 no19 p45 D 8 2016

Times Book Review p16 Ag 13 2017

Stanton: Lincoln's War Secretary W. R. Mead *Foreign Affairs* v96 no6 p159 N/D 2017

Stain removers

K2R SPOT-LIFTER: NO PAIN, NO STAIN C. LEU color *Wired* v25 no9 p36 S 2017

Stain removers—Evaluation

HOLI DAY STAIN Guide [Cover story] C. FORTÉ color *Good Housekeeping* v263 no6 p89 D 2016

SOLUTIONS chart color *Horse & Rider* v56 no1 p20 Ja 2017

Stainier, Didier Y. R.

Injury-induced ctgfa directs glial bridging and spinal cord regeneration in zebrafish bibl graph *Science* v354 no6312 p630 N 4 2016

Stainless steel

See also

Ferritic steel

Drilling Stainless Steel C. Lawson color *Sail* v48 no5 p49 My 2017

Stains & staining

See also

Varnish & varnishing

Fixing Wood Floors M. Ellen Polson color *Log Home Living* v33 no7 p75 S 2016

Outdoor Stains & Paints D. HOWLAND color *Cabin Living* p14 Ap 2017

REMOVING GRASS STAINS C. Barakat and M. Freckleton *Equus* no475 p32 Ap 2017

Stains & staining—Equipment & supplies

Inside Job color *Log Home Living* v33 no7 p15 S 2016

STAINTON, LESLIE

Things Sweet to Taste: MUCH TO MY REGRET, I NEVER TRULY KNEW THE WOMAN WHO HELPED RAISE ME *American Scholar* v86 no3 p72 Summ 2017

Stair design

Last Look E. Daigneau *Governing* v30 no3 p64 D 2016

Staircases

See also

Spiral staircases

THE DECIDERS AND THE DAMNED G. CARTER *Vanity Fair* v58 no12 p62 D 2016

RISE AND SHINE J. BREWSTER color *Cabin Living* p46 O 2017

Tradesman's Sample Staircase color *Magazine Antiques* v183 no6 p45 N/D 2016

Stairs

The Tulip Stairs in the Queen's House color *Magazine Antiques* v184 no3 pCover My/Je 2017

Staiti, Paul

PORTRAIT OF A REVOLUTION *MHQ: Quarterly Journal of Military History* v29 no2 p60 Wint 2017

The Rebels' Art A. HENDERSON cartoon *Weekly Standard* v22 no13 p26 D 5 2016

Stajic, Jelena

MANIPULATING ULTRACOLD MATTER [Cover story] color *Science* v357 no6355 p984 S 8 2017

Stakeholders

Boards Aren't the Right Way to Monitor Companies S. Boivie, M. Bednar et al *Harvard Business Review Digital Articles* p2 My 10 2016

Cities for People and by People S. Boonyabancha and T. Kerr *UN Chronicle* v53 no3 p1 2016

Why Decisions Get Second-Guessed, and What to Do About It R. M. Galford, B. Frisch et al *Harvard Business Review Digital Articles* p2 F 25 2016

Stakeholders—Attitudes

HOW TO GET ECOSYSTEM BUY-IN M. IHRIG and I. C. MACMILLAN chart img *Harvard Business Review* v95 no2 p102 Mr/Ap 2017

Stakeholders—Research

HOW TO GET ECOSYSTEM BUY-IN M. IHRIG and I. C. MACMILLAN chart img *Harvard Business Review* v95 no2 p102 Mr/Ap 2017

Staley, John C.—Interviews

Member Spotlight: John C. Staley V. Paynich *Parks & Recreation* v52 no2 p48 F 2017

STALEY, SAMUEL R.

The Infrastructure Bank We Need *National Review* v68 no24 p18 D 31 2016

Jane Jacobs, In Her Own Words bw color *Reason* v49 no4 p72 Ag/S 2017

Staley, Willy

Diddy Doesn't Like To Get Hot *New York Times Magazine* p58 Jl 9 2017

Stalin, Joseph, 1879-1953

Stalin at the Movies S. Kotkin bw *New York Review of Books* v64 no16 p39 O 26 2017

When Stalin Faced Hitler S. Kotkin cartoon *Foreign Affairs* v96 no6 p48 N/D 2017

Stalk, George, Jr.

Is Your Supply Chain Ready for the Congestion Crisis? *Harvard Business Review Digital Articles* p2 Je 22 2015

Stalker, Jim

Resistance to malaria through structural variation of red blood cell invasion receptors diag *Science* v356 no6343 p1139 Je 16 2017

STALL, JAMI

BUZZWORTHY *Indianapolis Monthly* p14 N 2017

STALL, SAM

Anderson Cooper *Indianapolis Monthly* v40 no7 p25 Mr 2017

BOOM OR BUST: Fireworks stores, Indiana roller coasters, and urban coyotes. Ask the Hoosierist *Indianapolis Monthly* v40 no11 p15 Jl 2017

CLEARING THE AIR: Hookah-smoking, motorboating, and immigrants *Indianapolis Monthly* v40 no10 p17 Je 2017

Criminal Minds *Indianapolis Monthly* v40 no10 p15 Je 2017

DYING TO KNOW color *Indianapolis Monthly* p17 Ap 2017

FIELD OF SCREAMS color *Indianapolis Monthly* v42 no2 p18 O 2017

FOWL AND FAIR: Backyard birds, neverending Vonnegut stories, and dining out on Thanksgiving. Ask the Hoosierist *Indianapolis Monthly* p22 N 2017

GIVE ME A BRAKE *Indianapolis Monthly* v40 no5 p13 Ja 2017

HERE'S THE DIRT *Indianapolis Monthly* p18 F 2017

HIGH ANXIETY: Daring orangutans, perfect weather, and food deserts. Ask the Hoosierist color *Indianapolis Monthly* v41 no2 p19 S 2017

Idina Menzel *Indianapolis Monthly* v12 no40 p25 Ag 2017

INQUIRING MINDS: CFI schools, open-air conventions, and Holliday Park ruins. Ask the Hoosierist *Indianapolis Monthly* v12 no40 p18 Ag 2017

Just for Clicks *Indianapolis Monthly* v40 no7 p20 Mr 2017

LET IT GLOW *Indianapolis Monthly* v40 no4 p22 D 2016

LIFE AND LIMB *Indianapolis Monthly* v40 no7 p19 Mr 2017

NAME-DROPPERS *Indianapolis Monthly* v40 no3 p22 N 2016

Patrick Monahan *Indianapolis Monthly* v40 no10 p23 Je 2017

Q+A *Indianapolis Monthly* v12 no40 p89 Ag 2017

RAY OF HOPE *Indianapolis Monthly* p17 My 2017

Terry Hilderbrand *Indianapolis Monthly* v40 no4 p29 D 2016

WHAT GOES UP *Indianapolis Monthly* v12 no40 p26 Ag 2017

Stallard, Avan Judd

The Myth of Symmetry and Balance *History Today* v67 no8 p12 Ag 2017

Stalling, Mary

Senior Games: Everybody Can Play *Parks & Recreation* v52 no1 p16 Ja 2017

STALLINS, J. ANTHONY

Crossing Scales: The Complexity of Barrier-Island Processes for Predicting Future Change *BioScience* v67 no1 p39 Ja 2017

Stallion 51 Corp.

MUSTANG TRIBUTE color *Flying* v144 no6 p82 Je 2017

Stallions

The 2017 Baroque Annual Gallery bw color *Dressage Today* v23 no11 p58 Ag 2017

2017 Egyptian Event RESULT *Arabian Horse World* v57 no11 p50 Ag 2017

Andreas Hausberger Brings Classical Dressage to America A. Heintzberger color *Dressage Today* v23 no9 p54 Je 2017

AWPA Nominated Stallions *Arabian Horse World* v57 no5 p82 F 2017

BACK TO HIS ROOTS MASTER DESIGN GA B. FINKE *Arabian Horse World* v57 no1 p122 O 2016

GREENER PASTURES: MAGIC DREAM CAHR N. VA-

LAITHAM *Arabian Horse World* v57 no12 p160 S 2017

Greener Pastures N. Valaitham *Arabian Horse World* v57 no3 p285 D 2016

IMPERIAL MADHEEN B. FINKE *Arabian Horse World* v57 no3 p36 D 2016

JC KLYM TO FAME B. FINKE *Arabian Horse World* v56 no12 p66 S 2016

Moments in Time A Walk IN THE Park B. FINKE *Arabian Horse World* v57 no3 p210 D 2016

SIRE LINE: SAKLAWI I PART I: A TALE OF IWO BROTHERS B. Finke *Arabian Horse World* v57 no10 p78 Jl 2017

SPORT HORSE NATIONALS AND THE RALVON ELIJAH INFLUENCE M. Moore *Arabian Horse World* v57 no4 p102 Ja 2017

STALLION Directory *Arabian Horse World* v57 no4 p190 Ja 2017

STALLION PROFILES *Arabian Horse World* v57 no3 p124 D 2016

U. S. Nationals AWPA Futurities G. Dearth *Arabian Horse World* v57 no3 p54 D 2016

WADEE AL SHAQAB D. Hearst *Arabian Horse World* v57 no9 p1 Je 2017

Stallions—Behavior

ZOBEYNI SIRE LINE - PART 2: MAHRUSS, RIJM, AND THE UNLIKELY BROTHERS B. Finke bw chart color *Arabian Horse World* v57 no7 p58 Ap 2017

Stallions—Competitions

Hariry Al Shaqab C. Reich color *Arabian Horse World* v57 no7 p113 Ap 2017

STALLO, CINDY

USA HALF MARATHON INVITATIONAL color *Runner's World* v51 no11 p98 D 2016

Stallone, Sistine

MUST-HAVES color *Harper's Bazaar* no3653 p176 My 2017

SLY'S ANGELS A. Spencer color *Harper's Bazaar* no3653 p167 My 2017

THE STALLONE SISTERS' BEAUTY HEROES color *Harper's Bazaar* no3653 p164 My 2017

Stallone, Sophia

editor's letter Glenda color *Harper's Bazaar* no3653 p162 My 2017

MUST-HAVES color *Harper's Bazaar* no3653 p176 My 2017

SLY'S ANGELS A. Spencer color *Harper's Bazaar* no3653 p167 My 2017

THE STALLONE SISTERS' BEAUTY HEROES color *Harper's Bazaar* no3653 p164 My 2017

Stallworth, Jacqueline

REFLECTING READERS AND THE REAL WORLD color *Literacy Today (2411-7862)* v34 no4 p32 Ja/F 2017

Stalnaker, Jason

Laser Experiments for Chemistry and Physics *Physics Today* v70 no1 p60 Ja 2017

Stamborski, Jim

Why There Is a Need to Discuss the Gap Between Research and Practice *Parks & Recreation* v52 no5 p12 My 2017

Stamell, Emmie Roe

How Mindfulness Improves Executive Coaching *Harvard Business Review Digital Articles* p2 Ja 29 2016

Stamford (England)

Stamford Celebrates Its Golden Georgian Heritage color *British Heritage Travel* v38 no5 p11 S/O 2017

Stamm, Peter, 1963-

To the Back of Beyond color *Publishers Weekly* v264 no34 p83 Ag 21 2017

Stamme, Cordula

Local amplifiers of IL-4Rα-mediated macrophage activation promote repair in lung and liver diag *Science* v356 no6342 p1076 Je 9 2017

STAMMERJOHN, SHARON

The Impact of a Large-Scale Climate Event on Antarctic Ecosystem Processes chart graph *BioScience* v66 no10 p848 O 1 2016

Responses of Antarctic Marine and Freshwater Ecosystems to Changing Ice Conditions color graph *BioScience* v66 no10 p864 O 1 2016

Stamos, John, 1963-

CHEERS & JEERS D. HOLBROOK *TV Guide* v65 no43 p88 O

16 2017

Stamoulis, Dean

How the Best CEOs Differ from Average Ones *Harvard Business Review Digital Articles* p2 N 15 2016

Stamp, Trent

Aging Societies Should Make More of Mentorship *Harvard Business Review Digital Articles* p2 Jl 6 2016

Stamp-n-Storage (Company)

Crafting a Big Business D. Bortz color *Money* v45 no10 p33 N 2016

STAMPER, KORY

CONFESSIONS OF A WORLD NERD color *Reader's Digest* v190 no1133 p112 S 2017

STAN, ADELE M.

First Family LLC *New Republic* v248 no7 p16 Jl 2017

Stanca, D.

Observation of a large-scale anisotropy in the arrival directions of cosmic rays above 8 × 1018 eV *Science* v357 no6357 p1266 S 22 2017

Stance Inc.

Skeptical Speculators Swoon for Socks S. McBride color *Bloomberg Businessweek* no4541 p21 O 9 2017

Stand by Me (Film)

Kiefer Sutherland C. Ianzito color *AARP: The Magazine* v60 no1A p64 D 2016/Ja 2017

Stand-up comedy

12. See Joe Mande *New York* v50 no16 p112 Ag 7 2017

ALI WONG *Washingtonian Magazine* v52 no6 p31 Mr 2017

ROCK IN A HARD PLACE [Cover story] S. Rodrick bw color *Rolling Stone* no1287 p28 My 18 2017

Stand-Up Finds a Home on Netflix A. Hoffman color *Time* v189 no10 p52 Mr 20 2017

Tig Notaro A. Hoffman color *Time* v190 no10/11 p116 S 18 2017

Standard & Poor's 500 Index

Why Your Portfolio Should Be Stocked With Global Shares P. J. Lim color *Time* v189 no20 p12 My 29 2017

Standard Chartered PLC

Diamonds Aren't A Bank's Best Friend F. Wild, T. Biesheuvel et al color *Bloomberg Businessweek* no4537 p26 S 11 2017

Standard operating procedure

OBSERVING A LOT JUST BY WATCHING J. King color *Flying* v144 no5 p30 My 2017

Standardization

Background Screening Methodology: Is your methodology leading the way or a best practice in attracting risk? *Parks & Recreation* v52 no10 p46 O 2017

Standardized tests

A Brief History of Imperial Examination and Its Influences K. Ko *Society* v54 no3 p272 Je 2017

THE NEW TURING TESTS J. Pavlus color *Scientific American* v316 no3 p61 Mr 2017

Testing R. J. Sternberg chart color *Phi Delta Kappan* v98 no4 p66 D 2016/Ja 2017

Standard Oil Sessions, The (Music)

Seventh Inning Stretch K. SILSBEE color *Downbeat* v84 no6 p76 Je 2017

Standards

See also

Dress codes

Professional standards

CREATIVITY IN COMMON T. Perkins color *Downbeat* v84 no6 p122 Je 2017

Finding your comfort zone T. Koester color *Model Railroader* v84 no11 p82 N 2017

The hard road to reproducibility L. A. Barba cartoon *Science* v354 no6308 p142 O 7 2016

Standards (Music)

A Trail of Cedars C. WOLFF bw *Downbeat* v84 no9 p70 S 2017

Standen, Clive

TAKEN C. Agard color *Entertainment Weekly* no1448 p43 Ja 13 2017

STANDER, EMILIE K.

Planning for the Future of Urban Biodiversity: A Global Review of City-Scale Initiatives *BioScience* v67 no4 p332 Ap 2017

Standfuss, Jörg

A three-dimensional movie of structural changes in bacteriorhodopsin bibl diag graph *Science* v354 no6319 p1552 D 23 2016

STANDIFORD, NATALIE

Somewhere Out There: In this middle-grade novel, a boy's quest to connect with alien life turns into a family affair *New York Times Book Review* p19 My 14 2017

Standing desks

YOU'LL GET USED TO IT diag *Fortune* v176 no1 p9 Jl 1 2017

Standing position

PUZZLED? T. Cooke and D. DeNunzio color *Golf Magazine* v59 no9 p47 S 2017

YOU'LL GET USED TO IT diag *Fortune* v176 no1 p9 Jl 1 2017

Standing Rock Indian Reservation (N.D. & S.D.)

Standing Rock Speaks W. Kirn *Harper's Magazine* v333 no1999 p4 D 2016

STANDING WITH STANDING ROCK S. KIRABO *Humanist* v77 no1 p25 Ja/F 2017

Still Defiant at Standing Rock D. MARTINDALE *In These Times* v40 no12 p32 D 2016

STANDISH, REID

A Silk Road Marriage color *Foreign Policy* no226 p8 S/O 2017

STANDOVÁR, TIBOR

Combining Biodiversity Resurveys across Regions to Advance Global Change Research *BioScience* v67 no1 p73 Ja 2017

Stands In Timber, John, 1882-1967

c. 1880: Tongue River, MT *Lapham's Quarterly* v10 no1 p177 Wint 2017

STANEK, AMIEL

36 HOURS [Cover story] color *Bon Appetit* v61 no11 p130 N 2016

Already Dressed color *Bon Appetit* v62 no2 p34 Mr 2017

Better Fish in the Sea color *Bon Appetit* no8 p20 Ag 2017

Breaking the Mold bw color *Bon Appetit* v61 no11 p34 N 2016

Cook Like a Pro: Summer Edition [Cover story] bw color diag *Bon Appetit* v62 no7 p56 Jl 2017

Dinner Tonight color *Bon Appetit* no8 p33 Ag 2017

EAT YOUR MEAT (AND FEEL BETTER ABOUT IT) cartoon color diag *Bon Appetit* no1 p88 F 2017

Home Shucked color *Bon Appetit* no11 p36 N 2017

Little Big Time color *Bon Appetit* v62 no4 p28 Ap 2017

NOSH IN THE NEW YEAR cartoon color *Bon Appetit* v61 no12 p120 D 2016 /Jan2017

PREP SCHOOL bw color *Bon Appetit* v61 no11 p153 N 2016

PUT AN EGG ON IT [Cover story] color *Bon Appetit* v62 no4 p66 Ap 2017

A Simple Roast Chicken color *Bon Appetit* v62 no10 p64 O 2017

starters color *Bon Appetit* p25 S 2017

starters color *Bon Appetit* v62 no6 p17 Je 2017

Sun Surf & Sumac bw color *Bon Appetit* no8 p68 Ag 2017

Thanksgiving LESSONS [Cover story] color *Bon Appetit* no11 p82 N 2017

This Month in Beer color *Bon Appetit* no8 p24 Ag 2017

TURN OVƎR A NoLII LƐAf color *Bon Appetit* p110 S 2017

A Very Organized Thanksgiving color *Bon Appetit* no11 p19 N 2017

WHIZ KID color *Bon Appetit* no1 p101 F 2017

Will It Miso? color *Bon Appetit* v62 no7 p34 Jl 2017

Stanfield, Keith

Keith Stanfield D. Kiper color *Current Biography* v78 no8 p73 Ag 2017

Stanfield, Lakeith Lee

The Breakout Star of 'Atlanta' D. FEAR color *Rolling Stone* no1293 p22 Ag 10 2017

HANG IN THERE, DUDE! B. Stephen color *Esquire* p96 Je/Jl 2017

Lakeith Stanfield, Contemporary Chameleon E. Berman color *Time* v190 no8 p47 Ag 28 2017

Stanfield's Hot Streak color *Rolling Stone* no1293 p22 Ag 10 2017

Stanford, Catherine M.

Discussion *Smithsonian* v48 no2 p8 My 2017

Stanford, Courtney

From Dissemination to Propagation: A New Paradigm for Education Developers *Change* v49 no4 p35 Jl/Ag 2017

STANFORD, JASON

BAD GIRLS GET OLD *Texas Monthly* v45 no7 p92 Jl 2017

Stanford, Lindsay B.

Evolution of protein phosphorylation across 18 fungal species bibl

graph *Science* v354 no6309 p229 O 14 2016

Stanford University

Issa Rae J. Crelin color *Current Biography* v78 no4 p68 Ap 2017

John Hennessy: The Exit Interview P. Robinson *Hoover Digest: Research & Opinion on Public Policy* no4 p170 Fall 2016

NATIONAL UNIVERSITIES chart *Washington Monthly* v49 no9/10 p82 S/O 2017

THROWING IN THE CHAIR J. WERTHEIM *Indianapolis Monthly* v40 no7 p80 Mr 2017

Stanford University—Sports

15 Stanford color *Sports Illustrated* v127 no5 p104 Ag 14 2017

Pool Cue J. Fuchs and T. Keith color *Sports Illustrated* v126 no16 p26 Je 5 2017

Week 13 color *Sports Illustrated* v127 no5 p84 Ag 14 2017

Stanger, Tobie

Faster, Fresher, Cheaper chart color il *Consumer Reports* v82 no7 p30 Jl 2017

A GIFT FOR KIDS THAT PAYS DIVIDENDS *Consumer Reports* v81 no12 p31 D 2016

Help With Home-Care Bills *Consumer Reports* v82 no12 p46 D 2017

How to Save on Car Insurance chart diag graph *Consumer Reports* v82 no3 p42 Mr 2017

The New Retirement [Cover story] color *Consumer Reports* v82 no1 p22 Ja 2017

THE RIGHT WAY TO PAY A CAREGIVER *Consumer Reports* v82 no12 p51 D 2017

Save Money il *Consumer Reports* v82 no3 p30 Mr 2017

Shop Online With Confidence graph il *Consumer Reports* v82 no12 p20 D 2017

Solving Family Money Fights chart il *Consumer Reports* v82 no5 p44 My 2017

Who Will Care for You? [Cover story] chart color map *Consumer Reports* v82 no10 p28 O 2017

Stangler, Cole

Lost amid Anxiety color *Commonweal* v144 no13 p33 Ag 11 2017

A Revolution Deferred *In These Times* v41 no4 p19 Ap 2017

STANGLER, DANE

Entrepreneurship at Home and Abroad *Washington Monthly* p5 Ja/F 2017

Politics of the platform economy color *Issues in Science & Technology* v33 no1 p19 Fall 2016

Stanglin, Doug

Russia's top court bans Jehovah's Witnesses *Christian Century* v134 no11 p14 My 24 2017

Stani., S.

Observation of a large-scale anisotropy in the arrival directions of cosmic rays above 8×1018 eV *Science* v357 no6357 p1266 S 22 2017

Staniszewski, Anna

Dogosaurus Rex color *Publishers Weekly* v264 no23 p50 Je 5 2017

Stankiewicz, Kevin

The Not-Talking Cure S. SCHULMAN color *Weekly Standard* v22 no15 p11 D 19 2016

Stanko, Tomasz

Tomasz Stańko's Solo on 'Suspended Variation VI' J. Durso bw color *Downbeat* v84 no4 p90 Ap 2017

Stankorb, Sarah

FIGHT CLUB *Cincinnati Magazine* v50 no12 p28 S 2017

Plot Twist *Cincinnati Magazine* v50 no5 p52 F 2017

RAPE CULTURE LIVES HERE *Cincinnati Magazine* p68 Je 2017

TECH RX *Cincinnati Magazine* v50 no4 p69 Ja 2017

Stanlaws, Penrhyn

LIMERICK LAUGHS *Saturday Evening Post* v289 no1 p104 Ja/F 2017

STANLEY, ALESSANDRA

THE ENDURING KENNEDYS color *New York Times Book Review* p70 D 4 2016

Rabbit Is Rich: Meryl Gordon's biography of Bunny Mellon reveals an aristocrat with a tumultuous private life *New York Times Book Review* p23 O 8 2017

Stanley, Amy

How HR can support a new leader *People Management* p50 Mr 2017

Stanley, Andrea

B×(M+F+A)+Att2 cartoon *Seventeen* v76 no2 p110 Mr 2017

Can Food Help You Feel Better? color *Seventeen* v75 no11 p62 N 2016

CHANGE IS GOOD bw color *Seventeen* v76 no4 p80 Jl/Ag 2017

Dancing Acting Taking Over the World [Cover story] bw color *Seventeen* v76 no4 p60 Jl/Ag 2017

FRESHMAN YEAR VS. SENIOR YEAR color *Seventeen* v76 no3 p102 My 2017

Get Your Posture Point color *Seventeen* v76 no5 p65 S 2017

Is Your Locker MAKING YOU SICK? color *Seventeen* v76 no2 p92 Mr 2017

Let's Talk About... BODY IMAGE cartoon color *Seventeen* v75 no11 p76 N 2017

"My View of the Country" color *Seventeen* v76 no5 p14 S 2017

Namaste Your Period Pain Away color *Seventeen* v75 no11 p57 N 2016

PERFECTLY ME bw cartoon color *Seventeen* v75 no11 p80 N 2016

QUAD GOALS! color *Seventeen* v76 no5 p76 S 2017

Sweat Out Your Blahs color *Seventeen* v76 no12 p65 D 2016/Ja 2017

UNDER(PROM) PRESSURE cartoon *Seventeen* v76 no3 p68 My 2017

"We Are STEM-ists" color *Seventeen* v75 no11 p22 N 2016

"What Would You Think If I Walked Into the Girls' Bathroom?" color *Seventeen* v76 no3 p20 My 2017

What Your SELFIE Says ABOUT YOU color *Seventeen* v76 no12 p68 D 2016/Ja 2017

YOUR CHEAT SHEET TO... Cramming Your Way to an A color *Seventeen* v75 no11 p102 N 2016

Stanley, Chris

THE TOP 10 *Sierra* v101 no5 p40 S/O 2016

Stanley, Jason

You Never Forget Your First Time diag il *Backpacker* v45 no2 p64 Mr 2017

Stanley, Jessamyn

The Beginner's Guide to Standing on Your Head S. Gaynes Levy color *Glamour* v114 no7 p90 Jl 2016

The Eye of the Beholder N. Spradley and A. Clarke color *Essence* v47 no9 p23 Ja 2017

Jessamyn Stanley, Internet Yogi M. Oaklander color *Time* v188 no20 p22 N 14 2016

stretch your limits K. Miller color *Good Housekeeping* v264 no5 p97 My 2017

Stanley, Jonathan

Child of the Pledge A. EBELING color *Forbes* v199 no5 p56 My 16 2017

Stanley, Lauren

10 TIPS FOR RANCH LOGS color *Horse & Rider* v56 no2 p54 F 2017

Stanley, Matthew

The enlightened empiricist color *Science* v356 no6345 p1341 Je 30 2017

Stanley, Ted, 1931-2016

Child of the Pledge A. EBELING color *Forbes* v199 no5 p56 My 16 2017

Stanley, Tiffany

MICHAEL TWITTY *Washingtonian Magazine* v52 no11 p43 Ag 2017

Stanley, Tim

The changing face of the GOP *History Today* v66 no11 p11 N 2016

Flying a Kite with Franklin *History Today* v67 no2 p62 F 2017

Stanley Black & Decker Inc.

AN OPEN LETTER TO THE MAN WHO BOUGHT CRAFTSMAN R. Berendsohn color *Popular Mechanics* p81 Jl 2017

Stanley Cup (Hockey)

STRENGTH VS. STRENGTH A. Prewitt color *Sports Illustrated* v126 no16 p62 Je 5 2017

Stanley Cup (Hockey)—History

Emperor PENGUINS A. Prewitt color *Sports Illustrated* v126 no17 p42 Je 19 2017

WILL CANADA'S 24-YEAR DROUGHT END? J. Fuchs color *Sports Illustrated* v127 no11 p45 O 9 2017

Stanley Cup (Hockey)—History—21st century

PRED ALERT A. Prewitt color *Sports Illustrated* v126 no15 p46 My 29 2017

Stanley Love Performance Group (Company)

DANCE *New Yorker* v93 no29 p24 S 25 2017

Stanley Robinson, Kim

THE GREAT UNKNOWN color *Scientific American* v315 no3 p80 S 2016

Stanton, Andrew

FINDING DORY C. Chiarella color *Sound & Vision* v82 no3 p70 Ap 2017

Stanton, Carol

Patriotism in the pews color *U.S. Catholic* v82 no11 p5 N 2017

Stanton, Charlotte Y.

Cash for carbon: A randomized trial of payments for ecosystem services to reduce deforestation bw chart *Science* v357 no6348 p267 Jl 21 2017

Stanton, Giancarlo, 1989-

The Case for ... GIANCARLO STANTON J. Dickey, T. Keith et al color *Sports Illustrated* v127 no7 p30 S 4 2017

HOT | NOT T. Keith color *Sports Illustrated* v127 no6 p17 Ag 28 2017

Stanton, Harry Dean, 1926-2017

1926-2017 Harry Dean Stanton D. Franich color *Entertainment Weekly* no1484 p17 S 29 2017

CHARACTER FLAWLESS D. Franich color *Entertainment Weekly* no1484 p17 S 29 2017

Stanton, J.

The Thread color *New York Times Magazine* p12 D 4 2016

Stanton, John

A place to run C. MCINTYRE color *Maclean's* v130 no8 p50 S 2017

Stanton, Joshua

Getting Tough on North Korea color *Foreign Affairs* v96 no3 p65 My/Je 2017

Stanton, Steve

How IBM, Intuit, and Rich Products Became More Customer-Centric *Harvard Business Review Digital Articles* p2 Je 17 2015

Stanzas

"The Moon Is Up ... A Single Star Is at Her Side" D. W. Olson bw color *Sky & Telescope* v134 no2 p68 Ag 2017

Stapczynski, Stephen

How to Lose $6 Billion color graph *Bloomberg Businessweek* no4512 p19 F 20 2017

India's Nuclear Industry Needs a Jolt color diag *Bloomberg Businessweek* no4526 p17 Je 12 2017

Nintendo's New Guard Tries to Switch It Up color *Bloomberg Businessweek* no4514 p35 Mr 13 2017

STAPEN, CANDYCE H.

Battle of the War Museums *Washingtonian Magazine* v52 no11 p90 Ag 2017

Staphylinidae

A new evolutionary classic E. Pennisi color *Science* v354 no6314 p813 N 18 2016

Staphylococcus

A WEED THAT BUSTS BACTERIA A. R. Williams color *National Geographic* v232 no3 p18 S 2017

Staphylococcus aureus

See also

Methicillin-resistant staphylococcus aureus

The cytotoxic Staphylococcus aureus PSMα3 reveals a cross-α amyloid-like fibril E. Tayeb-Fligelman, O. Tabachnikov et al bibl color diag graph *Science* v355 no6327 p831 F 24 2017

Stapinski, Helen

Original Sin M. BYRD *New York Times Book Review* p18 Je 25 2017

Staples & stapling machines—Evaluation

BEST STUFF OF THE YEAR 2016 color *GQ: Gentlemen's Quarterly* v86 no12 p63 D 2016

Staples, Andy

2017 SI'S (WAY TOO EARLY) TOP 10 color *Sports Illustrated* v126 no2 p33 Ja 16 2017

BIG TROUBLE IN THE BIG XII color diag *Sports Illustrated* v127 no5 p54 Ag 14 2017

CASE FOR ... ALABAMA color *Sports Illustrated* v125 no19 p38 D 12 2016

CHANGE FOR THE BETTER [Cover story] color diag *Sports*

Illustrated v125 no19 p42 D 12 2016

CHAOS THEORIES color *Sports Illustrated* v125 no17 p82 N 21 2016 Double Issue

THE FULL LEADED JACKET AT LEADBELLY color *Sports Illustrated* v127 no5 p74 Ag 14 2017

NEW TAKES ON TACKLING color *Sports Illustrated* v127 no5 p64 Ag 14 2017

NO ONE TO NO. 1 color *Sports Illustrated* v126 no14 p96 My 15-22 2017

Position Change color *Sports Illustrated* v126 no8 p20 Mr 20 2017

RUN IT BACK color *Sports Illustrated* v126 no1 p34 Ja 9 2017

SHOESTORM [Cover story] color *Sports Illustrated* v127 no11 p22 O 9 2017

Surprise, Surprise color *Sports Illustrated* v125 no14 p53 O 24-31 2016

THINK BIG color *Sports Illustrated* v126 no7 p56 Mr 6 2017

THROWN TO THE WOLVES color *Sports Illustrated* v127 no8 p56 S 18 2017

'TIS BETTER TO RECEIVE color *Sports Illustrated* v127 no6 p46 Ag 28 2017

TRUE GRIT color *Sports Illustrated* v126 no11 p36 Ap 17-24 2017

WHAT IF THE PIRATE NEVER LEFT THE ISLAND? color *Sports Illustrated* v127 no9 p36 S 25 2017

Staples, Brent

Portrait of Obama as a Young Man: A biography presents the former president as subordinating crucial aspects of his life—even love—to political expedience *New York Times Book Review* p14 My 21 2017

Staples, Jeffrey

Distribution and clinical impact of functional variants in 50,726 whole-exome sequences from the DiscovEHR study chart graph *Science* v354 no6319 paaf6814-1 D 23 2016

Staples, Mavis, 1939-

Mardi Gras With Mavis color *AARP: The Magazine* v59 no2A p11 F/Mr 2016

MAVIS STAPLES B. Zehme cartoon *Chicago* v65 no11 p168 N 2016

Staples, Vince

GOINGS ON ABOUT TOWN color *New Yorker* v93 no7 p7 Ap 3 2017

Vince Staples E. R. Brown color *Entertainment Weekly* no1472 p59 Je 30 2017

WAIT FOR THE DROP: THE YEAR THE SURPRISE ALBUM TOOK OVER MUSIC color *GQ: Gentlemen's Quarterly* v86 no12 p147 D 2016

Staples Inc.

SHIP SHAPE diag *Fortune* v75 no1 p15 Ja 1 2017

Staples Doesn't Want To Be Your Superstore M. Townsend color *Bloomberg Businessweek* no4517 p24 Ap 3 2017

STAPLETON, ANNECLAIRE

Rescuing The Police color *Reader's Digest* v189 no1129 p12 Ap 2017

Stapleton, Chris, 1978-

CHRIS STAPLETON'S TRUE GRIT M. Vain color *Entertainment Weekly* no1465 p52 My 12 2017

The Outlaw Soul of Chris Stapleton W. HERMES color *Rolling Stone* no1287 p53 My 18 2017

Stapleton, Lyssa C.

The Box Project: Works from the Lloyd Cotsen Collection J. SHAYKETT color *American Craft* v77 no2 p16 Ap/My 2017

Stapleton, Sullivan—Interviews

Blindspot D. Holbrook color *TV Guide* v64 no42 p35 O 10 2016

Stappenbeck, Thaddeus S.

The microbial metabolite desaminotyrosine protects from influenza through type I interferon graph *Science* v357 no6350 p498 Ag 4 2017

Star (TV program)

EMPIRE/STAR CROSSOVER M. Logan *TV Guide* v65 no39 p45 S 18 2017

Lenny Kravitz Gets Typecast on Star M. Logan *TV Guide* v64 no48 p10 N 21 2016

Star J. Jensen color *Entertainment Weekly* no1443 p50 D 9 2016

Star N. Abrams, B. L. Heldman et al color *Entertainment Weekly* no1482/1483 p76 S 22 2017

STAR, NANCY

Time to See A Shrink *Publishers Weekly* v263 no41 p84 O 10 2016

Star clusters

See also

Open clusters of stars

Caught in a spider's web color *Astronomy* v45 no3 p74 Mr 2017

Cluster Shots [Cover story] J. RAO color *Natural History* v125 no11 p44 N 2017

Deep-sky objects in Cancer P. HARRINGTON color *Astronomy* v45 no5 p66 My 2017

GALLERY *Sky & Telescope* v134 no3 p72 S 2017

How to observe colorful open clusters P. Harrington color *Astronomy* v44 no12 p32 D 2016

M17: The Nebula With Too Many Names: Follow this observers' guide to find one of the best H II regions in the night sky H. Banich *Sky & Telescope* v134 no3 p57 S 2017

The Queen's Finest: Look to Cassiopeia for her varied collection of celestial treasure S. French *Sky & Telescope* v134 no6 p55 D 2017

Rogue globular clusters P. HARRINGTON color *Astronomy* v45 no9 p68 S 2017

The secrets of off-season globular clusters F. M. Witkoski chart color *Astronomy* v45 no9 p50 S 2017

STAR DOME color *Astronomy* v45 no9 p38 S 2017

Target open clusters P. HARRINGTON color *Astronomy* v45 no1 p69 Ja 2017

Winter Departs F. Schaaf *Sky & Telescope* v133 no4 p45 Ap 2017

Star formation

Entropy redux J. HESTER color *Astronomy* v45 no11 p66 N 2017

Hunting the Galaxy Killer K. Cooper *Sky & Telescope* v134 no1 p22 Jl 2017

Lofty telescope will survey the cool universe G. Schilling color *Science* v356 no6340 p789 My 26 2017

Supernovae may leave dust behind color *Astronomy* v45 no11 p15 N 2017

Star maps (Astronomy)

Gaia Maps a 1,000,000,000+ Stars J. HATTENBACH *Sky & Telescope* v133 no1 p10 Ja 2017

The Return of Uranus and Neptune *Sky & Telescope* v134 no4 p50 O 2017

Star observations

Enter the Summer Citadel: The sights and scents of the season encourage a visit to an old friend F. Schaaf *Sky & Telescope* v134 no1 p45 Jl 2017

Explaining a few discoveries S. Tremaine, A. Garscadden et al *Physics Today* v70 no9 p12 S 2017

The final four G. CHAPLE bw color *Astronomy* v45 no9 p64 S 2017

FROM OUR READERS C. Simpson, T. Wright et al *Sky & Telescope* v133 no6 p6 Je 2017

Moon motion B. Berman color *Astronomy* v45 no7 p10 Jl 2017

The Most Mysterious Star in the Galaxy B. Montet and T. Boyajian *Sky & Telescope* v133 no6 p16 Je 2017

A Mystery for the Age P. Tyson *Sky & Telescope* v133 no6 p4 Je 2017

Star parties (Astronomy)

FUN AT AMERICA'S DARKEST SKY STAR PARTY color map *Astronomy* v45 no9 p60 S 2017

How FLAGSTAFF is preserving DARK SKIES C. Luginbuhl and J. Hall color graph *Astronomy* v45 no9 p54 S 2017

Star trackers—Evaluation

Portable Star Trackers J. Lodriguss *Sky & Telescope* v133 no5 p66 My 2017

Star Trek (TV program)

In a Quantum Leap, Star Trek Becomes a Female Enterprise E. Dockterman color *Time* v190 no13 p59 O 2 2017

William Shatner: Still Beaming After All These Years B. Newcott color *AARP: The Magazine* v59 no5A p14 Ag/S 2016

Star Trek Beyond (Film)

PARTY LINES J. Vineyard img *New York* v49 no15 p90 Jl 25 2016

Star Trek Beyond M. FELL *TV Guide* v65 no11 p49 Mr 6 2017

Star Trek films

ANTON YELCHIN J. J. Abrams and A. Breznican color *Entertainment Weekly* no1446/1447 p89 D 2016/Ja 2017

SCENE STEALERS R. CHUN color *Wired* v25 no3 p78 Mr 2017

Star Trek films—Charts, diagrams, etc.
A TIMELINE OF TREKS D. Franich color *Entertainment Weekly* no1476 p28 Ag 4 2017
Star Trek: Discovery (TV program)
AN ALIEN ENCOUNTER WITH DOUG JONES S. Li color *Entertainment Weekly* no1476 p27 Ag 4 2017
A STAR-FLEET IS BORN [Cover story] J. Hibberd color *Entertainment Weekly* no1476 p22 Ag 4 2017
STARFLEET RISING: The new prequel goes where no Star Trek series has gone before: gay romance, major crew conflicts and a Spock sister M. LOGAN *TV Guide* v65 no35 p18 Ag 21 2017
Star Trek: Discovery D. Franich color *Entertainment Weekly* no1485 p46 O 6 2017
Star Trek Discovery J. Hibberd, A. Bacle et al color *Entertainment Weekly* no1482/1483 p104 S 22 2017
Star Trek: Enterprise (TV program)
Strange New Worlds B. R. REYNOLDS color *Los Angeles Magazine* v62 no10 p104 O 2017
Star Trek: Into Darkness (Film)
STAR TREK INTO DARKNESS T. J. Norton color *Sound & Vision* v81 no9 p67 N 2016
Star Trek V: The Final Frontier (Film)
Sky Gods for Skeptics M. Shermer color *Scientific American* v317 no4 p88 O 2017
Star Wars Episode V: The Empire Strikes Back (Film)
GREAT UNKNOWNS cartoon color *Popular Mechanics* p22 Ap 2017
Star Wars Episode VI: Return of the Jedi (Film)
Revoltingly Real Cosplay M. GILES color *Popular Science* v288 no6 p92 N/D 2016
Star Wars Episode VIII: The Last Jedi (Film)
THE LAST JEDI: LUKE BREAKS HIS SILENCE A. Breznican color *Entertainment Weekly* no1463/1464 p18 Ap/My 2017
THE LAST OF LEIA A. Breznican color *Entertainment Weekly* no1478 / 1479 p35 Ag 18-25 2017
STAR WARS THE LAST JEDI [Cover story] A. Breznican color *Entertainment Weekly* no1478 / 1479 p30 Ag 18-25 2017
Who Is The Last Jedi? A. Breznican color *Entertainment Weekly* no1451/1452 p13 F 3-10 2017
Star Wars films
BY THE NUMBERS P. Treble bw color *Maclean's* v129 no51/52 p52 D 26 2016
Go far, far away color *Backpacker* p15 My 2017
KENNY BAKER A. Daniels color *Entertainment Weekly* no1446/1447 p91 D 2016/Ja 2017
Miss Universe [Cover story] G. Wood color *Vogue* v207 no11 p190 N 2017
Product Success Is Not About the Zeitgeist C. R. Sunstein *Harvard Business Review Digital Articles* p2 Je 22 2016
Solo Loses Duo A. Breznican color *Entertainment Weekly* no1472 p14 Je 30 2017
'Star Wars' at 40 D. Wallace and B. Burton bw color *AARP: The Magazine* v60 no3A p10 Ap/My 2017
STAR WARS' FEMINIST FORCE A. Breznican color *Entertainment Weekly* no1462 p12 Ap 21 2017
"Star Wars" Goes Rogue W. D. Gehring *USA Today Magazine* v145 no2858 p63 N 2016
Star Wars films—Collectibles
MUSEUM WARS A. Greenblatt *Governing* v30 no6 p9 Mr 2017
Star Wars Rebels (TV program)
ROGUE'S SECRET REBELS ROOTS A. Breznican color *Entertainment Weekly* no1446/1447 p32 D 2016/Ja 2017
Star Wars: Rogue One (Film)
FLIGHT OF THE U-WING A. Breznican color *Entertainment Weekly* no1442 p18 D 2 2016 Rebellious Special Issue
Going Rogue R. DOUTHAT color *National Review* v69 no1 p42 Ja 23 2017
Rogue One Rewinds-and-Rewrites-the Star Wars Legacy E. Dockterman color diag *Time* v188 no22-23 p100 N/D 2016
Star Wars: The Last Jedi (Film)
Gathering FORCE [Cover story] A. LEIBOVITZ bw color *Vanity Fair* v59 no7 p80 Summ 2017
Starboy (Music)
The Bullseye M. Snetiker color *Entertainment Weekly* no1443 p68 D 9 2016
The Playlist bw color *Rolling Stone* no1272 p10 O 20 2016

What to Stream color *Entertainment Weekly* no1442 p57 D 2 2016 Rebellious Special Issue
Starbucks Corp.
The Branding Logic Behind Google's Creation of Alphabet K. L. Keller *Harvard Business Review Digital Articles* p2 Ag 14 2015
A COFFEE STOCK LOSES ITS BUZZ R. Derousseau color diag *Fortune* v175 no3 p36 Mr 1 2017
HOWARD SCHULTZ HAS SOMETHING LEFT TO PROVE B. Kowitt chart color *Fortune* v175 no8 p114 Je 15 2017
How Starbucks's Culture Brings Its Strategy to Life P. Leinwand and V. Davidson *Harvard Business Review Digital Articles* p2 D 30 2016
MERE LATTES CANNOT SLAKE OUR THIRST FOR PUMPKIN SPICE color *Fortune* v176 no5 p19 O 1 2017
Purple Coffee, Rainbow Toast and the Politics of Unicorns N. Hopper color *Time* v189 no18 p27 My 15 2017
SMALL TOWN COFFEE P. Higbee *South Dakota Magazine* v33 no2 p64 Jl/Ag 2017
What Netflix and Starbucks Know About Cash Flow Eddie Yoon *Harvard Business Review Digital Articles* p2 Ja 22 2015
Starbursts (Astronomy)
Galaxies in Collision S. Gottlieb *Sky & Telescope* v133 no5 p28 My 2017
Starch metabolism
Early farmers expanded dogs' diet *Science* v354 no6313 p687 N 11 2016
Starck, Philippe, 1949-
PHILIPPE STARCK D. KAMP bw *Vanity Fair* v58 no12 p100 D 2016
StarCraft games
StarCraft Pros Are Ready to Battle AI E. Woyke and Yoochul Kim color *MIT Technology Review* v120 no5 p18 S/O 2017
Starcraft Marine LLC
Starcraft Star Step 221 E I/O *Boating World* v38 no1 p53 Ja 2017
Starfishes
Biological eigenstrokes *Physics Today* v70 no3 p84 Mr 2017
Starfishes—Behavior
Cost of Fast Food N. Wilson color *Natural History* v125 no3 p6 Mr 2017
Starflower (Music)
Rekindle Your Crush on Jennifer Paige N. Feeney color *Entertainment Weekly* no1462 p62 Ap 21 2017
STARGARDT, NICHOLAS
Power and Persecution *New York Times Book Review* p16 Ja 8 2017
STARIN, DAWN
Fighting Fit color *Natural History* v125 no10 p28 O 2017
Starin, Liz
Splashdance color *Publishers Weekly* v263 no49 p40 D 7 2016
Stark, Andrew
End Games D. Callahan color *Commonweal* v144 no4 p26 F 24 2017
Stark, Ellen
What to Do If You Can't File Your Taxes on Time color *Time* v189 no11 p18 Mr 27 2017
Who Will Care for You? [Cover story] chart color map *Consumer Reports* v82 no10 p28 O 2017
Stark, Freya, 1893-1993
1931: Baghdad F. Stark *Lapham's Quarterly* v10 no1 p83 Wint 2017
STARK, HERB
Chords & Discords color *Downbeat* v83 no11 p10 N 2016
Chords & Discords color *Downbeat* v84 no8 p10 Ag 2017
Stark, Jordan
You Don't Need a Promotion to Grow at Work *Harvard Business Review Digital Articles* p2 Je 24 2015
STARK, KIO
Talk to Strangers! *Reader's Digest* v189 no1128 p52 Mr 2017
Stark, Luke
Recognizing the Role of Emotional Labor in the On-Demand Economy *Harvard Business Review Digital Articles* p2 Ag 26 2016
Stark, Rodney, 1934-
The Triumph of Faith L. T. Johnson color *Commonweal* v144 no3 p35 F 10 2017
STARKE, JOHN

AN EVANGELICAL'S GUIDE TO THE ENNEAGRAM cartoon *Christianity Today* v60 no9 p54 N 2016

Starks, Misty

In Our Cities bw color *Ebony* v72 no9 p32 Jl/Ag 2017

Starlight Instruments LLC

State of the Art – Today: Here's a look at the cutting edge of telescope technology now J. Oltion color *Sky & Telescope* v134 no5 p72 N 2017

Starling, Simon—Exhibitions

Otherworldly J. Acocella cartoon *New Yorker* v92 no35 p20 O 31 2016

Starlings—Behavior

Under the Influence T. John color *Time* v188 no16/17 p8 O 24 2016

Starn, Doug

Like Minds V. LOWRY color *Architectural Digest* v74 no3 p56 Mr 2017

Starnone, Domenico

Interlocking Pieces R. DONADIO *New York Times Book Review* p10 Mr 26 2017

Starobin, Paul

Madness Rules the Hour: Charleston, 1860, and the Mania for War N. Tappan *MHQ: Quarterly Journal of Military History* v30 no1 p93 Aut 2017

Rebel Yells: How the Charleston elite brought on the American Civil War D. GOLDFIELD bw *New York Times Book Review* p22 Ap 23 2017

STAROBINSKY, ALEXEI

A COSMIC CONTROVERSY color *Scientific American* v317 no1 p5 Jl 2017

STARR, ALEXANDRA

OBAMA'S AMERICA img *New York* v49 no20 p12 O 3 2016

STARR, DOUGLAS

Sky Net cartoon map *Wired* v25 no3 p38 Mr 2017

Starr, Joshua P.

Leadership color *Phi Delta Kappan* v98 no8 p70 My 2017

Leadership il *Phi Delta Kappan* v98 no6 p70 Mr 2017

Leadership il *Phi Delta Kappan* v99 no2 p72 O 2017

Leadership *Phi Delta Kappan* v98 no3 p72 N 2016

Spending dollars to make a difference color *Phi Delta Kappan* v98 no5 p72 F 2017

STARR, KEN

The Persecution of Ting Xue bw cartoon *Weekly Standard* v22 no42 p8 Jl 17 2017

Starr, Kevin, 1940-2017

THE COLONIAL BEGINNINGS OF NORTH AMERICAN CATHOLICISM T. J. Shelley color diag *America* v216 no9 p38 Ap 24 2017

Here from the Beginning L. Tentler bw *Commonweal* v144 no8 p38 My 5 2017

Starr, Ringo, 1940——Interviews

Ringo Starr A. GREENE color *Rolling Stone* no1294 p20 Ag 24 2017

Starr, S. Frederick

THE INVENTION OF WORLD HISTORY *History Today* v67 no7 p36 Jl 2017

Starr, Stephen—Interviews

STEPHEN STARR L. M. M. BLUME bw *Vanity Fair* v59 no2 p48 F 2017

Starrett, Kelly

UNLOCK YOUR STRENGTH T. GRAHAM color diag *Men's Health* v32 no7 p94 S 2017

Starrett, Michael J.

Reactivation of latent working memories with transcranial magnetic stimulation bibl graph *Science* v354 no6316 p1136 D 2 2016

Stars

See also

Alpha Centauri

Black holes (Astronomy)

Dwarf stars

Magellanic clouds

Neutron stars

Planetary nebulae

Protostars

Red giants

Sun

Supergiant stars

Variable stars

75, 50 & 25 YEARS AGO R. W. Sinnott *Sky & Telescope* v134 no1 p8 Jl 2017

ASTRONOMERS HAVE COMBINED C. M. CARLISLE *Sky & Telescope* v133 no4 p12 Ap 2017

Be Starstruck: Remote Primland Resort is off the grid yet finely attuned to creature comforts, outdoor fun, and the human fascination with stars in the night sky D. LEATHERMAN *Washingtonian Magazine* v52 no11 p92 Ag 2017

Building Blocks L. SCHLEY color *Discover* v38 no9 p18 N 2017

Dark Galaxies C. Crockett cartoon color *Science News* v190 no12 p18 D 10 2016

The final four G. CHAPLE bw color *Astronomy* v45 no9 p64 S 2017

A fishy tale in the fall sky S. JAMES O'MEARA color *Astronomy* v45 no11 p16 N 2017

How high-speed stars escape the galaxy [Cover story] B. Dorminey color *Astronomy* v45 no3 p22 Mr 2017

HOW STARS VISIT THE SOLAR NEIGHBORHOOD *Physics Today* v70 no6 p24 Je 2017

HUBBLE GONE WILD E. MASTROIANNI color *Discover* v38 no7 p20 S 2017

INTRODUCING WASHINGTONIAN'S Best Moms *Washingtonian Magazine* v52 no9 p116 Je 2017

My Shot *National Geographic Kids* no466 p39 D 2016/Ja 2017

Occulting the Little King J. RAO color *Natural History* v125 no10 p45 O 2017

Party of One C. S. POWELL color graph *Discover* v27 no10 p60 D 2016

Quantum effect passes space test E. CONOVER *Science News* v191 no1 p12 Ja 21 2017

READER GALLERY color *Astronomy* v45 no8 p88 Ag 2017

READER GALLERY J. Fisanotti, D. Crowson et al color *Astronomy* v44 no12 p70 D 2016

'Runaway' stars fled nearby galaxy color *Science* v357 no6346 p8 Jl 7 2017

The secrets of off-season globular clusters F. M. Witkoski chart color *Astronomy* v45 no9 p50 S 2017

Seeing Stars C. S. POWELL color *Discover* v38 no3 p62 Ap 2017

Solar Eclipse Geometry M. E. BAKICH diag *Discover* v38 no7 p34 S 2017

A spinning, star-eating black hole color *Science* v354 no6318 p1358 D 16 2016

STAR DOME chart color *Astronomy* v45 no5 p38 My 2017

STAR DOME chart map *Astronomy* v45 no10 p38 O 2017

STAR DOME chart map *Astronomy* v45 no1 p38 Ja 2017

STAR DOME color *Astronomy* v45 no9 p38 S 2017

staring into Earth's past S. Fecht cartoon *Popular Science* v289 no5 p20 S/O 2017

Star-Powered Fun color *Good Housekeeping* v265 no2 p133 Ag 2017

Stellar Splendor: A deepest, darkest sky offers an extraordinary encounter with the stars F. Schaaf *Sky & Telescope* v134 no4 p45 O 2017

The strange star discovered by Planet Hunters B. E. Schaefer *Physics Today* v70 no3 p82 Mr 2017

TRAPPIST-1 Star Is Old C. M. CARLISLE *Sky & Telescope* v134 no6 p10 D 2017

Twice-setting stars S. J. O'MEARA color *Astronomy* v45 no3 p20 Mr 2017

Stars to the Rescue (TV program)

Gimme Shelter S. Apstein and T. Keith color *Sports Illustrated* v126 no5 p22 F 13 2017

Stars—Age

Faraway galaxy has oldest known dust A. YEAGER color *Science News* v191 no6 p13 Ap 1 2017

Stars—Color

STAR DOME chart map *Astronomy* v45 no3 p38 Mr 2017

Stars—Formation

Black holes may make good neighbors A. YEAGER *Science News* v191 no4 p8 Mr 4 2017

The First Black Holes C. M. Carlisle *Sky & Telescope* v133 no1 p24 Ja 2017

Stars—Globular clusters

v71 no2 p8 F 2017

State universities & colleges—Finance

Best State Schools for Out-of-Staters K. Clark chart *Money* v45 no11 p31 D 2016

State universities & colleges—Mergers

ZERO DEGREES OF SEPERATION P. Bridges cartoon color *Snowboarder* v29 no4 p26 D 2016

State University of New York at Buffalo—Sports

Willie Evans (1937-2017) J. Fuchs and T. Keith color *Sports Illustrated* v126 no3 p18 Ja 23 2017

State University of New York College at Fredonia

State University of New York at Fredonia *Dance Magazine* v90 p64 2016/2017 Supplement College Guide

Statehood (American politics)

1867 - The Time of our Birth C. Amundson *Nebraska Life* v21 no1 p9 Ja/F 2017

Dream On *Weekly Standard* v22 no11 p2 N 21 2016

A Quest for the Best Man: Missouri's First Governors R. SOODALTER color map *Missouri Life* v44 no4 p52 Je 2017

State laws—Charts, diagrams, etc.

Biometrics Regulation: The State (by State) of Play *Bloomberg Businessweek* no4531 p42 Jl 24 2017

Stateless persons

Universally Undocumented T. MARLAN cartoon *Walrus* v14 no3 p20 Ap 2017

Staten Island (New York, N.Y.)

Where the Fish and the Fisher-People Are img *New York* v50 no13 p60 Je 26 2017

States' rights (American politics)

Not My Philosopher R. R. Reilly *Claremont Review of Books* v17 no3 p47 Summ 2017

Statesmen

See also

Diplomats

Founders of nations

Heads of state

Legislators

Politicians

Static stretching (Physiology)

5 WAYS... To Warm Up L. McGLASHAN color *Muscle & Performance* v9 no9 p66 S 2017

Statins (Cardiovascular agents)

Statin Denialism H. HALL *Skeptical Inquirer* v41 no3 p40 My/Je 2017

Statins (Cardiovascular agents)—Therapeutic use

March highlights questions about benefits of science *Science News* v191 no9 p2 My 13 2017

THE STATIN UMBRELLA L. Beil cartoon diag graph *Science News* v191 no9 p22 My 13 2017

Station wagons

Stations of the Wagon color *Car & Driver* v63 no4 p71 O 2017

WARM WHEELS G. FREKING *Cincinnati Magazine* v50 no6 p30 Mr 2017

Stationery

See also

Envelopes (Stationery)

Notable Addiction M. W. Spencer *New Orleans Homes & Lifestyles* v20 no1 p104 Wint 2016

STYLE *New Orleans Homes & Lifestyles* v20 no2 p16 Spr 2017

Stationery—Evaluation

Early Bird Gift Guide S. JEAN SHELTON color *Redbook* p112 N 2017

Moving Stationery color *American History* v52 no3 p29 Ag 2017

Stations of the Cross

Disrupting the Cradle to Prison Pipeline, by Ndume Olatushani L. Copan color *Christian Century* v134 no8 p1 Ap 12 2017

Statistical astronomy

Black hole census results in big tally E. CONOVER *Science News* v192 no4 p7 S 16 2017

Statistical decision making

Hiring Algorithms Are Not Neutral G. Mann and C. O'Neil *Harvard Business Review Digital Articles* p2 D 9 2016

Statistical reliability

Lies, Damn Lies, and Financial Statistics P. Coy, S. Kishan et al cartoon *Bloomberg Businessweek* no4518 p8 Ap 10 2017

Statistical significance

A Refresher on Statistical Significance A. Gallo *Harvard Business Review Digital Articles* p2 F 16 2016

Statisticians

MIDCENTURY-MODERN POTTERY color *Indianapolis Monthly* v42 no2 p64 O 2017

Statistics

See also

Data science (Information science)

Decision making

Forecasting

Statisticians

How Stat Got Stuck J. B. Wogan *Governing* v30 no7 p32 Ap 2017

P-Hacker Confessions: Daryl Bern and Me S. VYSE *Skeptical Inquirer* v41 no5 p25 S/O 2017

Statistics—Methodology

Measurement error and the replication crisis E. Loken and A. Gelman bibl graph *Science* v355 no6325 p584 F 10 2017

Statman, Meir

Investing Can Be About Feelings Too color *Money* v46 no5 p30 Je 2017

Staton, Michael

When a Fancy Degree Scares Employers Away *Harvard Business Review Digital Articles* p2 Ja 6 2015

Statovci, Pajtim

Balkan Ghosts: Even in exile, a Kosovan mother and son hold on to their dreams T. OBREHT color *New York Times Book Review* p9 Ap 23 2017

Stattmann, Dean

The Guys Next Door color *Women's Health* v14 no4 p20 My 2017

Statue of Liberty (New York, N.Y.)

Ask Smithsonian K. Nodjimbadem color *Smithsonian* v47 no10 p96 Mr 2017

FXFOWLE Museum Breaks Ground on Liberty Island A. FIXSEN *Architectural Record* v204 no11 p28 N 2016

Mind-Blowing Facts About The Statue Of Liberty B. SPECKTOR *Reader's Digest* v188 no1124 p122 O 2016

Statues

A Confederate Monument Solution, With Context J. Sanburn color *Time* v190 no1 p17 Jl 3 2017

How to Pull Down a Statue M. Wollan *New York Times Magazine* p32 S 17 2017

THE JESUS LADY *Washingtonian Magazine* v52 no12 p70 S 2017

JULIA STREET WITH POYDRAS THE PARROT J. STREET bw *New Orleans Magazine* v51 no2 p24 D 2016

Monumental BATTLE: Why a movement to topple Confederate monuments has sparked debate, protests, and even violence [Cover story] *New York Times Upfront* p6 S 18 2017

The Monument MEN J. N. LOMAX *Texas Monthly* v45 no8 p31 Ag 2017

Rated PC J. LILEKS *National Review* v69 no17 p33 S 11 2017

REASON IN BRONZE: CLARENCE DARROW to Reunite with WILLIAM JENNINGS BRYAN at Dayton Courthouse J. MELCHIOR *Humanist* v77 no4 p32 Jl/Ag 2017

The Return of Jefferson Davis D. COURTNEY *Texas Monthly* v45 no6 p48 Je 2017

Tear Down This Colloseum! Taki *American Conservative* v16 no4 p66 Jl/Ag 2017

Statues—Conservation & restoration

BLADE BONNER R. CARTAGENA *Washingtonian Magazine* v52 no3 p16 D 2016

Brazil's iconic statue Christ the Redeemer is in need of restoration J. T. Coelho color *Christian Century* v134 no3 p14 F 2017

Statues—New York (State)

See also

Statue of Liberty (New York, N.Y.)

Statues—United States

Decommissioning Lee: The controversial removal of a prominent New Orleans statue W. CURTIS *American Scholar* v86 no4 p97 Aut 2017

Monuments to What? R. WILSON *American Scholar* v86 no4 p2 Aut 2017

Stature

Choose the Best Warmblood Hunter J. Winkel color *Practical Horseman* v45 no2 p13 F 2017

Stature—Social aspects

My best Halloween costume ever was ... map *Reader's Digest* v190 no1134 p26 O 2017

Status attainment

Improving Opportunities for Economic Mobility R. Chetty *Bridges (Federal Reserve Bank of St. Louis)* p1 Fall 2016

Statutes

See also

Repeal of legislation

HOW SHOULD CONFEDERATE STATUES IN PUBLIC SPACES BE TREATED? color *America* v217 no6 p6 S 18 2017

Staub, Sandy

Chrestia Staub Pierce P. Marquis *New Orleans Homes & Lifestyles* v20 no1 p92 Wint 2016

Staub, Wendy Corsi

Dead of Winter: A Lily Dale Mystery *Publishers Weekly* v264 no38 p55 S 18 2017

St. Aubyn, Edward, 1960-

Dunbar color *British Heritage Travel* v38 no5 p72 S/O 2017

Staudte, André

Tailored semiconductors for high-harmonic optoelectronics graph *Science* v357 no6348 p303 Jl 21 2017

Staudter, Thomas

New Album Chronicles Pastorius in '82 color *Downbeat* v84 no6 p20 Je 2017

Odradek's Juried Art bw *Downbeat* v84 no3 p18 Mr 2017

Stauffer, Carolyn

Witnesses to war color *Christian Century* v133 no25 p36 D 7 2016

STAUFFER, GEORGE B.

Symphonic Range color *Weekly Standard* v22 no31 p34 Ap 17 2017

Staunton (Va.)

SENSE OF PLACE: THREE TOWNS WHERE YOU CAN GET A TASTE OF THE VALLEY'S HISTORY, ARCHITECTURE, FOOD SCENE-AND PRIDE L. Ward *Washingtonian Magazine* v53 no1 p98 O 2017

Stavanger (Norway)

Norwegian Tags G. Haraldseth color *Art in America* v104 no10 p51 N 2016

Staves, The (Performer)

March Forth M. Griffith color *New Orleans Magazine* v51 no5 p50 Mr 2017

Stavitsky, Gail

Regarding Henri Matisse cartoon *Magazine Antiques* v184 no1 p180 Ja/F 2017

Stavridis, James

The Cuban Litmus Test *Time* v188 no24 p49 D 12 2016

Dealing With North Korea Is a Team Sport, and the U.S. Needs China on Its Side color *Time* v189 no6 p24 F 20 2017

FIND TIME TO SERVE OTHERS *Vital Speeches of the Day* v83 no8 p244 Ag 2017

Geopolitics: Trump's Top Priority Must Be a Strong China Strategy *Time* v188 no27-28 p30 D 26 2016

How to Ease Europe's Fears About the New U.S.-Russia Relationship color *Time* v190 no6 p28 Ag 7 2017

The Iran Paradox color *Time* v188 no16/17 p33 O 24 2016

It's Time to Plan for Civil War In Venezuela color *Time* v190 no10/11 p35 S 18 2017

President Trump Should Send More Troops to Afghanistan color *Time* v189 no22 p43 Je 12 2017

Terrorists Have Been All Too Effective by Air and Land. What If They Hit by Sea? color *Time* v190 no2/3 p29 Jl 10-17 2017

U.S. Security Hinges on Getting Foggy Bottom Back In the Game color *Time* v189 no11 p32 Mr 27 2017

The U.S. Should Form a Closer Military Alliance With Israel color *Time* v189 no3 p20 Ja 16 2017

When the Commander in Chief Disrespects His Commanders color *Time* v190 no16/17 p36 O 23 2017

When the Military Does Battle With Nature color *Time* v190 no12 p45 S 25 2017

Stax Records (Company)

Stax Celebrateds 60 Years A. Cohen color *Downbeat* v84 no9 p18 S 2017

Stay-at-home fathers

What It's Like When a Stay-at-Home Dad Goes Back to Work W. Johnson *Harvard Business Review Digital Articles* p2 Ap 19 2016

Stay Human Band (Performer)

JON BATISTE: 'Reservoir of Positivity' [Cover story] A. Morrison color *Downbeat* v84 no4 p28 Ap 2017

Stay With Me (Music)

Shawn Mendes D. Kiper color *Current Biography* v78 no4 p59 Ap 2017

Stayer, Ralph F., 1915-2007

Making Sense of Zappos' War on Managers G. Petriglieri *Harvard Business Review Digital Articles* p2 My 19 2015

St. Clair, Jessica

Jessica St. Clair and Lennon Parham A. Wilkinson color *Entertainment Weekly* no1473 p16 Jl 7 2017

St. Clair, Kassia

The Secret Lives of Color color *Publishers Weekly* v264 no25 p100 Je 19 2017

Stead, Philip

The Steads: Reconstructing Mark Twain's Only Picture Book S. Corbett bw color *Publishers Weekly* v264 no11 p23 Mr 13 2017

Steadicam (Trademark)

AMAZING GRACE J. BAILEY bw color *Film Comment* v52 no6 p24 N/D 2016

CENTER OF GRAVITY E. HYNES color *Film Comment* v52 no6 p28 N/D 2016

Steak (Beef)

Cheesesteaks for All B. LEONE, C. MOROCCO et al color *Bon Appetit* no1 p36 F 2017

Cream of the Crop color *Martha Stewart Living* p29 S 2017

Dinner Tonight A. STANEK color *Bon Appetit* no8 p33 Ag 2017

FIRE UP THE GRILL! [Cover story] color *Good Housekeeping* v265 no2 p58 Ag 2017

A Man, a Pan, a Plan color *Men's Health* v31 no10 p34 D 2016

On Your Way to Your New Year's Self G. Hamilton *New York Times Magazine* p20 Ja 1 2017

Perfect Indoor Steak color *American Cowboy* v23 no6 p68 Ap/ My 2017

Raise the Steaks T. Keith color *Sports Illustrated* v126 no16 p28 Je 5 2017

SHARPEN YOUR KNIVES [Cover story] C. BOERS, P. POLLACK et al color *Chicago* v66 no11 p60 N 2017

THIN-POUNDED VENISON STEAKS J. Miles color *Field & Stream* v122 no3 p20 Ag 2017

When Too Much Is Just Enough S. Sifton *New York Times Magazine* p26 S 3 2017

Steak houses

BEST OF WASHINGTON HALL OF FAME *Washingtonian Magazine* v52 no6 p186 Mr 2017

DINING GUIDE *Cincinnati Magazine* v50 no3 p139 D 2016

THE SKINNY ON BLACK COW FAT PIG S. W. KANSTEINER color *Nebraska Life* v21 no2 p28 Mr/Ap 2017

Steak houses—Evaluation

DOWNTOWN *Indianapolis Monthly* v42 no2 p114 O 2017

GOING DUTCH A. AHUJA *Cincinnati Magazine* v50 no3 p126 D 2016

High Five P. SHARPE *Texas Monthly* v45 no5 p36 My 2017

In the SUNSET KITCHEN color *Sunset* v239 no3 p100 S 2017

Selling the Sizzle J. SPALDING *Indianapolis Monthly* p40 F 2017

STEAKHOUSE img *New York* p77 Mr 6 2017

STEAKS *Cincinnati Magazine* v50 no8 p125 My 2017

United Steaks J. Sens and J. Passov color *Golf Magazine* v58 no11 p96 N 2016

Steam automobiles

See also

Doble steam automobiles

Doble Talk *American History* v52 no1 p31 Ap 2017

STEAM education

'In Tune' with the Community M. Acquino *Parks & Recreation* v52 no8 p80 Ag 2017

Steam generators—Efficiency

Solar steam generator needs no lenses or mirrors J. Miller *Physics Today* v69 no11 p17 N 2016

Steam locomotives

How to Make... EXTINCT STEEL K. DUPZYK color *Popular Mechanics* p78 S 2017

New sound for an old brass steamer L. Puckett color *Model Railroader* v84 no1 p66 Ja 2017

Operating with Digital Command Control L. Puckett color *Model*

Railroader v84 no2 p66 F 2017

Steam locomotives—Congresses

How to Make... EXTINCT STEEL K. DUPZYK color *Popular Mechanics* v193 no7 p78 S 2016

Steam locomotives—Evaluation

NEWS & PRODUCTS C. Grivno bw color *Model Railroader* v84 no2 p10 F 2017

Steam therapy

Enlarged prostate: New surgical options *Mayo Clinic Health Letter* v35 no10 p7 O 2017

Salt Saunas: Healthy or Hype? color *Health* v31 no6 p14 Jl 2017

Steam Whistle Brewing Inc.

For beer drinkers, by beer drinkers S. NIEDOBA color *Maclean's* v130 no4 p56 My 2017

Steamboat disasters

The Bertrand M. GARRIOTT bw cartoon color diag *Nebraska Life* v21 no1 p72 Ja/F 2017

Steamboats

THE BIG PICTURES: RED ROCK COUNTRY R. Stieve *Arizona Highways* v93 no11 p16 N 2017

Steaming (Cooking)

Steam Power C. CHAEY color *Bon Appetit* v62 no4 p46 Ap 2017

Stearn, Jonathan M.

How to Design Work Projects for Maximum Learning *Harvard Business Review Digital Articles* p2 Jl 22 2015

Steckel, Barbara

IT'S NOT THE TOOLS ...IT'S THE TEACHING color *Literacy Today (2411-7862)* v34 no3 p22 N/D 2016

STECKER, TIFFANY

Guess Who's Ghostwriting Monsanto's Safety Reviews color *Bloomberg Businessweek* no4534 p14 Ag 14 2017

Roundup: The Usual Suspect color graph *Bloomberg Businessweek* no4530 p42 Jl 17 2017

Steckler, Michael

Bangladesh Sits Atop Potential Major Quake Zone G. TARLACH color map *Discover* v38 no1 p22 Ja/F 2017

STEDMAN, NANCY

PHYSICIAN BURNOUT: The number of overworked, emotionally exhausted doctors has reached epidemic proportions. Stressed-out doctors have less time with patients and are more prone to making medical errors. Fixing the problem is a matter of national... *Saturday Evening Post* v289 no4 p46 Jl/Ag 2017

Stedman, Rich

THE PATH LESS TRAVELED color *New York State Conservationist* v71 no2 p24 O 2016

Stedman, Stephen John

Civil Wars & the Post–Cold War International Order *Daedalus* v146 no4 p33 Fall 2017

Steed, Ashley L.

The microbial metabolite desaminotyrosine protects from influenza through type I interferon graph *Science* v357 no6350 p498 Ag 4 2017

STEED, EDWARD

COMIC STRIP cartoon *New Yorker* v93 no14 p65 My 22 2017

THE GREAT AMERICAN ECLIPSE OF 2017 cartoon *New Yorker* v93 no27 p65 S 11 2017

Steegborn, Clemens

A conserved NAD+ binding pocket that regulates protein-protein interactions during aging bibl graph *Science* v355 no6331 p1312 Mr 24 2017

Steege, Hanster

Forest conservation: Humans' handprints bibl color *Science* v355 no6324 p466 F 3 2017

Steel

See also

Damascus steel

Nickel steel

Steel, Alix

Tillerson's Got a Private State Department *Bloomberg Businessweek* no4505 p30 D 26 2016

STEEL, E. ASHLEY

Envisioning, Quantifying, and Managing Thermal Regimes on River Networks *BioScience* v67 no6 p506 Je 2017

Steel, Piers

Research: The Biggest Culture Gaps Are Within Countries, Not Between Them *Harvard Business Review Digital Articles* p2

My 18 2016

Steel corrosion

NAIL FALL COLOR color *Women's Health* v14 no8 p34 O 2017

Steel industry—China

China Gets Serious About Shrinking Steel *Bloomberg Businessweek* no4505 p18 D 26 2016

Steel industry—Employees

500,000 Tons of Steel. 14 Jobs T. Biesheuvel color *Bloomberg Businessweek* no4528 p16 Je 26 2017

Steel industry—Government policy

China Gets Serious About Shrinking Steel *Bloomberg Businessweek* no4505 p18 D 26 2016

Steel industry—Mergers

IN BRIEF K. Stock bw color *Bloomberg Businessweek* no4539 p10 S 25 2017

Steel industry—United States—History—21st century

American Producers See an Election Boost J. Deaux color *Bloomberg Businessweek* no4500 p22 N 21 2016

Steel manufacture

U.S. Steel's Revitalization J. Deaux color *Bloomberg Businessweek* no4536 p42 S 4 2017

Steel mills

RUST: Inside the hulking structure that was once the Bethlehem Steel Works, a photographer finds beauty in decay J. WALDMAN *Saturday Evening Post* v289 no4 p50 Jl/Ag 2017

Socialism in the Basement M. Z. MARVIT *In These Times* v41 no4 p44 Ap 2017

Steele, Allen

Avengers of the Moon *Publishers Weekly* v263 no51 p127 D 12 2016

Steele, Brendan

Brendan Steele C. Barrett color *Golf Magazine* v59 no6 p23 Je 2017

Steele, Cameron

TOYOTAS GO FULL MOON IN BAJA S. OCHSNER color *Dirt Sports + Off-Road* v51 no3 p58 Mr 2017

Steele, David

The Best Boots of 2018 color *Powder* p95 S 2017

Steele, Diana

Artist's amnesia could unlock brain mysteries color *Science News* v191 no3 p28 F 18 2017

Steele, Elisa

What Kind of Thinker Are You? *Harvard Business Review Digital Articles* p2 N 23 2015

Steele, Glenn D., Jr.

A Proven New Model for Reimbursing Physicians *Harvard Business Review Digital Articles* p2 S 15 2015

Steele, Jonathan

Turkey and the Kurds: A Chance for Peace? color *New York Review of Books* v64 no7 p20 Ap 20 2017

Steele, Judy

REMEMBERING PEARL HARBOR *Saturday Evening Post* v288 no6 p6 N/D 2016

Steele, Kim

The Thread color *New York Times Magazine* p14 O 9 2016

Steele, Shelby

End of the Line for the Shame Train: White self-congratulation, disguised as penance, has informed American liberalism for decades. Now liberalism is at last exhausted--and that's a very good thing *Hoover Digest: Research & Opinion on Public Policy* no3 p35 Summ 2017

The Soft Bigotry of Political Correctness: President Trump has never bowed to the culture of victimization. His lack of deference could be liberating *Hoover Digest: Research & Opinion on Public Policy* no2 p54 Spr 2017

What's the Story? J. EPSTEIN *Weekly Standard* v23 no3 p27 S 25 2017

Steele, Taylor

Editor's Note T. PRODANOVICH color *Surfer* v58 no3 p10 Je 2017

THE PROXIMITY TAPES N. MEYERS and A. GOGGANS bw color *Surfer* v58 no3 p56 Je 2017

Steel—Export & import trade

Does Foreign Steel Threaten U.S. Security? J. Deaux color *Bloomberg Businessweek* no4524 p31 My 29 2017

Steelhead fishing

Stir It Up: In this oral biography of Bob Marley, friends and family recall his generosity, spiritual force and hard work TOURÉ *New York Times Book Review* p10 Jl 30 2017

Steffenson, Brian

Wild emmer genome architecture and diversity elucidate wheat evolution and domestication color *Science* v357 no6346 p93 Jl 7 2017

Steffes, P.

Jupiter's interior and deep atmosphere: The initial pole-to-pole passes with the Juno spacecraft [Cover story] color graph *Science* v356 no6340 p821 My 26 2017

STEFFY, LOREN

Big Oil Roars Back *Texas Monthly* v45 no2 p60 F 2017

Black Elk Down *Texas Monthly* v45 no4 p82 Ap 2017

The Pot of Cold *Texas Monthly* v44 no12 p78 D 2016

Why, That Son of a Steak! *Texas Monthly* v45 no1 p56 Ja 2017

Stefka, Andrew T.

Neonatal acquisition of Clostridia species protects against colonization by bacterial pathogens diag *Science* v356 no6335 p315 Ap 21 2017

Stegemann, Eileen

Celebrating ADIRONDACK PARK'S 125th ANNIVERSARY *New York State Conservationist* v71 no6 p2 Je 2017

POND HOPPING *New York State Conservationist* v72 no1 p6 Ag 2017

Steger, Brooke

WHEEL AND DEAL *Harper's Magazine* no2007 p19 Ag 2017

Stegerhoek, Ward

HOLD STEADY color *Vogue* v206 no12 p266 D 2016

Stegle, Oliver

Single-cell epigenomics: Recording the past and predicting the future diag *Science* v357 no6359 p69 O 6 2017

Stegman, Mary Ruth

KNOWN UNKNOWNS *Commonweal* v144 no4 p4 F 24 2017

Stegmann, Martin

The receptor kinase FER is a RALF-regulated scaffold controlling plant immune signaling graph *Science* v355 no6322 p287 Ja 20 2017

Stegner, Lynn

Merging paleobiology with conservation biology to guide the future of terrestrial ecosystems color *Science* v355 no6325 p594 F 10 2017

Stehlik, Mark

How to Prepare the Next Generation for Jobs in the AI Economy color *Harvard Business Review Digital Articles* p2 Je 5 2017

STEHR, NICO

Too much democracy? *Issues in Science & Technology* v33 no1 p5 Fall 2016

Trusting the Climate: Catastrophe Vs. Stability graph *Society* v53 no6 p573 D 2016

Steidel, C.

iPTF16geu: A multiply imaged, gravitationally lensed type Ia supernova color diag graph *Science* v356 no6335 p291 Ap 21 2017

Steidl (Film)

Through a Glass Darkly N. PINKERTON bw *Film Comment* v52 no6 p90 N/D 2016

Steidl, Gerhard, 1950-

THE BOOK MONK R. MEAD cartoon color *New Yorker* v93 no14 p60 My 22 2017

Steig, William, 1907-2003

Building blocks color *U.S. Catholic* v82 no2 p19 F 2017

Steigerwald, Bill

Separate and Unequal J. HILL bw *Weekly Standard* v22 no38 p38 Je 12 2017

Steigman, Gary

Gary Steigman R. Scherrer, J. Beacom et al *Physics Today* v70 no8 p72 Ag 2017

Steiker, Carol S.

Will the Death Penalty Ever Die? J. S. Rakoff color *New York Review of Books* v64 no10 p46 Je 8 2017

STEIKER, VALERIE

Behind the Scenes color *Vogue* v207 no3 p386 Mr 2017

Girl on the RUN color *Vogue* v207 no1 p42 Ja 2017

Long RANGE bw *Vogue* v207 no1 p43 Ja 2017

Object Lesson bw cartoon *Vogue* v207 no3 p388 Mr 2017

On the Bright Side color *Vogue* v207 no3 p384 Mr 2017

On the Road color *Vogue* v207 no3 p390 Mr 2017

Story Time *Vogue* v207 no3 p392 Mr 2017

Steiker-Ginzberg, Kate

THE FAIRY TALE AND THE NIGHTMARE color *Sports Illustrated* v127 no3 p104 Jl 24 2017

STEIL, BENN

Of Debt and Detriment *Weekly Standard* v22 no22 p22 F 13 2017

Steimatsky, Noa

Head On M. J. ROWIN bw *Film Comment* v53 no1 p92 Ja/F 2017

Stein, Alexander

NEXT GIN J. Kell color *Fortune* v175 no2 p28 F 1 2017

Stein, C.

A nontoxic pain killer designed by modeling of pathological receptor conformations bibl diag graph *Science* v355 no6328 p966 Mr 3 2017

Stein, Charles

BlackRock Fights A Price War, Selectively graph *Bloomberg Businessweek* no4520 p39 My 1 2017

Fidelity Fires a Shot in The Fund Price War *Bloomberg Businessweek* no4533 p26 Ag 7 2017

Schwab's Cut-Rate ETFs Are Catching On color graph *Bloomberg Businessweek* no4494 p39 O 10 2016

When Bad Things Happen to Good Funds cartoon *Bloomberg Businessweek* no4507 p32 Ja 16 2017

STEIN, ELIOT

INSTAGRAM EVERYWHERE color *Wired* v24 no12 p91 D 2016

SLEEP TIGHT cartoon *Wired* v24 no12 p90 D 2016

Sleep Up In a Tree: Fulfill a childhood fantasy and branch out on your next getaway by renting a treehouse *Washingtonian Magazine* v52 no11 p86 Ag 2017

STEIN, EWAN

Islamists and Liberal Values in the Middle East *Current History* v115 no785 p363 D 2016

Stein, Gila E.

Surprising states of order for linear diblock copolymers diag *Science* v356 no6337 p487 My 5 2017

STEIN, HARRY

Elective Surgery cartoon *Weekly Standard* v22 no19 p14 Ja 23 2017

Stein, Isaac

SAND HILL ROAD: AN ORAL HISTORY color *Wired* v25 no9 p24 S 2017

Stein, Jill

Jill Stein's Recounts Are Destructive to Democracy T. B. Olson *Time* v188 no24 p18 D 12 2016

Stein, Joel

15 Minutes color *Time* v188 no25-26 p30 D 19 2016 Double Issue

The 2018 Time 100 color *Time* v189 no16/17 p151 My 1-8 2017

American Wine? Whine Not! *Los Angeles Magazine* p44 F 2017

Bummed About the Election? Finding a New Country Is a Lot Harder Than It Looks color *Time* v188 no22-23 p111 N/D 2016

Change Thy Ways: A LITTLE FRIENDLY ADVICE FOR NEW YORK CHEFS OPENING OUTPOSTS HERE color *Los Angeles Magazine* v62 no7 p33 Jl 2017

Château Murdoch bw *Bloomberg Businessweek* no4530 p63 Jl 17 2017

Fire Fighter *Los Angeles Magazine* p48 Ap 2017

Hacking Myself Is the Most Surprisingly Humiliating Decision I've Ever Made color *Time* v189 no12 p63 Ap 3 2017

Hello, Darkness *Los Angeles Magazine* v62 no9 p49 S 2017

I'm a Football Fan. I Just Didn't Know It color *Time* v188 no15 p63 O 17 2016

In 2016, Lies, the Whole Lies and Nothing but the Lies color *Time* v188 no25-26 p158 D 19 2016 Double Issue

A KINDER, GENTLER REDDIT cartoon color *Bloomberg Businessweek* no4503 p65 D 12 2016

Life *Reader's Digest* v188 no1124 p40 O 2016

Me, My Liberal Wife and What Happened When We Went to a Gun Range color *Time* v190 no9 p62 S 4 2017

Mr. President, I Demand You Do Your Duty and Insult Me. Please? color *Time* v190 no5 p64 Jl 31 2017

MY DIGITAL color *Men's Health* v32 no9 p104 N 2017

My Son Doesn't Care About the Super Bowl. So I Brought In a Ringer color *Time* v189 no4 p59 F 6 2017

6 2017

Martyrs & Saints bw *Commonweal* v144 no5 p28 Mr 10 2017

A Turn That Went a Long Way *Commonweal* v144 no6 p12 Mr 24 2017

The War against Just War color *Commonweal* v144 no11 p15 Je 16 2017

Steingarten, Jeffrey

COAST TO COAST color *Vogue* v207 no11 p208 N 2017

HAND to MOUTH cartoon *Vogue* v207 no3 p474 Mr 2017

Steingoltz, Maria

Virtual and Augmented Reality Will Reshape Retail *Harvard Business Review Digital Articles* p2 S 9 2016

Steinhage, Anna

The Pros and Cons of Competition Among Employees *Harvard Business Review Digital Articles* p2 Mr 20 2017

Steinhagen, Ruth Ann

BEYOND OBSESSION R. Cohen color *Sports Illustrated* v127 no8 p50 S 18 2017

Steinhardt, Paul J.

POP goes the universe color graph *Scientific American* v316 no2 p32 F 2017

STEINHAUER, OLEN

Along Came a Death Squad *New York Times Book Review* p13 O 9 2016

Steinherr, Alessandra

Bold Always Wins bw color *Glamour* v115 no11 p150 N 2017

Steinke, Kirt

MONTANA MAYHEM color *Spin to Win Rodeo* v21 no1 p18 Mr 2017

Steinkraus, Bill

Confessions of a Nitpicker color *Practical Horseman* v45 no2 p20 F 2017

Steinmetz, Katy

7 Food Trends for 2017 color *Time* v188 no27-28 p86 D 26 2016

The California Republic Comes Roaring Back color diag map *Time* v189 no5 p34 F 13 2017

The Campus Culture Wars color *Time* v190 no16/17 p48 O 23 2017

Emotional Divide color diag *Time* v189 no7/8 p38 F 27 2017

Fighting Words color *Time* v189 no22 p32 Je 12 2017

The Fire Season color map *Time* v190 no16/17 p40 O 23 2017

Going After the 'Really Bad Dudes' color *Time* v190 no2/3 p12 Jl 10-17 2017

The Golden State's Big Green Bet color *Time* v188 no20 p38 N 14 2017

How Political Language Got So Coded *Time* v188 no16/17 p65 O 24 2016

Infinite Identities [Cover story] color *Time* v189 no11 p48 Mr 27 2017

A Monumental Fight color *Time* v190 no9 p30 S 4 2017

Next Generation Leaders color *Time* v189 no9 p38 Mr 13 2017

The Other Side [Cover story] color diag *Time* v189 no4 p24 F 6 2017

The Philosopher King color *Time* v190 no10/11 p58 S 18 2017

Sniffing Out Dog Whistles *Time* v188 no16/17 p65 O 24 2016

Startups Are Laser-Focused on Helping Self-Driving Cars See color *Time* v190 no9 p26 S 4 2017

Uber Fail [Cover story] color diag *Time* v189 no24 p22 Je 26 2017

Unthinkable. Unspeakable. The Language of Tragedy *Time* v190 no15 p25 O 16 2017

The U.S. Continues to Come Apart In the Wake of a Divisive Election color diag *Time* v188 no22-23 p9 N/D 2016

Steinmetz, Nicholas A.

Selective modulation of cortical state during spatial attention bibl graph *Science* v354 no6316 p1140 D 2 2016

Steinruecken, Christian

We will have to decide whether to hire humans or machines: Cambridge University's Christian Steinruecken on how AI will reshape HR's role *People Management* p13 My 2017

Steinshnider, Robin

The Challenge of Renovating Historic Aquatic Facilities: How the Dallas Park & Recreation Department is preserving community history and memories *Parks & Recreation* v52 no9 p104 S 2017

Steitz, Joan

Not just Salk color *Science* v357 no6356 p1105 S 15 2017

Stekel, Dov

Microbial mass movements color *Science* v357 no6356 p1099 S 15 2017

Stella & Dot LLC

Style Star M. Santos color *Working Mother* v40 no3 p10 Ag/S 2017

Stella, F.

Superficial layers of the medial entorhinal cortex replay independently of the hippocampus bibl graph *Science* v355 no6321 p1 Ja 13 2017

STELLA, FRANK

The Year in Reading [Cover story] *New York Times Book Review* p8 D 25 2016

Stella, Luigi

An accreting pulsar with extreme properties drives an ultraluminous x-ray source in NGC 5907 bibl chart graph *Science* v355 no6327 p817 F 24 2017

Stella McCartney Ltd.

ARM CANDY: Totes used to be more function than form, but these fall bags don't sacrifice details or style H. G. Phillips *Washingtonian Magazine* v53 no1 p109 O 2017

my style color *InStyle* v24 no5 p122 My 2017

Nail Your Holiday Style! color *Glamour* v114 no12 p91 D 2016

Stellar black holes

Black hole census results in big tally E. CONOVER *Science News* v192 no4 p7 S 16 2017

Stellar density (Stellar population)

The Queen's Finest: Look to Cassiopeia for her varied collection of celestial treasure S. French *Sky & Telescope* v134 no6 p55 D 2017

Stellar magnetic fields

See also

Solar magnetic fields

Reconciling solar and stellar magnetic cycles with nonlinear dynamo simulations A. Strugarek, P. Beaudoin et al diag *Science* v357 no6347 p185 Jl 14 2017

Stellar magnitudes

Astronomy's ATLAS OF TOTALITY M. E. Bakich color map *Astronomy* v45 no8 p54 Ag 2017

December 2016: Inner planet convention M. RATCLIFFE and A. LING chart color *Astronomy* v44 no12 p36 D 2016

Don't blame aliens for star's flickering L. GROSSMAN *Science News* v192 no5 p11 S 30 2017

Stellar rhythm B. BERMAN color *Astronomy* v45 no2 p10 F 2017

Tabby's Star Dims on Cue M. YOUNG *Sky & Telescope* v134 no3 p13 S 2017

Tabby's Star Gets Weirder M. YOUNG *Sky & Telescope* v133 no1 p18 Ja 2017

Stellar masses

HOW DOES A BLACK HOLE FORM? color diag *Astronomy* v45 no7 p15 Jl 2017

Light-bending by distant star seen L. GROSSMAN color *Science News* v191 no13 p10 Jl 8 2017

Stellar mergers

Red nova explosion predicted for 2022 color *Astronomy* v45 no5 p13 My 2017

Stellar parallax

STILL IN THE FAMILY J. Bochanski, R. Shubinski et al color *Astronomy* v45 no1 p34 Ja 2017

Stellar populations

Brown Dwarfs Mimic Stellar Siblings J. BOCHANSKI *Sky & Telescope* v134 no4 p10 O 2017

Stellar rotation

'PUMPKIN STARS' CARVE OUT A NICHE IN THE UNIVERSE J. Wenz color *Astronomy* v45 no3 p12 Mr 2017

Stellarvue (Company)

Stellarvue's Optimus eyepieces tested T. Hallas color *Astronomy* v45 no5 p62 My 2017

Stelling, Jörg

β-cell–mimetic designer cells provide closed-loop glycemic control bibl graph *Science* v354 no6317 p1296 D 9 2016

Stelzer, Irwin

HORSE AND RABBIT STEW *Claremont Review of Books* v17 no1 p82 Wint 2016/2017

Stelzer, Irwin M.

The Cartel That Failed color *Weekly Standard* v22 no29 p11 Ap 3 2017

A Case for Caution *Weekly Standard* v22 no25 p20 Mr 6 2017

New Yorkers bw *Weekly Standard* v22 no46 p5 Ag 14 2017

An Opportunity for Environmentalists color *Weekly Standard* v22 no26 p16 Mr 13 2017

Retaliation Nation color *Weekly Standard* v22 no36 p26 My 29 2017

Teaching by Numbers color *Weekly Standard* v22 no29 p32 Ap 3 2017

Trump and Trade color *Weekly Standard* v22 no15 p27 D 19 2016

Why Not an Auction? color *Weekly Standard* v22 no28 p20 Mr 27 2017

Stem, Peter

THE FUTURE OF PAIN RESEARCH color *Science* v354 no6312 p565 N 4 2016

Stem cell culture

Embryogenesis in a dish M. Pera color *Science* v356 no6334 p137 Ap 14 2017

Stem cell research

COPD Treatment Takes Center Stage D. Ebner *Saturday Evening Post* v288 no6 p115 N/D 2016

Hearts On Demand: Mass General Surgeon Makes Critical Strides in Regenerating Organs R. SINE color *Forbes* v200 no3 p56 S 28 2017

Key Discoveries on Cellular Regeneration *USA Today Magazine* v145 no2865 p14 Je 2017

Stem Cell Research W. F. Vitulli and T. O. Diener *Skeptical Inquirer* v41 no3 p63 My/Je 2017

Stem cell research—United States

STEM CELL RESEARCH R. BARGLOW and M. SCHAEFER *Skeptical Inquirer* v41 no1 p34 Ja/F 2017

Stem cell transplantation

Stem cells help sterile mice grow eggs L. HAMERS color *Science News* v191 no12 p13 Je 24 2017

Stem cell treatment

Challenging the Status Quo with Stem Cells C. TOMPOT bw color *National Review* v68 no20 p9 N 7 2016

THE END OF PAIN? [Cover story] B. STULBERG cartoon color *Runner's World* v52 no2 p50 Mr 2017

Mending a Broken Heart D. Fine Maron color *Scientific American* v317 no2 p19 Ag 2017

STEM CELL THERAPY AND WILLIE NELSON: Rebels by Their Own Rules M. Reinstetle *Saturday Evening Post* v289 no2 p92 Mr/Ap 2017

Texas signals support for unproven stem cell therapies K. Servick *Science* v356 no6344 p1219 Je 23 2017

Stem cells

Cardiac regeneration strategies: Staying young at heart E. Tzahor and K. D. Poss diag *Science* v356 no6342 p1035 Je 9 2017

COPD Treatment Takes Center Stage D. Ebner *Saturday Evening Post* v288 no6 p115 N/D 2016

Linking stem cells to germ cells Vielle-Calzada color *Science* v356 no6336 p378 Ap 28 2017

Managing cell and human identity J. Moreno, J. Gearhart et al cartoon *Science* v356 no6334 p139 Ap 14 2017

Stem cell approach for cataracts challenged K. Servick color *Science* v356 no6345 p1318 Je 30 2017

THE STEM CELL SKEPTIC K. Servick color graph *Science* v357 no6350 p441 Ag 4 2017

STEM CELLS MAY HELP HEAL SOFT-TISSUE INJURIES AND ARTHRITIS C. Barakat and M. McCluskey color *Equus* no477 p16 Je 2017

VARIETY AMONG CLONES E. MASTROIANNI color *Discover* v38 no7 p9 S 2017

Stem cells—Research—Political aspects

STEM CELL RESEARCH R. BARGLOW and M. SCHAEFER *Skeptical Inquirer* v41 no1 p34 Ja/F 2017

STEM education

The Benefits of Encouraging STEM to Young Girls A. Yu color *Maclean's* v130 no3 p63 Ap 2017

Build STEM Skills, but Don't Neglect the Humanities J. Roos *Harvard Business Review Digital Articles* p2 Je 24 2015

The Effectiveness of Class Size Reduction W. J. MATHIS *Education Digest* v82 no5 p60 Ja 2017

Helping less-prepared students excel A. Sessoms color *Science* v357 no6352 p654 Ag 18 2017

I'll have a Cosmo L. Kruesi cartoon color *Astronomy* v44 no12 p58 D 2016

Increasing Student Success in STEM: Summary of A Guide to Systemic Institutional Change S. Elrod and A. Kezar *Change* v49 no4 p26 Jl/Ag 2017

Insights into Student Gains from Undergraduate Research Using Pre- and Post-Assessments A. L. MCDEVITT, M. V. PATEL et al *BioScience* v66 no12 p1070 D 1 2016

Kazoo Magazine Aims to Encourage Girls in Science B. RADFORD *Skeptical Inquirer* v41 no3 p7 My/Je 2017

Longitudinal Analysis of a Diversity Support Program in Biology: A National Call for Further Assessment C. J. BALLEN and N. A. MASON *BioScience* v67 no4 p367 Ap 2017

Making Math Count More for Young Latinos D. Murphey, R. Madill et al bw *Education Digest* v83 no1 p8 S 2017

STEAM-POWERED READERS R. B. Jackson color *Literacy Today (2411-7862)* v34 no4 p14 Ja/F 2017

TALKING TO KIDS BOOSTS TEST SCORES, CAREERS [Cover story] *USA Today Magazine* v145 no2865 p1 Je 2017

Toward a More Diverse Research Community Models of Success: A forward-looking group of colleges and universities are demonstrating effective ways to educate underrepresented minorities for careers in science and engineering F. A. HRABOWSKI III and P. H. HENDERSON *Issues in Science & Technology* v33 no3 p33 Spr 2017

We Have So Much Power! A. Reign color *Essence* v47 no9 p94 Ja 2017

Young science officers lead by example D. Iyer bibl color *Science* v355 no6322 p256 Ja 20 2017

STEM education—Congresses

Students seek scientific solutions at Broadcom MASTERS International color *Science News* v191 no13 p40 Jl 8 2017

STEM education—Finance

Society seeks new sponsor for International Science and Engineering Fair color *Science News* v191 no5 p29 Mr 18 2017

STEM education—Social aspects

Without inclusion, diversity initiatives may not be enough C. Puritty, L. R. Strickland et al color *Science* v357 no6356 p1101 S 15 2017

STEM education—Study & teaching

The candidates are out there A. DOMISE *Maclean's* p10 Je 2017

StemCells Inc.

Failed spinal cord trial offers cautionary tale K. Servick color *Science* v355 no6326 p679 F 17 2017

Stemme, Nina, 1963-

The Ten Best Classical Music Performances of the Year J. Davidson img *New York* v49 no25 p130 D 12 2016

Stemme AG

STEMME S12 [Cover story] R. MARK chart color *Flying* v144 no6 p52 Je 2017

Stempeck, Matt

Are Uber and Facebook Turning Users into Lobbyists? *Harvard Business Review Digital Articles* p2 Ag 11 2015

Stenberg, Amandla, 1998-

Harris DICKINSON *Interview* v47 no5 p61 Je/Jl 2017

Stencel-Baerenwald, Jennifer E.

Reovirus infection triggers inflammatory responses to dietary antigens and development of celiac disease color diag *Science* v356 no6333 p44 Ap 7 2017

Stencil work

the pleasures of Handwork M. E. Polson color *Arts & Crafts Homes & the Revival* v11 no5 p33 Wint 2017

Steneck, Nick

Addressing scientific integrity scientifically *Science* v357 no6357 p1248 S 22 2017

Stenger, Sebastien

What a Study of French Auditors Shows About Homophobia at Work *Harvard Business Review Digital Articles* p2 Mr 29 2017

Stengl, Suzanne

The Thurston Heirloom *Publishers Weekly* v264 no35 p77c Ag 28 2017

Stengler, Mark

NATURAL REMEDIES FOR COLD SORES color *Amazing Wellness* v9 no3 p32 EarlySumm 2017

Natural Remedies for Cold Sores color *Better Nutrition* v79 no1 p30 Ja 2017

Stenson, Henrik, 1976-

What CEOs Think of Trump R. T. Beckwith color *Time* v189 no6 p10 F 20 2017

Stephenson, Sam

DEPTH OF FIELD M. Dolan bw color *American History* v52 no4 p70 O 2017

STEPHENSON, WEN

Normalizing Deceit *Nation* v304 no2 p4 Ja 16 2017

Stephens-Reed, Laura

SURPRISE *Christian Century* v134 no12 p22 Je 7 2017

Stepinski, Adam

Why Unicorns Are Struggling *Harvard Business Review Digital Articles* p2 Ap 21 2016

Stepmom (Film)

MOTHER'S DAY WEEKEND M. FELL *TV Guide* v65 no19 p44 My 1 2017

Stepmothers

Fitting a family together color *Redbook* p112 S 2017

Stepparents & stepchildren

THE WORK OF LOVE R. Mawhood Lee color *America* v216 no3 p32 F 6 2017

Steppke, Alexander

Strong peak in Tc of Sr2RuO4 under uniaxial pressure bibl color graph *Science* v355 no6321 p1 Ja 13 2017

Steptoe, Javaka, 1971-

Javaka Steptoe C. Mari *Current Biography* v78 no8 p78 Ag 2017

Stepwells

INDIA'S LOST WONDERS N. RHEE color *Chicago* v66 no4 p94 Ap 2017

STERBINI, CESARE

Il Barbiere di Siviglia *Opera News* v81 no7 p57 Ja 2017

Sterchi, Matthew

Not Your Grandfather's Log Cabin P. Peebles color *Log Home Living* v34 no2 p66 Mr 2017

Stereochemistry

See also

   Asymmetry (Chemistry)

   Atoms

   Chirality

   Stereoselective reactions

Enantioselective photochemistry through Lewis acid–catalyzed triplet energy transfer T. R. Blum, Z. D. Miller et al bibl chart diag graph *Science* v354 no6318 p1391 D 16 2016

Stereographs

The Illusion of Reality: The shocking power of virtual reality was all the buzz once before--about 150 years ago C. Thompson *Smithsonian* v48 no6 p18 O 2017

Stereoscope

NATURAL MAGIC S. JOHNSON *New York Times Magazine* p48 N 6 2016

Stereoselective reactions

An artificial metalloenzyme with the kinetics of native enzymes P. Dydio, H. M. Key et al bibl diag graph *Science* v354 no6308 p102 O 7 2016

Stereospecificity

Macrocyclic bis-thioureas catalyze stereospecific glycosylation reactions Yongho Park, K. C. Harper et al bibl diag *Science* v355 no6321 p1 Ja 13 2017

Stereotype threat

Why Women Feel More Stress at Work A. S. Kramer and A. B. Harris *Harvard Business Review Digital Articles* p2 Ag 4 2016

Stereotypes (Social psychology)

See also

   Gender stereotypes

The Great Beauty Shake-Up M. Singer bw color *Vogue* v207 no3 p436 Mr 2017

How We'll Stereotype Our Robot Coworkers T. Park *Harvard Business Review Digital Articles* p2 O 2 2014

Older Workers Need to Stop Believing Stereotypes About Themselves S. Taneva and J. Arnold *Harvard Business Review Digital Articles* p2 Je 20 2016

THE POLARIZATION EXPRESS *Psychology Today* v50 no3 p9 My/Je 2017

To Stand And Deliver J. HERBST *Los Angeles Magazine* p19 F 2017

Why Aren't There More Asian Americans in Leadership Positions? S. K. Johnson and T. Sy *Harvard Business Review Digital*

Articles p2 D 19 2016

STERGAR, DAVE

The Skis of the Year color *Powder* p82 S 2017

Sterile neutrinos

Making a statement about parameter ranges A. Caldwell *Physics Today* v70 no8 p12 Ag 2017

Sterile neutrinos give IceCube and other experiments the cold shoulder Sung Chang *Physics Today* v69 no10 p15 O 2016

Sterilis LLC

Innovation: Needle Grinder C. Winter color *Bloomberg Businessweek* no4531 p21 Jl 24 2017

Sterilization (Birth control)—Finance

Pro-Life Goals Need to Be More Ambitious Than Opposing Abortion *America* v216 no11 p8 My 15 2017

Sterilization (Disinfection)

X-ray sterilization with accelerators is viable in US C. Boulware *Physics Today* v70 no1 p11 Ja 2017

Sterilization (Disinfection)—Equipment & supplies

a chemical-free clean *Parents* v92 no4 p105 Ap 2017

Sterios, Peter

REVOLVE TO EVOLVE color *Yoga Journal* p90 2017 Special Issue

Sterling, Adina

How Having an MBA vs. a Law Degree Shapes Your Network *Harvard Business Review Digital Articles* p2 F 19 2016

Research: Black Employees Are More Likely to Be Promoted When They Were Referred by Another Employee color *Harvard Business Review Digital Articles* p2 F 28 2017

Sterling, Cara

The Harvard Contest That's Trying to Improve Health Care Delivery *Harvard Business Review Digital Articles* p2 O 2 2015

STERLING, ELEANOR

Society Is Ready for a New Kind of Science--Is Academia? *BioScience* v67 no7 p591 Jl 2017

Sterling, Lisa

Internal Hires Need Orientation Too *Harvard Business Review Digital Articles* p2 N 4 2016

Stern, A. D.

How economics can shape precision medicines bibl color *Science* v355 no6330 p1131 Mr 17 2017

Stern, Alan

Pioneers [Cover story] color *Time* v189 no16/17 p14 My 1-8 2017

Stern, Alexander

The Art of Thinking in Other People's Heads *Humanities* v38 no1 p1 Wint 2017

For More than 100 Years, D.C. Has Drawn People to Protest *Humanities* v37 no4 p1 Fall 2016

Stern, Alexander L.

Chiral Majorana fermion modes in a quantum anomalous Hall insulator–superconductor structure diag *Science* v357 no6348 p294 Jl 21 2017

STERN, ALEXANDRA MINNA

Eugenics warning *Issues in Science & Technology* v33 no1 p15 Fall 2016

STERN, AMANDA

Durga CHEW--BOSE: THE CANADIAN WRITER'S FIRST BOOK OF ESSAYS SYNTHESIZES PUBLIC AND PRIVATE THOUGHTS INTO AN ANTHEM OF A DIFFICULT AGE *Interview* v47 no3 p32 Ap 2017

Stern, Andy, 1950-

AT LABOR'S CROSSROADS R. YESELSON bw color *Nation* v304 no10 p27 Mr 27 2017

Stern, Chantal

Howard Eichenbaum (1947–2017) color *Science* v357 no6354 p875 S 1 2017

Stern, Claire

DUA LIPA color *InStyle* v24 no6 p33 Je 2017

Great Escapes color *InStyle* v24 no8 p163 Ag 2017

the life color *InStyle* v24 no5 p249 My 2017

the life color *InStyle* v24 no7 p131 Jl 2017

the life color *InStyle* v24 no9 p425 S 2017

THANKSGIVING WITH A VIEW color *InStyle* v24 no11 p211 N 2017

YARA SHAHIDI color *InStyle* v24 no8 p57 Ag 2017

Stern, Dana

Fresh COAT K. MOLVAR color *Vogue* v207 no7 p56 Jl 2017

Stern, Dave
Born a Crime bw *Publishers Weekly* v263 no44 p(Sp)26 O 31 2016
Strange New Worlds color *Publishers Weekly* v263 no44 p(Sp)17 O 31 2016

Stern, Eric A.
Global Arsenic Contamination: Living With the Poison Nectar bibl color map *Environment* v59 no2 p24 Mr/Ap 2017

Stern, Gerald, 1925-
Coal Barons *Progressive* v81 no2 p43 F 2017
Evermore D. KIRBY *New York Times Book Review* p14 Ag 27 2017
GELATO *New Yorker* v93 no8 p46 Ap 10 2017

Stern, Grete
GRETE STERN J. Thurman cartoon *New Yorker* v92 no42 p100 D 19 2016

STERN, JEFFREY E.
THE POISON FLOWER color *Atlantic* v319 no1 p74 Ja/F 2017

STERN, JERRY
Defining Jewish Conservatism *Commentary* v144 no1 p4 Jl/Ag 2017

STERN, MARK JOSEPH
NO CONGRESS? NO PROBLEM *Advocate* no1088 p12 D 2016/ Ja 2017
SIX THINGS WE MUST DO TO SURVIVE TRUMP'S AMERI-CA color *Advocate* no1089 p42 F/Mr 2017

STERN, MELANIE
Will shared parental leave ever work? *People Management* p8 F 2017

Stern, Molly R.
42 new ALL-STAR PRODUCTS of the year [Cover story] color *Redbook* p27 Jl/Ag 2017
PLAY UP YOUR natural beauty [Cover story] P. STABLES bw color *Redbook* p50 F 2017

Stern, Omri
How Israeli Startups Can Scale *Harvard Business Review Digital Articles* p2 S 10 2015

Stern, Robert
Pushback to NHL records demand *Science* v355 no6326 p671 F 17 2017

Stern, Robert A. M., 1939-
The Battle for History D. LIND *Architectural Record* v205 no7 p77 Jl 2017

Stern, Robin
Teaching Teenagers to Develop Their Emotional Intelligence *Harvard Business Review Digital Articles* p2 My 19 2015

Stern, S. Alan
PUZZLED BY PLUTO [Cover story] bw color *Astronomy* v45 no9 p22 S 2017

STERN, STEVE
Spyless in Gaza: A disgraced Israeli agent offers tragicomic reflections on the broken promises of the Promised Land *New York Times Book Review* p12 S 17 2017

STERNBERG, HANNAH
So Many Books *Publishers Weekly* v264 no7 p80 F 13 2017

Sternberg, Libby
Death Is the Cool Night and Lost to the World color *Publishers Weekly* v263 no43 p50a O 24 2016

Sternberg, Mary Ann
Close Quarters color *AARP: The Magazine* v60 no1A p54 D 2016/ Ja 2017

Sternberg, Robert J.
Testing chart color *Phi Delta Kappan* v98 no4 p66 D 2016/Ja 2017

Sternbergh, Adam
Andrea Martin's Big Break img *New York* v50 no8 p122 Ap 17 2017
The Blinds *Publishers Weekly* v264 no24 p41 Je 12 2017
Every Home Needs a Wig Wall img *New York* v50 no18 p74 S 4 2017
"Every Man Has to Go Through Hell to Reach Paradise" img *New York* p114 Mr 6 2017
I Am Not Interchangeable img *New York* v50 no11 p109 My 29 2017
New York Would Never Dream of Building a Wall img *New York* v49 no25 p62 D 12 2016
OBAMA'S AMERICA img *New York* v49 no20 p12 O 3 2016

THE ONE QUESTION INTERVIEW: ADAM STERNBERGH J. SALAMON *Texas Monthly* v45 no8 p42 Ag 2017
This Magic Moment: For more than 50 years, photographer Jean-Pierre Laffont has proved that in New York, you never know what you might see img *New York* v50 no15 p64 Jl 24 2017
Tony's Dead, Walt's Not, and Phoebe's Hooked on Meth img *New York* v50 no12 p102 Je 12 2017
Turned Upside Down img *New York* v50 no17 p88 Ag 21 2017

Sterne, Peter
'Put the camera down' color *Columbia Journalism Review* v56 no2 p21 Fall 2017

Sterner, T.
Best cost estimate of greenhouse gases *Science* v357 no6352 p655 Ag 18 2017

Stern-Ginossar, Noam
Global mRNA polarization regulates translation efficiency in the intestinal epithelium diag *Science* v357 no6357 p1299 S 22 2017

Stethoscopes—History—19th century
THOU SIMPLE TUBE M. Dickson *History Today* v67 no5 p66 My 2017

Stettheimer, Florine, 1871-1944
THE ROARING STETTIES P. SCHJELDAHL color *New Yorker* v93 no13 p90 My 15 2017
To All Tomorrow's Parties A. RUSSETH bw cartoon *ARTnews* v116 no1 p26 Spr 2017

Stettheimer, Florine, 1871-1944—Exhibitions
ART bw *New Yorker* v93 no18 p9 Je 26 2017
ART color *New Yorker* v93 no23 p8 Ag 7 2017
An avant-garde patron and peer at the Jewish Museum bw color *Magazine Antiques* v184 no4 p26 Jl/Ag 2017
Taking Her Place in American Art S. Schwartz color *New York Review of Books* v64 no12 p11 Jl 13 2017

Steuck, Sarah
What it takes to breed horses color *Equus* no475 p15 Ap 2017

Steuer, Eric
The Customer-Service Rep *New York Times Magazine* p43 F 26 2017
THE #FREEBASSEL EFFECT color *Wired* v25 no10 p17 O 2017

Steurer, Stefan
A pathogenic role for T cell–derived IL-22BP in inflammatory bowel disease bibl graph *Science* v354 no6310 p358 O 21 2016

Stevanović, Sanja
Landscape of immunogenic tumor antigens in successful immunotherapy of virally induced epithelial cancer graph *Science* v356 no6334 p200 Ap 14 2017

Steve at the Party (Short story)
STEVE AT THE PARTY C. NISSAN cartoon *New Yorker* v93 no19 p29 Jl 3 2017

Steve Harvey's Funderdome (TV program)
Entrepreneurs Wanted for Steve Harvey's New Competition Show On ABC color *Black Enterprise* v47 no3 p16 O 2016

Steven, Arian
Flash Frozen D. L. NG bw *Field & Stream* v121 no8 p10 F/Mr 2017

Steven Madden Ltd.
All-Star Stashes! K. FOSTER color *Seventeen* v76 no3 p41 My 2017

Steven Lucas, Matthew
Harvesting electrical energy from carbon nanotube yarn twist diag graph *Science* v357 no6353 p773 Ag 25 2017

Stevens, Amanda
Smart Trail-Ride Prep color *Horse & Rider* v56 no6 p75 Je 2017

Stevens, Becca
BECCA STEVENS: Regal Strength A. Morrison color *Downbeat* v84 no8 p52 Ag 2017
Singer-Songwriters Follow Their Muses A. MORRISON color *Downbeat* v84 no5 p60 My 2017

Stevens, Brad, 1976-
Brad Stevens J. Crelin color *Current Biography* v77 no11 p82 N 2016

Stevens, Chevy
Never Let You Go color *Publishers Weekly* v264 no4 p55 Ja 23 2017

Stevens, Claire H.
Site-specific phosphorylation of tau inhibits amyloid-β toxicity in

Alzheimer's mice bibl graph *Science* v354 no6314 p904 N 18 2016

Stevens, Craig

Why the rest of the world is marching color *Science* v356 no6334 p119 Ap 14 2017

Stevens, Dan

DAN STEVENS TRANSFORMS LIKE THE DICKENS C. Collis color *Entertainment Weekly* no1459 p12 Mr 31 2017

Legion J. Hibberd color *Entertainment Weekly* no1448 p40 Ja 13 2017

VESTING OPTIONS color *GQ: Gentlemen's Quarterly* v97 no4 p106 Ap 2017

X MARKS THE SPOT E. NUSSBAUM cartoon *New Yorker* v92 no49 p98 F 13 2017

Stevens, Dana

Bookends *New York Times Book Review* p31 N 27 2016

What's the best book, new or old, you read this year? *New York Times Book Review* p27 D 25 2016

Stevens, David

POWER [Cover story] color *Christian Century* v134 no1 p22 Ja 4 2017

Stevens, Fisher

The Messenger J. Hahn *Sierra* v102 no1 p11 Ja/F 2017

Stevens, Katie

THE 20-WORD REVIEW S. Highfill color *Entertainment Weekly* no1473 p50 Jl 7 2017

Stevens, Laura

Scientists Find Trigger That Cracks lakes color *Oceanus* v51 no2 p20 Wint 2016

Stevens, Lindsey

CHANGE the CITY *Indianapolis Monthly* p55 Ap 2017

Hot on the TRAILS: A ROAD-FREE GUIDE TO EXPLORING CENTRAL INDIANA *Indianapolis Monthly* v40 no10 p59 Je 2017

Stevens, Madelyn

Get It, Girls! color *Glamour* v115 no4 p30 Ap 2017

Stevens, Martin

The biology of color color *Science* v357 no6350 p470 Ag 4 2017

STEVENS, MICHAEL T.

Origins of Science Faculty with Education Specialties: Hiring Motivations and Prior Connections Explain Institutional Differences in the SFES Phenomenon *BioScience* v67 no5 p452 My 2017

Stevens, Molly M.

Extracting the contents of living cells color *Science* v356 no6336 p379 Ap 28 2017

Stevens, Nell

I Am a ROCK color *Vogue* v207 no3 p228 Mr 2017

Stevens, R. Paul

Aging Matters: Finding Your Calling for the Rest of Your Life B. Mink *Christian Century* v133 no23 p41 N 9 2016

Stevens, Sufjan

Cosmic meditations from Sufjan Stevens C. E. McCarthy color *America* v217 no3 p49 Ag 7 2017

Stevens Arms (Company)

THE AMERICAN SIDE-BY-SIDE T. WIELAND and J. M. TAYLOR color *Outdoor Life* v224 no5 p72 Je/Jl 2017

Stevens Institute of Technology

School of Quant M. SCHIFRIN and J. BROWN color *Forbes* v200 no2 p54 S 5 2017

Stevenson, Bryan

Genius at Work K. F. DANIELS and S. TIABROWN color *Ebony* v72 no4 p80 F 2017

A Presumption of Guilt color *New York Review of Books* v64 no12 p8 Jl 13 2017

REMEMBER WHEN A. OLSEN *Christianity Today* v61 no7 p7 S 2017

Stevenson, D.

Jupiter's interior and deep atmosphere: The initial pole-to-pole passes with the Juno spacecraft [Cover story] color graph *Science* v356 no6340 p82l My 26 2017

Stevenson, David

In defense of Crazy Ideas *Physics Today* v70 no4 p10 Ap 2017

Stevenson, Deborah

LIGHT OF THE WORLD color *ARTnews* v115 no4 p141 Wint 2016/2017

Stevenson, J. P.

Case Study: Competing Against Bling il *Harvard Business Review* v95 no3 p155 My/Je 2017

Case Study: How Should an Understated Luxury Brand Compete Against Bling? color *Harvard Business Review Digital Articles* p2 F 28 2017

Stevenson, James

Into the Wild Blue Yonder with the Air National Guard S. W. KANSTEINER color *Nebraska Life* v21 no4 p20 Jl/Ag 2017

Stevenson, Jane

7 Tenets of a Good CEO Succession Process *Harvard Business Review Digital Articles* p2 D 7 2016

Stevenson, Karen

Red squirrels in the British Isles are infected with leprosy bacilli bibl color diag map *Science* v354 no6313 p744 N 11 2016

STEVENSON, KATHERINE

Petnet SmartFeeder: Robot pet feeder meets smartphone app with mostly good results color *PCWorld* v35 no7 p155 Jl 2017

Stevenson, Kathryn

How Kids Learn in Nature *Parks & Recreation* v52 no5 p36 My 2017

Stevenson, Matthew

KILLING BILL O'REILLY: The disgraced broadcaster's distortions of history *Harper's Magazine* v335 no2006 p69 Jl 2017

Stevenson, Mercedes

THE QUEEN PASSED ON, BUT THE QUEEN LIVES ON D. J. JENNINGS bw color *Louisiana Life* v37 no2 p40 N/D 2016

Stevenson, P. R.

Persistent effects of pre-Columbian plant domestication on Amazonian forest composition bibl chart graph map *Science* v355 no6328 p925 Mr 3 2017

Stevenson, Robert

When It's Time To Go Home color *Powder* v45 no3 p152 N 2016

STEVENSON, ROBERT D.

Communicating the Science and Human Significance of Climate Change *BioScience* v67 no3 p306 Mr 2017

STEVENSON, SAMANTHA

Glow Sticks color *Indianapolis Monthly* v41 no2 p29 S 2017

HOW ROUGE! Scarlet, crimson, ruby, fire-engine—whatever you call it, this season's hottest hue will have you seeing red color *Indianapolis Monthly* v42 no2 p30 O 2017

MAKING WAVES: From dainty frills to major flounces, fashion is currently rife with ruffles bw color *Indianapolis Monthly* v41 no2 p30 S 2017

WAX ELOQUENT: You can't hold a candle to these entrepreneurs and their fast-growing business color *Indianapolis Monthly* v41 no2 p34 S 2017

STEVENSON, VERITY

HOW TO GET A JOB AT GOOGLE color *Maclean's* v129 no47 p48 N 28 2016

Steverman, Ben

401(k) Nation: Who's Left Out color *Bloomberg Businessweek* no4540 p49 O 2 2017

Blowing Down That Fiduciary Rule color *Bloomberg Businessweek* no4511 p35 F 13 2017

The Case for Not Overstocking Your IRA *Bloomberg Businessweek* no4516 p41 Mr 27 2017

Living on 4 Percent—Or Less cartoon *Bloomberg Businessweek* no4493 p56 O 3 2016

Monetizing Lost Vacation Time color *Bloomberg Businessweek* no4495 p33 O 17 2016

New Gender New Finances color *Bloomberg Businessweek* no4502 p56 D 5 2016

Retirement's Scariest Question: How Long? bw *Bloomberg Businessweek* no4498 p51 N 7 2016

Time to Rethink Early Retirement graph *Bloomberg Businessweek* no4516 p40 Mr 27 2017

Steves, Brian P.

Tsunami-driven rafting: Transoceanic species dispersal and implications for marine biogeography color graph *Science* v357 no6358 p1402 S 29 2017

Stevia—Research

SUGAR RUSH B. Kowitt color diag *Fortune* v175 no3 p102 Mr 1 2017

Steward, Austin

Currents of Race and Religion Flowing Along the Waters Of the

Erie Canal S. Brent Rodriguez Plate color graph *America* v217 no6 p46 S 18 2017

Steward, Michelle D.

Business Professors Need to Spend Time in Companies *Harvard Business Review Digital Articles* p2 N 27 2015

Corporate Ethics Can't Be Reduced to Compliance *Harvard Business Review Digital Articles* p2 Ap 29 2016

Steward, Tina

The Healing Power of Dressage color *Dressage Today* v23 no9 p20 Je 2017

Stewards

Karen Golding Is a Steward for the Horse: This horse show icon believes that safeguarding equine welfare is her No. 1 priority as a steward K. Rover *In Stride* v12 no3 p37 My 2017

STEWART, ALEX

AMAZING MAIZE MAZES *Missouri Life* v43 no6 p50 O/N 2016

A GROWING TREND *Missouri Life* v43 no6 p84 O/N 2016

Stewart, Andrea

20-MINUTE SUPPERS color *Good Housekeeping* v265 no4 p117 O 2017

Stewart, Dan

Britain Stumbles Toward Exit Talks With a Reinvigorated Europe color *Time* v189 no24 p7 Je 26 2017

How Diana Became Britain's 'Queen of the Heart' color *Time* v190 no9 p23 S 4 2017

London Strives to Remain a Place the World Will Call Home color *Time* v189 no23 p18 Je 19 2017

Savagery In the U.K. Britain Comes Under Attack at a Turning Point color *Time* v189 no21 p34 Je 5 2017

Should Mercenaries Take Over In Afghanistan? color *Time* v190 no7 p11 Ag 21 2017

TIME's Foreign Correspondents on How the World Sees the U.S. Election *Time* v188 no16/17 p34 O 24 2016

Stewart, David

After weeks of terrorism and tragedy, divisions emerge in Britain color *America* v217 no2 p15 Jl 24 2017

BUBBLING UNDER color *America* v215 no15 p30 N 14 2016

Europe's far right attempts to harass refugees on Mediterranean color *America* v217 no5 p16 S 4 2017

Saving the Skyline *America* v215 no12 p11 O 24 2016

Unaccompanied Minors Neglected As Calais Camp Is Demolished color *America* v215 no16 p8 N 21 2016

Stewart, Fiona

THE BEST BET img *New York* v50 no6 p55 Mr 20 2017

Stewart, Frank

I, SNOW LEOPARD J. MAJIA *Orion Magazine* v35 no4/5 p82 Jl-O 2016

STEWART, FRED

READERS' THOUGHTS ON PAST ISSUES color *Motor Trend* v69 no2 p26 F 2017

Stewart, Haley

In the new adaptation of Anne of Green Gables, hope is replaced by horror color *America* v216 no13 p56 Je 12 2017

Stewart, Henry

CHRISTINE GOERKE *Opera News* v81 no10 p28 Ap 2017

JOHAN BOTHA. RUSTENBERG, SOUTH AFRICA, AUGUST 19,1965—VIENNA, AUSTRIA, SEPTEMBER 8, 2016 *Opera News* v81 no5 p60 N 2016

Kamala Sankaram *Opera News* v81 no7 p10 Ja 2017

Redefining the Gold Standard: As he winds down his New York Philharmonic tenure with Das Rheingold, Alan Gilbert looks forward to new beginnings *Opera News* v81 no12 p51 Je 2017

Sean Michael Plumb *Opera News* v81 no10 p12 Ap 2017

Stewart, Ian

Calculating the Cosmos: How Mathematics Unveils the Universe *Publishers Weekly* v263 no39 p77 S 26 2016

Significant Figures: The Lives and Works of Great Mathematicians color *Publishers Weekly* v264 no31 p79 Jl 31 2017

STEWART, JACK

DRIVE IN THE SKY color *Wired* v25 no10 p54 O 2017

STEWART, JAMES B.

Profit or Loss: How Harvard Business School has reshaped American capitalism *New York Times Magazine* p11 Ap 30 2017

Stewart, John R.

Neandertal and Denisovan DNA from Pleistocene sediments bw color *Science* v356 no6338 p605 My 12 2017

Reconstruction of CES time series: implementing the 2010 OMB metropolitan area delineations bibl chart color graph *Monthly Labor Review* p1 O 2016

Stewart, Jon, 1962-

BEE NOT AFRAID D. CORN *Mother Jones* v42 no3 p62 My/Je 2017

Jon Stewart, Superboss S. Finkelstein *Harvard Business Review Digital Articles* p2 Jl 30 2015

Points to Ponder color *Reader's Digest* v189 no1130 p31 My 2017

STRONG FOR LIFE A. Heffernan color diag *Men's Health* v31 no10 p98 D 2016

Stewart, Jude

How to Cut in Line color *Atlantic* v320 no2 p22 S 2017

Make Time for Boredom cartoon *Atlantic* v319 no5 p23 Je 2017

Stewart, Julie

Gabrielle Union color *Men's Health* v32 no2 p28 Mr 2017

LOOK YOUNG, FEEL EVEN YOUNGER [Cover story] cartoon color *Men's Health* v32 no1 p126 Ja/F 2017

Put Your Best Foot Forward color *Men's Health* v32 no2 p78 Mr 2017

Save Your Butt cartoon *Men's Health* v32 no1 p88 Ja/F 2017

The Six Smartest Fast-Food Lunches bw color *Men's Health* v32 no5 p94 Je 2017

The STI You Already Have cartoon *Men's Health* v32 no3 p78 Ap 2017

Why You Cough color *Men's Health* v31 no10 p86 D 2016

Winning the Prostate Cancer War color *Men's Health* v32 no4 p75 My 2017

Stewart, Justin

The Art of Selling Movies bw *Film Comment* v53 no1 p92 Ja/F 2017

Stewart, Kristen, 1990-

CERTAIN WOMEN C. ELLENBERG bw color *Vogue* v207 no6 p72 Je 2017

THE ESCAPE ARTIST S. Vilkomerson color *Entertainment Weekly* no1457/1458 p44 Mr 17 2017

Halter Dresses E. Wilson color *InStyle* v24 no5 p74 My 2017

Kristen Stewart color *InStyle* v23 no12 p189 N 2016

Kristen Stewart HER BEST EVER T. Swennen and K. Stewart's color *InStyle* v24 no2 p60 F 2017

Kristen Stewart Sets Personal Shopper Ablaze S. Zacharek color *Time* v189 no10 p51 Mr 20 2017

Pop Chart R. Bruner, C. Lang et al color *Time* v189 no6 p54 F 20 2017

Separated at Death img *New York* p121 Mr 6 2017

Yeah, Bra E. Wilson color *InStyle* v24 no9 p182 S 2017

Stewart, Martha, 1941-

A Feast for the Senses color *Martha Stewart Living* p13 My 2017

LIFE, ACCORDING TO MARTHA color *Fortune* v175 no8 p44 Je 15 2017

The Life of Trees *Martha Stewart Living* no269 p19 N 2016

Martha's Month *Martha Stewart Living* no267 p2 S 2016

Martha's October chart color *Martha Stewart Living* p4 O 2017

SIGHTS ON SUCCESS bw color *Martha Stewart Living* no271 p13 Ja/F 2017

TRUE-BLUE WINNERS E. Moody, M. Ozawa et al color *Martha Stewart Living* no271 p76 Ja/F 2017

Stewart, Martin

MARTIN STEWART S. CORBETT color *Publishers Weekly* v263 no52 p67 D 19 2016

Stewart, Michael

Eastman ETR824S Trumpet color *Downbeat* v84 no4 p93 Ap 2017

Stewart, Michelle

OF DIGITAL SELVES AND DIGITAL SOVEREIGNTY: OF THE NORTH *Film Quarterly* v70 no4 p23 Summ 2017

Stewart, Patrick

patrick stewart will look great forever C. WEAVER bw color *GQ: Gentlemen's Quarterly* v97 no3 p146 Mr 2017

STEWART, REBECCA FELSENTHAL

drop-off jitters *Parents* v92 no4 p130 Ap 2017

HOW TO Wipe Out Whining *Parents* v92 no11 p120 N 2017

Stewart, Rod, 1945-

COAL AND STEEL FOR Rod Stewart's masterpiece [Cover story] C. Swanson color *Model Railroader* v84 no6 p42 Je 2017

Stewart, Rory

He Saw the Marches Differently on the March A. Motion color *New York Review of Books* v64 no5 p49 Mr 23 2017

Stewart, Scott

Catch Me Is Uncatchable T. Booker *In Stride* v12 no2 p18 Mr 2017

Playbook Draft & Victory in the $218,04 Platinum Performance/ USJHA Green Hunter Incentive Championship T. Booker *In Stride* v12 no5 p20 S 2017

Stewart, Tom

Going Once, Going Twice J. Passov color *Golf Magazine* v59 no4 p124 Ap 2017

Stewart, Tyler

TARGET PRACTICE K. BIRCHMIER *Successful Farming* v114 no12 p52 Mid-N 2016

Stewart, Vincent

THE AGE OF COGNITIVE WAR *Vital Speeches of the Day* v83 no10 p293 O 2017

WHAT WILL YOUR STORY BE? *Vital Speeches of the Day* v83 no9 p267 S 2017

Stewart Filmscreen Corp.

Photon Menace M. P. Hamilton chart color *Sound & Vision* v82 no8 p62 O 2017

Stewart-Halevy, Jacob

Copy That bw *Art in America* v105 no3 p61 Mr 2017

Stewart-Spears, Genie

The 62nd, Tevis Cup *Arabian Horse World* v57 no12 p128 S 2017

aerc National Awards: Endurance riders and horses honored at the 2016 AERC Convention *Arabian Horse World* v57 no10 p58 Jl 2017

American Endurance Ride Conference *Arabian Horse World* v57 no3 p72 D 2016

Biltmore Challenge Endurance Rides: What's happening in the world of Arabian horses *Arabian Horse World* v57 no10 p104 Jl 2017

enduring partners—Stagg and Cheryl Newman *Arabian Horse World* v57 no8 p122 My 2017

OLD DOMINION: Endurance Race *Arabian Horse World* v57 no11 p142 Ag 2017

TEVIS CUP *Arabian Horse World* v56 no12 p164 S 2016

Stews

See also

Compotes (Stewed fruit)

Gumbo (Soup)

Oxtail stew

Garne Guisada C. BOND *Texas Monthly* v45 no2 p36 F 2017

Larger Than Life S. Sifton *New York Times Magazine* p22 Ap 2 2017

Steyer, Tom, 1957-——Interviews

The Man Who Fell for Earth N. STOCKTON bw color graph *Wired* v25 no4 p46 Ap 2017

Steyger, Peter S.

Community network for deaf scientists color *Science* v356 no6336 p386 Ap 28 2017

ST. FÉLIX, DOREEN

KARA WALKER, AFTER SUBTLETY [Cover story] img *New York* v50 no8 p34 Ap 17 2017

St. George, Zach

BULLDOZERS VS. CHAINSAWS color *Powder* v45 no3 p50 N 2016

Return of Giants color *Orion Magazine* v36 no1 p7 Ja/F 2017

St George-Hyslop, Peter H.

Deciphering microglial diversity in Alzheimer's disease color *Science* v356 no6343 p1123 Je 16 2017

Sti International Inc.

STI 211 HEX TACTICAL J. B. SNOW chart color *Outdoor Life* v224 no1 pR13 D 2016/Ja 2017

Stibel, Jeff

Why the Falling U.S. Unemployment Rate Matters *Harvard Business Review Digital Articles* p2 N 18 2014

Stibitz, Sara

Get What You Need from Your Hands-Off Boss *Harvard Business Review Digital Articles* p2 Je 12 2015

How to Get a New Employee Up to Speed *Harvard Business Review Digital Articles* p2 My 22 2015

How to Really Listen to Your Employees *Harvard Business Re-*

view Digital Articles p2 Ja 30 2015

How to Spot a Bad Boss During an Interview *Harvard Business Review Digital Articles* p2 D 21 2015

Stich, Kai Petra

Cognition-mediated evolution of low-quality floral nectars bibl graph *Science* v355 no6320 p1 Ja 6 2017

Sticklebacks—Behavior—Research

One's True Nature J. G. Goldman color *Scientific American* v315 no6 p24 D 2016

Stickler, Haley—Interviews

MEET HALEY STICKLER *Sea Magazine* v108 no10 pCA-9 O 2016

Stickney, Tom

MIND YOUR MISS color *Golf Magazine* v59 no2 p49 F 2017

Sticky notes

The Surprising Persuasiveness of a Sticky Note K. Hogan *Harvard Business Review Digital Articles* p2 My 26 2015

Stid, Daniel

Why the GOP Congress Will Stop Trump from Going Too Far *Washington Monthly* p17 Ja/F 2017

Stieb, Matt

...AND NINE THEY NEED TO PROTECT *New York* v50 no7 p31 Ap 3 2017

TO UNDERSTAND THIS NEW RIGHT, IT HELPS TO SEE IT NOT AS A FRINGE MOVEMENT, BUT A POWERFUL COUNTERCULTURE img *New York* v50 no9 p24 My 1 2017

Stiebale, Joel

Research: Innovation Suffers When Drug Companies Merge *Harvard Business Review Digital Articles* p2 Ag 3 2016

STIEFEL, STEVEN

5 Fat-Loss Hacks color *Muscle & Performance* v9 no7 p24 Jl 2017

Stiefvater, Maggie

The Raven King color *Publishers Weekly* v263 no49 p110 D 7 2016

Stieg, Cory

SAY AMEN TO GOOD HEALTH bw *Good Housekeeping* v263 no5 p150 N 2016

Stielstra, Megan

BOOK OF FEARS N. PARSI color *Chicago* v66 no8 p42 Ag 2017

The Wrong Way to Save Your Life: Essays *Publishers Weekly* v264 no20 p48 My 15 2017

Stier, Molly

Nation Voices 2016 *Nation* v304 no2 p8 Ja 16 2017

STIEVE, ROBERT

THE BIG PICTURES: RED ROCK COUNTRY *Arizona Highways* v93 no11 p16 N 2017

CAMPBELL MESA LOOP *Arizona Highways* v92 no7 p54 Jl 2016

CIBECUE FALLS *Arizona Highways* v96 no7 p46 Jl 2017

CREATIVE ENVIRONMENT *Arizona Highways* v93 no2 p50 F 2017

DEVIL'S BRIDGE TRAIL color map *Arizona Highways* v93 no5 p54 My 2017

editor's LETTER *Arizona Highways* v92 no7 p2 Jl 2016

editor's LETTER *Arizona Highways* v93 no6 p2 Je 2017

editor's LETTER *Arizona Highways* v93 no9 p2 S 2017

Emily Dickinson wrote poems *Arizona Highways* v96 no7 p2 Jl 2017

For the most determined *Arizona Highways* v93 no8 p2 Ag 2017

GRANDVIEW TRAIL *Arizona Highways* v92 no11 p54 N 2016

HOPE CAMP TRAIL *Arizona Highways* v93 no2 p54 F 2017

HUNTER TRAIL *Arizona Highways* v93 no3 p54 Mr 2017

I don't have a favorite place *Arizona Highways* v93 no11 p2 N 2017

THE INSIDERS CALL IT PEFO *Arizona Highways* v93 no2 p2 F 2017

It seemed like such a simple *Arizona Highways* v92 no12 p1 D 2016

I watched the sun set with one *Arizona Highways* v92 no8 p3 Ag 2016

JOE'S CANYON TRAIL: Of the five trails in Coronado National Memorial, the best is arguably Joe's Canyon, which winds through waves of grama grasses that dispel stereotypes and come alive with the summer rains *Arizona Highways* v93 no8 p54 Ag 2017

JUNIPER SPRINGS TRAIL *Arizona Highways* v93 no11 p54 N

2017

MOUNT BALDY CROSSOVER TRAIL Although it's overshadowed by its celebrated neighbors, the Mount Baldy Crossover Trail is the epitome of a gorgeous walk in the woods *Arizona Highways* v93 no6 p54 Je 2017

PACKARD MESA TRAIL *Arizona Highways* v93 no1 p54 Ja 2017

PITCH A TENT & HIT THE TRAIL: Lewis and Clark, Simon and Garfunkel, peanut butter and chocolate... there's a long list of great combinations. In the summer in the Santa Catalina Mountains, the best combo might be hiking and camping. Here's a little... *Arizona Highways* v93 no6 p38 Je 2017

PUMPHOUSE WASH *Arizona Highways* v93 no10 p54 O 2017

QUIET ON THE SET *Arizona Highways* v93 no11 p42 N 2017

Rodgers and Hammerstein *Arizona Highways* v93 no4 p2 Ap 2017

SECRET MOUNTAIN TRAIL *Arizona Highways* v93 no9 p54 S 2017

The topography *Arizona Highways* v93 no5 p2 My 2017

WALNUT CANYON TRAIL: You could spend all summer hiking the Arizona Trail If you only have a day, this scenic stroll to Fisher Point is a great option *Arizona Highways* v96 no7 p54 Jl 2017

WE KNOW IT'S COMING *Arizona Highways* v93 no3 p2 Mr 2017

WOODCHUTE TRAIL *Arizona Highways* v93 no4 p54 Ap 2017

Stiff, Lee V.
Less is more diag graph *Phi Delta Kappan* v98 no7 p55 Ap 2017

Stiff, Michael
Posthole color *Powder* v45 no4 p146 D 2016

Stiffelman, Susan
Paternidad consciente/Parenting with Presence *Publishers Weekly* v263 no46 p23 N 14 2016

Stifle joint
3 STEPS TO STRONGER STIFLES K. L. Marcella color diag *Practical Horseman* v45 no4 p48 Ap 2017

Stifter, John
THE FAMILY bw *Powder* v45 no6 p34 F 2017
Fated bw cartoon color *Powder* v45 no5 p52 Ja 2017

Stiglitz, Joseph E., 1943-
The Brutal Battle over the Euro R. Foroohar color *New York Review of Books* v63 no19 p20 D 8 2016
MONEY TRAP J. LANCHESTER cartoon *New Yorker* v92 no34 p73 O 24 2016
Titans color *Time* v189 no16/17 p94 My 1-8 2017

Stigma (Social psychology)—Prevention
THE VLOGGING CURE C. Lanning *Psychology Today* v50 no3 p68 My/Je 2017

STILES, ANDREW
Happy Warrior *National Review* v69 no2 p48 F 6 2017
The Tiny Violin *National Review* v68 no22 p52 D 5 2016

Stiles, Jackie
Breaking Points color *Sports Illustrated* v126 no7 p80 Mr 6 2017

Stiles, Julia
Riviera A. Bacle, K. Connolly et al color *Entertainment Weekly* no1482/1483 p106 S 22 2017

Stiles, Mike
Caring for Aging Loved Ones color *Consumer Reports* v82 no12 p6 D 2017

Stiles, T. J.
The ghost that haunts the book of Grant *New York Times Book Review* p15 O 15 2017
A Man of Moral Courage *New York Times Book Review* p12 O 23 2016

Still, Christopher D.
Distribution and clinical impact of functional variants in 50,726 whole-exome sequences from the DiscovEHR study chart graph *Science* v354 no6319 paaf6814-1 D 23 2016

Still hunting
Still-Hunt Rule Breaker A. Jennings color *Field & Stream* v121 no6 pW7 N 2016

Still Life With Trouble (Music)
Chords & Discords V. SNIECKUS, H. DWYER et al color *Downbeat* v84 no7 p10 Jl 2017

Still video cameras—Evaluation
Photo shootout: We tested Portrait mode with an iPhone 7 Plus fashion shoot S. OCHS and A. P. MURRAY color *Macworld -*

Digital Edition p47 D 2016

Stillbirth—Risk factors
Strep B pigment attacks placenta R. EHRENBERG bw *Science News* v190 no10 p8 N 12 2016

Stiller, John B.
Evolutionary drivers of thermoadaptation in enzyme catalysis [Cover story] bibl color graph *Science* v355 no6322 p289 Ja 20 2017

STILLER, KAREN
Lonelier Than Thou color *Walrus* v14 no8 p66 O 2017

Stillinger, Elizabeth
Revisiting The Art of the Common Man bw cartoon *Magazine Antiques* v184 no1 p110 Ja/F 2017

Stillman, Amy
Violence Raises Oil Risk in Mexico color *Bloomberg Businessweek* no4532 p31 Jl 31 2017

Stillman, David
How to Work With Generation Z S. Begley color *Time* v189 no11 p24 Mr 27 2017

STILLMAN, SARAH
GOOD BEHAVIOR cartoon *New Yorker* v92 no46 p46 Ja 23 2017

Stillman, Whit
Love & Friendship F. S. Nehme *Film Comment* v53 no1 p51 Ja/F 2017
Metropolitan *New Yorker* v92 no39 p20 N 28 2016
The Witty, Wistful Films of Whit Stillman A. PALETTA *American Conservative* v16 no5 p46 S/O 2017

STILLPASS, ZOE
Julie BEAUFILS *Interview* v46 no10 p108 D 2016/Ja 2017

Stills, Stephen, 1945-
FLAMES J. Seabrook cartoon *New Yorker* v93 no29 p38 S 25 2017

Still Star-Crossed (TV program)
America's top TV critic Matt Roush answers your burning questions M. Roush *TV Guide* v65 no31 p2 Jl 24 2017
Still Star-Crossed M. Logan *TV Guide* v65 no23 p20 My 29 2017
Still Star-Crossed M. Logan *TV Guide* v65 no31 p32 Jl 24 2017
What to Watch R. Rahman, D. Franich et al color *Entertainment Weekly* no1468/1469 p94 Je 2-9 2017

Stilz, Peter
How glass fronts deceive bats color diag *Science* v357 no6355 p977 S 8 2017

Stimson, Ellen
Christmas in New England *Yankee* v80 no6 p35 N/D 2016
A Vermont Family Christmas L. Tucker color *Yankee* v80 no6 p33 N/D 2016

Stimulants
ADDERALL C. Schwartz *New York Times Magazine* p54 O 16 2016
BUZZ WORTHY L. MCGLASHAN color *Muscle & Performance* v9 no6 p26 Je 2017

Stimulus & response (Psychology)
GETTING INSIDE FIDO'S HEAD N. Strochlic color *National Geographic* v232 no4 p16 O 2017

Stine, R. L., 1943-
R.L. STINE I. Biedenharn color *Entertainment Weekly* no1477 p62 Ag 11 2017
R.L. Stine's First Comics Work Is on Marvel's Man-Thing H. MacDonald color *Publishers Weekly* v263 no51 p8 D 12 2016
Slappy Birthday to You *Publishers Weekly* v263 no47 p108 N 21 2016

Stinear, Timothy P.
Leprosy in red squirrels bibl color diag *Science* v354 no6313 p702 N 11 2016

Stines, Yvelette
The Forgotten color *Ebony* v72 no9 p60 Jl/Ag 2017
Railroad Leads to Pulitzer for Gifted Author color *Ebony* v72 no9 p28 Jl/Ag 2017

Sting (Anatomy)
a sea of hurt A. Dance bw chart color diag *Science News* v191 no8 p28 Ap 29 2017

Sting (Performer), 1951-
The Sons Also Rise A. LANGER *Texas Monthly* v45 no2 p70 F 2017
Sting Makes a Surprise Return to Rock & Roll J. DOLAN color *Rolling Stone* no1274 p58 N 17 2016

Sting's Rock & Roll Salvation S. RODRICK bw color *Rolling Stone* no1276 p48 D 15 2016

Stingray Boats (Company)
Find your Center A. JONES *Boating World* v38 no3 p40 Mr 2017

Stingray Inc.
Stingray 186cc Deck Boat *Boating World* v38 no1 p54 Ja 2017

STINSON, LANI T.
Addressing the Gender Gap in Distinguished Speakers at Professional Ecology Conferences *BioScience* v67 no5 p464 My 2017

Stinson, Liz
FETISH ART ROCK color *Wired* v25 no4 p35 Ap 2017
GEARHEAD: STEAM POWER color *Wired* v25 no9 p46 S 2017
NEXT LIST 2017 bw graph *Wired* v25 no5 p63 My 2017
WISH LIST 2016 color *Wired* v24 no12 p45 D 2016

STINSON, MATTHEW
Salesman Xi *National Review* v69 no12 p18 Je 26 2017

STINSON, RIVAN
CALENDAR: 11/2017 color *Kiplinger's Personal Finance* v71 no11 p14 N 2017
DON'T OVERSHARE YOUR MOBILE NUMBER color *Kiplinger's Personal Finance* v71 no10 p12 O 2017
WATCH OUT FOR FLOOD-DAMAGED CARS cartoon *Kiplinger's Personal Finance* v71 no12 p11 D 2017

STINSON, TAMIA
Seoul Pocket *Cincinnati Magazine* v50 no2 p121 N 2016

Stintzi, Annick
Precursor processing for plant peptide hormone maturation by subtilisin-like serine proteinases bibl color graph *Science* v354 no6319 p1594 D 23 2016

Stipek, Deborah
advice every new mom needs [Cover story] color *Parents* v92 no7 p32 Jl 2017

Stipes, Jesse
Hockin' Nation [Cover story] J. Mankin color *Spin to Win Rodeo* v21 no4 p50 Je 2017

Stirling, Andy
Nuclear power: Serious risks *Science* v354 no6316 p1112 D 2 2016

Stirling, Lindsey, 1986-
Lindsey Stirling M. Hagan color *Current Biography* v78 no9 p76 S 2017

Stirling, Mark
Complex multifault rupture during the 2016 Mw 7.8 Kaikōura earthquake, New Zealand color map *Science* v356 no6334 p154 Ap 14 2017

Stirling Prize
Newport Street Art Gallery Wins 2016 RIBA Stirling Prize A. KLIMOSKI *Architectural Record* v204 no11 p29 N 2016

Stirone, Shannon
HOW AN INTERPLANETARY MISSION CHANGED THE WORLD cartoon *Astronomy* v45 no10 p56 O 2017
The New Star Wars color *New Republic* v248 no6 p10 Je 2017

Stirrups
Margaret's Blog M. Freeman *Dressage Today* p14 My 2017
Three Good Seats, One Jumping Ahead G. H. Morris color *Practical Horseman* v45 no1 p10 Ja 2017
'What the Horse Takes, the Rider Gives' G. H. Morris color *Practical Horseman* v45 no4 p12 Ap 2017

Stirrups—Evaluation
Stirrup Style color *American Cowboy* v23 no6 p42 Ap/My 2017
Tack Room color *Practical Horseman* v45 no3 p70 Mr 2017

Stitch Fix Inc.
How One Clothing Company Blends AI and Human Expertise H. J. Wilson, P. Daugherty et al *Harvard Business Review Digital Articles* p2 N 21 2016
What Stitch Fix Figured Out About Mass Customization S. Ahuja *Harvard Business Review Digital Articles* p2 My 26 2015

Stitches (Sewing)
the pleasures of Handwork M. E. Polson color *Arts & Crafts Homes & the Revival* v11 no5 p33 Wint 2017

Stites, Jessica
40 More Years... color *In These Times* v40 no11 p50 N 2016
The Handmaid and the Despot *In These Times* v41 no5 p38 My 2017

Stith, Susan
Country Lore *Mother Earth News* no281 p84 Ap/My 2017

Stivers, Valerie
FROM RUSSIA WITH LATTES color *Bloomberg Businessweek* no4534 p42 Ag 14 2017

St. James, Dorothy
Asking for Truffle: A Southern Chocolate Shop Mystery *Publishers Weekly* v264 no31 p64 Jl 31 2017

St. John, Allen
The Real Voice Behind Siri il *Consumer Reports* v82 no3 p50 Mr 2017
Shop Online With Confidence graph il *Consumer Reports* v82 no12 p20 D 2017

St. John, David
The Way It Is *New York Times Magazine* p15 Ag 13 2017

St. John's University (Collegeville, Minn.)
His Bleak Materials J. Meyers bw *Commonweal* v144 no12 p18 Jl 7 2017
Week 4 color *Sports Illustrated* v127 no5 p62 Ag 14 2017

St. Laurent, Ron
Mount a switch motor horizontally color *Model Railroader* v84 no6 p56 Je 2017

Stochastic Fancy (Short story)
STOCHASTIC FANCY C. J. ANDERS cartoon *Wired* v25 no1 p34 Ja 2017

Stock, James
Reforming the U.S. coal leasing program color graph *Science* v354 no6316 p1096 D 2 2016

Stock, Kyle
Americas bw color *Bloomberg Businessweek* no4529 p8 Jl 3 2017
Americas color *Bloomberg Businessweek* no4535 p9 Ag 28 2017
Asia color *Bloomberg Businessweek* no4538 p11 S 18 2017
Asia color graph *Bloomberg Businessweek* no4529 p9 Jl 3 2017
Cost of Running Harvard color diag *Bloomberg Businessweek* no4535 p19 Ag 28 2017
Downs color *Bloomberg Businessweek* no4494 p15 O 10 2016
Europe color *Bloomberg Businessweek* no4529 p8 Jl 3 2017
Europe color *Bloomberg Businessweek* no4530 p9 Jl 17 2017
The Future of Fishing color *Bloomberg Businessweek* no4531 p63 Jl 24 2017
IN BRIEF color *Bloomberg Businessweek* no4528 p6 Je 26 2017
IN BRIEF color graph *Bloomberg Businessweek* no4531 p6 Jl 24 2017
JUST DO IT REDO IT TRY NOT TO UNDO IT DON'T LOSE TO ADIDAS color *Bloomberg Businessweek* no4523 p42 My 22 2017
Movers bw cartoon color *Bloomberg Businessweek* no4497 p15 O 31 2016
Movers color *Bloomberg Businessweek* no4509 p11 Ja 30 2017
Movers color graph *Bloomberg Businessweek* no4524 p13 My 29 2017
This Is What Climate Change Sounds Like color *Bloomberg Businessweek* no4535 p20 Ag 28 2017
Ups color *Bloomberg Businessweek* no4494 p15 O 10 2016
Walk the Walk color *Bloomberg Businessweek* no4503 p72 D 12 2016

Stock car drivers
WALL? WHAT WALL? A. Lawrence color *Sports Illustrated* v126 no5 p74 F 13 2017

Stock car racing
See also
   NASCAR (Association)
Watch Legendary Pro Stocks From the 1970s and 1980s Run Again T. Taylor color *Hot Rod* v70 no7 p70 Jl 2017

Stock cars (Automobiles)
THE GLORY OF PENSKE AND DONOHUE color *Road & Track* v68 no5 p18 D 2016/Ja 2017

Stock charts (Finance)
Blue Chips Gain Advantage chart diag *Money* v46 no9 p88 O 2017
Focus Shifts Back to Income chart diag *Money* v46 no7 p78 Ag 2017
Stocks Hit a Small Glitch I. Salisbury chart *Money* v46 no9 p89 O 2017

Stock exchanges
See also
   Bull markets
   Stock exchanges & current events
ASH CASH'S LAWS FOR FINANCIAL SUCCESS J. MCKIN-

NEY color *Black Enterprise* v47 no8 p24 Jl/Ag 2017

The Factors That Lead to High CEO Pay G. Gavett *Harvard Business Review Digital Articles* p2 My 22 2015

How to Thrive as Market Cycles Return J. K. GLASSMAN color *Kiplinger's Personal Finance* v71 no6 p20 Je 2017

IS THE STOCK MARKET TOO HOT? map *Fortune* v176 no3 p15 S 1 2017

Milking Your Stocks J. DOBOSZ color *Forbes* v199 no7 p132 Je 29 2017

Stock-Market Highs Pose Vexing Questions for the Soon-to-Be Retired L. Shen color *Time* v190 no12 p28 S 25 2017

WHEN WILL TRENDS CHANGE? A. Kluis *Successful Farming* v115 no5 p18 Mid-Mr 2017

Why Am I Lagging? Blame It on 2015 K. KRISTOF chart *Kiplinger's Personal Finance* v70 no12 p56 D 2016

WORRIED ABOUT THE STOCK MARKET? D. FONDA cartoon *Kiplinger's Personal Finance* v71 no6 p13 Je 2017

Stock exchanges & current events

MORE UPS THAN DOWNS A. GARA color graph *Forbes* v200 no3 p52 S 28 2017

Stock exchanges—China

A Dozen Ways to Cash In on China J. K. GLASSMAN color *Kiplinger's Personal Finance* v71 no12 p14 D 2017

Where It's Still a Mom and Pop Market color *Bloomberg Businessweek* no4540 p30 O 2 2017

Why China's Market Crash Is So Unsurprising L. Yueh *Harvard Business Review Digital Articles* p2 Ja 12 2016

Stock exchanges—History—21st century

TRUMP, BREXIT, AND THE CHINA SLOWDOWN G. Smith color *Fortune* v174 no8 p24 D 15 2016

Stock exchanges—News briefs

The Sky's the Limit for Amazon's Stock J. Milliot chart *Publishers Weekly* v264 no28 p11 Jl 10 2017

Stock exchanges—United States

DONOR-ADVISED FUNDS SOAR ALONG WITH MARKETS E. Wine color *Forbes* v198 no7 p82 N 29 2016

GRAIN DROPS TO BARGAIN-BASEMENT PRICES: EXPECT GLOBAL DEMAND TO SOAR A. Kluis *Successful Farming* v115 no11 p18 S 2017

A STOCK-MARKET SKEPTIC EYES THE TRUMP BUMP color *Fortune* v175 no8 p40 Je 15 2017

When Everything Is Working, Sit Tight J. R. KOSNETT color *Kiplinger's Personal Finance* v71 no7 p53 Jl 2017

Where to Invest in 2017 A. K. SMITH cartoon graph *Kiplinger's Personal Finance* v71 no1 p42 Ja 2017

Stock exchanges—United States—History—21st century

TRUMP-IMPERVIOUS MARKET K. FISHER *Forbes* v198 no9 p100 D 30 2016

TRUMP'S MARKET RALLY J. Surowiecki cartoon *New Yorker* v93 no3 p25 Mr 6 2017

Why the Stock Market Is Stacked Against Him S. Tully color diag *Fortune* v174 no8 p88 D 15 2016

Stock funds

See also

Exchange traded funds

Be Patient With This Dividend Fund N. S. HUANG chart *Kiplinger's Personal Finance* v71 no10 p61 O 2017

The Fed Primes the Stock Pump T. Tepper chart *Money* v45 no10 p96 N 2016

Funds That Let Their Brood Grow J. Waggoner color *Money* v45 no10 p42 N 2016

Politics Afflicts Our Favorite Health Fund N. S. HUANG chart *Kiplinger's Personal Finance* v71 no4 p61 Ap 2017

We Welcome a New Dividend Fund N. S. HUANG chart *Kiplinger's Personal Finance* v71 no1 p55 Ja 2017

Stock funds—Management

A Fidelity Manager Takes a Break N. S. HUANG chart *Kiplinger's Personal Finance* v71 no7 p59 Jl 2017

Stock options

CEOs with Lots of Stock Options Are More Likely to Break Laws D. Minor *Harvard Business Review Digital Articles* p2 My 26 2016

Milking Your Stocks J. DOBOSZ color *Forbes* v199 no7 p132 Je 29 2017

Research: Firms Give More Stock Options When They're Committing Fraud A. Call, S. Kedia et al color *Harvard Business*

Review Digital Articles p2 Ja 26 2017

Stock ownership—United States

Warren Buffett Is Betting the Airline Oligopoly Is Here to Stay M. Schmalz *Harvard Business Review Digital Articles* p2 N 17 2016

Stock price forecasting

4 BIG TRENDS YOU CAN RIDE FOR YEARS J. Waggoner color diag *Money* v46 no1 p70 Ja/F 2017

Investors: Don't Fear Higher Rates J. J. SIEGEL *Kiplinger's Personal Finance* v70 no12 p52 D 2016

TOP PICKS FROM TOP PROS C. Bigda color diag *Money* v46 no1 p58 Ja/F 2017

What to Own in an Expensive Market color *Kiplinger's Personal Finance* v71 no7 p50 Jl 2017

You Can't Retire On the Trump Bump S. Woolley cartoon *Bloomberg Businessweek* no4514 p38 Mr 13 2017

Stock price indexes

A Financial Fund Heats Up D. FONDA chart *Kiplinger's Personal Finance* v71 no6 p56 Je 2017

Indexes graph *Bloomberg Businessweek* no4522 p46 My 15 2017

Industry Stocks Were Mixed in 2016 J. Milliot chart *Publishers Weekly* v264 no2 p11 Ja 9 2017

My 10 Top Stock Picks for 2017 J. K. GLASSMAN chart *Kiplinger's Personal Finance* v71 no1 p19 Ja 2017

Who's Afraid of Low Volatility? P. Coy and W. Soong cartoon graph *Bloomberg Businessweek* no4533 p23 Ag 7 2017

Stock prices

See also

Price-earnings ratio

AIRLINES' STOCK RALLY SHOWS IT'S BETTER TO BE GOOD THAN NICE A. Vandermey diag *Fortune* v175 no7 p16 Je 1 2017

Amazon Is the Big First-Quarter Winner J. Milliot chart *Publishers Weekly* v264 no15 p16 Ap 10 2017

How to Invest When Rates Rise J. Waggoner diag *Money* v46 no5 p38 Je 2017

Investing With a Conscience A. K. SMITH chart color *Kiplinger's Personal Finance* v71 no7 p54 Jl 2017

Join the Race to $1 Trillion Stocks J. K. GLASSMAN chart color *Kiplinger's Personal Finance* v71 no10 p18 O 2017

The Sky's the Limit for Amazon's Stock J. Milliot chart *Publishers Weekly* v264 no28 p11 Jl 10 2017

When Is a Bubble Not a Bubble? Why This Tech-Stock Boom Is Different P. J. Lim color *Time* v189 no24 p20 Je 26 2017

Stock prices—United States

5 Signals to Look For If You're Worried About the Market I. Salisbury *Money* v46 no8 p35 S 2017

"It's Going to Collapse" and Other Dire Warnings About Stocks A. Nova color *Money* v46 no8 p33 S 2017

Stock repurchasing

GM's Stock Buyback Is Bad for America and the Company W. Lazonick and M. Hopkins *Harvard Business Review Digital Articles* p2 Mr 11 2015

Numbers Show Apple Shareholders Have Already Gotten Plenty W. Lazonick *Harvard Business Review Digital Articles* p2 O 16 2014

Stock Buybacks Aren't Hurting Innovation G. Satell *Harvard Business Review Digital Articles* p2 Mr 31 2015

STOCKS THAT DODGE THE BUYBACK BLUES R. Derousseau chart color diag *Fortune* v175 no6 p29 My 1 2017

Stock repurchasing—Government policy

Clinton's Proposals on Stock Buybacks Don't Go Far Enough W. Lazonick *Harvard Business Review Digital Articles* p2 Ag 11 2015

Stockbrokers

SHOWCASE: FEATURED BROKERAGE BOATS color *Sea Magazine* v109 no7 p53 Jl 2017

SHOWCASE FEATURED BROKERAGE BOATS *Sea Magazine* v108 no12 p57 D 2016

Welcome Home *Washingtonian Magazine* v52 no1 p188 O 2016

When Your Broker Goes Rogue K. LANKFORD *Kiplinger's Personal Finance* v71 no3 p36 Mr 2017

Stockbrokers—China

Where It's Still a Mom and Pop Market color *Bloomberg Businessweek* no4540 p30 O 2 2017

Stockbrokers—Corrupt practices

A STOCK TRADER LOSES IN COURT. IT'S NO REASON TO CELEBRATE S. Gandel color *Fortune* v174 no6 p14 N 1 2016

Stockbrokers—Employment

Where a Graying Herd Still Thunders H. Son cartoon *Bloomberg Businessweek* no4503 p34 D 12 2016

Stock car drivers—Charts, diagrams, etc.

Magnificent Sevens T. Keith chart color *Sports Illustrated* v125 no18 p19 D 5 2016

STOCKEN, NICOLA

A ROSE FOR ROMANCE color diag *House Beautiful* p148 Ag 2017

Stock exchanges—Charts, diagrams, etc.

Markets Reactions D. Burger and L. Kawa graph *Bloomberg Businessweek* no4536 p31 S 4 2017

Stock funds—Charts, diagrams, etc.

Trump Bump Suffers Slump T. Tepper chart *Money* v46 no5 p76 Je 2017

A Value Fund Leaps Ahead of Its Rivals R. ERMEY chart *Kiplinger's Personal Finance* v71 no2 p62 F 2017

Stockholder, Jessica

The Artist's Artist A Rauschenberg Symposium color *Art in America* v105 no1 p44 Ja 2017

Stockholder wealth

All Hail Medium-Term Planning D. Houlder and N. Nandkishore *Harvard Business Review Digital Articles* p2 Je 23 2016

The False Premise of the Shareholder Value Debate R. L. Martin *Harvard Business Review Digital Articles* p2 S 26 2016

Reclaiming the Idea of Shareholder Value M. J. Mauboussin and A. Rappaport *Harvard Business Review Digital Articles* p2 Jl 1 2016

WHEN SHAREHOLDERS ARE SPECTATORS R. Derousseau color diag *Fortune* v175 no2 p40 F 1 2017

Stockholders

Are We Giving Shareholders Too Much Power? A. Ignatius *Harvard Business Review* v95 no3 p8 My/Je 2017

Serving Shareholders Doesn't Mean Putting Profit Above All Else O. Hart and L. Zingales *Harvard Business Review Digital Articles* p2 O 12 2017

Stockholders—Legal status, laws, etc.

What's Missing from Annual Reports G. Kenny *Harvard Business Review Digital Articles* p2 D 19 2014

Stockholders—United States

HOW INVESTORS WIN IF CASH COMES HOME S. Tully diag *Fortune* v175 no2 p36 F 1 2017

Stockholm (Sweden)—Description & travel

taking stockholm E. Goldberg bw color *Bon Appetit* v61 no11 p84 N 2016

Stockholm (Sweden)—Buildings, structures, etc.

Color Theory A. MARTINS *Architectural Record* v205 no9 p98 S 2017

Stockman, David Alan, 1946-

David Stockman's Latest Target: The feisty contrarian takes on the 'War Party' R. W. MERRY *American Conservative* v16 no5 p9 S/O 2017

Stock price indexes—Charts, diagrams, etc.

Economic Data Slows Stocks chart diag *Money* v46 no5 p74 Je 2017

Focus Shifts Back to Income chart diag *Money* v46 no7 p78 Ag 2017

Stocks Look Past Decent Earnings chart diag *Money* v45 no11 p88 D 2016

Tech Shares on a Tear chart diag *Money* v46 no6 p76 Jl 2017

We Welcome a New Dividend Fund N. S. HUANG chart *Kiplinger's Personal Finance* v71 no1 p55 Ja 2017

Stocks (Cooking)

Building a Better Dumpling img *New York* v49 no25 p109 D 12 2016

Stocks (Finance)

See also

Blue chip stocks

Dividends

Large capitalization stocks

Mid-capitalization stocks

10 Great All-Weather Stocks D. FONDA chart color *Kiplinger's Personal Finance* v71 no2 p52 F 2017

The Best Investment I Ever Made K. PALMER color *AARP: The Magazine* v59 no2A p34 F/Mr 2016

THE BEST LIST [Cover story] bw color *Kiplinger's Personal Finance* v71 no12 p58 D 2017

Big-Cap Growth Stocks Are Back N. S. HUANG chart *Kiplinger's Personal Finance* v71 no6 p55 Je 2017

A Bird in the Hand D. WESTON, P. SCHMIDT et al color graph *Kiplinger's Personal Finance* v71 no2 p6 F 2017

BITCOIN INVESTORS ARE FEELING GOLDEN, FOR NOW R. Hackett diag *Fortune* v176 no5 p17 O 1 2017

Buy Retail Stocks at Wholesale Prices J. K. GLASSMAN chart *Kiplinger's Personal Finance* v71 no5 p18 My 2017

Can This Fallen Biotech Be Revived? K. KRISTOF *Kiplinger's Personal Finance* v71 no5 p61 My 2017

A GIFT FOR KIDS THAT PAYS DIVIDENDS T. Stanger *Consumer Reports* v81 no12 p31 D 2016

I'm Still Cheering for GM and Gilead K. KRISTOF color *Kiplinger's Personal Finance* v71 no2 p61 F 2017

It's Okay to Reach for Yield J. R. KOSNETT *Kiplinger's Personal Finance* v71 no10 p60 O 2017

The Kip 25 Funds DELIVER N. S. HUANG chart color *Kiplinger's Personal Finance* v71 no5 p50 My 2017

Low Fees, Low Minimum, Big Return R. ERMEY chart *Kiplinger's Personal Finance* v71 no6 p57 Je 2017

Our Top Dividend Picks D. FONDA chart color *Kiplinger's Personal Finance* v71 no12 p50 D 2017

Profit From Being a Patient Investor J. K. GLASSMAN chart *Kiplinger's Personal Finance* v71 no8 p17 Ag 2017

Ray DALIO A. Carter color *Esquire* p62 O 2017

Riding the Highs and Lows of a Fickle Market E. AMBROSE color *AARP: The Magazine* v59 no4A p24 Je/Jl 2016

An Rx for Healthier Gains D. FONDA chart *Kiplinger's Personal Finance* v71 no12 p54 D 2017

SAVING FOR YOUR LONG-TERM GOAL: Q&A WITH A FINANCIAL EXPERT *Scholastic Choices* p4 O 2017 Supplement

TAKING STOCK K. Olsen color *Washingtonian Magazine* v52 no7 p129 Ap 2017

Tech IPOs Want to Get Ahead of Trump A. Barinka *Bloomberg Businessweek* no4500 p33 N 21 2016

Three Ways to Join in Europe's Recovery R. ERMEY chart *Kiplinger's Personal Finance* v71 no8 p55 Ag 2017

UNDERSTANDING HOW MY MONEY CAN GROW *Scholastic Choices* p6 O 2017 Supplement

The Very First Mistake Most Startup Founders Make N. Wasserman and T. Hellmann *Harvard Business Review Digital Articles* p2 F 23 2016

What I'm Telling Worried Readers J. R. KOSNETT *Kiplinger's Personal Finance* v71 no5 p62 My 2017

When to Step Back From Stocks J. Waggoner diag *Money* v46 no9 p51 O 2017

When Will the Bull Market End? A. K. SMITH color *Kiplinger's Personal Finance* v71 no10 p59 O 2017

Where to Invest Now A. K. SMITH cartoon graph *Kiplinger's Personal Finance* v71 no7 p46 Jl 2017

Why I Think Apple Is a Bargain *Kiplinger's Personal Finance* v71 no12 p49 D 2017

Stocks (Finance)—China

A Dozen Ways to Cash In on China J. K. GLASSMAN color *Kiplinger's Personal Finance* v71 no12 p14 D 2017

WHERE BULLS ARE CHINA-SHOPPING L. Shen color diag *Fortune* v176 no2 p23 Ag 1 2017

Stocks (Finance)—Evaluation

Cheap Stocks for a Pricey Market T. PETRUNO color *Kiplinger's Personal Finance* v71 no8 p50 Ag 2017

Finding Bargains Across the Pond N. S. HUANG chart *Kiplinger's Personal Finance* v71 no8 p54 Ag 2017

Stock X-Ray: Priceline P. J. Lim color diag *Money* v46 no9 p52 O 2017

What 7 Top Pros Are Doing Now D. FONDA color *Kiplinger's Personal Finance* v71 no8 p42 Ag 2017

Stocks (Finance)—Law & legislation

Alphabet Soup N. S. HUANG *Kiplinger's Personal Finance* v71 no7 p58 Jl 2017

Stocks (Finance)—Management

Index everything? Not so fast N. S. HUANG cartoon *Kiplinger's Personal Finance* v71 no3 p44 Mr 2017

Stocks (Finance)—Marketing

Don't Let Current Events Spook You K. KRISTOF *Kiplinger's Personal Finance* v71 no11 p57 N 2017

Stocks (Finance)—Prices

10 GREAT STOCKS FOR THE NEXT 10 YEARS D. FONDA color *Kiplinger's Personal Finance* v70 no12 p46 D 2016

8 STOCKS TO BUY NOW D. FONDA color *Kiplinger's Personal Finance* v71 no1 p50 Ja 2017

After the Polls graph *Bloomberg Businessweek* no4500 p38 N 21 2016

... AND 5 TO SELL D. FONDA cartoon *Kiplinger's Personal Finance* v71 no1 p51 Ja 2017

AVOIDING A STEEP DESCENT R. Derousseau color diag *Fortune* v175 no4 p44 Mr 15 2017

A COFFEE STOCK LOSES ITS BUZZ R. Derousseau color diag *Fortune* v175 no3 p36 Mr 1 2017

The False Premise of the Shareholder Value Debate R. L. Martin *Harvard Business Review Digital Articles* p2 S 26 2016

Foreign Funds Stay on a Roll T. Tepper chart *Money* v46 no3 p77 Ap 2017

Movers K. Stock cartoon color *Bloomberg Businessweek* no4518 p13 Ap 10 2017

PLAY YOUR CARDS RIGHT M. Heimer color diag *Fortune* v174 no7 p30 D 1 2016

STOCKS THAT ARE BETTER-OFF SINGLE L. Shen color *Fortune* v175 no4 p48 Mr 15 2017

Stocks to Keep a Nest Egg Growing J. Wieczner color diag *Fortune* v174 no8 p108 D 15 2016

TOP PICKS FROM TOP PROS C. Bigda color diag *Money* v46 no1 p58 Ja/F 2017

Under new management J. Quigley and B. Bartenstein color *Bloomberg Businessweek* no4496 p18 O 24 2016

Wall Street Rewards CEOs Who Talk About Their Strategies R. Whittington, B. Yakis-Douglas et al *Harvard Business Review Digital Articles* p2 D 28 2015

Why Data Breaches Don't Hurt Stock Prices E. Kvochko and R. Pant *Harvard Business Review Digital Articles* p2 Mr 31 2015

Worrying About the Bear? Don't J. K. GLASSMAN chart *Kiplinger's Personal Finance* v71 no4 p16 Ap 2017

Stocks (Finance)—Prices—Economic aspects

The Fed Keeps Its Eye on Swings in the Stock Market M. Boesler color *Bloomberg Businessweek* no4518 p15 Ap 10 2017

Stocks (Finance)—Prices—United States

SNAP IS CLOWN CAR 2.0 D. Lyons color *Fortune* v175 no4 p72 Mr 15 2017

Stock X-Ray: H&R Block I. Salisbury diag *Money* v46 no4 p36 My 2017

Stocks (Finance)—Rate of return

See also

Small capitalization stocks—Rate of return

HERE ARE FIVE STOCKS—TO BE HOPEFUL FOR K. FISHER *Forbes* v198 no7 p62 N 29 2016

Stocks (Finance)—Ratings & rankings

Stocks Hit a Small Glitch I. Salisbury chart *Money* v46 no9 p89 O 2017

Stocks (Finance)—Research

One Very Important Footnote S. H. e. Costa bw *Bloomberg Businessweek* no4493 p51 O 3 2016

Stocks (Finance)—Social aspects

HOW TO INVEST, WHOEVER WINS T. Tepper diag *Fortune* v174 no6 p43 N 1 2016

Stocks (Finance)—Study & teaching

Everybody Into The Dark Pool A. Massa color *Bloomberg Businessweek* no4519 p45 Ap 24 2017

Stocks (Finance)—Taxation

Clinton's Proposals on Stock Buybacks Don't Go Far Enough W. Lazonick *Harvard Business Review Digital Articles* p2 Ag 11 2015

Stocks (Finance)—United States

7 Great All-American Stocks T. PETRUNO chart color *Kiplinger's Personal Finance* v71 no5 p58 My 2017

8 STOCKS TO BUY NOW D. FONDA color *Kiplinger's Personal Finance* v71 no1 p50 Ja 2017

... AND 5 TO SELL D. FONDA cartoon *Kiplinger's Personal Finance* v71 no1 p51 Ja 2017

Don't Dump Your Dividend Stocks J. R. KOSNETT *Kiplinger's Personal Finance* v71 no3 p60 Mr 2017

Great Dividends, Fair Prices T. PETRUNO color *Kiplinger's Personal Finance* v71 no10 p56 O 2017

HOW TO INVEST, WHOEVER WINS T. Tepper diag *Fortune* v174 no6 p43 N 1 2016

INVESTOR'S MIDYEAR GUIDE J. Wieczner diag *Fortune* v175 no7 p49 Je 1 2017

Research: How Investors' Reading Habits Influence Stock Prices A. Fedyk *Harvard Business Review Digital Articles* p2 S 2 2016

U.S. Stocks Win Again M. SCHIFFRES chart *Kiplinger's Personal Finance* v71 no3 p52 Mr 2017

Why I'm Hanging On to a Loser K. KRISTOF *Kiplinger's Personal Finance* v71 no10 p62 O 2017

STOCKS, CHRISTOPHER

Act of Faith color *Architectural Digest* v74 no4 p76 Ap 2017

Stocks (Finance)—Charts, diagrams, etc.

13 STOCKS FOR THE TECH REVOLUTION D. FONDA cartoon chart color *Kiplinger's Personal Finance* v71 no4 p52 Ap 2017

Investors Focus on Fundamentals chart diag *Money* v46 no4 p70 My 2017

U.S. Stocks Win Again M. SCHIFFRES chart *Kiplinger's Personal Finance* v71 no3 p52 Mr 2017

Stocks (Finance)—Prices—Charts, diagrams, etc.

THE FUND REPORT D. I. Salisbury diag *Money* v46 no1 p108 Ja/F 2017

Tech Moves to Head of the Class chart diag *Money* v46 no3 p76 Ap 2017

WATCHING THE DOW LEAP J. Wieczner diag *Fortune* v175 no2 p84 F 1 2017

Stocks (Finance)—United States—Charts, diagrams, etc.

The New Bond King Is Stressing Safety N. S. HUANG chart *Kiplinger's Personal Finance* v71 no3 p61 Mr 2017

We Add a Real Estate Fund D. FONDA chart *Kiplinger's Personal Finance* v71 no3 p62 Mr 2017

Stockton, Angela

One church? *U.S. Catholic* v82 no7 p5 Jl 2017

Stockton, Frank

A meal for many color *U.S. Catholic* v82 no6 p5 Je 2017

STOCKTON, NICK

The Man Who Fell for Earth bw color graph *Wired* v25 no4 p46 Ap 2017

THE NEW FOMO cartoon *Wired* v25 no9 p68 S 2017

OUT OF THIS WORLD: SCOTT KELLY'S YEAR IN SPACE bw color *Wired* v25 no9 p15 S 2017

Stockwell, Norman

An Appeal for Thoughtfulness bw cartoon color *Progressive* v81 no4 p63 Ap/My 2017

Assassination of a Saint: The Plot to Murder Óscar Romero and the Quest to Bring His Killers to Justice/Transitional Justice in Latin America: The Uneven Road from Impunity towards Accountability/The Blood of Emmett Till color *Progressive* p60 D 2016/Ja 2017

Disaster Area: U.S. Policy in the Middle East color *Progressive* v81 no2 p37 F 2017

'Every Day, There Is Some New Shock': An Interview with Naomi Klein, on Her New Book and Donald Trump color *Progressive* v81 no6 p60 Ag/S 2017

'Great Things Come Out of Discomfort': An Interview with Our Revolution's Nina Turner color *Progressive* v81 no7 p60 O/N 2017

'It's a Scary Time' bw *Progressive* v81 no4 p60 Ap/My 2017

The Progressive color *Progressive* v81 no4 p2 Ap/My 2017

The Progressive color *Progressive* v81 no7 p37 O/N 2017

Public Broadcasting at Fifty: From a Proud Beginning to an Uncertain Future bw *Progressive* v81 no7 p54 O/N 2017

Retrieving Bones, Reviving Memories color *Progressive* v81 no2 p32 F 2017

The Russian Revolution at 100 Years color *Progressive* v81 no6 p63 Ag/S 2017

'This Country Is at a Tipping Point' cartoon color *Progressive* v81 no10 p35 N 2016

'This Is like My 9/11 All Over Again' color *Progressive* p37 D 2016/Ja 2017

Tough Love for White America *Progressive* v81 no3 p38 Mr 2017

Stockwell, Rebecca E.

Emergence and spread of a human-transmissible multidrug-resistant nontuberculous mycobacterium bibl diag graph *Science* v354 no6313 p751 N 11 2016

Stoddard, Mary Caswell

Avian egg shape: Form, function, and evolution color diag *Science* v356 no6344 p1249 Je 23 2017

Stoddard, Stephen

#trailchat color *Backpacker* v45 no2 p10 Mr 2017

Stodden, Victoria

Enhancing reproducibility for computational methods bibl color *Science* v354 no6317 p1240 D 9 2016

Stodder, Sarah

19 THINGS YOU REALLY OUGHT TO DO THIS MONTH *Washingtonian Magazine* v52 no1 p33 O 2016

STOECKL, KRISTINA

The Russian Orthodox Church's Conservative Crusade *Current History* v116 no792 p271 O 2017

STOFFERS, CARL

Are We Heading Toward a New COLD WAR? *New York Times Upfront* v149 no3 p18 O 10 2016

Equal Pay for Equal Play? *New York Times Upfront* v149 no7 p16 Ja 9 2017

FAKE NEWS FOOLING MILLIONS! *New York Times Upfront* v149 no7 p6 Ja 9 2017

Hidden AD-gendas? *New York Times Upfront* v149 no11 p14 Ap 3 2017

A Painful Legacy *New York Times Upfront* v149 no8 p6 Ja 30 2017

Smoke Signals *New York Times Upfront* v149 no5 p10 N 21 2016

Star-Spangled PROTEST [Cover story] *New York Times Upfront* v149 no3 p8 O 10 2016

STOFFREGEN, NEIL

Simmer In Style color *Treasures* v5 no5 p38 Ap/My 2016

Stohl, Margaret

Royce Rolls *Publishers Weekly* v264 no5 p205 Ja 30 2017

Stohr, Greg

A Cake Dispute Rises To the Highest Court color *Bloomberg Businessweek* no4539 p43 S 25 2017

Stoicism

AT HOME WITH THE STOICS: Do Stoic philosophy and the family mix? The writings of Seneca show how the model Stoic, relying on nothing but his own mind, can still be a loving family man L. Gloyn *History Today* v67 no9 p48 S 2017

Waiting With Kipling R. HADAS *American Scholar* v86 no1 p18 Wint 2017

Stoin, Stoin M.

BORN OF THE MUD: THE STORY OF A COLLECTION B. PAUL color *Phi Kappa Phi Forum* v97 no1 p13 Spr 2017

Stojic, Lovorka

Aging increases cell-to-cell transcriptional variability upon immune stimulation color diag graph *Science* v355 no6332 p1433 Mr 31 2017

Neurodevelopmental protein Musashi-1 interacts with the Zika genome and promotes viral replication diag *Science* v357 no6346 p83 Jl 7 2017

Stoker, Bram

IS THAT WHAT THEY SHOULD LOOK LIKE? bw color *Reader's Digest* v190 no1134 p98 O 2017

STOKES, COLIN

TRANSLATING THE NOISES MY RADIATOR MAKES cartoon *New Yorker* v92 no47 p29 Ja 30 2017

Stokes, Dale

Turbulence in breaking waves *Physics Today* v69 no10 p86 O 2016

STOKES, DOUGLAS M.

Chicken Acceleration? APA Puts Imprimatur on Credulous Psi Book *Skeptical Inquirer* v41 no3 p6 My/Je 2017

Genetic Engineering through Music? *Skeptical Inquirer* v41 no5 p11 S/O 2017

Stokes, Jon

Railway Post Office color *Model Railroader* v84 no4 p22 Ap 2017

Stokes, Kendal

Dream Buddy on a Trail Ride cartoon *Horse & Rider* v56 no3 p72 Mr 2017

STOKES, LINDSAY

WHY OUR BODY DESTROY ITSELF bw color *Christianity Today* v61 no1 p60 Ja/F 2017

STOKESBURY, MICHAEL J. W.

Envisioning the Future of Aquatic Animal Tracking: Technology, Science, and Application *BioScience* v67 no10 p884 O 2017

Stokke, Katherine

Staying Ahead of the Curve *Parks & Recreation* v52 no3 p18 Mr 2017

Stoklosa, Alexander

STRANGER THINGS color *Car & Driver* v62 no10 p13 Ap 2017

Stokstad, Erik

Engineered crops could have it made in the shade color *Science* v354 no6314 p816 N 18 2016

European bee study fuels debate over pesticide ban color *Science* v356 no6345 p1321 Je 30 2017

HOW TO BE HEARD *Science* v355 no6325 p572 F 10 2017

A lifeline for Greek science—or living on borrowed time? color *Science* v353 no6307 p1481 S 30 2016

New crop pest takes Africa at lightning speed color map *Science* v356 no6337 p473 My 5 2017

Norway seeks to stamp out prion disease color map *Science* v356 no6333 p12 Ap 7 2017

Revelations about rhythm of life rewarded color *Science* v357 no6359 p18 O 6 2017

SAVING EUROPE'S SALAMANDERS color map *Science* v357 no6348 p242 Jl 21 2017

Sea trash traps face doubts *Science* v356 no6339 p671 My 19 2017

Surge in right whale deaths raises alarms color map *Science* v357 no6353 p740 Ag 25 2017

TAMING RABIES color graph map *Science* v355 no6322 p238 Ja 20 2017

U.K. scientists gird for future break with EU color graph *Science* v355 no6330 p1107 Mr 17 2017

U.N. biodiversity group confronts cash crunch color *Science* v355 no6332 p1358 Mr 31 2017

Who will watch the Amazon? *Science* v356 no6338 p569 My 12 2017

Stolarski, Richard

Ralph J. Cicerone *Physics Today* v70 no2 p67 F 2017

Stole, Bryn

THREE DAYS IN AMERICA color *Wired* v24 no12 p114 D 2016

Stoll, Corey

The Strain J. Halterman *TV Guide* v65 no31 p36 Jl 24 2017

Stoll, Steven

Ramp Hollow: The Ordeal of Appalachia S. JONES color *Publishers Weekly* v264 no36 p79 S 4 2017

Stolle, Fred

The extent of forest in dryland biomes [Cover story] chart map *Science* v356 no6338 p635 My 12 2017

Stoller, James K.

Why The Best Hospitals Are Managed by Doctors *Harvard Business Review Digital Articles* p2 D 27 2016

STOLLER, MATT

AFTER THE FUMBLE color *Nation* v304 no9 p49 Mr 20 2017

THE RETURN OF MONOPOLY color *New Republic* v248 no8/9 p18 Ag/S 2017

Stoller, Nick

Friends From College I. Ratledge *TV Guide* v65 no25 p24 Je 2017

Stolling, Russ

Railway Post Office color *Model Railroader* v84 no6 p18 Je 2017

Stolovitzky, Gustavo

Predicting human olfactory perception from chemical features of odor molecules bibl diag graph *Science* v355 no6327 p820 F 24 2017

Stoltz, Steve

CUTT AND RUN 2.0 B. LOVETT and G. BETHGE color *Outdoor Life* v224 no3 pT1 Ap 2017

Stolzenburg, Sabine

Click chemistry enables preclinical evaluation of targeted epigenetic therapies diag *Science* v356 no6345 p1397 Je 30 2017

Stomach

TUMMY TROUBLE TOOLBOX S. LIAO *Better Homes & Gardens* v94 no12 p144 D 2016

Stomach ulcers

GASTRIC ULCERS: THE TRUE STORY B. Crabbe color *Horse & Rider* v56 no8 p78 Ag 2017

Stomach—Cancer

Urgent need for implementation of precision medicine in gastric cancer in China Shuqin Jia, Lianhai Zhang et al bibl chart *Sci-*

ence v354 no6319 p39 D 23 2016

Stomach—Physiology

What to eat when you have chronic heartburn *Harvard Health Letter* v42 no4 p6 F 2017

Stomach—Ulcers—Treatment

ULCERS PART ONE M. DEPAOLO *Arabian Horse World* v57 no2 p138 N 2016

Stomata

How plants learned to breathe E. Pennisi color *Science* v355 no6330 p1110 Mr 17 2017

Making more of your stomata color *Science* v355 no6330 p1169 Mr 17 2017

Stomps, Kelly

Kelly Stomps S. RAVITS color *Louisiana Life* v37 no3 p58 Ja/F 2017

Stomski, Lorraine

What Makes Someone an Engaging Leader *Harvard Business Review Digital Articles* p2 N 7 2014

Stone

17 Sound Design Ideas for Every Room in the House color *Log Home Living* v34 no1 p48 F 2017

A story in STONE G. E. CLARKE bw color *Canadian Geographic* v137 no4 p42 Jl/Ag 2017

Totally Rockin' Idea color *Good Housekeeping* v265 no1 p121 Jl 2017

Stone, A. Douglas

Einstein's Greatest Mistake: A Biography *Physics Today* v70 no5 p58 My 2017

Stone, Brad

AMAZON WON'T KNOW WHAT HIT 'EM! [Cover story] color graph *Bloomberg Businessweek* no4521 p42 My 8 2017

How Uber and Airbnb Fought City Halls, Won Over the Citizenry, Outlasted Rivals, and Figured Out the Sharing Economy bw color graph *Bloomberg Businessweek* no4509 p44 Ja 30 2017

OUT-UBERING Uber How CHENG WEI, founder of China's DIDI, drove the Americans OFF THE ROAD in CHINA color *Bloomberg Businessweek* no4494 p60 O 10 2016

Silicon Valley's New Reality Show color *Bloomberg Businessweek* no4505 p6 D 26 2016

Summer of Samsung bw color diag graph *Bloomberg Businessweek* no4532 p42 Jl 31 2017

TENCENT GOES GLOBAL MAYBE color diag *Bloomberg Businessweek* no4529 p50 Jl 3 2017

Stone, Brad—Interviews

Why Uber and Airbnb Needed a Different Kind of CEO D. McGinn color *Harvard Business Review Digital Articles* p2 Ja 31 2017

Stone, Christian

Hoop for Thought color *Sports Illustrated* v125 no14 p16 O 24-31 2016

Stone, Curtis

Catch Your FANCY color *O, The Oprah Magazine* p110 Jl 2017

HARVEST FEAST *Saturday Evening Post* v289 no5 p76 S/O 2017

SIMPLY SUMMER: Take alfresco dining to the next level with light, must-try recipes from the celebrity chef and author *Saturday Evening Post* v289 no4 p78 Jl/Ag 2017

SPRING FLING *Saturday Evening Post* v289 no2 p74 Mr/Ap 2017

WILD ABOUT SALMON! *Saturday Evening Post* v289 no3 p76 My/Je 2017

WINTER SOUPS TAKE ROOT *Saturday Evening Post* v289 no1 p78 Ja/F 2017

Stone, Daniel

BIG ADVANCES diag *National Geographic* v231 no6 p10 Je 2017

BUGS ARE IN OUR FOOD—AND THAT'S OK color *National Geographic* v231 no2 p22 F 2017

A FAMILY ON THE HIGH SEAS color *National Geographic* v232 no1 p16 Jl 2017

FOR CITRUS, IT'S ALL RELATIVE color *National Geographic* v231 no2 p20 F 2017

FRESHWATER AT THE SOURCE color *National Geographic* v231 no4 p18 Ap 2017

HOW TO KNOW URINE PARIS color *National Geographic* v232 no5 p16 N 2017

A Last Glance at North Korea color map *National Geographic* v232 no5 p136 N 2017

Pollution on the Move graph map *National Geographic* v230 no4 p22 O 2016

Riding in a Rickshaw With a Hostage Orangutan color *National Geographic* v230 no5 p25 N 2016

SAVING OCEAN SPECIES, FROM TOP TO BOTTOM color *National Geographic* v231 no6 p12 Je 2017

THE SECRET LIFE OF PLANTS color *National Geographic* v231 no5 p26 My 2017

STRAWBERRIES PRESERVED color *National Geographic* v232 no5 p20 N 2017

Tracking a tornado's damage from every angle color map *National Geographic* v230 no4 p24 O 2016

TROUBLED WATERS map *National Geographic* v231 no4 p20 Ap 2017

UP AND OVER diag *National Geographic* v231 no3 p22 Mr 2017

Stone, Dorian

A Step-by-Step Plan to Improve CMO-COO Collaboration *Harvard Business Review Digital Articles* p2 Ja 28 2015

Stone, E.

Jupiter's interior and deep atmosphere: The initial pole-to-pole passes with the Juno spacecraft [Cover story] color graph *Science* v356 no6340 p821 My 26 2017

STONE, EMILY

The Meaning of Zelda *Commentary* v144 no1 p6 Jl/Ag 2017

Stone, Emma, 1988-

150 MOST FASHIONABLE WOMEN color *Harper's Bazaar* no3650 p127 F 2017

5 ways to ditch the winter blahs color *Redbook* p121 D 2016

EMMA STONE J. McGovern color *Entertainment Weekly* no1444/1445 p21 D 16 2016

Emma Stone's Hollywood Ending [Cover story] J. Weiner color *Rolling Stone* no1278/1279 p34 Ja 12 2017

Hollywood On Hollywood R. DOUTHAT color *National Review* v69 no2 p47 F 6 2017

How Emma Stone Got Ripped S. Dreisbach color *Glamour* v115 no9 p114 S 2017

La La Land: Haters Shall Be Lovers S. Zacharek color *Time* v188 no24 p62 D 12 2016

MIXED SINGLES A. Carter color *Esquire* p28 O 2017

A Musical Triumph P. Travers color *Rolling Stone* no1276 p64 D 15 2016

A Night They' ll Remember color *Vanity Fair* v59 no5 p72 Ap 2017

NINA'S BEAUTY HEROES color *Harper's Bazaar* no3656 p335e S 2017

On with the Show J. Gay color *Vogue* v206 no11 p212 N 2016

PARTY LINES img *New York* p128 Mr 6 2017

Petal Pushers E. Wilson color *InStyle* v24 no4 p76 Ap 2017

RED CARPET INTELLIGENCE I. Biedenharn color *Entertainment Weekly* no1456 p50 Mr 10 2017

Steve Carell M. ZIMMERMAN *Men's Health* v32 no8 p128 O 2017

Venus and Mars Duke It Out on the Tennis Court S. Zacharek color *Time* v190 no13 p64 O 2 2017

Who Won Fashion? J. Ferrise color *InStyle* v24 no5 p82 My 2017

WONDER WOMEN A. LEIBOVITZ and J. WOLCOTT bw color *Vanity Fair* p126 Hollywood 2017 Supplement

Stone, Emma, 1988-—Awards

SOLID GOLD K. Peiffer, B. Fowler et al color *InStyle* v24 no3 p153 Mr 2017

Stone, Emma, 1988-—Interviews

A WINNING BATTLE L. J. Wertheim color *Sports Illustrated* v127 no9 p32 S 25 2017

Stone, Geoffrey R.

Naked Justice M. KINSLEY *New York Times Book Review* p21 Ap 2 2017

Sex and the Constitution: Sex, Religion, and Law from America's Origins to the Twenty-First Century *Publishers Weekly* v264 no1 p49 Ja 2 2017

THE WORK OF EQUALITY A. NORTH bw *Nation* v304 no16 p39 My 22 2017

Stone, Greg

For Better Presentations, Start with a Villain *Harvard Business Review Digital Articles* p2 N 12 2015

Stone, Howard

OUTREACH YIELDS REWARDS IN VAIL P. de Barros color *Downbeat* v84 no6 p132 Je 2017

Stone, Jeremy J. (Jeremy Judah), 1935-2017

Everyone should try J. Berg bw *Science* v355 no6322 p227 Ja 20 2017

Stone, Kim

PLAN. WORK. ACHIEVE K. NAVARRA color *Horse & Rider* v56 no8 p71 Ag 2017

STONE, LOIS GREENE

A LADDER IS TO CLIMB *Humanist* v77 no3 p40 My/Je 2017

Stone, Lyman

UPWARD MOBILITY STALLS E. BLOXHAM color *Phi Kappa Phi Forum* v96 no4 p16 Wint 2016

STONE, MARCIA

Gut Reaction: Bacteria to Autism in Four (Not-So-) Easy Steps *BioScience* v66 no11 p1004 N 1 2016

Microbial Targets Can Help Make Parkinson's History *BioScience* v67 no5 p484 My 2017

Moving Back to Stay Ahead: Phage Research Comes Out of Storage *BioScience* v67 no2 p188 F 2017

Taming the Wild Carrot *BioScience* v66 no10 p912 O 1 2016

Tree-Killing Fungus Continues to Spread on Hawaii's Biggest Island *BioScience* v67 no8 p776 Ag 2017

Stone, Matt

THE GENESIS OF THE BOOK OF MORMON *Cincinnati Magazine* v50 no8 p24 My 2017

Stone, Matthew B.

Neutron scattering in the proximate quantum spin liquid a-RuCl3 bw diag *Science* v356 no6342 p1055 Je 9 2017

STONE, MICHAEL

Where's the Beef? color *Discover* v38 no4 p17 My 2017

Stone, Michael K.

Discussion color *Smithsonian* v47 no10 p8 Mr 2017

Stone, Oliver, 1946-

Full Pardon D. EDELSTEIN img *New York* v49 no19 p94 S 19 2016

LEAK, PAY, LOVE J. ANDERSON color *America* v215 no10 p43 O 10 2016

Stone, Pat

Grow a Community GIVING GARDEN *Mother Earth News* no279 p46 D/Ja 2017

Stone, Rachel Marie

The Man Who Never Stopped Sleeping: A Novel *Christian Century* v134 no13 p40 Je 21 2017

Stone, Richard

ATOMIC BONDING color *Science* v357 no6354 p862 S 1 2017

Dam-building threatens Mekong fisheries color map *Science* v354 no6316 p1084 D 2 2016

Grad students, postdocs with U.S. visas face uncertainty color *Science* v355 no6325 p557 F 10 2017

Immigration order threatens overseas talent color *Science* v355 no6324 p439 F 3 2017

PREDICTION AND ITS LIMITS [Cover story] color *Science* v355 no6324 p468 F 3 2017

Raising the drawbridge graph *Science* v355 no6328 p896 Mr 3 2017

SOME LIKE IT HOT color map *Science* v354 no6318 p1366 D 16 2016

Test blasts simulate a nuclear attack on a port color *Science* v355 no6328 p897 Mr 3 2017

Travel ban would slam university in North Korea color *Science* v357 no6349 p342 Jl 28 2017

Stone, Roger—Interviews

Roger Stone A. Altman color *Time* v189 no6 p56 F 20 2017

Stone, S.

Mars' atmospheric history derived from upper-atmosphere measurements of 38 Ar/36Ar diag *Science* v355 no6332 p1408 Mr 31 2017

Stone, Sharon, 1958-

Leading Ladies M. Rochlin color *AARP: The Magazine* v59 no4A p38 Je/Jl 2016

Stone, Terry

Incremental Fixes Won't Save the U.S. Health Care System *Harvard Business Review Digital Articles* p2 D 6 2016

Stone, Yael

Murder Most Foul D. ANDERSON-MINSHALL color *Advocate* no1090 p57 Ap 2017

Stone age

The Dismal Swamp: One Road out of Slavery Took You Straight into the Boggiest Place You've Ever Been W. H. Funk *Humanities* v38 no2 p5 Spr 2017

Stone Age people treated cavities B. BOWER color *Science News* v191 no9 p15 My 13 2017

Stone bridges

DEVIL'S BRIDGE TRAIL R. STIEVE color map *Arizona Highways* v93 no5 p54 My 2017

Stone building

See also

Stone bridges

Stone circles

Neolithic stone ring site holds new surprise: a buried square monument color *Science* v356 no6345 p1315 Je 30 2017

Stone cladding

Understanding Anchorage Systems for Natural Stone Cladding A. A. Hunt color *Architectural Record* v204 no12 p198 D 2016

Stone implements

Early Civilization Uncovered in Southeast *USA Today Magazine* v145 no2865 p11 Je 2017

THE NEW ORIGINS OF TECHNOLOGY [Cover story] K. Wong color map *Scientific American* v316 no5 p28 My 2017

Oldest members of our species discovered in Morocco A. Gibbons color map *Science* v356 no6342 p993 Je 9 2017

Stone Cold Science B. ALEX bw color *Discover* v38 no9 p64 N 2017

Stone pines

See also

Whitebark pine

Guardian of the Blood Moon J. BALDWIN *American Forests* v123 no3 p48 Fall 2017

Stone walls

The Perfect Marriage color *Log Home Living* v34 no7 p8 S 2017

Stone walls—Design & construction

Stone by Stone J. E. DAVIS color *Orion Magazine* v36 no2 p8 Mr/Ap 2017

Stonebrook, Shelley

BIRD FRIENDLY *Mother Earth News* no281 p10 Ap/My 2017

Groundbreaking Solar Roof Panels *Mother Earth News* no281 p9 Ap/My 2017

National GMO Labeling Bill Signed Into Law *Mother Earth News* no279 p6 D/Ja 2017

Online Courses for Homestead Herbalists *Mother Earth News* no281 p9 Ap/My 2017

Organic Seed Cultivars to Try This Year *Mother Earth News* no281 p8 Ap/My 2017

Potential for Wind Energy in All 50 States *Mother Earth News* no280 p8 F/Mr 2017

Sunny Outlook for Solar Growth *Mother Earth News* no279 p7 D/Ja 2017

Take a Free Course on Organic Seed *Mother Earth News* no279 p7 D/Ja 2017

UNCONVENTIONAL GARDENING METHODS Pros and Cons *Mother Earth News* no280 p14 F/Mr 2017

Stonefield, Sean

Serious Lawyers, Serious Results img *New York* v49 no25 p19 D 12 2016

Stone House, The (Music)

The Stone House J. Ephland color *Downbeat* v84 no7 p51 Jl 2017

Stonemason, The (Play)

Children of God? M. Boudway bw color *Commonweal* v143 no18 p18 N 11 2016

StoneMill Log & Timber Homes Inc.

Better Together J. BREWSTER color *Cabin Living* p44 Ja/F 2017

Two Houses in One color diag *Log Home Living* p56 2017 SpecialIssue

Stoner, James R., Jr.

TEACH YOUR CHILDREN WELL *Claremont Review of Books* v17 no2 p91 Spr 2017

Stones Throw Records (Company)

BONUS LEVEL: With Hazy Moods, DJ Harrison reveals his perfect pitch D. HARRISON *Virginia Living* v15 no6 p29 O 2017

Stoneware—United States

The Met snares a splendid piece of southern stoneware S. Archer color *Magazine Antiques* v184 no5 p48 S/O 2017

STONEY, KIMBERLY
fooled you! color *Parents* v92 no4 p74 Ap 2017

St-Onge, Elizabeth
Why Women Aren't Making It to the Top of Financial Services Firms *Harvard Business Review Digital Articles* p2 O 25 2016

Stooß, V.
Observing the ultrafast buildup of a Fano resonance in the time domain bibl graph *Science* v354 no6313 p738 N 11 2016

STOOKSBERRY, JAY
NOW HIRING: TEEN CIGARETTE NARCS bw *Reason* v49 no6 p14 N 2017

Stools (Furniture)
BEST BETS img *New York* v50 no8 p82 Ap 17 2017
FEVERED DAZE B. Schott color *Powder* v45 no5 p102 Ja 2017
Gift SETS *Interview* v46 no10 p52 D 2016/Ja 2017
The Outside Scoop R. C. Orrell *Architectural Record* v205 no6 p61 Je 2017
SURPRISE, SURPRISE K. Hunhoff *South Dakota Magazine* v32 no4 p6 N/D 2016

Stools (Furniture)—Evaluation
4 Could This Be in Your Living Rooms Future? T. Rami img *New York* v49 no21 p92 O 17 2016
Adam's Home STYLE SHEET color *O, The Oprah Magazine* p66 F 2017
HOME UNDER $100 color *Redbook* p106 Jl/Ag 2017
HOME UNDER $150 color *Redbook* p136 S 2017

STOOP, CHATANIKA
Grant-Writing Bootcamp: An Intervention to Enhance the Research Capacity of Academic Women in STEM *BioScience* v67 no7 p638 Jl 2017

Stoos, William Kevin
Bittersweet in the Preserve *South Dakota Magazine* v33 no3 p93 S/O 2017

Stop codons
Translational termination without a stop codon N. R. James, A. Brown et al bibl color *Science* v354 no6318 p1437 D 16 2016

Stoppers (Implements)
THE FIX E. Johnson cartoon *Old House Journal* v45 no6 p56 S 2017

Storage
STORAGE SOLUTIONS: EMPLOY COMMON DEVICES IN UNCOMMON WAYS TO STORE TOOLS, CORDS, AND STRAPS D. Mowitz *Successful Farming* v115 no6 p28 Ap 2017

Storage batteries
See also
Lithium-ion batteries
Aftermarket Accessories R. GIMENEZ color *Trail Rider* v29 no4 p18 My 2017
ASK SAIL D. CASEY, G. WEST et al *Sail* v48 no5 p50 My 2017
Breakthrough battery hinged on funding from program in Trump's crosshairs D. Kramer *Physics Today* v70 no6 p34 Je 2017
Charging the Future S. Gaidos bw color diag *Science News* v191 no1 p22 Ja 21 2017
Q + A *Boating World* v38 no1 p30 Ja 2017
Rechargeable nickel–3D zinc batteries: An energy-dense, safer alternative to lithium-ion J. F. Parker, C. N. Chervin et al bw chart diag *Science* v356 no6336 p415 Ap 28 2017
Tesla's New Strategy Is Over 100 Years Old J. Suskewicz *Harvard Business Review Digital Articles* p2 My 19 2015
Why We Still Don't Have Better Batteries R. Martin il *MIT Technology Review* v119 no6 p22 N/D 2016

Storage batteries—Design & construction
A BETTER BATTERY E. Tingwall cartoon *Car & Driver* v62 no8 p18 F 2017
Building a Better Battery D. Pogue color *Scientific American* v316 no5 p26 My 2017

Storage batteries—Performance
Charged Up N. Calder color *Sail* v47 no12 p46 D 2016

Storage batteries—Recycling
NEW LIFE FOR DEAD BATTERIES P. Constantakes and V. Minocha *New York State Conservationist* v71 no3 p26 D 2016

Storage fragmentation (Computer science)
When to defrag a hard drive, TRIM an SSD and perform other storage tasks, or not J. NOREM color *PCWorld* v35 no6 p157

Je 2017

Storage in the home
Louisiana Custom Closets: Don Wise P. Marquis *New Orleans Homes & Lifestyles* v20 no3 p96 Summ 2017

Storage in the home—Equipment & supplies
product spotlight color *Timber Home Living* v27 no5 p31 O 2017

Storage racks
A CLEAN, WELL-LIGHTED WORKROOM R. D'AGOSTINO cartoon color *Popular Mechanics* p103 D 2016/Ja 2017
In the World of OHJ P. Poore color *Old House Journal* v45 no5 p8 Ag 2017

Storage racks—Evaluation
Garage Utility color *Old House Journal* v45 no1 p50 F 2017
Paddlecraft Racks D. ARMITAGE color *Cabin Living* p59 Ap 2017

Storage—Equipment & supplies
ASK JEFFREY J. PHILLIP color *Good Housekeeping* v264 no2 p54 F 2017
new products color *Science* v357 no6349 p418 Jl 28 2017

Storage—Equipment & supplies—Evaluation
WHEELS UP M. Khemsurov color *Bloomberg Businessweek* no4507 p65 Ja 16 2017

Storchmann, Karl
TAKE THAT, WINE SNOBS E. REYNOLDS *USA Today Magazine* v145 no2862 p58 Mr 2017

Store decoration
The Return of the Squiggle L. SCHWARTZBERG img *New York* v50 no11 p96 My 29 2017

Store location
Gottwals Books Turns 10, Adds 15th Store J. Rosen color *Publishers Weekly* v264 no10 p5 Mr 6 2017

Stored-value cards
Show Me the Money *Consumer Reports* v81 no12 p25 D 2016
What the Heck Is Rewards for Good ? cartoon *AARP: The Magazine* v60 no5A p66 Ag/S 2017

Storey, Erik
Nothing Short of Dying: A Clyde Barr Novel *Publishers Weekly* v263 no40 p117 O 3 2016

Storey, John D.
Systems-level analysis of mechanisms regulating yeast metabolic flux bibl diag graph *Science* v354 no6311 paaf2786-1 O 28 2016

STOREY, KENNETH B.
Anesthesia and Euthanasia of Amphibians and Reptiles Used in Scientific Research: Should Hypothermia and Freezing Be Prohibited? *BioScience* v67 no1 p53 Ja 2017

STOREY, STEVE
AN UNCERTAIN ROAD bw color *Bike Magazine* v24 no2 p56 Mr 2017

Stork, Travis
Honor America's Amazing Nurses color *Prevention* v68 no12 p19 D 2016

Storm, Shaye
Spiral density waves in a young protoplanetary disk bibl graph *Science* v353 no6307 p1519 S 30 2016

Storm, The (Music)
The Playlist bw *Rolling Stone* no1299 p11 N 2 2017

Storm reconstruction
Cleaning up in the wake of hurricanes, tornadoes, and other catastrophes has become a lucrative business for companies such as Cavalry P. Gopal color *Bloomberg Businessweek* no4538 p17 S 18 2017

Storm shelters
HOW to STOP the WIND B. HARGROVE color *Popular Mechanics* p86 S 2017

Storm surges—Prevention
On the Waterfront M. Cockram *Architectural Record* v205 no10 p123 O 2017

Storme: The Lady of the Jewel Box (Film)
Club King H. Als cartoon *New Yorker* v92 no48 p6 F 6 2017

Storms
See also
Rainstorms
Windstorms
Winter storms
99 fried weather balloons Cici Zhang cartoon *Popular Science* v289 no4 p87 Jl/Ag 2017

alaskan weather R. Thoman, M. Stuefer et al *Weatherwise* v70 no5 p48 S/O 2017

the night we evacuated Oroville M. B. Griggs cartoon *Popular Science* v289 no4 p84 Jl/Ag 2017

'Parasitic' strangler figs can help trees weather a storm color *Science* v356 no6342 p991 Je 9 2017

The second time around H. Ellis-Ashburn color *Equus* no473 p72 F 2017

STORM'S COMING J. Brown color *Popular Science* v289 no4 p6 Jl/Ag 2017

Storms & the environment

A Perfect Storm Shot color *Reader's Digest* v190 no1134 p36 O 2017

Storms—Environmental aspects

IT'S A HARD RAIN T. TEMPEST WILLIAMS and B. WILLIAMS *Arizona Highways* v92 no7 p36 Jl 2016

Storrar, William

From Scotland to Sicily [Cover story] color *Commonweal* v144 no17 p9 O 20 2017

From Wittenberg to Brexit cartoon *Commonweal* v143 no18 p34 N 11 2016

Storring, Kathryn

Walk with Me color *Alternatives Journal (A.J) - Canada's Environmental Voice* v42 no3 p26 2016

Story, Jared

Lee Cake *Idaho Magazine* v16 no1 p57 O 2016

Story, Michael

On the value of carbon-ion therapy *Physics Today* v69 no11 p14 N 2016

Story, Rob

HERE'S TO No. 83 color *Skiing* p18 Wint 2017

RESURRECTION bw color *Skiing* p66 Wint 2017

SKIING IS THE BESTEST color *Powder* v45 no5 p22 Ja 2017

THE TRUTH ABOUT PENGUINS color *Skiing* p24 D 2016

Story, Tomasz

Robust spin-polarized midgap states at step edges of topological crystalline insulators bibl graph *Science* v354 no6317 p1269 D 9 2016

Story of G.I. Joe, The (Film)

RUNNING DEEP I. S. SMITH bw *Film Comment* v53 no5 p38 S/O 2017

Story of Us, The (TV program)

The Story of Us [Cover story] D. Snierson color *Entertainment Weekly* no1435 p18 O 14 2016

Story of Us With Morgan Freeman, The (TV program)

The Story of Us With Morgan Freeman K. Hahn *TV Guide* v65 no41 p35 O 2 2017

Storytelling

See also

Transmedia storytelling

Adding Rattlesnake To Our Journalism L. D'VORKIN *Forbes* v200 no2 p12 S 5 2017

Black Gotham J. L. HESTER bw color map *Atlantic* v320 no1 p30 Jl/Ag 2017

Creating better stories M. Dodd color *Christian Century* v134 no20 p10 S 27 2017

THE MARGINALIZATION OF CINEMA K. JONES color *Film Comment* v52 no6 p54 N/D 2016

A NARRATIVE ACROSS PLATFORMS: Transmedia, politics, and encouraging youth authorship anywhere and anytime A. Garcia *Literacy Today (2411-7862)* v35 no2 p34 S/O 2017

SEPTEMBER 2017 *Idaho Magazine* v16 no12 p58 S 2017

Sketchbook A. Nilsen *New York Times Book Review* p27 Je 25 2017

SNEAK PEEK *Idaho Magazine* v16 no11 p63 Ag 2017

Storytelling in business

The Best Data Storytellers Aren't Always the Numbers People A. Samuel *Harvard Business Review Digital Articles* p2 O 28 2015

A Refresher on Storytelling 101 J. D. Schramm *Harvard Business Review Digital Articles* p2 O 8 2014

Use Storytelling to Explain Your Company's Purpose J. Coleman *Harvard Business Review Digital Articles* p2 N 24 2015

Why Your Brain Loves Good Storytelling P. J. Zak *Harvard Business Review Digital Articles* p2 O 28 2014

Storytelling—Social aspects

HORROR STORIES H. Tuma *Lapham's Quarterly* v10 no3 p151

Summ 2017

Storz, Gisela

Not just Salk color *Science* v357 no6356 p1105 S 15 2017

Storz, Jay F.

Predictable convergence in hemoglobin function has unpredictable molecular underpinnings bibl graph *Science* v354 no6310 p336 O 21 2016

Rewiring metabolism under oxygen deprivation color *Science* v356 no6335 p248 Ap 21 2017

STOSSEL, JOHN

Is free speech under threat IN THE UNITED STATES? WE RECEIVED TWENTY-SEVEN RESPONSES. WE PUBLISH THEM HERE, IN ALPHABETICAL ORDER *Commentary* v144 no1 p13 Jl/Ag 2017

Stossel, John, 1947——Interviews

The Man. The Myth. The Moustache K. MANGU-WARD bw color *Reason* v48 no10 p36 Mr 2017

Stoudemire, Amar'e, 1982——Travel

FRESH START IN THE OLD CITY L. J. Wertheim color *Sports Illustrated* v126 no2 p46 Ja 16 2017

Stoumpos, C. C.

Extremely efficient internal exciton dissociation through edge states in layered 2D perovskites bibl graph *Science* v355 no6331 p1288 Mr 24 2017

Stourton, James

Critic, curator, broadcaster, scoundrel R. Hosmer bw *America* v216 no8 p42 Ap 17 2017

Defender of civilisation D. Seward *History Today* v67 no1 p61 Ja 2017

Of Arts and the Man T. LEE SIMMONS color *Weekly Standard* v22 no21 p30 F 6 2017

Stout, James

BREAD IS NOT THE ENEMY color *Bicycling* v58 no8 p36 S 2017

Stout, Justin

Stop Noise from Ruining Your Open Office *Harvard Business Review Digital Articles* p2 Mr 16 2015

Stout, Katie

Girl Just Wants to Have Fun S. COCHRAN color *Architectural Digest* v74 no9 p94 S 2017

STOUT, MIKE

THE DREAM ISLANDS color map *Sail* v48 no1 p30 Ja 2017

STOUT, ROBIN

THE DREAM ISLANDS color map *Sail* v48 no1 p30 Ja 2017

STOVALL, ERIN

17 hairstyles that slay color *Seventeen* p112 Ja 1 2017

cheap THRILLS color *Seventeen* v76 no12 p54 D 2016/Ja 2017

cheap THRILLS color *Seventeen* v76 no2 p84 Mr 2017

cheap THRILLS color *Seventeen* v76 no5 p62 S 2017

Find Your SPF OTP color diag *Seventeen* v76 no3 p62 My 2017

Fun 1st-Day STYLES color *Seventeen* v76 no5 p42 S 2017

Organize Like a VLOGGER color *Seventeen* v76 no2 p74 Mr 2017

Skin-TERTAINMENT color *Seventeen* v76 no4 p43 Jl/Ag 2017

Stove design & construction

How to Make a... ROCKET STOVE color *Popular Mechanics* v193 no7 p74 S 2016

Stover, Brooks

CHANGING SEASONS on a finished layout color *Model Railroader* v83 no12 p32 D 2016

SCRATCHBUILD A DIESEL SHELL from styrene color diag *Model Railroader* v84 no1 p54 Ja 2017

Stover, Dawn

Kerry Emanuel: A climate scientist for nuclear energy bibl *Bulletin of the Atomic Scientists* v73 no1 p7 Ja 2017

Paul Hawken: "Game on" for global warming bibl color *Bulletin of the Atomic Scientists* v73 no3 p145 My 2017

Stoves

See also

Range cookers

Cooking in an OUTDOOR OVEN: Go beyond bread and pizza. Learn strategies for firing your hand-built clay oven and baking casseroles, vegetables, meats, and more W. Rubel *Mother Earth News* no282 p44 Je/Jl 2017

Fast Fixes for a Sparkling Kitchen color *Good Housekeeping* v263 no5 p58 N 2016

How to Make a... ROCKET STOVE color *Popular Mechanics* p74 S 2017

ON THE RISE: A CADRE OF NEW ENGLAND WHEAT GROWERS AND ARTISAN BAKERS WHO PROUDLY CALL THEMSELVES "GRAINIACS" ARE CREATING SOME OF THE BEST BREADS IN THE COUNTRY R. JACOBSEN *Yankee* v81 no5 p118 S/O 2017

Stoves—Evaluation

A CHEF'S TEST: THE AUTOMATIC OVEN W. DUFRESNE color *Popular Mechanics* p77 My 2017

A SLICE OF ALFRESCO EATING C. HASLAM bw color *House Beautiful* p144 Ag 2017

What's cooking? color *Backpacker* v45 no1 p50 Ja 2017

STOWE, JAY

DOG DAZE *Cincinnati Magazine* v50 no10 p52 Jl 2017

LETTER FROM THE EDITOR: AUGUST 2017 *Cincinnati Magazine* v50 no11 p16 Ag 2017

LETTER FROM THE EDITOR *Cincinnati Magazine* p14 Je 2017

LETTER FROM THE EDITOR *Cincinnati Magazine* v50 no4 p16 Ja 2017

LETTER FROM THE EDITOR *Cincinnati Magazine* v50 no5 p14 F 2017

LETTER FROM THE EDITOR MARCH 2017 *Cincinnati Magazine* v50 no6 p18 Mr 2017

Tom Selleck color *Men's Health* v32 no9 p124 N 2017

Stowell, Caleb

Better Value in Health Care Requires Focusing on Outcomes *Harvard Business Review Digital Articles* p2 S 17 2015

STOWELL, JOHN

Country House 2.0 *Cincinnati Magazine* v50 no3 p56 D 2016

ENCYCLOPEDIA CINCINNATI bw cartoon color *Cincinnati Magazine* v51 no1 p42 O 2017

Swing Shift *Cincinnati Magazine* v50 no12 p48 S 2017

VIEW FROM THE BRIDGE *Cincinnati Magazine* v50 no2 p70 N 2016

WORLD OF WAR *Cincinnati Magazine* v50 no7 p20 Ap 2017

Stozkhov, Yuri

Global atmospheric particle formation from CERN CLOUD measurements bibl graph map *Science* v354 no6316 p1119 D 2 2016

St. Pe, Kerry

Cajun Son: A Louisiana native has spent his career working to save the state's coastline and the communities he loves S. Netter *Sierra* v102 no4 p24 Jl/Ag 2017

St. Pierre, Brian

Fix It Faster with Food K. Morell bw cartoon *Men's Health* v32 no3 p62 Ap 2017

St. Pierre, David

David St. Pierre T. C. FISHMAN color *Chicago* v66 no6 p90 Je 2017

Strabo, 64/63 B.C.-ca. 24 A.D.

c. 20: Rome *Lapham's Quarterly* v10 no2 p113 Spr 2017

Stracquadanio, Giovanni

Bug mapping and fitness testing of chemically synthesized chromosome X diag *Science* v355 no6329 p1048 Mr 10 2017

Deep functional analysis of synII, a 770-kilobase synthetic yeast chromosome diag *Science* v355 no6329 p1047 Mr 10 2017

Design of a synthetic yeast genome bibl chart color graph *Science* v355 no6329 p1040 Mr 10 2017

"Perfect" designer chromosome V and behavior of a ring derivative diag *Science* v355 no6329 p1046 Mr 10 2017

Synthesis, debugging, and effects of synthetic chromosome consolidation: synVI and beyond color *Science* v355 no6329 p1045 Mr 10 2017

Stradal, J. Ryan

FOOD CONNECTS US *South Dakota Magazine* p9 S/O 2017 Supplement

Stradano, Giovanni

Crucifixion H. J. Hornik and M. C. Parsons color *Christian Century* v133 no23 p47 N 9 2016

Straetker, Riyana

How Families Throw Birthday Parties color graph *Parents* v92 no4 p18 Ap 2017

How to Swear in Front of Your Kids color *Parents* v92 no4 p20 Ap 2017

Your Backseat Could Be Safer color *Parents* v92 no9 p25 S 2017

Strafella, F.

Observation of a large-scale anisotropy in the arrival directions of cosmic rays above 8 × 1018 eV *Science* v357 no6357 p1266 S 22 2017

Strah, Tiffany

Guardian Angels School *Cincinnati Magazine* v51 no1 p109 O 2017

Strahan, Michael, 1971-——Interviews

JUST MY TYPE D. Patrick and T. Keith color *Sports Illustrated* v125 no18 p25 D 5 2016

LIFE'S WORK: An Interview with MICHAEL STRAHAN ATHLETE/TV HOST color *Harvard Business Review* v95 no5 p156 S/O 2017

Strahs, Kathy

The Lemonade Stand Cookbook: Step-by-Step Recipes and Crafts for Kids to Make—and Sell! *Publishers Weekly* v264 no26 p146f Je 26 2017

Straight Ahead From Havana (Music)

Berroa's Jazz Crossroads J. Potter color *Downbeat* v84 no9 p22 S 2017

Straight No Chaser (Performer)

Note-Worthy *Indianapolis Monthly* v40 no4 p17 D 2016

Speed Read K. KENDALL *Indianapolis Monthly* v40 no4 p18 D 2016

Straight Outta Compton (Film)

Long RANGE A. GREEN and V. STEIKER bw *Vogue* v207 no1 p43 Ja 2017

Straight Up (Music)

Paula Abdul's Greatest Hits A. Bacle color *Entertainment Weekly* no1465 p55 My 12 2017

Strain (Physiology)

Head in Hand S. RAVELLA color *Discover* v38 no3 p22 Ap 2017

STRAIN, ELISABETH

Assessing National Biodiversity Trends for Rocky and Coral Reefs through the Integration of Citizen Science and Scientific Monitoring Programs *BioScience* v67 no2 p134 F 2017

Strain, The (TV program)

The Strain J. Halterman *TV Guide* v65 no31 p36 Jl 24 2017

Strait, George, 1952-

Meet the Texas Gentlemen A. LANGER *Texas Monthly* v45 no9 p36 S 2017

Strait, George, 1952-——Interviews

Legendary Texans color *American Cowboy* p18 LEGENDS OF TEXAS Special Issue 2017

Strait, Steven

The Best Sci-Fi Show You Aren't Watching D. Ross and R. Rahman color *Entertainment Weekly* no1453 p53 F 17 2017

STRAKA, THOMAS

THE BIG QUESTION cartoon *Atlantic* v319 no5 p96 Je 2017

Obama's Monuments *Commentary* v143 no2 p6 F 2017

Those '60s Flashbacks *Commentary* v142 no4 p10 N 2016

Stramer, Susan L.

Enhancement of Zika virus pathogenesis by preexisting antiflavivirus immunity graph *Science* v356 no6334 p175 Ap 14 2017

Strand, Ginger

The Brothers Vonnegut C. Barnett *Orion Magazine* v35 no3 p54 My/Je 2016

Strand, Oliver

MAN of the WORLD color *Vogue* v206 no11 p236 N 2016

Setting the Mood color *Vogue* v207 no7 p112 Jl 2017

Strandburg, K.

Fostering reproducibility in industry-academia research color *Science* v357 no6353 p759 Ag 25 2017

Stranding of ships

ASK SAIL D. CASEY, G. WEST et al color *Sail* v48 no3 p58 Mr 2017

Making Sound Choices P. FREDERIKSEN color *Power & Motoryacht* v34 no7 p22 Jl 2017

Strang, Cameron

Spheres of Influence E. GRAHAM *American Scholar* v86 no2 p15 Spr 2017

Strange, Stephen (Fictitious character)

NO. 26 Doctor Strange C. Collis color *Entertainment Weekly* no1436/1437 p64 O 21 2016

Strange Fruit (Theatrical production)

Before #BlackLivesMatter: A Timeline E. M. THEYS *Dance Magazine* v90 no12 p43 D 2016

color *Harvard Business Review Digital Articles* p2 Mr 10 2017

How to Know Whether You're Giving Your Team Needless Work M. Valcour *Harvard Business Review Digital Articles* p2 Ag 26 2016

How to Prioritize Your Company's Projects A. Nieto-Rodriguez *Harvard Business Review Digital Articles* p2 D 13 2016

How to Tell if You've Made a Good Decision J. Fox *Harvard Business Review Digital Articles* p2 N 21 2014

IBM's Emerging Market Strategy Has 3 Pillars J. Berman *Harvard Business Review Digital Articles* p2 N 27 2014

If Snap's Strategy Is Building New Products, It Won't Live Up to Its IPO Price N. Furr *Harvard Business Review Digital Articles* p2 F 17 2017

Is Your Company Experiencing Good Times? Time for a Plan B W. Johnson *Harvard Business Review Digital Articles* p2 N 18 2016

A List of Goals Is Not a Strategy G. Kenny *Harvard Business Review Digital Articles* p2 N 19 2014

Longitudinal Analysis of a Diversity Support Program in Biology: A National Call for Further Assessment C. J. BALLEN and N. A. MASON *BioScience* v67 no4 p367 Ap 2017

Many Companies Still Don't Know How to Compete in the Digital Age R. Adner *Harvard Business Review Digital Articles* p2 Mr 28 2016

Navigating the Dozens of Different Strategy Options M. Reeves, K. Haanaes et al *Harvard Business Review Digital Articles* p2 Je 24 2015

Piecing Together the Tesla Strategy Puzzle B. Halla *Harvard Business Review Digital Articles* p2 S 16 2015

President Trump's ties to Russia matter. Here's why M. Malone *America* v216 no4 p3 F 20 2017

Professionalize a Startup Without Stifling It J. Allen *Harvard Business Review Digital Articles* p2 Jl 29 2016

Question What You "Know" About Strategy M. Chussil *Harvard Business Review Digital Articles* p2 Jl 30 2015

Reid Hoffman's Two Rules for Strategy Decisions B. Casnocha *Harvard Business Review Digital Articles* p2 Mr 5 2015

A Simple Way to Test Your Company's Strategic Alignment J. Trevor and B. Varcoe *Harvard Business Review Digital Articles* p2 My 16 2016

SOULCYCLE'S CEO ON SUSTAINING GROWTH IN A FADDISH INDUSTRY: It's all about friendship and community M. Whelan color img *Harvard Business Review* v95 no4 p37 Jl/Ag 2017

Stop Distinguishing Between Execution and Strategy R. L. Martin *Harvard Business Review Digital Articles* p2 Mr 13 2015

Stop Letting Quarterly Numbers Dictate Your Strategy D. Hersh *Harvard Business Review Digital Articles* p2 D 13 2016

Stop Using Battle Metaphors in Your Company Strategy F. V. Cespedes *Harvard Business Review Digital Articles* p2 D 19 2014

A Story from Google Shows You Don't Need Power to Drive Strategy A. K. Olson and K. Simerson *Harvard Business Review Digital Articles* p2 Ap 29 2015

Strategic Choices Need to Be Made Simultaneously, Not Sequentially R. L. Martin color diag *Harvard Business Review Digital Articles* p2 Ap 3 2017

Strategic Plans Are Less Important than Strategic Planning G. Kenny *Harvard Business Review Digital Articles* p2 Je 21 2016

Strategy Lessons From Jean Tirole J. Fox *Harvard Business Review Digital Articles* p2 O 15 2014

To Change Your Strategy, First Change How You Think M. Bonchek and B. Libert *Harvard Business Review Digital Articles* p2 My 17 2017

To Jumpstart Growth, Flip the Company's Priorities R. ". Wang *Harvard Business Review Digital Articles* p2 My 11 2015

To Make Money with Digital, Be an Innovator - Not a Strategist J. Dyer and N. Furr *Harvard Business Review Digital Articles* p2 Ja 8 2015

Too Much Profit Can Doom Your Company B. Power and R. Merrifield *Harvard Business Review Digital Articles* p2 Je 1 2015

Top-Down Solutions Like Holacracy Won't Fix Bureaucracy G. Hamel and M. Zanini *Harvard Business Review Digital Articles* p2 Mr 22 2016

What Companies Should Ask Before Embracing Wearables A. Spicer and C. Cederström *Harvard Business Review Digital Articles* p2 My 20 2015

What Economists Get Wrong About Measuring Productivity R. L. Martin *Harvard Business Review Digital Articles* p2 S 14 2015

What Is Strategy, Again? A. Ovans *Harvard Business Review Digital Articles* p2 My 12 2015

What Makes a Great Chief Strategy Officer M. Birshan, E. Gibbs et al *Harvard Business Review Digital Articles* p2 My 14 2015

What Mark Zuckerberg Understands About Corporate Purpose G. Serafeim *Harvard Business Review Digital Articles* p2 F 22 2017

When Transparency Backfires, and How to Prevent It D. De Cremer *Harvard Business Review Digital Articles* p2 Jl 21 2016

Why Being Unpredictable Is a Bad Strategy M. Chussil color *Harvard Business Review Digital Articles* p2 Ja 5 2017

Why Digital Companies Grow Without Adding Headcount T. Perrault *Harvard Business Review Digital Articles* p2 F 11 2016

Why Some Digital Companies Should Delay Profitability for as Long as They Can M. Wessel, A. Levie et al *Harvard Business Review Digital Articles* p2 My 4 2017

Why Talking About Strategy "Execution" Is Still Dangerous R. L. Martin *Harvard Business Review Digital Articles* p2 S 15 2015

Your Network's Structure Matters more than Its Size K. Libert *Harvard Business Review Digital Articles* p2 F 23 2016

Strategic planning—Psychological aspects

Mindfulness Can Improve Strategy, Too J. Talbot-Zorn and F. Edgette *Harvard Business Review Digital Articles* p2 My 2 2016

Strategic planning—Charts, diagrams, etc.

The Data: Where Long-Termism Pays Off D. BARTON, J. MANYIKA et al graph img *Harvard Business Review* v95 no3 p67 My/Je 2017

Strategy games

Games Can Make You a Better Strategist M. Reeves and G. Wittenburg *Harvard Business Review Digital Articles* p2 S 7 2015

Stratton, Christy

Ask anything bw color *Women's Health* v14 no4 p18 My 2017

STRATTON, DONALD

All the Gallant Men *Reader's Digest* v188 no1126 p82 D 2016/Ja 2017

Stratton, Layne

THE UNION bw color *Surfing Magazine* v53 no3 p22 Mr 2017

Stratton, Michael R.

Mutational signatures associated with tobacco smoking in human cancer bibl graph *Science* v354 no6312 p618 N 4 2016

Straub, Emma, 1980——Interviews

Emma Straub *New York Times Book Review* p8 Je 25 2017

Straub, Richard

Managing in an Age of Winner-Take-All *Harvard Business Review Digital Articles* p2 Ap 7 2015

Meaningful Work Should Not Be a Privilege of the Elite color *Harvard Business Review Digital Articles* p2 Ap 3 2017

The Promise of a Truly Entrepreneurial Society *Harvard Business Review Digital Articles* p2 Mr 25 2016

Straub, Richard E.

Intersection of diverse neuronal genomes and neuropsychiatric disease: The Brain Somatic Mosaicism Network color *Science* v356 no6336 p395 Ap 28 2017

Straudt, Kurt

Succulent Savvy *Atlanta* v56 no12 p43 Ap 2017

Straus, Brian

OUT OF THE SHADOWS [Cover story] color *Sports Illustrated* v127 no4 p28 Ag 7 2017

Straus, Joe, 1959-

THE DIPLOMAT *Texas Monthly* v45 no2 p88 F 2017

Straus, Mary

Homemade Dog Food *Mother Earth News* no280 p78 F/Mr 2017

Strausfogel, Sherrie

Absolutely Essential color *Amazing Wellness* v9 no1 p74 Wint 2017

BB & CC Cream Benefits color *Better Nutrition* v79 no9 p28 S 2017

Beauty Secrets of the Desert color *Better Nutrition* v79 no11 p38 N 2017

Beauty Tools color *Better Nutrition* v79 no4 p38 Ap 2017

Face Scrubs to Leave You Glowing color *Better Nutrition* p30 My 2017

Feng Shui Beauty color *Better Nutrition* v79 no1 p54 Ja 2017

Island-Inspired Skin & Hair Care color *Better Nutrition* v79 no3

p34 Mr 2017

Natural Eye Creams color *Better Nutrition* v79 no10 p34 O 2017

Stop Wrestling with Your Razor color *Better Nutrition* v79 no6 p52 Je 2017

Toxin-Free Hair Care color *Better Nutrition* v78 no11 p38 N 2016

Strauss, Anne McCarthy

Saratoga Springs/New York bw color *Old House Journal* v45 no5 p34 Ag 2017

STRAUSS, DARIN

Lord of the Flaws *New York Times Book Review* p9 Mr 12 2017

Strauss, Elissa

The Academy Will See Us Now color *Glamour* v115 no3 p50 Mr 2017

Strauss, Leo, 1899-1973—Political & social views

Leo Strauss's Forgotten Letter S. B. Smith *Commentary* v142 no3 p17 O 2016

STRAUSS, LOUISA

FIRST CLASS bw color *Vanity Fair* v58 no12 p84 D 2016

WHAT YOU SHOULD KNOW ABOUT PAUL BETTANY bw *Vanity Fair* v59 no9 p142 S 2017

Strauss, Lowell

HOGS WILD color *Canadian Wildlife* v23 no4 p28 S/O 2017

Strauss, Mark

Planet Earth to get a daily selfie color graph *Science* v355 no6327 p782 F 24 2017

STRAUSS, NEIL

THE AGE OF FEAR color *Rolling Stone* no1272 p42 O 20 2016

Strauss, Robert

THE BUMBLINGEST R. Winn color *American History* v52 no4 p66 O 2017

Straussman, Ravid

Potential role of intratumor bacteria in mediating tumor resistance to the chemotherapeutic drug gemcitabine diag *Science* v357 no6356 p1156 S 15 2017

Stravinsky, Igor, 1882-1971

Stravinsky: Threni, Requiem Canticles *Opera News* v81 no7 p50 Ja 2017

Strawberries

CREAM OF THE CROP S. DRY color *Louisiana Life* v37 no4 p24 Mr/Ap 2017

GET PUMPED R. Meltzer Warren color *Women's Health* v14 no4 p108 My 2017

HOMEGROWN STRAWBERRIES M. HUGHES color *Better Homes & Gardens* v95 no5 p94 My 2017

JUST ADD FRIENDS *Martha Stewart Living* no275 p8 Je 2017

Strawberry Cookies color *Vegetarian Today* no2 p46 Ap 2017

Strawberry Shortcake Bars color *Vegetarian Today* no2 p48 Ap 2017

Strawberries—Research

This Just In J. Zorthian *Time* v189 no11 p27 Mr 27 2017

Strawberries—Sales & prices

STRAWBERRY VALLEY D. GOODYEAR cartoon *New Yorker* v93 no24 p30 Ag 21 2017

Strawberry growing

BERRY GOOD: PAUL AND SHELLY DETWILER WELCOME THE PUBLIC TO THEIR OHIO STRAWBERRY AND RASP-BERRY FARM K. Bernick color *Successful Farming* v115 no7 p50 My 2017

HOMEGROWN STRAWBERRIES M. HUGHES color *Better Homes & Gardens* v95 no5 p94 My 2017

STRAWSER, JESSICA

When an Editor Writes Fiction *Publishers Weekly* v264 no13 p104 Mr 27 2017

Stray, Jonathan

The age of the cyborg color *Columbia Journalism Review* p70 Fall/Wint 2016

Strayed, Cheryl

ASK-HOLE M. Schulman cartoon *New Yorker* v92 no41 p24 D 12 2016

The Summer Job I'll Never Forget color *Time* v190 no2/3 p55 Jl 10-17 2017

We Three *New York Times Book Review* p16 My 7 2017

Wild Writer Walks on Washington J. Goodman color *Entertainment Weekly* no1451/1452 p18 F 3-10 2017

Stream restoration

RIVER REBORN K. Davidson, D. Skaros et al *New York State Conservationist* v71 no4 p10 F 2017

Streambank planting

TREES FOR TRIBS TURNS 10 S. Walsh *New York State Conservationist* v71 no4 p20 F 2017

Streaming audio

BLUES STREAK A. BRANDT *Cincinnati Magazine* v50 no10 p26 Jl 2017

How Streaming Is Changing Music (Again) M. Luca and C. McFadden *Harvard Business Review Digital Articles* p2 D 12 2016

Inside the War Over Album Exclusives S. KNOPPER color *Rolling Stone* no1272 p13 O 20 2016

Music Goes Freemium Z. O'MALLEY bw *Forbes* v199 no7 p96 Je 29 2017

THE NEXT NAPSTER? Major record labels take on Spinrilla, an Atlanta music streaming service G. GODFREY *Atlanta* v57 no2 p28 Je 2017

NOW STREAMING! A. TINUBU color *Ebony* v72 no11 p86 S 2017

WHAT STREAMS ARE MADE OF N. SANTOS color *Ebony* v72/73 no12/1 p86 O/N 2017

What to Stream color *Entertainment Weekly* no1442 p57 D 2 2016 Rebellious Special Issue

Why Apple Music Missed a Beat M. Bonchek and W. Patrick *Harvard Business Review Digital Articles* p2 S 25 2015

Streaming audio—Computer network resources

No One Wants to Pay $9.99 for Your Remixes A. Satariano and L. Shaw color *Bloomberg Businessweek* no4506 p25 Ja 9 2017

Streaming audio—Economic aspects

THE RECORD INDUSTRY SEES A SAVIOR IN STREAMING diag *Fortune* v174 no6 p11 N 1 2016

Taylor Swift and the Economics of Music as a Service K. R. Lakhani and M. Iansiti *Harvard Business Review Digital Articles* p2 N 6 2014

Streaming audio—Equipment & supplies

streaming devices D. DICKINSON color diag *Better Homes & Gardens* v95 no2 p68 F 2016

Streaming audio—Equipment & supplies—Evaluation

Roku Ultra Streaming Player B. Gonzalez color *Sound & Vision* v82 no2 p48 F/Mr 2017

Streaming technology (Telecommunications)

See also

Streaming audio

Streaming video

360° CAMERAS color *Popular Mechanics* p80 D 2016/Ja 2017

5 Streaming Networks to Check Out Now A. D'Arminio *TV Guide* v65 no21 p10 My 15 2017

Bingeing on CBS Assets M. ANTONOFF color *Sound & Vision* v82 no6 p25 Jl/Ag 2017

The Gratitude Meter Z. Donaldson bw color *O, The Oprah Magazine* p22 F 2017

LEARNING FROM HORROR C. Benson-Allott *Film Quarterly* v70 no2 p58 Wint 2016

MONEY SAVING GUIDE [Cover story] N. SAPORITA, C. FORTÉ et al cartoon color *Good Housekeeping* v264 no2 p79 F 2017

WHAT STREAMS ARE MADE OF N. SANTOS color *Ebony* v72/73 no12/1 p86 O/N 2017

Streaming technology (Telecommunications)—Equipment & supplies

streaming devices D. DICKINSON color diag *Better Homes & Gardens* v95 no2 p68 F 2016

Streaming technology (Telecommunications)—Equipment & supplies—Evaluation

New Streaming Devices A. D'ARMINIO *TV Guide* p14 D 5 2016

Streaming on a Shoestring L. Eadicicco color *Money* v46 no4 p15 My 2017

Streaming technology (Telecommunications)—Evaluation

Best Bets for Cord Cutting E. Samuel color *Entertainment Weekly* no1442 p33 D 2 2016 Rebellious Special Issue

CuriosityStream is for science-hungry viewers E. Conover color *Science News* v191 no12 p27 Je 24 2017

The Download on Netflix M. ANTONOFF color *Sound & Vision* v82 no4 p25 My 2017

Streaming video

THE COMPLETE HISTORY OF VIDEO bw color *Popular Mechanics* p13 O 2017

Cutting the Cord G. DELL'ABATE color *Popular Mechanics* p16

Ap 2017

Does Anyone Still Need Cable? [Cover story] J. K. Willcox chart color diag graph il *Consumer Reports* v82 no8 p24 Ag 2017

Everybody Must Get Streamed F. Gillette color *Bloomberg Businessweek* no4504 p30 D 19 2016

The Golden Girls BINGE A. Wilkinson color *Entertainment Weekly* no1453 p40 F 17 2017

The Great Library D. GIRISH bw *Film Comment* v53 no1 p91 Ja/F 2017

How streaming TV services are coping with ISP data caps J. NEWMAN color *Macworld - Digital Edition* v34 no8 p120 Ag 2017

How to cut the cord without resorting to a pricey streaming-TV bundle J. NEWMAN color *PCWorld* v35 no6 p47 Je 2017

How to stream media from your PC to your HDTV over Wi-Fi L. SPECTOR and I. PAUL color *PCWorld* v35 no10 p112 O 2017

How to watch Netflix offline on your PC I. PAUL color *PCWorld* v35 no6 p155 Je 2017

Live from Pebble Beach E. Loh color *Motor Trend* v68 no12 p12 D 2016

NETFLIX FOR FILM NERDS K. Staskiewicz bw color *Bloomberg Businessweek* no4506 p62 Ja 9 2017

Streaming S. Li color *Entertainment Weekly* no1442 p46 D 2 2016 Rebellious Special Issue

Streaming S. Li color *Entertainment Weekly* no1451/1452 p94 F 3-10 2017

Streaming S. Li color *Entertainment Weekly* no1463/1464 p91 Ap/My 2017

Streaming S. Li color *Entertainment Weekly* no1477 p44 Ag 11 2017

Swimming Upstream: The advent of streaming film and television has brought untold freedom and opportunity to creators--and an unprecedented chance to get lost in the Peak TV shuffle D. Marchese img *New York* v50 no11 p111 My 29 2017

What Disney's Netflix Snub Means M. Lev-ram color *Fortune* v176 no3 p18 S 1 2017

Streaming video—Economic aspects

Cord cutting is a bigger bargain than ever J. NEWMAN cartoon color *PCWorld* p123 O 2016

Stepping Out of YouTube's Shadow S. CARPENTER color *Forbes* v198 no6 p52 N 8 2016

Streaming video—Equipment & supplies

New Gear color *Sound & Vision* v82 no4 p28 My 2017

Streaming on a Budget A. D'Arminio *TV Guide* v65 no27 p6 Je 26 2017

Streb, Elizabeth

What's Not Okay to Ask a Dancer to Do? C. ESCOYNE, S. FRISCIA et al *Dance Magazine* v91 no4 p31 Ap 2017

Streep, Abe

THE BEAUTY OF IT IS THAT *New York Times Magazine* p31 O 2 2016

Is Coal No Longer King? *New Republic* v247 no12 p8 D 2016

The Meat Cutter *New York Times Magazine* p44 F 26 2017

Streep, Meryl, 1949-

7 Things You Didn't See L. Rice, M. Snetiker et al color *Entertainment Weekly* no1449 p14 Ja 20 2017

BEAUTY'S NEW BALLER K. Diamond color *InStyle* v24 no5 p228 My 2017

FEAR NOT *USA Today Magazine* v145 no2860 p64 Ja 2017

Icons color *Time* v189 no16/17 p122 My 1-8 2017

My Obsessions... *TV Guide* v65 no39 p14 S 18 2017

Streep, Meryl, 1949-——Awards

WINNING STREEP J. Nolfi *Entertainment Weekly* no1449 p14 Ja 20 2017

Streep, Meryl, 1949-——Political & social views

Movie Stars and the Perils of the Podium D. Von Drehle color *Time* v189 no4 p21 Ja 23 2017

Street, Ian

Adaptation *Science* v356 no6335 p243 Ap 21 2017

Sunshine outside the ivory tower bw *Science* v357 no6357 p1322 S 22 2017

STREET, JULIA

JULIA STREET WITH POYDRAS THE PARROT bw *New Orleans Magazine* v51 no2 p24 D 2016

JULIA STREET / WITH POYDRAS THE PARROT bw *New Orleans Magazine* v51 no3 p20 Ja 2017

JULIA STREET WITH POYDRAS THE PARROT bw *New Orleans Magazine* v51 no4 p22 F 2017

JULIA STREET | WITH POYDRAS THE PARROT bw *New Orleans Magazine* v51 no6 p22 Ap 2017

WITH POYDRAS THE PARROT color *New Orleans Magazine* v51 no1 p24 N 2016

WITH POYDRAS THE PARROT color *New Orleans Magazine* v51 no7 p22 My 2017

STREET, MIKELLE

MOSAIC OF CULTURES color *Ebony* v72 no8 p42 Je 2017

SNATCH That STYLE: Breaking Down Looks of Lyrical Trendsetters color *Ebony* v72 no8 p44 Je 2017

Street, Randy

What 20 Years as a Remote Organization Has Taught Us About Managing Remote Teams *Harvard Business Review Digital Articles* p2 F 20 2017

Street art—Exhibitions

MORE THAN MURALS D. Michaud *Atlanta* v57 no5 p28 S 2017

Street design & construction

AHEAD OF THE CURRENT R. Annis, S. Bahr et al color *Indianapolis Monthly* v41 no2 p68 S 2017

Street Fighter games

Thai Temple Soundtrack Tangle M. SCARLES color *Tricycle: The Buddhist Review* v27 no1 p17 Fall 2017

Street food

The Urbanist: Chefs Search Out the Best Street Food B. CUSHING img *New York* v49 no19 p24 S 19 2016

Street lighting

Case Study: Should You Adjust Your Business Model for a Major Customer? M. Weiss *Harvard Business Review Digital Articles* p2 My 5 2016

Let There Be Dark D. HURLEY cartoon *Discover* v27 no10 p70 D 2016

Street names

See also

Street signs

13 Coveted Streets *Washingtonian Magazine* v52 no7 p96 Ap 2017

Street photographers

FLEETING GRACE D. Grossman color *Popular Photography* v81 no2 p32 Mr/Ap 2017

Street railroads

Worth a stop N. Walker color *Canadian Geographic* v135 no6 p50 D 2015

Street railroads—Rolling stock

BUILD A SINGLE-POINT TURNOUT [Cover story] J. F. Cordaro color *Model Railroader* v84 no7 p48 Jl 2017

Street signs

Q + A *Cincinnati Magazine* v50 no12 p30 S 2017

SECRET FILES *TV Guide* v65 no4 p22 Ja 16 2017

Signs Of The Times bw color *National Geographic Kids* no474 p30 O 2017

Street vendors

Flower Men K. HERMANN color map *National Geographic* v231 no5 p112 My 2017

NFR NUMBERS color *Horse & Rider* v56 no11 p85 N 2017

The Side Effect A. ROBERT color *National Geographic* v231 no6 p128 Je 2017

Streetball

We'll Get Write on That *Los Angeles Magazine* p6 Ag 2017

Streeter, Karen

SADDLE CHAT bw color graph *Horse & Rider* v56 no11 p21 N 2017

Street of Bugles, A (Short story)

A Street of Bugles A. Tyler *Saturday Evening Post* v289 no3 p60 My/Je 2017

Streets

Broad Ripple Avenue A. LYNCH *Indianapolis Monthly* p32 My 2017

DR. KNOW *Cincinnati Magazine* v50 no11 p28 Ag 2017

Streets—California

See also

Rodeo Drive (Beverly Hills, Calif.)

Buds Light *Los Angeles Magazine* p34 D 2016

Where the Rubber Meets the Road M. SEGAL *Los Angeles Maga-*

Stress (Psychology) in children

Early life stress confers lifelong stress susceptibility in mice via ventral tegmental area OTX2 C. J. Peña, H. G. Kronman et al diag *Science* v356 no6343 p1185 Je 16 2017

Stress (Psychology)—Alternative treatment

THE GOODS C. COX *Atlanta* v56 no9 p41 Ja 2017

Stress (Psychology)—Prevention

Ashwagandha V. TWEED color *Better Nutrition* v79 no10 p26 O 2017

Attention, office workers! color *Health* v31 no9 p10 N 2017

beat the clock R. RABKIN PEACHMAN *Parents* v92 no2 p44 F 2017

BETH BEHRS "Healthy Doesn't Have to Be So Stressful" J. Andriakos color *Health* v31 no6 p21 Jl 2017

Cat Calm and Carry On J. HOFVE color *Better Nutrition* v78 no11 p42 N 2016

Drugstore shopping is my therapy E. Seidman color *Health* v31 no9 p65 N 2017

Go Ahead and Really Relax C. McHugh color *Health* v31 no6 p6 Jl 2017

gotta have it! J. BENJAMIN *Parents* p134 2015

HOMEOPATHIC STRESS RELIEF I. Eliaz *Better Nutrition* v79 no9 p42 S 2017

How My Horse De-Stresses Me E. Quillen, K. Pierce et al color *Horse & Rider* v55 no12 p72 D 2016

Mark your calendar now with these can't-miss offerings! color *Yoga Journal* no295 p8 O 2017

No Joke color *GQ: Gentlemen's Quarterly* v87 no1 p20 Ja 2017

One Minute to a Healthier You J. Migala color *Health* v31 no6 p63 Jl 2017

Power Days Start Here C. McHugh color *Health* v31 no2 p8 Mr 2017

Pressure Doesn't Have to Turn into Stress N. Petrie *Harvard Business Review Digital Articles* p2 Mr 16 2017

RELIEF FOR STRESS J. Susser *Dressage Today* v23 no4 p16 D 2016

Rough Day? Hit Reset M. HUTSON *Psychology Today* v50 no1 p16 Ja/F 2017

Skip the Stress color *Health* v30 no10 p8 D 2016

Staying positive with age: Attitude as a route to health and happiness *Mayo Clinic Health Letter* v358 p1 2017 SpecialIssue

STRESS LESS TO SLIM S. Powers color *Yoga Journal* p108 2017 Special Issue

THIS WORKOUT IS ALL WET color *Health* v31 no9 p20 N 2017

WHAT'S THE DEAL WITH ADULT COLORING BOOKS? E. SILBER *Psychology Today* v49 no5 p20 S/O 2016

YOUR FARM C. Tevis *Successful Farming* v115 no11 p14 S 2017

Stress (Psychology)—Prevention—Research

Simple Moves Can Lead to a Less Stressed-Out You M. Oaklander color *Time* v189 no4 p56 F 6 2017

Stress (Psychology)—Social aspects

... And There's an Invisible Workload That Drags Men Down Too J. Levs color *Money* v46 no4 p66 My 2017

How Stressing Out Can Help You Succeed I. Robertson *Time* v189 no4 p23 Ja 23 2017

Stress management

5 Ways to Minimize Office Distractions J. Grenny *Harvard Business Review Digital Articles* p2 D 17 2015

6 Ways to Reduce the Stress of Presenting J. Grenny *Harvard Business Review Digital Articles* p2 Ag 31 2015

ALL IN A Day's Work U. MCCAMLEY, C. BUSSEY cartoon *Reader's Digest* v190 no1132 p54 Jl/Ag 2017

Banish Back Pain the Natural Way K. ALEISHA FETTERS color *Men's Health* v32 no7 p75 S 2017

De-Stress Your Life S. BLOCK cartoon *Kiplinger's Personal Finance* v71 no2 p64 F 2017

Don't Stress About It N. Brechka *Better Nutrition* v79 no9 p6 S 2017

Express Yourself! color *Kiplinger's Personal Finance* v70 no12 p70 D 2016

Handle Your Stress Better by Knowing What Causes It A. Grady *Harvard Business Review Digital Articles* p1 Je 21 2017

Help Your Overwhelmed, Stressed-Out Team J. Mosow *Harvard Business Review Digital Articles* p2 Ja 16 2015

Here's What Mindfulness Is (and Isn't) Good For D. Goleman

Harvard Business Review Digital Articles p2 S 28 2017

HOW CAN I AVOID BUCKLING UNDER SEASONAL STRESS? bw *Prevention* v68 no12 p10 D 2016

How to Bounce Back After Getting Laid Off R. Knight *Harvard Business Review Digital Articles* p2 Jl 31 2015

How to Conduct an Effective Job Interview R. Knight *Harvard Business Review Digital Articles* p2 Ja 23 2015

How to Evaluate, Manage, and Strengthen Your Resilience D. Kopans *Harvard Business Review Digital Articles* p2 Je 14 2016

HOW TO GET OVER IT S. KOGAN *USA Today Magazine* v146 no2866 p28 Jl 2017

How to Stop Overplanning (Even If You're a Perfectionist) E. G. Saunders *Harvard Business Review Digital Articles* p2 Ag 24 2015

How to Use Stress to Your Advantage S. David *Harvard Business Review Digital Articles* p2 Ag 10 2016

If Mindfulness Makes You Uncomfortable, It's Working A. J. Su *Harvard Business Review Digital Articles* p2 Ag 29 2015

Journaling: A Timeless Tool for Growth C. V. CLARKE color *Black Enterprise* v47 no2 p31 S 2016

Managing the Hidden Stress of Emotional Labor S. David *Harvard Business Review Digital Articles* p2 S 8 2016

MOOD MAKEOVER L. Turner color *Amazing Wellness* v9 no4 p28 Summ 2017

Move into meditation color *Yoga Journal* p76 2016 Special Issue

A One-Page Exercise to Get Stress Under Control A. Rimm *Harvard Business Review Digital Articles* p2 S 15 2015

Pampering with Purpose H. Dowdle color *Yoga Journal* p100 2017 Special Issue

The Powerful Effect of Noticing Good Things at Work T. M. Glomb and J. E. Bono *Harvard Business Review Digital Articles* p2 S 4 2015

Prevent Burnout by Making Compassion a Habit A. McKee and K. Wiens *Harvard Business Review Digital Articles* p1 My 11 2017

Q: For stress relief, what is your go-to practice or pose? A. Owens, C. Owerko et al color *Yoga Journal* no294 p14 S 2017

RELIEF FOR STRESS J. Susser *Dressage Today* v23 no4 p16 D 2016

Resilience Is About How You Recharge, Not How You Endure S. Achor and M. Gielan *Harvard Business Review Digital Articles* p2 Je 24 2016

SECRETS TO ZEN [Cover story] J. Bowden color *Amazing Wellness* v9 no6 p36 EarlyWint 2017

SECRET STRESS BUSTERS of the Stars C. GOYANES *Scholastic Choices* v32 no7 p16 Ap 2017

The Snacking Diaries K. Dold, C. Apovian et al color *Women's Health* v14 no2 p106 Mr 2017

So Happy Together [Cover story] N. HORVATH bw color *Prevention* v69 no2 p96 F 2017

Stress Can Be a Good Thing If You Know How to Use It A. Crum and T. Crum *Harvard Business Review Digital Articles* p2 S 3 2015

Stress Is Your Brain Trying to Avoid Something A. Markman *Harvard Business Review Digital Articles* p2 Ag 26 2015

Think It, Speak It, Live It J. CHAPMAN *USA Today Magazine* v145 no2860 p69 Ja 2017

To Reduce Stress, Embrace Your Inner Type-B V. Lipman *Harvard Business Review Digital Articles* p2 S 22 2017

Try the nature cure color *Parents* v92 no5 p80 My 2017

Ways to Enhance Your "Thought Life" *USA Today Magazine* v146 no2869 p13 O 2017

What Not to Say to a Stressed-Out Colleague H. Weeks *Harvard Business Review Digital Articles* p2 Ag 23 2016

Why Leaders Don't Brag About Successfully Managing Stress J. R. Bailey *Harvard Business Review Digital Articles* p2 O 29 2014

Why Some People Get Burned Out and Others Don't K. Wiens and A. McKee *Harvard Business Review Digital Articles* p2 N 23 2016

You Can Improve Your Default Response to Stress M. Gielan bw *Harvard Business Review Digital Articles* p2 Ja 5 2017

YOUR BODY ON... A CONFESSION J. Migala color *Women's Health* v14 no2 p88 Mr 2017

Stress relieving (Materials)

One-Minute Stress Tips [Cover story] color *Prevention* v69 no1

p16 Ja 2017

Stressman, Karl

Back to the Future G. R. Schiavino color *Spin to Win Rodeo* v21 no6 p104 Ag 2017

Stretch (Physiology)

See also

Static stretching (Physiology)

between the lines color *Yoga Journal* p90 2017 Special Issue

Bright Ideas B. O'Dair *Prevention* v69 no11 p3 N 2017

COMPLEX MOBILITY L. McGLASHAN color *Muscle & Performance* v9 no5 p24 My 2017

The Flexibility Factor L. MCGLASHAN color *Muscle & Performance* v9 no11 p28 N 2017

Gentle Moves A. FERRETTI color *Prevention* v69 no11 p64 N 2017

heart wide open J. RODRIGUE color *Yoga Journal* p40 2017 Special Issue

A home practice to find peace & possibility E. Finn color *Yoga Journal* no292 p66 Je 2017

How STRETCHING Can BENEFIT Your Horse [Cover story] K. Pavicic and B. Baumert color *Dressage Today* p32 My 2017

lightness of being color *Yoga Journal* p70 2017 Special Issue

nourish yourself J. RODRIGUE color *Yoga Journal* p102 2017 Special Issue

playing with power color *Yoga Journal* p74 2017 Special Issue

play leads the way E. WINTER color *Yoga Journal* p36 2017 Special Issue

Poses of the month C. Owerko color *Yoga Journal* no290 p47 Mr 2017

simple everyday practice K. HOLCOMBE color *Yoga Journal* p12 2017 Special Issue

Supta Padangusthasana to Ardha Chandra Chapasana [Cover story] A. Ippoliti color *Yoga Journal* no295 p55 O 2017

turn up the torque color *Yoga Journal* p78 2017 Special Issue

UNLOCK YOUR STRENGTH T. GRAHAM color diag *Men's Health* v32 no7 p94 S 2017

WARM UP LIKE A PRO L. BOYCE color *Muscle & Performance* v8 no12 p26 D 2016

Stretch marks treatment

STRETCH MARK SMOOTHERS L. Turner color *Amazing Wellness* v8 no2 p76 Spr 2016

Streur, John

Stop Waiting for Governments to Close the Skills Gap color *Harvard Business Review Digital Articles* p2 Ja 11 2017

Striccoli, Marinella

Photolithography based on nanocrystals color *Science* v357 no6349 p353 Jl 28 2017

Stricker, Steve, 1967-

THIS YOUNG GUN HAS FIREPOWER D. M. Clarke color *Golf Magazine* v59 no7 p11 Jl 2017

Stricker, Steve, 1967——Interviews

strick-ly speaking J. Marksbury color *Golf Magazine* v59 no7 p64 Jl 2017

STRICKLAND, BILL

"HOW MUCH TRAVEL DO I NEED?" color *Bicycling* v58 no3 p44 Ap 2017

"I JUST SIGNED UP FOR DIRTY KANZA. WTF DO I DO NOW?!" color *Bicycling* v58 no3 p88 Ap 2017

"I LIKE RIDING FAST, BUT I DON'T RACE." color *Bicycling* v58 no3 p20 Ap 2017

"I LOVE OLD-SCHOOL STEEL BIKES." color *Bicycling* v58 no3 p78 Ap 2017

"I'M GOING THROUGH A MIDLIFE CRISIS AND WANT SOMETHING BETTER THAN A CORVETTE." color *Bicycling* v58 no3 p96 Ap 2017

"I NEED A YETI." color *Bicycling* v58 no3 p64 Ap 2017

"I QUIT MY JOB, AND I WANT TO RIDE ACROSS THE COUNTRY." color *Bicycling* v58 no3 p62 Ap 2017

"I'VE GOT $3,000. CAN I GET A BIKE WITH NICE WHEELS?" color *Bicycling* v58 no3 p56 Ap 2017

"I WANT A BIANCHI." color *Bicycling* v58 no3 p98 Ap 2017

"I WANT A BIKE THAT GIVES ME EVERY SPEED ADVANTAGE." color *Bicycling* v58 no3 p104 Ap 2017

"I WANT A BIKE THAT MAKES CLIMBING EASY." color *Bicycling* v58 no3 p34 Ap 2017

"I WANT A BIKE THAT WILL LAST ME 15 YEARS." color *Bicycling* v58 no3 p52 Ap 2017

"I WANT A BIKE THAT WILL STAND OUT." color *Bicycling* v58 no3 p22 Ap 2017

"I WANT A BIKE WITH HERITAGE." color *Bicycling* v58 no3 p58 Ap 2017

"I WANT A GOOD ROAD BIKE, BUT I DON'T WANT TO SPEND MORE THAN $1,000." color *Bicycling* v58 no3 p50 Ap 2017

"I WANT TO DRINK MY COFFEE WHILE I RIDE TO WORK." color *Bicycling* v58 no3 p40 Ap 2017

"I WANT TO GET AWAY." color *Bicycling* v58 no3 p82 Ap 2017

"I WANT TO GO BIKE CAMPING." color *Bicycling* v58 no3 p24 Ap 2017

"I WANT TO GO FAST." color *Bicycling* v58 no3 p68 Ap 2017

"I WANT TO GO ON DIRT-ROAD ADVENTURES." color *Bicycling* v58 no3 p42 Ap 2017

"I WANT TO TAKE MORE RISKS." color *Bicycling* v58 no3 p70 Ap 2017

"I WANT TO TRY CYCLOCROSS." color *Bicycling* v58 no3 p66 Ap 2017

"I WISH MY RIDES COULD GO ON FOREVER." color *Bicycling* v58 no3 p110 Ap 2017

OFFICINA BATTAGLIN POWER+ color *Bicycling* v58 no4 p92 My 2017

ON THE MOUNTAIN color *Bicycling* v58 no3 p84 Ap 2017

THE SELECTION *Bicycling* v58 no4 p12 My 2017

THE SELECTION cartoon color *Bicycling* v58 no1 p10 Ja/F 2017

"SHOULD I GET A DROP-BAR OR A FLAT-BAR ROAD BIKE?" color *Bicycling* v58 no3 p108 Ap 2017

"SHOULD I GET A FULL-SUSPENSION OR HARDTAIL MOUNTAIN BIKE?" color *Bicycling* v58 no3 p28 Ap 2017

"SHOULD I GET AN ENDURO BIKE?" color *Bicycling* v58 no3 p94 Ap 2017

"SHOULD I GET A PLUS BIKE OR A 29ER?" color *Bicycling* v58 no3 p100 Ap 2017

"SHOULD I GET A ROAD BIKE WITH DISC BRAKES? color diag *Bicycling* v58 no3 p30 Ap 2017

"SHOULD I GET A ROAD BIKE WITH SUSPENSION?" color *Bicycling* v58 no3 p86 Ap 2017

WHAT BIKE SHOULD I BUY? color *Bicycling* v58 no3 p16 Ap 2017

"WHAT'S A GOOD BIKE FOR RIDING HOME FROM THE BAR?" color *Bicycling* v58 no3 p54 Ap 2017

"WHAT'S A GOOD FIRST ROAD BIKE?" color *Bicycling* v58 no3 p18 Ap 2017

"WHERE DO I WANT TO RIDE? DUH, EVERYWHERE." color *Bicycling* v58 no3 p48 Ap 2017

"WHY SHOULD I SPEND $5,000 ON A BIKE?" color *Bicycling* v58 no3 p46 Ap 2017

WHY WHEELS MATTER color *Bicycling* v58 no3 p57 Ap 2017

Strickland, Eliza

Beyond the Radio Collar *Sierra* v101 no4 p28 Jl/Ag 2016

The Biochar Solution *Sierra* v102 no4 p25 Jl/Ag 2017

Charge of the Light Brigade color *Foreign Policy* no222 p24 Ja/F 2017

Fishy Business color *Foreign Policy* no222 p24 Ja/F 2017

Seeing the Forest Through the Trees color *Foreign Policy* no221 p28 N/D 2016

Taking In the Trash *Sierra* v102 no1 p24 Ja/F 2017

Strickland, Hugh

1849: Downe C. Darwin *Lapham's Quarterly* v10 no2 p127 Spr 2017

Strickland, Lynette R.

Without inclusion, diversity initiatives may not be enough color *Science* v357 no6356 p1101 S 15 2017

STRICKLAND, PATRICK

A FOUR-STAR RESPONSE TO THE REFUGEE CRISIS *In These Times* v41 no7 p44 Jl 2017

STRICKLAND, PAUL

A TALE OF TWO FAAS color *Flying* v144 no7 p56 Jl 2017

Stricklin, Joe

No-Nonsense Soundness C. Shaffer color *Team Roping Journal* p80 S 2017

Strief, Zach

Zach Strief: Brewing success, both on the field and off A. McLellan color *New Orleans Magazine* v51 no10 p40 Ag 2017

Strikeouts (Baseball)
GO FIGURE T. Keith color *Sports Illustrated* v126 no14 p22 My 15-22 2017
SPECIAL K T. Verducci color *Sports Illustrated* v126 no18 p40 Je 26 2017
STRIKE FORCE color *Sports Illustrated* v126 no18 p43 Je 26 2017

Strikes & lockouts
See also
Demonstrations (Collective behavior)

Strikes & lockouts—Brazil
Brazilian Police Strike, And Violence Spikes D. Biller and W. Brandimarte color *Bloomberg Businessweek* no4512 p14 F 20 2017

Strikes & lockouts—Prevention
Writers' Strike Averted! J. Russell *TV Guide* v65 no21 p11 My 15 2017

Strikes & lockouts—United States
Female Privilege M. A. MIRANDA ALCAZAR and K. D. GRIFFITHS *Nation* v304 no10 p4 Mr 27 2017

STRINER, RICHARD
A Brief History of Secession [Cover story] *American Scholar* v86 no2 p20 Spr 2017
Culture Clash *Weekly Standard* v22 no40 p36 Je 26 2017

String
THE FINE PRINT B. HEAVEY color *Field & Stream* v122 no5 p90 O 2017

String Quartet 1931 (Music)
Woman, Interrupted R. Platt color *New Yorker* v93 no33 p26 O 23 2017

Stringed instrument music
Strings in Jazz: Learning To Swing & Articulate in Style A. DIXON bw color *Downbeat* v84 no10 p186 O 2017

Stringed instruments—Evaluation
Campellone Deluxe Series Archtop K. Baumann color *Downbeat* v84 no10 p194 O 2017

STRINGER, TOM
DESIGN DILEMMA: My Home Has Tiny Closets. How Do I Store My Stuff? color *Chicago* v66 no9 p89 S 2017

Stringfellow, Jamie
From the Forest to the Sea *Yankee* p99 Mr 2017

Stringham, Jim
EYE HEALTH IN THE DIGITAL AGE color *Amazing Wellness* p26 Fall 2017

Strip shopping centers
SAIGON SUPERSTORE K. RANDALL *Washingtonian Magazine* v52 no8 p28 My 2017

Stripe (Company)
THE CLOUD 100 *Forbes* v200 no1 p81 Jl 27 2017

Stripe Inc.
CELTIC TIGERS A. Vance color *Bloomberg Businessweek* no4533 p38 Ag 7 2017

Striped bass fishing
Current Trends J. Cermele color *Field & Stream* v122 no1 pF7 My 2017

Stripes
STRIPE RIGHT K. O'SHEA-EVANS color *House Beautiful* p21 Jl 2017
Top of the LINE color *Vogue* v206 no12 p140 D 2016

Stripped (Music)
MACY GRAY S. J. O'Connell bw *Downbeat* v83 no12 p23 D 2016

Striptease
TOP BRASS A. BROWNLEE *Cincinnati Magazine* v50 no8 p53 My 2017

Striptease clubs—Evaluation
TOP BRASS A. BROWNLEE *Cincinnati Magazine* v50 no8 p53 My 2017

Stritzke, Jerry
A RETAILER FINDS ITS VOICE C. Zillman color *Fortune* v176 no4 p46 S 15 2017

Strochlic, Nina
The Anti-Indiana Jones Measures the Pyramids color *National Geographic* v230 no5 p27 N 2016
ARTISTIC LIBERTY AT THE TABLE color *National Geographic* v231 no2 p16 F 2017

CHANGING THE WORLD KIDS SEE color *National Geographic* v231 no3 p24 Mr 2017
COLORING SPACE color *National Geographic* v232 no1 p152 Jl 2017
DEEP-SEA VINO color *National Geographic* v231 no4 p22 Ap 2017
DO YOU REALLY KNOW YOUR CAT? color *National Geographic* v232 no4 p12 O 2017
DREAM CATCHERS color *National Geographic* v231 no5 p22 My 2017
ECLIPSED BY WAR bw *National Geographic* v232 no2 p26 Ag 2017
GETTING INSIDE FIDO'S HEAD color *National Geographic* v232 no4 p16 O 2017
HIGH-FLYING HELP color *National Geographic* v231 no6 p6 Je 2017
HOLO BONES color *National Geographic* v231 no6 p4 Je 2017
PICTURES OF MENTAL HEALTH color *National Geographic* v232 no3 p16 S 2017
PLANTING PEACE color *National Geographic* v232 no5 p22 N 2017
Sahara's Coolest Ants color *National Geographic* v230 no5 p19 N 2016
SAND TRICKS color *National Geographic* v232 no5 p144 N 2017
THE SPORT THAT SOARS—AND KILLS color *National Geographic* v232 no1 p18 Jl 2017
WATER COLLECTIVE color *National Geographic* v231 no4 p24 Ap 2017
A WATERY SHRINE color *National Geographic* v231 no4 p26 Ap 2017
When croc babies become teenagers color *National Geographic* v230 no4 p24 O 2016

Stroessner, Alfredo, 1912-2006
PERSONAL THOUGHTS ON MY DAYS IN THE ARCHIVES P. Encina *Film Quarterly* v70 no4 p47 Summ 2017

Stroeve, Julienne
Observed Arctic sea-ice loss directly follows anthropogenic CO_2 emission bibl graph *Science* v354 no6313 p747 N 11 2016

Strohm, C.
Spectral narrowing of x-ray pulses for precision spectroscopy with nuclear resonances diag *Science* v357 no6349 p375 Jl 28 2017

Strohm, Chris
The Fall Guy bw *Bloomberg Businessweek* no4523 p24 My 22 2017
Fired. But Not Finished bw *Bloomberg Businessweek* no4522 p30 My 15 2017

Strohm, Emily
Seacrest IN! color *Entertainment Weekly* no1465 p17 My 12 2017

Strojny, Chelsee
Dopamine oxidation mediates mitochondrial and lysosomal dysfunction in Parkinson's disease graph *Science* v357 no6357 p1255 S 22 2017

Stroke
Get Smart About Stroke G. deGROOT REDFORD cartoon *AARP: The Magazine* v60 no1A p18 D 2016/Ja 2017
HEART BEAT D. Zipes *Saturday Evening Post* v289 no2 p72 Mr/Ap 2017
Long-Distance Service D. Pelz and C. Barrett color *Golf Magazine* v59 no4 p40 Ap 2017
STROKE AWARENESS color *New Orleans Magazine* v51 no6 p140 Ap 2017

Stroke patients
NOW WHAT? E. Marko color *Tricycle: The Buddhist Review* v26 no4 p68 Summ 2017
A Tip From a Stroke Expert D. Chiu color *Prevention* v69 no5 p8 My 2017

Stroke patients—Medical care
Nice Stent If You Can Get It M. Cortez color diag *Bloomberg Businessweek* no4518 p34 Ap 10 2017

Stroke treatment
Advances in emergency stroke care *Mayo Clinic Health Letter* v35 no9 p4 S 2017
Screen Savers *Virginia Living* v15 no1 p105 D 2016

Stroke—Case studies
When Time is Brain K. RIDDERBUSCH *Atlanta* v56 no7 p215

N 2016

Stroke—Prevention

FIVE FACTS: STROKE F. Esker *Louisiana Life* v37 no5 p12 My/Je 2017

Losing Big Saved My Life L. Murray color *Health* v30 no9 p54 N 2016

Seven Ways to Prevent a Stroke L. TURNER color *Better Nutrition* p26 My 2017

Stopping Stroke Karla, Rob et al color *Ebony* v72 no6 p64 Ap/My 2017

Stroke Awareness N. Brechka *Better Nutrition* p6 My 2017

Stroke—Psychological aspects

a stroke erased my sense of past or future S. Bushwick cartoon *Popular Science* v289 no5 p75 S/O 2017

strokes, tess weaver

shelter from the storm color *Bike Magazine* v24 no3 p40 My 2017

solid as steel bw color *Bike Magazine* v24 no6 p42 Ag 2017

TATUM MONOD color *Skiing* p34 D 2016

Strokes, The (Performer)

The Last Moment of the Last Great Rock Band L. Goodman img *New York* v50 no10 p86 My 15 2017

Stroma, Freddie

Time After Time D. Holbrook *TV Guide* v65 no8 p32 F 27 2017

Stromatolites

IN THE NEWS map *Scientific American* v315 no5 p18 N 2016

Stromback, Rich—Interviews

99% of Networking Is a Waste of Time G. McKeown *Harvard Business Review Digital Articles* p2 Ja 22 2015

Stromberg, Lisen

Work Pause Thrive: How to Pause for Parenthood Without Killing Your Career *Publishers Weekly* v263 no52 p121 D 19 2016

Stromseth, Jonathan R.

China's Governance Puzzle: Enabling Transparency and Participation in a Single-Party State YUEN YUEN ANG and A. J. Nathan *Foreign Affairs* v96 no6 p172 N/D 2017

Strong, Bruce A.

How Employees Shaped Strategy at the New York Public Library *Harvard Business Review Digital Articles* p2 D 5 2016

Strong, Kate

TOUCH WOOD S. SMITH color *House Beautiful* p128 Ag 2017

Stronger (Film)

DAN BRISSE T. Monterosso color *Snowboarder* v29 no2 p38 O 2016

Gyllenhaal Only Gets Stronger S. Zacharek color *Time* v190 no14 p50 O 9 2017

JAKE GYLLENHAAL IN Stronger J. McGovern color *Entertainment Weekly* no1478 / 1479 p39 Ag 18-25 2017

The Must List color *Entertainment Weekly* no1484 p9 S 29 2017

Stropp, J.

Persistent effects of pre-Columbian plant domestication on Amazonian forest composition bibl chart graph map *Science* v355 no6328 p925 Mr 3 2017

Stroscio, Joseph A.

An on/off Berry phase switch in circular graphene resonators diag graph *Science* v356 no6340 p845 My 26 2017

STROUD, DAVID A.

The Arctic in the Twenty-First Century: Changing Biogeochemical Linkages across a Paraglacial Landscape of Greenland *BioScience* v67 no2 p118 F 2017

Stroud, Matt

MISTAKEN IDENTITIES *Harper's Magazine* v334 no2001 p48 F 2017

Private Prisons Get A Boost From Trump color *Bloomberg Businessweek* no4500 p28 N 21 2016

Strouse, Sunshine

I Wish My Horse's Mentor Could Be... color *Horse & Rider* v56 no6 p88 Je 2017

Strout, Elizabeth

Class Action A. BARRETT *New York Times Book Review* p10 My 14 2017

Hot Type S. CROSLEY color *Vanity Fair* v59 no6 p54 My 2017

A LONG HOMECOMING A. LEVY bw color *New Yorker* v93 no11 p22 My 1 2017

Witness to suffering J. G. Phelan *America* v217 no7 p49 O 2 2017

Strout, Elizabeth—Interviews

Elizabeth Strout S. Begley color *Time* v189 no18 p60 My 15 2017

Strout, Erin

COUCH TO 50K color *Runner's World* v52 no3 p34 Ap 2017

IN THE ZONE [Cover story] bw color *Runner's World* v52 no6 p20 Jl 2017

KATE THE GREAT color *Runner's World* v51 no11 p44 D 2016

Long Trails to Recovery color *Runner's World* v52 no8 p46 S 2017

MATTHEW CENTROWITZ color *Runner's World* v52 no1 p82 Ja/F 2017

RUN AWAY! [Cover story] color *Runner's World* v52 no7 p54 Ag 2017

Strout, Preston G.

BENNY MILAM color *Snowboarder* v29 no2 p46 O 2016

CAM FITZPATRICK cartoon color *Snowboarder* v29 no4 p48 D 2016

JUDD HENKES color *Snowboarder* v29 no5 p40 Ja 2017

Strovink, Kurt

What Makes a Great Chief Strategy Officer *Harvard Business Review Digital Articles* p2 My 14 2015

Strowig, Till

The DNA-sensing AIM2 inflammasome controls radiation-induced cell death and tissue injury bibl color graph *Science* v354 no6313 p765 N 11 2016

A pathogenic role for T cell–derived IL-22BP in inflammatory bowel disease bibl graph *Science* v354 no6310 p358 O 21 2016

Strüber, Christian

Angular momentum–induced delays in solid-state photoemission enhanced by intra-atomic interactions chart color graph *Science* v357 no6357 p1274 S 22 2017

Struck, Doug

Idaho town stares down so-called Aryan church *Christian Century* v134 no22 p19 O 25 2017

Structural colors

A whole new (tiny) ball game for color L. Hamers color *Science News* v192 no6 p32 O 14 2017

Structural frame design & construction

How to Make a... CONCRETE FRAME B. LOSLEBEN chart color *Popular Mechanics* v193 no7 p82 S 2016

Structural frames

See also
    Metal-organic frameworks

Metal-organic framework extracts water from thin air J. Miller *Physics Today* v70 no6 p16 Je 2017

Structural geology

Weatherscapes: The Grand Canyon of the Colorado River – Earth's Dynamic Past Opened by the Sky E. Darack *Weatherwise* v70 no2 p8 Mr/Ap 2017

Structural panels (Construction)

SIPS cartoon *Timber Home Living* p44 2017 Annual Buyers

Strength Meets Sustainability color *Timber Home Living* v27 no5 p14 O 2017

Structural steel workers

A preacher builds bridges B. K. Modahl color *Christian Century* v134 no3 p24 F 2017

Strugarek, A.

Reconciling solar and stellar magnetic cycles with nonlinear dynamo simulations diag *Science* v357 no6347 p185 Jl 14 2017

Strugatskiĭ, Boris Natanovich, 1933-2012

Monday Starts on Saturday color *Publishers Weekly* v264 no35 p109 Ag 28 2017

Strugnell, Jan M.

Biodiversity redistribution under climate change: Impacts on ecosystems and human well-being color *Science* v355 no6332 p1389 Mr 31 2017

Struhl, Gary

Causal role for inheritance of H3K27me3 in maintaining the OFF state of a Drosophila HOX gene diag *Science* v356 no6333 p41 Ap 7 2017

Struijs, Jeroen N.

How Bundled Health Care Payments Are Working in the Netherlands *Harvard Business Review Digital Articles* p2 O 12 2015

Strupp, Julie

WHERE & WHEN *Washingtonian Magazine* v52 no8 p35 My 2017

Strut Commander (Company)

Reed Section W. Brantley color *Field & Stream* v121 no9 pT8 Ap 2017

Struth, Thomas
End of an Era bw *Art in America* p41 O 2017
Nature and Politics T. Brorby color *Orion Magazine* v36 no1 p62
Ja/F 2017
Strycker, Noah
Birding Without Borders: An Obsession, a Quest, and the Biggest
Year in the World color *Publishers Weekly* v264 no35 p114 Ag
28 2017
Strzelecki, Marek
Christ, King, and Corporate Savior bw *Bloomberg Businessweek*
no4531 p33 Jl 24 2017
In Poland, the Stench Of Swamp Clearing color map *Bloomberg
Businessweek* no4505 p17 D 26 2016
St. Thomas, Mike
Pedagogy of the Distracted bw *Commonweal* v144 no7 p32 Ap
14 2017
St. Midas' Prep bw *Commonweal* v114 no14 p9 S 8 2017
Stuart, Brad
Giving Seriously Ill Patients More Choices About Their Care *Har-
vard Business Review Digital Articles* p2 My 23 2017
STUART, EDEN
AMERICAN DREAMING: Take a sophisticated approach to pa-
triotic fashion *Virginia Living* v15 no4 p37 Je 2017
between the LINES *Virginia Living* v15 no3 p37 Ap 2017
COMING IN clutch *Virginia Living* v15 no1 p35 D 2016
Minimalist Cool *Virginia Living* v15 no1 p48 D 2016
PLAID TO THE BONE: A fall trend as versatile as it is classic
Virginia Living v15 no6 p37 O 2017
RAISING THE BAR *Virginia Living* v15 no3 p23 Ap 2017
western PROMISES *Virginia Living* v15 no2 p29 F 2017
Stuart, Jan
Debut Novels color *New York Times Book Review* p27 Ja 29 2017
GINNY MOON *New York Times Book Review* p26 Je 18 2017
STUART, KEVIN E.
Trump Has Given Us an Opportunity *America* v215 no18 p15 D
5 2016
STUART, RALPH
THE FAST TRACK color *Outdoor Life* v224 no1 p46 D 2016/
Ja 2017
FRESH TRACKS IN THE BIG WOODS bw *Outdoor Life* v224
no1 p40 D 2016/Ja 2017
stuart, ryan
dirty in dodge color *Bike Magazine* v24 no6 p36 Ag 2017
the missing link color *Bike Magazine* v24 no2 p34 Mr 2017
Reindeer games color map *Canadian Geographic* v135 no6 p28
D 2015
School of tides color *Canadian Geographic* v137 no5 p24 S/O
2017
STUART, TAYLOR JR.
The Persistently Misleading Media color graph *Weekly Standard*
v22 no46 p17 Ag 14 2017
STUART, TESSA
Kirsten Gillibrand color *Rolling Stone* no1295 p44 S 7 2017
The Liar in Chief color *Rolling Stone* no1285 p46 Ap 20 2017
Stuart-Fox, Devi
The biology of color color *Science* v357 no6350 p470 Ag 4 2017
Stuart period, Great Britain, 1603-1714
Entwined and Engaged *British Heritage Travel* v38 no3 p28 My/
Je 2017
Stuart-Pontier, Zac
A different kind of family in Providence K. Weber color *America*
v216 no3 p49 F 6 2017
STUART-SMITH, RICK D.
Assessing National Biodiversity Trends for Rocky and Coral
Reefs through the Integration of Citizen Science and Scientific
Monitoring Programs *BioScience* v67 no2 p134 F 2017
STUB, SARA TOTH
Expanding the Story [Cover story] bw color *Archaeology* v69 no6
p26 N/D 2016
Mending Their Lives: Through sewing and design, survivors of
Israel's sex industry begin anew *Ms.* v27 no2 p12 Summ 2017
Stubbes, John, 1543-1591
Swift Beyond Satire J. MCNAMARA *New York Times Book Re-
view* p20 F 26 2017
Stubbington, Michael J. T.
Aging increases cell-to-cell transcriptional variability upon im-

mune stimulation color diag graph *Science* v355 no6332 p1433
Mr 31 2017
Single-cell transcriptomics to explore the immune system in
health and disease diag *Science* v357 no6359 p58 O 6 2017
Stubblefield, Clyde, 1943-2017
Secrets of the Funky Drummer C. R. WEINGARTEN bw color
Rolling Stone no1283 p12 Mr 23 2017
Stubbs, Erin Laray
TEA OFF: Inspirations for afternoon tea, that most Anglophilic of
traditions color *Virginia Living* v15 no5 p23 Ag 2017
Stubbs, John
How Swift Saw It M. FORBES *Weekly Standard* v22 no31 p41
Ap 17 2017
Jonathan Swift: The Reluctant Rebel *Publishers Weekly* v263
no40 p108 O 3 2016
STUBBS, MICHAEL
Along with Tom *Idaho Magazine* v16 no2 p18 N 2016
Stuber, Scott
family FIRST M. Sims color *Good Housekeeping* v265 no5 p48
N 2017
Stubner, Stephan
What BMW's Corporate VC Offers That Regular Investors Can't
Harvard Business Review Digital Articles p2 Jl 27 2017
Stucker, Hal
40 Years IN THE Dark bw color *Popular Photography* v81 no2
p62 Mr/Ap 2017
Stuckey, Bobby
LOVIN' THE OVEN J. DRILLING *Cincinnati Magazine* v50 no2
p122 N 2016
Stuckey, Darrell
Fortune Brainstorm HEALTH C. Leaf and D. B. Agus color *For-
tune* v175 no7 p20 Je 1 2017
STUCKY, JANAKA
I Am Flying Into Myself: Selected Poems, 1960-2014 color *Pub-
lishers Weekly* v264 no3 p38 Ja 16 2017
Studebaker Corp.
GOING IN STYLE J. OBER bw *Dirt Sports + Off-Road* v51 no5
p74 My 2017
Student activism
See also
Student strikes
THE OLD NEW LEFT AND THE NEW NEW LEFT C. R. Kesler
Claremont Review of Books v17 no3 p31 Summ 2017
The Uncomfortable Truth Z. R. WOOD *Weekly Standard* v22 no8
p13 O 31 2016
The Whole World Was Watching [Cover story] C. ALLEN color
Weekly Standard v22 no39 p26 Je 19 2017
Student activism—Research
Teach the Moment J. Ahern-Dodson *Change* v48 no6 p24 N/D
2016
Student activism—United States
The Crisis at Berkeley S. F. HAYWARD bw color *Weekly Stan-
dard* v22 no34 p26 My 15 2017
Student activism—United States—History—20th century
Joe College Is Dead: In an essay directed at bewildered '60s-era
parents, a noted historian attempts to explain the roots of student
unrest A. SCHLESINGER JR. *Saturday Evening Post* v289 no4
p44 Jl/Ag 2017
Student activities
5 Fantastic Ideas *Scholastic Choices* pT1 S 2017 Supplement
CAMP Grandma ...AND GRANDPAA. TOO P. MEAD color
Cabin Living p120 Ja/F 2017
More time for learning A. Magaña, M. Saab et al color *Phi Delta
Kappan* v98 no4 p26 D 2016/Ja 2017
YOUR CHEAT SHEET TO... School! Money! Jobs! C. THORP
cartoon color *Seventeen* v76 no5 p72 S 2017
Student assignments
How Can I Rock a... Group Project? *Scholastic Choices* v32 no3
p24 N/D 2016
The Right Way to Do Redos R. WORMELI *Education Digest* v82
no9 p29 My 2017
Student attitudes
See also
Student engagement
Countering Students' Negative Narratives J. D. DeHart bw *Educa-
tion Digest* v83 no3 p4 N 2017

Making Math Count More for Young Latinos D. Murphey, R. Madill et al bw *Education Digest* v83 no1 p8 S 2017

Student awards

Student Music Award Listings color *Downbeat* v84 no6 p96 Je 2017

Student-centered learning

LITERACY IS THE KEY C. P. Clark *Literacy Today (2411-7862)* v35 no1 p3 Jl/Ag 2017

STANDING UP FOR OUR STUDENTS R. W. GOODE and S. Hill color *Black Enterprise* v47 no7 p28 My/Je 2017

Student Conservation Association

THE AUDACITY OF LIZ PUTNAM M. ALLEN and M. FLEMING bw color *Yankee* p86 My/Je 2017

Student counselors

A COLLEGE ADVISER IN EVERY SCHOOL G. Edelman color *Washington Monthly* v49 no9/10 p62 S/O 2017

Student development

Bethany School S. Snavely *Cincinnati Magazine* v51 no1 p105 O 2017

Guardian Angels School T. Strah *Cincinnati Magazine* v51 no1 p109 O 2017

Physics education research and student development J. Winfrey *Physics Today* v70 no2 p10 F 2017

St. Ursula Academy J. Cahill *Cincinnati Magazine* v51 no1 p113 O 2017

St. Ursula Villa M. Runnels *Cincinnati Magazine* v51 no1 p114 O 2017

Student engagement

Countering Students' Negative Narratives J. D. DeHart bw *Education Digest* v83 no3 p4 N 2017

E is for Enrichment E. M. Wood color *Cincinnati Magazine* v51 no1 p100 O 2017

Going outdoors E. G. Merritt color *Phi Delta Kappan* v99 no2 p21 O 2017

Paths to Engagement: PROVOKING INTELLECTUAL FERMENT through Pedagogies of Social Participation W. M. Sullivan *Change* v49 no3 p52 My/Je 2017

Student Success Built on a Positive School Climate L. WARNER and P. HEINDEL *Education Digest* v82 no7 p10 Mr 2017

Three Ways the Flipped Classroom Leads to Better Subject Mastery A. SAMS and J. AGLIO *Education Digest* v82 no5 p52 Ja 2017

To engage students, give them meaningful choices in the classroom F. Parker, J. Novak et al il *Phi Delta Kappan* v99 no2 p37 O 2017

Student ethics

See also

Students' conduct of life

Classes of Kindergarteners F. M. HESS and G. ADDISON il *National Review* v69 no19 p36 O 16 2017

Student exchange programs

GETTING STARTED color *Maclean's* v129 no44 p47 N 7 2016

Student financial aid

See also

Scholarships

Student loans

FINANCIAL AID C. WAYLOCK *Atlanta* v56 no7 p113 N 2016

FIVE STEPS TO WIN MORE AID K. Clark color *Money* v46 no3 p52 Ap 2017

Student health

The distracted student mind — enhancing its focus and attention L. D. Rosen chart color diag graph il *Phi Delta Kappan* v99 no2 p8 O 2017

Student housing

See also

Dormitories

Student leadership

INSPIRATION, REWARDED M. CAMPBELL color *Maclean's* v130 no10 p74 N 2017

Student loan debt

The Affordability Factor A. RIDNER *USA Today Magazine* v145 no2864 p64 My 2017

Climb Out of Student Debt K. Mulhere chart color *Money* v45 no10 p29 N 2016

HEAVY DEBT R. HENAGER color *Phi Kappa Phi Forum* v97 no2 p15 Summ 2017

Research: Millennials Can't Afford to Job Hop S. A. Hewlett and J. S. Kuhl *Harvard Business Review Digital Articles* p2 Ag 31 2016

Retirees Shoulder a Bigger Share of Student Debt H. S. Edwards color *Time* v189 no6 p22 F 20 2017

Student Debt Blamed For Falling Homeownership *America* v217 no4 p8 Ag 21 2017

STUDENT DEBT: Good, Bad, and Misunderstood S. Baum *Change* v49 no3 p60 My/Je 2017

Who's Picking Up the Education Tab? H. S. Edwards color *Time* v188 no16/17 p76 O 24 2016

Student loan debt—Economic aspects

Student Loans S. Nasiripour and J. Lorin color graph *Bloomberg Businessweek* no4509 p33 Ja 30 2017

Student loan debt—Government policy

Defrauded For-Profit Grads Seek Relief S. Nasiripour bw color *Bloomberg Businessweek* no4505 p30 D 26 2016

Student loans

CALENDAR R. ERMEY color *Kiplinger's Personal Finance* v71 no6 p18 Je 2017

Every Student a Bond Seller J. HARTLEY color *National Review* v68 no19 p37 O 24 2016

Student loans—Government policy

5 Things to Know About the New FAFSA K. Clark and K. Mulhere *Money* v45 no10 p37 N 2016

Student Lenders Get a Chance to Cut Loose S. Nasiripour *Bloomberg Businessweek* no4500 p37 N 21 2016

Student loans—United States

DeVos, Trump Make the Student Loan Crisis Worse S. Ross color *Progressive* v81 no6 p44 Ag/S 2017

A Guide to Borrowing for Your Kid's College Degree K. Mulhere color *Money* v46 no7 p20 Ag 2017

HEAVY DEBT R. HENAGER color *Phi Kappa Phi Forum* v97 no2 p15 Summ 2017

Should colleges use collection agencies for overdue student bills? K. KIPLINGER *Kiplinger's Personal Finance* v71 no11 p12 N 2017

Student Loans S. Nasiripour and J. Lorin color graph *Bloomberg Businessweek* no4509 p33 Ja 30 2017

Student loans—United States—Government policy

Movers K. Stock color graph *Bloomberg Businessweek* no4502 p17 D 5 2016

Student mobility

See also

College student mobility

ON THE MOVE M. TODD *Phi Kappa Phi Forum* v96 no4 p1 Wint 2016

Student protesters

'Shut Up, Already!': The New Battle Over Campus Free Speech B. Lueders color *Progressive* v81 no6 p52 Ag/S 2017

Student publications

The Importance of Scholarship N. MITCHELL and P. BERKERY *Publishers Weekly* v264 no38 p76 S 18 2017

Student records—Access control—United States

Under The Law J. Underwood *Phi Delta Kappan* v98 no8 p74 My 2017

Student rights—Lawsuits & claims

High Court Ruling color *Weekly Standard* v22 no40 p4 Je 26 2017

Student speech

In the Debate Over Campus Free Speech, Who Are the Real Special Snowflakes? E. S. J. Glaude color *Time* v190 no14 p25 O 9 2017

Speak Your Piece C. MALONEY JR. *USA Today Magazine* v146 no2868 p31 S 2017

Student strikes

Evergreen State Blues: How George Bridges fostered his own humiliation [Cover story] G. HERRINGTON *American Conservative* v16 no5 p13 S/O 2017

Strike disrupts research at Puerto Rico's top university J. Mervis color *Science* v356 no6340 p793 My 26 2017

Student suspension

One Key to Reducing School Suspension: A Little Respect S. D. SPARKS *Education Digest* v82 no4 p8 D 2016

Student teachers

PDK Connection *Phi Delta Kappan* v98 no6 p79 Mr 2017

TOUCHING ON VOCABULARY: Using multiple methods to

Students

energize vocabulary instruction S. Craig *Literacy Today (2411-7862)* v35 no2 p32 S/O 2017

See also

Adult students

Architecture students

Bilingual students

Black students

Boarding school students

Business students

College students

Homecoming queens

Low-income students

Muslim students

Older students

School children

Science students

4 steps for redesigning time for student and teacher learning b. L. Nazareno diag il *Phi Delta Kappan* v98 no4 p21 D 2016/Ja 2017

7 common questions about applying for college: Advice from parents, dancers, and directors A. RIVERS *Dance Magazine* p12 2016/2017

ALWAYS A STUDENT E. Graves color *Martha Stewart Living* p8 S 2017

The big picture K. Marshall chart color diag *Phi Delta Kappan* v99 no2 p42 O 2017

BUZZWORTHY J. H. NEWMAN, J. STALL et al *Indianapolis Monthly* p14 N 2017

College and Career Readiness Starts With Essential Skills R. DALTON *Education Digest* v82 no9 p41 My 2017

Dancing Through Language Barriers G. HENDERSON *Dance Magazine* v91 no6 p48 Je 2017

How Can I Make a... Tough Decision? *Scholastic Choices* v32 no8 p24 My 2017

Taking Student Success to Scale R. R. Martin *Change* v49 no1 p38 Ja/F 2017

Why Fraternities and Sororities Have Houses O. B. Waxman *Time* v190 no10/11 p29 S 18 2017

Students' conduct of life

See also

Hazing

Busting the School-to-Prison Pipeline J. LANGBERG and A. CIOLFI *Education Digest* v82 no5 p42 Ja 2017

no average day K. BRADY *Dance Magazine* p18 2016/2017

STORIES WITH VALUE: Inspiring positive student conduct with children's picture books C. A. Jones *Literacy Today (2411-7862)* v35 no1 p28 Jl/Ag 2017

WHY ARE COPS PUTTING KIDS IN CUFFS? R. SOAVE and T. KOTESKEY color *Reason* v48 no10 p46 Mr 2017

Students for a Democratic Society (U.S.)

Protest, Then and Now C. R. Kesler *Claremont Review of Books* v17 no3 p33 Summ 2017

A Sui Generis Radical M. DAVIS *Nation* v303 no20 p8 N 14 2016

Students' sexual behavior

Consensual Sex Under Title IX M. LISSACK *USA Today Magazine* v145 no2864 p67 My 2017

Students with disabilities

Heterogeneous education output measures for public school students with and without disabilities S. G. Powers bibl chart color graph *Monthly Labor Review* p1 S 2016

It's instruction over place — not the other way around! J. M. Kauffman and J. Badar color diag il *Phi Delta Kappan* v98 no4 p55 D 2016/Ja 2017

Students—Abuse of

My Friend Is Bankrupting Herself. Should I Speak Up? K. A. Appiah *New York Times Magazine* p18 Ap 2 2017

Students—Academic workload

Is Home work Out of Control? *Scholastic Choices* v32 no4 p2 Ja 2017

Students—Attitudes

See also

College students—Attitudes

Student engagement

Real confusion about fake news color *Phi Delta Kappan* v98 no5 p6 F 2017

Students—China

Filling Empty Seats A. J. ZAVAGNIN color *America* v215 no13 p25 O 31 2016

Students—China—History

Tsinghua University founded *History Today* v67 no4 p8 Ap 2017

Students—Mental health

Busting the School-to-Prison Pipeline J. LANGBERG and A. CIOLFI *Education Digest* v82 no5 p42 Ja 2017

Students—Rating of

Less is more V. Faulkner, P. L. Marshall et al diag graph *Phi Delta Kappan* v98 no7 p55 Ap 2017

The VALUE of Assessment: Transforming the Culture of Learning T. L. Rhodes *Change* v48 no5 p36 S/O 2016

Students—Services for

Flipping Student Support Services to Improve Outcomes P. Wheelan *Change* v48 no6 p36 N/D 2016

Students—Social aspects

CJA Sets Students on Positive Path with Music J. Hale color *Downbeat* v84 no5 p142 My 2017

LITERATURE AS AN AGENT OF SOCIAL CHANGE: Promoting awareness of critical social issues in schools K. C. Kao color *Literacy Today (2411-7862)* v34 no6 p40 My/Je 2017

Students—Training of

The land is the classroom M. ROSANO color *Canadian Geographic* v137 no2 p58 Mr/Ap 2017

The ROTC Freakout *Weekly Standard* v22 no6 p2 O 17 2016

Students—United States

Building a 21st Century Workforce T. J. DONOHUE *Weekly Standard* v22 no48 p9 S 4 2017

CHARTER-ING A NEW COURSE D. Wilson color *New Orleans Magazine* v51 no8 p82 Je 2017

Helping less-prepared students excel A. Sessoms color *Science* v357 no6352 p654 Ag 18 2017

History Is for Making Great Citizens A. SARGEANT *National Review* v69 no19 p42 O 16 2017

Studer, Armido

Radical-polar crossover reactions of vinylboron ate complexes bibl diag *Science* v355 no6328 p936 Mr 3 2017

Studer, Romain A.

Evolution of protein phosphorylation across 18 fungal species bibl graph *Science* v354 no6309 p229 O 14 2016

Studio 54 (Nightclub)

Life of the Party M. ROZZO bw color *Architectural Digest* v74 no9 p98 S 2017

Studio Fever B. COLACELLO bw color *Vanity Fair* v59 no9 p134 S 2017

Studio Bergtraun Architects (Company)

house of the month M. SITZ *Architectural Record* v205 no1 p27 Ja 2017

Studio D Radiodurans (Company)

Postcards From The Edge J. Pavlus color *Bloomberg Businessweek* no4494 p44 O 10 2016

Studio Drift (Company)

A Bar Lamp Like No Other E. HILL-AGNUS *D: The Magazine of Dallas* v43 no10 p52 O 2016

Studio Four NYC (Company)

UNCOMMON THREADS K. HACKETT color *Better Homes & Gardens* v95 no2 p102 F 2016

Studio Neat LLC

GLIF TRIPOD ADAPTER FOR iPHONE G. FLEISHMAN color *Macworld - Digital Edition* v34 no8 p48 Ag 2017

Studio Swine (Company)

Studio Swine H. MARTIN bw color *Architectural Digest* v74 no10 p100 O 1 2017

Study & teaching of ballet

See also

Ballet dancing

the case for ballet in college: How a ballet degree can lead to a performance career K. RICHTER *Dance Magazine* v90 p14 2016/2017 Supplement College Guide

Indiana University Jacobs School of Music *Dance Magazine* v90 p74 2016/2017 Supplement College Guide

La Roche College *Dance Magazine* v90 p80 2016/2017 Supplement College Guide

Marygrove College *Dance Magazine* v90 p81 2016/2017 Supplement College Guide

Mercyhurst University *Dance Magazine* v90 p82 2016/2017 Sup-

Subchapter S corporations
Shrink Your Salary K. PHILLIPS ERB color *Forbes* v199 no7 p138 Je 29 2017

Subconsciousness
See also
Dreams
Hallucinations & illusions
Sleep
SUB HERO T. J. Tomasi and D. DeNunzio color *Golf Magazine* v59 no4 p68 Ap 2017

Subduction (Geology)
Graveyard of cold slabs mapped in Earth's mantle P. Voosen color map *Science* v354 no6315 p954 N 25 2016
Release of mineral-bound water prior to subduction tied to shallow seismogenic slip off Sumatra A. Hüpers, M. E. Torres et al graph *Science* v356 no6340 p841 My 26 2017

Subedi, Kiran
Restored iron transport by a small molecule promotes absorption and hemoglobinization in animals color graph *Science* v356 no6338 p608 My 12 2017

Subgroup analysis (Experimental design)
When It Comes to Data, Skepticism Matters T. C. Redman *Harvard Business Review Digital Articles* p2 O 22 2014

Subject headings
Information Bias in Library Catalogs T. BINGA *Skeptical Inquirer* v41 no3 p9 My/Je 2017

Subliminal perception
Why Executives Should Talk About Racial Bias at Work M. M. Wilkins *Harvard Business Review Digital Articles* p2 Ap 20 2015

Submarine cables
The Digital Cloud Is Underwater-and Vulnerable K. Vick and E. Barone color diag map *Time* v188 no15 p16 O 17 2016
Get Your Own Broadband M. Chafkin and D. Bass cartoon map *Bloomberg Businessweek* no4496 p38 O 24 2016

Submarine disasters
CLUES SURFACE TO LOCATION OF ILL-FATED INDIANAPOLIS B. Manley *Military History* v33 no5 p10 Ja 2017

Submarine topography
See also
Hydrothermal vents
Mid-ocean ridges
Ocean bottom
Submarine trenches
Pop Goes the Seafloor Rock: RESEARCHERS HUNT FOR SEAFLOOR LAVAS TO REVEAL THE INNER WORKINGS OF OUR PLANET *Oceanus* v52 no2 p22 Spr 2017

Submarine trenches
The Hunt for Fresh Water Below the Seafloor E. Lubofsky *Oceanus* v52 no2 p40 Spr 2017

Submarine volcanoes—North Pacific Ocean
See also
Axial Seamount
Seismic constraints on caldera dynamics from the 2015 Axial Seamount eruption W. S. D. Wilcock, M. Tolstoy et al bibl color graph *Science* v354 no6318 p1395 D 16 2016

Submarine volcanoes—Research
COLIN DEVEY K. SHEIKH cartoon *Popular Science* p53 Ja/F 2017

Submarines (Ships)
FORLORN VICTORY [Cover story] R. Soodalter bw color map *Military History* v34 no4 p38 N 2017
MACHINES OF THE ABYSS K. ATHERTON diag *Popular Science* p26 Ja/F 2017
Now Boarding For the Titanic Tour J. Dean color *Bloomberg Businessweek* no4537 p54 S 11 2017

Submarines (Ships)—History
THAT SINKING FEELING B. Hogan color *MHQ: Quarterly Journal of Military History* v29 no4 p28 Summ 2017
A U-BOAT'S U-TURN [Cover story] W. Bernard bw color map *MHQ: Quarterly Journal of Military History* v29 no4 p40 Summ 2017

Submarine topography—Mexico, Gulf of
See also
Chicxulub Crater
DEVASTATION DETECTIVES T. Sumner color diag map *Science News* v191 no2 p16 F 4 2017

Submersibles
See also
Submarines (Ships)
Innovation A. Popescu color *Bloomberg Businessweek* no4525 p34 Je 5 2017
The Open-Top Submarine J. Zorthian color *Time* v188 no20 p19 N 14 2016
Technology *Oceanus* v52 no1 p19 Summ 2016
When the Hunter Became the Hunted V. LaCapra *Oceanus* v52 no1 p21 Summ 2016

Subprime automobile loans
It's happening again G. Coppola and J. Butters color graph *Bloomberg Businessweek* no4531 p23 Jl 24 2017

Subprime loans
E-Z Auto Loans Are A Tough Business T. Metcalf color graph *Bloomberg Businessweek* no4521 p37 My 8 2017

Subrahmanian, V. S.
Predicting human behavior: The next frontiers bibl color *Science* v355 no6324 p489 F 3 2017

Subramani, Gauri
Lessons from Yelp's Empirical Approach to Diversity *Harvard Business Review Digital Articles* p2 S 20 2017

Subramaniam, Mohan
Are You Using APIs to Gain Competitive Advantage? *Harvard Business Review Digital Articles* p2 Ap 13 2015
Corporate Alliances Matter Less Thanks to APIs *Harvard Business Review Digital Articles* p2 Je 8 2015
The Next Battle in Antitrust Will Be About Whether One Company Knows Everything About You *Harvard Business Review Digital Articles* p2 Jl 6 2017
The Strategic Value of APIs *Harvard Business Review Digital Articles* p2 Ja 7 2015

SUBRAMANIAN, DIVYA
Facing the Flood bw *Publishers Weekly* v264 no36 p81 S 4 2017

Subramanian, R.
Spectral narrowing of x-ray pulses for precision spectroscopy with nuclear resonances diag *Science* v357 no6349 p375 Jl 28 2017

Subramanian, Samanth
Bangalore was once the icon of a globalized, high tech future. Now it's the thirsty sign of a global catastrophe color *Wired* v25 no5 p110 My 2017
The Eurocrat Who Makes Corporate America Tremble bw color *Bloomberg Businessweek* no4522 p68 My 15 2017
UP & OUT *New York Times Magazine* p46 Ap 23 2017
Welcome to Macedonia, Fake News Factory to the World color graph *Wired* v25 no3 p68 Mr 2017

Subramanian, Santhosh
CANCER SCANNERS L. BELLOWS *Atlanta* v56 no10 p22 F 2017

Subramanian, Sundar
Personalized Technology Will Upend the Doctor-Patient Relationship *Harvard Business Review Digital Articles* p2 Je 19 2015

Subramanian, Sushma
My Forgotten Language color *Discover* v38 no9 p28 N 2017
SHRINK YOUR GUT WITH GASTROPHYSICS color *Men's Health* v32 no2 p63 Mr 2017

Subscription services
See also
Subscription gift-box services
Subscriptions to serial publications
3 tools that easily unsubscribe you from emails M. ANSALDO color *PCWorld* v35 no6 p44 Je 2017
GIVE THE GIFT OF TIME color *Money* v45 no11 p15 D 2016
How Subscriptions Are Creating Winners and Losers in Retail C. Randall, A. Lewis et al *Harvard Business Review Digital Articles* p2 Ja 8 2016
LIVE LARGE ON A SUBSCRIPTION PLAN T. H. BLANTON color *Kiplinger's Personal Finance* v71 no7 p15 Jl 2017
Subscription Business Models Are Great for Some Businesses and Terrible for Others R. K. Baxter *Harvard Business Review Digital Articles* p2 Jl 13 2016

Subscription services—Evaluation
EVERY-SIZE STYLE color *Good Housekeeping* v264 no3 p18 Mr 2017

Subscription gift-box services

Boxed In G. Barkho and Jing Cao color graph *Bloomberg Businessweek* no4535 p23 Ag 28 2017

Subscriptions to serial publications

WELCOME, MS. PARTNERS AND LIFETIME MEMBERS! *Ms.* v26 no4 p34 Wint 2016

Subscription services—Charts, diagrams, etc.

CELLPHONE ACCESS HAS SKYROCKETED. THE WORLD IS BETTER FOR IT M. Tupy graph *Reason* v49 no5 p44 O 2017

Subsidiarity—Religious aspects

Locally grown K. Clarke color *U.S. Catholic* v82 no3 p42 Mr 2017

Subsidiary corporations—Finance

WHEN SHAREHOLDERS ARE SPECTATORS R. Derousseau color diag *Fortune* v175 no2 p40 F 1 2017

Subsidies

UNDER WATER B. Jarvis *New York Times Magazine* p64 Ap 23 2017

Wasting time: Subsidies, operating reactors, and melting ice P. A. Bradford *Bulletin of the Atomic Scientists* v73 no1 p13 Ja 2017

Subsidies—China

Will Trump Crush China Over Aluminum? J. Deaux color *Bloomberg Businessweek* no4510 p22 F 6 2017

Subsidies—Italy

When La Dolce Vita Starts to Sour J. Follain color *Bloomberg Businessweek* no4536 p33 S 4 2017

Subsistence farming

Country Lore S. Stith, S. M. Furl et al *Mother Earth News* no281 p84 Ap/My 2017

Substance abuse

Lights, Camera, Therapy A. KRAFT color *Discover* v38 no5 p24 Je 2017

SOLUTIONS IN RECOVERY *Psychology Today* v50 no1 p1 Ja/F 2017

WRITTEN INTERACTIONS PREDICT INCARCERATION *USA Today Magazine* v145 no2860 p10 Ja 2017

Substance abuse treatment

How Can Families Develop Resilience Against Patient Relapse Behaviors? M. Powers *Psychology Today* v50 no1 p14 Ja/F 2017

TREATING ADDICTED WOMEN during pregnancy D. Gilbert *Psychology Today* v50 no3 p25 My/Je 2017

Substance-induced disorders—Treatment

The effect of state parity laws on how providers treat substance use disorder K. Harris *Monthly Labor Review* p1 Je 2017

Substitute players

14 HANDY MEN S. Apstein color diag *Sports Illustrated* v126 no9 p67 Mr 27 2017

BEING NO. 2 A. Prewitt color *Sports Illustrated* v125 no17 p98 N 21 2016 Double Issue

RESERVE AND PROTECT R. Nadkarni color *Sports Illustrated* v126 no12 p33 My 1 2017

Subterranean civilization

HIDDEN FROM VIEW B. DONAHUE color *Archaeology* v70 no2 p48 Mr/Ap 2017

Subtext (Short story)

SUBTEXT® C. YU cartoon color *Wired* v25 no1 p46 Ja 2017

Suburban homes—Sales & prices

SUBURBAN SAFARI T. Perrotta cartoon *New Yorker* v92 no41 p28 D 12 2016

Suburban life

I Love My Collections color *House Beautiful* v158 no10 p104 D 2016/Ja 2017

Suburban sprawl

Pockets of Growth: Suburban counties are once again gaining population at the expense of the cities around them M. Maciag *Governing* v30 no9 p56 Je 2017

Suburbanization

SUBURBAN FUTURISM G. Kroeber bw color *Art in America* v104 no11 p106 D 2016

Suburbicon (Film)

SUBURBICON C. Collis color *Entertainment Weekly* no1478 / 1479 p51 Ag 18-25 2017

Suburbs

Are Cities Growing or Not? W. Fulton *Governing* v30 no1 p24 O 2016

SORRY, URBANITES: PEOPLE STILL LOVE SUNBELT SUBURBS diag map *Fortune* v175 no8 p36 Je 15 2017

Where the Wild Things Are In the Suburbs E. BASTOS color *Reader's Digest* v189 no1130 p56 My 2017

Suburbs—United States—Economic conditions

THE POSTWAR DREAM: NOV. 15, 1947 A. BROWN bw color *Forbes* v200 no4 p30 O 24 2017

Subversive activities

    See also

    Espionage

    Spies

    Terrorism

Subway stations—New York (State)

The Subterranean Scene M. Guerber color il *American Craft* v77 no3 p80 Je/Jl 2017

Subways

Worth a stop N. Walker color *Canadian Geographic* v135 no6 p50 D 2015

Subways—California—Los Angeles

FORWARD MOTION D. L. ULIN *Los Angeles Magazine* p90 My 2017

Subways—Design & construction

ALL ABOARD N. PAUMGARTEN cartoon *New Yorker* v92 no49 p36 F 13 2017

Now Arriving (Really!) on Second Avenue img *New York* v49 no25 p18 D 12 2016

Second Avenue Subway J. Gonchar *Architectural Record* v205 no4 p200 Ap 2017

Subways—New York (State)—New York

ALL ABOARD N. PAUMGARTEN cartoon *New Yorker* v92 no49 p36 F 13 2017

MILLION-DOLLAR SUBWAY FIXES E. WAITE and R. CLEGG cartoon *New Yorker* v93 no24 p29 Ag 21 2017

Notes from Underground R. BROOKHISER il *National Review* v69 no3 p55 F 20 2017

Second Avenue Subway J. Gonchar *Architectural Record* v205 no4 p200 Ap 2017

Subway Napping A. Deutsch *New York Times Magazine* p18 F 26 2017

Subwoofers

Bluesound Pulse Soundbar and Pulse Sub D. Kumin color graph *Sound & Vision* v82 no5 p52 Je 2017

Decorator-Friendly Bass J. SCIACCA color *Sound & Vision* v82 no6 p23 Jl/Ag 2017

Hi-Res Streams A. L. GRIFFIN color *Sound & Vision* v82 no5 p19 Je 2017

JL Audio Fathom IWS-SYS-1 In-Wall Subwoofer System D. Wilkinson color *Sound & Vision* v82 no6 p50 Jl/Ag 2017

New Gear color *Sound & Vision* v82 no7 p32 S 2017

What's the Frequency? A. GRIFFIN color *Sound & Vision* v82 no3 p23 Ap 2017

Subwoofers—Evaluation

Gift Guide *Boating World* v37 no9 p43 N/D 2016

JL Audio Dominion d110 Subwoofer D. Vaughn color graph *Sound & Vision* v82 no3 p64 Ap 2017

PSB SubSeries 450 Subwoofer D. Vaughn color graph *Sound & Vision* v81 no10 p60 D 2016

SVS PB16-Ultra and SB16-Ultra Subwoofers D. Vaughn color graph *Sound & Vision* v82 no2 p50 F/Mr 2017

Sucato, Steve

A New Home for Choreograpers: NCCAkron launches its first official residency this month *Dance Magazine* v91 no7 p16 Jl 2017

On the Move: Two American artistic directors are taking over major international troupes *Dance Magazine* v91 no9 p20 S 2017

Success

    See also

    Academic achievement

    Success in business

AMERICAN HUSTLERS L. SCHWARTZBERG color *Wired* v25 no6 p86 Je 2017

Commit to Under-Scheduling in 2016 E. G. Saunders *Harvard Business Review Digital Articles* p2 D 21 2015

DEAR Younger me M. FOYE *Scholastic Choices* v33 no1 p20 S 2017

Following my lucky star N. G. Roman color *Science* v354 no6317

p1346 D 9 2016

THE GOOD BUSINESS ISSUE *Bloomberg Businessweek* no4505 p53 D 26 2016

The Joy of Sharing S. Gregory color *Time* v189 no7/8 p62 F 27 2017

The League of Extraordinary LOSERS [Cover story] J. PRESS *Scholastic Choices* v32 no5 p10 F 2017

PLANTING A NEW HOBBY, OUTLOOK ON LIFE D. HEITMAN *Phi Kappa Phi Forum* v96 no4 p36 Wint 2016

Sadness: A Love Story J. Klausner color *InStyle* v24 no9 p218 S 2017

Stop Reading Lists of Things Successful People Do E. Soyer and R. M. Hogarth *Harvard Business Review Digital Articles* p2 Mr 13 2017

(VIRTUAL) REALITY BITES E. Griffith color *Fortune* v175 no2 p45 F 1 2017

Which Woman Powers Your Success? bw color *Glamour* v115 no2 p20 F 2017

Write a Failure Résumé to Learn What Makes You Succeed B. Taylor *Harvard Business Review Digital Articles* p2 My 3 2016

Success in business

3 Things Driving Entrepreneurial Growth in Africa R. Klingebiel and C. Stadler color *Harvard Business Review Digital Articles* p2 F 1 2017

4 Factors That Predict Startup Success, and One That Doesn't T. J. Marion *Harvard Business Review Digital Articles* p2 My 3 2016

The 4 Things It Takes to Succeed in the Digital Economy L. Anderson and I. Wladawsky-Berger *Harvard Business Review Digital Articles* p2 Mr 24 2016

The 5 Elements of a Strong Leadership Pipeline J. Bersin *Harvard Business Review Digital Articles* p2 O 6 2016

7 SECRETS OF A SIDE HUSTLER K. Johnson color *Black Enterprise* v47 no7 p14 My/Je 2017

A business doing pleasure M. CAMPBELL *Maclean's* v130 no7 p12 Ag 2017

Companies Can't Be Great Unless They've Almost Failed B. Taylor *Harvard Business Review Digital Articles* p2 Mr 21 2016

Cooking in My Own Voice: Chowder-soaked toast is a dish any chef would want to claim G. Hamilton *New York Times Magazine* p36 My 21 2017

Develop Deep Knowledge in Your Organization—and Keep It D. Leonard *Harvard Business Review Digital Articles* p2 S 29 2016

Does Your Company Have What It Takes to Go Global? D. Quackenbos, R. Ettenson et al *Harvard Business Review Digital Articles* p2 Ap 11 2016

Don't Let Your Company Get Trapped by Success M. Reeves and J. Harnoss *Harvard Business Review Digital Articles* p2 N 19 2015

Driving Sales Success This Quarter, This Year, and Beyond A. A. Zoltners, P. K. Sinha et al *Harvard Business Review Digital Articles* p2 D 1 2016

FIVE TRENDS THAT COULD CHANGE YOUR FARM G. Johnston *Successful Farming* v114 no11 p54 N 2016

Germany's Midsize Manufacturers Outperform Its Industrial Giants W. W. Weber *Harvard Business Review Digital Articles* p2 Ag 12 2016

Growth Needs to Come from the Entire Company P. Leinwand, C. Mainardi et al *Harvard Business Review Digital Articles* p2 Je 17 2016

How Dell, HP, and Apple Rediscovered Their Founders' Vision C. Zook *Harvard Business Review Digital Articles* p2 Jl 15 2016

How Did I Get Here? A. Cohen bw color *Bloomberg Businessweek* no4526 p72 Je 12 2017

How to Know If a Spin-Off Will Succeed H. Vantrappen and E. Polastro *Harvard Business Review Digital Articles* p2 F 24 2015

IT WAS BUZZ AT FIRST SIGHT E. Griffith color *Fortune* v174 no8 p81 D 15 2016

Most Likely to succeed bw color *Bloomberg Businessweek* no4526 p67 Je 12 2017

OUT WITH THE OLD P. Marx cartoon *New Yorker* v92 no44 p22 Ja 9 2017

PENNEY WISE A. Gumbs color *Black Enterprise* v47 no2 p34 S 2016

Stop Believing That You Have to Be Perfect D. Clark *Harvard Business Review Digital Articles* p2 O 8 2014

Strategies for Succeeding in Today's Brazil P. G. Alonso *Harvard Business Review Digital Articles* p2 N 19 2015

Successful Movements All Have 3 Acts N. Duarte *Harvard Business Review Digital Articles* p2 Mr 24 2016

A Survey of 3,000 Executives Reveals How Businesses Succeed with AI J. Bughin, B. McCarthy et al *Harvard Business Review Digital Articles* p2 Ag 28 2017

To Manage a Platform, Think of It as a Micromarket U. Haque *Harvard Business Review Digital Articles* p2 Ap 13 2016

We've Forgotten What "Greatness" Really Means D. Seidman *Harvard Business Review Digital Articles* p2 Mr 4 2016

What Do You Do Well That Others Don't? W. Johnson *Harvard Business Review Digital Articles* p2 O 6 2015

What Resilience Means, and Why It Matters A. Ovans *Harvard Business Review Digital Articles* p2 Ja 5 2015

When Opportunity Resides Along the Edges A. Lewis and D. McKone *Harvard Business Review Digital Articles* p2 F 1 2016

When You've Made Enough Money to Cause Family Tension J. Baron, R. Lachenauer et al *Harvard Business Review Digital Articles* p2 Ja 8 2016

Success in business—Economic aspects

THE MAGIC IN THE WAREHOUSE N. Gabler color diag *Fortune* v174 no8 p182 D 15 2016

Success in business—History—21st century

The Best in Business 2016 color diag *Fortune* v174 no8 p18 D 15 2016

Success in business—United States

How U.S. Businesses Can Succeed in India in 2015 V. Govindarajan and G. Bagla *Harvard Business Review Digital Articles* p2 D 22 2014

How WD-40 Created a Learning-Obsessed Company Culture B. Taylor *Harvard Business Review Digital Articles* p2 S 16 2016

Success in business—United States—Research

THE NEW ORGANIZATION MEN (AND WOMEN) graph img *Harvard Business Review* v95 no2 p30 Mr/Ap 2017

Successful aging

Oral Health for Healthy Aging D. Scott color *Maclean's* v129 no40 p59 O 10 2016

Successful people

The Best Leaders Allow Themselves to Be Persuaded A. Pittampalli *Harvard Business Review Digital Articles* p2 Mr 3 2016

Finding the Healthy Tension Between Being Confident and Collaborative L. Levy bw *Harvard Business Review Digital Articles* p2 Ja 10 2017

GLOBAL GAME CHANGERS bw *Forbes* v199 no6 p38 Je 13 2017

Great Performers Make Their Personal Lives a Priority S. Friedman *Harvard Business Review Digital Articles* p2 O 6 2016

How Successful People Network with Each Other D. Clark *Harvard Business Review Digital Articles* p2 Ja 21 2016

Succession planning

A CEO's Personality Can Undermine Succession Planning B. Dattner and T. Chamorro-Premuzic *Harvard Business Review Digital Articles* p2 S 15 2016

FARM TRANSITIONS: AG'S DOWN CYCLE MAY OFFER A SLOW BUT STEADY SUCCESSION ROUTE C. Tevis *Successful Farming* v115 no9 p18 Ag 2017

How to Get on the Shortlist for the C-Suite C. Frangos color *Harvard Business Review Digital Articles* p2 Mr 2 2017

Outsider CEOs Are on the Rise at the World's Biggest Companies C. Nickisch *Harvard Business Review Digital Articles* p2 Ap 19 2016

What Next? Succession Planning for Nonprofits A. Fraizer *Bridges (Federal Reserve Bank of St. Louis)* p5 Fall 2016

Why Boards Get C-Suite Succession So Wrong C. Fernández-Aráoz *Harvard Business Review Digital Articles* p2 My 15 2015

Why Family Firms in East Asia Struggle with Succession C. Fernández-Aráoz, S. Iqbal et al *Harvard Business Review Digital Articles* p2 Mr 24 2015

Success—Psychological aspects

How Stressing Out Can Help You Succeed I. Robertson *Time* v189 no4 p23 Ja 23 2017

SLAY YOUR SETBACKS M. NICOLE NAZZARO color *Runner's World* v52 no8 p24 S 2017

Success—Social aspects

How to Create More from What You Already Have S. Sonenshein *Time* v189 no7/8 p28 F 27 2017

Success—United States

The Case for ... The White Sox J. Fuchs and T. Keith color *Sports Illustrated* v126 no12 p21 My 1 2017

Succulent plants

Ask Martha *Martha Stewart Living* no267 p62 S 2016

Can't. Look. Away Z. Schaeffer color *Women's Health* v14 no2 p78 Mr 2017

GREEN THUMB F. SUN *Atlanta* v56 no12 p44 Ap 2017

Such A Boy (Music)

THE ULTIMATE SUMMER SINGLES SWAP N. Feeney color *Entertainment Weekly* no1477 p54 Ag 11 2017

Suchanková, Alžběta

Higher predation risk for insect prey at low latitudes and elevations graph *Science* v356 no6339 p742 My 19 2017

SUCHER, SANDRA

CASE STUDY: FOLLOW DUBIOUS ORDERS OR SPEAK UP? AN INTERN CONTEMPLATES WHETHER SHE SHOULD COMPROMISE HER VALUES FOR A JOB il *Harvard Business Review* v95 no4 p139 Jl/Ag 2017

Suchyta, S.

Observation of coherent elastic neutrino-nucleus scattering diag *Science* v357 no6356 p1123 S 15 2017

SUCKLING, KIERÁN

An Ecoregion-Based Approach to Protecting Half the Terrestrial Realm *BioScience* v67 no6 p534 Je 2017

Suckling in animals

Wild orangutans set nursing record S. MILIUS color *Science News* v191 no12 p8 Je 24 2017

Sucov, Jenny

Eat Clean, Stay Lean [Cover story] M. TAYLOR color *Prevention* v68 no11 p42 N 2016

Sucrose

DISAPPOINTING RESULTS FOR ULCER BLOOD TEST C. Barakat and M. McCluskey color *Equus* no477 p17 Je 2017

Sudanese refugees

Aid groups seek funds as Sudan crisis worsens F. Nzwili color *Christian Century* v134 no20 p14 S 27 2017

Suddath, Claire

Alakazam! color diag *Bloomberg Businessweek* no4495 p56 O 17 2016

Americas color map *Bloomberg Businessweek* no4532 p7 Jl 31 2017

Asia color *Bloomberg Businessweek* no4532 p6 Jl 31 2017

At Work With U.S. Coast Guard Ice Patrol color *Bloomberg Businessweek* no4528 p37 Je 26 2017

BIG MAC ATTACK color *Bloomberg Businessweek* no4508 p62 Ja 23 2017

CRAZY FOR CAULIFLOWER color *Bloomberg Businessweek* no4521 p66 My 8 2017

Europe color *Bloomberg Businessweek* no4532 p6 Jl 31 2017

I LOVE LAGUARDIA color *Bloomberg Businessweek* no4514 p72 Mr 13 2017

'I mean, is there anti-murder training?' *Bloomberg Businessweek* no4501 p42 N 28 2016

Liberal Nonprofits Ride The Anti-Trump Wave color *Bloomberg Businessweek* no4500 p30 N 21 2016

Paid In Semi Full color diag *Bloomberg Businessweek* no4528 p42 Je 26 2017

Sudden infant death syndrome prevention

Think About Pacifiers L. Anastasia *Parents* v92 no9 p163 S 2017

Sudeikis, Jason, 1975-

Jason SUDEIKIS *Vanity Fair* v59 no2 p128 F 2017

QUOTE MACHINE M. Schulman cartoon *New Yorker* v92 no40 p24 D 5 2016

Suderman, Peter

AMERICAN GODS *Reason* v49 no4 p76 Ag/S 2017

THE COST OF CARRYING DEBT *Reason* v48 no11 p9 Ap 2017

DEMOCRATS DEFECT FROM OBAMACARE bw cartoon color graph *Reason* v48 no9 p26 F 2017

GOVERNMENT ALMOST KILLED THE COCKTAIL color *Reason* v49 no5 p54 O 2017

HEALTH CARE AND THE POLITICS OF DISRUPTION color *Reason* v49 no4 p7 Ag/S 2017

THE HIDDEN MIND color *Reason* v48 no8 p50 Ja 2017

REPUBLICANS DON'T LACK A PLAN TO REPLACE OBAMACARE. THEY LACK A UNIFIED THEORY color *Reason* v49 no2 p14 Je 2017

Young Men Are Playing Video Games Instead of Getting Jobs. That's OK. (For Now.) color *Reason* v49 no3 p16 Jl 2017

Sudholz, T.

Observation of a large-scale anisotropy in the arrival directions of cosmic rays above 8×10^{18} eV *Science* v357 no6357 p1266 S 22 2017

Sudjic, Olivia

Sympathy *Publishers Weekly* v264 no6 p42 F 6 2017

Sudol, Alison

ALISON SUDOL K. SMITH color *Vanity Fair* v58 no12 p73 D 2016

SUED, YAMIL

RUGER LCP II color *Outdoor Life* v224 no4 pP1 My 2017

Süel, Gürol M.

Coupling between distant biofilms and emergence of nutrient time-sharing bw color graph *Science* v356 no6338 p638 My 12 2017

Suellentrop, Chris

BEANTOWN BAEDEKER bw color *American History* v52 no2 p68 Je 2017

Suesse, Ned

2017 DUCATI MULTISTRADA 950 color *Cycle World* v56 no2 p14 Mr 2017

Suetonius, ca. 69-ca. 122

TYRANNUS REX Suetonius *Lapham's Quarterly* v10 no3 p41 Summ 2017

Suffering

See also

Loneliness

"How Bad Is Your Pain?" Notes on the nature of suffering R. TELHAN *American Scholar* v86 no4 p20 Aut 2017

How to Talk to a Loved One Who Is Suffering S. Sandberg and A. Grant color *Time* v189 no15 p43 Ap 24 2017

Suffolk (England)

Wild Vacation R. DAVIDSON *National Geographic Kids* no468 p11 Mr 2017

Suffrage

See also

Ballot

Ex-convicts—Suffrage

Women's suffrage

RIGHT TO VOTE? WRONG A. BERMAN *Sierra* v101 no5 p34 S/O 2016

Suffrage—Lawsuits & claims

MESSING WITH TEXAS P. Levy *Mother Jones* v42 no5 p32 S/O 2017

Suffrage—United States

Ballot Blockers P. Levy *Mother Jones* v42 no6 p27 N/D 2017

The Case for Re-Enfranchisement J. Lewis Berg *Humanist* v76 no6 p6 N/D 2016

THE FIGHT TO VOTE J. Toobin cartoon *New Yorker* v92 no41 p23 D 12 2016

HOW TO DEFLATE A DEMAGOGUE M. BAUERLEIN and C. JEFFERY *Mother Jones* v42 no6 p4 N/D 2017

Should You Have the Right to Vote Now? *Scholastic Choices* p2 O 2017

Suffragists

Owning Your Vote M. Clark cartoon *Glamour* v114 no11 p36 N 2016

Suffragists—History

SUFFRAGE SHIFT N. TAPPAN bw color *American History* v52 no3 p14 Ag 2017

Sufism

THE LILA OF THE GNAWA K. GREENSPAN bw color *Natural History* v125 no3 p34 Mr 2017

Suga, Kishio

KISHIO SUGA J. S. Li color *Art in America* v105 no5 p135 My 2017

Sugar

See also

Food—Sugar content

FAMILY HEALTH GUIDE L. Turner color *Amazing Wellness* v9 no4 p58 Summ 2017

Sugar rush *Science* v355 no6326 p706 F 17 2017

Sugar, Rachel

What You Should Read This Spring color *Fortune* v175 no5 p16 Ap 1 2017

Sugar beet

SUGAR CITY: SWEET TOWN, IDAHO J. D. EDLEFSEN *Idaho Magazine* v16 no11 p32 Ag 2017

Sugar content of beverages

Should soft-drink makers be held liable for the health risks of sugar? K. KIPLINGER *Kiplinger's Personal Finance* v71 no10 p14 O 2017

Sugar Land (Tex.)

Blood and SUGAR M. HARDY *Texas Monthly* v45 no1 p47 Ja 2017

Sugar maple—Tapping

SAP TO SYRUP E. M. Jennings *New York State Conservationist* v71 no4 p14 F 2017

Sugar pine

Protecting One of America's Premier Wildernesses: American Re-Leaf in Tahoe National Forest D. Irvin *American Forests* v123 no1 p7 Wint/Spr 2017

Sugar substitutes

CAN YOU BUILD A BETTER SUGAR? M. Stacey color *Women's Health* v14 no4 p112 My 2017

SUGAR RUSH B. Kowitt color diag *Fortune* v175 no3 p102 Mr 1 2017

SUGARBAKER, SANDRA

ROAR OF THE CROWD *Texas Monthly* v45 no1 p8 Ja 2017

SugarCreek Packing Co.

The Meat Cutter A. Streep *New York Times Magazine* p44 F 26 2017

Sugar—History

Sugar Rush: The unsavory history of an insatiable American craving J. R. GRITZ *Smithsonian* v48 no2 p16 My 2017

Sugarman, Joe

THE EASTERN SHORE color *Washingtonian Magazine* v52 no7 p149 Ap 2017

Hit the Trail: Perhaps nothing helps clear the head more than an exhilarating day of exertion--such as a 41-mile hike across Maryland *Washingtonian Magazine* v52 no11 p98 Ag 2017

THE ITINERARY: FREDERICK *Washingtonian Magazine* v52 no2 p237 N 2016

JOLLY GOOD FELLAS *Washingtonian Magazine* v52 no3 p94 D 2016

Keep It Simple *Washingtonian Magazine* v52 no11 p88 Ag 2017

MY TOWN color *Washingtonian Magazine* v52 no7 p159 Ap 2017

TAKE A DRIVE: FELLS POINT: Even if you love our town, it's nice to get away. This month-new reasons to visit a historic waterfront neighborhood in Baltimore *Washingtonian Magazine* v52 no12 p106 S 2017

Sugar—Physiological effect

Let's get granular about SUGAR S. KUZEMCHAK color *Redbook* p96 Ap 2017

Unsweetened N. Buhayar and P. Clark bw color *Bloomberg Businessweek* no4516 p27 Mr 27 2017

Sugars in human nutrition

Not-So-Sweet Heart J. MIGALA cartoon color *AARP: The Magazine* v60 no2A p23 F/Mr 2017

Where Sugar Bombs Hide cartoon chart color *Men's Health* v32 no1 p64 Ja/F 2017

Sugars—Physiological effect

CANCER'S Sweet Cloak [Cover story] E. Landhuis color diag graph *Science News* v191 no6 p24 Ap 1 2017

Sugden, John

The merry dance of the HIGHWAYMAN *History Today* v67 no3 p48 Mr 2017

Sugg, Richard

The Search for the Soul *History Today* v67 no4 p48 Ap 2017

Suggestion systems

Employee Suggestion Schemes Don't Have to Be Exercises in Futility E. R. Burris *Harvard Business Review Digital Articles* p2 Ja 26 2016

Suggs, Carroll—Awards

ADL presents Torch awards to Isaacson, Suggs *Successful Farming* v115 no1 p14 Ja 2017

Sugiyama, Hiroshi

Holliday junction resolvases mediate chloroplast nucleoid segre-

gation diag *Science* v356 no6338 p631 My 12 2017

Sugiyama, Masaaki

Crystal structure of the overlapping dinucleosome composed of hexasome and octasome graph *Science* v356 no6334 p205 Ap 14 2017

SUGRUE, THOMAS J.

In Praise of a City: Herb Boyd's 'Black Detroit' celebrates the freedom fighters on history's margins *New York Times Book Review* p10 S 10 2017

The Language of the Unheard: Fifty years on, the flames of the 1967 Detroit uprising still burn *In These Times* v41 no8 p25 Ag 2017

Suh, B.

Observation of coherent elastic neutrino-nucleus scattering diag *Science* v357 no6356 p1123 S 15 2017

Suh, Lisa S.

Site-specific phosphorylation of tau inhibits amyloid-β toxicity in Alzheimer's mice bibl graph *Science* v354 no6314 p904 N 18 2016

Suhrie, Garret

FORESTS IN FOCUS *American Forests* v123 no1 p40 Wint/Spr 2017

Suicidal behavior

    See also

    Suicide

Cause for Hope S. POLAN *Psychology Today* v50 no1 p21 Ja/F 2017

Suicide in the workplace R. Harris *Monthly Labor Review* p1 D 2016

Suicidal behavior in military personnel

A Lifesaving Golf Date with His Dad D. CHRISINGER color *Reader's Digest* v190 no1134 p48 O 2017

Suicidal behavior in youth—Prevention

Confronting Student Suicide G. W. ". McGee cartoon *Education Digest* v82 no8 p4 Ap 2017

Why Schools Need to Step Up Suicide Prevention Efforts M. Swanbrow Becker *Education Digest* v83 no2 p17 O 2017

Suicide

    See also

    Assisted suicide

Bridge Builder A. JUNG color *Reader's Digest* v190 no1133 p8 S 2017

Lack of Means Doesn't Justify End L. Featherstone color *Nation* v305 no10 p5 O 23 2017

An Open Letter To the Shoppers Who Consoled Me [Cover story] D. GREENE *Reader's Digest* v188 no1125 p94 N 2016

Who Saved Whom? W. Sheridan bw *Commonweal* v144 no4 p31 F 24 2017

Suicide bombers

The Known Wolf D. GREEN color *Weekly Standard* v22 no38 p20 Je 12 2017

Suicide bombings

Egypt's Copts face rising fears, divisions J. Wirtschafter, M. Nader et al color *Christian Century* v134 no10 p14 My 10 2017

Suicide notes

SUICIDE NOTES D. Merkin *Harper's Magazine* v334 no2000 p17 Ja 2017

Suicide prevention

Cause for Hope S. POLAN *Psychology Today* v50 no1 p21 Ja/F 2017

How to spot the warning signs of suicide L. Aston *People Management* p48 Jl 2017

Suicide Squad (Film)

LET'S PLAY JOKER'S WILD! K. P. Sullivan color *Entertainment Weekly* no1444/1445 p64 D 16 2016

Suicide Squad M. FELL *TV Guide* v65 no14 p43 Ap 3 2017

VIOLA DAVIS N. Sperling color *Entertainment Weekly* no1444/1445 p36 D 16 2016

Suicide statistics

Suicide in the workplace R. Harris *Monthly Labor Review* p1 D 2016

Suicide Rates of U.S. Farmers and Agriculture Workers, 1992-2010 L. SCHLEY graph *Discover* v38 no8 p14 O 2017

Suicide victims

CAST AWAYS *Harper's Magazine* v335 no2006 p15 Jl 2017

FINDINGS *Harper's Magazine* no2007 p96 Ag 2017

Stefan Zweig's Ordeal J. P. O'MALLEY bw *American Conservative* v16 no3 p39 My/Je 2017

Suitcases

Back to the Future color *Conde Nast Traveler* v52 no7 p21 Ag 2017

MAKING THE CASE FOR PROTECTION T. HANSEN color *Outdoor Life* v224 no8 pB4 O 2017

STUPID OR AMAZING? color *Popular Mechanics* p76 D 2016/ Ja 2017

Suitcases—Design & construction

A Suitcase That Follows Its Owner J. Zorthian color *Time* v189 no6 p21 F 20 2017

Suitcases—Evaluation

2016 GIFT GUIDE K. Flaim color *Fortune* v174 no7 p43 D 1 2016

Die Hard E. FLORIO color *Conde Nast Traveler* v52 no1 p116 Ja 2017

FORCES OF NATURE color *Harper's Bazaar* no3649 p170 D 2016/Ja 2017

Gimme, Gimme! bw color *Glamour* v114 no7 p30 Jl 2016

High Rollers H. ROLLERS color *Forbes* v198 no8 p22 D 20 2016

Rimowa Topas Suitcase color *Bloomberg Businessweek* no4536 p71 S 4 2017

Suits (Clothing)

BLACK IS THE NEW BLACK K. Soller color *Bloomberg Businessweek* no4521 p63 My 8 2017

Finding Her LEGS M. HOLGATE and M. GUIDUCCI color *Vogue* v207 no7 p40 Jl 2017

Find Your Strong Suit B. BOYÉ cartoon color *Men's Health* v32 no4 p57 My 2017

Is Your Suit Too Tight? N. SULLIVAN color *Esquire* v167 no1 p34 F 2017

Only If It SUITS YOU A. Bilmes bw color *Esquire* p66 BigBlackBook

Our Hyper-Evolutionary Moment J. Fielden color *Esquire* p18 2017 BigBlackBook

Out of the Warehouse S. Eide color *Weekly Standard* v22 no33 p45 My 8 2017

"PANTSUIT" /PANT SOOT/ B. PETERSON *Washingtonian Magazine* v52 no3 p18 D 2016

P. JOHNSON MAKES COOL SUITS YOU ACTUALLY WANT TO WEAR color *Esquire* p54 Je/Jl 2017

Three Young Designers Bring Back Custom Suits—and They're Actually Affordable M. A. GREEN and N. MARINO bw color *GQ: Gentlemen's Quarterly* v97 no4 p42 Ap 2017

The Wright Way to Keep Your Cool C. Flammia and P. Kita color *Men's Health* v32 no2 p25 Mr 2017

Suits (Clothing)—Evaluation

60 FOR 60 color *GQ: Gentlemen's Quarterly* v97 no10 p134 O 2017

CAN YOU SAY 'GLENURQUHART'? bw color *Esquire* p82 Ag 2017

Double Vision T. Patterson chart color *Bloomberg Businessweek* no4535 p61 Ag 28 2017

HANG LOOSE J. Roth bw color *Esquire* v167 no2 p128 Mr 2017

How the Style Guy Turns $1,000 into $3,000 M. A. GREEN color *GQ: Gentlemen's Quarterly* v87 no1 p10 Ja 2017

THE NEW SUITING color *Harper's Bazaar* no3655 p132 Ag 2017

Suits (TV program)

Suits D. Holbrook *TV Guide* v65 no4 p38 Ja 16 2017

What to Watch R. Rahman, C. Agard et al color *Entertainment Weekly* no1480 p46 S 1 2017

Suits, Arthur G.

Synthesis of mixed hypermetallic oxide BaOCa+ from laser-cooled reagents in an atom-ion hybrid trap diag graph *Science* v357 no6358 p1370 S 29 2017

Sujin Jang

To Connect Across Cultures, Find Out What You Have in Common *Harvard Business Review Digital Articles* p2 Ja 20 2017

Sukachev, D. D.

An integrated diamond nanophotonics platform for quantum-optical networks bibl graph *Science* v354 no6314 p847 N 18 2016

Suki Kim

LAND OF DARKNESS *Lapham's Quarterly* v10 no3 p205 Summ 2017

Sukiya (Company)

Bowled Over C. SORVINO color *Forbes* v199 no5 p26 My 16 2017

Sukkot

SMALL WORLD S. ORR *Better Homes & Gardens* v95 no10 p10 O 2017

SULA, MIKE

THE ULTIMATE TAILGATE GRILL TEST color *Popular Mechanics* p34 Jl 2017

Sulcov, Michelle Rose

Welcome Back, Bobby Pins color *Glamour* v115 no4 p46 Ap 2017

Suleiman, Susan Rubin

A Marvelous Writer in a Hopeless Situation A. Muhlstein bw *New York Review of Books* v63 no20 p40 D 22 2016

Selected for Death *New York Times Book Review* p20 O 23 2016

Suleyman I, Sultan of the Turks, 1494 or 5-1566

DISASTER AT DJERBA: During a period of European peace, Spain sought to establish control of the Mediterranean. Yet a disastrous attempt to oust the Ottomans from North Africa threatened to accelerate the westward advance of Islam B. W. Allen *History Today* v67 no6 p24 Je 2016

Sulfonamides

Anticancer sulfonamides target splicing by inducing RBM39 degradation via recruitment to DCAF15 T. Han, M. Goralski et al color diag *Science* v356 no6336 p397 Ap 28 2017

Sulfur

Putting the spotlight on organic sulfur N. M. Levine bibl color diag *Science* v354 no6311 p418 O 28 2016

Sulfur & the environment

Sulfur injections for a cooler planet U. Niemeier and S. Tilmes color graph *Science* v357 no6348 p246 Jl 21 2017

Sull, Donald

Where Disruptive Innovation Came From *Harvard Business Review Digital Articles* p2 N 10 2015

Sulla, Angela

KITCHEN-TESTED TIPS color *Vegetarian Today* no1 p4 F 2017

Sullivan, Alaina

Socca Star color *Bon Appetit* no1 p42 F 2017

Sullivan, Amanda

A Bountiful Life color *Nebraska Life* v21 no4 p76 Jl/Ag 2017

PUT YOUR YEAR IN GEAR L. GOLDMAN color *Better Homes & Gardens* v95 no9 p158 S 2017

Sullivan, Andrew

America Is Still the Future img *New York* p16 Ja 23 2017

Bokeh C. Nashawaty color *Entertainment Weekly* no1459 p48 Mr 31 2017

I Used to Be a Human Being img *New York* v49 no19 p32 S 19 2016

OBAMA'S AMERICA img *New York* v49 no20 p12 O 3 2016

The Republic Repeals Itself *New York* v49 no23 p22 N 14 2016

A Right to Live *New York Times Book Review* p1 N 27 2016

Sounds of Silence *New Republic* v248 no3 p4 Mr 2017

Sullivan, Andrew, 1963-

The Fate of Republics: Does the Roman story pose lessons for America? R. W. MERRY *American Conservative* v16 no4 p13 Jl/Ag 2017

REACTIONARIES MUST BE TAKEN SERIOUSLY: A tricky exercise in our political climate—but a necessary one img *New York* v50 no9 p28 My 1 2017

Sullivan, Barry

It's Time to Tie Executive Compensation to Sustainability *Harvard Business Review Digital Articles* p2 2017

Why Companies Should Measure "Share of Growth," Not Just Market Share color *Harvard Business Review Digital Articles* p1 Je 2 2017

Sullivan, Bo

CURTIS PORCHWORK cartoon *Arts & Crafts Homes & the Revival* v12 no3 p72 Summ 2017

Gordon-Van Tine Homes: Davenport, Iowa: "The Kitchen," 1926 color *Arts & Crafts Homes & the Revival* v12 no5 p72 Wint 2018

HENRY BOSCH CO cartoon *Arts & Crafts Homes & the Revival* v11 no5 p72 Wint 2017

L. & J.G. STICKLEY: Fayetteville, N.Y. "A Living Room," 1912 color *Arts & Crafts Homes & the Revival* v12 no4 p72 Fall 2017

TAPESTRY PORTIÈRES color *Arts & Crafts Homes & the Re-*

vival v12 no2 p72 Spr 2017

Sullivan, C.C.

Cutting-Edge Elevator Technology: Elevating architecture with destination dispatch controls color *Architectural Record* v205 no8 p152 Ag 2017

Sullivan, Caroline

No More Flu Shot Excuses! J. SINRICH color *Reader's Digest* v190 no1135 p46 N 2017

SULLIVAN, CATEY

54 GREAT THINGS TO DO THIS MONTH color *Chicago* v66 no1 p117 Ja 2017

58 GREAT THINGS TO DO THIS MONTH color *Chicago* v66 no2 p101 F 2017

62 GREAT THINGS TO DO THIS MONTH color *Chicago* v66 no6 p97 Je 2017

63 GREAT THINGS TO DO THIS MONTH color *Chicago* v66 no7 p87 Jl 2017

63 GREAT THINGS TO DO THIS MONTH color *Chicago* v66 no8 p105 Ag 2017

65 GREAT THINGS TO DO THIS MONTH color *Chicago* v65 no11 p115 N 2016

66 GREAT THINGS TO DO THIS MONTH color *Chicago* v66 no9 p139 S 2017

67 GREAT THINGS TO DO THIS MONTH color *Chicago* v66 no3 p129 Mr 2017

68 GREAT THINGS TO DO THIS MONTH color *Chicago* v66 no5 p119 My 2017

GO: 69 GREAT THINGS TO DO THIS MONTH color *Chicago* v66 no11 p103 N 2017

GO bw color *Chicago* v66 no10 p105 O 2017

GO color *Chicago* v65 no12 p119 D 2016

GO color *Chicago* v66 no4 p113 Ap 2017

Sullivan, Charlie

How to Know Which Digital Trends Are Worth Chasing *Harvard Business Review Digital Articles* p2 Jl 7 2016

SULLIVAN, CLAIRE

HOW TO GET RID OF ANYTHING cartoon color *Martha Stewart Living* p118 Ap 2017

Meatball Makeovers color *Martha Stewart Living* p83 O 2017

RAISING YOUR HOME'S IQ color *Martha Stewart Living* p80 S 2017

SULLIVAN, DAN

PREACHING WHAT YOU PRACTICE bw color *Film Comment* v52 no6 p78 N/D 2016

Sullivan, Daniel F.

Big Progress in Authentic Assessment, But by Itself Not Enough *Change* v49 no1 p14 Ja/F 2017

Sullivan, Devin P.

A subcellular map of the human proteome color *Science* v356 no6340 p820 My 26 2017

Sullivan, Eric

THE BOMBER SQUAD bw color *Esquire* p86 My 2017

GEORGE SAUNDERS bw *Esquire* v167 no1 p58 F 2017

A Gym of Angels cartoon color *Esquire* v167 no1 p48 F 2017

KARL OVE KNAUSGAARD: THREE BOOKS THAT CHANGED MY LIFE color *Esquire* p48 S 2017

ROCKIN' THE FULL TRUMP color *Esquire* p44 Ap 2017

STOP RIGHT THERE, MISTER color *Esquire* p108 Je/Jl 2017

Sullivan, Erin E.

How One California Medical Group Is Decreasing Physician Burnout color *Harvard Business Review Digital Articles* p2 Je 7 2017

Strong Patient-Provider Relationships Drive Healthier Outcomes *Harvard Business Review Digital Articles* p2 O 9 2015

Sullivan, Felicia C.

Follow Me into the Dark *Publishers Weekly* v264 no5 p175 Ja 30 2017

Sullivan, J. Courtney

On Camp *New York Times Book Review* p13 Je 4 2017

The Roads Both Taken: A time-traveling novel follows two immigrant sisters on their very different paths S. BERNE *New York Times Book Review* p13 Jl 9 2017

Saints, Elsewhere S. Begley color *Time* v189 no19 p55 My 22 2017

Sullivan, J. R.

2016 BEST OF THE BEST bw color *Field & Stream* v121 no7

p96 D 2016/Ja 2017

DAMAGE CONTROL color *Field & Stream* v121 no8 p40 F/Mr 2017

EARLY BIRDS cartoon chart *Field & Stream* v121 no8 p28 F/Mr 2017

SEARCHING FOR SILVER color *Field & Stream* v122 no2 p26 Je/Jl 2017

THE SHIPWRECK OF SAN LEON cartoon *Field & Stream* v121 no7 p56 D 2016/Ja 2017

THIS LAND WAS YOUR LAND cartoon color diag map *Field & Stream* v122 no1 p40 My 2017

THE VANISHING [Cover story] color *Field & Stream* v122 no6 p64 N 2017

SULLIVAN, JENNA

Long-Term Studies Contribute Disproportionately to Ecology and Policy *BioScience* v67 no3 p271 Mr 2017

SULLIVAN, JENNY

Healing Hands color *Trail Rider* v29 no4 p26 My 2017

Horse Owner's Spring Notebook color *Trail Rider* v29 no4 p38 My 2017

Ride for a Cause color *Trail Rider* v29 no2 p28 Mr 2017

SULLIVAN, JEREMIAH

PRINCE *New York Times Magazine* p48 D 25 2016

Sullivan, Jeremiah D.

IN MEMORIAM *Phi Kappa Phi Forum* v97 no1 p33 Spr 2017

Sullivan, John

6 Ways to Screen Job Candidates for Strategic Thinking *Harvard Business Review Digital Articles* p2 D 13 2016

7 Rules for Job Interview Questions That Result in Great Hires *Harvard Business Review Digital Articles* p2 F 10 2016

Sullivan, Kara

Workforce growth in community-based care: meeting the needs of an aging population *Monthly Labor Review* p1 D 2016

Sullivan, Katherine

Local news on public airways graph *Columbia Journalism Review* v56 no1 p101 Spr 2017

Sullivan, Kevin P.

10 — THE NYC CHASE *Entertainment Weekly* no1444/1445 p61 D 16 2016

THE 25 MOST PATRIOTIC MOVIES OF ALL TIME color *Entertainment Weekly* no1472 p30 Je 30 2017

3 — "WOULD THAT IT WERE SO SIMPLE" color *Entertainment Weekly* no1444/1445 p58 D 16 2016

50 YEARS OF ARTHUR color *Entertainment Weekly* no1450 p37 Ja 27 2017

ALIEN AWAKENS color *Entertainment Weekly* no1467 p44 My 26 2017

Amanda Knox color *Entertainment Weekly* no1434 p42 O 7 2016

ATTACK OF THE KILLER WHITE PEOPLE color *Entertainment Weekly* no1454/1455 p80 F 24 2017

THE BATTLE OF CHRISTOPHER NOLAN color *Entertainment Weekly* no1474/1475 p56 Jl 21-28 2017

BEST ACTOR color diag *Entertainment Weekly* no1451/1452 p54 F 3-10 2017

Best and Most Beautiful Things color *Entertainment Weekly* no1443 p48 D 9 2016

THE BEST, BADDEST ACTION HERO NAMES color *Entertainment Weekly* no1449 p44 Ja 20 2017

The Deuce color *Entertainment Weekly* no1482/1483 p29 S 22 2017

THE DEUCE IS WILD! color *Entertainment Weekly* no1456 p18 Mr 10 2017

Don of the Planet of the Apes color *Entertainment Weekly* no1474/1475 p94 Jl 21-28 2017

DUNKIRK color *Entertainment Weekly* no1446/1447 p50 D 2016/Ja 2017

DUNKIRK color *Entertainment Weekly* no1463/1464 p66 Ap/My 2017

GAMBLING MAN color *Entertainment Weekly* no1477 p34 Ag 11 2017

A GHOST STORY color *Entertainment Weekly* no1463/1464 p68 Ap/My 2017

The Good Knight color *Entertainment Weekly* no1466 p22 My 19 2017

Good Time color *Entertainment Weekly* no1478 / 1479 p84 Ag 18-25 2017

THE GREATEST DISNEY SONGS OF ALL TIME color *Entertainment Weekly* no1454/1455 p36 F 24 2017

The Handmaiden color *Entertainment Weekly* no1436/1437 p87 O 21 2016

Hey, These Beasts Are Fantastic! color *Entertainment Weekly* no1441 p37 N 25 2016

How Iron Fist Packs a Punch color *Entertainment Weekly* no1457/1458 p84 Mr 17 2017

JOHN CENA: UNDER FIRE color *Entertainment Weekly* no1466 p41 My 19 2017

Justin Timberlake and Jonathan Demme color *Entertainment Weekly* no1435 p42 O 14 2016

KING ARTHUR: LEGEND OF THE SWORD color *Entertainment Weekly* no1463/1464 p40 Ap/My 2017

LET'S PLAY JOKER'S WILD! color *Entertainment Weekly* no1444/1445 p64 D 16 2016

THE LOST CITY OF Z color *Entertainment Weekly* no1446/1447 p57 D 2016/Ja 2017

THE MAN HOLLYWOOD CAN'T STOP READING color *Entertainment Weekly* no1462 p64 Ap 21 2017

MARY J. BLIGE IN Mudbound color *Entertainment Weekly* no1478 / 1479 p61 Ag 18-25 2017

MR. ROBOT color *Entertainment Weekly* no1474/1475 p66 Jl 21-28 2017

A NEW KING WILL RISE color *Entertainment Weekly* no1450 p34 Ja 27 2017

NO. 28 SILVER SURFER color *Entertainment Weekly* no1436/1437 p64 O 21 2016

NO. 6 IRON MAN color *Entertainment Weekly* no1436/1437 p49 O 21 2016

THE PROS OF CON color *Entertainment Weekly* no1476 p32 Ag 4 2017

R.I.P. VINE: THE SIX-SECOND OBITUARY color *Entertainment Weekly* no1439 p11 N 11 2016

Ron Glass 1945-2016 color *Entertainment Weekly* no1443 p17 D 9 2016

THE TEENY-TINY NOLAN MOVIE color *Entertainment Weekly* no1474/1475 p60 Jl 21-28 2017

WAR FOR THE PLANET OF THE APES color *Entertainment Weekly* no1446/1447 p54 D 2016/Ja 2017

WarReN BEAtty An ORAL HISTORY color *Entertainment Weekly* no1440 p30 N 18 2016

WHAT'S NEXT FOR WOLVERINE? color *Entertainment Weekly* no1457/1458 p16 Mr 17 2017

What's the Most Bingeworthy Show? color *Entertainment Weekly* no1443 p21 D 9 2016

What to Watch color *Entertainment Weekly* no1436/1437 p94 O 21 2016

What to Watch color *Entertainment Weekly* no1451/1452 p100 F 3-10 2017

What to Watch color *Entertainment Weekly* no1470 p52 Je 16 2017

What to Watch color *Entertainment Weekly* no1485 p52 O 6 2017

WHO WOULD WIN? WOLVERINE VS. IRON MAN *Entertainment Weekly* no1436/1437 p49 O 21 2016

Will Dunkirk Score Nolan His First Oscar? color *Entertainment Weekly* no1476 p16 Ag 4 2017

WOLVERINE NO MORE [Cover story] color *Entertainment Weekly* no1456 p22 Mr 10 2017

THE WORST FILMS OF THE YEAR color *Entertainment Weekly* no1444/1445 p62 D 16 2016

THE WORST — WIG GAME! color *Entertainment Weekly* no1444/1445 p60 D 16 2016

Your Sunshiny, Stupendous, Seriously Spectacular SUMMER BUCKET LIST color *Entertainment Weekly* no1470 p32 Je 16 2017

Sullivan, Leonard

LIVING HISTORY L. Cutrone color *Louisiana Life* v37 no5 p24 My/Je 2017

Sullivan, Louis H., 1856-1924

Reflections on the lectionary S. Swain *Christian Century* v134 no19 p19 S 13 2017

Sullivan, M.

iPTF16geu: A multiply imaged, gravitationally lensed type Ia supernova color diag graph *Science* v356 no6335 p291 Ap 21 2017

Sullivan, Margaret

Game, Set, Match E. Alterman *Nation* v304 no13 p6 Ap 17 2017

Spin, Span, Spun color *Weekly Standard* v22 no24 p3 F 27 2017

Trump and the Watergate effect bw *Columbia Journalism Review* v56 no2 p27 Fall 2017

Sullivan, Margaret—Interviews

Q&A MARGARET SULLIVAN il *Nation* v303 no25/26 p5 D 19 2016

Sullivan, Mary

Treat *Publishers Weekly* v263 no49 p42 D 7 2016

Sullivan, Matthew

Midnight at the Bright Ideas Bookstore *Publishers Weekly* v264 no15 p52 Ap 10 2017

SULLIVAN, MICHELLE

NEWPORT *Cincinnati Magazine* v50 no7 p33 Ap 2017

Sullivan, Molly

Have You Thought About Certification as an Alternative Educational Experience? *Parks & Recreation* v52 no2 p42 F 2017

SULLIVAN, NICK

THE ABROAD-ROBE bw color *Esquire* p46 My 2017

BOOT UP color *Esquire* p60 S 2017

CARE LESS, LOOK BETTER bw cartoon color *Esquire* v167 no2 p66 Mr 2017

THE CHINO GETS ITS BALLS BACK bw color *Esquire* p44 Je/Jl 2017

COOLER THREADS PREVAIL color *Esquire* p40 Ag 2017

Dressed to Chill bw color *Esquire* v166 no5 p64 D 2016/Ja 2017

A FEW GOOD FINDS color *Esquire* p58 Ap 2017

FLOATS LIKE A BUTTERFLY color *Esquire* p41 O 2017

Ground Control color *Esquire* v166 no4 p66 N 2016

hitting the BIG TIME bw color *Esquire* p38 2017 BigBlackBook

HORSE POWER bw color *Esquire* p104 2017 BigBlackBook

THE IMPOSSIBLE LIST bw cartoon color *Esquire* v167 no1 p70 F 2017

Is Your Suit Too Tight? color *Esquire* v167 no1 p34 F 2017

Leather Heads color *Esquire* v166 no4 p52 N 2016

The New ETERNALS color *Esquire* p36 BigBlackBook

One Tough MUDDER bw color *Esquire* p48 BigBlackBook

Physical Graffiti cartoon color *Esquire* v167 no1 p31 F 2017

RESTRAIN YOURSELF bw color *Esquire* p46 N 2017

Space Race bw color *Esquire* v166 no4 p60 N 2016

THE TEST OF TIME color *Esquire* p42 N 2017

this Way In: HIT THE LINKS FLASH SOME GREEN color *Esquire* p27 S 2017

THREE WISE MEN bw color *Esquire* p88 2017 BigBlackBook

THE TIP SHEET color *Esquire* p36 Ag 2017

WELCOME TO PEAK STYLE SEASON color *Esquire* p61 S 2017

SULLIVAN, PAUL

cabin capers cartoon *Cabin Living* p88 Ap 2017

Sullivan, Robert

DEALER'S CHOICE color *Vogue* v207 no4 p124 Ap 2017

Face OF Bass color *Vogue* v207 no7 p44 Jl 2017

FACING HISTORY cartoon *New Yorker* v93 no17 p20 Je 19 2017

Home of the Brave bw color *Vogue* v207 no1 p60 Ja 2017

In It to Win It color *Vogue* v207 no9 p330 S 2017

Model BEHAVIOR color *Vogue* v207 no1 p30 Ja 2017

Nathan Benderson Park: A Classic Reclamation Project *Parks & Recreation* v51 no10 p28 O 2016

OBJECTS of their DESIRE color *Vogue* v207 no3 p326 Mr 2017

Our Invasive Species *New York Times Book Review* p31 D 11 2016

Reigning Supreme bw color *Vogue* v207 no9 p710 S 2017

Riley Keough color *Vogue* v207 no9 p372 S 2017

Triple Bull's-Eye color *Vogue* v207 no9 p624 S 2017

Sullivan, Robert David

Bloc the Vote [Cover story] color graph map *America* v215 no13 p16 O 31 2016

The Change Is Us *America* v215 p23 N 28 2016

DEMOCRATS STUMBLE OVER ABORTION POLITICS IN OMAHA color graph *America* v216 no11 p12 My 15 2017

Ending Civil Death *America* v215 no11 p18 O 17 2016

The real bubble protects elected officials *America* v216 no13 p3 Je 12 2017

SCORCHED EARTH DAY? color graph *America* v216 no8 p12 Ap 17 2017

STAYING PUT IN A MOBILE ERA chart color graph map *Amer-*

ica v217 no2 p12 Jl 24 2017

SULLIVAN, ROSEANNE

SYMBOLIC GESTURES *Commonweal* v144 no13 p2 Ag 11 2017

Sullivan, Terry

How to Shoot Great Video chart color *Consumer Reports* v82 no5 p18 My 2017

Sullivan, Tim

BLOCKBUSTER MAGIC bw color il img *Harvard Business Review* v95 no1 p164 Ja/F 2017

Entrepreneurs, Economic Growth, and the Enlightenment *Harvard Business Review Digital Articles* p2 Ag 10 2015

Everything We Know About Platforms We Learned from Medieval France *Harvard Business Review Digital Articles* p2 Mr 24 2016

If Your Argument Is Based on Economics, You've Already Lost *Harvard Business Review Digital Articles* p2 Je 24 2016

The Internet of "Stuff Your Mom Won't Do for You Anymore" *Harvard Business Review Digital Articles* p2 Jl 26 2016

The Philanthropist's Burden color il *Harvard Business Review* v94 no12 p114 D 2016

A Super Bowl Ad Is the Equivalent of Lighting Money on Fire (Which Can Be More Strategic Than It Sounds) color *Harvard Business Review Digital Articles* p2 F 3 2017

What Economists Don't Get About Uber's Surge Pricing *Harvard Business Review Digital Articles* p2 D 17 2014

Sullivan, William M.

Paths to Engagement: PROVOKING INTELLECTUAL FERMENT through Pedagogies of Social Participation *Change* v49 no3 p52 My/Je 2017

STUDENTS ON THE WAY G. D. O'BRIEN *America* v215 no18 p36 D 5 2016

SULLUM, JACOB

CAN YOU GO TO JAIL FOR HANDING OUT PAMPHLETS? bw *Reason* v49 no6 p8 N 2017

DOES LEGALIZATION BOOST TEEN MARIJUANA USE? cartoon *Reason* v49 no1 p12 My 2017

ENLISTING MARIJUANA AND MDMA TO FIGHT PTSD color *Reason* v49 no6 p32 N 2017

FROM THE ARCHIVES bw cartoon *Reason* v48 no11 p70 Ap 2017

FROM THE ARCHIVES bw color *Reason* v49 no3 p70 Jl 2017

FROM THE ARCHIVES bw *Reason* v49 no6 p78 N 2017

IS KRATOM THE NEW MARIJUANA? color *Reason* v48 no8 p8 Ja 2017

ISRAEL DECRIMINALIZES POT POSSESSION color *Reason* v49 no2 p8 Je 2017

JEFF SESSIONS, GLUTTON FOR PUNISHMENT *Reason* v49 no5 p6 O 2017

OBAMA FINALLY FINDS HIS CLEMENCY PEN graph *Reason* v48 no11 p44 Ap 2017

Obama's Belated Drug War Retreat *Reason* v48 no9 p6 F 2017

Putin's Biggest Fan *Reason* v48 no7 p14 D 2016

Reefer Madness at The New York Times color *Reason* v49 no4 p42 Ag/S 2017

THE SEARCH FOR A PLACE TO TOKE UP color *Reason* v49 no3 p6 Jl 2017

SEX AND KIDS color *Reason* v48 no11 p26 Ap 2017

SHOULD YOU TELL THE COPS YOU HAVE A GUN? color graph *Reason* v49 no5 p7 O 2017

A TIMELINE OF MARIJUANA IN THE NEW YORK TIMES bw color *Reason* v49 no4 p52 Ag/S 2017

Trump's Troubling Attorney General Pick color *Reason* v48 no10 p6 Mr 2017

WHAT AMERICA TAUGHT A MURDEROUS DRUG WARRIOR color *Reason* v49 no4 p12 Ag/S 2017

Sully (Film)

How to Dramatize Heroism—and How Not To R. Alleva color *Commonweal* v143 no17 p27 O 21 2016

HUMAN PRESENCE S. KLAWANS *Nation* v303 no17 p36 O 24 2016

SULLY A. Greengart color *Sound & Vision* v82 no4 p67 My 2017

Sully *New Yorker* v92 no33 p14 O 17 2016

Sulmers, Claire—Interviews

LEADERS OF THE NEW COOL A. LUCAS and J. R. LOVE II bw color *Ebony* v72 no6 p35 Ap/My 2017

Sulmeyer, Michael

What the Rise of Russian Hackers Means for Your Business *Harvard Business Review Digital Articles* p2 My 12 2017

Sulong Xiao

Generation of influenza A viruses as live but replication-incompetent virus vaccines bibl graph *Science* v354 no6316 p1170 D 2 2016

Sultan, Donald—Exhibitions

DISASTER AS DESTINY *USA Today Magazine* v146 no2866 p46 Jl 2017

Sultan, Sonia E.

A UNIFIED VIEW OF DEVELOPMENT: MAKING EVO-DEVO OPERATIONAL M. MANGEL *BioScience* v67 no5 p478 My 2017

Sulzberger, Arthur Gregg, 1980-

A. G. Sulzberger M. Hagan color *Current Biography* v78 no9 p80 S 2017

Twilight Times E. Alterman *Nation* v304 no17 p6 Je 5 2017

Sulzberger, Gregg

Keeping Up with the Times G. Snyder bw cartoon color graph *Wired* v25 no3 p50 Mr 2017

Sum 41 (Performer)

The Resuscitation of Sum 41 A. GREENE color *Rolling Stone* no1273 p17 N 3 2016

Sumaila, U. Rashid

Science-based management in decline in the Southern Ocean bibl map *Science* v354 no6309 p185 O 14 2016

Sumanth, John J.

Get Your Employees to Make Better Suggestions *Harvard Business Review Digital Articles* p2 Mr 5 2015

Sumatra Earthquake, 2004

Deep heat intensified mega-quake L. HAMERS *Science News* v191 no12 p7 Je 24 2017

Sumba Island (Indonesia)

Sumba Island INDONESIA color *Sports Illustrated* v126 no6 p112 F 20 2017

TRAVEL Sumba Island color *Sports Illustrated* v126 no6 p130 F 20 2017

Sumbal, Marni

BEST FOODS FOR RUNNERS [Cover story] cartoon color *Runner's World* v52 no3 p54 Ap 2017

SUMELL, MATT

AND THEN SHE APPEARED color *Popular Mechanics* p32 O 2017

Sumiya, Hitoshi

Nanoscale nuclear magnetic resonance with chemical resolution diag *Science* v357 no6346 p67 Jl 7 2017

Sumlin, Christopher M.

TECH TRENDS CHANGING OUR WORLD color *Black Enterprise* v47 no2 p46 S 2016

Summer

BEST Summer Ever! [Cover story] color *Chicago* v66 no7 p48 Jl 2017

The Case for ... Boxing's Big Summer G. Bishop and T. Keith color *Sports Illustrated* v126 no17 p30 Je 19 2017

The Dos of Summer Hair K. Erickson color *Glamour* v114 no7 p80 Jl 2016

forecast center T. Vasquez *Weatherwise* v70 no5 p60 S/O 2017

FUN IN THE SUN color *Field & Stream* v122 no2 p65 Je/Jl 2017

HEALTH color *Horse & Rider* v56 no6 p26 Je 2017

Here We Go! Oprah color *O, The Oprah Magazine* p17 Je 2017

Hot-Weather Trail Hazards H. S. Thomas color *Horse & Rider* v56 no6 p64 Je 2017

I'M 44 AND I WANT TO GET RAD J. LINDSEY color *Bicycling* v58 no9 p48 O 2017

IT TAKES A VILLAGE R. O'CONNOR color *Chicago* v66 no8 p32 Ag 2017

Q: Who's your trusty sidekick for summer adventures, and why? R. FICKE, W. MOORE et al color *O, The Oprah Magazine* p14 Je 2017

South Florida's Toxic Summer M. SHAW color *Surfer* v58 no4 p42 Ag 2017

Summer Beauty 911 color *O, The Oprah Magazine* p60 Je 2017

SUMMER GETAWAYS: IT'S POSSIBLE TO ENJOY MINI-CRUISES IN THE SEA OF CORTEZ WHILE STAYING CLOSE TO A HURRICANE HOLE P. RAINS color map *Sea*

Magazine v109 no7 p12 Jl 2017

Summer Living C. Rose cartoon *New Orleans Magazine* v51 no8 p44 Je 2017

That FIRST WARM DAY S. M. Danler color *Esquire* p78 My 2017

TRANS COMMUNITY AND SUMMER DRESS CODES [Cover story] *USA Today Magazine* v146 no2867 p1 Ag 2017

WHY I HATE SUMMER T. CHIARELLA color *Chicago* v66 no7 p63 Jl 2017

wildlife quiz cartoon color *Cabin Living* p11 Je 2017

Summer, Eugenia

IN MEMORIAM *Phi Kappa Phi Forum* v96 no4 p33 Wint 2016

Summer cooking

In the SUNSET KITCHEN color *Sunset* v238 no6 p98 Je 2017

SHOW TIME I. Edwards color *Sunset* v238 no6 p6 Je 2017

SINGULAR Sensation M. Kiesel color *O, The Oprah Magazine* p106 Jl 2017

Summer employment

Hunting for a Summer SM Job D. J. McGraw *Stage Directions* v30 no1 p16 Ja 2017

The Summer Job I'll Never Forget Miranda, J. Patterson et al color *Time* v190 no2/3 p55 Jl 10-17 2017

What I Learned AT MY Summer Job T. CHIARELLA, H. ROLLINS et al cartoon *Popular Mechanics* p64 Je 2017

What You Said About ... color map *Time* v190 no4 p5 Jl 24 2017

Where Did America's Summer Jobs Go? K. Vick, M. Fabry color diag *Time* v190 no2/3 p52 Jl 10-17 2017

Summer festivals

MEET RICHARD ANDERSEN *Sea Magazine* v108 no8 pPNW-8 Ag 2016

Summer Hawk Optics Inc.

FLYING EYES SUNGLASSES cartoon color *Flying* v144 no1 p14 Ja 2017

Summer reading programs

SIDE-BY-SIDE LEARNING: A summer program focused on science disciplinary literacy C. Condie and J. Ippolito *Literacy Today (2411-7862)* v35 no1 p30 Jl/Ag 2017

Summer school curriculum

Live and Learn: As kids return to school, here's a lesson on education: A lot of it happens during summer, and theory has nothing to do with it P. GULLEY *Indianapolis Monthly* v12 no40 p50 Ag 2017

Summer schools

Summer learning that sticks D. Browne color *Phi Delta Kappan* v98 no4 p15 D 2016/Ja 2017

Summer squash

YELLOW SUMMER SQUASH *South Dakota Magazine* v33 no3 p33 S/O 2017

Summer vacations

50 WAYS TO GET LOST IN SUMMER E. N. GAGE color *Martha Stewart Living* p83 Jl/Ag 2017

CAN'T AFFORD A VACATION? BLAME THE STATE! V. D. RUGY color *Reason* v49 no4 p10 Ag/S 2017

The Importance of Being Idle P. Coy color *Bloomberg Businessweek* no4532 p8 Jl 31 2017

MAKE SOME AMAZING MEMORIES A. BARTZ and J. Press color *Redbook* p88 Jl/Ag 2017

A PLACE IN THE SUN C. Kearns color *Field & Stream* v122 no2 p10 Je/Jl 2017

SMALL WORLD S. ORR *Better Homes & Gardens* v95 no10 p10 O 2017

THE SOUNDS OF VACATION L. MYERS cartoon *Missouri Life* v44 no5 p66 Ag 2017

THE SUMMER EFFECT L. KAMPS color *Martha Stewart Living* p50 Jl/Ag 2017

TAKE A FAMILY 'FIELD' TRIP: MAKE AG A PART OF YOUR VACATION PLANS - NO MATTER WHERE YOU'RE HEADED L. F. Prater color *Successful Farming* v115 no7 p57 My 2017

THRILL RIDES color *Field & Stream* v122 no2 p37 Je/Jl 2017

Summer vacations (Schools)

The Citified Origins of Summer Vacation O. B. Waxman *Time* v190 no5 p27 Jl 31 2017

From Studio to Summertime L. WINGENROTH *Dance Magazine* v91 no1 p122 Ja 2017

SUMMER BRAIN DRAIN: FIND A FUN WAY TO HELP YOUR

KIDS KEEP THEIR MINDS ENGAGED ONCE SCHOOL IS OUT color *Successful Farming* v115 no7 p60 My 2017

Weight Gain Occurs When School Is Out *USA Today Magazine* v145 no2861 p5 F 2017

Summerhays, Daniel, 1984-

Daniel Summerhays J. Marksbury color *Golf Magazine* v59 no10 p25 O 2017

Summer King, The (Theatrical production)

King of Diamonds A. KOZINN *Opera News* v81 no10 p18 Ap 2017

Summer—Psychological aspects

20 Quirky Summer Health Tips (That Actually Work) B. Howard, J. Migala et al color *AARP: The Magazine* v59 no4A p19 Je/Jl 2016

SUMMERS, B. F.

Halloween Under The Sea color *National Geographic Kids* no474 p26 O 2017

Summers, Christopher

Targeted Ads Don't Just Make You More Likely to Buy—They Can Change How You Think About Yourself *Harvard Business Review Digital Articles* p2 Ap 4 2016

Summers, Clint

BUCKLE UP with Clint Summers K. Gustave color *Team Roping Journal* p22 S 2017

Summers, Lawrence H., 1954-

How Uber and the Sharing Economy Can Win Over Regulators *Harvard Business Review Digital Articles* p2 O 13 2014

Is Corporate Short-Termism Really a Problem? The Jury's Still Out *Harvard Business Review Digital Articles* p2 F 16 2017

Yes, Short-Termism Really Is a Problem R. L. Martin *Harvard Business Review Digital Articles* p2 O 9 2015

Summers, Lawrence H., 1954—Interviews

Larry Summers: Business Leaders Should Stand Up to President Trump A. Ignatius bw *Harvard Business Review Digital Articles* p2 F 1 2017

Larry Summers on What Business Can Do to Save the Middle Class W. Frick *Harvard Business Review Digital Articles* p2 F 9 2015

Summers, Marina

real style color *InStyle* v24 no3 p66 Mr 2017

Summers, Nick

ALONG CAME A SCAPEGOAT color *Bloomberg Businessweek* no4516 p66 Mr 27 2017

Making Their Bets *Bloomberg Businessweek* no4499 p31 N 14 2016

Summers, Z.

Fostering reproducibility in industry-academia research color *Science* v357 no6353 p759 Ag 25 2017

Summerscales, Owen

Middle of Somewhere color *Climbing* no357 p36 N 2017

Summer Wishes, Winter Dreams (Film)

The Little Guy S. Mears color *Film Comment* v53 no4 p18 Jl/Ag 2017

Summit Adventure Guide (Company)

TRUE WILDERNESS *Iceland Review* v54 no6 p110 N/D 2016

Summit meetings

The Tipping Point: When Do Female Leaders Become the Norm? S. Schrobsdorff color *Time* v190 no16/17 p38 O 23 2017

Summitt, Pat, 1952-2016

PAT SUMMITT E. WEIL *New York Times Magazine* p60 D 25 2016

Sumner, Christie

Christmas in the country S. S. SORIA *Better Homes & Gardens* v94 no12 p39 D 2016

Sumner, D. Y.

Redox stratification of an ancient lake in Gale crater, Mars color *Science* v356 no6341 p922 Je 1 2017

Sumner, Jason

HOW CYCLING WORKS cartoon diag *Bicycling* v58 no9 p21 O 2017

Keep It Fresh color *Bicycling* v58 no6 p30 Jl 2017

OXYGEN IS OVERRATED color *Bicycling* v58 no8 p22 S 2017

SUMNER, THOMAS

2016 shattered Earth's heat record map *Science News* v191 no3 p9 F 18 2017

Anthropocene has begun, group says color graph *Science News*

v190 no8 p14 O 15 2016

Arctic summer may be iceless by 2050 chart *Science News* v190 no12 p15 D 10 2016

Asteroid barrage not linked to boom in ancient marine life *Science News* v191 no3 p18 F 18 2017

Atlantic ocean gets its first U.S. national monument map *Science News* v190 no8 p5 O 15 2016

Big quake hopscotched across faults *Science News* v191 no8 p14 Ap 29 2017

Budget proposal would slash science *Science News* v191 no7 p15 Ap 15 2017

Climate-friendly coolants needed *Science News* v190 no11 p13 N 26 2016

Computer defeats master at ancient Chinese game color *Science News* v190 no13 p28 D 24 2016

Data show no sign of methane boost *Science News* v191 no1 p15 Ja 21 2017

DEVASTATION DETECTIVES color diag map *Science News* v191 no2 p16 F 4 2017

Earth's big oxygen boost pushed back *Science News* v191 no4 p9 Mr 4 2017

Earth's mantle is cooling fast color *Science News* v191 no1 p14 Ja 21 2017

Fossils contain earliest signs of shells color *Science News* v190 no9 p9 O 29 2016

How Earth Got its MOON color *Science News* v191 no7 p18 Ap 15 2017

Mars may feature a stagnant interior color *Science News* v191 no4 p12 Mr 4 2017

Microbes quick to occupy impact site *Science News* v191 no1 p15 Ja 21 2017

Mystery over methane rise deepens *Science News* v191 no9 p14 My 13 2017

New device harvests water from air color *Science News* v191 no9 p10 My 13 2017

New proposal reimagines Mars' origin color *Science News* v191 no10 p14 My 27 2017

New tests reveal hotter mantle color *Science News* v191 no6 p9 Ap 1 2017

Nobels honor the small and exotic cartoon color *Science News* v190 no9 p6 O 29 2016

Pollution reaches old groundwater *Science News* v191 no10 p12 My 27 2017

Rocks hint at early oxygen oases *Science News* v191 no3 p16 F 18 2017

Rocks retain bits of Earth's early crust color *Science News* v191 no7 p8 Ap 15 2017

Sunspot cycle may be ancient routine color *Science News* v191 no3 p16 F 18 2017

Wind is an asteroid's deadliest weapon color graph *Science News* v191 no9 p12 My 13 2017

Zealandia may be eighth continent map *Science News* v191 no5 p11 Mr 18 2017

Sumner, William Graham

OLD and RIGHT *American Conservative* v15 no6 p26 N/D 2016

Sumo

Some Things You Should Know About Sumo [Cover story] D. Lowry color *Black Belt* v55 no2 p24 F/Mr 2017

Sun

   See also
      Helioseismology
      Solar technology

Eclipse time! P. HARRINGTON color *Astronomy* v45 no8 p78 Ag 2017

Hello, Moon S. J. O'MEARA color *Astronomy* v45 no10 p66 O 2017

LAST PAGE P. STEFÁNSSON color *Iceland Review* v54 no5 p128 S-O 2016

Syzygy L. SCHLEY color *Discover* v38 no5 p20 Je 2017

Sun, Elizabeth Wen

Lipid transport by TMEM24 at ER-plasma membrane contacts regulates pulsatile insulin secretion diag *Science* v355 no6326 p709 F 17 2017

SUN, FEIFEI

Bertille Sefolosha *Atlanta* v56 no11 p46 Mr 2017

BEST OF ATLANTA *Atlanta* v56 no8 p106 D 2016

COCO AND MISCHA *Atlanta* v56 no10 p44 F 2017

GREEN THUMB *Atlanta* v56 no12 p44 Ap 2017

Party Animals *Atlanta* v56 no7 p47 N 2016

SAVE FACE *Atlanta* v57 no1 p38 My 2017

Sun, Hongtao

Three-dimensional holey-graphene/niobia composite architectures for ultrahigh-rate energy storage color diag graph *Science* v356 no6338 p599 My 12 2017

Sun, I-Fang

Plant diversity increases with the strength of negative density dependence at the global scale diag *Science* v356 no6345 p1389 Je 30 2017

SUN, IRENE YUAN

The World's Next Great Manufacturing Center color *Harvard Business Review* v95 no3 p122 My/Je 2017

Sun, Lin

Clathrate colloidal crystals bibl color *Science* v355 no6328 p931 Mr 3 2017

Sun, Lixing

Pairing off color *Science* v357 no6356 p1103 S 15 2017

Sun, Lulu

The microbial metabolite desaminotyrosine protects from influenza through type I interferon graph *Science* v357 no6350 p498 Ag 4 2017

Sun, Ming-An

A placental growth factor is silenced in mouse embryos by the zinc finger protein ZFP568 color graph *Science* v356 no6339 p757 My 19 2017

Sun, Walter

Where Predictive Analytics Is Having the Biggest Impact *Harvard Business Review Digital Articles* p2 My 25 2016

Sun, Xiangnan

A molecular spin-photovoltaic device color diag *Science* v357 no6352 p677 Ag 18 2017

Sun, Yan-Gang

A central neural circuit for itch sensation color graph *Science* v357 no6352 p695 Ag 18 2017

Sun, Yingjie

Treadmilling by FtsZ filaments drives peptidoglycan synthesis and bacterial cell division bibl graph *Science* v355 no6326 p739 F 17 2017

SUN, YUELUN

Asia's Rising Stars color *Forbes* v199 no5 p20 My 16 2017

Sun, Yugang

Quantitative 3D evolution of colloidal nanoparticle oxidation in solution diag graph *Science* v356 no6335 p303 Ap 21 2017

Sun Ling Wang

Productivity Growth Is Still the Major Driver in Growing U.S. Agricultural Output *Amber Waves: The Economics of Food, Farming, Natural Resources, & Rural America* p5 S 2016

Sun observations

Mercury Maxes Out F. Schaaf *Sky & Telescope* v133 no4 p46 Ap 2017

OBSERVING April 2017r M. Wedel *Sky & Telescope* v133 no4 p41 Ap 2017

What to Expect During the Eclipse L. A. ADDINGTON color map *Missouri Life* v44 no4 p26 Je 2017

Sun Records (TV program)

Sun Records A. D'arminio color *TV Guide* v65 no7 p42 F 13 2017

Sun Valley (Idaho)—Description & travel

POWDER PLAY J. Pugh, M. Mccrea et al chart color diag *Sunset* v238 no1 p22 Ja 2017

Sunadome, Kazunori

Multipotent peripheral glial cells generate neuroendocrine cells of the adrenal medulla color *Science* v357 no6346 p46 Jl 7 2017

Sunbelt States

Jammed Cities W. Fulton *Governing* v30 no5 p25 F 2017

Migration The Sun Belt Rises Again S. Matthews graph map *Bloomberg Businessweek* no4521 p15 My 8 2017

Sunbelt States—Economic conditions

The Sun Belt's Urban Reality: The region grapples with familiar issues that need unique solutions W. Fulton color *Governing* v30 no11 p23 Ag 2017

Sunbelt States—History

The Sun Belt's Urban Reality: The region grapples with familiar issues that need unique solutions W. Fulton color *Governing*

SULE COLLECTION color *Harper's Bazaar* no3656 p156 S 2017
ICY STARE A. Westenfeld color *Esquire* p38 N 2017
My Shot color *National Geographic Kids* no470 p35 My 2017
The New ETERNALS N. Sullivan color *Esquire* p36 BigBlack-Book
Nice to See You color *Glamour* v115 no7 p110 Jl 2017
Sunglasses—Evaluation
16 ways to do CREAMSICLE color *Good Housekeeping* v265 no1 p48D Jl 2017
$50 & UNDER SUMMER STYLE color *Seventeen* v76 no4 p14 Jl/Ag 2017
Accent the BOATER *Sea Magazine* v108 no12 p42 D 2016
ADIDAS PROTEAN R. Missel color *Bicycling* v58 no9 p64 O 2017
BATTLE LA BREEZE D. Canet color *Cycle World* v56 no3 p20 Ap 2017
Bright Future L. BECKETT color *Power & Motoryacht* v33 no2 p58 F 2017
CLUTCH MOVE color *Esquire* p42 Je/Jl 2017
The Cover color *InStyle* v23 no13 p36 D 2016
DEEP PURPLE J. MOAZAMI color *Chicago* v66 no10 p42 O 2017
digital directory color *InStyle* v24 no6 p18 Je 2017
DOWN BY THE SEA T. Ebony color *Ebony* v72 no9 p41 Jl/Ag 2017
Fall into Festival Fashion M. CAMERAN color *New Orleans Magazine* v52 no1 p44 S 2017
FASHION UNDER $100 color *Redbook* p65 O 2017
FLYING EYES SUNGLASSES cartoon color *Flying* v144 no1 p14 Ja 2017
THE FREE SPIRIT J. BLAKENEY color *Martha Stewart Living* p56 Jl/Ag 2017
GEAR OF THE YEAR [Cover story] J. Dengate color *Runner's World* v51 no11 p56 D 2016
How the Style Guy Turns $1,000 into $3,000 M. A. GREEN color *GQ: Gentlemen's Quarterly* v87 no1 p10 Ja 2017
instant style color *InStyle* v24 no6 p63 Je 2017
In the Driver's Seat A. O. SCOTT color *Esquire* v167 no2 p100 Mr 2017
IRON MAN L. IMMEDIATO *Los Angeles Magazine* p27 My 2017
IT'S SPRING! GO BIG OR GO HOME color *Essence* v47 no12 p94 Ap 2017
The Joy of Specs color *O, The Oprah Magazine* p47 Je 2017
The LIST color *Harper's Bazaar* no3653 p85 My 2017
MEANS TO A LENS S. Horaczek color *Popular Science* v289 no4 p36 Jl/Ag 2017
my style color *InStyle* v24 no6 p79 Je 2017
Off to the Races J. B. Hager color *Southern Living* v52 no4 p62 Ap 2017
O'S FALL FASHION Look Book color *O, The Oprah Magazine* p55 S 2017
RANDOLPH SUNGLASSES color *Flying* v144 no5 p13 My 2017
real style color *InStyle* v24 no10 p32 O 2017
ROCK STEADY J. MOAZAMI color *Chicago* v66 no4 p48 Ap 2017
Save $500 on a Single Outfit D. Michel bw color *Men's Health* v31 no10 p74 D 2016
SILVER LINING color *Harper's Bazaar* no3655 p118 Ag 2017
SO BAZAAR color *Harper's Bazaar* no3653 p296 My 2017
Street Style: FITNESS EDITION K. Bacher color *Women's Health* v14 no3 p18 Ap 2017
Summer Lovers color *InStyle* v24 no5 p125 My 2017
Sunny Sunnies color *Good Housekeeping* v264 no6 p13 Je 2017
Tinted Love color *GQ: Gentlemen's Quarterly* v97 no7 p72 Jl 2017
Twice? Nice! S. P. Nadella color *Glamour* no8 p58 Ag 2017
Untie Him J. Passov color *Golf Magazine* v59 no6 p106 Jc 2017
VISION QUEST [Cover story] J. DENGATE color *Runner's World* v52 no6 p34 Jl 2017
a week of AWESOME OUTFITS color *Good Housekeeping* v264 no1 p34 Ja 1 2017
What to Know Now L. Chan color *Glamour* v115 no6 p52 Je 2017
WHEN OPPOSITES ATTRACT J. Roth color *Esquire* p35 Je/Jl

2017
THE WOMAN Priyanka Chopra E. Wilson color *InStyle* v24 no11 p82 N 2017
Wrap It Up! J. Passov color *Golf Magazine* v59 no1 p88 Ja 2017
YOUR AIRPORT SECURITY UPGRADE color *Esquire* v167 no2 p148 Mr 2017
Your Spring Look Is Here F. Kane, S. P. Nadella et al color *Glamour* v115 no3 p59 Mr 2017
YVONNE ORJI O. J. Williams color *Ebony* v72 no9 p44 Jl/Ag 2017
Sungsik Lee
Subthreshold Schottky-barrier thin-film transistors with ultralow power and high intrinsic gain bibl graph *Science* v354 no6310 p302 O 21 2016
Sungyoon Kim
A chemical biology route to site-specific authentic protein modifications bibl diag graph *Science* v354 no6312 p623 N 4 2016
SUNIM, HAEMIN
The Things You Can See Only When You Slow Down cartoon *Tricycle: The Buddhist Review* v26 no3 p120 Spr 2017
Suniva Inc.
A Solar Trade Case Tailor-Made for Trump J. Ryan and J. A. Dlouhy color graph *Bloomberg Businessweek* no4527 p49 Je 19 2017
Sunkara, Bhaskar, 1989-
Bhaskar Sunkara M. Hagan *Current Biography* v77 no11 p86 N 2016
Is Russia a Red Herring? *In These Times* v41 no3 p12 Mr 2017
Sunny, Steffi
Preventing mussel adhesion using lubricant-infused materials color diag graph *Science* v357 no6352 p668 Ag 18 2017
Sun Ra, 1914-1993
Magic on the Bandstand M. LONGLEY bw *Downbeat* v84 no5 p64 My 2017
Sunrise (Film)
Dirt Beneath the Daydreams D. Girish color *Film Comment* v53 no4 p74 Jl/Ag 2017
Sunrise, Sunset (Short story)
SUNRISE, SUNSET E. Danticat cartoon *New Yorker* v93 no28 p54 S 18 2017
Sunrise Strategic Partners (Company)
Searching for New Ideas in the Curious Things Your Customers Do T. Hall and E. Yoon *Harvard Business Review Digital Articles* p2 Ap 13 2017
Sun—Rising & setting
MARCH color *Martha Stewart Living* p75 Mr 2017
squinting into the sunset m. ferrentino color *Bike Magazine* v24 no1 p66 Ja/F 2017
Your True Stories L. ELSNER, J. L. DAVIS et al *Reader's Digest* v188 no1124 p22 O 2016
Sunroofs
Shattered J. Plungis and T. Germain chart color diag graph *Consumer Reports* v82 no12 p30 D 2017
Sunsail (Company)
Specialty Charters Z. Prochazka color *Sail* v48 no5 p59 My 2017
Sunscreens (Cosmetics)
BEAUTY SCIENTIST S. Wizemann color *Good Housekeeping* v264 no5 p15 My 2017
Best DEFENSE color *O, The Oprah Magazine* p88 My 2017
Do worry, be happy color *Redbook* p103 O 2017
Driving Home the Safety Discussion S. Longo, M. Mase et al il *Consumer Reports* v82 no9 p6 S 2017
I WISH SOMEONE WOULD INVENT... S. Chodosh, M. Koziol et al cartoon *Popular Science* p98 Ja/F 2017
My Skin N. Richie and C. Whitney color *InStyle* v24 no5 p240 My 2017
THE NEW CLASSICS color *Harper's Bazaar* no3656 p416 S 2017
OUT OF THE SHADOWS K. Donahue Hodes color *Women's Health* v14 no4 p45 My 2017
Secrets of a 52-year-old beauty V. Kirby color *Redbook* p48 S 2017
Skinlike Sunscreen M. Sedacca color *Scientific American* v317 no3 p15 S 2017
THE SKINNY with Val V. Monroe *O, The Oprah Magazine* p64 Je 2017

SUN SCREENED *Cincinnati Magazine* v50 no10 p35 Jl 2017

Sunscreen Smarts V. TWEED color *Better Nutrition* v79 no7 p64 Jl 2017

This Just In J. Zorthian *Time* v190 no5 p27 Jl 31 2017

THE TRUTH ABOUT SUNSCREEN A. FRANZINO color *Good Housekeeping* v264 no6 p24 Je 2017

What doctors tell their friends about the sun S. WOOD color *Redbook* p66 Je 2017

your get-real SUN-CARE GUIDE M. R. CHADWICK cartoon color *Better Homes & Gardens* v95 no6 p18 Je 2017

Sunscreens (Cosmetics)—Evaluation

10 New Rules of Southern Style A. R. Williams color *Southern Living* v52 no3 p45 Mr 2017

Beauty & the Beach color *InStyle* v24 no6 p84 Je 2017

BODY SUNSCREEN color *Good Housekeeping* v264 no6 p28 Je 2017

Don't Get Burned! T. Calvo chart color *Consumer Reports* v82 no7 p8 Jl 2017

DOWN BY THE SEA T. Ebony color *Ebony* v72 no9 p41 Jl/Ag 2017

Editors Tell All! A. Keller, A. Austen et al bw color *Women's Health* v14 no2 p60 Mr 2017

Find Your SPF OTP E. STOVALL color diag *Seventeen* v76 no3 p62 My 2017

Side Hustlers color *Women's Health* v14 no2 p58 Mr 2017

Skin Guards A. Aguillard color *Southern Living* v52 no6 p50 Je 2017

SMARTER SCREENS M. M. GOLDSTEIN color *Martha Stewart Living* no275 p38 Je 2017

Sunscreen Saviors color *Essence* v48 no3 p38 Jl 2017

WE'VE GOT YOU COVERED A. Finney *Women's Health* v14 no5 p138 Je 2017

Sunseeker International Ltd.

Out from the Crowd A. HARPER chart color *Power & Motoryacht* v34 no9 p58 S 2017

Small Wonder A. HARPER chart color *Power & Motoryacht* v32 no11 p108 N 2016

Smart and Stylish A. HARPER chart color *Power & Motoryacht* v33 no4 p62 Ap 2017

Style and Substance J. WOOLDRIDGE color *Power & Motoryacht* v33 no2 p100 F 2017

Sunset Boulevard (Theatrical production)

MAD ABOUT THE BOY H. ALS cartoon *New Yorker* v93 no2 p76 F 27 2017

READY FOR HER CLOSE-UP AGAIN C. Collis color *Entertainment Weekly* no1451/1452 p34 F 3-10 2017

Sunshine

the elusive green flash M. D. Kaufman color *Popular Science* v289 no4 p93 Jl/Ag 2017

exposure color *Canadian Geographic* v137 no4 p14 Jl/Ag 2017

Improving photosynthesis and crop productivity by accelerating recovery from photoprotection J. Kromdijk, K. Głowacka et al bibl chart color graph *Science* v354 no6314 p857 N 18 2016

New device harvests water from air T. SUMNER color *Science News* v191 no9 p10 My 13 2017

Sunshine—Therapeutic use

Light Activated A. Hadhazy color *Natural History* v125 no3 p8 Mr 2017

Sunski (Company)

EYEWEAR M. HORJUS color diag *Backpacker* v45 no3 p112 Ap 2017

Sunspots

Flares hold clues to solar mystery L. GROSSMAN color *Science News* v192 no5 p6 S 30 2017

Sunstein, Cass R.

Amazon Is Right That Disagreement Results in Better Decisions *Harvard Business Review Digital Articles* p2 Ag 18 2015

Deliberative Democracy in the Trenches *Daedalus* v146 no3 p129 Summ 2017

Great Teams Need Social Intelligence, Equal Participation, and More Women *Harvard Business Review Digital Articles* p2 D 16 2014

Listen, Economists! color *New York Review of Books* v63 no17 p53 N 10 2016

Product Success Is Not About the Zeitgeist *Harvard Business Review Digital Articles* p2 Je 22 2016

Sunstein, Sara

WE HEAR YOU *Progressive* v81 no7 p9 O/N 2017

Suntan products

Self-Tanners, Decoded E. Reimel color *Glamour* v115 no6 p78 Je 2017

Skinlike Sunscreen M. Sedacca color *Scientific American* v317 no3 p15 S 2017

Sunless tanner could protect skin A. CUNNINGHAM color *Science News* v191 no13 p11 Jl 8 2017

Suntan products—Evaluation

Does It Really Work? color *InStyle* v24 no4 p166 Ap 2017

SUNY, RONALD GRIGOR

The Empire that Dared Not Speak Its Name: Making Nations in the Soviet State *Current History* v116 no792 p251 O 2017

Sunyaev2, Shamil R.

Negative selection in humans and fruit flies involves synergistic epistasis chart graph *Science* v356 no6337 p539 My 5 2017

Sunzi, 6th century B.C.

It's Not a War on Science C. A. MILLER *Issues in Science & Technology* v33 no3 p26 Spr 2017

Suo, Z.

Tough adhesives for diverse wet surfaces diag *Science* v357 no6349 p378 Jl 28 2017

Suomijarvi, T.

Observation of a large-scale anisotropy in the arrival directions of cosmic rays above 8 × 1018 eV *Science* v357 no6357 p1266 S 22 2017

Supanitsky, A. D.

Observation of a large-scale anisotropy in the arrival directions of cosmic rays above 8 × 1018 eV *Science* v357 no6357 p1266 S 22 2017

Supapannachart, Rarinthip June

Regeneration of fat cells from myofibroblasts during wound healing bibl color graph *Science* v355 no6326 p748 F 17 2017

Super Bowl (Football game)

See also

Super Bowl (Football game) halftime show

BY THE NUMBERS *TV Guide* v65 no6 p12 Ja 30 2017

The Case of The Lousy Super Bowl Seats V. GLEMBOCKI *Reader's Digest* v189 no1127 p35 F 2017

The NFL in Decline G. NORMAN *Weekly Standard* v22 no8 p16 O 31 2016

WAS THAT THE MOST POLITICAL SUPER BOWL EVER? D. Coggan color *Entertainment Weekly* no1453 p17 F 17 2017

Why Everyone Loves the Big Game T. AIKMAN and K. Rosen *TV Guide* v65 no6 p16 Ja 30 2017

Super Bowl (Football game) advertisements

A Super Bowl Ad Is the Equivalent of Lighting Money on Fire (Which Can Be More Strategic Than It Sounds) T. Sullivan and R. Fisman color *Harvard Business Review Digital Articles* p2 F 3 2017

Super Bowl (Football game) halftime show

GOING GAGA AT HALFTIME! K. ROSEN *TV Guide* v65 no6 p48 Ja 30 2017

INSIDE LADY GAGA'S SUPER-SECRET SUPER BOWL SET N. Feeney color *Entertainment Weekly* no1451/1452 p14 F 3-10 2017

Super Bowl (Football game)—History

BIG GAME, BIG MYTH L. J. Wertheim color *Sports Illustrated* v126 no4 p46 Ja 30 2017

FIVE WILL GET YOU ZEN P. King color *Sports Illustrated* v126 no7 p74 Mr 6 2017

Super Bowl (Football game)—History—21st century

THE FOX FOCUS color *Sports Illustrated* v126 no4 p29 Ja 30 2017

Leading Off color *Sports Illustrated* v126 no5 p6 F 13 2017

My Son Doesn't Care About the Super Bowl. So I Brought In a Ringer J. Stein color *Time* v189 no4 p59 F 6 2017

SUPER BOWL LI: THE PICK G. A. Bedard color *Sports Illustrated* v126 no4 p39 Ja 30 2017

SUSPENDED DISBELIEF [Cover story] G. Bishop, B. Baskin et al color *Sports Illustrated* v126 no5 p26 F 13 2017

Tom Brady's Payback Play S. Gregory color *Time* v189 no4 p55 F 6 2017

WIN ONE MORE? ROGER T. Layden color *Sports Illustrated* v126 no4 p31 Ja 30 2017

Super Dark Times (Film)
Super Dark Times C. Nashawaty color *Entertainment Weekly* no1485 p42 O 6 2017

Super Mario Bros. (Game)
TRENDING color *Forbes* v198 no8 p49 D 20 2016

Superbank (Qld.)
THE SERPENTINE PACT A. GOGGANS color *Surfer* v58 no1 p90 Ap 2017

Superbikes—Competitions
FASTEST ON THE FLIPSIDE G. Ritchie color *Cycle World* v56 no3 p64 Ap 2017

Superbikes—Equipment & supplies
WHERE IS WORLD SUPERBIKE GOING? K. Cameron color *Cycle World* v56 no9 p50 O 2017

Superbikes—Evaluation
BRUSH YOUR TEETH WITH GASOLINE J. Snyder color *Esquire* v167 no2 p28 Mr 2017
OF STYLE AND SUBSTANCE S. MacDonald chart color *Cycle World* v56 no8 p38 S 2017
RIDING WITH THE KING D. Canet cartoon chart color *Cycle World* v56 no8 p22 S 2017

Supercapacitors
Charge of the Light Brigade E. STRICKLAND color *Foreign Policy* no222 p24 Ja/F 2017

Superchargers
See also
    Automobile engines—Superchargers
Does More Boost Always Make More Power? M. Davis color *Hot Rod* v70 no9 p92 S 2017
New Teslas Get Autonomous Tech with a Temporary Catch A. Nishimoto and E. Tahaney color *Motor Trend* v69 no2 p18 F 2017
PARTS & STUFF color *Hot Rod* v70 no8 p116 Ag 2017

Superchargers—Evaluation
TRANS-PLANT K. C. Colwell diag *Car & Driver* v62 no11 p26 My 2017

Superclusters
The cosmic bullies next door L. Kruesi color *Astronomy* v45 no7 p28 Jl 2017
LANIAKEA SUPERCLUSTER P. FRIEDLANDER *Scientific American* v315 no5 p6 N 2016

Supercomputer design & construction
Platforms, Codes, and Facilities Form a Three-Pronged Supercomputing Strategy M. McCoy *Science & Technology Review* p3 Mr 2017

Supercomputers
Building a New Brain-Inspired Supercompu *Science & Technology Review* p2 S 2016

Superconducting Super Collider
A BRIDGE TOO FAR The demise of the Superconducting Super Collider M. Riordan *Physics Today* v69 no10 p48 O 2016
Issues that pushed the SSC's demise C. Milner *Physics Today* v70 no8 p12 Ag 2017

Superconductivity
See also
    Low temperature superconductivity
    Superconductors
Evidence for bulk superconductivity in pure bismuth single crystals at ambient pressure O. Prakash, A. Kumar et al bibl color graph *Science* v355 no6320 p1 Ja 6 2017

Superconductivity—History
BETWEEN RESEARCH AND DEVELOPMENT: IBM AND JOSEPHSON COMPUTING C. C. M. Mody *Physics Today* v69 no10 p32 O 2016

Superconductors
At low temps, bismuth superconducts E. CONOVER color *Science News* v190 no13 p14 D 24 2016
Discovery of orbital-selective Cooper pairing in FeSe P. O. Sprau, A. Kostin et al diag *Science* v357 no6346 p75 Jl 7 2017
Hunting down unconventional superconductors Lee diag *Science* v357 no6346 p32 Jl 7 2017
Putting the squeeze on superconductivity K. M. Shen bibl diag *Science* v355 no6321 p133 Ja 13 2017
Strong peak in Tc of Sr2RuO4 under uniaxial pressure Lishan Zhao, M. E. Barber et al bibl color graph *Science* v355 no6321 p1 Ja 13 2017

A twist on the Majorana fermion V. S. Pribiag graph *Science* v357 no6348 p252 Jl 21 2017

Superfluidity
See also
    Bose-Einstein condensation
The new era of POLARITON CONDENSATES D. W. Snoke and J. Keeling *Physics Today* v70 no10 p54 O 2017
Superfluid behaves like black holes E. CONOVER *Science News* v191 no7 p11 Ap 15 2017

Supergiant stars
In Good Company M. BARTUSIAK color *Natural History* v125 no10 p10 O 2017
RECIPE FOR A SUPERNOVA diag *Astronomy* v45 no10 p17 O 2017
Story of a supernova D. J. EICHER *Astronomy* v45 no3 p6 Mr 2017
SUPERNOVA 1987A 30 years later L. Kruesi color *Astronomy* v45 no3 p28 Mr 2017

Supergirl (Fictitious character)
NO. 23 Supergirl N. Abrams color *Entertainment Weekly* no1436/1437 p62 O 21 2016
WHO WOULD WIN? SUPERGIRL VS. THE THING N. Abrams and J. McGovern *Entertainment Weekly* no1436/1437 p63 O 21 2016

Supergirl (TV program)
CHEERS & JEERS D. HOLBROOK *TV Guide* v64 no48 p88 N 21 2016
Supergirl D. Holbrook *TV Guide* v65 no6 p35 Ja 30 2017
Supergirl N. Abrams, C. Holub et al *Entertainment Weekly* no1482/1483 p49 S 22 2017
Superheroes Break Into Song D. HOLBROOK *TV Guide* v65 no13 p6 Mr 20 2017
What to Watch R. Rahman, L. Greenblatt et al color *Entertainment Weekly* no1459 p56 Mr 31 2017

Supergoop (Company)
"Go Get Your Elephant" A. FELDMAN color *Forbes* v199 no7 p56 Je 29 2017

Superheavy elements
GETTING TO THE END OF THE MATTER *Science & Technology Review* p12 D 2016

Superhero films
THE BRIEF CRUSADE OF THE RED HAWK P. Higbee *South Dakota Magazine* v33 no3 p62 S/O 2017
PLEASE SEND HELP N. Pinkerton color *Film Comment* v53 no4 p46 Jl/Ag 2017
Superheroes at Bay J. PODHORETZ color *Weekly Standard* v22 no27 p43 Mr 20 2017

Superhero television programs
616 PUBLIC ENEMIES DEFENDERS [Cover story] S. Li color *Entertainment Weekly* no1449 p26 Ja 20 2017
ALL IN THE FAMILY [Cover story] J. Jensen and N. Abrams color *Entertainment Weekly* no1440 p20 N 18 2016
JONESING ON JONES J. Jensen color *Entertainment Weekly* no1436/1437 p73 O 21 2016

Superhero comic books, strips, etc.
Jeremy Lin R. WIEDEMANN img *New York* v49 no22 p18 O 31 2016

Superheroes
The Bullseye M. Snetiker color *Entertainment Weekly* no1436/1437 p108 O 21 2016
CARTOONS *In These Times* v41 no2 p34 F 2017
How to Take the Plunge J. BILLS *Yankee* v81 no1 p26 Ja/F 2017
I NEED A (BLACK) HERO W. K. BELL bw *Wired* v25 no6 p15 Je 2017
Johnny Canuck R. Fawkes color *Canadian Geographic* v137 no4 p82 Jl/Ag 2017
NO. 24 The Thing J. McGovern color *Entertainment Weekly* no1436/1437 p62 O 21 2016
NO. 27 CAPTAIN MARVEL C. Agard color *Entertainment Weekly* no1436/1437 p64 O 21 2016
NO. 33 Human Torch C. Collis color *Entertainment Weekly* no1436/1437 p69 O 21 2016
NO. 35 Falcon D. Coggan color *Entertainment Weekly* no1436/1437 p70 O 21 2016
NO. 36 NIGHTCRAWLER J. McGovern color *Entertainment Weekly* no1436/1437 p70 O 21 2016

NO. 37 ANT-MAN C. Collis color *Entertainment Weekly* no1436/1437 p72 O 21 2016

NO. 38 Vision N. Sperling color *Entertainment Weekly* no1436/1437 p72 O 21 2016

NO. 41 Mr. Fant astic C. Agard color *Entertainment Weekly* no1436/1437 p74 O 21 2016

NO. 42 BLADE C. Agard color *Entertainment Weekly* no1436/1437 p75 O 21 2016

NO. 43 Beast C. Holub color *Entertainment Weekly* no1436/1437 p75 O 21 2016

NO. 45 Cyclops S. Vilkomerson color *Entertainment Weekly* no1436/1437 p76 O 21 2016

NO. 47 Shazam J. Jensen color *Entertainment Weekly* no1436/1437 p78 O 21 2016

NO. 50 DR. MANHATTAN J. Jensen color *Entertainment Weekly* no1436/1437 p79 O 21 2016

Powered UP A. MARRA color *Vogue* v207 no4 p130 Ap 2017

SUPER FUNNY A. Breznican color *Entertainment Weekly* no1436/1437 p52 O 21 2016

WHO WOULD WIN? CYCLOPS VS. INVISIBLE WOMAN N. Terrero and S. Vilkomerson *Entertainment Weekly* no1436/1437 p77 O 21 2016

WHO WOULD WIN? SUPERGIRL VS. THE THING N. Abrams and J. McGovern *Entertainment Weekly* no1436/1437 p63 O 21 2016

WORST POTENTIAL ROOM MATES D. Franich color *Entertainment Weekly* no1436/1437 p50 O 21 2016

Superheroes—Charts, diagrams, etc.

Show Me a Superhero E. Dockterman color *Time* v189 no11 p60 Mr 27 2017

SUPERHERO POWER INDEX chart color *Entertainment Weekly* no1436/1437 p80 O 21 2016

Superheroes—In art

PLEASE SEND HELP N. Pinkerton color *Film Comment* v53 no4 p46 Jl/Ag 2017

Superhydrophobic surfaces

Superhydrophobic L. SCHLEY cartoon *Discover* v38 no3 p14 Ap 2017

Superior, Lake

RAMBLING AROUND THE BIG LAKE B. MARR *American Forests* v123 no1 p24 Wint/Spr 2017

Superior Aloeswood (Poem)

SUPERIOR ALOESWOOD P. Muldoon *New York Review of Books* v64 no1 p30 Ja 19 2017

Superior Donuts (TV program)

JERMAINE FOWLER C. M. Smith color *Entertainment Weekly* no1451/1452 p97 F 3-10 2017

JOKERS WILD J. RUSSELL *TV Guide* v65 no6 p30 Ja 30 2017

Superior Donuts N. Abrams, C. Holub et al color *Entertainment Weekly* no1482/1483 p52 S 22 2017

Superior Hiking Trail (Minn.)

Light Up Your Life K. FERRARO color *Backpacker* v45 no1 p24 Ja 2017

Superior-subordinate relationship

5 Questions to Help Your Employees Find Their Inner Purpose K. Hedges *Harvard Business Review Digital Articles* p2 2017

Don't Let Your Stressed- Out Boss Stress You Out A. McKee *Harvard Business Review Digital Articles* p2 S 11 2015

How Adobe Structures Feedback Conversations D. Burkus *Harvard Business Review Digital Articles* p2 Jl 20 2017

How to Ask for a Raise C. O'Hara *Harvard Business Review Digital Articles* p2 Mr 5 2015

How to Deal with a Boss Who Stresses You Out T. Chamorro-Premuzic *Harvard Business Review Digital Articles* p2 Jl 19 2017

How to Disagree with Someone More Powerful than You A. Gallo *Harvard Business Review Digital Articles* p2 Mr 17 2016

How to Earn Your Manager's Respect R. Knight *Harvard Business Review Digital Articles* p2 D 2 2016

How to Handle Your First Meeting With a New Boss L. McCreary *Harvard Business Review Digital Articles* p2 D 10 2014

How to Succeed at Work When Your Boss Doesn't Respect You C. Porath *Harvard Business Review Digital Articles* p2 Je 22 2016

Make Sure Your Employees Have Good Things to Say About You Behind Your Back N. T. Washburn and B. Galvin *Harvard Business Review Digital Articles* p2 S 22 2016

Managing Police Departments Post-Ferguson S. Wolfe and J. Nix *Harvard Business Review Digital Articles* p2 S 13 2016

Navigating the Transition from Friend to Boss B. Gentry *Harvard Business Review Digital Articles* p2 F 24 2015

Overcome Resistance to Change by Enlisting the Right People T. Warner *Harvard Business Review Digital Articles* p2 S 13 2016

Overcoming the Peter Principle A. Ovans *Harvard Business Review Digital Articles* p2 D 22 2014

The Right Way to Bring a Problem to Your Boss A. Gallo *Harvard Business Review Digital Articles* p2 D 5 2014

Team Leaders Should Play Favorites (but Only in Moderation) B. Kirkman, Yang Sui et al *Harvard Business Review Digital Articles* p2 Ja 13 2016

Two-Thirds of Managers Are Uncomfortable Communicating with Employees L. Solomon *Harvard Business Review Digital Articles* p2 Mr 9 2016

What Everyone Should Know About Managing Up D. Rousmaniere *Harvard Business Review Digital Articles* p2 Ja 23 2015

What to Do If Your Boss Asks You to Break the Rules P. T. Coleman and R. Ferguson *Harvard Business Review Digital Articles* p2 Ja 7 2016

What to Do If You're Smarter than Your Boss A. Gallo *Harvard Business Review Digital Articles* p2 D 12 2014

What To Do When the Boss Gives You Baseless Feedback J. Zenger and J. Folkman *Harvard Business Review Digital Articles* p2 Mr 4 2015

What to Do When You and Your Boss Aren't Getting Along R. Knight *Harvard Business Review Digital Articles* p2 Ag 18 2016

What to Do When Your Boss Is Socially Awkward R. Knight *Harvard Business Review Digital Articles* p2 D 7 2016

What to Do When Your Peer Becomes Your Boss A. Gallo *Harvard Business Review Digital Articles* p2 O 24 2016

When It's Tough to Speak Up, Get Help from Your Coworkers J. R. Detert and E. R. Burris *Harvard Business Review Digital Articles* p2 Mr 4 2016

When to Solve Your Team's Problems, and When to Let Them Sort It Out J. Grenny *Harvard Business Review Digital Articles* p2 Jl 20 2017

Why It's Dangerous to Love Your Boss A. McKee *Harvard Business Review Digital Articles* p2 D 4 2014

Superkul Inc.

house of the month M. SITZ *Architectural Record* v204 no11 p35 N 2016

Superlattices

Ballistic miniband conduction in a graphene superlattice J. R. Wallbank, P. Gallagher et al bibl graph *Science* v353 no6307 p1526 S 30 2016

Superman (Fictitious character)

NO. 4 SUPERMAN N. Sperling color *Entertainment Weekly* no1436/1437 p47 O 21 2016

Supermarkets

OUT-SMART THE SUPER-MARKET P. FLAX color *Prevention* v69 no8 p60 Ag 2017

Prevention. Stronger Barbara *Prevention* v69 no8 p3 Ag 2017

Whole Foods' Misguided Play for Millennials R. Bolton *Harvard Business Review Digital Articles* p2 My 14 2015

Supermarkets—Great Britain

Why Tesco's Strengths Are No Longer Good Enough J. Wells *Harvard Business Review Digital Articles* p2 O 6 2014

Supermarkets—United States

Faster, Fresher, Cheaper T. Stanger, S. Wadyka et al chart color il *Consumer Reports* v82 no7 p30 Jl 2017

Low-Income Areas With Low Supermarket Access Increased in Urban Areas, But Not in Rural Areas, Between 2010 and 2015 A. Rhone *Amber Waves: The Economics of Food, Farming, Natural Resources, & Rural America* p22 Ap 2017

Supermassive black holes

Coming soon: Our first picture of a black hole A. Klesman color *Astronomy* v45 no8 p13 Ag 2017

The First Black Holes C. M. Carlisle *Sky & Telescope* v133 no1 p24 Ja 2017

Global telescope gears up to image black holes D. Clery color map *Science* v355 no6328 p893 Mr 3 2017

How to Swallow a Sun S. B. Cenko and N. Gehrels color *Scientific American* v316 no4 p38 Ap 2017

Observations hint at a new recipe for giant black holes J. Sokol color *Science* v355 no6321 p120 Ja 13 2017

Supernatural
See also
Spirits
At the Boundary of Knowledge M. Shermer color *Scientific American* v315 no3 p88 S 2016

Supernatural (TV program)
Supernatural S. Highfill, N. Abrams et al color *Entertainment Weekly* no1482/1483 p84 S 22 2017

Supernatural on television
THE 8-SECOND REVIEW N. Serrao color *Entertainment Weekly* no1470 p46 Je 16 2017

Supernova 1987A
Stellar storyteller color *Science News* v191 no6 p31 Ap 1 2017
SUPERNOVA 1987A 30 years later L. Kruesi color *Astronomy* v45 no3 p28 Mr 2017
The Supernova of a Lifetime R. R. Kirshner *Sky & Telescope* v133 no2 p36 F 2017

Supernova 1987A—Research
The Stellar Storyteller C. Crockett color *Science News* v191 no3 p20 F 18 2017
Supernova story continues, just like science journalism *Science News* v191 no3 p2 F 18 2017

Supernovae
RECIPE FOR A SUPERNOVA diag *Astronomy* v45 no10 p17 O 2017
Stars Explode in Earthly Skies K. HAYNES color *Discover* v38 no3 p12 Ap 2017
The stellar shreds of supernovas C. Crockett color *Science News* v191 no3 p32 F 18 2017
Superluminous event caused by spinning black hole swallowing star color *Astronomy* v45 no4 p16 Ap 2017
Supernovae may leave dust behind color *Astronomy* v45 no11 p15 N 2017
The Supernova of a Lifetime R. R. Kirshner *Sky & Telescope* v133 no2 p36 F 2017
Witnessing a Supernova P. Tyson *Sky & Telescope* v133 no2 p4 F 2017

Supernovae—Research
Supernova Shocker! Y. CENDES color *Discover* v38 no1 p84 Ja/F 2017
Waiting for a Supernova E. Conover color diag *Science News* v191 no3 p24 F 18 2017

Superposition principle (Physics)
Potential signs of quantum collapse E. CONOVER *Science News* v192 no5 p10 S 30 2017

Supersonic plane design & construction
NASA says it's got the secret to quiet supersonic planes. Now comes the hard part T. Black color *Bloomberg Businessweek* no4532 p19 Jl 31 2017

Supersonic planes—Design & construction
SUPERSONIC TRAVEL IS BOOMING C. Dillow color *Fortune* v174 no8 p34 D 15 2016

Superstition
See also
Omens
Never Fear! There's History Behind These Superstitions B. SPECKTOR color *Reader's Digest* v190 no1134 p130 O 2017
THE POLITICIZATION of Scientific Issues: Looking through Galileo's Lens or through the Imaginary Looking Glass J. GOLDBERG *Skeptical Inquirer* v41 no5 p34 S/O 2017
SAINTS, RABBITS' FEET, GARTERS AND BOOMERANGS M. Lunken bw color *Flying* v144 no2 p62 F 2017

Superstore (TV program)
CHEERS & JEERS D. HOLBROOK *TV Guide* v65 no43 p88 O 16 2017
Superstore M. Roffman *TV Guide* v64 no40 p59 O 3 2016
Superstore M. Roffman *TV Guide* v65 no19 p39 My 1 2017
Superstore N. Abrams, B. L. Heldman et al color *Entertainment Weekly* no1482/1483 p84 S 22 2017

SUPERTRAMP, DEVIN
DRONES chart color *Popular Mechanics* p78 O 2017

Superunion Architects (Company)
Tipping the Scales A. FIXSEN *Architectural Record* v204 no10 p33 O 2016

Supervet, The (TV program)

ANIMALS ON DEMAND S. Weldon color *Entertainment Weekly* no1478 / 1479 p90 Ag 18-25 2017

Supervillains
The Greatest Villains of All Time D. Franich color *Entertainment Weekly* no1436/1437 p66 O 21 2016

Superville, Denisa R.
As Schools Tackle Poverty, Attendance Goes Up, but Academic Gains Are Tepid *Education Digest* v83 no2 p46 O 2017
Few Women Run the Nation's School Districts. Why? *Education Digest* v82 no6 p14 F 2017

Supervision
THE LARGEST PARISH IN AMERICA [Cover story] L. Libresco color *America* v216 no10 p18 My 1 2017

Supervision of employees
See also
Goal setting in personnel management
How to Get Your Team to Follow Through After a Meeting P. Axtell color *Harvard Business Review Digital Articles* p2 Mr 30 2017
PUTTING A PRICE ON "PEOPLE PROBLEMS" graph img *Harvard Business Review* v94 no12 p28 D 2016

Supervisors
Do You Hate Your Boss? M. F. R. Kets de Vries color il *Harvard Business Review* v94 no12 p98 D 2016
FLYING THE BOSS D. Karl color *Flying* v144 no5 p70 My 2017
How to Tell Your Boss to Stop Doing Your Job R. Carucci color *Harvard Business Review Digital Articles* p2 Mr 27 2017
What Separates High- Performing Leaders from Average Ones T. Warner *Harvard Business Review Digital Articles* p2 N 11 2015
What to Do When Your Boss Says No S. Sonenshein color *Harvard Business Review Digital Articles* p2 F 6 2017
WHEN TECHNICAL SKILL BEATS EMOTIONAL INTELLIGENCE *Harvard Business Review* v95 no3 p36 My/Je 2017
When Your Boss Is Terrible at Leading Meetings P. Axtell *Harvard Business Review Digital Articles* p2 My 16 2016

Supervisors—Attitudes
Research: Shifting the Power Balance with an Abusive Boss Hui Liao, E. Wee et al *Harvard Business Review Digital Articles* p2 O 9 2017

Supervisors—Training of
Why Do We Spend So Much Developing Senior Leaders and So Little Training New Managers? V. Lipman *Harvard Business Review Digital Articles* p2 Je 28 2016

SUPP, SARAH R.
Skills and Knowledge for Data-Intensive Environmental Research *BioScience* v67 no6 p546 Je 2017

Supper at Emmaus (Art)
The Supper at Emmaus H. J. Hornik and M. C. Parsons color *Christian Century* v134 no7 p47 Mr 29 2017

Suppers
20-MINUTE SUPPERS color *Good Housekeeping* v264 no4 p120 Ap 2017
HEAD TO TAIL E. SIGURÐARDÓTTIR and Z. ROBRET *Iceland Review* v55 no2 p26 Mr/Ap 2017
HOLIDAY MEAL M. Shih *Martha Stewart Living* no270 p104 D 2016
SPECIAL DELIVERY E. Graves *Martha Stewart Living* no270 p10 D 2016

Supplemental Nutrition Assistance Program (U.S.)
Changes in Food-At-Home Spending by SNAP Participants After the Stimulus Act of 2009 C. Tuttle bw chart color graph *Amber Waves: The Economics of Food, Farming, Natural Resources, & Rural America* p8 D 2016
Organic for Everyone Z. SCHAEFFER color *Rodale's Organic Life* v3 no1 p33 Ja 2017

Supplementary employment
Multiple jobholding in states in 2015 S. Campolongo bibl chart color map *Monthly Labor Review* p1 F 2017

Suppliers
50 TOP COMPANIES FOR SUPPLIER DIVERSITY J. McKinney color *Black Enterprise* v47 no7 p32 My/Je 2017
Hidden Suppliers Can Make or Break Your Operations T. Y. Choi, B. B. M. Shao et al *Harvard Business Review Digital Articles* p2 My 29 2015
Theatrical Retailers & Suppliers *Stage Directions* v30 no7 p59 Jl 1 2017

Supply & demand
See also
> Labor supply
> Production (Economic theory)
Fashion's Great Handbag Crash P. Wahba color *Fortune* v175 no4 p18 Mr 15 2017
Improving Alignment between Educational Supply and Labor Market Needs P. Kelly, B. T. Prescott et al *Change* v49 no1 p34 Ja/F 2017
PRICES *Economic Indicators* p22 Mr 2017
Your New Hit Product Might Be Underpriced M. Ramanujam and G. Tacke *Harvard Business Review Digital Articles* p2 My 24 2016

Supply & demand of teachers
Solving the teacher shortage B. Berry and P. M. Shields color *Phi Delta Kappan* v98 no8 p8 My 2017
Sub Shortage Leaves Schools Scrambling T. García Mathewson *Education Digest* v83 no3 p24 N 2017

Supply chain management
How Coty Reinvigorated Its Supply Chain T. Halton and K. Perlman *Harvard Business Review Digital Articles* p2 My 19 2016
Is Your Supply Chain Ready for the Congestion Crisis? G. Stalk Jr. and P. Paranikas *Harvard Business Review Digital Articles* p2 Je 22 2015
Rethinking Your Supply Chain in an Era of Protectionism J. Rose and M. Reeves *Harvard Business Review Digital Articles* p2 Mr 22 2017
TIFFANY'S CEO ON CREATING A SUSTAINABLE SUPPLY CHAIN F. Cumenal color graph img *Harvard Business Review* v95 no2 p41 Mr/Ap 2017

Supply chains
See also
> Supply chain management
Hidden Suppliers Can Make or Break Your Operations T. Y. Choi, B. B. M. Shao et al *Harvard Business Review Digital Articles* p2 My 29 2015
Is Your Supply Chain Ready for a NAFTA Overhaul? J. Terino *Harvard Business Review Digital Articles* p2 Je 30 2017
It's OK to Move Down (Yes, Down) the Value Chain B. Staats and D. M. Upton *Harvard Business Review Digital Articles* p2 Je 2 2015
The Rise of FinTech in Supply Chains D. Rogers, R. Leuschner et al *Harvard Business Review Digital Articles* p2 Je 22 2016
State of the Industry A. Dennis color *Climbing* no352 p14 Ap 2017
Toiling for King Cotton M. KRESE *In These Times* v41 no4 p22 Ap 2017
Using Supply Chains to Grow Your Businesss D. Isenberg and T. Coates *Harvard Business Review Digital Articles* p2 N 20 2015

Supply chains—Economic aspects
Labor Rights in the Age of Global Supply Chains L. MOSLEY *Current History* v116 no786 p17 Ja 2017

Support (Domestic relations)
SPEAKING OF FIRST DAUGHTERS... D. BLASBERG color *Vanity Fair* v59 no10 p190 O 2017

Support groups
LISTEN TO THE VOICES IN YOUR HEAD S. M. SHAPIRO color map *Foreign Policy* no222 p56 Ja/F 2017
You Can't Achieve Your Goals Without the Right Support A. Jen Su *Harvard Business Review Digital Articles* p2 Ja 15 2016

Supportive communication
To Develop Teachers, Look to Other Teachers A. A. Arnett *Education Digest* v83 no1 p50 S 2017

Suppressor mutations in fungi
Exploring genetic suppression interactions on a global scale J. van Leeuwen, C. Pons et al diag *Science* v354 no6312 p599 N 4 2016

Suppuration—Treatment
HEALTH color *Horse & Rider* v56 no1 p19 Ja 2017

Suprachiasmatic nucleus
Molecular and neural basis of contagious itch behavior in mice Yu, D. M. Barry et al bibl diag *Science* v355 no6329 p1072 Mr 10 2017

Supreme (Company)
Reigning Supreme R. Sullivan bw color *Vogue* v207 no9 p710 S 2017
Sickest Collaborations on the Planet, Part 2 > Louis Vuitton

x Supreme M. A. Green color *GQ: Gentlemen's Quarterly* v97 no6 p36 Je 2017
this Way In bw color *Esquire* p5 Je/Jl 2017

Supreme Court justices (U.S.)
COURTROOM DRAMAS [Cover story] P. SMITH *New York Times Upfront* v149 no8 p8 Ja 30 2017
How Neil Gorsuch Is Shaking Up the Supreme Court T. Berenson color *Time* v190 no15 p9 O 16 2017
The Ninth Justice P. M. Barrett color *Bloomberg Businessweek* no4499 p33 N 14 2016
ONE CHEER FOR JUSTICE SOTOMAYOR D. ROOT color *Reason* v48 no9 p11 F 2017
Supreme Court 'Manterruption' J. Zorthian color *Time* v189 no22 p17 Je 12 2017

Supreme Court justices (U.S.)—Education (Graduate)
Higher Justice [Cover story] A. J. White color *Weekly Standard* v22 no23 p20 F 20 2017

Supreme Court justices (U.S.)—Selection & appointment
Angling for a Supreme Pick F. BARNES *Weekly Standard* v22 no22 p10 F 13 2017
CASE STUDIES J. Toobin cartoon *New Yorker* v93 no7 p33 Ap 3 2017
The Dangers of an Empty Seat D. Verrilli color *Time* v188 no16/17 p80 O 24 2016
A Great Scalia Successor T. Eastland *Weekly Standard* v22 no22 p8 F 13 2017
Make 50 the New 60 W. Kristol color *Weekly Standard* v22 no22 p6 F 13 2017
Under the Law J. Underwood color *Phi Delta Kappan* v98 no7 p76 Ap 2017
The Value of Life M. Hemingway *Weekly Standard* v22 no22 p9 F 13 2017

Supreme Court justices (U.S.)—Selection & appointment—History—20th century
The Gorsuch Triumph R. PONNURU il *National Review* v69 no8 p14 My 2017

Supreme Court justices (U.S.)—Selection & appointment—History—21st century
The Gorsuch Triumph R. PONNURU il *National Review* v69 no8 p14 My 2017
Trump's Supreme Court Pick Puts Democrats In a Bind T. Berenson and S. Frizell color diag *Time* v189 no5 p10 F 13 2017

Suqi, Rima
Pimp My Office Plant color *Bloomberg Businessweek* no4525 p60 Je 5 2017

Sur La Table Inc.
Chef's Knives [Cover story] color *Good Housekeeping* v265 no3 p99 S 2017

SURANA, KAVITHA
The Elephant in the Comedy Club color *Foreign Policy* no225 p23 Jl/Ag 2017
fulCan Stories About Food Upend Familiar Narratives of War? bw *Foreign Policy* no225 p16 Jl/Ag 2017
Undocumented on Patrol color *Foreign Policy* no226 p11 S/O 2017
Why Do Some Countries Get Away With Taking Fewer Refugees? bw *Foreign Policy* no226 p14 S/O 2017

Surane, Jenny
Disputing Credit Card Charges Gets Easy color *Bloomberg Businessweek* no4529 p28 Jl 3 2017
Piecing Together A Credit Fraud color *Bloomberg Businessweek* no4538 p26 S 18 2017

Surappaeva, Venera
The extent of forest in dryland biomes [Cover story] chart map *Science* v356 no6338 p635 My 12 2017

Surcharges
TONI'S SODA TAX SPIRAL C. FELSENTHAL color *Chicago* v66 no10 p21 O 2017

Surendra, Rajiv
The Elephants in My Backyard: A Memoir *Publishers Weekly* v263 no39 p78 S 26 2016

Suresh, Subra
Business backs the basics color *Science* v354 no6309 p151 O 14 2016
This Program Uses Lean Startup Techniques to Turn Scientists into Entrepreneurs G. Satell color *Harvard Business Review*

Digital Articles p2 Mr 7 2017

Suretyship & guaranty

See also

Bail

Read This Before You Cosign J. Chatzky *AARP: The Magazine* v59 no6A p27 O/N 2016

Surf scoter

CHOMPING AT NATURE'S BIT E. Knapp *New York State Conservationist* v71 no6 p7 Je 2017

Surface chemistry

Optical imaging of surface chemistry and dynamics in confinement C. Macias-Romero, I. Nahalka et al color *Science* v357 no6353 p784 Ag 25 2017

A water window on surface chemistry J. Hunger and S. H. Parekh diag *Science* v357 no6353 p755 Ag 25 2017

Surface coatings

See also

Acrylic coatings

Paint

Protective coatings

cabin maintenance ELASTO-WHAT? J. Cooper color *Cabin Living* p69 S 2017

Install Yacht-like Non-Skid J. JOHNSON *Boating World* v38 no2 p22 F 2017

Surface coatings—Evaluation

COLOR FULL K. RENDA color *House Beautiful* v158 no9 p41 N 2016

Surface cracks

Filling in the Gaps B. PIKE color *Power & Motoryacht* v32 no12 p72 D 2016

Surface fault ruptures

Complex multifault rupture during the 2016 Mw 7.8 Kaikōura earthquake, New Zealand I. J. Hamling, S. Hreinsdóttir et al color map *Science* v356 no6334 p154 Ap 14 2017

Surface of Europa

Enceladus's Hydrothermal Heating, Europa's Leaks C. M. Carlisle color *Sky & Telescope* v134 no2 p10 Ag 2017

Surface of the earth

The Myth of Symmetry and Balance A. J. Stallard *History Today* v67 no8 p12 Ag 2017

Surface plasmons

Anti-coalescence of bosons on a lossy beam splitter B. Vest, Dheur et al bw chart diag graph *Science* v356 no6345 p1373 Je 30 2017

Surface-to-air missiles

THE (NEW) TROUBLE WITH RUSSIA J. Pappalardo color *Popular Mechanics* p72 Mr 2017

Surfaces (Geometry)

Secrets of the Canine Mind J. Kluger color *Time* v189 no19 p42 My 22 2017

Surfboards

See also

Longboards

Carving Giants D. LATOURRETTE bw color *Surfer* v58 no2 p46 My 2017

DO SOMETHING J. HOUSMAN bw color *Surfer* v58 no6 p32 O 2017

SHAPIN' SAFARI M. CALORE color *Wired* v25 no7 p46 Jl 2017

Sons of Sam A. GOGGANS color *Surfer* v58 no2 p34 My 2017

TORREN MARTYN A. DOUGLAS color *Surfer* v58 no3 p42 Je 2017

WARREN SMITH A. GOGGANS color *Surfer* v58 no3 p44 Je 2017

Warts and All J. HOUSMAN color *Surfer* v58 no6 p42 O 2017

Surfboards—Design & construction

BEACH PEOPLE color *Popular Mechanics* p76 Ap 2017

The Featherweight Future Z. MORTON color *Surfer* v58 no4 p40 Ag 2017

On the Nose Z. MORTON color *Surfer* v58 no5 p44 S 2017

A Parallel Universe M. SHAW bw color *Surfer* v58 no1 p32 Ap 2017

THE SHAPE OF THINGS TO COME J. HOUSMAN color *Surfer* v58 no2 p64 My 2017

Shaper Hall of Fame A. GOGGANS color *Surfer* v58 no2 p40 My 2017

Whither the Thruster? J. HOUSMAN cartoon color *Surfer* v57

no12 p30 Ja/F 2017

Surfboards—Evaluation

2017 Surfboard & Accessory Guide bw color *Surfer* v58 no2 p1 My 2017

2017 SURFBOARD GUIDE bw cartoon color *Surfing Magazine* v53 no3 p85 Mr 2017

Proctor Worldwide Custom color *Surfer* v58 no4 p126 Ag 2017

Surfer (Periodical)

Time Capsule M. WARSHAW bw color *Surfer* v58 no1 p30 Ap 2017

Surfer photography

Along for the Ride G. Ellis color *Surfer* v57 no13 p14 Mr 2017

Lining Up W. Skudin color *Surfer* v58 no2 p18 My 2017

PEAKING bw color *Surfer* v58 no4 p106 Ag 2017

Perfect Day, Somewhere M. Jones color *Surfer* v58 no2 p134 My 2017

Screen, I Wish I Knew How to Quit You J. HOUSMAN cartoon color *Surfer* v57 no13 p30 Mr 2017

SURFING OUTTAKES color *Surfing Magazine* v53 no3 p96 Mr 2017

TAYLOR KNOX, NORTHERN BAJA color *Surfer* v57 no13 p12 Mr 2017

Surfers

See also

Wakeboarders

1968 PETER TROY M. Warshaw bw *Surfer* v57 no11 p30 D 2016

ALL TO YOURSELF bw color *Surfer* v58 no6 p62 O 2017

Billy "Mystic" Wilmot, 57 A. DOUGLAS bw *Surfer* v58 no5 p40 S 2017

The Challenge from Down Under M. WARSHAW color *Surfer* v58 no4 p38 Ag 2017

DO SOMETHING J. HOUSMAN bw color *Surfer* v58 no6 p32 O 2017

Editor's Note color *Surfer* v58 no5 p10 S 2017

Editor's Note T. PRODANOVICH color *Surfer* v58 no1 p10 Ap 2017

For the Record T. PRODANOVICH color *Surfer* v58 no5 p46 S 2017

Geiselman (There Are Two) B. FLEMISTER color *Surfing Magazine* v53 no3 p32 Mr 2017

Gut Check Z. MORTON color *Surfer* v58 no5 p28 S 2017

IN SESSION T. PRODANOVICH color *Surfer* v58 no1 p48 Ap 2017

IN THE SHADOW OF GIANTS A. GOGGANS color *Surfer* v58 no5 p70 S 2017

In the Wind W. Bendix and A. Van Gysen bw color *Surfing Magazine* v53 no3 p50 Mr 2017

IRISH CROSS ROADS T. PAUL color *Surfing Magazine* v53 no3 p68 Mr 2017

Javanese Blend M. SHAW color *Surfer* v58 no5 p48 S 2017

John Severson: 1933-2017 T. PRODANOVICH bw *Surfer* v58 no4 p132 Ag 2017

THE LAGOSIAN OASIS W. BENDIX color *Surfer* v58 no5 p54 S 2017

Lessons From John D. KAMPION bw color *Surfer* v58 no6 p56 O 2017

Lining Up color *Surfer* v58 no5 p16 S 2017

MASON HO Z. MORTON color *Surfer* v58 no3 p38 Je 2017

MIND CONTROL T. PRODANOVICH bw color *Surfer* v58 no3 p46 Je 2017

More (or Less) Core Division J. HOUSMAN color *Surfer* v58 no4 p34 Ag 2017

Oscar Billy Pippen Wright, 41 S. DOHERTY color *Surfer* v58 no6 p40 O 2017

OUTTAKES bw color *Surfing Magazine* v53 no2 p94 F 2017

Perfect Day, Papua New Guinea color *Surfer* v58 no6 p96 O 2017

Perfect Day, Sumba, Indonesia color *Surfer* v58 no5 p94 S 2017

THE PROXIMITY TAPES N. MEYERS and A. GOGGANS bw color *Surfer* v58 no3 p56 Je 2017

Rise of the Machines T. PRODANOVICH color *Surfer* v58 no6 p28 O 2017

Rizal Tanjung, 42 Z. MORTON color *Surfer* v58 no4 p36 Ag 2017

SAFETY NOT GUARANTEED J. HOUSMAN color *Surfer* v58 no1 p68 Ap 2017

SAN FRANCISCO color *Surfer* v57 no13 p94 Mr 2017

SPIRIT ANIMAL K. TAYLOR bw color *Surfer* v57 no11 p54 D

2016

UNNAMED SLAB NORTHERN ITALY Z. MORTON color *Surfer* v58 no4 p64 Ag 2017

The #VanLife Checklist H. VANDERSMITH color *Surfer* v58 no2 p132 My 2017

Warts and All J. HOUSMAN color *Surfer* v58 no6 p42 O 2017

What's So Great About the Great Outdoors? J. HOUSMAN cartoon color *Surfer* v57 no11 p32 D 2016

WILD MAN OF A CERTAIN AGE C. Ballard color *Sports Illustrated* v127 no10 p48 O 2 2017

Surfers—Attitudes

The Other SURFER Poll color *Surfer* v57 no12 p96 Ja/F 2017

Splitting the Political Peak J. HOUSMAN cartoon *Surfer* v58 no1 p42 Ap 2017

Surfers—Awards

YOUTH-FUL EXUBERANCE Z. Morton color *Surfing Magazine* v53 no1 p12 Ja 2017

Surfers—Crimes against

BATTLE FOR THE BAY A. DOUGLAS color *Surfer* v58 no5 p62 S 2017

Surfers—Interviews

CONFIRMATION Z. Morton color *Surfing Magazine* v53 no2 p18 F 2017

DISTANCE BETWEEN DREAMS T. Paul color *Surfing Magazine* v53 no2 p80 F 2017

extra hours A. Van Gysen color *Surfing Magazine* v53 no2 p52 F 2017

Surfers—Wounds & injuries

SHOCK WAVES J. HOUSMAN color *Surfer* v57 no12 p42 Ja/F 2017

Surfing

30 Cool Things About Winter A. SILEN color *National Geographic Kids* no475 p22 N 2017

"All decisions, even those of a traveler roaming the world, require a compromise." A. GOGGANS color *Surfer* v58 no2 p38 My 2017

Can't We All Just Get Along(board)? T. Prodanovich color *Surfer* v57 no12 p14 Ja/F 2017

The Challenge from Down Under M. WARSHAW color *Surfer* v58 no4 p38 Ag 2017

CURSED LAND color *Surfer* v57 no11 p72 D 2016

Don't Call It "Alternative" Z. MORTON color *Surfer* v58 no3 p32 Je 2017

THE DROWNING ISLES A. DOUGLAS color *Surfer* v58 no4 p76 Ag 2017

Editor's Note color *Surfer* v58 no6 p10 O 2017

Editor's Note T. PRODANOVICH color *Surfer* v58 no2 p12 My 2017

Editor's Note T. PRODANOVICH color *Surfer* v58 no3 p10 Je 2017

EMBRACING COLOSSUS J. HOUSMAN bw color *Surfer* v58 no4 p96 Ag 2017

FOCAL POINTS color *Surfer* v57 no13 p74 Mr 2017

Forgotten Island Of Santosha M. WARSHAW bw color *Surfer* v58 no2 p30 My 2017

THE GOOD SAMARITAN K. TAYLOR bw color *Surfer* v57 no11 p44 D 2016

AN ICY RESOLVE A. DOUGLAS bw color *Surfer* v58 no2 p56 My 2017

IF YOU BUILD IT, They Will Surf T. PRODANOVICH color *Surfer* v58 no6 p48 O 2017

IN THE SHADOW OF GIANTS A. GOGGANS color *Surfer* v58 no5 p70 S 2017

KAI LENNY Z. MORTON color *Surfer* v58 no3 p40 Je 2017

THE LAGOSIAN OASIS W. BENDIX color *Surfer* v58 no5 p54 S 2017

Lining Up D. Agius color *Surfer* v58 no3 p16 Je 2017

Lining Up W. Skudin color *Surfer* v58 no2 p18 My 2017

LIQUID IDEALS color *Surfer* v58 no1 p76 Ap 2017

MATT "ARCHY" ARCHBOLD 47, SAN CLEMENTE, CALIFORNIA G. James bw *Surfer* v57 no12 p34 Ja/F 2017

Nat Young, 69 A. DOUGLAS bw *Surfer* v58 no1 p40 Ap 2017

NEW PIER DURBAN, SOUTH AFRICA Z. MORTON color *Surfer* v58 no4 p60 Ag 2017

The OCEAN IS SALTY m. Diffee bw cartoon color *Esquire* p106 O 2017

ON YAGO T. Paul color *Surfing Magazine* v53 no2 p66 F 2017

The Other SURFER Poll color *Surfer* v57 no12 p96 Ja/F 2017

OUT OF BOUNDS A. GOGGANS color *Surfer* v57 no12 p74 Ja/F 2017

THE PATH OF MOST RESISTANCE Z. Morton color *Surfing Magazine* v53 no2 p10 F 2017

Perfect Day, New South Wales, Australia R. Bierke color *Surfer* v58 no3 p90 Je 2017

Perfect Day, Papua New Guinea color *Surfer* v58 no6 p96 O 2017

Perfect Day, Somewhere M. Jones color *Surfer* v58 no2 p134 My 2017

Perfect Day, Sumba, Indonesia color *Surfer* v58 no5 p94 S 2017

Rise of the Machines T. PRODANOVICH color *Surfer* v58 no6 p28 O 2017

Saving San Miguel A. DOUGLAS color *Surfer* v58 no2 p32 My 2017

SEBASTIAN INLET FLORIDA, UNITED STATES OF AMERICA Z. MORTON color *Surfer* v58 no4 p62 Ag 2017

SOUTH AFRICA color *Surfer* v57 no12 p94 Ja/F 2017

Stopover of a Lifetime: Nemberala Beach Resort J. Honscheid bw color *Surfer* v57 no11 p35 D 2016

Surf Bashed D. L. NG color *Field & Stream* v122 no6 p10 N 2017

SURFING OUTTAKES color *Surfing Magazine* v53 no3 p96 Mr 2017

Surf's Up L. McGLASHAN bw color *Muscle & Performance* v9 no7 p34 Jl 2017

Taking Off color *Surfer* v57 no12 p12 Ja/F 2017

THOMAS CAMPBELL 47, FILMMAKER/PHOTOGRAPHER/ ARTIST M. Shaw color *Surfer* v57 no13 p34 Mr 2017

Time Capsule M. WARSHAW bw color *Surfer* v58 no1 p30 Ap 2017

The Ultimate Surf Selfie color *Surfer* v57 no13 p96 Mr 2017

UNNAMED SLAB NORTHERN ITALY Z. MORTON color *Surfer* v58 no4 p64 Ag 2017

Welcome to the Pizote House T. Prodanovich color *Surfer* v57 no11 p12 D 2016

Whither the Thruster? J. HOUSMAN cartoon color *Surfer* v57 no12 p30 Ja/F 2017

WONDERLAND J. FIELDEN color *Esquire* p22 O 2017

Surfing competitions

DON'T MISS LIST FEBRUARY 2017 *Sea Magazine* v109 no2 pCA-7 F 2017

Going Off Script A. DOUGLAS color *Surfer* v57 no12 p52 Ja/F 2017

GROM GAMES 2016 T. Paul color *Surfing Magazine* v53 no1 p76 Ja 2017

HER BROTHER'S KEEPER S. DOHERTY color *Surfer* v58 no1 p58 Ap 2017

LET THEM LOG A. GOGGANS bw color *Surfer* v57 no12 p62 Ja/F 2017

SURFER OF THE MONTH: ANDREW NEIMANN M. Ciaramella color *Surfing Magazine* v53 no3 p84 Mr 2017

Surfing equipment

See also

Surfboards

Proctor Worldwide Custom color *Surfer* v58 no4 p126 Ag 2017

Summer Gear Guide color *Surfer* v58 no3 p84 Je 2017

Surfing techniques

The Beach Boys D. COURTNEY *Texas Monthly* v45 no5 p224 My 2017

Surfing—Accidents

POINT BREAK V. von Pfetten *Women's Health* v14 no5 p136 Je 2017

Surfing—California

Wet Hot American Mixtape J. HOUSMAN cartoon *Surfer* v58 no5 p42 S 2017

Surfing—Equipment & supplies

See also

Surfboards

Even a Shark Attack Can't Stop This Surfer J. RENDON color *Popular Science* v288 no6 p90 N/D 2016

THE SHAPE OF THINGS TO COME J. HOUSMAN color *Surfer* v58 no2 p64 My 2017

Sons of Sam A. GOGGANS color *Surfer* v58 no2 p34 My 2017

TOM MOREY 1971 M. Warshaw cartoon *Surfer* v57 no12 p36 Ja/F 2017

Surfing—Equipment & supplies—Evaluation

2017 Surfboard & Accessory Guide bw color *Surfer* v58 no2 p1 My 2017

Surfboard Accessory Guide color *Surfer* v58 no2 p42 My 2017

Surfing—Hawaii

Wet Hot American Mixtape J. HOUSMAN cartoon *Surfer* v58 no5 p42 S 2017

Surfing—History

The Significance of the Frontier in Surfing History J. HOUSMAN color *Surfer* v58 no2 p40 My 2017

Surfing—Periodicals

BE HERE NOW color *Surfing Magazine* v53 no3 p12 Mr 2017

SURFTONE, SUSAN

The Soft Warrior Spreads Her Wings *USA Today Magazine* v146 no2868 p60 S 2017

Surgeons

> *See also*
> Orthopedists
> Plastic surgeons

BIKE BLUR S. Cravatts color *Popular Photography* v80 no11 p24 D 2016

Black Man, White Coat J. Thompson *D: The Magazine of Dallas* v43 no10 p126 O 2016

Smooth Operators color *Prevention* v69 no11 p9 N 2017

Vivek Murthy Thinks We Need to Learn How to Deal With Stress A. M. Cox *New York Times Magazine* p58 Ja 1 2017

Surgeons—Awards

People A. M. Banks color *Christian Century* v134 no2 p19 Ja 18 2017

Surgeons—Malpractice

Paolo Macchiarini's academic afterlife in Russia ends A. Astak-hova and M. Enserink color *Science* v356 no6339 p672 My 19 2017

Surgery

> *See also*
> Abortion
> Artificial implants
> Veterinary surgery

What Nurses Know (THAT CAN SAVE YOUR LIFE) L. Pepper cartoon *Prevention* p70 Mr 2017

Surgery—Psychological aspects

HOW MY BODY CHANGED... AND HOW IT CHANGED ME color *Women's Health* v14 no7 p117 S 2017

Surgical complications

THE POST-OP BRAIN M. Leslie color *Science* v356 no6341 p898 Je 1 2017

Surgical operations

> *See also*
> Elective surgery

4 Things to Do Before You Have Surgery color *Prevention* v69 no8 p8 Ag 2017

Surgical robots

Artificial intelligence in research J. Sills, M. Musib et al color *Science* v357 no6346 p28 Jl 7 2017

Surgical stents

Nice Stent If You Can Get It M. Cortez color diag *Bloomberg Businessweek* no4518 p34 Ap 10 2017

Suri, Himanshu, 1985-

the artists bw color *Foreign Policy* no221 p67 N/D 2016

SURI, MANIL

An Illicit Past color *New York Times Book Review* p9 S 25 2016

Suri, Siddharth

The Humans Working Behind the AI Curtain bw *Harvard Business Review Digital Articles* p2 Ja 9 2017

Suri, Tavneet

The long-run poverty and gender impacts of mobile money bibl chart graph *Science* v354 no6317 p1288 D 9 2016

Making Microfinance More Effective *Harvard Business Review Digital Articles* p2 O 5 2016

Surka, Christine

Xist recruits the X chromosome to the nuclear lamina to enable chromosome-wide silencing bibl graph *Science* v354 no6311 p468 O 28 2016

Surmeier, D. James

Dopamine oxidation mediates mitochondrial and lysosomal dys-function in Parkinson's disease graph *Science* v357 no6357

p1255 S 22 2017

Surowiecki, James

BIG-TICKET TRANSIT cartoon *New Yorker* v92 no46 p21 Ja 23 2017

THE CORRUPTION CONUNDRUM cartoon *New Yorker* v92 no48 p19 F 6 2017

DOCTOR'S ORDERS cartoon *New Yorker* v92 no42 p50 D 19 2016

Fine Dining for the Masses color *Bon Appetit* no11 p28 N 2017

THE HIDDEN COST OF RACE cartoon *New Yorker* v92 no32 p39 O 10 2016

ROBOPOCALYPSE NOT: EVERYONE THINKS THAT AUTO-MATION WILL TAKE AWAY OUR JOBS. THE EVIDENCE DISAGREES cartoon color graph *Wired* v25 no9 p60 S 2017

SHOP TILL THEY DROP cartoon *New Yorker* v92 no44 p23 Ja 9 2017

TRUMP'S BUDGET BLUFF cartoon *New Yorker* v92 no49 p34 F 13 2017

TRUMP SETS PRIVATE PRISONS FREE cartoon *New Yorker* v92 no40 p26 D 5 2016

TRUMP'S INFRASTRUCTURE PROMISES cartoon *New York-er* v92 no39 p35 N 28 2016

TRUMP'S MARKET RALLY cartoon *New Yorker* v93 no3 p25 Mr 6 2017

TRUMP'S OTHER TAX PLOY cartoon *New Yorker* v92 no33 p29 O 17 2016

UNEASY LIES THE HEAD cartoon *New Yorker* v92 no36 p19 N 7 2016

VISIONARIES color il *MIT Technology Review* v120 no5 p42 S/O 2017

WHAT'S IN A NAME? cartoon *New Yorker* v92 no37 p35 N 14 2016

Why Tesla Is Worth More Than GM *MIT Technology Review* v120 no4 p28 Jl/Ag 2017

Surplus (Economics)

FEDERAL FINANCE *Economic Indicators* p32 Mr 2017

Surprenant, Leslie

ORIGINAL WOODSWOMAN: Preserving the legacy of Anne LaBastille *New York State Conservationist* v71 no3 p10 D 2016

Surprise

Caught by surprise P. W. Marty *Christian Century* v134 no12 p3 Je 7 2017

SURPRISE S. Sorensen, W. H. Griffith et al *Christian Century* v134 no12 p22 Je 7 2017

Surrealism

Master of The Surreal J. J. MILLER color *National Review* v69 no11 p38 Je 12 2017

What makes an image surreal is not the artful crafting of illusion but the eruption of the accidental into the everyday *New York Times Magazine* p16 O 23 2016

Surrender (Military)

How Israel Wins F. Ehrman *Commentary* v143 no3 p7 Mr 2017

Surrogate mothers

MADE IN AMERICA M. WEIGEL color *New Republic* v248 no11 p32 N 2017

WHO ASKED YOU? WE DID! *Parents* v91 no12 p16 D 2016

Surround-sound systems

All About Atmos A. L. GRIFFIN diag *Sound & Vision* v82 no6 p19 Jl/Ag 2017

Soundbar Shortcomings A. L. GRIFFIN color *Sound & Vision* v81 no10 p22 D 2016

Surveillance (Poem)

Surveillance A. MOTION *American Scholar* v86 no4 p55 Aut 2017

Surveys

> *See also*
> Internet surveys
> Public opinion polls
> Work environment surveys

An "Age" - Old Problem K. PARKER and J. HOROWITZ *USA Today Magazine* v145 no2860 p28 Ja 2017

and the survey says *U.S. Catholic* v82 no8 p19 Ag 2017

Feeling Powerful at Work Makes Us Feel Worse When We Get Home T. A. Foulk and K. Lanaj *Harvard Business Review Digital Articles* p2 Je 13 2017

HOW TO GOVERN YOUR CHURCH EFFECTIVELY color

graph *Christianity Today* v60 no8 p22 O 2016

(I DON'T WANT NO) SATISFACTION SURVEY E. Dwyer *Saturday Evening Post* v289 no5 p28 S/O 2017

In the Spirit of Friendship W. Damon *Hoover Digest: Research & Opinion on Public Policy* no4 p185 Fall 2016

Park Agencies: s to Sustainability in Their Communities K. Roth *Parks & Recreation* v52 no4 p12 Ap 2017

We've made giving a damn surprisingly affordable *Skeptical Inquirer* v40 no6 p10 N/D 2016

What would you like your parish to make a higher priority? graph *America* v216 no7 p6 Ap 3 2017

Survival

See also

Airplane crash survival

DEEP TIME, DEEP SURVIVAL D. Grinspoon color *Scientific American* v315 no3 p76 S 2016

FIFTY-FIFTY E. O. Wilson *Sierra* v102 no1 p28 Ja/F 2017

I Survived! [Cover story] J. RIOS, C. S. GRANT et al *Reader's Digest* v189 no1128 p62 Mr 2017

I SURVIVED D. O'NEIL and A. DAWSON color *Men's Health* v32 no6 p128 Ag 2017

Survival & emergency equipment

See also

Lifesaving—Equipment & supplies

HEALTHY TRAVELS K. P. S. Khalsa color *Amazing Wellness* v8 no6 p36 Early Winter2016

Survival behavior (Animals)

Panda Patrol J. KIFFEL-ALCHEH color map *National Geographic Kids* no472 p12 Ag 2017

Survival behavior (Humans)

All the Gallant Men D. STRATTON and K. GIRE *Reader's Digest* v188 no1126 p82 D 2016/Ja 2017

THE HEIGHTS WE GO TO K. COATES color *Archaeology* v70 no5 p38 S/O 2017

Monuments to Catastrophe L. Spinney *History Today* v67 no4 p72 Ap 2017

SCHOOL SURVIVAL GUIDE R. Lynes *Harper's Magazine* p43 S 2017

SEX: OUR WONDERFUL GIFT M. WERNER *Humanist* v77 no4 p41 Jl/Ag 2017

THE WORST PLACES LIFE LOVES TO LIVE C. MALDARELLI cartoon *Popular Science* p30 Ja/F 2017

Survival skills training

Professor Caveman R. SCHIFFMAN color *Atlantic* v319 no3 p18 Ap 2017

SURVIVE ANYWHERE C. ALLEN, T. MACWELCH et al bw cartoon color diag *Outdoor Life* v224 no3 p33 Ap 2017

Survivalist movement

SURVIVAL OF THE RICHEST E. OSNOS cartoon color *New Yorker* v92 no47 p36 Ja 30 2017

Survival—Religious aspects

Survival is sacred N. Ripatrazone *Christian Century* v134 no16 p24 Ag 2 2017

Survivor (TV program)

Ask Matt M. Roush *TV Guide* v64 no40 p4 O 3 2016

CHEERS & JEERS D. HOLBROOK *TV Guide* v65 no19 p88 My 1 2017

Will These Five Survive? D. Ross color *Entertainment Weekly* no1454/1455 p19 F 24 2017

Survivor: Heroes vs. Healers vs. Hustlers (TV program)

LIKE FATHER, LIKE DAUGHTER color *Entertainment Weekly* no1484 p49 S 29 2017

Survivor: Heroes vs. Healers vs. Hustlers N. Abrams, B. L. Heldman et al *Entertainment Weekly* no1482/1483 p75 S 22 2017

Survivors' benefits

When You Need Cash Quick E. AMBROSE color *AARP: The Magazine* v60 no4A p21 Je/Jl 2017

Sushi

Conic Boom J. SPALDING *Indianapolis Monthly* p45 N 2017

Sushi restaurants

IS THIS GUY THE MOST HATED RESTAURATEUR IN AMERICA? J. Gordinier cartoon color *Esquire* v167 no2 p56 Mr 2017

The Nobu Effect: HOW AMERICA'S MOST INFLUENTIAL SUSHI CHEF REDEFINED JAPANESE FOOD IN L.A P. KUH *Los Angeles Magazine* v62 no9 p106 S 2017

SUSHI FOR ADULTS J. RUBY color *Chicago* v66 no8 p60 Ag 2017

Sushkevich, Vitaly L.

Selective anaerobic oxidation of methane enables direct synthesis of methanol diag graph *Science* v356 no6337 p523 My 5 2017

Sushko, Maria L.

Direction-specific van der Waals attraction between rutile TiO_2 nanocrystals diag *Science* v356 no6336 p434 Ap 28 2017

Sushkov, Alexander O.

Probing the frontiers of particle physics with tabletop-scale experiments color graph *Science* v357 no6355 p990 S 8 2017

Suskewicz, Josh

Tesla's New Strategy Is Over 100 Years Old *Harvard Business Review Digital Articles* p2 My 19 2015

Suskind, Ron

A Character Among Characters: Judith Newman's moving memoir of life with an autistic son *New York Times Book Review* p13 Ag 20 2017

NO ONE CARES ABOUT CRAZY PEOPLE *New York Times Book Review* p1 Ap 9 2017

Suspects (Criminal justice)

In India, a legal group defends Muslims accused in terrorism cases B. Dore color *Christian Century* v134 no7 p16 Mr 29 2017

THE MURDER OF ROGER ACKROYED L. Pham *New York Times Book Review* p27 Ja 22 2017

Suspended Night (Music)

Tomasz Stańko's Solo on 'Suspended Variation VI' J. Durso bw color *Downbeat* v84 no4 p90 Ap 2017

Suspense (Film)

Majority Rule D. Eagan bw *Film Comment* v53 no4 p77 Jl/Ag 2017

Suspense fiction

Despite Some Editors' Weariness, Psychological Suspense Is Still Hot R. Deahl *Publishers Weekly* v263 no41 p5 O 10 2016

Golden Prey *Publishers Weekly* v264 no9 p74 F 27 2017

iBook Bestsellers chart color *Publishers Weekly* v264 no20 p17 My 15 2017

SUMMER'S CHILLIEST THRILLERS I. Biedenharn and L. Greenblatt color *Entertainment Weekly* no1473 p60 Jl 7 2017

Suspension bridges

Bridge to the Future E. Barone color *Time* v189 no13 p42 Ap 10 2017

Suspicion

British strive to build interfaith bridges amid terrorist attacks C. Traub and S. M. Llana color *Christian Century* v134 no15 p14 Jl 19 2017

Susser, Jenny

Coping with Judgment *Dressage Today* v23 no8 p16 Ap 2017

Coping with the Loss of an Equine Partner color *Dressage Today* v23 no12 p16 S 2017

Energize Yourself for Competition color *Dressage Today* p20 My 2017

Free Yourself from Feelings Of Guilt Over Barn Time *Dressage Today* v24 no2 p16 N 2017

How Can I Maximize Rides When I Have Minimal Time? *Dressage Today* v23 no6 p16 F 2017

How Can I Move Past Training Ruts? *Dressage Today* v23 no5 p18 Ja 2017

How to Break Your Goals Into Manageable Pieces *Dressage Today* v23 no7 p16 Mr 2017

Is the Tough Trainer Worth It? *Dressage Today* v23 no11 p16 Ag 2017

Prevent Disappointment in the Saddle color *Dressage Today* v23 no9 p18 Je 2017

Rediscover the Joy of Riding *Dressage Today* v24 no1 p18 O 2017

RELIEF FOR STRESS *Dressage Today* v23 no4 p16 D 2016

Susskind, Daniel

IF YOU THOUGHT YOU KNEW L&D... THINK AGAIN: Discover new ideas and trends at this year's CIPD Learning and Development Show *People Management* p42 My 2017

Susskind, Leonard

A COSMIC CONTROVERSY color *Scientific American* v317 no1 p5 Jl 2017

David Ritz Finkelstein *Physics Today* v70 no2 p68 F 2017

Sussman, Adeena

COLD SUMMER SOUPS color *Sunset* v239 no1 p89 Jl 2017

THE NORMAN color *Conde Nast Traveler* v52 no9 p34 O 2017

Sussman, Matt

Casemore Kirkeby color *Art in America* v105 no6 p144 Je/Jl 2017

LIBBY BLACK *Art in America* v104 no9 p161 O 2016

Sustainability

10 Sustainable Business Stories That Shaped 2015 A. Winston *Harvard Business Review Digital Articles* p2 D 23 2015

9 Sustainable Business Stories That Shaped 2016 A. Winston *Harvard Business Review Digital Articles* p2 D 20 2016

Brother Act H. Smith *Sierra* v102 no5 p62 St/O 2017

BUILDING YOUR FARM'S BRAND: YOUR BRAND IS A TOOL THAT CAN HELP YOU ACHIEVE YOUR FARM'S GOALS J. Scott *Successful Farming* v115 no12 p18 O 2017

The Comprehensive Business Case for Sustainability T. Whelan and C. Fink *Harvard Business Review Digital Articles* p2 O 21 2016

A Different Carbon Tax: The Sustainable Green Tariff P. Lorenzi *Society* v54 no4 p342 Ag 2017

Faith that grows W. Massey color *U.S. Catholic* v82 no6 p22 Je 2017

The Fastest-Growing Cause for Shareholders Is Sustainability G. Serafeim *Harvard Business Review Digital Articles* p2 Jl 12 2016

FOREWORD M. Nasser *UN Chronicle* v53 no2 p4 2016

Golden J. HORNER color *Idaho Magazine* v16 no1 p10 O 2016

How Industrial Firms Invest in Renewable Energy, Affordably A. Winston *Harvard Business Review Digital Articles* p2 Ag 5 2016

How Target Is Taking Sustainable Products Mainstream A. Winston *Harvard Business Review Digital Articles* p2 Ag 4 2015

How to Quantify Sustainability's Impact on Your Bottom Line T. Whelan, B. Zappa et al *Harvard Business Review Digital Articles* p2 S 13 2017

It's Time for Companies to Be Strategic About Energy A. Winston *Harvard Business Review Digital Articles* p2 Je 14 2016

It's Time to Tie Executive Compensation to Sustainability S. Burchman and B. Sullivan *Harvard Business Review Digital Articles* p2 2017

Luxury Brands Can No Longer Ignore Sustainability A. Winston *Harvard Business Review Digital Articles* p2 F 8 2016

NATURE LOVER J. Lovell bw color *Conde Nast Traveler* v52 no4 p54 Ap 2017

A New Vision for Business N. Gibbs color *Time* v188 no24 p4 D 12 2016

The Next Stage of Sustainability D. Gould color *Bloomberg Businessweek* no4502 p10 D 5 2016

OUT OF THE BOX L. Rao color *Fortune* v174 no7 p22 D 1 2016

Planning for the Future of Urban Biodiversity: A Global Review of City-Scale Initiatives C. H. NILON, M. F. J. ARONSON et al *BioScience* v67 no4 p332 Ap 2017

Raw Appeal C. Leu *Sierra* v101 no4 p8 Jl/Ag 2016

Saving the Planet from Ecological Disaster Is a $12 Trillion Opportunity J. Elkington *Harvard Business Review Digital Articles* p2 My 4 2017

Selling out science? K. F. Boehnke cartoon *Science* v354 no6314 p934 N 18 2016

State of the Industry A. Dennis color *Climbing* no352 p14 Ap 2017

SUSTAINABILITY color *National Geographic* v232 no5 p10 N 2017

SUSTAINABILITY KEY FOR CITIES S. Goldberg *National Geographic* v232 no4 p2 O 2017

Transforming Health Care Takes Continuity and Consistency M. Britnell *Harvard Business Review Digital Articles* p2 D 28 2015

Two Buzzwords, Same Meaning? 'Zero waste' and 'circular economy' are often used together E. Daigneau *Governing* v30 no10 p20 Jl 2017

USING SPORT TO END HUNGER AND ACHIEVE FOOD SECURITY J. BREWER *UN Chronicle* v53 no2 p39 2016

Will Today's Devastating Weather Change Business the Way Hurricane Katrina Did? A. Winston *Harvard Business Review Digital Articles* p2 S 13 2017

Sustainability—Congresses

20 million sustainability leaders by 2025 color *National Wildlife (World Edition)* v55 no2 p44 F/Mr 2017

Sustainability—Economic aspects

Sustainable Business Will Move Ahead With or Without Trump's

Support A. Winston *Harvard Business Review Digital Articles* p2 N 19 2016

Sustainability—Government policy

What's Sustainability, Anyhow? E. Daigneau *Governing* v30 no3 p20 D 2016

Sustainability—Management

Green from the Get-Go: At 24, Atlanta's new sustainability director has already spent a lifetime in the field E. Daigneau *Governing* v31 no1 p20 O 2017

The sustainable scientist J. J. Mcdonnell color *Science* v357 no6356 p1202 S 15 2017

Sustainable agriculture

Agriculture in 2050: Recalibrating Targets for Sustainable Intensification M. C. HUNTER, R. G. SMITH et al *BioScience* v67 no4 p386 Ap 2017

Patagonia: For climbing Everest, diving the Great Barrier Reef, and saving the planet on a beer run B. Wieners color *Bloomberg Businessweek* no4494 p54 O 10 2016

SUSTAINABLE COTTON D. Kessenides color *Bloomberg Businessweek* no4496 p62 O 24 2016

Time for responsible peatland agriculture L. S. Wijedasa, S. E. Page et al bibl *Science* v354 no6312 p562 N 4 2016

Sustainable architecture

Campuses Go Green K. Logan *Architectural Record* v204 no11 p134 N 2016

PYRAMID POWER S. COCHRAN color *Architectural Digest* v73 no11 p208 N 2016

Suite Life K. Logan color *Architectural Record* v204 no12 p105 D 2016

What the New Administration Could Mean for Green Buildings C. VON KAENEL *Architectural Record* v205 no1 p19 Ja 2017

Sustainable architecture—Evaluation

Psychology Of Green L. Halley color *Alternatives Journal (AJ) - Canada's Environmental Voice* v42 no3 p51 2016

Sustainable buildings

Designing Green Mosques U. MIRZA *Islamic Horizons* v46 no1 p42 Ja/F 2017

Last Look D. Kidd *Governing* v30 no4 p64 Ja 2017

The Microbiome of Green Design C. BEANS color *BioScience* v66 no10 p801 O 1 2016

Sustainable buildings—Design & construction

Psychology Of Green L. Halley color *Alternatives Journal (AJ) - Canada's Environmental Voice* v42 no3 p51 2016

Sustainable communities

FEATURED FELLOW: GORDON HARRIS M. Rosano color *Canadian Geographic* v137 no3 p78 My 2017

Sustainable development

See also

Green infrastructure (Economics)

The 10 Most Important Sustainable Business Stories from 2014 A. Winston *Harvard Business Review Digital Articles* p2 D 19 2014

10 SUCCESSFUL FARMERS: RANDY CONSTANT J. Henke *Successful Farming* v115 no8 p28 Je/Jl 2017

10 Sustainable Business Stories That Shaped 2015 A. Winston *Harvard Business Review Digital Articles* p2 D 23 2015

Bridging the Gaps between Science and Policy for the Sustainable Management of Rangeland Resources in the Developing World SHIKUI DONG, S. A. WOLF et al *BioScience* v67 no7 p656 Jl 2017

Companies That Don't Manage Utilities Strategically Are Throwing Money Away J. Jia *Harvard Business Review Digital Articles* p2 Mr 22 2016

A Conference to #SaveOurOcean W. Hongbo *UN Chronicle* v54 no1/2 p1 2017

Dubai's Audacious Goal R. KUNZIG color map *National Geographic* v232 no4 p52 O 2017

Global Fund lessons for Sustainable Development Goals J. D. Sachs and G. Schmidt-Traub color *Science* v356 no6333 p32 Ap 7 2017

Global Marine Governance and Oceans Management for the Achievement of SDG 14 M. Vierros *UN Chronicle* v54 no1/2 p1 2017

HOW CITIES COULD SAVE US W. McDonough color *Scientific American* v317 no1 p44 Jl 2017

Improving Environmental Outcomes at the State Level *Governing*

v30 no4 p10 Ja 2017

The Ocean Conference: a Game-Changer P. Thomson *UN Chronicle* v54 no1/2 p1 2017

The Role of Sport in Achieving the Sustainable Development Goals W. LEMKE *UN Chronicle* v53 no2 p6 2016

SPORT AS A MEANS OF ADVANCING INTERNATIONAL DEVELOPMENT S. DARNELL *UN Chronicle* v53 no2 p27 2016

What Businesses Need to Know About Sustainable Development Goals B. Chakravorti *Harvard Business Review Digital Articles* p2 N 20 2015

Sustainable Development Goals (United Nations)

Achieving SDG 14: the Role of the United Nations Convention on the Law of the Sea M. d. S. Soares *UN Chronicle* v54 no1/2 p1 2017

The Arctic Ocean and the Sea Ice Is Our Nuna O. Eegeesiak *UN Chronicle* v54 no1/2 p1 2017

Global Marine Governance and Oceans Management for the Achievement of SDG 14 M. Vierros *UN Chronicle* v54 no1/2 p1 2017

How Companies Can Champion Sustainable Development B. Chakravorti *Harvard Business Review Digital Articles* p2 Mr 14 2017

Maintaining Healthy Ocean Fisheries to Support Livelihoods: Achieving SDG 14 in Europe K. Vella *UN Chronicle* v54 no1/2 p1 2017

Making SDGs Work for Climate Change Hotspots S. Szabo, R. J. Nicholls et al bibl *Environment* v58 no6 p24 N/D 2016

Making the Ocean a Partner in Our Quest for a Sustainable Future J. G. d. Silva *UN Chronicle* v54 no1/2 p1 2017

Mobilizing the Global Community to Achieve SDG 14 A. J. Mohammed *UN Chronicle* v54 no1/2 p1 2017

The New Urban Agenda's Road Map for Planning Urban Spatial Development: Tangible, Manageable and Measurable E. L. Birch *UN Chronicle* v53 no3 p18 2016

A Sea of Islands: How a Regional Group of Pacific States Is Working to Achieve SDG 14 D. M. Taylor *UN Chronicle* v54 no1/2 p1 2017

What Businesses Need to Know About Sustainable Development Goals B. Chakravorti *Harvard Business Review Digital Articles* p2 N 20 2015

Sustainable development reporting

A Better Scorecard for Your Company's Sustainability Efforts M. Thomas and M. W. McElroy *Harvard Business Review Digital Articles* p2 D 10 2015

Sustainable fisheries

Reform China's fisheries subsidies H. Yang, M. Ma et al color *Science* v356 no6345 p1343 Je 30 2017

"The Importance of Benthic Habitats for Coastal Fisheries" (Kritzer et al. 2016): Soft Bottoms Are Biologically Productive, Not "Abiotic" L. B. CAHOON *BioScience* v67 no9 p781 S 2017

Sustainable living

Hey Mr. Green! What's a good ecofriendly tile cleaner? B. Schildgen *Sierra* v102 no1 p14 Ja/F 2017

Sustainable tourism

Destination: Making a Difference D. POINTDUJOUR color *Ebony* v72 no5 p60 Mr 2017

NYT: Lather, Rinse, Repeat color *Weekly Standard* v22 no38 p2 Je 12 2017

Sustainable agriculture—Societies, etc.

Take a Free Course on Organic Seed S. Stonebrook *Mother Earth News* no279 p7 D/Ja 2017

Susumu Sakata

Methane production from coal by a single methanogen bibl graph *Science* v354 no6309 p222 O 14 2016

Susumu Tonegawa

Ventral CA1 neurons store social memory bibl graph *Science* v353 no6307 p1536 S 30 2016

Sutanto, Clarinda N.

Preventing mussel adhesion using lubricant-infused materials color diag graph *Science* v357 no6352 p668 Ag 18 2017

Sutcliffe, Kathleen M.

The Next Wave of Hospital Innovation to Make Patients Safer *Harvard Business Review Digital Articles* p2 Ag 8 2016

When Health Care Providers Look at Problems from Multiple Perspectives, Patients Benefit *Harvard Business Review Digital*

Articles p2 Je 23 2017

SUTER, LESLEY BARGAR

THE FAST-»FOOD« REMEDY *Los Angeles Magazine* p98 Ja 2017

Golden Girls *Los Angeles Magazine* p46 Ap 2017

Group Effort *Los Angeles Magazine* v62 no6 p40 Je 2017

THE HOT LIST *Los Angeles Magazine* p132 D 2016

Kanpai Cool *Los Angeles Magazine* p41 My 2017

MIRY WHITEHILL-BEN ATAR: THE FOUNDER OF MIRY'S LIST HAS HELPED MORE THAN 100 RESETTLED FAMILIES MAKE A LIFE IN THE U.S. HERE'S WHERE HER INSPIRATION CAME FROM *Los Angeles Magazine* v62 no9 p94 S 2017

Taste The New Hope *Los Angeles Magazine* p48 My 2017

Suter, Robert

Multiscale measurements for materials modeling diag *Science* v356 no6339 p704 My 19 2017

Suter Racing Technology (Company)

DADDY, WHAT'S A CARBURETOR? K. CAMERON color *Cycle World* v56 no10 p22 N 2017

Sutherland, Greg

Site-specific phosphorylation of tau inhibits amyloid-β toxicity in Alzheimer's mice bibl graph *Science* v354 no6314 p904 N 18 2016

Sutherland, Jeff

The Secret History of Agile Innovation *Harvard Business Review Digital Articles* p2 Ap 20 2016

Sutherland, John

He Loved Opium, Murder and Wordsworth *New York Times Book Review* p22 O 30 2016

You Don't Know Jane: A new reading of Jane Austen's novels depicts her as a critic of her society *New York Times Book Review* p11 Jl 16 2017

Sutherland, Kiefer, 1966-

DESIGNATED SURVIVOR I. RATLEDGE *TV Guide* p26 Ap 17 2017

Designated Survivor J. Jensen color *Entertainment Weekly* no1440 p48 N 18 2016

Designated Survivor L. Rice, N. Abrams et al color *Entertainment Weekly* no1482/1483 p74 S 22 2017

Kiefer Sutherland C. Ianzito color *AARP: The Magazine* v60 no1A p64 D 2016/Ja 2017

Sutherland, Kiefer, 1966-—Interviews

DESIGNATED SURVIVOR I. Ratledge *TV Guide* v65 no39 p42 S 18 2017

Sutherland, Sarah

Sarah SUTHERLAND M. MULLEN *Interview* v47 no3 p18 Ap 2017

Sutherland, Tara E.

Local amplifiers of IL-4Rα-mediated macrophage activation promote repair in lung and liver diag *Science* v356 no6342 p1076 Je 9 2017

Sutherland, Will

The Vanhandlers color *Popular Mechanics* p59 Je 2017

Sutoris, Peter

Visions of Development: Films Division of India and the Imagination of Progress, 1948-1975 N. VACHANI *Film Quarterly* v70 no4 p127 Summ 2017

Sutphin, Eric

Half color *Art in America* v105 no1 p81 Ja 2017

PETER LINDE BUSK *Art in America* v104 no9 p152 O 2016

Shrine color *Art in America* v105 no6 p131 Je/Jl 2017

TERESA BURGA color *Art in America* p120 O 2017

THOMAS TROSCH color *Art in America* p121 O 2017

Zahra Al-Ghamdi color *Art in America* v105 no5 p31 My 2017

Sutro Baths (San Francisco, Calif.)

A Splash from the Past: Sutro Baths M. Hsu *Parks & Recreation* p8 Aquatics Guide 2017

Sutter, Markus

Assembly principles and structure of a 6.5-MDa bacterial microcompartment shell color diag *Science* v356 no6344 p1293 Je 23 2017

Sutterfield, Ragan

Hope that flows color *Christian Century* v134 no3 p32 F 2017

Suttmeier, Richard P.

Challenges of S&T system reform in China bibl color *Science* v355 no6329 p1019 Mr 10 2017

Sutton, Adrian P.

Nanocrystalline copper films are never flat diag graph *Science* v357 no6349 p397 Jl 28 2017

Sutton, Cyrus

CYRUS SUTTON J. HOUSMAN color *Surfer* v58 no3 p36 Je 2017

Sutton, Jason

DRIVE IT A MILE! color *Golf Magazine* v59 no8 p43 Ag 2017

HIT THE BRAKES AT IMPACT color *Golf Magazine* v59 no7 p46 Jl 2017

Sutton, Jeannette—Interviews

Putting the Right Information on Twitter in a Crisis S. G. Carmichael *Harvard Business Review Digital Articles* p2 N 20 2015

Sutton, Katie

Game Changer color *House Beautiful* v159 no2 p45 Mr 2017

Resources *House Beautiful* v159 no2 p126 Mr 2017

SUTTON, KEITH

CAT HACKS color *Outdoor Life* v224 no6 p35 Ag 2017

Sutton, Kelly

What a tiny house can teach you color *Redbook* p148 S 2017

Sutton, Matthew Avery

Faith in the New Millennium: The Future of Religion and American Politics R. Balmer *Christian Century* v133 no22 p41 O 26 2016

Sutton, Mike

The Big Show color *Car & Driver* v63 no1 p102 Jl 2017

Fleet Files color diag *Car & Driver* v63 no1 p88 Jl 2017

Haymaker color *Car & Driver* v62 no8 p84 F 2017

Sutton, Patrice

Estimating the health benefits of environmental regulations color *Science* v357 no6350 p457 Ag 4 2017

Sutton, Paul S.

A schoolwide investment in problem-based learning chart il *Phi Delta Kappan* v99 no2 p65 O 2017

Sutton, Rebecca J.

Perovskite-perovskite tandem photovoltaics with optimized band gaps bibl chart graph *Science* v354 no6314 p861 N 18 2016

Sutton, Robert I.

The Asshole Survival Guide: How to Deal with People Who Treat You like Dirt *Publishers Weekly* v264 no20 p46 My 15 2017

Better Service, Faster: A Design Thinking Case Study *Harvard Business Review Digital Articles* p2 Ja 6 2016

What Design Thinking Is Doing for the San Francisco Opera *Harvard Business Review Digital Articles* p2 Je 3 2016

Sutton, Robert K.

Stark Mad Abolitionists: Lawrence, Kansas, and the Battle over Slavery in the Civil War Era *Publishers Weekly* v264 no22 p57 My 29 2017

Sutton, Roxanne

NRPA's Wildlife Explorer Program *Parks & Recreation* v51 no10 p82 O 2016

Sutton Hoo Ship Burial (England)

SOMETHING NEW FOR SUTTON HOO J. URBANUS bw color *Archaeology* v70 no2 p14 Mr/Ap 2017

Suvà, Mario L.

Decoupling genetics, lineages, and microenvironment in IDH-mutant gliomas by single-cell RNA-seq diag *Science* v355 no6332 p1391 Mr 31 2017

Suwanee (Ga.)

Sugar Rush E. JACKSON *Atlanta* v56 no7 p59 N 2016

Suzman, James

What's next for the Ju/'hoansi? A. Barnard color *Science* v356 no6345 p1340 Je 30 2017

Suzuki, Ichiro, 1973-

Ichiro SUZUKI A. Belth bw *Esquire* p70 Ap 2017

Suzuki, Keiichiro

Integration of CpG-free DNA induces de novo methylation of CpG islands in pluripotent stem cells diag *Science* v356 no6337 p503 My 5 2017

Suzuki Marine (Company)

Positive Spin: Suzuki raises the bar on high-horsepower outboards with a testosterone-laced engine that has a pair … of propellers A. JONES *Boating World* v38 no8 p20 S/O 2017

Suzuki motorcycle

2017 SUZUKI GSX-R1000 TRACK CLUB SPECIAL M. Hoyer

color *Cycle World* v56 no6 p12 Jl 2017

2018 SUZUKI GSX-S750 D. Canet color *Cycle World* v56 no10 p16 N 2017

MAN, VAN, CHAMPIONSHIP PLAN M. HOYER color *Cycle World* v56 no4 p6 My 2017

SERVICE R. NIERLICH color *Cycle World* v56 no1 p54 Ja/F 2017

SLIPSTREAM color *Cycle World* v55 no10 p66 N 2016

Suzuki motorcycle—Evaluation

2016 SUZUKI GSX-S1000 D. Canet chart color *Cycle World* v56 no1 p52 Ja/F 2017

2017 SUZUKI GSX-R1000R [Cover story] B. Adams color *Cycle World* v56 no4 p36 My 2017

SUZUKI'S NEW SWORLD [Cover story] K. Cameron color *Cycle World* v55 no10 p30 N 2016

Svalbard Global Seed Vault (Svalbard, Norway)

ARKS OF THE APOCALYPSE M. WOLLAN *New York Times Magazine* p34 Jl 16 2017

Svensson, Erik I.

Precipitation drives global variation in natural selection bibl chart diag map *Science* v355 no6328 p959 Mr 3 2017

Svirgun, Anna

RIVER REBORN *New York State Conservationist* v71 no4 p10 F 2017

Svirsky, Mario

Cochlear implants and electronic hearing *Physics Today* v70 no8 p52 Ag 2017

Svoboda, Dillon C.

Restored iron transport by a small molecule promotes absorption and hemoglobinization in animals color graph *Science* v356 no6338 p608 My 12 2017

Svoboda, Valerie

More time for learning color *Phi Delta Kappan* v98 no4 p26 D 2016/Ja 2017

Svoboda, Vit

Time-resolved x-ray absorption spectroscopy with a water window high-harmonic source bibl graph *Science* v355 no6322 p264 Ja 20 2017

SVP Yachts d.o.o.

Changing the Game [Cover story] J. Y. WOOD chart color diag *Power & Motoryacht* v34 no6 p66 Je 2017

Swaab, Roderick I.

Having Too Many Options Can Make You a Worse Negotiator *Harvard Business Review Digital Articles* p2 My 24 2017

SWABY, RACHEL

Herd Mentality color *Runner's World* v52 no8 p44 S 2017

Swaddling

SLEEP LIKE A BABY color *Prevention* v69 no6 p10 Je 2017

Swafford, Jan

Symphonic Range G. B. STAUFFER color *Weekly Standard* v22 no31 p34 Ap 17 2017

Swail, Conor

Longines FEI World Cup North American League News color *Practical Horseman* v45 no11 p65 N 2017

Swails, Kelsey

Speak Your Truth bw color *Glamour* v115 no6 p22 Je 2017

Swaim, Barton

Bill de Blasio, Culture-meister color *Weekly Standard* v22 no46 p14 Ag 14 2017

Did You Ever See a Dreamer Walking? color *Weekly Standard* v23 no2 p9 S 18 2017

The Expertocracy color *Weekly Standard* v22 no35 p26 My 22 2017

Good Writer's Disease? color *Weekly Standard* v23 no5 p42 O 9 2017

It Can't Happen Here color *Weekly Standard* v23 no1 p9 S 11 2017

The Masculine Case B. SWAIM *Weekly Standard* v22 no8 p41 O 31 2016

The Meaning of Stupid cartoon *Weekly Standard* v22 no45 p5 Ag 7 2017

Through Glasses, Darkly cartoon *Weekly Standard* v22 no48 p5 S 4 2017

Swain, Amanda

Ductal sex determination diag *Science* v357 no6352 p648 Ag 18 2017

Swain, Bernie

Successful Leaders Know What Made Them Who They Are *Harvard Business Review Digital Articles* p2 S 5 2016

Swain, Carol
The Cassandra of Vanderbilt A. B. LLOYD color *Weekly Standard* v22 no34 p32 My 15 2017

SWAIN, HILARY M.
Teaching Biology in the Field: Importance, Challenges, and Solutions *BioScience* v67 no6 p558 Je 2017

Swain, J.
Observation of a large-scale anisotropy in the arrival directions of cosmic rays above 8×1018 eV *Science* v357 no6357 p1266 S 22 2017

SWAIN, JEANNETTE
Check out these outrageous facts *National Geographic Kids* no469 p4 Ap 2017
Weird but true! color map *National Geographic Kids* no470 p4 My 2017
Weird But True! color *National Geographic Kids* no473 p4 S 2017

Swain, Stacy
Reflections on the lectionary *Christian Century* v134 no19 p19 S 13 2017

SWAMINATHAN, NIKHIL
PROTEINS SOLVE A HOMININ PUZZLE color *Archaeology* v70 no1 p11 Ja/F 2017
SHOPPED AROUND color *Mother Jones* v42 no5 p50 S/O 2017
STANDING STILL IN BERINGIA? *Archaeology* v70 no3 p19 My/Je 2017
TOP 10 DISCOVERIES OF 2016 bw cartoon color *Archaeology* v70 no1 p26 Ja/F 2017

Swaminathan, Vanitha
What 100,000 Tweets About the Volkswagen Scandal Tell Us About Angry Customers *Harvard Business Review Digital Articles* p2 S 2 2016

Swamp Fever (Music)
Sweeter Than Honey HADLEY bw *Downbeat* v84 no8 p75 Ag 2017

Swamps
PARODY *Weekly Standard* v22 no17 p40 Ja 2 2017
The Swamp Lover H. David color *Atlantic* v320 no4 p122 N 2017
Swamps G. TARLACH color *Discover* v38 no5 p74 Je 2017

Swan, Astrid
One minute to a better butt cartoon color *Redbook* p99 My 2017

SWAN, JAMES A.
THE HEROIC WORK OF THIN GREEN LINE GAME WARDENS *American Forests* v122 no3 p32 Fall 2016

SWAN, JENNIFER HUBERT
Outsiders *New York Times Book Review* p33 N 13 2016

Swan, Mara
The Big Disconnect in Your Talent Strategy and How to Fix It *Harvard Business Review Digital Articles* p2 D 23 2016
It's the Company's Job to Help Employees Learn *Harvard Business Review Digital Articles* p2 Jl 18 2016

Swan, Serinda
Marvel's Inhumans D. Franich color *Entertainment Weekly* no1484 p48 S 29 2017

SWAN, SUSAN
Boat Trouble color *Walrus* v14 no6 p50 Jl/Ag 2017

Swan Lake (Theatrical production)
DANCE *New Yorker* v93 no17 p13 Je 19 2017

Swanbrow Becker, Marty
Why Schools Need to Step Up Suicide Prevention Efforts *Education Digest* v83 no2 p17 O 2017

Swanepoel, Candice
BEAUTY DIARIES color *Harper's Bazaar* no3656 p380 S 2017

Swaney, Danielle L.
Evolution of protein phosphorylation across 18 fungal species bibl graph *Science* v354 no6309 p229 O 14 2016

Swanigan, Caleb
PROJECT BIGGIE L. Winn color *Sports Illustrated* v126 no5 p82 F 13 2017

SWANN, MAXINE
It Takes TWO bw color *Conde Nast Traveler* v52 no10 p114 N 2017

Swans
    See also
    Trumpeter swan

Tundra swan
SWAN SONG H. Macdonald *New York Times Magazine* p24 Ja 8 2017

SWANSBURG, JOHN
Men of Summer *New York Times Book Review* p14 Ap 2 2017

Swans—Congresses
Feed the Birds A. LAHEY color *Walrus* v14 no8 p21 O 2017

Swanson, Barrett
Pistol Pete's Homework Basketball *New York Times Magazine* p20 Ap 30 2017

Swanson, Carisha
Big Ideas for Tight Spots color *House Beautiful* v159 no5 p59 Je 2017
Fancy Cocktails? A Breeze! color *House Beautiful* v159 no4 p65 My 2017
for 2018 [Cover story] color *House Beautiful* v159 no9 p29 N 2017
In Perfect Harmony color *House Beautiful* v158 no10 p49 D 2016/Ja 2017
STEPS IN TIME bw color *House Beautiful* v158 no9 p95 N 2016
Top This Ice Cream color *House Beautiful* v159 no7 p74 S 2017
Tricks of the Trade color *House Beautiful* v159 no2 p69 Mr 2017
Wash and Wow color *House Beautiful* v159 no7 p69 S 2017

SWANSON, CARL
92 MINUTES WITH ... Glenn Close img *New York* p16 F 20 2017
All Those Cranes in Queens img *New York* v50 no18 p64 S 4 2017
ANT FARM TO TABLE img *New York* v49 no15 p36 Jl 25 2016
COAL AND STEEL FOR Rod Stewart's masterpiece [Cover story] color *Model Railroader* v84 no6 p42 Je 2017
Dan Doctoroff img *New York* v50 no17 p34 Ag 21 2017
home & help img *New York* p96 Mr 6 2017
IS POLITICAL ART THE ONLY ART THAT MATTERS NOW? THE ART WORLD IS GOING TO WAR WITH TRUMP. IF IT DOESN'T SHOOT ITSELF IN THE FOOT FIRST img *New York* v50 no8 p60 Ap 17 2017
Life on Mars img *New York* p58 Ja 23 2017
THE MAKING OF BARRY JENKINS img *New York* v49 no24 p122 N 28 2016
Marina Abramovic at 70 img *New York* v49 no21 p99 O 17 2016
PANDAS WILL FIX EVERYTHING img *New York* p54 Mr 6 2017
Seducing Robert Pattinson: How directors Josh and Benny Safdie landed the star for their heist thriller Good Time img *New York* v50 no16 p97 Ag 7 2017
VACCARELLO'S VISION bw color *Harper's Bazaar* no3655 p152 Ag 2017
The Willy Wonka of Hudson Yards img *New York* v49 no19 p79 S 19 2016

Swanson, Clare
HMH Looks for More in Culinary, Lifestyle color *Publishers Weekly* v264 no16 p6 Ap 17 2017
Home on the Range bw color *Publishers Weekly* v264 no10 p20 Mr 6 2017
Weise Reimagines Charlesbridge's Imagine *Publishers Weekly* v263 no39 p14 S 26 2016

Swanson, Larry W.
The Beautiful Brain: The Drawings of Santiago Ramón y Cajal C. Moskowitz color *Scientific American* v316 no1 p68 Ja 2017

Swanson, Michael
FROM OUR READERS color *Sky & Telescope* v134 no2 p6 Ag 2017

SWANSON, PETER
The Refit That Sparked Revolution bw color *Power & Motoryacht* v34 no8 p74 Ag 2017

Swanson, Wendy Sue
advice every new mom needs [Cover story] color *Parents* v92 no7 p32 Jl 2017

Swanton, Charles
Origins of lymphatic and distant metastases in human colorectal cancer diag graph *Science* v357 no6346 p55 Jl 7 2017

Swap, Walter
Artificial Intelligence Can't Replace Hard-Earned Knowledge - Yet *Harvard Business Review Digital Articles* p2 N 17 2014
What's Lost When Experts Retire *Harvard Business Review Digital Articles* p2 D 2 2014

SwapBots (Company)

Meet SwapBots, an augmented-reality toy that pairs with the iPad L. YAMSHON color *Macworld - Digital Edition* v34 no4 p51 My 2017

Swapna, G. V. T.

Principles for designing proteins with cavities formed by curved β sheets bibl color graph *Science* v355 no6321 p1 Ja 13 2017

Sward, Anna

POW(D)ER UP YOUR MEALS L. McGLASHAN color *Muscle & Performance* v9 no7 p51 Jl 2017

Swarm intelligence

The 'Wisdom of the Crowd' Has a Pretty Bad Track Record at Predicting Jobs Reports D. Cassino *Harvard Business Review Digital Articles* p2 Jl 8 2016

Swarming (Zoology)

Crabs Swarm on the Seafloor V. LaCapra *Oceanus* v52 no1 p6 Summ 2016

Swarnkar, Abhishek

Quantum dot–induced phase stabilization of α-CsPbI3 perovskite for high-efficiency photovoltaics bibl chart graph *Science* v354 no6308 p92 O 7 2016

Swarts, Kelly

Genomic estimation of complex traits reveals ancient maize adaptation to temperate North America diag *Science* v357 no6350 p512 Ag 4 2017

Swartz, Aimee

8 Ways to Ruin Your Summer cartoon color *Men's Health* v32 no6 p94 Ag 2017

Is Your Liver Cooked? color *Men's Health* v32 no1 p90 Ja/F 2017

Swartz, Dan

DAN ABOUT TOWN *Washingtonian Magazine* v52 no9 p30 Je 2017

Swartz, Jonas J.

Protecting unauthorized immigrant mothers improves their children's mental health diag *Science* v357 no6355 p1041 S 8 2017

SWARTZ, MIMI

Denton A. Cooley, 1920-2016 *Texas Monthly* v45 no1 p54 Ja 2017

IT CAN'T ALL BE ENERGY *Texas Monthly* v45 no5 p79 My 2017

Not So Special Ed *Texas Monthly* v45 no3 p26 Mr 2017

OUT OF Africa *Texas Monthly* v44 no12 p74 D 2016

Towering Debts *Texas Monthly* v45 no2 p20 F 2017

Swartz, Wilf

Committing to socially responsible seafood color *Science* v356 no6341 p912 Je 1 2017

Swartzlander, Anne

ANNE SWARTZLANDER *Phi Kappa Phi Forum* v97 no2 p33 Summ 2017

Swastikas

DIALOGUE A. Russell bw *New Yorker* v93 no24 p18 Ag 21 2017

The embattled swastika C. MCINTYRE color *Maclean's* v130 no10 p15 N 2017

S.W.A.T. (TV program)

S.W.A.T A. D'Arminio *TV Guide* v65 no37 p36 S 4 2017

Swatch watches

WRIST CANDY color *Esquire* p43 My 2017

Swayne, David E.

Role for migratory wild birds in the global spread of avian influenza H5N8 bibl graph map *Science* v354 no6309 p213 O 14 2016

SWEANY, BRIAN D.

EDITOR'S LETTER *Texas Monthly* v44 no11 p24 N 2016

THE HOBBY NAME IS ONE *Texas Monthly* v44 no12 p24 D 2016

Where Do We Go From Here? *Texas Monthly* v44 no12 p26 D 2016

Swearing (Profanity)

This Just In J. Zorthian *Time* v189 no19 p19 My 22 2017

Sweat (Play)

Closing TIME B. Reesman *Stage Directions* v30 no5 p12 My 2017

THE LISTENER M. SCHULMAN cartoon color *New Yorker* v93 no6 p30 Mr 27 2017

Sweat gland diseases

Keep Your Cool A. Weil color *Prevention* v69 no8 p26 Ag 2017

Sweat glands

Sweat: The Details J. COVERT and J. DEMELO bw graph *Men's Health* v32 no6 p92 Ag 2017

Sweat suits

Some Like It Aught J. Harman color *Glamour* v114 no12 p84 D 2016

Sweatbaths

Sensoriality and Wendat Steams S. DORLAND *American Indian Quarterly* v41 no1 p1 Wint 2017

Sweaters

See also

Pullovers (Sweaters)

BEST BETS img *New York* v50 no6 p56 Mr 20 2017

black POWER O. J. WILLIAMS color *Ebony* v72/73 no12/1 p44 O/N 2017

DIY Celeb Style J. Radosevich color *Seventeen* v76 no12 p30 D 2016/Ja 2017

Extreme Weirdness A. SANDLIN color *National Geographic Kids* no471 p10 Je/Jl 2017

FAIR PLAY color *Vogue* v207 no11 p214 N 2017

GREAT BUYS: UNDER $100 color *O, The Oprah Magazine* p64 N 2017

In This Issue *Vogue* v206 no11 p262 N 2016

MILLENNIAL PINK: THE LASTING COLOR OF NOW T. M. FERGUSON color *Ebony* v72 no11 p40 S 2017

The New ETERNALS N. Sullivan color *Esquire* p36 BigBlack-Book

Sweater WEATHER H. Rolfe *Dance Spirit* v20 no10 p54 D 2016

WORK DOMINATION color *Women's Health* v14 no8 p54 O 2017

Sweaters—Evaluation

17 Ways to... SLAY SUMMER STYLE color *Seventeen* v76 no3 p32 My 2017

Adam's HOLIDAY GIFT GUIDE color *O, The Oprah Magazine* p106 D 2016

BARE ESSENTIALS color *Indianapolis Monthly* p26 Ap 2017

BECKHAM THE YOUNGER S. BALL color *GQ: Gentlemen's Quarterly* v97 no9 p160 S 2017

The Blueprint J. LOVE and M. BOBO color *Ebony* v72 no5 p50 Mr 2017

CAN YOU SAY 'GLENURQUHART'? bw color *Esquire* p82 Ag 2017

Casual Glam cartoon color *Seventeen* v76 no12 p43 D 2016/Ja 2017

CHECK YOUR COAT C. SKIPPER color *GQ: Gentlemen's Quarterly* v97 no9 p172 S 2017

Fashion FORMULA OVERSIZE SWEATER + SLIP SKIRT color *InStyle* v23 no12 p130 N 2016

THE FRESH FACE OF BEAUTY M. OZAWA color *Martha Stewart Living* no271 p40 Ja/F 2017

The Get-It Guide *Glamour* v114 no11 p182 N 2016

GLOBAL Warmth M. HOLGATE and M. GUIDUCCI color *Vogue* v207 no1 p34 Ja 2017

GOING GRAPHIC color *Harper's Bazaar* no3649 p166 D 2016/Ja 2017

GREAT BUYS UNDER $100: IN THE NAVY color *O, The Oprah Magazine* p62 O 2017

HIGH SCORE *Interview* v46 no8 p52 O 2016

HOOP Dreams color *Vogue* v206 no12 p174 D 2016

Now meet 39 more beauty game changers—each defining themselves [Cover story] S. Kitchens, J. Harman et al bw color *Glamour* v115 no4 p166 Ap 2017

PACKING FOR THE ADIRONDACKS BRING ON THE KNITS AND HOT TODDYS L. DECARLO color *Conde Nast Traveler* v52 no10 p46 N 2017

Self-less Portrait C. L'HEUREUX img *New York* v49 no22 p65 O 31 2016

STRIPED JOGGERS color *Good Housekeeping* v264 no1 p16 Ja 1 2017

The Superhero Sweater J. CHEN color *Esquire* v166 no5 p55 D 2016/Ja 2017

THREE WISE MEN N. Sullivan, J. Roth et al bw color *Esquire* p88 2017 BigBlackBook

TOVE LOVE A. Salazar color *InStyle* v24 no1 p22 Ja 2017

Tree Huggers, Unite! A Guide to Sustainable Style J. GROFF color *GQ: Gentlemen's Quarterly* v97 no10 p59 O 2017

We Found the Perfect Fall Sweater J. MOORE bw *GQ: Gentlemen's Quarterly* v97 no10 p66 O 2017

THE WELL-SPENT $ DOLLAR bw *Harper's Bazaar* no3652

p124 Ap 2017

WHO WEARS THE PANTS? color *Esquire* p96 N 2017

Why Does This Sweater Cost $4,925? E. Wilson color *InStyle* v24 no10 p71 O 2017

WISH LIST 2016 B. Barrett, J. Bien-Kahn et al color *Wired* v24 no12 p45 D 2016

YARA SHAHIDI C. Stern color *InStyle* v24 no8 p57 Ag 2017

SWEATMAN, HUGH

Assessing National Biodiversity Trends for Rocky and Coral Reefs through the Integration of Citizen Science and Scientific Monitoring Programs *BioScience* v67 no2 p134 F 2017

Sweatshirts—Evaluation

BIG, BOLD & BEAUTIFUL color *O, The Oprah Magazine* p118 O 2017

CREW UP *Interview* v46 no10 p62 D 2016/Ja 2017

Gifts for a Fangirl cartoon color *Seventeen* v76 no12 p19 D 2016/Ja 2017

HOOP Dreams color *Vogue* v206 no12 p174 D 2016

MASTER CLASS WITH R. McKNIGHT bw cartoon color *Esquire* v166 no5 p69 D 2016/Ja 2017

NINE NEW COLLABS: Coming soon img *New York* v49 no23 p52 N 14 2016

SOLDIER ON color *Harper's Bazaar* no3657 p141 O 2017

Style for Miles C. KUZMA cartoon color *Runner's World* v52 no4 p46 My 2017

THE TRADE-UP color *Esquire* p38 Je/Jl 2017

Sweazy, Larry D.

See Also Murder *Publishers Weekly* v264 no5 p196 Ja 30 2017

Sweden—Description & travel

GUCCI WESTMAN K. MOLVAR color *Conde Nast Traveler* v52 no8 p24 S 2017

Sweden—Emigration & immigration

THE APATHETIC R. AVIV cartoon color *New Yorker* v93 no7 p68 Ap 3 2017

The Truth About Sweden P. Neuding color *Weekly Standard* v22 no26 p27 Mr 13 2017

Sweden—Social conditions

The Best Countries For Business K. BADENHAUSEN color *Forbes* v199 no2 p22 F 28 2017

Swedes—United States

FACES IN THE CROWD T. Keith color *Sports Illustrated* v126 no1 p18 Ja 9 2017

Swedish Academy (Organization)

The Lyrics Laureate D. ORR *New York Times Book Review* p22 Mr 26 2017

Sweeder, Ryan D.

Updating the Two Cultures: How Structures Can Promote Interdisciplinary Cultures *Change* v48 no6 p28 N/D 2016

Sweeney, A. M.

Eye patches: Protein assembly of index-gradient squid lenses bw color graph *Science* v357 no6351 p564 Ag 11 2017

Sweeney, Alison, 1976-

4 little moves that work wonders color *Redbook* p24 N 2017

Can a gadget make you skinny? color *Redbook* p26 Ap 2017

DAYS OF OUR LIVES M. LOGAN *TV Guide* v65 no41 p42 O 2 2017

Do this to meet your goals color *Redbook* p19 S 2017

Don't let winter drag you down! [Cover story] color *Redbook* p36 F 2017

Feel your best under stress color *Redbook* p30 D 2016

How to drink, relax, snack... and slim down color *Redbook* p20 Jl/Ag 2017

Little steps to total body confidence color *Redbook* p28 My 2017

Overcome any setback color *Redbook* p27 O 2017

Weight-loss numbers that truly matter *Redbook* p17 Mr 2017

Sweeney, Alison, 1976—Interviews

Confidence Lessons [Cover story] T. BLACKSTONE color *Redbook* p70 Je 2017

Sweeney, Bill

Cybersecurity Is Every Executive's Job *Harvard Business Review Digital Articles* p2 S 13 2016

SWEENEY, CHRIS

The FEATHER DETECTIVE *Audubon* v118 no6 p28 Wint 2016

Sweeney, F.

Direct observation of individual hydrogen atoms at trapping sites in a ferritic steel bibl diag *Science* v355 no6330 p1196 Mr 17

2017

Sweeney, James L.

Energy Efficiency: Still Low-hanging Fruit: There are still plenty of ways we can use energy more efficiently. Simple changes would produce large effects *Hoover Digest: Research & Opinion on Public Policy* no2 p121 Spr 2017

Sweeney, Jon M.

Bresson on Bresson: Interviews 1943–1983 *Christian Century* v134 no12 p41 Je 7 2017

From the academy, books that think (and a few that sell) color *America* v216 no5 p40 Mr 6 2017

Last Testament: In His Own Words *Christian Century* v134 no5 p40 Mr 1 2017

WHY READ FICTION? color *America* v215 no14 p27 N 7 2016

Sweeney, Michael J.

A friar turned detective color *America* v217 no4 p50 Ag 21 2017

Sweeney, Peggy

Water-Trough Raised Beds *Mother Earth News* no282 p84 Je/Jl 2017

Sweeney, Trevor R.

Neurodevelopmental protein Musashi-1 interacts with the Zika genome and promotes viral replication diag *Science* v357 no6346 p83 Jl 7 2017

Sweeney Todd: The Demon Barber of Fleet Street (Theatrical production)

GOINGS ON ABOUT TOWN color *New Yorker* v93 no3 p8 Mr 6 2017

PARTNERS H. ALS color *New Yorker* v93 no4 p82 Mr 13 2017

SWeeNey ToDD R. Minetor *Stage Directions* v29 no11 p40 N 2016

Sweeny, Elizabeth A.

Ratchet-like polypeptide translocation mechanism of the AAA+ disaggregase Hsp104 diag *Science* v357 no6348 p273 Jl 21 2017

Sweepstakes

Having More Options Can Make Us Evaluate Risk Differently U. Khan and D. Kupor color *Harvard Business Review Digital Articles* p2 F 9 2017

Sweepstakes color *Nebraska Life* v21 no1 p13 Ja/F 2017

Sweet, Bob

Class Is in Session color *Power & Motoryacht* v34 no9 p24 S 2017

Sweet, Elizabeth

GIRLS, BOYS, AND GENDERED TOYS N. Daly color *National Geographic* v231 no1 p17 Ja 2017

Sweet, Julie

Access to Digital Technology Accelerates Global Gender Equality *Harvard Business Review Digital Articles* p2 My 17 2016

Sweet, Julie—Awards

Women of Excellence color *Working Mother* p48 F/Mr 2017

Sweet, Melissa

Magic in a Web A. GOPNIK *New York Times Book Review* p24 N 13 2016

Sweet Charity (Theatrical production)

DEAR HEART H. ALS color *New Yorker* v92 no40 p84 D 5 2016

Sweet Jane

How to Tell Someone to Shut Up About Alta, Already color *Powder* v46 no2 p38 O 2017

Lessons In Ego Checking cartoon *Powder* p44 S 2017

Sweet potatoes

Dig in to über tubers color *Good Housekeeping* v265 no5 p67 N 2017

HERE'S HOW YOU MAKE AN "AUTHENTIC" AMERICAN TACO W. AVILA color *Bon Appetit* v62 no2 p68 Mr 2017

Stuff That Sweet Potato B. Lipton color *Health* v30 no10 p136 D 2016

Sweet Potatoes vs. Yams color *Prevention* v68 no12 p14 D 2016

Will It Miso? A. STANEK color *Bon Appetit* v62 no7 p34 Jl 2017

Sweet potatoes—Storage

SWEET POTATOES & SHALLOTS to Savor in Winter *Mother Earth News* no279 p10 D/Ja 2017

Sweetman, Kate

Embracing Change Means Disrupting Your Day *Harvard Business Review Digital Articles* p2 Jl 22 2016

Sweetnam, Shane

Back-to-Back Wins for Ireland color *Practical Horseman* v45 no5

zine v59 no10 p38 O 2017

HIT ROPES OFF THE TEE E. a. Tischler, O. Fields et al color *Golf Magazine* v59 no2 p55 F 2017

HOOK-PROOF YOUR SWING M. Blackburn, Birmingham et al color diag *Golf Magazine* v59 no2 p54 F 2017

HOT FOR TEACHER color *Golf Magazine* v59 no11 p68 N 2017

How to Build a Swing You Can Believe in K. Kirk color *Golf Magazine* v59 no9 p71 S 2017

Is My Setup Hurting My Swing? M. Chuck and D. DeNunzio *Golf Magazine* v59 no6 p42 Je 2017

MIND YOUR MISS D. Denunzio and T. Stickney color *Golf Magazine* v59 no2 p49 F 2017

OH, SNAP! M. Hunt and D. DeNunzio color *Golf Magazine* v59 no9 p52 S 2017

ONE LENGTH ONLY? R. Sauerhaft and R. Sauerhaft color *Golf Magazine* v58 no11 p86 N 2016

PARADISE LOST J. King and D. Denunzio color *Golf Magazine* v59 no10 p51 O 2017

PASS PARALLEL M. Durland and D. Denunzio color diag *Golf Magazine* v59 no10 p47 O 2017

POWER CORD T. Ruggiero and D. DeNunzio color *Golf Magazine* v59 no7 p44 Jl 2017

Practice Like a Pro [Cover story] D. Berger color *Golf Magazine* v59 no3 p65 Mr 2017

private LESSONS color *Golf Magazine* v59 no10 p101 O 2017

private LESSONS color *Golf Magazine* v59 no1 p93 Ja 2017

private LESSONS color *Golf Magazine* v59 no3 p113 Mr 2017

private LESSONS color *Golf Magazine* v59 no8 p99 Ag 2017

Pulling Out All the Flops D. Pelz and C. Barrett color *Golf Magazine* v59 no7 p35 Jl 2017

SAVING PAR: GRIND OVER MATTER G. Weir and D. DeNunzio color *Golf Magazine* v59 no3 p45 Mr 2017

SEVEN HEAVEN D. Doniger and D. Denunzio color *Golf Magazine* v59 no11 p43 N 2017

STARE WAY TO HEAVEN S. Munroe and D. DeNunzio color *Golf Magazine* v59 no6 p49 Je 2017

STOP YOUR CHOP! J. Dunigan and D. Denunzio color *Golf Magazine* v59 no11 p54 N 2017

SURVIVAL TACTICS M. Jacobs and D. DeNunzio color *Golf Magazine* v59 no9 p60 S 2017

TEE SHEET E. Ibarguen and D. DeNunzio color *Golf Magazine* v59 no1 p47 Ja 2017

"The Greatest Shot I Ever Saw" S. Zak color *Golf Magazine* v59 no2 p65 F 2017

THIS SWEET-SWINGING JUNIOR ADDED THIRTY YARDS ALMOST OVERNIGHT WITH A NEW FINISH. HERE'S HOW D. DeNunzio color *Golf Magazine* v59 no7 p46 Jl 2017

TRY THIS! STRONG & LONG S. Munroe and D. Denunzio color *Golf Magazine* v59 no11 p50 N 2017

TURN STYLE K. Sprecher and D. DeNunzio color *Golf Magazine* v59 no6 p42 Je 2017

Watch + Learn J. Tattersall and C. Barrett color *Golf Magazine* v59 no7 p32 Jl 2017

Why Can't I Get My Pitches to Bite? B. Manzella and D. Denunzio color *Golf Magazine* v59 no5 p54 N 2017

YOU DA AQUAMAN! J. Carbone, Springfield et al color *Golf Magazine* v59 no2 p48 F 2017

YOUR EXIT PLAN M. Jacobs and D. DeNunzio color *Golf Magazine* v59 no6 p50 Je 2017

ZEN AT WORK J. Sieckmann and D. DeNunzio color *Golf Magazine* v59 no7 p41 Jl 2017

Swing states (United States politics)

Go Ahead, Throw Your Vote Away T. W. Hazlett color *Reason* v48 no7 p62 D 2016

Swingin' With Oscar (Music)

Dispatches from the Great White North K. MCDOWALL color *Downbeat* v84 no7 p53 Jl 2017

Swings

CURTIS PORCHWORK B. Sullivan cartoon *Arts & Crafts Homes & the Revival* v12 no3 p72 Summ 2017

How to Make a... PORCH SWING chart color *Popular Mechanics* p75 S 2017

Indoor, Outdoor M. E. Polson color *Old House Journal* v45 no4 p76 Je 2017

Swings—Design & construction

Full Circle Swing A. Fixsen *Architectural Record* v205 no4 p211

Ap 2017

How to Make a... PORCH SWING chart color *Popular Mechanics* v193 no7 p75 S 2016

Swinson, David

Crime Song *Publishers Weekly* v264 no12 p54 Mr 20 2017

Swinton, Scott M.

Cellulosic biofuel contributions to a sustainable energy future: Choices and outcomes color *Science* v356 no6345 p1349 Je 30 2017

Swiss, Jamy Ian

Science Education, Communication on Display at CSICon S. Vyse *Skeptical Inquirer* v41 no2 p15 Mr/Ap 2017

Swiss chard

15-Minute Meal under $15 color *Prevention* v69 no1 p14 Ja 2017

GREAT GREENS MADE EASY C. Thompson color *Men's Health* v31 no10 p61 D 2016

Swiss exercise balls

15 MINUTE WORKOUT color *Women's Health* v14 no8 p76 O 2017

The Three-B Workout L. McGLASHAN chart color *Muscle & Performance* v9 no8 p16 Ag 2017

Why Your Hammies Are Tight C. ROSSI chart color *Muscle & Performance* v9 no8 p28 Ag 2017

Swiss Reinsurance Co. Ltd.

When Nature Gets An Insurance Policy C. Flavelle color *Bloomberg Businessweek* no4531 p26 Jl 24 2017

Swistak, Peggy

Eat YOUR HEART OUT O. Manno color *Dance Spirit* v20 no9 p32 N 2016

NUTRITION LABEL Breakdown O. Manno chart img *Dance Spirit* v21 no3 p28 Mr 2017

Switch, The (TV program)

11 THINGS THAT GOT US THROUGH THIS ISSUE: Movies, a bitchin' album, paper dolls, and some celebrity comings out helped our editors get through the making of this issue *Advocate* no1093 p50 O/N 2017

Switching power supplies

a pretty SMART HOME C. Knobloch color *Good Housekeeping* v265 no4 p54 O 2017

A SHELF TRACK PLAN for a switching line P. Boehlert map *Model Railroader* v84 no2 p64 F 2017

Switchplates (Electric switchgear)

Mount a switch motor horizontally R. St. Laurent color *Model Railroader* v84 no6 p56 Je 2017

Switchplates (Electric switchgear)—Evaluation

SWITCH THE PLATES color *Old House Journal* v45 no3 p23 My 2017

Switek, Brian

Fossil Octopus Is a Jurassic Jewel color *Scientific American* v316 no3 p21 Mr 2017

Switkes, Josh

IN THE DRAFT P. LERNER color *Road & Track* v69 no4 p62 N 2017

Switzer, Jay A.

Epitaxial lift-off of electrodeposited single-crystal gold foils for flexible electronics bibl bw diag *Science* v355 no6330 p1203 Mr 17 2017

Switzer, Kathrine

A Woman's Place Is in the Marathon V. BURTON color *Reader's Digest* v189 no1129 p20 Ap 2017

Switzerland—Description & travel

Lucerne is 'Essence of Switzerland' D. Heimburger color *Christianity Today* v61 no5 p7 Je 2017

ON THE GRAND LAKE A. Erace color *Fortune* v175 no8 p90 Je 15 2017

SWITZERLAND D. Heimburger color *Christianity Today* v61 no5 p6 Je 2017

Swivel (Music)

Swivel P. Margasak color *Downbeat* v83 no11 p52 N 2016

SWOBODA, A. J.

God Is a Homemaker bw color *Christianity Today* v61 no4 p62 My 2017

Swonk, Diane—Interviews

WHAT A WEAKER DOLLAR MEANS TO YOU D. FONDA color *Kiplinger's Personal Finance* v71 no11 p10 N 2017

Sworakowski, Witold Saturnin

Historical Harvest M. Siekierski *Hoover Digest: Research & Opinion on Public Policy* no1 p209 Wint 2017

Swordfish

Mother Knows Best G. Hamilton *New York Times Magazine* p24 F 26 2017

Sword in the Stone, The (Film)

50 YEARS OF ARTHUR K. P. Sullivan color *Entertainment Weekly* no1450 p37 Ja 27 2017

Sword of Doom, The (Film)

Army of One I. S. SMITH bw *Film Comment* v53 no1 p16 Ja/F 2017

Swordplay

50 Reasons to Love Being 50+ color *AARP: The Magazine* v60 no2A p67 F/Mr 2017

Swords

BLADE BONNER R. CARTAGENA *Washingtonian Magazine* v52 no3 p16 D 2016

A Trafalgar Square Deal color *Forbes* v199 no4 p20 Ap 25 2017

SWOT analysis

Prioritize Your Opportunities with This Checklist D. Andrew *Harvard Business Review Digital Articles* p2 S 22 2017

Swuec, Paolo

A supramolecular assembly mediates lentiviral DNA integration bibl color *Science* v355 no6320 p1 Ja 6 2017

SY, ELIZABETH

The Question *O, The Oprah Magazine* p16 My 2017

Sy, Thomas

Why Aren't There More Asian Americans in Leadership Positions? *Harvard Business Review Digital Articles* p2 D 19 2016

Syberberg, Hans-Jürgen, 1935-

First Person Singular R. Brody bw *New Yorker* v92 no36 p9 N 7 2016

Sycalik, Bill

The Great Escape: Bill Sycalik walked away from an unfulfilling corporate job. Now he is on a quest to complete marathons in all 59 national parks K. SIBER *National Parks* v91 no3 p16 Summ 2017

Sycamore Partners LP

Shopping the Retail Apocalypse D. Carey and L. Coleman-Lochner color *Bloomberg Businessweek* no4523 p37 My 22 2017

Sycamores

THE AXIS AND THE SYCAMORE P. KINGSNORTH color *Orion Magazine* v36 no1 p34 Ja/F 2017

Syd tha Kyd (Performer)

SOLO STAR A. Solomon color *Essence* v47 no12 p67 Ap 2017

Sydell Group (Company)

Game Changer: ANDREW ZOBLER N. Ekstein color *Bloomberg Businessweek* no4534 p68 Ag 14 2017

Sydney (N.S.W.)—Description & travel

Great Escapes C. Stern color *InStyle* v24 no8 p163 Ag 2017

Sydney Theatre Co.

CHEKHOV MATES A. Green bw *Vogue* v206 no12 p252 D 2016

Sydnor Romm, Eliza

Finding the Ideal Free Walk color *Dressage Today* v23 no12 p28 S 2017

Syed, Adnan—Trials, litigation, etc.

Simplify The Law B. H. BARTON and S. BIBAS color *National Review* v69 no15 p20 Ag 14 2017

SYED, SHAKEEL

Is Mass Distribution of the Qur'an Useful? *Islamic Horizons* v45 no6 p44 N/D 2016

Syeed, Nafeesa

The Fight for Syria's Future Has Only Begun map *Bloomberg Businessweek* no4525 p28 Je 5 2017

Microsoft Isn't Feeling Any Russian Thaw *Bloomberg Businessweek* no4500 p35 N 21 2016

Tillerson Hits The Road and Finds His Feet color *Bloomberg Businessweek* no4530 p38 Jl 17 2017

Trump and Tech Companies Make Nice color *Bloomberg Businessweek* no4514 p43 Mr 13 2017

The War in Yemen Tests Saudi Arabia's Clout color *Bloomberg Businessweek* no4508 p12 Ja 23 2017

Syeed, Sayyid

ISNA OUTREACH *Islamic Horizons* v45 no6 p9 N/D 2016

Shifting Gears J. WILLOUGHBY *Islamic Horizons* v46 no2 p14 Mr/Ap 2017

SYHABOUT, JAMES

YOU WON'T FIND THIS IN LAOS. AND THAT'S THE POINT color *Bon Appetit* v62 no2 p72 Mr 2017

Sykes, Charles J.

Charlie Sykes Is Unsure About The Future Of the G.O.P A. M. Cox *New York Times Magazine* p66 Ag 27 2017

Providence and Predestination *Commentary* v142 no5 p36 D 2016

Righteousness M. LASSWELL *Commentary* v144 no3 p46 O 2017

The Right Stuff: Charlie Sykes and the Practice of Sane Conservatism B. Lueders color *Progressive* v81 no7 p63 O/N 2017

Sykes, Ephraim

17 QUESTIONS WITH THE CAST OF Hairspray Live! color *Seventeen* v76 no12 p16 D 2016/Ja 2017

SYKES, PLUM

BUILDING A DREAM color *Vogue* v206 no11 p228 N 2016

Fit to be KING color *Vogue* v206 no11 p174 N 2016

Queen V color *Vogue* v207 no1 p74 Ja 2017

STELLA McCARTNEY color *Vogue* v207 no3 p402 Mr 2017

Sykes, S. D.

Masks and Murder L. PICKER *Publishers Weekly* v264 no19 p37 My 8 2017

Sykes, Tanisha A.

BLACK WOMEN'S MENTOR IN YOUR POCKET color *Essence* v47 no12 p100 Ap 2017

Sylvan, Derek

What Counts as Climate Consensus? *National Review* v69 no11 p2 Je 12 2017

SYLVESTER, CAM

No Cars Go color *Walrus* v14 no7 p18 S 2017

SYLVESTRE, BERLIN

HPV: THE HEALTH CRISIS WE'RE NOT TALKING ABOUT color *Advocate* no1089 p23 F/Mr 2017

Symantec Corp.

The best consumer antivirus products of 2016 are Avira and Norton M. HACHMAN chart color *PCWorld* p33 Mr 2017

Symbiosis

Ancestral alliances: Plant mutualistic symbioses with fungi and bacteria F. M. Martin, S. Uroz et al color *Science* v356 no6340 p819 My 26 2017

Symbolism

See also

Animals—Symbolic aspects

Christian art & symbolism

Ciphers

Hindu art & symbolism

Islamic art & symbolism

Swastikas

Extinction Risk and Conservation of the Earth's National Animal Symbols N. HAMMERSCHLAG and A. J. GALLAGHER *BioScience* v67 no8 p744 Ag 2017

Symbolism in art

See also

Islamic art & symbolism

Logos (Symbols) in art

Symbolism in literature

The Secret Jews of The Hobbit *Commentary* v142 no1 p1 Jl/Ag 2016

Symbolism—Exhibitions

Under a Spell E. White color *New York Review of Books* v64 no14 p66 S 28 2017

Symbolism—History

GLOSSARY L. Wittgenstein *History Today* v67 no7 p110 Jl 2017

Symbolist movement (Art)—Exhibitions

Charmed circle: A new exhibition at the Guggenheim examines the supernatural symbolist artists of late nineteenth-century France J. Gardner color *Magazine Antiques* v184 no4 p102 Jl/Ag 2017

SYME, RACHEL

All of Her *New Republic* v247 no11 p56 N 2016

The Big Short *New Republic* v248 no3 p66 Mr 2017

Eyes on the Guys color *New Republic* v248 no5 p60 My 2017

Mean Streets color *New Republic* v248 no10 p54 O 2017

Mom, Interrupted il *New Republic* v248 no11 p58 N 2017

Self-Made Woman bw color *New Republic* v248 no7 p56 Jl 2017

Strange Seer color *New Republic* v248 no8/9 p66 Ag/S 2017

Symmes, Patrick

Dreams of Argentina: The naturalist W.H. Hudson wrote one of the 20th century's greatest memoirs after a fever rekindled visions of his childhood *Smithsonian* v48 no2 p58 My 2017

Symmetry

Choose the Best Young Prospect J. Winkel color *Practical Horseman* v45 no3 p13 Mr 2017

The Myth of Symmetry and Balance A. J. Stallard *History Today* v67 no8 p12 Ag 2017

Symonette, Precious

WRITING YOURSELF INTO EXISTENCE C. Patrice Clark color *Literacy Today (2411-7862)* v34 no5 p20 Mr/Ap 2017

Symons, Lesley

How Women Are Faring at Business Schools Worldwide *Harvard Business Review Digital Articles* p2 Ap 27 2015

Only 11% of Top Business School Case Studies Have a Female Protagonist *Harvard Business Review Digital Articles* p2 Mr 9 2016

Sympathetic nervous system

Max Out With Capsaicin D. JACKSON and J. WUEBBEN color *Muscle & Performance* v9 no11 p33 N 2017

Sympathy

See also

Empathy

THE ART THAT OPENS D. PENICK color *Tricycle: The Buddhist Review* v27 no1 p82 Fall 2017

Everyone Calm Down About My Being Single, Please C. Fisher color *Glamour* v114 no11 p132 N 2016

Symptoms

See also

Hot flashes

Pain

African Horse Sickness—Could It Be Our Next West Nile? C. Reich *Arabian Horse World* v57 no8 p155 My 2017

Eye redness *Mayo Clinic Health Letter* v35 no5 p7 My 2017

Got Tummy Troubles? A. Patz color diag *Health* v30 no10 p85 D 2016

Symptoms—Prevention

Orthostatic hypotension *Mayo Clinic Health Letter* v35 no2 p6 F 2017

Syms, Martine—Exhibitions

ART bw *New Yorker* v93 no18 p9 Je 26 2017

Synagogues

Conservative synagogues can now officially accept non-Jews as members L. Markoe *Christian Century* v134 no8 p1 Ap 12 2017

Critics with Bombs J. BOTTUM color *Weekly Standard* v22 no20 p21 Ja 30 2017

Synagogues—Design & construction

In Uganda, a new synagogue for tiny Jewish community L. Markoe color *Christian Century* v133 no21 p16 O 12 2016

Synagogues—Government policy

To promote diversity, Egypt plans to restore Alexandria synagogue J. Wirtschafter color *Christian Century* v134 no18 p13 Ag 30 2017

Synagogues—Italy

After 500 years, a new synagogue opens in Sicily J. McKenna color *Christian Century* v134 no4 p15 F 15 2017

Synapses

Energy pulses reveal possible new state of memory J. Boddy *Science* v354 no6316 p1089 D 2 2016

Homer1a drives homeostatic scaling-down of excitatory synapses during sleep G. H. Diering, R. S. Nirujogi et al bibl graph *Science* v355 no6324 p511 F 3 2017

Synaptic scaling in sleep L. Acsády and K. D. Harris bibl color *Science* v355 no6324 p457 F 3 2017

Synaptics Inc.

New Synaptics fingerprint sensor sits under glass for smoother phone screens M. WILLIAMS color *PCWorld* v35 no1 p31 Ja 2017

Synchronicity (Short story)

SYNCHRONICITY J. Keeble *Harper's Magazine* p75 S 2017

Synchronization

The Science Behind How Leaders Connect with Their Teams S. Pillay *Harvard Business Review Digital Articles* p2 Mr 31 2016

Synchronized swimming

50 Reasons to Love Being 50+ color *AARP: The Magazine* v60

no4A p57 Je/Jl 2017

Synchrotron radiation

SHOCKING COLLISIONS of Cosmological Proportions A. Parker *Science & Technology Review* p20 Jl/Ag 2017

Synchrotrons

Biology and Light Sources R. BLAUSTEIN *BioScience* v67 no3 p201 Mr 2017

SESAME and beyond S. K. Mtingwa and H. Winick color *Science* v356 no6340 p785 My 26 2017

Syndergaard, Noah, 1992-

Noah Syndergaard J. Crelin color *Current Biography* v78 no9 p85 S 2017

SYNDERELLA B. Reiter color *Sports Illustrated* v126 no5 p64 F 13 2017

Synechococcus

A Green Thumb for Synechococcus K. Hunter-Cevera color *Oceanus* v51 no2 p64 Wint 2016

Physiological and ecological drivers of early spring blooms of a coastal phytoplankter K. R. Hunter-Cevera, M. G. Neubert et al bibl graph *Science* v354 no6310 p326 O 21 2016

A plankton bloom shifts as the ocean warms A. Z. Worden and S. Wilken bibl color diag *Science* v354 no6310 p287 O 21 2016

Synnott, Amy

The Art of Being Blunt [Cover story] color *InStyle* v23 no12 p238 N 2016

BEAUTY'S NEW EXPERIMENT color *Women's Health* v14 no9 p124 N 2017

Charlize Theron color *InStyle* v24 no1 p60 Ja 2017

Do You Have SKINNY GENES? color *InStyle* v24 no1 p64 Ja 2017

I AM THAT GIRL Cate Blanchett color *InStyle* v23 no13 p282 D 2016

Synnott, Mark

Into the Deep color map *National Geographic* v231 no3 p104 Mr 2017

The Last Honey Hunter color map *National Geographic* v232 no1 p80 Jl 2017

Synonyms—Study & teaching

IT PAYS TO INCREASE YOUR Word Power E. COX and H. RATHVON *Reader's Digest* v189 no1131 p133 Je 2017

Synovial fluid

WARM UP LIKE A PRO L. BOYCE color *Muscle & Performance* v8 no12 p26 D 2016

Synthesis (Chemistry)

A general catalytic β-C–H carbonylation of aliphatic amines to β-lactams D. Willcox, B. G. N. Chappell et al bibl diag *Science* v354 no6314 p851 N 18 2016

A general, modular method for the catalytic asymmetric synthesis of alkylboronate esters J. Schmidt, Junwon Choi et al bibl color *Science* v354 no6317 p1265 D 9 2016

Polynitrogen chemistry enters the ring K. O. Christe bibl diag *Science* v355 no6323 p351 Ja 27 2017

Synthesis Centers as Critical Research Infrastructure J. S. BARON, A. SPECHT et al *BioScience* v67 no8 p750 Ag 2017

Synthesis of a carbon nanobelt G. Povie, Y. Segawa et al diag graph *Science* v356 no6334 p172 Ap 14 2017

Synthesis of resveratrol tetramers via a stereoconvergent radical equilibrium M. H. Keylor, B. S. Matsuura et al bibl diag graph *Science* v354 no6317 p1260 D 9 2016

Synthesizer (Musical instrument)—Evaluation

GEAR BOX color *Downbeat* v84 no9 p100 S 2017

Synthesizer music

Hot New Wave Austin Synth Rock C. R. WEINGARTEN bw color *Rolling Stone* no1274 p39 N 17 2016

Synthetic antibodies

Unnatural Responsibilities K. M. Esvelt color *Scientific American* v316 no4 p50 Ap 2017

Synthetic aperture radar

SATELLITE PICS FOR CHEAP!! A. Vance bw *Bloomberg Businessweek* no4522 p37 My 15 2017

Synthetic biology

CANCER KILLERS A. D. J. Posey, C. H. June et al color *Scientific American* v316 no3 p38 Mr 2017

Labmade smallpox is possible, study shows K. Kupferschmidt color *Science* v357 no6347 p115 Jl 14 2017

Mapping the Landscape of Public Attitudes on Synthetic Biology

H. AKIN, K. M. ROSE et al *BioScience* v67 no3 p290 Mr 2017

Synthesis, debugging, and effects of synthetic chromosome consolidation: synVI and beyond L. A. Mitchell, A. Wang et al color *Science* v355 no6329 p1045 Mr 10 2017

Synthetic Biology and the Marketplace B. BAKER *BioScience* v67 no10 p877 O 2017

Yeast genome, by design K. Kannan and D. G. Gibson bibl color *Science* v355 no6329 p1024 Mr 10 2017

Synthetic drugs

Synthetic Drugs Pose Hidden Risk *USA Today Magazine* v145 no2861 p8 F 2017

Synthetic fertilizers

BEST ORGANIC FERTILIZERS [Cover story] H. Garrett *Mother Earth News* no281 p16 Ap/My 2017

Synthetic fibers

NYLON RIOT color *Spin to Win Rodeo* v20 no9 p96 N 2016

Synthetic fuels

Introduction: International security in the age of renewables J. Mecklin *Bulletin of the Atomic Scientists* v72 no6 p377 N 2016

Synthetic genes

Unnatural Responsibilities K. M. Esvelt color *Scientific American* v316 no4 p50 Ap 2017

Synthetic lubricants

THE BUYER'S GUIDE color *Hot Rod* v70 no7 p84 Jl 2017

Synthetic products

See also

Plastics

Synthetic drugs

Synthetic textiles

BUGS ARE IN OUR FOOD—AND THAT'S OK D. Stone color *National Geographic* v231 no2 p22 F 2017

Synthetic textiles

THE RISE OF SYNTHETIC DNA J. Alsever color *Fortune* v175 no2 p19 F 1 2017

Synucleins

See also

Alpha-synuclein

β2-Adrenoreceptor is a regulator of the a-synuclein gene driving risk of Parkinson's disease S. Mittal, K. Bjørnevik et al cartoon chart graph *Science* v357 no6354 p891 S 1 2017

Immune receptor for pathogenic α-synuclein M. Jucker and M. Heikenwalder bibl diag *Science* v353 no6307 p1498 S 30 2016

Sypnier, Craig

VINYL J. LYNCH color *Popular Mechanics* p35 My 2017

Syracuse (N.Y.)

Is Syracuse Necessary? Some want to save a fiscally challenged city by effectively abolishing it A. Ehrenhalt *Governing* v30 no8 p14 My 2017

Syracuse University

Syracuse Music Students Keep Options Wide Open P. Lutz color *Downbeat* v84 no4 p94 Ap 2017

Syracuse University—Sports

15 SYRACUSE ORANGE P. Thamel chart color *Sports Illustrated* v125 no15 p74 N 7 2016

Week 7 color *Sports Illustrated* v127 no5 p70 Ag 14 2017

Syrdal, Holly

How to Design a Return Policy *Harvard Business Review Digital Articles* p2 Ag 2 2016

Syrén, Karin

SV Delos A. Schell color *Sail* v48 no11 p12 N 2017

Syrett, Alison

Ave Maria color *InStyle* v24 no9 p394 S 2017

cuff love color *InStyle* v24 no2 p128 F 2017

ELLIE BAMBER color *InStyle* v24 no3 p121 Mr 2017

EYE OF THE BEHOLDER color *InStyle* v24 no5 p218 My 2017

Heidi Klum color *InStyle* v24 no4 p96 Ap 2017

HOOP DREAMS color *InStyle* v24 no8 p158 Ag 2017

Lily Aldridge color *InStyle* v24 no3 p172 Mr 2017

Miranda Kerr color *InStyle* v24 no10 p113 O 2017

THE MODERN GIRL color *InStyle* v24 no7 p110 Jl 2017

off the chain color *InStyle* v24 no1 p82 Ja 2017

PRETTY IS BACK color *InStyle* v24 no3 p354 Mr 2017

Rachel Zoe color *InStyle* v24 no9 p197 S 2017

Rosie Assoulin color *InStyle* v24 no5 p98 My 2017

Super Fine color *InStyle* v24 no10 p236 O 2017

Syria

EMERGENCY CINEMA AND THE DIGNIFIED IMAGE: CELL PHONE ACTIVISM AND FILMMAKING IN SYRIA C. Elias *Film Quarterly* v71 no1 p18 Fall 2017

Syriac Christians—Social conditions—21st century

Hell on Earth A. R. KHAN color *Maclean's* v129 no46 p16 N 21 2016

Syria—Foreign relations—United States

Arms Shipment Lunacy *American Conservative* v16 no4 p5 Jl/Ag 2017

Cleaning Up Obama's Syria Mess *Commentary* v141 no9 p1 N 2016

Cleaning Up Obama's Syria Mess *Commentary* v142 no4 p1 N 2016

The Fight for Syria's Future Has Only Begun H. Meyer, N. Syeed et al map *Bloomberg Businessweek* no4525 p28 Je 5 2017

Let Him Eat Cake *Commonweal* v144 no8 p5 My 5 2017

Mad, Democrats? Blame the Iran Deal *Commentary* p1 Ja 2017

Mad, Democrats? Blame the Iran Deal *Commentary* v143 no1 p1 Ja 2017

More Violence Should Not Be Our Response to Atrocities in Syria *America* v216 no10 p8 My 1 2017

The Origins and Consequences of US Nonintervention in Syria F. ITANI *Current History* v115 no785 p337 D 2016

Superheroes and the Sacking of Cities G. NORMAN color *Weekly Standard* v22 no17 p15 Ja 2 2017

Who We Are and Who He Is S. F. Hayes color *Weekly Standard* v22 no16 p7 D 26 2016

Syria—History—Anti-ISIL intervention, 2014-

What Trump Should Do in Syria K. Roth color *New York Review of Books* v63 no20 p50 D 22 2016

Syria—History—Civil War, 2011-

Assad Allies Profit Off UN Money For Syria K. Foroohar bw *Bloomberg Businessweek* no4533 p34 Ag 7 2017

Donald Trump Heads For the War in Syria bw *Bloomberg Businessweek* no4510 p8 F 6 2017

The Fight for Syria's Future Has Only Begun H. Meyer, N. Syeed et al map *Bloomberg Businessweek* no4525 p28 Je 5 2017

Middle East img *New York Times Upfront* v149 no6 p25 D 12 2016

My Family Is Stuck in Aleppo A. Haglage color *Glamour* v115 no5 p149 My 2017

No-Win War in Syria P. J. BUCHANAN *American Conservative* v15 no6 p11 N/D 2016

The Origins and Consequences of US Nonintervention in Syria F. ITANI *Current History* v115 no785 p337 D 2016

SCIENCE, INTERRUPTED J. HATTAM bw color graph map *Discover* v38 no7 p42 S 2017

Syria's First Responders N. Gibbs color *Time* v188 no15 p3 O 17 2016

TO THE ASSAD REGIME, RUSSIA, AND IRAN: IT IS YOUR NOOSE AROUND SYRIAN CIVILIANS *Vital Speeches of the Day* v83 no2 p49 F 2017

Trump's War Fever K. V. HEUVEL color *Nation* v304 no15 p4 My 8 2017

What Syrians Want D. Corstange *Hoover Digest: Research & Opinion on Public Policy* no1 p136 Wint 2017

What You Said About ... color *Time* v188 no16/17 p2 O 24 2016

When Home Isn't Where the Heart Is A. Baker, H. Roonemaa et al color map *Time* v189 no21 p40 Je 5 2017

With Aleppo's Fall, Syria's Civil War Reaches a Grim Turning Point J. Malsin color diag *Time* v188 no27-28 p11 D 26 2016

Syria—History—Civil War, 2011—American participation

Lament for Aleppo *Christian Century* v134 no2 p7 Ja 18 2017

Speaking Up for Standing Down M. O. Steinfels color *Commonweal* v143 no19 p6 D 2 2017

TRUMP'S INTERVENTION S. Coll cartoon *New Yorker* v93 no9 p19 Ap 17 2017

The U.S. Has a Weak Hand In Syria-and Russia Knows It I. Bremmer *Time* v188 no14 p10 O 10 2016

Syria—History—Civil War, 2011—Foreign participation

See also

Syria—History—Civil War, 2011—American participation

THE ANARCHISTS VS. ISIS S. HARP color *Rolling Stone* no1281/1282 p42 F 23 2017

Syria—History—Civil War, 2011—International cooperation

BAD NEWS color *Maclean's* v129 no41 p9 O 17 2016

p76 EarlySumm 2017

Szabó, Magda, 1917-
AN EDUCATION *Harper's Magazine* p18 S 2017
A Soul Uprooted L. GROFF *New York Times Book Review* p39 N 13 2016

Szabo, Sylvia
Making SDGs Work for Climate Change Hotspots bibl *Environment* v58 no6 p24 N/D 2016

Szadkowski, Z.
Observation of a large-scale anisotropy in the arrival directions of cosmic rays above 8 × 1018 eV *Science* v357 no6357 p1266 S 22 2017

Szalai, Bence
Predicting human olfactory perception from chemical features of odor molecules bibl diag graph *Science* v355 no6327 p820 F 24 2017

Szalai, Jennifer
The Education of Ellen Pao: How one Silicon Valley executive came to question the culture of the industry *New York Times Book Review* p18 S 24 2017
IN THE SHADE *Harper's Magazine* v334 no2000 p98 Ja 2017
Kids Today: A senator's solution for moral decline: Get tough on your offspring *New York Times Book Review* p15 My 21 2017
The Shortlist: Argentine Fiction *New York Times Book Review* p22 Mr 5 2017

Szalavitz, Maia
Breaking Addicts in Order to Fix Them color *Reason* v49 no5 p72 O 2017
hope riseS color *Women's Health* v14 no5 p154 Je 2017

Szalay, David, 1974-
David Szalay C. Mari color *Current Biography* v78 no1 p81 Ja 2017
DONA NOBIS PACEM *Harper's Magazine* v334 no2002 p75 Mr 2017
MALE GAZE J. WOOD cartoon *New Yorker* v92 no32 p98 O 10 2016
Nine Lives M. Gorra color *New York Review of Books* v64 no11 p47 Je 22 2017
Wandering Men G. GREENWELL *New York Times Book Review* p16 O 9 2016

Szalay, J. R.
Jupiter's interior and deep atmosphere: The initial pole-to-pole passes with the Juno spacecraft [Cover story] color graph *Science* v356 no6340 p821 My 26 2017

Szathmáry, Eörs
Beyond Hamilton's rule color *Science* v356 no6337 p485 My 5 2017
Transient compartmentalization of RNA replicators prevents extinction due to parasites bibl chart graph *Science* v354 no6317 p1293 D 9 2016

Szczech, Barb
pontoon mania color *Cabin Living* p60 Je 2017

Szczerbakow, Andrzej
Robust spin-polarized midgap states at step edges of topological crystalline insulators bibl graph *Science* v354 no6317 p1269 D 9 2016

Szczesiul, Stacy
What real high performance looks like chart diag *Phi Delta Kappan* v98 no7 p38 Ap 2017

Szczytko, Rachel
How Kids Learn in Nature *Parks & Recreation* v52 no5 p36 My 2017

Sze, Sarah
Underground Art J. Gardner color *Weekly Standard* v22 no24 p39 F 27 2017

Szeto, Hayden
The New Crush D. Coggan color *Entertainment Weekly* no1440 p18 N 18 2016

Szigethy, Les
Backfires: The joyful noise of the commentariat, rebutted sporadically by Ed color *Car & Driver* v62 no11 p9 My 2017

Szilágyi, András
Transient compartmentalization of RNA replicators prevents extinction due to parasites bibl chart graph *Science* v354 no6317 p1293 D 9 2016

Szimhart, Joe

Astrology's Bait of a Caring Cosmos *Skeptical Inquirer* v40 no6 p62 N/D 2016

SZIRTES, GEORGE
Love and Violence *New York Times Book Review* p23 N 27 2016

Szöke, Abraham
Abraham Szöke S. B. Libby and M. D. Rosen *Physics Today* v70 no10 p76 O 2017

Szolgay, Jan
Changing climate shifts timing of European floods color graph *Science* v357 no6351 p588 Ag 11 2017

Szostak, Jack
Not just Salk color *Science* v357 no6356 p1105 S 15 2017

Szostak, Veronika
Seeds of Change cartoon *Alternatives Journal (AJ) - Canada's Environmental Voice* v42 no3 p54 2016

Szot, Paulo
ROAD SHOW: Paulo Szot in Marseilles M. R. MERCADO *Opera News* v81 no9 p18 Mr 2017

Szpylczyn, Fran Rossi
Did you receive support from your faith community while you were experiencing depression and/or anxiety? graph *America* v216 no12 p6 My 29 2017

Szul, Michael
COMMENT color *Canadian Geographic* v137 no4 p72 Jl/Ag 2017

T

T cell receptors
T cell costimulatory receptor CD28 is a primary target for PD-1–mediated inhibition E. Hui, J. Cheung et al color diag graph *Science* v355 no6332 p1428 Mr 31 2017

T cells
Can T cells be too exhausted to fight back? S. J. Turner and B. E. Russ bibl diag *Science* v354 no6316 p1104 D 2 2016
Costimulation, a surprising connection for immunotherapy D. L. Clouthier and P. S. Ohashi color diag *Science* v355 no6332 p1373 Mr 31 2017
The epigenetic landscape of T cell exhaustion D. R. Sen, J. Kaminski et al bibl graph *Science* v354 no6316 p1165 D 2 2016
Epigenetic stability of exhausted T cells limits durability of reinvigoration by PD-1 blockade K. E. Pauken, M. A. Sammons et al bibl graph *Science* v354 no6316 p1160 D 2 2016
A Fresh Approach to Fighting MS D. Ferry color *AARP: The Magazine* v30 no6A p29 O/N 2017
Genetic biomarker for cancer immunotherapy S. Goswami and P. Sharma diag *Science* v357 no6349 p358 Jl 28 2017
Lactobacillus reuteri induces gut intraepithelial CD4+CD8αα+ T cells L. Cervantes-Barragan, J. N. Chai et al diag graph *Science* v357 no6353 p806 Ag 25 2017
Nose's flu fighters have long memories T. HESMAN SAEY color *Science News* v191 no13 p16 Jl 8 2017
A pathogenic role for T cell–derived IL-22BP in inflammatory bowel disease P. Pelczar, M. Witkowski et al bibl graph *Science* v354 no6310 p310 O 21 2016
Visualizing dynamic microvillar search and stabilization during ligand detection by T cells E. Cai, K. Marchuk et al color *Science* v356 no6338 p598 My 12 2017

T cells—Therapeutic use
Harnessing Cellular Tools from Immune Systems to Help Prevent Graft Rejection M. Levings and L. J. West color *Maclean's* v130 no9 p34 O 2017

T helper cells
Aerobic glycolysis promotes T helper 1 cell differentiation through an epigenetic mechanism Min Peng, Na Yin et al bibl graph *Science* v354 no6311 p481 O 28 2016
Warburg meets epigenetics C. H. Patel and J. D. Powell bibl diag *Science* v354 no6311 p419 O 28 2016

T-L Irrigation Co.
PMDI SUCCESS T. Gaines *Successful Farming* v115 no4 p50 Mr 2017

T La Rock (Performer)
THE PATIENT WHO FORGOT HE WAS A RAP LEGEND J. BEARMAN bw color *GQ: Gentlemen's Quarterly* v97 no10 p126 O 2017

ALL ABOUT YVES H. MARTIN color *Architectural Digest* v73 no12 p34 D 2016

All Set for Thanksgiving B. H. Miller color *Southern Living* v51 no11 p19 N 2016

ASK CAROLYN C. FORTÉ color diag *Good Housekeeping* v264 no1 p48 Ja 1 2017

Get Creative with Turkey Plates Z. Gowen and F. Keenan color *Southern Living* v52 no11 p15 N 2017

Tables (Furniture)—Design & construction

AIR HOCKEY TABLE! J. SCHADEWALD color diag *Popular Mechanics* p114 Ap 2017

HIGH GLOSS L. HOWARD color *Better Homes & Gardens* v95 no4 p18 Ap 2017

Reclaimed Wood Tables B. D. Coleman color *Old House Journal* v45 no3 p56 My 2017

A Side Table That Can Charge Your Phone A. GEORGE color *Popular Mechanics* p110 Ap 2017

Tables (Furniture)—Evaluation

The Cocktail Hour A. HEROLD *Los Angeles Magazine* v61 no11 p52 N 2016

LA BREA *Los Angeles Magazine* v62 no6 p70 Je 2017

PETAL TO THE METAL *Cincinnati Magazine* v50 no6 p38 Mr 2017

Slab City L. IMMEDIATO color *Los Angeles Magazine* v62 no10 p34 O 2017

sofa table update A. PALANJIAN *Better Homes & Gardens* v95 no1 pN6 Ja 2017

SOFT FOCUS color *House Beautiful* p64 Ag 2017

Statement Chair, 2 Ways color *Good Housekeeping* v264 no1 p45 Ja 1 2017

STYLE *New Orleans Homes & Lifestyles* v20 no4 p18 Aut 2017

Tiny Tables: Petite, portable and posh, accent tables put your drink in easy reach from every seat in the house L. Tudor *New Orleans Homes & Lifestyles* v20 no4 p33 Aut 2017

Underrated Icon: Jens Quistgaard B. LIBBY *Treasures* v6 no3 p22 D 2016/Ja 2017

Welcome Effects A. Kwun *Architectural Record* v205 no4 p93 Ap 2017

WITH an ARTIST'S EYE A. PANOS color *Better Homes & Gardens* v95 no4 p120 Ap 2017

Tables (Furniture)—History

Foot Fetish H. MARTIN bw color *Architectural Digest* no11 p30 N 1 2017

Tablet computers

See also

iPad (Computer)

A moonlit trek V. Ingurgio bibl color *Science* v355 no6323 p358 Ja 27 2017

Tablet computers—Equipment & supplies

iOS Accessories J. Mathis color *Macworld - Digital Edition* v34 no10 p60 O 2017

Tablet computers—Evaluation

10.5-INCH iPAD PRO: IF ANY iPAD REPLACES THE MAC-BOOK, IT'S THIS ONE O. RAYMUNDO color *Macworld - Digital Edition* v34 no8 p69 Ag 2017

DITCH THE LAPTOP? K. Sintumuang cartoon color *Esquire* p52 S 2017

The iPad Pro: Now a true photographer's tool J. CARLSON color *Macworld - Digital Edition* v34 no8 p57 Ag 2017

The iPad's popularity is on the rise, and it's all thanks to cheaper prices D. MOREN color *Macworld - Digital Edition* v34 no10 p42 O 2017

Lenovo's ThinkPad X1 Tablet modules add features but limit functionality M. HACHMAN color *PCWorld* p128 D 2016

Lenovo Yoga Book: Unique touch features let you be hands-on creative M. RIOFRIO color *PCWorld* v35 no11 p82 N 2016

LG V20: The Android phone for hard-core enthusiasts J. PHIL-LIPS color *PCWorld* v35 no1 p108 Ja 2017

Surface Book i7: Still unique and still blazing fast G. MAHUNG color graph *PCWorld* p64 D 2016

WACOM BAMBOO SLATE J. DOVE color *Macworld - Digital Edition* p44 D 2016

Tablet computers—Mobile apps—Evaluation

MARBOTIC SMART LETTERS AND SMART NUMBERS: TOYS + TABLETS = EDUCATIONAL FUN J. R. BOOK-WALTER color *Macworld - Digital Edition* p53 Mr 2017

Tabletop hockey (Game)

AIR HOCKEY TABLE! J. SCHADEWALD color diag *Popular Mechanics* p114 Ap 2017

Tableware

See also

Bowls (Tableware)

Metal tableware

Tureens

6 Things to Eat, Drink, & Buy This Month color *Bon Appetit* v62 no10 p19 O 2017

Crystal Visions P. LAFFOON IV *Cincinnati Magazine* v50 no6 p50 Mr 2017

DOWN PAT F. VIGNA *Martha Stewart Living* no269 p152 N 2016

Hang some plates on the wall color *Redbook* p105 Jl/Ag 2017

HIGH or LOW? color *Good Housekeeping* v265 no5 p42 N 2017

PUNCH LIST K. SELZER color *Better Homes & Gardens* v95 no5 p60 My 2017

Tableware design

The bouillabaisse of design influences on an early American silver soup tureen D. Zimmermann color *Magazine Antiques* v184 no3 p68 My/Je 2017

Tableware—Evaluation

15 Reasons to Become a Morning Person J. J. CONDON color *House Beautiful* v159 no7 p48 S 2017

BOWLED OVER: Noodling around in the studio led one talented potter to a design for a hot new ramen restaurant V. FORD *Indianapolis Monthly* p38 N 2017

Earthly Pleasures N. BRARA color *Vogue* v207 no11 p166 N 2017

AN ENCHANTED GARDEN H. BROWN color *House Beautiful* p34 Jl 2017

FORAGED FINDS *Better Homes & Gardens* v94 no11 p12 N 2016

going green color *Better Homes & Gardens* v95 no3 p50 Mr 2017

A HOLIDAY SOIREE H. BROWN color *House Beautiful* v158 no10 p36 D 2016/Ja 2017

A LADIES' BRUNCH H. BROWN color *House Beautiful* v159 no2 p58 Mr 2017

The Life Aquatic J. JONES CONDON color *House Beautiful* p24 Jl 2017

OBSESSED WITH TILE MOTIFS E. S. SOTO color *Better Homes & Gardens* v95 no4 p6 Ap 2017

Rise & Dine J. J. CONDON color *House Beautiful* v159 no7 p46 S 2017

TABLESCAPE: A WELCOME BRUNCH W. M. Porter color *House Beautiful* v159 no9 p42 N 2017

The Wild Things color *House Beautiful* v159 no2 p36 Mr 2017

Taboada, A.

Observation of a large-scale anisotropy in the arrival directions of cosmic rays above 8×10^{18} eV *Science* v357 no6357 p1266 S 22 2017

Taboada, Marcela

Consecrated in Mexico color map *National Geographic* v230 no5 p130 N 2016

Taboo

Here We Go! Oprah color *O, The Oprah Magazine* p21 My 2017

Taboo (TV program)

Taboo D. Franich color *Entertainment Weekly* no1448 p54 Ja 13 2017

Taboo's Biggest Taboo R. Rahman color *Entertainment Weekly* no1450 p53 Ja 27 2017

Tabor, Nick

Federal employees contemplate what would make them leave *New York* v50 no17 p50 Ag 21 2017

Government By Gazzillionaires img *New York* p30 Ja 23 2017

OBAMA'S AMERICA img *New York* v49 no20 p12 O 3 2016

THEY'RE WITH HIM img *New York* v49 no22 p60 O 31 2016

TO UNDERSTAND THIS NEW RIGHT, IT HELPS TO SEE IT NOT AS A FRINGE MOVEMENT, BUT A POWERFUL COUNTERCULTURE img *New York* v50 no9 p24 My 1 2017

When the President Is Your Landlord img *New York* p52 F 20 2017

Taborda, O. A.

Observation of a large-scale anisotropy in the arrival directions of cosmic rays above 8×10^{18} eV *Science* v357 no6357 p1266 S 22 2017

Taborn, Craig

CRAIG TABORN: 'GO INSIDE THE SOUND' [Cover story] K. MICALLEF color *Downbeat* v84 no3 p26 Mr 2017

Ghost Notes: Craig Taborn has become one of the best jazz pianists alive—by disappearing almost completely into his music A. Shatz *New York Times Magazine* p54 Je 25 2017

Tabouret, Claire, 1981-

Pray Tell M. OWENS color *Architectural Digest* no11 p162 N 1 2017

Tabrizi, Behnam

75% of Cross-Functional Teams Are Dysfunctional *Harvard Business Review Digital Articles* p2 Je 23 2015

Carly Fiorina's Legacy as CEO of Hewlett Packard *Harvard Business Review Digital Articles* p2 S 25 2015

The Key to Change Is Middle Management *Harvard Business Review Digital Articles* p2 O 27 2014

Tabuchi, Masashi

Branch-specific plasticity of a bifunctional dopamine circuit encodes protein hunger graph *Science* v356 no6337 p534 My 5 2017

Tacchetti, Carlo

Reticulon 3–dependent ER-PM contact sites control EGFR nonclathrin endocytosis color diag graph *Science* v356 no6338 p617 My 12 2017

Tacconelli, Evelina

Fighting the enemy within bibl diag *Science* v355 no6326 p689 F 17 2017

Tachibana, Chris

Five reasons to leave your science bubble color *Science* v357 no6353 p823 Ag 25 2017

New tools for measuring academic performance color *Science* v355 no6325 p651 F 10 2017

The scientific swerve: Changing your research focus color *Science* v357 no6359 p126 O 6 2017

Tachometer

See also

Speedometers

Service R. NIERLICH color *Cycle World* v56 no2 p62 Mr 2017

Tacitus, Cornelius, 56-117

Tacitus' Perfect Man E. Southon *History Today* v67 no8 p18 Ag 2017

TACK, KAREN

one dough, six cookies *Parents* p94 2015

Tacke, Georg

In Product Development, Let Your Customers Define Perfection *Harvard Business Review Digital Articles* p2 My 9 2016

Your New Hit Product Might Be Underpriced *Harvard Business Review Digital Articles* p2 My 24 2016

Tackett, Tim

BLACK BELT HALL OF FAME [Cover story] cartoon color *Black Belt* v55 no5 p32 Ag/S 2017

KICKING TOOLS OF JKD color *Black Belt* v55 no4 p46 Je/Jl 2017

Tackett, Timothy

Did Emotions Cause the Terror? C. Jones bw *New York Review of Books* v64 no11 p38 Je 22 2017

Tackie, Hilary

Through our eyes Perspectives from black teachers color *Phi Delta Kappan* v98 no5 p36 F 2017

Tacking

CRUISING TIPS T. Cunliffe color *Sail* v47 no12 p16 D 2016

Tackling (Football)—Universities & colleges

NEW TAKES ON TACKLING A. Staples color *Sports Illustrated* v127 no5 p64 Ag 14 2017

Tacoma (Wash.)—Description & travel

ART, HISTORY AND FUN D. HISLOP *Sea Magazine* v109 no1 pPNW-8 Ja 2017

Tacoma truck

Exit Strategery S. SMITH bw color *Road & Track* v68 no8 p24 My 2017

Tacos

15-Minute All-Organic Meal Under $15 color *Prevention* v69 no9 p14 O 2017

BUZZER BEATERS [Cover story] A. CANTOR color *Runner's World* v52 no5 p32 Je 2017

Cinco de Mayo San Antonio Style P. Disbrowe and J. Hernandez color *Southern Living* v52 no5 p110 My 2017

Cooking the Pinterest Way S. Dreisbach color *Glamour* v115 no6 p88 Je 2017

Deviled Egg Taco color *Indianapolis Monthly* p47 Ap 2017

The Harder They Come: The hard-shell tacos of childhood still bring joy to the dinner table S. Sifton *New York Times Magazine* p26 My 14 2017

Itty-Bitty Taco Cups color *Good Housekeeping* v264 no5 p111 My 2017

MIRACULOUS, MULTITASKING RECIPES D. Hay color *Redbook* p130 S 2017

Sauce Boss J. K. WOLFE *Cincinnati Magazine* v50 p141 Ag 2017 Supplement

SHELL GAME T. Keith and S. Kwak color *Sports Illustrated* v127 no7 p26 S 4 2017

Sizzling Steak Tacos R. Melvin color *Southern Living* v52 no7 p112 Jl 2017

A Sunny Start to the Day C. MOROCCO color *Bon Appetit* no11 p52 N 2017

TACO-TASTIC! color *O, The Oprah Magazine* p162 My 2017

Taco Time color *Backpacker* p32 Je 2017

#taco tuesday color *Good Housekeeping* v265 no2 p113 Ag 2017

A Taste for Sprouts V. Willis color *Southern Living* v52 no1 p126 Ja 2017

Tactile maps

Navigating by Touch A. Marks color *Scientific American* v317 no3 p22 S 2017

Tactile sensors

How Apple can bring the Touch Bar and Touch ID to desktop Macs J. SNELL color *Macworld - Digital Edition* p11 Mr 2017

TADA, RICHARD

Alternate Exodus bw *Weekly Standard* v22 no11 p37 N 21 2016

TADAKI, MARC

ECONOMIZING NATURE AS A POLITICAL STRATEGY: IS IT WORKING? *BioScience* v67 no8 p770 Ag 2017

Tadd, Ellen

The Infinite View: A Guidebook for Life on Earth color *Publishers Weekly* v264 no7 p69 F 13 2017

Taddia, F.

iPTF16geu: A multiply imaged, gravitationally lensed type Ia supernova color diag graph *Science* v356 no6335 p291 Ap 21 2017

Tado (Company)

TADO SMART AC REMOTE J. D'APRILE color *Macworld - Digital Edition* v34 no11 p37 N 2017

Tadpoles—Physiology

Diet Change K. Moore color *Natural History* v125 no3 p6 Mr 2017

Tadross, Michael R.

Deconstructing behavioral neuropharmacology with cellular specificity color *Science* v356 no6333 p42 Ap 7 2017

Tae-In Kam

A nuclease that mediates cell death induced by DNA damage and poly(ADP-ribose) polymerase-1 bw graph *Science* v354 no6308 paad6872-1 O 7 2016

Pathological α-synuclein transmission initiated by binding lymphocyte-activation gene 3 bibl graph *Science* v353 no6307 paah3374-1 S 30 2016

Tae kwon do

From the Archives J. Chong color *Black Belt* v55 no6 p82 O/N 2017

Name Fights, IRL T. Keith color diag *Sports Illustrated* v127 no1 p16 Jl 3 2017

Tae kwon do training

ROAR OF THE TIGER J. E. SWIFT bw cartoon color *Black Belt* v55 no4 p60 Je/Jl 2017

Taeuber-Arp, Sophie, 1889-1943

ARTISTIC AFFINITIES C. Bauer color *Magazine Antiques* v183 no6 p98 N/D 2016

Tafreshi, Ali M.

HEALTH CARE NEEDS REAL COMPETITION: INTERACTION img *Harvard Business Review* v95 no2 p19 Mr/Ap 2017

Tag Heuer SA

The Essential: Watch J. TUNG *Martha Stewart Living* no269 p52 N 2016

TAG Heuer Connected Modular 45: Hands on with the swankiest Wear watch of all J. PHILLIPS color *PCWorld* v35 no5 p140

dopsin bibl diag graph *Science* v354 no6319 p1552 D 23 2016

TAKACS-VESBACH, CRISTINA

Microbial Community Dynamics in Two Polar Extremes: The Lakes of the McMurdo Dry Valleys and the West Antarctic Peninsula Marine Ecosystem chart color graph *BioScience* v66 no10 p829 O 1 2016

Takahashi, Maiko

Changes On Tap for Japan's Beer Tax color *Bloomberg Businessweek* no4513 p29 Mr 6 2017

Takahashi, Yuta

Integration of CpG-free DNA induces de novo methylation of CpG islands in pluripotent stem cells diag *Science* v356 no6337 p503 My 5 2017

Takahiro Inagaki

A coherent Ising machine for 2000-node optimization problems bibl diag graph *Science* v354 no6312 p603 N 4 2016

A fully programmable 100-spin coherent Ising machine with all-to-all connections bibl diag graph *Science* v354 no6312 p614 N 4 2016

Takahiro Osada

Causal neural network of metamemory for retrospection in primates bibl diag graph *Science* v355 no6321 p1 Ja 13 2017

Takaki Hatsui

A three-dimensional movie of structural changes in bacteriorhodopsin bibl diag graph *Science* v354 no6319 p1552 D 23 2016

Takako Taniguchi

Japan Isn't Getting Its Share Of Gaming Gold bw color *Bloomberg Businessweek* no4539 p23 S 25 2017

Takanori Nakane

A three-dimensional movie of structural changes in bacteriorhodopsin bibl diag graph *Science* v354 no6319 p1552 D 23 2016

Takao Fujiwara

THE SECRET LIFE OF PLANTS color *National Geographic* v231 no5 p26 My 2017

Takar, Mehmet

Exploring genetic suppression interactions on a global scale diag *Science* v354 no6312 p599 N 4 2016

Takase, Aki

Cherry–Sakura J. Corbett color *Downbeat* v84 no5 p49 My 2017

Takashi Kameshima

A three-dimensional movie of structural changes in bacteriorhodopsin bibl diag graph *Science* v354 no6319 p1552 D 23 2016

Takashi Kitamura

Ventral CA1 neurons store social memory bibl graph *Science* v353 no6307 p1536 S 30 2016

Takashi Nomura

A three-dimensional movie of structural changes in bacteriorhodopsin bibl diag graph *Science* v354 no6319 p1552 D 23 2016

Takashi Taniguchi

Ballistic miniband conduction in a graphene superlattice bibl graph *Science* v353 no6307 p1526 S 30 2016

Electron optics with p-n junctions in ballistic graphene bibl graph *Science* v353 no6307 p1522 S 30 2016

Takata Corp.—Finance

Deal Snapshot: Takata Corp Ma Jie chart *Bloomberg Businessweek* no4529 p21 Jl 3 2017

Take Me (Film)

ALSO PLAYING: MAY J. Nolfi color *Entertainment Weekly* no1463/1464 p40 Ap/My 2017

Take-Two Interactive Software Inc.

Using Graphic Novels, Bill Jemas Resurrects 'Night of the Living Dead' C. Reid *Publishers Weekly* v263 no40 p6 O 3 2016

Takeda, Masaki

Conversion of object identity to object-general semantic value in the primate temporal cortex color graph *Science* v357 no6352 p687 Ag 18 2017

Takei, George

Pioneers [Cover story] color *Time* v189 no16/17 p14 My 1-8 2017

Taken (TV program)

TAKEN C. Agard color *Entertainment Weekly* no1448 p43 Ja 13 2017

Taken I. Rudolph *TV Guide* v65 no2 p36 Ja 2 2017

Takeshi Umeki

A coherent Ising machine for 2000-node optimization problems bibl diag graph *Science* v354 no6312 p603 N 4 2016

Takeshi Yoshizumi

Photoactivation and inactivation of Arabidopsis cryptochrome 2 bibl graph *Science* v354 no6310 p343 O 21 2016

Taketa, M.

Structural basis of the redox switches in the NAD+-reducing soluble [NiFe]-hydrogenase diag *Science* v357 no6354 p928 S 1 2017

Takeuchi, Hirotaka

The Secret History of Agile Innovation *Harvard Business Review Digital Articles* p2 Ap 20 2016

TAKEYH, RAY

The Myths of 1953 bw *Weekly Standard* v22 no43 p21 Jl 24 2017

Taking On Iran [Cover story] *National Review* v68 no24 p28 D 31 2016

West of Suez bw *Weekly Standard* v22 no9 p36 N 7 2016

Taki

The Art of Lying *American Conservative* v16 no3 p58 My/Je 2017

Tear Down This Colloseum! *American Conservative* v16 no4 p66 Jl/Ag 2017

Takla Makan Desert (China)

XINJIANG, CHINA J. CHEN color *Conde Nast Traveler* v52 no1 p32 Ja 2017

Takubo, Masa

Closing Japan's Monju fast breeder reactor: The possible implications bibl *Bulletin of the Atomic Scientists* v73 no3 p182 My 2017

Takumi Kobayashi

Buffer-gas cooling of antiprotonic helium to 1.5 to 1.7 K, and antiproton-to-electron mass ratio bibl chart diag graph *Science* v354 no6312 p610 N 4 2016

Tal, Alon

The Land Is Full: Addressing Overpopulation in Israel J. Waterbury *Foreign Affairs* v96 no1 p173 Ja/F 2017

Tal, Aner

Beware the Truthiness of Charts *Harvard Business Review Digital Articles* p2 N 19 2015

Tal, Diana

Sleeping Beauties of Political Science: The Case of AF Bentley chart graph *Society* v54 no4 p355 Ag 2017

Talapin, Dmitri V.

Direct optical lithography of functional inorganic nanomaterials diag graph *Science* v357 no6349 p385 Jl 28 2017

Talas, Laszlo

The biology of color color *Science* v357 no6350 p470 Ag 4 2017

Talbert, David E.

Almost Christmas D. Coggan color *Entertainment Weekly* no1440 p43 N 18 2016

Talbert, Mark

Empowering Youth to Care for Local Parks and Their Neighborhoods *Parks & Recreation* v52 no8 p30 Ag 2017

Talbot, David

The Hole in the Digital Economy color graph map *MIT Technology Review* v120 no1 p88 Ja/F 2017

TALBOT, MARGARET

THE ADDICTS NEXT DOOR bw cartoon *New Yorker* v93 no16 p74 Je 5 2017

OBSTACLE COURSE cartoon *New Yorker* v93 no7 p86 Ap 3 2017

TAKING TROLLS TO COURT cartoon color *New Yorker* v92 no40 p56 D 5 2016

THAT'S WHAT HE SAID cartoon *New Yorker* v92 no34 p19 O 24 2016

WOMEN IN THE WHITE HOUSE cartoon *New Yorker* v92 no42 p43 D 19 2016

Talbott, John E.

WAR IN HISTORY AND MEMORY *History Today* v67 no3 p18 Mr 2017

Talbot-Zorn, Justin

The Busier You Are, the More You Need Quiet Time *Harvard Business Review Digital Articles* p2 Mr 17 2017

Mindfulness Can Improve Strategy, Too *Harvard Business Review Digital Articles* p2 My 2 2016

Talcott, Richard

The Grand Tour diag *Astronomy* v45 no10 p50 O 2017

In pursuit of PLUTO color *Astronomy* v45 no7 p56 Jl 2017

PATH OF THE PLANETS chart color *Astronomy* v45 no11 p40 N 2017

PLANETARY WEIGHT LOSS color *Astronomy* v45 no4 p34 Ap 2017

SIZING UP PLANETARY NEBULAE color *Astronomy* v45 no1 p44 Ja 2017

STAR DOME color *Astronomy* v45 no11 p38 N 2017

STAR DOME/PATH OF THE PLANETS chart color *Astronomy* v45 no7 p38 Jl 2017

STAR DOME/PATH OF THE PLANETS chart color graph map *Astronomy* v45 no8 p46 Ag 2017

STAR DOME/PATH OF THE PLANETS color diag *Astronomy* v45 no6 p38 Je 2017

A step-by-step guide to the Great American Eclipse bw color *Astronomy* v45 no8 p26 Ag 2017

STILL IN THE FAMILY color *Astronomy* v45 no1 p34 Ja 2017

Talebian, Sheeva

Ask anything [Cover story] cartoon color *Women's Health* v13 no10 p22 D 2016

Talent agents

ABE BURNS, CELEBRITY TECHSPLAINER S. MARIKAR color *Bloomberg Businessweek* no4519 p82 Ap 24 2017

Talent development

Jon Stewart, Superboss S. Finkelstein *Harvard Business Review Digital Articles* p2 Jl 30 2015

Nonprofits Can't Keep Ignoring Talent Development L. Landles-Cobb, K. Kramer et al *Harvard Business Review Digital Articles* p2 D 17 2015

Talent management

3 Reasons Why Talent Management Isn't Working Anymore T. Warner *Harvard Business Review Digital Articles* p2 Jl 5 2016

The 3 Simple Rules of Managing Top Talent R. L. Martin *Harvard Business Review Digital Articles* p2 F 24 2017

The 3 Things CEOs Worry About the Most B. Groysberg and K. Connolly *Harvard Business Review Digital Articles* p2 Mr 16 2015

The Best Companies Don't Have More Stars — They Cluster Them Together M. Mankins color *Harvard Business Review Digital Articles* p2 F 3 2017

The Big Disconnect in Your Talent Strategy and How to Fix It J. Boudreau, M. Swan et al *Harvard Business Review Digital Articles* p2 D 23 2016

Companies Are Bad at Identifying High-Potential Employees J. Zenger and J. Folkman *Harvard Business Review Digital Articles* p2 F 20 2017

A Guide to Finding and Hiring the Best Contractors A. Merwin *Harvard Business Review Digital Articles* p2 Jl 17 2017

How to Manage Your Star Employee R. Knight *Harvard Business Review Digital Articles* p2 Je 30 2017

The Inescapable Paradox of Managing Creativity L. A. Hill, G. Brandeau et al *Harvard Business Review Digital Articles* p2 D 12 2014

LGBT-Inclusive Companies Are Better at 3 Big Things Sylvia Ann Hewlett and Kenji Yoshino *Harvard Business Review Digital Articles* p2 F 2 2016

Managing On-Demand Talent J. Younger and N. Smallwood *Harvard Business Review Digital Articles* p2 Ja 28 2016

PE Firms Are Creating a New Role: Leadership Capital Partner D. Ulrich and J. Allen *Harvard Business Review Digital Articles* p2 Ag 11 2017

Performance Management in the Gig Economy J. Younger and N. Smallwood *Harvard Business Review Digital Articles* p2 Ja 11 2016

The Portable Leader Is the New "Organization Man" G. Petriglieri *Harvard Business Review Digital Articles* p2 Ag 10 2017

REINVENTING TALENT MANAGEMENT: HOW GE USES ANALYTICS TO GUIDE A MORE DIGITAL, FAR-FLUNG WORKFORCE S. PROKESCH *Harvard Business Review* v95 no5 p54 S/O 2017

The Solution to the Skills Gap Could Already Be Inside Your Company E. Harrell *Harvard Business Review Digital Articles* p2 S 27 2016

What I Learned from Transforming the U.S. Military's Approach to Talent A. Carter *Harvard Business Review Digital Articles* p2 My 23 2017

WHAT WORKERS WANT cartoon diag map *Forbes* v199 no4 p76 Ap 25 2017

You Can't Delegate Talent Management to the HR Department

R. Ashkenas *Harvard Business Review Digital Articles* p2 S 23 2016

Talent shows

The Gong Show K. Freeze *TV Guide* v65 no27 p30 Je 26 2017

Talese, Gay, 1932-

Good Old New Journalism M. GORDON color *New York Times Book Review* p15 Ja 29 2017

The Lady and the Scamp E. PERETZ bw color *Vanity Fair* v59 no5 p128 Ap 2017

Talese, Nan

The Lady and the Scamp E. PERETZ bw color *Vanity Fair* v59 no5 p128 Ap 2017

Tales of Hoffman, The (Theatrical production)

Operapedia: Tales of Hoffmann *Opera News* v81 no5 p14 N 2016

Talev, Margaret

Fired. But Not Finished bw *Bloomberg Businessweek* no4522 p30 My 15 2017

TALIAFERRO, TIM

CALLED to Lead *Texas Monthly* v45 no9 p42 S 2017

CONFESSION: BEFORE I WAS *Texas Monthly* v45 no8 p14 Ag 2017

EDITOR'S LETTER *Texas Monthly* v45 no2 p14 F 2017

EDITOR'S LETTER *Texas Monthly* v45 no5 p14 My 2017

EVALUATING A MAGAZINE *Texas Monthly* v45 no3 p22 Mr 2017

FORTY YEARS AGO *Texas Monthly* v45 no4 p16 Ap 2017

A Guide to Our New Dining Guide *Texas Monthly* v45 no9 p6 S 2017

Taliban

A Fateful Decision T. Joscelyn color *Weekly Standard* v22 no47 p7 Ag 21 2017

Lost in Translation T. A. FRAIL *Smithsonian* v47 no7 p68 N 2016

MY LONGEST DAY J. LIENHARD *Humanist* v77 no1 p34 Ja/F 2017

THE PATIENT WAR May Jeong *Harper's Magazine* v334 no2001 p51 F 2017

Taliente, Davide

How Multinationals Can Adapt to a Political Mood That Doesn't Care for Them at All *Harvard Business Review Digital Articles* p2 My 23 2017

Talkoff, Emma

No Good Options on North Korea color *Time* v190 no4 p10 Jl 24 2017

The Secret History of Election 2016 [Cover story] color map *Time* v190 no5 p32 Jl 31 2017

Tall building design & construction

See also

Skyscraper design & construction

Tall building fires & fire prevention

Grenfell Tower Fire Tragedy Sparks Safety Dispute P. REINA and A. WRIGHT color *Architectural Record* v205 no8 p17 Ag 2017

Tall people

ALL RISE [Cover story] S. Apstein chart color *Sports Illustrated* v126 no14 p76 My 15-22 2017

A Tale of Two Kates G. WOOD bw *Missouri Life* v44 no2 p122 Ap 2017

Tall stature

THINK BIG A. Staples color *Sports Illustrated* v126 no7 p56 Mr 6 2017

TALLAMY, DOUG W.

Using Plant-Animal Interactions to Inform Tree Selection in Tree-Based Agroecosystems for Enhanced Biodiversity *BioScience* v66 no12 p1046 D 1 2016

Tallent, Gabriel

My Absolute Darling *Publishers Weekly* v264 no26 p149 Je 26 2017

Tallinn (Estonia)

Estonia color *National Geographic* v231 no3 p6 Mr 2017

Tallis, Nicola

Crown of Blood: The Deadly Inheritance of Lady Jane Grey *Publishers Weekly* v263 no41 p69 O 10 2016

Crown of Blood W. Moore *History Today* v67 no3 p59 Mr 2017

Talmud—Versions

Nonprofit offers Talmud in English online for free M. Chabin *Christian Century* v134 no8 p1 Ap 12 2017

TALTY, ALEXANDRA

Q&A: PW TALKS WITH HELEN THORPE: Refugees and Me color *Publishers Weekly* v264 no40 p126 O 2 2017

Talty, Stephan

The Surprising Power of 400-Year-Old Paintings E. Mitchell *Smithsonian* v48 no3 p28 Je 2017

TALU, YONCA

APPETITE FOR DESTRUCTION bw color *Film Comment* v53 no5 p62 S/O 2017

THE LONG GOODBYE color *Film Comment* v53 no2 p27 Mr/Ap 2017

THE SETTING SUN color *Film Comment* v53 no2 p24 Mr/Ap 2017

The Son of Joseph color *Film Comment* v53 no1 p85 Ja/F 2017

Wealth Management bw color *Film Comment* v53 no3 p77 My/Je 2017

Tam, Charmaine

Reprogramming my career color *Science* v357 no6346 p102 Jl 7 2017

Tam, Simon—Interviews

THE SLANTS M. BRAGG color *Reason* v48 no11 p36 Ap 2017

Tamaki, Jillian

Sketchbook *New York Times Book Review* p27 Ag 20 2017

This Scribbly Stuff S. ROGERS cartoon *Walrus* v14 no6 p70 Jl/Ag 2017

Tamanaha, E. K.

Persistent effects of pre-Columbian plant domestication on Amazonian forest composition bibl chart graph map *Science* v355 no6328 p925 Mr 3 2017

Tamarack Aerospace Group Inc.

ATLAS WINGLETS CERTIFIED color *Flying* v144 no3 p18 Mr 2017

TAMARACK'S ACTIVE WINGLETS P. Bergqvist color diag *Flying* v143 no12 p14 D 2016

Tamassia, Giovanna

Love's Labor color *O, The Oprah Magazine* p24 F 2017

Tamaya, Tomohiro

High-harmonic generation in graphene enhanced by elliptically polarized light excitation color graph *Science* v356 no6339 p736 My 19 2017

TAMBA, YANA

Q: Who's your trusty sidekick for summer adventures, and why? color *O, The Oprah Magazine* p14 Je 2017

Tambellini, Aldo

Character Study bw *Art in America* v105 no3 p57 Mr 2017

Tamblyn, Michael—Interviews

SHARJAH INTERNATIONAL BOOK FAIR Q&A WITH MICHAEL TAMBLYN *Publishers Weekly* v263 no43 p(Sp)22 O 24 2016

Tambor, Jeffrey, 1944-

BARGAIN BASEMENT I. Parker cartoon *New Yorker* v93 no23 p20 Ag 7 2017

By the Book M. WAKIM *Los Angeles Magazine* p58 My 2017

Transparent A. Bacle, K. Connolly et al color *Entertainment Weekly* no1482/1483 p109 S 22 2017

Tambor, Jeffrey, 1944-—Interviews

Jeffrey Tambor *New York Times Book Review* p8 My 21 2017

TAMBURRINI, ANDREA

ROOM WITH A VIEW color *Conde Nast Traveler* v52 no10 p142 N 2017

Tambyraja, Sherine

THE LITERACY LINK: Reading activities as a mechanism to strengthen family engagement *Literacy Today (2411-7862)* v35 no1 p12 Jl/Ag 2017

Tameem, Abdul Fattah

The Syrians Next Door R. Shulman color *Time* v188 no20 p40 N 14 2016

TAMER, FILIZ

Breaking Ground and Glass Ceilings cartoon *Alternatives Journal (AJ) - Canada's Environmental Voice* v42 no2 p49 2016

Tamerat, Jalene

Critical consciousness A key to student achievement bw il *Phi Delta Kappan* v98 no5 p18 F 2017

Tamiasciurus

Leprosy in red squirrels R. Brosch and T. P. Stinear bibl color diag *Science* v354 no6313 p702 N 11 2016

Red squirrels harbor leprosy bacteria L. HAMERS color *Science*

News v190 no12 p9 D 10 2016

Red squirrels in the British Isles are infected with leprosy bacilli C. Avanzi, J. del-Pozo et al bibl color diag map *Science* v354 no6313 p744 N 11 2016

Tamil (Indic people)—Sri Lanka

Fragile Peace R. Draper color map *National Geographic* v230 no5 p108 N 2016

Tamilila Vitutalaippulikal (Organization)

The Tangled Politics of Postwar Justice in Sri Lanka J. GOODHAND and O. WALTON *Current History* v116 no789 p130 Ap 2017

Tamir, Lois

Younger and Older Executives Need Different Things from Coaching *Harvard Business Review Digital Articles* p2 Jl 6 2017

TAMKIN, EMILY

Happy Birthday, Marie Jana Korbelova *Foreign Policy* no225 p25 Jl/Ag 2017

TAMMEMAG, HANS

The magnificent SEVEN color *Canadian Geographic* v136 no6 p54 D 2016

Tammet, Daniel

Every Word Is a Bird We Teach to Sing: Encounters with Language *Publishers Weekly* v264 no28 p77 Jl 10 2017

Tamoxifen—Therapeutic use

An eye-opening role for a cancer drug B. Brookshire color *Science News* v191 no11 p4 Je 10 2017

Tampa (Fla.)

Discover Saddlebrook *Tennis* v53 no1 p74 Ja/F 2017

Tampa Bay Buccaneers (Football team)

2 Tampa Bay Buccaneers color *Sports Illustrated* v127 no7 p97 S 4 2017

Tampa Bay Lightning (Hockey team)

EASTERN CONFERENCE POWER RANKINGS A. Prewitt color *Sports Illustrated* v125 no12 p56 O 10 2016

Tampa Bay Rays (Baseball team)

4 RAYS color *Sports Illustrated* v126 no9 p80 Mr 27 2017

Tampons

PERIOD OF ADJUSTMENT A. MASTROMONACO color *Washingtonian Magazine* v52 no7 p200 Ap 2017

Tampons—Evaluation

Special DELIVERY J. ABIDOR color *Seventeen* v75 no11 p60 N 2016

Tampons—Marketing

Period Drama K. LAIDLAW color *Walrus* v14 no3 p18 Ap 2017

Tampopo (Film)

23. See Tampopo *New York* v49 no21 p122 O 17 2016

Tamron Co. Ltd.

TELE TITAN J. Silber color *Popular Photography* v81 no1 p102 Ja/F 2017

Tamte, Megan

Style in Store color *Working Mother* v40 no4 p14 O/N 2017

Tamulaitis, Gintautas

A cyclic oligonucleotide signaling pathway in type III CRISPR-Cas systems *Science* v357 no6351 p605 Ag 11 2017

Tamura, Keita

Conversion of object identity to object-general semantic value in the primate temporal cortex color graph *Science* v357 no6352 p687 Ag 18 2017

TAMURA, TODD

Too much democracy? *Issues in Science & Technology* v33 no1 p5 Fall 2016

Tam Wu, Karen

GO WEST TO SEE THE FUTURE OF GREEN BUILDINGS color *Maclean's* v129 no50 p39 D 19 2016

Tan, Amy, 1952-

Discovering the Past K. E. LIVINGSTON color *Publishers Weekly* v264 no41 p54 O 9 2017

PEN PALS bw color *O, The Oprah Magazine* p34 N 2017

the profound delight in PERSONAL EXPRESSION [Cover story] B. D. COLEMAN color *Arts & Crafts Homes & the Revival* v12 no4 p40 Fall 2017

Tan, Cheng

Tuning quantum nonlocal effects in graphene plasmonics bw diag *Science* v357 no6347 p187 Jl 14 2017

Tan, Cheryl Lu-Lien

For the Love of Welsh Rarebit color *Foreign Policy* no225 p84 Jl/Ag 2017

A Shorter Road to Singapore F. Lam *New York Times Magazine* p34 O 30 2016

Tan, Fengji

Deep functional analysis of synII, a 770-kilobase synthetic yeast chromosome diag *Science* v355 no6329 p1047 Mr 10 2017

Tan, Gang

Scalable-manufactured randomized glass-polymer hybrid metamaterial for daytime radiative cooling bibl diag *Science* v355 no6329 p1062 Mr 10 2017

Tan, Hairen

Efficient and stable solution-processed planar perovskite solar cells via contact passivation bibl graph *Science* v355 no6326 p722 F 17 2017

Tan, Longzhi

Single-cell whole-genome analyses by Linear Amplification via Transposon Insertion (LIANTI) graph *Science* v356 no6334 p189 Ap 14 2017

Tan, Meng How

Deficiency of microRNA miR-34a expands cell fate potential in pluripotent stem cells diag *Science* v355 no6325 p596 F 10 2017

TAN, TERI

The Academic Book Market in China color *Publishers Weekly* v264 no39 p(Sp)3 S 25 2017

Educational and STM Publishing in SINGAPORE *Publishers Weekly* v263 no41 p31 O 10 2016

A Gallery of Hot Titles from China color *Publishers Weekly* v264 no12 p32 Mr 20 2017

Gearing Up for the Shifts and Twists in the Digital Content Industry color *Publishers Weekly* v264 no27 p(Sp)4 Jl 3 2017

Hot Topics in Chinese Academic Publishing *Publishers Weekly* v264 no39 p(Sp)26 S 25 2017

Literary Publishing in SINGAPORE *Publishers Weekly* v263 no41 p23 O 10 2016

Marie Kondo's Global Appeal *Publishers Weekly* v263 no41 p13 O 10 2016

More Self-Help Bestsellers Coming from Japan color *Publishers Weekly* v264 no35 p17 Ag 28 2017

New Titles from Chinese Academic Presses *Publishers Weekly* v264 no39 p(Sp)28 S 25 2017

An Overview of the Children's Book Market in China color *Publishers Weekly* v264 no12 p3 Mr 20 2017

Retooling the HONG KONG & CHINA Print Business color *Publishers Weekly* v264 no35 p78 Ag 28 2017

Social Media Marketing Takes Center Stage color *Publishers Weekly* v264 no12 p30 Mr 20 2017

Taiwan's Indie Booksellers and Publishers Join Forces to Tackle Challenges color *Publishers Weekly* v264 no8 p6 F 20 2017

A Time to Embrace: Uncertainties and Inconsistencies *Publishers Weekly* v264 no27 p(Sp)3 Jl 3 2017

Tan, Xiaojun

Keeping in touch with the ER network color *Science* v356 no6338 p584 My 12 2017

Tan, Yuan Yuan

The Arc of Artistry J. CARMAN *Dance Magazine* v91 no1 p91 Ja 2017

Tanabe, Ariana

the return of the HOUSEPLANT M. HUGHES *Better Homes & Gardens* v95 no1 p57 Ja 2017

Tanaka, Koichiro

High-harmonic generation in graphene enhanced by elliptically polarized light excitation color graph *Science* v356 no6339 p736 My 19 2017

Tanaka, Mina

A peptide hormone required for Casparian strip diffusion barrier formation in Arabidopsis roots color graph *Science* v355 no6322 p284 Ja 20 2017

Tanas, Olga

For Manufacturers, Russia Is Now a Bargain graph *Bloomberg Businessweek* no4501 p15 N 28 2016

The Trouble Brewing In Putin's Heartland color graph *Bloomberg Businessweek* no4538 p36 S 18 2017

Tanderup, Art

THE FIGHT OF OUR LIFETIME K. ARONOFF *In These Times* v41 no3 p20 Mr 2017

Tandrup, Hans

GREAT DANE J. DRILLING *Cincinnati Magazine* v50 no10 p122 Jl 2017

Taneja, Hemant

Why Startups Are More Successful than Ever at Unbundling Incumbents *Harvard Business Review Digital Articles* p2 Je 18 2015

TANENBAUM, LAURA

Bohemian Fantasy bw *New York Times Book Review* p18 S 25 2016

Tale of Two Fathers *New York Times Book Review* p23 Mr 12 2017

Tanenbaum, Robert K.

Without Fear or Favor *Publishers Weekly* v264 no25 p93 Je 19 2017

TANENHAUS, SAM

The Architect of the Radical Right color *Atlantic* v320 no1 p40 Jl/Ag 2017

CHARGE OF THE RIGHT BRIGADE bw color *Esquire* p80 My 2017

THE RIGHT IDEA bw cartoon *New Yorker* v92 no34 p77 O 24 2016

Shimmering Visions bw color *New Republic* v248 no6 p66 Je 2017

STORIES WE TELL OURSELVES S. BRAMMER, S. L. SEITZ et al color *Vanity Fair* v58 no11 p88 N 2016

The White House Mythmaker color *Atlantic* v320 no4 p46 N 2017

Who Stopped McCarthy? bw color *Atlantic* v319 no3 p34 Ap 2017

Taneva, Stanimira

Older Workers Need to Stop Believing Stereotypes About Themselves *Harvard Business Review Digital Articles* p2 Je 20 2016

Taneyhill, Lisa A.

Precaution and governance of emerging technologies bibl color *Science* v354 no6313 p710 N 11 2016

Tang, C.

Intonational speech prosody encoding in the human auditory cortex diag *Science* v357 no6353 p797 Ag 25 2017

Tang, Chi-Hsien

Imaging the distribution of transient viscosity after the 2016 Mw 7.1 Kumamoto earthquake map *Science* v356 no6334 p163 Ap 14 2017

Tang, Dingzhong

Plants transfer lipids to sustain colonization by mutualistic mycorrhizal and parasitic fungi diag graph *Science* v356 no6343 p1172 Je 16 2017

Tang, H.

Improving global integration of crop research color *Science* v357 no6349 p359 Jl 28 2017

Tang, Jau

Imaging rotational dynamics of nanoparticles in liquid by 4D electron microscopy bibl diag graph *Science* v355 no6324 p494 F 3 2017

Tang, Sindy K. Y.

Self-repairing cells: How single cells heal membrane ruptures and restore lost structures diag *Science* v356 no6342 p1022 Je 9 2017

Tang, Stephen J.

Community network for deaf scientists color *Science* v356 no6336 p386 Ap 28 2017

Tang, Wenfang

Populist Authoritarianism: Chinese Political Culture and Regime Sustainability A. J. Nathan *Foreign Affairs* v96 no3 p173 My/Je 2017

TANG, WILSON

"I'm That Guy Who Kept Old Chinatown Old." color *Bon Appetit* v62 no2 p60 Mr 2017

Tang, Zuojian

Synthesis, debugging, and effects of synthetic chromosome consolidation: synVI and beyond color *Science* v355 no6329 p1045 Mr 10 2017

Tang Long

THE FLAWED PERFECT GENERAL *Military History* v33 no6 p48 Mr 2017

Tangari, Joe

'It's Always Music First' THUNDERCAT color *Downbeat* v84 no6 p52 Je 2017

Tangent Scale Models (Company)
Tangent HO 40-foot Mini Hy-Cube boxcar C. Grivno *Model Railroader* v84 no9 p63 S 2017

Tanghe, S.
Inhibitors of PEX14 disrupt protein import into glycosomes and kill Trypanosoma parasites chart color diag graph *Science* v355 no6332 p1416 Mr 31 2017

Tangirala, Subra
How to Get Men Involved with Gender Parity Initiatives *Harvard Business Review Digital Articles* p2 S 13 2017

Tangled Before Ever After (Film)
Tangled Before Ever After M. Logan *TV Guide* v65 no11 p39 Mr 6 2017

Tangley, Laura
Arrested Recovery color *National Wildlife (World Edition)* v55 no5 p34 Ag/S 2017
Bringing Back the Light color *National Wildlife (World Edition)* v55 no4 p12 Je/Jl 2017

Taniguchi, T.
Magnetic resonance spectroscopy of an atomically thin material using a single-spin qubit bibl color diag graph *Science* v355 no6324 p503 F 3 2017

Taniguchi, Takako
Why Japan's Idemitsu Isn't Feeling Blue color *Bloomberg Businessweek* no4520 p34 My 1 2017

Taniguchi, Takashi
An on/off Berry phase switch in circular graphene resonators diag graph *Science* v356 no6340 p845 My 26 2017
Tuning quantum nonlocal effects in graphene plasmonics bw diag *Science* v357 no6347 p187 Jl 14 2017

Tanikella, Anand
Industry-Academic Partnerships Can Solve Bigger Problems *Harvard Business Review Digital Articles* p2 My 2 2016

Tanis, Justin
HOW DO YOU HOLD TOGETHER YOUR TRANS IDENTITY AND YOUR LIFE OF FAITH? color *Christian Century* v134 no2 p22 Ja 18 2017

Tanjung, Rizal
Rizal Tanjung, 42 Z. MORTON color *Surfer* v58 no4 p36 Ag 2017

Tank cars—Export & import trade
Ask MR S. Otte color *Model Railroader* v84 no5 p18 My 2017

Tanker accidents
THE HIJACKING OF THE BRILLANTE VIRTUOSO K. CHELLEL, M. CAMPBELL et al color map *Bloomberg Businessweek* no4532 p48 Jl 31 2017

Tankers
WEST COAST FOCUS S. SHIBATA *Sea Magazine* v108 no12 p12 D 2016

Tankersley, Jennifer
A Way to Assess and Prioritize Your Change Efforts *Harvard Business Review Digital Articles* p2 Jl 9 2015

Tanks
Floating in Space J. DeBold color *New Orleans Magazine* v51 no5 p150 Mr 2017
The New Quiet Time K. Massicot color *New Orleans Magazine* v51 no5 p36 Mr 2017

Tanks (Military science)
Hardware Char B1 bis J. Guttman color *Military History* v34 no4 p20 N 2017
WHEN FRANCE DEFIED HITLER'S PANZERS [Cover story] J. Koster bw color map *Military History* v34 no4 p30 N 2017

Tanks—Evaluation
STRATEGIST img *New York* v50 no15 p41 Jl 24 2017

Tannenbaum, Andrew
Why Do IoT Companies Keep Building Devices with Huge Security Flaws? [Cover story] *Harvard Business Review Digital Articles* p2 Ap 27 2017

Tannenbaum, Barbara
From specimens to souls bw color *Magazine Antiques* v183 no6 p68 N/D 2016

Tanner, Henry Ossawa, 1859-1937
A difficult choice J. Bleem color *U.S. Catholic* v82 no3 p50 Mr 2017

Tanner, Kathryn
From God-talk to God's work A. P. Pauw *Christian Century* v134 no14 p22 Jl 5 2017

TANNER, KIMBERLY D.
Origins of Science Faculty with Education Specialties: Hiring Motivations and Prior Connections Explain Institutional Differences in the SFES Phenomenon *BioScience* v67 no5 p452 My 2017

TANNER, LES
The Butterfly, in Fact: Stuff You Probably Didn't Know *Idaho Magazine* v16 no10 p46 Jl 2017
In Praise of Smallness: Fishing the Little Creeks *Idaho Magazine* v16 no8 p6 My 2017
Pickleballed *Idaho Magazine* v16 no5 p6 F 2017

Tanner, Lydia
#BIKECRUSH color *Bicycling* v58 no7 p65 Ag 2017
#BIKECRUSH color *Bicycling* v58 no8 p53 S 2017
CANYON SPECTRAL CF 9.0 EX color *Bicycling* v58 no7 p78 Ag 2017
FACTOR O2 DISC color *Bicycling* v58 no9 p76 O 2017
GET LIT! color *Bicycling* v58 no10 p76 N/D 2017
"I'VE GOT $3,000. CAN I GET A BIKE WITH NICE WHEELS?" color *Bicycling* v58 no3 p56 Ap 2017
"I WANT TO GO ON DIRT-ROAD ADVENTURES." color *Bicycling* v58 no3 p42 Ap 2017
Let's Talk About Socks color *Bicycling* v58 no4 p74 My 2017
Totally Worth It! color *Bicycling* v58 no4 p22 My 2017
YOU SHOULD KNOW color *Bicycling* v58 no7 p104 Ag 2017

Tanner, Tim
Inviting and Efficient color *Old House Journal* v44 no8 p70 D 2016

Tanning (Hides & skins)—Equipment & supplies
Self-Tanners, Decoded E. Reimel color *Glamour* v115 no6 p78 Je 2017

Tanning (Suntan) beds
TEMPTED TO TAN? Read This First! L. BALSAMO color *Seventeen* v76 no2 p80 Mr 2017

Tannon, Jerome—Interviews
AV CLUB WITH B. Merrill color *Snowboarder* v29 no3 p33 N 2016

Tanoesoedibjo, Hary
THE TRUMP CLONE [Cover story] A. BROWN, D. Sirtori-Cortina et al bw color *Forbes* v199 no3 p50 Mr 28 2017

Tanon, Jerome
Hymns of the Western Peaks: Loose Change in India D. Crosilla bw color *Snowboarder* v29 no2 p82 O 2016

Tanquary, Kathryn
The Night Parade color *Publishers Weekly* v263 no49 p79 D 7 2016

Tansill, Frederick J.
BEST IN WEALTH MANAGEMENT *Washingtonian Magazine* v52 no3 p112 D 2016

Tantalum
Rarest nucleus reluctant to decay E. CONOVER *Science News* v190 no9 p11 O 29 2016

Tantaros, Andrea, 1978-
OUT–FOXED D. Bacher color *Esquire* v166 no4 p86 N 2016

Tantimedh, Adi
Gods and Monsters L. PICKER color *Publishers Weekly* v264 no41 p44 O 9 2017

Tantric Buddhism
INSEPARABLE ACROSS LIFETIMES H. Gayley color *Tricycle: The Buddhist Review* v27 no1 p76 Fall 2017
WHERE THE THINKING STOPS K. MCLEOD color *Tricycle: The Buddhist Review* v26 no2 p66 Wint 2016

Tantry, Sathvik
Making Personalized Marketing Work *Harvard Business Review Digital Articles* p2 F 29 2016

Tanz, Jason
Fact: diag *Wired* v25 no3 p48 Mr 2017
A TO-DO LIST FOR THE TECH INDUSTRY cartoon *Wired* v24 no11 p92 N 2016

Tao, Ran
"Perfect" designer chromosome V and behavior of a ring derivative diag *Science* v355 no6329 p1046 Mr 10 2017

Tao Cheng
Ultrafine jagged platinum nanowires enable ultrahigh mass activity for the oxygen reduction reaction bibl chart graph *Science* v354 no6318 p1414 D 16 2016

Tao Lin

A chemical genetic roadmap to improved tomato flavor bibl graph *Science* v355 no6323 p391 Ja 27 2017

Tao Wu

Biaxially strained PtPb/Pt core/shell nanoplate boosts oxygen reduction catalysis bibl color graph *Science* v354 no6318 p1410 D 16 2016

Tao Yue

Case Study: Is Holacracy for Us? *Harvard Business Review Digital Articles* p2 D 8 2016

Tap dancers

by Jared Grimes Tap dancer *Dance Magazine* v91 no10 p80 O 2017

by Melinda Sullivan: Tap dancer *Dance Magazine* v91 no6 p88 Je 2017

Emma WYLIE N. Loeffler-Gladstone *Dance Spirit* v21 no1 p95 Ja 2017

Tap dancing—Reviews

HAPPY FEET J. ACOCELLA cartoon *New Yorker* v92 no40 p82 D 5 2016

Tapalansky, Nick

Cast No Shadow *Publishers Weekly* v264 no38 p74 S 18 2017

Tapbots LLC

PASTEBOT 2: MAC UTILITY COMBINES A DEEP CLIPBOARD WITH CLEVER CONVERSIONS G. FLEISHMAN color *Macworld - Digital Edition* p19 F 2017

Tape 10 (Music)

RAP SESSION A. KONERMANN *Cincinnati Magazine* v50 no7 p19 Ap 2017

Tape craft

A Little Tape'll Do Ya! B. PIKE color *Power & Motoryacht* v33 no4 p104 Ap 2017

Tapestry

On the Horizon M. Moses color *American Craft* v76 no6 p36 D 2016-Ja 2017

Tapestry design

WRITTEN IN THE STARS J. FOUMBERG cartoon *Chicago* v65 no11 p44 N 2016

Tapestry—Exhibitions

WRITTEN IN THE STARS J. FOUMBERG cartoon *Chicago* v65 no11 p44 N 2016

Tapeworm infections—Diagnosis

New DIY Tapeworm Test S. Wenholz color *Practical Horseman* v45 no5 p76 My 2017

Tapeworms

NEW TEST FOR TAPEWORMS C. Barakat and M. McCluskey color *Equus* no481 p14 O 2017

Tapia, A.

Observation of a large-scale anisotropy in the arrival directions of cosmic rays above 8 × 1018 eV *Science* v357 no6357 p1266 S 22 2017

Tapirs—Behavior

Made for Each Other P. Edmonds color *National Geographic* v230 no4 p31 O 2016

Tapley, Brian

COMMENT color *Canadian Geographic* v137 no4 p72 Jl/Ag 2017

Tapp, P. Gaye

P. GAYE TAPP ON ICONIC STYLE K. O'Shea-Evans bw color *House Beautiful* v159 no4 p56 My 2017

TAPPAN, NANCY

AMERICA'S STAND ON SELF-DEFENSE bw *American History* v52 no4 p16 O 2017

ELUSIVE BALANCE *American History* v51 no6 p12 F 2017

Madness Rules the Hour: Charleston, 1860, and the Mania for War *MHQ: Quarterly Journal of Military History* v30 no1 p93 Aut 2017

PLUCKING OUT JIM CROW *American History* v52 no1 p12 Ap 2017

SUFFRAGE SHIFT bw color *American History* v52 no3 p14 Ag 2017

WAR BY TELEPHONE bw color *American History* v52 no3 p68 Ag 2017

WATER WARS color map *American History* v52 no2 p16 Je 2017

Woodford Reserve Distillery *American History* v51 no6 p72 F 2017

Tapper, Jake, 1969-

Jake Tapper: So, how'd you get so fit? D. WALTERS color *Bon Appetit* no8 p106 Ag 2017

The Realest Face in "Fake News" T. BRODESSER-AKNER color *GQ: Gentlemen's Quarterly* v97 no5 p56 My 2017

Tapper, Jake, 1969-—Interviews

Jake Tapper A. GREENE bw *Rolling Stone* no1294 p62 Ag 24 2017

Tapscott, Alex

Blockchain Could Help Artists Profit More from Their Creative Works *Harvard Business Review Digital Articles* p2 Mr 22 2017

How Blockchain Is Changing Finance color *Harvard Business Review Digital Articles* p2 Mr 1 2017

The Impact of the Blockchain Goes Beyond Financial Services *Harvard Business Review Digital Articles* p2 My 10 2016

Tapscott, Don

After 20 Years, It's Harder to Ignore the Digital Economy's Dark Side *Harvard Business Review Digital Articles* p2 Mr 11 2016

Blockchain Could Help Artists Profit More from Their Creative Works *Harvard Business Review Digital Articles* p2 Mr 22 2017

How Blockchain Is Changing Finance color *Harvard Business Review Digital Articles* p2 Mr 1 2017

The Impact of the Blockchain Goes Beyond Financial Services *Harvard Business Review Digital Articles* p2 My 10 2016

Tara, Sylvia

In Defense of Fat R. M. HENIG *New York Times Book Review* p23 Ja 8 2017

The Secret Life of FAT bw color *Discover* v38 no2 p50 Mr 2017

Tarango, Alanna—Interviews

THE DIRT with Alanna Tarango *Dance Spirit* v21 no4 p16 Ap 2017

TARANTO, JAMES

FROM THE ARCHIVES cartoon *Reason* v49 no2 p70 Je 2017

Taranto, Tim

Ars Botanica *Publishers Weekly* v264 no16 p56 Ap 17 2017

Tarantulas

From The Pages Of Quiz Whiz: Stump Your Parents cartoon color *National Geographic Kids* no474 p33 O 2017

Nature's Jewels A. Bolen color *National Wildlife (World Edition)* v55 no4 p22 Je/Jl 2017

Taras, Vas

Research: The Biggest Culture Gaps Are Within Countries, Not Between Them *Harvard Business Review Digital Articles* p2 My 18 2016

Taraska, Julie

Air Supply *Architectural Record* v204 no10 p63 O 2016

All the Right Moves color *Architectural Record* v205 no2 p124 F 2017

Bright Ideas *Architectural Record* v204 no11 p159 N 2016

Get Schooled *Architectural Record* v204 no11 p61 N 2016

Inside Job color *Architectural Record* v205 no2 p48 F 2017

Open and Shut *Architectural Record* v204 no10 p57 O 2016

Over Our Heads color *Architectural Record* v205 no2 p46 F 2017

Record Products 2016 color *Architectural Record* v204 no12 p113 D 2016

Safe and Sound *Architectural Record* v205 no1 p53 Ja 2017

TARAZI, BASSAM

Link 10 Peaks in a Day il *Backpacker* p36 Ag 2017

Tarbell, Edmund Charles, 1862-1938

Mary Josephine color *Magazine Antiques* v183 no6 p21 N/D 2016

Tarbell, Jim

Growing Up P. LAFFOON IV color *Cincinnati Magazine* v51 no1 p38 O 2017

Tardigrada

Tardigrades aren't genetic mash-ups T. H. SAEY color *Science News* v192 no2 p13 Ag 19 2017

Tardiness

Later start time for teens improves grades, mood, and safety K. L. Wahlstrom chart color diag *Phi Delta Kappan* v98 no4 p8 D 2016/Ja 2017

Tarditi, Federico Rodriguez

The Benefits of Taking a Slower Approach to Innovation *Harvard Business Review Digital Articles* p2 Je 26 2017

Target Corp.

Target Slips Up M. Boyle color graph *Bloomberg Businessweek* no4528 p13 Je 26 2017

Why Target's Canadian Expansion Failed D. Dahlhoff *Harvard Business Review Digital Articles* p2 Ja 20 2015

Target marketing

Getting the Most from an Online Customer Community C. Trevail *Harvard Business Review Digital Articles* p2 Je 3 2016

Targeted Ads Don't Just Make You More Likely to Buy—They Can Change How You Think About Yourself R. W. Reczek, C. Summers et al *Harvard Business Review Digital Articles* p2 Ap 4 2016

Target practice

The Jump Shot P. Bourjaily color *Field & Stream* v122 no4 pF10 S 2017

Targeting (Nuclear strategy)

US cities are not medically prepared for a nuclear detonation J. M. Hauer *Bulletin of the Atomic Scientists* v73 no4 p215 Jl 2017

Targets (Sports)

See also

Holes (Golf)

A GOLF MAGAZINE STUDY IT'S TIME TO CHANGE YOUR AIM B. Christina and E. Alpenfels color *Golf Magazine* v59 no11 p76 N 2017

How to Break Your Goals Into Manageable Pieces J. Susser *Dressage Today* v23 no7 p16 Mr 2017

Targhetta, N.

Persistent effects of pre-Columbian plant domestication on Amazonian forest composition bibl chart graph map *Science* v355 no6328 p925 Mr 3 2017

Taricha granulosa

Rough-skinned newt color *Canadian Wildlife* v23 no2 p9 My/Je 2017

TARICO, VALERIE

CAN BACTERIA Help Us Understand RELIGION? *Humanist* v77 no3 p16 My/Je 2017

Tariff

The Questions Executives Should Ask About 3D Printing C. Flynn *Harvard Business Review Digital Articles* p2 Ap 19 2016

Tariff Act of 1909 (U.S.)

Chilly Trade Winds J. McCORMACK color *Weekly Standard* v22 no21 p10 F 6 2017

Tariff—Canada

TITANS of the Great Lakes I. COUTTS color map *Canadian Geographic* v137 no4 p34 Jl/Ag 2017

Tariff—United States

HOW A BORDER TAX WOULD AFFECT YOU S. BLOCK color *Kiplinger's Personal Finance* v71 no5 p11 My 2017

A Tax Showdown At the Border L. Browning and S. Kapur cartoon *Bloomberg Businessweek* no4514 p25 Mr 13 2017

VW's Latest Woe: A Reliance on Mexico R. Beene, C. Rauwald et al *Bloomberg Businessweek* no4512 p20 F 20 2017

Tariff—United States—History—21st century

Will the BAT Be the Tax That Changes Everything? H. S. Edwards color diag *Time* v189 no11 p28 Mr 27 2017

TARIQ, AMBREEN

Tents, Trails and Tranquility *Islamic Horizons* v46 no1 p44 Ja/F 2017

Tarkington, Ed

TARNISHED IDEALS: A young boy emerges from the dark shadow cast by his ne'er-do-well half-brother B. GLOSE *Virginia Living* v15 no4 p29 Je 2017

Tarkus (Music)

EMERSON, LAKE & PALMER M. Mettler color *Sound & Vision* v81 no10 p72 D 2016

TARLACH, GEMMA

20 Things You Didn't Know About ... Animal Domestication color *Discover* v38 no8 p82 O 2017

20 Things You Didn't Know About... Metabolism color *Discover* v38 no2 p74 Mr 2017

Ancient Monkey Teeth Change Evolutionary Timeline bw color diag *Discover* v38 no1 p76 Ja/F 2017

Bangladesh Sits Atop Potential Major Quake Zone color map *Discover* v38 no1 p22 Ja/F 2017

Bears bw color *Discover* v38 no10 p74 D 2017

Beyond DNA color *Discover* v38 no7 p64 S 2017

BOOKS color *Discover* v38 no10 p18 D 2017

Did Lucy Fall and Not Get Up? color *Discover* v38 no1 p21 Ja/F 2017

Earthquakes color *Discover* v38 no4 p74 My 2017

A Happy Feat for Antarctica color *Discover* v38 no1 p75 Ja/F 2017

In Search of King Arthur's Roots color *Discover* v38 no1 p86 Ja/F 2017

A Leg Up on Arachnid Evolution color *Discover* v38 no1 p80 Ja/F 2017

More Hobbitses, Precious! color *Discover* v38 no1 p25 Ja/F 2017

The Origins of Dogs bw cartoon color graph map *Discover* v27 no10 p32 D 2016

Rain color *Discover* v38 no3 p74 Ap 2017

Rock-a-Bye Baby's Rocky Roots color *Discover* v38 no5 p66 Je 2017

SMACKDOWN! cartoon *Discover* v38 no1 p50 Ja/F 2017

Swamps color *Discover* v38 no5 p74 Je 2017

Traffic color *Discover* v38 no7 p74 S 2017

T. rex Evolution: Smarts First, Size Second color diag map *Discover* v38 no1 p42 Ja/F 2017

When Dinosaurs Went Bad bw color *Discover* v38 no4 p66 My 2017

When We Left Water bw color *Discover* v38 no6 p44 Jl/Ag 2017

Yoga color *Discover* v38 no6 p98 Jl/Ag 2017

Tarmy, James

40 and Under (and Underperforming) bw *Bloomberg Businessweek* no4502 p88 D 5 2016

And the Nominees For Best New Bill Are... color *Bloomberg Businessweek* no4502 p60 D 5 2016

Blurring the Clean Lines of MODERNISM color *Bloomberg Businessweek* no4533 p55 Ag 7 2017

The Castle Matchmaker bw color *Bloomberg Businessweek* no4536 p67 S 4 2017

Conrad Shawcross *Bloomberg Businessweek* no4530 p68 Jl 17 2017

Game of Kings color *Bloomberg Businessweek* no4539 p67 S 25 2017

In the Shadow Of a Bear color *Bloomberg Businessweek* no4541 p66 O 9 2017

MOVING TO: Munich color *Bloomberg Businessweek* no4531 p68 Jl 24 2017

Riots at the Museum color *Bloomberg Businessweek* no4539 p72 S 25 2017

Technicolor Dreams color *Bloomberg Businessweek* no4532 p66 Jl 31 2017

Tarn, Nathaniel

Gondwana and Other Poems *Publishers Weekly* v264 no20 p35 My 15 2017

Tarnawski, Miroslaw

Engineering extrinsic disorder to control protein activity in living cells bibl color *Science* v354 no6318 p1441 D 16 2016

Tarpley, Webster G.—Trials, litigation, etc.

WHO IS WEBSTER G. TARPLEY? B. Freed *Washingtonian Magazine* v52 no2 p20 N 2016

Tarpon fishing

A Conch's Life J. BROWNLEE color *Power & Motoryacht* v34 no7 p64 Jl 2017

TARR, D. ELLEN K.

Everything You Know about Being Rh-Negative Is Wrong *Skeptical Inquirer* v41 no3 p53 My/Je 2017

Tarr, Patricia

Defining quality in visual art education for young children: Building on the position statement of the Early Childhood Art Educators bibl *Arts Education Policy Review* v118 no3 p154 2017

Tarrant, Rhona

Abortion on the Agenda *America* v215 no16 p11 N 21 2016

Armagh Archbishop Martin contemplates changing times in Ireland color *America* v216 no4 p15 F 20 2017

Tarrant, Shira

LIGHTS. CAMERA. ACTION K. FORRESTER cartoon color *New Yorker* v92 no30 p64 S 26 2016

Tarselli, Michael A.

Artificial intelligence in research color *Science* v357 no6346 p28 Jl 7 2017

Research night owls color *Science* v354 no6315 p964 N 25 2016

Tart, Chris

Blending Skill Sets color *Downbeat* v84 no9 p16 S 2017

Lashes color *Downbeat* v83 no12 p70 D 2016

Marrying Genres color *Downbeat* v84 no3 p62 Mr 2017

Rubicon/Rumi Songs color *Downbeat* v83 no11 p66 N 2016

Tartaglia, Lawrence J.

Trispecific broadly neutralizing HIV antibodies mediate potent SHIV protection in macaques color graph *Science* v357 no6359 p85 O 6 2017

Tartakoff, Laura

Synagogues, Cemeteries, and Frontiers: Anti-Semitism in Switzerland *Society* v54 no1 p56 F 2017

Tartakovsky, Joseph

ZERO SHADES OF GRAY *Claremont Review of Books* v17 no2 p90 Spr 2017

Tartar, Andre

Brexit Could Hurt the Most Here graph map *Bloomberg Businessweek* no4527 p20 Je 19 2017

The Navigable Northwest Passage graph map *Bloomberg Businessweek* no4537 p73 S 11 2017

Outlook Where the Growth Is map *Bloomberg Businessweek* no4517 p17 Ap 3 2017

Tarte Inc.

Val's Guide to GORGEOUS V. Monroe color *O, The Oprah Magazine* p56 Jl 2017

Tarter, Brent

VERY TAXING TIMES M. Oppenheim color *American History* v52 no2 p70 Je 2017

Tarter, Jill

Jill Tarter: E.T. Whisperer, Possible Martian Descendant *Skeptical Inquirer* v41 no2 p12 Mr/Ap 2017

Tarttelin, Abigail

Modern Love bw color *Glamour* v115 no7 p94 Jl 2017

Tarvin, Rebecca D.

Interacting amino acid replacements allow poison frogs to evolve epibatidine resistance chart diag graph *Science* v357 no6357 p1261 S 22 2017

Tascent (Company)

BLINK OF AN EYE J. J. Roberts color *Fortune* v175 no4 p36 Mr 15 2017

Taschner, Rudolf

Fun and games C. J. Phillips color *Science* v357 no6359 p54 O 6 2017

TASER International Inc.

Forget the Taser, Says Taser K. Weise bw diag *Bloomberg Businessweek* no4518 p35 Ap 10 2017

Tash, Sarvenaz

The Geek's Guide to Unrequited Love *Publishers Weekly* v263 no49 p95 D 7 2016

Tashlin, Frank

A Funny Direction *USA Today Magazine* v145 no2858 p62 N 2016

Task, Aaron

The Trump Economy color *Fortune* v174 no8 p90 D 15 2016

Task forces

Idaho town stares down so-called Aryan church D. Struck *Christian Century* v134 no22 p19 O 25 2017

UNSUNG SAVIORS *Atlanta* v56 no9 p122 Ja 2017

Task performance

8 Android gestures that speed up everyday tasks B. PATTERSON color *PCWorld* v35 no1 p192 Ja 2017

Accomplish More by Committing to Less E. G. Saunders *Harvard Business Review Digital Articles* p2 Ja 30 2015

Manage Your Team's Attention J. Birkinshaw *Harvard Business Review Digital Articles* p2 Ja 29 2015

The Pros and Cons of Doing One Thing at a Time A. O'Connell *Harvard Business Review Digital Articles* p2 Ja 20 2015

Stop Trying to Please Everyone R. Ashkenas and M. McCreight *Harvard Business Review Digital Articles* p2 Jl 29 2015

Tasker, Elizabeth

Other Worlds: THE PLANET FACTORY: Exoplanets and the Search for a Second Earth S. N. JOHNSON-ROEHR *Sky & Telescope* v134 no6 p39 D 2017

The Planet Factory: Exoplanets And the Search for a Second Earth *Publishers Weekly* v264 no34 p100 Ag 21 2017

TASKER, KAITLIN

TEXAS IN-MIGRATION AND OUT-MIGRATION *Texas Monthly* v45 no2 p50 F 2017

TaskRabbit Inc.—Officials & employees

PERSON OF INTEREST K. Kokalitcheva color *Fortune* v174 no8 p40 D 15 2016

Tasks—Management

THINGS 3 color *Macworld - Digital Edition* p57 Je 13 2017

Tasler, Nick

Explain Your New Strategy By Emphasizing What It Isn't *Harvard Business Review Digital Articles* p2 My 18 2015

Stop Using the Excuse "Organizational Change Is Hard" *Harvard Business Review Digital Articles* p2 Jl 19 2017

You Don't Need Charisma to Be an Inspiring Leader *Harvard Business Review Digital Articles* p2 O 27 2015

Tasman, Abel Janszoon, ca. 1603-1659

1642: Batavia *Lapham's Quarterly* v10 no2 p55 Spr 2017

Tasmania

TWO TOWERS B. R. AND and M. SMITH-GOBAT color *Climbing* no349 p58 N 2016

Tasmanian devil

See also

Devil facial tumor disease

Benign Selection A. Braun *Natural History* v125 no1 p7 D 2016/Ja 2017

Weird but true! M. HARRIS and J. BEER color *National Geographic Kids* no465 p4 N 2016

Tasmanian devil—Diseases

New cancer strikes Tasmanian devils color *Science* v357 no6347 p112 Jl 14 2017

Tassels—Evaluation

Fringe Festival color *Martha Stewart Living* no275 p22 Je 2017

TRY THE TREND color *Better Homes & Gardens* v95 no10 p18 O 2017

TASSEY, GREGORY

A Technology-Based Growth Policy graph *Issues in Science & Technology* v33 no2 p80 Wint 2017

Taste

See also

Flavor

A MATTER OF TASTE D. DICKINSON chart color *Better Homes & Gardens* v95 no5 p98 My 2017

The Science of Making Food Taste Better T. John color *Time* v189 no5 p12 F 13 2017

Taste of Thai (Company)

Food & Drink *Virginia Living* p145 2017 Best 20of Virginia

Tata Power Delhi Distribution Ltd.

Rich Returns From Poor Women Collecting Debts B. Shrivastava and R. K. Singh color *Bloomberg Businessweek* no4541 p18 O 9 2017

Tata Teleservices Ltd.

The Prenup That Didn't Stick B. Einhorn, I. Marlow et al chart color *Bloomberg Businessweek* no4498 p25 N 7 2016

Tataria, Monika

New imaging center by women, for women *Successful Farming* v115 no1 p41 Ja 2017

Tate, Carson

Differing Work Styles Can Help Team Performance *Harvard Business Review Digital Articles* p2 Ap 3 2015

Your Team May Have Too Many Prioritizers and Planners *Harvard Business Review Digital Articles* p2 My 15 2015

Tate, Deborah

The Snacking Diaries color *Women's Health* v14 no2 p106 Mr 2017

Tate, Golden—Interviews

JUST MY TYPE D. Patrick and T. Keith color *Sports Illustrated* v125 no20 p28 D 19 2016

TATE, GREG

SNMAAHC in the Middle of the Mall color *ARTnews* v115 no4 p30 Wint 2016/2017

Wards Matter M. AGRESTA *Texas Monthly* v44 no12 p84 D 2016

'We the People . . .' *New York Times Magazine* p26 Mr 12 2017

Tate, James

DRIVE A WEDGE color *Car & Driver* v63 no5 p17 N 2017

Tate, James, 1943-2015

Inexhaustible & Brilliant C. Simic bw color *New York Review of Books* v64 no3 p26 F 23 2017

Tate, Jessica Jo

Here's How color diag graph *Practical Horseman* v45 no9 p66 S 2017

23 2016

Taubman, William, 1940-

Forces He Could Not Control: The biography of a transformational leader who was celebrated abroad, reviled at home P. BAKER *New York Times Book Review* p11 S 10 2017

Regime Change D. PRYCE-JONES *National Review* v69 no18 p35 O 2 2017

Taubman Museum of Art

SOUTHWEST REGION *Virginia Living* p114 2017 Best 20of Virginia

Taucer, Marco

Tailored semiconductors for high-harmonic optoelectronics graph *Science* v357 no6348 p303 Jl 21 2017

Taufer, Michela

Enhancing reproducibility for computational methods bibl color *Science* v354 no6317 p1240 D 9 2016

Taufour, V.

Discovery of orbital-selective Cooper pairing in FeSe diag *Science* v357 no6346 p75 Jl 7 2017

Tavakolian, Newsha

VACATION IN IRAN color map *New Yorker* v93 no10 p74 Ap 24 2017

Tavani, Rebecca

Positive biodiversity-productivity relationship predominant in global forests bibl chart graph map *Science* v354 no6309 paaf8957-1 O 14 2016

Tavares, Matt

Red & Lulu *Publishers Weekly* v264 no36 p94 S 4 2017

Tavares, Stephen

To Understand Whether Your Company Is Inclusive, Map How Your Employees Interact *Harvard Business Review Digital Articles* p2 Jl 19 2017

Tavassoli, Nader

Case Study: When You Have to Choose Between Core and New Customers: An extreme sports company considers a VIP tier il *Harvard Business Review* v95 no5 p143 S/O 2017

Case Study: When You Have to Choose Between Core and New Customers *Harvard Business Review Digital Articles* p2 Je 26 2017

Taverns (Inns)—Evaluation

Tavern Hotel N. AUSTIN *Arizona Highways* v92 no11 p14 N 2016

Taviani, Paolo, 1931-

Mother Tongue R. Brody color *New Yorker* v92 no45 p14 Ja 16 2017

TAVRIS, CAROL

Why We Believe--Long After We Shouldn't *Skeptical Inquirer* v41 no2 p51 Mr/Ap 2017

Tawada, Yoko, 1960-

Bear Hugs R. AUSUBEL *New York Times Book Review* p11 N 27 2016

IMAGINE THAT R. Galchen *New York Times Magazine* p66 O 30 2016

Tawfiq, Hisham

The Blacklist I. Rudolp *TV Guide* p37 Ap 17 2017

Tax administration & procedure—United States

Tax Reform For the Working Class H. OLSEN *National Review* v69 no9 p16 My 15 2017

Tax base

Five Paths for the EU D. GREEN color *Weekly Standard* v22 no28 p14 Mr 27 2017

Tax benefits

Cut Your Tax Bill Now S. BLOCK color *Kiplinger's Personal Finance* v70 no12 p36 D 2016

Tax collection—United States

Board of Confusion A. Greenblatt *Governing* v30 no10 p9 Jl 2017

Tax credits

See also

Earned income tax credit

"Drive Clean" at a Discount *New York State Conservationist* v71 no6 p28 Je 2017

Elements of a Blueprint for ACA Replacement O. Spurgeon, III *Parks & Recreation* v52 no3 p22 Mr 2017

The New Markets Tax Credit O. Spurgeon III *Parks & Recreation* v51 no11 p24 N 2016

The Right Way to Repeal M. Hemingway *Weekly Standard* v22

no26 p10 Mr 13 2017

Tax cuts

If They Only Had a Brain S. MOORE color *Weekly Standard* v22 no36 p16 My 29 2017

The U.S. Needs Tax Reform, Not Tax Cuts E. Toder *Harvard Business Review Digital Articles* p2 2017

Tax cuts—Economic aspects

WHY THE TRUMP TAX CUT SHOULD BE BIG AND BOLD S. FORBES *Forbes* v198 no9 p11 D 30 2016

Tax cuts—Texas

FIVE ISSUES TO WATCH *Texas Monthly* v45 no2 p89 F 2017

Tax cuts—United States

2017 INVESTMENT GUIDE [Cover story] color *Forbes* v198 no9 p87 D 30 2016

401(k) Interrupted A. EBELING color *Forbes* v199 no1 p58 Ja 24 2017

8 Money Moves Before the Ball Drops K. A. Renzulli color *Money* v45 no11 p26 D 2016

The Big 4 F. BARNES color *Weekly Standard* v23 no2 p14 S 18 2017

How should I handle a tax windfall that I don't want? K. KIPLINGER *Kiplinger's Personal Finance* v71 no3 p15 Mr 2017

Republican Heaven C. R. Morris cartoon *Commonweal* v144 no9 p6 My 19 2017

Sizing Up Trump's Tax Proposal L. Braham color graph *Bloomberg Businessweek* no4520 p42 My 1 2017

Tax Cuts. As Easy As ... P. Coy *Bloomberg Businessweek* no4521 p24 My 8 2017

A Taxing Debate R. L. BOROSAGE color *Nation* v305 no5 p3 Ag 28 2017

TRUMP THE IRS [Cover story] W. BALDWIN color graph *Forbes* v198 no9 p90 D 30 2016

Trump vows to cut the corporate tax rate from 35% to 15%. Suppose Republicans could raise $2 trillion to pay for cuts (not an easy task). That would require hiking other taxes or ending popular deductions. And it can't all go to corporate giants, so... S. Kapur and P. Coy *Bloomberg Businessweek* no4538 p34 S 18 2017

Untaxing the Rich R. PONNURU color *National Review* v69 no19 p21 O 16 2017

WHY THE TRUMP TAX CUT SHOULD BE BIG AND BOLD S. FORBES *Forbes* v198 no9 p11 D 30 2016

Tax deductions

HOW A BORDER TAX WOULD AFFECT YOU S. BLOCK color *Kiplinger's Personal Finance* v71 no5 p11 My 2017

Trim Your Tax Bill S. BLOCK color *Kiplinger's Personal Finance* v71 no12 p38 D 2017

Tax evasion

The Great Indian Tax Dodge of 2016 A. Antony *Bloomberg Businessweek* no4503 p14 D 12 2016

Research: Moral Appeals Can Help Reduce Tax Evasion K. Bott, A. W. Cappelen et al *Harvard Business Review Digital Articles* p2 Jl 20 2017

Tax evasion—International cooperation

Data Mining to Find Tax Cheaters D. Voreacos and C. Berthelsen color *Bloomberg Businessweek* no4524 p41 My 29 2017

Tax evasion—Prevention

Can Puerto Rico Corral Its Tax Dodgers? P. Laya, J. Levin et al color graph *Bloomberg Businessweek* no4524 p17 My 29 2017

Tax evasion—United States

All the President's LLCs L. Browning, J. McCormick et al color *Bloomberg Businessweek* no4534 p24 Ag 14 2017

Should I Turn In My Tax-Cheating Relative? K. A. Appiah *New York Times Magazine* p24 Ag 27 2017

Tax free exchanges

See also

Like kind exchange

ORCHESTRATING 1031 AND REVERSE 1031 EXCHANGES S. Williamson *Successful Farming* v115 no2 p16 F 2017

Tax havens

Could Puerto Rico Be the Next Tax Haven? T. Metcalf color *Bloomberg Businessweek* no4535 p28 Ag 28 2017

Tax incentives

See also

Tax credits

Where the Money Is M. Funkhouser *Governing* v30 no2 p4 N

Management p10 Ag 2017

Taxation of dividends

A Tax with a Twist: A novel idea to distribute carbon dividends that's both fair and workable G. P. Shultz and T. Halstead *Hoover Digest: Research & Opinion on Public Policy* no3 p73 Summ 2017

Taxation—China

Could Tesla Run Out of Gas in Hong Kong? B. Einhorn *Bloomberg Businessweek* no4517 p25 Ap 3 2017

Taxation—Europe

Europeans Cheer Move Toward Flexible VAT for E-books E. Nawotka color *Publishers Weekly* v264 no4 p8 Ja 23 2017

Taxation—India

The ABCs of India's GST U. Krishnan and J. Rodrigues color graph *Bloomberg Businessweek* no4496 p19 O 24 2016

One Tax To Rule Them All I. Marlow, E. Curran et al color *Bloomberg Businessweek* no4528 p28 Je 26 2017

Taxation—Japan

Changes On Tap for Japan's Beer Tax G. Huang, G. Reidy et al color *Bloomberg Businessweek* no4513 p29 Mr 6 2017

Taxation—Law & legislation

THE BANK *Texas Monthly* v45 no2 p92 F 2017

Taxation—Law & legislation—United States

JOHN MAYNARD TRUMP B. GREELEY bw *Bloomberg Businessweek* no4500 p44 N 21 2016

This Tax Do-Over Could Be Handy P. Wang color diag *Money* v46 no4 p26 My 2017

WHAT TO WATCH FOR IN TRUMP'S TAX PLAN T. Newmyer *Fortune* v75 no1 p14 Ja 1 2017

Taxation—Puerto Rico

Could Puerto Rico Be the Next Tax Haven? T. Metcalf color *Bloomberg Businessweek* no4535 p28 Ag 28 2017

Taxation—Societies, etc.

Delaware's Odd, Beautiful, Contentious, Private Utopia J. WALKER bw color *Reason* v49 no6 p62 N 2017

Taxation—Texas

On the Defensive A. Greenblatt *Governing* v31 no1 p9 O 2017

Taxation—United States

THE APPROVAL MATRIX Our deliberately oversimplified guide to who falls where on our taste hierarchies img *New York* v50 no9 p124 My 1 2017

COUNTING COINS J. J. Roberts *Fortune* v175 no5 p15 Ap 1 2017

Getting Tax Reform Done—and Done Right T. J. DONOHUE *Weekly Standard* v22 no27 p25 Mr 20 2017

Give Your Best K. A. Renzulli color diag *Money* v45 no11 p82 D 2016

The Great Pretender M. Konczal *Nation* v304 no17 p5 Je 5 2017

How Long to Hang on to Tax Records K. LANKFORD *Kiplinger's Personal Finance* v71 no5 p42 My 2017

How to Find a Home's Claims History K. LANKFORD color *Kiplinger's Personal Finance* v71 no10 p42 O 2017

IN BRIEF K. Stock color graph *Bloomberg Businessweek* no4540 p14 O 2 2017

It's the Corporate Tax Rate, Stupid T. MECIA graph *Weekly Standard* v23 no4 p10 O 2 2017

Republican Heaven C. R. Morris cartoon *Commonweal* v144 no9 p6 My 19 2017

Revising Retirement S. Woolley color *Bloomberg Businessweek* no4522 p43 My 15 2017

The Right Cure L. B. Lindsey color *Weekly Standard* v22 no23 p10 F 20 2017

Simplify, Simplify, Simplify F. BARNES color *Weekly Standard* v22 no30 p9 Ap 10 2017

The Smart Person's Guide To Paying Taxes J. Drucker color *Bloomberg Businessweek* no4494 p10 O 10 2016

Snuggly Vestments cartoon *Weekly Standard* v22 no25 p3 Mr 6 2017

Top Heavy C. R. Morris chart *Commonweal* v144 no5 p6 Mr 10 2017

Two Flawed Tax Plans R. PONNURU *National Review* v68 no20 p18 N 7 2016

WE COULD ALL HAVE BEEN CANADIANS A. GOPNIK cartoon *New Yorker* v93 no13 p79 My 15 2017

WHY DON'T WE HAVE MORE BILLIONAIRES? S. FORBES color *Forbes* v199 no3 p25 Mr 28 2017

Taxation—United States—History—21st century

33 WAYS TO CUT YOUR TAXES [Cover story] K. Mulhere, E. O'brien et al color diag *Money* v46 no2 p52 Mr 2017

HOW WASHINGTON TAX CUTS WILL AFFECT YOUR WALLET I. Salisbury color diag *Money* v46 no2 p60 Mr 2017

Taxation—United States—Law & legislation

That 'Huge' Tax Cut May Take a While T. Newmyer color *Fortune* v175 no4 p19 Mr 15 2017

Taxation—United States—States

Capitol Hardball A. Greenblatt color *Governing* v30 no11 p9 Ag 2017

STATE TAXES SPIRAL UPWARD S. BLOCK cartoon *Kiplinger's Personal Finance* v71 no1 p13 Ja 2017

Tax cuts—Charts, diagrams, etc.

ANATOMY OF A TRUMP TAX CUT C. Matthews diag *Fortune* v174 no8 p17 D 15 2016

Taxi (TV program)

It Is Not About Race cartoon *New Orleans Magazine* v51 no12 p22 O 2017

Taxi Driver (Film)

ALONE WITH YOU N. PINKERTON color *Film Comment* v53 no3 p33 My/Je 2017

Taxi service

D.C. Is Building an Uber-Fighting Test Lab J. Brustein color *Bloomberg Businessweek* no4524 p34 My 29 2017

Kiddie Car Service [Cover story] J. Bianchi color *Working Mother* v40 no2 p22 Je/Jl 2017

Uber's Travis Kalanick Shows How Growing Up Is Much Harder Than Simply Growing A. Lashinsky color *Time* v189 no24 p29 Je 26 2017

Taxicab design & construction

Flying Jet Taxis J. Zorthian color *Time* v189 no18 p25 My 15 2017

Taxicab drivers

THE ACCIDENTAL GETAWAY DRIVER P. KIX cartoon color *GQ: Gentlemen's Quarterly* v97 no5 p110 My 2017

Taxicab industry

The Taxi Industry Can Innovate, Too R. Mohammed *Harvard Business Review Digital Articles* p2 F 13 2015

Taxicabs

Kiddie Car Service [Cover story] J. Bianchi color *Working Mother* v40 no2 p22 Je/Jl 2017

Uber Fail [Cover story] K. Steinmetz, M. Vella et al color diag *Time* v189 no24 p22 Je 26 2017

Taxicabs—Sales & prices

POCKET PRICE GUIDE: Action Prices On Class 7 Day Cab Semitrucks chart *Successful Farming* v115 no7 p19 My 2017

Taxidermists

Joanna Suitors Taxidermist: A Putnam County artisan cutting it in a male-dominated industry L. Wright *Indianapolis Monthly* v40 no10 p48 Je 2017

What Makes a Creep? L. SCHLEY cartoon *Discover* v27 no10 p8 D 2016

Taxonomy

THE FALLACY FORK: Why It's time to Get Rid of Fallacy Theory M. BOUDRY *Skeptical Inquirer* v41 no5 p46 S/O 2017

Specimen collection crucial to taxonomy E. E. Gutiérrez and R. H. Pine bibl *Science* v355 no6331 p1275 Mr 24 2017

Taxpayer compliance

Research: Moral Appeals Can Help Reduce Tax Evasion K. Bott, A. W. Cappelen et al *Harvard Business Review Digital Articles* p2 Jl 20 2017

Tax rates & tables—Charts, diagrams, etc.

Overhauling the Tax Code H. S. Edwards color diag *Time* v188 no22-23 p28 N/D 2016

Tay, Alicia

Mapping the human DC lineage through the integration of high-dimensional techniques diag *Science* v356 no6342 p1044 Je 9 2017

Tay, Andy

Learning from rejections color *Science* v355 no6331 p1342 Mr 24 2017

Tay, Isabelle

AnD WHat a MasqUeRaDe H. Rolfe *Dance Spirit* v21 no1 p48 Ja 2017

Tayan, Brian

We Studied 38 Incidents of CEO Bad Behavior and Measured

Their Consequences *Harvard Business Review Digital Articles* p2 Je 9 2016

What It's Like to Be Owned by Berkshire Hathaway *Harvard Business Review Digital Articles* p2 D 14 2015

Why Is CEO Pay Rising? Maybe There Aren't Enough Good CEOs *Harvard Business Review Digital Articles* p2 O 5 2017

Tayeb-Fligelman, Einav

The cytotoxic Staphylococcus aureus PSMα3 reveals a cross-α amyloid-like fibril bibl color diag graph *Science* v355 no6327 p831 F 24 2017

Tayeh, Sonya

In the Books J. Ouellette bw color *Dance Spirit* v20 no9 p50 N 2016

Tayler, Christopher

LIKELY STORY *Harper's Magazine* v333 no1999 p84 D 2016

TAYLER, JEFFREY

Where the Waters Speak of Love *American Scholar* v86 no3 p5 Summ 2017

Tayler, Jon

12 ETA: RIGHT NOW color *Sports Illustrated* v126 no9 p60 Mr 27 2017

Biter Beware color *Sports Illustrated* v127 no1 p22 Jl 3 2017

CAN TREA TURNER SAVE THE STEAL? color diag *Sports Illustrated* v126 no14 p82 My 15-22 2017

Tayloe, R.

Observation of coherent elastic neutrino-nucleus scattering diag *Science* v357 no6356 p1123 S 15 2017

Taylor, Alison

We Shouldn't Always Need a "Business Case" to Do the Right Thing *Harvard Business Review Digital Articles* p2 S 19 2017

Taylor, Andrew

Model a modern log-grasping lift color *Model Railroader* v84 no6 p53 Je 2017

Taylor, Angela

Feminist Force color *Glamour* v115 no3 p38 Mr 2017

TAYLOR, APRIL

LET THE EXPERIMENTS BEGIN! color *Black Belt* v55 no4 p66 Je/Jl 2017

Taylor, Ashley P.

THE Magic OF Massage color *Dance Spirit* v21 no2 p32 F 2017

Taylor, Astra

Q&A: JESSICA BRUDER *Nation* v305 no9 p5 O 16 2017

Taylor, B. Kim

Alpine Escapes [Cover story] color *Vegetarian Times* v43 no2 p70 N/D 2016

Taylor, Barbara Brown

WRITERS' FEAST color *Christian Century* v134 no10 p30 My 10 2017

Taylor, Ben

Can AI Ever Be as Curious as Humans? color *Harvard Business Review Digital Articles* p2 Ap 5 2017

Taylor, Benjamin

Self-Portrait With Jack: Meeting Kennedy on that November day shapes a boy's world S. HARRIGAN *New York Times Book Review* p16 Jl 9 2017

Taylor, Bill

4 Kinds of Workplaces, and How to Know Which Is Best for You *Harvard Business Review Digital Articles* p2 Ap 10 2017

The 4 Leadership Styles, and How to Identify Yours *Harvard Business Review Digital Articles* p2 Ag 3 2016

5 Questions to Ask About Corporate Culture to Get Beyond the Usual Meaningless Blather *Harvard Business Review Digital Articles* p2 Je 1 2017

Amazon, Whole Foods, and the Future of the (Old) New Economy *Harvard Business Review Digital Articles* p2 Je 16 2017

The Best Entrepreneurs Are Missionaries, Not Mercenaries *Harvard Business Review Digital Articles* p2 Ap 11 2016

Companies Can't Be Great Unless They've Almost Failed *Harvard Business Review Digital Articles* p2 Mr 21 2016

How Domino's Pizza Reinvented Itself *Harvard Business Review Digital Articles* p2 N 28 2016

How One Fast-Food Chain Keeps Its Turnover Rates Absurdly Low *Harvard Business Review Digital Articles* p2 Ja 26 2016

How WD-40 Created a Learning-Obsessed Company Culture *Harvard Business Review Digital Articles* p2 S 16 2016

There's No Such Thing As an Average Business, Just Average

Ways to Do Business *Harvard Business Review Digital Articles* p2 Ag 11 2016

True Leaders Believe Dissent Is an Obligation bw *Harvard Business Review Digital Articles* p2 Ja 12 2017

What the Best Change Leaders Know, and Why They're So Hard to Copy *Harvard Business Review Digital Articles* p2 D 21 2016

Why Sports Are a Terrible Metaphor for Business bw *Harvard Business Review Digital Articles* p2 F 3 2017

Why the Future Belongs to Tough-Minded Optimists *Harvard Business Review Digital Articles* p2 Mr 3 2016

Will Wall Street (or the Rest of Us) Ever Learn? *Harvard Business Review Digital Articles* p2 Ap 10 2017

Write a Failure Résumé to Learn What Makes You Succeed *Harvard Business Review Digital Articles* p2 My 3 2016

Taylor, Brandon

Runyan and Taylor Nab USTRC's Chisholm Trail Classic #10 Win chart color *Team Roping Journal* p30 O 2017

Taylor, Brian

STILL CLIMBING J. WILLIAMS *Cincinnati Magazine* v50 no2 p22 N 2016

Taylor, Brian D.

The Russian Siloviki & Political Change *Daedalus* v146 no2 p53 Spr 2017

Taylor, Carolyn

HOW TO: Assemble a Sketch-Comedy Troupe From Scratch S. LISS img *New York* v50 no15 p63 Jl 24 2017

Taylor, Chris

BEWARE OF HAPPY MEMORIES color diag *Fortune* v175 no3 p40 Mr 1 2017

TIMES CHANGE, BUT 'GREEN' FUNDS KEEP GROWING color diag *Fortune* v176 no4 p48 S 15 2017

Untangling Dividend Stocks color diag *Fortune* v174 no8 p132 D 15 2016

WORLD'S 50 GREATEST LEADERS [Cover story] color *Fortune* v175 no5 p46 Ap 1 2017

Taylor, Claude

SOURCE OF DEBATE: Twitter star Claude Taylor says he has juicy inside info about Trump investigations. Should we take him seriously? B. Peterson *Washingtonian Magazine* v53 no1 p20 O 2017

TAYLOR, CORY

Dying while Alive color *Tricycle: The Buddhist Review* v27 no1 p86 Fall 2017

TAYLOR, CRAIG

Better Than Siberia color *New York Times Book Review* p10 S 25 2016

Steeled to the Storm: Jim Shepard's stories course toward crisis points, amid whipping winds and rising water *New York Times Book Review* p8 Mr 5 2017

Taylor, Dame Meg

A Sea of Islands: How a Regional Group of Pacific States Is Working to Achieve SDG 14 *UN Chronicle* v54 no1/2 p1 2017

Taylor, Dennis

Intimate Warfare: The True Story of the Arturo Gatti and Micky Ward Boxing Trilogy color *Publishers Weekly* v263 no42 p58 O 17 2016

Taylor, Derek

FOR GENERATIONS color *Powder* v45 no3 p40 N 2016

TAYLOR, ELAINE

Dump the Emotional Manure *USA Today Magazine* v145 no2860 p61 Ja 2017

Taylor, Elizabeth Dowling

Upwardly Minded L. O. GRAHAM *New York Times Book Review* p10 F 5 2017

Taylor, Elizabeth, 1932-2011

SUGAR Taylor *Interview* v46 no8 p128 O 2016

Taylor, Ella

Marjorie Prime color *Film Comment* v53 no4 p72 Jl/Ag 2017

TAYLOR, EMILY

AHEAD OF THE CURRENT color *Indianapolis Monthly* v41 no2 p68 S 2017

BRIDGE TO THE PAST color *Indianapolis Monthly* v41 no2 p70 S 2017

Broad RIPPLE color map *Indianapolis Monthly* v41 no2 p66 S 2017

CAN YOU DIG IT? diag *Indianapolis Monthly* v41 no2 p72 S

A DAM SHAME *Indianapolis Monthly* v41 no2 p64 S 2017

Downtown color map *Indianapolis Monthly* v41 no2 p73 S 2017

Farther Downstream color map *Indianapolis Monthly* v41 no2 p77 S 2017

Girls Gone Wild color *Indianapolis Monthly* v42 no2 p36 O 2017

GM STAMPING PLANT color map *Indianapolis Monthly* v41 no2 p75 S 2017

Hamilton COUNTY color map *Indianapolis Monthly* v41 no2 p63 S 2017

MAKING A SPLASH color *Indianapolis Monthly* v41 no2 p76 S 2017

Mounds STATE PARK color map *Indianapolis Monthly* v41 no2 p60 S 2017

Riverside PARK color map *Indianapolis Monthly* v41 no2 p68 S 2017

TOUR OF DOODY diag *Indianapolis Monthly* v41 no2 p65 S 2017

WHERE THE WILD THINGS ARE color *Indianapolis Monthly* v41 no2 p62 S 2017

THE White RIVER diag *Indianapolis Monthly* v41 no2 p59 S 2017

Taylor, F.

Seasonal exposure of carbon dioxide ice on the nucleus of comet 67P/Churyumov-Gerasimenko bibl bw graph *Science* v354 no6319 p1563 D 23 2016

Taylor, Fallon

Barrel Arc and Counter-Arc [Cover story] color *Horse & Rider* v55 no12 p25 D 2016

Fallon Taylor's Best Advice for Any Rider color *Horse & Rider* v56 no11 p118 N 2017

Taylor, Frank J.

THE PEOPLE NOBODY WANTS *Saturday Evening Post* v289 no3 p34 My/Je 2017

Taylor, G. Jeffrey

Formation of the Orientale lunar multiring basin bibl graph *Science* v354 no6311 p441 O 28 2016

Gravity field of the Orientale basin from the Gravity Recovery and Interior Laboratory Mission bibl graph *Science* v354 no6311 p438 O 28 2016

Taylor, Gabe

GABE TAYLOR T. Bird color *Snowboarder* v29 no2 p36 O 2016

Taylor, Henry

HENRY TAYLOR C. Moloney cartoon *Art in America* v104 no11 p125 D 2016

Taylor, Ian A.

A supramolecular assembly mediates lentiviral DNA integration bibl color *Science* v355 no6320 p1 Ja 6 2017

Taylor, J. Edward

Research: Refugees Can Bolster a Region's Economy *Harvard Business Review Digital Articles* p2 O 5 2016

Taylor, J. M.

Quantum correlations from a room-temperature optomechanical cavity color diag graph *Science* v356 no6344 p1265 Je 23 2017

Taylor, James E.—Interviews

Meet 'Mr. Diversity' James E. Taylor T. Townsend and K. MEEKS chart color *Black Enterprise* v47 no3 p43 O 2016

Taylor, Jared

Rise of the Alt-Right S. McCONNELL *American Conservative* v15 no6 p12 N/D 2016

Taylor, Jeremy

BLUEBIRD COUNTRY *New York State Conservationist* v71 no5 p6 Ap 2017

Taylor, Jessica L.

Mythic Frontiers: Remembering, Forgetting, and Profiting with Cultural Heritage Tourism *American Indian Quarterly* v41 no2 p187 Spr 2017

Taylor, Joan—Interviews

Desert Guardian W. Becktold *Sierra* v101 no4 p67 Jl/Ag 2016

Taylor, Joanne

Lee Rubin: Our mentor and role model *Science* v355 no6327 p806 F 24 2017

Taylor, John

TOP SHOTS chart color *Outdoor Life* v223 no9 p77 N 2016

Taylor, John D.

Profiles in Courage *Sierra* v102 no4 p4 Jl/Ag 2017

TAYLOR, JOHN M.

THE AMERICAN SIDE-BY-SIDE color *Outdoor Life* v224 no5 p72 Je/Jl 2017

Taylor, Justin

FLESH AND BLOOD *Harper's Magazine* v333 no1998 p87 N 2016

Taylor, Katherine

HUMANITARIANS E. Gent, N. Byrnes et al color il *MIT Technology Review* v120 no5 p62 S/O 2017

SOUTH OF THE WALL bw *Forbes* v199 no3 p74 Mr 28 2017

Taylor, Keeanga-Yamahtta—Interviews

Q&A: KEEANGA-YAMAHTTA TAYLOR S. Leonard bw *Nation* v304 no8 p5 Mr 13 2017

TAYLOR, KIMBALL

THE GOOD SAMARITAN bw color *Surfer* v57 no11 p44 D 2016

OF WAVES AND WHITE ELEPHANTS color *Surfer* v58 no4 p86 Ag 2017

SPIRIT ANIMAL bw color *Surfer* v57 no11 p54 D 2016

TAYLOR, KIMBERLY HAYES

In Our Cities bw color *Ebony* v72 no6 p32 Ap/My 2017

Taylor, Laini

Strange the Dreamer *Publishers Weekly* v264 no22 p63 My 29 2017

Taylor, Louise

Competition & Camaraderie in the Children's and Adult Amateur Jumper Championships *In Stride* v11 no6 p36 N 2016

Longeing Needs to Come Full Circle *In Stride* v12 no4 p14 Jl 2017

A Passion for Horses and Horsemanship Lead Alix Morrison to Gold *In Stride* v12 no1 p26 Ja 2017

Rachel Long Is Making a Splash *In Stride* v12 no2 p49 Mr 2017

Trainers Will Have 2 Tracks & 4 Levels for Certification *In Stride* v12 no3 p24 My 2017

Taylor, Maral

NEVER GOING BACK TO MY OLD SCHOOL bw color *American History* v52 no4 p67 O 2017

Taylor, Marcus J.

T cell costimulatory receptor CD28 is a primary target for PD-1–mediated inhibition color diag graph *Science* v355 no6332 p1428 Mr 31 2017

Taylor, Mark

A chemical genetic roadmap to improved tomato flavor bibl graph *Science* v355 no6323 p391 Ja 27 2017

Taylor, Mark R.

Railway Post Office color *Model Railroader* v84 no4 p22 Ap 2017

Taylor, Marquis

OUR 11TH ANNUAL APPRECIATION OF Angels AMONG US I. Aldrich and D. Smith color *Yankee* v80 no6 p130 N/D 2016

TAYLOR, MARYGRACE

Dr. Oz's favorite superfoods color *Redbook* p96 O 2017

Eat Clean, Stay Lean [Cover story] color *Prevention* v68 no11 p42 N 2016

Eat these for better sleep color *Redbook* p84 D 2016

Eat these for healthier eyes color *Redbook* p82 S 2017

Eat these to fight allergies cartoon *Redbook* p88 My 2017

Eat these to hit your perfect weight color *Redbook* p82 N 2017

Eat these to stress less cartoon *Redbook* p92 F 2017

Exactly how to FILL your PLATE color *Redbook* p90 Ap 2017

Fruit with huge health benefits color *Redbook* p72 Jl/Ag 2017

Herbs and spices with benefits cartoon *Redbook* p87 Mr 2017

Hive to Table color *Women's Health* v14 no3 p91 Ap 2017

Taylor, Matthew A.

Fabrication of fillable microparticles and other complex 3D microstructures color diag *Science* v357 no6356 p1138 S 15 2017

Taylor, Nike

Winning Pair C. SHMERLER *Tennis* v52 no6 p40 N/D 2016

Taylor, Otis

Otis Taylor: 'TRIUMPH IS THE KEY' J. Johnson color *Downbeat* v84 no4 p40 Ap 2017

Taylor, P. Craig

EXOTIC FORMS of SILICON *Physics Today* v69 no12 p34 D 2016

TAYLOR, PAUL

HERE'S LOOKING AT YOU, 2050 cartoon graph map *Foreign Policy* no222 p30 Ja/F 2017

TAYLOR, PETER SHAWN

Taylor, Zachary, 1784-1850
INTERESTING AND UPSETTING M. D. Köhn color *American History* v52 no2 p12 Je 2017

Taylor Made Golf Co. Inc.
Designated Drivers A. Shipnuck and C. Barrett color *Golf Magazine* v59 no3 p28 Mr 2017
DISTANCE BLADES M. Chwasky color *Golf Magazine* v59 no11 p82 N 2017

Taylor-Bubes, Nancy
HOW TO SELL A $12 MILLION HOUSE C. ALTER color *Washingtonian Magazine* v52 no7 p52 Ap 2017

Taylor-Joy, Anya, 1996-
STYLE CRUSH Anya Taylor-Joy S. Simon color *InStyle* v24 no4 p94 Ap 2017
Suit Yourself E. Wilson color *InStyle* v24 no6 p42 Je 2017

Taylor Perron, J.
Global drainage patterns and the origins of topographic relief on Earth, Mars, and Titan diag graph *Science* v356 no6339 p727 My 19 2017

Taylor Rhodes, M.
Regulation, Market Signals, and the Provision of Food Safety in Meat and Poultry *Amber Waves: The Economics of Food, Farming, Natural Resources, & Rural America* p1 My 2017

TAYLOR-VAISEY, NICK
FRIENDS OF GERRY bw *Maclean's* v130 no10 p28 N 2017
The perfect voters color *Maclean's* v129 no43 p33 O 31 2016
Wooing America color graph *Maclean's* v130 no8 p20 S 2017

Taylor-Washington, Lakya
Eliminating Grade Levels M. Jo Madda *Education Digest* v83 no2 p61 O 2017

Taymor, Julie, 1952-
Julie Taymor Flies Again R. MILZOFF img *New York* v50 no17 p130 Ag 21 2017

Tazzari, Marco
Spiral density waves in a young protoplanetary disk bibl graph *Science* v353 no6307 p1519 S 30 2016

Tchebakova, Nadja
Positive biodiversity-productivity relationship predominant in global forests bibl chart graph map *Science* v354 no6309 paaf8957-1 O 14 2016

Tcherniakov, Dmitri
THE MUSIC OF TIME NO 3: THE SOUND OF SILENCE: How and why did concert-going change from a raucous, noisy affair to one of hushed appreciation? A. Lee *History Today* v67 no9 p86 S 2017

Tchernichovski, Ofer
Encoding vocal culture bibl color *Science* v354 no6317 p1234 D 9 2016

Tci Auto (Company)
PARTS & STUFF color *Hot Rod* v70 no10 p100 O 2017

TD Bank NA
The BEST BANK FOR YOU M. Leonhardt, A. Adamczyk et al color diag map *Money* v45 no10 p86 N 2016

Tea
See also
Caffeine
Green tea
A Dish of Tea M. Kaufman *British Heritage Travel* v38 no4 p76 Jl/Ag 2017
GREAT GIFTS UNDER $20 color *Better Homes & Gardens* v95 no11 p16 N 2017
My LIST L. Christensen color *Harper's Bazaar* no3652 p106 Ap 2017
my style color *InStyle* v24 no3 p221 Mr 2017
Props has a Drinking Problem J. Duckworth *Stage Directions* v30 no4 p28 Ap 2017
TEA OFF: Inspirations for afternoon tea, that most Anglophilic of traditions E. L. Stubbs color *Virginia Living* v15 no5 p23 Ag 2017
Which Teas Are Healthiest? A. Levi color *Health* v31 no7 p151 S 2017

Tea & coffee services (Tableware)
Tiffany Applied Japanese Influence Coffee Set color *Magazine Antiques* v183 no6 p24 N/D 2016

Tea & health
ICED TEA color *Women's Health* v14 no5 p164 Je 2017

Tea, Michelle
Bohemian Fantasy L. TANENBAUM bw *New York Times Book Review* p18 S 25 2016

Tea advertising
The Sales of Summertime color *Consumer Reports* v82 no7 p67 Jl 2017

Tea Party movement (U.S.)
BACK TO BASICS A. GREENBLATT *Governing* v30 no6 p26 Mr 2017
Copy the Tea Party A. NABAUM *New Republic* v248 no3 p32 Mr 2017
The Tea Party Centrists: A lot of the governors elected as hardliners in 2010 have surprised their states A. Ehrenhalt *Governing* v30 no9 p14 Je 2017

Tea strainers—Evaluation
The Coffeeization of Tea C. MUHLKE color *GQ: Gentlemen's Quarterly* v86 no12 p108 D 2016

Teach Us All (Film)
TRANSFORMING THE NARRATIVE: The director and producer of Teach Us All on literacy's role in the fight for educational equity S. Lowman *Literacy Today (2411-7862)* v35 no1 p10 Jl/Ag 2017

Teacher burnout
Burnout factories M. Fusco color il *Phi Delta Kappan* v98 no8 p26 My 2017

Teacher burnout—Prevention
How to Beat Teacher Burnout: With More Education L. Farmer bw *Education Digest* v83 no2 p13 O 2017

Teacher certification
Putting paraeducators on the path to teacher certification J. Morrison and L. Lightner color *Phi Delta Kappan* v98 no8 p43 My 2017
Why make it hard for teachers to cross state borders? D. Goldhaber, C. Grout et al color il *Phi Delta Kappan* v98 no5 p55 F 2017

Teacher collaboration
The right network for the right problem L. M. Gomez, J. L. Russell et al color diag *Phi Delta Kappan* v98 no3 p8 N 2016

Teacher development
Alternatives to Workshops K. BAUM and D. KRULWICH *Education Digest* v82 no6 p38 F 2017
Microcredentials B. Berry, K. M. Airhart et al color il *Phi Delta Kappan* v98 no3 p34 N 2016
Promoting Student Academic Achievement Through Faculty Development about Inclusive Teaching M. E. Schmid, D. L. Gillian-Daniel et al *Change* v48 no5 p16 S/O 2016
Think Globally, Act Locally D. C. Paris *Change* v49 no4 p4 Jl/Ag 2017
To Develop Teachers, Look to Other Teachers A. A. Arnett *Education Digest* v83 no1 p50 S 2017
Volunteers boost careers support: Members share their HR expertise with local schools to help young people prepare for work *People Management* p56 Mr 2017

Teacher education
Backtalk S. van der Veen and E. M. Furtak color *Phi Delta Kappan* v98 no8 p80 My 2017
Community arts: (Re)contextualizing the narrative of teaching and learning R. H. Schlemmer bibl *Arts Education Policy Review* v118 no1 p27 2017
Cultivating a school-university partnership for teacher learning C. H. Reischl, D. Khasnabis et al color *Phi Delta Kappan* v98 no8 p48 My 2017
DOE Removes Requirements Around Selectivity to Diversify the Teaching Force J. MADER cartoon *Education Digest* v82 no6 p30 F 2017
The Editor's Note J. Richardson *Phi Delta Kappan* v98 no3 p4 N 2016
get more yj color *Yoga Journal* no290 p8 Mr 2017
Making teaching visible through learning opportunities B. A. Ermeling, R. Gallimore et al color *Phi Delta Kappan* v98 no8 p54 My 2017
The power and potential of teacher residencies R. Guha, M. E. Hyler et al color graph *Phi Delta Kappan* v98 no8 p31 My 2017
Shifting discourses in teacher education: Performing the advocate bilingual teacher B. Caldas bibl *Arts Education Policy Review* v118 no4 p190 2017
The Teacher Residency R. Guha, M. E. Hyler et al *Education Di-*

gest v83 no2 p38 O 2017

Teacher educators

Backtalk L. S. Goldstein diag *Phi Delta Kappan* v98 no6 p80 Mr 2017

BOYS ON THE SIDE N. PARSI color *Chicago* v66 no1 p31 Ja 2017

Teacher effectiveness

Backtalk J. Eckert *Phi Delta Kappan* v98 no3 p80 N 2016

Teacher evaluation

Coaching to Evaluate Teachers [Cover story] K. E. FOUAD *Islamic Horizons* v46 no2 p26 Mr/Ap 2017

Making teaching visible through learning opportunities B. A. Ermeling, R. Gallimore et al color *Phi Delta Kappan* v98 no8 p54 My 2017

Teacher evaluation methods

All sizzle and no steak A. Amrein-Beardsley and T. Geiger color graph il *Phi Delta Kappan* v99 no2 p53 O 2017

Teacher leadership

Helping Teachers Become Leaders E. Mack Trapanese *Education Digest* v83 no3 p37 N 2017

Observing peers develops practice, changes culture K. A. Reilly il *Phi Delta Kappan* v98 no6 p13 Mr 2017

Teacher pensions

For teachers, a better kind of pension plan M. A. Winters graph il *Phi Delta Kappan* v99 no2 p32 O 2017

Teacher recruitment

The power and potential of teacher residencies R. Guha, M. E. Hyler et al color graph *Phi Delta Kappan* v98 no8 p31 My 2017

Sticky schools A. Podolsky, T. Kini et al color graph *Phi Delta Kappan* v98 no8 p19 My 2017

The Teacher Residency R. Guha, M. E. Hyler et al *Education Digest* v83 no2 p38 O 2017

Teacher retirement

For teachers, a better kind of pension plan M. A. Winters graph il *Phi Delta Kappan* v99 no2 p32 O 2017

Teacher role

Helping Teachers Become Leaders E. Mack Trapanese *Education Digest* v83 no3 p37 N 2017

Teacher-student communication

THE ROOT OF CONNECTION J. Sanacore color *Literacy Today (2411-7862)* v34 no4 p8 Ja/F 2017

TEACHER TALK AS AN INSTRUCTIONAL TOOL: Tips for making use of the "third turn" E. Ford-Connors and D. A. Robertson *Literacy Today (2411-7862)* v35 no1 p34 Jl/Ag 2017

Teacher-student relationships

See also

Classroom environment

10 THINGS WE'RE TALKING ABOUT T. A. Christian color *Essence* v48 no2 p67 Je 2017

The big picture K. Marshall chart color diag *Phi Delta Kappan* v99 no2 p42 O 2017

Growing mastery in NYC J. Nolan chart color il *Phi Delta Kappan* v98 no3 p41 N 2016

How to Correct Your Teacher D. Lowry color *Black Belt* v55 no3 p24 Ap/My 2017

THE ROOT OF CONNECTION J. Sanacore color *Literacy Today (2411-7862)* v34 no4 p8 Ja/F 2017

Top of the Class D. Wilson color *New Orleans Magazine* v51 no9 p32 Jl 2017

Trauma and learning in America's classrooms S. Terrasi and P. C. de Galarce chart color graph *Phi Delta Kappan* v98 no6 p35 Mr 2017

Teacher-student relationships—Moral & ethical aspects

Love IN THE YOGA STUDIO S. Herrington color *Yoga Journal* no296 p40 N 2017

Teacher-student relationships—United States

OUT OF BOUNDS A. McCook color *Science* v355 no6323 p339 Ja 27 2017

Teachers

See also

Bilingual teachers

Black teachers

College teachers

Male teachers

Public school teachers

Reading teachers

Student teachers

back to SCHOOL color *Yoga Journal* no292 p51 Je 2017

Beauty Boss M. Santos color *Working Mother* v40 no2 p16 Je/Jl 2017

Chasing contentment J. Hanson Lasater color *Yoga Journal* no296 p14 N 2017

The Editor's Note J. Richardson *Phi Delta Kappan* v98 no4 p4 D 2016/Ja 2017

The Energizing Impact of Micro-Credentials in Kettle Moraine P. Deklotz *Education Digest* v82 no9 p24 My 2017

How Do You CHOOSE? color *Literacy Today (2411-7862)* v34 no6 p51 My/Je 2017

IF YOU'RE NOT MAKING MISTAKES, YOU'RE NOT LIVING N. OFFERMAN *Vital Speeches of the Day* v83 no8 p239 Ag 2017

IGNITING THE FLAME K. Lett *Literacy Today (2411-7862)* v35 no2 p12 S/O 2017

Kat Fowler M. RABBITT color *Yoga Journal* no296 p10 N 2017

Local Strategies: Creating and Nurturing Collaborative Communities of Practice D. Bauer, E. Beaulieu et al *Change* v49 no4 p20 Jl/Ag 2017

Make this the best year for every kid J. PRESS color *Redbook* p110 S 2017

Meet your next teacher: Carrie Owerko color *Yoga Journal* no294 p83 S 2017

Meet your next teacher: Shiva Rea [Cover story] color *Yoga Journal* no292 p83 Je 2017

Meria Carstarphen *Atlanta* v57 no2 p93 Je 2017

A MOST DESERVING RECOGNITION C. P. Clark *Literacy Today (2411-7862)* v35 no2 p2 S/O 2017

Q: For stress relief, what is your go-to practice or pose? A. Owens, C. Owerko et al color *Yoga Journal* no294 p14 S 2017

Rules of the Game: How to get more than just a medal out of competitions C. THOMPSON *Dance Magazine* v91 no10 p48 O 2017

Teachers are designers D. Henriksen and C. Richardson color il *Phi Delta Kappan* v99 no2 p60 O 2017

Tips for Getting the New School Year Rolling S. SOWERS *Education Digest* v82 no9 p49 My 2017

Whither the Faculty? M. J. Finkelstein, V. M. Conley et al *Change* v49 no4 p43 Jl/Ag 2017

Teachers Insurance & Annuity Association

Q&A: Roger Ferguson, CEO of TIAA bw cartoon *Bloomberg Businessweek* no4496 p54 O 24 2016

Teachers' unions—Illinois

The Other Chicago Teachers Union M. UETRICHT *In These Times* v41 no5 p10 My 2017

Teachers' unions—United States

The Media Wouldn't Look for the Union Label M. Continetti *Commentary* v143 no3 p64 Mr 2017

Teachers—Attitudes

One Key to Reducing School Suspension: A Little Respect S. D. SPARKS *Education Digest* v82 no4 p8 D 2016

Opening your door to research M. Zoch and A. D. David color *Phi Delta Kappan* v98 no3 p28 N 2016

Pathways to Adulthood J. KNOLL *Education Digest* v82 no4 p13 D 2016

Teachers—China

HERE A CITY SHALL BE WROUGHT: What's forgotten in China's time-lapse urbanism D. Brook color *Harper's Magazine* v335 no2005 p49 Je 2017

Teachers—Congresses

Attendees selected for 2017 Research Teachers Conference color *Science News* v192 no5 p28 S 30 2017

Teachers—Interviews

Funding Teachers' Dreams for Their Students S. MAUGHAN color *Publishers Weekly* v264 no34 p64 Ag 21 2017

Jill Franco A. BRANDT color *Cincinnati Magazine* v51 no1 p32 O 2017

Teachers—Malpractice

MEAN GIRLS: A committed team player is falsely accused of dealing drugs *People Management* p66 Je 2017

Teachers—Massachusetts

Natasha Rizopoulos color *Yoga Journal* no296 p83 N 2017

Teachers—Pensions

Highlighted & Underlined color *Phi Delta Kappan* v98 no7 p6

Ap 2017

Teachers—Pensions—Law & legislation

Highlighted & Underlined color *Phi Delta Kappan* v98 no7 p6 Ap 2017

Teachers—Societies, etc.

FROM TEACHER to leader S. Kaplan color *Literacy Today (2411-7862)* v34 no3 p44 N/D 2016

Teachers—Training of

Time for teacher learning, planning critical for school reform E. G. Merritt color *Phi Delta Kappan* v98 no4 p31 D 2016/Ja 2017

True Teaching Expertise B. MASCIO cartoon *Education Digest* v82 no4 p17 D 2016

Teachers—United States

Attendees selected for 2017 Research Teachers Conference color *Science News* v192 no5 p28 S 30 2017

GOLF Magazine's Top 100 Teachers in America D. DeNunzio color *Golf Magazine* v59 no3 p56 Mr 2017

Teachers receive $100,000 in STEM Research Grants color *Science News* v192 no1 p28 Ag 5 2017

Teaching

See also

Direct instruction

Questioning

Teacher-student relationships

ALL IN A Day's Work color *Reader's Digest* v189 no1129 p60 Ap 2017

Highlighted & Underlined J. Richardson color *Phi Delta Kappan* v98 no8 p6 My 2017

Let's be honest color *Yoga Journal* no295 p12 O 2017

Meet your next teacher Colleen Saidman Yee [Cover story] color *Yoga Journal* no295 p85 O 2017

The Right Way to Do Redos R. WORMELI *Education Digest* v82 no9 p29 My 2017

seekers WANTED C. GORRELL color *Yoga Journal* no288 p15 D 2016

TEACHING A PEDAGOGY OF PEACE: Starting a dialogue by engaging one's differences A. O'Donnell *Literacy Today (2411-7862)* v35 no2 p38 S/O 2017

Teaching personal initiative beats traditional training in boosting small business in West Africa F. Campos, M. Frese et al chart graph *Science* v357 no6357 p1287 S 22 2017

Transcending Apathy Towards Writing: A Love Letter to Henry David Thoreau C. O'Sullivan Sachar *Change* v49 no4 p55 Jl/Ag 2017

True Teaching Expertise B. MASCIO cartoon *Education Digest* v82 no4 p17 D 2016

Valuing differences: B. Rentenbach, L. Prislovsky et al color *Phi Delta Kappan* v98 no8 p59 My 2017

What I Know for Sure O. Winfrey color *O, The Oprah Magazine* p140 S 2017

WHAT IT TAKES TO TEACH T. EICHENSEHER color *Yoga Journal* no287 p48 N 2016

Your True Stories IN 100 WORDS A. ASHBY, P. RAE et al color *Reader's Digest* v189 no1131 p32 Je 2017

Teaching aids & devices

Buyer — Be informed B. Noll color il *Phi Delta Kappan* v98 no4 p60 D 2016/Ja 2017

DIGITAL COLLABORATORS B. Cook color *Literacy Today (2411-7862)* v34 no4 p28 Ja/F 2017

Teaching awards

Top of the Class D. Wilson color *New Orleans Magazine* v51 no9 p32 Jl 2017

YEAR IN REVIEW: Catching up with some of our ILA 30 Under 30 honorees M. C. Ciccarelli *Literacy Today (2411-7862)* v35 no2 p14 S/O 2017

Teaching experience

Literature by Degree B. MARKOVITS *New York Times Book Review* p15 Mr 12 2017

Teaching hospitals

Teaching Hospitals Are the Best Place to Test Health Innovation L. A. Shapiro and C. M. Angelo *Harvard Business Review Digital Articles* p2 N 21 2014

Teaching methodology

See also

Teaching methods

BUILDING A COMMUNITY OF LIFELONG LEARNING T.

McKAY color *Phi Kappa Phi Forum* v97 no2 p10 Summ 2017

Moving readers from struggling to proficient D. Wolter color *Phi Delta Kappan* v99 no1 p37 S 2017

Teaching methods

See also

Direct instruction

Group work in education

CONFESSION: BEFORE I WAS T. TALIAFERRO *Texas Monthly* v45 no8 p14 Ag 2017

EDUCATIONAL options JULIE YOUNG *Indianapolis Monthly* v40 no3 p107 N 2016

Getting better together K. MacConnell and S. Caillier color il *Phi Delta Kappan* v98 no3 p16 N 2016

Teaching office of the Catholic Church

Can Catholics dissent from Pope Francis' teaching on the family? Wrong question P. Folan color *America* v216 no8 p36 Ap 17 2017

Teaching—Standards

How to Turn Around a Failing School A. Hill, L. Mellon et al *Harvard Business Review Digital Articles* p2 Ag 5 2016

Teaching—United States

RECOGNIZE, RESIST, REPORT J. REEVES cartoon *Reason* v49 no1 p38 My 2017

TEACHOUT, TERRY

Broadway's Tiny Giant *Commentary* v143 no4 p49 Ap 2017

Class Act color *National Review* v68 no19 p46 O 24 2016

The Darkness of Hank Williams *Commentary* v143 no2 p49 F 2017

The Great Man That Was Toscanini *Commentary* v144 no2 p48 S 2017

Is It Here to Stay? Rock'n'roll considered *Commentary* v142 no2 p66 S 2016

Jack Benny's Comic Program *Commentary* v144 no3 p56 O 2017

'Masterpieces' Without Masters *Commentary* v142 no1 p56 Jl/Ag 2016

Orchestras and Nazis: When music could not transcend evil *Commentary* v144 no1 p58 Jl/Ag 2017

Remember These Forgotten Men *Commentary* v143 no1 p58 Ja 2017

The Tragic Trumpeter *Commentary* v143 no6 p52 Je 2017

A Troubadour in the Age of Trump *Commentary* v142 no5 p51 D 2016

The Two Billie Holidays *Commentary* v140 no2 p66 S 2015

Two Kinds Of People bw *National Review* v69 no16 p41 Ag 28 2017

Van Cliburn, To Russia With Love *Commentary* v142 no3 p50 O 2016

Waitresses and Witches: Broadway's new formula for success *Commentary* v142 no4 p49 N 2016

Teachout, Zephyr

HER REVOLUTION Zephyr Teachout S. JAFFE bw color *Nation* v303 no20 p12 N 14 2016

In Foreign Pay color *Nation* v304 no4 p21 F 6 2017

PRO CANVASSER C. Bethea cartoon *New Yorker* v93 no10 p38 Ap 24 2017

Tea—Evaluation

The Coffeeization of Tea C. MUHLKE color *GQ: Gentlemen's Quarterly* v86 no12 p108 D 2016

ONE FRESH CUP color *Good Housekeeping* v264 no3 p160 Mr 2017

Teague, Matthew

RACING THE STORM *Smithsonian* v48 no4 p64 Jl/Ag 2017

the SWEETNESS of AN AGE color *Southern Living* v52 no9 p100 S 2017

Teague, Richard

Shoestring Styling T. Taylor bw *Hot Rod* v70 no9 p90 S 2017

Tea—History

It's Always Time for Tea C. Hopley *British Heritage Travel* v38 no1 p68 Ja/F 2017

Tea's Noble Afternoon Ritual M. Kaufman color *British Heritage Travel* v38 no5 p76 S/O 2017

TEAL, TRACY K.

Skills and Knowledge for Data-Intensive Environmental Research *BioScience* v67 no6 p546 Je 2017

Teale, William

Mission Impossible *Literacy Today (2411-7862)* v34 no6 p6 My/

Je 2017

Teall, Geoff

Are You Qualified Just Because You Qualified? *In Stride* v12 no1 p48 Ja 2017

Team building

The Benefits of Unplugging as a Team Z. First *Harvard Business Review Digital Articles* p2 Ap 8 2015

How to Plan a Team Offsite That Actually Works B. Dattner *Harvard Business Review Digital Articles* p2 Je 25 2015

How U.S. Army Basic Training Turns Diverse Groups into Teams R. Farnell *Harvard Business Review Digital Articles* p2 Jl 18 2016

Team roping

THE ADVANTAGES OF YEAR-ROUND ROPING K. Santos color *Spin to Win Rodeo* v20 no11 p34 Ja 2017

(At home with) G. R. SCHIAVINO color *Team Roping Journal* p44 O 2017

THE BAR JUST KEEPS BEING RAISED K. Santos color *Spin to Win Rodeo* v20 no11 p26 Ja 2017

BFI BOUND color *Spin to Win Rodeo* v21 no3 p12 My 2017

BIG REACH color *Spin to Win Rodeo* v20 no12 p16 F 2017

BUCKLE UP C. Toy color *Spin to Win Rodeo* v21 no3 p17 My 2017

BUCKLE UP G. Rogers and C. Toy *Spin to Win Rodeo* v21 no2 p19 Ap 2017

Caldwell Kings color *Team Roping Journal* p22 O 2017

CASE CLOSED color *Spin to Win Rodeo* v21 no2 p60 Ap 2017

THE CASTRO BROTHERS B. Welch bw *Spin to Win Rodeo* v21 no2 p96 Ap 2017

COUSINS TRAVIS AND CHASE TRYAN WIN SAN ANGELO color *Spin to Win Rodeo* v21 no2 p20 Ap 2017

FIVE FLAT C. Toy color *Spin to Win Rodeo* v21 no2 p33 Ap 2017

FREEZE FRAME C. Toy color *Spin to Win Rodeo* v21 no2 p44 Ap 2017

Freeze Frame Junior Nogueira color *Team Roping Journal* p70 O 2017

FREEZE FRAME WITH JUSTIN DAVIS C. Toy color *Spin to Win Rodeo* v21 no4 p42 Je 2017

FREEZE FRAME WITH LEVI SIMPSON C. Toy color *Spin to Win Rodeo* v20 no12 p44 F 2017

GAME PLAN for Gaining Success J. Barnes and K. Santos color *Team Roping Journal* p54 S 2017

GETTING STARTED ON THE RIGHT (ROPING) FOOT J. BARNES color *Spin to Win Rodeo* v21 no2 p38 Ap 2017

GETTING THE MOST OUT OF EVERY HORSE C. O. COOPER color *Spin to Win Rodeo* v21 no2 p46 Ap 2017

GOLD RUSH [Cover story] K. Santos color *Spin to Win Rodeo* v21 no4 p56 Je 2017

GO-TO GIRL S. Sorensen chart color *Team Roping Journal* p64 S 2017

HANDLES ARE SPEEDING UP WITH THE TIMES K. Santos color *Spin to Win Rodeo* v20 no12 p38 F 2017

HAPPY BIRTHDAY [Cover story] K. Santos color *Spin to Win Rodeo* v21 no1 p54 Mr 2017

Hass Takes Aim in Two Events K. Santos color *Spin to Win Rodeo* v21 no5 p22 Jl 2017

Hockin' Nation [Cover story] J. Mankin color *Spin to Win Rodeo* v21 no4 p50 Je 2017

IN IT FOR THE LONG HAUL K. Santos color *Spin to Win Rodeo* v21 no1 p38 Mr 2017

Knowing How to Win K. Driggers color *Team Roping Journal* p74 O 2017

LEARNING BY WATCHING AND LISTENING TO OTHERS [Cover story] K. Santos color *Spin to Win Rodeo* v21 no4 p44 Je 2017

MAKING IT HAPPEN color *Spin to Win Rodeo* v21 no2 p16 Ap 2017

Match Made in Houston C. Toy color *Spin to Win Rodeo* v21 no3 p54 My 2017

MAXIMIZING THE BENEFITS of Minimal Practice C. O'Brien and K. Santos color *Team Roping Journal* p56 S 2017

No-Nonsense Soundness C. Shaffer color *Team Roping Journal* p80 S 2017

NTR Finals Cap Off Arizona Winter color *Spin to Win Rodeo* v21 no3 p18 My 2017

OUT OF TOWNERS color *Spin to Win Rodeo* v21 no2 p14 Ap

2017

Patience and Perseverance Pay for Long K. Santos color *Spin to Win Rodeo* v21 no4 p28 Je 2017

Raising the Bar [Cover story] C. Shaffer color *Team Roping Journal* p82 S 2017

Small Shifts Gears from Steers to School K. Santos *Spin to Win Rodeo* v21 no2 p30 Ap 2017

STRAIT Chemistry J. Mankin color *Spin to Win Rodeo* v21 no3 p60 My 2017

Swing Consistency T. Graves and C. Shaffer color *Team Roping Journal* p58 O 2017

Thorp Thrives on Team Roping K. Santos *Spin to Win Rodeo* v21 no3 p30 My 2017

Tierney Trifecta at the Timed Event K. Santos color *Spin to Win Rodeo* v21 no3 p64 My 2017

Truman House A. Gentry color *Spin to Win Rodeo* v21 no3 p28 My 2017

THE USTRC NATIONAL FINALS REMIX D. Gentry *Team Roping Journal* p10 S 2017

WHAT'S YOUR NUMBER A. Gentry color *Spin to Win Rodeo* v20 no9 p22 N 2016

WHAT'S YOUR NUMBER? A. Gentry color *Spin to Win Rodeo* v21 no4 p26 Je 2017

WHAT'S YOUR NUMBER? C. Toy color *Spin to Win Rodeo* v21 no2 p28 Ap 2017

WHAT'S YOUR NUMBER with LORIE PATTERSON A. Gentry color *Spin to Win Rodeo* v20 no10 p30 D 2016

WORLD SERIES FINALE XI B. WELCH color *Spin to Win Rodeo* v20 no11 p56 Ja 2017

Wrangler TRC color *Spin to Win Rodeo* v20 no10 p28 D 2016

YOUNG GUNS C. Toy color *Spin to Win Rodeo* v21 no2 p24 Ap 2017

Team roping—Awards

YOU PICKED 'EM! [Cover story] B. WELCH and C. TOY color *Spin to Win Rodeo* v20 no12 p54 F 2017

Team roping—Competitions

ABNEY AND KELLER BANK color *Team Roping Journal* p26 O 2017

BUCKLE UP with Clint Summers K. Gustave color *Team Roping Journal* p22 S 2017

CANADIAN CASH color *Team Roping Journal* p10 O 2017

FALL FIGHT to the finish J. Barnes and K. Santos color *Team Roping Journal* p48 O 2017

Going, Going, Gone K. Santos color *Team Roping Journal* p84 O 2017

GO-TO GIRL B. Cannizzaro chart color *Team Roping Journal* p56 O 2017

Iconic Moments in US Finals History C. Shaffer color *Team Roping Journal* p90 O 2017

IVY AND HAWKINS GET A GRIPP K. Gustave chart color *Team Roping Journal* p18 O 2017

LEGENDARY CONNECTION color *Team Roping Journal* p12 O 2017

LIFELONG PASSION J. Mankin color *Team Roping Journal* p52 O 2017

LONE-STAR STATE OF MIND color *Team Roping Journal* p8 O 2017

NOT TOO SHABBY color *Spin to Win Rodeo* v20 no12 p15 F 2017

Runyan and Taylor Nab USTRC's Chisholm Trail Classic #10 Win chart color *Team Roping Journal* p30 O 2017

SHARP SHOOTING color *Spin to Win Rodeo* v21 no1 p15 Mr 2017

USTRC Midwest Regional Finals Wrap Up chart color *Team Roping Journal* p36 O 2017

Why do I rope? G. Miller color *Team Roping Journal* p152 O 2017

The World of TEAM ROPING G. R. Schiavino chart color map *Team Roping Journal* p96 O 2017

Team roping—Equipment & supplies

NEW PRODUCTS color *Spin to Win Rodeo* v21 no2 p26 Ap 2017

NEW PRODUCTS color *Spin to Win Rodeo* v21 no3 p26 My 2017

Team sports

See also

Baseball

Basketball

Soccer

Volleyball

Strength IN NUMBERS A. FRIEDMAN *Tennis* v53 no4 p56 Jl/ Ag 2017

There's No 'I' in Tone House J. Kelly color *Bloomberg Businessweek* no4528 p72 Je 26 2017

Team roping—Societies, etc.

Iconic Moments in US Finals History C. Shaffer color *Team Roping Journal* p90 O 2017

Teams

> *See also*
>
> Sports teams
>
> Team building
>
> Teams in the workplace

Great Leaders Can Think Like Each Member of Their Team B. Uzzi *Harvard Business Review Digital Articles* p2 Jl 8 2015

Teams in the workplace

> *See also*
>
> Brainstorming
>
> Self-directed work teams
>
> Task forces

3 Improv Exercises That Can Change the Way Your Team Works T. Yorton *Harvard Business Review Digital Articles* p2 Mr 9 2015

3 Things the Most Creative Leaders Do T. Kelley *Harvard Business Review Digital Articles* p2 D 10 2015

3 Ways Leaders Accidentally Undermine Their Teams' Creativity D. Burkus *Harvard Business Review Digital Articles* p2 Jl 7 2015

3 Ways to Encourage Smarter Teamwork J. Whitehurst *Harvard Business Review Digital Articles* p2 S 7 2015

A 4-Step Process to Help Senior Teams Prioritize Decisions P. Hopper and J. Sakuja color *Harvard Business Review Digital Articles* p2 Mr 27 2017

75% of Cross-Functional Teams Are Dysfunctional B. Tabrizi *Harvard Business Review Digital Articles* p2 Je 23 2015

8 Ways to Get a Difficult Conversation Back on Track M. Valcour *Harvard Business Review Digital Articles* p2 My 22 2017

The Ballooning Executive Team J. Neatby *Harvard Business Review Digital Articles* p2 Jl 21 2016

Being a Strategic Leader Is About Asking the Right Questions L. Lai color *Harvard Business Review Digital Articles* p2 Ja 18 2017

Create a "Mastermind Group" to Help Your Career D. Clark *Harvard Business Review Digital Articles* p2 Ag 13 2015

CULTURED TO EXCEL T. VELOCCI color *Forbes* v198 no9 p38 D 30 2016

Debriefing: A Simple Tool to Help Your Team Tackle Tough Problems D. Sundheim *Harvard Business Review Digital Articles* p2 Jl 2 2015

Develop Your Company's Cross-Functional Capabilities P. Leinwand, C. Mainardi et al *Harvard Business Review Digital Articles* p2 F 2 2016

Does Diversity Actually Increase Creativity? T. Chamorro-Premuzic *Harvard Business Review Digital Articles* p2 Je 28 2017

The Emotional Impulses That Poison Healthy Teams A. McKee *Harvard Business Review Digital Articles* p2 Jl 16 2015

An Experiment in Enlivening Stagnant Teams P. Wadors *Harvard Business Review Digital Articles* p2 Jl 3 2015

GE's Real-Time Performance Development L. Baldassarre and B. Finken *Harvard Business Review Digital Articles* p2 Ag 12 2015

Get Rid of Unhealthy Competition on Your Team A. C. Edmondson *Harvard Business Review Digital Articles* p2 Je 26 2015

Great Teams Need Social Intelligence, Equal Participation, and More Women C. R. Sunstein and R. Hastie *Harvard Business Review Digital Articles* p2 D 16 2014

Help Your Overwhelmed, Stressed-Out Team J. Mosow *Harvard Business Review Digital Articles* p2 Ja 16 2015

Help Your Team Agree on How They'll Collaborate M. Shapiro *Harvard Business Review Digital Articles* p2 S 8 2015

Help Your Team Spend Time on the Right Things R. Ashkenas and A. McDougall *Harvard Business Review Digital Articles* p2 O 23 2014

Hire the Best People, and Let Them Work from Wherever They Are C. Frangos *Harvard Business Review Digital Articles* p2 F 8 2016

How Structured Debate Helps Your Team Grow B. Dattner *Harvard Business Review Digital Articles* p2 D 10 2015

How to Boost Your Team's Productivity R. Knight *Harvard Business Review Digital Articles* p2 Ja 29 2016

How to Break Through Deadlock on Your Team R. Schwarz *Harvard Business Review Digital Articles* p2 Jl 7 2015

How to Build Trust on Your Cross-Cultural Team A. Molinsky and E. Gundling *Harvard Business Review Digital Articles* p2 Je 28 2016

How to Capture Value from Collaboration, Especially If You're Skeptical About It H. K. Gardner and H. Ibarra *Harvard Business Review Digital Articles* p2 My 2 2017

How to Get Experts to Work Together Effectively S. Kudaravalli, S. Faraj et al *Harvard Business Review Digital Articles* p2 My 10 2017

How to Get Your Team to Follow Through After a Meeting P. Axtell color *Harvard Business Review Digital Articles* p2 Mr 30 2017

How to Give Feedback to Someone Who Gets Crazy Defensive H. Weeks *Harvard Business Review Digital Articles* p2 Ag 12 2015

How to Handle a Disagreement on Your Team J. Brett and S. B. Goldberg *Harvard Business Review Digital Articles* p2 Jl 10 2017

How to Make a Team of Stars Work C. Fernández-Aráoz *Harvard Business Review Digital Articles* p2 Jl 17 2015

How to Manage a Narcissist M. F. R. Kets de Vries *Harvard Business Review Digital Articles* p2 My 10 2017

How to Manage a Team of B Players T. Chamorro-Premuzic *Harvard Business Review Digital Articles* p2 Jl 13 2015

How to Plan a Team Offsite That Actually Works B. Dattner *Harvard Business Review Digital Articles* p2 Je 25 2015

How to Pull Your Company Out of a Tailspin C. Zook *Harvard Business Review Digital Articles* p2 S 8 2016

How to Put the Right Amount of Pressure on Your Team L. Davey *Harvard Business Review Digital Articles* p2 Jl 1 2016

How to Work with Someone Who Isn't a Team Player C. O'Hara *Harvard Business Review Digital Articles* p2 Ap 21 2017

If Your Team Agrees on Everything, Working Together Is Pointless L. Davey color *Harvard Business Review Digital Articles* p2 Ja 31 2017

Improving Customer Satisfaction with Simple Analytics P. Jain *Harvard Business Review Digital Articles* p2 N 17 2015

Improving On-the-Fly Teamwork in Health Care M. Valentine and A. C. Edmondson *Harvard Business Review Digital Articles* p2 N 30 2016

Innovate Without Diluting Your Core Idea J. Campbell *Harvard Business Review Digital Articles* p2 Mr 25 2015

In the Best Sales Teams, About Half of the People Are in Support Roles M. Viertler, D. Sprengel et al *Harvard Business Review Digital Articles* p2 My 25 2016

Is Your Team Coordinating Too Much, or Not Enough? R. Schwarz *Harvard Business Review Digital Articles* p2 Mr 23 2017

Keep Employees from Leaving by Emphasizing Teamwork C. Fernández-Aráoz and R. Vasudeva *Harvard Business Review Digital Articles* p2 N 7 2016

The Kinds of Teams Health Care Needs A. C. Edmondson *Harvard Business Review Digital Articles* p2 D 16 2015

The Leadership Behaviors That Make or Break a Global Team D. Champion *Harvard Business Review Digital Articles* p2 Je 22 2015

Make Sure Your Team's Workload Is Divided Fairly R. Knight *Harvard Business Review Digital Articles* p2 N 14 2016

A Manager's Job Is Making Sure Employees Have a Life Outside Work A. D. Arora and R. Frey *Harvard Business Review Digital Articles* p2 Mr 25 2016

Managing a Team That's Been Asked to Do Too Much L. Davey color *Harvard Business Review Digital Articles* p2 Ja 9 2017

Measure Your Team's Intellectual Diversity *Harvard Business Review Digital Articles* p2 My 21 2015

My Competitiveness Was Hurting My Sales Team. Here's How I Realized It R. Harris *Harvard Business Review Digital Articles* p2 S 29 2017

Overcome Your Biases and Build a Great Team R. Gupta *Harvard Business Review Digital Articles* p2 D 25 2014

THE OVERCOMMITTED ORGANIZATION: WHY IT'S HARD TO SHARE PEOPLE ACROSS MULTIPLE TEAMS—AND

How You Define the Problem Determines Whether You Solve It
A. Markman color *Harvard Business Review Digital Articles* p2
Je 6 2017

THE HUSTLE M. HANSEN bw color *Powder* p72 S 2017

IGNORANCE WAS BLISS S. Manguso bw *O, The Oprah Magazine* p32 D 2016

In Defense Of Robots R. D. ATKINSON *National Review* v69
no7 p35 Ap 17 2017

Informational overload? P. Nielsen color *Sail* v48 no5 p4 My 2017

Innovation Isn't the Answer to All Your Problems S. Anthony, D.
S. Duncan et al *Harvard Business Review Digital Articles* p2
Je 2 2015

Invention Ambassadors take on society's challenge color *Science*
v357 no6353 p766 Ag 25 2017

The iPhone's Home button is gone: What's next to go? D. MOREN
color *Macworld - Digital Edition* v34 no11 p56 N 2017

IT'S AN INDUSTRY THING P. D'ORLÉANS *Cycle World* v56
no7 p26 Ag 2017

It's Time to Bury the Idea of the Lone Genius Innovator G. Satell
Harvard Business Review Digital Articles p2 Ap 6 2016

Let's Stop Arguing About Whether Disruption Is Good or Bad G.
Satell *Harvard Business Review Digital Articles* p2 My 21 2015

The List color *MIT Technology Review* v120 no4 p56 Jl/Ag 2017

Many CEOs Aren't Breakthrough Innovators (and That's OK) F.
Barber and J. Bistrova *Harvard Business Review Digital Articles* p2 S 4 2015

The Many Ways to Innovate M. Fischetti diag *Scientific American*
v315 no5 p80 N 2016

A moonlit trek V. Ingurgio bibl color *Science* v355 no6323 p358
Ja 27 2017

The More We Learn, the More We Grow S. ECKELBERRY *Parks
& Recreation* v51 no11 p6 N 2016

MOST PROMISING TECHNOLOGY E. Tingwall and D. Beard
cartoon color diag *Car & Driver* v62 no7 p28 Ja 2017

THE MYTH OF TECHNOLOGICAL UNEMPLOYMENT D. N.
MCCLOSKEY color *Reason* v49 no4 p8 Ag/S 2017

Nearly Half of Companies Say They Don't Have the Digital Skills
They Need J. Goldman *Harvard Business Review Digital Articles* p1 Jl 28 2017

Nothing New P. GULLEY *Indianapolis Monthly* p46 F 2017

Now Is the Greatest Time To Shed Your Pathetic Flesh Siri cartoon
Bloomberg Businessweek no4496 p28 O 24 2016

Oilfield Cleanup Tools D. Wethe chart *Bloomberg Businessweek*
no4503 p31 D 12 2016

An Online Medical Database Is Reducing Diagnostic Errors R.
Weintraub, Y. K. Valtis et al *Harvard Business Review Digital
Articles* p2 O 27 2015

On Technology J. Wortham color *New York Times Magazine* p16
Ja 29 2017

Out From the Shadow of the Valley S. Lynn, D. T. Dingle et al
color *Black Enterprise* v47 no4 p18 N/D 2016

PATENTLY ABSURD? B. Preston bw *Car & Driver* v62 no6 p26
D 2016

Precaution and governance of emerging technologies G. E. Kaebnick, E. Heitman et al bibl color *Science* v354 no6313 p710 N
11 2016

The Problem with Tech Copycats D. Pogue cartoon *Scientific
American* v315 no5 p23 N 2016

Pulitzer-winning author Tracy Kidder: Looking for the soul of the
machine makers D. Drollette color *Bulletin of the Atomic Scientists* v73 no2 p74 Mr 2017

REALITY CHECK: Will your next surgery be done with virtual
reality? More area hospitals are employing this cutting-edge
technology C. Cunningham *Washingtonian Magazine* v52 no12
p115 S 2017

A Refresher on Discovery-Driven Planning A. Gallo *Harvard
Business Review Digital Articles* p2 F 13 2017

Relying on--or Recoiling from--Reproductive Enhancement P.
LEVINE *USA Today Magazine* v145 no2864 p62 My 2017

Research: Family Firms Are More Innovative Than Other Companies N. Kammerlander and M. van Essen color *Harvard Business Review Digital Articles* p2 Ja 25 2017

Right Tech, Wrong Time R. Adner and R. Kapoor color img *Harvard Business Review* v94 no11 p60 N 2016

The Right to Cognitive Liberty M. Ienca color *Scientific American*
v317 no2 p10 Ag 2017

SILVER IS THE NEW OIL D. M. Engstrom graph *Kiplinger's
Personal Finance* v71 no4 p43 Ap 2017

A Skier's Must-Have: THE BIG DUMPS TI 5000 2 J. C. Davies
diag *Powder* p46 S 2017

Society Is Ready for a New Kind of Science--Is Academia? B. L.
KEELER, R. CHAPLIN-KRAMER et al *BioScience* v67 no7
p591 Jl 2017

Sometimes, Less Innovation Is Better S. Berinato *Harvard Business Review* v95 no3 p38 My/Je 2017

THE SOUL IN THE MACHINE W. ISAACSON color *Vanity
Fair* v59 no11 p110 N 2017

The Soundtrack of Our Lives T. Golson color *Dressage Today* v24
no1 p60 O 2017

Successful Innovators Don't Care About Innovating D. Sundheim
Harvard Business Review Digital Articles p2 O 22 2014

Technology as Magic D. Pogue color *Scientific American* v317
no2 p26 Ag 2017

Technology assessment and the social and human impact of innovation F. Y. Phillips and Oh bibl diag *Bulletin of the Atomic
Scientists* v72 no6 p402 N 2016

Technology Progresses When Business, Government, and Academia Work Together G. Satell *Harvard Business Review Digital Articles* p2 Je 16 2016

TECH TRENDS CHANGING OUR WORLD S. Lynn, R. Leslie
et al color *Black Enterprise* v47 no2 p46 S 2016

A Testable Idea Is Better than a Good Idea M. Schrage *Harvard
Business Review Digital Articles* p2 D 24 2014

THIRTY YEARS LATER… C. Iozzio color *Popular Science*
v289 no6 p8 N/D 2017

A Tradition of Technological Breakthroughs with Commercial
Success *Science & Technology Review* p3 Je 2017

TREKKIE TECH C. HARRINGTON color *Wired* v25 no10 p32
O 2017

THE TRUTH ABOUT BLOCKCHAIN M. IANSITI and K. R.
LAKHANI bw color diag img *Harvard Business Review* v95
no1 p118 Ja/F 2017

WANTED: FRESH SOLUTIONS FOR AGE-OLD PROBLEMS
J. Alsever, V. Zarya et al color diag *Fortune* v175 no6 p68 My
1 2017

WE FEEL IT TOO A. MARSHALL cartoon color *Wired* v25 no9
p56 S 2017

What a Study of 33 Countries Found About Aging Populations
and Innovation A. Irmen and A. Litina bw *Harvard Business
Review Digital Articles* p2 Ja 18 2017

What Driverless Cars Mean for Today's Automakers M. Wessel
Harvard Business Review Digital Articles p2 Ag 27 2015

What Innovative Companies Can Learn from Keurig's Highs and
Lows V. Govindarajan *Harvard Business Review Digital Articles* p2 Je 20 2016

WHAT TECHNOLOGY SHOULD I USE TO ENSURE MY
LEGACY LIVES ON? R. CAPPS diag *Wired* v25 no8 p96 Ag
2017

What Your Moonshot Can Learn from the Apollo Program J.
Geraci *Harvard Business Review Digital Articles* p2 Ap 4 2017

When Old Technologies Create New Industries J. P. V. Sampere
Harvard Business Review Digital Articles p2 Jl 18 2016

WHEN SEEING IS FEELING R. ITO *Los Angeles Magazine* p98
F 2017

Where Disruptive Innovation Came From D. Sull *Harvard Business Review Digital Articles* p2 N 10 2015

Why B2B Companies Struggle with Collaborative Innovation A.
Di Fiore and J. Vetter *Harvard Business Review Digital Articles*
p2 Mr 16 2016

Why Silicon Valley Shouldn't Be the Model for Innovation D.
Breznitz *Harvard Business Review Digital Articles* p2 N 18
2014

You don't have to lose your job if you lose your sight M. Schuman
Bloomberg Businessweek no4508 p6 Ja 23 2017

Your Innovation Team Shouldn't Run Like a Well-Oiled Machine
R. Ashkenas and M. Spiegel *Harvard Business Review Digital
Articles* p2 O 28 2015

Technological innovations management

Why Preventing Disruption in 2017 Is Harder Than It Was When
Christensen Coined the Term M. Wessel *Harvard Business Review Digital Articles* p2 S 4 2017

Technological innovations—Awards

A Time to Embrace: Uncertainties and Inconsistencies T. TAN *Publishers Weekly* v264 no27 p(Sp)3 Jl 3 2017

A TRANSFORMATION IN PROGRESS *Governing* v30 no1 p34 O 2016

Wake Up Happy—with Tech! color *Health* v31 no7 p90 S 2017

What Makes Tech Tick E. Perkins color *Hot Rod* v70 no11 p6 N 2017

Why Unicorns Are Struggling V. Govindarajan, T. Govindarajan et al *Harvard Business Review Digital Articles* p2 Ap 21 2016

Technology & children

Codebreakers M. Gunch cartoon *New Orleans Magazine* v51 no9 p42 Jl 2017

Technology & economics

NEW KIDS ON THE BLOCKCHAIN C. Leaf color *Fortune* v176 no3 p9 S 1 2017

Technology & society

See also

Sociotechnical systems

Eliminating the Human D. Byrne il *MIT Technology Review* v120 no5 p8 S/O 2017

Hope in the Humanless Economy K. Brown and S. Mcmullen color *Christianity Today* v61 no6 p30 Jl/Ag 2017

Is Tech Making Our Sex Lives Better or Worse? D. Friedman color *Glamour* v115 no7 p71 Jl 2017

Technology & state

30 Years of Disruption: Technology evolves rapidly, but that's not always true for states and localities T. Newcombe *Governing* v31 no1 p60 O 2017

The Benefits of Technocracy in China LIU YONGMOU *Issues in Science & Technology* v33 no1 p25 Fall 2016

E Pluribus Unum And The Blockchain L. BRODY color *Forbes* v200 no1 p78 Jl 27 2017

Technology & state—United States

The U.S. Government Needs to Hire More Geeks J. P. Farmer *Harvard Business Review Digital Articles* p2 S 3 2015

Technology assessment

Technology assessment and the social and human impact of innovation F. Y. Phillips and Oh bibl diag *Bulletin of the Atomic Scientists* v72 no6 p402 N 2016

Technology education

See also

Technology education (Middle school)

THE #FREEBASSEL EFFECT E. STEUER color *Wired* v25 no10 p17 O 2017

Technology education (Middle school)

CODING: The New 21st-Century Literacy? S. Lafee *Education Digest* v83 no2 p25 O 2017

Technology in the theater

Weaving Conductive Threads R. Dionne *Stage Directions* v30 no1 p28 Ja 2017

Technology research

New Genetic Engineering Techniques: Precaution, Risk, and the Need to Develop Prior Societal Technology Assessment R. A. Steinbrecher and H. Paul bibl *Environment* v59 no5 p38 S/O 2017

Technology Review (Periodical)

INNOVATORS UNDER 35 *MIT Technology Review* v120 no5 p40 S/O 2017

Technology transfer

See also

New product development

Nuclear nonproliferation

Navigating technology transfer issues A. G. Levine color *Science* v355 no6328 p975 Mr 3 2017

Technology—Congresses

Out From the Shadow of the Valley S. Lynn, D. T. Dingle et al color *Black Enterprise* v47 no4 p18 N/D 2016

Technology—Economic aspects

A Cheap Way to Own Tech D. FONDA chart *Kiplinger's Personal Finance* v70 no12 p59 D 2016

The Slow-Motion Bust M. Chafkin cartoon graph *Bloomberg Businessweek* no4496 p30 O 24 2016

A TO-DO LIST FOR THE TECH INDUSTRY J. Tanz cartoon *Wired* v24 no11 p92 N 2016

THE VALUE PROPOSITION L. Bedord *Successful Farming* v114 no12 p6 Mid-N 2016

Technology—European Union countries

Euro Trip To Hell A. Satariano and A. White cartoon diag *Bloomberg Businessweek* no4496 p34 O 24 2016

Technology—Evaluation

Go to bed with Alexa color *Health* v31 no9 p18 N 2017

new products color *Science* v356 no6340 p867 My 26 2017

Technology—History—21st century

DIGITAL DEATH STAR R. KARLGAARD color *Forbes* v198 no6 p44 N 8 2016

Technology—Law & legislation

Euro Trip To Hell A. Satariano and A. White cartoon diag *Bloomberg Businessweek* no4496 p34 O 24 2016

Evidence in the Precautionary Assessment of Novel Substances A. Chapman bibl *Environment* v59 no5 p16 S/O 2017

New Genetic Engineering Techniques: Precaution, Risk, and the Need to Develop Prior Societal Technology Assessment R. A. Steinbrecher and H. Paul bibl *Environment* v59 no5 p38 S/O 2017

Technology—Mexico—History

Give Us Your Coders Yearning to Be Free A. Navarro color graph *Bloomberg Businessweek* no4518 p16 Ap 10 2017

Technology—News briefs

Now Is the Greatest Time To Shed Your Pathetic Flesh Siri cartoon *Bloomberg Businessweek* no4496 p28 O 24 2016

Quick Hits A. Marks map *Scientific American* v316 no4 p20 Ap 2017

Sony Projectors M. Fleischmann color *Sound & Vision* v82 no3 p17 Ap 2017

Technology—Psychological aspects

See also

Persuasive technology

the health nut A. Brightfield color *Better Homes & Gardens* v95 no8 p178 Ag 2017

Technology—Social aspects

See also

Educational technology—Social aspects

Information technology—Social aspects

Paleo-Tech L. A. HENION *Sierra* v102 no1 p104 Ja/F 2017

Seizing Our Brand's Destiny L. D'VORKIN *Forbes* v198 no7 p16 N 29 2016

Technology Is Not Threatening Our Humanity—We Are G. Petriglieri *Harvard Business Review Digital Articles* p2 O 30 2015

Technology—Study & teaching

MASTERS OF TECH J. Santiago color *Literacy Today (2411-7862)* v34 no3 p12 N/D 2016

Technology—United States

Get Your Own Broadband M. Chafkin and D. Bass cartoon map *Bloomberg Businessweek* no4496 p38 O 24 2016

Tech Industry, Meet Donald color *Popular Mechanics* p18 S 2017

TQ TECH QUOTIENT M. SMITH *Foreign Policy* no221 p104 N/D 2016

Teclemariam, Laura

TECH REBELS [Cover story] color *Black Enterprise* v47 no2 p52 S 2016

TECH TRENDS CHANGING OUR WORLD color *Black Enterprise* v47 no2 p46 S 2016

TED Conference

Tapping into TED B. WARNER *Publishers Weekly* v264 no35 p64 Ag 28 2017

TED GOES CORPORATE L. Entis color *Fortune* v175 no6 p20 My 1 2017

THE TED TALK AN ORAL HISTORY E. G. ELLIS bw diag *Wired* v25 no5 p26 My 2017

Ted Inc.

Tapping into TED B. WARNER *Publishers Weekly* v264 no35 p64 Ag 28 2017

Ted Yu

Ultrafine jagged platinum nanowires enable ultrahigh mass activity for the oxygen reduction reaction bibl chart graph *Science* v354 no6318 p1414 D 16 2016

Tedder, Michael

ELISABETH MOSS'S MAD WORLD color *Esquire* p26 My 2017

Tedder, Ryan—Interviews

Ryan Tedder S. Lansky color *Time* v188 no15 p55 O 17 2016

Teddy bears

Play color *Backpacker* p72 Je 2017

Teder, Tiit

Higher predation risk for insect prey at low latitudes and elevations graph *Science* v356 no6339 p742 My 19 2017

TEDESCHI, CHRISTOPHER

Under Pressure color *Discover* v38 no6 p18 Jl/Ag 2017

Tedesco, Laura

5 LESSONS FROM THE NEW PALEO color *Men's Health* v32 no7 p104 S 2017

Patient in Training color *Women's Health* v14 no9 p78 N 2017

Spring for Hygge [Cover story] color *Women's Health* v14 no3 p78 Ap 2017

Track Meet color *Women's Health* v14 no1 p108 Ja/F 2017

Tedesco, Selina

TECH OF ALL TRADES color *Good Housekeeping* v265 no2 p6 Ag 2017

TEEMAN, JENNIFER

innocent mistakes *Parents* v92 no5 p121 My 2017

Teen Vogue (Periodical)

Refashionista J. HUGHES *New York Times Magazine* p28 S 3 2017

Teen Wolf (TV program)

THE 22-WORD REVIEW D. Rovenstine color *Entertainment Weekly* no1476 p50 Ag 4 2017

ONE LAST HOWL S. Highfill color *Entertainment Weekly* no1480 p30 S 1 2017

Teenage actors—Interviews

Insecure A. D'Arminio *TV Guide* v65 no35 p33 Ag 21 2017

Teenage businesspeople

Meet the Teenagers Who Found Their Own Startups J. Esteves and G. de Haro *Harvard Business Review Digital Articles* p2 D 5 2016

Teenage Emotions (Music)

Q&A: Lil Yachty A. GREENE color *Rolling Stone* no1290 p24 Je 29 2017

Teenage girls

Amrita took action when she discovered a local school was low on laptops *Scholastic Choices* p24 O 2017

Teenage girls—Medical care

To Talk About Sex to Teens In Zambia, Play the Diva J. Scanlon and T. C. Mitimingi color *Bloomberg Businessweek* no4494 p42 O 10 2016

Teenage girls—Religious life

Through the Motions N. BAZIS color *America* v215 p27 N 28 2016

Teenage girls—Social conditions

10 THINGS WE'RE TALKING ABOUT T. A. Christian color *Essence* v47 no11 p67 Mr 2017

Teenage girls—United States

THEY CHANGED THEIR SCHOOL. Could You? J. PRESS *Scholastic Choices* v33 no1 p6 S 2017

Teenage girls—United States—Psychology

MISS UNDERSTOOD G. Bishop color *Sports Illustrated* v127 no7 p128 S 4 2017

Teenage Mutant Ninja Turtles (Fictitious characters)

NO. 21 RAPHAEL OF TEENAGE MUTANT NINJA TURTLES S. Li color *Entertainment Weekly* no1436/1437 p60 O 21 2016

Teenage Mutant Ninja Turtles: Out of the Shadows (Film)

TEENAGE MUTANT NINJA TURTLES: OUT OF THE SHADOWS C. Gunnestad color *Sound & Vision* v82 no2 p71 F/Mr 2017

Teenage pregnancy—Prevention

The Condom Campaign C. RIOS *Ms.* v26 no4 p10 Wint 2016

Teenage pregnancy—Prevention—Government policy

Teen Pregnancy Prevention *Congressional Digest* v96 no7 p30 S 2017

Teenage pregnancy—Research

Teen Pregnancy Prevention *Congressional Digest* v96 no7 p30 S 2017

Teenagers

See also

Cell phones & teenagers

Muslim teenagers

Teenage girls

All Your Likes color *Seventeen* v75 no11 p14 N 2016

The Friedman Pharmacy *Commentary* v141 no9 p1 N 2016

The Friedman Pharmacy *Commentary* v142 no4 p1 N 2016

How School MESSES WITH YOUR SKIN K. CASTAÑON color *Seventeen* v75 no11 p52 N 2016

How Should You Spend Your HOLIDAY HANG TIME? H. VIGGIANI color *Seventeen* v75 no11 p68 N 2016

I would tell my teenage self ... *Reader's Digest* v188 no1125 p48 N 2016

THE MATH POLYMATH B. Peterson *Washingtonian Magazine* v52 no4 p45 Ja 2017

Meet the Class of 2016 A. Park, S. Gregory et al color *Time* v188 no18 p22 O 31 2016

PERFECTLY ME A. STANLEY bw cartoon color *Seventeen* v75 no11 p80 N 2016

TEENS: PHONES OVER FRIES color *Fortune* v175 no6 p12 My 1 2017

TRAUMARAMA color *Seventeen* v75 no11 p104 N 2016

TRAUMARAMA color *Seventeen* v76 no2 p132 Mr 2017

The Urbanist: The Teens of Havana T. MACMILLAN and R. MORGAN img *New York* v49 no21 p30 O 17 2016

Would You Rather... color *Seventeen* v76 no2 p136 Mr 2017

YOUR CHEAT SHEET TO... Cramming Your Way to an A L. MARCHANT and A. STANLEY color *Seventeen* v75 no11 p102 N 2016

Your Relationships: They Changed Their School *Scholastic Choices* pT4 S 2017 Supplement

Teenagers' health

All Your Likes cartoon color *Seventeen* v76 no2 p16 Mr 2017

Debate: Do Teens Need Recess? *Scholastic Choices* pT3 S 2017 Supplement

SCREEN GRAB M. BRADY *Psychology Today* v50 no3 p20 My/Je 2017

Teenagers—Alcohol use

This Just In J. Zorthian color *Time* v189 no20 p19 My 29 2017

Teenagers—Attitudes

B×(M+F+A)+Att2 A. STANLEY cartoon *Seventeen* v76 no2 p110 Mr 2017

Teenagers—Canada

In praise of teenagers (really) *Maclean's* v130 no7 p4 Ag 2017

Teenagers—Drug use

TEEN SUBSTANCE USE SHOWS DECLINE *USA Today Magazine* v145 no2862 p6 Mr 2017

Teenagers—Drug use—United States

DOES LEGALIZATION BOOST TEEN MARIJUANA USE? J. SULLUM cartoon *Reason* v49 no1 p12 My 2017

Teenagers—Employment

COSTUME DRAMA G. Flynn cartoon *New Yorker* v92 no32 p78 O 10 2016

NOW HIRING: TEEN CIGARETTE NARCS J. STOOKSBERRY bw *Reason* v49 no6 p14 N 2017

SCOOP DREAMS S. Rhimes color *New Yorker* v92 no32 p64 O 10 2016

Teaching Teenagers to Develop Their Emotional Intelligence M. Brackett, D. Divecha et al *Harvard Business Review Digital Articles* p2 My 19 2015

Teen labor force participation before and after the Great Recession and beyond T. L. Morisi bibl chart color graph *Monthly Labor Review* p1 F 2017

Why Today's Teens Are More Entrepreneurial than Their Parents W. Johnson *Harvard Business Review Digital Articles* p2 My 25 2015

Teenagers—Growth

Your Body Right Now! Is this weird? Is that normal? And perhaps most important—is that me I smell? Here, answers to a few of your most pressing puberty-related questions (ones you're maybe too afraid to ask!) M. Foye and M. Walker *Scholastic Choices* v32 no5 p6 F 2017

Teenagers—Humor

PI A LA MOAN *Reader's Digest* v189 no1131 p97 Je 2017

Teenagers—Interviews

"We Are STEM-inists" A. STANLEY color *Seventeen* v75 no11 p22 N 2016

Teenagers—Salaries, wages, etc.

Should Teens Earn Less Than Adults? Some lawmakers believe that lowering the minimum wage for young people will encourage more businesses to hire them. Would you say this is a smart move to help teens get jobs—or is it fundamentally unfair?

Scholastic Choices v32 no5 p2 F 2017

Teenagers—Sleep

Generation Z Z Z Z Z Z Z Z M. CROUCH img Scholastic Choices v33 no1 p10 S 2017

Your Health: Generation Zzzzzzzz Scholastic Choices pT6 S 2017 Supplement

Teenagers—Suicidal behavior

Confronting Student Suicide G. W. ". McGee cartoon Education Digest v82 no8 p4 Ap 2017

Teenagers—Tobacco use

Smoke Signals C. STOFFERS New York Times Upfront v149 no5 p10 N 21 2016

Teenagers—United States

A Bronx Tale American Scholar v86 no4 p14 Aut 2017

Should You Have the Right to Vote Now? Scholastic Choices p2 O 2017

Teenagers—United States—Education

Team of Dreamers H. Harper color AARP: The Magazine v59 no5A p70 Ag/S 2016

Teenagers—United States—Mental health

The Kids Are Not All Right [Cover story] S. Schrobsdorff color diag Time v188 no19 p44 N 7 2016

Teenagers—United States—Political activity

My Household Get-out-the-vote Campaign Hits a Teen Roadblock K. Van Ogtrop color Time v188 no16/17 p95 O 24 2016

Teeter, Lara

"Failing" in the Classroom K. M. Mitchell Stage Directions v29 no10 p34 O 2016

Teeth

the Separation R. K. JOHNSON cartoon New Yorker v93 no7 p76 Ap 3 2017

Teeth abnormalities

Protect Your Teeth [Cover story] A. Weil color Prevention v69 no5 p24 My 2017

Teeth—Anatomy

Advances in dental care Mayo Clinic Health Letter v35 p1 My 2017 Supplement

Teeth—Care & hygiene

happy teeth A. OGLETHORPE color Better Homes & Gardens v95 no3 p152 Mr 2017

Teeth—Size

Check out these outrageous facts A. E. HURT and J. SWAIN National Geographic Kids no469 p4 Ap 2017

Teeth—Surgery

PARTY LINES img New York p76 F 20 2017

Tegel, Hanna

A subcellular map of the human proteome color Science v356 no6340 p820 My 26 2017

TEGLER, ERIC

THE MILITARY'S NEW WORKHORSE chart color Popular Mechanics p8 Jl 2017

TEGMARK, MAX

OUR NEXT BILLION YEARS color Discover v38 no9 p58 N 2017

Postmodern Prometheus H. Hirsh bw color Science v357 no6350 p460 Ag 4 2017

TEH, IAN

A River at Risk color map National Geographic v232 no1 p142 Jl 2017

Teh, Lydia C. L.

Committing to socially responsible seafood color Science v356 no6341 p912 Je 1 2017

Tehlar, Andres

Time-resolved x-ray absorption spectroscopy with a water window high-harmonic source graph Science v355 no6322 p264 Ja 20 2017

Tei Shi (Performer)

GOINGS ON ABOUT TOWN color New Yorker v93 no12 p4 My 8 2017

Teicher, Craig Morgan

Chapters on Verse: New books by Robert Hass and Louise Glück examine the finer points of poetic form and practice bw New York Times Book Review p22 Ag 6 2017

Half-Light: Collected Poems, 1965–2016 color Publishers Weekly v264 no29 p194 Jl 17 2017

Homeschooling: New Creative Writing Guides bw color Publish-

ers Weekly v263 no42 p23 O 17 2016

The Poetic Is Political bw color Publishers Weekly v264 no14 p38 Ap 3. 2017

Politics Was Front and Center At This Year's AWP Conference color Publishers Weekly v264 no8 p4 F 20 2017

The Trembling Answers Publishers Weekly. v264 no8 p61 F 20 2017

Teichmann, Sarah A.

Aging increases cell-to-cell transcriptional variability upon immune stimulation color diag graph Science v355 no6332 p1433 Mr 31 2017

Single-cell transcriptomics to explore the immune system in health and disease diag Science v357 no6359 p58 O 6 2017

Teigen, Chrissy, 1985-

digital directory color InStyle v24 no11 p28 N 2017

Eye of the Teigen [Cover story] C. Bagley color InStyle v24 no11 p172 N 2017

Hello! L. Brown color InStyle v24 no11 p30 N 2017

In the Nude color InStyle v24 no3 p292 Mr 2017

Kimono A-Go-Go E. Wilson color InStyle v24 no10 p88 O 2017

What you don't know about... me [Cover story] bw color Glamour v115 no4 p160 Ap 2017

Teigen, Chrissy, 1985-—Interviews

TWO COURSES WITH Chrissy Teigen N. Feeney color Entertainment Weekly no1443 p40 D 9 2016

TEIRSTEIN, PAUL

MY LONGEST TRIP TO VEGAS color Flying v143 no12 p20 D 2016

Teissandier, Aurélie

The DNA methyltransferase DNMT3C protects male germ cells from transposon activity bibl diag graph Science v354 no6314 p909 N 18 2016

TEITELBAUM, EMMANUEL

India's Weakened Unions Face a Push for Reform Current History v116 no789 p142 Ap 2017

Teitelbaum, Jacob

FEELING THE BURN? color Amazing Wellness v8 no6 p28 Early Winter2016

SIBO SOLUTIONS color Amazing Wellness v9 no4 p32 Summ 2017

Stay Sharp color Better Nutrition v78 no11 p34 N 2016

Teitler, Lucy

To Do img New York v49 no15 p91 Jl 25 2016

Teixeira, Ruy

The End of the Clintons M. Continetti Commentary v142 no5 p56 D 2016

Teixeira, Thales S.

When People Pay Attention to Video Ads and Why Harvard Business Review Digital Articles p2 O 14 2015

Tejani, Viral D.

Community network for deaf scientists color Science v356 no6336 p386 Ap 28 2017

Teknetics (Company)

DIGGING UP THE PAST R. Verger color Popular Science v289 no5 p26 S/O 2017

Tektite

75, 50 & 25 YEARS AGO R. W. Sinnott Sky & Telescope v133 no5 p6 My 2017

TELAROLI, GINA

Free for All bw color Film Comment v53 no5 p77 S/O 2017

Tele Vue Optics Inc.

NEW PRODUCTS bw color Astronomy v45 no2 p71 F 2017

Telebrands Corp.

tangle-free lights color Good Housekeeping v263 no6 p49 D 2016

Telecommunication

See also

Artificial satellites in telecommunication

Image transmission

Podcasting

Transponders

Video on demand

Virtual networks

ANALOG CHURCH R. MERCER SCHUCHARDT bw color Christianity Today v60 no8 p40 O 2016

Fast Forward D. B. CLARK color graph Wired v25 no10 p58 O 2017

NEW PRODUCTS color *Astronomy* v45 no8 p85 Ag 2017

NEW PRODUCT SHOWCASE *Sky & Telescope* v133 no4 p64 Ap 2017

The Other 130-mm Tabletops *Sky & Telescope* v132 no6 p62 D 2016

Portable Star Trackers J. Lodriguss *Sky & Telescope* v133 no5 p66 My 2017

A quick guide to scopes for kids T. Trusock color *Astronomy* v45 no11 p60 N 2017

Sky-Watcher USA's new COMPOUND SCOPE P. Harrington color *Astronomy* v45 no3 p62 Mr 2017

Smart Astronomy: The NexStar Evolution 9,25 R. Mollise *Sky & Telescope* v133 no5 p60 My 2017

TELESCOPE K. Dupzyk color diag *Popular Mechanics* p18 F 2017

Telescopes—Maintenance & repair

How to care for your telescope P. Harrington color *Astronomy* v45 no3 p54 Mr 2017

Restoring an Ellison Reflector *Sky & Telescope* v133 no5 p26 My 2017

Telescopes—Management

In pursuit of PLUTO R. Talcott color *Astronomy* v45 no7 p56 Jl 2017

Telescopes—Sales & prices

Hitching a ride G. Chaple bw *Astronomy* v45 no7 p66 Jl 2017

Telescopic gun sights

LIGHTS OUT FOR HOGS G. BETHGE color *Outdoor Life* v224 no8 p24 O 2017

Telesnitsky, Alice

Not just Salk color *Science* v357 no6356 p1105 S 15 2017

Televangelists

The Born-Again Scoundrel M. OPPENHEIMER bw cartoon *GQ: Gentlemen's Quarterly* v97 no3 p140 Mr 2017

Televised debates—Social aspects

The Debate Stage Reveals Character, Preparation and the Candidate Who Is Still a Child J. Klein color *Time* v188 no14 p28 O 10 2016

Television

　See also

　　Characters & characteristics on television

　　Gay men on television

　　High definition television

　　Interactive television

　　Internet television

　　Police on television

　　Politics on television

　　Television programs

　　Video on demand

I Have a Dream, Too S. CARR *Idaho Magazine* v16 no1 p54 O 2016

No Rest for the Wicked M. Z. SEITZ img *New York* p76 F 9 2017

On and Off Script S. Lipscomb *History Today* v66 no12 p31 D 2016

watch this way *Parents* v91 no11 p29 N 2016

YOGA TV color *Yoga Journal* no292 p23 Je 2017

Television & politics

The National Interest: Jonathan Chait J. Chait img *New York* v50 no8 p15 Ap 17 2017

Political Hardball color *Weekly Standard* v22 no34 p3 My 15 2017

TV IN THE TRUMP AGE L. Rice color *Entertainment Weekly* no1441 p9 N 25 2016

WHO'S LAUGHING NOW? The tragicomedy of Donald Trump on Saturday Night Live T. Bissell *Harper's Magazine* p61 O 2017

Television acting

Killer Instinct J. POWERS color *Vogue* v207 no6 p81 Je 2017

Television actors & actresses

Ben Higgins Reality Star M. RUBINO *Indianapolis Monthly* v40 no3 p62 N 2016

Cover *Entertainment Weekly* no1435 pC1 O 14 2016

DAYS OF OUR LIVES M. LOGAN *TV Guide* v65 no8 p38 F 27 2017

LUKE PERRY MY LIFE ON TV D. HOLBROOK *TV Guide* v65 no8 p26 F 27 2017

Out & About *TV Guide* v65 no25 p2 Je 2017

RED-CARPET INTELLIGENCE Emmys Edition C. Sosenko,

J. Heyman et al color *Entertainment Weekly* no1484 p22 S 29 2017

Simon Helberg C. Mari color *Current Biography* v78 no5 p35 My 2017

Studio City J. HERBST *Los Angeles Magazine* p76 Mr 2017

THE THINKING MAN DAVID HARBOUR M. Khidekel bw *Women's Health* v14 no9 p104 N 2017

TOASTING THIS IS US color *Entertainment Weekly* no1486 p49 O 13 2017

Television actors & actresses—Congresses

TOASTING FALL TV H. Goldblatt color *Entertainment Weekly* no1467 p12 My 26 2017

Television actors & actresses—Interviews

The Duke of Diversion M. BAZER *Chicago* v66 no10 p72 O 2017

Q&A WITH CUSH JUMBO M. M. Toby color *Essence* v47 no11 p60 Mr 2017

Television actors & actresses—United States

Better Call Tina Parker K. LEMIEUX *Texas Monthly* v45 no6 p52 Je 2017

CARRIE FISHER M. Roush *TV Guide* v65 no4 p14 Ja 16 2017

GENERAL HOSPITAL M. LOGAN *TV Guide* v64 no40 p62 O 3 2016

Grey's Anatomy M. Logan *TV Guide* v65 no4 p35 Ja 16 2017

IT'S GOOD TO BE QUEEN M. LOGAN *TV Guide* v65 no4 p24 Ja 16 2017

My Obsessions... *TV Guide* v65 no4 p8 Ja 16 2017

Paris Jackson Is a Star *TV Guide* v65 no8 p10 F 27 2017

The Young Pope A. D'Arminio *TV Guide* v65 no4 p41 Ja 16 2017

Television adaptations

"GET ME ANOTHER HANDMAID'S TALE!" I. Biedenharn color *Entertainment Weekly* no1472 p60 Je 30 2017

Television advertising

　See also

　　Super Bowl (Football game) advertisements

A Super Bowl Ad Is the Equivalent of Lighting Money on Fire (Which Can Be More Strategic Than It Sounds) T. Sullivan and R. Fisman color *Harvard Business Review Digital Articles* p2 F 3 2017

When Upbeat Commercials Backfire N. M. Puccinelli, D. Grewal et al *Harvard Business Review Digital Articles* p2 O 23 2015

Television advertising—United States

Ad Nauseam M. Rubino *Indianapolis Monthly* p12 F 2017

Television antennas

TERK TRINITY XTEND: THIS TV ANTENNA TRIES TO PULL DOUBLE-DUTY AS A WI-FI RANGE EXTENDER J. CIPRIANI and M. BROWN color *Macworld - Digital Edition* v34 no11 p25 N 2017

Television art directors

DAVID KORINS bw color *Bloomberg Businessweek* no4521 p68 My 8 2017

Television authorship

IN THE FALL OF 2011 *Atlanta* v57 no1 p90 My 2017

THE NEVER-ENDING STORY S. Highfill color *Entertainment Weekly* no1450 p11 Ja 27 2017

Television broadcasting

　See also

　　Cable television industry

　　Television broadcasting of sports

　　Television networks

　　Television programs

CHEERS & JEERS D. HOLBROOK *TV Guide* v65 no39 p107 S 18 2017

THE END OF THE EARLY ADOPTER R. SABIN color *Sound & Vision* v82 no4 p8 My 2017

OTT Video Is Creating Cord-Extenders, Not Cord-Cutters J. Samit *Harvard Business Review Digital Articles* p2 Jl 17 2015

WIMBLEDON HOLDS SERVE R. A. BERENZ *TV Guide* v65 no27 p41 Je 26 2017

Yep, There Are Books C. JOHNSON color *Publishers Weekly* v264 no32 p76 Ag 7 2017

Television broadcasting of films

ROYAL PAIN: King Charles III S. Gutierrez *British Heritage Travel* v38 no3 p70 My/Je 2017

Television broadcasting of news

　See also

　　Television press conferences

AT RT. NEWS BREAKS YOU S. van Zuylen-Wood color *Bloomberg Businessweek* no4521 p48 My 8 2017

Television broadcasting of news—Government policy

REMOTE CONTROLLED A. KROLL and R. Choma color graph *Mother Jones* v42 no6 p48 N/D 2017

Television broadcasting of sports

MLB'S "SURREAL" SEASON OPENER R. A. BERENZ *TV Guide* v65 no13 p48 Mr 20 2017

NFL WARM-UP R. A. BERENZ *TV Guide* v65 no31 p43 Jl 24 2017

Political Football R. Deitsch and T. Keith color *Sports Illustrated* v125 no13 p18 O 17 2016

THE SOX'S NEW VOICE W. MOSER color *Chicago* v66 no8 p26 Ag 2017

Television broadcasting of sports—Equipment & supplies

THE REVOLUTION [WILL NOT BE TELEVISED] A. Wolff chart color diag *Sports Illustrated* v125 no19 p112 D 12 2016

Television broadcasting of sports—History—21st century

The Reckoning L. J. Wertheim and T. Keith color *Sports Illustrated* v126 no14 p17 My 15-22 2017

Television broadcasting—Awards

THE TELEVISION INDUSTRY ADVOCACY AWARDS, LOS ANGELES *TV Guide* v65 no41 p2 O 2 2017

Television broadcasting—Awards—United States

See also
Emmy Awards

Television broadcasting—Europe

Where YouTube Meets The Boob Tube S. Nicola, A. Boksenbaum-Granier et al graph *Bloomberg Businessweek* no4512 p44 F 20 2017

Television broadcasting—United States

America's top TV critic Matt Roush answers your burning questions M. Roush color *TV Guide* v64 no42 p6 O 10 2016

CHEERS & JEERS D. HOLBROOK *TV Guide* v65 no8 p68 F 27 2017

HOLLYWOOD GIVES BACK K. Hahn *TV Guide* v65 no39 p22 S 18 2017

Teri Arvesu N. RHEE color *Chicago* v66 no6 p81 Je 2017

W.W.E. THE PEOPLE N. Klein *Harper's Magazine* p11 S 2017

Television broadcasting—United States—News briefs

This Just In... M. Fleischmann color *Sound & Vision* v82 no4 p17 My 2017

Television comedies

See also
Situation comedies (Television programs)

black-ish I. Ratledge *TV Guide* v65 no19 p28 My 1 2017

Is Your Favorite Show Safe? M. ROFFMAN *TV Guide* v65 no21 p6 My 15 2017

THE MAYOR J. Russell *TV Guide* v65 no37 p29 S 4 2017

NO JOKE V. LUCCA color *Film Comment* v53 no2 p52 Mr/Ap 2017

The Politics of Late-Night Comedy M. Gerson, T. Noah et al color *Atlantic* v320 no1 p10 Jl/Ag 2017

The Workaholics' Finest Work A. Bacle color *Entertainment Weekly* no1449 p52 Ja 20 2017

Television commercials

BARGAIN BASEMENT I. Parker cartoon *New Yorker* v93 no23 p20 Ag 7 2017

Television consultants

LIKE FATHER, LIKE DAUGHTER color *Entertainment Weekly* no1484 p49 S 29 2017

Television cooking programs

Bon Appétit M. Rubino *Indianapolis Monthly* p10 My 2017

A Sea Change at America's Test Kitchen A. Green *Publishers Weekly* v264 no27 p10 Jl 3 2017

Television crime programs

See also
Gangsters on television

ANIMAL KINGDOM: The Cody clan at the center of the California-set crime drama often get into hot water. But on set, they know how to keep it cool J. HALTERMAN *TV Guide* v65 no27 p20 Je 26 2017

CELL BLOCK GQ color *GQ: Gentlemen's Quarterly* v86 no12 p138 D 2016

LAW AND DISORDER E. LANDAU bw *GQ: Gentlemen's Quarterly* v86 no12 p131 D 2016

Why Viewers Love True-Crime Shows I. RUDOLPH *TV Guide* v64 no40 p10 O 3 2016

Television crime programs—Reviews

NCIS A. D'Arminio color *TV Guide* v64 no42 p34 O 10 2016

With Mindhunter, Fincher Perfects the Art of Darkness D. D'addario color *Time* v190 no16/17 p99 O 23 2017

Television critics

Emily Nussbaum J. Johnson color *Current Biography* v77 no10 p82 O 2016

THE PLATINUM AGE OF TELEVISION *TV Guide* v65 no25 p10 Je 2017

TCA *TV Guide* v64 no15 p17 Ap 4 2016

Television Critics Association (U.S.)

COMING SOON TO A TV NEAR YOU N. Abrams color *Entertainment Weekly* no1477 p16 Ag 11 2017

TCA *TV Guide* v64 no15 p17 Ap 4 2016

WHAT YOU'LL BE WATCHING IN 2017 (AND BEYOND) J. Hibberd color *Entertainment Weekly* no1450 p18 Ja 27 2017

Television equipment—Evaluation

New Gear color *Sound & Vision* v82 no8 p32 O 2017

Television film—Reviews

THE WILD BUNC D. HOLBROOK color *TV Guide* v64 no42 p24 O 10 2016

Television game programs

LONG LIVE GAME SHOWS! I. Rudolph color *TV Guide* v64 no42 p16 O 10 2016

What's Up With the Game Show Boom? L. Rice color *Entertainment Weekly* no1472 p16 Je 30 2017

Television hosts

1921-2017 REMEMBERING MONTY HALL L. Rice color *Entertainment Weekly* no1486 p50 O 13 2017

Afternoons and Popeye Cartoons M. W. SCHWARTZ *Missouri Life* v43 no7 p38 D 2016/Ja 2017

Dave Is Back! S. Vilkomerson color *Entertainment Weekly* no1478 / 1479 p18 Ag 18-25 2017

THE DEVIL'S ADVOCATE S. RODRICK bw color *Esquire* p58 Ag 2017

GARRY SHANDLING B. Maher and D. Franich color *Entertainment Weekly* no1446/1447 p98 D 2016/Ja 2017

GETTING TO KNOW JOHNNY CARSON *Saturday Evening Post* v288 no6 p105 N/D 2016

HAPPY SUMMER! [Cover story] color *Redbook* p85 Jl/Ag 2017

How Did I Get Here?: WENDY WILLIAMS bw color *Bloomberg Businessweek* no4516 p72 Mr 27 2017

James Corden M. Rich color *Current Biography* v78 no2 p21 F 2017

Jimmy Kimmel D. BROWNE bw *Rolling Stone* no1281/1282 p58 F 23 2017

Mr. Popular T. BRODESSER-AKNER *New York Times Magazine* p34 Ja 15 2017

Reza Aslan Thinks TV Can End Bigotry A. M. Cox *New York Times Magazine* p94 Mr 26 2017

RICH KOZ B. Zehme color *Chicago* v66 no10 p152 O 2017

RYAN SEACREST D. WALTERS color *Bon Appetit* v61 no12 p174 D 2016 /Jan2017

THE TALK M. LOGAN *TV Guide* v65 no27 p40 Je 26 2017

"THE POLITICAL EQUIVALENT OF ENRICHED URANIUM" A. RICHARD ALBANESE color *Publishers Weekly* v263 no52 p50 D 19 2016

Ziya Tong T. Hall color *Canadian Geographic* v137 no5 p82 S/O 2017

Television hosts—Attitudes

Glenn Beck Is Sorry About All That A. M. Cox color *New York Times Magazine* p70 N 27 2016

Megyn KELLY color *Vanity Fair* v59 no1 p125 Holiday 2017

Television hosts—Interviews

By the Book T. Noah *New York Times Book Review* p8 N 6 2016

Glenn Beck B. Luscombe color *Time* v189 no3 p64 Ja 16 2017

Is Bigotry a Parking Ticket or a Capital Offense? R. Carroll *New York* v49 no23 p27 N 14 2016

Jake Tapper A. GREENE bw *Rolling Stone* no1294 p62 Ag 24 2017

LIFE'S WORK: An Interview with MICHAEL STRAHAN ATHLETE/TV HOST color *Harvard Business Review* v95 no5 p156 S/O 2017

Television in security systems

13 Home Security Secrets You Should Know M. CROUCH color *Reader's Digest* v189 no1130 p130 My 2017

LOGITECH CIRCLE 2 HOME SECURITY CAMERA M. ANSALDO color *Macworld - Digital Edition* v34 no10 p37 O 2017

PEACE OF MIND [Cover story] J. Cooper color *Cabin Living* p68 O 2017

REOLINK KEEN: BATTERY-POWERED CAMERA OFFERS WIRELESS SECURITY FOR CHEAP J. R. BOOKWALTER color *Macworld - Digital Edition* p23 Je 13 2017

Your Security Cam Is Watching You D. Pogue color *Scientific American* v317 no4 p30 O 2017

Television in security systems—Evaluation

Always Watching G. DELL'ABATE and B. BOOEY color *Popular Mechanics* p38 Mr 2017

D-Link DCS-8200LH HD 180-Degree Wi-Fi Camera: An all-seeing eye for large spaces M. ANSALDO color *PCWorld* p125 Mr 2017

THE WELL-MONITORED HOME T. CHIARELLA color *Popular Mechanics* p78 My 2017

Television journalists

See also

Television news anchors

Television monitors

Big-screen blowout S. HORACZEK color *Popular Science* v289 no6 p22 N/D 2017

Photon Menace M. P. Hamilton chart color *Sound & Vision* v82 no8 p62 O 2017

Television musicals

You Can't Stop the Chic M. Snetiker color *Entertainment Weekly* no1442 p51 D 2 2016 Rebellious Special Issue

Television musicals—Reviews

Hairspray Live! Promises Retro Fun With Little Risk D. D'Addario color *Time* v188 no24 p68 D 12 2016

Television networks

5 SMALLER NETWORKS YOU NEED TO KNOW ABOUT D. HOLBROOK *TV Guide* v65 no31 p6 Jl 24 2017

5 Streaming Networks to Check Out Now A. D'Arminio *TV Guide* v65 no21 p10 My 15 2017

As Television Expands, the Emmys Are Becoming a Battlefield D. D'addario color *Time* v190 no10/11 p30 S 18 2017

W.W.E. THE PEOPLE N. Klein *Harper's Magazine* p11 S 2017

Television networks—Finance

AT RT. NEWS BREAKS YOU S. van Zuylen-Wood color *Bloomberg Businessweek* no4521 p48 My 8 2017

The Kremlin's New Disinformation Machine H. Meyer, C. Matlack et al *Bloomberg Businessweek* no4512 p27 F 20 2017

Television news anchors

CHANNEL 7, WHERE ARE YOU? A. Beaujon *Washingtonian Magazine* v52 no6 p49 Mr 2017

JIM VANCE: The newsman's life traced the history of our region--and we loved him for it. But in today's TV world, there can't be another like him A. Beaujon *Washingtonian Magazine* v52 no12 p48 S 2017

THE NEW JIM A. Beaujon *Washingtonian Magazine* v52 no3 p45 D 2016

PARODY color *Weekly Standard* v22 no30 p40 Ap 10 2017

The Realest Face in "Fake News" T. BRODESSER-AKNER color *GQ: Gentlemen's Quarterly* v97 no5 p56 My 2017

Television news anchors—Interviews

Bret Baier J. Marksbury and C. Barrett color *Golf Magazine* v58 no11 p37 N 2016

Television news consultants

FOX'S LIBERAL: Pundit Jessica Tarlov on playing the villain on America's most watched cable network A. Whiting *Washingtonian Magazine* v52 no8 p51 My 2017

Television personalities

See also

Reality television program participants

Television actors & actresses

Television news anchors

Television talk show hosts

CHEERS & JEERS D. HOLBROOK *TV Guide* v65 no25 p80 Je 2017

I Was a Child Star--and Lived to Tell About It A. JOHNSON and D. Holbrook *TV Guide* v65 no19 p13 My 1 2017

LITTLE MAN, STRONG WOMAN G. Zee color *Women's*

Health v14 no7 p78 S 2017

Omarosa Manigault Changed Parties For Trump A. M. Cox *New York Times Magazine* p78 O 30 2016

ZAZIE BEETZ S. Pulia color *InStyle* v24 no1 p44 Ja 2017

Television personalities—Employment

Easy Listening J. Traina and T. Keith color *Sports Illustrated* v127 no6 p17 Ag 28 2017

Television personalities—Interviews

Charlamagne Tha God Loves Telling Middle America About Black Privilege J. Hughes color *New York Times Magazine* p82 My 21 2017

INTERVIEW: KENNEDY K. Mangu-Ward color *Reason* v49 no5 p46 O 2017

JIMMY KIMMEL LIVE! L. ACKEN color *TV Guide* v64 no42 p47 O 10 2016

Television personalities—United States

Glenn Beck's Regrets E. Hedegaard color *Rolling Stone* no1273 p44 N 3 2016

JOURNEYMAN P. R. KEEFE cartoon color *New Yorker* v92 no49 p52 F 13 2017

L'Affaire Kardashian M. SEAL color *Vanity Fair* v59 no1 p150 Holiday 2017

Television premieres

Westworld: Fall TV's Biggest Mystery J. Hibberd color *Entertainment Weekly* no1435 p8 O 14 2016

Television press conferences

EMBEDDED A. Marantz cartoon *New Yorker* v93 no2 p23 F 27 2017

Television previews

George Michael: Freedom I. Ratledge *TV Guide* v65 no43 p34 O 16 2017

Television producers & directors

See also

Women television producers & directors

5 THINGS TO KNOW ABOUT. . . THE GUEST BOOK J. RUSSELL *TV Guide* v65 no31 p20 Jl 24 2017

Chuck Barris 1929-2017 M. Roush *TV Guide* v65 no14 p13 Ap 3 2017

CRANSTON COMES ALIVE [Cover story] J. PRESSLER bw color *Esquire* p80 N 2017

David Lynch Is Rolling Off a Log D. Marchese img *New York* v50 no10 p94 My 15 2017

GRANT TINKER J. L. Brooks and L. Rice color *Entertainment Weekly* no1446/1447 p89 D 2016/Ja 2017

JOSH BERMAN J. HALTERMAN *TV Guide* v64 no40 p14 O 3 2016

JULIE PLEC I. RUDOLPH *TV Guide* v65 no13 p11 Mr 20 2017

PETE NOWALK M. LOGAN *TV Guide* v65 no4 p12 Ja 16 2017

Roger Ailes J. Dickey color *Time* v189 no21 p14 Je 5 2017

THE STRATEGY OF TRUTH J. Lepore cartoon *New Yorker* v93 no16 p37 Je 5 2017

WELCOME TO HAWLEYWOOD D. RILEY color *GQ: Gentlemen's Quarterly* v86 no12 p140 D 2016

Television producers & directors—Interviews

'This Country Is at a Tipping Point' N. Stockwell cartoon color *Progressive* v81 no10 p35 N 2016

Television producers & directors—United States

ADAM HOROWITZ AND EDWARD KITSIS M. LOGAN *TV Guide* v65 no8 p12 F 27 2017

Gary Glasberg A. D'Arminio color *TV Guide* v64 no42 p17 O 10 2016

Television producers & directors—United States—Interviews

STEVEN MOLARO J. HALTERMAN color *TV Guide* v64 no42 p12 O 10 2016

Television production & direction

See also

Television programs—Casting

29 Reasons Why BuzzFeed Is Getting Into the TV Game G. Smith and F. Gillette color *Bloomberg Businessweek* no4526 p60 Je 12 2017

New Myths, New Busters J. LYNCH color *Popular Mechanics* p22 N 2017

Out & About *TV Guide* v65 no8 p3 F 27 2017

"Peak TV" Is Further Away Than We Think T. J. Huddleston color *Fortune* v176 no1 p10 Jl 1 2017

SHARON HORGAN A. D'ARMINIO *TV Guide* v64 no46 p8 N

27 2017

BETTER LATE THAN NEVER R. Rahman color *Entertainment Weekly* no1457/1458 p14 Mr 17 2017

Politics = Big Ratings I. RUDOLPH *TV Guide* v65 no11 p7 Mr 6 2017

Rock of the aged J. J. WEINEMAN color *Maclean's* v129 no40 p72 O 10 2016

WINNERS AND LOSERS L. Rice color *Entertainment Weekly* no1440 p12 N 18 2016

Television programs—Reviews

Trumped up TV J. WEINMAN color *Maclean's* v129 no51/52 p70 D 26 2016

WIKIPEDIA BROWN E. NUSSBAUM cartoon *New Yorker* v92 no42 p126 D 19 2016

Television programs—Social aspects

John Oliver is good for the Republic. Or not J. Martin and Z. Davis color *America* v216 no6 p47 Mr 20 2017

Television programs—Syndication

THE DEATH OF Syndicated Reruns G. SMITH cartoon color *Bloomberg Businessweek* no4496 p68 O 24 2016

Television programs—United States

America's top TV critic Matt Roush answers your burning questions Jordan and Gerry *TV Guide* v65 no8 p4 F 27 2017

America's top TV critic Matt Roush answers your burning questions M. Roush color *TV Guide* v64 no42 p6 O 10 2016

Ask Matt M. Roush *TV Guide* v64 no46 p5 N 7 2016

Bones' Big Send-Off M. Roffman *TV Guide* v65 no8 p10 F 27 2017

CHEERS & JEERS D. HOLBROOK *TV Guide* v65 no8 p68 F 27 2017

Inside Scorpion's Nest M. ROFMAN *TV Guide* v64 no40 p48 O 3 2016

THE NEW TV SHOWS YOU CAN'T GET ENOUGH OF J. Hibberd color *Entertainment Weekly* no1436/1437 p20 O 21 2016

The Scenes That Changed Everything J. Kantor and S. Leach color *Glamour* v115 no10 p50 O 2017

STRANGER THINGS PANEL *TV Guide* v64 no42 p4 O 10 2016

TV'S WINNERS AND LOSERS BY THE NUMBERS *TV Guide* v64 no40 p16 O 3 2016

TV Will Save Us All C. Leive color *Glamour* v115 no10 p28 O 2017

Why Viewers Love True-Crime Shows I. RUDOLPH *TV Guide* v64 no40 p10 O 3 2016

Television remakes

Bill SKARSGÅRD A. Skarsgard *Interview* v47 no5 p58 Je/Jl 2017

THE NEVER-ENDING STORY S. Highfill color *Entertainment Weekly* no1450 p11 Ja 27 2017

ONCE MORE, WITH FEELING! S. Highfill color *Entertainment Weekly* no1450 p12 Ja 27 2017

OUR CHARMED REBOOT WISH LIST N. Abrams color *Entertainment Weekly* no1449 p22 Ja 20 2017

PEAKS 'N' FREAKS [Cover story] J. Jensen color *Entertainment Weekly* no1459 p20 Mr 31 2017

QUEER EYE RETURNS! J. Hibberd color *Entertainment Weekly* no1451/1452 p20 F 3-10 2017

REBOOTS, REVIVALS & ROCKY BALBOA! N. Abrams and D. Snierson color *Entertainment Weekly* no1478 / 1479 p20 Ag 18-25 2017

WHY YOU'LL (PROBABLY) NEVER SEE A LOST REBOOT S. Highfill color *Entertainment Weekly* no1450 p15 Ja 27 2017

Television reruns

THE DEATH OF Syndicated Reruns G. SMITH cartoon color *Bloomberg Businessweek* no4496 p68 O 24 2016

Television script writing

GOING OUT WITH A BANG N. Abrams, B. L. Heldman et al color *Entertainment Weekly* no1463/1464 p10 Ap/My 2017

Striking Out J. Hibberd color *Entertainment Weekly* no1465 p9 My 12 2017

Television scripts

"Peak TV" Is Further Away Than We Think T. J. Huddleston color *Fortune* v176 no1 p10 Jl 1 2017

A Very Timeless Script S. Li color *Entertainment Weekly* no1436/1437 p92 O 21 2016

Television sequels

The L Word Returns! T. Stack color *Entertainment Weekly*

no1474/1475 p18 Jl 21-28 2017

Television series

See also

    Television soap operas

America's Most Watched 25 TOP SHOWS *TV Guide* v65 no41 p10 O 2 2017

America's top TV critic Matt Roush answers your burning questions *TV Guide* v65 no41 p3 O 2 2017

Do Endings Matter Anymore? Yes, but not nearly as much as they used to. TV is moving away from finale fever—which is making for better TV M. Z. Seitz *New York* v50 no12 p92 Je 12 2017

EXAMINING THE ALLURE OF THE ANTIHERO *USA Today Magazine* v146 no2867 p10 Ag 2017

FALL TV MATH D. Holbrook *TV Guide* v65 no41 p6 O 2 2017

Five Rejected Ideas for How to End The Leftovers img *New York* v50 no12 p98 Je 12 2017

Forever and Ever, Amen img *New York* v50 no12 p96 Je 12 2017

Goodbyes Are Hard B. Kachka img *New York* v50 no12 p84 Je 12 2017

HOW THE FUGITIVE FINALE MADE TV BETTER D. Bianculli *TV Guide* v65 no35 p8 Ag 21 2017

Must Listening *Weekly Standard* v22 no20 p4 Ja 30 2017

Must-See TV E. Rampell *Sierra* v101 no6 p9 N/D 2016

The Postmortem *New York* v50 no12 p104 Je 12 2017

THE SIMPSONS M. Logan *TV Guide* v65 no43 p26 O 16 2017

Specials, Movies & Marathons D. Holbrook *TV Guide* v65 no43 p27 O 16 2017

Tony's Dead, Walt's Not, and Phoebe's Hooked on Meth A. STERNBERGH img *New York* v50 no12 p102 Je 12 2017

Television series—Reviews

Horror Show M. Bayles *Claremont Review of Books* v16 no4 p87 Fall 2016

The Keepers Avoids True Crime's Ghastliest Pitfalls D. D'Addario color *Time* v189 no21 p63 Je 5 2017

The Rise of the Telenovela S. MARSHALL color *New Republic* v248 no1/2 p64 Ja/F 2017

Television set top boxes

Streaming on a Budget A. D'Arminio *TV Guide* v65 no27 p6 Je 26 2017

Television sets

See also

    Organic light-emitting diode televisions

    Smart television devices

HOME ENTERTAINMENT G. GRAJEK and R. ROTHMAN color *Good Housekeeping* v263 no5 p144 N 2016

Poolside Video J. SCIACCA color *Sound & Vision* v81 no9 p19 N 2016

Television sets—Evaluation

Sony's Bravia OLED: the first flat-screen TV with sound that doesn't suck M. BROWN color *PCWorld* v35 no2 p21 F 2017

Television soap operas

The Collection A. D'arminio color *TV Guide* v65 no7 p45 F 13 2017

Santa Barbara Forevah! M. IOSSEL color *Foreign Policy* no225 p54 Jl/Ag 2017

A SENTIMENTAL EDUCATION D. PINCKNEY cartoon *New Yorker* v93 no26 p58 S 4 2017

Television soundtracks

The Best Small-Screen Soundtracks C. Agard and A. Bacle color *Entertainment Weekly* no1439 p53 N 11 2016

Television talk programs

Classic Conversation F. P. DRISCOLL *Opera News* v81 no7 p18 Ja 2017

THE LATE LATE SHOW WITH JAMES CORDEN M. ROFFMAN *TV Guide* p45 Ap 17 2017

The Most Trusted Name in News L. Brown color *InStyle* v24 no9 p386 S 2017

Television talk show hosts

King of The Nerds M. WAKIM *Los Angeles Magazine* p72 Mr 2017

MEDIA Maven in the Making T. A. Christian color *Essence* v48 no5 p82 S 2017

ON THE CONTRARY K. SANNEH cartoon color *New Yorker* v93 no8 p50 Ap 10 2017

The Pyne Tree K. Cook *Smithsonian* v48 no3 p18 Je 2017

WENDY WILLIAMS IS MORE THAN JUST TALK V. Zarya

color *Fortune* v175 no2 p34 F 1 2017

Television viewers

MARIA BARTIROMO: GLOBAL MARKETS EDITOR, FOX BUSINESS NETWORK bw color *Harvard Business Review* v95 no4 p144 Jl/Ag 2017

Television viewers—Attitudes

HOW WE WATCH FOOTBALL J. Feldman color *Sports Illustrated* v125 no18 p36 D 5 2016

WINNERS AND LOSERS L. Rice color *Entertainment Weekly* no1440 p12 N 18 2016

Television viewers—Psychology

What's Up With the Game Show Boom? L. Rice color *Entertainment Weekly* no1472 p16 Je 30 2017

Television viewers—United States

Outside the Box T. Keith chart *Sports Illustrated* v127 no2 p20 Jl 17 2017

Television viewing

smart ENTERTAINMENT N. SAPORITA diag *Good Housekeeping* v263 no5 p143 N 2016

A WESTEROS TEST(EROS) R. Kinane color *Entertainment Weekly* no1480 p44 S 1 2017

What's Normal? B. ROWEN cartoon *Atlantic* v320 no4 p28 N 2017

Television viewing—Equipment & supplies

HOW TO WATCH R. Deitsch color *Sports Illustrated* v126 no8 p61 Mr 20 2017

Television viewing—History—21st century

VIEWERS TUNE IN FOR CUBS' EPIC WIN, TUNE OUT THE REST T. J. Huddleston color *Fortune* v174 no8 p22 D 15 2016

Television viewing—Psychological aspects

The Ninja Cure for Anxiety J. PARKER color *Atlantic* v319 no1 p30 Ja/F 2017

Television writers

Los Angeles ICON P. BROWNFIELD *Los Angeles Magazine* p110 F 2017

NORMAN LEAR M. Paterniti color *GQ: Gentlemen's Quarterly* v97 no6 p120 Je 2017

When Writers Rule, TV Gets Wonderfully Weird E. Dockterman color *Time* v189 no7/8 p102 F 27 2017

Will TV Go Dark This Summer? What a possible writers' strike means for viewers J. RUSSELL *TV Guide* v65 no19 p6 My 1 2017

Television—Antennas—Evaluation

Gear P. Nielsen color *Sail* v48 no3 p30 Mr 2017

Television—Awards

Introducing: TV for Grownups color *AARP: The Magazine* v60 no5A p14 Ag/S 2017

Television—Congresses

Editor's Note H. Goldblatt color *Entertainment Weekly* no1471 p10 Je 23 2017

The Rest of the ATX Fest N. Abrams color *Entertainment Weekly* no1471 p15 Je 23 2017

A REUNION OF GALACTICA PROPORTIONS J. Hibberd color diag *Entertainment Weekly* no1471 p14 Je 23 2017

Television—Evaluation

I Hired a Sleep Coach E. Listfield color *Health* v31 no6 p74 Jl 2017

Ultra-HD 55" TVs color *Good Housekeeping* v264 no3 p97 Mr 2017

Welcome to 'Wow!' TV J. K. Willcox chart color graph *Consumer Reports* v82 no11 p44 N 2017

Television—Influence of

Q: What did you let go of that changed your life? P. JOHNSON, M. LANGE et al color *O, The Oprah Magazine* p16 Ag 2017

Television—News briefs

Cheers & Jeers D. HOLBROOK *TV Guide* v65 no2 p84 Ja 2 2017

WHAT YOU'LL BE WATCHING IN 2017 (AND BEYOND) J. Hibberd color *Entertainment Weekly* no1450 p18 Ja 27 2017

Television programs—Charts, diagrams, etc.

America's Most Watched 25 TOP SHOWS *TV Guide* v65 no43 p11 O 16 2017

Is American Gods the Most Outrageous Show on TV? M. Snetiker color *Entertainment Weekly* no1467 p53 My 26 2017

TV'S WINNERS AND LOSERS BY THE NUMBERS *TV Guide* v65 no11 p16 Mr 6 2017

Why Is Rick and Morty So Fun? It's All About the References L.

Eadicicco color *Time* v190 no6 p53 Ag 7 2017

Television programs—Plots, themes, etc.

Covfefe: The Show color *Entertainment Weekly* no1470 p10 Je 16 2017

Seinfeld's Lost Story Lines D. Snierson color *Entertainment Weekly* no1460/1461 p64 Ap 7-17 2017

TOGETHER WE STAND J. HALTERMAN *TV Guide* v65 no8 p22 F 27 2017

Television programs—Rating—Charts, diagrams, etc.

50 TOP SHOWS *TV Guide* v65 no25 p11 Je 2017

America's Most Watched 25 TOP SHOWS *TV Guide* v65 no37 p16 S 4 2017

Television—Sales & prices

Best TVs for Your Buck J. K. Willcox chart color diag graph *Consumer Reports* v82 no2 p30 F 2017

Television series—Charts, diagrams, etc.

America's Most Watched 25 TOP SHOWS *TV Guide* v65 no43 p11 O 16 2017

Television—Sound transmission

The 5.1 Basics of Surround Audio J. SCIACCA diag *Sound & Vision* v82 no2 p19 F/Mr 2017

Television—Stage-setting & scenery

See also

Stage props

BULL A. D'ARMINIO *TV Guide* v65 no8 p28 F 27 2017

REBUILDING THE VATICAN C. Agard color *Entertainment Weekly* no1449 p49 Ja 20 2017

Television viewers—Charts, diagrams, etc.

Attention Is Our Business cartoon *Wired* v25 no3 p60 Mr 2017

Television writers—Salaries, wages, etc.

Writers' Strike Averted! J. Russell *TV Guide* v65 no21 p11 My 15 2017

Telfair, Tula

Tula Telfair: Invented Landscapes color *Art in America* v104 no10 p55 N 2016

Telford (England)

How the Pieces all Came Together in Ironbridge Gorge *British Heritage Travel* v37 no6 p49 N/D 2016

TELHAN, RAJ

"How Bad Is Your Pain?" Notes on the nature of suffering *American Scholar* v86 no4 p20 Aut 2017

Telis, Natalie

Detection of human adaptation during the past 2000 years bibl graph *Science* v354 no6313 p760 N 11 2016

Tell Me You Love Me (Music)

Demi Lovato R. Bruner color *Time* v190 no14 p54 O 9 2017

Tell Them We Are Rising (Film)

FULL FRAME 2017: Twentieth Anniversary Retrospective B. Cook *Film Quarterly* v71 no1 p91 Fall 2017

Tellado, Marta L.

The Compassionate Care You Need *Consumer Reports* v82 no10 p4 O 2017

A Diet of Good Information *Consumer Reports* v82 no11 p4 N 2017

Fighting for Fairness on Every Front *Consumer Reports* v82 no8 p4 Ag 2017

A Legacy of Safety Lives On color *Consumer Reports* v82 no2 p5 F 2017

A Prescription for Better Health *Consumer Reports* v82 no9 p4 S 2017

Steering You Right *Consumer Reports* v82 no4 p5 Ap 2017

There's No Place Like Home *Consumer Reports* v82 no3 p5 Mr 2017

'Tis the Season for Stress-Free Shopping *Consumer Reports* v82 no12 p4 D 2017

When Hidden Algorithms Lead to Higher Prices *Consumer Reports* v82 no7 p4 Jl 2017

A Year of Celebration *Consumer Reports* v81 no12 p5 D 2016

Your Partner for Every Stage of Life *Consumer Reports* v82 no1 p5 Ja 2017

Teller

Houdini's Handcuffs *AARP: The Magazine* v60 no4A p62 Je/Jl 2017

Teller, Adam

HE KNOWS WHAT HE'S TALKING ABOUT M. JAFFE *Arizona Highways* v93 no10 p46 O 2017

Teller, Astro
WHAT'S EVERYBODY SO AFRAID OF? color *Popular Mechanics* p72 N 2017

Teller, Miles
A Comeback King Fights His Way Back Into the Ring E. Berman color *Time* v188 no22-23 p102 N/D 2016

Teller, Richard
Shooting Life BELOW ZERO color *Nebraska Life* v21 no1 p36 Ja/F 2017

TELLING, JON
The Arctic in the Twenty-First Century: Changing Biogeochemical Linkages across a Paraglacial Landscape of Greenland *BioScience* v67 no2 p118 F 2017

Tellman, Beth
Without inclusion, diversity initiatives may not be enough color *Science* v357 no6356 p1101 S 15 2017

Tello, J. Sebastián
Plant diversity increases with the strength of negative density dependence at the global scale diag *Science* v356 no6345 p1389 Je 30 2017

Telomerase
See also
Telomerase reverse transcriptase
Mutations in the promoter of the telomerase gene TERT contribute to tumorigenesis by a two-step mechanism K. Chiba, F. K. Lorbeer et al diag *Science* v357 no6358 p1416 S 29 2017

Telomerase reverse transcriptase
New insights into melanoma development J. W. Shay diag *Science* v357 no6358 p1358 S 29 2017

Telomeres
TZAP: A telomere-associated protein involved in telomere length control J. S. Zhou Li, J. Miralles Fusté et al bibl diag graph *Science* v355 no6325 p638 F 10 2017

Telomeres—Research
TZAP or not to zap telomeres G. Lossaint and J. Lingner bibl diag *Science* v355 no6325 p578 F 10 2017

Temer, Michel, 1940——Political & social views
Unpresidential Palaces T. John color *Time* v189 no11 p14 Mr 27 2017

Temkin, Brad
Rooftop T. Brorby *Orion Magazine* v35 no4/5 p111 Jl-O 2016

Temkin, Max
SECRET HITLER J. WALKER color *Reason* v49 no4 p76 Ag/S 2017

Temme, Mark
STRONG MUSCLES, HEALTHY JOINTS A. C. SHILTON color *Runner's World* v51 no10 p58 N 2016

Temming, Maria
Archaea fold DNA like animals do color *Science News* v192 no3 p14 S 2 2017
Continents' bottoms found diag *Science News* v192 no4 p11 S 16 2017
DNA reveals Canaanites' fate color *Science News* v192 no3 p8 S 2 2017
FAIR-MINDED MACHINES color graph map *Science News* v192 no4 p26 S 16 2017
Fossil DNA shakes up elephant history bw color *Science News* v191 no13 p8 Jl 8 2017
Green Bank Goes Independent *Sky & Telescope* v133 no2 p12 F 2017
How gut bacteria may affect anxiety *Science News* v192 no5 p12 S 30 2017
Humans' arrival in Australia redated color *Science News* v192 no2 p10 Ag 19 2017
Magma under volcanoes is largely solid *Science News* v191 no13 p11 Jl 8 2017
Origami outfits help bots retool color *Science News* v192 no7 p13 O 28 2017
Original asteroids came only in size XL *Science News* v192 no3 p8 S 2 2017
Quantum storage device fits on a chip color *Science News* v192 no5 p8 S 30 2017
Tiny antennas read signals in new way *Science News* v192 no4 p17 S 16 2017
You missed a spot, bee color *Science News* v192 no5 p32 S 30 2017

Temp, J.
A nontoxic pain killer designed by modeling of pathological receptor conformations bibl diag graph *Science* v355 no6328 p966 Mr 3 2017

Temper
Viral Anger Spreads Like a Disease—and It's Making the Country Sick S. Schrobsdorff color *Time* v190 no2/3 p19 Jl 10-17 2017

Temperament
Adopting the Right Cat for You J. Singer *Catnip* v24 no10 p10 O 2016

Temperance
Why Is Everybody Suddenly Fasting? (And How Can I Fast Better Than Them?) J. VRABEL color *GQ: Gentlemen's Quarterly* v97 no6 p38 Je 2017

Temperature
See also
High temperatures
Low temperatures
COLD CUTS color *Women's Health* v14 no6 p32 Jl 2017
Metamaterials for perpetual cooling at large scales X. Zhang bibl color *Science* v355 no6329 p1023 Mr 10 2017
one crazy month in Montana S. Chodosh color *Popular Science* v289 no4 p18 Jl/Ag 2017
so you want to terraform Mars M. B. Griggs color *Popular Science* v289 no4 p14 Jl/Ag 2017
Too Hot to Stomach L. Evans Ogden color *Natural History* v125 no10 p7 O 2017

Temperature control equipment
Your Summer Savior J. Paulson *Horse & Rider* v56 no6 p15 Je 2017

Temperature measurements
See also
Ocean temperature—Measurement
The Day Warming Began D. FOX bw cartoon color *Discover* v27 no10 p54 D 2016

Temperature sensors
POWER FROM THE PEOPLE E. MASTROIANNI color *Discover* v38 no10 p16 D 2017

Tempest (Theatrical production)
Summer: The Tempest J. Rosenblum *Opera News* v81 no9 p51 Mr 2017

Temple, Craig
TWO IMAGERS are better than one color *Astronomy* v45 no1 p50 Ja 2017

Temple, James
The Growing Case for Geoengineering chart color graph map *MIT Technology Review* v120 no3 p28 My/Je 2017
Hot SOLAR Cells color *MIT Technology Review* v120 no2 p52 Mr/Ap 2017
INVENTORS color il *MIT Technology Review* v120 no5 p56 S/O 2017
Obama's Energy Secretary Addresses Trump's Attacks on His Legacy il *MIT Technology Review* v120 no5 p15 S/O 2017
Reinventing Rice for a World Transformed by Climate Change color *MIT Technology Review* v120 no4 p15 Jl/Ag 2017
Why Bad Things Happen to Clean-Energy Startups il *MIT Technology Review* v120 no4 p92 Jl/Ag 2017

Temple, Stanley A.
Quantify endangered species listings color *Science* v356 no6345 p1342 Je 30 2017

Temple, Tammy
TWO IMAGERS are better than one color *Astronomy* v45 no1 p50 Ja 2017

Temple Mount (Jerusalem)
Archaeologists restore floor from Second Temple period on Jerusalem mount C. Beck *Christian Century* v133 no21 p17 O 12 2016

Temple of Apollo (Delphi)
VESSELS OF THE GODS [Cover story] L. Ruffle *History Today* v67 no5 p50 My 2017

Temple of the Dog (Music)
TEMPLE OF THE DOG M. Mettler bw color *Sound & Vision* v82 no1 p72 Ja 2017

Temple of the Dog (Performer)
TEMPLE OF THE DOG M. Mettler bw color *Sound & Vision* v82 no1 p72 Ja 2017

Temple University

THE SUMMER EFFECT L. KAMPS color *Martha Stewart Living* p50 Jl/Ag 2017

"You have to tell yourself you're enough" E. Mahaney bw *Glamour* v115 no9 p142 S 2017

Temple Bombing, The (Theatrical production)

THE TEMPLE BOMBING D. SCHECHTER *Atlanta* v56 no10 p41 F 2017

Temples

See also

Buddhist temples

Where Is God at Work? M. Simone *America* v217 no6 p60 S 18 2017

Temples—Conservation & restoration

Archaeologists restore floor from Second Temple period on Jerusalem mount C. Beck *Christian Century* v133 no21 p17 O 12 2016

Of Form and Folly J. TUPPONCE *Virginia Living* v15 no1 p41 D 2016

Temples—Jerusalem

Clashes over security at Jerusalem Temple Mount M. Chabin, L. Markoe et al *Christian Century* v134 no17 p14 Ag 16 2017

Temple-Wood, Emily

THE BLOGGER AND THE TROLLS color *Scientific American* v317 no3 p70 S 2017

The Online Troll Patrol A. SIMMONS *Reader's Digest* v189 no1127 p12 F 2017

Templin, R. M.

A microtubule-organizing center directing intracellular transport in the early mouse embryo diag *Science* v357 no6354 p925 S 1 2017

Tempo, Roberto

Network science on belief system dynamics under logic constraints bibl diag graph *Science* v354 no6310 p321 O 21 2016

Temporal lobes

See also

Entorhinal cortex

Ventral CA1 neurons store social memory Teruhiro Okuyama, Takashi Kitamura et al bibl graph *Science* v353 no6307 p1536 S 30 2016

Temporary employees

How to Turn an Interim Role into a Permanent Job B. Dattner color *Harvard Business Review Digital Articles* p2 Ja 16 2017

What Motivates Gig Economy Workers A. Rosenblat *Harvard Business Review Digital Articles* p2 N 17 2016

Temporary employees—Social conditions

How to Make Employment Fair in an Age of Contracting and Temp Work D. Weil *Harvard Business Review Digital Articles* p2 Mr 24 2017

Temporary stores

Pop-Up Bookstores Proliferate E. Nawotka color *Publishers Weekly* v264 no21 p11 My 22 2017

Temporomandibular disorders—Treatment

Treat TMJ Naturally J. Martin color *Amazing Wellness* v9 no1 p26 Wint 2017

Temporomandibular joint

WHY IS MY JAW CLICKING AND POPPING? P. Marzban *Washingtonian Magazine* v52 no12 p116 S 2017

Temprana, Silvio G.

A disynaptic feedback network activated by experience promotes the integration of new granule cells bibl graph *Science* v354 no6311 p459 O 28 2016

Tempura

(THE JAPANESE FOOD LOVERS GUIDE) RAMEN! TEMPURA! SUSHI! YAKITORI! MOCHI! *Los Angeles Magazine* v62 no9 p104 S 2017

Ten Arquitectos (Company)

Triple Play D. MADSEN *Architectural Record* v205 no10 p114 O 2017

Ten commandments

Clock out J. Ryan color *U.S. Catholic* v82 no7 p25 Jl 2017

Commentary on Commentary *Commentary* v143 no4 p14 Ap 2017

Ten Days in the Valley (TV program)

Ten Days in the Valley: Getting hooked on a nail-biter that would feel at home on cable M. ROUSH *TV Guide* v65 no43 p14 O 16 2017

Tenant farmers

This Land Ain't My Land K. Angel color *Bloomberg Businessweek* no4503 p38 D 12 2016

Tencent Holdings Ltd.

18 PONY MA N. Varchaver color *Fortune* v174 no7 p89 D 1 2016

TENCENT GOES GLOBAL MAYBE B. Stone and Lulu Chen color diag *Bloomberg Businessweek* no4529 p50 Jl 3 2017

Tendons—Anatomy

Get to know ... Your IT band [Cover story] J. Miller color *Yoga Journal* no295 p62 O 2017

Teng, Andrew

Why and How to Build an In-House Consulting Team *Harvard Business Review Digital Articles* p2 S 11 2015

Tenkara fly fishing

Learn Minimalist Fly-Fishing C. GERARD il *Backpacker* p36 My 2017

Tennant, David A.

Neutron scattering in the proximate quantum spin liquid a-RuCl3 bw diag *Science* v356 no6342 p1055 Je 9 2017

Tennant, David, 1971-

Broadchurch I. Rudolph *TV Guide* v65 no27 p29 Je 26 2017

DuckTales for a New Generation M. Snetiker color *Entertainment Weekly* no1470 p10 Je 16 2017

Tennant, Nancy

The 5 Requirements of a Truly Innovative Company *Harvard Business Review Digital Articles* p2 Ap 27 2015

TENNEFOSS, KEN

BROKEN WINDOWS *Sea Magazine* v109 no1 p24 Ja 2017

Tennent, Rose

ALT DANCE-OFF A. Marantz cartoon *New Yorker* v93 no13 p34 My 15 2017

Tennessee

Swimming in Sustainability in Loretto T. Doherty *Parks & Recreation* v51 no10 p40 O 2016

Tennessee Titans (Football team)

1 Tennessee Titans color *Sports Illustrated* v127 no7 p74 S 4 2017

Tennessee—Description & travel

LOG HOME ROAD TRIP: Tennessee color map *Log Home Living* v34 no2 p52 Mr 2017

Tennessee—History—Civil War, 1861-1865

See also

Battle of Franklin, Tenn., 1864

What We Learned From... The Battle of Franklin, 1864 J. Byrne *Military History* v33 no5 p18 Ja 2017

Tenney, Leah

10 TIPS FROM U.S. OLYMPIAN LISA WILCOX color *Dressage Today* p44 My 2017

Tennis

See also

Doubles tennis

Table tennis

Tennis for women

AMERICAN DREAM S. TIGNOR *Tennis* v52 no6 p26 N/D 2016

Belinda Bencic S. TIGNOR *Tennis* v53 no4 p70 Jl/Ag 2017

BREAK THE RULES G. MORAN bw color *Tennis* v53 no2 p66 Mr/Ap 2017

How to Play Like You Practice A. Fox *Tennis* v53 no3 p10 My/Je 2017

The Power of Focus A. Fox *Tennis* v53 no4 p12 Jl/Ag 2017

Tennis, Joe

CIDER HOUSE RULES: Foggy Ridge Cider founder Diane Flynt earns third nod from James Beard *Virginia Living* v15 no6 p21 O 2017

Tennis clubs

Long Island City's Slow Sizzle C. Bonanos img *New York* v50 no18 p12 S 4 2017

Tennis clubs—Management

The Social Network *Tennis* v52 no6 p52 N/D 2016

Tennis coaches

Captain Kathy N. Patltic *Tennis* v53 no3 p8 My/Je 2017

A Legacy Lives On *Tennis* v52 no6 p46 N/D 2016

A Tennis Mecca C. Evert bw color *Tennis* v53 no2 p2 Mr/Ap 2017

Tennis coaching

Captain Kathy N. Patltic *Tennis* v53 no3 p8 My/Je 2017

Farm Team G. Mackin *Tennis* v52 no6 p33 N/D 2016

MOST IMPROVED color *Tennis* v53 no2 p41 Mr/Ap 2017

MOST USER-FRIENDLY color *Tennis* v53 no2 p34 Mr/Ap 2017

Multiple Personalities J. LEVEY color *Tennis* v53 no2 p12 Mr/Ap 2017

THE SPECS chart *Tennis* v53 no2 p54 Mr/Ap 2017

THE STRING GUIDE color *Tennis* v53 no2 p38 Mr/Ap 2017

Tennis resorts—Evaluation

Nirvana with NETS C. SHMERLER color *Tennis* v53 no2 p56 Mr/Ap 2017

Tennis rules

COURT of APPEALS R. GOOD color *Tennis* v53 no2 p8 Mr/Ap 2017

COURT of APPEALS WITH REBEL GOOD Bo-hae Yu, T. Lykins et al *Tennis* v52 no6 p6 N/D 2016

In Box E. Bukzin, R. GOOD et al *Tennis* v53 no4 p14 Jl/Ag 2017

The Rules of the Game *Tennis* v52 no6 p62 N/D 2016

Tennis teams

Learn how to cover the lob—and ensure that your team will van the point G. Fernandez bw color *Tennis* v53 no2 p76 Mr/Ap 2017

Tennis techniques

See also

Tennis—Forehand

Belinda Bencic S. TIGNOR *Tennis* v53 no4 p70 Jl/Ag 2017

Bernard Tomic's Downward Swing J. YANDELL *Tennis* v53 no3 p76 My/Je 2017

COURT of APPEALS J. Bogle color *Tennis* v53 no5 p10 S/O 2017

GAME, SET...NAPTIME B. Eckstein cartoon *Esquire* p46 S 2017

Garbine Muguruza's First Serve J. YANDELL *Tennis* v53 no4 p66 Jl/Ag 2017

How to Cover a Lob G. Moran *Tennis* v53 no3 p72 My/Je 2017

LEARNING FROM... KAROLINA PLISKOVA S. Tignor *Tennis* v53 no1 p55 Ja/F 2017

One Shining Backhand S. TIGNOR *Tennis* v53 no3 p80 My/Je 2017

The PRO SHOP J. LEVEY *Tennis* v53 no5 p12 S/O 2017

RAFAEL NADAL'S FOREHAND EXTENSION J. YANDELL *Tennis* v53 no1 p29 Ja/F 2017

Sam Stosur's Kick Serve J. YANDELL *Tennis* v53 no4 p68 Jl/Ag 2017

Serving strategies while in formation G. Fernandez *Tennis* v53 no4 p76 Jl/Ag 2017

Three ways your team can break serve G. Fernandez *Tennis* v53 no3 p74 My/Je 2017

Tennis tournaments

See also

U.S. Open (Tennis tournament)

Wimbledon Championships

13 MUST-SEE EVENTS R. A. BERENZ *TV Guide* v65 no23 p44 My 29 2017

2017 Tennis Calendar chart *Tennis* v53 no1 p80 Ja/F 2017

COURT of APPEALS R. GOOD *Tennis* v53 no1 p6 Ja/F 2017

COURT of APPEALS R. GOOD *Tennis* v53 no3 p12 My/Je 2017

COURTSIDE CHRONiCLeS G. Dyer *New York Times Magazine* p50 Ag 27 2017

The Crown Jewel of the Queen City *Tennis* v52 no6 p68 N/D 2016

DIARY OF A SEASON S. Johnson *Tennis* v53 no1 p36 Ja/F 2017

THE ETERNAL SECOND S. TIGNOR *Tennis* v53 no3 p68 My/Je 2017

Fact: You have what it takes color *Redbook* p97 S 2017

OPEN SEASON *Atlanta* v57 no3 p23 Jl 2017

Sunny Forecast C. Evert *Tennis* v53 no1 p4 Ja/F 2017

THE TENNIS ROUNDTABLE chart *Tennis* v53 no1 p42 Ja/F 2017

Tour Guide: An inside look at upcoming ATP and WTA tournaments color *Tennis* v53 no5 p27 S/O 2017

Tour Guide: ATP color *Tennis* v53 no2 p14 Mr/Ap 2017

Tour Guide: ATP E. D. McGROGAN *Tennis* v53 no1 p70 Ja/F 2017

Tour Guide *Tennis* v53 no4 p34 Jl/Ag 2017

Tour Guide: WTA color *Tennis* v53 no2 p16 Mr/Ap 2017

Tour Guide: WTA E. D. McGROGAN *Tennis* v53 no1 p72 Ja/F 2017

US Open Special A. FRIEDMAN, J. ARIAS et al bw color *Tennis* v53 no5 p30 S/O 2017

When Bobby Met Billie Jean C. Bonanos img *New York* v50 no17 p28 Ag 21 2017

Your Serve, Elisabeth color *AARP: The Magazine* v60 no5A p11 Ag/S 2017

Tennis tournaments—England

See also

Wimbledon Championships

Tennis training

The Future of Tennis C. SHMERLER *Tennis* v53 no3 p62 My/Je 2017

Student Union *Tennis* v52 no6 p74 N/D 2016

Tennis umpires

Calling the Shots *Tennis* v52 no6 p44 N/D 2016

Tennis—Backhand

Alexander Zverev's Two-Handed Backhand J. YANDELL color *Tennis* v53 no2 p72 Mr/Ap 2017

Belinda Bencic's Running Backhand L. ROLLEY bw chart color *Tennis* v53 no2 p64 Mr/Ap 2017

A Game Changer S. TIGNOR bw color *Tennis* v53 no2 p80 Mr/Ap 2017

Tennis—Competitions

Finishing Strong C. Evert *Tennis* v52 no6 p4 N/D 2016

THE KYRGIOS ENIGMA L. THOMAS cartoon color *New Yorker* v93 no20 p28 Jl 10 2017

Tennis—Finance

The Sun Rises Again B. Henley *Tennis* v52 no6 p12 N/D 2016

Tennis—Forehand

Gael Monfils' Swinging Forehand Volley J. YANDELL chart color *Tennis* v53 no5 p72 S/O 2017

Venus Williams' Forehand J. YANDELL color *Tennis* v53 no5 p74 S/O 2017

Tennis—Officiating

The $200 All-Seeing Line Judge A. Vance color *Bloomberg Businessweek* no4513 p37 Mr 6 2017

Tennis players—Charts, diagrams, etc.

THE TENNIS ROUNDTABLE chart *Tennis* v53 no1 p9 Ja/F 2017

Tennis—Serve

Garbine Muguruza's First Serve J. YANDELL *Tennis* v53 no4 p66 Jl/Ag 2017

Hold Strong G. Moran *Tennis* v53 no4 p72 Jl/Ag 2017

How to Cover a Lob G. Moran *Tennis* v53 no3 p72 My/Je 2017

Sam Stosur's Kick Serve J. YANDELL *Tennis* v53 no4 p68 Jl/Ag 2017

Serving strategies while in formation G. Fernandez *Tennis* v53 no4 p76 Jl/Ag 2017

Tennis—Social aspects

Tennis, Everyone Adaptive tennis programs in the parks can bring future players off the sidelines and into the game: M. H. Sprecher *Parks & Recreation* v52 no9 p74 S 2017

Tennis—Study & teaching

Tennis, Everyone Adaptive tennis programs in the parks can bring future players off the sidelines and into the game: M. H. Sprecher *Parks & Recreation* v52 no9 p74 S 2017

Tenofovir

Vaginal bacteria modify HIV tenofovir microbicide efficacy in African women N. R. Klatt, R. Cheu et al chart graph *Science* v356 no6341 p938 Je 1 2017

Vaginal microbes hamper HIV drug A. CUNNINGHAM *Science News* v191 no13 p8 Jl 8 2017

Tenors (Singers)

American Identity: Tenor Nicholas Phan, who sings Berlioz's Roméo et Juliette with San Francisco Symphony this month, thrives on exploring an eclectic repertoire J. Malafronte *Opera News* v81 no12 p1 Je 2017

JOHAN BOTHA. RUSTENBERG, SOUTH AFRICA, AUGUST 19,1965—VIENNA, AUSTRIA, SEPTEMBER 8, 2016 H. Stewart *Opera News* v81 no5 p60 N 2016

MATTHEW POLENZANI M. Mazzaro *Opera News* v81 no10 p24 Ap 2017

Tenosynovitis

Your Body on a Cell Phone color *Prevention* p11 Mr 2017

Tentacles (Animal anatomy)

Ancient fossils feature tube feet L. HAMERS color *Science News* v192 no6 p12 O 14 2017

Tentler, Leslie

Here from the Beginning bw *Commonweal* v144 no8 p38 My 5

See also

Harbors

WHILE YOU ARE WAITING R. LORENZI color *Archaeology* v70 no4 p12 Je-Ag 2017

Terminator 2: Judgment Day (Film)

TERMINATOR 2: JUDGMENT DAY 3D C. Collis color *Entertainment Weekly* no1480 p34 S 1 2017

Termites—Behavior

Termites and plants both shape fairy circles color *Science* v355 no6322 p229 Ja 20 2017

Terms & phrases

See also

Clichés

Slogans

The Adults in the Room [Cover story] J. Mann *New York Review of Books* v64 no16 p6 O 26 2017

Confessions of a Nitpicker B. Steinkraus color *Practical Horseman* v45 no2 p20 F 2017

GLOSSARY *History Today* v67 no5 p110 My 2017

IT PAYS TO INCREASE YOUR Word Power E. COX and H. RATHVON *Reader's Digest* v188 no1125 p145 N 2016

Know Thyself (And Try to Understand Everyone Else): Our 101 guide to gender identities and sexual orientations R. NEIRENE and J. ANDERSON-MINSHALL *Advocate* no1093 p17 O/N 2017

NAKED [Cover story] color *Women's Health* v14 no7 p31 S 2017

THE PERIODIC TABLE OF CYCLING *Bicycling* v58 no7 p34 Ag 2017

'Plus Size' Goes Out of Fashion K. Samuelson color *Time* v190 no12 p14 S 25 2017

Undo the Chains A. A. BAFAQUIH *Islamic Horizons* v46 no1 p36 Ja/F 2017

Terms & phrases—History

What's in a Name? A. Morrow bw color *American History* v52 no3 p48 Ag 2017

Terms of Endearment (Theatrical production)

To Do img *New York* v49 no23 p90 N 14 2016

Tern Bicycles (Company)

TERN CARGO NODE R. KOCH color *Bicycling* v58 no1 p70 Ja/F 2017

Ternion Quartet (Music)

Round Trip/Ternion Quartet Y. Kato color *Downbeat* v84 no9 p65 S 2017

Terra-cotta

ADDITIONAL LISTINGS *Arts & Crafts Homes & the Revival* v12 no1 p40 2017 Resouce Guide

Terra Firma Development Pvt. Ltd.

ARTFUL TILE color *Arts & Crafts Homes & the Revival* v12 no1 p39 2017 Resouce Guide

Terra Firma Tiles Ltd.

Tile Everywhere M. E. Polson color *Old House Journal* v45 no6 p76 S 2017

TERRA-BERNS, MARY

Mischief on High: Investigating the Mysterious Wolverine *Idaho Magazine* v16 no7 p27 Ap 2017

MURRAY *Idaho Magazine* v16 no6 p32 Mr 2017

You Are Not a Salt Lick *Idaho Magazine* v16 no3 p6 D 2016

Terracotta army (Xi'an Shi, China)

Clay army made from custom pastes B. BOWER color *Science News* v192 no4 p19 S 16 2017

Terrasi, Salvatore

Trauma and learning in America's classrooms chart color graph *Phi Delta Kappan* v98 no6 p35 Mr 2017

Terrazzo

Terrazzo color *Old House Journal* v45 no3 p46 My 2017

Terrell, Edwin Holland, 1848-1910

The Man Who Killed Quantrill R. J. GREEN bw cartoon *Missouri Life* v44 no3 p50 My 2017

TERRELL, MARILYN

Weird But True! color map *National Geographic Kids* no471 p4 Je/Jl 2017

Terrell, Mary Church, 1863-1954

PLUCKING OUT JIM CROW N. TAPPAN *American History* v52 no1 p12 Ap 2017

Terrer, César

Response to Comment on "Mycorrhizal association as a primary

control of the CO2 fertilization effect" bibl graph *Science* v355 no6323 p358 Ja 27 2017

Terrero, Nina

Going for Impact color *Entertainment Weekly* no1436/1437 p22 O 21 2016

NO. 15 Storm color *Entertainment Weekly* no1436/1437 p56 O 21 2016

NO. 46 INVISIBLE WOMAN color *Entertainment Weekly* no1436/1437 p77 O 21 2016

What to Watch color *Entertainment Weekly* no1436/1437 p94 O 21 2016

WHO WOULD WIN? CYCLOPS VS. INVISIBLE WOMAN *Entertainment Weekly* no1436/1437 p77 O 21 2016

Terriers

Amazing Animals G. S. Hennessey and S. Schwartz color map *National Geographic Kids* no473 p12 S 2017

Terrill, Gregston

Publish openly but responsibly color *Science* v357 no6347 p141 Jl 14 2017

Terrill, Ross

A Beijing Model? color *Weekly Standard* v22 no23 p18 F 20 2017

Territorial waters

See also

Fishery law & legislation

WE HEAR YOU J. R. Poole, R. D. Sanchez et al *Progressive* v81 no6 p9 Ag/S 2017

Why the Boundary Waters Matter M. Ingram color *Progressive* v81 no5 p31 Je/Jl 2017

Terrones, Mauricio

Mildred S. Dresselhaus *Physics Today* v70 no6 p73 Je 2017

Terrorism

See also

Cyberterrorism

September 11 Terrorist Attacks, 2001

'Afghanistan Is the Front Line' N. Kumar and F. Shoaib color *Time* v189 no22 p38 Je 12 2017

After weeks of terrorism and tragedy, divisions emerge in Britain D. Stewart color *America* v217 no2 p15 Jl 24 2017

THE APPROVAL MATRIX img *New York* p92 F 20 2017

BEFORE DAWN ON A SUNDAY LATE J. VERINI *New York Times Magazine* p48 N 20 2016

Between the Lines A. Wintour color *Vogue* v207 no10 p128 O 2017

Don't Let's Roll cartoon *Weekly Standard* v22 no18 p3 Ja 16 2017

Is the World Getting More Dangerous? *New York Times Upfront* v149 no6 p12 D 12 2016

Lightbox color *Time* v188 no27-28 p18 D 26 2016

Postcard from the EDGE S. HANSEN color *Vogue* v207 no1 p26 Ja 2017

The Story of Islam D. Pinault cartoon color *Commonweal* v144 no6 p14 Mr 24 2017

TERROR AROUND THE GLOBE color *Maclean's* v129 no48/49 p52 D 5 2016

The terrorists on the right S. GILMORE color *Maclean's* v130 no9 p12 O 2017

Terror's Afterlife: Do suicide bombers think their victims are headed to paradise as well? B. Challman *Humanist* v77 no4 p6 Jl/Ag 2017

Turmoil in Turkey hits science T. Feder *Physics Today* v69 no12 p30 D 2016

Terrorism—Afghanistan

President Trump Should Send More Troops to Afghanistan A. J. Stavridis color *Time* v189 no22 p43 Je 12 2017

Terrorism—England

See also

Manchester Arena Bombing, Manchester, England, 2017

CENTURY marks *Christian Century* v134 no14 p8 Jl 5 2017

OUR VALUES WILL ALWAYS PREVAIL T. MAY *Vital Speeches of the Day* v83 no7 p196 Jl 2017

Terrorism—England—London

Notes from an Un-Reeling Island E. D. Huntley bw color *British Heritage Travel* v38 no5 p26 S/O 2017

Terrorism—Finance

Can Bankers Fight Terrorism? M. Levitt, K. Bauer et al *Foreign Affairs* v96 no6 p144 N/D 2017

Terrorism—Finance—Prevention

Don't Follow the Money P. R. Neumann color *Foreign Affairs* v96 no4 p93 Jl/Ag 2017

Terrorism—France

The French State of Emergency J. FREDETTE *Current History* v116 no788 p101 Mr 2017

Terrorism—Government policy

Another Mideast Debacle: How America armed terrorists in Syria G. PORTER *American Conservative* v16 no4 p20 Jl/Ag 2017

Terrorism—Great Britain

An Attack on Girlhood C. Alter color *Time* v189 no21 p37 Je 5 2017

British strive to build interfaith bridges amid terrorist attacks C. Traub and S. M. Llana color *Christian Century* v134 no15 p14 Jl 19 2017

Savagery In the U.K. Britain Comes Under Attack at a Turning Point D. Stewart, T. John et al color *Time* v189 no21 p34 Je 5 2017

Terror and the Failure of the Liberal Imagination: Three attacks in Britain highlight the West's inability to see the threat clearly J. Foreman *Commentary* v144 no1 p34 Jl/Ag 2017

Terrorism—Iraq

LIFE AFTER ISIS J. Verini color map *National Geographic* v231 no4 p96 Ap 2017

Lightbox I. Bremmer color *Time* v190 no4 p14 Jl 24 2017

Terrorism—Israel

The Department of Pay-for-Slay: How the Palestinian Authority not only incites terrorist murder—but supports it with U.S. tax dollars D. J. Feith and S. Gerber *Commentary* v143 no4 p19 Ap 2017

Netanyahu, the Almost-American *Commentary* v142 no1 p1 Jl/Ag 2016

Terrorism—Korea (North)

An Outlaw State E. Epstein color *Weekly Standard* v22 no25 p9 Mr 6 2017

Terrorism—Law & legislation

See also

   State-sponsored terrorism—Law & legislation

Another Dispute Over The Sept. 11 Lawsuit Bill P. M. Barrett color *Bloomberg Businessweek* no4495 p22 O 17 2016

Honorable Bobby Scott *Congressional Digest* v95 no9 p23 N 2016

Honorable Jerrold Nadler *Congressional Digest* v95 no9 p20 N 2016

Honorable Sheila Jackson Lee *Congressional Digest* v95 no9 p22 N 2016

Justice Against Sponsors of Terrorism Act *Congressional Digest* v95 no9 p9 N 2016

Legislative Background on Redress for Terrorism Victims *Congressional Digest* v95 no9 p11 N 2016

Stunts & Punts cartoon *Commonweal* v143 no17 p5 O 21 2016

Terrorism—Psychological aspects

Life under ISIS [Cover story] A. R. KHAN color *Maclean's* v129 no51/52 p22 D 26 2016

Why People Keep Saying, "That's What the Terrorists Want" M. Abrahms *Harvard Business Review Digital Articles* p2 N 20 2015

Terrorism—Religious aspects

Remembering 9/11 *America* v217 no4 p3 Ag 21 2017

Terrorism—Research

Challenges in researching terrorism from the field S. Atran, R. Axelrod et al bibl color *Science* v355 no6323 p352 Ja 27 2017

Terrorism—Social aspects

People J. Bell *Christian Century* v134 no14 p19 Jl 5 2017

Terrorism—Spain

Spain Is Different R. L. BARDAJÍ color *Weekly Standard* v22 no48 p15 S 4 2017

Terrorism—Turkey

January 2017 *Current History* v116 no788 p120 Mr 2017

Lightbox J. Malsin color *Time* v189 no3 p12 Ja 16 2017

The Real Challenge to Turkey's Economy Isn't Terrorism H. A. Unver *Harvard Business Review Digital Articles* p2 Jl 8 2016

Terrorism—United States

See also

   September 11 Terrorist Attacks, 2001

Infinite Quagmire M. JEONG il *New Republic* v247 no11 p6 N 2016

Obama's Terror 'Narrative' M. Hemingway *Weekly Standard* v22 no4 p7 O 3 2016

We Got Lucky...This Time T. JOSCELYN *Weekly Standard* v22 no4 p8 O 3 2016

Terrorism—United States—Government policy

MAKE AMERICA KIND AGAIN C. F. NAFF *Humanist* v77 no1 p12 Ja/F 2017

Terrorism—United States—Lawsuits & claims

Redress for Victims of Terrorism *Congressional Digest* v95 no9 p1 N 2016

Terrorism—United States—Charts, diagrams, etc.

U.S.-Saudi Arabia Relations Timeline *Congressional Digest* v95 no9 p2 N 2016

Terrorist organizations

Another Mideast Debacle: How America armed terrorists in Syria G. PORTER *American Conservative* v16 no4 p20 Jl/Ag 2017

The Growing Lone Wolf Threat from ISIS and Other Players M. E. NATHANSON *USA Today Magazine* v145 no2860 p48 Ja 2017

Terrorist organizations—Security measures

How to Defeat ISIS L. Smith *Weekly Standard* v22 no29 p8 Ap 3 2017

Terrorists

See also

   Lone wolves (Terrorists)

   Terrorist organizations

Arizona's Manufactured Terrorism Threat B. Hodai color *Progressive* v81 no5 p51 Je/Jl 2017

BEFORE DAWN ON A SUNDAY LATE J. VERINI *New York Times Magazine* p48 N 20 2016

On Witches and Terrorists M. Shermer color *Scientific American* v316 no5 p77 My 2017

Terror and the Failure of the Liberal Imagination: Three attacks in Britain highlight the West's inability to see the threat clearly J. Foreman *Commentary* v144 no1 p34 Jl/Ag 2017

Terrorists—Psychology

Why People Keep Saying, "That's What the Terrorists Want" M. Abrahms *Harvard Business Review Digital Articles* p2 N 20 2015

Terry, Andrew

Backfires: The joyful noise of the commentariat, rebutted sporadically by Ed color *Car & Driver* v62 no11 p9 My 2017

Terry, Candis

Perfect for You: Sunshine Creek Vineyard, Book 2 color *Publishers Weekly* v264 no2 p46 Ja 9 2017

Terry, Ellie

Forget Me Not *Publishers Weekly* v264 no3 p60 Ja 16 2017

Terry, Luke

HOT | NOT T. Keith color *Sports Illustrated* v126 no14 p22 My 15-22 2017

Terry Crews Saves Christmas (TV program)

MOVIES AND SPECIALS *TV Guide* p31 D 5 2016

Tersoff, Jerry

Carbon nanotube transistors scaled to a 40-nanometer footprint color graph *Science* v356 no6345 p1369 Je 30 2017

ter Steege, H.

Persistent effects of pre-Columbian plant domestication on Amazonian forest composition bibl chart graph map *Science* v355 no6328 p925 Mr 3 2017

Teruhiro Okuyama

Ventral CA1 neurons store social memory bibl graph *Science* v353 no6307 p1536 S 30 2016

Teruya-Feldstein, Julie

Self-renewal of a purified Tie2+ hematopoietic stem cell population relies on mitochondrial clearance bibl graph *Science* v354 no6316 p1156 D 2 2016

Terzian, Philip

All in the (Presidential) Family color *Weekly Standard* v22 no44 p15 Jl 31 2017

The Art of Losing Gracefully bw *Weekly Standard* v23 no4 p12 O 2 2017

The Biden Trial Balloon color *Weekly Standard* v22 no46 p21 Ag 14 2017

Celebrity in Chief color *Weekly Standard* v22 no18 p13 Ja 16 2017

Don't Blame the Message color *Weekly Standard* v22 no16 p14 D 26 2016

Feeding the Crocodile color *Weekly Standard* v23 no1 p17 S 11 2017

The Great Day-Care Sexual-Abuse Panic bw *Weekly Standard* v22 no42 p12 Jl 17 2017

Huddled Masses Through the Ages bw *Weekly Standard* v22 no47 p20 Ag 21 2017

Killer Celebrities bw *Weekly Standard* v23 no6 p19 O 16 2017

Let Trump Be Trump? color *Weekly Standard* v23 no3 p12 S 25 2017

Permanent Crisis bw *Weekly Standard* v22 no32 p20 My 1 2017

Pioneering Press Critic bw *Weekly Standard* v22 no26 p14 Mr 13 2017

The Veneration of Cool *Weekly Standard* v22 no8 p12 O 31 2016

Why Argue About a Day Off? color *Weekly Standard* v23 no2 p19 S 18 2017

Tesar, Alexander

Bigfoot on Four Paws cartoon *Walrus* v14 no2 p22 Mr 2017

Imagining Exoplanets color *Walrus* v14 no5 p59 Je 2017

Tesauro, Jason

DREAM WEAVER color *Better Homes & Gardens* v95 no9 p120 S 2017

THE IMPOSSIBLE LIST bw cartoon color *Esquire* v167 no1 p70 F 2017

Tesco PLC

Tesco's Downfall Is a Warning to Data-Driven Retailers M. Schrage *Harvard Business Review Digital Articles* p2 O 28 2014

Why Tesco's Strengths Are No Longer Good Enough J. Wells *Harvard Business Review Digital Articles* p2 O 6 2014

Teshigahara, Hiroshi

WOMAN IN THE DUNES J. Krebs bw *Sound & Vision* v82 no4 p70 My 2017

Tesla, Nikola, 1856-1943

1899: Colorado Springs *Lapham's Quarterly* v10 no2 p24 Spr 2017

Nikola Tesla E. BETZ color *Discover* v38 no4 p43 My 2017

Tesla automobiles

The Everyman Ride For the Upper Half D. Hull, J. Butters et al bw *Bloomberg Businessweek* no4533 p14 Ag 7 2017

FOR THE LOVE OF CARS: THE BEST RIDES OF 2017 Esquire K. SINTUMUANG, M. Prince et al color *Esquire* p65 O 2017

TESLA'S GOOD DEED SPARKS A (MISPLACED) BACKLASH K. Korosec color *Fortune* v176 no5 p14 O 1 2017

Tesla automobiles—Evaluation

FIRST DRIVE: Tesla Model 3 K. Reynolds and S. Evans color *Motor Trend* v69 no10 p16 O 2017

Tesla coils

Nikola Tesla E. BETZ color *Discover* v38 no4 p43 My 2017

Tesla Motors Inc.

0-60 MPH in 2.3 Seconds! F. Markus color graph *Motor Trend* v69 no5 p12 My 2017

2015 TESLA MODEL S P85D E. Tingwall bw color *Car & Driver* v62 no10 p72 Ap 2017

Don't Blame the Robots; Blame Us C. DIANA color *Popular Science* v288 no6 p46 N/D 2016

Fast and Flawed *Consumer Reports* v82 no1 p59 Ja 2017

FOR THE LOVE OF CARS: THE BEST RIDES OF 2017 Esquire K. SINTUMUANG, M. Prince et al color *Esquire* p65 O 2017

THE FUTURE ACCORDING TO MUSK T. Randall bw color *Bloomberg Businessweek* no4529 p48 Jl 3 2017

The Future of Electric Vehicles Is Golf Carts, Not Tesla T. Bartman *Harvard Business Review Digital Articles* p2 My 14 2015

Getting Juiced by the Roadside C. SMITH *Weekly Standard* v22 no6 p14 O 17 2016

How Tesla, Under Armour, and Sonos Do Branding R. B. Hansen *Harvard Business Review Digital Articles* p2 O 8 2015

Investors Watch Tesla L. Boggild *Alternatives Journal (AJ) - Canada's Environmental Voice* v42 no3 p11 2016

Is Tesla Really a Disruptor? (And Why the Answer Matters) L. Downes and P. Nunes *Harvard Business Review Digital Articles* p2 2017

Lightning in a Bottle E. Loh color *Motor Trend* v69 no5 p8 My 2017

The Many Ways to Innovate M. Fischetti diag *Scientific American* v315 no5 p80 N 2016

New Teslas Get Autonomous Tech with a Temporary Catch A. Nishimoto and E. Tahaney color *Motor Trend* v69 no2 p18 F 2017

Piecing Together the Tesla Strategy Puzzle B. Halla *Harvard Business Review Digital Articles* p2 S 16 2015

Rocket plan C. SORENSEN cartoon color *Maclean's* v129 no48/49 p64 D 5 2016

Tesla Is Betting on Solar, Not Just Batteries G. Battisti and M. Giulietti *Harvard Business Review Digital Articles* p2 Jl 2 2015

TESLA MAKES A U-TURN IN CHINA S. Cendrowski chart color diag *Fortune* v175 no8 p128 Je 15 2017

Tesla Model S 60/75 chart color *Motor Trend* v69 no1 p144 Ja 2017

Tesla Model X chart color *Motor Trend* v69 no1 p68 Ja 2017

Tesla Shows How Traditional Business Metrics Are Outdated E. Yoon *Harvard Business Review Digital Articles* p2 Ag 8 2017

Tesla's New Strategy Is Over 100 Years Old J. Suskewicz *Harvard Business Review Digital Articles* p2 My 19 2015

Why Elon Musk's New Strategy Makes Sense J. Gans *Harvard Business Review Digital Articles* p2 Jl 25 2016

Why Tesla Won't Be Able to Scale T. Bartman *Harvard Business Review Digital Articles* p2 Ap 23 2015

Why the Tesla model isn't replicable M. Rechtin color *Motor Trend* v69 no4 p28 Ap 2017

Tesla Motors Inc.—Finance

Could Tesla Run Out of Gas in Hong Kong? B. Einhorn *Bloomberg Businessweek* no4517 p25 Ap 3 2017

Stock X-Ray: Tesla T. Tepper color diag *Money* v46 no7 p36 Ag 2017

Tesla's Electric Shock M. Vella color *Time* v189 no15 p13 Ap 24 2017

Tesla Roadster automobile

High Voltage [Cover story] C. Seabaugh chart color graph *Motor Trend* v69 no2 p30 F 2017

Tesser, Lewis

IN DEFENSE OF LAWYERS: The widely held belief that lawyers are untrustworthy and unprincipled is dead wrong *Saturday Evening Post* v289 no5 p12 S/O 2017

Tessin, Carl Gustaf, 1695-1770

Man of distinction J. Gardner cartoon *Magazine Antiques* v184 no1 p174 Ja/F 2017

TESTA, JEREMY M.

Ecological Forecasting and the Science of Hypoxia in Chesapeake Bay *BioScience* v67 no7 p614 Jl 2017

Submersed Aquatic Vegetation in Chesapeake Bay: Sentinel Species in a Changing World *BioScience* v67 no8 p698 Ag 2017

Teste, François P.

Plant-soil feedback and the maintenance of diversity in Mediterranean-climate shrublands bibl graph *Science* v355 no6321 p1 Ja 13 2017

Testi, Leonardo

Spiral density waves in a young protoplanetary disk bibl graph *Science* v353 no6307 p1519 S 30 2016

Testimony (Law)

A Memo-rable Hearing M. WARREN color *Weekly Standard* v22 no39 p10 Je 19 2017

Testing

A Refresher on A/B Testing A. Gallo *Harvard Business Review Digital Articles* p2 Je 28 2017

SURVIVAL TRAINING ENTER THE CHAMBER A. MARSHALL color *Wired* v25 no5 p38 My 2017

Testing—Equipment & supplies

Focus on test and measurement A. Mandelis *Physics Today* v70 no3 p68 Mr 2017

Testosterone

STRONGER EVERYTHING! M. HEID cartoon color *Men's Health* v32 no4 p102 My 2017

Testosterone—Therapeutic use—Research

Testosterone therapy is a mixed bag M. ROSEN graph *Science News* v191 no6 p8 Ap 1 2017

Testudinidae—Behavior

FRED EVERLASTING H. Yanagihara color *New York Times Magazine* p58 My 21 2017

Tetalli, Vamsi

What 20 Years as a Remote Organization Has Taught Us About Managing Remote Teams *Harvard Business Review Digital Articles* p2 F 20 2017

Tetanus vaccination

VACCINES ON TRIAL M. Wadman color *Science* v356 no6336 p370 Ap 28 2017

Tetlock, Philip E.
Bringing probability judgments into policy debates via forecasting tournaments bibl color *Science* v355 no6324 p481 F 3 2017

Tetlow, Karin
Horizontal Sliding Fire Doors: Architectural Design Freedom color diag *Architectural Record* v204 no12 p188 D 2016

Teton Gravity Research (Company)
THE DOWNSLIDE color *Skiing* p10 Wint 2017

Tetramers (Oligomers)
Synthesis of resveratrol tetramers via a stereoconvergent radical equilibrium M. H. Keylor, B. S. Matsuura et al bibl diag graph *Science* v354 no6317 p1260 D 9 2016

Tetrapods
When We Left Water G. TARLACH bw color *Discover* v38 no6 p44 Jl/Ag 2017

Tetrick, Josh
The Mayo Mogul B. Bosker color *Atlantic* v320 no4 p76 N 2017

Tetrodes
Dynamics of cortical dendritic membrane potential and spikes in freely behaving rats J. J. Moore, P. M. Ravassard et al diag *Science* v355 no6331 p1281 Mr 24 2017

Tetsunari Kimura
A three-dimensional movie of structural changes in bacteriorhodopsin bibl diag graph *Science* v354 no6319 p1552 D 23 2016

TETT, GILLIAN
The Emperor Has No Clothes cartoon *Foreign Policy* no222 p70 Ja/F 2017
Gender Hack diag *Foreign Policy* no223 p68 Mr/Ap 2017
The Productivity Imperative color *Foreign Policy* no221 p98 N/D 2016

TETZLAFF, CHRISTIAN
Points to Ponder *Reader's Digest* v188 no1124 p39 O 2016

Teubner, Brett J. W.
Restoring auditory cortex plasticity in adult mice by restricting thalamic adenosine signaling graph *Science* v356 no6345 p1352 Je 30 2017

Teuchmann, H. L.
Gliogenic LTP spreads widely in nociceptive pathways bibl graph *Science* v354 no6316 p1144 D 2 2016

Teva Pharmaceutical Industries Ltd.
The Difficulties Of Cloning A CEO D. Leonard and Y. Benmeleh color graph *Bloomberg Businessweek* no4535 p50 Ag 28 2017

Tevet, Nahum
Bertha and Karl Leubsdorf Art Gallery R. Rubinstein color *Art in America* v105 no1 p84 Ja 2017

Tevis, Cheryl
FARM TRANSITIONS: AG'S DOWN CYCLE MAY OFFER A SLOW BUT STEADY SUCCESSION ROUTE *Successful Farming* v115 no9 p18 Ag 2017
YOUR FARM *Successful Farming* v115 no11 p14 S 2017

Tevis Cup Ride
The 62nd, Tevis Cup G. STEWART-SPEARS *Arabian Horse World* v57 no12 p128 S 2017
Artist Designs New Wendell Robie Trophy for Tevis Cup M. Melde *Arabian Horse World* v57 no11 p163 Ag 2017
If Adversity Builds Character I Have Plenty D. WHYTE *Arabian Horse World* v57 no12 p146 S 2017
OLD DOMINION: Endurance Race G. STEWART-SPEARS *Arabian Horse World* v57 no11 p142 Ag 2017
TEVIS CUP G. Stewart-Spears *Arabian Horse World* v56 no12 p164 S 2016
TEVIS journey D. Whyte *Arabian Horse World* v56 no12 p178 S 2016
What Head Veterinarian Greg Fellers Says about the Tevis G. Fellers *Arabian Horse World* v56 no12 p171 S 2016

Tewa, Sophia
The BEST BANK FOR YOU color diag map *Money* v45 no10 p86 N 2016

Texans
On Being Texan J. R. Erickson color *American Cowboy* p8 LEGENDS OF TEXAS Special Issue 2017

Texas
TEXAS WELCOME H. Anders bw color *Louisiana Life* v38 no1 p48 S/O 2017

Texas & Pacific Railway Co.
It Happened Here: Ranger, Texas S. Klomhaus bw *American Cowboy* p54 LEGENDS OF TEXAS Special Issue 2017

Texas, Virgil
TALKING HEADS A. Marantz cartoon *New Yorker* v92 no32 p36 O 10 2016

Texas A & M University
CONFESSION: BEFORE I WAS T. TALIAFERRO *Texas Monthly* v45 no8 p14 Ag 2017

Texas A & M University—Sports
25 Texas A&M color *Sports Illustrated* v127 no5 p114 Ag 14 2017
Week 11 color *Sports Illustrated* v127 no5 p77 Ag 14 2017

Texas blind salamander
Amphibious Assault C. HOOKS *Texas Monthly* v45 no2 p52 F 2017

Texas Christian University
CHANGE OF PLANS color *Flying* v144 no6 p24 Je 2017

Texas Gentlemen (Performer)
Meet the Texas Gentlemen A. LANGER *Texas Monthly* v45 no9 p36 S 2017

Texas Library Association—Congresses
TIME TO BE A TEXAN A. R. ALBANESE *Publishers Weekly* v264 no14 p22 Ap 3. 2017
TLA Program Highlights> bw color *Publishers Weekly* v264 no14 p24 Ap 3. 2017

Texas Monthly (Periodical)
BEST AND WORST *Texas Monthly* v45 no7 p10 Jl 2017
EDITOR'S LETTER B. D. SWEANY *Texas Monthly* v45 no1 p14 Ja 2017

Texas Panhandle (Tex.)—Environmental conditions
LOVE AND LOSS ON THE PLAINS: The day the fire came to the Franklin Ranch S. HOLLANDSWORTH *Texas Monthly* v45 no8 p60 Ag 2017

Texas Rangers (Baseball team)
2 RANGERS color *Sports Illustrated* v126 no9 p90 Mr 27 2017
HOT | NOT T. Keith color *Sports Illustrated* v126 no15 p19 My 29 2017
Who Would Vote Against This? E. CELESTE *D: The Magazine of Dallas* v43 no10 p82 O 2016

Texas Woman's University
BEST BANG FOR THE BUCK SOUTHERN COLLEGES chart *Washington Monthly* v49 no9/10 p52 S/O 2017
Texas Woman's University *Dance Magazine* v90 p121 2016/2017 Supplement College Guide

Texas—Description & travel
18.70 color *Horse & Rider* v56 no11 p30 N 2017
3 Days in… San Angelo, Texas G. R. SCHIAVINO color *American Cowboy* v23 no6 p34 Ap/My 2017
5 East Texas Hideaways color *American Cowboy* p55 LEGENDS OF TEXAS Special Issue 2017
DESERT HISTORIES H. HAWORTH *Orion Magazine* v35 no3 p64 My/Je 2016
The Great Guadalupe J. C. Smith color *Southern Living* v52 no7 p45 Jl 2017
It Happened Here: Nacogdoches, Texas G. R. Schiavino color *American Cowboy* v23 no6 p36 Ap/My 2017
The North Texas Loop G. R. SCHIAVINO map *American Cowboy* v23 no6 p35 Ap/My 2017
Pay Your Respects A. SAIKIN color map *Backpacker* p28 My 2017
TNT color *Vogue* v207 no6 p68 Je 2017

Texas—History
It Happened Here: Ranger, Texas S. Klomhaus bw *American Cowboy* p54 LEGENDS OF TEXAS Special Issue 2017
TEXAS TITANS bw *American Cowboy* p58 LEGENDS OF TEXAS Special Issue 2017

Texas—History—19th century
Come Along Boys and Listen to My Tale… color *American Cowboy* p56 LEGENDS OF TEXAS Special Issue 2017

Texas—Politics & government
THE FUTURE IS TEXAS L. WRIGHT bw cartoon *New Yorker* v93 no20 p40 Jl 10 2017
A Genius, If You Can Keep Him bw *Weekly Standard* v23 no4 p2 O 2 2017
TEXAS IS THE FUTURE A. Cockburn *Harper's Magazine* v334 no2002 p26 Mr 2017

Turning Blue A. Cockburn *Harper's Magazine* v334 no2004 p2 My 2017

Texas—Politics & government—21st century

MESSING WITH TEXAS P. Levy *Mother Jones* v42 no5 p32 S/O 2017

YES SHE CAN: WOMEN ARE POWERING TEXAS' PROGRESSIVE COMEBACK A. Dejean *Mother Jones* v42 no5 p28 S/O 2017

Texas—Politics & government—History

THE HOBBY NAME IS ONE B. D. SWEANY *Texas Monthly* v44 no12 p24 D 2016

Texas—Social conditions

EDITOR'S LETTER T. TALIAFERRO *Texas Monthly* v45 no2 p14 F 2017

THE FUTURE IS TEXAS L. WRIGHT bw cartoon *New Yorker* v93 no20 p40 Jl 10 2017

Text Cloud Anthology (Poem)

Text Cloud Anthology K. ALI *New Republic* v248 no7 p63 Jl 2017

Text messages (Telephone systems)

See also

Text messaging & driving

14 Totally Legit Expectations in Love K. Bonnell and P. R. Satran color *Glamour* v115 no2 p127 F 2017

day tripping J. BLEYER *Psychology Today* v49 no6 p96 N/D 2016

How to turn on/off read receipts in macOS Sierra's Messages R. LOYOLA cartoon color *Macworld - Digital Edition* v33 no11 p127 N 2016

Texting Is Turning Into Serious Business M. C. White color *Money* v46 no2 p20 Mr 2017

Text messages (Telephone systems)—Software

What Marketers Need to Know About Chat Apps M. W. Schaefer *Harvard Business Review Digital Articles* p2 Je 14 2016

Text messaging & driving

Don't Text and Drive, Grown-Ups color *Prevention* v69 no7 p11 Jl 2017

MEET THE TEXTALYZER P. Smith *New York Times Upfront* v149 no10 p13 Mr 13 2017

Quick Hits L. Nemo map *Scientific American* v317 no3 p20 S 2017

Textbooks

See also

Electronic textbooks

Buyer — Be informed B. Noll color il *Phi Delta Kappan* v98 no4 p60 D 2016/Ja 2017

Textbooks—Sales & prices

Unit Sales Slide 3% from 2016 chart *Publishers Weekly* v264 no38 p6 S 18 2017

Texter, Cory

Indian FTR750 Is On Track color *Cycle World* v55 no11 p34 D 2016

Textile arts

Editor's Letter L. POLLOCK bw *Art in America* v105 no4 p14 Ap 2017

Stitches of change J. Bleem color *U.S. Catholic* v81 no11 p50 N 2016

Textile arts—Exhibitions

SEEING WAR THROUGH ROSE PETALS A. WILLIS *In These Times* v41 no2 p41 F 2017

Textile design

My New Career H. BOWLES color *Vogue* v207 no11 p142 N 2017

Textile exhibitions

Events bw color *Virginia Living* v15 no5 p33 Ag 2017

TRENDY TEXTILE *Iceland Review* v55 no3 p12 My/Je 2017

Textile factories—Great Britain

Weaving Life at Quarry Bank mill *British Heritage Travel* v37 no6 p54 N/D 2016

Textile industry

See also

Cotton trade

Textile design

Weaving

At Archive Edition M. Ellen Polson color *Arts & Crafts Homes & the Revival* v12 no4 p50 Fall 2017

Textile industry—Economic aspects

Pins and Needles in The Heart of the Alps C. Bosley and C. Gretler color *Bloomberg Businessweek* no4531 p31 Jl 24 2017

Textile patterns

See also

Plaid

1975 PLAID L. HEDRICK color *Better Homes & Gardens* v95 no11 p156 N 2017

Textiles

See also

Animal prints (Decoration & ornament)

Camouflage print (Textiles)

Carpets

Corduroy

Linen

Plaid

Rugs

Towels

ADDITIONAL LISTINGS *Arts & Crafts Homes & the Revival* v12 no1 p21 2017 Resouce Guide

The Art of Science L. Dern color *InStyle* v24 no11 p96 N 2017

a happy medium J. GARLOCK color diag *Better Homes & Gardens* v95 no5 p30 My 2017

Skate color *Architectural Digest* v73 no11 p102c N 2016

A STUDY IN CONTRAST K. RENDA color *House Beautiful* v159 no2 p16 Mr 2017

WELCOME TO THE ISSUE color *Harper's Bazaar* no3655 p26 Ag 2017

Textiles in interior decoration

BARBARA WESTBROOK ON "FEEL" K. O'SHEA-EVANS color *House Beautiful* p38 Jl 2017

Textiles—Evaluation

COME RAIN OR SHINE color *House Beautiful* p19 Ag 2017

INSTANT ROOM: A DAPPER FAMILY SALON M. Aiduss color *House Beautiful* v159 no9 p46 N 2017

Make the Cut color *House Beautiful* v159 no5 p44 Je 2017

MICROFIBER CLOTH color *Good Housekeeping* v264 no2 p144 F 2017

The Plush Life color *Architectural Digest* v74 no10 p39 O 1 2017

Rhapsody in BLUE color *House Beautiful* p20 Ag 2017

Wanted L. BAILEY *Indianapolis Monthly* v40 no3 p33 N 2016

WORK IN PROGRESS E. Ross and H. BROWN color *House Beautiful* v159 no1 p42 F 2017

TEXTOR, TED

LOST SOUL OR GUARDIAN ANGEL? color *Flying* v144 no4 p30 Ap 2017

Textron Aviation Inc.

CULTURED TO EXCEL T. VELOCCI color *Forbes* v198 no9 p38 D 30 2016

DIESEL SKYHAWK JT-A ENTERS THE MARKET color *Flying* v144 no8 p18 Ag 2017

Innovation J. Bachman color *Bloomberg Businessweek* no4517 p37 Ap 3 2017

Texture in interior decoration

BARBARA WESTBROOK ON "FEEL" K. O'SHEA-EVANS color *House Beautiful* p38 Jl 2017

Texture of cosmetics

COLOR Coded M. Fuhrer *Dance Spirit* v21 no7 p98 S 2017

Textured woven textiles—Evaluation

Woven WORKS A. NEASON color *House Beautiful* p126 Ag 2017

Textures

What In The World? color *National Geographic Kids* no472 p31 Ag 2017

Tezel, Tunç

TARGETING THE "Tutulemma" *Sky & Telescope* v132 no6 p66 D 2016

Tgif (TV program)

TGIF A. D'ARMINIO *TV Guide* v65 no39 p63 S 18 2017

Thacker, Paul D.

Consumers Deserve to Know Who's Funding Health Research *Harvard Business Review Digital Articles* p2 D 2 2014

Flacking for GMOs: How the Biotech Industry Cultivates Positive Media color *Progressive* v81 no6 p34 Ag/S 2017

Thackrey, Sean

A Century of Style M. GOULET and J. Roth bw color *Esquire* p77 O 2017

Thaggard, Holly

"Go Get Your Elephant" A. FELDMAN color *Forbes* v199 no7 p56 Je 29 2017

Thai, Loi

The Elegance of Alliums Z. Gowen color *Southern Living* v52 no5 p48 My 2017

Thai restaurants

THAT ONE TIME I NEARLY DESTROYED THE FAMILY BUSINESS K. YENBAMROONG bw color *Bon Appetit* v62 no2 p74 Mr 2017

Thai restaurants—Evaluation

THE DINING GUIDE *Atlanta* v56 no8 p189 D 2016

Doctor's Orders J. K. WOLFE *Cincinnati Magazine* v50 no10 p121 Jl 2017

Pato Thai Cuisine J. LENNERS *Arizona Highways* v92 no7 p12 Jl 2016

Spice Island J. DRILLING *Cincinnati Magazine* v50 no3 p130 D 2016

THAI *Cincinnati Magazine* v50 no8 p126 My 2017

Thailand—Description & travel

Balling on a Budget G. ATANMO color *Ebony* v72 no8 p54 Je 2017

ONE TRIP, TWO WAYS: THAILAND D. Pointdujour color *Ebony* v72 no9 p56 Jl/Ag 2017

ORIENT Excess P. NIELSEN color map *Sail* v48 no10 p44 O 2017

Thailand—Politics & government—20th century

The Tightening Authoritarian Grip on Thailand C. SOPRANZETTI *Current History* v116 no791 p230 S 2017

Thaisomboonsuk, Butsaya

Dengue diversity across spatial and temporal scales: Local structure and the effect of host population size bibl graph *Science* v355 no6331 p1302 Mr 24 2017

Thaiss, Christoph A.

Potential role of intratumor bacteria in mediating tumor resistance to the chemotherapeutic drug gemcitabine diag *Science* v357 no6356 p1156 S 15 2017

Thaker, Nikhil G.

Measuring and Communicating Health Care Value with Charts *Harvard Business Review Digital Articles* p2 O 26 2015

Thakker, Krishna

WORLD'S LARGEST CORPORATIONS chart diag *Fortune* v176 no2 pF1 Ag 1 2017

Thakor, Manisha

Ask anything bw color *Women's Health* v14 no2 p18 Mr 2017

The Pause THAT REFRESHES F. TORABI cartoon *O, The Oprah Magazine* p40 Ap 2017

THE THOUSAND DOLLAR PAGE bw color *Men's Health* v32 no7 p42 S 2017

Thaler, Richard H., 1945-

Milestones color *Time* v190 no16/17 p20 O 23 2017

Thaman, Mary Beth

The 'Why' for the National Gold Medal Award *Parks & Recreation* v52 no1 p42 Ja 2017

Thamel, Pete

10 ARIZONA WILDCATS chart color *Sports Illustrated* v125 no15 p69 N 7 2016

15 SYRACUSE ORANGE chart color *Sports Illustrated* v125 no15 p74 N 7 2016

Big Man on Campus color *Sports Illustrated* v125 no13 p16 O 17 2016

CASE FOR ... OHIO STATE color *Sports Illustrated* v125 no19 p41 D 12 2016

THE CRAB WHO PULLS OTHERS UP color *Sports Illustrated* v126 no11 p30 Ap 17-24 2017

High STAKES color *Sports Illustrated* v126 no9 p32 Mr 27 2017

A LION IN SUMMER color *Sports Illustrated* v127 no3 p92 Jl 24 2017

NEW YORK JET color *Sports Illustrated* v125 no21 p38 D 26 2016

THE STREAM TEAMS color *Sports Illustrated* v126 no4 p62 Ja 30 2017

The System Is the Star chart color *Sports Illustrated* v125 no14 p50 O 24-31 2016

Three and Out color *Sports Illustrated* v125 no16 p16 N 14 2016

WHO DAK? [Cover story] color *Sports Illustrated* v125 no13 p24

O 17 2016

Thames, Eric

15 HOME SWEET HOMERS T. Verducci color *Sports Illustrated* v126 no9 p68 Mr 27 2017

HOT | NOT T. Keith color *Sports Illustrated* v126 no13 p19 My 8 2017

International Harvest Z. Pereles and T. Keith chart color *Sports Illustrated* v126 no15 p16 My 29 2017

Thames River (England)—History

Take a Walk on the South Side S. Lawrence *British Heritage Travel* v38 no3 p26 My/Je 2017

Thamizhavel, A.

Evidence for bulk superconductivity in pure bismuth single crystals at ambient pressure bibl color graph *Science* v355 no6320 p1 Ja 6 2017

Thanabalasuriar, Ajitha

Visualizing the function and fate of neutrophils in sterile injury and repair color graph *Science* v357 no6359 p111 O 6 2017

Thane, Pat

MORE THAN FREE LOVE AND SANDALS: The lives of six Victorian radicals shed light on the struggle to establish feminism, social reform and the Labour movement *History Today* v67 no7 p102 Jl 2017

THANGE, MUSADDIQUE

Standing against Islamophobia in California School Curricula *Islamic Horizons* v45 no6 p32 N/D 2016

Thank-you notes

7 Ways to Thank People in Your Network E. Baehr *Harvard Business Review Digital Articles* p2 D 1 2015

Thanksgiving cooking

36 HOURS [Cover story] C. SAFFITZ and A. STANEK color *Bon Appetit* v61 no11 p130 N 2016

BAO WOW J. WALKER and D. LI color *Bon Appetit* v61 no11 p118 N 2016

BEST SUPPORTING DISH C. K. Jackson color *Essence* v47 no7 p113 N 2016

A BLOODY GOOD TIME A. RAPOPORT color *Bon Appetit* no11 p10 N 2017

FANCY THAT! A. REDDING and M. DANZER color *Bon Appetit* v61 no11 p104 N 2016

FOOD + MEMORY I. Edwards color *Sunset* v237 no5 p8 N 2016

full house W. Williams color *Bon Appetit* v61 no11 p96 N 2016

HOME AGAIN J. BLACK color *Better Homes & Gardens* v95 no11 p106 N 2017

it's not all gravy J. Bainbridge and A. Jones color *Bon Appetit* v61 no11 p58 N 2016

Mila Kunis: What's on your Thanksgiving table? D. WALTERS color *Bon Appetit* no11 p136 N 2017

PREP SCHOOL C. MOROCCO, A. STANEK et al bw color *Bon Appetit* v61 no11 p153 N 2016

SARAH JESSICA PARKER M. KUTNER WALTERS color *Bon Appetit* v61 no11 p162 N 2016

Thanksgiving LESSONS [Cover story] B. LEONE, C. MOROCCO et al color *Bon Appetit* no11 p82 N 2017

there's an app for that C. Saffitz bw color *Bon Appetit* v61 no11 p76 N 2016

THE ULTIMATE MAKE-AHEAD THANKSGIVING color *Redbook* p115 N 2017

A Very Organized Thanksgiving A. BEGGS, A. STANEK et al color *Bon Appetit* no11 p19 N 2017

WITH LOVE AND GRATITUDE C. HONG and G. LOFTS *Martha Stewart Living* no269 p98 N 2016

Thanksgiving Day

13 Things You Didn't Know About the Macy's Thanksgiving Parade B. SPECKTOR bw color *Reader's Digest* v190 no1135 p124 N 2017

Apple Pie, Solo M. Miskimen *Saturday Evening Post* v288 no6 p62 N/D 2016

APPRECIATE C. K. Jackson color *Essence* v47 no7 p124 N 2016

A BLOODY GOOD TIME A. RAPOPORT color *Bon Appetit* no11 p10 N 2017

Bloody Thursday D. MENAKER color *Esquire* v166 no4 p13 N 2016

Can I Get an Amen? R. Bragg color *Southern Living* v51 no11 p172 N 2016

CHILL-GIVING J. BAINBRIDGE color *Bon Appetit* v61 no11

Production Partners M. S. Eddy *Stage Directions* v30 no7 p3 Jl 1 2017

Theater Needs Tomorrow's Technicians Today W. Djerf *Stage Directions* v30 no10 p34 O 2017

THE THEATRE *New Yorker* v92 no42 p20 D 19 2016

Touring with Stage Automation – Part 2 S. Cox *Stage Directions* v29 no12 p18 D 2016

We Are Connected M. S. Eddy *Stage Directions* v30 no6 p2 Je 2017

Theater awards

See also

Tony Awards

Expanding to Improve J. Coakley *Stage Directions* v29 no10 p30 O 2016

REDEMPTION SONG A. GREEN color *Vogue* v207 no10 p288 O 2017

Theater commercials (Motion pictures)

When People Pay Attention to Video Ads and Why T. S. Teixeira *Harvard Business Review Digital Articles* p2 O 14 2015

Theater curtains

The Evolving World of Fabrics and Soft Goods K. M. Mitchell *Stage Directions* v29 no11 p32 N 2016

Theater design & construction

Historic and Thriving: Ford's Theatre: A hallowed past meets a modern aesthetic L. Mulcahy *Stage Directions* v30 no6 p11 Je 2017

Setting the stage E. M. Kahn bw color *Magazine Antiques* v184 no3 p74 My/Je 2017

SOAR LIKE AN Eagle: Opera Theatre of St. Louis? production of Titus takes light M. S. Eddy *Stage Directions* v30 no9 p18 S 2017

Theater education

The Learning Curve of Theater M. S. Eddy *Stage Directions* v30 no10 p2 O 2017

Theater education in universities & colleges

Education Directory *Stage Directions* v30 no10 p36 O 2017

Theater equipment industry

Golden Age of Gear J. Coakley *Stage Directions* v29 no12 p2 D 2016

In the Greenroom *Stage Directions* v29 no11 p4 N 2016

Theater lighting

To See; To Hear M. Bissett *Stage Directions* v30 no10 p14 O 2017

Theater production & direction

Early Days M. S. Eddy *Stage Directions* v29 no10 p12 O 2016

Illuminations Debuts Online J. Coakley *Stage Directions* v29 no10 p2 O 2016

In the Greenroom *Stage Directions* v29 no10 p4 O 2016

LCT's Associate PM Kevin Orzechowski talks integrating Ghost Light into the Claire Tow Theater *Stage Directions* v30 no10 p9 O 2017

Play by Play: Lawrenceville's Aurora Theatre finds inspiration in the diversity of its audience T. MALONE *Atlanta* v57 no6 p82 O 2017

Your Fall To-Do List: Mark your calendars for these can't-miss artsy autumn events C. COX *Atlanta* v57 no6 p83 O 2017

Theater remodeling

Another Opening... Finally!: Broadway's Oldest Theater, The Hudson, Returns as Broadway's Newest Space M. S. Eddy *Stage Directions* v30 no6 p30 Je 2017

Theater schools

Education Directory *Stage Directions* v29 no10 p36 O 2016

"You have to tell yourself you're enough" E. Mahaney bw *Glamour* v115 no9 p142 S 2017

Theater sound designers & design

Mixing Without Leading B. Reesman *Stage Directions* v29 no10 p18 O 2016

Theater tickets

Hamilton's $849 Tickets Are Priced Too Low R. Mohammed *Harvard Business Review Digital Articles* p2 Je 24 2016

Theater—Congresses

Career is the Operative Word M. S. Eddy *Stage Directions* v30 no4 p2 Ap 2017

Theater—Equipment & supplies

Drapery & Tracking *Stage Directions* v30 no7 p24 Jl 1 2017

Flooring & Seating *Stage Directions* v30 no7 p34 Jl 1 2017

Golden Age of Gear J. Coakley *Stage Directions* v29 no12 p2 D

2016

Lighting Design, Service & Rentals *Stage Directions* v30 no7 p35 Jl 1 2017

Lighting & Electrical Equipment Manufacturers & Distributors *Stage Directions* v30 no7 p38 Jl 1 2017

Platforms, Risers & Stage Lifts *Stage Directions* v30 no7 p45 Jl 1 2017

Projection *Stage Directions* v30 no7 p47 Jl 1 2017

Props *Stage Directions* v30 no7 p48 Jl 1 2017

(Re)Creating The Encounter [Cover story] B. Reesman *Stage Directions* v29 no12 p12 D 2016

Rigging & Safety Equipment *Stage Directions* v30 no7 p50 Jl 1 2017

Special Effects *Stage Directions* v30 no7 p53 Jl 1 2017

Stage Automation *Stage Directions* v30 no7 p58 Jl 1 2017

Theatrical Retailers & Suppliers *Stage Directions* v30 no7 p59 Jl 1 2017

Tools of the Trade *Stage Directions* v30 no4 p6 Ap 2017

Touring with Stage Automation S. Cox *Stage Directions* v29 no11 p18 N 2016

Theater—Equipment & supplies—Evaluation

Buyer's Guide J. Coakley *Stage Directions* v30 no1 p12 Ja 2017

Elation - The Latest in Theatre-Optimized Lighting *Stage Directions* v30 no3 p25 Mr 2017

ETC ColorSource Consoles B. Creel *Stage Directions* v29 no12 p26 D 2016

It is a dark and stormy night... *Stage Directions* v30 no5 p24 My 2017

Next-Gen Par C. Rutherford *Stage Directions* v29 no12 p24 D 2016

See Clearly N. Schoenfeld and J. Coakley *Stage Directions* v29 no12 p20 D 2016

Tools: Products for your Consideration *Stage Directions* v30 no10 p6 O 2017

Theater—Evaluation

THE THEATRE *New Yorker* v93 no27 p14 S 11 2017

Theater—New York (State)—New York

GOINGS ON ABOUT TOWN color *New Yorker* v92 no33 p5 O 17 2016

Russian Unorthodox M. Schulman cartoon *New Yorker* v92 no34 p9 O 24 2016

Spring Preview M. Schulman cartoon *New Yorker* v93 no4 p15 Mr 13 2017

THE THEATRE cartoon *New Yorker* v92 no45 p10 Ja 16 2017

THE THEATRE *New Yorker* v92 no49 p24 F 13 2017

Theater—New York (State)—New York—Reviews

GOINGS ON ABOUT TOWN color *New Yorker* v92 no30 p6 S 26 2016

THE THEATRE *New Yorker* v92 no30 p12 S 26 2016

Theater—Production & direction—Equipment & supplies

Tools of the Trade *Stage Directions* v29 no10 p6 O 2016

Theater—Reviews

See also

Opera—Reviews

THE THEATRE *New Yorker* v93 no20 p12 Jl 10 2017

Theaters

See also

Amphitheaters

Motion picture theaters

Music halls (Variety-theaters, cabarets, etc.)

Barbizon Lighting Company Your Trusted Partner in Production *Stage Directions* v30 no3 p62 Mr 2017

Gateway Set Rentals - Sets worthy of your stage *Stage Directions* v30 no3 p37 Mr 2017

What Design Thinking Is Doing for the San Francisco Opera D. Hoyt and R. I. Sutton *Harvard Business Review Digital Articles* p2 Je 3 2016

Theaters—Argentina

open house M. R. MERCADO *Opera News* v81 no6 p29 D 2016

Theaters—California

Making Art Accessible L. Mulcahy *Stage Directions* v29 no10 p28 O 2016

Theaters—Design & construction

See also

Music halls (Variety-theaters, cabarets, etc.)—Design & construction

Grand Opera N. R. POLLOCK color diag *Architectural Record* v204 no12 p60 D 2016

Mark Cavagnero Associates L. Lee *Architectural Record* v205 no4 p130 Ap 2017

York Theatre Royal C. Foges *Architectural Record* v204 no11 p150 N 2016

Theaters—England—Design & construction

BEHIND THE CURTAIN M. BROWN *Archaeology* v70 no2 p17 Mr/Ap 2017

Theaters—Equipment & supplies

Audio Design, Service & Rentals *Stage Directions* v30 no7 p5 Jl 1 2017

Audio Equipment, Manufacturers & Distributors *Stage Directions* v30 no7 p6 Jl 1 2017

Backdrops, Sets & Scenic Supplies *Stage Directions* v30 no7 p10 Jl 1 2017

Theaters—Evaluation

POINTS of INTEREST *Texas Monthly* v45 no3 p110 Mr 2017

Theaters—Missouri

CURTAIN CALL A. BURGER color *Missouri Life* v44 no2 p46 Ap 2017

Theaters—New York (State)

Setting the stage E. M. Kahn bw color *Magazine Antiques* v184 no3 p74 My/Je 2017

Theaters—Ohio

Show Business A. Brownlee *Cincinnati Magazine* v50 no5 p62 F 2017

Theaters—Sound effects

Sounds From Under the Sea G. Petersen *Stage Directions* v30 no5 p16 My 2017

Theaters—United States

'O' the drama color *Nebraska Life* v20 no6 p65 N/D 2016

Theaters—Utah

AUTHENTIC for the festival J. Coakley *Stage Directions* v29 no10 p22 O 2016

Theater—Training of

A Moment and a Space T. H. Freeman *Stage Directions* v30 no1 p6 Ja 2017

Theater—United States

CENTER STAGE A. Green color *Vogue* v207 no6 p126 Je 2017

HOT SEATS L. VACCARIELLO *Indianapolis Monthly* p34 F 2017

Theatre Communications Group Inc.

Edgerton Foundation New Play Awards *Stage Directions* v30 no8 p4 Ag 2017

TheatreWorld Backdrops LLC

TheatreWorld Backdrops Artful. Intelligent. Vivid Colorization *Stage Directions* v30 no3 p26 Mr 2017

Theatrical companies

Enter Stage Right . . M. S. Eddy *Stage Directions* v30 no3 p2 Mr 2017

Theatrical companies—Officials & employees

We Can't Remain Silent K. M. Mitchell *Stage Directions* v30 no4 p4 Ap 2017

Theatrical costume

Costume Craftsperson Elizabeth Flauto's Tips on Thermoplastics *Stage Directions* v30 no8 p24 Ag 2017

Curating the Character's Closet J. Kucharski *Stage Directions* v30 no8 p20 Ag 2017

Theatrical makeup

See also

Film makeup

GOOD AT LOOKING BAD *Stage Directions* v30 no5 p23 My 2017

Theatrical producers & directors

See also

Musical theater producers & directors

Director Kate Whoriskey brings intellect and compassion to Sweat L. Mulcahy *Stage Directions* v30 no5 p8 My 2017

The Good Fight K. M. Mitchell *Stage Directions* v30 no10 p12 O 2017

RISE UP R. MEAD cartoon color *New Yorker* v93 no5 p44 Mr 20 2017

ROBERT FALLS B. Zehme cartoon *Chicago* v66 no3 p148 Mr 2017

Susan Booth *Atlanta* v57 no2 p92 Je 2017

Theatrical producers & directors—Interviews

"Look What We Did!" B. Boritt, T. Yarden et al *Stage Directions* v30 no10 p19 O 2017

Theatrical scenery

See also

Set design

Stage props

Backdrops Beautiful® Custom-Designed Backdrops that Set the Stage *Stage Directions* v30 no3 p46 Mr 2017

Color and Light L. Mulcahy *Stage Directions* v30 no2 p20 F 2017

Teaching Aesthetics R. Minetor *Stage Directions* v30 no4 p10 Ap 2017

Theatrical scenery—Design & construction

SCENE UNSEEN L. VACCARIELLO *Cincinnati Magazine* v50 no3 p96 D 2016

The skills of scenic artists can take a design to the next level J. Coakley *Stage Directions* v30 no2 p16 F 2017

Theatrical scenery—Equipment & supplies

Staging Concepts - Elevate Your Experience *Stage Directions* v30 no3 p36 Mr 2017

Tools of the Trade *Stage Directions* v30 no1 p6 Ja 2017

Theatrical stages—Design & construction

Evolution and Elevation: Staging Concepts Continues to Grow and Expand *Stage Directions* v30 no9 p10 S 2017

Thede, Robin

ROCKIN' ROBIN R. R. Robertson color *Essence* v48 no5 p61 S 2017

When Kanye Met Donald cartoon color *Wired* v25 no4 p66 Ap 2017

Theft

See also

Identity theft

Wage theft

Time Bandits J. BOTTUM color *Weekly Standard* v22 no30 p5 Ap 10 2017

WHO COMES TO STEAL KILL AND DESTROY? C. KEENER *Christianity Today* p48 Ap 2017

Theft from motor vehicles

HOT CARS C. Atiyeh chart graph *Car & Driver* v63 no5 p22 N 2017

Theft prevention

Chicago's Plan to Stop Wage Theft J. MILLER *In These Times* v41 no4 p10 Ap 2017

Protect Your Rig From Theft: Every year, about 5,000 boats are stolen. Here's how to keep it from happening A. JONES *Boating World* v38 no8 p14 S/O 2017

Theillet, Francois-Xavier

Opposing effects of Elk-1 multisite phosphorylation shape its response to ERK activation bibl graph *Science* v354 no6309 p233 O 14 2016

Their Finest (Film)

ANGLO-FILE S. Gutierrez *British Heritage Travel* v38 no4 p12 Jl/Ag 2017

The Ministry of Information: Parsing the Facts of Fiction A. Hastie *Film Quarterly* v71 no1 p65 Fall 2017

Theism

CLASSIC HUMANIST *Humanist* v76 no6 p10 N/D 2016

Thelen, Ashley M.

Lysosomal cholesterol activates mTORC1 via an SLC38A9–Niemann-Pick C1 signaling complex bibl diag graph *Science* v355 no6331 p1306 Mr 24 2017

Thelen, Kurt D.

Cellulosic biofuel contributions to a sustainable energy future: Choices and outcomes color *Science* v356 no6345 p1349 Je 30 2017

Thelonius Monk With John Coltrane: The Complete 1957 Riverside Recordings (Music)

Monk & Coltrane Reissue Unites Architects of Jazz K. MICALLEF bw *Downbeat* v84 no10 p24 O 2017

Theme Building (Los Angeles, Calif.)

Theme Building *Los Angeles Magazine* v62 no6 p20 Je 2017

Themed environments

TO BOLDLY CRUISE WHERE NO COUPLE HAS CRUISED BEFORE F. GOLDEN color *Bloomberg Businessweek* no4512 p75 F 20 2017

Themes in art

See also

Themes in sculpture

Works of art in art

POETRY & PAINT D. T. MORAN *Humanist* v77 no5 p40 S/O 2017

The Return L. Copan color *Christian Century* v134 no18 p47 Ag 30 2017

Themes in sculpture

Art Watch: Three artists moving the Atlanta art scene forward F. FEASTER *Atlanta* v57 no6 p76 O 2017

Themine (Company)

COLOR GOURD GREENS M. B. EYERS color *Better Homes & Gardens* v95 no10 p34 O 2017

Theo Wanne (Company)

Theo Wanne Slant Sig B. Gibson color *Downbeat* v84 no1 p106 Ja 2017

Theobald, Douglas L.

Evolutionary drivers of thermoadaptation in enzyme catalysis [Cover story] bibl color graph *Science* v355 no6322 p289 Ja 20 2017

Theodoracopulos, Mandolyna

PEAK SEASON color *Vanity Fair* v59 no1 p93 Holiday 2017

Theodore Roosevelt National Park (N.D.)

The Greatest Places to See Wild Horses color *American Cowboy* v23 no6 p67 Ap/My 2017

Theodore Roosevelt National Park R. H. MOHLENBROCK color map *Natural History* v125 no3 p42 Mr 2017

Visiting Theodore Roosevelt National Park with my Father T. T. Williams color *Progressive* v81 no5 p34 Je/Jl 2017

Theodoro, V. M.

Observation of a large-scale anisotropy in the arrival directions of cosmic rays above 8 × 1018 eV *Science* v357 no6357 p1266 S 22 2017

THEOHARIS, ATHAN

God and Man at the FBI bw color *Reason* v49 no3 p66 Jl 2017

Theoharis, Liz

The poor we have with us bw *Christian Century* v134 no9 p26 Ap 26 2017

Theologians—United States

A Life Lived in God's Love C. González-Andrieu color *America* v216 no5 p18 Mr 6 2017

Realism without despair J. Sabella *Christian Century* v134 no18 p10 Ag 30 2017

Theological liberalism

WHY CHRISTIANITY TODAY REVISITED T. OLSEN color *Christianity Today* v60 no8 p46 O 2016

Theological seminaries

See also

Episcopalian theological seminaries

Habit forming P. W. Marty *Christian Century* v134 no4 p3 F 15 2017

Reimaging Seminary C. SCHAREN cartoon color *Christianity Today* v61 no1 p75 Ja/F 2017

Seminary at the megachurch R. Lockhart and J. Byassee color *Christian Century* v134 no4 p24 F 15 2017

Theological virtues

See also

Charity

Faith

Hope—Religious aspects—Christianity

Faith Matters M. C. Barnes *Christian Century* v134 no12 p40 Je 7 2017

Why I stay D. Thomas *Christian Century* v134 no14 p13 Jl 5 2017

Theology

See also

Bible

Church

Doctrinal theology

Borg's Jesus S. King *Christian Century* v134 no17 p6 Ag 16 2017

I WASTED MY TIME WITH THIS. So should you M. Galli color *Christianity Today* v61 no6 p74 Jl/Ag 2017

THE MAINLINE'S SAVING GRACE? Even in secular Canada's declining denominations, conservative theology correlates with church growth K. SHELLNUTT color *Christianity Today* v61 no4 p13 My 2017

OUR FAVORITE HERESIES graph *Christianity Today* v60 no9

p19 N 2016

Survey: U.S. Protestants and Catholics have more in common than not E. M. Miller *Christian Century* v134 no20 p16 S 27 2017

Theology & philosophy

Churched Philosophy J. J. CONLEY *America* v215 no11 p26 O 17 2016

Theology—History

THE FUTURE OF BELIEF K. Tippett color *America* v216 no4 p32 F 20 2017

Theology—Study & teaching (Higher)

The dance of faith A. Papanikolaou color *Christian Century* v134 no4 p36 F 15 2017

Theophilos, Emperor of Constantinople, d. 842

Death of the Byzantine Emperor Theophilus *History Today* v67 no1 p8 Ja 2017

Theory

See also

Systems theory

REPUBLICANS DON'T LACK A PLAN TO REPLACE OBAM-ACARE. THEY LACK A UNIFIED THEORY P. SUDERMAN color *Reason* v49 no2 p14 Je 2017

Theory of constraints (Management)

Constraints and Community: To get things done, leaders need to focus on the bigger picture M. Funkhouser *Governing* v30 no12 p61 S 2017

Theory of knowledge

See also

Analogy

Belief & doubt

Common sense

Error

Experience

Expertise

Idea (Philosophy)

Ideology

Ignorance (Theory of knowledge)

Intuition (Psychology)

Judgment (Psychology)

Values (Ethics)

The Editor's Note J. Richardson *Phi Delta Kappan* v98 no3 p4 N 2016

How to Make Better Decisions with Less Data T. Menon and L. Thompson *Harvard Business Review Digital Articles* p2 N 7 2016

THE INSULATED LEADER A. IGNATIUS bw img *Harvard Business Review* v95 no2 p12 Mr/Ap 2017

Let Your Questioning Start with Wikipedia S. GERBIC *Skeptical Inquirer* v41 no2 p24 Mr/Ap 2017

The Virtuous Skeptic M. PIGLIUCCI *Skeptical Inquirer* v41 no2 p54 Mr/Ap 2017

Theory of wave motion

Dynamics of a human spiral wave A. J. Welsh, E. F. Greco et al *Physics Today* v70 no2 p78 F 2017

Theory of self-knowledge

A Way of Knowing bw *American Craft* v76 no6 p8 D 2016-Ja 2017

Theranos Inc.

THE RISE AND FALL OF THERANOS S. VOLK color *Discover* v38 no1 p44 Ja/F 2017

Therapeutic use of antineoplastic agents

Potential role of intratumor bacteria in mediating tumor resistance to the chemotherapeutic drug gemcitabine L. T. Geller, M. Barzily-Rokni et al diag *Science* v357 no6356 p1156 S 15 2017

Therapeutic use of antioxidants

Put Purple on Your Plate color *Health* v31 no6 p9 Jl 2017

Therapeutic use of capsaicin

Max Out With Capsaicin D. JACKSON and J. WUEBBEN color *Muscle & Performance* v9 no11 p33 N 2017

Therapeutic use of coffee

30 Superfoods for a Healthier Life K. KLOSS color *Prevention* v69 no11 p44 N 2017

Therapeutic use of essential oils

Is Your Pet Stressed Out? J. SZABO color *Better Nutrition* v79 no10 p36 O 2017

Therapeutic use of ginseng

CASH CROP R. J. Smith *Cincinnati Magazine* v50 no12 p70 S

2017

Therapeutic use of lasers
MBODY—MODERN BODY CONTOURING & LASER CEN-
TER *Washingtonian Magazine* v53 no1 p112 O 2017

Therapeutic use of LSD
A DOORWAY TO CHANGE J. Bleyer *Psychology Today* v50 no3
p60 My/Je 2017

Therapeutic use of meditation
Of Mice and Mindfulness: Putting mice into something like a
meditative state may shed light on the human brain G. Reynolds
color *New York Times Magazine* p24 My 21 2017

Therapeutic use of minerals
Minerals in Medicine Prove a Perfect Prescription *USA Today
Magazine* v145 no2865 p16 Je 2017

Therapeutic use of probiotics
A Bug in the System H. ESTROFF MARANO *Psychology Today*
v50 no3 p31 My/Je 2017
Probiotics for Less Stress color *Prevention* v69 no8 p13 Ag 2017

Therapeutic use of vitamin C
FRESHER THAN EVER: VITAMIN C FOR YOUR SKIN color
Health v31 no9 p14 N 2017

Therapeutic use of vitamin D
Dairy-Free Do's and Don'ts color *Health* v31 no6 p16 Jl 2017

Therapeutics
See also
Drug therapy
Fluid therapy
Gene therapy
Immunotherapy
Music therapy
Physical therapy
Placebos (Medicine)
Treatment effectiveness
Precision Medicine *Congressional Digest* v96 no2 p3 F 1 2017

Therapeutics—Economic aspects
It's Easier to Measure the Cost of Health Care than Its Value D.
Goldman, A. Chandra et al *Harvard Business Review Digital
Articles* p2 N 18 2014

Therapy dogs
Comfort & Joy S. A. SMITH color *Missouri Life* v44 no4 p58
Je 2017

There Goes Rhymin' Simon (Music)
Essential Paul Simon D. Fricke bw color *Rolling Stone* no1275
p62 D 1 2016

'There Was a Great Want of Civility' (Poem)
'There Was a Great Want of Civility' J. Suarez *New York Times
Magazine* p17 F 5 2017

Thérèse, de Lisieux, Saint, 1873-1897
Learning to love Thérèse S. Guthrie *Christian Century* v133 no25
p10 D 7 2016

Thermal conductivity
Anomalously low electronic thermal conductivity in metallic vanadium dioxide K. Hippalgaonkar, K. Wang et al bibl graph *Science* v355 no6323 p371 Ja 27 2017

Thermal imaging cameras
NEW ELECTRONICS J. Y. WOOD color *Power & Motoryacht*
v34 no6 p26 Je 2017

Thermal imaging cameras—Evaluation
new products color *Science* v355 no6325 p648 F 10 2017

Thermal properties of solids
Oxidation at the atomic scale D. Cadavid and A. Cabot diag *Science* v356 no6335 p245 Ap 21 2017

Thermal stability
Cell-wide analysis of protein thermal unfolding reveals determi-
nants of thermostability P. Leuenberger, S. Ganscha et al color
Science v355 no6327 p812 F 24 2017

Thermo Fisher Scientific Inc.
new products: cell culture color *Science* v356 no6333 p99 Ap 7
2017
new products *Science* v356 no6342 p1088 Je 9 2017

Thermoelectric materials
Advances in thermoelectric materials research: Looking back and
moving forward J. He and T. M. Tritt diag *Science* v357 no6358
p1369 S 29 2017

Thermography
new products color *Science* v355 no6325 p648 F 10 2017

THERMAL IMAGERS HAVE BECOME BETTER AND
CHEAPER. HERE'S WHY J. B. SNOW color diag *Outdoor
Life* v224 no2 p42 F/Mr 2017

Thermometers
get in gear color *Bon Appetit* v61 no11 p72 N 2016

Thermometers—Evaluation
iOS Accessories J. MATHIS color *Macworld - Digital Edition* p74
D 2016
PRODUCT TEST TEAM D. MOWITZ *Successful Farming* v115
no2 p34 F 2017

Thermoplastics
See also
Polyethylene
Costume Craftsperson Elizabeth Flauto's Tips on Thermoplastics
Stage Directions v30 no8 p24 Ag 2017
High-performance vitrimers from commodity thermoplastics
through dioxaborolane metathesis M. Röttger, T. Domenech et
al color diag *Science* v356 no6333 p62 Ap 7 2017
IN SCIENCE JOURNALS color *Science* v356 no6333 p37 Ap 7
2017

Thermos bottles—Evaluation
SOMETHING COOL FOR EVERYONE color *Popular Mechanics* p94 D 2016/Ja 2017

Thermostat
Adam's Home STYLE SHEET Adam color *O, The Oprah Maga-
zine* p56 Ag 2017
Internal Affairs K. L. Beamon *Architectural Record* v205 no10
p61 O 2017
Q+A G. Michal, Z. Prochazka et al *Boating World* v38 no5 p26
My 2017

Thermostat—Evaluation
Nexia Smart Home Control System D. Wilkinson color *Sound &
Vision* v81 no9 p62 N 2016
A Smarter Way to Heat and Cool Your Home P. M. ESSWEIN
color *Kiplinger's Personal Finance* v70 no12 p39 D 2016

Thermotherapy
See also
Phototherapy
Rotator cuff injury [Cover story] *Mayo Clinic Health Letter* v35
no3 p1 Mr 2017

Thernstrom, Melanie
Grief and Reckoning *New York Times Book Review* p16 F 5 2017
The Playborhood *New York Times Magazine* p42 O 23 2016

Theron, Charlize, 1975-
Atomic Blonde C. Nashawaty color *Entertainment Weekly* no1476
p48 Ag 4 2017
BLONDE AMBITION: FILMING A KILLER ACTION SE-
QUENCE M. YARM bw color *Wired* v25 no8 p16 Ag 2017
EW AT COMIC-CON color *Entertainment Weekly* p8 Jl 24 2017
A Fierce Role Model S. ERICKSON *Los Angeles Magazine* v62
no9 p72 S 2017
GAME PLAN M. Zimmerman color diag map *Men's Health* v32
no6 p10 Ag 2017
Going Theronuclear J. Podhoretz color *Weekly Standard* v22 no47
p47 Ag 21 2017
Lethally Blonde E. Dockterman color *Time* v190 no6 p46 Ag 7
2017

Theron, Charlize, 1975—Interviews
BLONDE, SWEAT & TEARS [Cover story] S. Vilkomerson color
Entertainment Weekly p12 Jl 24 2017
Charlize Theron A. Synnott color *InStyle* v24 no1 p60 Ja 2017
"You've got to break your back!" A. Eler, L. Brody et al color
Glamour v115 no4 p153 Ap 2017

Theroux, Justin, 1971-
THE BOMBER SQUAD E. Sullivan bw color *Esquire* p86 My
2017
THE LEFTOVERS J. Hibberd color *Entertainment Weekly*
no1446/1447 p58 D 2016/Ja 2017
What's Left for The Leftovers? J. Hibberd color *Entertainment
Weekly* no1466 p47 My 19 2017
A wild ride with The Leftovers K. Reklis color *Christian Century*
v134 no15 p44 Jl 19 2017

Theroux, Louis
The British Michael Moore investigates the Church of Scientology E. Blondiau color *America* v216 no6 p46 Mr 20 2017

THEROUX, MARCEL

Pitch of Dreams color *New York Times Book Review* p10 Ja 29 2017

Theroux, Paul
HALEIWA, HAWAII *Harper's Magazine* p35 O 2017
Life Magazine *New York Times Magazine* p20 Ap 2 2017
Maternal Claws: It isn't Mother's Day in Paul Theroux's portrait of dysfunction running in the family S. KING *New York Times Book Review* p13 My 14 2017

Théry, Manuel
Microtubules acquire resistance from mechanical breakage through intralumenal acetylation diag graph *Science* v356 no6335 p328 Ap 21 2017

Thessaly (Greece)—History
A SURPRISE CITY IN THESSALY J. URBANUS color *Archaeology* v70 no2 p16 Mr/Ap 2017

Thetford, Adam
Identification of single-site gold catalysis in acetylene hydrochlorination bw diag graph *Science* v355 no6332 p1399 Mr 31 2017

Thetford, Tamra
Entrepreneurship and Re-entry: Aspire Entrepreneurship Initiative *Bridges (Federal Reserve Bank of St. Louis)* p8 Spr 2017

Theulier, Cyril A.
A catalytic fluoride-rebound mechanism for C(sp3)-CF3 bond formation diag *Science* v356 no6344 p1272 Je 23 2017

Thevamaran, Ramathasan
Dynamic creation and evolution of gradient nanostructure in single-crystal metallic microcubes bibl bw *Science* v354 no6310 p312 O 21 2016

Thèves, Catherine
Ancient genomic changes associated with domestication of the horse color diag *Science* v356 no6336 p442 Ap 28 2017

They Live by Night (Film)
GOINGS ON ABOUT TOWN cartoon *New Yorker* v93 no23 p6 Ag 7 2017

THEYS, EMILY MACEL
Before #BlackLivesMatter: A Timeline *Dance Magazine* v90 no12 p43 D 2016

Theyskens, Olivier
Olivier's TWIST L. YAEGER bw color *Vogue* v206 no12 p142 D 2016

Thézénas, Marie-Laëtitia
Posttranslational mutagenesis: A chemical strategy for exploring protein side-chain diversity diag *Science* v354 no6312 p597 N 4 2016

THIAGARAJAN, MAYA
are asian kids really better at math? *Parents* v91 no9 p58 S 2016

Thibaud, Blanka M.
Job openings, hires, and separations rise, but at a slower pace, in 2016 bibl *Monthly Labor Review* p1 Ag 2017

Thibodeaux, Jeremy—Interviews
French Quarter Festival color *New Orleans Magazine* v51 no6 p27 Ap 2017

Thibodeaux, Todd
Smart Cities Are Going to Be a Security Nightmare *Harvard Business Review Digital Articles* p2 Ap 28 2017

Thich Nhat Hanh, 1926-
THICH NHAT HANH color *Tricycle: The Buddhist Review* v26 no4 p20 Summ 2017

Thicke, Alan, 1947-2016
Alan Thicke: 1947-2016 M. Roush *TV Guide* v65 no2 p10 Ja 2 2017
Alan Thicke D. D'addario color *Time* v188 no27-28 p17 D 26 2016

Thiel, Peter A., 1967-
FLIGHT 1040 M. Mechanic color *Mother Jones* v42 no3 p46 My/Je 2017
THE PRESIDENT'S MEN PART I: Frenemy of the State A. CIRALSKY color *Vanity Fair* v59 no11 p118 N 2017
THE RECKONING G. CARTER *Vanity Fair* v59 no11 p46 N 2017
V.C. FOR VENDETTA D. MARGOLICK color *Vanity Fair* v59 no1 p108 Holiday 2017
The Winner-Take-All Economy A. M. Renn *Governing* v30 no4 p22 Ja 2017

THIEL, RICHARD
ALL-AMERICAN chart color diag *Power & Motoryacht* v33 no3 p90 Mr 2017
A Different Breed of Cat chart color *Power & Motoryacht* v33 no4 p78 Ap 2017
The Family Way cartoon chart color *Power & Motoryacht* v32 no12 p56 D 2016
Farewell, My Friend B. PIKE color *Power & Motoryacht* v32 no11 p72 N 2016
A Man You Could Count On L. Burke color *Power & Motoryacht* v32 no11 p34 N 2016
READY & ABLE chart color diag *Power & Motoryacht* v33 no3 p76 Mr 2017
STRONG SILENT TYPE chart color diag *Power & Motoryacht* v33 no2 p94 F 2017
Temperature Check color *Power & Motoryacht* v32 no11 p46 N 2016

THIEL, RICHARD R.
An Unparalleled Opportunity for an Important Ecological Study *BioScience* v67 no10 p875 O 2017

Thiele, Alexander
Selective modulation of cortical state during spatial attention bibl graph *Science* v354 no6316 p1140 D 2 2016

Thielen, Laura
Sundance Film Festival's Focus on Syria *Film Quarterly* v70 no4 p109 Summ 2017

Thiem, Dominic
The BIG TWO L. Thomas color *Vogue* v207 no9 p722 S 2017
Dominic Thiem *Tennis* v53 no1 p26 Ja/F 2017

Thien, Madeleine, 1974-
Dogs at the Perimeter color *Publishers Weekly* v264 no34 p80 Ag 21 2017
Madeleine Thien D. Kiper color *Current Biography* v78 no3 p73 Mr 2017
'Never such a thing as arrival' B. BETHUNE color *Maclean's* v129 no43 p47 O 31 2016
When Music Was Life and Death J. FAN *New York Times Book Review* p21 N 6 2016

Thieneman, R. J.
Hikes Gone Wrong: We all love the trail. Sometimes love hurts color il *Backpacker* p69 S 2017

Thierry, Agnès
3D organization of synthetic and scrambled chromosomes diag *Science* v355 no6329 p1050 Mr 10 2017

Thies, Bill—Awards
Three Society alumni named MacArthur Fellows color *Science News* v190 no12 p29 D 10 2016

Thieves
See also
Robbers
DOG NABS THIEF S. McCollum *National Geographic Kids* no467 p13 F 2017
How to Carry Your Wife: Giving new meaning to "spousal support" Elliot and Giana Storey share their secrets for winning a sports competition like no other J. BILLS *Yankee* v81 no5 p28 S/O 2017

Thigh exercises
Simply Toned J. B. SOUTHERLAND color *Prevention* v69 no9 p74 O 2017
Thigh Sweep color *Prevention* v69 no7 p17 Jl 2017
Tone up while watching TV color *Redbook* p70 Jl/Ag 2017

Thigh muscles
See also
Biceps femoris
15 MINUTE WORKOUT M. Gainsburg color *Women's Health* v14 no1 p90 Ja/F 2017
Leg Drop With Abduction color *Prevention* v69 no6 p16 Je 2017
Standing Star color *Prevention* v69 no9 p16 O 2017

Thigh—Anatomy
Get to know ... Your IT band [Cover story] J. Miller color *Yoga Journal* no295 p62 O 2017

Thigh blood-vessels
Roll for the Flow L. McGlashan and J. WUEBBEN color *Muscle & Performance* v9 no11 p21 N 2017

Thill, Gary
HAVEN'T PLANNED FOR RETIREMENT? HERE ARE THREE PITFALLS TO AVOID *Washingtonian Magazine* v52 no8 p144 My 2017

How God Befriends Us B. Davies bw *Commonweal* v143 no17 p36 O 21 2016

Thomas, Ayanna K.
Retrieval practice protects memory against acute stress bibl chart graph *Science* v354 no6315 p1046 N 25 2016

Thomas, Beth A.
Language policy, language ideology, and visual art education for emergent bilingual students bibl *Arts Education Policy Review* v118 no4 p228 2017

Thomas, Biju
Feed Your Soul J. Lindsey color *Bicycling* v58 no6 p26 Jl 2017

THOMAS, BRAD
Hoarder Control color *Forbes* v200 no2 p42 S 5 2017

THOMAS, BRIAN
THE FORGOTTEN HISTORY OF U STREET *Washingtonian Magazine* v52 no5 p60 F 2017

Thomas, Briana
19 THINGS YOU REALLY OUGHT TO DO THIS MONTH *Washingtonian Magazine* v52 no1 p33 O 2016

THOMAS, CANDACE
The Question color *O, The Oprah Magazine* p14 N 2017

THOMAS, CARLA
Asia's Rising Stars color *Forbes* v199 no5 p20 My 16 2017

Thomas, Chad
A Continental Retreat color map *Bloomberg Businessweek* no4514 p23 Mr 13 2017
This Just Got Awkward color graph *Bloomberg Businessweek* no4532 p36 Jl 31 2017

THOMAS, CHRIS
LET THE EXPERIMENTS BEGIN! color *Black Belt* v55 no4 p66 Je/Jl 2017

Thomas, Chris D.
Adapting to the Anthropocene A. Mooers color *Science* v357 no6354 p878 S 1 2017

Thomas, Christopher
How to Do Walking Meetings Right *Harvard Business Review Digital Articles* p2 Ag 5 2015

Thomas, Clarence, 1948-
Full Disclosure A. BEATTIE *American Scholar* v86 no2 p18 Spr 2017
Redoubting Thomas color *Weekly Standard* v23 no5 p4 O 9 2017

Thomas, Corey E.
Why Companies Shouldn't Try to Hack Their Hackers *Harvard Business Review Digital Articles* p2 My 24 2017

THOMAS, DANA
ALL THE RAJ color *Architectural Digest* v74 no4 p146 Ap 2017
DARK KNIGHT bw color *Architectural Digest* v73 no12 p48 D 2016
A Fine Vintage color *Architectural Digest* v74 no8 p94 Ag 2017
SHIP TO SHORE color *Architectural Digest* v74 no1 p196 Ja 2017

Thomas, Danny
Charitable Giving May Be in Your Genes J. BODNAR color *Kiplinger's Personal Finance* v71 no7 p24 Jl 2017

THOMAS, DARREN
Opportunities for Improved Transparency in the Timber Trade through Scientific Verification *BioScience* v66 no11 p990 N 1 2016

Thomas, Debie
Reflections on the lectionary *Christian Century* v134 no20 p21 S 27 2017
Why I stay *Christian Century* v134 no14 p13 Jl 5 2017

THOMAS, DOROTHY DEE
A Little Bit Braver Now color *O, The Oprah Magazine* p18 D 2016

Thomas, Duncan W.
Plant diversity increases with the strength of negative density dependence at the global scale diag *Science* v356 no6345 p1389 Je 30 2017

Thomas, Dylan, 1914-1953
Hear Here! S. PHILLIPS *Smithsonian* v47 no8 p17 D 2016

Thomas, Eddie Kaye
Scorpion M. Roffman color *TV Guide* v64 no42 p39 O 10 2016
Toby and Happy's Scorpion Wedding! M. Roffman *TV Guide* p9 Ap 17 2017

Thomas, Edwin L.

Dynamic creation and evolution of gradient nanostructure in single-crystal metallic microcubes bibl bw *Science* v354 no6310 p312 O 21 2016

Thomas, Etan
What Kaepernick Started bw *Progressive* v81 no10 p29 N 2016

THOMAS, EVAN
Staying Out *New York Times Book Review* p17 O 16 2016

THOMAS, GILLIAN
Turning Point *New York Times Book Review* p12 Mr 12 2017

Thomas, Grace
Our Bodies. No Shame color *Glamour* v115 no9 p32 S 2017

THOMAS, GREG
FIRE BUGS color *Field & Stream* v121 no9 p53 Ap 2017

Thomas, Heather Smith
6 Things you may not have known about Pigeon fever color *Equus* no470 p44 N 2016
Barn-Bored to Trail-Ready [Cover story] color *Horse & Rider* v56 no5 p44 My 2017
Barn Life, Made Easy color *Horse & Rider* v56 no4 p43 Ap 2017
BEYOND INSULIN RESISTANCE color *Equus* no475 p42 Ap 2017
Boost Your Wildlife Savvy color *Horse & Rider* v56 no7 p72 Jl 2017
CHOOSE THE RIGHT FENCE color *Equus* no476 p70 My 2017
A field guide to HOOF CRACKS color *Equus* no474 p26 Mr 2017
Hot-Weather Trail Hazards color *Horse & Rider* v56 no6 p64 Je 2017
What to do about Enteroliths color *Equus* no481 p36 O 2017

THOMAS, HON. W. NEIL III
Free Speech on College Campuses *American Scholar* v86 no3 p4 Summ 2017

Thomas, Isaiah
LITTLE MAN, BIG SHOTS T. Layden color *Sports Illustrated* v126 no5 p52 F 13 2017

Thomas, Isaiah, 1989-
BIG LITTLE MAN L. Jenkins color *Sports Illustrated* v127 no12 p42 O 16 2017
Isaiah Thomas M. Hagan color *Current Biography* v78 no8 p82 Ag 2017

Thomas, Jeni
"SHAMPOOING" CONDITIONERS color *Good Housekeeping* v263 no5 p28 N 2016

Thomas, Jerushah
A transcription factor hierarchy defines an environmental stress response network diag *Science* v354 no6312 p598 N 4 2016

Thomas, June
Between the Lines bw color *Advocate* no1089 p62 F/Mr 2017
Masters of Link color *Bloomberg Businessweek* no4536 p63 S 4 2017
Pedro Almodóvar Grows Up *Advocate* no1088 p60 D 2016/Ja 2017

Thomas, Justin
FIVE KEYS FOR SPEED [Cover story] color *Golf Magazine* v59 no7 p58 Jl 2017
THIS YOUNG GUN HAS FIREPOWER D. M. Clarke color *Golf Magazine* v59 no7 p11 Jl 2017
Watch + Learn M. Perpich and C. Barrett color *Golf Magazine* v59 no2 p34 F 2017

Thomas, Justin—Interviews
Justin Thomas J. Marksbury and C. Barrett color *Golf Magazine* v59 no3 p42 Mr 2017

Thomas, Keith
Will They Really Leave, and How? cartoon *New York Review of Books* v63 no16 p40 O 27 2016

Thomas, Latham
TAKE YOUR SEAT ON THE THRONE color *Essence* v48 no6 p126 O 2017

Thomas, Leo
BUILDING A FRANCHISE EMPIRE J. McKinney color *Black Enterprise* v47 no7 p13 My/Je 2017

Thomas, Liz
Find your Stride: Hiking in the Zone color *Backpacker* v45 no1 p16 Ja 2017
Go the Distance color *Backpacker* v45 no1 p6 Ja 2017
Toughen Up color *Backpacker* v45 no1 p31 Ja 2017

THOMAS, LLEWELLYN

Chords & Discords color *Downbeat* v84 no3 p10 Mr 2017

Thomas, Louisa

The BIG TWO color *Vogue* v207 no9 p722 S 2017

THE KYRGIOS ENIGMA cartoon color *New Yorker* v93 no20 p28 Jl 10 2017

Thomas, Lyn

KITCHEN-TESTED TIPS color *Vegetarian Today* no2 p4 Ap 2017

Thomas, Marlo, 1937-

Charitable Giving May Be in Your Genes J. BODNAR color *Kiplinger's Personal Finance* v71 no7 p24 Jl 2017

That Girl Grows Up bw color *AARP: The Magazine* v60 no1A p58 D 2016/Ja 2017

THOMAS, MARTHA

THE POWER OF Touch color *AARP: The Magazine* v59 no1A p38 D 2015/Ja 2016

Thomas, Martin

A Better Scorecard for Your Company's Sustainability Efforts *Harvard Business Review Digital Articles* p2 D 10 2015

Thomas, Maura

4 Organizational Mistakes That Plague Modern Knowledge Workers *Harvard Business Review Digital Articles* p2 My 10 2016

Fixing Our Unhealthy Obsession with Work Email *Harvard Business Review Digital Articles* p2 S 24 2015

Time Management Training Doesn't Work *Harvard Business Review Digital Articles* p2 Ap 22 2015

Until You Have Productivity Skills, Productivity Tools Are Useless *Harvard Business Review Digital Articles* p2 Ag 1 2016

Vacation Policy in Corporate America Is Broken *Harvard Business Review Digital Articles* p2 Je 26 2015

Why New Personal Productivity Efforts Don't Stick *Harvard Business Review Digital Articles* p2 Ja 19 2016

Your Late-Night Emails Are Hurting Your Team *Harvard Business Review Digital Articles* p2 Mr 16 2015

Your Team's Time Management Problem Might Be a Focus Problem color *Harvard Business Review Digital Articles* p2 F 27 2017

THOMAS, MIKE

PENNY POLLACK color *Chicago* v66 no11 p164 N 2017

THEY OWNED THE NIGHT bw color *Chicago* v66 no11 p96 N 2017

Thomas, N.

Rosetta's comet 67P/Churyumov-Gerasimenko sheds its dusty mantle to reveal its icy nature bibl graph *Science* v354 no6319 p1566 D 23 2016

Surface changes on comet 67P/Churyumov-Gerasimenko suggest a more active past bw graph *Science* v355 no6332 p1392 Mr 31 2017

Thomas, Nancy E.

Cash for carbon: A randomized trial of payments for ecosystem services to reduce deforestation bw chart *Science* v357 no6348 p267 Jl 21 2017

Thomas, Neethi Mary

Relearning the Art of Asking Questions *Harvard Business Review Digital Articles* p2 Mr 27 2015

Thomas, Nicole

INVEST IN YOURSELF IN 2017 color *Black Enterprise* v47 no5 p46 Ja/F 2017

Thomas, Pat

Who I am *People Management* p49 S 2017

Thomas, Patrick

Saving the saola from extinction color *Science* v357 no6357 p1248 S 22 2017

Thomas, Peter O.

Dams threaten rare Mekong dolphins bibl color *Science* v355 no6327 p805 F 24 2017

Thomas, Phillip

140-MPH, Slot-Car Drag Racing color *Hot Rod* v70 no7 p12 Jl 2017

ANATOMY OF A DRIFT CAR color *Hot Rod* v70 no8 p60 Ag 2017

Big Red Redemption color *Hot Rod* v70 no12 p18 D 2017

Bowling Green's Variable-Cam Brawler color graph *Hot Rod* v70 no7 p34 Jl 2017

Chasing the SUMMIT bw color *Hot Rod* v69 no12 p26 D 2016

The Diesel Weasel Mow-Kart! chart color *Hot Rod* v70 no6 p12

Je 2017

Frame-Draggin' Brat Rod color *Hot Rod* v70 no9 p12 S 2017

Hot Rod Anything! Clearing Snow With 4,000 HP bw color *Hot Rod* v70 no3 p10 Mr 2017

Hot Rod Anything! Medieval One bw color *Hot Rod* v70 no8 p12 Ag 2017

Inside a Fuel Car's 3,700-Degree Slider Clutch color *Hot Rod* v70 no12 p76 D 2017

JEFF OPPENHEIM WINS SPIRIT OF DRAG WEEK color *Hot Rod* v70 no2 p48 F 2017

Joe Carroll Pulls Spec Puzzle Pieces Together at Engine Masters Challenge color *Hot Rod* v70 no4 p72 Ap 2017

Kawasaki's Hellcat for the Water color *Hot Rod* v70 no11 p10 N 2017

More Doors, More Fun color *Hot Rod* v70 no5 p8 My 2017

NOT YOUR FATHER'S SHOEBOX color *Hot Rod* v70 no5 p46 My 2017

Petersen's Toast to "THE KING" color *Hot Rod* v70 no10 p60 O 2017

Power Tour's ROAD TO RECOVERY color *Hot Rod* v70 no11 p38 N 2017

POWER TOUR'S Sun-Powered Hot Rod color *Hot Rod* v70 no12 p66 D 2017

TWO YEARS, TWO TURBOS: THE AUSSIE CHEVELLE RETURNS! color *Hot Rod* v70 no2 p38 F 2017

Under Pressure color *Hot Rod* v70 no12 p26 D 2017

Until Next Time color *Hot Rod* v70 no12 p6 D 2017

THOMAS, R. ERIC

More Than Words: A speechwriter for Barack Obama recalls coming of age at the White House *New York Times Book Review* p19 S 24 2017

Thomas, Rachel

BE YOUR OWN COLORIST G. MONSMA cartoon color *Better Homes & Gardens* v95 no4 p12 Ap 2017

Thomas, Rob, 1972-

Rob Thomas Belts It Out on iZombie M. Roffman *TV Guide* v64 no15 p15 Ap 4 2016

Veronica Mars: Evil, Loner...and a Dude? J. Jensen color *Entertainment Weekly* no1460/1461 p100 Ap 7-17 2017

Thomas, Robert J.

How Artificial Intelligence Will Redefine Management *Harvard Business Review Digital Articles* p2 N 2 2016

How Smart CEOs Use Social Tools to Their Advantage *Harvard Business Review Digital Articles* p2 Mr 9 2015

Your Leadership Development Program Needs an Overhaul *Harvard Business Review Digital Articles* p2 D 5 2016

Thomas, Rosanne J.

Excuse Me: The Survival Guide to Modern Business Etiquette *Publishers Weekly* v264 no26 p170 Je 26 2017

THOMAS, SALI

ALL IN A Day's Work cartoon color *Reader's Digest* v190 no1134 p54 O 2017

Thomas, Shawn

Why New Personal Productivity Efforts Don't Stick *Harvard Business Review Digital Articles* p2 Ja 19 2016

Thomas, Steven

UNSOLICITED BETA *Climbing* no355 p14 Ag 2017

THOMAS, SUE

City of Sand bw *Orion Magazine* v35 no6 p9 N/D 2016

Thomas, Tommy

GRAND TOUR OF THE RED ROCK COUNTRY *Arizona Highways* v93 no11 p32 N 2017

Thomas, Tudor H.

High-performance light-emitting diodes based on carbene-metalamides chart graph *Science* v356 no6334 p159 Ap 14 2017

Thomas Cook Group PLC

A German, a Swede, and A Brit Walk Into a Hotel... C. Jasper cartoon chart *Bloomberg Businessweek* no4518 p18 Ap 10 2017

Thomas Jefferson Memorial (Washington, D.C.)

Memorial for the Future E. RUSH color *Orion Magazine* v36 no1 p9 Ja/F 2017

Thomas-Kennedy, Jackie

There's a Reason We Don't Say Certain Things Out Loud color *Publishers Weekly* v263 no48 p58 N 28 2016

Thomason, Bobbi

Research: When Men Have Lower Status at Work, They're Less

Likely to Negotiate *Harvard Business Review Digital Articles* p2 S 8 2017

Thomason, Bruce

Perception of Power *Publishers Weekly* v263 no40 p102 O 3 2016

Thomasson, Lynn

Should Farmers Fear Him? color graph *Bloomberg Businessweek* no4512 p13 F 20 2017

Thomas-Tran, Rhiannon

Asymmetric synthesis of batrachotoxin: Enantiomeric toxins show functional divergence against NaV bibl diag graph *Science* v354 no6314 p865 N 18 2016

Thomas Williamson, R.

Unequivocal determination of complex molecular structures using anisotropic NMR measurements color *Science* v356 no6333 p43 Ap 7 2017

Thome, Karen

International Food Security Assessment, 2017-2027 *Amber Waves: The Economics of Food, Farming, Natural Resources, & Rural America* p26 Je 2017

Thomke, Stefan

High-Tech Tools Won't Automatically Improve Your Operations *Harvard Business Review Digital Articles* p2 Je 10 2015

THE SURPRISING POWER OF ONLINE EXPERIMENTS: GETTING THE MOST OUT OF A/B AND OTHER CONTROLLED TESTS color diag graph img *Harvard Business Review* v95 no5 p74 S/O 2017

Thompson, Alexis, 1995-

TITANIC THOMPSON D. Denunzio color *Golf Magazine* v59 no11 p10 N 2017

Thompson, Alexis, 1995----Interviews

Lexi Thompson J. Marksbury and J. Marksbury color *Golf Magazine* v59 no11 p34 N 2017

Thompson, Anne Bahr

The Intangible Things Employees Want from Employers *Harvard Business Review Digital Articles* p2 D 3 2015

Thompson, Bo

Being a Bird L. TONINO *Orion Magazine* v36 no2 p7 Mr/Ap 2017

Thompson, Bobby Charles

THE STRANGE, SPECTACULAR CON OF BOBBY CHARLES THOMPSON D. FROMSON *Washingtonian Magazine* v52 no6 p62 Mr 2017

Thompson, Bryan

THE EXPEDITIONS color map *Canadian Geographic* v137 no4 p49 Jl/Ag 2017

Thompson, Candice

DIY Ballet: Five former Atlanta Ballet dancers have taken their careers into their own hands *Dance Magazine* v91 no10 p14 O 2017

Grin and Bear It *Dance Magazine* v90 no12 p108 D 2016

How to Choose the Right Summer Program: A Checklist *Dance Magazine* v91 no1 p132 Ja 2017

One for the Ladies: Cincinnati Ballet shows even more love for women choreographers this season *Dance Magazine* v91 no9 p18 S 2017

THE REBIRTH OF DAVID HALLBERG *Dance Magazine* v91 no6 p26 Je 2017

Rules of the Game: How to get more than just a medal out of competitions *Dance Magazine* v91 no10 p48 O 2017

(Virtually) Part of the Ballet color *Dance Magazine* v91 no3 p14 Mr 2017

Thompson, Chris

GREAT GREENS MADE EASY color *Men's Health* v31 no10 p61 D 2016

Thompson, Christine Marmé

Defining quality in visual art education for young children: Building on the position statement of the Early Childhood Art Educators bibl *Arts Education Policy Review* v118 no3 p154 2017

THOMPSON, CHUCK

OFF the BEATEN PATH color *GQ: Gentlemen's Quarterly* v97 no9 p154 S 2017

THOMPSON, CLIVE

BUSY BODY cartoon *Wired* v25 no6 p30 Je 2017

CAPITOL IDEA: SCIENTISTS, PLEASE RUN FOR OFFICE color *Wired* v25 no8 p34 Ag 2017

CODE IS KING cartoon *Wired* v24 no12 p40 D 2016

FLOOD OF MONEY cartoon *Wired* v25 no4 p32 Ap 2017

History's Most Misleading Maps: Today's high-tech devices aren't the only tools leading voyagers astray. And some "mistakes" were made deliberately *Smithsonian* v48 no4 p18 Jl/Ag 2017

The Illusion of Reality: The shocking power of virtual reality was all the buzz once before--about 150 years ago *Smithsonian* v48 no6 p18 O 2017

IN MATH WE TRUST HOW DATA CAN SAVE DEMOCRACY cartoon *Wired* v25 no5 p40 My 2017

PAID TO PLAY cartoon *Wired* v25 no3 p31 Mr 2017

Rage Against the Machines *Smithsonian* v47 no9 p21 Ja/F 2017

STOP THE CHITCHAT cartoon *Wired* v25 no10 p44 O 2017

TOO MUCH INFORMATION color *Mother Jones* v42 no3 p66 My/Je 2017

UNDER THE HOOD: MAKE CODE MORE TINKER-FRIENDLY cartoon *Wired* v25 no7 p34 Jl 2017

VERTICAL REALITY: PHONES HAVE TILTED OUR WORLDVIEW cartoon *Wired* v25 no9 p40 S 2017

The Whole World in Your Hands: Are high-tech maps ruining our sense of direction--or giving us a new awareness of where we are? *Smithsonian* v48 no4 p16 Jl/Ag 2017

Thompson, Danny

A RECORD 48 YEARS IN THE MAKING B. Gillogly color *Hot Rod* v70 no1 p34 Ja 2017

Thompson, David

Broadway's Next Bets: The stars and stories hitting stages soon S. GOLD *Dance Magazine* v91 no9 p24 S 2017

How the Social Sector Can Attract More Young Talent *Harvard Business Review Digital Articles* p2 D 7 2016

The Right Kind of Conflict Leads to Better Products *Harvard Business Review Digital Articles* p2 D 23 2016

Thompson, Deanna A.

Cancer Is Funny: Keeping Faith in Stage-Serious Chemo color *Christian Century* v134 no10 p34 My 10 2017

Gigabytes of grace A. Van Wyk *Christian Century* v134 no6 p38 Mr 15 2017

The Virtual Body of Christ in a Suffering World A. Van Wyk color *Christian Century* v134 no6 p38 Mr 15 2017

Thompson, Derek

BLOCKBUSTER MAGIC T. SULLIVAN bw color il img *Harvard Business Review* v95 no1 p164 Ja/F 2017

BUSINESSES THAT REALLY (REALLY) KNOW THEIR CUSTOMERS color *Fortune* v175 no2 p17 F 1 2017

INSIDE GOOGLE'S MOONSHOT FACTORY cartoon color *Atlantic* v320 no4 p60 N 2017

The Myth of 'Going Viral' on the Internet *Time* v189 no6 p21 F 20 2017

WHAT MAKES THINGS COOL color *Atlantic* v319 no1 p68 Ja/F 2017

Why You Click on Those Cat Videos color *Fortune* v175 no2 p17 F 1 2017

Thompson, Don

THE ORANGE BALLOON DOG B. BETHUNE color *Maclean's* v130 no3 p68 Ap 2017

Thompson, Dorothy, 1923-2011

REALITY SHOW D. Thompson *Lapham's Quarterly* v10 no3 p70 Summ 2017

THOMPSON, DOUG

BUYING OR SELLING SOLO *Sea Magazine* v108 no8 p46 Ag 2016

DON'T BE ALL WET *Sea Magazine* v108 no10 p42 O 2016

Finish the Job *Boating World* v37 no9 p14 N/D 2016

West Coast "Winterization" *Sea Magazine* v108 no10 p54 O 2016

Thompson, Elizabeth Laing

When God Says "Wait": Navigating Life's Detours and Delays Without Losing Your Faith, Your Friends, or Your Mind *Publishers Weekly* v264 no2 p63 Ja 9 2017

THOMPSON, EMILY

Thanksgiving LESSONS [Cover story] color *Bon Appetit* no11 p82 N 2017

Thompson, Emma, 1959-

Toronto Must List S. Vilkomerson color *Entertainment Weekly* no1480 p36 S 1 2017

Thompson, Erin L.

THE BIG QUESTION cartoon *Atlantic* v320 no3 p100 O 2017

Thompson, Phillip
Outside the Law *Publishers Weekly* v263 no45 p39 N 7 2016
Thompson, Ruth
AT THEIR PEAK D. Timberlake *Virginia Living* v15 no2 p48 F 2017
Thompson, Samantha J.
How Do You Find an Exoplanet? *Physics Today* v69 no11 p59 N 2016
Thompson, Shaddah
TONAL VISION N. Spradley color *Essence* v47 no12 p51 Ap 2017
THOMPSON, SHARON
Bet you didn't know color *National Geographic Kids* no465 p10 N 2016
Thompson, Sharyl
My golden mare color *Equus* no474 p64 Mr 2017
Thompson, Steve
Don't Turn Your Sales Team Loose Without a Strategy *Harvard Business Review Digital Articles* p2 D 15 2015
THOMPSON, SUSAN PEIRCE
Follow the "Bright Line" *USA Today Magazine* v146 no2868 p62 S 2017
Thompson, Susan Russell
A Tea Drinker's Novel: Chilverton Park *Publishers Weekly* v264 no40 p115 O 2 2017
Thompson, Tessa
my style color *InStyle* v24 no2 p88 F 2017
Thompson, Theresa
News Briefs *Publishers Weekly* v263 no42 p10 O 17 2016
Thompson, Trudy
MICKEY & TRUDY THOMPSON J. OBER color *Dirt Sports + Off-Road* v51 no10 p74 O 2017
Thompson, Valerie
Al Gore's inconvenient update color *Science* v357 no6349 p361 Jl 28 2017
Thompsonville (Mich.)
COLD COMFORT K. SCHNEIDER *Indianapolis Monthly* v40 no4 p46 D 2016
Thomsen, L.
An ecosystem-based deep-ocean strategy bibl color map *Science* v355 no6324 p452 F 3 2017
Thomson, Alex
A Separate Reality C. J. Doane color *Sail* v48 no3 p96 Mr 2017
Thomson, David Ker, 1958-
Babylon Illustrated bw *Film Comment* v52 no6 p94 N/D 2016
HER WAY bw color *Film Comment* v53 no4 p50 Jl/Ag 2017
The Producers: The film critic David Thomson takes on the Warner brothers, especially one irresistible showman and show-off T. SHONE *New York Times Book Review* p12 S 3 2017
Thomson, Jason
Interfaith support rises along with attacks color *Christian Century* v134 no7 p12 Mr 29 2017
THOMSON, LIZ
Bringing The Nobel Back Home color *Publishers Weekly* v263 no43 p80 O 24 2016
IMPRESSIONS OF A LIFE bw color *Publishers Weekly* v264 no21 p43 My 22 2017
NOTES ON A SCANDAL *Publishers Weekly* v263 no41 p51 O 10 2016
Oneworld Piles Up the Wins color *Publishers Weekly* v264 no20 p5 My 15 2017
Still Vibrant After All These Years bw color *Publishers Weekly* v264 no27 p47 Jl 3 2017
Thomson, Peter
The Ocean Conference: a Game-Changer *UN Chronicle* v54 no1/2 p1 2017
Thomson, Rachel
Emergence and spread of a human-transmissible multidrug-resistant nontuberculous mycobacterium bibl diag graph *Science* v354 no6313 p751 N 11 2016
THOMSON, RUSSELL
Assessing National Biodiversity Trends for Rocky and Coral Reefs through the Integration of Citizen Science and Scientific Monitoring Programs *BioScience* v67 no2 p134 F 2017
Thomson, Simon
HIGHWAY RUN S. Mait bw color *Skiing* p30 Wint 2017

THOMSON, SUSAN
The Long Shadow of Genocide in Rwanda *Current History* v116 no790 p183 My 2017
Thomson Reuters Corp.
How Thomson Reuters Is Creating a Culture of Innovation R. Ashkenas and C. Burch *Harvard Business Review Digital Articles* p2 O 2 2014
Thong Song (Music)
We Like Big Hits and We Cannot Lie E. R. Brown color *Entertainment Weekly* no1480 p51 S 1 2017
Thor (Fictitious character : Marvel)
NO. 13 Thor C. Holub color *Entertainment Weekly* no1436/1437 p56 O 21 2016
Thor (Norse deity)
OFF THE GRID M. GRUNBERG-BANYASZ color *Archaeology* v70 no4 p10 Je-Ag 2017
Thor, Andrea
ChromEMT: Visualizing 3D chromatin structure and compaction in interphase and mitotic cells color *Science* v357 no6349 p370 Jl 28 2017
Thor: Ragnarok (Film)
THE Anticipation Index: What we're excited about right now *New York* v50 no9 p81 My 1 2017
IF HE HAD A HAMMER... [Cover story] T. Stack color *Entertainment Weekly* no1457/1458 p28 Mr 17 2017
THOR: RAGNAROK T. Stack color *Entertainment Weekly* no1478 / 1479 p62 Ag 18-25 2017
Thoracic vertebrae
Core Twist and Press chart *Men's Health* v32 no8 p60 O 2017
Spinal T(ap) E. CALDERONE color *Muscle & Performance* v9 no10 p28 O 2017
Thorarensen, Hildur Sif—Interviews
FINE PRINT L. KYZER *Iceland Review* v55 no2 p62 Mr/Ap 2017
Thoreau, Henry David, 1817-1862
7 BEARDS FROM THE CONSERVATION HALL OF FAME L. TONINO *Orion Magazine* v35 no4/5 p6 Jl-O 2016
The Abolitionist of Walden Pond *In These Times* v41 no8 p38 Ag 2017
Henry David Thoreau: a man of solitude seeking connection R. Harper color *America* v217 no3 p38 Ag 7 2017
Mary Moody Emerson Was a Scholar, a Thinker, and an Inspiration N. A. Baker and S. H. Petrulionis *Humanities* v38 no1 p1 Wint 2017
Open Book J. WILLIAMS *New York Times Book Review* p4 Ja 15 2017
PINE SENSE A. Ryder color *Popular Photography* v81 no2 p26 Mr/Ap 2017
Reading Thoreau at 200: WHY IS THE SEMINAL WORK OF THE GREAT AMERICAN TRANSCENDENTALIST HELD IN SUCH SCORN TODAY? W. HOWARTH *American Scholar* v86 no3 p44 Summ 2017
The Swamp Lover H. David color *Atlantic* v320 no4 p122 N 2017
Thoreau and the Legacy of Wilderness D. Brinkley *New York Times Book Review* p12 Jl 9 2017
Thoreau for the Ages B. T. MAURER *American Scholar* v86 no4 p3 Aut 2017
What Thoreau Saw A. WULF color *Atlantic* v320 no4 p106 N 2017
Thoreson, Katie
You Never Forget Your First Time diag il *Backpacker* v45 no2 p64 Mr 2017
Thoreson, Sallie
THE GATEWAY TO ACTIVE SENIORS *Parks & Recreation* v52 no1 p32 Ja 2017
Thorien, Kalen
A GIRL ON THE ROAD T. Neville color *Skiing* p42 D 2016
Thorisson, Mimi
THE COUNTRY CUISINIÉRE *Martha Stewart Living* no269 p58 N 2016
Thorisson, Oddur
Gran TORINO bw color *Conde Nast Traveler* v52 no2 p84 F 2017
THORKELSON, BERIT
AT YOUR SERVICE color *Better Homes & Gardens* v95 no9 p48 S 2017
a case for coding *Parents* v92 no7 p130 Jl 2017

India's Movie Industry Gets a New Script color graph *Bloomberg Businessweek* no4525 p20 Je 5 2017

Thorpe, Jasen
38 REASONS TO GO GA-GA FOR THE TOUR DE FRANCE color *Bicycling* v58 no7 p24 Ag 2017

Thorpe, Jeremy
Intersection of diverse neuronal genomes and neuropsychiatric disease: The Brain Somatic Mosaicism Network color *Science* v356 no6336 p395 Ap 28 2017

Thorpe, Nick
On Today's Refugee Road color map *New York Review of Books* v63 no18 p27 N 24 2016

Thorstensen, J. R.
An unusual white dwarf star may be a surviving remnant of a sub-luminous Type Ia supernova chart diag *Science* v357 no6352 p680 Ag 18 2017

Thorvilson, Leah
STRAIGHT TO THE BIG TIME M. HURFORD color *Bicycling* v58 no6 p42 Jl 2017

Thought & thinking
See also
Attention
Critical thinking
Design thinking
Ideology
Judgment (Psychology)
Memory
32 Weirdly Random Thoughts We've Had During Yoga K. Bonnell and P. R. Satran color *Glamour* v115 no9 p215 S 2017
4 Ways to Improve Your Strategic Thinking Skills N. Bowman *Harvard Business Review Digital Articles* p2 D 27 2016
Are We All Racists? M. Shermer color *Scientific American* v317 no2 p81 Ag 2017
Back Talk color *National Geographic Kids* no475 p32 N 2017
The Cognitive Usefulness of the Internet of Things H. J. Wilson *Harvard Business Review Digital Articles* p2 N 17 2014
Design How Your Team Thinks M. Bonchek *Harvard Business Review Digital Articles* p2 Je 24 2016
Don't be bored P. W. Marty *Christian Century* v134 no20 p3 S 27 2017
THE GRAVE IS A GATEWAY C. W. KEGLEY and D. J. KEGLEY *USA Today Magazine* v145 no2862 p48 Mr 2017
I WAS CRAZY NOW I'M NOT cartoon color *Men's Health* v32 no3 p118 Ap 2017
Linear Thinking in a Nonlinear World B. DE LANGHE, S. PUNTONI et al bw chart diag graph img *Harvard Business Review* v95 no3 p130 My/Je 2017
Mindfulness Isn't Much Harder than Mindlessness E. Langer *Harvard Business Review Digital Articles* p2 Ja 13 2016
Mind-reading great apes V. Morell color *Science* v354 no6319 p1520 D 23 2016
The Science of Sounding Smart J. Schroeder and N. Epley *Harvard Business Review Digital Articles* p2 O 7 2015
Take it all in R. Miller cartoon *Yoga Journal* no288 p38 D 2016
To Change Your Strategy, First Change How You Think M. Bonchek and B. Libert *Harvard Business Review Digital Articles* p2 My 17 2017
Ways to Enhance Your "Thought Life" *USA Today Magazine* v146 no2869 p13 O 2017
What Kind of Thinker Are You? M. Bonchek and E. Steele *Harvard Business Review Digital Articles* p2 N 23 2015
When the Mind Wanders J. PELINI color *Atlantic* v320 no3 p26 O 2017

Thouless, D. J., 1934—Awards
Trio wins Nobel for effects of topology on exotic matter A. Cho color *Science* v354 no6308 p21 O 7 2016

Thrall, Nathan
The Middle East Puzzle's Missing Piece K. Vick color *Time* v189 no22 p53 Je 12 2017

Thread
See also
Dental floss
the SURPRISE inside color *Better Homes & Gardens* v95 no2 p46 F 2016

Threadgill, Henry, 1944-
Henry Threadgill M. Hagan color *Current Biography* v77 no10

p87 O 2016

Threats
Dangerous Liaisons: In the current climate, violence is seeping into politics A. Greenblatt *Governing* v30 no10 p17 Jl 2017
The Fire's Edge B. L. HOWELL *American Forests* v122 no3 p16 Fall 2016

Threats—Social aspects
The Incredible Shrinking Power of the President's Threats M. Scherer and S. Frizell color *Time* v189 no14 p9 Ap 17 2017

Three-dimensional imaging
Handheld 3D Mapper M. Belfiore color *Bloomberg Businessweek* no4514 p37 Mr 13 2017
THE MAN WHO ONLY EXISTS ON VIDEO color *Popular Mechanics* p74 O 2017

Three-dimensional imaging in archaeology
THE FACTORY OF FAKES D. ZALEWSKI cartoon color *New Yorker* v92 no39 p66 N 28 2016

Three-dimensional imaging in biology
Three-dimensional Ca2+ imaging advances understanding of astrocyte biology E. Bindocci, I. Savtchouk et al diag *Science* v356 no6339 p715 My 19 2017

Three-dimensional imaging—Equipment & supplies
Hands-on: ShapeScale 3D color *PCWorld* v35 no6 p162 Je 2017

Three-dimensional imaging—History
The Illusion of Reality: The shocking power of virtual reality was all the buzz once before--about 150 years ago C. Thompson *Smithsonian* v48 no6 p18 O 2017

Three-dimensional integrated circuits
The carbon nanotube integrated circuit goes three-dimensional: Chip makers have a mantra: smaller, cheaper, and faster. They may now need a new adjective--taller M. Wilson *Physics Today* v70 no9 p14 S 2017

Three-dimensional printing
1940s cement mixers from 3-D printed parts E. White color *Model Railroader* v84 no6 p24 Je 2017
3-D Classes Showing the industry a new way to design and build cars F. Markus bw *Motor Trend* v69 no3 p32 Mr 2017
3D PRINTED FOOD L. SOROKANICH color *Popular Mechanics* p78 D 2016/Ja 2017
3D Printing Is Already Changing Health Care D. Hendricks *Harvard Business Review Digital Articles* p2 Mr 4 2016
3D Printing Is Changing the Way We Think T. J. McCue *Harvard Business Review Digital Articles* p2 Jl 21 2015
3D Printing Reaches the Ocean Floor L. SOROKANICH color *Popular Mechanics* p18 Mr 2017
3D Printing Will Revive Conglomerates R. D'Aveni *Harvard Business Review Digital Articles* p2 My 19 2015
Carbon K. Bourzac color il *MIT Technology Review* v120 no4 p62 Jl/Ag 2017
DESKTOP METAL THINKS ITS MACHINES WILL GIVE DESIGNERS AND MANUFACTURERS A PRACTICAL AND AFFORDABLE WAY TO PRINT METAL PARTS [Cover story] D. Rotman chart color *MIT Technology Review* v120 no3 p42 My/Je 2017
FINE PRINT C. Atiyeh color *Car & Driver* v63 no1 p22 Jl 2017
FIT TO PRINT B. YEOMAN *Atlanta* v56 no7 p90 N 2016
Get Your Organization Ready for 3D Printing R. D'Aveni *Harvard Business Review Digital Articles* p2 Je 1 2015
Innovation O. Kharif color *Bloomberg Businessweek* no4513 p39 Mr 6 2017
The Limits of 3D Printing M. Holweg *Harvard Business Review Digital Articles* p2 Je 23 2015
Metal Devices, in Miniature M. Belfiore bw *Scientific American* v316 no3 p16 Mr 2017
A MIGHTY WIND M. JANCER diag *Wired* v25 no6 p28 Je 2017
Model a LARGE STATION using 3-D PRINTING B. Kingsnorth color *Model Railroader* v84 no8 p24 Ag 2017
Multiprocess 3D printing for increasing component functionality E. MacDonald and R. Wicker bibl bw color *Science* v353 no6307 paaf2093-1 S 30 2016
My Dentist 3D Printed My Crown S. Kaplan *Harvard Business Review Digital Articles* p2 O 24 2014
A NEW COMPOSITE-MANUFACTURING Approach Takes Shape R. Hansen *Science & Technology Review* p16 Je 2017
Pick these flowers! color *Redbook* p61 My 2017
The Questions Executives Should Ask About 3D Printing C. Fly-

nn *Harvard Business Review Digital Articles* p2 Ap 19 2016

Rare Jewelry That Isn't So Rare Anymore O. Kharif color *Bloomberg Businessweek* no4514 p36 Mr 13 2017

RESEARCH color *Science* v356 no6338 p594 My 12 2017

The Time to Think About the 3D-Printed Future Is Now R. D'Aveni *Harvard Business Review Digital Articles* p2 My 6 2015

Virtual Plan, Real Surgery L. BRODY color *Forbes* v198 no9 p82 D 30 2016

Three-dimensional printing—Equipment & supplies

DESKTOP METAL THINKS ITS MACHINES WILL GIVE DESIGNERS AND MANUFACTURERS A PRACTICAL AND AFFORDABLE WAY TO PRINT METAL PARTS [Cover story] D. Rotman chart color *MIT Technology Review* v120 no3 p42 My/Je 2017

Innovation 3D-Printing Recycler M. Purves color *Bloomberg Businessweek* no4498 p46 N 7 2016

Three-dimensional printing—Finance

ETFs Are Hot. So's 3D Printing... I Got an Idea! A. Massa color *Bloomberg Businessweek* no4497 p43 O 31 2016

Three Futures (Music)

WHAT TO STREAM color *Entertainment Weekly* no1485 p57 O 6 2017

Three Generations (Film)

3 GENERATIONS J. Nolfi color *Entertainment Weekly* no1463/1464 p37 Ap/My 2017

Three-point shooting (Basketball)

GOING GREEN R. Nadkarni color *Sports Illustrated* v126 no12 p37 My 1 2017

Three Questions (Poem)

Three questions J. L. Moore *Christian Century* v133 no23 p12 N 9 2016

Three Sisters Wilderness (Or.)

What's the Rush? L. ". C. LANCASTER color *Backpacker* v45 no1 p28 Ja 2017

Three Stooges (Comedy team)

Life IN THESE UNITED STATES Y. BRODD, E. BOGAERT et al *Reader's Digest* v189 no1128 p38 Mr 2017

Three Wonder Walks (Poem)

Three Wonder Walks M. Jensen *Orion Magazine* v35 no4/5 p57 Jl-O 2016

Three Billboards Outside Ebbing, Missouri (Film)

FRANCES McDORMAND IN Three Billboards Outside Ebbing, Missouri J. McGovern color *Entertainment Weekly* no1478 / 1479 p66 Ag 18-25 2017

Three Caballeros, The (Film)

Crossing Artistic Borders M. WAKIM *Los Angeles Magazine* v62 no9 p59 S 2017

Threespine stickleback

Déjà Vu A. Hadhazy color *Natural History* v125 no7 p8 Jl/Ag 2017

Threlkeld, Leslie

10 BLANKETING TIPS FROM EMMA FORD color *Practical Horseman* v45 no10 p60 O 2017

BENEATH THE SURFACE OF RAIN ROT color *Practical Horseman* v45 no6 p54 Je 2017

Coast to Coast for a Cause color *Practical Horseman* v45 no3 p72 Mr 2017

COMBATING JOINT DISEASE color *Practical Horseman* v45 no9 p56 S 2017

DEEP BREATH: EQUINE RESPIRATORY DISEASE color diag *Practical Horseman* v45 no8 p48 Ag 2017

Little Horse, Big Heart color *Practical Horseman* v45 no5 p80 My 2017

PRINCIPLES OF CROSS-COUNTRY RIDING color *Practical Horseman* v45 no3 p42 Mr 2017

Threni, Requiem Canticles (Music)

Stravinsky: Threni, Requiem Canticles *Opera News* v81 no7 p50 Ja 2017

Threshing machines

COMBINE TLC: HOW TO SCRUTINIZE YOUR COMBINE TO SHORT-CIRCUIT BREAKDOWNS D. MOWITZ *Successful Farming* v115 no11 p28 S 2017

Thriftiness

BUSTING THE RECYCLING MYTH P. TREBLE color *Maclean's* v129 no40 p53 O 10 2016

Philosophers Who Like Stuff: Their case against frugality E. Westacott *Humanities* v38 no4 p1 Fall 2017

Thriller (Film)

"WE CAN MAKE SOMETHING OUT OF ANYTHING": SALLY POTTER'S THRILLER AND LONDON'S HISTORY OF QUEER FEMINIST FILM SPACES S. Mayer and S. Robertson *Film Quarterly* v70 no4 p39 Summ 2017

Thriller (TV program)

STREAMING A. D'ARMINIO *TV Guide* v65 no37 p50 S 4 2017

Thrillers (Motion pictures)

HARDCORE HENRY C. Gunnestad color *Sound & Vision* v82 no4 p70 My 2017

JASON BOURNE C. Gunnestad color *Sound & Vision* v82 no4 p69 My 2017

Thrillers (Motion pictures)—Reviews

XXX: RETURN OF XANDER CAGE D. Vaughn color *Sound & Vision* v82 no8 p70 O 2017

Thrillers (Television programs)

5 THINGS TO KNOW ABOUT... ZOO: A decade after rabid animals nearly conquered the world, Jackson Oz and Co. reunite to save mankind from even deadlier beasties in the thriller's third season A. D'ARMINIO *TV Guide* v65 no27 p18 Je 26 2017

THE RIGHT PATH I. RUDOLPH *TV Guide* v65 no6 p28 Ja 30 2017

Tick... Tick... BOOM! [Cover story] M. ROFFMAN *TV Guide* v65 no6 p20 Ja 30 2017

Training Day L. Acken *TV Guide* v65 no6 p34 Ja 30 2017

Throat diseases

How can I soothe my sore throat? [Cover story] T. L. Dog color *Prevention* v69 no2 p26 F 2017

IT'S ALIIIIVE! color *Women's Health* v14 no1 p33 Ja/F 2017

Throat diseases—Treatment

6 WAYS TO SUCK IT UP WHEN COUGH, COLD, OR FLU STRIKE K. Donohue color *Maclean's* v129 no40 p70 O 10 2016

Throm, Roger

Popular piety color *U.S. Catholic* v82 no2 p5 F 2017

Thrombophlebitis prevention

Pulmonary embolism: Common, life-threatening condition [Cover story] *Mayo Clinic Health Letter* v35 no11 p1 N 2017

Thrombosis treatment

A Critical Gap in Cancer Care A. Papmehl bw color *Maclean's* v130 no9 p38 O 2017

Thrombosis—Prevention

ASK THE DOCTOR A. L. KOMAROFF *Harvard Health Letter* v42 no6 p2 Ap 2017

Compression stockings *Mayo Clinic Health Letter* v35 no2 p7 F 2017

Throntveit, Trygve

Power Without Victory: Woodrow Wilson and the American Internationalist Experiment G. J. Ikenberry *Foreign Affairs* v96 no6 p151 N/D 2017

Throws (Coverlets)—Evaluation

Designers' Favorites UNDER $150 color *Redbook* p140 O 2017

Mother's Day gifts UNDER $50 color *Redbook* p132 My 2017

ONYX AND ECRU L. BIRCH color *House Beautiful* p17 Ag 2017

Thrun, Sebastian

LAUNCH color *Wired* v25 no8 p5 Ag 2017

Thuan Pham

How Did I Get Here? THUAN PHAM bw color *Bloomberg Businessweek* no4499 p88 N 14 2016

Thubagere, Anupama J.

A cargo-sorting DNA robot color *Science* v357 no6356 p1112 S 15 2017

Thubron, Colin, 1939-

Eternal Flames W. LESSER *New York Times Book Review* p16 F 12 2017

Life as a Burning House J. Banville color *New York Review of Books* v64 no9 p16 My 25 2017

A River Runs Through It color *New York Review of Books* v64 no16 p47 O 26 2017

Where Globalization Began? color *New York Review of Books* v64 no10 p28 Je 8 2017

Thubten Chodron, 1950-

THUBTEN CHODRON Dharmarakshita *Tricycle: The Buddhist*

Review v26 no2 p23 Wint 2016

Thul, Peter J.
A subcellular map of the human proteome color *Science* v356 no6340 p820 My 26 2017

Thumb—Diseases
For years, her arthritis was under control, and she could work in her garden. But then a rash appeared and crippled her hand. Why? L. Sanders *New York Times Magazine* p22 Mr 5 2017

Thumbnail images (Image processing)
How Babelsoft Media Preview reveals less-common file types in Explorer J. JACOBI color *PCWorld* v35 no4 p152 Ap 2017

Thumbtzen, Matt
FIT TO PRINT bw color *Wired* v25 no5 p14 My 2017

Thunder
Unlike most people I'm not afraid of... *Reader's Digest* v188 no1124 p30 O 2016

Thunder, Little
For Lack of a Handshake B. HUNHOFF *South Dakota Magazine* v32 no4 p30 N/D 2016

Thunder Bay (Ont.)
A RIVER OF TEARS [Cover story] N. Macdonald color *Maclean's* v130 no7 p38 Ag 2017

Thunderbird automobile
Shattered J. Plungis and T. Germain chart color diag graph *Consumer Reports* v82 no12 p30 D 2017

Thunderbolt & Lightfoot (Film)
On the Wild Side R. Brody color *New Yorker* v93 no19 p12 Jl 3 2017

Thundercat (Performer)
'It's Always Music First' THUNDERCAT J. Tangari color *Downbeat* v84 no6 p52 Je 2017

Thunderstorm forecasting
Forecast Center T. Vasquez map *Weatherwise* v70 no4 p54 Jl/Ag 2017

Thunderstorms
Lightbox color *Time* v189 no20 p14 My 29 2017
More tornadoes in the most extreme U.S. tornado outbreaks M. K. Tippett, C. Lepore et al bibl chart graph *Science* v354 no6318 p1419 D 16 2016
THUNDERSTORM AVOIDANCE, PENETRATION AND SURVIVAL R. Lengel color *Flying* v144 no6 p28 Je 2017

Thunderstorms in art
Weathered... *South Dakota Magazine* v33 no2 p67 Jl/Ag 2017

THUNES, CLAIR
Promoting Weight Gain After Illness *Horse & Rider* v56 no3 p12 Mr 2017

Thungkasemvathana, Pimrapee
Passion's Frontier *Psychology Today* v50 no1 p12 Ja/F 2017

Thurber, Christopher M.
Combining polyethylene and polypropylene: Enhanced performance with PE/iPP multiblock polymers bibl chart graph *Science* v355 no6327 p814 F 24 2017

Thurber, James, 1894-1961
1936: New York City J. Thurber *Lapham's Quarterly* v10 no1 p111 Wint 2017

Thurber, Rawson Marshall, 1975-
CENTRAL INTELLIGENCE D. Vaughn color *Sound & Vision* v82 no2 p70 F/Mr 2017

Thurman, Dawn
'ME TIME' FOR MOMS Z. HUGHES and S. T. BROWN cartoon *Ebony* v72 no6 p66 Ap/My 2017

Thurman, Judith
BEAUTY QUEEN BEES cartoon *New Yorker* v93 no8 p21 Ap 10 2017
GRETE STERN cartoon *New Yorker* v92 no42 p100 D 19 2016
ROTH ON TRUMP cartoon *New Yorker* v92 no47 p18 Ja 30 2017
WORLD OF INTERIORS cartoon color *New Yorker* v93 no23 p48 Ag 7 2017

THURMAN, PATRICK
#Climbing Training color *Climbing* no352 p9 Ap 2017

Thursday Night Football (TV program)
The Case for ... Killing TNF J. Dickey and T. Keith color *Sports Illustrated* v125 no18 p26 D 5 2016

Thusi, Pearl—Interviews
FRESH FACE: PEARL THUSI color *Essence* v47 no10 p38 F 2017

Thwaites, Thomas—Awards
Ig Nobels honor goat man, mirror scratching color *Science* v353 no6307 p1475 S 30 2016

THX Ltd.
The Future of Audio C. Crowley color *Sound & Vision* v81 no9 p16 N 2016

Thygesen, Kristian S.
Making the most of materials computations bibl diag *Science* v354 no6309 p180 O 14 2016

Thylacine
Lost then Loved: The Case of the Tasmanian Tiger S. B. Gmelch and M. Z. Gmelch bw color map *Natural History* v125 no4 p36 Ap 2017

Thyne, T. J.
BONES M. Roffman *TV Guide* v64 no15 p54 Ap 4 2016

Thyroid disease diagnosis
My thyroid went totally haywire W. Meer color *Health* v31 no9 p77 N 2017

Thyroid gland
Diagnosis L. Sanders *New York Times Magazine* p20 Je 11 2017

Thyroid gland physiology
Give Your Thyroid Some TLC L. TURNER color *Better Nutrition* v79 no9 p66 S 2017

Thyroid hormones
Your body's got something to tell you L. KRIEGER *Redbook* p92 S 2017

Thyroid hormones—Regulation
ASK THE EXPERT A. Romm *Prevention* v69 no1 p10 Ja 2017

Thyroiditis—Treatment
THE THYROID MISTAKE J. Bowden color *Amazing Wellness* v9 no3 p34 EarlySumm 2017

Tiafoe, Frances
GUEST LIST: A monthly roundup of people we'd like to have over for drinks, food, and conversation *Washingtonian Magazine* v53 no1 p24 O 2017

Tian, Bin
Tudor-SN–mediated endonucleolytic decay of human cell microRNAs promotes G1/S phase transition graph *Science* v356 no6340 p859 My 26 2017

Tian, Geng
UBE2O remodels the proteome during terminal erythroid differentiation diag *Science* v357 no6350 p471 Ag 4 2017

Tian, Kai-Ren
"Perfect" designer chromosome V and behavior of a ring derivative diag *Science* v355 no6329 p1046 Mr 10 2017

Tian, Maoqun
Decarboxylative borylation color *Science* v356 no6342 p1045 Je 9 2017

Tian, Yancong
Experimentally realized mechanochemistry distinct from force-accelerated scission of loaded bonds diag graph *Science* v357 no6348 p299 Jl 21 2017

Tian Tao
Huawei: A Case Study of When Profit Sharing Works *Harvard Business Review Digital Articles* p2 S 24 2015
Huawei's Culture Is the Key to Its Success *Harvard Business Review Digital Articles* p2 Je 11 2015

Tianyu Chen
Ocean mixing and ice-sheet control of seawater 234U/238U during the last deglaciation bibl graph *Science* v354 no6312 p626 N 4 2016

Tiara (Company)
TIARA 53 COUPE M. WERLING *Sea Magazine* v109 no2 p34 F 2017

Tiara Yachts Inc.
The Family Way R. THIEL cartoon chart color *Power & Motoryacht* v32 no12 p56 D 2016
TIARA 44 FLYBRIDGE: A COUPLES COUPE GETS A FLYBRIDGE ADDITION AND GOES TO A WHOLE NEW LEVEL, LITERALLY AND FIGURATIVELY M. WERLING color *Sea Magazine* v109 no8 p42 Ag 2017

Tiaras
Oh, and Tiaras Too?! J. Harman color *Glamour* no8 p36 Ag 2017

Tibbetts, Elizabeth
The biology of color color *Science* v357 no6350 p470 Ag 4 2017

TIBBETTS, JOHN H.

no4 p62 Ap 2017

TOTALLY TIFFANY color *Architectural Digest* v74 no10 p152 O 1 2017

Tiffany & Co.—Officials & employees

TIFFANY'S CEO ON CREATING A SUSTAINABLE SUPPLY CHAIN F. Cumenal color graph img *Harvard Business Review* v95 no2 p41 Mr/Ap 2017

Tiffany, Connor R.

Microbiota-activated PPAR-γ signaling inhibits dysbiotic Enterobacteriaceae expansion graph *Science* v357 no6351 p570 Ag 11 2017

TIGAR, LINDSAY

Water—To Your Health! color *Reader's Digest* v190 no1133 p33 S 2017

Tigé Boats Inc.

Locked and Loaded A. JONES *Boating World* v38 no6 p38 Je 2017

Tiger, John

CONTROLLING LAKE WEEDS color *Cabin Living* p67 Ap 2017

HELP! MY OUTBOARD WON'T START! color *Cabin Living* p72 Mr 2017

SAFE ON THE water color *Cabin Living* p56 Ap 2017

Tiger attacks

TIGER TOMBSTONE K. RANDALL *Washingtonian Magazine* v52 no9 p24 Je 2017

Tigers

30 Cool THINGS ABOUT BIG CATS J. BEER *National Geographic Kids* no467 p18 F 2017

Art Zone *National Geographic Kids* no466 p36 D 2016/Ja 2017

Back to the Wild K. Samuelson color *Time* v190 no12 p12 S 25 2017

Rise of the Tiger J. KIFFEL-ALCHEH *National Geographic Kids* no466 p14 D 2016/Ja 2017

THE TIGER WATCHERS M. BENANAV *Sierra* v102 no4 p36 Jl/Ag 2017

Tigers—Behavior

Splish Splash color *Reader's Digest* v189 no1131 p16 Je 2017

Tight ends (Football)

TRAVIS KELCE DOES A VERY TRAVIS KELCE THING D. Greene color *Sports Illustrated* v127 no12 p26 O 16 2017

Tightrope walking

Hanging Out, Extreme Edition *New York Times Upfront* v149 no4 p2 O 31 2016

#NGMADVENTURE color *National Geographic* v232 no1 p14 Jl 2017

Tights (Hosiery)

Men in tights M. CAMPBELL color *Maclean's* v129 no43 p63 O 31 2016

Tights (Hosiery)—Evaluation

TRY-ONS *Interview* v46 no8 p78 O 2016

TIGNOR, STEPHEN

AMERICAN DREAM *Tennis* v52 no6 p26 N/D 2016

Belinda Bencic *Tennis* v53 no4 p70 Jl/Ag 2017

THE BEST OF RIVALS, THE BEST OF FRIENDS *Tennis* v53 no4 p60 Jl/Ag 2017

Class Act *Tennis* v52 no6 p57 N/D 2016

THE ETERNAL SECOND *Tennis* v53 no3 p68 My/Je 2017

A Game Changer bw color *Tennis* v53 no2 p80 Mr/Ap 2017

HEART OF THE CITY: Roger Federer's connection to New York is unmistakable, both on and off the court color *Tennis* v53 no5 p42 S/O 2017

I'll be in the Room color *Tennis* v53 no5 p64 S/O 2017

LEARNING FROM... DOMINIKA CIBULKOVA *Tennis* v53 no1 p53 Ja/F 2017

LEARNING FROM... KAROLINA PLISKOVA *Tennis* v53 no1 p55 Ja/F 2017

LEARNING FROM... MILOS RAONIC *Tennis* v53 no1 p17 Ja/F 2017

Miss America *Tennis* v53 no4 p42 Jl/Ag 2017

One Shining Backhand *Tennis* v53 no3 p80 My/Je 2017

Ready to Launch *Tennis* v53 no4 p52 Jl/Ag 2017

Roger's New Chapter *Tennis* v53 no4 p80 Jl/Ag 2017

THE SOPHOMORE *Tennis* v53 no3 p52 My/Je 2017

The Spirit of the Sisters bw color *Tennis* v53 no5 p80 S/O 2017

The SUMMER of 1977 bw color *Tennis* v53 no5 p68 S/O 2017

Who's the Greatest CLAY COURTER of the mall? *Tennis* v53 no3 p42 My/Je 2017

WORLD ON A STRING color *Tennis* v53 no2 p42 Mr/Ap 2017

Tikoo, Sonia

The formation of peak rings in large impact craters bibl color graph *Science* v354 no6314 p878 N 18 2016

TIKU, NITASHA

Tales From the Dark Web: The downfall of the Silk Road's creator is the startup hero's journey in a black mirror *New York Times Book Review* p13 Je 18 2017

Til They Bang on the Door (Music)

Til They Bang On The Door S. J. O'Connell color *Downbeat* v83 no11 p63 N 2016

Tilak Ratnanather, J.

Community network for deaf scientists color *Science* v356 no6336 p386 Ap 28 2017

Tilberis, Liz

THE LEGEND OF LIZ TILBERIS S. Mooallem bw color *Harper's Bazaar* no3657 p222 O 2017

Tilcsik, András

Research: How Subtle Class Cues Can Backfire on Your Resume *Harvard Business Review Digital Articles* p2 D 21 2016

The Unintended Consequences of Diversity Statements *Harvard Business Review Digital Articles* p2 Mr 29 2016

When Having Too Many Experts on the Board Backfires *Harvard Business Review Digital Articles* p2 Ag 29 2016

Tile construction

Last Look E. Daigneau *Governing* v30 no3 p64 D 2016

Tile flooring

ATLAS OBSCURA BERBER LODGE IS A HIP OASIS HIDDEN AMONG OLIVE AND CITRUS GROVES NEAR THE MOUNTAINS OUTSIDE MARRAKECH A. GIACOBBE color *Conde Nast Traveler* v52 no10 p30 N 2017

Faux Finishes D. HOWLAND color *Cabin Living* p14 D 2016

Tile pavements

FIT TO BE tiled J. Dorris color *Martha Stewart Living* p122 O 2017

Tiles

See also

Ceiling tiles

Ceramic tiles

Tile flooring

Tile pavements

BACK splash PROGRESSION M. ELLEN POLSON color *Arts & Crafts Homes & the Revival* v12 no5 p28 Wint 2018

A CRAFTSMAN HOME in Perfect Pitch [Cover story] D. PIZZI color *Arts & Crafts Homes & the Revival* v12 no5 p40 Wint 2018

AN EXPLOSION OF COLORFUL TILE color *Old House Journal* v45 no7 p30 O 2017

Peachy! A surviving bathroom, ca. 1922 P. Poore color *Old House Journal* v45 no3 p74 My 2017

RANCH REDEMPTION P. POORE color *Arts & Crafts Homes & the Revival* v11 no5 p48 Wint 2017

revival baths *Design Center Sourcebook* p30 2017

SPANISH & ART DECO tile FANTASY P. POORE color *Arts & Crafts Homes & the Revival* v12 no4 p28 Fall 2017

Tiles in interior decoration

make a SPLASH J. BREWSTER color *Cabin Living* p52 Ap 2017

Tiles—Design & construction

Cersaie 2016 A. Fixsen *Architectural Record* v204 no11 p59 N 2016

A Mosaic Tile Floor M. E. Polson color *Arts & Crafts Homes & the Revival* v12 no2 p34 Spr 2017

Tiles—Evaluation

ARTFUL TILE color *Arts & Crafts Homes & the Revival* v12 no1 p39 2017 Resouce Guide

Cersaie 2016 A. Fixsen *Architectural Record* v204 no11 p59 N 2016

Enduring Finish M. E. Polson color *Old House Journal* v45 no2 p76 Ap 2017

In the Western HOME color *Sunset* v239 no3 p58 S 2017

KITCHENS & BATHS color *Arts & Crafts Homes & the Revival* v12 no1 p36 2017 Resouce Guide

A Luxury Bath of 1924 G. Louise cartoon color *Old House Journal* v45 no2 p72 Ap 2017

LUXURY LOOK A. MANLEY color *House Beautiful* p127 Ag 2017

MAKE IT LIGHTER, BRIGHTER, BIGGER S. EMSLIE color *House Beautiful* p70 Ag 2017

Make your bathroom beautiful color *Redbook* p142 S 2017

MOSAIC PATTERNS for Serviceable Floors B. D. COLEMAN color *Arts & Crafts Homes & the Revival* v12 no2 p29 Spr 2017

Tile Everywhere M. E. Polson color *Old House Journal* v45 no6 p76 S 2017

ULTIMATE GUIDE TO REVAMP BUYS C. RODRIGUES color *House Beautiful* p102 Ag 2017

Ups and Downs color *Log Home Living* v34 no6 p38 Ag 2017

Tilghman, Shirley
Not just Salk color *Science* v357 no6356 p1105 S 15 2017

Tilker, Andrew
Saving the saola from extinction color *Science* v357 no6357 p1248 S 22 2017

Till, Christy B.
Rapid cooling and cold storage in a silicic magma reservoir recorded in individual crystals color diag graph *Science* v356 no6343 p1154 Je 16 2017

Till, Emmett, 1941-1955
EMMETT, STILL S. WELLER bw *Vanity Fair* p179 Hollywood 2017 Supplement

Emmett Till Revisited V. MAJEROL, A. Blinder et al img *New York Times Upfront* v149 no11 p16 Ap 3 2017

A Missing Memorial C. ALESSIO bw color *America* v215 no19 p21 D 19 2016

Till, Emmett, 1941-1955—Trials, litigation, etc.
A BLACK AND WHITE CASE J. Edgar Wideman bw color *Esquire* v166 no4 p100 N 2016

Till, Lucas, 1990-
MacGyver N. Abrams, S. Highfill et al *Entertainment Weekly* no1482/1483 p99 S 22 2017

Till, Lucas, 1990-—Interviews
MACGYVER I. Rudolph *TV Guide* v65 no39 p52 S 18 2017

MACGYVER'S DYNAMIC DUO I. RUDOLPH *TV Guide* v64 no46 p26 N 7 2016

Tillage
FALL TILLAGE VALUES: THERE ARE OPPORTUNITIES TO BUY LITTLE-USED TILLAGE IMPLEMENTS AT MUCH-USED PRICES D. Mowitz *Successful Farming* v115 no12 p36 O 2017

SOIL STEALER: TILLAGE IS A STEALTHY ERODER THAT ROBS YOUR PRECIOUS TOPSOIL. HERE'S HOW TO FIX IT G. GULLICKSON *Successful Farming* v115 no12 p44 O 2017

Tiller, Bryson, 1993-
Bryson Tiller M. Rich color *Current Biography* v78 no3 p78 Mr 2017

Tillerson, Rex W., 1952-
The Boy Scout Leading State R. Ratnesar color *Bloomberg Businessweek* no4513 p14 Mr 6 2017

Dealt a Weak Hand, Rex Tillerson Is Still In the Game at State I. Bremmer color *Time* v190 no7 p12 Ag 21 2017

Iran on Notice L. Smith color *Weekly Standard* v22 no32 p8 My 1 2017

No Press? No Problem N. Wadhams color *Bloomberg Businessweek* no4516 p22 Mr 27 2017

Objectively Speaking, Rand Is History: The recent presidential race made it obvious: conservatives have shrugged off Ayn Rand J. Burns *Hoover Digest: Research & Opinion on Public Policy* no3 p170 Summ 2017

PARODY color *Weekly Standard* v23 no6 p48 O 16 2017

Rex's Right-Hand Woman N. Wadhams *Bloomberg Businessweek* no4525 p25 Je 5 2017

Tillerson Hits The Road and Finds His Feet N. Wadhams and N. Syeed color *Bloomberg Businessweek* no4530 p38 Jl 17 2017

Tillerson's Got a Private State Department J. Carroll and A. Steel *Bloomberg Businessweek* no4505 p30 D 26 2016

Trump and Russia: Nothing to See Here? B. LUEDERS color *Progressive* v81 no6 p14 Ag/S 2017

Trump and Tillerson: Conflict Ahead? J. Ball color *Fortune* v75 no1 p20 Ja 1 2017

The United States of Exxon A. JUHASZ *In These Times* v41 no2 p18 F 2017

The Week color il *National Review* v68 no24 p4 D 31 2016

Will Beijing Also Have A Friend at State? T. Shi, D. Tweed et al bw *Bloomberg Businessweek* no4504 p26 D 19 2016

TILLERY, ALISHA
Bae Watch color *Ebony* v72 no4 p82 F 2017

Total Boz Moves color *Ebony* v72 no5 p72 Mr 2017

When Things Aren't 'OK' color *Ebony* v72 no3 p90 D 2016/Ja 2017

TILLET, SALAMISHAH
Now She's Done It color *New York Times Book Review* p15 S 25 2016

TILLEY, AARON
Battling Giants chart color *Forbes* v200 no1 p50 Jl 27 2017

THE NEW INTEL color graph *Forbes* v198 no8 p78 D 20 2016

Tilley, Jonathan
The Age of Smart, Safe, Cheap Robots Is Already Here *Harvard Business Review Digital Articles* p2 Je 15 2015

Tilley, Louise
Resistance to malaria through structural variation of red blood cell invasion receptors diag *Science* v356 no6343 p1139 Je 16 2017

TILLEY, TERRENCE W.
LANDING IN DULLES *America* v215 p34 N 28 2016

Tillich, Paul, 1886-1965
UNHOLY DREAD *Lapham's Quarterly* v10 no3 p116 Summ 2017

Tillinghast, Joel
Big Money Thinks Small: Biases, Blind Spots, and Smarter Investing *Publishers Weekly* v264 no22 p55 My 29 2017

TILLMAN, JOI
The Way Forward color *O, The Oprah Magazine* p18 My 2017

Tillman, Josh—Interviews
Q&A: Father John Misty A. GREENE *Rolling Stone* no1284 p20 Ap 6 2017

Tillman, Michael
Imagine Dragons bw *Current Biography* v78 no9 p42 S 2017

Perfume Genius bw *Current Biography* v78 no9 p66 S 2017

Tillman, Robert
Kendrick Cabin: Built around 1960, this rustic, three-bedroom cabin features pine flooring, mugh-hewn pine ceiling beams and, best of all, a front porch adorned with Adirondack chairs aimed at distant mountains A. McGIVNEY *Arizona Highways* v96 no7 p14 Jl 2017

Tilmes, Simone
Sulfur injections for a cooler planet color graph *Science* v357 no6348 p246 Jl 21 2017

Timbaland, 1971-
Timbaland N. Feeney color *Entertainment Weekly* no1460/1461 p96 Ap 7-17 2017

Timber
Opportunities for Improved Transparency in the Timber Trade through Scientific Verification A. J. LOWE, E. E. DORMONTT et al *BioScience* v66 no11 p990 N 1 2016

plan color *Timber Home Living* p16 2017 Annual Buyers

q&a color *Timber Home Living* v27 no3 p20 Je 2017

your DREAM HOME STARTS HERE *Timber Home Living* p17 2017 Annual Buyers

Timber Block (Thermo Structure Inc.)—Awards
Timber Block Wins at America's Biggest Building Show color *Log Home Living* v34 no4 p16 My 2017

Timberbuilt (Company)
Come Together color *Timber Home Living* p42 2017 SpecialIssue

Timber—Grading
Why Buy From A Log and Timber Homes Council Member? D. Perry color *Log Home Living* v33 no9 p71 D 2016

Timberhaven Log & Timber Homes LLC
the retreat that love built F. SIGURDSSON color diag *Cabin Living* p56 Ja/F 2017

Timberlake, Deveran
AT THEIR PEAK *Virginia Living* v15 no2 p48 F 2017

TIMBERLAKE, JONATHAN
An Ecoregion-Based Approach to Protecting Half the Terrestrial Realm *BioScience* v67 no6 p534 Je 2017

Timberlake, Justin, 1981-—Interviews
Justin Timberlake and Jonathan Demme K. P. Sullivan color *Entertainment Weekly* no1435 p42 O 14 2016

Timberpeg (Company)

Coastal Charm color *Timber Home Living* p34 2017 SpecialIssue

Timbers, Alex

RISE UP R. MEAD cartoon color *New Yorker* v93 no5 p44 Mr 20 2017

Timbuk2 (Company)

TIMBUK2 AUTHORITY PACK O. RAYMUNDO color *Macworld - Digital Edition* v34 no9 p36 S 2017

Time

    See also

    Cycles

    Midnight

Borrowed Time D. Paul bw *Indianapolis Monthly* p120 Ap 2017

EAT EARLY, STAY SLIM color *Health* v31 no8 p13 O 2017

Physicists make 'time crystal' in lab E. CONOVER *Science News* v190 no10 p12 N 12 2016

Poses of the month [Cover story] T. Little color *Yoga Journal* no291 p49 My 2017

STANDSTILL T. Verducci color *Sports Illustrated* v126 no18 p36 Je 26 2017

Take Back Your Lunch Break color *Health* v31 no7 p20 S 2017

TIME DIFFERENCES J. Brown *Popular Science* v289 no5 p5 S/O 2017

Why does time seem to fly when we're having fun? P. Simen and M. Matell bibl color *Science* v354 no6317 p1231 D 9 2016

Time & the Conways (Theatrical production)

Theater img *New York* v50 no17 p126 Ag 21 2017

Time (Periodical)

A FIVE-MINUTE GUIDE TO FIVE MILLENNIA OF HUMAN HISTORY K. Andersen cartoon *Esquire* p123 S 2017

Jefferson's Warning to the White House N. Gibbs color *Time* v189 no5 p4 F 13 2017

On Leaders E. Felsenthal color *Time* v190 no16/17 p4 O 23 2017

TIME's Second Century E. Felsenthal color *Time* v190 no13 p6 O 2 2017

Time, In Whales (Poem)

TIME, IN WHALES E. J. Yoon *New Yorker* v93 no13 p58 My 15 2017

Time After Time (TV program)

Time After Time D. Holbrook *TV Guide* v65 no8 p32 F 27 2017

Time capsules

WHY I'M SENDING A TIME CAPSULE TO MARS color *National Geographic* v230 no6 pc13 D 2016

Time delay systems

To slow or not? Challenges in subsecond networks N. F. Johnson bibl color graph *Science* v355 no6327 p801 F 24 2017

Time management

    See also

    Deadlines

    Human multitasking

    Work-life balance

3 Ways to Get More Done Right Now K. Sehgal *Harvard Business Review Digital Articles* p2 F 23 2017

3 Ways to Make Time for the Little Tasks You Never Make Time For D. Clark *Harvard Business Review Digital Articles* p2 F 14 2017

4 steps for redesigning time for student and teacher learning b. L. Nazareno diag il *Phi Delta Kappan* v98 no4 p21 D 2016/Ja 2017

5 Steps to Investing Your Energy More Wisely P. Bregman *Harvard Business Review Digital Articles* p2 Mr 8 2016

9 Productivity Tips from People Who Write About Productivity R. Friedman *Harvard Business Review Digital Articles* p2 D 31 2015

Are You Proud of How You're Spending Your Time? E. G. Saunders *Harvard Business Review Digital Articles* p2 F 13 2015

BEAT GENEROSITY BURNOUT A. GRANT and R. REBELE color *Harvard Business Review Digital Articles* p3 Ja 1 2017

a brief history of time(keeping) K. Atherton bw color *Popular Science* v289 no5 p14 S/O 2017

Cancelling One-on-One Meetings Destroys Your Productivity E. G. Saunders *Harvard Business Review Digital Articles* p2 Mr 9 2015

Commit to Under-Scheduling in 2016 E. G. Saunders *Harvard Business Review Digital Articles* p2 D 21 2015

Companies with a Formal Sales Process Generate More Revenue J. Jordan and R. Kelly *Harvard Business Review Digital Articles* p2 Ja 21 2015

Conquer Your To-Do List with Your Phone A. Samuel *Harvard Business Review Digital Articles* p2 D 1 2014

Don't Wait Until After the Meeting to Start Your Action Items K. S. Milway *Harvard Business Review Digital Articles* p2 Ap 28 2016

The Editor's Note J. Richardson *Phi Delta Kappan* v98 no4 p4 D 2016/Ja 2017

editor's note. THE MIND'S WHITE SPACE K. Perina *Psychology Today* v50 no5 p3 S/O 2017

EVERY DAY I'M SIDE-HUSTLIN' C. Cardinal, B. J. Novak et al cartoon color *GQ: Gentlemen's Quarterly* v97 no4 p60 Ap 2017

A Formula to Stop You from Overcommitting Your Time E. G. Saunders *Harvard Business Review Digital Articles* p2 F 19 2015

Get More Done by Focusing Less on Work S. Friedman *Harvard Business Review Digital Articles* p2 F 5 2015

Give Yourself Permission to Work Fewer Hours E. G. Saunders *Harvard Business Review Digital Articles* p2 Jl 13 2016

Help Your Team Spend Time on the Right Things R. Ashkenas and A. McDougall *Harvard Business Review Digital Articles* p2 O 23 2014

How Do You Waste Time at Work? K. Morell color *Bloomberg Businessweek* no4494 p70 O 10 2016

How to Beat Procrastination C. Webb *Harvard Business Review Digital Articles* p2 Jl 29 2016

How to Create More from What You Already Have S. Sonenshein *Time* v189 no7/8 p28 F 27 2017

How to Get into a Rhythm at Work If You Can't Stick to a Schedule E. G. Saunders *Harvard Business Review Digital Articles* p2 Ap 14 2016

How to get more time in your day cartoon *Redbook* p140 Ap 2017

How to Protect Your Time Without Alienating Your Network D. Clark *Harvard Business Review Digital Articles* p2 F 6 2015

How to Use Your Travel Time Productively D. Clark *Harvard Business Review Digital Articles* p2 N 5 2015

If You Dread Deadlines, You're Thinking About Them All Wrong E. G. Saunders *Harvard Business Review Digital Articles* p2 Mr 18 2016

IS THIS THE YEAR? *Successful Farming* v115 no1 p68 Ja 2017

The Magic of 30-Minute Meetings P. Bregman *Harvard Business Review Digital Articles* p2 F 22 2016

messy no more! *Parents* v92 no1 p55 Ja 2017

Rescuing my time from science L. Rinaldi color *Science* v354 no6319 p1666 D 23 2016

A scientist on any schedule A. L. Mayer color *Science* v355 no6323 p426 Ja 27 2017

SEIZE THE DAY! [Cover story] color *O, The Oprah Magazine* p102 O 2017

Show-Time COUNTDOWN B. Jewett and A. Boatwright color *Horse & Rider* v55 no11 p56 N 2016

Stop Doing Low-Value Work P. Claman *Harvard Business Review Digital Articles* p2 Je 1 2016

Stop Letting Email Control Your Work Day P. A. Argenti *Harvard Business Review Digital Articles* p2 S 7 2017

Stop Playing the Victim with Your Time E. G. Saunders *Harvard Business Review Digital Articles* p2 Ja 21 2015

Strategies for Every Type of Email Pain A. Samuel *Harvard Business Review Digital Articles* p2 My 20 2015

THE ultimate guide to SAVING TIME & FEELING IN CONTROL S. M. FERNÁNDEZ color *Redbook* p99 S 2017

A Way to Plan If You're Bad at Planning E. G. Saunders *Harvard Business Review Digital Articles* p2 Jl 4 2017

When More Is Too Much S. Sonenshein color *Time* v189 no7/8 p28 F 27 2017

where does the day go? S. Chodosh color *Popular Science* v289 no5 p12 S/O 2017

You May Hate Planning, But You Should Do It Anyway E. G. Saunders color *Harvard Business Review Digital Articles* p2 S 19 2016

Your Calendar Needs an Upgrade M. Schrage *Harvard Business Review Digital Articles* p2 Jl 9 2015

Time management software

CONSTRUCTION SIMULATOR 2 J. MATHIS color *Macworld - Digital Edition* v34 no4 p59 My 2017

Timely: Time tracking Mac app hampered by required Internet connection J. BATTERSBY color *Macworld - Digital Edition*

v34 no10 p89 O 2017

Time management surveys

Americans Spend an Average of 37 Minutes a Day Preparing and Serving Food and Cleaning Up K. Hamrick *Amber Waves: The Economics of Food, Farming, Natural Resources, & Rural America* p26 N 2016

Time management—Humor

STRATEGIC HUMOR il *Harvard Business Review* v94 no12 p21 D 2016

Time management—Social aspects

Q: If you had an extra hour in your day, what would you do with it? N. Naar, S. Cordova et al color *O, The Oprah Magazine* p18 O 2017

Time measurements

See also

Geochronometry

the 10-second marathon M. Shieh color *Popular Science* v289 no5 p16 S/O 2017

a brief history of time(keeping) K. Atherton bw color *Popular Science* v289 no5 p14 S/O 2017

SHOT TIMERS R. MANN and J. B. SNOW color *Outdoor Life* v224 no5 pR10 Je/Jl 2017

WATCHING THE CLOCKS B. GARDINER, E. F. ARIAS et al *Popular Science* v289 no5 p45 S/O 2017

Time-of-flight mass spectrometers

A brief overview of matrix-assisted laser desorption/ionization time-of-flight mass spectrometry (MALDI-TOF MS) applications in clinical microbiology in China Meng Xiao, T. Kudinha et al *Science* v354 no6319 p55 D 23 2016

Application of MALDI-TOF mass spectrometry for identifying clinical microorganisms Xiaowei Zhan, Jun Yang et al bibl *Science* v354 no6319 p58 D 23 2016

Time outs (Sports)

HOT | NOT T. Keith color *Sports Illustrated* v127 no3 p24 Jl 24 2017

Time perception

Borrowed Time D. Paul bw *Indianapolis Monthly* p120 Ap 2017

Time Warp R. Li *Natural History* v124 no10 p7 N 2016

where does the day go? S. Chodosh color *Popular Science* v289 no5 p12 S/O 2017

Time perception in animals

The Remarkable Timing of Seals J. G. Goldman color *Scientific American* v316 no1 p17 Ja 2017

Time perspective

WATCHING THE CLOCKS B. GARDINER, E. F. ARIAS et al *Popular Science* v289 no5 p45 S/O 2017

What's special about instructions? J. Dziedzic color *Model Railroader* v84 no9 p68 S 2017

Time travel

THE LAST LAUGH B. RADFORD *Skeptical Inquirer* v41 no4 p66 Jl/Ag 2017

Time Warner Inc.—Finance

THE AT&T-TIME WARNER MERGER (UNLESS ...) A. Pressman diag *Fortune* v174 no8 p20 D 15 2016

Where the Future's AT(&T) G. Smith cartoon *Bloomberg Businessweek* no4497 p22 O 31 2016

Time—Charts, diagrams, etc.

Actionable Offenses T. Verducci, T. Keith et al color diag *Sports Illustrated* v126 no7 p20 Mr 6 2017

WAITING GAME chart color *Sports Illustrated* v126 no18 p39 Je 26 2017

Timeless (TV program)

Meet the crew... I. Rudolph *TV Guide* v64 no48 p12 N 21 2016

Timeless I. Rudolph *TV Guide* p40 D 5 2016

Timeless I. Rudolph *TV Guide* v65 no4 p34 Ja 16 2017

A Very Timeless Script S. Li color *Entertainment Weekly* no1436/1437 p92 O 21 2016

Timeley AS

Timely: Time tracking Mac app hampered by required Internet connection J. BATTERSBY color *Macworld - Digital Edition* v34 no10 p89 O 2017

Time—Psychological aspects

PRESENT TENSE A. BURDICK cartoon *New Yorker* v92 no42 p68 D 19 2016

Times Have Changed (Music)

Personal Strains of the Blues HADLEY color *Downbeat* v84 no3

p60 Mr 2017

Time's Person of the Year selections

What You Said About ... color *Time* v188 no27-28 p8 D 26 2016

Times-Picayune (Newspaper)

THE T-P AND THE ADVOCATE cartoon *New Orleans Magazine* v51 no1 p22 N 2016

Times Are Racing, The (Theatrical production)

Bobby Pins Come Loose J. Acocella cartoon *New Yorker* v93 no12 p11 My 8 2017

Time—Social aspects

What You Said About ... chart color *Time* v189 no4 p6 Ja 23 2017

Times Square (New York, N.Y.)

Times Square Reconstruction New York J. Minutillo *Architectural Record* v205 no4 p210 Ap 2017

Timestamps

Using Blockchain to Keep Public Data Public B. Forde *Harvard Business Review Digital Articles* p2 Mr 31 2017

Time—Systems & standards

See also

Daylight saving

Timex Corp.

THE TEST OF TIME N. Sullivan color *Esquire* p42 N 2017

Timlin, Addison

From Marilyn Manson to Marian prayer T. Donnellan color *America* v216 no5 p45 Mr 6 2017

TIMM, JONATHAN

"Clopening" Time *In These Times* v40 no12 p10 D 2016

Timm, Robert

BEYOND ENDURANCE P. Garrison color *Flying* v144 no2 p80 F 2017

Timme, Elizabeth—Interviews

HELEN LEUNG + ELIZABETH TIMME: THE "WONKISH" URBAN PLANNER AND "ARCHITECTURE GEEK" ARE OUT TO SOLVE SOME OF L.A.'S TOUGHEST HOUSING AND SMALL-BUSINESS PROBLEMS J. HERBST *Los Angeles Magazine* v62 no9 p93 S 2017

Timmerman, Robert

On the value of carbon-ion therapy *Physics Today* v69 no11 p14 N 2016

Timmermans, C.

Observation of a large-scale anisotropy in the arrival directions of cosmic rays above 8×1018 eV *Science* v357 no6357 p1266 S 22 2017

Timms, Henry

TED's Shift from Old to New Power *Harvard Business Review Digital Articles* p2 D 1 2014

Timna Site (Israel)

ISRAEL UPRISING S. DAVIS color *Climbing* no349 p38 N 2016

TIMSON, JUDITH

GENIUS, SQUARED bw *Maclean's* v130 no9 p78 O 2017

Tin

WHEN TIN CEILINGS WERE HIGH-TECH V. Postrel *Reason* v49 no5 p16 O 2017

Tin Star (TV program)

Tin Star A. Bacle, K. Connolly et al *Entertainment Weekly* no1482/1483 p109 S 22 2017

Tinariwen (Performer)

TINARIWEN C. MUSMECI *Interview* v47 no2 p76 Mr 2017

Tinashe (Performer)

Hot Pop Tinashe B. SPANOS color *Rolling Stone* no1274 p35 N 17 2014

Tinctures (Pharmacy)

Dr. Low Dog [Cover story] T. L. Dog color *Prevention* p26 Mr 2017

Tindall, Gillian

Are you related to Charlemagne? *History Today* v66 no10 p56 O 2016

Through the Fog and Filthy Air *History Today* v67 no2 p65 F 2017

Tindell, Kip

The Container Store's CEO on Finding and Keeping Front-Line Talent *Harvard Business Review Digital Articles* p2 N 19 2014

Tinder (Web resource)

THE APPROVAL MATRIX img *New York* v49 no24 p180 N 28 2016

BRING BEER, TOILET PAPER, SOAP S. Jane cartoon *Powder* v45 no3 p58 N 2016

A WHIFF OF CULTURE color *Wired* v25 no4 p28 Ap 2017

Tittle, Y. A. (Yelberton Abraham), 1926-2017

Y.A. TITTLE (1926-2017) S. Kwak color *Sports Illustrated* v127 no12 p22 O 16 2017

Y.A. Tittle S. Gregory color *Time* v190 no16/17 p20 O 23 2017

Titus, Ella

GET HER LOOK: Ella Titus H. Rolfe *Dance Spirit* v21 no7 p96 S 2017

Tivey, Maurice—Interviews

Attracted to Magnetics L. Lippsett *Oceanus* v52 no1 p52 Summ 2016

Tivoli Audio LLC

Tivoli Audio Model One Digital review: Big sound from a small footprint M. BROWN color *Macworld - Digital Edition* v34 no8 p124 Ag 2017

Tizon, Alex, 1959-2017

THE CONVERSATION A. Bonifacio, V. Rafael et al color *Atlantic* v320 no2 p8 S 2017

Lola's Story bw color *Atlantic* v319 no5 p64 Je 2017

A REPORTER'S STORY J. Goldberg bw *Atlantic* v319 no5 p8 Je 2017

Tjan, Anthony K.

5 Things New Managers Should Focus on First *Harvard Business Review Digital Articles* p2 My 9 2017

5 Ways to Become More Self-Aware *Harvard Business Review Digital Articles* p2 F 11 2015

6 Rules for Building and Scaling Company Culture *Harvard Business Review Digital Articles* p2 Mr 23 2015

Before You Respond to that Email, Pause *Harvard Business Review Digital Articles* p2 O 21 2014

Good People: The Only Leadership Decision That Really Matters color *Publishers Weekly* v264 no10 p51 Mr 6 2017

Strategy as Jazz vs. Symphony *Harvard Business Review Digital Articles* p2 Mr 3 2017

What the Best Mentors Do bw *Harvard Business Review Digital Articles* p2 F 27 2017

Tjian, Robert

Not just Salk color *Science* v357 no6356 p1105 S 15 2017

TJM (Company)

Where a Graying Herd Still Thunders H. Son cartoon *Bloomberg Businessweek* no4503 p34 D 12 2016

Tjossem, Paul J. H.

Learning the Art of Electronics: A Hands-On Lab Course *Physics Today* v70 no5 p61 My 2017

TK Group LLC

Laos' New Breed of Entrepreneurs *Foreign Affairs* v95 no6 p(Sp)17 N/D 2016

TKACH, VASYL V.

Transformational Principles for NEON Sampling of Mammalian Parasites and Pathogens: A Response to Springer and Colleagues *BioScience* v66 no11 p917 N 1 2016

Tkačik, Gašper

Biased partitioning of the multidrug efflux pump AcrAB-TolC underlies long-lived phenotypic heterogeneity diag *Science* v356 no6335 p311 Ap 21 2017

Decoding of position in the developing neural tube from antiparallel morphogen gradients diag *Science* v356 no6345 p1379 Je 30 2017

TKACIK, MOE

The Bankers Take Manhattan *In These Times* v41 no6 p34 Je 2017

Tkaczyk, Filip

CORDAGE *Mother Earth News* no279 p50 D/Ja 2017

TLC (Performer)

TLC STORIES BEHIND THE SONGS C. Arnold color *Entertainment Weekly* no1472 p28 Je 30 2017

Tlon, Uqbar, Orbis Tertius (Short story)

1935: Ramos Mejía J. L. Borges *Lapham's Quarterly* v10 no2 p151 Spr 2017

To, John W. F.

Highly stretchable polymer semiconductor films through the nanoconfinement effect bibl graph *Science* v355 no6320 p1 Ja 6 2017

To, Nhien

Consumer Expenditure Surveys Methods Symposium and Microdata Users' Workshop, July 12-15, 2016 bibl *Monthly Labor Review* p1 My 2017

To an Immigrant (Poem)

To an Immigrant J. M. Pitas il *U.S. Catholic* v82 no5 p11 My 2017

To Die For (Film)

THE ESSENTIAL NICOLE KIDMAN L. Greenblatt color *Entertainment Weekly* no1472 p44 Je 30 2017

To Kill a Mockingbird (Film)

In Honor of Atticus C. Nashawaty color *Entertainment Weekly* no1470 p40 Je 16 2017

To Pimp a Butterfly (Music)

LARRY YANDO J. BERG color *Chicago* v65 no12 p56 D 2016

To the Bone (Film)

ALSO PLAYING: JULY J. Nolfi color *Entertainment Weekly* no1463/1464 p66 Ap/My 2017

BONE DEEP D. Coggan color *Entertainment Weekly* no1476 p30 Ag 4 2017

To the Bone L. Greenblatt color *Entertainment Weekly* no1474/1475 p98 Jl 21-28 2017

To the Ghost (Poem)

To the Ghost C. A. Lawrence *America* v216 no11 p49 My 15 2017

To Walk Invisible: The Brontë Sisters (TV program)

Behind the Scenes J. POWERS and V. STEIKER color *Vogue* v207 no3 p386 Mr 2017

Toads

The Case for Cannibalism B. SCHUTT cartoon *Discover* v38 no3 p56 Ap 2017

TOADZILLA! B. Wright *National Geographic Kids* no469 p13 Ap 2017

Toal, Gerard

Near Abroad: Putin, the West, and the Contest over Ukraine and the Caucasus *Publishers Weekly* v263 no45 p52 N 7 2016

Near Abroad: Putin, the West, and the Contest Over Ukraine and the Caucasus R. Legvold *Foreign Affairs* v96 no2 p183 Mr/Ap 2017

Toast (Bread)

The Fawning Over Avocado Toast *Los Angeles Magazine* v61 no11 p66 N 2016

Terrific Toasters color *Good Housekeeping* v265 no4 p81 O 2017

Why I Have Takeout On Speed Dial D. THORNE color *Reader's Digest* v190 no1133 p16 S 2017

Toaster oven cooking—Equipment & supplies

For the Family Chef [Cover story] color *Consumer Reports* v81 no12 p18 D 2016

Toasters—Evaluation

For the Family Chef [Cover story] color *Consumer Reports* v81 no12 p18 D 2016

Terrific Toasters color *Good Housekeeping* v265 no4 p81 O 2017

Toasts

June All-star color *Women's Health* v14 no5 p16 Je 2017

Tobacco industry—United States

BRIGHT LEAF LEGACY: THE PAST, PRESENT AND FUTURE OF VIRGINIA'S TOBACCO INDUSTRY E. J. WALLACE *Virginia Living* v15 no4 p104 Je 2017

Tobacco products—Marketing

The new world of tobacco A. McShane *History Today* v67 no4 p41 Ap 2017

Tobacco products—Sales & prices

Marlboro F. Gillette, J. Kaplan et al color *Bloomberg Businessweek* no4514 p46 Mr 13 2017

Tobaccowala, Rishad

Extracting Insights from Vast Stores of Data *Harvard Business Review Digital Articles* p2 Ag 30 2016

Tobah, Yvonne Butler

How Mayo Clinic Is Simplifying Prenatal Care for Low-Risk Patients *Harvard Business Review Digital Articles* p2 Je 19 2017

Tobben, Sheela

U.S. OIL'S $10 BILLION VENEZUELAN THREAT color *Bloomberg Businessweek* no4534 p28 Ag 14 2017

Tobey, Pamela

USHERING IN THE NEXT GOLDEN DECADE *Bloomberg Businessweek* no4536 p4 S 4 2017

TOBIAS, JIMMY

BANKING ON RESISTANCE color *Nation* v304 no16 p24 My 22 2017

Tobias, Joseph A.

Avian egg shape: Form, function, and evolution color diag *Science* v356 no6344 p1249 Je 23 2017

Tobin, Celia Talbot
RAVALLI COUNTY, MONTANA *Harper's Magazine* p27 O 2017

TOBIN, JONATHAN S.
A False Theatrical Peace *Commentary* v143 no2 p52 F 2017

Tobin, Joseph
Cardinal Tobin calls on church leaders to 'put a face' on deportation crisis W. Massey color *America* v216 no13 p17 Je 12 2017
Discerning a New Role M. O'LOUGHLIN color *America* v215 no14 p8 N 7 2016

Tobin, Joseph—Interviews
Faith in real life J. C. Tobin color *U.S. Catholic* v82 no7 p18 Jl 2017

Tobler, Michael
Swimming in polluted waters bibl diag *Science* v354 no6317 p1232 D 9 2016

Tobolowsky, Stephen—Interviews
GROUNDHOG Deus D. MARTINEZ *Texas Monthly* v45 no4 p74 Ap 2017

TOBON, WOLKE
National Ecosystem Assessments in Europe: A Review chart *BioScience* v66 no10 p813 O 1 2016

Toby, Mekeisha Madden
Q&A WITH CUSH JUMBO color *Essence* v47 no11 p60 Mr 2017

Tocca (Company)
The Essence of Spring A. Aguillard color *Southern Living* v52 no5 p68 My 2017

Toch, Thomas
Has D.C. Teacher Reform Been Successful? *Washington Monthly* v49 no9/10 p16 S/O 2017
Hot for Teachers color *Washington Monthly* v49 no6-8 p47 Je-Ag 2017

Tochka, Zachary L.
Fabrication of fillable microparticles and other complex 3D microstructures color diag *Science* v357 no6356 p1138 S 15 2017

tocker, Benjamin D.
Response to Comment on "Mycorrhizal association as a primary control of the CO2 fertilization effect" bibl graph *Science* v355 no6323 p358 Ja 27 2017

TOCKNER, KLEMENT
Freshwater Megafauna: Flagships for Freshwater Biodiversity under Threat *BioScience* v67 no10 p919 O 2017

Tocqueville, Alexis de 1805-1859
"FEVER GRIPS THE ENTIRE NATION" A. GOLDHAMMER bw color il map *Nation* v303 no16 p10 O 17 2016
HOME INSECURITY *Lapham's Quarterly* v10 no3 p65 Summ 2017

Today Show (TV program)
Morning Glory I. Rudolph *TV Guide* v65 no7 p20 F 13 2017
Today by the Numbers bw *TV Guide* v65 no7 p22 F 13 2017
Today's Most Memorable Moments E. Aslanian bw color *TV Guide* v65 no7 p24 F 13 2017

TodayTix Inc.—Finance
MAKING IT ON BROAD-WAY T. J. Huddleston color *Fortune* v174 no8 p75 D 15 2016

TODD, ANDREA
DEATH BY PREGNANCY bw color *Women's Health* v14 no9 p128 N 2017

Todd, Chuck, 1972-
CHUCK TODD C. Bethea color *Runner's World* v52 no2 p96 Mr 2017
My Obsessions... *TV Guide* v65 no25 p7 Je 2017

Todd, Chuck, 1972-—Interviews
Chuck Todd Thinks It's Important to Stay Neutral A. M. Cox *New York Times Magazine* p70 O 8 2017

Todd, Jessica E.
USDA's FoodAPS: Providing Insights Into U.S. Food Demand and Food Assistance Programs *Amber Waves: The Economics of Food, Farming, Natural Resources, & Rural America* p42 Ag 2017

Todd, John-Paul
Rapid development of a DNA vaccine for Zika virus bibl graph *Science* v354 no6309 p237 O 14 2016
Trispecific broadly neutralizing HIV antibodies mediate potent SHIV protection in macaques color graph *Science* v357 no6359 p85 O 6 2017

TODD, KIM
THOSE Magnificent Women AND THEIR TYPING MACHINES *Smithsonian* v47 no7 p60 N 2016

TODD, MARY
DIGGING IN THE DIRT *Phi Kappa Phi Forum* v97 no1 p1 Spr 2017
ON THE MOVE *Phi Kappa Phi Forum* v96 no4 p1 Wint 2016
TAKING IT TO THE STREETS color *Phi Kappa Phi Forum* v97 no2 p2 Summ 2017

Todd, Matthew—Interviews
Morning Glory I. Rudolph *TV Guide* v65 no7 p20 F 13 2017

TODD, STEPHEN
WIZARD OF OZ color *Conde Nast Traveler* v52 no9 p22 O 2017

Todd Snyder (Company)
MODERN CLASSIC M. BERLINGER color *Bloomberg Businessweek* no4494 p67 O 10 2016

Toddlers
For crying out loud R. M. McKenny color *U.S. Catholic* v82 no4 p36 Ap 2017

Toddlers—Development
This Just In J. Zorthian *Time* v189 no3 p19 Ja 16 2017

Toder, Eric
The U.S. Needs Tax Reform, Not Tax Cuts *Harvard Business Review Digital Articles* p2 2017
We Need to Raise Taxes for Shareholders and Cut Them for Companies *Harvard Business Review Digital Articles* p2 N 1 2016

Todero Peixoto, C. J.
Observation of a large-scale anisotropy in the arrival directions of cosmic rays above 8×10^{18} eV *Science* v357 no6357 p1266 S 22 2017

Todman, Daniel
BOMBED INTO DEMOCRACY T. Downing *History Today* v67 no8 p104 Ag 2017

Todor, Andrei
mTOR regulates metabolic adaptation of APCs in the lung and controls the outcome of allergic inflammation graph *Science* v357 no6355 p1014 S 8 2017

Todorov, Alexander
About face J. Antonakis color *Science* v357 no6348 p259 Jl 21 2017
FACE VALUE: THE IRRESISTIBLE INFLUENCE OF FIRST IMPRESSION C. Smallwood *Harper's Magazine* v334 no2004 p80 My 2017

Tod's SpA
Save $500 on a Single Outfit D. Michel bw color *Men's Health* v31 no10 p74 D 2016

Toe abnormalities
See also
Bunion
For Feet's sake [Cover story] A. Weil color *Prevention* v69 no7 p22 Jl 2017

Toegel, Ginka
3 Situations Where Cross-Cultural Communication Breaks Down *Harvard Business Review Digital Articles* p2 Je 8 2016

TOENSING, AMY
CITY OF HOPE color *Yankee* p118 Mr 2017

Toer, Pramoedya Ananta, 1925-2006
A Flawed Portrait M. C. Ricklefs, *History Today* v67 no7 p6 Jl 2017
PORTRAIT OF THE AUTHOR AS A HISTORIAN NO. 11: PRAMOEDYA ANANTA TOER A. Lee *History Today* v67 no5 p86 My 2017

Toes
Horses traded toes for speed, strength E. UNDERWOOD color *Science News* v192 no5 p12 S 30 2017
How horses evolved just one toe color *Science* v357 no6353 p737 Ag 25 2017

TOFFEL, MICHAEL W.
MANAGING CLIMATE CHANGE: LESSONS FROM THE U.S. NAVY color il img *Harvard Business Review* v95 no4 p102 Jl/Ag 2017
Starbucks' "Race Together" Campaign and the Upside of CEO Activism *Harvard Business Review Digital Articles* p2 Mr 24 2015

Tofino (B.C.)
Sarah McLachlan V. Hrvatin cartoon *Canadian Geographic* v137

no1 p82 F 2017

Tofu

Conic Boom J. SPALDING *Indianapolis Monthly* p45 N 2017

WHAT'S IN THEIR FRIDGE? [Cover story] C. schedler color *Chicago* v66 no7 p72 Jl 2017

Together at Last (Music)

Three Alt-Country Stars Align With New Albums M. Ayers color *Time* v189 no24 p51 Je 26 2017

Togetherness (TV program)

What's Love Got To Do With It? E. GOULD color *New Republic* v247 no11 p50 N 2016

TOHT, DAVE

Restoring the Beauty in the Beast *Treasures* v6 no5 p22 Ap/My 2017

Toia, Sam

THE NEW SODA TAX H. CONICK color *Chicago* v66 no7 p18 Jl 2017

Tóibín, Colm

The Class Renegade color *New York Review of Books* v64 no12 p21 Jl 13 2017

Shadows & Ghosts bw color *New York Review of Books* v64 no8 p37 My 11 2017

The Year in Reading [Cover story] *New York Times Book Review* p8 D 25 2016

Toilet design & construction

Powder Rooms & Half Baths B. D. Coleman color diag *Old House Journal* v45 no6 p64 S 2017

Toilet paper

Bottom Story of the Day color *Weekly Standard* v22 no45 p2 Ag 7 2017

Popular money-saving strategies prove elusive for low-income households S. Carter *Monthly Labor Review* p1 S 2016

Toilet paper—Evaluation

Toilet Paper *Good Housekeeping* v265 no2 p89 Ag 2017

Toilet preparations

See also

Hair care products

Perfumes

Skin care products

DOUBLE HEADER M. Goldberg color *O, The Oprah Magazine* p92 N 2017

HOW TO AVOID A Travel Hangover J. DeMelo color *O, The Oprah Magazine* p97 N 2017

Toilet preparations industry

See also

Cosmetics industry

We Need to Talk About Your Eye Bags G. MUNCE color *GQ: Gentlemen's Quarterly* v97 no5 p48 My 2017

Toilet preparations—Evaluation

These Fall Perfumes Gave Us All the Feels A. Rambharose bw color *Glamour* v115 no10 p98 O 2017

Travel at a moment's notice color *Good Housekeeping* v264 no3 p20 Mr 2017

Toilet training

Comic Relief for Tired Potty Trainers color *Parents* v92 no11 p20 N 2017

Toilets

Is It Germier To...? K. KLOSS *Reader's Digest* v188 no1124 p48 O 2016

Toilets—Maintenance & repair

A Second Biffy color *Cabin Living* p69 Ja/F 2017

Tok, Jeffery B.-H.

Highly stretchable polymer semiconductor films through the nanoconfinement effect bibl graph *Science* v355 no6320 p1 Ja 6 2017

Tokamaks

Necessary and sufficient conditions for practical fusion power R. L. Hirsch *Physics Today* v70 no10 p11 O 2017

Tokens

CHUCK'S NEW CHEDDAR M. Pilon color *Bloomberg Businessweek* no4494 p74 O 10 2016

TOKUMITSU, MIYA

The United States of Work color *New Republic* v248 no5 p52 My 2017

Tokyo (Japan)—Description & travel

STARCATION: TOKYO O. J. WILLIAMS and S. E. JAMISON

color *Ebony* v72/73 no12/1 p68 O/N 2017

Toledo (Ohio)

Restorative Healing at Youth Visions Relection Park S. Bartram *Parks & Recreation* v51 no10 p58 O 2016

TOLEDO, DAVID

Incorporating Sociocultural Phenomena into Ecosystem-Service Valuation: The Importance of Critical Pluralism *BioScience* v67 no3 p233 Mr 2017

Toledo, M.

Persistent effects of pre-Columbian plant domestication on Amazonian forest composition bibl chart graph map *Science* v355 no6328 p925 Mr 3 2017

Tolentino, Jia

AFTERMATH bw cartoon *New Yorker* v92 no38 p48 N 21 2016

A WOMAN'S WORK bw cartoon *New Yorker* v93 no30 p38 O 2 2017

Toler, Pamela D.

ARTISTS: THREADS OF HISTORY color *MHQ: Quarterly Journal of Military History* v30 no1 p84 Aut 2017

DEMING'S LAST STAND *MHQ: Quarterly Journal of Military History* v29 no2 p87 Wint 2017

EYEWITNESS TO HORROR color *MHQ: Quarterly Journal of Military History* v29 no4 p86 Summ 2017

HELL ON THE RIVER KWAI *MHQ: Quarterly Journal of Military History* v29 no3 p89 Spr 2017

Toleration

The Barça Foundation J. C. CASAUS *UN Chronicle* v53 no2 p44 2016

A Big Wet Kiss to Bigots D. Wycliff *Commonweal* v114 no14 p6 S 8 2017

Hello, Cruel World M. TRUONG bw color *O, The Oprah Magazine* p146 My 2017

Malign Marcuse D. FRENCH il *National Review* v69 no7 p32 Ap 17 2017

Safe Spaces and the Spiritual Exercises *America* v216 no7 p8 Ap 3 2017

Too Much Tolerance *Governing* v30 no6 p12 Mr 2017

Toleration—Social aspects

The Soft Bigotry of Political Correctness: President Trump has never bowed to the culture of victimization. His lack of deference could be liberating S. Steele *Hoover Digest: Research & Opinion on Public Policy* no2 p54 Spr 2017

Tolinski, Brad

Electrifying Saga B. Milkowski color *Downbeat* v83 no12 p93 D 2016

Tolkien, J. R. R. (John Ronald Reuel), 1892-1973

Points of Interest: Even the most obscure topic can be fascinating, and fascination can be found in the most unlikely places E. Parker *History Today* v67 no9 p106 S 2017

The Secret Jews of The Hobbit M. SOLOVEICHIK *Commentary* v142 no2 p62 S 2016

Tolley, Stewart

THE WORST PRISON IN THE COUNTRY: An informative and stimulating biography of a prison which became a microcosm of society *History Today* v67 no6 p98 Je 2016

Tolman, Allison, 1981-

Allison Tolman C. Mari color *Current Biography* v78 no3 p82 Mr 2017

Downward Dog I. Ratledge *TV Guide* v65 no21 p35 My 15 2017

Tolmé, Paul

Going... Going...? color *National Wildlife (World Edition)* v55 no2 p22 F/Mr 2017

Malheur Refuge on the Rebound color *National Wildlife (World Edition)* v55 no1 p14 D/Ja 2016

Scorched Earth color *National Wildlife (World Edition)* v55 no4 p38 Je/Jl 2017

tolnai, dave

missed connections color *Bike Magazine* v24 no7 p40 S 2017

Tolnick, Matt

A Kickstarter Business Takes Off K. KRISTOF color *Kiplinger's Personal Finance* v71 no1 p72 Ja 2017

TOLOKONNIKOVA, NADYA

PUTIN TRUMP *Foreign Policy* no223 p72 Mr/Ap 2017

Tolonen, Tuutikki

Monster Nanny *Publishers Weekly* v264 no39 p105 S 25 2017

Tolson, Ben

Snow BOUND color *Cabin Living* p41 D 2016

Tolstoy, Leo, graf, 1828-1910

1880: St. Petersburg L. Tolstoy *Lapham's Quarterly* v10 no1 p76 Wint 2017

Tolstoy, Maya

Seismic constraints on caldera dynamics from the 2015 Axial Seamount eruption bibl color graph *Science* v354 no6318 p1395 D 16 2016

Tolstoy, Victoria

VIKTORIA TOLSTOY J. Ephland color *Downbeat* v84 no3 p25 Mr 2017

Tolstukhin, I.

Observation of coherent elastic neutrino-nucleus scattering diag *Science* v357 no6356 p1123 S 15 2017

Tolzmann, Don Heinrich

VIEW FROM THE BRIDGE J. STOWELL *Cincinnati Magazine* v50 no2 p70 N 2016

Tom, Kip—Interviews

Q&A L. BEDORD *Successful Farming* v114 no12 p56 Mid-N 2016

Tom, Steve

Brickbats C. Oliver cartoon *Reason* v48 no7 p9 D 2016

Tom Ford International LLC

SUNNY SIDE UP color *O, The Oprah Magazine* p55 Jl 2017

this Way In: HIT THE LINKS FLASH SOME GREEN N. Sullivan color *Esquire* p27 S 2017

Tom Gun Live: A Maverick's Homage (Theatrical production)

Step Into Tom's Shoes M. WAKIM *Los Angeles Magazine* p54 My 2017

Tom Osborne: A Legacy Beyond the Game (TV program)

Documentary reveals Osborne in his own words A. J. BARTELS bw color *Nebraska Life* v21 no4 p14 Jl/Ag 2017

TOMA, GLENDA

Asia's Rising Stars color *Forbes* v199 no5 p20 My 16 2017

TOMAINE, GINA

FUNDIES GALORE! color *Rodale's Organic Life* v3 no1 p16 Ja 2017

The GREENEST HOLIDAY color *Rodale's Organic Life* v2 no7 p52 D 2016/Ja 2017

TOMAN, NICHOLAS

THE NEW SALES IMPERATIVE color diag il img *Harvard Business Review* v95 no2 p118 Mr/Ap 2017

Tománek, David

Mildred S. Dresselhaus *Physics Today* v70 no6 p73 Je 2017

Tomankova, L.

Observation of a large-scale anisotropy in the arrival directions of cosmic rays above 8 × 1018 eV *Science* v357 no6357 p1266 S 22 2017

Tomás Colette, Marisol

Show Up. Be You color *Glamour* v115 no5 p18 My 2017

Tomasek, Kathrin

Biased partitioning of the multidrug efflux pump AcrAB-TolC underlies long-lived phenotypic heterogeneity diag *Science* v356 no6335 p311 Ap 21 2017

Tomasello, Michael

Great apes anticipate that other individuals will act according to false beliefs bibl chart diag graph *Science* v354 no6308 p110 O 7 2016

LANGUAGE IN A NEW KEY cartoon *Scientific American* v315 no5 p70 N 2016

Tomasetti, Cristian

Genes, environment, and "bad luck" M. A. Nowak and B. Waclaw bibl color *Science* v355 no6331 p1266 Mr 24 2017

Stem cell divisions, somatic mutations, cancer etiology, and cancer prevention bibl chart diag graph *Science* v355 no6331 p1330 Mr 24 2017

Tomasi, T. J.

SIGHT CLUB color *Golf Magazine* v59 no5 p62 My 2017

SUB HERO color *Golf Magazine* v59 no4 p68 Ap 2017

Tomasic, Stephanie

Fabrication of fillable microparticles and other complex 3D microstructures color diag *Science* v357 no6356 p1138 S 15 2017

Tomasky, Michael

A Consequential Presidency D. Greenberg color *Washington Monthly* v49 no3-5 p58 Mr-My 2017

The Great Democratic Divide il *New Republic* v248 no6 p14 Je

2017

The Republican Anti-Trump? color *New York Review of Books* v64 no14 p34 S 28 2017

The Resistance So Far bw color *New York Review of Books* v64 no17 p42 N 9 2017

Susan Rice: Talking Trump and tennis with the former national-security adviser *New York* v50 no13 p16 Je 26 2017

That Other Clinton J. KELLY *New York Times Book Review* p7 Ja 22 2017

Trump: The Gang cartoon color *New York Review of Books* v64 no1 p4 Ja 19 2017

Trump: The Scramble color *New York Review of Books* v64 no6 p12 Ap 6 2017

Tomato diseases & pests

THE GRUMPY GARDENER S. Bender color *Southern Living* v52 no7 p31 Jl 2017

Tomato farming

Companion Planting E. Millard color *Log Home Living* v34 no1 p24 F 2017

PEAK FRUIT C. SCHEDLER color *Chicago* v66 no9 p61 S 2017

The Tomato Man J. Borden color *Southern Living* v52 no7 p24 Jl 2017

Tomato sauces

WE SAY TOMATOES B. P. KATZ color *Martha Stewart Living* p102 Jl/Ag 2017

Tomato varieties

TOO MANY TO EAT! L. HECK color *Missouri Life* v44 no5 p68 Ag 2017

Tomatoes

THE 5-INGREDIENT Farmers' Market Cookbook L. Cericola, K. Hammonds et al color *Southern Living* v52 no7 p61 Jl 2017

Good Enough to Eat E. Millard color *Log Home Living* v34 no4 p36 My 2017

Go SPLAT! On the Tee Box E. A. Tischler and D. DeNunzio color *Golf Magazine* v58 no12 p82 D 2016

Got Extra Tomatoes? B. Lipton color *Health* v31 no7 p141 S 2017

MARINARA S. PUCKETT *Atlanta* v56 no10 p60 F 2017

PURE AND SIMPLE A. RAPOPORT color *Bon Appetit* no8 p12 Ag 2017

SL COOKING SCHOOL color *Southern Living* v52 no6 p140 Je 2017

TERRIFIC TOMATOES for Spectacular Sauces and Creative Canning C. LeHoullier *Mother Earth News* no280 p20 F/Mr 2017

Trudie Styler's Tuscany color *AARP: The Magazine* v60 no3A p68 Ap/My 2017

Weird but true! J. SWAIN and A. E. HURT color map *National Geographic Kids* no470 p4 My 2017

You Say Tomato... *Martha Stewart Living* no267 p15 S 2016

Tomatoes—Flavor & odor

Tastier tomatoes through chemistry S. MILIUS color *Science News* v191 no3 p12 F 18 2017

Tomatoes—Genetics

A chemical genetic roadmap to improved tomato flavor D. Tieman, M. F. R. Resende Jr. et al bibl graph *Science* v355 no6323 p391 Ja 27 2017

Tomatoes—Research

Tastier tomatoes through chemistry S. MILIUS color *Science News* v191 no3 p12 F 18 2017

Tomb Raider (Film)

TOMB RAIDER J. McGovern color *Entertainment Weekly* no1474/1475 p45 Jl 21-28 2017

Tombs

See also

Mounds (Archaeology)

Delhi, the Forever City N. Gupta *UN Chronicle* v53 no3 p3 2016

TOMB COUTURE D. WEISS color *Archaeology* v70 no4 p16 Je-Ag 2017

Tombs—Mexico

Predicting where victims of Mexico's violence are buried L. Wade color map *Science* v356 no6345 p1317 Je 30 2017

Tombstone (Ariz.)

EXPLORERS, GUNFIGHTERS & SMUGGLERS [Cover story] J. KOPYCINSKI color *Dirt Sports + Off-Road* v51 no10 p30 O 2017

Tomé, Antonio

Global atmospheric particle formation from CERN CLOUD measurements bibl graph map *Science* v354 no6316 p1119 D 2 2016

Tome, B.

Observation of a large-scale anisotropy in the arrival directions of cosmic rays above 8 × 1018 eV *Science* v357 no6357 p1266 S 22 2017

Tomei, Joe

A meal for many color *U.S. Catholic* v82 no6 p5 Je 2017

Tomesco, Frederic

Bombardier's Painful Double Whammy *Bloomberg Businessweek* no4540 p23 O 2 2017

The Habs, Poutine, Jobs: Welcome to Quebec graph *Bloomberg Businessweek* no4508 p16 Ja 23 2017

Tometi, Opal

4 Steps for the Next President color *Time* v188 no16/17 p63 O 24 2016

Now What? color *Time* v188 no21 p42 N 21 2016

Tomic, Milena

FRANZ ERHARD WALTHER color *Art in America* v104 no10 p159 N 2016

SHARON HAYES *Art in America* v104 no9 p162 O 2016

YDESSA HENDELES color *Art in America* v105 no8 p128 S 2017

Tomii, Reiko

Multiple Originals E. Heartney cartoon color *Art in America* v104 no11 p63 D 2016

Tominaga, Masako

Masako Tominaga P. HESS cartoon *Popular Science* p52 Ja/F 2017

TOMINE, ADRIAN

Bad Boys: Akhil Sharma's story collection is a cultural exposé and a lacerating critique of a certain type of male ego *New York Times Book Review* p15 Ag 20 2017

TOMKINS, CALVIN

ART WITHOUT WALLS cartoon *New Yorker* v92 no40 p34 D 5 2016

TROUBLING PICTURES cartoon color *New Yorker* v93 no8 p30 Ap 10 2017

Tomlin, Annie

FOR OUR GENERATION color *Women's Health* v14 no5 p134 Je 2017

TOMLIN, C. M.

COOL inventions cartoon color *National Geographic Kids* no470 p11 My 2017

COOL inventions *National Geographic Kids* no466 p5 D 2016/ Ja 2017

Dare To Explore color *National Geographic Kids* no473 p28 S 2017

DARE to EXPLORE *National Geographic Kids* no468 p6 Mr 2017

TOMLIN, CAROLYN

FAR FROM THE MADDING CROWD cartoon color *Missouri Life* v44 no4 p30 Je 2017

Tomlin, Lily, 1939——Interviews

Lily at Large H. HALTERMAN *TV Guide* v65 no4 p6 Ja 16 2017

Tomlinson, Jean

At Peace in the Sun color *Money* v45 no11 p92 D 2016

Tomlinson, Rick

Rick Tomlinson A. Schell color *Sail* v48 no7 p12 Jl 2017

Tommy Hilfiger Corp.

STYLE AHOY! color *Seventeen* v75 no11 p27 N 2016

Tommy's Honour (Film)

Jason Connery J. Marksbury and C. Barrett color *Golf Magazine* v59 no4 p44 Ap 2017

Pairs for The Course T. Keith chart color *Sports Illustrated* v126 no11 p21 Ap 17-24 2017

THE TEES THAT BIND S. Gutierrez *British Heritage Travel* v38 no2 p34 Mr/Ap 2017

Tomohiro Nishizawa

A three-dimensional movie of structural changes in bacteriorhodopsin bibl diag graph *Science* v354 no6319 p1552 D 23 2016

Tomohiro Sonobe

A coherent Ising machine for 2000-node optimization problems bibl diag graph *Science* v354 no6312 p603 N 4 2016

TOMORROW, TOM

THE MODERN WORLD *Nation* v304 no11 p8 Ap 3 2017

THIS MODERN WORLD il *Nation* v305 no8 p8 O 9 2017

THIS MODERN WORLD *In These Times* v41 no1 p6 Ja 2017

THIS MODERN WORLD *In These Times* v41 no2 p6 F 2017

Tomosynthesis

This Is Not Your Mother's Mammogram. It's a... 3-D Medical Breakthrough S. KLEIN bw *Prevention* v69 no2 p32 F 2017

Tomoyuki Tanaka

A three-dimensional movie of structural changes in bacteriorhodopsin bibl diag graph *Science* v354 no6319 p1552 D 23 2016

Tompkins, Caroline

KICK IT WITH YOUR COLLEAGUES color *Bloomberg Businessweek* no4525 p55 Je 5 2017

Pimp My Office Plant color *Bloomberg Businessweek* no4525 p60 Je 5 2017

Tompkins, Paul

Panama's impotent mangrove laws bibl *Science* v355 no6328 p918 Mr 3 2017

Tompot, Cara

Challenging the Status Quo with Stem Cells bw color *National Review* v68 no20 p9 N 7 2016

CHALLENGING THE STATUS QUO WITH STEM CELLS *Saturday Evening Post* v289 no1 p70 Ja/F 2017

Tomuschat, Christian

Protection of Human Rights under Universal International Law *UN Chronicle* v53 no4 p1 2016

Protection of Human Rights under Universal International Law *UN Chronicle* v54 no4 p23 2017

Ton, Zeynep

4 Reasons Retail Jobs Are About to Get Better *Harvard Business Review Digital Articles* p2 S 4 2015

How 4 Retailers Became "Best Places to Work" color *Harvard Business Review Digital Articles* p2 Ja 2 2017

How Low-Paying Retailers Can Adapt to Higher Minimum Wages *Harvard Business Review Digital Articles* p2 Ag 23 2016

A New Way to Rate Retailers on Providing Good Jobs *Harvard Business Review Digital Articles* p2 S 3 2015

Transforming Today's Bad Jobs into Tomorrow's Good Jobs *Harvard Business Review Digital Articles* p2 Je 12 2017

Tone, Joe

Blood Brothers: Two siblings—a bricklayer in Texas and a drug cartel boss in Mexico—get involved in money laundering at the racetrack I. GRILLO *New York Times Book Review* p23 S 24 2017

Tonegawa, Susumu

Engrams and circuits crucial for systems consolidation of a memory diag *Science* v356 no6333 p73 Ap 7 2017

Tong, Kevin

CROSSING THE CHASM cartoon *Wired* v25 no1 p92 Ja 2017

Tong, Kwing

Highly efficient electrocaloric cooling with electrostatic actuation bw diag *Science* v357 no6356 p1130 S 15 2017

Tongue

One Fine Piece of Meat: Braised tongue with sauce gribiche can make you appreciate a cut you might otherwise avoid G. Hamilton *New York Times Magazine* p20 Jl 16 2017

Tongue diseases

THE ORAL REPORT N. BARR color *Martha Stewart Living* p42 My 2017

Tongue twisters

Just Joking *National Geographic Kids* no469 p32 Ap 2017

TONGUETTE, PETER

Classics of Conspiracy color *National Review* v69 no19 p56 O 16 2017

A Man for All Seasons At 50 bw *National Review* v68 no21 p45 N 21 2016

Toni Erdmann (Film)

Candid CAMERA color *Vogue* v206 no12 p210 D 2016

Don't Let Your Babies Grow Up to Be Consultants M. ATKINSON *In These Times* v40 no12 p38 D 2016

The End color *Film Comment* v53 no1 p44 Ja/F 2017

SPOTTING BIGFOOT AT LINCOLN CENTER S. KLAWANS color *Nation* v303 no22 p35 N 28 2016

TONI ERDMANN, FAUX PA: INTERVIEW WITH MAREN ADE M. Ratner *Film Quarterly* v70 no3 p43 Spr 2017

TONI ERDMANN R. R. Cooper color *Commonweal* v144 no5 p26 Mr 10 2017

Tonight Show, The (TV program)
That's Not Funny *Weekly Standard* v22 no4 p2 O 3 2016
THE TONIGHT SHOW STARRING JIMMY FALLON J. Halterman *TV Guide* v65 no11 p47 Mr 6 2017
When Harry Met Late Night J. WALSH bw color *Nation* v304 no7 p20 Mr 6 2017

Toninato, Alisa
American Skillet Co D. DANIEL color map *American Craft* v77 no3 p14 Je/Jl 2017

Tonino, Leath
7 BEARDS FROM THE CONSERVATION HALL OF FAME *Orion Magazine* v35 no4/5 p6 Jl-O 2016
The Ancient Art of Imbibing color *Tricycle: The Buddhist Review* v27 no1 p30 Fall 2017
Being a Bird *Orion Magazine* v36 no2 p7 Mr/Ap 2017
Bonfire Buddha cartoon color *Tricycle: The Buddhist Review* v26 no3 p24 Spr 2017
The Doe's Song color *Orion Magazine* v36 no1 p14 Ja/F 2017
WHERE NATURE & MIND MEET color *Tricycle: The Buddhist Review* v26 no4 p76 Summ 2017

Tonko, Paul D.
Time to codify scientific integrity *Science* v356 no6344 p1241 Je 23 2017

Tonnerre, Pierre
The epigenetic landscape of T cell exhaustion bibl graph *Science* v354 no6316 p1165 D 2 2016

TONNIGES, KYLE
Ink Stains bw *Publishers Weekly* v264 no5 p171 Ja 30 2017

Tononi, Giulio
Ultrastructural evidence for synaptic scaling across the wake/sleep cycle bibl diag graph *Science* v355 no6324 p507 F 3 2017

Tony Awards
Dawn Chiang Named to Tony Nominating Committee *Stage Directions* v30 no10 p4 O 2017
Hot Takes and Cold Shoulders M. Snetiker color *Entertainment Weekly* no1465 p10 My 12 2017
Our Ridiculously Early Tony Preview M. Snetiker color *Entertainment Weekly* no1462 p14 Ap 21 2017
The Regional Theatre Tony Award Goes To ... *Stage Directions* v30 no6 p4 Je 2017
The Tonys You Didn't See J. Derschowitz color *Entertainment Weekly* no1471 p16 Je 23 2017

Tony Bennett Celebrates 90: The Best Is Yet to Come (TV program)
Tony Turns 90 D. Ross color *Entertainment Weekly* no1443 p21 D 9 2016

Too Far North (Poem)
Too Far North T. Hayes *New York Times Magazine* p17 Jl 9 2017

Too Good At Goodbyes (Music)
The Playlist color *Rolling Stone* no1297 p8 O 5 2017

Toobin, Jeffrey
AFTERMATH bw cartoon *New Yorker* v92 no38 p48 N 21 2016
ANOTHER ROUND cartoon *New Yorker* v92 no37 p31 N 14 2016
CASE STUDIES cartoon *New Yorker* v93 no7 p33 Ap 3 2017
FEEDING THE BEAST bw cartoon *New Yorker* v93 no19 p38 Jl 3 2017
THE FIGHT TO VOTE cartoon *New Yorker* v92 no41 p23 D 12 2016
FULL-COURT PRESS cartoon color *New Yorker* v93 no9 p24 Ap 17 2017
LATE BLOOMER cartoon *New Yorker* v93 no32 p23 O 16 2017
THE SILENT MAJORITY cartoon *New Yorker* v93 no14 p27 My 22 2017
THIS TIME, IT'S PERSONAL cartoon *New Yorker* v93 no23 p19 Ag 7 2017
TIPPED SCALES cartoon *New Yorker* v93 no2 p22 F 27 2017
WHEN TRUTH IS NOT ENOUGH cartoon *New Yorker* v92 no42 p96 D 19 2016

Toogood, Faye
In Her Element H. MARTIN bw color *Architectural Digest* v74 no3 p46 Mr 2017

Tooker, John
Taking Nebraska Life Doorstep to Doorstep C. Amundson *Nebraska Life* v20 no6 p9 N/D 2016

Tookes, Jasmine
So What Do You Do, JASMINE TOOKES? color *InStyle* v24 no4 p158 Ap 2017

TOOKEY, JESSICA
ART IS LIFE: AND LACK OF IT ALMOST KILLED ME *Idaho Magazine* v16 no9 p12 Je 2017

Tool design & construction
See also
Woodworking tools—Design & construction
Introducing the New Park Champion Toolkit! J. Rasmusse *Parks & Recreation* v52 no5 p26 My 2017

Tool use in animals
ANIMAL HACKS R. H. Shea color *National Geographic* v231 no3 p18 Mr 2017

Toolboxes
Outfitting a Custom Toolkit J. SCIACCA color *Sound & Vision* v82 no8 p28 O 2017

TOOLE, MICHAEL J.
Polio's Last Stand? color *Natural History* v125 no9 p32 S 2017

Tools
See also
Carpentry tools
Cutlery
Handles
Against the Grain color *AARP: The Magazine* v59 no2A p73 F/Mr 2016
ANIMAL HACKS R. H. Shea color *National Geographic* v231 no3 p18 Mr 2017
CLEVER STORAGE J. KOPYCINSKI color *Dirt Sports + Off-Road* v51 no7 p64 Jl 2017
CREATE A WORKSHOP ON WHEELS R. BERENDSOHN color *Popular Mechanics* p16 Je 2017
How to Skin a Cat R. D'AGOSTINO *Popular Mechanics* p8 N 2017
MOVING DIRT & GRAVEL M. Boncher color *Cabin Living* p68 S 2017
RATCHETING SCREWDRIVERS color *Popular Mechanics* p26 Jl 2017
THE Right TOOL R. BERENDSOHN and R. ROMANSKI color *Popular Mechanics* p80 N 2017
TOOLS THEY USE color *Popular Mechanics* p108 Mr 2017

Tools—Equipment & supplies
Wire Strippers color *Popular Mechanics* p36 Mr 2017

Tools—Evaluation
CORDLESS ELECTRIC CHAINSAWS R. ROMANSKI color *Popular Mechanics* p94 N 2017
full service r. cleek color *Bike Magazine* v24 no6 p126 Ag 2017
PRACTICAL PRODUCTS L. Back color *Trail Rider* v29 no2 p57 Mr 2017
WELDING INNOVATIONS D. Mowitz *Successful Farming* v115 no9 p36 Ag 2017

Tools—Management
One Tool Box Is Never Enough B. Pike color *Power & Motoryacht* v34 no11 p152 N 2017

Tools—Storage
A FARM SHOP ON-THE-GO A. McConnell *Successful Farming* v115 no3 p49 Mid-F 2017

Toomey, Pat, 1961-
The View From Pennsylvania J. LERNER color *National Review* v68 no22 p27 D 5 2016

Toomey, Taryn
GETTING IT OUT S. Marikar cartoon *New Yorker* v93 no2 p24 F 27 2017

Toon, Ann
at the SHARP END color diag *Earth Island Journal* v32 no4 p30 Wint 2017

TOON, GREG
On the SPLIT LEVEL color *House Beautiful* p137 Ag 2017

Toon, Steve
at the SHARP END color diag *Earth Island Journal* v32 no4 p30 Wint 2017

Tooth care & hygiene
See also
Dental floss
cheat sheet: Backcountry Hygiene C. BUHAY *Backpacker* p30 S 2017
Teeth: an owner's manual J. CHEN color *Redbook* p77 Jl/Ag 2017

Toothache

A Bad Bite Concerns More than Your Grin *USA Today Magazine* v146 no2869 p8 O 2017

Toothbrushes

JOKES *Saturday Evening Post* v288 no6 p34 N/D 2016

Toothbrushes—Evaluation

GOOD-FOR-YOU GIFT GUIDE color *Prevention* v68 no12 p68 D 2016

GOOD MORNING, NEAL! N. POLLACK color *Popular Mechanics* p72 My 2017

Toothpaste

Does It Really Work? color *InStyle* v24 no3 p281 Mr 2017

Toothpaste—Evaluation

SHAKE UP YOUR MORNING ROUTINE color *Prevention* v69 no4 p11 Ap 2017

Toothpicks

A Toothpick When You're Hungry D. Lowry color *Black Belt* v55 no6 p26 O/N 2017

Tooze, Sharon A.

A switch from canonical to noncanonical autophagy shapes B cell responses bibl graph *Science* v355 no6325 p641 F 10 2017

Top Chef (TV program)

Offal Behavior color *Weekly Standard* v22 no47 p3 Ag 21 2017

Top Chef I. Ratledge *TV Guide* v64 no48 p41 N 21 2016

Top Gear (TV program)

How to Make a Great TV Show About Cars E. DYER color *Popular Mechanics* p24 N 2017

Top of the Lake (TV program)

Diving into the Wreck N. Davis color *Film Comment* v53 no5 p10 S/O 2017

Returning TV That Deserves a Second Chance E. Dockterman color *Time* v190 no14 p49 O 9 2017

Topgolf Entertainment Group (Company)

GET IN THE HOLE! I. Boudway cartoon color *Bloomberg Businessweek* no4497 p63 O 31 2016

Topiary work

THE BRITISH HERITAGE TRAVEL PUZZLER *British Heritage Travel* v38 no4 p78 Jl/Ag 2017

THE BRITISH HERITAGE TRAVEL PUZZLER T. Allen, M. Trinder et al color *British Heritage Travel* v38 no5 p78 S/O 2017

Garden States color *House Beautiful* v159 no2 p32 Mr 2017

Have a Ball color *House Beautiful* v159 no2 p34 Mr 2017

THE SHAPE OF THINGS T. MARTIN bw color *Better Homes & Gardens* v95 no11 p118 N 2017

Shaping Up: Add interest, whimsy and elegance to the garden with topiary P. Marquis *New Orleans Homes & Lifestyles* v20 no4 p26 Aut 2017

SHEAR GENIUS M. OWENS color *Architectural Digest* no11 p146 N 1 2017

STRANGE & WONDERFUL TOPIARY GARDENS V. Johnson color *Old House Journal* v45 no4 p20 Je 2017

Topical rubs

Sunless tanner could protect skin A. CUNNINGHAM color *Science News* v191 no13 p11 Jl 8 2017

Topilko, Piotr

Multipotent peripheral glial cells generate neuroendocrine cells of the adrenal medulla color *Science* v357 no6346 p46 Jl 7 2017

Toplis, M. J.

Extensive water ice within Ceres' aqueously altered regolith: Evidence from nuclear spectroscopy bibl graph *Science* v355 no6320 p1 Ja 6 2017

Topo Athletic (Company)

SOLID FOOTING J. DENGATE and M. SHORTEN cartoon color graph *Runner's World* v52 no3 p83 Ap 2017

Topography

See also

Earth topography

Ocean surface topography

Submarine topography

Defining the topography of a planetary body D. Burr map *Science* v356 no6339 p708 My 19 2017

How glaciers shaped the sea floor color *Science* v356 no6336 p354 Ap 28 2017

NASA armada targets thaw in Arctic soil P. Voosen color map *Science* v357 no6346 p12 Jl 7 2017

The topography R. STIEVE *Arizona Highways* v93 no5 p2 My 2017

Topol, Sarah A.

THE BOYS FROM BAGA: THE FOUR OF THEM, CHILDREN FROM A FISHING VILLAGE IN NORTHEASTERN NIGERIA, WERE AMONG THOUSANDS ABDUCTED BY BOKO HARAM AND TRAINED AS CHILD SOLDIERS. THEY LEARNED TO SURVIVE, BUT ONLY BY FORGETTING WHO THEY WERE *New York Times Magazine* p42 Je 25 2017

SONS AND DAUGHTERS *Harper's Magazine* no2007 p25 Ag 2017

The Thread *New York Times Magazine* p9 Jl 9 2017

Topology

See also

Surfaces (Geometry)

Quantized electric multipole insulators W. A. Benalcazar, B. Andrei Bernevig et al bw color graph *Science* v357 no6346 p61 Jl 7 2017

Topor, Roland

GRAPHIC DETAIL A. Curry color *Film Comment* v53 no3 p80 My/Je 2017

TOPRAN, MARTA

JUST camila color *Seventeen* v76 no2 p102 Mr 2017

Topsy (Company)

What the Death of Topsy Tells Us About Today's Social Web A. Samuel *Harvard Business Review Digital Articles* p2 D 23 2015

Topychkanov, Petr

Nuclear disarmament summits: A proposal to break the international impasse bibl *Bulletin of the Atomic Scientists* v73 no4 p264 Jl 2017

Tor Books (Company)

Deals R. DEAHL color *Publishers Weekly* v264 no15 p14 Ap 10 2017

Tor Project Inc.

Anonymous browsing with Tor reduces exposure but still has risks G. FLEISHMAN cartoon color *Macworld - Digital Edition* p99 Mr 2017

Torabi, Farnoosh

advice every new mom needs [Cover story] color *Parents* v92 no7 p32 Jl 2017

FINDING THAT Special Someone color *O, The Oprah Magazine* p41 Je 2017

Give Well, Give Wisely cartoon color graph *O, The Oprah Magazine* p56 D 2017

Let's Get Digital color *O, The Oprah Magazine* p33 Ja 2017

The Pause THAT REFRESHES cartoon *O, The Oprah Magazine* p40 Ap 2017

Spending to Save cartoon *O, The Oprah Magazine* p48 My 2017

Stage APPROPRIATE color *O, The Oprah Magazine* p46 F 2017

When Less Is More Money cartoon *O, The Oprah Magazine* p40 Mr 2017

Torbert, R. B.

Structure, force balance, and topology of Earth's magnetopause diag graph *Science* v356 no6341 p960 Je 1 2017

Torch Song (Theatrical production)

GOINGS ON ABOUT TOWN bw *New Yorker* v93 no31 p4 O 9 2017

Torchetti, Mia Kim

Role for migratory wild birds in the global spread of avian influenza H5N8 bibl graph map *Science* v354 no6309 p213 O 14 2016

Tordrillo Mountains (Alaska)

SHOOTING GALLERY bw color *Powder* v45 no6 p20 F 2017

TORGERSEN, CHRISTIAN E.

Envisioning, Quantifying, and Managing Thermal Regimes on River Networks *BioScience* v67 no6 p506 Je 2017

Torgoff, Martin

Bohemian Rhapsodies J. Mcdonough color *Downbeat* v84 no4 p67 Ap 2017

TORJUSSEN, MARY

Truth and Memory color *Publishers Weekly* v264 no7 p50 F 13 2017

Torn, M. S.

The whole-soil carbon flux in response to warming [Cover story] chart graph *Science* v355 no6332 p1420 Mr 31 2017

Tornado damage

Forecast Center T. Vasquez map *Weatherwise* v70 no4 p54 Jl/Ag

2017

IF CLASSIC BOOKS BECAME CLICKBAIT *Reader's Digest* v190 no1133 p65 S 2017

Tracking a tornado's damage from every angle D. Stone color map *National Geographic* v230 no4 p24 O 2016

Tornadoes

10 FREAKY FORCES OF NATURE D. E. RICHARDS color *National Geographic Kids* no465 p26 N 2016

More tornadoes in the most extreme U.S. tornado outbreaks M. K. Tippett, C. Lepore et al bibl chart graph *Science* v354 no6318 p1419 D 16 2016

not a weather girl R. Feltman cartoon *Popular Science* v289 no4 p81 Jl/Ag 2017

Pillar of fire K. Dickman color *Popular Science* v289 no4 p48 Jl/Ag 2017

supersize supercell supersimulation R. Verger color *Popular Science* v289 no4 p16 Jl/Ag 2017

The Tucson Tornado N. AUSTIN *Arizona Highways* v93 no1 p8 Ja 2017

weather gets weird M. D. Kaufman diag *Popular Science* v289 no4 p10 Jl/Ag 2017

Tornadoes—Colorado

Weatherscapes: Denver, Colorado — The "Mile High City" E. Darack color *Weatherwise* v70 no4 p8 Jl/Ag 2017

Tornadoes—History

Q | A *Cincinnati Magazine* v50 no6 p32 Mr 2017

Tornadoes—Oklahoma

Tracking a tornado's damage from every angle D. Stone color map *National Geographic* v230 no4 p24 O 2016

Tornadoes—Texas

Lightbox color *Time* v189 no20 p14 My 29 2017

Tornatore, Guiseppe

CINEMA PARADISO B. A. DuHamel color *Sound & Vision* v82 no5 p68 Je 2017

Toro, Benicio del, 1967-

Benicio Del Toro C. Ianzito color *AARP: The Magazine* v60 no2A p82 F/Mr 2017

TORO, FRANCISCO

UGANDA'S BAD SEEDS color *Reason* v48 no10 p24 Mr 2017

Toro, Guillermo del, 1964-

The Master of Highbrow Horror T. RAFFERTY cartoon *Atlantic* v318 no4 p48 N 2016

Pacific Rim Uprising A. Breznican color *Entertainment Weekly* no1486 p44 O 13 2017

Toro, Noel

Speak up color *U.S. Catholic* v82 no4 p5 Ap 2017

Toroczkai, Zoltán

Network Science *Physics Today* v70 no4 p55 Ap 2017

Toronado automobile

Thom On Design T. Taylor bw *Hot Rod* v70 no2 p84 F 2017

Toronto (Ont.)—Description & travel

TORONTO ... FOR WASHINGTONIANS J. Clark *Washingtonian Magazine* v52 no2 p241 N 2016

Toronto Blue Jays (Baseball team)

2 BLUEJAYS color *Sports Illustrated* v126 no9 p78 Mr 27 2017

Toronto Maple Leafs (Hockey team)—History

AUSTON'S POWERS A. Prewitt color diag *Sports Illustrated* v127 no11 p38 O 9 2017

Dear Auston ... W. Clark color *Sports Illustrated* v125 no12 p60 O 10 2016

Toronto Raptors (Basketball team)

3 Raptors R. Nadkarni, B. Golliver et al color *Sports Illustrated* v125 no14 p75 O 24-31 2016

4 RAPTORS color *Sports Illustrated* v127 no12 p60 O 16 2017

Toronto Zoo

Photos from the Field *Mother Earth News* no280 p112 F/Mr 2017

Toronto International Film Festival (Toronto, Ont.)

PARTY IN THE USA* (AND CANADA!) H. Goldblatt color *Entertainment Weekly* no1484 p6 S 29 2017

Torotrak PLC

TRANS-PLANT K. C. Colwell diag *Car & Driver* v62 no11 p26 My 2017

Torpedo-boats

LIFE ON A TORPEDO BOAT M. McDowell *MHQ: Quarterly Journal of Military History* v29 no2 p84 Wint 2017

Torpey, Elka

Data on display Women in management *Career Outlook* p1 Mr 2017

Finding hot jobs: Using data to locate career opportunities *Career Outlook* p1 D 2016

Interview with a ... Park interpreter *Career Outlook* p1 Jl 2017

Jobs for people who love being outdoors *Career Outlook* p1 Jl 2017

New year, new career: 5 tips for changing occupations *Career Outlook* p4 F 2017

Part-time jobs that pay more than $20 per hour chart color img *Career Outlook* p1 Je 2017

Water work: Jobs related to water utilities chart color *Career Outlook* p1 Ap 2017

Will I need a license or certification for my job? color graph *Career Outlook* p2 S 2017

You're a what? Social media specialist color *Career Outlook* p1 N 2016

Torqeedo Inc.

Power Trip A. JONES *Boating World* v38 no2 p20 F 2017

Torque

Degrees of Separation E. Perkins chart color graph *Hot Rod* v70 no6 p72 Je 2017

What's the Crossover Point Between a "Torque" Cam Versus One Ground to Maximize Top-End Power? M. Davis color *Hot Rod* v70 no1 p92 Ja 2017

Torque control

Pam Jacoby's 700-R4 Trans Won't Lock Up the Torque Converter. We're Gonna Fix It M. Davis chart color diag *Hot Rod* v70 no11 p110 N 2017

Torralba Elipe, G.

Observation of a large-scale anisotropy in the arrival directions of cosmic rays above 8 × 1018 eV *Science* v357 no6357 p1266 S 22 2017

Torrance, Kelly Jane

Afghanistan and Its Neighbors color *Weekly Standard* v22 no48 p6 S 4 2017

Epic of the Midlands *National Review* v69 no2 p45 F 6 2017

Meanwhile, Up North color *Weekly Standard* v22 no36 p22 My 29 2017

Misreporting Iran color *Weekly Standard* v22 no37 p16 Je 5 2017

Tortured by 'Moderates' color *Weekly Standard* v22 no47 p34 Ag 21 2017

Torrão, João Miguel Varela

ACTIVATE YOUR HORSE'S MOTOR color *Dressage Today* v23 no7 p22 Mr 2017

Torre, E. V.

Persistent effects of pre-Columbian plant domestication on Amazonian forest composition bibl chart graph map *Science* v355 no6328 p925 Mr 3 2017

Torre, Tom

Hire Extra Muscle to Reduce Monthly Bills J. Chatzky cartoon *AARP: The Magazine* v60 no1A p25 D 2016/Ja 2017

Torrella, Sebastián

Forest conservation: Remember Gran Chaco bibl color *Science* v355 no6324 p465 F 3 2017

Torrens, Pip

PREACHER C. Collis color *Entertainment Weekly* no1474/1475 p74 Jl 21-28 2017

Torrente, Mariana P.

Ratchet-like polypeptide translocation mechanism of the AAA+ disaggregase Hsp104 diag *Science* v357 no6348 p273 Jl 21 2017

Torrent-Sucarrat, Miquel

Angular momentum–induced delays in solid-state photoemission enhanced by intra-atomic interactions chart color graph *Science* v357 no6357 p1274 S 22 2017

Torres, Aurora

A looming tragedy of the sand commons color *Science* v357 no6355 p970 S 8 2017

Torres, Craig

Dollar So Ripped, It Might Actually Rip color *Bloomberg Businessweek* no4506 p12 Ja 9 2017

How Rational Are Rational Expectations? *Bloomberg Businessweek* no4501 p13 N 28 2016

Trump And Yellen: Besties? color *Bloomberg Businessweek* no4502 p12 D 5 2016

Torres, Diego
In Colombia, peace dividend for science proves elusive L. Wade color graph *Science* v357 no6355 p958 S 8 2017

Torres, Gina
Suits D. Holbrook *TV Guide* v65 no4 p38 Ja 16 2017

Torres, José M.
Backtalk *Phi Delta Kappan* v98 no7 p80 Ap 2017

Torres, Justin
Hustle and Flow *New York Times Book Review* p10 Mr 19 2017
LEASHED color *New Yorker* v92 no32 p60 O 10 2016

Torres, Marta E.
Release of mineral-bound water prior to subduction tied to shallow seismogenic slip off Sumatra graph *Science* v356 no6340 p841 My 26 2017

Torres, Nicole
The H-1B Visa Debate, Explained *Harvard Business Review Digital Articles* p2 My 4 2017
It's Better to Avoid a Toxic Employee than Hire a Superstar *Harvard Business Review Digital Articles* p2 D 9 2017
Just Hearing Your Phone Buzz Hurts Your Productivity *Harvard Business Review Digital Articles* p2 Jl 10 2015
Looking for Problems Makes Us Tired *Harvard Business Review Digital Articles* p2 Mr 30 2015
MBAS ARE MORE SELF-SERVING THAN OTHER CEOS color *Harvard Business Review* v94 no12 p32 D 2016
Mindfulness Mitigates Biases You May Not Know You Have *Harvard Business Review Digital Articles* p2 D 24 2014
Narcissistic Students Get Better Grades from Narcissistic Professors *Harvard Business Review Digital Articles* p2 Mr 4 2016
No, the Best Science Students Aren't Becoming Financiers *Harvard Business Review Digital Articles* p2 D 22 2015
Private Equity Can Make Firms More Innovative *Harvard Business Review Digital Articles* p2 Je 29 2015
Proof That Women Get Less Credit for Teamwork *Harvard Business Review Digital Articles* p2 F 9 2016
Research: Technology Is Only Making Social Skills More Important *Harvard Business Review Digital Articles* p2 Ag 26 2015
To Recover Faster from Rejection, Shift Your Mindset *Harvard Business Review Digital Articles* p2 Ap 6 2016
What Angel Investors Value Most When Choosing What to Fund *Harvard Business Review Digital Articles* p2 Ag 6 2015
What Executive Assistants Know About Managing Up *Harvard Business Review Digital Articles* p2 D 23 2014
What Generous People's Brains Do Differently *Harvard Business Review Digital Articles* p2 O 1 2015
Why Do So Few Women Edit Wikipedia? *Harvard Business Review Digital Articles* p2 Je 2 2016
Why It's So Hard for Us to Visualize Uncertainty *Harvard Business Review Digital Articles* p2 N 11 2016
Why Sex and Violence Don't Sell *Harvard Business Review Digital Articles* p2 S 4 2015
Why Sourcing Local Food Is So Hard for Restaurants *Harvard Business Review Digital Articles* p2 Je 15 2016

Torres, Ricardo
Forest conservation: Remember Gran Chaco bibl color *Science* v355 no6324 p465 F 3 2017

Torres, Ritchie
BRONX TALE J. GONNERMAN cartoon color *New Yorker* v92 no41 p36 D 12 2016

Torres, Roselinde
How to Regain the Lost Art of Reflection *Harvard Business Review Digital Articles* p2 S 25 2017
The Rise of the Not-So- Experienced CEO *Harvard Business Review Digital Articles* p2 D 26 2014

Torres, Teresa P.
Microbiota-activated PPAR-γ signaling inhibits dysbiotic Enterobacteriaceae expansion graph *Science* v357 no6351 p570 Ag 11 2017

Torres-Lezama, A.
Persistent effects of pre-Columbian plant domestication on Amazonian forest composition bibl chart graph map *Science* v355 no6328 p925 Mr 3 2017

TORRES SIDERS, JENNIFER
cultivate caring *Parents* v91 no12 p122 D 2016

Torrey, E. Fuller (Edwin Fuller), 1937-
The Death Of Freud color *National Review* v69 no17 p35 S 11 2017
Evolving Brains, Emerging Gods: Early Humans and the Origins of Religion color *Publishers Weekly* v264 no31 p76 Jl 31 2017

Torrey, Richard
HAPPY RETURNS color *Publishers Weekly* v264 no29 p219 Jl 17 2017

Torrice, Andrea
THEY PERSISTED A. BRANDT bw *Cincinnati Magazine* v51 no1 p20 O 2017

Torsoli, Albertina
J&J Plays the Spurned Suitor cartoon *Bloomberg Businessweek* no4503 p20 D 12 2016

Torta, Federico
Characterization of a dynamic metabolon producing the defense compound dhurrin in sorghum bibl graph *Science* v354 no6314 p890 N 18 2016
Lipid transport by TMEM24 at ER-plasma membrane contacts regulates pulsatile insulin secretion diag *Science* v355 no6326 p709 F 17 2017

Tortilla chips
Bonfire Pizza Chips A. Larson *Idaho Magazine* v16 no9 p56 Je 2017
Sizzlin' Campfire Nachos P. KITA bw color *Men's Health* v32 no6 p36 Ag 2017

Tortillas
Fast and Flavorful L. TYRELL color *Martha Stewart Living* p88 O 2017
Make America **eat Again C. CALDWELL cartoon *Weekly Standard* v22 no19 p5 Ja 23 2017

Tortorella, Domenico
Enhancement of Zika virus pathogenesis by preexisting antiflavivirus immunity graph *Science* v356 no6334 p175 Ap 14 2017

Tortorello, Michael
AT THE WHEEL OVER 65: Driving Safer, Driving Longer [Cover story] chart color graph *Consumer Reports* v82 no7 p18 Jl 2017

TORTORICI, DAYNA
Zadie Smith's Dance of Ambivalence color *Atlantic* v318 no5 p32 D 2016

Torts—United States—Law & legislation
Will the GOP Finally Crush Class Actions? P. M. Barrett *Bloomberg Businessweek* no4514 p28 Mr 13 2017

Torture
TRUMP AND THE TRIUMPH OF FEAR IN AMERICAN POLITICS S. ABRAMSKY bw color *Nation* v305 no8 p18 O 9 2017

Tory Burch LLC
Love Is in the Air! color *O, The Oprah Magazine* p69 F 2017
Signature Style color *O, The Oprah Magazine* p59 My 2017
TORY BURCH'S Icons M. Robin color *InStyle* v24 no3 p264 Mr 2017

Tory Party (Great Britain)
Sorry, Tories J. MILLER *In These Times* v41 no8 p41 Ag 2017

Tosa, Yukio
Evolution of the wheat blast fungus through functional losses in a host specificity determinant diag map *Science* v357 no6346 p80 Jl 7 2017

Tosca (Theatrical production)
Dateline *Opera News* v81 no10 p10 Ap 2017
Lebanon, NH D. Shengold *Opera News* v81 no5 p44 N 2016

Toscanini, Arturo, 1867-1957
The Great Man That Was Toscanini T. TEACHOUT *Commentary* v144 no2 p48 S 2017

Toshi Arima
A three-dimensional movie of structural changes in bacteriorhodopsin bibl diag graph *Science* v354 no6319 p1552 D 23 2016

Toshiaki Hosaka
A three-dimensional movie of structural changes in bacteriorhodopsin bibl diag graph *Science* v354 no6319 p1552 D 23 2016

Toshiba KK—Finance
How to Lose $6 Billion J. Clenfield, Y. Nakamura et al color graph *Bloomberg Businessweek* no4512 p19 F 20 2017

Toshihide Mizoguchi
Self-renewal of a purified Tie2+ hematopoietic stem cell population relies on mitochondrial clearance bibl graph *Science* v354 no6316 p1156 D 2 2016

Toshimori Honjo

A coherent Ising machine for 2000-node optimization problems bibl diag graph *Science* v354 no6312 p603 N 4 2016

Toshio Suda

Self-renewal of a purified Tie2+ hematopoietic stem cell population relies on mitochondrial clearance bibl graph *Science* v354 no6316 p1156 D 2 2016

Tosi, Christina

MORE the MERRIER color *Vogue* v206 no12 p264 D 2016

Tosi, F.

Localized aliphatic organic material on the surface of Ceres bibl graph *Science* v355 no6326 p719 F 17 2017

Seasonal exposure of carbon dioxide ice on the nucleus of comet 67P/Churyumov-Gerasimenko bibl bw graph *Science* v354 no6319 p1563 D 23 2016

Toska, Eneda

PI3K pathway regulates ER-dependent transcription in breast cancer through the epigenetic regulator KMT2D bibl graph *Science* v355 no6331 p1324 Mr 24 2017

Toskovich, John

ship shape K. BARNES *Better Homes & Gardens* v94 no12 pN8 D 2016

Toste, F. Dean

Redox-based reagents for chemoselective methionine bioconjugation bibl diag graph *Science* v355 no6325 p597 F 10 2017

Total Eclipse of the Heart (Music)

5 Great Songs Almost Ruined by Their Original Titles B. SPECKTOR *Reader's Digest* v188 no1124 p134 O 2016

Total hip replacement

BONE TIRED M. Hannan Davant *Washingtonian Magazine* v52 no5 p129 F 2017

Boomers Go Bionic P. MERTZ ESSWEIN color *Kiplinger's Personal Finance* v71 no5 p64 My 2017

"I felt pride, and that changed everything." S. Kitchens color *Glamour* v115 no6 p72 Je 2017

Moving Forward *Virginia Living* v15 no1 p107 D 2016

Total knee replacement

BONE TIRED M. Hannan Davant *Washingtonian Magazine* v52 no5 p129 F 2017

Less Pain, More Gain K. H. QUEEN color *Forbes* v200 no4 p(Sp)1 O 24 2017

Total Seal Inc.

TESTED: TOTAL SEAL'S 110V RING FILER B. Gillogly color *Hot Rod* v70 no2 p72 F 2017

Total solar eclipses

1925 AN ECLIPSE LIKE NO OTHER E. Maor *Sky & Telescope* v133 no1 p66 Ja 2017

The 2017 Total Solar Eclipse J. Rao *Weatherwise* v70 no2 p12 Mr/Ap 2017

20 HOT SPOTS to view the eclipse M. E. Bakich color map *Astronomy* v45 no8 p38 Ag 2017

75, 50 & 25 YEARS AGO R. W. Sinnott color *Sky & Telescope* v134 no2 p8 Ag 2017

All eyes on the eclipse L. Grossman color *Science News* v192 no1 p4 Ag 5 2017

Astronomy's ATLAS OF TOTALITY M. E. Bakich color map *Astronomy* v45 no8 p54 Ag 2017

August 2017: Totality comes to America M. RATCLIFFE and A. LING color *Astronomy* v45 no8 p44 Ag 2017

DARKNESS FALLS E. Conant color map *National Geographic* v232 no2 p24 Ag 2017

The Day the Sun Disappears C. Fulco color map *National Wildlife (World Edition)* v55 no4 p18 Je/Jl 2017

The Deeper Meaning of the Great American Eclipse J. Kluger color map *Time* v190 no7 p19 Ag 21 2017

Eclipse, At Last: The "Great American" total solar eclipse is this month's star attraction F. Schaaf color *Sky & Telescope* v134 no2 p46 Ag 2017

The eclipse of a generation A. Speck *Physics Today* v70 no8 p10 Ag 2017

Expert tips on imaging M. Reynolds color *Astronomy* v45 no8 p70 Ag 2017

Here's every total solar eclipse from now to 2040 E. DeMarco map *Science News* v192 no1 p32 Ag 5 2017

Keep your eyes on the eclipse G. CHAPLE color *Astronomy* v45 no8 p84 Ag 2017

LET THE COUNTDOWN TO 2024 BEGIN M. E. Bakich map

Astronomy v45 no8 p74 Ag 2017

Lightbox J. Kluger color *Time* v190 no9 p18 S 4 2017

Love affair with a saros B. BERMAN color *Astronomy* v45 no11 p10 N 2017

A Moment of Darkness J. RAO color *Natural History* v125 no7 p43 Jl/Ag 2017

Navigating the sky M. E. Bakich color *Astronomy* v45 no8 p52 Ag 2017

Nebraska's magical moment in the shade 2017 ECLIPSE A. J. BARTELS color *Nebraska Life* v21 no6 p14 N/D 2017

Perfect totality B. BERMAN color *Astronomy* v45 no6 p10 Je 2017

POPULAR MECHANICS EVERYWHERE color *Popular Mechanics* p8 S 2017

Prepping for the Really Big Show M. W. SCHWARTZ chart color diag *Missouri Life* v44 no2 p28 Ap 2017

Shadow From Beyond Our World: How can we describe the wonder and awe we experience during a total solar eclipse? F. Schaaf color *Sky & Telescope* v134 no2 p45 Ag 2017

Solar Eclipse City Event Guide *Missouri Life* v44 no4 p27 Je 2017

The Sun's 'shimmering' corona S. JAMES O'MEARA color *Astronomy* v45 no6 p60 Je 2017

Talking totality B. BERMAN *Astronomy* v45 no1 p9 Ja 2017

Through Glasses, Darkly B. SWAIM cartoon *Weekly Standard* v22 no48 p5 S 4 2017

TOTAL ECLIPSE OF HOTEL AVAILABILITY J. Alsever color *Fortune* v176 no1 p11 Jl 1 2017

TOTALLY J. Kersten cartoon *New Yorker* v93 no25 p28 Ag 28 2017

VIDEO STRATEGIES FOR ECLIPSE DAY M. E. Bakich color *Astronomy* v45 no8 p68 Ag 2017

What to Expect During the Eclipse L. A. ADDINGTON color map *Missouri Life* v44 no4 p26 Je 2017

Totalitarianism

See also

Communism

BRICKBATS C. Oliver bw color *Reason* v49 no5 p80 O 2017

Totalitarian Noir: It Happened Here L. PICKER color *Publishers Weekly* v264 no31 p63 Jl 31 2017

Tote bags

ARM CANDY: Totes used to be more function than form, but these fall bags don't sacrifice details or style H. G. Phillips *Washingtonian Magazine* v53 no1 p109 O 2017

HOMESTEAD HACKS: Our readers share clever projects that will help you live a self-sufficient life in the country, the suburbs, or the city R. D. Copeland *Mother Earth News* no282 p72 Je/Jl 2017

The LIST color *Harper's Bazaar* no3651 p197 Mr 2017

MAY@GH bw color *Good Housekeeping* v264 no5 p13 My 2017

Mixing Bowl color *O, The Oprah Magazine* p108 Jl 2017

SHAPE SHIFTERS L. IMMEDIATO color *Los Angeles Magazine* v62 no10 p32 O 2017

The Well-Edited Tote color *Esquire* p133 BigBlackBook

Tote bags—Evaluation

Adam's STYLE SHEET A. Glassman color *O, The Oprah Magazine* p50 Jl 2017

THE A-LIST color *O, The Oprah Magazine* p59 Mr 2017

IN THE BAG color *Harper's Bazaar* no3648 p95 N 2016

the life C. Stern color *InStyle* v24 no9 p425 S 2017

Lug your stuff in style color *Redbook* p67 F 2017

MAGIC HOUR color *Conde Nast Traveler* v52 no10 p29 N 2017

MUSEUM GIFT GUIDE *Los Angeles Magazine* p89 D 2016

Start With Your Bag color *Glamour* v115 no10 p56 O 2017

Thoroughly Modern Charlotte color *House Beautiful* v159 no1 p35 F 2017

Tote Couture color *O, The Oprah Magazine* p53 Mr 2017

Tuscan Olive K. RENDA and B. REYNAERT color *House Beautiful* v159 no8 p21 O 2017

Va-Va-Va Velvet S. P. Nadella color *Glamour* v114 no12 p92 D 2016

Totem poles

Stand to Reason E. MERCADO *Los Angeles Magazine* p156 D 2016

Totems

WITH STRANGE TOTEMS ... img *New York* v50 no9 p38 My 1 2017

p79 D 2016

SOUTH DAKOTA TRIVIA *South Dakota Magazine* v32 no4 p16 N/D 2016

Summer Solitude J. KEHOE color *Backpacker* p19 S 2017

Summit Fever: MacIntyre Range, New York O. DWYER color *Backpacker* p26 S 2017

Tourism: Committed to Preserving Life below Water T. Rifai *UN Chronicle* v54 no1/2 p1 2017

UNITED WAYPOINTS A. FISHER *Wired* v24 no12 p90 D 2016

Why You Shouldn't Skip the Duty-Free Shop bw color *Conde Nast Traveler* v52 no10 p138 N 2017

Tourism advertising

Summertime Slipups color *Consumer Reports* v82 no8 p63 Ag 2017

Tourism in Asia

10 TRIPS TO ASIA THAT WON'T COST A FORTUNE M. Leonhardt and K. A. Renzulli color map *Money* v46 no7 p71 Ag 2017

Tourism in Europe

TOP 10 EUROPE TRIPS FOR YOUR MONEY M. Leonhardt, K. A. Renzulli et al color *Money* v46 no5 p48 Je 2017

Tourism—Bahamas

island time T. DeBacco and K. Payne color *Power & Motoryacht* v34 no10 p84 O 2017

Tourism—Burma

Myanmar's Hotel Room Glut P. Heijmans color *Bloomberg Businessweek* no4528 p29 Je 26 2017

Tourism—California

WIN A SOCAL BEACH GETAWAY! T. Enriquez color *Sunset* v238 no5 p106 My 2017

Tourism—Canada

BRITISH COLUMBIA'S EAST VANCOUVER E. Ehmsen color map *Sunset* v239 no3 p36 S 2017

SHELTER AT THE EDGE OF THE WORLD A. Scott color *Sunset* v239 no3 p62 S 2017

Tourism—Colombia

Americans Are Traveling More E. Fry map *Fortune* v75 no1 p15 Ja 1 2017

Tourism—Congresses

NORDIC NEIGHBORS UNITE color *Iceland Review* v54 no5 p98 S-O 2016

Tourism—Cuba

Cruises Could Be Big Winners in Cuba C. Palmeri color graph *Bloomberg Businessweek* no4522 p23 My 15 2017

Here Comes the Wave C. Gorney color map *National Geographic* v230 no5 p82 N 2016

ISLAND HOP P. GUZMÁN color *Conde Nast Traveler* v51 no10 p34 N 2016

A Tale of Two Cubas [Cover story] R. RADOSH and A. RADOSH color *Weekly Standard* v22 no40 p17 Je 26 2017

Tourism—Egypt

Five-Star Pilgrimage J. Casper *Christianity Today* v61 no6 p18 Jl/Ag 2017

Tourism—Florida

A Key West Road Trip A. FLANGO *Cincinnati Magazine* p57 Je 2017

Tourism—France

Comme des Gascons P. Guzmán color *Conde Nast Traveler* v52 no3 p74 Mr 2017

Tourism—France—Paris

A SANCTUARY FROM TERROR L. Tramuta color *Fortune* v176 no2 p40 Ag 1 2017

Tourism—Georgia

Meet Me in Savannah A. R. Williams color *Southern Living* v52 no2 p79 F 2017

Tourism—Germany

Travel to Germany with PDK color *Phi Delta Kappan* v98 no5 p79 F 2017

Tourism—Greece

MILOS'S MOMENT E. N. Gage color *Conde Nast Traveler* v52 no5 p108 My 2017

Tourism—Hawaii

NEW HAWAII P. Orenstein color *Sunset* v237 no6 p23 D 2016

Tourism—Iceland

WISDOM OF GOÐAFOSS J. Visco *Iceland Review* v55 no2 p22 Mr/Ap 2017

Tourism—Illinois—Chicago

SOUTH SHORE J. REESE color map *Chicago* v66 no6 p28 Je 2017

Tourism—Korea (South)

Tourists: China's New Political Weapon C. Dillow color *Fortune* v175 no8 p42 Je 15 2017

Tourism—Louisiana

Tour Score K. Finn color *New Orleans Magazine* v51 no5 p30 Mr 2017

Tourism—Maine

A Masterpiece by the Ocean S. Jermanok *Yankee* p96 Mr 2017

A Walk That Says Maine A. GRAVES color *Yankee* p88 Mr 2017

Tourism—Marketing

How Much Is an Instagram Story Worth? N. Ekstein color *Bloomberg Businessweek* no4513 p38 Mr 6 2017

Tourism—Massachusetts

A Gift for All I. A. LDRICH *Yankee* p99 Mr 2017

The Picture-Perfect Stroll I. A. LDRICH color *Yankee* p94 Mr 2017

Solitude by the Seashore J. K. DeFoe *Yankee* p89 Mr 2017

Tourism—Mexico

San Miguel Modern S. Deseran color *Sunset* v237 no6 p52 D 2016

Tourism—New York (State)

Notebook: Here Come the Tourists: Visiting New York has never felt so politically fraught J. D. Stein and J. Rothman img *New York* v50 no9 p18 My 1 2017

Tourism—North Carolina

Asheville, North Carolina A. BRANDT *Cincinnati Magazine* p60 Je 2017

Tourism—Pennsylvania

Pittsburgh A. FLANGO *Cincinnati Magazine* p62 Je 2017

Tourism—Romania—Transylvania

ROMANIA'S PROBLEM WITH DRACULA D. Light *History Today* v67 no5 p62 My 2017

Tourism—Rwanda

Rwanda Reborn S. Hepola color *Bloomberg Businessweek* no4540 p71 O 2 2017

Tourism—Social aspects

A SANCTUARY FROM TERROR L. Tramuta color *Fortune* v176 no2 p40 Ag 1 2017

Tourism—Southeast Asia

Towards a World-Class Destination *Foreign Affairs* v95 no6 p(Sp)19 N/D 2016

Tourism—Spain

Spain Is Different R. L. BARDAJÍ color *Weekly Standard* v22 no48 p15 S 4 2017

Tourism—Sweden

taking stockholm E. Goldberg bw color *Bon Appetit* v61 no11 p84 N 2016

Tourism—Switzerland

From Our Editor color *House Beautiful* v159 no7 p8 S 2017

Tourism—Taiwan

The Taiwan Strait Freezes E. EPSTEIN *Weekly Standard* v22 no4 p16 O 3 2016

Tourism—Texas—San Antonio

Deep in the Heart T. Ethington color *American Cowboy* v23 no6 p24 Ap/My 2017

Tourism—United States

The Best Walk in Newport M. Allen *Yankee* p91 Mr 2017

A Respite from the Crowds A. Graves color *Yankee* p86 Mr 2017

Tourism Woes Threaten Retail P. Wahba color diag *Fortune* v175 no5 p15 Ap 1 2017

Where Are All the Tourists? H. Goldman and D. Biller color diag *Bloomberg Businessweek* no4514 p15 Mr 13 2017

Tourism—United States—States

State Secrets map *Canadian Geographic* v135 no6 p21 D 2015

Tourism—Virginia

Back to The northern neck T. Ward *Virginia Living* v15 no6 p74 O 2017

Our Boys in Blue color *Weekly Standard* v22 no42 p2 Jl 17 2017

Tourism—Washington (State)

UNPLUGGING IN PREVOST HARBOR D. HISLOP *Sea Magazine* v108 no8 pPNW-1 Ag 2016

Tourism—West Bank

Room With a View (of a Wall and Barbed Wire) J. Ferziger and F. Hodali color *Bloomberg Businessweek* no4516 p14 Mr 27 2017

Tourist attractions

2017 A Look Ahead D. Harding Jr., B. Pike et al color map *Power & Motoryacht* v32 no12 p38 D 2016

3 Days in... Kearney, Neb color *American Cowboy* v23 no4 p40 D 2016/Ja 2017

7 Days of LOCURA L. Hittmeier color *Skiing* p58 Wint 2017

AUSTIN, TEXAS A. JOHNSTON *Atlanta* v56 no9 p50 Ja 2017

BAY AREA BOAT STOP: REDWOOD CITY IS A LUXURIOUS AND WELCOMING RETREAT IN THE HEART OF SILICON VALLEY color map *Sea Magazine* v109 no6 pCA-6 Je 2017

Be More Pacific J. VOELKER *Indianapolis Monthly* p38 My 2017

Blue Whale Nurtures Creativity K. Silsbee color *Downbeat* v84 no2 p51 F 2017

Bogotá, Colombia L. DIXON color *Foreign Policy* no224 p82 My/Je 2017

Bonjour, Montréal R. WALLWORK *Tennis* v53 no4 p30 Jl/Ag 2017

BRINGING VIKING-ERA ICELAND TO LIFE color *Iceland Review* v54 no5 p106 S-O 2016

THE BRITISH HERITAGE TRAVEL PUZZLER *British Heritage Travel* v37 no6 p87 N/D 2016

Broad RIPPLE R. Annis, S. Bahr et al color map *Indianapolis Monthly* v41 no2 p66 S 2017

Bull City E. WARTZMAN color *Bon Appetit* no11 p74 N 2017

CALIFORNIA S. Doyle color map *Canadian Geographic* v135 no6 p32 D 2015

Cascadia H. Hansman color *Powder* v45 no3 p108 N 2016

CHATTANOOGA, TENNESSEE R. J. Smith *Cincinnati Magazine* v50 no12 p38 S 2017

Colombo, Sri Lanka A. PERERA color *Foreign Policy* no222 p74 Ja/F 2017

COLOURFUL NUUK: JUST THREE HOURS FROM ICELAND color *Iceland Review* v54 no5 p104 S-O 2016

Come in for a landing color *Backpacker* p20 S 2017

THE DARK AND THE LIGHT J. C. Davies bw color *Powder* v45 no3 p94 N 2016

DELIGHT ON THE NORTH YORKSHIRE COAST D. Huntley *British Heritage Travel* v38 no1 p60 Ja/F 2017

Do the Charleston B. PORTER KATZ color *Martha Stewart Living* p110 My 2017

Downtown R. Annis, S. Bahr et al color map *Indianapolis Monthly* v41 no2 p73 S 2017

EAST ATLANTA VILLAGE G. CHAPMAN *Atlanta* v56 no10 p50 F 2017

El Paso J. BREAL *Texas Monthly* v45 no5 p30 My 2017

ESTONIA *New York Times Magazine* p48 S 24 2017

FIELD GUIDE: ELMHURST J. REESE color map *Chicago* v66 no9 p41 S 2017

Find Bliss in Bermuda *New York* v50 no17 p149 Ag 21 2017

FINE CHINA K. GLOWCZEWSKA bw color map *Harper's Bazaar* no3655 p95 Ag 2017

Galveston: NEITHER SHIFTING SANDS NOR FLUCTUATING FORTUNES CAN ERODE THIS ISLAND TOWN'S INDOMITABLE SPIRIT J. BREAL *Texas Monthly* v45 no7 p28 Jl 2017

GAS WORKS PARK color *Sea Magazine* v109 no6 pPNW-5 Je 2017

GHOSTS IN WINTER V. M. Kotz color *Popular Photography* v80 no11 p20 D 2016

Goes Down Easy E. FLORIO color *Conde Nast Traveler* v52 no2 p54 F 2017

GRAND TOUR OF THE RED ROCK COUNTRY T. Thomas *Arizona Highways* v93 no11 p32 N 2017

The Great British Day Off C. MUHLKE color *Bon Appetit* v62 no7 p70 Jl 2017

THE GREAT LOBSTER ROLL ADVENTURE: WE SENT FOOD EDITOR UP THE MAINE COAST, FROM KITTERY TO EASTPORT, TO SAMPLE NEARLY TWO | DOZEN ROLLS AND CROWN A CHAMPION A. TRAVERSO chart color *Yankee* p78 Jl 2017

The Great North L. WARNER color *Backpacker* p13 O 2017

GUINEA *New York Times Magazine* p54 S 24 2017

Hamilton COUNTY R. Annis, S. Bahr et al color map *Indianapolis Monthly* v41 no2 p63 S 2017

Hand in Hand M. McCowan color map *American Craft* v76 no6 p82 D 2016-Ja 2017

HOST FOR THE HOLIDAYS P. RAINS *Sea Magazine* v108 no12 p16 D 2016

HOUSTON: THE AMERICAN CITY OF THE FUTURE T. M. FERGUSON color *Ebony* v72 no11 p30 S 2017

In Search of Middle England *British Heritage Travel* v38 no1 p18 Ja/F 2017

Intel bw chart *Conde Nast Traveler* v52 no7 p96 Ag 2017

IRAN *New York Times Magazine* p70 S 24 2017

ITALIAN OASIS S. SHIBATA *Sea Magazine* v108 no12 pCA-1 D 2016

ITALY *New York Times Magazine* p62 S 24 2017

JULIAETTA: WHERE THERE IS THERE AGAIN S. PETTICORD *Idaho Magazine* v16 no7 p32 Ap 2017

Last Look E. Daigneau *Governing* v30 no1 p64 O 2016

Life Finds a Way: Gifford Pinchot National Forest, Washington L. LANCASTER color map *Backpacker* p22 S 2017

LIGHT & FOG J. Wignall color *Popular Photography* v81 no1 p44 Ja/F 2017

LOGAN CIRCLE AND SHAW *Washingtonian Magazine* v52 no5 p151 F 2017

LOG HOME ROAD TRIP: Tennessee color map *Log Home Living* v34 no2 p52 My 2017

The Magic of Maui: Turn your summer vacation into a wellness retreat on this laid-back Hawaiian isle R. WALLWORK color *Tennis* v53 no5 p22 S/O 2017

The Majestic Ahwahnee Hotel A. Andrews *Sierra* v101 no4 p17 Jl/Ag 2016

Meet Me in ST. LOUIS P. M. Jacoby-Garrett *Parks & Recreation* v51 no10 p60 O 2016

MELLOW OUT IN THE MILE HIGH CITY Z. HILL color *Ebony* v72/73 no12/1 p28 O/N 2017

Memories gathered by the mile in Western Nebraska color *Nebraska Life* v21 no6 p71 N/D 2017

MEMORY LANE P. F. STAHLS JR. color *Louisiana Life* v37 no3 p34 Ja/F 2017

MOUNT BALDY CROSSOVER TRAIL Although it's overshadowed by its celebrated neighbors, the Mount Baldy Crossover Trail is the epitome of a gorgeous walk in the woods R. STIEVE *Arizona Highways* v93 no6 p54 Je 2017

MOUNT LEMMON C. ABBOTT *Arizona Highways* v93 no6 p42 Je 2017

NAPA VALLEY, A CONNOISSEUR'S PARADISE O. J. WILLIAMS color *Ebony* v72 no11 p62 S 2017

Narragansett, Rhode Island: In this town, a mile-long beach is the local playground A. GRAVES color map *Yankee* p56 Jl 2017

NEAH BAY *Sea Magazine* v108 no12 pPNW-8 D 2016

The new Barbados T. HALL color map *Canadian Geographic* v135 no6 p9 D 2015

The New Dallas J. M. Frazier color *Southern Living* v51 no11 p73 N 2016

NEW PIER DURBAN, SOUTH AFRICA Z. MORTON color *Surfer* v58 no4 p60 Ag 2017

NEXT EXIT: AMERICANA: FROM FIBERGLASS DINOSAURS TO STONEWALL JACKSON'S STUFFED HORSE TO PATSY CLINE'S ICE-CREAM SCOOP, SHENANDOAH IS HOME TO SOME PARTICULARLY AMERICAN ATTRACTIONS B. Jensen *Washingtonian Magazine* v53 no1 p104 O 2017

NORTH CENTER J. REESE color map *Chicago* v66 no11 p29 N 2017

Oakland J. HERBST *Los Angeles Magazine* v62 no9 p68 S 2017

One Step Beyond K. LAGRAVE color *Conde Nast Traveler* v52 no7 p41 Ag 2017

Open House *Arizona Highways* v92 no11 p56 N 2016

OUT OF THIS WORLD K. SCHNEIDER *Indianapolis Monthly* v40 no7 p36 Mr 2017

Pebble Beach The Golfer's Ultimate Guide J. Passov and J. Sens color *Golf Magazine* v59 no2 p84 F 2017

The Perfect Day S. Murray color *Power & Motoryacht* v34 no9 p56 S 2017

PITCH A TENT & HIT THE TRAIL: Lewis and Clark, Simon and Garfunkel, peanut butter and chocolate... there's a long list of great combinations. In the summer in the Santa Catalina Mountains, the best combo might be hiking and camping. Here's a little... R. STIEVE and K. VAUGHN *Arizona Highways* v93 no6 p38 Je 2017

QUIET ON THE SET R. STIEVE *Arizona Highways* v93 no11 p42 N 2017

QUIET THE MIND C. Menzel bw color *Powder* v45 no3 p64 N 2016

QUILT TO LAST A. LYNCH *Indianapolis Monthly* v40 no3 p48 N 2016

Remote Argentina G. LONGO color *Conde Nast Traveler* v52 no7 p16 Ag 2017

Retro Summer-Fun Spots: Where a vintage vibe and timeless appeal keep the generations coming back K. K. BECKIUS color *Yankee* p66 Jl 2017

ROAD TRIP J. Wignall bw *Popular Photography* v80 no11 p38 D 2016

ROOM WITH A VIEW color *O, The Oprah Magazine* p113 Ja 2017

RUTLAND AND HIDDEN ENGLAND *British Heritage Travel* v38 no3 p40 My/Je 2017

SAVANNAH, GEORGIA A. BROWNLEE *Cincinnati Magazine* v50 no5 p40 F 2017

See the World, Be the World color *Climbing* no357 p13 N 2017

SHOW OFF SIN CITY bw color *Runner's World* v52 no3 p24 Ap 2017

SIGHTS UNSEEN J. BREAL *Texas Monthly* v45 no3 p100 Mr 2017

Snowmen, ice skates and lights make Nebraska's holiday bucket list D. LEFEVERS color *Nebraska Life* v21 no6 p68 N/D 2017

SOUND BOUND D. Hislop *Sea Magazine* v108 no12 p18 D 2016

SOUTH SHORE J. REESE color map *Chicago* v66 no6 p28 Je 2017

Summer Solitude J. KEHOE color *Backpacker* p19 S 2017

SURVIVAL OF THE FINNISH IN SOINTULA D. HISLOP *Sea Magazine* v108 no12 p116 D 2016

THE SYMMETRY OF 50 S. FENNESSY *Atlanta* v57 no2 p18 Je 2017

TAKE A DRIVE: INTO THE HIGHLANDS R. Sklarew *Washingtonian Magazine* v52 no6 p100 Mr 2017

TAKING THE TOUR 2017 K. MONTGOMERY *Arizona Highways* v93 no11 p40 N 2017

THE Trip M. Rapkin and M. Salcido color *Sunset* v238 no1 p48 Ja 2017

WALES IN THE YEAR OF LEGENDS S. Ellis *British Heritage Travel* v38 no3 p64 My/Je 2017

Water's Edge: Pictured Rocks National Lakeshore, Michigan E. KWAK-HEFFERAN color *Backpacker* p12 S 2017

Water to Wine P. Brady bw color diag *Conde Nast Traveler* v52 no7 p72 Ag 2017

We Remember J. BILLS and M. SEAMANS color *Yankee* v80 no6 p96 N/D 2016

Where we go A. Kylie color *Canadian Geographic* v135 no6 p4 D 2015

WHERE WE'RE SKIING AND EATING IN EUROPE color *Conde Nast Traveler* v52 no2 p42 F 2017

WONDERLAND J. Brown bw color *Powder* v45 no3 p82 N 2016

WORKING FOR THE WEEKEND A. Poe *Washingtonian Magazine* v52 no5 p161 F 2017

Yes, You Can Do Low-Key St. Barts A. Brooks color *Conde Nast Traveler* v52 no1 p60 Ja 2017

Tourist camps, hostels, etc.

See also

Bed & breakfast accommodations

Park lodging facilities

Doubling Down on DTLA M. WILLIAMS color *Conde Nast Traveler* v52 no9 p24 O 2017

Tourist camps, hostels, etc.—Evaluation

Up the Creek B&B N. AUSTIN *Arizona Highways* v92 no7 p14 Jl 2016

Tourists

EUROPE'S BEST AIRPORT color *Iceland Review* v54 no5 p36 S-O 2016

From Our Editor color *House Beautiful* v159 no7 p8 S 2017

GRAND TOUR OF THE RED ROCK COUNTRY T. Thomas *Arizona Highways* v93 no11 p32 N 2017

HARQUAHALA MOUNTAIN N. AUSTIN *Arizona Highways* v92 no11 p52 N 2016

THE LOOK BOOK A. SWERDLOFF img *New York* v49 no21 p75 O 17 2016

Meet Me in ST. LOUIS P. M. Jacoby-Garrett *Parks & Recreation* v51 no10 p60 O 2016

The Taiwan Strait Freezes E. EPSTEIN *Weekly Standard* v22 no4 p16 O 3 2016

Tour Score K. Finn color *New Orleans Magazine* v51 no5 p30 Mr 2017

WE SET UP SHOP IN THE MIDDLE OF A NATURAL WONDER A. McGIVNEY *Arizona Highways* v92 no11 p43 N 2016

Why You Shouldn't Skip the Duty-Free Shop bw color *Conde Nast Traveler* v52 no10 p138 N 2017

Tourists—Attitudes

A German, a Swede, and A Brit Walk Into a Hotel... C. Jasper cartoon chart *Bloomberg Businessweek* no4518 p18 Ap 10 2017

LOOK EAST *Iceland Review* v55 no4 p102 Jl/Ag 2017

Tourists—Services for

Welcome to America? A. HUTCHINS color *Maclean's* v130 no4 p14 My 2017

Tournament fishing

THE CHAMPS B. RUZZO and G. BETHGE color *Outdoor Life* v224 no5 p34 Je/Jl 2017

DON'T MISS LIST FEBRUARY 2017 BOAT SHOWS *Sea Magazine* v109 no2 pPNW-10 F 2017

DON'T MISS LIST FEBRUARY 2017 *Sea Magazine* v109 no2 pCA-7 F 2017

Tournament of Roses

Buds Light *Los Angeles Magazine* p34 D 2016

Tours

See also

Concert tours

Package tours

The best of the west with Nebraska Life color *Nebraska Life* v21 no4 p89 Jl/Ag 2017

FAMILY *Sierra* v102 no1 p82 Ja/F 2017

HOT ROD Power Tour 2017 color *Hot Rod* v70 no11 p18 N 2017

INSTAGRAM EVERYWHERE E. STEIN color *Wired* v24 no12 p91 D 2016

The Not-So-Grand Tour G. WISHARD cartoon *Weekly Standard* v22 no42 p5 Jl 17 2017

On the Road with the Hachette Book Group A. Green chart color *Publishers Weekly* v264 no32 p8 Ag 7 2017

Power Tour's ROAD TO RECOVERY P. Thomas color *Hot Rod* v70 no11 p38 N 2017

QUAD GOALS! A. STANLEY color *Seventeen* v76 no5 p76 S 2017

THE SEXIEST TOUR OF PARIS color *Advocate* no1091 p118 Je/Jl 2017

TNT color *Vogue* v207 no6 p68 Je 2017

We're Headed to the Big Eassy P. M. Jacoby-Garrett *Parks & Recreation* v52 no9 p78 S 2017

Touryalai, Halah

America's Top 100 Wealth Advisors chart *Forbes* v200 no4 p105 O 24 2017

LESSONS AND IDEAS BY THE 100 GREATEST LIVING BUSINESS MINDS bw color *Forbes* v200 no3 p115 S 28 2017

Toussaint, John S.

Hospitals Are Finally Starting to Put Real-Time Data to Use *Harvard Business Review Digital Articles* p2 N 12 2014

Hospitals Can't Improve Without Better Management Systems *Harvard Business Review Digital Articles* p2 O 21 2015

How Atrius Health Is Making the Shift from Volume to Value *Harvard Business Review Digital Articles* p2 D 13 2016

Improve the Affordable Care Act, Don't Repeal It *Harvard Business Review Digital Articles* p2 N 16 2016

To Radically Redesign Health Care, Start with One Unit *Harvard Business Review Digital Articles* p2 D 9 2015

What a Bipartisan Approach to U.S. Health Care Could Look Like color *Harvard Business Review Digital Articles* p2 Mr 30 2017

Toussaint, Ted

How Atrius Health Is Making the Shift from Volume to Value *Harvard Business Review Digital Articles* p2 D 13 2016

Tovani, Cris

news & notes *Literacy Today (2411-7862)* v35 no2 p42 S/O 2017

Tove Lo (Performer)

COOL GIRL INTERRUPTED N. Feeney color *Entertainment*

Toxemia of pregnancy
> *See also*
> Preeclampsia
Circulating peptide prevents preeclampsia R. C. Wirka and T. Quertermous diag *Science* v357 no6352 p643 Ag 18 2017

Toxic algae
Toxic algae may be culprit in mysterious dinosaur deaths C. Gramling *Science* v357 no6354 p857 S 1 2017

Toxic substance exposure
THE PRICE OF A DIGITAL WORLD C. Simpson, B. Elgin et al color *Bloomberg Businessweek* no4527 p58 Je 19 2017

Toxic substance exposure—Law & legislation
A CALL FOR BETTER Toxics Policy Reform J. Wilson and O. A. Ogunseitan color diag *Environment* v59 no1 p30 2017

Toxicity testing
Policy reforms to update chemical safety testing A. E. Nel and T. F. Malloy bibl color *Science* v355 no6329 p1016 Mr 10 2017

Toxins
> *See also*
> Plant toxins
> Venom
The balance between immunity and inflammation D. L. Wiesner and B. S. Klein diag *Science* v357 no6355 p973 S 8 2017
Botulism L. Bonner color *Equus* no481 p31 O 2017
I-3-C and DIM V. Tweed color *Amazing Wellness* p12 Fall 2017
IS YOUR SUPPLEMENT TOXIC? L. Beil color *Men's Health* v32 no3 p86 Ap 2017
SPRING detox PLAN I. Eliaz color *Amazing Wellness* v9 no2 p46 Spr 2017
STINK: THE REAL STORY OF TOXINS V. Tweed color *Amazing Wellness* v8 no2 p14 Spr 2016

Toxoplasma gondii
Parasites fight for nutrients A. Cunningham color *Science News* v192 no6 p16 O 14 2017

Toxvaerd, Laura
Graphic Designs P. MARGASAK bw *Downbeat* v84 no5 p18 My 2017

Toy, Chelsea
ALL IN THE FAMILY color *Spin to Win Rodeo* v21 no2 p54 Ap 2017
BUCKLE UP color *Spin to Win Rodeo* v21 no5 p15 Jl 2017
BUCKLE UP *Spin to Win Rodeo* v21 no2 p19 Ap 2017
BUCKLE UP with Derrick Begay color *Spin to Win Rodeo* v20 no11 p15 Ja 2017
BUCKLE UP with Dustin Egusquiza color *Spin to Win Rodeo* v21 no6 p19 Ag 2017
BUCKLE UP with Jackie Hobbs-Crawford color *Spin to Win Rodeo* v20 no12 p19 F 2017
BUCKLE UP with Jeremy Buhler color *Spin to Win Rodeo* v20 no10 p25 D 2016
BUCKLE UP with Tom Richards color *Spin to Win Rodeo* v21 no1 p21 Mr 2017
The Cinch Timed Event Championship of the World color *American Cowboy* v23 no5 p29 F/Mr 2017
CORKILL'S SAN ANTONIO ROSE color diag *Spin to Win Rodeo* v21 no2 p52 Ap 2017
DALLYING TECHNIQUES with Brock Hanson color *Spin to Win Rodeo* v20 no11 p21 Ja 2017
DEAR ROPER color *Spin to Win Rodeo* v21 no5 p6 Jl 2017
ELITE HARDWARE color *Spin to Win Rodeo* v20 no11 p42 Ja 2017
FIVE FLAT color *Spin to Win Rodeo* v21 no2 p33 Ap 2017
FIVE FLAT color *Spin to Win Rodeo* v21 no5 p25 Jl 2017
FIVE FLAT with Dakota Kirchenschlager color *Spin to Win Rodeo* v20 no12 p33 F 2017
FIVE FLAT with Paul David Tierney color *Spin to Win Rodeo* v21 no1 p33 Mr 2017
FIVE FLAT with Zane Bruce color *Spin to Win Rodeo* v21 no6 p31 Ag 2017
FREEZE FRAME color *Spin to Win Rodeo* v20 no10 p52 D 2016
FREEZE FRAME color *Spin to Win Rodeo* v21 no2 p44 Ap 2017
FREEZE FRAME WITH BILLIE JACK SAEBENS color *Spin to Win Rodeo* v20 no11 p32 Ja 2017
FREEZE FRAME WITH CESAR DE LA CUZ color *Spin to Win Rodeo* v21 no3 p44 My 2017
FREEZE FRAME WITH CHRIS GLOVER color *Spin to Win Ro-*
deo v21 no5 p38 Jl 2017
FREEZE FRAME WITH JUSTIN DAVIS color *Spin to Win Rodeo* v21 no4 p42 Je 2017
FREEZE FRAME WITH LEVI SIMPSON color *Spin to Win Rodeo* v20 no12 p44 F 2017
FREEZE FRAME WITH PAUL EAVES color *Spin to Win Rodeo* v21 no1 p44 Mr 2017
Golden Oldie color *Spin to Win Rodeo* v21 no5 p46 Jl 2017
LESSONS LEARNED bw color *Spin to Win Rodeo* v21 no1 p66 Mr 2017
Mare Magic color diag *Spin to Win Rodeo* v21 no3 p52 My 2017
Mastering the Entering Game color *Spin to Win Rodeo* v21 no3 p22 My 2017
Match Made in Houston color *Spin to Win Rodeo* v21 no3 p54 My 2017
Mysterious Foot Injuries color *Spin to Win Rodeo* v21 no6 p52 Ag 2017
Power of Goal Setting color *Spin to Win Rodeo* v21 no4 p22 Je 2017
Retirement Gig color diag *Spin to Win Rodeo* v21 no6 p50 Ag 2017
SILVER STANDARD color *Spin to Win Rodeo* v21 no6 p70 Ag 2017
Spring Veterinary Checklist color *Spin to Win Rodeo* v21 no1 p52 Mr 2017
Weathering the Storm [Cover story] color *Spin to Win Rodeo* v21 no4 p60 Je 2017
WHAT'S YOUR NUMBER? color *Spin to Win Rodeo* v21 no2 p28 Ap 2017
WPRA MOVES TO WELCOME 18 & UNDER ROPERS color *Spin to Win Rodeo* v20 no12 p28 F 2017
THE X FACTOR color *Spin to Win Rodeo* v21 no5 p48 Jl 2017
YOUNG GUNS color *Spin to Win Rodeo* v21 no2 p24 Ap 2017
YOUNG GUNS with Kyle Lockett color *Spin to Win Rodeo* v21 no6 p24 Ag 2017
YOUNG GUNS with Travis Graves color *Spin to Win Rodeo* v21 no1 p28 Mr 2017
YOU PICKED 'EM! [Cover story] color *Spin to Win Rodeo* v20 no12 p54 F 2017

Toy guns
BRICKBATS C. OLIVER color *Reason* v49 no4 p80 Ag/S 2017

Toy industry—Congresses
What Technology Companies Can Learn from Toy Makers A. Samuel *Harvard Business Review Digital Articles* p2 Mr 30 2016

Toy industry—Equipment & supplies
Make Room on the Shelf cartoon *Good Housekeeping* v263 no6 p77 D 2016

Toy industry—United States
THE TOY INDUSTRY IS A RETAIL BRIGHT SPOT *Fortune* v175 no3 p11 Mr 1 2017

Toy making
PAPER AIRPLANE LAUNCHER! J. SCHADEWALD cartoon color *Popular Mechanics* p104 Je 2017

Toy manufacturing
Why Suppliers Will Still Play With Toys 'R' Us M. Townsend, E. Ronalds-Hannon et al color *Bloomberg Businessweek* no4539 p17 S 25 2017

Toy robots—Evaluation
LEGO BOOST CREATIVE TOOLBOX: YUP, TABLET-CONNECTED LEGO ROBOTS ARE AS COOL AS THEY SOUND S. OCHS color *Macworld - Digital Edition* v34 no11 p67 N 2017

Toy stores
54th and Monon T. BRAND *Indianapolis Monthly* p30 F 2017
From Beanie Babies to fidget spinners, the evolution of toy fads shows how technology has thrown the consumer economy into chaos C. Duhigg *New York Times Magazine* p12 Ag 20 2017
Magic in Miniature T. SANCTON bw color *Vanity Fair* v59 no9 p98 S 2017
shopping img *New York* p86 Mr 6 2017

Toyokazu Endo
Injury-induced ctgfa directs glial bridging and spinal cord regeneration in zebrafish bibl graph *Science* v354 no6312 p630 N 4 2016

Toyota 4Runner sport utility vehicle

ANZA ADVENTURES C. SPRAGUE color *Dirt Sports + Off-Road* v51 no6 p8 Je 2017

RUNNING WILD [Cover story] D. SCANLON and M. EMERY color *Dirt Sports + Off-Road* v51 no12 p40 D 2017

Toyota automobiles
See also
Camry automobile

Toyota automobiles—Evaluation
25 CARS WORTH WAITING FOR J. Gall, D. Pund et al color *Car & Driver* v62 no10 p32 Ap 2017

BOLDLY GOING F. Markus chart color *Motor Trend* v69 no9 p80 S 2017

GARAGE M. Rechtin, K. Pleskot et al chart color diag *Motor Trend* v69 no8 p96 Ag 2017

Hydrogen-Powered Hipness T. Mirai color *Consumer Reports* v82 no10 p62 O 2017

IDENTITY CRISIS S. Evans chart color *Motor Trend* v69 no6 p66 Je 2017

It's Alive! R. Ceppos color *Car & Driver* v63 no4 p104 O 2017

Space Invader J. Pearley Huffman color *Car & Driver* v63 no5 p118 N 2017

T100 SALVATION M. EMERY color *Dirt Sports + Off-Road* v51 no11 p54 N 2017

TECTONIC SHIFT [Cover story] cartoon color *Motor Trend* v69 no3 p38 Mr 2017

Toyota FT-4X Concept M. Cantu color *Motor Trend* v69 no7 p22 Jl 2017

TREND S. Evans color *Motor Trend* v69 no2 p15 F 2017

WINTER is here C. Seabaugh chart color *Motor Trend* v69 no2 p84 F 2017

Toyota Motor Corp.
25 CARS WORTH WAITING FOR J. Gall, D. Pund et al color *Car & Driver* v62 no10 p32 Ap 2017

GARAGE cartoon chart color *Motor Trend* v69 no4 p86 Ap 2017

Hydrogen-Powered Hipness T. Mirai color *Consumer Reports* v82 no10 p62 O 2017

Space Invader J. Pearley Huffman color *Car & Driver* v63 no5 p118 N 2017

T100 SALVATION M. EMERY color *Dirt Sports + Off-Road* v51 no11 p54 N 2017

TECTONIC SHIFT [Cover story] cartoon color *Motor Trend* v69 no3 p38 Mr 2017

Toyota FT-4X Concept M. Cantu color *Motor Trend* v69 no7 p22 Jl 2017

Toyota Highlander SE chart color *Motor Trend* v69 no1 p58 Ja 2017

Toyota Land Cruiser chart color *Motor Trend* v69 no1 p60 Ja 2017

Toyota Prius Two Eco chart color *Motor Trend* v69 no1 p133 Ja 2017

Toyota RAV4 chart color *Motor Trend* v69 no1 p61 Ja 2017

TREND S. Evans color *Motor Trend* v69 no2 p15 F 2017

A TUN OF FUN M. EMERY color *Dirt Sports + Off-Road* v51 no5 p40 My 2017

WINTER is here C. Seabaugh chart color *Motor Trend* v69 no2 p84 F 2017

Toyota Motor Sales USA Inc. Lexus Division
LEXUS RISING J. H. HARPER color *Road & Track* v68 no7 p32 Mr/Ap 2017

Toyota MR2 automobile
Mr. Toyoda, please bring back MR2 E. Loh *Motor Trend* v69 no7 p12 Jl 2017

Toyota Racing Development USA Inc.
Exit Strategery S. SMITH bw color *Road & Track* v68 no8 p24 My 2017

Toyota RAV4 sport utility vehicle—Evaluation
Toyota RAV4 chart color *Motor Trend* v69 no1 p61 Ja 2017

Toyota trucks
See also
Highlander sport utility vehicle
Family-Friendly Road Warrior *Consumer Reports* v82 no7 p63 Jl 2017

Toys
See also
Blocks (Toys)
Fidget spinners
Kites

LEGO toys
Slinky (Toy)

Toys "R" Us Inc.
PLAYED OUT S. Kolhatkar color *New Yorker* v93 no31 p23 O 9 2017

Toys 'R' Us Might Be Dying, but Physical Retail Isn't G. Satell *Harvard Business Review Digital Articles* p2 S 20 2017

Why Suppliers Will Still Play With Toys 'R' Us M. Townsend, E. Ronalds-Hannon et al color *Bloomberg Businessweek* no4539 p17 S 25 2017

Toys for dogs—Evaluation
Get Your Dog To Behave Around Company N. B. McGough and P. York color *Southern Living* v52 no4 p50 Ap 2017

Puppy love color *Equus* no481 p65 O 2017

Toys for pets
Country Lore *Mother Earth News* no279 p83 D/Ja 2017

Toys—Evaluation
5 SMART Toys C. BOYER *National Geographic Kids* no466 p18 D 2016/Ja 2017

BEST TOY AWARDS 2016 cartoon color *Good Housekeeping* v263 no5 p121 N 2016

BEST TOY AWARDS 2017 N. SAPORITA color *Good Housekeeping* v265 no5 p85 N 2017

GEARHEAD: STEAM POWER L. STINSON color *Wired* v25 no9 p46 S 2017

Make Room on the Shelf cartoon *Good Housekeeping* v263 no6 p77 D 2016

November @ GH cartoon color *Good Housekeeping* v263 no5 p14 N 2016

Pop Chart M. Mccluskey color *Time* v190 no16/17 p110 O 23 2017

The Shoddy Science Behind Fidget Spinners S. Gregory color *Time* v189 no19 p17 My 22 2017

WHAT'S NEW? *USA Today Magazine* v145 no2860 p74 Ja 2017

Toys—Exhibitions
Consolidation in Book Plus And the Evolution of Coloring K. Raugust color *Publishers Weekly* v264 no9 p7 F 27 2017

Things That Go *Treasures* v6 no3 p12 D 2016/Ja 2017

Tozzi, G. P.
Seasonal exposure of carbon dioxide ice on the nucleus of comet 67P/Churyumov-Gerasimenko bibl bw graph *Science* v354 no6319 p1563 D 23 2016

Tozzi, John
Health Care Has A Goldilocks Problem graph *Bloomberg Businessweek* no4532 p38 Jl 31 2017

Trump Slows Efforts to Cut Health-Care Costs color graph *Bloomberg Businessweek* no4541 p38 O 9 2017

Where County Lines Mean Life and Death graph *Bloomberg Businessweek* no4538 p31 S 18 2017

Tozzo, Effie
Systemic pan-AMPK activator MK-8722 improves glucose homeostasis but induces cardiac hypertrophy graph *Science* v357 no6350 p507 Ag 4 2017

TPG Capital LP
IF I RAN THE CIRCUS M. Lev-ram color *Fortune* v175 no3 p132 Mr 1 2017

TPI Composites Inc.
A Rust Belt Town Goes Green--And Non-Union Y. KUNICHOFF *In These Times* v41 no10 p9 O 2017

Traband, Elizabeth
Traband Receives Hamel Scholarship *In Stride* v12 no5 p10 S 2017

Trace elements in nutrition
EAT GREAT & LOSE WEIGHT H. LEVINE *Better Homes & Gardens* v95 no1 p116 Ja 2017

Got vitamins? J. WUEBBEN bw color *Muscle & Performance* v9 no7 p14 Jl 2017

POWER-PACKED VITAMINS D. N. JACKSON color *Muscle & Performance* v9 no10 p56 O 2017

Trace gases
Let There Be Laser Light G. Schanker *Oceanus* v52 no1 p26 Summ 2016

Tracer, Zachary
Obamacare's Problems Still Need Solving map *Bloomberg Businessweek* no4531 p37 Jl 24 2017

Repeal and _____ *Bloomberg Businessweek* no4509 p22 Ja

DRIVEN TO DISTRACTION P. SMITH, N. E. Bondette et al *New York Times Upfront* v149 no10 p10 Mr 13 2017

Insurers Ding Innocent Drivers After Accidents M. Leonhardt color *Money* v46 no3 p18 Ap 2017

Learning to Dance in the Rain L. Ostrander color *Horse & Rider* v56 no5 p14 My 2017

Right Aid D. MANN *Texas Monthly* v44 no11 p26 N 2016

Tesla, Autopilot, and the Challenge of Trusting Machines W. Frick *Harvard Business Review Digital Articles* p2 Jl 11 2016

WHEEL OF FORTUNE color *Road & Track* v68 no7 p98 Mr/Ap 2017

Traffic cameras

WHERE RADAR CAMERAS FEAR TO TREAD J. D. TUCCILLE bw *Reason* v49 no1 p10 My 2017

Traffic congestion

Citywide effects of high-occupancy vehicle restrictions: Evidence from "three-in-one" in Jakarta R. Hanna, G. Kreindler et al chart graph map *Science* v357 no6346 p89 Jl 7 2017

GIVE ME A BRAKE S. STALL *Indianapolis Monthly* v40 no5 p13 Ja 2017

How to beat the traffic M. Anderson color *Science* v357 no6346 p36 Jl 7 2017

Is Your Supply Chain Ready for the Congestion Crisis? G. Stalk Jr. and P. Paranikas *Harvard Business Review Digital Articles* p2 Je 22 2015

Jammed Cities W. Fulton *Governing* v30 no5 p25 F 2017

Traffic G. TARLACH color *Discover* v38 no7 p74 S 2017

Why the Future of ECommerce Depends on Better Roads E. Humes *Harvard Business Review Digital Articles* p2 Ap 8 2016

Traffic congestion—Humor

08:01:30 G. EICHLER cartoon *New Yorker* v93 no8 p29 Ap 10 2017

Traffic engineering—United States

Why the Future of ECommerce Depends on Better Roads E. Humes *Harvard Business Review Digital Articles* p2 Ap 8 2016

Traffic flow—Management

ZEBRAS IN THE STREETS I. Henderson color *Atlantic* v319 no2 p26 Mr 2017

Traffic incident management

Making Trains Run on Time J. Sanburn color diag *Time* v189 no13 p38 Ap 10 2017

Traffic regulations

See also

Drugged driving—Law & legislation

Traffic safety

1-PERCENT FASTER J. L. Stein color *Cycle World* v56 no4 p30 My 2017

A Decision That Could Save Your Life M. Monticello color graph *Consumer Reports* v82 no8 p52 Ag 2017

Ezra Dyer color *Car & Driver* v62 no6 p36 D 2016

GOING PLACES? Z. Robert color *Iceland Review* v54 no5 p76 S-O 2016

HOW TO Arrive alive color *Good Housekeeping* v264 no4 p83 Ap 2017

A Path to Safer Roadways color *Consumer Reports* v82 no12 p5 D 2017

The Road Ahead: BIKE LANES, CROSSWALKS, RAMPED-UP POLICE ENFORCEMENT— THERE'S LOTS OF CHANGE AFOOT AS LOS ANGELES MOVES TO REDUCE TRAFFIC-RELATED DEATHS S. CARPENTER *Los Angeles Magazine* v62 no9 p76 S 2017

The Thread H. S. Moffic, H. Cohen et al *New York Times Magazine* p9 Ja 22 2017

TICKLE TUMMY HILL J. ARTERBURN *Outdoor Life* v224 no9 p78 N 2017

Unsafe at Any Speed J. PELINI cartoon *Atlantic* v319 no2 p22 Mr 2017

Traffic signs & signals

Signs Of The Times bw color *National Geographic Kids* no474 p30 O 2017

Trager, Eric

Springtime for Morsi *Commentary* v141 no10 p1 D 2016

Springtime for Morsi M. J. TOTTEN *Commentary* v142 no5 p45 D 2016

Tragically Hip (Performer)

A farewell for the ages M. BARCLAY color *Maclean's* v129

no48/49 p70 D 5 2016

Traiger, Lisa

The More Things Change... *Dance Magazine* v90 no11 p16 N 2016

A New Funding Model for Dance? *Dance Magazine* v91 no6 p18 Je 2017

TRAIL, JESSE VERNON

EDIBLE TREES *American Forests* v123 no1 p16 Wint/Spr 2017

Trail, Pepper

The FEATHER DETECTIVE C. SWEENEY *Audubon* v118 no6 p28 Wint 2016

Trail bike trails

LINES IN THE DIRT [Cover story] D. O'NEIL bw color *Bike Magazine* v24 no7 p60 S 2017

Trail bikes

analysis paralysis r. palmer color *Bike Magazine* v24 no1 p21 Ja/F 2017

RACING THE LONG WAY TO RENO [Cover story] S. OCHSNER color *Dirt Sports + Off-Road* v51 no1 p10 Ja 2017

RIDING IN THE CLOUDS S. Macdonald color *Cycle World* v56 no5 p50 Je 2017

ROB MACCACHREN M. EMERY color *Dirt Sports + Off-Road* v51 no9 p20 S 2017

Trail bikes—Evaluation

CANNONDALE SCALPEL SE 2 M. Yozell color *Bicycling* v58 no8 p62 S 2017

FIRST LOOK: 2017 YAMAHA WOLVERINE R-SPEC EPS SPECIAL EDITION [Cover story] M. EMERY color *Dirt Sports + Off-Road* v51 no1 p16 Ja 2017

Liv Pique L. Kemp color *Bike Magazine* v24 no5 p92 Jl 2017

THINGS COME APART K. Dupzyk color *Popular Mechanics* p24 S 2017

Trail bikes—Maintenance & repair

RETRO OFFROAD RACING TO RESTORE TEAM CAR FOR ORMHOF INDUCTEE VALENTA color *Dirt Sports + Off-Road* v51 no1 p8 Ja 2017

Trail horse class

Barn-Bored to Trail-Ready [Cover story] H. S. Thomas color *Horse & Rider* v56 no5 p44 My 2017

Blazing a New Trail R. E. Riley *Trail Rider* v29 no4 p6 My 2017

Fix Showmanship Dullness color *Horse & Rider* v56 no5 p73 My 2017

Hind-End 'L' [Cover story] L. Place and J. Paulson color *Horse & Rider* v56 no5 p31 My 2017

The 'Man of Trail' SHARES HIS TIPS T. Kimura and N. Chirico color *Horse & Rider* v55 no12 p52 D 2016

Trail riding

8 Great Gaited Getaways A. PAVIA color *Horse & Rider* v56 no10 p80 O 2017

Alone on the Trail J. GOODNIGHT and H. MELOCCO color *Horse & Rider* v56 no11 p46 N 2017

Around the Campfire D. H. Sempter, K. B. Allen et al color *Trail Rider* v29 no1 p6 Ja/F 2017

BREED-ASSOCIATION TRAIL-RIDING PROGRAMS color *Trail Rider* v29 no3 p67 Ap 2017

Celebrate Earth Day R. EVERSOLE color *Trail Rider* v29 no3 p16 Ap 2017

Dream Buddy on a Trail Ride S. Savage, E. Gilbreath et al cartoon *Horse & Rider* v56 no3 p72 Mr 2017

Guest-Ranch Guide color *Trail Rider* v29 no3 p84 Ap 2017

High-Desert Adventure C. KAYANO color *Trail Rider* v29 no4 p58 My 2017

How to Change a Trailer Tire R. GIMENEZ color *Trail Rider* v29 no1 p18 Ja/F 2017

The 'Man of Trail' SHARES HIS TIPS T. Kimura and N. Chirico color *Horse & Rider* v55 no12 p52 D 2016

New for You J. Paulson *Horse & Rider* v56 no7 p14 Jl 2017

Open a Trail Gate J. GOODNIGHT and H. MELOCCO color *Horse & Rider* v56 no8 p46 Ag 2017

The Open Road T. SCHEVE and N. K. SCHEVE color *Trail Rider* v29 no1 p56 Ja/F 2017

ORGANIZED TRAIL RIDES *Trail Rider* v29 no3 p76 Ap 2017

Oskar the Invisible Horse B. GODDARD color *Trail Rider* v29 no4 p72 My 2017

Ride for a Cause J. Sullivan color *Trail Rider* v29 no2 p28 Mr 2017

front lines n. formosa bw *Bike Magazine* v24 no7 p23 S 2017

See the Forest for the Trees L. LANCASTER map *Backpacker* v45 no1 p25 Ja 2017

Trails—Canada

See also

Trans Canada Trail

FROM SEA TO SHINING SEA, MORE OR LESS J. MARKU-SOFF color *Maclean's* v130 no9 p29 O 2017

The great Canadian road trip map *Maclean's* no1 p15 F 17 2017

WHERE NOBODY KNOWS YOUR TRAIL NAME T. Alvarez color *Backpacker* v45 no1 p80 Ja 2017

Trails—Colorado

See also

Colorado Trail (Colo.)

Discomfort Zone D. LEWON color *Backpacker* v45 no2 p8 Mr 2017

Trails—Design & construction

Slow Children C. KALMAN color *Climbing* no350 p26 D 2016/Ja 2017

Trails—Evaluation

PACKARD MESA TRAIL R. STIEVE *Arizona Highways* v93 no1 p54 Ja 2017

Trails—Georgia

SCOUT ABOUT TOWN L. SCHOLZ *Atlanta* v56 no12 p44 Ap 2017

Trails—Idaho

Along with Tom M. STUBBS *Idaho Magazine* v16 no2 p18 N 2016

Trails—Maintenance & repair

GIVING BACK S. RICHARDS color *Dirt Sports + Off-Road* v51 no9 p58 S 2017

MOVING DIRT & GRAVEL M. Boncher color *Cabin Living* p68 S 2017

Year-Round, Paved-Trail Surface Maintenance T. Houck *Parks & Recreation* v51 no11 p22 N 2016

Trails—Missouri

THE ROAD TO RIDE B. BRYAN bw color *Missouri Life* v44 no5 p48 Ag 2017

Trails—Montana

THE LONG WAY 'ROUND E. KWAK-HEFFERAN il *Backpacker* p83 My 2017

Trails—New Hampshire

EATON, NEW HAMPSHIRE color *Runner's World* v52 no8 p8 S 2017

Trails—North Carolina

Mystery, Adventure, and Julia B. Miller color *Climbing* no357 p28 N 2017

NECESSARY RISKS J. Plunkett *Climbing* no357 p32 N 2017

Trails—Oregon

WILD EAST N. FORMOSA bw color *Bike Magazine* v24 no7 p80 S 2017

Trails—Public use

Protect Private Trails D. Moyer color *Trail Rider* v29 no2 p30 Mr 2017

Trails—Safety measures

Boost Your Wildlife Savvy H. S. Thomas color *Horse & Rider* v56 no7 p72 Jl 2017

Trails—Societies, etc.

Protect Private Trails D. Moyer color *Trail Rider* v29 no2 p30 Mr 2017

Trails—United States

See also

Appalachian Trail

10 BEST WALKS IN AMERICA K. Benjamin cartoon *Prevention* p46 Mr 2017

America's Wildest Hikes T. VanderMolen color *Backpacker* p61 Ag 2017

The Best Walk in Newport M. Allen *Yankee* p91 Mr 2017

Exploring a 'Last Great Place' P. Voskamp *Yankee* p93 Mr 2017

Go Big: Superhike A. DRUMMOND map *Backpacker* p28 Ag 2017

HIKE MORE, DRIVE LESS P. CHISHOLM color *Backpacker* p56 My 2017

Local Hikes Just Got Better D. LEWON *Backpacker* p10 Ag 2017

MIND THE GAPS W. ". Kemsley Jr. *Backpacker* v45 no1 p75 Ja 2017

THE PATH LESS TRAVELED C. Gerard color *Backpacker* v45 no1 p86 Ja 2017

ROOF OF AMERICA M. Horjus color *Backpacker* v45 no1 p68 Ja 2017

ROOM WITH A VIEW M. Horjus color *Backpacker* v45 no1 p78 Ja 2017

Saddle Up for Spring R. Eversole color *Trail Rider* v29 no2 p24 Mr 2017

Trails—Washington (D.C.)

Cure summit fever color *Backpacker* p14 Ag 2017

Goat Lake Loop, Gifford-Pinchot National Forest, Washington [Cover story] T. VANDERMOLEN diag *Backpacker* p96 Ag 2017

PARK YOURSELF HERE M. Graham color *Washingtonian Magazine* v52 no7 p116 Ap 2017

Train (Performer)

Patrick Monahan S. Stall *Indianapolis Monthly* v40 no10 p23 Je 2017

Traina, Jimmy

Easy Listening color *Sports Illustrated* v127 no6 p17 Ag 28 2017

Traina, Vanessa

my style color *InStyle* v24 no3 p221 Mr 2017

Training

See also

Occupational training

Finding Carawich J. Wofford bw *Practical Horseman* v45 no2 p16 F 2017

Ja, Ja — Muskeln Machen! J. CISSIK bw chart *Muscle & Performance* v9 no7 p18 Jl 2017

MENTAL CHILLNESS [Cover story] B. Stulberg cartoon color *Runner's World* v52 no3 p46 Ap 2017

News BITS color *Practical Horseman* v45 no11 p66 N 2017

P-Hacker Confessions: Daryl Bern and Me S. VYSE *Skeptical Inquirer* v41 no5 p25 S/O 2017

Teaching personal initiative beats traditional training in boosting small business in West Africa F. Campos, M. Frese et al chart graph *Science* v357 no6357 p1287 S 22 2017

Two Types of Diversity Training That Really Work A. Lindsey, E. King et al *Harvard Business Review Digital Articles* p1 Jl 28 2017

Training Day (TV program)

ALSO COMING . . J. Russell *TV Guide* v65 no2 p39 Ja 2 2017

Everything New Is Old Again E. Dockterman color *Time* v189 no4 p49 F 6 2017

Training Day L. Acken *TV Guide* v65 no6 p34 Ja 30 2017

Training of athletes

Roll for the Flow L. McGlashan and J. WUEBBEN color *Muscle & Performance* v9 no11 p21 N 2017

Tsewang Rinzing W. Joan Biddlecombe color *Tricycle: The Buddhist Review* v26 no4 p22 Summ 2017

Training of boxers (Sports)

Poverty vs. Professional Fighting in Southeast Asia A. Graceffo color *Black Belt* v55 no6 p22 O/N 2017

YOUNG GLOVE M. M. KASHINO *Washingtonian Magazine* v53 no1 p26 O 2017

Training of dogs

BEAST MODE A. ROBINSON color *Outdoor Life* v224 no8 pW5 O 2017

FIVE WAYS TO KILL YOUR DOG color *Outdoor Life* v224 no6 p39 Ag 2017

FOWL PLAY T. E. NICKENS color *Field & Stream* v122 no2 p84 Je/Jl 2017

Get Your Dog To Behave Around Company N. B. McGough and P. York color *Southern Living* v52 no4 p50 Ap 2017

A Helping Paw M. W. Schwartz color *Missouri Life* v44 no2 p16 Ap 2017

LACEY AND THE LION B. FITZPATRICK color *Outdoor Life* v224 no6 p53 Ag 2017

THE UNDERDOG T. DOKKEN and T. PETERSON color *Outdoor Life* v224 no6 p46 Ag 2017

WONDER DOGS color *Outdoor Life* v224 no6 p44 Ag 2017

YOUR PUP'S FIRST YEAR S. LINDEN color *Outdoor Life* v224 no3 p28 Ap 2017

Training of hockey players

ICE FLOW J. Fuchs and T. Keith color *Sports Illustrated* v127 no9 p16 S 25 2017

COUNTRY'S GREATEST REVOLUTIONARIES. SO WHY DO AMERICANS KEEP FORGETTING WE EXIST? J. ANDERSON-MINSHALL bw color *Advocate* no1091 p74 Je/Jl 2017

SAY HER NAME: As one murder case is closed, another begins, marking 16 trans women killed before August N. BROVERMAN and D. GUERRERO *Advocate* no1093 p8 O/N 2017

Transgender rights

New Gender New Finances B. Steverman color *Bloomberg Businessweek* no4502 p56 D 5 2016

Transgender rights—Lawsuits & claims

Trans Rights at the High Court color *Advocate* no1089 p37 F/Mr 2017

Transgender students

"What Would You Think If I Walked Into the Girls' Bathroom?" A. STANLEY color *Seventeen* v76 no3 p20 My 2017

Transgender teenagers

In Her Skin: Growing Up Trans color *Publishers Weekly* v263 no47 p76f N 21 2016

Transgenderism

Womanhood Redefined N. VARGAS-COOPER *American Conservative* v16 no1 p27 Ja/F 2017

Transgender people—United States—Legal status, laws, etc.

Bathroom Foofaraw *Reason* v48 no7 p6 D 2016

Transgenic insects

Mosquitoes to the Rescue J. Hsu color diag map *Scientific American* v315 no5 p17 N 2016

Transgenic mice

Mighty Mouse J. Adler *Smithsonian* v47 no8 p54 D 2016

Transgenic organisms

See also
    Transgenic plants

AGED POPCORN *Successful Farming* v115 no4 p10 Mr 2017

Changes in the microbiota cause genetically modified Anopheles to spread in a population A. Pike, Y. Dong et al graph *Science* v357 no6358 p1396 S 29 2017

EASY CHAIR: The Spaceship and the Moose W. Kirn *Harper's Magazine* p5 O 2017

Flacking for GMOs: How the Biotech Industry Cultivates Positive Media P. D. Thacker color *Progressive* v81 no6 p34 Ag/S 2017

Genome Fidelity and the American Chestnut E. BRISTER *Issues in Science & Technology* v33 no4 p41 Summ 2017

GET BEYOND THE SCIENCE J. Scott *Successful Farming* v115 no1 p17 Ja 2017

GMOs J. HIRSCH color *Popular Mechanics* p108 S 2017

Hey Mr. Green! What's the greenest way to weatherize? B. Schildgen *Sierra* v102 no5 p12 St/O 2017

THE NEXT GENERATION OF GMOs D. PERLS *Nation* v305 no11 p17 O 30 2017

YEAST OF BURDEN M. ZARASKA cartoon *Mother Jones* v41 no6 p64 N/D 2016

Transgenic organisms—Risk assessment

Engineered Food Holds Our Future H. Jahren color *Time* v188 no16/17 p78 O 24 2016

Transgenic plants

Although Small, Markets Have Been Expanding for GE Crops With Traits That Increase Nutrient Content or Improve Taste J. McFadden *Amber Waves: The Economics of Food, Farming, Natural Resources, & Rural America* p19 Ag 2017

China aims to sow a revolution with GM seed takeover M. Hvistendahl color *Science* v356 no6333 p16 Ap 7 2017

Genetically Modified Alfalfa Production in the United States S. J. Wechsler and D. Milkove *Amber Waves: The Economics of Food, Farming, Natural Resources, & Rural America* p1 My 2017

Message Control B. Borel color graph *Scientific American* v317 no4 p68 O 2017

THE NEXT GENERATION OF GMOs D. PERLS *Nation* v305 no11 p17 O 30 2017

Quick Hits A. Marks map *Scientific American* v317 no1 p22 Jl 2017

Raising Lettuce, Buddhist Style J. D. OLIVER color *Tricycle: The Buddhist Review* v27 no1 p28 Fall 2017

Traits Under the Lens G. Gullickson *Successful Farming* v115 no2 p44 F 2017

Transgenic plants—Export & import trade

CHINA SLOWS DOWN APPROVAL OF GMO VARIETIES *Successful Farming* v115 no7 p9 My 2017

Transgenic plants—Law & legislation

CHINA SLOWS DOWN APPROVAL OF GMO VARIETIES *Successful Farming* v115 no7 p9 My 2017

Transhumanism

THE BIONIC CANDIDATE A. Marantz cartoon *New Yorker* v92 no37 p34 N 14 2016

Do-It-Yourself Transhumanism A. Popescu bw color *Bloomberg Businessweek* no4512 p34 F 20 2017

Transhumanism Is Inevitable R. Bailey *Reason* v48 no7 p18 D 2016

Transient ischemic attack—Risk factors

Possible stroke warning signs *Mayo Clinic Health Letter* v34 no11 p6 N 2016

Transient ischemic attack—Treatment

Possible stroke warning signs *Mayo Clinic Health Letter* v34 no11 p6 N 2016

Transients (Electricity)—Equipment & supplies

Geeni Surge: This smart surge protector falls short on automation and documentation G. FLEISHMAN color *Macworld - Digital Edition* v34 no10 p92 O 2017

Transistors

See also
    Thin film transistors

MoS2 transistors with 1-nanometer gate lengths S. B. Desai, S. R. Madhvapathy et al bibl color graph *Science* v354 no6308 p99 O 7 2016

Transit of Mercury (Planet)

Three Centuries, One Scope J. Church and W. Murray *Sky & Telescope* v132 no6 p84 D 2016

Transition Bike Co.

TRANSITION PATROL CARBON A. Smith color *Bike Magazine* v23 no9 p86 D 2016

Transitional justice

The Long Shadow of Genocide in Rwanda S. THOMSON *Current History* v116 no790 p183 My 2017

Transitional justice—History

Remembrance of Things Past S. Lipscomb *History Today* v67 no4 p40 Ap 2017

Translating & interpreting

Hard data and human empathy D. Collins color *Science* v357 no6359 p142 O 6 2017

THE TURNING SKY S. B. Morrow *Lapham's Quarterly* v10 no2 p199 Spr 2017

Translational research

The need for a translational science of democracy M. A. Neblo, W. Minozzi et al bibl color *Science* v355 no6328 p914 Mr 3 2017

Translations

Eleven Pleasures of Translating L. Davis bw *New York Review of Books* v63 no19 p22 D 8 2016

Hard data and human empathy D. Collins color *Science* v357 no6359 p142 O 6 2017

Translators

See also
    Translating & interpreting

BRINGING BANDAR HOME J. COON color *Reason* v49 no6 p26 N 2017

FORTY QUESTIONS *Harper's Magazine* no2007 p11 Ag 2017

Lost in Translation T. A. FRAIL *Smithsonian* v47 no7 p68 N 2016

Translators (Computer programs)

The End of the Language Barrier D. GERSHGORN and L. KRATOCHWILL color *Popular Science* v288 no6 p84 N/D 2016

Translocation (Genetics)

Ratchet-like polypeptide translocation mechanism of the AAA+ disaggregase Hsp104 S. N. Gates, A. L. Yokom et al diag *Science* v357 no6348 p273 Jl 21 2017

Transmedia storytelling

A NARRATIVE ACROSS PLATFORMS: Transmedia, politics, and encouraging youth authorship anywhere and anytime A. Garcia *Literacy Today (2411-7862)* v35 no2 p34 S/O 2017

Transmission electron microscopes

A droplet that won't freeze harbors a crystal that won't melt A. G. Smart *Physics Today* v69 no10 p18 O 2016

Transmission electron microscopes—Design & construction

Electron microscopy gets a multicolor makeover Sung Chang

Physics Today v70 no1 p14 Ja 2017

Transmission of texts

See also

Errata (Publishing)

Transmitters (Communication)

Tag, They're It L. SCHLEY color *Discover* v38 no4 p18 My 2017

Transmitters (Communication)—Evaluation

Lectrosonics is Dedicated to Pushing the Envelope on Wireless Technology *Stage Directions* v30 no3 p40 Mr 2017

Transparency (Optics)

A Forum for Integrating the Life Sciences J. M. VERDIER and S. L. COLLINS *BioScience* v67 no10 p871 O 2017

Transparency in government

OPEN CITY M. FUNK *New York Times Magazine* p31 O 23 2016

'The Most Transparent Administration in History' C. J. CIARAMELLA color *Reason* v48 no9 p10 F 2017

Transparency and Truth D. C. Dennett *NPQ: New Perspectives Quarterly* v34 no2 p44 My 2017

Transparency in government—History—21st century

The Real Cost of 'Forced Transparency' I. Bremmer *Time* v189 no11 p14 Mr 27 2017

Transparency in organizations

The Case Against Pay Transparency T. Zenger *Harvard Business Review Digital Articles* p1 S 30 2016

Climate scientists open up their black boxes to scrutiny P. Voosen color *Science* v354 no6311 p401 O 28 2016

Health Care Transparency Should Be About Strategy, Not Marketing T. H. Lee *Harvard Business Review Digital Articles* p2 My 21 2015

How to foster an open and honest culture A. Heal *People Management* p50 Je 2017

How Well Is Vanguard's Boss Paid? A. Melin graph *Bloomberg Businessweek* no4508 p33 Ja 23 2017

Keeping Up with the "Clean Label" Movement A. Winston *Harvard Business Review Digital Articles* p2 O 30 2015

McDonald's and the Challenges of a Modern Supply Chain S. New *Harvard Business Review Digital Articles* p2 F 4 2015

We used to withhold information from staff - now we tell them the truth: Why transparent communication means the charitys HR director can cross the car park without facing angry employees *People Management* p20 My 2017

What Makes Doctors Value Patient Feedback D. E. Mylod and T. H. Lee *Harvard Business Review Digital Articles* p2 N 30 2015

Why Cleveland Clinic Shares Its Outcomes Data with the World M. W. Kattan *Harvard Business Review Digital Articles* p2 S 22 2015

Why Keeping Salaries a Secret May Hurt Your Company D. Burkus *Harvard Business Review Digital Articles* p2 Mr 10 2016

Transparent (TV program)

My Obsessions... *TV Guide* v65 no14 p12 Ap 3 2017

Transparent A. Bacle, K. Connolly et al color *Entertainment Weekly* no1482/1483 p109 S 22 2017

Transplantation of organs, tissues, etc.

See also

Heart transplantation

Kidney transplants

Plastic surgery

Canadian Innovations in Organ Donation and Transplantation A. Humar color *Maclean's* v130 no9 p34 O 2017

Fall into a new book color *Science* v357 no6355 p964 S 8 2017

HUMAN ORGANS FROM ANIMAL BODIES J. C. Izpisúa Belmonte cartoon color diag *Scientific American* v315 no5 p32 N 2016

Transplantation of organs, tissues, etc.—Economic aspects

THE COST OF TRANSPLANTS color diag *Fortune* v176 no4 p23 S 15 2017

Transponders

DOCK BOX color *Sea Magazine* v109 no8 p32 Ag 2017

Transport for London (Organization)

Who I am *People Management* p49 S 2017

Transport of sick & wounded

See also

Ambulance service

Transport planes

Hot Wings Z. MATTHEW color *Los Angeles Magazine* v62 no10

p20 O 2017

Transportation

See also

Air travel

Bus transportation

Delivery of goods

Ocean travel

Public transit

Railroad travel

Railroads

BUSINESS OR PLEASURE C. WARE cartoon *New Yorker* v93 no16 p72 Je 5 2017

Clearing the Line: In the Railroad's Heyday T. WAITE *Idaho Magazine* v16 no10 p27 Jl 2017

FUTURE WORLD: Transportation K. DE SEVE color *National Geographic Kids* no470 p20 My 2017

Last Look D. Kidd *Governing* v30 no12 p64 S 2017

ROUTE RECALCULATION: NAVIGATING WHERE WE ARE, WHERE WE'RE GOING, AND WHAT WE'VE MISSED ALONG THE WAY R. SHAKLEE diag *Phi Kappa Phi Forum* v97 no1 p23 Spr 2017

Sick Transit D. C. Vock *Governing* v30 no2 p46 N 2016

Technology Is Changing Transportation, and Cities Should Adapt S. M. Knupfer, E. Hannon et al *Harvard Business Review Digital Articles* p2 S 13 2017

Too Many Infrastructure Projects Go It Alone R. M. Kanter *Harvard Business Review Digital Articles* p2 My 14 2015

What the Auto Industry Can Learn from Cloud Computing M. Wessel *Harvard Business Review Digital Articles* p2 Jl 29 2015

Transportation & state—Texas

Taken for a Ride M. HEMINGWAY color *Weekly Standard* v22 no41 p14 Jl 3 2017

Transportation & the environment

Next Stop: Anybody's Guess: There are no crystal balls in transportation. Some judges don't understand that A. Ehrenhalt color *Governing* v30 no11 p14 Ag 2017

Transportation industry

See also

Scenic transportation

Bringing the Dream Horse Home D. E. Barber color *Dressage Today* v23 no4 p48 D 2016

How to Think About the Future of Cars M. Wessel *Harvard Business Review Digital Articles* p2 Jl 27 2015

TAKING THE INFORMATION AGE ON THE ROAD D. F. McCourt color *Maclean's* v129 no51/52 p15 D 26 2016

Transportation of school children

UBER, BUT FOR SCHOOL BUSES T. KOTESKEY color *Reason* v49 no3 p10 Jl 2017

Transportation—California

Where the Rubber Meets the Road M. SEGAL *Los Angeles Magazine* p14 F 2017

Transportation—Computer network resources

¿Cómo se dice 'Uber'? E. Newcomer color *Bloomberg Businessweek* no4495 p25 O 17 2016

Transportation—New York (State)—New York

Just Build It *Commonweal* v144 no12 p5 Jl 7 2017

A Look at New York's Ambitious Infrastructure Plans F. A. BERNSTEIN color *Architectural Record* v205 no2 p20 F 2017

Transportation—Rates

Everyone Hates Uber's Surge Pricing - Here's How to Fix It U. M. Dholakia *Harvard Business Review Digital Articles* p2 D 21 2015

Transportation—Safety measures

GA AND THE NTSB'S MOST WANTED LIST S. Pope *Flying* v144 no3 p10 Mr 2017

Transportation—Social aspects

A Fare Deal M. Haiken *Sierra* v101 no4 p47 Jl/Ag 2016

Transportation—United States—Planning

Growing Smart: The right kind of transit is crucial for growing cities S. Beyer *Governing* v30 no12 p23 S 2017

Transposons

The Difference Makers [Cover story] T. Hesman Saey color diag *Science News* v191 no10 p22 My 27 2017

Jumping genes are part of all that makes us human E. Quill color *Science News* v191 no10 p2 My 27 2017

Poisons, antidotes, and selfish genes N. Phadnis diag *Science* v356

no6342 p1013 Je 9 2017

Transversus abdominis muscle

RECTUS THE RIGHT WAY K. A. FETTERS chart color *Muscle & Performance* v8 no12 p24 D 2016

Trant, Andrew

Humanity for Habitat K. Moore *Natural History* v125 no1 p6 D 2016/Ja 2017

Trapanese, Erin Mack

Helping Teachers Become Leaders *Education Digest* v83 no3 p37 N 2017

Trapezius muscle

2 Exercises to Prevent "Dowager's Hump" cartoon *Prevention* v69 no1 p17 Ja 2017

Traphagan, John

We're Thinking About Organizational Culture All Wrong color *Harvard Business Review Digital Articles* p2 Ja 6 2017

Why "Company Culture" Is a Misleading Term *Harvard Business Review Digital Articles* p2 Ap 21 2015

Trapnell, Cole

Comprehensive single-cell transcriptional profiling of a multicellular organism diag *Science* v357 no6352 p661 Ag 18 2017

TRAPPIST-1

7 Earth-sized planets circle nearby star A. YEAGER chart *Science News* v191 no5 p6 Mr 18 2017

7 Earth-Size Planets Orbit Dim Star C. M. Carlisle *Sky & Telescope* v133 no6 p12 Je 2017

Are We Alone? S. W. DRIMMER color *National Geographic Kids* no474 p16 O 2017

DETAILS ARRIVE ON TRAPPIST-1'S OUTERMOST PLANET N. Kiefert color *Astronomy* v45 no9 p12 S 2017

Finding aliens B. BERMAN color *Astronomy* v45 no9 p10 S 2017

Like This World of Ours M. BARTUSIAK color *Natural History* v125 no5 p10 My 2017

staring into Earth's past S. Fecht cartoon *Popular Science* v289 no5 p20 S/O 2017

A system of seven worlds D. J. Eicher color *Astronomy* v45 no7 p8 Jl 2017

TRAPPIST-1's planets may trade life color *Astronomy* v45 no10 p15 O 2017

Trappists

Conducive Atmosphere A. Hadhazy *Natural History* v124 no10 p6 N 2016

Trapsoul (Music)

Bryson Tiller M. Rich color *Current Biography* v78 no3 p78 Mr 2017

Trash bags

Discovery C. Lyons color *Backpacker* p70 Je 2017

Trashed (Theatrical production)

KINETIC CLUTTER L. WARNECKE color *Chicago* v66 no3 p52 Mr 2017

Trasi, Amita

The Color of Our Sky *Publishers Weekly* v264 no7 p47 F 13 2017

Trask, Harry

Game Changer bw *Yankee* p144 Mr 2017

Trason, Ann

ASK THE EXPERTS color *Runner's World* v52 no1 p50 Ja/F 2017

Traub, Courtney

British strive to build interfaith bridges amid terrorist attacks color *Christian Century* v134 no15 p14 Jl 19 2017

Traub, James

MAKE POLAND GREAT AGAIN *New York Times Magazine* p42 N 6 2016

The Strangely Contentious Lives of the Quincy Adamses G. S. Wood color *New York Review of Books* v63 no19 p55 D 8 2016

Think Locally, Act Locally: Michael Ignatieff questions whether universalist values can survive the disruptive forces of globalization *New York Times Book Review* p19 O 15 2017

Trauger, Sunia A.

Potential role of intratumor bacteria in mediating tumor resistance to the chemotherapeutic drug gemcitabine diag *Science* v357 no6356 p1156 S 15 2017

Traumatology

COLD REMEDY N. TWILLEY cartoon color *New Yorker* v92 no39 p36 N 28 2016

Traurig, Christine

PUSHING AWAY FROM THE BIT [Cover story] color *Dressage Today* v23 no4 p24 D 2016

Trautman, Brian

SV Delos A. Schell color *Sail* v48 no11 p12 N 2017

TRAUTMAN, SUSAN K.

Restoration and Renewal *Parks & Recreation* v51 no10 p8 O 2016

Travel

See also

    Adventure travel

    Air travel

    Authors—Travel

    Automobile travel

    Bus travel

    Business travel

    College student travel

    Luxury travel

    Motorcycle touring

    Ocean travel

    Packing luggage

    Railroad travel

    River travel

    Travel with horses

10 Tips for Traveling Solo with your horse H. Ellis-Ashburn bw color *Equus* no472 p54 Ja 2017

18 GREAT SUMMER ESCAPES *Cincinnati Magazine* p50 Je 2017

3 GIRLFRIEND GETAWAYS color *Health* v30 no9 p20 N 2016

Age of Experience color *Conde Nast Traveler* v52 no8 p16 S 2017

ALL AROUND Missouri S. LOUIS *Missouri Life* v43 no6 p95 O/N 2016

ARDENT SPRITS M. W. Spencer color *Louisiana Life* v37 no6 p8 Jl/Ag 2017

ask REDBOOK color *Redbook* p16 My 2017

AUSTIN, TEXAS A. FLANGO *Cincinnati Magazine* v50 no6 p46 Mr 2017

BANKS *Interview* v46 no10 p32 D 2016/Ja 2017

Beautiful Bequia Z. Prochazka color *Sail* v48 no10 p93 O 2017

BEING PRESENT C. Moss color *House Beautiful* v159 no2 p57 Mr 2017

better *Better Homes & Gardens* v94 no12 p143 D 2016

BOTANICAL BEVERLY HILLS A. Preiser color *Sunset* v238 no5 p32 My 2017

BRINGING VIKING-ERA ICELAND TO LIFE *Iceland Review* v54 no6 p104 N/D 2016

Buckeye Street: Get to know the darling of Kokomo's historic district L. FISHER *Indianapolis Monthly* v12 no40 p38 Ag 2017

College! Money! Jobs! C. THORP color *Seventeen* v76 no4 p58 Jl/Ag 2017

DESERT COOL J. Scatena chart color *Sunset* v238 no5 p26 My 2017

THE DUCKS STOP HERE G. BETHGE color *Outdoor Life* v224 no1 p70 D 2016/Ja 2017

THE EXPEDITIONS J. Heinerth, N. Martinez et al color map *Canadian Geographic* v137 no4 p49 Jl/Ag 2017

FALL HIKINGS & BIKING P. N. MORAN *Missouri Life* v43 no6 p63 O/N 2016

Food Fright D. Paul *Indianapolis Monthly* v40 no5 p132 Ja 2017

Frigid Embrace: A Backcountry Winter Introduction J. DALME *Idaho Magazine* v16 no10 p49 Jl 2017

FROM THE COURTHOUSE STEPS *Missouri Life* v43 no6 p10 O/N 2016

GARIBALDI LAKE, BRITISH COLUMBIA color *Runner's World* v52 no5 p8 Je 2017

GATEWAY TO THE ISLANDS: CHANNEL ISLANDS HARBOR IS FAMILY AND FOODIE FRIENDLY, AND ITS LOCATION IS IDEAL FOR A TRIP TO THE OFFSHORE PARK AND SANCTUARY S. SHIBATA color map *Sea Magazine* v109 no7 pCA-1 Jl 2017

Go Fly with Her color *O, The Oprah Magazine* p23 Mr 2017

gringo syndrome m. ferrentino bw *Bike Magazine* v24 no5 p50 Jl 2017

Guide to Missouri Bed-and-Breakfasts Unique Hotels *Missouri Life* v43 no6 p92 O/N 2016

HARD BALL R. NELSON *Virginia Living* v15 no3 p100 Ap 2017

have a nicer trip R. RABKIN PEACHMAN *Parents* v91 no11 p142 N 2016

The United States of Dogs G. Norman color *Weekly Standard* v22 no24 p30 F 27 2017

Travel with horses

Road-Ready Tips B. Avila and J. Paulson color *Horse & Rider* v56 no7 p47 Jl 2017

socially speaking color *Horse & Rider* v56 no10 p24 O 2017

Travel writing

THE SEVEN-YEAR ITCH P. Leigh Fermor *Harper's Magazine* p16 S 2017

Travel bans, 2017 (U.S.)

AAAS Members Stand Up for Science M. Jarvis color *Science* v357 no6349 p365 Jl 28 2017

America, Be Beautiful C. González-Andrieu *America* v217 no2 p54 Jl 24 2017

BANNED TOGETHER T. MURPHY color *Mother Jones* v42 no4 p39 Jl/Ag 2017

BEFORE THE BAN A. A. ABRAHAMIAN bw color *New Republic* v248 no4 p26 Ap 2017

Executive Disorder J. LILEKS *National Review* v69 no3 p41 F 20 2017

EYE ON 45 color *Science* v356 no6343 p1105 Je 16 2017

The Justices Agree to Grapple With Travel Bans and Phantoms D. V. Drehle color *Time* v190 no2/3 p7 Jl 10-17 2017

Legislative Background on Immigration *Congressional Digest* v96 no3 p11 Mr 2017

New Travel Ban Helps U.S.-Iraq Relations but Still Stings Elsewhere J. Malsin and R. Collard color *Time* v189 no10 p7 Mr 20 2017

New travel ban still anti-Muslim, critics charge *Christian Century* v134 no8 p1 Ap 12 2017

Over 150 Scientific Organizations, Sixty-Two Nobel Laureates Urge Repeal of Controversial Immigration Ban K. FRAZIER *Skeptical Inquirer* v41 no3 p5 My/Je 2017

The Pros and Cons of the President's Immigrant Travel Ban C. Higgins *Congressional Digest* v96 no3 p26 Mr 2017

Revised Travel Ban *Congressional Digest* v96 no4 p30 Ap 2017

ROCKIN' THE FULL TRUMP E. Sullivan color *Esquire* p44 Ap 2017

Second Nature B. Gage *New York Times Magazine* p11 Mr 26 2017

Sheer Lunacy D. FOSTER *National Review* v69 no3 p56 F 20 2017

Travel ban confusion continues even after Supreme Court weighs in K. Clarke color *America* v217 no2 p16 Jl 24 2017

Travel ban would slam university in North Korea R. Stone color *Science* v357 no6349 p342 Jl 28 2017

Trump's Travel Ban Could Hit Colleges E. Fry color diag *Fortune* v175 no4 p14 Mr 15 2017

Trump's Travel Ban Might Escape Judgment T. Berenson map *Time* v190 no14 p12 O 9 2017

TRUMP'S TRAVEL BAN P. SMITH, T. Erdbrink et al *New York Times Upfront* v149 no10 p6 Mr 13 2017

The Week color il *National Review* v69 no19 p4 O 16 2017

Travel—Competitions

WIN A YOSEMITE ADVENTURE! T. Enriquez color *Sunset* v238 no4 p106 Ap 2017

Travel—Economic aspects

Cuba Libre A. Ellin color *Money* v45 no10 p100 N 2016

save on bucket-list trips K. CICERO *Parents* v91 no9 p64 S 2016

Travel—Equipment & supplies

See also

Luggage

Travel paraphernalia

AHEAD OF THE PACK S. Feinstein color *Consumer Reports* v81 no12 p12 D 2016

The HELLO, WORLD O List color *O, The Oprah Magazine* p37 Ja 2017

Travel—Equipment & supplies—Evaluation

See also

Luggage—Evaluation

Airweave Traveler color *Bloomberg Businessweek* no4533 p63 Ag 7 2017

HONOR ROLL D. FOX color *Men's Health* v32 no7 p(Sp)9 S 2017

TAKE IT WITH YOU M. DURAN color *Wired* v24 no12 p84 D 2016

TOWN AND COUNTRY C. Dash color *Sunset* v239 no3 p32 S 2017

Travelers

See also

Backpackers

LGBT travelers

Pilgrims & pilgrimages

Tourists

THE ACCIDENTAL BOOKSHOP D. KAMP color *Vanity Fair* v58 no12 p112 D 2016

Beach bonanza *Canadian Geographic* v137 p50 2017 Travel

BORDER to BORDER 1-80 Adventure A. J. BARTELS bw color *Nebraska Life* v21 no1 p18 Ja/F 2017

Dear Yankee bw color *Yankee* p8 Jl 2017

Move over Lonely Planet J. MCCARTNEY color *Publishers Weekly* v264 no26 p131 Je 26 2017

Where You Lead P. Guzmán bw *Conde Nast Traveler* v52 no2 p12 F 2017

Your Feedback S. Leveene, T. Buchman et al color il *Consumer Reports* v82 no8 p6 Ag 2017

Travelers (TV program)

STREAMING A. D'ARMINIO *TV Guide* p42 D 19 2016

Travelers' writings

THE GJØA DIARIES COME TO CANADA N. Walker bw *Canadian Geographic* v137 no3 p74 My 2017

Travelers—Humor

Laugh Lines color *Reader's Digest* v189 no1131 p111 Je 2017

Travelers—Management

Remember, It's Your Vacation D. T. PUTERBAUGH *USA Today Magazine* v146 no2866 p82 Jl 2017

Travelers—Safety measures

Don't Leave Home Without It D. DAVIS *Sierra* v102 no1 p18 Ja/F 2017

Travelers—Services for

See also

Tourists—Services for

Travel—Exhibitions

SOUTH BEACH IN SOUTHWEST B. L. Smith *Washingtonian Magazine* v52 no1 p47 O 2016

Travel—Finance

GIFTS THAT GO THE DISTANCE D. Rosato color *Consumer Reports* v81 no12 p45 D 2016

Travel—Health aspects

SAVE YOUR VACATION D. Keating color *Maclean's* v129 no50 p54 D 19 2016

Your Best Health While Traveling S. Goldberg *Cincinnati Magazine* v50 no4 p88 Ja 2017

Traveling theater

ROAD SHOW: Bryan Hymel in New Orleans M. R. MERCADO *Opera News* v81 no6 p16 D 2016

Traveling Wilburys, The (Music)

THE TRAVELING WILBURYS M. Mettler color *Sound & Vision* v81 no9 p72 N 2016

Travel—Management

The Long Haul to a New Home K. NAVARRA color *Horse & Rider* v56 no11 p126 N 2017

WE'RE TURNING 30 R. MISNER, E. FLORIO et al bw chart color *Conde Nast Traveler* v52 no8 p55 S 2017

Travel—Psychological aspects

Around the World in 2,557 Days... Paul Salopek G. DREVITCH *Psychology Today* v49 no6 p27 N/D 2016

FINDINGS *Harper's Magazine* v334 no2002 p96 Mr 2017

Travel—Safety measures

Equine Traveling Papers R. GIMENEZ color *Trail Rider* v29 no3 p10 Ap 2017

The No-GPS Road Trip E. DYER and A. Langer color *Popular Mechanics* p32 S 2017

Notes from an Un-Reeling Island E. D. Huntley bw color *British Heritage Travel* v38 no5 p26 S/O 2017

TRAVELERS NEED TO EXERCISE CAUTION *USA Today Magazine* v146 no2869 p12 O 2017

Travel—Social aspects

STREET VIEW *New York Times Magazine* p42 Ja 22 2017

TRAVERS, BEN

Forced Confessions color *Walrus* v14 no4 p42 My 2017

Travers, Peter

American Horror Story color *Rolling Stone* no1294 p56 Ag 24 2017

Fast-Food Godfather color *Rolling Stone* no1280 p56 F 9 2017

The Guardians Return color *Rolling Stone* no1287 p56 My 18 2017

He's One Weird Dude color *Rolling Stone* no1274 p60 N 17 2016

A Hillbilly 'Ocean's 11' color *Rolling Stone* no1295 p56 S 7 2017

How to Replicate a Hit color *Rolling Stone* no1298 p53 O 19 2017

Joyride of Summer! color *Rolling Stone* no1291/1292 p67 Jl 13 2017

Love Is a Battlefield color *Rolling Stone* no1290 p55 Je 29 2017

Middle Age in Revolt color *Rolling Stone* no1284 p54 Ap 6 2017

MOVIES OF THE YEAR color *Rolling Stone* no1276 p24 D 15 2016

A Musical Triumph color *Rolling Stone* no1276 p64 D 15 2016

Old Man Wolverine color *Rolling Stone* no1283 p54 Mr 23 2017

Oscar Shows Its Colors color *Rolling Stone* no1281/1282 p54 F 23 2017

Party Girl, Godzilla Girl color *Rolling Stone* no1285 p55 Ap 20 2017

'Pirates 5' Scrapes the Franchise Bottom color *Rolling Stone* no1289 p60 Je 15 2017

Racial Fury Unleashed color *Rolling Stone* no1272 p52 O 20 2016

Scorsese's Passion color *Rolling Stone* no1278/1279 p52 Ja 12 2017

Summer's New Heroes color *Rolling Stone* no1288 p52 Je 1 2017

Traverso, Amy

Apple Custard Cake: Re-creating a recipe from memory ... when the memory isnt yours *Yankee* v81 no5 p68 S/O 2017

Barnard General Store color *Yankee* p64 My/Je 2017

CHRISTMAS in Boston color *Yankee* v80 no6 p108 N/D 2016

EDITORS' CHOICE FOOD AWARDS 2016 color *Yankee* v80 no6 p73 N/D 2016

THE GREAT LOBSTER ROLL ADVENTURE: WE SENT FOOD EDITOR UP THE MAINE COAST, FROM KITTERY TO EASTPORT, TO SAMPLE NEARLY TWO | DOZEN ROLLS AND CROWN A CHAMPION chart color *Yankee* p78 Jl 2017

GRILLING 101 with Andy Husbands color *Yankee* p54 My/Je 2017

HOLIDAY KITCHEN color *Yankee* v80 no6 p58 N/D 2016

HOW TO MAKE THE WINNING LOBSTER ROLL color *Yankee* p90 Jl 2017

Maple Dumplings (Grandpères) color *Yankee* p64 Mr 2017

Modern Diner *Yankee* v81 no1 p62 Ja/F 2017

Outside-In Burgers: Reviving a family recipe with a tip for anyone seeking perfection color *Yankee* p54 Jl 2017

Palace Diner: With the greatest tuna melt in lunch counter history, a 15-seat dining car becomes an anchor for a Maine mill town's revival color *Yankee* p50 Jl 2017

Poorhouse Pies: Baked in a farmhouse and sold on the honor system, these pies are a Vermont slice of life *Yankee* v81 no5 p64 S/O 2017

Strawberry-Rhubarb Coffee Cake color *Yankee* p68 My/Je 2017

"WEEKENDS" WARRIOR color *Yankee* p50 Mr 2017

TRAVIS, ALEXANDER J.

Society Is Ready for a New Kind of Science--Is Academia? *Bio-Science* v67 no7 p591 Jl 2017

Travis, John

FRONTIERS IN CANCER THERAPY *Science* v355 no6330 p1143 Mr 17 2017

ON THE CLOCK color *Science* v354 no6315 p986 N 25 2016

Travis, Kate

Charting genetic diversity around the world map *Science News* v190 no9 p32 O 29 2016

Travis, Ken—Interviews

A Cappella Adventures B. Reesman *Stage Directions* v30 no2 p12 F 2017

Travis, Lisa

Changing the World, One Reader at a Time M. BURNETT color *Publishers Weekly* v264 no35 p60 Ag 28 2017

Mystery of the Troubled Toucan *Publishers Weekly* v264 no9 p66k F 27 2017

TRAVIS, SUTTON

VITAL SIGNS *Texas Monthly* v45 no9 p62 S 2017

Travnicek, P.

Observation of a large-scale anisotropy in the arrival directions of cosmic rays above 8×10^{18} eV *Science* v357 no6357 p1266 S 22 2017

Travolta, John, 1954-

CHEERS & JeeRS D. HOLBROOK *TV Guide* v64 no15 p96 Ap 4 2016

TRAVOLTA HOLDS COURT C. WEAVER color *GQ: Gentlemen's Quarterly* v86 no12 p182 D 2016

Trawlers (Vessels)

Guardian Angels B. PIKE cartoon *Power & Motoryacht* v33 no1 p168 Ja 2017

Trays

GATHER ROUNDS F. VIGNA color *Martha Stewart Living* p140 Ap 2017

Out of Africa K. O'SHEA-EVANS color *House Beautiful* v159 no5 p39 Je 2017

The Plastic Inevitable T. PRODANOVICH color *Surfer* v58 no1 p28 Ap 2017

SHINE ON color *Bon Appetit* v61 no11 p128 N 2016

Trays—Evaluation

4 pretty, mini updates for your home color *Redbook* p136 F 2017

For Your Favorite Foodie color *Consumer Reports* v81 no12 p34 D 2016

NEBRASKA MADE D. VAN BUREN color *Nebraska Life* v20 no6 p54 N/D 2016

Trays—Research

STICKY MAT FOR TOOLS color *Flying* v144 no4 p16 Ap 2017

Traywick, Catherine

Don't Frack on Me color *Bloomberg Businessweek* no4541 p24 O 9 2017

Hidden Hand: Neil Chatterjee bw *Bloomberg Businessweek* no4541 p39 O 9 2017

Treadaway, Harry

MR. MERCEDES A. Breznican color *Entertainment Weekly* no1474/1475 p70 Jl 21-28 2017

TREADGOLD, WARREN

Is free speech under threat IN THE UNITED STATES? WE RECEIVED TWENTY-SEVEN RESPONSES. WE PUBLISH THEM HERE, IN ALPHABETICAL ORDER *Commentary* v144 no1 p13 Jl/Ag 2017

Treadmill exercise

GO LONG K. LOREN chart color *Muscle & Performance* v9 no5 p20 My 2017

SWEAT TO SUCCEED A. C. Shilton cartoon *Runner's World* v51 no11 p40 D 2016

Treadmills (Exercise equipment)

AMIN EL GAMAL D. Meltzer Zepeda bw *Runner's World* v52 no9 p96 O 2017

Ask Our Experts color *Consumer Reports* v82 no1 p21 Ja 2017

Treadmills (Exercise equipment)—Evaluation

Choose the Right Machine for You bw *Kiplinger's Personal Finance* v71 no1 p70 Ja 2017

INSIDER TRAINING J. DENGATE color *Runner's World* v52 no1 p90 Ja/F 2017

TECH RX *Cincinnati Magazine* v50 no4 p77 Ja 2017

Treasure, Alyxandria—Interviews

DIGESTIVE HEALTH color *Maclean's* v129 no48/49 p75 D 5 2016

Treasure troves

PLOT OF GOLD A. Abel color *Maclean's* v130 no10 p40 N 2017

Treasury bills—United States

How Offshore Is All That Overseas Cash? M. Mossman color *Bloomberg Businessweek* no4541 p28 O 9 2017

TREAT, JEREMY

God Is Not Out to Get You color *Christianity Today* v60 no9 p64 N 2016

Treaties

See also

Commercial treaties

International arbitration

Peace treaties

A comprehensive nuclear test ban E. J. Moniz bibl color *Science* v354 no6316 p1081 D 2 2016

With Peace, Colombia Is Poised for Greater Prosperity R. H. K. Vietor *Harvard Business Review Digital Articles* p2 Jl 7 2016

Treatment duration (Medical care)

Charlie Gard and other precious lives graph *Christian Century* v134 no18 p7 Ag 30 2017

Treatment effectiveness

Charlie Gard and other precious lives graph *Christian Century* v134 no18 p7 Ag 30 2017

Gene Therapy 2.0 E. MULLIN bw color *MIT Technology Review* v120 no2 p48 Mr/Ap 2017

Testosterone therapy is a mixed bag M. ROSEN graph *Science News* v191 no6 p8 Ap 1 2017

Treatment effectiveness—Evaluation

Soothe a headache C. Lee color *Yoga Journal* p30 2017 SpecialIssue

Treatment for burns & scalds

Second opinion *Mayo Clinic Health Letter* v35 no6 p8 Je 2017

SOOTHE YOURSELF C. ZULKEY color *Runner's World* v52 no7 p28 Ag 2017

Treatment of addictions

Toward a targeted treatment for addiction M. C. Creed color diag *Science* v357 no6350 p464 Ag 4 2017

Treatment of autism spectrum disorders

Autism Spectrum Disorder M. BARNA color diag *Discover* v38 no6 p62 Jl/Ag 2017

Treatment of backaches

Oh, My Aching Back H. VanEs and R. Harvey *USA Today Magazine* v146 no2868 p23 S 2017

Yog-ahhh N. PAIN color *Yoga Journal* p6 2017 SpecialIssue

Treatment of cataracts

Stem cell approach for cataracts challenged K. Servick color *Science* v356 no6345 p1318 Je 30 2017

Treatment of colic in horses

COLIC SURGERY [Cover story] S. D. Wenholz color *Practical Horseman* v45 no7 p52 Jl 2017

Treatment of constipation

Problem Solved Constipation R. LALIBERTE *Prevention* v69 no9 p24 O 2017

Treatment of dental caries

Stone Age people treated cavities B. BOWER color *Science News* v191 no9 p15 My 13 2017

Treatment of drug addiction

THE ADDICTED BRAIN [Cover story] F. Smith color *National Geographic* v232 no3 p30 S 2017

Follow the "Bright Line" S. P. THOMPSON *USA Today Magazine* v146 no2868 p62 S 2017

Treatment of dysmenorrhea

YOGI HEAL THYSELF S. WADYKA color *Yoga Journal* p106 2017 SpecialIssue

Treatment of eczema

HIDING IN PLAIN SIGHT K. Booker color *Women's Health* v14 no8 p46 O 2017

Treatment of edema

My legs sometimes become swollen, but they don't hurt and it doesn't feel like anything else is wrong. Why might this be happening? *Mayo Clinic Health Letter* v35 no7 p8 Jl 2017

Treatment of heart diseases

Watermelon's Effect on Blood Vessels *USA Today Magazine* v146 no2869 p2 O 2017

Treatment of hemorrhoids

Anal and rectal discomfort *Mayo Clinic Health Letter* v35 no10 p4 O 2017

Treatment of HIV infections

We still need to beat HIV F. Dabis and Bekker color *Science* v357 no6349 p335 Jl 28 2017

Treatment of horse diseases

INJECTABLE ULCER DRUG MAY SOON BE AVAILABLE C. Barakat and M. McCluskey color *Equus* no478 p17 Jl 2017

Treatment of memory loss

KEEP YOUR MIND SHARP J. Challem color *Amazing Wellness* v8 no2 p32 Spr 2016

Treatment of mental depression

Cognitive behavioral therapy *Mayo Clinic Health Letter* v35 no7 p7 Jl 2017

Depressed Without Knowing It: Even when we know what depression looks like, we can miss it in ourselves S. J. GILLIHAN *Psychology Today* v50 no5 p50 S/O 2017

Hope from a Strange Source [Cover story] M. Oaklander color *Time* v190 no6 p38 Ag 7 2017

Treatment of mental illness

See also

Psychotherapy

Does My Ex Owe Anything To Our Grown Kids? K. A. Appiah *New York Times Magazine* p24 Je 11 2017

What Veterans Need: Caring for those who served *Psychology Today* v50 no4 p14 Ag 2017

Treatment of mountain sickness

The Ups (and Downs) of Mountain Travel A. WISLOWSKI chart diag *Climbing* no355 p48 Ag 2017

Treatment of sexual disorders

Pleasure Principal S. Barmak color *Walrus* v14 no5 p38 Je 2017

Treatment of spinal muscular atrophy

How a Boy's Lazarus-like Revival Points to a New Generation of Drugs K. Weintraub color *MIT Technology Review* v120 no4 p24 Jl/Ag 2017

Treatment of post-traumatic stress disorder

Dance floor drug could treat PTSD color *Science* v357 no6354 p850 S 1 2017

ENLISTING MARIJUANA AND MDMA TO FIGHT PTSD J. SULLUM color *Reason* v49 no6 p32 N 2017

Treaty on Principles Governing the Activities of States in the Exploration & Use of Outer Space, Including the Moon & Other Celestial Bodies (1967)

Space Prospecting J. Dunietz color *Scientific American* v317 no4 p14 O 2017

Treaty tested by space miners D. Clery color *Science* v357 no6359 p19 O 6 2017

TREBLE, PATRICIA

Around the world color map *Maclean's* v129 no51/52 p44 D 26 2016

BEAUTY STOLE THE ROYAL SHOW color *Maclean's* v129 no41 p46 O 17 2016

BUSTING THE RECYCLING MYTH color *Maclean's* v129 no40 p53 O 10 2016

BY THE NUMBERS bw color *Maclean's* v129 no51/52 p52 D 26 2016

A changing of the guard color *Maclean's* v129 no48/49 p62 D 5 2016

COLOUR, MADE IN CANADA color *Maclean's* v129 no48/49 p68 D 5 2016

HARRY'S NEXT GAMES color *Maclean's* v129 no51/52 p47 D 26 2016

Hashtags, memes and viral hits cartoon color *Maclean's* v129 no48/49 p68 D 5 2016

Keep calm and adventure on bw color *Maclean's* v129 no40 p56 O 10 2016

The little prince color *Maclean's* v129 no40 p52 O 10 2016

NEWSMAKERS: ANIMAL EDITION color *Maclean's* v129 no48/49 p63 D 5 2016

Not your daughter's Harry Potter color *Maclean's* v129 no46 p61 N 21 2016

The ones the war forgot color *Maclean's* v129 no43 p45 O 31 2016

A Protestant miracle color graph *Maclean's* v129 no47 p54 N 28 2016

RASPUTIN color *Maclean's* v129 no47 p60 N 28 2016

The royal treatment color *Maclean's* v129 no44 p111 N 7 2016

Sharing the limelight color *Maclean's* v129 no40 p48 O 10 2016

Slacking, royally color graph *Maclean's* v129 no40 p49 O 10 2016

Taking them on tour bw color *Maclean's* v129 no40 p50 O 10 2016

UNEASY LIES THE HEAD THAT WEARS THE CROWN color *Maclean's* no1 p58 F 17 2017

The year of Diana color *Maclean's* v129 no51/52 p46 D 26 2016

Trebosc, Vincent

Reversion of antibiotic resistance in Mycobacterium tuberculosis by spiroisoxazoline SMARt-420 bibl diag *Science* v355 no6330 p1206 Mr 17 2017

TREDICK, CATHERINE A.

A Rubric to Evaluate Citizen-Science Programs for Long-Term Ecological Monitoring *BioScience* v67 no9 p834 S 2017

Tree (Poem)

A Tree Grows on the Marne M. S. J. Malone *America* v216 no10 p3 My 1 2017

Tree climbing

Lightbox color *Time* v190 no2/3 p16 Jl 10-17 2017

Tree crickets—Behavior

TRILLING INTRUDER M. A. Ronconi color *New York State Conservationist* v71 no2 p22 O 2016

Tree farms

HOLIDAY SPIRIT I. Edwards color *Sunset* v237 no6 p8 D 2016

O CHRISTMAS TREE [Cover story] C. Lamers and K. Smoot color *Sunset* v237 no6 p62 D 2016

Tree growth

A matter of tree longevity C. Körner bibl color *Science* v355 no6321 p130 Ja 13 2017

Tree houses

Sleep Up In a Tree: Fulfill a childhood fantasy and branch out on your next getaway by renting a treehouse E. STEIN *Washingtonian Magazine* v52 no11 p86 Ag 2017

Timber Treehouse Makes One Girl's Dreams Come True color *Timber Home Living* v27 no2 p7 Ap 2017

WASHINGTON N. Walker color map *Canadian Geographic* v135 no6 p26 D 2015

Tree of life in art

Tree of Life *Archaeology* v69 no6 pCover N/D 2016

Tree planting

AROUND THE GARDEN S. Bender color map *Southern Living* v51 no11 p54 N 2016

Jad Daley, Vice President of Conservation Programs *American Forests* v123 no3 p9 Fall 2017

Joan and Mike Diggs *American Forests* v123 no2 p8 Summ 2017

Justin Hynicka, Manager of Forest Conservation *American Forests* v123 no3 p8 Fall 2017

The Life of Trees *Martha Stewart Living* no269 p19 N 2016

Made in the Shade P. GULLEY cartoon *Indianapolis Monthly* v42 no2 p51 O 2017

Optimal Tree Canopy Cover during Ecological Restoration: A Case Study of Possible Ecological Thresholds in Changting, China SHIXIONG CAO, CHENXI LU et al *BioScience* v67 no3 p221 Mr 2017

POT LUCK L. HEDRICK color *Better Homes & Gardens* v95 no4 p46 Ap 2017

Protecting One of America's Premier Wildernesses: American Re-Leaf in Tahoe National Forest D. Irvin *American Forests* v123 no1 p7 Wint/Spr 2017

SHADY POLITICS A. Greenblatt *Governing* v30 no1 p11 O 2016

Tree planting & the environment

A TREE GROWS IN CHINA V. BEISER color *Mother Jones* v42 no5 p38 S/O 2017

Tree tapping

See also
Sugar maple—Tapping

SAP TO SYRUP E. M. Jennings *New York State Conservationist* v71 no4 p14 F 2017

Trees

See also
Landscape gardening
National trees

30 Secrets of an Affordable Log Home color *Log Home Living* v34 no6 p74 Ag 2017

Bacteria Beef Up New Tree of Life J. KEATS diag *Discover* v38 no1 p90 Ja/F 2017

Carbon sequestration beyond tree longevity L. C. R. Silva bibl *Science* v355 no6330 p1141 Mr 17 2017

EDIBLE TREES J. V. TRAIL *American Forests* v123 no1 p16 Wint/Spr 2017

The everything-proof house H. Murphy color *Popular Science* v289 no4 p56 Jl/Ag 2017

Ian Leahy, Director of Urban Forests Programs *American Forests* v122 no3 p8 Fall 2016

Japan color *National Geographic* v231 no4 p8 Ap 2017

last look *American Forests* v123 no1 p48 Wint/Spr 2017

Tallying the tropical toll on trees from lightning M. Price color *Science* v356 no6344 p1222 Je 23 2017

That Was Then *National Parks* v91 no2 p68 Spr 2017

Trees, Saws, and Ladders Do Not Mix *USA Today Magazine* v146 no2867 p7 Ag 2017

The Wisdom of TREES C. NEWMAN color *National Geographic* v231 no3 p52 Mr 2017

Trees in cities

Benefits of trees in tropical cities X. Ping Song, D. Richards et al color *Science* v356 no6344 p1241 Je 23 2017

The natural capital of city trees K. J. Willis and G. Petrokofsky color *Science* v356 no6336 p374 Ap 28 2017

Trees—Diseases & pests

High Country Rescue C. WALKER *National Parks* v91 no1 p14 Wint 2017

Trees—History

HEARTS OF OAK S. Lawrence *British Heritage Travel* v38 no3 p54 My/Je 2017

The magnificent SEVEN H. TAMMEMAG color *Canadian Geographic* v136 no6 p54 D 2016

Trees—Measurement

The Virtual Forest V. SCHIPANI *American Scholar* v86 no2 p16 Spr 2017

Trees—Nebraska

Nebraska's long love affair with Trees color *Nebraska Life* v21 no4 p32 Jl/Ag 2017

Treestands (Hunting)

ONE FELL SWOOP D. W. Grable cartoon *Outdoor Life* v223 no9 p16 N 2016

Treffeisen, Elsa

Regeneration of fat cells from myofibroblasts during wound healing bibl color graph *Science* v355 no6326 p748 F 17 2017

Trefonas, Peter

Double-heterojunction nanorod light-responsive LEDs for display applications bibl color graph *Science* v355 no6325 p616 F 10 2017

Tregillis, Ian

The Liberation *Publishers Weekly* v263 no41 p61 O 10 2016

Tregoing, Ben

EVERY DAY I'M SIDE-HUSTLIN' cartoon color *GQ: Gentlemen's Quarterly* v97 no4 p60 Ap 2017

Treherne, Tish

WILD AT HEART E. Jardina color *Sunset* v238 no3 p66 Mr 2017

Trei, Michael

Gallons of Sound, Pint-Sized Speaker color *Sound & Vision* v82 no4 p46 My 2017

Samsung HW-K950 Soundbar System color graph *Sound & Vision* v81 no9 p48 N 2016

TREISMAN, DEBORAH

Rebel In the House *Los Angeles Magazine* v62 no6 p60 Je 2017

Treisman, Richard

Opposing effects of Elk-1 multisite phosphorylation shape its response to ERK activation bibl graph *Science* v354 no6309 p233 O 14 2016

Trek Bicycle Corp.

#BIKECRUSH M. Yozell, M. Phillips et al color *Bicycling* v58 no8 p53 S 2017

CHAMOIS UP S. Yeager, M. Yozell et al color *Bicycling* v58 no8 p60 S 2017

EVEN FLOW T. Engel, R. Cleek et al bw color *Bike Magazine* v24 no1 p94 Ja/F 2017

"I WANT A BIKE THAT MAKES CLIMBING EASY." M. Phillips and B. STRICKLAND color *Bicycling* v58 no3 p34 Ap 2017

"I WANT TO GO FAST." G. Liu and B. STRICKLAND color *Bicycling* v58 no3 p68 Ap 2017

"SHOULD I GET CARBON OR ALUMINUM?" color *Bicycling* v58 no3 p36 Ap 2017

SUPER COMMUTER+ 8S J. Sherry color *Bicycling* v58 no8 p(Sp)16 S 2017

TAKE WINTER BY STORM color *Men's Health* v31 no10 p(Sp)14 D 2016

TREK ÉMONDA SLR 9 DISC, PROJECT ONE M. Yozell color *Bicycling* v58 no9 p74 O 2017

TREK FUEL EX 9.8 WOMEN'S N. Formosa color *Bike Magazine* v23 no9 p90 D 2016

TREK SILQUE SLR 7 S. Yeager color *Bicycling* v58 no4 p64 My 2017

Treleaven, Sarah

Home Wrecker cartoon *Walrus* v14 no6 p28 Jl/Ag 2017

HOUSE HUNTERS TRANSNATIONAL *Harper's Magazine* v334 no2000 p48 Ja 2017

Trelstad, Brian

Making Sense of the Many Kinds of Impact Investing *Harvard*

Changing of the Guard color *Walrus* v14 no9 p20 N 2017

Tretiak, S.
Extremely efficient internal exciton dissociation through edge states in layered 2D perovskites bibl graph *Science* v355 no6331 p1288 Mr 24 2017

Treu, Kayci
FOLLOW Like a Boss C. Bohen *Dance Spirit* v21 no7 p100 S 2017

Trevail, Charles
The Brands That Make Customers Feel Respected *Harvard Business Review Digital Articles* p2 N 1 2016
Getting the Most from an Online Customer Community *Harvard Business Review Digital Articles* p2 Je 3 2016

Treverton, Gregory F.
North Korea: How to Stop Kim Jong Un color *Time* v189 no12 p40 Ap 3 2017

TREVES, ADRIAN
Conserving the World's Megafauna and Biodiversity: The Fierce Urgency of Now *BioScience* v67 no3 p197 Mr 2017
Saving the World's Terrestrial Megafauna color *BioScience* v66 no10 p807 O 1 2016

Trevigne, Talise
It's a Wonderful Life G. Barnett *Opera News* v81 no9 p38 Mr 2017

Trevor, Jonathan
How Aligned Is Your Organization? color *Harvard Business Review Digital Articles* p2 F 7 2017
A Simple Way to Test Your Company's Strategic Alignment *Harvard Business Review Digital Articles* p2 My 16 2016

Trevor, William, 1928-2016
THE PIANO TEACHER'S PUPIL W. TREVOR cartoon *New Yorker* v93 no18 p56 Je 26 2017

Trevorrow, Colin, 1976-
The Book of Henry J. McGovern color *Entertainment Weekly* no1471 p50 Je 23 2017

Trial & Error (TV program)
Getting Med-ucated M. Snetiker color *Entertainment Weekly* no1462 p53 Ap 21 2017
Trial & Erro's stunt double Arthur Davis J. Russell *TV Guide* p15 Ap 17 2017

Trial, The (Theatrical production)
Sound Bites: Theo Hoffman: A native New Yorker returns to Missouri F. P. Driscoll *Opera News* v81 no12 p58 Je 2017

Trial consultants (Law)
Nancy Rafuse *Atlanta* v57 no2 p102 Je 2017

Trials (Fraud)—United States
Indictment? What Indictment? A. Greenblatt *Governing* v31 no1 p11 O 2017

Trials (Law)
See also
Trials (Murder)
Benghazi at the Bar J. LIFHITS color *Weekly Standard* v23 no6 p14 O 16 2017

Trials (Law)—Texas
THE TROUBLE WITH INNOCENCE M. Hall *Texas Monthly* v45 no4 p96 Ap 2017

Trials (Murder)
Sketchbook: Graphic Review H. Bliss *New York Times Book Review* p31 S 24 2017

Trials (Murder)—South Carolina
United States v. Dylann Roof E. Ball color *New York Review of Books* v64 no4 p4 Mr 9 2017

Trials (Rape)
THE DECISION E. WEST *Indianapolis Monthly* p74 F 2017

Trials (Terrorism)—United States
CRIME AND PUNISHMENT Will the 9/11 case finally go to trial? A. Cockburn *Harper's Magazine* p41 O 2017

Triangles (Interpersonal relations)
Crowdsource This J. Valenti, K. Mark et al color *Glamour* v115 no9 p124 S 2017

Triangle Shirtwaist factory fire, New York (N.Y.), 1911
The Triangle Disaster: How a fire a century ago at a New York clothing factory changed U.S. labor laws P. Smith *New York Times Upfront* v150 no1 p11 S 4 2017

Triangulum Galaxy
M33 in a 10-inch Scope S. French *Sky & Telescope* v132 no6 p54

D 2016

Trianni, Francesca
Children of No Nation [Cover story] color map *Time* v188 no27-28 p38 D 26 2016
Promised Land color *Time* v190 no14 p40 O 9 2017
When the Call Comes color map *Time* v189 no6 p32 F 20 2017

Triantafyllou, Michael S.
Tuna fin hydraulics inspire aquatic robotics [Cover story] diag *Science* v357 no6348 p251 Jl 21 2017

Triantis, Kostas A.
Island biogeography: Taking the long view of nature's laboratories map *Science* v357 no6354 p885 S 1 2017

TRIANTOGIANNIS, LENA
Onboarding Isn't Enough color diag graph il img *Harvard Business Review* v95 no3 p78 My/Je 2017

Triathletes
AMANDA CHARNEY C. FENNESSY color *Runner's World* v52 no1 p89 Ja/F 2017

Triathlon
ASK RW C. ZILBERMAN, R. KNAPP et al color *Runner's World* v52 no4 p35 My 2017
A Family Reunion with a Twist [Cover story] S. KELLY bw color *Cabin Living* p46 Ag 2017
SEPTEMBER 2017 color *Missouri Life* v44 no6 p81 S 2017

Triathlon training
IRONMAN TRAINING V. Tweed color *Amazing Wellness* v9 no4 p74 Summ 2017
THE TRIATHLON: YES, YOU CAN DO THIS! J. B. Polloreno cartoon color *Men's Health* v32 no2 p39 Mr 2017

Tribal tattoos—Social aspects
ABOUT THAT TATTOO N. MACDONALD color *Maclean's* v129 no44 p25 N 7 2016

Tribe Called Quest (Performer)
'We the People . . . .' G. TATE *New York Times Magazine* p26 Mr 12 2017

Tribeca Film Festival
PARTY LINES S. W. Hunt img *New York* v50 no9 p98 My 1 2017

Tribes
LOSING HOME Z. Loftus-Farren color *Earth Island Journal* v32 no1 p19 Spr 2017
Navajo Nation Council Chamber N. AUSTIN *Arizona Highways* v93 no6 p6 Je 2017
No-Collateral Damage N. S. RILEY color *Weekly Standard* v22 no36 p15 My 29 2017
TRIBAL LEGACY M. Hill color *Louisiana Life* v37 no6 p64 Jl/Ag 2017
WANT TO SPREAD THE WORD ABOUT YOUR WORK? FIND YOUR TRIBE K. Johnson *Black Enterprise* v47 no8 p32 Jl/Ag 2017

Tribes—Social aspects
Hope and Honor: Lakota Women Warriors inspire reservation youth *South Dakota Magazine* v33 no3 p18 S/O 2017

Tribord (Company)
Breathe Easy S. MURRAY color *Power & Motoryacht* v34 no7 p39 Jl 2017

Tribune (Newspaper)
HOOKER COUNTY TRIBUNE C. Spike bw *Columbia Journalism Review* v56 no1 p95 Spr 2017

Tribune Publishing Co.
Tronc's Data Delusion G. Satell *Harvard Business Review Digital Articles* p2 Je 23 2016

Triceps—Physiology
TONE YOUR TRICEPS V. Tweed color *Amazing Wellness* v9 no3 p74 EarlySumm 2017

Triceratops
DINOSAUR COWBOY M. Sager *Smithsonian* v48 no4 p52 Jl/Ag 2017

Trichodesmium
The complex effects of ocean acidification on the prominent N2-fixing cyanobacterium Trichodesmium H. Hong, R. Shen et al graph *Science* v356 no6337 p527 My 5 2017

TRICK, SARAH
No Vacancy cartoon *Walrus* v13 no10 p22 D 2016

Trickster (Music)
Outside the Box B. Milkowski color *Downbeat* v84 no6 p32 Je 2017

Trieb, Erin
Life With ISIS & After ISIS color *Glamour* no8 p117 Ag 2017
What's the Biggest Risk You've Ever Taken? bw color *Glamour* no8 p26 Ag 2017

Triebner, Mat
7 Factors of Great Office Design *Harvard Business Review Digital Articles* p2 My 20 2016

Trier, Allonzo
Ready SET, ZO! L. Winn color *Sports Illustrated* v126 no9 p37 Mr 27 2017

Trifecta (Company)
Triple Threat A. JONES *Boating World* v38 no3 p36 Mr 2017

Trifluoromethyl compounds
A catalytic fluoride-rebound mechanism for C(sp3)-CF3 bond formation M. D. Levin, T. Q. Chen et al diag *Science* v356 no6344 p1272 Je 23 2017

Trifonov, Daniil
CLASSICAL MUSIC *New Yorker* v92 no37 p16 N 14 2016
SLEIGHT OF HAND A. ROSS cartoon *New Yorker* v92 no44 p74 Ja 9 2017

Trigeminal nerve
NERVE'S ROLE IN HEADSHAKING INVESTIGATED C. Barakat and M. McCluskey color *Equus* no481 p12 O 2017

Trigeminal neuralgia
Trigeminal neuralgia *Mayo Clinic Health Letter* v358 no8 p7 Ag 2017

Trigilio, Merri Lisa
WATER WARS N. TAPPAN color map *American History* v52 no2 p16 Je 2017

Trillin, Calvin, 1935-
FINAL CUT cartoon color *New Yorker* v93 no27 p28 S 11 2017
HUMORISTS ON HUMOR: CRACKING THE CODE ON WHAT CRACKS US UP R. WARREN *Saturday Evening Post* v289 no5 p38 S/O 2017
THE IRISH CONSTELLATION color *New Yorker* v93 no11 p27 My 1 2017
The Scariest Word *New York Times Book Review* p29 N 27 2016
TOSSING AND TURNING cartoon *New Yorker* v92 no45 p33 Ja 16 2017

Trillin, Calvin, 1935—Interviews
Calvin Trillin *New York Times Book Review* p10 Jl 23 2017

Trim of ships (Equilibrium)
Attitude Adjustment T. Serio *Boating World* v37 no9 p50 N/D 2016

Trimarans
Battle of the One-Design Tris color *Sail* v48 no5 p8 My 2017

Trimble, Chris
The Best Way to Improve Health Care Delivery Is with a Small, Dedicated Team *Harvard Business Review Digital Articles* p2 Mr 9 2016

Trimbuch, Thorsten
Loss of a mammalian circular RNA locus causes miRNA deregulation and affects brain function color *Science* v357 no6357 p1254 S 22 2017

Trimm, Wayne
The Lasting Images of Wayne Trimm *New York State Conservationist* v72 no1 p10 Ag 2017
Recollections of Wayne Trimm W. Jones *New York State Conservationist* v72 no1 p14 Ag 2017

Trinchero, Mariela F.
A disynaptic feedback network activated by experience promotes the integration of new granule cells bibl graph *Science* v354 no6311 p459 O 28 2016

Trinder, Mark
Human health color *Science* v356 no6338 p590 My 12 2017

Trinder, Michael
THE BRITISH HERITAGE TRAVEL PUZZLER color *British Heritage Travel* v38 no5 p78 S/O 2017

Tringides, Michael C.
Robert Gomer *Physics Today* v70 no5 p67 My 2017

TRINH, JEAN
IT'S PARTY TIME! WHERE'S THE CAKE? *Los Angeles Magazine* v61 no11 p128 N 2016

Trini, M.
Observation of a large-scale anisotropy in the arrival directions of cosmic rays above 8 × 1018 eV *Science* v357 no6357 p1266 S 22 2017

Trinity
See also
Jesus Christ
Formed in Their Likeness M. Simone *America* v216 no12 p56 My 29 2017
Show Us the Father M. S. J. Simone *America* v216 no10 p53 My 1 2017

Trinity Alps Wilderness (Calif.)
Hit the high country color *Backpacker* p10 S 2017

Trinity Sunday
LIVING BY The Word *Christian Century* v134 no11 p20 My 24 2017

Trinity Wall Street (Performer)
To Lou, with Love A. Ross color *New Yorker* v93 no10 p18 Ap 24 2017

Trinkaus, Erik
Late Pleistocene archaic human crania from Xuchang, China bibl color diag graph *Science* v355 no6328 p969 Mr 3 2017

Trinko, Therese
Did you receive support from your faith community while you were experiencing depression and/or anxiety? graph *America* v216 no12 p6 My 29 2017

Trio A With Flags (Theatrical production)
Naked Flag Dance J. Acocella bw *New Yorker* v93 no6 p10 Mr 27 2017

Trip (Music)
WHAT TO STREAM color *Entertainment Weekly* no1484 p57 S 29 2017

Tripathi, Sarvind
Structural basis of the day-night transition in a bacterial circadian clock bibl diag *Science* v355 no6330 p1174 Mr 17 2017

Tripathi, Shashank
Enhancement of Zika virus pathogenesis by preexisting antiflavivirus immunity graph *Science* v356 no6334 p175 Ap 14 2017

Tripeptides
Polymeric peptide pigments with sequence-encoded properties A. Lampel, S. A. McPhee et al color graph *Science* v356 no6342 p1064 Je 9 2017
RESEARCH color *Science* v356 no6342 p1040 Je 9 2017

Triple Crown (U.S. horse racing)
A role model G. Schramm color *Equus* no482 p72 N 2017

Triple Five Corp.
Supermall, Superstalled S. BERFIELD, I. MARRITZ et al color *Bloomberg Businessweek* no4504 p44 D 19 2016

Triplicate (Music)
Dylan, Deep in the Wee Small Hours M. GILMORE color *Rolling Stone* no1284 p51 Ap 6 2017

Tripodi, Joseph V., 1967-
REFLECTIONS OF A SIX-TIME CMO: A CONVERSATION WITH JOE TRIPODI D. MCGINN color *Harvard Business Review* v95 no4 p56 Jl/Ag 2017

Tripp, Aili Mari
Women and Power in Postconflict Africa N. van de Walle *Foreign Affairs* v95 no6 p194 N/D 2016

Tripp, Thomas
Research: The More Essential Your Job Is to Your Company, the Happier You'll Be *Harvard Business Review Digital Articles* p2 My 10 2017

Tripp family
The Roses of Fairhope R. BRAGG color *Reader's Digest* v189 no1130 p22 My 2017

Trippy, Ruth
The Language of Music *Publishers Weekly* v264 no21 p65a My 22 2017

Tripsianes, K.
Inhibitors of PEX14 disrupt protein import into glycosomes and kill Trypanosoma parasites chart color diag graph *Science* v355 no6332 p1416 Mr 31 2017

Trip to Spain, The (Film)
The Trip to Spain C. Nashawaty color *Entertainment Weekly* no1478 / 1479 p85 Ag 18-25 2017

Tristan und Isolde (Theatrical production)
CLASSICAL MUSIC *New Yorker* v92 no30 p15 S 26 2016
WAGNER WEEKEND A. ROSS cartoon *New Yorker* v92 no33 p104 O 17 2016

BREAK OUT! W. BRANTLEY, J. CERMELE et al cartoon color *Field & Stream* v121 no9 p35 Ap 2017

PAIN, SUFFERING & MUSKIES D. KARCZYNSKI color *Outdoor Life* v224 no8 p63 O 2017

WEATHER STRIPPING J. CERMELE cartoon color *Field & Stream* v121 no9 p16 Ap 2017

TROUT, CHRISTINA

USA HALF MARATHON INVITATIONAL color *Runner's World* v51 no11 p98 D 2016

Trout, Mike

TROUT'S POND K. Ducey chart *Sports Illustrated* v126 no9 p45 Mr 27 2017

Trout fishing

See also

Brown trout fishing

Lake trout fishing

All Spun Up M. Modoski color *Field & Stream* v121 no9 pF5 Ap 2017

ATLANTA'S BLUE-RIBBON TROUT STREAM C. Scalley *Atlanta* v57 no4 p50 Ag 2017

BRING ON THE NIGHT D. KARCZYNSKI and G. BETHGE color *Outdoor Life* v224 no5 p36 Je/Jl 2017

RELISH THE WEENIE J. Cermele color *Field & Stream* v122 no3 p22 Ag 2017

WATER: CAST A LURE, GRAB A TUBE, AND PADDLE AN OAR J. GREEN *Atlanta* v57 no4 p51 Ag 2017

THE WISHING TREE K. McCafferty color *Field & Stream* v122 no2 p56 Je/Jl 2017

Trout fishing—New York (State)

SING ABOUT SPRING R. Preall *New York State Conservationist* v71 no5 p2 Ap 2017

Trouwborst, Arie

Europe's biodiversity avoids fatal setback color *Science* v355 no6321 p140 Ja 13 2017

International Wildlife Law: Understanding and Enhancing Its Role in Conservation *BioScience* v67 no9 p784 S 2017

Trovatore (Music)

Operapedia: La Traviata G. VERDI *Opera News* v81 no6 p12 D 2016

Trow, M. J.

Eleventh Hour: A Kit Marlowe Mystery *Publishers Weekly* v264 no20 p41 My 15 2017

Troy, Gil

Jimmy Breslin color *Time* v189 no12 p18 Ap 3 2017

Troy, Lindsey

DEAP VALLY D. EHRLICH *Interview* v46 no8 p32 O 2016

Troy, Peter

1968 PETER TROY M. Warshaw bw *Surfer* v57 no11 p30 D 2016

Troy, Tevi

BEFORE THERE WAS NERD PROM color *Washingtonian Magazine* v52 no7 p16 Ap 2017

CLEANING UP OBAMA'S HEALTH-CARE MESS *Commentary* v142 no4 p25 N 2016

Deep State of Affairs *Commentary* v143 no4 p4 Ap 2017

Five-Alarm Fire J. GEDMIN color *Weekly Standard* v22 no16 p30 D 26 2016

Help Isn't on the Way *Commentary* v141 no10 p1 D 2016

Help Isn't on the Way *Commentary* v142 no5 p1 D 2016

How Republicans Might Bring About Single-Payer Health Care: The long-term consequences of the failure of 2017 *Commentary* v144 no3 p31 O 2017

Lives of the Mind *Commentary* v143 no6 p49 Je 2017

Mastering Disaster A. S. FELZENBERG bw color *National Review* v68 no21 p43 N 21 2016

ObamaCare: What Can a Republican President Do About It in 2017? *Commentary* v140 no2 p30 S 2015

ObamaCare: What Can a Republican President Do About It in 2017? Pursue repeal, but have a Chinese menu of reforms in your back pocket just in case *Commentary* v140 no2 p22 S 2015

Out of the Shadow *Weekly Standard* v22 no41 p35 Jl 3 2017

Trivia *Washingtonian Magazine* v52 no4 p104 Ja 2017

WILL THERE BE AN INTERNAL REVOLT AGAINST TRUMP? color *Commentary* v143 no2 p12 F 2017

Will There Be An Internal Revolt Against Trump? color *Commentary* v143 no2 p1 F 2017

Troye, Edward, 1808-1874

FROM THE ARTISTS: EDWARD TROYE color *Arabian Horse World* v57 no7 p138 Ap 2017

Troyer, Matthias

Solving the quantum many-body problem with artificial neural networks bibl diag *Science* v355 no6325 p602 F 10 2017

Troy University (Troy, Ala.)—Sports

Week 10 color *Sports Illustrated* v127 no5 p76 Ag 14 2017

Truax, Laura Sumner

Take this $500 and do good in the world color *Christian Century* v134 no8 p1 Ap 12 2017

Truax, Robert Collins, 1917-2010

Rocket Redux D. KEISER *Idaho Magazine* v16 no2 p40 N 2016

TRUBETSKOY, SASHA

THE URBAN PILEUP *Texas Monthly* v45 no5 p46 My 2017

Truck campers—Evaluation

BIG-IRON BOONDOCKING [Cover story] J. CAPPA color *Dirt Sports + Off-Road* v51 no12 p34 D 2017

Truck customizing

CLEANING UP M. EMERY color *Dirt Sports + Off-Road* v51 no10 p52 O 2017

IN THE COMFORT ZONE B. W. SMITH color *Dirt Sports + Off-Road* v51 no9 p46 S 2017

Truck drivers

The Chariots of My People R. Bragg color *Southern Living* v52 no1 p132 Ja 2017

GREAT UNKNOWNS cartoon *Popular Mechanics* p26 My 2017

HUCKING IT AT HAVOC 4 M. KAUSCH color *Dirt Sports + Off-Road* v51 no2 p54 F 2017

Truck engines (Diesel)

POST-TIER 4 SEMITRUCKS ARE THE BEST BUY: SURE, MOST TRUCKS MADE AFTER 2007 USE DEF, BUT SUCH SEMIS OFFER A FAR BETTER BUY *Successful Farming* v115 no7 p17 My 2017

Truck racing

2017 SCHEDULE chart color *Dirt Sports + Off-Road* v51 no1 p73 Ja 2017

Truck sales

POST-TIER 4 SEMITRUCKS ARE THE BEST BUY: SURE, MOST TRUCKS MADE AFTER 2007 USE DEF, BUT SUCH SEMIS OFFER A FAR BETTER BUY *Successful Farming* v115 no7 p17 My 2017

Truck tires—Evaluation

TRUCK TIRE TECH M. Cantu, J. Udy et al color *Motor Trend* v69 no10 p80 O 2017

Truck drivers—Salaries, wages, etc.

SELF-DRIVING Trucks D. H. FREEDMAN color *MIT Technology Review* v120 no2 p62 Mr/Ap 2017

Trucking

Alice Tarjan's RISE TO THE TOP N. Jaffer color *Dressage Today* v23 no12 p44 S 2017

Trucking—United States

Changing Lanes M. Chafkin and J. Eidelson color *Bloomberg Businessweek* no4528 p60 Je 26 2017

LONG-HAUL TRUCKING U.S.A map *Fortune* v175 no6 p9 My 1 2017

Trucks

See also

Dodge trucks

Ford trucks

General Motors trucks

Pickup trucks

AFFORDABLE OFF-ROADING D. SCANLON color *Dirt Sports + Off-Road* v51 no5 p58 My 2017

The Chariots of My People R. Bragg color *Southern Living* v52 no1 p132 Ja 2017

Daniel Pund D. Pund color *Car & Driver* v63 no5 p30 N 2017

Instant Cattle-Panel Cage R. Hackenberg *Mother Earth News* no282 p86 Je/Jl 2017

The New Luxury Trucks E. DYER color *Popular Mechanics* v193 no7 p50 S 2016

PICKIN' OFF THE CHERRY PRE-TIER 4 SEMIS *Successful Farming* v114 no10 p26 O 2016

September F. ESKER color *New Orleans Magazine* v52 no1 p26 S 2017

Snake! S. BUTCHER *Texas Monthly* v45 no3 p90 Mr 2017

Trucks, Butch, 1947-2017

Ap 2017

TRUITT, DUANE

Trump Theory *Commentary* v142 no1 p6 Jl/Ag 2016

Trujillo, Chad

ASK ASTRO color diag *Astronomy* v45 no3 p34 Mr 2017

Trujillo, Maria

Systemic pan-AMPK activator MK-8722 improves glucose homeostasis but induces cardiac hypertrophy graph *Science* v357 no6350 p507 Ag 4 2017

TRULSSON, NORA BURBA

Big Earl's Greasy Eats: Although its building is listed on the National Register of Historic Places, the food at Big Earl's is anything but dated. The burgers are made with Harris Ranch or Kobe beef, and the delicious home made buns are baked daily *Arizona Highways* v93 no11 p12 N 2017

The Downtown Clifton *Arizona Highways* v93 no2 p14 F 2017

Truman, Harry S., 1884-1972

WHEN COURTS KILL EXECUTIVE ORDERS D. ROOT bw *Reason* v49 no1 p12 My 2017

Truman Doctrine

A New Truman Doctrine T. Kaine color *Foreign Affairs* v96 no4 p36 Jl/Ag 2017

Trumbull, Douglas

Restoring the Allure of the Movie Theater E. Woyke color *MIT Technology Review* v119 no6 p90 N/D 2016

Trumka, Richard L., 1949-

THE NEXT FEW YEARS WILL DEFINE WHO AND WHAT WE REALLY ARE R. L. TRUMKA *Vital Speeches of the Day* v83 no3 p81 Mr 2017

Trump, Donald, 1946-

100 Days of Resistance J. NICHOLS color *Nation* v304 no15 p3 My 8 2017

The 10 best days in journalism P. Vernon color *Columbia Journalism Review* v56 no2 p50 Fall 2017

10 QUESTIONS FOR SONNY PERDUE *Successful Farming* v115 no8 p6 Je/Jl 2017

10 to watch J. MARKUSOFF color *Maclean's* v129 no46 p37 N 21 2016

117 Days, A Million Trump Jokes A First Draft of History, With Punch Lines *New York* p42 Mr 6 2017

The 140-character president M. Ingram and P. Vernon color graph *Columbia Journalism Review* v56 no2 p76 Fall 2017

the 2016 HALL of FAME J. WOLCOTT bw cartoon color *Vanity Fair* v59 no1 p117 Holiday 2017

2016 Person of the Year Donald Trump color *Time* v188 no25-26 p42 D 19 2016 Double Issue

2017 The Year Ahead *Time* v188 no27-28 p37 D 26 2016

The 2017 Time 100 N. Gibbs color *Time* v189 no16/17 p6 My 1-8 2017

THE 30-SECOND CAMPAIGN P. SMITH *New York Times Upfront* v149 no3 p14 O 10 2016

42 Months to Go... K. Pollitt *Nation* v305 no4 p6 Ag 14 2017

The $4.5 Billion Cabinet C. PETERSON-WITHORN, J. WANG et al color *Forbes* v199 no1 p26 Ja 24 2017

73 MINUTES WITH ... Eric Schneiderman A. RICE img *New York* v50 no10 p22 My 15 2017

7 Great All-American Stocks T. PETRUNO chart color *Kiplinger's Personal Finance* v71 no5 p58 My 2017

7 PREDICTIONS: How long will President Trump survive? Nobody knows, but everyone's guessing *New York* v50 no13 p25 Je 26 2017

Aasif Mandvi Knows How To Make America Great Again A. M. Cox color *New York Times Magazine* p86 O 9 2016

About That Cover img *New York* v49 no23 p10 N 14 2016

ACADEMIA ON THE MOVE A. MORETTI *Phi Kappa Phi Forum* v96 no4 p10 Wint 2016

ACCESS 2 PREZ WHILE U WAIT: THE BUCKS START HERE N. Confessore *New York Times Magazine* p32 S 3 2017

The ACLU Is Ready to Rumble A. RICE img *New York* v49 no23 p59 D 12 2016

ACROSS THE GREAT DIVIDE: On the Road in Trump's America N. Phillips color *Progressive* v81 no7 p18 O/N 2017

Act for science R. Holt color *Science* v355 no6325 p551 F 10 2017

AN ACTION LIST FOR THE (UN) GAITHFUL C. T. QUAM *Humanist* v77 no1 p20 Ja/F 2017

The Administrative State on the Chopping Block J. W. EMORD *USA Today Magazine* v145 no2864 p18 My 2017

Adolescent Politics H. WILHELM diag *National Review* v69 no5 p28 Mr 20 2017

The Adults in the Room [Cover story] J. Mann *New York Review of Books* v64 no16 p6 O 26 2017

AFTER BANNON J. Cobb cartoon *New Yorker* v93 no26 p19 S 4 2017

After Charlottesville *Commonweal* v114 no14 p5 S 8 2017

After Fidel P. KORNBLUH bw color *Nation* v303 no25/26 p4 D 19 2016

After the Polls graph *Bloomberg Businessweek* no4500 p38 N 21 2016

After Trump W. Kristol color *Weekly Standard* v22 no34 p6 My 15 2017

Against Russian Fever B. SHAPIRO *Nation* v304 no12 p4 Ap 10 2017

AGAINST THE CURRENT A. Marantz cartoon *New Yorker* v93 no22 p18 Jl 31 2017

Against Trumpian Triumphalism E. J. Dionne color *Commonweal* v143 no19 p8 D 2 2016

AG FORECAST: GLUM BUT SUNNY AT THE SAME TIME *Successful Farming* v115 no4 p16 Mr 2017

AG IN THE BALANCE *Successful Farming* v115 no3 p10 Mid-F 2017

Alienating Friends and Comforting Enemies J. Klein color *Bloomberg Businessweek* no4527 p16 Je 19 2017

The Ali We Need Today D. ZIRIN bw *Progressive* v81 no2 p45 F 2017

Allies First, Mr. President M. A. McFaul *Hoover Digest: Research & Opinion on Public Policy* no1 p77 Wint 2017

ALL THE PRESIDENT'S MEN 2.0 G. CARTER *Vanity Fair* v59 no8 p34 Ag 2017

All the President's Neighbors C. PETERSON-WITHORN color *Forbes* v199 no4 p18 Ap 25 2017

All the President's Phantoms J. WALKER color *New Republic* v248 no3 p14 Mr 2017

The Alt-Right Doesn't Care About the Constitution J. Ehrett color *Washington Monthly* v49 no3-5 p8 Mr-My 2017

#Always Trump J. HEER color *New Republic* v248 no10 p28 O 2017

AMAZING DISGRACE S. POSNER *New Republic* v248 no4 p34 Ap 2017

AMERICA FIRST D. TRUMP *Vital Speeches of the Day* v83 no3 p66 Mr 2017

The America I believe in H. A. Lashuel cartoon *Science* v355 no6326 p706 F 17 2017

AMERICA IN AFGHANISTAN: THREE FUNDAMENTAL CONCLUSIONS *Vital Speeches of the Day* v83 no10 p282 O 2017

America Is Finally Winning Again(TM)! F. FIORENTINI color *Nation* v304 no9 p28 Mr 20 2017

American Carnage *Commonweal* v144 no3 p5 F 10 2017

AMERICAN DUCE R. O. Paxton *Harper's Magazine* v334 no2004 p38 My 2017

AMERICA NEEDS HIGH-SKILLED FOREIGN WORKERS S. DALMIA color *Reason* v49 no1 p17 My 2017

American Illiberalism T. M. WIGHT *Commentary* v142 no3 p6 O 2016

AMERICANISMS A. Gopnik cartoon *New Yorker* v92 no49 p29 F 13 2017

AMERICAN NIGHTMARE W. Yang *Harper's Magazine* v334 no2001 p27 F 2017

Americans Can Unify Around Economic Growth T. J. DONOHUE *Weekly Standard* v22 no11 p9 N 21 2016

AMERICAN VALUES BY THE NUMBERS cartoon *Rolling Stone* no1281/1282 p31 F 23 2017

Ana Navarro Wants the G.O.P. to Stand Up to Trump A. M. Cox *New York Times Magazine* p62 O 2 2016

Anger Management J. Lustig *New York Times Magazine* p15 O 30 2016

Another Abu Ghraib? S. O'Brien Margaret color *Commonweal* v144 no6 p7 Mr 24 2017

Another Brief (ONE HOPES) Shining (PERHAPS) Moment? B. HANDY color *Vanity Fair* v59 no2 p40 F 2017

Another Election Day Loser: Corporate Media [Cover story] A.

Can This Relationship Survive? F. BARNES cartoon *Weekly Standard* v22 no28 p10 Mr 27 2017

Can Trump Clean Up His Messy World of Conflicts? M. Calabresi color *Time* v188 no24 p13 D 12 2016

Can Trump Handle Putin? P. R. Gregory *Hoover Digest: Research & Opinion on Public Policy* no1 p103 Wint 2017

Can Trump 'Scrap' Green Rules? J. Worland color *Time* v188 no27-28 p95 D 26 2016

Can U.S. states and cities overcome Paris exit? W. Cornwall graph *Science* v356 no6342 p1000 Je 9 2017

Can Wall Street Save Trump From Himself? W. D. COHAN color *Atlantic* v319 no3 p22 Ap 2017

Capitalism and Climate C. RORKE *American Conservative* v16 no1 p18 Ja/F 2017

The 'Car 54' Model W. Kristol bw *Weekly Standard* v22 no27 p10 Mr 20 2017

THE CARROT, THE STICK, AND THE BUGGY WHIP K. MANGU-WARD *Reason* v48 no10 p4 Mr 2017

Cartoons *New York Times Upfront* v149 no10 p24 Mr 13 2017

A Case for Caution I. M. STELZER *Weekly Standard* v22 no25 p20 Mr 6 2017

The Case for Trump's Foreign Policy M. Kroenig color *Foreign Affairs* v96 no3 p30 My/Je 2017

Celebrate the Occasion M. J. GAYNOR and S. DALPHONSE *Washingtonian Magazine* v52 no4 p104 Ja 2017

CENTRAL INTELLIGENCE P. COLLOFF *Texas Monthly* v45 no2 p106 F 2017

Centrist Pundits Prepared Way for Trump Smear of 'Alt-Left' A. Johnson *Extra!* v30 no8 p1 O 2017

CEOs Face Off Against Trump (or Not) D. McGinn bw *Harvard Business Review Digital Articles* p2 Ja 31 2017

The CEO Who Went Too Far T. Noah color *New York Review of Books* v64 no6 p37 Ap 6 2017

The Challenges Ahead *Islamic Horizons* v46 no1 p6 Ja/F 2017

The changing face of the GOP T. Stanley *History Today* v66 no11 p11 N 2016

CHANGING The Conversation C. HOOKS *Texas Monthly* v45 no8 p44 Ag 2017

Changing Tides B. LUTZ *Road & Track* v68 no9 p100 Je 2017

CHARGE OF THE RIGHT BRIGADE S. TANENHAUS bw color *Esquire* p80 My 2017

Charlie Rose talks to... Glenn Beck bw *Bloomberg Businessweek* no4497 p29 O 31 2016

A children's guide to parenting S. FESCHUK color *Maclean's* v130 no3 p72 Ap 2017

Chiling Effect color *National Review* v68 no24 p14 D 31 2016

China's Moment L. Billings graph *Scientific American* v317 no4 p72 O 2017

The Choice N. Gibbs map *Time* v188 no25-26 p44 D 19 2016 Double Issue

CHRISTIAN HEGEMONY IN THE AGE OF TRUMP M. Kuhlenbeck *Humanist* v77 no3 p12 My/Je 2017

Christians and Donald Trump R. Munch color *Progressive* v81 no4 p21 Ap/My 2017

THE CHURCH'S INTEGRITY IN THE TRUMP YEARS M. GALLI cartoon *Christianity Today* v61 no1 p23 Ja/F 2017

CITIES GO ROGUE T. ANDERSON *In These Times* v41 no3 p24 Mr 2017

Citizenship on Its Knees P. J. Williams *Nation* v305 no10 p10 O 23 2017

Citizens, United J. Chait img *New York* v49 no23 p12 N 14 2016

Citizen Trump Upends: The Oval Office L. D'VORKIN *Forbes* v200 no5 p14 N 14 2017

The City Is Still Ours D. Wallace-Wells img *New York* v49 no25 p40 D 12 2016

CLEAN ENERGY D. C. Vock *Governing* v30 no4 p36 Ja 2017

Cleveland: Four Days in Donald Trump's America J. Chait and D. W. Frazier img *New York* v49 no15 p13 Jl 25 2016

Click Bait A. Hess *New York Times Magazine* p11 Mr 5 2017

Climate Denialism Kills M. HERTSGAARD *Nation* v305 no7 p3 S 25 2017

A Climate of Denial E. Alterman color il *Nation* v305 no1 p6 Jl 3 2017

Climate's Trump Card M. HERTSGAARD *Nation* v304 no13 p4 Ap 17 2017

A CLOSE LOOK AT TWO ADS *New York Times Upfront* v149

no3 p14 O 10 2016

THE CLOSER'S CLOSING ARGUMENT color *GQ: Gentlemen's Quarterly* v86 no11 p164 N 2016

Coach Pop vs. Donald Trump D. ZIRIN color *Progressive* v81 no3 p45 Mr 2017

Coal and Climate Change in Kentucky T. Cole color *Progressive* v81 no2 p16 F 2017

Cold Climate M. Philips *Bloomberg Businessweek* no4499 p31 N 14 2016

The Collapse of Fair-Minded Journalism M. GOODWIN *USA Today Magazine* v146 no2868 p12 S 2017

The Comey Misfire D. V. Drehle, A. Altman et al color *Time* v189 no19 p20 My 22 2017

Comey, Trump, and the GOP S. F. Hayes color *Weekly Standard* v22 no35 p6 My 22 2017

COMICS T. LABAN, K. BABIS et al *In These Times* v41 no10 p46 O 2017

COMIC TRIP C. WINTER color *Bloomberg Businessweek* no4516 p58 Mr 27 2017

Commander in confusion [Cover story] A. ABEL color *Maclean's* v129 no51/52 p40 D 26 2016

COMMENT: FIGHTING WORDS E. Osnos bw *New Yorker* v93 no33 p35 O 23 2017

Comments img *New York* v49 no25 p16 D 12 2016

Comments img *New York* v50 no6 p6 Mr 20 2017

The Common Sense of Oklahomans L. Granados *Humanist* v77 no1 p6 Ja/F 2017

Congress Confronts a Daunting to-Do List N. Jenkins color *Time* v190 no10/11 p16 S 18 2017

Conjectures from the Swamp P. A. Harkness *Governing* v30 no4 p16 Ja 2017

Consequences R. WILSON *American Scholar* v86 no1 p2 Wint 2017

CONTAINING TRUMP J. RAUCH cartoon color *Atlantic* v319 no2 p60 Mr 2017

Containing Trump P. Leach *Atlantic* v319 no5 p10 Je 2017

The Contest For the Senate R. PONNURU *National Review* v68 no19 p18 O 24 2016

CONVERSATION A. WILSON color *Forbes* v199 no4 p30 Ap 25 2017

COOKIE MONSTER ON THE DOLE H. ALFORD cartoon *New Yorker* v93 no9 p29 Ap 17 2017

The Cost of Repealing Obamacare J. WEST color *Progressive* v81 no4 p10 Ap/My 2017

Could this get any worse? [Cover story] J. Gatehouse color *Maclean's* v129 no43 p28 O 31 2016

Counter Offensive: The American far right has become remarkably adept at commandeering ideas from its enemies. Now it's pulling off its trickiest switch yet: billing itself as the new 'alternative' culture J. Herrman *New York Times Magazine* p11 Jl 2 2017

Country First [Cover story] M. Duffy, A. Altman et al color *Time* v190 no7 p26 Ag 21 2017

COURTROOM DRAMAS [Cover story] P. SMITH *New York Times Upfront* v149 no8 p8 Ja 30 2017

The Courts Fight Trump D. COLE *Nation* v304 no16 p4 My 22 2017

Covering History N. Gibbs color *Time* v188 no21 p4 N 21 2016

Covfefe: The Show color *Entertainment Weekly* no1470 p10 Je 16 2017

The Crackdown Has Begun A. Gupta color *Progressive* v81 no4 p56 Ap/My 2017

Crisis of the Conservative House Divided S. F. HAYWARD *Weekly Standard* v22 no8 p20 O 31 2016

Critical but Not Serious W. Kristol *Weekly Standard* v22 no26 p8 Mr 13 2017

THE CROSSING K. WALKER cartoon *New Yorker* v92 no49 p72 F 13 2017

Crossover Act C. Homans *New York Times Magazine* p15 N 6 2016

A DACA Deal R. VERBRUGGEN color *National Review* v69 no18 p26 O 2 2017

Dakota pipeline to go on, president orders, despite concerns of Sioux people color *Christian Century* v134 no5 p14 Mr 1 2017

The Damage Done K. Wright color *Nation* v305 no4 p10 Ag 14 2017

John Legend Can't Pretend Times Are Normal A. M. Cox *New York Times Magazine* p66 F 26 2017

John Paulson's Long Bet on Trump Pays Off J. Light color graph *Bloomberg Businessweek* no4501 p33 N 28 2016

A JOKE CERTAINLY, but NO LAUGHING MATTER G. CARTER *Vanity Fair* v59 no5 p40 Ap 2017

Journalism in Trump's America M. MASSING color diag *Nation* v304 no4 p24 F 6 2017

The Justices Agree to Grapple With Travel Bans and Phantoms D. V. Drehle color *Time* v190 no2/3 p7 Jl 10-17 2017

Just Say No to Just Say No J. B. JUDIS color *New Republic* v248 no5 p14 My 2017

Kafka Wouldn't Dare E. Alterman il *Nation* v304 no11 p6 Ap 3 2017

Keeping the Deal and Cracking Down on Iran color *Bloomberg Businessweek* no4504 p8 D 19 2016

Keep Your Panic Dry W. Kristol cartoon *Weekly Standard* v22 no13 p7 D 5 2016

KELLY ANNE CONWAY IS A STAR O. NUZZI img *New York* v50 no6 p26 Mr 20 2017

KELLYANNE'S ALTERNATIVE UNIVERSE M. BALL color *Atlantic* v319 no3 p44 Ap 2017

Kill This Idea E. Epstein color *Weekly Standard* v22 no19 p6 Ja 23 2017

KIM JONG-UN NO PATSY B. McCALL cartoon *New Yorker* v93 no6 p29 Mr 27 2017

The King of Debt *Commonweal* v144 no9 p5 My 19 2017

Kings of the Hill (and the White House) [Cover story] P. SMITH *New York Times Upfront* v149 no9 p6 F 20 2017

The Kiss-Up That Wasn't A. FERGUSON color *Weekly Standard* v22 no40 p8 Je 26 2017

The Kleptocracy Preps for Pennsylvania Avenue J. Chait img *New York* v49 no24 p29 N 28 2016

THE KNIGHT'S MOVE G. LEWIS-KRAUS il *Nation* v304 no15 p27 My 8 2017

Know Your Trumps K. BENNETT *Washingtonian Magazine* v52 no4 p98 Ja 2017

THE KREMLIN CONNECTION H. BLUM color *Vanity Fair* v59 no5 p85 Ap 2017

LAND OF CONFUSION: THE RELIGIOUS RIGHT, TRUMP, AND 'POST-TRUTH' AMERICA R. BOSTON *Humanist* v77 no2 p32 Mr/Ap 2017

Language Games P. J. Williams *Nation* v304 no17 p10 Je 5 2017

last word E. Smeal *Ms.* v26 no3 p16 Fall 2016

Lawmakers balk at most Trump cuts D. Malakoff and J. Mervis color *Science* v357 no6346 p11 Jl 7 2017

The Leak War M. Hemingway color *Weekly Standard* v22 no20 p6 Ja 30 2017

LEGAL JEOPARDY T. Schoenberg, S. Pettypiece et al bw color *Bloomberg Businessweek* no4541 p35 O 9 2017

Legislative Background on Deregulation *Congressional Digest* v96 no4 p11 Ap 2017

LESSONS FROM THE LAST FIGHT S. Schulman *Harper's Magazine* v334 no2001 p34 F 2017

Let Him Eat Cake *Commonweal* v144 no8 p5 My 5 2017

Let's Give the Stimulus Its Due: It saved the economy, but that isn't always acknowledged P. A. Harkness *Governing* v30 no10 p16 Jl 2017

A Letter to Washington color *Scientific American* v316 no2 p7 F 2017

Let the market freak-out begin C. SORENSEN color *Maclean's* v129 no46 p35 N 21 2016

Let Trump Be Trump? P. TERZIAN color *Weekly Standard* v23 no3 p12 S 25 2017

Let Us Now Praise Homemakers R. STEIN bw *National Review* v69 no2 p18 F 6 2017

The Leveling of Tehran *USA Today Magazine* v145 no2860 p16 Ja 2017

Liar and Lunatic E. Alterman *Nation* v305 no11 p8 O 30 2017

The Liar in Chief T. STUART color *Rolling Stone* no1285 p46 Ap 20 2017

Liberalism is founded on the belief that we should tolerate one another's error A. Kirsch *New York Times Book Review* p27 O 1 2017

Liberal Nonprofits Ride The Anti-Trump Wave I. Boudway, C. Suddath et al color *Bloomberg Businessweek* no4500 p30 N 21 2016

LIBIDINAL POLITICS K. Forrester *Harper's Magazine* v334 no2001 p30 F 2017

A life with loss F. W. Nichols, M. Griffith et al color *U.S. Catholic* v82 no1 p5 Ja 2017

Lightbox K. Vick color *Time* v189 no21 p22 Je 5 2017

The Limits of Spending More M. Thompson color *Time* v188 no22-23 p31 N/D 2016

The Little Guy and the Billionaire F. BARNES color *Weekly Standard* v22 no11 p10 N 21 2016

LIVE AND LEARN P. King color *Sports Illustrated* v127 no10 p34 O 2 2017

Long Shots That May Pay Off Big M. Abelson and Z. R. Mider bw *Bloomberg Businessweek* no4499 p23 N 14 2016

The Long View R. LONG il *National Review* v68 no19 p40 O 24 2016

The Long View R. LONG il *National Review* v69 no17 p34 S 11 2017

The Long View R. LONG il *National Review* v69 no6 p38 Ap 3 2017

Look to Cities and States G. Newsom *New Republic* v248 no3 p33 Mr 2017

The Looming Trump Trade Disaster cartoon *Bloomberg Businessweek* no4508 p8 Ja 23 2017

The Loser W. Kristol *Weekly Standard* v22 no8 p6 O 31 2016

Losing Hearts and Minds B. POWERS *New Republic* v248 no10 p8 O 2017

Louder Than Bombs J. NELSON color *GQ: Gentlemen's Quarterly* v97 no6 p16 Je 2017

Lower Your Expectations color *Kiplinger's Personal Finance* v71 no1 p45 Ja 2017

Low-Key Villainy K. Wright color il *Nation* v304 no15 p10 My 8 2017

The Loyalty Freak J. B. JUDIS color *New Republic* v248 no7 p14 Jl 2017

THE LYING GAME J. WOLCOTT color *Vanity Fair* v59 no8 p56 Ag 2017

The Lying Golfer-in-Chief B. LUEDERS color *Progressive* v81 no7 p14 O/N 2017

Machine Error L. SMILEY il *New Republic* v247 no11 p8 N 2016

Mad, Democrats? Blame the Iran Deal *Commentary* p1 Ja 2017

Mad, Democrats? Blame the Iran Deal *Commentary* v143 no1 p1 Ja 2017

MAD LIBS color map *Mother Jones* v42 no3 p11 My/Je 2017

MADMEN THEORIES S. Coll cartoon *New Yorker* v93 no30 p17 O 2 2017

MAD SCIENTISTS GET EVEN N. BAJWA *In These Times* v41 no3 p11 Mr 2017

Make America Gipper Again F. BARNES color *Weekly Standard* v23 no5 p10 O 9 2017

MAKE AMERICA HATE AGAIN J. HARKINSON, S. Posner et al bw cartoon *Mother Jones* v42 no1 p24 Ja/F 2017

Make Medicine Great Again K. S. HELD *USA Today Magazine* v145 no2860 p65 Ja 2017

Making Airports and Bridges Great Again S. Frizell color *Time* v188 no22-23 p33 N/D 2016

Making ALA Great Again A. Richard Albanese color *Publishers Weekly* v264 no8 p21 F 20 2017

Making Their Bets N. Summers *Bloomberg Businessweek* no4499 p31 N 14 2016

Making Trump Pay D. COLE *Nation* v304 no17 p3 Je 5 2017

Making Use of Donald Trump M. CONTINETTI *Commentary* v140 no2 p72 S 2015

Manufacturing's loss, Trump's gain R. ATKINSON color *Issues in Science & Technology* v33 no1 p5 Fall 2016

The Man Who Knew Too Little [Cover story] M. W. O'Reilly bw *Commonweal* v144 no17 p6 O 20 2017

Man Without a Plan M. Konczal diag il *Nation* v304 no10 p5 Mr 27 2017

MAR-A-LAGO RULES S. Kolhatkar cartoon *New Yorker* v93 no5 p34 Mr 20 2017

A March for Science Is Not Enough color *Scientific American* v316 no5 p9 My 2017

The Markets In the Age of Trump R. Foroohar color *Time* v188 no21 p24 N 21 2016

The Martyr Complex J. Marley color *Commonweal* v144 no6 p19

p6 S/O 2016

Trump, Donald, 1946——Psychology

The Counterpuncher F. BARNES cartoon *Weekly Standard* v22 no19 p9 Ja 23 2017

TRUMP, BETWEEN TAKES N. BILTON color *Vanity Fair* v59 no2 p52 F 2017

The Trump Tweetometer graph *New Republic* v248 no5 p9 My 2017

Trump, Donald, 1946——Trials, litigation, etc.

ALL THE PRESIDENT'S LAWYERS: DONALD TRUMP'S LIFE AND CAREER HAVE BEEN DEFINED BY HIS LEGAL BATTLES. BUT DO THE ATTORNEYS WHO GUIDED HIM THROUGH THE COURTROOMS OF NEW YORK AND NEW JERSEY KNOW HOW TO NAVIGATE WASHINGTON? J. MAHLER *New York Times Magazine* p28 Jl 9 2017

THE NAGGING WHEELS OF JUSTICE *New York* v50 no12 p43 Je 12 2017

A Trump Lawsuit Gets a Boost From Restaurants B. Van Voris color *Bloomberg Businessweek* no4519 p34 Ap 24 2017

Trump, Donald, Jr., 1977-

AGENTS AND ASSETS A. Davidson color *New Yorker* v93 no22 p21 Jl 31 2017

Cover *Time* v190 no4 pC1 Jl 24 2017

DONNY AND ERIC MIND THE STORE P. Robison, M. Smith et al color *Bloomberg Businessweek* no4535 p54 Ag 28 2017

Do You Love It Now? P. M. Barrett, S. Pettypiece et al color *Bloomberg Businessweek* no4530 p36 Jl 17 2017

How Donald Trump Jr.'s Emails Have Cranked Up the Heat on His Family [Cover story] D. V. Drehle, M. Calabresi et al color *Time* v190 no4 p22 Jl 24 2017

Ms-Speaking color *Weekly Standard* v22 no43 p2 Jl 24 2017

What You Said About ... color *Time* v190 no5 p5 Jl 31 2017

Trump, Eric

DONNY AND ERIC MIND THE STORE P. Robison, M. Smith et al color *Bloomberg Businessweek* no4535 p54 Ag 28 2017

"Everybody Gets Billed" [Cover story] D. ALEXANDER color *Forbes* v199 no7 p104 Je 29 2017

Trump, Friedrich, 1869-1918

The Best Former Whorehouse in Canada N. O. Pearson color *Bloomberg Businessweek* no4497 p28 O 31 2016

THE EMIGRANTS *Harper's Magazine* v334 no2002 p18 Mr 2017

Trump's wild Canadian past J. MARKUSOFF bw *Maclean's* v129 no42 p30 O 24 2016

Trump, Ivana

TRUMP REBOOT J. Mayer cartoon *New Yorker* v92 no34 p20 O 24 2016

Trump, Ivanka, 1981-

BLAND AMBITION S. ELLISON color *Vanity Fair* v59 no10 p174 O 2017

Born Trump M. BRENDAN DOUGHERTY il *National Review* v69 no12 p27 Je 26 2017

Brand Names: Amy Larocca img *New York* p18 F 20 2017

China Makes Nice With Ivanka and Jared *Bloomberg Businessweek* no4511 p27 F 13 2017

DISOWNING IVANKA N. FREEMAN cartoon color *ARTnews* v116 no1 p98 Spr 2017

The Family Leave Dilemma A. B. LLOYD color graph *Weekly Standard* v22 no48 p21 S 4 2017

FATHER ISSUES A. ABEL color *Maclean's* p40 Je 2017

Ivana Trump Has Her Say B. Luscombe color *Time* v190 no16/17 p94 O 23 2017

IVANKA'S APPRENTICE S. ELLISON and E. J. Fox color *Vanity Fair* v59 no2 p70 F 2017

JARED & IVANKA'S GUIDE TO MINDFUL MARRIAGE P. RUDNICK cartoon *New Yorker* v93 no17 p29 Je 19 2017

Lightbox color *Time* v189 no12 p20 Ap 3 2017

The People's Princess C. FLANAGAN and T. O'Brien img *New York* v50 no10 p46 My 15 2017

The queen of spin H. Seligson color *Columbia Journalism Review* v56 no2 p100 Fall 2017

Send in the Clones W. D. COHAN color *Vanity Fair* v59 no2 p76 F 2017

THIS PARTICULAR DADDY'S GIRL A. WILENTZ color *Nation* v304 no5 p14 F 20 2017

TRUMP FAMILY VALUES G. CARTER *Vanity Fair* v59 no6 p40 My 2017

Trump Family Values S. DOYLE *In These Times* v41 no5 p24 My 2017

WELCOME TO TRUMPISTAN G. CARTER *Vanity Fair* v59 no2 p20 F 2017

Why America's First Daughter Is a Hit In China C. Campbell color *Time* v190 no2/3 p36 Jl 10-17 2017

Trump, Melania, 1970-

The Bess Is Yet to Come color *Weekly Standard* v22 no22 p2 F 13 2017

Brand Names: Amy Larocca img *New York* p18 F 20 2017

Bully, Bully cartoon *Weekly Standard* v22 no29 p3 Ap 3 2017

Don't Cry for Me, Paparazzi color *Weekly Standard* v22 no30 p2 Ap 10 2017

HE COMES FIRST E. PERETZ color *Vanity Fair* v59 no6 p92 My 2017

Know Your Trumps K. BENNETT *Washingtonian Magazine* v52 no4 p98 Ja 2017

MELANIA'S DIARY 1/21/2017 P. RUDNICK cartoon *New Yorker* v92 no48 p27 F 6 2017

THE MOUSE PACK J. WOLCOTT color *Vanity Fair* v59 no6 p63 My 2017

Sixteen Trumps C. Bonanos img *New York* v49 no22 p12 O 31 2016

WHEREVER WOMEN ARE DIMINISHED, THE ENTIRE WORLD IS DIMINISHED WITH THEM *Vital Speeches of the Day* v83 no6 p184 Je 2017

Trump, Melania, 1970——Trials, litigation, etc.

WHO IS WEBSTER G. TARPLEY? B. Freed *Washingtonian Magazine* v52 no2 p20 N 2016

Trump Hotels & Casino Resorts Inc.

TRUMP HOTELS' WEIRD PITCH A. Davidson color *New Yorker* v93 no18 p21 Je 26 2017

Trumper, Stephen

Wheelchair Parkour color *Walrus* v14 no5 p21 Je 2017

Trumpet players

Alpert Shines Spotlight on Community College Programs B. Zimmerman color *Downbeat* v84 no1 p96 Ja 2017

DIZZY GILLESPIE T. Panken bw *Downbeat* v84 no1 p34 Ja 2017

Friendship Through Mentorship J. Murph color *Downbeat* v84 no10 p30 O 2017

He's Funny That Way: THE LIFE, TIMES, AND PICKLED GARLIC OF ALAN KIGER K. LAUR *Cincinnati Magazine* v50 no11 p40 Ag 2017

JONATHAN FINLAYSON P. Lutz color *Downbeat* v84 no1 p46 Ja 2017

PETER ASPLUND J. Ephland color *Downbeat* v84 no4 p20 Ap 2017

REIN MEN *Los Angeles Magazine* v62 no6 p100 Je 2017

The Tragic Trumpeter T. TEACHOUT *Commentary* v143 no6 p52 Je 2017

WALLACE RONEY TAKING THE HARD TRAIL [Cover story] T. Panken color *Downbeat* v84 no2 p40 F 2017

Trumpet playing

Latin Lead Trumpet vs. Jazz Soloist: Developing Different Concepts S. KUEHN color *Downbeat* v84 no6 p82 Je 2017

Trumpeter swan

Feed the Birds A. LAHEY color *Walrus* v14 no8 p21 O 2017

ON THE RISE *South Dakota Magazine* v32 no4 p110 N/D 2016

Safe Harbour? color *Canadian Wildlife* v22 no5 p12 N/D 2016

Trumpet—Evaluation

B&S MBX3 Heritage X-Line Trumpet B. Zimmerman color *Downbeat* v84 no10 p194 O 2017

Eastman ETR824S Trumpet M. Stewart color *Downbeat* v84 no4 p93 Ap 2017

Kanstul 1603 Committee Trumpet B. Zimmerman color *Downbeat* v84 no4 p92 Ap 2017

Trump International Hotel & Tower (Chicago, Ill.)

THE URBANIST: MY SUPER CLASSY SPA DAY R. O'CONNOR color *Chicago* v66 no9 p44 S 2017

Trump Organization (New York, N.Y.)

THE DONALD OF THE DESERT A. BROWN color *Forbes* v199 no3 p62 Mr 28 2017

Foreign Entanglements D. McLAUGHLIN il *National Review* v69 no4 p13 Mr 6 2017

See also

Charitable uses, trusts, & foundations (Law)

Trusts & trustees—Accounting

Trump Vs. The Rule Of Law M. Levine color *Bloomberg Businessweek* no4510 p6 F 6 2017

Trust—Social aspects

POLICING M. Maciag *Governing* v30 no4 p34 Ja 2017

Trusting the Climate: Catastrophe Vs. Stability N. Stehr and A. Machin graph *Society* v53 no6 p573 D 2016

Understanding Trust, In China and the West D. De Cremer *Harvard Business Review Digital Articles* p2 F 11 2015

Trut, Lyudmila

HOW TO BUILD A DOG color *Scientific American* v316 no5 p68 My 2017

Truth

See also

Error

Evidence

Reality

Alternative facts and the coming constitutional crisis M. Malone *America* v216 no3 p3 F 6 2017

Can Trump Handle the Truth? [Cover story] M. Scherer, S. Frizell et al color *Time* v189 no12 p32 Ap 3 2017

Fake News: Tamar Wilner Is the Hero We Need *Skeptical Inquirer* v41 no2 p11 Mr/Ap 2017

FIND THE TRUTH AND PRINT IT S. Goldberg color *National Geographic* v231 no6 pC7 Je 2017

Living truthfully *Christian Century* v134 no1 p7 Ja 4 2017

Take a Deep Breath K. FINNERAN *Issues in Science & Technology* v33 no2 p17 Wint 2017

There's a Word for Using Truthful Facts to Deceive: Paltering F. Gino *Harvard Business Review Digital Articles* p2 O 5 2016

TOWARDS A POST-LIES FUTURE: FIGHTING "ALTERNATIVE FACTS" AND "POST-TRUTH" POLITICS G. TSIPURSKY *Humanist* v77 no2 p12 Mr/Ap 2017

What Is Truth, Anyway? M. Shermer color *Scientific American* v316 no4 p78 Ap 2017

When a President Can't Be Taken at His Word N. Gibbs color *Time* v189 no12 p5 Ap 3 2017

Why We Believe--Long After We Shouldn't C. TAVRIS and E. ARONSON *Skeptical Inquirer* v41 no2 p51 Mr/Ap 2017

Truth, Liberty & Soul-Live In NYC: The Complete 1982 NPR Jazz Alive! Recording (Music)

New Album Chronicles Pastorius in '82 T. Staudter color *Downbeat* v84 no6 p20 Je 2017

Truthfulness & falsehood

See also

Deception

Error

7 Things to Say When a Conversation Turns Negative K. K. Reardon *Harvard Business Review Digital Articles* p2 My 11 2016

The Big Reveal M. BECK cartoon *O, The Oprah Magazine* p40 My 2017

Credibility Counts [Cover story] J. KIRCHICK bw color *Weekly Standard* v22 no16 p18 D 26 2016

THE END OF FACTS M. Taibbi cartoon *Rolling Stone* no1281/1282 p28 F 23 2017

How and Why We Lie at Work T. Chamorro-Premuzic *Harvard Business Review Digital Articles* p2 Ja 2 2015

How to Fake It When You're Not Feeling Confident R. Knight *Harvard Business Review Digital Articles* p2 Je 7 2016

Leading Across Cultures Is More Complicated for Women S. A. Hewlett and R. Rashid *Harvard Business Review Digital Articles* p2 D 2 2015

The Liar in Chief T. STUART color *Rolling Stone* no1285 p46 Ap 20 2017

A Man I Know Faked His Academic Credentials. Should I Tell His Fiancée? K. A. Appiah *New York Times Magazine* p20 O 23 2016

Talk: Christian Lorentzen img *New York* p13 F 20 2017

Ten Practical Tactics to Unravel the Uncanny M. POLIDORO *Skeptical Inquirer* v41 no1 p25 Ja/F 2017

Why Lying Is So Easy for Trump B. ADLER color *New Republic* v248 no4 p10 Ap 2017

WHY WE LIE Y. BHATTACHARJEE cartoon color graph *National Geographic* v231 no6 p30 Je 2017

Truthfulness & falsehood in politics

All the News That Causes Fits *America* v215 no18 p5 D 5 2016

The Truth Is Out There C. Alter, M. Scherer et al color *Time* v188 no15 p28 O 17 2016

Truthfulness & falsehood—Psychological aspects

The Truth About Lies color *Prevention* v69 no7 p15 Jl 2017

Truthfulness & falsehood—Religious aspects

The 'no cross talk' rule A. B. Robinson *Christian Century* v134 no10 p10 My 10 2017

Truthfulness & falsehood—Research

Apes recognize others' false beliefs B. BOWER *Science News* v190 no10 p8 N 12 2016

Truth—Moral & ethical aspects

CONFESSING color *Women's Health* v14 no2 p160 Mr 2017

Truth—Religious aspects—Christianity

Godly play with adults S. Wells *Christian Century* v134 no15 p35 Jl 19 2017

Truth—Research

Frequent lying alters brain activity L. SANDERS *Science News* v190 no11 p12 N 26 2016

Tryan, Brady

NORTHERN EXPOSURE color *Spin to Win Rodeo* v20 no11 p12 Ja 2017

Tryan, Chase

FIVE FLAT [Cover story] C. Toy color *Spin to Win Rodeo* v21 no4 p31 Je 2017

Tryan, Clay, 1979-

ELITE HARDWARE C. TOY color *Spin to Win Rodeo* v20 no11 p42 Ja 2017

Tryan and Graves Hit for $22K at RHR color *Spin to Win Rodeo* v21 no5 p16 Jl 2017

Tryan, Travis

COUSINS TRAVIS AND CHASE TRYAN WIN SAN ANGELO color *Spin to Win Rodeo* v21 no2 p20 Ap 2017

Trygstad, Ryan

Sneaky strategies for better hair M. OLIVA *Redbook* p50 N 2017

Trying to Figure It Out (Music)

JAZZ ALBUM OF THE YEAR bw color *Downbeat* v83 no12 p38 D 2016

Tryon (N.C.)

Margaret's Blog *Dressage Today* v23 no5 p12 Ja 2017

Tryon, Jay—Interviews

Member Spotlight: Jay Tryon V. Paynich *Parks & Recreation* v52 no5 p69 My 2017

Trypanosoma

Inhibitors of PEX14 disrupt protein import into glycosomes and kill Trypanosoma parasites M. Dawidowski, L. Emmanouilidis et al chart color diag graph *Science* v355 no6332 p1416 Mr 31 2017

Trypanosomatidae

When stop makes sense B. Zinshteyn and R. Green bibl diag *Science* v354 no6316 p1106 D 2 2016

Tryptophan

Kynurenines: Tryptophan's metabolites in exercise, inflammation, and mental health I. Cervenka, L. Z. Agudelo et al color *Science* v357 no6349 p369 Jl 28 2017

TSABARI, AYELET

Hit and Run *New York Times Book Review* p22 Mr 19 2017

Tsai, Charlie

Direct and continuous strain control of catalysts with tunable battery electrode materials bibl graph *Science* v354 no6315 p1031 N 25 2016

Tsai, H.

Extremely efficient internal exciton dissociation through edge states in layered 2D perovskites bibl graph *Science* v355 no6331 p1288 Mr 24 2017

Tsai, Jill

TZAP: A telomere-associated protein involved in telomere length control bibl diag graph *Science* v355 no6325 p638 F 10 2017

Tsai, Ming, 1964-

Fast Hands! color *AARP: The Magazine* v60 no3A p66 Ap/My 2017

Tsai, Ming-Jer

Elimination of the male reproductive tract in the female embryo is promoted by COUP-TFII in mice color graph *Science* v357 no6352 p717 Ag 18 2017

Tsai, Sophia Y.

Elimination of the male reproductive tract in the female embryo is promoted by COUP-TFII in mice color graph *Science* v357 no6352 p717 Ag 18 2017

Tsai, Waysun Johnny

A GURU FOR THE END OF DAYS R. O'CONNOR color *Chicago* v66 no11 p32 N 2017

Tsai Ing-wen, 1956-

Taipei Calling E. Epstein cartoon *Weekly Standard* v22 no15 p6 D 19 2016

Tsakmakidis, K. L.

Breaking Lorentz reciprocity to overcome the time-bandwidth limit in physics and engineering bw diag graph *Science* v356 no6344 p1260 Je 23 2017

Tsao, Han-Fei

In situ architecture, function, and evolution of a contractile injection system color diag *Science* v357 no6352 p713 Ag 18 2017

Tsatskis, Yonit

Drosophila insulin release is triggered by adipose Stunted ligand to brain Methuselah receptor bibl graph *Science* v353 no6307 p1553 S 30 2016

Tsatsouline, Pavel

When a 130-Pound Girl Can Lift More Than You T. FERRISS cartoon color *Men's Health* v32 no4 p28 My 2017

Tsawwassen (B.C.)

A First Nation For the 21st Century N. O. Pearson color *Bloomberg Businessweek* no4541 p30 O 9 2017

Tschoepe, Ray

Avoiding Paint Buildup cartoon *Old House Journal* v44 no8 p58 D 2016

Do you need a chimney liner? color *Old House Journal* v45 no7 p42 O 2017

Fixing Sagging Floor Joists diag *Old House Journal* v45 no7 p56 O 2017

Hanging Heavy Ceiling Fixtures cartoon *Old House Journal* v45 no1 p58 F 2017

Installing Clapboards diag *Old House Journal* v45 no4 p58 Je 2017

Running New Plumbing Lines cartoon *Old House Journal* v45 no2 p58 Ap 2017

Securing Loose Stretchers diag *Old House Journal* v45 no6 p60 S 2017

Subbing Materials for Wood diag *Old House Journal* v45 no3 p58 My 2017

Tschöp, Matthias H.

Fat controls U bibl diag *Science* v355 no6330 p1124 Mr 17 2017

Tse, Terence

Companies Are Working with Consumers to Reduce Waste *Harvard Business Review Digital Articles* p2 Je 7 2016

How Businesses Can Support a Circular Economy *Harvard Business Review Digital Articles* p2 F 1 2016

Tse, Tommy

READER GALLERY bw color *Astronomy* v45 no11 p72 N 2017

Tseng, Roger

Structural basis of the day-night transition in a bacterial circadian clock bibl diag *Science* v355 no6330 p1174 Mr 17 2017

Tseng Kwong Chi

PAINT BY NUMBERS bw *Advocate* no1091 p93 Je/Jl 2017

Tserkovnyak, Yaroslav

Control and local measurement of the spin chemical potential in a magnetic insulator bw diag *Science* v357 no6347 p195 Jl 14 2017

Tsewang Rinzing—Interviews

Tsewang Rinzing W. Joan Biddlecombe color *Tricycle: The Buddhist Review* v26 no4 p22 Summ 2017

Tse-Wei Wang, Jacob

Perovskite-perovskite tandem photovoltaics with optimized band gaps bibl chart graph *Science* v354 no6314 p861 N 18 2016

TSHIKORORO, "TEPSII" THENDO

GIFTS that UPLIFT! cartoon *O, The Oprah Magazine* p148 D 2016

Tshiuetin Rail Transportation Inc.

Riding the Tshiuetin C. ELLINGSON bw color *Walrus* v14 no9 p54 N 2017

Tsien, Roger Y., 1952-2016

Roger Y. Tsien (1952–2016) S. J. Lippard color *Science* v354 no6308 p41 O 7 2016

Tsikurishvili, Irina

SLEEPING BEAUTY R. f. RITZEL *Virginia Living* v15 no1 p33 D 2016

Tsinigine, Aaron

SILVER CITY SWING color *Spin to Win Rodeo* v21 no6 p13 Ag 2017

TSIPURSKY, GLEB

TOWARDS A POST-LIES FUTURE: FIGHTING "ALTERNATIVE FACTS" AND "POST-TRUTH" POLITICS *Humanist* v77 no2 p12 Mr/Ap 2017

Tsolakis, Elena

A Star Wars-Inspired Observatory J. Zorthian color *Time* v190 no12 p23 S 25 2017

Tsolis, Renée M.

Microbiota-activated PPAR-γ signaling inhibits dysbiotic Enterobacteriaceae expansion graph *Science* v357 no6351 p570 Ag 11 2017

Tsolkas, Christos

What It Was Like to Be a Manager in Ukraine *Harvard Business Review Digital Articles* p2 Je 2 2015

Tsoukalis, Loukas

Canary in the Union J. PSAROPOULOS color *Weekly Standard* v22 no15 p33 D 19 2016

TSOULIS-REAY, ALEXA

The New York Liberty's Dancers, the Timeless Torches, Are All 40-Plus img *New York* v49 no25 p54 D 12 2016

OBAMA'S AMERICA img *New York* v49 no20 p12 O 3 2016

One Building, 41 Moon Shots img *New York* v49 no21 p64 O 17 2016

One Couple, Two Pregnancies, One Year Later img *New York* v49 no26 p10 D 26 2016

Tsubota, Tadashi

Conversion of object identity to object-general semantic value in the primate temporal cortex color graph *Science* v357 no6352 p687 Ag 18 2017

Tsuchiya, Keiichi

COMPETITION color *Road & Track* v69 no2 p12 S 2017

Tsui, Bonnie

Mapping Melodies *Audubon* v119 no1 p14 Spr 2017

The poet editor of West Marin color *Columbia Journalism Review* v56 no1 p74 Spr 2017

Tsui, Carlson

A switch from canonical to noncanonical autophagy shapes B cell responses bibl graph *Science* v355 no6325 p641 F 10 2017

TSUI, CLARENCE

Jean-Marie Straub & Danièle Huillet *Film Quarterly* v70 no2 p103 Wint 2016

Tsujimura, Taka

OLED Turns 30 C. Crowley color *Sound & Vision* v82 no6 p16 Jl/Ag 2017

Tsukiori, Yoshiko

Stylish Wraps Sewing Book: Ponchos, Capes, Coats and More *Publishers Weekly* v264 no29 p213 Jl 17 2017

Tsunami damage

Tsunami-driven rafting: Transoceanic species dispersal and implications for marine biogeography J. T. Carlton, J. W. Chapman et al color graph *Science* v357 no6358 p1402 S 29 2017

Tsunamis

AFTER THE SKY FELL S. Armington color *Progressive* v81 no5 p22 Je/Jl 2017

A New Tsunami Warning System K. Madin *Oceanus* v52 no2 p53 Spr 2017

The Tsunamis of Mars S. PALUS bw color *Discover* v38 no1 p61 Ja/F 2017

Tsunamis—Indonesia

How the Himalayas primed the Indonesian tsunami P. Voosen color *Science* v356 no6340 p794 My 26 2017

On Mecca's Front Porch D. Pinault color *Commonweal* v144 no7 p8 Ap 14 2017

Tsuzaki, Kaneaki

Bone-like crack resistance in hierarchical metastable nanolaminate steels bibl color diag *Science* v355 no6329 p1055 Mr 10 2017

Tsvangirai, Morgan, 1952-

This One Huge Heroic Act of Togetherness: TODAY WE HAVE

PUT THIS REGIME ON NOTICE *Vital Speeches of the Day* v83 no9 p263 S 2017

Tsvetkov, N.
Chronic exposure to neonicotinoids reduces honey bee health near corn crops diag *Science* v356 no6345 p1395 Je 30 2017

Tsybovsky, Yaroslav
Rapid development of a DNA vaccine for Zika virus bibl graph *Science* v354 no6309 p237 O 14 2016

TTM Technologies Inc.
Mother and Daughter Score With Micro Caps R. ERMEY chart *Kiplinger's Personal Finance* v70 no12 p61 D 2016

Tuan, Christopher
I WISH SOMEONE WOULD INVENT... Cici Zhang, E. Cummins et al cartoon *Popular Science* v289 no4 p102 Jl/Ag 2017

Tuan, Tai-Lan
Regeneration of fat cells from myofibroblasts during wound healing bibl color graph *Science* v355 no6326 p748 F 17 2017

Tuanmu, Mao-Ning
Biodiversity redistribution under climate change: Impacts on ecosystems and human well-being color *Science* v355 no6332 p1389 Mr 31 2017

TUBB, KATIE
Unleashing Energy Winners il *American Conservative* v16 no1 p20 Ja/F 2017

Tuberculosis
In My Solitude C. CALDWELL *Weekly Standard* v22 no8 p5 O 31 2016
TB exploits zombie cells *Science* v356 no6334 p150 Ap 14 2017
WHERE HEALTH CARE WON'T GO: A tuberculosis crisis in the Black Belt Helen Ouyang color *Harper's Magazine* v335 no2005 p27 Je 2017

Tuberculosis—Drug therapy
Limiting a Drug's Use To Maintain Its Efficacy A. Altstedter and U. Trivedi *Bloomberg Businessweek* no4507 p20 Ja 16 2017

Tuberculosis—Treatment
Easier cure for resistant TB J. Cohen color *Science* v355 no6326 p677 F 17 2017
Limiting a Drug's Use To Maintain Its Efficacy A. Altstedter and U. Trivedi *Bloomberg Businessweek* no4507 p20 Ja 16 2017

Tuberosa, Roberto
Wild emmer genome architecture and diversity elucidate wheat evolution and domestication color *Science* v357 no6346 p93 Jl 7 2017

Tubers
Dig in to über tubers color *Good Housekeeping* v265 no5 p67 N 2017

Tubes—Equipment & supplies
Clog-Free Nation B. PIKE cartoon *Power & Motoryacht* v33 no2 p232 F 2017

Tubiana, C.
Rosetta's comet 67P/Churyumov-Gerasimenko sheds its dusty mantle to reveal its icy nature bibl graph *Science* v354 no6319 p1566 D 23 2016
Surface changes on comet 67P/Churyumov-Gerasimenko suggest a more active past bw graph *Science* v355 no6332 p1392 Mr 31 2017

Tubman, Harriet, ca. 1820-1913
ALL About MONEY! K. B. RATTINI color *National Geographic Kids* no465 p8 N 2016
Behind the Story R. Marech *National Parks* v91 no4 p4 Fall 2017
Fighting Harder T. Pierno *National Parks* v91 no4 p3 Fall 2017
Remember Aunt Harriet [Cover story] R. KOBELL *National Parks* v91 no4 p26 Fall 2017
Tubman Time S. Richardson bw *American History* v52 no2 p6 Je 2017

Tubulins—Research
GTPase activity-coupled treadmilling of the bacterial tubulin FtsZ organizes septal cell wall synthesis X. Yang, Z. Lyu et al bibl graph *Science* v355 no6326 p744 F 17 2017

Tucci, Andrea
Macrophage function in tissue repair and remodeling requires IL-4 or IL-13 with apoptotic cells diag *Science* v356 no6342 p1072 Je 9 2017

Tuccille, J. D.
Living Without Banks color *Reason* v48 no10 p62 Mr 2017
MY KID PACKS HEAT color *Reason* v48 no8 p10 Ja 2017

NOT OFF THE GRID, BUT WE CAN SEE THE EDGE FROM HERE color *Reason* v48 no10 p16 Mr 2017
RIP JEROME TUCCILLE, AUTHOR OF IT USUALLY BEGINS WITH AYN RAND bw *Reason* v49 no2 p16 Je 2017
SELF-DRIVING CARS ARE COOL, BUT THEY'RE NOT FOR EVERYONE color *Reason* v49 no5 p12 O 2017
UNDER THE STARS AND UNDER THE RADAR color *Reason* v49 no3 p14 Jl 2017
WHERE RADAR CAMERAS FEAR TO TREAD bw *Reason* v49 no1 p10 My 2017

Tuck, Janna
SCRATCH AND SNIFFLE E. BATTAGLIA color *Martha Stewart Living* no275 p56 Je 2017

Tuck, Lily
Over Her Shoulder: A contemporary 'Rebecca,' Lily Tuck's new novel exposes a second wife's obsession with the woman who got to her husband first K. HARRISON *New York Times Book Review* p20 O 8 2017

Tuck, Melanie
Driving Home the Safety Discussion il *Consumer Reports* v82 no9 p6 S 2017

Tucker, Abigail
Books in Brief M. POTEMRA color *National Review* v68 no20 p45 N 7 2016
Hail to the Chieftain *Smithsonian* v47 no9 p11 Ja/F 2017
In Gourd We Trust: How our most symbolic squash grew to bizarre proportions and took over the world *Smithsonian* v48 no6 p11 O 2017
SPACE ARCHAEOLOGIST *Smithsonian* v47 no8 p38 D 2016
Trails and Tribulations: In 1948, a haunted Army veteran became the first to hike the entire Appalachian Trail *Smithsonian* v48 no4 p26 Jl/Ag 2017
Why Cats Rule the World S. Begley color *Time* v188 no15 p14 O 17 2016

Tucker, Allen C., 1866-1939
October Shadows color *Magazine Antiques* v183 no6 p17 N/D 2016

TUCKER, ANCEL
The Brilliance of Colored Light color *Yankee* v80 no6 p38 N/D 2016

Tucker, Catherine
The 4 Mistakes Most Managers Make with Analytics *Harvard Business Review Digital Articles* p2 Jl 12 2016
When early adopters don't adopt graph *Science* v357 no6347 p135 Jl 14 2017

Tucker, Johnny
This Gravedigger Saves Lives D. COOK color *Reader's Digest* v189 no1130 p10 My 2017

TUCKER, KEN
First Editions: Stolen Fitzgerald manuscripts jump-start John Grisham's thriller *New York Times Book Review* p18 Je 18 2017

Tucker, Lindsay
A Vermont Family Christmas color *Yankee* v80 no6 p33 N/D 2016

Tucker, Nicholas
Darkness Visible: Philip Pullman and His Dark Materials color *Publishers Weekly* v264 no31 p74 Jl 31 2017

Tucker, Reed
Pow! to the People D. Leonard color *Bloomberg Businessweek* no4540 p78 O 2 2017

Tucker, T. J.
BEST AND WORST *Texas Monthly* v45 no7 p10 Jl 2017

Tucker, Wallace
X-Ray Revelations S. N. Johnson-Roehr color *Sky & Telescope* v134 no2 p57 Ag 2017

TUCKER, WILLIAM
FROM THE ARCHIVES cartoon *Reason* v49 no2 p70 Je 2017

Tucson (Ariz.)
TUCSON, ARIZONA F. Cantú *Harper's Magazine* p28 O 2017

Tucson (Ariz.)—Description & travel
WHY ARE PEOPLE TALKING ABOUT TUCSON? *Los Angeles Magazine* p132 Mr 2017

Tucson Pressed Brick Co.
I JUST STARTED READING THE T. A. Johnson, M. McQuaid et al *Arizona Highways* v92 no11 p4 N 2016

Tuddenham, Susan
A microbiome variable in the HIV-prevention equation color *Sci-*

ence v356 no6341 p907 Je 1 2017

Tudor, Lisa

CHIC STREET color *New Orleans Magazine* v51 no12 p84 O 2017

Fancy Feast *New Orleans Homes & Lifestyles* v20 no3 p33 Summ 2017

FEST FORWARD color *New Orleans Magazine* v51 no6 p76 Ap 2017

Fountain Fancy *New Orleans Homes & Lifestyles* v20 no2 p33 Spr 2017

Global Warming *New Orleans Homes & Lifestyles* v20 no1 p32 Wint 2016

heartfelt color *New Orleans Magazine* v51 no4 p72 F 2017

Tiny Tables: Petite, portable and posh, accent tables put your drink in easy reach from every seat in the house *New Orleans Homes & Lifestyles* v20 no4 p33 Aut 2017

Tudor architecture

BEAMS & in between P. Poore color *Arts & Crafts Homes & the Revival* v11 no5 p28 Wint 2017

Living the Tudor Life at Kentwell Hall S. Lawrence *British Heritage Travel* v38 no4 p68 Jl/Ag 2017

TUDOR 101 J. BALL color *Indianapolis Monthly* v42 no2 p32 O 2017

Tudyk, Alan

MR. ROBOT J. KEHE color *Wired* v24 no12 p30 D 2016

TUETH, MICHAEL

THE SECRET LIFE OF THE AMERICAN MUSICAL color *America* v215 no12 p34 O 24 2016

Tufano, Victoria M.

Where do hosts come from? *U.S. Catholic* v82 no6 p49 Je 2017

Why do priests wear green in Ordinary Time? color *U.S. Catholic* v82 no1 p49 Ja 2017

Tufas

Telltale 'Bathtub Rings' Reveal Ancient Rainfall N. Murthy *Oceanus* v52 no1 p30 Summ 2016

Tuğal, Cihan

The Fall of the Turkish Model: How the Arab Uprisings Brought Down Islamic Liberalism J. Waterbury *Foreign Affairs* v96 no2 p184 Mr/Ap 2017

Tugboats—Conservation & restoration

DON'T OVERLOOK THE OUTBOARD D. HISLOP *Sea Magazine* v108 no10 p30 O 2016

TUGEND, ALINA

THE A.P. CALCULUS *New York Times Magazine* p66 S 10 2017

Tugwell, Paul

THE HIJACKING OF THE BRILLANTE VIRTUOSO color map *Bloomberg Businessweek* no4532 p48 Jl 31 2017

TUHUS-DUBROW, REBECCA

AN AD HOC AFFAIR bw *Nation* v304 no5 p27 F 20 2017

Tuition

ALL THE PLACES YOU CAN GO TO COLLEGE FOR FREE K. Mulhere color *Money* v46 no9 p82 O 2017

The Higher and Higher Cost of Higher Ed J. SENGENBERGER color *Weekly Standard* v22 no35 p19 My 22 2017

Making College Free Again S. E. SMITH *In These Times* v41 no4 p8 Ap 2017

Student Debt Blamed For Falling Homeownership *America* v217 no4 p8 Ag 21 2017

Tuition—Economic aspects

consider COMMUNITY COLLEGE A. SMITH *Dance Magazine* p16 2016/2017

Tuition—Universities & colleges

Dream-School Debt color *Money* v45 no10 p22 N 2016

HIGHER EDUCATION J. B. Wogan *Governing* v30 no4 p39 Ja 2017

Research: Want More Entrepreneurs? Make College Cheaper W. Frick *Harvard Business Review Digital Articles* p2 Jl 7 2016

We Could Still Win Free College J. SCHUHRKE *In These Times* v40 no12 p8 D 2016

Tukel, Onur

Catfight *New Yorker* v93 no4 p6 Mr 13 2017

Tulane University

Tulane, Emory, Vandy make best-of list for Jewish students *Successful Farming* v115 no1 p36 Ja 2017

Tulane University—Sports

Week 9 color *Sports Illustrated* v127 no5 p76 Ag 14 2017

TULATHIMUTTE, TONY

MEET THE NU-NERDS color *Wired* v25 no5 p100 My 2017

The Missing Millennial Novel *New York Times Book Review* p37 D 11 2016

Tulip Fever (Film)

Love in a Bubble J. Weisenthal cartoon *Bloomberg Businessweek* no4536 p70 S 4 2017

Tulipane, Barbara

Activate Your Parks and Your People *Parks & Recreation* v52 no6 p8 Je 2017

Controlling Your Future Savings *Parks & Recreation* v52 no2 p8 F 2017

The Future of Community Recreation *Parks & Recreation* v52 no9 p8 S 2017

Rural Park and Recreation Agencies Struggle to Find Funding *Parks & Recreation* v51 no12 p6 D 2016

Speak Up *Parks & Recreation* v52 no4 p8 Ap 2017

Tulips

EDITOR'S LETTER S. ORR *Better Homes & Gardens* v95 no3 p4 Mr 2017

GARDEN VARIETY K. RANDALL *Washingtonian Magazine* v52 no9 p28 Je 2017

Tulip Time Martha color *Martha Stewart Living* p19 S 2017

Tulips—Varieties

bloom time color *Better Homes & Gardens* v95 no3 p106 Mr 2017

Tullis, Paul

An Account of Clayton Valley and the Great Nevada LITHIUM RUSH color graph *Bloomberg Businessweek* no4517 p60 Ap 3 2017

Tulloch, Janet

New Narratives on Women's History S. Dunant *History Today* v67 no3 p65 Mr 2017

Tully, Colleen Fisher

Paddling Forward color *Walrus* v14 no9 p41 N 2017

Q&A color *Walrus* v14 no9 p40 N 2017

Tully, Damien C.

The epigenetic landscape of T cell exhaustion bibl graph *Science* v354 no6316 p1165 D 2 2016

Tully, Shawn

20 OSCAR MUNOZ color diag *Fortune* v174 no7 p90 D 1 2016

AT LENDINGTREE, IT'S ALL FIST BUMPS—AND HYPER-GROWTH color diag *Fortune* v176 no4 p166 S 15 2017

HOW INVESTORS WIN IF CASH COMES HOME diag *Fortune* v175 no2 p36 F 1 2017

THE LAST RAILROAD TYCOON color diag map *Fortune* v176 no3 p84 S 1 2017

MARRIOTT GOES ALL IN chart color diag *Fortune* v175 no8 p200 Je 15 2017

THE PROMISE AND THE PERIL OF THE TRUMP ECONO-MY [Cover story] color diag *Fortune* v175 no3 p80 Mr 1 2017

Why the Stock Market Is Stacked Against Him color diag *Fortune* v174 no8 p88 D 15 2016

Tully monsters

The Tully Monster Mystery E. BETZ color *Discover* v38 no1 p56 Ja/F 2017

Tulman, Sarah

Nearly 14,000 USDA Microloans Issued Between 2013 and 2015 *Amber Waves: The Economics of Food, Farming, Natural Resources, & Rural America* p12 Mr 2017

TULOWIECKI, PAUL

Chords & Discords bw color *Downbeat* v84 no10 p10 O 2017

Tulsa World (Newspaper)

The pleasure and pain of going nonprofit D. Lee color *Columbia Journalism Review* v56 no1 p54 Spr 2017

Tulum Site (Mexico)

Mexico TULUM color *Sports Illustrated* v126 no6 p62 F 20 2017

Tuma, Hama

HORROR STORIES *Lapham's Quarterly* v10 no3 p151 Summ 2017

Tumas, William

Terawatt-scale photovoltaics: Trajectories and challenges chart graph *Science* v356 no6334 p141 Ap 14 2017

TUMMINELLO, NICK

CLOSING THE (THIGH) GAP cartoon *Muscle & Performance* v9 no5 p22 My 2017

EGREGIOUS ACTS OF EXERCISE color *Muscle & Perfor-*

mance v9 no10 p46 O 2017

PERFECTING THE REP color *Muscle & Performance* v9 no10 p52 O 2017

Tumor antigens—Therapeutic use

Landscape of immunogenic tumor antigens in successful immunotherapy of virally induced epithelial cancer S. Stevanović, A. Pasetto et al graph *Science* v356 no6334 p200 Ap 14 2017

Tumor markers

Tumor aneuploidy correlates with markers of immune evasion and with reduced response to immunotherapy T. Davoli, H. Uno et al diag *Science* v355 no6322 p261 Ja 20 2017

Tumor treatment

Fighting cancer from within *Mayo Clinic Health Letter* v35 no9 p4 S 2017

Targeting nonviral antigens in viral-driven cancer color *Science* v356 no6334 p149 Ap 14 2017

Tumors

See also

Sarcoidosis

Soft tissue tumors

Origins of lymphatic and distant metastases in human colorectal cancer K. Naxerova, J. G. Reiter et al diag graph *Science* v357 no6346 p55 Jl 7 2017

What's the best treatment for my uterine fibroids? A. Weil color *Prevention* v69 no2 p24 F 2017

Tumors—Genetic aspects

Decoupling genetics, lineages, and microenvironment in IDH-mutant gliomas by single-cell RNA-seq A. S. Venteicher, I. Tirosh et al diag *Science* v355 no6332 p1391 Mr 31 2017

Tumors—Prevention

The benefits of vitamin pills and chocolate A. L. KOMAROFF color *Harvard Health Letter* v41 no12 p2 O 2016

Keep Cancer from Coming Back *Tufts University Health & Nutrition Letter* v35 no2 p6 2017

Weighing in *Mayo Clinic Health Letter* v35 no3 p4 Mr 2017

Tumors—Risk factors

Build a better cookout *Harvard Health Letter* v42 no9 p3 Jl 2017

Tumors—Treatment

Good News About the "Bad" Cancers G. Graves color *Health* v30 no9 p97 N 2016

Tumuhamye, Nathan

Applying Deliberative Democracy in Africa: Uganda's First Deliberative Polls *Daedalus* v146 no3 p140 Summ 2017

Tuna

See also

Albacore

Bluefin tuna

Hydraulic control of tuna fins: A role for the lymphatic system in vertebrate locomotion V. Pavlov, B. Rosental et al color *Science* v357 no6348 p310 Jl 21 2017

Tuna fishing

Rigged for Tuna J. BROWNLEE color *Power & Motoryacht* v34 no6 p24 Je 2017

SUMMER CRUSH J. CERMELE color *Field & Stream* v122 no2 p18 Je/Jl 2017

Tuna—Behavior

Tuna fin hydraulics inspire aquatic robotics [Cover story] M. S. Triantafyllou diag *Science* v357 no6348 p251 Jl 21 2017

Tundra swan

THE DITCH T. E. Nickens cartoon color *Field & Stream* v121 no7 p38 D 2016/Ja 2017

Tundra truck—Evaluation

SHAPE SHIFTER M. EMERY color *Dirt Sports + Off-Road* v51 no3 p46 Mr 2017

Tune, Tommy

35 Years Ago This Month *Dance Magazine* v91 no9 p67 S 2017

TUNG, FAWZIA MAI

Rejuvenation through Nature [Cover story] *Islamic Horizons* v46 no2 p36 Mr/Ap 2017

TUNG, JENNIFER

BEAUTIFUL CREATURES *Martha Stewart Living* no268 p33 O 2016

THE BEST-LAID (KITCHEN) PLANS *Martha Stewart Living* no268 p98 O 2016

The Essential: Watch *Martha Stewart Living* no269 p52 N 2016

The Essential: Workbag *Martha Stewart Living* no267 p36 S 2016

a grateful spread *Martha Stewart Living* no269 p114 N 2016

LIGHTING THE WAY *Martha Stewart Living* no267 p114 S 2016

RAISING THE BAR *Martha Stewart Living* no269 p38 N 2016

TRUE-BLUE WINNERS color *Martha Stewart Living* no271 p76 Ja/F 2017

The Wild and Wonderful *Martha Stewart Living* no267 p54 S 2016

WORK THE ROOM *Martha Stewart Living* no267 p29 S 2016

Tung, Jenny

Social status alters immune regulation and response to infection in macaques bibl graph *Science* v354 no6315 p1041 N 25 2016

Tungodden, Bertil

Is It OK to Get Paid More for Being Lucky? color graph *Harvard Business Review Digital Articles* p2 Mr 9 2017

Research: Moral Appeals Can Help Reduce Tax Evasion *Harvard Business Review Digital Articles* p2 Jl 20 2017

Tungsten

The long and winding road to methane color *Science* v354 no6308 p77 O 7 2016

Tungsten isotopes

Tungsten-182 heterogeneity in modern ocean island basalts A. Mundl, M. Touboul et al chart diag *Science* v356 no6333 p66 Ap 7 2017

Tunics

DYNAMIC DUO color *Essence* v48 no2 p15 Je 2017

Give Em the Boot bw color *Glamour* v115 no7 p100 Jl 2017

Tunics—Evaluation

Signature Style color *O, The Oprah Magazine* p59 My 2017

Tunisia. Ministry of Higher Education

What I Learned from Leading a Tunisian Ministry During the Arab Spring T. Jelassi *Harvard Business Review Digital Articles* p2 My 16 2016

Tunisian Revolution, 2010-2011

WOMEN AND THE ARAB SPRING T. KARMAN *UN Chronicle* v54 no4 p21 2017

Tunisia—Politics & government

Can Tunisia Remain a Beacon of Democracy for the Arab World? I. Bremmer color *Time* v190 no5 p21 Jl 31 2017

Tunnard, Christopher

Where the Digital Economy Is Moving the Fastest *Harvard Business Review Digital Articles* p2 F 19 2015

Tunnel design & construction

Tunneling to Brooklyn: The first rapid-transit tunnel linking the teeming waterfronts of Manhattan and Brooklyn was completed in January 1908. A century on, the Lexington Avenue subway lines still use the tunnel, carrying tens of thousands of riders daily J. MCKENDRY *Smithsonian* v48 no2 p42 My 2017

Tunnels—Design & construction

Totally Bored R. NUWER *Smithsonian* v47 no7 p19 N 2016

Tunnel Vision *Los Angeles Magazine* p32 Mr 2017

Tunnels—Evaluation

JOURNEY TO THE CENTER OF THE GLACIER *Iceland Review* v54 no6 p108 N/D 2016

Tunnels—New York (State)

ON THE MAP B. McGrath cartoon *New Yorker* v92 no38 p31 N 21 2016

Tunnels—Switzerland

Innovation by the Numbers *Popular Science* v288 no6 p6 N/D 2016

Totally Bored R. NUWER *Smithsonian* v47 no7 p19 N 2016

Tunnel Through the Alps S. PALUS and J. SCHWARTZ color *Popular Science* v288 no6 p78 N/D 2016

Tuntsov, A. V.

The magnetic field and turbulence of the cosmic web measured using a brilliant fast radio burst bibl chart graph *Science* v354 no6317 p1249 D 9 2016

Tunuguntla, Ramya H.

Enhanced water permeability and tunable ion selectivity in sub-nanometer carbon nanotube porins chart color *Science* v357 no6353 p792 Ag 25 2017

Tuo Qiao

A Silurian maxillate placoderm illuminates jaw evolution bibl color *Science* v354 no6310 p334 O 21 2016

Tuominen, Angelia

I Wish My Horse's Mentor Could Be... color *Horse & Rider* v56 no6 p88 Je 2017

Tupayachi, R.

Airborne laser-guided imaging spectroscopy to map forest trait diversity and guide conservation bibl chart graph *Science* v355 no6323 p385 Ja 27 2017

Tupper, Seth

FIRST IMPRESSIONS: Bringing President Calvin Coolidge to the Black Hills wasn't easy *South Dakota Magazine* v33 no3 p60 S/O 2017

TUPPONCE, JOAN

Of Form and Folly *Virginia Living* v15 no1 p41 D 2016

SPARC OF GENIUS *Virginia Living* v15 no3 p33 Ap 2017

Tupy, Marian

CELLPHONE ACCESS HAS SKYROCKETED. THE WORLD IS BETTER FOR IT graph *Reason* v49 no5 p44 O 2017

Tur, Katy

Enduring Trump: Katy Tur describes life on the front lines during the Trump presidential campaign J. ABRAMSON *New York Times Book Review* p10 S 17 2017

The Making of a News Junkie color *Glamour* v115 no10 p141 O 2017

Tura, Dennis

And the Winning Photo Is... *British Heritage Travel* v38 no4 p80 Jl/Ag 2017

Turandot (Theatrical production)

ON WITH THE Encore *Atlanta* v57 no2 p130 Je 2017

Operapedia: Turandot *Opera News* v81 no9 p12 Mr 2017

Puccini/Hao: Turandot M. Mandel *Opera News* v81 no9 p50 Mr 2017

Turbine pumps—Evaluation

Focus on materials, semiconductors, vacuum, and cryogenics A. Mandelis *Physics Today* v69 no10 p62 O 2016

Turbines

Turbines can use CO2 to cut CO2 L. Irwin and Y. Le Moullec diag *Science* v356 no6340 p805 My 26 2017

Turbiville, Charles

WELCOME... Festival of Books Visitors *South Dakota Magazine* p4 S/O 2017 Supplement

Turbomachines

See also
  Compressors

Outboard Towing Magic: Installing TurboSwing to tow skiers behind an outboard-powered boat is one-person simple K. HARRIS *Boating World* v38 no8 p22 S/O 2017

Turboprop airplanes

AUTO-THROTTLES R. Mark color *Flying* v144 no9 p20 S 2017

PILATUS PC-12 NG P. BERGQVIST chart color *Flying* v144 no8 p42 Ag 2017

Turboprop airplanes—Evaluation

BEECHCRAFT: KING AIR 250 S. POPE chart color *Flying* v144 no10 p42 O 2017

CESSNA 206 [Cover story] R. MARK chart color *Flying* v144 no9 p42 S 2017

MAHINDRA'S AIRVAN 10 GETS CERTIFIED color *Flying* v144 no9 p18 S 2017

Turbulence

Classical precursor to turbulence observed in a superfluid M. Wilson *Physics Today* v70 no1 p19 Ja 2017

The magnetic field and turbulence of the cosmic web measured using a brilliant fast radio burst V. Ravi, R. M. Shannon et al bibl chart graph *Science* v354 no6317 p1249 D 9 2016

Turbulence in breaking waves G. B. Deane, D. Stokes et al *Physics Today* v69 no10 p86 O 2016

Turbulent flow

Transition from turbulent to coherent flows in confined three-dimensional active fluids Wu, J. Bernard Hishamunda et al color *Science* v355 no6331 p1284 M 24 2017

The turbulent cascade in five dimensions J. I. Cardesa, A. Vela-Martín et al color *Science* v357 no6353 p782 Ag 25 2017

Turco, Richard

Nuclear foreboding: Shadows cast by nuclear winter bibl *Bulletin of the Atomic Scientists* v73 no4 p240 Jl 2017

Turcotte, Paul

Out & About *TV Guide* v64 no40 p6 O 3 2016

Turcotte, Raphaël

Self-renewal of a purified Tie2+ hematopoietic stem cell population relies on mitochondrial clearance bibl graph *Science* v354

no6316 p1156 D 2 2016

Turd (Music)

The Playlist color *Rolling Stone* no1276 p10 D 15 2016

Tureens

The bouillabaisse of design influences on an early American silver soup tureen D. Zimmermann color *Magazine Antiques* v184 no3 p68 My/Je 2017

Turek, Fred W.

Circadian clocks: Not your grandfather's clock bibl diag *Science* v354 no6315 p992 N 25 2016

Turekian, Vaughan

Empowering science advice color *Science* v357 no6353 p735 Ag 25 2017

Turfgrasses

How to model tall grass easily D. Popp color diag *Model Railroader* v84 no2 p32 F 2017

A Rare Tuft K. SIBER *National Parks* v91 no1 p26 Wint 2017

Turin (Italy)—Description & travel

Gran TORINO O. Thorisson bw color *Conde Nast Traveler* v52 no2 p84 F 2017

Turing test

AM I HUMAN? [Cover story] G. Marcus color *Scientific American* v316 no3 p58 Mr 2017

Turiv, Taras

Command of active matter by topological defects and patterns bibl graph *Science* v354 no6314 p882 N 18 2016

Turka, Laurence A.

Rescue of exhausted CD8 T cells by PD-1–targeted therapies is CD28-dependent bw diag graph *Science* v355 no6332 p1423 Mr 31 2017

Turkey

COOKING SCHOOL L. Cericola color *Southern Living* v52 no11 p132 N 2017

Erdogan's Counter-Revolution [Cover story] E. EDELMAN color *Weekly Standard* v22 no32 p26 My 1 2017

The White Helmets of Syria [Cover story] color *Time* v188 no15 p20 O 17 2016

Turkey farming

Where Your Thanksgiving Turkey Comes From *New York Times Upfront* v149 no5 p2 N 21 2016

Turkey hunting

Boom and Bloom D. L. NG color *Field & Stream* v121 no9 p12 Ap 2017

DIRTY BIRDS G. Bethge color *Outdoor Life* v223 no9 pH14 N 2016

DOUBLE-TEAM GOBBLER DRAG B. RUZZO cartoon *Outdoor Life* v224 no3 p26 Ap 2017

The Easy Bird S. Bestul color *Field & Stream* v121 no9 pT1 Ap 2017

FOUR OF A KIND W. Brantley cartoon *Field & Stream* v121 no9 p30 Ap 2017

GET YOUR GOBBLER T. CARPENTER, R. SPOMER et al color *Outdoor Life* v224 no4 p43 My 2017

Gobblers When It Blows G. Almy color *Field & Stream* v121 no9 pT4 Ap 2017

Not Worth a Sit D. Draper color *Field & Stream* v121 no9 pT7 Ap 2017

RETHINK YOUR TURKEY VEST T. CARPENTER and G. BETHGE color *Outdoor Life* v224 no3 pT5 Ap 2017

SUPER SCATTERS D. HART color *Outdoor Life* v224 no8 pH7 O 2017

TURKEY RECOVERY G. BETHGE color *Outdoor Life* v224 no3 pT7 Ap 2017

Turkey hunting—Equipment & supplies—Evaluation

CHOKE JOB G. BETHGE and T. HANSEN chart color *Outdoor Life* v224 no2 p20 F/Mr 2017

NEXT-LEVEL TURKEY CALLS J. ARTERBURN, S. Wagner et al color *Outdoor Life* v224 no3 p50 Ap 2017

Reed Section W. Brantley color *Field & Stream* v121 no9 pT8 Ap 2017

RETHINK YOUR TURKEY VEST T. CARPENTER and G. BETHGE color *Outdoor Life* v224 no3 pT5 Ap 2017

Turkey. Ministry of Education

CFI, Richard Dawkins, Teachers Slam as 'Unconscionable' Turkey's Decision to Ban Teaching Evolution K. FRAZIER *Skeptical Inquirer* v41 no5 p7 S/O 2017

Turner, Giles

A Reputation for Badoo Behavior color *Bloomberg Businessweek* no4526 p30 Je 12 2017

When Coders Become Stickup Artists color *Bloomberg Businessweek* no4517 p35 Ap 3 2017

Will Britain Keep Investing in a Sex Offender's Venture Fund? *Bloomberg Businessweek* no4539 p22 S 25 2017

Turner, Hester

Pioneer in American Forests' Boardroom L. SLOAN *American Forests* v123 no1 p46 Wint/Spr 2017

Turner, James M. A.

Fertile offspring from sterile sex chromosome trisomic mice chart diag *Science* v357 no6354 p932 S 1 2017

TURNER, JOE M.

A LABRADOR OF LOVE cartoon *Outdoor Life* v224 no1 p16 D 2016/Ja 2017

Turner, Joe—Interviews

Reflections on a Career T. Dellner *Parks & Recreation* v52 no3 p44 Mr 2017

TURNER, JOHN

LIFE AS LITURGY *American Conservative* v15 no6 p4 N/D 2016

Turner, John L.

WONDERFUL WOODPECKERS: Of the 22 species found in North America, we have 9 woodpecker species that inhabit the forests of New York *New York State Conservationist* v72 no2 p20 O 2017

Turner, Jonathan

Sergeant Turner's Ride Home A. SIMMONS color *Reader's Digest* v190 no1132 p12 Jl/Ag 2017

TURNER, JULIA

Into the Woods: Four new picture books take young readers on adventures in gorgeously illustrated forests *New York Times Book Review* p20 My 14 2017

Turner, Kathleen, 1954-

SERIAL MOM C. Collis color *Entertainment Weekly* no1465 p42 My 12 2017

Turner, Kevin

Maybe a Good Manager Can't Run Everything M. Leising and A. Massa *Bloomberg Businessweek* no4510 p32 F 6 2017

TURNER, LEANNE

STORIES WE TELL OURSELVES color *Vanity Fair* v58 no11 p88 N 2016

Turner, Lisa

10 Foods to Tame Your Pain color *Better Nutrition* v79 no10 p68 O 2017

30 Ways to EAT MORE VEGGIES [Cover story] color *Better Nutrition* v79 no11 p60 N 2017

5 Ways to Use Charcoal color *Better Nutrition* v79 no7 p30 Jl 2017

7 COMMON NUTRIENT DEFICIENCIES color *Better Nutrition* v79 no3 p48 Mr 2017

7 COMMON VITAMIN DEFICIENCIES color *Amazing Wellness* v9 no4 p52 Summ 2017

7 supplements for better sleep color *Better Nutrition* v79 no10 p52 O 2017

allergy SURVIVAL GUIDE color *Better Nutrition* v79 no4 p56 Ap 2017

All in the Family color *Better Nutrition* v79 no9 p32 S 2017

Baby on Board color *Better Nutrition* v79 no1 p26 Ja 2017

BEAUTIFUL CHOICES color *Amazing Wellness* p74 Fall 2017

Beauty's More than Skin Deep color *Better Nutrition* v79 no4 p62 Ap 2017

Beyond The Blender color *Better Nutrition* v79 no6 p26 Je 2017

BLACK MAGIC color *Amazing Wellness* v9 no4 p66 Summ 2017

CBD Oil: Anxiety Aid & Much More [Cover story] color *Better Nutrition* v79 no11 p34 N 2017

CBD OIL color *Amazing Wellness* p22 Fall 2017

Cinco de Mayo SPA CUISINE color *Better Nutrition* p46 My 2017

Comfort-Food Makeovers color *Amazing Wellness* p90 Fall 2017

CONSTANT CRAVINGS [Cover story] color *Amazing Wellness* v9 no6 p44 EarlyWint 2017

customize YOUR HEALTH [Cover story] color *Amazing Wellness* v9 no3 p54 EarlySumm 2017

DIY RECIPE KITS color *Amazing Wellness* v8 no6 p90 Early Winter2016

DIY SPA FACIAL color *Amazing Wellness* v9 no3 p70 Early-Summ 2017

EXOTIC OILS [Cover story] color *Amazing Wellness* v9 no6 p82 EarlyWint 2017

FAMILY HEALTH GUIDE color *Amazing Wellness* v9 no4 p58 Summ 2017

Feel-Good Foods color *Better Nutrition* v79 no1 p58 Ja 2017

Foodie Fun in the Sun color *Better Nutrition* v79 no7 p58 Jl 2017

fully functional color *Amazing Wellness* v9 no1 p62 Wint 2017

Give Your Thyroid Some TLC color *Better Nutrition* v79 no9 p66 S 2017

healthy & hearty color *Better Nutrition* v78 no11 p68 N 2016

Heal Your Gut [Cover story] color *Better Nutrition* v79 no11 p68 N 2017

HENNA 101 color *Amazing Wellness* v9 no2 p70 Spr 2017

holiday gift kits color *Better Nutrition* v78 no12 p45 D 2016

It's a Guy Thing color *Better Nutrition* v79 no6 p54 Je 2017

LISA TURNER J. Chen color *Bloomberg Businessweek* no4509 p63 Ja 30 2017

MOOD MAKEOVER color *Amazing Wellness* v9 no4 p28 Summ 2017

NOW HEAR THIS! color *Amazing Wellness* v8 no6 p64 Early Winter2016

THE PALEO VEGAN color *Amazing Wellness* v8 no2 p84 Spr 2016

The Paleo Vegan color *Better Nutrition* v78 no11 p78 N 2016

Prevent, Treat, & Recover: A FLU GUIDE color *Better Nutrition* v79 no1 p44 Ja 2017

PROTEIN POWDERS FOR EVERYDAY PEOPLE [Cover story] color *Better Nutrition* v79 no7 p46 Jl 2017

READY FOR YOUR CLOSE-UP? color *Amazing Wellness* v8 no6 p82 Early Winter2016

Seven Ways to Prevent a Stroke color *Better Nutrition* p26 My 2017

SEX AFTER 40 color *Amazing Wellness* v9 no2 p30 Spr 2017

SLIM DOWN IN 2017 color *Better Nutrition* v79 no1 p36 Ja 2017

STRETCH MARK SMOOTHERS color *Amazing Wellness* v8 no2 p76 Spr 2016

Summer Slim Down color *Better Nutrition* p54 My 2017

What Is Aquafaba? color *Better Nutrition* p60 My 2017

Your Brain on Food color *Better Nutrition* v79 no3 p64 Mr 2017

Turner, Michael

Gary Steigman *Physics Today* v70 no8 p72 Ag 2017

TURNER, MICHAEL S.

A COSMIC CONTROVERSY color *Scientific American* v317 no1 p5 Jl 2017

TURNER, MONICA G.

When, Where, and How Nature Matters for Ecosystem Services: Challenges for the Next Generation of Ecosystem Service Models *BioScience* v67 no9 p820 S 2017

Turner, Nat, ca. 1800-1831

STORIES WE TELL OURSELVES S. BRAMMER, S. L. SEITZ et al color *Vanity Fair* v58 no11 p88 N 2016

Turner, Nathan

California dreamy K. P. Badal color *Sunset* v238 no6 p46 Je 2017

Turner, Nina—Interviews

'Great Things Come Out of Discomfort': An Interview with Our Revolution's Nina Turner N. Stockwell color *Progressive* v81 no7 p60 O/N 2017

Turner, Rebecca

The Congressional Review Act: Congress Putting Our Forests in Jeopardy *American Forests* v123 no2 p10 Summ 2017

Countering the President's Budget Proposal *American Forests* v123 no3 p14 Fall 2017

Proposed Endangered Species Delisting of Yellowstone Grizzly Bears *American Forests* v122 no3 p15 Fall 2016

Turner, Scott

KICK-ASS CUSTOMER SERVICE chart color graph il img *Harvard Business Review* v95 no1 p110 Ja/F 2017

Turner, Sophie, 1996-

BLONDE Ambition G. WILLIAMS color *Vogue* v207 no7 p53 Jl 2017

A HOUSE UNDIVIDED [Cover story] J. Hibberd color *Entertainment Weekly* no1468/1469 p28 Je 2-9 2017

Sophie Turner M. Hagan color *Current Biography* v77 no10 p92

Tuthill, Matthew
Making a difference, differently cartoon *Science* v354 no6316 p1194 D 2 2016

Tutino, Marco
Tutino: Le Braci J. Rosenblum *Opera News* v81 no5 p56 N 2016

Tutoring services
The revitalized tutoring center J. koselak chart color graph *Phi Delta Kappan* v98 no5 p61 F 2017

Tutsi (African people)—Crimes against—Rwanda—History—20th century
Duty Bound Killings B. Bower bw chart color map *Science News* v192 no2 p22 Ag 19 2017

Tuttle, Becky
Working Together for a Healthier Wichita *Parks & Recreation* v52 no1 p28 Ja 2017

Tuttle, Brad
36 APPS THAT WILL SAVE YOU MONEY color *Money* v46 no4 p46 My 2017
5 Ways to Save Money on Amazon color *Money* v46 no8 p21 S 2017
FROM USA TO EUR [Cover story] color *Money* v46 no5 p42 Je 2017
HOW TO FIND 2017'S CHEAPEST FLIGHTS color *Money* v46 no2 p21 Mr 2017
THE MONEY CHAMPIONS [Cover story] color *Money* v45 no11 p52 D 2016
Secrets of the Kingdom [Cover story] color *Money* v46 no6 p44 Jl 2017
Smart Speakers: Which Is the Best Buy? color *Money* v46 no8 p14 S 2017

Tuttle, Charlotte
Changes in Food-At-Home Spending by SNAP Participants After the Stimulus Act of 2009 bw chart color graph *Amber Waves: The Economics of Food, Farming, Natural Resources, & Rural America* p8 D 2016
Percent of Income Spent on Food Falls as Income Rises *Amber Waves: The Economics of Food, Farming, Natural Resources, & Rural America* p31 S 2016
Unexpected Hikes in Energy Prices Increase the Likelihood of Food Insecurity *Amber Waves: The Economics of Food, Farming, Natural Resources, & Rural America* p9 Jl 2017

TUTTLE, IAN
Acts of Undermining *National Review* v69 no9 p38 My 15 2017
Doctor Doom *National Review* v69 no3 p23 F 20 2017
Race and Trumpism *National Review* v68 no22 p18 D 5 2016
The Religious Right's Demise color *National Review* v68 no20 p20 N 7 2016
Where Time Wears Thin color *National Review* v68 no21 p24 N 21 2016
Who Critiques The Critic? color *National Review* v69 no16 p21 Ag 28 2017

TUTTLE, MERLIN D.
Give Bats a Break *Issues in Science & Technology* v33 no3 p41 Spr 2017

Tuttle, Robert
Reviving Keystone XL Is No Sure Thing *Bloomberg Businessweek* no4510 p23 F 6 2017

Tuttle, Tell
Polymeric peptide pigments with sequence-encoded properties color graph *Science* v356 no6342 p1064 Je 9 2017

Tuxedos
New York R. Roye *New York Times Magazine* p39 N 20 2016

Tu Youyou, 1930-
Tu Youyou K. Vezina *Current Biography* v78 no2 p90 F 2017

TV Guide (Periodical)
FIRST LOOKS color *TV Guide* v65 no7 p12 F 13 2017

TVERSKY, AMOS
Quotable Quotes bw color *Reader's Digest* v190 no1132 p140 Jl/Ag 2017

Twain, Mark, 1835-1910
1847: Florida, MO M. Twain *Lapham's Quarterly* v10 no1 p70 Wint 2017
Life on His Mississippi C. BUCKLEY *New York Times Book Review* p14 N 20 2016
Mark Twain Country R. EVERSOLE color *Trail Rider* v29 no4 p22 My 2017

MISCELLANY *Lapham's Quarterly* v10 no1 p212 Wint 2017
WHEN TITANS TANGLED S. Kinzer bw cartoon color *American History* v52 no4 p40 O 2017

Twain, Shania, 1965-
THE 28-WORD REVIEW K. O'donnell color *Entertainment Weekly* no1472 p56 Je 30 2017
ROCK THIS COUNTRY *USA Today Magazine* v146 no2868 p58 S 2017
Shania's Hard Road Back A. GREENE color *Rolling Stone* no1281/1282 p15 F 23 2017
SHANIA TWAIN K. O'Donnell color *Entertainment Weekly* no1446/1447 p72 D 2016/Ja 2017
Sound Bites color *Entertainment Weekly* no1484 p3 S 29 2017
Still the One S. Cristobal color *InStyle* v24 no10 p118 O 2017

Twardziok, Sven O.
Wild emmer genome architecture and diversity elucidate wheat evolution and domestication color *Science* v357 no6346 p93 Jl 7 2017

Twaronite, Karyn
A Global Survey on the Ambiguous State of Employee Trust *Harvard Business Review Digital Articles* p2 Jl 22 2016

Twedt, Paul
The Long Haul R. MARECH *National Parks* v91 no1 p18 Wint 2017
Packing It Out A. Carnes *Sierra* v102 no2 p25 Mr/Ap 2017

Tweed, David
Border Trouble: China and India Face Off bw map *Bloomberg Businessweek* no4534 p32 Ag 14 2017
Will Beijing Also Have A Friend at State? bw *Bloomberg Businessweek* no4504 p26 D 19 2016

Tweed, Vera
10 Trending Supplements FOR 2017 color *Better Nutrition* v79 no1 p16 Ja 2017
10 WEIGHT-LOSS MYTHS BUSTED color *Amazing Wellness* v8 no2 p54 Spr 2016
30% color *Amazing Wellness* v9 no2 p18 Spr 2017
3 hidden food sources of mercury (besides fish) color *Amazing Wellness* p14 Fall 2017
3 Mediterranean Diet Myths, Busted color *Better Nutrition* p8 My 2017
3 More Reasons to Exercise color *Amazing Wellness* v8 no6 p12 Early Winter2016
7 NEW WAYS TO USE PROTEIN POWDERS color *Amazing Wellness* v9 no4 p20 Summ 2017
7 REASONS YOU HAVE SORE MUSCLES color *Amazing Wellness* p78 Fall 2017
7 WAYS TO LOWER BLOOD SUGAR cartoon graph *Better Nutrition* v78 no11 p62 N 2016
7 WAYS TO LOWER BLOOD SUGAR color diag graph *Amazing Wellness* v8 no6 p58 Early Winter2016
AGING gracefully color *Amazing Wellness* p58 Fall 2017
AMAZING AMINOS color *Amazing Wellness* v8 no2 p28 Spr 2016
AMAZING NEWS *Amazing Wellness* v8 no2 p12 Spr 2016
AMAZING NEWS color *Amazing Wellness* v9 no1 p14 Wint 2017
AMAZING NEWS color *Amazing Wellness* v9 no6 p14 Early-Wint 2017
Are Your Joints Healthy? color *Better Nutrition* v79 no10 p80 O 2017
Are You Wasting Food? color *Better Nutrition* v78 no11 p92 N 2016
Ashwagandha color *Better Nutrition* v79 no10 p26 O 2017
Ayurvedic HERB GUIDE color *Amazing Wellness* v9 no2 p38 Spr 2017
The Beauty of Keratin color *Better Nutrition* v79 no6 p22 Je 2017
BEST DEAL ON HEALTH CARE: exercise color *Better Nutrition* v78 no11 p14 N 2016
Best Ways to Take Mineral Supplements color *Better Nutrition* v79 no3 p10 Mr 2017
BUG OFF! color *Amazing Wellness* v9 no4 p26 Summ 2017
Busting the Multivitamin Myth color *Better Nutrition* v79 no9 p8 S 2017
Calcium Myths and Facts [Cover story] chart color *Better Nutrition* v79 no11 p26 N 2017
Calories Count color *Better Nutrition* v79 no3 p72 Mr 2017
carnitine color *Amazing Wellness* v9 no4 p12 Summ 2017

TWEEDY, DAMON

Twenge, Jean

Twentieth century

Twenty-Four Hours From Home (Poem)

Twenty20 cricket

Twiggs, Leo

Twilight

Twilight Saga film series

Twilight Zone: The Movie (Film)

Twilight Zone, The (TV program)

TWILLEY, NICOLA

Twin Metals Minnesota LLC

v81 no5 p27 Je/Jl 2017

Twin Peaks (Film)

Can Twin Peaks Make a Comeback? C. R. MORGAN bw *American Conservative* v16 no3 p52 My/Je 2017

Deep in the Forest N. PINKERTON color *Film Comment* v53 no3 p18 My/Je 2017

Strange Seer R. SYME color *New Republic* v248 no8/9 p66 Ag/S 2017

Twin Peaks (Performer)

WHICH CHICACQ INDIE BAHB SHOULD YOU SEE THIS MONTH? *Washingtonian Magazine* v52 no8 p36 My 2017

Twin Peaks (TV program)

America's top TV critic Matt Roush answers your burning questions M. ROUSH *TV Guide* v65 no27 p2 Je 26 2017

DAVID LYNCH'S MIND GAMES J. Jensen color *Entertainment Weekly* no1468/1469 p90 Je 2-9 2017

HORROR SHOW: The nightmare logic of Twin Peaks M. Dean *Harper's Magazine* p86 O 2017

How Twin Peaks Changed TV Forever E. Dockterman color *Time* v189 no19 p51 My 22 2017

HOW TWIN PEAKS INFLUENCED MY WORK: Fargo and Legion creator Noah Hawley pays homage to Peaks' mastermind, David Lynch N. HAWLEY and A. D'Arminio *TV Guide* v65 no35 p10 Ag 21 2017

How Twin Peaks Invented Modern Television J. PARKER color *Atlantic* v319 no5 p28 Je 2017

PEAKS 'N' FREAKS [Cover story] J. Jensen color *Entertainment Weekly* no1459 p20 Mr 31 2017

The Season's Peak [Cover story] R. SHEFFIELD color *Rolling Stone* no1289 p29 Je 15 2017

The Slowness of 'Twin Peaks' A. Kleeman *New York Times Magazine* p38 O 8 2017

Small-Town Noir A. Thirlwell color *New York Review of Books* v64 no17 p4 N 9 2017

So Far, Twin Peaks' Mysteries Remain Unsatisfying D. D'Addario color *Time* v189 no21 p62 Je 5 2017

To Do: Twenty-five things to see, hear, watch, and read D. EDELSTEIN, M. Z. SEITZ et al img *New York* v50 no10 p106 My 15 2017

TWIN PEAKS A to Z [Cover story] D. HOLBROOK *TV Guide* v65 no21 p18 My 15 2017

Twin Peaks Cheat Sheet: Showtime's revival has (finally!) ended--here's a guide to the essential episodes J. Clark *TV Guide* v65 no39 p18 S 18 2017

Twin Peaks *TV Guide* v65 no13 p39 Mr 20 2017

Uncompromised J. Podhoretz *Weekly Standard* v22 no37 p39 Je 5 2017

AN UNRIVALED REVIVAL color *Entertainment Weekly* no1480 p42 S 1 2017

YOUR GUIDE TO (ALMOST) UNDERSTANDING TWIN PEAKS J. Jensen and D. Franich color *Entertainment Weekly* no1466 p32 My 19 2017

You Were Expecting Pie? In his scalding Twin Peaks revisit, David Lynch doubles down on being David Lynch M. Z. SEITZ img *New York* v50 no11 p124 My 29 2017

Twin sisters

Sister Act K. Lafferty color *Glamour* v115 no5 p188 My 2017

Twine

Zip Ties K. Tingley *New York Times Magazine* p30 S 17 2017

Twins

The Truth About Twins A. MENCEL color *Parents* v92 no8 p26 Ag 2017

TWINNING AS BOSSES IS A LIFESTYLE B. VIERA color *Ebony* v72/73 no12/1 p26 O/N 2017

When There's Another You L. B. Ray color *InStyle* v24 no10 p116 O 2017

Twins—Charts, diagrams, etc.

Is the Rise in Twin Births Cresting? K. Peek graph *Scientific American* v315 no6 p88 D 2016

Twitchen, D. J.

Entanglement distillation between solid-state quantum network nodes diag *Science* v356 no6341 p928 Je 1 2017

Twitter (Web resource)

50 Companies That Get Twitter - and 50 That Don't B. Parmar *Harvard Business Review Digital Articles* p2 Ap 27 2015

The 8 Digital Productivity Tools Everyone Should Adopt A.

Samuel *Harvard Business Review Digital Articles* p2 Je 20 2016

Apple investigates iPhone 7 Plus that 'blew up' O. Raymundo color *Macworld - Digital Edition* p15 Ap 2017

Dana Delany M. Rochlin color *AARP: The Magazine* v59 no6A p19 O/N 2016

First the Cold War, Now the Flame War L. Kinstler color *Fortune* v176 no2 p19 Ag 1 2017

From the Twitter feed of Kim Jong Un, @youthcaptain R. LONG il *National Review* v69 no1 p34 Ja 23 2017

How Bots Took Over Twitter A. Samuel *Harvard Business Review Digital Articles* p2 Je 19 2015

How I Survived The Election A. Shields color *Nation* v33 no21 p10 N 21 2016

How Trump Could Change America P. SMITH, D. E. Sanger et al *New York Times Upfront* v149 no7 p8 Ja 9 2017

In Case of Low Revenue B. Elgin, P. Robison et al cartoon *Bloomberg Businessweek* no4497 p50 O 31 2016

Laugh Lines F. SCOTT FITZGERALD color *Reader's Digest* v189 no1129 p104 Ap 2017

The Lifestyle of Protest C. ROSEN *Commentary* v144 no1 p7 Jl/Ag 2017

POPPING THE RED PILL E. G. ELLIS color graph *Wired* v25 no10 p28 O 2017

Reading and tweeting Augustine C. Zaleski *Christian Century* v134 no10 p59 My 10 2017

The Reason Twitter's Losing Active Users U. Haque *Harvard Business Review Digital Articles* p2 F 12 2016

SOCIAL INSECURITY F. Manjoo *New York Times Magazine* p38 Ap 30 2017

Taking on the Haters J. KAY *Walrus* v13 no10 p74 D 2016

The Trump Tweetometer map *New Republic* v248 no6 p9 Je 2017

Tweeter in Chief F. BARNES cartoon *Weekly Standard* v22 no13 p11 D 5 2016

WE LOVE HEARING FROM YOU! color diag *Essence* v47 no12 p14 Ap 2017

Why D.C.'s Missing Children Became a Political Rallying Cry M. Rhodan color *Time* v189 no13 p17 Ap 10 2017

Twitter (Web resource)—Social aspects

The Trump Tweetometer graph *New Republic* v248 no5 p9 My 2017

Twitter Inc.

How the Market Ruined Twitter J. Fox *Harvard Business Review Digital Articles* p2 O 31 2014

Jack Dorsey Is Losing Control of Twitter S. Frier and A. Sherman cartoon graph *Bloomberg Businessweek* no4495 p26 O 17 2016

Why Twitter's Mission Statement Matters J. Fox *Harvard Business Review Digital Articles* p2 N 13 2014

Twitter Inc.—Management

NOW TRENDING: #ethicalproblems J. J. Roberts color *Fortune* v174 no8 p42 D 15 2016

Twitto, Anna

Country Lore *Mother Earth News* no280 p85 F/Mr 2017

Country Lore *Mother Earth News* no281 p84 Ap/My 2017

Fresh, Homemade SALAD DRESSINGS *Mother Earth News* no281 p36 Ap/My 2017

PICKLE RECIPES for the Picking: Ferment or quick-pickle your harvest with this assortment of ideas from Mother Earth News bloggers *Mother Earth News* no282 p56 Je/Jl 2017

Twitty, Michael

Feeding the Soul N. Schlager *Sierra* v102 no5 p10 St/O 2017

MICHAEL TWITTY T. Stanley *Washingtonian Magazine* v52 no11 p43 Ag 2017

Two Bit Circus (Company)

Los Angeles's New Circus Act N. Piper color *Bloomberg Businessweek* no4517 p44 Ap 3 2017

Two-dimensional materials (Nanotechnology)

See also

Graphene

Magnetic resonance spectroscopy of an atomically thin material using a single-spin qubit I. Lovchinsky, J. D. Sanchez-Yamagishi et al bibl color diag graph *Science* v355 no6324 p503 F 3 2017

Two Hands (Film)

DESERT ROSE L. Brown color *InStyle* v24 no8 p144 Ag 2017

Two-photon-spectroscopy

Revealing the subfemtosecond dynamics of orbital angular mo-

Tyrese, 1978-
　Tyrese Gibson P. G. Cooper *Current Biography* v78 no6 p47 Je 2017

Tyson, Bernard J.
　6 CEOs on How Business Can Do Better color *Time* v190 no13 p34 O 2 2017

Tyson, Cicely, 1933-—Awards
　EBONY POWER 100 Celebrated Black Excellence, Community and Creativity L. CROSS and M. KIMBLE color *Ebony* v72 no4 p26 F 2017

Tyson, Clayton
　UNSOLICITED BETA color *Climbing* no352 p8 Ap 2017

Tyson, Joel
　Pathological α-synuclein transmission initiated by binding lymphocyte-activation gene 3 bibl graph *Science* v353 no6307 paah3374-1 S 30 2016

Tyson, Mike, 1966-
　Sound Bites color *Entertainment Weekly* no1474/1475 p4 Jl 21-28 2017
　When Migos Met Mike Tyson color *GQ: Gentlemen's Quarterly* v97 no5 p138 My 2017

Tyson, Mike, 1966-—Trials, litigation, etc.
　THE DECISION E. WEST *Indianapolis Monthly* p74 F 2017

Tyson, Neil deGrasse, 1958-
　The Discerning Doodler N. deGrasse Tyson color *AARP: The Magazine* v59 no6A p64 O/N 2016
　From TV to Lab, and Back color *National Geographic* v231 no6 p26 Je 2017
　Geek in Space color *National Geographic* v230 no6 p26 D 2016
　Getting Out the Word bw *Discover* v38 no4 p51 My 2017
　Neil DeGRASSE TYSON L. WILMORE *Interview* v46 no9 p25 N 2016
　A Pocket-Size Primer to the Universe color *Popular Mechanics* p20 Je 2017
　The Science of Jazz color *National Geographic* v231 no3 p26 Mr 2017
　She Favors Seas, He Prefers Stars color *National Geographic* v232 no5 p24 N 2017
　SPACE JAM C. COX *Atlanta* v57 no2 p34 Je 2017
　Stardom & Sci-Fi bw color *National Geographic* v231 no2 p24 F 2017

Tyson, Neil deGrasse, 1958-—Interviews
　LATE NIGHT L. ACKEN *TV Guide* p45 D 19 2016

Tyson, Peter
　Eclipse Day's Big Unknown color *Sky & Telescope* v134 no2 p4 Ag 2017
　A Mystery for the Age *Sky & Telescope* v133 no6 p4 Je 2017
　A New Cosmopolitanism color *Sky & Telescope* v134 no5 p4 N 2017
　On the Alert for Apparitions *Sky & Telescope* v133 no4 p4 Ap 2017
　The Stone Tree *Sky & Telescope* v134 no4 p4 O 2017
　A Taste of Relativity *Sky & Telescope* v134 no1 p4 Jl 2017
　This Is, and No Mistake *Sky & Telescope* v133 no5 p4 My 2017
　Welcoming New Staff *Sky & Telescope* v134 no6 p4 D 2017
　Witnessing a Supernova *Sky & Telescope* v133 no2 p4 F 2017
　Written in the Star *Sky & Telescope* v134 no4 p22 O 2017

Tyson, Timothy B.
　The Blood of Emmett Till D. Bendis *Christian Century* v134 no12 p36 Je 7 2017
　False Witness J. PARHAM *New York Times Book Review* p11 F 12 2017
　Justice In Slow Motion *New York Times Book Review* p1 My 21 2017
　The lynching that shook the conscience of the world S. Dee Williams bw *America* v216 no12 p48 My 29 2017

Tyson, Timothy B.—Interviews
　Remembering Emmett Till E. Holley Jr. color *Publishers Weekly* v264 no2 p52 Ja 9 2017

Tyson, Zachary—Interviews
　Tyson Construction P. Marquis *New Orleans Homes & Lifestyles* v20 no2 p86 Spr 2017

Tyson Construction (Company)
　Tyson Construction P. Marquis *New Orleans Homes & Lifestyles* v20 no2 p86 Spr 2017

Tyszko, Jason A.
　Employer-led Quality Assurance *Change* v49 no1 p26 Ja/F 2017

Tytell, John
　An Illegal Immigrant *Commonweal* v144 no10 p8 Je 2 2017

TYUKAVINA, ALEXANDRA
　An Ecoregion-Based Approach to Protecting Half the Terrestrial Realm *BioScience* v67 no6 p534 Je 2017

Tyx, Daniel Blue
　Smells Like Teen Spirit *Sierra* v101 no5 p62 S/O 2016

Tzahor, Eldad
　Cardiac regeneration strategies: Staying young at heart diag *Science* v356 no6342 p1035 Je 9 2017

Tzeng, Stephany Y.
　Fabrication of fillable microparticles and other complex 3D microstructures color diag *Science* v357 no6356 p1138 S 15 2017

Tzou, C.-Y.
　Xenon isotopes in 67P/Churyumov-Gerasimenko show that comets contributed to Earth's atmosphere diag *Science* v356 no6342 p1069 Je 9 2017

U

U2 (Performer)
　How U2 Got Back to 'The Joshua Tree' A. GREENE bw *Rolling Stone* no1280 p11 F 9 2017
　THE JOSHUA TREE – SUPER DELUXE EDITION M. Mettler color *Sound & Vision* v82 no7 p72 S 2017
　Random Notes color *Rolling Stone* no1291/1292 p35 Jl 13 2017
　Random Notes color *Rolling Stone* no1293 p30 Ag 10 2017
　U2 Reinvent 'The Joshua Tree' [Cover story] A. GREENE bw color *Rolling Stone* no1289 p16 Je 15 2017
　U2's New Fire [Cover story] A. GREENE color *Rolling Stone* no1297 p11 O 5 2017
　The Unbearable Lightness Of Being U2 D. Dark bw color *America* v217 no4 p38 Ag 21 2017

uAvionix Corp.
　UAVIONIX ADS-B PRODUCTS color *Flying* v144 no2 p16 F 2017

Ubachs, Wim
　A testing time for antimatter bibl color diag *Science* v354 no6312 p546 N 4 2016

Ubbink, Job
　There's more to a meal color *Science* v356 no6343 p1129 Je 16 2017

Uber Technologies Inc.
　15 TRAVIS KALANICK A. Lashinsky color *Fortune* v174 no7 p88 D 1 2016
　Bozoma Saint John Wants To Humanize Uber A. M. Cox *New York Times Magazine* p58 S 3 2017
　¿Cómo se dice 'Uber'? E. Newcomer color *Bloomberg Businessweek* no4495 p25 O 17 2016
　THE DRUMBEAT FOR A PILOTLESS AIR TAXI CONTINUES color *Flying* v144 no4 p24 Ap 2017
　Everyone Hates Uber's Surge Pricing - Here's How to Fix It U. M. Dholakia *Harvard Business Review Digital Articles* p2 D 21 2015
　Everything We Know About Platforms We Learned from Medieval France R. Fisman and T. Sullivan *Harvard Business Review Digital Articles* p2 Mr 24 2016
　Flexible jobs give workers choices M. S. Hicks *Monthly Labor Review* p1 My 2017
　How Uber and the Sharing Economy Can Win Over Regulators S. Cannon and L. H. Summers *Harvard Business Review Digital Articles* p2 O 13 2014
　How Uber ran afoul of Apple's privacy rules C. McGARRY color *Macworld - Digital Edition* v34 no6 p63 Je 2017
　Investors Fawning over Uber Should Recall AOL's Stumbles R. G. McGrath *Harvard Business Review Digital Articles* p2 Ja 9 2015
　The Latest Victim of Uber's Bold Disruption May Be Itself R. Hackett color *Time* v189 no10 p22 Mr 20 2017
　LESSONS IN UBER'S ROUGH RIDE E. Griffith color *Fortune* v175 no6 p32 My 1 2017
　Lots of Employees Get Misclassified as Contractors. Here's Why It Matters D. Weil *Harvard Business Review Digital Articles* p2 Jl 5 2017

p264 O 2017

Uelmen, Amy
More hyperbole for the culture wars *America* v216 no10 p48 My 1 2017

Ueno, Masaki
Control of species-dependent cortico-motoneuronal connections underlying manual dexterity diag graph *Science* v357 no6349 p400 Jl 28 2017

UETRICHT, MICAH
The Local Labor Leader Who Defied Trump *In These Times* v41 no2 p32 F 2017
The Other Chicago Teachers Union *In These Times* v41 no5 p10 My 2017

Uffington White Horse (England)
WHITE HORSE OF THE SUN E. A. POWELL color *Archaeology* v70 no5 p9 S/O 2017

Ufot, Sonia
The Hair Braider J. Hughes *New York Times Magazine* p40 F 26 2017

Uganda
DOING GOOD S. Pulia color map *InStyle* v24 no8 p68 Ag 2017

Uganda—History
NATIONAL GALLERY UGANDA R. Griffiths *History Today* v67 no7 p78 Jl 2017

Ugarenko, Michal
PAF1 regulation of promoter-proximal pause release via enhancer activation color *Science* v357 no6357 p1294 S 22 2017

Ugarte, Adriana, 1985-
THE BREAK-OUTS 2016 S. Ball, Z. Baron et al color *GQ: Gentlemen's Quarterly* v86 no12 p198 D 2016

Ugaz, José Carlos
Icons color *Time* v189 no16/17 p122 My 1-8 2017

Uglow, Jenny
Collecting for the Glory of God color *New York Review of Books* v64 no15 p34 O 12 2017

Ugochukwu, Zim
Go Fly with Her color *O, The Oprah Magazine* p23 Mr 2017

Ugrešić, Dubravka
THE SHAMING OF THE SHREW *Harper's Magazine* v334 no2000 p23 Ja 2017

Uhalt, Lynne—Interviews
READY, FETE, GO ! L. CREGAN color *House Beautiful* v158 no10 p92 D 2016/Ja 2017

UHL, JENNIFER
CAR TALK *Indianapolis Monthly* p18 My 2017
G Is for Gains *Indianapolis Monthly* v40 no7 p34 Mr 2017

Uhl, Michael
Innovation Is as Much About Finding Partners as Building Products *Harvard Business Review Digital Articles* p2 Jl 20 2017

Uhlen, Mathias
Agreeable antibodies: Antibody validation challenges and solutions A. Dove color *Science* v357 no6356 p1165 S 15 2017
A pathology atlas of the human cancer transcriptome diag *Science* v357 no6352 p660 Ag 18 2017
A subcellular map of the human proteome color *Science* v356 no6340 p820 My 26 2017

Uhlmann, Frank
Building chromosomes without bricks [Cover story] diag *Science* v356 no6344 p1233 Je 23 2017

Uhlmann, Michael M.
THE LEFT'S DIRTY LITTLE SECRET *Claremont Review of Books* v17 no3 p20 Summ 2017

UJHÁZY, KAROL
Combining Biodiversity Resurveys across Regions to Advance Global Change Research *BioScience* v67 no1 p73 Ja 2017

UK Independence Party (Political party : Great Britain)
How People Power Is Splitting Europe S. Shuster and V. Walt color diag *Time* v188 no25-26 p80 D 19 2016 Double Issue
Trump Finds Support in Britain's Brexit Capital C. Randall *Wilson Quarterly* p5 Spr 2017

Ukeles, Mierle Laderman
Editor's Letter L. POLLOCK bw *Art in America* v105 no1 p14 Ja 2017
LABOR RELATIONS M. Heddaya color map *Art in America* v105 no1 p66 Ja 2017

Ukeles, Mierle Laderman—Exhibitions

Labor Intensive A. K. Scott color *New Yorker* v92 no36 p6 N 7 2016

Ukraine. Ministerstvo oborony
LIGHTS OUT A. GREENBERG color map *Wired* v25 no7 p52 Jl 2017

Ukraine Conflict, 2014-
BOOM That You Hear Is Ukraine's Agriculture A. Bjerga and V. Verbyany color *Bloomberg Businessweek* no4495 p12 O 17 2016
CONTAINING PUTIN'S RUSSIA R. E. POWASKI *USA Today Magazine* v146 no2868 p28 S 2017
Everyday Life in Ukraine's War Zone G. UEHLING *Current History* v116 no792 p264 O 2017
OLIGARCHY 2.0 J. YAFFA cartoon color *New Yorker* v93 no15 p46 My 29 2017
Will Ukraine Ever Change? T. Judah color *New York Review of Books* v64 no9 p47 My 25 2017

Ukraine—Description & travel
UKRAINE J. Lowe *New York Times Magazine* p22 S 24 2017

Ukraine—History—21st century
The Battle for Historical Memory in Postrevolutionary Ukraine O. SHEVEL *Current History* v115 no783 p258 O 2016

Ukraine—Politics & government—1991-
First the Cold War, Now the Flame War L. Kinstler color *Fortune* v176 no2 p19 Ag 1 2017

Ukulele
PERSONA color *New Orleans Magazine* v51 no12 p27 O 2017

Ulam, Adam B., 1922-2000
Governing Matters Most W. Kristol color *Weekly Standard* v22 no14 p7 D 12 2016

Ulanovsky, Nachum
Vectorial representation of spatial goals in the hippocampus of bats bibl graph *Science* v355 no6321 p1 Ja 13 2017

Ulate, Giselle
The Thread cartoon color *New York Times Magazine* p10 My 21 2017

ULATOWSKI, LEAH
She Adopts Babies Who Are Dying Alone [Cover story] *Reader's Digest* v188 no1125 p88 N 2016

Ulbricht, Ross William, 1985-
THE APPROVAL MATRIX img *New York* v50 no11 p148 My 29 2017
BRAVE NEW UNDERWORLD N. BILTON color *Vanity Fair* v59 no6 p68 My 2017

Ulcers
See also
Abscesses
Ulcers in the Dressage Horse E. Hardy *Dressage Today* v23 no4 p14 D 2016

Ulcers—Diagnosis
ULGERS PART TWO M. DEPAOLO *Arabian Horse World* v57 no3 p286 D 2016

Ulijn, Rein V.
Polymeric peptide pigments with sequence-encoded properties color graph *Science* v356 no6342 p1064 Je 9 2017

Ulin, David L.
The Bostonian: Novelist Dennis Lehane is drawn to restless characters who aren't quite sure where they fit in. It's a feeling he can relate to *New York* v50 no9 p88 My 1 2017
FORWARD MOTION *Los Angeles Magazine* p90 My 2017

Ulinich, Anya
IMAGINE WANTING ONLY THIS *New York Times Book Review* p29 My 21 2017
IN-BETWEEN DAYS: A Memoir About Living With Cancer *New York Times Book Review* p28 My 21 2017

Ullambana
Light it up A. POPE color map *Canadian Geographic* v137 p38 2017 Travel

Ullberg, Susann Baez
The Relevance of Soft Infrastructure in Disaster Management and Risk Reduction *UN Chronicle* v53 no3 p20 2016

Ullian, Jessica
A Ticket to Write color *Money* v46 no1 p140 Ja/F 2017

Ullman, Ellen
GENDER BINARY *Harper's Magazine* v335 no2006 p11 Jl 2017
Life in Code L. Greenblatt color *Entertainment Weekly* no1478 /

1479 p108 Ag 18-25 2017

Tech Decoder: The pioneering programmer Ellen Ullman discusses her career and the dangers the internet poses to privacy and civility J. D. BIERSDORFER *New York Times Book Review* p14 Ag 20 2017

Ullman, Tracey, 1959-

TRACEY ULLMAN J. McGovern color *Entertainment Weekly* no1439 p52 N 11 2016

Ullrich, J.

Ultrafast electron diffraction imaging of bond breaking in di-ionized acetylene bibl graph *Science* v354 no6310 p308 O 21 2016

Ullrich, Volker

The Führer Without Myth A. KIRSCH *New York Times Book Review* p12 O 16 2016

Hitler: Ascent, 1889-1939 A. Moravcsik *Foreign Affairs* v96 no2 p176 Mr/Ap 2017

Lessons from Hitler's Rise C. R. Browning bw cartoon *New York Review of Books* v64 no7 p10 Ap 20 2017

A WARNING FROM HISTORY R. J. EVANS bw *Nation* v304 no9 p43 Mr 20 2017

Ulm, Roman

A photoreceptor's on-off switch bibl diag *Science* v354 no6310 p282 O 21 2016

Ulrich, Brian

Rhode Island *New York Times Magazine* p45 N 20 2016

Ulrich, David, 1953-

Calculating the Market Value of Leadership *Harvard Business Review Digital Articles* p2 Ap 3 2015

PE Firms Are Creating a New Role: Leadership Capital Partner *Harvard Business Review Digital Articles* p2 Ag 11 2017

Private Equity's New Phase *Harvard Business Review Digital Articles* p2 Ag 9 2016

Victory Through Organization: *People Management* p52 Ap 2017

Your Company Culture Can't Be Disconnected from Your Customers *Harvard Business Review Digital Articles* p2 Mr 18 2016

Ulrich, David, 1953——Interviews

"YOUR EMPLOYEES ARE THE PEOPLE WHO MAKE YOU WIN": Organisations are too focused on great players, says HR guru Dave Ulrich - it's time to start playing a team game G. GYTON *People Management* p40 Ap 2017

Ulrich, Jochen

In the Best Sales Teams, About Half of the People Are in Support Roles *Harvard Business Review Digital Articles* p2 My 25 2016

Ulrich, Lars, 1963——Interviews

Lars Ulrich K. GROW cartoon *Rolling Stone* no1274 p62 N 17 2016

METALLICA'S LARS ULRICH D. Snierson color *Entertainment Weekly* no1442 p58 D 2 2016 Rebellious Special Issue

Ulrich, Laurel Thatcher

Book of Mormons B. GAGE *New York Times Book Review* p12 Ja 29 2017

A House Full of Women *Publishers Weekly* v263 no46 p50 N 14 2016

One Man, Many Wives, Full House L. Rothman color *Time* v189 no4 p49 Ja 23 2017

ULRICH, LAWRENCE

the 10 best new family cars [Cover story] cartoon color *Parents* v92 no7 p100 Jl 2017

Ulrich, R.

Observation of a large-scale anisotropy in the arrival directions of cosmic rays above 8×10^{18} eV *Science* v357 no6357 p1266 S 22 2017

ULTA Salon Cosmetics & Fragrance Inc.

3 MARY DILLON P. Wahba color *Fortune* v174 no7 p75 D 1 2016

Ultimate (Game)—Competitions

On Our Honour H. Roderique color *Walrus* v14 no5 p24 Je 2017

Ultimate Ears LLC

ULTIMATE EARS MEGABOOM BLUETOOTH SPEAKER BUILT TO BE THE LIFE OF THE PARTY T. NICOLAKIS color *Macworld - Digital Edition* v33 no11 p48 N 2016

Ultimate Fighting Championship (Organization)

Cage Match A. SHEPHARD il *New Republic* v247 no11 p11 N 2016

GARDEN PARTY L. J. Wertheim color *Sports Illustrated* v125 no17 p102 N 21 2016 Double Issue

Ultimate Fighting Championship (Organization)—Officials & employees

Demetrious Johnson L. J. Wertheim color *Sports Illustrated* v126 no15 p44 My 29 2017

Ultra-high energy cosmic rays

Cosmic rays raid the Milky Way L. GROSSMAN color *Science News* v192 no6 p7 O 14 2017

Ultra high net worth individuals

THE FORBES 400 bw color *Forbes* v200 no5 p86 N 14 2017

Forbes 400 index *Forbes* v200 no5 p166 N 14 2017

Ultra-Orthodox Jews

APOSTATES ANONYMOUS T. Brodesser-Akner *New York Times Magazine* p36 Ap 2 2017

Ultracold molecules

Synthesis of mixed hypermetallic oxide $BaOCa^+$ from laser-cooled reagents in an atom-ion hybrid trap P. Puri, M. Mills et al diag graph *Science* v357 no6358 p1370 S 29 2017

Ultrahigh definition television

Sony Spiffed Up PS4 Pro M. Fleischmann and C. Crowley color *Sound & Vision* v82 no1 p17 Ja 2017

Soundbar Shortcomings A. L. GRIFFIN color *Sound & Vision* v81 no10 p22 D 2016

ULTRA HD SETTLES IN R. SABIN *Sound & Vision* v82 no1 p8 Ja 2017

Ultrahigh definition television—Evaluation

2016 TOP PICKS OF THE YEAR R. Sabin color *Sound & Vision* v82 no2 p32 F/Mr 2017

Hisense 50H8C LCD Ultra HDTV A. Griffin color graph *Sound & Vision* v81 no9 p40 N 2016

LG 65UH8500 LCD Ultra HDTV R. Sabin color graph *Sound & Vision* v82 no1 p46 Ja 2017

LG OLED65E6P OLED Ultra HDTV T. J. Norton color graph *Sound & Vision* v82 no2 p54 F/Mr 2017

Not Your Father's HDTV T. J. Norton color *Sound & Vision* v82 no7 p42 S 2017

Sony XBR-65Z9D LCD Ultra HDTV T. J. Norton color graph *Sound & Vision* v82 no1 p36 Ja 2017

Ultra-HD 55" TVs color *Good Housekeeping* v264 no3 p97 Mr 2017

Ultramarathon running

2,190 MILES, 1,102 HOURS, 348,000 CALORIES, AND 1 WORLD RECORD B. HANSEN-BUNDY bw color *GQ: Gentlemen's Quarterly* v86 no12 p152 D 2016

COLD CALCULATIONS color *Runner's World* v52 no3 p80 Ap 2017

Go The Distance M. BERG chart color *Muscle & Performance* v9 no8 p20 Ag 2017

NO DOGS ALLOWED K. FOX color map *Runner's World* v52 no3 p76 Ap 2017

SO FAR. SO GOOD K. VAUGHN *Arizona Highways* v93 no1 p40 Ja 2017

Ultramarathon running—Training

ASK THE EXPERTS A. Trason, J. Hamilton et al color *Runner's World* v52 no1 p50 Ja/F 2017

Ultrasonic equipment

Christmas Island bat is officially no more color *Science* v357 no6357 p1216 S 22 2017

Ultrasonic imaging

MEET A WARRIOR V. Jonas color *Essence* v48 no6 p118 O 2017

Ultrasonic waves

Boom Box A. Hadhazy *Natural History* v125 no1 p8 D 2016/Ja 2017

Ultraviolet radiation

Best DEFENSE color *O, The Oprah Magazine* p88 My 2017

Bifurcating electron-transfer pathways in DNA photolyases determine the repair quantum yield Meng Zhang, Lijuan Wang et al bibl graph *Science* v354 no6309 p209 O 14 2016

Flu Season J. RAO color *Natural History* v125 no9 p46 S 2017

Safe Foraging d. mother il *Backpacker* p48 Ag 2017

Vitamin D Essentials V. TWEED *Better Nutrition* v79 no1 p68 Ja 2017

WE'VE GOT YOU COVERED A. Finney *Women's Health* v14 no5 p138 Je 2017

Ulvestad, Andrew

Bragg coherent diffractive imaging of single-grain defect dynamics in polycrystalline films color graph *Science* v356 no6339

College freshmen
College sophomores
Beyond the Transcript: The Need to Showcase More G. Wienhausen and K. Elias *Change* v49 no4 p14 Jl/Ag 2017
Genial Screw-Off J. Epstein *Claremont Review of Books* v17 no3 p64 Summ 2017
My lessons in mentorship S. Jain Goodwin color *Science* v356 no6344 p1302 Je 23 2017

Underground (Film)
Powered Up K. Kyles color *Ebony* v72 no3 p20 D 2016/Ja 2017

Underground (Short story)
UNDERGROUND D. Gilbert cartoon *New Yorker* v92 no48 p60 F 6 2017

Underground (TV program)
5 BINGE-WORTHY SHOWS WE LOVE color *Essence* v47 no8 p70 D 2016
John's Legendary Role M. LOGAN *TV Guide* v65 no11 p8 Mr 6 2017
March! T. PAYNE color *Ebony* v72 no5 p24 Mr 2017
One Legend Plays Another C. Holub and A. Wilkinson color *Entertainment Weekly* no1456 p61 Mr 10 2017
Underground M. Logan *TV Guide* p41 Ap 17 2017

Underground architecture
WHILE YOU ARE WAITING R. LORENZI color *Archaeology* v70 no4 p12 Je-Ag 2017

Underground construction
See also
Subways
Tunnels—Design & construction

Underground music
Bone Records K. C. POHLMANN and C. Crowley color *Sound & Vision* v81 no9 p26 N 2016

Underground nuclear explosions
SPYING ON NUCLEAR BLASTS [Cover story] A. Witze color graph *Science News* v192 no1 p18 Ag 5 2017

Undershirts
Runnerhood of the Traveling Singlet K. FOX color *Runner's World* v52 no7 p50 Ag 2017

Underside of Power, The (Music)
What to Stream color *Entertainment Weekly* no1472 p58 Je 30 2017

Undertakers & undertaking
THE MORTUARY MOGUL: Willie Watkins will bury you in style--its his calling G. GODFREY *Atlanta* v57 no6 p23 O 2017

Underwater (Film)
CERTAIN WOMEN C. ELLENBERG bw color *Vogue* v207 no6 p72 Je 2017

Underwater (Poem)
Underwater E. Lund *Christian Century* v133 no22 p13 O 26 2016

Underwater acoustics
Communicating Under Sea Ice: ENGINEERS USE OCEAN CHANNEL TO RELAY SOUND EFFICIENTLY K. Madin *Oceanus* v52 no2 p48 Spr 2017
A New Tsunami Warning System K. Madin *Oceanus* v52 no2 p53 Spr 2017

Underwater acoustics—Measurement
Ultrasounds for Coral Reefs? M. Kaplan color *Oceanus* v51 no2 p36 Wint 2016

Underwater archaeology
DECEMBER 7, 1941 S. S. PATEL bw color diag *Archaeology* v70 no1 p40 Ja/F 2017
Town Beneath the Waves D. WEISS color *Archaeology* v70 no2 p30 Mr/Ap 2017

Underwater cameras
LOOK OUT BELOW S. PENNAZ and G. BETHGE color *Outdoor Life* v224 no5 p38 Je/Jl 2017
A New Eye on Deep-Sea Fisheries L. Lippsett *Oceanus* v52 no1 p23 Summ 2016

Underwater construction
STRATEGIST img *New York* v49 no21 p73 O 17 2016

Underwater exploration
See also
Deep diving
THE DEEP SEA SIX color *Popular Science* p45 Ja/F 2017
A Luxury-Laden Shipwreck from 65 B.C E. Koenig *Oceanus* v52 no1 p12 Summ 2016

MACHINES OF THE ABYSS K. ATHERTON diag *Popular Science* p26 Ja/F 2017
She Favors Seas, He Prefers Stars N. DEGRASSE TYSON color *National Geographic* v232 no5 p24 N 2017
Sylvia Earle M. B. GRIGGS cartoon *Popular Science* p46 Ja/F 2017
WHALES OF ICELAND: Visit an Underwater World *Iceland Review* v55 no3 p101 My/Je 2017

Underwater navigation—Research
Seal Whiskers Inspire Marine Technology H. Beem color *Oceanus* v51 no2 p82 Wint 2016

Underwear
See also
T-shirts
Captain Underpants: The First Epic Movie K. DE SEVE color *National Geographic Kids* no471 p26 Je/Jl 2017
MALE Order *Interview* v47 no5 p37 Je/Jl 2017
UNDER ARMOR M. T. Goldman cartoon *O, The Oprah Magazine* p122 Mr 2017
Would You Rather... cartoon chart color *Seventeen* v76 no12 p112 D 2016/Ja 2017

Underwear—Evaluation
emporium bw color *Dressage Today* v23 no5 p62 Ja 2017
FUNDIES GALORE! G. TOMAINE color *Rodale's Organic Life* v3 no1 p16 Ja 2017
MORE UNDER STATEMENTS! color *Women's Health* v14 no7 p54 S 2017
Take COVER: FASHION'S RECONFIGURATIONS OF THE WIND-BREAKER BREATHE A FUTURISTIC LOOK INTO THE UTILITARIAN STAPLE FOR THOSE COOL NIGHTS OUT *Interview* v47 no3 p46 Ap 2017

Underwood, Beth
BLINDING SADDAM *Military History* v33 no6 p38 Mr 2017
THE RELIC HUNTER color *MHQ: Quarterly Journal of Military History* v29 no4 p24 Summ 2017

Underwood, Brian
Custom EYES color *O, The Oprah Magazine* p86 N 2017

Underwood, Cone S.
Thoughts on previous issues color *American Cowboy* v23 no4 p26 D 2016/Ja 2017

UNDERWOOD, DEBORAH
If We Ran the World (Or at Least the Country): A children's author's love letter to her colleagues' character, knowledge, and empathy *Publishers Weekly* v264 no29 p224 Jl 17 2017

Underwood, Emily
4.5 billion years of human history color *Science News* v190 no10 p28 N 12 2016
Bumblebees exhibit signs of emotions *Science News* v190 no9 p12 O 29 2016
Horses traded toes for speed, strength color *Science News* v192 no5 p12 S 30 2017
How ApoE4 endangers brains color *Science* v357 no6357 p1224 S 22 2017
How the body learns to hurt color *Science* v354 no6313 p694 N 11 2016
Mind the Monkey Business *Smithsonian* v47 no8 p21 D 2016
THE PAIN OF EXILE color diag *Science* v356 no6339 p682 My 19 2017
THE POLLUTED BRAIN color diag *Science* v355 no6323 p342 Ja 27 2017
Vanishing Act *Smithsonian* v47 no9 p16 Ja/F 2017

Underwood, Julie
Speak freely to the school board color *Phi Delta Kappan* v98 no5 p76 F 2017
Under the Law color *Phi Delta Kappan* v98 no3 p76 N 2016
Under the Law color *Phi Delta Kappan* v98 no7 p76 Ap 2017
Under The Law *Phi Delta Kappan* v98 no8 p74 My 2017
Under the Law *Phi Delta Kappan* v99 no1 p44 S 2017

Underwood, Matt
DIVERSE BY DESIGN T. Wheatley *Atlanta* v57 no5 p23 S 2017

UNDERWOOD, NORA
BACK TO THE (DIGITAL) DRAWING BOARD bw color *Maclean's* v129 no42 p48 O 24 2016

Underwood, Paul L.
HOW I GOT MY STYLE: LARRY McGUIRE color *Esquire* p55 N 2017

color graph *Monthly Labor Review* p1 Mr 2017
UNEMPLOYMENT IS REALLY LOW K. Bahler color map *Money* v46 no6 p70 Jl 2017
Why the Falling U.S. Unemployment Rate Matters J. Stibel *Harvard Business Review Digital Articles* p2 N 18 2014

Unemployment insurance—Law & legislation
Changes in federal and state unemployment insurance legislation in 2016 L. Lancaster *Monthly Labor Review* p1 Ag 2017

Unemployment insurance—United States
EMPLOYMENT, UNEMPLOYMENT, AND WAGES *Economic Indicators* p11 O 2016
Why the U.S. Needs Wage Insurance L. G. Kletzer *Harvard Business Review Digital Articles* p2 Ja 25 2016

Unemployment statistics
The Jobs Problem A. SMARICK bw color *Weekly Standard* v23 no4 p22 O 2 2017
Restoring Work and Wages K. A. HASSETT graph *National Review* v69 no6 p6 Ap 3 2017
Underemployment among Hispanics: the case of involuntary part-time work J. R. Young and M. J. Mattingly *Monthly Labor Review* p1 D 2016

Unerman, Sue
The Glass Wall *People Management* p55 O 2016

UNESCO
RIGA, LATVIA S. Kerrick Sullivan color *Snowboarder* v29 no2 p104 O 2016
SESAME and beyond S. K. Mtingwa and H. Winick color *Science* v356 no6340 p785 My 26 2017

Unfair labor practices
In the Greenroom *Stage Directions* v29 no10 p4 O 2016

Unferth, Deb Olin
Flash Friction: Thirty-nine offbeat stories find humor among the ruins H. PHILLIPS *New York Times Book Review* p16 Ap 30 2017

Unfold (Music)
Something From Nothing: My obsession with the Necks, the greatest trio on earth G. Dyer *New York Times Magazine* p52 O 8 2017

Unforgiven (Film : 1992)
UNFORGIVEN B. A. DuHamel color *Sound & Vision* v82 no8 p67 O 2017

UNG, GORDON MAH
Acer Predator 21 X: The most insane laptop ever built [Cover story] color graph *PCWorld* v35 no10 p48 O 2017
Acer's Switch 7 could overpower the Surface Pro and MacBook Pro color *PCWorld* v35 no10 p12 O 2017
AMD busts Ryzen performance myths, clearing Windows 10 from blame color graph *PCWorld* v35 no4 p9 Ap 2017
AMD Ryzen Threadripper: Everything we know so far about this monster CPU [Cover story] color *PCWorld* v35 no6 p9 Je 2017
Dell XPS 13 Kaby Lake: Yes, this is the best one so far color graph *PCWorld* v35 no1 p67 Ja 2017
Best cheap laptops: We rate the best-sellers on Amazon and Best Buy color *PCWorld* v35 no9 p56 S 2017
Facepalm: Intel's upcoming Coffee Lake CPUs won't work with today's motherboards color *PCWorld* v35 no9 p11 S 2017
FINSIX DART-C CHARGER: TINY, POWERFUL, AND WORTH THE EXPENSE chart color *Macworld - Digital Edition* v34 no6 p33 Je 2017
Finsix Dart-C charger: Tiny, powerful, and worth the expense chart color *PCWorld* v35 no7 p145 Jl 2017
Gigabyte Aero 15: A near-perfect power user's laptop color graph *PCWorld* v35 no8 p87 Ag 2017
Hands-on: AMD's Radeon Vega Frontier Edition vs Nvidia Titan Xp color *PCWorld* v35 no8 p105 Ag 2017
Here's proof that Ryzen can benefit from optimized game code color graph *PCWorld* v35 no5 p120 My 2017
How much will AMD's Zen cost? Here's what we think chart color *PCWorld* v35 no1 p24 Ja 2017
HP Spectre x360: Faster, smaller, and better than before color graph *PCWorld* v35 no1 p77 Ja 2017
Intel Core i9: The fastest consumer CPU prepares for Ryzen war chart color graph *PCWorld* v35 no8 p42 Ag 2017
Intel Optane Memory has a mission: Make hard drives faster than SSDs color graph *PCWorld* v35 no5 p33 My 2017
MacBook Pro's 'terrible' battery life tested color graph *Macworld*

- *Digital Edition* p20 Ap 2017
Official Intel 7th-gen Kaby Lake: One big change makes up for smaller ones chart color diag graph *PCWorld* v35 no2 p49 F 2017
Ryzen 5 vs. Core i5: Ryzen 5 1600X wins for best mainstream power CPU chart color graph *PCWorld* v35 no5 p107 My 2017
Ryzen review: AMD is back [Cover story] chart color diag graph map *PCWorld* v35 no4 p49 Ap 2017
Ryzen Threadripper: AMD's monster stomps on other CPUs chart color graph *PCWorld* v35 no9 p27 S 2017
SURFACE BOOK i7 vs. MACBOOK PRO: FIGHT! color graph *PCWorld* v35 no1 p155 Ja 2017
TESTED: THE TRUTH BEHIND THE MACBOOK PRO'S TERRIBLE BATTERY LIFE cartoon color graph *Macworld - Digital Edition* p68 Mr 2017
Tested: The truth behind the MacBook Pro's 'terrible' battery life color graph *PCWorld* p53 Mr 2017
What we know about AMD's Ryzen so far chart color graph *PCWorld* v35 no1 p18 Ja 2017

Ungar, Peter S.
Chew on this K. Christopher Beard color *Science* v356 no6339 p710 My 19 2017
Evolution's Bite: A Story of Teeth, Diet, and Human Origins L. A. MARSCHALL color *Natural History* v125 no5 p47 My 2017

Ungar, Richard
Yitzi and the Giant Menorah *Publishers Weekly* v263 no39 p93 S 26 2016

UNGAR, SANFORD J.
In Circular Pursuit bw *Weekly Standard* v22 no19 p33 Ja 23 2017

UNGER, CRAIG
Trump's Russian Laundromat color *New Republic* v248 no8/9 p26 Ag/S 2017

Unger, M.
Observation of a large-scale anisotropy in the arrival directions of cosmic rays above 8×1018 eV *Science* v357 no6357 p1266 S 22 2017

Unichef: Uniting Through Food (TV program)
UNICHEF: Uniting Through Food K. Hahn *TV Guide* v64 no46 p35 N 7 2016

Unicorns
Faires, Feasting & Fun J. B. PATTON chart color *Missouri Life* v44 no5 p42 Ag 2017

Unicorns (Finance)
A Few Unicorns Are No Substitute for a Competitive, Innovative Economy G. Hamel and M. Zanini color graph *Harvard Business Review Digital Articles* p2 F 8 2017
What Big Companies Can Learn from the Success of the Unicorns A. De Massis, F. Frattini et al *Harvard Business Review Digital Articles* p2 Mr 14 2016

Unicorns (Finance)—Charts, diagrams, etc.
What's in a Valley Valuation? A. Vandermey diag *Fortune* v176 no3 p19 S 1 2017

Unidentified flying objects
'UFO Disclosure' Fizzles Again in 2016 R. SHEAFFER *Skeptical Inquirer* v41 no2 p32 Mr/Ap 2017

Unidentified flying objects—Humor
PARODY diag *Weekly Standard* v22 no18 p44 Ja 16 2017

Uniforms
See also
Military uniforms
ATLANTA IN 50 OBJECTS T. MALONE *Atlanta* v56 no8 p50 D 2016
A CLASSIC COAT GOES ROGUE color *Esquire* p48 O 2017
The D.C. Working Man's True Power Suit S. Jefferies color *Washington Monthly* v49 no3-5 p6 Mr-My 2017
SCHOOL UNIFORMS WE WISH EXISTED *Parents* v91 no9 p104 S 2016

Uniforms—Evaluation
ESSENTIAL GEAR color *Black Belt* v55 no6 p72 O/N 2017

Uniforms—Sales & prices
The Border Patrol Wants to Buy American L. Etter color *Bloomberg Businessweek* no4497 p31 O 31 2016

Unilever Group (Company)
The Fresh Scent of Success T. Buckley and M. Campbell color *Bloomberg Businessweek* no4536 p46 S 4 2017
How Unilever Reaches Rural Consumers in Emerging Markets

V. Mahajan *Harvard Business Review Digital Articles* p2 D 14 2016

IT ISN'T EASY BEING GREEN B. Kowitt color *Fortune* v174 no7 p100 D 1 2016

Off-Color Ads by Beauty Brands K. Samuelson color *Time* v190 no16/17 p16 O 23 2017

SELLING SOAP AND SAVING THE WORLD V. Walt color *Fortune* v175 no3 p122 Mr 1 2017

Unilever's Big Strategic Bet on the Dollar Shave Club B. Chakravorti *Harvard Business Review Digital Articles* p2 Jl 28 2016

Unilever United States Inc.

super sticks color *Good Housekeeping* v265 no2 p140 Ag 2017

Uninstaller software

Our favorite Mac cleanup tips color *Macworld - Digital Edition* v34 no4 p81 My 2017

Union, Gabrielle, 1972-

Gabrielle Union J. STEWART and P. Kita color *Men's Health* v32 no2 p28 Mr 2017

THE GIFT OF GAB [Cover story] C. Connors color *Women's Health* v14 no2 p115 Mr 2017

"I won't be defined by my hair choices" A. Gardner and Ying Chu color *Glamour* v115 no4 p102 Ap 2017

Static Bling E. Wilson color *InStyle* v24 no4 p74 Ap 2017

THEN AND NOW Drama Queens C. Murray and B. Danielle color *Essence* v48 no5 p64 S 2017

Union, Gabrielle, 1972——Interviews

Being Mary Jane T. Stack color *Entertainment Weekly* no1448 p37 Ja 13 2017

FLAWLESS BEAUTY K. CHANEY and A. LUCAS bw color *Ebony* v72 no6 p42 Ap/My 2017

Gabrielle Union E. Berman color *Time* v188 no18 p56 O 31 2016

Q&A:Gabrielle Union's inspiring advice V. Kirby color *Redbook* p48 N 2017

STATE OF THE UNION [Cover story] C. Murray color *Essence* v47 no7 p76 N 2016

Union Binding Co.

UNION STRIKE MISSION E-STONE cartoon color *Snowboarder* v29 no5 p58 Ja 2017

Union of European Football Associations

CHANGING THE GAME FOR YOUNG PEOPLE IN HEALTH AND DEVELOPMENT M. SIDIBE *UN Chronicle* v53 no2 p22 2016

Union Pacific Railroad Co. Inc.

CAPTURING THE MIDWEST in HO scale [Cover story] P. K. Søeborg color diag *Model Railroader* v84 no5 p40 My 2017

The Legend Comes to Town: And I Will Get That Ride A. SCHENK *Idaho Magazine* v16 no10 p42 Jl 2017

Trackside Photos color *Model Railroader* v84 no5 p66 My 2017

Union Pacific's Spine Line in HO and N B. Sprague color diag map *Model Railroader* v84 no4 p72 Ap 2017

Union Square Hospitality Group LLC—Officials & employees

Q&A: DANNY MEYER A. Lappé *Nation* v305 no11 p5 O 30 2017

Union Theological Seminary (New York, N.Y.)

Episcopal Divinity School to affiliate with Union Theological in New York C. Kennel-Shank *Christian Century* v134 no7 p13 Mr 29 2017

Uniqlo Co. Ltd.

This Jacket Is the Bomb(er) color *Esquire* v166 no4 p56 N 2016

Unitarian Universalist Association of Congregations

People A. M. Banks *Christian Century* v134 no16 p16 Ag 2 2017

Unitarian Universalist head resigns amid controversy about staff diversity A. M. Banks color *Christian Century* v134 no9 p15 Ap 26 2017

United Airlines Inc.

Airlines Like United Can Underpay Bumped Passengers Because of a Government Rule R. Mohammed *Harvard Business Review Digital Articles* p2 Ap 12 2017

Companies Like United Need to Cultivate Good Judgment, and Free Their Employees to Use It J. Deighton *Harvard Business Review Digital Articles* p2 Ap 14 2017

United's No Good, Very Bad Day-and What It Means for All of Us N. Hopper color *Time* v189 no15 p22 Ap 24 2017

United Arab Emirates

European Racing Report S. Andersen *Arabian Horse World* v57 no1 p150 O 2016

United Arab Emirates Space Agency

Small Gulf nation aims for big splash on Mars S. El-Showk color *Science* v355 no6320 p12 Ja 6 2017

United Arab Emirates—Description & travel

The Great Escape D. POINTDUJOUR color *Ebony* v72 no3 p78 D 2016/Ja 2017

United Church of Christ

Shared space, shared vision C. H. Merritt *Christian Century* v134 no1 p45 Ja 4 2017

United Continental Holdings Inc.

20 OSCAR MUNOZ S. Tully color diag *Fortune* v174 no7 p90 D 1 2016

United Methodist Church (U.S.)

UMC court rules against consecrating gay bishops K. L. Gilbert, L. Bloom et al color *Christian Century* v134 no11 p13 My 24 2017

United Nations

The Barça Foundation J. C. CASAUS *UN Chronicle* v53 no2 p44 2016

Editor's note L. Crowder *Bulletin of the Atomic Scientists* v73 no3 p196 My 2017

The Evolving Role of the United Nations in Securing Human Rights Z. R. Al Hussein *UN Chronicle* v53 no4 p1 2016

The Evolving Role of the United Nations in Securing Human Rights Z. R. AL HUSSEIN *UN Chronicle* v54 no4 p6 2017

Faith-based groups, others put pressure on UN for its role in Haiti cholera deaths C. Kennel-Shank *Christian Century* v133 no24 p15 N 23 2016

Foreword M. Nasser *UN Chronicle* v53 no4 p1 2016

FOREWORD M. Nasser *UN Chronicle* v54 no4 p5 2017

How Companies Can Champion Sustainable Development B. Chakravorti *Harvard Business Review Digital Articles* p2 Mr 14 2017

NYT: Lather, Rinse, Repeat color *Weekly Standard* v22 no38 p2 Je 12 2017

THE OLYMPIC MOVEMENT THE UNITED NATIONS AND THE PURSUIT OF COMMON IDEALS T. BACH *UN Chronicle* v53 no2 p14 2016

PARODY color *Weekly Standard* v22 no39 p44 Je 19 2017

PHOTO color *Reason* v48 no8 p9 Ja 2017

SPORT AS A MEANS OF ADVANCING INTERNATIONAL DEVELOPMENT S. DARNELL *UN Chronicle* v53 no2 p27 2016

The U.N., Hard at Work color *Weekly Standard* v22 no31 p3 Ap 17 2017

USING SPORT TO END HUNGER AND ACHIEVE FOOD SECURITY J. BREWER *UN Chronicle* v53 no2 p39 2016

WORTH NOTING K. A. GAJEWSKI *Humanist* v77 no4 p48 Jl/Ag 2017

United Nations Framework Convention on Climate Change (1992)

Climate adaptation funding: Getting the money to those who need it M. Mostafa, M. F. Rahman et al bibl *Bulletin of the Atomic Scientists* v72 no6 p396 N 2016

The trouble with negative emissions K. Anderson and G. Peters bibl graph *Science* v354 no6309 p182 O 14 2016

United Nations. General Assembly

U.N. declares war on superbugs *Science* v353 no6307 p1474 S 30 2016

United Nations. General Assembly—Proceedings

UN-Convincing: Trump Goes Rogue on Iran N. Wadhams and K. Foroohar graph *Bloomberg Businessweek* no4540 p44 O 2 2017

United Nations. Security Council

Human Rights, Mass Atrocity Prevention and the United Nations Security Council: The Long Road Ahead H. S. Puri *UN Chronicle* v53 no4 p1 2016

'Tough Love'—The First and Last Obama Lie J. PODHORETZ *Commentary* v143 no2 p1 F 2017

United Nations—Appropriations & expenditures

Assad Allies Profit Off UN Money For Syria K. Foroohar bw *Bloomberg Businessweek* no4533 p34 Ag 7 2017

United Nations—Congresses

Calendar: Power T. Berenson and J. Shapiro color *Time* v188 no27-28 p62 D 26 2016

United Nations—Peacekeeping forces

What Trump Got Right About The UN C. MacDougall color

Bloomberg Businessweek no4516 p6 Mr 27 2017

United Nations—Peacekeeping forces—Congo (Democratic Republic)

What We Learned From... U.N. Peacekeepers in the Congo D. T. Zabecki bw *Military History* v34 no1 p18 My 2017

United Negro College Fund

Designing the Next Generation of Business Leaders D. T. Dingle color *Black Enterprise* v47 no4 p24 N/D 2016

United Parcel Service Inc.

BECOMING VISIBLE: INSIGHTS FOR WORKING WOMEN FROM THE WOMEN OF HIDDEN FIGURES *Vital Speeches of the Day* v83 no10 p304 O 2017

IF EVER THERE WERE A TIME WHEN WE NEED TO WORK WITH AND THROUGH EACH OTHER, IT'S NOW *Vital Speeches of the Day* v83 no9 p270 S 2017

United States

Besting The Bullies T. PATKIN *USA Today Magazine* v145 no2860 p36 Ja 2017

BOOTLEGGER'S MAP OF THE UNITED STATES, 1926 K. Wiles *History Today* v67 no6 p4 Je 2016

A Call for Hope D. YARNOLD *Audubon* v118 no6 p8 Wint 2016

The Century's First Big Craze: Ping-Pong *Saturday Evening Post* v289 no5 p97 S/O 2017

Could You Pass the U.S. CITIZENSHIP TEST? *New York Times Upfront* v149 no11 p10 Ap 3 2017

THE FUTURE OF VEGANISM D. Wasserman and C. Stabler *Vegetarian Journal* v36 no1 p4 2017

Grail Bird K. Kaufman *Audubon* v118 no6 p46 Wint 2016

Looking Downstream to "Troubled Waters" *USA Today Magazine* v146 no2867 p9 Ag 2017

made in america [Cover story] color *Parents* v92 no7 p68 Jl 2017

Now More Than Ever [Cover story] P. J. BOYER color *Weekly Standard* v23 no5 p21 O 9 2017

OUR CIVIC DNA S. FENNESSY *Atlanta* v56 no11 p16 Mr 2017

THE PERFECT WATERFALL *Saturday Evening Post* v289 no5 p23 S/O 2017

Places Worth Preserving G. Wuerthner *Sierra* v101 no4 p48 Jl/Ag 2016

RISK *Cycle World* v56 no7 p8 Ag 2017

STRESSED OUT K. MOORE *Natural History* v125 no1 p2 D 2016/Ja 2017

Top 10 States for Well-Being map *Prevention* v69 no4 p13 Ap 2017

THE UNITED STATES OF MOVIES color *Entertainment Weekly* no1477 p40 Ag 11 2017

The Urbanist: The Teens of Havana T. MACMILLAN and R. MORGAN img *New York* v49 no21 p30 O 17 2016

U.S. immigration ban undermines scientists M. Hassan bibl color *Science* v355 no6326 p704 F 17 2017

The View from Center Ring G. Dearth *Arabian Horse World* v57 no1 p74 O 2016

Way Down South N. ZEVNIK color *Better Nutrition* v78 no11 p82 N 2016

You know you're in America when ... map *Reader's Digest* v190 no1132 p28 Jl/Ag 2017

You Say Tomato ... J. KATZ map *Reader's Digest* v190 no1132 p124 Jl/Ag 2017

United States armed forces

See also

United States. Air Force

United States. Army

United States. Coast Guard

United States. Navy

AMERICA ENTERS THE GREAT WAR M. YOCKELSON *Prologue* v49 no1 p6 Spr 2017

BRAVERY AT THE BATTLE OF THE BULGE A. M. FLYNN *USA Today Magazine* v145 no2864 p44 My 2017

CHOSIN RESERVOIR *AARP: The Magazine* v59 no3A p66 Ap/My 2016

Life Lessons From Boot Camp J. MARK JACKSON color *Reader's Digest* v190 no1135 p26 N 2017

OFF-TARGET M. KLARE and P. A. DUR *Foreign Affairs* v95 no6 p196 N/D 2016

Remembering WORLD WAR I D. S. Ferriero *Prologue* v49 no1 p2 Spr 2017

Restoring Solvency H. BRANDS and E. EDELMAN color *Weekly*

Standard v22 no25 p23 Mr 6 2017

The Soldier and the State: We thank you for your service--sucker! M. C. DESCH *American Conservative* v16 no5 p38 S/O 2017

Trump's Fake Defense Buildup T. Donnelly and G. Schmitt color *Weekly Standard* v22 no26 p9 Mr 13 2017

An Uncertain Trumpet T. Donnelly and G. Schmitt *Weekly Standard* v22 no17 p8 Ja 2 2017

War Games *Military History* v33 no6 p78 Mr 2017

Warriors and Citizens R. Brooks *Hoover Digest: Research & Opinion on Public Policy* no4 p73 Fall 2016

What Good Is Military Force? J. BERGNER *Weekly Standard* v22 no6 p16 O 17 2016

United States armed forces—Civilian employees

World War What? A. ABEL color *Maclean's* v130 no4 p44 My 2017

United States Attorney's Office

A RIGHTEOUS CASE W. FINNEGAN cartoon color *New Yorker* v93 no13 p66 My 15 2017

United States census

Is Bigger Always Better? Population growth doesn't necessarily mean a city is thriving J. B. Wogan *Governing* v30 no12 p24 S 2017

United States climate change policy

A MARCH FOR THE FUTURE PEOPLE'S CLIMATE MOBILIZATION B. McKIBBEN color *Nation* v304 no15 p12 My 8 2017

United States Commission on Civil Rights

Freedom to Serve color *America* v215 no10 p5 O 10 2016

United States Commission on International Religious Freedom

U.S. commission: Russia among worst violators of religious freedom L. Markoe *Christian Century* v134 no11 p15 My 24 2017

United States Dressage Federation

Coaching Youth Toward USDF MEDALS [Cover story] K. Brittle color *Dressage Today* v24 no2 p30 N 2017

Dressage Movers and Shakers Gather in St. Louis J. O. Bryant color *Practical Horseman* v45 no3 p64 Mr 2017

INSIGHTS from Lilo Fore and Hans-Christian Matthiesen B. Baumert color graph *Dressage Today* v23 no8 p36 Ap 2017

United States Equestrian Federation (Organization)

Build a Fan Base *Practical Horseman* v45 no4 p59 Ap 2017

COMING HOME N. Jaffer color *Dressage Today* v23 no6 p58 F 2017

Dressage Movers and Shakers Gather in St. Louis J. O. Bryant color *Practical Horseman* v45 no3 p64 Mr 2017

Keeping It LEGAL J. M. Keeler color *Dressage Today* v23 no8 p60 Ap 2017

USEF Agrees to Rehearing Request *Practical Horseman* v45 no5 p68 My 2017

USEF Reveals New Vision color *Practical Horseman* v45 no4 p58 Ap 2017

United States federal budget

CAPITOL IDEA: SCIENTISTS, PLEASE RUN FOR OFFICE C. THOMPSON color *Wired* v25 no8 p34 Ag 2017

Check the budget K. Clarke *U.S. Catholic* v82 no7 p42 Jl 2017

Politics/Policy P. Coy color graph *Bloomberg Businessweek* no4524 p27 My 29 2017

Rich Man, Poor City K. PHILLIPS-FEIN *New Republic* v248 no8/9 p8 Ag/S 2017

A Social Security Proposal We Can All Live With R. C. Pozen *Harvard Business Review Digital Articles* p2 Je 17 2017

The Strength of a Nation L. E. Panetta *America* v216 no12 p58 My 29 2017

Trump budget proposal: gloomy, but just a proposal M. Hourihan and D. Parkes *Issues in Science & Technology* v33 no4 p21 Summ 2017

United States federal budget—Computer network resources

Wharton's Policy Tool Isn't Just for Wonks P. Coy color *Bloomberg Businessweek* no4522 p52 My 15 2017

United States Grand Prix Race

Start Your Engines! F. Seidel color *New York Review of Books* v64 no1 p16 Ja 19 2017

United States gross domestic product

TOTAL OUTPUT, INCOME, AND SPENDING *Economic Indicators* p1 Ap 2017

United States gubernatorial elections

Blue on Blue in Virginia A. FERGUSON color *Weekly Standard* v22 no35 p15 My 22 2017

United States Highway 66

ROUTE 66: SELIGMAN TO KINGMAN N. AUSTIN *Arizona Highways* v93 no2 p52 F 2017

United States Hunter Jumper Association (Organization)

Applications Open for EAP Regional Training Sessions *In Stride* v12 no2 p10 Mr 2017

Bill Moroney Sets Sail for New Challenges N. Jaffer *In Stride* v11 no6 p50 N 2016

CORE Clinics K. Rover *In Stride* v11 no6 p43 N 2016

Cuba: Conquers the $268,550 USHJA International Hunter Derby Championship T. Booker *In Stride* v12 no5 p12 S 2017

The EAP Regionals Open Eyes--and Doors--Throughout the Country K. Rover *In Stride* v12 no5 p27 S 2017

Emerging Jumper Rider Program Launched *In Stride* v12 no4 p8 Jl 2017

Expanding Opportunities for Derby and Green Hunters R. Danta *In Stride* v12 no5 p6 S 2017

Horsemanship, Front and Center W. Allen *In Stride* v12 no5 p36 S 2017

Hunter Championships Conclude in the North K. Rover *In Stride* v11 no6 p47 N 2016

Making the Most of a Once-in-a-Lifetime Experience G. Marlowe *In Stride* v12 no2 p31 Mr 2017

Marley Jordan's 'Village' Expands to Florida and Beyond K. Cattani *In Stride* v12 no3 p41 My 2017

Mary Babick Arrives for the 'Formative Years' T. Booker *In Stride* v11 no6 p32 N 2016

Millions of Reasons to Celebrate the USHJA International Hunter Derby Program: After less than a decade, the program pays out more than $10 million--and the numbers are only increasing T. Booker *In Stride* v12 no4 p20 Jl 2017

Nancy Crary Jones: An Amateur with a Professional Mindset T. Booker *In Stride* v12 no4 p39 Jl 2017

Navigating the Purchase Process M. Lacy *In Stride* v12 no4 p24 Jl 2017

News BITS color *Practical Horseman* v44 no12 p67 D 2016

News BITS color *Practical Horseman* v45 no7 p64 Jl 2017

Old Dominion and Strapless Find Fame N. Jaffer *In Stride* v12 no5 p45 S 2017

Pony Derby Established *In Stride* v11 no6 p14 N 2016

Pony Finals Dreams Come True *In Stride* v12 no5 p8 S 2017

Remember: The Word 'Horse' Comes First in the Horse Business A. Thornbury *In Stride* v12 no4 p6 Jl 2017

Remember to Sport Your Integrity M. Babick *In Stride* v12 no4 p34 Jl 2017

Taking Ownership: Tips for the New or Longtime Horse Owner M. Lacy *In Stride* v12 no2 p45 Mr 2017

Thank You for the Honor B. Moroney *In Stride* v11 no6 p8 N 2016

The Top Three Derby Contenders: A Conformation Analysis J. Winkel *In Stride* v11 no6 p44 N 2016

Where Do You Stand? M. Babick *In Stride* v12 no2 p8 Mr 2017

United States Hunter Jumper Association (Organization)—Congresses

USHJA Focuses on Growth and Sport Integrity K. F. Miller color *Practical Horseman* v45 no3 p66 Mr 2017

United States legislators

See also

Senators (U.S.)

10 THINGS WE'RE TALKING ABOUT T. A. Christian color *Essence* v48 no2 p67 Je 2017

Congress Confronts a Daunting to-Do List N. Jenkins color *Time* v190 no10/11 p16 S 18 2017

The Importance of Being Idle P. Coy color *Bloomberg Businessweek* no4532 p8 Jl 31 2017

A Local Pol with A Global Profile G. KAHN color *Los Angeles Magazine* v62 no7 p58 Jl 2017

RICHER AND POORER: How could the nation's wealthiest state become a fiscal basket case? A. Greenblatt *Governing* v30 no12 p30 S 2017

Scarborough Fare color *Weekly Standard* v22 no41 p4 Jl 3 2017

Self-Inflicted Carnage G. Orfalea color *Commonweal* v144 no13 p17 Ag 11 2017

Senator Jeff Merkley, Working-Class Hero Z. CARPENTER color *Nation* v304 no17 p22 Je 5 2017

United States Playing Card Co.

NAMED FOR A CRAZE *Saturday Evening Post* v289 no2 p98 Mr/Ap 2017

United States political parties

BARE, RUINED CHOIRS: HOW BARACK OBAMA WRECKED THE DEMOCRATIC PARTY [Cover story] J. PODHORETZ and N. C. ROTHMAN *Commentary* v142 no5 p12 D 2016

THE BATTLE LINES HAVE BEEN DRAWN R. L. FISCHER *USA Today Magazine* v146 no2866 p14 Jl 2017

Democracy vs. Math E. Bazelon *New York Times Magazine* p48 S 3 2017

None of the Above: Have 2016's candidates made room for third parties? A. Greenblatt *Governing* v30 no12 p17 S 2017

Warning: Semantic Traps Ahead: Environmental politics are littered with language that obscures meaning and hinders good policy T. L. Anderson and K. R. Leube *Hoover Digest: Research & Opinion on Public Policy* no3 p77 Summ 2017

United States presidential elections

Let the Investigation Begin [Cover story] color *Weekly Standard* v22 no36 p6 My 29 2017

STRANGERS IN A STRANGE LAND L. BLADES and S. T. BROWN color *Ebony* v72 no6 p69 Ap/My 2017

United States Steel Corp.

U.S. Steel's Revitalization J. Deaux color *Bloomberg Businessweek* no4536 p42 S 4 2017

United States Tennis Association

COURT of APPEALS R. GOOD color *Tennis* v53 no2 p8 Mr/Ap 2017

The Future of Tennis C. SHMERLER *Tennis* v53 no3 p62 My/Je 2017

James Blake's Next Challenge B. KALLET *Tennis* v52 no6 p22 N/D 2016

Student Union *Tennis* v52 no6 p74 N/D 2016

A Tennis Mecca C. Evert bw color *Tennis* v53 no2 p2 Mr/Ap 2017

United States. Advanced Research Projects Agency—Finance

A Cloud Hangs Over a Clean-Energy Fund A. Natter color graph *Bloomberg Businessweek* no4513 p33 Mr 6 2017

United States. Age Discrimination in Employment Act of 1967

Age Discrimination Claim by Beach Patrol Chief J. C. Kozlowski *Parks & Recreation* v51 no11 p26 N 2016

United States. Air Force

backstory color *New Republic* v248 no10 p68 O 2017

BLINDING SADDAM B. Underwood *Military History* v33 no6 p38 Mr 2017

Completing a career G. Andrew Mickley color *Science* v356 no6337 p554 My 5 2017

DISPOSABLE DRONES J. PAPPALARDO cartoon *Popular Mechanics* p9 Je 2017

The Response: A SPACE-DEFENSE TELESCOPE color *Popular Mechanics* p72 Mr 2017

United States. Air Force—Airmen

Hump Days L. G. MacNicol *MHQ: Quarterly Journal of Military History* v29 no3 p10 Spr 2017

United States. Air Traffic Control System

TRUMP ENVISIONS "BIG CHANGES" IN AVIATION color *Flying* v144 no4 p22 Ap 2017

United States. American Recovery & Reinvestment Act of 2009

Capitalism Behaving Badly D. Rotman il *MIT Technology Review* v119 no6 p96 N/D 2016

United States. Americans with Disabilities Act of 1990

ADA Accessibility Rules for Alterations to Existing Facilities J. C. Kozlowski *Parks & Recreation* v52 no8 p24 Ag 2017

United States. Army

Army now allows soldiers to wear turbans, beards, and headscarves A. M. Banks color *Christian Century* v134 no4 p14 F 15 2017

RESEARCHERS SEEK TO ID MEXICAN WAR REMAINS B. Manley *Military History* v33 no6 p8 Mr 2017

The Response: THE LIGHTWEIGHT PERSONAL BAZOOKA color *Popular Mechanics* p75 Mr 2017

A SOLDIER'S LAST BEDTIME Story K. MILLER *Reader's Digest* v189 no1128 p80 Mr 2017

A U.S. Commander's Year on the Front Line Against ISIS In Iraq and Syria J. Malsin color *Time* v190 no10/11 p14 S 18 2017

War Games *Military History* v33 no6 p78 Mr 2017

United States. Army Rangers

SPECIAL OPS FITNESS SECRETS [Cover story] B. COURT cartoon color *Men's Health* v32 no4 p94 My 2017

United States. Army. Special Forces

A Veteran's Son Goes to VIETNAM G. SHELBY *Reader's Digest* v188 no1125 p114 N 2016

United States. Army—Medical care

How the U.S. Army Personalized Its Mental Health Care J. Srinivasan, M. D. Brown et al *Harvard Business Review Digital Articles* p2 D 7 2016

United States. Bureau of Immigration & Customs Enforcement

How do I respond when ICE comes for my flock? R. P. Roden color *America* v216 no10 p38 My 1 2017

United States. Bureau of Indian Affairs

The Big Black Box of Indian Country V. LAMBERT *American Indian Quarterly* v40 no4 p333 Fall 2016

United States. Bureau of Labor Statistics

Consumer Expenditure Surveys Methods Symposium and Microdata Users' Workshop, July 12-15, 2016 G. D. Paulin and N. To bibl *Monthly Labor Review* p1 My 2017

Corporate America Ready for Social Workers *USA Today Magazine* v145 no2863 p11 Ap 2017

Data on display More education: Lower unemployment, higher earnings A. Chen graph *Career Outlook* p1 Ap 2017

DOES YOUR CHOICE MEASURE UP? Check out the numbers surrounding popular degree choices and careers J. H. REDMOND *Cincinnati Magazine* v50 no11 pCG8 Ag 2017

Finding hot jobs: Using data to locate career opportunities E. Torpey *Career Outlook* p1 D 2016

Job openings, hires, and separations rise, but at a slower pace, in 2016 B. M. Thibaud bibl *Monthly Labor Review* p1 Ag 2017

Jobs for people who love being outdoors E. Torpey *Career Outlook* p1 Jl 2017

One hundred years of Current Employment Statistics: busting CES myths M. Calvillo and T. Downing bibl chart color graph *Monthly Labor Review* p1 O 2016

Reconstruction of CES time series: implementing the 2010 OMB metropolitan area delineations S. M. Mance and J. R. Stewart bibl chart color graph *Monthly Labor Review* p1 O 2016

An update on SOII undercount research activities M. M. Gunter bibl chart color graph *Monthly Labor Review* p1 S 2016

Water work: Jobs related to water utilities E. Torpey chart color *Career Outlook* p1 Ap 2017

United States. Bureau of Land Management

warm front d. o'neil color *Bike Magazine* v24 no5 p34 Jl 2017

United States. Bureau of Ocean & Energy Management

WINDS OF CHANGE J. McMURRAY and G. BETHGE color map *Outdoor Life* v224 no5 p33 Je/Jl 2017

United States. Bureau of the Census

COUNTING AMERICANS IN REAL TIME *Saturday Evening Post* v289 no2 p96 Mr/Ap 2017

How to Avoid the 2020 Census Fiasco bw *Bloomberg Businessweek* no4526 p10 Je 12 2017

Ng *Washingtonian Magazine* v52 no4 p74 Ja 2017

Social Science and the Public Interest *Society* v54 no3 p213 Je 2017

Why the Census Matters Now More Than Ever H. S. Edwards color *Time* v189 no20 p17 My 29 2017

United States. Bureau of the Census—Finance

Scientists fear pending attack on federal statistics collection J. Mervis color *Science* v355 no6320 p16 Ja 6 2017

United States. Central Intelligence Agency

The CIA, Post-Obama R. M. GERECHT color *Weekly Standard* v22 no15 p24 D 19 2016

The CIA's Hackers Find Their Secrets Posted Online K. Vick color *Time* v189 no10 p12 Mr 20 2017

DEEP BACKGROUND P. GIRALDI *American Conservative* v16 no1 p36 Ja/F 2017

How Intelligence Works (When It Does) H. E. MEYER *USA Today Magazine* v145 no2864 p10 My 2017

Human Resource Exploitation Training Manual *Lapham's Quarterly* v10 no3 p210 Summ 2017

THE MONTH IN REVIEW: March 2017 *Current History* v116 no790 p200 My 2017

Those Hacking Charges color *Nation* v304 no2 p3 Ja 16 2017

Trump Got This One Right T. JOSCELYN color *Weekly Standard* v22 no45 p14 Ag 7 2017

WikiLeaks dump brings CIA spying powers into the spotlight M. KAN color *PCWorld* v35 no4 p33 Ap 2017

United States. Chemical Safety & Hazard Investigation Board

Chemical safety K. REST *Issues in Science & Technology* v33 no1 p17 Fall 2016

United States. Civil Aeronautics Board

On the House C. BONANOS color *Conde Nast Traveler* v52 no7 p98 Ag 2017

United States. Civil Rights Act of 1964

Judges Rule Queers Have Civil Rights J. ANDERSON-MINSHALL color *Advocate* no1091 p21 Je/Jl 2017

United States. Coast Guard

IT'S HERE! M. Werling *Sea Magazine* v109 no5 p6 My 2017

MEET COMMANDER BRIAN MEIER *Sea Magazine* v108 no9 pPNW-10 S 2016

Mission Ready J. Y. WOOD color *Power & Motoryacht* v34 no9 p36 S 2017

OFF THE CHARTERS: AUTHORITIES ARE CRACKING DOWN ON UNAUTHORIZED PASSENGER-FOR-HIRE ACTIVITIES IN SOUTHERN CALIFORNIA color *Sea Magazine* v109 no7 pCA-6 Jl 2017

Polar Ice Squad J. Hsu color *Scientific American* v316 no6 p10 Je 2017

Take It Easy B. PIKE cartoon *Power & Motoryacht* v34 no9 p184 S 2017

United States. Commodity Futures Trading Commission

Dirty Deeds Hidden In a Mess of Data M. Leising *Bloomberg Businessweek* no4512 p38 F 20 2017

United States. Congress

2011: Washington, DC *Lapham's Quarterly* v10 no2 p102 Spr 2017

The Blight of ObamaCare Will Not Vanish J. M. ORIENT *USA Today Magazine* v146 no2868 p16 S 2017

The Border Wall: Immigration, Security, and U.S.-Mexico Relations *Congressional Digest* v96 no8 p2 O 2017

Broadband Industry Self-Regulation: Federal Trade Commission Consumer Privacy Principles *Congressional Digest* v96 no5 p7 My 2017

By number, Christians overrepresented in Congress D. Iaconangelo and F. Kiefer color *Christian Century* v134 no3 p12 F 2017

Clock Is Ticking for DACA Solution T. J. DONOHUE *Weekly Standard* v23 no5 p14 O 9 2017

Congress and War S. R. Weissman cartoon *Foreign Affairs* v96 no1 p132 Ja/F 2017

Dr. Obama Remains On Call--for Now *USA Today Magazine* v145 no2864 p28 My 2017

Ensuring scientific integrity in the Age of Trump G. T. Goldman, E. Berman et al bibl cartoon *Science* v355 no6326 p696 F 17 2017

Female Athletics Continues to Grow *USA Today Magazine* v146 no2867 p14 Ag 2017

Free the Copyright Office M. RASENBERGER *Publishers Weekly* v264 no19 p64 My 8 2017

How to Remove A President 101 P. M. Barrett color *Bloomberg Businessweek* no4523 p26 My 22 2017

If sports betting is legalized, could its hunger for analytics restore an older, purer version of fandom? J. C. Kang *New York Times Magazine* p16 Ap 30 2017

In Congress, It's Do-or-Die Time for the GOP E. Wasson, A. Edgerton et al cartoon *Bloomberg Businessweek* no4530 p39 Jl 17 2017

Interview Veterans Advocate Congressman Charles Rangel *Military History* v33 no5 p14 Ja 2017

John Lewis L. Rothman color *Time* v189 no13 p56 Ap 10 2017

Legislative Background on Border Security: Legislative Background on Border Security *Congressional Digest* v96 no8 p7 O 2017

Legislative Background on Broadband Privacy: Recent Action by Congress on the FCC Rulemaking *Congressional Digest* v96 no5 p9 My 2017

Lobbyists Are Behind the Rise in Corporate Profits J. Bessen *Harvard Business Review Digital Articles* p2 My 26 2016

Play Hardball in Congress T. E. Mann *New Republic* v248 no3 p32 Mr 2017

The Pros and Cons of the President's Deregulation Agenda *Congressional Digest* v96 no4 p12 Ap 2017

United States. Dept. of Agriculture

ANOTHER 4-BILLION-BUSHEL SOYBEAN CROP? *Successful Farming* v115 no1 p14 Ja 2017

Applications for the Noninsured Crop Disaster Program Increased After the Agricultural Act of 2014 A. Hungerford and G. Astill *Amber Waves: The Economics of Food, Farming, Natural Resources, & Rural America* p5 Jl 2017

Changes in Food-At-Home Spending by SNAP Participants After the Stimulus Act of 2009 C. Tuttle bw chart color graph *Amber Waves: The Economics of Food, Farming, Natural Resources, & Rural America* p8 D 2016

Cotton Fields in Scottsdale K. MONTGOMERY *Arizona Highways* v93 no2 p8 F 2017

Educating the New Administration and Congress About Park & Rec Programs K. Sims *Parks & Recreation* v52 no9 p28 S 2017

EYE ON 45 color *Science* v355 no6331 p1245 Mr 24 2017

FOUR INSIGHTS INTO LAND OWNERSHIP B. Spiegel *Successful Farming* v115 no1 p22 Ja 2017

Green Gazette *Mother Earth News* no280 p10 F/Mr 2017

HEMP COMES HOME R. Kobell color *Reason* v49 no5 p38 O 2017

LONELY AT THE TOP: ASIDE FROM SONNY PERDUE, USDA IS SHORT OF LEADERS *Successful Farming* v115 no9 p14 Ag 2017

Nearly 14,000 USDA Microloans Issued Between 2013 and 2015 S. Tulman *Amber Waves: The Economics of Food, Farming, Natural Resources, & Rural America* p12 Mr 2017

ON THE RISE: USDA FORECASTS FIRST UPTURN IN FARM INCOME IN FOUR YEARS. WILL IT LAST? *Successful Farming* v115 no12 p12 O 2017

Redeeming WIC Benefits at California Farmers' Markets P. McLaughlin *Amber Waves: The Economics of Food, Farming, Natural Resources, & Rural America* p25 Jl 2017

USDA's FoodAPS: Providing Insights Into U.S. Food Demand and Food Assistance Programs J. E. Todd, L. Tiehen et al *Amber Waves: The Economics of Food, Farming, Natural Resources, & Rural America* p42 Ag 2017

USDA's National School Lunch Program Reduces Food Insecurity K. Ralston and A. Coleman-Jensen *Amber Waves: The Economics of Food, Farming, Natural Resources, & Rural America* p38 Ag 2017

USDA sued on animal data *Science* v355 no6326 p670 F 17 2017

WIC Participation Continues To Decline V. Oliveira *Amber Waves: The Economics of Food, Farming, Natural Resources, & Rural America* p53 Je 2017

United States. Dept. of Agriculture. Economic Research Service

Americans' Seafood Consumption Below Recommendations L. Kantor *Amber Waves: The Economics of Food, Farming, Natural Resources, & Rural America* p1 O 2016

FoodAPS Data Now Available to the General Public E. Larimore, E. Page et al chart color graph *Amber Waves: The Economics of Food, Farming, Natural Resources, & Rural America* p27 D 2016

A Look at Calorie Sources in the American Diet S. Rehkamp color graph *Amber Waves: The Economics of Food, Farming, Natural Resources, & Rural America* p23 D 2016

Newly Updated ERS Data Show 2016 Production, Trade Volume, and Per Capita Availability of Vegetables and Pulses T. Minor *Amber Waves: The Economics of Food, Farming, Natural Resources, & Rural America* p11 Ag 2017

Productivity Growth Is Still the Major Driver in Growing U.S. Agricultural Output Sun Ling Wang, E. Ball et al *Amber Waves: The Economics of Food, Farming, Natural Resources, & Rural America* p5 S 2016

Using the ERS County Economic Types To Explore Demographic and Economic Trends in Rural Areas L. Kusmin color graph *Amber Waves: The Economics of Food, Farming, Natural Resources, & Rural America* p1 D 2016

United States. Dept. of Agriculture—History—20th century

Steady Diet of Depression J. Zegelman and A. Coe *American History* v52 no1 p56 Ap 2017

United States. Dept. of Agriculture—Officials & employees

AN 8-YEAR RUN T. Vilsack *Successful Farming* v114 no13 p28 D 2016

United States. Dept. of Commerce

An Internet Whole and Free K. Raustiala color *Foreign Affairs*

v96 no2 p140 Mr/Ap 2017

United States. Dept. of Commerce—History—21st century

MAN OF THE (VERY RICH) PEOPLE [Cover story] M. Abelson and D. Carey color *Bloomberg Businessweek* no4509 p38 Ja 30 2017

United States. Dept. of Defense

Boost for manufacturing labor *Science* v355 no6320 p10 Ja 6 2017

Building the Third Offset A. FRANK *Commentary* v142 no3 p8 O 2016

The Creative, Unpredictable, and Terrifying (to Enemies) Genius That Is Mad Dog *USA Today Magazine* v145 no2860 p17 Ja 2017

THE GREATEST ASSIGNMENT C. Leaf color *Fortune* v175 no5 p6 Ap 1 2017

NEWS LETTERS M. Gaffney *Washingtonian Magazine* v52 no6 p199 Mr 2017

United States nuclear forces, 2017 H. M. Kristensen and R. S. Norris bibl *Bulletin of the Atomic Scientists* v73 no1 p48 Ja 2017

THE WARRIOR MONK D. FILKINS cartoon *New Yorker* v93 no15 p34 My 29 2017

United States. Dept. of Education

Choice for Secretary of Education M. FERGUSON color *Phi Delta Kappan* v98 no5 p74 F 2017

Civil Rights Survey Underscores Need for Continued Focus on Equity *Education Digest* v82 no6 p53 F 2017

THE COMMON CORE CONUNDRUM H. ARABADJIS *USA Today Magazine* v145 no2864 p54 My 2017

Decline in Diplomas: Students aren't seeking public service careers the way they used to M. Maciag *Governing* v30 no8 p56 My 2017

DOE Removes Requirements Around Selectivity to Diversify the Teaching Force J. MADER cartoon *Education Digest* v82 no6 p30 F 2017

Federal Budget Cuts Threaten Educational Funding K. Sims *Parks & Recreation* v52 no6 p18 Je 2017

Giving Every Student a Fair Shot J. B. KING JR. *Education Digest* v82 no7 p16 Mr 2017

Indianola Promise Community: Improving Academic Outcomes in the Delta D. Moore *Bridges (Federal Reserve Bank of St. Louis)* p1 Wint 2016/2017

Media Embrace of Ed 'Reform' Paved Way for Betsy DeVos M. Knefel *Extra!* v30 no2 p3 Mr 2017

A Note on Methodology: 4-year Colleges and Universities *Washington Monthly* p1 S/O 2016

A NOTE ON METHODOLOGY: 4-YEAR COLLEGES AND UNIVERSITIES *Washington Monthly* v49 no9/10 p120 S/O 2017

The Title IX Lives of Christian Colleges S. E. ZYLSTRA *Christianity Today* v60 no10 p24 D 2016

Why Charter School Leader Eva Moskowitz Endorses Betsy DeVos C. Feldman *Education Digest* v83 no1 p15 S 2017

United States. Dept. of Energy

THE 5TH RISK M. LEWIS color *Vanity Fair* v59 no9 p192 S 2017

Can a trusting relationship between DOE and its labs be restored? D. Kramer *Physics Today* v70 no3 p27 Mr 2017

DOE freezes millions in awards J. Mervis color *Science* v356 no6337 p471 My 5 2017

From the Laboratory to the WORLD L. L. Helms *Science & Technology Review* p12 Je 2017

HIGH-PERFORMANCE COMPUTING TAKES AIM AT CANCER A. Heller color *Science & Technology Review* p4 O/N 2016

"Home-Grown" Efforts Thrive at Livermore color *Science & Technology Review* p11 O/N 2016

Laying the Groundwork for EXTREME-SCALE COMPUTING R. Hansen *Science & Technology Review* p5 S 2016

Looking Forward to New Generations of Supercomputers color *Science & Technology Review* p8 O/N 2016

Potential for Wind Energy in All 50 States S. Stonebrook *Mother Earth News* no280 p8 F/Mr 2017

Unleashing Energy Winners K. TUBB il *American Conservative* v16 no1 p20 Ja/F 2017

United States. Dept. of Energy. National Ignition Facility

Fabricating the World's Thinnest Plastic Wrap L. Casonhua color *Science & Technology Review* p16 Ja/F 2017

Mighty ATLAS Supports Precise Alignment A. Heller *Science &*

Technology Review p16 Mr 2017

United States. Dept. of Energy—Officials & employees

EYE ON 45 color *Science* v357 no6348 p233 Jl 21 2017

Governor Goodhair Goes to Washington J. HIGHTOWER cartoon *Progressive* v81 no3 p46 Mr 2017

Obama's Energy Secretary Addresses Trump's Attacks on His Legacy J. Temple il *MIT Technology Review* v120 no5 p15 S/O 2017

United States. Dept. of Health & Human Services

A Disaster That Will Tar the GOP M. ASTRUE color *Weekly Standard* v22 no32 p12 My 1 2017

DOCTOR'S ORDERS J. Surowiecki cartoon *New Yorker* v92 no42 p50 D 19 2016

Empowering Older Adults to Age Out Loud! C. Gilchrist and L. Spencer-Brown *Parks & Recreation* v52 no5 p38 My 2017

HOW YOU'LL MODERNIZE HHS SYSTEMS *Governing* v30 no1 p20 O 2016

MODERN MEDICINE MESS E. LEE VLIET and M. SINGLE-TON *USA Today Magazine* v145 no2862 p52 Mr 2017

Price Takes a Beating F. BARNES color *Weekly Standard* v22 no21 p7 F 6 2017

A TRANSFORMATION IN PROGRESS *Governing* v30 no1 p34 O 2016

Where HIV and Housing Intersect M. Quinn *Governing* v30 no7 p18 Ap 2017

United States. Dept. of Health & Human Services. Office for Human Research Protections

What do revised U.S. rules mean for human research? L. Nichols, L. Brako et al color *Science* v357 no6352 p650 Ag 18 2017

United States. Dept. of Homeland Security

Why the U.S. Is Cracking Down on Gadgets In Airplane Cabins Z. J. Miller, K. Reilly et al color *Time* v189 no12 p11 Ap 3 2017

United States. Dept. of Housing & Urban Development

Ben Carson Is Right H. Husock *Commentary* v143 no3 p34 Mr 2017

Is Anybody Home at HUD? A. MacGillis img *New York* v50 no17 p40 Ag 21 2017

Shelter and the Storm F. Shafroth *Governing* v30 no6 p62 Mr 2017

United States. Dept. of Justice

Attorney General Sessions A. C. MCCARTHY il *National Review* v68 no23 p20 D 19 2016

Beyond Affirmative Action B. COVERT and M. KONCZAL *Nation* v305 no6 p5 S 11 2017

CIVIL LIBERTIES C. J. CIARAMELLA bw *Reason* v48 no8 p8 Ja 2017

DEPARTMENT OF JUSTIFICATION E. Bazelon *New York Times Magazine* p36 Mr 5 2017

Forensic Science Must Be Scientific S. Sah color *Scientific American* v317 no4 p12 O 2017

'Law and Order' Should Not Mean Wiping Out Civil Rights Protections *America* v216 no11 p8 My 15 2017

Private Prisons Fail S. FREED WESSLER color *Nation* v304 no3 p6 Ja 30 2017

Undocumented Immigrants May Get Less Time to Make Their Case T. Berenson map *Time* v190 no8 p12 Ag 28 2017

What's Jeff Sessions Up To? T. Schoenberg color *Bloomberg Businessweek* no4529 p34 Jl 3 2017

United States. Dept. of Justice—Officials & employees

GUEST LIST: A monthly roundup of people we'd like to have over for drinks, food, and conversation *Washingtonian Magazine* v52 no12 p22 S 2017

United States. Dept. of Labor

Alphabet Soup N. S. HUANG *Kiplinger's Personal Finance* v71 no7 p58 Jl 2017

Keeping Work Flexible, Even with Changes to U.S. Overtime Rules L. Morris *Harvard Business Review Digital Articles* p2 F 12 2016

Taking DOL's Overtime Rule to Court T. J. Donohue *Weekly Standard* v22 no6 p11 O 17 2016

Trump Vs. The Rule Of Law M. Levine color *Bloomberg Businessweek* no4510 p6 F 6 2017

United States. Dept. of Labor—Officials & employees

REVOLUTION AT LABOR A. SHLAES, P. JOHNSON et al *Forbes* v199 no1 p32 Ja 24 2017

Robert Reich's Plan To Save the Democrats J. BLEIFUSS *In These Times* v41 no1 p30 Ja 2017

United States. Dept. of State

Affairs of State J. BERGNER color *Weekly Standard* v22 no20 p12 Ja 30 2017

How I Led Change in the U.S. State Department Bureaucracy T. Cochran color *Harvard Business Review Digital Articles* p2 Ja 4 2017

The United States of Exxon A. JUHASZ *In These Times* v41 no2 p18 F 2017

WHEREVER WOMEN ARE DIMINISHED, THE ENTIRE WORLD IS DIMINISHED WITH THEM *Vital Speeches of the Day* v83 no6 p184 Je 2017

United States. Dept. of State—Management

Rex's Right-Hand Woman N. Wadhams *Bloomberg Businessweek* no4525 p25 Je 5 2017

U.S. Security Hinges on Getting Foggy Bottom Back In the Game A. J. Stavridis color *Time* v189 no11 p32 Mr 27 2017

United States. Dept. of the Interior

Legislative Background on Public Land Use: Recent Action by Congress on Federal Land Management *Congressional Digest* v96 no6 p9 Je 2017

Seizing Our Energy Potential T. J. DONOHUE *Weekly Standard* v22 no14 p29 D 12 2016

United States. Dept. of the Treasury

Hellllp! S. Mohsin and R. Schmidt color *Bloomberg Businessweek* no4526 p22 Je 12 2017

United States. Dept. of the Treasury—Officials & employees

A Hillary Fan Inside Trump's Treasury R. Schmidt color *Bloomberg Businessweek* no4517 p30 Ap 3 2017

United States. Dept. of Transportation

7 Times The Airline Likely Owes You Money J. LABIANCA color *Reader's Digest* v190 no1134 p46 O 2017

Ramen Is My Copilot M. SEGAL *Los Angeles Magazine* v62 no9 p14 S 2017

United States. Dept. of Veterans Affairs

A Transformation Is Underway at U.S. Veterans Affairs. We Got an Inside Look R. W. Buell *Harvard Business Review Digital Articles* p2 D 22 2016

United States. Drug Enforcement Administration

THE DEA'S WARRANTLESS CASH GRAB C. J. CIARAMELLA color *Reason* v49 no3 p13 Jl 2017

IS KRATOM THE NEW MARIJUANA? J. SULLUM color *Reason* v48 no8 p8 Ja 2017

United States. Education Amendments of 1972. Title IX

Overruled K. C. JOHNSON and S. J. TAYLOR color *Weekly Standard* v23 no5 p15 O 9 2017

The Title IX Lives of Christian Colleges S. E. ZYLSTRA *Christianity Today* v60 no10 p24 D 2016

United States. Elementary & Secondary Education Act of 1965

Every Student Succeeds Act: Federal Elementary and Secondary Education Policy *Congressional Digest* v96 no7 p4 S 2017

United States. Employee Retirement Income Security Act of 1974

GLEANINGS graph *Christianity Today* v61 no7 p18 S 2017

United States. Endangered Species Act of 1973

Is the Endangered Species Act in Danger? B. PALMER *Audubon* v119 no1 p19 Spr 2017

Monkey species may be listed as 'threatened' color *Science* v355 no6330 p1104 Mr 17 2017

Overcoming Challenges to the Recovery of Declining Amphibian Populations in the United States S. C. WALLS, L. C. BALL et al *BioScience* v67 no2 p156 F 2017

Quantify endangered species listings T. David Male and S. A. Temple color *Science* v356 no6345 p1342 Je 30 2017

visual statement PARISEAU color *Foreign Policy* no221 p26 N/D 2016

United States. Energy Information Administration

Q&A N. S. Malik color *Bloomberg Businessweek* no4496 p85 O 24 2016

United States. Energy Research & Development Administration

INVESTING IN THE NATION'S FUTURE: The Laboratory Directed Research and Development Program has been a significant engine of scientific discovery for 25 years A. Heller *Science & Technology Review* p4 Ap/My 2017

Program Supports BLAZING NEW TRAILS A. Chen *Science & Technology Review* p13 Ap/My 2017

United States. Environmental Protection Agency

Another Illegal Power Grab T. Eastland *Weekly Standard* v22 no5
p8 O 10 2016

Bill helps restore clean water to Flint, Michigan color *National
Wildlife (World Edition)* v55 no3 p48 Ap/My 2017

Budget proposal would slash science L. Hamers, M. Rosen et al
Science News v191 no7 p15 Ap 15 2017

DIRTY POWER PLAN D. SLATER *Sierra* v101 no5 p36 S/O
2016

The dishonest HONEST Act D. Michaels and T. Burke color *Science* v356 no6342 p989 Je 9 2017

EYE ON 45 color *Science* v356 no6344 p1215 Je 23 2017

Industry Giveaway M. F. Jacobson *Nutrition Action Health Letter*
v44 no4 p2 My 2017

New Law Lets EPA Ban Toxic Chemicals E. BETZ color *Discover*
v38 no1 p78 Ja/F 2017

Pick Yer Poison: Recirculated CO2 or "fresh" pollution? F.
Markus color *Motor Trend* v69 no11 p28 N 2017

The Pruitt Backlash A. Greenblatt *Governing* v30 no5 p9 F 2017

Pruitt Faces Fire on Climate Views J. A. Dlouhy bw *Bloomberg
Businessweek* no4508 p25 Ja 23 2017

Radioactivity in Drinking Water *Mother Earth News* no279 p8 D/
Ja 2017

Research on a razor's edge E. Dexter *Science* v356 no6342 p1094
Je 9 2017

SCOTT PRUITT'S CRIMES AGAINST NATURE J. GOODELL
color *Rolling Stone* no1293 p44 Ag 10 2017

Trump's Starvation Budget M. BURK *Ms.* v27 no2 p35 Summ
2017

Trump targets environmental science for cuts D. Malakoff and W.
Cornwall color graph *Science* v355 no6329 p1000 Mr 10 2017

Water rule on the chopping block color *Science* v355 no6328 p890
Mr 3 2017

**United States. Environmental Protection Agency—Officials &
employees**

With Climate Denial in the White House, Will Media Echo Official Know-Nothingism? R. Richardson *Extra!* v30 no4 p4 My
2017

United States. Espionage Act of 1917

WHEN THE GOVERNMENT DECLARED WAR ON THE
FIRST AMENDMENT D. Root color *Reason* v49 no5 p18 O
2017

United States. Executive Office of the President

The Obama Administration's Roadmap for AI Policy A. Agrawal,
J. Gans et al *Harvard Business Review Digital Articles* p2 D
21 2016

United States. Family & Medical Leave Act of 1993

Stop Punishing the Family Man J. Levs *Harvard Business Review
Digital Articles* p2 My 14 2015

Why Paid Leave Matters for the Future of Business S. Friedman
Harvard Business Review Digital Articles p2 S 16 2015

United States. Farm Service Agency

MICROLOANS D. Keller *Successful Farming* v114 no10 p61 O
2016

United States. Federal Aviation Administration

ACS MAKES MY HEAD ACHE M. Lunken chart graph *Flying*
v144 no4 p74 Ap 2017

THE ADS-B MANDATE: WHY YOU NEED A PLAN S. Pope
Flying v143 no12 p8 D 2016

ATLAS WINGLETS CERTIFIED color *Flying* v144 no3 p18 Mr
2017

BELONGING M. Lunken *Flying* v144 no11 p66 N 2017

BRAVE NEW WORLD S. Weigel color *Flying* v144 no11 p36
N 2017

The Debate Over Drone IDs A. Levin bw *Bloomberg Businessweek* no4534 p36 Ag 14 2017

GAMEBIRD FAA CERTIFIED bw color *Flying* v144 no11 p20
N 2017

GETTING TO YES color *Flying* v144 no6 p8 Je 2017

HANGIN' TOUGH M. Jancer color *Car & Driver* v63 no1 p24
Jl 2017

IS THE FA A PULLING A FAST ONE? M. Lunken *Flying* v144
no10 p67 O 2017

LOOKING FOR A NEW AIRPLANE D. Karl color *Flying* v144
no11 p68 N 2017

SAFETY CAUSE DU JOUR M. King color *Flying* v144 no3 p32
Mr 2017

THE SANTA MONICA PRECEDENT S. Pope color *Flying* v144
no4 p10 Ap 2017

SHAKING THINGS UP AT BRISTOL VILLAGE M. Lunken
color *Flying* v144 no6 p66 Je 2017

A TALE OF TWO FAAS P. STRICKLAND color *Flying* v144
no7 p56 Jl 2017

TAMARACK'S ACTIVE WINGLETS P. Bergqvist color diag
Flying v143 no12 p14 D 2016

Want a Drone of Your Own? M. Frank *Consumer Reports* v82
no1 p48 Ja 2017

Why There's Still an Ashtray on Your Airplane J. Hincks *Time*
v190 no14 p23 O 9 2017

You won't have to hear about the Galaxy Note7 on flights anymore M. SIMON color *PCWorld* v35 no2 p33 F 2017

United States. Federal Bureau of Investigation

THE BIG BUST T. WEINER bw color *Esquire* v167 no1 p102
F 2017

THE BOMB DETECTIVE P. FLAX color *Popular Mechanics*
p104 Ap 2017

Christopher Wray M. Calabresi color *Time* v189 no23 p15 Je 19
2017

The Curious Case of the Disappearing Laptop A. C. McCARTHY
National Review v69 no18 p16 O 2 2017

Donald Trump's Loyalty Pledge for the FBI Challenges the Nation
M. Calabresi color *Time* v189 no23 p11 Je 19 2017

A FARCE TO BE RECKONED WITH G. CARTER color *Vanity
Fair* v59 no7 p32 Summ 2017

FBI report shows surge in anti-Muslim attacks, rise in hate crimes
L. Markoe *Christian Century* v133 no26 p15 D 21 2016

FREE AGENTS: How the F.B.I. understands its relationship to the
president - and how Donald Trump misunderstands the F.B.I T.
Weiner *New York Times Magazine* p26 Jl 2 2017

How the Apple/FBI Fight Risks the Whole U.S. Tech Industry
J. Allworth *Harvard Business Review Digital Articles* p2 F 24
2016

It's Mueller Time [Cover story] M. WARREN and J. LIFHITS
color *Weekly Standard* v22 no36 p18 My 29 2017

THE KILLER NEXT DOOR J. BOND color *Reader's Digest*
v189 no1130 p122 My 2017

Secrets the FBI May Not Want You to Know B. DREHER *Reader's Digest* v188 no1125 p144 N 2016

THE STING OF THE TRUTH J. WOLCOTT color *Vanity Fair*
v59 no7 p62 Summ 2017

Summer 2017: America Is on the Road Again *USA Today Magazine* v146 no2867 p8 Ag 2017

What James Comey Did D. Cole color *New York Review of Books*
v63 no19 p4 D 8 2016

Why James Comey Couldn't Keep the FBI Above Politics S. Frizell and M. Calabresi color *Time* v188 no20 p7 N 14 2016

Yes, She Is Guilty color *National Review* v68 no21 p13 N 21 2016

**United States. Federal Bureau of Investigation—Officials &
employees**

On Patrol with America's Top Bioterror Cop A. Regalado color
diag *MIT Technology Review* v120 no1 p15 Ja/F 2017

United States. Federal Communications Commission

GOP Rolls Back Online Privacy Rules A. Altman *Time* v189 no13
p8 Ap 10 2017

How Not to Regulate The Internet bw *Bloomberg Businessweek*
no4498 p16 N 7 2016

Internet Privacy *Congressional Digest* v96 no4 p31 Ap 2017

Internet Regulation Is About the Common Good, Not Just Competition *America* v216 no8 p8 Ap 17 2017

United States. Federal Emergency Management Agency

STORMY WATERS: The fight over New York City's flood lines
R. Elliott and E. Rush map *Harper's Magazine* v335 no2005
p46 Je 2017

United States. Federal Energy Regulatory Commission

Consider climate, courts say *Science* v357 no6354 p850 S 1 2017

Hidden Hand: Neil Chatterjee C. Traywick bw *Bloomberg Businessweek* no4541 p39 O 9 2017

United States. Federal Motor Carrier Safety Administration

AXLES TO GRIND C. Atiyeh and J. Gall color graph *Car &
Driver* v62 no6 p28 D 2016

United States. Federal Railroad Administration

Fine locomotives inspired fine models K. Wills color *Model Railroader* v84 no2 p30 F 2017

United States. Federal Trade Commission

Detoxing Foot Pads [Cover story] color *Prevention* v69 no2 p13 F 2017

FTC Will Regulate Marketing of Homeopathic Drugs R. A. Lindsay *Skeptical Inquirer* v41 no2 p6 Mr/Ap 2017

U.S. charges journal publisher with misleading authors J. Bohannon *Science* v354 no6308 p23 O 7 2016

United States. Food & Drug Administration

AMERICAN HIGH J. FIELDEN color *Esquire* p16 N 2017

Are These Remedies Safe? [Cover story] J. COOK color *Prevention* v69 no6 p74 Je 2017

Available Drugs, Affordable Drugs P. HOWARD color *National Review* v69 no6 p34 Ap 3 2017

Bad Diagnosis S. Nash color *Progressive* v81 no3 p34 Mr 2017

Before You Take It S. KLEIN color *Prevention* p22 Mr 2017

Before You Take It S. KLEIN color *Prevention* v69 no2 p22 F 2017

Cells that kill cancer [Cover story] C. Harvey and C. Maldarelli color *Popular Science* v289 no6 p12 N/D 2017

FDA Nutrition Guidelines *Congressional Digest* v95 no10 p12 D 2016

A Fight Worth Having S. F. Hayes color *Weekly Standard* v22 no28 p6 Mr 27 2017

GETTING TO YES! YES! YES! G. Graves cartoon *O, The Oprah Magazine* p128 D 2016

Hard to Swallow [Cover story] B. Howard color *Prevention* v69 no9 p42 O 2017

In a major shift, cancer drugs go 'tissue-agnostic' K. Garber chart color *Science* v356 no6343 p1111 Je 16 2017

Influence, integrity, and the FDA: An ethical framework S. Phillips Hey, I. Glenn Cohen et al color *Science* v357 no6354 p876 S 1 2017

Is a Cigarette Without the Nicotine Still A Smoke? A. Edney and J. Kaplan cartoon graph *Bloomberg Businessweek* no4533 p37 Ag 7 2017

Needed: A Spine Transplant for the FDA: The new chief of the Food and Drug Administration must move fast, avoid politics, and confront overregulation H. I. Miller *Hoover Digest: Research & Opinion on Public Policy* no3 p45 Summ 2017

THE NEW RULES OF FEED ANTIBIOTICS G. Johnston *Successful Farming* v115 no1 p60 Ja 2017

Next Up for FDA Approval: Fewer FDA Rules S. Mukherjee color *Fortune* v175 no5 p14 Ap 1 2017

Not Racing for the Cure M. ASTRUE *Weekly Standard* v23 no3 p18 S 25 2017

Shortcut for stem cell therapies color *Science* v354 no6318 p1356 D 16 2016

Should Drugs Do Double Duty? T. Carr il *Consumer Reports* v82 no2 p12 F 2017

Texas signals support for unproven stem cell therapies K. Servick *Science* v356 no6344 p1219 Je 23 2017

Vaccine Safety *Congressional Digest* v96 no5 p30 My 2017

When Medical Tests Mislead C. Schmidt color *Scientific American* v315 no6 p28 D 2016

YOUR SUPPLEMENT QUESTIONS, ANSWERED! T. Low Dog color *Amazing Wellness* p50 Fall 2017

United States. Foreign Intelligence Surveillance Act of 1978 Amendments Act of 2008 or the FISA Amendments Act of 2008

The 702 Problem J. LIFHITS color *Weekly Standard* v23 no4 p14 O 2 2017

United States. Forest Service

Greetings from MIDEWIN NATIONAL TALLGRASS PRAIRIE D. Newman color *Practical Horseman* v44 no12 p62 D 2016

It Starts With a Fever A. WISNIEWSKI *American Forests* v123 no3 p46 Fall 2017

Trial by Fire M. BLACKBIRD color *Idaho Magazine* v16 no1 p14 O 2016

United States. Freedom of Information Act

THE NAGGING WHEELS OF JUSTICE *New York* v50 no12 p43 Je 12 2017

United States. Immigration & Nationality Act

DO YOU LIVE IN A BORDER ZONE? C. J. CIARAMELLA color map *Reason* v49 no1 p36 My 2017

United States. Internal Revenue Service

CAN STEVE MNUCHIN MAKE THE IRS GREAT AGAIN? J.

Wieczner color *Fortune* v175 no5 p13 Ap 1 2017

FROM 9/11 to 11/9 G. CARTER *Vanity Fair* v59 no1 p42 Holiday 2017

United States. Marine Corps

THE BATTLE OF NEW YORK C. Buzzell color *Popular Mechanics* p80 My 2017

How the U.S. Marines Encourage Service-Based Leadership A. Morgan and C. Lynch color *Harvard Business Review Digital Articles* p2 F 2 2017

LOVE IN A WAR ZONE C. COLIN bw color *Men's Health* v32 no6 p124 Ag 2017

"NCIS: NEW ORLEANS" A. JOHNSON JR. color *New Orleans Magazine* v51 no1 p40 N 2016

SCREEN SHOT E. ACKERMAN color *Esquire* p76 Ag 2017

United States. Marine Corps—Training of

THE MAKING—AND BREAKING—OF MARINES: THE DEATH OF A MUSLIM RECRUIT LAST YEAR HAS DRAWN SCRUTINY TO THE U.S. MARINES' TRAINING BASE AT PARRIS ISLAND, WHERE BRUTAL HAZING HAS FLOURISHED. IS THIS REALLY THE ONLY WAY TO CREATE A WARRIOR? J. Reitman *New York Times Magazine* p32 Jl 9 2017

United States. National Aeronautics & Space Administration

ASTEROID MISSION S. MURPHY and LAURETTA *Scientific American* v315 no6 p8 D 2016

Astrophysics missions vie for NASA money D. Clery color *Science* v357 no6352 p634 Ag 18 2017

Cassini's Closing Act E. MASTROIANNI color *Discover* v38 no7 p14 S 2017

COLORING SPACE N. Strochlic color *National Geographic* v232 no1 p152 Jl 2017

The Crisis in Astronomy: One NASA flagship mission at a time hurts astrophysics and planetary science. Here's a solution M. Elvis *Sky & Telescope* v134 no3 p84 S 2017

Earth science a 'no-brainer' for NASA's science chief P. Voosen color *Science* v355 no6330 p1112 Mr 17 2017

Eyes In the Sky J. Kluger color *Time* v190 no1 p42 Jl 3 2017

FANTASTIC VOYAGE T. Ferris color diag *National Geographic* v232 no2 p22 Ag 2017

A fiery finish to Cassini's long run at Saturn P. Voosen color *Science* v357 no6357 p1219 S 22 2017

Fire in the Sky C. Klosterman color *AARP: The Magazine* v59 no1A p26 D 2015/Ja 2016

Future of space J. JOHNSON-FREESE and C. BOARDMAN color *Issues in Science & Technology* v33 no1 p15 Fall 2016

THE GRID: HERE COMES THE SUN A. Hollandbeck *Saturday Evening Post* v289 no4 p26 Jl/Ag 2017

HOW IT WORKS NASA's Venus Machine J. PAPPALARDO color *Popular Mechanics* p72 F 2017

How Juno Met Jupiter B. ANDREWS color *Discover* v38 no1 p73 Ja/F 2017

How NASA Uses Telemedicine to Care for Astronauts in Space A. S. Menon, S. Moynihan et al *Harvard Business Review Digital Articles* p2 Jl 6 2017

How to... DESTROY ANYTHING cartoon color *Popular Mechanics* v193 no7 p83 S 2016

Inside the Historic Mission to Europa E. BETZ bw color *Discover* v38 no2 p58 Mr 2017

LAUNCHED INTO MEMORY A. Crawford *Smithsonian* v48 no3 p14 Je 2017

Let NASA Take Flight color *Scientific American* v316 no1 p7 Ja 2017

Man vs. Machine: Space Medicine color *Bloomberg Businessweek* no4534 p23 Ag 14 2017

Mars scientists close in on sites for 2020 landing color *Science* v355 no6326 p670 F 17 2017

Meet the Next-Generation Space Telescope K. HAYNES color diag *Discover* v38 no6 p84 Jl/Ag 2017

MISSION INTO THE HEAT OF THE SUN R. Hartigan Shea color *National Geographic* v232 no2 p29 Ag 2017

NASA Fights Flight Delays J. Hsu color *Scientific American* v316 no4 p26 Ap 2017

NASA Hopes to Make History With Its Latest Mission—to the Sun J. Kluger color *Time* v189 no22 p7 Je 12 2017

NASA pushes for diversity in planetary science P. Voosen diag *Science* v356 no6337 p475 My 5 2017

no4493 p16 O 3 2016

Downs K. Stock color *Bloomberg Businessweek* no4494 p15 O 10 2016

NSA DOCUMENT EXTRACT 111016: 00:45GMT R. LONG *National Review* v68 no22 p50 D 5 2016

The NSA's foreign surveillance: 5 things to know G. GROSS color *PCWorld* v35 no4 p37 Ap 2017

NSA SURVEILLANCE INTERCEPT R. LONG *National Review* v69 no8 p34 My 2017

SNOWDEN'S BOX J. Bruder and D. Maharidge *Harper's Magazine* v334 no2004 p25 My 2017

The Surveillance We Need cartoon *Weekly Standard* v23 no4 p6 O 2 2017

The Swedish Kings of Cyberwar H. Eakin color map *New York Review of Books* v64 no1 p56 Ja 19 2017

United States. National Transportation Safety Board

AVIATE, NAVIGATE, COMMUNICATE - THEN RECORD! J. Zimmerman color *Flying* v144 no2 p30 F 2017

HUMAN, ALL TOO HUMAN P. Garrison *Flying* v144 no6 p34 Je 2017

HURRY HOME P. Garrison *Flying* v143 no12 p30 D 2016

A SHORT HOP P. Garrison *Flying* v144 no5 p34 My 2017

WHAT HAPPENS AFTER A CRASH? G. Silveira color *Flying* v144 no5 p60 My 2017

United States. National Weather Service

Hurricane Harvey provides lab for U.S. forecast experiments P. Voosen and J. Rosen *Science* v357 no6354 p854 S 1 2017

A Moment of Darkness J. RAO color *Natural History* v125 no7 p43 Jl/Ag 2017

United States. Natural Resources Conservation Service

The Earth Below S. BUTCHER *Texas Monthly* v45 no1 p64 Ja 2017

An Economic Perspective on Soil Health M. Bowman, S. Wallander et al *Amber Waves: The Economics of Food, Farming, Natural Resources, & Rural America* p18 S 2016

Forest Frontiers *American Forests* v123 no1 p4 Wint/Spr 2017

United States. Navy

becoming a navy master diver J. EMERSON and M. Koziol cartoon *Popular Science* v289 no2 p80 Mr/Ap 2017

MANAGING CLIMATE CHANGE: LESSONS FROM THE U.S. NAVY F. L. REINHARDT and M. W. TOFFEL chart color il img *Harvard Business Review* v95 no4 p102 Jl/Ag 2017

NAVY MARKS 75TH ANNIVERSARY OF PIVOTAL BATTLE OF MIDWAY B. Manley bw *Military History* v34 no4 p10 N 2017

PILOTS OF THE CARIBBEAN R. MARK color *Flying* v144 no11 p58 N 2017

The Response: A CREWLESS TRACKING SHIP color *Popular Mechanics* p76 Mr 2017

Scientists and the Navy Join Forces: NATO SEEKS ADVICE TO AVOID COLLATERAL ENVIRONMENTAL DAMAGE L. Lippsett *Oceanus* v52 no2 p6 Spr 2017

Valor He Built, He Fought J. W. Brown bw color *Military History* v34 no2 p16 Jl 2017

United States. Navy. SEALs

A New Mission S. HOLLAND MURPHY *D: The Magazine of Dallas* v43 no10 p54 O 2016

United States. Navy—Congresses

In Praise of the Aircraft Carrier G. Norman color *Weekly Standard* v22 no37 p20 Je 5 2017

United States. No Child Left Behind Act of 2001

School Choice 2017-2018 Policy Debate Topic *Congressional Digest* v96 no7 p2 S 2017

United States. Office of Science & Technology Policy

Trump's science shop is small and waiting for leadership J. Mervis color *Science* v357 no6347 p117 Jl 14 2017

United States. Office of Strategic Services

HIGHLY INEFFECTIVE PEOPLE *Harper's Magazine* v334 no2002 p19 Mr 2017

OSS VETERANS RECEIVE CONGRESSIONAL GOLD MEDAL B. Manley bw *Military History* v34 no1 p10 My 2017

TROUBLED WATERS P. X. Rutz bw color map *Military History* v34 no1 p40 My 2017

United States. Patent & Trademark Office

PATENTLY ABSURD? B. Preston bw *Car & Driver* v62 no6 p26 D 2016

United States. Patient Protection & Affordable Care Act

3 Health Care Trends That Don't Hinge on the ACA F. Baitman and K. Karpay *Harvard Business Review Digital Articles* p2 My 25 2017

AS IF ANY FURTHER *Texas Monthly* v45 no4 p8 Ap 2017

Ask a Doctor: A feminist-founded group of Ohio doctors is vocal in its support of health care and abortion rights C. HAHN *Ms.* v27 no3 p12 Fall 2017

Bearing Burdens After Obamacare K. SHELLNUTT *Christianity Today* v61 no4 p18 My 2017

The Best Cure for Obamacare Woes L. Zamosky color *Money* v45 no10 p36 N 2016

Beware Delay M. Hemingway *Weekly Standard* v22 no15 p10 D 19 2016

Beyond Repeal and Replace P. Elliott, A. Park et al color diag map *Time* v190 no2/3 p30 Jl 10-17 2017

A Biologic Problem cartoon *Weekly Standard* v22 no38 p3 Je 12 2017

The Blight of ObamaCare Will Not Vanish J. M. ORIENT *USA Today Magazine* v146 no2868 p16 S 2017

Bringing the Senate to Heel J. COST color *Weekly Standard* v23 no1 p15 S 11 2017

CALENDAR: 11/2017 R. STINSON color *Kiplinger's Personal Finance* v71 no11 p14 N 2017

Catholic hospitals' C.E.O. ready to fix health care after G.O.P. 'skinny repeal' fails K. Clarke color *America* v217 no4 p17 Ag 21 2017

Church leaders urge Senate fix on G.O.P. Obamacare repeal K. Clarke color *America* v216 no12 p17 My 29 2017

Cleaning Up Obama's HealthCare Mess *Commentary* v141 no9 p1 N 2016

Cleaning Up Obama's HealthCare Mess *Commentary* v142 no4 p1 N 2016

CLEANING UP OBAMA'S HEALTH-CARE MESS T. TROY *Commentary* v142 no4 p25 N 2016

Consumers Deserve to Know Who's Funding Health Research P. D. Thacker *Harvard Business Review Digital Articles* p2 D 2 2014

The Cost of Repealing Obamacare J. WEST color *Progressive* v81 no4 p10 Ap/My 2017

Critical but Not Serious W. Kristol *Weekly Standard* v22 no26 p8 Mr 13 2017

Delayed but Not Dead *Nation* v305 no2 p3 Jl 17 2017

DELISLE, MISSISSIPPI J. Ward *Harper's Magazine* p32 O 2017

DEMOCRATS DEFECT FROM OBAMACARE P. SUDERMAN bw cartoon color graph *Reason* v48 no9 p26 F 2017

Democrats Look for an Upside In Obamacare's Repeal H. S. Edwards and S. Frizell color diag *Time* v189 no3 p5 Ja 16 2017

A Disappointing Start *National Review* v69 no6 p9 Ap 3 2017

A Disaster That Will Tar the GOP M. ASTRUE color *Weekly Standard* v22 no32 p12 My 1 2017

End the Assault on Women's Health color *Scientific American* v317 no3 p9 S 2017

'Everybody Says How Cool I Am' A. Ferguson color *Commentary* v143 no2 p1 F 2017

Everybody's Fault J. COST color *Weekly Standard* v22 no30 p10 Ap 10 2017

Failure, Bigly diag *Commonweal* v144 no7 p5 Ap 14 2017

FARMING WITHOUT A NET: HEALTH INSURANCE CAN SAVE THE FARM, BUT BETWEEN THE COMPLICATED PROCESS AND THE EXPENSE, SOME FARMERS ARE GOING WITHOUT L. F. Prater *Successful Farming* v115 no11 p58 S 2017

Fixing Obamacare *Congressional Digest* v96 no8 p30 O 2017

For the Record color *Time* v189 no13 p6 Ap 10 2017

GOP HEALTHCARE FAILURE: RESISTANCE IS STILL NOT FUTILE G. CHRISTINA *Humanist* v77 no3 p36 My/Je 2017

'Have You Read the Bill?' *Weekly Standard* v22 no41 p6 Jl 3 2017

Health care after Obama *Christian Century* v134 no9 p7 Ap 26 2017

Health Care Needs the Individual Mandate cartoon *Bloomberg Businessweek* no4515 p10 Mr 20 2017

THE HEALTH CARE SCHMOZZLE C. R. Kesler *Claremont Review of Books* v17 no3 p5 Summ 2017

Here's How to Save Obamacare K. DRUM *Mother Jones* v42 no1 p19 Ja/F 2017

United States. Patient Protection & Affordable Care Act—Economic aspects

United States. President's Emergency Plan for AIDS Relief

United States. Public Health Service. Office of the Surgeon General

United States. Reserve Officers' Training Corps

The ROTC Freakout *Weekly Standard* v22 no6 p2 O 17 2016

United States. Securities & Exchange Commission—Officials & employees

SEC's Acting Chair Acts Like He Runs the Place R. Schmidt and B. Bain bw *Bloomberg Businessweek* no4512 p29 F 20 2017

United States. Social Security Administration

Happy Birthday to Me! L. Myers color *Missouri Life* v44 no6 p64 S 2017

United States. Supreme Court

A Cake Dispute Rises To the Highest Court G. Stohr color *Bloomberg Businessweek* no4539 p43 S 25 2017

Christians Started the Wedding Wars S. SLADE cartoon *Reason* v48 no11 p56 Ap 2017

Code of Silence R. Wexler color *Washington Monthly* v49 no6-8 p18 Je-Ag 2017

The Court Moves Right D. COLE *Nation* v305 no2 p4 Jl 17 2017

The Democrats v. Gorsuch color *National Review* v69 no7 p13 Ap 17 2017

INSIDER-TRADING LAW: A SUPREME COURT RULING GIVES PROSECUTORS A BOOST J. J. Roberts *Fortune* v75 no1 p94 Ja 1 2017

Movers cartoon color *Bloomberg Businessweek* no4503 p11 D 12 2016

Myriad take two: Can genomic databases remain secret? C. J. Guerrini, A. L. McGuire et al color *Science* v356 no6338 p586 My 12 2017

Supreme Court allows parts of travel ban to proceed before hearing case P. Grier and H. Gass *Christian Century* v134 no16 p13 Ag 2 2017

The Supreme Court, the Senate and the Filibuster P. H. Douglas *America* v216 no10 p40 My 1 2017

Under the Law J. Underwood *Phi Delta Kappan* v99 no1 p44 S 2017

The U.S. Supreme Court Is Reining in Patent Trolls, Which Is a Win for Innovation L. Downes color *Harvard Business Review Digital Articles* p1 Je 2 2017

A Voting-Rights Victory A. BERMAN *Nation* v304 no17 p4 Je 5 2017

WHAT CAN WE EXPECT FROM THE SUPREME COURT'S NEW TERM? E. K. BOEGEL color *America* v215 no12 p13 O 24 2016

What Young vs. UPS Means for Pregnant Workers and Their Bosses L. Morris, C. T. Calvert et al *Harvard Business Review Digital Articles* p2 Mr 26 2015

United States. Transportation Security Administration

The Best Way to Beat the Lines M. Leonhardt and M. C. White diag *Money* v46 no3 p26 Ap 2017

United States. Voting Rights Act of 1965

COLORBLIND JUSTICE S. MENCIMER color *Mother Jones* v41 no6 p45 N/D 2016

United States. Warren Commission

Dallas Revisited G. L. AGUILAR and C. WECHT *American Scholar* v86 no1 p4 Wint 2017

JFK CONSPIRACY COVERUP? *Saturday Evening Post* v289 no1 p100 Ja/F 2017

United States. White House Office

The Day America Went Global G. NORMAN bw *Weekly Standard* v22 no15 p19 D 19 2016

Editor's note A. ASTLEY color *Architectural Digest* v73 no12 p32 D 2016

Executive Order [Cover story] M. RUS color *Architectural Digest* v73 no12 p78 D 2016

THE NEW WHITE HOUSE REPORTERS A. Beaujon *Washingtonian Magazine* v52 no4 p49 Ja 2017

A Very Goldman White House W. D. COHAN color *Vanity Fair* v59 no8 p90 Ag 2017

What You Said About ... color *Time* v189 no23 p6 Je 19 2017

United States—Armed Forces—Appropriations & expenditures

How to Sustain Our Military G. Roughead *Hoover Digest: Research & Opinion on Public Policy* no4 p90 Fall 2016

Ready or Not? Not T. Donnelly *Hoover Digest: Research & Opinion on Public Policy* no4 p83 Fall 2016

Which Side Is Gen. Mattis On? J. McCORMACK color *Weekly Standard* v22 no27 p15 Mr 20 2017

United States—Armed Forces—History

PATRIOT GAMES A. Lawrence color *Sports Illustrated* v126 no3

p52 Ja 23 2017

United States—Civilization—French influences

Vive la Différence C. Kolb color *New Orleans Magazine* v51 no7 p40 My 2017

United States—Climate

Forecast Center T. Vasquez *Weatherwise* v70 no1 p66 Ja/F 2017

United States—Commerce

If Trump Abandons the TPP, China Will Be the Biggest Winner P. Ghemawat *Harvard Business Review Digital Articles* p2 D 12 2016

United States—Commercial treaties

America's Uneasy History with Free Trade I. M. Destler *Harvard Business Review Digital Articles* p2 Ap 28 2016

The Looming Trump Trade Disaster cartoon *Bloomberg Businessweek* no4508 p8 Ja 23 2017

MEET THE FREE TRADERS WHO DON'T LIKE GLOBAL TRADE AGREEMENTS M. WELCH cartoon *Reason* v48 no10 p12 Mr 2017

United States—Defenses

Unfinished Business [Cover story] T. Joscelyn color map *Weekly Standard* v22 no37 p22 Je 5 2017

United States—Description & travel

Celebrate Earth Day R. EVERSOLE color *Trail Rider* v29 no3 p16 Ap 2017

Eagle's View Of a Nation R. BROOKHISER il *National Review* v68 no23 p43 D 19 2016

MOST OF THE COAST [Cover story] C. Coen color *New Orleans Magazine* v51 no5 p60 Mr 2017

NONSTOP TRAVEL A. RODERIQUE-JONES color *Louisiana Life* v37 no4 p100 Mr/Ap 2017

VOYAGES S. ANDERSON, J. L. KEILES et al *New York Times Magazine* p37 Mr 26 2017

YOUR ONE WILD AND PRECIOUS SUMMER C. DOKA and M. SIMMS color *O, The Oprah Magazine* p86 Je 2017

United States—Economic aspects

AN OPEN LETTER TO OUR NEXT PRESIDENT A. McKEAN cartoon color *Outdoor Life* v224 no1 p56 D 2016/Ja 2017

Tax Reform First F. Barnes color *Weekly Standard* v22 no23 p9 F 20 2017

United States—Economic conditions

Our Miserable 21st Century *Commentary* v143 no3 p15 Mr 2017

To Form a Mo re Corporate Union C. LEHMANN *In These Times* v41 no4 p53 Ap 2017

Turning Walls Into Bridges M. BRUNE *Sierra* v102 no1 p6 Ja/F 2017

The U.S. Economy Is Doing Only Half Its Job J. W. Rivkin *Harvard Business Review Digital Articles* p2 D 17 2015

What It Will Take to Rebuild America [Cover story] D. Von Drehle, B. Goldberger et al color *Time* v189 no13 p22 Ap 10 2017

Will the Liberal Order Survive? J. S. Nye Jr. color *Foreign Affairs* v96 no1 p10 Ja/F 2017

THE YEAR IN REVIEW AND THE YEARS AHEAD *Economic Indicators* p51 S 2016

United States—Economic conditions—21st century

AMERICA WITHOUT MIGRANTS D. W. GIBSON color il *Nation* v303 no16 p20 O 17 2016

For the Record color *Time* v188 no18 p8 O 31 2016

GRANDPA, WHAT'S A RATE HIKE? J. KIRBY color *Maclean's* v129 no51/52 p48 D 26 2016

It's the Jobs, Stupid M. Muro il *MIT Technology Review* v120 no1 p10 Ja/F 2017

The Missing Political Debate Over the Digital Economy B. Chakravorti *Harvard Business Review Digital Articles* p2 O 6 2016

Only a Clean Sweep Will Do J. H. Cochrane *Hoover Digest: Research & Opinion on Public Policy* no4 p9 Fall 2016

PITY PARTY diag *Fortune* v75 no1 p15 Ja 1 2017

The Road Back from France? K. A. HASSETT graph *National Review* v69 no4 p8 Mr 6 2017

United States—Economic policy

40 More Years... J. STITES color *In These Times* v40 no11 p50 N 2016

The Courage Deficit S. F. Hayes color *Weekly Standard* v22 no26 p7 Mr 13 2017

United States—Economic policy—21st century

Fact Finders J. Chait *New Republic* v248 no5 p4 My 2017

2016

Donald Trump's Long Tail J. Kurlantzick color *Bloomberg Businessweek* no4495 p6 O 17 2016

A Free Hand on Immigration J. Eidelson and K. Weise graph *Bloomberg Businessweek* no4499 p32 N 14 2016

How Much Is Trump Really Disrupting Politics-as-Usual? J. Gans *Harvard Business Review Digital Articles* p2 Mr 1 2016

How Wikipedia Keeps Political Discourse from Turning Ugly S. Greenstein and Feng Zhu *Harvard Business Review Digital Articles* p2 N 7 2016

Left Out B. Raushenbush *Harper's Magazine* v334 no2000 p2 Ja 2017

OBAMA, RACE, AND AMERICA'S FUTURE J. Goldberg color *Atlantic* v319 no1 p8 Ja/F 2017

OBAMA'S FEEBLE APOLOGIA FOR THE ECONOMY S. FORBES *Forbes* v198 no6 p23 N 8 2016

Politics/Policy P. Coy and E. Wasson color *Bloomberg Businessweek* no4505 p27 D 26 2016

snapshot P. KARMAN *In These Times* v41 no1 p7 Ja 2017

STATES VS. TRUMP J. Cobb cartoon *New Yorker* v92 no39 p31 N 28 2016

The swamp creatures A. ABEL color *Maclean's* v129 no48/49 p24 D 5 2016

Trump Is About to Test Our Theory of When Leaders Actually Matter G. Mukunda *Harvard Business Review Digital Articles* p2 N 9 2016

U.S. Where Washington Fails to Drive Progress, Cities Will Act M. Bloomberg color *Time* v188 no27-28 p28 D 26 2016

The Way Forward J. LILEKS *National Review* v68 no21 p37 N 21 2016

The Week color il *National Review* v68 no21 p4 N 21 2016

United States—Politics & government—2009-2017

IS IT 1968? [Cover story] D. FRUM *Commentary* v142 no2 p15 S 2016

Maintaining Perspective on the Economic Issues of Today D. Lindauer *Society* v54 no1 p2 F 2017

Westminster, D.C.? No, the United States does not need a prime minister D. Brady *Commentary* v142 no2 p51 S 2016

Whose Violence Is It? The left excused violent protest away when it was ideologically useful to do so. And then came Trump N. C. Rothman *Commentary* v142 no2 p20 S 2016

United States—Politics & government—2009-2017—News briefs

The Week color il *National Review* v69 no7 p6 Ap 17 2017

United States—Politics & government—2009—Economic aspects

THE 2017 WASHINGTON WISH LIST K. Clark, M. Leonhardt et al color diag *Money* v46 no1 p96 Ja/F 2017

United States—Politics & government—2009—Social aspects

Making Up Is Hard to Do C. FRIEDERSDORF color *Atlantic* v318 no4 p19 N 2016

United States—Politics & government—2017-

100 Days of Resistance J. NICHOLS color *Nation* v304 no15 p3 My 8 2017

42 Months to Go... K. Pollitt *Nation* v305 no4 p6 Ag 14 2017

ACROSS THE GREAT DIVIDE: On the Road in Trump's America N. Phillips color *Progressive* v81 no7 p18 O/N 2017

After Comey, Keeping a Sense of Balance *America* v216 no12 p8 My 29 2017

After Trump W. Kristol color *Weekly Standard* v22 no34 p6 My 15 2017

Alternative facts and the coming constitutional crisis M. Malone *America* v216 no3 p3 F 6 2017

Audubon, Now More Than Ever D. YARNOLD *Audubon* v119 no1 p8 Spr 2017

Can He Be Tamed? Z. J. Miller and M. ScHerer color *Time* v189 no24 p36 Je 26 2017

Chaos Theory [Cover story] P. Elliott, S. Frizell et al color *Time* v189 no7/8 p32 F 27 2017

THE CLIMATE TEST B. McKibben *Rolling Stone* no1291/1292 p43 Jl 13 2017

CONTAINING TRUMP J. RAUCH cartoon color *Atlantic* v319 no2 p60 Mr 2017

THE CONTENDER J. Van Meter color *Vogue* v207 no11 p198 N 2017

The Damage Done K. Wright color *Nation* v305 no4 p10 Ag 14

2017

THE DIVIDER D. Remnick cartoon *New Yorker* v93 no25 p27 Ag 28 2017

EGO INFLATION bw cartoon graph *Mother Jones* v42 no2 p5 Mr/Ap 2017

THE ENABLERS S. ELLISON color *Vanity Fair* v59 no8 p78 Ag 2017

EYE ON 45 color *Science* v355 no6324 p437 F 3 2017

Game On!!! R. J. BRESLER *USA Today Magazine* v145 no2862 p10 Mr 2017

Get Out And Vote *Los Angeles Magazine* p18 Mr 2017

The Great Carter Mystery A. Schlesinger Jr. *New Republic* v248 no6 p4 Je 2017

The Great Democratic Divide M. TOMASKY il *New Republic* v248 no6 p14 Je 2017

THE GREAT UNRAVELING J. W. EMORD *USA Today Magazine* v145 no2862 p16 Mr 2017

The Hatreds They Share E. Alterman *Nation* v305 no6 p10 S 11 2017

How It Begins ... J. MEACHAM *New York Times Book Review* p14 Ja 22 2017

How to Revive Democracy J. NICHOLS *Nation* v305 no3 p3 Jl 31 2017

How to Use A Majority L. THOMPSON color il *National Review* v69 no8 p26 My 2017

How to Win the Culture War L. Lalami il *Nation* v305 no5 p10 Ag 28 2017

How Trump's Fifth Avenue Shooting Plays Out W. DURST cartoon *Progressive* v81 no7 p66 O/N 2017

A Hundred Days *National Review* v69 no9 p12 My 15 2017

If Democrats Want to Challenge Trump, They Need a New Strategy G. Mukunda *Harvard Business Review Digital Articles* p2 F 23 2017

IN SEARCH OF AMERICA L. Collins cartoon *New Yorker* v93 no32 p22 O 16 2017

Low-Key Villainy K. Wright color il *Nation* v304 no15 p10 My 8 2017

Maintaining Perspective on the Economic Issues of Today D. Lindauer *Society* v54 no1 p2 F 2017

MILLENNIALS NEED THIS (GOP) BREAK A. SHLAES *Forbes* v199 no2 p40 F 28 2017

THE MODERN WORLD T. TOMORROW *Nation* v304 no11 p8 Ap 3 2017

Mr. Worldwide color il *Nation* v304 no7 p11 Mr 6 2017

The New Blue S. JONES *New Republic* v248 no10 p27 O 2017

NO COMMENT cartoon *Progressive* v81 no7 p8 O/N 2017

NO COMMENT color *Progressive* v81 no6 p8 Ag/S 2017

No Refuge from Trump M. Lough color *Commonweal* v144 no11 p9 Je 16 2017

NSA SURVEILLANCE INTERCEPT R. LONG *National Review* v69 no8 p34 My 2017

On Infighting and Real Fighting D. FOSTER *National Review* v69 no15 p48 Ag 14 2017

On Your Honor J. GELERNTER *Weekly Standard* v22 no22 p38 F 13 2017

Over the Wall R. CONNIFF *Progressive* v81 no7 p5 O/N 2017

THE POLITICS OF ANGER S. Coll cartoon *New Yorker* v93 no18 p17 Je 26 2017

PRESENT AT THE DESTRUCTION? G. Rose color *Foreign Affairs* v96 no3 pviii My/Je 2017

President-Elect Trump: Is the Past Prologue? T. Gallagher *Society* v54 no1 p10 F 2017

REACTIONARIES MUST BE TAKEN SERIOUSLY: A tricky exercise in our political climate—but a necessary one A. SULLIVAN img *New York* v50 no9 p28 My 1 2017

The Real Cost of 'Forced Transparency' I. Bremmer *Time* v189 no11 p14 Mr 27 2017

Red State, Blue City D. A. GRAHAM cartoon *Atlantic* v319 no2 p24 Mr 2017

The Right Way to Reform Health Care S. Hathi and B. Kocher color *Foreign Affairs* v96 no4 p17 Jl/Ag 2017

'She Said What?' J. LILEKS *National Review* v69 no8 p33 My 2017

Should Democratic Socialists Be Democrats? *In These Times* v41 no5 p12 My 2017

Slow Confirmations Are Thwarting Progress T. J. DONOHUE

Weekly Standard v23 no6 p9 O 16 2017

Splitting the Political Peak J. HOUSMAN cartoon *Surfer* v58 no1 p42 Ap 2017

Taunting a Tyrant color *Commonweal* v144 no17 p5 O 20 2017

This Land Is Their Land D. DEVOSS color *Weekly Standard* v22 no22 p20 F 13 2017

THIS MODERN WORLD T. TOMORROW il *Nation* v305 no8 p8 O 9 2017

TOWARDS A POST-LIES FUTURE: FIGHTING "ALTERNATIVE FACTS" AND "POST-TRUTH" POLITICS G. TSIPURSKY *Humanist* v77 no2 p12 Mr/Ap 2017

Trumping Trumpism B. LUEDERS *Progressive* v81 no7 p6 O/N 2017

Trump on the Menu A. FERGUSON *Commentary* v143 no4 p9 Ap 2017

Trump's Triumph Should Show the Way L. P. ARN *USA Today Magazine* v145 no2862 p12 Mr 2017

THE WAR IN THE WHITE HOUSE M. Taibbi color *Rolling Stone* no1287 p24 My 18 2017

Washington Hasn't Changed C. Deaton cartoon *Weekly Standard* v22 no30 p6 Ap 10 2017

What Bannon Wrought R. L. BOROSAGE *Nation* v305 no6 p6 S 11 2017

WHICH MEANS THE NEW RIGHT IS NOT GOING ANYWHERE M. READ img *New York* v50 no9 p50 My 1 2017

WILL THE TRUMP BUMP GO THUNK? P. Coy graph *Bloomberg Businessweek* no4520 p16 My 1 2017

WINNER TAKES ALL [Cover story] R. LANE color *Forbes* v200 no5 p38 N 14 2017

United States—Politics & government—Charts, diagrams, etc.

The Three Branches of Government *New York Times Upfront* v149 no7 p27 Ja 9 2017

United States presidential election, 1916

Preamble H. E. Blake color *Orion Magazine* v35 no6 p1 N/D 2016

United States presidential election, 1972

RAGE AGAINST - THE - DEMOCRATIC MACHINE: A grassroots revolt from the left is wresting control of the party away from the corporate establishment, one state at a time T. ANDERSON *In These Times* v41 no7 p18 Jl 2017

United States presidential election, 2016

The 2016 Election as a 'Sputnik' Moment for Character Education J. VALENT *Education Digest* v82 no7 p57 Mr 2017

ACTIVE MEASURES E. OSNOS, D. REMNICK et al cartoon color *New Yorker* v93 no3 p40 Mr 6 2017

Between the Lines A. Wintour color *Vogue* v207 no10 p128 O 2017

The Biden Trial Balloon P. TERZIAN color *Weekly Standard* v22 no46 p21 Ag 14 2017

A Call to (Emotional) Arms F. RICH *New York* v49 no15 p20 Jl 25 2016

The Case for Optimism In These Strange Times J. Kerry color *Time* v189 no22 p20 Je 12 2017

Citizen Clinton: The surreal postelection life of the woman who would have been president R. Traister img *New York* v50 no11 p26 My 29 2017

Collusion Confusion A. C. MCCARTHY *National Review* v69 no15 p26 Ag 14 2017

Commentary on Commentary J. PODHORETZ *Commentary* v143 no4 p1 Ap 2017

The Eagle Has Landed K. CLINTON color *Progressive* v81 no4 p67 Ap/My 2017

Fixing Electoral Mechanics J. BLEIFUSS *In These Times* v41 no2 p5 F 2017

For the Record color *Time* v189 no18 p8 My 15 2017

Frank Rich: NO SYMPATHY FOR THE HILLBILLY img *New York* v50 no6 p18 Mr 20 2017

A GOOD CONVERSATION B. HOUGHTON *Commonweal* v144 no12 p4 Jl 7 2017

HACKER, BANKER, SOLDIER, SPY A. Dejean, H. Levintova et al bw color *Mother Jones* v42 no4 p19 Jl/Ag 2017

Hacking Democracy Inside Russia's Social Media War on America M. Calabresi and P. Rebala color *Time* v189 no20 p30 My 29 2017

HACKS, LEAKS, AND TWEETS H. Levintova, A. Dejean et al color *Mother Jones* v42 no4 p22 Jl/Ag 2017

Hold to the Center! W. Egyoku Nakao Roshi color *Tricycle: The*

Buddhist Review v26 no4 p36 Summ 2017

How the Attacks on Trump Reinforce His Strategy R. L. Martin color *Harvard Business Review Digital Articles* p2 Ja 12 2017

How to Make the Electoral College Work for Everyone S. Silberstein graph map *Washington Monthly* v49 no3-5 p11 Mr-My 2017

How Will They Know, And When Will They Know It? S. T. Dennis diag *Bloomberg Businessweek* no4518 p28 Ap 10 2017

The Impeach-Trump Conspiracy P. J. BUCHANAN *American Conservative* v16 no4 p12 Jl/Ag 2017

INSIDE THE RECOUNT S. FRIESS bw color *New Republic* v248 no3 p46 Mr 2017

It's gut-check time M. Malone *America* v216 no5 p3 Mr 6 2017

THE KREMLIN CONNECTION H. BLUM color *Vanity Fair* v59 no5 p85 Ap 2017

THE LOOK BOOK A. SWERDLOFF img *New York* p41 Ja 23 2017

Mad, Democrats? Blame the Iran Deal *Commentary* v143 no1 p1 Ja 2017

The Meaning of Trump R. W. MERRY bw *American Conservative* v16 no2 p20 Mr/Ap 2017

Moscow on the Potomac M. BAUERLEIN and C. JEFFERY color *Mother Jones* v42 no4 p5 Jl/Ag 2017

The National Interest: Jonathan Chait img *New York* v49 no19 p15 S 19 2016

Needs Some Plaid color *Weekly Standard* v22 no22 p2 F 13 2017

THE Never-Ending Pursuit of Religious Liberty S. Slade bw color *America* v216 no6 p18 Mr 20 2017

NO COMMENT cartoon *Progressive* v81 no3 p8 Mr 2017

ON KOMPROMAT A. Dejean, H. Levintova et al bw *Mother Jones* v42 no4 p24 Jl/Ag 2017

Peace Over Politics M. PATTERSON *America* v215 no19 p14 D 19 2016

A Perfect Storm: American Media, Russian Propaganda S. OATES *Current History* v116 no792 p282 O 2017

Readers of the Year C. JEFFERY *Mother Jones* v42 no3 p3 My/Je 2017

Realism on Russia K. V. HEUVEL *Nation* v305 no4 p4 Ag 14 2017

Redoing the Electoral Math J. B. JUDIS color *New Republic* v248 no10 p16 O 2017

Red Vs. Pink: The Politics of Fashion and Why a Hat Is No Longer Just a Hat S. Schrobsdorff color *Time* v189 no6 p55 F 20 2017

Reinhold Niebuhr's Trump Prophecy S. Bates *Society* v54 no1 p4 F 2017

The Revolt Against the Elites [Cover story] P. J. O'ROURKE *Weekly Standard* v22 no22 p26 F 13 2017

RIGGED [Cover story] A. BERMAN and P. Levy color map *Mother Jones* v42 no6 p24 N/D 2017

A SEASON IN PURGATORY L. ANOLIK color *Vanity Fair* v59 no7 p66 Summ 2017

The Secret History of Election 2016 [Cover story] M. Calabresi, J. Brewster et al color map *Time* v190 no5 p32 Jl 31 2017

The Soap Opera Comes to an End N. EMERY color *Weekly Standard* v22 no20 p23 Ja 30 2017

STILL HERE D. REMNICK cartoon color *New Yorker* v93 no29 p58 S 25 2017

Those '60s Flashbacks *Commentary* v142 no4 p1 N 2016

Trump and His Allies Stumble As Russia Probe Moves Closer to the White House M. Calabresi, Z. J. Miller et al color *Time* v189 no21 p9 Je 5 2017

Trump Fills the Vacuum *Commentary* v142 no5 p1 D 2016

Trump's First 100 Days W. DURST *Progressive* v81 no3 p44 Mr 2017

TRUMP TIME *Foreign Affairs* v96 no2 pC9 Mr/Ap 2017

The U.S. Media's Problems Are Much Bigger than Fake News and Filter Bubbles B. N. Anand color *Harvard Business Review Digital Articles* p2 Ja 5 2017

Wandering in the Wilderness G. NORMAN color *Weekly Standard* v22 no20 p20 Ja 30 2017

We Ain't Seen Nothin' Yet J. PODHORETZ *Commentary* v143 no1 p1 Ja 2017

When Rhetoric Wanders in Wacky Ways R. E. VATZ *USA Today Magazine* v145 no2862 p20 Mr 2017

You Can't Handle the Post-Truth C. ROSEN *Commentary* v143 no1 p4 Ja 2017

United States presidential election, 2016—Economic aspects

Secondary Offerings Take Center Stage D. Singer graph *Bloomberg Businessweek* no4520 p43 My 1 2017

You Can't Retire On the Trump Bump S. Woolley cartoon *Bloomberg Businessweek* no4514 p38 Mr 13 2017

United States presidential election, 2016—Humor

PARODY color *Weekly Standard* v22 no22 p40 F 13 2017

United States presidential election, 2016—Psychological aspects

Brave New World S. MAUGHAN color *Publishers Weekly* v264 no14 p30 Ap 3. 2017

United States presidential election, 2016—Social aspects

Are We Up to the Job? J. Cost color *Weekly Standard* v22 no26 p18 Mr 13 2017

Brave New World S. MAUGHAN color *Publishers Weekly* v264 no14 p30 Ap 3. 2017

FIRED UP M. Singer cartoon *New Yorker* v92 no48 p18 F 6 2017

IF I HAD AN AXE R. Wiedeman cartoon *New Yorker* v92 no48 p17 F 6 2017

United States Senate Chamber (United States Capitol, Washington, D.C.)

LIMITED LIABILITY P. R. KEEFE cartoon color *New Yorker* v93 no22 p28 Jl 31 2017

United States—Social conditions—1980-

Continental Divide T. Layden and T. Keith color *Sports Illustrated* v125 no17 p20 N 21 2016 Double Issue

United States—Trials, litigation, etc.

KIDS GET THEIR DAY IN COURT J. MARK *Sierra* v101 no5 p42 S/O 2016

Unite the Right rally, Charlottesville, Va., 2017

American Hate, a History J. Meacham and A. Abrams color *Time* v190 no8 p36 Ag 28 2017

A Beating in Berkeley [Cover story] M. LABASH color *Weekly Standard* v23 no1 p18 S 11 2017

Bigots, Boosted by the Bully Pulpit M. Scherer, A. Altman et al color *Time* v190 no8 p30 Ag 28 2017

BIRTH OF A SUPREMACIST A. MARANTZ cartoon color *New Yorker* v93 no32 p26 O 16 2017

The Case for Cultural Nationalism M. LIND *National Review* v69 no17 p27 S 11 2017

Clergy on the front lines in Charlottesville C. Kennel-Shank color *Christian Century* v134 no19 p12 S 13 2017

EDITOR'S LETTER D. ANDERSON-MINSHALL *Advocate* no1093 p7 O/N 2017

From Selma to Charlottesville, the Ghosts of Our Past T. Smiley *Time* v190 no8 p45 Ag 28 2017

GATEKEEPERS A. Marantz cartoon *New Yorker* v93 no25 p32 Ag 28 2017

Hate In America [Cover story] N. Gibbs color *Time* v190 no8 p24 Ag 28 2017

IN CASE YOU MISSED IT *In These Times* v41 no10 p10 O 2017

Never Again *In These Times* v41 no10 p3 O 2017

The 'N' Word K. D. WILLIAMSON color *National Review* v69 no17 p22 S 11 2017

Rated PC J. LILEKS *National Review* v69 no17 p33 S 11 2017

A Town Violated J. Grisham color *Time* v190 no8 p44 Ag 28 2017

Unity Will Take Generations I. Omar *Time* v190 no8 p44 Ag 28 2017

What White America Must Do Next E. S. J. Glaude color *Time* v190 no8 p42 Ag 28 2017

WHEN THE K.K.K. CAME TO CHARLOTTESVILLE HOW SHOULD CATHOLICS RESPOND TO THE SIN OF RACISM? [Cover story] N. M. Flores color *America* v217 no5 p34 S 4 2017

The White Nationalist House The GOP once drew the line at Nazis J. Chait img *New York* v50 no17 p31 Ag 21 2017

WHITE SUPREMACIST VIOLENCE IS ALL TOO AMERICAN R. GREENE II *In These Times* v41 no10 p26 O 2017

Units of measurement

Constant Connections E. Conover chart color diag *Science News* v190 no10 p24 N 12 2016

I Know That Name bw *Discover* v38 no4 p41 My 2017

Plot to redefine the kilogram nears climax A. Cho color *Science* v356 no6339 p670 My 19 2017

Units of measurement—History

MASS HYSTERIA T. Folger color diag *Scientific American* v316 no2 p46 F 2017

Units of measurement—Standards

MASS HYSTERIA T. Folger color diag *Scientific American* v316 no2 p46 F 2017

Universal Audio Inc.

UA Apollo Twin MkII K. Baumann color *Downbeat* v84 no6 p89 Je 2017

Universal Beat (Music)

Matthew Garrison D. OUELLETTE color *Downbeat* v84 no8 p98 Ag 2017

Universal design

How Long Is a Year? S. BUSHWICK bw color graph *Popular Science* v289 no5 p50 S/O 2017

Universe

COSMOS CONSENSUS? J. A. SCLATER *Scientific American* v317 no4 p8 O 2017

CuriosityStream is for science-hungry viewers E. Conover color *Science News* v191 no12 p27 Je 24 2017

Hubble Spies Faint Galaxies in Early Universe G. SCHILLING *Sky & Telescope* v133 no6 p8 Je 2017

Imagine No Universe M. Shermer color *Scientific American* v316 no2 p73 F 2017

Many Planets, Not Much Life P. Davies color *Scientific American* v315 no3 p8 S 2016

OUR NEXT BILLION YEARS M. TEGMARK color *Discover* v38 no9 p58 N 2017

Our trillion-galaxy universe [Cover story] C. J. Conselice and A. Klesman color *Astronomy* v45 no6 p18 Je 2017

Picturing the Universe P. MURDIN color *Natural History* v125 no11 p24 N 2017

Singularities may reveal themselves E. CONOVER *Science News* v191 no11 p12 Je 10 2017

WHAT CAME BEFORE THE BIG BANG? R. FELTMAN and M. R. FRANCIS color *Popular Science* v289 no5 p52 S/O 2017

Why we need dark matter F. Reddy color *Astronomy* v45 no11 p30 N 2017

Universe—Research

GAME OVER Y. CENDES cartoon *Discover* v38 no2 p46 Mr 2017

Universidad Nacional Autónoma de México

Gas changes signal eruptions J. Rosen color graph *Science* v354 no6315 p952 N 25 2016

Underwater pollinators color *National Wildlife (World Edition)* v55 no4 p8 Je/Jl 2017

Universidade do Estado do Rio de Janeiro

Brazil's public universities in crisis C. C. Siqueira, C. Frederico et al color *Science* v356 no6340 p812 My 26 2017

Universität für Musik und Darstellende Kunst Graz

Mirga Gražinytė-Tyla J. Crelin color *Current Biography* v78 no4 p25 Ap 2017

Université du Québec

Denis Villeneuve M. Hagan color *Current Biography* v78 no4 p90 Ap 2017

Universiteit Maastricht

Goodbye Farm. Hello Lab K. Wong *Sierra* v102 no2 p24 Mr/Ap 2017

Universities & colleges

See also

Catholic universities & colleges

College campuses

Community & college

Historically black colleges & universities

Addressing scientific integrity scientifically T. Mayer, L. Bouter et al *Science* v357 no6357 p1248 S 22 2017

The Bargain D. C. Paris *Change* v48 no5 p4 S/O 2016

BEYOND MERE SURVIVAL: Transforming Independent Colleges and Universities M. B. Marcy *Change* v49 no3 p36 My/Je 2017

BIG NEWS ON CAMPUS H. M. CAULEY *Atlanta* v56 no11 p128 Mr 2017

In guns we trust? F. A. Fitzgerald color *U.S. Catholic* v82 no2 p24 F 2017

INTERNATIONAL color *Downbeat* v84 no10 p180 O 2017

IUPUI T. KIRTS *Indianapolis Monthly* v40 no4 p40 D 2016

The Long March to Bedlam R. J. BRESLER *USA Today Magazine* v146 no2866 p13 Jl 2017

More Universities Need to Teach Sales F. V. Cespedes and D.

Design for Social Animals C. McGuigan *Architectural Record* v204 no11 p21 N 2016

The Doctor Is In J. COST color *Weekly Standard* v22 no20 p5 Ja 30 2017

Full House J. GAUER *Architectural Record* v204 no11 p104 N 2016

Genial Screw-Off J. Epstein *Claremont Review of Books* v17 no3 p64 Summ 2017

A Great Deal J. Epstein *Claremont Review of Books* v17 no3 p67 Summ 2017

Lisa Lucas J. Crelin color *Current Biography* v78 no3 p40 Mr 2017

Modest Cultural Literacy J. Epstein *Claremont Review of Books* v17 no3 p66 Summ 2017

No Soft Spots J. Epstein *Claremont Review of Books* v17 no3 p66 Summ 2017

Scruffy Bohemianism J. Epstein *Claremont Review of Books* v17 no3 p65 Summ 2017

UNIVERSITY OF CHICAGO DAYS J. Epstein *Claremont Review of Books* v17 no3 p64 Summ 2017

University of Cincinnati

A MESSAGE FROM THE DEAN G. Glazer *Cincinnati Magazine* v50 no8 p68 My 2017

Plot Twist S. STANKORB *Cincinnati Magazine* v50 no5 p52 F 2017

Q&A: A "See" Change S. Goldberg *Cincinnati Magazine* v51 no1 p144 O 2017

RAPE CULTURE LIVES HERE S. STANKORB *Cincinnati Magazine* p68 Je 2017

STORY TIME A. KONERMANN *Cincinnati Magazine* v50 no7 p22 Ap 2017

A Whole Lot to Celebrate color *Cincinnati Magazine* v51 no1 p84 O 2017

University of Cincinnati. College of Nursing & Health

THE HIGHEST STANDARDS V. PREVISH *Cincinnati Magazine* v50 no8 p72 My 2017

University of Cincinnati. Medical Center

PRIMING THE PUMP L. MURTHA *Cincinnati Magazine* v50 no4 p66 Ja 2017

University of Cincinnati—Sports

NEW COACH, OLD DREAM G. Freking *Cincinnati Magazine* v50 no12 p23 S 2017

University of Colorado Hospital

How We Transformed Emergency Care at Our Hospital R. Zane *Harvard Business Review Digital Articles* p2 D 17 2015

University of Dayton

Cheer to Eternity A. Gray and T. Keith color *Sports Illustrated* v126 no9 p23 Mr 27 2017

University of Florida

University of Florida *Dance Magazine* v90 p63 2016/2017 Supplement College Guide

University of Florida—Sports

18 Florida color *Sports Illustrated* v127 no5 p107 Ag 14 2017

University of Georgia

HOME AGAIN S. ONEY *Atlanta* v56 no8 p136 D 2016

University of Georgia *Dance Magazine* v90 p66 2016/2017 Supplement College Guide

University of Georgia—Sports

16 Georgia color *Sports Illustrated* v127 no5 p105 Ag 14 2017

University of Hawaii (Honolulu)—Sports

HOT | NOT T. Keith color *Sports Illustrated* v126 no17 p20 Je 19 2017

University of Hawaii at Manoa

University of Hawai'i at Manoa *Dance Magazine* v90 p69 2016/2017 Supplement College Guide

University of Idaho

Week 10 color *Sports Illustrated* v127 no5 p76 Ag 14 2017

University of Idaho—Curricula

University of Idaho *Dance Magazine* v90 p72 2016/2017 Supplement College Guide

University of Iowa

University of Iowa *Dance Magazine* v90 p76 2016/2017 Supplement College Guide

University of Kansas—Sports

2 KANSAS JAYHAWKS D. Gardner chart color *Sports Illustrated* v125 no15 p61 N 7 2016

Leading Off color *Sports Illustrated* v126 no9 p6 Mr 27 2017

University of Kentucky—Sports

3 KENTUCKY WILDCATS S. Davis chart color *Sports Illustrated* v125 no15 p62 N 7 2016

University of Louisiana at Lafayette

Collection in limbo *Science* v356 no6333 p9 Ap 7 2017

University of Louisville—Sports

13 LOUISVILLE CARDINALS S. Davis chart color *Sports Illustrated* v125 no15 p72 N 7 2016

14 Louisville color *Sports Illustrated* v127 no5 p102 Ag 14 2017

University of Manitoba—Curricula

Hunting for credit M. ROBINSON color *Maclean's* v129 no44 p70 N 7 2016

University of Maryland at College Park—Sports

Week 6 color *Sports Illustrated* v127 no5 p64 Ag 14 2017

University of Memphis—Sports

Week 9 color *Sports Illustrated* v127 no5 p76 Ag 14 2017

University of Miami—Sports

20 Miami color *Sports Illustrated* v127 no5 p109 Ag 14 2017

GO FIGURE T. Keith color *Sports Illustrated* v126 no16 p24 Je 5 2017

University of Michigan

University of Michigan *Dance Magazine* v90 p118 2016/2017 Supplement College Guide

University of Michigan—Sports

11 Michigan color *Sports Illustrated* v127 no5 p99 Ag 14 2017

High STAKES P. Thamel color *Sports Illustrated* v126 no9 p32 Mr 27 2017

Week 8 color *Sports Illustrated* v127 no5 p75 Ag 14 2017

University of Minnesota

University of Minnesota—Twin Cities *Dance Magazine* v90 p84 2016/2017 Supplement College Guide

University of Mississippi

Entrepreneurship and Economic Development Fueled by Students and Faculty J. R. Love *Bridges (Federal Reserve Bank of St. Louis)* p10 Summ 2016

University of Missouri

Protests Get Results color *Weekly Standard* v22 no36 p2 My 29 2017

Toe-Tapping to Better Arteries *Saturday Evening Post* v288 no6 p81 N/D 2016

What's on the Mizzou Training Table? M. Crossman color *Missouri Life* v44 no6 p66 S 2017

University of Nebraska at Kearney

Tyronn Lue C. Cullen color *Current Biography* v78 no3 p45 Mr 2017

University of New Mexico

IRON MAN B. COLVIN color *Phi Kappa Phi Forum* v96 no4 p3 Wint 2016

University of New Mexico—Sports

Week 11 color *Sports Illustrated* v127 no5 p77 Ag 14 2017

Week 3 color *Sports Illustrated* v127 no5 p61 Ag 14 2017

University of North Carolina at Chapel Hill—Sports

6 NORTH CAROLINA TAR HEELS B. Hamilton chart color *Sports Illustrated* v125 no15 p65 N 7 2016

Full SWING [Cover story] M. Rosenberg color *Sports Illustrated* v126 no10 p36 Ap 10 2017

University of North Dakota

Member Spotlight: John C. Staley V. Paynich *Parks & Recreation* v52 no2 p48 F 2017

University of Notre Dame—Sports

Week 13 color *Sports Illustrated* v127 no5 p84 Ag 14 2017

University of Notre Dame—Students

Big Man on Campus P. Thamel and T. Keith color *Sports Illustrated* v125 no13 p16 O 17 2016

University of Oklahoma—Sports

6 Oklahoma color *Sports Illustrated* v127 no5 p94 Ag 14 2017

University of Oregon—Sports

4 OREGON DUCKS L. Winn chart color *Sports Illustrated* v125 no15 p63 N 7 2016

University of Oxford

And The Winning Photo Is.... S. Saxby *British Heritage Travel* v37 no6 p88 N/D 2016

Riz Ahmed J. Crelin color *Current Biography* v78 no4 p3 Ap 2017

SHE IS US T. S. Young color *Essence* v48 no6 p67 O 2017

Summa Cum Lettuce G. SINGER color *Walrus* v14 no9 p82 N

v125 no19 p38 D 12 2016
RUN IT BACK A. Staples color *Sports Illustrated* v126 no1 p34
Ja 9 2017
University of Basel (Basel, Switzerland)
Epidemics database gets top prize *Science* v355 no6329 p998 Mr
10 2017
University of California, Berkeley
AND EVEN UC BERKELEY HAS BECOME A POWER CEN-
TER B. CRAIR img *New York* v50 no9 p49 My 1 2017
Berkeley Goes Offline color *Weekly Standard* v22 no27 p13 Mr
20 2017
Color vision strategy defies textbooks T. H. SAEY color *Science
News* v190 no8 p10 O 15 2016
Thwarting the Grievance-Industrial Complex cartoon *Weekly
Standard* v22 no28 p2 Mr 27 2017
University of California, Berkeley—Students
OUT AND UP L. MACFARQUHAR cartoon *New Yorker* v92
no41 p54 D 12 2016
University of California, Davis
GENETIC BASIS FOR "TIGER EYE" IDENTIFIED C. Barakat
and M. McCluskey color *Equus* no480 p15 S 2017
The Hangover J. MINUTILLO color diag *Architectural Record*
v204 no12 p69 D 2016
HEALTH color *Horse & Rider* v55 no11 p19 N 2016
University of California, Irvine
YOUR HAIR IS AWARE bw *Prevention* v69 no11 p6 N 2017
University of California, Los Angeles
THE OLD COLLEGE TRY C. FEHRMAN *Cincinnati Magazine*
v50 no2 p17 N 2016
What's Your Plan? K. Cicero color graph *Prevention* v68 no12
p86 D 2016
University of California, Los Angeles—Officials & employees
Master of Her Domain M. WAKIM *Los Angeles Magazine* p60
Ja 2017
University of California, Los Angeles—Sports
16 UCLA BRUINS B. Hamilton chart color *Sports Illustrated*
v125 no15 p75 N 7 2016
Fun & Gun L. Jenkins color *Sports Illustrated* v126 no3 p44 Ja
23 2017
Week 12 color *Sports Illustrated* v127 no5 p78 Ag 14 2017
University of California, Los Angeles—Students
Students Develop Modular Homeless Shelters for L.A J. ZARA
color *Architectural Record* v205 no2 p24 F 2017
University of California, San Francisco
Bitter Truth color *Prevention* v68 no12 p17 D 2016
University of California, Santa Barbara
Safe to Swim color *Earth Island Journal* v32 no2 p7 Summ 2017
Victoria Orphan J. Crelin color *Current Biography* v78 no4 p63
Ap 2017
University of Colorado, Boulder
sleep under the stars for better zzz's color *Good Housekeeping*
v264 no6 p83 Je 2017
University of Connecticut (Storrs, Conn.)—Sports
Taking HER SHOT S. Apstein color *Sports Illustrated* v126 no8
p62 Mr 20 2017
UCONN WOMEN'S WINNING STREAK 11/23/14 A. Ross and
T. Keith color diag *Sports Illustrated* v126 no2 p15 Ja 16 2017
Unbeatable C. P. Pierce and T. Keith color *Sports Illustrated* v126
no2 p14 Ja 16 2017
WHO CAN BEAT UCONN? R. Deitsch color *Sports Illustrated*
v126 no8 p65 Mr 20 2017
University of Greenland (Nuuk, Greenland)
Growing Greenland's archaeologists color *Science* v354 no6313
p700 N 11 2016
University of Hong Kong (Hong Kong, China)
Popular HKU president resigns *Science* v355 no6325 p553 F 10
2017
University of Illinois at Urbana-Champaign
University of Illinois at Urbana-Cnampaign *Dance Magazine* v90
p73 2016/2017 Supplement College Guide
University of Nevada, Las Vegas
Specializing in Unique *Stage Directions* v30 no3 p68 Mr 2017
University of Nevada, Reno
We're Number One! D. L. Wheeler, T. Murarik et al color *Back-
packer* v45 no1 p8 Ja 2017
University of Regina (Regina, Sask.)

More Than the Little Publisher on the Prairie E. Nawotka *Publish-
ers Weekly* v264 no14 p10 Ap 3. 2017
University of Rochester (Rochester, N.Y.)
Garth Greenwell M. Hagan bw *Current Biography* v78 no3 p24
Mr 2017
University of St. Thomas (Saint Paul, Minn.)—Sports
Week 4 color *Sports Illustrated* v127 no5 p62 Ag 14 2017
University of Tennessee, Knoxville
Twitter Tyranny *Weekly Standard* v22 no4 p3 O 3 2016
University of the Arts (Philadelphia, Pa.)
The University of the Arts *Dance Magazine* v90 p105 2016/2017
Supplement College Guide
University of Waterloo (Waterloo, Ont.)
FIX IT WITH THE BACK MECHANIC L. Schuler cartoon color
Men's Health v32 no1 p43 Ja/F 2017
The secret to a relationship that lasts color *Redbook* p99 F 2017
University of West Virginia (Morgantown, W. Va.)—Sports
LOCAL HERO D. Greene color *Sports Illustrated* v126 no9 p39
Mr 27 2017
University of Wisconsin (Green Bay, Wis.)
Challenge the Mind. Engage the Heart. Delight the Senses. UW
Green Bay Theatre and Dance Program *Stage Directions* v30
no3 p72 Mr 2017
University of Wisconsin (Madison, Wis.)
'Shut Up, Already!': The New Battle Over Campus Free Speech
B. Lueders color *Progressive* v81 no6 p52 Ag/S 2017
University of Wisconsin (Madison, Wis.)—Sports
12 Wisconsin color *Sports Illustrated* v127 no5 p100 Ag 14 2017
8 WISCONSIN BADGERS L. Winn chart color *Sports Illustrated*
v125 no15 p67 N 7 2016
W STARTS WITH D J. Niesen color *Sports Illustrated* v125 no13
p36 O 17 2016
University of Wisconsin (Stevens Point, Wis.)
University of Wisconsin— Stevens Point *Dance Magazine* v90
p111 2016/2017 Supplement College Guide
Univision Communications Inc.
$10,000,000 Says Hillary Wins [Cover story] D. LEONARD col-
or *Bloomberg Businessweek* no4495 p44 O 17 2016
Unjust judge (Parable)
Prepare for Battle J. W. MARTENS il *America* v215 no10 p47
O 10 2016
Unknown Girl, The (Film)
INQUIRING MINDS A. LANE cartoon *New Yorker* v93 no27
p82 S 11 2017
The Outsider C. LORENTZEN *New Republic* v248 no10 p60 O
2017
Unkrich, Lee, 1967-
COCO M. Snetiker color *Entertainment Weekly* no1446/1447 p46
D 2016/Ja 2017
COCO M. Snetiker color *Entertainment Weekly* no1478 / 1479
p58 Ag 18-25 2017
Unlawful entry—Lawsuits & claims
NIGHTMARE IN MCLEAN J. FAGONE *Washingtonian Maga-
zine* v52 no1 p66 O 2016
Unlimited 1 (Music)
The Hot Box J. Corbett, J. Macnie et al chart *Downbeat* v84 no2
p71 F 2017
Unlimited 1 J. McDonough color *Downbeat* v84 no2 p69 F 2017
Unmarried couples
See also
Single parents
THE MARRIAGE BIAS J. NELSON color *GQ: Gentlemen's
Quarterly* v86 no12 p40 D 2016
Unnikrishnan, Deepak
Temporary People *Publishers Weekly* v264 no2 p38 Ja 9 2017
Unwelcome Guests S. MATHEW *New York Times Book Review*
p18 Mr 26 2017
Unnraptured (Poem)
UNRAPTURED D. Levering *Commonweal* v144 no15 p38 S 22
2017
Uno, Hajime
Tumor aneuploidy correlates with markers of immune evasion and
with reduced response to immunotherapy diag *Science* v355
no6322 p261 Ja 20 2017
Unoson, Cecilia
Kinetics of dCas9 target search in Escherichia coli diag *Science*

v357 no6358 p1420 S 29 2017

Unpublished materials

Is Poetry "the New Adult Coloring Book"? J. Boog color *Publishers Weekly* v264 no35 p12 Ag 28 2017

Unreconstructed Rebel (Music)

America's Top 240 img *New York* v49 no19 p92 S 19 2016

Unruh, Gregory

Coastal Cities Are Increasingly Vulnerable, and So Is the Economy that Relies on Them *Harvard Business Review Digital Articles* p2 S 7 2017

Pittsburgh's Transformation Is a Model for Clean Energy Innovation color *Harvard Business Review Digital Articles* p2 Je 6 2017

Unruh, Jack, 1935-2016

The One *Texas Monthly* v44 no11 p12 N 2016

Unruh effect

Traveler in a vacuum might heat up E. CONOVER *Science News* v192 no6 p12 O 14 2017

Unsafe sex

MORE THAN 40% OF GAY AND BI MEN ARE HAVING CONDOMLESS SEX J. ANDERSON-MINSHALL *Advocate* no1088 p27 D 2016/Ja 2017

Unver, H. Akin

The Real Challenge to Turkey's Economy Isn't Terrorism *Harvard Business Review Digital Articles* p2 Jl 8 2016

Unwanted pregnancy

200 YEARS OF ABORTION J. LARSON img *New York* p32 F 9 2017

Unwin, Mike

The Enigma of the Owl: An Illustrated Natural History C. Moskowitz color *Scientific American* v316 no3 p76 Mr 2017

Upadhyay, Samrat

Below Base Camp R. BLACK *New York Times Book Review* p22 My 7 2017

Upadhyaya, Pramey

Control and local measurement of the spin chemical potential in a magnetic insulator bw diag *Science* v357 no6347 p195 Jl 14 2017

UPCHURCH, MICHAEL

The Long Shadow color *New York Times Book Review* p21 S 25 2016

Updegrave, Walter

3 Tips From Millionaires That Can Improve Your Retirement color diag *Money* v46 no9 p35 O 2017

5 Ways Retirement Savers Put Their Dreams at Risk color *Money* v46 no7 p28 Ag 2017

Go Ahead—Invest Already color diag *Money* v46 no4 p31 My 2017

A Simple Habit With a Big Payoff diag *Money* v46 no9 p41 O 2017

Updike, John, 1932-2009

Live Your Best Life color *O, The Oprah Magazine* p21 F 2017

Upgrading of computer software

CDW And Dell Team Up To Offer Optimal Windows 10 Migration M. RONEY color *Forbes* v200 no4 p(Sp)1 O 24 2017

The iOS 11 To-Do List D. Pogue color *Scientific American* v316 no6 p26 Je 2017

Microsoft slips four more features into the Fall Creators Update with Build 16251 M. HACHMAN color *PCWorld* v35 no9 p14 S 2017

Old Windows PCs can stop WannaCry ransomware with new Microsoft patch M. KAN color map *PCWorld* v35 no6 p22 Je 2017

Upham, Charles

Valor Remarkable Exploits C. Lyons *Military History* v33 no5 p16 Ja 2017

Upham, J.

Breaking Lorentz reciprocity to overcome the time-bandwidth limit in physics and engineering bw diag graph *Science* v356 no6344 p1260 Je 23 2017

Upholstery

Call of the Wild D. BRENNER color *House Beautiful* p76 Jl 2017

SCREEN MAGIC E. N. GAGE color *Martha Stewart Living* p25 S 2017

Sea Change C. KELLY color *House Beautiful* p86 Jl 2017

Upholstery repair

Easy Fixes for your Furniture L. Elliott color *Old House Journal*

v45 no6 p48 S 2017

Uploading of data—Software

GRIDS 4.0 FOR INSTAGRAM: POST PHOTOS FROM MAC, BUT SHARING IS LIMITED J. R. BOOKWALTER color *Macworld - Digital Edition* p36 F 2017

Uppaluru, Maya

The Untapped Potential of Health Care APIs *Harvard Business Review Digital Articles* p2 D 23 2015

Upper Peninsula (Mich.)

Log Home Fixer Upper D. Peak color diag *Log Home Living* v33 no7 p24 S 2016

Upside Down & Inside Out (Music)

HIGH FLIERS J. MACGREGOR *Smithsonian* v47 no8 p52 D 2016

Upside Travel Co. LLC

AN UPSIDE FOR BUSINESS TRAVELERS A. Nusca color *Fortune* v175 no7 p30 Je 1 2017

Upson, Kaari—Interviews

Kaari UPSON: THE MONUMENTAL WORK OF THE LOS ANGELES MIXED-MEDIA ARTIST TURNS THE AMERICAN DREAM INSIDE OUT AND LETS ALL THE MESSY PARTS SPILL OUT KAARI UPSON MAY JUST BE THE ARTIST OF OUR AGE J. LUCAS *Interview* v47 no3 p101 Ap 2017

Upton, David M.

The Flaws in Obama's Cybersecurity Initiative *Harvard Business Review Digital Articles* p2 Ja 20 2015

It's OK to Move Down (Yes, Down) the Value Chain *Harvard Business Review Digital Articles* p2 Je 2 2015

Upton, Kate, 1992-

MY BEAUTY MARK ... Kate Upton color *InStyle* v24 no6 p106 Je 2017

UPTON, PETER

FROM THE ARTISTS *Arabian Horse World* v57 no6 p144 Mr 2017

Upward mobility (Social sciences)

Improving Opportunities for Economic Mobility R. Chetty *Bridges (Federal Reserve Bank of St. Louis)* p1 Fall 2016

Upwelling (Oceanography)

How deep water surfaces around Antarctica E. DeMarco color graph *Science News* v192 no4 p36 S 16 2017

Upworthy (Company)

How Upworthy Gets Its Staff to Bond H. Monarth *Harvard Business Review Digital Articles* p2 N 11 2015

Ural, Arda

Predictive Medicine Depends on Analytics *Harvard Business Review Digital Articles* p2 O 23 2014

Ural Motorcycles (Company)

Built for War, Just as Fun on a Trip to the Coffee Shop D. CURCURITO color *Popular Mechanics* p58 My 2017

EDITOR'S LETTER K. WOLFKILL color *Road & Track* v68 no6 p19 F 2017

Uranium

Bottom-up construction of a superstructure in a porous uranium-organic crystal P. Li, N. A. Vermeulen et al color graph *Science* v356 no6338 p624 My 12 2017

Lunar Birth H. Leifert bw *Natural History* v125 no4 p6 Ap 2017

Marie Curie L. SCHLEY color *Discover* v38 no4 p38 My 2017

The secret search for URANIUM IN COLD WAR MOROCCO M. Adamson *Physics Today* v70 no6 p54 Je 2017

Uranium isotopes

Deep-sea corals feel the flow Yusuke Yokoyama and T. M. Esat bibl color *Science* v354 no6312 p550 N 4 2016

LION Hunts for Nuclear Forensics Clues A. Chen color graph *Science & Technology Review* p19 Ja/F 2017

Uranium mines & mining

STATES OF DECAY: A journey through America's nuclear heartland B. Mauk *Harper's Magazine* p48 O 2017

Uranus (Planet)

October 2017: Uranus glows brightly M. RATCLIFFE and A. LING bw chart color *Astronomy* v45 no10 p36 O 2017

Quick Uranus Spotter: Can You Detect the "Secret Naked-Eye Planet"? *Sky & Telescope* v132 no6 p49 D 2016

The unsolved mysteries of the ICE GIANTS K. Haynes bw color *Astronomy* v45 no10 p46 O 2017

Urbach, E. K.

Magnetic resonance spectroscopy of an atomically thin material using a single-spin qubit bibl color diag graph *Science* v355 no6324 p503 F 3 2017

Urbahn, Keith

Upstart D.C. Agents Making Waves in N.Y.C R. Deahl color *Publishers Weekly* v264 no36 p5 S 4 2017

Urban, Alexander E.

Intersection of diverse neuronal genomes and neuropsychiatric disease: The Brain Somatic Mosaicism Network color *Science* v356 no6336 p395 Ap 28 2017

URBAN, DEAN L.

Mapping Conservation Strategies under a Changing Climate *BioScience* v67 no6 p494 Je 2017

Urban, Jeffrey J.

Anomalously low electronic thermal conductivity in metallic vanadium dioxide bibl graph *Science* v355 no6323 p371 Ja 27 2017

Urban, Linda

Weekends with Max and His Dad color *Publishers Weekly* v263 no49 p66 D 7 2016

Urban, M.

Observation of a large-scale anisotropy in the arrival directions of cosmic rays above 8 × 1018 eV *Science* v357 no6357 p1266 S 22 2017

URBAN, MISTY

The View from Abroad bw *Publishers Weekly* v264 no24 p52 Je 12 2017

Urban agriculture

Edible Schoolyard New York J. Minutillo *Architectural Record* v205 no4 p186 Ap 2017

Farm City D. COPELAND color *Alternatives Journal (AJ) - Canada's Environmental Voice* v42 no2 p70 2016

Urban agriculture—Law & legislation

Urban Farming *Congressional Digest* v95 no9 p13 N 2016

Urban animals

VALLEY CATS D. GOODYEAR cartoon color *New Yorker* v92 no49 p44 F 13 2017

Wild in the City color *Canadian Wildlife* v23 no2 p42 My/Je 2017

Urban Armor Gear Inc.

URBAN ARMOR GEAR RUGGED CASE: AN EXCELLENT TOUGH CASE FOR YOUR DELICATE FLOWER OF A LAPTOP S. BELLAMY color *Macworld - Digital Edition* v34 no9 p33 S 2017

URBAN ARMOR GEAR RUGGED CASE S. BELLAMY color *Macworld - Digital Edition* v34 no8 p49 Ag 2017

Urban biodiversity

Biodiversity in the City: Fundamental Questions for Understanding the Ecology of Urban Green Spaces for Biodiversity Conservation C. A. LEPCZYK, M. F. J. ARONSON et al *BioScience* v67 no9 p799 S 2017

THE TREE GUARDIANS OF KYOTO W. BIRD color *Tricycle: The Buddhist Review* v27 no1 p66 Fall 2017

Urban Decay Cosmetics LLC

The New Matte K. Erickson and Y. Chu color *Glamour* v115 no1 p38 Ja 2017

Wrap. Me. Up [Cover story] M. Lynch, G. Porcaro et al color *Women's Health* v13 no10 p110 D 2016

Urban decline

Tales From Motor City L. BERNSTEIN-MACHLAY *American Scholar* v86 no1 p82 Wint 2017

Urban density

China's 'Mountain' Skyscrapers J. Zorthian color *Time* v190 no13 p23 O 2 2017

Urban ecology (Biology)

See also

Urban biodiversity

Benefits of trees in tropical cities X. Ping Song, D. Richards et al color *Science* v356 no6344 p1241 Je 23 2017

Biodiversity in the City: Fundamental Questions for Understanding the Ecology of Urban Green Spaces for Biodiversity Conservation C. A. LEPCZYK, M. F. J. ARONSON et al *BioScience* v67 no9 p799 S 2017

Connecting the Collective M. Church color *Canadian Wildlife* v23 no4 p42 S/O 2017

Urban ecology (Sociology)

Chicago Gets a Fitbit T. Newcombe *Governing* v30 no2 p60 N 2016

Urban economics—History—21st century

CITIES ARE THE FUTURE R. KARLGAARD *Forbes* v198 no7 p38 N 29 2016

Urban forestry

Doubling Down on Urban Forests D. Irvin *American Forests* v123 no2 p7 Summ 2017

Laurence Wiseman *American Forests* v123 no3 p4 Fall 2017

Vibrant Cities Lab: A State-of-the-Art Platform to Connect Urban Forest Leaders I. LEAHY *American Forests* v123 no3 p40 Fall 2017

Urban forestry—Arizona

SHADY POLITICS A. Greenblatt *Governing* v30 no1 p11 O 2016

Urban gardens

HIGH-RISE GREENS I. FRAZIER cartoon *New Yorker* v92 no44 p52 Ja 9 2017

The Urban Wild A. Gem color *Chicago* v66 no8 p90 Ag 2017

Urban growth

1970: St. Louis *Lapham's Quarterly* v10 no1 p62 Wint 2017

All Those Cranes in Queens C. Swanson img *New York* v50 no18 p64 S 4 2017

HOW CITIES COULD SAVE US W. McDonough color *Scientific American* v317 no1 p44 Jl 2017

How to Manage The Sprawl P. Coy map *Bloomberg Businessweek* no4534 p8 Ag 14 2017

What Inclusive Urban Development Can Look Like R. Florida and J. W. McLean *Harvard Business Review Digital Articles* p2 Jl 11 2017

Urban heat islands

A Commitment to Greenspace Takes Root in Dallas *American Forests* v122 no3 p6 Fall 2016

Urban land use

See also

Urban planning

FROM PARKING LOT TO PARADISE C. Ratti and A. Biderman color diag *Scientific American* v317 no1 p54 Jl 2017

Urban life

EDITOR'S LETTER G. Cerio color *Magazine Antiques* v184 no3 p16 My/Je 2017

Urban Outfitters Inc.

CUTE REBOOT L. BAILEY *Indianapolis Monthly* p26 F 2017

Urban parks

Collaborating with Communities Strengthens Green Infrastructure Outcomes L. Robertson *Parks & Recreation* v52 no8 p32 Ag 2017

JULIA STREET WITH POYDRAS THE PARROT bw color *New Orleans Magazine* v52 no1 p22 S 2017

Wandering into the Past G. WOOD color *Missouri Life* v44 no6 p90 S 2017

WILDLIFE color *Canadian Geographic* v137 no3 p22 My 2017

Urban planning

See also

Housing

5 Simple Urban Fixes A. Marshall *Governing* v30 no5 p24 F 2017

Architecture and the Future of the Public Realm C. McGuigan *Architectural Record* v205 no4 p24 Ap 2017

Can't Go Home A. Konermann *Cincinnati Magazine* v50 no5 p64 F 2017

Capital considerations B. BANKS map *Canadian Geographic* v137 no3 p32 My 2017

The Demand for Responsive Architectural Planning and Production in Rapidly Urbanizing Regions: the Case of Ethiopia Z. C. Mamo *UN Chronicle* v53 no3 p15 2016

Designing the City of Tomorrow Today M. DiChristina color *Scientific American* v317 no1 p4 Jl 2017

Design of the PUBLIC REALM *Architectural Record* v205 no4 p175 Ap 2017

Dream Team J. KRAJESKI bw color *Nation* v305 no4 p20 Ag 14 2017

Fighting Diabetes in the 21st Century L. R. Sørensen *Harvard Business Review Digital Articles* p2 D 29 2015

Form Versus Function: L.A.'S DIRECTOR OF PLANNING, VINCE BERTONI, OFFERS INSIGHTS ON THE CITY TAKING SHAPE BEFORE OUR EYES M. SEGAL *Los Angeles Magazine* p18 Ag 2017

On Interventions that Catalyze Greater Change M. Murphy *Architectural Record* v205 no4 p212 Ap 2017

On the Waterfront M. Cockram *Architectural Record* v205 no10 p123 O 2017

Planning for the Future of Urban Biodiversity: A Global Review of City-Scale Initiatives C. H. NILON, M. F. J. ARONSON et al *BioScience* v67 no4 p332 Ap 2017

The Rise of Urban Innovation Districts B. J. Katz and J. Wagner *Harvard Business Review Digital Articles* p2 N 12 2014

A Second Chance *Governing* v30 no2 p12 N 2016

Two Major Heatherwick Projects Nixed A. KLIMOSKI *Architectural Record* v205 no6 p26 Je 2017

UNCOMMON GROUND N. SAVAL *New York Times Magazine* p72 N 13 2016

Urban planning—China

Adapting Chinese cities to climate change Qinhua Fang bibl *Science* v354 no6311 p425 O 28 2016

Urban planning—Florida

30 Years Later A. Ehrenhalt *Governing* v31 no1 p26 O 2017

Urban planning—Indiana

AHEAD OF THE CURRENT R. Annis, S. Bahr et al color *Indianapolis Monthly* v41 no2 p68 S 2017

Urban planning—United States

What Inclusive Urban Development Can Look Like R. Florida and J. W. McLean *Harvard Business Review Digital Articles* p2 Jl 11 2017

Urban policy—United States

Cities and the People Left Behind: What should we be doing for the casualties of 'winner-take-all urbanism'? A. Marshall *Governing* v30 no9 p22 Je 2017

Urban renewal

Can't Go Home A. Konermann *Cincinnati Magazine* v50 no5 p64 F 2017

A Data-Driven Approach to Revitalizing the L.A. River A. FIXSEN *Architectural Record* v205 no4 p34 Ap 2017

THE GEOGRAPHY OF MEMORY A. B. WALTERS *Cincinnati Magazine* v50 no5 p72 F 2017

Smart Cities Are Going to Be a Security Nightmare T. Thibodeaux *Harvard Business Review Digital Articles* p2 Ap 28 2017

Urban renewal—Michigan—Detroit

Detroit: The Remix C. MCGUIGAN *Architectural Record* v205 no4 p84 Ap 2017

Urban renewal—United States

Civic Lesson D. LIND *Architectural Record* v205 no4 p176 Ap 2017

Urban runoff management

Quantifying Green Infrastructure's Stormwater Capture Potential S. Ozbenian *Parks & Recreation* v52 no9 p42 S 2017

Urban tourism

GOING LOCAL S. Hansen *New York Times Magazine* p16 S 24 2017

Urban transportation

See also

Public transit

The Autonomobile and the City M. SORKIN *Architectural Record* v205 no4 p64 Ap 2017

Urban transportation—China—Beijing

OVER THE HANDLEBARS C. Larson color *Bloomberg Businessweek* no4534 p50 Ag 14 2017

Urban transportation—Florida—Miami

A lesson from Pope Francis for Miami's gridlocked streets T. Padgett color *America* v217 no6 p16 S 18 2017

Urban women

Transforming Settlements in Africa S. NANDUDU *UN Chronicle* v53 no3 p23 2016

Urbanization

AMERICAN PLACES *American Scholar* v86 no3 p128 Summ 2017

Cities for People and by People S. Boonyabancha and T. Kerr *UN Chronicle* v53 no3 p1 2016

CITY OF GILT T. Gold *Harper's Magazine* v334 no2002 p67 Mr 2017

EYE on the PRIZE E. J. WALLACE *Virginia Living* v15 no3 p90 Ap 2017

FEAR OF ARRIVAL I. Vladislavić *Lapham's Quarterly* v10 no3 p193 Summ 2017

Foreword M. Nasser *UN Chronicle* v53 no3 p5 2016

GM STAMPING PLANT R. Annis, S. Bahr et al color map *Indianapolis Monthly* v41 no2 p75 S 2017

Habitat III Is the Citizens' Conference of the United Nations J. Clos *UN Chronicle* v53 no3 p9 2016

How did a scientific Siberia turn into AstroBoulder? J. P. Bassi *Physics Today* v70 no2 p36 F 2017

Managing in an Age of Winner-Take-All R. Straub *Harvard Business Review Digital Articles* p2 Ap 7 2015

No Place Like Home M. Zucca bw cartoon color *O, The Oprah Magazine* p162 D 2016

PARODY color *Weekly Standard* v22 no21 p40 F 6 2017

A River at Risk I. TEH color map *National Geographic* v232 no1 p142 Jl 2017

Side Effects of 'The Great Inversion': Low pay and long, pricey commutes often go hand in hand W. Fulton *Governing* v30 no9 p23 Je 2017

WHIMSY ON MAIN *South Dakota Magazine* v33 no3 p24 S/O 2017

Urbanization—Africa

The Contentious Politics of African Urbanization J. W. PALLER *Current History* v116 no790 p163 My 2017

Transforming Settlements in Africa S. NANDUDU *UN Chronicle* v53 no3 p23 2016

Urbanization—California

Form Versus Function: L.A.'S DIRECTOR OF PLANNING, VINCE BERTONI, OFFERS INSIGHTS ON THE CITY TAKING SHAPE BEFORE OUR EYES M. SEGAL *Los Angeles Magazine* p18 Ag 2017

Urbanization—China

China Gambles on Modernizing Through Urbanization M. RITHMIRE and K. LOONEY *Current History* v116 no791 p203 S 2017

Urbanization—Illinois

Head Space color *Popular Photography* v81 no2 p12 Mr/Ap 2017

URBANSKI, DEBBIE

6 COMPENSATIONS FOR SLEEPLESSNESS *Orion Magazine* v35 no3 p4 My/Je 2016

URBANUS, JASON

A DANGEROUS ISLAND [Cover story] color *Archaeology* v70 no4 p14 Je-Ag 2017

FIRE IN THE FENS color *Archaeology* v70 no1 p34 Ja/F 2017

A LAST DAY, RECLAIMED bw color *Archaeology* v69 no6 p48 N/D 2016

Looking Beyond the Hillforts [Cover story] color *Archaeology* v70 no4 p38 Je-Ag 2017

Murder on the Mountain? bw color *Archaeology* v69 no6 p14 N/D 2016

Ötzi's Sartorial Splendor color *Archaeology* v69 no6 p18 N/D 2016

A PHARAOH'S LAST FLEET color *Archaeology* v70 no1 p13 Ja/F 2017

A PRINCELY UPDATE color *Archaeology* v70 no5 p16 S/O 2017

SOMETHING NEW FOR SUTTON HOO bw color *Archaeology* v70 no2 p14 Mr/Ap 2017

A SURPRISE CITY IN THESSALY color *Archaeology* v70 no2 p16 Mr/Ap 2017

TAKE ME OUT TO THE BALL GAME [Cover story] color *Archaeology* v70 no4 p16 Je-Ag 2017

TOP 10 DISCOVERIES OF 2016 bw cartoon color *Archaeology* v70 no1 p26 Ja/F 2017

THE VIKINGS' WIDE REACH color *Archaeology* v70 no3 p20 My/Je 2017

WORLD ROUNDUP color map *Archaeology* v70 no2 p24 Mr/Ap 2017

WORLD ROUNDUP color map *Archaeology* v70 no4 p24 Je-Ag 2017

WORLD ROUNDUP color map *Archaeology* v70 no5 p24 S/O 2017

Urías, Julio, 1996-

Julio Urias M. Hagan *Current Biography* v78 no4 p86 Ap 2017

Uribe, Mauricio—Interviews

What I Wear to Work: MAURICIO URIBE J. Chen color *Bloomberg Businessweek* no4507 p67 Ja 16 2017

Uridine

An adipo-biliary-uridine axis that regulates energy homeostasis Y. Deng, Z. V. Wang et al diag *Science* v355 no6330 p1173 Mr 17 2017

SEPTEMBER bw chart color *Popular Mechanics* p6 S 2017

The SUMMER of 1977 S. TIGNOR bw color *Tennis* v53 no5 p68 S/O 2017

UNBREAKABLE S. l. Price color *Sports Illustrated* v127 no8 p38 S 18 2017

US Open Special A. FRIEDMAN, J. ARIAS et al bw color *Tennis* v53 no5 p30 S/O 2017

U.S. states

Informally Grading the States K. Barrett and R. Greene *Governing* v30 no7 p58 Ap 2017

THE SHAPE WE'RE IN *Texas Monthly* v45 no3 p62 Mr 2017

States Lead the Way with Renewable Energy Policy *Mother Earth News* no284 p6 O/N 2017

WE MARCHED EVERYWHERE *Ms.* v27 no1 p20 Spr 2017

Which state has the happiest couples? color *Women's Health* v14 no4 p34 My 2017

U.S. states—Politics & government

Computers Made Gerrymandering Worse. Can They Fix It? E. Barone diag map *Time* v190 no14 p14 O 9 2017

U.S. states—Politics & government—21st century

States Lean Left on Local Votes J. Sanburn color *Time* v188 no21 p16 N 21 2016

USA Water Polo Inc.

Head Shots: Just Part of the Game J. C. Kozlowski *Parks & Recreation* v52 no2 p22 F 2017

US Airways Flight 1549 Crash Landing, Hudson River, N.Y. & N.J., 2009

THE SULLENBERGER-SKILES EFFECT L. Abend color *Flying* v144 no1 p66 Ja 2017

SULLY AND MARVIN S. Weigel bw *Flying* v144 no1 p34 Ja 2017

Ušaj, Matej

Exploring genetic suppression interactions on a global scale diag *Science* v354 no6312 p599 N 4 2016

Ušaj, Mojca Mattiazzi

Exploring genetic suppression interactions on a global scale diag *Science* v354 no6312 p599 N 4 2016

USB (Computer bus)

Apricorn Aegis Secure Key 3z: This USB thumbdrive is small, secure, and device-agnostic J. L. JACOBI color graph *PCWorld* p79 Mr 2017

Asus ZenBook Flip: A sleek, affordable 2-in-1 for everyday tasks J. NOREM color graph *PCWorld* p84 Mr 2017

free the mouse S. Horaczek color *Popular Science* v289 no6 p84 N/D 2017

USB (Computer bus)—Equipment & supplies

CALDIGIT USB-C DOCK: A FULLFEATURED USB-C DOCK WITH BOTH DISPLAYPORT AND HDMI PORTS G. FLEISHMAN color *Macworld - Digital Edition* p25 Mr 2017

iOS Accessories J. Mathis color *Macworld - Digital Edition* v34 no4 p60 My 2017

NONDA USB-C TO HDMI ADAPTER G. FLEISHMAN color *Macworld - Digital Edition* v34 no10 p35 O 2017

USB (Computer bus)—Evaluation

AudioQuest DragonFly Red and DragonFly Black Amp/DACs M. Fleischmann color *Sound & Vision* v81 no10 p66 D 2016

AUKEY MULTIPORT USB-C HUB G. FLEISHMAN color *Macworld - Digital Edition* v34 no6 p47 Je 2017

CABLE MATTERS 72W 4-PORT USB CHARGER WITH USB-C POWER DELIVERY G. FLEISHMAN color *Macworld - Digital Edition* v34 no9 p38 S 2017

GEARHEAD AWAY GAME D. PIERCE bw color *Wired* v25 no6 p34 Je 2017

USB flash drives

TECH VS. TYRANNY color *Reason* v49 no2 p9 Je 2017

Why your USB drive's file format matters: FAT32 vs. exFAT vs. NTFS J. NOREM color *PCWorld* p165 O 2016

USB flash drives—Evaluation

Best USB-C memory card readers J. CARLSON color graph *Macworld - Digital Edition* v34 no9 p71 S 2017

CABLE MATTERS 72W 4-PORT USB CHARGER WITH USB-C POWER DELIVERY G. FLEISHMAN color *Macworld - Digital Edition* v34 no9 p38 S 2017

K'ABLEKEY REVIEW: VERSATILE IPHONE FLASH DRIVE DOUBLES AS LIGHTNING CHARGE CABLE J. R. BOOKWALTER color *Macworld - Digital Edition* p51 Je 13 2017

USCINSKI, JOSEPH E.

FAKE NEWS FREAKOUT bw *Reason* v48 no10 p54 Mr 2017

U.S. Consumer Product Safety Commission—Trials, litigation, etc.

The Regulators' Bad Day in Court A. W. SCHACHTER color *Weekly Standard* v22 no14 p17 D 12 2016

Used aircraft—Sales & prices

LOOKING FOR A NEW AIRPLANE D. Karl color *Flying* v144 no11 p68 N 2017

Used car sales & prices

Best and Worst Used Cars J. Linkov color *Consumer Reports* v82 no9 p52 S 2017

Ezra Dyer E. Dyer color *Car & Driver* v63 no2 p34 Ag 2017

Used cars

1989 Isuzu Trooper RS color *Popular Mechanics* p44 Je 2017

WATCH OUT FOR FLOOD-DAMAGED CARS R. STINSON cartoon *Kiplinger's Personal Finance* v71 no12 p11 D 2017

Used cars—Economic aspects

Deals on Wheels E. AMBROSE color *AARP: The Magazine* v59 no5A p27 Ag/S 2017

Used cars—Evaluation

Best and Worst Used Cars J. Linkov color *Consumer Reports* v82 no9 p52 S 2017

Steering You Right M. L. Tellado *Consumer Reports* v82 no4 p5 Ap 2017

Used Car Winners & Losers chart color *Consumer Reports* v82 no4 p49 Ap 2017

Used cars—Sales & prices

Deals on Wheels E. AMBROSE color *AARP: The Magazine* v59 no5A p27 Ag/S 2016

John Phillips color *Car & Driver* v62 no6 p30 D 2016

Used clothing

A Real Mr. Fusion Feeds on Used Clothing P. Alpeyev *Bloomberg Businessweek* no4509 p29 Ja 30 2017

Used clothing industry

The Six Best Secondhand Stores in the World color *Esquire* p110 BigBlackBook

Used tractors—Sales & prices

DEERE DEALERS' DEALS ON 4WDs D. Mowitz *Successful Farming* v115 no3 p20 Mid-F 2017

USEEM, JERRY

Power Causes Brain Damage color *Atlantic* v320 no1 p24 Jl/Ag 2017

When Working From Home Doesn't Work cartoon *Atlantic* v320 no4 p26 N 2017

Useem, Michael

How CEOs Can Best Manage Their Boards *Harvard Business Review Digital Articles* p2 D 9 2014

Your Board Should Think Like Activists *Harvard Business Review Digital Articles* p2 F 9 2015

User-centered system design

Pokémon Go, Amazon Dash, and the Future of User Interaction M. Schrage *Harvard Business Review Digital Articles* p2 Jl 14 2016

User charges

See also

Surcharges

Hidden Bank Fees L. LAZARONY cartoon *AARP: The Magazine* v60 no5A p25 Ag/S 2017

Usher, Shaun

HUXLEY TO ORWELL: MY DYSTOPIA IS BETTER THAN YOURS bw *Atlantic* v319 no1 p17 Ja/F 2017

YOURS SINCERELY, DAVID BOWIE color *Entertainment Weekly* no1435 p60 O 14 2016

Ushiba, Junichi

Help, hope, and hype: Ethical dimensions of neuroprosthetics color *Science* v356 no6345 p1338 Je 30 2017

Ushio, Sam

Final salute in Alliance: Nebraska Veterans Cemetery E. Case *Nebraska Life* v20 no6 p17 N/D 2016

Usoskin, Dmitry

miR-183 cluster scales mechanical pain sensitivity by regulating basal and neuropathic pain genes diag graph *Science* v356 no6343 p1168 Je 16 2017

Multipotent peripheral glial cells generate neuroendocrine cells of the adrenal medulla color *Science* v357 no6346 p46 Jl 7 2017

aimed at distant mountains A. McGIVNEY *Arizona Highways* v96 no7 p14 Jl 2017

THE LAKE HOUSE T. George cartoon *Cabin Living* p88 Mr 2017

LET'S COZY UP TO small CABINS! M. R. JOHNSON bw color *Cabin Living* p5 Mr 2017

Marinating in the Moment C. HEITGER-EWING color *Cabin Living* p18 Mr 2017

Oh! The Stories They Tell M. R. JOHNSON *Cabin Living* p5 S 2017

One Wright Pilgrimage R. Cole color *Arts & Crafts Homes & the Revival* v12 no3 p20 Summ 2017

Open House *Arizona Highways* v92 no11 p56 N 2016

our happy place K. BLAYLOCK and J. BLAYLOCK color map *Cabin Living* p15 S 2017

Out of the Woods B. BOEHLERT color *Architectural Digest* v74 no10 p44 O 1 2017

Party TIME L. READIE MAYER color *Cabin Living* p58 D 2016

Perfect Fit D. NETTO color *Architectural Digest* v74 no10 p120 O 1 2017

Picking Grapes J. THOMPSON color *Cabin Living* p80 S 2017

A place of first permission J. WILKINS *Orion Magazine* v35 no4/5 p73 Jl-O 2016

SCARY THINGS S. M. BRADLEY color *Cabin Living* p80 O 2017

Snow BOUND color *Cabin Living* p41 D 2016

Star-Spangled Style K. O'SHEA-EVANS color *House Beautiful* p50 Jl 2017

Sweet and low down color *Cabin Living* p25 S 2017

an unexpected gift K. ENGEL color map *Cabin Living* p14 S 2017

Using History to Activate a Neighborhood Green Space C. G. Wallace *Parks & Recreation* v52 no10 p24 O 2017

we asked you answered R. Bridge, A. Reynolds et al color *Cabin Living* p8 D 2016

Yoga at the CABIN C. HEITGER-EWING color *Cabin Living* p56 Je 2017

Vacation homes—California

Resort Camping color *Cabin Living* p29 Je 2017

Vacation homes—Colorado

OUR CABIN SURVIVED A WILDFIRE N. Fay and K. Fay color *Cabin Living* p69 Je 2017

Vacation homes—Design & construction

13 TIPS FOR GETTING THE MOST FROM A COZY CABIN color *Cabin Living* p8 Mr 2017

5 Forever Futuristic W. Goodman img *New York* v49 no21 p96 O 17 2016

all-inclusive space SAVERS J. BREWSTER color *Cabin Living* p54 Mr 2017

BUILDING small J. BREWSTER color *Cabin Living* p42 Mr 2017

Cabin Patterns D. MULFINGER color *Cabin Living* p20 Mr 2017

cabins For Snow play K. BASTONE color *Cabin Living* p52 D 2016

circle j lodge P. JACOT color *Cabin Living* p16 D 2016

Coping with Steep Slopes J. COOPER color *Cabin Living* p64 Ap 2017

cozy MOUNTAIN CABIN [Cover story] M. MYLCHREEST color *Cabin Living* p42 D 2016

Decluttering the Cabin D. HOWLAND color *Cabin Living* p14 Mr 2017

DESIGNING a dream J. BREWSTER color diag *Cabin Living* p66 D 2016

Faux Finishes D. HOWLAND color *Cabin Living* p14 D 2016

Hardworking ISLANDS D. Howland color *Cabin Living* p7 Mr 2017

Hearth of the Matter color *Cabin Living* p51 D 2016

home sweet cabin J. DOYLE color *Cabin Living* p18 Ap 2017

Off-Grid in Alaska F. SIGURDSSON color *Cabin Living* p22 D 2016

Outdoor Stains & Paints D. HOWLAND color *Cabin Living* p14 Ap 2017

reclaimed cabin R. ZWIRZ color *Cabin Living* p17 Mr 2017

TREASURE ISLAND J. Chamberlain color *Sunset* v238 no3 p29 Mr 2017

A TRULY Special PLACE M. PAULSEN bw color diag *Cabin Living* p46 Mr 2017

Unique Challenges of Building on an Island K. Paulsen color *Cabin Living* p51 Mr 2017

What is a cabin? M. R. JOHNSON color *Cabin Living* p5 Ap 2017

Winter Wonderland WEEKEND M. FREITAG bw color *Cabin Living* p88 D 2016

Vacation homes—Evaluation

in harmony L. WATERMAN color *Architectural Digest* v74 no7 p52 Jl 2017

Vacation homes—Interior decoration

All Together Now K. HACKETT color *House Beautiful* p68 Jl 2017

"Camp Off the Grid" F. SIGURDSSON color *Cabin Living* p24 Ja/F 2017

GETAWAY CABINS: NETFLIX AND CHILL, MINUS THE NETFLIX J. WILLIAMS *Cincinnati Magazine* v50 no10 p42 Jl 2017

ReTRO-A-Go-Go J. BREWSTER color *Cabin Living* p38 D 2016

SPLASH PAD: This Lake Monroe vacation home lives in a whole different league J. Payton *Indianapolis Monthly* v40 no10 p34 Je 2017

Vacation homes—Maintenance & repair

Decluttering the Cabin D. HOWLAND color *Cabin Living* p14 Mr 2017

TIME TO RE-STAIN THE DECK color *Cabin Living* p70 Mr 2017

What is a cabin? M. R. JOHNSON color *Cabin Living* p5 Ap 2017

Vacation homes—Michigan

A 15-Year Passion Project C. HEITGER-EWING color *Cabin Living* p26 S 2017

cabin in training C. HEITGER-EWING bw cartoon color *Cabin Living* p30 Je 2017

Vacation homes—Remodeling

DIY cabin remodel M. MYLCHREEST color *Cabin Living* p30 D 2016

DOCKS BUILT TO LAST color *Cabin Living* p68 Ap 2017

Vacation homes—Sales & prices

Time-Share Bandits D. Shadel color *AARP: The Magazine* v60 no4A p48 Je/Jl 2017

Vacation homes—United States

THE BARN BY THE BEACH M. M. Kashino *Washingtonian Magazine* v52 no9 p151 Je 2017

Cabin Details [Cover story] D. MULFINGER color *Cabin Living* p18 O 2017

cabin real estate chart *Cabin Living* p9 O 2017

home sweet cabin J. DOYLE color *Cabin Living* p18 Ap 2017

home to roost A. NICHOLS color map *Cabin Living* p19 Je 2017

Off-Grid in the Catskills F. SIGURDSSON color *Cabin Living* p24 Ap 2017

snowbound but beautiful D. MCMILLEN color map *Cabin Living* p18 Je 2017

Vacation homes—Vermont

Off-Grid in Vermont's Northeast Kingdom F. SIGURDSSON color *Cabin Living* p26 Je 2017

Vacation homes—Wisconsin

birds of a feather D. JOHNSON color *Cabin Living* p19 Ap 2017

Building at the Water's Edge D. MULFINGER bw color *Cabin Living* p20 Ap 2017

The PURSUIT of Life S. UMLAND color *Cabin Living* p88 Je 2017

Vacation rentals

BE OUR GUEST L. F. Prater *Successful Farming* v115 no5 p61 Mid-Mr 2017

Enjoy a Senior Term Abroad I. Case color *Money* v46 no2 p43 Mr 2017

A Warm Welcome color *Cabin Living* p28 Ja/F 2017

Vacations

See also

Employee vacations

Family vacations

Summer vacations

3 Ways to Control Your Phone Addiction on Vacation R. Walsh *Harvard Business Review Digital Articles* p2 Jl 31 2017

7 Amazing Adventures That Won't Cost a Fortune M. Leonhardt and K. A. Renzulli color *Money* v46 no6 p12 Jl 2017

An Alluring Compromise M. BLYTH color *AARP: The Magazine* v60 no2A p42 F/Mr 2017

At Peace in the Sun J. Tomlinson color *Money* v45 no11 p92 D 2016

Bet the Ranch R. Lizza *New Republic* v248 no8/9 p5 Ag/S 2017

Cabin Fever? C. HEITGER-EWING color *Cabin Living* p18 D 2016

CAN NAVY PIER EVER BE COOL? J. REESE color *Chicago* v66 no8 p21 Ag 2017

CLOSE ENCOUNTERS C. Colin color *Sunset* v238 no3 p20 Mr 2017

College! Money! Jobs! C. THORP color *Seventeen* v76 no4 p58 Jl/Ag 2017

Dear Readers B. Kelley *Reader's Digest* v189 no1131 p4 Je 2017

The Difference Matters G. MICHAL *Boating World* v38 no2 p30 F 2017

Great American Cruises color *AARP: The Magazine* v60 no2A p40 F/Mr 2017

Guest Ranch Redefined: EVERYTHING OLD IS NEW AGAIN AT THIS HILL COUNTRY HIDEAWAY L. SMITH FORD *Texas Monthly* v45 no9 p13 S 2017

HAPPY RETURNS K. MOLVAR color *Conde Nast Traveler* v52 no7 p26 Ag 2017

Haunted Hikes M. Horjus color *Backpacker* p10 O 2017

Here, Here! P. Guzmán color *Conde Nast Traveler* v52 no7 p14 Ag 2017

Hillingdon Street Blues E. S. MACLEAN *Weekly Standard* v22 no5 p5 O 10 2016

Hire a Pro to Plan Your Trip M. CROSS color *Kiplinger's Personal Finance* v71 no11 p70 N 2017

How to Keep Email from Ruining Your Vacation A. Huffington *Harvard Business Review Digital Articles* p2 2017

How to Take a Productive Yet Refreshing Vacation [Cover story] D. Clark *Harvard Business Review Digital Articles* p2 Je 4 2015

If I had an extra vacation day, I would… map *Reader's Digest* v189 no1131 p30 Je 2017

Intel bw chart *Conde Nast Traveler* v52 no7 p96 Ag 2017

Last-Minute Spring Break Trips K. Cicero *Parents* v92 no2 p16 F 2017

Laura Dern D. WALTERS bw color *Conde Nast Traveler* v52 no6 p40 Je/Jl 2017

Let yourself be astonished M. Rollins *Redbook* p8 Mr 2017

Lonelier Than Thou K. STILLER color *Walrus* v14 no8 p66 O 2017

One Step Beyond K. LAGRAVE color *Conde Nast Traveler* v52 no7 p41 Ag 2017

OPEN SEASON E. Graves *Martha Stewart Living* p14 Jl/Ag 2017

pack and play *Parents* v91 no10 p29 O 2016

Picking Grapes J. THOMPSON color *Cabin Living* p80 S 2017

Plan the Perfect Vacation J. Kita and E. Gundersen cartoon color *AARP: The Magazine* v59 no6A p46 O/N 2016

Remember, It's Your Vacation D. T. PUTERBAUGH *USA Today Magazine* v146 no2866 p82 Jl 2017

Remote Argentina G. LONGO color *Conde Nast Traveler* v52 no7 p16 Ag 2017

The Rest Stop Road Trip M. ROACH color *Reader's Digest* v189 no1131 p72 Je 2017

Sigourney Weaver D. WALTERS color *Conde Nast Traveler* v51 no10 p62 N 2016

The Stunning Beauty of a Pacific Northwest Sea M. GRANT color *AARP: The Magazine* v60 no2A p44 F/Mr 2017

THE SWEET SPOT J. FIELDEN color *Esquire* p8 Ag 2017

SWITZERLAND D. Heimburger color *Christianity Today* v61 no4 p24 My 2017

Take a break A. Scobey color *U.S. Catholic* v82 no5 p43 My 2017

TAKE A VACAY A. Reliford color *Good Housekeeping* v265 no1 p90 Jl 2017

This Vacation Could Save Your Life! M. Reyes and M. Kreizman color *Bloomberg Businessweek* no4522 p81 My 15 2017

THE TREE FUNERAL M. W. Spencer color *Louisiana Life* v38 no1 p10 S/O 2017

Two Tickets to Paradise A. EDWARDS color *AARP: The Magazine* v60 no2A p43 F/Mr 2017

Vacation! [Cover story] color *Reader's Digest* v189 no1131 p66 Je 2017

VACATION ON THE ROAD LESS TRAVELED: Big things happen in small towns … Welcome to Lemmon, SD! *South Dakota Magazine* v33 no3 p9 S/O 2017

WE SET UP SHOP IN THE MIDDLE OF A NATURAL WONDER A. McGIVNEY *Arizona Highways* v92 no11 p43 N 2016

ZARA LARSSON color *Seventeen* v76 no2 p37 Mr 2017

Vacations—Economic aspects

the Disney park that's right for your family [Cover story] K. CICERO chart color *Parents* v92 no3 p34 Mr 2017

Secrets of the Kingdom [Cover story] B. Tuttle color *Money* v46 no6 p44 Jl 2017

Vacations—Humor

Laugh Lines color *Reader's Digest* v189 no1131 p111 Je 2017

Vacations—Psychological aspects

Why Some of Us Dread Going on Vacation A. Markman *Harvard Business Review Digital Articles* p2 Je 16 2015

Vaccarello, Anthony, 1982-

VACCARELLO'S VISION C. Swanson bw color *Harper's Bazaar* no3655 p152 Ag 2017

VACCARIELLO, LINDA

Cold Comfort *Cincinnati Magazine* v50 no5 p176 F 2017

DOUBLET TROUBLE *Cincinnati Magazine* v50 no12 p59 S 2017

ENCYCLOPEDIA CINCINNATI bw cartoon color *Cincinnati Magazine* v51 no1 p42 O 2017

Glory Bound *Cincinnati Magazine* v50 no6 p160 Mr 2017

Heavenly Host *Cincinnati Magazine* v50 no7 p168 Ap 2017

HOT SEATS *Indianapolis Monthly* p34 F 2017

IN THE ASHES *Cincinnati Magazine* v50 no5 p70 F 2017

Look Sharp *Cincinnati Magazine* v50 no4 p160 Ja 2017

Nanny State *Cincinnati Magazine* v50 no10 p132 Jl 2017

Nobody's Home *Cincinnati Magazine* v50 no8 p128 My 2017

ON THE ROCKS *Indianapolis Monthly* v40 no5 p30 Ja 2017

Raising Canes *Cincinnati Magazine* v50 no2 p136 N 2016

Savannah and Her Stories color *Parents* v92 no11 p8 N 2017

SCENE UNSEEN *Cincinnati Magazine* v50 no3 p96 D 2016

Talon Show *Cincinnati Magazine* v50 no3 p160 D 2016

When We Were Very Young bw color *Cincinnati Magazine* v51 no1 p58 O 2017

Yes, I'm Playing Favorites bw *Parents* v92 no9 p8 S 2017

Vaccariello, Liz

"Call Back Anytime" *Reader's Digest* v188 no1126 p34 D 2016/Ja 2017

Fatima's Freedom *Reader's Digest* v188 no1124 p32 O 2016

guess my power move *Parents* v92 no3 p6 Mr 2017

How "Claire's Day" Began *Reader's Digest* v188 no1125 p35 N 2016

it's twins! color *Parents* v92 no4 p8 Ap 2017

the kind of mom i am *Parents* v92 no2 p10 F 2017

my write space *Parents* v92 no7 p10 Jl 2017

On the Trail Of a Fairy Queen *Reader's Digest* v189 no1127 p32 F 2017

stories on sanibel bw *Parents* v92 no8 p8 Ag 2017

that time i won parenting *Parents* v92 no5 p6 My 2017

Vaccarino, Flora M.

Intersection of diverse neuronal genomes and neuropsychiatric disease: The Brain Somatic Mosaicism Network color *Science* v356 no6336 p395 Ap 28 2017

Vaccination

See also
Vaccine refusal

ask the experts K. Rowse and M. H. Bell color *Dressage Today* v23 no6 p64 F 2017

BOOSTER CLUB L. Krieger color *O, The Oprah Magazine* p78 Ag 2017

The Dangerous Delusion about Vaccines and Autism J. RANDI *Skeptical Inquirer* v41 no2 p29 Mr/Ap 2017

A Farmer's Best Friend B. Hewitt and M. FLEMING color *Yankee* p104 Mr 2017

Improving vaccine trials in infectious disease emergencies M. Lipsitch and N. Eyal graph *Science* v357 no6347 p153 Jl 14 2017

TO VACCINATE OR NOT? A. Constantinides color *Amazing Wellness* p36 Fall 2017

Vaccinating Your Dressage Horse K. Brittle color *Dressage Today* v23 no7 p58 Mr 2017

THE VACCINE WARS [Cover story] M. Wadman and J. You color *Science* v356 no6336 p364 Ap 28 2017

Why Vaccines Matter C. Gorney color graph *National Geographic*

v232 no5 p114 N 2017

Vaccination of animals

ADDITIONAL APPROVAL FOR LEPTOSPIROSIS VACCINE
C. Barakat and M. McCluskey *Equus* no471 p12 D 2016

CREATURE COMFORTS E. BATTAGLIA color *Martha Stewart Living* no271 p48 Ja/F 2017

Horse Owner's Spring Notebook J. Jahiel, H. Melocco et al color *Trail Rider* v29 no4 p38 My 2017

Vaccination of children

My Sister Won't Vaccinate Her Son. Can I Help Him? K. A. Appiah *New York Times Magazine* p18 Ja 1 2017

Vaccination—United States

To Increase Vaccination Rates, Share Information on Disease Outbreaks A. B. Jena and D. Khullar *Harvard Business Review Digital Articles* p2 F 22 2017

Winning the Vaccine War M. NISBET *Skeptical Inquirer* v40 no6 p27 N/D 2016

Vaccine effectiveness

Atomic structure of the human cytomegalovirus capsid with its securing tegument layer of pp150 X. Yu, J. Jih et al color *Science* v356 no6345 p1350 Je 30 2017

Vaccine Safety *Congressional Digest* v96 no5 p30 My 2017

Vaccine manufacturing—Economic aspects

The Flu Shot's Chicken-And-Egg Problem B. Einhorn color *Bloomberg Businessweek* no4493 p43 O 3 2016

Vaccine refusal

Can I Spread The Word About an Unvaccinated Child? K. A. Appiah *New York Times Magazine* p18 O 1 2017

Vaccine testing

Cholera vaccine faces major test in Yemen K. Kupferschmidt color *Science* v356 no6345 p1316 Je 30 2017

Vaccines

A Cure for Diabetes? M. Munson color *O, The Oprah Magazine* p104 N 2017

Drones to the Rescue B. Y. Lee *MIT Technology Review* v120 no4 p12 Jl/Ag 2017

A half-billion-dollar bid to head off emerging diseases J. Cohen color *Science* v355 no6322 p237 Ja 20 2017

Vaccines, Autism, and the Promotion of Irrelevant Research: A Science-Pseudoscience Analysis C. A. FOSTER and S. M. ORTIZ *Skeptical Inquirer* v41 no3 p44 My/Je 2017

VACCINES ON TRIAL M. Wadman color *Science* v356 no6336 p370 Ap 28 2017

THE VACCINE WARS [Cover story] M. Wadman and J. You color *Science* v356 no6336 p364 Ap 28 2017

Why Debunking Myths About Vaccines Hasn't Convinced Dubious Parents C. Graves *Harvard Business Review Digital Articles* p2 F 20 2015

Why is the flu vaccine so mediocre? J. Cohen color graph *Science* v357 no6357 p1222 S 22 2017

Vaccines—Biotechnology

The Flu Shot's Chicken-And-Egg Problem B. Einhorn color *Bloomberg Businessweek* no4493 p43 O 3 2016

Vaccines—Physiological effect

No More Flu Shot Excuses! J. SINRICH color *Reader's Digest* v190 no1135 p46 N 2017

Vaccines—Social aspects

Why Vaccines Matter C. Gorney color graph *National Geographic* v232 no5 p114 N 2017

Vaccinium vitis-idaea

FROM Forest TO Table V. Walsh and S. McCallum color *Canadian Wildlife* v22 no5 p30 N/D 2016

Vacha, John

THE CIVIL WARRIOR bw *MHQ: Quarterly Journal of Military History* v30 no1 p74 Aut 2017

VACHANI, NILITA

Visions of Development: Films Division of India and the Imagination of Progress, 1948-1975 *Film Quarterly* v70 no4 p127 Summ 2017

Vacheron Constantin SA

Fresh FACES color *Esquire* p86 BigBlackBook

Vacuum

HOW IT WORKS NASA's Venus Machine J. PAPPALARDO color *Popular Mechanics* p72 F 2017

Vacuum cleaner design & construction

FIGHTING HIS WAY OUT OF A PAPER BAG D. Eng color *For-*

tune v176 no4 p40 S 15 2017

Vacuum cleaners

See also
Roomba vacuum cleaner

ASK CAROLYN C. FORTÉ color *Good Housekeeping* v264 no3 p53 Mr 2017

Vacuum cleaners—Evaluation

SAFE ECO STARS color *Good Housekeeping* v264 no4 p94 Ap 2017

Vacuum ultraviolet spectroscopy

Unique free electron laser laboratory opens in China D. Normile color *Science* v355 no6322 p235 Ja 20 2017

Vadakkepuliyambatta, S.

Massive blow-out craters formed by hydrate-controlled methane expulsion from the Arctic seafloor graph map *Science* v356 no6341 p948 Je 1 2017

VADUKUL, ALEX

THE EVERYTHING GUIDE TO: Catching Your Lunch img *New York* v50 no13 p58 Je 26 2017

Vaghi, Peter J.

Inside the Cenacle T. J. Scirghi *America* v216 no12 p50 My 29 2017

Vagina

See also
Vaginal discharge

YOUR VAGINA WILL SEE YOU NOW W. L. Wilson color *Essence* v48 no5 p109 S 2017

Vaginal discharge

HOW TO Decode Your Discharge T. REECE color *Parents* v92 no11 p117 N 2017

Vaginal diseases

4 Times Your Vagina Needs to See a Doctor M. Masters color *Health* v30 no10 p80 D 2016

Vaginal diseases—Diagnosis

Our Doc Will See You Now R. Rajapaksa color *Health* v31 no6 p71 Jl 2017

VAGLE, SVEIN

Envisioning the Future of Aquatic Animal Tracking: Technology, Science, and Application *BioScience* v67 no10 p884 O 2017

Vaglica, Sal

CORDLESS YARD GEAR color *Men's Health* v32 no3 p26 Ap 2017

Craft a New Coffee Rig color *Men's Health* v32 no2 p34 Mr 2017

Vagts, Summer

What My Horse Wears on His Feet cartoon *Horse & Rider* v56 no5 p80 My 2017

Vahedi, Golnaz

Epigenetic stability of exhausted T cells limits durability of reinvigoration by PD-1 blockade bibl graph *Science* v354 no6316 p1160 D 2 2016

Vahedifard, Farshid

Lessons from the Oroville dam bibl *Science* v355 no6330 p1139 Mr 17 2017

Vaid, Champa Rani

A Life in the Family K. CLINTON color *Progressive* v81 no7 p67 O/N 2017

VAIDHYANATHAN, SIVA

The Silicon President color *Nation* v304 no1 p74 Ja 2 2017 The Obama Years

VAIDYA, ANJALI

NATIVE or INVASIVE: What it means to adapt in a postcolonial world color *Orion Magazine* v36 no2 p52 Mr/Ap 2017

Vail Resorts Inc.

WHISTLER HITS A PEAK N. O. Pearson color *Bloomberg Businessweek* no4541 p62 O 9 2017

Vail Resorts Inc.—Finance

Peak Performance D. FISHER color graph *Forbes* v198 no8 p44 D 20 2016

VAILL, AMANDA

'Just What You Are to Me' *New York Times Book Review* p11 O 16 2016

Vaillancourt, William

The Great Destroyer: Donald Trump's Contempt for Aesthetics color *Progressive* v81 no6 p24 Ag/S 2017

Vain, Madison

10 ARTISTS WHO WILL RULE 2017 color *Entertainment Week-*

efit-cost methodology that is used to calculate marginal costs of environmental regulations should not be used for long-lasting greenhouse gases *Issues in Science & Technology* v33 no4 p43 Summ 2017

Vaitiekėnas, S.
Majorana bound state in a coupled quantum-dot hybrid-nanowire system bibl graph *Science* v354 no6319 p1557 D 23 2016

Vakakis, A. F.
Breaking Lorentz reciprocity to overcome the time-bandwidth limit in physics and engineering bw diag graph *Science* v356 no6344 p1260 Je 23 2017

Vakhrusheva, Olga A.
Negative selection in humans and fruit flies involves synergistic epistasis chart graph *Science* v356 no6337 p539 My 5 2017

Vakil, Sanam
Iran's Next Supreme Leader color *Foreign Affairs* v96 no3 p76 My/Je 2017

Vakis, Renos
Left Behind: Chronic Poverty in Latin America and the Caribbean R. Feinberg *Foreign Affairs* v96 no3 p167 My/Je 2017

VAKOCH, DOUGLAS
HOW TO MAKE ANYTHING [Cover story] color diag *Popular Mechanics* p56 S 2017

Valaitham, Nakashen
AT THE WATERHOLE *Arabian Horse World* v56 no12 p244 S 2016
Greener Pastures *Arabian Horse World* v57 no3 p285 D 2016
Greener Pastures *Arabian Horse World* v57 no10 p107 Jl 2017
GREENER PASTURES: MAGIC DREAM CAHR *Arabian Horse World* v57 no12 p160 S 2017

Valances (Windows)
A DARLING SITTING ROOM K. Istomin and H. BROWN color *House Beautiful* v159 no1 p38 F 2017

Valantine, Hannah A.
Science Has a Gender Problem color *Scientific American* v315 no6 p12 D 2016

Valberg, Michelle
big picture color *Canadian Geographic* v136 no6 p10 D 2016

Valberg, Stephanie
Deciphering Shivers color *Practical Horseman* v44 no12 p69 D 2016

Valby, Karen
Felicity Goes Rogue color *Glamour* v115 no1 p88 Ja 2017

Valcour, Monique
A 10-Minute Meditation to Help You Solve Conflicts at Work *Harvard Business Review Digital Articles* p2 Ap 27 2015
4 Ways to Become a Better Learner *Harvard Business Review Digital Articles* p2 D 31 2015
8 Ways to Get a Difficult Conversation Back on Track *Harvard Business Review Digital Articles* p2 My 22 2017
Beating Burnout il img *Harvard Business Review* v94 no11 p98 N 2016
How to Give Tough Feedback That Helps People Grow *Harvard Business Review Digital Articles* p2 Ag 11 2015
How to Know Whether You're Giving Your Team Needless Work *Harvard Business Review Digital Articles* p2 Ag 26 2016
The Kind of Homework That Helps Coaching Stick *Harvard Business Review Digital Articles* p2 Mr 3 2015
Leaving a Stable Job to Create Your Dream Career *Harvard Business Review Digital Articles* p2 Ja 26 2016
Navigating Tradeoffs in a Dual-Career Marriage *Harvard Business Review Digital Articles* p2 Ap 14 2015
People Won't Grow If You Think They Can't Change *Harvard Business Review Digital Articles* p2 Ap 21 2016
A Simple Yet Powerful Way to Handle a Stress Episode *Harvard Business Review Digital Articles* p2 Ag 27 2015
Steps to Take When You're Starting to Feel Burned Out *Harvard Business Review Digital Articles* p2 Je 20 2016
What We Can Learn About Resilience from Female Leaders of the UN *Harvard Business Review Digital Articles* p2 S 28 2017

Valdés, Chucho, 1941-
Arturo O'Farrill & Chucho Valdés: SONGS FOR OUR FATHERS T. Panken color *Downbeat* v84 no10 p40 O 2017

Valdes, Marcela
The Book of Disquiet color *Publishers Weekly* v264 no27 p51 Jl 3 2017

Florida *New York Times Magazine* p44 N 20 2016

Valdes Galicia, J. F.
Observation of a large-scale anisotropy in the arrival directions of cosmic rays above 8×1018 eV *Science* v357 no6357 p1266 S 22 2017

Valdesolo, Fiorella
BODY AND SOUL... SKIN LIKE THIS bw color *Women's Health* v13 no10 p126 D 2016
THE HEALING POWER OF LIPSTICK color *Women's Health* v14 no3 p(Sp)6 Ap 2017
home & help img *New York* p96 Mr 6 2017
"I'm complicated, but my beauty routine is simple" color *Glamour* v115 no9 p94 S 2017
Is "Sensitive Skin" B.S.? color *Glamour* v115 no9 p86 S 2017
"My Mom Taught Me Less Is More" color *Glamour* v115 no5 p69 My 2017
Perfect Pare color *Vogue* v207 no9 p450 S 2017
Secrets of the Foundation Free color *Glamour* v115 no6 p66 Je 2017
The Skin We're In color *Glamour* v115 no11 p95 N 2017
Tighten Up color *Vogue* v207 no4 p172 Ap 2017
The Ultimate Beauty How-tos... color *Glamour* v115 no4 p204 Ap 2017
The World According to Huda color *Glamour* v115 no11 p82 N 2017

Valdes-Perez, Raul
Smart Benchmarking Starts with Knowing Whom to Compare Yourself To *Harvard Business Review Digital Articles* p2 O 30 2015

Valdez, Dana
KAY-TRANADA color *Surfing Magazine* v53 no1 p30 Ja 2017

Valdez, Javier
Milestones *Time* v189 no20 p11 My 29 2017

VALDIVIA, WALTER D.
Are Moonshots Giant Leaps of Faith? *Issues in Science & Technology* v33 no3 p51 Spr 2017

Valdivieso, Maria
Why Salespeople Need to Develop "Machine Intelligence" *Harvard Business Review Digital Articles* p2 Je 10 2016

Vale, Malcolm
Renaissance Hal J. M. BANNER JR. cartoon *Weekly Standard* v22 no13 p34 D 5 2016

Vale, Mariana M.
A global map of roadless areas and their conservation status bibl color graph map *Science* v354 no6318 p1423 D 16 2016

Vale, Ronald
Not just Salk color *Science* v357 no6356 p1105 S 15 2017
T cell costimulatory receptor CD28 is a primary target for PD-1–mediated inhibition color diag graph *Science* v355 no6332 p1428 Mr 31 2017

Valeant Pharmaceuticals International Inc.
ANATOMY OF A VERY BAD DEAL J. Wieczner *Fortune* v175 no5 p12 Ap 1 2017
A Felled Sequoia Works to Recover N. S. HUANG chart *Kiplinger's Personal Finance* v70 no12 p57 D 2016

Valek, P.
Jupiter's magnetosphere and aurorae observed by the Juno spacecraft during its first polar orbits diag graph *Science* v356 no6340 p826 My 26 2017

Valencia, Jordana
How Founders Can Recognize and Combat Depression *Harvard Business Review Digital Articles* p2 F 17 2017

Valencia, Renato
Positive biodiversity-productivity relationship predominant in global forests bibl chart graph map *Science* v354 no6309 paaf8957-1 O 14 2016

Valent, Barbara
Durable resistance to rice blast bibl color *Science* v355 no6328 p906 Mr 3 2017
Evolution of the wheat blast fungus through functional losses in a host specificity determinant diag map *Science* v357 no6346 p80 Jl 7 2017

VALENT, JON
The 2016 Election as a 'Sputnik' Moment for Character Education *Education Digest* v82 no7 p57 Mr 2017

Valente, Catherynne M.

The Refrigerator Monologues G. BOND color *Publishers Weekly* v264 no16 p50 Ap 17 2017

Valente, Judith

Budget Fight Bruises the Needy *America* v215 no10 p12 O 10 2016

Street matriculation: Chicago student finds a way out of homelessness color *America* v216 no5 p15 Mr 6 2017

True Stories *America* v215 no18 p11 D 5 2016

When sexual assault goes viral *America* v216 no10 p16 My 1 2017

Valenti, Jessica

Crowdsource This color *Glamour* v115 no9 p124 S 2017

Valentin, de Boulogne, 1591-1632

BEFORE REALISM R. Neer color *Art in America* v105 no1 p58 Ja 2017

An old master, newly arrived J. Gardner color *Magazine Antiques* v183 no6 p116 N/D 2016

Valentine, Denzel

RAGING BULL J. WUEBBEN chart color *Muscle & Performance* v9 no10 p38 O 2017

Valentine, Melissa

Improving On-the-Fly Teamwork in Health Care *Harvard Business Review Digital Articles* p2 N 30 2016

Valentinelli, Monica

Upside Down: Inverted Tropes in Storytelling *Publishers Weekly* v263 no42 p55 O 17 2016

Valentines

Laugh Lines MY FUNNY VALENTINE *Reader's Digest* v189 no1127 p103 F 2017

Valentine's Day

CRIMSON CUTOUTS color *Better Homes & Gardens* v95 no2 p74 F 2016

February! T. PAYNE and L. CROSS cartoon color *Ebony* v72 no4 p24 F 2017

Martha's Winter chart color *Martha Stewart Living* no271 p2 Ja/F 2017

STROKES OF GENIUS E. N. GAGE color *Martha Stewart Living* no271 p19 Ja/F 2017

Valentini, Fabio Benedetti

Paris and Frankfurt Vie For Brexit's Spoils *Bloomberg Businessweek* no4530 p30 Jl 17 2017

VALENTINI, KRISTI

THE GIRLFRIEND GETAWAY GUIDE color *Redbook* p118 O 2017

THE NO-FLY, ALL-FUN VACATION [Cover story] color diag *Redbook* p97 Jl/Ag 2017

This country is incredible [Cover story] color *Redbook* p105 Mr 2017

Valentino, 1932-

EN PLEIN AIR D. GILMORE color *Vanity Fair* v59 no9 p145 S 2017

Valentino, Claudia

The Architecture of Belief color *Archaeology* v69 no6 p4 N/D 2016

HUMAN WHYS AND WHEREFORES color *Archaeology* v70 no2 p4 Mr/Ap 2017

NO LONGER LOST color *Archaeology* v70 no5 p4 S/O 2017

NO PLACE LIKE HOME color *Archaeology* v70 no4 p4 Je-Ag 2017

SPEAKING VOLUMES *Archaeology* v70 no3 p4 My/Je 2017

Valenza, Joyce Kasman

Building a Digital Toolbox color *Publishers Weekly* v264 no34 p46 Ag 21 2017

POWERFUL PARTNERSHIPS: Literacy, your librarian, and you *Literacy Today (2411-7862)* v35 no1 p14 Jl/Ag 2017

Valenzuela, Luisa, 1938-

IT HAPPENS HERE *Lapham's Quarterly* v10 no3 p99 Summ 2017

Valérian & the City of a Thousand Planets (Film)

Face of Change [Cover story] A. Aboah bw color *Glamour* no8 p124 Ag 2017

Space Oddity A. Bhattacharji color *Bloomberg Businessweek* no4531 p70 Jl 24 2017

Things to Do! R. Mosely color *Seventeen* v76 no4 p8 Jl/Ag 2017

VALERIAN AND THE CITY OF A THOUSAND PLANETS J. McGovern color *Entertainment Weekly* no1463/1464 p72 Ap/My 2017

Valerian's Half-Crazed Space Race S. Zacharek color *Time* v190 no5 p59 Jl 31 2017

Valerian (Film)

Rihanna's Out-of-This-World Role J. McGovern color *Entertainment Weekly* no1440 p17 N 18 2016

Valerio, Alejandro

When Should Multinationals Move Back into Venezuela? *Harvard Business Review Digital Articles* p2 S 1 2017

Valerio, Anna Marie

The Men Who Mentor Women *Harvard Business Review Digital Articles* p2 D 7 2016

Valerio, Wendy H.

Early childhood arts education in the United States: A special issue of Arts Education Policy Review bibl *Arts Education Policy Review* v118 no3 p133 2017

Valine

Could a Special Diet Replace Chemotherapy? K. Weintraub color *Scientific American* v316 no1 p14 Ja 2017

Depleting dietary valine permits nonmyeloablative mouse hematopoietic stem cell transplantation Yuki Taya, Yasunori Ota et al bibl graph *Science* v354 no6316 p1152 D 2 2016

Valino, I.

Observation of a large-scale anisotropy in the arrival directions of cosmic rays above 8×1018 eV *Science* v357 no6357 p1266 S 22 2017

Valiunas, Algis

Big Plans *Claremont Review of Books* v17 no3 p71 Summ 2017

Building Against Doomsday *Claremont Review of Books* v17 no3 p73 Summ 2017

EDISONIAN DEMOCRACY *Claremont Review of Books* v17 no1 p89 Wint 2016/2017

Hearth and Home *Claremont Review of Books* v17 no3 p72 Summ 2017

Kraus Revisited bw color *Weekly Standard* v22 no24 p41 F 27 2017

Levelling Opponents *Claremont Review of Books* v17 no3 p74 Summ 2017

MASTER BUILDER *Claremont Review of Books* v17 no3 p71 Summ 2017

Modernity and Genius *Claremont Review of Books* v17 no3 p73 Summ 2017

Other Rivals *Claremont Review of Books* v17 no3 p76 Summ 2017

Reading her novels on the bicentennial of her death color *Weekly Standard* v22 no42 p28 Jl 17 2017

VOICE OF CIVILIZATION *Claremont Review of Books* v16 no4 p65 Fall 2016

Waugh's Gift bw *Weekly Standard* v22 no16 p34 D 26 2016

Valladares, Fernando

Positive biodiversity-productivity relationship predominant in global forests bibl chart graph map *Science* v354 no6309 paaf8957-1 O 14 2016

Valladares, Michelle Renée

Learning from schools that close opportunity gaps *Phi Delta Kappan* v99 no1 p8 S 2017

Vallance, Brandy

Within the Veil *Publishers Weekly* v264 no11 p66 Mr 13 2017

VALLE, SABRINA

DEPT. OF SHELL COMPANIES CLANDESTINE ACCOUNTS, & BRIBERY cartoon color *Bloomberg Businessweek* no4526 p46 Je 12 2017

Vallejo (Calif.)

Splish Splash color *Reader's Digest* v189 no1131 p16 Je 2017

Vallejo, Fred

Former Kickboxing Champ Lou Neglia Is Proof of the Power of Martial Arts color *Black Belt* v55 no3 p22 Ap/My 2017

Vallejos, Catalina A.

Aging increases cell-to-cell transcriptional variability upon immune stimulation color diag graph *Science* v355 no6332 p1433 Mr 31 2017

Valles, Sean A.

Updating the Two Cultures: How Structures Can Promote Interdisciplinary Cultures *Change* v48 no6 p28 N/D 2016

Valletta, Amber

The many shades of AMBER L. Sandell color *InStyle* p88 Home & Design 2016

THE ROAD HOME color *Vogue* v207 no9 p650 S 2017

Valletti, Tommaso M.
Net Neutrality Rules Will Make Winners and Losers Out of Businesses *Harvard Business Review Digital Articles* p2 Je 27 2016

Valley County (Idaho)
Ditch Rider F. A. LOOMIS *Idaho Magazine* v16 no1 p28 O 2016

Valley Irrigation Co.
SMART PIVOT CONTROLS T. Gaines *Successful Farming* v115 no4 p49 Mr 2017

Valleys
A BRACE IN THE SUN P. BOURJAILY color *Field & Stream* v121 no8 p16 F/Mr 2017
Valley Girl G. DOYLE MELTON color *O, The Oprah Magazine* p36 Je 2017

Valleys—Arizona
MIDDLEMARCH ROAD N. AUSTIN *Arizona Highways* v93 no11 p52 N 2017

Vallgren, Carl-Johan
The Tunnel: A Danny Katz Thriller *Publishers Weekly* v264 no15 p53 Ap 10 2017

Vallier, R. D.
Darkshine *Publishers Weekly* v264 no4 p62 Ja 23 2017

Vallieres, Robert
Birds for the Battle-worn P. SAHA color *Audubon* v119 no3 p26 Fall 2017

Valls, Manuel, 1962-
Manuel Valls B. Lightner *Current Biography* v77 no11 p90 N 2016

Valor (TV program)
Primetime Combat T. Appelo color *AARP: The Magazine* v30 no6A p15 O/N 2017
Valor N. Abrams, C. Holub et al color *Entertainment Weekly* no1482/1483 p52 S 22 2017

Valore, L.
Observation of a large-scale anisotropy in the arrival directions of cosmic rays above 8×1018 eV *Science* v357 no6357 p1266 S 22 2017

Valter, Sarah
THE PD NEXT DOOR: The impact of observation in our own schools *Literacy Today (2411-7862)* v35 no2 p18 S/O 2017

Valters, Christine
Lauds C. V. Paintner *U.S. Catholic* v82 no10 p51 O 2017

Valtin, Tom
Confluence *Sierra* v101 no4 p52 Jl/Ag 2016

Valtis, Yannis K.
An Online Medical Database Is Reducing Diagnostic Errors *Harvard Business Review Digital Articles* p2 O 27 2015

Valuation
See also
  Corporations—Valuation
The Elements of Value: Interaction C. O'Connor, R. J. Dreyfus et al *Harvard Business Review* v94 no11 p18 N 2016
Got data? Now what? L. Bedord *Successful Farming* v114 no12 p10 Mid-N 2016

Valuation of corporations
Stock Investors Nervously Do the Math K. Burton, K. Porzecanski et al color *Bloomberg Businessweek* no4520 p41 My 1 2017

Value (Economics)
See also
  Net worth
  Value creation
The Elements of Value: Interaction C. O'Connor, R. J. Dreyfus et al *Harvard Business Review* v94 no11 p18 N 2016
Predict the Future of Your Business M. Wessel *Harvard Business Review Digital Articles* p2 Ap 13 2015

Value added (Marketing)
Where Does Ben Franklin Go Furthest? *New York Times Upfront* v149 no3 p5 O 10 2016

Value-added assessment (Education)
All sizzle and no steak A. Amrein-Beardsley and T. Geiger color graph il *Phi Delta Kappan* v99 no2 p53 O 2017

Value-added tax
The ABCs of India's GST U. Krishnan and J. Rodrigues color graph *Bloomberg Businessweek* no4496 p19 O 24 2016
One Tax To Rule Them All I. Marlow, E. Curran et al color *Bloomberg Businessweek* no4528 p28 Je 26 2017

Value-based purchasing (Medical care)

The Mayo Clinic Model for Running a Value-Improvement Program D. A. Haas, R. A. Helmers et al *Harvard Business Review Digital Articles* p2 O 22 2015
Turning Value-Based Health Care into a Real Business Model L. S. Kaiser and T. H. Lee *Harvard Business Review Digital Articles* p2 O 8 2015
U.S. Health Care Reform Can't Wait for Quality Measures to Be Perfect B. J. Marcotte, A. G. Fildes et al *Harvard Business Review Digital Articles* p2 O 4 2017

Value chains
It's OK to Move Down (Yes, Down) the Value Chain B. Staats and D. M. Upton *Harvard Business Review Digital Articles* p2 Je 2 2015
What Is a Business Model? A. Ovans *Harvard Business Review Digital Articles* p2 Ja 23 2015

Value creation
The 7 Laws of Regenerative Enterprises K. C. Korn and B. J. Pine II *Harvard Business Review Digital Articles* p2 N 17 2014
Finally, Proof That Managing for the Long Term Pays Off D. Barton, J. Manyika et al color graph *Harvard Business Review Digital Articles* p2 F 7 2017
A Testable Idea Is Better than a Good Idea M. Schrage *Harvard Business Review Digital Articles* p2 D 24 2014

Value proposition
Any Value Proposition Hinges on the Answer to One Question F. V. Cespedes *Harvard Business Review Digital Articles* p2 Ja 13 2015
THE VALUE PROPOSITION L. Bedord *Successful Farming* v114 no12 p6 Mid-N 2016
Why the Fail-Fast Approach Isn't Right for Breakthrough Ventures H. Kressel and N. Winarsky *Harvard Business Review Digital Articles* p2 N 6 2015

Values (Ethics)
See also
  Dignity
  Work values
4 Ways CEOs Can Conquer Short-Termism K. Isaacs, D. Langstaff et al *Harvard Business Review Digital Articles* p2 F 24 2017
Counterprotesters greet "free speech rally" H. Gass and S. Hinckley *Christian Century* v134 no19 p13 S 13 2017
Leadership J. P. Starr *Phi Delta Kappan* v98 no3 p72 N 2016

Values (Ethics)—History
ON THE SPOT CAROLINE DODDS PENNOCK: We ask leading historians 20 questions on why their research matters, one book everyone should read and their views on the Tudors ... C. D. Pennock *History Today* v67 no7 p112 Jl 2017

Values (Ethics)—Social aspects
THE EDITORIAL *Maclean's* v129 no46 p5 N 21 2016

Valve Corp.
Gabe Newell's Reddit Q&A: on Half-Life 3, Steam support, and more H. DINGMAN color *PCWorld* v35 no2 p25 F 2017

Valve maintenance & repair
Seacocks D. Everitt color *Sail* v48 no10 p84 O 2017

Valverde, F. C.
Persistent effects of pre-Columbian plant domestication on Amazonian forest composition bibl chart graph map *Science* v355 no6328 p925 Mr 3 2017

Valverde, Spencer
Speak up color *U.S. Catholic* v82 no4 p5 Ap 2017

Valves
Can Your Refrigerator Help? B. Pike color *Power & Motoryacht* v33 no3 p120 Mr 2017
No Regrets K. Ward *Earth Island Journal* v32 no2 p56 Summ 2017
Scott A. Sawyer From Pacifica, California, Asks... M. Davis color *Hot Rod* v70 no2 p96 F 2017

Valves—Maintenance & repair
VALVE STEM VITALS J. KOPYCINSKI color *Dirt Sports + Off-Road* v51 no4 p64 Ap 2017

Vampa, Giulio
Tailored semiconductors for high-harmonic optoelectronics graph *Science* v357 no6348 p303 Jl 21 2017

Vampire Diaries, The (TV program)
THERE WILL BE TEARS S. Highfill color *Entertainment Weekly* no1454/1455 p54 F 24 2017

The Vampire Diaries I. Rudolph *TV Guide* v65 no11 p38 Mr 6 2017

Van der Graaf Generator (Performer)
Van der Graaf Generator Disturbs the Sonic Wavelength (But in a Good Way) M. METTLER bw color *Sound & Vision* v82 no4 p26 My 2017

Van der Waals forces
Direction-specific van der Waals attraction between rutile $TiO2$ nanocrystals X. Zhang, Y. He et al diag *Science* v356 no6336 p434 Ap 28 2017
Polaritons in van der Waals materials D. N. Basov, M. M. Fogler et al bibl chart color diag graph *Science* v354 no6309 paag1992-1 O 14 2016

Van Halen (Performer)
Sammy Hagar A. GREENE color *Rolling Stone* no1290 p58 Je 29 2017

van Aar, G.
Observation of a large-scale anisotropy in the arrival directions of cosmic rays above 8×1018 eV *Science* v357 no6357 p1266 S 22 2017

Vanadium dioxide
Anomalously low electronic thermal conductivity in metallic vanadium dioxide K. Hippalgaonkar, K. Wang et al bibl graph *Science* v355 no6323 p371 Ja 27 2017

Van Aelst, Peter
The Trump Conundrum color graph *Columbia Journalism Review* v56 no2 p42 Fall 2017

Van Alstyne, Marshall W.
4 Mistakes That Kill Crowdsourcing Efforts *Harvard Business Review Digital Articles* p2 Jl 21 2017
6 Reasons Platforms Fail *Harvard Business Review Digital Articles* p2 Mr 31 2016
The Best Platforms Are More than Matchmakers *Harvard Business Review Digital Articles* p2 Ag 2 2016

van Amerongen, Herbert
The complex that conquered the land diag *Science* v357 no6353 p752 Ag 25 2017

van Andel, T. R.
Persistent effects of pre-Columbian plant domestication on Amazonian forest composition bibl chart graph map *Science* v355 no6328 p925 Mr 3 2017

VanArendonk, Kathryn
I Can't Believe It's Not TV! img *New York* v50 no7 p80 Ap 3 2017

Vanasco, Jeannie
The Glass Eye I. Biedenharn color *Entertainment Weekly* no1486 p62 O 13 2017

Van Bavel, Jay
The Problem with Rewarding Individual Performers *Harvard Business Review Digital Articles* p2 D 27 2016

Van Berkel, Ben
Rules of the Game A. Vidler *Architectural Record* v205 no1 p41 Ja 2017

van Bever, Derek
AFRICA'S NEW GENERATION OF INNOVATORS color il img *Harvard Business Review* v95 no1 p128 Ja/F 2017
Uber Needs Our Permission to Grow *Harvard Business Review Digital Articles* p2 F 9 2015

Van Biema, David
Museum exhibit reveals many sides of Jerusalem in Middle Ages and today color *Christian Century* v133 no22 p17 O 26 2016

Van Biesen, Koen, 1964-
Roger Is Going Fishing color *Publishers Weekly* v264 no34 p111 Ag 21 2017

Van Biljon, Zak
Seeing Red A. CRAWFORD *Smithsonian* v47 no7 p14 N 2016

van Bodegom, P.
Observation of a large-scale anisotropy in the arrival directions of cosmic rays above 8×1018 eV *Science* v357 no6357 p1266 S 22 2017

Van Boeckel, Thomas P.
Reducing antimicrobial use in food animals color graph *Science* v357 no6358 p1350 S 29 2017

van Bokhoven, Jeroen A.
Selective anaerobic oxidation of methane enables direct synthesis of methanol diag graph *Science* v356 no6337 p523 My 5 2017

van BREUGEL, PAULO

An Ecoregion-Based Approach to Protecting Half the Terrestrial Realm *BioScience* v67 no6 p534 Je 2017

VAN BUREN, DAVINA
NEBRASKA MADE color *Nebraska Life* v20 no6 p54 N/D 2016

VAN BUSEN, CHRISTINE
#SQUAD GOALS *Atlanta* v56 no9 p118 Ja 2017

Vance, Ashlee
The $200 All-Seeing Line Judge color *Bloomberg Businessweek* no4513 p37 Mr 6 2017
AI Speed-Reading For the Masses cartoon *Bloomberg Businessweek* no4512 p33 F 20 2017
CELTIC TIGERS color *Bloomberg Businessweek* no4533 p38 Ag 7 2017
FURY ROAD color *Bloomberg Businessweek* no4515 p54 Mr 20 2017
Google's Other Founder Wants to Fly, Too color *Bloomberg Businessweek* no4521 p32 My 8 2017
In Ads We Trust color *Bloomberg Businessweek* no4521 p6 My 8 2017
Life, Or Something Like It color *Bloomberg Businessweek* no4537 p42 S 11 2017
SATELLITE PICS FOR CHEAP!! bw *Bloomberg Businessweek* no4522 p37 My 15 2017
THEY CAME FOR OUTER SPACE color graph map *Bloomberg Businessweek* no4529 p40 Jl 3 2017

Vance, Brian
GARAGE chart color diag *Motor Trend* v69 no11 p106 N 2017
GARRAGE cartoon chart color *Motor Trend* v69 no3 p86 Mr 2017

Vance, Erik
LOOK INTO MY EYES: THE FANTASTICAL HISTORY, MYSTERIOUS HEALING POWER, AND EMERGENT NEUROSCIENCE OF HYPNOSIS *Saturday Evening Post* v289 no5 p48 S/O 2017
Mind Over Matter color diag *National Geographic* v230 no6 p30 D 2016
Requiem for the Vaquita color map *Scientific American* v317 no2 p36 Ag 2017
Stewards of the Sea color map *National Geographic* v232 no3 p56 S 2017

Vance, J. D.
Albion's Ashes K. D. WILLIAMSON *Commentary* v142 no3 p42 O 2016
The Book of Jobs *Commentary* v143 no6 p40 Je 2017
Hillbilly Elegy: A Memoir of a Family and Culture in Crisis W. Russell Mead *Foreign Affairs* v95 no6 p179 N/D 2016
Hillbilly Energy R. DREHER *American Conservative* v16 no1 p42 Ja/F 2017
Now What? color *Time* v188 no21 p42 N 21 2016
Q: What is the most interesting family in history? color *Atlantic* v318 no5 p96 D 2016

Vance, J. D.—Interviews
J.D. Vance T. Berenson color *Time* v188 no20 p60 N 14 2016
Rust Belt Prophet P. Robinson *Hoover Digest: Research & Opinion on Public Policy* no1 p154 Wint 2017

Vance, Jim, 1942-2017
JIM VANCE: The newsman's life traced the history of our region-and we loved him for it. But in today's TV world, there can't be another like him A. Beaujon *Washingtonian Magazine* v52 no12 p48 S 2017

Vance, Russell E.
Intracellular innate immune surveillance devices in plants and animals chart color diag graph *Science* v354 no6316 paaf6395-1 D 2 2016

Vanchieri, Cori
Farm tale warns against antibiotics color *Science News* v192 no5 p30 S 30 2017

Van Clief, Ron
RON VAN CLIEF THE BLACK DRAGON [Cover story] color *Black Belt* v55 no2 p10 F/Mr 2017

Van Court, Tanya
Mixing Dollars and Sense L. D. JOHNSON and S. T. BROWN color *Ebony* v72 no5 p74 Mr 2017

Vancouver (B.C.)
perspective house of the month A. WEDER *Architectural Record* v205 no4 p39 Ap 2017

Vancouver (B.C.)—Description & travel

BRITISH COLUMBIA'S EAST VANCOUVER E. Ehmsen color map *Sunset* v239 no3 p36 S 2017

SURVIVAL OF THE FINNISH IN SOINTULA D. HISLOP *Sea Magazine* v108 no12 p116 D 2016

Vancouver (B.C.)—Economic conditions

Chinese Buyers Move On From Vancouver K. Dmitrieva chart *Bloomberg Businessweek* no4504 p37 D 19 2016

Vancouver (B.C.)—Economic conditions—21st century

Hedge City Blues P. ROBERTS color graph *Mother Jones* v42 no3 p40 My/Je 2017

JUST CALL IT SILICON COAST C. Dillow color *Fortune* v176 no2 p30 Ag 1 2017

Vancouver (B.C.)—History

Rebranding Canada 150 N. MACDONALD *Maclean's* v130 no3 p14 Ap 2017

Vancouver (B.C.)—Politics & government

LOCKED IN B. SOLOMON and D. ALEXANDER bw color *Forbes* v199 no3 p76 Mr 28 2017

Vancouver (B.C.)—Social conditions—21st century

MONEY CAN'T BUY HAPPY KIDS C. GILLIS color *Maclean's* v129 no44 p21 N 7 2016

Vancouver Island (B.C.)

Women Who Ride L. Brooks-Dalton *New York Times Magazine* p25 Ja 15 2017

Vandalism

Election tensions lead to rise in anti-Semitic incidents color *America* v216 no11 p17 My 15 2017

Interfaith support rises along with attacks K. Winston, L. Markoe et al color *Christian Century* v134 no7 p12 Mr 29 2017

van Dam, Nick

There's a Proven Link Between Effective Leadership and Getting Enough Sleep *Harvard Business Review Digital Articles* p2 F 16 2016

Vandebroek, Sophie—Interviews

When Personal Tragedy Strikes, Downshifting at Work Doesn't Always Help D. McGinn *Harvard Business Review Digital Articles* p2 My 15 2015

van den Berg, A. M.

Observation of a large-scale anisotropy in the arrival directions of cosmic rays above 8 × 1018 eV *Science* v357 no6357 p1266 S 22 2017

Vandenberg, Katrina

Hell Is a Very Small Place *Orion Magazine* v35 no3 p56 My/Je 2016

van den Berg, Leonard H.

Negative selection in humans and fruit flies involves synergistic epistasis chart graph *Science* v356 no6337 p539 My 5 2017

Vandenberg Air Force Base (Calif.)

Of missile bases and drag races M. Rechtin color *Motor Trend* v69 no11 p24 N 2017

Vanden Berghe, Pieter

Lineage-dependent spatial and functional organization of the mammalian enteric nervous system color graph *Science* v356 no6339 p722 My 19 2017

van den Bosch, Frank

Searching for the Oldest Stars *Physics Today* v69 no10 p56 O 2016

Vanden Bout, Paul A.

Kwok-Yung Lo *Physics Today* v70 no8 p71 Ag 2017

VANDEN HEUVEL, KATRINA

The GOP Tax Scam *Nation* v305 no7 p4 S 25 2017

Realism on Russia *Nation* v305 no4 p4 Ag 14 2017

Trump's War Fever color *Nation* v304 no15 p4 My 8 2017

van den Pol, Anthony N.

Rapid binge-like eating and body weight gain driven by zona incerta GABA neuron activation graph *Science* v356 no6340 p853 My 26 2017

VANDE PANNE, VALERIE

Detroit's Underground Economy *In These Times* v41 no7 p8 Jl 2017

Van der Beek, James, 1977-

What Would Diplo Do? D. Holbrook *TV Guide* v65 no31 p35 Jl 24 2017

Vanderbilt, Cornelius, 1898-1974

Uber's CEO Has a Little Bit of Vanderbilt in Him J. Fox *Harvard Business Review Digital Articles* p2 N 25 2014

Vanderbilt, Tom

Attention Must Be Paid color *New Republic* v247 no11 p60 N 2016

auto no mo' us bw color diag graph *Car & Driver* v63 no5 p58 N 2017

Have You Read This? color *Bicycling* v58 no9 p38 O 2017

Vanderham, Thomas

BUZZ bw color *Bike Magazine* v23 no9 p24 D 2016

van der Heijde, Roel

How Design Thinking Turned One Hospital into a Bright and Comforting Place *Harvard Business Review Digital Articles* p2 D 2 2016

van der Heijden, G.

Persistent effects of pre-Columbian plant domestication on Amazonian forest composition bibl chart graph map *Science* v355 no6328 p925 Mr 3 2017

van der Helm, Els

There's a Proven Link Between Effective Leadership and Getting Enough Sleep *Harvard Business Review Digital Articles* p2 F 16 2016

Van der Heyden, Ludo

VW's Board Needed More Outsiders *Harvard Business Review Digital Articles* p2 N 17 2015

VANDERHOOF, ERIN

10 TILES TO PICK UP NOW color *O, The Oprah Magazine* p112 My 2017

10 TITLES TO PICK UP NOW color *O, The Oprah Magazine* p93 Ap 2017

AN EAR FOR THE MOMENT color *Nation* v304 no7 p35 Mr 6 2017

van der Hoven, Julia

Site-specific phosphorylation of tau inhibits amyloid-β toxicity in Alzheimer's mice bibl graph *Science* v354 no6314 p904 N 18 2016

Vanderkam, Laura

Points to Ponder color *Reader's Digest* v190 no1134 p35 O 2017

The Problem with Part- Time Work Is That It's Rarely Part-Time *Harvard Business Review Digital Articles* p2 My 26 2015

SEIZE THE DAY! [Cover story] color *O, The Oprah Magazine* p102 O 2017

VANDERKLIFT, MATHEW

Accelerating Tropicalization and the Transformation of Temperate Seagrass Meadows *BioScience* v66 no11 p938 N 1 2016

van der Kroeg, Mark

Activity-based protein profiling reveals off-target proteins of the FAAH inhibitor BIA 10-2474 chart color graph *Science* v356 no6342 p1084 Je 9 2017

van der LEUN, JUSTINE

Facing Her Monsters: A law intern finds unexpected connections when her firm takes on the case of a pedophile *New York Times Book Review* p25 Jl 23 2017

The Purest Bond *New York Times Book Review* p9 Ja 29 2017

Van der Lugt, Frans, 1938-2014

Still, the world is good J. Denari Duffner il *U.S. Catholic* v81 no11 p45 N 2016

VanderMeer, Jeff

Climate Changed WAI CHEE DIMOCK *New York Times Book Review* p18 My 7 2017

The Girl On Fire *New York Times Magazine* p1 Ap 30 2017

A LITTLE STRANGER L. MILLER color *New Yorker* v93 no10 p96 Ap 24 2017

Vandermey, Anne

100 BEST COMPANIES TO WORK FOR 2017 [Cover story] color diag map *Fortune* v175 no4 p79 Mr 15 2017

10-HOUR LAYOVER? LUCKY YOU color *Fortune* v174 no6 p70 N 1 2016

THE 2017 Fortune Crystal Ball color diag *Fortune* v174 no7 p11 D 1 2016

50 BEST WORKPLACES FOR DIVERSITY color *Fortune* v174 no8 p45 D 15 2016

AIRLINES' STOCK RALLY SHOWS IT'S BETTER TO BE GOOD THAN NICE diag *Fortune* v175 no7 p16 Je 1 2017

APPLE REBOOTS IN CHINA color *Fortune* v176 no5 p106 O 1 2017

As Oceans Rise, Insurers Flee color *Fortune* v176 no2 p18 Ag

The Mayor of Mogadishu: A Story of Chaos and Redemption in the Ruins of Somalia *Foreign Affairs* v96 no2 p189 Mr/Ap 2017

Morning in South Africa *Foreign Affairs* v95 no6 p193 N/D 2016

The Paradox of Traditional Chiefs in Democratic Africa *Foreign Affairs* v96 no1 p179 Ja/F 2017

Spies in the Congo: America's Atomic Mission in World War II *Foreign Affairs* v96 no1 p178 Ja/F 2017

This Present Darkness: A History of Nigerian Organized Crime *Foreign Affairs* v96 no1 p178 Ja/F 2017

Understanding Zimbabwe: From Liberation to Authoritarianism *Foreign Affairs* v96 no3 p176 My/Je 2017

Violent Nonstate Actors in Africa: Terrorists, Rebels, and Warlords *Foreign Affairs* v96 no6 p173 N/D 2017

Women and Power in Postconflict Africa *Foreign Affairs* v95 no6 p194 N/D 2016

Van de Water, Frederic Franklyn
CAST AWAY *Harper's Magazine* v333 no1999 p73 D 2016

van de Water, Jeroen A. J. M.
Seagrass ecosystems reduce exposure to bacterial pathogens of humans, fishes, and invertebrates bibl graph *Science* v355 no6326 p731 F 17 2017

Vandeweghe, CoCo
Miss America S. TIGNOR *Tennis* v53 no4 p42 Jl/Ag 2017
Ones to Watch N. PANTIC *Tennis* v53 no1 p66 Ja/F 2017

van de Wetering, Marc
Origins of lymphatic and distant metastases in human colorectal cancer diag graph *Science* v357 no6346 p55 Jl 7 2017

van de Zande, Louis
Male sex in houseflies is determined by Mdmd, a paralog of the generic splice factor gene CWC22 bw color *Science* v356 no6338 p642 My 12 2017

van Dijk, Marie
ELABELA deficiency promotes preeclampsia and cardiovascular malformations in mice color diag graph *Science* v357 no6352 p707 Ag 18 2017

Van Dissen, Russ
Complex multifault rupture during the 2016 Mw 7.8 Kaikōura earthquake, New Zealand color map *Science* v356 no6334 p154 Ap 14 2017

Van Doninck, Helene
Leading the Way Against Lead color *Canadian Wildlife* v23 no2 p12 My/Je 2017

Van Dover, Cindy Lee
CINDY LEE VAN DOVER S. CHODOSH cartoon *Popular Science* p48 Ja/F 2017
An ecosystem-based deep-ocean strategy bibl color map *Science* v355 no6324 p452 F 3 2017

Van Draanen, Wendelin, 1965-
Wild Bird *Publishers Weekly* v264 no27 p77 Jl 3 2017

Vandrei, Charles
Chuck Vandrei: DEC Researcher With An Historical View *New York State Conservationist* v72 no1 p21 Ag 2017
Clues in the Forest--Archaeology at Florence Hill State Forest *New York State Conservationist* v72 no1 p18 Ag 2017

Van Duppen, Ben
Tuning quantum nonlocal effects in graphene plasmonics bw diag *Science* v357 no6347 p187 Jl 14 2017

Van Durme, Matthias
RETINOBLASTOMA RELATED1 mediates germline entry in Arabidopsis color diag *Science* v356 no6336 p396 Ap 28 2017

Van Dusen, Caitlin
Meditation App Roundup color *Tricycle: The Buddhist Review* v26 no2 p88 Wint 2016
Meditation App Roundup color *Tricycle: The Buddhist Review* v26 no4 p92 Summ 2017
Meditation App Roundup color *Tricycle: The Buddhist Review* v27 no1 p98 Fall 2017
TAKE A CHILL color *Tricycle: The Buddhist Review* v26 no3 p90 Spr 2017

Van Dusen, Chris
Adventures in Illustrating *South Dakota Magazine* p8 S/O 2017 Supplement

VAN DUSEN, CHRISTINE
THE COMET PUB & LANES *Atlanta* v56 no7 p60 N 2016
FOODSTUFFS *Atlanta* v56 no9 p54 Ja 2017
RADICAL REMEDIES *Atlanta* v56 no9 p43 Ja 2017

The Soccer Mom's Lament *Atlanta* v56 no11 p93 Mr 2017
Soccer's gender gap *Atlanta* v56 no11 p94 Mr 2017
TOP DOCS 2017: Every year we present a roster of the best metro Atlanta doctors, as chosen by their peers. On the following pages, find 720 of the area's most trusted physicians--our biggest list ever *Atlanta* v57 no3 p65 Jl 2017
WORK OUT LIKE A PRO *Atlanta* v56 no9 p112 Ja 2017

Vandvik, Vigdis
Higher predation risk for insect prey at low latitudes and elevations graph *Science* v356 no6339 p742 My 19 2017

Van Dyken, Rachel
Fraternize *Publishers Weekly* v264 no28 p72 Jl 10 2017

Van Eaton, Alexa R.
Volcanic tremor and plume height hysteresis from Pavlof Volcano, Alaska bibl graph *Science* v355 no6320 p1 Ja 6 2017

van Eijkeren, Robert J.
Lysosomal cholesterol activates mTORC1 via an SLC38A9–Niemann-Pick C1 signaling complex bibl diag graph *Science* v355 no6331 p1306 Mr 24 2017

Van Eldere, Johan
De novo design of a biologically active amyloid bibl graph *Science* v354 no6313 paah4949-1 N 11 2016

Van Erp, Harrie
Fatty acids in arbuscular mycorrhizal fungi are synthesized by the host plant diag graph *Science* v356 no6343 p1175 Je 16 2017

Vanes, Howard
Oh, My Aching Back *USA Today Magazine* v146 no2868 p23 S 2017

van Esbroeck, Annelot C. M.
Activity-based protein profiling reveals off-target proteins of the FAAH inhibitor BIA 10-2474 chart color graph *Science* v356 no6342 p1084 Je 9 2017

Vanessa (Theatrical production)
Rediscovering a Neglected Treasure S. Williams *Opera News* v81 no5 p40 N 2016

van Essen, Marc
Research: Family Firms Are More Innovative Than Other Companies color *Harvard Business Review Digital Articles* p2 Ja 25 2017

Van Gelder, Rudy, 1924-2016
Remembering Rudy Van Gelder, Who Defined the Sound of Jazz bw *Downbeat* v83 no11 p23 N 2016

van Gelder, Sarah
Creating Communities of Change *Progressive* v81 no4 p26 Ap/My 2017

VanGilder, Suzanne
gold standard color *Yoga Journal* p114 2017 Special Issue

VANGOOL, JANINE
Who is pushing the craft field forward? color *American Craft* v76 no6 p26 D 2016-Ja 2017

VAN GORDER, BRYAN
HAWAII FOR FAMILY color *Advocate* no1089 p54 F/Mr 2017

Van Gorder, Chris
A No-Layoffs Policy Can Work, Even in an Unpredictable Economy *Harvard Business Review Digital Articles* p2 Ja 26 2015

Vangsness, Kirsten
Criminal Minds N. Abrams, B. L. Heldman et al color *Entertainment Weekly* no1482/1483 p79 S 22 2017

Vanguard Group of Investment Cos.
A Mutual Fund Giant Flexes Its Muscles E. Fry color diag *Fortune* v174 no8 p126 D 15 2016

Vanguard Health Services Inc.
Politics Afflicts Our Favorite Health Fund N. S. HUANG chart *Kiplinger's Personal Finance* v71 no4 p61 Ap 2017

Van Gysen, Alan
extra hours color *Surfing Magazine* v53 no2 p52 F 2017
In the Wind bw color *Surfing Magazine* v53 no3 p50 Mr 2017

Van Halen, Eddie, 1957-
AN ALL-AMERICAN STREET RACE D. CURCURITO color *Popular Mechanics* p48 Jl 2017

Van Harpen, Iris
TRANSFORMER R. MEAD cartoon color *New Yorker* v93 no29 p42 S 25 2017

Vanhée-Cybulski, Nadège—Interviews
NADÈGE Vanhée-Cybulski S. STEIN *Interview* v46 no10 p136 D 2016/Ja 2017

van Heek, Margaret
Systemic pan-AMPK activator MK-8722 improves glucose homeostasis but induces cardiac hypertrophy graph *Science* v357 no6350 p507 Ag 4 2017

Vanheems, Benedict
Country Lore *Mother Earth News* no280 p85 F/Mr 2017

VANHELDER, MIKE
12 Free Utilities THAT CAN GIVE YOU MORE CONTROL OVER YOUR PC [Cover story] color diag graph *PCWorld* v35 no7 p167 Jl 2017

VanHise, James L.
Nonviolence, Power, and Possibility bw *Progressive* v81 no4 p51 Ap/My 2017

VANHOENACKER, MARK
WORKING EVERY DAY AT 35,000 FEET color *Reader's Digest* v189 no1130 p114 My 2017

Van Horn, Cameo
I AM A WOMAN FARMER A. MCCONNELL *Successful Farming* v115 no3 p35 Mid-F 2017

VAN HORN, GAVIN
City Creatures *Orion Magazine* v35 no4/5 p9 Jl-O 2016

Van Horne, Mark
Driving Home the Safety Discussion il *Consumer Reports* v82 no9 p6 S 2017

Van Hout, Cristopher V.
Distribution and clinical impact of functional variants in 50,726 whole-exome sequences from the DiscovEHR study chart graph *Science* v354 no6319 paaf6814-1 D 23 2016

Van Hove, Ivo
10 — THE CRUCIBLE M. Snetiker *Entertainment Weekly* no1444/1445 p118 D 16 2016

van Hummel, Annika
Site-specific phosphorylation of tau inhibits amyloid-β toxicity in Alzheimer's mice bibl graph *Science* v354 no6314 p904 N 18 2016

Vanian, Jonathan
THE 2017 Fortune Crystal Ball color diag *Fortune* v174 no7 p11 D 1 2016
7 JEN-HSUN HUANG color *Fortune* v174 no7 p84 D 1 2016
CHANGE THE WORLD !!!! color diag map *Fortune* v176 no4 p74 S 15 2017
DATA CENTERS GO EXOTIC color *Fortune* v175 no5 p20 Ap 1 2017
FLASH FORWARD color *Fortune* v175 no8 p60 Je 15 2017
THE REVOLUTION STARTS HERE color *Fortune* v174 no7 p26 D 1 2016
RISING STARS color *Fortune* v176 no4 p89 S 15 2017
VIRTUAL REALITY'S MONEY QUEST color *Fortune* v75 no1 p28 Ja 1 2017

Vanilla
HOW TO MAKE ICE CREAM J. BRITTON BAUER, J. Lynch et al bw color diag *Popular Mechanics* p80 S 2017
SL cooking school K. Hammonds color *Southern Living* v51 no12 p230 D 2016
Synthetic Biology and the Marketplace B. BAKER *BioScience* v67 no10 p877 O 2017

Vanilla Workshop (Company)
SPEEDVAGEN ROAD DISC M. Phillips color *Bicycling* v58 no4 p61 My 2017

van Ingen, Jakko
Emergence and spread of a human-transmissible multidrug-resistant nontuberculous mycobacterium bibl diag graph *Science* v354 no6313 p751 N 11 2016

Van Isacker, Piet
Group Theory in a Nutshell for Physicists *Physics Today* v70 no1 p58 Ja 2017

Vanity Fair (Periodical)
ALL THE PRESIDENT'S MEN 2.0 G. CARTER *Vanity Fair* v59 no8 p34 Ag 2017
The Palace Intrigue Obsession A. FERGUSON *Commentary* v143 no6 p11 Je 2017

Van Kirk, Kat
My boyfriend of four years doesn't want to move in together color *Glamour* v115 no3 p144 Mr 2017

Van Kranendonk, Martin J.
life springs [Cover story] color *Scientific American* v317 no2 p28

Ag 2017

VanLaer, Scott
Mountain Rescue *New York State Conservationist* v71 no4 p2 F 2017

Van Landingham, Corey
GILLY'S BOWL & GRILLE *New Yorker* v92 no45 p58 Ja 16 2017

Vanlandingham, Dana L.
Rapid development of a DNA vaccine for Zika virus bibl graph *Science* v354 no6309 p237 O 14 2016

VANLANDINGHAM, ERIC
Cheers & Jeers cartoon color *Field & Stream* v121 no9 p14 Ap 2017

van Leeuwen, Jolanda
Exploring genetic suppression interactions on a global scale diag *Science* v354 no6312 p599 N 4 2016

van Leeuwen, Thomas
Locked synchronous rotor motion in a molecular motor diag *Science* v356 no6341 p964 Je 1 2017

Van Lennep, Erik
TRENDING NOW color *Wired* v25 no4 p12 Ap 2017

van Lieshout, Natascha
Exploring genetic suppression interactions on a global scale diag *Science* v354 no6312 p599 N 4 2016

Vanlife
#VANLIFE R. MONROE cartoon color *New Yorker* v93 no10 p40 Ap 24 2017

Van Lith, Jessica Sailer
Four Truths About Dressing Your Shape color *Glamour* v114 no11 p90 N 2016
Hey, Jenna! color *Glamour* v114 no11 p70 N 2016
What to Know NOW color *Glamour* v114 no11 p72 N 2016
Winter Is Coming [Cover story] color *Glamour* v114 no11 p53 N 2016

Van Loo, Peter
Mutational signatures associated with tobacco smoking in human cancer bibl graph *Science* v354 no6312 p618 N 4 2016

VAN LOON, ANDRÉ
Talking Heads color *Weekly Standard* v22 no16 p31 D 26 2016

VAN LOTRINGEN, INGEBORG
GLOW ALL OUT color diag *Seventeen* v76 no5 p100 S 2017
Simple EYELASH Hacks color *Seventeen* v76 no12 p52 D 2016/Ja 2017

Van Lustbader, Eric—Interviews
Q&A WITH ERIC VAN LUSTBADER bw *Publishers Weekly* v263 no43 p(Sp)13 O 24 2016

Vanmechelen, Koen
et al *Phi Kappa Phi Forum* v96 no4 p4 Wint 2016

Van Meter, Jonathan
Big Return color *Vogue* v207 no4 p202 Ap 2017
THE CONTENDER color *Vogue* v207 no11 p198 N 2017
ON the FRONT LINES bw color *Vogue* v207 no7 p84 Jl 2017
OPRAH'S BLISS color *Vogue* v207 no9 p666 S 2017
UNFORGETTABLE [Cover story] color *Vogue* v206 no12 p219 D 2016

VAN MIERLO, PETER
CASE STUDY: IS HOLACRACY FOR US? color il *Harvard Business Review* v95 no2 p151 Mr/Ap 2017

van Moorsel, G. A.
Molecular gas in the halo fuels the growth of a massive cluster galaxy at high redshift bibl graph *Science* v354 no6316 p1128 D 2 2016

VANN, DAVID
If He Writes It, She Will Come *New York Times Book Review* p18 O 16 2016

Van Ngoc, Thinh
Saving the saola from extinction color *Science* v357 no6357 p1248 S 22 2017

van Niel, Guillaume
Tubular clathrin/AP-2 lattices pinch collagen fibers to support 3D cell migration color *Science* v356 no6343 p1138 Je 16 2017

Van Nieuwenhze, Michael S.
Treadmilling by FtsZ filaments drives peptidoglycan synthesis and bacterial cell division bibl graph *Science* v355 no6326 p739 F 17 2017

Van Noten, Dries, 1958-

the life C. Stern and A. Vorrasi color *InStyle* v24 no3 p363 Mr 2017

The Magic Numbers M. HOLGATE color *Vogue* v207 no11 p134 N 2017

van Nouhuys, Saskya

Higher predation risk for insect prey at low latitudes and elevations graph *Science* v356 no6339 p742 My 19 2017

Vannucchi, Paola

Release of mineral-bound water prior to subduction tied to shallow seismogenic slip off Sumatra graph *Science* v356 no6340 p841 My 26 2017

Van Ogtrop, Kristin

The Crucial Difference Between Christmas and a Trip to the Store color *Time* v188 no24 p71 D 12 2016

Hey! You! Get Off of My Cloud! And Other Tales from the Family-Data-Sharing Economy color *Time* v190 no14 p55 O 9 2017

How I Learned to Stop Worrying and Love the Roomba color *Time* v189 no13 p55 Ap 10 2017

How This Family of Worrywarts Copes In an Age of Anxiety color *Time* v190 no6 p59 Ag 7 2017

How to Recover from This No Good, Very Bad Election Season and All Its Spooky Horrors color *Time* v188 no21 p73 N 21 2016

Invasion of the Garden Snatcher and Other Tales of Suburban Apocalypse color *Time* v189 no23 p55 Je 19 2017

A Letter of Apology to a Son Graduating from College color *Time* v189 no15 p55 Ap 24 2017

The Most Important Difference Between an Elite Athlete and a Middle-Aged Writer color *Time* v189 no9 p59 Mr 13 2017

My Household Get-out-the-vote Campaign Hits a Teen Roadblock color *Time* v188 no16/17 p95 O 24 2016

Safe Gun Policy Doesn't Have to Mean No Guns—Or No Safety color *Time* v190 no16/17 p111 O 23 2017

What Do I Do Now? A Midlife Career Change May Be Just the Challenge You Need color *Time* v190 no8 p59 Ag 28 2017

VANOOSTING, JAMES

The Last Bursts of Memory *American Scholar* v86 no1 p87 Wint 2017

Van Patten, Grace

GRACE VAN PATTEN K. SMITH color *Vanity Fair* v59 no10 p89 O 2017

van Putten, Alexander

How to Set More-Realistic Growth Targets *Harvard Business Review Digital Articles* p2 Jl 12 2017

Vanquish Boats (Company)

WEST COAST FOCUS S. SHIBATA *Sea Magazine* v108 no10 p10 O 2016

van Ree, Janine H.

Cyclin A2 is an RNA binding protein that controls Mre11 mRNA translation bibl graph *Science* v353 no6307 p1549 S 30 2016

Van Reenen, John

Research: The Rise of Superstar Firms Has Been Better for Investors than for Employees *Harvard Business Review Digital Articles* p1 My 11 2017

WHY DO WE UNDERVALUE COMPETENT MANAGEMENT? NEITHER GREAT LEADERSHIP NOR BRILLIANT STRATEGY MATTERS WITHOUT OPERATIONAL EXCELLENCE graph il img *Harvard Business Review* v95 no5 p120 S/O 2017

van Rees, Wim M.

Complete measurement of helicity and its dynamics in vortex tubes color diag graph *Science* v357 no6350 p487 Ag 4 2017

van Rens, Thijs

Paying Skilled Workers More Would Create More Skilled Workers *Harvard Business Review Digital Articles* p2 My 19 2016

Van Rheene, Erin

Conservation Lessons from a Still-Wild River: Be Known, Spread the Word, and Get Creative *Humanist* v77 no5 p6 S/O 2017

VAN RIPER, CARENA J.

Incorporating Sociocultural Phenomena into Ecosystem-Service Valuation: The Importance of Critical Pluralism *BioScience* v67 no3 p233 Mr 2017

Van Roekel, Ryan

DON'T FORGET SULFUR K. Birchmier *Successful Farming* v115 no1 p49 Ja 2017

Van Ryk, Donald

Sustained virologic control in SIV+ macaques after antiretrovi-

ral and α4β7 antibody therapy bibl graph *Science* v354 no6309 p197 O 14 2016

Vans

Mercedes-Benz Vision Van Concept A. MacKenzie color *Motor Trend* v68 no12 p20 D 2016

Van's Aircraft Inc.

SHOULD YOU BUY AN LSA? S. POPE color *Flying* v144 no1 p52 Ja 2017

Vansina, Jan, 1929-2017

Social Science and the Public Interest *Society* v54 no4 p313 Ag 2017

Van Skalk, Patricia

HIVE MIND B. COLEMAN *Cincinnati Magazine* p20 Je 2017

Van Syckle, Katie

10 Apps to Make You Productive color *Money* v46 no9 p22 O 2017

PARTY LINES img *New York* v50 no11 p127 My 29 2017

PARTY LINES img *New York* v50 no12 p112 Je 12 2017

PARTY LINES img *New York* v50 no15 p73 Jl 24 2017

PARTY LINES img *New York* v50 no16 p110 Ag 7 2017

VAN THULL, JODY

Lion in Wait *Sierra* v101 no4 p18 Jl/Ag 2016

VanTine, Julia

AGE PROOF YOUR BRAIN [Cover story] cartoon chart *Prevention* v69 no5 p60 My 2017

Vantrappen, Herman

How to (Gradually) Become a Different Company *Harvard Business Review Digital Articles* p2 O 15 2014

How to Know If a Spin-Off Will Succeed *Harvard Business Review Digital Articles* p2 F 24 2015

Joint Ventures Reduce the Risk of Major Capital Investments *Harvard Business Review Digital Articles* p2 Ap 6 2016

Making Matrix Organizations Actually Work *Harvard Business Review Digital Articles* p2 Mr 1 2016

VAN VALKENBURGH, BLAIRE

Conserving the World's Megafauna and Biodiversity: The Fierce Urgency of Now *BioScience* v67 no3 p197 Mr 2017

Saving the World's Terrestrial Megafauna color *BioScience* v66 no10 p807 O 1 2016

Van Vechten, Carl, 1880-1964

SPRING SHOWS color *Popular Photography* v81 no2 p20 Mr/Ap 2017

Vanveen, Yolanda

BRIGHT BULB *Saturday Evening Post* v289 no1 p25 Ja/F 2017

van Vliet, A.

Observation of a large-scale anisotropy in the arrival directions of cosmic rays above 8 × 1018 eV *Science* v357 no6357 p1266 S 22 2017

Van Voris, Bob

Hot Tickets and Wall Street Marks *Bloomberg Businessweek* no4540 p33 O 2 2017

A Trump Lawsuit Gets a Boost From Restaurants color *Bloomberg Businessweek* no4519 p34 Ap 24 2017

Van Wassenhove, Luk N.

Europe Can Find Better Ways to Get Refugees into Workforces *Harvard Business Review Digital Articles* p2 O 5 2015

What's Europe's Long-Term Plan for Integrating Refugees? *Harvard Business Review Digital Articles* p2 S 22 2015

van Wessum, Rob

There Are No Shortcuts color *Dressage Today* p22 My 2017

van Wijk, Kasper

Apple seismology *Physics Today* v70 no10 p94 O 2017

Van Winkle, Edwin

SECRET PASSAGE L. MURTHA *Cincinnati Magazine* v50 no3 p46 D 2016

Van Wyk, Alan

Gigabytes of grace *Christian Century* v134 no6 p38 Mr 15 2017

The Virtual Body of Christ in a Suffering World color *Christian Century* v134 no6 p38 Mr 15 2017

van Zadelhoff, Marc

Cybersecurity Has a Serious Talent Shortage. Here's How to Fix It *Harvard Business Review Digital Articles* p2 My 4 2017

Van Zadelhoff, Marc—Interviews

Why Cybersecurity Is So Difficult to Get Right J. M. Olejarz *Harvard Business Review Digital Articles* p2 Jl 27 2015

VAN ZANDT, BABS

PUT YOUR CARDS ON THE DINING TABLE bw color *Louisiana Life* v38 no1 p36 S/O 2017

Van Zandt, J. T.

The art of Sight-Casting L. SMITH FORD *Texas Monthly* v45 no9 p16 S 2017

Van Zandt, Steve, 1950-

Little Steven Heads Back to the Garage, Emerges With the Eclectic Sounds of Soulfire M. METTLER color *Sound & Vision* v82 no8 p30 O 2017

Little Steven Is His Own Boss Again B. HIATT bw color *Rolling Stone* no1288 p16 Je 1 2017

Vanzant, Iyanla—Interviews

THREE MOST IMPORTANT MONEY LESSONS C. M. Brown color *Black Enterprise* v47 no2 p18 S 2016

Van Zeebroeck, Nicholas

6 Digital Strategies, and Why Some Work Better than Others *Harvard Business Review Digital Articles* p2 Jl 31 2017

Van Zoggel, Karl H.

La Divina Redux F. P. Driscoll *Opera News* v81 no9 p62 Mr 2017

Van Zuiden, Audrey Millicent

Audrey Millicent van Zuiden A. A. DAVIS color *Maclean's* no1 p66 F 17 2017

van Zuylen-Wood, Simon

AT RT. NEWS BREAKS YOU color *Bloomberg Businessweek* no4521 p48 My 8 2017

ED RECKONING: The Republican candidate for governor of Virginia comes straight from the national GOP establishment. Not long ago, his résumé could have been a plus. These days, it might be Ed Gillespie's biggest challenge *Washingtonian Magazine* v53 no1 p84 O 2017

GET OUT color *Bloomberg Businessweek* no4495 p50 O 17 2016

Oy, the TRAFFIC. And it's POURING! Do I hear SIRENS? color *Columbia Journalism Review* v56 no1 p96 Spr 2017

TO UNDERSTAND THIS NEW RIGHT, IT HELPS TO SEE IT NOT AS A FRINGE MOVEMENT, BUT A POWERFUL COUNTERCULTURE img *New York* v50 no9 p24 My 1 2017

Van Zweden, Jaap

Wagner: Die Walküre F. Cohn *Opera News* v81 no9 p51 Mr 2017

van Zwoll, Wayne

THE RETURN OF RIGBY bw *Outdoor Life* v224 no2 p63 F/Mr 2017

VAPNYAR, LARA

Click Bait: A debut novel about the pitfalls of startup culture *New York Times Book Review* p11 My 14 2017

DEAF AND BLIND bw cartoon color *New Yorker* v93 no10 p82 Ap 24 2017

Vapor compression cycle

The refrigerant is also the pump Q. M. Zhang and T. Zhang diag *Science* v357 no6356 p1094 S 15 2017

Vappiani, Johanna

Click chemistry enables preclinical evaluation of targeted epigenetic therapies diag *Science* v356 no6345 p1397 Je 30 2017

Vaquero (Music)

Vaquero color *American Cowboy* v23 no6 p43 Ap/My 2017

Vara, Vauhini

BEE--BRAINED *Harper's Magazine* v334 no2004 p54 My 2017

How Frackers Beat OPEC color *Atlantic* v319 no1 p20 Ja/F 2017

The New Advertising, As Seen on TV color *Bloomberg Businessweek* no4502 p41 D 5 2016

The new meaning of new media color *Columbia Journalism Review* v56 no1 p104 Spr 2017

Silicon Valley, USA bw diag graph map *Wired* v25 no6 p76 Je 2017

Startup Types Build Ready-Made Activism *Bloomberg Businessweek* no4511 p32 F 13 2017

The Toll of Cheap Clothing color *Bloomberg Businessweek* no4497 p10 O 31 2016

Varadarajan, Tunku

"There's No Optimism": Hoover fellow Michael A. McFaul, former ambassador to Moscow, reflects on fading democratic hopes for Russia *Hoover Digest: Research & Opinion on Public Policy* no3 p97 Summ 2017

Varadkar, Leo

A New Face for the Republic of Ireland T. John color *Time* v189 no23 p13 Je 19 2017

A Portrait of the Prime Minister As a Young Man J. Duggan color

Time v190 no4 p36 Jl 24 2017

YOUTH REVOLT V. Walt, A. Vandermey et al color *Fortune* v176 no3 p64 S 1 2017

Varadkar, Leo—Political & social views

More Bridges and Fewer Borders: THIS COMMON EUROPEAN IDENTITY IS NOT VALUED BY EVERYONE ON THESE ISLANDS *Vital Speeches of the Day* v83 no9 p241 S 2017

Varanda (Music)

The Beautiful Sound A. MORRISON bw *Downbeat* v84 no7 p59 Jl 2017

Varchaver, Nicholas

12 MARY BARRA color *Fortune* v174 no7 p86 D 1 2016

18 PONY MA color *Fortune* v174 no7 p89 D 1 2016

Varcoe, Barry

How Aligned Is Your Organization? color *Harvard Business Review Digital Articles* p2 F 7 2017

A Simple Way to Test Your Company's Strategic Alignment *Harvard Business Review Digital Articles* p2 My 16 2016

Varda, Agnès, 1928-

Faces Places: Two Artists Hit the Road S. Zacharek color *Time* v190 no15 p56 O 16 2017

Varda, Agnès, 1928-—Interviews

WE CAN BE HEROES WANG MUYAN color *Film Comment* v53 no5 p24 S/O 2017

Vardi, Moshe

SELF-DRIVING CARS ARE COOL, BUT THEY'RE NOT FOR EVERYONE J. D. Tuccille color *Reason* v49 no5 p12 O 2017

VARDI, NATHAN

AUSTIN POWERED color *Forbes* v200 no1 p98 Jl 27 2017

The Bitterest Pill cartoon color *Forbes* v199 no4 p38 Ap 25 2017

Faceless Returns color *Forbes* v199 no7 p148 Je 29 2017

Hedge Fund Resurrection color *Forbes* v198 no8 p58 D 20 2016

LESSONS AND IDEAS BY THE 100 GREATEST LIVING BUSINESS MINDS bw color *Forbes* v200 no3 p115 S 28 2017

Moderna's Mystery Medicines color *Forbes* v198 no9 p46 D 30 2016

THE WORLD'S BILLIONAIRES bw color diag graph map *Forbes* v199 no3 p84 Mr 28 2017

Varela, E.

Observation of a large-scale anisotropy in the arrival directions of cosmic rays above 8×1018 eV *Science* v357 no6357 p1266 S 22 2017

VARGAS, CESAR

¡En la Lucha! *Nation* v303 no23/24 p6 D 5 2016

Vargas, Fred

A Climate of Fear *Publishers Weekly* v264 no2 p43 Ja 9 2017

Vargas, P. Núñez

Persistent effects of pre-Columbian plant domestication on Amazonian forest composition bibl chart graph map *Science* v355 no6328 p925 Mr 3 2017

VARGAS, VANESSA

Ecological Forecasting and the Science of Hypoxia in Chesapeake Bay *BioScience* v67 no7 p614 Jl 2017

Vargas Cardenas, B.

Observation of a large-scale anisotropy in the arrival directions of cosmic rays above 8×1018 eV *Science* v357 no6357 p1266 S 22 2017

Vargas-Cooper, Natasha

RED HOT color *InStyle* v23 no12 p244 N 2016

Womanhood Redefined *American Conservative* v16 no1 p27 Ja/F 2017

Vargas Llosa, Mario, 1936-

TRUTH HURTS *Lapham's Quarterly* v10 no3 p155 Summ 2017

Varghese, Neha

Protein structure determination using metagenome sequence data bibl color graph *Science* v355 no6322 p294 Ja 20 2017

VARGO, JOE

r.s.v.p bw color *Bon Appetit* v62 no7 p12 Jl 2017

Variable stars

75, 50 & 25 YEARS AGO R. W. Sinnott *Sky & Telescope* v133 no2 p8 F 2017

The First Pulsing White Dwarf Hambsch *Sky & Telescope* v133 no1 p84 Ja 2017

The Inconstant Star: The joys of observing variable stars are predictably wonderful S. French *Sky & Telescope* v134 no4 p54 O 2017

The star clusters of Puppis P. HARRINGTON color *Astronomy* v45 no3 p68 Mr 2017

Varicose veins

Image of God B. Haile color *U.S. Catholic* v82 no11 p10 N 2017

Varin, Caroline

Violent Nonstate Actors in Africa: Terrorists, Rebels, and War-lords N. van de Walle *Foreign Affairs* v96 no6 p173 N/D 2017

Varisco, Michel

MICHEL VARISCO J. R. Kemp bw color *Louisiana Life* v37 no6 p16 Jl/Ag 2017

Varlamov, Andrey A.

Alexei Alexeyevich Abrikosov *Physics Today* v70 no10 p73 O 2017

Varma, Anand

SEEING BEAUTY VIA TECHNOLOGY color *National Geographic* v232 no1 p8 Jl 2017

Varma, Mukund

Reovirus infection triggers inflammatory responses to dietary anti-gens and development of celiac disease color diag *Science* v356 no6333 p44 Ap 7 2017

Varner, G.

Observation of a large-scale anisotropy in the arrival directions of cosmic rays above 8 × 1018 eV *Science* v357 no6357 p1266 S 22 2017

VARNER, JAMIE

NPCA AT WORK: TRASH SOLUTIONS *National Parks* v91 no1 p19 Wint 2017

Varner, Jeff

Survivor: an Outing and an Ousting N. Serrao, P. Gomez et al color *Entertainment Weekly* no1463/1464 p21 Ap/My 2017

Varner, R. L.

Observation of coherent elastic neutrino-nucleus scattering diag *Science* v357 no6356 p1123 S 15 2017

Varnish & varnishing

FINISHING TOUCH color *Timber Home Living* v27 no3 p32 Je 2017

Varoufakis, Yanis, 1961-

A New Deal for Europe color *Nation* v305 no10 p22 O 23 2017

Yanis VAROUFAKIS A. Carter color *Esquire* p58 N 2017

Varvaloucas, Emma

How to Get Through These Times [Cover story] bw *Tricycle: The Buddhist Review* v26 no4 p34 Summ 2017

Varvatos, John

DETROIT ENDURES bw *Men's Health* v32 no2 p(Sp)6 Mr 2017

Vasarely, Victor

Victor Vasarely Sculpture from Leah Gordaon color *Magazine Antiques* v183 no6 p33 N/D 2016

Vasavada, A. R.

Redox stratification of an ancient lake in Gale crater, Mars color *Science* v356 no6341 p922 Je 1 2017

Vasavada, Ashwin R.

Our changing view of MARS *Physics Today* v70 no3 p34 Mr 2017

Vase painting—Exhibitions

EMILY MULLIN J. Kreimer color *Art in America* v105 no3 p124 Mr 2017

Vases

Art + Craft color *Arts & Crafts Homes & the Revival* v12 no5 p11 Wint 2018

Vases—Design & construction

Glass Vases by Ettore Sotsass: The late Italian architect and de-signer, known as much for his product designs as his buildings, was a master of color and shape E. GAUKEL *Treasures* v6 no6 p40 Je/Jl 2017

Q&A WITH BRAD PEARCE *Texas Monthly* v44 no11 p36 N 2016

Vases—Evaluation

15 WAYS TO DO tinsell color *Good Housekeeping* v263 no6 p74A D 2016

17 WAYS TO ADD COLOR TO EVERY ROOM A. LONGO-BUCCO color *Good Housekeeping* v264 no4 p50 Ap 2017

the best of THE BEST 120 K. O'SHEA-EVANS and H. BROWN color *House Beautiful* v158 no9 p57 N 2016

BOHO LOUNGE B. L. GRANT color *Chicago* v66 no4 p68 Ap 2017

Brad Pearce Glass L. S. FORD *Texas Monthly* v44 no11 p35 N 2016

COLOR GOURD GREENS M. B. EYERS color *Better Homes & Gardens* v95 no10 p34 O 2017

garden IN A VASE J. CHAI color *Better Homes & Gardens* v95 no5 p80 My 2017

Give It a Swirl color *Martha Stewart Living* no275 p20 Je 2017

Keith Kreeger Studios L. S. FORD *Texas Monthly* v45 no1 p25 Ja 2017

PALE PINK + CAFÉ AU LAIT color *Martha Stewart Living* no271 p29 Ja/F 2017

SARAH STORMS M. B. EYERS color *Better Homes & Gardens* v95 no9 p18 S 2017

SULTRY OPULENCE color *House Beautiful* v159 no8 p125 O 2017

Vases—Exhibitions

EVENTS + EXHIBITS color *Arts & Crafts Homes & the Revival* v12 no5 p16 Wint 2018

Vasilyev, N. V.

Tough adhesives for diverse wet surfaces diag *Science* v357 no6349 p378 Jl 28 2017

Vasodilation

POMEGRANATE PUMP J. WUEBBEN cartoon *Muscle & Performance* v9 no4 p10 Ap 2017

VASQUEZ, JACQUELINE

vocabulary lessons *Parents* v92 no7 p126 Jl 2017

Vásquez, Juan Gabriel, 1973-

Poison Pen YIYUN LI *New York Times Book Review* p11 O 9 2016

Vasquez, Rodolfo M.

Persistent effects of pre-Columbian plant domestication on Ama-zonian forest composition bibl chart graph map *Science* v355 no6328 p925 Mr 3 2017

Positive biodiversity-productivity relationship predominant in global forests bibl chart graph map *Science* v354 no6309 paaf8957-1 O 14 2016

Vasquez, Tim

Forecast Center map *Weatherwise* v70 no4 p54 Jl/Ag 2017

Forecast Center *Weatherwise* v70 no1 p66 Ja/F 2017

Forecast Center *Weatherwise* v70 no2 p54 Mr/Ap 2017

forecast center *Weatherwise* v70 no5 p60 S/O 2017

Vassall, Anna

When an emerging disease becomes endemic color *Science* v357 no6347 p156 Jl 14 2017

Vassanji, M. G., 1950-

NOSTALGIA Z. SCHWARTZ color *Maclean's* v129 no40 p76 O 10 2016

Vassen, Wim

The proton radius revisited graph *Science* v357 no6359 p39 O 6 2017

Vassilopoulos, Stéphane

Tubular clathrin/AP-2 lattices pinch collagen fibers to support 3D cell migration color *Science* v356 no6343 p1138 Je 16 2017

Vasta, Stephen Francis

Jenkins: Cantata Memoria *Opera News* v81 no10 p55 Ap 2017

Vasudeva, Rajeev

Keep Employees from Leaving by Emphasizing Teamwork *Harvard Business Review Digital Articles* p2 N 7 2016

Vaswani, Balram

Hot Weed Mogul Balram Vaswani D. BROWNE color *Rolling Stone* no1274 p44 N 17 2016

Vatanka, Alex

How Deep Is Iran's State? *Foreign Affairs* v96 no4 p155 Jl/Ag 2017

Vater, Linda

The Ultimate Plot Twist L. M. Minor color *Southern Living* v52 no3 p28 Mr 2017

Vatican Council (2nd : 1962-1965)

No 'Reform of the Reform' G. O'CONNELL *America* v215 no19 p24 D 19 2016

Pope Francis says Vatican II liturgical reform is 'irreversible' G. O'Connell color *America* v217 no6 p17 S 18 2017

Vatnajökull (Iceland)

COLD CASE P. STEFÁNSSON *Iceland Review* v54 no6 p26 N/D 2016

Vatner, Dorothy E.

Minority investigators lack NIH funding color *Science* v356 no6342 p1018 Je 9 2017

Vatner, Stephen F.

Minority investigators lack NIH funding color *Science* v356 no6342 p1018 Je 9 2017

Vattel, Emer de, 1714-1767

LAWS OF WAR: FOUNDING FATHERS J. A. Haymond color *MHQ: Quarterly Journal of Military History* v30 no1 p16 Aut 2017

VATTER, WALTER

A Man, A Plan bw color *Weekly Standard* v22 no27 p41 Mr 20 2017

VATZ, RICHARD E.

Papa Was a Rolling Stone *USA Today Magazine* v146 no2868 p35 S 2017

When Rhetoric Wanders in Wacky Ways *USA Today Magazine* v145 no2862 p20 Mr 2017

Vaudeville—United States—History

VAUDEVILLE TONITE! JOHNSON *Treasures* v6 no4 p38 F/ Mr 2017

VAUGEN, KELLY

The Bones of a Saguaro *Arizona Highways* v93 no3 p34 Mr 2017

Vaughan, Carson

The GRAND DAME of Cowboy Poetry cartoon color *American Cowboy* v23 no5 p58 F/Mr 2017

Vaughan, Geoffrey

Anthony Daniels, Good and Evil in the Garden of Art: Discrimination as the Guarantor of Civilization *Society* v54 no4 p375 Ag 2017

Vaughan, Liam

Why the U.K.'s Whistles Remain Mostly Unblown color *Bloomberg Businessweek* no4525 p38 Je 5 2017

Vaughan, Ryan

MOTOR CITY MADE B. Boyé bw color *Men's Health* v32 no2 p(Sp)20 Mr 2017

Vaughan-Marra, Jessica C.

Teaching music in the flat world: Reflections on the work of Darling-Hammond and Rothman bibl *Arts Education Policy Review* v118 no2 p123 2017

VAUGHAN-NICHOLS, STEVEN J.

Microsoft: Don't worry, MS-DOS will live on after all color *PC-World* v35 no1 p29 Ja 2017

Vaughn, Daniel

Barbecue Italian Style *Texas Monthly* v45 no4 p34 Ap 2017

THE GOLDEN AGE OF BBQ *Texas Monthly* v45 no6 p94 Je 2017

KNIVES OUT *Texas Monthly* v44 no12 p90 D 2016

Smoke Over the Water *Texas Monthly* v45 no8 p26 Ag 2017

Vaughn, David

ALLEGIANT color *Sound & Vision* v81 no9 p67 N 2016

Anthem MRX 1120 A/V Receiver chart color graph *Sound & Vision* v81 no9 p36 N 2016

ATI AT527NC and AT524NC Amplifiers chart color graph *Sound & Vision* v82 no3 p48 Ap 2017

BILLY LYNN'S LONG HALFTIME WALK color *Sound & Vision* v82 no6 p69 Jl/Ag 2017

CENTRAL INTELLIGENCE color *Sound & Vision* v82 no2 p70 F/Mr 2017

DEEPWATER HORIZON color *Sound & Vision* v82 no5 p65 Je 2017

HACKSAW RIDGE color *Sound & Vision* v82 no7 p67 S 2017

HUMPBACK WHALES color *Sound & Vision* v81 no10 p69 D 2016

THE HUNTSMAN: WINTER'S WAR color *Sound & Vision* v82 no1 p69 Ja 2017

INFERNO color *Sound & Vision* v82 no5 p68 Je 2017

JL Audio Dominion d110 Subwoofer color graph *Sound & Vision* v82 no3 p64 Ap 2017

JOHN WICK – CHAPTER 2 color *Sound & Vision* v82 no8 p67 O 2017

THE MAGFINICENT SEVEN (2016) color *Sound & Vision* v82 no4 p68 My 2017

NOW YOU SEE ME 2 color *Sound & Vision* v82 no5 p66 Je 2017

PLANET EARTH II color *Sound & Vision* v82 no7 p71 S 2017

PSB SubSeries 450 Subwoofer color graph *Sound & Vision* v81 no10 p60 D 2016

THE SHALLOWS color *Sound & Vision* v82 no2 p69 F/Mr 2017

SING STREET color *Sound & Vision* v81 no10 p71 D 2016

STAR TREK BEYOND color *Sound & Vision* v82 no3 p69 Ap 2017

SUICIDE SQUAD color *Sound & Vision* v82 no4 p67 My 2017

SVS PB16-Ultra and SB16-Ultra Subwoofers color graph *Sound & Vision* v82 no2 p50 F/Mr 2017

XXX: RETURN OF XANDER CAGE color *Sound & Vision* v82 no8 p70 O 2017

Vaughn, Dona D.

La Clemenza di Tito J. Malafronte *Opera News* v81 no9 p36 Mr 2017

Vaughn, Kelly

American Bison *Arizona Highways* v93 no4 p13 Ap 2017

BALANCING ACT *Arizona Highways* v93 no2 p30 F 2017

Bobby D's BBQ color *Arizona Highways* v93 no5 p12 My 2017

CABIN LOOP *Arizona Highways* v92 no7 p32 Jl 2016

THE CALL OF THE CANYON *Arizona Highways* v93 no1 p28 Ja 2017

Coyotes *Arizona Highways* v93 no2 p13 F 2017

FROM A DISTANCE *Arizona Highways* v93 no8 p28 Ag 2017

Gambel's Quail *Arizona Highways* v93 no3 p13 Mr 2017

INSIDE OUT *Arizona Highways* v93 no10 p32 O 2017

IT'S GOOD TO BE Home *Arizona Highways* v93 no4 p44 Ap 2017

LIKE A MOUNTAIN *Arizona Highways* v96 no7 p30 Jl 2017

MASTER OF THE ARTS *Arizona Highways* v92 no11 p22 N 2016

THE MAVERICK. "Doc" "Doc" "Luce" "The Maverick Doctor"... these are just some of the names people use when referring to Sam Luce. The names vary, but the regal'd is the same: Sam Luce is a legend down in the Blue *Arizona Highways* v96 no7 p34 Jl 2017

MY LADY OF THE DESERT *Arizona Highways* v93 no6 p28 Je 2017

PITCH A TENT & HIT THE TRAIL: Lewis and Clark, Simon and Garfunkel, peanut butter and chocolate... there's a long list of great combinations. In the summer in the Santa Catalina Mountains, the best combo might be hiking and camping. Here's a little... *Arizona Highways* v93 no6 p38 Je 2017

POSTCARDS FROM THE CANYON *Arizona Highways* v93 no10 p28 O 2017

The Shady Dell *Arizona Highways* v93 no9 p16 S 2017

SMALL WONDERS *Arizona Highways* v93 no9 p30 S 2017

SO FAR. SO GOOD *Arizona Highways* v93 no1 p40 Ja 2017

A Song FOR Katie bw *Arizona Highways* v93 no5 p50 My 2017

Tratto *Arizona Highways* v92 no11 p12 N 2016

WAITING FOR WATER *Arizona Highways* v93 no11 p28 N 2017

Vaughn, Matthew, 1971-

KINGSMAN: THE GOLDEN CIRCLE J. McGovern color *Entertainment Weekly* no1462 p46 Ap 21 2017

KINGSMAN: THE GOLDEN CIRCLE J. McGovern color *Entertainment Weekly* no1474/1475 p48 Jl 21-28 2017

Return of the Kingsman S. Zacharek color *Time* v190 no13 p65 O 2 2017

Vaughn, N. R.

Airborne laser-guided imaging spectroscopy to map forest trait diversity and guide conservation bibl chart graph *Science* v355 no6323 p385 Ja 27 2017

Vaughn, Robert, 1932-2016

Robert Vaughn, 1932-2016 cartoon color *Weekly Standard* v22 no12 p3 N 28 2016

Vaught, Richard

Backfires: The joyful noise of the commentariat, rebutted sporadically by Ed bw color *Car & Driver* v62 no10 p7 Ap 2017

Vaught, Vanessa—Interviews

Hatton Henry *Texas Monthly* v44 no12 p35 D 2016

Vaught, Wilma—Interviews

Interview U.S. Air Force Brigadier General Wilma Vaught (Ret.) cartoon color *Military History* v34 no1 p14 My 2017

Vauraste, Tero

An Investment Model for the Arctic color *Wilson Quarterly* p1 Summ 2017

Vaux, Calvert, 1824-1895

GARDEN STATE OF MIND D. BRENNER color *House Beautiful* v159 no4 p80 My 2017

Vavilina, Anastasia

Assembly of a nucleus-like structure during viral replication in bacteria bibl color graph *Science* v355 no6321 p1 Ja 13 2017

Vavouri, Tanya
Transgenerational transmission of environmental information in C. elegans diag *Science* v356 no6335 p320 Ap 21 2017

VAVREK, ROYCE
From Screen to Stage *Opera News* v81 no6 p20 D 2016

Vayreda, Jordi
Positive biodiversity-productivity relationship predominant in global forests bibl chart graph map *Science* v354 no6309 paaf8957-1 O 14 2016

Vaziev, Makhar—Interviews
Makhar Vaziev: The Bolshoi's ballet director talks future plans ahead of the company's Lincoln Center appearance C. PAWLICK *Dance Magazine* v91 no7 p18 Jl 2017

VAZNIS, BILL
WHEN YOU SPOOK A BUCK color *Outdoor Life* v224 no8 pH13 O 2017

VAZQUEZ, BERTHA
Helping Teachers Teach Evolution in the United States *Skeptical Inquirer* v41 no3 p49 My/Je 2017

Vazquez, R. A.
Observation of a large-scale anisotropy in the arrival directions of cosmic rays above 8 × 1018 eV *Science* v357 no6357 p1266 S 22 2017

Vazquez Sampere, Juan Pablo
The Reason Air Travel Is Terrible and So Few Airlines Are Profitable *Harvard Business Review Digital Articles* p2 My 27 2016
We Shouldn't Be Dazzled by Apple's Earnings Report *Harvard Business Review Digital Articles* p2 F 4 2015
Why Big Companies Struggle to Market Online *Harvard Business Review Digital Articles* p2 O 15 2015
Why Estonia Is Letting Entrepreneurs Become "E-Residents" *Harvard Business Review Digital Articles* p2 Mr 9 2016
Why Platform Disruption Is So Much Bigger than Product Disruption *Harvard Business Review Digital Articles* p2 Ap 8 2016
Xiaomi, Not Apple, Is Changing the Smartphone Industry *Harvard Business Review Digital Articles* p2 O 14 2014
Zappos and the Connection Between Structure and Strategy *Harvard Business Review Digital Articles* p2 Je 3 2015

Veazey, Trey
A WAVE OF GENEROSITY: Just one example of how the ILA network and book lovers everywhere helped restore libraries--and hope color *Literacy Today (2411-7862)* v34 no6 p42 My/Je 2017

Veberi., D.
Observation of a large-scale anisotropy in the arrival directions of cosmic rays above 8 × 1018 eV *Science* v357 no6357 p1266 S 22 2017

Vecchiatto, Paul
THE MAYOR IS IN color *Bloomberg Businessweek* no4534 p66 Ag 14 2017
The Race to Lead South Africa Is On color *Bloomberg Businessweek* no4524 p15 My 29 2017

Vecsi, Elizabeth
No Time Like the Present *Catnip* v24 no10 p2 O 2016

Vector beams
Vortex generation reaches a new plateau Qiu and Y. Yang color *Science* v357 no6352 p645 Ag 18 2017

Vedantham, H. K.
The magnetic field and turbulence of the cosmic web measured using a brilliant fast radio burst bibl chart graph *Science* v354 no6317 p1249 D 9 2016

Vedder, Richard
YOU DIDN'T BUILD THAT *Claremont Review of Books* v17 no1 p79 Wint 2016/2017

Veenstra, Alan
Solo Distance Racing on the Great Lakes color *Sail* v48 no11 p18 N 2017

Veep (TV program)
Julia Louis-Dreyfus R. SHEFFIELD color *Rolling Stone* no1287 p20 My 18 2017
The Must List color *Entertainment Weekly* no1462 p1 Ap 21 2017
New Sentences N. Abebe *New York Times Magazine* p16 My 21 2017
Out of Office S. MARSHALL il *New Republic* v248 no6 p56 Je 2017
Sarah SUTHERLAND M. MULLEN *Interview* v47 no3 p18 Ap 2017
Veep A. D'Arminio *TV Guide* v65 no25 p35 Je 2017
'Veep' in the Age of Trump R. SHEFFIELD color *Rolling Stone* no1285 p17 Ap 20 2017
VEEP'S SAM RICHARDSON GETS OUR VOTE N. Maslow color *Entertainment Weekly* no1467 p52 My 26 2017

Veeramachaneni, Kalyan
Why You're Not Getting Value from Your Data *Science Harvard Business Review Digital Articles* p2 D 7 2016

VEERMAN, FRANS
UNDER DISCUSSION *Christianity Today* p17 Ap 2017

Veesler, David
Local protein kinase A action proceeds through intact holoenzymes color diag graph *Science* v356 no6344 p1288 Je 23 2017

Veeva Systems Inc.
Big Pharma's Friend A. KONRAD color *Forbes* v199 no6 p46 Je 13 2017

Vega (Company)
Plant-Based Power J. WUEBBEN color *Muscle & Performance* v9 no11 p33 N 2017

Vega, Michelle
Deals D. LEFFERTS color *Publishers Weekly* v263 no52 p10 D 19 2016

VEGA, MURIEL
Pile On the PICKLES *Atlanta* v56 no7 p84 N 2016
Zero Forks Given: Forget what your mother taught you and roll up your sleeves; these dishes are meant to be eaten with nothing but your hands *Atlanta* v57 no4 p35 Ag 2017

Vega, Suzanne
LEONARD COHEN color *Entertainment Weekly* no1446/1447 p98 D 2016/Ja 2017

Vegans
THE LOOK BOOK img *New York* v49 no26 p53 D 26 2016

Vegemite (Trademark)
the cover color *InStyle* v24 no7 p18 Jl 2017

Vegetable farming
See also
  Lettuce growing
  Pumpkin growing
A Brief History of Improbably Large Produce K. Frischkorn *Smithsonian* v48 no6 p13 O 2017
Digging It *Martha Stewart Living* no268 p14 O 2016

Vegetable gardening
See also
  Edible greens
  Lettuce growing
  Pumpkin growing
GREEN GIANT E. E. OGDEN color *Better Homes & Gardens* v95 no3 p118 Mr 2017
THE GRUMPY GARDENER S. Bender color *Southern Living* v52 no5 p58 My 2017
HOW TO PLANT A VEGETABLE GARDEN M. Ozawa cartoon chart color *Martha Stewart Living* p76 Mr 2017
The Vole's Fate: Eat and Be Eaten F. RUDEBUSCH *Idaho Magazine* v16 no11 p20 Ag 2017

Vegetable juices
ASK THE EXPERT A. Romm *Prevention* v69 no1 p10 Ja 2017
JUST CHILL M. C. Cairns color *Southern Living* v52 no6 p106 Je 2017
Ready, Set, Blend! L. TYRELL color *Martha Stewart Living* p86 Ap 2017

Vegetable marketing
SMALL FARM, REAL PROFIT: This inspiring half-acre urban farm in Oregon is proving that size doesn't matter when it comes to profitability J. Volk *Mother Earth News* no284 p40 O/N 2017

Vegetable oils
In the SUNSET KITCHEN color *Sunset* v238 no1 p90 Ja 2017

Vegetable oils—Therapeutic use
Smashing the Coconut Oil Myth color *Health* v31 no2 p11 Mr 2017

Vegetable soup
The Best Soups for Men cartoon color *Men's Health* v32 no9 p62 N 2017
NEW WAYS WITH AVOCADO M. GLISAN color *Better Homes & Gardens* v95 no8 p104 Ag 2017

PARTY HEARTY! S. DRY color *Louisiana Life* v37 no3 p22 Ja/F 2017

Vegetable trade

Postcard From the Moon J. MILLER *In These Times* v41 no3 p42 Mr 2017

Vegetables

See also

Edible greens

2 weeks is all it takes to feel an energy boost after upping your intake of FRUITS & VEGGIES S. LIAO color *Better Homes & Gardens* v95 no6 p150 Je 2017

30 Ways to EAT MORE VEGGIES [Cover story] L. Turner color *Better Nutrition* v79 no11 p60 N 2017

All wrapped up J. Iserloh color *Yoga Journal* no289 p68 F 2017

ASK SUSAN S. WESTMORELAND color *Good Housekeeping* v264 no1 p114 Ja 1 2017

Back to Your Roots R. Bashinsky color *Health* v30 no9 p122 N 2016

Crunch It Out B. Lipton color *Health* v31 no3 p114 Ap 2017

Delish dips A. Young color *Yoga Journal* no295 p26 O 2017

Farmers' Market [Cover story] M. CROUCH color *Prevention* v69 no7 p20 Jl 2017

FLL-FLAVORED & FUNKY C. KETTLEWELL *Virginia Living* v15 no3 p21 Ap 2017

Get Sneaky With Squash color *Parents* v92 no9 p28 S 2017

Holiday Escape color *Bon Appetit* v61 no12 p80 D 2016 /Jan2017

Incredible Eggs color *Vegetarian Today* no2 p30 Ap 2017

Learning Chinese K. SHERWOOD *Nutrition Action Health Letter* v44 no5 p12 Je 2017

Must-Have Salads K. SHERWOOD *Nutrition Action Health Letter* v44 no4 p12 My 2017

My stay-slim faves color *Health* v31 no8 p122 O 2017

NEW WAY TO EAT E. N. GAGE and S. BOCAR color *Martha Stewart Living* p92 Ap 2017

RECIPE: ORANGE-SESAME CHICKEN STIR-FRY WITH BROCCOLI & PEPPERS *Tufts University Health & Nutrition Letter* p3 S 2017 Supplement

RICH & SKINNY D. Wise color *Health* v31 no8 p102 O 2017

Southern Veggie Burgers color *Vegetarian Today* no2 p24 Ap 2017

SPRING FLING C. Stone *Saturday Evening Post* v289 no2 p74 Mr/Ap 2017

vegetable LOVE *Martha Stewart Living* no267 p106 S 2016

Veggie Steaks R. Bashinsky color *Health* v31 no4 p88 My 2017

Veg In! K. SHERWOOD *Nutrition Action Health Letter* v44 no1 p12 Ja/F 2017

YELLOW SUMMER SQUASH *South Dakota Magazine* v33 no3 p33 S/O 2017

Your CHECKLIST E. Jardina and C. Salwitz color *Sunset* v238 no2 p44 F 2017

Your CHECKLIST E. Jardina color *Sunset* v238 no3 p40 Mr 2017

Zoodle Ramen Bowl J. BOWDEN and J. BESSINGER color *Better Nutrition* v79 no3 p70 Mr 2017

Vegetables—Prices

Magic Greens K. Krader color *Bloomberg Businessweek* no4527 p88 Je 19 2017

Vegetarian cooking

Abiodun Henderson J. BAINBRIDGE *Atlanta* v57 no2 p54 Je 2017

THE PALEO VEGAN L. Turner color *Amazing Wellness* v8 no2 p84 Spr 2016

Vegetarian foods

PLANT-Powered J. D. Hench color *Dance Spirit* v21 no8 p50 O 2017

Vegetarian restaurants—Evaluation

By Chloe N. Niarchos color *New Yorker* v93 no12 p13 My 8 2017

THE HOT LIST *Los Angeles Magazine* v62 no6 p86 Je 2017

NIGHT *Atlanta* v56 no12 p77 Ap 2017

VEG OUT E. WARTZMAN color *Bon Appetit* no1 p64 F 2017

Vegetarianism

Baguette Basics color *Vegetarian Today* no1 p38 F 2017

Cheesy Broccoli Soup color *Vegetarian Today* no1 p8 F 2017

Chicago-Style Pizza color *Vegetarian Today* no1 p20 F 2017

Chili fest J. Iserloh color *Yoga Journal* no287 p64 N 2016

Chocolate Cheesecake color *Vegetarian Today* no1 p48 F 2017

COMMUNITY color *Vegetarian Times* v43 no2 p10 N/D 2016

COOK THE BOOKS M. M. Chappell color *Vegetarian Times* v43

no2 p58 N/D 2016

Culinary Power Plants P. KUH *Los Angeles Magazine* p62 D 2016

diet for a green planet K. Kelly color *Yoga Journal* p117 2017 Special Issue

DIY Delicious [Cover story] S. Morrow and M. M. Chappell color *Vegetarian Times* v43 no2 p45 N/D 2016

FATHER PFLEGER B. Zehme color *Chicago* v65 no12 p152 D 2016

THE FUTURE OF VEGANISM D. Wasserrman and C. Stabler *Vegetarian Journal* v36 no1 p4 2017

Golden Risotto color *Vegetarian Today* no1 p24 F 2017

GOOD FOOD FOR the holidays *Vegetarian Times* v43 no2 p4 N/D 2016

Key Lime Cookies color *Vegetarian Today* no1 p46 F 2017

Let Them Eat veGan Cake l. mcguiness *Vegetarian Journal* v35 no4 p16 2016

Make Your Own Vegan Condiments N. Berkoff *Vegetarian Journal* v36 no1 p6 2017

NOTES FROM THE VRG SCIENTIFIC DEPARTMENT *Vegetarian Journal* v36 no1 p29 2017

Nutritional Yeast Dishes D. Wasserman *Vegetarian Journal* v36 no3 p13 2017

Oat-standing color *Vegetarian Today* no1 p30 F 2017

Party Time! R. Best color *Vegetarian Times* v43 no2 p52 N/D 2016

PETA'S VEGAN COLLEGE COOKBOOK D. Wasserman *Vegetarian Journal* v36 no2 p31 2017

Portable Picnic Feasts N. Berkoff *Vegetarian Journal* v36 no2 p6 2017

QUESTION: Can I be vegetarian and still gain muscle? E. SHAW color *Muscle & Performance* v9 no11 p38 N 2017

Quick and Easy Pear Dishes N. Berkoff *Vegetarian Journal* v36 no1 p10 2017

reviews. EAT AND RUN: MY UNLIKELY JOURNEY TO ULTRAMARATHON GREATNESS S. Lawrence *Vegetarian Journal* v36 no3 p31 2017

reviews. STREET VEGAN D. Wasserman *Vegetarian Journal* v35 no1 p31 2016

reviews. SUPERFOODS FOR LIFE, CACAO R. Mangels *Vegetarian Journal* v35 no1 p31 2016

SCRUMPTIOUS SAMPLER A. Wolfe color *Vegetarian Times* v43 no2 p80 N/D 2016

Stuffed Poblanos color *Vegetarian Today* no1 p18 F 2017

Tomato Soup color *Vegetarian Today* no1 p10 F 2017

Transform Yourself N. BRECHKA color *Better Nutrition* v79 no7 p62 Jl 2017

VEGAN BURGER Condiments *Vegetarian Journal* v35 no2 p12 2016

A Vegan in a Refugee Camp on the Thai-Burma Border Y. Radbod *Vegetarian Journal* v35 no2 p6 2016

Vegetable Soup color *Vegetarian Today* no1 p12 F 2017

The Vegetarian Journal's 2016 Essay Contest Winner *Vegetarian Journal* v35 no4 p11 2016

Veggie Nice! K. SHERWOOD *Nutrition Action Health Letter* v43 no9 p11 N 2016

VRG Catalog *Vegetarian Journal* v35 no2 p33 2016

Weight Loss Strategies That Work color *Prevention* v69 no9 p15 O 2017

WINTER Warmer color *Vegetarian Times* v43 no2 p88 N/D 2016

Vegetarianism—History

You Are What You Eat E. Fudge *History Today* v67 no2 p41 F 2017

Vegetarianism—Societies, etc.

35 Year of Vegan Activism *Vegetarian Journal* v36 no3 p18 2017

Help Create a Veggie World *Vegetarian Journal* v36 no1 p32 2017

Help Create a Veggie World *Vegetarian Journal* v36 no3 p32 2017

NOTE FROM THE COORDINATORS. 35 YEARS OF VEGAN ACTIVISM BY THE VEGETARIAN RESOURCE GROUP D. Wasserman and C. Stahler *Vegetarian Journal* v36 no3 p4 2017

NOTES FROM THE VRG SCIENTIFIC DEPARTMENT *Vegetarian Journal* v35 no4 p23 2016

Where Are They Now? Cathing Up with the Past VRG Interns and Scholarships Winners C. Brown and H. Francis *Vegetarian Journal* v36 no3 p9 2017

Vegetarians—Humor

Just Joking bw color *National Geographic Kids* no474 p32 O

2017
Laughter *Reader's Digest* v188 no1124 p98 O 2016

Vegetation & climate
See also
Growing season (Agriculture)
A human-driven decline in global burned area N. Andela, D. C. Morton et al chart graph map *Science* v356 no6345 p1356 Je 30 2017

Vegetation & climate—Research
Flora finders J. BENNETT color *Canadian Geographic* v136 no6 p31 D 2016

Vehicle design & construction
See also
Bicycle design & construction
Motor vehicle design & construction
Hot Rod Anything! Medieval One P. Thomas bw color *Hot Rod* v70 no8 p12 Ag 2017

Vehicle models
See also
Freight car models
Locomotive models
Model airplanes
Railroad cars—Models
InterMountain N scale SD40-2 with sound D. Kawala color *Model Railroader* v84 no9 p60 S 2017

Vehicle models—Evaluation
TOP THREE: ENJOY THE RIDE A. DAVIES color *Wired* v25 no10 p48 O 2017

Vehicle motors
See also
Motorcycle engines
MY INDIAN TAMING A THOROUGHBRED SCOUT IS TOUGH BUT FTR750 GRATIFYING EXPERIENCE A. Colton color *Cycle World* v56 no9 p44 O 2017
SERVICE R. NIERLICH and K. Cameron color *Cycle World* v56 no7 p54 Ag 2017
Small Wonders Two promising boosters for our ever-shrinking engines F. Markus bw *Motor Trend* v69 no8 p30 Ag 2017

Vehicles
See also
Airplanes
Autonomous vehicles
Carriages & carts
Four-wheel drive vehicles
Railroad trains
Space vehicles
Trailers
Wheels
A Farm Forever A. Woldt *New York State Conservationist* v71 no6 p32 Je 2017

Vehicles—Design & construction
See also
Bicycles—Design & construction
Ezra Dyer color *Car & Driver* v62 no6 p36 D 2016
Ray Evernham R. Evernham color *Car & Driver* v62 no6 p38 D 2016

Vehicles—Evaluation
Steering You Right M. L. Tellado *Consumer Reports* v82 no4 p5 Ap 2017

Vehicles—Sales & prices
How to Get a Great Deal on a Lease D. MUHLBAUM *Kiplinger's Personal Finance* v71 no1 p38 Ja 2017

Veiga, Christina
Special Ed Teacher Puts His Background to Work in the Classroom bw *Education Digest* v83 no2 p21 O 2017

Veillette, Beth
The SAILING SCENE color *Sail* v48 no6 p6 Je 2017

Veillette, Pat
The SAILING SCENE color *Sail* v48 no6 p6 Je 2017

VEISSIEÈE, SAMUEL
WHEN HEALING IS A NO-BRAINER *Psychology Today* v50 no4 p62 Ag 2017

VEITCH, JAMES
Scamming The Scammers *Reader's Digest* v189 no1128 p15 Mr 2017

Veiteberg, Jorunn

Making Spaces G. Haraldseth color *Art in America* v105 no5 p37 My 2017

Veith, Michael
De-extinction, nomenclature, and the law color *Science* v356 no6342 p1016 Je 9 2017

Vekrellis, Kostas
Lee Rubin: Our mentor and role model *Science* v355 no6327 p806 F 24 2017

Vela, C. I. A.
Persistent effects of pre-Columbian plant domestication on Amazonian forest composition bibl chart graph map *Science* v355 no6328 p925 Mr 3 2017

Vela, Filemon
UP AGAINST the Wall E. BENSON *Texas Monthly* v44 no11 p66 N 2016

Vela-Martín, Alberto
The turbulent cascade in five dimensions color *Science* v357 no6353 p782 Ag 25 2017

Velamuri, S. Ramakrishna
Being an Ethical Business in a Corrupt Environment *Harvard Business Review Digital Articles* p2 Mr 23 2017

Velarde-Felix, Jesùs S.
Red squirrels in the British Isles are infected with leprosy bacilli bibl color diag map *Science* v354 no6313 p744 N 11 2016

Velasco, Jorge
Christopher Speakers CSP1 Reference Monitors color *Downbeat* v84 no2 p98 F 2017

Velasquez-Manoff, Moises
DOCTOR WHO? color *New York Times Magazine* p68 My 21 2017

VELA-WILLIAMSON, MELISSA
The Question *O, The Oprah Magazine* p16 My 2017

VELAZQUEZ, ERIC
STRENGTH GONE SIMPLE color *Muscle & Performance* v9 no4 p14 Ap 2017

Velde, Greetje Vande
De novo design of a biologically active amyloid bibl graph *Science* v354 no6313 paah4949-1 N 11 2016

Veldhuis, Tyas
An interactive three-dimensional digital atlas and quantitative database of human development bibl color graph *Science* v354 no6315 paag0053-1 N 25 2016

Veldink, Jan H.
Negative selection in humans and fruit flies involves synergistic epistasis chart graph *Science* v356 no6337 p539 My 5 2017

Vélez, Jennifer
Heavens to Betsy cartoon chart map *Mother Jones* v42 no2 p30 Mr/Ap 2017

Vélez, Saùl
A molecular spin-photovoltaic device color diag *Science* v357 no6352 p677 Ag 18 2017

Vella, Karmenu
Maintaining Healthy Ocean Fisheries to Support Livelihoods: Achieving SDG 14 in Europe *UN Chronicle* v54 no1/2 p1 2017

Vella, Matt
Fast & Furious: The Completist's Guide color *Time* v189 no14 p54 Ap 17 2017
Gilbert Baker color *Time* v189 no14 p15 Ap 17 2017
The Hackers color diag *Time* v188 no25-26 p102 D 19 2016 Double Issue
A Shocking Internet Attack Shows America's Vulnerability color diag *Time* v188 no19 p7 N 7 2016
Summer Movie Preview: August color *Time* v189 no20 p58 My 29 2017
Summer Movie Preview: July color *Time* v189 no20 p56 My 29 2017
Summer Movie Preview: June color *Time* v189 no20 p50 My 29 2017
Summer Movie Preview: May color *Time* v189 no20 p48 My 29 2017
Tesla's Electric Shock color *Time* v189 no15 p13 Ap 24 2017
Uber Fail [Cover story] color diag *Time* v189 no24 p22 Je 26 2017
A Utopian Idea Whose Time May Finally Have Arrived color *Time* v189 no15 p17 Ap 24 2017
What Silicon Valley Can Learn from Travis Kalanick's Uber Fail color *Time* v190 no1 p23 Jl 3 2017

Food for Thought M. Nandini Mitra *Earth Island Journal* v32 no3 p2 Aut 2017

Venezuela—Social conditions—1999-

An Elegy for Venezuela's Revolution M. GONZALEZ *In These Times* v41 no7 p15 Jl 2017

What's Really Going Down in Venezuela R. Erlich color *Progressive* v81 no7 p45 O/N 2017

Vengroff, Harvey

A Sarasota Scenario: One developer's battle to build affordable housing *Governing* v30 no8 p27 My 2017

Venice (Italy)

Splendor in the Glass C. FOGES *Architectural Record* v205 no9 p104 S 2017

Venice (Italy)—History—Republic, 697-1797

Why Innovators Should Study the Rise and Fall of the Venetian Empire P. Formica color *Harvard Business Review Digital Articles* p2 Ja 17 2017

Venice (Los Angeles, Calif.)

Minimalist Appeal P. KUH *Los Angeles Magazine* p42 Ja 2017

Venice (Los Angeles, Calif.)—Social conditions

Fun Filters Don't Make Good Neighbors S. Frier, A. Ito et al color *Bloomberg Businessweek* no4513 p35 Mr 6 2017

Venkatachari, Dilip

Messaging Apps Are Changing How Companies Talk with Customers *Harvard Business Review Digital Articles* p2 S 23 2016

Venkatakrishnan, Natarajan (Venkat)

How GE Appliances Built an Innovation Lab to Rapidly Prototype Products *Harvard Business Review Digital Articles* p2 Jl 18 2017

Venkataraman, S.

Being an Ethical Business in a Corrupt Environment *Harvard Business Review Digital Articles* p2 Mr 23 2017

Venkatasubba Sreekantan, Badanaval

M. G. K. Menon (1928–2016) color *Science* v355 no6325 p586 F 10 2017

Venkatesan, Rajkumar

A Better Way to Calculate the ROI of Your Marketing Investment *Harvard Business Review Digital Articles* p2 N 10 2015

Venkatesh, Vinodh

New Maricón Cinema: Outing Latin American Film M. BETANCOURT *Film Quarterly* v70 no3 p95 Spr 2017

Venkatraman, N. Venkat

Alphabet Isn't a Typical Conglomerate *Harvard Business Review Digital Articles* p2 Ag 18 2015

What Comes After Smart Products *Harvard Business Review Digital Articles* p2 Jl 1 2015

Venker, Suzanne

Inviting controversy D. Bendis color *Christian Century* v134 no15 p10 Jl 19 2017

Vennes, S.

An unusual white dwarf star may be a surviving remnant of a subluminous Type Ia supernova chart diag *Science* v357 no6352 p680 Ag 18 2017

Vennestrøm, Peter N. R.

A molecular dance to cleaner air color *Science* v357 no6354 p866 S 1 2017

Vens, Celine

Predicting human olfactory perception from chemical features of odor molecules bibl diag graph *Science* v355 no6327 p820 F 24 2017

Venson, George

Voutsa S. COCHRAN color *Architectural Digest* v74 no10 p102 O 1 2017

Venteicher, Andrew S.

Decoupling genetics, lineages, and microenvironment in IDH-mutant gliomas by single-cell RNA-seq diag *Science* v355 no6332 p1391 Mr 31 2017

Venter, J. Craig, 1946-

HOW TO CHEAT DEATH [Cover story] M. HERPER color map *Forbes* v199 no2 p74 F 28 2017

NEWSMAKERS *Science* v357 no6358 p1333 S 29 2017

What A $25,000 Medical Test Can't Tell You C. Chen bw *Bloomberg Businessweek* no4539 p21 S 25 2017

Ventilation

See also

Natural ventilation

How Transom Windows Work A. Santantonio color *Old House Journal* v45 no7 p50 O 2017

THE TOLL TRAVEL TAKES C. Barakat and M. Freckleton color *Equus* no477 p22 Je 2017

Ventilating an Attic M. E. Polson color diag *Old House Journal* v45 no4 p52 Je 2017

WINTER BARN VENTILATION C. Barakat and M. Freckleton color *Equus* no470 p24 N 2016

Winterize Your Home color *Good Housekeeping* v265 no5 p59 N 2017

Ventilation design & construction

Breath of Fresh Air K. Logan *Architectural Record* v205 no7 p126 Jl 2017

Ventimiglia, Milo

THE BEST TV OF 2016 [Cover story] M. ROUSH *TV Guide* p20 D 19 2016

Family fears J. Chu color *Christian Century* v134 no3 p37 F 2017

Laughter and tears flow freely in the season's most moving new show M. ROUSH color *TV Guide* v64 no42 p18 O 10 2016

Lighten Your Workload B. CARLEY color *GQ: Gentlemen's Quarterly* v97 no7 p84 Jl 2017

THIS IS US I. Ratledge *TV Guide* v65 no39 p36 S 18 2017

Ventoux Mountain (France)

WHAT IT TAKES TO RIDE... MONT VENTOUX J. See and S. Yeager color *Bicycling* v58 no9 p36 O 2017

Ventrudo, Brian

The Father of Southern Astronomy *Sky & Telescope* v134 no4 p34 O 2017

Ventura, C.

Observation of a large-scale anisotropy in the arrival directions of cosmic rays above 8×1018 eV *Science* v357 no6357 p1266 S 22 2017

Ventura, Eduardo

AROUND RIO DE JANEIRO C. RIGBY cartoon color *ARTnews* v115 no3 p150 Fall 2016

Ventura, Miguel

FROM PORTUGAL WITH LOVE W. BOLAND and M. SAMET bw color *Climbing* no353 p66 My/Je 2017

Ventura, Yordano, 1991-2017

Milestones *Time* v189 no4 p13 F 6 2017

Mourning After T. Verducci and T. Keith color *Sports Illustrated* v126 no4 p14 Ja 30 2017

Ventura County (Calif.)

BEST VALUE TOWNS 2017 [Cover story] C. Ryan color *Sunset* v238 no2 p48 F 2017

Venture capital

BALLERS I. BOUDWAY color *Bloomberg Businessweek* no4535 p44 Ag 28 2017

Expand innovation finance via crowdfunding O. Sorenson, V. Assenova et al bibl color graph map *Science* v354 no6319 p1526 D 23 2016

FEDERAL FINANCE *Economic Indicators* p32 Mr 2017

How Talent Pulls One Over on the Capitalists R. L. Martin *Harvard Business Review Digital Articles* p2 Ag 4 2015

ONCE CODDLED, NOW CURBED E. Griffith color *Fortune* v176 no3 p40 S 1 2017

The Other Brother [Cover story] S. BERTONI color *Forbes* v199 no4 p70 Ap 25 2017

VR STARTUPS ARE A HOT COMMODITY diag *Fortune* v175 no7 p11 Je 1 2017

We Recorded VCs' Conversations and Analyzed How Differently They Talk About Female Entrepreneurs M. Malmstrom, J. Johansson et al *Harvard Business Review Digital Articles* p2 My 17 2017

What Big Companies Can Learn from the Success of the Unicorns A. De Massis, F. Frattini et al *Harvard Business Review Digital Articles* p2 Mr 14 2016

What BMW's Corporate VC Offers That Regular Investors Can't G. Gimmy, D. Kanbach et al *Harvard Business Review Digital Articles* p2 Jl 27 2017

Why Sexual Harassment Is More of a Problem in Venture Capital J. C. Williams *Harvard Business Review Digital Articles* p2 Jl 12 2017

Venture capital—California—Santa Clara Valley

Oh, the Places You'll Go! S. ADAMS color *Forbes* v198 no7 p52 N 29 2016

Verden (Germany)
DRESSAGE SNAPSHOTS color *Dressage Today* v23 no4 p13 D 2016

Verdi, Giuseppe, 1813-1901
La Traviata *Opera News* v81 no9 p58 Mr 2017
Nabucco *Opera News* v81 no7 p54 Ja 2017
Operapedia: La Traviata *Opera News* v81 no6 p12 D 2016

Verdieck, Eileen
the WAY WE ARE *Arabian Horse World* v57 no6 p48 Mr 2017

VERDIER, JAMES M.
The Coming Era of Open Data *BioScience* v67 no3 p191 Mr 2017
A Forum for Integrating the Life Sciences *BioScience* v67 no10 p871 O 2017
Science Communication *BioScience* v67 no6 p487 Je 2017

Verdin, Monique
Her Louisiana Love A. R. HARRISON bw *New Orleans Magazine* v52 no1 p28 S 2017

Verdine, Vanessa
Nucleic acid detection with CRISPR-Cas13a/C2c2 color diag *Science* v356 no6336 p438 Ap 28 2017

Verdon, Charles
A Stellar Experimental Facility for Stockpile Sustainment and Fundamental Science *Science & Technology Review* p3 D 2016

Verdu, Elena F.
How infection can incite sensitivity to food diag *Science* v356 no6333 p29 Ap 7 2017

Verdu, Paul
Dispersals and genetic adaptation of Bantu-speaking populations in Africa and North America diag *Science* v356 no6337 p543 My 5 2017

Verducci, Tom
15 HOME SWEET HOMERS color *Sports Illustrated* v126 no9 p68 Mr 27 2017
16 PITCH WHISPERERS color *Sports Illustrated* v126 no9 p69 Mr 27 2017
17 MACRO MANAGING color *Sports Illustrated* v126 no9 p70 Mr 27 2017
1 THE NEW TESTAMENT color *Sports Illustrated* v126 no9 p40 Mr 27 2017
7 AFTER BIG PAPI, THE LITTLE THINGS color *Sports Illustrated* v126 no9 p49 Mr 27 2017
9 BORN TO WIN [Cover story] color diag *Sports Illustrated* v126 no9 p52 Mr 27 2017
Actionable Offenses color diag *Sports Illustrated* v126 no7 p20 Mr 6 2017
C of Joy color *Sports Illustrated* v125 no17 p32 N 21 2016 Double Issue
CONTACT HIGH color diag *Sports Illustrated* v127 no8 p44 S 18 2017
THE CUBS WAY color *Sports Illustrated* v126 no8 p78 Mr 20 2017
Ghostbusters [Cover story] color *Sports Illustrated* v125 no12 p24 O 10 2016
In Tom We Trust color *Sports Illustrated* v126 no9 p12 Mr 27 2017
LOVE SPRINGS ETERNAL color *Sports Illustrated* v127 no4 p38 Ag 7 2017
Mourning After color *Sports Illustrated* v126 no4 p14 Ja 30 2017
The Rainmaker color *Sports Illustrated* v125 no20 p110 D 19 2016
REAL MEN HAVE CURVES [Cover story] color *Sports Illustrated* v126 no15 p36 My 29 2017
SEVENTH SONS color *Sports Illustrated* v127 no10 p40 O 2 2017
SPECIAL K color *Sports Illustrated* v126 no18 p40 Je 26 2017
STANDSTILL color *Sports Illustrated* v126 no18 p36 Je 26 2017
Summer Madness color *Sports Illustrated* v126 no8 p20 Mr 20 2017
WORLD SERIES It Happened [Cover story] color *Sports Illustrated* v125 no16 p24 N 14 2016
WORLD SERIES Timeless color *Sports Illustrated* v125 no15 p30 N 7 2016

Verdugo, Claudio
A genetic signature of the evolution of loss of flight in the Galapagos cormorant color diag *Science* v356 no6341 p921 Je 1 2017

Verfaillie, Catherine

De novo design of a biologically active amyloid bibl graph *Science* v354 no6313 paah4949-1 N 11 2016

Vergara, Sofia, 1972-
DAMN, SOFIA! [Cover story] L. Majewski color *Women's Health* v14 no7 p49 S 2017

Vergara Quispe, I. D.
Observation of a large-scale anisotropy in the arrival directions of cosmic rays above 8×1018 eV *Science* v357 no6357 p1266 S 22 2017

Vergauwe, Jasmine
Too Much Charisma Can Make Leaders Look Less Effective *Harvard Business Review Digital Articles* p2 S 26 2017

Verger, Rob
COUNTING SLEEP color *Popular Science* v289 no5 p35 S/O 2017
DIGGING UP THE PAST color *Popular Science* v289 no5 p26 S/O 2017
Downhill dynamo color *Popular Science* v289 no6 p34 N/D 2017
FIND YOUR INNER PREPPER color *Popular Science* v289 no4 p32 Jl/Ag 2017
A MIGHTY (QUIET) WIND color *Popular Science* v289 no4 p26 Jl/Ag 2017
STORM BRAIN color *Popular Science* v289 no4 p30 Jl/Ag 2017
supersize supercell supersimulation color *Popular Science* v289 no4 p16 Jl/Ag 2017
These skis fold in half! color diag *Popular Science* v289 no6 p30 N/D 2017
This AI flushes out trolls color *Popular Science* v289 no6 p65 N/D 2017
WAIT A SECOND (AND A HALF) color *Popular Science* v289 no5 p24 S/O 2017

Vergés, Adriana
Accelerating Tropicalization and the Transformation of Temperate Seagrass Meadows *BioScience* v66 no11 p938 N 1 2016
Biodiversity redistribution under climate change: Impacts on ecosystems and human well-being color *Science* v355 no6332 p1389 Mr 31 2017

VERGHESE, ABRAHAM
Baby Steps *New York Times Book Review* p16 Je 25 2017

Verghese, Abraham, 1955-—Awards
Abraham Verghese E. W. Gutting *Humanities* v37 no4 p1 Fall 2016

Vergil, Polydore, ca. 1470-1555
1499: Padua P. Vergil *Lapham's Quarterly* v10 no2 p91 Spr 2017

VERHAGEN, WILLEM
Harmonizing Biodiversity Conservation and Productivity in the Context of Increasing Demands on Landscapes graph *BioScience* v66 no10 p890 O 1 2016

VERHEGGEN, FRANÇOIS
The Odor of Death: An Overview of Current Knowledge on Characterization and Applications *BioScience* v67 no7 p600 Jl 2017

Verheyen, Erik
Oil extraction imperils Africa's Great Lakes bibl color *Science* v354 no6312 p561 N 4 2016

VERHEYEN, KRIS
Combining Biodiversity Resurveys across Regions to Advance Global Change Research *BioScience* v67 no1 p73 Ja 2017

Verhoef, Lisette G. G. C.
Reticulon 3–dependent ER-PM contact sites control EGFR non-clathrin endocytosis color diag graph *Science* v356 no6338 p617 My 12 2017

Verhoeven, Paul
AGENTS PROVOCATEURS M. HASKELL color *Film Comment* v52 no6 p38 N/D 2016
Elle C. Nashawaty color *Entertainment Weekly* no1440 p47 N 18 2016
Elle's Belle: Huppert Resounds In Verhoeven's Latest S. Zacharek color *Time* v188 no21 p67 N 21 2016
Judging The Art And Not The Artist S. ERICKSON *Los Angeles Magazine* p86 D 2016
Rape comedy? Really? J. SEMLEY color *Maclean's* v129 no47 p63 N 28 2016

Verhoogen, Eric
How Labor Standards Can Be Good for Growth *Harvard Business Review Digital Articles* p2 Ap 27 2016

Verhovek, Sam Howe

Shoot for the moon. Again color diag *National Geographic* v232 no2 p32 Ag 2017

Verily Life Sciences LLC

Downsizing Google's Dream C. Chen and M. Bergen color *Bloomberg Businessweek* no4519 p36 Ap 24 2017

Verini, James

BEFORE DAWN ON A SUNDAY LATE *New York Times Magazine* p48 N 20 2016

LIFE AFTER ISIS color map *National Geographic* v231 no4 p96 Ap 2017

THE LIVING AND THE DEAD *New York Times Magazine* p36 Jl 23 2017

Verismo (Music)

Anna Netrebko: Verismo J. S. Lessner *Opera News* v81 no9 p54 Mr 2017

Veritas Genetics (Company)

Baby Genome Sequencing for Sale in China A. Regalado il *MIT Technology Review* v120 no5 p13 S/O 2017

VERIVE, JOHN M.

99 Cans Of Beer On the Wall *Los Angeles Magazine* p48 Ja 2017

HOPS OVER THE HILL *Los Angeles Magazine* p46 My 2017

Verizon Communications Inc.

CAR SMARTIFIER color *Good Housekeeping* v264 no6 p77 Je 2017

Watching Your DVR From Anywhere M. ANTONOFF and C. Crowley color *Sound & Vision* v81 no9 p24 N 2016

Verizon Communications Inc.—Officials & employees

VERIZON'S STRIKE SETTLEMENT A. Pressman color *Fortune* v174 no8 p20 D 15 2016

Verlander, Justin, 1983-

PER ASPERA AD ASTRO B. Reiter color *Sports Illustrated* v127 no9 p20 S 25 2017

Verma, Deepshikha

Emergence and spread of a human-transmissible multidrug-resistant nontuberculous mycobacterium bibl diag graph *Science* v354 no6313 p751 N 11 2016

Verma, Seema

The Medicaid Flexibility Puzzle: How much freedom should states have to tailor the program to local conditions? M. Quinn *Governing* v30 no12 p18 S 2017

Verma, Varun

Nanophotonic rare-earth quantum memory with optically controlled retrieval diag graph *Science* v357 no6358 p1392 S 29 2017

Vermeer, Johannes, 1632-1675

EDITOR'S LETTER G. Cerio *Magazine Antiques* v184 no5 p14 S/O 2017

Vermeren, Peter

The Accidental Bike Shop M. HURFORD color *Bicycling* v58 no4 p50 My 2017

Vermette, Stephen

Chains of Connection: Alexander Von Humboldt's Meteorological Legacy Lives On color map *Weatherwise* v69 no6 p32 N-D 2016

Vermeule, Adrian

Pangloss And the Bureaucrats J. H. ADLER color *National Review* v69 no2 p35 F 6 2017

Vermeulen, Freek

3 Steps to Break Out in a Tired Industry *Harvard Business Review Digital Articles* p2 My 1 2015

5 Strategy Questions Every Leader Should Make Time For *Harvard Business Review Digital Articles* p2 S 3 2015

Stop Comparing Management to Sports *Harvard Business Review Digital Articles* p2 Je 2 2016

Stop Paying Executives for Performance *Harvard Business Review Digital Articles* p2 F 23 2016

What Happens When All Employees Work When They Feel Like It *Harvard Business Review Digital Articles* p2 D 17 2014

What So Many Strategists Get Wrong About Disruption color *Harvard Business Review Digital Articles* p2 Ja 3 2017

Vermeulen, Nicolaas A.

Bottom-up construction of a superstructure in a porous uranium-organic crystal color graph *Science* v356 no6338 p624 My 12 2017

Vermont

CAST AWAY F. F. Van de Water *Harper's Magazine* v333 no1999

p73 D 2016

The Meandering Poultney River R. H. MOHLENBROCK *Natural History* v125 no1 p36 D 2016/Ja 2017

Vermont—Description & travel

Holiday Shopping Towns K. K. BECKIUS color *Yankee* v80 no6 p94 N/D 2016

VERMONT *Yankee* p140 My/Je 2017

Vermouth

The No-Frills NEGRONI A. Rapoport and J. Harman color *Glamour* v115 no1 p96 Ja 2017

PINK IS THE NEW BLACK: We could sip Etto's sprightly vermouth cocktail all afternoon long *Washingtonian Magazine* v52 no8 p134 My 2017

Vermund, Sten H.

Fund global health: Save lives and money color *Science* v356 no6342 p1018 Je 9 2017

Verna, Harmony

Beneath the Apple Leaves *Publishers Weekly* v264 no19 p34 My 8 2017

Vernal equinox

Saddle Up for Spring R. Eversole color *Trail Rider* v29 no2 p24 Mr 2017

Vernalization

RESEARCH bw color *Science* v357 no6356 p1108 S 15 2017

Vernazza (Italy)

Room 8 Albergo Barbara L. LAUCHT color *Conde Nast Traveler* v52 no8 p122 S 2017

Verne, Jules, 1828-1905

A Brief History of the Future P. O'Donnell *Smithsonian* v48 no3 p12 Je 2017

Vernet, Carle, 1758-1836

MEMORIES OF Carle Vernet J. WICH-WENNING *Arabian Horse World* v57 no9 p148 Je 2017

Vernet, J.

Molecular gas in the halo fuels the growth of a massive cluster galaxy at high redshift bibl graph *Science* v354 no6316 p1128 D 2 2016

Vernon, Art

The Thread *New York Times Magazine* p9 F 12 2017

Vernon, Carla

Champion of Breakfasts bw color *Working Mother* v40 no2 p12 Je/Jl 2017

VERNON, JOHN

The Emperor Makes a Friend *New York Times Book Review* p27 O 23 2016

Vernon, Pete

The 10 best days in journalism color *Columbia Journalism Review* v56 no2 p50 Fall 2017

The 140-character president color graph *Columbia Journalism Review* v56 no2 p76 Fall 2017

Hey, big funder color *Columbia Journalism Review* v56 no1 p60 Spr 2017

OCRACOKE OBSERVER bw *Columbia Journalism Review* v56 no1 p33 Spr 2017

What if the right-wing media wins? bw color *Columbia Journalism Review* v56 no2 p52 Fall 2017

Where the digital dollars have gone graph *Columbia Journalism Review* p58 Fall/Wint 2016

Veron, Fabrice

OCEAN SPRAY: AN OUTSIZED INFLUENCE ON WEATHER AND CLIMATE *Physics Today* v69 no11 p34 N 2016

Veronica Mars (TV program)

Veronica Mars: Evil, Loner...and a Dude? J. Jensen color *Entertainment Weekly* no1460/1461 p100 Ap 7-17 2017

Ver Ploeg, Michele

ERS's Updated Food Access Research Atlas Shows an Increase in Low-Income and Low-Supermarket Access Areas in 2015 *Amber Waves: The Economics of Food, Farming, Natural Resources, & Rural America* p1 F 2017

Verreault, Jonathan

Northern exposure J. BENNETT color *Canadian Geographic* v135 no6 p33 D 2015

Verreum (Company)

A Fresh Breath for Czech Glass C. Matlack color *Bloomberg Businessweek* no4535 p42 Ag 28 2017

Verrilli, Donald

The Dangers of an Empty Seat color *Time* v188 no16/17 p80 O 24 2016

OBAMA'S AMERICA img *New York* v49 no20 p12 O 3 2016

Verrone, Patric

COMPLETE SET D. Steinberg cartoon *New Yorker* v93 no3 p23 Mr 6 2017

Versace, Donatella, 1955-

ALWAYS on MY MIND bw color *Vogue* v207 no9 p320 S 2017

DONATELLA VERSACE S. SINGER bw color *Vogue* v207 no3 p424 Mr 2017

Versace, Donatella, 1955-—Interviews

Donatella Versace E. Wilson color *InStyle* v23 no12 p97 N 2016

Verschuur, Gerrit L.

Arecibo Under the Gun *Sky & Telescope* v133 no5 p84 My 2017

Versed, Gina

Spectacle of Lights *Sierra* v102 no4 p14 Jl/Ag 2017

Verso Books (Company)

Leftist Indies Put Politics First J. Maher color *Publishers Weekly* v264 no26 p3 Je 26 2017

Verstappen, Max, 1997-

Max Verstappen J. Crelin color *Current Biography* v78 no8 p86 Ag 2017

Vertebrate anatomy

The inside story on 20,000 vertebrates R. Cross color *Science* v357 no6353 p742 Ag 25 2017

Vertebrate evolution

The "tao" of integuments Yung Chih Lai and Cheng-Ming Chuong bibl color diag *Science* v354 no6319 p1533 D 23 2016

Vertebrates

See also

Amphibians

Birds

Fishes

Mammals

Multicluster Pcdh diversity is required for mouse olfactory neural circuit assembly G. Mountoufaris, W. V. Chen et al diag *Science* v356 no6336 p411 Ap 28 2017

Rewiring metabolism under oxygen deprivation J. F. Storz and G. B. McClelland color *Science* v356 no6335 p248 Ap 21 2017

The sacral autonomic outflow is sympathetic I. Espinosa-Medina, O. Saha et al bibl color diag *Science* v354 no6314 p893 N 18 2016

Vertical farming

The Future Of Farming Is Looking Up Selina Wang color *Bloomberg Businessweek* no4537 p62 S 11 2017

Vertical gardening

1925 VERTICAL GARDENS M. MANNARINO color *Better Homes & Gardens* v95 no6 p168 Je 2017

Grow Up E. Millard color *Log Home Living* v34 no6 p36 Ag 2017

Vertical jump

BARE MINIMUM [Cover story] M. Gainsburg color *Women's Health* v14 no7 p73 S 2017

Vertically rising aircraft

XTI SWITCHES TO HYBRID — ELECTRIC PROPULSION color *Flying* v144 no5 p16 My 2017

Verutes, Gregory M.

Poor fisheries struggle with U.S. import rule bibl color *Science* v355 no6329 p1031 Mr 10 2017

Verve Wine (Company)

THE PERFECT POUR I. Frisch cartoon *Bloomberg Businessweek* no4499 p82 N 14 2016

Verweij, P. A.

The impact of hunting on tropical mammal and bird populations graph map *Science* v356 no6334 p180 Ap 14 2017

Very Large Telescope (Chile)

Starshot has ESO telescope time *Science* v355 no6321 p113 Ja 13 2017

Very light jets

WE FLY: CIRRUS VISION [Cover story] S. POPE chart color *Flying* v144 no7 p44 Jl 2017

Very light jets—Evaluation

550 ONE AVIATION'S ECLIPSE R. MARK bw chart color *Flying* v144 no2 p38 F 2017

Very Kacey Christmas, A (Music)

The Best Stocking Stuffers (And A Few Lumps Of Coal) E. R. Brown color *Entertainment Weekly* no1442 p56 D 2 2016 Re-

bellious Special Issue

Very Sordid Wedding, A (Film)

A Very Sordid Return N. Serrao color *Entertainment Weekly* no1462 p47 Ap 21 2017

Verzemnieks, Inara

Homeland: Revisiting her roots in Latvia, a woman learns what happened to her family in World War II D. BEZMOZGIS *New York Times Book Review* p8 S 17 2017

IN THE DEAD ZONE color *New York Times Magazine* p82 D 11 2016

Verzi, V.

Observation of a large-scale anisotropy in the arrival directions of cosmic rays above 8 × 1018 eV *Science* v357 no6357 p1266 S 22 2017

Vesicular-arbuscular mycorrhizas

Plants transfer lipids to sustain colonization by mutualistic mycorrhizal and parasitic fungi Y. Jiang, W. Wang et al diag graph *Science* v356 no6343 p1172 Je 16 2017

Vesper, Inga

Alien fungus blights Hawaii's native trees color *Science* v354 no6310 p273 O 21 2016

Continental Divide color *Scientific American* v317 no4 p70 O 2017

Vespers (Liturgy)

Evening's light M. Centore color *U.S. Catholic* v82 no7 p45 Jl 2017

Vest, Benjamin

Anti-coalescence of bosons on a lossy beam splitter bw chart diag graph *Science* v356 no6345 p1373 Je 30 2017

Vestager, Margrethe, 1968-

The Eurocrat Who Makes Corporate America Tremble S. SUB-RAMANIAN and A. White bw color *Bloomberg Businessweek* no4522 p68 My 15 2017

Vesterlund, Lise

New Research: Women Who Don't Negotiate Might Have a Good Reason *Harvard Business Review Digital Articles* p2 Ap 12 2016

Vestfirdir (Iceland)

STRANDED P. Stefánsson *Iceland Review* v54 no6 p92 N/D 2016

Vests—Evaluation

ALMOST NAKED! J. LINDSEY color *Bicycling* v58 no7 p72 Ag 2017

Hunt Down the Next Camo B. CARLEY color *GQ: Gentlemen's Quarterly* v97 no10 p68 O 2017

ONYX color *Canoe & Kayak Magazine* v45 no1 p96 Wint 2017

VEST IN CLASS color *Runner's World* v52 no3 p53 Ap 2017

Vesuvius (Italy)—History

The Map K. Wiles *History Today* v67 no4 p26 Ap 2017

Veterans

Birds for the Battle-worn P. SAHA color *Audubon* v119 no3 p26 Fall 2017

Changing of the Guard L. TRETHEWEY color *Walrus* v14 no9 p20 N 2017

EXPERIENCE: THE INSURGENT color *MHQ: Quarterly Journal of Military History* v30 no1 p18 Aut 2017

FIGHTER TO FARMER: NOMINATE FARMER VETERANS YOU KNOW FOR THE 2017 CONTEST J. Scott *Successful Farming* v115 no6 p54 Ap 2017

A (Frightening) Bird's Eye View R. R. RYDER *USA Today Magazine* v145 no2858 p41 N 2016

FROM FIGHTER TO FARMER J. Scott *Successful Farming* v114 no11 p50 N 2016

GIVING BACK R. Cartagena *Washingtonian Magazine* v52 no3 p106 D 2016

He Paints Their Final Portraits J. LABIANCA *Reader's Digest* v188 no1124 p8 O 2016

MEET THE FIGHTER TO FARMER RECIPIENTS J. Scott *Successful Farming* v114 no10 p58 O 2016

Solar-Ready Vet P. Rauber *Sierra* v102 no2 p26 Mr/Ap 2017

WE OWE A LOT TO OUR VETERANS D. KURNS *Successful Farming* v114 no11 p6 N 2016

Veterans' benefits—United States

The Military's Got a New Spin on Retirement D. Kadlec color diag *Money* v46 no6 p28 Jl 2017

Veterans Day

ABOVE & BEYOND cartoon *New Yorker* v92 no37 p28 N 14

2017

DAYTONA GRAND PRIX color *Road & Track* v68 no7 p16 Mr/Ap 2017

Vetter, Jonas

Why B2B Companies Struggle with Collaborative Innovation *Harvard Business Review Digital Articles* p2 Mr 16 2016

Vetus BV

Smooth Operator D. HARDING JR. color *Power & Motoryacht* v33 no1 p95 Ja 2017

Veugelers, Reinhilde

Crossing borders along an endless frontier color *Science* v356 no6339 p694 My 19 2017

Vevers, Stuart

COACH'S DINO-MITE YEAR S. Cristobal color *Harper's Bazaar* no3649 p322 D 2016/Ja 2017

Physical Graffiti N. SULLIVAN cartoon color *Esquire* v167 no1 p31 F 2017

VEVO LLC—Finance

Stepping Out of YouTube's Shadow S. CARPENTER color *Forbes* v198 no6 p52 N 8 2016

Veyne, Paul

Goodbye, Palmyra B. Allen color *Weekly Standard* v22 no33 p38 My 8 2017

LOST TREASURE RECAPTURED IN WORDS: The destruction of Palmyra robbed us of one of antiquity's great trading cities. A slim but evocative study reminds us of its importance L. Gregoratti *History Today* v67 no10 p96 O 2017

THE OASIS OF PALMYRA *Lapham's Quarterly* v10 no1 p214 Wint 2017

Vezina, Kenrick

Tu Youyou *Current Biography* v78 no2 p90 F 2017

VF Corp.

WRANGLES *Texas Monthly* v45 no1 p70 Ja 2017

VHF devices

BELT & SUSPENDERS Z. Prochazka *Sea Magazine* v108 no10 p60 O 2016

Viale, Telma

How to Select the Right Freelancer for the Work *Harvard Business Review Digital Articles* p2 F 23 2016

Viall, Nick

Sound Bites color *Entertainment Weekly* no1448 p6 Ja 13 2017

Viana, Blandina

Ten policies for pollinators bibl color *Science* v354 no6315 p975 N 25 2016

Viana, Helder

Positive biodiversity-productivity relationship predominant in global forests bibl chart graph map *Science* v354 no6309 paaf8957-1 O 14 2016

Viar, Lori

Why People Quit Their Jobs: Interaction *Harvard Business Review* v94 no11 p18 N 2016

Viard, Alan D.

We Need to Raise Taxes for Shareholders and Cut Them for Companies *Harvard Business Review Digital Articles* p2 N 1 2016

Viboud, Cécile

Death March of 1918 bw color *Natural History* v125 no9 p11 S 2017

First flu is forever bibl diag *Science* v354 no6313 p706 N 11 2016

Vibrans, Alexander C.

Positive biodiversity-productivity relationship predominant in global forests bibl chart graph map *Science* v354 no6309 paaf8957-1 O 14 2016

Vibraphonists

The 'Always Striving' Bobby Hutcherson: 1941-2016 Y. Kato bw *Downbeat* v83 no11 p16 N 2016

Vibrations of foundations

Taking six-dimensional spectra in finite time J. Goodknight and A. Aspuru-Guzik diag *Science* v356 no6345 p1333 Je 30 2017

Vibrators (Massage)

THE NEW TURN-ONS C. CARTER and K. CARTER color *Men's Health* v32 no7 p114 S 2017

The Sex Toy Awards color *Glamour* v115 no10 p125 O 2017

Vicca, Sara

Response to Comment on "Mycorrhizal association as a primary control of the CO2 fertilization effect" bibl graph *Science* v355 no6323 p358 Ja 27 2017

Vice Media LLC—Finance

GONZO GOLD RUSH N. ROBEHMED color *Forbes* v200 no1 p24 Jl 27 2017

Vice-Presidential candidates

KAINE COUNTRY E. OSNOS bw cartoon *New Yorker* v92 no34 p40 O 24 2016

Vice-Presidential candidates—Attitudes

For the Record color *Time* v188 no15 p4 O 17 2016

Vice-Presidents

All That I Can and Would Like to Do Is to Make You All Speak and Act to Enable Effective Functioning of the House: I CERTAINLY CAN'T BE LIKE A HEADMASTER HERDING THE ERRANT STUDENTS ON THE PATH OF DISCIPLINE *Vital Speeches of the Day* v83 no9 p261 S 2017

Meet Venezuela's New Iron-Fisted No. 2 A. Rosati, F. Zerpa et al color *Bloomberg Businessweek* no4511 p16 F 13 2017

Who's Afraid of President Pence? J. ZENGERLE color *GQ: Gentlemen's Quarterly* v97 no9 p124 S 2017

Vice-Presidents—United States

A Heartbeat Away P. SMITH *New York Times Upfront* v149 no4 p14 O 31 2016

LIFE IS WINNING IN AMERICA M. PENCE *Vital Speeches of the Day* v83 no3 p92 Mr 2017

PACKING HIS BAGGAGE C. FEHRMAN *Indianapolis Monthly* v40 no5 p46 Ja 2017

The Persistent Passion of Vice President Mike Pence P. Elliott color *Time* v189 no21 p18 Je 5 2017

THE PRESIDENT PENCE DELUSION J. MAYER bw color *New Yorker* v93 no33 p54 O 23 2017

TO DEFEND THE LIBERAL INTERATIONAL ORDER J. BIDEN *Vital Speeches of the Day* v83 no3 p75 Mr 2017

UNDER PRESIDENT TRUMP, AMERICA STANDS WITH IS-RAEL *Vital Speeches of the Day* v83 no5 p143 My 2017

When Politics Get Personal S. Detrow *America* v217 no7 p54 O 2 2017

When The Vice President Is Not a Political Prop S. Pettypiece and E. Wasson color *Bloomberg Businessweek* no4535 p34 Ag 28 2017

Vice-Presidents—United States—Attitudes

WHAT WOULD BILLY DO? L. Collins cartoon *New Yorker* v93 no8 p20 Ap 10 2017

Vice-Presidents—United States—Elections

Assistant Presidents D. F. Kettl *Governing* v30 no1 p16 O 2016

Why Pence Matters W. Kristol *Weekly Standard* v22 no6 p6 O 17 2016

Vicem Yachts Inc.

ODYSSEY AT THE CROSSROADS [Cover story] D. J. HARDING chart color diag *Power & Motoryacht* v34 no6 p40 Je 2017

VICENS, A. J.

DEFENSE OF THE NERDS color *Mother Jones* v42 no6 p57 N/D 2017

HACKER, BANKER, SOLDIER, SPY bw color *Mother Jones* v42 no4 p19 Jl/Ag 2017

HACKS, LEAKS, AND TWEETS color *Mother Jones* v42 no4 p22 Jl/Ag 2017

THE KREMLIN'S GREMLINS color *Mother Jones* v42 no4 p20 Jl/Ag 2017

ON KOMPROMAT bw *Mother Jones* v42 no4 p24 Jl/Ag 2017

PUTIN'S LONG GAME color *Mother Jones* v42 no4 p26 Jl/Ag 2017

THE RUSSIAN CONNECTION color *Mother Jones* v42 no4 p16 Jl/Ag 2017

WIKILEAKS' ROLE *Mother Jones* v42 no4 p30 Jl/Ag 2017

Viceroy's House (Film)

ALSO PLAYING color *Entertainment Weekly* no1478 / 1479 p41 Ag 18-25 2017

Vices

OLD and RIGHT A. SMITH *American Conservative* v16 no2 p29 Mr/Ap 2017

Vicha, J.

Observation of a large-scale anisotropy in the arrival directions of cosmic rays above 8×10^{18} eV *Science* v357 no6357 p1266 S 22 2017

VICK, JULIE

math word problems for today's parents color *Parents* v92 no5 p124 My 2017 reasons your baby isn't sleeping (abridged) color *Parents* v92 no4 p136 Ap 2017

Vick, Karl

The 8,000-Mile Shortcut color map *Time* v188 no16/17 p69 O 24 2016

Another Innocent Abroad color *Time* v190 no8 p58 Ag 28 2017

Between Two Worlds color *Time* v188 no18 p36 O 31 2016

The Burning Sands of Iraq color *Time* v189 no24 p30 Je 26 2017

The CIA's Hackers Find Their Secrets Posted Online color *Time* v189 no10 p12 Mr 20 2017

The Death of Iran's Ultimate Political Insider Gives Hard-Liners an Edge color *Time* v189 no4 p13 Ja 23 2017

The Digital Cloud Is Underwater-and Vulnerable color diag map *Time* v188 no15 p16 O 17 2016

Emotional Divide color diag *Time* v189 no7/8 p38 F 27 2017

Family First [Cover story] color *Time* v189 no22 p24 Je 12 2017

The Home of the Future color *Time* v189 no12 p46 Ap 3 2017

How Castro Will Be Trump's First Foreign Policy Test color *Time* v188 no24 p46 D 12 2016

Internet for All color *Time* v189 no13 p34 Ap 10 2017

The Island and the Storm color *Time* v190 no14 p26 O 9 2017

Lightbox color *Time* v189 no21 p22 Je 5 2017

The Lost Colony color *Time* v190 no15 p32 O 16 2017

The Middle East Puzzle's Missing Piece color *Time* v189 no22 p53 Je 12 2017

The Other Side [Cover story] color diag *Time* v189 no4 p24 F 6 2017

The Person of the Year [Cover story] color diag map *Time* v188 no25-26 p46 D 19 2016 Double Issue

Shimon Peres Could Change. Can the Israelis and the Palestinians? color *Time* v188 no14 p7 O 10 2016

Smoldering Ruins color *Time* v189 no22 p53 Je 12 2017

Trump's Great Faith In the Military Does Not a Strategy Make color diag *Time* v190 no1 p9 Jl 3 2017

Trump's Penchant for Chaos Brings Less World Order color *Time* v190 no8 p9 Ag 28 2017

The U.S. and Iran's New Relationship Status: Enemies, With Benefits color *Time* v189 no6 p9 F 20 2017

The U.S. Continues to Come Apart In the Wake of a Divisive Election color diag *Time* v188 no22-23 p9 N/D 2016

The War That Broke the Country color *Time* v190 no12 p46 S 25 2017

Where Did America's Summer Jobs Go? color diag *Time* v190 no2/3 p52 Jl 10-17 2017

The White Helmets of Syria [Cover story] color *Time* v188 no15 p20 O 17 2016

VICK, LANCE

10! cartoon color *Field & Stream* v122 no1 p30 My 2017

Vick, Michael, 1980-

Lost and Found J. Fuchs and T. Keith color *Sports Illustrated* v126 no12 p20 My 1 2017

Vick, Michael, 1980——Trials, litigation, etc.

MIKED VICK R. Deitsch, T. Keith et al color *Sports Illustrated* v127 no7 p20 S 4 2017

VICKARY, JOHN R.

Chords & Discords bw color *Downbeat* v84 no6 p10 Je 2017

VICKBERG, SUZANNE M. JOHNSON

PIONEERS, DRIVERS, INTEGRATORS, AND GUARDIANS: INTERACTION color *Harvard Business Review* v95 no4 p18 Jl/Ag 2017

PIONEERS, DRIVERS, INTEGRATORS, & GUARDIANS [Cover story] bw graph il img *Harvard Business Review* v95 no2 p50 Mr/Ap 2017

Vickers, Brian

Can We Ever Master King Lear? S. Greenblatt cartoon color *New York Review of Books* v64 no3 p34 F 23 2017

Vickery, Heather

Finding Herself at 36 K. BOLONIK color *Prevention* v69 no1 p38 Ja 2017

VICK-MAJORS, TRISTA J.

Microbial Community Dynamics in Two Polar Extremes: The Lakes of the McMurdo Dry Valleys and the West Antarctic Peninsula Marine Ecosystem chart color graph *BioScience* v66 no10 p829 O 1 2016

VICKREY, BOB

In Memoriam: Dave Dutton color *Publishers Weekly* v264 no5 p208 Ja 30 2017

Vic's Auto Glass (Poem)

VIC'S AUTO GLASS, for Rachel Sens *Commonweal* v144 no16 p26 O 6 2017

Victim compensation

LIVING BY The Word *Christian Century* v134 no12 p20 Je 7 2017

Victims

See also

Accident victims

Child victims

Disaster victims

The Modern Bully *USA Today Magazine* v145 no2860 p35 Ja 2017

PEOPLE OF THE YEAR: THE HEROES OF PULSE M. LAMBERT *Advocate* no1088 p34 D 2016/Ja 2017

Victims of terrorism

London Strives to Remain a Place the World Will Call Home D. Stewart color *Time* v189 no23 p18 Je 19 2017

ORLANDO: THE DAY AFTER S. Flynn color *GQ: Gentlemen's Quarterly* v86 no12 p190 D 2016

Victims of terrorism—Legal status, laws, etc.

Honorable John Conyers *Congressional Digest* v95 no9 p15 N 2016

Honorable Mac Thornberry *Congressional Digest* v95 no9 p17 N 2016

Honorable Peter King *Congressional Digest* v95 no9 p18 N 2016

Stunts & Punts cartoon *Commonweal* v143 no17 p5 O 21 2016

Victor, Daniel

Supreme BATTLE *New York Times Upfront* v149 no10 p14 Mr 13 2017

Victor, David G.

Climate Control *MIT Technology Review* v120 no1 p11 Ja/F 2017

Making climate science more relevant bibl color *Science* v354 no6311 p421 O 28 2016

The Next Energy Revolution color *Foreign Affairs* v96 no4 p124 Jl/Ag 2017

Victor Huang, Cheng Lai

Design of a synthetic yeast genome bibl chart color graph *Science* v355 no6329 p1040 Mr 10 2017

Victoria & Abdul (Film)

Director Stephen Frears on Victoria and Abdul, Judi and More S. Gutierrez color *British Heritage Travel* v38 no5 p66 S/O 2017

UNRELIABLE HISTORIES A. LANE cartoon *New Yorker* v93 no30 p78 O 2 2017

VICTORIA & ABDUL J. McGovern color *Entertainment Weekly* no1478 / 1479 p46 Ag 18-25 2017

Victoria & Albert Museum

HAT TIP A. Russell cartoon *New Yorker* v93 no10 p36 Ap 24 2017

Victoria (B.C.)

MODERN ROYALS E. Malter color *Sunset* v239 no1 p36 Jl 2017

Victoria (TV program)

A Game of Throne E. Dockterman color diag *Time* v189 no3 p51 Ja 30 2017

Queen V P. Sykes color *Vogue* v207 no1 p74 Ja 2017

'They Are Not Themselves': The Lives of the English Queens A. A. O'Donnell color *America* v216 no7 p38 Ap 3 2017

Victoria J. Russell *TV Guide* v65 no2 p34 Ja 2 2017

Victoria: The teenage queen's early reign gets the Masterpiece treatment M. ROUSH *TV Guide* v65 no2 p18 Ja 2 2017

YOUR NEXT ROYAL OBSESSION C. Collis color *Entertainment Weekly* no1449 p53 Ja 20 2017

Victoria, Queen of Great Britain, 1819-1901

Daisy Goodwin on Victoria, Victoria and Victoria-The Queen, Novel and Show S. Gutierrez *British Heritage Travel* v38 no1 p38 Ja/F 2017

NEVERTHELESS, HER MAJESTY PERSISTED D. GOODWIN color *Foreign Policy* no223 p46 Mr/Ap 2017

Victoria: The Queen S. Gutierrez *British Heritage Travel* v37 no6 p12 N/D 2016

Victorian architecture

Case of the Missing Piazza P. Poore color *Old House Journal* v45 no7 p8 O 2017

house of sunshine M. E. POLSON color *Old House Journal* v45 no6 p14 S 2017

Stick and Shingle color *Old House Journal* v45 no5 p36 Ag 2017

Victorian architecture—Conservation & restoration
Renovating a Victorian? P. Poore cartoon color *Old House Journal* v45 no2 p64 Ap 2017

Victorian glassware
DOWN PAT F. VIGNA *Martha Stewart Living* no269 p152 N 2016

Victorian tiles
WALL & FLOOR TILES color *Old House Journal* v44 p33 2016 Design Center source Book

Victoria's Secret Fashion Show, The (TV program)
What to Watch R. Rahman, D. Snierson et al color *Entertainment Weekly* no1443 p56 D 9 2016

Victorinox AG
WRIST ROCK IT color *Popular Science* p13 Ja/F 2017

VICTORY, HANNAH
The Skis of the Year color *Powder* p82 S 2017

Victory motorcycle—Evaluation
93 OCTANE S. MacDonald color *Cycle World* v56 no2 p36 Mr 2017
PERPENDICULAR TWINS D. Canet chart color *Cycle World* v56 no2 p42 Mr 2017

Vida, Melissa
New cardinal wants to revive legacy of Óscar Romero in El Salvador color *America* v217 no5 p15 S 4 2017

Vidal, Jorge
Both Clinton and Trump are trying to win over Latinos in Florida, about 16 percent of all registered voters. Democrats have an advantage of 284,000 among them color *Bloomberg Businessweek* no4498 p36 N 7 2016

Video art
A MOVIE color *Art in America* v104 no10 p20 N 2016

Video art—Exhibitions
IMMERSE YOURSELF W. S. Smith color *Art in America* v105 no1 p74 Ja 2017

Video art—Exhibitions—Reviews
On Message A. K. Scott color *New Yorker* v92 no46 p13 Ja 23 2017

Video astronomy
VIDEO STRATEGIES FOR ECLIPSE DAY M. E. Bakich color *Astronomy* v45 no8 p68 Ag 2017

Video blogs
Growing Up In Public B. Luscombe color *Time* v189 no20 p42 My 29 2017
A WINDOW INTO FARMING *Successful Farming* v115 no3 p16 Mid-F 2017

Video chat services (Internet)
Can I video-chat with my kids even though I have an iPhone and they all have Androids? il *Consumer Reports* v82 no5 p23 My 2017
How to use Skype without an account I. PAUL color *PCWorld* v35 no1 p198 Ja 2017
Quantum video chat links Asia, Europe E. CONOVER *Science News* v192 no7 p14 O 28 2017

Video compression
The Windows 10 Anniversary Update is breaking webcams I. PAUL color *PCWorld* p50 O 2016

Video editing—Software
CONSTRUCTION SIMULATOR 2 J. MATHIS color *Macworld - Digital Edition* v34 no4 p59 My 2017
Hands-on with Apple Clips: How to use the iOS videoediting app and why you'd want to C. McGARRY color *Macworld - Digital Edition* v34 no6 p49 Je 2017
How to create powerful presentations with Adobe Spark Video J. DOVE color *Macworld - Digital Edition* p99 F 2017

Video equipment
See also
Video recordings
Videocassettes
Analog Video Bites the Dust K. C. POHLMANN color *Sound & Vision* v82 no1 p28 Ja 2017

Video game addiction
Young Men Are Playing Video Games Instead of Getting Jobs. That's OK. (For Now.) P. SUDERMAN color *Reason* v49 no3 p16 Jl 2017

Video game consoles
See also

PlayStation video game consoles
9 REASONS WHY PC GAMING IS A BETTER VALUE THAN CONSOLES H. DINGMAN bw color *PCWorld* p131 O 2016

Video game consoles—Design & construction
Nintendo's New Guard Tries to Switch It Up Y. Nakamura and S. Stapczynski color *Bloomberg Businessweek* no4514 p35 Mr 13 2017

Video game consoles—Evaluation
For the Home Entertainment Aficionado bw color *Consumer Reports* v81 no12 p52 D 2016
Holiday Gift Guide D. HOLBROOK *TV Guide* p20 D 5 2016
Nintendo Switch console details revealed H. DINGMAN color *PCWorld* v35 no2 p28 F 2017
A real console, really mobile S. Horaczek and A. Smith color *Popular Science* v289 no6 p18 N/D 2017
TOO FUN TO FAIL K. Sintumuang cartoon color *Esquire* p32 Ap 2017
Xbox One X: Everything you need to know about this powerful gaming console H. DINGMAN chart color *PCWorld* v35 no7 p32 Jl 2017

Video game design
BLOWN COVER T. Keith and S. Kwak color *Sports Illustrated* v127 no7 p22 S 4 2017
'Torment: Tides of Numenera': The 'Planescape' successor you've been waiting for H. DINGMAN color *PCWorld* v35 no4 p103 Ap 2017

Video game equipment
AMD Threadripper grab: Dell's Alienware shuts out other major vendors for 2017 GORDON MAH UNG color *PCWorld* v35 no7 p19 Jl 2017

Video game equipment—Evaluation
GAEMS M155 PERFORMANCE MONITOR: PORTABLE DISPLAY SHOWS ITS PROMISE—AND FAULTS S. BELLAMY color graph *Macworld - Digital Edition* p19 Je 13 2017
How to use the Nintendo Switch's Joy-Cons with your Mac—and why you'd want to A. HAYWARD color *Macworld - Digital Edition* v34 no4 p13 My 2017

Video game industry
AMD Threadripper grab: Dell's Alienware shuts out other major vendors for 2017 GORDON MAH UNG color *PCWorld* v35 no7 p19 Jl 2017
A GIANT ENTERS A NEW ARENA M. Lev-ram chart color *Fortune* v175 no8 p192 Je 15 2017

Video game industry—Finance
THE TALKING CAT AND THE PEROXIDE CORPORATION A. SATARIANO, D. Ramli et al color *Bloomberg Businessweek* no4523 p54 My 22 2017

Video gamers
Gunning For eSports Equality P. GREEN *Los Angeles Magazine* p26 Mr 2017
How to judge the time commitment of your next video game I. PAUL color *PCWorld* p167 Mr 2017
The Lure of Virtual Reality K. PITSKER color *Kiplinger's Personal Finance* v71 no7 p41 Jl 2017
Sugar Mama L. D. JOHNSON and S. T. BROWN color *Ebony* v72 no6 p75 Ap/My 2017
WHY EVER STOP PLAYING VIDEO GAMES F. Guan img *New York* p28 F 20 2017

Video gamers—Health
Gamer Shape S. Apstein and T. Keith color *Sports Illustrated* v127 no6 p18 Ag 28 2017

Video gamers—Psychology
Video games: The bad, the ugly, and the (potentially) good M. Jarvis color *Science* v355 no6332 p1385 Mr 31 2017

Video games
See also
NBA 2K (Game)
Nintendo video games
Street Fighter games
The Best of Everything This Year-So Far E. Berman, R. Bruner et al color *Time* v189 no21 p61 Je 5 2017
Dell XPS Tower Special Edition: It's faster than it looks J. NOREM color graph *PCWorld* p67 Mr 2017
Feel Great After a Bad Night of Sleep J. COVERT cartoon *Men's Health* v32 no4 p80 My 2017
Film Criticism in the Era of Algorithms R. Rich *Film Quarterly*

v70 no2 p5 Wint 2016

FUN AND GAMES *Cincinnati Magazine* v50 no8 p42 My 2017

Here Comes Another Round of Everyone's favorites *USA Today Magazine* v145 no2860 p78 Ja 2017

How Gaming Is Shaping the Future of Work K. Tynan *Harvard Business Review Digital Articles* p2 My 2 2016

PAID TO PLAY C. THOMPSON cartoon *Wired* v25 no3 p31 Mr 2017

The Quiz T. BALAZO *Maclean's* v130 no10 p126 N 2017

RACE, GENDER, AND GENRE IN SPEC OPS: THE LINE S. Murray *Film Quarterly* v70 no2 p38 Wint 2016

The Smartest Machines Are Playing Games J. Kahn color *Bloomberg Businessweek* no4517 p34 Ap 3 2017

THE STORY TELLER R. D'Agostino color *Popular Mechanics* p68 O 2017

WHY EVER STOP PLAYING VIDEO GAMES F. Guan img *New York* p28 F 20 2017

Video games—Competitions
See also
Esports

Japan Isn't Getting Its Share Of Gaming Gold Yuji Nakamura and Takako Taniguchi bw color *Bloomberg Businessweek* no4539 p23 S 25 2017

ROMANCING THE DRONE R. O'CONNOR color *Chicago* v66 no6 p30 Je 2017

Video games—Computer network resources—Evaluation
How to judge the time commitment of your next video game I. PAUL color *PCWorld* p167 Mr 2017

Video games—Equipment & supplies—Evaluation
MINECRAFT APPLE TV EDITION: BLOCK BUILDING ON THE BIG SCREEN A. HAYWARD color *Macworld - Digital Edition* p59 F 2017

Video games—Psychological aspects—Congresses
Video games: The bad, the ugly, and the (potentially) good M. Jarvis color *Science* v355 no6332 p1385 Mr 31 2017

Video games—Religious aspects
A Virtual Faith E. DRESCHER color *America* v215 no10 p22 O 10 2016

Video games—Reviews
10 — NO MAN'S SKY D. Franich color *Entertainment Weekly* no1444/1445 p123 D 16 2016

The 15 best new PC games of 2017, and their release dates H. DINGMAN color *PCWorld* v35 no9 p70 S 2017

2 — DISHONORED 2 A. Morales color *Entertainment Weekly* no1444/1445 p122 D 16 2016

3 — THE LAST GUARDIAN A. Morales color diag *Entertainment Weekly* no1444/1445 p122 D 16 2016

4 — TITANFALL 2 A. Morales *Entertainment Weekly* no1444/1445 p122 D 16 2016

5 — FIREWATCH D. Franich *Entertainment Weekly* no1444/1445 p122 D 16 2016

6 — UNCHARTED 4: A THIEF'S END A. Morales *Entertainment Weekly* no1444/1445 p122 D 16 2016

7 — REZ INFINITE A. Morales color *Entertainment Weekly* no1444/1445 p122 D 16 2016

8 — THE WITNESS D. Franich *Entertainment Weekly* no1444/1445 p122 D 16 2016

9 — DOOM A. Morales color *Entertainment Weekly* no1444/1445 p123 D 16 2016

The best PC games of 2017 (so far) H. DINGMAN color *PCWorld* v35 no8 p25 Ag 2017

Forza Horizon 3 (PC): Get ready to make your graphics card sweat H. DINGMAN color *PCWorld* v35 no11 p114 N 2016

Hot Digital Psychedelia Rez Infinite and Thumper E. SHAMOON color *Rolling Stone* no1274 p47 N 17 2016

Latest Mac games A. Hayward bw color *Macworld - Digital Edition* p81 Ap 2017

No. 1 INSIDE D. Franich and A. Morales color *Entertainment Weekly* no1444/1445 p120 D 16 2016

Round-up: Latest Mac games A. Hayward color diag *Macworld - Digital Edition* p89 Ja 2017

Ulysses: The Video Game E. GRAHAM *American Scholar* v86 no1 p17 Wint 2017

Video Killed the Radio Star (Music)
"Video Killed the Radio Star" E. R. Brown color *Entertainment Weekly* no1460/1461 p45 Ap 7-17 2017

Video monitors
GAEMS M155 PERFORMANCE MONITOR: PORTABLE DISPLAY SHOWS ITS PROMISE—AND FAULTS S. BELLAMY color graph *Macworld - Digital Edition* p19 Je 13 2017

Video on demand
HOW TO WATCH IT ALL D. PIERCE cartoon color *Wired* v25 no4 p42 Ap 2017

OTT Video Is Creating Cord-Extenders, Not Cord-Cutters J. Samit *Harvard Business Review Digital Articles* p2 Jl 17 2015

PUT UP OR SHUT UP E. Loh color *Motor Trend* v69 no10 p12 O 2017

Video production & direction
THE COMPLETE HISTORY OF VIDEO bw color *Popular Mechanics* p13 O 2017

Video recording
See also
Digital video recording
High-speed video recording
Video surveillance

2016 BY THE NUMBERS *TV Guide* p14 D 19 2016

ARTIFICIAL INTELLIGENCE, REAL FOOD *Harvard Business Review Digital Articles* p30 Jl 1 2017

GREAT MOMENTS IN VIDEO TUTORIALS J. LYNCH and L. SOROKANICH color *Popular Mechanics* p94 O 2017

Teacher self-captured video M. G. Sherin and E. B. Dyer color il *Phi Delta Kappan* v98 no7 p49 Ap 2017

Will Your Video Go Viral? color *Popular Mechanics* p100 O 2017

Video recording piracy
See also
Television program piracy

MR. KNOW-IT-ALL J. MOOALLEM cartoon *Wired* v25 no9 p34 S 2017

Video recording—Equipment & supplies
See also
Digital video recorders

Blackmagic Design Helps Theatres Capture the Magic *Stage Directions* v29 no11 p22 N 2016

Video recording—Equipment & supplies—Evaluation
GoPro cartoon color *Snowboarder* v29 no4 p113 D 2016

iOS Accessories J. Mathis color *Macworld - Digital Edition* p66 F 2017

Video recordings
See also
Documentary films
Experimental films
Internet videos
Podcasts
Streaming video

ALL WORK AND REPLAY A. Prewitt color *Sports Illustrated* v126 no11 p87 Ap 17-24 2017

Bright lights, big history A. Gunadie and H. Wilson color *Canadian Geographic* v137 no3 p26 My 2017

The easy way to save Facebook videos J. NOREM color *PCWorld* p190 D 2016

How to save your Vine videos right now I. PAUL color *PCWorld* p184 D 2016

How to Shoot Great Video T. Sullivan chart color *Consumer Reports* v82 no5 p18 My 2017

METHOD TO THE MADNESS b. minnigh bw color *Bike Magazine* v24 no1 p42 Ja/F 2017

Orbs as Plasma Life B. RADFORD *Skeptical Inquirer* v41 no5 p28 S/O 2017

Video recordings industry—News briefs
HDR Is Getting Support From M. Fleischmann and C. Crowley color *Sound & Vision* v82 no2 p17 F/Mr 2017

Video recordings—Exhibitions
AMIE SIEGEL G. Coxhead color *Art in America* v105 no4 p122 Ap 2017

THE BRIEF bw color *Art in America* v105 no3 p25 Mr 2017

JAMES COLEMAN A. Considine color *Art in America* v105 no4 p110 Ap 2017

KEN OKIISHI T. Ballard color *Art in America* v105 no4 p113 Ap 2017

LILI REYNAUD-DEWAR M. Heddaya color *Art in America* v105 no4 p123 Ap 2017

"PERPETUAL REVOLUTION: THE IMAGE AND SOCIAL

CHANGE" E. Heartney color *Art in America* v105 no4 p114 Ap 2017

SEEING JUSTICE DONE *USA Today Magazine* v145 no2864 p48 My 2017

"THE STAND" D. Markus color *Art in America* v105 no4 p115 Ap 2017

Video surveillance

EVERY NIGHT PERFECT K. Dupzyk and J. Lynch bw color *Popular Mechanics* p84 O 2017

HOW TO DO EVERY THING WITH VIDEO M. Wilson and D. Dubno bw color diag *Popular Mechanics* p58 O 2017

INSIDE NASCAR'S VIDEO REVIEW TRAILER E. HILDEB-RANDT color *Popular Mechanics* p28 O 2017

MY GOPRO LIFE color *Popular Mechanics* p92 O 2017

Overseeing What's Overheard J. LIFHITS color *Weekly Standard* v22 no28 p16 Mr 27 2017

Video tapes

Rules Aren't Made to Be Broken M. Bamberger color *Golf Magazine* v59 no6 p124 Je 2017

Videocassettes

What to Do with All Those Cassettes D. Pogue color *Scientific American* v315 no3 p27 S 2016

Videoconferencing

Technology Alone Won't Solve Our Collaboration Problems M. Mortensen *Harvard Business Review Digital Articles* p2 Mr 26 2015

Videoconferencing—Software—Evaluation

Easy Family Reunions D. Pogue color *AARP: The Magazine* v59 no6A p12 O/N 2016

Videographers

chemtrails b. minnigh bw *Bike Magazine* v24 no5 p42 Jl 2017

Vidler, Anthony

Rules of the Game *Architectural Record* v205 no1 p41 Ja 2017

Vieira, I. C. Guimarães

Persistent effects of pre-Columbian plant domestication on Amazonian forest composition bibl chart graph map *Science* v355 no6328 p925 Mr 3 2017

Viéitez, Cristina

Evolution of protein phosphorylation across 18 fungal species bibl graph *Science* v354 no6309 p229 O 14 2016

Vielle-Calzada, Jean-Philippe

Linking stem cells to germ cells color *Science* v356 no6336 p378 Ap 28 2017

Vienna Boys Choir (Performer)

MARCH'S COOLEST EVENTS *Indianapolis Monthly* v40 no7 p24 Mr 2017

Vieques Island (P.R.)—Description & travel

THE GIRLFRIEND GETAWAY GUIDE K. VALENTINI and S. Humphreys Collins color *Redbook* p118 O 2017

Vieques National Wildlife Refuge (P.R.)

Vieques refuge: Not for sale color *National Wildlife (World Edition)* v54 no6 p44 O/N 2016

VIERA, BENÉ

BLACK-ISH STARS ACT LIKE REAL-LIFE HUSBAND & WIFE [Cover story] color *Ebony* v72 no11 p58 S 2017

CELEBRITIES AREN'T REQUIRED TO BE ACTIVISTS color *Ebony* v72 no11 p26 S 2017

DONALD TRUMP IS FAILING BLACK PEOPLE... WHERE DO WE GO FROM HERE? *Ebony* v72/73 no12/1 p24 O/N 2017

TWINNING AS BOSSES IS A LIFESTYLE color *Ebony* v72/73 no12/1 p26 O/N 2017

A WOMAN ON THE RISE color *Ebony* v72 no11 p22 S 2017

Vierheilig, Julia

Giant viruses with an expanded complement of translation system components diag *Science* v356 no6333 p82 Ap 7 2017

Vierros, Marjo

Global Marine Governance and Oceans Management for the Achievement of SDG 14 *UN Chronicle* v54 no1/2 p1 2017

Vierstra, Richard D.

Phytochrome B integrates light and temperature signals in Arabidopsis bibl graph *Science* v354 no6314 p897 N 18 2016

Viertel, Benjamin

Cinema Scope H. Als cartoon *New Yorker* v93 no2 p16 F 27 2017

Viertel, Jack

THE SECRET LIFE OF THE AMERICAN MUSICAL M. TU-

ETH color *America* v215 no12 p34 O 24 2016

Viertler, Michael

In the Best Sales Teams, About Half of the People Are in Support Roles *Harvard Business Review Digital Articles* p2 My 25 2016

Vietnam—Description & travel

Balling on a Budget G. ATANMO color *Ebony* v72 no8 p54 Je 2017

SEARCHING FOR TIA: In modern Vietnam, memories of the war still linger J. K. ROBINSON *Saturday Evening Post* v289 no4 p56 Jl/Ag 2017

Wild Vacation R. DAVIDSON color *National Geographic Kids* no465 p6 N 2016

Vietnamese authors

Viet Thanh Nguyen D. Kiper color *Current Biography* v78 no6 p73 Je 2017

Vietnamese cooking

Pho Keeps A. BRANDT *Cincinnati Magazine* p111 Je 2017

Vietnamese refugees—Attitudes

A refugee's gift P. W. Marty *Christian Century* v134 no6 p3 Mr 15 2017

Vietnamese restaurants

Chè Sundae R. Patronite and R. Raisfeld img *New York* v50 no6 p67 Mr 20 2017

Vietnamese restaurants—Evaluation

THE DINING GUIDE *Atlanta* v56 no12 p137 Ap 2017

MASTER OF FIRE J. R. FULLER color *Chicago* v66 no8 p51 Ag 2017

Pho Keeps A. BRANDT *Cincinnati Magazine* p111 Je 2017

Pho Real N. Niarchos color *New Yorker* v93 no23 p17 Ag 7 2017

Phô With Soul and Style: The Vietnamese cooking at Hanoi House tastes fresh, homespun, and inventive all at once A. PLATT img *New York* v50 no13 p56 Je 26 2017

Vietnam—Foreign economic relations

Vietnam Shrugs Off the Loss of a Trade Pact N. Dieu Tu Uyen and K. Lester *Bloomberg Businessweek* no4512 p15 F 20 2017

Vietnam—History

Vietnam before the War C. Goscha *History Today* v67 no2 p20 F 2017

Vietnam Moratorium, 1969

If Nixon Could Tweet S. J. DOUGLAS *In These Times* v41 no3 p18 Mr 2017

Vietnam War, 1961-1975

ESCAPE FROM VIETNAM K. Luu *Saturday Evening Post* v289 no2 p16 Mr/Ap 2017

A Good Resister G. NORMAN bw color *Weekly Standard* v22 no9 p17 N 7 2016

How Americans Lost Faith in the Presidency K. BURNS and L. NOVICK bw *Atlantic* v320 no3 p24 O 2017

Lasting Images color *Time* v190 no12 p50 S 25 2017

My Father's Vietnam J. Meacham color *Time* v190 no12 p52 S 25 2017

OZ IN 'NAM R. Willis bw color map *Military History* v34 no5 p54 Ja 2018

SEARCHING FOR TIA: In modern Vietnam, memories of the war still linger J. K. ROBINSON *Saturday Evening Post* v289 no4 p56 Jl/Ag 2017

Still Resonating a Half-Century Later F. KREBSBACH *USA Today Magazine* v145 no2864 p40 My 2017

Studying the Vietnam War: How the scholarship has changed M. A. Lawrence *Humanities* v38 no4 p1 Fall 2017

The War That Broke the Country K. Vick color *Time* v190 no12 p46 S 25 2017

Vietnam War, 1961-1975—Exhibitions

ARCHIVES Events & News *Prologue* v49 no1 p68 Spr 2017

Vietnam War, 1961-1975—Motion pictures & the war

INTO THE VOID P. KLAY bw cartoon color *Mother Jones* v42 no5 p56 S/O 2017

Vietnam War, 1961-1975—Protest movements—United States

THE FORGOTTEN POWER OF THE VIETNAM PEACE MOVEMENT T. HAYDEN bw color *Nation* v304 no3 p18 Ja 30 2017

HELL, NO, WE WON'T GO! B. Davidson *Saturday Evening Post* v289 no4 p42 Jl/Ag 2017

Vietnam War, The (TV program)

Documentarian Ken Burns on How Vietnam Explains the Current Political Moment N. Gillespie color *Reason* v49 no5 p79

O 2017

Ken Burns revisits the division and bloodshed wrought by 'a barbaric war' R. A. Schroth bw *America* v217 no7 p50 O 2 2017

GOOD EVENING, VIETNAM D. KAMP bw *Vanity Fair* v59
no8 p58 Ag 2017

THE VIETNAM WAR: How the film story of the most divisive
event in America since the Civil War came to life in a small New
Hampshire town M. ALLEN *Yankee* v81 no5 p136 S/O 2017

The Vietnam War: Ken Burns's moving history of the grueling
war that divided America M. ROUSH *TV Guide* v65 no39 p26
S 18 2017

Vietor, Richard H. K.
With Peace, Colombia Is Poised for Greater Prosperity *Harvard
Business Review Digital Articles* p2 Jl 7 2016

View, The (TV program)
CLINTON KELLY M. LOGAN *TV Guide* v65 no19 p14 My 1
2017

FINDING YOUR REAL VOICE S. Hostin color *Essence* v48 no2
p118 Je 2017

THE VIEW M. LOGAN *TV Guide* v64 no46 p40 N 7 2016

THE VIEW M. LOGAN *TV Guide* v65 no11 p46 Mr 6 2017

Views
CREATIVE ENVIRONMENT R. STIEVE *Arizona Highways*
v93 no2 p50 F 2017

Vigalondo, Nacho
Big Monsters, Bigger Feelings S. Zacharek color *Time* v189 no14
p53 Ap 17 2017

Monster Mash J. PODHORETZ color *Weekly Standard* v22 no32
p43 My 1 2017

VIGGIANI, HEATHER
How Should You Spend Your HOLIDAY HANG TIME? color
Seventeen v75 no11 p68 N 2016

Vigilance (Psychology)
Research: Being in a Group Makes Us Less Likely to Fact-Check
R. Meng, Youjung Jun et al *Harvard Business Review Digital
Articles* p2 Ag 1 2017

Vigilant, Linda
Chimpanzee genomic diversity reveals ancient admixture with
bonobos bibl diag graph map *Science* v354 no6311 p477 O 28
2016

Vigils (Poem)
Vigils C. V. Paintner color *U.S. Catholic* v82 no11 p11 N 2017

Viglione, Alberto
Changing climate shifts timing of European floods color graph
Science v357 no6351 p588 Ag 11 2017

VIGNA, FRANCES
All Keyed Up color *Martha Stewart Living* p144 O 2017

ANIMAL ATTRACTION color *Martha Stewart Living* p116 My
2017

BOX SET color *Martha Stewart Living* p120 Mr 2017

CASE STUDIES color *Martha Stewart Living* p120 S 2017

A CUT ABOVE *Martha Stewart Living* no268 p148 O 2016

DOWN PAT *Martha Stewart Living* no269 p152 N 2016

FUN SIZE color *Martha Stewart Living* p124 Jl/Ag 2017

GATHER ROUNDS color *Martha Stewart Living* p140 Ap 2017

GLASS ACTS color *Martha Stewart Living* no275 p120 Je 2017

A GOOD CLIP *Martha Stewart Living* no270 p166 D 2016

LOVE STORY color *Martha Stewart Living* no271 p116 Ja/F
2017

TRUE-BLUE WINNERS color *Martha Stewart Living* no271 p76
Ja/F 2017

WORTH THEIR WEIGHT *Martha Stewart Living* no267 p132
S 2016

Vignali, Dario A. A.
Pathological α-synuclein transmission initiated by binding lymphocyte-activation gene 3 bibl graph *Science* v353 no6307
paah3374-1 S 30 2016

Vignaud, Hélène
Gene duplication can impart fragility, not robustness, in the yeast
protein interaction network bibl color graph *Science* v355
no6325 p630 F 10 2017

Vignelli, leila
Designers We'll Miss E. Gaukel *Treasures* v6 no4 p4 F/Mr 2017

Vignieri, Sacha
ECOSYSTEM EARTH [Cover story] color *Science* v356 no6335
p258 Ap 21 2017

Vigoreaux, Gabriella
5-minute PIE CRUST color *Good Housekeeping* v265 no5 p33
N 2017

Vigorito, Rosaria
Using Their Noodles E. Petrini color *AARP: The Magazine* v59
no1A p50 D 2015/Ja 2016

Viitasaari, Ville
THE BLOCKCHAIN REVOLUTION: INTERACTION color
Harvard Business Review v95 no2 p20 Mr/Ap 2017

Vijayaraghavan, Vineeta
2 Myths About Engaging B-Players *Harvard Business Review
Digital Articles* p2 N 28 2014

Vikan, Gary
Of Saints and Vandals J. GARDNER color *Weekly Standard* v22
no18 p41 Ja 16 2017

Viking (Military aircraft)
BOATASHORE G. FREKING *Cincinnati Magazine* v50 no3 p32
D 2016

Viking antiquities
HOARDS OF THE VIKINGS D. WEISS color *Archaeology* v70
no1 p48 Ja/F 2017

News Roundup V. HAFSTAÐ *Iceland Review* v54 no6 p18 N/D
2016

THE VIKINGS' WIDE REACH J. URBANUS color *Archaeology*
v70 no3 p20 My/Je 2017

Viking Yacht Co.
BATTLE TESTED G. CAPUTI chart color diag *Power & Motoryacht* v33 no2 p76 F 2017

Reinventing a Classic J. BROWNLEE chart color *Power & Motoryacht* v34 no7 p60 Jl 2017

Viking 37 Billfish B. Pike color *Power & Motoryacht* v34 no6
p30 Je 2017

Viking 93 MY S. Murray color *Power & Motoryacht* v34 no11
p76 N 2017

Vikings
GREENLAND'S VANISHED VIKINGS Z. Zorich color map
Scientific American v316 no6 p66 Je 2017

Magic, medicine and the Viking way of war B. Burfield *History
Today* v67 no4 p19 Ap 2017

NEW VISIONS OF THE VIKINGS H. Pringle color *National
Geographic* v231 no3 p30 Mr 2017

Norse Knarr J. Guttman cartoon *Military History* v34 no1 p20 My
2017

Skeleton ignites Viking warrior debate B. BOWER bw *Science
News* v192 no6 p6 O 14 2017

Viking Invasion K. B. RATTINI *National Geographic Kids* no468
p26 Mr 2017

Vikings (TV program)
Travis Fimmel D. Franich color *Entertainment Weekly* no1448
p55 Ja 13 2017

VIKINGS D. Franich color *Entertainment Weekly* p24 Jl 24 2017

Vikings K. Hahn *TV Guide* v64 no48 p38 N 21 2016

VIKINGS' NEW ERA D. Franich color *Entertainment Weekly*
no1448 p54 Ja 13 2017

Vikings—Research
DARKNESS AT THE EDGE OF THE WORLD T. Folger color
map *Smithsonian* v47 no10 p28 Mr 2017

VILADAS, PILAR
house of the month *Architectural Record* v205 no10 p31 O 2017

Overdue Notice bw color *Architectural Digest* no11 p57 N 1 2017

Vilanova, John
Music's Scary New Reality color *Rolling Stone* no1289 p13 Je
15 2017

Vilches, Harold
HOW TO BECOME AN INTERNATIONAL GOLD SMUG-
GLER M. SMITH and J. FRANKLIN color *Bloomberg Busi-
nessweek* no4514 p54 Mr 13 2017

VILD, ONDREJ
Combining Biodiversity Resurveys across Regions to Advance
Global Change Research *BioScience* v67 no1 p73 Ja 2017

Vile, Kurt, 1980-
Kurt and Courtney: Indie Rock's Superduo S. VOZICK-LEVIN-
SON bw *Rolling Stone* no1295 p18 S 7 2017

VILENKIN, ALEXANDER
A COSMIC CONTROVERSY color *Scientific American* v317
no1 p5 Jl 2017

VILIBERT, DIANA
The wise woman's guide to booze color *Redbook* p89 D 2016
VILJOEN, MARIE
WINDOWSILL GINGER color *Better Homes & Gardens* v95 no2 p72 F 2016
Vilkeviciute, Edita
MICHAEL KORS'S Icons A. Serrano color *InStyle* v24 no8 p108 Ag 2017
Vilkomerson, Sara
THE 25 MOST PATRIOTIC MOVIES OF ALL TIME color *Entertainment Weekly* no1472 p30 Je 30 2017
3 Rounds WITH TARAN Killam & COUBIE Smulders color *Entertainment Weekly* no1457/1458 p50 Mr 17 2017
AFTER GLOW color *Entertainment Weekly* no1473 p24 Jl 7 2017
ALIEN color *Entertainment Weekly* no1460/1461 p28 Ap 7-17 2017
ALIEN: COVENANT color *Entertainment Weekly* no1446/1447 p53 D 2016/Ja 2017
ALIEN: COVENANT color *Entertainment Weekly* no1463/1464 p42 Ap/My 2017
ANOTHER SIDE OF MATT SMITH color *Entertainment Weekly* no1439 p24 N 11 2016
ARRIVAL color *Entertainment Weekly* no1438 p40 N 4 2016
Ben Affleck color *Entertainment Weekly* no1444/1445 p20 D 16 2016
BEST ACTOR color diag *Entertainment Weekly* no1451/1452 p54 F 3-10 2017
BEST ACTRESS color diag *Entertainment Weekly* no1451/1452 p44 F 3-10 2017
BEST DIRECTOR color diag *Entertainment Weekly* no1451/1452 p66 F 3-10 2017
BEST SUPPORTING ACTOR color diag *Entertainment Weekly* no1451/1452 p50 F 3-10 2017
BEST SUPPORTING ACTRESS color diag *Entertainment Weekly* no1451/1452 p62 F 3-10 2017
Big Little Lies color *Entertainment Weekly* no1448 p34 Ja 13 2017
BLADE NEW WORLD color *Entertainment Weekly* no1486 p32 O 13 2017
BLADE RUNNER 2049 color *Entertainment Weekly* p18 Jl 24 2017
BLONDE, SWEAT & TEARS [Cover story] color *Entertainment Weekly* p12 Jl 24 2017
DANNY McBRIDE color *Entertainment Weekly* no1467 p45 My 26 2017
Dave Is Back! color *Entertainment Weekly* no1478 / 1479 p18 Ag 18-25 2017
THE ESCAPE ARTIST color *Entertainment Weekly* no1457/1458 p44 Mr 17 2017
A FERRY TALE color *Entertainment Weekly* no1473 p22 Jl 7 2017
A GAY Old Timeline color diag *Entertainment Weekly* no1471 p32 Je 23 2017
GENTLEMEN BEWARE BLONDES color *Entertainment Weekly* no1474/1475 p50 Jl 21-28 2017
Ghost's Clay Foreplay color *Entertainment Weekly* no1460/1461 p81 Ap 7-17 2017
GLOW color *Entertainment Weekly* no1468/1469 p52 Je 2-9 2017
THE GOODBYE GIRLS color *Entertainment Weekly* no1449 p22 Ja 20 2017
THE GREATEST DISNEY SONGS OF ALL TIME color *Entertainment Weekly* no1454/1455 p36 F 24 2017
The Handmaid's Tale color *Entertainment Weekly* no1442 p13 D 2 2016 Rebellious Special Issue
Hannah and Her Sisters color *Entertainment Weekly* no1463/1464 p95 Ap/My 2017
KUMAIL NANJIANI color *Entertainment Weekly* no1463/1464 p54 Ap/My 2017
MANCHESTER by the SEA color *Entertainment Weekly* no1438 p43 N 4 2016
MARC MARON color *Entertainment Weekly* no1468/1469 p53 Je 2-9 2017
MOTHER! color *Entertainment Weekly* no1478 / 1479 p40 Ag 18-25 2017
NASTY WOMEN color *Entertainment Weekly* no1463/1464 p76 Ap/My 2017
NO. 30 Aquaman color *Entertainment Weekly* no1436/1437 p68

O 21 2016
NO. 34 Rogue color *Entertainment Weekly* no1436/1437 p70 O 21 2016
NO. 45 Cyclops color *Entertainment Weekly* no1436/1437 p76 O 21 2016
Oh, mother! color *Entertainment Weekly* no1484 p16 S 29 2017
OSCAR RACE TAKES SHAPE color *Entertainment Weekly* no1484 p38 S 29 2017
PICTURE color diag *Entertainment Weekly* no1451/1452 p70 F 3-10 2017
THE PROS OF CON color *Entertainment Weekly* no1476 p32 Ag 4 2017
REAL OR REPLICANT? color *Entertainment Weekly* no1446/1447 p45 D 2016/Ja 2017
REBORN TO RUN [Cover story] color *Entertainment Weekly* no1446/1447 p40 D 2016/Ja 2017
RIDLEY SCOTT A LIFE IN PICTURES color *Entertainment Weekly* no1465 p34 My 12 2017
ROLE CALL JEAN SMART color *Entertainment Weekly* no1449 p34 Ja 20 2017
RYAN GOSLING IN Blade Runner 2049 color *Entertainment Weekly* no1478 / 1479 p52 Ag 18-25 2017
Sam Shepard color *Entertainment Weekly* no1477 p14 Ag 11 2017
SAVING SPIDER-MAN [Cover story] color *Entertainment Weekly* no1473 p18 Jl 7 2017
SNATCHED color *Entertainment Weekly* no1463/1464 p37 Ap/My 2017
THE SNOWMAN color *Entertainment Weekly* no1478 / 1479 p55 Ag 18-25 2017
SPIDER-MAN: HOMECOMING color *Entertainment Weekly* no1463/1464 p65 Ap/My 2017
SPIDEY SQUAD color *Entertainment Weekly* no1473 p21 Jl 7 2017
Toronto Must List color *Entertainment Weekly* no1480 p36 S 1 2017
Trainspotting's Toilet Dive color *Entertainment Weekly* no1460/1461 p71 Ap 7-17 2017
TV chart color *Entertainment Weekly* no1444/1445 p66 D 16 2016
WarReN BEAtty An ORAL HISTORY color *Entertainment Weekly* no1440 p30 N 18 2016
What Light color *Entertainment Weekly* no1438 p63 N 4 2016
What to Watch color *Entertainment Weekly* no1451/1452 p100 F 3-10 2017
What to Watch color *Entertainment Weekly* no1467 p54 My 26 2017
Who's A PRETTY Girl? [Cover story] color *Entertainment Weekly* no1462 p20 Ap 21 2017
WHO'S THE BOSS? 1984-1992 color *Entertainment Weekly* no1434 p34 O 7 2016
WHO WOULD WIN? CYCLOPS VS. INVISIBLE WOMAN *Entertainment Weekly* no1436/1437 p77 O 21 2016
Your Sunshiny, Stupendous, Seriously Spectacular SUMMER BUCKET LIST color *Entertainment Weekly* no1470 p32 Je 16 2017

Villa, Elizabeth
Assembly of a nucleus-like structure during viral replication in bacteria bibl color graph *Science* v355 no6321 p1 Ja 13 2017
VILLA, HEATHER
Stake Your Claim *Publishers Weekly* v264 no12 p76 Mr 20 2017
Villa Capri (Film)
ALSO PLAYING color *Entertainment Weekly* no1478 / 1479 p73 Ag 18-25 2017
Villages
Arizona Nordic Village: Yurts are cool. Period. But they're even better when they're located in an alpine meadow that's alive with wildflowers, songbirds and browsing elk A. McGIVNEY *Arizona Highways* v93 no6 p14 Je 2017
Creighton creates magic in holiday SantaLand B. SCHWINDT color *Nebraska Life* v21 no6 p69 N/D 2017
LIFE ON THE EDGE R. Rivera *Sierra* v102 no4 p42 Jl/Ag 2017
SONS AND DAUGHTERS S. A. Topol *Harper's Magazine* no2007 p25 Ag 2017
Villages—China
MURDER VILLAGES AND SCAM TOWNS R. Foyle Hunwick color *Atlantic* v319 no3 p21 Ap 2017
Villages—Great Britain

p197 O 14 2016

Vilorio, Dennis

Space careers: A universe of options chart color *Career Outlook* p1 N 2016

Vilsack, Tom, 1950-

AN 8-YEAR RUN T. Vilsack *Successful Farming* v114 no13 p28 D 2016

Vinaigrettes

Mint's Moment K. O'SHEA-EVANS color *House Beautiful* v159 no3 p73 Ap 2017

VINAL, KELLIE

THE ATLANTA SCIENCE FESTIVAL IS BACK *Atlanta* v56 no11 p148 Mr 2017

From the Front Lines of Science *Atlanta* v56 no11 p154 Mr 2017

Vincenot, Christian E.

Can we protect island flying foxes? color *Science* v355 no6332 p1368 Mr 31 2017

Vincent, J.-B.

Rosetta's comet 67P/Churyumov-Gerasimenko sheds its dusty mantle to reveal its icy nature bibl graph *Science* v354 no6319 p1566 D 23 2016

Surface changes on comet 67P/Churyumov-Gerasimenko suggest a more active past bw graph *Science* v355 no6332 p1392 Mr 31 2017

Vincent, Jason

HIP TO BE SQUARE M. HENNESSY color *Chicago* v66 no1 p56 Ja 2017

Vincent, Lynne C.

Why Creative People Are More Likely to Be Dishonest *Harvard Business Review Digital Articles* p2 N 23 2015

VINCENT, MATT

ALIVE AND FISHING color *Outdoor Life* v224 no3 p67 Ap 2017

GET TO THE POINT cartoon *Outdoor Life* v224 no2 p32 F/Mr 2017

THE UGLY FISH color *Outdoor Life* v224 no3 p62 Ap 2017

Vincent, Nicholas

A Medieval Royal Rollercoaster *History Today* v67 no3 p58 Mr 2017

Vincent, Rachel

Spectacle *Publishers Weekly* v264 no16 p51 Ap 17 2017

VINCENZ, MARC

Crossing Fingers, Kissing Hands *Nation* v305 no6 p36 S 11 2017

Vinculin

Vinculin forms a directionally asymmetric catch bond with F-actin D. L. Huang, N. A. Bax et al chart color *Science* v357 no6352 p703 Ag 18 2017

Vindolanda Site (Chesterholme, England)

LIFE ON THE FRONTIER color *Archaeology* v70 no3 p34 My/Je 2017

Vine (Web resource)

Dying on the Vine T. Keith color *Sports Illustrated* v125 no15 p22 N 7 2016

VINE'S FATAL LESSON FOR THE TECH WORLD A. DOMISE *Maclean's* v129 no45 p12 N 14 2016

VINE, KATY

GET THE PICTURE? *Texas Monthly* v45 no5 p88 My 2017

Vine Co.

R.I.P. VINE: THE SIX-SECOND OBITUARY K. P. Sullivan color *Entertainment Weekly* no1439 p11 N 11 2016

Vinegar

See also

Cider vinegar

Gillian's Valentine Advice color *AARP: The Magazine* v60 no2A p11 F/Mr 2017

Quick Hits L. Nemo map *Scientific American* v317 no4 p22 O 2017

Vinegar, Michael—Interviews

Michael Vinegar A. FLANGO *Cincinnati Magazine* v50 no6 p40 Mr 2017

Vinegar—Evaluation

In the SUNSET KITCHEN color *Sunset* v237 no5 p96 N 2016

Vineis, Paolo

Mutational signatures associated with tobacco smoking in human cancer bibl graph *Science* v354 no6312 p618 N 4 2016

Vineyard, Jennifer

PARTY LINES img *New York* v50 no6 p88 Mr 20 2017

Vineyards

BAJA ON FIRE S. Schneider color *Sunset* v239 no4 p70 O 2017

BEST OF HALL OF FAME *Washingtonian Magazine* v52 no12 p164 S 2017

BEST OF WASHINGTON HALL OF FAME *Washingtonian Magazine* v52 no8 p209 My 2017

Southern sippin' M. Rosano color *Canadian Geographic* v137 p16 2017 Travel

Stomping Ground C. TATTOLI color *Conde Nast Traveler* v52 no5 p22 My 2017

Sweet Georgia E. FLORIO color *Conde Nast Traveler* v52 no9 p38 O 2017

TRAILS AND TOURS: WHERE IN THE VALLEY TO RIDE A BIKE, PADDLE A CANOE, SIP GOOD WINE AND BEER, OR SNUGGLE A BABY GOAT *Washingtonian Magazine* v53 no1 p106 O 2017

Vineyards—California

IN Season L. RAMZI color *Vogue* v206 no12 p212 D 2016

Vineyards—Evaluation

LET'S GO WINETASTING N. BAUER *Washingtonian Magazine* v52 no8 p90 My 2017

Trek and Toast T. BROWN color *Backpacker* p19 My 2017

Vineyards—France

WHAT A SOMMELIER DRINKS AT HOME color *Esquire* p60 BigBlackBook

Vineyards—Management

THE VINE LIFE M. D. G. Kaplan *Washingtonian Magazine* v52 no1 p205 O 2016

Vineyards—New York (State)

A HOUSE UNITED BY ROSÉ J. Kell color *Fortune* v176 no2 p44 Ag 1 2017

Vinjamuri, Leslie

The Distant Promise of a Negotiated Justice *Daedalus* v146 no1 p100 Wint 2017

VINOPAL, COURTNEY

VITAL SIGNS: Amid Washington's visual cacophony, some signage stands out. An expert weighs in on a few of the area's significant images *Washingtonian Magazine* v53 no1 p18 O 2017

WHERE & WHEN: 17 THINGS YOU REALLY OUGHT TO DO THIS MONTH *Washingtonian Magazine* v53 no1 p31 O 2017

WHERE & WHEN: 18 THINGS YOU REALLY OUGHT TO DO THIS MONTH *Washingtonian Magazine* v52 no12 p29 S 2017

Vinson, Charles

Impact of cytosine methylation on DNA binding specificities of human transcription factors diag *Science* v356 no6337 p502 My 5 2017

Vinson, Nick

My LIST color *Harper's Bazaar* no3649 p144 D 2016/Ja 2017

Vinson, Tripp

NOT-SO-INTELLECTUAL PROPERTY A. FRENCH *New York Times Magazine* p30 Jl 30 2017

Vintage clothing

New Wave S. BAHR color *Indianapolis Monthly* v42 no2 p31 O 2017

Supremely Retro C. Ianzito color *AARP: The Magazine* v59 no5A p69 Ag/S 2016

Thoroughly Modern Millinery B. L. Walls color *AARP: The Magazine* v59 no2A p72 F/Mr 2016

Vintage Doors LLC

Going Dutch color *Log Home Living* v34 no7 p20 S 2017

Vintage Hardware & Lighting (Company)

STAIR RODS & DUST CORNERS color *Old House Journal* v45 no1 p78 F 2017

Vintcent, Toby

Crash color *Publishers Weekly* v264 no10 p42 Mr 6 2017

Vinther, Jakob

THE True Colors OF DINOSAURS [Cover story] color *Scientific American* v316 no3 p50 Mr 2017

Vintners

LODI LEADS S. Schneider color *Sunset* v239 no3 p102 S 2017

Vintner's Daughter (Company)

the cover color *InStyle* v24 no2 p20 F 2017

Vintners—Interviews

Q&A: Genevieve Janssens K. DOANE *Cincinnati Magazine* v50 no6 p118 Mr 2017

VINTON, KATE

The $4.5 Billion Cabinet color *Forbes* v199 no1 p26 Ja 24 2017

Paymasters color *Forbes* v198 no9 p20 D 30 2016

THE PLANET'S RICHEST PERSON bw color graph *Forbes* v200 no2 p30 S 5 2017

Ringmaster of the Universe color *Forbes* v198 no8 p50 D 20 2016

THE WORLD'S MOST INNOVATIVE COMPANIES chart color *Forbes* v200 no2 p72 S 5 2017

The Young and the Restless color *Forbes* v199 no3 p32 Mr 28 2017

The Young and the Rich color graph *Forbes* v198 no5 p40 O 25 2016

Viola, Matt

Posthole color *Powder* v45 no3 p148 N 2016

Violence

See also

Violence in the workplace

After Charlottesville *Commonweal* v114 no14 p5 S 8 2017

Battle Cry A. Hess *New York Times Magazine* p9 Ag 20 2017

Between Violence and Responsibility: Peering at Protests through a Dual Lens [Cover story] I. QAIYIM *Islamic Horizons* v46 no1 p24 Ja/F 2017

GEORGIAN RUGBY UNiTES TO END VIOLENCE AGAINST WOMEN AND GIRLS I. JAPHARIDZE *UN Chronicle* v53 no2 p33 2016

Helping Kids Cope T. ANDERSON and D. POINTDUJOUR color *Ebony* v72 no4 p70 F 2017

Is the World Getting More Dangerous? *New York Times Upfront* v149 no6 p12 D 12 2016

Man's Best Fiend T. D. Parry *History Today* v66 no12 p50 D 2016

Marching to City Hall A. J. Johnson color *New Orleans Magazine* v51 no5 p38 Mr 2017

Organized Crime, Illicit Economies, Civil Violence & International Order: More Complex Than You Think V. Felbab-Brown *Daedalus* v146 no4 p98 Fall 2017

Our Bigot in Chief S. ABRAMSKY *Nation* v305 no6 p3 S 11 2017

TRUMP AND THE TRIUMPH OF FEAR IN AMERICAN POLITICS S. ABRAMSKY bw color *Nation* v305 no8 p18 O 9 2017

Violent Portland M. Hemingway *Weekly Standard* v22 no39 p9 Je 19 2017

The War That Broke the Country K. Vick color *Time* v190 no12 p46 S 25 2017

Yemen's Tragic Civil War Reaches a New Level of Violence J. Malsin color *Time* v188 no16/17 p7 O 24 2016

YOUR LIFE *USA Today Magazine* v145 no2862 p6 Mr 2017

Violence against gay men

An anti-gay campaign turns deadly in Chechnya, and journalists are also in danger R. Denber *America* v216 no13 p10 Je 12 2017

Violence against women

François-Henri Pinault A. B. -B. bw *Vanity Fair* v58 no12 p137 D 2016

GUARDIAN OF THE GIRL-CHILD S. O'GRADY color *Foreign Policy* no223 p36 Mr/Ap 2017

The Rapist's Loophole: Marriage R. MELLEN map *Foreign Policy* no223 p20 Mr/Ap 2017

Violence against women—Prevention

WORTH NOTING K. A. GAJEWSKI *Humanist* v77 no1 p48 Ja/F 2017

Violence in hockey

THE EDITORIAL *Maclean's* v129 no43 p5 O 31 2016

Violence in mass media

The Geography of Mercy V. J. MILLER color *America* v215 no11 p14 O 17 2016

Violence in music

The Case of The Violent Rap Lyrics V. GLEMBOCKI color *Reader's Digest* v189 no1129 p23 Ap 2017

Violence in the Bible

Does the Bible condone violence? E. Sanna *U.S. Catholic* v82 no10 p49 O 2017

Violence in the community

Post-traumatic ministry [Cover story] L. Kraus, D. Holyan et al color *Christian Century* v134 no7 p22 Mr 29 2017

Violence in the workplace

Modified Limited Hangouts D. HARSANYI *National Review* v69 no18 p44 O 2 2017

Violence on television

IS TV NEWS TOO VIOLENT? I. RUDOLPH *TV Guide* v65 no25 p6 Je 2017

Violence prevention

Attacking the Roots of Violence L. S. Wen and M. C. Lloyd cartoon *Scientific American* v315 no5 p9 N 2016

Consider This color *Yoga Journal* no291 p14 My 2017

INTERNAL AFFAIRS D. Gunn *Psychology Today* v50 no2 p64 Mr/Ap 2017

Violence—Congo (Democratic Republic)

Congo's churches face rising violence C. Kennel-Shank *Christian Century* v134 no13 p12 Je 21 2017

Violence—Economic aspects

Violence Raises Oil Risk in Mexico A. Stillman color *Bloomberg Businessweek* no4532 p31 Jl 31 2017

Violence—Forecasting

Predicting armed conflict: Time to adjust our expectations? Cederman and N. B. Weidmann bibl color map *Science* v355 no6324 p474 F 3 2017

Violence—Mexico

Three Priests Killed Over Two Days color *America* v215 no10 p10 O 10 2016

Violence—Mexico—History—21st century

Violence Raises Oil Risk in Mexico A. Stillman color *Bloomberg Businessweek* no4532 p31 Jl 31 2017

Violence—Psychological aspects

Papa Was a Rolling Stone R. E. VATZ *USA Today Magazine* v146 no2868 p35 S 2017

Violence—Religious aspects—Christianity

Does the Bible condone violence? E. Sanna *U.S. Catholic* v82 no10 p49 O 2017

God among the gangs P. Jenkins *Christian Century* v133 no24 p45 N 23 2016

Violence—United States

What could 'free speech' possibly mean when a mob is bullying and beating people with whom they don't agree? F. Prose *New York Times Book Review* p27 O 1 2017

Violence—United States—Prevention

Buried Alive: Stories from Inside Solitary Confinement N. PENN color map *GQ: Gentlemen's Quarterly* v97 no3 p154 Mr 2017

Violent criminals

A Glimpse Inside a Violent Gang T. MECIA color *Weekly Standard* v22 no46 p19 Ag 14 2017

Violent deaths

See also

Asphyxia

Drowning

Murder

One Family's Tragic Tale: Their story became a symbol of the nation's collapse N. Casey *New York Times Upfront* v149 no13 p15 My 15 2017

VENEZUELA IN CRISIS: With its economy in free fall and a government looking more and more like a dictatorship, Venezuela is on the brink of disaster P. SMITH *New York Times Upfront* v149 no13 p12 My 15 2017

Violets

IN PRAISE of VIOLAS A. MAZE color *Better Homes & Gardens* v95 no4 p126 Ap 2017

Violin—Study & teaching

My Family Is Stuck in Aleppo A. Haglage color *Glamour* v115 no5 p149 My 2017

Violists

Empire State of Mind P. MARGASAK color *Downbeat* v84 no1 p16 Ja 2017

Viper automobile

Chasing the SUMMIT P. Thomas bw color *Hot Rod* v69 no12 p26 D 2016

DODGE VIPER J. Jacquot color graph *Car & Driver* v63 no5 p26 N 2017

VIPKid (Company)

When the Teacher Is An Ocean Away P. Elstrom and D. Ramli color graph *Bloomberg Businessweek* no4505 p22 D 26 2016

VIRA, BHASKAR

Society Is Ready for a New Kind of Science--Is Academia? *BioScience* v67 no7 p591 Jl 2017

Viral antibodies

Maternal antibodies' role in immunity H. Lemke, K. M. Gostic et al bibl color *Science* v355 no6326 p704 F 17 2017

Science suffers as China plugs holes in Great Firewall D. Normile color *Science* v357 no6354 p856 S 1 2017

Why Apple withdrew VPN apps from its China App Store G. FLEISHMAN color *Macworld - Digital Edition* v34 no10 p46 O 2017

Why Linux users should worry about malware and what they can do about it A. CAMPBELL color *PCWorld* p40 Mr 2017

Virtual prototypes—Software

NEW PRODUCTS *Physics Today* v70 no6 p68 Je 2017

Virtual reality

See also

Avatars (Virtual reality)

Barbara Rothbaum *Atlanta* v57 no2 p106 Je 2017

Can journalism be virtual? T. Owen cartoon *Columbia Journalism Review* p102 Fall/Wint 2016

Can VR Find a Seat In the Parlor? A. Sakoui color *Bloomberg Businessweek* no4524 p22 My 29 2017

CELEBRATING PEBBLE BEACH CAR WEEK color *Motor Trend* v69 no11 p95 N 2017

EVERYTHING WORTH KNOWING color *Discover* v38 no6 p28 Jl/Ag 2017

FUTURE AUSTEN ADAPTATIONS B. ROBERSON cartoon *New Yorker* v93 no23 p29 Ag 7 2017

THE GREAT INDOORS B. Wieners color *Bloomberg Businessweek* no4495 p71 O 17 2016

How Alienware's 20-year history with PC gaming can help drive the future of VR A. SHAH color *PCWorld* v35 no11 p21 N 2016

How Gaming Is Shaping the Future of Work K. Tynan *Harvard Business Review Digital Articles* p2 My 2 2016

How to Run a Great Virtual Meeting K. Ferrazzi *Harvard Business Review Digital Articles* p2 Mr 27 2015

Inside Facebook's Big VR Lawsuit color *Time* v189 no3 p8 Ja 30 2017

The Lure of Virtual Reality K. PITSKER color *Kiplinger's Personal Finance* v71 no7 p41 Jl 2017

REALITY CHECK: Will your next surgery be done with virtual reality? More area hospitals are employing this cutting-edge technology C. Cunningham *Washingtonian Magazine* v52 no12 p115 S 2017

The Region's Newest Sales Tool: Virtual reality cartoon *Washingtonian Magazine* v52 no7 p92 Ap 2017

Science journalists don't use the science of 'nudge' E. Quill *Science News* v191 no5 p2 Mr 18 2017

Seeing into the Future [Cover story] J. MOSER color *Power & Motoryacht* v34 no6 p22 Je 2017

THE SETUP UNREAL ESTATE P. SARCONI cartoon *Wired* v25 no4 p40 Ap 2017

TECH QUIZ P. McCartney *Popular Mechanics* p72 O 2017

A Thought Experiment D. Byrne color *National Geographic* v231 no6 p14 Je 2017

Total Immersion M. LEIGHTON BEAMAN *Architectural Record* v204 no11 p57 N 2016

Virtual and Augmented Reality Will Reshape Retail D. McKone, R. Haslehurst et al *Harvard Business Review Digital Articles* p2 S 9 2016

(Virtually) Part of the Ballet C. Thompson color *Dance Magazine* v91 no3 p14 Mr 2017

VIRTUAL REALITY IN REAL TIME: A CONVERSATION S. Frilot and H. King *Film Quarterly* v71 no1 p51 Fall 2017

Virtual Reality S. ORNES color *Discover* v38 no6 p48 Jl/Ag 2017

A VR SPACE ODYSSEY color *Entertainment Weekly* no1441 p54 N 25 2016

VR STARTUPS ARE A HOT COMMODITY diag *Fortune* v175 no7 p11 Je 1 2017

What Everyone Should Know About Running Virtual Meetings P. Axtell *Harvard Business Review Digital Articles* p2 Ap 14 2016

WHEN SEEING IS FEELING R. ITO *Los Angeles Magazine* p98 F 2017

Why Physical Things Matter In a Digital World D. Sax *Time* v188 no20 p19 N 14 2016

Windows 10 Creators Update FAQ: Everything you need to know [Cover story] B. CHACOS color *PCWorld* v35 no5 p9 My 2017

Virtual reality—Equipment & supplies

REAL SICK [Cover story] B. Mason color *Science News* v191 no5 p24 Mr 18 2017

THE REVOLUTION [WILL NOT BE TELEVISED] A. Wolff

chart color diag *Sports Illustrated* v125 no19 p112 D 12 2016

Rock Band VR: Rock Band's roaring PC debut showcases Oculus Touch's potential H. DINGMAN color *PCWorld* v35 no5 p125 My 2017

Virtual reality raises nausea risk B. MASON color *Science News* v191 no1 p7 Ja 21 2017

VIRTUAL REALITY'S MONEY QUEST J. Vanian color *Fortune* v75 no1 p28 Ja 1 2017

WE HAVE SEEN THE LIGHT color *Men's Health* v31 no10 p(Sp)32 D 2016

When League Pass Takes You Courtside I. Boudway color *Bloomberg Businessweek* no4498 p42 N 7 2016

Virtual reality—Equipment & supplies—Evaluation

Daydream View: Sparse content is all that stands between Google and VR greatness J. CROSS color *PCWorld* v35 no1 p145 Ja 2017

First Windows Mixed Reality headsets color *PCWorld* v35 no10 p132 O 2017

VIRTUAL REALITY, ONE YEAR OUT: What went right, what didn't B. CHACOS color *PCWorld* p141 Mr 2017

VR GOALS N. SANTOS color *Ebony* v72/73 no12/1 p93 O/N 2017

Virtual reality—Equipment & supplies—Sales & prices

Making VR Matter J. Brustein cartoon color *Bloomberg Businessweek* no4496 p23 O 24 2016

Time for a (Virtual) Reality Check J. J. Roberts color *Fortune* v175 no3 p14 Mr 1 2017

Virtual reality—Exhibitions—Reviews

BIG TIME VIRTUAL REALITY E. Hancox *Iceland Review* v55 no1 p6 Ja/F 2017

Virtual reality—Marketing

STILL BAKING R. SABIN color *Sound & Vision* v82 no8 p8 O 2017

Virtual reality—Social aspects

Virtually Yours M. Burns and T. Keith color *Sports Illustrated* v125 no17 p30 N 21 2016 Double Issue

(VIRTUAL) REALITY BITES E. Griffith color *Fortune* v175 no2 p45 F 1 2017

Virtual Reality's Missing Element: Other People R. Metz color *MIT Technology Review* v120 no4 p84 Jl/Ag 2017

Virtual Trolls M. Mossey il *MIT Technology Review* v120 no4 p10 Jl/Ag 2017

Virtual reality in art—Exhibitions

A HISTORY OF VIOLENCE N. FREEMAN bw color *ARTnews* v116 no1 p20 Spr 2017

Virtual reality in education

Educators Share 10 Best Teaching, Technology Practices M. LEVITT *Education Digest* v82 no8 p56 Ap 2017

Virtual reality in management

Reimagining the Boardroom for an Age of Virtual Reality and AI D. Lancefield and C. Gagliardi *Harvard Business Review Digital Articles* p2 Ap 3 2015

Virtual reality in medicine

Innovation M. Cortez bw color *Bloomberg Businessweek* no4502 p43 D 5 2016

Virtual Plan, Real Surgery L. BRODY color *Forbes* v198 no9 p82 D 30 2016

Virtual reality in motion pictures

Beyond the Nickel Ride N. PINKERTON color *Film Comment* v53 no2 p36 Mr/Ap 2017

Virtual reality therapy

Real Trauma, Virtual Therapy A. Popescu color *Bloomberg Businessweek* no4515 p28 Mr 20 2017

Virtual work teams

Communication Tips for Global Virtual Teams P. Berry *Harvard Business Review Digital Articles* p2 O 30 2014

A First-Time Manager's Guide to Leading Virtual Teams M. Mortensen *Harvard Business Review Digital Articles* p2 S 25 2015

What 20 Years as a Remote Organization Has Taught Us About Managing Remote Teams R. Street, D. Wang et al *Harvard Business Review Digital Articles* p2 F 20 2017

Working Smoothly with a Virtual Boss K. Ferrazzi *Harvard Business Review Digital Articles* p2 D 11 2014

Virtue, C. J.

Observation of coherent elastic neutrino-nucleus scattering diag

Science v357 no6356 p1123 S 15 2017

Virtue Labs (Company)

the COMPACT N. Spradley color *Essence* v47 no10 p42 F 2017

Virtues

See also

Generosity

Gratitude

Humility

Toleration

Corporate Ethics Can't Be Reduced to Compliance P. Rea, A. Kolp et al *Harvard Business Review Digital Articles* p2 Ap 29 2016

OLD and RIGHT A. SMITH *American Conservative* v16 no2 p29 Mr/Ap 2017

Virulence (Microbiology)

See also

Bacteriophages—Virulence

Inflammation boosts bacteriophage transfer between Salmonella spp M. Diard, E. Bakkeren et al bibl diag *Science* v355 no6330 p1211 Mr 17 2017

Viruses

Bats and human health A. L. BAUCELLS *Issues in Science & Technology* v33 no4 p16 Summ 2017

Give Bats a Break M. D. TUTTLE *Issues in Science & Technology* v33 no3 p41 Spr 2017

A Tangled Food Web A. Hadhazy *Natural History* v125 no2 p7 F 2017

Viruses—Morphology

Zika's baby photo snapped M. Rosen color *Science News* v191 no4 p32 Mr 4 2017

Visages Villages (Film)

The Speed of Light in a Vacuum A. Taubin bw color *Film Comment* v53 no4 p54 Jl/Ag 2017

Visas

See also

Foreign investment visas

Plan forming for EU visas *People Management* p10 N 2016

Real News, Fake Panic J. LILEKS *National Review* v69 no5 p39 Mr 20 2017

Visas—Government policy

Why a Visa Crackdown Is Bad for Business J. Ellison color *Bloomberg Businessweek* no4528 p34 Je 26 2017

Visas—United States

The H-1B Visa Debate, Explained N. Torres *Harvard Business Review Digital Articles* p2 My 4 2017

Visas—United States—Government policy

Turkey-U.S. Relations are Going from Bad to Much, Much Worse I. Bremmer *Time* v190 no16/17 p16 O 23 2017

Visceral pain

POP QUIZ C. Barakat and M. Freckleton color *Equus* no471 p14 D 2016

Vischer, Robert K.

Agreeing on How to Disagree color *Commonweal* v144 no16 p33 O 6 2017

Catholic Universities And #BlackLivesMatter color *America* v215 no12 p24 O 24 2016

Visco, Jason

DISCOVERING THE SUBLIME *Iceland Review* v54 no6 p36 N/D 2016

WISDOM OF GOÐAFOSS *Iceland Review* v55 no2 p22 Mr/Ap 2017

Viscosimeters—Evaluation

new products: metabolomics color *Science* v356 no6338 p649 My 12 2017

Viscosity

Constraining lithospheric flow B. J. P. Kaus bibl color graph *Science* v353 no6307 p1495 S 30 2016

High-resolution lithosphere viscosity and dynamics revealed by magnetotelluric imaging Lijun Liu and D. Hasterok bibl graph *Science* v353 no6307 p1515 S 30 2016

Imaging the distribution of transient viscosity after the 2016 Mw 7.1 Kumamoto earthquake J. D. P. Moore, H. Yu et al map *Science* v356 no6334 p163 Ap 14 2017

A MAP OF EARTH'S VISCOUS CRUST *Physics Today* v69 no12 p24 D 2016

Viscosity—Measurement

OIL VISCOSITY DEBATE R. Bohacz *Successful Farming* v115 no3 p29 Mid-F 2017

Viscusi, Gregory

Après le Champagne, More Campaign color graph *Bloomberg Businessweek* no4522 p34 My 15 2017

In France, an Election Veers Off the Rails graph *Bloomberg Businessweek* no4511 p17 F 13 2017

Macron vs. The Unions graph *Bloomberg Businessweek* no4529 p30 Jl 3 2017

Viscusi, W. Kip

Consumer Warning Labels Aren't Working *Harvard Business Review Digital Articles* p2 N 30 2016

Vishneva, Diana

Alfa Romeo J. Acocella bw *New Yorker* v93 no17 p12 Je 19 2017

Vishneva, Diana—Interviews

Diana Vishneva W. PERRON *Dance Magazine* v90 no11 p18 N 2016

Vishnoi, Abhishek

South Korea Tries to Curb the Chaebol color *Bloomberg Businessweek* no4504 p15 D 19 2016

Vishwanatha, Jamboor

NIH's mentoring makes progress bibl *Science* v354 no6314 p840 N 18 2016

Visibility

ENHANCED VISION SYSTEM R. Mark color *Flying* v144 no7 p22 Jl 2017

Vision

THE DREAMERS color *Road & Track* v69 no4 p56 N 2017

FORGED ACCURACY T. E. Nickens bw cartoon *Field & Stream* v121 no6 p26 N 2016

Good Food: Protect Your vision P. ORMONT BLUMBERG color *Prevention* v69 no8 p34 Ag 2017

Still-Hunt Rule Breaker A. Jennings color *Field & Stream* v121 no6 pW7 N 2016

Veggies with Vision M. Zaraska color *Scientific American* v316 no1 p18 Ja 2017

Vision-Box SA

Small to Big Vision-Box color diag graph *Bloomberg Businessweek* no4495 p40 O 17 2016

Vision disorders

Blind Spots A. PATZ bw color *Women's Health* v14 no9 p72 N 2017

Check His Eyes at the Movies *Parents* v91 no9 p34 S 2016

FROM LOSS TO ABILITY J. Barratt color *Maclean's* v129 no42 p35 O 24 2016

Vision disorders—Prevention

Say Goodbye to Contact Lenses and Glasses with PiXLTM — the New Non-Invasive Vision Improvement Procedure M. Sponagle color *Maclean's* v129 no42 p36 O 24 2016

trend WATCH V. Tweed *Better Nutrition* v79 no11 p12 N 2017

Vision disorders—Treatment

Electronic screen alert: Avoid this vision risk *Harvard Health Letter* v42 no10 p3 Ag 2017

Vision of Love (Music)

1990 L. Greenblatt color *Entertainment Weekly* no1476 p60 Ag 4 2017

Vision statements

Communicating a Corporate Vision to Your Team K. Decker and B. Decker *Harvard Business Review Digital Articles* p2 Jl 10 2015

Vision testing

TARGET TRANSITIONS J. B. SNOW color *Outdoor Life* v224 no1 pR9 D 2016/Ja 2017

Vision—Physiological aspects

An eye-opening role for a cancer drug B. Brookshire color *Science News* v191 no11 p4 Je 10 2017

Vision—Religious aspects

Seeing Is Believing C. Nelson bw *Commonweal* v143 no18 p14 N 11 2016

Visions

See also

Dreams

A Brief History of the Future P. O'Donnell *Smithsonian* v48 no3 p12 Je 2017

DREAMS THAT MOVIES ARE MADE OF A. M. Ingham *Iceland Review* v55 no3 p14 My/Je 2017

Visit From St. Winfricholas, A (Poem)
A Visit from St. Winfricholas N. McGOVERN color *O, The Oprah Magazine* p14 D 2016

Visiting (Social interaction)
Gracious Guests N. B. McGough and P. S. York color *Southern Living* v52 no11 p47 N 2017
Take a friend to the barn cartoon *Equus* no474 p72 Mr 2017

Visitors' centers
Go With the Flow A. MARTINS color *Architectural Record* v205 no8 p84 Ag 2017
New Visitor Center at Five Rivers *New York State Conservationist* v72 no1 p36 Ag 2017
The Power of Persuasion R. CAMPBELL color *Architectural Record* v205 no8 p90 Ag 2017

Visits of state
The grittiest royal tour N. MACDONALD color map *Maclean's* v129 no40 p44 O 10 2016
The royals on tour [Cover story] color *Maclean's* v129 no40 p38 O 10 2016
Sharing the limelight P. TREBLE color *Maclean's* v129 no40 p48 O 10 2016
Slacking, royally P. PATRICIA color graph *Maclean's* v129 no40 p49 O 10 2016
Taking them on tour P. TREBLE bw color *Maclean's* v129 no40 p50 O 10 2016
Trailblazing Trip C. ZEIGLER bw *Indianapolis Monthly* p20 Ap 2017

Visits of state—United States
Made-to-Please Religious Reforms: Egyptian strongman El-Sisi seeks ways to please Western supporters M. KOSABA *Islamic Horizons* v46 no4 p50 Jl/Ag 2017

Visotzky, Burton L.
Rome and Jerusalem *Commentary* v141 no10 p1 D 2016
Rome and Jerusalem *Commentary* v142 no5 p1 D 2016

Visscher, S.
Improving global integration of crop research color *Science* v357 no6349 p359 Jl 28 2017

Vista Equity Partners (Company)
Philanthropy Paves Road to Riches M. S. Hopkins color *Ebony* v72 no9 p76 Jl/Ag 2017

Vista Outdoor Inc.
GRAND OPENING J. B. SNOW color *Outdoor Life* v224 no1 p95 D 2016/Ja 2017

Visual analytics
3 Things Are Holding Back Your Analytics, and Technology Isn't One of Them T. Clark and D. Wiesenfeld *Harvard Business Review Digital Articles* p2 Je 9 2017

Visual Apex (Company)
VApex PRO Fixed Frame Screen A. Griffifin chart color *Sound & Vision* v81 no10 p64 D 2016

Visual communication
See also
Signs & signboards
Written communication
People Remember What You Say When You Paint a Picture A. M. Carton *Harvard Business Review Digital Articles* p2 Je 12 2015
Signs Of The Times color *National Geographic Kids* no471 p30 Je/Jl 2017

Visual cortex
coloring inside the lines color *Popular Science* v289 no2 p89 Mr/Ap 2017

Visual optics
See also
Optical illusions
Xtreme Illusions *National Geographic Kids* no469 p26 Ap 2017

Visual perception
See also
Optical illusions
Visualization
Visualization—or "Pre-Visualization" J. KIDA *Arizona Highways* v93 no2 p9 F 2017

Visual Food Encyclopedia, The (Poem)
The Visual Food Encyclopedia G. CAMPANO *America* v215 no11 p30 O 17 2016

Visualization
Harnessing the Power Of Observation [Cover story] T. Johnston

color *Practical Horseman* v45 no7 p20 Jl 2017
Love Quest S. MILAN *USA Today Magazine* v145 no2860 p58 Ja 2017

Vita-mix Corp.
Vitamix A3500 Blender color *Bloomberg Businessweek* no4541 p67 O 9 2017

Vital, Not—Exhibitions
NOT VITAL W. Saunders and A. Rochette bw *Art in America* v105 no4 p124 Ap 2017

Vital force
Claims of Chi: Besting a Tai Chi Master J. NICKELL *Skeptical Inquirer* v41 no1 p20 Ja/F 2017

Vital signs
See also
Blood pressure
Respiration
Help in the Office: The Physician Extender Will See You Now B. Lutz color *New Orleans Magazine* v51 no10 p46 Ag 2017

VITALE, AMI
Warriors to the Rescue color map *National Geographic* v232 no2 p76 Ag 2017

Vitality
PURE ENERGY! V. Tweed color *Amazing Wellness* v9 no4 p38 Summ 2017

Vital records (Births, deaths, etc.)
See also
Wills
News Roundup V. HAFSTAÐ *Iceland Review* v55 no3 p8 My/Je 2017

Vitamin A
Body WISE color *O, The Oprah Magazine* p72 F 2017
SUPERCHARGE YOUR SKINCARE A. HERTZIG color *Redbook* p38 O 2017

Vitamin B complex
See also
Folic acid
THE A-Z ON VITAMIN B D. JACKSON color *Muscle & Performance* v9 no4 p26 Ap 2017
A Vitamin for Depression? color *O, The Oprah Magazine* p71 Jl 2017
What is the Nutritional Yeast *Vegetarian Journal* v36 no3 p14 2017

Vitamin B deficiency
How To "B" Smart E. SILBER *Psychology Today* v49 no6 p31 N/D 2016
NIACIN DEFICIENCY RULED OUT AS GRASS SICKNESS CAUSE C. Barakat and M. McCluskey *Equus* no470 p20 N 2016

Vitamin B1
THE A-Z ON VITAMIN B D. JACKSON color *Muscle & Performance* v9 no4 p26 Ap 2017
How To "B" Smart E. SILBER *Psychology Today* v49 no6 p31 N/D 2016

Vitamin B12 deficiency—Prevention
Is Your B12 Status at Risk? *Tufts University Health & Nutrition Letter* v35 no2 p7 2017

Vitamin B12 deficiency—Risk factors
DEFICIENCY NATION B12 K. Dold color *Women's Health* v14 no7 p82 S 2017

Vitamin B12—Therapeutic use
trend WATCH V. TWEED color *Better Nutrition* v79 no4 p10 Ap 2017

Vitamin C—Physiological effect
the cold (and flu) truth T. G. HOPE *Better Homes & Gardens* v94 no11 p150 N 2016

Vitamin C—Therapeutic use
Can vitamin C prevent a cold? *Harvard Health Letter* v42 no4 p7 F 2017

Vitamin D
BE SMART ABOUT Supplements M. OZ color *O, The Oprah Magazine* p84 Ap 2017
SKIING IS THE BESTEST R. Story color *Powder* v45 no5 p22 Ja 2017

Vitamin D deficiency—Prevention
Do you need a supplement? *Mayo Clinic Health Letter* v35 no9 p6 S 2017

Vitamin deficiency
7 COMMON VITAMIN DEFICIENCIES L. Turner color *Amazing Wellness* v9 no4 p52 Summ 2017
REBOOT! A. Nix *Amazing Wellness* v9 no4 p8 Summ 2017

Vitamin deficiency—Risk factors
What Are You Missing? N. Brechka color *Better Nutrition* v79 no3 p6 Mr 2017

Vitamin K
AND THE WINNERS ARE... [Cover story] color *Amazing Wellness* v9 no6 p50 EarlyWint 2017

Vitamin Shoppe Inc.
A WHEY BETTER (BLEND) PROTEIN M. FARRAR color *Muscle & Performance* v9 no6 p34 Je 2017

Vitamin therapy
Get Your Vita-Fix P. E. Christiani color *Essence* v47 no7 p36 N 2016

Vitamins
See also
Dietary supplements
Eat for Endurance C. Gerard color *Backpacker* v45 no1 p36 Ja 2017
Got vitamins? J. WUEBBEN bw color *Muscle & Performance* v9 no7 p14 Jl 2017
mykind ORGANICS A. Silverstone color *Amazing Wellness* p1 Fall 2017
POWER-PACKED VITAMINS D. N. JACKSON color *Muscle & Performance* v9 no10 p56 O 2017
A Tip From a Stroke Expert D. Chiu color *Prevention* v69 no5 p8 My 2017
Too Many Meds? [Cover story] T. Carr, R. R. Peachman et al color *Consumer Reports* v82 no9 p24 S 2017

Vitamins—Evaluation
ANAVITE R. GASPARI color *Muscle & Performance* v8 no12 p62 D 2016
customize YOUR HEALTH [Cover story] L. Turner color *Amazing Wellness* v9 no3 p54 EarlySumm 2017
THE EVOLUTION OF THE MULTIVITAMIN V. Tweed chart color *Amazing Wellness* v9 no3 p62 EarlySumm 2017
Garden of Life A. Silverstone color *Amazing Wellness* v9 no4 p1 Summ 2017
mykind ORGANICS GUMMIES A. Silverstone color *Amazing Wellness* v9 no6 pC1 EarlyWint 2017

Vitiligo
The Skin We're In F. Valdesolo color *Glamour* v115 no11 p95 N 2017

Vitobello, Antonio
Gene bivalency at Polycomb domains regulates cranial neural crest positional identity diag *Science* v355 no6332 p1390 Mr 31 2017

Vitorica-Yrezabal, Iñigo J.
Braiding a molecular knot with eight crossings bibl diag graph *Science* v355 no6321 p1 Ja 13 2017

Vitorino, Ana Paula
Portugal and the Ocean Economy *UN Chronicle* v54 no1/2 p1 2017

Vitruvius Pollio
c. 27 BC: Rome *Lapham's Quarterly* v10 no2 p163 Spr 2017

VITTER, DAVID
Should Birthright Citizenship Be Abolished? *New York Times Upfront* v149 no3 p22 O 10 2016

Vittori, Jodi
Can Bankers Fight Terrorism? *Foreign Affairs* v96 no6 p144 N/D 2017

VITULE, JEAN R. S.
Nonnative Fish to Control Aedes Mosquitoes: A Controversial, Harmful Tool *BioScience* v67 no1 p84 Ja 2017

Vitulli, William F.
Stem Cell Research *Skeptical Inquirer* v41 no3 p63 My/Je 2017

Vivaldi Album, The (Music)
Diva Playlist F. P. DRISCOLL *Opera News* v81 no5 p18 N 2016

Viviano, Frank
A tiny country feeds the world color graph map *National Geographic* v232 no3 p82 S 2017

Vivier, Karl
C'est Bon Bon *Atlanta* v57 no1 p60 My 2017

Viviscal (Company)
HAIR IT IS GROOMING J. WUEBBEN color *Muscle & Performance* v9 no8 p12 Ag 2017

Vizard, Rebecca—Interviews
RETURN TO EDEN M. K. QUINLAN color *House Beautiful* v159 no3 p84 Ap 2017

Vizguerra, Jeanette
CENTURY marks *Christian Century* v134 no12 p8 Je 7 2017

VIZIO Inc.
This Just In... M. Fleischmann color *Sound & Vision* v82 no8 p19 O 2017
Vizio M65-D0 Ultra HD Display A. Griffin color graph *Sound & Vision* v81 no10 p56 D 2016

Vizzard, William J.
Are We Any Safer? color *Atlantic* v318 no4 p14 N 2016

Vlachonis, Vicky
Ask anything bw color *Women's Health* v14 no4 p18 My 2017
Ask anything [Cover story] cartoon color *Women's Health* v13 no10 p22 D 2016

Vlachoutsicos, Charalambos
Need to Change? Keep a Diary *Harvard Business Review Digital Articles* p2 N 27 2014

Vladislav
The Love Nest cartoon *Walrus* v14 no6 p60 Jl/Ag 2017

Vladislavić, Ivan
2006: Johannesburg *Lapham's Quarterly* v10 no1 p183 Wint 2017
FEAR OF ARRIVAL *Lapham's Quarterly* v10 no3 p193 Summ 2017
A View of South Africa M. SEIDEL bw *Publishers Weekly* v264 no12 p45 Mr 20 2017

VLAHOS, JAMES
A SON'S QUEST TO GIVE HIS DYING FATHER ARTIFICIAL IMMORTALITY color *Wired* v25 no8 p56 Ag 2017

VLAHOS, KELLEY BEAUCAR
Cory Booker's Challenge *American Conservative* v16 no3 p28 My/Je 2017

VLASITS, ANNA
A BUMPER CROP OF FRUIT-PICKING BOTS diag *Wired* v25 no9 p38 S 2017
CHILL OUT: FIXES FOR A HOT PLANET cartoon *Wired* v25 no9 p32 S 2017
GENE GENIES color *Wired* v25 no6 p18 Je 2017
SEA OF LOUVRE ABU DHABI'S NEW ISLAND MUSEUM bw color *Wired* v25 no5 p28 My 2017

Vlassak, J. J.
Tough adhesives for diverse wet surfaces diag *Science* v357 no6349 p378 Jl 28 2017

VLIET, ELIZABETH LEE
MODERN MEDICINE MESS *USA Today Magazine* v145 no2862 p52 Mr 2017
Will ObamaCare Kill Medicare? *USA Today Magazine* v145 no2858 p30 N 2016

Vocabulary
In Praise of $%!#?! J. Murph cartoon chart *AARP: The Magazine* v60 no1A p12 D 2016/Ja 2017
The Intricacies of Power D. Lowry color *Black Belt* v55 no4 p26 Je/Jl 2017
IT PAYS TO INCREASE YOUR Word Power E. COX and H. RATHVON *Reader's Digest* v189 no1128 p131 Mr 2017
IT PAYS TO INCREASE YOUR Word Power E. COX and H. RATHVON *Reader's Digest* v189 no1129 p133 Ap 2017
IT PAYS TO INCREASE YOUR Word Power E. COX and H. RATHVON *Reader's Digest* v190 no1134 p133 O 2017
The Logophile *Saturday Evening Post* v289 no1 p28 Ja/F 2017
A LOVE ACQUIRED C. Agra Deedy bw *Literacy Today (2411-7862)* v34 no5 p32 Mr/Ap 2017
New Words for a New World K. Samuelson *Time* v190 no13 p16 O 2 2017
Speaking Freely M. Helprin *Claremont Review of Books* v17 no2 p98 Spr 2017
Word Inflation S. MILLER *Weekly Standard* v22 no34 p47 My 15 2017
Word Power E. COX and H. RATHVON *Reader's Digest* v188 no1126 p131 D 2016/Ja 2017

Vocabulary education
SO MANY WORDS, SO LITTLE TIME: How morphological awareness can help young learners with their vocabulary com-

prehension S. L. Hall *Literacy Today (2411-7862)* v35 no1 p26 Jl/Ag 2017

TOUCHING ON VOCABULARY: Using multiple methods to energize vocabulary instruction S. Craig *Literacy Today (2411-7862)* v35 no2 p32 S/O 2017

Vocabulary tests

IT PAYS TO INCREASE YOUR Word Power E. COX and H. RATHVON *Reader's Digest* v189 no1131 p133 Je 2017

Vocabulary—Study & teaching

IT'S NOT THE TOOLS ...IT'S THE TEACHING B. Steckel and V. Harlow Shinas color *Literacy Today (2411-7862)* v34 no3 p22 N/D 2016

Vocal cord dysfunction

Your Body on an Argument color *Prevention* v68 no11 p17 N 2016

Vocal cord dysfunction—Risk factors

Make your voice heard! *Harvard Health Letter* v42 no7 p4 My 2017

Vocal cords—Care & hygiene

Cracking the Voice img *New York* v49 no20 p113 O 3 2016

Researching Reflux and Its Link to Inflammation S. D. Wenholz color *Practical Horseman* v45 no3 p69 Mr 2017

Where the Top Notes Go J. Davidson img *New York* v49 no20 p114 O 3 2016

Vocational education

Career and Technical Education for Youth at Park & Rec Agencies K. Sims *Parks & Recreation* v52 no8 p22 Ag 2017

Have You Thought About Certification as an Alternative Educational Experience? M. Sullivan *Parks & Recreation* v52 no2 p42 F 2017

Vocational guidance

See also

    Career changes

    Career development

    Employment in foreign countries

    Job qualifications

Developing a Strategy for a Life of Meaningful Labor B. Fetherstonhaugh *Harvard Business Review Digital Articles* p2 S 5 2016

Don't Set Too Many Goals for Yourself D. Clark *Harvard Business Review Digital Articles* p2 D 16 2016

Get to Know Your Campus Career Development Office R. W. Goode color *Black Enterprise* v47 no3 p32 O 2016

Having the Here's-What-IWant Conversation With Your Boss R. Shambaugh *Harvard Business Review Digital Articles* p2 N 20 2015

How to Build a Meaningful Career A. Gallo *Harvard Business Review Digital Articles* p2 F 4 2015

How to Launch a Successful Portfolio Career M. Greenspan *Harvard Business Review Digital Articles* p2 My 4 2017

How to Turn an Interim Role into a Permanent Job B. Dattner color *Harvard Business Review Digital Articles* p2 Ja 16 2017

How to Use Stretch Assignments to Support Social Good M. Horoszowski *Harvard Business Review Digital Articles* p2 N 13 2015

If You're Fed Up with Your Job, Try Working More Pauses into Your Day R. O'Meara *Harvard Business Review Digital Articles* p2 Ap 7 2017

My First Lilith L. Dunham color *Glamour* no8 p146 Ag 2017

Research: The More Essential Your Job Is to Your Company, the Happier You'll Be Lixin Jiang, T. Tripp et al *Harvard Business Review Digital Articles* p2 My 10 2017

Taking Longer to Reach the Top Has Its Benefits K. Firestone *Harvard Business Review Digital Articles* p2 D 30 2015

Think Strategically About Your Career Development D. Clark *Harvard Business Review Digital Articles* p2 D 6 2016

To Get Promoted, Get Feedback from Your Critics S. Nawaz *Harvard Business Review Digital Articles* p2 N 10 2016

What Do I Do Now? A Midlife Career Change May Be Just the Challenge You Need K. V. Ogtrop color *Time* v190 no8 p59 Ag 28 2017

What Parents Should Tell Their Kids About Finding a Career J. M. Citrin *Harvard Business Review Digital Articles* p2 My 15 2015

Will Refusing an International Assignment Derail Your Career? M. C. Bolino, A. C. Klotz et al *Harvard Business Review Digital Articles* p2 Ap 18 2017

You Need to Practice Being Your Future Self P. Bregman *Harvard Business Review Digital Articles* p2 Mr 28 2016

Vocational guidance counselors

THE HAPPINESS FACTOR: A look at career satisfaction *Cincinnati Magazine* v50 no11 pCG10 Ag 2017

Vocational guidance—United States

MISSION: RETHINK HIGHER ED E. BLOXHAM color *Phi Kappa Phi Forum* v97 no2 p14 Summ 2017

Vocational interests

Stop Fantasizing About the Perfect Job J. Lees *Harvard Business Review Digital Articles* p2 Ap 22 2015

Vocation—Christianity

Walk of life J. Molyneux *U.S. Catholic* v82 no8 p4 Ag 2017

Vocation (in religious orders, congregations, etc.)

Discerning Desire A. HEYER color *America* v216 no1 p30 Ja 2 2017

Vock, Daniel C.

Banding Together: New public-private partnerships may finally help bridge the digital divide *Governing* v30 no8 p44 My 2017

CLEAN ENERGY *Governing* v30 no4 p36 Ja 2017

COUNTING DOWN TO ZERO *Governing* v30 no5 p38 F 2017

Defense with Dignity *Governing* v30 no6 p50 Mr 2017

INFRASTRUCTURE SPENDING *Governing* v30 no4 p33 Ja 2017

Lone Country: Navajos in Utah are used to having to fight for basic government services. But they'd at least like to see some roads that don't turn every trip into an endurance test *Governing* v30 no10 p48 Jl 2017

MARIJUANA *Governing* v30 no4 p34 Ja 2017

A PLACE OF REFUGE: A small Idaho city has endured many months of anti-immigrant hostility--and emerged stronger as a result *Governing* v30 no9 p36 Je 2017

The Politics of IDENTIFICATION *Governing* v30 no1 p34 O 2016

Project Runway *Governing* v30 no3 p48 D 2016

PUBLIC OFFICIALS OF THE YEAR *Governing* v30 no3 p26 D 2016

REROUTED: Big-city bus systems are finding ways to dig out from decades of stagnation *Governing* v30 no12 p38 S 2017

Road Rage *Governing* v30 no7 p44 Ap 2017

Sick Transit *Governing* v30 no2 p46 N 2016

Voting for Change *Governing* v30 no1 p17 O 2016

Vodianova, Natalia

Date with DIANE color *InStyle* v24 no5 p118 My 2017

Mad Plaids E. Wilson color *InStyle* v24 no11 p72 N 2017

Vodka

13 Things That Should Be A Thing K. Bonnell and P. R. Satran color *Glamour* v114 no11 p183 N 2016

Make the Perfect Summer Drink J. Momose color *Chicago* v66 no7 p62 Jl 2017

NOSH IN THE NEW YEAR A. STANEK and C. SAFFITZ cartoon color *Bon Appetit* v61 no12 p120 D 2016 /Jan2017

Shake, Pour and Chill Out: The Saltwater T. McNally color *New Orleans Magazine* v51 no10 p178 Ag 2017

Vodou

VODOU AND THE RAINBOW B. AHMED *Advocate* no1088 p56 D 2016/Ja 2017

Voegeli, William

Autopsies *Claremont Review of Books* v17 no3 p8 Summ 2017

Calling the Shots *Claremont Review of Books* v17 no3 p11 Summ 2017

Caution Ahead *Claremont Review of Books* v17 no3 p13 Summ 2017

Class Dismissed [Cover story] color *National Review* v69 no12 p24 Je 26 2017

THE DEMOCRATIC PARTY'S IDENTITY CRISIS *Claremont Review of Books* v17 no1 p30 Wint 2016/2017

DIVERSITY AND ITS DISCONTENTS *Claremont Review of Books* v17 no3 p8 Summ 2017

Is Nationhood Obsolete? *Claremont Review of Books* v17 no3 p9 Summ 2017

Moving Way Left *Claremont Review of Books* v17 no3 p9 Summ 2017

Near and Far *Claremont Review of Books* v17 no3 p11 Summ 2017

A New Us *Claremont Review of Books* v17 no3 p12 Summ 2017

WHAT'S LEFT? *Claremont Review of Books* v16 no4 p10 Fall 2016

Voelkel, Bret

The HOT ROD Archives D. Wallace color *Hot Rod* v70 no1 p18 Ja 2017

VOELKER, JESSICA

Be More Pacific *Indianapolis Monthly* p38 My 2017

VOGE, MAIANNA

An Ecoregion-Based Approach to Protecting Half the Terrestrial Realm *BioScience* v67 no6 p534 Je 2017

Vogel, Christine

Quantifying protein (dis)order bibl diag *Science* v355 no6327 p794 F 24 2017

Vogel, Daniel

Nuclear Power and the Psychology of Evaluating Risk *Skeptical Inquirer* v40 no6 p56 N/D 2016

Nuclear Power and Risk Psychology *Skeptical Inquirer* v41 no2 p64 Mr/Ap 2017

Vogel, Gretchen

Are labmade human eggs coming soon? color *Science* v354 no6310 p272 O 21 2016

Europe's top court alarms vaccine experts color *Science* v356 no6345 p1320 Je 30 2017

German researchers start 2017 without Elsevier journals color *Science* v355 no6320 p17 Ja 6 2017

Germany seeks 'big flip' in publishing model color graph *Science* v357 no6353 p744 Ag 25 2017

How to listen to your horse color *Equus* no470 p55 N 2016

Mouse eggs made in the lab color *Science* v354 no6319 p1520 D 23 2016

New Ebola outbreak rings alarm bells early color map *Science* v356 no6340 p788 My 26 2017

One year later, Zika scientists prepare for a long war graph *Science* v354 no6316 p1088 D 2 2016

Parasitic worm may trigger mystery nodding syndrome color *Science* v355 no6326 p678 F 17 2017

PUSHING THE LIMIT color *Science* v354 no6311 p404 O 28 2016

Revelations about rhythm of life rewarded color *Science* v357 no6359 p18 O 6 2017

WHERE HAVE ALL THE INSECTS GONE? color graph *Science* v356 no6338 p576 My 12 2017

Vogel, John P.

Mobile MUTE specifies subsidiary cells to build physiologically improved grass stomata bibl diag *Science* v355 no6330 p1215 Mr 17 2017

Vogel, Justine

Big Daddies chart color *Team Roping Journal* p36 S 2017

Vogel, Mike

The Brave N. Abrams, C. Holub et al color *Entertainment Weekly* no1482/1483 p55 S 22 2017

The case for (and problem with) Christian movies P. S. J. Lickteig color *America* v216 no10 p50 My 1 2017

Vogel, Nicolas

Preventing mussel adhesion using lubricant-infused materials color diag graph *Science* v357 no6352 p668 Ag 18 2017

Vogel, Paula

I Would Like to Thank... *Stage Directions* v30 no6 p34 Je 2017

STAGE OF ENLIGHTENMENT S. CROSLEY color *Vanity Fair* v59 no6 p74 My 2017

Vogel, Wendy

ANTEK WALCZAK color *Art in America* v104 no10 p153 N 2016

CARL CHENG *Art in America* v104 no9 p159 O 2016

CHOU YU-CHENG color *Art in America* v104 no11 p133 D 2016

LARRY WALKER *Art in America* v104 no9 p155 O 2016

LAURA COTTINGHAM color *Art in America* v105 no8 p120 S 2017

LILLIAN SCHWARTZ cartoon *Art in America* v104 no11 p119 D 2016

Swiss In situ color *Art in America* v105 no6 p133 Je/Jl 2017

Vogelpohl, Ruth

They vs. Them R. J. SMITH *Cincinnati Magazine* v50 no7 p42 Ap 2017

Vogelsang, Jessica

Ask anything bw color *Women's Health* v14 no4 p18 My 2017

Vogelstein, Bert

Mismatch repair deficiency predicts response of solid tumors to PD-1 blockade chart graph *Science* v357 no6349 p409 Jl 28 2017

Stem cell divisions, somatic mutations, cancer etiology, and cancer prevention bibl chart diag graph *Science* v355 no6331 p1330 Mr 24 2017

VOGT, JUSTIN

The Deep State: What were the nation's plans to govern after a nuclear strike? *New York Times Book Review* p18 Je 18 2017

Vogt, Michele

SOLUTIONS chart color *Horse & Rider* v56 no5 p24 My 2017

Vogt-Roberts, Jordan

Gorilla Theater J. Podhoretz color *Weekly Standard* v22 no29 p39 Ap 3 2017

Kong: Skull Island *New Yorker* v93 no7 p23 Ap 3 2017

Vogue (Periodical)

The Age of Canlandia J. JOHNSON cartoon *Walrus* v13 no10 p26 D 2016

Always in Vogue N. EMERY color *Weekly Standard* v22 no15 p17 D 19 2016

first BLUSH color *Vogue* v207 no6 p112 Je 2017

HAPPY BIRTHDAY TO US! color *Vogue* v207 no9 p464 S 2017

VOHR, ERIC

ISLAND Fling color map *Sail* v48 no9 p40 S 2017

Staying Connected color *Sail* v48 no10 p24 O 2017

Voice

    See also

       Vocal cords

Where the Top Notes Go J. Davidson img *New York* v49 no20 p114 O 3 2016

Why Your Cell Phone Sounds Female J. HEMPEL *Reader's Digest* v189 no1127 p54 F 2017

Voice, The (TV program)

CHEERS & JEERS D. HOLBROOK *TV Guide* p88 Ap 17 2017

CHEERS & JEERS D. HOLBROOK *TV Guide* v64 no40 p88 O 3 2016

The Voice N. Abrams, C. Holub et al color *Entertainment Weekly* no1482/1483 p49 S 22 2017

The Voice Soars M. ROFFMAN *TV Guide* v65 no19 p20 My 1 2017

Winners' Club *TV Guide* v65 no19 p23 My 1 2017

Voice analysis—Software

Should Your Voice Determine Whether You Get Hired? T. Chamorro-Premuzic and S. Adler *Harvard Business Review Digital Articles* p2 Ap 20 2015

Voice change

Tangled Up in Bob P. Candler color *Commonweal* v144 no10 p21 Je 2 2017

Voice of America (Organization)

TRUTH TALKERS C. ROSE *Cincinnati Magazine* v50 no8 p23 My 2017

The Voice of Trump C. IOVENKO *New Republic* v248 no5 p12 My 2017

Voice recognition software

COP TALK: THE SOUND OF BIAS L. MURROW color *Wired* v25 no8 p20 Ag 2017

Department of Wit Paging Dr. Malaprop! M. WOLFE cartoon *Reader's Digest* v190 no1134 p19 O 2017

Voice—Psychological aspects

LEARNING TO SPEAK THE TRUTH D. HERNÁNDEZ bw *Tricycle: The Buddhist Review* v27 no1 p55 Fall 2017

Voice—Social aspects

I'm a Female Author, So Why Did I Want a Man to Narrate My Audiobook? W. Johnson *Harvard Business Review Digital Articles* p2 N 25 2015

Voigt, Erich P.

Got a Cold? Do This M. Santos color *Working Mother* p57 F/Mr 2017

Volante, José N.

Forest conservation: Remember Gran Chaco bibl color *Science* v355 no6324 p465 F 3 2017

Volatile organic compounds

Emission of volatile organic compounds from petunia flowers is facilitated by an ABC transporter F. Adebesin, J. R. Widhalm et al diag *Science* v356 no6345 p1386 Je 30 2017

Releasing plant volatiles, as simple as ABC F. Eberl and J. Gershenzon color *Science* v356 no6345 p1334 Je 30 2017

Volatile organic compounds & the environment

The Odor of Death: An Overview of Current Knowledge on Characterization and Applications F. VERHEGGEN, K. A. PERRAULT et al *BioScience* v67 no7 p600 Jl 2017

Volatility (Finance)

The Dark Side of Efficient Markets R. L. Martin *Harvard Business Review Digital Articles* p2 O 15 2014

Gold Gets Its Own Flash Crash S. Barton and E. van der Walt graph *Bloomberg Businessweek* no4529 p26 Jl 3 2017

How to Brace Yourself C. Bigda color diag *Money* v45 no11 p45 D 2016

Maybe the Flash Boys Are the Good Guys C. Russo and J. Detrixhe graph *Bloomberg Businessweek* no4498 p49 N 7 2016

Riding the Highs and Lows of a Fickle Market E. AMBROSE color *AARP: The Magazine* v59 no4A p24 Je/Jl 2016

We Tracked Every Dollar 235 U.S. Households Spent for a Year, and Found Widespread Financial Vulnerability J. Morduch and R. Schneider *Harvard Business Review Digital Articles* p2 Ap 12 2017

Why China's Market Crash Is So Unsurprising L. Yueh *Harvard Business Review Digital Articles* p2 Ja 12 2016

Volatility (Securities)

Who's Afraid of Low Volatility? P. Coy and W. Soong cartoon graph *Bloomberg Businessweek* no4533 p23 Ag 7 2017

Volcanic activity prediction

Detecting the Next Volcanic Eruption [Cover story] D. M. PYLE color map *Natural History* v125 no6 p24 Je 2017

Volcanic ash clouds

ICE AND FIRE *Sierra* v101 no5 p2 S/O 2016

Volcanic craters

Fields of Fire R. JUSKALIAN color map *Discover* v38 no9 p32 N 2017

Volcanic eruptions

Changes Real and (Mostly) Imagined: Even renowned lunar observers have sometimes been fooled by tricks of lighting and resolution C. A. Wood color *Sky & Telescope* v134 no2 p52 Ag 2017

Detecting the Next Volcanic Eruption [Cover story] D. M. PYLE color map *Natural History* v125 no6 p24 Je 2017

Fire and Ice S. Hall color *Scientific American* v317 no2 p22 Ag 2017

Hawaii's Lava Waterfall *New York Times Upfront* v149 no12 p2 Ap 24 2017

HEAVEN AND EARTH E. MASTROIANNI color *Discover* v38 no4 p9 My 2017

Inflation-predictable behavior and co-eruption deformation at Axial Seamount S. L. Nooner and W. W. Chadwick Jr. bibl graph map *Science* v354 no6318 p1399 D 16 2016

Vertically extensive and unstable magmatic systems: A unified view of igneous processes K. V. Cashman, R. S. J. Sparks et al color *Science* v355 no6331 p1280 Mr 24 2017

Warning Signs color *Natural History* v125 no6 p5 Je 2017

Volcanic eruptions—Environmental aspects

Volcanic Skies A. Macrobert color *Sky & Telescope* v134 no2 p73 Ag 2017

Volcanic eruptions—History

See also

Mount Vesuvius Eruption, 79 AD

The Lost City Of Pompeii K. B. RATTINI cartoon color map *National Geographic Kids* no471 p20 Je/Jl 2017

Volcanic fields

Online Exhibitions color *Natural History* v125 no10 p5 O 2017

Volcanic plumes

Volcanic tremor and plume height hysteresis from Pavlof Volcano, Alaska A. R. Van Eaton, D. Fee et al bibl graph *Science* v355 no6320 p1 Ja 6 2017

Volcanic soils

LAVA CENTRE: The Epic Forces that Created Iceland *Iceland Review* v55 no3 p100 My/Je 2017

Volcanic ash, tuff, etc.

The Big Pictures: THE CHIRICAHUA MOUNTAINS *Arizona Highways* v93 no9 p18 S 2017

Chapel of the Holy Dove N. AUSTIN *Arizona Highways* v93 no9 p6 S 2017

Hell's Half Acre: Strolling the Lava Trails B. BASH *Idaho Magazine* v16 no11 p15 Ag 2017

Volcanism

See also

Magmatism

Volcanic eruptions

Earth's big oxygen boost pushed back T. SUMNER *Science News* v191 no4 p9 Mr 4 2017

Volcanoes

The Lava Catcher M. BARNA color *Discover* v38 no7 p16 S 2017

Weird but true! J. BEER and M. HARRIS *National Geographic Kids* no466 p4 D 2016/Ja 2017

WHATEVER HAPPENED TO THAT VOLCANO ON LOST? J. Jensen color *Entertainment Weekly* no1460/1461 p101 Ap 7-17 2017

Volcanoes—Iceland

ICE AND FIRE *Sierra* v101 no5 p2 S/O 2016

Volcanoes—Indonesia—Java

INDONESIA color *National Geographic* v232 no5 p8 N 2017

Volcanoes—Mexico

Lightbox color *Time* v189 no5 p14 F 13 2017

Volcanoes—Nicaragua

The Dragon's Lair V. LILLO color map *Backpacker* p16 Ag 2017

Volcanology

CRYSTAL CLOCKS J. Rosen color diag *Science* v354 no6314 p822 N 18 2016

Volckhausen, Willie

The Farmer I. Fohrman color *Powder* v45 no4 p38 D 2016

Vold, Harry

DEAR ROPER B. Welch *Spin to Win Rodeo* v21 no3 p8 My 2017

HARRY VOLD color *Horse & Rider* v56 no11 p86 N 2017

Harry Vold: Jan. 29, 1924-March 13, 2017 color *Spin to Win Rodeo* v21 no3 p20 My 2017

In Memory... color *American Cowboy* v24 no1 p25 Je/Jl 2017

Voles

The Vole's Fate: Eat and Be Eaten F. RUDEBUSCH *Idaho Magazine* v16 no11 p20 Ag 2017

Volf, Miroslav

Flourishing L. T. Johnson bw *Commonweal* v144 no3 p37 F 10 2017

Volk, Gregory

Instituto de Visión color *Art in America* v105 no1 p89 Ja 2017

Lehmann Maupin color *Art in America* v105 no6 p134 Je/Jl 2017

SLAVS AND TATARS cartoon *Art in America* v104 no11 p123 D 2016

Volk, Josh

SMALL FARM, REAL PROFIT: This inspiring half-acre urban farm in Oregon is proving that size doesn't matter when it comes to profitability *Mother Earth News* no284 p40 O/N 2017

VOLK, PATRICIA

A Family Affair bw color *Publishers Weekly* v264 no2 p36 Ja 9 2017

VOLK, STEVE

BUZZKILL color graph map *Discover* v38 no2 p30 Mr 2017

Carbon Dioxide and the New Stone Age color *Discover* v38 no1 p74 Ja/F 2017

THE RISE AND FALL OF THERANOS color *Discover* v38 no1 p44 Ja/F 2017

Volkerling, Alexander

Site-specific phosphorylation of tau inhibits amyloid-β toxicity in Alzheimer's mice bibl graph *Science* v354 no6314 p904 N 18 2016

Volkman, Paul

POST SCRIPT: HOW A SMALL-TIME CHICAGO DOCTOR CAME TO THE SOUTHEASTERN OHIO TOWN OF PORTSMOUTH AND HELPED SPUR AN EPIDEMIC P. EIL *Cincinnati Magazine* v50 no10 p66 Jl 2017

Volkswagen AG

1983 Volkswagen Rabbit GTi color *Popular Mechanics* p45 F 2017

2017 Volkswagen Golf Alltrack S. Evans color *Motor Trend* v69 no2 p67 F 2017

2018 Volkswagen Arteon F. Markus color *Motor Trend* v69 no3 p24 Mr 2017

2018 Volkswagen Atlas J. Cammisa color *Motor Trend* v69 no8 p26 Ag 2017

2018 Volkswagen Tiguan F. Markus color *Motor Trend* v69 no3 p22 Mr 2017

BIG TIG M. Cortina color *Motor Trend* v69 no10 p92 O 2017

Dieselgate and Dollars M. Rechtin cartoon *Motor Trend* v68 no12 p28 D 2016

THE FIX IS IN J. SABATINI, D. Sherman et al chart color graph *Car & Driver* v63 no1 p50 Jl 2017

GREED, GUILE & LIES D. BURNETT *Reader's Digest* v188 no1124 p100 O 2016

Like a Bus, But Better color *Consumer Reports* v82 no10 p62 O 2017

Milestones *Time* v189 no5 p13 F 13 2017

The Moral Cost of Dieselgate E. Loh color *Motor Trend* v69 no4 p14 Ap 2017

Reinventing These Wheels C. Rauwald and C. Reiter color graph *Bloomberg Businessweek* no4504 p19 D 19 2016

Road Test chart color *Consumer Reports* v82 no12 p62 D 2017

Three-Row Hero K. C. Colwell color *Car & Driver* v63 no1 p94 Jl 2017

VOLKSWAGEN GOES UPMARKET C. Clonts chart color *Motor Trend* v69 no9 p96 S 2017

VW's Problem Is Bad Management, Not Rogue Engineers M. Schrage *Harvard Business Review Digital Articles* p2 O 15 2015

What VW Didn't Understand About Trust A. Winston *Harvard Business Review Digital Articles* p2 S 23 2015

Volkswagen AG—Finance

VW's Latest Woe: A Reliance on Mexico R. Beene, C. Rauwald et al *Bloomberg Businessweek* no4512 p20 F 20 2017

Volkswagen automobiles

People Management 10 BEST ECO FLEET CARS: The writing's on the wall for petrol and diesel cars - so what should your staff be driving? *People Management* p45 S 2017

Volkswagen automobiles—Evaluation

10 Cars Worth Waiting For color *Consumer Reports* v82 no4 p38 Ap 2017

1983 Volkswagen Rabbit GTi color *Popular Mechanics* p45 F 2017

2017 EV BUYERS' GUIDE J. Motavalli *Sierra* v102 no5 p40 St/O 2017

2017 Volkswagen Golf Alltrack S. Evans color *Motor Trend* v69 no2 p67 F 2017

2018 Volkswagen Arteon F. Markus color *Motor Trend* v69 no3 p24 Mr 2017

2018 Volkswagen Atlas J. Cammisa color *Motor Trend* v69 no8 p26 Ag 2017

2018 Volkswagen Tiguan F. Markus color *Motor Trend* v69 no3 p22 Mr 2017

BIG TIG M. Cortina color *Motor Trend* v69 no10 p92 O 2017

Like a Bus, But Better color *Consumer Reports* v82 no10 p62 O 2017

Neither Snow nor Rain nor Heat nor Gloom of Night J. Sabatini color *Car & Driver* v62 no6 p100 D 2016

SIZE MATTERS J. H. HARPER color *Road & Track* v69 no1 p86 Ag 2017

Three-Row Hero K. C. Colwell color *Car & Driver* v63 no1 p94 Jl 2017

Volkswagen B-SUV F. Markus color *Motor Trend* v68 no12 p22 D 2016

VOLKSWAGEN GOES UPMARKET C. Clonts chart color *Motor Trend* v69 no9 p96 S 2017

Volkswagen Beetle automobile

HOW I DISCOVERED MY STYLE M. JACOBSON and J. Roth cartoon color *Esquire* p48 My 2017

Volkswagen AG—Trials, litigation, etc.

Can You Say Class Action in German? Nein K. Matussek and M. Cronin Fisk color *Bloomberg Businessweek* no4505 p39 D 26 2016

Voller, Ronald L.

Mount Wilson's famous telescope celebrates a century bw color *Astronomy* v45 no5 p28 My 2017

Volleyball

SWEATY, SANDY, SCULPTED M. Gainsburg color *Women's Health* v14 no5 p136 Je 2017

WHAT'S NEW AT THE APP STORE color *Macworld - Digital Edition* v34 no10 p59 O 2017

Volleyballs—Evaluation

The BEST OF SUMMER O List color *O, The Oprah Magazine* p43 Je 2017

Volman, Kay

MOTORCYCLE ROAD: The making of a photo essay color *Virginia Living* v15 no5 p13 Ag 2017

Volner, Ian

An Architect for All Seasons P. Goldberger *Architectural Record* v205 no10 p49 O 2017

Cadaval & Solà-Morales color *Architectural Digest* v74 no10 p114 O 1 2017

Volokhonsky, Larissa

LOST IN TRANSLATION E. ALTER bw color *Publishers Weekly* v264 no1 p31 Ja 2 2017

Volonakis, George

Perovskite-perovskite tandem photovoltaics with optimized band gaps bibl chart graph *Science* v354 no6314 p861 N 18 2016

Volpe, Tristan

Keine Atombombe, Bitte color *Foreign Affairs* v96 no4 p103 Jl/Ag 2017

Volpi, Elena

Changing climate shifts timing of European floods color graph *Science* v357 no6351 p588 Ag 11 2017

Volpp, Kevin G.

Use Behavioral Economics to Achieve Wellness Goals *Harvard Business Review Digital Articles* p2 D 1 2014

Volt automobile—Evaluation

Chevrolet Volt chart color *Motor Trend* v69 no1 p122 Ja 2017

Tortoise and the Hare T. QUIROGA chart color *Car & Driver* v62 no8 p48 F 2017

Voltaggio, Bryan

TASTE Baltimore's TRANSFORMATION *Washingtonian Magazine* v53 no1 p12 O 2017

Voltaire, 1694-1778

CONVERSATIONS *Lapham's Quarterly* v10 no2 p205 Spr 2017

Volterra, Andrea

Three-dimensional Ca2+ imaging advances understanding of astrocyte biology diag *Science* v356 no6339 p715 My 19 2017

Volunteer recruitment

How the Social Sector Can Attract More Young Talent K. Sanders and D. Thompson *Harvard Business Review Digital Articles* p2 D 7 2016

NRPA Update. It's Easier Than Ever to Get Involved with NRPA *Parks & Recreation* v52 no6 p42 Je 2017

Volunteer service

See also

Volunteers

Built-in Peril M. N. MITRA color *Earth Island Journal* v32 no1 p27 Spr 2017

Can volunteering be made compulsory? *People Management* p55 Je 2017

Destination: Making a Difference D. POINTDUJOUR color *Ebony* v72 no5 p60 Mr 2017

Empowering Volunteers to Take the Lead L. Robertson *Parks & Recreation* v51 no11 p32 N 2016

Feeding the Spirit D. SACHS bw *Rodale's Organic Life* v2 no7 p36 D 2016/Ja 2017

GO FOR A "HELPER'S HIGH" A. Reliford color *Good Housekeeping* v264 no6 p84 Je 2017

HIGH STAKES N. Schmidle cartoon *New Yorker* v93 no23 p22 Ag 7 2017

How to Use Stretch Assignments to Support Social Good M. Horoszowski *Harvard Business Review Digital Articles* p2 N 13 2015

I Love My Park Day *New York State Conservationist* v71 no5 p37 Ap 2017

Planning to Live to 100? Volunteer! E. J. Schneidewind *AARP: The Magazine* v60 no4A p65 Je/Jl 2017

Stronger together H. Khouri color *Yoga Journal* no295 p19 O 2017

The Summer of Change C. GRISE *Scholastic Choices* v32 no8 p20 My 2017

Summer service A. Scobey color *U.S. Catholic* v82 no6 p43 Je 2017

What volunteering did for me: HR professionals share their experiences of giving something back G. GYTON *People Management* p12 S 2017

Volunteer service—Management

A Guide to Managing a Volunteer Workforce J. McCannon and H. Han *Harvard Business Review Digital Articles* p2 Mr 2 2016

Volunteer service—United States

MAKING TIME FOR FUN: Retirement is a great time to take up new interests and activities C. Barker *Washingtonian Magazine* v52 no8 p145 My 2017

TRUMP and CONSEQUENCES M. LEWIS color *Vanity Fair* v59 no2 p58 F 2017

Volunteer tourism

Save While You Serve S. Kelso color *Money* v46 no2 p24 Mr 2017

Volunteer workers in urban planning

I Love My Park Day *New York State Conservationist* v71 no5 p37 Ap 2017

Volunteers

See also

Caregivers

Women volunteers

Young volunteers

The Cat Named Morphine S. Jaszberenyi *New York Times Magazine* p23 F 19 2017

CENTURY marks bw graph *Christian Century* v134 no20 p8 S 27 2017

Christopher Horn, Director of Communications *American Forests* v123 no1 p8 Wint/Spr 2017

Class Dismissed *Arizona Highways* v93 no6 p56 Je 2017

Florence's Mud Angels R. I. Jobs *History Today* v67 no8 p8 Ag 2017

HIGH STAKES N. Schmidle cartoon *New Yorker* v93 no23 p22 Ag 7 2017

PASSING THE TORCH: Volunteers Keep Outdoor Traditions Alive P. J. Chaisson *New York State Conservationist* v72 no2 p26 O 2017

PAYING IT FORWARD D. Kingsland *New York State Conservationist* v71 no5 p11 Ap 2017

STOCKING FISH + SAVING A LIFE S. Robb *New York State Conservationist* v71 no5 p18 Ap 2017

Water Wizard J. Spring *Sierra* v102 no1 p103 Ja/F 2017

Welcome to St. Louis *Parks & Recreation* v51 no10 p72 O 2016

The Women of Baylor K. DONNELLY il *America* v215 no14 p25 N 7 2016

Volunteers—Awards

Scotland stalwart given top accolade *People Management* p56 F 2017

Volunteer service—Societies, etc.

Save While You Serve S. Kelso color *Money* v46 no2 p24 Mr 2017

Volvo (Company)

New-look VOR Boats B. Hancock color *Sail* v48 no8 p20 Ag 2017

Volvo automobile

Cross Country Dresser D. Pund color *Car & Driver* v63 no2 p92 Ag 2017

ON THE WAGON K. Sintumuang color *Esquire* p18 Je/Jl 2017

SPA TREATMENT F. Markus chart color *Motor Trend* v69 no8 p62 Ag 2017

THE VOLVO WAGON B. Berk bw color *Car & Driver* v62 no8 p20 F 2017

Volvo automobile—Evaluation

2018 Volvo V90 DOING WHAT VOLVO DOES BEST A. Mackenzie color *Motor Trend* v69 no2 p64 F 2017

The Finalists... color *Motor Trend* v69 no1 p134 Ja 2017

FOURS TO BE RECKONED WITH J. Gall color graph *Car & Driver* v62 no7 p94 Ja 2017

Volvo S90 chart color *Motor Trend* v69 no1 p145 Ja 2017

WAKE UP: MONTEREY UTILIZES FORWARD DRIVE TO LAUNCH A SURFING BOAT WITH PIZZAZZ S. SHIBATA *Boating World* v38 no8 p6 S/O 2017

Volvo XC90 automobile—Evaluation

GARAGE cartoon chart color *Motor Trend* v68 no12 p106 D 2016

Volz, Jürgen

Quantum optical circulator controlled by a single chirally coupled atom bibl graph *Science* v354 no6319 p1577 D 23 2016

Vomiting

A college student experienced stomach pain and vomiting that quickly devolved into something much worse. No one could figure out what it was until it was too late L. Sanders *New York Times Magazine* p24 Ap 30 2017

von Arx, Jeffrey S.J.

Pilate as an agent of salvation *America* v216 no10 p48 My 1 2017

von Baeyer, Hans Christian

Pseudoscience versus science *Physics Today* v69 no11 p10 N 2016

VON BENEDIKT, ARAM

SURVIVE ANYWHERE bw cartoon color diag *Outdoor Life* v224 no3 p33 Ap 2017

von Benedikt, Joseph

ROUND DOWN color *Field & Stream* v122 no5 p25 O 2017

YOUR Wildest DREAMS color *Field & Stream* v122 no5 p38 O 2017

von Borzyskowski, Lennart Schada

A synthetic pathway for the fixation of carbon dioxide in vitro bibl graph *Science* v354 no6314 p900 N 18 2016

Von Bruenchenhein, Eugene, 1910-1983—Exhibitions

Art out of boundaries at the Kohler Arts Center color *Magazine Antiques* v184 no4 p34 Jl/Ag 2017

von Conta, Aaron

Time-resolved x-ray absorption spectroscopy with a water window high-harmonic source bibl graph *Science* v355 no6322 p264 Ja 20 2017

Vonderach, Matthias

Local protein kinase A action proceeds through intact holoenzymes color diag graph *Science* v356 no6344 p1288 Je 23 2017

von Dietze, Susanne

The Clinic color *Dressage Today* v23 no10 p24 Jl 2017

The Clinic color *Dressage Today* v23 no5 p20 Ja 2017

The Clinic color *Dressage Today* v23 no7 p19 Mr 2017

The Clinic PHOTO CRITIQUES color *Dressage Today* p26 My 2017

The Clinic: PHOTO CRITIQUES color *Dressage Today* v23 no11 p20 Ag 2017

The Clinic PHOTO CRITIQUES color *Dressage Today* v23 no12 p26 S 2017

The Clinic PHOTO CRITIQUES color *Dressage Today* v23 no6 p19 F 2017

The Clinic PHOTO CRITIQUES color *Dressage Today* v23 no9 p22 Je 2017

The Clinic PHOTO CRITIQUES color *Dressage Today* v24 no2 p24 N 2017

To help stabilize and deepen your upper body while giving your hands a more forward tendency... color *Dressage Today* v23 no9 p72 Je 2017

Von Drehle, David

Anne-Marie Slaughter color *Time* v189 no11 p64 Mr 27 2017

Arnold Palmer color *Time* v188 no14 p12 O 10 2016

The Comey Misfire color *Time* v189 no19 p20 My 22 2017

The Fight for the Meaning of America color *Time* v188 no16/17 p82 O 24 2016

How Donald Trump Jr.'s Emails Have Cranked Up the Heat on His Family [Cover story] color *Time* v190 no4 p22 Jl 24 2017

Is Telecommuting Work? The Answer Isn't In the Fridge. (I Already Looked.) color *Time* v188 no19 p63 N 7 2016

John F. Kennedy's America Answered a Call to Leadership No Longer Given Voice color *Time* v189 no21 p32 Je 5 2017

The Justices Agree to Grapple With Travel Bans and Phantoms color *Time* v190 no2/3 p7 Jl 10-17 2017

The Last Act color *Time* v189 no18 p44 My 15 2017

The Lasting Legacy of a Life Devoted to Loving the Sinner color *Time* v190 no5 p31 Jl 31 2017

Message Delivered [Cover story] color *Time* v188 no21 p28 N 21 2016

Movie Stars and the Perils of the Podium color *Time* v189 no4 p21 Ja 23 2017

Never Mind Trump. We Need Shakespeare More Than Ever color *Time* v189 no24 p17 Je 26 2017

The Second Most Powerful Man In the World? [Cover story] color *Time* v189 no5 p24 F 13 2017

Trump's American Vision [Cover story] color *Time* v189 no3 p24 Ja 30 2017

What It Will Take to Rebuild America [Cover story] color *Time* v189 no13 p22 Ap 10 2017

Will Bob Mueller Separate Fact from Fiction? [Cover story] color *Time* v190 no1 p24 Jl 3 2017

The World May Little Note, but Kansas City Still Remembers

We Have a Villain. We Need a Vision L. C. GOODMAN *In These Times* v41 no3 p16 Mr 2017

Voters—Attitudes

At a Loss C. BARRIA color *Nation* v303 no22 p11 N 28 2016

The perfect voters N. TAYLOR-VAISEY color *Maclean's* v129 no43 p33 O 31 2016

THE VOTE color *New Yorker* v92 no35 p62 O 31 2016

Voters—Education

In Spite of Education ... R. S. LAWRENCE and C. R. ADAMS JR. *American Scholar* v86 no1 p3 Wint 2017

Voters—Psychology

Losers, Weepers B. ROWEN cartoon *Atlantic* v318 no4 p33 N 2016

Voth, Christine

Remedies Against the Devil and Dementia: The medical advice in Bald's Leechbook outlasted the language in which it was written *History Today* v67 no10 p18 O 2017

Voting

See also

    Absentee voting
    Ballot
    Early voting
    Popular vote
    Postal voting
    Referendum
    Voter turnout
    Voting age
    Voting machines
    Voting registers

Beat the Lines at the Polls R. F. MANDELBAUM color *Popular Science* v288 no6 p96 N/D 2016

Closing Argument: Why Hillary Clinton Is the Only Choice to Keep America Great J. Klein color *Time* v188 no20 p24 N 14 2016

Editor's Letter M. Breen *Advocate* no1088 p8 D 2016/Ja 2017

In Spite of Education ... R. S. LAWRENCE and C. R. ADAMS JR. *American Scholar* v86 no1 p3 Wint 2017

Virginia G. Howard *New York Times Magazine* p40 N 20 2016

Will There Be Peace in Colombia? J. Laun and C. Zárate-Laun color *Progressive* p45 D 2016/Ja 2017

Voting age

We Need More Voters P. B. Denison *Humanist* v77 no1 p47 Ja/F 2017

Voting—California

There Is Such a Thing As Too Much Voting, and It's Going on In My Neighborhood J. Stein color *Time* v188 no20 p59 N 14 2016

Voting—Government policy

RIGHT TO VOTE? WRONG A. BERMAN *Sierra* v101 no5 p34 S/O 2016

Voting—History

TAKING a STAND FOR VOTING RIGHTS *Prologue* v48 no3 p72 Fall 2016

Voting machines

Crappy, Buggy, Obsolete Voting Technology We Trust M. Riley, J. Robertson et al color *Bloomberg Businessweek* no4493 p60 O 3 2016

Falling Apart at the Polls [Cover story] J. B. Wogan *Governing* v30 no2 p26 N 2016

Voting machines—Security measures

Demo: Hacking a voting machine color *PCWorld* v35 no11 p162 N 2016

What's the likelihood that a national U.S. election could be hacked? color *Popular Mechanics* p104 N 2017

Voting—Methodology

7 Ideas from Other Countries That Could Improve U.S. Elections K. Samuelson color *Time* v188 no20 p11 N 14 2016

Voting—Moral & ethical aspects

THIRD PARTY REVOLUTION R. McCULLOUGH color *America* v215 no12 p24 O 24 2016

Voting—United States

Go Ahead, Throw Your Vote Away T. W. Hazlett color *Reason* v48 no7 p62 D 2016

Great White Hopes A. RUSSELL HOCHSCHILD il *New Republic* v248 no1/2 p16 Ja/F 2017

The Politics of IDENTIFICATION D. C. VOCK *Governing* v30 no1 p34 O 2016

Vote for Jobs and Growth T. J. DONOHUE *Weekly Standard* v22 no10 p21 N 14 2016

Voting Trends by Age Group *Congressional Digest* v96 no1 p12 Ja 2017

Voting—United States—History

Electrious and the ELECTORAL COLLEGE J. Kratz *Prologue* v48 no3 p34 Fall 2016

INTERESTING AND UPSETTING M. D. Köhn color *American History* v52 no2 p12 Je 2017

Voting—United States—History—19th century

Back When Everyone Knew How You Voted P. Wasley *Humanities* v37 no4 p1 Fall 2016

Voting—United States—Law & legislation

Democrats Are Winning the Battle to Expand Voting Access S. Frizell color *Time* v188 no15 p5 O 17 2016

The Real Voter Fraud Z. ROTH color *New Republic* v248 no8/9 p10 Ag/S 2017

Some Cities Want Their Immigrants to Vote C. Winter *Bloomberg Businessweek* no4497 p27 O 31 2016

Votruba, James C.

Inspired Lives R. Bird *Cincinnati Magazine* v50 no10 p71 Jl 2017

Votto, Joey

13 THE REDS' BIG MACHINE J. Dickey color *Sports Illustrated* v126 no9 p66 Mr 27 2017

Voulgaris, Nick

Your DREAM KITCHEN is right here color *Redbook* p134 My 2017

Voutsa (Company)

Voutsa S. COCHRAN color *Architectural Digest* v74 no10 p102 O 1 2017

Voyage of Time: Life's Journey (Film)

18. See Voyage of Time *New York* v49 no21 p121 O 17 2016

Form and Void E. HYNES color *Film Comment* v53 no1 p14 Ja/F 2017

Voyage of Time: The IMAX Experience (Film)

Voyage of Time more art film than documentary E. Wayman color *Science News* v190 no9 p29 O 29 2016

Voyager Project

FANTASTIC VOYAGE T. Ferris color diag *National Geographic* v232 no2 p22 Ag 2017

The Grand Tour R. Talcott diag *Astronomy* v45 no10 p50 O 2017

HOW AN INTERPLANETARY MISSION CHANGED THE WORLD S. Stirone cartoon *Astronomy* v45 no10 p56 O 2017

Memories from a BACKYARD OBSERVER R. Shubinski color *Astronomy* v45 no10 p62 O 2017

Nostalgic documentary relives triumphs of the Voyager mission L. Grossman color *Science News* v192 no2 p26 Ag 19 2017

Reflections on Voyager D. J. Eicher color *Astronomy* v45 no10 p8 O 2017

UNVEILING A GIANT [Cover story] F. Reddy bw chart color diag *Astronomy* v45 no10 p20 O 2017

VOYAGER REVEALED! J. Wenz color diag graph *Astronomy* v45 no10 p34 O 2017

Voyager's great legacy D. J. EICHER color *Astronomy* v45 no10 p6 O 2017

Voyages & travels

See also

    Aeronautical flights
    Air travel
    Excursions (Travel)
    Ocean travel
    Papal visits
    Pilgrims & pilgrimages
    Railroad travel
    Scientific expeditions
    Shipwrecks
    Underwater exploration

3 COUPLES, ONE 45-FOOT CATAMARAN, 9 MEDITERRANEAN ISLANDS, 6 PORTS, COUNTLESS EMPTY BEACHES, AND 7 NIGHTS SPENT SIPPING ROSÉ AND BLASTING THE SMITHS UNDER THE STARS [Cover story] R. Misner color *Conde Nast Traveler* v52 no7 p60 Ag 2017

ACCESSORIES AND JEWELRY DESIGNER KENDALL CONRAD A. WHITTLE color *Conde Nast Traveler* v52 no7 p28 Ag 2017

Along for the Ride R. Bragg color *Southern Living* v52 no6 p146

No Press? No Problem color *Bloomberg Businessweek* no4516 p22 Mr 27 2017

Rex's Right-Hand Woman *Bloomberg Businessweek* no4525 p25 Je 5 2017

Tillerson Hits The Road and Finds His Feet color *Bloomberg Businessweek* no4530 p38 Jl 17 2017

UN-Convincing: Trump Goes Rogue on Iran graph *Bloomberg Businessweek* no4540 p44 O 2 2017

'We Must As a Nation Be More Unpredictable' *Bloomberg Businessweek* no4503 p12 D 12 2016

Wadhams, Peter

CHILL OUT: FIXES FOR A HOT PLANET A. VLASITS cartoon *Wired* v25 no9 p32 S 2017

Wadhwa, Vivek

SAND HILL ROAD: AN ORAL HISTORY color *Wired* v25 no9 p24 S 2017

Wadis—Jordan

THE DESCENT J. LUCAS color *Climbing* no351 p80 F/Mr 2017

Wadkins, Lanny

TEEING OFF J. Sens color *Golf Magazine* v59 no8 p16 Ag 2017

Wadkins, Timothy

A guide to holy places and people color *America* v217 no2 p46 Jl 24 2017

Wadlow, Jeff

True Memoirs of an International Assassin C. Nashawaty color *Entertainment Weekly* no1440 p44 N 18 2016

Wadman, Meredith

Antisense rescues babies from killer disease color diag *Science* v354 no6318 p1359 D 16 2016

Battle over rare disease drug ensnares NIH color *Science* v354 no6308 p18 O 7 2016

Brain health should be top of mind color *Science* v354 no6310 p277 O 21 2016

Courts ponder how public animal reports must be color *Science* v356 no6340 p790 My 26 2017

Culture Research: The Vaccine Race: Science, Politics, and the Human Costs of Defeating Disease K. B. Nelson *Issues in Science & Technology* v33 no4 p85 Summ 2017

Documents detail gender-related tensions at Salk *Science* v357 no6353 p741 Ag 25 2017

For chronic fatigue syndrome, a 'shifting tide' at NIH color *Science* v354 no6313 p691 N 11 2016

Gender discrimination lawsuit at Salk ignites controversy color *Science* v357 no6348 p237 Jl 21 2017

Grad students, postdocs with U.S. visas face uncertainty color *Science* v355 no6325 p557 F 10 2017

Immigration order threatens overseas talent color *Science* v355 no6324 p439 F 3 2017

Mauritius invites primate research labs to set up shop chart color *Science* v356 no6337 p472 My 5 2017

Mental health chief to stress neural circuits color *Science* v354 no6311 p405 O 28 2016

NIH quietly shelves gun research program *Science* v357 no6356 p1082 S 15 2017

Our best shot E. C. Jonlin bw *Science* v355 no6324 p464 F 3 2017

Rogue protein's partners offer hope in Parkinson's disease color *Science* v354 no6315 p956 N 25 2016

A trans-Atlantic transparency gap on animal experiments color graph *Science* v357 no6347 p119 Jl 14 2017

VACCINES ON TRIAL color *Science* v356 no6336 p370 Ap 28 2017

THE VACCINE WARS [Cover story] color *Science* v356 no6336 p364 Ap 28 2017

ZAPPING COCAINE ADDICTION color *Science* v357 no6355 p960 S 8 2017

Wadors, Pat

Diversity Efforts Fall Short Unless Employees Feel That They Belong *Harvard Business Review Digital Articles* p2 Ag 10 2016

An Experiment in Enlivening Stagnant Teams *Harvard Business Review Digital Articles* p2 Jl 3 2015

Letting Good People Go When It's Time *Harvard Business Review Digital Articles* p2 O 2 2015

To Stay Relevant, Your Company and Employees Must Keep Learning *Harvard Business Review Digital Articles* p2 Mr 7 2016

Wadyka, Sally

THE CHECKUP CHECKLIST *Martha Stewart Living* no268 p70 O 2016

Eat Smarter, Eat Healthier [Cover story] color *Consumer Reports* v82 no11 p18 N 2017

Faster, Fresher, Cheaper chart color il *Consumer Reports* v82 no7 p30 Jl 2017

MINDING YOUR MEMORY *Martha Stewart Living* no269 p62 N 2016

YOGI HEAL THYSELF color *Yoga Journal* p106 2017 Special-Issue

Waechter, Ben

Waechter Architecture D. De Koff bw color *Architectural Record* v204 no12 p40 D 2016

Waffle House Inc.

Ponce de León Dept cartoon *Weekly Standard* v22 no27 p3 Mr 20 2017

Wagamese, Richard, 1955-2017

Embers: One Ojibway's Meditations *Publishers Weekly* v264 no6 p57 F 6 2017

Medicine Walk A. Weldon *Orion Magazine* v35 no4/5 p106 Jl-O 2016

Wage bargaining

Gender Can Be a Bigger Factor than Race in Raise Negotiations K. Jones *Harvard Business Review Digital Articles* p2 S 1 2016

Setting the Record Straight on Negotiating Your Salary A. Gallo *Harvard Business Review Digital Articles* p2 Mr 9 2015

Wage decreases

How can I tell staff about pay rate cuts? PM's Fixer Samantha Sales tackles readers big issues *People Management* p53 Ap 2017

Why Some People Intentionally Take a Pay Cut When Resuming Their Careers C. F. Cohen *Harvard Business Review Digital Articles* p2 Ja 28 2016

Wage decreases—Law & legislation

Can he sue us over pay cut? *People Management* p52 D 2016/ Ja 2017

Wage differentials

Ace the Money Question M. Leonhardt color *Money* v46 no8 p20 S 2017

Cartoons *New York Times Upfront* v150 no1 p24 S 4 2017

Disabled veterans and veterans with service-connected disabilities: are they the same? C. M. Irby *Monthly Labor Review* p1 D 2016

How the Gender Pay Gap Widens as Women Get Promoted L. Frank *Harvard Business Review Digital Articles* p2 N 5 2015

Research: When Men Have Lower Status at Work, They're Less Likely to Negotiate H. R. Bowles, B. Thomason et al *Harvard Business Review Digital Articles* p2 S 8 2017

Wage differentials—Great Britain

PAY GAP J. FARAGHER *People Management* p26 F 2017

Tackling the gender pay gap P. Cheese *People Management* p5 Ap 2017

Wage differentials—United States

(The Big)Salary Reveal [Cover story] L. Brody, J. Militare et al bw color *Glamour* v115 no3 p146 Mr 2017

Wage and job-skill distributions in the National Compensation Survey C. M. Cunningham and R. D. Mohr bibl chart color graph *Monthly Labor Review* p1 F 2017

Wage increases

Asking for a Raise When You're Afraid To L. Daskal *Harvard Business Review Digital Articles* p2 N 18 2015

The Business Investments That Freak People Out A. Winston *Harvard Business Review Digital Articles* p2 My 6 2015

Corrections & Clarifications *Bloomberg Businessweek* no4524 p6 My 29 2017

Do CEOs Really Have the Power to Raise Wages? W. Frick *Harvard Business Review Digital Articles* p2 Ap 23 2015

Get the money you deserve N. Lapin color *Redbook* p26 S 2017

How Jamie Dimon's Minimum Wage Hike Could Backfire W. Frick *Harvard Business Review Digital Articles* p2 Jl 13 2016

How Low-Paying Retailers Can Adapt to Higher Minimum Wages Z. Ton *Harvard Business Review Digital Articles* p2 Ag 23 2016

How to Ask for a Raise C. O'Hara *Harvard Business Review Digital Articles* p2 Mr 5 2015

How to Respond When Your Employee Asks for a Raise A. Gallo *Harvard Business Review Digital Articles* p2 F 17 2016

Let's Get You Your Raise! E. L. Gross and C. Drell cartoon *Glamour* v115 no11 p110 N 2017

New Research: Women Who Don't Negotiate Might Have a Good Reason C. Exley, M. Niederle et al *Harvard Business Review Digital Articles* p2 Ap 12 2016

Not So Fast, Blue Cities C. CHANG il *New Republic* v248 no6 p12 Je 2017

Restoring Work and Wages K. A. HASSETT graph *National Review* v69 no6 p6 Ap 3 2017

Setting the Record Straight: Using an Outside Offer to Get a Raise A. Gallo *Harvard Business Review Digital Articles* p2 Jl 5 2016

Survival of the Hippest color *Weekly Standard* v22 no33 p4 My 8 2017

When You Find Out a Coworker Makes More Money than You Do R. Knight *Harvard Business Review Digital Articles* p2 Mr 7 2016

Why Are Some Whistleblowers Vilified and Others Celebrated? D. M. Mayer *Harvard Business Review Digital Articles* p2 S 1 2016

YOUR NEXT PAY RAISE WILL LOOK FAMILIAR S. BLOCK *Kiplinger's Personal Finance* v71 no11 p9 N 2017

Wage increases—Government policy

Can the public sector survive a 1% pay rise? HR professionals are concerned about concerned about their and motivate staff - yet engagement levels have hit new highs *People Management* p8 My 2017

Wage increases—Law & legislation

Repeal and Replace C. CHANG il *New Republic* v248 no11 p12 N 2017

Wage surveys

Disabled veterans and veterans with service-connected disabilities: are they the same? C. M. Irby *Monthly Labor Review* p1 D 2016

Wage theft

Chicago's Plan to Stop Wage Theft J. MILLER *In These Times* v41 no4 p10 Ap 2017

Wage theory (Economics)

THE PROBLEM: HOW CAN PAY BE USED TO LEAD AND KEEP VALUED EMPLOYEES? D. J. Jonovic color *Successful Farming* v115 no7 p56 My 2017

Wagers

How to Bet Smarter *Kiplinger's Personal Finance* v71 no8 p35 Ag 2017

Wages

　　See also

　　Employee fringe benefits

　　Equal pay for equal work

　　Executive compensation

　　Lawyers—Salaries, wages, etc.

　　Minimum wage

　　Overtime

　　Pay equity

　　Tips & tipping (Gratuities)

　　Wage decreases

　　Wage differentials

　　Wage increases

　　Women's wages

10 Myths About Negotiating Your First Salary L. Babcock and J. Bear *Harvard Business Review Digital Articles* p2 Jl 3 2017

America's Happiest Incomes D. Johnson color *Time* v189 no19 p11 My 22 2017

Asking for a Raise When You're Afraid To L. Daskal *Harvard Business Review Digital Articles* p2 N 18 2015

Big Companies Don't Pay as Well as They Used To W. Frick *Harvard Business Review Digital Articles* p2 F 13 2017

BLACK WOMEN'S MENTOR IN YOUR POCKET T. A. Sykes color *Essence* v47 no12 p100 Ap 2017

EMPLOYMENT, UNEMPLOYMENT, AND WAGES *Economic Indicators* p11 Mr 2017

Estimating the U.S. labor share M. D. Giandrea and S. A. Sprague bibl chart color graph *Monthly Labor Review* p1 F 2017

Fake Lives, Real Paydays C. Agard color *Entertainment Weekly* no1485 p48 O 6 2017

HEALTH CARE COSTS ARE THE REASON YOU'RE NOT GETTING A RAISE V. De Rugy bw *Reason* v49 no5 p11 O 2017

HELPING THE PLANET V. Tweed color *Amazing Wellness* v9 no1 p12 Wint 2017

How should we define "low-wage" work? An analysis using the Current Population Survey V. A. Fusaro and H. L. Shaefer bibl chart color graph *Monthly Labor Review* p1 O 2016

Overcome Your Reluctance and Start Negotiating Your Salary J. White *Harvard Business Review Digital Articles* p2 My 19 2016

Paying Skilled Workers More Would Create More Skilled Workers T. van Rens *Harvard Business Review Digital Articles* p2 My 19 2016

Performance-Based Pay for Executives Still Works A. Edmans *Harvard Business Review Digital Articles* p2 F 23 2016

Research: How Incentive Pay Affects Employee Engagement, Satisfaction, and Trust C. Ogbonnaya, K. Daniels et al *Harvard Business Review Digital Articles* p2 Mr 15 2017

Research: When Men Have Lower Status at Work, They're Less Likely to Negotiate H. R. Bowles, B. Thomason et al *Harvard Business Review Digital Articles* p2 S 8 2017

Thank You, American Workers T. J. DONOHUE *Weekly Standard* v23 no1 p8 S 11 2017

What Matters More to Your Workforce than Money A. Chamberlain color *Harvard Business Review Digital Articles* p2 Ja 17 2017

When Paper Beats Cash W. BALDWIN color *Forbes* v199 no7 p142 Je 29 2017

Which MBAs Make More: Consultants or Small-Business Owners? R. S. Ruback and R. Yudkoff *Harvard Business Review Digital Articles* p2 Je 28 2016

Why Banning Questions About Salary History May Not Improve Pay Equity L. Frank *Harvard Business Review Digital Articles* p1 S 5 2017

Why Isn't Jamie Dimon Telling Clients to Raise Wages Too? T. A. Kochan *Harvard Business Review Digital Articles* p2 Jl 20 2016

Why Keeping Salaries a Secret May Hurt Your Company D. Burkus *Harvard Business Review Digital Articles* p2 Mr 10 2016

Wages—Advances

"Clopening" Time J. TIMM *In These Times* v40 no12 p10 D 2016

Wages—College graduates—Research

Is a degree losing its value at work? *People Management* p11 O 2016

Wages—History—21st century

Why Wages Aren't Growing M. J. Schuman *Bloomberg Businessweek* no4539 p12 S 25 2017

Wages—Law & legislation—United States

Why the U.S. Decided That Managers Deserve Overtime Too P. Cappelli *Harvard Business Review Digital Articles* p2 My 26 2016

Wages—Management

Why It's So Hard to Figure Out What to Pay Top Talent T. Low *Harvard Business Review Digital Articles* p2 F 19 2015

Wages—Mexico

A Raise for Mexican Workers? G. Quinn, E. Martin et al graph *Bloomberg Businessweek* no4534 p29 Ag 14 2017

Wages of Fear, The (Film)

EVERY PEBBLE CAN BLOW US SKY-HIGH J. Hoberman *Lapham's Quarterly* v10 no3 p198 Summ 2017

Wages—Social aspects

What HR Can Do to Fix the Gender Pay Gap D. Ashton *Harvard Business Review Digital Articles* p2 D 2 2014

Wages—United States

10 Years of Data on Baseball Teams Shows When Pay Transparency Backfires A. D. Hill, F. Aime et al *Harvard Business Review Digital Articles* p2 My 9 2017

4 Reasons Retail Jobs Are About to Get Better Z. Ton *Harvard Business Review Digital Articles* p2 S 4 2015

6 Things New Grads Should Know Before Joining a Startup L. Berger *Harvard Business Review Digital Articles* p1 My 1 2017

"Clopening" Time J. TIMM *In These Times* v40 no12 p10 D 2016

Excuse Me, Sir, How Much Do You Make? C. Bonanos img *New York* v50 no10 p14 My 15 2017

Gig Work Doesn't Have to Be Isolating and Unstable C. M. Lane *Harvard Business Review Digital Articles* p2 My 4 2017

How Much Room to Grow? P. Coy and P. Laya color *Bloomberg Businessweek* no4511 p8 F 13 2017

The Mystery of Tepid Wage Growth P. Coy graph *Bloomberg*

Businessweek no4523 p17 My 22 2017

Paid Parent Leave: Rare A. Adamczyk color *Money* v46 no1 p21 Ja/F 2017

Still worried F. Lesko, F. Koob et al *U.S. Catholic* v82 no10 p5 O 2017

Wages—Women

How the Gender Pay Gap Widens as Women Get Promoted L. Frank *Harvard Business Review Digital Articles* p2 N 5 2015

Measuring Up L. YOUNG *Ms.* v26 no4 p12 Wint 2016

More Reasons Women Need to Negotiate Their Salaries M. A. Neale and T. Z. Lys *Harvard Business Review Digital Articles* p2 Je 29 2015

New Research: Women Who Don't Negotiate Might Have a Good Reason C. Exley, M. Niederle et al *Harvard Business Review Digital Articles* p2 Ap 12 2016

Pay Fairness Isn't Just About Teaching Employees to Negotiate C. H. Arscott *Harvard Business Review Digital Articles* p2 My 4 2016

Waggoner, John

4 BIG TRENDS YOU CAN RIDE FOR YEARS color diag *Money* v46 no1 p70 Ja/F 2017

Alexa: Is There a Safer Way to Bet on the Amazon Economy? diag *Money* v46 no8 p38 S 2017

Funds That Let Their Brood Grow color *Money* v45 no10 p42 N 2016

Hedging Inflation Without Gold color diag *Money* v46 no4 p34 My 2017

How to Invest When Rates Rise diag *Money* v46 no5 p38 Je 2017

How to Use ETFs to Pick Other ETFs diag *Money* v46 no6 p40 Jl 2017

Spring-Clean Your Portfolio color diag *Money* v46 no2 p49 Mr 2017

When Dividends Don't Pay diag *Money* v46 no7 p34 Ag 2017

When to Step Back From Stocks diag *Money* v46 no9 p51 O 2017

Waggoner, Stacy

UNCOMMON THREADS K. HACKETT color *Better Homes & Gardens* v95 no2 p102 F 2016

WAGLEY, CATHERINE G.

EVERYBODY LOVES THE SUNSHINE cartoon color diag *ARTnews* v115 no3 p106 Fall 2016

WAGMAN, DIANA

Moon Maiden *New York Times Book Review* p20 O 9 2016

WAGNER, ALEX

HOW FRANKLIN LEONARD CREATED THE HOLLYWOOD LIST EVERYONE WANTS TO BE ON color *Atlantic* v319 no2 p66 Mr 2017

Wagner, Anne J.

Click chemistry enables preclinical evaluation of targeted epigenetic therapies diag *Science* v356 no6345 p1397 Je 30 2017

Wagner, Ashley

FIGURE SKATING SHOWDOWN! K. Rosen *TV Guide* v65 no13 p49 Mr 20 2017

Wagner, Bill

Head toward the Island map *Sail* v48 no9 p26 S 2017

Wagner, Bob

How Do You Know When It's Time to Give Up? color *Sail* v48 no2 p13 F 2017

Wagner, David

Winning Pair C. SHMERLER *Tennis* v52 no6 p40 N/D 2016

Wagner, Erica

Over the River: A man known for his engineering legacy endured hardships throughout his life J. Alexiou *New York Times Book Review* p9 Ag 13 2017

Wagner, Gert G.

A nod to public open access infrastructures *Science* v356 no6344 p1242 Je 23 2017

Wagner, Jim

TEEING OFF J. Passov color *GolfMagazine* v59 no1 p14 Ja 2017

Wagner, Julie

The Rise of Urban Innovation Districts *Harvard Business Review Digital Articles* p2 N 12 2014

Wagner, Kate

GUEST LIST: A monthly roundup of people we'd like to have over for drinks, food, and conversation *Washingtonian Magazine* v52 no11 p22 Ag 2017

Wagner, Mary

The Making of a Leader in Forestry L. SLOAN *American Forests* v122 no3 p46 Fall 2016

Wagner, Michael

Giant viruses with an expanded complement of translation system components diag *Science* v356 no6333 p82 Ap 7 2017

Wagner, Morgan

Without limits T. Rice color *Equus* no472 p63 Ja 2017

Wagner, Norman

De-extinction, nomenclature, and the law color *Science* v356 no6342 p1016 Je 9 2017

Wagner, Paul E.

Global atmospheric particle formation from CERN CLOUD measurements bibl graph map *Science* v354 no6316 p1119 D 2 2016

Wagner, Richard, 1813-1883

Senta's CHOICE P. KENNICOTT *Opera News* v81 no10 p32 Ap 2017

Wagner, Rodd

Stop Using Employee Friendships to Measure Engagement *Harvard Business Review Digital Articles* p2 Ag 7 2015

Wagner, Roger

The Penultimate Curiosity: How Science Swims in the Slipstream of Ultimate Questions P. Kulkarni color *Issues in Science & Technology* v33 no1 p94 Fall 2016

WAGNER, SARA

I Survived! [Cover story] *Reader's Digest* v189 no1128 p62 Mr 2017

Wagner, Steve

NEXT-LEVEL TURKEY CALLS color *Outdoor Life* v224 no3 p50 Ap 2017

Wagner, Tristan

The methanogenic CO_2 reducing-and-fixing enzyme is bifunctional and contains 46 [4Fe-4S] clusters bibl diag *Science* v354 no6308 p114 O 7 2016

Methanogenic heterodisulfide reductase (HdrABC-MvhAGD) uses two noncubane [4Fe-4S] clusters for reduction color *Science* v357 no6352 p699 Ag 18 2017

Wagner-Peck, Kari

Not Always Happy: An Unusual Parenting Journey *Publishers Weekly* v264 no16 p64 Ap 17 2017

Wagoneer automobile

1987 Jeep Grand Wagoneer color *Popular Mechanics* p66 D 2016/ Ja 2017

Wagons—Design & construction

Kitbashing an early B&O wagontop boxcar D. Kawala color *Model Railroader* v84 no9 p22 S 2017

Wahba, Phil

17 BARBARA RENTLER *Fortune* v174 no7 p89 D 1 2016

THE 2017 Fortune Crystal Ball color diag *Fortune* v174 no7 p11 D 1 2016

3 MARY DILLON color *Fortune* v174 no7 p75 D 1 2016

APPLE REBOOTS IN CHINA color *Fortune* v176 no5 p106 O 1 2017

As Oceans Rise, Insurers Flee color *Fortune* v176 no2 p18 Ag 1 2017

THE BLACK CEILING color *Fortune* v176 no5 p94 O 1 2017

BOXED IN color diag *Fortune* v176 no5 p86 O 1 2017

BYE-BYE, DISCOUNTS. HELLO, MARGINS color *Fortune* v176 no4 p30 S 15 2017

CHANGE THE WORLD !!!! color diag map *Fortune* v176 no4 p74 S 15 2017

COACH THINKS OUTSIDE THE BAG color diag *Fortune* v175 no7 p80 Je 1 2017

The Death of Retail Is Greatly Exaggerated color diag *Fortune* v175 no8 p33 Je 15 2017

DREAM WEAVER color *Fortune* v176 no3 p74 S 1 2017

E-COMMERCE: BETTER LATE THAN NEVER color diag *Fortune* v176 no3 p18 S 1 2017

EVERYTHING MUST GO color diag *Fortune* v175 no3 p94 Mr 1 2017

EXPECT MORE STORE CLOSURES IN 2017 diag *Fortune* v175 no2 p12 F 1 2017

Fashion's Great Handbag Crash color *Fortune* v175 no4 p18 Mr 15 2017

FORTY UNDER FORTY 2017 color *Fortune* v176 no3 p62 S 1 2017

HOW E-COMMERCE IS MAKING STORES RELEVANT

29 2017

Wal-Mart Stores Inc.

Bed Bath & Beyond's Persistent Coupons and the Return of Thrifty Consumers R. Mohammed *Harvard Business Review Digital Articles* p2 O 6 2015

Blockchain May Help Walmart Stop Bad Food O. Kharif cartoon *Bloomberg Businessweek* no4501 p20 N 28 2016

Bring Your Smartphone Shopping E. AMBROSE color *AARP: The Magazine* v59 no6A p23 O/N 2016

Can Walmart Get Us to Buy Sustainable Products? A. Winston *Harvard Business Review Digital Articles* p2 F 24 2015

Corrections & Clarifications *Bloomberg Businessweek* no4522 p6 My 15 2017

Movers K. Stock cartoon color *Bloomberg Businessweek* no4520 p15 My 1 2017

Wal-Mart Cracks the Whip on Suppliers M. Boyle *Bloomberg Businessweek* no4531 p14 Jl 24 2017

Walmart Won't Stay on Top If Its Strategy Is "Copy Amazon" D. L. Yohn *Harvard Business Review Digital Articles* p2 Mr 21 2017

Why GE, Boeing, Lowe's, and Walmart Are Directly Buying Health Care for Employees J. R. Slotkin, O. A. Ross et al *Harvard Business Review Digital Articles* p2 Je 9 2017

WORLD'S LARGEST CORPORATIONS L. Fu and K. Thakker chart diag *Fortune* v176 no2 pF1 Ag 1 2017

Wal-Mart Stores Inc.—Finance

AMAZON WON'T KNOW WHAT HIT 'EM! [Cover story] B. Stone, M. Boyle et al color graph *Bloomberg Businessweek* no4521 p42 My 8 2017

X-Ray: Walmart C. Bigda diag *Money* v45 no10 p43 N 2016

Walbott, Hélène

Crystal structures of a group II intron lariat primed for reverse splicing color diag *Science* v354 no6316 paaf9258-1 D 2 2016

Walcott, Derek, 1930-2017

Derek Walcott S. Begley color *Time* v189 no12 p19 Ap 3 2017

Derek Walcott's Timeless Fable I. Hutchinson bw *New York Times Book Review* p27 Ag 6 2017

Southern Sublime J. Lucas color *New York Review of Books* v64 no6 p8 Ap 6 2017

Walczak, Antek

ANTEK WALCZAK W. Vogel color *Art in America* v104 no10 p153 N 2016

Waldbieser, Jill

BRIGHT YOUNG THINGS color *Women's Health* v14 no5 p85 Je 2017

Ciao Time! [Cover story] color *Women's Health* v13 no10 p89 D 2016

Curve Balls color *Women's Health* v14 no9 p81 N 2017

EARTHLY TREASURES color *Women's Health* v14 no8 p93 O 2017

Fiery Ideas color *Women's Health* v14 no5 p146 Je 2017

LUNCH BOXES [Cover story] color *Women's Health* v14 no6 p87 Jl 2017

Silver PLATTERS [Cover story] color *Women's Health* v14 no3 p140 Ap 2017

SPRING CHICKEN color *Women's Health* v14 no4 p101 My 2017

"This Is Amazing! What's In It?" color *Women's Health* v14 no2 p95 Mr 2017

Wrap. Me. Up [Cover story] color *Women's Health* v13 no10 p110 D 2016

Waldburger, D.

Dual-comb spectroscopy of water vapor with a free-running semiconductor disk laser diag *Science* v356 no6343 p1164 Je 16 2017

Walden, Dana

BONES BIDS ADIEU M. ROFFMAN *TV Guide* v65 no13 p16 Mr 20 2017

Walden, Libby

Bear Hugs *Publishers Weekly* v264 no5 p202 Ja 30 2017

Walden, Patricia

practice safely color *Yoga Journal* p16 2017 SpecialIssue

WALDEN, TIFFANY

HEF AS CHANGE AGENT color *Chicago* v66 no4 p44 Ap 2017

WHY We LOVE CHICAGO bw cartoon color *Chicago* v66 no3 p75 Mr 2017

Walden Pond State Reservation (Mass.)

Man and Nature bw color *Architectural Record* v205 no8 p12 Ag 2017

The Power of Persuasion R. CAMPBELL color *Architectural Record* v205 no8 p90 Ag 2017

Walden Woods (Mass.)

Transcendigital B. PETERSON color *Smithsonian* v47 no10 p14 Mr 2017

Waldgirmes (Germany)

FROM OUR READERS S. Lower, C. McGee et al *Archaeology* v70 no3 p8 My/Je 2017

The Road Almost Taken A. CURRY color *Archaeology* v70 no2 p32 Mr/Ap 2017

Waldhauser, Felix

Seismic constraints on caldera dynamics from the 2015 Axial Seamount eruption bibl color graph *Science* v354 no6318 p1395 D 16 2016

Waldholz, Michael

2017 Future of Medicine TRANSFORMERS color diag *Scientific American* v316 no4 p46 Ap 2017

Waldia, Manuja

Cover Girl M. FERNANDEZ *Indianapolis Monthly* v40 no4 p20 D 2016

Waldman, Adelle

The Novel in the Age of Obama img *New York* p69 F 9 2017

Pride and Principle: Richard Russo's collection turns from his familiar blue-collar types to cast a sympathetic eye on upper-middle-class professionals *New York Times Book Review* p13 Je 11 2017

Waldman, Ayelet

NOT A NORMAL WORK TRIP C. Battan color *Bloomberg Businessweek* no4504 p60 D 19 2016

A Trip of One's Own C. VAYE WATKINS color *New Republic* v248 no1/2 p50 Ja/F 2017

Waldman, Ayelet—Interviews

AYELET WALDMAN L. Greenblatt color *Entertainment Weekly* no1448 p62 Ja 13 2017

Ayelet Waldman *New York Times Book Review* p6 Ja 22 2017

Battling Depression with LSD C. JUMPERTZ color *Publishers Weekly* v263 no52 p110 D 19 2016

WALDMAN, JONATHAN

RUST: Inside the hulking structure that was once the Bethlehem Steel Works, a photographer finds beauty in decay *Saturday Evening Post* v289 no4 p50 Jl/Ag 2017

WALDMAN, PETER

DON'T LET THE MONSTER EAT YOU UP' color *Bloomberg Businessweek* no4516 p46 Mr 27 2017

Good Deals Make Good Neighbors color map *Bloomberg Businessweek* no4510 p36 F 6 2017

Guess Who's Ghostwriting Monsanto's Safety Reviews color *Bloomberg Businessweek* no4534 p14 Ag 14 2017

The Plucky Little Emirate Vs. Old Foes color *Bloomberg Businessweek* no4535 p36 Ag 28 2017

Roundup: The Usual Suspect color graph *Bloomberg Businessweek* no4530 p42 Jl 17 2017

WALDMAN, RACHEL

BRIGHT YOUNG THINGS bw color *Vogue* v206 no11 p246 N 2016

DRESS TO IMPRESS color *Vogue* v206 no12 p268 D 2016

Fully STACKED color *Vogue* v206 no11 p120 N 2016

Hot Rocks color *Vogue* v207 no4 p162 Ap 2017

Kindred SOLES color *Vogue* v206 no12 p158 D 2016

Mansur Gavriel Coats color *Vogue* v207 no9 p386 S 2017

Show of Strength cartoon color *Vogue* v207 no11 p226 N 2017

Statement Belts color *Vogue* v207 no9 p382 S 2017

Waldner, Aaron

ALL AROUND THE FARM® color *Successful Farming* v115 no7 p67 My 2017

Waldner, George

ALL AROUND THE FARM® *Successful Farming* v114 no13 p88 D 2016

Waldner, Liz

ON DISTANCE (QUONDAM/QUANTUM OVERDUE NOTICE) *New Yorker* v92 no46 p63 Ja 23 2017

Waldoch, Marta

Photostat: Krakow's Hottest Accessory color *Bloomberg Busi-*

READERS' GUIDE TO PERIODICAL LITERATURE 2017

nessweek no4528 p30 Je 26 2017

WALDRON, ARTHUR

All Quiet(ed) on the Eastern Front *Weekly Standard* v22 no5 p14 O 10 2016

Waldron, Jeremy

The Battle for War Powers *New York Times Book Review* p25 N 20 2016

Our Timeless, Timely Constitution bw cartoon *New York Review of Books* v64 no7 p50 Ap 20 2017

Waldron, Peter

Running a Red Light *History Today* v67 no3 p62 Mr 2017

WALDRON, SHAWN

AN EYE TO REMEMBER bw *Vanity Fair* v59 no2 p69 F 2017

WALDROP, ANTHONY M.

Ecological Forecasting and the Science of Hypoxia in Chesapeake Bay *BioScience* v67 no7 p614 Jl 2017

Waldrop, Jonathan

The Patent Troll Hunter: Jonathan Waldrop S. Lynn color *Black Enterprise* v47 no3 p28 O 2016

Waldseemüller, Martin, 1470-1519

CIRCLING LHASA J. HERTOG bw *Tricycle: The Buddhist Review* v26 no3 p74 Spr 2017

Waldstein, Margarete

Escape Artist J. MacGregor *Smithsonian* v47 no7 p13 N 2016

Waldstreicher, David

BOTH SIDES THEN R. Culver color *American History* v52 no3 p66 Ag 2017

Wales—Description & travel

Bryn Eryr Iron Age Farmstead at St Fagans *British Heritage Travel* v37 no6 p7 N/D 2016

once upon a time in Wales: Life in the Valleys of Glamorganshire D. Huntley *British Heritage Travel* v38 no4 p56 Jl/Ag 2017

Spring Breezes on the Open Road *British Heritage Travel* v38 no4 p28 Jl/Ag 2017

WALES IN THE YEAR OF LEGENDS S. Ellis *British Heritage Travel* v38 no3 p64 My/Je 2017

Walgreen Co.

JULIA STREET WITH POYDRAS THE PARROT J. STREET bw *New Orleans Magazine* v51 no4 p22 F 2017

stellar serum color *Good Housekeeping* v265 no4 p136 O 2017

Walk Against Wind (Music)

The Hot Box chart *Downbeat* v84 no6 p63 Je 2017

Walk Against Wind J. Corbett color *Downbeat* v84 no6 p61 Je 2017

Walkability

No Car, No Problem W. P. BARRETT and L. GENSLER color *Forbes* v199 no2 p99 F 28 2017

Walken, Christopher, 1943-

Christopher Walken J. V. Houlihan Jr. color *AARP: The Magazine* v60 no2A p20 F/Mr 2017

Walker, A. P.

Comment on "Mycorrhizal association as a primary control of the CO2 fertilization effect" bibl graph *Science* v355 no6323 p358 Ja 27 2017

Walker, Aaron

SYSTEMIC SUCCESS M. Hill color *Louisiana Life* v37 no5 p64 My/Je 2017

Walker, Amanda

How to Cash In on Cash-Back Credit Cards color graph *Consumer Reports* v82 no9 p46 S 2017

Walker, Andrew T.

Joy in the Mourning *Weekly Standard* v22 no26 p36 Mr 13 2017

Respecting Religion *Weekly Standard* v22 no45 p31 Ag 7 2017

Walker, Ashley Edwards

All the Feels color *Glamour* v115 no6 p142 Je 2017

Inside the Making of Women of the Year color *Glamour* v114 no12 p67 D 2016

Oh Hey, Thongs: Welcome Back! color *Glamour* v114 no7 p40 Jl 2016

Your New Summer Uniform: The Doily Dress color *Glamour* v114 no7 p35 Jl 2016

Walker, Bill

SOUTH SIDE STORY J. FOUMBERG color *Chicago* v66 no11 p42 N 2017

Walker, Brian

Social norms as solutions bibl color *Science* v354 no6308 p42 O

7 2016

Walker, Bryan

Changing Company Culture Requires a Movement, Not a Mandate *Harvard Business Review Digital Articles* p2 Je 20 2017

WALKER, CAM

POSTHOLE color *Powder* v46 no2 p94 O 2017

WALKER, CAMERON

High Country Rescue *National Parks* v91 no1 p14 Wint 2017

True Colors: Learning about evolution from the white lizards of White Sands *National Parks* v91 no3 p22 Summ 2017

Walker, Carol A.

New Managers Need a Philosophy About How They'll Lead *Harvard Business Review Digital Articles* p2 S 15 2015

Why Delegating Tasks Before a Vacation Never Works *Harvard Business Review Digital Articles* p2 Ag 2 2017

Walker, Catherine

The Interstate Passport: A New Framework for Seamless Student Transfer *Change* v48 no5 p44 S/O 2016

Walker, Colin

FROM ACROSS THE POND E. Perkins color *Hot Rod* v70 no1 p42 Ja 2017

Walker, Darren

Progressives, Inc J. PIERESON and N. SCHAEFER RILEY color *Weekly Standard* v22 no31 p24 Ap 17 2017

Walker, David H.

TIME TO WORRY ABOUT ANTHRAX AGAIN color diag *Scientific American* v316 no4 p70 Ap 2017

Walker, Deena M.

Early life stress confers lifelong stress susceptibility in mice via ventral tegmental area OTX2 diag *Science* v356 no6343 p1185 Je 16 2017

Walker, Elle

Cute Ways to Organize Toys color *Parents* v92 no4 p106 Ap 2017

Walker, George, 1922-

An American Outsider J. NORDLINGER *National Review* v69 no9 p40 My 15 2017

Walker, Greg

MICHAEL D. ECHANIS HONORED POSTHUMOUSLY color *Black Belt* v55 no5 p12 Ag/S 2017

Walker, J. P.—Interviews

JP WALKER T. Monterosso color *Snowboarder* v29 no5 p33 Ja 2017

Walker, Jamie Rae

THE DIRT *Dance Spirit* v21 no3 p16 Mr 2017

Walker, Jay

Connect Inventors with the Right Problems *Harvard Business Review Digital Articles* p2 Ap 1 2015

Walker, Jay S., 1955—Interviews

AN UPSIDE FOR BUSINESS TRAVELERS A. Nusca color *Fortune* v175 no7 p30 Je 1 2017

Walker, Jeff

Why Social Ventures Need Systems Thinking *Harvard Business Review Digital Articles* p2 Jl 25 2016

Walker, Jesse

All the President's Phantoms color *New Republic* v248 no3 p14 Mr 2017

Delaware's Odd, Beautiful, Contentious, Private Utopia bw color *Reason* v49 no6 p62 N 2017

The Indestructible IDEA of the Basic INCOME color *Reason* v49 no3 p32 Jl 2017

SECRET HITLER color *Reason* v49 no4 p76 Ag/S 2017

Seeing Trump on the Silver Screen bw *Reason* v48 no7 p40 D 2016

Walker, Jimmy

Finishing Rush A. Shipnuck, T. Keith et al color *Sports Illustrated* v127 no5 p26 Ag 14 2017

TEEING OFF C. Morfit color *Golf Magazine* v58 no11 p16 N 2016

Walker, Jimmy—Interviews

playing with fire R. Asselta color *Golf Magazine* v59 no8 p76 Ag 2017

WALKER, JOSH

BAO WOW color *Bon Appetit* v61 no11 p118 N 2016

Walker, Kara, 1969-

KARA WALKER, AFTER SUBTLETY [Cover story] D. ST. FÉLIX img *New York* v50 no8 p34 Ap 17 2017

THE CROSSING cartoon *New Yorker* v92 no49 p72 F 13 2017

Walker, Kara, 1969-—Exhibitions

The American Artist J. SALTZ img *New York* v50 no18 p82 S 4 2017

Black Lives Matter D. Pinckney bw color *New York Review of Books* v64 no17 p55 N 9 2017

Walker, Karen

Vision Statements J. DeLeon bw color *Conde Nast Traveler* v51 no11 p60 D 2016

Walker, Kéla

KÉLA WALKER J. Wilson color *Essence* v48 no6 p34 O 2017

Walker, Kelley—Exhibitions

Editor's Letter L. POLLOCK color *Art in America* v104 no11 p18 D 2016

Walker, Ken

Love in the Time of YouTube: De'arra and Ken 4 Life are just your typical couple trying to live their lives. Except they're doing it in public, for millions of fans S. I. Rosenbaum img *New York* v50 no16 p100 Ag 7 2017

Walker, Larry

LARRY WALKER W. Vogel *Art in America* v104 no9 p155 O 2016

Walker, Laurel

Yes—You Can Develop Feel [Cover story] color *Horse & Rider* v56 no1 p34 Ja 2017

Walker, Lawrence

The Board Game That Is Bringing Conversation Back C. M. Brown color *Black Enterprise* v47 no4 p10 N/D 2016

Walker, Marley

Better Than Ever color *Wired* v24 no11 p48 N 2016

Walker, Martin

The Templars' Last Secret: A Bruno, Chief of Police Novel color *Publishers Weekly* v264 no17 p67 Ap 24 2017

Walker, Melissa

A new family activism color *U.S. Catholic* v82 no11 p12 N 2017

Your Body Right Now! Is this weird? Is that normal? And perhaps most important—is that me I smell? Here, answers to a few of your most pressing puberty-related questions (ones you're maybe too afraid to ask!) *Scholastic Choices* v32 no5 p6 F 2017

Walker, Mitchell

From the Front Lines of Science K. VINAL *Atlanta* v56 no11 p154 Mr 2017

WALKER, NAOMI

The Public Sector on Trial *In These Times* v41 no6 p15 Je 2017

Walker, Nick

THE BALD EAGLES OF BESNARD LAKE color *Canadian Geographic* v137 no5 p63 S/O 2017

CANADA'S NATIONAL BIRD THE GRAY JAY [Cover story] color map *Canadian Geographic* v136 no6 p36 D 2016

Christi Belcourt color *Canadian Geographic* v135 no6 p23 D 2015

CLIMATE CHANGE AND THE ECONOMY diag *Canadian Geographic* v137 no2 p69 Mr/Ap 2017

ᐸᐸᐧᑕᑦ color map *Canadian Geographic* v137 no2 p52 Mr/Ap 2017

THE GJØA DIARIES COME TO CANADA bw *Canadian Geographic* v137 no3 p74 My 2017

Gordon Lightfoot color *Canadian Geographic* v136 no6 p82 D 2016

Harvey wants half color map *Canadian Geographic* v137 no1 p42 F 2017

Montebello monument color map *Canadian Geographic* v137 no1 p26 F 2017

A NEW HOME FOR THE RCGS: 50 SUSSEX color *Canadian Geographic* v136 no6 p74 D 2016

On our radar color *Canadian Geographic* v135 no6 p12 D 2015

RCGS AND PARTNERS ANNOUNCE THE INDIGENOUS PEOPLES ATLAS OF CANADA color *Canadian Geographic* v137 no4 p75 Jl/Ag 2017

Root wars color *Canadian Geographic* v137 no5 p26 S/O 2017

Star struck color *Canadian Geographic* v137 no4 p28 Jl/Ag 2017

Sway solution bw *Canadian Geographic* v137 no3 p28 My 2017

Taking on Tahoe color map *Canadian Geographic* v137 p14 2017 Travel

Their native land map *Canadian Geographic* v135 no6 p26 D 2015

To preserve and protect graph map *Canadian Geographic* v137 no1 p32 F 2017

THE ULTIMATE CANADIAN GEOGRAPHY QUIZ CITIES EDITION color map *Canadian Geographic* v137 no3 p41 My 2017

WASHINGTON color map *Canadian Geographic* v135 no6 p26 D 2015

Worth a stop color *Canadian Geographic* v135 no6 p50 D 2015

Walker, Noel

Dark Beauty color *Ebony* v72 no9 p45 Jl/Ag 2017

Walker, Richard J.

Tungsten-182 heterogeneity in modern ocean island basalts chart diag *Science* v356 no6333 p66 Ap 7 2017

Walker, Rob

Can Lemonade Lure Insurance Skeptics? *Bloomberg Businessweek* no4503 p40 D 12 2016

Giving New Yorkers a Real Feel For Flooding color *Bloomberg Businessweek* no4539 p46 S 25 2017

How Adobe Got Its Customers Hooked color graph *Bloomberg Businessweek* no4526 p37 Je 12 2017

LIFE MADE EASIER color *AARP: The Magazine* v60 no1A p34 D 2016/Ja 2017

MAKE-OVER MANIA color *New York Times Magazine* p26 N 13 2016

THE MOST IMPORTANT QUARTER-INCH IN BUSINESS LOGO color *Fortune* v175 no8 p210 Je 15 2017

WALKER, ROSS V.

This Little Piggy: Did Not Make It All the Way Home *Idaho Magazine* v16 no7 p6 Ap 2017

Walker, Roy

3D organization of synthetic and scrambled chromosomes diag *Science* v355 no6329 p1050 Mr 10 2017

Bug mapping and fitness testing of chemically synthesized chromosome X diag *Science* v355 no6329 p1048 Mr 10 2017

Deep functional analysis of synII, a 770-kilobase synthetic yeast chromosome diag *Science* v355 no6329 p1047 Mr 10 2017

Engineering the ribosomal DNA in a megabase synthetic chromosome diag *Science* v355 no6329 p1049 Mr 10 2017

"Perfect" designer chromosome V and behavior of a ring derivative diag *Science* v355 no6329 p1046 Mr 10 2017

Synthesis, debugging, and effects of synthetic chromosome consolidation: synVI and beyond color *Science* v355 no6329 p1045 Mr 10 2017

WALKER, RYAN

a strong tradition color map *Cabin Living* p17 Ag 2017

Walker, Sam

The Captain Class: The Hidden Force That Creates the World's Greatest Teams *Publishers Weekly* v264 no15 p65 Ap 10 2017

The Hidden Stars of Champion Teams S. Begley color *Time* v189 no18 p22 My 15 2017

MOBILE PIVOT PAYOFF: TOWABLE SPRINKLERS ARE A LOWER INVESTMENT PER ACRE WHILE STILL OFFERING THE YIELD POTENTIAL FROM IRRIGATION T. Gaines *Successful Farming* v115 no12 p56 O 2017

Walker, Samuel Hamilton

THE GUN THAT WON THE WEST N. Solheim bw cartoon color *American Cowboy* p46 LEGENDS OF TEXAS Special Issue 2017

Walker, Sara I.

The Emergence of the Fourth Geosphere *Physics Today* v70 no9 p58 S 2017

Walker, Scott, 1967-

Climate Change, What Climate Change? B. Lueders color *Progressive* v81 no5 p43 Je/Jl 2017

Two Paths Diverged in the Midwest. Here's Where They Led T. ANDERSON *In These Times* v41 no8 p20 Ag 2017

Walker Used Group to Snare Corporate Cash B. LUEDERS diag *Progressive* v81 no10 p12 N 2016

Walker, Scott, 1967-—Political & social views

Who Moved My Teachers? P. CALDWELL cartoon *Mother Jones* v42 no2 p36 Mr/Ap 2017

Walker, Sean

Explore Scientific's 92° Long Eye Relief Eyepieces *Sky & Telescope* v133 no6 p61 Je 2017

Sky Guide: Here's a great app for casual and experienced stargazers alike color *Sky & Telescope* v134 no2 p62 Ag 2017

Walker, Shannon
HOMESTEAD HACKS *Mother Earth News* no280 p66 F/Mr 2017
Shannon Walker B. Lightner *Current Biography* v77 no11 p93 N 2016

Walker, Sirdeaner
SIRDEANER WALKER S. DOMINUS *New York Times Magazine* p47 D 25 2016

Walker, Steve
FROM ACROSS THE POND E. Perkins color *Hot Rod* v70 no1 p42 Ja 2017

Walker, Taylor
The Board Game That Is Bringing Conversation Back C. M. Brown color *Black Enterprise* v47 no4 p10 N/D 2016

Walker, Terry
Gary Steigman *Physics Today* v70 no8 p72 Ag 2017

Walker, Tristan—Awards
And the Award Goes to... S. Lynn color *Black Enterprise* v47 no2 p22 S 2016

Walker, William
GARAGE chart color diag *Motor Trend* v69 no8 p96 Ag 2017
GARRAGE cartoon chart color *Motor Trend* v69 no3 p86 Mr 2017
THE KAISER'S GRIM REAPER bw *MHQ: Quarterly Journal of Military History* v30 no1 p48 Aut 2017
MYSTERY AT MONTFAUCON *MHQ: Quarterly Journal of Military History* v29 no3 p28 Spr 2017
Pershing's Crusaders: The American Soldier in World War I *MHQ: Quarterly Journal of Military History* v29 no4 p92 Summ 2017

Walker, William S.
Are We Any Safer? color *Atlantic* v318 no4 p14 N 2016

Walker, William, 1824-1860
IMPERIAL WALKER P. CARLSON bw color *American History* v52 no3 p16 Ag 2017

Walker-Diallo, Carolyn
Muslims in the Halls of Justice J. KOZAK *Islamic Horizons* v45 no6 p46 N/D 2016

Walkers (Orthopedic apparatus)
Innovation Walker-Chair N. Leiber color *Bloomberg Businessweek* no4501 p31 N 28 2016

Walking
See also
Hiking
ASK THE EXPERTS H. Lynn, K. Everett et al color *Runner's World* v52 no3 p42 Ap 2017
Don't let winter drag you down! [Cover story] A. Sweeney color *Redbook* p36 F 2017
Finding the Ideal Free Walk E. Sydnor Romm and A. Morris color *Dressage Today* v23 no12 p28 S 2017
A FISH IN THE TREE J. LANDRETTI color *Orion Magazine* v36 no2 p45 Mr/Ap 2017
Home Sweet Home Office T. Bufete color graph il *Consumer Reports* v82 no9 p8 S 2017
I Tried Dieting Like My Mom B. Hauser color *Health* v30 no10 p55 D 2016
OKLAHOMA CITY, OKLAHOMA color *Washington Monthly* v49 no3-5 p29 Mr-My 2017
Rihanna's Midnight Magic F. Kane color *Glamour* v114 no11 p40 N 2016
STRIDE WITH PRIDE C. KUZMA color *Runner's World* v52 no9 p26 O 2017
This Just In J. Zorthian *Time* v190 no1 p19 Jl 3 2017
TIMBERLINE I. VORSTER *American Forests* v123 no3 p32 Fall 2017
The Walking Cure [Cover story] S. FRIEDMAN cartoon color *Prevention* p40 Mr 2017
Walking South Dakota: Rollie Noem saw the state one step at a time *South Dakota Magazine* v33 no2 p18 Jl/Ag 2017
Walk This Way B. O'Dair *Prevention* p3 Mr 2017

Walking Dead, The (TV program)
Ask Matt M. Roush *TV Guide* v64 no46 p5 N 7 2016
BACK FROM THE DEAD D. Ross color *Entertainment Weekly* no1450 p30 Ja 27 2017
CLASH OF THE TITANS: What zombies?! Rick and Negan prepare to battle each other on The Walking Dead M. LOGAN *TV Guide* v65 no43 p20 O 16 2017

Gone Glenn [Cover story] D. Ross color *Entertainment Weekly* no1438 p22 N 4 2016
GUESS WHO'S COMING TO DINNER... [Cover story] D. Ross color *Entertainment Weekly* no1484 p24 S 29 2017
Horror Show M. Bayles *Claremont Review of Books* v16 no4 p87 Fall 2016
NEW WORLD ORDER M. LOGAN *TV Guide* v64 no48 p20 N 21 2016
RICK GRIMES' WATCH M. Romero color *Entertainment Weekly* no1460/1461 p94 Ap 7-17 2017
Skybound's Walking Dead Graphic Novel Sales Won't Die C. Reid chart color *Publishers Weekly* v263 no45 p5 N 7 2016
A Song for Abraham D. Ross color *Entertainment Weekly* no1438 p26 N 4 2016
The Walking Dead Deals a Grisly Blow M. McCluskey color *Time* v188 no16/17 p91 O 24 2016
THE WALKING DEAD M. Logan *TV Guide* v65 no39 p55 S 18 2017
The Walking Dead's Brutal Return E. Lewis *TV Guide* v64 no46 p11 N 7 2016
What's Next for the Survivors D. Ross color *Entertainment Weekly* no1438 p27 N 4 2016
WHAT TO PACK FOR THE ZOMBIE APOCALYPSE M. WELLS *Atlanta* v56 no10 p38 F 2017
Why I Still Love The Walking Dead Y. N. BROWN and J. Russell *TV Guide* v65 no11 p18 Mr 6 2017

Walking—Evaluation
EASIEST MOOD BOOST EVER color *Health* v31 no2 p12 Mr 2017

WALKS, ALAN
Our Mortgaged Future color graph *Alternatives Journal (AJ) - Canada's Environmental Voice* v42 no2 p22 2016

Walkup, Daniel
An on/off Berry phase switch in circular graphene resonators diag graph *Science* v356 no6340 p845 My 26 2017

WALL, ALIX
GREEN GODDESS color *Rodale's Organic Life* v3 no1 p43 Ja 2017

Wall, Debra
FREE FOR ALL color *O, The Oprah Magazine* p20 O 2017

Wall, John, 1990-
WONDER WALL L. Jenkins color *Sports Illustrated* v126 no12 p30 My 1 2017

Wall, Kim
THE WEEKLY PACKAGE: How Cubans deliver culture without internet *Harper's Magazine* v335 no2006 p59 Jl 2017

Wall, Mick
Foo Fighters: Learning to Fly color *Publishers Weekly* v264 no25 p102 Je 19 2017

Wall, Pam
Pam Wall A. Schell color *Sail* v48 no5 p14 My 2017

Wall, Patrick
GUESS WHO'S COMING TO KINDERGARTEN *Mother Jones* v42 no5 p17 S/O 2017

Wall, The (Film)
JOHN CENA: UNDER FIRE K. P. Sullivan color *Entertainment Weekly* no1466 p41 My 19 2017

Wall, Travis
Travis Wall: Puts His Stamp on Ballet C. Bowers *Dance Spirit* v21 no7 p41 S 2017

Wall, V.
UNSOLICITED BETA color *Climbing* no352 p8 Ap 2017

Wall clocks—Evaluation
HOME STYLE *Cincinnati Magazine* v50 no4 p36 Ja 2017

Wall coverings
See also
Wallpaper
From Our Editor S. Donelson color *House Beautiful* p2 Jl 2017
PEEL-OFF WALLPAPER E. MOODY color *Martha Stewart Living* p29 Mr 2017
Resources color *House Beautiful* v159 no9 p110 N 2017

Wall coverings—Design & construction
Facades color *Architectural Record* v204 no12 p114 D 2016

Wall design & construction
How to Make a... WALL color *Popular Mechanics* v193 no7 p80 S 2016

Wallander, Steven
An Economic Perspective on Soil Health *Amber Waves: The Economics of Food, Farming, Natural Resources, & Rural America* p18 S 2016
Farmers Employ Strategies To Reduce Risk of Drought Damages *Amber Waves: The Economics of Food, Farming, Natural Resources, & Rural America* p57 Je 2017
Gathering Experimental Evidence To Improve the Design of Agricultural Programs *Amber Waves: The Economics of Food, Farming, Natural Resources, & Rural America* p1 Ag 2017

Wallans, Connor
Backfires: The joyful noise of the commentariat, rebutted sporadically by Ed color *Car & Driver* v62 no11 p9 My 2017

Wallarab, Brent
The Exposed Melodic Use OF BASS TROMBONE IN A BIG BAND color *Downbeat* v84 no4 p82 Ap 2017

Wallbank, John R.
Ballistic miniband conduction in a graphene superlattice bibl graph *Science* v353 no6307 p1526 S 30 2016

Wallenberg, Jacob
Hello, Ericsson. 'The Butcher' Is on the Line N. Rolander, V. Ek et al color *Bloomberg Businessweek* no4526 p35 Je 12 2017

Wallenberg, Raoul, 1912-1952
Milestones *Time* v188 no20 p11 N 14 2016

WALLER, DONALD M.
Combining Biodiversity Resurveys across Regions to Advance Global Change Research *BioScience* v67 no1 p73 Ja 2017

Waller, Donald Scott
Neutralizing North Korea color *Atlantic* v320 no3 p10 O 2017

Waller-Bridge, Phoebe
DIRTY BIRD E. NUSSBAUM cartoon *New Yorker* v92 no30 p76 S 26 2016
Hot Cringe Queen Phoebe Waller-Bridge D. FEAR color *Rolling Stone* no1274 p43 N 17 2016
NASTY WOMEN S. Vilkomerson color *Entertainment Weekly* no1463/1464 p76 Ap/My 2017
TELEVISION'S COMEDY AUTEURS S. Larson bw *New Yorker* v93 no26 p62 S 4 2017

WalletHub (Company)
Cities for Vets to Flock to—and Avoid *USA Today Magazine* v145 no2859 p5 D 2016

Wallets
YOU SHOULD KNOW cartoon *Bicycling* v58 no1 p12 Ja/F 2017

Wallets—Evaluation
FORGET THE BAG color *Conde Nast Traveler* v52 no2 p28 F 2017
Living in the Present D. POINTDUJOUR color *Ebony* v72 no3 p72 D 2016/Ja 2017
SMALL BATCH, HIGH YIELD D. MICHEL color *Men's Health* v32 no2 p(Sp)14 Mr 2017

Walleye fishing
Drop It Like It's Hot R. Robertson color *Field & Stream* v121 no9 pF1 Ap 2017

WALLIS, EVAN
CRUISE CONTROL *Cincinnati Magazine* v50 no3 p48 D 2016

Wallis, Michael, 1945-
Unhappy Trails: A look at the Donners and the dark side of Manifest Destiny D. PRESTON *New York Times Book Review* p16 Jl 9 2017

Wallis, Quvenzhané, 2003-
A Night Out with Mama *Publishers Weekly* v264 no35 p125 Ag 28 2017
Shai & Emmie Star in Break an Egg! *Publishers Weekly* v264 no35 p128 Ag 28 2017

Wallis, R.
Grace Davie, Religion in Britain: a Persistent Paradox *Society* v53 no6 p665 D 2016

WALLIS, STEPHEN
Cloud Nine color *Architectural Digest* v74 no1 p224 Ja 2017
Noble Spirit color *Architectural Digest* no11 p62 N 1 2017
Renaissance Man color *Architectural Digest* v74 no1 p80 Ja 2017

Wallisch, Kristi—Interviews
BATTLE OF NEW ORLEANS ANNIVERSARY color *New Orleans Magazine* v51 no3 p25 Ja 2017

WALLJASPER, JAY
ARLINGTON, VIRGINIA color *Washington Monthly* v49 no3-5

p25 Mr-My 2017
Ask Our Experts *Mother Earth News* no281 p91 Ap/My 2017

Walljasper, Matt
BEST OF ATLANTA *Atlanta* v56 no8 p106 D 2016

WALLMAN, REINI
#Climbing Training color *Climbing* no352 p9 Ap 2017

Wallonia (Belgium)—Politics & government
Why Wallonia wobbled S. HAYDEN color *Maclean's* v129 no45 p43 N 14 2016

Wallpaper
EDGEWOOD HALL: Welcome to Edgewood Hall color *House Beautiful* v159 no9 p50 N 2017
House Beautiful GUIDE TO Family Style color *House Beautiful* v159 no7 p21 S 2017
PEEL-OFF WALLPAPER E. MOODY color *Martha Stewart Living* p29 Mr 2017
qenevieve GORDER N. DAYTON *Better Homes & Gardens* v94 no11 p14 N 2016
Resources *Old House Journal* v44 no8 p95 D 2016
Stroke of Genius K. O'SHEA-EVANS color *House Beautiful* p31 Jl 2017
walls & ceilings *Design Center Sourcebook* p76 2017

Wallpaper design
AT HOME WITH MORRIS: PATTERNS NEVER OUT OF STYLE bw color *Old House Journal* v45 no6 p22 S 2017

Wallpaper—Evaluation
Adam's Home STYLE SHEET Adam color *O, The Oprah Magazine* p52 Jl 2017
Adam's Home STYLE SHEET color *O, The Oprah Magazine* p67 My 2017
ALL ATWITTER L. MOWRY *Atlanta* v57 no2 p44 Je 2017
The Belle Is Back K. O'SHEA-EVANS color *House Beautiful* v159 no8 p53 O 2017
debut: On a Roll M. OWENS color *Architectural Digest* no11 p50 N 1 2017
Finishing Touch J. J. CONDON color *House Beautiful* v159 no4 p38 My 2017
MAKE IT LIGHTER, BRIGHTER, BIGGER S. EMSLIE color *House Beautiful* p70 Ag 2017
MARTYN LAWRENCE BULLARD ON CEILINGS K. O'SHEA-EVANS color *House Beautiful* v159 no7 p60 S 2017
Paper Trail L. RAMZI and C. SCHAMA color *Vogue* v207 no9 p614 S 2017
WALLS & CEILINGS cartoon color *Arts & Crafts Homes & the Revival* v12 no1 p18 2017 Resouce Guide
Whirlwind color *Architectural Digest* v74 no2 p19 F 2017

Wallraff, Barbara
Improve Your Writing to Improve Your Credibility *Harvard Business Review Digital Articles* p2 Jl 29 2015

Wallroth, Alexander
mTORC1 activity repression by late endosomal phosphatidylinositol 3,4-bisphosphate diag *Science* v356 no6341 p968 Je 1 2017

Walls
See also
Concrete walls
Stone walls
How to Make a... WALL color *Popular Mechanics* p80 S 2017
it's coming from inside the house S. Bushwick color *Popular Science* v289 no6 p88 N/D 2017
On the Surface K. Wilburn *New Orleans Homes & Lifestyles* v20 no1 p96 Wint 2016

Walls (Music)
Kings of Leon K. O'Donnell color *Entertainment Weekly* no1436/1437 p99 O 21 2016

Walls, Barbranda Lumpkins
Thoroughly Modern Millinery color *AARP: The Magazine* v59 no2A p72 F/Mr 2016

WALLS, JEANNETTE
THOUGHTS ON Property *Forbes* v199 no5 p124 My 16 2017

Walls, Laura Dassow
American Surveyor: A new life of Thoreau on his 200th birthday shows that his time at Walden Pond was far from solitary F. MONTAIGNE *New York Times Book Review* p17 Jl 23 2017
INTO THE WILD: Henry David Thoreau as prophet, naturalist, and stealth comedian J. Marcus *Harper's Magazine* p90 O 2017
A RADICAL FOR ALL SEASONS J. PURDY il *Nation* v304

no18 p29 Je 19 2017

The Radical M. D. AESCHLIMAN *National Review* v69 no15 p38 Ag 14 2017

Walls, Robert E.

Imprints: The Pokagon Band of Potawatomi Indians and the City of Chicago *American Indian Quarterly* v41 no3 p292 Summ 2017

WALLS, SUSAN C.

Overcoming Challenges to the Recovery of Declining Amphibian Populations in the United States *BioScience* v67 no2 p156 F 2017

Walls—Equipment & supplies

How to Make a... WALL color *Popular Mechanics* v193 no7 p80 S 2016

Wallweber, Heidi A.

T cell costimulatory receptor CD28 is a primary target for PD-1–mediated inhibition color diag graph *Science* v355 no6332 p1428 Mr 31 2017

WALLWORK, REBECCA

Bonjour, Montréal *Tennis* v53 no4 p30 Jl/Ag 2017

The Magic of Maui: Turn your summer vacation into a wellness retreat on this laid-back Hawaiian isle color *Tennis* v53 no5 p22 S/O 2017

Next Stop, Newport *Tennis* v53 no3 p28 My/Je 2017

Walmsley, Jim

Long Trails to Recovery E. STROUT color *Runner's World* v52 no8 p46 S 2017

Walnut

EAT MO NUTS! D. BRESHEARS *Missouri Life* v43 no7 p70 D 2016/Ja 2017

Missouriana M. W. SCHWARTZ *Missouri Life* v43 no7 p98 D 2016/Ja 2017

Walnut Canyon National Monument (Ariz.)

WALNUT CANYON TRAIL: You could spend all summer hiking the Arizona Trail If you only have a day, this scenic stroll to Fisher Point is a great option R. STIEVE *Arizona Highways* v96 no7 p54 Jl 2017

Walpole, Horace, 1717-1797

1783: London *Lapham's Quarterly* v10 no2 p157 Spr 2017

WALRATH, TOBY

THE COYOTE SCALE color *Outdoor Life* v224 no2 p78 F/Mr 2017

FEEL THE BURN color *Outdoor Life* v224 no7 pH5 S 2017

GET IT ALL OUT color *Outdoor Life* v224 no7 pH12 S 2017

MULEYS ON YOUR OWN color *Outdoor Life* v223 no9 pH5 N 2016

Walraven, Jook T. M.

Ultrafast many-body interferometry of impurities coupled to a Fermi sea bibl diag graph *Science* v354 no6308 p96 O 7 2016

Walrus Islands (Alaska)

Prehistoric walrus hunting site shielded color *Science* v355 no6322 p228 Ja 20 2017

Walrus—Behavior

FEEDING FRENZY *Sierra* v102 no1 p2 Ja/F 2017

Walsh, Blair

MISS UNDERSTOOD G. Bishop color *Sports Illustrated* v127 no7 p128 S 4 2017

Walsh, Bryan

How the Enlightenment Predicted Modern Populism color *Time* v189 no6 p19 F 20 2017

How Zika Could Change the Politics of Abortion color *Time* v188 no16/17 p58 O 24 2016

The Right to Speech Vs. the Right to Censor color *Time* v189 no9 p19 Mr 13 2017

A Safer, Smarter Grid color *Time* v189 no13 p30 Ap 10 2017

Trump's Presidency Could Mean the End of a Livable Climate color *Time* v188 no22-23 p17 N/D 2016

Warning: The Next Global Security Threat Isn't What You Think [Cover story] color diag *Time* v189 no18 p32 My 15 2017

Walsh, Christopher A.

Intersection of diverse neuronal genomes and neuropsychiatric disease: The Brain Somatic Mosaicism Network color *Science* v356 no6336 p395 Ap 28 2017

Walsh, Courtney

Just Look Up *Publishers Weekly* v264 no21 p79 My 22 2017

Walsh, Dan

Fin color *Art in America* v105 no1 p11 Ja 2017

WALSH, DANIELLE

Brave Hearts color *O, The Oprah Magazine* p14 Mr 2017

WALSH, DAVID

PURSUIT OF JUSTICE *America* v215 no11 p34 O 17 2016

Walsh, Declan

A DEATH IN CAIRO *New York Times Magazine* p26 Ag 20 2017

Walsh, Don

SPECIAL EXPERIENCE K. Krause *Lapham's Quarterly* v10 no2 p192 Spr 2017

Walsh, Heather Gowen

bored no more *Parents* v92 no4 p132 Ap 2017

Brush Up on Mealtime Manners *Parents* v92 no9 p170 S 2017

fair ground *Parents* v91 no11 p146 N 2016

let's pretend *Parents* p136 2015

the sleep fix *Parents* v91 no11 p58 N 2016

Walsh, Ian

OUTTAKES bw color *Surfing Magazine* v53 no2 p94 F 2017

Walsh, Ian—Interviews

DISTANCE BETWEEN DREAMS T. Paul color *Surfing Magazine* v53 no2 p80 F 2017

Walsh, James D.

The Bullet, the Cop, the Boy img *New York* v50 no12 p46 Je 12 2017

Government By Gazzillionaires img *New York* v30 Ja 23 2017

OBAMA'S AMERICA img *New York* v49 no20 p12 O 3 2016

TO UNDERSTAND THIS NEW RIGHT, IT HELPS TO SEE IT NOT AS A FRINGE MOVEMENT, BUT A POWERFUL COUNTERCULTURE img *New York* v50 no9 p24 My 1 2017

TRUMP'S CAMPAIGN HAS BEEN SO INSANE *New York* v49 no22 p46 O 31 2016

WALSH, JANE

FIELDS OF Gold: CELEBRATING THE SWEET CORN HARVEST IN THE BERKSHIRES AND BEYOND color map *Yankee* p44 Jl 2017

Walsh, Jason

The Unboring Workout S. G. Levy color *Glamour* v114 no12 p154 D 2016

Walsh, Jessica J.

Gating of social reward by oxytocin in the ventral tegmental area color graph *Science* v357 no6358 p1406 S 29 2017

Walsh, Joan

The Arc Bent color diag il *Nation* v304 no1 p52 Ja 2 2017 The Obama Years

FIRST THEY MARCHED... NOW WHAT HAPPENS WHEN WOMEN RUN? bw color *Nation* v305 no5 p12 Ag 28 2017

People Lead the Pols *Nation* v304 no5 p10 F 20 2017

Q&A il *Nation* v304 no18 p5 Je 19 2017

Resistance Is Not Enough [Cover story] color *Nation* v304 no17 p16 Je 5 2017

Trump Exposed il *Nation* v303 no16 p3 O 17 2016

When Harry Met Late Night bw color *Nation* v304 no7 p20 Mr 6 2017

Whitelash color *Nation* v303 no22 p4 N 28 2016

Walsh, Joe, 1947-—Interviews

Joe Walsh A. GREENE bw *Rolling Stone* no1293 p58 Ag 10 2017

Walsh, Kate, 1967-

KATE WALSH STANDS WITH WOMEN D. Coggan color *Entertainment Weekly* no1457/1458 p16 Mr 17 2017

Walsh, Kenneth

Clonal hematopoiesis associated with TET2 deficiency accelerates atherosclerosis development in mice bibl diag *Science* v355 no6327 p842 F 24 2017

Walsh, Kevin

Identification of a primordial asteroid family constrains the original planetesimal population diag graph *Science* v357 no6355 p1026 S 8 2017

Walsh, Mary

HOLY BOWLY MAMMOTH MTN, CA color *Snowboarder* v29 no4 p104 D 2016

Walsh, Matt

PARTY LINES img *New York* v49 no20 p134 O 3 2016

WALSH, MEGAN

CAN'T KEEP HER DOWN bw color *Climbing* no356 p54 S/O 2017

Walsh, Peter

Letting Go color *Prevention* v69 no4 p54 Ap 2017

Walsh, Regan

3 Ways to Control Your Phone Addiction on Vacation *Harvard Business Review Digital Articles* p2 Jl 31 2017

Before You Agree to Take on New Work, Ask 3 Questions *Harvard Business Review Digital Articles* p2 My 23 2017

Walsh, Robb

Island Life in Galveston color *Southern Living* v52 no3 p69 Mr 2017

Walsh, Sara

FINDING FITNESS: Incorporating exercise and wellness can increase years of happiness and health *Washingtonian Magazine* v52 no8 p146 My 2017

Walsh, Sarah

TINY INSECT—BIG IMPACT *New York State Conservationist* v71 no3 p14 D 2016

TREES FOR TRIBS TURNS 10 *New York State Conservationist* v71 no4 p20 F 2017

WALSH, TERRY

How to overclock your PC's CPU color *PCWorld* v35 no6 p139 Je 2017

Walsh, Victoria

FROM Forest TO Table color *Canadian Wildlife* v22 no5 p30 N/D 2016

Walsh, Vincent

THERE IS NO SUCH THINGS AS BEING GOOD UNDER PRESSURE: Brain research professor Vincent Walsh on how we can get smarter at making better decisions *People Management* p38 My 2017

Walshaw, Martin

Emergence and spread of a human-transmissible multidrug-resistant nontuberculous mycobacterium bibl diag graph *Science* v354 no6313 p751 N 11 2016

Walsworth, Ronald L.

Control and local measurement of the spin chemical potential in a magnetic insulator bw diag *Science* v357 no6347 p195 Jl 14 2017

Walt, Vivienne

The Business Guide to Europe's Wild Year chart color diag *Fortune* v175 no5 p9 Ap 1 2017

DREAM WEAVER color *Fortune* v176 no3 p74 S 1 2017

FORTY UNDER FORTY 2017 color *Fortune* v176 no3 p62 S 1 2017

France's Youngest Leader Since Napoleon Takes the Stage color *Time* v189 no19 p9 My 22 2017

How People Power Is Splitting Europe color diag *Time* v188 no25-26 p80 D 19 2016 Double Issue

MINING COMEDY GOLD color *Fortune* v176 no3 p70 S 1 2017

Not All Russian Hackers Are Bad color *Fortune* v175 no2 p12 F 1 2017

Notre Dame Cathedral Is Crumbling. Who Will Help Save It? color *Time* v190 no6 p26 Ag 7 2017

The Power of Le Pen color *Time* v189 no11 p34 Mr 27 2017

SELLING SOAP AND SAVING THE WORLD color *Fortune* v175 no3 p122 Mr 1 2017

WELCOME TO TOMORROW LAND color map *Fortune* v175 no6 p60 My 1 2017

YOUTH REVOLT color *Fortune* v176 no3 p64 S 1 2017

YOU'VE NEVER HEARD OF *HNA GROUP. HERE'S WHY YOU WILL color diag *Fortune* v176 no2 p86 Ag 1 2017

Walt Disney Co.

Beauty and the Bakeware Set C. Palmeri and M. Townsend color graph *Bloomberg Businessweek* no4515 p20 Mr 20 2017

CRUISE LINES color *Conde Nast Traveler* v52 no10 p74 N 2017

DISNEY'S GALACTIC GAMBIT D. LEONARD and C. PALMERI color diag *Bloomberg Businessweek* no4519 p56 Ap 24 2017

Healing presence J. M. Griffith *U.S. Catholic* v82 no4 p38 Ap 2017

How Disney Found Its Way Back to Creative Success V. Govindarajan *Harvard Business Review Digital Articles* p2 Je 3 2016

How Pixar Lost Its Way C. ORR cartoon *Atlantic* v319 no5 p34 Je 2017

Market Rules J. PODHORETZ color *Weekly Standard* v22 no38 p39 Je 12 2017

May 1, 1971: Financing Fantasyland A. BROWN bw color *Forbes*

v199 no4 p28 Ap 25 2017

A NEW HOPE D. WILSON color *Film Comment* v53 no2 p56 Mr/Ap 2017

PELICAN BRIEFS L. LeBlanc-Berry bw color *Louisiana Life* v38 no1 p12 S/O 2017

What Disney's Netflix Snub Means M. Lev-ram color *Fortune* v176 no3 p18 S 1 2017

Walt Disney Co.—Finance

One for Mickey's Mantel A. GARA color *Forbes* v199 no6 p24 Je 13 2017

WALT DISNEY BREAKS RECORDS T. J. Huddleston color *Fortune* v174 no8 p21 D 15 2016

Walt Disney World (Fla.)

FINDINGS *Harper's Magazine* v333 no1999 p96 D 2016

Secrets of the Kingdom [Cover story] B. Tuttle color *Money* v46 no6 p44 Jl 2017

Walt Disney World (Fla.)—Finance

May 1, 1971: Financing Fantasyland A. BROWN bw color *Forbes* v199 no4 p28 Ap 25 2017

WALTER, COURTNEY

SPARKLE & SHINE, TWINKLE TOES! color *Ebony* v72 no11 p41 S 2017

WALTER, DEREK

Transfer everything from your old Android phone to your new one bw color *PCWorld* v35 no8 p134 Ag 2017

WALTER, JESS

Smorgasbord of Champions: Before he became famous as a novelist and countercultural guru, Kurt Vonnegut wrote a lot of short stories *New York Times Book Review* p12 O 15 2017

Walter, John

MAN OF STEEL A. Ryder color *Popular Photography* v81 no2 p90 Mr/Ap 2017

SUPERFORECASTING FOR THE FARM *Successful Farming* v115 no1 p38 Ja 2017

There's An Ag App For That *Successful Farming* v114 no12 p70 Mid-N 2016

Walter, Lutz

Sustained virologic control in SIV+ macaques after antiretroviral and $\alpha 4\beta 7$ antibody therapy bibl graph *Science* v354 no6309 p197 O 14 2016

Walter, Rob

Backfires: The joyful noise of the commentariat, rebutted sporadically by Ed color *Car & Driver* v62 no11 p9 My 2017

Walter, Sarah

16 ways to do COPPER color *Good Housekeeping* v264 no4 p76E Ap 2017

20 WAYS TO DO PLUM color *Good Housekeeping* v263 no5 p56C N 2016

38 Easy Ways to CLEAN HOUSE color *Good Housekeeping* v265 no3 p60A S 2017

48 hours in VANCOUVER color *Good Housekeeping* v264 no2 p35 F 2017

FLAB-FREE ARMS color *Good Housekeeping* v264 no6 p87 Je 2017

TIGHTER TUSH color *Good Housekeeping* v264 no4 p103 Ap 2017

A WEEK OF Awesome Outfits color *Good Housekeeping* v264 no4 p38 Ap 2017

WALTERS, AMANDA BOYD

DOG DAZE *Cincinnati Magazine* v50 no10 p52 Jl 2017

ENCYCLOPEDIA CINCINNATI bw cartoon color *Cincinnati Magazine* v51 no1 p42 O 2017

THE GEOGRAPHY OF MEMORY *Cincinnati Magazine* v50 no5 p72 F 2017

HAVE IT YOUR WAY *Cincinnati Magazine* v50 no2 p58 N 2016

NIGHT MOVES *Cincinnati Magazine* v50 no8 p40 My 2017

NO FILTER *Cincinnati Magazine* p24 Je 2017

U.S. 127 Yard Sale *Cincinnati Magazine* p58 Je 2017

Walters, Barbara, 1931-

Today's Most Memorable Moments E. Aslanian bw color *TV Guide* v65 no7 p24 F 13 2017

Walters, Ben

KRISTEN & BEN WALTERS 2245 PARK AVE., WALNUT HILLS *Cincinnati Magazine* v50 no11 p75 Ag 2017

Walters, Dan

Romancing the Water color *Audubon* v119 no3 p49 Fall 2017

Walters, David

Armie Hammer Has Two Turkeys color *Bon Appetit* no11 p24 N 2017

CHILD IN CHARGE color *Bloomberg Businessweek* no4517 p71 Ap 3 2017

Christian Slater: How do you navigate a dinner party? bw color *Bon Appetit* v62 no10 p112 O 2017

David Sedaris What's your cooking philosophy? bw color *Bon Appetit* v62 no6 p114 Je 2017

Debbie Harry What's your backstage essential? color *Bon Appetit* v62 no4 p118 Ap 2017

FISHING FROM THE SKY cartoon color *Popular Mechanics* p88 Mr 2017

Jake Tapper: So, how'd you get so fit? color *Bon Appetit* no8 p106 Ag 2017

Laura Dern bw color *Conde Nast Traveler* v52 no6 p40 Je/Jl 2017

Mila Kunis: What's on your Thanksgiving table? color *Bon Appetit* no11 p136 N 2017

REALITY BITES color *Bloomberg Businessweek* no4501 p62 N 28 2017

RYAN SEACREST color *Bon Appetit* v61 no12 p174 D 2016 / Jan2017

Scarlett Johansson: What's your go-to movie snack? color *Bon Appetit* v62 no7 p108 Jl 2017

Sigourney Weaver color *Conde Nast Traveler* v51 no10 p62 N 2016

starters color *Bon Appetit* no1 p13 F 2017

Steve Coogan If you were a critic, what would get four stars? color *Bon Appetit* p154 S 2017

THE SUNDANCE KID color *Bloomberg Businessweek* no4507 p59 Ja 16 2017

THERE'S A GIRL IN MY SWEATER bw color *Esquire* v166 no4 p108 N 2016

WILL IT KILL YOU? bw color *Popular Mechanics* p88 Jl 2017

WALTERS, JOHN P.

The Opioid Crisis color graph *Weekly Standard* v22 no9 p19 N 7 2016

Walters, Laura

My Look *Indianapolis Monthly* v40 no10 p29 Je 2017

RANCH DRESSING: Styles that are right at home on the range (and beyond) *Indianapolis Monthly* v12 no40 p32 Ag 2017

Walters, LeeAnne

WHISTLEBLOWERS J. MCQUAID *Smithsonian* v47 no8 p48 D 2016

WALTERS, MAURA KUTNER

SARAH JESSICA PARKER color *Bon Appetit* v61 no11 p162 N 2016

Walters, R.

iPTF16geu: A multiply imaged, gravitationally lensed type Ia supernova color diag graph *Science* v356 no6335 p291 Ap 21 2017

Walters-Storyk Design Group (Company)

DAILY DOUBLE [Cover story] R. Sabin bw color *Sound & Vision* v82 no3 p34 Ap 2017

Waltham, Chris

American Luthier Carleen Hutchins—the Art and Science of the Violin *Physics Today* v70 no2 p60 F 2017

Walther, Franz Erhard

FRANZ ERHARD WALTHER M. Tomic color *Art in America* v104 no10 p159 N 2016

WALTHER, MATTHEW

A Better Brew color *National Review* v69 no6 p23 Ap 3 2017

Winnie-the-Pooh at 90 color *National Review* v69 no1 p22 Ja 23 2017

Walther, Michael

Measurement of the small-scale structure of the intergalactic medium using close quasar pairs diag graph *Science* v356 no6336 p418 Ap 28 2017

Walther, Peter

Image of a Decade J. WEISER bw *Weekly Standard* v22 no36 p37 My 29 2017

Waltl, Josef

How Investors React When Companies Announce They're Moving to a SaaS Business Model color *Harvard Business Review Digital Articles* p2 Ja 12 2017

Walton, Andre

Resolving the Paradox of Group Creativity *Harvard Business Review Digital Articles* p2 Ja 25 2016

Walton, Bill

When a MAN with a checkered past gets to make the RULES M. Abelson and D. Voreacos color *Bloomberg Businessweek* no4502 p33 D 5 2016

Walton, Bill, 1952-

WHAT IF? ... WALTON AND ODEN AND ROY HAD STAYED HEALTHY? (DON'T EVEN START ON MJ) B. Golliver and J. Feldman color *Sports Illustrated* v126 no11 p67 Ap 17-24 2017

Walton, Chris

2018 Dodge Challenger SRT Demon color *Motor Trend* v69 no10 p18 O 2017

911 WEAPONS-GRADE EDITION chart color *Motor Trend* v69 no5 p82 My 2017

THE BEST NEVER REST chart color *Motor Trend* v69 no6 p76 Je 2017

COMBO PLATE chart color *Motor Trend* v69 no9 p88 S 2017

eins, zwei, drei, quattros! chart color *Motor Trend* v69 no8 p76 Ag 2017

EVERYBODY'S EVERYTHING color *Motor Trend* v69 no1 p38 Ja 2017

FIRST DRIVE "1963" Superformance Corvette Grand Sport color *Motor Trend* v68 no12 p46 D 2016

GARAGE chart color diag *Motor Trend* v69 no8 p96 Ag 2017

INCREMENTAL BUSINESS OR NEXT BIG THING? chart color *Motor Trend* v69 no3 p70 Mr 2017

Karma Revero Back to the future color *Motor Trend* v69 no9 p18 S 2017

Leading from the Front chart color *Motor Trend* v69 no3 p52 Mr 2017

the leftovers... [Cover story] chart color *Motor Trend* v69 no4 p36 Ap 2017

MONSTER-ATI chart color *Motor Trend* v69 no5 p56 My 2017

Walton, Crystal

Arms of Promise *Publishers Weekly* v264 no5 p187 Ja 30 2017

Walton, James

All That Shite bw color *New York Review of Books* v64 no17 p44 N 9 2017

Myths, Tribes & Troubles bw *New York Review of Books* v64 no12 p34 Jl 13 2017

Shake Those Dice Again bw *New York Review of Books* v63 no19 p38 D 8 2016

Walton, Keith

Summer Storm Batters OSTAR P. Gelder color *Sail* v48 no8 p18 Ag 2017

Walton, Lester

Wit and Wisdom from our Early Breeders M. J. PARKINSON *Arabian Horse World* v57 no5 p158 F 2017

WALTON, OLIVER

The Tangled Politics of Postwar Justice in Sri Lanka *Current History* v116 no789 p130 Ap 2017

Walton, Steuart

trail wizards k. butcher color *Bike Magazine* v24 no1 p56 Ja/F 2017

Waltz, Margrit

In Depth D. PIMENTEL color *Flying* v143 no12 p66 D 2016

Waltz, Sasha

Upheaval at Staatsballett Berlin L. Cappelle *Dance Magazine* v91 no1 p40 Ja 2017

WALWYN, MEL

Gulf of St Lawrence Beach Pinweed color *Canadian Wildlife* v23 no4 p37 S/O 2017

Nodding Onion color *Canadian Wildlife* v23 no1 p37 Mr/Ap 2017

Pineapple Weed color *Canadian Wildlife* v23 no2 p37 My/Je 2017

Walz, D.

Observation of a large-scale anisotropy in the arrival directions of cosmic rays above 8 × 1018 eV *Science* v357 no6357 p1266 S 22 2017

Walz, Emily

19 THINGS YOU REALLY OUGHT TO 00 THIS MONTH *Washingtonian Magazine* v52 no3 p31 D 2016

19 THINGS YOU REALLY OUGHT TO DO THIS MONTH *Washingtonian Magazine* v52 no1 p33 O 2016

FOTOWEEKDC *Washingtonian Magazine* v52 no2 p35 N 2016

WHERE & WHEN color *Washingtonian Magazine* v52 no7 p31

Ap 2017

Walz, Kevin

THE LOOK BOOK K. WALZ and A. SWERDLOFF img *New York* v50 no10 p69 My 15 2017

Walzer, Michael

Does Betrayal Still Matter? color *New York Review of Books* v64 no8 p52 My 11 2017

Evaluating the Revisionist Critique of Just War Theory S. Lazar *Daedalus* v146 no1 p113 Wint 2017

Wamala, I.

Tough adhesives for diverse wet surfaces diag *Science* v357 no6349 p378 Jl 28 2017

Wambach, Abby, 1980-

THE WOMEN'S FUND – A CONVERSATION WITH ABBY WAMBACH *Cincinnati Magazine* p42 Je 2017

Wamego, Michael McKee

DEAR MOTHER *Mother Earth News* no283 p7 Ag/S 2017

Wampler, Rosalie

TRUE VINTAGE STYLE color *Old House Journal* v45 no2 p32 Ap 2017

Wan, Siyuan

All-oxide–based synthetic antiferromagnets exhibiting layer-resolved magnetization reversal diag *Science* v357 no6347 p191 Jl 14 2017

Wan, Yan

Long-range hot-carrier transport in hybrid perovskites visualized by ultrafast microscopy diag graph *Science* v356 no6333 p59 Ap 7 2017

Wan, Z.

Observation of coherent elastic neutrino-nucleus scattering diag *Science* v357 no6356 p1123 S 15 2017

Wanda (Film)

HER WAY D. Thomson bw color *Film Comment* v53 no4 p50 Jl/Ag 2017

STRONGER TOGETHER S. ENELOW bw color *Film Comment* v53 no5 p50 S/O 2017

Wanda *New Yorker* v93 no9 p12 Ap 17 2017

WANDEL, JEFFREY

Check Out These Outrageous Facts color *National Geographic Kids* no475 p4 N 2017

WANDESFORDE-SMITH, GEOFFREY

International Wildlife Law: Understanding and Enhancing Its Role in Conservation *BioScience* v67 no9 p784 S 2017

WANG, ALEXANDER

NIC GALWAY *Interview* v47 no2 p246 Mr 2017

Wang, Alexander, 1983-

Alexander Wang T. Patterson color *Bloomberg Businessweek* no4535 p72 Ag 28 2017

cool customer A. BEVAN color *Architectural Digest* v74 no9 p130 S 2017

Fashion Moments A. ASTLEY color *Architectural Digest* v74 no9 p28 S 2017

STYLE CRUSH Nicola Peltz S. Simon color *InStyle* v24 no2 p62 F 2017

Wang, Andrea

The Nian Monster *Publishers Weekly* v263 no40 p122 O 3 2016

WANG, ANDY

From Dawn Till Dusk color *Los Angeles Magazine* v62 no10 p46 O 2017

Wang, Ann

Engineering the ribosomal DNA in a megabase synthetic chromosome diag *Science* v355 no6329 p1049 Mr 10 2017

Synthesis, debugging, and effects of synthetic chromosome consolidation: synVI and beyond color *Science* v355 no6329 p1045 Mr 10 2017

Wang, Anne

Regeneration of fat cells from myofibroblasts during wound healing bibl color graph *Science* v355 no6326 p748 F 17 2017

Wang, Bo

THE BIG QUESTION cartoon *Atlantic* v319 no5 p96 Je 2017

FOR SHAOLIN MONK WANG BO, THE MESSAGE REMAINS THE SAME color *Black Belt* v55 no1 p12 D 2016/Ja 2017

Wang, Changjian

China can lead on climate change color *Science* v357 no6353 p764 Ag 25 2017

Wang, Chen

Three-dimensional holey-graphene/niobia composite architectures for ultrahigh-rate energy storage color diag graph *Science* v356 no6338 p599 My 12 2017

Wang, Chongmin

Direction-specific van der Waals attraction between rutile TiO2 nanocrystals diag *Science* v356 no6336 p434 Ap 28 2017

Wang, Dapeng

Plants transfer lipids to sustain colonization by mutualistic mycorrhizal and parasitic fungi diag graph *Science* v356 no6343 p1172 Je 16 2017

Wang, Daren

The Hidden Light of Northern Fires *Publishers Weekly* v264 no27 p51 Jl 3 2017

Wang, David Der-wei

Manifestations N. Haggerty *Commonweal* v144 no15 p43 S 22 2017

Wang, David Henry

BUTTERFLY STROKE D. STUMPF color *Vanity Fair* v59 no11 p142 N 2017

Wang, Dina

The Dangers of Hiring a Nice CEO *Harvard Business Review Digital Articles* p2 Je 7 2016

What 20 Years as a Remote Organization Has Taught Us About Managing Remote Teams *Harvard Business Review Digital Articles* p2 F 20 2017

What Sets Successful CEOs Apart [Cover story] color *Harvard Business Review* v95 no3 p70 My/Je 2017

Wang, En-Xu

"Perfect" designer chromosome V and behavior of a ring derivative diag *Science* v355 no6329 p1046 Mr 10 2017

Wang, Ertao

Epigenetic regulation of antagonistic receptors confers rice blast resistance with yield balance bibl diag *Science* v355 no6328 p962 Mr 3 2017

Plants transfer lipids to sustain colonization by mutualistic mycorrhizal and parasitic fungi diag graph *Science* v356 no6343 p1172 Je 16 2017

Wang, Evelyn N.

Water harvesting from air with metal-organic frameworks powered by natural sunlight diag *Science* v356 no6336 p430 Ap 28 2017

Wang, Fei

China can lead on climate change color *Science* v357 no6353 p764 Ag 25 2017

History of winning remodels thalamo-PFC circuit to reinforce social dominance color *Science* v357 no6347 p162 Jl 14 2017

Wang, Feng

Artificial intelligence in research color *Science* v357 no6346 p28 Jl 7 2017

Wang, Gang

Inactivation of porcine endogenous retrovirus in pigs using CRISPR-Cas9 diag *Science* v357 no6357 p1303 S 22 2017

VISIONARIES J. Surowiecki, M. Orcutt et al color il *MIT Technology Review* v120 no5 p42 S/O 2017

Wang, Ging-Ji Nathan

Highly stretchable polymer semiconductor films through the nanoconfinement effect bibl graph *Science* v355 no6320 p1 Ja 6 2017

Wang, Guo-Liang

Durable resistance to rice blast bibl color *Science* v355 no6328 p906 Mr 3 2017

Wang, Haiyan

Why Xiaomi Can't Succeed Without India *Harvard Business Review Digital Articles* p2 Je 29 2015

Wang, Han

Global climatic drivers of leaf size [Cover story] graph *Science* v357 no6354 p917 S 1 2017

Wang, Hao

Mismatch repair deficiency predicts response of solid tumors to PD-1 blockade chart graph *Science* v357 no6349 p409 Jl 28 2017

Wang, Hongwu

Systemic pan-AMPK activator MK-8722 improves glucose homeostasis but induces cardiac hypertrophy graph *Science* v357 no6350 p507 Ag 4 2017

Wang, Huapei

Lifetime of the solar nebula constrained by meteorite paleomagnetism bibl graph *Science* v355 no6325 p623 F 10 2017

WANG, JENNIFER

The $4.5 Billion Cabinet color *Forbes* v199 no1 p26 Ja 24 2017

The Class of 2016 cartoon chart *Forbes* v198 no5 p36 O 25 2016

THE DEFINITIVE LOOK AT DONALD TRUMP'S WEALTH color *Forbes* v198 no5 p80 O 25 2016

THE GREATEST GIVERS color graph *Forbes* v200 no5 p30 N 14 2017

HOW MUCH IS PRESIDENT TRUMP WORTH NOW? color *Forbes* v199 no3 p82 Mr 28 2017

SOUTH OF THE WALL bw *Forbes* v199 no3 p74 Mr 28 2017

TRUMP AMERICA bw *Forbes* v199 no3 p72 Mr 28 2017

Wang, Jennifer E.

A nuclease that mediates cell death induced by DNA damage and poly(ADP-ribose) polymerase-1 bw graph *Science* v354 no6308 paad6872-1 O 7 2016

Wang, Jiajun

Lifetime of the solar nebula constrained by meteorite paleomagnetism bibl graph *Science* v355 no6325 p623 F 10 2017

Wang, Jian

Deep functional analysis of synII, a 770-kilobase synthetic yeast chromosome diag *Science* v355 no6329 p1047 Mr 10 2017

Wang, Jianlin, 1954-

16 WANG JIANLIN S. Cendrowski color *Fortune* v174 no7 p88 D 1 2016

Wang, Jian-Yu

Satellite-based entanglement distribution over 1200 kilometers diag graph *Science* v356 no6343 p1140 Je 16 2017

Wang, Jie

ATP as a biological hydrotrope color graph *Science* v356 no6339 p753 My 19 2017

Decarboxylative borylation color *Science* v356 no6342 p1045 Je 9 2017

Wang, Jing

Chiral Majorana fermion modes in a quantum anomalous Hall insulator–superconductor structure diag *Science* v357 no6348 p294 Jl 21 2017

Visualizing the function and fate of neutrophils in sterile injury and repair color graph *Science* v357 no6359 p111 O 6 2017

Wang, Jinlan

An organic-inorganic perovskite ferroelectric with large piezoelectric response graph *Science* v357 no6348 p306 Jl 21 2017

Wang, Jun

Lifetime of the solar nebula constrained by meteorite paleomagnetism bibl graph *Science* v355 no6325 p623 F 10 2017

Wang, Junjun

Global roadless areas: Consider terrain color *Science* v355 no6332 p1381 Mr 31 2017

Wang, Kang L.

Chiral Majorana fermion modes in a quantum anomalous Hall insulator–superconductor structure diag *Science* v357 no6348 p294 Jl 21 2017

Wang, Kevin

Anomalously low electronic thermal conductivity in metallic vanadium dioxide bibl graph *Science* v355 no6323 p371 Ja 27 2017

Wang, Keyun

Trispecific broadly neutralizing HIV antibodies mediate potent SHIV protection in macaques color graph *Science* v357 no6359 p85 O 6 2017

Wang, Liangyan

Behavior management color *Science* v356 no6335 p244 Ap 21 2017

Wang, Lihui

Bug mapping and fitness testing of chemically synthesized chromosome X diag *Science* v355 no6329 p1048 Mr 10 2017

Engineering the ribosomal DNA in a megabase synthetic chromosome diag *Science* v355 no6329 p1049 Mr 10 2017

Wang, Lin-Ting

"Perfect" designer chromosome V and behavior of a ring derivative diag *Science* v355 no6329 p1046 Mr 10 2017

Wang, Liyang

Systemic pan-AMPK activator MK-8722 improves glucose homeostasis but induces cardiac hypertrophy graph *Science* v357

no6350 p507 Ag 4 2017

Wang, M.

Coseismic rupturing stopped by Aso volcano during the 2016 Mw 7.1 Kumamoto earthquake, Japan bibl color graph *Science* v354 no6314 p869 N 18 2016

Wang, Marina

FEATURED FELLOW: BRIAN KEATING color *Canadian Geographic* v137 no5 p78 S/O 2017

Wang, Meimei

Bone-like crack resistance in hierarchical metastable nanolaminate steels bibl color diag *Science* v355 no6329 p1055 Mr 10 2017

Wang, Na

Satellite-based entanglement distribution over 1200 kilometers diag graph *Science* v356 no6343 p1140 Je 16 2017

Wang, O.

Persistent effects of pre-Columbian plant domestication on Amazonian forest composition bibl chart graph map *Science* v355 no6328 p925 Mr 3 2017

Wang, Peggy I.

Mutation of a nucleosome compaction region disrupts Polycomb-mediated axial patterning bibl chart diag *Science* v355 no6329 p1081 Mr 10 2017

Wang, Penelope

33 WAYS TO CUT YOUR TAXES [Cover story] color diag *Money* v46 no2 p52 Mr 2017

5 WAYS YOUR 401(K) IS HELPING YOU SAVE BETTER color diag *Money* v46 no1 p78 Ja/F 2017

ASK THE EXPERT chart *Money* v46 no1 p29 Ja/F 2017

California's Big IRA Push color *Money* v45 no10 p21 N 2016

Getting Help at Home color *Consumer Reports* v82 no12 p40 D 2017

Mom, Dad: Your House Isn't Safe color *Money* v46 no5 p22 Je 2017

THE MONEY CHAMPIONS [Cover story] color *Money* v45 no11 p52 D 2016

The Next President's Financial Imperative: Fixing Social Security color *Time* v188 no20 p20 N 14 2016

States Try to Save Retirement While Washington Waits color diag *Time* v188 no14 p14 O 10 2016

This Tax Do-Over Could Be Handy color diag *Money* v46 no4 p26 My 2017

The Ultimate Guide to Retirement: Couples Edition [Cover story] color diag *Money* v45 no10 p48 N 2016

Who Will Care for You? [Cover story] chart color map *Consumer Reports* v82 no10 p28 O 2017

Wang, Pengfei

Reconfiguration of DNA molecular arrays driven by information relay diag *Science* v357 no6349 p371 Jl 28 2017

Wang, R.

Improving global integration of crop research color *Science* v357 no6349 p359 Jl 28 2017

Wang, R. "Ray"

To Jumpstart Growth, Flip the Company's Priorities *Harvard Business Review Digital Articles* p2 My 11 2015

What a Visit to an AIEnabled Hospital Might Look Like *Harvard Business Review Digital Articles* p2 N 16 2016

Wang, Rachael

Outfits for Days color *Glamour* v115 no9 p74 S 2017

Wang, Run

Harvesting electrical energy from carbon nanotube yarn twist diag graph *Science* v357 no6353 p773 Ag 25 2017

Wang, Sam

Five reasons to leave your science bubble C. Tachibana color *Science* v357 no6353 p823 Ag 25 2017

Wang, Selina

It's the U.S. Army Vs. the Drone Army *Bloomberg Businessweek* no4536 p26 S 4 2017

Wang, Shouqi

Inactivation of porcine endogenous retrovirus in pigs using CRISPR-Cas9 diag *Science* v357 no6357 p1303 S 22 2017

Wang, Sibao

Driving mosquito refractoriness to Plasmodium falciparum with engineered symbiotic bacteria color graph *Science* v357 no6358 p1399 S 29 2017

Wang, Su

Wang Xiaobo

Sexual Life in Modern China I. Johnson color *New York Review of Books* v64 no16 p63 O 26 2017

Wangchuk, Sonam

A WATERY SHRINE N. Strochlic color *National Geographic* v231 no4 p26 Ap 2017

Wanjiru, Rahab

People F. Nzwili color *Christian Century* v134 no1 p18 Ja 4 2017

Wanunu, Meni

Enhanced water permeability and tunable ion selectivity in sub-nanometer carbon nanotube porins chart color *Science* v357 no6353 p792 Ag 25 2017

Wapner, Jessica

Cancer Gene Tests Provide Few Answers color *Scientific American* v315 no3 p24 S 2016

Wappler, Margaret

MISS lily color *InStyle* v24 no3 p189 Mr 2017

Woman Warrior color *Glamour* v115 no6 p106 Je 2017

Wapstra, Erik

Biodiversity redistribution under climate change: Impacts on ecosystems and human well-being color *Science* v355 no6332 p1389 Mr 31 2017

War

See also

Battles

Chemical warfare

Civil war

Combat

Information warfare

Irregular warfare

Nuclear warfare

Revolutions

War & society

Women in war

AMERICA FIRST, FIRST img *New York* v49 no22 p39 O 31 2016

AT THE FRONT bw *MHQ: Quarterly Journal of Military History* v29 no4 p13 Summ 2017

FINAL EXAM J. D. Frank *Lapham's Quarterly* v10 no3 p144 Summ 2017

Goodbye, Obama G. HEALY color *Reason* v48 no9 p18 F 2017

I Told Steve Bannon: 'We Are Not At War With Islam.' He Disagreed F. Rose *NPQ: New Perspectives Quarterly* v34 no2 p17 My 2017

SAFETY IN NUMBERS? The mathematics of predicting war G. Greenberg chart color *Harper's Magazine* v335 no2005 p67 Je 2017

A Vision of Trump at War P. Gordon color *Foreign Affairs* v96 no3 p10 My/Je 2017

WAR IN HISTORY AND MEMORY J. E. Talbott *History Today* v67 no3 p18 Mr 2017

What to Do About The Koreas M. Thompson *Bloomberg Businessweek* no4519 p10 Ap 24 2017

War & emergency legislation

The French State of Emergency J. FREDETTE *Current History* v116 no788 p101 Mr 2017

War & emergency powers

Congress and War S. R. Weissman cartoon *Foreign Affairs* v96 no1 p132 Ja/F 2017

War & ethics

See also

Just war doctrine

BEYOND "JUST CAUSE" M. P. GILLEO, P. STEINFELS et al color *Commonweal* v144 no16 p4 O 6 2017

LEGITIMATE DEFENSE T. HUGHSON *Commonweal* v144 no16 p2 O 6 2017

THE NUCLEAR THIRD RAIL M. GALLAGHER *Commonweal* v144 no16 p2 O 6 2017

War & society

Everyday Life in Ukraine's War Zone G. UEHLING *Current History* v116 no792 p264 O 2017

War (International law)

See also

Humanitarian law

International mediation

Military law

Sanctions (International law)

backstory color *New Republic* v248 no1/2 p72 Ja/F 2017

Outlaw Nation M. PATTERSON *America* v215 no12 p12 O 24 2016

War casualties

The Epidemiologic Challenge to the Conduct of Just War: Confronting Indirect Civilian Casualties of War P. H. Wise *Daedalus* v146 no1 p139 Wint 2017

War correspondents

See also

Military journalism

Women war correspondents

WAR REPORTER FOR A DAY E. DYER color *Popular Mechanics* p24 O 2017

War crimes

Remember Malmedy G. SCHOENFELD bw *Weekly Standard* v22 no39 p36 Je 19 2017

THE RESPONSIBILITY TO PROTECT I. ŠIMONOVIĆ *UN Chronicle* v54 no4 p18 2017

Stop the War Party Now P. J. BUCHANAN *American Conservative* v16 no3 p11 My/Je 2017

War Crimes in Yemen M. T. KLARE *Nation* v33 no21 p4 N 21 2016

War criminals

Stay the Hand of Justice? Evaluating Claims that War Crimes Trials Do More Harm than Good M. S. Martins and J. Bronsther *Daedalus* v146 no1 p83 Wint 2017

War for the Planet of the Apes (Film)

Ape Overload R. DOUTHAT *National Review* v69 no15 p47 Ag 14 2017

THE APES ARE COMING T. GRIERSON color *Popular Mechanics* p12 Jl 2017

Do Humans Even Deserve War for the Planet of the Apes? S. Zacharek color *Time* v190 no4 p47 Jl 24 2017

STEVE ZAHN GOES APE D. Franich color *Entertainment Weekly* no1471 p52 Je 23 2017

War for the Planet of the Apes C. Nashawaty color *Entertainment Weekly* no1474/1475 p95 Jl 21-28 2017

WAR FOR THE PLANET OF THE APES D. Franich color *Entertainment Weekly* no1463/1464 p70 Ap/My 2017

WAR FOR THE PLANET OF THE APES K. P. Sullivan color *Entertainment Weekly* no1446/1447 p54 D 2016/Ja 2017

War game software

Total War Saga series focused on smaller 'powder-keg' moments in history H. DINGMAN color *PCWorld* v35 no8 p37 Ag 2017

War games

A New Level: When Gen Con lands on planet Indianapolis August 17 and turns 50, the annual gathering of gamers will look quite different than it did during the beta phase L. JOSS *Indianapolis Monthly* v12 no40 p16 Ag 2017

War in the Bible

Prepare for Battle J. W. MARTENS il *America* v215 no10 p47 O 10 2016

War Machine (Film)

Brad Pitt Takes on the Runaway General In War Machine S. Zacharek color *Time* v189 no21 p58 Je 5 2017

PULVERIZER T. Friend cartoon *New Yorker* v93 no17 p21 Je 19 2017

WAR MACHINE T. Stack color *Entertainment Weekly* no1463/1464 p34 Ap/My 2017

War memorials—Washington (D.C.)

OVER HERE M. W. SCHWARTZ bw color *Missouri Life* v44 no2 p32 Ap 2017

War of 1812

Retrospect: August 24–25, 1814: Burning of Washington, D.C S. Potter il *Weatherwise* v70 no4 p10 Jl/Ag 2017

War on Drugs (Performer)

THINK PIECES A. PETRUSICH cartoon *New Yorker* v93 no24 p78 Ag 21 2017

War Paint (Theatrical production)

BEAUTY QUEENS A. F. COLLINS color *Vanity Fair* v59 no4 p200 Mr 2017

GOINGS ON ABOUT TOWN bw *New Yorker* v93 no6 p4 Mr 27 2017

Scattered Brushstrokes of Beauty J. GREEN img *New York* v50 no8 p134 Ap 17 2017

War posters

EVIL EYE *MHQ: Quarterly Journal of Military History* v29 no3 p96 Spr 2017

"Over There" Becomes "Over Here" *USA Today Magazine* v146 no2866 p38 Jl 2017

War profiteering

War Profiteering Ain't Physics L. C. GOODMAN *In These Times* v41 no6 p12 Je 2017

War victims

See also

Holocaust survivors

Prisoners of war

My Father's Vietnam J. Meacham color *Time* v190 no12 p52 S 25 2017

Warady, Natalie

TRUE-BLUE WINNERS color *Martha Stewart Living* no271 p76 Ja/F 2017

Warao (South American people)

INTO THE URBAN JUNGLE D. Biller color *Bloomberg Businessweek* no4534 p60 Ag 14 2017

Warblers

Mapping Melodies B. TSUI *Audubon* v119 no1 p14 Spr 2017

Warblers—Research

Microtracker maps a rare bird's migration color *Science* v355 no6329 p998 Mr 10 2017

WARBURTON, JESSE

Moose Amour *Idaho Magazine* v17 no1 p24 Ja 2017

Warchus, Matthew, 1966-

ET TU, MURRAY? A. Carter cartoon *Esquire* v167 no2 p58 Mr 2017

Time After Time A. Green color *Vogue* v207 no4 p240 Ap 2017

Warcraft (Film)

WARCRAFT C. Gunnestad color *Sound & Vision* v82 no2 p69 F/Mr 2017

Ward, Aden

WORD EXCHANGE *Natural History* v125 no2 p9 F 2017

Ward, Amanda Eyre

WHAT'S GOING DOWN IN ROOM 312 *Texas Monthly* v45 no2 p52 F 2017

WARD, ANDY

starters bw color diag *Bon Appetit* v62 no2 p19 Mr 2017

Ward, Annie

THREE COMPONENTS TO READING SUCCESS: Guide readers from striving to thriving through reading volume color *Literacy Today (2411-7862)* v34 no6 p10 My/Je 2017

Ward, Aoife

Click chemistry enables preclinical evaluation of targeted epigenetic therapies diag *Science* v356 no6345 p1397 Je 30 2017

Ward, Bronagh

How Laws and Culture Hold Back Socially Minded Companies *Harvard Business Review Digital Articles* p2 My 18 2017

Ward, Carol

Beyond George Washington bw cartoon color *Magazine Antiques* v184 no1 p188 Ja/F 2017

Ward, Catriona

The Girl from Rawblood color *Publishers Weekly* v264 no2 p44 Ja 9 2017

Ward, Cefestia

All the Skeptic Ladies *Skeptical Inquirer* v41 no3 p66 My/Je 2017

WARD, CELESTIA

A History of Physics Worth Fifty-One Thousand Words *Skeptical Inquirer* v41 no5 p58 S/O 2017

Ward, David C.

Celebrate the Occasion M. J. GAYNOR and S. DALPHONSE *Washingtonian Magazine* v52 no4 p104 Ja 2017

WARD, DOUGLAS

A Global Assessment of Inland Wetland Conservation Status *BioScience* v67 no6 p523 Je 2017

Ward, Ed

Guitar Hero, Chicago Born J. JOHNSON color *Downbeat* v83 no12 p80 D 2016

Ward, Fay E.

Cowboy Chronicler B. Welch color *American Cowboy* v23 no5 p21 F/Mr 2017

Ward, Geoffrey C.

The War That Never Ends: Vietnam divided Americans 50 years ago. It continues to divide us today D. GREENBERG *New York*

Times Book Review p16 S 17 2017

Ward, George

Does Work Make You Happy? Evidence from the World Happiness Report *Harvard Business Review Digital Articles* p2 Mr 20 2017

Ward, Jared

Fleet Geek K. FOX color *Runner's World* v52 no4 p39 My 2017

Ward, Jay

THE CREATIVE GENIUSES BEHIND "CARS" D. Hakim color *Hot Rod* v70 no8 p42 Ag 2017

Ward, Jesmyn

AFTER THE FLOOD V. CUNNINGHAM cartoon *New Yorker* v93 no27 p69 S 11 2017

Catching Up to James Baldwin D. Pinckney color *New York Review of Books* v64 no9 p22 My 25 2017

DELISLE, MISSISSIPPI *Harper's Magazine* p32 O 2017

DREAD RECKONING color *O, The Oprah Magazine* p140 My 2017

Ghosts On the Bayou T. K. Smith *New York Times Book Review* p1 S 24 2017

Jesmyn Ward, Heir to Faulkner, Probes the Specter of Race In the South S. Begley color *Time* v190 no9 p58 S 4 2017

Jesmyn Ward *New York Times Book Review* p7 S 3 2017

Ward, Jesmyn—Interviews

HEARING VOICES M. Oatman color *Mother Jones* v42 no5 p59 S/O 2017

Ward, Jill

A Serious Pounding color *Bloomberg Businessweek* no4497 p17 O 31 2016

Ward, Joseph

Disciple for Dakota: Joseph Ward came to Yankton to spread Congregationalism, but he also built schools and helped create a state J. ANDREWS *South Dakota Magazine* v33 no2 p32 Jl/Ag 2017

Ward, Kay

ENEMY color *Christian Century* v134 no5 p20 Mr 1 2017

Ward, Ken

No Regrets *Earth Island Journal* v32 no2 p56 Summ 2017

Ward, Logan

Deep Cuts *Virginia Living* v15 no1 p54 D 2016

National Treasure *Washingtonian Magazine* v53 no1 p91 O 2017

Rediscovering Bogotá *Virginia Living* v15 no3 p62 Ap 2017

ROAD SHOWS: FOUR SCENIC DRIVES WHERE YOU CAN TAKE IN FALL LEAVES, SAMPLE WINES, EXPLORE HISTORY, AND GET A TASTE OF THE VALLEY *Washingtonian Magazine* v53 no1 p94 O 2017

SENSE OF PLACE: THREE TOWNS WHERE YOU CAN GET A TASTE OF THE VALLEY'S HISTORY, ARCHITECTURE, FOOD SCENE-AND PRIDE *Washingtonian Magazine* v53 no1 p98 O 2017

Ward, McLain

Facebook Feeds *In Stride* v12 no3 p19 My 2017

McLain Ward's Flawless World Cup Finish Was No Fluke T. Booker *In Stride* v12 no3 p16 My 2017

WARD, PETER L.

THE HEAT IS ON *USA Today Magazine* v145 no2862 p56 Mr 2017

Ward, Ray

Nicely Subversive *Skeptical Inquirer* v41 no5 p65 S/O 2017

Ward, Sela—Interviews

THE GOOD WIFE: She has our vote! Sela Ward makes a power play in the dramatic new season of Graves J. HALTERMAN *TV Guide* v65 no43 p16 O 16 2017

Ward, Susan

Business with a Cause K. F. Miller color *Practical Horseman* v45 no10 p72 O 2017

Ward, Terry

Back to The northern neck *Virginia Living* v15 no6 p74 O 2017

RETURN TO THE RIVER: Finding something new in a familiar place E. PARKHURST *Virginia Living* v15 no6 p11 O 2017

WARD, VICKY

The Money Pit: America's largest private home and the history of its inhabitants *New York Times Book Review* p21 O 15 2017

THE PLOT AGAINST AMERICA cartoon color *Esquire* v166 no5 p130 D 2016/Ja 2017

WARDAK, ARZO

Island Escape *Ms.* v27 no2 p24 Summ 2017

Wardeh, Amr H.

Genetic identification of familial hypercholesterolemia within a single U.S. health care system chart graph *Science* v354 no6319 paaf7000-1 D 23 2016

Wardell, Brandon

Hot Comedian Brandon Wardell B. HIATT color *Rolling Stone* no1274 p43 N 17 2016

Warden, Mellisa Davis

Little Horse, Big Heart L. Threlkeld color *Practical Horseman* v45 no5 p80 My 2017

Wardian, Mike—Interviews

Running Man Challenge C. Chavez and T. Keith color *Sports Illustrated* v126 no5 p20 F 13 2017

Wardle, David A.

Plant-soil feedback and the maintenance of diversity in Mediterranean-climate shrublands bibl graph *Science* v355 no6321 p1 Ja 13 2017

Wardle, Glenda M.

Publish openly but responsibly color *Science* v357 no6347 p141 Jl 14 2017

Wardle, Patrick

Report: Security hole in macOS Keychain puts passwords at risk R. LOYOLA color *Macworld - Digital Edition* v34 no11 p22 N 2017

Wardley, Duncan

The Pros and Cons of Competition Among Employees *Harvard Business Review Digital Articles* p2 Mr 20 2017

Wardrobes (Furniture)—Evaluation

FURNITURE color *Arts & Crafts Homes & the Revival* v12 no1 p24 2017 Resouce Guide

WARE, CHRIS

BUSINESS OR PLEASURE cartoon *New Yorker* v93 no16 p72 Je 5 2017

SNAPCHAT cartoon *New Yorker* v92 no37 p44 N 14 2016

Ware, Mark

IN THE WEEDS H. Wallace color *Vogue* v206 no12 p181 D 2016

Wareheim, Eric

Sex, Drugs, Comedy J. WEINER color *Rolling Stone* no1297 p17 O 5 2017

Warehouse design & construction

ADD A STORAGE BUILDING J. Cooper color *Cabin Living* p65 O 2017

Warehouse management

The Airbnb Of Warehousing S. Soper *Bloomberg Businessweek* no4523 p32 My 22 2017

Warehouses

See also

Self-service storage facilities

BeltLine BREWERS S. Henry *Atlanta* v56 no11 p114 Mr 2017

Yes!!! C. O'CONNELL *Texas Monthly* v45 no8 p48 Ag 2017

WARGAS, ROBERT

Charm Offensive bw *Weekly Standard* v22 no11 p39 N 21 2016

Wargo, Jennifer A.

Potential role of intratumor bacteria in mediating tumor resistance to the chemotherapeutic drug gemcitabine diag *Science* v357 no6356 p1156 S 15 2017

War—Government policy

Cheney Was Right E. EDELMAN and R. JOSEPH color *Weekly Standard* v23 no5 p27 O 9 2017

White House Divided P. J. Boyer color *Weekly Standard* v22 no47 p9 Ag 21 2017

Warheads

A botnet vaccine [Cover story] K. D. Atherton and R. Feltman color *Popular Science* v289 no6 p49 N/D 2017

THE MONTH IN REVIEW *Current History* v115 no784 p328 N 2016

Pakistani nuclear forces, 2016 H. M. Kristensen and R. S. Norris bibl chart *Bulletin of the Atomic Scientists* v72 no6 p368 N 2016

War—History

The Epidemiologic Challenge to the Conduct of Just War: Confronting Indirect Civilian Casualties of War P. H. Wise *Daedalus* v146 no1 p139 Wint 2017

ON THE TRAIL OF THE INDIANS color *MHQ: Quarterly Journal of Military History* v29 no4 p20 Summ 2017

What Comes Next A. Chayes and J. E. Nolan *Daedalus* v146 no1

p125 Wint 2017

Warhol, Andy, 1928-1987

Frank ANDREWS F. ANDREWS *Interview* v46 no10 p46 D 2016/Ja 2017

SELF-PORTRAIT A. KARNES *Texas Monthly* v44 no11 p101 N 2016

Self-Portrait (Fright Wig) bw *Art in America* v104 no10 p47 N 2016

WARING, GORDON T.

Google Haul Out: Earth Observation Imagery and Digital Aerial Surveys in Coastal Wildlife Management and Abundance Estimation *BioScience* v67 no8 p760 Ag 2017

Warinner, Christina

Ancient tales from teeth H. Thompson color *Science News* v192 no6 p18 O 14 2017

War—International cooperation

Why We Need Cyberwar Rules of Engagement Now L. Bershidsky *Bloomberg Businessweek* no4531 p40 Jl 24 2017

War—Iraq

GOODBYE MY BROTHER E. ACKERMAN color map *Esquire* p84 Ap 2017

REMAINS OF THE DAY C. Wolf *Harper's Magazine* v334 no2002 p11 Mr 2017

War—Law & legislation

THE BLOODY CODE J. A. Haymond *MHQ: Quarterly Journal of Military History* v29 no2 p14 Wint 2017

War—Law & legislation—History

Rebellion, War Aims & the Laws of War T. M. Fazal *Daedalus* v146 no1 p71 Wint 2017

Warmbier, Otto F., 1994-2017

Otto Warmbier N. Jenkins color *Time* v190 no1 p13 Jl 3 2017

Warmup

5 WAYS... To Warm Up L. McGLASHAN color *Muscle & Performance* v9 no9 p66 S 2017

Capturing your BEST FIRST Arabesque H. FOSTER *Dance Magazine* p8 2016/2017

CONFESSIONS OF A FITNESS EDITOR color *Women's Health* v14 no2 p132 Mr 2017

REACH FOR MORE A. Ippoliti color *Yoga Journal* p38 2017 Special Issue

SHOW-JUMPING WARM-UP STRATEGIES THAT WORK S. Taylor color *Practical Horseman* v45 no2 p50 F 2017

THIS IS YOUR BODY ON CYCLING A. C. SHILTON cartoon color *Bicycling* v58 no1 p17 Ja/F 2017

To Fast or To Feed? B. BRAZIER color *Muscle & Performance* v9 no9 p64 S 2017

Warnecke, Lauren

54 GREAT THINGS TO DO THIS MONTH color *Chicago* v66 no1 p117 Ja 2017

58 GREAT THINGS TO DO THIS MONTH color *Chicago* v66 no2 p101 F 2017

63 GREAT THINGS TO DO THIS MONTH color *Chicago* v66 no8 p105 Ag 2017

65 GREAT THINGS TO DO THIS MONTH color *Chicago* v65 no11 p115 N 2016

66 GREAT THINGS TO DO THIS MONTH color *Chicago* v66 no9 p139 S 2017

67 GREAT THINGS TO DO THIS MONTH color *Chicago* v66 no3 p129 Mr 2017

68 GREAT THINGS TO DO THIS MONTH color *Chicago* v66 no5 p119 My 2017

GO: 69 GREAT THINGS TO DO THIS MONTH color *Chicago* v66 no11 p103 N 2017

GO bw color *Chicago* v66 no10 p105 O 2017

GO color *Chicago* v65 no12 p119 D 2016

GO color *Chicago* v66 no4 p113 Ap 2017

John Neumeier: Hamburg Ballet's artistic director brings his work back to the Midwest *Dance Magazine* v91 no9 p22 S 2017

KINETIC CLUTTER color *Chicago* v66 no3 p52 Mr 2017

Training Wheels *Dance Magazine* v91 no8 p14 Ag 2017

Warner, Bernhard

INVASION OF THE PUNKS color *Fortune* v174 no8 p176 D 15 2016

WARNER, BROOKE

HEAD OF THE HOUSE A. GROSS bw color *Publishers Weekly* v264 no18 p22 My 1 2017

Slaying the Green-Eyed Monster color *Publishers Weekly* v264 no17 p41 Ap 24 2017

Tapping into TED *Publishers Weekly* v264 no35 p64 Ag 28 2017

Warner, Bruce E.

Breakthroughs Advance U.S. Competitiveness *Science & Technology Review* p3 Ja/F 2017

Warner, Chloe

#2: In California, decorator Chloe Warner transforms a modernist glass box into a family house that is both beautiful and kid-proof. All it takes is pattern-andcolor confidence—and 200 yards of sheer pink fabric D. A. KEEPS color *House Beautiful* v159 no2 p90 Mr 2017

Warner, Gary A.

COLLEGE TOWN SMACKDOWN color *Sunset* v239 no3 p28 S 2017

RODEO A-GO-GO color *Sunset* v239 no1 p38 Jl 2017

Warner, Harold

Blow-Up Bomb Shelter E. BOODMAN bw color *Discover* v27 no10 p16 D 2016

Warner, Jack L., 1892-1978

BOGIE'S DARK SIDE *Saturday Evening Post* v289 no3 p93 My/Je 2017

Warner, Jeroen

The Relevance of Soft Infrastructure in Disaster Management and Risk Reduction *UN Chronicle* v53 no3 p20 2016

WARNER, JOEL

A BUD-TO-BLUNT PATH TO LEGAL WEED chart color *Wired* v25 no3 p24 Mr 2017

Warner, John J.

How Our Community Designed a Better Hospital *Harvard Business Review Digital Articles* p2 D 7 2015

Warner, Kade

FACES IN THE CROWD T. Keith color *Sports Illustrated* v125 no13 p20 O 17 2016

WARNER, LINDSAY

The Great North color *Backpacker* p13 O 2017

WARNER, LIZ

Student Success Built on a Positive School Climate *Education Digest* v82 no7 p10 Mr 2017

Warner, Marina

Legends of the Fall [Cover story] bw color *New York Review of Books* v64 no14 p22 S 28 2017

Otherworldly Ties *New York Times Book Review* p10 My 7 2017

Warner, Mark R., 1954-

DAN ABOUT TOWN D. Swartz *Washingtonian Magazine* v52 no9 p30 Je 2017

DAN ABOUT TOWN *Washingtonian Magazine* v52 no6 p26 Mr 2017

Warner, Meredith

SOLDIERING ON M. HILL color *Louisiana Life* v37 no4 p112 Mr/Ap 2017

Warner, Todd

3 Reasons Why Talent Management Isn't Working Anymore *Harvard Business Review Digital Articles* p2 Jl 5 2016

Overcome Resistance to Change by Enlisting the Right People *Harvard Business Review Digital Articles* p2 S 13 2016

To Address Gender Bias at Your Company, Start with Teams color *Harvard Business Review Digital Articles* p2 Ja 27 2017

What Separates High- Performing Leaders from Average Ones *Harvard Business Review Digital Articles* p2 N 11 2015

Warner, Tom

A FAIRY TALE L. MURTHA color *Cincinnati Magazine* v51 no1 p30 O 2017

Warner Theatre (Washington, D.C.)

DAN ABOUT TOWN *Washingtonian Magazine* v52 no4 p28 Ja 2017

Warnick, Garrett, 1994-

CHAMPERY, SWITZERLAND A. Povich color *Snowboarder* v29 no5 p86 Ja 2017

Warning labels

Consumer Warning Labels Aren't Working L. A. Robinson, W. K. Viscusi et al *Harvard Business Review Digital Articles* p2 N 30 2016

War on Terrorism, 2001-2009

OUR WARLORDS IN AFGHANISTAN M. JEONG *In These Times* v41 no10 p28 O 2017

Warp (Music)

JON BALKE J. Ephland bw *Downbeat* v84 no4 p24 Ap 2017

Warraich, Haider

Modern Death: How Medicine Changed the End of Life *Publishers Weekly* v263 no50 p61 D 5 2016

Warrants (Law)

Dispatching with track warrants J. Dziedzic chart *Model Railroader* v84 no8 p65 Ag 2017

Warranty—Evaluation

Everything you need to know about Apple's extended warranty program S. OCHS color *Macworld - Digital Edition* v34 no11 p10 N 2017

Warren, Anita

How Amazon Adapted Its Business Model to India *Harvard Business Review Digital Articles* p2 Jl 20 2016

Warren, Bill

FROM OUR READERS *Sky & Telescope* v134 no6 p6 D 2017

Warren, Bonnie

DOCTOR'S ORDER color *New Orleans Magazine* v51 no1 p60 N 2016

GLITZ ON THE RITZ color *New Orleans Magazine* v51 no2 p58 D 2016

Looking Sharpe color *New Orleans Magazine* v51 no4 p54 F 2017

PEACEFUL GRANDEUR color *New Orleans Magazine* v51 no3 p52 Ja 2017

A Study in Good Taste color *New Orleans Magazine* v51 no5 p56 Mr 2017

Warren, David B.

Lone star bw cartoon *Magazine Antiques* v184 no1 p160 Ja/F 2017

Warren, Elizabeth, 1949-

All That's Left P. KRUGMAN *New York Times Book Review* p12 My 7 2017

For the Record color *Time* v189 no6 p8 F 20 2017

Milestones *Ms.* v27 no1 p5 Spr 2017

Trump vs. Warren A. ZAITCHIK color *New Republic* v248 no4 p12 Ap 2017

Warren, Elizabeth, 1949—Interviews

Elizabeth Warren S. Frizell color *Time* v189 no21 p68 Je 5 2017

Warren, Elizabeth, 1949—Political & social views

For the Record color *Time* v188 no19 p6 N 7 2016

Nevertheless, She Persisted M. Halpin color *Glamour* v115 no5 p162 My 2017

Warren, Emily

WHO'S THAT GIRL? N. Feeney color *Entertainment Weekly* no1465 p54 My 12 2017

WARREN, GENE

Chatter *Indianapolis Monthly* v12 no40 p11 Ag 2017

WARREN, JAMES

TWO RIVALS, ONE TRUTH bw color *Vanity Fair* v59 no9 p210 S 2017

Warren, Jim

THE ACTOR'S LIFE: Behind the scenes at Staunton's American Shakespeare Center E. J. WALLACE *Virginia Living* v15 no6 p31 O 2017

Warren, Kelcy, 1955-

THE BALLAD OF KELCY WARREN J. H. Richardson cartoon *Mother Jones* v42 no2 p12 Mr/Ap 2017

Warren, Lynne

NATURE'S WITNESSES bw color *National Wildlife (World Edition)* v55 no1 p20 D/Ja 2016

Notorious—or Not? Reeking reputation aside, skunks are full of surprises, as science is showing color *National Wildlife (World Edition)* v55 no3 p40 Ap/My 2017

Out of Time? color *National Wildlife (World Edition)* v55 no6 p40 O/N 2017

WARREN, MARK

THE PARTY PLANNERS bw color diag map *Popular Mechanics* p82 Ap 2017

Warren, Mark E.

Authoritarian Deliberation in China *Daedalus* v146 no3 p155 Summ 2017

Warren, Michael

The Adult in the Room color *Weekly Standard* v22 no26 p12 Mr 13 2017

'Decius' Comes in from the Cold *Weekly Standard* v22 no22 p11 F 13 2017

'Extremely Unfair' color *Weekly Standard* v22 no44 p12 Jl 31 2017

The Firing That Misfired color *Weekly Standard* v22 no35 p10 My 22 2017

Getting to No color *Weekly Standard* v23 no6 p24 O 16 2017

He Still Hasn't Torn It Up color *Weekly Standard* v22 no43 p9 Jl 24 2017

It's Mueller Time [Cover story] color *Weekly Standard* v22 no36 p18 My 29 2017

A Memo-rable Hearing color *Weekly Standard* v22 no39 p10 Je 19 2017

Not so Blue-grass color *Weekly Standard* v22 no13 p14 D 5 2016

Obamacare color *Weekly Standard* v22 no15 p14 D 19 2016

Resisting Trump's Voter Fraud Inquiry color *Weekly Standard* v22 no42 p10 Jl 17 2017

The Voice in His Ear color *Weekly Standard* v22 no34 p20 My 15 2017

Warren, Morgan
COMMENT color *Canadian Geographic* v137 no1 p72 F 2017

WARREN, NATALIE
CLOSE TO HOME color *Canoe & Kayak Magazine* v45 no1 p36 Wint 2017

Warren, Rachel Meltzer
The Cereal Aisle chart color *Men's Health* v32 no5 p78 Je 2017

Eat Smarter, Eat Healthier [Cover story] color *Consumer Reports* v82 no11 p18 N 2017

Faster, Fresher, Cheaper chart color il *Consumer Reports* v82 no7 p30 Jl 2017

GET PUMPED color *Women's Health* v14 no4 p108 My 2017

Get the Party Started! color *Consumer Reports* v82 no1 p9 Ja 2017

The New Super Bowls chart color *Consumer Reports* v82 no10 p42 O 2017

A New Twist on Pasta chart color *Consumer Reports* v82 no5 p14 My 2017

WARREN, RICH
HUMORISTS ON HUMOR: CRACKING THE CODE ON WHAT CRACKS US UP *Saturday Evening Post* v289 no5 p38 S/O 2017

Warren, Rita
THE JESUS LADY *Washingtonian Magazine* v52 no12 p70 S 2017

WARREN, TISH HARRISON
The Privilege Enforcers color *Christianity Today* p72 Ap 2017

Warren, Wesley C.
The genomic landscape of rapid repeated evolutionary adaptation to toxic pollution in wild fish bibl graph *Science* v354 no6317 p1305 D 9 2016

Warren Easton Charter High School (New Orleans, La.)
Alexina Medley D. R. WILSON *New Orleans Magazine* v52 no1 p38 S 2017

Warrick, Phil
Get it right the first time! chart color *Phi Delta Kappan* v98 no6 p58 Mr 2017

Warsh, Jonathan
Getting Bundled Payments Right in Health Care *Harvard Business Review Digital Articles* p2 O 19 2015

Warshaw, Matt
1968 PETER TROY bw *Surfer* v57 no11 p30 D 2016

California's Lost Bliss color *Surfer* v57 no13 p52 Mr 2017

The Challenge from Down Under color *Surfer* v58 no4 p38 Ag 2017

Forgotten Island Of Santosha bw color *Surfer* v58 no2 p30 My 2017

For the Record T. PRODANOVICH color *Surfer* v58 no5 p46 S 2017

Time Capsule bw color *Surfer* v58 no1 p30 Ap 2017

TOM MOREY 1971 cartoon *Surfer* v57 no12 p36 Ja/F 2017

Warships
See also
Aircraft carriers

Warships-Exhibitions
BOATASHORE G. FREKING *Cincinnati Magazine* v50 no3 p32 D 2016

Warthog
True north? color *National Wildlife (World Edition)* v55 no2 p8 F/Mr 2017

Wartman, Lukas
SURVIVING THE CURE J. Cohen color diag *Science* v357 no6347 p122 Jl 14 2017

Warts
Problem Solved: Warts R. LALIBERTE *Prevention* v69 no11 p20 N 2017

WARTZMAN, EMMA
Bull City color *Bon Appetit* no11 p74 N 2017

ШЕЛСОМɘ TO CUTLЄT COUИTRЧ color *Bon Appetit* p124 S 2017

r.s.v.p.: BEST NEW RESTAURANTS EDITION bw color *Bon Appetit* p16 S 2017

Simple Pleasures color *Bon Appetit* no8 p22 Ag 2017

starters color *Bon Appetit* p25 S 2017

starters color *Bon Appetit* v62 no6 p17 Je 2017

Thanksgiving LESSONS [Cover story] color *Bon Appetit* no11 p82 N 2017

VEG OUT color *Bon Appetit* no1 p64 F 2017

Wartzman, Rick
What Business Can Learn from Government *Harvard Business Review Digital Articles* p2 Ja 12 2015

What Peter Drucker Had to Say About Automation *Harvard Business Review Digital Articles* p2 N 2 2015

What Peter Drucker Knew About 2020 *Harvard Business Review Digital Articles* p2 O 16 2014

Warwick, Genevieve
Seeing Renaissance Art Anew *History Today* v67 no2 p61 F 2017

Wasden, Becky
OH, SHUCKS! M. HILL color *Louisiana Life* v37 no2 p104 N/D 2016

WASEF, BASEM
BEST PORSCHE of the Year bw color *Esquire* v166 no4 p75 N 2016

Washburn, Nathan T.
The Decline of the Rural American Hospital and How to Reverse It *Harvard Business Review Digital Articles* p2 Ja 30 2015

Followers Don't See Their Leaders as Real People color *Harvard Business Review Digital Articles* p2 Ja 23 2017

Make Sure Your Employees Have Good Things to Say About You Behind Your Back *Harvard Business Review Digital Articles* p2 S 22 2016

Washchyshyn, Marika
The New Queen Bee color *Golf Magazine* v59 no10 p21 O 2017

Under Pressure color *Golf Magazine* v59 no7 p25 Jl 2017

Washing machines—Evaluation
Can Your Washing Machine Work Harder? K. Janeway chart color il *Consumer Reports* v82 no10 p14 O 2017

DO I NEED A SMART... S. Franke, C. Forté et al color *Popular Mechanics* p76 My 2017

Dynamic Duos K. Janeway chart color graph *Consumer Reports* v82 no8 p12 Ag 2017

Washington & Lee University
BEST BANG FOR THE BUCK SOUTHEAST COLLEGES chart *Washington Monthly* v49 no9/10 p54 S/O 2017

LIBERAL ARTS COLLEGES chart *Washington Monthly* v49 no9/10 p96 S/O 2017

Washington (D.C.)
BINDAAS A. Limpert *Washingtonian Magazine* v52 no2 p255 N 2016

HELLO, AMERICAN J. Green and Z. Mider color *Bloomberg Businessweek* no4503 p50 D 12 2016

IN DEFENSE OF 2016 B. Freed *Washingtonian Magazine* v52 no3 p13 D 2016

THE NEW RETIREMENT AGE S. Sataline *Washingtonian Magazine* v52 no3 p109 D 2016

Outposts of Rationality P. A. Harkness *Governing* v30 no6 p16 Mr 2017

SEASON TICKETS R. Cooper *Washingtonian Magazine* v52 no3 p96 D 2016

SMALL WONDERS *Washingtonian Magazine* v52 no6 p153 Mr 2017

SOUTH'S BEST MUSEUM V. Gregory color *Southern Living* v52 no4 p84 Ap 2017

The Suite of Power [Cover story] A. Altman, T. Berenson et al color *Time* v189 no23 p22 Je 19 2017

Where Does Ben Franklin Go Furthest? *New York Times Upfront*

v149 no3 p5 O 10 2016
Why D.C.'s Missing Children Became a Political Rallying Cry M.
Rhodan color *Time* v189 no13 p17 Ap 10 2017
Washington (D.C.). Court of Appeals
A Setback for Free Speech *National Review* v69 no1 p12 Ja 23
2017
Washington (D.C.)—Description & travel
6 WEIRD WINTER SITES AROUND WASHINGTON M. Blitz
Washingtonian Magazine v52 no4 p18 Ja 2017
ANYTIME GETAWAY S. SHIBATA *Sea Magazine* v109 no2
pPNW-1 F 2017
BEST OF WASHINGTON *Washingtonian Magazine* v52 no9 p80
Je 2017
LOGAN CIRCLE AND SHAW *Washingtonian Magazine* v52
no5 p151 F 2017
THE MORE THINGS CHANGE... D. HISLOP *Sea Magazine*
v109 no2 pPNW-6 F 2017
Too Cool to Fail: Why Trump Can't Kill D.C.'s Mojo M. BYRNE
color *GQ: Gentlemen's Quarterly* v97 no4 p52 Ap 2017
Washington, D.C M. Rosano color *Canadian Geographic* v137
p20 2017 Travel
What to Do and See in DC *New York* v50 no17 p147 Ag 21 2017
Washington (D.C.)—History
BEST & WORST OF WASHINGTON K. OLSEN *Washingtonian
Magazine* v52 no9 p12 Je 2017
IS DC BECOMING THE GAY CAPITAL OF AMERICA? K.
OLSEN *Washingtonian Magazine* v53 no1 p10 O 2017
RED STARE E. CARTER *Washingtonian Magazine* v52 no3 p22
D 2016
Washington (D.C.)—Maps
RED STARE E. CARTER *Washingtonian Magazine* v52 no3 p22
D 2016
Washington (D.C.)—Politics & government
RON FOURNIER A. Beaujon *Washingtonian Magazine* v52 no1
p43 O 2016
Washington (D.C.)—Residents
Ng *Washingtonian Magazine* v52 no4 p74 Ja 2017
WASHINGTONIANS OF THE YEAR L. MILK *Washingtonian
Magazine* v52 no4 p54 Ja 2017
Welcome to Washington PRESIDENT TRUMP *Washingtonian
Magazine* v52 no4 p92 Ja 2017
Washington (State)—Description & travel
A COMMUNITY EFFORT D. HISLOP *Sea Magazine* v109 no1
pPNW-14 Ja 2017
FIRE AND ICE D. HISLOP *Sea Magazine* v108 no12 pPNW-1
D 2016
NEAH BAY *Sea Magazine* v108 no12 pPNW-8 D 2016
SOUND BOUND D. Hislop *Sea Magazine* v108 no12 p18 D 2016
WASHINGTON N. Walker color map *Canadian Geographic*
v135 no6 p26 D 2015
WILDLIFE ADVENTURES AT EAGLE HARBOR:FIND AN
UNTOUCHED ISLAND THAT IS A HIKER'S PARADISE D.
HISLOP *Sea Magazine* v109 no5 pPNW-1 My 2017
Washington (State)—Politics & government—1951
A Strategy for Conflict M. Funkhouser *Governing* v30 no4 p4 Ja
2017
WASHINGTON, C. J.
DESIGNATED RIDES color *Ebony* v72 no11 p91 S 2017
Washington, Denzel, 1954-
FENCES N. Sperling color *Entertainment Weekly* no1438 p42 N
4 2016
GIVING US LIFE I. ARCHER color *Film Comment* v53 no1 p32
Ja/F 2017
LUKE GRIMES B. COOPER *Interview* v46 no8 p108 O 2016
Shallow Fences J. PODHORETZ *Weekly Standard* v22 no20 p39
Ja 30 2017
THE TIES THAT BIND [Cover story] R. R. Robertson color *Es-
sence* v47 no8 p94 D 2016
Washington, Denzel, 1954——Awards
OSCARS TURNED UPSIDE DOWN N. Sperling color *Enter-
tainment Weekly* no1453 p13 F 17 2017
Washington, Eldredge E.
Minding Our Business L. d. JOHNSON color *Ebony* v72 no3
p108 D 2016/Ja 2017
Washington, George, 1732-1799
Building a Nation M. Fabry *Time* v189 no13 p24 Ap 10 2017

Curious About George J. SHATWELL *Yankee* v81 no1 p111 Ja/F
2017
LAST GASPS B. Hogan *MHQ: Quarterly Journal of Military
History* v29 no2 p20 Wint 2017
THE PLOT TO KIDNAP WASHINGTON [Cover story] C. Mc-
Burney color map *MHQ: Quarterly Journal of Military History*
v29 no4 p30 Summ 2017
Presidents of the United States *New York Times Upfront* v149 no7
p25 Ja 9 2017
WASHINGTON, KAMASI
The Year in Reading [Cover story] *New York Times Book Review*
p8 D 25 2016
Washington, Kamasi, 1981-
Kamasi Turns Bay Residency into Party Y. Kato color *Downbeat*
v84 no3 p20 Mr 2017
Washington, Karen
Love Story, With Lettuce color *AARP: The Magazine* v60 no4A
p59 Je/Jl 2017
Washington, Kerry, 1977-
Artists color *Time* v189 no16/17 p40 My 1-8 2017
CAUSE & EFFECT D. Gluck color *InStyle* v24 no2 p52 F 2017
Confirmation M. ROUSH *TV Guide* v64 no15 p20 Ap 4 2016
A DIFFERENT DIRECTION T. A. Christian color *Essence* v48
no3 p51 Jl 2017
In Check E. Wilson color *InStyle* v24 no9 p178 S 2017
Justice M. LOGAN *TV Guide* v64 no15 p40 Ap 4 2016
Kerry Washington color *InStyle* v24 no5 p150 My 2017
SCANDAL L. Rice color *Entertainment Weekly* no1448 p40 Ja
13 2017
Scandal M. Logan *TV Guide* v65 no14 p39 Ap 3 2017
SCANDAL N. Abrams color *Entertainment Weekly* no1477 p30
Ag 11 2017
This Is Our Time A. Behm and E. Krapcha color *Glamour* v115
no7 p14 Jl 2017
Washington, Kerry, 1977-——Interviews
Kerry's Got This [Cover story] P. Mendoza color *Glamour* v115
no5 p156 My 2017
Washington Ballet (Company)
FROM BARRE TO BOSS A. Whiting *Washingtonian Magazine*
v52 no6 p16 Mr 2017
Washington Capitals (Hockey team)
WHO CAN END THE PENGUINS' REIGN? J. Fuchs color
Sports Illustrated v127 no11 p43 O 9 2017
Washington Cathedral
AFTER SHOCK B. FREED *Washingtonian Magazine* v52 no1
p28 O 2016
NAVE-GAZING K. OLSEN color *Washingtonian Magazine* v52
no7 p24 Ap 2017
People C. Kennel-Shank color *Christian Century* v133 no21 p19
O 12 2016
Washington County (Me.)
A PLACE TO GET AWAY W. CURTIS and W. L. Duncan color
Yankee p92 My/Je 2017
Washington Dulles International Airport
A BRILLIANT PROPOSAL TO SOLVE OUR AIRPORT PROB-
LEMS A. WHITING *Washingtonian Magazine* v52 no2 p12 N
2016
Destination: The Airports C. Cunningham, M. J. Gaynor et al
Washingtonian Magazine v52 no2 p80 N 2016
How I Spent 24 Hours at Dulles M. J. Gaynor *Washingtonian
Magazine* v52 no2 p87 N 2016
Washington Metropolitan Area Transit Authority
The D.C. Subway System Banned These Ads C. J. CIARAMEL-
LA color *Reason* v49 no6 p54 N 2017
Washington Nationals (Baseball team)
1 NATIONALS color *Sports Illustrated* v126 no9 p94 Mr 27 2017
WHOLE NEW BALL GAME T. Wendel *Washingtonian Maga-
zine* v52 no5 p125 F 2017
Washington Post (Newspaper)
Democracy's Eulogists *Weekly Standard* v22 no25 p3 Mr 6 2017
Don't Cry for Me, Paparazzi color *Weekly Standard* v22 no30 p2
Ap 10 2017
MY HOMETOWN PAPER: Lauren Williams L. Williams color
Columbia Journalism Review v56 no1 p46 Spr 2017
Robots Wrote This Story J. Keohane cartoon *Wired* v25 no3 p62
Mr 2017

Trumpoplectic Tees color *Weekly Standard* v22 no28 p4 Mr 27 2017

TWO RIVALS, ONE TRUTH J. WARREN bw color *Vanity Fair* v59 no9 p210 S 2017

WaPo Spun Scoop to Shelter Sessions J. Naureckas *Extra!* v30 no3 p4 Ap 2017

Washington Redskins (Football team)

4 Washington Redskins color *Sports Illustrated* v127 no7 p90 S 4 2017

Washington State University—Sports

22 Washington State color *Sports Illustrated* v127 no5 p111 Ag 14 2017

Washington Wizards (Basketball team)

3 WIZARDS color *Sports Illustrated* v127 no12 p59 O 16 2017

8 Wizards R. Mahoney, B. Golliver et al color *Sports Illustrated* v125 no14 p82 O 24-31 2016

Washingtonian (Periodical)

FREAKY FANTASTIC GEORGETOWN K. OLSEN *Washingtonian Magazine* v52 no11 p10 Ag 2017

Washington Monument (Washington, D.C.)

First Drafts of History B. SPECKTOR bw *Reader's Digest* v190 no1132 p130 Jl/Ag 2017

FOGGY BOTTOM A. WHITING *Washingtonian Magazine* v52 no6 p24 Mr 2017

Washington Senators (Baseball team : 1886-1960)

THE MISFITS OF SUMMER F. J. FROMMER *Washingtonian Magazine* v52 no8 p70 My 2017

WASIK, JOHN F.

9 Upgrades That Pay You Back color *AARP: The Magazine* v59 no3A p21 Ap/My 2016

Waskul, Michele

What Ghosts Mean B. RADFORD *Skeptical Inquirer* v41 no2 p62 Mr/Ap 2017

Wasley, Paula

Back When Everyone Knew How You Voted *Humanities* v37 no4 p1 Fall 2016

Chicken Soup and Other Remedies *Humanities* v37 no4 p1 Fall 2016

Prison University Project *Humanities* v37 no4 p1 Fall 2016

WASLIN, MICHELE

Should Birthright Citizenship Be Abolished? *New York Times Upfront* v149 no3 p22 O 10 2016

Wasps

One Sting Too Many J. MAPES *USA Today Magazine* v145 no2858 p37 N 2016

WATCH OUT FOR WASPS C. Barakat and M. Freckleton color *Equus* no481 p20 O 2017

Wasps—Behavior—Research

Wasps are experts at crypt escape S. Milius color *Science News* v191 no6 p4 Ap 1 2017

WASSER, LEAH A.

Skills and Knowledge for Data-Intensive Environmental Research *BioScience* v67 no6 p546 Je 2017

Wasser, Sam

The Elephant Detective E. KOLBERT *Smithsonian* v47 no9 p29 Ja/F 2017

Wasser, Samantha

This Old Boardinghouse: A once-abandoned Boerum Hill building got stripped down to its bones and built back up again W. GOODMAN img *New York* v50 no13 p63 Je 26 2017

WASSERMAN, ADAM

His Dark Materials *Opera News* v81 no7 p14 Ja 2017

Luminous *Opera News* v81 no9 p28 Mr 2017

Pale Caesar *Opera News* v81 no5 p54 N 2016

Room for Interpretation *Opera News* v81 no6 p22 D 2016

Wasserman, Debra

NOTE FROM THE COORDINATORS. 35 YEARS OF VEGAN ACTIVISM BY THE VEGETARIAN RESOURCE GROUP *Vegetarian Journal* v36 no3 p4 2017

NOTE FROM THE COORDINATORS. VEGAN TAKES VOWS *Vegetarian Journal* v35 no4 p4 2016

Nutritional Yeast Dishes *Vegetarian Journal* v36 no3 p13 2017

PETA'S VEGAN COLLEGE COOKBOOK *Vegetarian Journal* v36 no2 p31 2017

reviews. CROSSROADS *Vegetarian Journal* v35 no4 p30 2016

reviews. EATING EARTH *Vegetarian Journal* v35 no4 p30 2016

VEGETARIAN DIETS AND WATER *Vegetarian Journal* v36 no2 p4 2017

Wasserman, Harvey

The Last Energy War: King CONG vs. Solartopia cartoon *Progressive* p50 D 2016/Ja 2017

The Unstoppable Green Power Revolution cartoon color *Progressive* v81 no5 p40 Je/Jl 2017

Wasserman, Lee

The Rockefeller Family Fund Takes on ExxonMobil color *New York Review of Books* v63 no20 p60 D 22 2016

The Rockefeller Family Fund vs. Exxon color *New York Review of Books* v63 no19 p31 D 8 2016

Wasserman, Noam

The Very First Mistake Most Startup Founders Make *Harvard Business Review Digital Articles* p2 F 23 2016

Wasserrnan, Debra

THE FUTURE OF VEGANISM *Vegetarian Journal* v36 no1 p4 2017

NOTE FROM THE COORDINATORS. NATURAL FOODS: UPSCALE OR DOWNSCALE? MANY ROLES FOR PROMOTING VEGANISM *Vegetarian Journal* v35 no2 p4 2016

reviews. STREET VEGAN *Vegetarian Journal* v35 no1 p31 2016

WASSERSTROM, JEFFREY

CHAPTERS IN CHINA'S LONG HISTORY J. Altehenger *History Today* v67 no5 p104 My 2017

Success Finds the Ex *New York Times Book Review* p38 N 13 2016

Xi Jinping's Authoritarianism Does a Disservice to China's Nuanced Political Tradition *NPQ: New Perspectives Quarterly* v33 no4 p15 O 2016

Wasson, Erik

In Congress, It's Do-or-Die Time for the GOP cartoon *Bloomberg Businessweek* no4530 p39 Jl 17 2017

Politics/Policy color *Bloomberg Businessweek* no4505 p27 D 26 2016

When The Vice President Is Not a Political Prop color *Bloomberg Businessweek* no4535 p34 Ag 28 2017

Wasta, Michael J.

PLCs on steroids Moving teacher practice to the center of data teams chart il *Phi Delta Kappan* v98 no5 p67 F 2017

Waste (Economics)

A BLOOD-SOAKED MONEY-WASTING SCANDAL color *Forbes* v199 no5 p15 My 16 2017

How the U.S. Can Reduce Waste in Health Care Spending by $1 Trillion N. Sahni, A. Chigurupati et al *Harvard Business Review Digital Articles* p2 O 13 2015

Waste disposal in the ocean

GARBAGE SWELL C. Zuckerman color *National Geographic* v231 no4 p14 Ap 2017

Waste lands

GM STAMPING PLANT R. Annis, S. Bahr et al color map *Indianapolis Monthly* v41 no2 p75 S 2017

Waste management

See also

Electronic waste

Electronic waste disposal

Recycling (Waste, etc.)

Wastewater treatment

13 Things Garbage Collectors Want You to Know M. CROUCH color *Reader's Digest* v190 no1134 p128 O 2017

Cleanup of Cold War nuclear waste drags on: Despite billions of dollars spent preparing to treat and stabilize liquid radioactive wastes, cleaning out leaking tanks at the former nuclear production site in Hanford, Washington, will take decades more D. Kramer *Physics Today* v70 no7 p28 Jl 2017

GARBAGE MEN C. Webber color *Backpacker* v45 no1 p63 Ja 2017

Lost and Found M. SIMMS color *O, The Oprah Magazine* p21 Ja 2017

NAHMS SNAPSHOT: HOW WE MANAGE MANURE C. Barakat and M. McCluskey chart color *Equus* no477 p20 Je 2017

That's Outrageous! cartoon *Reader's Digest* v190 no1134 p117 O 2017

The Truth About Our Trash L. SCHLEY color graph *Discover* v38 no9 p18 N 2017

Waste management—California

THE WORST OF TINES J. LUNA color *Mother Jones* v42 no4

Water reuse
the water (re)cycle S. Chodosh diag *Popular Science* v289 no2 p14 Mr/Ap 2017

Water salinization
How Salt Chlorination Systems Work S. Pearce *Parks & Recreation* p4 Aquatics Guide 2017

Water security
Water and food security in a changing world Brian I.6Baker *Monthly Labor Review* p1 Mr 2017

Water shortages
THE AQUANAUTS S. FECHT cartoon *Popular Science* v289 no2 p47 Mr/Ap 2017

Flint: a day by the bottle R. Feltman color *Popular Science* v289 no2 p11 Mr/Ap 2017

HIGH AND DRY L. KAUFMAN color *Popular Science* v289 no2 p36 Mr/Ap 2017

KING OF THRONES S. Chodosh color *Popular Science* v289 no2 p33 Mr/Ap 2017

la's far-ranging roots A. Schellenbaum map *Popular Science* v289 no2 p17 Mr/Ap 2017

LIFE IS THIRSTY J. Brown *Popular Science* v289 no2 p6 Mr/Ap 2017

PARCHED S. SCOLES color *Popular Science* v289 no2 p58 Mr/Ap 2017

Solving the Twin Crises of Energy and Water Scarcity K. Moss and D. Frodl *Harvard Business Review Digital Articles* p2 Ja 25 2016

stressed out: gauging global water worries M. B. Griggs map *Popular Science* v289 no2 p8 Mr/Ap 2017

Water skiing
WATERSPORTS HOTSPOTS Z. BILAS color *Boating World* v38 no7 p46 Jl 2017

Water supply
See also
Water use
The Bison Deep Well Hand Pump S. Maxwell *Mother Earth News* no280 p78 F/Mr 2017

Digging Deeper B. Jo Lieberman color diag *Equus* no478 p60 Jl 2017

Eutrophication will increase during the 21st century as a result of precipitation changes E. Sinha, A. M. Michalak et al map *Science* v357 no6349 p405 Jl 28 2017

Pipe Dreams B. LUTZ color *New Orleans Magazine* v51 no12 p42 O 2017

Pitch the Perfect Camp color *Backpacker* p33 My 2017

Precipitation drives global variation in natural selection A. M. Siepielski, M. B. Morrissey et al bibl chart diag map *Science* v355 no6328 p959 Mr 3 2017

Tuba City Water Tower N. AUSTIN *Arizona Highways* v92 no11 p6 N 2016

WATER COLLECTIVE N. Strochlic color *National Geographic* v231 no4 p24 Ap 2017

Water supply management
Protecting water resources calls for international efforts A. Q. Hoy color *Science* v356 no6340 p814 My 26 2017

Water supply—Bolivia
HIGH AND DRY L. KAUFMAN color *Popular Science* v289 no2 p36 Mr/Ap 2017

Water supply—California
California's Stressed Water System: A Primer J. Null *Weatherwise* v70 no1 p12 Ja/F 2017

From the Editor M. Benner Smidt *Weatherwise* v70 no1 p4 Ja/F 2017

la's far-ranging roots A. Schellenbaum map *Popular Science* v289 no2 p17 Mr/Ap 2017

Water supply—China
How China Could Weaponize Water T. John color *Time* v190 no13 p14 O 2 2017

Water supply—Equipment & supplies
UNDER PRESSURE C. Iozzio color *Popular Science* v289 no2 p32 Mr/Ap 2017

Water supply—Government policy
Water strategies for the next administration P. H. Gleiek bibl graph *Science* v354 no6312 p555 N 4 2016

Water supply—India
Bangalore was once the icon of a globalized, high tech future.

Now it's the thirsty sign of a global catastrophe S. Subramanian color *Wired* v25 no5 p110 My 2017

Water supply—Peru
stressed out: gauging global water worries M. B. Griggs map *Popular Science* v289 no2 p8 Mr/Ap 2017

Water supply—United States
the case of the cat-scented faucet A. DIETRICH and S. Chodosh cartoon *Popular Science* v289 no2 p82 Mr/Ap 2017

Water temperature
Envisioning, Quantifying, and Managing Thermal Regimes on River Networks E. A. STEEL, T. J. BEECHIE et al *BioScience* v67 no6 p506 Je 2017

Water temperature & the environment
IN HOT WATER A. Witze color graph map *Science News* v191 no9 p18 My 13 2017

Water testing
The Water Taste Test img *New York* p58 F 9 2017

Water towers
Tuba City Water Tower N. AUSTIN *Arizona Highways* v92 no11 p6 N 2016

Water treatment plants
See also
Saline water conversion plants
the water (re)cycle S. Chodosh diag *Popular Science* v289 no2 p14 Mr/Ap 2017

Water use
Ecomaniacs M. HUTSON cartoon *Atlantic* v320 no1 p26 Jl/Ag 2017

THE SUCCESSFUL INTERVIEW D. Looker *Successful Farming* v114 no13 p10 D 2016

Water—To Your Health! M. LALIBERTE and L. TIGAR color *Reader's Digest* v190 no1133 p33 S 2017

Water utilities
FIELD OF DREAMS: How a city girl-turned-accidental farmhand discovered heaven on earth S. DUGGER *Indianapolis Monthly* v12 no40 p78 Ag 2017

Water work: Jobs related to water utilities E. Torpey chart color *Career Outlook* p1 Ap 2017

Water utilities—United States
ALMOST FAMOUS: Waterfront the Blue Ridge hasn't won any contests--yet R. NELSON *Virginia Living* v15 no6 p112 O 2017

Water vapor
anatomy of a hurricane S. Fecht color *Popular Science* v289 no4 p12 Jl/Ag 2017

Hydrolytically stable fluorinated metal-organic frameworks for energy-efficient dehydration A. Cadiau, Y. Belmabkhout et al diag *Science* v356 no6339 p731 My 19 2017

Water waves
Editor's Note color *Surfer* v58 no4 p12 Ag 2017

Lining Up color *Surfer* v58 no4 p18 Ag 2017

SKELETON BAY NAMIBIA Z. MORTON color *Surfer* v58 no4 p58 Ag 2017

Water well drilling
Good Well Hunting B. HEWITT and P. HEWITT color *Yankee* p16 My/Je 2017

Waterboarding
Get Board S. O'BRIEN *Boating World* v38 no1 p12 Ja 2017

Waterborne infection
battling a waterborne plague R. GELTING and C. Maldarelli cartoon *Popular Science* v289 no2 p78 Mr/Ap 2017

I WISH SOMEONE WOULD INVENT... S. Chodosh and C. Maldarelli cartoon *Popular Science* v289 no2 p98 Mr/Ap 2017

Waterborne infection—Prevention
Operations. Recreational Water Disinfection: Avoiding disease outbreaks E. Meyer *Parks & Recreation* v52 no6 p46 Je 2017

Waterbury, John
America's Dream Palace: Middle East Expertise and the Rise of the National Security State *Foreign Affairs* v96 no2 p183 Mr/Ap 2017

Citizen Hariri: Lebanon's Neoliberal Reconstruction *Foreign Affairs* v96 no6 p168 N/D 2017

Debriefing the President: The Interrogation of Saddam Hussein *Foreign Affairs* v96 no3 p171 My/Je 2017

Democratic Transitions in the Arab World *Foreign Affairs* v96 no6 p167 N/D 2017

The Fall of the Turkish Model: How the Arab Uprisings Brought

Down Islamic Liberalism *Foreign Affairs* v96 no2 p184 Mr/Ap 2017

Ike's Gamble: America's Rise to Dominance in the Middle East *Foreign Affairs* v96 no2 p185 Mr/Ap 2017

The Iran Wars: Spy Games, Bank Battles, and the Secret Deals That Reshaped the Middle East *Foreign Affairs* v96 no1 p174 Ja/F 2017

ISIS: A History *Foreign Affairs* v95 no6 p188 N/D 2016

The Land Is Full: Addressing Overpopulation in Israel *Foreign Affairs* v96 no1 p173 Ja/F 2017

The New Sectarianism: The Arab Uprisings and the Rebirth of the Shi'a-Sunni Divide *Foreign Affairs* v95 no6 p189 N/D 2016

The New Sultan: Erdogan and the Crisis of Modern Turkey *Foreign Affairs* v96 no6 p168 N/D 2017

A Path to Peace: A Brief History of Israeli-Palestinian Negotiations and a Way Forward in the Middle East *Foreign Affairs* v96 no1 p172 Ja/F 2017

A People Without a State: The Kurds From the Rise of Islam to the Dawn of Nationalism/The Kurds: A Modern History *Foreign Affairs* v96 no3 p171 My/Je 2017

Political Islam in Tunisia: The History of Ennahda *Foreign Affairs* v96 no6 p169 N/D 2017

The Rope *Foreign Affairs* v96 no1 p173 Ja/F 2017

Shadow Wars: The Secret Struggle for the Middle East *Foreign Affairs* v96 no2 p185 Mr/Ap 2017

Vanguard of the Imam: Religion, Politics, and Iran's Revolutionary Guards *Foreign Affairs* v96 no1 p174 Ja/F 2017

The Way of the Strangers: Encounters With the Islamic State/The Master Plan: ISIS, al-Qaeda, and the Jihadi Strategy for Final Victory *Foreign Affairs* v96 no3 p170 My/Je 2017

Watercolor

SERVE CHILLED E. N. GAGE color *Martha Stewart Living* p25 Jl/Ag 2017

Watercolor painting—Exhibitions

GLADYS NILSSON J. Kreimer cartoon *Art in America* v105 no4 p112 Ap 2017

JANUARY'S COOLEST EVENTS *Indianapolis Monthly* v40 no5 p18 Ja 2017

Water—Distribution

See also

Water towers

Case Study: How Would You Save This Farm? F. L. Reinhardt and A. Beard *Harvard Business Review Digital Articles* p2 Ag 12 2016

Waterfalls

CIBECUE FALLS R. STIEVE *Arizona Highways* v96 no7 p46 Jl 2017

Enter fantasyland color *Backpacker* p22 Ag 2017

FOOTSTEPS *Iceland Review* v55 no4 p36 Jl/Ag 2017

ICEFALL E. MASTROIANNI color *Discover* v38 no10 p9 D 2017

IMAGES OF A LOST WORLD T. NICHOLS bw *Arizona Highways* v93 no5 p40 My 2017

Let There Be Light *Arizona Highways* v96 no7 p5 Jl 2017

McCloud Falls, Shasta-Trinity National Forest, California [Cover story] diag *Backpacker* p96 My 2017

OUT WEST *Iceland Review* v54 no6 p98 N/D 2016

Passing It Down E. OSBORN *Sierra* v101 no5 p64 S/O 2016

THE PERFECT WATERFALL *Saturday Evening Post* v289 no5 p23 S/O 2017

Running Water *Arizona Highways* v92 no11 p5 N 2016

When It Rains *Arizona Highways* v93 no11 p56 N 2017

WISDOM OF GOÐAFOSS J. Visco *Iceland Review* v55 no2 p22 Mr/Ap 2017

Waterfalls—Switzerland

SWITZERLAND D. Heimburger color *Christianity Today* v61 no5 p6 Je 2017

Waterfield (Company)

WATERFIELD iPAD PRO SLEEVECASE S. J. PUREWAL *Macworld - Digital Edition* v34 no9 p37 S 2017

Waterfield Designs Inc.

WATERFIELD DESIGNS iPAD PRO GEAR CASE L. YAMSHON color *Macworld - Digital Edition* p33 Je 13 2017

Water—Filtration—Equipment & supplies

YOUR VISION QUEST PACKING LIST R. KOCH color *Bicycling* v58 no1 p78 Ja/F 2017

Waterfowl

A pattern most fowl H. Wilson map *Canadian Geographic* v136 no6 p24 D 2016

Waterfowl shooting

See also

Duck shooting

Goose shooting

BEAST MODE A. ROBINSON color *Outdoor Life* v224 no8 pW5 O 2017

DUCKING THE GREAT SALT LAKE A. Mckean cartoon color *Outdoor Life* v223 no9 p31 N 2016

HUNT THE PUDDLE DIVER T. CARPENTER color *Outdoor Life* v224 no8 pW6 O 2017

START WITH A BANG A. ROBINSON color *Outdoor Life* v224 no7 pW1 S 2017

THE WATERFOWL FRONTIER W. BRANTLEY color diag *Field & Stream* v121 no7 p76 D 2016/Ja 2017

Waterfowl shooting—Equipment & supplies

GREAT DUCK GUNS J. SPILGER color *Outdoor Life* v224 no8 p32 O 2017

THE RED ZONE B. Fitzpatrick color *Outdoor Life* v223 no9 pH11 N 2016

Waterfronts

BREMERTON IS BOOMING: AN INTERESTING AND LIKABLE PORT OF CALL FOR PUGET SOUND BOATERS IS NOT FAR FROM SEATTLE D. HISLOP color map *Sea Magazine* v109 no8 pPNW-1 Ag 2017

RELAX YOURSELF IN LANGLEY D. HISLOP *Sea Magazine* v108 no10 pPNW-4 O 2016

A SHORE THING J. BREWSTER color *Cabin Living* p38 Ap 2017

Waterfronts—Design & construction

Building at the Water's Edge D. MULFINGER bw color *Cabin Living* p20 Ap 2017

Watergate Affair, 1972-1974

The Eternal Scandal D. HARSANYI *National Review* v69 no11 p44 Je 12 2017

Waterhouse, Suki, 1992-

LEG Work M. GUIDUCCI and M. HOLGATE color *Vogue* v207 no3 p338 Mr 2017

SUKI WATERHOUSE K. SMITH color *Vanity Fair* v59 no5 p45 Ap 2017

Waterhouse Press (Company)

Waterhouse Press Prepares for Misadventures J. Milliot chart color *Publishers Weekly* v264 no18 p6 My 1 2017

Waterloo (Ont.)

Waterloo Region map *Alternatives Journal (AJ) - Canada's Environmental Voice* v42 no3 p16 2016

WATERMAN, HILLARY

This Means War! color *Discover* v38 no3 p68 Ap 2017

WATERMAN, JONATHAN

Cabin Convert color *Backpacker* p51 O 2017

WATERMAN, LAUREN

in harmony color *Architectural Digest* v74 no7 p52 Jl 2017

Watermelon varieties

NATIONAL WATERMELON DAY S. LIAO color *Better Homes & Gardens* v95 no8 p167 Ag 2017

Watermelons

Big SPLASH Z. RUFFNER color *Vogue* v207 no6 p74 Je 2017

Delicious Hydration Tips L. DIAMOND color *Reader's Digest* v189 no1131 p52 Je 2017

Easy Backyard BBQ [Cover story] K. Hymore color *Prevention* v69 no6 p82 Je 2017

GET PUMPED R. Meltzer Warren color *Women's Health* v14 no4 p108 My 2017

My Shot color *National Geographic Kids* no470 p35 My 2017

Super Mom color *AARP: The Magazine* v59 no5A p9 Ag/S 2016

Watermelon's Effect on Blood Vessels *USA Today Magazine* v146 no2869 p2 O 2017

Water.org (Organization)

MATT DAMON'S WATER FIGHT D. Coggan color *Entertainment Weekly* no1467 p14 My 26 2017

TALKING TOILETS WITH MATT DAMON S. Goldberg *National Geographic* v232 no2 p6 Ag 2017

Waterproof clothing

Waterproof Gear : Don't Get Soaked bw color *Men's Health* v32

no7 p32 S 2017

Waterproof clothing—Evaluation

BAMBOO-MERINO HENLEY color *Bike Magazine* v24 no4 p106 Je 2017

BECAUSE DOGS LOVE WINTER, TOO J. Schnuer color *Rodale's Organic Life* v2 no7 p16 D 2016/Ja 2017

Waterproofing

ROOF PREP M. E. POLSON color diag *Old House Journal* v45 no4 p39 Je 2017

SHOP NOTES cartoon chart color *Popular Mechanics* v193 no7 p36 S 2016

Streamin' in the Shower M. ANTONOFF cartoon color *Sound & Vision* v81 no10 p28 D 2016

Water—Psychological aspects

WAITING FOR WATER K. VAUGHN *Arizona Highways* v93 no11 p28 N 2017

Water—Purification—Equipment & supplies

starters M. Perello, L. MENNIES et al color *Bon Appetit* no1 p13 F 2017

Water—Religious aspects—Christianity

Living Waters M. Malone *America* v217 no6 p3 S 18 2017

Waters, Alice, 1944-

Coming to My Senses: The Making of a Counterculture Cook *Publishers Weekly* v264 no29 p209 Jl 17 2017

Prep Work: How Alice Waters came to create Chez Panisse and lead a revolution in American food P. WELLS *New York Times Book Review* p15 S 24 2017

Waters, Alice, 1944-—Interviews

Cheap Food is a Myth Z. LOFTUS-FARREN color *Earth Island Journal* v32 no4 p45 Wint 2017

Life's Work: An Interview with Alice Waters A. Beard color *Harvard Business Review* v95 no3 p176 My/Je 2017

Waters, Cam

LEAN ON ME color *Runner's World* v52 no3 p26 Ap 2017

Waters, Dawn

HAPPY CAMPERS J. Haddad *Virginia Living* v15 no1 p23 D 2016

Waters, Don

Faith and Science at a Crossroad *Sky & Telescope* v134 no3 p6 S 2017

Waters, Jessica

LEAN ON ME color *Runner's World* v52 no3 p26 Ap 2017

Waters, John

MY CHILDHOOD HOME *Lapham's Quarterly* v10 no1 p206 Wint 2017

SERIAL MOM C. Collis color *Entertainment Weekly* no1465 p42 My 12 2017

Waters, John—Interviews

By the Book color *New York Times Book Review* p8 Ap 23 2017

WATERS, MARY C.

Crime and Immigration New Forms of Exclusion and Discrimination color *Issues in Science & Technology* v33 no1 p29 Fall 2016

Waters, Maxine, 1938-—Interviews

Maxine Waters Is Learning From Millennials A. M. Cox *New York Times Magazine* p58 Jl 23 2017

Waters, Roger, 1943-

BRICKBATS C. OLIVER and T. COLON color *Reason* v49 no6 p80 N 2017

Roger Waters' Fight D. FRICKE color *Rolling Stone* no1295 p13 S 7 2017

Roger Waters Returns to Rock K. GROW color *Rolling Stone* no1283 p11 Mr 23 2017

Watersheds

Amazon Atlantis A. Posada-Swafford color map *Scientific American* v317 no1 p12 Jl 2017

Watersheds—Asia

Can South Asia Share Its Rivers? G. PRICE and S. MITTRA *Current History* v116 no789 p148 Ap 2017

Waterston, Katherine

girl on top J. Doll color *InStyle* v23 no13 p242 D 2016

Waterston, Robert H.

Comprehensive single-cell transcriptional profiling of a multicellular organism diag *Science* v357 no6352 p661 Ag 18 2017

Waterstudio.nl (Company)

Noah's Ark-itecture K. Logan *Architectural Record* v205 no4

p217 Ap 2017

Waterton Lakes National Park (Alta.)

INTO THE ROCKY MOUNTAIN WILD A. Shoalts color *Canadian Geographic* v136 no6 p34 D 2016

Water Trees, The (Poem)

TWO POEMS A. Amsterdam *Harper's Magazine* no2007 p67 Ag 2017

Waterways

See also

Grassed waterways

Water Hazard D. Mother il *Backpacker* p39 Je 2017

Waterways—Design & construction

TAKE THEM TO THE RIVER M. LAWLER color map *Chicago* v66 no6 p26 Je 2017

Waterways—History

WET AND WILD: New York's waterfront, once home to pirates and robber barons, fell into dangerous decline. But with a new wave of money and creativity the city is rediscovering its maritime spirit T. PERROTTET *Smithsonian* v48 no2 p26 My 2017

Waterways—Illinois

TAKE THEM TO THE RIVER M. LAWLER color map *Chicago* v66 no6 p26 Je 2017

Waterways—Maintenance & repair

Pick a Lock J. Sanburn color *Time* v189 no13 p33 Ap 10 2017

Waterways—United States

WATERSPORTS HOTSPOTS Z. BILAS color *Boating World* v38 no7 p46 Jl 2017

Waterways—Virginia

See also

James River Batteau Festival Trail (Va.)

JOURNEY DOWN THE JAMES: James River Batteau Festival gears up for its 32nd trip downriver E. J. Wallace *Virginia Living* v15 no4 p25 Je 2017

WATKINS, CLAIRE VAYE

A Trip of One's Own color *New Republic* v248 no1/2 p50 Ja/F 2017

Watkins, Denny

Conquer Aches Without Drugs *AARP: The Magazine* v30 no6A p32 O/N 2017

Watkins, Eileen

The Persian Always Meows Twice *Publishers Weekly* v264 no35 p105 Ag 28 2017

WATKINS, JAMES E., JR.

Sex and the Single Gametophyte: Revising the Homosporous Vascular Plant Life Cycle in Light of Contemporary Research *BioScience* v66 no11 p928 N 1 2016

Watkins, Kenna

You Never Forget Your First Time diag il *Backpacker* v45 no2 p64 Mr 2017

Watkins, Michael D.

Internal Hires Need Just as Much Support as External Ones *Harvard Business Review Digital Articles* p2 Ap 4 2016

Onboarding Isn't Enough color diag graph il img *Harvard Business Review* v95 no3 p78 My/Je 2017

Watkins, Michael M.

Gravity field of the Orientale basin from the Gravity Recovery and Interior Laboratory Mission bibl graph *Science* v354 no6311 p438 O 28 2016

WATKINS, ROWBOAT

Children's Books *New York Times Book Review* p14 F 12 2017

Watkins, Sherron

Enron and On And On... *Texas Monthly* v44 no12 p60 D 2016

Watkins, Tim

Human health color *Science* v356 no6338 p590 My 12 2017

Watkins, Willie A.

THE MORTUARY MOGUL: Willie Watkins will bury you in style--its his calling G. GODFREY *Atlanta* v57 no6 p23 O 2017

Watrous, Nancy

Glimpses of Home *American Scholar* v86 no4 p17 Aut 2017

Watson (Computer)

IBM D. H. Freedman color il *MIT Technology Review* v120 no4 p72 Jl/Ag 2017

INVESTORS TAKE A SHINE TO WATSON D. FONDA color *Kiplinger's Personal Finance* v71 no4 p12 Ap 2017

Watson, A. A.

Observation of a large-scale anisotropy in the arrival directions

of cosmic rays above 8 × 1018 eV *Science* v357 no6357 p1266 S 22 2017

Watson, Aaron
EVALUATING A MAGAZINE T. TALIAFERRO *Texas Monthly* v45 no3 p22 Mr 2017
THE UNDERDOG'S ON TOP A. ROUSH *Texas Monthly* v45 no3 p112 Mr 2017
Vaquero color *American Cowboy* v23 no6 p43 Ap/My 2017

Watson, Alan A.
James W. Cronin (1931–2016) bw *Science* v353 no6307 p1501 S 30 2016

WATSON, ANDREA V.
CELEBRATING 28 YEARS OF REAL MEN COOK color *Ebony* v72 no8 p48 Je 2017
In Our Cities bw color *Ebony* v72 no4 p42 F 2017

Watson, Andrew J.
Oceans on the edge of anoxia bibl diag *Science* v354 no6319 p1529 D 23 2016

Watson, Bradley C. S.
SECOND-CLASS CITIZENS *Claremont Review of Books* v16 no4 p44 Fall 2016

Watson, Brynn
A Look Inside Lockheed Martin's Space-Age Operations *Harvard Business Review Digital Articles* p2 Je 25 2015

Watson, Charles S.
Exposing Unfair Pricing in Auto Insurance Rates color *Consumer Reports* v82 no5 p6 My 2017

Watson, Danie
Emergence and spread of a human-transmissible multidrug-resistant nontuberculous mycobacterium bibl diag graph *Science* v354 no6313 p751 N 11 2016

Watson, David
Killer Commodes N. LUND *National Parks* v91 no1 p22 Wint 2017

Watson, Deshaun
HOT | NOT S. Kwak color *Sports Illustrated* v127 no11 p20 O 9 2017
INTO THE FIRE A. Benoit color *Sports Illustrated* v126 no13 p40 My 8 2017
Lightbox color *Time* v189 no4 p18 Ja 23 2017
TRUE GRIT A. Staples color *Sports Illustrated* v126 no11 p36 Ap 17-24 2017

Watson, Emma, 1990-
Beauty and the Beast Is Wonderfully Out of Step With the Times S. Zacharek color *Time* v189 no11 p57 Mr 27 2017
The Rebel Belle D. BLASBERG bw color *Vanity Fair* v59 no4 p152 Mr 2017

Watson, Emma, 1990—Interviews
Emma Watson K. B. Brown color *InStyle* v24 no5 p152 My 2017
REBEL BELLE [Cover story] A. Breznican color *Entertainment Weekly* no1454/1455 p24 F 24 2017

Watson, George
Talkin' 'bout a revolution D. Armitage *History Today* v67 no2 p72 F 2017

Watson, James E. M.
Australia needs a wake-up call bibl color *Science* v355 no6328 p918 Mr 3 2017
The broad footprint of climate change from genes to biomes to people bibl chart color *Science* v354 no6313 paaf7671-1 N 11 2016

Watson, James V.
Positive biodiversity-productivity relationship predominant in global forests bibl chart graph map *Science* v354 no6309 paaf8957-1 O 14 2016

WATSON, JOE, JR.
The End of Despair il *America* v215 no19 p25 D 19 2016

Watson, Kittie W.
How Your Company Can Better Retain Employees Who Are Veterans *Harvard Business Review Digital Articles* p2 Jl 11 2017

Watson, Larry
Thom On Design: Whatever Happened to Customizing? T. Taylor color *Hot Rod* v70 no12 p92 D 2017

Watson, Lorena
On Rebels and Role Models color *Glamour* v115 no10 p34 O 2017

Watson, Marshall—Interviews
WATER COLORS M. READ color *House Beautiful* v158 no9

p138 N 2016

Watson, Mary Anne
Case Study: Should He Be Fired for That Facebook Post? *Harvard Business Review Digital Articles* p2 D 11 2015

Watson, Micah
SEEKING REFUGE color *Christianity Today* v61 no1 p55 Ja/F 2017

Watson, Mike
An accreting pulsar with extreme properties drives an ultraluminous x-ray source in NGC 5907 bibl chart graph *Science* v355 no6327 p817 F 24 2017

Watson, Murray
The WATSON FILES L. Heaton bw color *Foreign Policy* no224 p46 My/Je 2017

Watson, Olivia
SCARVES AS HAIR ACCESSORIES cartoon *Women's Health* v14 no9 p34 N 2017

Watson, Paul
Frozen Folly A. HENDERSON color *Weekly Standard* v22 no43 p33 Jl 24 2017
Frozen I. Mcguire *New York Times Book Review* p12 Ap 9 2017
Ice Ghosts: The Epic Hunt for the Lost Franklin Expedition *Publishers Weekly* v264 no7 p63 F 13 2017

Watson, Peter, 1943-
Universal Joint J. L. HEILBRON *New York Times Book Review* p22 Mr 12 2017

Watson, Philip A.
SOX2 promotes lineage plasticity and antiandrogen resistance in TP53- and RB1-deficient prostate cancer bibl graph *Science* v355 no6320 p1 Ja 6 2017

Watson, Robert P.
The Ghost Ship of Brooklyn: An Untold Story of the American Revolution K. M. Kostyal bw *MHQ: Quarterly Journal of Military History* v30 no1 p92 Aut 2017

Watson, Robert, 1953-
BOBBY WATSON G. Himes color *Downbeat* v84 no7 p34 Jl 2017

Watson, Sammy
FACES IN THE CROWD T. Keith color *Sports Illustrated* v126 no9 p26 Mr 27 2017

Watson, Sara Kiley
I WISH SOMEONE WOULD INVENT... cartoon *Popular Science* v289 no5 p98 S/O 2017
WE WISH SOMEONE WOULD INVENT... color *Popular Science* v289 no6 p98 N/D 2017

Watson, Sarah
The Bold Type's IRL Inspo S. Highfill color *Entertainment Weekly* no1478 / 1479 p89 Ag 18-25 2017

Watson, Stephen
ALTITUDE ADJUSTMENT color *Esquire* p29 Ag 2017
GET IN GEAR color *Esquire* p50 Ap 2017
WANNA BUY A WATCH? color *Esquire* p46 Je/Jl 2017
A Well-Oiled Machine color *Esquire* v167 no1 p38 F 2017

Watson, Susan Kelechi
KEEPING UP WITH THE PEARSONS color *Entertainment Weekly* no1468/1469 p92 Je 2-9 2017
SHE IS US T. S. Young color *Essence* v48 no6 p67 O 2017
This Is Us *TV Guide* v65 no41 p33 O 2 2017

WATSON, TRACI
A Residence Fit for a President [Cover story] color *Archaeology* v70 no4 p34 Je-Ag 2017

Watson-Schütze, Eva
Pictorialist photography at the Palmer bw *Magazine Antiques* v184 no1 p46 Ja/F 2017

Watson-Shada, Janice
FREE FOR ALL color *O, The Oprah Magazine* p20 O 2017

Watt, Elizabeth Bauer
#3: How to softly turn up the volume on a classic Connecticut family farmhouse? Elizabeth Bauer Watt goes all out with mirror-like aqua walls and a dining room wrapped in shimmering chinoiserie J. LASKY color *House Beautiful* v159 no2 p100 Mr 2017

Watt, J. J., 1989-
Leading Off B. Reiter color *Sports Illustrated* v127 no8 p6 S 18 2017

Watt, J. J., 1989-—Finance

Disaster Relief T. Keith and S. Kwak color *Sports Illustrated* v127 no7 p20 S 4 2017

Watt, James

INVASION OF THE PUNKS B. Warner color *Fortune* v174 no8 p176 D 15 2016

Watt, Marie

Gather Round J. Lovelace bw color *American Craft* v77 no2 p36 Ap/My 2017

WATT, RIAN

THE WHITE SOX PUZZLE color graph *Chicago* v66 no4 p21 Ap 2017

Watters, Caitlin—Interviews

Is It Safe to Talk Politics Yet? S. E. Cupp, K. Ball et al bw color *Glamour* v115 no2 p77 F 2017

Watters, Ellen Leah Isabel

Ellen Leah Isabel Watters A. A. DAVIS color *Maclean's* v130 no2 p74 Mr 2017

Watters, Harper

HARPER WATTERS *Dance Spirit* v21 no3 p41 Mr 2017

Watterston, George, 1783-1854

HOUSES WITH HISTORY K. Randall *Washingtonian Magazine* v52 no9 p172 Je 2017

Wattpad (Company)

Wattpad Grows from Reading Site to Multiplatform Entertainment Venue C. Reid color *Publishers Weekly* v263 no50 p10 D 5 2016

Watts, Corinne

SAVING THE 'GOD OF UGLY THINGS' E. Pennisi color *Science* v356 no6342 p1001 Je 9 2017

Watts, D.

Fostering reproducibility in industry-academia research color *Science* v357 no6353 p759 Ag 25 2017

Watts, Duncan J.

Prediction and explanation in social systems bibl diag graph *Science* v355 no6324 p486 F 3 2017

Watts, Irene N.

Seeking Refuge *Publishers Weekly* v264 no3 p62 Ja 16 2017

Watts, Jon

SAVING SPIDER-MAN [Cover story] S. Vilkomerson color *Entertainment Weekly* no1473 p18 Jl 7 2017

Spider-Man ... Again *Weekly Standard* v22 no43 p39 Jl 24 2017

SPIDER-MAN: HOMECOMING S. Vilkomerson color *Entertainment Weekly* no1463/1464 p65 Ap/My 2017

Watts, Julian

Julian Watts D. BISHOP color *American Craft* v76 no6 p12 D 2016-Ja 2017

Watts, Melissa

'I can help you transform a fixer-upper, but how do I go from architect to real estate agent?' K. Palmer color *AARP: The Magazine* v59 no5A p36 Ag/S 2016

Watts, Naomi, 1968-

Bazaar's Best-Dressed LIST N. Silva-Jelly color *Harper's Bazaar* no3656 p230 S 2017

Best-Dressed LIST L. McCarthy color *Harper's Bazaar* no3648 p118 N 2016

Best Dress E. Wilson color *InStyle* v23 no12 p61 N 2016

Gypsy A. D'ARMINIO *TV Guide* v65 no27 p37 Je 26 2017

Naomi Watts' Deceptive Therapist Just Can't Help Herself on Gypsy D. D'addario color *Time* v190 no1 p53 Jl 3 2017

Watts, Naomi, 1968—Interviews

Gypsy M. Logan *TV Guide* v65 no25 p22 Je 2017

Naomi Watts E. Dockterman color *Time* v190 no2/3 p93 Jl 10-17 2017

Watts, Sarah

BEHIND THE BUNS bw *Chicago* v65 no11 p26 N 2016

haikus for parents color *Parents* v92 no8 p108 Ag 2017

Special Dolls for Special Kids color *Parents* v92 no3 p18 Mr 2017

Turn Off Your Fat Switch cartoon color diag *Men's Health* v32 no6 p85 Ag 2017

Watts, Stephanie Powell

No One Is Coming to Save Us *Publishers Weekly* v264 no8 p54 F 20 2017

South of West Egg J. Chang *New York Times Book Review* p17 Ap 9 2017

Watts, Steven

HE WASN'T ALL RIGHT AFTER ALL, JACK M. Dolan *Ameri-*

can History v52 no1 p70 Ap 2017

Watts, Zoe

I'm a comp Kid. Zoe Watts color *Dance Spirit* v21 no8 p66 O 2017

Waugh, Evelyn, 1903-1966

Waugh's Gift A. VALIUNAS bw *Weekly Standard* v22 no16 p34 D 26 2016

Waugh, Kevin

DeepStack: Expert-level artificial intelligence in heads-up no-limit poker [Cover story] chart diag *Science* v356 no6337 p508 My 5 2017

Waugh, William

NAME THE BOAT S. SHIBATA *Sea Magazine* v108 no8 p10 Ag 2016

Wave Books (Company)

Indie House Rides the Pulitzer Wave J. Maher color *Publishers Weekly* v264 no22 p7 My 29 2017

Wave functions

Potential signs of quantum collapse E. CONOVER *Science News* v192 no5 p10 S 30 2017

Waveguides

A low-loss origami plasmonic waveguide F. Vetrone and F. Rosei diag *Science* v357 no6350 p452 Ag 4 2017

Wavelength dispersive X-ray spectroscopy

NEW PRODUCTS *Physics Today* v70 no10 p67 O 2017

Wavelengths

[C II] 158-μm emission from the host galaxies of damped Lyman-alpha systems M. Neeleman, N. Kanekar et al bibl color graph *Science* v355 no6331 p1285 Mr 24 2017

the elusive green flash M. D. Kaufman color *Popular Science* v289 no4 p93 Jl/Ag 2017

EYE HEALTH IN THE DIGITAL AGE J. Stringham color *Amazing Wellness* p26 Fall 2017

Waves (Physics)

See also

Atmospheric waves

Gravitational waves

Gravity waves

Dynamics of a human spiral wave A. J. Welsh, E. F. Greco et al *Physics Today* v70 no2 p78 F 2017

Waves (Poem)

Waves C. OH-HYUN color *Tricycle: The Buddhist Review* v26 no2 p116 Wint 2016

Wavves (Performer)

The Playlist color *Rolling Stone* no1288 p8 Je 1 2017

Wawrinka, Stanislas, 1985-

Stan Wawrinka *Tennis* v53 no1 p18 Ja/F 2017

Wax, Trevin

Make Holiness Great Again color *Christianity Today* p73 Ap 2017

Wax figures

The Bullseye M. Snetiker color *Entertainment Weekly* no1453 p64 F 17 2017

WAXLER, CAROLINE

CA$HING IN color *Publishers Weekly* v263 no50 p34 D 5 2016

WAXMAN, DOV

Is Israeli Democracy in Danger? *Current History* v115 no785 p360 D 2016

Waxman, Harlan S.

New Male Potency Formula Makes "The Little Blue Pill" Obsolete *Saturday Evening Post* v289 no2 p103 Mr/Ap 2017

Waxman, Matthew C.

The Other Forever War *Hoover Digest: Research & Opinion on Public Policy* no1 p92 Wint 2017

Waxman, Olivia B.

America's 'Real' Independence Day Is Not July 4 *Time* v190 no2/3 p23 Jl 10-17 2017

The Birth of America's Flag Obsession *Time* v189 no23 p21 Je 19 2017

The Birth of the Bachelorette Party *Time* v190 no1 p19 Jl 3 2017

The Birth of the U.S. Police Force *Time* v189 no20 p19 My 29 2017

The Citified Origins of Summer Vacation *Time* v190 no5 p27 Jl 31 2017

The Dark Origins of Dog Breeding *Time* v189 no7/8 p27 F 27 2017

The Fight to Change How Hurricanes Are Named *Time* v190 no12

p23 S 25 2017

Firsts & Lasts color diag *Time* v188 no25-26 p23 D 19 2016 Double Issue

The Forgotten Origins of Father's Day *Time* v189 no24 p19 Je 26 2017

The Forgotten Parent Behind Mother's Day *Time* v189 no19 p19 My 22 2017

How Sharks Became So Scary *Time* v189 no22 p17 Je 12 2017

Name Game *Time* v189 no16/17 p152 My 1-8 2017

The Original Point of Daylight Saving Time *Time* v189 no10 p21 Mr 20 2017

The Origins of Pumpkin-Spice Mania *Time* v190 no13 p23 O 2 2017

The Political History of St. Patrick's Day Green *Time* v189 no11 p27 Mr 27 2017

The Results: Congress color diag map *Time* v188 no21 p14 N 21 2016

The Scoop on Ice Cream's Health-Food Origins *Time* v190 no8 p21 Ag 28 2017

The Surprising Evolution of Cinco de Mayo *Time* v189 no18 p25 My 15 2017

The Surprising History of Cherry Blossoms *Time* v189 no12 p25 Ap 3 2017

The Surprising History of Women's Tattoos *Time* v189 no9 p23 Mr 13 2017

The Surprising Origin of Canada's Thanksgiving *Time* v190 no15 p19 O 16 2017

Where the Easter-Egg Tradition Comes From *Time* v189 no15 p19 Ap 24 2017

Why Fraternities and Sororities Have Houses *Time* v190 no10/11 p29 S 18 2017

The Women Who Won Elections Before Suffrage *Time* v190 no9 p25 S 4 2017

Waxwings

do you know your waxwings? color *Cabin Living* p10 Mr 2017

WAY, GINA

42 new ALL-STAR PRODUCTS of the year [Cover story] color *Redbook* p27 Jl/Ag 2017

BEAUTY LESSONS FROM AMAZING-LOOKING WOMEN [Cover story] color *Redbook* p38 Mr 2017

BE HAPPIER IN YOUR SKIN color *Redbook* p93 My 2017

THE DAY & NIGHT GUIDE TO GORGEOUS SKIN color *Redbook* p1c O 2017

Softer skin for everyone color *Redbook* p58 F 2017

WHY SO DRY? color *Martha Stewart Living* p44 Mr 2017

Way, Lucan Ahmad

Is America Still Safe for Democracy? color *Foreign Affairs* v96 no3 p20 My/Je 2017

Way, Susanne

The Clinic S. von Dietze color *Dressage Today* v23 no5 p20 Ja 2017

Wayans, Damon

LETHAL WEAPON J. Halterman *TV Guide* v65 no39 p39 S 18 2017

Wayans, Marlon—Interviews

ONE WAYANS WAY T. M. FERGUSON color *Ebony* v72 no11 p58 S 2017

WAYCOTT, MICHELLE

Environmental Change and Human Health: Can Environmental Proxies Inform the Biodiversity Hypothesis for Protective Microbial-Human Contact? *BioScience* v66 no12 p1023 D 1 2016

Wayfair LLC

PUNCH LIST K. SELZER color *Better Homes & Gardens* v95 no10 p62 O 2017

Way It Is, The (Poem)

The Way It Is D. St. John *New York Times Magazine* p15 Ag 13 2017

WAYLOCK, CANDY

FINANCIAL AID *Atlanta* v56 no7 p113 N 2016

Wayman, Erin

Budget proposal would slash science *Science News* v191 no7 p15 Ap 15 2017

Fiction meets fact in science adventure tale color *Science News* v191 no2 p28 F 4 2017

Voyage of Time more art film than documentary color *Science News* v190 no9 p29 O 29 2016

Waymo (Company)

A Slow-Motion, Self-Driving Car Crash J. Rosenblatt and M. Bergen *Bloomberg Businessweek* no4537 p22 S 11 2017

Wayne, Jimmy

LITTLE BOY LOST... & FOUND G. GRAVES color *Good Housekeeping* v263 no5 p105 N 2016

Wayne, Teddy

Unhinged at Harvard L. ROSENFELD color *New York Times Book Review* p20 S 25 2017

Wayne State University

Wayne State Faces Bright Future J. Hale color *Downbeat* v84 no9 p102 S 2017

Waytz, Adam

The Dangers of "Mandatory Fun" *Harvard Business Review Digital Articles* p2 O 4 2017

The Strange Relationship Between Power and Loneliness *Harvard Business Review Digital Articles* p2 Ap 27 2016

WHY We LOVE CHICAGO bw cartoon color *Chicago* v66 no3 p75 Mr 2017

Wayward Sisters (TV program)

Supernatural's Sister Act S. Highfill color *Entertainment Weekly* no1472 p16 Je 30 2017

Way We Were, The (Film)

Barbra Streisand's 75th Birthday M. FELL *TV Guide* p47 Ap 17 2017

Way You Look Tonight, The (Music)

Gentlemen Prefer Song K. SILSBEE color *Downbeat* v83 no11 p54 N 2016

Waze Inc.

Waze Wants to Help You Hitch a Ride A. Satariano and M. Bergen *Bloomberg Businessweek* no4523 p34 My 22 2017

WCELA, EMIL A.

Songs on the Wing *America* v216 no1 p29 Ja 2 2017

WD-40 Co.

How WD-40 Created a Learning-Obsessed Company Culture B. Taylor *Harvard Business Review Digital Articles* p2 S 16 2016

We All Want The Same Things (Music)

The Must List color *Entertainment Weekly* no1459 p2 Mr 31 2017

We Collect Things (Short story)

We Collect Things E. CRANE *Commentary* v142 no3 p30 O 2016

We Have Gone Too Far (Poem)

c. 1945: Austerlitz, NY E. S. V. Millay *Lapham's Quarterly* v10 no2 p176 Spr 2017

We the People (Music)

'We the People . . . .' G. TATE *New York Times Magazine* p26 Mr 12 2017

We Were So Beloved (Film)

Sanctuary City R. Brody bw *New Yorker* v92 no49 p12 F 13 2017

Weadick, Elizabeth

I Wish My Horse's Mentor Could Be... color *Horse & Rider* v56 no6 p88 Je 2017

When I Was a Horse-Crazy Kid, I... color *Horse & Rider* v56 no2 p72 F 2017

Weakley, Sue

21 TRAINING TIPS FROM 3 OLYMPIANS color *Practical Horseman* v45 no4 p34 Ap 2017

Weakly interacting massive particles

In search for unseen matter, physicists turn to dark sector A. Cho color diag *Science* v355 no6331 p1251 Mr 24 2017

Weakly interacting massive particles—Research

Dark matter searches come up empty E. CONOVER color *Science News* v190 no10 p14 N 12 2016

Wealth

See also

Income

Saving & investment

Stockholder wealth

FROM THE EDITOR P. Laif *History Today* v67 no3 p2 Mr 2017

METROPOLIS M. Roemers color *National Geographic* v231 no3 p120 Mr 2017

Prosperity bw color *Forbes* v199 no3 p152 Mr 28 2017

Wealth management services

2017 CINCINNATI AWARD WINNERS color *Cincinnati Magazine* v51 no1 p1 O 2017

BEST IN WEALTH MANAGEMENT *Washingtonian Magazine* v52 no3 p112 D 2016

Articles p2 Jl 29 2016
How to Tell a Coworker They're Annoying You *Harvard Business Review Digital Articles* p2 Mr 10 2016

Webb, Dave
Mr. Nomad: Tales of a Traveling Teacher *Publishers Weekly* v263 no52 p90e D 19 2016

Webb, Elizabeth
Facts on the ground *America* v217 no7 p48 O 2 2017

Webb, Jimmy
THE ELEMENTS S. Larson cartoon *New Yorker* v93 no12 p19 My 8 2017
The Hits and Heartache of Jimmy Webb J. DOLAN bw *Rolling Stone* no1285 p14 Ap 20 2017

Webb, Nicole K.
4 CAREER GEMS FROM BLACK BUSINESS MASTER-MINDS color *Black Enterprise* v47 no7 p25 My/Je 2017

Webber, Carolyn
GARBAGE MEN color *Backpacker* v45 no1 p63 Ja 2017
A New Joe's color *Climbing* no353 p22 My/Je 2017
out alive: lost & blind color *Backpacker* p43 My 2017
out alive: mauled by a grizzly. twice color diag *Backpacker* p35 Je 2017
survival bw color *Backpacker* v45 no2 p39 Mr 2017

Webber, Katherine
The Heartbeats of Wing Jones *Publishers Weekly* v264 no4 p80 Ja 23 2017

Webber, Michael E.
Liquid Assets W. MCKENZIE *Weekly Standard* v22 no8 p37 O 31 2016
TAPPING THE TRASH color diag *Scientific American* v317 no1 p48 Jl 2017

WEBBER, REBECCA
THE REAL NARCISSISTS [Cover story] *Psychology Today* v49 no5 p52 S/O 2016

WEBB-HEHN, KATHERINE
The Political Revolution's Southern Front *In These Times* v41 no10 p6 O 2017

Webcams
Why you should cover up your laptop's webcam J. NOREM color *PCWorld* p172 Mr 2017

Webcasting
See also
Internet television
Podcasting
Does Anyone Still Need Cable? [Cover story] J. K. Willcox chart color diag graph il *Consumer Reports* v82 no8 p24 Ag 2017

Weber, Alexander
Are Banking Rules About To Go the Other Way? color *Bloomberg Businessweek* no4520 p37 My 1 2017

Weber, Ann
Systemic pan-AMPK activator MK-8722 improves glucose homeostasis but induces cardiac hypertrophy graph *Science* v357 no6350 p507 Ag 4 2017

Weber, Beckey
MEMBER SPOTLIGHT color *Literacy Today (2411-7862)* v34 no5 p50 Mr/Ap 2017

Weber, Bruce
Current and coming bw color *Magazine Antiques* v184 no5 p26 S/O 2017

Weber, Chris
Does stressing performance goals lead to too much, well, stress? color il *Phi Delta Kappan* v98 no6 p31 Mr 2017

Weber, Eicke R.
Terawatt-scale photovoltaics: Trajectories and challenges chart graph *Science* v356 no6334 p141 Ap 14 2017

Weber, Elke U.
Social norms as solutions bibl color *Science* v354 no6308 p42 O 7 2016

Weber, Greta
19 THINGS YOU REALLY OUGHT TO DO THIS MONTH *Washingtonian Magazine* v52 no1 p33 O 2016
CARLA HAYDEN *Washingtonian Magazine* v52 no3 p39 D 2016
HOW TO BE A BLEACHER-STOMPING, BEER-TOSSING D.C. UNITED FAN *Washingtonian Magazine* v52 no6 p70 Mr 2017
MONEYGAMI *Washingtonian Magazine* v52 no4 p23 Ja 2017

"WHERE ARE MY PEOPLE?" At Montpelier, descendents of James Madison's slaves are reviving their ancestors' history *Washingtonian Magazine* v52 no12 p19 S 2017
WHERE & WHEN: 17 THINGS YOU REALLY OUGHT TO DO THIS MONTH *Washingtonian Magazine* v53 no1 p31 O 2017
WHERE & WHEN: 18 THINGS YOU REALLY OUGHT TO DO THIS MONTH *Washingtonian Magazine* v52 no12 p29 S 2017
WOMEN AT WAR: A new book about female codebreakers during WWII captures a unique Washington moment that still reverberates *Washingtonian Magazine* v53 no1 p44 O 2017

Weber, J. Cynthia
STATE OF PRESERVATION *Archaeology* v70 no5 p8 S/O 2017

Weber, Jennifer
Hoop Dreams A. R. Fleming color *Good Housekeeping* v264 no3 p71 Mr 2017

WEBER, JEREMY
OUTPACING PERSECUTION [Cover story] color *Christianity Today* v60 no9 p38 N 2016

Weber, Jon
Commencal color *Bike Magazine* v24 no4 p98 Je 2017
DOUBLE DUTY color *Bike Magazine* v24 no1 p88 Ja/F 2017
EVEN FLOW bw color *Bike Magazine* v24 no1 p94 Ja/F 2017
flat out color *Bike Magazine* v24 no3 p112 My 2017
How to Know Which Digital Trends Are Worth Chasing *Harvard Business Review Digital Articles* p2 Jl 7 2016
IBIS RIPLEY LS color *Bike Magazine* v23 no9 p92 D 2016
Kona Honzo color *Bike Magazine* v24 no6 p118 Ag 2017
pack mentality color *Bike Magazine* v24 no7 p44 S 2017
Salsa Deadwood color *Bike Magazine* v24 no5 p84 Jl 2017
Santa Cruz: HIGHTOWER LT X01/CARBON CC W/ RESERVE 30 WHEEL UPGRADE color *Bike Magazine* v24 no8 p66 N 2017
STEADY PULL: SHIMANO'S SLX BRAKES ARE SO GOOD, IT'S ALMOST BORING color *Bike Magazine* v24 no7 p120 S 2017
X-FUSION MANIC color *Bike Magazine* v24 no2 p86 Mr 2017

Weber, Julie
How Southwest Airlines Hires Such Dedicated People *Harvard Business Review Digital Articles* p2 D 2 2015

Weber, Kerry
At a time of real division, how can we help clear the air? First, breathe *America* v216 no6 p3 Mr 20 2017
A different kind of family in Providence color *America* v216 no3 p49 F 6 2017
HEALING A MOTHER'S PAIN [Cover story] color il *America* v216 no11 p18 My 15 2017
OF MANY THINGS *America* v215 no16 p2 N 21 2016
A patchwork quilt *America* v217 no5 p48 S 4 2017

Weber, M.
A nontoxic pain killer designed by modeling of pathological receptor conformations bibl diag graph *Science* v355 no6328 p966 Mr 3 2017
Observation of a large-scale anisotropy in the arrival directions of cosmic rays above 8×10^{18} eV *Science* v357 no6357 p1266 S 22 2017

WEBER, MARCIA
Jail Birds *Orion Magazine* v35 no6 p11 N/D 2016

Weber, Max, 1864-1920
MAX WEBER WAS WRONG D. NANSEN MCCLOSKEY color *Reason* v49 no6 p12 N 2017

Weber, Nancy
HER SISTER'S KEEPER? A. Day color *O, The Oprah Magazine* p76 Je 2017

WEBER, NICHOLAS FOX
TURNER'S CLASSICS color *New York Times Book Review* p74 D 4 2016

WEBER, NICOLA
Using Social Network Measures in Wildlife Disease Ecology, Epidemiology, and Management *BioScience* v67 no3 p245 Mr 2017

Weber, Richard
ICE CYCLE A. HALPERN color *Wired* v25 no6 p26 Je 2017

Weber, Roy E.
Predictable convergence in hemoglobin function has unpredictable molecular underpinnings bibl graph *Science* v354 no6310 p336 O 21 2016

Weber, Stanley

BEHIND THE SCENES E. PARKHURST *Virginia Living* v15 no2 p7 F 2017

Bella Sicilia H. BOWLES color *Vogue* v207 no9 p408 S 2017

CAITI & JACK V. HUBBARD *Virginia Living* v15 no2 p96 F 2017

Get Together D. Grossman color *Popular Photography* v80 no11 p66 D 2016

Hold your lamp high A. Camille color *U.S. Catholic* v82 no11 p47 N 2017

I Feel Bad About Paula Deen A. MACLIN *O, The Oprah Magazine* p145 My 2017

Love that can't be shamed L. G. Irwin *Christian Century* v133 no24 p12 N 23 2016

REAL WEDDINGS *Virginia Living* v15 no2 p77 F 2017

REMEMBERING DIANA D. ARBITER, S. B. SMITH et al color *AARP: The Magazine* v60 no5A p50 Ag/S 2017

A sorta CATHOLIC'S very CATHOLIC WEDDING [Cover story] T. Wigfield bw *America* v216 no10 p34 My 1 2017

A WEDDING bw *Women's Health* v14 no5 p78 Je 2017

Weddings—Costs

keep calm AND MARRY ON J. Young *Indianapolis Monthly* v40 no5 p21 Ja 2017

Weddings—Planning

2017 WASHINGTONIAN BRIDE & GROOM UNVEILED color *Washingtonian Magazine* v52 no7 p158 Ap 2017

keep calm AND MARRY ON J. Young *Indianapolis Monthly* v40 no5 p21 Ja 2017

Weddle, Eric

Here's an Idea: Rethink Your Rest Day cartoon color *Men's Health* v32 no8 p50 O 2017

Wedel, Mathew

Against the Wall of Night *Sky & Telescope* v134 no1 p42 Jl 2017

A Cluster of Clusters *Sky & Telescope* v133 no1 p41 Ja 2017

Eyes of the Dragon bw chart color diag *Sky & Telescope* v134 no2 p22 Ag 2017

Four for the Road *Sky & Telescope* v134 no4 p42 O 2017

A Galaxy in the Giraffe *Sky & Telescope* v132 no6 p42 D 2016

Hail to the King *Sky & Telescope* v133 no5 p41 My 2017

Lucy in the Sky color *Sky & Telescope* v134 no2 p42 Ag 2017

OBSERVING April 2017r *Sky & Telescope* v133 no4 p41 Ap 2017

OBSERVING December 2017 *Sky & Telescope* v134 no6 p41 D 2017

Odd One Out *Sky & Telescope* v134 no3 p43 S 2017

The Silver Coin chart color *Sky & Telescope* v134 no5 p42 N 2017

Twelve Steps to Infinity *Sky & Telescope* v132 no6 p24 D 2016

WEDELL-WEDELLSBORG, THOMAS

ARE YOU SOLVING THE RIGHT PROBLEMS? color diag *Harvard Business Review* v95 no1 p76 Ja/F 2017

Get More Actionable Ideas from Your Employees *Harvard Business Review Digital Articles* p2 N 25 2014

What It Really Means to Be a Chief Innovation Officer *Harvard Business Review Digital Articles* p2 D 5 2014

WEDEMAN, ANDREW

China's Corruption Crackdown: War Without End? *Current History* v116 no791 p210 S 2017

WEDER, ADELE

Lightly on the Land color diag *Architectural Record* v204 no12 p84 D 2016

perspective house of the month *Architectural Record* v205 no4 p39 Ap 2017

Wedge shot (Golf)

The Crisp Wedge Secret D. Pelz and J. Marksbury color *Golf Magazine* v59 no11 p33 N 2017

Flight School S. Munroe and D. DeNunzio color *Golf Magazine* v59 no1 p52 Ja 2017

MAKE LAYUPS A SLAM DUNK J. Plecker and D. DeNunzio color *Golf Magazine* v59 no7 p52 Jl 2017

MAKE YOUR GAME PRESSURE-PROOF D. M. Clarke color *Golf Magazine* v58 no11 p10 N 2016

NIX YOUR CHILI-DIP M. Chuck and D. DeNunzio color *Golf Magazine* v59 no9 p64 S 2017

private LESSONS color *Golf Magazine* v58 no11 p99 N 2016

WIN WITH YOUR WEDGES D. Denunzio color *Golf Magazine* v58 no11 p41 N 2016

Your Lucky Number: 13 M. Broadie and C. Barrett color *Golf Magazine* v59 no7 p34 Jl 2017

Wedge shot (Golf)—Equipment & supplies

Sole Mates A. Johnson color *Golf Magazine* v59 no10 p98 O 2017

Wedges

All Mixed Up M. Broadie and J. Marksbury color *Golf Magazine* v59 no9 p36 S 2017

Henrik Stenson C. Barrett color *Golf Magazine* v59 no8 p31 Ag 2017

Jon Rahm C. Barrett color *Golf Magazine* v59 no7 p29 Jl 2017

WEDGES M. Chwasky, M. Dee et al color *Golf Magazine* v59 no6 p98 Je 2017

Wedgwood (Company)

shopping: Moody Blooms color *Architectural Digest* no11 p52 N 1 2017

Wee, Elijah

Research: Shifting the Power Balance with an Abusive Boss *Harvard Business Review Digital Articles* p2 O 9 2017

Weed control

FIGHTING BACK K. Birchmier *Successful Farming* v114 no10 p42 O 2016

GQHQ bw color *GQ: Gentlemen's Quarterly* v97 no9 p54 S 2017

Nanny State L. VACCARIELLO *Cincinnati Magazine* v50 no10 p132 Jl 2017

Organic Parks: The challenge of managing and maintaining well-manicured landscapes S. Ozbenian *Parks & Recreation* v52 no10 p26 O 2017

SUMMER BUMMERS: PESTS, WEEDS, STRESSED PLANTS. EVERY YEAR, THEY SHOW UP OUT OF NOWHERE. SEND THEM PACKING WITH THESE EASY TIPS E. Liskey color *Successful Farming* v115 no7 p54 My 2017

WEED-CONTROL TECHNOLOGY UPDATE: NO TRULY NEW HERBICIDES ARE SLATED FOR 2017, BUT DICAMBA-TOLERANT SOYBEANS ARE READY TO COMPLETELY ROLL OUT THIS YEAR G. Gullickson color *Successful Farming* v115 no7 p36 My 2017

Weeds Be Gone! color *Cabin Living* p21 S 2017

Weed control equipment

FLEX-WING ROTARY CUTTERS: TACKLE TALL WEEDS WITH THESE VERSATILE MACHINES B. Freese *Successful Farming* v115 no11 p34 S 2017

Weed Science Society of America—Congresses

Calendar of meetings *BioScience* v67 no1 p95 Ja 2017

Calendar of meetings *BioScience* v67 no2 p183 F 2017

Weedall, Lynne—Interviews

HR should be the experts in managing and leading change C. NEWBERY *People Management* p13 O 2016

WEEDEN, DON

An Ecoregion-Based Approach to Protecting Half the Terrestrial Realm *BioScience* v67 no6 p534 Je 2017

WEEDMAN, MARY JANE

Bottled Water img *New York* p56 F 9 2017

THE EVERYTHING GUIDE TO: Bottled Water img *New York* p56 Ja 9 2017

Guilin Mi Fen Noodles img *New York* v50 no16 p95 Ag 7 2017

home & help img *New York* p96 Mr 6 2017

New Bars for Everyone img *New York* v50 no17 p84 Ag 21 2017

Pickled Napa Cabbage img *New York* v49 no15 p67 Jl 25 2016

PUT SOME FETA AT THE BOTTOM img *New York* v49 no20 p106 O 3 2016

So, You Want a Grain Bowl img *New York* v49 no20 p110 O 3 2016

Weeds

See also

    Amaranthus palmeri

    Host plants

THE EIGHTH PHASE C. LISKA bw cartoon color *Snowboarder* v29 no4 p54 D 2016

Pineapple Weed M. WALWYN color *Canadian Wildlife* v23 no2 p37 My/Je 2017

Root Causes M. Gunch color *New Orleans Magazine* v51 no6 p44 Ap 2017

Weeds (TV program)

Late Bloomer S. FRIEDMAN color *AARP: The Magazine* v59 no2A p52 F/Mr 2016

Weeds—Risk assessment

CONTROLLING LAKE WEEDS J. Tiger color *Cabin Living* p67 Ap 2017

Weekend, The (Music)

The Playlist bw color *Rolling Stone* no1272 p10 O 20 2016

Weekends

Don't let the Smondays* ruin your life K. Schaefer color *Bloomberg Businessweek* no4495 p67 O 17 2016

great weekend getaways *Washingtonian Magazine* v52 no11 p80 Ag 2017

How to Plan Your Week to Keep Your Weekend Free E. G. Saunders *Harvard Business Review Digital Articles* p2 Ap 27 2015

Reclaim Your Weekends! M. C. White color *Money* v46 no9 p28 O 2017

silver linings J. Francisco *Good Housekeeping* v264 no4 p16 Ap 2017

Weekends with Yankee (TV program)

"WEEKENDS" WARRIOR A. Traverso, M. FLEMING et al color *Yankee* p50 Mr 2017

Weekends—Social aspects

I Have a Dream, Too S. CARR *Idaho Magazine* v16 no1 p54 O 2016

Weekly Standard, The (Periodical)

PARODY color *Weekly Standard* v22 no20 p40 Ja 30 2017

Weeknd, The, 1990-

Random Notes color *Rolling Stone* no1280 p24 F 9 2017

WEEKND UPDATE B. Mazurek bw *Harper's Bazaar* no3656 p398 S 2017

Weeks, Amy M.

Redox-based reagents for chemoselective methionine bioconjugation bibl diag graph *Science* v355 no6325 p597 F 10 2017

Weeks, Elizabeth

Improving Alignment between Educational Supply and Labor Market Needs *Change* v49 no1 p34 Ja/F 2017

Weeks, Holly

How to Give Feedback to Someone Who Gets Crazy Defensive *Harvard Business Review Digital Articles* p2 Ag 12 2015

Make It Easier for Your Boss to Say Yes to a Vacation Request *Harvard Business Review Digital Articles* p2 Je 3 2015

What Not to Say to a Stressed-Out Colleague *Harvard Business Review Digital Articles* p2 Ag 23 2016

Weeks, Kelly Pledger

Every Generation Wants Meaningful Work—but Thinks Other Age Groups Are in It for the Money *Harvard Business Review Digital Articles* p2 Jl 31 2017

Weeks, Kevin

DOUBLE PLAY color *Golf Magazine* v59 no1 p46 Ja 2017

Weeks, Stephen

The Countess of Prague: Book 1 of the Countess of Prague Mysteries *Publishers Weekly* v264 no27 p54 Jl 3 2017

Weeks, William B.

Patient-Reported Data Can Help People Make Better Health Care Choices *Harvard Business Review Digital Articles* p2 S 21 2015

Weems, Carrie Mae, 1953-

"BLACKNESS IN ABSTRACTION" E. Buhe *Art in America* v104 no9 p151 O 2016

Wegener, Dawn

DONKEY LIVES IN HOUSE K. Jazynka *National Geographic Kids* no469 p12 Ap 2017

Wegener, Martin

Hall-effect metamaterials and "anti-Hall bars" *Physics Today* v70 no10 p14 O 2017

Wegman, Jay

MAI: Lil Buck and Jon Boogz W. Perron *Dance Magazine* v91 no9 p13 S 2017

We Got It From Here, Thank You for Your Service (Music)

Marrying Genres C. TART color *Downbeat* v84 no3 p62 Mr 2017

Wehner, Peter

The Political Meaning of Christianity color *Christianity Today* v60 no8 p82 O 2016

Salt and Leaven color *National Review* v69 no6 p40 Ap 3 2017

Weiß, Clemens L.

Neandertal and Denisovan DNA from Pleistocene sediments bw color *Science* v356 no6338 p605 My 12 2017

Wei, Daniela

The Chinese Rediscover Luxury color *Bloomberg Businessweek* no4509 p15 Ja 30 2017

Japan's Big Bet color *Bloomberg Businessweek* no4505 p20 D 26 2016

Philippine Casinos Are Cleaning Up color graph *Bloomberg Businessweek* no4521 p19 My 8 2017

What Happens in Vegas Doesn't Stay There color *Bloomberg Businessweek* no4497 p24 O 31 2016

Wei, Ge

Driving mosquito refractoriness to Plasmodium falciparum with engineered symbiotic bacteria color graph *Science* v357 no6358 p1399 S 29 2017

Wei, H.

Observing the ultrafast buildup of a Fano resonance in the time domain bibl graph *Science* v354 no6313 p738 N 11 2016

Wei, Hong

Inactivation of porcine endogenous retrovirus in pigs using CRISPR-Cas9 diag *Science* v357 no6357 p1303 S 22 2017

Wei, Hong-Jiang

Inactivation of porcine endogenous retrovirus in pigs using CRISPR-Cas9 diag *Science* v357 no6357 p1303 S 22 2017

Wei, Kuangyi

If Data Is Money, Why Don't Businesses Keep It Secure? *Harvard Business Review Digital Articles* p2 F 10 2015

Wei, Lilly

From Disciple to Master bw *Art in America* v105 no6 p69 Je/Jl 2017

Second Sight bw *Art in America* v104 no10 p83 N 2016

Wei, Ronnie R.

Trispecific broadly neutralizing HIV antibodies mediate potent SHIV protection in macaques color graph *Science* v357 no6359 p85 O 6 2017

Wei, Shengji

Imaging the distribution of transient viscosity after the 2016 Mw 7.1 Kumamoto earthquake map *Science* v356 no6334 p163 Ap 14 2017

Wei, Xiao-Tong

"Perfect" designer chromosome V and behavior of a ring derivative diag *Science* v355 no6329 p1046 Mr 10 2017

Wei, Xuepeng

Structure and assembly mechanism of plant C2S2M2-type PSII-LHCII supercomplex color *Science* v357 no6353 p815 Ag 25 2017

Wei, Y.

A prominent glycyl radical enzyme in human gut microbiomes metabolizes trans-4-hydroxy-L-proline diag *Science* v355 no6325 p595 F 10 2017

Wei Cai

Highly stretchable polymer semiconductor films through the nanoconfinement effect bibl graph *Science* v355 no6320 p1 Ja 6 2017

WEI LI

Responses of Antarctic Marine and Freshwater Ecosystems to Changing Ice Conditions color graph *BioScience* v66 no10 p864 O 1 2016

Wei Liu

Photoactivation and inactivation of Arabidopsis cryptochrome 2 bibl graph *Science* v354 no6310 p343 O 21 2016

Wei Lu

Where the Living Is Easy map *Bloomberg Businessweek* no4514 p41 Mr 13 2017

Wei Peng

Structural basis for the gating mechanism of the type 2 ryanodine receptor RyR2 bibl color graph *Science* v354 no6310 paah5324-1 O 21 2016

Wei Shi

Research: When CEOs Don't Win Awards, They Make More Acquisitions *Harvard Business Review Digital Articles* p2 Mr 27 2017

Wei-Shin Lai—Interviews

Her Headphones Lull You to Sleep P. M. ESSWEIN color *Kiplinger's Personal Finance* v71 no3 p17 Mr 2017

Wei Sun

Realization of two-dimensional spin-orbit coupling for Bose-Einstein condensates bibl graph *Science* v354 no6308 p83 O 7 2016

Wei Wang

Glycomics and its application potential in precision medicine bibl diag *Science* v354 no6319 p36 D 23 2016

Growing pains for global monitoring of societal events bibl graph *Science* v353 no6307 p1502 S 30 2016

Weight loss & psychology

Weight loss preparations
THE RIGHT STUFF color *Muscle & Performance* v9 no4 p64 Ap 2017

Weight loss preparations—Evaluation
WEIGHT-LOSS SUPPORTERS color *Amazing Wellness* v9 no1 p42 Wint 2017

Weight loss—Equipment & supplies—Evaluation
NOT YOUR FATHER'S FAT BURNER J. WUEBBEN color *Muscle & Performance* v8 no12 p14 D 2016

Weight loss—Research
TRACKING YOUR WEIGHT LOSS M. Farrar and J. WUEBBEN color *Muscle & Performance* v8 no12 p15 D 2016

Weight training
See also
Bench press
Dead lift (Weight lifting)
Powerlifting
Squat (Weight lifting)
Weight lifting
10 WEIGHT-LOSS MYTHS BUSTED V. Tweed color *Amazing Wellness* v8 no2 p54 Spr 2016
BARBELL BENT-OVER ROW J. WUEBBEN color *Muscle & Performance* v9 no5 p13 My 2017
CYNTHIA ERIVO N. Weldon color *Runner's World* v51 no11 p108 D 2016
FULL FRONTAL J. CISSIK chart color *Muscle & Performance* v9 no5 p18 My 2017
Head in Hand S. RAVELLA color *Discover* v38 no3 p22 Ap 2017
JUST 3 MOVES FIRM UP, FAST! bw color *Good Housekeeping* v263 no5 p156 N 2016
Martha's Month chart color *Martha Stewart Living* no275 p1 Je 2017
Martha's Month chart color *Martha Stewart Living* p1 My 2017
[RE]BALANCING ACT M. BERG chart color *Muscle & Performance* v9 no1 p20 Ja 2017
Simone Missick N. Habtezghi color *Essence* v47 no12 p44 Ap 2017

Weight training equipment & supplies
See also
Dumbbells
5 WAYS... TO USE A SMITH MACHINE J. WUEBBEN color *Muscle & Performance* v9 no6 p66 Je 2017
Core Moves You've Never Tried L. BOYCE color *Muscle & Performance* v9 no7 p41 Jl 2017

Weight loss—Charts, diagrams, etc.
And Down 140 Pounds! color *Women's Health* v14 no3 p114 Ap 2017

Weight of These Wings, The (Music)
Miranda Lambert: Blonde on the Tracks W. HERMES color *Rolling Stone* no1275 p59 D 1 2016
Miranda Lambert L. Greenblatt color *Entertainment Weekly* no1441 p52 N 25 2016
PINK LEMONADE K. SANNEH cartoon *New Yorker* v92 no37 p89 N 14 2016
To Do img *New York* v49 no23 p90 N 14 2016

Weights & measures
See also
Body weight
WEIGHT & BALANCE R. Lengel diag *Flying* v144 no3 p30 Mr 2017

Weights & measures of horses
Playing the Hay Odds B. CRABBE color *Horse & Rider* v56 no11 p102 N 2017

Weigl, Andrea
SOUTH'S BEST ISLAND color *Southern Living* v52 no4 p82 Ap 2017

Weike Wang
Chemistry L. Greenblatt color *Entertainment Weekly* no1468/1469 p107 Je 2-9 2017

Weikert, Katherine
VALIANT LOSERS *History Today* v66 no10 p34 O 2016

Weil, Andrew
Better Bones color *Prevention* v69 no11 p22 N 2017
Dr. Weil [Cover story] cartoon color *Prevention* p24 Mr 2017
Dr. Weil [Cover story] color *Prevention* v69 no1 p24 Ja 2017
For Feet's sake [Cover story] color *Prevention* v69 no7 p22 Jl

2017
Keep Your Cool color *Prevention* v69 no8 p26 Ag 2017
Our Antibiotics Problem [Cover story] color *Prevention* v69 no4 p24 Ap 2017
Protect Your Teeth [Cover story] color *Prevention* v69 no5 p24 My 2017
Save Your Scalp [Cover story] color *Prevention* v69 no6 p24 Je 2017
Should I be eating less salt? color graph *Prevention* v68 no12 p26 D 2016
Under Pressure [Cover story] color *Prevention* v69 no9 p30 O 2017
What's the best treatment for my uterine fibroids? color *Prevention* v69 no2 p24 F 2017

Weil, David
How to Make Employment Fair in an Age of Contracting and Temp Work *Harvard Business Review Digital Articles* p2 Mr 24 2017
Lots of Employees Get Misclassified as Contractors. Here's Why It Matters *Harvard Business Review Digital Articles* p2 Jl 5 2017

WEIL, ELIZABETH
The Curse of the Bahia Emerald cartoon *Wired* v25 no3 p84 Mr 2017
PAT SUMMITT *New York Times Magazine* p60 D 25 2016

Weil, Liz
Lab Fab color *Vogue* v207 no9 p446 S 2017

Weil, Peter—Interviews
PETER WEIL A. Brandt *Dance Spirit* v21 no3 p38 Mr 2017

Weil, Simone, 1909-1943
CONVERSATIONS *Lapham's Quarterly* v10 no2 p205 Spr 2017

Weiland, Reid
BUILDING YOUR FARM'S BRAND: YOUR BRAND IS A TOOL THAT CAN HELP YOU ACHIEVE YOUR FARM'S GOALS J. Scott *Successful Farming* v115 no12 p18 O 2017

Weiman Products LLC
MICROFIBER CLOTH color *Good Housekeeping* v264 no2 p144 F 2017

Weimin Li
Quality management for precision medicine clinical applications: A consensus from the China Precision Medicine Clinical Research and Application Association bibl *Science* v354 no6319 p11 D 23 2016

Weinacker, Henry
An Essential Heart-Surgery Device Has a Rare But Deadly Side Effect J. Interlandi color *Consumer Reports* v82 no1 p41 Ja 2017

Weinberg, Bill
CUBA VERDE [Cover story] color *Earth Island Journal* v32 no3 p18 Aut 2017

Weinberg, Caroline
From a tweet, a March for Science is born L. Wessel color *Science* v355 no6325 p556 F 10 2017
THE MYTH OF SUPERFOOD color *Men's Health* v32 no2 p53 Mr 2017

Weinberg, Craig
VPD STUDIO *South Dakota Magazine* v33 no3 p24 S/O 2017

Weinberg, David E.
CAT-tailing as a fail-safe mechanism for efficient degradation of stalled nascent polypeptides diag *Science* v357 no6349 p414 Jl 28 2017

Weinberg, Neil
The $90 Billion Investor Who Can't Shake Wall Street color *Bloomberg Businessweek* no4518 p38 Ap 10 2017
Drug Costs Too High? Fire the Middleman *Bloomberg Businessweek* no4513 p28 Mr 6 2017
How Fancy Private Bankers Cross-Sell graph *Bloomberg Businessweek* no4510 p35 F 6 2017

Weinberg, Steven
A COSMIC CONTROVERSY color *Scientific American* v317 no1 p5 Jl 2017
The Trouble with Quantum Mechanics cartoon color *New York Review of Books* v64 no1 p51 Ja 19 2017

Weinberger, Daniel R.
Intersection of diverse neuronal genomes and neuropsychiatric disease: The Brain Somatic Mosaicism Network color *Science*

v356 no6336 p395 Ap 28 2017

Weinberger, David

How Reddit the Business Lost Touch With Reddit the Culture *Harvard Business Review Digital Articles* p2 Jl 14 2015

How Yahoo Betrayed Its Users by Doing What They Asked *Harvard Business Review Digital Articles* p2 D 16 2014

Weinberger, Sharon

Geniuses, Bureaucrats and Nuts: The story of Darpa, sponsor of scientific projects from the brilliant to the ridiculous F. KAPLAN *New York Times Book Review* p21 Jl 2 2017

Weinczok, David C.

TOWERS OF POWER *History Today* v66 no11 p34 N 2016

Weindl, A.

Observation of a large-scale anisotropy in the arrival directions of cosmic rays above 8 × 1018 eV *Science* v357 no6357 p1266 S 22 2017

WEINEMAN, JAIME J.

Rock of the aged color *Maclean's* v129 no40 p72 O 10 2016

Weiner (Film)

The 21 Documentaries from the 21st Century Every Man Should See bw color *GQ: Gentlemen's Quarterly* v86 no11 p84 N 2016

Flies on the wall D. D. Collum color *U.S. Catholic* v81 no11 p38 N 2016

No. 8 WEINER C. Nashawaty color *Entertainment Weekly* no1444/1445 p55 D 16 2016

Weiner, Allen S.

Just War Theory & the Conduct of Asymmetric Warfare *Daedalus* v146 no1 p59 Wint 2017

Weiner, Anthony D., 1964-

For the Record *Time* v189 no21 p7 Je 5 2017

WEINER, ELIZABETH

The Question color *O, The Oprah Magazine* p14 N 2017

WEINER, ERIC

FINANCIAL AIDE *Smithsonian* v47 no8 p44 D 2016

Renaissance Florence Was a Better Model for Innovation than Silicon Valley Is *Harvard Business Review Digital Articles* p2 Ja 25 2016

Weiner, G.

Jesse Norman, ed., Edmund Burke: Reflections on the Revolution in France and Other Writings *Society* v54 no4 p377 Ag 2017

Weiner, Jeff, 1971-

THE WORLD ACCORDING TO Gayle Gayle color *O, The Oprah Magazine* p38 O 2017

Weiner, Jennifer, 1970-

75 ways to be a grown-up *Parents* v91 no11 p95 N 2016

Hungry Heart T. Jordan color *Entertainment Weekly* no1436/1437 p106 O 21 2016

JENNIFER WEINER D. Meltzer Zepeda color *Runner's World* v52 no7 p92 Ag 2017

The Littlest Bigfoot *Publishers Weekly* v264 no5 p199 Ja 30 2017

Outsiders J. H. SWAN *New York Times Book Review* p33 N 13 2016

WEINER, JONAH

DUDES OF THE DANCE color *Rolling Stone* no1272 p38 O 20 2016

Emma Stone's Hollywood Ending [Cover story] color *Rolling Stone* no1278/1279 p34 Ja 12 2017

Fleet Foxes' New Harmony [Cover story] color *Rolling Stone* no1289 p18 Je 15 2017

Fleetwood Mac's New Spinoff bw color *Rolling Stone* no1290 p19 Je 29 2017

GOING SOLO *New York Times Magazine* p26 F 19 2017

HIP-HOP'S FAB THREE color *Rolling Stone* no1281/1282 p38 F 23 2017

Hip-Hop's King of Chaos color *Rolling Stone* no1297 p40 O 5 2017

Hot Rebel MC Lil Yachty bw color *Rolling Stone* no1274 p38 N 17 2016

"I feel like I got woken up this year. I'm really alive." color *Glamour* v114 no12 p202 D 2016

Khalid's Teen Spirit color *Rolling Stone* no1293 p32 Ag 10 2017

Mike D's Endless Summer bw *Rolling Stone* no1275 p20 D 1 2016

The New Norah bw color *Rolling Stone* no1273 p18 N 3 2016

'Pinky and the Brain' *New York Times Magazine* p22 N 6 2016

Sex, Drugs, Comedy color *Rolling Stone* no1297 p17 O 5 2017

Sisters in Arms bw color *Rolling Stone* no1287 p40 My 18 2017

Star Wars' Secret Weapon color *Rolling Stone* no1278/1279 p20 Ja 12 2017

Weiner, Kevin S.

Microstructural proliferation in human cortex is coupled with the development of face processing bibl graph *Science* v355 no6320 p1 Ja 6 2017

WEINER, LAUREN

The Soul of Mencken color *National Review* v69 no1 p35 Ja 23 2017

Weiner, Randy

Happenings M. Schulman color *New Yorker* v93 no11 p8 My 1 2017

Weiner, Tim

THE BIG BUST bw color *Esquire* v167 no1 p102 F 2017

FREE AGENTS: How the F.B.I. understands its relationship to the president - and how Donald Trump misunderstands the F.B.I *New York Times Magazine* p26 Jl 2 2017

Weinersmith, Kelly

Soonish C. McCormick *Science* v357 no6355 p965 S 8 2017

Weinert-Kendt, Rob

'A HEAVEN SOMEWHERE' color *America* v215 no12 p30 O 24 2016

August Wilson will not go quietly: revisiting "Fences" and "Jitney" color *America* v216 no5 p44 Mr 6 2017

Sam Shepard: America's cowboy Jeremiah color *America* v217 no5 p51 S 4 2017

Weinfurter, Daniel

The Best Ways to Hire Salespeople *Harvard Business Review Digital Articles* p2 N 2 2015

More Universities Need to Teach Sales *Harvard Business Review Digital Articles* p2 Ap 26 2016

Weingarten, Christopher R.

THE 50 GREATEST CONCERTS OF THE LAST 50 YEARS bw color *Rolling Stone* no1286 p30 My 4 2017

Charli XCX Gets Down With the Robots color *Rolling Stone* no1284 p52 Ap 6 2017

FALL ALBUM PREVIEW *Rolling Stone* no1297 p12 O 5 2017

Hot New Wave Austin Synth Rock bw color *Rolling Stone* no1274 p39 N 17 2016

Secrets of the Funky Drummer bw color *Rolling Stone* no1283 p12 Mr 23 2017

WEINMAN, JAIME

Adapting the unadaptable color *Maclean's* v129 no42 p56 O 24 2016

The movie is the message bw color *Maclean's* v129 no45 p52 N 14 2016

The prize, it is a-changing bw *Maclean's* v129 no43 p59 O 31 2016 Trumped up TV color *Maclean's* v129 no51/52 p70 D 26 2016

WILL NATO NOW BE 'OBSOLETE'? color *Maclean's* v129 no47 p30 N 28 2016

Weinman, Sam

Use Failure as Fuel color *Men's Health* v31 no10 p36 D 2016

Win at Losing: How Our Biggest Setbacks Can Lead to Our Greatest Gains *Publishers Weekly* v263 no41 p71 O 10 2016

Weinmann, Jens

The 3 Stages of a Country Embracing Renewable Energy *Harvard Business Review Digital Articles* p2 Ap 17 2017

Weinstein, Adam

THE TRUMP BUMP cartoon *Esquire* v167 no1 p54 F 2017

WEINSTEIN, ALEXANDER

Digital Fatigue *Publishers Weekly* v263 no42 p72 O 17 2016

They Deleted Their Kids J. WILWOL *New York Times Book Review* p16 O 9 2016

Weinstein, Austin

Trump Threatens to Undo Nafta's Auto Alley bw graph *Bloomberg Businessweek* no4509 p25 Ja 30 2017

Weinstein, Bruce

All-Time Favorite Sheet Cakes & Slab Pies: Easy to Make, Easy to Serve *Publishers Weekly* v264 no29 p212 Jl 17 2017

Weinstein, Emily

How America Lost Its Mind color *Atlantic* v320 no4 p12 N 2017

Weinstein, Harvey, 1952-

How Do You Solve a Problem Like Harvey Weinstein? [Cover story] S. Zacharek color *Time* v190 no16/17 p27 O 23 2017

Titans color *Time* v189 no16/17 p94 My 1-8 2017

What Weinstein's Downfall Means for Other Predators J. Filipovic *Time* v190 no16/17 p29 O 23 2017

Weinstein, James

40 Years J. BLEIFUSS bw *In These Times* v40 no11 p9 N 2016

Weinstein, James M.

Reducing Health Disparities and Promoting Health Equity *Parks & Recreation* v52 no5 p40 My 2017

Weinstein, James N.

Patient-Reported Data Can Help People Make Better Health Care Choices *Harvard Business Review Digital Articles* p2 S 21 2015

Weinstein, Jason S.

Macrophage function in tissue repair and remodeling requires IL-4 or IL-13 with apoptotic cells diag *Science* v356 no6342 p1072 Je 9 2017

Weinstein, Jimmy

BEHIND THE SCENES C. AARON, M. HARVEY et al bw color *In These Times* v40 no11 p48 N 2016

Weinstein, Joshua Z.

So When Are You Getting Married? R. Margalit color *New York Review of Books* v64 no16 p12 O 26 2017

Weinstein, Michael

Of Scorched Earth and Skyscrapers G. KAHN *Los Angeles Magazine* v61 no11 p26 N 2016

Weinstein, Paul V.

Make It Easy for Decision Makers to Approve Your Deal *Harvard Business Review Digital Articles* p2 Ja 16 2015

Win Over the Person Blocking Your Deal *Harvard Business Review Digital Articles* p2 N 4 2014

WEINSTEIN, PHILIP

Environmental Change and Human Health: Can Environmental Proxies Inform the Biodiversity Hypothesis for Protective Microbial-Human Contact? *BioScience* v66 no12 p1023-D 1 2016

Weinstein, Russell

How Geography Affects Where Elite Consulting Firms Recruit J. M. Olejarz *Harvard Business Review Digital Articles* p2 Jl 5 2016

Weintraub, Joseph R.

4 Reasons Managers Should Spend More Time on Coaching *Harvard Business Review Digital Articles* p2 My 29 2015

Weintraub, Karen

Could a Special Diet Replace Chemotherapy? color *Scientific American* v316 no1 p14 Ja 2017

How a Boy's Lazarus-like Revival Points to a New Generation of Drugs color *MIT Technology Review* v120 no4 p24 Jl/Ag 2017

Rejuvenating the Chance of Motherhood? color il *MIT Technology Review* v120 no1 p44 Ja/F 2017

Revenge of the Super Lice color *Scientific American* v316 no6 p24 Je 2017

Stomach Upset color *Scientific American* v316 no2 p22 F 2017

WEINTRAUB, PAMELA

HIDDEN INVADERS cartoon color diag *Discover* v38 no3 p46 Ap 2017

Weintraub, Rebecca

11 Things the Health Care Sector Must Do to Improve Cybersecurity *Harvard Business Review Digital Articles* p2 Je 1 2017

An Online Medical Database Is Reducing Diagnostic Errors *Harvard Business Review Digital Articles* p2 O 27 2015

Weiping Xie

A selective insecticidal protein from Pseudomonas for controlling corn rootworms bibl chart graph *Science* v354 no6312 p634 N 4 2016

Weir, Amelia—Interviews

All in the Fund Family J. BODNAR color *Kiplinger's Personal Finance* v70 no12 p21 D 2016

Weir, Andy—Interviews

Geek in Space N. deGrasse Tyson color *National Geographic* v230 no6 p26 D 2016

Weir, Bob—Interviews

Bob Weir D. BROWNE bw *Rolling Stone* no1273 p58 N 3 2016

Weir, Candace King—Interviews

All in the Fund Family J. BODNAR color *Kiplinger's Personal Finance* v70 no12 p21 D 2016

Weir, Fred

Persecution in Russia and Kazakhstan worsens for Jehovah's Witnesses *Christian Century* v134 no13 p13 Je 21 2017

State museum or church? Russians debate future of iconic cathedral color *Christian Century* v134 no7 p14 Mr 29 2017

Weir, Gary

POINT AND SHOOT color *Golf Magazine* v59 no4 p66 Ap 2017

SAVING PAR: GRIND OVER MATTER color *Golf Magazine* v59 no3 p45 Mr 2017

WEIR, JONAS

MORE GOOD READS *Missouri Life* v43 no6 p20 O/N 2016

Vintage Sounds *Missouri Life* v43 no6 p17 O/N 2016

Weir, Rachel

Music for the people: the role of music in the southern textile strikes of 1929-34 *Monthly Labor Review* p1 My 2017

Weirauch, Matthew T.

Control of species-dependent cortico-motoneuronal connections underlying manual dexterity diag graph *Science* v357 no6349 p400 Jl 28 2017

Weis, Judith S.

What lies beneath color *Science* v356 no6336 p384 Ap 28 2017

Weis, William I.

Vinculin forms a directionally asymmetric catch bond with F-actin chart color *Science* v357 no6352 p703 Ag 18 2017

Weisberg, Danielle

Carly Zakin And Danielle Weisberg Want You to Get The News A. M. Cox *New York Times Magazine* p66 Ap 30 2017

Weisberg, Jacob

How Megyn Kelly Won bw color *New York Review of Books* v64 no5 p8 Mr 23 2017

They've Got You, Wherever You Are color *New York Review of Books* v63 no16 p12 O 27 2016

What Are Impeachable Offenses? [Cover story] color *New York Review of Books* v64 no14 p16 S 28 2017

Weisberg, Jessica

THE BOY WITHOUT A COUNTRY *Harper's Magazine* p73 Ap 2017

Weisberg, Joe—Interviews

COLD WAR CONFIDENTIAL S. Li color *Entertainment Weekly* no1457/1458 p36 Mr 17 2017

WEISBERG, SAUL

Teaching Biology in the Field: Importance, Challenges, and Solutions *BioScience* v67 no6 p558 Je 2017

Weise, 1966-

How Tibet Is Being Crushed—While the Dalai Lama Survives J. Mirsky color *New York Review of Books* v63 no20 p95 D 22 2016

Weise, Don

Weise Reimagines Charlesbridge's Imagine C. Swanson *Publishers Weekly* v263 no39 p14 S 26 2016

Weise, Karen

Forget the Taser, Says Taser bw diag *Bloomberg Businessweek* no4518 p35 Ap 10 2017

A Free Hand on Immigration graph *Bloomberg Businessweek* no4499 p32 N 14 2016

MY, WHAT GREAT BIG SYMBOLIC VALUE YOU HAVE! [Cover story] bw color *Bloomberg Businessweek* no4505 p54 D 26 2016

Reno-vating color *Bloomberg Businessweek* no4528 p18 Je 26 2017

So you want to move to the U.S color diag graph *Bloomberg Businessweek* no4538 p48 S 18 2017

Thank You For Calling Equifax, Your Business Is Not Important to Us *Bloomberg Businessweek* no4538 p38 S 18 2017

Weise, Michelle

The Real Revolution in Online Education Isn't MOOCs *Harvard Business Review Digital Articles* p2 O 17 2014

WEISENBURGER, EDWARD J.

Payday Predators *America* v215 no15 p24 N 14 2016

Weisenthal, Joe

Love in a Bubble cartoon *Bloomberg Businessweek* no4536 p70 S 4 2017

Weiser (Idaho)

Memorial Hike B. MORGAN color *Idaho Magazine* v16 no1 p24 O 2016

WEISER, JAY

Image of a Decade bw *Weekly Standard* v22 no36 p37 My 29 2017

Weiskopf, Tom

DEAD AT AUGUSTA J. Passov color *Golf Magazine* v59 no4 p72 Ap 2017

TOWER OF POWER B. Riggs, D. Denunzio color *Golf Magazine* v59 no11 p48 N 2017

Weisman, Alex

ALMOST FAMOUS N. PARSI color *Chicago* v66 no11 p37 N 2017

WEISMAN, WENDY

Nashville Opera *Opera News* v81 no5 p16 N 2016

WEISS, ALEXANDRA

Aldous HARDING *Interview* v47 no6 p24 Ag 2017

Weiss, Andrew S.

Trump and Russia color *Foreign Affairs* v96 no2 p12 Mr/Ap 2017

Weiss, Benjamin P.

Lifetime of the solar nebula constrained by meteorite paleomagnetism bibl graph *Science* v355 no6325 p623 F 10 2017

WEISS, DANIEL

AFTER THE BATTLE bw color *Archaeology* v70 no3 p50 My/Je 2017

China's Legendary Flood color *Archaeology* v69 no6 p21 N/D 2016

A CORNUCOPIA OF CONDIMENTS color *Archaeology* v70 no3 p12 My/Je 2017

DISCOVERING TERROR color *Archaeology* v70 no1 p14 Ja/F 2017

DISPOSABLE GODS color *Archaeology* v70 no5 p16 S/O 2017

HOARDS OF THE VIKINGS color *Archaeology* v70 no1 p48 Ja/F 2017

KA-CHING! color *Archaeology* v70 no4 p9 Je-Ag 2017

LAST STAND OF THE BLUE BRIGADE color *Archaeology* v70 no5 p14 S/O 2017

LOST KINGDOM OF THE BRITONS color *Archaeology* v70 no5 p32 S/O 2017

ROYAL GAMS color *Archaeology* v70 no2 p18 Mr/Ap 2017

SCROLL SEARCH color *Archaeology* v70 no3 p9 My/Je 2017

TOMB COUTURE color *Archaeology* v70 no4 p16 Je-Ag 2017

TOP 10 DISCOVERIES OF 2016 bw cartoon color *Archaeology* v70 no1 p26 Ja/F 2017

Town Beneath the Waves color *Archaeology* v70 no2 p30 Mr/Ap 2017

Weiss, David, 1964-

Weiss Explores 'Fusion-Blues' Sounds with Point of Departure T. Panken color *Downbeat* v84 no7 p17 Jl 2017

Weiss, Emily

Gloss Castle K. Branch color *Vogue* v207 no10 p219 O 2017

Pioneers [Cover story] color *Time* v189 no16/17 p14 My 1-8 2017

Weiss, Gregor L.

In situ architecture, function, and evolution of a contractile injection system color diag *Science* v357 no6352 p713 Ag 18 2017

WEISS, HALEY

New RIDE *Interview* v46 no9 p45 N 2016

Ray BLK *Interview* v47 no1 p18 F 2017

SEVDALIZA: FOR THE IRANIAN DITCH SINGER-SONGWRITER, BOUNDARIES IN HER LIFE AND ART ARE MEANT TO BE BROKEN *Interview* v47 no3 p32 My 2017

SIGRID *Interview* v47 no6 p12 Ag 2017

WEISS, HEDY

The Best of 2016 *Dance Magazine* v90 no12 p84 D 2016

Weiss, Jed

A Fidelity Manager Takes a Break N. S. HUANG chart *Kiplinger's Personal Finance* v71 no7 p59 Jl 2017

Weiss, Jeff

How to Cool Down a Heated Negotiation *Harvard Business Review Digital Articles* p2 F 16 2016

Weiss, Jeffrey

My friends are praying for me. Does God care? *Christian Century* v134 no8 p1 Ap 12 2017

Weiss, Jeffrey S., 1958-

Relationship Investing: Stock Market Therapy for Your Money *Publishers Weekly* v263 no44 p64 O 31 2016

Weiss, Kenneth R.

Can deep reefs rescue shallow ones? *Science* v355 no6328 p903 Mr 3 2017

INTO THE TWILIGHT ZONE [Cover story] color graph *Science* v355 no6328 p900 Mr 3 2017

Weiss, Leah

A Simple Way to Stay Grounded in Stressful Moments *Harvard Business Review Digital Articles* p2 N 18 2016

Stop Mindlessly Going Through Your Work Day *Harvard Business Review Digital Articles* p2 Mr 23 2017

Weiss, Leonard

Safeguards and the NPT: Where our current problems began bibl *Bulletin of the Atomic Scientists* v73 no5 p328 2017

Weiss, Mitchell

Case Study: Should You Adjust Your Business Model for a Major Customer? *Harvard Business Review Digital Articles* p2 My 5 2016

Lessons from Boston's Experiment with The One Fund *Harvard Business Review Digital Articles* p2 Ja 22 2016

UBE2O remodels the proteome during terminal erythroid differentiation diag *Science* v357 no6350 p471 Ag 4 2017

WEISS, RAINER

A COSMIC CONTROVERSY color *Scientific American* v317 no1 p5 Jl 2017

Trio surfs gravitational waves to Nobel glory A. Cho color *Science* v357 no6359 p17 O 6 2017

Weiss, Richard

Achtung, Berlin: Your Flight Is Five Years Late color *Bloomberg Businessweek* no4517 p18 Ap 3 2017

Adidas Automates to Make Shoes Faster bw color *Bloomberg Businessweek* no4541 p17 O 9 2017

Europe's Big Airlines Struggle for Altitude color graph *Bloomberg Businessweek* no4503 p19 D 12 2016

How a 70-Year-Old in Nerdy Shoes Got Cool color *Bloomberg Businessweek* no4521 p20 My 8 2017

Racing to Run A Two-Hour Marathon color graph *Bloomberg Businessweek* no4538 p18 S 18 2017

WEISS, SASHA

THE REVEALER *New York Times Magazine* p28 Mr 5 2017

Weissberg, Roger P.

Social Emotional Learning in Elementary School: Preparation for Success *Education Digest* v83 no1 p36 S 2017

Weisser, Cybele

RETIRE EARLY: HOW THEY CAN DO IT chart color diag *Money* v46 no3 p44 Ap 2017

Weissflog, Anita

Higher predation risk for insect prey at low latitudes and elevations graph *Science* v356 no6339 p742 My 19 2017

Weissman, Elissa Brent

'OUR STORY BEGINS' bw color *Publishers Weekly* v264 no5 p19 Ja 30 2017

Weissman, Jonathan S.

CAT-tailing as a fail-safe mechanism for efficient degradation of stalled nascent polypeptides diag *Science* v357 no6349 p414 Jl 28 2017

CRISPRi-based genome-scale identification of functional long noncoding RNA loci in human cells bibl graph *Science* v355 no6320 p1 Ja 6 2017

Weissman, Stephen R.

Congress and War cartoon *Foreign Affairs* v96 no1 p132 Ja/F 2017

Weissmueller, Zach

Is Recreational Pot Coming to Cali? color *Reason* v48 no7 p11 D 2016

Neuropsychopharmacologist David Nutt on Alcohol, LSD, and Getting Sacked for His Findings color *Reason* v49 no4 p79 Ag/S 2017

Weiss-Wolf, Jennifer

Seeing Red: Periods Gone Public: Taking a Stand for Menstrual Equity M. M. GINTY *Ms.* v27 no3 p53 Fall 2017

WEISUL, KIMBERLY

Credit Check cartoon color *Rodale's Organic Life* v2 no7 p18 D 2016/Ja 2017

Weisz, Claire

On Connecting People in Public Space *Architectural Record* v205 no4 p191 Ap 2017

Weitekamp, Margaret A.

The image of scientists in The Big Bang Theory *Physics Today* v70 no1 p40 Ja 2017

Weitz, Joshua S.

How microbes survive in the open ocean color diag *Science* v357 no6352 p646 Ag 18 2017

Quantitative Viral Ecology M. C. Lagomarsino *Physics Today* v70 no6 p65 Je 2017

Weitzer, Ronald

Recent Ethnographies of the Criminal Justice System *Society* v54 no3 p292 Je 2017

Weitzman, Steven

WASHINGTON MONUMENT: A statue honoring Marion Barry will-of course--be larger than life A. Whiting *Washingtonian Magazine* v52 no12 p18 S 2017

WEI-VITAL, DENISE

Q: Who's your trusty sidekick for summer adventures, and why? color *O, The Oprah Magazine* p14 Je 2017

Weizman, Tomer

Global mRNA polarization regulates translation efficiency in the intestinal epithelium diag *Science* v357 no6357 p1299 S 22 2017

Welburn, Ed—Interviews

What I'd Do Differently Ed Welburn, 66 J. P. HUFFMAN color *Car & Driver* v62 no11 p120 My 2017

Welby, Justin, 1956-

The Hardest Word? Is it ahistorical for public figures to say sorry for events that took place before they were born? The issue cuts to the heart of the relationship between the living and the dead S. Lipscomb *History Today* v67 no6 p106 Je 2016

Welch, Amanda

Sunshine outside the ivory tower bw *Science* v357 no6357 p1322 S 22 2017

welch, betsy

divide and conquer bw color *Bike Magazine* v23 no9 p36 D 2016

Welch, Bob

2016 PRORODEO WORLD CHAMPS color *Spin to Win Rodeo* v20 no11 p54 Ja 2017

2016 WRANGLER NATIONAL FINALS RODEO PREVIEW color *Spin to Win Rodeo* v20 no10 p78 D 2016

At Home With... bw *American Cowboy* v23 no5 p17 F/Mr 2017

At Home With... color *American Cowboy* v24 no1 p16 Je/Jl 2017

Bigger Picture color *American Cowboy* v23 no4 p8 D 2016/Ja 2017

BUCKLE UP color *Spin to Win Rodeo* v20 no9 p19 N 2016

THE CASTRO BROTHERS bw *Spin to Win Rodeo* v21 no2 p96 Ap 2017

CLUTCH color *Spin to Win Rodeo* v20 no9 p50 N 2016

Cowboy Chronicler color *American Cowboy* v23 no5 p21 F/Mr 2017

Cow College color *American Cowboy* v23 no4 p24 D 2016/Ja 2017

DEAR ROPER color *Spin to Win Rodeo* v20 no11 p8 Ja 2017

Dreams bw *Horse & Rider* v56 no11 p17 N 2017

Family-Style bw *Horse & Rider* v56 no8 p17 Ag 2017

Finding Your Lane bw *Horse & Rider* v56 no7 p17 Jl 2017

FIVE FLAT color *Spin to Win Rodeo* v20 no9 p29 N 2016

FIVE FLAT with Jake Long color *Spin to Win Rodeo* v20 no10 p41 D 2016

FREEZE FRAME color *Spin to Win Rodeo* v20 no9 p40 N 2016

John Blocker's Road Brand color *American Cowboy* v23 no6 p72 Ap/My 2017

Legends in the Making color *American Cowboy* p72 LEGENDS OF TEXAS Special Issue 2017

Less Me, More We color *Horse & Rider* v56 no9 p17 S 2017

More of the Same color *Spin to Win Rodeo* v21 no2 p70 Ap 2017

My Collection color *Horse & Rider* v56 no7 p112 Jl 2017

My Favorite Brand color *American Cowboy* v24 no1 p72 Je/Jl 2017

NEW LIVING ARRANGEMENTS color *Spin to Win Rodeo* v20 no11 p88 Ja 2017

The Old CHISHOLM TRAIL [Cover story] color map *American Cowboy* v23 no6 p54 Ap/My 2017

PICKING THE FAVORITES color *American Cowboy* v23 no4 p64 D 2016/Ja 2017

Reaching the Next Level color *American Cowboy* v24 no1 p20 Je/Jl 2017

Salute to Service color *American Cowboy* v23 no5 p8 F/Mr 2017

A SHORT HISTORY OF THE RNCFR map *Spin to Win Rodeo* v21 no4 p88 Je 2017

The Spirit of the West *American Cowboy* v24 no1 p8 Je/Jl 2017

Tapped Off color *American Cowboy* v24 no1 p42 Je/Jl 2017

That Old Time Feeling color *American Cowboy* v23 no6 p38 Ap/My 2017

Trail Broke bw color *American Cowboy* v23 no6 p62 Ap/My 2017

Wagonhound Land and Livestock color *American Cowboy* v23 no4 p96 D 2016/Ja 2017

whatever IT Takes color *Spin to Win Rodeo* v21 no1 p62 Mr 2017

WORLD SERIES FINALE XI color *Spin to Win Rodeo* v20 no11 p56 Ja 2017

THE WYOMING COWBOY color *Spin to Win Rodeo* v21 no1 p96 Mr 2017

The XIT Ranch bw color *American Cowboy* p88 LEGENDS OF TEXAS Special Issue 2017

The Young'ns color *Horse & Rider* v56 no10 p17 O 2017

YOU PICKED 'EM! [Cover story] color *Spin to Win Rodeo* v20 no12 p54 F 2017

Welch, Craig

The Grass-Eating Monkeys of Ethiopia cartoon color map *National Geographic* v231 no4 p72 Ap 2017

Snorkeling With the President color *National Geographic* v231 no2 p76 F 2017

Welch, David

ALL ABOUT THE Benjamins chart color *Bloomberg Businessweek* no4523 p20 My 22 2017

Come for the Treadmill Desk, Stay for the ... color *Bloomberg Businessweek* no4522 p40 My 15 2017

A Continental Retreat color map *Bloomberg Businessweek* no4514 p23 Mr 13 2017

The Real Cause of the U.S. Car Slide: SUVs diag *Bloomberg Businessweek* no4518 p24 Ap 10 2017

This Hospital Operator Needs A Prescription graph *Bloomberg Businessweek* no4539 p18 S 25 2017

Trump Threatens to Undo Nafta's Auto Alley bw graph *Bloomberg Businessweek* no4509 p25 Ja 30 2017

Where Cadillac Is Still Prized color graph *Bloomberg Businessweek* no4510 p16 F 6 2017

Why Mexico's Autoworkers Aren't Prospering color graph *Bloomberg Businessweek* no4521 p12 My 8 2017

WELCH, GREG

REDUCING CMO TURNOVER: A Recruiter's Prescription color *Harvard Business Review* v95 no4 p59 Jl/Ag 2017

WELCH, JULIA

STORIES WE TELL OURSELVES color *Vanity Fair* v58 no11 p88 N 2016

Welch, Karla

Where the Red-Carpet Madness Begins [Cover story] J. Harman color *Glamour* v115 no3 p47 Mr 2017

Welch, Lynn

Calling the Shots *Tennis* v52 no6 p44 N/D 2016

Welch, Matt

BILL WELD'S WEIRD TUESDAY *Reason* v48 no9 p56 F 2017

The Collectivist Election *Reason* v48 no7 p12 D 2016

THE DEMOCRATS' DULLARD DYNASTY color *Reason* v49 no3 p10 Jl 2017

THE DEREGULATOR? color *Reason* v49 no2 p18 Je 2017

DID THE LIBERTARIAN PARTY BLOW IT IN 2016? color *Reason* v48 no9 p44 F 2017

FROM THE ARCHIVES bw color *Reason* v49 no3 p70 Jl 2017

FROM THE ARCHIVES cartoon *Reason* v49 no2 p70 Je 2017

Is free speech under threat IN THE UNITED STATES? WE RE-CEIVED TWENTY-SEVEN RESPONSES. WE PUBLISH THEM HERE, IN ALPHABETICAL ORDER *Commentary* v144 no1 p13 Jl/Ag 2017

JOHN MCCAIN: THE ANTI-TRUMP color *Reason* v49 no5 p10 O 2017

MEET THE FREE TRADERS WHO DON'T LIKE GLOBAL TRADE AGREEMENTS cartoon *Reason* v48 no10 p12 Mr 2017

POLITICIANS WILL DISAPPOINT YOU color *Reason* v49 no4 p14 Ag/S 2017

TRUMP'S SCHWARZENEGGER PROBLEM color *Reason* v48 no11 p14 Ap 2017

THE UNKILLABLE TWO-PARTY SYSTEM *Reason* v48 no8 p7 Ja 2017

WELCH, MEGGIE

BUTLER BLUE III, AKA TRIP *Indianapolis Monthly* p24 N 2017

Welch, Tana Jean

'Leda' Burning, Immendorf Palace, 1945 *New York Times Maga-*

zine p21 Ja 15 2017

Welch, Tyler
  Celebrating S&T's 75th Anniversary *Sky & Telescope* v133 no2 p6 F 2017

Welcome to Jamrock (Music)
  DAMIAN MARLEY J. Black color *Esquire* p37 My 2017

Weld, William F., 1945-
  BILL WELD'S WEIRD TUESDAY M. WELCH *Reason* v48 no9 p56 F 2017

Welding equipment
  ALL AROUND THE FARM® D. Foster, H. Fratzke et al color *Successful Farming* v115 no7 p67 My 2017
  ALL AROUND THE FARM P. Barbour *Successful Farming* v115 no8 p62 Je/Jl 2017

Welding instruction
  THE NEW SHOP CLASS color *Popular Mechanics* p59 Jl 2017

Welding shops
  THE NEW SHOP CLASS color *Popular Mechanics* p59 Jl 2017

Weldon, Amy
  Apple Eaters *Orion Magazine* v35 no6 p12 N/D 2016
  Medicine Walk *Orion Magazine* v35 no4/5 p106 Jl-O 2016

Weldon, Fay, 1931-
  Size Matters S. COLL *New York Times Book Review* p11 Mr 12 2017

Weldon, Nick
  Chin Losers color *Runner's World* v52 no9 p45 O 2017
  CYNTHIA ERIVO color *Runner's World* v51 no11 p108 D 2016
  DOMESTIQUE BLISS color *Runner's World* v51 no11 p22 D 2016
  JON GLASER color *Runner's World* v52 no1 p112 Ja/F 2017
  KRISTEN SCHAAL color *Runner's World* v52 no5 p96 Je 2017
  MAKOROBONDO "DEE" SALUKOMBO color *Runner's World* v52 no1 p84 Ja/F 2017
  NEW ORLEANS bw color map *Runner's World* v52 no1 p76 Ja/F 2017
  POLITICAL RACE color *Runner's World* v51 no10 p26 N 2016
  Roads Less Traveled bw color *Runner's World* v52 no5 p54 Je 2017
  RW 2016 COVER SEARCH [Cover story] color *Runner's World* v51 no11 p62 D 2016
  SAM RYAN color *Runner's World* v52 no4 p78 My 2017
  SHE'S GOING THE DISTANCE bw color *Runner's World* v52 no4 p53 My 2017
  STEVE SPENCE color *Runner's World* v51 no10 p36 N 2016
  THE UNSTOPPABLES color *Runner's World* v51 no10 p112 N 2016
  WHAT IT TAKES TO... RUN RELAYS ALL YEAR color *Runner's World* v52 no1 p34 Ja/F 2017

Weldon, Sarah
  ANIMALS ON DEMAND color *Entertainment Weekly* no1478 / 1479 p90 Ag 18-25 2017

Welfare recipients—Employment
  More Than Just a Job J. B. Wogan *Governing* v30 no1 p46 O 2016

Welin, Eric R.
  Photosensitized, energy transfer-mediated organometallic catalysis through electronically excited nickel(II) bibl diag graph *Science* v355 no6323 p380 Ja 27 2017

Welky, David
  POLAR VORTEX S. WHEELER *New York Times Book Review* p73 D 4 2016

Well-being
  See also
    Employee well-being
  Finding a fresh start M. Rollins *Redbook* p21 F 2017
  Forgive: Your Life Could Depend on It G. Roberts-Grey color *Essence* v48 no2 p111 Je 2017
  Human Well-Being and Historical Ecosystems: The Environmentalist's Paradox Revisited L. E. DELGADO and V. H. MARÍN *BioScience* v67 no1 p5 Ja 2017
  INTO THE GREAT UNKNOWN *Governing* v30 no1 p4 O 2016
  My Ex Is Advertising For Sugar Daddies. Can I Tell Her Mother? K. A. Appiah *New York Times Magazine* p18 O 30 2016
  A Plea to America's Adults A. POWELL and C. POWELL color *Reader's Digest* v190 no1132 p20 Jl/Ag 2017
  Rethinking the BOX STALL N. Moffitt color *Equus* no478 p34 Jl 2017

SIMPLE PLEASURES V. K. De Luca color *Essence* v47 no11 p14 Mr 2017
  This Just In J. Zorthian *Time* v190 no6 p25 Ag 7 2017
  Top 10 States for Well-Being map *Prevention* v69 no4 p13 Ap 2017
  WHAT IT MEANS TO BE HEALTHY color *National Geographic* v232 no3 p8 S 2017
  Why Fitness Trackers Aren't Making Us Healthier M. Oaklander color *Time* v188 no18 p19 O 31 2016
  You just woke up and already feel behind P. Moffitt color *Yoga Journal* p38 2016 Special Issue
  You're Never Done Finding Purpose at Work [Cover story] D. Pontefract *Harvard Business Review Digital Articles* p2 Mr 20 2016

Well-being—Psychological aspects
  MIDLIFE CRISIS APPARENTLY IS A MYTH *USA Today Magazine* v145 no2859 p1 D 2016

Well-being—Social aspects
  Personal Best M. Singer color *Vogue* v207 no11 p160 N 2017

Well Made Home (Company)
  Made to Measure J. J. CONDON color *House Beautiful* v159 no7 p51 S 2017

Wellaway, Christopher R.
  Click chemistry enables preclinical evaluation of targeted epigenetic therapies diag *Science* v356 no6345 p1397 Je 30 2017

Weller, Corry
  2016 YAMAHA WALL OF CHAMPIONS INDUCTEE CEREMONY color *Dirt Sports + Off-Road* v51 no5 p8 My 2017

WELLER, DONALD E.
  Submersed Aquatic Vegetation in Chesapeake Bay: Sentinel Species in a Changing World *BioScience* v67 no8 p698 Ag 2017

Weller, Jason—Interviews
  Forest Frontiers *American Forests* v123 no1 p4 Wint/Spr 2017

WELLER, ROBERT P.
  Chronicles of China's Spiritual Revival *Current History* v116 no791 p244 S 2017

WELLER, SHEILA
  EMMETT, STILL bw *Vanity Fair* p179 Hollywood 2017 Supplement
  IT HAPPENED IN 1967 bw color *Vanity Fair* v59 no4 p192 Mr 2017
  SEX AGE MADONNA cartoon color *AARP: The Magazine* v60 no2A p60 F/Mr 2017

Wellers, Dan
  8 Ways Machine Learning Is Improving Companie's Work Processes *Harvard Business Review Digital Articles* p2 My 31 2017

Wellerstein, Alex
  NUKEMAP creator Alex Wellerstein puts nuclear risk on the radar E. Eaves color *Bulletin of the Atomic Scientists* v73 no4 p211 Jl 2017
  The secret of the SOVIET HYDROGEN BOMB *Physics Today* v70 no4 p40 Ap 2017

Wellesley College (Wellesley, Mass.)
  YOU DIDN'T CREATE THESE CIRCUMSTANCES BUT YOU HAVE THE POWER TO CHANGE THEM H. R. CLINTON *Vital Speeches of the Day* v83 no7 p202 Jl 2017

Wellman, Natalia
  KITCHEN-TESTED TIPS color *Vegetarian Today* no1 p4 F 2017

Wells
  The Bison Deep Well Hand Pump S. Maxwell *Mother Earth News* no280 p78 F/Mr 2017
  Good Well Hunting B. HEWITT and P. HEWITT color *Yankee* p16 My/Je 2017
  Pollution reaches old groundwater T. SUMNER *Science News* v191 no10 p12 My 27 2017

Wells, Angela
  forest TLC M. MYLCHREEST color *Cabin Living* p52 O 2017

WELLS, IRA
  Socialism Is Back color *Walrus* v14 no7 p14 S 2017

Wells, James A.
  Redox-based reagents for chemoselective methionine bioconjugation bibl diag graph *Science* v355 no6325 p597 F 10 2017

Wells, Jerry
  #trailchat color *Backpacker* v45 no2 p10 Mr 2017

Wells, John
  Why Tesco's Strengths Are No Longer Good Enough *Harvard*

Business Review Digital Articles p2 O 6 2014

Wells, Kristen Fuhs
Fall Creek Place: A neighborhood once known as "Dodge City" thrives anew *Indianapolis Monthly* v40 no10 p32 Je 2017
Greencastle: Reasons to cheer the charming college town this month *Indianapolis Monthly* p40 N 2017

Wells, Linda
The Beauty Queen of QVC img *New York* v49 no26 p44 D 26 2016
SKIN IN THE GAME color *Harper's Bazaar* no3651 p333 Mr 2017
What Happens Between Before and After: A rarely seen side of plastic surgery img *New York* v50 no11 p46 My 29 2017
What to Do About Getting Old img *New York* p32 Ja 23 2017

Wells, Martha
The Harbors of the Sun *Publishers Weekly* v264 no23 p34 Je 5 2017

Wells, Mary Shannon
Fall Color, Four Ways color *Southern Living* v52 no10 p15 O 2017

Wells, Myrydd
BEST OF ATLANTA *Atlanta* v56 no8 p106 D 2016
POKÉMANIA! *Atlanta* v56 no7 p44 N 2016
WHAT TO PACK FOR THE ZOMBIE APOCALYPSE *Atlanta* v56 no10 p38 F 2017

Wells, Patricia
4 lovely ways to happy up your home color *Redbook* p132 Mr 2017

WELLS, PAUL
2,816 dead Canadians and counting color *Maclean's* v130 no10 p20 N 2017
Donald Trump's gilded cage color *Maclean's* v130 no4 p38 My 2017
THE INTERVIEW color *Maclean's* v130 no7 p20 Ag 2017
In Trump they trust color *Maclean's* v130 no9 p39 O 2017
It's not so bad. Really [Cover story] color *Maclean's* p24 Je 2017
JUSTIN TRUDEAU'S LONG GAME color *Maclean's* v130 no7 p36 Ag 2017
The newest new NDP color *Maclean's* v130 no10 p8 N 2017
Who we are chart color *Maclean's* v130 no6 p10 Jl 2017

WELLS, PETE
Prep Work: How Alice Waters came to create Chez Panisse and lead a revolution in American food *New York Times Book Review* p15 S 24 2017

Wells, Pete, ca. 1964-
Pete Wells J. Crelin *Current Biography* v78 no1 p91 Ja 2017

Wells, Peter P.
Identification of single-site gold catalysis in acetylene hydrochlorination bw diag graph *Science* v355 no6332 p1399 Mr 31 2017

Wells, Samuel
Clutter counselor *Christian Century* v134 no11 p35 My 24 2017
Faith Matters *Christian Century* v133 no24 p44 N 23 2016
Faith Matters *Christian Century* v134 no13 p2 Je 21 2017
Godly play with adults *Christian Century* v134 no15 p35 Jl 19 2017
Hovering over the deep *Christian Century* v134 no17 p28 Ag 16 2017
How evils wins *Christian Century* v134 no7 p35 Mr 29 2017
Love becomes fruitful *Christian Century* v134 no19 p35 S 13 2017
Partial depravity *Christian Century* v133 no21 p57 O 12 2016
The Politics of Virtue: Post-Liberalism and the Human Future color *Christian Century* v134 no10 p45 My 10 2017
We are God's artwork *Christian Century* v134 no3 p31 F 2017
What Brexit is revealing color *Christian Century* v133 no25 p35 D 7 2016

Wells, William
Caring for Aging Loved Ones color *Consumer Reports* v82 no12 p6 D 2017

Wells Fargo & Co.
CAN WELLS FARGO GET WELL? G. Colvin chart color diag *Fortune* v175 no8 p138 Je 15 2017
The Lawless Suites R. L. BOROSAGE *Nation* v303 no16 p4 O 17 2016
The Leadership Blind Spots at Wells Fargo S. M. Ochs *Harvard Business Review Digital Articles* p2 O 6 2016
WELLS FARGO'S CHEATING HEART B. McLEAN color *Van-*

ity Fair v59 no7 p70 Summ 2017

Wells Fargo & Co.—Finance
X-Ray: Wells Fargo R. Derousseau diag *Money* v45 no11 p47 D 2016

Wells Fargo & Co.—Officials & employees
Executive Clawbacks J. Zorthian *Time* v189 no15 p19 Ap 24 2017

Wells-Barnett, Ida B., 1862-1931
UNWRITTEN LAW *Lapham's Quarterly* v10 no3 p43 Summ 2017

Wells—Evaluation
A Well That Sucks Water from Air J. Zorthian color *Time* v188 no19 p17 N 7 2016

Wells Rowe, Deborah
EARLY WRITING EXPERIENCES: What every teacher and parent should know about why young children need to write *Literacy Today (2411-7862)* v35 no2 p30 S/O 2017

Welner, Kevin
Learning from schools that close opportunity gaps *Phi Delta Kappan* v99 no1 p8 S 2017

Welsh, Andrea J.
Dynamics of a human spiral wave *Physics Today* v70 no2 p78 F 2017

Welsh, Gary
BUZZWORTHY *Indianapolis Monthly* v40 no3 p14 N 2016

Welsh, Irvine
WHY We LOVE CHICAGO bw cartoon color *Chicago* v66 no3 p75 Mr 2017

Welsh, Johnny
Weedgalized in Colorado: True Tales from the High Country *Publishers Weekly* v264 no9 p66j F 27 2017

Welsh, Michael
Contingent valuation: Flawed logic? color *Science* v357 no6349 p363 Jl 28 2017
Putting a value on injuries to natural assets: The BP oil spill chart *Science* v356 no6335 p253 Ap 21 2017

Welsh Borders (England & Wales)
Touring the Welsh Marches: Land of Cider Apples, Offa's Dyke and Ancient Battles *British Heritage Travel* v38 no4 p21 Jl/Ag 2017

Welsh cooking
Sunken Hundred B. Cooper color *New Yorker* v92 no41 p21 D 12 2016

Welshans, Phillip
THE BIG QUESTION cartoon *Atlantic* v320 no4 p124 N 2017

Welte, Cornelia U.
A microbial route from coal to gas bibl color *Science* v354 no6309 p184 O 14 2016

Welteroth, Elaine, 1986-
Elaine Welteroth J. Crelin color *Current Biography* v78 no2 p83 F 2017
Refashionista J. HUGHES *New York Times Magazine* p28 S 3 2017

Wemple, Erik
Innovation gone bad *Columbia Journalism Review* p30 Fall/Wint 2016

Wen, Bo
Deep functional analysis of synII, a 770-kilobase synthetic yeast chromosome diag *Science* v355 no6329 p1047 Mr 10 2017

Wen, Leana S.
Attacking the Roots of Violence cartoon *Scientific American* v315 no5 p9 N 2016

Wen, Ming
Mapping the human DC lineage through the integration of high-dimensional techniques diag *Science* v356 no6342 p1044 Je 9 2017

Wen, Xiaodong
Atomic-layered Au clusters on α-MoC as catalysts for the low-temperature water-gas shift reaction chart diag graph *Science* v357 no6349 p389 Jl 28 2017

Wen, Zuozhu
The complex effects of ocean acidification on the prominent N2-fixing cyanobacterium Trichodesmium graph *Science* v356 no6337 p527 My 5 2017

Wen Geng Zhang
Quality management for precision medicine clinical applications: A consensus from the China Precision Medicine Clinical Re-

search and Application Association bibl *Science* v354 no6319 p11 D 23 2016

Wen Ma

Perovskite-perovskite tandem photovoltaics with optimized band gaps bibl chart graph *Science* v354 no6314 p861 N 18 2016

Wenchuan Earthquake, China, 2008

HERE A CITY SHALL BE WROUGHT: What's forgotten in China's time-lapse urbanism D. Brook color *Harper's Magazine* v335 no2005 p49 Je 2017

Wende, Sandra

A pathogenic role for T cell–derived IL-22BP in inflammatory bowel disease bibl graph *Science* v354 no6310 p358 O 21 2016

Wendel, Theodore, 1859-1932

Dealers' choice J. Gardner color *Magazine Antiques* v183 no6 p102 N/D 2016

Wendel, Tim

GETTING INTO THE SWING color *Washingtonian Magazine* v52 no7 p126 Ap 2017

WHOLE NEW BALL GAME *Washingtonian Magazine* v52 no5 p125 F 2017

Wenderoth, Michael Chang

Great Leaders Embrace Office Politics *Harvard Business Review Digital Articles* p2 Ap 11 2016

WENDERS, WIM

Paul AUSTER *Interview* v47 no1 p26 F 2017

Wendle, John

The World Nomad Games color *Atlantic* v318 no5 p18 D 2016

Wendler, Andrew

$80K+ CARS color *Car & Driver* v62 no7 p22 Ja 2017

Wendler, Gerd

Weatherwatch color map *Weatherwise* v70 no4 p38 Jl/Ag 2017

Weatherwatch *Weatherwise* v70 no1 p50 Ja/F 2017

Weatherwatch *Weatherwise* v70 no2 p38 Mr/Ap 2017

Wendling, Chanin D.

Why This Health System Offers Refunds to Dissatisfied Patients *Harvard Business Review Digital Articles* p2 N 16 2016

Wendowski, Jen

BEND AWAY THE BLUES diag *Rodale's Organic Life* v2 no7 p28 D 2016/Ja 2017

Wendricks, Angie

COTTAGE INDUSTRY K. FRANZMAN color *Indianapolis Monthly* v41 no2 p82 S 2017

Wendt, Bill

THE INDY OFFY LAND-SPEED MASH-UP T. Taylor bw color *Hot Rod* v70 no3 p30 Mr 2017

Wendt, Henry

PUT AWAY WET S. Lachenauer bw color *Hot Rod* v70 no3 p40 Mr 2017

Wendt, Kathleen A.

Response to Comments on "Reconciliation of the Devils Hole climate record with orbital forcing" bibl chart graph *Science* v354 no6310 p296-e O 21 2016

Wenger, Daniel

Aska color *New Yorker* v93 no2 p19 F 27 2017

Flora Bar color *New Yorker* v93 no11 p15 My 1 2017

Günter Seeger color *New Yorker* v92 no40 p19 D 5 2016

Pondicheri color *New Yorker* v92 no34 p17 O 24 2016

Wenger, Tisa

Whose religious freedom? [Cover story] color *Christian Century* v134 no22 p24 O 25 2017

WENGERT, BRIANA

BUG throwback GOT YOU COVERED *Better Homes & Gardens* v94 no12 p156 D 2016

Wenholz, Sushil Dulai

Can Algae Fight Ulcers? color *Practical Horseman* v45 no7 p68 Jl 2017

Can Your Horse Ask You For Help? color *Practical Horseman* v45 no4 p67 Ap 2017

COLIC SURGERY [Cover story] color *Practical Horseman* v45 no7 p52 Jl 2017

Diet Does Matter In OCD Development color *Practical Horseman* v45 no6 p76 Je 2017

New DIY Tapeworm Test color *Practical Horseman* v45 no5 p76 My 2017

New Horse Headset Records EEGs color *Practical Horseman* v45 no8 p68 Ag 2017

Pressure-Testing Equine Leg Wraps color *Practical Horseman* v45 no1 p69 Ja 2017

Researching Reflux and Its Link to Inflammation color *Practical Horseman* v45 no3 p69 Mr 2017

Wenjack, Chanie

'I believe that Chanie Wenjak chose me' J. BOYDEN bw color *Maclean's* v129 no44 p16 N 7 2016

Wenjin Zhao

A Silurian maxillate placoderm illuminates jaw evolution bibl color *Science* v354 no6310 p334 O 21 2016

Wenk, Markus R.

Characterization of a dynamic metabolon producing the defense compound dhurrin in sorghum bibl graph *Science* v354 no6314 p890 N 18 2016

Lipid transport by TMEM24 at ER-plasma membrane contacts regulates pulsatile insulin secretion diag *Science* v355 no6326 p709 F 17 2017

Wenmei Li

Expert consensus on point-of-care testing *Science* v354 no6319 p15 D 23 2016

Recommendations on the management and use of POCT in medical institutions (nosocomial) *Science* v354 no6319 p13 D 23 2016

Wenner, Jann S.

Between the Covers J. HAGAN bw color *Vanity Fair* v59 no11 p144 N 2017

A Conversation With President Obama [Cover story] color *Rolling Stone* no1276 p34 D 15 2016

Jann Wenner color *AARP: The Magazine* v30 no6A p16 O/N 2017

The Story of 'Rolling Stone' bw color *Rolling Stone* no1289 p26 Je 15 2017

Wenner Moyer, Melinda

THE LOOMING THREAT OF FACTORY — FARM SUPERBUGS color diag *Scientific American* v315 no6 p70 D 2016

Wennersten, John R.

Refugees of rising seas H. Wiegel color *Science* v357 no6346 p41 Jl 7 2017

Wensinger, Terri Sue

A DIFFERENT Kind of Ride J. Keeler color *Dressage Today* v23 no8 p52 Ap 2017

Wenting Guo

Structural basis for the gating mechanism of the type 2 ryanodine receptor RyR2 bibl color graph *Science* v354 no6310 paah5324-1 O 21 2016

Wentworth (TV program)

LIKE THAT? TRY THIS! A. D'Arminio *TV Guide* v65 no25 p24 Je 2017

Wentworth, Ali

Ali Wentworth Talks the Talk D. Coggan color *Entertainment Weekly* no1440 p16 N 18 2016

Wentworth Inc.

BUILDER PROFILES *Washingtonian Magazine* v52 no8 p187 My 2017

Custom Home Builders Directory *Washingtonian Magazine* v52 no8 p186 My 2017

Wenu Wenu (Music)

The Wedding Singer M. Trammell cartoon *New Yorker* v93 no26 p15 S 4 2017

Wenxin, Fan

So you want to move to the U.S color diag graph *Bloomberg Businessweek* no4538 p48 S 18 2017

Wenxin Xu

Systems-level analysis of mechanisms regulating yeast metabolic flux bibl diag graph *Science* v354 no6311 paaf2786-1 O 28 2016

Wen Yu, Chung

Predicting human olfactory perception from chemical features of odor molecules bibl diag graph *Science* v355 no6327 p820 F 24 2017

Wenyuan Li

Quality management for precision medicine clinical applications: A consensus from the China Precision Medicine Clinical Research and Application Association bibl *Science* v354 no6319 p11 D 23 2016

Wenz, John

16 TIMES WE DIDN'T FIND E.T cartoon *Astronomy* v45 no9 p34 S 2017

CAN TONS OF XENON FINALLY FIND DARK MATTER? color *Astronomy* v45 no7 p12 Jl 2017

CERES HAS AN ABUNDANCE OF ICE color *Astronomy* v45 no4 p12 Ap 2017

COULD PLANET NINE TILT OUR SOLAR SYSTEM? color *Astronomy* v45 no2 p12 F 2017

Get ready for the next generation planet hunter color *Astronomy* v45 no7 p44 Jl 2017

'PUMPKIN STARS' CARVE OUT A NICHE IN THE UNIVERSE color *Astronomy* v45 no3 p12 Mr 2017

VOYAGER REVEALED! color diag graph *Astronomy* v45 no10 p34 O 2017

WENZL, ROY

My Father Was the BTK Killer *Reader's Digest* v188 no1126 p112 D 2016/Ja 2017

Wepf, R. A.

Direct observation of individual hydrogen atoms at trapping sites in a ferritic steel bibl diag *Science* v355 no6330 p1196 Mr 17 2017

Wepner, Chuck

Chuck Redux T. Keith color *Sports Illustrated* v126 no13 p22 My 8 2017

We're in This Together (Music)

THE ESSENTIALS M. Vain *Entertainment Weekly* no1454/1455 p22 F 24 2017

WERKER, ERIC

MAPPING FRONTIER ECONOMIES [Cover story] chart color diag graph il img *Harvard Business Review* v94 no12 p40 D 2016

WERLING, MIKE

ANCHORS, OBEY *Sea Magazine* v109 no9 p6 S 2017

CHANGE OF VENUE, CHANGE OF NAME *Sea Magazine* v108 no9 p6 S 2016

CRUISERS 60 CANTIUS FLYBRIDGE *Sea Magazine* v108 no10 p40 O 2016

CUTWATER: 302 SPORT COUPE THIS OUTBOARD-POWERED CRUISER CAN HIT 50 MPH AND HOST A DOCKSIDE SUNSET DINNER color *Sea Magazine* v109 no6 p34 Je 2017

DON'T GET HOLIDAZED *Sea Magazine* v108 no12 p5 D 2016

DUFFIELD 58: TRADITIONAL LINES AND A DOUG ZURN DESIGN CREATE A COUPLES CRUISER WITH RANGE AND COMFORT color *Sea Magazine* v109 no6 p38 Je 2017

ESCAPE TO AVALON *Sea Magazine* v108 no10 pCA-1 O 2016

FORMIDABLE FEATURES *Sea Magazine* v109 no7 p4 Jl 2017

FOUR WINNS HORIZON 350 *Sea Magazine* v108 no12 p28 D 2016

A FRESH LOOK *Sea Magazine* v108 no10 p6 O 2016

GALEON 445 HTS *Sea Magazine* v108 no8 p34 Ag 2016

Gettin' Better *Sea Magazine* v109 no5 p54 My 2017

GETTING BETTER *Sea Magazine* v109 no1 p6 Ja 2017

HAMPTON 650 PILOTHOUSE *Sea Magazine* v108 no10 p38 O 2016

HELP CREATE THE NEXT GENERATION OF BOATERS *Sea Magazine* v108 no8 p5 Ag 2016

IT'S HERE! *Sea Magazine* v109 no5 p6 My 2017

JEANNEAU LEADER 30 *Sea Magazine* v109 no2 p38 F 2017

JEANNEAU NC 895: A NEW CONCEPT GETS AN OUTBOARD REDESIGN BUT KEEPS ITS PERFORMANCE CHOPS AND WEEKEND CRUISING ABILITY *Sea Magazine* v109 no9 p38 S 2017

LOCAL DEBUT color *Sea Magazine* v109 no6 p6 Je 2017

Mini-Crulse *Sea Magazine* v109 no5 p20 My 2017

NORDHAVN 59 COASTAL PILOT *Sea Magazine* v108 no8 p30 Ag 2016

NORDHAVN N96: AWARD-WINNING DESIGN AND OCEAN-CROSSING RANGE FIND A HOME IN ONE NEAR-100-FOOT YACHT *Sea Magazine* v109 no9 p42 S 2017

OCEAN ALEXANDER 70 EVOLUTION *Sea Magazine* v108 no12 p32 D 2016

OCEAN PRESERVATION TAKES SHAPE *Sea Magazine* v109 no2 p4 F 2017

POCKETS GET POPULAR color *Sea Magazine* v109 no8 p4 Ag 2017

RIVIERA 4800 SPORT YACHT: THE LATEST IN TECHNOLOGY AND PROPULSION COMBINE WITH STYLE AND

STRENGTH color *Sea Magazine* v109 no7 p28 Jl 2017

SCANDINAVIAN STYLE *Boating World* v38 no1 p6 Ja 2017

TAKE THE BEACH *Sea Magazine* v109 no4 p6 Ap 2017

THINKING CAP *Sea Magazine* v108 no10 p6 O 2016

TIARA 44 FLYBRIDGE: A COUPLES COUPE GETS A FLYBRIDGE ADDITION AND GOES TO A WHOLE NEW LEVEL, LITERALLY AND FIGURATIVELY color *Sea Magazine* v109 no8 p42 Ag 2017

TIARA 53 COUPE *Sea Magazine* v109 no2 p34 F 2017

Wernberg, Thomas

Accelerating Tropicalization and the Transformation of Temperate Seagrass Meadows *BioScience* v66 no11 p938 N 1 2016

Biodiversity redistribution under climate change: Impacts on ecosystems and human well-being color *Science* v355 no6332 p1389 Mr 31 2017

Werner, Brian

Should You Finally Get It Fixed? M. HEID and M. DITROLIO color *Men's Health* v31 no10 p114 D 2016

Werner, C.

Comment on "Mycorrhizal association as a primary control of the CO_2 fertilization effect" bibl graph *Science* v355 no6323 p358 Ja 27 2017

WERNER, DOUG

BATTLING CHILDHOOD OBESITY *USA Today Magazine* v146 no2866 p62 Jl 2017

Werner, Finn

The architecture of transcription elongation diag *Science* v357 no6354 p871 S 1 2017

Werner, Harry W.

How to Deal with Choke color *Dressage Today* v23 no8 p18 Ap 2017

Werner, Kimi

GOING DEEP J. Dean color *Sunset* v238 no5 p19 My 2017

WERNER, MICHAEL

HOPE *Humanist* v76 no6 p42 N/D 2016

LET'S CELEBRATE! (AKA HOW WE CAN BE OF SERVICE TO THE SECULAR COMMUNITY) *Humanist* v77 no3 p38 My/Je 2017

REMAKING OURSELVES *Humanist* v77 no2 p38 Mr/Ap 2017

SEX: OUR WONDERFUL GIFT *Humanist* v77 no4 p41 Jl/Ag 2017

WERNER, PETER

Planning for the Future of Urban Biodiversity: A Global Review of City-Scale Initiatives *BioScience* v67 no4 p332 Ap 2017

Werner, Thilo

Click chemistry enables preclinical evaluation of targeted epigenetic therapies diag *Science* v356 no6345 p1397 Je 30 2017

Werner, Tillmann

LAUNCH color *Wired* v25 no4 p3 Ap 2017

Werner, W. J.

Long-term pattern and magnitude of soil carbon feedback to the climate system in a warming world chart graph *Science* v357 no6359 p101 O 6 2017

Werner, William

A Berry Good Idea A. MASON color *Bon Appetit* no8 p28 Ag 2017

Werris, Wendy

Beyond High Heels and Lipstick color *Publishers Weekly* v264 no19 p48 My 8 2017

Good Vibrations *Publishers Weekly* v263 no41 p67 O 10 2016

MURDER AND RACE IN EAST TEXAS color *Publishers Weekly* v264 no28 p58 Jl 10 2017

Werth, Isabell

ISABELL WERTH TAKES TOP HONORS AT THE FEI WORLD CUP DRESSAGE FINAL OMAHA 2017 color *Dressage Today* v23 no9 p14 Je 2017

Tips From a World Cup Champion B. Baumert color *Dressage Today* v23 no9 p40 Je 2017

WERTHEIM, JON

TENNIS, ANYONE? *Indianapolis Monthly* v40 no4 p96 D 2016

THROWING IN THE CHAIR *Indianapolis Monthly* v40 no7 p80 Mr 2017

Wertheim, L. Jon

The AFTER-PARTY color *Sports Illustrated* v127 no1 p48 Jl 3 2017

Artist IN RESIDENCE [Cover story] color *Sports Illustrated*

v127 no6 p32 Ag 28 2017

BATTER, INTERRUPTED color *Sports Illustrated* v126 no11 p50 Ap 17-24 2017

Beyond Words color *Sports Illustrated* v125 no12 p16 O 10 2016

BIG GAME, BIG MYTH color *Sports Illustrated* v126 no4 p46 Ja 30 2017

The Case for ... Peak NBA color *Sports Illustrated* v127 no2 p27 Jl 17 2017

The Case for ... Time Off color *Sports Illustrated* v127 no1 p28 Jl 3 2017

Demetrious Johnson color *Sports Illustrated* v126 no15 p44 My 29 2017

Draw Of Lots color *Sports Illustrated* v127 no6 p36 Ag 28 2017

Eighth WONDER color *Sports Illustrated* v127 no3 p58 Jl 24 2017

Fading Fast color *Sports Illustrated* v127 no1 p14 Jl 3 2017

FRESH START IN THE OLD CITY color *Sports Illustrated* v126 no2 p46 Ja 16 2017

GARDEN PARTY color *Sports Illustrated* v125 no17 p102 N 21 2016 Double Issue

HAVE IT BOTH WAYS color *Sports Illustrated* v126 no11 p92 Ap 17-24 2017

Hot Spot color *Sports Illustrated* v126 no13 p16 My 8 2017

INDYCAP VICE color *Sports Illustrated* v126 no2 p54 Ja 16 2017

INTERSTATE 5 KILLER color *Sports Illustrated* v125 no17 p108 N 21 2016 Double Issue

More Perfect Unions color *Sports Illustrated* v125 no19 p19 D 12 2016

Players Of the Year color *Sports Illustrated* v125 no20 p92 D 19 2016

The Reckoning color *Sports Illustrated* v126 no14 p17 My 15-22 2017

SEA OF DREAMS color map *Sports Illustrated* v126 no18 p54 Je 26 2017

Sports and Autism color *Sports Illustrated* v125 no16 p52 N 14 2016

Team of Rivals color *Sports Illustrated* v125 no19 p100 D 12 2016

TIME TO BE RELEASED? color *Sports Illustrated* v126 no5 p70 F 13 2017

A WINNING BATTLE color *Sports Illustrated* v127 no9 p32 S 25 2017

WON FOR THE AGED color *Sports Illustrated* v126 no5 p60 F 13 2017

Wertheimer, Neil

Lessons From the Rich chart color *AARP: The Magazine* v60 no2A p38 F/Mr 2017

To Lose Weight, Put Your Home on a Diet color *AARP: The Magazine* v60 no4A p14 Je/Jl 2017

Werther (Theatrical production)

Werther *Opera News* v81 no9 p57 Mr 2017

Werthwein, Harold

A modeling ambassador T. Koester color *Model Railroader* v84 no2 p90 F 2017

Wertmüller, Lina, 1928-—Interviews

O, Pioneer N. Rapold bw *Film Comment* v53 no2 p10 Mr/Ap 2017

Wery, Paige

Outsider Art's Inner Santum D. HARVEY *Los Angeles Magazine* p30 Mr 2017

Wesch, Charlotte

De-extinction, nomenclature, and the law color *Science* v356 no6342 p1016 Je 9 2017

Weschler, Lawrence

Waves Passing in the Night: Walter Murch in the Land of the Astrophysicists *Publishers Weekly* v263 no42 p59 O 17 2016

Wesley, Eric—Exhibitions

ERIC WESLEY G. Kroeber color *Art in America* v105 no3 p135 Mr 2017

Wesley, John, 1703-1791

At Home with the Wesleys *British Heritage Travel* v37 no6 p70 N/D 2016

Wesley, Rutina, 1979-

A VIBRANT LEGACY A. Tinubu color *Ebony* v72 no9 p78 Jl/Ag 2017

Wesley College (Dover, Del.)

Sentence First... cartoon *Weekly Standard* v22 no7 p3 O 24 2016

WESS, YOLANDA

LOOKING BACK *Cincinnati Magazine* v50 no8 p73 My 2017

Wessel, Kipp—Interviews

Meet the Finalists for the booklife Prize in Fiction N. AUDREY SPECTOR color *Publishers Weekly* v263 no52 p78 D 19 2016

Wessel, Lindzi

From a tweet, a March for Science is born color *Science* v355 no6325 p556 F 10 2017

On eve of science march, planners look ahead color *Science* v356 no6334 p118 Ap 14 2017

Wessel, Maxwell

3 Questions to Get the Most Out of Your Company's Data *Harvard Business Review Digital Articles* p2 Ja 29 2015

How Big Data Is Changing Disruptive Innovation *Harvard Business Review Digital Articles* p2 Ja 27 2016

How to Think About the Future of Cars *Harvard Business Review Digital Articles* p2 Jl 27 2015

Making Sense of Uber's $40 Billion Valuation *Harvard Business Review Digital Articles* p2 D 10 2014

The Most Innovative Companies Don't Worry About Consensus *Harvard Business Review Digital Articles* p2 O 3 2014

The Most Innovative Companies Have Long- Term Leadership *Harvard Business Review Digital Articles* p2 D 30 2014

Most On-Demand Businesses Aren't Actually Disruptive *Harvard Business Review Digital Articles* p2 S 29 2015

Old Management Systems Stifle New Business Models *Harvard Business Review Digital Articles* p2 Ap 28 2015

Predict the Future of Your Business *Harvard Business Review Digital Articles* p2 Ap 13 2015

The President's Policy Changes Are Already Hurting U.S. Innovation color *Harvard Business Review Digital Articles* p2 F 1 2017

The Problem with Legacy Ecosystems il *Harvard Business Review* v94 no11 p68 N 2016

What Driverless Cars Mean for Today's Automakers *Harvard Business Review Digital Articles* p2 Ag 27 2015

What Net Present Value Can't Tell You *Harvard Business Review Digital Articles* p2 N 20 2014

What the Auto Industry Can Learn from Cloud Computing *Harvard Business Review Digital Articles* p2 Jl 29 2015

What VCs Can Teach Executives About What Drives Returns *Harvard Business Review Digital Articles* p2 Je 25 2015

Why Preventing Disruption in 2017 Is Harder Than It Was When Christensen Coined the Term *Harvard Business Review Digital Articles* p2 S 4 2017

Why Some Digital Companies Should Delay Profitability for as Long as They Can *Harvard Business Review Digital Articles* p2 My 4 2017

You Don't Need Big Data—You Need the Right Data *Harvard Business Review Digital Articles* p2 N 3 2016

Wesselman, Hank

The Re-Enchantment: A Shamanic Path to a Life of Wonder color *Publishers Weekly* v263 no51 p144 D 12 2016

Wessels, Dean

ALL AROUND THE FARM® *Successful Farming* v115 no6 p77 Ap 2017

WESSLER, SETH FREED

Private Prisons Fail color *Nation* v304 no3 p6 Ja 30 2017

TRUMP'S 3 MILLION CRIMINALS color *Nation* v303 no25/26 p16 D 19 2016

Wessling-Resnick, Marianne

Restored iron transport by a small molecule promotes absorption and hemoglobinization in animals color graph *Science* v356 no6338 p608 My 12 2017

Wesson, Rob

Darwin's First Theory: Exploring Darwin's Quest to Find a Theory of the Earth L. A. MARSCHALL color *Natural History* v125 no5 p46 My 2017

West (U.S.)—Description & travel

FOLLOW YOUR GUT J. Battilana chart color *Sunset* v238 no6 p30 Je 2017

West, Adam, 1928-2017

Adam West (1928-2017) M. Roush *TV Guide* v65 no27 p3 Je 26 2017

Adam West J. McGovern color *Entertainment Weekly* no1471 p20 Je 23 2017

West, Andrew J.

Inside Once Upon a Time's Big Reset N. Abrams color *Entertainment Weekly* no1467 p52 My 26 2017

Once Upon a Time N. Abrams, S. Highfill et al color *Entertainment Weekly* no1482/1483 p96 S 22 2017

West, Audrey

Reflections on the lectionary *Christian Century* v134 no22 p21 O 25 2017

West, Dan

Take this $500 and do good in the world L. S. Truax and A. Campbell color *Christian Century* v134 no8 p1 Ap 12 2017

West, Dominic

STATE OF THE AFFAIR J. RUSSELL *TV Guide* v64 no48 p26 N 21 2016

West, Evan

AHEAD OF THE CURRENT color *Indianapolis Monthly* v41 no2 p68 S 2017

best of Indy *Indianapolis Monthly* v40 no4 p73 D 2016

Broad RIPPLE color map *Indianapolis Monthly* v41 no2 p66 S 2017

CAN YOU DIG IT? diag *Indianapolis Monthly* v41 no2 p72 S 2017

A DAM SHAME *Indianapolis Monthly* v41 no2 p64 S 2017

DAN WEEKEND NEEDS A RIDE *Indianapolis Monthly* v40 no5 p60 Ja 2017

THE DECISION *Indianapolis Monthly* p74 F 2017

Downtown color map *Indianapolis Monthly* v41 no2 p73 S 2017

Farther Downstream color map *Indianapolis Monthly* v41 no2 p77 S 2017

GM STAMPING PLANT color map *Indianapolis Monthly* v41 no2 p75 S 2017

Hamilton COUNTY color map *Indianapolis Monthly* v41 no2 p63 S 2017

MAKING A SPLASH color *Indianapolis Monthly* v41 no2 p76 S 2017

Mounds STATE PARK color map *Indianapolis Monthly* v41 no2 p60 S 2017

Riverside PARK color map *Indianapolis Monthly* v41 no2 p68 S 2017

TOUR OF DOODY diag *Indianapolis Monthly* v41 no2 p65 S 2017

WHERE THE WILD THINGS ARE color *Indianapolis Monthly* v41 no2 p62 S 2017

THE White RIVER diag *Indianapolis Monthly* v41 no2 p59 S 2017

West, Geoffrey

The elegant law that governs us all Barabási color *Science* v357 no6347 p138 Jl 14 2017

WEST, GORDON

ASK SAIL color *Sail* v48 no1 p58 Ja 2017

ASK SAIL color *Sail* v48 no4 p68 Ap 2017

West, Jerry, 1938-

GOLDEN DAYS J. McCallum color *Sports Illustrated* v127 no12 p98 O 16 2017

WEST, JIM

Activists Work to Stop Militarization of the Border color *Progressive* p12 D 2016/Ja 2017

The Cost of Repealing Obamacare color *Progressive* v81 no4 p10 Ap/My 2017

West, Joe

THE LAST COWBOY M. Rosenberg color *Sports Illustrated* v127 no3 p84 Jl 24 2017

West, Julian G.

Fortune favors the well read color *Science* v355 no6329 p1090 Mr 10 2017

West, Kanye, 1977-

The Bullseye M. Snetiker color *Entertainment Weekly* no1466 p64 My 19 2017

'Fade' T. C. WILLIAMS *New York Times Magazine* p53 Mr 12 2017

Pop Chart R. Bruner, C. Lang et al color *Time* v189 no4 p58 F 6 2017

What's Next for Kanye West? E. R. Brown, J. Rubenstein et al color *Entertainment Weekly* no1443 p17 D 9 2016

When Kanye Met Donald R. THEDE cartoon color *Wired* v25 no4 p66 Ap 2017

West, Kevin

KIND OF BLUE color *Conde Nast Traveler* v51 no10 p148 N 2016

West, Lindy

On the PLUS SIDE color *InStyle* v24 no9 p404 S 2017

West, Lori J.

Harnessing Cellular Tools from Immune Systems to Help Prevent Graft Rejection color *Maclean's* v130 no9 p34 O 2017

West, Maura—Interviews

DAYTIME M. LOGAN *TV Guide* v65 no35 p42 Ag 21 2017

West, Michael

When Galaxies Become Cannibals color *Discover* v38 no8 p70 O 2017

When galaxies become CANNIBALS [Cover story] color *Astronomy* v44 no12 p20 D 2016

West, Michael E.

Getting Bundled Payments Right in Health Care *Harvard Business Review Digital Articles* p2 O 19 2015

West, Michael J.

THE RIGHT MOVE color *Downbeat* v84 no3 p48 Mr 2017

Winter Jazzfest Artists Address Social Justice color *Downbeat* v84 no3 p14 Mr 2017

West, Noreen

Emergence and spread of a human-transmissible multidrug-resistant nontuberculous mycobacterium bibl diag graph *Science* v354 no6313 p751 N 11 2016

West, Phil

The United States of Soccer: MLS and the Rise of American Soccer Fandom *Publishers Weekly* v263 no39 p80 S 26 2016

West, Stuart

#trailchat color il map *Backpacker* p6 Je 2017

West, Suzanne

Whose Side Are You On, Anyway? L. MCKEON cartoon *Walrus* v13 no10 p32 D 2016

WEST, VAN

CHANGE the CITY *Indianapolis Monthly* p55 Ap 2017

West Africa

EPIDEMIC INSURANCE J. Cohen and J. Gerberding color graph *Science* v356 no6334 p125 Ap 14 2017

Strange Fruit K. GOLDYNIA *Psychology Today* v50 no3 p34 My/Je 2017

West Canyon Limestone (Utah)

IMAGES OF A LOST WORLD T. NICHOLS bw *Arizona Highways* v93 no5 p40 My 2017

West Clear Creek Wilderness (Ariz.)

Cool off color *Backpacker* p18 Ag 2017

West Indian cooking

FRESH DIRECT S. CLEMENCE color *Conde Nast Traveler* v52 no9 p32 O 2017

West Indies—Description & travel

FRESH DIRECT S. CLEMENCE color *Conde Nast Traveler* v52 no9 p32 O 2017

West Nile fever

West Nile encephalitis L. Bonner bw color *Equus* no475 p36 Ap 2017

West Nile virus

AIR SICKNESS M. McKenna *New York Times Magazine* p42 Ap 23 2017

West Side Story (Film)

MAKING WEST SIDE STORY'S "AMERICA" J. McGovern color *Entertainment Weekly* no1473 p46 Jl 7 2017

West Virginia University

MEMBER NEWS *Phi Kappa Phi Forum* v97 no1 p7 Spr 2017

West Virginia University—Sports

21 West Virginia color *Sports Illustrated* v127 no5 p110 Ag 14 2017

West Virginia—Description & travel

The Other Charleston C. Balestier color *Southern Living* v52 no10 p67 O 2017

TAKE A DRIVE: SNOWSHOE D. A. Leatherman *Washingtonian Magazine* v52 no4 p116 Ja 2017

West Virginia—Economic conditions—21st century

In Coal Country, Signing Bonuses Are the Buzz T. Loh color graph *Bloomberg Businessweek* no4521 p28 My 8 2017

West Virginia—Environmental conditions

Protecting the "Birthplace of Rivers" and beyond color *National Wildlife (World Edition)* v55 no6 p46 O/N 2017

Westacott, Emrys
Philosophers Who Like Stuff: Their case against frugality *Humanities* v38 no4 p1 Fall 2017
The Simpler Life L. KLEPP *Weekly Standard* v22 no22 p35 F 13 2017

Westad, Odd Arne
Cold War World P. IBER bw color il *New Republic* v248 no11 p60 N 2017

Westbrook, Barbara—Interviews
BACK TO THE LAND D. Brenner color *House Beautiful* v159 no8 p96 O 2017

Westbrook, Ken
Backfires: The joyful noise of the commentariat, rebutted sporadically by Ed color *Car & Driver* v62 no11 p9 My 2017

Westbrook, Robert
I choose, therefore I am color *Christian Century* v133 no26 p30 D 21 2016
The price of modernity *Christian Century* v134 no22 p33 O 25 2017

Westbrook, Russell, 1988-
April/May T. PAYNE color *Ebony* v72 no6 p18 Ap/My 2017
AROUND the WORLD, ONE PARTY at a TIME color *Vanity Fair* v59 no10 p135 O 2017
Confidence D. Riley color *GQ: Gentlemen's Quarterly* v86 no11 p114 N 2016
For the Record color *Time* v189 no15 p6 Ap 24 2017
HOT | NOT T. Keith color *Sports Illustrated* v125 no19 p24 D 12 2016
THE MYSTERiES OF AN EVERYTHiNG MAN S. ANDERSON *New York Times Magazine* p32 F 5 2017
Staying Power [Cover story] L. Jenkins color *Sports Illustrated* v125 no14 p56 O 24-31 2016
WHO IS RUSSELL WESTBROOK? B. DANIELLE color *Ebony* v72 no6 p76 Ap/My 2017
The World Is Yours K. Kyles color *Ebony* v72 no6 p14 Ap/My 2017

West Building of the National Gallery of Art (Washington, D.C.)
Neglected viewpoints at the National Gallery of Art color *Magazine Antiques* v184 no3 p30 My/Je 2017

Westbury, Chris
What Makes a Funny Word Funny M. HINGSTON *Reader's Digest* v189 no1128 p124 Mr 2017

Westchester County (N.Y.)
UNDOCUMENTED IN AMERICA K. Clarke and R. David Sullivan chart color graph *America* v216 no4 p12 F 20 2017

Westech Automotive (Company)
Time to Fix It—Again M. Davis chart color *Hot Rod* v70 no8 p102 Ag 2017

WESTEN, ROBIN
Checkup for Your Medicine Cabinet *AARP: The Magazine* v59 no5A p20 Ag/S 2016
Fast Fixes for What Ails You cartoon chart color *AARP: The Magazine* v60 no1A p16 D 2016/Ja 2017

West End (London, England)—History
A CORNUCOPIA OF CONDIMENTS D. WEISS color *Archaeology* v70 no3 p12 My/Je 2017

Westenfeld, Adrienne
2017 MaVeRicks OF Style bw color *Esquire* p81 S 2017
BITTERSWEET ESCAPE color *Esquire* p21 Ag 2017
THE CLAMPDOWN color *Esquire* v167 no2 p52 Mr 2017
DEEP DIVES color *Esquire* p50 S 2017
DIFFICULT MEN color *Esquire* p38 O 2017
THE GREAT OZ color *Esquire* p22 N 2017
ICY STARE color *Esquire* p38 N 2017

Wester, Philippus
Making SDGs Work for Climate Change Hotspots bibl *Environment* v58 no6 p24 N/D 2016

Westerbeck, Colin
Photography and Paradox *Art in America* v104 no9 p65 O 2016

Westerberg, Paul
FOR THE CULTURE J. WILLIAMS *Cincinnati Magazine* v50 no11 p22 Ag 2017

Westergaard, Nick
Your Content Marketing Strategy Doesn't Have to Be Complicated *Harvard Business Review Digital Articles* p2 My 26 2016

Westerman, George

The Best Digital Business Models Put Evolution Before Revolution *Harvard Business Review Digital Articles* p2 Ja 20 2015
The Internet-Connected Engine Will Change Trucking *Harvard Business Review Digital Articles* p2 N 4 2014

Westerman, Josefa
Current and coming bw color *Magazine Antiques* v184 no5 p26 S/O 2017

Western Canada
Western Colleges: Career Take-off J. Southerst color *Maclean's* v130 no10 p111 N 2017

Western corn rootworm
CORNBOY VS. THE BILLION-DOLLAR BUG [Cover story] H. Nordhaus color *Scientific American* v316 no3 p64 Mr 2017
A selective insecticidal protein from Pseudomonas for controlling corn rootworms U. Schellenberger, J. Oral et al bibl chart graph *Science* v354 no6312 p634 N 4 2016
Tips for battling billion-dollar beetles B. E. Tabashnik bibl color graph *Science* v354 no6312 p552 N 4 2016

Western countries—History
The Globalization of Rage P. Mishra color *Foreign Affairs* v95 no6 p46 N/D 2016

Western countries—Politics & government
A Republic, If We Can Renew It F. BAUER color *National Review* v69 no5 p16 Mr 20 2017

Western countries—Politics & government—21st century
Populism on the March F. Zakaria color *Foreign Affairs* v95 no6 p9 N/D 2016

Western Edges (Music)
Born In An Urban Ruin J. D. Considine bw *Downbeat* v84 no2 p81 F 2017

Western horses
Running Martingale A. Dunning and J. Paulson color *Horse & Rider* v55 no12 p30 D 2016

Western Pacific Railroad Co.
FOUR ERAS OVER WP'S FEATHER RIVER ROUTE R. W. Scott color diag *Model Railroader* v83 no12 p46 D 2016

Western Portland Cement Co.
River Ruins *South Dakota Magazine* v32 no6 p48 Mr/Ap 2017

Western redcedar
Giant Red D. PENCE color *Idaho Magazine* v16 no1 p6 O 2016

Western riding—Competitions
Get Through the Line L. Lange and N. Chirico color *Horse & Rider* v56 no7 p86 Jl 2017

Western Sahara—Politics & government
Africa's Last Colony C. ROSS bw color *New Republic* v248 no5 p46 My 2017

Western society
The Era of Post-Party Politics: New Institutions That Embrace Participation Without Populism N. GARDELS *NPQ: New Perspectives Quarterly* v33 no4 p2 O 2016
Pitirim Sorokin Revisited: He predicted the West's societal deterioration G. T. SEWALL *American Conservative* v16 no5 p42 S/O 2017

Western Union Co.—Finance
Refugees, immigrants, expatriates. For some politicians, they're scapegoats. For Western Union, they're customers D. Bennett and L. Etter color *Bloomberg Businessweek* no4527 p74 Je 19 2017

Westerners (Western society)
See also
    Americans
    Canadians
    Europeans
Code of the West, History vs. Hollywood R. Soodalter cartoon *American Cowboy* v24 no1 p22 Je/Jl 2017

Westfall, Carroll William
Blind Venetians color *Weekly Standard* v22 no29 p34 Ap 3 2017

Westfall, Catherine
The Pope of Physics *Physics Today* v69 no12 p57 D 2016

Westfall, Stephen
LOS ANGELES — Los Angeles County Museum of Art color *Art in America* v105 no6 p143 Je/Jl 2017

Westfront 1918 (Film)
Between Two Fires M. Nelson bw *Film Comment* v53 no1 p11 Ja/F 2017

Westhof, Eric

Crystal structures of a group II intron lariat primed for reverse splicing color diag *Science* v354 no6316 paaf9258-1 D 2 2016

WESTHOFF, BEN

CALIFORNIA LOVE *Los Angeles Magazine* v61 no11 p78 N 2016

Westley, Curt

Barn Parties *Arabian Horse World* v57 no11 p48 Ag 2017

WESTLIND, DOUGLAS J.

Physiological Stress and Ethanol Accumulation in Tree Stems and Woody Tissues at Sublethal Temperatures from Fire *BioScience* v67 no5 p443 My 2017

Westmacott, Garrett

Vaginal bacteria modify HIV tenofovir microbicide efficacy in African women chart graph *Science* v356 no6341 p938 Je 1 2017

Westman, Gucci

GUCCI WESTMAN K. MOLVAR color *Conde Nast Traveler* v52 no8 p24 S 2017

Westman, Karl

When stuff happens... cartoon *Sail* v48 no4 p30 Ap 2017

Westminster Palace (London, England)

Renovations at the Houses of Parliament *British Heritage Travel* v38 no2 p6 Mr/Ap 2017

WESTMORELAND, SUSAN

ASK SUSAN color *Good Housekeeping* v264 no1 p114 Ja 1 2017

ASK SUSAN color *Good Housekeeping* v264 no4 p112 Ap 2017

ASK SUSAN color *Good Housekeeping* v264 no5 p112 My 2017

GH TEST KITCHEN color *Good Housekeeping* v265 no4 p105 O 2017

Westoby, Mark

Global climatic drivers of leaf size [Cover story] graph *Science* v357 no6354 p917 S 1 2017

Weston, Carol

Advice Needed: A teenager faces the sudden loss of her mother and her dad's new dating life M. RABB *New York Times Book Review* p15 Je 18 2017

WESTON, DAVID

A Bird in the Hand color graph *Kiplinger's Personal Finance* v71 no2 p6 F 2017

Weston, Liz

Live large for less K. ROCKWOOD color *Redbook* p109 S 2017

Westover, Mike

Quantifying the Impact of Marketing Analytics *Harvard Business Review Digital Articles* p2 N 5 2015

Westover, Steve

Diamondback Clutch color *Bike Magazine* v24 no6 p122 Ag 2017

Westphal, James

Research: Executives Who Flatter Their CEOs Are More Likely to Criticize Them to the Press bw *Harvard Business Review Digital Articles* p2 Ap 5 2017

Westphal, Ruth

Outdoorsy Types D. Grant color *Commonweal* v144 no1 p28 Ja 6 2017

Westphal, Volker

Nanometer resolution imaging and tracking of fluorescent molecules with minimal photon fluxes bibl graph *Science* v355 no6325 p606 F 10 2017

Westport Yachts (Company)

Westport 125 J. Y. Wood color *Power & Motoryacht* v34 no7 p32 Jl 2017

WESTRICK, A. B.

Bibles Across the Spectrum color *Publishers Weekly* v263 no45 p12 N 7 2016

Educating the New Activists color *Publishers Weekly* v263 no45 p4 N 7 2016

West-Rosenthal, Lauren Brown

Meet the New Money Experts color *Glamour* v115 no9 p134 S 2017

Westrup, Greg

BELOW AND ABOVE bw *MHQ: Quarterly Journal of Military History* v29 no4 p10 Summ 2017

West Village (New York, N.Y.)

There Goes the Neighborhood Restaurant: A regular's lament M. SHERATON img *New York* v50 no9 p76 My 1 2017

Westward Leaning (Company)

HIS & HERS color *Women's Health* v14 no1 p72 Ja/F 2017

West Wing, The (TV program)

Sorkin's West Wing Swan Song C. Agard color *Entertainment Weekly* no1460/1461 p95 Ap 7-17 2017

WESTWOOD, ROSEMARY

THE BIG UNEASY color *Maclean's* v130 no4 p42 My 2017

Westworld (TV program)

The Awakening of Evan Rachel Wood A. MORRIS color *Rolling Stone* no1275 p46 D 1 2016

HBO Offers a West-Ward Expansion of the Mind D. D'addario color *Time* v188 no14 p61 O 10 2016

Killer Reboot J. HEER il *New Republic* v247 no12 p67 D 2016

Marx in Westworld E. JONES *In These Times* v41 no1 p34 Ja 2017

Pop Chart R. Bruner, C. Lang et al color *Time* v190 no5 p63 Jl 31 2017

Robots of the West K. Reklis color *Christian Century* v134 no1 p43 Ja 4 2017

Sci-fi Evolves Into Disturbing Reality In Black Mirror and Westworld E. Dockterman color *Time* v188 no16/17 p90 O 24 2016

SECOND WORLD E. NUSSBAUM cartoon *New Yorker* v92 no34 p82 O 24 2016

TV'S NEW AWARDS SHOW DARLINGS C. Agard color *Entertainment Weekly* no1446/1447 p24 D 2016/Ja 2017

Westworld: Fall TV's Biggest Mystery J. Hibberd color *Entertainment Weekly* no1435 p68 O 14 2016

Westworld M. ROUSH *TV Guide* v64 no40 p22 O 3 2016

When 'Blade Runner' Meets 'Deadwood' R. SHEFFIELD color *Rolling Stone* no1273 p23 N 3 2016

Wet Hot American Summer: Ten Years Later (TV program)

HAPPY CAMPERS: The funny franchise's new sequel heads into the 1990s--Big Chill style--with a bevy of fresh Camp Firewood faces worth a hearty salute I. RATLEDGE *TV Guide* v65 no31 p24 Jl 24 2017

The Must List color *Entertainment Weekly* no1477 p6 Ag 11 2017

Wet Hot's Face-off D. Snierson color *Entertainment Weekly* no1476 p52 Ag 4 2017

Wethe, David

Drilling Is Back. What About the Workers? graph *Bloomberg Businessweek* no4509 p14 Ja 30 2017

How Exxon Is Learning To Let Go color *Bloomberg Businessweek* no4519 p49 Ap 24 2017

Oilfield Cleanup Tools chart *Bloomberg Businessweek* no4503 p31 D 12 2016

Wetherbe, James C.

Making Business School Research More Relevant *Harvard Business Review Digital Articles* p2 D 24 2014

Wetherell, Tim

A Gentleman's Observatory *Sky & Telescope* v134 no4 p30 O 2017

WETHERELL, WES

Ride Off the Rail color *Horse & Rider* v56 no8 p92 Ag 2017

Wethersfield (Conn.)—Description & travel

Old Wethersfield, Connecticut A. GRAVES color map *Yankee* p68 Mr 2017

Wetland conservation

A Cleansing Fire S. COSIER *Audubon* v119 no2 p14 Summ 2017

A Global Assessment of Inland Wetland Conservation Status V. REIS, V. HERMOSO et al *BioScience* v67 no6 p523 Je 2017

Wetland restoration

U.S.-Mexico water pact aims for a greener Colorado delta W. Cornwall color *Science* v357 no6352 p635 Ag 18 2017

Wetlands

See also

Marshes

Riparian areas

Swamps

chinatown J. HERBST color *Los Angeles Magazine* v62 no7 p70 Jl 2017

Chiricahua Leopard Frogs E. Balli color *Arizona Highways* v93 no5 p13 My 2017

Swamps G. TARLACH color *Discover* v38 no5 p74 Je 2017

Wonderful Wetlands B. Friedlander *USA Today Magazine* v146 no2866 p68 Jl 2017

Wetsuits

COOL inventions C. M. TOMLIN *National Geographic Kids* no466 p5 D 2016/Ja 2017

Wettlaufer, Elizabeth Tracey Mae

BAD NEWS color *Maclean's* v129 no44 p9 N 7 2016

Wetzler, Rachel

Autocorrect color *ARTnews* v115 no3 p38 Fall 2016

DIANE SIMPSON color *Art in America* v105 no3 p129 Mr 2017

Dominique Lévy color *Art in America* v105 no1 p78 Ja 2017

Gavin Brown's enterprise color *Art in America* v105 no6 p135 Je/Jl 2017

GELATIN color *Art in America* p124 O 2017

KASSEL Dislocated Loot color *Art in America* v105 no8 p43 S 2017

KATHARINA GROSSE cartoon *Art in America* v105 no4 p112 Ap 2017

MONICA BONVICINI color *Art in America* v105 no5 p126 My 2017

"WITH THE EYES OF OTHERS: HUNGARIAN ARTISTS OF THE SIXTIES AND SEVENTIES" color *Art in America* v105 no8 p123 S 2017

Wetzstein, Hazel Y.

Emission of volatile organic compounds from petunia flowers is facilitated by an ABC transporter diag *Science* v356 no6345 p1386 Je 30 2017

Wework Cos. Inc.

THE WAY WE WORK [Cover story] S. BERTONI color *Forbes* v200 no4 p64 O 24 2017

"We're always glad it's Monday morning": Keeping things positive is key for the co-working start-up. But how can it stay happy as it goes global? *People Management* p20 Jl 2017

WEX, MICHAEL

Yiddish for Everyone *New York Times Book Review* p37 N 13 2016

Wexler, Celia Viggo

Where and who you are color *U.S. Catholic* v82 no1 p12 Ja 2017

Wexler, Mark

Celebrating America's "Great Land" [Cover story] color *National Wildlife (World Edition)* v55 no6 p22 O/N 2017

Coping with Chronic Clamor color *National Wildlife (World Edition)* v55 no2 p40 F/Mr 2017

Worth Their Weight in Gold color *National Wildlife (World Edition)* v55 no5 p12 Ag/S 2017

Wexler, Rebecca

Code of Silence color *Washington Monthly* v49 no6-8 p18 Je-Ag 2017

WEXLER, SARAH Z.

Tracy Morgan What's your favorite restaurant in the world? cartoon color *Bon Appetit* v62 no2 p104 Mr 2017

Wey, Tunde

The Urbanist: Chefs Search Out the Best Street Food B. CUSHING img *New York* v49 no19 p24 S 19 2016

Weyl, E. Glen

What If Socially Useful Jobs Were Taxed Less Than Other Jobs? *Harvard Business Review Digital Articles* p2 O 11 2017

Wezowski, Kasia

6 Ways to Look More Confident During a Presentation [Cover story] *Harvard Business Review Digital Articles* p2 Ap 6 2017

The Secret to Negotiating Is Reading People's Faces *Harvard Business Review Digital Articles* p2 Je 16 2017

Whale shark

DNA in seawater reveals shark numbers color *Science* v354 no6315 p949 N 25 2016

Whalen, Amelia

Amelia's Big Fish R. Redman *New York State Conservationist* v71 no5 p40 Ap 2017

Whalen, Bill

Alpha Dog Days *Hoover Digest: Research & Opinion on Public Policy* no4 p49 Fall 2016

Change for a Dollar? *Hoover Digest: Research & Opinion on Public Policy* no1 p180 Wint 2017

Whalen, C. Benjamin

Backfires: The joyful noise of the commentariat, rebutted sporadically by Ed bw color *Car & Driver* v62 no10 p7 Ap 2017

WHALEN, CHRISTOPHER

Big-Bank Hegemony: They have seized control of their own regulators *American Conservative* v16 no5 p25 S/O 2017

An Economic Primer for Stagnant Times *American Conservative* v16 no2 p47 Mr/Ap 2017

WHALEN, JENNIFER KYLE

I BATHE IN A RIVER AND DON'T GIVE A SHIT color *Bicycling* v58 no7 p45 Ag 2017

Whalen, Michael

The formation of peak rings in large impact craters bibl color graph *Science* v354 no6314 p878 N 18 2016

Whalen, Rita

The Thread bw cartoon *New York Times Magazine* p14 D 11 2016

Whales

See also

Baleen whales

A Call to Action R. Bates *Canadian Wildlife* v23 no1 p5 Mr/Ap 2017

Cetacean seeker A. Pope color graph *Canadian Geographic* v136 no6 p28 D 2016

Cutting the Lines N. Hawkins color *Canadian Wildlife* v23 no1 p18 Mr/Ap 2017

FOOTPRINT IN MOUTH LIND cartoon *Alternatives Journal (AJ) - Canada's Environmental Voice* v42 no3 p10 2016

LONG WAY HOME *Phi Kappa Phi Forum* v96 no4 p5 Wint 2016

A New Whale Species Is Discovered in the Wild E. Koenig *Oceanus* v52 no1 p10 Summ 2016

The Politics of Rotting Blubber S. LEWSEN color *Walrus* v14 no3 p59 Ap 2017

SAVE THE WHALE: HARDENING A HEART M. NGUYEN bw color *Wired* v25 no7 p30 Jl 2017

Surge in right whale deaths raises alarms E. Stokstad color map *Science* v357 no6353 p740 Ag 25 2017

WHALES OF ICELAND: Visit an Underwater World *Iceland Review* v55 no3 p101 My/Je 2017

Whales—Food

Living Large A. Marks color *Scientific American* v317 no3 p18 S 2017

Whales—Physiology

Living Large A. Marks color *Scientific American* v317 no3 p18 S 2017

Our Ailing Oceans map *Earth Island Journal* v32 no3 p10 Aut 2017

Whales—Population biology

Species IN THE Making R. Riesch color diag *Scientific American* v315 no5 p54 N 2016

Whaling

Cutting the Lines N. Hawkins color *Canadian Wildlife* v23 no1 p18 Mr/Ap 2017

The Hunt: In Native Alaska, whaling ties people to history, culture, and one another M. M. LANE color *Orion Magazine* v36 no1 p24 Ja/F 2017

The Inuit Whale Hunter Emmanuel Adam E. ANSELMI color *Foreign Policy* no224 p24 My/Je 2017

Wham! (Performer)

The Genius of George Michael R. SHEFFIELD bw *Rolling Stone* no1280 p16 F 9 2017

George Michael M. Johnston color *Time* v189 no3 p11 Ja 16 2017

Wharton, Edith, 1862-1937

A Hundred Years of Summer K. HALL color *Weekly Standard* v22 no48 p34 S 4 2017

Losing the American Tone M. Gorra bw *New York Review of Books* v64 no9 p40 My 25 2017

A PATCH OF BEAUTY C. Moss and K. O'SHEA-EVANS color *House Beautiful* v159 no4 p52 My 2017

Wharton, Mark

PEREGRINE BLOODSTOCK *Arabian Horse World* v57 no5 p1 F 2017

Wharton School

A Reckoning At Trump's Alma Mater K. Porzecanski color *Bloomberg Businessweek* no4502 p64 D 5 2016

Wharton's Policy Tool Isn't Just for Wonks P. Coy color *Bloomberg Businessweek* no4522 p52 My 15 2017

What Happens at the Abbey (TV program)

THE 8-SECOND REVIEW N. Maslow color *Entertainment Weekly* no1466 p46 My 19 2017

What Would Diplo Do? (TV program)

What Would Diplo Do? D. Holbrook *TV Guide* v65 no31 p35 Jl 24 2017

WhatsApp Inc.

How to improve your security with WhatsApp G. FLEISHMAN color *Macworld - Digital Edition* p103 Mr 2017

WhatsApp Grew to One Billion Users by Focusing on Product, Not Technology Baculard *Harvard Business Review Digital Articles* p2 Jl 1 2016

Wheat

AG FROM ABOVE B. SPIEGEL *Successful Farming* v114 no12 p38 Mid-N 2016

THE MYTH OF MUMMY WHEAT: Despite a total lack of evidence, the belief that grains of wheat found in Ancient Egyptian tombs could produce bountiful crops was surprisingly hardy G. Moshenska *History Today* v67 no9 p36 S 2017

Wild emmer genome architecture and diversity elucidate wheat evolution and domestication R. Avni, M. Nave et al color *Science* v357 no6346 p93 Jl 7 2017

Wheat farming

WHEAT HELPS A NO-TILL ROTATION: WINTER WHEAT DIVERSIFIES CROPS AND ADDS CARBON TO THE SOIL R. Nickel *Successful Farming* v115 no6 p40 Ap 2017

Wheat harvesting

Streets of Gold *Saturday Evening Post* v289 no4 p100 Jl/Ag 2017

Wheatcroft, Geoffrey

How Bad Was Tony Blair? bw *New York Review of Books* v64 no1 p64 Ja 19 2017

THE WAR TO END ALL WARS color *Nation* v305 no10 p35 O 23 2017

Wheater, Ashley

HOW TO Reboot a Holiday Classic N. RHEE color *Chicago* v65 no12 p92 D 2016

Wheatland, Thomas

Richard H. King, Arendt and America *Society* v54 no2 p199 Ap 2017

Wheatley, Ben, 1972-

Free Fire C. Nashawaty color *Entertainment Weekly* no1463/1464 p89 Ap/My 2017

Free Fire N. PINKERTON color *Film Comment* v53 no2 p67 Mr/Ap 2017

WHEATLEY, THOMAS

CABBAGE TOWN 1996 *Atlanta* v57 no2 p160 Je 2017

DIVERSE BY DESIGN *Atlanta* v57 no5 p23 S 2017

EMPIRE BUILDING, MARIETTA & BROAD 1900 *Atlanta* v57 no5 p160 S 2017

THE FUTURE OF THE CHATTAHOOCHEE: Long overlooked, the river s segment along Atlanta's west side has endless opportunity *Atlanta* v57 no4 p57 Ag 2017

HYATT REGENCY 1967 *Atlanta* v57 no3 p176 Jl 2017

LOOK UP *Atlanta* v56 no11 p22 Mr 2017

MAKE NO LITTLE PLANS *Atlanta* v57 no1 p17 My 2017

NORTHLAKE MALL 1993 *Atlanta* v57 no6 p144 O 2017

RIVER: SIGNS OF CIVILIZATIONS PAST *Atlanta* v57 no4 p55 Ag 2017

SAVING MORRIS BROWN *Atlanta* v56 no12 p92 Ap 2017

SAVING THE BIG CHICKEN 1993 *Atlanta* v57 no4 p128 Ag 2017

THAT'S A STRETCH *Atlanta* v57 no2 p26 Je 2017

THERE'S SOMETHING ABOUT MARY: The implausible and inevitable rise of the woman who could be mayor *Atlanta* v57 no6 p28 O 2017

Whedon, Joss, 1964-

UNDEAD AGAIN [Cover story] T. Stack color *Entertainment Weekly* no1460/1461 p50 Ap 7-17 2017

Wheel of Fortune (TV program)

Game Show Philosophy J. S. J. Conley *America* v216 no10 p54 My 1 2017

Wheelan, Pete

Flipping Student Support Services to Improve Outcomes *Change* v48 no6 p36 N/D 2016

Wheelbarrows—Evaluation

kinder gardening J. A. BAGGETT color *Better Homes & Gardens* v95 no8 p98 Ag 2017

Wheelchair tennis

Coaching With Purpose *Tennis* v52 no6 p75 N/D 2016

Wheelchairs

Wheelchair Parkour S. Trumper color *Walrus* v14 no5 p21 Je 2017

Wheelchairs—Design & construction

Innovation Walker-Chair N. Leiber color *Bloomberg Businessweek* no4501 p31 N 28 2016

Wheeler (Film)

THAT TIME RYAN ROSS DANCED WITH WINONA RYDER J. DEFORE *Texas Monthly* v45 no2 p46 F 2017

Wheeler, Amy

Sweet Deal P. SAHA *Audubon* v119 no1 p17 Spr 2017

Wheeler, Brian

From school newsletter to nonprofit newsroom B. Fitzgerald *Columbia Journalism Review* v56 no1 p57 Spr 2017

Wheeler, Clark

Cheers & Jeers color *Field & Stream* v121 no6 p12 N 2016

Wheeler, Cole

BACK TO BACK J. Mankin color *Spin to Win Rodeo* v21 no6 p64 Ag 2017

Wheeler, Debora Ligaya

We're Number One! color *Backpacker* v45 no1 p8 Ja 2017

Wheeler, Edward T.

When Art & Spirit Meet color *Commonweal* v144 no16 p35 O 6 2017

Wheeler, Heather

Lipid transport by TMEM24 at ER-plasma membrane contacts regulates pulsatile insulin secretion diag *Science* v355 no6326 p709 F 17 2017

Wheeler, Jeffrey

Navigating national regulations and global changes: international and comparative employment *Monthly Labor Review* p1 Je 2017

Wheeler, John Archibald, 1911-2008

Birth of the QUBIT T. Siegfried bw color *Science News* v191 no13 p34 Jl 8 2017

Wheeler, Martin

Der Freischütz *Opera News* v81 no7 p44 Ja 2017

Wheeler, Michael

Get in the Right State of Mind for Any Negotiation *Harvard Business Review Digital Articles* p2 My 5 2015

WHEELER, SARA

Adventures in Quinine: A magic realist mission in the forests of the Andes *New York Times Book Review* p18 S 17 2017

POLAR VORTEX *New York Times Book Review* p73 D 4 2016

Wheeler-Dubas, Maria

How I found my outreach niche color *Science* v357 no6353 p837 Ag 25 2017

Wheelock, Katherine

Of Land and Sea color map *Conde Nast Traveler* v52 no6 p60 Je/Jl 2017

Wheelock, Stefan M.

Critics of a savage empire E. J. Blum *Christian Century* v133 no24 p36 N 23 2016

Wheels

See also

Axles

Gearing

Tires

Create a User-Friendly Trailer C. CASWELL *Boating World* v38 no2 p14 F 2017

full circle r. palmer color *Bike Magazine* v24 no5 p96 Jl 2017

momentum r. palmer color *Bike Magazine* v24 no7 p46 S 2017

Wheels of Time (Company)

Wheels of Time HO 62-foot bulkhead flatcar S. Otte color *Model Railroader* v84 no5 p64 My 2017

Wheels—Evaluation

GEARBOX bw color *Dirt Sports + Off-Road* v51 no2 p68 F 2017

PARTS & STUFF color *Hot Rod* v70 no12 p108 D 2017

Stan's NoTubes ZTR Avion Pro Wheels M. Yozell color *Bicycling* v58 no4 p78 My 2017

WHEELWRIGHT, JEFF

High Consequences color map *Discover* v38 no7 p50 S 2017

This Old Brain [Cover story] bw color *Discover* v38 no8 p26 O 2017

WHEEN, FRANCIS

Little Shop of Hoarders bw color *Vanity Fair* v59 no2 p100 F 2017

Whelan, Brian

Holy Cities B. G. Prusak color *Commonweal* v143 no20 p20 D 16 2016

WHELAN, ELIZABETH M.

FROM THE ARCHIVES bw *Reason* v49 no1 p70 My 2017

Whelan, Jon

STINK: THE REAL STORY OF TOXINS V. Tweed color *Amazing Wellness* v8 no2 p14 Spr 2016

Whelan, Matt

A New View of Playboy E. Aslanian *TV Guide* v65 no11 p14 Mr 6 2017

Whelan, Melanie

Q: What is the most significant fad of all time? color *Atlantic* v319 no3 p96 Ap 2017

SOULCYCLE'S CEO ON SUSTAINING GROWTH IN A FADDISH INDUSTRY: It's all about friendship and community color img *Harvard Business Review* v95 no4 p37 Jl/Ag 2017

Whelan, Tensie

The Comprehensive Business Case for Sustainability *Harvard Business Review Digital Articles* p2 O 21 2016

How to Quantify Sustainability's Impact on Your Bottom Line *Harvard Business Review Digital Articles* p2 S 13 2017

WHELDON, WYNN

Cheek to Jowl *Commentary* v142 no5 p53 D 2016

Tribal Dress *Commentary* v143 no4 p52 Ap 2017

When Death Comes (Poem)

When Death Comes C. Innes color *U.S. Catholic* v81 no11 p11 N 2016

When the Bough Breaks (Film)

THAT'S A WRAP L. LEBLANC-BERRY *Louisiana Life* v37 no2 p14 N/D 2016

When the Heart Emerges Glistening (Music)

NIGHT LIFE *New Yorker* v92 no48 p8 F 6 2017

When the Levees Broke (Film)

The 21 Documentaries from the 21st Century Every Man Should See bw color *GQ: Gentlemen's Quarterly* v86 no11 p84 N 2016

When We Rise (TV program)

EDITOR'S LETTER D. ANDERSON-MINSHAL bw color *Advocate* no1090 p8 Ap 2017

EYES ON THE RISE M. Snetiker color *Entertainment Weekly* no1454/1455 p87 F 24 2017

TOGETHER WE STAND J. HALTERMAN *TV Guide* v65 no8 p22 F 27 2017

When We Rise M. ROUSH *TV Guide* v65 no8 p16 F 27 2017

Where in the World Is Matt Lauer? (TV program)

Today by the Numbers bw *TV Guide* v65 no7 p22 F 13 2017

Where Windows Should Be (Poem)

WHERE WINDOWS SHOULD BE Tongo Eisen-Martin *Harper's Magazine* v334 no2001 p21 F 2017

Wherry, E. John

The epigenetic landscape of T cell exhaustion bibl graph *Science* v354 no6316 p1165 D 2 2016

Epigenetic stability of exhausted T cells limits durability of reinvigoration by PD-1 blockade bibl graph *Science* v354 no6316 p1160 D 2 2016

Whetstones—Evaluation

Cut 'Em Loose S. MURRAY color *Power & Motoryacht* v34 no11 p84 N 2017

Whey proteins

Ascent Protein color *Muscle & Performance* v9 no10 p36 O 2017

Gain Strength, Power and More color *Muscle & Performance* v9 no7 p64 Jl 2017

Inner Armour Isolate Zero color *Muscle & Performance* v9 no7 p62 Jl 2017

IT'S WHEY BETTER WITH LEUCINE J. WUEBBEN bw *Muscle & Performance* v9 no10 p17 O 2017

PICKING THE PERFECT PROTEIN D. N. JACKSON color *Muscle & Performance* v9 no6 p51 Je 2017

Supplement Strategy D. N. JACKSON color diag *Muscle & Performance* v9 no6 p57 Je 2017

Whey proteins—Evaluation

GET TO KNOW: INNER ARMOUR J. SCHILDHOUSE color *Muscle & Performance* v9 no1 p34 Ja 2017

GO ALL OUT color *Muscle & Performance* v9 no1 p64 Ja 2017

NATIVE PRO 100 color *Muscle & Performance* v9 no1 p62 Ja 2017

Whibley, Deryck

The Resuscitation of Sum 41 A. GREENE color *Rolling Stone* no1273 p17 N 3 2016

Whipped Cream (Theatrical production)

DANCE *New Yorker* v93 no19 p8 Jl 3 2017

SPUN SUGAR J. ACOCELLA color *New Yorker* v93 no17 p72 Je 19 2017

Whipped toppings

PIPE DOWN C. SAFFITZ color *Bon Appetit* v61 no12 p165 D 2016 /Jan2017

Whipple, Brian

How People Are Actually Using the Internet of Things *Harvard Business Review Digital Articles* p2 O 28 2015

Whipple, Chris

Chief of Staff: Master of One M. Duffy color *Time* v189 no14 p56 Ap 17 2017

NIXON'S S.O.B bw color *American History* v52 no4 p48 O 2017

Some Advice for Reince Priebus M. O'Donnell bw *Washington Monthly* v49 no3-5 p53 Mr-My 2017

Whipple, Fred L. (Fred Lawrence), 1906-2004

Collecting cosmic dust D. J. Eicher bw *Astronomy* v45 no4 p8 Ap 2017

Whippman, Ruth

But Am I Happy Enough? H. ROSIN *New York Times Book Review* p8 O 30 2016

"FOR THE FIRST TIME IN MY LIFE, I didn't have any friends" bw color *Good Housekeeping* v264 no3 p75 Mr 2017

This Is Only a Test *New York Times Book Review* p21 Mr 19 2017

Whirlpool Corp.

THE FINANCIAL PAGE: CLEANING UP A. Davidson color *New Yorker* v93 no33 p40 O 23 2017

Whirlwind Music Distributors Inc.

Whirlwind's 42 Years of Rock-Solid Reliability and Diversity *Stage Directions* v30 no3 p13 Mr 2017

Whiskey

See also

Bourbon whiskey

Rye whiskey

Common Threads D. Coggins color map *Conde Nast Traveler* v52 no3 p64 Mr 2017

FALL FORWARD *Martha Stewart Living* no268 p56 O 2016

A Maker's Guide to... LOUISVILLE F. MAROUKIAN color map *Popular Mechanics* p22 S 2017

The Secret to Drinking More Is... Drinking Less M. BYRNE color *GQ: Gentlemen's Quarterly* v97 no6 p42 Je 2017

Whiskey industry

CAN WHITE WHISKEY GROW UP? A. Hurly color *Bloomberg Businessweek* no4495 p74 O 17 2016

Whiskey Tango Foxtrot (Film)

WHISKEY TANGO FOXTROT B. A. DuHamel color *Sound & Vision* v81 no9 p70 N 2016

Whiskey—Evaluation

American Spirits J. deBary color *Bloomberg Businessweek* no4528 p73 Je 26 2017

A CONUNDRUM IN A BOTTLE color *Esquire* p14 Ap 2017

Multi-Flasking J. Passov color *Golf Magazine* v59 no7 p95 Jl 2017

Pants on Fireball color *Weekly Standard* v22 no25 p2 Mr 6 2017

Whistle speech

THE whistled WORD J. Meyer color graph map *Scientific American* v316 no2 p60 F 2017

Whistleblowers

Blowing the Whistle E. K. BOEGEL *America* v215 no13 p20 O 31 2016

How Does Tax Avoidance Play in Peoria? B. Gruley, D. Voreacos et al color *Bloomberg Businessweek* no4525 p42 Je 5 2017

THE OUTSIDE MAN M. GLADWELL cartoon color *New Yorker* v92 no42 p119 D 19 2016

When Fighting (Alleged) Crime Doesn't Pay A. Satariano *Bloomberg Businessweek* no4522 p38 My 15 2017

Whistleblowing

Managers Aren't Doing Enough to Encourage Whistleblowing S. Rajgopal bw *Harvard Business Review Digital Articles* p2 F 7 2017

Whistleblowing—Computer network resources

Widening the Whistleblower's Reach G. PURDOM *American Scholar* v86 no1 p16 Wint 2017

Whistleblowing—Lawsuits & claims

Court rules small groups can bring whistleblowing claims: Landmark case could influence future decisions defining what is in the public interest *People Management* p14 Ag 2017

Whistler, James McNeill, 1834-1903

Harmony in Blue and Pearl: The Sands, Dieppe color *Magazine Antiques* v183 no6 p138 N/D 2016

Railroader v84 no1 p32 Ja 2017

Atlas O Maxi-IV well cars pack a heavy punch color *Model Railroader* v84 no3 p68 Mr 2017

Bachmann HO scale lighted passenger cars *Model Railroader* v84 no10 p62 O 2017

Bachmann introduces new N scale lighted streamlined passenger cars color *Model Railroader* v84 no1 p72 Ja 2017

Bachmann Sound Value HO scale PCC trolley chart color diag *Model Railroader* v84 no8 p60 Ag 2017

BENCHWORK AND TRACK for the Beer Line addition color diag *Model Railroader* v84 no2 p36 F 2017

MTH HO scale New York City subway cars chart color *Model Railroader* v84 no4 p94 Ap 2017

New paint schemes for smooth-running Atlas N scale General Electric B36-7 bw color *Model Railroader* v83 no12 p68 D 2016

Not quite a DROP-IN DECODER color diag *Model Railroader* v84 no11 p28 N 2017

Rapido brings feature-packed New Haven FL9 commuter locomotive to N scale chart color diag *Model Railroader* v84 no2 p70 F 2017

Rapido HO New Haven cars *Model Railroader* v84 no7 p63 Jl 2017

ScaleTrains.com HO scale SD40-2 chart color *Model Railroader* v84 no11 p62 N 2017

Spring Mills Depot HO wagontop hopper color *Model Railroader* v84 no6 p66 Je 2017

Using multiple techniques to build a CEMENT PLANT color *Model Railroader* v84 no6 p34 Je 2017

WalthersProto HO scale EMD GP35 diesel color *Model Railroader* v84 no9 p58 S 2017

WHITE, ETHAN P.
Skills and Knowledge for Data-Intensive Environmental Research *BioScience* v67 no6 p546 Je 2017

White, Gillian B.
Fixing Tech's "Loss Points" *Atlantic* v319 no5 p11 Je 2017

White, Gregory
Putin's Rival Targets Provincial Russians color *Bloomberg Businessweek* no4517 p28 Ap 3 2017

White, Isaac
TRENDING NOW color *Wired* v25 no4 p12 Ap 2017

White, J. Kevin
BY THE sea color *Cabin Living* p27 Ap 2017

White, Jack, 1975-
THE POLYMATH A. WILKINSON bw cartoon *New Yorker* v93 no4 p42 Mr 13 2017

White, Jaleel—Interviews
Family Matters G. Hall color *Entertainment Weekly* no1485 p24 O 6 2017

White, James
Arctic odysseys H. Wilson cartoon map *Canadian Geographic* v137 no2 p22 Mr/Ap 2017

WHITE, JENNY
Takeaways from the 2016 Blended and Personalized Learning Conference *Education Digest* v82 no6 p42 F 2017

White, Jerry
John Berger of the Haute-Savoie *Film Quarterly* v70 no4 p93 Summ 2017

Part Seminar, Part Something Else: The 69th Festival del Film, Locarno *Film Quarterly* v70 no2 p74 Wint 2016

THE WORST PRISON IN THE COUNTRY: An informative and stimulating biography of a prison which became a microcosm of society S. Tolley *History Today* v67 no6 p98 Je 2016

White, Jesse, 1934-
JESSE WHITE B. Zehme color *Chicago* v66 no5 p148 My 2017

White, Jessica
TRENDING FRIENDS K. NEITZ color *Runner's World* v52 no1 p28 Ja/F 2017

WHITE, JONATHAN
WE'RE TURNING 30 bw chart color *Conde Nast Traveler* v52 no8 p55 S 2017

White, Judith
Overcome Your Reluctance and Start Negotiating Your Salary *Harvard Business Review Digital Articles* p2 My 19 2016

White, Kate
Q: What is the most significant fad of all time? color *Atlantic* v319

no3 p96 Ap 2017

WHITE, KAY
CHAPTER UPDATE color *Phi Kappa Phi Forum* v96 no4 p8 Wint 2016

CHAPTER UPDATE color *Phi Kappa Phi Forum* v97 no2 p6 Summ 2017

PHI KAPPA PHI color *Phi Kappa Phi Forum* v97 no1 p8 Spr 2017

White, M. D.
A microtubule-organizing center directing intracellular transport in the early mouse embryo diag *Science* v357 no6354 p925 S 1 2017

White, Maria Mallory
Reflections on the lectionary *Christian Century* v134 no15 p21 Jl 19 2017

White, Martha C.
137% This Year's Spike in Online Fraud color *Money* v45 no10 p19 N 2016

33 WAYS TO CUT YOUR TAXES [Cover story] color diag *Money* v46 no2 p52 Mr 2017

AMERICANS' $2 BILLION GAS MISTAKE color *Money* v45 no10 p20 N 2016

ASK THE EXPERT diag *Money* v46 no2 p31 Mr 2017

BEST CREDIT CARDS color *Money* v46 no9 p72 O 2017

The Best Way to Beat the Lines diag *Money* v46 no3 p26 Ap 2017

Bundled Policies Can Save You a Lot ... Sometimes color *Money* v45 no10 p20 N 2016

GET A BETTER JOB NOW color diag *Money* v46 no2 p76 Mr 2017

How to Click Your Way to Cash color *Money* v46 no5 p24 Je 2017

Limit Your Exposure color map *Money* v46 no2 p29 Mr 2017

Reclaim Your Weekends! color *Money* v46 no9 p28 O 2017

REGRETS: YOU'VE HAD A FEW color *Money* v46 no1 p20 Ja/F 2017

Texting Is Turning Into Serious Business color *Money* v46 no2 p20 Mr 2017

Want the Most for Your Home? Buyers Favor Bold Colors color diag *Money* v46 no8 p12 S 2017

WORK TAKES A HIT FROM POLITICS color *Money* v46 no3 p18 Ap 2017

White, Martin
Measurement of the small-scale structure of the intergalactic medium using close quasar pairs diag graph *Science* v356 no6336 p418 Ap 28 2017

WHITE, MEL
Music Lovers' Mecca color *AARP: The Magazine* v59 no5A p59 Ag/S 2016

Out on a Limb color map *National Geographic* v230 no6 p56 D 2016

White, Michael
Tribute to Satchmo J. Berry color *New Orleans Magazine* v51 no7 p54 My 2017

White, Mike
ENVY T. Friend cartoon *New Yorker* v93 no28 p20 S 18 2017

Measuring Up J. PODHORETZ color *Weekly Standard* v23 no4 p39 O 2 2017

White, Nancy
POP GOES BAZAAR S. Mooallem color *Harper's Bazaar* no3654 p132 Je/Jl 2017

WHITE, NATHANIEL
Here's How color *Practical Horseman* v45 no8 p56 Ag 2017

WHITE, OGUNGBEMI
Chords & Discords color *Downbeat* v84 no8 p10 Ag 2017

WHITE, PAMELA GAYLE
Real Belief color *Tricycle: The Buddhist Review* v27 no1 p31 Fall 2017

White, Patricia
BODIES THAT MATTER: BLACK GIRLHOOD IN THE FITS *Film Quarterly* v70 no3 p23 Spr 2017

White, Rachel
Building a better measure of school quality color il *Phi Delta Kappan* v98 no7 p43 Ap 2017

White, Raven
Celebrate Good Times K. A. BACKER and D. POINTDUJOUR color *Ebony* v72 no3 p74 D 2016/Ja 2017

White, Richard, 1947-

Misfortunes Multiplied: Richard White's history of late-19th-century America describes a country lashed by greed and brutality S. WILENTZ *New York Times Book Review* p21 S 24 2017

WHITE, ROGER

ART APPRECIATION *New York Times Book Review* p57 D 4 2016

White, Ronald C. (Ronald Cedric), 1939-

The Enigma of Ulysses S. Grant A. C. Guelzo *Washington Monthly* p8 N/D 2016

A Man of Moral Courage T. J. STILES *New York Times Book Review* p12 O 23 2016

The Napoleon of Modesty J. STEELE GORDON *Commentary* v143 no1 p52 Ja 2017

White, Rossandra

Monkey's Wedding *Publishers Weekly* v264 no29 p192 Jl 17 2017

White, Ryan, 1981-

In 'The Keepers,' the Hopes of Vatican II Crumble Amid Sexual Abuse and Murder N. Ripatrazone bw color *America* v216 no13 p42 Je 12 2017

YOUR NEXT TRUE-CRIME OBSESSION IS HERE C. Agard color *Entertainment Weekly* no1466 p48 My 19 2017

White, Sam

An Icy Conquest S. Dunn bw color *New York Review of Books* v64 no17 p52 N 9 2017

White, Shaun, 1986-

"Get Me Marty Singer!" D. MARGOLICK color *Vanity Fair* p154 Hollywood 2017 Supplement

White, Simone

IN END TIME *Harper's Magazine* v334 no2001 p36 F 2017

Push and Pull: Matthew Zapruder and Jill Bialosky tackle the question of what readers can get out of verse color *New York Times Book Review* p11 Ag 6 2017

White, Slaton L.

COLD COMFORT color *Field & Stream* v121 no6 p80 N 2016

FIELD TEST color *Field & Stream* v122 no2 p99 Je/Jl 2017

HOLIDAY GIFT GUIDE 2016 color *Field & Stream* v121 no7 p92 D 2016/Ja 2017

LIGHT ON YOUR FEET color *Field & Stream* v121 no9 p74 Ap 2017

White, Stanley G.

Stanley G. White Sr. July 31, 1936-April 3, 2017 G. DEARTH *Arabian Horse World* v57 no8 p90 My 2017

White, Stephen D.

CONSULTANTS color *Equus* no472 p67 Ja 2017

White, Susanna

OUR KIND OF TRAITOR J. Krebs color *Sound & Vision* v82 no3 p70 Ap 2017

A Truly Timeless Love color *Practical Horseman* v45 no1 p72 Ja 2017

White, Timothy D.

Kilogram-scale prexasertib monolactate monohydrate synthesis under continuous-flow CGMP conditions chart diag *Science* v356 no6343 p1144 Je 16 2017

White, Tyler R.

Nuclear Weapons in a Changing Climate: Probability, Increasing Risks, and Perception bibl chart color graph *Environment* v59 no4 p22 Jl-Ag 2017

White, Victor

THE PREACHER AND THE SHERIFF N. RICH color *New York Times Magazine* p28 F 12 2017

White, Whitney

Merry Manes N. Spradley color *Essence* v47 no8 p61 D 2016

White collar crimes

See also

Tax evasion

SWINDLERS LIST M. SOLOMON color *Forbes* v200 no3 p62 S 28 2017

White collar workers

See also

Clerks

White dwarf stars

HUBBLE WEIGHS A WHITE DWARF A. Klesman color *Astronomy* v45 no10 p12 O 2017

Light-bending by distant star seen L. GROSSMAN color *Science News* v191 no13 p10 Jl 8 2017

On the Alert for Apparitions P. Tyson *Sky & Telescope* v133 no4

p4 Ap 2017

The White Dwarf That Survived The Blast J. BARBUZANO *Sky & Telescope* v134 no6 p11 D 2017

White-faced saki

Incredible Animal Friends E. DEFFNER *National Geographic Kids* no468 p5 Mr 2017

White Famous (TV program)

Season of the Weird R. SHEFFIELD color *Rolling Stone* no1297 p21 O 5 2017

White Famous I. Ratledge *TV Guide* v65 no41 p34 O 2 2017

White Gold (TV program)

STREAMING A. D'ARMINIO *TV Guide* v65 no43 p42 O 16 2017

White House Correspondents' Association

The Fourth Estate Dines Out color *Weekly Standard* v22 no23 p2 F 20 2017

White men

Corporate Diversity Initiatives Should Include White Men A. Wittenberg-Cox *Harvard Business Review Digital Articles* p2 S 6 2016

White Mountain Apache (North American people)

from our archives [July 1962] *Arizona Highways* v93 no11 p10 N 2017

White Mountain National Forest (N.H. & Me.)

Get a fresh perspective color *Backpacker* p16 Je 2017

Victory Lap C. BUHAY *Backpacker* v45 no2 p20 Mr 2017

White Mountains (Ariz.)

AT HOME IN THE WOODS J. Baeza *Arizona Highways* v96 no7 p48 Jl 2017

The Big Pictures: THE WHITE MOUNTAINS *Arizona Highways* v96 no7 p18 Jl 2017

BLUE RANGE LOOP N. AUSTIN *Arizona Highways* v92 no7 p52 Jl 2016

CIBECUE FALLS R. STIEVE *Arizona Highways* v96 no7 p46 Jl 2017

EXPLORE THE WHITE MOUNTAINS *Arizona Highways* v96 no7 p16 Jl 2017

White Mountain Country J. R. MUENCH *Arizona Highways* v96 no7 p40 Jl 2017

White nationalism

See also

Alt-Right (Political science)

White supremacy movements

Blood and Faith: Christianity in American White Nationalism *Publishers Weekly* v264 no28 p81 Jl 10 2017

CHARLOTTESVILLE AND THE PERILS OF COLLECTIVISM E. BOEHM color *Reason* v49 no6 p7 N 2017

Southern Baptists condemn white supremacy, call for 'moral character' in officials A. M. Banks color *Christian Century* v134 no15 p15 Jl 19 2017

White parents

GUESS WHO'S COMING TO KINDERGARTEN P. Wall *Mother Jones* v42 no5 p17 S/O 2017

White privilege

POLITICAL PEROXIDE: Blonde privilege A. LAROCCA img *New York* v50 no16 p44 Ag 7 2017

White River (Ind. : River)

BRIDGE TO THE PAST E. Taylor color *Indianapolis Monthly* v41 no2 p70 S 2017

Broad RIPPLE R. Annis, S. Bahr et al color map *Indianapolis Monthly* v41 no2 p66 S 2017

THE White RIVER R. Annis, S. Bahr et al diag *Indianapolis Monthly* v41 no2 p59 S 2017

White-rumped shama

LOVED TO DEATH R. Conniff color graph *Scientific American* v317 no4 p40 O 2017

White Sands National Monument (N.M.)

True Colors: Learning about evolution from the white lizards of White Sands C. WALKER *National Parks* v91 no3 p22 Summ 2017

White shark

Gray Seals and White Sharks Meet Anew G. B. SKOMAL and S. A. WOOD color *Natural History* v125 no7 p22 Jl/Ag 2017

White spot syndrome virus

8 Ways to Ruin Your Summer A. SWARTZ cartoon color *Men's Health* v32 no6 p94 Ag 2017

White supremacy movements
Co-Opted by Co-Eds *Weekly Standard* v23 no3 p3 S 25 2017
THE NEW MILITANTS M. Pauly *Mother Jones* v42 no3 p22 My/Je 2017
Sand in the Gears E. Epstein *Weekly Standard* v22 no48 p10 S 4 2017

White supremacy movements—United States
BIRTH OF A SUPREMACIST A. MARANTZ cartoon color *New Yorker* v93 no32 p26 O 16 2017
Denouncing the evil lie of white supremacy *Christian Century* v134 no19 p7 S 13 2017
DONALD TRUMP IS FAILING BLACK PEOPLE... WHERE DO WE GO FROM HERE? B. VIERA *Ebony* v72/73 no12/1 p24 O/N 2017
Marching Orders S. Chapin *New York Times Magazine* p11 S 10 2017
Stop a Bigot: A five-step tool kit for dealing with white supremacists in the era of Trump M. LANGELAN *Ms.* v27 no3 p56 Fall 2017
"The Only Good Muslim Is a Dead Muslim" T. GENOWAYS color *New Republic* v248 no6 p30 Je 2017
WHITE SUPREMACIST VIOLENCE IS ALL TOO AMERICAN R. GREENE II *In These Times* v41 no10 p26 O 2017

White-tailed deer
84 Great Days A. Licata color *Field & Stream* v121 no6 p8 N 2016
Nooner Booner D. Draper color *Field & Stream* v121 no6 pW5 N 2016
Read the Beans S. Bestul color *Field & Stream* v122 no4 pW5 S 2017
Seven BEST DAYS of The Rut S. BESTUL color map *Field & Stream* v121 no6 p39 N 2016
WHITE-TAILED DEER FAWN color *Canadian Wildlife* v23 no2 p6 My/Je 2017

White-tailed deer behavior
THE BUCK PROFILE F. MINITER bw color *Outdoor Life* v224 no7 p43 S 2017
SCUFFLE IN THE LOOP C. Begeman *South Dakota Magazine* v33 no3 p94 S/O 2017

White-tailed deer hunting
DAZE OF THE RUT B. Heavey cartoon *Field & Stream* v121 no6 p90 N 2016
A Free Trip D. HURTEAU and T. J. Peterson color *Field & Stream* v122 no4 p40 S 2017
Fresh Takes S. Bestul color *Field & Stream* v122 no6 pW1 N 2017
TAIL TALES T. CARPENTER color *Outdoor Life* v224 no7 pH14 S 2017
YEAR OF THE GIANT S. Bestul color graph *Field & Stream* v122 no3 p30 Ag 2017

White-tailed deer—Reproduction
wildlife quiz color *Cabin Living* p10 O 2017

White whale
Ziya Tong T. Hall color *Canadian Geographic* v137 no5 p82 S/O 2017

White whale hunting
The Inuit Whale Hunter Emmanuel Adam E. ANSELMI color *Foreign Policy* no224 p24 My/Je 2017

White whale—Research
WILDLIFE color *Canadian Geographic* v135 no6 p24 D 2015

White wines—Evaluation
SUMMER WHITES S. Schneider color *Sunset* v238 no6 p100 Je 2017

White women—Social conditions
White Women and the Specter of Islam R. ZAKARIA color il *Nation* v305 no5 p20 Ag 28 2017

Whitebark pine
Blisters, Beetles and British Columbia: Global ReLeaf in Canada D. Irvin *American Forests* v123 no1 p6 Wint/Spr 2017
Guardian of the Blood Moon J. BALDWIN *American Forests* v123 no3 p48 Fall 2017
High Country Rescue C. WALKER *National Parks* v91 no1 p14 Wint 2017
ONE TREE, MANY FUTURES D. IRVIN *American Forests* v123 no3 p24 Fall 2017

Whiteboards
RECALLS color *Consumer Reports* v82 no10 p26 O 2017

WHITECLOUD-BRASS, STEPHANIE

Celebrate Canada? Not yet chart color *Maclean's* v130 no6 p21 Jl 2017

Whitecross, Christine
'We just can't have this' S. PROUDFOOOT color *Maclean's* v129 no45 p26 N 14 2016

Whited, Brittany
Science in litigation, the third branch of U.S. climate policy graph *Science* v357 no6355 p979 S 8 2017

WHITEFORD, ERIKA J.
The Arctic in the Twenty-First Century: Changing Biogeochemical Linkages across a Paraglacial Landscape of Greenland *BioScience* v67 no2 p118 F 2017

Whitehall (N.Y.)
A TOWN, A TEAM AND FOOTBALL T. Layden color *Sports Illustrated* v127 no11 p46 O 9 2017

Whitehall, Jack, 1988-
Eva Goes Retro *TV Guide* v65 no19 p11 My 1 2017

WHITEHALL, KETIMA
LOVE HURTS—AND SO DOES BETRAYAL *USA Today Magazine* v145 no2862 p66 Mr 2017

Whitehead, Andrew
The genomic landscape of rapid repeated evolutionary adaptation to toxic pollution in wild fish bibl graph *Science* v354 no6317 p1305 D 9 2016

Whitehead, Colson
BESTSELLERS C. JURIS chart color graph *Publishers Weekly* v264 no17 p13 Ap 24 2017
DAVID BOWIE C. WHITEHEAD *New York Times Magazine* p18 D 25 2016
Railroad Leads to Pulitzer for Gifted Author Y. Stines color *Ebony* v72 no9 p28 Jl/Ag 2017
The Ten Best Books of the Year C. Lorentzen img *New York* v49 no25 p122 D 12 2016
The Underground Railroad: A Novel P. Christman color *Christian Century* v133 no21 p36 O 12 2016
When Spirits Linger *New York Times Book Review* p1 F 12 2017

WHITEHEAD, MARGARET REDMOND
HOME ECONOMICS FOR REFUGEES color map *Reason* v49 no2 p48 Je 2017

WHITEHORN, KATHARINE
Laugh Lines color *Reader's Digest* v189 no1130 p107 My 2017

WHITEHOUSE, ELAINE
Humor in Uniform *Reader's Digest* v189 no1127 p135 F 2017

Whitehouse, Joanna
Emergence and spread of a human-transmissible multidrug-resistant nontuberculous mycobacterium bibl diag graph *Science* v354 no6313 p751 N 11 2016

Whitehouse, Mark
How Screwed Is Your Job? diag *Bloomberg Businessweek* no4528 p50 Je 26 2017

Whitehouse, Sheldon
The Climate Movement Needs More Corporate Lobbyists *Harvard Business Review Digital Articles* p2 F 25 2016

White House (Washington, D.C.)
The Adult in the Room M. Warren color *Weekly Standard* v22 no26 p12 Mr 13 2017
A Big Deal? E. Abrams color *Weekly Standard* v22 no24 p9 F 27 2017
Haunted White House K. B. RATTINI color *National Geographic Kids* no474 p24 O 2017
Research: Companies See a Stock Bump After Executives Visit the White House G. Gavett *Harvard Business Review Digital Articles* p2 Jl 5 2017
What You Said About ... color *Time* v189 no3 p4 Ja 30 2017
The White House Selfie: The Visual Web's Latest Victory P. Hewitt *Harvard Business Review Digital Articles* p2 Jl 2 2015

White House (Washington, D.C.)—History—21st century
In Defense of an Open, Fair and Free Press N. Gibbs color *Time* v189 no9 p4 Mr 13 2017

White House (Washington, D.C.)—Interior decoration
PARODY color *Weekly Standard* v22 no47 p48 Ag 21 2017

White House (Washington, D.C.)—Officials & employees
The House As a Home K. A. Brower color *Time* v189 no4 p37 Ja 23 2017
NORMALIZE THIS M. Leibovich color *New York Times Magazine* p40 N 27 2016

Whitehurst, Jim
3 Ways to Encourage Smarter Teamwork *Harvard Business Review Digital Articles* p2 S 7 2015
Be a Leader Who Can Admit Mistakes *Harvard Business Review Digital Articles* p2 Je 2 2015
Create a Culture Where Difficult Conversations Aren't So Hard *Harvard Business Review Digital Articles* p2 Ag 14 2015
Decisions Are More Effective When More People Are Involved from the Start *Harvard Business Review Digital Articles* p2 Mr 15 2016
Despite What Zappos Says, Middle Managers Still Matter *Harvard Business Review Digital Articles* p2 My 28 2015
How to Build a Passionate Company *Harvard Business Review Digital Articles* p2 F 15 2016
How to Earn Respect as a Leader *Harvard Business Review Digital Articles* p2 My 20 2015
Managing Performance When It's Hard to Measure *Harvard Business Review Digital Articles* p2 My 11 2015
The Real Power of Platforms Is Helping People Self-Organize *Harvard Business Review Digital Articles* p2 Ap 25 2016

Whiteley, Larry
6 Must-Haves to Turn Your Pontoon Into a Fishing Machine color *Cabin Living* p12 Ag 2017
Autumn isn't just the end of summertime, it's bonus time color *Cabin Living* p13 S 2017

White Princess, The (TV program)
The White Princess B. Oates *TV Guide* v65 no13 p36 Mr 20 2017

White River State Park (Indianapolis, Ind.)
Farther Downstream R. Annis, S. Bahr et al color map *Indianapolis Monthly* v41 no2 p77 S 2017

Whites
        See also
        White men
Empire's Other Whites W. Jackson *History Today* v66 no12 p43 D 2016
New Orleans Confronts Its Confederate History J. Sanburn color *Time* v189 no19 p12 My 22 2017

Whites—Attitudes
White like me J. RICHARDSON *Phi Delta Kappan* v98 no5 p4 F 2017

Whitesell, Luke
Susan Lindquist (1949–2016) color *Science* v354 no6315 p974 N 25 2016

Whiteside, James
why i dance *Dance Magazine* v90 no11 p72 N 2016

Whiteside, Janey
PLATINUM REWARDS N. Silva-Jelly color *Harper's Bazaar* no3657 p163 O 2017

Whitesides, George M.
John D. Roberts (1918–2016) color *Science* v354 no6318 p1382 D 16 2016

Whitesides, Jonathan
Posthole color *Powder* v45 no3 p148 N 2016

Whites—United States—Political activity
Whitelash J. WALSH color *Nation* v303 no22 p4 N 28 2016

Whites—United States—Social conditions
Don't Forget High Earners H. OLSEN *National Review* v69 no19 p32 O 16 2017

Whitewashing in mass media
In a Handbasket Dept color *Weekly Standard* v23 no1 p2 S 11 2017

Whitewater kayaking
Bringing Whitewater Kayaking to Your Community B. Bevacqua *Parks & Recreation* v52 no4 p20 Ap 2017

Whitfeld, Christina
The Production and Migration of Educational Capital *Change* v49 no3 p71 My/Je 2017

Whitfield, Bethany
INSIDE ADS-B color *Flying* v143 no12 p16 D 2016

Whitfield, Fredricka
Fredricka Whitfield *Atlanta* v57 no2 p96 Je 2017
A "Marvelous" Family Legacy N. PARKER bw *Ebony* v72 no8 p84 Je 2017

Whitfield, Jonny
Lee Rubin: Our mentor and role model *Science* v355 no6327 p806 F 24 2017

Whitfield, Lynn—Interviews
KINDRED SPIRITS M. LOGAN *TV Guide* v65 no11 p22 Mr 6 2017

Whitfield, Mal, 1924-2015
A "Marvelous" Family Legacy N. PARKER bw *Ebony* v72 no8 p84 Je 2017

WHITFIELD, TERRYLYNN
Living Out Loud: On good food, great reads, and strong women color *O, The Oprah Magazine* p20 S 2017

Whiting, Alyse
Essential Framework for Adaptive Aquatics *Parks & Recreation* v52 no10 p54 O 2017

Whiting, Amanda
19 THINGS YOU REALLY OUGHT TO 00 THIS MONTH *Washingtonian Magazine* v52 no3 p31 D 2016
AND NOW FOR THE NEXT COURSE *Washingtonian Magazine* v52 no1 p10 O 2016
A BRILLIANT PROPOSAL TO SOLVE OUR AIRPORT PROBLEMS *Washingtonian Magazine* v52 no2 p12 N 2016
EXTREME ANNAPOLIS: A spurned action-sports starwoos his hometown *Washingtonian Magazine* v52 no12 p20 S 2017
FEEDING AND READING *Washingtonian Magazine* v52 no3 p17 D 2016
FOGGY BOTTOM *Washingtonian Magazine* v52 no6 p24 Mr 2017
FOX'S LIBERAL: Pundit Jessica Tarlov on playing the villain on America's most watched cable network *Washingtonian Magazine* v52 no8 p51 My 2017
FROM BARRE TO BOSS *Washingtonian Magazine* v52 no6 p16 Mr 2017
HOW TO BE A BLEACHER-STOMPING, BEER-TOSSING D.C. UNITED FAN *Washingtonian Magazine* v52 no6 p70 Mr 2017
IN DEFENSE OF EXPERTISE *Washingtonian Magazine* v52 no5 p15 F 2017
INN THE MONEY *Washingtonian Magazine* v52 no8 p20 My 2017
MUSIC IS LIFE *Washingtonian Magazine* v52 no9 p22 Je 2017
MY TOWN *Washingtonian Magazine* v52 no5 p156 F 2017
MY TOWN *Washingtonian Magazine* v52 no9 p174 Je 2017
The NATION of FLYING DOG *Washingtonian Magazine* v52 no4 p68 Ja 2017
PARK AND SIGH *Washingtonian Magazine* v52 no8 p12 My 2017
The Tyranny of Tennis Rackets *Washingtonian Magazine* v52 no6 p54 Mr 2017
WASHINGTON MONUMENT: A statue honoring Marion Barry will-of course--be larger than life *Washingtonian Magazine* v52 no12 p18 S 2017

WHITING, SCOTT
Accelerating Tropicalization and the Transformation of Temperate Seagrass Meadows *BioScience* v66 no11 p938 N 1 2016

WHITLER, KIMBERLY A.
EXECUTIVE SUMMARIES bw color *Harvard Business Review* v95 no4 p146 Jl/Ag 2017
THE POWER PARTNERSHIP: CMO & CIO *Harvard Business Review* v95 no4 p55 Jl/Ag 2017
WHY CMOs NEVER LAST AND WHAT TO DO ABOUT IT chart color graph img *Harvard Business Review* v95 no4 p46 Jl/Ag 2017

Whitley, Angus
China Challenges the Giants With Low Fares color graph *Bloomberg Businessweek* no4504 p22 D 19 2016

Whiting, Natasha
Animal CSI [Cover story] color *Scientific American* v316 no1 p56 Ja 2017

Whitlock, Sharon
Feminist Force color *Glamour* v115 no3 p38 Mr 2017

Whitman, Alan
FROM OUR READERS *Sky & Telescope* v134 no4 p6 O 2017

WHITMAN, ARDIS
Overtaken by Joy *Reader's Digest* v189 no1128 p94 Mr 2017

Whitman, James Q.
What America Taught the Nazis I. KATZNELSON color *Atlantic* v320 no4 p42 N 2017
What Uncle Sam and Jim Crow Taught Hitler M. HARWOOD bw

Reason v49 no1 p64 My 2017

Whitman, Meg, 1956-
BOXED IN J. Wieczner, K. Bellstrom et al color diag *Fortune* v176 no5 p86 O 1 2017

Whitman, Walt, 1819-1892
The Walt Whitman Workout Plan N. Hopper color *Time* v189 no5 p53 F 13 2017

Whitman Ongstad, Anne
10 SUCCESSFUL FARMERS: ANNE WHITMAN ONGSTAD A. McConnell *Successful Farming* v115 no8 p20 Je/Jl 2017

Whitmarsh, Alan J.
Multisite phosphorylation by MAPK bibl diag *Science* v354 no6309 p179 O 14 2016

WHITMER, ERIN
7 heart-pumping facts *National Geographic Kids* no467 p10 F 2017
8 totally wild facts about animals *National Geographic Kids* no469 p10 Ap 2017
8 ways people try to get good luck around the world *National Geographic Kids* no468 p10 Mr 2017
Bet You Didn't Know color map *National Geographic Kids* no472 p6 Ag 2017
Bet You Didn't Know color *National Geographic Kids* no473 p11 S 2017
Bet you didn't know *National Geographic Kids* no466 p10 D 2016/Ja 2017
Funny Fill-In cartoon *National Geographic Kids* no471 p31 Je/Jl 2017

Whitmire, Jason K.
MAVS-dependent host species range and pathogenicity of human hepatitis A virus bibl graph *Science* v353 no6307 p1541 S 30 2016

Whitmire, Richard
Sharing the Wealth W. MCKENZIE *Weekly Standard* v22 no38 p35 Je 12 2017

Whitmore, Lisa
FIGHT LINES AT EVERY AGE color *Health* v31 no4 p94 My 2017

Whitney (Music)
WHITNEY HOUSTON'S WHITNEY TURNS 30 K. O'donnell color *Entertainment Weekly* no1468/1469 p103 Je 2-9 2017

Whitney, Christine
Clemons' Time color *InStyle* v24 no9 p221 S 2017
My Skin color *InStyle* v24 no5 p240 My 2017

Whitney, Joel
Literary Agents P. IBER color il *New Republic* v248 no1/2 p68 Ja/F 2017

Whitney, Quincy
American Luthier Carleen Hutchins—the Art and Science of the Violin C. Waltham *Physics Today* v70 no2 p60 F 2017

Whitney, Tim
The SAILING SCENE color *Sail* v48 no11 p6 N 2017

Whitney Biennial
GOINGS ON ABOUT TOWN color *New Yorker* v93 no5 p9 Mr 20 2017
Objets d'Art H. MARTIN cartoon color *Architectural Digest* v74 no4 p62 Ap 2017
TNT M. HOLGATE and M. GUIDUCCI cartoon color *Vogue* v207 no3 p342 Mr 2017
WHAT'S NEW? P. SCHJELDAHL cartoon *New Yorker* v93 no6 p76 Mr 27 2017

Whitney: Can I Be Me (Film)
Whitney: Can I Be Me I. Ratledge *TV Guide* v65 no35 p32 Ag 21 2017

Whitney Museum of American Art
Art In the Age of Trump: The Whitney Biennial Takes a First Crack E. Berman color *Time* v189 no13 p47 Ap 10 2017
FRESH PAINT P. SCHJELDAHL cartoon *New Yorker* v92 no48 p76 F 6 2017
Live Wire A. K. Scott cartoon *New Yorker* v93 no19 p10 Jl 3 2017
WHAT'S NEW? P. SCHJELDAHL cartoon *New Yorker* v93 no6 p76 Mr 27 2017
Your $1,000 New York Weekend color map *GQ: Gentlemen's Quarterly* v87 no1 p14 Ja 2017

WHITSON, PEGGY
WHERE ARE YOU GOING? color *O, The Oprah Magazine* p128

S 2017

Whitt, Margaret
THE BIG QUESTION cartoon *Atlantic* v319 no5 p96 Je 2017

Whittaker, Ashley
BETTER WITH AGE K. RENDA color *House Beautiful* v159 no3 p76 Ap 2017

Whittaker, Linda
Isabella and the Tale of the Unanswered Question *Publishers Weekly* v263 no52 p103 D 19 2016

Whittaker, Robert J.
Island biogeography: Taking the long view of nature's laboratories map *Science* v357 no6354 p885 S 1 2017

Whitten, Barbara L.
The Only Woman in the Room *Physics Today* v69 no10 p55 O 2016

Whittenburg, Zachary
10 MINUTES WITH . . . Mark Morris *Dance Magazine* v90 no12 p30 D 2016
Gone Viral *Dance Magazine* v90 no12 p59 D 2016
Like No Place Else *Dance Magazine* v90 no12 p102 D 2016
Marketing Mistakes *Dance Magazine* v91 no6 p52 Je 2017
The MOST INFLUENTIAL PEOPLE IN DANCE TODAY: THE MOVERS, SHAKERS AND CHANGEMAKERS HAVING THE BIGGEST IMPACT ON DANCE RIGHT NOW *Dance Magazine* v91 no7 p27 Jl 2017

Whittington, Richard
Wall Street Rewards CEOs Who Talk About Their Strategies *Harvard Business Review Digital Articles* p2 D 28 2015

WHITTLE, ANDREA
ACCESSORIES AND JEWELRY DESIGNER KENDALL CONRAD color *Conde Nast Traveler* v52 no7 p28 Ag 2017
BLOGGER AND DESIGNER MARLIEN RENTMEESTER color *Conde Nast Traveler* v52 no10 p38 N 2017
Contact High color *Conde Nast Traveler* v51 no10 p182 N 2016
Flight Deck color *Conde Nast Traveler* v52 no2 p110 F 2017
"FLYING ALONE FOR WORK IS LIKE A VACATION. FLYING WITH MY SON IS DEFINITELY WORK." color *Conde Nast Traveler* v52 no6 p30 Je/Jl 2017
GQ STYLE FASHION DIRECTOR MOBOLAJI DAWODU color *Conde Nast Traveler* v52 no8 p30 S 2017
HELLO, TOKYO color *Conde Nast Traveler* v52 no4 p24 Ap 2017
Hotel de Russie, Rome color *Conde Nast Traveler* v52 no7 p36 Ag 2017
"IF YOU PACK EVERYTHING IN ONE COLOR PALETTE, YOU'LL BRING 30 PERCENT LESS" color *Conde Nast Traveler* v52 no2 p24 F 2017
IN HIS ELEMENT BRUNELLO CUCINELLI FINDS CASHMERE AND PEACE IN MONGOLIA color *Conde Nast Traveler* v52 no10 p44 N 2017
Le Bristol Paris color *Conde Nast Traveler* v51 no11 p62 D 2016
"MY PACKING ADVICE? ROLL EVERYTHING AND BRING A DRY SHAMPOO" color *Conde Nast Traveler* v52 no4 p26 Ap 2017
"NEVER LOOK LIKE A TOURIST. ACT LIKE YOU KNOW WHERE YOU ARE." color *Conde Nast Traveler* v52 no3 p32 Mr 2017
"NO ONE WILL HELP YOU RUSH THROUGH SECURITY IF YOU LOOK LIKE YOU JUST ROLLED OUT OF BED." color *Conde Nast Traveler* v52 no5 p28 My 2017
NORTHERN MOROCCO color map *Conde Nast Traveler* v52 no4 p64 Ap 2017
PRIME CUT color *Conde Nast Traveler* v52 no2 p30 F 2017
RWANDA + UGANDA color *Conde Nast Traveler* v52 no4 p32 Ap 2017
San Francisco color map *Conde Nast Traveler* v52 no6 p50 Je/Jl 2017
Sunset Tower Hotel, Los Angeles color *Conde Nast Traveler* v52 no1 p58 Ja 2017
Take a Left At the Fork bw color map *Conde Nast Traveler* v52 no9 p50 O 2017

WHITTLE, MADELINE
Beyond Illusion color *Film Comment* v53 no1 p93 Ja/F 2017

Whittle, Ricky
American Gods J. Halterman *TV Guide* v65 no13 p34 Mr 20 2017
AMERICAN GODS P. SUDERMAN *Reason* v49 no4 p76 Ag/S

MEMORIES OF Carle Vernet *Arabian Horse World* v57 no9 p148 Je 2017

Wick, Abbey

ABBEY WICK: SOIL HEALTH SPECIALIST KNOWS HOW TO CONNECT WITH FARMERS G. Gullickson bw *Successful Farming* v115 no7 p5 My 2017

Wick, Marion

Fresh, Homemade SALAD DRESSINGS *Mother Earth News* no281 p36 Ap/My 2017

Wicked (Theatrical production)

Waitresses and Witches: Broadway's new formula for success T. TEACHOUT *Commentary* v142 no4 p49 N 2016

Waitresses and Witches *Commentary* v141 no9 p1 N 2016

Waitresses and Witches *Commentary* v142 no4 p1 N 2016

Wicker, Marcus

Film Noir at Gallop Park, On the Edge *Nation* v303 no23/24 p37 D 5 2016

Silencer *Publishers Weekly* v264 no34 p87 Ag 21 2017

Wicker, Ryan

Multiprocess 3D printing for increasing component functionality bibl bw color *Science* v353 no6307 paaf2093-1 S 30 2016

Wicker furniture

Dream Weavers H. MARTIN color *Architectural Digest* no6 p48 Je 1 2017

Wicker Park (Chicago, Ill.)

THE GREAT ESCAPE R. O'CONNOR color *Chicago* v65 no12 p40 D 2016

Wicki, Bernhard

La Notte *New Yorker* v93 no14 p21 My 22 2017

WICKS, AMANDA

HEARTFELT VOCALS color *Louisiana Life* v37 no3 p112 Ja/F 2017

Wicks, Maris

FORECASTING THE FUTURE OF FISH *Oceanus* v51 no2 p94 Wint 2016

Wickstrand, Cecilia

A three-dimensional movie of structural changes in bacteriorhodopsin bibl diag graph *Science* v354 no6319 p1552 D 23 2016

Wickstrom, Stefanie

Mestizaje and Globalization: Transformations of Identity and Power M. Milazzo *American Indian Quarterly* v40 no4 p379 Fall 2016

Widdicombe, Lizzie

CITIZENS IN TRAINING cartoon *New Yorker* v92 no49 p32 F 13 2017

DEM BONES cartoon *New Yorker* v93 no8 p18 Ap 10 2017

FROZEN cartoon *New Yorker* v92 no32 p34 O 10 2016

HIGH CUISINE cartoon color *New Yorker* v93 no10 p48 Ap 24 2017

MUSLIM SISTERHOOD cartoon *New Yorker* v92 no38 p30 N 21 2016

TOP DOGS cartoon *New Yorker* v92 no46 p18 Ja 23 2017

THE UNSOCIALIZED SELF cartoon *New Yorker* v92 no34 p22 O 24 2016

Wide-angle lenses

D-Link DCS-8200LH HD 180-Degree Wi-Fi Camera: An all-seeing eye for large spaces M. ANSALDO color *PCWorld* p125 Mr 2017

Wide receivers (Football)

ALL ABOUT CONNECTIONS [Cover story] T. Layden color *Sports Illustrated* v126 no3 p22 Ja 23 2017

American Voices Pierre Garçon J. Feldman and T. Keith color *Sports Illustrated* v125 no17 p26 N 21 2016 Double Issue

Wide receivers (Football)—Universities & colleges

'TIS BETTER TO RECEIVE A. Staples color *Sports Illustrated* v127 no6 p46 Ag 28 2017

Wideman, John Edgar, 1941-

A BLACK AND WHITE CASE bw color *Esquire* v166 no4 p100 N 2016

CRIMES OF BEING J. C. WILLIAMS bw color *New York Times Magazine* p30 Ja 29 2017

Fathers and Sons E. EUGENE HOLLEY JR. color *Publishers Weekly* v263 no43 p35 O 24 2016

In Emmett Till's Shadow G. L. BUCKLEY *New York Times Book Review* p11 D 18 2016

JB & FD J. E. Wideman *Harper's Magazine* v334 no2001 p73 F 2017

When is silence a lie S. Anderson *New York Times Magazine* p15 Ap 30 2017

WIDEMAN'S GHOSTS J. McCARTHY color *Nation* v303 no25/26 p27 D 19 2016

Writing to Save a Life: The Louis Till File A. Frykholm *Christian Century* v134 no6 p39 Mr 15 2017

Widener, Michael

DESERT-READY HOT ROD M. EMERY color *Dirt Sports + Off-Road* v51 no7 p52 Jl 2017

Widge, Alik S.

Behavior management color *Science* v356 no6335 p244 Ap 21 2017

Widgerow, Alan D.

Regeneration of fat cells from myofibroblasts during wound healing bibl color graph *Science* v355 no6326 p148 F 17 2017

Widhalm, Joshua R.

Emission of volatile organic compounds from petunia flowers is facilitated by an ABC transporter diag *Science* v356 no6345 p1386 Je 30 2017

WIDNER, KITTY

BIG CREEK: A FAMILY RECALLS YEARS AT THE LODGE *Idaho Magazine* v16 no10 p32 Jl 2017

Sing the Hero: A Hole in the Boat, And Ice in the Water *Idaho Magazine* v16 no7 p21 Ap 2017

A TOWN RECYCLED AND ITS MASTERFUL MOVER *Idaho Magazine* v17 no1 p42 Ja 2017

Widom, Michael

Segregation-induced ordered superstructures at general grain boundaries in a nickel-bismuth alloy color *Science* v357 no6359 p97 O 6 2017

Widows—Legal status, laws, etc.

Life After Loss C. GORNEY color map *National Geographic* v231 no2 p78 F 2017

WHAT WIDOWS LOSE—AND KEEP S. Goldberg color *National Geographic* v231 no2 p2 F 2017

Widows—Social conditions

Life After Loss C. GORNEY color map *National Geographic* v231 no2 p78 F 2017

WHAT WIDOWS LOSE—AND KEEP S. Goldberg color *National Geographic* v231 no2 p2 F 2017

Wiebe, David

Washing COLOR into Nebraska skies N. Buck cartoon color *Nebraska Life* v21 no2 p76 Mr/Ap 2017

Wiebe, Joseph R.

Racism in Port William K. B. Heidelberger *Christian Century* v134 no18 p36 Ag 30 2017

Wiebe, Krystalee

Wild emmer genome architecture and diversity elucidate wheat evolution and domestication color *Science* v357 no6346 p93 Jl 7 2017

Wiech, Katja

Deconstructing the sensation of pain: The influence of cognitive processes on pain perception bibl diag graph *Science* v354 no6312 p584 N 4 2016

Wieczner, Jen

100 FASTEST-GROWING COMPANIES chart color diag map *Fortune* v176 no4 p157 S 15 2017

19 LARRY FINK color *Fortune* v174 no7 p89 D 1 2016

THE 21ST-CENTURY BANK ROBBERY color *Fortune* v176 no3 p52 S 1 2017

ANATOMY OF A VERY BAD DEAL *Fortune* v175 no5 p12 Ap 1 2017

APPLE REBOOTS IN CHINA color *Fortune* v176 no5 p106 O 1 2017

THE BLACK CEILING color *Fortune* v176 no5 p94 O 1 2017

BOXED IN color diag *Fortune* v176 no5 p86 O 1 2017

CAN STEVE MNUCHIN MAKE THE IRS GREAT AGAIN? color *Fortune* v175 no5 p13 Ap 1 2017

DEFENDING YOUR PORTFOLIO color diag *Fortune* v175 no8 p78 Je 15 2017

EPIPEN PANIC color *Fortune* v174 no8 p21 D 15 2016

HOW THE FTC GOT THE HERBALIFE SETTLEMENT DISASTROUSLY WRONG color *Fortune* v175 no3 p12 Mr 1 2017

HOW TO SNAG A STOCK TICKER *Fortune* v75 no1 p20 Ja

1 2017

Investors Go Long on Slime color *Fortune* v175 no7 p12 Je 1 2017

INVESTOR'S MIDYEAR GUIDE diag *Fortune* v175 no7 p49 Je 1 2017

MOST POWERFUL WOMEN color *Fortune* v176 no5 p54 O 1 2017

MOST POWERFUL WOMEN INTERNATIONAL color *Fortune* v176 no5 p111 O 1 2017

THE QUEEN OF POP [Cover story] color diag *Fortune* v176 no5 p70 O 1 2017

THE REVOLUTION STARTS HERE color *Fortune* v174 no7 p26 D 1 2016

Snap's Audacious Wall Street Play *Time* v189 no9 p30 Mr 13 2017

STEVE COHEN HAS NOTHING TO PROVE (BUT HE'S GOING TO PROVE IT ANYWAY) color diag *Fortune* v174 no6 p94 N 1 2016

Stocks to Keep a Nest Egg Growing color diag *Fortune* v174 no8 p108 D 15 2016

TECH TAKEOVER IN TOYLAND color diag *Fortune* v176 no5 p76 O 1 2017

WATCHING THE DOW LEAP diag *Fortune* v175 no2 p84 F 1 2017

WHEN THE BEST WORKPLACES ARE THE BEST INVESTMENTS color diag *Fortune* v175 no4 p137 Mr 15 2017

WORLD'S 50 GREATEST LEADERS [Cover story] color *Fortune* v175 no5 p46 Ap 1 2017

Wieczorek, Mark A.

Formation of the Orientale lunar multiring basin bibl graph *Science* v354 no6311 p441 O 28 2016

Gravity field of the Orientale basin from the Gravity Recovery and Interior Laboratory Mission bibl graph *Science* v354 no6311 p438 O 28 2016

Wiedeman, Reeves

As American as Refusing to Stand for the National Anthem img *New York* p34 F 20 2017

The Dirtbag Left's Man in Syria img *New York* v50 no7 p40 Ap 3 2017

Hot Do-Gooder Svante Myrick color *Rolling Stone* no1274 p46 N 17 2016

IF I HAD AN AXE cartoon *New Yorker* v92 no48 p17 F 6 2017

IN THE DARK cartoon *New Yorker* v92 no42 p49 D 19 2016

Jeremy Lin img *New York* v49 no22 p18 O 31 2016

The No. 2 College-Football Recruit in the Country Is From Canarsie and Wears a SpongeBob Backpack img *New York* v49 no25 p76 D 12 2016

Uber, But for Melt downs: Sexual harassment, corporate-espionage charges, taking advantage of drivers: The company that practically courts bad PR has an even greater, more existential dilemma img *New York* v50 no11 p34 My 29 2017

"WE SAVE THE WORLD AGAIN!" color *Popular Mechanics* p96 Ap 2017

Wiedemann, Julius

The Art of National Geographic I. Biedenharn color *Entertainment Weekly* no1450 p62 Ja 27 2017

Wieden + Kennedy (Company)

THE REWARDS OF RISK T. Foster color *Men's Health* v32 no1 p40 Ja/F 2017

WIEDENHOEFT, ALEX

Opportunities for Improved Transparency in the Timber Trade through Scientific Verification *BioScience* v66 no11 p990 N 1 2016

Wiederin, Alex

HORSE POWER bw color *Esquire* p104 2017 BigBlackBook

Wiegard, Anika

Structures of the cyanobacterial circadian oscillator frozen in a fully assembled state bibl diag *Science* v355 no6330 p1181 Mr 17 2017

Wiegel, Hanne

Refugees of rising seas color *Science* v357 no6346 p41 Jl 7 2017

Wieland, Andreas

Rescue of exhausted CD8 T cells by PD-1–targeted therapies is CD28-dependent bw diag graph *Science* v355 no6332 p1423 Mr 31 2017

WIELAND, TERRY

THE AMERICAN SIDE-BY-SIDE color *Outdoor Life* v224 no5

p72 Je/Jl 2017

Wieliczko, Patty—Interviews

Member Spotlight: Patty Wieliczko V. Paynich *Parks & Recreation* v51 no12 p44 D 2016

Wiencke, L.

Observation of a large-scale anisotropy in the arrival directions of cosmic rays above 8 × 1018 eV *Science* v357 no6357 p1266 S 22 2017

Wiener, Aaron

THAT TOWN color *Mother Jones* v42 no4 p6 Jl/Ag 2017

Wiener, Anna

Only Human color *New Republic* v248 no3 p68 Mr 2017

SAN FRANCISCO *Harper's Magazine* p31 O 2017

The Shine Comes Off Silicon Valley cartoon color *Atlantic* v319 no2 p44 Mr 2017

WIENER, JOCELYN

rough reads *Parents* v92 no3 p112 Mr 2017

talking to strangers *Parents* v92 no7 p128 Jl 2017

Wieners, Brad

THE GREAT INDOORS color *Bloomberg Businessweek* no4495 p71 O 17 2016

An island moneymaker that knows everybody's secrets *Columbia Journalism Review* v56 no1 p80 Spr 2017

Patagonia: For climbing Everest, diving the Great Barrier Reef, and saving the planet on a beer run color *Bloomberg Businessweek* no4494 p54 O 10 2016

Wienhausen, Gabriele

Beyond the Transcript: The Need to Showcase More *Change* v49 no4 p14 Jl/Ag 2017

Wienke, Tiffany

FOR THE RECORD H. Ribons color *Field & Stream* v121 no7 p17 D 2016/Ja 2017

Wiens, Jenna

PIONEERS E. Mullin, S. Parkin et al color il *MIT Technology Review* v120 no5 p50 S/O 2017

Wiens, Kandi

Prevent Burnout by Making Compassion a Habit *Harvard Business Review Digital Articles* p1 My 11 2017

Why Some People Get Burned Out and Others Don't *Harvard Business Review Digital Articles* p2 N 23 2016

Wiens, Kyle

The Weird Rules Governing What We Download *Harvard Business Review Digital Articles* p2 N 3 2015

Wiens, R. C.

Redox stratification of an ancient lake in Gale crater, Mars color *Science* v356 no6341 p922 Je 1 2017

Wientge, Kristi

Karma Khullar's Mustache *Publishers Weekly* v264 no23 p52 Je 5 2017

WIER, GEORGIA

Textiles to Ride: The Saddle Blanket Weaver *Idaho Magazine* v16 no9 p7 Je 2017

Wiersema, Margarethe

What Board Directors Really Think of Gender Quotas *Harvard Business Review Digital Articles* p2 N 14 2016

WIERSMA, YOLANDA F.

Scientific Evidence for Fifty Percent? *BioScience* v67 no9 p781 S 2017

Wiesenfeld, Dan

3 Things Are Holding Back Your Analytics, and Technology Isn't One of Them *Harvard Business Review Digital Articles* p2 Je 8 2017

3 Things Are Holding Back Your Analytics, and Technology Isn't One of Them *Harvard Business Review Digital Articles* p2 Je 9 2017

Wiesenfeldt, Mario P.

Hydrogenation of fluoroarenes: Direct access to all-cis-(multi)fluorinated cycloalkanes diag *Science* v357 no6354 p908 S 1 2017

Wiesner, Darin L.

The balance between immunity and inflammation diag *Science* v357 no6355 p973 S 8 2017

Wiewiora, Rafal

Posttranslational mutagenesis: A chemical strategy for exploring protein side-chain diversity diag *Science* v354 no6312 p597 N 4 2016

Wife abuse

A Disobedient Woman L. Schenkman *New York Times Magazine* p34 Mr 26 2017

Wigdor, Douglas

The Trump-Loving Lawyer Who Won't Stop Suing Fox News F. Gillette color *Bloomberg Businessweek* no4540 p60 O 2 2017

Wigfield, Tracey

A sorta CATHOLIC'S very CATHOLIC WEDDING [Cover story] bw *America* v216 no10 p34 My 1 2017

Wigge, Philip A.

Phytochrome B integrates light and temperature signals in Arabidopsis bibl graph *Science* v354 no6314 p897 N 18 2016

Phytochromes function as thermosensors in Arabidopsis bibl graph *Science* v354 no6314 p886 N 18 2016

Wigger, John—Interviews

Fall from Grace H. CLUTTERBUCK-COOK bw *Publishers Weekly* v264 no31 p75 Jl 31 2017

Wiggins, Kaye

Will Britain Keep Investing in a Sex Offender's Venture Fund? *Bloomberg Businessweek* no4539 p22 S 25 2017

Wiggins, Patrick

Celebrating S&T's 75th Anniversary *Sky & Telescope* v133 no2 p6 F 2017

Wigginton, N.

Fostering reproducibility in industry-academia research color *Science* v357 no6353 p759 Ag 25 2017

WIGHT, THEODORE M.

American Illiberalism *Commentary* v142 no3 p6 O 2016

Wigley, Mark—Interviews

Mark Wigley and Beatriz Colomina F. A. BERNSTEIN *Architectural Record* v204 no10 p28 O 2016

Wignall, Jeff

HOT SPOT color *Popular Photography* v81 no2 p34 Mr/Ap 2017

LIGHT & FOG color *Popular Photography* v81 no1 p44 Ja/F 2017

ROAD TRIP bw *Popular Photography* v80 no11 p38 D 2016

Wigs

THE WORST — WIG GAME! K. P. Sullivan color *Entertainment Weekly* no1444/1445 p60 D 16 2016

Wiig, Kristen, 1973—Interviews

RENAISSANCE Woman A. Grant color *Esquire* p56 O 2017

Wijedasa, Lahiru S.

Time for responsible peatland agriculture bibl *Science* v354 no6312 p562 N 4 2016

Wijeratne, Sagara

Control of species-dependent cortico-motoneuronal connections underlying manual dexterity diag graph *Science* v357 no6349 p400 Jl 28 2017

Wijnaldum, Yasmin

GIRLS *Interview* v47 no2 p178 Mr 2017

Wijnker, Erik

RETINOBLASTOMA RELATED1 mediates germline entry in Arabidopsis color diag *Science* v356 no6336 p396 Ap 28 2017

Wijnsma, Leanne

A Data Breach You Can Smell J. Zorthian color *Time* v188 no18 p21 O 31 2016

Wijshake, Tobias

Senescent intimal foam cells are deleterious at all stages of atherosclerosis bibl *Science* v354 no6311 p472 O 28 2016

WikiLeaks (Organization)

The CIA's Hackers Find Their Secrets Posted Online K. Vick color *Time* v189 no10 p12 Mr 20 2017

MAN WITHOUT A COUNTRY R. KHATCHADOURIAN cartoon color *New Yorker* v93 no24 p36 Ag 21 2017

THE MONTH IN REVIEW: March 2017 *Current History* v116 no790 p200 My 2017

Unpardonable *Weekly Standard* v22 no4 p2 O 3 2016

WikiLeaks dump brings CIA spying powers into the spotlight M. KAN color *PCWorld* v35 no4 p33 Ap 2017

WIKILEAKS' ROLE A. Dejean, H. Levintova et al *Mother Jones* v42 no4 p30 Jl/Ag 2017

Wiking, Mikaela

A subcellular map of the human proteome color *Science* v356 no6340 p820 My 26 2017

Wikipedia

Academics can help shape Wikipedia T. Shafee, D. Mietchen et al *Science* v357 no6351 p557 Ag 11 2017

Discovery Happens Here A. R. ALBANESE color *Publishers Weekly* v264 no38 p40 S 18 2017

How Wikipedia Keeps Political Discourse from Turning Ugly S. Greenstein and Feng Zhu *Harvard Business Review Digital Articles* p2 N 7 2016

IS WIKIPEDIA WOKE? D. KESSENIDES and M. CHAFKIN color *Bloomberg Businessweek* no4505 p70 D 26 2016

Let Your Questioning Start with Wikipedia S. GERBIC *Skeptical Inquirer* v41 no2 p24 Mr/Ap 2017

Why Do So Few Women Edit Wikipedia? N. Torres *Harvard Business Review Digital Articles* p2 Je 2 2016

Wikipedia Is More Biased Than Britannica, but Don't Blame the Crowd W. Frick *Harvard Business Review Digital Articles* p2 D 3 2014

WIKRAMANAYAKE, ERIC

An Ecoregion-Based Approach to Protecting Half the Terrestrial Realm *BioScience* v67 no6 p534 Je 2017

Wikstrom, Darcie

Posthole color *Powder* v45 no5 p108 Ja 2017

Wilbanks, Thomas J.

Thomas J. Wilbanks *Environment* v59 no4 p3 Jl-Ag 2017

Wilber, Charles

Free-Market Folly color *Commonweal* v144 no9 p15 My 19 2017

Wilber, Ken

The Religion of Tomorrow: A Vision for the Future of the Great Traditions; More Inclusive, More Comprehensive, More Complete *Publishers Weekly* v264 no11 p79 Mr 13 2017

Wilburn, Kelcy

Décor Fresh for Spring *New Orleans Homes & Lifestyles* v20 no2 p88 Spr 2017

The Great Outdoors: Creating backyard living spaces fit for your indoor style *New Orleans Homes & Lifestyles* v20 no3 p100 Summ 2017

Mix and Match: Incerporating art and antiques with style and panache *New Orleans Homes & Lifestyles* v20 no4 p102 Aut 2017

On the Surface *New Orleans Homes & Lifestyles* v20 no1 p96 Wint 2016

Wilby, Robert L.

Measuring the changing pulse of rivers color *Science* v357 no6351 p552 Ag 11 2017

Wilce, James M.

How to Lament M. Wollan diag *New York Times Magazine* p25 Ag 6 2017

Wilcock, William S. D.

Seismic constraints on caldera dynamics from the 2015 Axial Seamount eruption bibl color graph *Science* v354 no6318 p1395 D 16 2016

Wilcove, David S.

The pet trade's role in defaunation color *Science* v356 no6341 p916 Je 1 2017

WILCOX, ANDREW C.

Applying Functional Traits to Ecogeomorphic Processes in Riparian Ecosystems *BioScience* v67 no8 p729 Ag 2017

WILCOX, DAVID J.

Submersed Aquatic Vegetation in Chesapeake Bay: Sentinel Species in a Changing World *BioScience* v67 no8 p698 Ag 2017

Wilcox, Eileen

FREE FOR ALL color *O, The Oprah Magazine* p20 O 2017

Wilcox, Helen

George Herbert: 100 Poems R. Lischer color *Christian Century* v133 no21 p55 O 12 2016

Wilcox, Keith

When Upbeat Commercials Backfire *Harvard Business Review Digital Articles* p2 O 23 2015

Wilcox, Lael

divide and conquer b. welch bw color *Bike Magazine* v23 no9 p36 D 2016

no free rides b. minnigh color *Bike Magazine* v23 no9 p19 D 2016

Wilcox, Lisa

COMING (Back) TO AMERICA E. Iliff Prax color *Practical Horseman* v45 no9 p30 S 2017

WILCZEK, FRANK

A COSMIC CONTROVERSY color *Scientific American* v317 no1 p5 Jl 2017

Wild, Franz

Diamonds Aren't A Bank's Best Friend color *Bloomberg Busi-*

nessweek no4537 p26 S 11 2017

Wild, Meredith
INTRODUCING A WORLD of ENDLESS MISADVENTURES *Publishers Weekly* v264 no9 pC1 F 27 2017

Wild animal trade
See also
Primate trade

Wild animal trade—Corrupt practices
THE TANGLED WEB D. Hayes cartoon *Canadian Wildlife* v22 no5 p18 N/D 2016

Wild boar
The Challenge of Invasives R. J. Bates *Canadian Wildlife* v23 no4 p5 S/O 2017

Wild boar hunting
HOG, WILD C. KEARNS color *Field & Stream* v121 no7 p68 D 2016/Ja 2017
THE MOST UNUSUAL GAME N. Krebs bw color *Outdoor Life* v223 no9 p14 N 2016

Wild boar—Environmental aspects
HOGS WILD L. Strauss color *Canadian Wildlife* v23 no4 p28 S/O 2017

Wild flowers
Arizona Nordic Village: Yurts are cool. Period. But they're even better when they're located in an alpine meadow that's alive with wildflowers, songbirds and browsing elk A. McGIVNEY *Arizona Highways* v93 no6 p14 Je 2017
Understanding Aperture R. BURRESS *Arizona Highways* v93 no6 p9 Je 2017

Wild foods
WILD EDIBLES color *Missouri Life* v44 no4 p70 Je 2017

Wild horses
The Greatest Places to See Wild Horses color *American Cowboy* v23 no6 p67 Ap/My 2017

Wild leek
FLL-FLAVORED & FUNKY C. KETTLEWELL *Virginia Living* v15 no3 p21 Ap 2017

Wild Rye (Company)
KIAH TEE N. Formosa color *Bike Magazine* v24 no4 p104 Je 2017

Wild turkey
Boom and Bloom D. L. NG color *Field & Stream* v121 no9 p12 Ap 2017

Wild turkey—Behavior
Boost Your Wildlife Savvy H. S. Thomas color *Horse & Rider* v56 no7 p72 Jl 2017

Wild west shows
Lost Skills L. FELDMAN bw *American Cowboy* v24 no1 p66 Je/Jl 2017

Wilde, Fran
Horizon *Publishers Weekly* v264 no30 p45 Jl 24 2017

WILDE, JIM
HOW TO MAKE ANYTHING [Cover story] color diag *Popular Mechanics* p56 S 2017

Wilde, Oscar, 1854-1900
DIVINE SALOMÉ: Wild yet chaste, impudent and ageless, Sarah Bernhardt was inescapably Oscar Wilde's Salomé, 'the most splendid creation' E. Fitzsimons *History Today* v67 no7 p66 Jl 2017
Oscar Wilde's 'Living Death' I. Buruma bw *New York Review of Books* v63 no18 p66 N 24 2016
The Wilde Bunch D. LUTZ *New York Times Book Review* p20 D 11 2016

Wilder, Gene, 1933-2016
GENE WILDER C. Kane and D. Coggan color *Entertainment Weekly* no1446/1447 p90 D 2016/Ja 2017

Wilder, Kali
50 BEST COMPANIES FOR DIVERSITY [Cover story] color *Black Enterprise* v47 no3 p52 O 2016
The American Black Film Festival Celebrates 20 Years with #ABFF20 color *Black Enterprise* v47 no2 p42 S 2016
How Juicing Changed My Life color *Black Enterprise* v47 no4 p46 N/D 2016
THE MOST POWERFUL WOMEN IN BUSINESS [Cover story] color *Black Enterprise* v47 no5 p56 Ja/F 2017

Wilder, Laura Ingalls, 1867-1957
BREATHE color *Prevention* v69 no9 p18 O 2017

LITTLE MANOR ON THE PRAIRIE K. HUNHOFF *South Dakota Magazine* v32 no4 p58 N/D 2016

Wilder-James, Edd
Breaking Down Data Silos *Harvard Business Review Digital Articles* p2 D 5 2016

Wildermuth, Todd A.
Green the Vote *Harper's Magazine* p2 O 2017

Wilderness areas
THE ARTS | a cultural showcase *Texas Monthly* v44 no11 p80 N 2016
GET AWAY CLOSE TO HOME *Sierra* v102 no3 p45 My/Je 2017
Nature's Pied Piper J. I. Keith color *AARP: The Magazine* v59 no3A p82 Ap/My 2016
Preamble H. E. Blake *Orion Magazine* v35 no4/5 p1 Jl-O 2016
Take Back the Parks R. JAGO bw *Walrus* v14 no8 p14 O 2017
THE WILDERNESS OUT YOUR FRONT DOOR G. KAMIYA *Sierra* v102 no3 p42 My/Je 2017

Wilderness areas—Arizona
WOODCHUTE TRAIL R. STIEVE *Arizona Highways* v93 no4 p54 Ap 2017

Wilderness areas—Minnesota
In the Deep Dark: Stargazing F. BURES color *Backpacker* p18 My 2017
THE STAKES A. FREEMAN color *Canoe & Kayak Magazine* v45 no1 p32 Wint 2017

Wilderness areas—Montana
See also
Rattlesnake National Recreation Area (Mont.)
Get the Drift D. L. NG color *Field & Stream* v122 no1 p8 My 2017

Wilderness areas—United States
Hike It All N. PIPENBERG *Backpacker* p24 Ag 2017
Human noises invade wilderness L. HAMERS color map *Science News* v191 no11 p14 Je 10 2017

Wilders, Geert, 1963-
Dutch election highlights divisions about religion and immigration M. Richards and Z. F. Parvez *Christian Century* v134 no8 p1 Ap 12 2017

Wildfire prevention
THE ANCIENT ECOLOGY OF FIRE A. PIERUCCI color *Archaeology* v70 no5 p55 S/O 2017

Wildfires
After Chile's fires, reforest private land M. J. Martinez-Harms, H. Caceres et al color *Science* v356 no6334 p147 Ap 14 2017
Agony and hope in the ashes N. MACDONALD color *Maclean's* v130 no8 p11 S 2017
The Fire's Edge B. L. HOWELL *American Forests* v122 no3 p16 Fall 2016
Spared by the blaze M. HEMMADI color *Maclean's* v130 no8 p18 S 2017
The Spirit of the West B. Welch *American Cowboy* v24 no1 p8 Je/Jl 2017
There for ewe A. HUTCHINS color *Maclean's* v130 no9 p13 O 2017
WANING WILDFIRES *Earth Island Journal* v32 no3 p5 Aut 2017

Wildfires & the environment
Scorched Earth P. Tolmé color *National Wildlife (World Edition)* v55 no4 p38 Je/Jl 2017

Wildfires—California
The Fire Season K. Steinmetz and M. Chan color map *Time* v190 no16/17 p40 O 23 2017

Wildfires—Climatic factors
Weatherwatch B. Rippey, J. B. Halverson et al color map *Weatherwise* v70 no4 p38 Jl/Ag 2017

Wildfires—Colorado
OUR CABIN SURVIVED A WILDFIRE N. Fay and K. Fay color *Cabin Living* p69 Je 2017

Wildfires—New Mexico
Pillar of fire K. Dickman color *Popular Science* v289 no4 p48 Jl/Ag 2017

Wildfires—Prevention
Wildfire watch J. PEARCE and H. WILSON map *Canadian Geographic* v137 no5 p30 S/O 2017

Wildfires—Prevention & control
ARE YOU FIREWISE? K. Preece and M. R. Johnson color *Cabin*

Living p72 Ap 2017

Fighting the beast C. GILLIS color *Maclean's* v129 no48/49 p54 D 5 2016

FIRE-RESISTANT PLANTS K. Preece color *Cabin Living* p73 Ap 2017

Wildfires—Risk factors

Downsizing the dream J. MARKUSOFF color *Maclean's* v130 no4 p24 My 2017

Wildfires—Texas

A CITY SLICKER in the PANHANDLE J. SALAMON *Texas Monthly* v45 no8 p6 Ag 2017

LOVE AND LOSS ON THE PLAINS: The day the fire came to the Franklin Ranch S. HOLLANDSWORTH *Texas Monthly* v45 no8 p60 Ag 2017

Wildfires—United States

Baptism by Fire T. HANEY color *Backpacker* p84 Ag 2017

Fires blaze in mountain forests color *Science* v354 no6317 p1208 D 9 2016

How Do You Save a Species? Save Its Habitat C. O'MARA *National Wildlife (World Edition)* v55 no4 p6 Je/Jl 2017

LETTING A Wildfire BURN OVER YOU B. MOCKENHAUPT color *Reader's Digest* v189 no1131 p112 Je 2017

Scorched Earth P. Tolmé color *National Wildlife (World Edition)* v55 no4 p38 Je/Jl 2017

Seeing Silver Linings *Mother Earth News* no282 p5 Je/Jl 2017

TRENDING L. SCHLEY graph map *Discover* v38 no5 p16 Je 2017

Weatherwatch B. Rippey, J. B. Halverson et al color map *Weatherwise* v70 no4 p38 Jl/Ag 2017

WILDGEN, MICHELLE

This Old House *New York Times Book Review* p9 F 12 2017

Who Are You Wearing? color *O, The Oprah Magazine* p119 Mr 2017

Wild Heart, The (Music)

WHAT THE HEART SAYS A. PETRUSICH bw cartoon *New Yorker* v92 no39 p82 N 28 2016

Wildhood, M. Nicole R.

Embracing the Homeless Woman Selling Papers *America* v216 no7 p43 Ap 3 2017

Wild Life, The (Film)

NEWLY AVAILABLE MOVIES M. FELL *TV Guide* v65 no13 p46 Mr 20 2017

Wildlife Acoustics Inc.

This Is What Climate Change Sounds Like K. Stock color *Bloomberg Businessweek* no4535 p20 Ag 28 2017

Wildlife as food

Kill What You Eat J. RICHLER color *Walrus* v14 no4 p15 My 2017

Wildlife conservation

> See also
>
> Amphibian conservation
> Bird conservation
> Fish conservation
> Marine parks & reserves
> Wildlife refuges
> Wildlife reintroduction
> Wildlife rescue

Adopting a New Vision for Wildlife C. O'MARA color *National Wildlife (World Edition)* v54 no6 p6 O/N 2016

Arrested Recovery L. Tangley color *National Wildlife (World Edition)* v55 no5 p34 Ag/S 2017

Beyond the Radio Collar E. Strickland *Sierra* v101 no4 p28 Jl/Ag 2016

BORN TO BE WILD J. Actman color *National Geographic* v232 no4 p22 O 2017

bush beat E. C. Alberts color *Earth Island Journal* v32 no4 p36 Wint 2017

Conservation Biology: A New Hope? L. E. OGDEN *BioScience* v66 no12 p1088 D 1 2016

Conserving Megafauna or Sacrificing Biodiversity? A. T. FORD, S. J. COOKE et al *BioScience* v67 no3 p193 Mr 2017

Conserving the World's Megafauna and Biodiversity: The Fierce Urgency of Now W. J. RIPPLE, G. CHAPRON et al *BioScience* v67 no3 p197 Mr 2017

De-extinction, nomenclature, and the law N. Wagner, A. Hochkirch et al color *Science* v356 no6342 p1016 Je 9 2017

Do not publish D. Lindenmayer and B. Scheele color diag *Science* v356 no6340 p800 My 26 2017

Editorial S. L. COLLINS *BioScience* v67 no1 p3 Ja 2017

Flag a Fence, Save a Sage-Grouse L. Moore color *National Wildlife (World Edition)* v55 no5 p18 Ag/S 2017

Flamingo Road M. BARTELS *Audubon* v119 no2 p20 Summ 2017

A Flight for Their Lives D. Cubie color *National Wildlife (World Edition)* v54 no6 p30 O/N 2016

From Alaska, a Lesson on the Value of Conservation Partnerships With Indigenous Communities H. P. Huntington color *Environment* v59 no1 p34 2017

From Field and Stream to Table L. Gross color *National Wildlife (World Edition)* v54 no6 p16 O/N 2016

From the Community *American Forests* v123 no3 p12 Fall 2017

Global Rush to Harness Drones Yields Ups and Downs J. CESSNA *BioScience* v67 no10 p944 O 2017

Home at Last [Cover story] J. Kohler color *National Wildlife (World Edition)* v55 no5 p22 Ag/S 2017

Home on the Sage [Cover story] T. Williams color map *National Wildlife (World Edition)* v54 no6 p22 O/N 2016

Let's Show a Little Love R. Bates *Canadian Wildlife* v22 no5 p5 N/D 2016

Modernization, Risk, and Conservation of the World's Largest Carnivores J. T. BRUSKOTTER, J. A. VUCETICH et al *BioScience* v67 no7 p646 Jl 2017

NATURE'S WITNESSES L. Warren bw color *National Wildlife (World Edition)* v55 no1 p20 D/Ja 2016

New Administration and New Congress Provide Opportunities and Challenges *American Forests* v123 no1 p14 Wint/Spr 2017

New Zealand Shouldn't Ignore Feral Cats C. ROUCO, R. DE TORRE-CEIJAS et al *BioScience* v67 no8 p686 Ag 2017

NRPA's Wildlife Explorer Program R. Sutton *Parks & Recreation* v51 no10 p82 O 2016

Oases in a Dry Land D. OWEN *Audubon* v119 no2 p22 Summ 2017

Our Disappearing Wildlife: What Parks Can Do About It R. J. Dolesh *Parks & Recreation* v52 no1 p26 Ja 2017

Out of Time? L. Warren color *National Wildlife (World Edition)* v55 no6 p40 O/N 2017

OUT ON A LIMB A. E. HURT color *National Geographic Kids* no465 p18 N 2016

Re: Conservation color *Canadian Wildlife* v23 no2 p11 My/Je 2017

Regional wins for people and wildlife in 2016 color *National Wildlife (World Edition)* v55 no1 p48 D/Ja 2016

Research color *Canadian Wildlife* v23 no2 p10 My/Je 2017

'Safe spaces' may save the European mink K. Karáth color *Science* v357 no6352 p636 Ag 18 2017

Shrinking birds color *National Wildlife (World Edition)* v54 no6 p8 O/N 2016

Sponge Buffet color *National Wildlife (World Edition)* v54 no6 p20 O/N 2016

Tree-Climbing Foxes and Other Success Stories K. R. FAULKNER and C. Graham *Natural History* v125 no2 p18 F 2017

Vanishing Life *Change* v82 no3 p9 Mr 2017

Winter storms drive rapid phenotypic, regulatory, and genomic shifts in the green anole lizard S. C. Campbell-Staton, Z. A. Cheviron et al graph *Science* v357 no6350 p495 Ag 4 2017

Wildlife conservation laws

International Wildlife Law: Understanding and Enhancing Its Role in Conservation A. TROUWBORST, A. BLACKMORE et al *BioScience* v67 no9 p784 S 2017

Wildlife conservation—Alberta

BACK WHERE THEY BELONG N. WILSON color map *Canadian Geographic* v137 no5 p32 S/O 2017

Build habitats, not fences, for caribou G. Proulx and R. A. Powell bibl *Science* v353 no6307 p1506 S 30 2016

Wildlife conservation—Arctic regions

GAME OF THRONES [Cover story] S. OOSTHOEK color map *Canadian Geographic* v135 no6 p36 D 2015

Wildlife conservation—California

Beavers as Ecopartners A. Bolen color *National Wildlife (World Edition)* v55 no5 p14 Ag/S 2017

Wildlife conservation—Canada

Wildlife utilization

The Complex Business of Sustainable Exploitation of Wildlife: Researchers grapple with the many unknowns L. E. OGDEN *BioScience* v67 no8 p691 Ag 2017

Wildman, Charlotte

A FORENSIC TAKE ON DEVIANCE: Microhistories, examining a range of notorious and mundane crimes, can help recover marginalised fi gures and forge links to wider cultural histories *History Today* v67 no9 p94 S 2017

Wildman, Sarah

MAKING HISTORY color *Washingtonian Magazine* v52 no7 p147 Ap 2017

Wild Party, The (Theatrical production)

EVENT CALENDAR *Washingtonian Magazine* v53 no1 p216 O 2017

Wilds, Mack, 1989-

Calling the Shots, Making an Impact C. Agard color *Entertainment Weekly* no1457/1458 p80 Mr 17 2017

FIRST LOOK: SHOTS FIRED L. CROSS color *Ebony* v72 no5 p26 Mr 2017

Wilds, Richard P.

The Dark Wolf of Summer *Sky & Telescope* v133 no6 p64 Je 2017

Wildstein, David, 1961-

Most Likely to Destroy a Governor A. Rice img *New York* v49 no19 p48 S 19 2016

Wile, David

The impact of business cycles on job mobility *Monthly Labor Review* p1 Je 2017

Wile, Rob

Channel Your Inner Bill Gates With These Beach Reads color *Money* v46 no7 p19 Ag 2017

He's the Youngest Self-Made Billionaire color *Money* v46 no5 p16 Je 2017

She Became a Billionaire at Age 82 color diag *Money* v46 no4 p14 My 2017

This Mansion Just Took a $66 Million Price Cut color diag map *Money* v46 no5 p18 Je 2017

What Uber Drivers Really Make color *Money* v46 no9 p20 O 2017

Wilen, James

Social norms as solutions bibl color *Science* v354 no6308 p42 O 7 2016

WILENSKY, DAN

A Note on the Big Picture color *Downbeat* v84 no3 p110 Mr 2017

WILENTZ, AMY

THIS PARTICULAR DADDY'S GIRL color *Nation* v304 no5 p14 F 20 2017

WILENTZ, SEAN

Misfortunes Multiplied: Richard White's history of late-19th-century America describes a country lashed by greed and brutality *New York Times Book Review* p21 S 24 2017

Wiles, Kate

'Atlantis at its Prime', 1896 *History Today* v66 no12 p18 D 2016

BERING STRAIT, 1860S *History Today* v67 no8 p4 Ag 2017

Beverly Hills Street Map, 1926 *History Today* v67 no1 p26 Ja 2017

BOOTLEGGER'S MAP OF THE UNITED STATES, 1926 *History Today* v67 no6 p4 Je 2016

A century of CONQUEST *History Today* v66 no10 p11 O 2016

The Map *History Today* v67 no3 p26 Mr 2017

The Map *History Today* v67 no4 p26 Ap 2017

THE MAP POLTAVA, 1709 *History Today* v67 no10 p4 O 2017

THE MAP ROME, 1942 *History Today* v67 no9 p4 S 2017

THE MAP THE MOON, 1647 *History Today* v67 no7 p4 Jl 2017

THE PRINCIPAL MOUNTAINS AND RIVERS OF THE WORLD, 1829 *History Today* v67 no5 p4 My 2017

Tenochtitlan, 1524 *History Today* v66 no10 p22 O 2016

TheMap *History Today* v66 no11 p32 N 2016

'The Road from London to Dover', 1675 *History Today* v67 no2 p18 F 2017

WILES, TIANA

HOW TO DELETE PORN FROM YOUR BRAIN color *Christianity Today* p11 Ap 2017

Wiley, Austin

The Case for ... Starting College Early S. Davis and T. Keith color *Sports Illustrated* v126 no3 p19 Ja 23 2017

Wiley, Frieda

Before Hillary *American History* v51 no6 p34 F 2017

Wiley, Samira, 1987——Interviews

EDITOR'S LETTER D. ANDERSON-MINSHAL bw color *Advocate* no1090 p8 Ap 2017

TALL TALES? D. ANDERSON-MINSHALL color *Advocate* no1090 p34 Ap 2017

Wiley, Sarah R.

best of Indy *Indianapolis Monthly* v40 no4 p73 D 2016

Hot on the TRAILS: A ROAD-FREE GUIDE TO EXPLORING CENTRAL INDIANA *Indianapolis Monthly* v40 no10 p59 Je 2017

Wiley, Steve

The Fairytale Chicago of Francesca Finnegan *Publishers Weekly* v264 no5 p185 Ja 30 2017

Wilf, Peter

Eocene lantern fruits from Gondwanan Patagonia and the early origins of Solanaceae bibl color diag *Science* v355 no6320 p1 Ja 6 2017

Global climatic drivers of leaf size [Cover story] graph *Science* v357 no6354 p917 S 1 2017

Wilfert, Stefan

Robust spin-polarized midgap states at step edges of topological crystalline insulators bibl graph *Science* v354 no6317 p1269 D 9 2016

Wilhelm, Dave

Built to Last *Arizona Highways* v93 no3 p56 Mr 2017

WILHELM, HEATHER

Adolescent Politics diag *National Review* v69 no5 p28 Mr 20 2017

Books for Children: A Symposium *National Review* v69 no19 p48 O 16 2017

Gibberish, Maya-Style *Commentary* v144 no3 p49 O 2017

The Great Unplugging color *National Review* v69 no11 p22 Je 12 2017

Happy Warrior *National Review* v68 no24 p44 D 31 2016

Home on the Ranch *National Review* v69 no17 p44 S 11 2017

The Kids Will Be Fine *National Review* v68 no22 p48 D 5 2016

Noisy Desperation *National Review* v69 no9 p44 My 15 2017

Revolution for What? *Commentary* v142 no2 p60 S 2016

Wilhelm, Steve

ONLY CONNECT color *Tricycle: The Buddhist Review* v26 no4 p84 Summ 2017

Wilhelm, T. 'Aualni

Committing to socially responsible seafood color *Science* v356 no6341 p912 Je 1 2017

Wilhite, Becca

Check Me Out *Publishers Weekly* v264 no27 p59 Jl 3 2017

Wilken, Susanne

A plankton bloom shifts as the ocean warms bibl color diag *Science* v354 no6310 p287 O 21 2016

Wilkerson, Gary

PORTERDALE MILL LOFTS/PORTERDALE 35 MILES SOUTHEAST OF ATLANTA J. GREEN *Atlanta* v56 no11 p232 Mr 2017

Wilkerson, Isabel

Isabel Wilkerson R. Early *Humanities* v37 no4 p1 Fall 2016

Wilkerson, Mike

Betsy DeVos and the Segregation of School Choice *Education Digest* v82 no8 p19 Ap 2017

Wilkerson, Travis

Living Proof E. HYNES bw color *Film Comment* v53 no3 p16 My/Je 2017

Wilkes, Sue

A (Working) Woman's Place: As the Industrial Revolution wrought widespread social changes, female cotton industry workers' lives changed dramatically *History Today* v67 no6 p16 Je 2016

WILKIN, JEN

The Church Is Not a Single-Parent Family *Christianity Today* v60 no10 p30 D 2016

How to Overcome Sibling Rivalry *Christianity Today* v61 no4 p32 My 2017

How to Prevent Bible Study Dropouts *Christianity Today* v61 no6 p28 Jl/Ag 2017

Let Bible Studies Be Bible Studies *Christianity Today* p26 Mr 2017

Where Kids Get Their Political Views *Christianity Today* v60 no8

p32 O 2016

Wilkin, Sam

Even for Companies, the U.S. Is Split Between Haves and Have-Nots *Harvard Business Review Digital Articles* p2 Ag 27 2015

Here's How the Backlash Against Tech Billionaires Will Play Out *Harvard Business Review Digital Articles* p2 Je 24 2016

WILKINS, CHARLES

'It's been raining! In the High Arctic!' color map *Canadian Geographic* v137 no4 p62 Jl/Ag 2017

TRASH NATION cartoon *Canadian Geographic* v137 no3 p48 My 2017

Wilkins, Dominique—Interviews

SI NOW M. Gray color *Sports Illustrated* v125 no14 p6 O 24-31 2016

Wilkins, Joe

Far Enough J. Shipley *Orion Magazine* v35 no3 p59 My/Je 2016

A place of first permission *Orion Magazine* v35 no4/5 p73 Jl-O 2016

WILKINS, KATE

Addressing the Gender Gap in Distinguished Speakers at Professional Ecology Conferences *BioScience* v67 no5 p464 My 2017

Wilkins, Muriel Maignan

Is Your Employee Coachable? *Harvard Business Review Digital Articles* p2 F 19 2015

Signs That You Lack Emotional Intelligence *Harvard Business Review Digital Articles* p2 D 31 2014

Signs That You're a Micromanager *Harvard Business Review Digital Articles* p2 N 11 2014

Signs That You're Being Too Stubborn *Harvard Business Review Digital Articles* p2 My 21 2015

Why Executives Should Talk About Racial Bias at Work *Harvard Business Review Digital Articles* p2 Ap 20 2015

Wilkins, Peter

Peter Cottontale M. POLLOCK color *Chicago* v66 no6 p94 Je 2017

Wilkins, Richard D.

Obama's Gift to Iran *Commentary* v141 no10 p1 D 2016

Obama's Gift to Iran *Commentary* v142 no5 p1 D 2016

Wilkins, Warren

The Locomotive of War: Money, Empire, Power and Guilt *Military History* v34 no5 p73 Ja 2018

Wilkins, William, 1778-1839

The 1794 Volcano on the Moon A. Livingston *Sky & Telescope* v134 no5 p30 N 2017

Wilkinson, Adam C.

Depleting dietary valine permits nonmyeloablative mouse hematopoietic stem cell transplantation bibl graph *Science* v354 no6316 p1152 D 2 2016

WILKINSON, ALEC

DEATH OF A DYSTOPIAN bw cartoon *New Yorker* v93 no8 p22 Ap 10 2017

THE POLYMATH bw cartoon *New Yorker* v93 no4 p42 Mr 13 2017

Wilkinson, Amy

THE 2016 POP CULTURE CHALLENGE color *Entertainment Weekly* no1444/1445 p40 D 16 2016

American Crime color *Entertainment Weekly* no1456 p58 Mr 10 2017

THE BIGGEST SUMMER BREAKOUTS (SO FAR) color diag *Entertainment Weekly* no1474/1475 p15 Jl 21-28 2017

The Cast of Grey's Anatomy color *Entertainment Weekly* no1439 p23 N 11 2016

CHRISTINE EVANGELISTA color *Entertainment Weekly* no1456 p59 Mr 10 2017

DEATH BECOMES THEM color *Entertainment Weekly* no1457/1458 p98 Mr 17 2017

Editor's Note color *Entertainment Weekly* no1439 p23 N 11 2016

Fantastic Beasts and Where to Find Them color *Entertainment Weekly* no1439 p18 N 11 2016

FRIENDS: PHOEBE'S SEDUCTION color *Entertainment Weekly* no1460/1461 p63 Ap 7-17 2017

Friends: The One With the Giant Turkey color *Entertainment Weekly* no1441 p48 N 25 2016

Fuller House *Entertainment Weekly* no1482/1483 p106 S 22 2017

Future Man *Entertainment Weekly* no1482/1483 p106 S 22 2017

Gilmore Girls: A Year in the Life color *Entertainment Weekly*

no1439 p18 N 11 2016

The Golden Girls BINGE color *Entertainment Weekly* no1453 p40 F 17 2017

HAPPY ENDINGS color *Entertainment Weekly* no1439 p20 N 11 2016

Hitting the Hamptons With Younger color *Entertainment Weekly* no1442 p22 D 2 2016 Rebellious Special Issue

IDRIS ELBA: THE RIGHTS STUFF color *Entertainment Weekly* no1462 p52 Ap 21 2017

Jessica St. Clair and Lennon Parham color *Entertainment Weekly* no1473 p16 Jl 7 2017

JOHN LITHGOW color *Entertainment Weekly* no1456 p60 Mr 10 2017

Marvel's The Punisher color *Entertainment Weekly* no1482/1483 p106 S 22 2017

Mindhunter color *Entertainment Weekly* no1482/1483 p107 S 22 2017

The Mindy Project *Entertainment Weekly* no1482/1483 p107 S 22 2017

MUSIC MADE THE PEOPLE COME TOGETHER color *Entertainment Weekly* no1439 p22 N 11 2016

One Legend Plays Another color *Entertainment Weekly* no1456 p61 Mr 10 2017

Reimagining Anne color *Entertainment Weekly* no1465 p47 My 12 2017

Riviera color *Entertainment Weekly* no1482/1483 p106 S 22 2017

Ryan Hansen Solves Crimes on Television* *Entertainment Weekly* no1482/1483 p109 S 22 2017

SARAH SILVERMAN I Love You, America color *Entertainment Weekly* no1482/1483 p108 S 22 2017

THE SCOOP, STARS & SONGS color *Entertainment Weekly* no1439 p16 N 11 2016

Star Trek Discovery color *Entertainment Weekly* no1482/1483 p104 S 22 2017

StartUp *Entertainment Weekly* no1482/1483 p109 S 22 2017

Sterling K. Brown color *Entertainment Weekly* no1444/1445 p30 D 16 2016

Stranger Things 2 color *Entertainment Weekly* no1482/1483 p100 S 22 2017

Suddenly Sutton color *Entertainment Weekly* no1440 p28 N 18 2016

Tin Star *Entertainment Weekly* no1482/1483 p109 S 22 2017

Transparent color *Entertainment Weekly* no1482/1483 p109 S 22 2017

What They Really Couldn't Do on You Can't Do That on Television color *Entertainment Weekly* no1460/1461 p41 Ap 7-17 2017

WHAT TO WATCH color *Entertainment Weekly* no1468/1469 p68 Je 2-9 2017

What to Watch color *Entertainment Weekly* no1484 p53 S 29 2017

Your Sunshiny, Stupendous, Seriously Spectacular SUMMER BUCKET LIST color *Entertainment Weekly* no1470 p32 Je 16 2017

Wilkinson, Ben

Carving Giants D. LATOURRETTE bw color *Surfer* v58 no2 p46 My 2017

Wilkinson, Charles

NO ARGUMENTS FOR NON-RENEWABLES J. GORDON color *Alternatives Journal (AJ) - Canada's Environmental Voice* v42 no2 p78 2016

Wilkinson, Darryl

Beryllium Makes It Better [Cover story] color graph *Sound & Vision* v82 no7 p48 S 2017

Control4 EA-1 Home Automation System color *Sound & Vision* v82 no1 p64 Ja 2017

JL Audio Fathom IWS-SYS-1 In-Wall Subwoofer System color *Sound & Vision* v82 no6 p50 Jl/Ag 2017

Nexia Smart Home Control System color *Sound & Vision* v81 no9 p62 N 2016

Phase Technology dARTS DFS-660-T Speaker System color *Sound & Vision* v82 no3 p38 Ap 2017

Sonos Playbase color *Sound & Vision* v82 no5 p40 Je 2017

Sophistication From Above color *Sound & Vision* v82 no8 p58 O 2017

Wilkinson, J. Harvie, 1944-

At Sea in The Sixties J. ROSEN color *National Review* v69 no6

p43 Ap 3 2017
Land of Disbelief T. EASTLAND color *Weekly Standard* v22 no28 p34 Mr 27 2017

Wilkinson, James, 1757-1825
A Quest for the Best Man: Missouri's First Governors R. SOODALTER color map *Missouri Life* v44 no4 p52 Je 2017

Wilkinson, Matt, 1988-
Can't We All Just Get Along(board)? T. Prodanovich color *Surfer* v57 no12 p14 Ja/F 2017
Going Off Script A. DOUGLAS color *Surfer* v57 no12 p52 Ja/F 2017

WILKINSON, PHILIP
Gator Growth and Reproduction color graph map *Natural History* v125 no7 p10 Jl/Ag 2017

WILKINSON, RACHEL
THE SAINTS OF PITTSBURGH: A TINY NEIGHBORHOOD CHURCH IS HOME TO THE GREATEST COLLECTION OF RELICS OUTSIDE OF THE VATICAN *Smithsonian* v48 no4 p98 Jl/Ag 2017

Wilkinson, Raven
The Photo That Changed My Life bw *Vanity Fair* v58 no11 p74 N 2016

Wilkinson, Todd
FRANK LLOYD WRIGHT [Cover story] *Saturday Evening Post* v289 no3 p36 My/Je 2017
THE GREAT DISCONNECT *Sierra* v102 no1 p34 Ja/F 2017
Master of the Seascape *Saturday Evening Post* v289 no2 p34 Mr/Ap 2017

Wilklow, Frank—Interviews
HEART TO HEART conversation with a cardiologist B. Lutz color *New Orleans Magazine* v51 no4 p76 F 2017

Will
See also
Will of God
WHITHER WILLPOWER? When entering disputed territory, you need a good guide T. OLSEN color *Christianity Today* v61 no4 p7 My 2017

Will & Grace (TV program)
Best Lineup of All Time M. Fell *TV Guide* v65 no37 p27 S 4 2017
The Bullseye M. Snetiker color *Entertainment Weekly* no1451/1452 p112 F 3-10 2017
EDITOR'S LETTER D. ANDERSON-MINSHALL *Advocate* no1093 p7 O/N 2017
THE FANTASTIC FOUR RETURN: Will. Grace. Karen. Jack. Need we say more? Behind the scenes of NBC's must-see revival [Cover story] J. HALTERMAN *TV Guide* v65 no41 p16 O 2 2017
HOLLYWOOD DISPATCH J. Halterman, D. Holbrook et al *TV Guide* v65 no35 p5 Ag 21 2017
IT'S GO TIME [Cover story] L. Rice color *Entertainment Weekly* no1477 p20 Ag 11 2017
A look back at Emmy wins, big moments and most memorable guest stars *TV Guide* v65 no41 p18 O 2 2017
MEGAN MULLALLY D. KAMP color *Vanity Fair* v59 no6 p60 My 2017
The Must List color *Entertainment Weekly* no1486 p9 O 13 2017
My TV Motto: You Go High; I'll Go Low C. Brody color *Glamour* v115 no10 p40 O 2017
TV YOU'LL FALL FOR L. Rice color *Entertainment Weekly* no1467 p10 My 26 2017
Will & Grace Hasn't Changed Much. And That's Just Fine D. D'addario color *Time* v190 no15 p57 O 16 2017
WILL & GRACE J. Halterman *TV Guide* v65 no37 p38 S 4 2017
Will & GRace: (KAREN, JACK, AND ROSARIO, TOO): THE NBC SITCOM'S MUCH-ANTICIPATED REVIVAL IS JUST WHAT AMERICA NEEDS NOW D. REYNOLDS *Advocate* no1093 p34 O/N 2017
Will & Grace L. Rice color *Entertainment Weekly* no1471 p44 Je 23 2017
Will & Grace Reunion! L. Beard color *Entertainment Weekly* no1434 p15 O 7 2016
Your Ridiculously Early Fall TV Preview J. Hibberd color *Entertainment Weekly* no1453 p10 F 17 2017

Will (TV program)
Ripped From the History Books? C. Agard color *Entertainment Weekly* no1473 p51 Jl 7 2017

'Will' explores the genesis of genius and Shakespeare's Catholic roots J. Anderson color *America* v217 no3 p48 Ag 7 2017
Will Has a Famous Name, but It Lacks Light-Footed Grace D. D'addario color *Time* v190 no4 p51 Jl 24 2017

Will, Elisa
Quantum optical circulator controlled by a single chirally coupled atom bibl graph *Science* v354 no6319 p1577 D 23 2016

Will, George F., 1941-
The Man Who Would Be Kempton A. FERGUSON color *Weekly Standard* v23 no6 p21 O 16 2017

Will, Hank
AGING GRACEFULLY on the Homestead *Mother Earth News* no280 p34 F/Mr 2017

Will, Jesse
This AI flushes out trolls color *Popular Science* v289 no6 p65 N/D 2017

Will, Oscar II. III
HATCH A FLOCK *Mother Earth News* no280 p42 F/Mr 2017

Will, Sebastian A.
Second-scale nuclear spin coherence time of ultracold 23Na40K molecules diag *Science* v357 no6349 p372 Jl 28 2017

Will of God
From the publisher P. W. Marty *Christian Century* v134 no13 p3 Je 21 2017

Willacy County (Tex.)
Prisonville Could Soon Be Back in Business K. Mehrotra color *Bloomberg Businessweek* no4520 p18 My 1 2017

Willamette Falls (Or.)
Fall down color *Backpacker* p17 My 2017

Willamette River Valley (Or.)—Description & travel
Gather I. Edwards color *Sunset* v237 no5 p54 N 2016

Willand, Nicolas
Reversion of antibiotic resistance in Mycobacterium tuberculosis by spiroisoxazoline SMARt-420 bibl diag *Science* v355 no6330 p1206 Mr 17 2017

Willard, Nancy, 1936-2017
Gum *Publishers Weekly* v264 no32 p72 Ag 7 2017

Willbold, Dieter
Fibril structure of amyloid-$\beta(1–42)$ by cryo–electron microscopy color diag *Science* v357 no6359 p116 O 6 2017
Mechanism of transmembrane signaling by sensor histidine kinases color *Science* v356 no6342 p1043 Je 9 2017

Willcocks, Leslie
What Knowledge Workers Stand to Gain from Automation *Harvard Business Review Digital Articles* p2 Je 19 2015

Willcox, Darren
A general catalytic β-C–H carbonylation of aliphatic amines to β-lactams bibl diag *Science* v354 no6314 p851 N 18 2016

Willcox, James
Best TVs for Your Buck chart color diag graph *Consumer Reports* v82 no2 p30 F 2017
Bring on the Joy chart il *Consumer Reports* v82 no3 p31 Mr 2017
Does Anyone Still Need Cable? [Cover story] chart color diag graph il *Consumer Reports* v82 no8 p24 Ag 2017
Welcome to 'Wow!' TV chart color graph *Consumer Reports* v82 no11 p44 N 2017

Willcox Playa (Ariz.)
Willcox Playa N. AUSTIN *Arizona Highways* v93 no8 p6 Ag 2017

Wille, Bart
Too Much Charisma Can Make Leaders Look Less Effective *Harvard Business Review Digital Articles* p2 S 26 2017

Wille, H.-C.
Spectral narrowing of x-ray pulses for precision spectroscopy with nuclear resonances diag *Science* v357 no6349 p375 Jl 28 2017

Willems, Mo
FAIL FUNNIER R. GALCHEN cartoon *New Yorker* v92 no48 p28 F 6 2017

Willens, Howard P.
Dallas Revisited G. L. AGUILAR and C. WECHT *American Scholar* v86 no1 p4 Wint 2017

Willers, Mary
pontoon mania color *Cabin Living* p60 Je 2017

Willerslev, Eske
Ancient genomic changes associated with domestication of the horse color diag *Science* v356 no6336 p442 Ap 28 2017

Willett, Danny, 1987-
CLOSE LIKE A CHAMP [Cover story] D. DeNunzio color *Golf Magazine* v59 no4 p96 Ap 2017
DANNY GETS HIS DUE D. M. Clarke color *Golf Magazine* v59 no4 p13 Ap 2017
Fringe Benefit D. Denunzio, B. Riggs et al color *Golf Magazine* v59 no2 p50 F 2017

Willett, Don
Lone Star Legal Show A. Greenblatt color *Governing* v30 no11 p38 Ag 2017

Willey, David
COVERING OURSELVES color *Runner's World* v51 no10 p14 N 2016
HITTING REFRESH color *Runner's World* v52 no4 p10 My 2017
LET'S RUN TOGETHER B. Wong Ortiz color *Runner's World* v52 no9 p10 O 2017
PREPARING TO LAUNCH color *Runner's World* v52 no3 p10 Ap 2017
THREE RABBITS AND A GUINEA PIG color *Runner's World* v52 no2 p10 Mr 2017
UNITED WE RUN color *Runner's World* v52 no1 p14 Ja/F 2017

Willey, Tristan
Pack a Wallop color *Bon Appetit* v61 no12 p56 D 2016 /Jan2017
SHOT IN A BEER color *Bon Appetit* v62 no6 p86 Je 2017

William, Joy
MY FIRST CAR J. William *Harper's Magazine* v334 no2004 p71 My 2017

William, Prince, Duke of Cambridge, 1982-
The royals on tour [Cover story] color *Maclean's* v129 no40 p38 O 10 2016

WILLIAM, TYLER
Conifer Cruising *American Forests* v122 no3 p24 Fall 2016

William Paterson University of New Jersey
ARCHIVES PROVIDE WINDOW TO JAZZ HISTORY color *Downbeat* v84 no10 p115 O 2017
WILLIAM PATERSON UNIVERSITY: 'WORKING TO MAKE PLAYERS' B. Pulliam bw color *Downbeat* v84 no10 p112 O 2017

William B. Hartsfield-Atlanta International Airport
FOREST GATE *Atlanta* v56 no8 p42 D 2016

William I, King of England, 1027 or 1028-1087
The Conqueror Reassessed M. Morris *History Today* v66 no10 p43 O 2016

William III, King of England, 1650-1702
A General State of Mourning R. Wilson *History Today* v67 no3 p7 Mr 2017

William McNeil, Jason
KARATE COLLEGE TRAINING CAMP BEGINS ITS THIRD DECADE bw color *Black Belt* v55 no6 p12 O/N 2017

Williams, A. R.
ANCIENT SITES AS SEEN FROM SPACE color *National Geographic* v232 no2 p138 Ag 2017
CSI TOOL FROM ANCIENT EGYPT color *National Geographic* v231 no5 p24 My 2017
Echoes of Pompeii Found in France color *National Geographic* v230 no4 p20 O 2016
NIT-PICKING IN ANCIENT CHILE color *National Geographic* v231 no3 p20 Mr 2017
RACING THE THAW color map *National Geographic* v231 no4 p134 Ap 2017
RECOVERING ERASED WISDOM color *National Geographic* v231 no3 p16 Mr 2017
REVIVING A RUINED CITY bw color *National Geographic* v232 no1 p28 Jl 2017
Secrets of the Terra-Cotta Warriors color *National Geographic* v230 no5 p23 N 2016
VOYAGES OF OLD color *National Geographic* v232 no1 p20 Jl 2017
A WEED THAT BUSTS BACTERIA color *National Geographic* v232 no3 p18 S 2017
WHERE STARDUST HIDES ON EARTH color *National Geographic* v232 no2 p14 Ag 2017

Williams, Adam
Who Gets to Drill Here? color *Bloomberg Businessweek* no4517 p15 Ap 3 2017

Williams, Allison

ALLISON WILLIAMS' HOPE ON THE HORIZON M. L. Lenker color *Entertainment Weekly* no1474/1475 p18 Jl 21-28 2017
Double Take E. Wilson color *InStyle* v24 no5 p68 My 2017

Williams, Allison—Interviews
In Girls We Trust L. Dunham and J. Konner color *Glamour* v115 no2 p98 F 2017
Later, Haters img *New York* p68 F 20 2017

Williams, Amanda
THE UPCYCLE ARTIST N. PARSI color *Chicago* v66 no7 p25 Jl 2017

Williams, Amber Lee
How to Speak Up If You See Bias at Work color *Harvard Business Review Digital Articles* p2 Ja 20 2017

Williams, Ann
PRIMARY-CARE PHYSICIANS *New York* v50 no11 p58 My 29 2017

Williams, Ashley Riddle
10 New Rules of Southern Style color *Southern Living* v52 no3 p45 Mr 2017
Arm Candy color *Southern Living* v52 no2 p67 F 2017
The Best Short Cut for You color *Southern Living* v52 no4 p53 Ap 2017
A CASE OF THE BLUES color *Southern Living* v52 no1 p39 Ja 2017
Colors of Summer color *Southern Living* v52 no6 p52 Je 2017
Dressed for the Season color *Southern Living* v51 no12 p65 D 2016
Fresh Faced color *Southern Living* v52 no5 p65 My 2017
Full Bloom color *Southern Living* v52 no2 p70 F 2017
The Getaway Dress color *Southern Living* v52 no7 p39 Jl 2017
Meet Me in Savannah color *Southern Living* v52 no2 p79 F 2017
MOISTURIZING MATTERS color *Southern Living* v52 no1 p43 Ja 2017
My Grandmother, the Beauty Icon color *Southern Living* v52 no7 p42 Jl 2017
MY MOM, THE BEAUTY ICON color *Southern Living* v51 no11 p66 N 2016
My Sister, the Beauty Icon color *Southern Living* v52 no5 p74 My 2017
Party-Ready Hair color *Southern Living* v51 no12 p74 D 2016
Puttin' on the Spritz color *Southern Living* v51 no12 p72 D 2016
SUIT YOURSELF color *Southern Living* v51 no11 p57 N 2016
Well Suited color *Southern Living* v52 no6 p45 Je 2017

WILLIAMS, BENNY
2017 HBCU QUEENS bw color *Ebony* v72/73 no12/1 p78 O/N 2017

Williams, Bill
Traveling exhibit remembers fallen Nebraskan heroes N. BUCK color *Nebraska Life* v21 no4 p84 Jl/Ag 2017

WILLIAMS, BOB
Should College Athletes Be Paid? *New York Times Upfront* v149 no10 p22 Mr 13 2017

Williams, Brandt
THREE DAYS IN AMERICA color *Wired* v24 no12 p114 D 2016

Williams, Brian
Black Man, White Coat J. Thompson *D: The Magazine of Dallas* v43 no10 p126 O 2016

WILLIAMS, BROOKE
IT'S A HARD RAIN *Arizona Highways* v92 no7 p36 Jl 2016

Williams, Bruce
Friendship Through Mentorship J. Murph color *Downbeat* v84 no10 p30 O 2017

Williams, Cassandra
Innovative Partnership Brings Hope to Small Towns *Bridges (Federal Reserve Bank of St. Louis)* p8 Summ 2016

Williams, Claudine
Bringing Luxury to Business Travel color *Black Enterprise* v47 no3 p70 O 2016

Williams, Cress
BLACK LIGHTNING N. Abrams color *Entertainment Weekly* no1474/1475 p73 Jl 21-28 2017

Williams, Daniel K.
When pro-lifers were progressives D. Heim color *Christian Century* v133 no23 p32 N 9 2016

WILLIAMS, DAR
Positive Proximity color *Publishers Weekly* v264 no34 p116 Ag

21 2017

Williams, David

The Amish after the end V. Weaver-Zercher *Christian Century* v134 no16 p26 Ag 2 2017

Survival Tactics: A dystopian novel about the utopian world of the Amish A. DEUTSCH *New York Times Book Review* p16 S 3 2017

Williams, David—Interviews

POST-APOCALYPTIC NOW E. Palmer *Christian Century* v134 no16 p27 Ag 2 2017

Williams, Deron

HOT | NOT T. Keith and R. Demak color *Sports Illustrated* v126 no7 p23 Mr 6 2017

Williams, Duncan Ryūken—Interviews

CAMP DHARMA M. Scarles bw color *Tricycle: The Buddhist Review* v26 no4 p54 Summ 2017

Williams, Durrel—Interviews

AV CLUB Davidaisy bw *Snowboarder* v29 no4 p34 D 2016

Williams, Eboni K.—Interviews

MEDIA Maven in the Making T. A. Christian color *Essence* v48 no5 p82 S 2017

Williams, Eduardo

The Human Surge M. NELSON color *Film Comment* v53 no1 p82 Ja/F 2017

Williams, Elanor F.

Research on Delegating Shows How Uncomfortable We Are Making Choices for Others *Harvard Business Review Digital Articles* p2 Ag 30 2016

Williams, Elizabeth

BREAKOUT PLAYERS *Atlanta* v57 no1 p34 My 2017

Williams, Elizabeth Johnson

Cattle Queen L. Feldman bw color *American Cowboy* v24 no1 p18 Je/Jl 2017

Williams, Florence

The Benefits of Biophilia G. LIDA color *Earth Island Journal* v32 · no2 p55 Summ 2017

EIGHT WAYS NATURE CAN HEAL YOU cartoon *Rodale's Organic Life* v3 no1 p83 Ja 2017

Happy Trails: Scientists examine the benefits of forests and birdsong J. MARK *New York Times Book Review* p14 Mr 5 2017

The Nature Cure color *Reader's Digest* v189 no1129 p106 Ap 2017

SOUND EFFECTS cartoon *Mother Jones* v42 no1 p53 Ja/F 2017

Urban Nature color *Natural History* v125 no4 p30 Ap 2017

Williams, Geisha

BLONDE Ambition color *Vogue* v207 no7 p53 Jl 2017

A BOLT OF ENERGY V. Zarya chart color *Fortune* v175 no8 p160 Je 15 2017

Williams, Greg

Railway Post Office color *Model Railroader* v84 no4 p22 Ap 2017

The Year of Small Things: Radical Faith for the Rest of Us *Christian Century* v134 no15 p42 Jl 19 2017

Williams, Hank, 1923-1953

The Darkness of Hank Williams T. TEACHOUT *Commentary* v143 no2 p49 F 2017

Williams, Hayley, 1988—Interviews

PARAMORE'S HAYLEY WILLIAMS A. Bacle color *Entertainment Weekly* no1466 p56 My 19 2017

Williams, Heather

Los Angeles Innovation Lab Tackles Homelessness *Parks & Recreation* v52 no3 p48 Mr 2017

Williams, Helen

COUTURE SHOCK G. BLACK bw *Ebony* v72 no6 p98 Ap/My 2017

Williams, Howard

OH, HOW I HAVE ENJOYED *Arizona Highways* v93 no10 p4 O 2017

Williams, Hype, 1970-

RAPTURE E. Wilson color *InStyle* v24 no9 p406 S 2017

Williams, Jack

HARNESSING MOTHER NATURE: The Storied History of Hurricane Control and Cloud Seeding *Weatherwise* v70 no5 p25 S/O 2017

The Missing J. Russell *TV Guide* v65 no6 p40 Ja 30 2017

Williams, James G.

Gravity field of the Orientale basin from the Gravity Recovery and

Interior Laboratory Mission bibl graph *Science* v354 no6311 p438 O 28 2016

Williams, Jason G.

ZATT (ZNF451)–mediated resolution of topoisomerase 2 DNA-protein cross-links diag *Science* v357 no6358 p1412 S 29 2017

Williams, Jayson, 1968—Substance use

Team of Rivals L. J. Wertheim color *Sports Illustrated* v125 no19 p100 D 12 2016

Williams, Jennifer

Help for a lonely mare color *Equus* no477 p80 Je 2017

PROVIDING DIRECTION *Literacy Today (2411-7862)* v34 no4 p16 Ja/F 2017

Williams, Jeremy

FIRE-STARTING TOOLS for Any Situation *Mother Earth News* no281 p67 Ap/My 2017

Williams, Jesse

JESSE WILLIAMS C. Glazek color *Esquire* v166 no5 p94 D 2016/Ja 2017

Williams, Jesse—Interviews

Grey's Anatomy M. Logan *TV Guide* v65 no11 p40 Mr 6 2017

Williams, Jessica, 1989-

8 — 2 DOPE QUEENS D. Jackson color *Entertainment Weekly* no1444/1445 p114 D 16 2016

Jessica Williams Gives You Permission to Chill img *New York* v50 no16 p105 Ag 7 2017

Williams, Jessica—Interviews

Two Peas in a Podcast color *O, The Oprah Magazine* p26 Ap 2017

Williams, Jim

HUSBAND AND WIFE HIT $200K JACKPOT at the Reno Million K. Santos color *Team Roping Journal* p91 S 2017

Williams, Joan C.

3 Ways Tech Companies Are Offering Parental Leave *Harvard Business Review Digital Articles* p2 N 19 2015

The 5 Biases Pushing Women Out of STEM *Harvard Business Review Digital Articles* p2 Mr 24 2015

Deplorables for Dummies K. HYMOWITZ *Commentary* v144 no1 p48 Jl/Ag 2017

Hillary Clinton, Bernie Sanders, and the Tug of War Between Women *Harvard Business Review Digital Articles* p2 F 22 2016

How the Imagined "Rationality" of Engineering Is Hurting Diversity—and Engineering *Harvard Business Review Digital Articles* p2 Ag 10 2017

Law Firms' Grueling Hours Are Turning Defectors into Competitors *Harvard Business Review Digital Articles* p2 Ag 25 2015

Need a Good Parental Leave Policy? Here It Is *Harvard Business Review Digital Articles* p2 N 23 2015

Pregnant Workers Have Rights, No Matter What the Supreme Court Says About UPS *Harvard Business Review Digital Articles* p2 D 18 2014

The Throwback Sexism of Kleiner Perkins *Harvard Business Review Digital Articles* p2 Mr 12 2015

Uber and Other Tech Companies Could Make Simple Changes to Avoid Driving Away Their Female Engineers color *Harvard Business Review Digital Articles* p2 F 28 2017

What So Many People Don't Get About the U.S. Working Class *Harvard Business Review Digital Articles* p2 N 10 2016

What Young vs. UPS Means for Pregnant Workers and Their Bosses *Harvard Business Review Digital Articles* p2 Mr 26 2015

Why Sexual Harassment Is More of a Problem in Venture Capital *Harvard Business Review Digital Articles* p2 Jl 12 2017

Williams, Jody, ca. 1963-

EAT, DRINK & BE FRIENDLY S. DANLER cartoon *O, The Oprah Magazine* p100 Ap 2017

WILLIAMS, JOHN

Long Live the Prince: A fan's appreciation takes the musical measure of Prince, the man and symbol *New York Times Magazine* p9 Ap 30 2017

Open Book *New York Times Book Review* p4 O 15 2017

Open Book *New York Times Book Review* p4 O 2 2016

Podcast Therapy *New York Times Book Review* p4 O 8 2017

THIS IS GLAM ROCK color *New York Times Book Review* p48 D 4 2016

A Timeless Observer/Writing With Sassigassity *New York Times Book Review* p6 S 25 2016

Williams, Joley

YVONNE ORJI color *Ebony* v72 no9 p44 Jl/Ag 2017

Williams, Oliver IV
Starcation: New Orleans color *Ebony* v72 no9 p58 Jl/Ag 2017

Williams, Paige
FIREWALL cartoon *New Yorker* v93 no7 p35 Ap 3 2017
HEAVY cartoon *New Yorker* v93 no16 p42 Je 5 2017
WILD WILD HORSES *Smithsonian* v47 no8 p56 D 2016

Williams, Patricia
13 AND COUNTING N. E. WILLIAMS color *Black Enterprise* v47 no8 p16 Jl/Ag 2017
Still Standing *Indianapolis Monthly* v12 no40 p86 Ag 2017

Williams, Patricia J.
Burning Down the House diag il *Nation* v305 no1 p12 Jl 3 2017
Citizenship on Its Knees *Nation* v305 no10 p10 O 23 2017
Cruel Intentions bw color *Nation* v304 no11 p10 Ap 3 2017
Decorum and Dissent bw diag *Nation* v304 no7 p10 Mr 6 2017
The "Hillary Effect" color il *Nation* v303 no17 p12 O 24 2016
Language Games *Nation* v304 no17 p10 Je 5 2017
Mrs. King and Coretta *New York Times Book Review* p9 Ja 15 2017
Our Panopticon, Ourselves color *Nation* v33 no21 p12 N 21 2016
The Road Not Taken color *Nation* v304 no1 p56 Ja 2 2017 The Obama Years
Serving God and Mammon il *Nation* v303 no25/26 p7 D 19 2016
You're Fired! diag *Nation* v304 no4 p10 F 6 2017

Williams, Patricia—Interviews
Q+A S. STALL *Indianapolis Monthly* v12 no40 p89 Ag 2017

Williams, Paul
Homes with A Pedigree A. HEROLD bw color *Los Angeles Magazine* v62 no10 p124 O 2017

Williams, Paul R., 1894-1980
Paul Revere Williams, Unsung Hero A. FIXSEN *Architectural Record* v205 no1 p21 Ja 2017

Williams, Peg
HUSBAND AND WIFE HIT $200K JACKPOT at the Reno Million K. Santos color *Team Roping Journal* p91 S 2017

Williams, Pete A.
Vitamin B3 modulates mitochondrial vulnerability and prevents glaucoma in aged mice bibl graph *Science* v355 no6326 p756 F 17 2017

Williams, Peter
The Master's Voice J. CHECK color *Weekly Standard* v22 no41 p36 Jl 3 2017

Williams, Peter Todd
Peer review as conflict *Physics Today* v70 no10 p17 O 2017

Williams, Pharrell, 1973-
ALL IN A. PETRUSICH color *New Yorker* v93 no4 p80 Mr 13 2017
MAKE AMERICA HAPPY AGAIN J. GORDINIER color *Esquire* v167 no1 p60 F 2017
Random Notes color *Rolling Stone* no1283 p23 Mr 23 2017
SPACE JAM D. Marchese img *New York* v49 no24 p133 N 28 2016

Williams, Philip R.
Building bridges to regenerate axons bibl color diag *Science* v354 no6312 p544 N 4 2016

Williams, R. Scott
An Odd Book: How the First Modern Pop Culture Reporter Conquered New York *Publishers Weekly* v264 no26 p146d Je 26 2017

Williams, Rachel
Lessons from Yelp's Empirical Approach to Diversity *Harvard Business Review Digital Articles* p2 S 20 2017

WILLIAMS, RAWLSTON
THE COUNTER JOINT AS COMMUNITY BOOSTER bw *Bon Appetit* v62 no2 p70 Mr 2017

WILLIAMS, RAYMOND A.
READERS' THOUGHTS ON PAST ISSUES color *Motor Trend* v69 no2 p26 F 2017

Williams, Rob
U.S. seafood import restriction presents opportunity and risk bibl color map *Science* v354 no6318 p1372 D 16 2016

Williams, Robert
A Fashion Empire's New Clothes color graph *Bloomberg Businessweek* no4535 p17 Ag 28 2017
The Taming of a Teen Emporium color *Bloomberg Businessweek*

no4518 p26 Ap 10 2017

WILLIAMS, SALLY
15-Minute All-Organic Meal Under $15 color *Prevention* v69 no11 p14 N 2017

WILLIAMS, SARAH C. P.
Garbage In, Garbage Out *National Parks* v91 no4 p22 Fall 2017
A Mission to Grow *National Parks* v91 no2 p16 Spr 2017

WILLIAMS, SEAN
Allow Me to Stipulate My Demands, Daddy bw color *Reader's Digest* v189 no1131 p13 Je 2017
#IHeartMyDictator *New Republic* v248 no1/2 p13 Ja/F 2017
TELLING TRABBIES FROM JUNKERS: Though fast-paced and refreshingly diff erent, this short study of Germany is more political manifesto than historical analysis *History Today* v67 no10 p104 O 2017

Williams, Sebastian
Sebastian Williams color *Surfing Magazine* v53 no1 p32 Ja 2017

Williams, Serena, 1981-
FORCES TO RECKON WITH M. HOLGATE and M. GUIDUCCI bw color *Vogue* v207 no3 p357 Mr 2017
Leading Off color *Sports Illustrated* v126 no4 p6 Ja 30 2017
Lewis HAMILTON *Interview* v47 no6 p68 Ag 2017
Milestones *Ms.* v26 no4 p7 Wint 2016
A New Doubles Partner: Staying active during pregnancy—such as by hitting the court—can be beneficial to a woman's health color *Tennis* v53 no5 p14 S/O 2017
SERENA SERENE R. Haskell color *Vogue* v207 no9 p672 S 2017
Serena's Love Match B. BUSSINGER bw color *Vanity Fair* v59 no8 p62 Ag 2017
Serena Williams *Tennis* v53 no1 p46 Ja/F 2017
The Spirit of the Sisters S. TIGNOR bw color *Tennis* v53 no5 p80 S/O 2017
Women Warriors L. GIBBS *Tennis* v52 no6 p16 N/D 2016

Williams, Serena, 1981-—Awards
WON FOR THE AGED L. J. Wertheim color *Sports Illustrated* v126 no5 p60 F 13 2017

Williams, Serena, 1981-—Interviews
World's Greatest Female Athlete [Cover story] M. Harris-Perry bw color *Glamour* v114 no7 p114 Jl 2016

Williams, Serena, 1981-—Political & social views
Pop Chart R. Bruner, C. Lang et al color *Time* v189 no4 p54 Ja 23 2017

Williams, Shawna
Foreign-born scientists find a home in China color *Science* v354 no6312 p644 N 4 2016

Williams, Simon
Macbeth *Opera News* v81 no6 p40 D 2016
Rediscovering a Neglected Treasure *Opera News* v81 no5 p40 N 2016
Wonderful Town *Opera News* v81 no9 p40 Mr 2017

Williams, Stephanie
Freedom Thirty-Five T. Henley color *Walrus* v14 no5 p16 Je 2017

Williams, Stephen E.
Biodiversity redistribution under climate change: Impacts on ecosystems and human well-being color *Science* v355 no6332 p1389 Mr 31 2017

Williams, Susan
Spies in the Congo: America's Atomic Mission in World War II N. van de Walle *Foreign Affairs* v96 no1 p178 Ja/F 2017

Williams, Tad
The Witchwood Crown: The Last King of Osten Ard, Book 1 color *Publishers Weekly* v264 no23 p36 Je 5 2017

Williams, Ted
Home on the Sage [Cover story] color map *National Wildlife (World Edition)* v54 no6 p22 O/N 2016

Williams, Ted, 1918-2002
BATTER, INTERRUPTED L. J. Wertheim and J. Feldman color *Sports Illustrated* v126 no11 p50 Ap 17-24 2017
Williams' Amazing Artistry B. Reed bw *Downbeat* v83 no12 p92 D 2016

Williams, Tennessee, 1911-1983
Tennessee Williams Stories E. Laborde bw cartoon *New Orleans Magazine* v51 no7 p152 My 2017

Williams, Teresa
SURPRISE *Christian Century* v134 no12 p22 Je 7 2017

Williams, Terry Tempest, 1955-

America's Evolving Idea *Sierra* v101 no4 p31 Jl/Ag 2016

BLIND FAITH *Audubon* v119 no2 p40 Summ 2017

The Hour of Land E. Kennedy *Orion Magazine* v35 no4/5 p106 Jl-O 2016

IT'S A HARD RAIN *Arizona Highways* v92 no7 p36 Jl 2016

Life on Earth R. CONNIFF *Progressive* v81 no5 p5 Je/Jl 2017

THIS LAND WAS MADE FOR YOU AND ME [Cover story] color *O, The Oprah Magazine* p78 Ja 2017

Visiting Theodore Roosevelt National Park with my Father color *Progressive* v81 no5 p34 Je/Jl 2017

WILLIAMS, THOMAS CHATTERTON

About a Boy color *New Republic* v247 no12 p62 D 2016

CRIMES OF BEING bw color *New York Times Magazine* p30 Ja 29 2017

'Fade' *New York Times Magazine* p53 Mr 12 2017

Portrait of a Hustler color *Esquire* v166 no4 p40 N 2016

RADICAL AMBITION *New York Times Magazine* p24 Ap 2 2017

Williams, Thomas N.

Resistance to malaria through structural variation of red blood cell invasion receptors diag *Science* v356 no6343 p1139 Je 16 2017

Williams, Tia

How to Look Less Tired bw color *Glamour* v115 no3 p120 Mr 2017

Meet Michelle Obama's Secret Weapon color *Glamour* v115 no2 p54 F 2017

WILLIAMS, TYLER

GROWING, GROWING, GONE *Arizona Highways* v93 no1 p44 Ja 2017

A JOURNEYMAN'S TALE color *Canoe & Kayak Magazine* v45 no1 p44 Wint 2017

Williams, Vanessa, 1963-

DAYTIME DIVAS C. Agard color *Entertainment Weekly* no1439 p12 N 11 2016

VANESSA + JILLIAN [Cover story] D. L. D'Oyley color *Essence* v47 no9 p58 Ja 2017

VANESSA WILLIAMS *TV Guide* v65 no27 p7 Je 26 2017

Williams, Venus, 1980-

Artists color *Time* v189 no16/17 p40 My 1-8 2017

The Spirit of the Sisters S. TIGNOR bw color *Tennis* v53 no5 p80 S/O 2017

Venus, Exonerated D. ZIRIN *Nation* v305 no3 p8 Jl 31 2017

VENUS VENERATED S. l. Price, T. Keith et al color *Sports Illustrated* v127 no7 p17 S 4 2017

Venus Williams' Forehand J. YANDELL color *Tennis* v53 no5 p74 S/O 2017

Women Warriors L. GIBBS *Tennis* v52 no6 p16 N/D 2016

Williams, Wendy

How Did I Get Here?: WENDY WILLIAMS bw color *Bloomberg Businessweek* no4516 p72 Mr 27 2017

WENDY WILLIAMS IS MORE THAN JUST TALK V. Zarya color *Fortune* v175 no2 p34 F 1 2017

Williams, Weston

Priests killed in Mexico as drug violence spirals color *Christian Century* v133 no23 p14 N 9 2016

Williams, Wyatt

full house color *Bon Appetit* v61 no11 p96 N 2016

NATIONAL BURDEN *New York Times Magazine* p26 Ja 22 2017

Williams International Corp.

PILATUS PC-24 ENGINE CERTIFIED color *Flying* v144 no10 p22 O 2017

Williamsburg (Va.)

ABOUT TOWN *Virginia Living* v15 no4 p41 Je 2017

NEW WORLD CHARM: A neoclassical waterfront home in Williamsburg is a stylish basis for the Fang family M. HERMANSON *Virginia Living* v15 no4 p60 Je 2017

Williamsburg (New York, N.Y.)

Silent Slurp img *New York* v49 no21 p78 O 17 2016

Williams-Garcia, Rita

Deep-Down Blues: This novel's young hero, an aspiring bluesman, finds a new beat as he learns to live with the loss of his grandfather M. MEDINA *New York Times Book Review* p25 My 14 2017

Williams-Goss, Nigel

OUTSIDE JOB L. Schnell color *Sports Illustrated* v126 no8 p46 Mr 20 2017

Williamson, Christina

Global atmospheric particle formation from CERN CLOUD measurements bibl graph map *Science* v354 no6316 p1119 D 2 2016

WILLIAMSON, EDWIN D.

Trump's Conflicts *Weekly Standard* v22 no19 p10 Ja 23 2017

Williamson, Eric

UPWARDLY MOBILE *Virginia Living* v15 no3 p24 Ap 2017

Williamson, James

The Gulf Opportunity Zone Helped Affected Counties Recover Economically After Hurricane Katrina *Amber Waves: The Economics of Food, Farming, Natural Resources, & Rural America* p1 O 2016

WILLIAMSON, KEVIN D.

Albion's Ashes *Commentary* v142 no3 p42 O 2016

Conservatism In Dissent *National Review* v68 no22 p42 D 5 2016

David Frum on Yuval Levin's 'The Fractured Republic' *Commentary* v142 no1 p1 Jl/Ag 2016

Enjoy the Silence *National Review* v69 no8 p16 My 2017

A Fiscal Collision Course *National Review* v68 no21 p17 N 21 2016

Hardly Working *Commentary* v144 no2 p39 S 2017

Help Them Move *National Review* v69 no2 p20 F 6 2017

The Inquisitor's Heirs color *National Review* v69 no9 p14 My 15 2017

KEVIN D. WILLIAMSON *Commentary* v142 no1 p38 Jl/Ag 2016

Litigating Politics color *National Review* v68 no23 p15 D 19 2016

Masters of The Game *National Review* v68 no20 p34 N 7 2016

Matthew Continetti on Yuval Levin's 'The Fractured Republic' *Commentary* v142 no1 p1 Jl/Ag 2016

Meir Soloveichik on Yuval Levin's 'The Fractured Republic' *Commentary* v142 no1 p1 Jl/Ag 2016

The NAACP And the GOP *National Review* v69 no12 p16 Je 26 2017

No, California [Cover story] color *National Review* v69 no7 p27 Ap 17 2017

The 'N' Word color *National Review* v69 no17 p22 S 11 2017

Professor Propaganda color *National Review* v69 no6 p28 Ap 3 2017

Progressivism in the Boardroom [Cover story] il *National Review* v69 no4 p24 Mr 6 2017

The Republican Civil War in Texas *National Review* v69 no15 p17 Ag 14 2017

Slanted Justice color *National Review* v68 no19 p19 O 24 2016

Sober, Seething Hollywood il *National Review* v69 no5 p33 Mr 20 2017

Superman Politics il *National Review* v68 no24 p16 D 31 2016

'To Perish in These Sordid, Abnormal Experiences' [Cover story] color *National Review* v69 no11 p24 Je 12 2017

Voice of America *National Review* v69 no3 p31 F 20 2017

'We Are as Gods and Might as Well Get Good at It' color *National Review* v69 no19 p29 O 16 2017

Wretched Refuse, Indeed bw *National Review* v69 no16 p14 Ag 28 2017

Williamson, Lauren

Can Arne Duncan Save Chicago? color *Chicago* v65 no11 p86 N 2016

McMANSIONS TO SPARE color *Chicago* v66 no11 p22 N 2017

THE PEANUT DOCTOR IS IN color *Chicago* v66 no10 p28 O 2017

Williamson, Sarah Keohane

The Data: Where Long-Termism Pays Off graph img *Harvard Business Review* v95 no3 p67 My/Je 2017

Finally, Proof That Managing for the Long Term Pays Off color graph *Harvard Business Review Digital Articles* p2 F 7 2017

Williamson, Shawn

THE FARM INSURANCE GAMBIT: DO YOU HAVE ENOUGH OR TOO MUCH INSURANCE? IT'S WORTH ASKING color *Successful Farming* v115 no7 p12 My 2017

ORCHESTRATING 1031 AND REVERSE 1031 EXCHANGES *Successful Farming* v115 no2 p16 F 2017

YEAR-END TIMING DECISIONS *Successful Farming* v114 no11 p20 N 2016

Williamson, Tim

What Makes New Orleans a Startup City to Rival the "Big Three" *Harvard Business Review Digital Articles* p2 Mr 8 2016

Williamson, Zion

Sent From Mount ZION C. Johnson color *Sports Illustrated* v127 no5 p40 Ag 14 2017

WILLICK, JASON

The Downside of Romneyism color *National Review* v68 no20 p42 N 7 2016

Willig, Lauren

THOUGHTS ON Inventions bw color *Forbes* v200 no2 p112 S 5 2017

Willig, Michael R.

Triumphs and Tribulations: An Intimate Account of How Long-Term Funding Affects the Lives of Scientists M. M. FULLER *BioScience* v67 no5 p477 My 2017

Willimon, William

The Witness of Religion in an Age of Fear *Christian Century* v134 no12 p39 Je 7 2017

WRITERS' FEAST color *Christian Century* v134 no10 p30 My 10 2017

Willimott, Andy

PEOPLE OF THE FUTURE: The October Revolution of 1917 inspired a generation of young Russians to embrace new ideals of socialist living *History Today* v67 no10 p24 O 2017

Willingness to pay

Let Your Customers Segment Themselves by What They're Willing to Pay S. Michel *Harvard Business Review Digital Articles* p2 Mr 11 2015

Willis, Andrew

An Energy Drink That Tastes of the Amazon graph *Bloomberg Businessweek* no4503 p39 D 12 2016

WILLIS, AVIANA

SEEING WAR THROUGH ROSE PETALS *In These Times* v41 no2 p41 F 2017

Willis, Brad

Find Calm amid the Chaos cartoon *Men's Health* v32 no1 p125 Ja/F 2017

Willis, Elizabeth

PLOT *New Yorker* v92 no37 p72 N 14 2016

WILLIS, JAY

THE CULTURAL SATURATION CHART bw cartoon color *GQ: Gentlemen's Quarterly* v97 no4 p59 Ap 2017

Musicals! (Now for Men!) bw color *GQ: Gentlemen's Quarterly* v97 no9 p116 S 2017

WILLIS, JIM

Refugees and the Reformation color *Christianity Today* v61 no7 p68 S 2017

Willis, Jon

All These Worlds Are Yours The Scientific Search for Alien Life P. Smith *Physics Today* v70 no3 p59 Mr 2017

Willis, Josh

WELLNESS Q+A *Atlanta* v57 no5 p119 S 2017

Willis, Katherine J.

The natural capital of city trees color *Science* v356 no6336 p374 Ap 28 2017

Willis, Richard

OZ IN 'NAM bw color map *Military History* v34 no5 p54 Ja 2018

Willis, Rumer, 1988-

Empire's Latest Rumer *TV Guide* v65 no13 p13 Mr 20 2017

Willis, Sam

The Struggle for Sea Power: A Naval History of the American Revolution A. Paletta *Military History* v34 no4 p72 N 2017

Willis, Susan

COMMON GROUND L. LEBLANC-BERRY color *Louisiana Life* v37 no3 p12 Ja/F 2017

Willis, Virginia

Beauty of the Beets color *Southern Living* v52 no3 p132 Mr 2017

Easy Okra color *Southern Living* v52 no9 p138 S 2017

IN PRAISE OF PECANS color *Southern Living* v51 no11 p150 N 2016

Juicy Little Gems color *Southern Living* v52 no5 p138 My 2017

A Taste for Sprouts color *Southern Living* v52 no1 p126 Ja 2017

TRADE KALE FOR COLLARDS color *Southern Living* v52 no11 p126 N 2017

Using All That Squash color *Southern Living* v52 no7 p114 Jl 2017

Williston (N.D.)

Boom and Bust *American Scholar* v86 no2 p12 Spr 2017

Willmetts, Simon

In Secrecy's Shadow: The OSS and CIA in Hollywood Cinema, 1941-1979 R. PRIME *Film Quarterly* v70 no3 p103 Spr 2017

Willmott, Kelly

SPACE QUEST C. FOSTER color *House Beautiful* p116 Ag 2017

Willot, Quentin

Sahara's Coolest Ants N. Strochlic color *National Geographic* v230 no5 p19 N 2016

Willoughby, CaraLea

from you, the reader color graph *Horse & Rider* v56 no8 p22 Ag 2017

WILLOUGHBY, JAY

Shifting Gears *Islamic Horizons* v46 no2 p14 Mr/Ap 2017

Willoughby, Martha

At Christie's color *Magazine Antiques* v184 no1 p84 Ja/F 2017

Willoughby Lake (Vt.)

Green Ice K. Rossiter color *Climbing* no350 p32 D 2016/Ja 2017

Willow Creek (Fremont County-Natrona County, Wyo.)

Colorful Wilderness *South Dakota Magazine* v33 no3 p91 S/O 2017

Wills

How to Talk About Getting a Will K. A. Renzulli color *Money* v46 no6 p20 Jl 2017

The Poisoned Will of Jean Meslier: A French priest's shocking attack on religion called for the fall of altars and the heads of kings M. Guinard *History Today* v67 no10 p12 O 2017

Wills, Garry

History's FIRST DRAFT color *Vanity Fair* v59 no10 p158 O 2017

Jesuits Admirable and Execrable bw cartoon *New York Review of Books* v64 no2 p39 F 9 2017

Remembering Bob Silvers: The legendary New York Review of Books editor knew everybody, had read everything, and oversaw every stage of what he published *American Scholar* v86 no3 p106 Summ 2017

Where Evangelicals Came From bw color *New York Review of Books* v64 no7 p26 Ap 20 2017

Wills, Keith

Finding ghosts in old layout photos bw *Model Railroader* v84 no4 p33 Ap 2017

Fine locomotives inspired fine models color *Model Railroader* v84 no2 p30 F 2017

How Märklin's 19th century Gauge 1 became the 20th century's LGB large scale *Model Railroader* v84 no10 p20 O 2017

Mantua's 4-4-0 Belle was a plain Jane color *Model Railroader* v83 no12 p26 D 2016

When O scale traction was popular bw diag *Model Railroader* v84 no8 p20 Ag 2017

Where are all the passengers? bw *Model Railroader* v84 no6 p23 Je 2017

Wills, Ken

The Conglomerate That Troubles China *Bloomberg Businessweek* no4533 p12 Ag 7 2017

Wills, Royal Barry, 1895-1962

ROYAL BARRY WILLS P. Poore bw color *Old House Journal* v45 no1 p23 F 2017

WILLSEY, SHAWN

A SHOCKING IMPACT: DISGUISED BY VOLCANOES AND CHALLIS *Idaho Magazine* v16 no12 p18 S 2017

Willson, Sam

NAME THE BOAT S. SHIBATA *Sea Magazine* v108 no9 p12 S 2016

Willy, Richard

JOINT ACTION [Cover story] A. C. Shilton color *Runner's World* v51 no10 p54 N 2016

Willyerd, Karie

How to Get Feedback When No One Is Volunteering It *Harvard Business Review Digital Articles* p2 Ag 14 2015

Millennials Want to Be Coached at Work *Harvard Business Review Digital Articles* p2 F 27 2015

What High Performers Want at Work *Harvard Business Review Digital Articles* p2 N 18 2014

Wilmette (Ill.)

WILMETTE J. REESE color map *Chicago* v65 no11 p29 N 2016

Wilmore, Larry

AFTERMATH bw cartoon *New Yorker* v92 no38 p48 N 21 2016

Neil DeGRASSE TYSON *Interview* v46 no9 p25 N 2016

Wilmot, Billy

Billy "Mystic" Wilmot, 57 A. DOUGLAS bw *Surfer* v58 no5 p40 S 2017

Wilms, Joern

An accreting pulsar with extreme properties drives an ultraluminous x-ray source in NGC 5907 bibl chart graph *Science* v355 no6327 p817 F 24 2017

Wilmshurst, Janet M.

Biodiversity losses and conservation responses in the Anthropocene color diag graph map *Science* v356 no6335 p270 Ap 21 2017

Wilner, David J.

Spiral density waves in a young protoplanetary disk bibl graph *Science* v353 no6307 p1519 S 30 2016

Wilner, Tamar

Fake News: Tamar Wilner Is the Hero We Need *Skeptical Inquirer* v41 no2 p11 Mr/Ap 2017

Wilsdon, James

UK science, post-Brexit color *Science* v355 no6331 p1243 Mr 24 2017

Wilser, Jeff

My boyfriend of four years doesn't want to move in together color *Glamour* v115 no3 p144 Mr 2017

WILSEY, BRENT M.

What to Do About Junior *USA Today Magazine* v145 no2864 p66 My 2017

WILSEY, JOHN D.

Whose Land? [Cover story] color *America* v215 p20 N 28 2016

Wilsie, Sharon

How to listen to your horse color *Equus* no470 p55 N 2016

Wilson (Film)

Lovably Unlikable D. EDELSTEIN img *New York* v50 no6 p85 Mr 20 2017

Only Connect R. R. Cooper color *Commonweal* v144 no8 p30 My 5 2017

Wilson C. Nashawaty color *Entertainment Weekly* no1459 p47 Mr 31 2017

Woody Harrelson Turns a Scowl Upside Down In Wilson S. Zacharek color *Time* v189 no12 p57 Ap 3 2017

WILSON, ALEXANDRA

CONVERSATION color *Forbes* v199 no4 p30 Ap 25 2017

CONVERSATION color *Forbes* v200 no4 p32 O 24 2017

CONVERSATION color graph *Forbes* v198 no8 p36 D 20 2016

CONVERSATION color graph *Forbes* v199 no7 p38 Je 29 2017

THE INTEREST GRAPH graph *Forbes* v199 no4 p30 Ap 25 2017

LESSONS AND IDEAS BY THE 100 GREATEST LIVING BUSINESS MINDS bw color *Forbes* v200 no3 p115 S 28 2017

OPERA: FOR THE ORDINARY: Despite popular misconceptions and its aristocratic origins, for part of its history opera was inextricably linked with popular culture - no more so than in the 1920s *History Today* v67 no9 p58 S 2017

Wilson, Amy

LIVIN' IT UP IN THE CITY color *Spin to Win Rodeo* v20 no10 p86 D 2016

LUKE BROWN'S "ROCKSTAR" color *Spin to Win Rodeo* v20 no12 p52 F 2017

The Storyteller color *American Cowboy* v23 no6 p69 Ap/My 2017

Wilson, Andrea

AMERICAN FLAT-TRACK REVIVAL color *Cycle World* v56 no2 p68 Mr 2017

WILSON, ANDREW

Good News Bears *Christianity Today* v61 no1 p26 Ja/F 2017

It's Not Only Bullies Who Boast *Christianity Today* v61 no7 p28 S 2017

The New Testament's Take on 'Equality' *Christianity Today* v60 no9 p28 N 2016

Our Spiritual Gifts Have an Expiration Date *Christianity Today* v61 no5 p22 Je 2017

A Tale of Two Churches *Christianity Today* p25 Ap 2017

What endures in Wittenberg *Christian Century* v133 no22 p11 O 26 2016

WILSON, ANNASUE MCCLEAVE

CRACKING THE TEACUP color *Publishers Weekly* v264 no7 p42 F 13 2017

WILSON, ASHLEE

THE THING THAT CHANGED IT ALL color *Bicycling* v58 no8 p17 S 2017

Wilson, August, 1945-2005

FIRST LOOK: FENCES D. PHILYAW and L. CROSS color *Ebony* v72 no3 p38 D 2016/Ja 2017

Wilson, Bill

BIGGER N. Paumgarten cartoon *New Yorker* v93 no12 p16 My 8 2017

Wilson, Brad

CHANGING THEIR TRAJECTORY color *Literacy Today (2411-7862)* v34 no5 p48 Mr/Ap 2017

Wilson, Brandi

Get to Know Your Campus Career Development Office R. W. Goode color *Black Enterprise* v47 no3 p32 O 2016

Wilson, Brian, 1942-

The Salvation of Brian Wilson J. Fine bw color *Rolling Stone* no1295 p48 S 7 2017

Wilson, Brian, 1942—-Interviews

Good Vibrations W. Werris *Publishers Weekly* v263 no41 p67 O 10 2016

Life's Work: An Interview with Brian Wilson A. Beard bw *Harvard Business Review* v94 no12 p120 D 2016

Wilson, Carolyn

STATEMENT OF OWNERSHIP, MANAGEMENT, AND CIRCULATION *BioScience* v66 no11 p1002 N 1 2016

Wilson, Casey

5 — BI2TCH SESH: A REAL HOUSEWIVES BREAKDOWN A. Sadlier color *Entertainment Weekly* no1444/1445 p114 D 16 2016

Can Fans Save The Sackett Sisters? R. Kinane color *Entertainment Weekly* no1468/1469 p92 Je 2-9 2017

Wilson, Chip, 1956-

Founder's Remorse A. BROWN color *Forbes* v198 no9 p40 D 30 2016

Wilson, Chris

America's Buzziest Baby Names color *Time* v189 no20 p9 My 29 2017

Can Trump Handle the Truth? [Cover story] color *Time* v189 no12 p32 Ap 3 2017

Getting Over My Divorce? Studying the Numbers Helped color diag *Time* v189 no7/8 p115 F 27 2017

The Grayest Professions In America color diag map *Time* v189 no15 p20 Ap 24 2017

Russia and the Trump Campaign color *Time* v189 no12 p36 Ap 3 2017

Which Harry Potter House Fits Your State? color map *Time* v190 no2/3 p98 Jl 10-17 2017

Wilson, Christopher

Evolutionary drivers of thermoadaptation in enzyme catalysis [Cover story] bibl color graph *Science* v355 no6322 p289 Ja 20 2017

Wilson, Cid

Nurturing Success J. Caplin color *Money* v46 no2 p26 Mr 2017

Wilson, Claggett, 1887-1952

Flower of Death–The Bursting of a Heavy Shell–Not as It Looks, but as It Feels and Sounds and Smells color *Art in America* v104 no10 p60 N 2016

Wilson, D.

iPTF16geu: A multiply imaged, gravitationally lensed type Ia supernova color diag graph *Science* v356 no6335 p291 Ap 21 2017

Wilson, Dawn Ruth

Alexina Medley *New Orleans Magazine* v52 no1 p38 S 2017

THE BUNGALOW BOOK LADY color *New Orleans Magazine* v51 no2 p34 D 2016

CHARTER-ING A NEW COURSE color *New Orleans Magazine* v51 no8 p82 Je 2017

Chartering the Course color *New Orleans Magazine* v51 no5 p32 Mr 2017

CHASING A MOVING TARGET cartoon *New Orleans Magazine* v51 no1 p34 N 2016

Remaking Public Schools color *New Orleans Magazine* v51 no6 p32 Ap 2017

Sci High Flies High color *New Orleans Magazine* v51 no12 p40 O 2017

Taking the Fast Track: Online links to higher education color *New Orleans Magazine* v51 no10 p44 Ag 2017

Top of the Class color *New Orleans Magazine* v51 no9 p32 Jl

2017

DOPE STUFF ON MY DESK color *Essence* v47 no7 p20 N 2016

DOPE STUFF ON MY DESK color *Essence* v48 no3 p26 Jl 2017

DOPE STUFF ON MY DESK color *Essence* v48 no6 p32 O 2017

ERICA M color *Essence* v47 no10 p26 F 2017

Face Forward color *Essence* v48 no3 p29 Jl 2017

the FENTY FACE color *Essence* v48 no6 p54 O 2017

Forever Tracy color *Essence* v48 no5 p96 S 2017

FULL EFFECT color *Essence* v47 no11 p28 Mr 2017

How fro can you go? color *InStyle* v24 no5 p242 My 2017

JAMEEL MOHAMMED color *Essence* v47 no12 p24 Ap 2017

JANELLE LANGFORD color *Essence* v48 no2 p26 Je 2017

KÉLA WALKER color *Essence* v48 no6 p34 O 2017

KIMBERLY DREW color *Essence* v47 no11 p30 Mr 2017

PRECIOUS LEE color *Essence* v47 no8 p38 D 2016

SARAH NAKINTU color *Essence* v47 no8 p40 D 2016

WHAT A SPECTACLE color *Essence* v47 no10 p24 F 2017

While You Were Sleeping color *Essence* v48 no6 p39 O 2017

Wilson, Justin E.

MAVS-dependent host species range and pathogenicity of human hepatitis A virus bibl graph *Science* v353 no6307 p1541 S 30 2016

WILSON, KAREN

Forever home color *House Beautiful* p54 Ag 2017

Wilson, Karma

Big Bear, Small Mouse *Publishers Weekly* v263 no40 p121 O 3 2016

Wilson, Kea

Schlock and Awe J. DEE color *New York Times Book Review* p14 S 25 2016

Wilson, Kevin

It Takes a Commune J. IRVING *New York Times Book Review* p9 F 5 2017

Perfect Little World L. Greenblatt color *Entertainment Weekly* no1450 p60 Ja 27 2017

Wilson, Kevin A.

How the Chaste Make Haste color *Car & Driver* v62 no6 p98 D 2016

Industrial, Heavy, and Magic color *Car & Driver* v62 no11 p114 My 2017

Wilson, Kinsey

PUB TECH CONNECT chart color *Publishers Weekly* v264 no15 p(Sp)3 Ap 10 2017

Wilson, Lauren Wesley—Interviews

Turning Networking On Its Head C. V. Clarke color *Black Enterprise* v47 no3 p40 O 2016

Wilson, Laurie

Inventing Nevelson C. Rosenberger bw *Art in America* v105 no4 p59 Ap 2017

Wilson, Lee

Hunted I. Ratledge *TV Guide* v65 no4 p36 Ja 16 2017

Wilson, Mark

Biological tissue can behave like a liquid crystal *Physics Today* v70 no6 p19 Je 2017

The carbon nanotube integrated circuit goes three-dimensional: Chip makers have a mantra: smaller, cheaper, and faster. They may now need a new adjective--taller *Physics Today* v70 no9 p14 S 2017

Circuitry made robust enough for Venus *Physics Today* v70 no3 p19 Mr 2017

Classical precursor to turbulence observed in a superfluid *Physics Today* v70 no1 p19 Ja 2017

Giant undersea craters were blown out by decomposing methane hydrates: Although the craters likely formed about 12 000 years ago, methane is still leaking profusely around and between them *Physics Today* v70 no8 p21 Ag 2017

Photonic doping tunes transparent media *Physics Today* v70 no5 p20 My 2017

Wilson, Mark E.

Social status alters immune regulation and response to infection in macaques bibl graph *Science* v354 no6315 p1041 N 25 2016

Wilson, Matt

MATT WILSON: LIFE'S CALLING D. Ouellette color *Downbeat* v84 no9 p44 S 2017

Wilson, Michael

HOW TO DO EVERY THING WITH VIDEO bw color diag *Popular Mechanics* p58 O 2017

MEET THE MAN WHO TOLD THE STORY OF NEW YORK CITY, ONE CRIME AT A TIME T. Donnellan color *America* v216 no9 p14 Ap 24 2017

WILSON, MICHELE

The Question color *O, The Oprah Magazine* p14 N 2017

Wilson, Mickey

High-Wire Act J. LABIANCA color *Reader's Digest* v189 no1129 p8 Ap 2017

Wilson, Niki

Active Perception *Natural History* v125 no2 p6 F 2017

Avoiding Overreaction color *Natural History* v125 no4 p7 Ap 2017

BACK WHERE THEY BELONG color map *Canadian Geographic* v137 no5 p32 S/O 2017

Can't Hurry Love color *Natural History* v125 no4 p48 Ap 2017

Cost of Fast Food color *Natural History* v125 no3 p6 Mr 2017

Dividends of Diversity color *Natural History* v125 no6 p8 Je 2017

Earliest Known Relative color *Natural History* v125 no5 p6 My 2017

Origin of Baleen color *Natural History* v125 no10 p6 O 2017

Orthopedic Exam *Natural History* v125 no1 p6 D 2016/Ja 2017

Triple Symbiosis *Natural History* v124 no10 p7 N 2016

AN UNCOMMON Snake color *Canadian Wildlife* v23 no2 p26 My/Je 2017

Very Distant Relative color *Natural History* v125 no7 p8 Jl/Ag 2017

Wilson, Norma

Born on the River *South Dakota Magazine* v32 no4 p61 N/D 2016

Wilson, Paul

THE COLLECTORS C. Neuhaus *Saturday Evening Post* v289 no3 p14 My/Je 2017

Estimating economic damage from climate change in the United States color graph *Science* v356 no6345 p1362 Je 30 2017

WILSON, PEGGY

Christmas at Bear *Idaho Magazine* v16 no3 p40 D 2016

WILSON, PETE

TRAILING THE HERD *Idaho Magazine* v16 no2 p48 N 2016

Wilson, Peter H.

Q: What is the most interesting family in history? color *Atlantic* v318 no5 p96 D 2016

Wilson, R.

Jupiter's interior and deep atmosphere: The initial pole-to-pole passes with the Juno spacecraft [Cover story] color graph *Science* v356 no6340 p821 My 26 2017

Wilson, Rachel

A General State of Mourning *History Today* v67 no3 p7 Mr 2017

Wilson, Rainn, 1968-

Star Trek Discovery J. Hibberd, A. Bacle et al color *Entertainment Weekly* no1482/1483 p104 S 22 2017

Wilson, Rebel, 1986-

Rebel Yell E. Wilson color *InStyle* v24 no8 p65 Ag 2017

Wilson, Rita, 1956-

RITA WILSON ON LIFE AFTER BREAST CANCER color *Harper's Bazaar* no3657 p196 O 2017

Wilson, Rob

The New World of Mini Consumer Packaged Goods *Harvard Business Review Digital Articles* p2 S 26 2016

WILSON, ROBERT

Breach of Faith *American Scholar* v86 no3 p2 Summ 2017

Consequences *American Scholar* v86 no1 p2 Wint 2017

Grace *American Scholar* v86 no2 p2 Spr 2017

Monuments to What? *American Scholar* v86 no4 p2 Aut 2017

Wilson, Russell, 1988-

INSIDE THE HUDDLE K. BADENHAUSEN, M. K. OZANIAN et al color *Forbes* v200 no4 p15 O 24 2017

Wilson, Ruth—Interviews

Ruth WILSON J. C. MITCHELL *Interview* v46 no9 p34 N 2016

Wilson, Sarah Hinlicky

Still reckoning with Luther *Christian Century* v134 no6 p22 Mr 15 2017

Wilson, Scott

BANISH IMBALANCES IN THE MOUTH color diag *Practical Horseman* v45 no1 p40 Ja 2017

WILSON, SHAUN

Accelerating Tropicalization and the Transformation of Temperate

Seagrass Meadows *BioScience* v66 no11 p938 N 1 2016

Wilson, Steve

THE BLOCKCHAIN REVOLUTION: INTERACTION color *Harvard Business Review* v95 no2 p20 Mr/Ap 2017

Reaching Full Digitization in the Classroom *Education Digest* v83 no3 p61 N 2017

WILSON, STEVE K.

The Thermal Edge color *Natural History* v125 no3 p48 Mr 2017

Wilson, Teddy

The Two Billie Holidays T. Teachout *Commentary* v140 no2 p63 S 2015

Wilson, Teri

Royally Roma: The Royals, Book 1 *Publishers Weekly* v264 no8 p71 F 20 2017

WILSON, TERRY L.

Cynthia Rothrock [Cover story] bw color *Black Belt* v55 no2 p26 F/Mr 2017

Gene LeBell [Cover story] color *Black Belt* v55 no2 p46 F/Mr 2017

Wilson, Tom

AS BUSINESSES, WE HAVE TO DEFINE OUR ROLE MORE BROADLY *Vital Speeches of the Day* v83 no5 p138 My 2017

Wilson, Wendy L..

DEAR TUPAC color *Essence* v48 no2 p58 Je 2017

Protection. PERIOD color *Essence* v48 no5 p112 S 2017

Sync With Your Cycle *Essence* v48 no5 p112 S 2017

YOUR VAGINA WILL SEE YOU NOW color *Essence* v48 no5 p109 S 2017

Wilson, William G.

Stormwater: A Resource for Scientists, Engineers, and Policy Makers A. L. MAYER *BioScience* v67 no2 p179 F 2017

Wilson, Woodrow, 1856-1924

Big Lie [Cover story] J. Connor bw *American History* v52 no2 p30 Je 2017

HATE SPEECH *Lapham's Quarterly* v10 no3 p60 Summ 2017

Weapon on the Wall: As World War I raged, posters encouraged, enticed, and even shamed young Americans into joining the great conflict J. M. Cannon *Hoover Digest: Research & Opinion on Public Policy* no2 p199 Spr 2017

Winning Women: Woodrow Wilson at first found himself scandalized by protesting women, but soon he championed their cause. How President Trump and feminists might likewise make common cause E. Cobbs *Hoover Digest: Research & Opinion on Public Policy* no2 p58 Spr 2017

Woodrow Wilson's War G. Norman bw *Weekly Standard* v22 no29 p26 Ap 3 2017

Wilson Sporting Goods Co.

MOST IMPROVED color *Tennis* v53 no2 p41 Mr/Ap 2017

Wilson-Grady, Joshua T.

UBE2O remodels the proteome during terminal erythroid differentiation diag *Science* v357 no6350 p471 Ag 4 2017

Wilt, Cara

Mismatch repair deficiency predicts response of solid tumors to PD-1 blockade chart graph *Science* v357 no6349 p409 Jl 28 2017

Wiltermuth, Scott

When You Shouldn't Try to Dominate a Negotiation *Harvard Business Review Digital Articles* p2 Ag 27 2015

Wiltz, Roger

PLEASE PASS THE DZ *South Dakota Magazine* v33 no3 p96 S/O 2017

WILWOL, JOHN

They Deleted Their Kids *New York Times Book Review* p16 O 9 2016

Wilwood Disc Brakes (Company)

BRAKE DOWN E. Perkins color *Hot Rod* v70 no5 p78 My 2017

WIMAN, CHRISTIAN

Still Wilderness: WHAT ARE WE FEELING WHEN WE ARE FEELING JOY? AND WHERE INSIDE US DOES THAT FEELING RESIDE? *American Scholar* v86 no4 p36 Aut 2017

Wimbledon Championships

THE BEST OF RIVALS, THE BEST OF FRIENDS S. TIGNOR *Tennis* v53 no4 p60 Jl/Ag 2017

COURTSIDE CHRONiCLeS G. Dyer *New York Times Magazine* p50 Ag 27 2017

From POW to SW19 P. PETRA and E. MCGROGAN *Tennis* v52 no6 p70 N/D 2016

Guessing Game C. Evert *Tennis* v53 no4 p6 Jl/Ag 2017

Sport's Centre N. Pantic *Tennis* v53 no4 p10 Jl/Ag 2017

Top of His Game T. PERROTTA color *Weekly Standard* v22 no44 p37 Jl 31 2017

A Tradition Unlike Any Other E. McGrogan *Tennis* v53 no4 p58 Jl/Ag 2017

WIMBLEDON HOLDS SERVE R. A. BERENZ *TV Guide* v65 no27 p41 Je 26 2017

Wimbledon Championships—History

Eighth WONDER L. J. Wertheim color *Sports Illustrated* v127 no3 p58 Jl 24 2017

Wimmer, Daniela

Global atmospheric particle formation from CERN CLOUD measurements bibl graph map *Science* v354 no6316 p1119 D 2 2016

Wimmer, Ernst A.

Male sex in houseflies is determined by Mdmd, a paralog of the generic splice factor gene CWC22 bw color *Science* v356 no6338 p642 My 12 2017

WINANT, GABRIEL

BIRTH OF AN IMPERIAL NATION color *Nation* v304 no3 p27 Ja 30 2017

Winarsky, Norman

Why the Fail-Fast Approach Isn't Right for Breakthrough Ventures *Harvard Business Review Digital Articles* p2 N 6 2015

WINBERG, JOANN

Soup's On color *Backpacker* v45 no2 p36 Mr 2017

WINBERY, ANNETTE

ROAR OF THE CROWD *Texas Monthly* v45 no6 p10 Je 2017

Wincent, Joakim

We Recorded VCs' Conversations and Analyzed How Differently They Talk About Female Entrepreneurs *Harvard Business Review Digital Articles* p2 My 17 2017

WINCH, GUY

Solutions For the Solitary: Loneliness requires courage and altered perception to escape, but it is possible *Psychology Today* v50 no4 p32 Ag 2017

Winches

JAKE KUZYK T. Monterosso cartoon color *Snowboarder* v29 no4 p42 D 2016

Winchester, Philip

Out & About *TV Guide* v65 no19 p4 My 1 2017

Winchester, Simon

COLLEGE OF FELLOWS ANNUAL DINNER color *Canadian Geographic* v137 no1 p76 F 2017

Confronting China *New York Times Book Review* p13 Ja 1 2017

Empire of Tolerance *New York Times Book Review* p14 D 11 2016

The Nature of Catastrophe bw color *New York Review of Books* v64 no17 p16 N 9 2017

Winchester Ammunition Co.

A 20 FOR TOM P. Bourjaily cartoon color *Field & Stream* v121 no9 p28 Ap 2017

Winchester rifle

THE BIG 1-5-0 D. E. PETZAL and P. BOURJAILY color *Field & Stream* v121 no6 p64 N 2016

Winckler, Cecile

IN FULL BLOOM M. GUIDUCCI, M. CARLOS et al color *Vogue* v207 no6 p114 Je 2017

Wind, Yoram (Jerry)

3 Ways to Get Your Own Digital Platform *Harvard Business Review Digital Articles* p2 Jl 22 2016

7 Questions to Ask Before Your Next Digital Transformation *Harvard Business Review Digital Articles* p2 Jl 14 2016

How to Navigate a Digital Transformation *Harvard Business Review Digital Articles* p2 Je 22 2016

Investors Today Prefer Companies with Fewer Physical As sets *Harvard Business Review Digital Articles* p2 S 29 2016

To Go Digital, Leaders Have to Change Some Core Beliefs *Harvard Business Review Digital Articles* p2 Je 1 2016

What Airbnb, Uber, and Alibaba Have in Common *Harvard Business Review Digital Articles* p2 N 20 2014

What Apple, Lending Club, and AirBnB Know About Collaborating with Customers *Harvard Business Review Digital Articles* p2 Jl 3 2015

Why Are We Still Classifying Companies by Industry? *Harvard Business Review Digital Articles* p2 Ag 18 2016

BARBARESCO J. McINERNEY bw color *Esquire* p32 2017 Big-BlackBook

Wine & wine making—Management

Cru Cut B. Morton *Cincinnati Magazine* v50 no12 p104 S 2017

Wine & wine making—Sales & prices

FORGET STEMWARE. BEHOLD THE RISE OF WINE IN A CAN J. Kell color *Fortune* v174 no6 p10 N 1 2016

GIVE THE GIFT OF TIME color *Money* v45 no11 p15 D 2016

TAKE THAT, WINE SNOBS E. REYNOLDS *USA Today Magazine* v145 no2862 p58 Mr 2017

Wine, Elizabeth

DONOR-ADVISED FUNDS SOAR ALONG WITH MARKETS color *Forbes* v198 no7 p82 N 29 2016

Wine, Jesse

BRIGHT YOUNG ARTISTS *Interview* v46 no10 p106 D 2016/Ja 2017

Jesse WINE A. PEASLEY *Interview* v46 no10 p110 D 2016/Ja 2017

Wine bars—Evaluation

The Hot List P. POLLACK color *Chicago* v66 no5 p74 My 2017

THE OTTOLENGHI GUIDE TO EATING AND DRINKING YOUR WAY AROUND GEORGIA color *Conde Nast Traveler* v52 no9 p40 O 2017

Pop the corks! T. McNally color *New Orleans Magazine* v51 no8 p106 Je 2017

THE ULTIMATE NATU RAL WINE BAR H. Wallace color *Rodale's Organic Life* v3 no1 p50 Ja 2017

Wine bottles

IN THE FIELD I. Edwards color *Sunset* v239 no4 p10 O 2017

Large and in Charge M. A. ROSS color *Bon Appetit* v61 no12 p58 D 2016 /Jan2017

Wine cellars

BOTTLE SERVICE color *Architectural Digest* v73 no11 p130 N 2016

DEEP-SEA VINO N. Strochlic color *National Geographic* v231 no4 p22 Ap 2017

HOT MOD M. LAWLER color *Chicago* v66 no5 p32 My 2017

Wine coolers (Beverage)

A Cooler Wine Cooler A. Erace color *Bloomberg Businessweek* no4515 p62 Mr 20 2017

Wine festivals

12th annual LAWineFest *Los Angeles Magazine* v62 no9 p86 S 2017

2017 CINCINNATI INTERNATIONAL *Cincinnati Magazine* v50 no6 p124 Mr 2017

Can't-Miss Fall Food Festivals *Atlanta* v57 no5 p148 S 2017

DON'T MISS LIST: JUNE 2017 color *Sea Magazine* v109 no6 pCA-10 Je 2017

Explore & Play Regional Festivals & Events color *New Orleans Magazine* v51 no6 p127 Ap 2017

NEW NEXT *Texas Monthly* v45 no3 p187 Mr 2017

NORTH J. FROIS color map *Louisiana Life* v37 no4 p94 Mr/Ap 2017

Wine flavor & odor

Rosé All Day K. MASSICOT color *New Orleans Magazine* v51 no12 p166 O 2017

Wine glasses

Brilliant Uses for Pennies B. SPECKTOR *Reader's Digest* v188 no1125 p68 N 2016

Wine glasses—Evaluation

DAZZLE THEM color *House Beautiful* v158 no10 p21 D 2016/Ja 2017

Wine industry

See also
Wine stores

Here, Here! P. Guzmán color *Conde Nast Traveler* v52 no7 p14 Ag 2017

Wine industry—China

For Chandon in China, a Kick From Champagne? B. Einhorn graph *Bloomberg Businessweek* no4501 p21 N 28 2016

Wine industry—France

Bacchus Takes an Ice Bath in Bordeaux G. Collins, R. Ruitenberg et al color *Bloomberg Businessweek* no4522 p24 My 15 2017

Wine stores

EVERYDAY ROSÉ S. Schneider color *Sunset* v238 no5 p98 My 2017

A Real-Life Guide to Buying Wine M. A. ROSS color *Bon Appetit* v62 no7 p22 Jl 2017

Wine stores—Evaluation

THE BIG CELEBRATION *Indianapolis Monthly* p63 F 2017

A SHOP OF YOUR OWN S. Schneider color *Sunset* v238 no4 p98 Ap 2017

Wine tasting

LA SOCIAL bw color *Los Angeles Magazine* v62 no10 p93 O 2017

PINOT FREEZIO J. Spalding *Indianapolis Monthly* v40 no10 p41 Je 2017

Rosé All Day K. MASSICOT color *New Orleans Magazine* v51 no12 p166 O 2017

A SHOP OF YOUR OWN S. Schneider color *Sunset* v238 no4 p98 Ap 2017

WINE TIME K. MASSICOT color *New Orleans Magazine* v51 no1 p183 N 2016

WINEAPPLE, BRENDA

America Transformed *New York Times Book Review* p12 D 18 2016

THE ROMANCE OF REFORM bw *Nation* v304 no15 p32 My 8 2017

Wineries

GIFT GUIDE H. Marsh *South Dakota Magazine* v32 no4 p67 N/D 2016

LET'S GO WINETASTING N. BAUER *Washingtonian Magazine* v52 no8 p90 My 2017

Southern sippin' M. Rosano color *Canadian Geographic* v137 p16 2017 Travel

Wineries—California

LODI LEADS S. Schneider color *Sunset* v239 no3 p102 S 2017

Wineries—Evaluation

BEST OF THE WEST J. Chamberlain, J. Ritz et al color *Sunset* v238 no4 p17 Ap 2017

PINOT FREEZIO J. Spalding *Indianapolis Monthly* v40 no10 p41 Je 2017

RUNE with a VIEW N. AUSTIN *Arizona Highways* v93 no4 p50 Ap 2017

Trek and Toast T. BROWN color *Backpacker* p19 My 2017

Winery design & construction

Set in Stone A. KLIMOSKI *Architectural Record* v205 no10 p74 O 2017

Wines, Michael

Are We Heading Toward a New COLD WAR? *New York Times Upfront* v149 no3 p18 O 10 2016

Russia: Friend, Enemy, or Frenemy? With relations between the U.S. and Russia at their lowest point in decades, President Trump has called for improving ties. But can Russian President Vladimir Putin be trusted? *New York Times Upfront* v149 no12 p8 Ap 24 2017

Winfield, Charlie—Interviews

CHARLIE WINFIELD J. Chen color *Bloomberg Businessweek* no4506 p67 Ja 9 2017

Winfree, Erik

A cargo-sorting DNA robot color *Science* v357 no6356 p1112 S 15 2017

Winfrey, John

Physics education research and student development *Physics Today* v70 no2 p10 F 2017

Winfrey, Oprah, 1954-

Adventure Starts Here! N. McGOVERN color *O, The Oprah Magazine* p12 Je 2017

Artists color *Time* v189 no16/17 p40 My 1-8 2017

BEHIND THE LENS T. Stack color *Entertainment Weekly* no1462 p34 Ap 21 2017

Behind the Scenes color *O, The Oprah Magazine* p12 N 2017

BODY AND SOUL bw color *O, The Oprah Magazine* p100 Ja 2017

For the Love of Henrietta Z. Donaldson bw color *O, The Oprah Magazine* p28 My 2017

A GREAT AHHH-VENTURE color *O, The Oprah Magazine* p12 Jl 2017

HAPPILY UNMARRIED S. E. JAMISON color *Ebony* v72 no11 p66 S 2017

Here We Go! color *O, The Oprah Magazine* p17 Ja 2017

Here We Go! color *O, The Oprah Magazine* p17 Mr 2017

WINSOR, DANIEL
#Climbing Training color *Climbing* no352 p9 Ap 2017
Winsor, Lynn
Winning Ways E. Laase and T. Keith color *Sports Illustrated* v127 no2 p26 Jl 17 2017
Winstead, Mary Elizabeth
Mercy Street M. Logan *TV Guide* v65 no4 p37 Ja 16 2017
Winston, Andrew
The 10 Most Important Sustainable Business Stories from 2014 *Harvard Business Review Digital Articles* p2 D 19 2014
10 Sustainable Business Stories That Shaped 2015 *Harvard Business Review Digital Articles* p2 D 23 2015
6 Ways the North American Clean Economy Agreement Will Affect Business *Harvard Business Review Digital Articles* p2 Jl 6 2016
9 Sustainable Business Stories That Shaped 2016 *Harvard Business Review Digital Articles* p2 D 20 2016
The Ambitious Business Goals Aiming to Change the World *Harvard Business Review Digital Articles* p2 F 5 2015
The Business Investments That Freak People Out *Harvard Business Review Digital Articles* p2 My 6 2015
Business Is Taking Action on LGBT Rights. Will Climate Change Be Next? *Harvard Business Review Digital Articles* p2 My 9 2016
Can Walmart Get Us to Buy Sustainable Products? *Harvard Business Review Digital Articles* p2 F 24 2015
Coca-Cola Met Its Water Goals Early. Were They Too Easy? *Harvard Business Review Digital Articles* p2 S 9 2015
The Data Says Climate Change Could Cost Investors Trillions *Harvard Business Review Digital Articles* p2 Ap 14 2016
The Drop in Oil Prices Might Be Bad for Business *Harvard Business Review Digital Articles* p2 D 3 2014
ENERGY STRATEGY FOR THE C-SUITE color graph img *Harvard Business Review* v95 no1 p138 Ja/F 2017
How General Mills and Kellogg Are Tackling Greenhouse Gas Emissions *Harvard Business Review Digital Articles* p2 Je 1 2016
How Industrial Firms Invest in Renewable Energy, Affordably *Harvard Business Review Digital Articles* p2 Ag 5 2016
How Target Is Taking Sustainable Products Mainstream *Harvard Business Review Digital Articles* p2 Ag 4 2015
Hurricane Sandy's Lesson: Resilience Isn't Enough *Harvard Business Review Digital Articles* p2 O 29 2014
An Inside View of How LVMH Makes Luxury More Sustainable color *Harvard Business Review Digital Articles* p2 Ja 11 2017
Is the End of GE Capital Good News for Ecomagination? *Harvard Business Review Digital Articles* p2 Ap 22 2015
It's Time for Companies to Be Strategic About Energy *Harvard Business Review Digital Articles* p2 Je 14 2016
Keeping Up with the "Clean Label" Movement *Harvard Business Review Digital Articles* p2 O 30 2015
Leading in a World of Resource Constraints and Extreme Weather *Harvard Business Review Digital Articles* p2 Je 16 2015
Luxury Brands Can No Longer Ignore Sustainability *Harvard Business Review Digital Articles* p2 F 8 2016
Pepsi, United, and the Speed of Corporate Shame *Harvard Business Review Digital Articles* p2 Ap 12 2017
Rolling Back Fuel Efficiency Is a Bad Deal for Everyone—Including U.S. Carmakers *Harvard Business Review Digital Articles* p2 Mr 17 2017
Sustainable Business Will Move Ahead With or Without Trump's Support *Harvard Business Review Digital Articles* p2 N 19 2016
Trump's Climate Rollback Will Hurt the Economy, Not Help It *Harvard Business Review Digital Articles* p2 Mr 29 2017
The U.S.-China Climate Goals Should be More Aggressive *Harvard Business Review Digital Articles* p2 N 12 2014
What Business Leaders Need to Know About the Paris Climate Conference *Harvard Business Review Digital Articles* p2 D 1 2015
What VW Didn't Understand About Trust *Harvard Business Review Digital Articles* p2 S 23 2015
Why the Keystone Pipeline Is the Wrong U.S. Energy Debate *Harvard Business Review Digital Articles* p2 Ja 30 2015
Will Today's Devastating Weather Change Business the Way Hurricane Katrina Did? *Harvard Business Review Digital Articles* p2 S 13 2017

WINSTON, DIANE
TWO SIDES OF THE SAME COIN color *Tricycle: The Buddhist Review* v26 no3 p60 Spr 2017
Winston, Fan
Coming Into Focus bw color *Conde Nast Traveler* v52 no3 p90 Mr 2017
Winston, Hella
Make America Make Again color *Foreign Affairs* v96 no1 p114 Ja/F 2017
Winston, Kimberly
Clashes over security at Jerusalem Temple Mount *Christian Century* v134 no17 p14 Ag 16 2017
HUMANIST PROFILE *Humanist* v77 no5 p2 S/O 2017
Interfaith support rises along with attacks color *Christian Century* v134 no7 p12 Mr 29 2017
Most of the unaffiliated just "stopped believing," according to new study graph *Christian Century* v133 no22 p16 O 26 2016
Religious Freedom Act also protects atheists *Christian Century* v134 no2 p15 Ja 18 2017
Sanctuary churches, cities may face consequences from federal authorities color *Christian Century* v134 no9 p13 Ap 26 2017
Winston, Tod
BIRDING *Audubon* v119 no1 p44 Spr 2017
Winter
    See also
    Automobile driving in winter
    Winter storms
30 Cool Things About Winter A. SILEN color *National Geographic Kids* no475 p22 N 2017
Ask Martha color *Martha Stewart Living* no271 p52 Ja/F 2017
BROWN UNIVERSITY D. KARCZYNSKI and G. BETHGE color *Outdoor Life* v224 no2 p28 F/Mr 2017
Christmas in New England E. Stimson *Yankee* v80 no6 p35 N/D 2016
Cisco Time K. MILLGATE *Idaho Magazine* v17 no1 p18 Ja 2017
COZY UP TO THIS R. DOLGIN *Martha Stewart Living* no268 p48 O 2016
DON'T BE DENIED *Boating World* v38 no3 p48 Mr 2017
Double Vision K. CORDES color *Climbing* no355 p26 Ag 2017
Gather color *Rodale's Organic Life* v2 no7 p15 D 2016/Ja 2017
Get Your House in Shape This Winter K. Close color *Money* v46 no1 p32 Ja/F 2017
Get Yourself Outside This Winter S. ECKELBERRY *Parks & Recreation* v52 no1 p8 Ja 2017
Holidays on the Square *South Dakota Magazine* v32 no4 p99 N/D 2016
Live Your Best Life color *O, The Oprah Magazine* p25 D 2016
On our radar M. Rosano, N. Walker et al color *Canadian Geographic* v135 no6 p12 D 2015
The Owl and the Photographer J. Bogo *Audubon* v118 no6 p48 Wint 2016
PERFECTLY Seasoned J. BREWSTER color *Cabin Living* p44 Je 2017
The Popular Mechanics WINTER OUTFITTER color *Popular Mechanics* p50 N 2017
Snow Day J. Youngerman and L. A. Miller bw *Art in America* v105 no4 p55 Ap 2017
The Snow People S. LOCKLEAR *Idaho Magazine* v17 no1 p27 Ja 2017
The Ultimate Winter Adventure Guide color *Conde Nast Traveler* v51 no11 p41 D 2016
Waiting on Winter A. J. BARTELS color *Nebraska Life* v20 no6 p20 N/D 2016
Wild Goose Chase J. DAVIS *Idaho Magazine* v17 no1 p21 Ja 2017
YAY WINTER! J. LINDSEY bw cartoon color *Bicycling* v58 no1 p30 Ja/F 2017
Winter, Amos
What Engineering a Reverse Innovation Looks Like *Harvard Business Review Digital Articles* p2 N 4 2015
Winter, Ariel, 1998-
BEHIND THE SCENES WITH Ariel Winter color *Seventeen* v75 no11 p10 N 2016
BODY CONFIDENCE SPECIAL color *Seventeen* v75 no11 p12 N 2016
Winter, Ariel, 1998—Interviews

KEEPING QUIET color *Seventeen* v75 no11 p70 N 2016

Winter, Brent

Blood Family *Publishers Weekly* v264 no34 p96 Ag 21 2017

Winter, Brian

Brazil's Never-Ending Corruption Crisis color *Foreign Affairs* v96 no3 p87 My/Je 2017

Winter, Caroline

COMIC TRIP color *Bloomberg Businessweek* no4516 p58 Mr 27 2017

Innovation: Needle Grinder color *Bloomberg Businessweek* no4531 p21 Jl 24 2017

Movers color graph *Bloomberg Businessweek* no4522 p13 My 15 2017

The Nestlé Bottled Water Cycle cartoon color *Bloomberg Businessweek* no4539 p56 S 25 2017

POWER WRAP color *Bloomberg Businessweek* no4505 p74 D 26 2016

SHE SELLS SEA SHELLS color *Bloomberg Businessweek* no4497 p68 O 31 2016

Some Cities Want Their Immigrants to Vote *Bloomberg Businessweek* no4497 p27 O 31 2016

We Have Lift Off! color diag *Bloomberg Businessweek* no4520 p67 My 1 2017

Winter, Clemens

Cognition-mediated evolution of low-quality floral nectars bibl graph *Science* v355 no6320 p1 Ja 6 2017

WINTER, ELIZABETH

play leads the way color *Yoga Journal* p36 2017 Special Issue

Winter, Jay

THE GENESIS OF 'GENOCIDE' *MHQ: Quarterly Journal of Military History* v29 no3 p17 Spr 2017

Winter, Kathleen

The Talking Dead M. DEAN color *Walrus* v14 no8 p61 O 2017

Winter, Kristy A.

Promoting human rights through science color *Science* v357 no6359 p34 O 6 2017

WINTER, MARTEN

Harmonizing Biodiversity Conservation and Productivity in the Context of Increasing Demands on Landscapes graph *BioScience* v66 no10 p890 O 1 2016

Planning for the Future of Urban Biodiversity: A Global Review of City-Scale Initiatives *BioScience* v67 no4 p332 Ap 2017

Synthesis Centers as Critical Research Infrastructure *BioScience* v67 no8 p750 Ag 2017

Winter, Meaghan

A MATTER OF LIFE & DEATH color *Essence* v48 no6 p106 O 2017

Winter, Sebastian E.

Paneth cells secrete lysozyme via secretory autophagy during bacterial infection of the intestine color diag *Science* v357 no6355 p1047 S 8 2017

Winter, W. Chris

The Most Important Hours of YOUR NIGHT color *O, The Oprah Magazine* p73 Jl 2017

The Sleep-Weight Connection color *Better Nutrition* v79 no10 p56 O 2017

WINTER, W. CHRISTOPHER

THE EXCHANGE cartoon chart color graph *Men's Health* v32 no9 p16 N 2017

Winter, York

Cognition-mediated evolution of low-quality floral nectars bibl graph *Science* v355 no6320 p1 Ja 6 2017

Winter festivals

CALENDAR OF EVENTS *Idaho Magazine* v17 no1 p58 Ja 2017

Events *Virginia Living* v15 no2 p33 F 2017

FUN FESTIVALS IN CABIN COUNTRY color *Cabin Living* p13 Mr 2017

LIGHTING UP REYKJAVÍK J. GOTTLIEB *Iceland Review* v55 no2 p6 Mr/Ap 2017

TINLEY PARK J. REESE color *Chicago* v65 no12 p37 D 2016

winter wonderlands L. BLEIBERG *Better Homes & Gardens* v94 no11 p166 N 2016

Winter gardening

Your CHECKLIST E. Jardina color *Sunset* v237 no5 p48 N 2016

Winter resorts

See also

Ski resorts

Yes, You Can Ski and Ride in October B. E. CLARK bw *Conde Nast Traveler* v51 no10 p172 N 2016

Winter solstice

Let the Stones Stand Again R. Erganbright *Sky & Telescope* v133 no4 p84 Ap 2017

Winter sports

See also

Skis & skiing

Snowshoes & snowshoeing

362" N. Paumgarten color graph *Powder* p68 S 2017

597" A. Barronian bw *Powder* p62 S 2017

FOR GENERATIONS D. Taylor color *Powder* v45 no3 p40 N 2016

Frigid Embrace: A Backcountry Winter Introduction J. DALME *Idaho Magazine* v16 no10 p49 Jl 2017

How Much Do You Love Your Skis? color *Powder* p136 S 2017

LUCAS STÅL-MADISON S. Davis color *Powder* v46 no2 p92 O 2017

MASHED M. Hansen color *Powder* v45 no3 p140 N 2016

Prep Your Legs for Winter L. BEDOSKY color *Men's Health* v32 no9 p54 N 2017

SHOOTING GALLERY color *Powder* p20 S 2017

Stiff AF color *Powder* p87 S 2017

What in the World? *National Geographic Kids* no466 p35 D 2016/Ja 2017

Winter storms

Mitigating coastal landslide damage B. Leshchinsky, M. J. Olsen et al color *Science* v357 no6355 p981 S 8 2017

Winter vacations

we asked you answered R. Bridge, A. Reynolds et al color *Cabin Living* p8 D 2016

Winterbottom, Michael, 1961-

The Trip to Spain C. Nashawaty color *Entertainment Weekly* no1478 / 1479 p85 Ag 18-25 2017

Winter—Equipment & supplies

GET KOSELIG! L. F. Prater *Successful Farming* v115 no2 p64 F 2017

Winterer, Caroline

REREADING THE ENLIGHTENMENT R. Lerner *Claremont Review of Books* v17 no2 p58 Spr 2017

Wintermute, Carol

HUMANIST PROFILE *Humanist* v76 no6 p2 N/D 2016

WINTERS, ALISON ACOSTA

The Cronyism Primer: Corporate welfare goes back at least to the Boston Tea Party *American Conservative* v16 no4 p34 Jl/Ag 2017

WINTERS, DAN

THE MAN IN THE BOX color *Wired* v25 no5 p56 My 2017

Winters, Dean

THE GREAT OZ A. Westenfeld color *Esquire* p22 N 2017

Winters, Emma

CHRISTIAN POETRY VS 'CHRISTIAN POETRY' bw *America* v217 no4 p46 Ag 21 2017

WINTERS, JONATHAN

Quotable Quotes bw color *Reader's Digest* v190 no1132 p140 Jl/Ag 2017

Winters, Marcus A.

For teachers, a better kind of pension plan graph il *Phi Delta Kappan* v99 no2 p32 O 2017

Winters, Michael Sean

Schools ... with superpowers color diag *U.S. Catholic* v82 no3 p12 Mr 2017

Winterson, Jeanette, 1959-

FALSTAFF: Give Me Life bw *New York Times Book Review* p1 Ap 23 2017

The Holly, the Ivy and the Sherry Trifle J. ROSENSTRACH *New York Times Book Review* p7 D 25 2016

Interiority Complex *New York Times Book Review* p21 O 23 2016

Wintersteen, Jeffrey

Al Rashediah Stud [Cover story] *Arabian Horse World* v57 no1 p105 O 2016

Arabian MEADOWS *Arabian Horse World* v57 no8 p1 My 2017

ARABIANS LTD *Arabian Horse World* v57 no3 p1 D 2016

Arabian U.S. Open central park show *Arabian Horse World* v57 no2 p90 N 2016

Retro Elegance B. Ankosko and C. Crowley color *Sound & Vision* v82 no5 p20 Je 2017

TURNIN' THE INSIDE OUT R. SABIN *Sound & Vision* v82 no6 p8 Jl/Ag 2017

Wireless technology in the home

See also

Smart speakers (Wireless technology)

WHEN YOUR STUFF SPIES ON YOU J. J. Roberts color *Fortune* v175 no7 p26 Je 1 2017

Wi-Fi Alliance introduces a certification program for new smart home construction M. BROWN color diag *PCWorld* v35 no7 p44 Jl 2017

Wireless telecommunication services industry—Africa

Mobile Carriers Start Hanging Up on Africa L. Prinsloo and J. Kew cartoon *Bloomberg Businessweek* no4530 p18 Jl 17 2017

Wirestone, Max

The Astonishing Mistakes of Dahlia Moss: A Dahlia Moss Mystery *Publishers Weekly* v264 no3 p43 Ja 16 2017

Wiretapping—United States

The Week color *National Review* v69 no6 p4 Ap 3 2017

Wirka, Robert C.

Circulating peptide prevents preeclampsia diag *Science* v357 no6352 p643 Ag 18 2017

WIRSING, AARON J.

Conserving the World's Megafauna and Biodiversity: The Fierce Urgency of Now *BioScience* v67 no3 p197 Mr 2017

Making a New Dog? *BioScience* v67 no4 p374 Ap 2017

Saving the World's Terrestrial Megafauna color *BioScience* v66 no10 p807 O 1 2016

Wirtschafter, Jacob

Egyptian Copts finally fulfilling dream of Jerusalem pilgrimage color *Christian Century* v134 no9 p15 Ap 26 2017

Egypt's Copts face rising fears, divisions color *Christian Century* v134 no10 p14 My 10 2017

To promote diversity, Egypt plans to restore Alexandria synagogue color *Christian Century* v134 no18 p13 Ag 30 2017

Wirtz, Frederic

Making Matrix Organizations Actually Work *Harvard Business Review Digital Articles* p2 Mr 1 2016

Wirtz, M.

Observation of a large-scale anisotropy in the arrival directions of cosmic rays above 8 × 1018 cV *Science* v357 no6357 p1266 S 22 2017

Wirtz, Rocky

WHY We LOVE CHICAGO bw cartoon color *Chicago* v66 no3 p75 Mr 2017

Wirtz, Sarah

De-extinction, nomenclature, and the law color *Science* v356 no6342 p1016 Je 9 2017

Wirtz International (Company)

Groundbreakers color *Architectural Digest* v74 no1 p146 Ja 2017

LUSH LIFE A. KORKEAKIVI color *Architectural Digest* v74 no1 p190 Ja 2017

Wirzba, Norman

Waking up to the Anthropocene [Cover story] color *Christian Century* v134 no20 p22 S 27 2017

Way of Love: Recovering the Heart of Christianity M. Z. Nelson color *Christian Century* v133 no25 p38 D 7 2016

Wisch, Ali

The Art of Sailing color *Sail* v47 no12 p34 D 2016

From the Atlantic to the Pacific color *Sail* v48 no5 p17 My 2017

GEAR UP FOR SUMMER color *Sail* v48 no7 p28 Jl 2017

HOLIDAY GIFT GUIDE color *Sail* v47 no12 p22 D 2016

No Man's Land: SHARPENING SAILING SKILLS ON A WOMEN-ONLY COURSE color map *Sail* v48 no8 p41 Ag 2017

See Change, Change Sea color *Sail* v48 no3 p10 Mr 2017

Stormy Seas color *Sail* v48 no2 p18 F 2017

Wisconsin. Dept. of Natural Resources

Communities Take the Lead in Battling Frac Sand Mines E. Ness color *Progressive* v81 no5 p19 Je/Jl 2017

Wisconsin. Supreme Court

Contempt for Democracy R. CONNIFF bw *Progressive* v81 no6 p6 Ag/S 2017

Wisconsin—Politics & government

HOW TO DEFLATE A DEMAGOGUE M. BAUERLEIN and C. JEFFERY *Mother Jones* v42 no6 p4 N/D 2017

Iron Man T. MURPHY bw *Mother Jones* v42 no6 p32 N/D 2017

Wisconsin—Politics & government—21st century

PLEA TO HIGH COURT: KNOW YOUR LIMITS S. FORBES color *Forbes* v200 no5 p17 N 14 2017

Wisdom

See also

Judgment (Psychology)

22 AVOIDABLE ON-THE-WATER MISTAKE D. T. CLARKE *Boating World* v38 no3 p54 Mr 2017

400 Years of Wisdom B. GREGORY bw *Men's Health* v32 no5 p12 Je 2017

What to Do When You Don't Know What's Next D. Tarchin Phillips color *Tricycle: The Buddhist Review* v26 no4 p40 Summ 2017

You Say You Want a Resolution... M. BECK color *O, The Oprah Magazine* p34 Ja 2017

Wisdom of the Crowd (TV program)

Wisdom of the Crowd A. Bacle, D. Coggan et al color *Entertainment Weekly* no1482/1483 p34 S 22 2017

Wise, Aaron

A transcription factor hierarchy defines an environmental stress response network diag *Science* v354 no6312 p598 N 4 2016

Wise, Chloe

SHE CAME FROM INSTAGRAM J. PRESSLER img *New York* v50 no8 p52 Ap 17 2017

WISE, DAVID

The Fake Russian *Smithsonian* v47 no7 p38 N 2016

Wise, Deb

Cupcakes à la Mode color *Southern Living* v52 no4 p144 Ap 2017

Easy as Peach Pie color *Southern Living* v52 no6 p138 Je 2017

EGGS BREAK OUT color *Health* v31 no1 p92 Ja 2017

Fried Delights color *Southern Living* v52 no6 p134 Je 2017

Pomegranate Power color *Health* v30 no10 p133 D 2016

Red, White & Berry Bars color *Southern Living* v52 no7 p124 Jl 2017

RICH & SKINNY color *Health* v31 no8 p102 O 2017

SUPERFOOD SWEETS color *Health* v31 no9 p98 N 2017

You Made Cranberry Sauce. Now What? color *Health* v30 no9 p144 N 2016

Wise, DeWanda

DeWanda Wise D. L. D'oyley color *Essence* v47 no11 p42 Mr 2017

Wise, Don

Louisiana Custom Closets: Don Wise P. Marquis *New Orleans Homes & Lifestyles* v20 no3 p96 Summ 2017

Wise, Frank W.

Spatiotemporal mode-locking in multimode fiber lasers color *Science* v357 no6359 p94 O 6 2017

Wise, Jeff

Better Typing Through Mind Control color *Bloomberg Businessweek* no4537 p74 S 11 2017

You Are Here (So Buy Something) *Bloomberg Businessweek* no4536 p24 S 4 2017

WISE, KATHY

A Fair to Remember *D: The Magazine of Dallas* v43 no10 p7 O 2016

The Lawyer, the Wife, and the Wardrobe *D: The Magazine of Dallas* v43 no10 p68 O 2016

Wise, Melonee

A Job Plan for Robots and Humans T. Simonite color *MIT Technology Review* v120 no4 p34 Jl/Ag 2017

Wise, Michael D.

Producing Predators: Wolves, Work, and Conquest in the Northern Rockies S. E. McFarland *American Indian Quarterly* v41 no3 p289 Summ 2017

Wise, Paul H.

Civil War & the Global Threat of Pandemics *Daedalus* v146 no4 p71 Fall 2017

The Epidemiologic Challenge to the Conduct of Just War: Confronting Indirect Civilian Casualties of War *Daedalus* v146 no1 p139 Wint 2017

Wise Solutions Inc.

ICELAND'S WISE SOLUTION *Iceland Review* v54 no6 p120 N/D 2016

Wiseman, Frederick, 1930-

BOOKISH A. LANE color *New Yorker* v93 no28 p72 S 18 2017

Wolfe, Matt
The Handshake color *New Republic* v248 no8/9 p36 Ag/S 2017
The Last Unknown Man color *New Republic* v247 no12 p40 D 2016
WOLFE, MIKE
50 Reasons to Love Being 50+ *AARP: The Magazine* v59 no4A p61 Je/Jl 2016
WOLFE, MK
Department of Wit Paging Dr. Malaprop! cartoon *Reader's Digest* v190 no1134 p19 O 2017
Wolfe, Scott
Managing Police Departments Post-Ferguson *Harvard Business Review Digital Articles* p2 S 13 2016
Wolfe, Suzanne M.
St. Augustine's love life K. Gilger *America* v216 no7 p46 Ap 3 2017
WOLFE, TOM
Scott Kelly color *Vanity Fair* v59 no9 p222 S 2017
Wolfe, Tom, 1931-
The Man in White D. BROWNE bw color *Rolling Stone* no1289 p24 Je 15 2017
Origins of Speech E. POWERS *Weekly Standard* v22 no6 p30 O 17 2016
We're Only Human A. Ferguson *Commentary* v142 no4 p46 N 2016
We're Only Human *Commentary* v141 no9 p1 N 2016
Wolfert, Paula
TIMELESS M. True color *Sunset* v238 no2 p82 F 2017
Wolff, Alexander
Frank Deford 1938-2017 color *Sports Illustrated* v126 no16 p19 Je 5 2017
THE REVOLUTION [WILL NOT BE TELEVISED] chart color diag *Sports Illustrated* v125 no19 p112 D 12 2016
Wolff Whistles color *Sports Illustrated* v125 no13 p14 O 17 2016
WOLFF, CARLO
At Home Anywhere color *Downbeat* v84 no1 p79 Ja 2017
The Declaration Of Musical Independence/Proximity color *Downbeat* v83 no12 p70 D 2016
ELEW Rejoins 'Jazz Republic' color *Downbeat* v83 no11 p19 N 2016
Jewish Jazz bw *Downbeat* v84 no3 p66 Mr 2017
Mightier Than the Sword color *Downbeat* v84 no4 p55 Ap 2017
A Trail of Cedars bw *Downbeat* v84 no9 p70 S 2017
Voices of a Golden Age color *Downbeat* v84 no10 p74 O 2017
Wolff, Catherine
An Ordinary Sunday [Cover story] color *Commonweal* v144 no15 p11 S 22 2017
Wolff, Daniel
The Connected Mysteries of Bob Dylan, Woody Guthrie, and the Calumet Massacre of 1913 J. Zinoman *New York Times Book Review* p58 Je 4 2017
Grown-Up Anger: The Connected Mysteries of Bob Dylan, Woody Guthrie, and the Calumet Massacre of 1913 *Publishers Weekly* v264 no17 p81 Ap 24 2017
WOLFF, EARL
I Survived! [Cover story] *Reader's Digest* v189 no1128 p62 Mr 2017
Wolff, Gerhard
Submillihertz magnetic spectroscopy performed with a nanoscale quantum sensor diag *Science* v356 no6340 p832 My 26 2017
Wolff, Larry
Signor Tambourrossini [Cover story] color *New York Review of Books* v64 no15 p17 O 12 2017
Wolff, Mark
THE EXCHANGE color graph *Men's Health* v32 no7 p16 S 2017
WOLFF, SUSANNA
IS THIS HYGGE? cartoon *New Yorker* v92 no49 p43 F 13 2017
WOLFFE, DANIELLE
WOMEN WITHOUT PAROLE color *Nation* v305 no1 p21 Jl 3 2017
Wolfgang (Performer)
Mozart: Le Nozze di Figaro F. Colin *Opera News* v81 no6 p51 D 2016
Wolfhard, Finn
THE KIDS OF STRANGER THINGS T. Stack, A. Bacle et al color *Entertainment Weekly* no1444/1445 p32 D 16 2016

Stranger Things 2 T. Stack, A. Bacle et al color *Entertainment Weekly* no1482/1483 p100 S 22 2017
Wolfinger, Russ
Predicting human olfactory perception from chemical features of odor molecules bibl diag graph *Science* v355 no6327 p820 F 24 2017
Wolfisberg, Raphael
Mouse models of acute and chronic hepacivirus infection *Science* v357 no6347 p204 Jl 14 2017
Wolfish, Mosheh
Defending the State *Commentary* v140 no2 p11 S 2015
WOLFKILL, KIM
EDITOR'S LETTER color *Road & Track* v68 no5 p31 D 2016/Ja 2017
EDITOR'S LETTER color *Road & Track* v68 no8 p20 My 2017
EDITOR'S LETTER *Road & Track* v68 no9 p186 Je 2017
EDITOR'S LETTER *Road & Track* v69 no2 p20 S 2017
EDITOR'S LETTER *Road & Track* v69 no3 p24 O 2017
EDITOR'S LETTER *Road & Track* v69 no4 p20 N 2017
MISSION ACCOMPLISHED [Cover story] chart color *Road & Track* v69 no1 p30 Ag 2017
Wolf OR-7 (Poem)
Wolf OR-7 N. Diaz *Orion Magazine* v36 no1 p57 Ja/F 2017
Wolford, Jerry
sun power [Cover story] S. FREED color *Cabin Living* p34 O 2017
Wolfson, Jordan—Exhibitions
A HISTORY OF VIOLENCE N. FREEMAN bw color *ARTnews* v116 no1 p20 Spr 2017
Wolfsthal, Jon
The political and military vulnerability of America's land-based nuclear missiles bibl *Bulletin of the Atomic Scientists* v73 no3 p150 My 2017
Wolinsky, Howard
'Specimens' goes behind the scenes color *Science News* v191 no7 p28 Ap 15 2017
WOLK, DOUGLAS
Dystopias, Fantasies, Memoirs *New York Times Book Review* p18 Ja 1 2017
Graphic Novels *New York Times Book Review* p50 Je 4 2017
Wild in the Streets *New York Times Book Review* p23 O 16 2016
Wolk, Lauren
Wolf Hollow color *Publishers Weekly* v263 no49 p82 D 7 2016
Wolk, Steven
Educating students for an outdated world bw color *Phi Delta Kappan* v99 no2 p46 O 2017
Wolke, Conrad T.
Spectroscopic snapshots of the proton-transfer mechanism in water bibl diag graph *Science* v354 no6316 p1131 D 2 2016
Wolkoff, Julia
JONATHAN GARDNER cartoon *Art in America* v104 no11 p124 D 2016
JORDAN KASEY color *Art in America* v105 no5 p126 My 2017
KEEGAN MONAGHAN color *Art in America* v104 no10 p150 N 2016
LESLIE HEWITT: IN THE STUDIO color *Art in America* v105 no8 p108 S 2017
Wollan, Malia
ARKS OF THE APOCALYPSE *New York Times Magazine* p34 Jl 16 2017
Brand new HUE *New York Times Magazine* p51 O 9 2016
How to Get Rid of Lice *New York Times Magazine* p19 My 14 2017
How to Handle a Sleepwalker *New York Times Magazine* p19 Ag 13 2017
How to Knot a Cherry Stem With Your Tongue *New York Times Magazine* p28 Je 25 2017
How to Lament diag *New York Times Magazine* p25 Ag 6 2017
How to Pull Down a Statue *New York Times Magazine* p32 S 17 2017
Wolly, Brian
THE BIG QUESTION cartoon *Atlantic* v319 no5 p96 Je 2017
Wolman, David
Mark My Word bw *Weekly Standard* v22 no25 p36 Mr 6 2017
Surf's SUP! color *Bloomberg Businessweek* no4518 p76 Ap 10 2017

Canadian Voices, Global Bestsellers E. NAWOTKA color *Publishers Weekly* v264 no41 p20 O 9 2017

Deborah Levy M. Rich color *Current Biography* v78 no5 p49 My 2017

Empire Building J. MCCARTNEY color *Publishers Weekly* v264 no21 p45 My 22 2017

The Fiction of Everyday Life E. ALTER color *Publishers Weekly* v264 no8 p52 F 20 2017

Generation Nomad [Cover story] A. Shamim color *Glamour* no8 p148 Ag 2017

GOING PLACES color *Harper's Bazaar* no3657 p169 O 2017

How to Reach Across the Aisle? Get a Dog L. Hartman bw *Publishers Weekly* v263 no44 p(Sp)12 O 31 2016

An Immigrant Experience A. GROSS color *Publishers Weekly* v263 no50 p41 D 5 2016

INDIAN SUMMER D. Beal color *Vogue* v207 no6 p130 Je 2017

A Jane Austen Kind of Guy: I GET IT THAT WOMEN FIND MY AFFINITY FOR THEIR WRITER INTRUSIVE, BUT HER WORLD HAS MUCH TO OFFER MEN, TOO W. DERESIEWICZ *American Scholar* v86 no4 p84 Aut 2017

Jennifer Egan *New York Times Book Review* p8 O 1 2017

Louise Penny *New York Times Book Review* p7 Ag 27 2017

Maggie Nelson D. Kiper color *Current Biography* v78 no5 p68 My 2017

'MY CURIOSITY FLARES UP WHEN I HEAR ABOUT...' B. BETHUNE color *Maclean's* v129 no45 p51 N 14 2016

"My face told me to stop partying" *Glamour* v115 no6 p76 Je 2017

THE SEEKERS R. Makkai color *O, The Oprah Magazine* p96 O 2017

SURVIVAL STORIES S. CORBETT color *Publishers Weekly* v264 no5 p24 Ja 30 2017

Susan Burton J. HERBST *Los Angeles Magazine* v62 no9 p92 S 2017

A WOMAN BY THE NAME OF Sedona L. S. HEIDINGER *Arizona Highways* v93 no11 p48 N 2017

Women authors—Biography

Dorit Rabinyan C. Mari color *Current Biography* v78 no9 p71 S 2017

Women authors—Interviews

Annalena McAfee, Author of Hame, on Her Love Letter to Scotland S. Gutierrez color *British Heritage Travel* v38 no5 p71 S/O 2017

Ayelet Waldman *New York Times Book Review* p6 Ja 22 2017

Battling Depression with LSD C. JUMPERTZ color *Publishers Weekly* v263 no52 p110 D 19 2016

CATE LINEBERRY: Be Free or Die K. DONOHUE *Prologue* v49 no2 p26 Summ 2017

Elizabeth WURTZEL L. Phair *Interview* v47 no5 p26 Je/Jl 2017

The Freedoms of Fiction A. Domestico bw *Commonweal* v144 no8 p26 My 5 2017

How Introverts Can Make the Most of Conferences D. Rousmaniere *Harvard Business Review Digital Articles* p2 O 9 2015

MAKING HISTORY S. Wildman color *Washingtonian Magazine* v52 no7 p147 Ap 2017

PW Talks with Sara Galindo L. Ahuile color *Publishers Weekly* v264 no23 p15 Je 5 2017

Women authors—Travel

'Never such a thing as arrival' B. BETHUNE color *Maclean's* v129 no43 p47 O 31 2016

Women automobile drivers

Saudi Women In the Driver's Seat T. John color *Time* v190 no14 p10 O 9 2017

Women automobile racing drivers

Amazing Race S. Schrobsdorff color *Sports Illustrated* v126 no11 p106 Ap 17-24 2017

Danica Patrick S. 1STALL *Indianapolis Monthly* v40 no11 p21 Jl 2017

DRIVER AVAILABLE J. Dean color *Bloomberg Businessweek* no4536 p58 S 4 2017

Women baseball players

Angel McCoughtry J. Crelin color *Current Biography* v78 no6 p64 Je 2017

OUT OF BOUNDS A. OKEOWO cartoon *New Yorker* v93 no27 p34 S 11 2017

Women basketball coaches

PAT SUMMITT E. WEIL *New York Times Magazine* p60 D 25 2016

Women basketball players

CAPPIE PONDEXTER H. MITCHELL color *Chicago* v66 no8 p46 Ag 2017

For the Record color *Time* v190 no10/11 p9 S 18 2017

Nneka Ogwumike B. Muteba color *Current Biography* v78 no8 p68 Ag 2017

Tina Charles M. Hagan color *Current Biography* v78 no5 p18 My 2017

Women basketball players—Attitudes

American Voices Nneka Ogwumike D. Greene and T. Keith color *Sports Illustrated* v125 no12 p20 O 10 2016

Women biologists

   See also

     Women microbiologists

Engineering better organs A. Witze color *Science News* v192 no6 p26 O 14 2017

Women boxers

The Good Fight color *O, The Oprah Magazine* p90 Jl 2017

Women broadcasters

The Voices of Truth E. Mahaney color *Glamour* v115 no5 p179 My 2017

Women capitalists & financiers

Beware the Gender Investing Gap S. Krawcheck color *Glamour* v115 no2 p74 F 2017

SURPRISE, SURPRISE WOMEN ARE OUTPERFORMING MEN A. Gumbs graph *Black Enterprise* v47 no7 p18 My/Je 2017

Women caregivers

The Social and etalk's Lainey Lui Turns Caregiver for Her Mother M. Sponagle color *Maclean's* v130 no9 p36 O 2017

Women cartoonists—United States

Vera Brosgol J. Crelin *Current Biography* v78 no8 p13 Ag 2017

Women cat owners

Cat Ladies, Unite! [Cover story] J. Lance color *Glamour* v114 no11 p45 N 2016

Women celebrities

Braless Nation [Cover story] K. Branch bw color *Glamour* v114 no11 p48 N 2016

These Are Your Sexual Rights C. ESPOSITO, N. GLASER et al color *Glamour* v114 no7 p94 Jl 2016

Velvet for Day color *Glamour* v114 no11 p184 N 2016

Women chief executive officers

BOXED IN J. Wieczner, K. Bellstrom et al color diag *Fortune* v176 no5 p86 O 1 2017

Carly Fiorina's Legacy as CEO of Hewlett Packard B. Tabrizi *Harvard Business Review Digital Articles* p2 S 25 2015

DOMINIQUE RACCAH J. MILLIOT color *Publishers Weekly* v263 no52 p20 D 19 2016

FORTUNE'S MPW VIPs C. Leaf color *Fortune* v176 no5 p10 O 1 2017

Lots of Companies Still Have No Senior Executives Who Are Women S. G. Carmichael color graph *Harvard Business Review Digital Articles* p2 Mr 8 2017

MOST POWERFUL WOMEN K. Bellstrom, B. Kowitt et al color *Fortune* v176 no5 p54 O 1 2017

NOT SO DUMB BLONDE color *Women's Health* v14 no4 p30 My 2017

THE QUEEN OF POP [Cover story] B. Kowitt, K. Bellstrom et al color diag *Fortune* v176 no5 p70 O 1 2017

Research: How Female CEOs Actually Get to the Top S. Dillard and V. Lipschitz *Harvard Business Review Digital Articles* p2 N 6 2014

Stephanie Klasky-Gamer M. WAKIM *Los Angeles Magazine* v62 no9 p96 S 2017

TECH TAKEOVER IN TOYLAND M. Lev-ram, K. Bellstrom et al color diag *Fortune* v176 no5 p76 O 1 2017

THE VALLEY'S FAVORITE BRITISH IMPORT L. Rao color *Fortune* v174 no6 p46 N 7 2016

Where Are the Women? A. Ignatius *Harvard Business Review* v94 no11 p12 N 2016

Women chief executive officers—United States

How the West Was Won D. M. EWALT and W. BALDWIN color *Forbes* v199 no6 p44 Je 13 2017

SUE DESMOND-HELLMANN color *Bloomberg Businessweek*

no4503 p76 D 12 2016

Women chief executive officers—United States—Interviews

"DON'T TRY TO PROTECT THE PAST": A CONVERSATION WITH IBM CEO GINNI ROMETTY A. IGNATIUS color graph img *Harvard Business Review* v95 no4 p126 Jl/Ag 2017

Women choreographers

60 Years Ago This Month *Dance Magazine* v91 no4 p67 Ap 2017

CAROLYN ADAMS R. Berman *Dance Magazine* v90 no12 p50 D 2016

One for the Ladies: Cincinnati Ballet shows even more love for women choreographers this season C. Thompson *Dance Magazine* v91 no9 p18 S 2017

What's on Your Mind? *Dance Magazine* v91 no7 p6 Jl 2017

Women choreographers—Interviews

Sonia Destri Lie S. E. Scherpf color *Dance Magazine* v91 no3 p18 Mr 2017

Women clergy

Jen Hatmaker B. Luscombe color *Time* v190 no8 p60 Ag 28 2017

Unprecedented Preaching M. O'LOUGHLIN *America* v215 no15 p10 N 14 2016

Women clergy—Employment

Pay gap for women clergy is decreasing D. Briggs color *Christian Century* v134 no18 p12 Ag 30 2017

Women college presidents

People color *Christian Century* v134 no11 p18 My 24 2017

Women college teachers

ANNE SWARTZLANDER *Phi Kappa Phi Forum* v97 no2 p33 Summ 2017

Women college teachers—Interviews

The Factors That Lead to a Pay Premium for Women G. Gavett *Harvard Business Review Digital Articles* p2 My 9 2016

Women comedians

A GIRL LIKE I H. ALS cartoon *New Yorker* v92 no32 p106 O 10 2016

The Girly Show P. Robinson cartoon *O, The Oprah Magazine* p120 Mr 2017

THE McKinnon Report L. ANOLIK color *Vanity Fair* v59 no11 p112 N 2017

Tiffany Haddish Doesn't Think Comedy Is a Game A. M. Cox *New York Times Magazine* p54 Ag 20 2017

Why it's COOL to be KIND [Cover story] E. BRIED color *Good Housekeeping* v265 no3 p85 S 2017

Women comedians—United States

Andrea Martin's Big Break A. Sternbergh img *New York* v50 no8 p122 Ap 17 2017

Women composers

Kamala Sankaram H. STEWART *Opera News* v81 no7 p10 Ja 2017

Women composers—United States

Still Having FUN! J. NEWMAN color *AARP: The Magazine* v59 no5A p42 Ag/S 2016

Women computer programmers

This Is My Job J. Militare bw cartoon color *Glamour* v115 no4 p146 Ap 2017

Women conductors (Musicians)

Leading Women M. YOUNG *Opera News* v81 no5 p22 N 2016

Susanna Mälkki J. Crelin color *Current Biography* v78 no5 p53 My 2017

Women construction workers

This Is My Job A. Swift and J. Militare color *Glamour* v114 no12 p176 D 2016

Women consultants

What I Learned About Helpfulness When I Used a Cane Instead of Crutches A. Rimm *Harvard Business Review Digital Articles* p2 D 30 2016

Women consumers

The Financial Services Industry's Untapped Market S. A. Hewlett and A. T. Moffitt *Harvard Business Review Digital Articles* p2 D 8 2014

TIME FOR SOMETHING MORE S. Perman color *Fortune* v176 no5 p43 O 1 2017

Women consumers—United States

The Health Care Industry Needs to Start Taking Women Seriously C. B. Luce and J. T. Kennedy *Harvard Business Review Digital Articles* p2 My 28 2015

Women cooks

AT MY HOUSE with Katie Lee L. Benoit and A. Chantim color *Good Housekeeping* v264 no6 p30 Je 2017

A Flair for Solar Cooking: And Distrust of the "Hippy" Method K. WRIGHT *Idaho Magazine* v16 no11 p48 Ag 2017

Graham Finale T. KIRTS color *Indianapolis Monthly* p39 Ap 2017

IN BLOOM C. MUHLKE bw color *Bon Appetit* v62 no6 p74 Je 2017

Niki Nakayama G. SNYDER *Los Angeles Magazine* v62 no9 p98 S 2017

SECOND ACT C. JAY color *Louisiana Life* v37 no3 p18 Ja/F 2017

WHERE ARE YOU GOING? color *O, The Oprah Magazine* p166 D 2016

Women cooks—Awards

Chef Hardette Harris C. JAY color *Louisiana Life* v37 no3 p54 Ja/F 2017

Women cooks—United States

Sweet Dreams Are Made of This M. GOLDBERG color *O, The Oprah Magazine* p30 D 2016

Women costume designers

CREATING EMERALD CITY COUTURE *Cincinnati Magazine* v50 no8 p22 My 2017

Women country musicians

Cam B. Muteba color *Current Biography* v78 no6 p20 Je 2017

Kelsea Ballerini J. Johnson color *Current Biography* v78 no5 p8 My 2017

Shania's Hard Road Back A. GREENE color *Rolling Stone* no1281/1282 p15 F 23 2017

WHERE I STOOD D. HARRISON *Virginia Living* v15 no2 p25 F 2017

Women country musicians—Interviews

Maren Morris D. BROWNE color *Rolling Stone* no1280 p20 F 9 2017

Women cyclists

Ellen Leah Isabel Watters A. A. DAVIS color *Maclean's* v130 no2 p74 Mr 2017

Tanya Quick color *Bicycling* v58 no1 p96 Ja/F 2017

Women dancers

See also

Ballerinas

Candy Land C. Bowers color *Dance Spirit* v21 no4 p15 Ap 2017

Jonalyn Saxer L. KAY *Dance Magazine* v90 no12 p34 D 2016

Leslie Andrea Williams S. BURKE *Dance Magazine* v91 no7 p22 Jl 2017

THE LOOK BOOK A. SWERDLOFF img *New York* p55 Ja 9 2017

why i dance S. Hutchings *Dance Magazine* v91 no1 p216 Ja 2017

Women dancers—United States

THE DIRT with Alanna Tarango *Dance Spirit* v21 no4 p16 Ap 2017

Kennadi BOESE H. Rolfe *Dance Spirit* v21 no7 p119 S 2017

Women deacons

A Neglected Order N. SCHNEIDER *America* v215 no11 p12 O 17 2016

Unprecedented Preaching M. O'LOUGHLIN *America* v215 no15 p10 N 14 2016

Women deans (Education)

What Still Makes Silicon Valley So Special J. Fox *Harvard Business Review Digital Articles* p2 D 5 2014

Women dermatologists

O's 2017 HEALTH HEROES J. THOMPSON, E. MOODY et al color *O, The Oprah Magazine* p57 Ja 2017

Women designers

See also

Women fashion designers

Women textile designers

Folk Revival H. MARTIN color *Architectural Digest* v74 no3 p40 Mr 2017

Women directors of corporations

FROSTY WELCOME Z. Robert color *Iceland Review* v54 no5 p72 S-O 2016

JOANNE HEYLER A. HEROLD *Los Angeles Magazine* v62 no9 p98 S 2017

PENNY POLLACK M. Thomas color *Chicago* v66 no11 p164 N 2017

Women Directors Change How Boards Work L. Liswood *Harvard*

MIRY WHITEHILL-BEN ATAR: THE FOUNDER OF MIRY'S LIST HAS HELPED MORE THAN 100 RESETTLED FAMILIES MAKE A LIFE IN THE U.S. HERE'S WHERE HER INSPIRATION CAME FROM L. B. SUTER *Los Angeles Magazine* v62 no9 p94 S 2017

MOST POWERFUL WOMEN K. Bellstrom, B. Kowitt et al color *Fortune* v176 no5 p54 O 1 2017

SAVING PUBLIC HIGHER EDUCATION *Vital Speeches of the Day* v82 no12 p362 D 2016

Step Up and Lead S. BARRY cartoon *Working Mother* p49 F/Mr 2017

A Study of the Champagne Industry Shows That Women Have Stronger Networks, and Profit from Them A. Ody-Brasier and I. Fernandez-Mateo *Harvard Business Review Digital Articles* p2 Jl 20 2017

TOP 60 COMPANIES FOR EXECUTIVE WOMEN 2017 *Working Mother* p28 F/Mr 2017

Why Men Have More Help Getting to the C-Suite S. Charas, L. L. Griffeth et al *Harvard Business Review Digital Articles* p2 N 16 2015

WOMEN'S WORK A. L. REVENGA and A. M. M. BOUDET color graph *Scientific American* v317 no3 p72 S 2017

Women executives—Attitudes

How to Negotiate for Yourself When People Don't Expect You To D. M. Kolb and D. A. Noumair *Harvard Business Review Digital Articles* p2 Je 17 2016

Women executives—Canada

PROMOTING WOMEN IN LEADERSHIP BENEFITS ALL S. Macgregor color *Maclean's* v130 no3 p58 Ap 2017

Women executives—Congresses

Build Your Own Company J. BODNAR cartoon *Kiplinger's Personal Finance* v71 no3 p37 Mr 2017

Women executives—Employment

Laws alone can't close boardroom gender gap *People Management* p55 F 2017

Lots of Companies Still Have No Senior Executives Who Are Women S. G. Carmichael color graph *Harvard Business Review Digital Articles* p2 Mr 8 2017

Women executives—Interviews

Income Inequality, by Chance or by Choice D. McGinn *Harvard Business Review Digital Articles* p2 Mr 28 2017

When Personal Tragedy Strikes, Downshifting at Work Doesn't Always Help D. McGinn *Harvard Business Review Digital Articles* p2 My 15 2015

Women executives—United States

Data on display Women in management E. Torpey *Career Outlook* p1 Mr 2017

Lisa Lucas: Executive Director, National Book Foundation C. Reid *Publishers Weekly* v263 no52 p29 D 19 2016

Only 11% of Top Business School Case Studies Have a Female Protagonist L. Symons *Harvard Business Review Digital Articles* p2 Mr 9 2016

STATE STREET'S GENDER SHOWDOWN A. Kurtz color diag *Fortune* v175 no7 p58 Je 1 2017

Study: Firms with More Women in the C-Suite Are More Profitable M. Noland and T. Moran *Harvard Business Review Digital Articles* p2 F 8 2016

Suzanne Nossel: PEN Executive Director J. Maher color *Publishers Weekly* v263 no52 p30 D 19 2016

top female achievers A. McLellan color *New Orleans Magazine* v51 no8 p70 Je 2017

Women explorers

CINDY LEE VAN DOVER S. CHODOSH cartoon *Popular Science* p48 Ja/F 2017

Women farmers

969,672 THE NUMBER OF WOMEN FARMERS *Successful Farming* v115 no9 p8 Ag 2017

FARMHERS ON FILM: LEARN MORE ABOUT THE FEMALE FARMERS AND RANCHERS IN THE FARMHER PROJECT M. Guyler-Alaniz *Successful Farming* v115 no12 p67 O 2017

Women fashion designers

Azéde Jean-Pierre J. Crelin color *Current Biography* v78 no6 p50 Je 2017

CAROLINA HERRERA A. CODINHA color *Vogue* v207 no3 p409 Mr 2017

COUTURE CURATOR M. BOBO color *Ebony* v72 no4 p56 F 2017

DIANE VON FURSTENBERG M. DOWD color *Vogue* v207 no3 p414 Mr 2017

MARIA GRAZIA CHIURI S. MOWER cartoon color *Vogue* v207 no3 p415 Mr 2017

MIUCCIA PRADA C. BARZINI color *Vogue* v207 no3 p406 Mr 2017

PHOEBE PHILO E. MACSWEENEY color *Vogue* v207 no3 p412 Mr 2017

Show of Strength color *Vogue* v207 no3 p399 Mr 2017

STELLA McCARTNEY P. SYKES color *Vogue* v207 no3 p402 Mr 2017

TASTEMAKER: CHRISTINA MONLEY H. MITCHELL color *Chicago* v66 no9 p58 S 2017

Women financial planners

Blazing a Trail in Finance J. BODNAR cartoon *Kiplinger's Personal Finance* v71 no1 p18 Ja 2017

Women fire fighters

IN THE LINE OF FIRE J. Lowe *New York Times Magazine* p40 S 3 2017

Women fishers

Fisherwomen--The Uncounted Dimension in Fisheries Management L. E. OGDEN *BioScience* v67 no2 p111 F 2017

HEROINES OF THE SEA E. S. ARNARSDÓTTIR color *Iceland Review* v54 no5 p78 S-O 2016

Women folklorists

Textiles to Ride: The Saddle Blanket Weaver G. WIER *Idaho Magazine* v16 no9 p7 Je 2017

Women generals

'We just can't have this' S. PROUDFOOOT color *Maclean's* v129 no45 p26 N 14 2016

Women golfers

Ariya Jutanugarn M. Hagan color *Current Biography* v78 no6 p54 Je 2017

Inbee Park M. Hagan color *Current Biography* v78 no2 p58 F 2017

Lexi Thompson J. Marksbury and J. Marksbury color *Golf Magazine* v59 no11 p34 N 2017

TITANIC THOMPSON D. Denunzio color *Golf Magazine* v59 no11 p10 N 2017

You're Up! color *Golf Magazine* v59 no8 p12 Ag 2017

Women golfers—United States

SWINGING LOW E. Laase and S. Kwak color *Sports Illustrated* v127 no11 p21 O 9 2017

Women graduate students

"I felt pride, and that changed everything." S. Kitchens color *Glamour* v115 no6 p72 Je 2017

Women gymnasts

The Ethics of Watching Gymnastics M. O'ROURKE and A. Kudacki img *New York* v49 no15 p54 Jl 25 2016

Simone BILES S. Dreisbach color *Glamour* v114 no12 p210 D 2016

Women gymnasts—Awards

American Voices Laurie Hernandez T. Keith color *Sports Illustrated* v125 no15 p24 N 7 2016

Women heads of state

See also

Women presidents

Women prime ministers

Would the World Be Different with Merkel, May, and Clinton in Charge? D. M. Kolb and M. Olekalns *Harvard Business Review Digital Articles* p2 S 12 2016

Women historians

Heather Ann Thompson J. Crelin color *Current Biography* v78 no9 p90 S 2017

LYNN GARAFOLA S. Burke *Dance Magazine* v90 no12 p52 D 2016

Women hockey players

Sports Funnies K. MILLER color *National Geographic Kids* no472 p9 Ag 2017

Women horse owners

Wonderful Women of World *Arabian Horse World* v57 no9 p164 Je 2017

Women human rights workers

My Stuff: BIANCA JAGGER color *Vanity Fair* v59 no9 p124 S 2017

COOL & COLLECTED C. KELLOGG color *House Beautiful* v158 no9 p150 N 2016

Women investment advisors
Amazon Woman A. GARA and W. BALDWIN color *Forbes* v200 no4 p52 O 24 2017

Women jazz musicians
Cécile McLorin Salvant: True Character [Cover story] P. Lutz color *Downbeat* v84 no10 p34 O 2017
Melodic Devotion G. Himes color *Downbeat* v84 no10 p28 O 2017

Women jazz singers
Deelee Dubé Wins Sarah Vaughan Jazz Vocal Competition M. Barris color *Downbeat* v84 no2 p13 F 2017
ELLEN ANDERSSON Leaving Spaces J. Ephland color *Downbeat* v84 no2 p23 F 2017

Women jockeys
WHAT IN THE WORLD *Arabian Horse World* v57 no9 p10 Je 2017

Women journalists
See also
    Women sportswriters
    Women television journalists
    Women war correspondents
Bonnie Angelo J. Schecter color *Time* v190 no13 p17 O 2 2017
DOROTHY LAWRENCE 4 OCTOBER 1896 - 4 OCTOBER 1964 J. Pollard and S. Pollard *History Today* v67 no10 p22 O 2017
Kate Walsh O'Beirne, R.I.P R. Ponnuru *National Review* v69 no9 p12 My 15 2017

Women journalists—History
THOSE Magnificent Women AND THEIR TYPING MACHINES K. TODD *Smithsonian* v47 no7 p60 N 2016

Women journalists—Interviews
Post Election—Dowd Dishes C. Kirch color *Publishers Weekly* v263 no44 p(Sp)23 O 31 2016
Q+A *Indianapolis Monthly* p44 F 2017

Women journalists—United States
Gwen Ifill M. Duffy color *Time* v188 no22-23 p13 N/D 2016
GWEN THE GREAT color *Essence* v47 no9 p44 Ja 2017
Kathryn Schulz D. Kiper *Current Biography* v78 no6 p92 Je 2017
MARY KATHARINE HAM E. PLOTT color *Washingtonian Magazine* v52 no7 p86 Ap 2017

Women landscape architects
Lara Zureikat [Cover story] M. OWENS color *Architectural Digest* v74 no10 p110 O 1 2017

Women lawyers
2017 NEW YORK'S WOMEN LEADERS IN THE LAW img *New York* v50 no8 p1 Ap 17 2017
Nina Shaw M. WAKIM *Los Angeles Magazine* v62 no9 p99 S 2017
Virginia's Best Women Lawyers *Virginia Living* v15 no5 p67 Ag 2017

Women leaders
See also
    Women executives
Beyond the Letter of the Law C. Kettlewell color *Virginia Living* v15 no5 p60 Ag 2017
Commitment to Diversity Puts Women in the Lead color *Maclean's* v130 no3 p57 Ap 2017
Getting More Women into Senior Management R. Shambaugh *Harvard Business Review Digital Articles* p2 My 25 2015
How One Law Measurably Lifted the Status of Women in India P. Kalsi *Harvard Business Review Digital Articles* p2 Mr 16 2017
In Good COMPANY L. ROMNEY color *Forbes* v200 no3 p85 S 28 2017
It's Time for Our Real-Life Female Leaders to Act Like Selina Meyer S. Schrobsdorff color *Time* v190 no4 p55 Jl 24 2017
KEY L.A. WOMAN MOMENTS OF 2017 *Los Angeles Magazine* v62 no9 p94 S 2017
Leaders S. Sandberg, I. Betancourt et al color *Time* v189 no16/17 p64 My 1-8 2017
NEVERTHELESS, HER MAJESTY PERSISTED D. GOODWIN color *Foreign Policy* no223 p46 Mr/Ap 2017
Research: We Are Way Harder on Female Leaders Who Make Bad Calls T. Huston *Harvard Business Review Digital Articles* p2 Ap 21 2016

We Are #PoweredByWomen bw color *Glamour* v115 no11 p14 N 2017
What to Do When a "Devil's Advocate" Tries to Derail Your Project J. Cleaver *Harvard Business Review Digital Articles* p2 Ja 18 2016
Why Some Women Negotiate Better Than Others S. Mor *Harvard Business Review Digital Articles* p2 O 8 2014
WOMAN in government J. Burrows *Governing* v30 no5 p48 F 2017
Women and Power M. Funkhouser *Governing* v30 no5 p4 F 2017

Women legislators—Canada
Rookie in the House S. PROUDFOOT color *Maclean's* v130 no2 p16 Mr 2017

Women legislators—United States
See also
    Women senators (U.S.)

Women librarians
Carla Hayden: U.S. Librarian of Congress A. Albanese *Publishers Weekly* v263 no52 p27 D 19 2016

Women lighthouse keepers
THE CHESAPEAKE'S FEMINIST LIGHTHOUSE K. Randall *Washingtonian Magazine* v52 no7 p157 Ap 2017

Women lyricists
WHO'S THAT GIRL? N. Feeney color *Entertainment Weekly* no1465 p54 My 12 2017

Women marines
SCREEN SHOT E. ACKERMAN color *Esquire* p76 Ag 2017

Women martial artists
AFGHANISTAN'S FEMALE KUNG FU FIGHTERS M. SCARLES color *Tricycle: The Buddhist Review* v27 no1 p16 Fall 2017

Women mayors
THERE'S SOMETHING ABOUT MARY: The implausible and inevitable rise of the woman who could be mayor T. WHEATLEY *Atlanta* v57 no6 p28 O 2017

Women microbiologists
Dianne Newman J. Crelin color *Current Biography* v78 no6 p68 Je 2017
Parasites fight for nutrients A. Cunningham color *Science News* v192 no6 p16 O 14 2017

Women military personnel
Death Battalions S. Wong and J. GUTTMAN *MHQ: Quarterly Journal of Military History* v29 no3 p11 Spr 2017
History's Greatest Hits K. BOATNER cartoon *National Geographic Kids* no473 p10 S 2017
THE INTERVIEW B. BETHUNE color *Maclean's* p20 Je 2017

Women military personnel—History
Skeleton ignites Viking warrior debate B. BOWER bw *Science News* v192 no6 p6 O 14 2017

Women military personnel—United States
The Female Soldiers Who've Already Joined Special Ops Teams G. T. Lemmon *Harvard Business Review Digital Articles* p2 Ag 21 2015

Women motion picture producers & directors
The 3-Minute Interview [Cover story] J. Kantor color *Glamour* v114 no11 p46 N 2016
ACTION HERO N. Sperling color *Entertainment Weekly* no1454/1455 p74 F 24 2017
THE UNBREAKABLE LEXI ALEXANDER B. RAFTERY color *Wired* v25 no8 p80 Ag 2017

Women motion picture producers & directors—Interviews
INVISIBLE SCRATCH LINES: AN INTERVIEW WITH JULIE DASH M. K. Holmes *Film Quarterly* v70 no2 p49 Wint 2016
The Superhero We've Been Waiting For L. Cornish and E. Mahaney color *Glamour* v115 no6 p110 Je 2017

Women motion picture producers & directors—United States
THE PRECISIONIST *New York Times Magazine* p36 O 16 2016

Women mountaineers
Climbing (Re)Structures J. FLASHMAN color *Climbing* no356 p20 S/O 2017
Future Female Crushers color *Climbing* no356 p19 S/O 2017
Gypsy Kitchen J. Lucas color *Climbing* no356 p28 S/O 2017
A League of Her Own C. Kalman color *Climbing* no351 p26 F/Mr 2017
No Man's Land N. PHILLIPS color *Climbing* no356 p22 S/O 2017
Sisterhood of the Rope K. LAMBERT *Climbing* no356 p26 S/O

2017

UNSOLICITED BETA C. Baird, M. Pervo et al color *Climbing* no353 p18 My/Je 2017

Women mountaineers—History

CAN'T KEEP HER DOWN M. WALSH bw color *Climbing* no356 p54 S/O 2017

Women mountaineers—Physiology

TRAIN LIKE A GIRL D. HIGGINS color *Climbing* no356 p60 S/O 2017

Women museum directors

VOX: ART FOR THE PEOPLE E. FISHMAN color *Chicago* v66 no9 p54 S 2017

Women musicians

See also

Women jazz musicians

Women singers

Women violinists

National Treasure P. G. DAVIS *Opera News* v81 no5 p24 N 2016

On Rebels and Role Models K. H. Biloxi, E. Wilson et al color *Glamour* v115 no10 p34 O 2017

Voices in My Head: I listened to only female singers all summer. Here's What I learned W. Morris *New York Times Magazine* p27 O 8 2017

Women musicians—United States

Angel Olsen [Cover story] M. Rich color *Current Biography* v78 no6 p83 Je 2017

Women novelists

Ali Benjamin R. Means color *Current Biography* v78 no5 p16 My 2017

Discovering the Past K. E. LIVINGSTON color *Publishers Weekly* v264 no41 p54 O 9 2017

WORLD OF INTERIORS J. THURMAN cartoon color *New Yorker* v93 no23 p48 Ag 7 2017

Women nutritionists

DO-IT-ALL DIETITIAN J. London color *Good Housekeeping* v265 no3 p10 S 2017

Women of a Certain Age (Theatrical production)

Real-Time Results J. GREEN *New York* v49 no23 p86 N 14 2016

Women of color

Powerful Partnerships K. BOWERS chart color graph *Working Mother* v40 no2 p28 Je/Jl 2017

Turning Networking On Its Head C. V. Clarke color *Black Enterprise* v47 no3 p40 O 2016

Women on television

The Revolution Is Being Televised *Glamour* v115 no10 p155 O 2017

The Scenes That Changed Everything J. Kantor and S. Leach color *Glamour* v115 no10 p50 O 2017

TV Will Save Us All C. Leive color *Glamour* v115 no10 p28 O 2017

Women-only events

REBELLES NAVIGATE THE ULTIMATE ADVENTURE S. OCHSNER color *Dirt Sports + Off-Road* v51 no4 p24 Ap 2017

Women painters

Agnes Martin's 'Summer, 1964 L. Shapton *New York Times Magazine* p39 O 8 2017

Bonnie Maygarden L. Cutrone *New Orleans Homes & Lifestyles* v20 no3 p22 Summ 2017

CANDIDA'S COLORING BOOK J. FOUMBERG color *Chicago* v66 no5 p43 My 2017

Columbus artist paints farm-fresh art A. J. BARTELS color *Nebraska Life* v21 no5 p74 S/O 2017

IMAGINATION TAKES FLIGHT A. ELLIOTT *Iceland Review* v54 no6 p8 N/D 2017

"Miss Dimock is not orthodox at all": The life and career of Edith Dimock Glackens A. Berman bw cartoon color *Magazine Antiques* v184 no5 p84 S/O 2017

VISIBLE DIFFERENCE D. KAZANJIAN color *Vogue* v207 no4 p208 Ap 2017

Women park rangers

Richmond's "Resident Rosie" C. Schuknecht *Sierra* v101 no4 p66 Jl/Ag 2016

Women periodical editors

Elaine Welteroth J. Crelin color *Current Biography* v78 no2 p83 F 2017

THE LEGEND OF LIZ TILBERIS S. Mooallem bw color *Harp-*

er's Bazaar no3657 p222 O 2017

NO FOOL M. Fischer *Harper's Magazine* v334 no2002 p91 Mr 2017

Women personal trainers

Street Style: FITNESS EDITION R. A. Darby color *Women's Health* v14 no5 p18 Je 2017

WHO WILL BE THE NEXT FITNESS STAR? [Cover story] M. Gainsburg color *Women's Health* v14 no6 p(Sp)2 Jl 2017

Women personnel directors

Who I am *People Management* p55 N 2016

Women philanthropists

Connecting With Melinda Gates color *Good Housekeeping* v265 no3 p14 S 2017

Women photographers

The Body Revolution bw color *Glamour* v115 no2 p94 F 2017

By Women, for Women S. Dreisbach color *Glamour* v115 no2 p86 F 2017

THE CUBAN CONNECTION color *Wired* v25 no8 p10 Ag 2017

In Defense of Body Hair K. Erickson color *Glamour* v115 no6 p60 Je 2017

LATOYA RUBY FRAZIER L. N. Williams color map *Essence* v47 no9 p48 Ja 2017

PICTURING TIME S. A. STEINBERG color *Iceland Review* v54 no5 p62 S-O 2016

Random Acts of Courage color *Glamour* no8 p24 Ag 2017

SHOWCASE A. GOGGANS color *Surfer* v58 no5 p78 S 2017

VIVA EL INTERNET A. G. Martínez color map *Wired* v25 no8 p68 Ag 2017

Woman Warrior M. Wappler and E. Mahaney color *Glamour* v115 no6 p106 Je 2017

Women photographers—Interviews

Annie Leibovitz bw *Rolling Stone* no1299 p82 N 2 2017

Women photographers—United States

Olivia Bee J. Johnson color *Current Biography* v78 no6 p10 Je 2017

SECRET SELVES A. LEVY cartoon color *New Yorker* v93 no4 p58 Mr 13 2017

Women physicists

Diversity in physics: Are you part of the problem? A. Nelson *Physics Today* v70 no5 p10 My 2017

Women poets

In the Palm of Her Hand A. LAHEY *Walrus* v14 no9 p72 N 2017

Women police chiefs

THE CHIEF C. PENDLEY *Atlanta* v57 no2 p23 Je 2017

Women political activists

THE RISE OF THE VALKYRIES: In the alt-right, women are the future, and the problem S. Darby *Harper's Magazine* p25 S 2017

Women political activists—History

After the Vote was Won J. Smith *History Today* v67 no1 p47 Ja 2017

Women political activists—United States

AFENI SHAKUR J. HUGHES *New York Times Magazine* p50 D 25 2016

COCA CRYSTAL S. DOLNICK *New York Times Magazine* p59 D 25 2016

A leap of fidelity M. Clark *U.S. Catholic* v82 no10 p10 O 2017

Masha Gessen P. NEIDL color *Rolling Stone* no1295 p46 S 7 2017

More than just safety pins A. KINGSTON color *Maclean's* v129 no47 p31 N 28 2016

THEY PERSISTED E. J. GRAFF color *Mother Jones* v42 no4 p34 Jl/Ag 2017

Women political candidates

SEE YVETTEY RUN L. MURTHA *Cincinnati Magazine* v50 no4 p82 Ja 2017

Why I'm Running H. Kelly color *Glamour* v115 no10 p146 O 2017

Women politicians

See also

Women political candidates

THIS LOSS HURTS, BUT PLEASE NEVER STOP BELIEVING THAT FIGHTING FOR WHAT'S RIGHT IS WORTH IT H. CLINTON *Vital Speeches of the Day* v83 no1 p4 Ja 2017

Women politicians—United States

Always in Vogue N. EMERY color *Weekly Standard* v22 no15 p17 D 19 2016

no1285 p38 Ap 20 2017

The Liberation of Kesha [Cover story] B. HIATT bw color *Rolling Stone* no1298 p26 O 19 2017

NATALIE COLE R. HOERBURGER *New York Times Magazine* p28 D 25 2016

SING IT STRONG N. Paumgarten cartoon *New Yorker* v92 no33 p26 O 17 2016

Women skiers

A GIRL ON THE ROAD T. Neville color *Skiing* p42 D 2016

A Mother's Nature S. Davis bw color *Powder* v45 no4 p94 D 2016

NEW STAR C. Menzel color *Powder* v45 no4 p144 D 2016

Toni: Gora Mamay, Russia J. CLARY DAVIES color *Powder* v46 no2 p9 O 2017

WHERE ARE YOU GOING? color *O, The Oprah Magazine* p126 F 2017

Women snowboarders

DESIRE MELANCON B. Merrill color *Snowboarder* v29 no3 p40 N 2016

Women soccer players

Carli Lloyd J. Crelin color *Current Biography* v78 no2 p44 F 2017

Eniola Aluko J. Crelin color *Current Biography* v77 no10 p3 O 2016

Women soccer players—Universities & colleges

NEW FOOTING E. Laase and T. Keith color *Sports Illustrated* v127 no9 p18 S 25 2017

Women social workers

Young Achievers *Islamic Horizons* v46 no4 p14 Jl/Ag 2017

Women softball players—Wounds & injuries

Rise Up J. Fuchs and T. Keith color *Sports Illustrated* v126 no17 p28 Je 19 2017

Women specialists—Interviews

Member Spotlight: Stephanie Gailes *Parks & Recreation* v52 no1 p41 Ja 2017

Women sportswriters

I TYPED AND DREAMED *Vital Speeches of the Day* v83 no9 p276 S 2017

Women stockbrokers

Blazing a Trail in Finance J. BODNAR cartoon *Kiplinger's Personal Finance* v71 no1 p18 Ja 2017

Women stunt performers

Fitness, According to Superheroes J. M. Goldstein and S. G. Levy bw chart color *Glamour* v115 no2 p63 F 2017

The World Is Her Playground [Cover story] M. STACEY color *Women's Health* v14 no8 p130 O 2017

Women superheroes

NO. 15 Storm N. Terrero color *Entertainment Weekly* no1436/1437 p56 O 21 2016

NO. 1 WONDER WOMAN A. Breznican color *Entertainment Weekly* no1436/1437 p42 O 21 2016

NO. 22 Black Widow N. Sperling color *Entertainment Weekly* no1436/1437 p61 O 21 2016

NO. 34 Rogue S. Vilkomerson color *Entertainment Weekly* no1436/1437 p70 O 21 2016

NO. 39 JESSICA JONES J. Jensen color *Entertainment Weekly* no1436/1437 p72 O 21 2016

NO. 40 KITTY PRYDE S. Li color *Entertainment Weekly* no1436/1437 p74 O 21 2016

NO. 46 INVISIBLE WOMAN N. Terrero color *Entertainment Weekly* no1436/1437 p77 O 21 2016

Wonder Woman Breaks Through E. Dockterman color *Time* v188 no27-28 p98 D 26 2016

Women superheroes—In literature

The World Needs More Sheroes J. MCCARTNEY cartoon color *Publishers Weekly* v264 no9 p41 F 27 2017

Women surfers

The American "Meh" J. HOUSMAN color *Surfer* v58 no3 p30 Je 2017

BEST FEMALE color *Surfing Magazine* v53 no1 p54 Ja 2017

Lisa Andersen A. DOUGLAS color *Surfer* v58 no3 p28 Je 2017

POINT BREAK V. von Pfetten *Women's Health* v14 no5 p136 Je 2017

Women swimmers

Beauty is Strength K. Greenidge color *Glamour* v115 no6 p134 Je 2017

Canada's champion A. HUTCHINS color *Maclean's* v129 no48/49 p66 D 5 2016

Free Style J. di Giovanni color *Vogue* v207 no4 p218 Ap 2017

MAKING WAVES B. COLVIN color *Phi Kappa Phi Forum* v97 no1 p6 Spr 2017

Women tattoo artists

Alice Guerin Tattoo Artist: A Fountain Square illustrator whose canvas is the human body L. WRIGHT color *Indianapolis Monthly* v41 no2 p48 S 2017

Women teachers

See also

Nuns as teachers

THE TEACHER J. WOOD cartoon *New Yorker* v92 no40 p28 D 5 2016

Women teachers—United States—History—19th century

Lost Skills of the frontier teacher L. FELDMAN bw color *American Cowboy* v23 no6 p66 Ap/My 2017

Women television journalists

How Did I Get Here? CHRISTIANE AMANPOUR bw color *Bloomberg Businessweek* no4520 p76 My 1 2017

The Making of a News Junkie K. Tur color *Glamour* v115 no10 p141 O 2017

Women television news anchors—Interviews

My Obsessions... *TV Guide* v65 no37 p15 S 4 2017

Women television personalities

DAYS OF OUR LIVES M. LOGAN *TV Guide* v65 no6 p44 Ja 30 2017

Katie RUSHWORTH A. CABLE color *House Beautiful* p178 Ag 2017

Women television producers & directors

ALISA BELLETTINI W. MORRIS *New York Times Magazine* p52 D 25 2016

NIEVES Zuberbühler M. GUIDUCCI color *Vogue* v207 no4 p156 Ap 2017

Shonda RHIMES color *Vanity Fair* v59 no11 p178 N 2017

Women television writers

(1922-2016) Agnes Nixon L. Rice color *Entertainment Weekly* no1435 p50 O 14 2016

HOW COMEDY'S SECRET WEAPON GOT SCHOOLED M. Snetiker color *Entertainment Weekly* no1463/1464 p96 Ap/My 2017

Women television writers—Interviews

5 Minutes With a TV Pioneer J. Konner *Glamour* v115 no10 p32 O 2017

Women tennis players

Fact: You have what it takes color *Redbook* p97 S 2017

Lightbox S. Gregory color *Time* v190 no12 p18 S 25 2017

A Match Made in Florida M. Sharapova and M. Ayers color *Money* v46 no9 p92 O 2017

Miss America S. TIGNOR *Tennis* v53 no4 p42 Jl/Ag 2017

PARTING SHOT *Tennis* v52 no6 p80 N/D 2016

Women tennis players—Interviews

Garbiñe Muguruza S. Gregory color *Time* v190 no9 p64 S 4 2017

World's Greatest Female Athlete [Cover story] M. Harris-Perry bw color *Glamour* v114 no7 p114 Jl 2016

Women tennis players—United States

Whit and Wisdom J. Fuchs and T. Keith color *Sports Illustrated* v126 no11 p28 Ap 17-24 2017

Women textile designers

SHAY spaniola A. MAZE color *Better Homes & Gardens* v95 no4 p34 Ap 2017

Women theatrical producers & directors

Gold Standard H. Freeman bw *Vogue* v207 no6 p120 Je 2017

Women track & field athletes—Interviews

DIGESTIVE HEALTH color *Maclean's* v129 no48/49 p75 D 5 2016

Women travelers—Safety measures

Female-Only Transport T. John color *Time* v189 no3 p10 Ja 30 2017

Women truck drivers

Taking Flight in Vegas color *O, The Oprah Magazine* p100 Je 2017

Women violinists

Saluting ELLA D. Ouellette color *Downbeat* v84 no10 p46 O 2017

Women volunteers

No Peace in the Peace Corps: Women volunteers face sexual assault and victim-blaming A. BUITRAGO *Ms.* v27 no3 p16 Fall

Women—Health—United States
Every Woman Is an Activist M. Kahn color *Glamour* v115 no3 p162 Mr 2017
Women—Honduras
A Dangerous Place for Women: Honduras is an epicenter of violence against women V. MAZATAUD *Ms.* v27 no2 p14 Summ 2017
Women in finance—Societies, etc.
IN GOOD Company L. ROMNEY color *Forbes* v198 no9 p67 D 30 2016
Women in science—Societies, etc.
Creating our own community C. Sánchez and A. Brown color *Science* v355 no6332 p1446 Mr 31 2017
Women—Israel—Social conditions
Mending Their Lives: Through sewing and design, survivors of Israel's sex industry begin anew S. T. STUB *Ms.* v27 no2 p12 Summ 2017
Women—Korea
No Safe Haven S. MCCLELLAND *Ms.* v26 no4 p14 Wint 2016
Women—Legal status, laws, etc.
See also
Husband & wife
Women's suffrage
CHALLENGING THE STATUS QUO WITH STEM CELLS C. Tompot *Saturday Evening Post* v289 no1 p70 Ja/F 2017
Women long-distance runners
CAROLYN MATHER A. BURFOOT color *Runner's World* v52 no2 p25 Mr 2017
MARATHON MOM S. L. Butler color *Runner's World* v52 no2 p34 Mr 2017
Women—Mental health
women struggling... "smiling depression" C. ARNOLD bw color *Women's Health* v14 no4 p144 My 2017
Women—Middle East—Social conditions
MUSLIM SISTERHOOD L. Widdicombe cartoon *New Yorker* v92 no38 p30 N 21 2016
Women—New York (State)
Nine Cool Girls L. Michael and R. RAMSEY img *New York* v50 no10 p60 My 15 2017
Women—News briefs
global *Ms.* v26 no4 p18 Wint 2016
Milestones *Ms.* v26 no4 p7 Wint 2016
Women—Nutrition
STOP THE SIGNS OF AGING V. Tweed color *Amazing Wellness* v8 no2 p48 Spr 2016
Women—Ontario
Mary Elizabeth Lynch: 1933 — 2016 E. SENGER color *Maclean's* v129 no46 p66 N 21 2016
Women—Periodicals
Get It, Girls! M. Stevens, A. Sanchez color *Glamour* v115 no4 p30 Ap 2017
Women politicians—Legal status, laws, etc.
Some days, it just isn't #2016 S. PROUDFOOT color *Maclean's* v129 no45 p24 N 14 2016
Women—Psychology
Sorry Not Sorry M. Ruiz *Women's Health* v14 no2 p128 Mr 2017
Women—Retirement
Does Having Grandchildren Persuade Women to Retire Early? K. Firestone *Harvard Business Review Digital Articles* p2 My 19 2015
Women's clothing
See also
Blouses
Dresses
Evening gowns
Petite clothing
Plus-size women's clothing
Skirts
Women's shoes
12 MORE INSTANT OUTFITS color *Redbook* p76 O 2017
The 2017 Essentials S. P. Nadella and E. Velluto color *Glamour* v115 no1 p23 Ja 2017
4 EASY PIECES ENDLESS OUTFITS color *Good Housekeeping* v263 no5 p47 N 2016
Accidental TOURIST *Interview* v47 no5 p34 Je/Jl 2017
The A-LIST J. Aniston bw color *Harper's Bazaar* no3657 p118

O 2017
All Hail Annie Hall F. Kane color *Glamour* v115 no4 p210 Ap 2017
Alma Bartos A. BRANDT *Cincinnati Magazine* v50 no4 p40 Ja 2017
AMERICAN DREAMING: Take a sophisticated approach to patriotic fashion E. STUART *Virginia Living* v15 no4 p37 Je 2017
The Art of Fashion P. Lefebure color *Working Mother* v40 no3 p14 Ag/S 2017
ATTENTION, PLEASE! color *Essence* v47 no9 p14 Ja 2017
AT YOUR LEISURE color *Women's Health* v14 no9 p134 N 2017
Ave Maria A. Syrett color *InStyle* v24 no9 p394 S 2017
Beach Bum cartoon color *Seventeen* v76 no12 p44 D 2016/Ja 2017
BEST DRESS E. Wilson color *InStyle* v24 no10 p87 O 2017
BEST DRESS E. Wilson color *InStyle* v24 no7 p41 Jl 2017
THE BEST OF WHAT'S NEW L. Armstrong color *Harper's Bazaar* no3656 p302 S 2017
Boho Mermaid cartoon color *Seventeen* v76 no12 p37 D 2016/Ja 2017
Calling All Crop Top Lovers color *Glamour* v114 no7 p65 Jl 2016
Can fashion be FEMINIST? E. Wilson color *InStyle* v24 no2 p49 F 2017
CHIC STREET L. TUDOR color *New Orleans Magazine* v51 no12 p84 O 2017
THE CLOSET IN THE CLOUD N. LISS-SCHULTZ cartoon *Mother Jones* v42 no1 p61 Ja/F 2017
Clothes Make the Man C. Edwards cartoon *O, The Oprah Magazine* p122 Mr 2017
Country Club E. ELWICK-BATES color *Vogue* v207 no11 p234 N 2017
DENIM WITH PERSONALITY color *Essence* v47 no12 p20 Ap 2017
Diamond in the Ruffle color *Vogue* v206 no12 p160 D 2016
DRESS THE PART H. ROLFE *Dance Spirit* v21 no3 p50 Mr 2017
EDITOR'S LETTER G. Bailey color *Harper's Bazaar* no3648 p94 N 2016
Escape Artistry color *Vogue* v207 no11 p180 N 2017
Express Yourself bw color *Glamour* v115 no3 p165 Mr 2017
FAIR PLAY color *Vogue* v207 no11 p214 N 2017
FANCY FREE J. Attenberg color *O, The Oprah Magazine* p118 Mr 2017
FUN & FESTIVE STREET STYLE color *Seventeen* v76 no12 p92 D 2016/Ja 2017
The Get-It Guide *Glamour* v115 no4 p209 Ap 2017
Girly Girl cartoon color *Seventeen* v76 no12 p42 D 2016/Ja 2017
The Girly Show P. Robinson cartoon *O, The Oprah Magazine* p120 Mr 2017
Glenda Bailey on the past and the future of Harper's Bazaar G. Bailey color *Harper's Bazaar* no3651 p180 Mr 2017
Hello! L. Brown color *InStyle* v24 no3 p58 Mr 2017
Her Style's in the Bag color *Working Mother* v40 no2 p18 Je/Jl 2017
Hey, Jenna! J. Lyons, J. K. de Valle et al color *Glamour* v114 no11 p70 N 2016
HIDING IN PLAIN SIGHT P. C. Dodson cartoon *O, The Oprah Magazine* p125 Mr 2017
HOW TO WEAR IT... K. SALADINO and L. BERGAMOTTO color *Good Housekeeping* v265 no2 p14 Ag 2017
In Bloom S. ZLOTNICK and H. G. PHILLIPS color *Washingtonian Magazine* v52 no7 p80 Ap 2017
THE JAZZ AGE bw color *Harper's Bazaar* no3650 p202 F 2017
Kate Hudson HER BEST EVER E. Wilson color *InStyle* v24 no10 p94 O 2017
Kicking It color *Vogue* v207 no11 p172 N 2017
Lady in Red M. G. Silver cartoon *O, The Oprah Magazine* p124 Mr 2017
LIKE A BOY color *Essence* v47 no9 p16 Ja 2017
THE LOOK OF THE Golden Globes E. Wilson color *InStyle* v24 no3 p148 Mr 2017
THE MAGIC OF A GREAT DRESS color *Redbook* p68 My 2017
A Match MADE IN Heaven color *O, The Oprah Magazine* p67 Mr 2017
NAVY IS THE NEW BLACK color *Essence* v47 no7 p13 N 2016
OFF THE SHOULDER bw color *Vogue* v207 no9 p400 S 2017
Olivia, Over Here! color *InStyle* v24 no9 p256 S 2017
Outfits for Days color *Glamour* v114 no11 p66 N 2016

Outfits for Days F. Kane, S. P. Nadella et al color *Glamour* v115 no3 p78 Mr 2017

Pineapples, Pineapples, Pineapples! color *Good Housekeeping* v265 no1 p13 Jl 2017

PLATINUM REWARDS N. Silva-Jelly color *Harper's Bazaar* no3657 p163 O 2017

POWER PUFF color *Vogue* v206 no11 p244 N 2016

Purple's Reign F. Kane, S. P. Nadella et al color *Glamour* v115 no3 p212 Mr 2017

The Question S. BUTLER, B. CLEVENGER et al *O, The Oprah Magazine* p12 Mr 2017

Quick, In the Trenches color *Glamour* v115 no10 p184 O 2017

Quiet Storm color *Essence* v47 no8 p106 D 2016

Quirky Chic cartoon color *Seventeen* v76 no12 p45 D 2016/Ja 2017

real style color *InStyle* v24 no2 p18 F 2017

real style color *InStyle* v24 no3 p66 Mr 2017

Red Carpet/Real Life color *InStyle* v24 no9 p230 S 2017

SHE'S GOT THE LOOK J. AMBROSE, J. PATTERSON et al *O, The Oprah Magazine* p121 Mr 2017

Show of Strength color *Vogue* v207 no3 p399 Mr 2017

Snow Bunny cartoon color *Seventeen* v76 no12 p38 D 2016/Ja 2017

Solange Knowles HER BEST EVER E. Wilson color *InStyle* v24 no9 p184 S 2017

Space COWBOY *Interview* v46 no9 p50 N 2016

Sporty Cool cartoon color *Seventeen* v76 no12 p41 D 2016/Ja 2017

Start Here S. P. Nadella and E. Velluto color *Glamour* v115 no1 p24 Ja 2017

Street APPEAL *Interview* v46 no9 p52 N 2016

STRONG GENES color *Women's Health* v14 no4 p162 My 2017

STYLE CRUSH Kenya Kinski-Jones S. Simon color *InStyle* v24 no3 p170 Mr 2017

STYLE CRUSH Laura Harrier J. Ferrise color *InStyle* v24 no10 p110 O 2017

SUPER Furry ANIMALS *Interview* v46 no9 p46 N 2016

SWEATER SONGS color *Vogue* v206 no11 p204 N 2016

Thank You color *InStyle* v24 no3 p76 Mr 2017

That FIRST WARM DAY S. M. Danler color *Esquire* p78 My 2017

The Tights Stuff K. Kankiewicz color *O, The Oprah Magazine* p126 Mr 2017

TOP OF THE ROCKS color *Vogue* v207 no11 p216 N 2017

THE VERY RED CARPET: And other trends that most caught our eye on the runways R. RAMSEY and I. BROWN img *New York* v50 no16 p58 Ag 7 2017

VISION OF LOVELINESS L. Godin color *O, The Oprah Magazine* p121 Mr 2017

a week of AWESOME OUTFITS color *Good Housekeeping* v265 no2 p32 Ag 2017

a week of AWESOME OUTFITS [Cover story] color *Good Housekeeping* v263 no5 p32 N 2016

a week of AWESOME OUTFITS L. Benoit color *Good Housekeeping* v265 no4 p34 O 2017

WELCOME TO THE ISSUE color *Harper's Bazaar* no3654 p26 Je/Jl 2017

Well Suited A. R. Williams color *Southern Living* v52 no6 p45 Je 2017

WHAT'S YOUR STYLE? color *Seventeen* v76 no2 p122 Mr 2017

WHERE TO BUY color *Essence* v47 no7 p118 N 2016

WHERE TO BUY color *Essence* v48 no5 p120 S 2017

WHERE TO BUY color *Harper's Bazaar* no3655 p166 Ag 2017

YOU WANT YOUR MTV? A. LUCAS color *Ebony* v72 no8 p35 Je 2017

Women's clothing design

All About Money! K. B. RATTINI color *National Geographic Kids* no473 p9 S 2017

Cat's Meow E. Wilson color *InStyle* v24 no1 p32 Ja 2017

Four Truths About Dressing Your Shape L. Chan, J. K. de Valle et al color *Glamour* v114 no11 p90 N 2016

"I feel my best in this dress" L. Garcia and F. Kane color *Glamour* v115 no4 p55 Ap 2017

NADÈGE Vanhée-Cybulski S. STEIN *Interview* v46 no10 p136 D 2016/Ja 2017

Women's clothing stores—Evaluation

GLOBE TROTTING: VENTURING AROUND THE WORLD FROM A COOL OTR SHOP B. GRANDISON *Cincinnati Magazine* v50 no10 p40 Jl 2017

Maternity Clothes N. ALCALA *Los Angeles Magazine* p38 Ap 2017

Women's clothing—Evaluation

10 new denim picks color *Seventeen* v76 no2 p42 Mr 2017

$50 & Under Graduation color *Seventeen* v76 no3 p38 My 2017

5 easy routes to style happiness color *Redbook* p78 My 2017

Adam's STYLE SHEET A. Glassman color *O, The Oprah Magazine* p64 O 2017

AMERICAN BEAUTY S. Trong color *InStyle* v24 no9 p376 S 2017

AMERICAN DAY DREAM color *Vogue* v207 no9 p684 S 2017

...And Even More Coats color *Glamour* v115 no11 p58 N 2017

Arms Race E. Wilson color *InStyle* v24 no4 p78 Ap 2017

BARELY THERE *Interview* v47 no2 p110 Mr 2017

Bazaar's Best-Dressed LIST color *Harper's Bazaar* no3654 p64 Je/Jl 2017

Beach Days color *Glamour* v115 no6 p38 Je 2017

Be Bold Ying Chu color *Glamour* v115 no3 p180 Mr 2017

Best-Dressed LIST B. Mazurek color *Harper's Bazaar* no3653 p100 My 2017

BEST DRESS E. Wilson color *InStyle* v24 no3 p141 Mr 2017

Between the Lines color *Vogue* v207 no6 p148 Je 2017

BOMBER JACKET color *Good Housekeeping* v264 no1 p18 Ja 1 2017

BRING THE NOISE color *Essence* v47 no9 p64 Ja 2017

CHARM SCHOOL M. BOBO color *Ebony* v72 no4 p45 F 2017

Check LIST color *Harper's Bazaar* no3653 p88 My 2017

CHECK, PLEASE color *Harper's Bazaar* no3653 p112 My 2017

Clemons' Time C. Whitney and K. Clemons color *InStyle* v24 no9 p221 S 2017

Coats for All Sizes L. CHAN color *Glamour* v114 no12 p104 D 2016

Coats of Many Colors M. M. Brown color *Southern Living* v52 no9 p48 S 2017

Cold Relief E. Wilson color *InStyle* v24 no3 p144 Mr 2017

COLLAR ME PRETTY color *InStyle* v24 no9 p296 S 2017

COLOR AND CONTRAST C. ROITFELD color *Harper's Bazaar* no3653 p195 My 2017

Color BALANCE *Interview* v47 no2 p108 Mr 2017

COMFORT & JOY color *Women's Health* v14 no6 p148 Jl 2017

the cover color *InStyle* v24 no3 p78 Mr 2017

THE CUT img *New York* v49 no24 p73 N 28 2016

Cut LOOSE *Interview* v47 no2 p208 Mr 2017

DAY TO NIGHT color *Redbook* p74 F 2017

Define Yourself F. Kane, S. P. Nadella et al color *Glamour* v115 no3 p60 Mr 2017

Denim, Your Way color *Glamour* no8 p45 Ag 2017

Designed by Women color *Glamour* v115 no11 p130 N 2017

DINERS, DRESSES & DIVES color *Chicago* v66 no3 p116 Mr 2017

DOING GOOD S. Pulia color *InStyle* v24 no10 p76 O 2017

the DRAMA of SPRING color *Essence* v47 no11 p80 Mr 2017

Dressed for the Season A. R. Williams color *Southern Living* v51 no12 p65 D 2016

DRESS TO IMPRESS R. WALDMAN color *Vogue* v206 no12 p268 D 2016

ELLIE BAMBER A. Syrett color *InStyle* v24 no3 p121 Mr 2017

Emma WATSON: THE FUTURE IS TERRIFYING. THE FUTURE IS UNCERTAIN. THE FUTURE IS ... HERE. AND IF EMMA WATSON HAS ANYTHING TO SAY ABOUT IT, THE FUTURE IS GOING TO BE MAGICAL J. CHASTAIN *Interview* v47 no3 p46 My 2017

Enter for a Chance to Win ... CUTE #OOTDS color *Seventeen* v76 no4 p95 Jl/Ag 2017

Extra SPECIAL color *InStyle* v24 no3 p250 Mr 2017

FABULOUS at Every Age color *Harper's Bazaar* no3653 p183 My 2017

FABULOUS at Every Age color *Harper's Bazaar* no3655 p85 Ag 2017

FALL FORWARD color *Essence* v48 no5 p27 S 2017

Fall's prettiest outfits B. Goreski color *Redbook* p21 O 2017

FANCY FOOTWORK color *O, The Oprah Magazine* p114 Ap 2017

FASHION Liftoff color *InStyle* v24 no9 p265 S 2017

FASHION UNDER $100 color *Redbook* p47 Je 2017

FASHION UNDER $100 color *Redbook* p65 O 2017

FASHION UNDER $100 [Cover story] color *Redbook* p63 My 2017

FASHION UNDER $100 [Cover story] color *Redbook* p69 F 2017

Feel Good, Look Great M. LOGAN BIKOFF *Atlanta* v56 no9 p106 Ja 2017

Femme FATALE: THE LITTLE BLACK CHAPEAU, WORN WITH A SUBVERSIVE TWIST, EMBRACES ITS HARD, DARK EDGE *Interview* v47 no3 p41 My 2017

Find Your Passion F. Kane, S. P. Nadella et al bw color *Glamour* v115 no3 p194 Mr 2017

Flower POWER color *Seventeen* v76 no2 p29 Mr 2017

FOOD FOR THOUGHT J. CAPITAIN color *O, The Oprah Magazine* p14 Ag 2017

For the Win F. Kane color *Glamour* v115 no4 p62 Ap 2017

FULL EFFECT J. Wilson color *Essence* v47 no11 p28 Mr 2017

GET DOWN color *Vogue* v207 no9 p698 S 2017

The Get-It Guide *Glamour* v115 no11 p157 N 2017

The Get-It Guide *Glamour* v115 no3 p211 Mr 2017

GET THESE looks for less color *Good Housekeeping* v265 no3 p42 S 2017

THE GIRL Gigi Hadid E. Wilson color *InStyle* v24 no3 p165 Mr 2017

THE GIRL Willow Smith E. Wilson color *InStyle* v24 no5 p91 My 2017

THE GIRL Zoë Kravitz E. Wilson color *InStyle* v24 no10 p97 O 2017

GOLD STANDARD color *Harper's Bazaar* no3655 p70 Ag 2017

Gwen Stefani HER BEST EVER E. Wilson color *InStyle* v24 no3 p162 Mr 2017

HAVANA NIGHTS chart color *O, The Oprah Magazine* p64 Mr 2017

HEAD TURNERS bw color *Vogue* v207 no10 p274 O 2017

her style color *InStyle* v24 no3 p84 Mr 2017

her style color *InStyle* v24 no9 p108 S 2017

Hey, Stores: Where's My Size? L. Chan and F. Kane cartoon color *Glamour* v115 no4 p76 Ap 2017

the HIT LIST A. Dorsey color *Essence* v48 no5 p32 S 2017

HOLDING COURT *Interview* v47 no2 p98 Mr 2017

Holidays Two Ways color *Seventeen* v76 no12 p28 D 2016/Ja 2017

HOW TO WEAR IT... anywhere! color *Good Housekeeping* v264 no4 p28 Ap 2017

HOW TO WEAR IT... anywhere! color *Good Housekeeping* v264 no6 p20 Je 2017

HOW TO WEAR IT... anywhere! color *Good Housekeeping* v265 no4 p18 O 2017

HOW TO WEAR IT K. SALADINO and L. BERGAMOTTO color *Good Housekeeping* v264 no2 p16 F 2017

If You're Gearing Up for Date Night S. P. Nadella and A. Hou color *Glamour* v115 no9 p48 S 2017

If You're Getting Your Girlboss On S. P. Nadella and A. Hou color *Glamour* v115 no9 p50 S 2017

IN SEARCH OF THE PERFECT TEE [Cover story] bw color *Women's Health* v14 no6 p56 Jl 2017

instant style color *InStyle* v24 no3 p207 Mr 2017

instant style color *InStyle* v24 no7 p57 Jl 2017

instant style color *InStyle* v24 no9 p235 S 2017

InSTYLE July 2017 color *InStyle* v24 no7 p103 Jl 2017

In the Spirit M. CAMERAN color *New Orleans Magazine* v51 no12 p46 O 2017

It's All in the Shoes E. Velluto color *Glamour* v115 no3 p66 Mr 2017

IT'S easy outfit SEASON color *Redbook* p56 Jl/Ag 2017

It's Spring! color *InStyle* v24 no3 p225 Mr 2017

JAM ROCK SWEETNESS bw color *Vogue* v207 no6 p150 Je 2017

JANE BIRKIN bw color *Harper's Bazaar* no3654 p82 Je/Jl 2017

La-Di-Dots E. Wilson color *InStyle* v24 no3 p142 Mr 2017

THE LADY Goldie Hawn E. Wilson color *InStyle* v24 no10 p100 O 2017

THE LADY Helen Mirren E. Wilson color *InStyle* v24 no5 p94 My 2017

THE LADY Tilda Swinton E. Wilson color *InStyle* v24 no3 p168

Mr 2017

Layer your way to more outfits B. Goreski color *Redbook* p30 F 2017

LET IT FLOW color *Essence* v47 no12 p17 Ap 2017

LIFE'S RICH TAPESTRY color *InStyle* v24 no10 p228 O 2017

Looking Fly K. KENDALL color *Indianapolis Monthly* v42 no2 p29 O 2017

Love your coat! color *Redbook* p57 N 2017

Lupita Nyong'o HER BEST EVER color *InStyle* v24 no4 p86 Ap 2017

Maria, Soo Joo & Emily invite you to Glamour's 2017 Kickoff Party! bw color *Glamour* v115 no1 p64 Ja 2017

Market SIMPLY STRIPES color *Vanity Fair* v59 no6 p50 My 2017

MAXIMUM GLAMOUR color *Harper's Bazaar* no3653 p191 My 2017

Mix and Remix F. Kane color *Glamour* v115 no4 p60 Ap 2017

Mod '60s color *Seventeen* v76 no2 p56 Mr 2017

MORE DREAM SUITS! color *Redbook* p60 Je 2017

my style color *InStyle* v24 no10 p134 O 2017

NATURAL SELECTION color *O, The Oprah Magazine* p58 Mr 2017

NEW ROMANTICS L. Clark color *Harper's Bazaar* no3654 p154 Je/Jl 2017

No Sweat E. Wilson color *InStyle* v24 no3 p146 Mr 2017

(not so) bad moms [Cover story] L. B. O'CONNELL color *Good Housekeeping* v265 no5 p26 N 2017

Now meet 39 more beauty game changers—each defining themselves [Cover story] S. Kitchens, J. Harman et al bw color *Glamour* v115 no4 p166 Ap 2017

ON THE DOT color *Essence* v48 no6 p27 O 2017

On the Spot E. Wilson color *InStyle* v24 no2 p57 F 2017

Outdoor Adventure A. Hou and M. Mendal color *Glamour* v115 no6 p36 Je 2017

Outfits for Days color *Glamour* v114 no12 p102 D 2016

Outfits for Days color *Glamour* v115 no7 p32 Jl 2017

OUTFITS FOR DAYS color *Redbook* p70 O 2017

Outfits for Days F. Kane color *Glamour* v115 no4 p74 Ap 2017

Out on the Town B. TURVETT color *Working Mother* p10 F/Mr 2017

Packing LIST G. Bailey color *Harper's Bazaar* no3653 p90 My 2017

Pack Your Bags F. Kane, S. P. Nadella et al color *Glamour* v115 no3 p206 Mr 2017

PETAL PUSHERS color *Harper's Bazaar* no3655 p71 Ag 2017

Pool PARTY color *Vogue* v207 no6 p156 Je 2017

Pop Art S. FRISCIA *Dance Magazine* v90 no12 p86 D 2016

POWER MOVE bw color *Harper's Bazaar* no3657 p157 O 2017

Pretty, Please! F. Kane color *Glamour* v115 no4 p58 Ap 2017

RANCH DRESSING: Styles that are right at home on the range (and beyond) L. WALTERS *Indianapolis Monthly* v12 no40 p32 Ag 2017

real style color *InStyle* v24 no9 p94 S 2017

REBOOT YOUR WARDROBE WITH FALL'S BEST JEANS color *Harper's Bazaar* no3657 p147 O 2017

Recycled Style F. Kane color *Glamour* v115 no4 p72 Ap 2017

Retro Sport color *O, The Oprah Magazine* p61 Mr 2017

ROSY ROMANCE color *Harper's Bazaar* no3653 p110 My 2017

RUNWAY TREND: NEW ROMANTICS color *Harper's Bazaar* no3650 p104 F 2017

SEE NOW, BUY NOW C. HORYN img *New York* v49 no19 p55 S 19 2016

SHE CAN DO IT! S. Trong color *InStyle* v24 no10 p214 O 2017

shoes you can't lose color *InStyle* v24 no3 p336 Mr 2017

Shop Guide color *O, The Oprah Magazine* p143 Mr 2017

SHOWSTOPPERS color *Essence* v48 no5 p90 S 2017

SIMPLY AMAZING! A. Dorsey color *Essence* v47 no11 p19 Mr 2017

Sleeve Game Strong F. Kane, S. P. Nadella et al color *Glamour* v115 no3 p62 Mr 2017

SNATCH That STYLE T. Ebony color *Ebony* v72 no9 p35 Jl/Ag 2017

SO BAZAAR color *Harper's Bazaar* no3657 p250 O 2017

So pretty, so useful color *Redbook* p45 Jl/Ag 2017

So What Do You Do, HILARY SWANK? color *InStyle* v24 no10 p182 O 2017

v92 no42 p43 D 19 2016

Women's rights—United States—History

200 YEARS OF ABORTION J. LARSON img *New York* p32 Ja 9 2017

Women's sexual behavior

THE HALF-GASM color *Women's Health* v14 no8 p36 O 2017

Women's shoes

Pineapples, Pineapples, Pineapples! color *Good Housekeeping* v265 no1 p13 Jl 2017

Silver and Gold for the Win E. Velluto color *Glamour* v114 no12 p100 D 2016

a week of AWESOME OUTFITS color *Good Housekeeping* v265 no2 p32 Ag 2017

WHAT WE LOVE color *Harper's Bazaar* no3657 p58 O 2017

Women's shoes—Evaluation

Adopt the new kitten heel color *Redbook* p63 O 2017

ALL IS NOT LOST - A MODERN WALLFLOWER FINDS HER WAY THROUGH A 70s LANDSCAPE OF FLORAL-WALLPAPER PRINTS AND SEPIA-TONED WARDROBE STAPLES. SHE INTERPRETS THE ERAS LOUNGE MOOD WITH A CASUAL NEW LANGUAGE THAT IS ALL HER OWN *Interview* v47 no3 p60 My 2017

BLACK-TIE AFFAIR color *Harper's Bazaar* no3649 p192 D 2016/Ja 2017

Bringing Booties Back! color *Glamour* v114 no11 p64 N 2016

Carry-ALLS: THE STANDOUT PRE-FALL BAGS PUT SOME PEP IN THE CROSSTOWN SCHLEP *Interview* v47 no3 p44 My 2017

Designed by Women color *Glamour* v115 no11 p130 N 2017

DOPE STUFF ON MY DESK J. Wilson color *Essence* v47 no11 p26 Mr 2017

Fall Re-Boot color *Seventeen* v76 no5 p34 S 2017

THE Fan Girl C. Brody color *Glamour* v115 no10 p172 O 2017

Feel Good, Look Great M. LOGAN BIKOFF *Atlanta* v56 no9 p106 Ja 2017

Find Your Shoe Style color *Glamour* v115 no10 p62 O 2017

FLAT-OUT FABULOUS color *Essence* v48 no3 p17 Jl 2017

Give 'Em The Slip *Los Angeles Magazine* v62 no6 p26 Je 2017

Go West! color *Glamour* v115 no10 p68 O 2017

IF THE SHOE FITS color *Vogue* v207 no1 p100 Ja 2017

The In/Out List color *Harper's Bazaar* no3648 p116 N 2016

The In/Out LIST color *Harper's Bazaar* no3655 p62 Ag 2017

It's All in the Shoes E. Velluto color *Glamour* v115 no3 p66 Mr 2017

Katherine WATERSTON: EMERGING, AS SHE HAS, FROM PRESTIGIOUS DIRECTOR-DRIVEN FILMS AND. BEFORE THAT, A WHOLE LOT OF HUSTLE AND TOIL. THE FIERCELY TALENTED ACTRESS IS BRINGING A LITTLE SCRAPPINESS BACK TO THE BLOCKBUSTER N. LYONNE *Interview* v47 no3 p80 My 2017

LET IT SLIDE color *Seventeen* v76 no4 p24 Jl/Ag 2017

The LIST color *Harper's Bazaar* no3655 p57 Ag 2017

MAGIC SLIPPERS color *Conde Nast Traveler* v52 no1 p38 Ja 2017

Manolo Blahnik boots, $1,065 V. SMITH color *Vogue* v207 no11 p240 N 2017

Market: FABULOUS 40S color *Vanity Fair* v59 no9 p116 S 2017

On Point! color *Glamour* no8 p64 Ag 2017

ON-THE-GO MUSTS color *Good Housekeeping* v264 no2 p87 F 2017

PEARLY WHITES J. MOAZAMI color *Chicago* v66 no8 p48 Ag 2017

Petal Pumps color *Good Housekeeping* v264 no3 p15 Mr 2017

Shoe Bling E. Velluto color *Glamour* v115 no6 p44 Je 2017

Sies Marjan Shoes C. NNADI, M. HOLGATE et al color *Vogue* v207 no9 p362 S 2017

A Sneaker for Every State J. Zorthian color *Time* v190 no5 p27 Jl 31 2017

TAKE IT TO THE STREETS: PRE-FALL'S COLLEGIATE-INSPIRED OUTERWEAR HAS A STRONG POINT OF VIEW. SPREAD THE MESSAGE *Interview* v47 no3 p42 My 2017

These Shoes Used to Be Water Bottles [Cover story] E. Velluto color *Glamour* v114 no11 p50 N 2016

Wall FLOWER: INTRICATE FLORAL PATTERNS ADORN THE SEASON'S MOST WELLCUT FEMININE PROPOSITIONS. A CLASSIC RE-BLOOMS *Interview* v47 no3 p40 Ap 2017

WHAT'S NEW color *Harper's Bazaar* no3649 p314 D 2016/Ja 2017

winter SHOE GUIDE J. DENGATE and M. SHORTEN cartoon chart color diag graph *Runner's World* v51 no11 p87 D 2016

Women's societies & clubs

See also

Sisterhoods

Fighting for Their Lives: In their first U.S. interview, Spain's hunger strikers against gender violence tell Ms. what motivates them I. R. Y MENDEZ *Ms.* v27 no3 p14 Fall 2017

Women's suffrage

How It All Began A. P. Dodson *USA Today Magazine* v146 no2866 p22 Jl 2017

PATRON OF THE PILL S. RICHARDSON *American History* v51 no6 p24 F 2017

"The suffragettes would not back down" A. Haglage and E. Mahaney color *Glamour* v115 no2 p80 F 2017

The Women Who Won Elections Before Suffrage O. B. Waxman *Time* v190 no9 p25 S 4 2017

Women's Tennis Association (Organization)

Tour Guide: WTA color *Tennis* v53 no2 p16 Mr/Ap 2017

Women's wages

969,672 THE NUMBER OF WOMEN FARMERS *Successful Farming* v115 no9 p8 Ag 2017

Let's Get You Your Raise! E. L. Gross and C. Drell cartoon *Glamour* v115 no11 p110 N 2017

Paid In Semi Full C. Suddath color diag *Bloomberg Businessweek* no4528 p42 Je 26 2017

WHITHER THE WAGE GAP? diag *Fortune* v176 no5 p15 O 1 2017

Women—Safety measures

No Peace in the Peace Corps: Women volunteers face sexual assault and victim-blaming A. BUITRAGO *Ms.* v27 no3 p16 Fall 2017

SAFETY FIRST color *Women's Health* v13 no10 p32 D 2016

SHORT TAKES *Ms.* v26 no4 p13 Wint 2016

Women—Saudi Arabia

IN BRIEF K. Stock color graph *Bloomberg Businessweek* no4540 p14 O 2 2017

To Reinvent Itself, Saudi Arabia Must Empower Its Women I. Bremmer *Time* v189 no10 p10 Mr 20 2017

Women—Sexual behavior

These Are Your Sexual Rights C. ESPOSITO, N. GLASER et al color *Glamour* v114 no7 p94 Jl 2016

Women's March on Washington, 2017

Beyond Words T. DARNELL, A. SLOAN et al color *O, The Oprah Magazine* p17 Ap 2017

FEET ON THE GROUND, NOT BACKING DOWN! *Ms.* v27 no1 p6 Spr 2017

First She Marched, Then She Ran: Alexis Frank, a 26-year-old political novice, never considered vying for Congress--until she saw Hillary Clinton lose M. COGAN img *New York* v50 no11 p42 My 29 2017

HAT TIP A. Russell cartoon *New Yorker* v93 no10 p36 Ap 24 2017

If Nixon Could Tweet S. J. DOUGLAS *In These Times* v41 no3 p18 Mr 2017

March On, Ladies N. DRAKE *USA Today Magazine* v146 no2866 p22 Jl 2017

New Friends, Common Foe C. Alter color *Time* v189 no3 p40 Ja 30 2017

The Other Side [Cover story] K. Vick, J. Sanburn et al color diag *Time* v189 no4 p24 F 6 2017

PROTEST NATION: From the Boston Tea Party to the modern-day Tea Party and the Women's March, America has been shaped by protest movements B. BROWN *New York Times Upfront* v149 no13 p16 My 15 2017

Relay the Message D. ZICKL bw color *Runner's World* v52 no6 p48 Jl 2017

Scientists speak out at Women's March color *Science* v355 no6323 p330 Ja 27 2017

Seeing Pink C. ALLEN color *Weekly Standard* v22 no21 p8 F 6 2017

Taking It to the Streets color *Progressive* v81 no3 p10 Mr 2017

A Time to Take Risks C. HASS *In These Times* v41 no3 p5 Mr 2017

WE MARCHED EVERYWHERE *Ms.* v27 no1 p20 Spr 2017

Wild Writer Walks on Washington J. Goodman color *Entertainment Weekly* no1451/1452 p18 F 3-10 2017

Women Marched. Now What? [Cover story] bw color *Glamour* v115 no4 p34 Ap 2017

Women—Social conditions—19th century

Fallen Women V. Leslie *History Today* v67 no1 p35 Ja 2017

Women—Social networks

NETWORKING AT NIGHT M. Koester color *Bloomberg Businessweek* no4501 p60 N 28 2016

TECH COMPANIES NEED WOMEN V. Zarya color *Fortune* v174 no6 p14 N 1 2016

Women—Socialization

Game Changers K. DOLD color *Women's Health* v14 no8 p122 O 2017

Women—Societies & clubs

A SUSTAINABLE SOLUTION J. BHATIA *Ms.* v27 no1 p38 Spr 2017

Women—Spain—Social conditions

Fighting for Their Lives: In their first U.S. interview, Spain's hunger strikers against gender violence tell Ms. what motivates them I. R. Y MENDEZ *Ms.* v27 no3 p14 Fall 2017

Women—Texas

Women bw cartoon color *American Cowboy* p34 LEGENDS OF TEXAS Special Issue 2017

Women—Time management

Here We Go! Oprah color *O, The Oprah Magazine* p23 O 2017

Women—Turkey—Legal status, laws, etc.

TURKISH WOMEN RISING S. JONES and C. ASQUITH *Ms.* v27 no1 p34 Spr 2017

Women—United States

    See also

      African American women

10 Women Who Changed My Life M. Markle color *Glamour* v115 no9 p36 S 2017

50-State Sisterhood color *Glamour* v115 no9 p30 S 2017

America's Richest Self-Made Women color *Forbes* v199 no6 p86 Je 13 2017

Are U.S. Millennial Men Just as Sexist as Their Dads? A. S. Kramer and A. B. Harris *Harvard Business Review Digital Articles* p2 Je 15 2016

Brave Hearts T. BROOKS, D. LANGFORD et al color *O, The Oprah Magazine* p14 Mr 2017

THE FEMMEPIRE STRIKES BACK bw color *GQ: Gentlemen's Quarterly* v86 no12 p160 D 2016

March 2017 color *O, The Oprah Magazine* p107 Mr 2017

OPRAH TALKS TO the Women of America color *O, The Oprah Magazine* p108 Mr 2017

STATES OF CHANGE *Vogue* v207 no9 p629 S 2017

THIS IS US color map *Glamour* v115 no9 p163 S 2017

This Just In J. Zorthian *Time* v188 no18 p21 O 31 2016

What I Know for Sure Oprah color *O, The Oprah Magazine* p144 Mr 2017

Women—United States—Economic conditions—21st century

CONVERSATION A. WILSON color graph *Forbes* v200 no1 p32 Jl 27 2017

Unequal Rights D. R. Wilson color *New Orleans Magazine* v51 no7 p32 My 2017

Women—United States—History

THE FEMINIST MYSTIQUE C. O'CONNOR color *Forbes* v200 no3 p68 S 28 2017

Mothers from the Past V. S. FLYNN color *Publishers Weekly* v264 no13 p68 Mr 27 2017

Women—United States—Social conditions

WOMEN ON THE RUN N. RABIN and R. BACON *Ms.* v27 no2 p18 Summ 2017

Women—United States—Social conditions—21st century

The Invisible Workload That Drags Women Down L. Wade color diag *Money* v46 no4 p64 My 2017

Women—Wounds & injuries

The Sky Is Falling T. John color *Time* v188 no22-23 p12 N/D 2016

Won-Yong Oh

K-Pop's Global Success Didn't Happen by Accident *Harvard Business Review Digital Articles* p2 N 10 2016

Wonder (Film)

A WONDERFUL WORLD M. Mechanic color *Mother Jones* v42

no6 p64 N/D 2017

WONDER I. Biedenharn color *Entertainment Weekly* no1478 / 1479 p65 Ag 18-25 2017

Wonder Forge Inc.—Officials & employees

Game On! D. Sax color *Bloomberg Businessweek* no4509 p55 Ja 30 2017

Wonder Lust (Music)

JAM SESH J. WILLIAMS bw *Cincinnati Magazine* v51 no1 p22 O 2017

Wonder Wheel (Film)

WONDER WHEEL J. Derschowitz and S. Li color *Entertainment Weekly* no1478 / 1479 p76 Ag 18-25 2017

Wonder Woman (Fictitious character)

NO. 1 WONDER WOMAN A. Breznican color *Entertainment Weekly* no1436/1437 p42 O 21 2016

SUPERHERO POWER INDEX chart color *Entertainment Weekly* no1436/1437 p80 O 21 2016

Wonder Woman Breaks Through E. Dockterman color *Time* v188 no27-28 p98 D 26 2016

WONDER WOMAN FOR PRESIDENT *Ms.* v27 no3 p33 Fall 2017

Wonder Woman (Film)

Blockbusting R. Alleva color *Commonweal* v144 no13 p21 Ag 11 2017

Comic Critics J. PODHORETZ *Weekly Standard* v22 no39 p43 Je 19 2017

FINALLY [Cover story] N. Sperling color *Entertainment Weekly* no1467 p20 My 26 2017

Gal Gadot N. Sperling color *Entertainment Weekly* no1444/1445 p52 D 16 2016

NOW PLAYING color *Entertainment Weekly* no1472 p45 Je 30 2017

Patty Jenkins B. Luscombe color *Time* v189 no24 p56 Je 26 2017

PEACE STRENGTH WISDOM WONDER A. DOVE-VIE-BAHN *Ms.* v27 no3 p31 Fall 2017

People of the Comic Book cartoon *Weekly Standard* v22 no38 p2 Je 12 2017

Summer Movie Preview S. Zacharek *Time* v189 no20 p46 My 29 2017

Summer's New Heroes P. Travers color *Rolling Stone* no1288 p52 Je 1 2017

SUMMER'S WINNERS AND LOSERS J. Nolfi color *Entertainment Weekly* no1477 p18 Ag 11 2017

Why Wonder Woman Broke Through E. Dockterman color *Time* v189 no23 p52 Je 19 2017

Woker Woman R. DOUTHAT color *National Review* v69 no12 p43 Je 26 2017

A woman at last: In Wonder Woman, accomplishment trumps beauty P. H. Nettleton color *U.S. Catholic* v82 no9 p38 S 2017

Woman of Wonder, God of War, Shortcomings of Yoga and Hero of India C. D. Reid color *Black Belt* v55 no6 p28 O/N 2017

The Wonder of Gal Gadot [Cover story] A. Morris color *Rolling Stone* no1295 p36 S 7 2017

Wonder Woman: A Perfect Paradox for the Generation That Expects to Have It All S. Schrobsdorff color *Time* v189 no22 p58 Je 12 2017

WONDER WOMAN N. Sperling color *Entertainment Weekly* no1446/1447 p56 D 2016/Ja 2017

WONDER WOMAN N. Sperling color *Entertainment Weekly* no1463/1464 p50 Ap/My 2017

WONDER WOMAN WINS N. Sperling color *Entertainment Weekly* no1470 p8 Je 16 2017

Wonderful Life (Film)

Santa Gets His Claws S. KASHNER bw cartoon color *Vanity Fair* v59 no1 p168 Holiday 2017

Wonderful Town (Theatrical production)

Wonderful Town S. Williams *Opera News* v81 no9 p40 Mr 2017

Wonderful Wonderful (Music)

THE KILLERS' WONDERFUL RETURN N. Feeney color *Entertainment Weekly* no1472 p56 Je 30 2017

WHAT TO STREAM color *Entertainment Weekly* no1484 p57 S 29 2017

Wonderstruck (Film)

ACROSS THE AGES A. LANE color *New Yorker* v93 no33 p98 O 23 2017

Wonderstruck M. KORESKY bw color *Film Comment* v53 no5

p68 S/O 2017

Wondrich, David
FIGHTING SPIRITS *Nation* v305 no11 p41 O 30 2017
The Well-Stocked Wet Bar chart color *Esquire* p140 BigBlack-Book

Wong, Ali, 1982-
ALI WONG *Washingtonian Magazine* v52 no6 p31 Mr 2017

WONG, ALIA
Why Kids Need Recess color *Atlantic* v318 no5 p22 D 2016

WONG, ANDREW
Home in the North color *Alternatives Journal (AJ) - Canada's Environmental Voice* v42 no2 p60 2016

Wong, Audris
Personalized Technology Will Upend the Doctor-Patient Relationship *Harvard Business Review Digital Articles* p2 Je 19 2015

WONG, B. D.
Most Peculiar *New York Times Book Review* p19 N 20 2016

Wong, Dale
Diamond's Space *Humanist* v77 no1 p5 Ja/F 2017

Wong, David
What the Hell Did I Just Read *Publishers Weekly* v264 no34 p95 Ag 21 2017

Wong, Fay
Mismatch repair deficiency predicts response of solid tumors to PD-1 blockade chart graph *Science* v357 no6349 p409 Jl 28 2017

Wong, George T. F.
21st-century rise in anthropogenic nitrogen deposition on a remote coral reef diag graph *Science* v356 no6339 p749 My 19 2017

Wong, H. -S. Philip
MoS2 transistors with 1-nanometer gate lengths bibl color graph *Science* v354 no6308 p99 O 7 2016

Wong, Jadyn
Scorpion M. Roffman *TV Guide* v65 no19 p24 My 1 2017

Wong, Jesse
UNSOLICITED BETA color *Climbing* no350 p16 D 2016/Ja 2017

WONG, JOANNE
The Resilience of Marine Ecosystems to Climatic Disturbances *BioScience* v67 no3 p208 Mr 2017

Wong, Joshua
August 2017 *Current History* v116 no792 p288 O 2017
Hong Kong Jails Its First Prisoners of Conscience F. Solomon color *Time* v190 no9 p13 S 4 2017

Wong, Kate
THE NEW ORIGINS OF TECHNOLOGY [Cover story] color map *Scientific American* v316 no5 p28 My 2017
The Oldest Homo sapiens? color *Scientific American* v317 no3 p12 S 2017
Our Cousin Neo color *Scientific American* v317 no2 p46 Ag 2017
Whose Tools Are These? color *Scientific American* v316 no1 p10 Ja 2017

Wong, Kristine
Goodbye Farm. Hello Lab *Sierra* v102 no2 p24 Mr/Ap 2017
Negative Energy *Sierra* v101 no6 p26 N/D 2016
Scaling New Heights *Sierra* v102 no3 p26 My/Je 2017
Sovereign Power *Sierra* v102 no4 p26 Jl/Ag 2017

Wong, Michael
How Merck Is Trying to Keep Disrupters at Bay *Harvard Business Review Digital Articles* p2 Je 8 2015
THE MAN BEHIND THE MASKS A. D. LITTLE *Cincinnati Magazine* v50 no10 p28 Jl 2017

Wong, Pindar
Global Supply Chains Are About to Get Better, Thanks to Blockchain *Harvard Business Review Digital Articles* p2 Mr 13 2017

Wong, Shirley
Death Battalions *MHQ: Quarterly Journal of Military History* v29 no3 p11 Spr 2017

Wong, Simon C. Y.
Improving the Way Boards, CEOs, and Shareholders Interact *Harvard Business Review Digital Articles* p2 Jl 28 2016
Public Pension Funds Perform Better When They Keep Politics at Bay *Harvard Business Review Digital Articles* p2 Jl 19 2016

Wong, Stephanie
In Style: Beauty Brands With Social Media Cred color *Bloomberg Businessweek* no4516 p18 Mr 27 2017
You're Smelling Different Again *Bloomberg Businessweek*

no4495 p19 O 17 2016

Wong, Victor
Community network for deaf scientists color *Science* v356 no6336 p386 Ap 28 2017

Wong, Yvette C.
Dopamine oxidation mediates mitochondrial and lysosomal dysfunction in Parkinson's disease graph *Science* v357 no6357 p1255 S 22 2017

Wong-Parodi, Gabrielle
A state of denial color *Science* v356 no6336 p385 Ap 28 2017

Wong-Rieger, Durhane
BLOOD HEALTH & ORGAN TRANSPLANTS *Maclean's* v130 no9 p31 O 2017

Wongvipat, John
SOX2 promotes lineage plasticity and antiandrogen resistance in TP53- and RB1-deficient prostate cancer bibl graph *Science* v355 no6320 p1 Ja 6 2017

Wonka, Willy (Fictitious character)
PARODY color *Weekly Standard* v22 no28 p44 Mr 27 2017

Woo, Carolyn Y.
Four ways to strengthen humanitarian aid *America* v216 no5 p10 Mr 6 2017

Woo, Jeremy
The Case for ... LOWERING THE NBA AGE MINIMUM color *Sports Illustrated* v127 no12 p24 O 16 2017

Wood
FIRE-STARTING TOOLS for Any Situation J. Williams *Mother Earth News* no281 p67 Ap/My 2017

Wood, Andrew
Priming HIV-1 broadly neutralizing antibody precursors in human Ig loci transgenic mice bibl graph *Science* v353 no6307 p1557 S 30 2016

Wood, Charles
Changes Real and (Mostly) Imagined: Even renowned lunar observers have sometimes been fooled by tricks of lighting and resolution color *Sky & Telescope* v134 no2 p52 Ag 2017
The Curious Case of Concentric Craters *Sky & Telescope* v133 no4 p52 Ap 2017
How Are Crater Rims Made? *Sky & Telescope* v133 no2 p52 F 2017
Lunar Hall of Fame: Beginning in 1645, obsessed observers drew maps of the Moon's face in ever-greater detail *Sky & Telescope* v134 no6 p52 D 2017
Mystery Ray in Serenitatis *Sky & Telescope* v132 no6 p52 D 2016
Peaks of "Eternal" Light *Sky & Telescope* v133 no6 p52 Je 2017
The Vagaries of Crater "Tweens": Some lunar impacts have characteristics that make them neither "simple" nor "complex." *Sky & Telescope* v134 no4 p52 O 2017

Wood, Charlie
Cave that housed Dead Sea Scrolls found color *Christian Century* v134 no6 p12 Mr 15 2017
CHARLIEWOOD color *ARTnews* v115 no4 p17 Wint 2016/2017

Wood, Chris
Born to be Wild color diag *Log Home Living* v34 no3 p52 Ap 2017
Built to Last color diag *Log Home Living* v34 no1 p28 F 2017
Changing the Iconic *Stage Directions* v29 no10 p60 O 2016
Living the Lake Life color diag *Log Home Living* v33 no9 p56 D 2016

Wood, Dan
3 A Solar-Powered Adobe J. Davidson img *New York* v49 no21 p90 O 17 2016

WOOD, DANITA ALLEN
BIRD BY BIRD color *Missouri Life* v44 no3 p10 My 2017
THE QUEEN WHO BECAME A WENCH color *Missouri Life* v44 no5 p10 Ag 2017
RIVER TALES color *Missouri Life* v44 no4 p10 Je 2017
ROAD TRIP color *Missouri Life* v44 no4 p19 Je 2017
A Shared Passion for Reading color *Missouri Life* v44 no6 p10 S 2017
SPRING MEANS VINTAGE HILL color *Missouri Life* v44 no2 p10 Ap 2017

WOOD, DAVID FLINT
ANGLO FILE bw color *Architectural Digest* no6 p110 Je 1 2017

Wood, Duncan
U.S.-Mexico Energy and Climate Collaboration *Wilson Quarterly* p1 Wint 2017

Wood, Elijah, 1981-
Sound Bites color *Entertainment Weekly* no1462 p7 Ap 21 2017

Wood, Elizabeth
When Coaching Finds That an Executive Isn't in the Right Role *Harvard Business Review Digital Articles* p2 Jl 31 2017

Wood, Elizabeth Miller
E is for Enrichment color *Cincinnati Magazine* v51 no1 p100 O 2017

Wood, Eric J. W.
Leo Leroy Beranek *Physics Today* v70 no10 p74 O 2017

WOOD, EVAN
DANCING IN THE DARK bw chart color map *Missouri Life* v44 no5 p32 Ag 2017
In Bloom color *Missouri Life* v44 no2 p56 Ap 2017
INNER HIGHWAYS color *Missouri Life* v44 no2 p20 Ap 2017
Whoa-o-oh, Listen to the Music color *Missouri Life* v44 no4 p14 Je 2017

Wood, Evan Rachel, 1987-
Arms Race E. Wilson color *InStyle* v24 no4 p78 Ap 2017
Artificial Grit M. Z. SEITZ img *New York* v49 no20 p128 O 3 2016
The Awakening of Evan Rachel Wood A. MORRIS color *Rolling Stone* no1275 p46 D 1 2016
SECOND WORLD E. NUSSBAUM cartoon *New Yorker* v92 no34 p82 O 24 2016
When 'Blade Runner' Meets 'Deadwood' R. SHEFFIELD color *Rolling Stone* no1273 p23 N 3 2016

Wood, Evan Rachel, 1987—Interviews
"They Said I Didn't Have the Face for Short Hair" S. Kitchens color *Glamour* v114 no7 p76 Jl 2016

Wood, Frank K.
What You Should NEVER Put in Your Will! *Saturday Evening Post* v289 no4 p85 Jl/Ag 2017

Wood, Gaby
Holding Court bw color *Vogue* v207 no9 p618 S 2017
May Day color *Vogue* v207 no4 p204 Ap 2017
Miss Universe [Cover story] color *Vogue* v207 no11 p190 N 2017
RUTH on the RISE bw color *Vogue* v207 no1 p80 Ja 2017

Wood, George J.
Discussion *Smithsonian* v48 no1 p10 Ap 2017

Wood, Gordon S.
The Inventor of the Presidency color *New York Review of Books* v64 no9 p34 My 25 2017
Prodigy of Freedom color *Weekly Standard* v22 no38 p30 Je 12 2017
The Strangely Contentious Lives of the Quincy Adamses color *New York Review of Books* v63 no19 p55 D 8 2016

Wood, Graeme
AMERICAN JIHADI cartoon color *Atlantic* v319 no2 p74 Mr 2017
HIS KAMPF bw *Atlantic* v319 no5 p40 Je 2017
On the Fringes of ISIS D. FILKINS *New York Times Book Review* p13 Ja 22 2017

WOOD, GREG
The Back Story color *Missouri Life* v44 no5 p98 Ag 2017
A Night at the Crossroads of America color *Missouri Life* v44 no4 p98 Je 2017
A Tale of Two Kates bw *Missouri Life* v44 no2 p122 Ap 2017
Wandering into the Past color *Missouri Life* v44 no6 p90 S 2017

Wood, Jacqueline MacInnes
THE BOLD AND THE BEAUTIFUL M. LOGAN *TV Guide* p48 D 5 2016

WOOD, JAMES
ENTANGLEMENT THEORY color *New Yorker* v93 no25 p83 Ag 28 2017
MALE GAZE cartoon *New Yorker* v92 no32 p98 O 10 2016
THE OTHER SIDE OF SILENCE bw cartoon *New Yorker* v93 no16 p90 Je 5 2017
PAUL IS DEAD color *New Yorker* v93 no20 p82 Jl 10 2017
SCRUTINY cartoon *New Yorker* v92 no41 p73 D 12 2016
STRANGERS AMONG US cartoon *New Yorker* v93 no29 p92 S 25 2017
THE TEACHER cartoon *New Yorker* v92 no40 p28 D 5 2016

Wood, Jason Y.
2017 A Look Ahead color map *Power & Motoryacht* v32 no12 p38 D 2016

Azimut Grande 35 Metri color *Power & Motoryacht* v34 no11 p74 N 2017
Azimut S7 color *Power & Motoryacht* v34 no6 p34 Je 2017
Beneteau Gran Turismo 46 color *Power & Motoryacht* v33 no2 p44 F 2017
Canados 808 Maximus color *Power & Motoryacht* v34 no11 p82 N 2017
Changing the Game [Cover story] chart color diag *Power & Motoryacht* v34 no6 p66 Je 2017
Climb Aboard chart color diag *Power & Motoryacht* v33 no1 p78 Ja 2017
C-MAP Genesis Edge Premium Marine-Mapping Service color *Power & Motoryacht* v34 no10 p58 O 2017
Cranchi E56F color *Power & Motoryacht* v34 no8 p32 Ag 2017
Danger Zone? color *Power & Motoryacht* v34 no11 p62 N 2017
Endless Possibilities [Cover story] chart color *Power & Motoryacht* v34 no10 p70 O 2017
Exploring Parts Unknown color *Power & Motoryacht* v33 no4 p24 Ap 2017
Fairline Squadron 53 color *Power & Motoryacht* v33 no3 p56 Mr 2017
FLIR One Smartphone Thermal-Imaging Attachment color *Power & Motoryacht* v33 no3 p46 Mr 2017
Forward Thinking color *Power & Motoryacht* v34 no10 p50 O 2017
Furuno TZTouch2 Software Update 4.01 color *Power & Motoryacht* v33 no3 p46 Mr 2017
Garmin InReach SE+ and Explorer+ Satellite Communication Devices color *Power & Motoryacht* v33 no3 p48 Mr 2017
Garmin Quatix 5 Marine GPS Smartwatch color *Power & Motoryacht* v34 no7 p28 Jl 2017
Greenline 65 OceanClass color *Power & Motoryacht* v34 no8 p34 Ag 2017
Helm Hacks color *Power & Motoryacht* v32 no11 p50 N 2016
ICOM IC-M605 VHF color *Power & Motoryacht* v34 no10 p54 O 2017
Living History color *Power & Motoryacht* v34 no6 p16 Je 2017
Minorca 42 Islander color *Power & Motoryacht* v34 no9 p50 S 2017
Mission Ready color *Power & Motoryacht* v34 no9 p36 S 2017
NEW ELECTRONICS bw color *Power & Motoryacht* v33 no4 p36 Ap 2017
NEW ELECTRONICS color *Power & Motoryacht* v32 no11 p54 N 2016
NEW ELECTRONICS color *Power & Motoryacht* v34 no6 p26 Je 2017
NEW ELECTRONICS color *Power & Motoryacht* v34 no9 p42 S 2017
Numarine 105HT color *Power & Motoryacht* v34 no10 p60 O 2017
Overmarine Mangusta Oceano 42 color *Power & Motoryacht* v32 no11 p66 N 2016
The Power of Proportion chart color *Power & Motoryacht* v33 no4 p92 Ap 2017
Prestige 460 color *Power & Motoryacht* v34 no6 p32 Je 2017
Pulling Back the Curtain color *Power & Motoryacht* v34 no7 p26 Jl 2017
Pursuit S 328 color *Power & Motoryacht* v34 no7 p30 Jl 2017
Put the Hammer Down color *Power & Motoryacht* v33 no1 p40 Ja 2017
Riva 76 Bahamas color *Power & Motoryacht* v32 no12 p30 D 2016
Sanlorenzo SL78 color *Power & Motoryacht* v33 no1 p48 Ja 2017
Sense of Duty bw color *Power & Motoryacht* v34 no8 p46 Ag 2017
THE SHAPE OF THINGS chart color *Power & Motoryacht* v32 no11 p102 N 2016
Sirena 64 color *Power & Motoryacht* v33 no4 p38 Ap 2017
Siren Marine MTC Boat-Monitoring System color *Power & Motoryacht* v34 no7 p28 Jl 2017
Skymate Mazu App and mSeries Satellite Communications System color *Power & Motoryacht* v34 no10 p56 O 2017
Sounds Terrific color *Power & Motoryacht* v33 no3 p42 Mr 2017
Stabilizing the Market color *Power & Motoryacht* v32 no11 p146 N 2016
THE STAR OF THE SHOW [Cover story] color *Power & Moto-*

ryacht v32 no11 p76 N 2016

To Each His Own cartoon chart color *Power & Motoryacht* v32 no12 p44 D 2016

Watch and Learn color *Power & Motoryacht* v34 no11 p68 N 2017

Westport 125 color *Power & Motoryacht* v34 no7 p32 Jl 2017

What's Next? color *Power & Motoryacht* v33 no2 p48 F 2017

Work in Progress color *Power & Motoryacht* v34 no8 p58 Ag 2017

A World Unfolding chart color diag *Power & Motoryacht* v33 no3 p106 Mr 2017

Wood, Jennifer Sheshko

Making The Knight of Mirrors *Stage Directions* v29 no11 p44 N 2016

Wood, Keith

CAN YOU GO TO JAIL FOR HANDING OUT PAMPHLETS? J. SULLUM bw *Reason* v49 no6 p8 N 2017

Wood, Lawrence

The Irrational Jesus: Leading the Fully Human Church *Christian Century* v134 no17 p39 Ag 16 2017

Wood, Maureen

House Mother: MAUREEN WOOD SPENT A LIFETIME CRE-ATING A SENSE OF HOME FOR OTHERS L. PIKE *Cincinnati Magazine* v50 no11 p44 Ag 2017

Wood, Michael

The Codebreaker M. PERLOFF bw *Weekly Standard* v22 no30 p32 Ap 10 2017

Finding Hardy at Last bw *New York Review of Books* v63 no20 p63 D 22 2016

In Praise of Ambiguity D. Bromwich bw *New York Review of Books* v64 no16 p50 O 26 2017

Wonderful Chances color *New York Review of Books* v64 no9 p45 My 25 2017

Wood, Michelle E.

Emergence and spread of a human-transmissible multidrug-re-sistant nontuberculous mycobacterium bibl diag graph *Science* v354 no6313 p751 N 11 2016

Wood, Paul

Arab Fling *Washington Monthly* p3 Ja/F 2017

Wood, Peter

Jon A. Shields and Joshua M. Dunn, Sr., Passing on the Right: Conservative Professors in the Progressive University *Society* v54 no1 p89 F 2017

Wood, Robert

THE SOFTER SIDE OF ROBOTICS N. Daly diag *National Geographic* v231 no5 p18 My 2017

Wood, Ron, 1947——Health

Random Notes color *Rolling Stone* no1297 p24 O 5 2017

Wood, Ryan

A LEAP OF FAITH J. Autry color *Practical Horseman* v45 no5 p30 My 2017

WOOD, STEPHANIE

What doctors tell their friends about birth control color *Redbook* p86 F 2017

What doctors tell their friends about bones color *Redbook* p82 D 2016

What doctors tell their friends about cancer color *Redbook* p77 N 2017

What doctors tell their friends about the sun color *Redbook* p66 Je 2017

What pediatricians tell their friends color *Redbook* p79 S 2017

WOOD, STEPHANIE A.

Gray Seals and White Sharks Meet Anew color *Natural History* v125 no7 p22 Jl/Ag 2017

WOOD, TARA

When Norah Met Mr. Dan color *Reader's Digest* v189 no1129 p94 Ap 2017

Wood, Zachary

Inviting controversy D. Bendis color *Christian Century* v134 no15 p10 Jl 19 2017

WOOD, ZACHARY R.

The Uncomfortable Truth *Weekly Standard* v22 no8 p13 O 31 2016

Wood carving

Crafted with a Purpose L. A. Addington color *Missouri Life* v44 no4 p16 Je 2017

A Cut Above J. BAINBRIDGE and N. Pomeroy color *Bon Appetit*

v61 no11 p38 N 2016

Julian Watts D. BISHOP color *American Craft* v76 no6 p12 D 2016-Ja 2017

make a WOODSY statement D. Howland color *Cabin Living* p7 S 2017

RIPE FOR DECORATING E. N. GAGE color *Martha Stewart Living* p104 S 2017

Wood carving——United States

Thomas Jefferson's Letter Rack: David Esterly carves our past E. Pochoda color *Magazine Antiques* v184 no5 p92 S/O 2017

Wood-cutting tools——Evaluation

Entry-Level Planers R. ROMANSKI color *Popular Mechanics* p40 D 2016/Ja 2017

Wood duck

HALF HOUR OF GLORY T. E. Nickens bw color *Field & Stream* v122 no4 p26 S 2017

Wood Duck color *Audubon* v119 no3 p48 Fall 2017

Wood floors

decorating: TRICKS OF THE TRADE [Cover story] J. LARSEN color *Timber Home Living* v27 no6 p46 D 2017

Family Tradition L. Cutrone color *New Orleans Magazine* v51 no9 p52 Jl 2017

finish color *Timber Home Living* p46 2017 Annual Buyers

Fixing Sagging Floor Joists R. Tschoepe diag *Old House Journal* v45 no7 p56 O 2017

FLOOR PLAN gallery color diag *Log Home Living* v34 no7 p44 S 2017

Go With the Grain E. MOODY chart color *Martha Stewart Living* p36 Mr 2017

Nice Save! color *Log Home Living* v34 no7 p20 S 2017

The Perfect Marriage color *Log Home Living* v34 no7 p8 S 2017

Wood floors——Design & construction

FLOORING color *Old House Journal* v44 p65 2016 Design Center source Book

Wood floors——Maintenance & repair

Fixing Wood Floors M. Ellen Polson color *Log Home Living* v33 no7 p75 S 2016

Wood pellets——Environmental aspects

THE BURNING QUESTION W. Cornwall color *Science* v355 no6320 p18 Ja 6 2017

Wood poles

Coat Rack from a Porch Post B. D. Coleman color *Old House Journal* v45 no6 p58 S 2017

VISIONS color *National Geographic* v231 no3 p6 Mr 2017

Wood products

See also

Plywood

A CUT ABOVE F. VIGNA *Martha Stewart Living* no268 p148 O 2016

Wood quality

Nice Save! color *Log Home Living* v34 no7 p20 S 2017

Wood recycling

Renewed Beauty L. Claverie *New Orleans Homes & Lifestyles* v20 no2 p28 Spr 2017

Wood sculpture

ESSENTIAL TRUTH S. SARGENT *Virginia Living* v15 no1 p31 D 2016

Wood sculpture——Exhibitions

ROSEMARY MAYER T. Ballard color *Art in America* v105 no3 p130 Mr 2017

Wood siding

CLAPBOARD, DUTCH LAP & OTHER NOVELTIES diag *Old House Journal* v45 no5 p21 Ag 2017

Exterior Finishes color *Cabin Living* p72 Ja/F 2017

Wood stoves

See also

Rocket mass heaters

HOMESTEAD HACKS: Our readers share clever projects that will help you live a self-sufficient life in the country, the sub-urbs, or the city *Mother Earth News* no284 p66 O/N 2017

Wood tar

Neandertal tar-making reconstructed B. BOWER color *Science News* v192 no5 p13 S 30 2017

Wood veneers & veneering

See also

Plywood

STUFF USE & TIME SCREWED UP T. Petty cartoon *Old House Journal* v45 no3 p54 My 2017

Wood warblers
See also
  Prothonotary warbler
Tuning up their vocal cords color *National Wildlife (World Edition)* v55 no4 p10 Je/Jl 2017
WANDERING WARBLERS: These featherweight frequent fliers go the distance C. KETTLEWELL *Virginia Living* v15 no4 p19 Je 2017

Woodard, Alfre, 1952-
Mother. Daughter. Repeat K. Brown color *Glamour* v115 no5 p189 My 2017

Woodard, Colin
Pluribus et Unum J. Miller *Washington Monthly* p6 N/D 2016

Woodard, George
CAN'T STOP NOW B. Donahue color *Backpacker* v45 no1 p70 Ja 2017

Woodard, Josef
The Art of Mosaic-Making at Vossa Jazz color *Downbeat* v84 no7 p20 Jl 2017
Bold in the Cold: Finland's Tampere Jazz Happening Makes an Impact color *Downbeat* v84 no2 p17 F 2017
CHARLIE HADEN: PURSUING LIBERATION bw *Downbeat* v84 no3 p36 Mr 2017
ERIC REVIS: Endless Possibilities color *Downbeat* v84 no10 p50 O 2017
FIMAV Covers Multiple Angles, with Solo Braxton on Top color *Downbeat* v84 no8 p14 Ag 2017
FLOATING & FLYING color *Downbeat* v83 no11 p36 N 2016
NILS ØKLAND color *Downbeat* v84 no1 p20 Ja 2017

Woodard, Monique
the moguls bw color *Foreign Policy* no221 p83 N/D 2016

Woodard, Walt
BIG SKY BONUS color *Team Roping Journal* p14 O 2017

Woodberry, Billy
DIGGING AND BLUING WITH BILLY WOODBERRY J. Luckett *Film Quarterly* v70 no4 p67 Summ 2017

Woodberry Forest School (Woodberry Forest, Virginia)
21st Century Know-How: WOODBERRY FOREST CREATES NEW LEARNING COMMONS *Virginia Living* v15 no6 p97 O 2017

Woodbury, Terrance
TECH TRENDS CHANGING OUR WORLD color *Black Enterprise* v47 no2 p46 S 2016

Woodcock, B. A.
Country-specific effects of neonicotinoid pesticides on honey bees and wild bees diag map *Science* v356 no6345 p1393 Je 30 2017

Woodcutting (Printmaking)
Treasure Map G. Pollard *Virginia Living* v15 no2 p35 F 2017

Wooden building
See also
  Log buildings
  Wood floors
8 STEPS TO A SMOOTH BUILD *Timber Home Living* p37 2017 Annual Buyers
The Accessible Home [Cover story] color *Timber Home Living* v27 no6 p20 D 2017
all in the details color *Timber Home Living* p50 2017 Annual Buyers
ask the editor color *Timber Home Living* p34 2017 Annual Buyers
BEST GREAT ROOMS color *Log Home Living* p24 2017 SpecialIssue
build color *Timber Home Living* p36 2017 Annual Buyers
COUNTRY PRIDE: Selling a log cabin to a military couple didn't come down to price A. GARDNER *Indianapolis Monthly* p42 N 2017
Log Your Vote *Log Home Living* p6 2017 SpecialIssue
Long Live the Log Home color diag *Log Home Living* p30 2017 SpecialIssue
THE LOOK FOR LESS color *Timber Home Living* p52 2017 Annual Buyers
Material Gain color *Timber Home Living* v27 no6 p8 D 2017
Revenge of the Trees J. DAVIDSON img *New York* v49 no26 p80 D 26 2016
Second Time's the Charm S. LOGAN color *Timber Home Living*

p54 2017 Annual Buyers
SIPS cartoon *Timber Home Living* p44 2017 Annual Buyers
SPACE SAVERS color *Timber Home Living* p35 2017 Annual Buyers
Standing Guard *Los Angeles Magazine* p20 Ag 2017
Timber Home Anatomy diag *Timber Home Living* p45 2017 Annual Buyers

Wooden building design & construction
The Beauty of Built-Ins color *Timber Home Living* v27 no2 p16 Ap 2017
A Change of Plans color diag *Log Home Living* p26 2017 SpecialIssue
THE GREAT ESCAPE color map *Timber Home Living* p66 2017 Annual Buyers
q&a color *Timber Home Living* v27 no2 p14 Ap 2017
Simple Addition color diag *Timber Home Living* v27 no2 p22 Ap 2017
tip color *Timber Home Living* v27 no2 p12 Ap 2017
Walk on Wood color *Timber Home Living* v27 no2 p26 Ap 2017

Wooden doors
HOUSE & GARDEN color *Old House Journal* v44 p109 2016 Design Center source Book

Wooden fences—Design & construction
Painting the Fence B. DONAHUE and C. RIZZA color *Yankee* p114 Mr 2017

Wooden-frame houses
barn style color *Timber Home Living* v27 no5 p54 O 2017
get the HOME you want diag *Timber Home Living* p15 2017 SpecialIssue
HOME ON THE RANGE [Cover story] color *Timber Home Living* v27 no5 p88 O 2017
HOUSE of STYLE color *Timber Home Living* p12 2017 SpecialIssue
Modern Mix S. LOGAN color *Timber Home Living* v27 no4 p44 Ag 2017
Reclaiming the Past N. E. BERRY color diag *Timber Home Living* v27 no6 p26 D 2017
resource guide color *Timber Home Living* p59 2017 SpecialIssue
waterfront retreats color *Timber Home Living* v27 no4 p80 Ag 2017
we asked you answered D. Henderson, W. Loder et al color *Timber Home Living* v27 no5 p18 O 2017

Wooden-frame houses—Design & construction
The Accessible Home [Cover story] color *Timber Home Living* v27 no6 p20 D 2017
BIG SKY BEAUTY color *Timber Home Living* v27 no2 p80 Ap 2017
Big Sky Beauty [Cover story] color *Timber Home Living* v27 no6 p34 D 2017
Country Craftsman C. Johnson color *Timber Home Living* v27 no6 p42 D 2017
decorating: TRICKS OF THE TRADE [Cover story] J. LARSEN color *Timber Home Living* v27 no6 p46 D 2017
Frame Time color diag *Timber Home Living* v27 no4 p10 Ag 2017
From Retreat to Forever C. Johnson color *Log Home Living* v34 no5 p(Sp)6 Jl 2017
Gathering Place color *Timber Home Living* v27 no5 p46 O 2017
Home with a View J. Brewster color diag *Log Home Living* v34 no5 p52 Jl 2017
HOUSE of STYLE color *Timber Home Living* p12 2017 SpecialIssue
In Great Demand color diag *Log Home Living* v34 no5 p46 Jl 2017
Making History color diag *Timber Home Living* v27 no5 p40 O 2017
New York State of Mind color *Timber Home Living* v27 no5 p32 O 2017
NOW & LATER color *Timber Home Living* v27 no4 p21 Ag 2017
Open House color diag *Timber Home Living* v27 no2 p36 Ap 2017
product spotlight color *Timber Home Living* v27 no5 p31 O 2017
Pure & Simple S. FREED color *Timber Home Living* v27 no2 p28 Ap 2017
regional resource guide color *Timber Home Living* v27 no5 p63 O 2017
Room with a View color *Timber Home Living* v27 no4 p38 Ag 2017
Strength Meets Sustainability color *Timber Home Living* v27 no5

p14 O 2017

WINNING COMBINATION [Cover story] color diag *Timber Home Living* v27 no6 p72 D 2017

your house your way color diag *Timber Home Living* v27 no4 p50 Ag 2017

Wooden spoons

Kitchen-Counter Couture color *Good Housekeeping* v264 no5 p57 My 2017

Wooden stairs—Design & construction

BEST STAIRWAY color *Timber Home Living* p26 2017 Special-Issue

Wooden tablets

Country Chic color *Architectural Digest* v73 no11 p116 N 2016

TOP 10 DISCOVERIES OF 2016 J. URBANUS, N. SWAMINA-THAN et al bw cartoon color *Archaeology* v70 no1 p26 Ja/F 2017

Wooden toys

holiday SURVIVAL GUIDE color *Good Housekeeping* v263 no6 p27 D 2016

INTO THE WOOD A. FLANGO *Cincinnati Magazine* v50 no8 p34 My 2017

Wooden windows

HOUSE & GARDEN *Design Center Sourcebook* p109 2016

Wood—Evaluation

Surface Value R. C. Orrell *Architectural Record* v205 no6 p57 Je 2017

Woodfield, Randall

INTERSTATE 5 KILLER L. J. Wertheim, M. Cohen et al color *Sports Illustrated* v125 no17 p108 N 21 2016 Double Issue

Woodford Reserve Distillery (Company)

Woodford Reserve Distillery N. Tappan *American History* v51 no6 p72 F 2017

Woodfox, Albert

From the publisher P. W. Marty *Christian Century* v134 no5 p3 Mr 1 2017

SURVIVING SOLITARY R. AVIV cartoon color *New Yorker* v92 no45 p54 Ja 16 2017

WOODHEAD, BEN

ROAR OF THE CROWD *Texas Monthly* v45 no6 p10 Je 2017

WOODHOUSE, LEIGHTON

Torching L.A.'s Olympic Plans *In These Times* v41 no10 p12 O 2017

Woodhouse, Michael

Terawatt-scale photovoltaics: Trajectories and challenges chart graph *Science* v356 no6334 p141 Ap 14 2017

Woodhouse Co.

Check, Please color *Timber Home Living* v27 no3 p14 Je 2017

Dream Destination color diag *Timber Home Living* v27 no3 p48 Je 2017

Woodie, Robert

SEARCHING FOR POPS color *Backpacker* p71 O 2017

WOODIWISS, BOB

The Man Who Spewed Too Much cartoon *Cincinnati Magazine* v51 no1 p70 O 2017

Woodland caribou

in a snap color *Canadian Geographic* v137 no5 p14 S/O 2017

Woodland Scenics (Company)

Woodland Scenics Built & Ready Work Shed D. Kawala *Model Railroader* v84 no6 p67 Je 2017

Woodland Scenics HO Just Plug vehicles S. Otte *Model Railroader* v84 no7 p65 Jl 2017

Woodle, Kathryne Sparks

A bridge between undergraduate and doctoral degrees *Physics Today* v70 no2 p50 F 2017

Woodley, Shailene, 1991-

Big Little Lies S. Vilkomerson color *Entertainment Weekly* no1448 p34 Ja 13 2017

War of the Greens color *Glamour* v114 no12 p244 D 2016

Woodpecker behavior

WONDERFUL WOODPECKERS: Of the 22 species found in North America, we have 9 woodpecker species that inhabit the forests of New York J. L. Turner *New York State Conservationist* v72 no2 p20 O 2017

Woodpeckers

See also

Red-bellied woodpecker

Conversing with a Sapsucker B. H. RICH *Natural History* v124 no10 p13 N 2016

Humor in Uniform T. HARNEY color *Reader's Digest* v189 no1129 p135 Ap 2017

Woodpeckers THE ENGINEERS OF ECOSYSTEMS J. LLOYD *American Forests* v123 no3 p16 Fall 2017

Woodriff, Piers

Shared Culture, Shared Beliefs *National Review* v69 no18 p2 O 2 2017

WOODRING, C. J.

Discussion *Smithsonian* v47 no7 p10 N 2016

WOODROFFE, ROSIE

Conserving the World's Megafauna and Biodiversity: The Fierce Urgency of Now *BioScience* v67 no3 p197 Mr 2017

Saving the World's Terrestrial Megafauna color *BioScience* v66 no10 p807 O 1 2016

Woodruff, H. Boyd

H. Boyd Woodruff (1917–2017) J. Wennstrom Bennett, D. Eveleigh et al bw *Science* v356 no6336 p381 Ap 28 2017

Woodruff, Judy

NewsHour Distracted by Distraction N. Solomon *Extra!* v30 no1 p3 Ja/F 2017

Woodruff, Teresa K.

Menstrual Cycle "on a Chip" D. Fine Maron color *Scientific American* v316 no6 p16 Je 2017

Woodruff, Tracey J.

Estimating the health benefits of environmental regulations color *Science* v357 no6350 p457 Ag 4 2017

Woods, C. Geoffrey

Neurodevelopmental protein Musashi-1 interacts with the Zika genome and promotes viral replication diag *Science* v357 no6346 p83 Jl 7 2017

Woods, Cheyenne

Cheyenne Woods J. Marksbury and C. Barrett color *Golf Magazine* v59 no6 p34 Je 2017

Woods, Damien

A cargo-sorting DNA robot color *Science* v357 no6356 p1112 S 15 2017

Woods, Eva

Something Like Happy color *Publishers Weekly* v264 no30 p38 Jl 24 2017

Woods, Grant

THE BEST DAYS OF THE Rut [Cover story] S. BESTUL color *Field & Stream* v122 no6 p37 N 2017

Woods, Jamila

HOOKED ON HER M. Nance color *Essence* v47 no7 p48 N 2016

Woods, Joel

Gifts of the Sea M. ALLEN *Yankee* v81 no1 p12 Ja/F 2017

A HARD LIFE MADE BEAUTIFUL *Yankee* v81 no1 p94 Ja/F 2017

Woods, Jonathan D.

The Angels of Irma [Cover story] color map *Time* v190 no12 p34 S 25 2017

WOODS, KERRY

Combining Biodiversity Resurveys across Regions to Advance Global Change Research *BioScience* v67 no1 p73 Ja 2017

WOODS, MATT

HOW TO MAKE ANYTHING [Cover story] color diag *Popular Mechanics* p56 S 2017

Woods, Phil, 1931-2015

81st READERS POLL COMPLETE RESULTS bw chart color *Downbeat* v83 no12 p56 D 2016

Hall of Fame PHIL WOODS 'A SOLIDER FOR JAZZ' T. Panken bw color *Downbeat* v83 no12 p34 D 2016

Seasons Change B. REED bw *Downbeat* v83 no12 p8 D 2016

Woods, Rick

FROM OUR READERS *Sky & Telescope* v133 no4 p6 Ap 2017

Woods, Tiger, 1975-

The 1997 Masters: My Story *Publishers Weekly* v264 no6 p61 F 6 2017

THE BALLAD OF A BIG CAT AND A GATOR M. Bamberger and J. Feldman color *Sports Illustrated* v126 no11 p64 Ap 17-24 2017

BY THE NUMBERS C. Mcdowell color *Golf Magazine* v59 no4 p84 Ap 2017

Game of Thrones A. Shipnuck and C. Barrett color *Golf Magazine*

Woojin Kwon
Spiral density waves in a young protoplanetary disk bibl graph *Science* v353 no6307 p1519 S 30 2016

Wook Lee Jeong
Nucleic acid detection with CRISPR-Cas13a/C2c2 color diag *Science* v356 no6336 p438 Ap 28 2017

Wook Choi, Jang
Highly elastic binders integrating polyrotaxanes for silicon microparticle anodes in lithium ion batteries diag *Science* v357 no6348 p279 Jl 21 2017

Wool
Wool Gathering M. ENGELHARD *Sierra* v101 no6 p64 N/D 2016

Wool industry
LUXE LAMBS: Gum Tree Farm wool blends rustic with luxury *Virginia Living* p88 2017 Best 20of Virginia

Wool textiles
COLD COMFORT S. L. White color *Field & Stream* v121 no6 p80 N 2016

Wool textiles—Evaluation
Cozy Comforts color *Martha Stewart Living* p50 O 2017
LUXE LAMBS: Gum Tree Farm wool blends rustic with luxury *Virginia Living* p88 2017 Best 20of Virginia

Woolaway, Michael
LEARNING FROM A MASTER S. MacDonald color *Cycle World* v56 no1 p48 Ja/F 2017

Wooldridge, Andrew
B.C. Presses Broaden Their Reach and Band Together A. GROSS color *Publishers Weekly* v263 no47 p44 N 21 2016

Wooldridge, Jeffrey M.
Contingent valuation: Flawed logic? color *Science* v357 no6349 p363 Jl 28 2017
Putting a value on injuries to natural assets: The BP oil spill chart *Science* v356 no6335 p253 Ap 21 2017

WOOLDRIDGE, JOHN
Against The Grain color *Power & Motoryacht* v34 no8 p70 Ag 2017
AMERICAN ICON chart color *Power & Motoryacht* v33 no1 p60 Ja 2017
Crafted for Cruising color *Power & Motoryacht* v34 no6 p62 Je 2017
Go Boldly color *Power & Motoryacht* v33 no1 p90 Ja 2017
THE GOOD LIFE color *Power & Motoryacht* v34 no11 p136 N 2017
HOME AND ABROAD color *Power & Motoryacht* v32 no11 p134 N 2016
LEADER OF THE PACK chart color *Power & Motoryacht* v32 no11 p114 N 2016
Miami Bound color *Power & Motoryacht* v33 no2 p62 F 2017
Pretty & Practical color *Power & Motoryacht* v34 no9 p78 S 2017
Style and Substance color *Power & Motoryacht* v33 no2 p100 F 2017
Yacht Royalty color *Power & Motoryacht* v33 no4 p74 Ap 2017

Woolen goods
Winter WARMER-UPPERS N. BUCK color *Nebraska Life* v21 no6 p64 N/D 2017

Woolen goods—Evaluation
Cashmere L. Indvik color *InStyle* v23 no12 p217 N 2016

Wooley, Nate
Language Games M. LONGLEY color *Downbeat* v84 no6 p66 Je 2017

WOOLF, AVI
The Expert Strikes Back *Commentary* v144 no1 p56 Jl/Ag 2017

Woolf, Clifford J.
Time for nonaddictive relief of pain bibl color *Science* v355 no6329 p1026 Mr 10 2017

Woolf, Virginia, 1882-1941
Faith Matters S. Paulsell color *Christian Century* v133 no25 p44 D 7 2016

Woolfson, Adrian
Inevitable or improbable? color *Science* v357 no6349 p362 Jl 28 2017
Tinkering with evolution color *Science* v354 no6313 p712 N 11 2016

Woolfson, Derek N.
How do miniproteins fold? diag *Science* v357 no6347 p133 Jl 14 2017

Woolfson, Michael Mark
Colour How We See It and How We Use It M. H. Brill *Physics Today* v70 no4 p56 Ap 2017

Woolhouse, Mark
Role for migratory wild birds in the global spread of avian influenza H5N8 bibl graph map *Science* v354 no6309 p213 O 14 2016

Woolley, Suzanne
The Fall of Warren's CFPB? bw *Bloomberg Businessweek* no4500 p36 N 21 2016
Revising Retirement color *Bloomberg Businessweek* no4522 p43 My 15 2017
Thank You For Calling Equifax, Your Business Is Not Important to Us *Bloomberg Businessweek* no4538 p38 S 18 2017
You Can't Retire On the Trump Bump cartoon *Bloomberg Businessweek* no4514 p38 Mr 13 2017

Woolly rhinoceros
Some woolly rhinos grew odd neck ribs S. MILIUS color *Science News* v192 no5 p10 S 30 2017

Woo Nam, Sae
Nanophotonic rare-earth quantum memory with optically controlled retrieval diag graph *Science* v357 no6358 p1392 S 29 2017

Woo Park, Jee
Second-scale nuclear spin coherence time of ultracold 23Na40K molecules diag *Science* v357 no6349 p372 Jl 28 2017

WOOSTER, MARTIN MORSE
FROM THE ARCHIVES bw cartoon *Reason* v48 no11 p70 Ap 2017
FROM THE ARCHIVES bw color *Reason* v49 no3 p70 Jl 2017
Thirst Cruncher color *Weekly Standard* v22 no12 p32 N 28 2016

Wooten, Eric C.
Tumor aneuploidy correlates with markers of immune evasion and with reduced response to immunotherapy diag *Science* v355 no6322 p261 Ja 20 2017

WORBY, REBECCA
Industrial Ecosystem *Orion Magazine* v35 no3 p7 My/Je 2016

WORCESTER, DAREN
Raise a Kid Who Loves Hiking il *Backpacker* v45 no2 p34 Mr 2017

Worcester, William
William the Wanderer N. Orme *History Today* v66 no12 p32 D 2016

Word (Linguistics)
Grammar School E. C. Peyton color *New Orleans Magazine* v51 no5 p48 Mr 2017
That's Outrageous! color *Reader's Digest* v190 no1133 p129 S 2017

Word games
Funny Fill-In S. YOUNGSON cartoon *National Geographic Kids* no472 p34 Ag 2017
IT PAYS TO INCREASE YOUR Word Power E. COX and H. RATHVON *Reader's Digest* v189 no1127 p132 F 2017
Stay Sharp M. DANESI color *Prevention* v69 no11 p96 N 2017
What in the World? *National Geographic Kids* no469 p34 Ap 2017
Word Play [Cover story] color *Prevention* v69 no6 p96 Je 2017

Word of God (Christian theology)
The Other Guy J. Ryan color *Commonweal* v144 no12 p39 Jl 7 2017

Word-of-mouth advertising
What Really Makes Customers Buy a Product H. N. Wilson, E. K. Macdonald et al *Harvard Business Review Digital Articles* p2 N 9 2015

Word-of-mouth communication
The Freelance Economy Still Runs on Word of Mouth J. Fox *Harvard Business Review Digital Articles* p2 O 9 2014
What to Do When Satisfied B2B Customers Refuse to Recommend You U. M. Dholakia *Harvard Business Review Digital Articles* p2 Ag 13 2015

Worden, Alexandra Z.
A plankton bloom shifts as the ocean warms bibl color diag *Science* v354 no6310 p287 O 21 2016

WordPress (Web resource)
Recent WordPress vulnerability used to deface 1.5 million pages L. CONSTANTIN color *PCWorld* p47 Mr 2017

2016

"My boss was secretly filming me" M. Elliott color *Glamour* v115 no4 p156 Ap 2017

Navigating Political Talk at Work D. W. Ballard color graph *Harvard Business Review Digital Articles* p2 Mr 2 2017

Office De-stress Ideas D. L. GORDON and D. L. KATZ color *Reader's Digest* v189 no1130 p49 My 2017

Our Biases Undermine Our Colleagues' Attempts to Be Authentic T. R. Opie and R. E. Freeman *Harvard Business Review Digital Articles* p2 Jl 5 2017

Pay Attention and Be Nice *USA Today Magazine* v145 no2859 p13 D 2016

Positive Teams Are More Productive E. Seppala *Harvard Business Review Digital Articles* p2 Mr 18 2015

The Powerful Effect of Noticing Good Things at Work T. M. Glomb and J. E. Bono *Harvard Business Review Digital Articles* p2 S 4 2015

Pumping on the Job *Glamour* v115 no5 p134 My 2017

The Real Cost of CHEAP FASHION: Many of our trendy, inexpensive clothes are made in places like Bangladesh, where workers--including children--toil under conditions that may shock you L. ANASTASIA *New York Times Upfront* v150 no1 p8 S 4 2017

Research: Political Polarization Is Changing How Americans Work and Shop C. McConnell, Y. Margalit et al *Harvard Business Review Digital Articles* p2 My 19 2017

Research: Workplace Injuries Are More Common When Companies Face Earnings Pressure J. Caskey and N. B. Ozel *Harvard Business Review Digital Articles* p2 My 18 2017

Rethinking What Masculinity Means at the Office A. Wittenberg-Cox *Harvard Business Review Digital Articles* p2 Je 16 2016

The Right and Wrong Ways to Help Pregnant Workers J. Clair, K. Jones et al *Harvard Business Review Digital Articles* p2 S 27 2016

Rules for Designing an Engaging Workplace S. Augustin *Harvard Business Review Digital Articles* p2 O 28 2014

SENSORY OVERLOAD R. Greenfield color *Bloomberg Businessweek* no4512 p82 F 20 2017

Should You Talk About Politics at Work? R. Knight *Harvard Business Review Digital Articles* p2 S 26 2016

SILICON VALLEY'S SEXUAL REVOLUTION J. SANCTON cartoon graph *Wired* v25 no4 p22 Ap 2017

A Simple Way to Be More Assertive (Without Being Pushy) A. Molinsky *Harvard Business Review Digital Articles* p2 Ag 31 2017

Stop Enabling Gossip on Your Team J. Grenny *Harvard Business Review Digital Articles* p2 Ja 9 2015

Stop "Protecting" Women from Challenging Work K. Jones and E. King *Harvard Business Review Digital Articles* p2 S 9 2016

TAKE YOUR SEAT ON THE THRONE L. Thomas color *Essence* v48 no6 p126 O 2017

Talking About Ethics Across Cultures M. C. Gentile *Harvard Business Review Digital Articles* p2 D 23 2016

UP IN THE AIR C. FISHMAN *Smithsonian* v48 no3 p32 Je 2017

Want to Be More Productive? Sit Next to Someone Who Is J. Corsello and D. Minor *Harvard Business Review Digital Articles* p2 F 14 2017

What It Really Takes to Attract Top Talent P. Cappelli *Harvard Business Review Digital Articles* p2 N 24 2015

Why Businesspeople Should Join Book Clubs J. Coleman *Harvard Business Review Digital Articles* p2 F 23 2016

Why Is It So Hard for Us to Admit Our Mistakes? K. Firestone *Harvard Business Review Digital Articles* p2 Mr 28 2016

Why You Should Tell Your Team to Take a Break and Go Outside E. Seppala and J. Berlin *Harvard Business Review Digital Articles* p2 Je 26 2017

A WORKPLACE TOO FUN TO EVER LEAVE *Los Angeles Magazine* p101 F 2017

Your New Hires Won't Succeed Unless You Onboard Them Properly A. M. Ellis, S. S. Nifadkar et al *Harvard Business Review Digital Articles* p2 Je 20 2017

Work environment surveys

The 10 Best Workplaces for Women C. Austin color *Fortune* v176 no5 p20 O 1 2017

THE MODERN WORKPLACE graph *Vanity Fair* v59 no1 p82 Holiday 2017

Work environment—Great Britain

MICHAEL JENKINS *People Management* p17 O 2016

Work environment—Humor

ALL IN A Day's Work color graph *Reader's Digest* v189 no1131 p58 Je 2017

Work environment—Law & legislation

When to Tell Your Employees to Stay Home K. Firestone *Harvard Business Review Digital Articles* p2 F 27 2015

Work environment—Management

"Don't Take It Personally" Is Terrible Work Advice D. Coombe *Harvard Business Review Digital Articles* p2 Mr 29 2016

How to Speak Up If You See Bias at Work A. L. Williams color *Harvard Business Review Digital Articles* p2 Ja 20 2017

Work environment—Psychological aspects

I'LL TELL YOU SOMETHING NICOLAS ARNAUD & THIBAUT BARDON: Happiness in the workplace is no laughing matter *People Management* p19 My 2017

Work environment—Research

INVESTING IN EMPLOYEES PAYS OFF graph img *Harvard Business Review* v95 no4 p26 Jl/Ag 2017

Work environment—Social aspects

How to support autistic employees *People Management* p48 My 2017

Work ethic

6 Traits That Predict Ethical Behavior at Work D. De Cremer *Harvard Business Review Digital Articles* p2 N 22 2016

Differing Work Styles Can Help Team Performance C. Tate *Harvard Business Review Digital Articles* p2 Ap 3 2015

Help Your Team Achieve Work-Life Balance—Even When You Can't R. Zucker *Harvard Business Review Digital Articles* p2 2017

How to Speak Up About Ethical Issues at Work A. Gallo *Harvard Business Review Digital Articles* p2 Je 4 2015

How to Work with a Bad Listener R. Knight *Harvard Business Review Digital Articles* p2 2017

The Pros and Cons of Competition Among Employees A. Steinhage, D. Cable et al *Harvard Business Review Digital Articles* p2 Mr 20 2017

Talking About Ethics Across Cultures M. C. Gentile *Harvard Business Review Digital Articles* p2 D 23 2016

What to Do When You Get a New Boss Every Few Months R. Knight *Harvard Business Review Digital Articles* p2 Jl 1 2016

Work ethic—Moral & ethical aspects

WORD PLAY R. Lederer *Saturday Evening Post* v289 no3 p28 My/Je 2017

Work experience (Employment)

Chelsea Boy N. Englander bw color *Vogue* v207 no11 p104 N 2017

Work-life balance

7 Simple Ways Working Parents Can Simultaneously Improve Their Careers, Their Families, and Themselves D. W. Dowling *Harvard Business Review Digital Articles* p2 Je 29 2017

The 8 Self-Assessments You Need to Improve at Work This Year A. Gallo *Harvard Business Review Digital Articles* p2 Ja 20 2016

and the survey says... *U.S. Catholic* v82 no7 p27 Jl 2017

The art of triage E. White color *Science* v357 no6351 p618 Ag 11 2017

Balancing Parenting and Work Stress: A Guide D. W. Dowling bw *Harvard Business Review Digital Articles* p2 Mr 9 2017

BARN PROBLEMS *Successful Farming* v114 no11 p64 N 2016

The Best Ways Your Organization Can Support Working Parents D. W. Dowling bw *Harvard Business Review Digital Articles* p2 Ja 31 2017

The Dangers of "Mandatory Fun" A. Waytz *Harvard Business Review Digital Articles* p2 O 4 2017

Dealing with the Unique Work-Life Challenges of Family Businesses J. Baron and R. Lachenauer *Harvard Business Review Digital Articles* p2 Mr 19 2015

Design a Work-Life Improvement Pilot Project C. W. Yost *Harvard Business Review Digital Articles* p2 Ap 9 2015

Don't Take Work Stress Home with You J. Coleman and J. Coleman *Harvard Business Review Digital Articles* p2 Jl 28 2016

FEEDING THE BEAST J. Scott *Successful Farming* v114 no11 p20 N 2016

Fixing Our Unhealthy Obsession with Work Email M. Thomas

Harvard Business Review Digital Articles p2 S 24 2015

Going on Vacation Doesn't Have to Stress You Out at Work E. G. Saunders *Harvard Business Review Digital Articles* p2 Je 2 2015

Great Performers Make Their Personal Lives a Priority S. Friedman *Harvard Business Review Digital Articles* p2 O 6 2016

Helping Workers Switch Off color *Time* v189 no3 p7 Ja 16 2017

Help! Sharing personal problems at work is no longer taboo. People Management examines what that means for employers - and how HR can help in eight key crises [Cover story] J. FARAGHER *People Management* p26 Jl 2017

Help Your Team Achieve Work-Life Balance—Even When You Can't R. Zucker *Harvard Business Review Digital Articles* p2 2017

How to Allow Flexible Work Without Playing Favorites E. Marescaux and S. De Winne *Harvard Business Review Digital Articles* p2 2017

How to Forget About Work When You're Not Working A. Markman *Harvard Business Review Digital Articles* p2 2017

How to Work from Home When You Have Kids D. Wademan Dowling *Harvard Business Review Digital Articles* p2 S 14 2017

If You're Fed Up with Your Job, Try Working More Pauses into Your Day R. O'Meara *Harvard Business Review Digital Articles* p2 Ap 7 2017

Keeping It Professional When You Work in a Family Business C. O'Hara *Harvard Business Review Digital Articles* p2 Je 14 2016

Law Firms' Grueling Hours Are Turning Defectors into Competitors J. C. Williams *Harvard Business Review Digital Articles* p2 Ag 25 2015

LIFE LESSONS V. K. De Luca color *Essence* v47 no7 p4 N 2016

Live your best life C. Gorrell *Yoga Journal* p5 2016 Special Issue

Looking for Life's MIDUS Touch *USA Today Magazine* v145 no2863 p14 Ap 2017

Millennials Say They'll Relocate for Work-Life Flexibility N. Fondas *Harvard Business Review Digital Articles* p2 My 7 2015

My second acts A. Mathur color *Science* v357 no6358 p1430 S 29 2017

Rescuing my time from science L. Rinaldi color *Science* v354 no6319 p1666 D 23 2016

Research: Keeping Work and Life Separate Is More Trouble than It's Worth D. Burkus *Harvard Business Review Digital Articles* p2 Ag 9 2016

Stop Putting Off Fun for After You Finish All Your Work E. O'Brien *Harvard Business Review Digital Articles* p2 Jl 7 2017

Strategies for Every Type of Email Pain A. Samuel *Harvard Business Review Digital Articles* p2 My 20 2015

strong /not-strong D. Points *Parents* v91 no9 p10 S 2016

Style Star M. Santos color *Working Mother* v40 no3 p10 Ag/S 2017

What Successful Work and Life Integration Looks Like S. Friedman *Harvard Business Review Digital Articles* p2 O 7 2014

What the U.S. Military Can Teach Companies About Supporting Employees' Families D. Wademan Dowling *Harvard Business Review Digital Articles* p1 My 11 2017

Who I am A. Preacher *People Management* p45 Ag 2017

Who I am Kimberley King *People Management* p49 Jl 2017

WORK-LIFE BALANCE IS A SHAM A. BRESLAW cartoon diag *Women's Health* v14 no3 p146 Ap 2017

Work Mistakes to Avoid in 2017 B. Levin color *Glamour* v115 no1 p59 Ja 2017

Your Calendar Needs an Upgrade M. Schrage *Harvard Business Review Digital Articles* p2 Jl 9 2015

You've Got a Job. And a Baby... ...And You're Gonna Be Fine L. Smith Brody color *Glamour* v115 no5 p126 My 2017

Work-life balance programs

The Best Ways Your Organization Can Support Working Parents D. W. Dowling bw *Harvard Business Review Digital Articles* p2 Ja 31 2017

Work-related injuries

Counting injuries and illnesses in the workplace: an international review [Cover story] bibl *Monthly Labor Review* p1 S 2017

DON'T LET THE MONSTER EAT YOU UP' P. WALDMAN color *Bloomberg Businessweek* no4516 p46 Mr 27 2017

Hospital workers: an assessment of occupational injuries and illnesses M. A. Dressner bibl *Monthly Labor Review* p1 Je 2017

How safe are the workers who process our food? S. M. Smith bibl *Monthly Labor Review* p1 Jl 2017

Research: Workplace Injuries Are More Common When Companies Face Earnings Pressure J. Caskey and N. B. Ozel *Harvard Business Review Digital Articles* p2 My 18 2017

The Triangle Disaster: How a fire a century ago at a New York clothing factory changed U.S. labor laws P. Smith *New York Times Upfront* v150 no1 p11 S 4 2017

Why Workplace Accidents Tend to Happen Late in a Project N. Swidey *Harvard Business Review Digital Articles* p2 F 20 2015

Work values

What to Do When You're Returning to a Company You Used to Work For R. Knight *Harvard Business Review Digital Articles* p2 Ag 4 2017

WORD PLAY R. Lederer *Saturday Evening Post* v289 no3 p28 My/Je 2017

Work visas

HACKING THE VISA RACKET M. Helft color *Forbes* v198 no5 p74 O 25 2016

Looking Beyond H-1B Visas to Find Tech Talent A. Mahmud *Harvard Business Review Digital Articles* p1 Je 22 2017

PICTURING AN H-1B OVERHAUL B. O'Keefe diag *Fortune* v175 no6 p88 My 1 2017

Work visas—Law & legislation

America's got NO Talent E. Huet and G. De Vynck color graph *Bloomberg Businessweek* no4500 p32 N 21 2016

The Trump-Valley Fight Starts to Take Shape P. Elstrom and S. Rai *Bloomberg Businessweek* no4510 p26 F 6 2017

WORKac (Company)

Edible Schoolyard New York J. Minutillo *Architectural Record* v205 no4 p186 Ap 2017

Workaholics

CELEBRATE C. K. Jackson color *Essence* v47 no8 p152 D 2016

How to Break Your Addiction to Work R. Knight *Harvard Business Review Digital Articles* p2 My 18 2016

How to Work for a Workaholic R. Knight *Harvard Business Review Digital Articles* p2 Mr 24 2016

Workaholics (TV program)

The Workaholics' Finest Work A. Bacle color *Entertainment Weekly* no1449 p52 Ja 20 2017

Workbenches

IDEA OF THE MONTH: CANS AND JUGS DISAPPEAR IN ROLLING WORKBENCH DOOR THAT ADDS STORAGE SPACE P. Barbour *Successful Farming* v115 no9 p80 Ag 2017

Work clothes—Charts, diagrams, etc.

What I Wear to Work J. Chen color *Bloomberg Businessweek* no4523 p67 My 22 2017

Workday Inc.

Build a Great Company Culture with Help from Technology A. Goldsmith and L. Levensaler *Harvard Business Review Digital Articles* p2 F 24 2016

MEET THE WORKPLACE CULTURE WARRIORS J. Kell color *Fortune* v175 no4 p117 Mr 15 2017

Workers' compensation—Rates

When Unequal Pay Is Actually Fair T. Low *Harvard Business Review Digital Articles* p2 Mr 31 2016

Workflow management systems

Apple's acquisition of Workflow could bring automation to iOS D. MOREN color *Macworld - Digital Edition* v34 no4 p45 My 2017

Workflow—Management

How Visual Systems Make It Easier to Track Knowledge Work D. Markovitz *Harvard Business Review Digital Articles* p2 S 24 2015

Until You Have Productivity Skills, Productivity Tools Are Useless M. Thomas *Harvard Business Review Digital Articles* p2 Ag 1 2016

Workforce planning

See also

Employee recruitment

3 Emerging Alternatives to Traditional Hiring Methods T. Chamorro-Premuzic *Harvard Business Review Digital Articles* p2 Je 26 2015

How Companies Are Using Simulations, Competitions, and Analytics to Hire D. Carey and M. Smith *Harvard Business Review Digital Articles* p2 Ap 22 2016

How I Hired an Entirely Remote Workforce K. Shalev *Harvard Business Review Digital Articles* p2 Ap 14 2016

Why Hiring for Cultural Fit Can Thwart Your Diversity Efforts C. de Anca *Harvard Business Review Digital Articles* p2 Ap 25 2016

Work—Humor

Is Telecommuting Work? The Answer Isn't In the Fridge. (I Already Looked.) D. Von Drehle color *Time* v188 no19 p63 N 7 2016

Working capital

B&N Keeps Its Focus On Revenue Growth J. Milliot chart *Publishers Weekly* v264 no26 p2 Je 26 2017

Scholastic Aims to Improve Profits J. Milliot chart color *Publishers Weekly* v264 no30 p5 Jl 24 2017

Working cats

Amazing Animals S. Schwartz and R. A. Musgrave color map *National Geographic Kids* no472 p10 Ag 2017

Working class

Bloc the Vote [Cover story] R. D. SULLIVAN color graph map *America* v215 no13 p16 O 31 2016

How should we define "low-wage" work? An analysis using the Current Population Survey V. A. Fusaro and H. L. Shaefer bibl chart color graph *Monthly Labor Review* p1 O 2016

Made in America J. DiMedio *Harper's Magazine* v335 no2005 p2 Je 2017

Millennials Are Actually Workaholics, According to Research S. G. Carmichael *Harvard Business Review Digital Articles* p2 Ag 17 2016

No Friend of the Worker E. J. J. Dionne bw *Commonweal* v144 no15 p7 S 22 2017

Rituals: The Last Pastrami J. D. Stein and J. Rothman img *New York* p18 F 9 2017

South Africa's Divided Working-Class Movements M. PARET *Current History* v116 no790 p176 My 2017

Working class—History

Working-Class Resilience in Russia J. MORRIS *Current History* v115 no783 p264 O 2016

Working class—Political activity

Great White Hopes A. RUSSELL HOCHSCHILD il *New Republic* v248 no1/2 p16 Ja/F 2017

Hangover Politics L. Featherstone diag *Nation* v305 no1 p5 Jl 3 2017

The Trouble Brewing In Putin's Heartland H. Meyer and O. Tanas color graph *Bloomberg Businessweek* no4538 p36 S 18 2017

Working class—United States

Middle Class Muddle K. FINNERAN *Issues in Science & Technology* v33 no1 p39 Fall 2016

POPULAR IDEAS ABOUT THE WORKING CLASS ARE WOEFULLY OUT OF DATE. HERE ARE NINE PEOPLE WHO TELL A TRUER STORY OF WHAT THE AMERICAN WORK FORCE DOES TODAY—AND WILL DO TOMORROW B. Appelbaum *New York Times Magazine* p36 F 26 2017

The Thread P. Feiner, D. Beck et al cartoon *New York Times Magazine* p12 Mr 12 2017

Trump's Vanishing Base B. MOSER il *New Republic* v248 no1/2 p6 Ja/F 2017

What So Many People Don't Get About the U.S. Working Class J. C. Williams *Harvard Business Review Digital Articles* p2 N 10 2016

Working hours

See also

Employee vacations

Flexible work arrangements

Holidays

Leave of absence

Overtime

Don't Call It the "End of the Siesta": What Spain's New Work Hours Really Mean M. Mayo *Harvard Business Review Digital Articles* p2 Ap 13 2016

Employee's time off is adding up S. Sales *People Management* p53 F 2017

Francesca Amfitheatrof E. Wilson color *InStyle* v23 no13 p124 D 2016

Give Yourself Permission to Work Fewer Hours E. G. Saunders *Harvard Business Review Digital Articles* p2 Jl 13 2016

How "Quality Time" Is Killing American Innovation M. J. Dun-

kelman *Harvard Business Review Digital Articles* p2 D 1 2014

Not So Picture Perfect color *Working Mother* v40 no3 p5 Ag/S 2017

The Remedy for Unproductive Busyness F. Gino and B. Staats *Harvard Business Review Digital Articles* p2 Ap 24 2015

What Great Managers Do Daily R. Fuller and N. Shikaloff *Harvard Business Review Digital Articles* p2 D 14 2016

What to Do When You Inherit a Team That Isn't Working Hard Enough J. Grenny bw *Harvard Business Review Digital Articles* p1 Je 2 2017

Why Overtime Pay Doesn't Change How Much We Work W. Frick *Harvard Business Review Digital Articles* p2 Jl 1 2015

Why Some Men Pretend to Work 80-Hour Weeks E. Reid *Harvard Business Review Digital Articles* p2 Ap 28 2015

Work Grind Killing You? E. Lowe and A. GUMBS color *Black Enterprise* v47 no4 p28 N/D 2016

Working Too Hard Makes Leading More Difficult R. Friedman *Harvard Business Review Digital Articles* p2 D 30 2014

Working hours—Law & legislation

French 'right to disconnect' law comes into force *People Management* p17 F 2017

Warning over huge holiday bill for workers: Paid leave or compensation may be due to those unable to take leave, says EU opinion *People Management* p17 Jl 2017

Working Mother (Periodical)

Less Guilt, More Sweet Success M. Bodgas color *Working Mother* v40 no2 p7 Je/Jl 2017

Working mothers

10 New Ways to Afford Fertility Treatments B. GADDIS color *Working Mother* v40 no3 p40 Ag/S 2017

career coach J. Barberio color *Working Mother* v40 no3 p6 Ag/S 2017

CATASTROPHE: Sharon is in meltdown over her return from maternity leave *People Management* p58 Mr 2017

Champion of Breakfasts C. Vernon bw color *Working Mother* v40 no2 p12 Je/Jl 2017

Company Profiles color *Working Mother* v40 no2 p38 Je/Jl 2017

Diary of a Working Mom's Date Night S. Heacock cartoon *Working Mother* v40 no3 p50 Ag/S 2017

family matters J. Barberio color *Working Mother* v40 no3 p38 Ag/S 2017

"I Feel Guilty When I Can't Help My Colleague Because of My Kids" [Cover story] M. Santos color *Working Mother* v40 no2 p14 Je/Jl 2017

THE JOY OF JUGGLING C. HONG color *Martha Stewart Living* p98 S 2017

Kids Incorporated K. REYNOLDS LEWIS color *Working Mother* v40 no4 p80 O/N 2017

Less Guilt, More Sweet Success M. Bodgas color *Working Mother* v40 no2 p7 Je/Jl 2017

mom wins... ...and fails A. L. Lewis, S. Pestel et al color *Working Mother* v40 no2 p8 Je/Jl 2017

mom wins & fails color *Working Mother* v40 no3 p46 Ag/S 2017

My brand: A "collaborative leader" fluent in two different cultures N. Granholm color *Working Mother* v40 no2 p2 Je/Jl 2017

my write space L. Vaccariello *Parents* v92 no7 p10 Jl 2017

Paying It Forward E. LEE color *Working Mother* v40 no2 p44 Je/Jl 2017

SWEET & STRONG [Cover story] J. D. Tatum color *Redbook* p104 My 2017

Top Wealth Adviser Moms J. BIANCHI chart color *Working Mother* v40 no4 p85 O/N 2017

WORKING MOTHERS OF THE YEAR 2017 *Working Mother* v40 no4 p82 O/N 2017

You've Got a Job. And a Baby... ...And You're Gonna Be Fine L. Smith Brody color *Glamour* v115 no5 p126 My 2017

Zen Master J. Barberio color *Working Mother* v40 no3 p47 Ag/S 2017

Working mothers—Services for

Family Planning E. Bazelon color *New York Times Magazine* p17 O 9 2016

Working mothers—United States

How Trump's Tax Proposals Will Affect Single Working Mothers S. Damaske *Harvard Business Review Digital Articles* p2 D 22 2016

Working parents

See also
Working mothers
7 Simple Ways Working Parents Can Simultaneously Improve Their Careers, Their Families, and Themselves D. W. Dowling *Harvard Business Review Digital Articles* p2 Je 29 2017
THE BEST PLACES FOR WORKING PARENTS K. Bahler color *Money* v45 no10 p21 N 2016
How to Handle Work When Your Child Is Sick D. W. Dowling *Harvard Business Review Digital Articles* p2 Jl 18 2017
When You're Leaving Your Job Because of Your Kids [Cover story] D. W. Dowling *Harvard Business Review Digital Articles* p2 Ap 11 2017

Working World Inc.
'Tech Is a New Place to Have an Old Battle' W. Meyer color *Progressive* p30 D 2016/Ja 2017

Workman, Creg J.
Pathological α-synuclein transmission initiated by binding lymphocyte-activation gene 3 bibl graph *Science* v353 no6307 paah3374-1 S 30 2016

Workman, Reggie—Interviews
Trio 3: SURVIVAL SYNDROME T. Panken color *Downbeat* v84 no4 p34 Ap 2017

Workmanship
The Back Story G. WOOD color *Missouri Life* v44 no3 p98 My 2017
A GARDEN DOWNEAST T. MARTIN color *Old House Journal* v45 no4 p14 Je 2017
RIPPLE EFFECT H. Yanagihara bw color *Conde Nast Traveler* v52 no5 p98 My 2017

Work—Moral & ethical aspects
See also
Work ethic
How to Speak Up About Ethical Issues at Work A. Gallo *Harvard Business Review Digital Articles* p2 Je 4 2015

Work—Philosophy
THE VIRTUE OF DOING LESS: BERTRAND RUSSELL'S IDLENESS S. M. SEAWARD *Humanist* v77 no1 p38 Ja/F 2017

Work—Physiological aspects
See also
Job stress
Work stress could be good for your health *People Management* p57 D 2016/Ja 2017

Workplace romance
How Do You Handle an Office Romance? K. Morell color *Bloomberg Businessweek* no4511 p62 F 13 2017

Works, Richard
Changes in the life cycle of women's employment *Monthly Labor Review* p1 Mr 2017
The impact of technology on labor markets *Monthly Labor Review* p1 Je 2017

Works of art in art
The ACCRA ART Scene C. BOLLEN *Interview* v46 no10 p44 D 2016/Ja 2017
Leon Polk Smith Works *Treasures* v5 no5 p12 Ap/My 2016
Why I Love DAN-AH KIM'S ARTWORK E. Moss color *InStyle* v24 no9 p440 S 2017

Workshops (Adult education)
INSIDE FACEBOOK'S AI WORKSHOP: At the social network behemoth, machine learning has become a platform for the platform S. Berinato *Harvard Business Review Digital Articles* p14 Jl 1 2017
More Robust Recalls color *Consumer Reports* v82 no11 p5 N 2017
THE NEW "SOLO" TRAVEL color *Conde Nast Traveler* v52 no3 p98 Mr 2017
Schedule of Events *South Dakota Magazine* p24 S/O 2017 Supplement
Workshop Builds Students' Writing Skills A. Kirby *Education Digest* v83 no2 p55 O 2017

Workshops (Facilities)
See also
Artists' studios
Hot shops (Glass blowing & working)
Fashion Forward J. Lovelace color *American Craft* v76 no6 p40 D 2016-Ja 2017
Peace Be upon You N. ROBERTS color *Walrus* p24 Ja\F 2017

Workshops (Facilities)—Equipment & supplies
See also
Workbenches
IDEA OF THE MONTH: CANS AND JUGS DISAPPEAR IN ROLLING WORKBENCH DOOR THAT ADDS STORAGE SPACE P. Barbour *Successful Farming* v115 no9 p80 Ag 2017

Workshops (Facilities)—History
Clay army made from custom pastes B. BOWER color *Science News* v192 no4 p19 S 16 2017

Work—Sociological aspects
See also
Coworker relationships
"CRAZY BUSY": THE NEW STATUS SYMBOL *Harvard Business Review* v95 no2 p28 Mr/Ap 2017
How to Build the Social Ties You Need at Work A. Gallo *Harvard Business Review Digital Articles* p2 S 23 2015
How to Succeed at Work When Your Boss Doesn't Respect You C. Porath *Harvard Business Review Digital Articles* p2 Je 22 2016
A Pool and Its Money color *Money* v46 no3 p16 Ap 2017
What to Do When a Coworker Goes Over Your Head A. Gallo *Harvard Business Review Digital Articles* p2 D 22 2016

Workweek
How to Plan Your Week to Keep Your Weekend Free E. G. Saunders *Harvard Business Review Digital Articles* p2 Ap 27 2015

Worland, Justin
Al Gore color *Time* v190 no5 p66 Jl 31 2017
The Angels of Irma [Cover story] color map *Time* v190 no12 p34 S 25 2017
As Drought Lets Up, California Faces New Water Struggles *Time* v189 no3 p10 Ja 30 2017
Beat Back the Sea color *Time* v189 no13 p41 Ap 10 2017
The Best 25 Inventions of 2016 color *Time* v188 no22-23 p43 N/D 2016
Better Batteries color *Time* v189 no13 p29 Ap 10 2017
Burning Questions color *Time* v189 no7/8 p88 F 27 2017
Can Trump 'Scrap' Green Rules? color. *Time* v188 no27-28 p95 D 26 2016
Charged Up: Batteries Are the Next Target In China's Clean-Energy Conquest color *Time* v190 no15 p20 O 16 2017
The Climate-Change Diet color *Time* v188 no27-28 p16 D 26 2016
Coal's Last Kick color diag *Time* v189 no14 p38 Ap 17 2017
Electric Vehicles Are Here. Now We Need to Figure Out How to Charge Them color *Time* v190 no16/17 p34 O 23 2017
A Fight Over the Electric Grid Could Reshape America's Green Power Boom color *Time* v190 no2/3 p26 Jl 10-17 2017
The Future of Zoos color *Time* v189 no7/8 p54 F 27 2017
A High-Plains Showdown Over the Dakota Access Pipeline color *Time* v188 no20 p12 N 14 2016
Houston After Harvey color *Time* v190 no10/11 p38 S 18 2017
How a War on Science Could Hurt the U.S.-and Its Citizens color *Time* v189 no5 p17 F 13 2017
How Bad Air Came Back color *Time* v188 no27-28 p94 D 26 2016
How Climate Change Became a Political Issue *Time* v190 no6 p25 Ag 7 2017
Inside Donald Trump's War Against the State [Cover story] color *Time* v189 no10 p26 Mr 20 2017
Inside the Fight for Cleaner Air color *Time* v188 no15 p13 O 17 2016
Lightbox color *Time* v188 no24 p22 D 12 2016
A Moment of Reckoning for a Soaring Solar Industry color *Time* v190 no12 p30 S 25 2017
New Deal on Pollutants Caps Good Year for Climate Action color *Time* v188 no18 p11 O 31 2016
The New Nissan Leaf Is Fun. Can It Transform the Electric-Vehicle Market? color *Time* v190 no13 p24 O 2 2017
Next Generation Leaders color *Time* v188 no15 p41 O 17 2016
Next Generation Leaders color *Time* v190 no16/17 p74 O 23 2017
The Perils of an Early Spring color *Time* v189 no10 p9 Mr 20 2017
The Perils of Pulling Out of Paris color *Time* v189 no22 p8 Je 12 2017
Planet Earth As Spectacle-and Cautionary Tale color *Time* v189 no7/8 p111 F 27 2017
A Small-Scale Power Solution Could Pay Big Dividends Across the U.S color *Time* v190 no7 p22 Ag 21 2017
A Tale of Two Pipelines color map *Time* v189 no5 p13 F 13 2017

Trump Takes Aim at Obama's Climate Legacy color *Time* v189 no13 p7 Ap 10 2017

U.S. Policies Informed by Science color *Time* v189 no5 p19 F 13 2017

Why Republicans Are Embracing Climate Change color *Time* v189 no11 p23 Mr 27 2017

Why Your Power Company Wants to Sell You More Than Electricity color *Time* v189 no20 p20 My 29 2017

Wind Power Catches a Mountain Breeze color *Time* v189 no21 p30 Je 5 2017

World AIDS day

December! T. PAYNE and L. CROSS color *Ebony* v72 no3 p34 D 2016/Ja 2017

World Bank

Fictional States & Atomized Public Spheres: A Non-Western Approach to Fragility W. Reno *Daedalus* v146 no4 p139 Fall 2017

WORTH NOTING K. A. GAJEWSKI *Humanist* v77 no1 p48 Ja/F 2017

World Baseball Classic

HOT NOT T. Keith color *Sports Illustrated* v126 no8 p24 Mr 20 2017

Summer Madness T. Verducci and T. Keith color *Sports Illustrated* v126 no8 p20 Mr 20 2017

Team Israel 17-1 J. Fuchs and T. Keith color *Sports Illustrated* v126 no9 p26 Mr 27 2017

World championships

32 The Facts color map *Horse & Rider* v56 no9 p30 S 2017

all or nothing p. gore bw *Bike Magazine* v24 no6 p50 Ag 2017

Bad Puns Are How Eye Roll P. RUBIN color *Reader's Digest* v190 no1135 p108 N 2017

NFR PREDICTIONS color *Horse & Rider* v56 no11 p80 N 2017

Wadee Al Shaqab B. Finke color *Arabian Horse World* v57 no7 p1 Ap 2017

WDAA World Show color *Horse & Rider* v56 no9 p28 S 2017

World Chess Championship

Checkmate A. Fenwick and T. Keith color *Sports Illustrated* v125 no19 p26 D 12 2016

Garry KASPAROV M. Potter color *Esquire* p124 Je/Jl 2017

World class companies

Higher Red J. Freedman color *Washington Monthly* p1 N/D 2016

World Cruising Club Ltd.

From the Atlantic to the Pacific A. Wisch color *Sail* v48 no5 p17 My 2017

World Cup (Dressage)

chantilly 2016 J. Wintersteen *Arabian Horse World* v56 no12 p198 S 2016

The Future of Midwestern Dressage N. Jaffer color *Dressage Today* v23 no10 p52 Jl 2017

World Cup (Show jumping)

7 Things to Do in APRIL *Practical Horseman* v45 no4 p58 Ap 2017

BRINGING THE BEST TO OMAHA N. Jaffer color *Practical Horseman* v45 no3 p53 Mr 2017

Facebook Feeds *In Stride* v12 no3 p19 My 2017

A KEY TO EVERY HORSE E. I. Prax color *Practical Horseman* v45 no4 p28 Ap 2017

McLain Ward's Flawless World Cup Finish Was No Fluke T. Booker *In Stride* v12 no3 p16 My 2017

Omaha: A World Cup Legacy N. Jaffer *In Stride* v12 no3 p20 My 2017

World Economic Forum

Alpine Disconnect M. Campbell and S. Kennedy cartoon *Bloomberg Businessweek* no4507 p35 Ja 16 2017

The Emperor Has No Clothes G. TETT cartoon *Foreign Policy* no222 p70 Ja/F 2017

Psychoanalyzing the World's Problems Won't Help Us Solve Them G. Petriglieri color *Harvard Business Review Digital Articles* p2 Ja 24 2017

A Specter Is Haunting Davos D. GREEN color *Weekly Standard* v22 no21 p14 F 6 2017

WHERE IN THE WORLD ARE WOMEN AND MEN MOST—AND LEAST—EQUAL? K. Nowakowski graph *National Geographic* v231 no1 p28 Ja 2017

World Equestrian Games

Margaret's Blog *Dressage Today* v23 no5 p12 Ja 2017

News BITS D. O'Connor *Practical Horseman* v45 no1 p64 Ja 2017

World Health Organization

Cholera crisis grows in Middle Eastern war zone color *Science* v356 no6340 p787 My 26 2017

Emergency Ebola vaccine backup *Science* v356 no6337 p468 My 5 2017

Finally, a Vaccine for Dengue [Cover story] A. FAVREAU and C. MALDARELLI color *Popular Science* v288 no6 p36 N/D 2016

From Contamination to Containment [Cover story] C. E. M. COLTART, A. M. JOHNSON et al color *Natural History* v125 no9 p40 S 2017

Hit Refresh N. Spradley color *Essence* v47 no12 p29 Ap 2017

LIVES OVER LANDFILLS C. REDDING *USA Today Magazine* v145 no2858 p34 N 2016

Misconduct found in fetal study fight color *Science* v354 no6311 p394 O 28 2016

Now Hear This! C. Thorp color *Seventeen* v76 no4 p51 Jl/Ag 2017

ROOM FOR EVERYONE B. SU *Foreign Affairs* v96 no6 p175 N/D 2017

Unhealthy Agency E. Epstein color *Weekly Standard* v22 no38 p8 Je 12 2017

What the World Health Organization's New Leader Must Tackle A. Sifferlin color *Time* v189 no21 p11 Je 5 2017

Who should direct WHO? D. L. Heymann color *Science* v354 no6313 p685 N 11 2016

World Health Organization—Officials & employees

Three left in race to head WHO *Science* v355 no6324 p437 F 3 2017

WHO selects African leader *Science* v356 no6340 p786 My 26 2017

World Heritage Sites

Milestones color *Time* v190 no4 p13 Jl 24 2017

World Heritage Sites—Evaluation

My Kind of Landscape K. Roosevelt III color *AARP: The Magazine* v59 no3A p76 Ap/My 2016

World history

See also

United States—History

THE INVENTION OF WORLD HISTORY S. F. Starr *History Today* v67 no7 p36 Jl 2017

World maps

Here's every total solar eclipse from now to 2040 E. DeMarco map *Science News* v192 no1 p32 Ag 5 2017

Points of Origin M. Fabry map *Time* v189 no16/17 p12 My 1-8 2017

World Meteorological Organization

The Fight to Change How Hurricanes Are Named O. B. Waxman *Time* v190 no12 p23 S 25 2017

World news briefs

See also

Asia—News briefs

Europe—News briefs

United States—News briefs

All the News That's Fit to Click M. Chafkin color *Bloomberg Businessweek* no4498 p81 N 7 2016

THE APPROVAL MATRIX img *New York* p96 Ja 9 2017

Around the world P. Treble color map *Maclean's* v129 no51/52 p44 D 26 2016

BAD NEWS color *Maclean's* v129 no51/52 p11 D 26 2016

Brickbats C. Oliver cartoon *Reason* v48 no7 p9 D 2016

CENTURY marks graph *Christian Century* v134 no6 p8 Mr 15 2017

et al il *Phi Kappa Phi Forum* v97 no2 p4 Summ 2017

GOOD NEWS color *Maclean's* v129 no42 p8 O 24 2016

IN BRIEF K. Stock color graph *Bloomberg Businessweek* no4531 p6 Jl 24 2017

Intel bw chart *Conde Nast Traveler* v52 no5 p129 My 2017

Milestones *Time* v189 no19 p13 My 22 2017

THE MONTH IN REVIEW *Current History* v115 no783 p287 O 2016

Movers K. Stock bw color *Bloomberg Businessweek* no4504 p11 D 19 2016

Movers K. Stock color *Bloomberg Businessweek* no4508 p11 Ja 23 2017

NEWS color *Science* v356 no6344 p1214 Je 23 2017

NEWSMAKERS *Science* v357 no6347 p113 Jl 14 2017

Weapon on the Wall: As World War I raged, posters encouraged, enticed, and even shamed young Americans into joining the great conflict J. M. Cannon *Hoover Digest: Research & Opinion on Public Policy* no2 p199 Spr 2017

When the World Went to War [Cover story] D. McMillen *Prologue* v49 no2 p6 Summ 2017

World War I campaigns—Belgium
    See also
      3rd Battle of Ypres, Ieper, Belgium, 1917
SAVING LIVES ON THE FRONT LINE C. E. Hallett *History Today* v67 no7 p24 Jl 2017

World War I in art—Exhibitions
FLOWERS OF DEATH E. Pochoda bw color *Magazine Antiques* v184 no3 p118 My/Je 2017
The moral blindness of war R. A. Schroth color *America* v217 no2 p49 Jl 24 2017

World War I—Exhibitions
ON THE MAP AT THE VIMY RIDGE CENTENNIAL color *Canadian Geographic* v137 no3 p76 My 2017

World War I, 1914-1918—American personal narratives
Letter from the Front B. Finlay *American History* v52 no1 p51 Ap 2017

World War I, 1914-1918—Armistices
THE HUMANITY IN LARGE NUMBERS *Vital Speeches of the Day* v83 no2 p59 F 2017

World War I, 1914-1918—Campaigns—Belgium
THE DAY THE EARTH BLEW OPEH E. G. Lengel *MHQ: Quarterly Journal of Military History* v29 no2 p51 Wint 2017

World War I, 1914-1918—Canada
Monumental event B. BETHUNE bw color *Maclean's* v129 no51/52 p38 D 26 2016

World War I, 1914-1918—Casualties
MYSTERY AT MONTFAUCON W. Walker *MHQ: Quarterly Journal of Military History* v29 no3 p28 Spr 2017

World War I, 1914-1918—Centennial celebrations, etc.
The World May Little Note, but Kansas City Still Remembers D. Von Drehle color *Time* v189 no14 p21 Ap 17 2017

World War I, 1914-1918—Great Britain
The Nation on its Honour J. Doyle *History Today* v67 no2 p3 F 2017

World War I, 1914-1918—Veterans
THE BATTLE OF ANACOSTIA FLATS B. Hogan *MHQ: Quarterly Journal of Military History* v29 no2 p66 Wint 2017

World War II
'Ain't Doing Right': NO MATTER YOUR AGE, BEING OPEN TO NEW LOVE IS NEVER EASY L. GOODSON color *Yankee* p122 Jl 2017

BATTLE OF ALL MOTHERS L. Smith color *Mother Jones* v42 no3 p12 My/Je 2017

BELOW AND ABOVE G. Westrup and R. Wright bw *MHQ: Quarterly Journal of Military History* v29 no4 p10 Summ 2017

BIG CREEK: A FAMILY RECALLS YEARS AT THE LODGE K. WIDNER *Idaho Magazine* v16 no10 p32 Jl 2017

THE BULGE *AARP: The Magazine* v59 no3A p64 Ap/My 2016

Child's Play *Reader's Digest* v188 no1124 p24 O 2016

Dissolving the Boundary Lines J. Shaheen *Tricycle: The Buddhist Review* v26 no4 p10 Summ 2017

DOT-DOT-DOT-DASH MEMORABILIA color *Indianapolis Monthly* v42 no2 p73 O 2017

A Good Germany? K. Graham *History Today* v67 no7 p8 Jl 2017

THE GOOD WAR C. R. Kesler *Claremont Review of Books* v16 no4 p5 Fall 2016

Hardware Type 94 Infantry Mortar J. Guttman *Military History* v33 no5 p20 Ja 2017

He Paints Their Final Portraits J. LABIANCA *Reader's Digest* v188 no1124 p8 O 2016

THE HEMINGWAY PATROLS: THE ENEMY IN THE MACHINE T. MORT bw *Power & Motoryacht* v33 no2 p110 F 2017

Hiroshima, His Amour B. McManus *Commentary* v142 no1 p32 Jl/Ag 2016

Hump Days L. G. MacNicol *MHQ: Quarterly Journal of Military History* v29 no3 p10 Spr 2017

In Decline *Change* v82 no3 p16 Mr 2017

Interview Jane Doyle Recognizing WASPs [Cover story] bw color *Military History* v34 no4 p14 N 2017

Judo Back in the Day H. NISHIOKA bw *Black Belt* v55 no4 p54 Je/Jl 2017

Living History J. Y. Wood color *Power & Motoryacht* v34 no6 p16 Je 2017

Malaria Dollars and Sense D. L. SMITH and J. M. COHEN bw color *Natural History* v125 no9 p28 S 2017

Nebraska at 150 A. J. BARTELS bw color *Nebraska Life* v21 no4 p56 Jl/Ag 2017

News Splash: Elated by the word that World War II had ended, Indy citizens took to the streets to cheer, party, wave flags—and even skivvies-dip on Monument Circle C. ZEIGLER bw *Indianapolis Monthly* v41 no2 p22 S 2017

OVER THERE, OVER HERE JOHNSON *Treasures* v6 no5 p30 Ap/My 2017

The Quiz T. BALAZO *Maclean's* v130 no4 p72 My 2017

SHOWDOWN IN THE ALEUTIANS D. Hammett *MHQ: Quarterly Journal of Military History* v29 no3 p54 Spr 2017

The Sinking of JAPAN M. Murfett *History Today* v66 no12 p20 D 2016

SURIGAO STRAIT color *AARP: The Magazine* v59 no3A p65 Ap/My 2016

Thunderbird Field N. AUSTIN *Arizona Highways* v93 no9 p8 S 2017

Valor Remarkable Exploits C. Lyons *Military History* v33 no5 p16 Ja 2017

The Veneration of Cool P. TERZIAN *Weekly Standard* v22 no8 p12 O 31 2016

WEAPONS CHECK: MG 42 C. McNab color *MHQ: Quarterly Journal of Military History* v30 no1 p27 Aut 2017

We Are Connected M. S. Eddy *Stage Directions* v30 no6 p2 Je 2017

What 'America First' Means Here W. Donahue color *Commonweal* v144 no12 p10 Jl 7 2017

WHEN FRANCE DEFIED HITLER'S PANZERS [Cover story] J. Koster bw color map *Military History* v34 no4 p30 N 2017

A YANK IN THE SS R. Soodalter *Military History* v33 no5 p40 Ja 2017

World War II, 1939-1945—Exhibitions
ARCHIVES Events *Prologue* v48 no3 p66 Fall 2016

World War II, 1939-1945—Jews—Rescue
THE ANGEL OF BUDAPEST R. Philpot *History Today* v67 no1 p21 Ja 2017

World War II, 1939-1945—Soviet Union
THE THIRD REICH'S ARCTIC OUTPOST E. A. POWELL bw color *Archaeology* v70 no3 p22 My/Je 2017

World War II, 1939-1945—Underground movements—France
True evangelical faith A. Frykholm bw *Christian Century* v133 no25 p28 D 7 2016

World War II—Japan
Guadalcanal Revisited: The official Japanese postmortem of World War II shows how rivalries, miscommunication, and poor leadership plagued the imperial military machine Yuma Totani *Hoover Digest: Research & Opinion on Public Policy* no3 p110 Summ 2017

World War II—Radio broadcasting & the war
Fighting the Nazis With Fake News M. SHAER *Smithsonian* v48 no1 p22 Ap 2017

World War II—Social aspects—United States
UNWANTED C. Omori *Saturday Evening Post* v289 no3 p30 My/Je 2017

World War II—Women
The Historian of the Soul N. Khrushcheva bw *Atlantic* v320 no2 p36 S 2017

World War II campaigns—France—Normandy
D-DAY THROUGH A GERMAN LENS R. M. Citino color *MHQ: Quarterly Journal of Military History* v29 no4 p68 Summ 2017

World War II campaigns—Germany
    See also
      Battle of Hürtgen, 1944
Slog Through the Hürtgen Forest M. Hull bw color map *Military History* v34 no5 p36 Ja 2018

World War II casualties
THE WAR COMES HOME TO WISCONSIN: In an indelible picture 50 years ago, one family faces a loss in Vietnam P. RHODEEN *Smithsonian* v48 no5 p26 S 2017

World War II Memorial (Washington, D.C.)

News B. Manley *Military History* v33 no6 p8 Mr 2017

World War II personal narratives

An Illegal Immigrant J. Tytell *Commonweal* v144 no10 p8 Je 2 2017

World War II Soviet personal narratives

The Historian of the Soul N. Khrushcheva bw *Atlantic* v320 no2 p36 S 2017

World Wide Technology Inc.

THE NATION'S LARGEST BLACK BUSINESSES *Black Enterprise* v47 no7 p51 My/Je 2017

World Wide Web

The Best Makeup Bags color *Health* v31 no7 p20 S 2017

Check Us Out on Social Media! cartoon *Better Nutrition* v78 no11 p8 N 2016

not your granny's slipcover color *Parents* v92 no6 p109 Je 2017

the right workout for you C. GRISE *Parents* v92 no1 p48 Ja 2017

Why Not... Master Meditation? color *Health* v30 no9 p10 N 2016

World Wide Web Consortium

Taking a Positive View of the IDPF-W3C Merger L. Dawson *Publishers Weekly* v264 no9 p19 F 27 2017

World Wide Web—Research

Science of the World Wide Web J. Hendler and W. Hall bibl color *Science* v354 no6313 p703 N 11 2016

World Wildlife Fund (U.S.)

PASSION IN ACTION M. Hill color *Louisiana Life* v38 no1 p64 S/O 2017

World Wrestling Entertainment Inc.

JUST ANOTHER MANIC SUNDAY color *Bloomberg Businessweek* no4519 p78 Ap 24 2017

Singapore, Part 2: Caught Up in Catch Wrestling A. Graceffo color *Black Belt* v55 no5 p22 Ag/S 2017

WorldPay PLC

Shop 'til Your Eyes Pop E. LAHEY *USA Today Magazine* v146 no2868 p79 S 2017

Worldpay US Inc.

YOUR LIFE *USA Today Magazine* v145 no2858 p6 N 2016

WorldRemit Ltd.

Changing the Way Cash Is Sent Home E. Robinson color graph *Bloomberg Businessweek* no4522 p44 My 15 2017

World Series (Baseball)—Charts, diagrams, etc.

What It Takes to Win It All E. Barone and S. Gregory color diag *Time* v188 no14 p24 O 10 2016

World's Greatest Lover, The (Film)

GENE WILDER C. Kane and D. Coggan color *Entertainment Weekly* no1446/1447 p90 D 2016/Ja 2017

Worldview

When Facts Backfire M. Shermer color *Scientific American* v316 no1 p69 Ja 2017

Worley, Katherine

Around the Campfire color *Trail Rider* v29 no4 p8 My 2017

Worley, Paul F.

Homer1a drives homeostatic scaling-down of excitatory synapses during sleep bibl graph *Science* v355 no6324 p511 F 3 2017

WORLEY, SAM

FRACTURED MEMORIES color *Chicago* v66 no9 p56 S 2017

WORMELI, RICK

The Right Way to Do Redos *Education Digest* v82 no9 p29 My 2017

Wormholes (Physics)

BLACK HOLES, WORMHO LES AND THE SECRETS OF QUANTUM SPACETIME J. Maldacena color diag *Scientific American* v315 no5 p26 N 2016

Worms—Anatomy

Acorn worms have a head for swimming E. DeMarco color *Science News* v191 no2 p5 F 4 2017

Wörner, Hans Jakob

Time-resolved x-ray absorption spectroscopy with a water window high-harmonic source graph *Science* v355 no6322 p264 Ja 20 2017

Worobey, Michael

Maternal antibodies' role in immunity bibl color *Science* v355 no6326 p704 F 17 2017

Potent protection against H5N1 and H7N9 influenza via childhood hemagglutinin imprinting bibl chart graph *Science* v354 no6313 p722 N 11 2016

Worrachate, Anchalee

Why Trump Is Making Bond Markets Nervous *Bloomberg Businessweek* no4500 p39 N 21 2016

Worry—Management

How This Family of Worrywarts Copes In an Age of Anxiety K. V. Ogtrop color *Time* v190 no6 p59 Ag 7 2017

WORSHAM, JAMES

EDITOR'S NOTE *Prologue* v49 no1 p1 Spr 2017

EDITOR'S NOTE *Prologue* v49 no2 p2 Summ 2017

Where Our WWII Leaders Spent WWI *Prologue* v49 no2 p18 Summ 2017

Worship programs

See also

Marriage service

EVANGELICAL CHURCH SHOPPING, EXPLAINED graph *Christianity Today* v60 no10 p21 D 2016

Worsley, Lucy

Jane's Addictions: A BBC presenter tells Austen's admirers what they want to know about how and where she lived A. Bloom *New York Times Book Review* p9 Jl 16 2017

Worsnop, Douglas R.

Global atmospheric particle formation from CERN CLOUD measurements bibl graph map *Science* v354 no6316 p1119 D 2 2016

Wortel, Verginia

Positive biodiversity-productivity relationship predominant in global forests bibl chart graph map *Science* v354 no6309 paaf8957-1 O 14 2016

Worth, Richard

an introduction to JERRY ANDRUS *Skeptical Inquirer* v41 no1 p65 Ja/F 2017

Worth, Robert F.

Libyan Ghosts color *Foreign Affairs* v96 no3 p127 My/Je 2017

OBAMA'S AMERICA img *New York* v49 no20 p12 O 3 2016

Wortham, Jenna

Artists, in their explorations of how tech companies violate our privacy, have begun to sound an alarm that we might not be ready to hear *New York Times Magazine* p12 Ja 1 2017

Barack Obama, the nation's first truly digital president, brought Silicon Valley ideas - and influence—to Washington. Is that a good thing? *New York Times Magazine* p22 O 30 2016

The disappearance of SoundCloud has become a real possibility. What would that mean for the music culture that thrives on the site? color *New York Times Magazine* p14 Ag 6 2017

Fitness feeds on Instagram can perpetuate harmful ideas about the perfect body—but they can also inspire us with bodies that are more like ours *New York Times Magazine* p14 Jl 9 2017

How should you deal with social media's constantly increasing demands? Be more like Beyoncé *New York Times Magazine* p20 O 2 2016

The internet should have made zines obsolete. Their resilience shows the limitations of the web as a place to nurture young creativity *New York Times Magazine* p14 Mr 5 2017

Marilyn Minter Finds Art In the Female Form *New York Times Magazine* p58 F 19 2017

MISS CLEO *New York Times Magazine* p17 D 25 2016

On Technology color *New York Times Magazine* p16 Ja 29 2017

On Technology *New York Times Magazine* p16 Je 11 2017

'REWIND' color *New York Times Magazine* p29 Mr 12 2017

We've heard about the power of social media to help us empathize with others. But what if, instead, it's just cocooning us with our friends? *New York Times Magazine* p20 N 27 2016

WORTHINGTON, MYLES

HEALTHY BROTHERHOOD color *Runner's World* v52 no1 p22 Ja/F 2017

Wortman, Marc

Fire on the Water: A newly discovered account of the biggest explosion of the pre-nuclear era surfaces after 100 years *Smithsonian* v48 no5 p15 S 2017

Wortz, Ron

Discussion *Smithsonian* v47 no7 p10 N 2016

Wound care

Anal and rectal discomfort *Mayo Clinic Health Letter* v35 no10 p4 O 2017

Wound healing

AN EQUITARIAN MISSION S. L. Bettison color map *Equus* no471 p32 D 2016

FAST FIXES J. Migala cartoon *Runner's World* v52 no1 p60 Ja/F

Raise Your Voice [Cover story] color *Glamour* v115 no3 p184 Mr 2017

Wright, IO Tillett, 1985—Interviews

THE RAW, REAL, AND UTTERLY INSPIRING STORY OF A NEW YORK KID WHO MADE HIS OWN RULES FOR LIVING, 10 TILLETT WRIGHT'S NEW MEMOIR IS A TRIBAL CRY FOR A WHOLE GENERATION N. GOLDIN *Interview* v46 no8 p116 O 2016

Wright, James

How Stable is the Condition of Family Homelessness? chart *Society* v54 no1 p46 F 2017

Wright, James D.

Impact ejecta at the Paleocene-Eocene boundary bibl bw graph *Science* v354 no6309 p225 O 14 2016

Wright, Jason

High-resolution interrogation of functional elements in the non-coding genome bibl graph *Science* v353 no6307 p1545 S 30 2016

Wright, Jason T.

Explaining a few discoveries *Physics Today* v70 no9 p12 S 2017

STRANGE NEWS FROM Another Star color diag graph *Scientific American* v316 no5 p36 My 2017

Wright, Jay

Life Lessons of the Anti-Coach L. PLATT bw color *GQ: Gentlemen's Quarterly* v97 no3 p100 Mr 2017

The Wright Way to Keep Your Cool C. Flammia and P. Kita color *Men's Health* v32 no2 p25 Mr 2017

Wright, Jeremy

The Canine Cottage K. Owen color diag *Southern Living* v52 no5 p54 My 2017

Wright, Kai

The Damage Done color *Nation* v305 no4 p10 Ag 14 2017

Devil's Choice *Nation* v305 no2 p10 Jl 17 2017

Dreamers in a Culture War bw diag *Nation* v304 no8 p10 Mr 13 2017

Low-Key Villainy color il *Nation* v304 no15 p10 My 8 2017

Race Against Time color *Nation* v304 no1 p46 Ja 2 2017 The Obama Years

We're All in Kansas Now il *Nation* v304 no12 p10 Ap 10 2017

Wright, Katherine

Sky Is the Limit color *Scientific American* v316 no4 p14 Ap 2017

WRIGHT, KHALIELA

ELK RIVER color *Idaho Magazine* v16 no1 p32 O 2016

A Flair for Solar Cooking: And Distrust of the "Hippy" Method *Idaho Magazine* v16 no11 p48 Ag 2017

No Janitor, No Lunch *Idaho Magazine* v16 no3 p12 D 2016

THE RAVAGES OF MARCH: A FAR-FLUNG FAMILY STRUCK BY FLOODS *Idaho Magazine* v16 no8 p48 My 2017

WRIGHT, KIMBERLY

Beyond Words color *O, The Oprah Magazine* p17 Ap 2017

Wright, Kiyah

your good-hair GAME PLAN G. MONSMA color *Better Homes & Gardens* v95 no10 p24 O 2017

WRIGHT, LAWRENCE

THE FUTURE IS TEXAS bw cartoon *New Yorker* v93 no20 p40 Jl 10 2017

Wright, Lawrence, 1947-

Seeing the Despair of Jihad A. Rashid cartoon color *New York Review of Books* v63 no18 p51 N 24 2016

Why They Hate Us J. Shepp color *Commonweal* v143 no18 p40 N 11 2016

Wright, Letitia

Letitia WRIGHT *Interview* v47 no5 p66 Je/Jl 2017

Wright, Lili

Alice Guerin Tattoo Artist: A Fountain Square illustrator whose canvas is the human body color *Indianapolis Monthly* v41 no2 p48 S 2017

Joanna Suitors Taxidermist: A Putnam County artisan cutting it in a male-dominated industry *Indianapolis Monthly* v40 no10 p48 Je 2017

Missy Hammond Casino Dealer: The longtime French Lick Resort employee is something of a card *Indianapolis Monthly* v12 no40 p48 Ag 2017

My Snow Angel color *Good Housekeeping* v264 no2 p63 F 2017

Tom Davis: Cemetery Guide *Indianapolis Monthly* p54 N 2017

Wright, Logan G.

Spatiotemporal mode-locking in multimode fiber lasers color *Science* v357 no6359 p94 O 6 2017

WRIGHT, MARK

TROUBLED WATERS *Indianapolis Monthly* v40 no3 p90 N 2016

Wright, Mary

How to Pay for Health Care/The Case for Capitation: Interaction *Harvard Business Review* v94 no11 p20 N 2016

Wright, Matthew

Gating of social reward by oxytocin in the ventral tegmental area color graph *Science* v357 no6358 p1406 S 29 2017

Wright, Mikey, 1998-

The Devil on My Shoulders T. PRODANOVICH color *Surfer* v58 no3 p94 Je 2017

Wright, Nikolas

BEST OF THE WEST color *Sunset* v238 no4 p17 Ap 2017

Wright, Richard

BELOW AND ABOVE bw *MHQ: Quarterly Journal of Military History* v29 no4 p10 Summ 2017

Wright, Richard S., Jr.

Imaging Adventure: Dry Tortugas *Sky & Telescope* v133 no2 p32 F 2017

Wright, Robert

AMERICAN NIRVANA A. GOPNIK cartoon *New Yorker* v93 no23 p69 Ag 7 2017

An End to Suffering: Can Buddhism create healthier individuals and communities? A. Damasio *New York Times Book Review* p17 Ag 13 2017

Illuminations M. B. DOUGHERTY color *National Review* v69 no17 p37 S 11 2017

Our Empathy Problem color *Nation* v304 no2 p16 Ja 16 2017

Toward a New Foreign Policy [Cover story] bw *Nation* v304 no2 p12 Ja 16 2017

Wright, Robert, 1957-

TRUDEAUMANIA A. LEVINE color *Maclean's* v129 no40 p76 O 10 2016

Why Buddhism Is True: The Science and Philosophy of Meditation and Enlightenment *Publishers Weekly* v264 no19 p53 My 8 2017

WRIGHT, ROBIN

AFTER THE ISLAMIC STATE cartoon *New Yorker* v92 no41 p30 D 12 2016

Wright, Robin, 1966-

REAL OR REPLICANT? S. Vilkomerson color *Entertainment Weekly* no1446/1447 p45 D 2016/Ja 2017

Wright, Ronald

A Short History of Progress color *Maclean's* v129 no42 p44 O 24 2016

Wright, Sarah Ressler

oops *Parents* v92 no7 p132 Jl 2017

Wright, Thomas J.

Harassment Strategy J. C. HIRSCH color *Weekly Standard* v22 no44 p32 Jl 31 2017

Wright, Tim J.

Complex multifault rupture during the 2016 Mw 7.8 Kaikōura earthquake, New Zealand color map *Science* v356 no6334 p154 Ap 14 2017

Wright, Todd

A Makeover on LAKE CHARLEVOIX P. POORE color *Arts & Crafts Homes & the Revival* v12 no3 p50 Summ 2017

Wright, Tom

FROM OUR READERS *Sky & Telescope* v133 no6 p6 Je 2017

Wright, Tom H.

Posttranslational mutagenesis: A chemical strategy for exploring protein side-chain diversity diag *Science* v354 no6312 p597 N 4 2016

Wright, Tracey

HOW COMEDY'S SECRET WEAPON GOT SCHOOLED M. Snetiker color *Entertainment Weekly* no1463/1464 p96 Ap/My 2017

Wright, Tyler

HER BROTHER'S KEEPER S. DOHERTY color *Surfer* v58 no1 p58 Ap 2017

Wright Brothers National Memorial (N.C.)

SOUTH'S BEST ISLAND A. Weigl color *Southern Living* v52 no4 p82 Ap 2017

TAKE A DRIVE: THE OUTER BANKS S. Herrada *Washingtonian Magazine* v52 no9 p133 Je 2017

Wrighton, Mark S.

CHALLENGES OF AN AGING GLOBAL POPULATION *Vital Speeches of the Day* v82 no12 p374 D 2016

Wrigley, William, 1861-1932

SEA OF DREAMS L. J. Wertheim color map *Sports Illustrated* v126 no18 p54 Je 26 2017

Wrigley Field (Chicago, Ill.)

Fair-Weather Fandom J. Gordon *New York Times Magazine* p28 Ja 15 2017

Wrinkle treatment

THE MASKERADE M. Goldberg color *O, The Oprah Magazine* p69 O 2017

STOP THE SIGNS OF AGING V. Tweed color *Amazing Wellness* v8 no2 p48 Spr 2016

Wrinkle in Time, A (Film)

A Wrinkle in Time M. Snetiker color *Entertainment Weekly* no1474/1475 p96 Jl 21-28 2017

Wrinkles (Skin)—Prevention

ASK APRIL A. FRANZINO color *Good Housekeeping* v264 no1 p20 Ja 1 2017

A Cure for the Ages M. Fabry color *Time* v189 no7/8 p86 F 27 2017

Smoother skin in seconds M. OLIVA color *Redbook* p47 Mr 2017

Wrist

DUCT-TAPE DEFENSE J. HANSON color *Black Belt* v55 no6 p58 O/N 2017

It's All in the Wrists L. McGLASHAN color *Muscle & Performance* v9 no9 p26 S 2017

Master class N. Rizopoulos color *Yoga Journal* p46 2017 SpecialIssue

Wrist watches

See also

Smartwatches

Sports watches

The Anatomy of the Watch color *Esquire* p135 BigBlackBook

Case Study: How Should an Understated Luxury Brand Compete Against Bling? S. Nason, J. Salvacruz et al color *Harvard Business Review Digital Articles* p2 F 28 2017

FABULOUS at Every Age color *Harper's Bazaar* no3656 p361 S 2017

FLOATS LIKE A BUTTERFLY N. Sullivan color *Esquire* p41 O 2017

Fresh FACES color *Esquire* p86 BigBlackBook

GOOD AS GOLD color *Forbes* v199 no7 p65 Je 29 2017

How Do You Sell A Priceless Watch? K. Kazakina color *Bloomberg Businessweek* no4535 p66 Ag 28 2017

THE IMPOSSIBLE LIST N. Sullivan, F. Arbona et al bw cartoon color *Esquire* v167 no1 p70 F 2017

LAPS OF LUXURY color *Conde Nast Traveler* v52 no4 p22 Ap 2017

RICK GRIMES' WATCH M. Romero color *Entertainment Weekly* no1460/1461 p94 Ap 7-17 2017

TIME FOR SOMETHING MORE S. Perman color *Fortune* v176 no5 p43 O 1 2017

TIME OUT G. SHTEYNGART cartoon *New Yorker* v93 no5 p36 Mr 20 2017

Up to the Minute H. MARTIN color *Architectural Digest* v74 no9 p62 S 2017

Wrist watches—Computer network resources

SMART WATCHES, DISSECTED D. GERSHGORN and A. GOLDBERG color *Popular Science* v288 no6 p20 N/D 2016

Wrist watches—Design & construction

Flight Time M. SOLOMON color *Forbes* v199 no1 p24 Ja 24 2017

Wrist watches—Equipment & supplies

NIKE DAY TO NIGHT APPLE WATCH BANDS R. LOYOLA color *Macworld - Digital Edition* p32 Je 13 2017

Wrist watches—Evaluation

100 YEARS OLD AND STILL A KNOCKOUT M. Hainey bw color *Esquire* p56 S 2017

2016 HOLIDAY GIFTS color *Flying* v143 no12 p48 D 2016

ABOUT FACE color *Harper's Bazaar* no3648 p164 N 2016

AUTOMATICS FOR THE PEOPLE color *Esquire* v167 no2 p78 Mr 2017

Bold-Faced Time J. MOORE color *GQ: Gentlemen's Quarterly* v97 no9 p63 S 2017

BREITLING'S LATEST color *Flying* v144 no6 p13 Je 2017

Bright Now color *Good Housekeeping* v264 no1 p15 Ja 1 2017

CHANDRA POINTER K. NEITZ color *Runner's World* v51 no10 p23 N 2016

DIVE IN color *Conde Nast Traveler* v52 no9 p30 O 2017

ENGINEER A BETTER BODY color *Men's Health* v31 no10 p(Sp)10 D 2016

The Essential: Watch J. TUNG *Martha Stewart Living* no269 p52 N 2016

FABULOUS at Every Age color *Harper's Bazaar* no3652 p163 Ap 2017

FACES OF INNOVATION D. MICHEL color *Men's Health* v32 no7 p(Sp)14 S 2017

Face TIME *Interview* v47 no5 p32 Je/Jl 2017

For the Man on a Mission J. Nosek cartoon color *Men's Health* v32 no4 p36 My 2017

GARMIN D2 CHARLIE color *Flying* v144 no10 p20 O 2017

GET IN GEAR S. Watson color *Esquire* p50 Ap 2017

Going Green T. Patterson color *Bloomberg Businessweek* no4533 p60 Ag 7 2017

THE HARD STUFF J. Roth color *Esquire* p47 Ap 2017

her style color *InStyle* v24 no7 p20 Jl 2017

hitting the BIG TIME N. SULLIVAN bw color *Esquire* p38 2017 BigBlackBook

HOLIDAY ON ICE color *Forbes* v198 no7 p65 N 29 2016

HORSE POWER S. Kneen, H. Leutwyler et al bw color *Esquire* p104 2017 BigBlackBook

If You Love a Good Throwback S. P. Nadella and A. Hou color *Glamour* v115 no9 p58 S 2017

LEATHER-BOUND S. Zlotnick *Washingtonian Magazine* v52 no2 p228 N 2016

The LIST color *Harper's Bazaar* no3652 p93 Ap 2017

The LIST color *Harper's Bazaar* no3657 p117 O 2017

Market: HIS OR HERS bw color *Vanity Fair* v59 no11 p60 N 2017

MATTIE JAMES L. CROSS color *Ebony* v72 no6 p27 Ap/My 2017

The O List color *O, The Oprah Magazine* p41 Jl 2017

on demand color *InStyle* v24 no6 p29 Je 2017

ONES TO WATCH color *Harper's Bazaar* no3652 p141 Ap 2017

Power Tools D. Michel color *Men's Health* v32 no2 p(Sp)26 Mr 2017

ROAD TESTING THE HUAWEI FIT color *Black Enterprise* v47 no5 p26 Ja/F 2017

THE SCENE MAKER H. BEACHLER color *Martha Stewart Living* p54 S 2017

The SCORE color *InStyle* v24 no1 p50 Ja 2017

SPEED RACER color *Harper's Bazaar* no3648 p129 N 2016

STAND OUT IN CAMO J. Roth bw color *Esquire* v167 no2 p114 Mr 2017

The Start color *InStyle* v24 no1 p11 Ja 2017

THE TEST OF TIME N. Sullivan color *Esquire* p42 N 2017

The Tick List J. Sens and J. Passov color *Golf Magazine* v59 no3 p108 Mr 2017

Time Honored B. BOYÉ color *Men's Health* v32 no5 p64 Je 2017

TIMELESS bw color *Vanity Fair* v58 no11 p78 N 2016

TIMELESS color *Road & Track* v69 no2 p96 S 2017

TOUGH ENOUGH *Los Angeles Magazine* p32 My 2017

THE UPGRADE color *Conde Nast Traveler* v52 no10 p44 N 2016

Weight Watches color *InStyle* v24 no4 p122 Ap 2017

A Well-Oiled Machine S. WATSON color *Esquire* v167 no1 p38 F 2017

THE WELL-SPENT $ DOLLAR color *Harper's Bazaar* no3655 p72 Ag 2017

What I Wear to Work J. Chen color *Bloomberg Businessweek* no4498 p91 N 7 2016

WISH LIST 2016 B. Barrett, J. Bien-Kahn et al color *Wired* v24 no12 p45 D 2016

WRIST CANDY color *Esquire* p43 My 2017

WRIST ROCK IT color *Popular Science* p13 Ja/F 2017

WRIST WATCH K. Dupzyk color *Popular Mechanics* p76 Jl 2017

Wrist watches—History

The Rolex President M. SOLOMON color *Forbes* v198 no5 p52 O 25 2016

Pcdhαc2 is required for axonal tiling and assembly of serotonergic circuitries in mice diag *Science* v356 no6336 p406 Ap 28 2017

Wu, Qing-Feng

Formation of α-chiral centers by asymmetric β-C(sp3)–H arylation, alkenylation, and alkynylation bibl diag *Science* v355 no6324 p499 F 3 2017

Wu, Qingyu

Engineering the ribosomal DNA in a megabase synthetic chromosome diag *Science* v355 no6329 p1049 Mr 10 2017

Wu, Ruidong

Global roadless areas: Consider terrain color *Science* v355 no6332 p1381 Mr 31 2017

Wu, Ruqian

Arthur J. Freeman *Physics Today* v69 no11 p69 N 2016

Wu, Shuangqing

Epigenetic regulation of antagonistic receptors confers rice blast resistance with yield balance bibl diag *Science* v355 no6328 p962 Mr 3 2017

Wu, Tim, ca. 1973-

THE ATTENTION MERCHANTS M. DOHERTY color *Maclean's* v129 no43 p61 O 31 2016

Content Confusion *New York Times Book Review* p21 N 27 2016

Net Neutrality Rules Will Make Winners and Losers Out of Businesses S. Greenstein, M. Peitz et al *Harvard Business Review Digital Articles* p2 Je 27 2016

Paying for Our Attention E. BELL *New York Times Book Review* p13 N 13 2016

We See You N. S. RILEY *Commentary* v143 no2 p44 F 2017

Wu, Wei

Global roadless areas: Consider terrain color *Science* v355 no6332 p1381 Mr 31 2017

Wu, Wenbin

All-oxide–based synthetic antiferromagnets exhibiting layer-resolved magnetization reversal diag *Science* v357 no6347 p191 Jl 14 2017

Wu, Xiao-Le

Bug mapping and fitness testing of chemically synthesized chromosome X diag *Science* v355 no6329 p1048 Mr 10 2017

"Perfect" designer chromosome V and behavior of a ring derivative diag *Science* v355 no6329 p1046 Mr 10 2017

Wu, Xiu-Jie

Late Pleistocene archaic human crania from Xuchang, China bibl color diag graph *Science* v355 no6328 p969 Mr 3 2017

Wu, Yalei

Deficiency of microRNA miR-34a expands cell fate potential in pluripotent stem cells diag *Science* v355 no6325 p596 F 10 2017

Wu, Yanli

Male sex in houseflies is determined by Mdmd, a paralog of the generic splice factor gene CWC22 bw color *Science* v356 no6338 p642 My 12 2017

Wu, Yi

3D organization of synthetic and scrambled chromosomes diag *Science* v355 no6329 p1050 Mr 10 2017

Bug mapping and fitness testing of chemically synthesized chromosome X diag *Science* v355 no6329 p1048 Mr 10 2017

Engineering the ribosomal DNA in a megabase synthetic chromosome diag *Science* v355 no6329 p1049 Mr 10 2017

"Perfect" designer chromosome V and behavior of a ring derivative diag *Science* v355 no6329 p1046 Mr 10 2017

Wu, Zhen-Yu

A central neural circuit for itch sensation color graph *Science* v357 no6352 p695 Ag 18 2017

Wu-Force (Performer)

KUNG-FU APPALACHIAN PUNK JAM color *Advocate* no1091 p34 Je/Jl 2017

Wu Man

CLASSICAL MUSIC *New Yorker* v93 no18 p9 Je 26 2017

Wu Qi

THE FLAWED PERFECT GENERAL Tang Long *Military History* v33 no6 p48 Mr 2017

Wu Tsang

356 Mission C. Moloney color *Art in America* v105 no1 p87 Ja 2017

Wudan Yan

Carbon monoxide, the silent killer, may have met its match *Science* v354 no6317 p1215 D 9 2016

WUEBBEN, JOE

5 WAYS... TO USE A SMITH MACHINE color *Muscle & Performance* v9 no6 p66 Je 2017

ASHWAGANDHA: One Quality Supplement color *Muscle & Performance* v9 no5 p11 My 2017

BARBELL BENT-OVER ROW color *Muscle & Performance* v9 no5 p13 My 2017

BECOME A PRO WITH PROBIOTICS color *Muscle & Performance* v9 no5 p12 My 2017

BOOST YOUR BENCH WITH CITRULLINE color *Muscle & Performance* v9 no9 p15 S 2017

BRAIN-BOOSTING SUPPLEMENT COMBO color *Muscle & Performance* v8 no12 p14 D 2016

BULGARIAN SPLIT SQUAT color *Muscle & Performance* v9 no8 p14 Ag 2017

CHLOROPHYLL color *Muscle & Performance* v9 no9 p17 S 2017

CITYWIDE EPIDEMIC color *Muscle & Performance* v9 no10 p19 O 2017

CROSS FAT GAIN OFF YOUR LIST color *Muscle & Performance* v8 no12 p16 D 2016

Don't Sleep on MELATONIN color *Muscle & Performance* v9 no6 p11 Je 2017

FAFQ color *Muscle & Performance* v9 no6 p13 Je 2017

FAFQ (FREQUENTLY ASKED FOOD QUESTIONS) color *Muscle & Performance* v9 no9 p18 S 2017

FAFQ *Muscle & Performance* v9 no5 p14 My 2017

Full-Body Fat Loss color *Muscle & Performance* v9 no11 p20 N 2017

Got vitamins? bw color *Muscle & Performance* v9 no7 p14 Jl 2017

HAIR IT IS GROOMING color *Muscle & Performance* v9 no8 p12 Ag 2017

IT'S WHEY BETTER WITH LEUCINE bw *Muscle & Performance* v9 no10 p17 O 2017

Max Out With Capsaicin color *Muscle & Performance* v9 no11 p33 N 2017

Milk Your Inflammation! color *Muscle & Performance* v9 no11 p32 N 2017

NOT YOUR FATHER'S FAT BURNER color *Muscle & Performance* v8 no12 p14 D 2016

OIL UP For Results color *Muscle & Performance* v8 no12 p13 D 2016

Plant-Based Power color *Muscle & Performance* v9 no11 p33 N 2017

POMEGRANATE PUMP cartoon *Muscle & Performance* v9 no4 p10 Ap 2017

PROTEIN PROTECTION color *Muscle & Performance* v9 no8 p11 Ag 2017

PROWLER (SLED) PUSHES color *Muscle & Performance* v9 no6 p14 Je 2017

PUSH PRESS color *Muscle & Performance* v9 no10 p21 O 2017

RAGING BULL chart color *Muscle & Performance* v9 no10 p38 O 2017

REAR-DELT MACHINE FLYE (AKA REVERSE PEC DECK) cartoon *Muscle & Performance* v8 no12 p16 D 2016

A Red-Hot Supplement color *Muscle & Performance* v9 no7 p13 Jl 2017

Roll for the Flow color *Muscle & Performance* v9 no11 p21 N 2017

RUNNING LIST color *Muscle & Performance* v9 no4 p12 Ap 2017

SEATED CALF RAISE color *Muscle & Performance* v9 no4 p13 Ap 2017

Sleep Tight with CASEIN color *Muscle & Performance* v9 no4 p9 Ap 2017

SPRINTS color *Muscle & Performance* v9 no9 p18 S 2017

TRACKING YOUR WEIGHT LOSS color *Muscle & Performance* v8 no12 p15 D 2016

Wuerl, Cardinal Donald

Looking for Answers to the World's Biggest Challenges In the Eternal City color *Time* v188 no24 p31 D 12 2016

Wuerthner, George

Places Worth Preserving *Sierra* v101 no4 p48 Jl/Ag 2016

Wuertz, Yoojin Grace

Big Little Lives C. HYUNG-OAK LEE *New York Times Book Re-

view p18 Mr 12 2017

Wuest, Craig—Awards

Patents and Awards *Science & Technology Review* p24 D 2016

WULF, ANDREA

Saving Nature, for the Joy of It *New York Times Book Review* p23 O 23 2016

What Thoreau Saw color *Atlantic* v320 no4 p106 N 2017

Wulf, Jane Bachman

Bambi Wulf 1954-2017 T. Keith color *Sports Illustrated* v126 no17 p18 Je 19 2017

WULF, MONIKA

Combining Biodiversity Resurveys across Regions to Advance Global Change Research *BioScience* v67 no1 p73 Ja 2017

Wulfhart, Nell McShane

BELFAST color *Runner's World* v52 no2 p64 Mr 2017

Viva Los Vino Pioneers color map *Conde Nast Traveler* v51 no10 p56 N 2016

WUNDERLICH, SHAILA

LIVING THE LOWE LIFE *Better Homes & Gardens* v94 no11 p128 N 2016

vintage couture color *Better Homes & Gardens* v95 no7 p64 Jl 2017

WUNDERMAN, ALI

GET CRACKIN' color *Backpacker* p14 Je 2017

Play hide-and-seek diag *Backpacker* p10 N 2017

Watch: The Bachelorette color *Backpacker* p22 S 2017

Wundheiler, B.

Observation of a large-scale anisotropy in the arrival directions of cosmic rays above 8×1018 eV *Science* v357 no6357 p1266 S 22 2017

Wünsch, Bettina

Molecular force spectroscopy with a DNA origami–based nanoscopic force clamp bibl diag graph *Science* v354 no6310 p305 O 21 2016

Wunsch, Eric—Interviews

Make Americana great again: The Wunsch family has a plan G. Adamson color *Magazine Antiques* v183 no6 p42 N/D 2016

Wunsch, Peter—Interviews

Make Americana great again: The Wunsch family has a plan G. Adamson color *Magazine Antiques* v183 no6 p42 N/D 2016

Wurlitzer, Rudolph H., 1873-1948

LAST WALTZ J. Vrabel *Indianapolis Monthly* v40 no11 p76 Jl 2017

Wurlitzer Co.

LAST WALTZ J. Vrabel *Indianapolis Monthly* v40 no11 p76 Jl 2017

Wurtz, B.

Rocks and Star Stuff color *Art in America* v104 no10 p58 N 2016

Wurtz, Benjamin

ALL AROUND THE FARM® *Successful Farming* v115 no6 p77 Ap 2017

Wurtz, Joseph

ALL AROUND THE FARM *Successful Farming* v115 no2 p79 F 2017

Wurtzel, Elizabeth

Elizabeth WURTZEL L. Phair *Interview* v47 no5 p26 Je/Jl 2017

Wurz, P.

Xenon isotopes in 67P/Churyumov-Gerasimenko show that comets contributed to Earth's atmosphere diag *Science* v356 no6342 p1069 Je 9 2017

Wuyi Wang

Large gem diamonds from metallic liquid in Earth's deep mantle bibl color *Science* v354 no6318 p1403 D 16 2016

Wuzubia, Steven

New Discovery for People with Failing Memory color *National Review* v69 no8 p9 My 2017

One Simple Trick to Reversing Memory Loss color *National Review* v68 no21 p7 N 21 2016

One Simple Trick to Reversing Memory Loss *Saturday Evening Post* v289 no2 p99 Mr/Ap 2017

One Simple Trick to Reversing Memory Loss *Saturday Evening Post* v289 no5 p94 S/O 2017

One Simple Trick to Reversing Memory Loss: World's Leading Brain Expert and Winner of the Prestigious Kennedy Award, Unveils Exciting News For the Scattered, Unfocused and Forgetful *Saturday Evening Post* v289 no4 p70 Jl/Ag 2017

WWW. (Music)

The Chosen One M. POLLOCK color *Chicago* v66 no10 p84 O 2017

Wxy Architecture + Urban Design (Company)

The Next New Astor Place J. DAVIDSON img *New York* p83 Ja 9 2017

Wyandot (North American people)—Rites & ceremonies

Sensoriality and Wendat Steams S. DORLAND *American Indian Quarterly* v41 no1 p1 Wint 2017

Wycliff, Don

A Big Wet Kiss to Bigots *Commonweal* v114 no14 p6 S 8 2017

Wyeth, Andrew, 1917-2009

'Wyeth World': On the centennial of the birth of Andrew Wyeth, a fellow artist and lifelong friend offers this one-of-a-kind remembrance P. RALSTON bw color *Yankee* p18 Jl 2017

Wyeth, Andrew, 1917-2009—Exhibitions

100th birthday tributes to Andrew Wyeth color *Magazine Antiques* v184 no3 p34 My/Je 2017

WYKES, SARA

What a Headache *USA Today Magazine* v145 no2858 p33 N 2016

Wyle, Noah, 1971-

The Librarians E. Aslanian *TV Guide* v64 no46 p37 N 7 2016

Wylie, Andrew

Andrew Wylie Makes First FIL Appearance L. Ahuile and E. Nawotka color *Publishers Weekly* v263 no50 p25 D 5 2016

Wylie, Candace Boyd

Spice Girl S. KROWIAK *Indianapolis Monthly* p43 F 2017

Wylie, Emma—Interviews

Emma WYLIE N. Loeffler-Gladstone *Dance Spirit* v21 no1 p95 Ja 2017

Wylie, Janice

Buzz M For Murder J. ELLROY bw color *Vanity Fair* v59 no11 p152 N 2017

Wylie, Leslie

REBECCA FARM: AMERICAN EVENTING'S FIELD OF DREAMS color *Practical Horseman* v45 no10 p36 O 2017

WYLIE, MADGE COOK

This Good Old Building: A Place Full of History *Idaho Magazine* v16 no12 p25 S 2017

Wyllie, Cheryl

16 Questions with INGRID KLIMKE color *Dressage Today* v23 no12 p52 S 2017

WYMA, CHLOE

HOCKNEY color *New York Times Book Review* p75 D 4 2016

WYNDHAM, SUSAN

The Circles of Hellhaus: A lonely British hiker goes dangerously walkabout in Germany *New York Times Book Review* p19 S 10 2017

Wynn, Patricia

Whisper of Death *Publishers Weekly* v264 no40 p119 O 2 2017

Wynn, Robin

When to Bring in a Professional Coach *Harvard Business Review Digital Articles* p2 F 20 2015

Wynn, Thomas A.

Inflammation and metabolism in tissue repair and regeneration diag *Science* v356 no6342 p1026 Je 9 2017

WYNN WHELDON

The Future Wasn't There *Commentary* v143 no1 p61 Ja 2017

WYNNE, MELANIE

TRAVEL SPECIALISTS 2016 color *Conde Nast Traveler* v51 no11 p78 D 2016

Wynn-Grant, Rae—Interviews

A RARE SPECIES R. W. Goode color *Black Enterprise* v47 no8 p31 Jl/Ag 2017

Wynonna Earp (TV program)

THE 8-SECOND REVIEW N. Serrao color *Entertainment Weekly* no1470 p46 Je 16 2017

Wyoming

COLDFRONT color *Snowboarder* v29 no2 p12 O 2016

Wyoming Range (Wyo.)

Get Lost on Wyoming's Edge B. GRAHAM color *Backpacker* p14 S 2017

Wyoming—Description & travel

The Long Way Home K. Siber *National Parks* v91 no2 p32 Spr 2017

Wyrick, Jonathan

An on/off Berry phase switch in circular graphene resonators diag graph *Science* v356 no6340 p845 My 26 2017

Wystrach, Mark

IT'S GOOD TO BE Home K. VAUGHN *Arizona Highways* v93 no4 p44 Ap 2017

Wytsma, Ken

The Myth of Equality: Uncovering the Roots of Injustice and Privilege *Publishers Weekly* v264 no15 p70 Ap 10 2017

X

X, Malcolm, 1925-1965

WHAT IF? ... MUHAMMAD ALI HAD NEVER MET MALCOLM X? R. O'Brien and J. Feldman color *Sports Illustrated* v126 no11 p61 Ap 17-24 2017

X chromosome

Xist recruits the X chromosome to the nuclear lamina to enable chromosome-wide silencing Chun-Kan Chen, M. Blanco et al bibl graph *Science* v354 no6311 p468 O 28 2016

X-Men: Apocalypse (Film)

X-MEN: APOCALYPSE C. Chiarella color *Sound & Vision* v82 no2 p71 F/Mr 2017

X-Men: Apocalypse M. FELL *TV Guide* v65 no8 p37 F 27 2017

X-ray absorption

Identification of single-site gold catalysis in acetylene hydrochlorination G. Malta, S. A. Kondrat et al bw diag graph *Science* v355 no6332 p1399 Mr 31 2017

RESEARCH M. S. Lcolor *Science* v355 no6322 p257 Ja 20 2017

Time-resolved x-ray absorption spectroscopy with a water window high-harmonic source Y. Pertot, C. Schmidt et al bibl graph *Science* v355 no6322 p264 Ja 20 2017

X-ray crystallography

The long and winding road to methane color *Science* v354 no6308 p77 O 7 2016

Rosalind Franklin color *Discover* v38 no4 p50 My 2017

Science and History Get Personal M. BOOTH *Skeptical Inquirer* v41 no3 p32 My/Je 2017

X-ray imaging

See also

X-ray crystallography

Novel Scintillator Improves X-Ray Imaging A. Chen color *Science & Technology Review* p12 Ja/F 2017

X-ray lasers

The Atomic Movie Machine J. KEATS color *Discover* v38 no7 p10 S 2017

X-ray optics—Research

RESEARCH color *Science* v357 no6349 p366 Jl 28 2017

X-ray spectroscopy

Following photoexcited electrons in reactions R. Sension color *Science* v356 no6333 p31 Ap 7 2017

X-ray telescopes

NEWS color *Science* v356 no6344 p1214 Je 23 2017

X-rays

See also

Soft X rays

Doctors, Nurses, and a World at War *USA Today Magazine* v146 no2869 p15 O 2017

Modern Medicine and the Great War *USA Today Magazine* v146 no2869 p16 O 2017

X-ray 'bump' hints at dark matter E. CONOVER color *Science News* v191 no4 p8 Mr 4 2017

X-ray mystery shrouds Pluto C. CROCKETT color *Science News* v190 no11 p15 N 26 2016

X-rays—Measurement

An accreting pulsar with extreme properties drives an ultraluminous x-ray source in NGC 5907 G. Luca Israel, A. Belfiore et al bibl chart graph *Science* v355 no6327 p817 F 24 2017

X-Yachts AS

X-Yachts X4 Z. Prochazka color *Sail* v48 no7 p22 Jl 2017

Xanadu Surfboards (Company)

The Featherweight Future Z. MORTON color *Surfer* v58 no4 p40 Ag 2017

Xantheas, Sotiris S.

Spying on the neighbors' pool bibl diag *Science* v354 no6316 p1101 D 2 2016

Xavier, Charles (Fictitious character)

NO. 19 PROFESSOR X T. Stack color *Entertainment Weekly* no1436/1437 p59 O 21 2016

Xavier, Ramnik J.

Paneth cells secrete lysozyme via secretory autophagy during bacterial infection of the intestine color diag *Science* v357 no6355 p1047 S 8 2017

Reovirus infection triggers inflammatory responses to dietary antigens and development of celiac disease color diag *Science* v356 no6333 p44 Ap 7 2017

Xavier Chen, Fei

PAF1 regulation of promoter-proximal pause release via enhancer activation color *Science* v357 no6357 p1294 S 22 2017

Xavier Prochaska, J.

[C II] 158-μm emission from the host galaxies of damped Lyman-alpha systems bibl color graph *Science* v355 no6331 p1285 Mr 24 2017

Measurement of the small-scale structure of the intergalactic medium using close quasar pairs diag graph *Science* v356 no6336 p418 Ap 28 2017

Xavier University (Cincinnati, Ohio)

A GLORIOUS LIFE M. Lunken color *Flying* v144 no1 p60 Ja 2017

SLICE OF LIFE J. COHEN *Cincinnati Magazine* v50 no2 p24 N 2016

A SOLDIER'S STORY G. MILLER JR. *Cincinnati Magazine* v50 no2 p76 N 2016

Xavier University (Cincinnati, Ohio)—Sports

12 XAVIER MUSKETEERS D. Greene chart color *Sports Illustrated* v125 no15 p71 N 7 2016

Xbox One (Video game console)

Xbox One X: Everything you need to know about this powerful gaming console H. DINGMAN chart color *PCWorld* v35 no7 p32 Jl 2017

Xbox One X PC Build: Can you do it for $500? A. YEE chart color *PCWorld* v35 no8 p112 Ag 2017

Xbox video game consoles

Xbox Project Scorpio specs revealed: Microsoft's next console is a Radeon-infused monster B. CHACOS chart color *PCWorld* v35 no5 p46 My 2017

Xenobiotics

Chemical transformation of xenobiotics by the human gut microbiota N. Koppel, V. Maini Rekdal et al diag *Science* v356 no6344 p1246 Je 23 2017

Xenografts

Advances in organ transplant from pigs [Cover story] J. Denner color *Science* v357 no6357 p1238 S 22 2017

Engineering better organs A. Witze color *Science News* v192 no6 p26 O 14 2017

Xenotransplant advances may prompt human trials K. Servick *Science* v357 no6358 p1338 S 29 2017

Xenon

Dark matter hunters raise the bar color *Science* v356 no6340 p786 My 26 2017

Xenon isotopes

Xenon isotopes in 67P/Churyumov-Gerasimenko show that comets contributed to Earth's atmosphere B. Marty, K. Altwegg et al diag *Science* v356 no6342 p1069 Je 9 2017

Xenophobia

EVIL MAY DAY 1517: Foreign traders were attracted to the City of London by England's prosperous trade in wool and cloth. They were not always made welcome D. Wilson *History Today* v67 no6 p66 Je 2016

Rising Fear *Change* v82 no3 p23 Mr 2017

Xenos, Michael A.

Mapping the Landscape of Public Attitudes on Synthetic Biology *BioScience* v67 no3 p290 Mr 2017

U.S. attitudes on human genome editing color graph *Science* v357 no6351 p553 Ag 11 2017

Xepapadeas, Anastasios

Social norms as solutions bibl color *Science* v354 no6308 p42 O 7 2016

XERAKIA, MARIA

BLOOD ORANGES *Better Homes & Gardens* v95 no1 p63 Ja 2017

FAST & FRESH color *Better Homes & Gardens* v95 no3 p98 Mr

2017

HANDY MIXERS color *Better Homes & Gardens* v95 no6 p124 Je 2017

ICE CREAM MAKERS color *Better Homes & Gardens* v95 no7 p154 Jl 2017

new ways with CHARD *Better Homes & Gardens* v94 no12 p92 D 2016

new ways with RED CABBAGE *Better Homes & Gardens* v95 no1 p70 Ja 2017

ROASTING PANS color *Better Homes & Gardens* v95 no11 p142 N 2017

VEGGIE TOOLS color *Better Homes & Gardens* v95 no8 p164 Ag 2017

Xeriscaping

Living Lab for Sustainable Cities E. BARTON *USA Today Magazine* v146 no2868 p69 S 2017

X-Files, The (TV program)

CHECKING IN ON THE X-FILES K. Connolly color *Entertainment Weekly* no1485 p44 O 6 2017

The Quiz T. BALAZO color *Maclean's* v130 no8 p64 S 2017

Xi, Jinping, 1953-

Can Xi Pacify a Restless Hong Kong? Ting Shi bw *Bloomberg Businessweek* no4529 p37 Jl 3 2017

The riddle of Xi D. Roberts color *Bloomberg Businessweek* no4496 p17 O 24 2016

Salesman Xi M. STINSON *National Review* v69 no12 p18 Je 26 2017

A Specter Is Haunting Davos D. GREEN color *Weekly Standard* v22 no21 p14 F 6 2017

Working Together to Usher In the Second "Golden Decade" of BRICS Cooperation *Vital Speeches of the Day* v83 no10 p277 O 2017

Xi Jinping's Authoritarianism Does a Disservice to China's Nuanced Political Tradition J. WASSERSTROM and K. MERKEL-HESS *NPQ: New Perspectives Quarterly* v33 no4 p15 O 2016

Xi, Jinping, 1953—Political & social views

A Beijing Model? R. Terrill color *Weekly Standard* v22 no23 p18 F 20 2017

Xi, Jinping, 1953—Travel

High Stakes: Can Trump and Xi Avoid War and Strike a North Korea Deal? G. Allison color *Time* v189 no14 p12 Ap 17 2017

Xi Zou

Charting China's Rising Individualism in Names, Songs, and Attitudes *Harvard Business Review Digital Articles* p2 Mr 11 2016

Xia, Jing

Chiral Majorana fermion modes in a quantum anomalous Hall insulator–superconductor structure diag *Science* v357 no6348 p294 Jl 21 2017

Xia, Yan

Mechanochemical unzipping of insulating polyladderene to semiconducting polyacetylene [Cover story] diag *Science* v357 no6350 p475 Ag 4 2017

Xia, Yeqiang

A paralogous decoy protects Phytophthora sojae apoplastic effector PsXEG1 from a host inhibitor bibl graph *Science* v355 no6326 p710 F 17 2017

Xia, Zheng-Bao

"Perfect" designer chromosome V and behavior of a ring derivative diag *Science* v355 no6329 p1046 Mr 10 2017

Xiahui Wang

Protecting China's soil by law bibl *Science* v354 no6312 p562 N 4 2016

Xi'an Shi (China)

10 TRIPS TO ASIA THAT WON'T COST A FORTUNE M. Leonhardt and K. A. Renzulli color map *Money* v46 no7 p71 Ag 2017

Xiang, Yang K.

β2-Adrenoreceptor is a regulator of the a-synuclein gene driving risk of Parkinson's disease cartoon chart graph *Science* v357 no6354 p891 S 1 2017

XIANG WANG

THE WORLD'S BILLIONAIRES bw color diag graph map *Forbes* v199 no3 p84 Mr 28 2017

Xiang Zhang

Anomalously low electronic thermal conductivity in metallic vanadium dioxide bibl graph *Science* v355 no6323 p371 Ja 27 2017

Xiangdong Lei

Positive biodiversity-productivity relationship predominant in global forests bibl chart graph map *Science* v354 no6309 paaf8957-1 O 14 2016

Xiangfeng Duan

Ultrafine jagged platinum nanowires enable ultrahigh mass activity for the oxygen reduction reaction bibl chart graph *Science* v354 no6318 p1414 D 16 2016

XIAO, DEREK

THE WORLD'S BILLIONAIRES bw color diag graph map *Forbes* v199 no3 p84 Mr 28 2017

Xiao, Huahua

Clean Combustion K. Moore *Natural History* v124 no10 p8 N 2016

Xiao, Jie

Flipping nanoscopy on its head bibl diag graph *Science* v355 no6325 p582 F 10 2017

GTPase activity-coupled treadmilling of the bacterial tubulin FtsZ organizes septal cell wall synthesis bibl graph *Science* v355 no6326 p744 F 17 2017

Xiao, Jing W.

Mouse models of acute and chronic hepacivirus infection *Science* v357 no6347 p204 Jl 14 2017

Xiao, Mengmeng

Scaling carbon nanotube complementary transistors to 5-nm gate lengths bibl chart graph *Science* v355 no6322 p271 Ja 20 2017

Xiao, Nianqing

Mismatch repair deficiency predicts response of solid tumors to PD-1 blockade chart graph *Science* v357 no6349 p409 Jl 28 2017

Xiao, Wen-Hai

Bug mapping and fitness testing of chemically synthesized chromosome X diag *Science* v355 no6329 p1048 Mr 10 2017

Xiao, Yibo

Engineering the ribosomal DNA in a megabase synthetic chromosome diag *Science* v355 no6329 p1049 Mr 10 2017

Xiao Jin Yang

Protecting China's soil by law bibl *Science* v354 no6312 p562 N 4 2016

Xiao Long

The formation of peak rings in large impact craters bibl color graph *Science* v354 no6314 p878 N 18 2016

Xiao Nan Yu

Xiao Nan Yu: The National Ballet of Canada principal knows that flexibility isn't always a blessing J. STAHL *Dance Magazine* v91 no7 p50 Jl 2017

Xiao-Tian Xu

Realization of two-dimensional spin-orbit coupling for Bose-Einstein condensates bibl graph *Science* v354 no6308 p83 O 7 2016

Xiaobo, Liu

Liu Xiaobo's Last Text bw *New York Review of Books* v64 no14 p8 S 28 2017

Xiaobo Hu

Expert consensus on point-of-care testing *Science* v354 no6319 p15 D 23 2016

Recommendations on the management and use of POCT in medical institutions (nosocomial) *Science* v354 no6319 p13 D 23 2016

Xiaobo Mao

Pathological α-synuclein transmission initiated by binding lymphocyte-activation gene 3 bibl graph *Science* v353 no6307 paah3374-1 S 30 2016

Xiaodan Gu

Highly stretchable polymer semiconductor films through the nanoconfinement effect bibl graph *Science* v355 no6320 p1 Ja 6 2017

Xiaojing Pan

Structural basis for the gating mechanism of the type 2 ryanodine receptor RyR2 bibl color graph *Science* v354 no6310 paah5324-1 O 21 2016

Xiaoli Yang

Expert consensus on point-of-care testing *Science* v354 no6319 p15 D 23 2016

Recommendations on the management and use of POCT in medi-

XTI SWITCHES TO HYBRID — ELECTRIC PROPULSION
color *Flying* v144 no5 p16 My 2017

XTO Energy Inc.
How Exxon Is Learning To Let Go J. Carroll and D. Wethe color *Bloomberg Businessweek* no4519 p49 Ap 24 2017

Xu, Bing
β2-Adrenoreceptor is a regulator of the a-synuclein gene driving risk of Parkinson's disease cartoon chart graph *Science* v357 no6354 p891 S 1 2017

Xu, C. Shan
Increased spatiotemporal resolution reveals highly dynamic dense tubular matrices in the peripheral ER bibl bw color graph *Science* v354 no6311 paaf3928-1 O 28 2016

Xu, Gege
Microbiota-activated PPAR-γ signaling inhibits dysbiotic Enterobacteriaceae expansion graph *Science* v357 no6351 p570 Ag 11 2017

Xu, Hang
"Perfect" designer chromosome V and behavior of a ring derivative diag *Science* v355 no6329 p1046 Mr 10 2017

Xu, Haoran
All-oxide–based synthetic antiferromagnets exhibiting layer-resolved magnetization reversal diag *Science* v357 no6347 p191 Jl 14 2017

Xu, Hong
Two-dimensional sp2 carbon–conjugated covalent organic frameworks diag graph *Science* v357 no6352 p673 Ag 18 2017

Xu, Jun
Combining polyethylene and polypropylene: Enhanced performance with PE/iPP multiblock polymers bibl chart graph *Science* v355 no6327 p814 F 24 2017

Xu, Ling
Trispecific broadly neutralizing HIV antibodies mediate potent SHIV protection in macaques color graph *Science* v357 no6359 p85 O 6 2017

Xu, Meng
Engineering the ribosomal DNA in a megabase synthetic chromosome diag *Science* v355 no6329 p1049 Mr 10 2017

Xu, Qing
Two-dimensional sp2 carbon–conjugated covalent organic frameworks diag graph *Science* v357 no6352 p673 Ag 18 2017

Xu, Shiyao
Systemic pan-AMPK activator MK-8722 improves glucose homeostasis but induces cardiac hypertrophy graph *Science* v357 no6350 p507 Ag 4 2017

Xu, Wenqian
Atomic-layered Au clusters on α-MoC as catalysts for the low-temperature water-gas shift reaction chart diag graph *Science* v357 no6349 p389 Jl 28 2017

Xu, Xian
Fabrication of fillable microparticles and other complex 3D microstructures color diag *Science* v357 no6356 p1138 S 15 2017

Xu, Xiao-Ran
"Perfect" designer chromosome V and behavior of a ring derivative diag *Science* v355 no6329 p1046 Mr 10 2017

Xu, Xu
Three-dimensional holey-graphene/niobia composite architectures for ultrahigh-rate energy storage color diag graph *Science* v356 no6338 p599 My 12 2017

Xu, Xuming
Control of species-dependent cortico-motoneuronal connections underlying manual dexterity diag graph *Science* v357 no6349 p400 Jl 28 2017

Xu, Xun
Deep functional analysis of synII, a 770-kilobase synthetic yeast chromosome diag *Science* v355 no6329 p1047 Mr 10 2017

Xu, Yu
Satellite-based entanglement distribution over 1200 kilometers diag graph *Science* v356 no6343 p1140 Je 16 2017

Xu, Zhenjie
Microtubules acquire resistance from mechanical breakage through intralumenal acetylation diag graph *Science* v356 no6335 p328 Ap 21 2017

Xu Hongci
XU HONGCI E. Osnos cartoon *New Yorker* v92 no42 p94 D 19 2016

Xu Tan—Exhibitions
ART'S SAKE: BRIGHT AND SHINY J. Fan bw *New Yorker* v93 no33 p38 O 23 2017

Xu Wang
Photoactivation and inactivation of Arabidopsis cryptochrome 2 bibl graph *Science* v354 no6310 p343 O 21 2016

Xu Yi
Microresonator soliton dual-comb spectroscopy bibl diag graph *Science* v354 no6312 p600 N 4 2016

Xu Zhang
Biaxially strained PtPb/Pt core/shell nanoplate boosts oxygen reduction catalysis bibl color graph *Science* v354 no6318 p1410 D 16 2016

Xu Zhu
Synthesis of resveratrol tetramers via a stereoconvergent radical equilibrium bibl diag graph *Science* v354 no6317 p1260 D 9 2016

Xuan, Zhenyu
Deficiency of microRNA miR-34a expands cell fate potential in pluripotent stem cells diag *Science* v355 no6325 p596 F 10 2017

Xue, Yali
A Neolithic expansion, but strong genetic structure, in the independent history of New Guinea diag *Science* v357 no6356 p1160 S 15 2017

Xue-peng Yang
The biosynthetic pathway of coenzyme F430 in methanogenic and methanotrophic archaea bibl diag graph *Science* v354 no6310 p339 O 21 2016

Xuejun Chen
Rapid development of a DNA vaccine for Zika virus bibl graph *Science* v354 no6309 p237 O 14 2016

Xuewei Bao
Fault activation by hydraulic fracturing in western Canada bibl graph map *Science* v354 no6318 p1406 D 16 2016

Xueying Zhou
Generation of influenza A viruses as live but replication-incompetent virus vaccines bibl graph *Science* v354 no6316 p1170 D 2 2016

Xuezhong Yu
Expert consensus on point-of-care testing *Science* v354 no6319 p15 D 23 2016
Recommendations on the management and use of POCT in medical institutions (nosocomial) *Science* v354 no6319 p13 D 23 2016

Xun, Lu
Jottings Under Lamplight *Publishers Weekly* v264 no27 p66 Jl 3 2017

Xuping Xie
Zika virus produces noncoding RNAs using a multi-pseudoknot structure that confounds a cellular exonuclease bibl color graph *Science* v354 no6316 p1148 D 2 2016

Xu Zhiyong, 1973-
To Build a Free China: A Citizen's Journey E. PILS *Foreign Affairs* v96 no3 p175 My/Je 2017

XX (Performer)
Downcast Brits Brew Up a Quiet Storm M. Johnston color *Time* v189 no4 p52 Ja 23 2017
The Playlist color *Rolling Stone* no1280 p8 F 9 2017
Secrets of the xx's Joyful New Sound M. Vain color *Entertainment Weekly* no1449 p57 Ja 20 2017
The xx N. Feeney color *Entertainment Weekly* no1449 p56 Ja 20 2017
The xx's Dreamy Late-Night Rapture J. DOLAN color *Rolling Stone* no1278/1279 p49 Ja 12 2017

XXL (Periodical)
FRESH C. Battan cartoon *New Yorker* v93 no18 p18 Je 26 2017

XXX: Return of Xander Cage (Film)
The Bullseye M. Snetiker color *Entertainment Weekly* no1450 p64 Ja 27 2017
the new girl H. Morrill color *InStyle* v24 no2 p146 F 2017
XXX: RETURN OF XANDER CAGE D. Vaughn color *Sound & Vision* v82 no8 p70 O 2017

Xyloglucans
A paralogous decoy protects Phytophthora sojae apoplastic effector PsXEG1 from a host inhibitor Z. Ma, L. Zhu et al bibl graph *Science* v355 no6326 p710 F 17 2017

p128 N 2016

Luxury Class: The smallest entry in the yacht line provides plenty of space, performance and luxury S. SHIBATA color *Sea Magazine* v109 no6 p10 Je 2017

Maritimo M54 *Sea Magazine* v108 no12 p52 D 2016

MODERN THROWBACK S. SHIBATA *Sea Magazine* v108 no12 p8 D 2016

Monte Carlo Yachts MCY70 *Sea Magazine* v108 no12 p50 D 2016

MORE THAN MEETS THE EYE S. SHIBATA *Sea Magazine* v109 no1 p10 Ja 2017

Nautitech 46 Fly [Cover story] T. Dove color *Sail* v48 no8 p22 Ag 2017

A NEW CLASS OF STABILITY-INTRODUCING THE SEA-KEEPER 3 *Sea Magazine* v108 no12 p10 D 2016

NEW FROM THE ETERNAL CITY: AN ITALIAN BUILDER RECALLS GLORIES PAST FOR ITS LATEST MODEL NAME, AND GLORIES PRESENT FOR ITS DESIGN AND BUILD S. SHIBATA color *Sea Magazine* v109 no7 p6 Jl 2017

THE NEW FRONTIER C. J. DOANE color diag *Sail* v48 no4 p34 Ap 2017

NEW TRADITIONS P. FREDERIKSEN chart color *Power & Motoryacht* v34 no9 p72 S 2017

NIMBUS 365 COUPE: A SWEDISH BUILDER COOKS UP A WEST COAST-WORTHY FAMILY COASTAL CRUISER color *Sea Magazine* v109 no7 p38 Jl 2017

NO LIMIT SHIPS 1550: THIS UNUSUAL BOAT FROM THE NETHERLANDS IS A GLOBAL TROTTER AND A LOCAL CRUISER T. SERIO color *Sea Magazine* v109 no6 p42 Je 2017

NORDHAVN 59 COASTAL PILOT M. WERLING *Sea Magazine* v108 no8 p30 Ag 2016

NORDHAVN N96: AWARD-WINNING DESIGN AND OCEAN-CROSSING RANGE FIND A HOME IN ONE NEAR-100-FOOT YACHT M. WERLING *Sea Magazine* v109 no9 p42 S 2017

NORTH PACIFIC *Sea Magazine* v109 no5 p34 My 2017

Numarine 105HT J. Y. Wood color *Power & Motoryacht* v34 no10 p60 O 2017

OCEAN ALEXANDER 70 EVOLUTION M. WERLING *Sea Magazine* v108 no12 p32 D 2016

Ocean Alexander *Sea Magazine* v108 no12 p50 D 2016

ODYSSEY AT THE CROSSROADS [Cover story] D. J. HARDING chart color diag *Power & Motoryacht* v34 no6 p40 Je 2017

ONE STEP IN THE RIGHT DIRECTION A. HARPER chart color diag *Power & Motoryacht* v33 no3 p62 Mr 2017

Open for Anything S. Shibata *Boating World* v37 no9 p8 N/D 2016

THE OTHER AMERICA C. CASWELL chart color *Power & Motoryacht* v34 no11 p92 N 2017

Outer Reef 610 MY D. Harding Jr. color *Power & Motoryacht* v34 no9 p46 S 2017

Overmarine Mangusta Oceano 42 J. Y. Wood color *Power & Motoryacht* v32 no11 p66 N 2016

Palmer Johnson 63 Sport S. Murray color *Power & Motoryacht* v33 no3 p58 Mr 2017

POWER TO CRUISE *Sea Magazine* v109 no5 p9 My 2017

Prestige 460 J. Y. Wood color *Power & Motoryacht* v34 no6 p32 Je 2017

Pretty & Practical J. WOOLDRIDGE color *Power & Motoryacht* v34 no9 p78 S 2017

PURSUIT OF PASSION D. HARDING JR. bw chart color *Power & Motoryacht* v34 no8 p52 Ag 2017

RANGER TUGS R-23 R. MCAFEE *Sea Magazine* v108 no10 p48 O 2016

READY & ABLE R. THIEL chart color diag *Power & Motoryacht* v33 no3 p76 Mr 2017

REGAL 42 FLY: WHO KNEW A GREAT PACIFIC NORTHWEST BOAT WOULD BE DESIGNED AND BUILT IN FLORIDA? R. McAFEE color *Sea Magazine* v109 no7 p32 Jl 2017

Reinventing a Classic J. BROWNLEE chart color *Power & Motoryacht* v34 no7 p60 Jl 2017

Return of a Legend B. PIKE chart color *Power & Motoryacht* v34 no7 p42 Jl 2017

Rio Yachts 58 GTS D. Harding color *Power & Motoryacht* v33 no2 p46 F 2017

RIVA'S REINVENTION A. HARPER chart color diag *Power & Motoryacht* v33 no2 p82 F 2017

Riviera 4800 Sport Yacht D. Harding color *Power & Motoryacht* v33 no2 p40 F 2017

RIVIERA 4800 SPORT YACHT: THE LATEST IN TECHNOLOGY AND PROPULSION COMBINE WITH STYLE AND STRENGTH M. WERLING color *Sea Magazine* v109 no7 p28 Jl 2017

RIVIERA 6000 SPORT YACHT R. MCAFEE *Sea Magazine* v108 no10 p44 O 2016

Riviera 68 Sports Motor Yacht D. J. Harding color *Power & Motoryacht* v34 no10 p62 O 2017

Room and a View C. CASWELL chart color diag *Power & Motoryacht* v33 no2 p70 F 2017

Sanlorenzo SL78 J. Y. Wood color *Power & Motoryacht* v33 no1 p48 Ja 2017

Schaefer Yachts 560 A. Parkinson color *Power & Motoryacht* v33 no3 p54 Mr 2017

Sea Ray SLX 400 B. Pike color *Power & Motoryacht* v34 no10 p64 O 2017

THE SHAPE OF THINGS J. y. Wood chart color *Power & Motoryacht* v32 no11 p102 N 2016

THE SHAPE OF THINGS TO COME A. HARPER chart color diag *Power & Motoryacht* v34 no10 p78 O 2017

SHOWCASE *Sea Magazine* v109 no1 p61 Ja 2017

The Show Goes On P. Nielsen color *Sail* v48 no4 p24 Ap 2017

SINCEREST FORM OF FLATTERY S. SHIBATA color *Sea Magazine* v109 no8 p8 Ag 2017

Small Wonder A. HARPER chart color *Power & Motoryacht* v32 no11 p108 N 2016

Solaris 50 C. J. Doane color *Sail* v48 no5 p20 My 2017

SPECIFICATIONS *Sea Magazine* v109 no1 p36 Ja 2017

THE STAR OF THE SHOW [Cover story] J. Y. Wood, B. Pike et al color *Power & Motoryacht* v32 no11 p76 N 2016

STRONG SILENT TYPE R. THIEL chart color diag *Power & Motoryacht* v33 no2 p94 F 2017

Style and Substance J. WOOLDRIDGE color *Power & Motoryacht* v33 no2 p100 F 2017

Sunreef Power Day Cat: Sunreef 's latest is a 60-knot, 41-foot catamaran with a penchant for dayboating S. SHIBATA *Sea Magazine* v109 no9 p10 S 2017

Sweet Summertime D. HARDING color *Power & Motoryacht* v33 no2 p88 F 2017

TIARA 44 FLYBRIDGE: A COUPLES COUPE GETS A FLYBRIDGE ADDITION AND GOES TO A WHOLE NEW LEVEL, LITERALLY AND FIGURATIVELY M. WERLING color *Sea Magazine* v109 no8 p42 Ag 2017

TIARA 53 COUPE M. WERLING *Sea Magazine* v109 no2 p34 F 2017

To Each His Own J. Y. WOOD cartoon chart color *Power & Motoryacht* v32 no12 p44 D 2016

Uncompromising Vision A. HARPER bw chart color *Power & Motoryacht* v34 no8 p64 Ag 2017

Viking 37 Billfish B. Pike color *Power & Motoryacht* v34 no6 p30 Je 2017

Westport 125 J. Y. Wood color *Power & Motoryacht* v34 no7 p32 Jl 2017

Whole New World B. PIKE chart color *Power & Motoryacht* v34 no8 p40 Ag 2017

A World Unfolding J. Y. WOOD chart color diag *Power & Motoryacht* v33 no3 p106 Mr 2017

X-Yachts X4 Z. Prochazka color *Sail* v48 no7 p22 Jl 2017

Yachts—Exhibitions

DON'T MISS LIST SEPTEMBER 2016 *Sea Magazine* v108 no9 pCA-7 S 2016

Yachts—Furniture, equipment, etc.

Superyacht Features S. SHIBATA *Sea Magazine* v108 no10 p12 O 2016

Yachts—History

The Refit That Sparked Revolution P. SWANSON bw color *Power & Motoryacht* v34 no8 p74 Ag 2017

Yachts—Maintenance & repair

DINGHIES DONE RIGHT G. MANSFIELD *Sea Magazine* v109 no1 p50 Ja 2017

Ground Rules [Cover story] J. Neeves color *Sail* v48 no8 p52 Ag 2017

Stay warm to beat a cold A. Iwasaki color *Redbook* p85 F 2017

Why Yale Owns a Forest J. Lorin color *Bloomberg Businessweek* no4536 p28 S 4 2017

Yale University—Sports

Handsome Is ... B. Marks, T. Keith et al color *Sports Illustrated* v127 no5 p28 Ag 14 2017

Yali Xue

Chimpanzee genomic diversity reveals ancient admixture with bonobos bibl diag graph map *Science* v354 no6311 p477 O 28 2016

Yalkın, Çar

Invented Myths in Contemporary Turkish Political Advertising *Society* v53 no6 p603 D 2016

YALLOP, MARIAN L.

The Arctic in the Twenty-First Century: Changing Biogeochemical Linkages across a Paraglacial Landscape of Greenland *BioScience* v67 no2 p118 F 2017

Yalom, Irvin David, 1931-

How to Die J. M. SMITH color *Atlantic* v320 no3 p20 O 2017

Yam, Kai Chi (Sam)

When Joking with Your Employees Leads to Bad Behavior *Harvard Business Review Digital Articles* p2 Mr 17 2017

Yamada, Frank M.

People C. Kennel-Shank color *Christian Century* v134 no5 p17 Mr 1 2017

Yamada, Kohji

Regulation of sugar transporter activity for antibacterial defense in Arabidopsis bibl diag graph *Science* v354 no6318 p1427 D 16 2016

Yamaguchi, Kosei E.

The formation of peak rings in large impact craters bibl color graph *Science* v354 no6314 p878 N 18 2016

Yamaguchi, Takafumi N.

Exploring genetic suppression interactions on a global scale diag *Science* v354 no6312 p599 N 4 2016

Yamaguchi, Yuhgo

Better Healing from Better Hospital Design *Harvard Business Review Digital Articles* p2 O 5 2015

Yamaha all terrain vehicles—Evaluation

FIRST LOOK: 2017 YAMAHA WOLVERINE R-SPEC EPS SPECIAL EDITION [Cover story] M. EMERY color *Dirt Sports + Off-Road* v51 no1 p16 Ja 2017

Yamaha Corp.

AVR Advice A. L. GRIFFIN color *Sound & Vision* v82 no1 p26 Ja 2017

Play Me a Tune B. Ankosko color *Sound & Vision* v82 no1 p74 Ja 2017

Yamaha 50th Anniversary Custom Z Alto Saxophone B. Gibson color *Downbeat* v84 no5 p85 My 2017

Yamaha Aventage RX-A3060 A/V Receiver M. Fleischmann chart color graph *Sound & Vision* v82 no1 p50 Ja 2017

Yamaha MX88 R. Gehrenbeck color *Downbeat* v84 no9 p98 S 2017

Yamaha Recording Custom Series M. Kern color *Downbeat* v83 no11 p81 N 2016

Yamaha Motor Co. Ltd.

2016 YAMAHA WALL OF CHAMPIONS INDUCTEE CEREMONY color *Dirt Sports + Off-Road* v51 no5 p8 My 2017

2017 YAMAHA FZ-09 B. Catterson color *Cycle World* v56 no4 p18 My 2017

2017 YAMAHA SCR950 B. Conner color *Cycle World* v55 no10 p14 N 2016

2018 YAMAHA STAR VENTURE TOURER J. Gustafson bw color *Cycle World* v56 no9 p14 O 2017

BACK TO THE FUTURE M. Emery *Dirt Sports + Off-Road* v51 no7 p6 Jl 2017

DT-07 STREET TRACKER [Cover story] B. Adams color *Cycle World* v56 no2 p30 Mr 2017

THE FIFTH VOICE M. Hoyer bw chart color graph *Cycle World* v56 no1 p30 Ja/F 2017

Fish It Up A. Jones *Boating World* v37 no9 p30 N/D 2016

GIVING BACK S. RICHARDS color *Dirt Sports + Off-Road* v51 no9 p58 S 2017

LOW DOWN AND DIRTY D. SCANLON color *Dirt Sports + Off-Road* v51 no2 p34 F 2017

ONE-HOUR WONDER S. RICHARDS color *Dirt Sports + Off-*

Road v51 no7 p58 Jl 2017

Propless Surfing A. JONES *Boating World* v38 no6 p46 Je 2017

Return of the Beast: Light weight converges with extreme power and channels a bit of checkered (flag) history A. JONES *Boating World* v38 no5 p38 My 2017

RUNNING WILD M. Emery color *Dirt Sports + Off-Road* v51 no8 p6 Ag 2017

YAMAHA CONTINUES TO SUPPORT SEAL-NAVAL SPECIAL WARFARE FAMILY color *Dirt Sports + Off-Road* v51 no10 p8 O 2017

You Can Have a V-8 A. Jones *Boating World* v37 no9 p20 N/D 2016

Yamaha motorcycle—Evaluation

2015 YAMAHA YZF-R1 B. Catterson color *Cycle World* v56 no5 p56 Je 2017

2017 YAMAHA FZ-09 B. Catterson color *Cycle World* v56 no4 p18 My 2017

2017 YAMAHA SCR950 B. Conner color *Cycle World* v55 no10 p14 N 2016

2017 YAMAHA YZF-R6 D. Canet color *Cycle World* v56 no5 p14 Je 2017

2018 YAMAHA STAR VENTURE TOURER J. Gustafson bw color *Cycle World* v56 no9 p14 O 2017

ANSWERING THE R QUESTION D. Canet chart color diag *Cycle World* v56 no10 p44 N 2017

DT-07 STREET TRACKER [Cover story] B. Adams color *Cycle World* v56 no2 p30 Mr 2017

THE FIFTH VOICE M. Hoyer bw chart color graph *Cycle World* v56 no1 p30 Ja/F 2017

HITTING A MARK B. Adams chart color *Cycle World* v56 no6 p56 Jl 2017

SUPER MIDDLEWEIGHT MATCHUP D. Canet chart color *Cycle World* v56 no6 p50 Jl 2017

THREE OF A KIND B. Adams chart color *Cycle World* v56 no4 p42 My 2017

Yamamura, Midori

BankART 1929 color *Art in America* v105 no1 p93 Ja 2017

Yamashita, Keith

Try This! cartoon *O, The Oprah Magazine* p152 My 2017

Yamashita, N.

Extensive water ice within Ceres' aqueously altered regolith: Evidence from nuclear spectroscopy bibl graph *Science* v355 no6320 p1 Ja 6 2017

Yamkovenko, Bogdan

To Understand Whether Your Company Is Inclusive, Map How Your Employees Interact *Harvard Business Review Digital Articles* p2 Jl 19 2017

Yampa River (Colo.)

Conservation Lessons from a Still-Wild River: Be Known, Spread the Word, and Get Creative E. Van Rheene *Humanist* v77 no5 p6 S/O 2017

Yampa River Valley (Colo.)

Conservation Lessons from a Still-Wild River: Be Known, Spread the Word, and Get Creative E. Van Rheene *Humanist* v77 no5 p6 S/O 2017

Yampolskiy, Roman V.

AI Is the Future of Cybersecurity, for Better and for Worse *Harvard Business Review Digital Articles* p2 My 8 2017

Yams

Sweet Potatoes vs. Yams color *Prevention* v68 no12 p14 D 2016

Yamshon, Leah

10.5- and 12.9in iPad Pros on the way color *Macworld - Digital Edition* p17 Ap 2017

8 times Google savagely burned Apple during the Pixel announcement cartoon color diag *PCWorld* v35 no11 p127 N 2016

BELKIN LIGHTNING AUDIO + CHARGE ROCKSTAR ADAPTER color *Macworld - Digital Edition* v33 no11 p53 N 2016

Meet Apple's complete MacBook lineup color *Macworld - Digital Edition* p13 D 2016

Meet SwapBots, an augmented-reality toy that pairs with the iPad color *Macworld - Digital Edition* v34 no4 p51 My 2017

MOPHIE WIRELESS CHARGING BASE color *Macworld - Digital Edition* v34 no11 p36 N 2017

WATERFIELD DESIGNS iPAD PRO GEAR CASE color *Macworld - Digital Edition* p33 Je 13 2017

Yan, J.-Q.

A parity-breaking electronic nematic phase transition in the spin-orbit coupled metal Cd2Re2O7 diag *Science* v356 no6335 p295 Ap 21 2017

Yan, Jian

Impact of cytosine methylation on DNA binding specificities of human transcription factors diag *Science* v356 no6337 p502 My 5 2017

Yan, Jiaqiang

Neutron scattering in the proximate quantum spin liquid a-RuCl3 bw diag *Science* v356 no6342 p1055 Je 9 2017

Yan, Judith

Woman of the Wand D. GROEN cartoon *Walrus* p44 Ja\F 2017

Yan, L.

iPTF16geu: A multiply imaged, gravitationally lensed type Ia supernova color diag graph *Science* v356 no6335 p291 Ap 21 2017

Yan, Lianke, 1958-

The Price of Prosperity J. FAN *New York Times Book Review* p38 N 13 2016

Yan, Ming

Decarboxylative borylation color *Science* v356 no6342 p1045 Je 9 2017

Yan, Nieng

Structure of a eukaryotic voltage-gated sodium channel at near-atomic resolution diag graph *Science* v355 no6328 p924 Mr 3 2017

Yan, Song

Using Longitudinal Data on Career Outcomes to Promote Improvements and Diversity in Graduate Education *Change* v48 no6 p42 N/D 2016

YAN, WUDAN

Group Effort *Discover* v38 no8 p16 O 2017

Yan, Yanfa

An organic-inorganic perovskite ferroelectric with large piezoelectric response graph *Science* v357 no6348 p306 Jl 21 2017

Yan, Zhang

So you want to move to the U.S color diag graph *Bloomberg Businessweek* no4538 p48 S 18 2017

Yan, Zoe Z.

Second-scale nuclear spin coherence time of ultracold 23Na40K molecules diag *Science* v357 no6349 p372 Jl 28 2017

Yan Anthea Zhang

Research: When CEOs Don't Win Awards, They Make More Acquisitions *Harvard Business Review Digital Articles* p2 Mr 27 2017

Yan Gu

Oral precision medicine: Identification of microbes from saliva by mass spectrometry bibl *Science* v354 no6319 p60 D 23 2016

Yan Li

Crystal structure of unlinked NS2B-NS3 protease from Zika virus bibl color graph *Science* v354 no6319 p1597 D 23 2016

Precision medicine for nasopharyngeal carcinoma bibl diag *Science* v354 no6319 p24 D 23 2016

Quality management for precision medicine clinical applications: A consensus from the China Precision Medicine Clinical Research and Application Association bibl *Science* v354 no6319 p11 D 23 2016

Yan Qun Xiao

Quality management for precision medicine clinical applications: A consensus from the China Precision Medicine Clinical Research and Application Association bibl *Science* v354 no6319 p11 D 23 2016

Yan Wang

Diagnosis and treatment of inherited metabolic diseases in China bibl *Science* v354 no6319 p52 D 23 2016

Generation of influenza A viruses as live but replication-incompetent virus vaccines bibl graph *Science* v354 no6316 p1170 D 2 2016

Recent progress in autism spectrum disorder research in China bibl chart diag *Science* v354 no6319 p48 D 23 2016

Yanagi, Yukinori

BankART 1929 M. Yamamura color *Art in America* v105 no1 p93 Ja 2017

Yanagihara, Hanya

FRED EVERLASTING color *New York Times Magazine* p58 My

21 2017

The GOLD List 2017 color *Conde Nast Traveler* v52 no1 p62 Ja 2017

Hula color *Conde Nast Traveler* v52 no1 p102 Ja 2017

More Is More color *Conde Nast Traveler* v52 no5 p50 My 2017

RIPPLE EFFECT bw color *Conde Nast Traveler* v52 no5 p98 My 2017

Staying Power color *Conde Nast Traveler* v52 no2 p38 F 2017

Why can't Americans cope with trauma? color *Foreign Policy* no221 p30 N/D 2016

Yanagisawa, Makoto

Emission of volatile organic compounds from petunia flowers is facilitated by an ABC transporter diag *Science* v356 no6345 p1386 Je 30 2017

Yanagitani, Kota

UBE2O is a quality control factor for orphans of multiprotein complexes diag *Science* v357 no6350 p472 Ag 4 2017

Yanbin Lu

Response to Comments on "Reconciliation of the Devils Hole climate record with orbital forcing" bibl chart graph *Science* v354 no6310 p296-e O 21 2016

Yancopoulos, George D.

Distribution and clinical impact of functional variants in 50,726 whole-exome sequences from the DiscovEHR study chart graph *Science* v354 no6319 paaf6814-1 D 23 2016

Genetic identification of familial hypercholesterolemia within a single U.S. health care system chart graph *Science* v354 no6319 paaf7000-1 D 23 2016

Yancy, William

7 FOODS DOCTORS PRESCRIBE B. Risher cartoon color *Men's Health* v32 no1 p55 Ja/F 2017

Yancy Lo

Going global by adapting local: A review of recent human adaptation bibl diag graph *Science* v354 no6308 p54 O 7 2016

YANDELL, JOHN

Alexander Zverev's Two-Handed Backhand color *Tennis* v53 no2 p72 Mr/Ap 2017

Bernard Tomic's Downward Swing *Tennis* v53 no3 p76 My/Je 2017

Gael Monfils' Swinging Forehand Volley chart color *Tennis* v53 no5 p72 S/O 2017

Garbine Muguruza's First Serve *Tennis* v53 no4 p66 Jl/Ag 2017

GARBINE MUGURUZA'S FOREHAND SWING *Tennis* v53 no1 p57 Ja/F 2017

KEI NISHIKORI'S TWO-HANDED BACKHAND *Tennis* v53 no1 p21 Ja/F 2017

RAFAEL NADAL'S FOREHAND EXTENSION *Tennis* v53 no1 p29 Ja/F 2017

Sam Stosur's Kick Serve *Tennis* v53 no4 p68 Jl/Ag 2017

Venus Williams' Forehand color *Tennis* v53 no5 p74 S/O 2017

Yanding Li

Formaldehyde stabilization facilitates lignin monomer production during biomass depolymerization bibl diag graph *Science* v354 no6310 p329 O 21 2016

Yando, Larry

LARRY YANDO J. BERG color *Chicago* v65 no12 p56 D 2016

Yáñez Murillo, Manu

CRITICS' CHOICE bw chart color *Film Comment* v53 no2 p12 Mr/Ap 2017

Yang, Aerin

A chemical biology route to site-specific authentic protein modifications bibl diag graph *Science* v354 no6312 p623 N 4 2016

Yang, Alan

ALAN YANG A. D'ARMINIO *TV Guide* v65 no23 p10 My 29 2017

Yang, Bing

Classic Conversation F. P. DRISCOLL *Opera News* v81 no7 p18 Ja 2017

Yang, Chen

Plants transfer lipids to sustain colonization by mutualistic mycorrhizal and parasitic fungi diag graph *Science* v356 no6343 p1172 Je 16 2017

Yang, Dali

Dirty Deeds color *Foreign Affairs* v96 no4 p149 Jl/Ag 2017

Yang, David

Fabrication of fillable microparticles and other complex 3D microstructures color diag *Science* v357 no6356 p1138 S 15 2017

Yang, Dongyong

Epigenetic regulation of antagonistic receptors confers rice blast resistance with yield balance bibl diag *Science* v355 no6328 p962 Mr 3 2017

Yang, Gene Luen, 1973-

CAUGHT BETWEEN TWO WORLDS D. CHENG-TOZUN cartoon *Christianity Today* p42 Mr 2017

Yang, Gene Luen, 1973—Awards

Eight Things We Love About Gene Luen Yang: The ILA 2017 Featured Speaker is a literacy advocate on a mission to diversify children's literature C. Maloney color *Literacy Today (2411-7862)* v34 no6 p32 My/Je 2017

Yang, Gene Luen, 1973—Interviews

Gene Luen Yang Thinks Superheroes Are For Everyone D. Itzkoff *New York Times Magazine* p66 N 20 2016

Yang, H.

Zones, spots, and planetary-scale waves beating in brown dwarf atmospheres color graph *Science* v357 no6352 p683 Ag 18 2017

Yang, Hong

Reform China's fisheries subsidies color *Science* v356 no6345 p1343 Je 30 2017

Yang, Hongchun

Distinct phases of Polycomb silencing to hold epigenetic memory of cold in Arabidopsis diag *Science* v357 no6356 p1142 S 15 2017

Yang, Huanming

3D organization of synthetic and scrambled chromosomes diag *Science* v355 no6329 p1050 Mr 10 2017

Bug mapping and fitness testing of chemically synthesized chromosome X diag *Science* v355 no6329 p1048 Mr 10 2017

Deep functional analysis of synII, a 770-kilobase synthetic yeast chromosome diag *Science* v355 no6329 p1047 Mr 10 2017

Engineering the ribosomal DNA in a megabase synthetic chromosome diag *Science* v355 no6329 p1049 Mr 10 2017

"Perfect" designer chromosome V and behavior of a ring derivative diag *Science* v355 no6329 p1046 Mr 10 2017

Yang, J.

Tough adhesives for diverse wet surfaces diag *Science* v357 no6349 p378 Jl 28 2017

Yang, Jeanne

China's Bridge and Tunnel Addiction color *Bloomberg Businessweek* no4513 p47 Mr 6 2017

"HOLLYWOOD" color *Bloomberg Businessweek* no4511 p18 F 13 2017

Yang, Kao Kalia, 1980-

The Song Poet: A Memoir of My Father S. Kielsmeier-Cook *Christian Century* v134 no12 p37 Je 7 2017

Yang, Kun

3D organization of synthetic and scrambled chromosomes diag *Science* v355 no6329 p1050 Mr 10 2017

Bug mapping and fitness testing of chemically synthesized chromosome X diag *Science* v355 no6329 p1048 Mr 10 2017

Deep functional analysis of synII, a 770-kilobase synthetic yeast chromosome diag *Science* v355 no6329 p1047 Mr 10 2017

Design of a synthetic yeast genome bibl chart color graph *Science* v355 no6329 p1040 Mr 10 2017

Engineering the ribosomal DNA in a megabase synthetic chromosome diag *Science* v355 no6329 p1049 Mr 10 2017

"Perfect" designer chromosome V and behavior of a ring derivative diag *Science* v355 no6329 p1046 Mr 10 2017

Synthesis, debugging, and effects of synthetic chromosome consolidation: synVI and beyond color *Science* v355 no6329 p1045 Mr 10 2017

Yang, Kunlun

An organic-inorganic perovskite ferroelectric with large piezoelectric response graph *Science* v357 no6348 p306 Jl 21 2017

Yang, L.

Observation of a large-scale anisotropy in the arrival directions of cosmic rays above 8 × 1018 cV *Science* v357 no6357 p1266 S 22 2017

YANG, LARRY

A Greater Whole *Orion Magazine* v35 no4/5 p50 Jl-O 2016

Yang, Le

High-performance light-emitting diodes based on carbene-metal-amides chart graph *Science* v356 no6334 p159 Ap 14 2017

Yang, Luhan

Inactivation of porcine endogenous retrovirus in pigs using CRISPR-Cas9 diag *Science* v357 no6357 p1303 S 22 2017

Yang, Mengjin

Long-range hot-carrier transport in hybrid perovskites visualized by ultrafast microscopy diag graph *Science* v356 no6333 p59 Ap 7 2017

Yang, Peng

A placental growth factor is silenced in mouse embryos by the zinc finger protein ZFP568 color graph *Science* v356 no6339 p757 My 19 2017

Yang, Q.

Tough adhesives for diverse wet surfaces diag *Science* v357 no6349 p378 Jl 28 2017

Yang, Qing-Zheng

Experimentally realized mechanochemistry distinct from force-accelerated scission of loaded bonds diag graph *Science* v357 no6348 p299 Jl 21 2017

YANG, RACHEL

r.s.v.p color *Bon Appetit* no8 p14 Ag 2017

Yang, Ronggui

Passive cooling doesn't cost the planet J. Miller *Physics Today* v70 no4 p16 Ap 2017

Scalable-manufactured randomized glass-polymer hybrid metamaterial for daytime radiative cooling bibl diag *Science* v355 no6329 p1062 Mr 10 2017

Yang, S.-J.

Femtosecond electron-phonon lock-in by photoemission and x-ray free-electron laser chart diag *Science* v357 no6346 p71 Jl 7 2017

Yang, Shi-Lan

"Perfect" designer chromosome V and behavior of a ring derivative diag *Science* v355 no6329 p1046 Mr 10 2017

Yang, Shu

Rescue of exhausted CD8 T cells by PD-1–targeted therapies is CD28-dependent bw diag graph *Science* v355 no6332 p1423 Mr 31 2017

Yang, Sungwoo

Water harvesting from air with metal-organic frameworks powered by natural sunlight diag *Science* v356 no6336 p430 Ap 28 2017

Yang, Tao

Release of mineral-bound water prior to subduction tied to shallow seismogenic slip off Sumatra graph *Science* v356 no6340 p841 My 26 2017

Yang, Wesley

AMERICAN NIGHTMARE *Harper's Magazine* v334 no2001 p27 F 2017

Only Human *New York Times Magazine* p9 F 19 2017

Yang, Woon Seok

Colloidally prepared La-doped BaSnO3 electrodes for efficient, photostable perovskite solar cells graph *Science* v356 no6334 p167 Ap 14 2017

Iodide management in formamidinium-lead-halide–based perovskite layers for efficient solar cells bw diag *Science* v356 no6345 p1376 Je 30 2017

Yang, Xiaodong

Systemic pan-AMPK activator MK-8722 improves glucose homeostasis but induces cardiac hypertrophy graph *Science* v357 no6350 p507 Ag 4 2017

Yang, Xiao-Na

"Perfect" designer chromosome V and behavior of a ring derivative diag *Science* v355 no6329 p1046 Mr 10 2017

Yang, Xiaoyu

Redox-based reagents for chemoselective methionine bioconjugation bibl diag graph *Science* v355 no6325 p597 F 10 2017

Yang, Xinxing

GTPase activity-coupled treadmilling of the bacterial tubulin FtsZ organizes septal cell wall synthesis bibl graph *Science* v355 no6326 p744 F 17 2017

Yang, Yang

Directing reconfigurable DNA nanoarrays color *Science* v357 no6349 p352 Jl 28 2017

THE UNFOLDING AND CONTROL OF NETWORK CASCADES *Physics Today* v70 no1 p32 Ja 2017

Yang, Yangyuchen

Liquefied gas electrolytes for electrochemical energy storage devices graph *Science* v356 no6345 p1351 Je 30 2017

Yang, Yanling

Synthesis, debugging, and effects of synthetic chromosome consolidation: synVI and beyond color *Science* v355 no6329 p1045 Mr 10 2017

Yang, Yingjun

Scaling carbon nanotube complementary transistors to 5-nm gate lengths chart graph *Science* v355 no6322 p271 Ja 20 2017

Yang, Yuanjie

Vortex generation reaches a new plateau color *Science* v357 no6352 p645 Ag 18 2017

Yang, Yuanzhu

Epigenetic regulation of antagonistic receptors confers rice blast resistance with yield balance bibl diag *Science* v355 no6328 p962 Mr 3 2017

Yang, Zhenyu

Efficient and stable solution-processed planar perovskite solar cells via contact passivation bibl graph *Science* v355 no6326 p722 F 17 2017

Yang, Zhi-yong

Trispecific broadly neutralizing HIV antibodies mediate potent SHIV protection in macaques color graph *Science* v357 no6359 p85 O 6 2017

Yang, Zhongfei

History of winning remodels thalamo-PFC circuit to reinforce social dominance color *Science* v357 no6347 p162 Jl 14 2017

Yang Gan

Footnote on femtochemistry *Physics Today* v70 no4 p14 Ap 2017

Yang Lin

Quality management for precision medicine clinical applications: A consensus from the China Precision Medicine Clinical Research and Application Association bibl *Science* v354 no6319 p11 D 23 2016

Yang Liu

CAR T-cell–based therapeutic modality in solid tumors: How to achieve precision bibl color *Science* v354 no6319 p27 D 23 2016

Yang Shao

Urgent need for implementation of precision medicine in gastric cancer in China bibl chart *Science* v354 no6319 p39 D 23 2016

Yang Sui

Team Leaders Should Play Favorites (but Only in Moderation) *Harvard Business Review Digital Articles* p2 Ja 13 2016

Yang-Yi Liu

Synthetic nacre by predesigned matrix-directed mineralization bibl bw diag graph *Science* v354 no6308 p107 O 7 2016

Yankee Barn Homes (Company)

New York State of Mind color *Timber Home Living* v27 no5 p32 O 2017

Yankee Boy Basin (San Juan Mountains, Colo.)

pass fail: Summit at Sunset A. GULSBY il *Backpacker* p32 S 2017

Yankee Stadium (New York, N.Y. : 1923-2009)

The Old Brawl Game L. SMITH color *Weekly Standard* v22 no40 p5 Je 26 2017

Yankee Stadium (New York, N.Y. : 2009-)

The Love Doctor Is In P. Mejia img *New York* v50 no18 p71 S 4 2017

Yanming Wang

Highly stretchable polymer semiconductor films through the nanoconfinement effect bibl graph *Science* v355 no6320 p1 Ja 6 2017

YANO, JANET

GIFTS that UPLIFT! cartoon *O, The Oprah Magazine* p148 D 2016

YANOELL, JOHN

TAYLOR FRITZ'S KICK SERVE *Tennis* v53 no3 p62 My/Je 2017

Yanosek, Kassia

The Next Energy Revolution color *Foreign Affairs* v96 no4 p124 Jl/Ag 2017

Yanosky, Alberto

Forest conservation: Remember Gran Chaco bibl color *Science* v355 no6324 p465 F 3 2017

YANOW, SCOTT

A Story Benind Every Song color *Downbeat* v84 no2 p82 F 2017

Yanowitz, Judith L.

Control of meiotic pairing and recombination by chromosomally tethered 26S proteasome bibl graph *Science* v355 no6323 p408 Ja 27 2017

Yanqing Wang

Rb1 and Trp53 cooperate to suppress prostate cancer lineage plasticity, metastasis, and antiandrogen resistance bibl graph *Science* v355 no6320 p1 Ja 6 2017

Yanran Xu

China's Strategic Partnerships in Latin America: Case Studies of China's Oil Diplomacy in Argentina, Brazil, Mexico, and Venezuela, 1991–2015 R. Feinberg *Foreign Affairs* v96 no3 p165 My/Je 2017

Yao (Southeast Asian people)

HUNGRY PLANET *Sierra* v102 no2 p4 Mr/Ap 2017

Yao, Humphrey H.-C.

Elimination of the male reproductive tract in the female embryo is promoted by COUP-TFII in mice color graph *Science* v357 no6352 p717 Ag 18 2017

Yao, Siyu

Atomic-layered Au clusters on α-MoC as catalysts for the low-temperature water-gas shift reaction chart diag graph *Science* v357 no6349 p389 Jl 28 2017

Yao, Yu

UBE2O remodels the proteome during terminal erythroid differentiation diag *Science* v357 no6350 p471 Ag 4 2017

Yao, Yun-Chiao

Enhanced water permeability and tunable ion selectivity in sub-nanometer carbon nanotube porins chart color *Science* v357 no6353 p792 Ag 25 2017

Yao Wang

CAR T-cell–based therapeutic modality in solid tumors: How to achieve precision bibl color *Science* v354 no6319 p27 D 23 2016

Yao Yang

Diagnosis and treatment of inherited metabolic diseases in China bibl *Science* v354 no6319 p52 D 23 2016

Yao Zhang

Single-molecule optomechanics in "picocavities" bibl graph *Science* v354 no6313 p726 N 11 2016

Yap, Cecilia

Philippine Casinos Are Cleaning Up color graph *Bloomberg Businessweek* no4521 p19 My 8 2017

Yap, Karl Lester

THE HIJACKING OF THE BRILLANTE VIRTUOSO color map *Bloomberg Businessweek* no4532 p48 Jl 31 2017

Philippine Leader Scares Off Investors color *Bloomberg Businessweek* no4493 p23 O 3 2016

Yap, Sandra

Plant diversity increases with the strength of negative density dependence at the global scale diag *Science* v356 no6345 p1389 Je 30 2017

YAQUB, SALIM

Ike's Gamble: America's Rise to Dominance in the Middle East *Foreign Affairs* v96 no2 p185 Mr/Ap 2017

YAR, CENGIZ

The Iraqis Who Fled Mosul color *Foreign Policy* no226 p5 S/O 2017

Yarbrough, Cedric, 1973-

My Obsessions? *TV Guide* v65 no6 p8 Ja 30 2017

Yarden, Tal

"Look What We Did!" *Stage Directions* v30 no10 p19 O 2017

Yardley, Jim

The Cultural Revolution *New York Times Upfront* v149 no5 p18 N 21 2016

States of Confusion *New York Times Magazine* p34 N 6 2016

YARM, MARK

BLONDE AMBITION: FILMING A KILLER ACTION SEQUENCE bw color *Wired* v25 no8 p16 Ag 2017

CHOOSE YOUR OWN SPACE ADVENTURE SAVING THE GALAXY ... AGAIN cartoon *Wired* v25 no5 p37 My 2017

HIGH RATINGS: DESUS & MERO JUDGE FALL TV cartoon color *Wired* v25 no9 p30 S 2017

MAGNIFICENT OBSESSION: A CULT AUTEUR'S NETFLIX DEBUT color *Wired* v25 no7 p16 Jl 2017

NOW (RE)PLAYING cartoon graph *Wired* v25 no3 p20 Mr 2017

v191 no10 p30 My 27 2017

Yekîneyên Parastina Gel (Kurdish military group)
THE ANARCHISTS VS. ISIS S. HARP color *Rolling Stone* no1281/1282 p42 F 23 2017

Yelchin, Anton, 1989-2016
ANTON YELCHIN J. J. Abrams and A. Breznican color *Entertainment Weekly* no1446/1447 p89 D 2016/Ja 2017
INTRODUCING TROLLHUNTERS C. Agard color *Entertainment Weekly* no1434 p16 O 7 2016

Yelle, R.
Mars' atmospheric history derived from upper-atmosphere measurements of 38 Ar/36Ar diag *Science* v355 no6332 p1408 Mr 31 2017

Yellen, Janet L. (Janet Louise), 1946-
FINANCIAL STABILITY A DECADE AFTER THE ONSET OF THE CRISIS *Vital Speeches of the Day* v83 no10 p288 O 2017
SCALING BACK ECONOMIC ACCOMMODATION *Vital Speeches of the Day* v83 no5 p153 My 2017
U.S. ECONOMY NEARS GOALS OF MAXIMUM EMPLOYMENT AND PRICE STABILITY *Vital Speeches of the Day* v82 no10 p307 O 2016

Yellen, Sheldon
SHELDON YELLEN'S BIG SECRET D. ALEXANDER bw color map *Forbes* v199 no2 p80 F 28 2017

Yellin, Adele
The Grand Central Market Cookbook: Cuisine and Culture from Downtown Los Angeles *Publishers Weekly* v264 no27 p69 Jl 3 2017

Yellin, Samuel, 1885-1940
Talking antiques At the WINTER ANTIQUES SHOW color *Magazine Antiques* v184 no1 p60 Ja/F 2017

Yellow
Goldenrod color *House Beautiful* v159 no9 p19 N 2017

Yellow-bellied marmot
Skiing for science D. T. Blumstein cartoon *Science* v356 no6334 p214 Ap 14 2017

Yellow birch
Rock-Solid Foundation B. HEINRICH *Natural History* v125 no2 p14 F 2017

Yellow fever
ON THE TRAIL OF YELLOW FEVER [Cover story] S. Kean color diag map *Science* v357 no6352 p637 Ag 18 2017

Yellow journalism
FAKE NEWS FOOLING MILLIONS! C. STOFFERS *New York Times Upfront* v149 no7 p6 Ja 9 2017

Yellow River (China)
A River at Risk I. TEH color map *National Geographic* v232 no1 p142 Jl 2017

Yellowfin tuna
Monster at Midnight K. Danielewicz color *Sail* v48 no7 p14 Jl 2017

YELLOWLEES, ANN
Estimation of Relative Potency from Bioassay Data that Include Values below the Limit of Quantitation *BioScience* v66 no11 p983 N 1 2016

Yellowstone Lake (Wyo.)
Features *Oceanus* v52 no2 p31 Spr 2017

Yellowstone National Park
Calendar MARCH chart color *Popular Mechanics* p10 Mr 2017
CROWNING GLORY E. Conant bw *National Geographic* v230 no6 p132 D 2016
The Hot Spot Beneath Yellowstone Park C. Linder *Oceanus* v52 no2 p54 Spr 2017
Join us for a new solar eclipse trip! D. J. EICHER color *Astronomy* v45 no2 p6 F 2017
WORKS IN PROGRESS *American Scholar* v86 no1 p12 Wint 2017
Yellowstone 2.0 J. ABRAHAMSON *Sierra* v101 no4 p36 Jl/Ag 2016

Yellowtail, Bethany
Bethany Yellowtail L. IMMEDIATO *Los Angeles Magazine* v62 no9 p95 S 2017

Yelp (Web resource)
City Governments Are Using Yelp to Tell You Where Not to Eat M. Luca and L. Lowe *Harvard Business Review Digital Articles* p2 F 12 2015

Yelp Inc.
Lessons from Yelp's Empirical Approach to Diversity R. Williams, G. Subramani et al *Harvard Business Review Digital Articles* p2 S 20 2017

Yemen (Republic)
War Crimes in Yemen M. T. KLARE *Nation* v33 no21 p4 N 21 2016

Yemen (Republic)—History—Civil War, 2015-
Battling for Yemen's survival C. Martin color *Science News* v192 no2 p4 Ag 19 2017
By the $ & £ We Live A. A. BAFAQUIH *Islamic Horizons* v46 no2 p47 Mr/Ap 2017
Yemen's Humanitarian Nightmare A. Orkaby color *Foreign Affairs* v96 no6 p93 N/D 2017

Yemen (Republic)—History—Civil War, 2015—Saudi participation
The War in Yemen Tests Saudi Arabia's Clout G. Carey and N. Syeed color *Bloomberg Businessweek* no4508 p12 Ja 23 2017
Yemen's Tragic Civil War Reaches a New Level of Violence J. Malsin color *Time* v188 no16/17 p7 O 24 2016

Yemen (Republic)—Politics & government
By the $ & £ We Live A. A. BAFAQUIH *Islamic Horizons* v46 no2 p47 Mr/Ap 2017

Yemeng Lu-Myers
When Health Care Providers Look at Problems from Multiple Perspectives, Patients Benefit *Harvard Business Review Digital Articles* p2 Je 23 2017

Yemeni cooking
Buttered Up: Sweet and supple, kubaneh is shot through with fat to create a melting, airy bread T. Rao *New York Times Magazine* p30 Je 25 2017

Yen, H. W.
High dislocation density–induced large ductility in deformed and partitioned steels bw color diag *Science* v357 no6355 p1029 S 8 2017

Yen Joe Tan
Seismic constraints on caldera dynamics from the 2015 Axial Seamount eruption bibl color graph *Science* v354 no6318 p1395 D 16 2016

YENBAMROONG, KRIS
THAT ONE TIME I NEARLY DESTROYED THE FAMILY BUSINESS bw color *Bon Appetit* v62 no2 p74 Mr 2017

Yende, Pretty
Born to Sing J. ALLISON *Opera News* v81 no6 p18 D 2016

Yende, Pretty—Interviews
Pretty Awesome M. GOLDBERG color *O, The Oprah Magazine* p26 My 2017

Yengo, Loic
Detection of human adaptation during the past 2000 years bibl graph *Science* v354 no6313 p760 N 11 2016

Yenor, Scott
CIVILITY AND ITS LIMITS *Claremont Review of Books* v17 no3 p59 Summ 2017
MAKING CHRISTIANITY SAFE FOR DEMOCRACY *Claremont Review of Books* v17 no1 p44 Wint 2016/2017

Yeo, Gene W.
Making the cut in the dark genome bibl diag *Science* v354 no6313 p705 N 11 2016

Yeoh, Michelle, 1963-
STAR TREK: DISCOVERY J. Hibberd color *Entertainment Weekly* no1474/1475 p71 Jl 21-28 2017

Yeom, Eun Joo
Colloidally prepared La-doped $BaSnO_3$ electrodes for efficient, photostable perovskite solar cells graph *Science* v356 no6334 p167 Ap 14 2017

Yeoman, Barry
DEMOCRACY ON THE LINE color map *Nation* v305 no9 p16 O 16 2017
FIT TO PRINT *Atlanta* v56 no7 p90 N 2016
Going Native color *National Wildlife (World Edition)* v55 no3 p28 Ap/My 2017
THE RADICATOR *Atlanta* v57 no4 p66 Ag 2017

Yeomans, Mike
What Every Manager Should Know About Machine Learning *Harvard Business Review Digital Articles* p2 Jl 7 2015

Yeong-seo, Kwon

A gesture for continual peace J. Bleem color *U.S. Catholic* v82 no2 p50 F 2017

Yersinia pestis
Tracking Ancient Plagues M. A. SPYROU and K. I. BOS bw color *Natural History* v125 no9 p18 S 2017

YESELSON, RICH
AT LABOR'S CROSSROADS bw color *Nation* v304 no10 p27 Mr 27 2017

Yeston, Jake
MANIPULATING ULTRACOLD MATTER [Cover story] color *Science* v357 no6355 p984 S 8 2017

YETI Coolers LLC
Day Tripper L. BECKETT color *Power & Motoryacht* v33 no3 p50 Mr 2017
The Pot of Cold L. STEFFY *Texas Monthly* v44 no12 p78 D 2016

Yeti Cycles (Company)
dreams of youth b. gavelda color *Bike Magazine* v23 no9 p44 D 2016
FORWARD MOMENTUM L. Kemp, K. Butcher et al color *Bike Magazine* v24 no1 p116 Ja/F 2017
"I NEED A YETI." T. Rojek and B. Strickland color *Bicycling* v58 no3 p64 Ap 2017
YETI SB5+ TURQ X01 EAGLE G. Liu color *Bicycling* v58 no4 p84 My 2017

Yeun, Steven, 1984-
ANDREW LINCOLN D. Ross color *Entertainment Weekly* no1438 p26 N 4 2016
Business Class color *GQ: Gentlemen's Quarterly* v86 no11 p148 N 2016
LAUREN COHAN D. Ross color *Entertainment Weekly* no1438 p25 N 4 2016
NEW WORLD ORDER M. LOGAN *TV Guide* v64 no48 p20 N 21 2016
NORMAN REEDUS D. Ross color *Entertainment Weekly* no1438 p26 N 4 2016

Yeun, Steven, 1984—Interviews
Gone Glenn [Cover story] D. Ross color *Entertainment Weekly* no1438 p22 N 4 2016

Yevtushenko, Yevgeny, 1933-2017
The Week bw color il *National Review* v69 no8 p4 My 2017

Yezerets, Aleksey
Dynamic multinuclear sites formed by mobilized copper ions in NOx selective catalytic reduction bw color diag graph *Science* v357 no6354 p898 S 1 2017

Yezidi women
Brave Hearts J. DI GIOVANNI color *Vogue* v206 no11 p94 N 2016

Yezidis—Crimes against
THE PAIN OF EXILE E. Underwood color diag *Science* v356 no6339 p682 My 19 2017

Yi, Anicka—Exhibitions
A WHIFF OF CULTURE A. TITTIGER color *Wired* v25 no4 p28 Ap 2017

Yi, Joseph
Evangelical Christian Discourse in South Korea on the LGBT: the Politics of Cross-Border Learning *Society* v54 no1 p29 F 2017

Yi, M.
Femtosecond electron-phonon lock-in by photoemission and x-ray free-electron laser chart diag *Science* v357 no6346 p71 Jl 7 2017

Yi, Shu
PICTURING TIME S. A. STEINBERG color *Iceland Review* v54 no5 p62 S-O 2016

Yi Cui
Direct and continuous strain control of catalysts with tunable battery electrode materials bibl graph *Science* v354 no6315 p1031 N 25 2016

Yi jing
c. 400 BC: China *Lapham's Quarterly* v10 no2 p107 Spr 2017
Locking Brows with BHARTRIHARI A. Schelling cartoon *Tricycle: The Buddhist Review* v26 no3 p72 Spr 2017

Yi Zhang
CAR T-cell–based therapeutic modality in solid tumors: How to achieve precision bibl color *Science* v354 no6319 p27 D 23 2016

Yi-Zhou Jiang

Breast cancer research in the era of precision medicine bibl color *Science* v354 no6319 p30 D 23 2016

Yi Zhu
When It's Smart to Copy Your Competitor's Brand Promise *Harvard Business Review Digital Articles* p2 Mr 23 2017

Yiadom-Boakye, Lynette
VISIBLE DIFFERENCE D. KAZANJIAN color *Vogue* v207 no4 p208 Ap 2017

Yiadom-Boakye, Lynette—Exhibitions
A BIRD OF FEW WORDS Z. SMITH cartoon color *New Yorker* v93 no17 p48 Je 19 2017

Yiannopoulos, Milo, 1984-
Defending Milo T. J. FLANNERY *Publishers Weekly* v264 no8 p88 F 20 2017
Readers Respond B. T. Greive and S. Kimmel bw *Publishers Weekly* v264 no2 p3 Ja 9 2017
Readers Respond P. Glassman color *Publishers Weekly* v264 no3 p2 Ja 16 2017

Yiannopoulos, Milo, 1984—Political & social views
Drawing the Line J. PESKIN *Publishers Weekly* v264 no6 p72 F 6 2017

Yien, Yvette Y.
Restored iron transport by a small molecule promotes absorption and hemoglobinization in animals color graph *Science* v356 no6338 p608 My 12 2017

Yifei Zhang
Oral precision medicine: Identification of microbes from saliva by mass spectrometry bibl *Science* v354 no6319 p60 D 23 2016

Yifeng Xu
Quality management for precision medicine clinical applications: A consensus from the China Precision Medicine Clinical Research and Application Association bibl *Science* v354 no6319 p11 D 23 2016

Yigong Shi
Structure of a yeast step II catalytically activated spliceosome bibl diag *Science* v355 no6321 p1 Ja 13 2017

YILDIZ-ODEH, ASLIHAN
Teaching Social Justice at Islamic Schools [Cover story] *Islamic Horizons* v46 no2 p30 Mr/Ap 2017

Yilmaz, Fulden Funda
A SPORT AND A PASSPORT *Harper's Magazine* p15 O 2017

Yilmaz, Omer
The DNA-sensing AIM2 inflammasome controls radiation-induced cell death and tissue injury bibl color graph *Science* v354 no6313 p765 N 11 2016

Yilong Li
The linker histone H1.0 generates epigenetic and functional intra-tumor heterogeneity bibl graph *Science* v353 no6307 paaf1644-1 S 30 2016

Yiming Wu
Generation of influenza A viruses as live but replication-incompetent virus vaccines bibl graph *Science* v354 no6316 p1170 D 2 2016

Yin, Denise
Segregation-induced ordered superstructures at general grain boundaries in a nickel-bismuth alloy color *Science* v357 no6359 p97 O 6 2017

Yin, Gen
Chiral Majorana fermion modes in a quantum anomalous Hall insulator–superconductor structure diag *Science* v357 no6348 p294 Jl 21 2017

Yin, Juan
Satellite-based entanglement distribution over 1200 kilometers diag graph *Science* v356 no6343 p1140 Je 16 2017

Yin, Xiaobo
Scalable-manufactured randomized glass-polymer hybrid metamaterial for daytime radiative cooling bibl diag *Science* v355 no6329 p1062 Mr 10 2017

Yin, Ya-Yun
Satellite-based entanglement distribution over 1200 kilometers diag graph *Science* v356 no6343 p1140 Je 16 2017

Yin, Yimeng
Impact of cytosine methylation on DNA binding specificities of human transcription factors diag *Science* v356 no6337 p502 My 5 2017

Yin Li

THE EXCHANGE bw cartoon *Men's Health* v32 no4 p14 My 2017

Find lasting peace [Cover story] R. Miller *Yoga Journal* no290 p28 Mr 2017

FIT FOR FREE L. SCHOLZ *Atlanta* v57 no1 p40 My 2017

Gather color *Rodale's Organic Life* v3 no1 p15 Ja 2017

get back on the mat H. Dowdle color *Yoga Journal* p8 2017 Special Issue

Get to know... your wrists R. Long color *Yoga Journal* p44 2017 SpecialIssue

Get Your Posture Point A. STANLEY color *Seventeen* v76 no5 p65 S 2017

A home practice for powerful legs N. Costello color *Yoga Journal* p98 2017 SpecialIssue

A home practice to get strong and empowered [Cover story] S. Nardini color *Yoga Journal* no290 p59 Mr 2017

A home practice to nix low-back pain A. Ferretti color *Yoga Journal* p63 2017 SpecialIssue

How Alternative Medicine Saved My Life S. E. Jamison color *Ebony* v72 no9 p62 Jl/Ag 2017

"I LOST 285 POUNDS" B. Gregory color *Men's Health* v31 no10 p24 D 2016

It Takes Two A. Eaves cartoon *Rodale's Organic Life* v3 no1 p30 Ja 2017

JUST 3 MOVES D. Burn color *Good Housekeeping* v265 no5 p74 N 2017

JUST ADD intensity [Cover story] T. Eichenseher color *Yoga Journal* no295 p74 O 2017

LAST LOOK A. SCHWEITZER color *Yoga Journal* p112 2017 SpecialIssue

Let go and allow C. Gorrell *Yoga Journal* no288 p12 D 2016

Listen within C. Gorrell color *Yoga Journal* no293 p10 Ag 2017

Martha's Month chart color *Martha Stewart Living* no275 p1 Je 2017

A Mass Shooting S. Frappier cartoon *Men's Health* v32 no4 p82 My 2017

May-June color *Yoga Journal* no292 p6 Je 2017

Meet the force WITHIN YOU [Cover story] L. Eckstrom color *Yoga Journal* no294 p74 S 2017

The mindful diet M. RABBITT color *Yoga Journal* p110 2016 Special Issue

Mindfulness, demystified bw *Yoga Journal* p8 2016 Special Issue

NAMASTAY AWHILE M. Gainsburg bw color diag *Women's Health* v14 no4 p78 My 2017

Namaste Your Period Pain Away A. STANLEY color *Seventeen* v75 no11 p57 N 2016

Neither Fight nor Flight C. DEDERER color *Rodale's Organic Life* v3 no1 p40 Ja 2017

NON-STOP Hilaria F. Penn color *InStyle* v24 no1 p58 Ja 2017

Performance Yoga S. MAIN color *Muscle & Performance* v9 no8 p24 Ag 2017

Poses of the month A. Palkhivala color *Yoga Journal* no288 p47 D 2016

Poses of the month [Cover story] T. Little color *Yoga Journal* no291 p49 My 2017

POSING OUTSIDE THE BOX cartoon chart color *AARP: The Magazine* v60 no3A p40 Ap/My 2017

practice imperfect C. Gorrell *Yoga Journal* p6 2017 Special Issue

practice safely B. Bell, A. Forrest et al color *Yoga Journal* p16 2017 SpecialIssue

REAL SLOW [Cover story] T. COCKBURN bw color *Runner's World* v52 no6 p24 Jl 2017

rise and RAVE M. RABBITT color *Yoga Journal* no289 p35 F 2017

rise and strrretch color *Parents* v92 no3 p15 Mr 2017

RULE THE WATER *Saturday Evening Post* v289 no4 p23 Jl/Ag 2017

A smart start to vinyasa N. Rizopoulos color *Yoga Journal* no296 p89 N 2017

sneaky practice plan cartoon color *Yoga Journal* p120 2017 Special Issue

Stand Strong R. Rosen color *Yoga Journal* p46 2017 Special Issue

Surprising Benefits of Aerial Yoga V. Tweed color *Amazing Wellness* v8 no2 p19 Spr 2016

take OM HOME A. Tust color *Yoga Journal* no287 p88 N 2016

Take your yoga to go M. Clarke color *Yoga Journal* no293 p24

Ag 2017

THIS IS WHAT SEVA LOOKS LIKE [Cover story] M. Rabbitt color *Yoga Journal* no295 p40 O 2017

A TO Z Guide to cues [Cover story] R. PEACOCK color *Yoga Journal* no293 p71 Ag 2017

Turn Your Practice UPSIDE DOWN [Cover story] C. ALYSSA color *Yoga Journal* no293 p82 Ag 2017

The United States of Yoga cartoon color *AARP: The Magazine* v60 no3A p36 Ap/My 2017

Voyages J. Lowe *New York Times Magazine* p24 N 6 2016

WHAT IT TAKES TO TEACH T. EICHENSEHER color *Yoga Journal* no287 p48 N 2016

What's So Wrong with Mindfulness? N. GAJAWEERA color *Tricycle: The Buddhist Review* v26 no2 p27 Wint 2016

WHAT'S YOUR FAVORITE YOGA READ? [Cover story] color *Yoga Journal* no292 p20 Je 2017

Yoga at the CABIN C. HEITGER-EWING color *Cabin Living* p56 Je 2017

Yoga G. TARLACH color *Discover* v38 no6 p98 Jl/Ag 2017

the Yoga Lesson R. K. JOHNSON cartoon *New Yorker* v93 no7 p58 Ap 3 2017

Yoga Moves We All Get Wrong K. McGee color *Health* v31 no7 p69 S 2017

The Yoga of Integrity [Cover story] color *Yoga Journal* no293 p97 Ag 2017

YOGA TV color *Yoga Journal* no292 p23 Je 2017

You find your job uninspiring S. Kempton color *Yoga Journal* p47 2016 Special Issue

You have too much stuff V. Reiss color *Yoga Journal* p49 2016 Special Issue

Yoga for children

Changing the World One Pose at a Time T. A. POWER *USA Today Magazine* v145 no2862 p40 Mr 2017

Yoga instruction

JIFFY MOVES S. ROUNTREE color *Runner's World* v52 no8 p22 S 2017

the Yoga Lesson R. K. JOHNSON cartoon *New Yorker* v93 no7 p58 Ap 3 2017

Yoga postures

Altogether Now H. Dowdle cartoon *Yoga Journal* p108 2017 Special Issue

ANNA GUEST-JELLEY color *Yoga Journal* no292 p16 Je 2017

the art of SEQUENCING J. Crandell color *Yoga Journal* p20 2017 Special Issue

BACK IN ACTION R. Yee color *Yoga Journal* p88 2017 Special Issue

BEND AWAY THE BLUES diag *Rodale's Organic Life* v2 no7 p28 D 2016/Ja 2017

Chart Your Depths M. Apt color *Yoga Journal* p60 2017 Special Issue

CHELSEA JACKSON ROBERTS color *Yoga Journal* no292 p12 Je 2017

THE COMPASSIONATE Backbend K. TREMBLAY color *Yoga Journal* p50 2017 Special Issue

Compassion in action M. KORN bw *Yoga Journal* p18 2016 Special Issue

DAN NEVINS color *Yoga Journal* no292 p14 Je 2017

Do the Twist C. Cummins color *Yoga Journal* p74 2017 Special Issue

DO THE TWIST S. Snyder color *Yoga Journal* p68 2017 Special Issue

Enjoy deep sleep color *Yoga Journal* p88 2016 Special Issue

Fab Abs R. Rosen color *Yoga Journal* p56 2017 Special Issue

Fight Gravity with Yoga A. Shaffer color *Health* v31 no1 p98 Ja 2017

FINAL THOUGHT color *Yoga Journal* p120 2016 Special Issue

Find fulfillment color *Yoga Journal* p82 2016 Special Issue

Find your faith in you color *Yoga Journal* p58 2016 Special Issue

Flow Motion J. Crandell color *Yoga Journal* p20 2017 Special Issue

Flying scares you S. Kaur color *Yoga Journal* p43 2016 Special Issue

Get Hip N. Rizopoulos color *Yoga Journal* p70 2017 Special Issue

happy days D. ANDERSON color *Yoga Journal* p44 2017 Special Issue

heart wide open J. RODRIGUE color *Yoga Journal* p40 2017

Special Issue

heavenly rest J. Hanc cartoon *Yoga Journal* p82 2017 Special Issue

A home practice to awaken your inner warrior [Cover story] D. Nevins color *Yoga Journal* no293 p65 Ag 2017

A home practice to awaken your sexual vitality [Cover story] L. Catone color *Yoga Journal* no289 p51 F 2017

A home practice to find peace & possibility E. Finn color *Yoga Journal* no292 p66 Je 2017

A home practice to get grounded and stable D. Burkman color *Yoga Journal* p93 2017 SpecialIssue

A home practice to get strong and empowered [Cover story] S. Nardini color *Yoga Journal* no290 p59 Mr 2017

in focus bw color *Yoga Journal* no290 p93 Mr 2017

in focus color *Yoga Journal* no289 p105 F 2017

INQUIRE WITHIN E. Marglin color diag *Yoga Journal* no289 p28 F 2017

IN THIS SECTION color *Yoga Journal* p70 2017 Special Issue

JUST 3 MOVES D. Burn color *Good Housekeeping* v265 no5 p74 N 2017

LIVE JOY N. Doane and E. Modestini color *Yoga Journal* p66 2017 Special Issue

Open up to love color *Yoga Journal* p70 2016 Special Issue

Peace Process M. Apt color *Yoga Journal* p78 2017 Special Issue

plumb Perfect R. Cole color *Yoga Journal* p34 2017 Special Issue

Poses of the month [Cover story] M. McCrary color *Yoga Journal* no293 p53 Ag 2017

Power Poses N. HORVATH color *Prevention* v69 no4 p96 Ap 2017

practice imperfect C. Gorrell *Yoga Journal* p6 2017 Special Issue

Quiet your mind color *Yoga Journal* p100 2016 Special Issue

REACH FOR MORE A. Ippoliti color *Yoga Journal* p38 2017 Special Issue

The Right Angle M. Apt color *Yoga Journal* p40 2017 Special Issue

SAGE MOVES FOR MEDITATION N. Isaacs color *Yoga Journal* p54 2017 Special Issue

Save your shoulders J. Crandell color *Yoga Journal* p40 2017 SpecialIssue

Seat of Power A. Carpenter color *Yoga Journal* p24 2017 Special Issue

September All-Star color *Women's Health* v14 no7 p18 S 2017

Serenity Now! C. Lee color *Yoga Journal* p90 2017 Special Issue

SHINE ON ME K. McGONIGAL color *Yoga Journal* p8 2017 Special Issue

A smart start to vinyasa N. Rizopoulos color *Yoga Journal* no296 p89 N 2017

Speed the Salutations G. Reynolds *New York Times Magazine* p22 F 12 2017

Stand Strong R. Rosen color *Yoga Journal* p46 2017 Special Issue

strike a ROYAL pose A. PALKHIVALA color *Yoga Journal* p64 2017 Special Issue

Tap your willpower color *Yoga Journal* p52 2016 Special Issue

Teacher's Pet N. Rizopoulos color *Yoga Journal* p14 2017 Special Issue

TEO DRAKE color *Yoga Journal* no292 p18 Je 2017

Turn Your Practice UPSIDE DOWN [Cover story] C. ALYSSA color *Yoga Journal* no293 p82 Ag 2017

Veg Out for Your HEALTH! L. Haney cartoon *O, The Oprah Magazine* p94 F 2017

ways of the Warrior H. DOWDLE bw color *Yoga Journal* p28 2017 Special Issue

Yoga Moves We All Get Wrong K. McGee color *Health* v31 no7 p69 S 2017

The Yoga of Integrity [Cover story] color *Yoga Journal* no293 p97 Ag 2017

Yoga That Will Kick Your Ass S. Dreisbach color *Glamour* v115 no11 p98 N 2017

Yoga vs. Back Pain K. McGee color *Health* v31 no4 p49 My 2017

Your greatest asset K. SIBER color *Yoga Journal* p80 2017 SpecialIssue

Yoga postures—Physiological aspects

STRIKE a Pose H. Rolfe, J. Brilliant et al *Dance Spirit* v21 no7 p56 S 2017

Yoga postures—Psychological aspects

A home practice to Cultivate contentment [Cover story] H. Archer

color *Yoga Journal* no295 p69 O 2017

Supta Padangusthasana to Ardha Chandra Chapasana [Cover story] A. Ippoliti color *Yoga Journal* no295 p55 O 2017

Yoga teachers

The Beginner's Guide to Standing on Your Head S. Gaynes Levy color *Glamour* v114 no7 p90 Jl 2016

Yoga techniques

    See also

    Yoga postures

Broga? D. Greene and T. Keith color *Sports Illustrated* v126 no14 p24 My 15-22 2017

FLAT ABS AFTER BABY M. Gainsburg color *Women's Health* v14 no2 p76 Mr 2017

Take Me To Church K. Massicot color *New Orleans Magazine* v51 no9 p134 Jl 2017

Yoga That Will Kick Your Ass S. Dreisbach color *Glamour* v115 no11 p98 N 2017

Yoga training & conditioning

Take Me To Church K. Massicot color *New Orleans Magazine* v51 no9 p134 Jl 2017

Yoga For Strength L. MCGLASHAN color *Muscle & Performance* v9 no1 p38 Ja 2017

Yoga—Charts, diagrams, etc.

Martha's Month chart color *Martha Stewart Living* p1 My 2017

Yoga—Congresses

ALA, Chicago Style B. KENNEY *Publishers Weekly* v264 no25 p40 Je 19 2017

Yoga—Equipment & supplies

GEAR ESSENTIALS H. Dowdle color *Yoga Journal* p18 2017 Special Issue

the Must List color *Yoga Journal* no296 p19 N 2017

My Live-Work Loft B. COOPER color *Indianapolis Monthly* p33 Ap 2017

Poses of the month [Cover story] J. Schumacher color *Yoga Journal* no289 p37 F 2017

Poses to last a lifetime [Cover story] M. Bolster color *Yoga Journal* p14 2017 Special Issue

Yoga—Physiological aspects

Is Beauty Self-Care? S. Kitchens color *Glamour* v115 no7 p55 Jl 2017

OUTSIDE INTERESTS color *Vogue* v207 no6 p78 Je 2017

POSE PRIORITIES C. KUZMA color *Runner's World* v52 no2 p46 Mr 2017

STRETCH YOUR LIMITS [Cover story] C. Kuzma color *Runner's World* v52 no2 p44 Mr 2017

Veg Out for Your HEALTH! L. Haney cartoon *O, The Oprah Magazine* p94 F 2017

Yoga For Strength L. MCGLASHAN color *Muscle & Performance* v9 no1 p38 Ja 2017

Yoga—Psychological aspects

Chasing contentment J. Hanson Lasater color *Yoga Journal* no296 p14 N 2017

Embodying the sutra color *Yoga Journal* no295 p51 O 2017

Fuel your WILLPOWER [Cover story] K. SIBER color *Yoga Journal* no289 p56 F 2017

Goodnight, SLEEP ISSUES T. Eichenseher color *Yoga Journal* p102 2017 Special Issue

HAPPY starts here A. Ferretti color *Yoga Journal* p80 2017 Special Issue

Have the time of your life N. Isaacs color *Yoga Journal* p69 2017 Special Issue

let it GO K. Siber color *Yoga Journal* p88 2017 Special Issue

Let's be honest color *Yoga Journal* no295 p12 O 2017

Live your best life C. Gorrell *Yoga Journal* p5 2016 Special Issue

love FOR LIFE S. Sexton color *Yoga Journal* p94 2017 Special Issue

refresh your soul retreat E. MARGLIN color *Yoga Journal* no287 p14 N 2016

United we practice C. Gorrell bw *Yoga Journal* no292 p10 Je 2017

Yoga—Social aspects

THE GOOD WITH THE BAAAD: Not tempted by traditional yoga? Perhaps you'd enjoy trying it with goats C. CUNNINGHAM *Washingtonian Magazine* v52 no11 p17 Ag 2017

Yoga—Study & teaching

The Power to Transform R. POLANECZKY color *Prevention* v69 no11 p82 N 2017

Yoga—Therapeutic use
Speed the Salutations G. Reynolds *New York Times Magazine* p22 F 12 2017

Yogic therapy
3 Steps to Holiday Stress Relief color *Prevention* v69 no11 p12 N 2017
The Power to Transform R. POLANECZKY color *Prevention* v69 no11 p82 N 2017
Surprising Benefits of Aerial Yoga V. Tweed color *Amazing Wellness* v8 no2 p19 Spr 2016
This Just In J. Zorthian *Time* v189 no19 p19 My 22 2017

Yogis, Jaimal
FROM BACKYARD TO BACKCOUNTRY [Cover story] color *Sunset* v238 no5 p60 My 2017
Love in a dumpling color *Yoga Journal* no296 p96 N 2017

Yogurt
See also
Greek yogurt
YO, YOGURT! M. MANNARINO color *Better Homes & Gardens* v95 no6 p166 Je 2017

Yogurt industry
GENERAL MILLS LOSES THE CULTURE WARS J. Kell color diag *Fortune* v175 no7 p66 Je 1 2017

Yogurt microbiology
THE TRUE COLORS OF PROBIOTICS L. BEIL color *Women's Health* v14 no6 p140 Jl 2017

Yogurt—Evaluation
INTERNATIONAL YOGURTS color *Women's Health* v14 no3 p38 Ap 2017
Is Whole-Milk Yogurt a Whole Lot Better? J. Calderone chart color *Consumer Reports* v82 no8 p18 Ag 2017

Yohei Murakami
Buffer-gas cooling of antiprotonic helium to 1.5 to 1.7 K, and antiproton-to-electron mass ratio bibl chart diag graph *Science* v354 no6312 p610 N 4 2016

Yohimbine
Are You Getting Stiffed? color *Men's Health* v31 no10 p30 D 2016

Yohn, Denise Lee
7 Steps to Deliver Better Customer Experiences *Harvard Business Review Digital Articles* p2 F 3 2015
The Best Salespeople Do What the Best Brands Do *Harvard Business Review Digital Articles* p2 Ag 15 2016
Big-Box Retailers Have Two Options If They Want to Survive *Harvard Business Review Digital Articles* p2 Je 22 2016
Design Your Employee Experience as Thoughtfully as You Design Your Customer Experience *Harvard Business Review Digital Articles* p2 D 8 2016
Is It Too Late for Sears to Save Itself? color *Harvard Business Review Digital Articles* p2 Mr 30 2017
Know When to Kill Your Brand *Harvard Business Review Digital Articles* p2 Jl 17 2015
Lilly Pulitzer's Target Disaster Was Actually a Success *Harvard Business Review Digital Articles* p2 My 22 2015
Retailers Can't Rely on Holiday-Season Gimmicks Like They Used To *Harvard Business Review Digital Articles* p2 N 3 2015
Should You Name Your Company After Yourself? *Harvard Business Review Digital Articles* p2 My 5 2017
To Stay Relevant, Professional Associations Must Rebrand *Harvard Business Review Digital Articles* p2 Ja 5 2016
Walmart Won't Stay on Top If Its Strategy Is "Copy Amazon" *Harvard Business Review Digital Articles* p2 Mr 21 2017
What Retail Sales Associates Still Do Better than Websites *Harvard Business Review Digital Articles* p2 D 15 2014
Why Companies Are Advertising Their Master Brand *Harvard Business Review Digital Articles* p2 Mr 28 2016
Why the Print Catalog Is Back in Style *Harvard Business Review Digital Articles* p2 F 25 2015
Why Your Company Culture Should Match Your Brand *Harvard Business Review Digital Articles* p2 Je 26 2017
Your Company Culture Shouldn't Just Be Great— It Should Be Distinctive *Harvard Business Review Digital Articles* p2 S 14 2015
Zumba's Success Arose from Long-Term Trends *Harvard Business Review Digital Articles* p2 O 14 2014

Yoho, Rachel
Artificial intelligence in research color *Science* v357 no6346 p28

Jl 7 2017

Yoho National Park (B.C.)
exposure color *Canadian Geographic* v137 no1 p14 F 2017
exposure color *Canadian Geographic* v137 no4 p14 Jl/Ag 2017

Yoichi Kamagata
Methane production from coal by a single methanogen bibl graph *Science* v354 no6309 p222 O 14 2016

Yokom, Adam L.
Ratchet-like polypeptide translocation mechanism of the AAA+ disaggregase Hsp104 diag *Science* v357 no6348 p273 Jl 21 2017

Yokose, Jun
Overlapping memory trace indispensable for linking, but not recalling, individual memories bibl graph *Science* v355 no6323 p398 Ja 27 2017

Yokoyama, Hideo
Crimes, Cover-Ups and Competition S. Begley color *Time* v189 no6 p53 F 20 2017
Inspector In the Labyrinth [Cover story] T. Rafferty *New York Times Book Review* p1 F 26 2017

Yokoyama, Shigeyuki
Structure of the complete elongation complex of RNA polymerase II with basal factors map *Science* v357 no6354 p921 S 1 2017

Yokoyama, Takeshi
Structure of the complete elongation complex of RNA polymerase II with basal factors map *Science* v357 no6354 p921 S 1 2017

Yoko Yazaki-Sugiyama
Mind the gap: Neural coding of species identity in birdsong prosody bibl graph *Science* v354 no6317 p1282 D 9 2016

Yokozuna USA (Company)
Yokozuna Motoko Road Disc Brake M. Phillips color *Bicycling* v58 no4 p82 My 2017

Yok Tan, Puay
Benefits of trees in tropical cities color *Science* v356 no6344 p1241 Je 23 2017

Yolen, Jane
ONCE UPON A TIME color *Publishers Weekly* v264 no41 p68 O 9 2017

YONAN, JOE
mothers' DAY color *Better Homes & Gardens* v95 no5 p122 My 2017
POT LUCK color *Better Homes & Gardens* v95 no10 p146 O 2017

Yoncheva, Sonya
Orange S. J. Mudge *Opera News* v81 no5 p52 N 2016
Soul SISTER F. COHN *Opera News* v81 no5 p26 N 2016

Yonck, Richard
The Upside of the AI Revolution S. Begley color *Time* v189 no7/8 p24 F 27 2017

Yoneyama, N.
Crystallization and vitrification of electrons in a glass-forming charge liquid bw *Science* v357 no6358 p1381 S 29 2017

Yong, Debbie
CHANGE THE WORLD !!!! color diag map *Fortune* v176 no4 p74 S 15 2017

Yong Cui
Quality management for precision medicine clinical applications: A consensus from the China Precision Medicine Clinical Research and Application Association bibl *Science* v354 no6319 p11 D 23 2016

Yongho Park
Macrocyclic bis-thioureas catalyze stereospecific glycosylation reactions bibl diag *Science* v355 no6321 p1 Ja 13 2017

Yonghua Chen
Gene expression profiling-guided clinical precision treatment for patients with endometrial carcinoma bibl color diag *Science* v354 no6319 p33 D 23 2016

Yong Kim, Sang
Deficiency of microRNA miR-34a expands cell fate potential in pluripotent stem cells diag *Science* v355 no6325 p596 F 10 2017

Yoo, Barney
Polymeric peptide pigments with sequence-encoded properties color graph *Science* v356 no6342 p1064 Je 9 2017

Yoo, J.
Observation of coherent elastic neutrino-nucleus scattering diag *Science* v357 no6356 p1123 S 15 2017

Yoon, Alicia
  what's the deal with K-BEAUTY? J. EDGAR *Better Homes & Gardens* v95 no1 p21 Ja 2017
Yoon, Carolyn
  Marketers Should Pay Attention to fMRI *Harvard Business Review Digital Articles* p2 N 3 2015
Yoon, Changkyu
  DNA sequence–directed shape change of photopatterned hydrogels via high-degree swelling color diag *Science* v357 no6356 p1126 S 15 2017
Yoon, Eddie
  The Benefits of Hiring Your Best Customers *Harvard Business Review Digital Articles* p2 D 20 2016
  Big Companies Should Collaborate with Startups *Harvard Business Review Digital Articles* p2 F 25 2016
  The Billion-Dollar Opportunity in Single-Serve Food *Harvard Business Review Digital Articles* p2 O 23 2015
  Don't Overlook the Small Brands You Already Own *Harvard Business Review Digital Articles* p2 D 30 2016
  The Forecasting Sweet Spot Between Micro and Macro *Harvard Business Review Digital Articles* p2 Ag 26 2016
  The Grocery Industry Confronts a New Problem: Only 10% of Americans Love Cooking *Harvard Business Review Digital Articles* p2 S 22 2017
  The Mistake Companies Make When Marketing to Different Cultures *Harvard Business Review Digital Articles* p2 F 17 2015
  Searching for New Ideas in the Curious Things Your Customers Do *Harvard Business Review Digital Articles* p2 Ap 13 2017
  Store Brands Aren't Just about Price *Harvard Business Review Digital Articles* p2 Ap 15 2015
  Tesla Shows How Traditional Business Metrics Are Outdated *Harvard Business Review Digital Articles* p2 Ag 8 2017
  What Netflix and Starbucks Know About Cash Flow *Harvard Business Review Digital Articles* p2 Ja 22 2015
  What Should an Apple Car Be? *Harvard Business Review Digital Articles* p2 Jl 4 2017
  Why Companies Should Measure "Share of Growth," Not Just Market Share color *Harvard Business Review Digital Articles* p1 Je 2 2017
  Why New Consumer Brands Must Scale Faster *Harvard Business Review Digital Articles* p2 Jl 8 2016
Yoon, Emily Jungmin
  TIME, IN WHALES *New Yorker* v93 no13 p58 My 15 2017
Yoon, In-Kyu
  Dengue diversity across spatial and temporal scales: Local structure and the effect of host population size bibl graph *Science* v355 no6331 p1302 Mr 24 2017
Yoon, Jean
  Convenience truth A. LEE color *Maclean's* v129 no42 p59 O 24 2016
Yoon, K-S.
  Structural basis of the redox switches in the NAD+-reducing soluble [NiFe]-hydrogenase diag *Science* v357 no6354 p928 S 1 2017
Yoon, Nicola
  THE BIG QUESTION cartoon *Atlantic* v320 no4 p124 N 2017
  CHILDREN'S BESTSELLERS chart *Publishers Weekly* v264 no22 p19 My 29 2017
  No. 8 THE SUN IS ALSO A STAR N. Serrao color *Entertainment Weekly* no1444/1445 p106 D 16 2016
  The Sun Is Also a Star color *Publishers Weekly* v263 no50 p67 D 5 2016
Yoon, Sangwon
  Mindfulness for the Hedge Fund Set color *Bloomberg Businessweek* no4494 p41 O 10 2016
  Patience You Must Have, My Young Investors color *Bloomberg Businessweek* no4503 p27 D 12 2016
YOON, TAESIK
  Google Slayer color *Forbes* v199 no6 p54 Je 13 2017
Yoon, Tehshik P.
  Enantioselective photochemistry through Lewis acid–catalyzed triplet energy transfer bibl chart diag graph *Science* v354 no6318 p1391 D 16 2016
YOOX SpA
  BEAUTIFUL DREAMERS D. KAZANJIAN color *Vogue* v207 no7 p100 Jl 2017

Yoox Net-a-Porter Group SpA
  DOUBLE VISION *Los Angeles Magazine* p30 My 2017
York, Adam
  Learning from schools that close opportunity gaps *Phi Delta Kappan* v99 no1 p8 S 2017
York, Kristen
  Rebel Yell S. KROWIAK color *Indianapolis Monthly* p42 Ap 2017
YORK, NADINE
  On Two Wheels *Idaho Magazine* v16 no6 p24 Mr 2017
York, Patricia
  Get Your Dog To Behave Around Company color *Southern Living* v52 no4 p50 Ap 2017
  Pups & Personal Space color *Southern Living* v52 no3 p26 Mr 2017
York, Patricia S.
  THE 5-INGREDIENT Farmers' Market Cookbook color *Southern Living* v52 no7 p61 Jl 2017
  Canine Campers color *Southern Living* v52 no7 p35 Jl 2017
  CHEERS to MOM color *Southern Living* v52 no5 p90 My 2017
  Dogs on the Town color *Southern Living* v52 no6 p43 Je 2017
  Gracious Guests color *Southern Living* v52 no11 p47 N 2017
  Hitting the Trails color *Southern Living* v52 no10 p42 O 2017
  Ripe for Easy Picking color *Southern Living* v52 no6 p29 Je 2017
  Seaside Suppers color *Southern Living* v52 no7 p101 Jl 2017
  Small-Space Living color *Southern Living* v52 no9 p33 S 2017
Yorkey, Brian
  Darkness Visible In 13 Reasons Why D. D'addario color *Time* v189 no13 p51 Ap 10 2017
  Does 13 Reasons Go Too Far? Inside the debate over Netflix's teen drama K. HAHN *TV Guide* v65 no21 p9 My 15 2017
YORKO, SCOTT
  APPAREL color *Backpacker* p55 N 2017
  EQUIPMENT color *Backpacker* p73 N 2017
  Gear for the Long Haul color *Backpacker* v45 no1 p43 Ja 2017
  Hall of Fame color *Backpacker* v45 no2 p45 Mr 2017
Yorkshire (England)—Description & travel
  DELIGHT ON THE NORTH YORKSHIRE COAST D. Huntley *British Heritage Travel* v38 no1 p60 Ja/F 2017
Yorton, Tom
  3 Improv Exercises That Can Change the Way Your Team Works *Harvard Business Review Digital Articles* p2 Mr 9 2015
Yosef, Nir
  The epigenetic landscape of T cell exhaustion bibl graph *Science* v354 no6316 p1165 D 2 2016
  Writ large: Genomic dissection of the effect of cellular environment on immune response bibl diag *Science* v354 no6308 p64 O 7 2016
Yosemite National Park (Calif.)
  Beyond the Bolt J. Lucas color *Climbing* no357 p60 N 2017
  Bouncing Back in Yosemite: After flirting with extinction, Sierra Nevada yellow-legged frogs are staging a remarkable—and unexpected—comeback N. LUND *National Parks* v91 no3 p24 Summ 2017
  Finding Home: What happens when a desert baby visits the meadows of Yosemite? M. BRANCH *National Parks* v91 no3 p18 Summ 2017
  out alive: stranded M. B. Skylis bw *Backpacker* p37 O 2017
  WIN A YOSEMITE ADVENTURE! T. Enriquez color *Sunset* v238 no4 p106 Ap 2017
Yosemite National Park (Calif.)—Description & travel
  YOSEMITE NATIONAL PARK, CALIFORNIA color *Runner's World* v52 no7 p8 Ag 2017
Yosemite Valley (Calif.)
  BATTLE GROUND P. Fish color *Sunset* v238 no5 p70 My 2017
  Beyond the Bolt J. Lucas color *Climbing* no357 p60 N 2017
  Yosemite Rockfall U. CHROBAK color *Climbing* no357 p24 N 2017
Yoshida, Kentaro
  Evolution of the wheat blast fungus through functional losses in a host specificity determinant diag map *Science* v357 no6346 p80 Jl 7 2017
Yoshida, Mike
  THE CASCADES, WASHINGTON bw color *Snowboarder* v29 no4 p100 D 2016
Yoshida, Naoki

Supersonic gas streams enhance the formation of massive black holes in the early universe diag graph *Science* v357 no6358 p1375 S 29 2017

Yoshida, Yutaka
Control of species-dependent cortico-motoneuronal connections underlying manual dexterity diag graph *Science* v357 no6349 p400 Jl 28 2017

Yoshihiro Sakoda
Role for migratory wild birds in the global spread of avian influenza H5N8 bibl graph map *Science* v354 no6309 p213 O 14 2016

Yoshihisa Yamamoto
A fully programmable 100-spin coherent Ising machine with all-to-all connections bibl diag graph *Science* v354 no6312 p614 N 4 2016

Yoshikawa, Naotaka
High-harmonic generation in graphene enhanced by elliptically polarized light excitation color graph *Science* v356 no6339 p736 My 19 2017

Yoshimura Research & Development of America Inc.
YOSHIMURA SIGNATURE SERIES ALPHA SLIP-ON D. Canet color *Cycle World* v56 no1 p19 Ja/F 2017

Yoshinaga, Satoshi
A crossroad of neuronal diversity to build circuitry color *Science* v356 no6336 p376 Ap 28 2017

Yoshino, Jun
An adipo-biliary-uridine axis that regulates energy homeostasis diag *Science* v355 no6330 p1173 Mr 17 2017

Yoshioka, Shin
Control of species-dependent cortico-motoneuronal connections underlying manual dexterity diag graph *Science* v357 no6349 p400 Jl 28 2017

Yoshitaka Haribara
A coherent Ising machine for 2000-node optimization problems bibl diag graph *Science* v354 no6312 p603 N 4 2016
A fully programmable 100-spin coherent Ising machine with all-to-all connections bibl diag graph *Science* v354 no6312 p614 N 4 2016

Yoshitaka Takano
Regulation of sugar transporter activity for antibacterial defense in Arabidopsis bibl diag graph *Science* v354 no6318 p1427 D 16 2016

Yoshiteru Maeno
Strong peak in Tc of Sr2RuO4 under uniaxial pressure bibl color graph *Science* v355 no6321 p1 Ja 13 2017

Yoshito Oka
Photoactivation and inactivation of Arabidopsis cryptochrome 2 bibl graph *Science* v354 no6310 p343 O 21 2016

Yosses, Bill
The Sweet Spot: Dialing Back Sugar and Amping Up Flavor *Publishers Weekly* v264 no36 p83 S 4 2017

Yost, Cali Williams
Design a Work-Life Improvement Pilot Project *Harvard Business Review Digital Articles* p2 Ap 9 2015

Yost, Dylan C.
The Rydberg constant and proton size from atomic hydrogen bw chart color diag graph *Science* v357 no6359 p79 O 6 2017

Yost, Whit
38 REASONS TO GO GA-GA FOR THE TOUR DE FRANCE color *Bicycling* v58 no7 p24 Ag 2017

You (The English word)
How "you" makes meaning A. Orvell, E. Kross et al bibl diag graph *Science* v355 no6331 p1299 Mr 24 2017

You, Edward
On Patrol with America's Top Bioterror Cop A. Regalado color diag *MIT Technology Review* v120 no1 p15 Ja/F 2017

You, Jia
A COSMIC CONTROVERSY diag *Science* v355 no6329 p1013 Mr 10 2017
Raising the drawbridge graph *Science* v355 no6328 p896 Mr 3 2017
THE VACCINE WARS [Cover story] color *Science* v356 no6336 p364 Ap 28 2017

You, Li
Deterministic entanglement generation from driving through quantum phase transitions bibl color graph *Science* v355 no6325 p620 F 10 2017

You, Yu-Meng
An organic-inorganic perovskite ferroelectric with large piezoelectric response graph *Science* v357 no6348 p306 Jl 21 2017

You Are Happy? (Short story)
You Are Happy? A. Sharma cartoon color *New Yorker* v93 no9 p58 Ap 17 2017

You Can't Do That on Television (TV program)
What They Really Couldn't Do on You Can't Do That on Television A. Wilkinson color *Entertainment Weekly* no1460/1461 p41 Ap 7-17 2017

You Can't Kill Light (Music)
YOU CAN'T KILL LIGHT DG bw *Advocate* no1091 p32 Je/Jl 2017

You Light up My Life (Music)
THE DARK SIDE OF "YOU LIGHT UP MY LIFE" D. Coggan color *Entertainment Weekly* no1451/1452 p78 F 3-10 2017

You Never Really Know (Short story)
YOU NEVER REALLY KNOW J. EISENBERG cartoon *New Yorker* v92 no46 p29 Ja 23 2017

You the Jury (TV program)
You the Jury *TV Guide* p36 Ap 17 2017

You Want It Darker (Music)
Last Rites P. IYER cartoon *Walrus* p67 Ja\F 2017
Leonard Cohen L. Greenblatt color *Entertainment Weekly* no1436/1437 p101 O 21 2016
Leonard Cohen's Golden Hour A. GREENE color *Rolling Stone* no1274 p15 N 17 2016
Leonard Cohen's Late-Night Serenade W. HERMES color *Rolling Stone* no1273 p49 N 3 2016
'You Want It Darker' J. MAHLER bw *New York Times Magazine* p20 Mr 12 2017

You Were Never Really Here (Film)
Catastrophes on Parade N. Rapold color *Film Comment* v53 no4 p64 Jl/Ag 2017

You-Xian Yan
Synthetic nacre by predesigned matrix-directed mineralization bibl bw diag graph *Science* v354 no6308 p107 O 7 2016

Youan Zhu
A Silurian maxillate placoderm illuminates jaw evolution bibl color *Science* v354 no6310 p334 O 21 2016

Youers, Rio
The Forgotten Girl *Publishers Weekly* v264 no36 p86 S 4 2017
Lost Memories L. PICKER color *Publishers Weekly* v264 no16 p44 Ap 17 2017

Youjin Deng
Realization of two-dimensional spin-orbit coupling for Bose-Einstein condensates bibl graph *Science* v354 no6308 p83 O 7 2016

Youjung Jun
Research: Being in a Group Makes Us Less Likely to Fact-Check *Harvard Business Review Digital Articles* p2 Ag 1 2017

Youn Jeong Lee
Role for migratory wild birds in the global spread of avian influenza H5N8 bibl graph map *Science* v354 no6309 p213 O 14 2016

Younan, Munib A.
People M. W. Qureshi and M. I. Pinsky color *Christian Century* v134 no18 p17 Ag 30 2017

Young & Hungry (TV program)
Betty White Gets Crazy on Young & Hungry E. Aslanian *TV Guide* v65 no8 p11 F 27 2017

Young & the Restless (TV program)
TV'S WINNERS AND LOSERS BY THE NUMBERS *TV Guide* v64 no40 p16 O 3 2016
THE YOUNG AND THE RESTLESS M. LOGAN *TV Guide* v65 no14 p44 Ap 3 2017

Young, Aden
DOING TIME E. NUSSBAUM cartoon *New Yorker* v92 no40 p74 D 5 2016

Young, Allison
BEST OF THE WEST color *Sunset* v239 no4 p13 O 2017
BODY SHOTS [Cover story] color *Women's Health* v14 no6 p96 Jl 2017
Delish dips color *Yoga Journal* no295 p26 O 2017
DINNER AND A SHOW [Cover story] color *Sunset* v238 no6 p58 Je 2017

Young, Andrew, 1932-
Andrew Young: Politician, activist, national treasure J. BAIN-

BRIDGE *Atlanta* v57 no3 p60 Jl 2017

Young, Ashley

My Deluxe Dream Barn Will Have... color *Horse & Rider* v56 no4 p80 Ap 2017

Young, Bellamy

Scandal N. Abrams, B. L. Heldman et al *Entertainment Weekly* no1482/1483 p88 S 22 2017

Young, Brett—Interviews

Meet the Celebrity Judge J. LABIANCA color *Reader's Digest* v190 no1135 p80 N 2017

Young, Carl S.

The Enemies of Data Security: Convenience and Collaboration *Harvard Business Review Digital Articles* p2 F 11 2015

Young, Carolin C.

Farther afield bw color *Magazine Antiques* v183 no6 p36 N/D 2016

YOUNG, CARRIE

Society Is Ready for a New Kind of Science--Is Academia? *BioScience* v67 no7 p591 Jl 2017

YOUNG, CATHY

Eternal Quadrangle color *Weekly Standard* v22 no16 p37 D 26 2016

False Friend *Weekly Standard* v22 no19 p16 Ja 23 2017

The Injustice of the 'Rape-Culture' Theory: For those in the grips of hysteria, proof is the enemy *Commentary* v144 no3 p26 O 2017

Is free speech under threat IN THE UNITED STATES? WE RECEIVED TWENTY-SEVEN RESPONSES. WE PUBLISH THEM HERE, IN ALPHABETICAL ORDER *Commentary* v144 no1 p13 Jl/Ag 2017

THE OTHER WOMEN'S MOVEMENT [Cover story] color *Foreign Policy* no223 p26 Mr/Ap 2017

The Russian We Need bw *Weekly Standard* v22 no46 p35 Ag 14 2017

RUSSIA'S GLOBAL ANTI-LIBERTARIAN CRUSADE [Cover story] color *Reason* v49 no4 p18 Ag/S 2017

Young, Charles

OKINAWA *AARP: The Magazine* v59 no3A p65 Ap/My 2016

Statin Denialism? *Skeptical Inquirer* v41 no5 p63 S/O 2017

Young, Chris—Interviews

SECURING MCAFEE M. Lev-Ram color *Fortune* v175 no6 p24 My 1 2017

Young, David

Murder in East Germany L. PICKER bw *Publishers Weekly* v264 no25 p92 Je 19 2017

Stasi Child: A Karin Müller Thriller color *Publishers Weekly* v264 no24 p39 Je 12 2017

YOUNG, DENISE

The Question color *O, The Oprah Magazine* p14 N 2017

YOUNG, DONALD R.

Crossing Scales: The Complexity of Barrier-Island Processes for Predicting Future Change *BioScience* v67 no1 p39 Ja 2017

Young, Elise

Connecticut Tells Amtrak to Slow Down color *Bloomberg Businessweek* no4493 p37 O 3 2016

Law Pushing Back on Public Dissent color *Bloomberg Businessweek* no4511 p26 F 13 2017

YOUNG, EMILY

The Accidental Collector *Los Angeles Magazine* p52 D 2016

Young, Erica—Interviews

ERICA M J. Wilson color *Essence* v47 no10 p26 F 2017

Young, Hester

The Shimmering Road *Publishers Weekly* v263 no51 p123 D 12 2016

YOUNG, HILLARY

Conserving the World's Megafauna and Biodiversity: The Fierce Urgency of Now *BioScience* v67 no3 p197 Mr 2017

Saving the World's Terrestrial Megafauna color *BioScience* v66 no10 p807 O 1 2016

Young, Jeff

America's top TV critic Matt Roush answers your burning questions Melissa, Florrie et al *TV Guide* p7 D 5 2016

Young, Jhana

Committing to socially responsible seafood color *Science* v356 no6341 p912 Je 1 2017

Young, John

HALO HUNTER E. MASTROIANNI color *Discover* v38 no8 p9 O 2017

Young, Jolyn

The Heart of Cowboy Camp bw color *American Cowboy* v23 no6 p48 Ap/My 2017

Lost Skills cartoon *American Cowboy* v23 no5 p66 F/Mr 2017

Young, Julia G.

Still Welcoming the Stranger color *Commonweal* v144 no5 p9 Mr 10 2017

YOUNG, JULIE

Back Home Again *Indianapolis Monthly* p94 F 2017

BANK ON IT color *Indianapolis Monthly* v41 no2 p30 S 2017

DITCH THE JITTERS! *Indianapolis Monthly* v40 no7 p86 Mr 2017

EDUCATIONAL options *Indianapolis Monthly* v40 no3 p107 N 2016

keep calm AND MARRY ON *Indianapolis Monthly* v40 no5 p21 Ja 2017

MISSION POSSIBLE color *Indianapolis Monthly* v41 no2 p33 S 2017

Paradise Reimagined *Indianapolis Monthly* p8 My 2017

Senior Living cartoon color *Indianapolis Monthly* v42 no2 p95 O 2017

TRAVEL bw color *Indianapolis Monthly* p79 Ap 2017

Work Hard, Play Hard *Indianapolis Monthly* p34 My 2017

Young, Justin R.

Underemployment among Hispanics: the case of involuntary part-time work *Monthly Labor Review* p1 D 2016

Young, K. R.

Persistent effects of pre-Columbian plant domestication on Amazonian forest composition bibl chart graph map *Science* v355 no6328 p925 Mr 3 2017

YOUNG, KAREN E.

Can the Saudi Economy Be Reformed? *Current History* v115 no785 p355 D 2016

YOUNG, KENNETH C.

PROGRAMMING FOR ALL color *Scientific American* v315 no6 p8 D 2016

Young, Kevin

BELIEVE IT OR NOT D. PATRICK color *Publishers Weekly* v264 no40 p111 O 2 2017

Young, La Rochelle

Full CIRCLE D. M. Owens color *Essence* v47 no10 p92 F 2017

YOUNG, LAUREN

Judge on Trial *Ms.* v26 no4 p8 Wint 2016

Measuring Up *Ms.* v26 no4 p12 Wint 2016

Real Representation: What if every voter in every election had the chance to cast a meaningful vote? *Ms.* v27 no3 p8 Fall 2017

They Held Their Own Hearts color *Reader's Digest* v190 no1133 p50 S 2017

Young, Laurence J.

De novo design of a biologically active amyloid bibl graph *Science* v354 no6313 paah4949-1 N 11 2016

Young, Lydia

De novo design of a biologically active amyloid bibl graph *Science* v354 no6313 paah4949-1 N 11 2016

YOUNG, MARCIA

Leading Women *Opera News* v81 no5 p22 N 2016

YOUNG, MARILYN

back in bloom color diag *Martha Stewart Living* no275 p92 Je 2017

Young, Marnin

FIELD GUIDE *Atlanta* v56 no11 p92 Mr 2017

Young, Melissa Scholes

A River Runs Through It L. Heck color *Missouri Life* v44 no6 p27 S 2017

YOUNG, MICAELA

Five Foods to Fend Off Cancer color *Men's Health* v32 no9 p64 N 2017

Grant-Writing Bootcamp: An Intervention to Enhance the Research Capacity of Academic Women in STEM *BioScience* v67 no7 p638 Jl 2017

The Secret Fuel Your Body Craves color *Men's Health* v32 no8 p92 O 2017

Young, Michael

Tomorrow: David Wallace-Wells img *New York* v49 no19 p20 S

19 2016

Young, Molly

Dear Diary, Now What? In the latest book in the series, Bridget Jones is pregnant but isn't sure of the father *New York Times Book Review* p10 O 23 2016

Help Wanted: In Catherine Lacey's novel, a famous actor tries to design the perfect partner piece by piece *New York Times Book Review* p16 Jl 30 2017

Instagram Explore *New York Times Magazine* p18 Ja 8 2017

Lighten Up, New York color *Bon Appetit* v62 no7 p46 Jl 2017

Young, Monica

Another Maunder Minimum? *Sky & Telescope* v133 no6 p9 Je 2017

Four Planets for Tau Ceti *Sky & Telescope* v134 no6 p11 D 2017

Is the Milky Way in a Void? *Sky & Telescope* v134 no4 p12 O 2017

Less Dark Matter in Young Galaxies? *Sky & Telescope* v134 no1 p13 Jl 2017

Machines Learning Astronomy: The new era of artificial intelligence & Big Data is changing how we do astronomy *Sky & Telescope* v134 no6 p20 D 2017

The Origin of the Milky Way's Mysterious Gamma Rays *Sky & Telescope* v134 no4 p14 O 2017

Potential "Failed Supernova" Discovered *Sky & Telescope* v134 no3 p10 S 2017

Spirits of Our Galaxy's Past *Sky & Telescope* v133 no4 p22 Ap 2017

Supermassive Black Holes in Close Dance *Sky & Telescope* v134 no4 p13 O 2017

Tabby's Star Dims on Cue *Sky & Telescope* v134 no3 p13 S 2017

Tabby's Star Gets Weirder *Sky & Telescope* v133 no1 p18 Ja 2017

Welcoming New Staff P. Tyson *Sky & Telescope* v134 no6 p4 D 2017

When Computers Wore Skirts *Sky & Telescope* v133 no6 p57 Je 2017

Young, Nat

Nat Young, 69 A. DOUGLAS bw *Surfer* v58 no1 p40 Ap 2017

YOUNG, NATHAN

Envisioning the Future of Aquatic Animal Tracking: Technology, Science, and Application *BioScience* v67 no10 p884 O 2017

Young, Neil, 1945-

Hitting the High(ish) Ones D. REILLY img *New York* v49 no20 p117 O 3 2016

Matters of Experience B. MEYER color *Downbeat* v84 no1 p77 Ja 2017

Neil Young Pulls a Lost Treasure Out of the Vault D. BROWNE bw *Rolling Stone* no1294 p54 Ag 24 2017

Neil Young: Restless as Ever B. HIATT color *Rolling Stone* no1278/1279 p19 Ja 12 2017

Young, Nic

Project Greenglow: How Horizon Lost the Message in the Medium J. EADES *Skeptical Inquirer* v41 no1 p52 Ja/F 2017

Young, Odessa

Odessa YOUNG *Interview* v47 no5 p65 Je/Jl 2017

Young, Paloma

Quick Change: Costume Designer Paloma Young takes us back to the 1940s M. S. Eddy *Stage Directions* v30 no6 p22 Je 2017

Young, Patricia

Short Takes on the Apocalypse *Publishers Weekly* v264 no13 p75 Mr 27 2017

YOUNG, PAUL

Hellboy's World: Comics and Monsters on the Margins *Film Quarterly* v70 no3 p99 Spr 2017

Young, Richard C.

Why I Read The American Conservative color *American Conservative* v16 no1 p2 Ja/F 2017

Young, Robert J.

Sensitive electromechanical sensors using viscoelastic graphene-polymer nanocomposites bibl graph *Science* v354 no6317 p1257 D 9 2016

Young, Robert W.

ANY DAMN FOOL color *Black Belt* v55 no2 p8 F/Mr 2017

A BIGGER AND BETTER BLACK BELT! bw *Black Belt* v55 no4 p8 Je/Jl 2017

BRUCE LEE ENTER THE COMIC BOOK - AND THEN ENTER THE TV! [Cover story] bw color *Black Belt* v55 no4 p32

Je/Jl 2017

CEASE AND DESIST, PLEASE color *Black Belt* v55 no3 p8 Ap/My 2017

Highlights From America's Premier Martial Arts Expo color *Black Belt* v55 no6 p76 O/N 2017

REMEMBER OUR ROOTS *Black Belt* v55 no6 p8 O/N 2017

Return of the Kicking Jeans color *Black Belt* v55 no4 p76 Je/Jl 2017

SHOT ACROSS THE BOW, KUK SOOL STYLE [Cover story] color *Black Belt* v55 no6 p32 O/N 2017

WHEN OLYMPIC GAMES MEET MARTIAL ARTS color *Black Belt* v55 no1 p8 D 2016/Ja 2017

Young, Steve, 1961-

YOUNG MONEY A. SHERMAN color *Bloomberg Businessweek* no4511 p54 F 13 2017

Young, Steven Tristan—Interviews

STEVEN TRISTAN YOUNG J. Chen color *Bloomberg Businessweek* no4511 p67 F 13 2017

Young, Taiia Smart

HARD AS NAILS color *Essence* v48 no3 p52 Jl 2017

How to Be Divorceproof cartoon *Ebony* v72 no4 p74 F 2017

Killer Crossover color *Ebony* v72 no6 p74 Ap/My 2017

SHE IS US color *Essence* v48 no6 p67 O 2017

SOMETHING NEW color *Essence* v48 no2 p76 Je 2017

Young, Taylor

Eyewitness J. Russell color *TV Guide* v64 no42 p36 O 10 2016

YOUNG, TRUMAN P.

Conserving Megafauna or Sacrificing Biodiversity? *BioScience* v67 no3 p193 Mr 2017

Young, Tyler

The Thread bw cartoon *New York Times Magazine* p14 D 11 2016

Young, Vince

Vince YOUNG G. Bishop color *Sports Illustrated* v127 no1 p40 Jl 3 2017

Young, William Paul

THE WEEKLY SCORECARD chart *Publishers Weekly* v264 no13 p5 Mr 27 2017

Young adult fiction

Juvenile Fiction Is a Bright Spot in a Down Week chart *Publishers Weekly* v264 no20 p5 My 15 2017

Revolution Devours Its Young Adult Fiction color *Weekly Standard* v22 no47 p2 Ag 21 2017

Titles With a Hook *Literacy Today (2411-7862)* v35 no2 p5 S/O 2017

Young adult literature

See also

Young adult fiction

Q&A WITH CASSANDRA CLARE bw *Publishers Weekly* v263 no43 p(Sp)12 O 24 2016

Shining a Light on YA, MG Fiction C. Kirch *Publishers Weekly* v264 no3 p11 Ja 16 2017

Titles With a Hook *Literacy Today (2411-7862)* v35 no2 p5 S/O 2017

Young adult literature—Congresses

The Prose of Cons S. CORBETT color *Publishers Weekly* v264 no19 p25 My 8 2017

Young adult literature—Social aspects

YA Authors Turn Advocates S. J. ROBBINS *Publishers Weekly* v263 no41 p40 O 10 2016

Young adults

A Community for Growth: A Community for Growth At John Volken Academy, students gain skills for life and love S. Gisler *Psychology Today* v50 no5 p18 S/O 2017

WE WERE RIGHT ALL ALONG color *Yankee* p26 Mr 2017

Why Your Late Twenties Is the Worst Time of Your Life R. Zilca *Harvard Business Review Digital Articles* p2 Mr 7 2016

Young adults—Canada

The three faces of id A. SAWHNEY color *Maclean's* v129 no44 p58 N 7 2016

Young adults—Finance

What Young Adults Need to Know About Buying Health Insurance A. Adamczyk color *Money* v46 no7 p17 Ag 2017

Young adults—Training of

Aging Societies Should Make More of Mentorship M. Freedman and T. Stamp *Harvard Business Review Digital Articles* p2 Jl 6 2016

Youngquist, Paul
The Orbit of Ra M. LONGLEY color *Downbeat* v83 no11 p64 N 2016

YOUNGSON, SARAH
Bet You Didn't Know color *National Geographic Kids* no474 p6 O 2017
Funny Fill-In cartoon *National Geographic Kids* no472 p34 Ag 2017
Funny Fill-In cartoon *National Geographic Kids* no474 p31 O 2017

Youngstown State University
Youngstown State University *Dance Magazine* v90 p112 2016/2017 Supplement College Guide

Young Victoria, The (Film)
TORI THE DOG S. Li color *Entertainment Weekly* no1454/1455 p88 F 24 2017

Younker, Jason
Culture clash color *Science* v356 no6335 p255 Ap 21 2017

Your Best American Girl (Music)
'YOUR BEST AMERICAN GIRL' J. ZHANG color *New York Times Magazine* p62 Mr 12 2017

You're Beautiful (Music)
James Blunt D. Snierson color *Entertainment Weekly* no1459 p60 Mr 31 2017

You're the Top (Music)
Cole Mining S. Rushin color *Sports Illustrated* v126 no8 p88 Mr 20 2017

You're the Worst (TV program)
Lou Diamond Phillips: Worst Dad Ever? M. Roffman *TV Guide* v65 no43 p7 O 16 2017

Yousafzai, Malala, 1997——Interviews
Malala Yousafzai R. Collard color *Time* v190 no4 p56 Jl 24 2017

Yousef, Deena Kamel
Long Reach, Big Problems bw *Bloomberg Businessweek* no4523 p22 My 22 2017
The No. 1 Airline Gets Its Wings Clipped bw color *Bloomberg Businessweek* no4531 p13 Jl 24 2017

Youssef, Assem——Interviews
'EGYPT'S JON STEWART' IN EXILE J. MONTICELLO color *Reason* v49 no6 p44 N 2017

Youssef, Bassem, 1974-
HECKLERS FOR HIRE A. Marantz cartoon *New Yorker* v93 no4 p29 Mr 13 2017

Youth
See also
> At-risk youth
> Homeless youth
> Internet & youth
> Teenagers
> Young adults

AND EVEN UC BERKELEY HAS BECOME A POWER CENTER B. CRAIR img *New York* v50 no9 p49 My 1 2017
Dear Readers A. Au Levitt color *Reader's Digest* v189 no1130 p4 My 2017
IDENTITY, EMPATHY, AND INQUIRY S. Ahmed and H. ". Daniels color *Literacy Today (2411-7862)* v34 no5 p44 Mr/Ap 2017
India's Youth and Liberty Are Looking Less Like Advantages Over China I. Bremmer color *Time* v190 no10/11 p17 S 18 2017
Super Summer Chefs M. Espinoza *Parks & Recreation* v51 no10 p56 O 2016

Youth & violence
True Stories J. VALENTE *America* v215 no18 p11 D 5 2016
Violence, boys, and the labor market S. Hyde *Monthly Labor Review* p1 O 2016

Youth culture
SLOUCHING TOWARDS BETHLEHEM J. DIDION *Saturday Evening Post* v289 no4 p38 Jl/Ag 2017

Youth development
The rise of creative youth development D. Montgomery bibl *Arts Education Policy Review* v118 no1 p1 2017

Youth——Congresses
Countering Violence in DC and Baltimore S. SWETZOFF *Islamic Horizons* v46 no1 p28 Ja/F 2017

Youth——Cuba
Night Creatures color *Foreign Policy* no221 p16 N/D 2016

STRIPES AND STICKERS color *Road & Track* v68 no8 p12 My 2017

Youthfulness
5 new ways to DEFY YOUR AGE A. FRANZINO color *Good Housekeeping* v264 no3 p27 Mr 2017

Youth—Political activity—United States
Voting Trends by Age Group *Congressional Digest* v96 no1 p12 Ja 2017

Youth—Political activity—United States—Research
Young and Apathetic M. Maciag *Governing* v30 no4 p56 Ja 2017

Youth—Psychology
Infinite Identities [Cover story] K. Steinmetz color *Time* v189 no11 p48 Mr 27 2017

Youth—Recreation
Stay on Your Smartphone! K. Schwab, S. H. Mackenzie et al *Parks & Recreation* v51 no11 p14 N 2016

Youth—Religious life
Faith away from home: Early faith formation prepares young adults for college--years before the admission letters arrive A. Scobey color *U.S. Catholic* v82 no9 p23 S 2017

Youth—Russia
THE PUTIN GENERATION J. Ioffe bw color graph map *National Geographic* v230 no6 p76 D 2016

Youths' attitudes
THE NEXT GENERATION: Join us as we meet a handful of Iceland's most promising young people P. STEFÁNSSON *Iceland Review* v55 no4 p72 Jl/Ag 2017

Youth—Social aspects
STEP RIGHT UP! SEE THE REINVENTION OF THE GREAT AMERICAN CIRCUS H. MILLEA *Smithsonian* v48 no4 p38 Jl/Ag 2017

Youth—Social life & customs
This Little Piggy: Did Not Make It All the Way Home R. V. WALKER *Idaho Magazine* v16 no7 p6 Ap 2017

Youth—United States
30 UNDER 30 [Cover story] color *Forbes* v199 no1 p68 Ja 24 2017
Career and Technical Education for Youth at Park & Rec Agencies K. Sims *Parks & Recreation* v52 no8 p22 Ag 2017
Challenges in researching terrorism from the field S. Atran, R. Axelrod et al bibl color *Science* v355 no6323 p352 Ja 27 2017
FACEBOOK FOR GRANDMA K. RANDALL *Washingtonian Magazine* v52 no9 p21 Je 2017
Guiding the Youth Amidst Islamophobia N. ALI *Islamic Horizons* v45 no6 p40 N/D 2016

YouTube (Web resource)
5 AWESOME YOUTUBE APP FEATURES R. WHITWAM color *PCWorld* v35 no10 p107 O 2017
Allow Me to Stipulate My Demands, Daddy S. WILLIAMS bw color *Reader's Digest* v189 no1131 p13 Je 2017
ASK A FLOWCHART R. CAPPS diag *Wired* v24 no12 p144 D 2016
Bank On Him P. Madden and C. Barrett color *Golf Magazine* v59 no3 p25 Mr 2017
BLAQUE OUT: BEING OUTED AS TRANS DIDN'T RUIN THIS YOUTUBE STAR. IT GAVE HER MORE FREEDOM D. GUERRERO color graph *Advocate* no1091 p78 Je/Jl 2017
Digital Business Models Should Have to Follow the Law, Too B. Edelman *Harvard Business Review Digital Articles* p2 Ja 6 2015
D.I.Y D. SPIOTTA cartoon *New Yorker* v93 no26 p42 S 4 2017
Free for All G. TELAROLI bw color *Film Comment* v53 no5 p77 S/O 2017
'Primitive Technology' J. Kahn color *New York Times Magazine* p24 D 4 2016
SHE'S ALL THAT: LESBIAN SENSATION GIGI GORGEOUS IS ALSO A MODEL, SPOKESPERSON, ACTIVIST, AND A TRANS WOMAN IN LOVE D. GUERRERO color *Advocate* no1091 p77 Je/Jl 2017
TALKING ABOUT MY GENERATION: CONNOR FRANTA MADE MILLIONS OFF BEING HIMSELF, AND IT'S ONLY THE BEGINNING D. ARTAVIA color *Advocate* no1091 p78 Je/Jl 2017
Tracking Tie-in Trends K. Raugust color *Publishers Weekly* v264 no16 p19 Ap 17 2017

YouTube (Web resource)—Economic aspects
Streaming Stars M. BERG color *Forbes* v198 no8 p28 D 20 2016

YouTube LLC
  THE MILLENNIAL CORD CUTTING SINGULARITY IS NIGH F. Gillette and L. Shaw color *Bloomberg Businessweek* no4513 p56 Mr 6 2017

Youxin Wang
  Glycomics and its application potential in precision medicine bibl diag *Science* v354 no6319 p36 D 23 2016

Yovanovitch, Pierre
  MAN OF THE WORLD J. LEVINE color *Architectural Digest* v74 no3 p132 Mr 2017

Yozell, Mike
  #BIKECRUSH color *Bicycling* v58 no7 p65 Ag 2017
  #BIKECRUSH color *Bicycling* v58 no8 p53 S 2017
  BULLS STURMVOGEL E EVO color *Bicycling* v58 no10 p68 N/D 2017
  CANNONDALE SCALPEL SE 2 color *Bicycling* v58 no8 p62 S 2017
  CHAMOIS UP color *Bicycling* v58 no8 p60 S 2017
  DeSalvo Builder Special color *Bicycling* v58 no1 p76 Ja/F 2017
  EASY ON, EASY OFF! color *Bicycling* v58 no7 p82 Ag 2017
  "I WANT A BIANCHI." color *Bicycling* v58 no3 p98 Ap 2017
  "I WANT A BIKE THAT WILL LAST ME 15 YEARS." color *Bicycling* v58 no3 p52 Ap 2017
  JAMIS ICON ELITE color *Bicycling* v58 no1 p68 Ja/F 2017
  PARK TOOL X BICYCLING PEDAL WRENCH color *Bicycling* v58 no9 p54 O 2017
  PINARELLO DOGMA F10 DISK color *Bicycling* v58 no9 p84 O 2017
  QUICK NEO color *Bicycling* v58 no8 p(Sp)4 S 2017
  RIDE HARD, LOUNGE HARDER color *Bicycling* v58 no10 p78 N/D 2017
  ROCKSHOX REVERB 1X REMOTE color *Bicycling* v58 no8 p66 S 2017
  "SHOULD I GET A FULL-SUSPENSION OR HARDTAIL MOUNTAIN BIKE?" color *Bicycling* v58 no3 p28 Ap 2017
  "SHOULD I GET A ROAD BIKE WITH SUSPENSION?" color *Bicycling* v58 no3 p86 Ap 2017
  SILCA PISTA FLOOR PUMP color *Bicycling* v58 no9 p80 O 2017
  Stan's NoTubes ZTR Avion Pro Wheels color *Bicycling* v58 no4 p78 My 2017
  THAT FRESH TIRE FEEL color *Bicycling* v58 no7 p84 Ag 2017
  TREK ÉMONDA SLR 9 DISC, PROJECT ONE color *Bicycling* v58 no9 p74 O 2017

Ypma, Sylvia
  RAILWAY POST OFFICE color *Model Railroader* v84 no2 p24 F 2017

YSL Beauté Inc.
  The Face STAZ Lindes C. ELLENBERG color *Vogue* v207 no1 p37 Ja 2017

Yttrup, Ginny L.
  Home *Publishers Weekly* v264 no7 p57 F 13 2017

Yu, Andrea
  The Benefits of Encouraging STEM to Young Girls color *Maclean's* v130 no3 p63 Ap 2017
  HOW MEDICINAL CANNABIS HELPED A CANCER SURVIVOR LIVE AGAIN color *Maclean's* v129 no40 p61 O 10 2016
  LIFE ON THE BIG SCREEN WITH TYPE 1 DIABETES color *Maclean's* v129 no48/49 p38 D 5 2016
  THE POWER OF MENTORS AND SPONSORS *Maclean's* v130 no3 p59 Ap 2017

Yu, Antony W.
  Decarboxylative borylation color *Science* v356 no6342 p1045 Je 9 2017

Yu, C.-h.
  Observation of coherent elastic neutrino-nucleus scattering diag *Science* v357 no6356 p1123 S 15 2017

YU, CHARLES
  SUBTEXT® cartoon color *Wired* v25 no1 p46 Ja 2017

YU, CHRISTINE
  Flight Club color *Runner's World* v52 no4 p48 My 2017

Yu, Hang
  Imaging the distribution of transient viscosity after the 2016 Mw 7.1 Kumamoto earthquake map *Science* v356 no6334 p163 Ap 14 2017

Yu, Hao

Yu, Hongbing
  Why Are they Silent? *Society* v53 no6 p625 D 2016

Yu, Hongtao
  Mitotic transcription and waves of gene reactivation during mitotic exit color graph *Science* v357 no6359 p119 O 6 2017

Yu, Howard
  AlphaGo and the Declining Advantage of Big Companies *Harvard Business Review Digital Articles* p2 Mr 24 2016
  The Best Companies Aren't Afraid to Replace Their Most Profitable Products *Harvard Business Review Digital Articles* p2 Jl 14 2016

Yu, Hui-yong
  Selling Trump's D.C. Hotel Wouldn't Be Easy *Bloomberg Businessweek* no4505 p40 D 26 2016

Yu, Jennifer—Interviews
  Author You'll Love JENNIFER YU color *Seventeen* v76 no3 p19 My 2017

Yu, Jing
  Restoring auditory cortex plasticity in adult mice by restricting thalamic adenosine signaling graph *Science* v356 no6345 p1352 Je 30 2017

Yu, Jin-Quan
  Formation of α-chiral centers by asymmetric β-C(sp3)–H arylation, alkenylation, and alkynylation bibl diag *Science* v355 no6324 p499 F 3 2017

Yu, Ke
  Rescue of exhausted CD8 T cells by PD-1–targeted therapies is CD28-dependent bw diag graph *Science* v355 no6332 p1423 Mr 31 2017

Yu, Kun-Hsing
  Artificial intelligence in research color *Science* v357 no6346 p28 Jl 7 2017
  Promoting human rights through science color *Science* v357 no6359 p34 O 6 2017

Yu, Lintao
  Linked In *Bloomberg Businessweek* no4538 pC1 S 18 2017

Yu, Peng
  Palladium-catalyzed carbon-sulfur or carbon-phosphorus bond metathesis by reversible arylation diag *Science* v356 no6342 p1059 Je 9 2017

Yu, Rin-rin
  HAVING "THE TALK ": How seniors can have a serious conversation with their adult children *Washingtonian Magazine* v52 no8 p154 My 2017
  A HELPING HAND: What to do when it's time to find care for your parents *Washingtonian Magazine* v52 no8 p156 My 2017
  Something Old, Something New [Cover story] color diag *Log Home Living* v34 no4 p60 My 2017
  TO YOUR HEALTH: Physicians and specialists recommend baseline health exams to prolong active lifestyle *Washingtonian Magazine* v52 no8 p150 My 2017

Yu, Shan
  Decarboxylative borylation color *Science* v356 no6342 p1045 Je 9 2017

Yu, Timothy
  Moon *New York Times Magazine* p19 Ap 30 2017

Yu, Verna
  I-Spy in China: a revival of Mao-era paranoia? color *America* v216 no12 p16 My 29 2017
  Rule of Law and 'Western' Notions Worry Beijing color *America* v216 no3 p15 F 6 2017

Yu, Xiaofei
  The intestinal microbiota regulates body composition through NFIL3 and the circadian clock diag *Science* v357 no6354 p912 S 1 2017

Yu, Xuekui
  Atomic structure of the human cytomegalovirus capsid with its securing tegument layer of pp150 color *Science* v356 no6345 p1350 Je 30 2017

Yu, Yao-Qing
  Molecular and neural basis of contagious itch behavior in mice bibl diag *Science* v355 no6329 p1072 Mr 10 2017

Yu, Yongjoon
  Double-heterojunction nanorod light-responsive LEDs for display

Hidden dynamics in the unfolding of individual bacteriorhodopsin proteins bibl diag *Science* v355 no6328 p945 Mr 3 2017

applications bibl color graph *Science* v355 no6325 p616 F 10 2017

Yu, Zhi-Chao

"Perfect" designer chromosome V and behavior of a ring derivative diag *Science* v355 no6329 p1046 Mr 10 2017

Yu, Zhiyang

Segregation-induced ordered superstructures at general grain boundaries in a nickel-bismuth alloy color *Science* v357 no6359 p97 O 6 2017

Yu Huang

Ultrafine jagged platinum nanowires enable ultrahigh mass activity for the oxygen reduction reaction bibl chart graph *Science* v354 no6318 p1414 D 16 2016

Yu Liang

Pathological α-synuclein transmission initiated by binding lymphocyte-activation gene 3 bibl graph *Science* v353 no6307 paah3374-1 S 30 2017

Yu-Qiu Zhang

Pain regulation by non-neuronal cells and inflammation bibl diag *Science* v354 no6312 p572 N 4 2016

Yu Yang

Cultural Stereotypes May Make You a Less Ethical Negotiator *Harvard Business Review Digital Articles* p2 Ja 8 2016

Yuan, Andy H.

A bacterial global regulator forms a prion bibl color diag graph *Science* v355 no6321 p1 Ja 13 2017

Yuan, Jada

Aziz Ansari Is From a Red State, Too: Even though he is the latest comic ambassador for New York neuroses img *New York* v50 no9 p79 My 1 2017

Elisabeth Moss: The Handmaid's Tale's star can't help turning her characters into feminist heroes, even if she's just trying to play a human img *New York* v50 no9 p16 My 1 2017

FINANCIAL ADVICE FROM THE STARS color *Bloomberg Businessweek* no4519 p86 Ap 24 2017

Glass Ceiling img *New York* p63 F 20 2017

It's Been Over a Year, and I Still Can't Decide on a Mattress *New York* v50 no9 p73 My 1 2017

NOW, THIS IS A SUPERMODEL: ASHLEY GRAHAM ISN'T A SAMPLE SIZE.: Which is exactly why she's become the face of a movement img *New York* v50 no16 p30 Ag 7 2017

One Part, Three Breakouts img *New York* v49 no21 p104 O 17 2016

PARTY LINES img *New York* v50 no10 p104 My 15 2017

TURN IT UP TO 11 img *New York* v49 no24 p114 N 28 2016

The Year of Living Publicly img *New York* v50 no6 p71 Mr 20 2017

Yuan, Kaiqing

Seismic evidence for partial melting at the root of major hot spot plumes diag graph *Science* v357 no6349 p393 Jl 28 2017

Yuan, Mingjian

Efficient and stable solution-processed planar perovskite solar cells via contact passivation bibl graph *Science* v355 no6326 p722 F 17 2017

Yuan, Peng

Extraordinary and poor color *Science* v356 no6345 p1406 Je 30 2017

Yuan, Yingjin

3D organization of synthetic and scrambled chromosomes diag *Science* v355 no6329 p1050 Mr 10 2017

Bug mapping and fitness testing of chemically synthesized chromosome X diag *Science* v355 no6329 p1048 Mr 10 2017

Deep functional analysis of synII, a 770-kilobase synthetic yeast chromosome diag *Science* v355 no6329 p1047 Mr 10 2017

Engineering the ribosomal DNA in a megabase synthetic chromosome diag *Science* v355 no6329 p1049 Mr 10 2017

"Perfect" designer chromosome V and behavior of a ring derivative diag *Science* v355 no6329 p1046 Mr 10 2017

Yuan Yang

Gene expression profiling–guided clinical precision treatment for patients with endometrial carcinoma bibl color diag *Science* v354 no6319 p33 D 23 2016

Yuanda Gao

Electron optics with p-n junctions in ballistic graphene bibl graph *Science* v353 no6307 p1522 S 30 2016

Yuankai Shi

Cancer precision medicine in China bibl *Science* v354 no6319 p20 D 23 2016

Yuanyang Yao

Gene expression profiling–guided clinical precision treatment for patients with endometrial carcinoma bibl color diag *Science* v354 no6319 p33 D 23 2016

Yubing Guo

Command of active matter by topological defects and patterns bibl graph *Science* v354 no6314 p882 N 18 2016

Yucatán (Mexico : State)—Description & travel

Where to go in 2017 S. Kelso color *Money* v46 no1 p124 Ja/F 2017

Yucca Mountain (Nev.)—Environmental conditions

How to Dispose Of Nuclear Waste color *Bloomberg Businessweek* no4522 p10 My 15 2017

Yuchun Lee

Your Sales Training Is Probably Lackluster. Here's How to Fix It *Harvard Business Review Digital Articles* p2 Je 12 2017

Yudkoff, Royce

BUYING YOUR WAY INTO ENTREPRENEURSHIP color il *Harvard Business Review* v95 no1 p149 Ja/F 2017

Which MBAs Make More: Consultants or Small-Business Owners? *Harvard Business Review Digital Articles* p2 Je 28 2016

Why Buying a Company Can Be Better than Starting One *Harvard Business Review Digital Articles* p2 Ap 5 2016

Why More MBAs Should Buy Small Businesses *Harvard Business Review Digital Articles* p2 Mr 25 2016

You Should Consider Buying a Small Business. But When? *Harvard Business Review Digital Articles* p2 F 15 2017

Yue, C.

A human-driven decline in global burned area chart graph map *Science* v356 no6345 p1356 Je 30 2017

Yue, Genevieve

Hoop Dreams color *Film Comment* v53 no1 p63 Ja/F 2017

Unknown Continents: A Conversation with Patricia Zimmermann and Scott MacDonald, authors of The Flaherty: Decades in the Cause of Independent Cinema *Film Quarterly* v71 no1 p104 Fall 2017

YUE, TAO

CASE STUDY: IS HOLACRACY FOR US? color il *Harvard Business Review* v95 no2 p151 Mr/Ap 2017

Yue Pan

Precision medicine development in Beijing *Science* v354 no6319 p61 D 23 2016

Yuefeng Tang

Principles for designing proteins with cavities formed by curved β sheets bibl color graph *Science* v355 no6321 p1 Ja 13 2017

Yueh, Linda

China's Growth: A Brief History *Harvard Business Review Digital Articles* p2 D 9 2015

Why China's Market Crash Is So Unsurprising *Harvard Business Review Digital Articles* p2 Ja 12 2016

YUEN, ISAAC

ME AND GRAVITY *Orion Magazine* v35 no4/5 p112 Jl-O 2016

Yuen, Michael

Exploring genetic suppression interactions on a global scale diag *Science* v354 no6312 p599 N 4 2016

YUEN YUEN ANG

China's Governance Puzzle: Enabling Transparency and Participation in a Single-Party State *Foreign Affairs* v96 no6 p172 N/D 2017

Yufeng Ding

Quality management for precision medicine clinical applications: A consensus from the China Precision Medicine Clinical Research and Application Association bibl *Science* v354 no6319 p11 D 23 2016

Yuguang Fu

Expert consensus on point-of-care testing *Science* v354 no6319 p15 D 23 2016

Recommendations on the management and use of POCT in medical institutions (nosocomial) *Science* v354 no6319 p13 D 23 2016

Yuhas, Daisy

Back to Basics color *Scientific American* v317 no4 p28 O 2017

Yuhgo Yamaguchi

What Health Care Can Learn from the Transformation of Finan-

p52 F 6 2017

I Am Michael Maps Painful Betrayal color *Time* v189 no4 p51 F 6 2017

I Don't Feel at Home Aims for the Heart color *Time* v189 no7/8 p110 F 27 2017

In Life, the Blob from Mars Is Small and Very Scary color *Time* v189 no12 p56 Ap 3 2017

It Comes at Night and the High Art of the New Horror color *Time* v189 no23 p49 Je 19 2017

Jackie Places the First Lady Under a Microscope color *Time* v188 no24 p63 D 12 2016

A Jersey Girl Dreams Big color *Time* v190 no8 p50 Ag 28 2017

Jonathan Demme color *Time* v189 no18 p15 My 15 2017

The Joneses Tries to Shake Up the 'Hood color *Time* v188 no18 p44 O 31 2016

The Kids of American Honey Hit the Road With a Sweet-and-Sour Hustle color *Time* v188 no14 p55 O 10 2016

King Arthur as a Knockabout Guy color *Time* v189 no19 p54 My 22 2017

Kristen Stewart Sets Personal Shopper Ablaze color *Time* v189 no10 p51 Mr 20 2017

La La Land: Haters Shall Be Lovers color *Time* v188 no24 p62 D 12 2016

Landline Is a Message from a Lost World: the 1990s color *Time* v190 no5 p58 Jl 31 2017

A Leading Man Saves Hacksaw Ridge from Hackdom color *Time* v188 no19 p56 N 7 2016

Lego Batman Finds the Funny In Existential Angst color *Time* v189 no6 p50 F 20 2017

The Light Touch color *Time* v189 no6 p38 F 20 2017

Love Takes Bravery Too color *Time* v190 no16/17 p103 O 23 2017

Medieval Laughs for the Modern Day color *Time* v190 no2/3 p90 Jl 10-17 2017

Minions, Delightfully Relegated to Their Proper Place color *Time* v190 no2/3 p90 Jl 10-17 2017

The Miracle of Dunkirk color *Time* v190 no5 p48 Jl 31 2017

A Monster Calls Offers a Big, Less-Friendly Giant color *Time* v189 no3 p57 Ja 16 2017

Moonlight Enchants by Revealing Itself In a Thousand Facets color *Time* v188 no18 p43 O 31 2016

More Notes of a Native Son color *Time* v189 no7/8 p109 F 27 2017

Newtown: A Vivid Portrait of a Grieving Community *Time* v188 no15 p52 O 17 2016

Oscar Nominee My Life As a Zucchini Is a Stop-Motion Marvel color *Time* v189 no7/8 p110 F 27 2017

Paterson Sings the Poetry of Everyday Life In the City color *Time* v189 no4 p50 Ja 23 2017

Pattinson Packs a Punch In Good Time color *Time* v190 no7 p51 Ag 21 2017

A Portrait of Male Beauty In Anguish color *Time* v190 no9 p56 S 4 2017

Return of the Kingsman color *Time* v190 no13 p65 O 2 2017

The Rights of the Heart, Interpreted With Beauty by Loving color *Time* v188 no20 p49 N 14 2016

Shane, With Claws and Bloodlust to Spare color *Time* v189 no9 p56 Mr 13 2017

A Slice of Childhood Heaven In the Sunshine State color *Time* v190 no15 p56 O 16 2017

The Soul of an Old Machine color *Time* v190 no9 p56 S 4 2017

Striking It Logan Lucky color *Time* v190 no8 p48 Ag 28 2017

A Sublime Farewell to Stanton In Lucky color *Time* v190 no14 p51 O 9 2017

Summer Movie Preview *Time* v189 no20 p46 My 29 2017

T2's Beloved Hooligans Get Older, but Not Wiser color *Time* v189 no11 p59 Mr 27 2017

Tiny Dancers Abound In Song to Song color *Time* v189 no12 p57 Ap 3 2017

Two Stars That Lived-and Shone-Orbiting Each Other color *Time* v189 no3 p10 Ja 16 2017

Valerian's Half-Crazed Space Race color *Time* v190 no5 p59 Jl 31 2017

Valley of Violence Is Hounded by Its True Star color *Time* v188 no19 p57 N 7 2016

Vengeance, the Slow Way color *Time* v189 no6 p50 F 20 2017

Venus and Mars Duke It Out on the Tennis Court color *Time* v190

no13 p64 O 2 2017

When the Film Greats Went to War color *Time* v189 no13 p50 Ap 10 2017

Whose Streets? Is a Ragged, Bracing Protest Document color *Time* v190 no7 p50 Ag 21 2017

The Women Behind Wonder Woman color *Time* v190 no16/17 p103 O 23 2017

Woody Harrelson Turns a Scowl Upside Down In Wilson color *Time* v189 no12 p57 Ap 3 2017

Zookeeper's Wife: Bravery In a Whisper color *Time* v189 no13 p50 Ap 10 2017

ZACHARIN, LINDA

Q: What was the greatest summer read of your life? color *O, The Oprah Magazine* p16 Jl 2017

Zacharis, Thomas

BEWARE THE FURIES *Military History* v33 no6 p62 Mr 2017

The Defence of Sevastopol, 1941-1942: The Soviet Perspective *Military History* v33 no5 p73 Ja 2017

The Spy in Hitler's Inner Circle: Hans-Thilo Schmidt and the Intelligence That Decoded Enigma *Military History* v33 no5 p73 Ja 2017

Titan: The Art of British Power in the Age of Revolution and Napoléon *Military History* v33 no5 p74 Ja 2017

Zachary, G. Pascal

The End of the Line: Cycles of Invention and Discovery: Rethinking the Endless Frontier *Issues in Science & Technology* v33 no4 p87 Summ 2017

Zachary, Julia

ASTRONOMERS HAVE COMBINED C. M. CARLISLE *Sky & Telescope* v133 no4 p12 Ap 2017

Zachary Koehn, J.

Committing to socially responsible seafood color *Science* v356 no6341 p912 Je 1 2017

Zaehle, S.

Comment on "Mycorrhizal association as a primary control of the CO_2 fertilization effect" bibl graph *Science* v355 no6323 p358 Ja 27 2017

Zaeta Motorcycles (Company)

ZAETA 530 SE B. Adams color *Cycle World* v56 no2 p34 Mr 2017

Zagajewski, Adam, 1945-

Double Focus A. Domestico bw *Commonweal* v144 no11 p37 Je 16 2017

Riffs and Displacements: Adam Zagajewski finds poetry a 'slight exaggeration, until we make our homes in it.' D. FRIED *New York Times Book Review* p25 Jl 23 2017

The Triumph of Mrs. L bw *New York Review of Books* v64 no5 p26 Mr 23 2017

WITHOUT A FIGHT A. Zagajewski *Harper's Magazine* v334 no2002 p15 Mr 2017

Zagare, Liena

Your tax dollars at work color *Columbia Journalism Review* v56 no1 p30 Spr 2017

Zagg Inc.

ZAGG RUGGED BOOK KEYBOARD CASE FOR THE iPAD PRO S. BELLAMY color *Macworld - Digital Edition* v33 no11 p54 N 2016

Zagorski, Marcin

Decoding of position in the developing neural tube from antiparallel morphogen gradients diag *Science* v356 no6345 p1379 Je 30 2017

Zagt, R.

Persistent effects of pre-Columbian plant domestication on Amazonian forest composition bibl chart graph map *Science* v355 no6328 p925 Mr 3 2017

Zaha Hadid Architects (Company)

Going It Alone C. TURNER *Architectural Record* v205 no4 p53 Ap 2017

Zahedi, Firooz

COLLECTED WISDOM V. LOWRY color *Architectural Digest* v73 no12 p96 D 2016

Zaheer, Atif

Mismatch repair deficiency predicts response of solid tumors to PD-1 blockade chart graph *Science* v357 no6349 p409 Jl 28 2017

ZAHL, DAVID

Justify Yourself bw cartoon *Christianity Today* v61 no1 p34 Ja/F 2017

Zahl, Simeon

Suggestions or Commands? bw *Commonweal* v143 no20 p9 D 16 2016

ZAHN, AMY

The Question *O, The Oprah Magazine* p18 S 2017

ZAHN, CLEMENS

Chords & Discords bw color *Downbeat* v84 no10 p10 O 2017

Zahn, Laura M.

BUILDING ON NATURE'S DESIGN [Cover story] color *Science* v355 no6329 p1038 Mr 10 2017

A FANTASTIC VOYAGE IN GENOMICS color *Science* v357 no6359 p56 O 6 2017

GENES UNDER PRESSURE color *Science* v354 no6308 p52 O 7 2016

Zahn, Steve, 1968——Interviews

STEVE ZAHN GOES APE D. Franich color *Entertainment Weekly* no1471 p52 Je 23 2017

Zahn, Timothy

Thrawn *Publishers Weekly* v264 no22 p61 My 29 2017

Zahner, L. William

The Elements of Value: Interaction *Harvard Business Review* v94 no11 p18 N 2016

Zahniser, Steven

Increased Demand for U.S. Agricultural Exports Would Likely Lead to More U.S. Jobs *Amber Waves: The Economics of Food, Farming, Natural Resources, & Rural America* p1 Je 2017

Zahradnik, Georg

Research: Arab Inventors Make the U.S. More Innovative *Harvard Business Review Digital Articles* p2 F 23 2017

Zaidi, Saima

CRACKING THE CONTENT AREAS color *Literacy Today (2411-7862)* v34 no3 p32 N/D 2016

Zaimi, Klodian

Changing climate shifts timing of European floods color graph *Science* v357 no6351 p588 Ag 11 2017

Zaino, Gene

Your Company Needs Independent Workers *Harvard Business Review Digital Articles* p2 N 23 2015

Zaiqi Pan

A selective insecticidal protein from Pseudomonas for controlling corn rootworms bibl chart graph *Science* v354 no6312 p634 N 4 2016

Zaire 74: The African Artists (Music)

International Studies HADLEY color *Downbeat* v84 no9 p68 S 2017

Zaiss, Dietmar M.

Local amplifiers of IL-4Rα-mediated macrophage activation promote repair in lung and liver diag *Science* v356 no6342 p1076 Je 9 2017

ZAITCHIK, ALEXANDER

Trump vs. Warren color *New Republic* v248 no4 p12 Ap 2017

Zajac, D. M.

Strong coupling of a single electron in silicon to a microwave photon bibl graph *Science* v355 no6321 p1 Ja 13 2017

Zak, D. R.

Comment on "Mycorrhizal association as a primary control of the CO2 fertilization effect" bibl graph *Science* v355 no6323 p358 Ja 27 2017

Zak, Dan

OUR NUCLEAR COMPLEX C. SCHAEFFER-DUFFY color *America* v215 no19 p35 D 19 2016

Zak, Marcelo

Forest conservation: Remember Gran Chaco bibl color *Science* v355 no6324 p465 F 3 2017

ZAK, PAUL J.

CAN NEUROSCIENCE HELP US UNDERSTAND TRUST AT WORK?: INTERACTION color *Harvard Business Review* v95 no2 p18 Mr/Ap 2017

THE NEUROSCIENCE OF TRUST color *Harvard Business Review* v95 no1 p84 Ja/F 2017

Why Your Brain Loves Good Storytelling *Harvard Business Review Digital Articles* p2 O 28 2014

Zak, Sean

Feels Like the First Time color *Golf Magazine* v59 no4 p76 Ap 2017

Grin to Win color *Golf Magazine* v58 no11 p23 N 2016

His Brother's Looper color *Golf Magazine* v59 no1 p76 Ja 2017

MASTER STROKES 4 shots to go low [Cover story] color *Golf Magazine* v59 no6 p75 Je 2017

Out of The Loop color *Sports Illustrated* v127 no1 p16 Jl 3 2017

"The Greatest Shot I Ever Saw" color *Golf Magazine* v59 no2 p65 F 2017

VINTAGE FORD color *Golf Magazine* v59 no4 p94 Ap 2017

What He's Really Like color *Golf Magazine* v59 no1 p67 Ja 2017

ZAKARIA, FAREED

Failing to Deliver: Edward Luce argues that the tradition of liberty is now under mortal threat *New York Times Book Review* p9 Jl 30 2017

Populism on the March color *Foreign Affairs* v95 no6 p9 N/D 2016

The Year in Reading [Cover story] *New York Times Book Review* p8 D 25 2016

ZAKARIA, RAFIA

Being Muslim at the airport *Christian Century* v134 no22 p12 O 25 2017

They'll Blame Us *New York Times Book Review* p9 N 13 2016

White Women and the Specter of Islam color il *Nation* v305 no5 p20 Ag 28 2017

Zakeeruddin, Shaik M.

Incorporation of rubidium cations into perovskite solar cells improves photovoltaic performance bibl graph *Science* v354 no6309 p206 O 14 2016

Zakharenko, Stanislav S.

Restoring auditory cortex plasticity in adult mice by restricting thalamic adenosine signaling graph *Science* v356 no6345 p1352 Je 30 2017

Zakharova, Maria

THE IMPORTANCE OF ASKING Questions K. Couric color *InStyle* v24 no9 p204 S 2017

Zakheim, Dov S.

Jerusalem's Reformer D. J. WOLPE *Weekly Standard* v22 no13 p29 D 5 2016

ZAKI, NORA

Teaching Arabic to Non-Native Speakers [Cover story] *Islamic Horizons* v46 no2 p32 Mr/Ap 2017

With More Than a Prayer *Islamic Horizons* v46 no1 p38 Ja/F 2017

Zakian, Virginia

Not just Salk color *Science* v357 no6356 p1105 S 15 2017

Zakin, Carly

A BOARDROOM OF ONE'S OWN D. GILMORE color *Vanity Fair* v59 no7 p55 Summ 2017

Carly Zakin And Danielle Weisberg Want You to Get The News A. M. Cox *New York Times Magazine* p66 Ap 30 2017

Zakon, Harold H.

Interacting amino acid replacements allow poison frogs to evolve epibatidine resistance chart diag graph *Science* v357 no6357 p1261 S 22 2017

ZALAN, KIRA

Breast Cancer Warrior *Ms.* v26 no4 p17 Wint 2016

Zalasiewicz, Jan

A HISTORY IN LAYERS [Cover story] color graph *Scientific American* v315 no3 p30 S 2016

Zalaznick, Matt

Use the News to Teach Reading Comprehension bw *Education Digest* v83 no3 p12 N 2017

ZALDARRIAGA, MATIAS

A COSMIC CONTROVERSY color *Scientific American* v317 no1 p5 Jl 2017

ZALESKI, ANDREW

GET OUT OF HIS LANE color *Fortune* v176 no3 p33 S 1 2017

THE JOY OF AX cartoon color *Men's Health* v32 no8 p100 O 2017

Zaleski, Carol

Anxious about anxiety *Christian Century* v134 no14 p35 Jl 5 2017

Blaise Pascal, blessed doubter *Christian Century* v134 no18 p35 Ag 30 2017

The Buddha and the Pantocrator *Christian Century* v134 no2 p33 Ja 18 2017

Faith Matters *Christian Century* v134 no11 p38 My 24 2017

Faith Matters *Christian Century* v134 no17 p42 Ag 16 2017

Faith Matters *Christian Century* v134 no2 p36 Ja 18 2017

Faith Matters C. Zaleski *Christian Century* v134 no17 p42 Ag 16 2017

Identity as a calling *Christian Century* v133 no24 p35 N 23 2016

Reading and tweeting Augustine *Christian Century* v134 no10 p59 My 10 2017

A toast to Ramanuja *Christian Century* v134 no6 p37 Mr 15 2017

What's worth saving *Christian Century* v134 no22 p37 O 25 2017

Zaleski, Glenn

GLENN ZALESKI B. Zimmerman color *Downbeat* v84 no5 p27 My 2017

ZALESKI, LUKE

What Kind of Father Lets His Son Play Football? color *GQ: Gentlemen's Quarterly* v97 no9 p132 S 2017

Zaleski, Olivia

Airbnb Finds China Is A Crowded House color *Bloomberg Businessweek* no4527 p23 Je 19 2017

Airbnb Inches Its Way Into China color *Bloomberg Businessweek* no4503 p30 D 12 2016

Jeff Bezos Goes Grocery Shopping color *Bloomberg Businessweek* no4517 p21 Ap 3 2017

Pet Food That Comes With an Oil Painting color *Bloomberg Businessweek* no4501 p30 N 28 2016

Uber's Campsites color *Bloomberg Businessweek* no4510 p24 F 6 2017

ZALEWSKI, DANIEL

THE FACTORY OF FAKES cartoon color *New Yorker* v92 no39 p66 N 28 2016

Zalik, David

THE MIDDLEMAN OF MIDDLE AMERICA L. GENSLER color *Forbes* v200 no2 p62 S 5 2017

ZAMAN, FARIHAH

The Bad Batch color *Film Comment* v53 no3 p70 My/Je 2017

Zamata, Sasheer, 1986-

ABOVE & BEYOND diag *New Yorker* v93 no24 p12 Ag 21 2017

Zamata, Sasheer, 1986——Interviews

Sasheer Zamata S. Pulia color *InStyle* v24 no7 p54 Jl 2017

Zambia

A Love Letter to Zambia P. Guzmán color *Conde Nast Traveler* v52 no2 p102 F 2017

Zambia—Description & travel

ZAMBIA + BOTSWANA P. GUZMAN color *Conde Nast Traveler* v52 no4 p44 Ap 2017

Zambians

Betiana Namambwe Mubili: 1988 – 2017 A. A. DAVIS color *Maclean's* v130 no10 p130 N 2017

Zambon, F.

Localized aliphatic organic material on the surface of Ceres bibl graph *Science* v355 no6326 p719 F 17 2017

Zamboni, Talia

And The Winning Photo Is... *British Heritage Travel* v38 no1 p80 Ja/F 2017

ZAMBRANO, JOSEPH

Ed Sheeran color *O, The Oprah Magazine* p25 Jl 2017

Issa Rae color *O, The Oprah Magazine* p28 Ag 2017

John Legend color *O, The Oprah Magazine* p23 Ja 2017

Kate Mara color *O, The Oprah Magazine* p23 Je 2017

Merle Dandridge color *O, The Oprah Magazine* p24 Mr 2017

Sterling K. Brown color *O, The Oprah Magazine* p30 S 2017

ZAMF, ZACHARY

STRAIGHT CIS FOLKS STILL DON'T GET US: Data reveals cisgender attitudes towards trans people haven't changed that much color *Advocate* no1091 p21 Je/Jl 2017

Zamir, Dani

A chemical genetic roadmap to improved tomato flavor bibl graph *Science* v355 no6323 p391 Ja 27 2017

ZAMMETT RUDDY, ERIN

deal with playdate drama color graph *Parents* v92 no4 p58 Ap 2017

raise a good sport color graph *Parents* v92 no5 p36 My 2017

when kids interrupt *Parents* v92 no2 p42 F 2017

Zamora, Javier

Unaccompanied *Publishers Weekly* v264 no34 p88 Ag 21 2017

Zamosky, Lisa

The Best Cure for Obamacare Woes color *Money* v45 no10 p36 N 2016

Keeping an Eye on Obamacare diag *Money* v46 no3 p23 Ap 2017

Zampelli, Angela

Transcriptional activation of RagD GTPase controls mTORC1 and promotes cancer growth diag *Science* v356 no6343 p1188 Je 16 2017

Zampese, Enrico

Dopamine oxidation mediates mitochondrial and lysosomal dysfunction in Parkinson's disease graph *Science* v357 no6357 p1255 S 22 2017

Zampieri, Luca

An accreting pulsar with extreme properties drives an ultraluminous x-ray source in NGC 5907 bibl chart graph *Science* v355 no6327 p817 F 24 2017

Zamudio, Natasha

The DNA methyltransferase DNMT3C protects male germ cells from transposon activity bibl diag graph *Science* v354 no6314 p909 N 18 2016

ZANDER, BOB

Chords & Discords color *Downbeat* v84 no7 p10 Jl 2017

Zander, Joakim

The Believer *Publishers Weekly* v263 no48 p48 N 28 2016

ZANDER, LISA

Teaching Biology in the Field: Importance, Challenges, and Solutions *BioScience* v67 no6 p558 Je 2017

Zandonatti, Michelle A.

Structural basis for antibody-mediated neutralization of Lassa virus [Cover story] color diag *Science* v356 no6341 p923 Je 1 2017

Zandvliet, Martin

Land of Mine M. J. ROWIN color *Film Comment* v53 no1 p86 Ja/F 2017

Land of Mine *New Yorker* v93 no3 p10 Mr 6 2017

Zane, Danny

Why Companies Are Blind to Child Labor *Harvard Business Review Digital Articles* p2 Ja 28 2016

Zane, Frank

Get to Know: GAT SPORT J. SCHILDHOUSE color *Muscle & Performance* v9 no7 p30 Jl 2017

Zane, Richard

How We Transformed Emergency Care at Our Hospital *Harvard Business Review Digital Articles* p2 D 17 2015

ZANE, ZACHARY

ALL ABOARD THE ZANDWAGON: Rising agency reflects the diversity of beauty with queer, trans, Muslim, punk, and plus-size models *Advocate* no1093 p9 O/N 2017

BLURRED LINES: CHEMSEX & CONSENT: It's time to talk about the elephant in the room *Advocate* no1093 p58 O/N 2017

Five Minutes to PrEP color *Advocate* no1090 p55 Ap 2017

HIV TESTING DOESN'T HAVE TO SUCK color *Advocate* no1091 p52 Je/Jl 2017

A LITTLE HELP FROM YOUR FRIENDS: Are friends with benefits actually benefiting you? color *Advocate* no1091 p107 Je/Jl 2017

Zanetti, Maurizio

Chromosomal chaos silences immune surveillance chart color *Science* v355 no6322 p249 Ja 20 2017

Zang, Ketao

Robust epitaxial growth of two-dimensional heterostructures, multiheterostructures, and superlattices color *Science* v357 no6353 p788 Ag 25 2017

Zangardi, Rob

Jennifer Lopez HER BEST EVER E. Wilson color *InStyle* v24 no8 p78 Ag 2017

Zangwill, Andrew

Maxwell's Enduring Legacy: A Scientific History of the Cavendish Laboratory *Physics Today* v70 no8 p60 Ag 2017

Zanichkowsky, Stephen

THE CONVERSATION color *Atlantic* v318 no5 p12 D 2016

Zanini, Michele

Excess Management Is Costing the U.S. $3 Trillion Per Year *Harvard Business Review Digital Articles* p2 S 5 2016

A Few Unicorns Are No Substitute for a Competitive, Innovative Economy color graph *Harvard Business Review Digital Articles* p2 F 8 2017

More of Us Are Working in Big Bureaucratic Organizations than Ever Before *Harvard Business Review Digital Articles* p2 Jl 5

Zasada, Christin

Fructose-driven glycolysis supports anoxia resistance in the naked mole-rat diag graph *Science* v356 no6335 p307 Ap 21 2017

Zaslav, David

THE YOUNG TRUMP A. Rice img *New York* p21 F 9 2017

Zaslavsky, Alan M.

Do Doctors Get Worse as They Get Older? *Harvard Business Review Digital Articles* p2 My 23 2017

ZAVAGNIN, ANTHONY J.

Filling Empty Seats color *America* v215 no13 p25 O 31 2016

ZAVALA-HURTADO, J. ALEJANDRO

The Role of Botanical Gardens in the Conservation of Cactaceae *BioScience* v66 no12 p1057 D 1 2016

Zaveloff, Rebekah

Tricks of the Trade C. Swanson color *House Beautiful* v159 no2 p69 Mr 2017

Zavislan, James

GO-TO GLASS color *Field & Stream* v121 no6 p75 N 2016

PEAK GLASS color *Field & Stream* v122 no4 p69 S 2017

Zavrtanik, D.

Observation of a large-scale anisotropy in the arrival directions of cosmic rays above 8×10^{18} eV *Science* v357 no6357 p1266 S 22 2017

Zavrtanik, M.

Observation of a large-scale anisotropy in the arrival directions of cosmic rays above 8×10^{18} eV *Science* v357 no6357 p1266 S 22 2017

Zawada, A.

Observation of coherent elastic neutrino-nucleus scattering diag *Science* v357 no6356 p1123 S 15 2017

Zawadzki, Matthew J.

The Two Main Sources of Stress for High-Status Workers *Harvard Business Review Digital Articles* p2 Ap 25 2016

Zawiła-Niedźwiecki, Tomasz

Positive biodiversity-productivity relationship predominant in global forests bibl chart graph map *Science* v354 no6309 paaf8957-1 O 14 2016

ZAYA, DAVID N.

Long-Term Trends in Midwestern Milkweed Abundances and Their Relevance to Monarch Butterfly Declines *BioScience* v67 no4 p343 Ap 2017

Zayed, A.

Chronic exposure to neonicotinoids reduces honey bee health near corn crops diag *Science* v356 no6345 p1395 Je 30 2017

Zaza (Theatrical production)

Leoncavallo: Zazà R. Pines *Opera News* v81 no5 p55 N 2016

ZAZO, ERICA

Up the River *Backpacker* v45 no2 p27 Mr 2017

Zderic, A. M.

Observation of coherent elastic neutrino-nucleus scattering diag *Science* v357 no6356 p1123 S 15 2017

Zea, Natalie

The Detour D. Holbrook color *TV Guide* v65 no7 p41 F 13 2017

Zeal Optics Inc.

EYEWEAR M. HORJUS color diag *Backpacker* v45 no3 p112 Ap 2017

Zealandia

Zealandia may be eighth continent T. SUMNER map *Science News* v191 no5 p11 Mr 18 2017

Zebker, Howard

Global drainage patterns and the origins of topographic relief on Earth, Mars, and Titan diag graph *Science* v356 no6339 p727 My 19 2017

Zebra danio

FISH'S FECUNDITY A BOON TO LABS P. Edmonds color *National Geographic* v232 no3 p25 S 2017

Macrophage, a long-distance middleman M. Guilliams bibl color *Science* v355 no6331 p1258 Mr 24 2017

Zebra finch

Lost in Translation M. L. Callaghan *Audubon* v119 no1 p15 Spr 2017

Zebra mussel

THE GREAT TAKEOVER D. EGAN color map *Discover* v38 no8 p56 O 2017

Zebras

What in the World? color *National Geographic Kids* no470 p29 My 2017

Zech, Charles

Get your money in order color graph *U.S. Catholic* v82 no1 p30 Ja 2017

Zecheng Zuo

Photoactivation and inactivation of Arabidopsis cryptochrome 2 bibl graph *Science* v354 no6310 p343 O 21 2016

Zecher, Linda

News Briefs *Publishers Weekly* v263 no39 p5 S 26 2016

Zeckhauser, Richard

Consumer Warning Labels Aren't Working *Harvard Business Review Digital Articles* p2 N 30 2016

Thomas Crombie Schelling (1921–2016) color *Science* v355 no6327 p800 F 24 2017

Zee, Anthony

Group Theory in a Nutshell for Physicists P. Van Isacker *Physics Today* v70 no1 p58 Ja 2017

Zee, Ginger

THE POPULAR MECHANICS GUIDE TO SELF-SUFFICIEN-CY [Cover story] color *Popular Mechanics* p55 F 2017

Zee, Ginger, 1981-

LITTLE MAN, STRONG WOMAN G. Zee color *Women's Health* v14 no7 p78 S 2017

Zeedyk, Genmyo Jana—Interviews

Anchorage Zen Community W. Joan Biddlecombe color *Tricycle: The Buddhist Review* v26 no4 p24 Summ 2017

Zegart, Amy B.

Trump Versus the Spies: All presidents clash with their intelligence experts, but the hostility the new administration has displayed is unusual--and risky *Hoover Digest: Research & Opinion on Public Policy* no2 p117 Spr 2017

Zegelman, Jane

Steady Diet of Depression *American History* v52 no1 p56 Ap 2017

Zegura, Dan

SWING SET M. Chwasky, M. Dee et al color *Golf Magazine* v59 no3 p96 Mr 2017

Zehme, Bill

CHILLI PEPPER cartoon *Chicago* v66 no1 p170 Ja 2017

CHRISTIE HEFNER cartoon *Chicago* v66 no2 p160 F 2017

FATHER PFLEGER color *Chicago* v65 no12 p152 D 2016

JEFF GARLIN [Cover story] color *Chicago* v66 no6 p132 Je 2017

JESSE WHITE color *Chicago* v66 no5 p148 My 2017

KAREN LEWIS *Chicago* v66 no9 p160 S 2017

MAVIS STAPLES cartoon *Chicago* v66 no11 p168 N 2016

RICH KOZ color *Chicago* v66 no10 p152 O 2017

RICH MELMAN *Chicago* v66 no7 p104 Jl 2017

ROBERT FALLS cartoon *Chicago* v66 no3 p148 Mr 2017

SUGAR RAUTBORD cartoon *Chicago* v66 no4 p132 Ap 2017

VICTOR SKREBNESKI color *Chicago* v66 no8 p132 Ag 2017

WHAT CANCER TAUGHT ME color *Chicago* v66 no1 p70 Ja 2017

Zehr, Jonathan P.

How microbes survive in the open ocean color diag *Science* v357 no6352 p646 Ag 18 2017

ZEICHNER, NAOMI

'Bad and Boujee' *New York Times Magazine* p65 Mr 12 2017

Zeid, Ahmed Abu

O Brotherhood, Where Art Thou? *Foreign Affairs* v96 no2 p164 Mr/Ap 2017

Zeidan, Rami

Meet Yr Match! R. Nelson color *Glamour* v115 no5 p116 My 2017

Zeidan, Rodrigo

How to Quantify Sustainability's Impact on Your Bottom Line *Harvard Business Review Digital Articles* p2 S 13 2017

Zeidler, Marian

BOLD BEAUTY color *Sunset* v238 no1 p42 Ja 2017

ZEIDNER, LISA

'The Most Honest Place' *New York Times Book Review* p20 O 2 2016

ZEIGLER, CONNIE

Drags to Riches color *Indianapolis Monthly* v42 no2 p20 O 2017

Extra! Extra! Pie-eating contests, swimming, junk food. For years, the annual Indianapolis Recorder picnics were a summertime highlight *Indianapolis Monthly* v12 no40 p22 Ag 2017

News Splash: Elated by the word that World War II had ended, Indy citizens took to the streets to cheer, party, wave flags—and even skivvies-dip on Monument Circle bw *Indianapolis Monthly* v41 no2 p22 S 2017

Queen for a Day: Starlet Norma Marla posed as Nefertiti for a bust by German sculptor Adolph Wolter, who made his mark on the local architectural scene *Indianapolis Monthly* p26 N 2017

A Short Ride *Indianapolis Monthly* p20 My 2017

Speed King: The first commissioner of NASCAR, "Cannon Ball" Baker, was already a legend in his own time *Indianapolis Monthly* v40 no11 p19 Jl 2017

Talk of the Town: In a city temporarily teeming with Shriners, silent-film star Harold Lloyd was the most famous man in a fez *Indianapolis Monthly* v40 no10 p21 Je 2017

Trailblazing Trip bw *Indianapolis Monthly* p20 Ap 2017

Zeihan, Peter

The Absent Superpower: The Shale Revolution and a World Without America *Publishers Weekly* v264 no26 p146c Je 26 2017

Zeisel, Eva

Eva Zeisel B. LIBBY color *Treasures* v5 no5 p19 Ap/My 2016

ZEISLER, ANDI

Mad Futures *New York Times Book Review* p15 D 11 2016

Zeiss International (Company)

PRIME WIDE J. Silber color diag *Popular Photography* v80 no11 p80 D 2016

Zeitler, Mary

LOONEY FUMES color *Women's Health* v14 no4 p40 My 2017

Zeitlin, Brigitte

FINISH STRONG color *Women's Health* v14 no8 p32 O 2017

Zeitz, Barney

People C. Kennel-Shank color *Christian Century* v133 no24 p20 N 23 2016

Zeleke, Aklilu

Updating the Two Cultures: How Structures Can Promote Interdisciplinary Cultures *Change* v48 no6 p28 N/D 2016

Zelenay, Piotr

Direct atomic-level insight into the active sites of a high-performance PGM-free ORR catalyst diag graph *Science* v357 no6350 p479 Ag 4 2017

Zelevinsky, Vladimir

Spartak Timofeevich Belyaev *Physics Today* v70 no6 p72 Je 2017

Zeller, Frauke

What a Hitchhiking Robot Can Teach Us About Automated Coworkers *Harvard Business Review Digital Articles* p2 D 18 2014

Zeller, Jared—Interviews

Bayou Boogaloo color *New Orleans Magazine* v51 no7 p27 My 2017

Zellers-Frederick, Andrew A.

CLOSE CALL AT CROOKED BILLET cartoon color map *Military History* v34 no1 p48 My 2017

Zellmer, Amanda

Family-friendly science cartoon *Science* v354 no6315 p1070 N 25 2016

Zellweger, Renée

WHY I LOVE color *InStyle* v24 no11 p220 N 2017

Zellweger, Renee, 1969-—Interviews

Renée ZELLWEGER cartoon *Vanity Fair* p196 Hollywood 2017 Supplement

Zemach, Itay

A chemical genetic roadmap to improved tomato flavor bibl graph *Science* v355 no6323 p391 Ja 27 2017

Zeman, Karel

Adventure Time M. SRAGOW color *Film Comment* v53 no5 p74 S/O 2017

ZEMANOVA, MIRIAM A.

More Training in Animal Ethics Needed for European Biologists *BioScience* v67 no3 p301 Mr 2017

Zemeckis, Robert, 1952-

ALLIED C. Chiarella color *Sound & Vision* v82 no6 p69 Jl/Ag 2017

Allied C. Nashawaty color *Entertainment Weekly* no1442 p40 D 2 2016 Rebellious Special Issue

CASABLANCA REVISITED D. Coggan color *Entertainment Weekly* no1441 p38 N 25 2016

Zemmel, Rodney

How the Best Board Directors Stay Involved *Harvard Business*

Review Digital Articles p2 F 23 2015

Zemmour, Éric

Les Déplorables C. CALDWELL *Weekly Standard* v22 no5 p23 O 10 2016

Zemunik, Graham

Plant-soil feedback and the maintenance of diversity in Mediterranean-climate shrublands bibl graph *Science* v355 no6321 p1 Ja 13 2017

Zen Buddhism

DIANE MUSHO HAMILTON cartoon *Tricycle: The Buddhist Review* v26 no3 p18 Spr 2017

THE MEETING H. SHUKMAN cartoon *Tricycle: The Buddhist Review* v26 no3 p78 Spr 2017

Zen Buddhism—China

Wild Mustard and the Way of Zen W. Johnson color *Tricycle: The Buddhist Review* v26 no4 p27 Summ 2017

Zen Buddhism—Clergy

Anchorage Zen Community W. Joan Biddlecombe color *Tricycle: The Buddhist Review* v26 no4 p24 Summ 2017

Zen Buddhism—Psychology

PERLE BESSERMAN AND MANFRED STEGER *Tricycle: The Buddhist Review* v26 no4 p19 Summ 2017

Zen Buddhists

Michelin Monastic M. Scarles color *Tricycle: The Buddhist Review* v26 no4 p17 Summ 2017

Zendaya, 1996-

My LIST L. McCarthy color *Harper's Bazaar* no3650 p80 F 2017

Tom HOLLAND *Interview* v47 no5 p50 Je/Jl 2017

Zendaya color *InStyle* v24 no7 p78 Jl 2017

ZENDAYA K. SMITH color *Vanity Fair* p87 Hollywood 2017 Supplement

THE Z FACTOR [Cover story] A. Aguirre color *Vogue* v207 no7 p74 Jl 2017

Zendaya, 1996-—Interviews

Generation Y. Shahidi bw color *Glamour* v115 no11 p124 N 2017

Zendaya A. Morris color *Glamour* v114 no12 p216 D 2016

Zeng, Bo-Xuan

"Perfect" designer chromosome V and behavior of a ring derivative diag *Science* v355 no6329 p1046 Mr 10 2017

Zeng, Mingshuo

A modular and enantioselective synthesis of the pleuromutilin antibiotics diag graph *Science* v356 no6341 p956 Je 1 2017

Zeng, Runxi

Promoting human rights through science color *Science* v357 no6359 p34 O 6 2017

Zenger, Jack

4 Ways to Be More Effective at Execution *Harvard Business Review Digital Articles* p2 My 23 2016

7 Things Leaders Do to Help People Change *Harvard Business Review Digital Articles* p2 Jl 20 2015

Are We More Productive When We Have More Time Off? *Harvard Business Review Digital Articles* p2 Je 17 2015

The Assumptions That Make Giving Tough Feedback Even Tougher *Harvard Business Review Digital Articles* p2 Ap 30 2015

Companies Are Bad at Identifying High-Potential Employees *Harvard Business Review Digital Articles* p2 F 20 2017

Do Women Make Bolder Leaders than Men? *Harvard Business Review Digital Articles* p2 Ap 27 2016

How Age and Gender Affect Self-Improvement *Harvard Business Review Digital Articles* p2 Ja 5 2016

How Managers Drive Results and Employee Engagement at the Same Time *Harvard Business Review Digital Articles* p2 Je 19 2017

How to Improve at Work When You're Not Getting Feedback *Harvard Business Review Digital Articles* p2 My 9 2017

If Your Boss Thinks You're Awesome, You Will Become More Awesome *Harvard Business Review Digital Articles* p2 Ja 27 2015

People Who Think They're Great Coaches Often Aren't *Harvard Business Review Digital Articles* p2 Je 23 2016

Research: 10 Traits of Innovative Leaders *Harvard Business Review Digital Articles* p2 D 15 2014

The Traits of Leaders Who Do Things Fast and Well *Harvard Business Review Digital Articles* p2 N 16 2016

The Trickle-Down Effect of Good (and Bad) Leadership *Harvard*

Business Review Digital Articles p2 Ja 14 2016

We Like Leaders Who Underrate Themselves *Harvard Business Review Digital Articles* p2 N 10 2015

What Great Listeners Actually Do *Harvard Business Review Digital Articles* p2 Jl 14 2016

What Separates Great HR Leaders from the Rest *Harvard Business Review Digital Articles* p2 Ag 17 2015

What To Do When the Boss Gives You Baseless Feedback *Harvard Business Review Digital Articles* p2 Mr 4 2015

What Younger Managers Should Know About How They're Perceived *Harvard Business Review Digital Articles* p2 S 29 2015

Why Middle Managers Are So Unhappy *Harvard Business Review Digital Articles* p2 N 24 2014

Why You Should Watch Out for Your 5-Year Job Anniversary *Harvard Business Review Digital Articles* p2 Ap 10 2015

You Have to Be Fast to Be Seen as a Great Leader *Harvard Business Review Digital Articles* p2 F 26 2015

Zenger, Todd

The Case Against Pay Transparency *Harvard Business Review Digital Articles* p1 S 30 2016

Do M&A Deals Ever Really Create Synergies? *Harvard Business Review Digital Articles* p2 Jl 6 2016

Trial and Error Is No Way to Make Strategy *Harvard Business Review Digital Articles* p2 Ap 24 2015

Why Google Became Alphabet *Harvard Business Review Digital Articles* p2 Ag 11 2015

Zengerle, Jason

BETTER TO BERN OUT *GQ: Gentlemen's Quarterly* v86 no12 p207 D 2016

Chris Christie's Last Fight bw color *GQ: Gentlemen's Quarterly* v97 no11 p74 N 2017

THE GAWKER STALKER color *GQ: Gentlemen's Quarterly* v86 no12 p164 D 2016

OBAMA'S AMERICA img *New York* v49 no20 p12 O 3 2016

PURPLE WITH RAGE: North Carolina is narrowly split between Democratic and Republican Parties that agree on virtually nothing. Are its scorched-earth politics what the rest of us have to look forward to? *New York Times Magazine* p36 Je 25 2017

THE SECOND-STRANGEST CAMPAIGN OF THE SEASON img *New York* v49 no15 p28 Jl 25 2016

The Thread *New York Times Magazine* p9 Jl 9 2017

Who's Afraid of President Pence? color *GQ: Gentlemen's Quarterly* v97 no9 p124 S 2017

Who Will Do What Harry Reid Did Now That Harry Reid Is Gone? img *New York* v49 no26 p32 D 26 2016

Zenith distance

Evening Entertainment: Go out early and stay out late to catch the best meteor shower of the year S. N. Johnson-Roehr *Sky & Telescope* v134 no6 p48 D 2017

Zenith SA

GET IN GEAR S. Watson color *Esquire* p50 Ap 2017

Zenk, Fides

Germ line–inherited H3K27me3 restricts enhancer function during maternal-to-zygotic transition diag *Science* v357 no6347 p212 Jl 14 2017

Zenker, J.

A microtubule-organizing center directing intracellular transport in the early mouse embryo diag *Science* v357 no6354 p925 S 1 2017

ZENLEA, DAVID

THE ALCHEMISTS color *Road & Track* v69 no3 p86 O 2017

CROSSBREEDING color *Road & Track* v69 no1 p88 Ag 2017

LABOR PAINS color *Road & Track* v68 no5 p76 D 2016/Ja 2017

REALITY CHECK color *Road & Track* v68 no5 p106 D 2016/Ja 2017

THUNDERSTRUCK color *Road & Track* v68 no9 p84 Je 2017

Zen Magnets LLC—Trials, litigation, etc.

The Regulators' Bad Day in Court A. W. SCHACHTER color *Weekly Standard* v22 no14 p17 D 12 2016

Zent, E. L.

Persistent effects of pre-Columbian plant domestication on Amazonian forest composition bibl chart graph map *Science* v355 no6328 p925 Mr 3 2017

Zent, S.

Persistent effects of pre-Columbian plant domestication on Amazonian forest composition bibl chart graph map *Science* v355

no6328 p925 Mr 3 2017

Zeolite catalysts—Research

"Ab initio" synthesis of zeolites for preestablished catalytic reactions E. María Gallego, M. T. Portilla et al bibl chart diag *Science* v355 no6329 p1051 Mr 10 2017

Beyond trial and error for zeolite catalysts R. Millini bibl diag *Science* v355 no6329 p1028 Mr 10 2017

RESEARCH color *Science* v355 no6329 p1035 Mr 10 2017

Zeolites

Dynamic multinuclear sites formed by mobilized copper ions in NOx selective catalytic reduction C. Paolucci, I. Khurana et al bw color diag graph *Science* v357 no6354 p898 S 1 2017

A molecular dance to cleaner air T. V. W. Janssens and P. N. R. Vennestrøm color *Science* v357 no6354 p866 S 1 2017

Zepeda, A.

Observation of a large-scale anisotropy in the arrival directions of cosmic rays above 8×10^{18} eV *Science* v357 no6357 p1266 S 22 2017

Zepeda, Dana Meltzer

AMIN EL GAMAL bw *Runner's World* v52 no9 p96 O 2017

ROBYN O'BRIEN color *Runner's World* v52 no3 p96 Ap 2017

STERLING K. BROWN color *Runner's World* v52 no8 p96 S 2017

TRAVIS BARKER color *Runner's World* v52 no6 p96 Jl 2017

Zepeda, Susan

To The Editor color *American Craft* v76 no6 p10 D 2016-Ja 2017

Zephyr Adventures (Company)

Rollerblading the Little Miami A. COHEN *Cincinnati Magazine* p62 Je 2017

Zeratsky, John

Sprints Are the Secret to Getting More Done *Harvard Business Review Digital Articles* p2 Mr 15 2016

Zerling, Andrew

COMPRESSION LOCKS color *Black Belt* v55 no6 p52 O/N 2017

Zermatt (Switzerland)

GLASS color *Powder* v45 no3 p26 N 2016

Zernicka-Goetz, Magdalena

Assembly of embryonic and extraembryonic stem cells to mimic embryogenesis in vitro diag *Science* v356 no6334 p153 Ap 14 2017

PUSHING THE LIMIT G. Vogel color *Science* v354 no6311 p404 O 28 2016

Zero-base budgeting

Zero-Based Budgeting Is Not a Wonder Diet for Companies D. Mahler *Harvard Business Review Digital Articles* p2 Je 30 2016

Zerofsky, Elisabeth

EVERYMAN'S WAR: The paramilitary fighters training to keep Russia out of the Baltics *Harper's Magazine* p69 O 2017

WHAT IS IT ASKING FOR? TO BE SOMETHING *New York Times Magazine* p50 Je 11 2017

Zerpa, Fabiola

Meet Venezuela's New Iron-Fisted No. 2 color *Bloomberg Businessweek* no4511 p16 F 13 2017

Photostat: Going Hungry in Venezuela color *Bloomberg Businessweek* no4540 p38 O 2 2017

Zervudachi, Tino

FRENCH EVOLUTION N. ARIKHA color *Architectural Digest* no11 p126 N 1 2017

Zerwick, Phoebe

Is This Pill the Future of Abortion? color *Glamour* v114 no7 p134 Jl 2016

Zeta-Jones, Catherine

CATHERINE THE GREAT A. D'ARMINIO *TV Guide* v65 no14 p24 Ap 3 2017

Zetka, Monique

When degradation spurs segregation bibl diag *Science* v355 no6323 p349 Ja 27 2017

Zetsche, Dieter, 1952——Interviews

Dieter Zetsche A. MacKenzie color *Motor Trend* v69 no6 p30 Je 2017

Zettl, Alex

Single-particle mapping of nonequilibrium nanocrystal transformations bibl bw graph *Science* v354 no6314 p874 N 18 2016

Zettlemoyer, J.

Observation of coherent elastic neutrino-nucleus scattering diag *Science* v357 no6356 p1123 S 15 2017

mosome X diag *Science* v355 no6329 p1048 Mr 10 2017

History of winning remodels thalamo-PFC circuit to reinforce social dominance color *Science* v357 no6347 p162 Jl 14 2017

Zhang, Michael Q.

PAF1 regulation of promoter-proximal pause release via enhancer activation color *Science* v357 no6357 p1294 S 22 2017

Zhang, Ming-Dong

miR-183 cluster scales mechanical pain sensitivity by regulating basal and neuropathic pain genes diag graph *Science* v356 no6343 p1168 Je 16 2017

Zhang, Q. M.

Accomplice to Memory bw *Publishers Weekly* v263 no51 p136 D 12 2016

The refrigerant is also the pump diag *Science* v357 no6356 p1094 S 15 2017

Zhang, Qi

A paralogous decoy protects Phytophthora sojae apoplastic effector PsXEG1 from a host inhibitor bibl graph *Science* v355 no6326 p726 F 17 2017

Zhang, Qianggong

Melting glaciers: Hidden hazards color *Science* v356 no6337 p495 My 5 2017

Zhang, Qihong

Biological control of aragonite formation in stony corals bw color graph *Science* v356 no6341 p933 Je 1 2017

Zhang, Rong

Quantum and isotope effects in lithium metal color diag graph *Science* v356 no6344 p1254 Je 23 2017

Zhang, Ruan

Rescue of exhausted CD8 T cells by PD-1–targeted therapies is CD28-dependent bw diag graph *Science* v355 no6332 p1423 Mr 31 2017

Zhang, Sarah

A MARKED MAN color *Wired* v24 no11 p46 N 2016

Zhang, Shou-Cheng

Chiral Majorana fermion modes in a quantum anomalous Hall insulator–superconductor structure diag *Science* v357 no6348 p294 Jl 21 2017

Zhang, Tian

The refrigerant is also the pump diag *Science* v357 no6356 p1094 S 15 2017

Zhang, Ting-Ting

"Perfect" designer chromosome V and behavior of a ring derivative diag *Science* v355 no6329 p1046 Mr 10 2017

Zhang, W.

A Fermi-degenerate three-dimensional optical lattice clock color diag graph *Science* v357 no6359 p90 O 6 2017

Zhang, Wei

"Perfect" designer chromosome V and behavior of a ring derivative diag *Science* v355 no6329 p1046 Mr 10 2017

Zhang, Weimin

3D organization of synthetic and scrambled chromosomes diag *Science* v355 no6329 p1050 Mr 10 2017

Engineering the ribosomal DNA in a megabase synthetic chromosome diag *Science* v355 no6329 p1049 Mr 10 2017

Zhang, Wei-Xiong

Controlling guest conformation for efficient purification of butadiene bw diag *Science* v356 no6343 p1193 Je 16 2017

Zhang, Wen-Qian

"Perfect" designer chromosome V and behavior of a ring derivative diag *Science* v355 no6329 p1046 Mr 10 2017

Zhang, Wenqing

Can we beat influenza? color *Science* v357 no6347 p111 Jl 14 2017

Zhang, Wen-Zheng

Bug mapping and fitness testing of chemically synthesized chromosome X diag *Science* v355 no6329 p1048 Mr 10 2017

"Perfect" designer chromosome V and behavior of a ring derivative diag *Science* v355 no6329 p1046 Mr 10 2017

Zhang, Xiang

Metamaterials for perpetual cooling at large scales bibl color *Science* v355 no6329 p1023 Mr 10 2017

Zhang, Xiao

Atomic-layered Au clusters on α-MoC as catalysts for the low-temperature water-gas shift reaction chart diag graph *Science* v357 no6349 p389 Jl 28 2017

Zhang, Xiaobing

Rapid binge-like eating and body weight gain driven by zona incerta GABA neuron activation graph *Science* v356 no6340 p853 My 26 2017

Zhang, Xiaopu

Nanocrystalline copper films are never flat diag graph *Science* v357 no6349 p397 Jl 28 2017

Zhang, Xiaowei

Plants transfer lipids to sustain colonization by mutualistic mycorrhizal and parasitic fungi diag graph *Science* v356 no6343 p1172 Je 16 2017

Zhang, Xiao-Xiang

Satellite-based entanglement distribution over 1200 kilometers diag graph *Science* v356 no6343 p1140 Je 16 2017

Zhang, Xin

Catalytic intermolecular hydroaminations of unactivated olefins with secondary alkyl amines bibl diag *Science* v355 no6326 p727 F 17 2017

Direction-specific van der Waals attraction between rutile TiO2 nanocrystals diag *Science* v356 no6336 p434 Ap 28 2017

Zhang, Xinzheng

Structure and assembly mechanism of plant C2S2M2-type PSII-LHCII supercomplex color *Science* v357 no6353 p815 Ag 25 2017

Zhang, Y.

Femtosecond electron-phonon lock-in by photoemission and x-ray free-electron laser chart diag *Science* v357 no6346 p71 Jl 7 2017

Zhang, Yan

Where Cadillac Is Still Prized color graph *Bloomberg Businessweek* no4510 p16 F 6 2017

Zhang, Yi

An organic-inorganic perovskite ferroelectric with large piezoelectric response graph *Science* v357 no6348 p306 Jl 21 2017

Zhang, Yuanyao

Segregation-induced ordered superstructures at general grain boundaries in a nickel-bismuth alloy color *Science* v357 no6359 p97 O 6 2017

Zhang, Zanbo, 1973-

Zhang Zanbo M. Hagan *Current Biography* v78 no2 p92 F 2017

Zhang, Zeda

SOX2 promotes lineage plasticity and antiandrogen resistance in TP53- and RB1-deficient prostate cancer bibl graph *Science* v355 no6320 p1 Ja 6 2017

Zhang, Zhao

Bone-like crack resistance in hierarchical metastable nanolaminate steels bibl color diag graph *Science* v355 no6329 p1055 Mr 10 2017

Zhang, Zhengwei

Robust epitaxial growth of two-dimensional heterostructures, multiheterostructures, and superlattices color *Science* v357 no6353 p788 Ag 25 2017

Zhang, Zhiyong

Scaling carbon nanotube complementary transistors to 5-nm gate lengths chart graph *Science* v355 no6322 p271 Ja 20 2017

Zhang, Ziyang

Highly efficient electrocaloric cooling with electrostatic actuation bw diag *Science* v357 no6356 p1130 S 15 2017

Zhao, C.

Structure, force balance, and topology of Earth's magnetopause diag graph *Science* v356 no6341 p960 Je 1 2017

Zhao, Chen

Stromal Gli2 activity coordinates a niche signaling program for mammary epithelial stem cells color *Science* v356 no6335 p284 Ap 21 2017

Zhao, Daxuan

The More Climate Skeptics There Are, the Fewer Climate Entrepreneurs *Harvard Business Review Digital Articles* p2 Mr 16 2017

Zhao, Dewei

An organic-inorganic perovskite ferroelectric with large piezoelectric response graph *Science* v357 no6348 p306 Jl 21 2017

Zhao, Dongliang

Scalable-manufactured randomized glass-polymer hybrid metamaterial for daytime radiative cooling bibl diag *Science* v355 no6329 p1062 Mr 10 2017

Zhao, Fei

Elimination of the male reproductive tract in the female embryo is promoted by COUP-TFII in mice color graph *Science* v357 no6352 p717 Ag 18 2017

Zhao, Guanghou

3D organization of synthetic and scrambled chromosomes diag *Science* v355 no6329 p1050 Mr 10 2017

Engineering the ribosomal DNA in a megabase synthetic chromosome diag *Science* v355 no6329 p1049 Mr 10 2017

Zhao, Guang-Rong

"Perfect" designer chromosome V and behavior of a ring derivative diag *Science* v355 no6329 p1046 Mr 10 2017

Zhao, Heng

Inactivation of porcine endogenous retrovirus in pigs using CRISPR-Cas9 diag *Science* v357 no6357 p1303 S 22 2017

Zhao, Hongcui

Deep functional analysis of synII, a 770-kilobase synthetic yeast chromosome diag *Science* v355 no6329 p1047 Mr 10 2017

Zhao, Hong-Ye

Inactivation of porcine endogenous retrovirus in pigs using CRISPR-Cas9 diag *Science* v357 no6357 p1303 S 22 2017

Zhao, Jenn

Globalism Is Alive and Well: Just Ask Carlos Ghosn color *Bloomberg Businessweek* no4531 p50 Jl 24 2017

Zhao, Jing

China's Bridge and Tunnel Addiction color *Bloomberg Businessweek* no4513 p47 Mr 6 2017

Zhao, Juan

"Perfect" designer chromosome V and behavior of a ring derivative diag *Science* v355 no6329 p1046 Mr 10 2017

Zhao, Li

Engineering the ribosomal DNA in a megabase synthetic chromosome diag *Science* v355 no6329 p1049 Mr 10 2017

Zhao, Meng

Bug mapping and fitness testing of chemically synthesized chromosome X diag *Science* v355 no6329 p1048 Mr 10 2017

"Perfect" designer chromosome V and behavior of a ring derivative diag *Science* v355 no6329 p1046 Mr 10 2017

Zhao, Xin'Ai

RETINOBLASTOMA RELATED1 mediates germline entry in Arabidopsis color diag *Science* v356 no6336 p396 Ap 28 2017

Zhao, Xixi

Release of mineral-bound water prior to subduction tied to shallow seismogenic slip off Sumatra graph *Science* v356 no6340 p841 My 26 2017

Zhao, Yan G.

A switch from canonical to noncanonical autophagy shapes B cell responses bibl graph *Science* v355 no6325 p641 F 10 2017

Zhao, Yicheng

Efficient and stable solution-processed planar perovskite solar cells via contact passivation bibl graph *Science* v355 no6326 p722 F 17 2017

Zhao, Yinan

China's Troubles Down on the Farm color *Bloomberg Businessweek* no4525 p16 Je 5 2017

Zhao, Yongbiao

Efficient and stable solution-processed planar perovskite solar cells via contact passivation bibl graph *Science* v355 no6326 p722 F 17 2017

Zhao, Yu

Synthesis, debugging, and effects of synthetic chromosome consolidation: synVI and beyond color *Science* v355 no6329 p1045 Mr 10 2017

Zhao, Yue

An on/off Berry phase switch in circular graphene resonators diag graph *Science* v356 no6340 p845 My 26 2017

Zhao, Z. Y.

A parity-breaking electronic nematic phase transition in the spin-orbit coupled metal Cd2Re2O7 diag *Science* v356 no6335 p295 Ap 21 2017

Zhao, Zipeng

Three-dimensional holey-graphene/niobia composite architectures for ultrahigh-rate energy storage color diag graph *Science* v356 no6338 p599 My 12 2017

Zhao Liang

BEHEMOTH color *Tricycle: The Buddhist Review* v27 no1 p7 Fall 2017

Zhao Ping

Quality management for precision medicine clinical applications: A consensus from the China Precision Medicine Clinical Research and Application Association bibl *Science* v354 no6319 p11 D 23 2016

Zhaohe Yang

Photoactivation and inactivation of Arabidopsis cryptochrome 2 bibl graph *Science* v354 no6310 p343 O 21 2016

Zhaohui Pan

A Silurian maxillate placoderm illuminates jaw evolution bibl color *Science* v354 no6310 p334 O 21 2016

Zhaoyang Lin

Ultrafine jagged platinum nanowires enable ultrahigh mass activity for the oxygen reduction reaction bibl chart graph *Science* v354 no6318 p1414 D 16 2016

Zhejiang Juvenile & Children's Publishing House (Company)

Zhejiang Juvenile & Children's Publishing House color *Publishers Weekly* v264 no39 p(Sp)24 S 25 2017

Zhejiang University (Hangzhou, China)

Zhejiang University Press color *Publishers Weekly* v264 no39 p(Sp)24 S 25 2017

Zheling Li

Sensitive electromechanical sensors using viscoelastic graphene-polymer nanocomposites bibl graph *Science* v354 no6317 p1257 D 9 2016

Zhen Cao

SOX2 promotes lineage plasticity and antiandrogen resistance in TP53- and RB1-deficient prostate cancer bibl graph *Science* v355 no6320 p1 Ja 6 2017

Zhenan Bao

Highly stretchable polymer semiconductor films through the nanoconfinement effect bibl graph *Science* v355 no6320 p1 Ja 6 2017

Zheng, Bijian, 1932-

China's 'One Belt, One Road' Plan Marks The Next Phase Of Globalization Z. Bijian *NPQ: New Perspectives Quarterly* v34 no3 p27 Jl 2017

Zheng, Shiwei

Single-cell RNA-seq reveals new types of human blood dendritic cells, monocytes, and progenitors color *Science* v356 no6335 p283 Ap 21 2017

Zheng, X.

Breaking Lorentz reciprocity to overcome the time-bandwidth limit in physics and engineering bw diag graph *Science* v356 no6344 p1260 Je 23 2017

Zheng, Xiaobo

A paralogous decoy protects Phytophthora sojae apoplastic effector PsXEG1 from a host inhibitor bibl graph *Science* v355 no6326 p710 F 17 2017

Zheng, Ying

Regeneration of fat cells from myofibroblasts during wound healing bibl color graph *Science* v355 no6326 p748 F 17 2017

Zheng Han

Electron optics with p-n junctions in ballistic graphene bibl graph *Science* v353 no6307 p1522 S 30 2016

Zhenlan Niu

Generation of influenza A viruses as live but replication-incompetent virus vaccines bibl graph *Science* v354 no6316 p1170 D 2 2016

Zhenyu Tian

Generation of influenza A viruses as live but replication-incompetent virus vaccines bibl graph *Science* v354 no6316 p1170 D 2 2016

Zhenzhen Zhang

Crystal structure of unlinked NS2B-NS3 protease from Zika virus bibl color graph *Science* v354 no6319 p1597 D 23 2016

Zhi-Chun Feng

Diagnosis and treatment of inherited metabolic diseases in China bibl *Science* v354 no6319 p52 D 23 2016

Zhi Min Du

Quality management for precision medicine clinical applications: A consensus from the China Precision Medicine Clinical Research and Application Association bibl *Science* v354 no6319 p11 D 23 2016

Zhi-Ming Shao

Breast cancer research in the era of precision medicine bibl color *Science* v354 no6319 p30 D 23 2016

Zhi Wei Seh

Combining theory and experiment in electrocatalysis: Insights into materials design bibl color graph *Science* v355 no6321 p1 Ja 13 2017

Zhi Xie

A nuclease that mediates cell death induced by DNA damage and poly(ADP-ribose) polymerase-1 bw graph *Science* v354 no6308 paad6872-1 O 7 2016

Zhi-Xue Zhang

What Chinese Companies Want from International Deals *Harvard Business Review Digital Articles* p2 F 12 2015

Zhibin Zhang

Merging paleobiology with conservation biology to guide the future of terrestrial ecosystems color *Science* v355 no6325 p594 F 10 2017

Zhigang He

Building bridges to regenerate axons bibl color diag *Science* v354 no6312 p544 N 4 2016

Zhiheng Wang

An Anthropocene map of genetic diversity bibl graph map *Science* v353 no6307 p1532 S 30 2016

Zhihua Wu

Quality management for precision medicine clinical applications: A consensus from the China Precision Medicine Clinical Research and Application Association bibl *Science* v354 no6319 p11 D 23 2016

ZHIHUI ZHANG

Technocracy Chinese style *Issues in Science & Technology* v33 no3 p18 Spr 2017

Zhiqi Wang

Gene expression profiling–guided clinical precision treatment for patients with endometrial carcinoma bibl color diag *Science* v354 no6319 p33 D 23 2016

Zhiqiang Wu

CAR T-cell–based therapeutic modality in solid tumors: How to achieve precision bibl color *Science* v354 no6319 p27 D 23 2016

Zhitenev, Nikolai B.

An on/off Berry phase switch in circular graphene resonators diag graph *Science* v356 no6340 p845 My 26 2017

Zhixin Zhang

Quality management for precision medicine clinical applications: A consensus from the China Precision Medicine Clinical Research and Application Association bibl *Science* v354 no6319 p11 D 23 2016

Zhiyun Xu

RPA binds histone H3-H4 and functions in DNA replication–coupled nucleosome assembly bibl graph *Science* v355 no6323 p415 Ja 27 2017

Zhong, Donglai

Scaling carbon nanotube complementary transistors to 5-nm gate lengths bibl chart graph *Science* v355 no6322 p271 Ja 20 2017

Zhong, Fan

Impact of cytosine methylation on DNA binding specificities of human transcription factors diag *Science* v356 no6337 p502 My 5 2017

Zhong, Tian

Nanophotonic rare-earth quantum memory with optically controlled retrieval diag graph *Science* v357 no6358 p1392 S 29 2017

Zhongguo ren min yin hang

China's Central Bank Has Begun Cautiously Testing a Digital Currency W. Knight color *MIT Technology Review* v120 no5 p22 S/O 2017

Zhongjie He

Expert consensus on point-of-care testing *Science* v354 no6319 p15 D 23 2016

Recommendations on the management and use of POCT in medical institutions (nosocomial) *Science* v354 no6319 p13 D 23 2016

Zhongsheng Sun

Recent progress in autism spectrum disorder research in China bibl chart diag *Science* v354 no6319 p48 D 23 2016

Zhongyuan Liu

A chemical genetic roadmap to improved tomato flavor bibl graph *Science* v355 no6323 p391 Ja 27 2017

Zhou, Baojin

Deep functional analysis of synII, a 770-kilobase synthetic yeast chromosome diag *Science* v355 no6329 p1047 Mr 10 2017

Zhou, Bo

Intersection of diverse neuronal genomes and neuropsychiatric disease: The Brain Somatic Mosaicism Network color *Science* v356 no6336 p395 Ap 28 2017

Zhou, Chris

Whose kids are these? M. CAMPBELL *Maclean's* p15 Je 2017

Zhou, Gaochao

Systemic pan-AMPK activator MK-8722 improves glucose homeostasis but induces cardiac hypertrophy graph *Science* v357 no6350 p507 Ag 4 2017

Zhou, Guangyu

Single-cell whole-genome analyses by Linear Amplification via Transposon Insertion (LIANTI) graph *Science* v356 no6334 p189 Ap 14 2017

Zhou, Jingtian

Single-cell methylomes identify neuronal subtypes and regulatory elements in mammalian cortex diag *Science* v357 no6351 p600 Ag 11 2017

Zhou, Kaile

Behavior management color *Science* v356 no6335 p244 Ap 21 2017

Zhou, Li-Ping

Late Pleistocene archaic human crania from Xuchang, China bibl color diag graph *Science* v355 no6328 p969 Mr 3 2017

Zhou, Naixie

Segregation-induced ordered superstructures at general grain boundaries in a nickel-bismuth alloy color *Science* v357 no6359 p97 O 6 2017

Zhou, Qionghua

An organic-inorganic perovskite ferroelectric with large piezoelectric response graph *Science* v357 no6348 p306 Jl 21 2017

Zhou, Quan

Chiral Majorana fermion modes in a quantum anomalous Hall insulator–superconductor structure diag *Science* v357 no6348 p294 Jl 21 2017

Zhou, Shibin

Mismatch repair deficiency predicts response of solid tumors to PD-1 blockade chart graph *Science* v357 no6349 p409 Jl 28 2017

Zhou, Si-Jie

Bug mapping and fitness testing of chemically synthesized chromosome X diag *Science* v355 no6329 p1048 Mr 10 2017

Zhou, Tingting

History of winning remodels thalamo-PFC circuit to reinforce social dominance color *Science* v357 no6347 p162 Jl 14 2017

Zhou, Tong

Engineering the ribosomal DNA in a megabase synthetic chromosome diag *Science* v355 no6329 p1049 Mr 10 2017

Zhou, Tongqing

Trispecific broadly neutralizing HIV antibodies mediate potent SHIV protection in macaques color graph *Science* v357 no6359 p85 O 6 2017

Zhou, Tony X.

Control and local measurement of the spin chemical potential in a magnetic insulator bw diag *Science* v357 no6347 p195 Jl 14 2017

Zhou, Wu

Atomic-layered Au clusters on α-MoC as catalysts for the low-temperature water-gas shift reaction chart diag graph *Science* v357 no6349 p389 Jl 28 2017

Zhou, Xiao

Bug mapping and fitness testing of chemically synthesized chromosome X diag *Science* v355 no6329 p1048 Mr 10 2017

Zhou, Xiaoyang

Inactivation of porcine endogenous retrovirus in pigs using CRISPR-Cas9 diag *Science* v357 no6357 p1303 S 22 2017

Zhou, Xin X.

Optical control of cell signaling by single-chain photoswitchable kinases bibl diag *Science* v355 no6327 p836 F 24 2017

Zhou, Yi-Lin

Satellite-based entanglement distribution over 1200 kilometers diag graph *Science* v356 no6343 p1140 Je 16 2017

Zhou, Z. Hong

Atomic structure of the human cytomegalovirus capsid with its securing tegument layer of pp150 color *Science* v356 no6345 p1350 Je 30 2017

Zhou Qiang

Rule of Law and 'Western' Notions Worry Beijing V. Yu color *America* v216 no3 p15 F 6 2017

Structure of a eukaryotic voltage-gated sodium channel at near-atomic resolution diag graph *Science* v355 no6328 p924 Mr 3 2017

Zhou Xiaoyan

USHERING IN THE NEXT GOLDEN DECADE *Bloomberg Businessweek* no4536 p4 S 4 2017

Zhou Li, Julia Su

TZAP: A telomere-associated protein involved in telomere length control bibl diag graph *Science* v355 no6325 p638 F 10 2017

Zhou Long, 1953-

The Ouroboros Trilogy J. S. Lessner *Opera News* v81 no6 p44 D 2016

Zhu, Cheng

Notch-Jagged complex structure implicates a catch bond in tuning ligand sensitivity bibl diag graph *Science* v355 no6331 p1320 Mr 24 2017

Zhu, D.

Femtosecond electron-phonon lock-in by photoemission and x-ray free-electron laser chart diag *Science* v357 no6346 p71 Jl 7 2017

Zhu, Dongjie

Structure and assembly mechanism of plant C2S2M2-type PSII-LHCII supercomplex color *Science* v357 no6353 p815 Ag 25 2017

Zhu, Hong

History of winning remodels thalamo-PFC circuit to reinforce social dominance color *Science* v357 no6347 p162 Jl 14 2017

Zhu, Jia-Qing

"Perfect" designer chromosome V and behavior of a ring derivative diag *Science* v355 no6329 p1046 Mr 10 2017

Zhu, Jing

T cell costimulatory receptor CD28 is a primary target for PD-1–mediated inhibition color diag graph *Science* v355 no6332 p1428 Mr 31 2017

Zhu, Jun-Qi

"Perfect" designer chromosome V and behavior of a ring derivative diag *Science* v355 no6329 p1046 Mr 10 2017

Zhu, Kai

Long-range hot-carrier transport in hybrid perovskites visualized by ultrafast microscopy diag graph *Science* v356 no6333 p59 Ap 7 2017

Zhu, Lin

A paralogous decoy protects Phytophthora sojae apoplastic effector PsXEG1 from a host inhibitor bibl graph *Science* v355 no6326 p710 F 17 2017

Zhu, Rui-Ying

Bug mapping and fitness testing of chemically synthesized chromosome X diag *Science* v355 no6329 p1048 Mr 10 2017

Zhu, Ru-Yi

Formation of α-chiral centers by asymmetric β-C(sp3)–H arylation, alkenylation, and alkynylation bibl diag *Science* v355 no6324 p499 F 3 2017

Zhu, Wei

Systemic pan-AMPK activator MK-8722 improves glucose homeostasis but induces cardiac hypertrophy graph *Science* v357 no6350 p507 Ag 4 2017

Zhu, Xiangwei

A molecular spin-photovoltaic device color diag *Science* v357 no6352 p677 Ag 18 2017

Zhu, Xiaolei

Mechanochemical unzipping of insulating polyladderene to semiconducting polyacetylene [Cover story] diag *Science* v357 no6350 p475 Ag 4 2017

Zhu, Xudong

Epigenetic regulation of antagonistic receptors confers rice blast resistance with yield balance bibl diag *Science* v355 no6328 p962 Mr 3 2017

Zhu, Yong-Guan

Microbial mass movements color *Science* v357 no6356 p1099 S 15 2017

Zhu, Yu

Carbon nanotube transistors scaled to a 40-nanometer footprint color graph *Science* v356 no6345 p1369 Je 30 2017

Zhu, Zhen-Cai

Satellite-based entanglement distribution over 1200 kilometers diag graph *Science* v356 no6343 p1140 Je 16 2017

Zhuang, Xiaoxi

Dopamine oxidation mediates mitochondrial and lysosomal dysfunction in Parkinson's disease graph *Science* v357 no6357 p1255 S 22 2017

Zhukovich, Vital

Higher predation risk for insect prey at low latitudes and elevations graph *Science* v356 no6339 p742 My 19 2017

Zhurbin, Roman

In Character M. HARSS *Dance Magazine* v91 no1 p128 Ja 2017

Zi, Jin

Deep functional analysis of synII, a 770-kilobase synthetic yeast chromosome diag *Science* v355 no6329 p1047 Mr 10 2017

Ziba (Company)

STOP THE CHITCHAT C. THOMPSON cartoon *Wired* v25 no10 p44 O 2017

ZICKL, DANIELLE

CAN'T TAKE THE HEAT? GET IN THE KITCHEN color *Runner's World* v52 no7 p30 Ag 2017

One-Trick Ponies color *Runner's World* v52 no5 p53 Je 2017

Relay the Message bw color *Runner's World* v52 no6 p48 Jl 2017

RUN AWAY! [Cover story] color *Runner's World* v52 no7 p54 Ag 2017

A Thing for Bling color *Runner's World* v52 no7 p46 Ag 2017

Ziebell, Don

KITCHEN OF THE MONTH: In With the Old World color *House Beautiful* v159 no9 p57 N 2017

Ziegler, Alfred

Join the Conversation *South Dakota Magazine* v32 no6 p19 Mr/Ap 2017

Ziegler, Deborah

Wild and Precious Life *Publishers Weekly* v263 no39 p81 S 26 2016

Ziegler, Dominic

A River Runs Through It C. Thubron color *New York Review of Books* v64 no16 p47 O 26 2017

ZIEGLER, GREGORY

Ecological Forecasting and the Science of Hypoxia in Chesapeake Bay *BioScience* v67 no7 p614 Jl 2017

Ziegler, Kelley

FUN & GAMES color *Backpacker* p71 Je 2017

Ziegler, Maddie

BEHIND THE SCENES WITH Maddie Ziegler color *Seventeen* v76 no4 p6 Jl/Ag 2017

Dancing Acting Taking Over the World [Cover story] A. STANLEY bw color *Seventeen* v76 no4 p60 Jl/Ag 2017

MILLIE BOBBY BROWN *Interview* v46 no9 p56 N 2016

Ziegler, Maddie—Interviews

Dear Diary C. Bowers *Dance Spirit* v21 no3 p15 Mr 2017

ZIEGLER, MARY ELLEN

Living Out Loud: On good food, great reads, and strong women color *O, The Oprah Magazine* p20 S 2017

Ziel, Erica

One speedy move for a toned core color *Redbook* p90 D 2016

Zielinski, Dina

DNA Fountain enables a robust and efficient storage architecture bibl chart diag *Science* v355 no6328 p950 Mr 3 2017

Zielinski, S.

THE SLUGGER THE SCOUT B. Reiter color *Sports Illustrated* v126 no13 p58 My 8 2017

Zieser, Rick

Posthole color *Powder* v45 no4 p146 D 2016

Ziettlow, Amy

Homeward Bound: Modern Families, Elder Care, and Loss S. G. Thornton *Christian Century* v134 no20 p41 S 27 2017

Reflections on the lectionary *Christian Century* v134 no17 p21 Ag 16 2017

ZIGMOND, DAN

The Last Dalai Lama color *Tricycle: The Buddhist Review* v27 no1 p94 Fall 2017

Zika virus

2016 Nobels: Science News fans read it here first *Science News* v190 no9 p2 O 29 2016

BABY'S FIRST ORGAN A. Erlebacher and S. J. Fisher color *Scientific American* v317 no4 p46 O 2017

THE BEST & WORST OF 2016 bw color *Men's Health* v31 no10 p90 D 2016

Case builds for another Zika vector S. MILIUS *Science News* v190 no9 p13 O 29 2016

Crystal structure of unlinked NS2B-NS3 protease from Zika virus Zhenzhen Zhang, Yan Li et al bibl color graph *Science* v354 no6319 p1597 D 23 2016

De novo assembly of the Aedes aegypti genome using Hi-C yields chromosome-length scaffolds O. Dudchenko, S. S. Batra et al chart color diag *Science* v356 no6333 p92 Ap 7 2017

In Sickness and in Health D. L. HEYMANN color *Natural History* v125 no9 p43 S 2017

Neurodevelopmental protein Musashi-1 interacts with the Zika genome and promotes viral replication P. L. Chavali, L. Stojic et al diag *Science* v357 no6346 p83 Jl 7 2017

A New Enemy Emerges L. MARSA color map *Discover* v38 no1 p12 Ja/F 2017

new products color *Science* v356 no6336 p446 Ap 28 2017

Rapid development of a DNA vaccine for Zika virus K. A. Dowd, Sung-Youl Ko et al bibl graph *Science* v354 no6309 p237 O 14 2016

RESEARCH color *Science* v357 no6346 p43 Jl 7 2017

A Thirst For Blood M. SEGAL bw *Los Angeles Magazine* v62 no10 p14 O 2017

U.S.-Cuba scientific collaboration advances M. Jarvis color *Science* v357 no6358 p1364 S 29 2017

ZIKA ON THE ADVANCE *Discover* v38 no1 p13 Ja/F 2017

Zika's baby photo snapped M. Rosen color *Science News* v191 no4 p32 Mr 4 2017

Zika virus devastates Brazil, spreads fear across Americas M. Rosen color *Science News* v190 no13 p19 D 24 2016

Zika virus produces noncoding RNAs using a multi-pseudoknot structure that confounds a cellular exonuclease B. M. Akiyama, H. M. Laurence et al bibl color graph *Science* v354 no6316 p1148 D 2 2016

Zika virus 'spillback' into monkeys raises risk of future outbreaks T. H. Saey color *Science News* v191 no4 p15 Mr 4 2017

Zika Virus Epidemic, 2015-

Flotsam from the Future G. Moreno color *Art in America* v104 no11 p31 D 2016

A New Enemy Emerges L. MARSA color map *Discover* v38 no1 p12 Ja/F 2017

South America img *New York Times Upfront* v149 no6 p35 D 12 2016

To Fight the Zika Pandemic, Learn from Ebola R. S. Dhillon, R. Glatter et al *Harvard Business Review Digital Articles* p2 F 4 2016

The World Is Completely Unprepared for a Global Pandemic R. S. Dhillon, D. Srikrishna et al *Harvard Business Review Digital Articles* p2 Mr 15 2017

THE ZIKA CRISIS: A RESULT OF NEGLECT S. SARKAR diag *Phi Kappa Phi Forum* v96 no4 p22 Wint 2016

ZIKA ON THE ADVANCE *Discover* v38 no1 p13 Ja/F 2017

Zika virus devastates Brazil, spreads fear across Americas M. Rosen color *Science News* v190 no13 p19 D 24 2016

Zika Virus Epidemic, 2015—Social aspects

Community Center. How to Keep Citizens Informed About the Threat of Zika in Your Community L. Schenck *Parks & Recreation* v52 no6 p16 Je 2017

How Zika Could Change the Politics of Abortion B. Walsh color *Time* v188 no16/17 p58 O 24 2016

Zika virus infections

BITING BACK M. Enserink and L. Roberts color *Science* v354 no6309 p162 O 14 2016

Concern grows over Zika birth defects M. ROSEN color diag *Science News* v190 no9 p14 O 29 2016

Data mount linking Zika, birth defects color *Science* v354 no6318 p1356 D 16 2016

Dengue may bring out the worst in Zika J. Cohen color *Science* v355 no6332 p1362 Mr 31 2017

Dengue may stoke Zika infections A. CUNNINGHAM graph *Science News* v191 no8 p14 Ap 29 2017

One year later, Zika scientists prepare for a long war G. Vogel graph *Science* v354 no6316 p1088 D 2 2016

Where has all the Zika gone? J. Cohen color graph *Science* v357 no6352 p631 Ag 18 2017

Zika hides out in hard-to-reach spots L. HAMERS color *Science News* v191 no10 p10 My 27 2017

Zika virus infections—Prevention

Community Center. How to Keep Citizens Informed About the Threat of Zika in Your Community L. Schenck *Parks & Recreation* v52 no6 p16 Je 2017

DNA vaccines for Zika show promise M. ROSEN color diag *Science News* v191 no5 p12 Mr 18 2017

EVEN IN THE AGE OF ZIKA, THE PEOPLE OF KEY WEST WANT NOTHING TO DO WITH OXITEC'S GENETICALLY MODIFIED MOSQUITOES [Cover story] R. KOLKER color *Bloomberg Businessweek* no4494 p48 O 10 2016

The Fight Against Zika Can't Wait for a Vaccine R. S. Dhillon, D. Srikrishna et al *Harvard Business Review Digital Articles* p2 Ag 18 2016

Zika rewrites maternal immunization ethics J. Cohen color *Science* v357 no6348 p241 Jl 21 2017

Zika virus infections—Transmission

BITE FRIGHT color *Missouri Life* v44 no3 p70 My 2017

Enhancement of Zika virus pathogenesis by preexisting antiflavivirus immunity S. V. Bardina, P. Bunduc et al graph *Science* v356 no6334 p175 Ap 14 2017

THE ZIKA CRISIS: A RESULT OF NEGLECT S. SARKAR diag *Phi Kappa Phi Forum* v96 no4 p22 Wint 2016

ZIKA M. Quinn *Governing* v30 no4 p33 Ja 2017

Zika virus went undetected for months L. BEIL map *Science News* v191 no12 p12 Je 24 2017

Zika virus infections—Vaccination

The Fight Against Zika Can't Wait for a Vaccine R. S. Dhillon, D. Srikrishna et al *Harvard Business Review Digital Articles* p2 Ag 18 2016

Zikic, Jelena

Being a Parent Made Me a Better Manager, and Vice Versa *Harvard Business Review Digital Articles* p2 My 9 2016

When Mentorship Crosses Cultures, Both Sides Learn *Harvard Business Review Digital Articles* p2 Ag 5 2016

ZILBERMAN, CAROLYN

ASK RW color *Runner's World* v52 no4 p35 My 2017

Zilca, Ran

Research: Millennials Think About Work Too Much *Harvard Business Review Digital Articles* p2 Jl 15 2016

Why Your Late Twenties Is the Worst Time of Your Life *Harvard Business Review Digital Articles* p2 Mr 7 2016

Zilinskas, Raymond A.

TIME TO WORRY ABOUT ANTHRAX AGAIN color diag *Scientific American* v316 no4 p70 Ap 2017

Zilis, Shivon

The Competitive Landscape for Machine Intelligence *Harvard Business Review Digital Articles* p2 N 2 2016

Machine Intelligence Will Let Us All Work Like CEOs *Harvard Business Review Digital Articles* p2 Je 13 2016

Zilles, Karl

Microstructural proliferation in human cortex is coupled with the development of face processing bibl graph *Science* v355 no6320 p1 Ja 6 2017

Zillman, Claire

100 BEST COMPANIES TO WORK FOR 2017 [Cover story] color diag map *Fortune* v175 no4 p79 Mr 15 2017

THE 2017 Fortune Crystal Ball color diag *Fortune* v174 no7 p11 D 1 2016

APPLE REBOOTS IN CHINA color *Fortune* v176 no5 p106 O 1 2017

CHANGE THE WORLD !!!! color diag map *Fortune* v176 no4 p74 S 15 2017

Fortune on the Global Stage color *Fortune* v176 no1 p18 Jl 1 2017

LEGENDS LIST color *Fortune* v175 no4 p92 Mr 15 2017

MOST POWERFUL WOMEN INTERNATIONAL color *Fortune* v176 no5 p111 O 1 2017

A RETAILER FINDS ITS VOICE color *Fortune* v176 no4 p46 S 15 2017

WEEKNIGHT COOKING color *Sunset* v238 no4 p90 Ap 2017

Zingales, Luigi

Serving Shareholders Doesn't Mean Putting Profit Above All Else *Harvard Business Review Digital Articles* p2 O 12 2017

Zingerman's Delicatessen Inc.

What Price Growth? B. BURLINGHAM color *Forbes* v198 no6 p56 N 8 2016

Zink, Nell

BONEBREAKER color *Harper's Magazine* v335 no2005 p77 Je 2017

Smokers Only E. McKENZIE *New York Times Book Review* p141 N 13 2016

The Untameable Nell Zink B. Kachka img *New York* v49 no20 p120 O 3 2016

The Year in Reading [Cover story] *New York Times Book Review* p8 D 25 2016

Zinke, Ryan, 1961-

The $4.5 Billion Cabinet C. PETERSON-WITHORN, J. WANG et al color *Forbes* v199 no1 p26 Ja 24 2017

Teddy or Not B. GOLDFARB *Audubon* v119 no2 p12 Summ 2017

U.S. monuments at risk color *Science* v357 no6357 p1216 S 22 2017

Zinman, Jonathan

Making Microfinance More Effective *Harvard Business Review Digital Articles* p2 O 5 2016

Zinnemann, Fred, 1907-1997

HIGH NOON C. Chiarella bw *Sound & Vision* v82 no5 p70 Je 2017

ZINNERT, JULIE C.

Crossing Scales: The Complexity of Barrier-Island Processes for Predicting Future Change *BioScience* v67 no1 p39 Ja 2017

Zinnia

THE GRUMPY GARDENER S. Bender color *Southern Living* v52 no4 p48 Ap 2017

Zinoman, Jason

Aaannnd now...DAVE diag *Indianapolis Monthly* p68 Ap 2017

Aaannnd now...DAVE J. ZINOMAN diag *Indianapolis Monthly* p68 Ap 2017

The Connected Mysteries of Bob Dylan, Woody Guthrie, and the Calumet Massacre of 1913 *New York Times Book Review* p58 Je 4 2017

Dystopia, Now Playing color *Bloomberg Businessweek* no4528 p74 Je 26 2017

Father of Dracula *New York Times Book Review* p19 O 30 2016

A TV Traditionalist With a Weird Streak D. D'Addario color *Time* v189 no14 p56 Ap 17 2017

Zinoman, Jason—Interviews

Q+A D. S. COMISKEY *Indianapolis Monthly* p73 Ap 2017

Zinoviev, Alexander

LORD OF THE FILES color *Harper's Magazine* v335 no2005 p15 Je 2017

Zinshteyn, Boris

When stop makes sense bibl diag *Science* v354 no6316 p1106 D 2 2016

Ziolkowski, M.

Observation of a large-scale anisotropy in the arrival directions of cosmic rays above 8 × 1018 eV *Science* v357 no6357 p1266 S 22 2017

ZIOLKOWSKI, THAD

Wish You Were Here: Money, murder and a missing heir combine on a Greek island in this literary thriller *New York Times Book Review* p8 Ag 20 2017

Ziolkowski, Theodore

Uses and Abuses of Moses: Literary Representations since the Enlightenment W. Brueggemann color *Christian Century* v133 no21 p54 O 12 2016

Zion National Park (Utah)

The Narrows: Zion National Park, Utah color *Backpacker* p88 S 2017

out alive: flooded color *Backpacker* p43 Ag 2017

Reality Check J. ELLISON color *Climbing* no350 p15 D 2016/ Ja 2017

WIN AN ESCAPE TO ZION! T. Enriquez color *Sunset* v239 no4 p130 O 2017

Zionism

See also

Christian Zionism

One Brief Kaddish, Summer 2017 M. Y. SOLOVEICHIK *Commentary* v144 no3 p11 O 2017

Zipcar Inc.

We Need to Expand the Definition of Disruptive Innovation R. Chase *Harvard Business Review Digital Articles* p2 Ja 7 2016

Zipeng Zhao

Ultrafine jagged platinum nanowires enable ultrahigh mass activity for the oxygen reduction reaction bibl chart graph *Science* v354 no6318 p1414 D 16 2016

Zipes, Douglas

ASK DR. ZIPES *Saturday Evening Post* v288 no6 p81 N/D 2016

BRAIN-ZAP WEIGHT LOSS PROGRAM *Saturday Evening Post* v289 no5 p69 S/O 2017

HEART BEAT *Saturday Evening Post* v289 no2 p72 Mr/Ap 2017

LEARNING FROM NATURE *Saturday Evening Post* v289 no4 p76 Jl/Ag 2017

Women at Higher Risk of Silent Heart Attack *Saturday Evening Post* v289 no3 p74 My/Je 2017

Zipfel, Cyril

The receptor kinase FER is a RALF-regulated scaffold controlling plant immune signaling bibl graph *Science* v355 no6322 p287 Ja 20 2017

Zipfel, Jaqueline

Glia relay differentiation cues to coordinate neuronal development in Drosophila color *Science* v357 no6354 p886 S 1 2017

Zipp, Samuel

Jane Jacobs, In Her Own Words S. R. STALEY bw color *Reason* v49 no4 p72 Ag/S 2017

Zippers

saved by: Lip Balm T. BROWN JR. color *Backpacker* p42 S 2017

Zippers—History

Made to Be Undone T. Patterson color *Bloomberg Businessweek* no4535 p70 Ag 28 2017

ZIPPLE, JEREMY

New U.S. Cardinals Condemn Polarization Inside the Church color *America* v215 no18 p8 D 5 2016

Zipple-Shedd, Kristin

Harvey brought new threats, and hope, to the undocumented in Houston *America* v217 no6 p10 S 18 2017

ZIRBEL, DICK

back at the lake color map *Cabin Living* p14 O 2017

Zircon

Rapid cooling and cold storage in a silicic magma reservoir recorded in individual crystals A. E. Rubin, K. M. Cooper et al color diag graph *Science* v356 no6343 p1154 Je 16 2017

Zircon analysis

Magma under volcanoes is largely solid M. TEMMING *Science News* v191 no13 p11 Jl 8 2017

ZIRIN, DAVE

The Ali We Need Today bw *Progressive* v81 no2 p45 F 2017

Ambassadors of Defiance color *Progressive* v81 no4 p68 Ap/My 2017

Coach Pop vs. Donald Trump color *Progressive* v81 no3 p45 Mr 2017

Getting Serious About Locker-Room Talk color *Progressive* p68 D 2016/Ja 2017

Kaepernick's Legacy Lives On color *Progressive* v81 no7 p68 O/N 2017

The Non-Virtue of Intolerance color *Progressive* v81 no6 p68 Ag/S 2017

The Season for Dissent *Progressive* v81 no10 p44 N 2016

Taking a Knee *Nation* v305 no9 p3 O 16 2017

Unsportsmanlike Conduct: College Football and the Politics of Rape/Long Shot: The Struggles and Triumphs of an NBA Freedom Fighter *Progressive* p60 D 2016/Ja 2017

Venus, Exonerated *Nation* v305 no3 p8 Jl 31 2017

When Raiders Become Traitors color *Progressive* v81 no5 p68 Je/ Jl 2017

Zirker, Jack B.

WHY IS THE SUN'S CORONA SO HOT? WHY ARE PROMINENCES SO COOL? *Physics Today* v70 no8 p35 Ag 2017

Zirogiannis, Beth

GO FORTH AND READ: How one Long Island school district started a literacy movement in its community color *Literacy Today (2411-7862)* v34 no6 p36 My/Je 2017

Zisa, Natalie
ACCEPTANCE Anxieties *Dance Spirit* v21 no3 p64 Mr 2017
Andrew WINGHART bw color *Dance Spirit* v21 no4 p24 Ap 2017

ZISSOU, REBECCA
A New Day for Cuba? *New York Times Upfront* v149 no7 p12 Ja 9 2017
NORTH KOREA VS. THE WORLD *New York Times Upfront* v149 no9 p14 F 20 2017
Trump Wins [Cover story] *New York Times Upfront* v149 no5 p6 N 21 2016
WILL A ROBOT TAKE YOUR JOB? *New York Times Upfront* v149 no3 p10 O 10 2016

Zitek, Emily
Research: Narcissists Don't Like Flat Organizations *Harvard Business Review Digital Articles* p2 Jl 27 2016

Zito, Salena
A White House on a War Footing P. J. BOYER color *Weekly Standard* v22 no38 p9 Je 12 2017

Zittrain, Jonathan
"Netwar": The unwelcome militarization of the Internet has arrived bibl *Bulletin of the Atomic Scientists* v73 no5 p300 2017

Zivin, Joshua Graff
Air Pollution Is Making Office Workers Less Productive *Harvard Business Review Digital Articles* p2 S 29 2016

Živković, Nenad
Changing climate shifts timing of European floods color graph *Science* v357 no6351 p588 Ag 11 2017

Ziwei Zhang
Generation of influenza A viruses as live but replication-incompetent virus vaccines bibl graph *Science* v354 no6316 p1170 D 2 2016

Ziyue Gao
Detection of human adaptation during the past 2000 years bibl graph *Science* v354 no6313 p760 N 11 2016

ŽIŽEK, SLAVOJ
From the Ashes of Liberal Democracy *In These Times* v41 no3 p17 Mr 2017
Zombie Lenin B. C. ANDERSON *National Review* v69 no18 p38 O 2 2017

Zlatopolsky, Ashley
Chris Cornell 1964-2017 [Cover story] bw color *Rolling Stone* no1289 p40 Je 15 2017

ZIMMERMAN, JULIE IRWIN
ENCYCLOPEDIA CINCINNATI bw cartoon color *Cincinnati Magazine* v51 no1 p42 O 2017

Zlotnick, Sarah
GIFT GUIDE 2016 *Washingtonian Magazine* v52 no3 p84 D 2016
In Bloom color *Washingtonian Magazine* v52 no7 p80 Ap 2017
LEATHER-BOUND *Washingtonian Magazine* v52 no2 p228 N 2016
LOOK CUTE ON YOUR COMMUTE *Washingtonian Magazine* v52 no5 p113 F 2017
PLEASE DON'T SAY CHEESE *Washingtonian Magazine* v52 no6 p97 Mr 2017
WHERE & WHEN *Washingtonian Magazine* v52 no5 p31 F 2017
WILD THINGS *Washingtonian Magazine* v52 no1 p107 O 2016

Zlotoff, Lee David
MacGyver J. Halterman color *TV Guide* v65 no7 p42 F 13 2017

ZOBENICA, JON
America in the Time of Kerouac's Travels il *American Conservative* v16 no2 p40 Mr/Ap 2017

Zobler, Andrew
Game Changer: ANDREW ZOBLER N. Ekstein color *Bloomberg Businessweek* no4534 p68 Ag 14 2017

Zoboi, Ibi
American Street color *Publishers Weekly* v263 no47 p110 N 21 2016
Spring Y.A.: Whole New Worlds: In these books, young people must break from the past to navigate first loves, troubled families, wartime travails and more *New York Times Book Review* p28 My 14 2017

Zobrist, Ben, 1981-
Ben Zobrist J. Crelin color *Current Biography* v78 no8 p91 Ag 2017

Zoch, Melody

Opening your door to research color *Phi Delta Kappan* v98 no3 p28 N 2016

Zodiac
See also
Aries (Astrology)
Leo (Astrology)
Pisces (Astrology)
Sagittarius (Astrology)
Scorpius (Constellation)
Virgo (Astrology)
Hair Horoscopes color *Essence* v47 no9 p36 Ja 2017
Surviving a Pisces M. ENGLISH *USA Today Magazine* v145 no2862 p70 Mr 2017

Zodiac Killer, The (Film)
To CATCH the ZODIAC Killer C. Collis color *Entertainment Weekly* no1468/1469 p72 Je 2-9 2017

Zoe, Rachel
Rachel Zoe A. Syrett color *InStyle* v24 no9 p197 S 2017

Zoeller, Gregory F., 1955-
Whose Law Is It? R. Cooper *Governing* v30 no11 p12 Ag 2017

ZOELLNER, TOM
From Here to Timbuktu *New York Times Book Review* p48 Je 4 2017

Zoellter, Juergen
On a Highway in Hell color *Car & Driver* v62 no6 p48 D 2016
Theater of the Absurd bw color diag *Car & Driver* v62 no11 p106 My 2017

Zoglin, Richard
The 10 Best Shows color *Time* v188 no25-26 p156 D 19 2016 Double Issue
A 9/11 Musical With Heart and Nostalgia color *Time* v189 no11 p62 Mr 27 2017

Zohari, Siamak
Role for migratory wild birds in the global spread of avian influenza H5N8 bibl graph map *Science* v354 no6309 p213 O 14 2016

Zolezzi, Francesca
Mapping the human DC lineage through the integration of high-dimensional techniques diag *Science* v356 no6342 p1044 Je 9 2017

Zollner, Patrick
Weather Front M. Branom *Weatherwise* v70 no1 p6 Ja/F 2017

Zoloth, Laurie
Managing cell and human identity cartoon *Science* v356 no6334 p139 Ap 14 2017

Zoltners, Andris A.
Are Sales Incentives Becoming Obsolete? *Harvard Business Review Digital Articles* p2 Ag 3 2017
Can Your Sales Team Actually Achieve Their Stretch Goals? *Harvard Business Review Digital Articles* p2 Jl 11 2016
Despite Dire Predictions, Salespeople Aren't Going Away *Harvard Business Review Digital Articles* p2 Mr 31 2016
Driving Sales Success This Quarter, This Year, and Beyond *Harvard Business Review Digital Articles* p2 D 1 2016
Great Salespeople Are Born, but Great Sales Forces Are Made *Harvard Business Review Digital Articles* p2 My 20 2016
Help Your Salespeople Spend Time on the Right Things *Harvard Business Review Digital Articles* p2 F 15 2016
How More Accessible Information Is Forcing B2B Sales to Adapt *Harvard Business Review Digital Articles* p2 Ja 6 2016
How to Spot Hidden Opportunities for Sales Growth *Harvard Business Review Digital Articles* p2 S 17 2015
Ineffective Sales Leaders Can Cause Lasting Damage color *Harvard Business Review Digital Articles* p2 Ja 30 2017
Sales Bonuses Are Supposed to Motivate, So Don't Waste Them on Easy Targets *Harvard Business Review Digital Articles* p2 S 14 2017
The Technology Trends That Matter to Sales Teams *Harvard Business Review Digital Articles* p2 My 7 2015
There's No One System for Paying Your Global Sales Force *Harvard Business Review Digital Articles* p2 N 13 2015
When Sales Incentives Should Be Based on Profit, Not Revenue *Harvard Business Review Digital Articles* p2 Je 10 2015
Why Sales Ops Is So Hard to Get Right *Harvard Business Review Digital Articles* p2 D 29 2014
Why Sales Teams Should Reexamine Territory Design *Harvard Business Review Digital Articles* p2 Ag 7 2015

2017

Zorrilla, Ana—Interviews

ANA ZORRILLA F. Dawson color *New Orleans Magazine* v51 no1 p30 N 2016

Zorthian, Julia

Apple's New Digs color *Time* v189 no9 p23 Mr 13 2017

The Bee Drone color *Time* v189 no11 p27 Mr 27 2017

The Best 25 Inventions of 2016 color *Time* v188 no22-23 p43 N/D 2016

Billboards That Don't Block the View color *Time* v189 no10 p21 Mr 20 2017

A Ceiling That Wirelessly Charges Devices color *Time* v189 no3 p21 Ja 30 2017

China's 'Mountain' Skyscrapers color *Time* v190 no13 p23 O 2 2017

A Data Breach You Can Smell color *Time* v188 no18 p21 O 31 2016

Denmark's Treetop Walkway color *Time* v190 no2/3 p23 Jl 10-17 2017

Electronic Play Dough color *Time* v189 no24 p19 Je 26 2017

The E.U.'s New Digs color *Time* v189 no3 p19 Ja 16 2017

Executive Clawbacks *Time* v189 no15 p19 Ap 24 2017

Floating Dorms color *Time* v188 no14 p23 O 10 2016

Flying Jet Taxis color *Time* v189 no18 p25 My 15 2017

A Glow-In-the-Dark Bike Path color *Time* v188 no16/17 p15 O 24 2016

A Laser That Prevents Bike Accidents color *Time* v189 no4 p21 F 6 2017

The Lego House color *Time* v190 no9 p25 S 4 2017

A Lego-Like Tape color *Time* v189 no12 p25 Ap 3 2017

A Mars Colony Near Dubai color *Time* v190 no15 p19 O 16 2017

Nasa's New 'Space Fabric' color *Time* v189 no19 p19 My 22 2017

A New Addition to the Glass Jungle color *Time* v189 no14 p23 Ap 17 2017

The Open-Top Submarine color *Time* v188 no20 p19 N 14 2016

Paris' Technicolor Basketball Court color *Time* v190 no4 p19 Jl 24 2017

A Parking Garage for Bikes color *Time* v190 no10/11 p29 S 18 2017

A Pizza-Making Robot color *Time* v189 no7/8 p27 F 27 2017

A Precarious but Picturesque Perch color *Time* v188 no22-23 p20 N/D 2016

Real-Life Robocops color *Time* v189 no21 p10 Je 5 2017

The 'Roboat' color *Time* v188 no15 p15 O 17 2016

Seoul's Garden In the Sky color *Time* v189 no22 p17 Je 12 2017

A Sneaker for Every State color *Time* v190 no5 p27 Jl 31 2017

The Solar-Power Road color *Time* v189 no4 p23 Ja 23 2017

A Star Wars-Inspired Observatory color *Time* v190 no12 p23 S 25 2017

A Suitcase That Follows Its Owner color *Time* v189 no6 p21 F 20 2017

Supreme Court 'Manterruption' color *Time* v189 no22 p17 Je 12 2017

Sweden's Solar Egg Sauna color *Time* v189 no20 p19 My 29 2017

Switzerland's New Medical Drones color *Time* v190 no14 p23 O 9 2017

This Just In *Time* v188 no16/17 p15 O 24 2016

This Just In *Time* v189 no13 p19 Ap 10 2017

This Just In *Time* v189 no24 p19 Je 26 2017

This Just In *Time* v190 no15 p19 O 16 2017

A Triumph Over Censorship color *Time* v190 no6 p25 Ag 7 2017

A Well That Sucks Water from Air color *Time* v188 no19 p17 N 7 2016

Window-Shopping Milan color *Time* v189 no15 p19 Ap 24 2017

World's Longest Suspension Footbridge color *Time* v190 no8 p21 Ag 28 2017

Zottarelli, Larry

Galaxy Quest K. Tingley color *New York Times Magazine* p28 Ag 6 2017

Zou, Manyun

WHERE & WHEN color *Washingtonian Magazine* v52 no7 p31 Ap 2017

Zou, Xinzhi

Engineering the ribosomal DNA in a megabase synthetic chromosome diag *Science* v355 no6329 p1049 Mr 10 2017

Zou, Yi-Quan

Deterministic entanglement generation from driving through quantum phase transitions bibl color graph *Science* v355 no6325 p620 F 10 2017

Zoumpoulis, Spyros

Run Field Experiments to Make Sense of Your Big Data *Harvard Business Review Digital Articles* p2 N 12 2015

Zsebők, Sándor

Acoustic mirrors as sensory traps for bats diag *Science* v357 no6355 p1045 S 8 2017

Zubcsek, Peter Pal

People Offer Better Ideas When They Can't See What Others Suggest *Harvard Business Review Digital Articles* p2 Jl 24 2015

Zuber, Maria T.

Formation of the Orientale lunar multiring basin bibl graph *Science* v354 no6311 p441 O 28 2016

Gravity field of the Orientale basin from the Gravity Recovery and Interior Laboratory Mission bibl graph *Science* v354 no6311 p438 O 28 2016

Zuberbühler, Nieves

NIEVES Zuberbühler M. GUIDUCCI color *Vogue* v207 no4 p156 Ap 2017

ZUBERI, HENA

40 Years and Counting *Islamic Horizons* v46 no2 p42 Mr/Ap 2017

Zucca, Mario

No Place Like Home bw cartoon color *O, The Oprah Magazine* p162 D 2016

Zuccarello, F.

Observation of a large-scale anisotropy in the arrival directions of cosmic rays above 8×1018 eV *Science* v357 no6357 p1266 S 22 2017

Zucchini

ALL AROUND Missouri color *Missouri Life* v44 no4 p81 Je 2017

THE WRINGER N. RICHARDSON color *Bon Appetit* no8 p102 Ag 2017

Zuchowski, Dave

Dave Zuchowski A. Priddle color *Motor Trend* v68 no12 p35 D 2016

Zucker, Arianne—Interviews

DAYS OF OUR LIVES M. LOGAN *TV Guide* v65 no8 p38 F 27 2017

Zucker, Jeff, 1965-

CNN K. R. Brooks and A. Heyman *New York Times Magazine* p10 Ap 23 2017

Zucker, Jeff, 1965-—Interviews

34 MINUTES WITH...Jeff Zucker G. SHERMAN img *New York* p12 Ja 23 2017

ZUCKER, LESLIE

Righting Words color *O, The Oprah Magazine* p17 Jl 2017

ZUCKER, MARSHALL

Chords & Discords bw color *Downbeat* v84 no10 p10 O 2017

ZUCKER, MEG

a rare condition, a beautiful legacy *Parents* v92 no2 p80 F 2017

Zucker, Rachel

And I Still Speak of It *Nation* v304 no8 p34 Mr 13 2017

I Can Barely Stand To R. ZUCKER *Nation* v304 no3 p35 Ja 30 2017

It's the World Committing Suicide Said One Mom R. ZUCKER *Nation* v304 no3 p30 Ja 30 2017

Zucker, Rebecca

Help Your Team Achieve Work-Life Balance—Even When You Can't *Harvard Business Review Digital Articles* p2 2017

Zuckerberg, Mark, 1984-

1 MARK ZUCKERBERG [Cover story] A. Lashinsky color diag *Fortune* v174 no7 p66 D 1 2016

America's relationship with Mark Zuckerberg is It's complicated M. Chafkin and S. Frier color graph *Bloomberg Businessweek* no4539 p50 S 25 2017

A drone for your thoughts color *U.S. Catholic* v81 no11 p10 N 2016

Red Meat from an Unexpected Source color *Weekly Standard* v22 no7 p4 O 24 2016

We Need More Alternatives to Facebook B. Bergstein color diag *MIT Technology Review* v120 no3 p86 My/Je 2017

When a Facebook Page Matters to Facebook S. Frier color *Bloomberg Businessweek* no4508 p28 Ja 23 2017

Why Mark Zuckerberg and Priscilla Chan Should Use Their Money for Fundraising D. Pallotta *Harvard Business Review Digital Articles* p2 D 3 2015

Zuckerberg, Mark, 1984—Political & social views
Touching Base A. Hess color *New York Times Magazine* p15 D 4 2016

Zuckerman, Catherine
ARRAY OF LIGHT color *National Geographic* v232 no2 p12 Ag 2017
ART THERAPY cartoon color *National Geographic* v231 no4 p154 Ap 2017
BABY STEPS bw *National Geographic* v231 no6 pC21 Je 2017
BACKUP BEES? color *National Geographic* v232 no4 p24 O 2017
CELEBRITY STATUS color *National Geographic* v232 no4 p29 O 2017
COLOR CODE color *National Geographic* v231 no1 p18 Ja 2017
EAT, DRINK, AND BE WARY color *National Geographic* v232 no3 p14 S 2017
FASHIONING FOOD WASTE color *National Geographic* v231 no5 p14 My 2017
FISH FOR THOUGHT color *National Geographic* v231 no4 p16 Ap 2017
FLASH POINTS graph map *National Geographic* v230 no6 p8 D 2016
GARBAGE SWELL color *National Geographic* v231 no4 p14 Ap 2017
KELP IS ON THE WAY color *National Geographic* v232 no5 p14 N 2017
LIP-READING color *National Geographic* v232 no3 p22 S 2017
NAME THAT STAR color *National Geographic* v232 no2 p16 Ag 2017
Speedy Delivery color *National Geographic* v230 no4 p18 O 2016
STING OPERATION color *National Geographic* v231 no6 p152 Je 2017
UNITED STATES OF CORN color *National Geographic* v231 no2 p18 F 2017

Zuckerman, Jocelyn C.
Oil Change color *Vogue* v207 no9 p454 S 2017

Zuckerman, Phil
Society's Books of Note *Society* v54 no2 p187 Ap 2017

Zuckerman, Suzanne
ADIR ABERGEL The Mane Man color *InStyle* v24 no11 p132 N 2017
Chloë Grace Moretz color *InStyle* v23 no12 p200 N 2016
Hung Vanngo color *InStyle* v24 no9 p342 S 2017
Kate Lee color *InStyle* v24 no5 p146 My 2017
Priyanka Chopra color *InStyle* v24 no2 p112 F 2017
Zoë Kravitz color *InStyle* v23 no13 p197 D 2016

Zucolotto, Maria E.
Lifetime of the solar nebula constrained by meteorite paleomagnetism bibl graph *Science* v355 no6325 p623 F 10 2017

Zuehlke, Sue
pontoon mania color *Cabin Living* p60 Je 2017

ZUERCHER, RACHEL
Long-Term Studies Contribute Disproportionately to Ecology and Policy *BioScience* v67 no3 p271 Mr 2017

Zuiker, Anthony E.
THE BIG QUESTION cartoon *Atlantic* v320 no3 p100 O 2017

ZUK, MARLENE
Fox and Friends *New York Times Book Review* p26 My 7 2017

Zukerman, Wendy
10 — SCIENCE VS C. Everett *Entertainment Weekly* no1444/1445 p114 D 16 2016

Zulawski, Andrzej
L'Important c'est d'aimer E. Bittencourt color *Film Comment* v53 no4 p71 Jl/Ag 2017

ZULKEY, CLAIRE
ASK AMY ABOUT HERSELF ALREADY color *Chicago* v66 no3 p30 Mr 2017
BOX-OFFICE MIND READERS color *Chicago* v66 no6 p24 Je 2017
COUCH CULTURE color *Chicago* v65 no12 p47 D 2016
IN PRAISE OF WALKING color *Chicago* v66 no1 p44 Ja 2017
Inside out: Can social emotional learning prevent bullying in Catholic middle schools? [Cover story] color *U.S. Catholic* v82 no9 p26 S 2017

READY, SET, SNOOZE color *Runner's World* v52 no9 p24 O 2017
Rules aren't enough color *U.S. Catholic* v82 no2 p12 F 2017
SOOTHE YOURSELF color *Runner's World* v52 no7 p28 Ag 2017
THE SUPERFAN color *Chicago* v65 no11 p24 N 2016
WHERE TO BUY NOW cartoon chart color graph *Chicago* v66 no4 p77 Ap 2017

Zulu (African people)
Adonis Expose L. Monk Carter color *New Orleans Magazine* v51 no4 p28 F 2017

Zuma, Jacob, 1942-
For the Record color *Time* v190 no7 p6 Ag 21 2017
In South Africa, more calls for Zuma to go A. Egan color *America* v216 no12 p15 My 29 2017
Patience Is Running Out in South Africa bw *Bloomberg Businessweek* no4518 p10 Ap 10 2017
The Race to Lead South Africa Is On M. Cohen, D. Malingha Doya et al color *Bloomberg Businessweek* no4524 p15 My 29 2017
South Africa's Graft Scandal Grows color *Time* v189 no23 p12 Je 19 2017

Zumba Fitness LLC
Zumba's Success Arose from Long-Term Trends D. L. Yohn *Harvard Business Review Digital Articles* p2 O 14 2014

ZUMMALLEN, RYAN
THE LAST LONG ROAD color *Road & Track* v69 no2 p64 S 2017

Zundel, Carole
When I Was a Horse-Crazy Kid, I... color *Horse & Rider* v56 no2 p72 F 2017

Zunger, Alex
Arthur J. Freeman *Physics Today* v69 no11 p69 N 2016

Zuniga, Tommy
Dahozy and Duby Win Sisters, Ore color *Spin to Win Rodeo* v21 no6 p22 Ag 2017

Zunyou Wu
The aftermath of AIDS in China K. Harper color *Science* v354 no6318 p1384 D 16 2016

Zuo, Xiaobing
Quantitative 3D evolution of colloidal nanoparticle oxidation in solution diag graph *Science* v356 no6335 p303 Ap 21 2017

Zuo, Zhijun
Atomic-layered Au clusters on α-MoC as catalysts for the low-temperature water-gas shift reaction chart diag graph *Science* v357 no6349 p389 Jl 28 2017

Zuo, Zongtang, 1812-1885
PARODY color *Weekly Standard* v22 no15 p40 D 19 2016

ZUPAN, MARTY
FROM THE ARCHIVES bw color *Reason* v49 no3 p70 Jl 2017

Zurbuchen, Thomas—Interviews
Earth science a 'no-brainer' for NASA's science chief P. Voosen color *Science* v355 no6330 p1112 Mr 17 2017

Zürcher, Erik
Opening and Closing of Turkey's Past *History Today* v66 no10 p72 O 2016

Zureikat, Lara
Lara Zureikat [Cover story] M. OWENS color *Architectural Digest* v74 no10 p110 O 1 2017

Zurek, Wojciech
Thomas Walter Bannerman Kibble *Physics Today* v69 no12 p68 D 2016

Zurenski, Matthew A.
Reovirus infection triggers inflammatory responses to dietary antigens and development of celiac disease color diag *Science* v356 no6333 p44 Ap 7 2017

ZURER, RACHEL
Increase your vocabulary *Backpacker* p14 S 2017
See the Light color *Backpacker* v45 no2 p21 Mr 2017

Zuriaga, María A.
Clonal hematopoiesis associated with TET2 deficiency accelerates atherosclerosis development in mice bibl diag *Science* v355 no6327 p842 F 24 2017

Zurla, Chiara
Sustained virologic control in SIV+ macaques after antiretroviral and α4β7 antibody therapy bibl graph *Science* v354 no6309

p197 O 14 2016

ZUTSHI, CHITRALEKHA

Seasons of Discontent and Revolt in Kashmir *Current History* v116 no789 p123 Ap 2017

Zuzana: Music Is Life (Film)

MUSIC IS LIFE A. Whiting *Washingtonian Magazine* v52 no9 p22 Je 2017

Zverev, Alexander, 1997-

Alexander Zverev's Two-Handed Backhand J. YANDELL color *Tennis* v53 no2 p72 Mr/Ap 2017

The BIG TWO L. Thomas color *Vogue* v207 no9 p722 S 2017

Zvesper, John

MISSION IMPOSSIBLE *Claremont Review of Books* v17 no3 p51 Summ 2017

Zvonarev, Mikhail B.

Bloch oscillations in the absence of a lattice graph *Science* v356 no6341 p945 Je 1 2017

Zwahlen, Martin

A subcellular map of the human proteome color *Science* v356 no6340 p820 My 26 2017

Zwang, Yaara

Potential role of intratumor bacteria in mediating tumor resistance to the chemotherapeutic drug gemcitabine diag *Science* v357 no6356 p1156 S 15 2017

Zwart, Peter H.

Principles for designing proteins with cavities formed by curved β sheets bibl color graph *Science* v355 no6321 p1 Ja 13 2017

Zwartjes, Arianne

My time at a refugee camp in Greece: Waiting in Malakasa color *Christian Century* v134 no2 p30 Ja 18 2017

Zweifel, Paul Frederick

Paul Frederick Zweifel N. J. McCormick, C. E. Siewert et al *Physics Today* v70 no8 p73 Ag 2017

Zweig, Stefan, 1881-1942

CATCH AND RELEASE S. Zweig *Lapham's Quarterly* v10 no3 p81 Summ 2017

Zwick, Ed—Interviews

Inside Nashville's Revamp S. Highfill color *Entertainment Weekly* no1443 p54 D 9 2016

Zwick, Edward

JACK REACHER: NEVER GO BACK C. Gunnestad color *Sound & Vision* v82 no5 p65 Je 2017

Zwiebel, Brian

AIM HIGH color *Audubon* v119 no3 p48 Fall 2017

Zwierlein, Martin W.

Second-scale nuclear spin coherence time of ultracold 23Na40K molecules diag *Science* v357 no6349 p372 Jl 28 2017

Two- and three-body contacts in the unitary Bose gas bibl diag graph *Science* v355 no6323 p377 Ja 27 2017

ZWIRZ, RICKY

reclaimed cabin color *Cabin Living* p17 Mr 2017

ZWO Co.

The ASI 1600MC Cooled Camera J. Horne *Sky & Telescope* v133 no4 p58 Ap 2017

Zya

MEET YOUR CHAKRAS color *Essence* v48 no5 p116 S 2017

Zylberman, William

The formation of peak rings in large impact craters bibl color graph *Science* v354 no6314 p878 N 18 2016

ZYLSTRA, SARAH EEKHOFF

ABANDONING THE ORPHANAGE color *Christianity Today* v61 no6 p54 Jl/Ag 2017

FREE EXERCISE color *Christianity Today* v61 no7 p15 S 2017

The Title IX Lives of Christian Colleges *Christianity Today* v60 no10 p24 D 2016

Together for the Gospels *Christianity Today* v61 no4 p20 My 2017

WHEN HELPING HURTS THE HELPERS color *Christianity Today* v61 no6 p13 Jl/Ag 2017

Zyman, Jennifer

50 Best, Refreshed *Atlanta* v56 no11 p2 Mr 2017

BAO, WOW! *Atlanta* v56 no12 p78 Ap 2017

BEST NEW RESTAURANTS *Atlanta* v57 no5 p78 S 2017

Brush Sushi Izakaya *Atlanta* v56 no11 p66 Mr 2017

Candy Land *Atlanta* v56 no8 p69 D 2016

DIM SUM AT BEST BBQ *Atlanta* v57 no3 p54 Jl 2017

The Federal *Atlanta* v56 no12 p66 Ap 2017

FOODSTUFFS *Atlanta* v56 no9 p54 Ja 2017

Food Terminal *Atlanta* v57 no2 p60 Je 2017

KFC (Korean Fried Chicken) *Atlanta* v57 no6 p53 O 2017

Pick Your Poké *Atlanta* v56 no10 p56 F 2017

Poor Hendrix *Atlanta* v57 no1 p68 My 2017

Sliced, Sealed, Delivered *Atlanta* v56 no9 p53 Ja 2017

Spring *Atlanta* v56 no9 p60 Ja 2017

VENKMAN'S PATTY MELT *Atlanta* v57 no2 p52 Je 2017

Zysk, Katarzyna

Nonstrategic nuclear weapons in Russia's evolving military doctrine bibl *Bulletin of the Atomic Scientists* v73 no5 p322 2017

Zywitza, Vera

Loss of a mammalian circular RNA locus causes miRNA deregulation and affects brain function color *Science* v357 no6357 p1254 S 22 2017

BOOK REVIEWS

America's Test Kitchen (Company) Food processor perfection. 2017
Publishers Weekly v264 no14 p68 Ap 3. 2017

America's Test Kitchen (Company) The complete Mediterranean cookbook. 2017
Publishers Weekly v263 no45 p55-6 N 7 2016

America's Test Kitchen (Company) and Crosby, G. Cook's science. 2016
Publishers Weekly v263 no40 p114 O 3 2016

Amini, M. and Gonzales, M. Yo soy Muslim. 2017
Publishers Weekly v264 no22 p67-8 My 29 2017

Amis, M. The Rachel papers. 1992
Esquire v167 no2 p108-13 Mr 2017

Ammerman, D. Waiting for the Voo. 2014
Publishers Weekly v263 no39 p94 S 26 2016
Publishers Weekly v263 no43 p50g O 24 2016

Amor, J. and others. One Week in the Library. 2016
Publishers Weekly v263 no50 p58 D 5 2016

Amstutz, M. R. Just immigration. 2017
Christianity Today v61 no4 p59-61 My 2017 S. D. James

Anālayo, B. Mindfully Facing Disease and Death. 2017
Tricycle: The Buddhist Review v26 no3 p92-3 Spr 2017 M. Scarles

Anastas, M. and others. Bob and Joss get lost. 2017
Publishers Weekly v263 no50 p71 D 5 2016

Anastasiu, H. and Brown, A. G. Girl Last Seen. 2016
Publishers Weekly v264 no15 p53 Ap 10 2017

Anbinder, T. City of Dreams. 2016
New York Times Book Review p12 N 6 2016 K. Hymowitz

Anchin, L. and Capucilli, A. S. I Will Love You. 2017
Publishers Weekly v264 no8 p83 F 20 2017

Anderer, P. Kurosawa's Rashomon. 2016
New York Times Book Review p30 D 4 2016 P. Lopate

Anders, A. In His Hands. 2017
Publishers Weekly v264 no26 p163 Je 26 2017

Anders, A. Under Her Skin. 2017
Publishers Weekly v263 no51 p131 D 12 2016

Andersen, C. and Peters, E. Indigenous in the city. 2013
American Indian Quarterly v40 no3 p283-5 Summ 2016 F. Delgado

Anderson, A. and Minier, B. Don't turn out the lights. 2016
Publishers Weekly v263 no39 p64 S 26 2016

Anderson, B. S. Chain of Mercy. 2014
Publishers Weekly v264 no4 p50a-b Ja 23 2017

Anderson, C. (. White Rage. 2016
Foreign Affairs v95 no6 p179 N/D 2016 W. Russell Mead

Anderson, C. The Christmas room. 2017
Publishers Weekly v264 no26 p110-4 Je 26 2017 R. Fox

Anderson, D. Imaginary cities. 2017
Publishers Weekly v264 no4 p70-1 Ja 23 2017

Anderson, E. and others. The book of greens. 2017
Publishers Weekly v263 no50 p59-64 D 5 2016

Anderson, G. and Nadel, J. We. 2017
Entertainment Weekly no1459 p63 Mr 31 2017 T. Jordan
Publishers Weekly v264 no4 p76 Ja 23 2017

Anderson, J. A. and Dyrness, W. A. Modern art and the life of a culture. 2016
Christianity Today v61 no1 p54 Ja/F 2017 W. Bearden

Anderson, J. D. Ms. Bixby's Last Day. 2016
Publishers Weekly v263 no49 p74 D 7 2016

Anderson, J. D. Posted. 2017
Publishers Weekly v264 no11 p84 Mr 13 2017

Anderson, J. L. and Klonsky, J. Midnight at the electric. 2017
Publishers Weekly v264 no16 p70 Ap 17 2017

Anderson, J. R. and others. Survivance, Sovereignty, and Story. 2015
American Indian Quarterly v41 no2 p190-2 Spr 2017 M. N. Boyer-Kelly

Anderson, L. H. Ashes. 2016
New York Times Book Review p32 N 13 2016 L. Bayard
Publishers Weekly v263 no49 p80-1 D 7 2016

Anderson, M. T. and Offermann, A. Yvain. 2017
New York Times Book Review p23 My 14 2017 M. Meloy
Publishers Weekly v263 no51 p150-1 D 12 2016

Anderson, M. T. Landscape With Invisible Hand. 2017
Publishers Weekly v264 no25 p113 Je 19 2017

Anderson, N. C. City of Saints & Thieves. 2017

Publishers Weekly v263 no45 p62-3 N 7 2016

Anderson, Q. The Other Five Percent. 2017
Publishers Weekly v264 no21 p79 My 22 2017

Anderson, S. and others. Animals Are Delicious. 2016
Publishers Weekly v263 no49 p56 D 7 2016

Anderson, S. The Hostage's Daughter. 2016
New York Times Book Review p20 N 27 2016 N. Burleigh

Anderson, T. and Allenby, V. Rhino rumpus. 2016
Publishers Weekly v263 no40 p121 O 3 2016

Anderson, T. The Dirty War on Syria. 2016
America v215 no14 p30-2 N 7 2016 J. Donnelly

Anderson, V. D. The martyr and the traitor. 2017
Publishers Weekly v264 no17 p83 Ap 24 2017

Andersson, K. and others. Pursuing sustainability. 2016
Environment v58 no6 p34-6 N/D 2016 T. O'Riordan

Andersson, M. The excavation. 2017
Publishers Weekly v264 no3 p47 Ja 16 2017

Andersson, P. J. and Holmwood, A. The Amazing Story of the Man Who Cycled from India to Europe for Love. 2017
Publishers Weekly v264 no3 p51 Ja 16 2017

Anderton, S. Lives of the Great Gardeners. 2016
Publishers Weekly v263 no42 p65 O 17 2016

Andison, F. S. Death of the Republic. 2011
Publishers Weekly v264 no9 p53-66 F 27 2017

Andreas, P. Rebel Mother. 2017
Foreign Affairs v96 no3 p165-6 My/Je 2017 R. Feinberg
New York Times Book Review p38 My 14 2017 J. Walker
Publishers Weekly v263 no51 p134 D 12 2016

Andrés, J. C. and others. My dad is a clown = : Mi papá es un payaso. 2017
Publishers Weekly v264 no47 p107-8 N 21 2016

Andrew, S. The satanic mechanic. 2017
Publishers Weekly v264 no17 p88 Ap 24 2017
Publishers Weekly v264 no5 p181 Ja 30 2017

Andrews, C. and Hirsheimer, C. The British Table. 2016
British Heritage Travel v37 no6 p79 N/D 2016 B. Patrick

Andrews, D. Die like and eagle. 2016
Publishers Weekly v263 no40 p117 O 3 2016

Andrews, D. Gone gull. 2017
Publishers Weekly v264 no25 p94-5 Je 19 2017

Andrews, I. White Hot. 2017
Publishers Weekly v264 no13 p87 Mr 27 2017

Andrews, R. and others. Hamlet. 2014
Weekly Standard v22 no31 p43 Ap 17 2017 C. Atamian

Andrews, R. and others. Romeo and Juliet. 2014
Publishers Weekly v263 no41 p79 O 10 2016

Andrews-Katz, E. Tartarus. 2016
Publishers Weekly v263 no45 p46 N 7 2016

Andrus, A. Botanical beauty. 2017
Publishers Weekly v264 no5 p206 Ja 30 2017

Angell, C. All the time in the world. 2016
New York Times Book Review p30 O 16 2016 S. Gilbert

Angell, T. and Calvez, L. The hidden lives of owls. 2016
Sierra v101 no6 p10 N/D 2016 S. Pagani

Angelou, M. Mom & me & mom. 2012
Entertainment Weekly no1454/1455 p30 F 24 2017 D. Coggan

Angleberger, T. and Bell, C. Inspector Flytrap. 2016
Publishers Weekly v263 no49 p66 D 7 2016

Anna, H. and Santos, G. Daisy Dreamer and the totally true imaginary friend. 2017
Publishers Weekly v264 no17 p93 Ap 24 2017

Annand, B. The girl from old Nichol. 2017
Publishers Weekly v263 no50 p58 D 5 2016

Anthony, B. and Walker, B. Abe Lincoln On Acid. 2016
Publishers Weekly v263 no51 p130 D 12 2016
Publishers Weekly v264 no4 p44 Ja 23 2017
Publishers Weekly v264 no4 p46-50 Ja 23 2017
Publishers Weekly v264 no4 p50a Ja 23 2017

Anthony, J. A Month of Mondays. 2017
Publishers Weekly v264 no3 p60 Ja 16 2017

Anthony, K. H. Defined by design. 2017
Publishers Weekly v264 no3 p52 Ja 16 2017

Antill, S. A bear's life. 2012
Publishers Weekly v264 no28 p87 Jl 10 2017

Antòn, J. and Brunellière, L. Deep in the forest. 2017
Publishers Weekly v264 no6 p67 F 6 2017

America v215 no15 p35-7 N 14 2016 M. C. McCarthy

Ashbery, J. Commotion of the Birds. 2016
  Publishers Weekly v263 no42 p47 O 17 2016

Ashburn, B. and Gee, K. The class. 2016
  Publishers Weekly v263 no49 p20 D 7 2016

Ashenden, J. In Bed With the Billionaire. 2016
  Publishers Weekly v263 no43 p63 O 24 2016

Ashenden, J. Wrong for Me. 2016
  Publishers Weekly v263 no41 p63 O 10 2016

Asher, J. Thirteen reasons why. 2007
  New York Times Book Review p25 Ap 30 2017
  New York Times Book Review p29 My 7 2017

Asher, J. What light. 2016
  Entertainment Weekly no1438 p63 N 4 2016 S. Vilkomerson
  New York Times Book Review p34 N 13 2016 J. Doll
  Publishers Weekly v264 no9 p98 F 27 2017

Asher, S. and Fearing, M. Chicken story time. 2016
  Publishers Weekly v263 no41 p77 O 10 2016

Ashford, J. Lord Sebastian's Secret. 2017
  Publishers Weekly v263 no48 p53 N 28 2016

Ashford, J. Nothing Like a Duke. 2017
  Publishers Weekly v264 no14 p59 Ap 3. 2017

Ashman, L. and Mulazzani, S. Rock-a-bye Romp. 2016
  Publishers Weekly v263 no44 D 7 2016

Ashton, B. and others. My Lady Jane. 2016
  Publishers Weekly v263 no49 p109-10 D 7 2016

Ashworth, A. R. Souls of Men. 2017
  Publishers Weekly v264 no6 p49 F 6 2017

Asim, J. and Lewis, E. B. Preaching to the chickens. 2016
  Publishers Weekly v263 no9 p50 D 7 2016

Aslam, N. The golden legend. 2017
  New York Times Book Review p10 My 21 2017 F. Prose
  Publishers Weekly v264 no9 p70 F 27 2017

Asma, S. T. The evolution of imagination. 2017
  Publishers Weekly v264 no17 p80 Ap 24 2017
  Science v356 no6344 p1240 Je 23 2017 M. Merritt

Aspden, R. Generation revolution. 2016
  New York Times Book Review p12 F 12 2017 T. Cambanis
  Publishers Weekly v263 no39 p75 S 26 2016

Aspelmeyer, M. and others. Cavity Optomechanics. 2016
  Physics Today v70 no2 p58-60 F 2017 P. Meystre

Asprey, D. Head strong. 2016
  Publishers Weekly v263 no45 p28-32 N 7 2016 D. L.

Assadi, H. L. Sonora. 2017
  New Yorker v93 no9 p72 Ap 17 2017
  Publishers Weekly v264 no3 p33-4 Ja 16 2017

Astin, A. W. Are you smart enough? 2016
  Change v49 no1 p7-13 Ja/F 2017 M. T. Huber

Aston, D. H. and Long, S. A beetle is shy. 2016
  Publishers Weekly v263 no49 p45 D 7 2016
  Science v354 no6317 p1224 D 9 2016 L. Kmec

Astor, L. and Weis, A. Blackwell. 2017
  New Orleans Magazine v51 no3 p48 Ja 2017 J. Debold

Astor, M. Life On Film. 1972
  New York Review of Books v64 no5 p39-42 Mr 23 2017 R. Gottlieb

Astor, M. My Story. 2011
  New York Review of Books v64 no5 p39-42 Mr 23 2017 R. Gottlieb

Atchison, M. Mellow Submarine. 2016
  Publishers Weekly v264 no20 p33 My 15 2017
  Publishers Weekly v264 no26 p146b Je 26 2017

Athill, D. A florence diary. 2016
  New York Times Book Review p16-7 Je 4 2017 L. Schillinger

Athitakis, M. The New Midwest. 2017
  Cincinnati Magazine v50 no5 p20-2 F 2017 C. Fehrman

Atkins, A. Robert B. Parker's Little White Lies. 2017
  Publishers Weekly v264 no10 p40 Mr 6 2017

Atkins, A. The fallen. 2017
  Publishers Weekly v264 no21 p73 My 22 2017

Atkins, D. and Fitzsimmons, A. Rethinking reputational risk. 2017
  People Management p52 F 2017

Atkinson, C. and Fergus, M. The day Santa stopped believing in Harold. 2016
  Publishers Weekly v263 no39 p90 S 26 2016

Atkinson, C. and Lodding, L. R. Little red riding sheep. 2017

Publishers Weekly v264 no23 p52 Je 5 2017

Atkinson, C. F. and Spengler, O. Man and technics. 1976
  American Conservative v15 no6 p51-3 N/D 2016 B. R. Myers

Atkinson, C. Plant craft. 2016
  Martha Stewart Living no271 p10 Ja/F 2017

Atogun, O. Taduno's song. 2017
  Publishers Weekly v264 no5 p174 Ja 30 2017

Atria, T. and Mayfield, T. Traveling soul. 2016
  Rolling Stone no1275 p14 D 1 2016 J. Dolan

Attebery, B. and Le Guin, U. K. The complete Orsinia. 2016
  Weekly Standard v22 no16 p36-7 D 26 2016 E. Mundahl

Attenberg, J. All Grown Up. 2017
  New York Times Book Review p18 Mr 19 2017 H. Schulman
  New York Times Book Review p23 Mr 26 2017
  O, The Oprah Magazine p91 Ap 2017 M. Filgate
  Publishers Weekly v264 no3 p34 Ja 16 2017

Atwood, M. and Christmas, J. Angel Catbird. 2016
  New York Times Book Review p18-9 Ja 1 2017 D. Wolk
  Publishers Weekly v264 no41 p65 O 10 2016

Atwood, M. and Petričić, D. A Trio of Tolerable Tales. 2017
  Publishers Weekly v264 no11 p84 Mr 13 2017

Atwood, M. Hag-Seed. 2016
  Maclean's v129 no41 p54-5 O 17 2016 B. Bethune
  New Yorker v92 no33 p85-9 O 17 2016 A. Gopnik
  New York Times Book Review p24 Je 11 2017 J. Khatib
  New York Times Book Review p9 O 30 2016 E. St. John Mandel
  Publishers Weekly v263 no50 p67 D 5 2016

Atwood, M. The Handmaid's tale. 2006
  America v216 no11 p46-9 My 15 2017 E. Blondiau
  Christian Century v134 no13 p42-3 Je 21 2017 K. Reklis
  Ms. v27 no2 p39-41 Summ 2017 M. Atwood
  New Yorker v93 no14 p78-80 My 22 2017 E. Nussbaum
  New York Times Book Review p1-15 Mr 19 2017 M. Atwood
  Publishers Weekly v264 no19 p11 My 8 2017 C. Juris

Auel, J. M. The Clan of the Cave Bear. 1980
  Walrus v14 no4 p63-5 My 2017 M. Meltzer

Auerbach, A. and Auerbach, A. Monkey brother. 2017
  Publishers Weekly v264 no18 p56 My 1 2017

Auerswald, P. E. The code economy. 2017
  Publishers Weekly v263 no43 p65-6 O 24 2016

Aughtmon, S. F. and Winz, B. One dress, one year. 2016
  Publishers Weekly v264 no17 p20-6 Ap 24 2017 L. Garrett

Aurell, B. and Cassidy, P. Scandikitchen Fika & Hygge. 2016
  New York Times Book Review p27 F 26 2017 J. Newman

Aures, V. and Meinecke, C. E. Your cabin in the woods. 2016
  Cabin Living p12 Ja/F 2017

Auslander, O. and Auslander, O. I feel bad ; all day, every day, about everything. 2017
  New York Times Book Review p29 My 21 2017 A. Ulinich

Auslin, M. R. The end of the Asian Century. 2016
  Claremont Review of Books v17 no1 p61-2 Wint 2016/2017 C. Horner
  Commentary v143 no4 p42-4 Ap 2017 D. Feith
  Foreign Affairs v96 no3 p146-53 My/Je 2017 B. Kausikan
  National Review v69 no3 p45-6 F 20 2017 J. Holmes
  Publishers Weekly v263 no44 p64 O 31 2016
  Weekly Standard v22 no37 p30-2 Je 5 2017 J. Psaropoulos

Austen, J. and Rogers, P. Pride and prejudice. 2006
  New York Times Book Review p25 D 25 2016 S. Chira

Austen, J. Sanditon. 2009
  New Yorker v93 no4 p77-9 Mr 13 2017 A. Lane

Auster, P. 4 3 2 1. 2017
  Esquire v167 no1 p20-1 F 2017 C. Beha
  Harper's Magazine v334 no2001 p88-93 F 2017 S. Sacks
  New Yorker v92 no47 p68-71 Ja 30 2017 L. Miller
  New York p68-9 Ja 23 2017 C. Lorentzen
  New York Review of Books v64 no6 p14-5 Ap 6 2017 N. Rich
  New York Times Book Review p24 F 19 2017 G. Cowles
  New York Times Book Review p8 F 5 2017 T. Perrotta
  O, The Oprah Magazine p100 F 2017 H. Cain
  Publishers Weekly v263 no39 p62 S 26 2016
  Publishers Weekly v263 no48 p26-7 N 28 2016 W. Smith
  Time v189 no4 p54 F 6 2017 S. Begley

Austin, M. and Rylant, C. Henny, Penny, Lenny, Denny, and Mike. 2017
  Publishers Weekly v264 no28 p86-8 Jl 10 2017

Austin, M. Maggie Austin cake. 2017
  Publishers Weekly v264 no3 p53-4 Ja 16 2017
Austin, R. and others. The girl who ran. 2017
  Publishers Weekly v264 no23 p51 Je 5 2017
Austrian, J. J. and Curato, M. Worm loves Worm. 2016
  Publishers Weekly v263 no49 p35 D 7 2016
Avagyan, S. The Hamburg score. 2017
  Publishers Weekly v263 no52 p115 D 19 2016
Avdic, A. and Willson-Broyles, R. The dying game. 2017
  Publishers Weekly v264 no23 p31-2 Je 5 2017
Aveni, A. In the shadow of the moon. 2017
  Natural History v125 no7 p47 Jl/Ag 2017 L. A. Marschall
  Publishers Weekly v264 no6 p58 F 6 2017
  Science News v191 no9 p28 My 13 2017 S. Perkins
Avent, R. The wealth of humans. 2016
  America v216 no11 p50-2 My 15 2017 J. Malesic
Avery, A. Sonata. 2017
  Publishers Weekly v264 no11 p75-6 Mr 13 2017
Avery, L. The memory book. 2016
  Publishers Weekly v263 no49 p99 D 7 2016
Avery, T. Not as we know it. 2016
  Publishers Weekly v263 no49 p69 D 7 2016
Avi, 1. The Most Important Thing. 2016
  Publishers Weekly v264 no9 p74 D 7 2016
Avi, The unexpected life of Oliver Cromwell Pitts. 2017
  Publishers Weekly v264 no12 p73 Mr 20 2017
Aviv, J. The acid watcher diet. 2017
  Publishers Weekly v263 no47 p102-3 N 21 2016
Avlon, J. Washington's farewell. 2017
  America v216 no7 p44-5 Ap 3 2017 W. Lanouette
  Foreign Affairs v96 no3 p161 My/Je 2017 W. Russell Mead
  New York Times Book Review p4 Ja 22 2017 J. Williams
Axat, F. and Frye, D. Kill the next one. 2016
  New York Times Book Review p25 D 18 2016 M. Stasio
  Publishers Weekly v263 no40 p101 O 3 2016
Aydin, A. and others. March. 2013
  New York Times Book Review p13 N 27 2016 J. Lucas
Aydin, C. The idea of the Muslim world. 2017
  Harper's Magazine v334 no2004 p82-7 My 2017 Y. Seale
Aykroyd, S. S. and Whaley, B. Practise to deceive. 2016
  Foreign Affairs v95 no6 p177 N/D 2016 L. D. Freedman
Ayris, A. A. The Kingstone Bible Trilogy. 2016
  Humanist v77 no2 p44-6 Mr/Ap 2017 F. Edwords

B

Baas, T. and others. The pied piper of Hamelin. 2016
  Publishers Weekly v263 no49 p28 D 7 2016
Baberowski, J. Scorched earth. 2016
  Publishers Weekly v263 no42 p61 O 17 2016
Bacal, N. Breakdown. 2017
  Walrus v14 no2 p63-6 Mr 2017 J. Kay
Bacevich, A. J. America's war for the greater Middle East. 2016
  Christian Century v133 no21 p28-31 O 12 2016 J. C. Danforth
  Claremont Review of Books v16 no4 p59-60 Fall 2016 C. Lord
  MHQ: Quarterly Journal of Military History v29 no2 p94 Wint 2017 M. S. Neiberg
  Progressive p60-4 D 2016/Ja 2017 B. Lueders
Bach, A. and Capucilli, A. S. Good Night, My Darling Baby. 2017
  Publishers Weekly v264 no5 p202 Ja 30 2017
Bacharach, J. The doorposts of your house and on your gates. 2017
  New York Times Book Review p14 Jl 9 2017 S. Deen
  Publishers Weekly v264 no4 p54-5 Ja 23 2017
Bacigalupi, P. and others. Cyber World. 2016
  Publishers Weekly v263 no40 p103 O 3 2016
Backhouse, S. Kierkegaard. 2016
  Christian Century v134 no11 p30-3 My 24 2017 E. Palmer
  Christianity Today v61 no1 p54-5 Ja/F 2017 J. Green
Backlund, J. R. Among the Dead. 2017
  Publishers Weekly v264 no24 p43-4 Je 12 2017
Backman, F. A man called Ove. 2014
  New York Times Book Review p24 D 25 2016
  New York Times Book Review p28 O 16 2016
  New York Times Book Review p80 D 4 2016
  Publishers Weekly v263 no46 p12-3 N 14 2016 E. Nawotka

Backman, F. and Menzies, A. And every morning the way home gets longer and longer. 2016
  Publishers Weekly v263 no40 p95 O 3 2016
Backman, F. and Smith, N. Beartown. 2017
  Publishers Weekly v264 no19 p11 My 8 2017 C. Juris
  Publishers Weekly v264 no26 p173 Je 26 2017
  Publishers Weekly v264 no9 p72 F 27 2017
Bacon, Q. and Batali, M. Mario Batali Big American cookbook. 2016
  New York Times Book Review p46-7 D 4 2016 L. Shapiro
Bacon, Q. and Garten, I. Cooking for Jeffrey. 2016
  Publishers Weekly v263 no45 p14 N 7 2016 C. Juris
Bacon, Q. and Santos, C. Share. 2017
  Publishers Weekly v264 no1 p52 Ja 2 2017
Baddeley, E. and Levy, D. I dissent. 2016
  American History v52 no3 p69 Ag 2017 G. Carrasco
Bader, J. Two Wizard Roulette. 2017
  Publishers Weekly v264 no23 p35 Je 5 2017
Baek, J. North Korea's hidden revolution. 2017
  New Yorker v92 no41 p77 D 12 2016
Baekgaard, B. B. A Colorful Way of Living. 2017
  Publishers Weekly v264 no9 p89 F 27 2017
Baer, M. The inconceivable life of Quinn. 2017
  Publishers Weekly v264 no6 p70 F 6 2017
Bagge, P. Fire! 2017
  Publishers Weekly v264 no3 p47 Ja 16 2017
  Reason v49 no3 p68 Jl 2017 B. Doherty
Baggini, J. The edge of reason. 2016
  Skeptical Inquirer v41 no1 p60-1 Ja/F 2017 K. Frazier
Baggott, J. Mass. 2017
  Publishers Weekly v264 no20 p48 My 15 2017
Bagley, J. and Bagley, J. Before I leave. 2016
  Publishers Weekly v263 no49 p11 D 7 2016
Bahrami, B. Café Neandertal. 2017
  Publishers Weekly v264 no4 p72 Ja 23 2017
Baier, B. and Whitney, C. Three days in January. 2017
  Publishers Weekly v264 no4 p10 Ja 23 2017 C. Juris
Bailey, C. The Official Chase 'n Yur Face Cookbook. 2016
  Publishers Weekly v263 no47 p102 N 21 2016
  Publishers Weekly v263 no52 p90f D 19 2016
Bailey, C. W. and Knebel, F. Seven days in May. 1970
  Good Housekeeping v265 no1 p67 Jl 2017
Bailey, R. American English, italian chocolate. 2017
  Publishers Weekly v264 no17 p77-8 Ap 24 2017
Bailey, T. Too Hot to Handle. 2016
  Publishers Weekly v263 no44 p59 O 31 2016
Bair, D. Al Capone. 2016
  New York Times Book Review p36 D 4 2016 J. A. Morone
Baird, J. Victoria the queen. 2016
  New York Times Book Review p20 D 4 2016 P. Parmar
Baird, J. Victoria. 2016
  Publishers Weekly v263 no40 p112 O 3 2016
  Saturday Evening Post v288 no6 p26 N/D 2016
Bajtlik, J. and Bajtlik, J. Alphadoodler. 2016
  Publishers Weekly v263 no49 p59 D 7 2016
Baker, A. Our Little Racket. 2017
  Publishers Weekly v264 no14 p46 Ap 3 2017
Baker, D. Cassandra at the wedding. 1962
  Nation v303 no18 p10 O 31 2016 M. Dean
Baker, J. and Baker, J. Circle. 2016
  Publishers Weekly v263 no49 p45-6 D 7 2016
Baker, J. R. and Bilbro, J. Wendell Berry and higher education. 2017
  Publishers Weekly v264 no17 p85 Ap 24 2017
Baker, K. and Dent, C. America the ingenius. 2016
  American History v51 no6 p70 F 2017 A. Barra
  New York Times Book Review p11 Ja 1 2017 R. Kurin
Baker, M. Phantom pains. 2017
  Publishers Weekly v264 no5 p183 Ja 30 2017
Baker, N. Substitute. 2016
  Commonweal v144 no7 p32-3 Ap 14 2017 M. S. Thomas
  Nation v303 no16 p27-31 O 17 2016 E. Kindley
  New Yorker v92 no36 p71 N 7 2016
Baker, P. Obama. 2017
  Foreign Affairs v96 no4 p134-40 Jl/Ag 2017 J. Klein
  New York Times Book Review p6 Je 18 2017 J. Williams

Budiansky, S. Code warriors. 2016
  Commentary v141 no10 p1-4 D 2016
  Commentary v142 no5 p1-4 D 2016
  Commentary v142 no5 p38-41 D 2016 H. Klehr
  Foreign Affairs v95 no6 p177 N/D 2016 L. D. Freedman
Budson, A. E. and O'Connor, M. K. Seven steps to managing your
  memory. 2017
  Publishers Weekly v264 no18 p54-5 My 1 2017
Buechinger-Schmid, G. and Wolf, N. Aging starts in your mind.
  2017
  Publishers Weekly v264 no17 p20-6 Ap 24 2017 L. Garrett
Buell, S. Capital Offenses. 2016
  Foreign Affairs v96 no1 p158 Ja/F 2017 R. N. Cooper
  Harvard Business Review v94 no11 p110-1 N 2016 J. Olejarz
Buettner, D. The Blue Zones of Happiness. 2017
  Publishers Weekly v264 no26 p64-71 Je 26 2017 E. Jones
Buettner, R. The Golden Gate. 2017
  Publishers Weekly v263 no48 p53 N 28 2016
Buffett, L. A. and Buffett, L. Gumbo love. 2017
  Publishers Weekly v264 no16 p62 Ap 17 2017
Bui, T. and Phi, B. A different pond. 2017
  Publishers Weekly v264 no24 p65 Je 12 2017
Bujold, L. M. Penric and the Shaman. 2017
  Publishers Weekly v263 no50 p53 D 5 2016
Bujold, L. M. Penric's Mission. 2017
  Publishers Weekly v264 no26 p160 Je 26 2017
Bukatman, S. Hellboy's world. 2016
  Film Quarterly v70 no3 p99-101 Spr 2017 P. Young
Bulla, D. W. and Sachsman, D. B. Sensationalism. 2013
  Skeptical Inquirer v41 no2 p62 Mr/Ap 2017 B. Radford
Bulliet, R. W. The wheel. 2015
  History Today v66 no10 p58 O 2016 H. Giffard
Bullough, T. Addlands. 2016
  New York Times Book Review p26 Ja 1 2017 M. Peed
Bundy, T. Walking with Miss Millie. 2017
  Publishers Weekly v264 no20 p56 My 15 2017
Bunge, M. Between two worlds. 2016
  Skeptical Inquirer v41 no2 p58-61 Mr/Ap 2017 J. E. Alcock
Bunker, J. True Grift. 2015
  Publishers Weekly v264 no26 p173-4 Je 26 2017
Bunker, L. Felix Yz. 2017
  Publishers Weekly v264 no19 p61 My 8 2017
Bunn, C. and others. The damned. 2017
  Publishers Weekly v264 no10 p48 Mr 6 2017
Bunn, D. Miramar Bay. 2017
  Publishers Weekly v264 no6 p40 F 6 2017
Bunnell, D. H. Good Friday on the Rez. 2017
  Publishers Weekly v263 no48 p57-8 N 28 2016
Buntin, J. Marlena. 2017
  New York Times Book Review p16 Ap 23 2017 D. Shapiro
  O, The Oprah Magazine p112 My 2017 E. Vanderhoof
  Publishers Weekly v263 no46 p31 N 14 2016
  Vogue v207 no4 p186 Ap 2017 M. O'Grady
Bunting, E. and Zimmer, K. Mr. Goat's valentine. 2016
  Publishers Weekly v263 no49 p64 D 7 2016
Buonomano, D. Your brain is a time machine. 2017
  Publishers Weekly v264 no8 p78-9 F 20 2017
Burach, R. and Hamburg, J. Billy Bloo is stuck in goo. 2017
  Publishers Weekly v264 no21 p92 My 22 2017
Burach, R. and others. I am not a chair. 2017
  Publishers Weekly v263 no50 p71 D 5 2016
Burak, A. and Parker, L. Power play. 2017
  Time v189 no3 p20 Ja 30 2017 S. Begley
Burbank, M. G. and others. Man of peace. 2016
  Publishers Weekly v264 no10 p48 Mr 6 2017
Burbridge, R. and others. Dior. 2016
  Vanity Fair v58 no11 p86 N 2016 S. H. G.
Burch, B. and Stimpson, E. The American Catholic almanac. 2014
  U.S. Catholic v82 no6 p41 Je 2017
Burdick, A. Why time flies. 2017
  Natural History v125 no3 p47 Mr 2017 L. A. Marschall
  New York Times Book Review p10 F 12 2017 C. Rovelli
  Publishers Weekly v263 no52 p117-8 D 19 2016
  Science News v191 no3 p28 F 18 2017 L. Sanders
  Science v355 no6321 p138 Ja 13 2017 C. Kemp
  Weekly Standard v22 no41 p34-5 Jl 3 2017 T. Ehrenfeld

Burger, W. C. Complexity. 2016
  BioScience v67 no1 p92-4 Ja 2017 N. H. Carter
Burgerman, J. and Burgerman, J. Splat! 2017
  Publishers Weekly v264 no19 p60 My 8 2017
Burgess, D. and Shepherd, M. The secret horses of Briar Hill.
  2016
  Time v188 no24 p66 D 12 2016 K. Salyer
Burgo, J. Grim. 2016
  Publishers Weekly v264 no13 p64e-f Mr 27 2017
  Publishers Weekly v264 no9 p97 F 27 2017
Burke, J. L. The jealous kind. 2016
  New York Times Book Review p26 Ja 1 2017 M. Peed
Burke, P. Secret History and Historical Consciousness. 2016
  History Today v67 no2 p57 F 2017 D. Snowman
Burke, Z. and Hall, C. Lines and triangles and squares, oh my!
  2017
  Publishers Weekly v264 no5 p202 Ja 30 2017
Burke, Z. Owls and loons. 2016
  Publishers Weekly v263 no42 p67 O 17 2016
Burleigh, R. and Colón, R. Solving the puzzle under the sea. 2016
  Science v354 no6317 p1223 D 9 2016 D. Chevlen
Burnet, G. M. His bloody project : documents relating to the case
  of Roderick Macrae : a novel. 2015
  New York Times Book Review p29 O 16 2016 M. Stasio
Burnet, G. M. His Bloody Project. 2016
  New York Times Book Review p29 O 16 2016 M. Stasio
Burnett, C. In such good company. 2016
  New York Times Book Review p16 N 20 2016 A. Jacobs
  Publishers Weekly v263 no44 p71 O 31 2016
Burnidge, C. L. A peaceful conquest. 2016
  Christian Century v134 no14 p36-7 Jl 5 2017 H. W. Carter
Burns, D. A New Leash on Love. 2017
  Publishers Weekly v264 no19 p44 My 8 2017
Burns, E. Someone to Watch over Me. 2017
  Publishers Weekly v264 no5 p194 Ja 30 2017
Burrington, I. Networks of New York. 2016
  New York v49 no25 p75 D 12 2016 M. Read
Burris, P. and Brown-Wood, J. Grandma's tiny house. 2016
  Publishers Weekly v264 no24 p64 Je 12 2017
Burrough, B. Days of Rage. 2015
  Commentary v140 no2 p48-9 S 2015 H. Klehr
  Commentary v140 no2 p61-3 S 2015 H. Klehr
Burrowes, G. The Trouble With Dukes. 2016
  Publishers Weekly v263 no42 p56 O 17 2016
Burrowes, G. Too Scot to Handle. 2017
  Publishers Weekly v264 no22 p51 My 29 2017
Burrows, M. S. The Paraclete poetry anthology, 2005-2016. 2016
  U.S. Catholic v82 no5 p41 My 2017 N. Ripatrazone
Burt, A. The good daughter. 2017
  Publishers Weekly v264 no47 p89 N 21 2016
Burton, J. and Rescek, S. The Itsy Bitsy Duckling. 2017
  Publishers Weekly v263 no50 p72 D 5 2016
Burton, J. Rules of contact. 2016
  Publishers Weekly v263 no45 p48 N 7 2016
Burton, S. and Lynn, C. Becoming Ms. Burton. 2017
  Publishers Weekly v264 no11 p71-2 Mr 13 2017
  Publishers Weekly v264 no3 p(Sp)18-26 Ja 16 2017
Burton, V. L. and Burton, V. L. Calico the Wonder Horse. 2016
  Publishers Weekly v263 no39 p85 S 26 2016
Burton, V. Successful women speak differently. 2016
  Essence v47 no9 p45 Ja 2017 Y. G. Caviness
Buruma, I. Their Promised Land. 2016
  New York Times Book Review p24 F 5 2017 J. Khatib
Bush, G. W. Portraits of Courage. 2017
  America v216 no7 p48-9 Ap 3 2017 J. Malesic
  Nation v304 no10 p10-1 Mr 27 2017 G. Younge
  New York Times Book Review p24 Mr 19 2017 G. Cowles
  Reason v49 no2 p69 Je 2017 S. Slade
  Texas Monthly v45 no3 p60 Mr 2017
  Weekly Standard v22 no41 p31-2 Jl 3 2017 J. Gardner
Busquets, B. and Lethem, M. F. The house of silence. 2016
  Publishers Weekly v263 no47 p92 N 21 2016
Busquets, M. and Miles, V. This too shall pass. 2016
  New York Times Book Review p28 Mr 12 2017 J. Khatib
Bussola, M. and Richards, J. Sleepless nights and kisses for
  breakfast. 2017

Callahan, D. The givers. 2017
  In These Times v41 no5 p37 My 2017 C. Lehmann
  New York Times Book Review p19 Ap 30 2017 M. Cottle
  Publishers Weekly v264 no6 p58-60 F 6 2017
  Time v189 no15 p18 Ap 24 2017 S. Begley
Callahan, M. The night she won Miss America. 2017
  New York Times Book Review p26 My 28 2017 C. Cain
  Vanity Fair v59 no5 p52 Ap 2017 S. C.
Callahan, T. Arnie. 2017
  Publishers Weekly v264 no7 p62 F 13 2017
  Weekly Standard v22 no41 p30-1 Jl 3 2017 G. Norman
Callahan, T. D. and Prothero, D. R. UFOs, chemtrails, and aliens. 2017
  Publishers Weekly v264 no23 p46 Je 5 2017
Callaway, K. and Batali, D. Watching TV religiously. 2016
  Publishers Weekly v263 no41 p76 O 10 2016
Calle, S. and Turner, M. Tiny creepy crawlers. 2017
  Publishers Weekly v263 no47 p106 N 21 2016
Callen, P. Fervent Charity. 2013
  South Dakota Magazine v32 no6 p44 Mr/Ap 2017
Callow, S. Orson Welles. 2016
  Weekly Standard v22 no12 p34-6 N 28 2016 D. A. Hoffman
Calvez, L. and Angell, T. The hidden lives of owls. 2016
  Sierra v101 no6 p10 N/D 2016 S. Pagani
Calvocoressi, G. Rocket fantastic. 2017
  Publishers Weekly v264 no29 p193 Jl 17 2017
Camden, E. A dangerous legacy. 2017
  Publishers Weekly v264 no35 p112 Ag 28 2017
Cameron, C. The last Neanderthal. 2017
  Publishers Weekly v264 no9 p67 F 27 2017
Cameron, J. B. Life lessons. 2017
  Publishers Weekly v264 no24 p60 Je 12 2017
Cameron, M. Field of Fire. 2016
  Publishers Weekly v263 no48 p50-1 N 28 2016
Cameron, M. The plague of swords. 2016
  Publishers Weekly v263 no43 p61 O 24 2016
Cameron, S. Lies that bind. 2017
  Publishers Weekly v264 no16 p49 Ap 17 2017
Cameron, W. B. A dog's purpose. 2010
  New York Times Book Review p22 F 5 2017
Camerota, A. Amanda Wakes Up. 2017
  O, The Oprah Magazine p92 S 2017 J. Milman
  Publishers Weekly v264 no21 p67 My 22 2017
Camilleri, A. and Sartarelli, S. A nest of vipers. 2017
  Publishers Weekly v264 no20 p36 My 15 2017
Campbell, A. and Linzey, T. We the people. 2016
  Earth Island Journal v32 no1 p55 Spr 2017 S. Sandronsky
Campbell, A. and Truax, L. Love let go. 2017
  Publishers Weekly v264 no4 p16-9 Ja 23 2017 L. Garrett
Campbell, B. and Sanborn, C. Hail to the Chin. 2017
  Publishers Weekly v264 no25 p105 Je 19 2017
  Publishers Weekly v264 no35 p21 Ag 28 2017 C. Juris
Campbell, C. C. and Konadu, K. The Ghana Reader. 2016
  Foreign Affairs v95 no6 p195 N/D 2016 N. Van De Walle
Campbell, D. Disappearance in Damascus. 2017
  New York Times Book Review p20 S 10 2017 S. Anderson
  Publishers Weekly v264 no32 p65 Ag 7 2017
Campbell, E. South Korea's new nationalism. 2016
  Foreign Affairs v95 no6 p191-2 N/D 2016 A. J. Nathan
Campbell, G. A short history of gardens. 2016
  Publishers Weekly v263 no42 p64-5 O 17 2016
Campbell, J. E. Polarized. 2016
  Claremont Review of Books v17 no3 p40-3 Summ 2017 H. C. Mansfield
Campbell, J. Morning in South Africa. 2016
  Foreign Affairs v95 no6 p193-4 N/D 2016 N. Van De Walle
Campbell, K. G. and others. Wee Sister Strange. 2016
  New York Times Book Review p16 O 8 2017 B. Handy
  Publishers Weekly v264 no28 p88 Jl 10 2017
Campbell, K. M. The Pivot. 2016
  Foreign Affairs v96 no3 p146-53 My/Je 2017 B. Kausikan
Campbell, L. N. Rollin' Down the River. 2017
  Missouri Life v44 no4 p19 Je 2017 D. A. Wood
Campbell, M. It's always the husband. 2017
  Publishers Weekly v264 no10 p40-1 Mr 6 2017
Campbell, N. J. Found Audio. 2017

Publishers Weekly v264 no15 p46 Ap 10 2017
Campbell, R. Blackmail. 2017
  Publishers Weekly v264 no15 p53 Ap 10 2017
Campbell, S. and Rex, A. XO, OX. 2017
  New York Times Book Review p18 Ja 15 2017 J. Livshin
  Publishers Weekly v263 no42 p66-8 O 17 2016
Campbell-Reed, E. R. Anatomy of a Schism. 2016
  Christian Century v133 no21 p25-7 O 12 2016
Campion, P. and Kiernan, P. Good morning, city. 2016
  Publishers Weekly v263 no49 p22 D 7 2016
Campion, P. and others. The unlikely story of a pig in the city. 2017
  Publishers Weekly v264 no35 p130 Ag 28 2017
Campisi, C. Blue on blue. 2017
  New York Times Book Review p34-5 Je 4 2017 M. Stasio
  Publishers Weekly v263 no47 p99 N 21 2016
Campolo, B. and Campolo, T. Why I left, why I stayed. 2017
  Humanist v77 no5 p44 S/O 2017 D. Chivers
Canadeo, A. Knit to kill. 2017
  Publishers Weekly v264 no39 p85-6 S 25 2017
Canavan, G. Octavia E. Butler. 2017
  Publishers Weekly v263 no44 p65 O 31 2016
Canfield, J. Dark Sky. 2015
  Publishers Weekly v264 no21 p76 My 22 2017
Cang Hui and Richardson, D. M. Invasion dynamics. 2017
  BioScience v67 no9 p860-1 S 2017 H. Mooney
Cannadine, D. Margaret Thatcher. 2017
  British Heritage Travel v38 no2 p72-3 Mr/Ap 2017 S. Gutierrez
  New York Times Book Review p26 Ap 30 2017 M. O'Donnell
  Weekly Standard v22 no25 p34-6 Mr 6 2017 G. Himmelfarb
Cannell, M. Incendiary. 2017
  Publishers Weekly v264 no9 p92 F 27 2017
Cannon, G. Trafalgar & Boone and the Books of Breathing. 2017
  Publishers Weekly v264 no32 p57 Ag 7 2017
Cannon, J. The Trouble With Goats and Sheep. 2016
  New York Times Book Review p24 O 1 2017 J. Khatib
Cano, V. The Rose Master. 2014
  Publishers Weekly v264 no31 p44 Jl 31 2017
Cantero, E. Meddling kids. 2017
  Publishers Weekly v264 no15 p56 Ap 10 2017
  Publishers Weekly v264 no31 p12 Jl 31 2017 C. Juris
Cantor, J. The hours count. 2015
  New York Times Book Review p28 S 25 2016 J. Khatib
Cantor, J. The lost letter. 2017
  Publishers Weekly v264 no16 p38 Ap 17 2017
Cantor, R. Good on paper. 2016
  New York Times Book Review p24 D 25 2016 J. Khatib
Canty, K. The underworld. 2017
  New York Times Book Review p30 My 7 2017 M. Bojanowski
  Publishers Weekly v264 no5 p170 Ja 30 2017
Cao, W. and others. Bronze and sunflower. 2017
  New York Times Book Review p21 My 14 2017 L. See
  Publishers Weekly v263 no52 p124-6 D 19 2016
Cao, W. and others. Feather. 2017
  Publishers Weekly v264 no31 p85 Jl 31 2017
Cao, Y. and others. To build a free China. 2017
  Foreign Affairs v96 no3 p175 My/Je 2017 E. Pils
Capaldi, G. and Goldin, B. D. The Passover cowboy. 2017
  Publishers Weekly v264 no4 p78 Ja 23 2017
Capetta, A. R. Echo After Echo. 2017
  Publishers Weekly v264 no36 p102 S 4 2017
Capouya, J. Florida soul. 2017
  Publishers Weekly v264 no32 p65 Ag 7 2017
Cappelli, P. and others. Fortune makers. 2017
  Harvard Business Review v95 no2 p156-7 Mr/Ap 2017 A. Ignatius
Capucilli, A. S. and Anchin, L. I Will Love You. 2017
  Publishers Weekly v264 no8 p83 F 20 2017
Capucilli, A. S. and Bach, A. Good Night, My Darling Baby. 2017
  Publishers Weekly v264 no5 p202 Ja 30 2017
Caputo, P. Some rise by sin. 2017
  New York Times Book Review p11 Je 25 2017 S. Akam
  Publishers Weekly v264 no12 p47 Mr 20 2017
Carafa, P. and Carandini, A. The atlas of Ancient Rome. 2017
  Magazine Antiques v184 no5 p42-4 S/O 2017 J. Gardner
  New York Review of Books v64 no12 p18-20 Jl 13 2017 M. Beard
Carbo, C. The weight of night. 2017

Vanity Fair v58 no12 p86 D 2016 S. Crosley

Carson, C. Orkney Twilight. 2017
Publishers Weekly v264 no17 p69-70 Ap 24 2017

Carson, C. The Salt Marsh. 2017
Publishers Weekly v264 no35 p108 Ag 28 2017

Carson, M. K. and Uhlman, T. Mission to Pluto. 2016
Publishers Weekly v263 no51 p149 D 12 2016

Cartaya, P. The epic fail of Arturo Zamora. 2017
Publishers Weekly v264 no27 p36-40 Jl 3 2017 K. P. Goddu
Publishers Weekly v264 no36 p90 S 4 2017

Carter, D. A. and Carter, D. A. Autumn. 2017
Publishers Weekly v264 no35 p126 Ag 28 2017

Carter, D. A. Brother Bill.
New York Review of Books v64 no10 p4-8 Je 8 2017 N. Lemann

Carter, E. Lucky You. 2017
O, The Oprah Magazine p90 Ap 2017 H. Cain
Publishers Weekly v264 no5 p171-2 Ja 30 2017

Carter, G. Vanity Fair's Schools for Scandal. 2017
Vanity Fair v59 no9 p138 S 2017 C. S.

Carter, G. Vanity fair's writers on writers. 2016
New York Times Book Review p61 D 4 2016 M. Schneier
Vanity Fair v58 no11 p96 N 2016 S. C.

Carter, J. E. Solomon D. Butcher. 2016
Nebraska Life v20 no6 p60 N/D 2016 E. Schwartz

Carter, K. and Crabbe, B. The comprehensive guide to equine veterinary medicine. 2007
Horse & Rider v55 no12 p19 D 2016

Carter, M. J. The Devil's feast. 2017
Publishers Weekly v264 no26 p174 Je 26 2017
Publishers Weekly v264 no2 p43 Ja 9 2017

Cartmel, A. The Run-out Groove. 2017
Publishers Weekly v264 no10 p42 Mr 6 2017

Caruso, M. The tethered mage. 2017
Publishers Weekly v264 no33 p56 Ag 14 2017

Carvalho, B. P. and Martins, I. M. Don't Cross the Line! 2016
New York Times Book Review p30 N 13 2016 R. Alam

Carvalho, B. P. and others. Outside. 2016
Science v354 no6317 p1226 D 9 2016 P. J. Hines

Carver, C. Immune. 2017
Publishers Weekly v264 no36 p82 S 4 2017

Carver, C. Soulful simplicity. 2017
Publishers Weekly v264 no39 p23-30 S 25 2017 L. Garrett

Carver, M. O. and others. Portmahomack on Tarbat Ness 2016. 2016
History Today v67 no9 p92-3 S 2017 R. Hodges

Carver, N. E. Discovering Public Parks in St. Louis, Missouri. 2017
Missouri Life v44 no4 p20 Je 2017 L. A. Addington

Caschetta, M. B. Pretend I'm your friend. 2016
Entertainment Weekly no1441 p62 N 25 2016 I. Biedenharn

Case, J. and others. Superman. 2016
Publishers Weekly v263 no44 p60 O 31 2016

Case, J. and White, L. Emma and the whale. 2017
Publishers Weekly v264 no1 p54 Ja 2 2017

Case, S. The third wave. 2016
Washington Monthly p5-1 Ja/F 2017 D. Stangler

Casella, J. and others. Hell is a very small place. 2016
New York Review of Books v63 no19 p24-6 D 8 2016 M. Garbus
Orion Magazine v35 no3 p56-9 My/Je 2016 K. Vandenberg

Casey, C. Little boxes. 2017
New York Times Book Review p6 S 10 2017 J. Williams

Casey, D. and Hall, A. Babushka. 2016
Publishers Weekly v263 no39 p91 S 26 2016

Casey, D. The return of the Raven Mocker. 2017
Publishers Weekly v263 no40 p98 O 3 2016

Casey, J. Let the Dead Speak. 2017
Publishers Weekly v264 no18 p39 My 1 2017

Casey, M. Art of mystery. 2018
Publishers Weekly v264 no39 p95 S 25 2017

Casey, S. The war beat, Europe. 2017
Foreign Affairs v96 no3 p158-9 My/Je 2017 L. D. Freedman

Cash, W. The last ballad. 2017
Publishers Weekly v264 no35 p100 Ag 28 2017

Cashore, K. Jane, unlimited. 2017
New York Times Book Review p26 O 15 2017 J. Giles
Publishers Weekly v264 no26 p183 Je 26 2017

Casner, S. Careful! 2017

Publishers Weekly v264 no8 p75 F 20 2017

Caspit, B. and Cummings, O. The Netanyahu years. 2017
Publishers Weekly v264 no18 p50-1 My 1 2017

Cassara, J. and Abdul-Jabbar, K. Mycroft Holmes and the Apocalypse handbook. 2017
Publishers Weekly v264 no38 p61 S 18 2017

Cassidy, C. and Doherty, P. And then you're dead. 2017
New York Times Book Review p4 Ap 23 2017 J. Williams

Cassidy, P. and Aurell, B. Scandikitchen Fika & Hygge. 2016
New York Times Book Review p27 F 26 2017 J. Newman

Castaldo, N. F. Beastly brains. 2017
Publishers Weekly v264 no6 p69 F 6 2017

Casteel, S. Pounce. 2016
Good Housekeeping v263 no5 p204 N 2016

Casteel, T. and Wood, M. B. The Science of Science Fiction. 2017
Publishers Weekly v263 no51 p149 D 12 2016

Castille, S. Fighting attraction. 2017
Publishers Weekly v264 no8 p72 F 20 2017

Castille, S. Luca. 2017
Publishers Weekly v264 no22 p50 My 29 2017

Castillo, L. and Graff, L. It is not time for sleeping. 2016
Publishers Weekly v263 no49 p44 D 7 2016

Castillo, L. and Herkert, B. A boy, a mouse, and a spider. 2017
Publishers Weekly v264 no41 p65 O 9 2017

Castillo, L. Down a dark road. 2017
New York Times Book Review p24 Jl 30 2017 G. Cowles
Publishers Weekly v264 no17 p66 Ap 24 2017
Publishers Weekly v264 no21 p75 My 22 2017 L. Castillo

Castle, A. Moriarty Meets His Match. 2016
Publishers Weekly v264 no33 p53 Ag 14 2017
Publishers Weekly v264 no35 p77b Ag 28 2017

Castle, F. and others. Lands of Long Ago. 2017
New York Times Book Review p40-1 Je 4 2017 C. Hong

Castle, J. The wishing wings. 2017
Publishers Weekly v264 no39 p107 S 25 2017

Castlemon, H. and Russell, C. M. Frank on the prairie. 2017
American Cowboy v24 no1 p47 Je/Jl 2017

Castrillón, M. and Laden, N. If I had a little dream. 2017
Publishers Weekly v264 no47 p107 N 21 2016

Castrovilla, S. and O'Brien, J. Revolutionary rogues. 2017
Publishers Weekly v264 no32 p71 Ag 7 2017

Catalano, K. Where the sun shines out. 2017
Publishers Weekly v264 no35 p106 Ag 28 2017

Catalinac, A. Electoral reform and national security in Japan. 2016
Foreign Affairs v96 no2 p187 Mr/Ap 2017

Cathcart, H. and others. The Palomar cookbook. 2016
Publishers Weekly v263 no50 p64-5 D 5 2016
Publishers Weekly v264 no10 p26 Mr 6 2017 C. S.

Catling, B. The Erstwhile. 2017
Publishers Weekly v263 no51 p128 D 12 2016

Catmull, K. The radiant road. 2016
Publishers Weekly v263 no49 p110 D 7 2016

Cato, B. Breath of earth. 2016
Publishers Weekly v263 no48 p54-5 N 28 2016

Cato, B. Call of Fire. 2017
Publishers Weekly v264 no26 p161 Je 26 2017

Catron, M. L. How to fall in love with anyone. 2017
New York Times Book Review p31 Jl 23 2017 M. Daum

Catts, M. Among the lesser gods. 2017
New York Times Book Review p26 Je 18 2017 J. Stuart

Catusanu, M. and Maurer, T. N. Noah Webster's fighting words. 2016
Publishers Weekly v264 no10 p60 Mr 6 2017

Cauchon, A. M. Nothing. 2013
Publishers Weekly v264 no26 p183 Je 26 2017

Cavallo, F. and Favilli, E. Good Night Stories for Rebel Girls. 2016
New York Times Book Review p28 Jl 23 2017 G. Cowles

Cavanagh, C. and Krynicki, R. Magnetic point. 2017
Publishers Weekly v264 no38 p51 S 18 2017 C. Simic

Cavanagh, C. and Zagajewski, A. Slight exaggeration. 2017
Commonweal v144 no11 p37-8 Je 16 2017 A. Domestico
New Yorker v93 no16 p97 Je 5 2017
New York Times Book Review p25 Jl 23 2017 D. Fried
Publishers Weekly v263 no51 p134 D 12 2016

Cave, N. and Joyce, A. The sick bag song. 2016

Chansky, A. Game changers. 2016
New York Times Book Review p58-60 D 4 2016 M. Tracy
Chaon, D. Ill will. 2017
Commonweal v144 no12 p35-6 Jl 7 2017 D. Preziosi
Entertainment Weekly no1456 p70 Mr 10 2017 I. Biedenharn
New York Times Book Review p12 Mr 26 2017 E. Brundage
Publishers Weekly v263 no50 p44 D 5 2016
Publishers Weekly v264 no3 p30-1 Ja 16 2017 M. Harvkey
Time v189 no6 p53 F 20 2017
Chaplin, H. Reckless years. 2017
New York Times Book Review p21 Ag 13 2017 J. Attenberg
Chapman, B. Shallow End. 2017
Publishers Weekly v264 no9 p81 F 27 2017
Chapman, J. and Wilson, K. Big bear, small mouse. 2016
Publishers Weekly v263 no40 p121-2 O 3 2016
Chapman, J. Date With Death. 2017
Publishers Weekly v264 no5 p179 Ja 30 2017
Chapman, S. and others. The girl who ran. 2017
Publishers Weekly v264 no23 p51 Je 5 2017
Chapnick, A. and Kukucha, C. J. The Harper era in Canadian foreign policy. 2016
Foreign Affairs v96 no1 p167-8 Ja/F 2017 R. Feinberg
Chapple, J. Mad Genius Tips. 2016
Publishers Weekly v263 no42 p63-4 O 17 2016
Charan, R. The high-potential leader. 2017
People Management p52 Ap 2017
Charap, S. and Colton, T. J. Everyone loses. 2017
Foreign Affairs v96 no3 p167-8 My/Je 2017 R. Legvold
Charbonneau, J. Dividing Eden. 2017
Publishers Weekly v264 no18 p60 My 1 2017
Charette, A. M. and Naivo, N. Beyond the rice fields. 2017
Publishers Weekly v264 no36 p62-3 S 4 2017
Charles, K. J. Wanted, a Gentleman. 2017
Publishers Weekly v263 no46 p38 N 14 2016
Charles, P. J. Armed in America. 2018
Publishers Weekly v264 no39 p95 S 25 2017
Charlesworth, L. and Reese, B. Amazing Animals. 2017
Publishers Weekly v263 no50 p72 D 5 2016
Charleyboy, L. and Leatherdale, M. B. #notyourprincess. 2017
Publishers Weekly v264 no34 p114 Ag 21 2017
Charman, I. The zoo. 2017
New York Times Book Review p8 Jl 9 2017 C. Casey
Publishers Weekly v264 no6 p61 F 6 2017
Science News v191 no6 p28 Ap 1 2017 M. Rosen
Charnwood, G. R. Abraham Lincoln. 1996
Christianity Today v60 no8 p82 O 2016 P. Wehner
Charyn, J. Jerzy. 2017
New Yorker v93 no6 p73-5 Mr 27 2017 R. Franklin
New York Times Book Review p22 Ap 9 2017
New York Times Book Review p9 Ap 2 2017 B. Markovits
Publishers Weekly v264 no4 p52-3 Ja 23 2017
Charyn, J. Winter warning. 2017
Publishers Weekly v264 no33 p49 Ag 14 2017
Chase, E. The Wildling sisters. 2017
British Heritage Travel v38 no4 p73 Jl/Ag 2017 S. Gutierrez
Chase, J. and Ullrich, V. Hitler. 2016
Foreign Affairs v96 no2 p176-7 Mr/Ap 2017 A. Moravcsik
Nation v304 no9 p43-8 Mr 20 2017 R. J. Evans
New York Review of Books v64 no7 p10-4 Ap 20 2017 C. R. Browning
New York Times Book Review p12 O 16 2016 A. Kirsch
New York Times Book Review p30 O 23 2016
Chase, J. Cat Got Your Cash. 2017
Publishers Weekly v264 no9 p78 F 27 2017
Chase, J. Cat Got Your Secrets. 2017
Publishers Weekly v264 no30 p44 Jl 24 2017
Chase, K. and Chase, K. Charlie's boat. 2017
New York Times Book Review p41 Je 4 2017 M. Russo
Chase, L. A Duke in Shining Armor. 2017
Publishers Weekly v264 no38 p59-60 S 18 2017
Chase, S. A Sky Full of Stars. 2017
Publishers Weekly v264 no15 p58-9 Ap 10 2017
Chase, S. One More Kiss. 2017
Publishers Weekly v263 no51 p132 D 12 2016
Chast, R. and Trillin, C. No fair! No fair! 2016
New York Times Book Review p20 N 13 2016 M. Ian Black

Chast, R. Going into town. 2017
Entertainment Weekly no1485 p63 O 6 2017
Publishers Weekly v264 no26 p34-40 Je 26 2017 H. Macdonald
Publishers Weekly v264 no27 p62 Jl 3 2017
Chatterjee, P. and Bendib, K. Verax. 2017
Publishers Weekly v264 no35 p113 Ag 28 2017
Chatterton, C. and others. In focus. 2016
Publishers Weekly v263 no41 p81 O 10 2016
Chatzikonstantis, M. and Kiros, T. Provence to Pondicherry. 2017
Publishers Weekly v264 no10 p56-7 Mr 6 2017
Chau, A. and Wang, A. The Nian monster. 2016
Publishers Weekly v263 no40 p122-3 O 3 2016
Publishers Weekly v263 no49 p64 D 7 2016
Chaudhuri, S. A midsummer night's dream. 2017
Publishers Weekly v264 no34 p14 Ag 21 2017 J. Milliot
Chaudry, R. Adnan's Story. 2016
Publishers Weekly v263 no44 p71 O 31 2016
Chazin, S. A Place in the Wind. 2017
Publishers Weekly v264 no35 p104 Ag 28 2017
Chbosky, S. The perks of being a wallflower. 1999
Seventeen v75 no11 p19 N 2016 J. Abidor
Chee, T. The Reader. 2016
Publishers Weekly v263 no49 p111 D 7 2016
Chemerinsky, E. Closing the courthouse door. 2017
Publishers Weekly v263 no43 p68-9 O 24 2016
Chen, A. K. and others. Free Speech Beyond Words. 2017
Publishers Weekly v263 no46 p42-3 N 14 2016
Chen, A. So many olympic exertions. 2017
Publishers Weekly v264 no23 p26-7 Je 5 2017
Chen, C. C. Kangaroo too. 2017
Publishers Weekly v264 no18 p41 My 1 2017
Chen, Z. and Umrigar, T. When I carried you in my belly. 2017
Publishers Weekly v264 no8 p83 F 20 2017
Cheney, B. Lightwood. 2014
Publishers Weekly v263 no44 p54 O 31 2016
Cheng, E. Beyond Infinity. 2017
Publishers Weekly v263 no51 p106-11 D 12 2016 A. Crowley
Cheng, J. See you in the Cosmos, Carl Sagan. 2017
Publishers Weekly v263 no50 p73-4 D 5 2016
Cheng, J. See you in the Cosmos. 2017
New York Times Book Review p19 My 14 2017 N. Standiford
Publishers Weekly v264 no31 p84 Jl 31 2017
Cheng Li Chinese politics in the Xi Jinping era. 2016
Foreign Affairs v96 no1 p177-8 Ja/F 2017 V. Shih
New York Review of Books v64 no2 p34-6 F 9 2017 A. J. Nathan
Chercover, S. The Savior's Game. 2017
Publishers Weekly v264 no24 p44 Je 12 2017
Chermayeff, I. and Vonnegut, K. Sun, moon, star. 1980
New York Times Book Review p19 D 18 2016 M. Russo
Publishers Weekly v263 no39 p85 S 26 2016
Chernow, R. Grant. 2017
Military History v34 no4 p72 N 2017
O, The Oprah Magazine p110 N 2017 J. Neber
Publishers Weekly v264 no33 p66 Ag 14 2017
Chesbro, G. C. Veil. 1986
Nation v305 no8 p25-30 O 9 2017 J. W. Scott
Cheshire, J. and Uberti, O. Where the animals go. 2017
Scientific American v317 no3 p88 S 2017 A. Gawrylewski
Chestnut, M. and Obadike, O. The cut. 2017
Publishers Weekly v264 no6 p64-5 F 6 2017
Cheung, R. New Hong Kong cinema. 2016
Film Quarterly v70 no2 p113-4 Wint 2016 G. Bettinson
Chevalier, T. New Boy. 2017
British Heritage Travel v38 no3 p74 My/Je 2017 S. Gutierrez
Maclean's p62-3 Je 2017 B. Bethune
Publishers Weekly v264 no13 p72 Mr 27 2017
Chew-Bose, D. Too much and not the mood. 2017
Interview v47 no3 p32 Ap 2017 A. Stern
New York Times Book Review p26 Ap 9 2017 K. Bolick
Chi-Young Kim and others. The things you can see only when you slow down. 2017
Publishers Weekly v263 no51 p143 D 12 2016
Tricycle: The Buddhist Review v26 no3 p92-3 Spr 2017 M. Scarles
Chiang, T. Stories of your life and others. 2010
Publishers Weekly v263 no48 p13 N 28 2016 C. Juris
Chiappe, L. M. and Meng Qingjin Birds of stone. 2016

Science News v190 no11 p29 N 26 2016

Chiavaroli, H. Freedom's ring. 2017
Publishers Weekly v264 no24 p49 Je 12 2017

Chichester Clark, E. and Blake, Q. Three Little Monkeys. 2017
Publishers Weekly v264 no38 p69 S 18 2017

Chichester Clark, E. and Chichester Clark, E. Plenty of love to go around. 2016
Publishers Weekly v263 no44 p74 O 31 2016

Chien, C. and Magliaro, E. Things to do. 2017
Publishers Weekly v263 no46 p54 N 14 2016

Child, L. Night school. 2016
New Yorker v92 no37 p85-8 N 14 2016 J. Lanchester
New York Times Book Review p10-1 O 30 2016 C. Finch
New York Times Book Review p78 D 4 2016

Child, L. No middle name. 2017
Publishers Weekly v264 no16 p43 Ap 17 2017

Child, L. The Midnight Line. 2017
Publishers Weekly v264 no36 p67 S 4 2017

Child, P. and others. France is a feast. 2016
Publishers Weekly v264 no38 p62-4 S 18 2017

Chilton, A. S. and Eckwall, J. The goblin's puzzle. 2016
Publishers Weekly v263 no49 p78-9 D 7 2016

Chin, E. My life with things. 2016
Christian Century v134 no1 p36-7 Ja 4 2017 L. H. Moses

Chin, R. The crisis of multiculturalism in Europe. 2017
Nation v305 no8 p25-30 O 9 2017 J. W. Scott
New York Times Book Review p20-1 S 17 2017 P. Mishra
Publishers Weekly v264 no21 p84 My 22 2017

Chinquee, K. Pretty. 2010
Publishers Weekly v264 no21 p93 My 22 2017

Chion, M. and others. Words on screen. 2017
Film Quarterly v71 no1 p119-21 Fall 2017 P. Rangan

Chiquet, M. Beyond the Label. 2017
Publishers Weekly v264 no8 p76-7 F 20 2017

Chirbes, R. and Costa, M. J. On the edge. 2016
New York Review of Books v63 no16 p18-20 O 27 2016 N. Rush

Chirovici, E. O. The book of mirrors. 2017
Publishers Weekly v263 no50 p49 D 5 2016

Chisholm, D. and Chisholm, D. Instrumental. 2017
Downbeat v84 no9 p16 S 2017 C. Tart
Publishers Weekly v264 no16 p54-5 Ap 17 2017

Chisholm, P. and Bang, M. Rivers of sunlight. 2016
Publishers Weekly v263 no51 p149 D 12 2016

Chistyakov, I. and Tait, A. The Day Will Pass Away. 2017
Publishers Weekly v264 no19 p48 My 8 2017

Chitara, J. and Flowers, A. Brer Rabbit Retold. 2017
Publishers Weekly v264 no33 p82 Ag 14 2017

Chittister, J. Radical spirit. 2017
U.S. Catholic v82 no6 p41 Je 2017 N. Ripatrazone

Chizmar, R. and King, S. Gwendy's button box. 2017
Publishers Weekly v264 no16 p51 Ap 17 2017
Publishers Weekly v264 no26 p173 Je 26 2017

Chizmar, R. Darkness Whispers. 2016
Publishers Weekly v264 no3 p45 Ja 16 2017

Chocano, C. You play the girl. 2017
New York Times Book Review p26 S 17 2017 H. Mlotek
O, The Oprah Magazine p90 S 2017 C. Luchette
Publishers Weekly v264 no19 p49 My 8 2017

Choi, L. and Russell, J. The Dragon Hunters. 2017
Publishers Weekly v264 no8 p82 F 20 2017

Chokshi, R. The star-touched queen. 2016
Publishers Weekly v263 no49 p111-2 D 7 2016

Choldenko, G. and Santat, D. Dad and the dinosaur. 2017
Publishers Weekly v263 no51 p146-8 D 12 2016

Chong, V. and Parker, K. J. Mightier Than the Sword. 2017
New York Times Book Review p23 Jl 16 2017 N. K. Jemisin
Publishers Weekly v264 no19 p43 My 8 2017

Chopra, D. and others. Home. 2017
Publishers Weekly v264 no33 p21 Ag 14 2017 S. Maughan

Chotiner, B. and Bower, G. A patch on the peak of Ararat. 2017
Publishers Weekly v263 no48 p70 N 28 2016

Choudhury, K. The Epic City. 2018
Publishers Weekly v264 no35 p46 Ag 28 2017 C. J.
Publishers Weekly v264 no39 p95-6 S 25 2017

Chrissopoulos, C. and Cullen, J. The Parthenon bomber. 2017
Publishers Weekly v264 no15 p49-50 Ap 10 2017

Christakis, E. The Importance of Being Little. 2016
Christian Century v134 no5 p36-8 Mr 1 2017 M. J. Bunge

Christelow, E. and Christelow, E. Robins! 2016
Publishers Weekly v264 no1 p57 Ja 2 2017

Christensen, E. and Christensen, N. Keeping Kyrie. 2016
Publishers Weekly v264 no17 p87 Ap 24 2017
Publishers Weekly v264 no21 p65d My 22 2017

Christensen, N. and Heivoll, G. Across the China sea. 2017
Publishers Weekly v264 no29 p189 Jl 17 2017

Christer, S. The House of Smoke. 2017
Publishers Weekly v264 no39 p88 S 25 2017

Christiansen, D. M. Planet A. 2016
Publishers Weekly v264 no17 p87 Ap 24 2017
Publishers Weekly v264 no21 p65d-e My 22 2017

Christie, A. Sleeping murder. 1976
New York Times Book Review p24 Ap 23 2017 P. Sehgal

Christie, R. G. and Corey, S. A time to act. 2017
Publishers Weekly v264 no8 p87 F 20 2017

Christie, S. The Icarus Show. 2017
Publishers Weekly v263 no43 p76 O 24 2016

Christie, W. A single spy. 2017
Publishers Weekly v264 no13 p25-36 Mr 27 2017 E. Norton
Publishers Weekly v264 no6 p47 F 6 2017

Christine, D. P. and Richards, E. J. The book of the city of ladies. 1982
New Yorker v93 no16 p102-6 Je 5 2017 J. Lepore

Christmas, J. and Atwood, M. Angel Catbird. 2016
New York Times Book Review p18-9 Ja 1 2017 D. Wolk
Publishers Weekly v263 no41 p65 O 10 2016

Christopher, A. Standard Hollywood Depravity. 2017
Publishers Weekly v264 no4 p61 Ja 23 2017

Christopher, N. On Jupiter place. 2016
New Yorker v92 no33 p99 O 17 2016

Christov-Bakargiev, C. and others. Parallel Views. 2015
Art in America v104 no11 p65 D 2016

Chrusciel, E. Of annunciations. 2017
Publishers Weekly v264 no38 p52-3 S 18 2017

Chu, A. and Moss, M. Kate Warne. 2017
Publishers Weekly v264 no10 p60 Mr 6 2017

Chu, C. and others. Kill them all. 2017
Publishers Weekly v264 no36 p77 S 4 2017

Chu, C. and others. The damned. 2017
Publishers Weekly v264 no10 p48 Mr 6 2017

Chu, C. and others. Time share. 2017
Publishers Weekly v264 no4 p67 Ja 23 2017

Chu, L. Little soldiers. 2017
New York Times Book Review p22 Ag 27 2017 A. Paul
Publishers Weekly v264 no30 p54 Jl 24 2017

Chu, M. and others. My Colors Book. 2017
Publishers Weekly v264 no31 p87 Jl 31 2017

Chung, A. and Chung, A. Ninja Claus! 2017
Publishers Weekly v264 no36 p96 S 4 2017

Chung, A. and Chung, A. Out. 2017
Publishers Weekly v264 no17 p91 Ap 24 2017

Chung, J. and others. Don't Move! 2017
Publishers Weekly v264 no5 p203 Ja 30 2017

Chung, J. and others. Superman. 2016
Publishers Weekly v263 no44 p60 O 31 2016

Chupeco, R. The bone witch. 2017
Publishers Weekly v264 no4 p80 Ja 23 2017

Church, C. J. and Church, C. J. I will love you forever. 2016
Publishers Weekly v264 no22 p66 My 29 2017

Church, E. J. The atomic weight of love. 2016
New York Times Book Review p24 Mr 26 2017 J. Khatib

Church, J. The gentleman from Japan. 2016
Publishers Weekly v263 no41 p57 O 10 2016

Churchman, J. and others. Brave little Finn. 2016
Publishers Weekly v263 no43 p75 O 24 2016

Churton, T. Deconstructing Gurdjieff. 2017
Publishers Weekly v264 no15 p68-9 Ap 10 2017

Cialdini, R. Pre-suasion. 2016
Fortune v174 no8 p70 D 15 2016 V. Harnish

Ciccarelli, K. The Last Namsara. 2017
Publishers Weekly v264 no41 p22-3 O 9 2017 S. Maughan

Cicchini, M. D. Convicting Avery. 2017
Publishers Weekly v264 no7 p62-3 F 13 2017

Cicciarelli, J. and others. Leo's gift. 2017
　Publishers Weekly v264 no36 p100 S 4 2017
Cicek, C. The Kurds of Turkey. 2017
　New York Review of Books v64 no7 p20-4 Ap 20 2017 J. Steele
Cicero, M. T. and Freeman, P. How to grow old. 2016
　Claremont Review of Books v16 no4 p83-6 Fall 2016 D. Wiser Jr.
Cihon, C. and Wiley, S. The Fairytale Chicago of Francesca
　Finnegan. 2017
　Publishers Weekly v264 no5 p185-6 Ja 30 2017
　Publishers Weekly v264 no9 p66c-d F 27 2017
Cimino-Isaacs, C. and Schott, J. J. Trans-Pacific Partnership.
　2016
　Foreign Affairs v95 no6 p174-5 N/D 2016 R. N. Cooper
Cinqualbre, O. and others. Pierre Chareau. 2016
　Publishers Weekly v263 no48 p57-64 N 28 2016
Ciraolo, S. and Ciraolo, S. The lines on Nana's face. 2016
　New York Times Book Review p29 N 13 2016
Ciraolo, S. and Knapman, T. Can't Catch Me! 2017
　Publishers Weekly v264 no39 p104 S 25 2017
Citro, A. and Lindsay, M. Dragons and Marshmallows. 2017
　Publishers Weekly v264 no9 p102 F 27 2017
Civil wars. 2017
　Publishers Weekly v263 no46 p41 N 14 2016
Claffey, B. and Bamford, L. Indoor green. 2017
　Publishers Weekly v263 no52 p120 D 19 2016
Clanton, B. and Berkner, L. We are the dinosaurs. 2017
　Publishers Weekly v264 no4 p79 Ja 23 2017
Clanton, B. and Clanton, B. Boo Who? 2017
　Publishers Weekly v264 no22 p65-7 My 29 2017
Clanton, B. and Clanton, B. Super Narwhal and Jelly Jolt. 2017
　Publishers Weekly v264 no18 p58 My 1 2017
Clare, A. A Rustle of Silk. 2017
　Publishers Weekly v263 no44 p53 O 31 2016
Clare, A. The Devil's Cup. 2017
　Publishers Weekly v264 no23 p33 Je 5 2017
Clare, O. Disasters in the first world. 2017
　New York Times Book Review p18 Jl 30 2017 A. Ervin
　Publishers Weekly v264 no16 p37 Ap 17 2017
Clark, C. D. The recovery revolution. 2017
　Reason v49 no5 p72-3 O 2017 M. Szalavitz
Clark, L. Blitzkrieg. 2016
　Military History v34 no4 p75 N 2017 M. Oppenheim
Clark, M. and Wolfinger, E. Dinner. 2017
　Martha Stewart Living p10 Mr 2017
　Publishers Weekly v263 no50 p64 D 5 2016
Clark, M. H. All by myself, alone. 2017
　Publishers Weekly v264 no9 p75 F 27 2017
Clark, M. H. and Lockhart, L. Me Museum. 2017
　Publishers Weekly v263 no48 p66 N 28 2016
Clark, M. Moral defense. 2016
　Publishers Weekly v264 no5 p196 Ja 30 2017
Clark, M. Snap Judgment. 2017
　Publishers Weekly v264 no26 p154 Je 26 2017
Clark, R. and Clark, R. Evolution. 2016
　Publishers Weekly v263 no39 p82 S 26 2016
Clark, W. C. and others. Pursuing sustainability. 2016
　Environment v58 no6 p34-6 N/D 2016 T. O'Riordan
Clarke, A. R. and Coelho, P. The alchemist. 2014
　New York Times Book Review p34 D 11 2016 G. Cowles
Clarke, C. R. and others. The Witch Who Came in from the Cold.
　2017
　Publishers Weekly v264 no17 p73 Ap 24 2017
Clarke, C. R. Magic of Blood and Sea. 2017
　Publishers Weekly v264 no1 p42 Ja 2 2017
Clarke, C. R. Star's end. 2017
　Publishers Weekly v264 no5 p184 Ja 30 2017
Clarke, D. J. and Dercon, S. Dull disasters? 2016
　Reason v48 no9 p66-7 F 2017 D. M. Rothschild
Clarke, J. and Birkett, G. How to bathe your little dino. 2016
　Publishers Weekly v264 no5 p203 Ja 30 2017
Clarke, J. and Blanco, M. Old Macdonald's Things That Go. 2016
　Publishers Weekly v264 no9 p99 F 27 2017
Clarke, K. Kind of Blue. 2016
　New York Review of Books v64 no16 p66-9 O 26 2017 F. Mount
Clarke, M. B. Foreign Soil. 2017
　O, The Oprah Magazine p103 F 2017

Clarke, N. Galactic empires. 2017
　New York Times Book Review p27 Ja 29 2017 N. K. Jemisin
　Publishers Weekly v263 no46 p37 N 14 2016
Clarke, N. More human than human. 2017
　Publishers Weekly v264 no40 p121 O 2 2017
Clarke, P. The locomotive of war. 2017
　MHQ: Quarterly Journal of Military History v29 no4 p92-4
　　Summ 2017 K. M. Kostyal
　Military History v34 no5 p73-4 Ja 2018 W. Wilkins
　Publishers Weekly v264 no18 p49 My 1 2017
Clarkson, A. Belonging. 2014
　Alternatives Journal (AJ) - Canada's Environmental Voice v42
　　no3 p46 2016 T. Barton
Clarkson, J. Bronx requiem. 2016
　Publishers Weekly v263 no39 p68 S 26 2016
Clarkson, N. and Clarkson, S. Different. 2016
　Publishers Weekly v264 no6 p12 F 6 2017 C. Juris
Claveloux, N. and others. The green hand and other stories. 2017
　Publishers Weekly v264 no36 p76 S 4 2017
Clavin, T. Dodge City. 2017
　American Cowboy v23 no6 p43 Ap/My 2017
　Publishers Weekly v264 no22 p63 My 29 2017
　Publishers Weekly v264 no5 p192-3 Ja 30 2017
Clay, C. Labyrinths. 2016
　New Yorker v92 no45 p79 Ja 16 2017
Claycomb, A. The Mermaid's Daughter. 2017
　Publishers Weekly v264 no5 p172-3 Ja 30 2017
Clayton, A. J. Writing with the words of others. 2010
　New York Review of Books v64 no16 p55-7 O 26 2017 N. Ascher-
　　son
Clayton, D. The Belles. 2018
　Publishers Weekly v264 no39 p34-54 S 25 2017 J. Maher
Clayton, J. Uproot. 2016
　Nation v33 no21 p20-4 N 21 2016 A. A. Abrahamian
　New York Times Book Review p26 D 18 2016 D. Kalotay
Clayton, J. Wonderlandscape. 2017
　Publishers Weekly v264 no21 p86 My 22 2017
Cleary, H. and others. Ikigai. 2017
　Publishers Weekly v264 no23 p48 Je 5 2017
　Publishers Weekly v264 no26 p64-71 Je 26 2017 E. Jones
Cleave, C. Everyone brave is forgiven. 2016
　New York Times Book Review p24 Ap 9 2017 J. Khatib
Cleave, P. A killer harvest. 2017
　Publishers Weekly v264 no22 p46 My 29 2017
Cleeton, C. On Broken Wings. 2017
　Publishers Weekly v263 no47 p97 N 21 2016
Cleeves, A. Cold earth. 2017
　Publishers Weekly v264 no8 p67 F 20 2017
Cleeves, A. The Crow Trap. 2017
　Publishers Weekly v263 no48 p46-7 N 28 2016
Clegg, B. Are numbers real? 2016
　Publishers Weekly v263 no41 p69 O 10 2016
Cleland, J. K. Glow of death. 2016
　Publishers Weekly v263 no39 p69 S 26 2016
Clement, B. and Clement, J. The Cat Sitter and the Canary. 2016
　Publishers Weekly v263 no42 p53 O 17 2016
Clement, J. and Miles, M. Screen schooled. 2017
　Publishers Weekly v264 no34 p107 Ag 21 2017
Clements, A. The Losers Club. 2017
　New York Times Book Review p27 Ag 27 2017 L. Bayard
　Publishers Weekly v264 no22 p68 My 29 2017
Clemmons, Z. What we lose. 2017
　Essence v48 no3 p56 Jl 2017 P. H. Bass
　New York Times Book Review p30 S 10 2017 V. V. Ganeshanan-
　　than
　O, The Oprah Magazine p84 Ag 2017 N. Dennis-Benn
　Publishers Weekly v264 no20 p32 My 15 2017
　Time v189 no22 p54 Je 12 2017 S. Begley
　Vanity Fair v59 no8 p48 Ag 2017 S. Crosley
　Vogue v207 no7 p59 Jl 2017 M. O'Grady
Clews Parsons, E. and others. The Origin Myth of Acoma Pueblo.
　2015
　New York Review of Books v63 no16 p58-60 O 27 2016 I. Frazier
Clickard, C. and Wu, K. Dumpling dreams. 2018
　Publishers Weekly v264 no32 p70 Ag 7 2017
Clicque, S. and others. A field guide to American houses. 2013

Cohen, E. A. The big stick. 2016
  Claremont Review of Books v17 no3 p23-6 Summ 2017 A. M.
    Codevilla
  Foreign Affairs v96 no1 p41-6 Ja/F 2017 K. Schake
  National Review v69 no6 p42-3 Ap 3 2017 A. Herman
  New York Review of Books v64 no2 p11-3 F 9 2017 J. T. Mathews
  Publishers Weekly v263 no43 p68 O 24 2016
  Weekly Standard v22 no18 p36-8 Ja 16 2017 M. T. Owens
Cohen, J. and Baram, N. A Land Without Borders. 2017
  America v217 no7 p48-9 O 2 2017 E. Webb
Cohen, J. and Grossman, D. A horse walks into a bar. 2016
  New York Review of Books v64 no7 p46-8 Ap 20 2017 S. Green-
    blatt
  New York Times Book Review p1-18 Mr 5 2017 G. Shteyngart
  New York Times Book Review p26 Mr 12 2017
Cohen, J. and Rabinyan, D. All the Rivers. 2017
  Publishers Weekly v264 no9 p71 F 27 2017
  Weekly Standard v22 no39 p39-40 Je 19 2017 D. Scharper
Cohen, J. Moving kings. 2017
  Esquire p21 Ag 2017 A. Westenfeld
  New York Times Book Review p11 Ag 13 2017 Z. Lazar
  Publishers Weekly v264 no18 p33 My 1 2017
  Time v190 no4 p54 Jl 24 2017 S. Begley
Cohen, L. and Parsons, K. The Yoga Kitchen. 2017
  Publishers Weekly v264 no1 p52 Ja 2 2017
Cohen, L. J. and others. Dreadnought And Shuttle. 2016
  Publishers Weekly v264 no4 p62 Ja 23 2017
  Publishers Weekly v264 no9 p66c F 27 2017
Cohen, M. A. American Maelstrom. 2016
  America v215 no15 p32-3 N 14 2016 J. P. Dolan
Cohen, M. A. and others. The Executive Coloring Book. 2017
  Fortune v175 no7 p18 Je 1 2017 A. Vandermey
Cohen, N. J. Facials can be fatal. 2017
  Publishers Weekly v263 no52 p102-3 D 19 2016
Cohen, R. and Sheringham, O. Encountering difference. 2016
  Current History v115 no784 p325-7 N 2016 F. J. Korom
Cohen, R. How to write like Tolstoy. 2016
  Commonweal v143 no19 p28-9 D 2 2016 D. Preziosi
  Harper's Magazine v334 no2002 p86-90 Mr 2017 N. Segnit
Cohen, R. The Chicago Cubs. 2017
  AARP: The Magazine v30 no6A p15 O/N 2017 C. Ianzito
Cohen, S. A. and Dunlap, J. Coming of Age at the End of Nature.
  2016
  Orion Magazine v36 no2 p59 Mr/Ap 2017 M. Landrigan
Cohen, S. and Hezroni, N. Three envelopes. 2017
  Publishers Weekly v264 no7 p48 F 13 2017
Cohen, S. S. and Delong, J. B. Concrete economics. 2016
  Claremont Review of Books v17 no1 p79-81 Wint 2016/2017 R.
    Vedder
Cohn, R. and Levithan, D. The Twelve Days of Dash & Lily. 2016
  Publishers Weekly v263 no39 p92 S 26 2016
Cohn, R. Kill all Happies. 2017
  Publishers Weekly v264 no36 p90 S 4 2017
Coken, J. When I Die, Take My Panties. 2016
  Publishers Weekly v264 no1 p51 Ja 2 2017
  Publishers Weekly v264 no4 p50f Ja 23 2017
Colak, M. and others. Kingsway West. 2017
  D: The Magazine of Dallas v43 no10 p58 O 2016 Z. Crain
  Publishers Weekly v264 no24 p50 Je 12 2017
Colbert, B. Little & Lion. 2017
  Publishers Weekly v264 no23 p55 Je 5 2017
Colby, R. and McClurkan, R. Captain Bling's Christmas plunder.
  2017
  Publishers Weekly v264 no36 p100 S 4 2017
Coldwell, D. F. and Douglas, G. Aeneid. 1964
  Weekly Standard v23 no2 p38-42 S 18 2017 S. Kristol
Cole, A. An Extraordinary Union. 2017
  Publishers Weekly v264 no8 p73 F 20 2017
Cole, D. Ragdoll. 2017
  Publishers Weekly v264 no3 p40 Ja 16 2017
Cole, I. F. and Hilbig, W. Old rendering plant. 2017
  Publishers Weekly v264 no38 p46 S 18 2017
Cole, I. F. and Kalka, J. Gaslight. 2017
  Harper's Magazine p91-3 Ap 2017 C. Smallwood
  Publishers Weekly v264 no6 p58 F 6 2017
Cole, L. Raven's Peak. 2016

  Publishers Weekly v264 no4 p50d Ja 23 2017
Cole, T. Blind spot. 2017
  New York Times Book Review p15 Je 4 2017 R. Pinsky
  New York Times Book Review p22 Je 11 2017
  Publishers Weekly v263 no51 p19-24 D 12 2016 A. Coreno
  Publishers Weekly v264 no20 p50 My 15 2017
Cole, T. Known and strange things. 2016
  New York Review of Books v64 no6 p23-4 Ap 6 2017 N. Rush
Cole, T. Open city. 2011
  New York p69-74 F 9 2017
Cole-Dai, P. and Wilson, R. R. Poetry of presence. 2017
  South Dakota Magazine p10 S/O 2017 Supplement
Coleman, G. Hacker, hoaxer, whistleblower, spy. 2014
  Publishers Weekly v264 no9 p98 F 27 2017
Coleman, J. W. The Buddha's dream of liberation. 2017
  Publishers Weekly v264 no15 p68 Ap 10 2017
Coleman, P. Introduction to many body physics. 2015
  Physics Today v70 no5 p59-60 My 2017 M. Randeria
Coleman, R. F. What you break. 2017
  Publishers Weekly v263 no47 p22-8 N 21 2016 J. Foster
  Publishers Weekly v263 no47 p89 N 21 2016
Coleman, S. and Thomas, B. Organizational change explained.
  2017
  People Management p50 My 2017
  People Management p52 Ap 2017
Coles, G. Single, gay, Christian. 2017
  Publishers Weekly v264 no24 p61-2 Je 12 2017
Colfer, C. and Dorman, B. The Land of stories. 2017
  Publishers Weekly v264 no31 p15 Jl 31 2017 C. Juris
Colfer, C. Stranger Than Fanfiction. 2017
  Publishers Weekly v264 no22 p64 My 29 2017
Colin, B. To capture what we cannot keep. 2016
  New York Times Book Review p26 F 5 2017 N. Kline
Colin, E. The Dream Keeper's Daughter. 2017
  Publishers Weekly v264 no23 p38 Je 5 2017
Collard, S. B. Catching air. 2017
  Publishers Weekly v264 no6 p69 F 6 2017
Collard, S. B. Hopping Ahead of Climate Change. 2016
  Science v354 no6317 p1226 D 9 2016 Y. Nusinovich
Collens, D. R. and Lawrence, N. Mark di Suvero. 2015
  Art in America v104 no10 p86 N 2016
Collett, C. A Good Death. 2017
  Publishers Weekly v263 no50 p52 D 5 2016
Collier, B. and Perkins, U. E. Hey black child. 2017
  Publishers Weekly v264 no39 p104-5 S 25 2017
Collier, D. Morton. 2017
  Publishers Weekly v264 no35 p113 Ag 28 2017
Collingham, L. The taste of empire. 2017
  Reason v49 no5 p77 O 2017 K. Mangu-Ward
  Time v190 no14 p22 O 9 2017 S. Begley
Collings, D. A. Stolen Future, Broken Present. 2014
  BioScience v67 no3 p306-9 Mr 2017 R. D. Stevenson
Collins, A. The most wonderful time of the year. 2016
  Publishers Weekly v263 no40 p84 O 3 2016 L. Garret
Collins, C. and others. Transitional justice in Latin America. 2016
  Progressive p60-6 D 2016/Ja 2017 N. Stockwell
Collins, C. J. and others. The teeth of the comb & other stories.
  2017
  New York Times Book Review p34 My 21 2017 L. Michel
  Publishers Weekly v264 no7 p47 F 13 2017
Collins, C. Lost treasures of St. Louis. 2016
  Missouri Life v44 no5 p21 Ag 2017 Z. Glasgow
Collins, H. Are We All Scientific Experts Now? 2014
  Issues in Science & Technology v33 no1 p89-90 Fall 2016 C. Mit-
    cham
Collins, J. Cravings. 2017
  Publishers Weekly v263 no48 p59-60 N 28 2016
Collins, K. Whatever Happened to Interracial Love? 2016
  Essence v47 no8 p72 D 2016 P. H. Bass
  Harper's Magazine v333 no1999 p81-3 D 2016 C. Smallwood
  New York Review of Books v64 no6 p28-30 Ap 6 2017 V. Gornick
  New York Times Book Review p22 D 18 2016
  New York Times Book Review p24 D 11 2016 M. Jerkins
  O, The Oprah Magazine p69 Ja 2017 D. Akintoye
  Vanity Fair v59 no1 p98 Holiday 2017 S. Crosley
Collins, L. When in French. 2016

Publishers Weekly v263 no49 p19-20 D 7 2016

Cyrus, K. and Cyrus, K. Shake a leg, egg! 2017
Publishers Weekly v264 no1 p57 Ja 2 2017

Czerski, H. Storm in a teacup. 2017
Physics Today v70 no8 p59-60 Ag 2017 B. Halfpap
Science v355 no6320 p33 Ja 6 2017 M. Engel
Scientific American v316 no1 p68 Ja 2017 C. Moskowitz
Skeptical Inquirer v41 no4 p61 Jl/Ag 2017

Czerwiec, M. K. and Czerwiec, M. K. Taking turns. 2017
Christian Century v134 no18 p43 Ag 30 2017

D

Dabney, R. S. The Soul Mender. 2016
Publishers Weekly v263 no45 p46 N 7 2016
Publishers Weekly v263 no47 p76c-d N 21 2016

D'Abo, C. Working It (Ringside Romance) 2017
Publishers Weekly v264 no1 p44 Ja 2 2017

Dacey, P. The outer cape. 2017
Publishers Weekly v264 no14 p46-8 Ap 3. 2017

DaCosta, P. Girl from Above. 2015
Publishers Weekly v264 no18 p43 My 1 2017
Publishers Weekly v264 no21 p65a My 22 2017

Dagan, D. and Teles, S. M. Prison break. 2016
Claremont Review of Books v17 no3 p15-9 Summ 2017 J. M. Bessette
Washington Monthly p1 S/O 2016 H. Schoenfeld

D'Agata, J. The making of the American essay. 2016
Atlantic v319 no1 p90-9 Ja/F 2017 W. Deresiewicz

D'Agostino, K. The Antiques. 2017
Publishers Weekly v263 no43 p52-3 O 24 2016

Dagostino, M. and others. The magnolia story. 2016
New York Times Book Review p20 D 25 2016
New York Times Book Review p24 F 5 2017
Publishers Weekly v263 no50 p69 D 5 2016

D'Agosto, A. and others. Hello, My Name is Ice Cream. 2017
Martha Stewart Living no275 p10 Je 2017

Dahl, K. O. and Bartlett, D. Faithless. 2017
Publishers Weekly v264 no28 p68 Jl 10 2017

Dahlstrom, S. and Wilke, C. The green colt. 2016
American Cowboy v24 no1 p47 Je/Jl 2017

Dailey, J. and others. Happy is the bride. 2017
Publishers Weekly v264 no17 p75 Ap 24 2017

Dailey, J. Just a Little Christmas. 2017
Publishers Weekly v264 no36 p73 S 4 2017

Dailey, J. Sunrise Canyon. 2017
Publishers Weekly v264 no5 p186 Ja 30 2017

Daines, J. Havencross. 2017
Publishers Weekly v264 no29 p204 Jl 17 2017

Dainty, S. The housekeeper. 2017
Publishers Weekly v263 no50 p50-1 D 5 2016

Dal Co, F. Centre Pompidou. 2016
Publishers Weekly v263 no42 p63 O 17 2016

Dal Co, F. The Guggenheim. 2017
Architectural Record v205 no7 p63 Jl 2017 S. Stephens

Dale, G. Karl Polanyi. 2016
Foreign Affairs v95 no6 p180-1 N/D 2016 A. Moravcsik
Nation v304 no2 p27-31 Ja 16 2017 N. Saval

Dale-Scott, L. and Lawler, J. Leaves. 2017
Publishers Weekly v264 no35 p126-7 Ag 28 2017

Daley, R. Prince of the city. 1978
Entertainment Weekly no1471 p65 Je 23 2017

Dalfonzo, G. One by one. 2017
Christianity Today v61 no5 p65-7 Je 2017 J. B. Smith

Dalí, S. and Moore, J. P. Les dîners de gala. 1973
Entertainment Weekly no1439 p62-3 N 11 2016 R. Kinane

Dallaire, R. Waiting for First Light. 2016
Maclean's v129 no43 p14-8 O 31 2016 B. Bethune

Dallek, R. Franklin D. Roosevelt. 2017
Publishers Weekly v264 no36 p80 S 4 2017

Daloz, K. We are as gods. 2016
Reason v48 no7 p56-9 D 2016 B. Doherty

Dalton, P. Under the silver moon. 2015
Publishers Weekly v264 no19 p58 My 8 2017

Daly, P. The Trophy Child. 2017

Publishers Weekly v264 no3 p40-1 Ja 16 2017

Damour, L. Untangled. 2016
Christian Century v133 no22 p32-4 O 26 2016 C. L. Hearlson

Dams, J. M. The missing masterpiece. 2017
Publishers Weekly v264 no29 p199 Jl 17 2017

Danaher, W. F. and Roscigno, V. J. The voice of southern labor. 2004
Monthly Labor Review p1-2 My 2017 R. Weir

Daniel, A. M. and Fitzgerald, F. S. I'd die for you. 2017
New York Times Book Review p22 Je 4 2017 B. Bailey

Daniel, K. R. Easy-to-make statement jewelry. 2017
Publishers Weekly v264 no23 p49 Je 5 2017

Daniel, R. Hacked. 2017
Publishers Weekly v264 no17 p71 Ap 24 2017

Daniels, C. and Bennardo, C. E. Evolution Revolution. 2016
Publishers Weekly v264 no39 p107 S 25 2017

Daniels, C. Graveyard Shift. 2017
Publishers Weekly v263 no45 p43 N 7 2016

Daniels, R. The Virgin Eye. 2016
America v216 no11 p54-5 My 15 2017 N. King

Danko, W. D. and Stanley, T. J. The millionaire next door. 1997
Black Enterprise v47 no5 p20 Ja/F 2017 D. D. Hughes

Danler, S. Sweetbitter. 2016
Commonweal v144 no13 p35-8 Ag 11 2017 A. Domestico

Dann, K. Expect great things. 2017
New York Times Book Review p13 Ja 15 2017 J. Kaag

Danner, M. Spiral. 2016
Nation v304 no12 p34-7 Ap 10 2017 K. J. Greenberg
Progressive p60-4 D 2016/Ja 2017 B. Lueders

Danois, A. The Boys of Dunbar. 2016
New York Times Book Review p58-60 D 4 2016 M. Tracy

Danticat, E. Art of death. 2017
Commonweal v114 no14 p29-30 S 8 2017 V. Sayers
New York Times Book Review p21 Ag 13 2017 W. Grimes
New York Times Book Review p22 Ag 20 2017
Publishers Weekly v264 no13 p90 Mr 27 2017

D'Antonio, M. A consequential president. 2017
America v216 no9 p25-6 Ap 24 2017 J. Berry
Foreign Affairs v96 no4 p134-40 Jl/Ag 2017 J. Klein
Publishers Weekly v263 no41 p71 O 10 2016

D'Antonio, M. The truth about Trump. 2016
Nation v303 no17 p32-6 O 24 2016 C. Lehmann

Dantzic, G. and Dantzic, J. Billie Holiday at Sugar Hill. 2016
Publishers Weekly v264 no14 p67 Ap 3. 2017

Danylko, K. Whispers in the windstorm. 2016
Publishers Weekly v264 no15 p71 Ap 10 2017
Publishers Weekly v264 no17 p58e-f Ap 24 2017

Danziger, M. Sing it! 2016
Publishers Weekly v263 no49 p85-6 D 7 2016

Dao, J. C. Forest of a thousand lanterns. 2017
Publishers Weekly v264 no34 p115 Ag 21 2017

Darcleight, D. Concrete carnival. 2016
Publishers Weekly v263 no39 p73 S 26 2016 N. P. R.

Darcy, D. and Telfer, T. Lady Killers. 2017
Publishers Weekly v264 no32 p61 Ag 7 2017

Dardik, H. and Dardik, H. The story of Noah's Ark. 2017
Publishers Weekly v264 no25 p111 Je 19 2017

Dare, W. How to Tame a Triceratops. 2017
Publishers Weekly v264 no17 p93 Ap 24 2017

Darke, R. and Oudolf, P. Gardens of the High Line. 2017
Architectural Record v205 no8 p51 Ag 2017 A. Shapiro

Darnielle, J. Universal harvester. 2017
Esquire v167 no1 p20-1 F 2017 C. Beha
New York Times Book Review p13 F 19 2017 J. Hill
O, The Oprah Magazine p105 Mr 2017
Publishers Weekly v263 no51 p119 D 12 2016

Darrow, G. and Miller, F. Hard boiled. 2017
Publishers Weekly v264 no39 p94 S 25 2017

Dascher, H. and Delisle, G. Hostage. 2017
Publishers Weekly v264 no18 p46 My 1 2017

Daswani, G. Looking back, moving forward. 2015
Christian Century v133 no21 p23-4 O 12 2016

Datlow, E. and Morton, L. Hallow's eve. 2017
Publishers Weekly v264 no32 p56 Ag 7 2017

Datlow, E. Black Feathers. 2017
Publishers Weekly v263 no44 p57 O 31 2016

Day, A. and Oh, E. Spirit hunters. 2017
   Publishers Weekly v264 no19 p61 My 8 2017
Day, J. A. and others. The Longevity Plan. 2017
   Publishers Weekly v264 no16 p63 Ap 17 2017
Daywalt, D. and Rex, A. The Legend of Rock Paper Scissors. 2017
   Publishers Weekly v264 no6 p68 F 6 2017
Dazieri, S. and Shugaar, A. Kill the father. 2017
   Publishers Weekly v263 no41 p56-7 O 10 2016
Deady, T. Haven. 2016
   Publishers Weekly v263 no44 p58 O 31 2016
Dean, C. and Kaliardos, J. Visionaire. 2016
   Interview v46 no9 p42 N 2016 M. Mullen
Dean, C. Making sense of science. 2017
   Publishers Weekly v264 no4 p74 Ja 23 2017
Dean, D. and others. The Barefoot Book of Children. 2016
   Publishers Weekly v263 no49 p45 D 7 2016
Dean, E. L. For the Love of Katie. 2017
   Publishers Weekly v264 no26 p164 Je 26 2017
Dean, J. and Holub, J. Tool school. 2017
   Publishers Weekly v264 no20 p53 My 15 2017
Dean, S. Thunder Road. 2016
   Publishers Weekly v263 no50 p55 D 5 2016
   Publishers Weekly v264 no4 p50d Ja 23 2017
Dear, B. The friendly orange glow. 2017
   Publishers Weekly v264 no33 p61 Ag 14 2017
Dearborn, M. V. Ernest Hemingway. 2017
   Claremont Review of Books v17 no3 p77-9 Summ 2017 M. Bauerlein
   National Review v69 no16 p41-2 Ag 28 2017 T. Teachout
   New York Review of Books v64 no11 p34-6 Je 22 2017 F. O'Toole
   New York Times Book Review p55 Je 4 2017
Death, S. and Lindgren, A. War Diaries, 1939-1945. 2016
   Atlantic v318 no4 p46 N 2016 A. Hulbert
Deaver, J. The burial hour. 2017
   Publishers Weekly v264 no8 p64-6 F 20 2017
de Bellaigue, C. The Islamic Enlightenment. 2017
   America v217 no6 p54 S 18 2017 P. B. Ely
   Harper's Magazine v334 no2004 p82-7 My 2017 Y. Seale
   New York Review of Books v64 no11 p22-5 Je 22 2017 M. Ruthven
   New York Times Book Review p20 Jl 23 2017 J. Goodwin
   Publishers Weekly v264 no7 p70 F 13 2017
De Bernières, L. The dust that falls from dreams. 2015
   New York Times Book Review p28 O 30 2016 J. Khatib
De Bodard, A. The house of binding thorns. 2017
   Publishers Weekly v264 no7 p54 F 13 2017
Debord, M. Return to Glory. 2017
   New York Times Book Review p18 Jl 9 2017 J. Kellerman
   New York Times Book Review p19 Jl 16 2017
Debos, M. Living by the Gun in Chad. 2016
   Foreign Affairs v96 no3 p176 My/Je 2017 N. Van De Walle
DeBuys, W. and Peck, M. Everglades. 2016
   Publishers Weekly v264 no7 p67 F 13 2017
   Publishers Weekly v264 no9 p66h F 27 2017
De Cataldo, G. and others. Suburra. 2017
   Publishers Weekly v264 no25 p94 Je 19 2017
Dech, S. and others. Mountains. 2016
   Natural History v125 no1 p40-3 D 2016/Ja 2017 L. A. Marschall
Décharné, M. Vulgar tongues. 2017
   New York Times Book Review p34 Ag 27 2017 P. Sokolowski
   Publishers Weekly v264 no9 p86 F 27 2017
DeCoste, J. Alone and on My Knees. 2016
   Publishers Weekly v263 no39 p52-9 S 26 2016
DeCristofano, C. C. Ultimate space atlas. 2017
   Publishers Weekly v264 no25 p114 Je 19 2017
DeCurtis, A. Lou Reed. 2017
   Publishers Weekly v264 no28 p76 Jl 10 2017
Dedek, P. B. The cemeteries of New Orleans. 2017
   New Orleans Magazine v52 no1 p58 S 2017
Dederer, C. Love and trouble. 2017
   Atlantic v319 no5 p31-3 Je 2017 L. Kipnis
   Entertainment Weekly no1468/1469 p109 Je 2-9 2017 T. Jordan
   New York Times Book Review p22-3 My 21 2017 H. Havrilesky
   Publishers Weekly v264 no13 p94-5 Mr 27 2017
Dee, J. The locals. 2018
   New York Times Book Review p11 Ag 27 2017 L. Rosenfeld
   Publishers Weekly v264 no25 p86 Je 19 2017

Deedy, C. A. and Yelchin, E. The rooster who would not be quiet! 2017
   Publishers Weekly v263 no46 p56 N 14 2016
Deering, A. and Lentz, B. Sandwiches! 2017
   Publishers Weekly v264 no22 p69 My 29 2017
Deering, J. Murder on the Moor. 2017
   Publishers Weekly v263 no47 p91 N 21 2016
Deetz, K. F. Bound to the fire. 2017
   Publishers Weekly v264 no36 p79-80 S 4 2017
DeFehr, B. and Boldt, P. Les marches Francais. 2016
   Publishers Weekly v264 no10 p56 Mr 6 2017
DeFelice, J. West Like Lightning. 2017
   American Cowboy v23 no5 p25 F/Mr 2017
DeForge, M. Sticks Angelica, Folk Hero. 2017
   Publishers Weekly v264 no4 p67 Ja 23 2017
De Giovanni, M. and Shugaar, A. Glass Souls. 2017
   Publishers Weekly v264 no22 p47 My 29 2017
De Givenchy, J. T. Taffin. 2016
   Vanity Fair v58 no12 p86 D 2016 J. Vitale
Degrand, D. and Keating, J. What makes a monster? 2017
   Publishers Weekly v264 no28 p87 Jl 10 2017
De Hahn, T. Swiss Vendetta. 2017
   Publishers Weekly v263 no50 p50 D 5 2016
De Hamel, C. Meetings with remarkable manuscripts. 2017
   American Scholar v86 no4 p118-20 Aut 2017 H. Hazen
   Publishers Weekly v264 no32 p61-2 Ag 7 2017
DeJong, D. H. American Indian treaties. 2015
   American Indian Quarterly v41 no2 p185-7 Spr 2017 J. C. Jurss
De Jong, P. and others. Saving Charlotte. 2017
   New Yorker v93 no31 p68 O 9 2017
De Jongh, A. and De Jongh, A. The Return of the Honey Buzzard. 2016
   Publishers Weekly v263 no41 p65 O 10 2016
Dek, M. and Dek, M. A walk in the forest. 2017
   New York Times Book Review p20 My 14 2017 J. Turner
   Publishers Weekly v264 no7 p76 F 13 2017
De la Bédoyère, G. Praetorian. 2017
   Military History v34 no2 p72-3 Jl 2017 R. A. Gabriel
Delacre, L. and others. Us, in progress. 2017
   Publishers Weekly v264 no22 p68 My 29 2017
De la Cruz, M. Pride and prejudice and mistletoe. 2017
   Publishers Weekly v264 no36 p73 S 4 2017
Delaney, J. P. The girl before. 2017
   Good Housekeeping v264 no3 p72 Mr 2017
   New York Times Book Review p24 F 12 2017 G. ^Cowles
   Publishers Weekly v264 no9 p96 F 27 2017
Delaney, K. Blood Red, White and Blue. 2017
   Publishers Weekly v264 no19 p40 My 8 2017
De Lange, N. and Oz, A. Judas. 2016
   America v216 no9 p52-4 Ap 24 2017 D. Vellucci
   Commonweal v144 no6 p25-6 Mr 24 2017 T. Novick
   Esquire v166 no4 p36 N 2016 J. Black
   New Yorker v92 no45 p79 Ja 16 2017
   New York Review of Books v64 no4 p35-6 Mr 9 2017 A. Margalit
   New York Times Book Review p26 D 11 2016 E. Barton
Delargy, M. and Tursten, H. Protected by the shadows. 2017
   Publishers Weekly v264 no41 p45 O 9 2017
Delauro, R. L. The least among us. 2017
   Foreign Affairs v96 no6 p159 N/D 2017 W. R. Mead
   Ms. v27 no2 p45 Summ 2017 R. Bacon
   Publishers Weekly v264 no17 p83 Ap 24 2017
Del Bosque, M. Bloodlines. 2017
   Texas Monthly v45 no9 p46-8 S 2017 S. Mahanta
Delbourgo, J. Collecting the world. 2017
   New York Review of Books v64 no15 p34-6 O 12 2017 J. Uglow
   New York Times Book Review p9 S 10 2017 B. Boucher
DeLillo, D. Zero K. 2016
   Commentary v142 no1 p59-61 Jl/Ag 2016 A. Greenwald
   New York Times Book Review p24 Je 11 2017 J. Khatib
Delisle, G. and Dascher, H. Hostage. 2017
   Publishers Weekly v264 no18 p46 My 1 2017
Dell, K. L. Tougher in Texas. 2017
   Publishers Weekly v264 no24 p47 Je 12 2017
Delogu, C. J. and others. Hannah's dress. 2017
   History Today v67 no7 p104-5 Jl 2017 A. Hájková
Delong, J. B. and Cohen, S. S. Concrete economics. 2016

Publishers Weekly v264 no25 p107 Je 19 2017

Desinger, K. The descent of man. 2011
Publishers Weekly v264 no14 p67 Ap 3, 2017

Desmond, J. and Desmond, J. The Polar Bear. 2016
New York Times Book Review p26-7 N 13 2016

Desmond, M. Evicted. 2016
Entertainment Weekly no1444/1445 p108 D 16 2016 T. Jordan
New York Times Book Review p24 F 26 2017 J. Khatib
Progressive p60-2 D 2016/Ja 2017 R. Conniff
Publishers Weekly v264 no17 p13 Ap 24 2017 C. Juris

Despommier, D. D. People, parasites, and plowshares. 2013
BioScience v66 no10 p907-8 O 1 2016 J. Moore

Dessen, S. Once and for all. 2017
Publishers Weekly v264 no17 p92 Ap 24 2017
Publishers Weekly v264 no25 p16 Je 19 2017 C. Juris
Publishers Weekly v264 no36 p89-90 S 4 2017
Seventeen v76 no4 p9 Jl/Ag 2017 R. Mosely

DeStefano, A. M. The Big Heist. 2017
Publishers Weekly v264 no18 p48 My 1 2017

De Stefano, C. and Harss, M. Oriana Fallaci. 2017
Publishers Weekly v264 no24 p51 Je 12 2017

Dettmar, K. and Lethem, J. Shake it up. 2017
New York Times Book Review p19 Je 4 2017 B. Handy
Rolling Stone no1290 p17 Je 29 2017 J. Dolan

Deutermann, P. T. Red swan. 2017
Publishers Weekly v264 no22 p45 My 29 2017

DeVecca, F. The nutting girl. 2017
Publishers Weekly v264 no24 p44 Je 12 2017

DeVega, M. R. Songs for the waiting. 2016
Publishers Weekly v263 no40 p84 O 3 2016 L. Garret

Devenish, R. and others. Particle physics in the LHC era. 2016
Physics Today v70 no6 p62 Je 2017 M. Cirelli

Devito, D. Cast Iron Pies. 2017
Publishers Weekly v264 no10 p32 Mr 6 2017

Devlin, C. Right where you left me. 2017
Publishers Weekly v264 no30 p62 Jl 24 2017

Devlin, K. Finding Fibonacci. 2017
New York Times Book Review p31 My 7 2017 J. Ryerson
Publishers Weekly v264 no9 p90 F 27 2017
Science News v191 no11 p28 Je 10 2017
Scientific American v316 no5 p74 My 2017 A. Marks

Devlin, P. Murray talks music. 2016
New Yorker v92 no33 p99 O 17 2016
Weekly Standard v22 no13 p36-7 D 5 2016 A. Tepper

Devore, L. How to break a boy. 2017
Publishers Weekly v263 no44 p79 O 31 2016

Dewdney, A. and Brown, M. W. Christmas in the barn. 2016
Publishers Weekly v263 no39 p91 S 26 2016

Dewdney, A. Little excavator. 2017
New York Times Book Review p22-3 My 14 2017 J. Sturm
Publishers Weekly v264 no15 p72 Ap 10 2017

DeWees, A. Sea of Secrets. 2012
Publishers Weekly v263 no41 p63-4 O 10 2016
Publishers Weekly v263 no43 p50c O 24 2016

DeWees, A. With This Curse. 2014
Publishers Weekly v263 no47 p98 N 21 2016
Publishers Weekly v263 no52 p90d-e D 19 2016

DeWitt, A. White nights in split town city. 2016
New York Times Book Review p30 N 6 2016 J. W. McCormack

DeWitt, S. H. and others. Let me tell you. 2015
New York Review of Books v63 no16 p47-51 O 27 2016 J. C. Oates

De Wolf, C. and Hoshino, T. Me. 2017
Publishers Weekly v264 no17 p63 Ap 24 2017

Dews, C. L. and McCullers, C. Carson McCullers. 2017
New York Review of Books v64 no14 p78-80 S 28 2017 J. C. Oates

DeYoe, J. K. Mindful Money. 2017
Publishers Weekly v263 no52 p116 D 19 2016

DeYoung, A. The exo project. 2017
Publishers Weekly v264 no6 p68-70 F 6 2017

Dhar, P. and others. Eat the sky, drink the ocean. 2014
Publishers Weekly v263 no52 p126-7 D 19 2016

Diacono, M. and Leendertz, L. My Tiny Veg Plot. 2017
Publishers Weekly v263 no47 p104 N 21 2016

Dial, C. The third hell. 2017
Publishers Weekly v263 no48 p47 N 28 2016

Diamant, A. The Jewish wedding now. 2017
Publishers Weekly v264 no15 p69-70 Ap 10 2017

Diamond, J. Dirty Like Me. 2016
Publishers Weekly v264 no3 p46 Ja 16 2017
Publishers Weekly v264 no9 p66c F 27 2017

Diamond, K. and others. The Cherry bombe cookbook. 2017
Publishers Weekly v264 no25 p106 Je 19 2017

Diamond, L. Kale & Caramel. 2017
Publishers Weekly v264 no8 p80 F 20 2017

Diamond, T. Such a Pretty Girl. 2017
Publishers Weekly v264 no36 p71 S 4 2017

Dias, M. A. and others. Outside. 2016
Science v354 no6317 p1226 D 9 2016 P. J. Hines

Diaz, E. and others. Indigo. 2017
Publishers Weekly v264 no16 p48 Ap 17 2017

Díaz, J. The brief wondrous life of Oscar Wao. 2007
America v216 no12 p42-7 My 29 2017 O. Segura

DiBattista, M. and Nord, D. E. At home in the world. 2017
Publishers Weekly v264 no4 p72 Ja 23 2017

DiBiase, D. D. Bound by mystery. 2017
Publishers Weekly v264 no7 p52 F 13 2017

DiCamillo, K. Raymie Nightingale. 2016
Publishers Weekly v263 no49 p76 D 7 2016

DiCampo, P. and others. Everyday Africa. 2016
Vanity Fair v59 no1 p98 Holiday 2017 A. Tepper

Dickerman, L. and Borchardt-Hume, A. Robert Rauschenberg. 2016
Publishers Weekly v264 no15 p66 Ap 10 2017

Dickerson, J. Whistlestop. 2016
New York Times Book Review p20 Jl 16 2017 J. Khatib

Dickey, C. Ghostland. 2016
New York Times Book Review p12 O 30 2016 T. Miles
Time v188 no18 p20 O 31 2016 S. Begley

Dickinson, A. Strangers tend to tell me things. 2016
Publishers Weekly v264 no26 p175 Je 26 2017
Publishers Weekly v264 no5 p194-5 Ja 30 2017

Dickinson, C. Words fail. 2016
Phi Kappa Phi Forum v97 no1 p31 Spr 2017

Dickson, A. Worlds elsewhere. 2016
New York Times Book Review p24 Ja 22 2017

Dickson, J. G. The Wild turkey. 1992
Outdoor Life v224 no2 p52-7 F/Mr 2017 J. Casada

Dickson, J. G. Wildlife of Southern Forests.
Outdoor Life v224 no2 p52-7 F/Mr 2017 J. Casada

Dickson, K. and Lahlum, H. O. Satellite People. 2016
Publishers Weekly v263 no39 p70 S 26 2016

Dickson, K. and Lahlum, H. O. The Catalyst Killing. 2017
Publishers Weekly v263 no51 p127 D 12 2016

Dickson, K. and Øyehaug, G. Knots. 2017
New Yorker v93 no25 p83-5 Ag 28 2017 J. Wood
Publishers Weekly v264 no18 p33 My 1 2017

Dickson, P. Leo Durocher. 2017
New York Times Book Review p14 Ap 2 2017 J. Swansburg
Publishers Weekly v263 no48 p59 N 28 2016

Didion, J. South and west. 2017
Esquire v167 no2 p52 Mr 2017 A. Westenfeld
New York p116-21 Mr 6 2017
Publishers Weekly v263 no51 p46-50 D 12 2016 E. Jones
Publishers Weekly v264 no12 p16 Mr 20 2017 C. Juris
Publishers Weekly v264 no2 p59 Ja 9 2017
Vogue v207 no3 p392 Mr 2017 V. Steiker

Didion, J. The white album. 2009
New York Review of Books v64 no14 p53-4 S 28 2017 M. Gorra

Diebenkorn, R. The sketchbooks revealed. 2015
New York Review of Books v64 no1 p12-4 Ja 19 2017 J. Perl

Diederich, P. Playing for the Devil's Fire. 2016
Publishers Weekly v263 no49 p100-1 D 7 2016

Dieterlé, N. and Rémond-Dalyac, E. Good night. 2017
Publishers Weekly v264 no25 p110 Je 19 2017

DiFelice, B. Almost There. 2017
Publishers Weekly v264 no19 p54 My 8 2017

DiGiacomo, K. and Naumann-Villemin, C. When a wolf is hungry. 2017
Publishers Weekly v264 no25 p112 Je 19 2017

Digitalis, R. Esoteric empathy. 2016
Publishers Weekly v263 no41 p74 O 10 2016

Dikötter, F. The Cultural Revolution. 2016

New York Review of Books v63 no16 p70-4 O 27 2016 I. Johnson

New York Times Book Review p24 Je 18 2017 J. Khatib

Dilke, L. The Outcast Spirit. 2016

Publishers Weekly v263 no39 p71-2 S 26 2016

Dill, J. Bluff. 2017

Publishers Weekly v263 no50 p74 D 5 2016

Dillard, A. The abundance. 2016

New York Times Book Review p24 F 26 2017 J. Khatib

Diller, J. and others. Mystery of the troubled toucan. 2015

Publishers Weekly v264 no3 p59 Ja 16 2017

Publishers Weekly v264 no9 p66k-l F 27 2017

Dillery, J. Clio's other sons. 2014

Weekly Standard v22 no11 p37-8 N 21 2016 R. Tada

Dillman, L. and Barba, A. Such small hands. 2017

Publishers Weekly v264 no7 p44 F 13 2017

Dillman, L. and Herrera, Y. Kingdom Cons. 2017

New York v50 no12 p116 Je 12 2017

Publishers Weekly v264 no14 p46 Ap 3, 2017

Dillon, E. Spies in the family. 2017

American Scholar v86 no3 p123-5 Summ 2017

Dillon, J. and Grant, M. Final Girls. 2017

Publishers Weekly v264 no21 p71 My 22 2017

Publishers Weekly v264 no9 p83 F 27 2017

DiLorenzo, B. and DiLorenzo, B. Renato and the Lion. 2017

Publishers Weekly v264 no16 p66-7 Ap 17 2017

Dinan, K. The yellow envelope. 2017

Cincinnati Magazine v50 no10 p24 Jl 2017 L. Murtha

Publishers Weekly v264 no4 p72 Ja 23 2017

Dinan, T. and others. The psychobiotic revolution. 2017

Publishers Weekly v264 no34 p106 Ag 21 2017

Dinerstein, J. The origins of cool in postwar America. 2017

New York Times Book Review p8 Je 4 2017 J. Williams

Weekly Standard v22 no35 p30-3 My 22 2017 J. Epstein

Dinh, V. After Disasters. 2016

New Yorker v92 no40 p78 D 5 2016

Dinnen, M. and Alder, M. Exceptional talent. 2017

People Management p53 Je 2017

Dionne, E. J. and others. One Nation After Trump. 2017

New York Times Book Review p22 O 1 2017 A. Berman

Dionne, K. The Marsh King's daughter. 2017

Publishers Weekly v264 no14 p52 Ap 3, 2017

Diouf, S. A. and Woodard, K. Black Power 50. 2016

New York Times Book Review p10 N 27 2016 R. Browne

Di Perna, A. and Tolinski, B. Play it loud. 2016

Downbeat v83 no12 p93 D 2016 B. Milkowski

Dipucchio, K. and Ford, A. G. Littles. 2017

Publishers Weekly v264 no17 p91 Ap 24 2017

Dipucchio, K. and Graegin, S. Super Manny stands up! 2017

Publishers Weekly v264 no19 p60 My 8 2017

Dipucchio, K. and Robinson, C. Antoinette. 2017

Publishers Weekly v263 no46 p54-5 N 14 2016

Dirand, A. and others. Joseph Dirand. 2017

Architectural Digest v74 no10 p48-50 O 1 2017 M. Owens

Dischell, S. Children with enemies. 2017

Publishers Weekly v264 no34 p85 Ag 21 2017

DiSilverio, L. That last weekend. 2017

Publishers Weekly v264 no31 p67 Jl 31 2017

Diski, J. In Gratitude. 2016

New York v49 no25 p122 D 12 2016 C. Lorentzen

Diski, J. The Vanishing Princess. 2017

Publishers Weekly v264 no40 p113 O 2 2017

Dismondy, M. and Brooks, P. S. The jelly donut difference. 2017

Publishers Weekly v264 no33 p78 Ag 14 2017

Publishers Weekly v264 no35 p77f Ag 28 2017

Disraeli, B. Sybil. 2017

American Conservative v16 no5 p62-5 S/O 2017 P. Gottfried

DiTerlizzi, A. and Smith, A. Seeking a Bunny. 2017

Publishers Weekly v264 no3 p58 Ja 16 2017

DiTerlizzi, A. and Smith, A. Seeking a Santa. 2016

Publishers Weekly v263 no39 p87 S 26 2016

DiTerlizzi, A. and Vukovic, E. I wanna be a cowgirl. 2017

Publishers Weekly v264 no38 p69 S 18 2017

Dittrich, L. Patient H.M. 2016

Entertainment Weekly no1466 p60-1 My 19 2017

Scientific American v315 no3 p86 S 2016 C. Moskowitz

Divakaruni, C. B. Before we visit the goddess. 2016

New York Times Book Review p24 Je 18 2017 J. Khatib

Dixon, A. and Mountford, K. J. Maurice the unbeastly. 2017

Publishers Weekly v264 no29 p215 Jl 17 2017

Dixon, F. R. and others. Crossing The Troll Bridge. 2015

Missouri Life v44 no2 p22 Ap 2017 M. W. Schwartz

Dixon, R. and Calasso, R. The Art of the Publisher. 2015

New York Times Book Review p24 Ja 15 2017 J. Khatib

Dixon, R. and Eco, U. Chronicles of a liquid society. 2017

Publishers Weekly v264 no33 p61 Ag 14 2017

Dixon, R. and Santagata, M. Dante. 2016

New York Review of Books v63 no16 p30-2 O 27 2016 R. P. Harrison

Weekly Standard v22 no20 p30-2 Ja 30 2017 J. Matthew Wilson

Djian, J. and others. The Baker Street Four. 2017

Publishers Weekly v264 no20 p45 My 15 2017

DK Publishing (Company) The Magic Show Book. 2016

Publishers Weekly v263 no41 p81 O 10 2016

DK Publishing (Company) Look, I'm a cook. 2017

Publishers Weekly v264 no22 p69 My 29 2017

DK Publishing (Company) Pillows, curtains, & shades step by step. 2017

Publishers Weekly v264 no6 p65 F 6 2017

DK Publishing (Company) Pop-up Peekaboo Pumpkin. 2017

Publishers Weekly v264 no26 p178 Je 26 2017

Doan, L. The Alarming Career of Sir Richard Blackstone. 2017

Publishers Weekly v263 no51 p148 D 12 2016

Doane, C. J. The Sea Is Not Full. 2017

Sail v48 no3 p15 Mr 2017 P. N.

Dobbs, L. and Born, J. O. Putin's Gambit. 2017

Publishers Weekly v264 no14 p53 Ap 3, 2017

Dobyns, S. Saratoga payback. 2017

New York Times Book Review p9 Mr 19 2017 M. Stasio

Publishers Weekly v264 no17 p88 Ap 24 2017

Publishers Weekly v264 no1 p37 Ja 2 2017

Dochuk, D. and Sutton, M. A. Faith in the new millennium. 2016

Christian Century v133 no22 p41-2 O 26 2016 R. Balmer

Docker, P. and others. Find your why. 2017

Publishers Weekly v264 no21 p35-42 My 22 2017 S. J. Robbins

Doctoroff, D. L. Greater than ever. 2017

Architectural Record v205 no10 p51 O 2017 D. Lind

New York v50 no17 p34-5 Ag 21 2017 C. Swanson

Doctorow, C. Little brother. 2008

New Yorker v93 no16 p102-6 Je 5 2017 J. Lepore

Doctorow, C. Walkaway. 2017

Publishers Weekly v264 no4 p61 Ja 23 2017

Doctorow, E. L. Doctorow. 2016

O, The Oprah Magazine p103 F 2017

Virginia Living v15 no4 p29 Je 2017 B. Glose

Doctorow, E. L. Ragtime. 2007

Publishers Weekly v264 no5 p197 Ja 30 2017

Dodd, C. The Woman Who Couldn't Scream. 2017

Publishers Weekly v264 no29 p197 Jl 17 2017

Dodd, E. and Dodd, E. Together. 2016

Entertainment Weekly no1438 p66 N 4 2016 I. Biedenharn

Dodds, J. Drakkar Noir. 2017

Walrus v14 no8 p65 O 2017 C. Starnino

Doerr, A. All the light we cannot see. 2014

New York Times Book Review p78 D 4 2016 G. Cowles

New York Times Book Review p8-17 D 25 2016 M. Hong Kingston

Doerrfeld, C. and Doerrfeld, C. Maggie and Wendel. 2016

Publishers Weekly v263 no49 p33 D 7 2016

Doerrfeld, C. and McNeil, K. Sleepy Toes. 2017

Publishers Weekly v263 no50 p72 D 5 2016

Dogi, F. and Riggs, K. Crowds of creatures. 2017

Publishers Weekly v264 no5 p203 Ja 30 2017

Doherty, P. and Cassidy, C. And then you're dead. 2017

New York Times Book Review p4 Ap 23 2017 J. Williams

Doi, K. and others. Chirri & Chirra in the Tall Grass. 2017

Publishers Weekly v264 no22 p66 My 29 2017

Doig, I. Last bus to wisdom. 2015

New York Times Book Review p28 O 2 2016 J. Khatib

Doig, P. and Walcott, D. Morning, Paramin. 2016

New York Review of Books v64 no6 p8-11 Ap 6 2017 J. Lucas

Doiron, P. Knife Creek. 2017

Publishers Weekly v264 no17 p66 Ap 24 2017

Dolan, C. Lies of the land. 2016

Publishers Weekly v263 no44 p56 O 31 2016
Dolan-Leach, C. Dead letters. 2017
Entertainment Weekly no1454/1455 p103 F 24 2017 I. Biedenharn
Publishers Weekly v264 no3 p34 Ja 16 2017
Publishers Weekly v264 no7 p20-7 F 13 2017 D. Lefferts
Dolce, J. Brave New Weed. 2016
New York Times Book Review p11 D 18 2016 M. Taibbi
Dolin, E. J. Brilliant beacons. 2016
Power & Motoryacht v33 no3 p34 Mr 2017 S. Murray
Dollenmayer, D. and Safranski, R. Goethe. 2017
New York Times Book Review p16 Je 18 2017 M. Hofmann
Publishers Weekly v264 no6 p55 F 6 2017
Doller, T. In a perfect world. 2017
Publishers Weekly v264 no14 p77-9 Ap 3. 2017
Dolman, E. C. Can science end war? 2015
Issues in Science & Technology v33 no1 p91-2 Fall 2016 B. R. Allenby
Dolnick, E. Seeds of life. 2017
Commentary v144 no2 p53-4 S 2017 J. S. Gordon
New York Times Book Review p16 Je 25 2017 A. Verghese
Publishers Weekly v264 no14 p65-6 Ap 3. 2017
Science News v191 no13 p38 Jl 8 2017
Science v356 no6342 p1009 Je 9 2017 S. Bay
Scientific American v316 no6 p74 Je 2017 C. Caruso
Dombrowski, C. Body of water. 2016
Orion Magazine v35 no6 p58 N/D 2016 T. Davis
Domet, S. The Guineveres. 2016
Cincinnati Magazine v50 no5 p20 F 2017 A. Konermann
New York Times Book Review p15 O 16 2016 M. Meloy
Dominguez, A. and Dominguez, A. How do you say? = ¿Como se dice? 2016
Publishers Weekly v263 no43 p77 O 24 2016
Dominguez, A. and others. Martí's song for freedom =. 2017
Publishers Weekly v264 no19 p59 My 8 2017
Dominski, J. and others. What is baby gorilla doing? 2017
Publishers Weekly v264 no25 p111 Je 19 2017
Domitrovic, B. and Kudlow, L. JFK and the Reagan revolution. 2016
Forbes v198 no7 p32 N 29 2016
National Review v69 no9 p37-8 My 15 2017 I. Brannon
Domnarski, W. Richard Posner. 2016
New York Times Book Review p27 O 9 2016 J. Fabian Witt
Donald, R. Hollywood enlists! 2017
Publishers Weekly v264 no3 p52-3 Ja 16 2017
Donaldson, G. A. When America liked Ike. 2016
Publishers Weekly v263 no43 p73 O 24 2016
Donaldson, J. and Oxenbury, H. The Giant Jumperee. 2017
Publishers Weekly v264 no5 p201 Ja 30 2017
Donaldson, J. and Voake, C. The further adventures of owl and the pussy-cat. 2017
Publishers Weekly v263 no45 p59 N 7 2016
Donaldson, S. R. Seventh decimate. 2017
Publishers Weekly v264 no34 p94 Ag 21 2017
Donath, O. Regretting motherhood. 2017
Publishers Weekly v264 no15 p62 Ap 10 2017
Donellan, J. M. Killing Adonis. 2016
Publishers Weekly v263 no41 p59 O 10 2016
Donlay, P. Seconds to Midnight. 2017
Publishers Weekly v264 no1 p38-9 Ja 2 2017
Donlea, C. The Girl Who Was Taken. 2017
Publishers Weekly v264 no3 p32 Ja 16 2017
Publishers Weekly v264 no6 p45 F 6 2017
Donnell, C. The Defence of Sevastopol 1941-1942. 2016
Military History v33 no5 p73 Ja 2017 T. Zacharis
Donnelly, L. E. Amberlough. 2017
Publishers Weekly v263 no51 p112-6 D 12 2016 R. Fox
Publishers Weekly v263 no51 p129 D 12 2016
Donoghue, E. and Hadilaksono, C. The Lotterys plus one. 2017
Publishers Weekly v263 no52 p124 D 19 2016
Donoghue, E. The wonder. 2016
New York Review of Books v64 no5 p53-5 Mr 23 2017 R. Scurr
New York Times Book Review p24 O 1 2017 J. Khatib
Publishers Weekly v264 no5 p198 Ja 30 2017
Donohue, M. Every Wild Heart. 2017
Publishers Weekly v264 no5 p175 Ja 30 2017
Donoso, J. and others. A house in the country. 1984

New York Times Book Review p22 D 4 2016 A. Becker
Donovan, K. Secret Life. 2016
Maclean's v129 no41 p10-1 O 17 2016 A. Kingston
Donovan, S. Do Not Open 'til Christmas. 2017
Publishers Weekly v264 no36 p76 S 4 2017
Dooley, S. Ashes to Asheville. 2017
Publishers Weekly v264 no8 p84-6 F 20 2017
Dooley, S. Free verse. 2016
Publishers Weekly v263 no49 p72 D 7 2016
Doran, A. and Treisman, D. The dream colony. 2017
Interview v47 no5 p30 Je/Jl 2017 C. Bollen
New Yorker v93 no33 p97 O 23 2017
New York Times Book Review p6 Je 18 2017 J. Williams
Doran, F. and Doran, F. Trial of Roger Casement. 2016
Publishers Weekly v263 no44 p60 O 31 2016
Doran, M. Ike's gamble. 2016
American Conservative v15 no6 p46-8 N/D 2016 J. M. Smith
Commentary v141 no10 p1-2 D 2016
Commentary v142 no5 p1-2 D 2016
Commentary v142 no5 p41-3 D 2016 O. Ceren
Foreign Affairs v96 no2 p185-6 Mr/Ap 2017 J. Waterbury
New York Times Book Review p16 O 16 2016 D. Frum
Weekly Standard v22 no9 p36-8 N 7 2016 R. Takeyh
Dori, F. and others. Gauguin. 2017
Entertainment Weekly no1465 p62-3 My 12 2017 N. Serrao
Publishers Weekly v264 no11 p67 Mr 13 2017
Dorje, O. T. and others. Interconnected. 2017
Publishers Weekly v263 no51 p140-1 D 12 2016
Dorling Kindersley Publishing Inc. Building Site. 2017
Publishers Weekly v264 no25 p111 Je 19 2017
Dorling Kindersley Publishing Inc. Counting. 2016
Publishers Weekly v263 no49 p56 D 7 2016
Dorling Kindersley Publishing Inc. Sharks. 2017
Publishers Weekly v263 no51 p149 D 12 2016
Dorman, B. and Colfer, C. The Land of stories. 2017
Publishers Weekly v264 no31 p15 Jl 31 2017 C. Juris
Dorman, J. and Lenkowsky, L. When ideas mattered. 2017
Commentary v143 no2 p46-8 F 2017 D. Disalvo
Dorman, S. R. Understanding Zimbabwe. 2016
Foreign Affairs v96 no3 p176-7 My/Je 2017 N. Van De Walle
Dormehl, L. Thinking machines. 2017
New York Times Book Review p13 Mr 19 2017 R. Kurzweil
Dorment, R. Exhibitionist. 2016
New York Review of Books v64 no8 p42-4 My 11 2017 J. Bell
Dormer, F. W. and Dormer, F. W. Firefighter duckies! 2017
Publishers Weekly v264 no12 p71 Mr 20 2017
Dornbusch, B. Enemy. 2017
Publishers Weekly v264 no1 p41 Ja 2 2017
Dorsey, T. Clownfish Blues. 2017
Publishers Weekly v263 no48 p47-8 N 28 2016
Doudna, J. A. and Sternberg, S. H. A crack in creation. 2017
Bloomberg Businessweek no4525 p62 Je 5 2017 R. Kolker
Natural History v125 no10 p46-7 O 2017 L. A. Marschall
New York Review of Books v64 no12 p31-4 Jl 13 2017 M. Cobb
Publishers Weekly v264 no15 p62-3 Ap 10 2017
Science News v192 no4 p32 S 16 2017
Science v356 no6342 p1005-6 Je 9 2017 K. Frischkorn
Dougherty, J. and Tazzyman, D. Stinkbomb & Ketchup-Face and the badness of badgers. 2014
Publishers Weekly v263 no46 p56 N 14 2016
Doughty, L. Apple Tree Yard. 2014
Publishers Weekly v264 no12 p22-3 Mr 20 2017 C. Juris
Douglas, C. Local Girl Missing. 2017
New York Times Book Review p26 Ag 20 2017 J. Carey
Publishers Weekly v264 no19 p38 My 8 2017
Douglas, E. A Season of You. 2017
Publishers Weekly v264 no36 p75-6 S 4 2017
Douglas, G. and Coldwell, D. F. Aeneid. 1964
Weekly Standard v23 no2 p38-42 S 18 2017 S. Kristol
Douglas, S. 100 things you can do to stay fit and healthy. 2017
Publishers Weekly v263 no47 p103 N 21 2016
Douglass, F. and Hamm, T. Frederick Douglass in Brooklyn. 2017
Publishers Weekly v263 no47 p100 N 21 2016
Doumanis, N. The Oxford handbook of European history, 1914-1945. 2016
History Today v66 no10 p62 O 2016 C. Baldoli

Forshaw, J. and Cox, B. Universal. 2017
  Publishers Weekly v264 no4 p71 Ja 23 2017
Forstchen, W. R. The Final Day. 2017
  Publishers Weekly v263 no43 p57 O 24 2016
Forsythe, M. and Hall, K. The Gold Leaf. 2017
  Publishers Weekly v264 no14 p75 Ap 3, 2017
Forsythe, M. and Snicket, L. The bad mood and the stick. 2017
  Publishers Weekly v264 no35 p125 Ag 28 2017
Fortey, R. The wood for the trees. 2016
  New York Times Book Review p35 D 4 2016 M. McCarthy
Fortier, J. and others. The market gardener. 2014
  Mother Earth News no280 p80-1 F/Mr 2017
Forward, T. Fireborn. 2013
  Publishers Weekly v263 no40 p103-4 O 3 2016
Fosberry, J. and Litwin, M. Isabella for president. 2016
  Publishers Weekly v263 no43 p75 O 24 2016
Foss, D. J. and others. Scientists making a difference. 2016
  Skeptical Inquirer v41 no2 p61 Mr/Ap 2017 B. Radford
Fossen, D. No Getting over a Cowboy. 2017
  Publishers Weekly v264 no10 p47 Mr 6 2017
Foster, A. D. Strange music. 2017
  Publishers Weekly v264 no34 p94 Ag 21 2017
Foster, C. Being a Beast. 2016
  Harper's Magazine v334 no2000 p94-7 Ja 2017 G. Greenberg
  New York Times Book Review p20 Jl 16 2017 J. Khatib
Foster, H. C. Ghost Cave. 2014
  Publishers Weekly v264 no26 p159-60 Je 26 2017
  Publishers Weekly v264 no31 p58b Jl 31 2017
Foster, J. J. and Joy, M. The schmuck in my office. 2017
  Louisiana Life v37 no5 p14 My/Je 2017
  Publishers Weekly v264 no3 p50 Ja 16 2017
  Time v189 no14 p22 Ap 17 2017 S. Begley
Foster, L. Hard Justice. 2017
  Publishers Weekly v264 no9 p85 F 27 2017
Foster, L. Under Pressure. 2017
  Publishers Weekly v263 no48 p55 N 28 2016
Foster, L. Worth the Wait. 2017
  Publishers Weekly v264 no23 p37 Je 5 2017
Foster, Y. Believe me. 2017
  Publishers Weekly v264 no30 p52 Jl 24 2017
Foster-Dimino, S. and Foster-Dimino, S. Sex Fantasy. 2017
  Publishers Weekly v264 no39 p94 S 25 2017
Foster-Lasser, S. and others. Grow happy. 2017
  Publishers Weekly v263 no52 p125 D 19 2016
Foudy, J. Choose to matter. 2017
  Publishers Weekly v264 no20 p57 My 15 2017
Fountain, H. The great quake. 2017
  Publishers Weekly v264 no23 p44 Je 5 2017
  Science News v192 no4 p32 S 16 2017 E. Demarco
  Science v357 no6351 p555 Ag 11 2017 R. J. Murnane
Fountain, T. Raising a Child with Autism. 2016
  South Dakota Magazine v33 no3 p58 S/O 2017
Fournier, R. Love that boy. 2016
  AARP: The Magazine v59 no3A p15 Ap/My 2016
Fowler, C. and others. Seeds on Ice. 2016
  Scientific American v315 no3 p86 S 2016 C. Moskowitz
Fowler, C. Bryant & May. 2016
  Publishers Weekly v263 no40 p98 O 3 2016
Fowler, S. L. Traveling with ghosts. 2017
  Publishers Weekly v263 no48 p61 N 28 2016
  Virginia Living v15 no6 p27 O 2017 B. Glose
Fowler, T. R. Combat mission Kandahar. 2016
  Military History v33 no5 p75 Ja 2017
Fowles, J. The tree. 2010
  New York Times Book Review p14 F 12 2017 R. Watkins
Fox, C. The Billionaires. 2017
  Publishers Weekly v264 no4 p63 Ja 23 2017
Fox, E. and Falcone, A. Unwrap My Heart. 2016
  Publishers Weekly v264 no26 p146c Je 26 2017
Fox, J. and Richards, K. Life. 2011
  New York Times Book Review p17 Jl 16 2017 M. Russo
  Publishers Weekly v264 no15 p72 Ap 10 2017
Fox, J. The charmed children of Rookskill Castle. 2016
  Publishers Weekly v263 no49 p78 D 7 2016
Fox, L. S. and others. Marriage as a fine art. 2016
  New Republic v248 no1/2 p56-8 Ja/F 2017 V. Gornick

Fox, M. and Brown, K. Tough Boris. 1994
  U.S. Catholic v82 no2 p19 F 2017
Fox, M. and Williams, B. The game don't change. 2016
  Publishers Weekly v264 no41 p60 O 10 2016
Fox, S. Fly Away With Me. 2017
  Publishers Weekly v264 no25 p98 Je 19 2017
Fox the modern family cookbook. 2015
  Entertainment Weekly no1484 p50 S 29 2017
Foy, G. M. Finding north. 2016
  Sail v48 no5 p18 My 2017 A. W.
Foyster, E. The trials of the King of Hampshire. 2016
  New York Times Book Review p14-5 O 30 2016 M. Stasio
Fracassi, P. and French, A. J. Behold the void. 2017
  New York Times Book Review p42-3 Je 4 2017 T. Rafferty
Fradkin, A. and Shepard, C. Citymakers. 2017
  Publishers Weekly v264 no35 p121 Ag 28 2017
Fraihat, I. and others. Libya's displacement crisis. 2016
  Christian Century v133 no25 p36-7 D 7 2016 C. Stauffer
Fraillon, Z. The Bone Sparrow. 2016
  Publishers Weekly v263 no40 p124 O 3 2016
  Publishers Weekly v263 no49 p70-1 D 7 2016
Frampton, M. and others. A Christmas to Remember. 2017
  Publishers Weekly v264 no36 p74 S 4 2017
Franaszek, A. and others. Milosz. 2017
  Foreign Affairs v96 no3 p169-70 My/Je 2017 R. Legvold
  Nation v304 no18 p12-6 Je 19 2017 S. Burt
  New Republic v248 no7 p60-3 Jl 2017 E. Hirsch
  New Yorker v93 no15 p67-71 My 29 2017 A. Kirsch
France, D. How to survive a plague. 2016
  New York Times Book Review p1-22 N 27 2016 A. Sullivan
  New York Times Book Review p28 O 8 2017 J. Khatib
  New York Times Book Review p78 D 4 2016
France, P. Time of gratitude. 2017
  Publishers Weekly v264 no36 p78 S 4 2017
Frances, A. Twilight of American Sanity. 2017
  Publishers Weekly v264 no32 p63 Ag 7 2017
Franceschelli, C. and Tullet, H. Say zoop! 2017
  Publishers Weekly v264 no23 p50 Je 5 2017
Franceschelli, C. Cityblock. 2016
  Publishers Weekly v263 no49 p56 D 7 2016
Francis, F. Pulse. 2017
  Publishers Weekly v264 no35 p104 Ag 28 2017
Francis, G. and others. Clark the shark loves Christmas. 2016
  Publishers Weekly v263 no39 p91 S 26 2016
Francis, P. Amoris Laetitia (La joie de l'amour) 2016
  Commonweal v144 no2 p18-21 Ja 27 2017 R. R. Gaillardetz
Francis, P. and Stransky, O. The name of God is mercy. 2016
  Christian Century v133 no23 p37-9 N 9 2016 R. P. Carbine
Francis, P. Dear Pope Francis. 2016
  Christian Century v133 no23 p37-9 N 9 2016 R. P. Carbine
Francis, R. Crane Pond. 2016
  New York Review of Books v64 no4 p22-3 Mr 9 2017 S. Schiff
Frank, D. B. Same Beach, Next Year. 2017
  Publishers Weekly v264 no22 p16-8 My 29 2017 C. Juris
Frank, L. C. An Uncommon Union. 2016
  Ms. v26 no4 p42 Wint 2016
Frank, M. The mighty Franks. 2017
  Entertainment Weekly no1468/1469 p110 Je 2-9 2017
  Publishers Weekly v264 no9 p87-8 F 27 2017
Frank, R. M. Sometimes we're all living in a foreign country. 2017
  Publishers Weekly v264 no38 p53-4 S 18 2017
Frank, T. Listen, liberal, or, What ever happened to the party of the
    people? 2016
  Nation v304 no9 p49-53 Mr 20 2017 M. Stoller
Frankel, G. High Noon. 2017
  American Cowboy v24 no1 p47 Je/Jl 2017
  American History v52 no3 p70 Ag 2017 M. Dolan
  New York Times Book Review p9 Mr 5 2017 P. Biskind
  Vanity Fair p100 Hollywood 2017 Supplement S. C.
Frankel, L. and others. Foraged flora. 2016
  American Craft v77 no2 p16 Ap/My 2017 M. Guerber
Frankel, L. This is how it always is. 2017
  New York Times Book Review p20 F 12 2017 H. Rosin
  Publishers Weekly v263 no48 p2 N 28 2016
Frankel, N. Oscar Wilde. 2017
  Publishers Weekly v264 no33 p67-8 Ag 14 2017

Friedman, T. L. Thank you for being late. 2016
  Bloomberg Businessweek no4499 p86 N 14 2016 P. M. Barrett
  Foreign Policy no221 p55-7 N/D 2016 D. Rothkopf
  Fortune v174 no6 p18 N 1 2016 T. Huddleston
  New York Times Book Review p1-14 D 18 2016 J. Micklethwait
Friedmann, P. An Organized Panic. 2017
  New Orleans Magazine v52 no1 p58 S 2017
Friedwald, W. The fifty greatest jazz and pop vocal albums. 2017
  Downbeat v84 no10 p74 O 2017 C. Wolff
  Publishers Weekly v264 no28 p76 Jl 10 2017
Friend, D. The naughty nineties. 2017
  Publishers Weekly v264 no22 p53 My 29 2017
  Publishers Weekly v264 no31 p92 Jl 31 2017 D. Friend
  Time v190 no12 p33 S 25 2017 J. Meacham
  Vanity Fair v59 no10 p128 O 2017 L. Jacobs
Friend, T. and others. Raising cooperative kids. 2017
  Publishers Weekly v264 no16 p65 Ap 17 2017
Fries, K. In the province of the gods. 2017
  Publishers Weekly v264 no35 p46 Ag 28 2017 C. J.
Friis, A. and Van Rooyen, L. F. What my body remembers. 2017
  New York Times Book Review p15 My 7 2017 M. Stasio
  Publishers Weekly v264 no11 p58-9 Mr 13 2017
Frisa, M. L. and others. Donatella Versace. 2017
  Saturday Evening Post v288 no6 p26 N/D 2016
Frisch, S. and Stach, R. Kafka. 2016
  Commonweal v144 no6 p27-8 Mr 24 2017 J. Meyers
  New York Times Book Review p4 N 6 2016 J. Szalai
Frith, N. J. and Frith, N. J. Hector and Hummingbird. 2016
  Publishers Weekly v263 no49 p13 D 7 2016
Fritze, R. H. Egyptomania. 2016
  New York Times Book Review p23 D 4 2016 B. Boucher
Fritzsche, P. An iron wind. 2016
  Military History v33 no6 p74 Mr 2017
  New York Times Book Review p14 N 27 2016 T. Snyder
Frohnen, B. P. and Carey, G. W. Constitutional morality and the rise of quasi-law. 2016
  Claremont Review of Books v17 no3 p54-8 Summ 2017 R. Epstein
Frolick, W. D. The Cabin. 2016
  Publishers Weekly v264 no17 p48-58 Ap 24 2017
Frolova-Walker, M. Stalin's music prize. 2016
  Opera News v81 no6 p62 D 2016 J. Melick
Fromm, P. The names of the stars. 2016
  Sierra v102 no2 p9 Mr/Ap 2017 J. Hahn
Fronsdal, G. and Fronsdal, G. The Buddha before Buddhism. 2016
  Tricycle: The Buddhist Review v26 no2 p90-1 Wint 2016 M. Scarles
Frost, J. Twelve Slays of Christmas. 2017
  Publishers Weekly v264 no35 p108 Ag 28 2017
Frost, M. The secret history of Twin Peaks. 2016
  Entertainment Weekly no1436/1437 p106 O 21 2016 D. Coggan
Frost, M. Twin Peaks. 2017
  Publishers Weekly v264 no40 p21-110 O 2 2017
Frost, T. and Singh, L. The Greatest Opposites Book on Earth. 2017
  Publishers Weekly v264 no35 p126 Ag 28 2017
Fry, M. and Fry, M. How to be a supervillain. 2017
  Publishers Weekly v264 no13 p99 Mr 27 2017
Frye, D. and Axat, F. Kill the next one. 2016
  New York Times Book Review p25 D 18 2016 M. Stasio
  Publishers Weekly v263 no40 p101 O 3 2016
Fucile, T. and Fucile, T. Poor Louie. 2017
  Publishers Weekly v264 no8 p82 F 20 2017
Fuentes, G. L. The sleeping world. 2016
  New York Times Book Review p30 N 6 2016 J. W. McCormack
Fuhrman, J. Eat to live quick and easy cookbook. 2017
  Publishers Weekly v264 no16 p62 Ap 17 2017
Fulford, J. and others. Lucky peach all about eggs. 2017
  Publishers Weekly v264 no10 p55 Mr 6 2017
Fulford, S. and Marche, S. The unmade bed. 2016
  New York Times Book Review p10 Ap 2 2017 S. T. Loh
Fulghum, R. It was on fire when I lay down on it. 1989
  Esquire p29 Je/Jl 2017 A. Carter
Fulk, K. Mr. Ken Fulk's Magical World. 2016
  Vanity Fair v58 no11 p94 N 2016 J. R.
Fuller, A. Quiet until the thaw. 2017

  New York Times Book Review p19 Jl 23 2017 E. Eakin
  Publishers Weekly v264 no17 p60-1 Ap 24 2017
Fuller, C. Swimming Lessons. 2017
  Publishers Weekly v263 no46 p28-9 N 14 2016
Fuller, R. The book that changed America. 2017
  American Scholar v86 no1 p113-5 Wint 2017 C. Irmscher
  Humanist v77 no3 p46 My/Je 2017 D. Chivers
  New York Times Book Review p10 Ja 22 2017 E. Foner
  Publishers Weekly v263 no45 p50 N 7 2016
  Science v355 no6323 p356 Ja 27 2017 M. P. Sheldon
  Weekly Standard v22 no30 p30-2 Ap 10 2017 S. Miller
Fuller, S. The academic Caesar. 2016
  Society v54 no1 p69 F 2017
Fuller, T. N. and Hodgson, R. A good day for a hat. 2017
  Publishers Weekly v264 no4 p77 Ja 23 2017
Fullerton, A. and La Fave, K. When the rain comes. 2017
  Publishers Weekly v263 no46 p56 N 14 2016
Fulton, K. and Berry, H. Long may she wave. 2017
  Publishers Weekly v264 no19 p59 My 8 2017
Fulton, S. and Martin, T. Rest in Power. 2017
  Ebony v72 no3 p44 D 2016/Ja 2017 L. Cross
  Entertainment Weekly no1457/1458 p106 Mr 17 2017
  New Republic v248 no7 p53-5 Jl 2017 M. D. Smith
Funakoshi, G. Karate-Do. 2013
  Black Belt v55 no6 p65-71 O/N 2017
Funk, J. and Kearney, B. The case of the stinky stench. 2017
  Publishers Weekly v264 no18 p58 My 1 2017
Füredi, F. What's happened to the university? 2017
  Claremont Review of Books v17 no3 p62-3 Summ 2017 K. C. Johnson
Furie, M. and Furie, M. Boy's Club. 2016
  New York v49 no25 p122 D 12 2016 A. Riesman
Furman, M. E. and others. A world of cookies for Santa. 2017
  Publishers Weekly v264 no36 p97 S 4 2017
Furmanczyk-Winogron, P. Giovanni. 2016
  Publishers Weekly v264 no39 p80d-e S 25 2017
Furniss, M. A new history of animation. 2016
  Film Quarterly v70 no4 p128-30 Summ 2017 J. C. Douglass
Fursland, R. and Gläser, M. The book jumper. 2017
  Publishers Weekly v263 no45 p62 N 7 2016
Furst, A. A Hero of France. 2016
  AARP: The Magazine v59 no4A p14 Je/Jl 2016 D. Donahue
Furtado, F. J. and Fergusson, J. G. Beyond Afghanistan. 2016
  Foreign Affairs v96 no1 p167-8 Ja/F 2017 R. Feinberg
Fusaro, D. and Impelluso, L. Gardens of Beauty. 2017
  Architectural Digest v74 no7 p96 Jl 2017 S. Cochran
Fussell, B. Eat, live, love, die. 2016
  New York Times Book Review p26 F 12 2017 J. R. Clark
Fynn, S. Chandigarh revealed. 2017
  Publishers Weekly v264 no8 p74-7 F 20 2017

G

Gaar, G. G. and others. Sgt. Pepper at Fifty. 2017
  British Heritage Travel v38 no3 p74 My/Je 2017 J. Hogan
Gabaldon, D. Seven stones to stand or fall. 2017
  British Heritage Travel v38 no3 p74 My/Je 2017 S. Gutierrez
GaBany, R. J. and others. Breakthrough! 2015
  Sky & Telescope v132 no6 p57 D 2016 M. Motta
Gabel, C. and Popovic, L. Wicked like a wildfire. 2017
  Publishers Weekly v264 no22 p70 My 29 2017
Gabler, N. Winchell. 1994
  New York Times Book Review p17 Ap 30 2017 J. Meacham
Gabriel, M. Ninth Street Women. 2017
  Art in America v105 no4 p61 Ap 2017
Gabriel, P. and Minato, K. Penance. 2017
  Publishers Weekly v264 no7 p49 F 13 2017
Gabriel, P. and others. Men without women. 2017
  New York Times Book Review p12 My 21 2017 J. Fielden
Gabriel, R. A. God's Generals. 2017
  Publishers Weekly v263 no46 p52 N 14 2016
Gage, T. Fully Alive. 2017
  Publishers Weekly v264 no23 p44 Je 5 2017
Gagne, T. The dog encyclopedia for kids. 2017
  Publishers Weekly v264 no1 p58 Ja 2 2017

New York Times Book Review p19 O 9 2016 S. Chainani
　　Publishers Weekly v263 no49 p82 D 7 2016
　　Publishers Weekly v264 no5 p200 Ja 30 2017
Gierach, J. and Wolff, G. A fly rod of your own. 2017
　　Publishers Weekly v264 no4 p70 Ja 23 2017
Giffard, H. Making jet engines in World War II. 2016
　　History Today v67 no9 p102 S 2017 J. A. Maiolo
Gifford, C. and McLelland, K. What's below? 2017
　　Publishers Weekly v263 no48 p69 N 28 2016
Giglio, V. L. and Sherman, S. Singing In My Own Key. 2016
　　Publishers Weekly v263 no45 p55 N 7 2016
　　Publishers Weekly v263 no47 p76f N 21 2016
Gilbert, A. Y. and Piper, S. Jesus Is Born. 2016
　　Publishers Weekly v263 no39 p90 S 26 2016
Gilbert, H. D. Forest Child. 2016
　　Publishers Weekly v264 no4 p44 Ja 23 2017
　　Publishers Weekly v264 no4 p50b Ja 23 2017
Gilbert, K. R. A pursued justice. 2016
　　Christian Century v134 no10 p42-4 My 10 2017 R. Lischer
Gilbert, M. One Pan & Done. 2017
　　Publishers Weekly v263 no47 p102 N 21 2016
Gilbert, M. The Churchill Documents. 2014
　　Commentary v143 no4 p47-8 Ap 2017 A. Roberts
Gilchrist, A. The Foetal Circulation. 2017
　　Publishers Weekly v264 no39 p70-80 S 25 2017
Gild, D. and Meehan, J. Meehan's bartender manual. 2017
　　Publishers Weekly v264 no29 p212 Jl 17 2017
Gilder, G. F. The scandal of money. 2016
　　Claremont Review of Books v17 no1 p75-8 Wint 2016/2017 B.
　　Domitrovic
Gilens, M. Affluence and influence. 2012
　　Monthly Labor Review p1-3 S 2016 E. C. Fasching
Giles, A. and Brosnan, R. Now is everything. 2017
　　Publishers Weekly v264 no38 p73 S 18 2017
Giles, J. The Edge of Everything. 2017
　　Entertainment Weekly no1446/1447 p82-3 D 2016/Ja 2017 I. Bie-
　　denham
　　Entertainment Weekly no1451/1452 p111 F 3-10 2017
　　New York Times Book Review p26 F 26 2017 M. Ingall
　　Publishers Weekly v263 no42 p71 O 17 2016
　　Time v189 no4 p54 F 6 2017 S. Begley
Giles, L. Overturned. 2017
　　Publishers Weekly v264 no4 p82 Ja 23 2017
Gilfillan, E. and others. Audubon. 2016
　　Earth Island Journal v32 no2 p54 Summ 2017 C. Ro
　　Publishers Weekly v264 no14 p61 Ap 3 2017
Gill, J. F. The gargoyle hunters. 2017
　　Entertainment Weekly no1459 p63 Mr 31 2017 I. Biedenharn
　　Publishers Weekly v264 no3 p34 Ja 16 2017
Gill, O. L. and Simon, F. The Monstrous Child. 2017
　　Publishers Weekly v264 no17 p92 Ap 24 2017
Gill, R. and Shakespeare, W. King Lear. 2013
　　New York Review of Books v64 no3 p34-6 F 23 2017 S. Greenblatt
Gillam, C. Whitewash. 2017
　　Publishers Weekly v264 no33 p64 Ag 14 2017
Gillespie, L. J. and Yukai Du 100 Steps for Science. 2017
　　Publishers Weekly v264 no12 p72 Mr 20 2017
Gillette, R. H. Escape to Virginia. 2016
　　Virginia Living v15 no1 p29 D 2016 B. Glose
Gillies, J. K. From hot mess to blessed. 2017
　　Publishers Weekly v264 no19 p54 My 8 2017
Gilligan, R. Nine folds make a paper swan. 2016
　　Publishers Weekly v263 no43 p52 O 24 2016
Gillingham, S. and Novesky, A. Love is a truck. 2016
　　Publishers Weekly v263 no67 O 17 2016
Gilliver, P. The making of the Oxford english dictionary. 2016
　　History Today v67 no5 p96 My 2017 J. Camplin
Gilman, S. L. and Thomas, J. M. Are racists crazy? 2016
　　Harper's Magazine v333 no1999 p81-3 D 2016 C. Smallwood
　　Publishers Weekly v263 no40 p110 O 3 2016
Gilmore, J. We were never here. 2016
　　Publishers Weekly v263 no49 p106 D 7 2016
Gilpin, S. and Katz, A. That stinks! 2016
　　Publishers Weekly v263 no49 p42 D 7 2016
Gilpin, S. and others. Pottymouth & Stoopid. 2016
　　Publishers Weekly v264 no18 p57 My 1 2017

Gilroy, J. Summer on Firefly Lake. 2017
　　Publishers Weekly v264 no25 p98 Je 19 2017
Gilroy, J. The Cottage at Firefly Lake. 2017
　　Publishers Weekly v264 no1 p44 Ja 2 2017
Gilroy, S. and Stockwell, R. The Prize. 2013
　　New York Times Book Review p32 O 23 2016 J. Khatib
Gilstrap, J. Final Target. 2017
　　Publishers Weekly v264 no18 p40 My 1 2017
Gilvarry, A. Eastman Was Here. 2017
　　Publishers Weekly v264 no27 p49-50 Jl 3 2017
Gimenez, J. The Fourth Power. 2017
　　Publishers Weekly v264 no3 p47 Ja 16 2017
Ginder, G. The people we hate at the wedding. 2017
　　Bloomberg Businessweek no4527 p90 Je 19 2017 T. Patterson
　　Publishers Weekly v264 no15 p50 Ap 10 2017
Gingiss, D. Winning at Social Customer Care. 2017
　　Publishers Weekly v264 no19 p53 My 8 2017
　　Publishers Weekly v264 no21 p65e My 22 2017
Gingrich, N. Lessons learned the hard way. 1998
　　New Republic v248 no10 p5 O 2017 D. Grann
Gingrich, N. Understanding Trump. 2017
　　New Republic v248 no10 p5 O 2017
　　Publishers Weekly v264 no26 p12 Je 26 2017 C. Juris
　　Weekly Standard v23 no3 p11-2 S 25 2017 F. Barnes
Ginsberg, A. and Morgan, B. The best minds of my generation.
　　2017
　　New York Times Book Review p18 Ag 6 2017 A. Douglas
　　Publishers Weekly v264 no2 p51 Ja 9 2017
Ginsburg, R. B. My own words. 2016
　　Ms. v26 no4 p39 Wint 2016 R. C. Bacon
　　Publishers Weekly v263 no50 p69 D 5 2016
Gioia, D. and Murphy, T. Devotions. 2017
　　O, The Oprah Magazine p109 N 2017 C. Luchette
　　Weekly Standard v23 no1 p42-3 S 11 2017 J. Matthew Wilson
Gioni, M. and Carrion-Murayari, G. Raymond Pettibon. 2017
　　Esquire p30 Ap 2017 J. Black
Giovanni, N. A Good Cry. 2017
　　Essence v48 no6 p74 O 2017 P. H. Bass
　　O, The Oprah Magazine p109 N 2017 C. Luchette
Giralt, S. and others. Lidia's celebrate like an Italian. 2017
　　Publishers Weekly v264 no36 p83 S 4 2017
Girard, G. Mary Rose. 2017
　　Publishers Weekly v264 no33 p56 Ag 14 2017
Girard, G. Truthers. 2017
　　Publishers Weekly v264 no23 p54-5 Je 5 2017
Girard, M. Girl Mans Up. 2016
　　Publishers Weekly v263 no49 p96 D 7 2016
Girard, P. Toussaint Louverture. 2016
　　Foreign Affairs v96 no1 p168 Ja/F 2017 R. Feinberg
　　Nation v33 no21 p40-4 N 21 2016 D. A. Bell
　　New Yorker v92 no44 p69 Ja 9 2017
　　New York Times Book Review p30 D 11 2016 P. Berman
Gisleson, A. The futilitarians. 2017
　　New York Times Book Review p25 O 8 2017 E. F. Gordon
　　Publishers Weekly v264 no18 p48 My 1 2017
Gisondi, J. Monster trek. 2015
　　Skeptical Inquirer v41 no4 p62-3 Jl/Ag 2017 J. Nickell
Gitlin, M. Powerful moments in sports. 2017
　　Publishers Weekly v264 no10 p53-4 Mr 6 2017
Gittins, I. The Periodic Table of Heavy Rock. 2017
　　New York Times Book Review p4 My 14 2017 J. Williams
Gittins, R. Investigating Mr Wakefield. 2016
　　Publishers Weekly v263 no41 p59-60 O 10 2016
Givhan, J. Protection spell. 2017
　　Publishers Weekly v264 no3 p38-40 Ja 16 2017
Gladding, J. and others. Rimbaud the son. 2013
　　New York Review of Books v64 no14 p47-9 S 28 2017 W. Mason
Gladding, J. and others. Small lives. 2008
　　New York Review of Books v64 no14 p47-9 S 28 2017 W. Mason
Gladding, J. and others. The eleven. 2013
　　New York Review of Books v64 no14 p47-9 S 28 2017 W. Mason
Gladding, J. and Pastoureau, M. Red. 2016
　　Weekly Standard v22 no40 p34-6 Je 26 2017 E. Powers
Gladstone, B. The trouble with reality. 2017
　　New Yorker v93 no16 p97 Je 5 2017
Gladstone, M. and others. Bookburners. 2017

Goldsmith, M. Sound. 2015
Physics Today v70 no6 p64-5 Je 2017 M. D. Greenfield
Goldsmith, W. The Bind. 2015
Publishers Weekly v263 no39 p74 S 26 2016
Goldstein, A. and Ferrante, E. Frantumaglia. 2016
Nation v33 no21 p14-6 N 21 2016 V. Gornick
New Republic v247 no12 p56-61 D 2016 A. Chee
New York Times Book Review p1-23 N 6 2016 E. Blair
Time v188 no20 p54-5 N 14 2016 S. Begley
Goldstein, A. and Ferrante, E. My brilliant friend. 2012
Nation v33 no21 p14-6 N 21 2016 V. Gornick
Goldstein, A. and Ferrante, E. The Story of a New Name. 2013
Nation v33 no21 p14-6 N 21 2016 V. Gornick
Goldstein, A. and others. The beach at night. 2016
New York Times Book Review p23 N 6 2016 M. Russo
Vanity Fair v58 no12 p86 D 2016 S. Crosley
Goldstein, A. Janesville. 2017
Commentary v143 no6 p40-2 Je 2017 J. D. Vance
Goldstein, B. The world broke in two. 2017
New York Times Book Review p13 Ag 13 2017 E. Bennett
Publishers Weekly v264 no21 p88 My 22 2017
Goldstein, D. and Schwartz, S. Y. Unplug. 2017
Glamour v115 no3 p130 Mr 2017 S. G. Levy
Goldstein, S. House of women. 2017
Publishers Weekly v264 no26 p34-40 Je 26 2017 H. Macdonald
Publishers Weekly v264 no28 p73-4 Jl 10 2017
Goldstone, L. Deadly Cure. 2017
Publishers Weekly v264 no38 p54 S 18 2017
Goldstone, L. Going Deep. 2017
American History v52 no3 p67 Ag 2017 M. Oppenheim
Publishers Weekly v264 no15 p64 Ap 10 2017
Goldstyn, J. and others. Letters to a prisoner. 2017
Publishers Weekly v264 no29 p218 Jl 17 2017
Goldswain, W. and others. Faster higher smarter. 2016
Science v354 no6317 p1224-5 D 9 2016 J. Mervis
Goldsworthy, A. Pax romana. 2016
Christian Century v134 no11 p41 My 24 2017 T. Jones
Foreign Affairs v95 no6 p178 N/D 2016 L. D. Freedman
History Today v67 no2 p56-7 F 2017 M. Leigh
MHQ: Quarterly Journal of Military History v29 no3 p92-3 Spr 2017 J. Lacey
Military History v34 no1 p71 My 2017 R. A. Gabriel
New York Times Book Review p40-1 N 13 2016 T. E. Ricks
Weekly Standard v22 no36 p36-7 My 29 2017 J. E. Lendon
Golio, G. and Riley-Webb, C. Strange fruit. 2017
Publishers Weekly v264 no7 p75 F 13 2017
Gomez, B. and Horowitz, R. Are we still friends? 2017
Publishers Weekly v263 no48 p65-7 N 28 2016
Gómez (Illustrator) and Lacasa, B. Bow-wow-meow. 2017
Publishers Weekly v264 no10 p59 Mr 6 2017
Gomi, T. and Gomi, T. Presents through the window. 2016
Publishers Weekly v263 no39 p85 S 26 2016
Publishers Weekly v263 no49 p64 D 7 2016
Gonzales, A. and others. Girl code. 2017
Publishers Weekly v264 no4 p83 Ja 23 2017
Gonzales, M. and Amini, M. Yo soy Muslim. 2017
Publishers Weekly v264 no22 p67-8 My 29 2017
Gonzalez, J. and others. Romeo and Juliet. 2012
Publishers Weekly v263 no41 p79 O 10 2016
González, J. L. A brief history of Sunday. 2017
Christianity Today v61 no5 p70 Je 2017 M. Barrett
González, J. L. Luke. 2010
Publishers Weekly v263 no44 p59 O 31 2016
González, J. L. The history of theological education. 2015
Christian Century v134 no4 p46-9 F 15 2017 C. Scharen
González, J. Reclaiming Gotham. 2017
Publishers Weekly v264 no27 p68 Jl 3 2017
Goo, M. I believe in a thing called love. 2017
Publishers Weekly v264 no14 p79 Ap 3. 2017
Gooch, B. Rumi's secret. 2017
New Yorker v92 no49 p95 F 13 2017
New York Times Book Review p18 Ja 22 2017 A. Moaveni
Publishers Weekly v263 no40 p109 O 3 2016
Goodavage, M. Secret Service Dogs. 2016
Time v188 no19 p16 N 7 2016 S. Begley
Goode, D. and Roberts, C. Ladies of Liberty. 2016

Publishers Weekly v263 no41 p83 O 10 2016
Goode, J. J. and Hollyman, H. Munchies. 2017
Publishers Weekly v264 no38 p65 S 18 2017
Goode, J. J. and others. Pok Pok. 2017
Publishers Weekly v264 no34 p105 Ag 21 2017
Goode, J. J. and others. State Bird Provisions. 2017
Publishers Weekly v264 no36 p83 S 4 2017
Goodell, J. The water will come. 2017
Publishers Weekly v264 no36 p81-2 S 4 2017
Goodhart, P. and Crane, R. My Very Own Space. 2017
Publishers Weekly v264 no19 p58-60 My 8 2017
Goodman, A. The chalk artist. 2017
Atlantic v319 no5 p39 Je 2017 A. Hulbert
New York Times Book Review p7 Ag 13 2017 J. Myerson
Publishers Weekly v264 no17 p59 Ap 24 2017
Goodman, A. The Dark Days Club. 2016
Publishers Weekly v263 no49 p107 D 7 2016
Goodman, C. The Metropolitans. 2017
Publishers Weekly v264 no2 p70 Ja 9 2017
Goodman, E. E. and Grindle, M. S. Reflections on Memory and Democracy. 2016
Foreign Affairs v95 no6 p184 N/D 2016 R. Feinberg
Goodman, J. A Touch of Frost. 2017
Publishers Weekly v264 no16 p53-4 Ap 17 2017
Goodman, K. and others. Praise the lard. 2017
Publishers Weekly v264 no6 p63 F 6 2017
Goodman, L. Meet me in the bathroom. 2017
Rolling Stone no1290 p17 Je 29 2017 A. Greene
Goodman, M. A. Whistleblower at the CIA. 2017
Publishers Weekly v264 no4 p71 Ja 23 2017
Goodman, M. Bucket of Blood. 2017
Publishers Weekly v264 no21 p56-65 My 22 2017
Goodman, R. and Soni, J. A mind at play. 2017
Fortune v176 no2 p17 Ag 1 2017 R. Hackett
Publishers Weekly v264 no18 p50 My 1 2017
Science News v192 no4 p32 S 16 2017
Goodrich, D. A Hole in the Wind. 2017
Publishers Weekly v264 no17 p82 Ap 24 2017
Goodwin, D. J. Left Bank of the Hudson. 2017
Publishers Weekly v264 no25 p100 Je 19 2017
Goodwin, D. Victoria. 2016
British Heritage Travel v37 no6 p78 N/D 2016 B. Patrick
Goodwin, G. Benjamin Franklin in London. 2016
History Today v67 no2 p62 F 2017 T. Stanley
New York Review of Books v63 no17 p42-3 N 10 2016 J. Brewer
Goodwin, M. D. Latin@ rising. 2016
Publishers Weekly v264 no1 p40-1 Ja 2 2017
Goop Inc. Goop clean beauty. 2016
Publishers Weekly v263 no45 p56 N 7 2016
Goossen, T. and others. Men without women. 2017
New York Times Book Review p12 My 21 2017 J. Fielden
Gopnik, A. At the strangers' gate. 2017
New York Times Book Review p14 O 1 2017 V. Gornick
New York Times Book Review p27 O 8 2017
O, The Oprah Magazine p99 O 2017 T. Lannamann
Publishers Weekly v264 no33 p70 Ag 14 2017
Gopnik, A. The gardener and the carpenter. 2016
Christian Century v133 no22 p42 O 26 2016
New York Review of Books v63 no17 p8-10 N 10 2016 M. Angell
Gorbachev, M. S. The new Russia. 2016
Foreign Affairs v95 no6 p186-7 N/D 2016 R. Legvold
Gorbachev, V. and Griswell, K. T. Rufus Blasts Off! 2017
Publishers Weekly v264 no34 p111 Ag 21 2017
Gorbman, C. and others. Words on screen. 2017
Film Quarterly v71 no1 p119-21 Fall 2017 P. Rangan
Gordis, D. Israel. 2016
Commentary v142 no3 p44-6 O 2016 A. Hernroth-Rothstein
National Review v68 no24 p36-8 D 31 2016 D. Green
Gordon, A. Death in D Minor. 2017
Publishers Weekly v264 no22 p48 My 29 2017
Gordon, E. The Invention of Angela Carter. 2016
Publishers Weekly v264 no2 p57-8 Ja 9 2017
Gordon, E. The invention of Angela Carter. 2017
New Yorker v93 no4 p71-6 Mr 13 2017 J. Acocella
New York Review of Books v64 no4 p16-8 Mr 9 2017 A. Lurie
New York Times Book Review p16 Mr 26 2017 R. Franklin

Weekly Standard v22 no9 p30-2 N 7 2016 W. Herbert

Graham, L. R. and others. Red star. 1984
In These Times v41 no10 p45 O 2017

Graham, L. Talking as fast as I can. 2016
Entertainment Weekly no1442 p62 D 2 2016 Rebellious Special Issue I. Biedenharn
New York Times Book Review p22 D 18 2016 G. Cowles
Publishers Weekly v263 no51 p9 D 12 2016

Graham, R. N. Beforelife. 2017
Publishers Weekly v264 no32 p57 Ag 7 2017

Grahame, K. and Banerjee, S. The wind in the willows. 2010
Publishers Weekly v264 no26 p176 Je 26 2017

Grahn, J. Hanging on our own bones. 2017
Publishers Weekly v264 no22 p32-4 My 29 2017

Grains, R. The Walking Bread. 2017
Entertainment Weekly no1484 p50 S 29 2017

Grande, L. Curators. 2017
Scientific American v316 no3 p76 Mr 2017 C. Moskowitz

Grande, P. The president will see you now. 2017
Publishers Weekly v264 no1 p51 Ja 2 2017

Grandin, G. Kissinger's Shadow. 2015
New York Times Book Review p32 O 23 2016 J. Khatib

Grandpré, M. and Rosenstock, B. Vincent Can't Sleep. 2017
Publishers Weekly v264 no41 p65 O 9 2017

Grandpré, M. and Rowling, J. K. Harry Potter and the Chamber of Secrets. 1999
New York Times Book Review p32-3 D 4 2016 J. Malouf

Grann, D. Killers of the Flower Moon. 2016
AARP: The Magazine v60 no3A p18 Ap/My 2017 D. Donahue
Entertainment Weekly no1462 p64-5 Ap 21 2017 K. P. Sullivan
Entertainment Weekly no1463/1464 p112 Ap/My 2017
Entertainment Weekly no1465 p63 My 12 2017
Entertainment Weekly no1466 p63 My 19 2017
Entertainment Weekly no1470 p60-1 Je 16 2017 L. Greenblatt
New York Times Book Review p16 My 14 2017 D. Eggers
New York Times Book Review p22 My 28 2017
Publishers Weekly v263 no41 p69 O 10 2016
Publishers Weekly v264 no22 p62-3 My 29 2017
Reason v49 no6 p72-3 N 2017 A. H. Sturgis
Time v189 no15 p53 Ap 24 2017 C. Howorth

Grant, A. and Sandberg, S. Option B. 2017
New York Times Book Review p14 My 14 2017 C. Flanagan
Publishers Weekly v264 no19 p11 My 8 2017 C. Juris

Grant, A. False friend. 2017
Publishers Weekly v263 no48 p48 N 28 2016

Grant, D. The Legend. 2017
Publishers Weekly v264 no21 p78 My 22 2017

Grant, D. The Protector. 2017
Publishers Weekly v263 no50 p56 D 5 2016

Grant, H. and others. Wee Sister Strange. 2016
New York Times Book Review p16 O 8 2017 B. Handy
Publishers Weekly v264 no28 p88 Jl 10 2017

Grant, M. and Dillon, J. Final Girls. 2017
Publishers Weekly v264 no21 p71 My 22 2017
Publishers Weekly v264 no9 p83 F 27 2017

Grant, M. and others. Indigo. 2017
Publishers Weekly v264 no16 p48 Ap 17 2017

Grant, M. and Tegen, K. Front Lines. 2016
Publishers Weekly v263 no49 p114 D 7 2016

Grant, M. Dusk or Dark or Dawn or Day. 2017
Publishers Weekly v263 no45 p44 N 7 2016

Grant, M. Into the drowning deep. 2017
Publishers Weekly v264 no40 p122-3 O 2 2017

Grant, P. and others. The ordinary man of cinema. 2016
Film Comment v52 no6 p95 N/D 2016 P. Fileri
Film Comment v52 no6 p96 N/D 2016 A. Curry

Grant, R. Cave dwellers. 2017
Publishers Weekly v264 no9 p67-8 F 27 2017

Grant, R. Tinderbox. 2017
Publishers Weekly v264 no29 p205 Jl 17 2017
Publishers Weekly v264 no31 p58c Jl 31 2017

Grant, V. 36 questions that changed my mind about you. 2017
Publishers Weekly v264 no35 p130 Ag 28 2017

Grass, G. and others. Of All That Ends. 2016
New York Review of Books v64 no10 p39-41 Je 8 2017 M. Hofmann

Publishers Weekly v263 no44 p61-6 O 31 2016

Grasset, L. and Mellor, B. How the Zebra Got its Stripes. 2016
Publishers Weekly v264 no12 p65 Mr 20 2017

Gratton, L. and Scott, A. The 100 Year Life. 2016
People Management p14 D 2016/Ja 2017

Gratz, A. Ban This Book. 2017
Publishers Weekly v264 no24 p65 Je 12 2017

Gratz, A. Refugee. 2017
Publishers Weekly v264 no21 p93 My 22 2017
Publishers Weekly v264 no24 p22 Je 12 2017 S. Maughan

Graudin, R. Invictus. 2017
Publishers Weekly v264 no27 p78-9 Jl 3 2017

Gravel, É. and others. Olga and the smelly thing from nowhere. 2017
Publishers Weekly v264 no2 p70 Ja 9 2017

Graves, L. Deciding what's true. 2016
Progressive v81 no3 p40-2 Mr 2017 B. Lueders

Graves, P. and Wegelius, J. The murderer's ape. 2017
Publishers Weekly v263 no44 p77 O 31 2016

Graves, V. Pressure Makes Diamonds. 2016
Essence v47 no9 p45 Ja 2017 Y. G. Caviness

Gravett, E. and Gravett, E. Little Mouse's big book of beasts. 2016
Publishers Weekly v263 no49 p39 D 7 2016

Gravett, E. and Gravett, E. Tidy. 2017
New York Times Book Review p16 Mr 12 2017 S. Hunt
Publishers Weekly v264 no1 p55 Ja 2 2017

Gray, A. Isadora. 2017
Publishers Weekly v264 no13 p80 Mr 27 2017

Gray, A. N. and Herbison, J. S. The Ghost Line. 2017
Publishers Weekly v264 no19 p42 My 8 2017

Gray, B. Seduced by Mrs. Robinson. 2017
Publishers Weekly v264 no33 p62 Ag 14 2017

Gray, C. Defy the stars. 2017
Publishers Weekly v264 no7 p79 F 13 2017

Gray, D. and Golding, E. A Moonlight Book. 2016
Publishers Weekly v263 no39 p89 S 26 2016

Gray, D. The Fourth Amendment in an age of surveillance. 2017
Weekly Standard v22 no48 p40-2 S 4 2017 M. Feeney

Gray, J. I am number 8. 2017
Publishers Weekly v263 no48 p20-4 N 28 2016 L. Garrett

Gray, R. The library book. 2012
Publishers Weekly v264 no38 p69 S 18 2017

Gray, S. S. Love held captive. 2017
Publishers Weekly v264 no35 p112-3 Ag 28 2017

Graydon, M. and others. Dining in. 2017
Publishers Weekly v264 no32 p67 Ag 7 2017

Grayling, A. C. Democracy and Its Crisis. 2017
Publishers Weekly v264 no35 p51 Ag 28 2017 J. Rosen

Grayling, A. C. War. 2017
America v217 no4 p50-1 Ag 21 2017 P. Lauritzen

Gray Smith, M. Speaking our truth. 2017
Publishers Weekly v264 no34 p114 Ag 21 2017

Grcevich, J. and others. The vacation guide to the solar system. 2017
Publishers Weekly v264 no14 p66-7 Ap 3. 2017

Greaney, M. Gunmetal gray. 2017
Publishers Weekly v263 no52 p98 D 19 2016

Greaney, M. Tom Clancy True Faith and Allegiance. 2016
Publishers Weekly v263 no44 p55 O 31 2016

Greaves, L. and Bosco, M. A. Death Going Down. 2017
Publishers Weekly v264 no4 p58 Ja 23 2017

Grebe, C. and Wessel, E. C. The ice beneath her. 2016
Publishers Weekly v263 no39 p70 S 26 2016

Greco, D. L. Making marriage beautiful. 2017
Publishers Weekly v263 no46 p51 N 14 2016

Green, D. How change happens. 2016
America v216 no5 p43 Mr 6 2017 A. J. Brown

Green, H. and Bronfman, C. Distilled. 2017
Maclean's v129 no44 p114 N 7 2016 A. Levine

Green, H. Back. 2016
Weekly Standard v22 no41 p42-3 Jl 3 2017 D. Heitman

Green, H. Loving ; Living ; Party going. 1978
Weekly Standard v22 no41 p42-3 Jl 3 2017 D. Heitman

Green, J. Devil's bargain. 2017
Foreign Affairs v96 no6 p158 N/D 2017 W. R. Mead

Publishers Weekly v264 no27 p54 Jl 3 2017
Griffiths, E. The chalk pit. 2017
 Publishers Weekly v264 no10 p41 Mr 6 2017
Griffiths, R. A. Iva Mae. 2017
 Missouri Life v44 no5 p22 Ag 2017 Z. Glasgow
Grigulis, K. and others. Plant functional diversity. 2016
 BioScience v66 no12 p1082-3 D 1 2016 M. J. Lechowicz
Grill, W. and Grill, W. The wolves of Currumpaw. 2016
 Publishers Weekly v263 no49 p18-9 D 7 2016
Grimes, N. and Cabrera, C. A. One last word. 2017
 New York Times Book Review p15 Ap 9 2017 M. Russo
 Publishers Weekly v263 no43 p79 O 24 2016
Grimes, N. Garvey's choice. 2016
 Publishers Weekly v263 no49 p72-3 D 7 2016
Grimwood, J. Moskva. 2017
 Publishers Weekly v264 no19 p38 My 8 2017
Grindle, D. How we won and lost the war in afghanistan. 2017
 Publishers Weekly v264 no39 p99-100 S 25 2017
Grindle, M. S. and Goodman, E. E. Reflections on Memory and
 Democracy. 2016
 Foreign Affairs v95 no6 p184 N/D 2016 R. Feinberg
Grine, C. Time Shifters. 2017
 Publishers Weekly v264 no15 p75 Ap 10 2017
Grinspoon, D. Earth in human hands. 2016
 Publishers Weekly v263 no41 p70-1 O 10 2016
 Scientific American v316 no1 p68 Ja 2017 L. Billings
Grippando, J. Most Dangerous Place. 2017
 Publishers Weekly v263 no48 p44-5 N 28 2016
Grippando, J. Need you now. 2011
 Publishers Weekly v264 no13 p87 Mr 27 2017
Grisetti, J. S. God in My Head. 2016
 Publishers Weekly v264 no7 p72 F 13 2017
 Publishers Weekly v264 no9 p66h-i F 27 2017
Grisham, J. Camino Island. 2017
 New York Times Book Review p18 Je 18 2017 K. Tucker
 New York Times Book Review p20 Jl 9 2017
 New York Times Book Review p22 Jl 30 2017
 Publishers Weekly v264 no25 p16 Je 19 2017 C. Juris
 Publishers Weekly v264 no31 p12 Jl 31 2017 C. Juris
 Publishers Weekly v264 no31 p13-4 Jl 31 2017 C. Juris
Grisham, J. The Whistler. 2016
 New York Times Book Review p13 N 6 2016 P. Lattman
 New York Times Book Review p20 D 25 2016
 New York Times Book Review p22 D 25 2016
 New York Times Book Review p46 N 13 2016 G. Cowles
 Publishers Weekly v263 no45 p14 N 7 2016 C. Juris
 Saturday Evening Post v288 no6 p26 N/D 2016
Grisham, T. and Grossman, J. Ida Lupino, director. 2017
 Film Quarterly v70 no4 p124-7 Summ 2017 C. Rickey
Grissom, E. and Connelly, C. The mark. 2017
 Publishers Weekly v264 no29 p223 Jl 17 2017
 Publishers Weekly v264 no31 p58d-e Jl 31 2017
Gristwood, S. Game of queens. 2016
 New York Times Book Review p51 D 4 2016 S. Dunant
 Publishers Weekly v263 no40 p112 O 3 2016
Griswell, K. T. and Gorbachev, V. Rufus Blasts Off! 2017
 Publishers Weekly v264 no34 p111 Ag 21 2017
Griswold, J. Feeling like a kid. 2006
 Walrus v14 no5 p56-7 Je 2017 K. Clare
Grøndahl, J. C. and Grøndahl, J. C. Often I am happy. 2017
 Publishers Weekly v264 no9 p67 F 27 2017
Grodstein, L. Our short history. 2017
 New York Times Book Review p17 Ap 9 2017 B. Anastas
 Publishers Weekly v264 no5 p176 Ja 30 2017
Groen, H. and Velmans, H. The secret diary of Hendrik Groen, 83
 1/4 years old. 2017
 Publishers Weekly v264 no22 p41-2 My 29 2017
Groenink, C. and Ashman, L. William's winter nap. 2017
 Publishers Weekly v264 no40 p138 O 2 2017
Groenink, C. and Kuhlman, E. Hank's big day. 2016
 Publishers Weekly v263 no49 p12-3 D 7 2016
Groenink, C. and Yeh, K. The Friend Ship. 2016
 Publishers Weekly v263 no40 p121 O 3 2016
Grogan, M. B. and Bradley, H. L. Switch off. 2016
 Christian Century v134 no6 p41-2 Mr 15 2017 C. Lindner
Grohl, V. H. From cradle to stage. 2017

Rolling Stone no1284 p19 Ap 6 2017 J. Dolan
Grolleau, F. and others. Audubon. 2016
 Earth Island Journal v32 no2 p54 Summ 2017 C. Ro
 Publishers Weekly v264 no14 p61 Ap 3. 2017
Groom, W. El Paso. 2016
 Publishers Weekly v263 no46 p12-3 N 14 2016 E. Nawotka
Gross, A. The one man. 2016
 Publishers Weekly v263 no44 p69 O 31 2016
Gross, A. The saboteur. 2017
 Publishers Weekly v264 no25 p91-2 Je 19 2017
Gross, G. P. and Zabecki, D. T. The myth and reality of German
 warfare. 2016
 Military History v34 no1 p74 My 2017 R. Guttman
Gross, K. N. Colored amazons. 2006
 Nation v33 no21 p11 N 21 2016 E. Hinton
Grossart, C. The Argus Deceit. 2017
 Publishers Weekly v264 no8 p70 F 20 2017
Grossberg, L. and others. Cultural studies 1983. 2016
 Nation v303 no20 p27-32 N 14 2016 B. Robbins
Grossman, D. and Cohen, J. A horse walks into a bar. 2016
 New York Review of Books v64 no7 p46-8 Ap 20 2017 S. Green-
 blatt
 New York Times Book Review p1-18 Mr 5 2017 G. Shteyngart
 New York Times Book Review p26 Mr 12 2017
Grossman, J. and Grisham, T. Ida Lupino, director. 2017
 Film Quarterly v70 no4 p124-7 Summ 2017 C. Rickey
Groth, A. The Kingdom of Happiness. 2017
 New York Times Book Review p18 F 19 2017 N. Bilton
 Publishers Weekly v264 no48 p60 N 28 2016
Groth, G. and Krassner, P. The realist cartoons. 2016
 Reason v48 no8 p61 Ja 2017 J. Walker
Grove, C. and Ransom, C. Amanda Panda quits kindergarten.
 2017
 Publishers Weekly v264 no20 p55 My 15 2017
Grove, T. Z. and Cortajarena, A. L. Protein-based engineered
 nanostructures. 2016
 Physics Today v70 no6 p66-7 Je 2017
Grover, L. A. and Parry, J. Bright Night. 2017
 Publishers Weekly v264 no36 p92 S 4 2017
Grubbs, V. Hundreds of Interlaced Fingers. 2017
 New York Times Book Review p26 Jl 2 2017 R. Pearson
Grubman, B. and Westermann, C. The Only Way I Can. 2017
 Publishers Weekly v264 no10 p61 Mr 6 2017
 Publishers Weekly v264 no20 p(Sp)46-54 My 15 2017
Grudova, C. The doll's alphabet. 2017
 Harper's Magazine p83-5 O 2017 C. Smallwood
 Publishers Weekly v264 no35 p98-9 Ag 28 2017
Grumet, R. S. First Manhattans. 2011
 American Indian Quarterly v40 no4 p382-4 Fall 2016 B. Rind-
 fleisch
Grunenwald, J. Running with a police escort. 2017
 New York Times Book Review p27 Ap 2 2017 M. Daum
 Publishers Weekly v263 no50 p65 D 5 2016
Guaracino, J. and Salvato, E. Handbook of LGBT tourism and
 hospitality. 2017
 Advocate no1093 p62 O/N 2017 D. Guerrero
Gubar, S. Reading and writing cancer. 2016
 Christian Century v133 no26 p42-3 D 21 2016 K. Saupe
Gubele, R. and others. Survivance, Sovereignty, and Story. 2015
 American Indian Quarterly v41 no2 p190-2 Spr 2017 M. N.
 Boyer-Kelly
Gubser, S. S. and Pretorius, F. The Little Book of Black Holes.
 2017
 Publishers Weekly v264 no26 p115-20 Je 26 2017 A. Crowley
 Publishers Weekly v264 no27 p67 Jl 3 2017
Gudenkauf, H. Not a Sound. 2017
 Publishers Weekly v264 no12 p55-6 Mr 20 2017
Gudeon, K. and Michelson, R. The language of angels. 2015
 Publishers Weekly v263 no48 p70-1 N 28 2016
Gueorguiev, D. D. and others. China's governance puzzle. 2017
 Foreign Affairs v96 no6 p172 N/D 2017 A. J. Nathan
Guerriero, L. Cuba on the Verge. 2017
 Publishers Weekly v264 no41 p56 O 9 2017
Guerrive, S. Dinosaur detective's search-and-find rescue miss.
 2017
 Publishers Weekly v264 no34 p113 Ag 21 2017

Heley, V. False Fire. 2017
Publishers Weekly v264 no9 p78 F 27 2017
Heley, V. Murder for Nothing. 2017
Publishers Weekly v264 no36 p68 S 4 2017
Helfand, D. J. A survival guide to the misinformation age. 2016
Physics Today v69 no12 p56-7 D 2016 K. B. Marvel
Helgeson, K. Say no to the bro. 2017
Publishers Weekly v264 no10 p63 Mr 6 2017
Helget, N. The end of the wild. 2017
New York Times Book Review p26 My 14 2017 J. L. Holm
Publishers Weekly v264 no5 p205 Ja 30 2017
Hellebrandt, T. and Mauro, P. World on the move. 2016
Foreign Affairs v96 no3 p156 My/Je 2017 R. N. Cooper
Heller, D. K. Jabotinsky's children. 2017
Publishers Weekly v264 no24 p58 Je 12 2017
Heller, J. and others. Cyber World. 2016
Publishers Weekly v263 no40 p103 O 3 2016
Heller, J. The Hunting Ground. 2016
Publishers Weekly v264 no5 p182-3 Ja 30 2017
Publishers Weekly v264 no9 p52 F 27 2017
Publishers Weekly v264 no9 p66d-e F 27 2017
Heller, P. Celine. 2017
Saturday Evening Post v289 no2 p22 Mr/Ap 2017
Vanity Fair v59 no5 p52 Ap 2017 S. Crosley
Hellman, P. In vino duplicitas. 2017
Maclean's v130 no7 p61 Ag 2017 B. Bethune
Publishers Weekly v264 no21 p87 My 22 2017
Hello, Sunshine. 2017
Publishers Weekly v264 no20 p59 My 15 2017
Publishers Weekly v264 no23 p29 Je 5 2017
Hellyer, H. A. A Revolution Undone. 2017
Foreign Affairs v96 no2 p184 Mr/Ap 2017 J. Waterbury
Helmholz, R. H. Natural law in court. 2015
Claremont Review of Books v16 no4 p31-4 Fall 2016 J. Dyer
Helmreich, J. The Return. 2017
Publishers Weekly v264 no5 p183 Ja 30 2017
Helquist, B. and Bell, J. The crooked sixpence. 2016
Publishers Weekly v263 no43 p76 O 24 2016
Helquist, B. and Bildner, P. Martina & Chrissie. 2017
Publishers Weekly v264 no7 p75 F 13 2017
Helquist, B. and others. The doll people's Christmas. 2016
Publishers Weekly v263 no39 p85 S 26 2016
Hemingway, E. and McAnulty, S. Mr. Fuzzbuster Knows He's the Favorite. 2017
Publishers Weekly v263 no47 p105 N 21 2016
Hemingway, E. Death in the afternoon. 1999
America v217 no7 p40-4 O 2 2017 A. A. O'Donnell
Hemingway, E. Men without women. 1997
Publishers Weekly v264 no12 p47 Mr 20 2017
Publishers Weekly v264 no21 p14 My 22 2017 C. Juris
Heminsley, A. Leap In. 2017
Publishers Weekly v264 no21 p87-8 My 22 2017
Hemming, H. Agent M. 2017
Publishers Weekly v264 no12 p64 Mr 20 2017
Weekly Standard v23 no3 p30-3 S 25 2017 H. Klehr
Hemstreet, P. The God Peak. 2017
Publishers Weekly v264 no24 p45 Je 12 2017
Hendershot, H. Open to debate. 2016
American Conservative v16 no1 p48-51 Ja/F 2017 J. R. Coyne Jr.
National Review v68 no19 p44-6 O 24 2016 N. B. Freeman
Henderson, B. Sons and soldiers. 2017
Maclean's v130 no7 p62 Ag 2017 B. Bethune
Publishers Weekly v264 no18 p51 My 1 2017
Publishers Weekly v264 no30 p10 Jl 24 2017 R. Deahl
Henderson, E. The twelve-mile straight. 2017
Publishers Weekly v264 no29 p191-2 Jl 17 2017
Hendrix, A. R. and Wohlforth, C. Beyond Earth. 2016
Publishers Weekly v263 no39 p77 S 26 2016
Science News v190 no11 p29 N 26 2016
Hendrix, G. The paperbacks from hell. 2017
New York Times Book Review p4 S 17 2017 J. Williams
Publishers Weekly v264 no31 p78 Jl 31 2017
Hendrix, S. H. Martin Luther. 2015
History Today v67 no1 p56-7 Ja 2017 E. Fulton
Henkes, K. and Henkes, K. Egg. 2017
Publishers Weekly v263 no43 p74-6 O 24 2016

Hennessy, K. Dorothy Day. 2017
Atlantic v319 no2 p32-4 Mr 2017 J. Parker
Commonweal v144 no5 p28-9 Mr 10 2017 P. Steinfels
Publishers Weekly v263 no46 p49 N 14 2016
U.S. Catholic v82 no4 p41 Ap 2017
Henrion, A. DIY dollhouse. 2017
Publishers Weekly v264 no32 p68 Ag 7 2017
Henriques, D. B. A first-class catastrophe. 2017
Publishers Weekly v264 no29 p210-1 Jl 17 2017
Henry, C. and Penhoat, G. I've got my period. so what? 2017
Publishers Weekly v264 no39 p109 S 25 2017
Henry, C. Back pocket pasta. 2017
Publishers Weekly v263 no50 p65 D 5 2016
Henry, C. Lost boy. 2017
Publishers Weekly v264 no21 p70 My 22 2017
Henry, D. Simple. 2016
New York Times Book Review p46-7 D 4 2016 L. Shapiro
Henry, F. B. and Fischer, J. Monkeytalk. 2017
Science News v191 no5 p30 Mr 18 2017 B. Bower
Henry, S. and Rylant, C. Herbert's first Halloween. 2017
Publishers Weekly v264 no26 p177 Je 26 2017
Hensher, J. and Bozo, F. French foreign policy since 1945. 2016
Foreign Affairs v96 no2 p178 Mr/Ap 2017 A. Moravcsik
Henson, P. Storm Season. 2017
Publishers Weekly v264 no1 p45 Ja 2 2017
Henson, T. P. Around the way girl. 2016
Essence v47 no7 p52 N 2016 T. P. Henson
Henthorne, C. The Queen of the North Disaster. 2017
Publishers Weekly v264 no4 p75 Ja 23 2017
Heos, B. and O'Kif Queen Dog. 2017
Publishers Weekly v263 no44 p73 O 31 2016
Heos, B. It's getting hot in here. 2016
Publishers Weekly v263 no49 p122-3 D 7 2016
Heos, B. Shell, beak, tusk. 2017
Publishers Weekly v264 no6 p69 F 6 2017
Hepinstall, K. The book of Polly. 2017
Publishers Weekly v264 no5 p172 Ja 30 2017
Heppermann, C. Ask Me How I Got Here. 2016
Publishers Weekly v263 no49 p92 D 7 2016
Herberger, B. Miss E. 2016
Publishers Weekly v264 no10 p62-3 Mr 6 2017
Publishers Weekly v264 no13 p64f Mr 27 2017
Herbert, K. and Lewis-Jones, H. Explorers' sketchbooks. 2017
Publishers Weekly v264 no8 p76 F 20 2017
Scientific American v316 no4 p76 Ap 2017 A. Gawrylewski
Herbison, J. S. and Gray, A. N. The Ghost Line. 2017
Publishers Weekly v264 no19 p42 My 8 2017
Herculano-Houzel, S. The human advantage. 2016
New York Review of Books v63 no18 p42-4 N 24 2016 S. Mithen
Herkert, B. and Castillo, L. A boy, a mouse, and a spider. 2017
Publishers Weekly v264 no41 p65 O 9 2017
Herman, A. Douglas MacArthur. 2016
Claremont Review of Books v17 no2 p68-73 Spr 2017 A. M. Codevilla
Commentary v142 no1 p48-50 Jl/Ag 2016 M. Boot
Herman, G. and Nathan, J. King Solomon's table. 2017
Martha Stewart Living p12 Ap 2017
Publishers Weekly v263 no52 p118 D 19 2016
Hernández, A. D. and Enstam, R. A. Sangama. 2014
Publishers Weekly v263 no46 p31 N 14 2016
Publishers Weekly v263 no52 p90c D 19 2016
Hernández, N. and others. My dad is a clown = : Mi papá es un payaso. 2017
Publishers Weekly v263 no47 p107-8 N 21 2016
Hernandez, R. I. and Obejas, A. Papi. 2016
Publishers Weekly v264 no22 p16-8 My 29 2017 C. Juris
Herod, A. Scale. 2010
New Yorker v93 no29 p97 S 25 2017
Science v357 no6347 p138 Jl 14 2017 A. Barabási
Herold, E. Beyond human. 2016
Reason v48 no7 p18-9 D 2016 R. Bailey
Herrera, R. and others. Not drunk enough. 2017
Publishers Weekly v264 no18 p46 My 1 2017
Herrera, R. and others. Our cats are more famous than us. 2017
Publishers Weekly v264 no3 p47 Ja 16 2017
Herrera, Y. and Dillman, L. Kingdom Cons. 2017

Publishers Weekly v263 no41 p82 O 10 2016
Publishers Weekly v263 no43 p50g O 24 2016
Hilty, S. L. Dirt, sweat, and diesel. 2016
Missouri Life v43 no6 p20 O/N 2016 J. Weir
Hiltzik, M. Big science. 2015
New York Times Book Review p28 N 27 2016 J. Khatib
Himes, J. L. Mikhail and Margarita. 2017
New Yorker v93 no14 p84 My 22 2017
Publishers Weekly v264 no5 p172 Ja 30 2017
Himmelfarb, G. Past and present. 2017
Weekly Standard v22 no34 p4 My 15 2017
Hinderaker, E. Boston's massacre. 2017
Publishers Weekly v264 no5 p191-2 Ja 30 2017
Hine, D. and others. Walking on lava. 2017
Publishers Weekly v264 no26 p172 Je 26 2017
Hinger, C. Fractured families. 2017
Publishers Weekly v264 no1 p38 Ja 2 2017
Hinton, E. From the war on poverty to the war on crime. 2016
Esquire v166 no5 p36 D 2016/Ja 2017
Nation v303 no16 p35-7 O 17 2016 J. Forman Jr.
Hinz, E. Heavy Weather Tactics. 2004
Sail v48 no10 p16 O 2017 F. Bone
Hippler, T. and Fernbach, D. Governing from the skies. 2017
Publishers Weekly v263 no46 p46-7 N 14 2016
Hirao, M. and Ogi, H. Electromagnetic acoustic transducers. 2016
Physics Today v70 no6 p66-7 Je 2017
Hirsch-Heisenberg, A. M. and others. My Dear Li. 2016
New York Review of Books v63 no20 p65-7 D 22 2016 T. Powers
Hirsch-Heisenberg, A. M. My Dear Li. 2016
Science News v190 no10 p28 N 12 2016
Hirschhorn, S. Y. City on a hilltop. 2017
Commentary v144 no2 p44-5 S 2017 E. Gordon
Hirsh, A. and others. Our cats are more famous than us. 2017
Publishers Weekly v264 no3 p47 Ja 16 2017
Hirsh, A. and Yuko Ota Lucky Penny. 2016
Publishers Weekly v263 no49 p123 D 7 2016
Hirsheimer, C. and Andrews, C. The British Table. 2016
British Heritage Travel v37 no6 p79 N/D 2016 B. Patrick
Hirsheimer, C. and others. Mozza at home. 2016
Martha Stewart Living no271 p10 Ja/F 2017
Hirsheimer, C. and others. Shake Shack. 2017
Publishers Weekly v264 no14 p68-9 Ap 3. 2017
Hirshfield, J. The beauty. 2015
Publishers Weekly v264 no40 p122 O 2 2017
Hirst, D. and Hirst, D. Alphonse, That Is Not Ok to Do! 2016
Publishers Weekly v263 no49 p35-6 D 7 2016
Hischak, T. S. 1939. 2017
Publishers Weekly v264 no15 p62 Ap 10 2017
Hitchmough, J. Sowing beauty. 2017
Publishers Weekly v263 no47 p104 N 21 2016
Ho, D. J. and others. Baco. 2017
Publishers Weekly v264 no34 p105 Ag 21 2017
Ho, J. and Ho, J. Bear and chicken. 2018
Publishers Weekly v264 no38 p68-9 S 18 2017
Ho, J. and Ho, J. Halloween ABC. 2017
Publishers Weekly v264 no26 p178 Je 26 2017
Ho-Ling Wong The Ginza Ghost. 2017
Publishers Weekly v264 no16 p48 Ap 17 2017
Hoagland, E. In the Country of the Blind. 2016
New York Review of Books v64 no5 p60-2 Mr 23 2017 F. Prose
New York Times Book Review p17 D 18 2016 R. Hoffman
Hoang, B. H. and Johnson, K. D. The justice calling. 2016
Christianity Today v61 no1 p55 Ja/F 2017 S. James
Publishers Weekly v263 no45 p4 N 7 2016 A. B. Westrick
Hoban, W. and Sloterdijk, P. Stress and freedom. 2015
New York Review of Books v64 no15 p22-4 O 12 2017 J. Gray
Hobb, R. Assassin's Fate. 2017
Publishers Weekly v264 no15 p57 Ap 10 2017
Hobbie, H. and Hobbie, H. A cat named Swan. 2017
Publishers Weekly v263 no50 p71 D 5 2016
Hobbs, L. Mr Chicken Arriva a Roma. 2017
Publishers Weekly v264 no22 p66 My 29 2017
Hobeika, N. and others. The pied piper of Hamelin. 2016
Publishers Weekly v263 no49 p28 D 7 2016
Hobsbawm, E. J. and Bethell, L. Viva la revolución. 2016
Foreign Affairs v96 no1 p168 Ja/F 2017 R. Feinberg

History Today v67 no3 p63 Mr 2017 P. Drinot
Hobsbawm, J. Fully connected. 2017
People Management p50 My 2017
Publishers Weekly v264 no17 p80-1 Ap 24 2017
Hochman, S. Loving Robert Lowell. 2017
Publishers Weekly v264 no17 p83 Ap 24 2017
Hochschild, A. R. Strangers in their own land. 2016
Christian Century v133 no26 p36-7 D 21 2016 A. B. Robinson
Nation v303 no16 p32-5 O 17 2016 J. B. Judis
New Yorker v92 no32 p101 O 10 2016
New York Review of Books v63 no17 p15-7 N 10 2016 N. Rich
New York Times Book Review p16 S 25 2016 J. Deparle
New York Times Book Review p26 N 27 2016 G. Cowles
Hochschild, A. Spain in our hearts. 2016
Commentary v142 no1 p52-4 Jl/Ag 2016 R. Radosh
MHQ: Quarterly Journal of Military History v29 no2 p92-3 Wint 2017 K. Baker
New York Times Book Review p24 Ap 30 2017 J. Khatib
Hockenos, P. Berlin calling. 2017
New York Times Book Review p49 Je 4 2017 J. Rockwell
Hockensmith, S. and Falco, L. Give the devil his due. 2017
Publishers Weekly v264 no9 p80 F 27 2017
Hocking, A. Freeks. 2017
Publishers Weekly v263 no43 p78 O 24 2016
Hockney, D. and Gayford, M. A history of pictures. 2016
History Today v67 no6 p96 Je 2016 D. Brady
New York Times Book Review p75 D 4 2016 C. Wyma
Hodge, S. Modern Art Mayhem. 2016
Publishers Weekly v263 no48 p66 N 28 2016
Hodges, C. and Fanning, R. Long Shot. 2017
Progressive p60-6 D 2016/Ja 2017 D. Zirin
Hodges, C. and others. The Perfect Present. 2017
Publishers Weekly v264 no36 p72 S 4 2017
Hodges, C. Deadly Rumors. 2017
New York Times Book Review p1-21 O 1 2017 R. Gottlieb
Publishers Weekly v264 no26 p110-4 Je 26 2017 R. Fox
Publishers Weekly v264 no39 p92 S 25 2017
Hodgkinson, L. A place to read. 2017
Publishers Weekly v264 no15 p72 Ap 10 2017
Hodgman, A. and Bingamon-Burt, K. Vegan food for the rest of us. 2017
Publishers Weekly v264 no23 p48 Je 5 2017
Hodgman, J. Vacationland. 2017
Publishers Weekly v264 no35 p121 Ag 28 2017
Publishers Weekly v264 no35 p46 Ag 28 2017 C. J.
Hodgson, R. and Fuller, T. N. A good day for a hat. 2017
Publishers Weekly v264 no4 p77 Ja 23 2017
Hoefler, K. and Bean, J. Real cowboys. 2015
American Cowboy v23 no5 p50 F/Mr 2017 L. F.
Publishers Weekly v263 no49 p16-7 D 7 2016
Hoekstra, M. and Nors, D. So much for that winter. 2016
Esquire v166 no5 p36 D 2016/Ja 2017
Hoena, B. and Bardin, D. Monster Heroes. 2017
Publishers Weekly v264 no23 p53 Je 5 2017
Hoerlin, B. and Segrè, G. The Pope of Physics. 2016
Issues in Science & Technology v33 no3 p93-4 Spr 2017 W. Lanouette
Natural History v124 no10 p46-7 N 2016 L. A. Marschall
New York Times Book Review p23 N 20 2016 G. Herken
New York Times Book Review p26 N 27 2016
Physics Today v69 no12 p57-8 D 2016 C. Westfall
Science News v191 no4 p28 Mr 4 2017 T. Siegfried
Hoey, J. K. Build Your Dream Network. 2017
Publishers Weekly v263 no44 p63 O 31 2016
Working Mother p7 F/Mr 2017
Hoffman, A. Faithful. 2016
New York Times Book Review p22 N 20 2016 H. Wecker
Hoffman, A. J. Finding Purpose. 2016
Earth Island Journal v32 no4 p55 Wint 2017 B. P. Beer
Hoffman, A. The rules of magic. 2017
Publishers Weekly v264 no34 p84 Ag 21 2017
Hoffman, C. Running. 2017
New York p131 Mr 6 2017
New York Times Book Review p10 Mr 19 2017 J. Torres
New York Times Book Review p23 Mr 26 2017
Hoffman, S. and Fleder, R. The Sports Bucket List. 2017

New York Times Book Review p76 D 4 2016
Publishers Weekly v263 no40 p115 O 3 2016
Honda, T. Soul Cage. 2017
Publishers Weekly v264 no21 p74 My 22 2017
Honeyman, G. Eleanor Oliphant Is Completely Fine. 2017
Publishers Weekly v264 no31 p82-3 Jl 31 2017
Time v189 no22 p54 Je 12 2017 S. Begley
Hong, J. and Han Yujoo The impossible fairy tale. 2017
New Yorker v93 no16 p97 Je 5 2017
Publishers Weekly v264 no2 p38 Ja 9 2017
Hong, J. and Hong, J. Lovely. 2017
Publishers Weekly v264 no35 p128 Ag 28 2017
Hong, N. and Hong, N. Days with Dad. 2017
Publishers Weekly v264 no39 p105 S 25 2017
Honigford, C. Homicide for the holidays. 2017
Publishers Weekly v264 no33 p52 Ag 14 2017
Hoock, H. Scars of independence. 2017
  MHQ: Quarterly Journal of Military History v29 no3 p93-4 Spr
  2017 M. W. Robbins
  New York Times Book Review p27 My 21 2017 J. Kamensky
  Publishers Weekly v264 no12 p66 Mr 20 2017
Hood, A. Morningstar. 2017
Publishers Weekly v264 no28 p79 Jl 10 2017
Hood, M. and Hood, M. Carrot and pea. 2017
Publishers Weekly v264 no5 p201 Ja 30 2017
Hood, S. and Comport, S. W. Ada's violin. 2016
Publishers Weekly v263 no49 p44 D 7 2016
Hood, S. and Fleck, J. Double take! a new look at opposites. 2017
New York Times Book Review p16 Jl 16 2017 J. Agee
Hoogstede, L. and others. Hieronymus Bosch, painter and draught-
  sman. 2016
  New York Times Book Review p19 D 25 2016 N. Siegal
Hooper, H. and Johnston, T. A small thing ... but big. 2016
Publishers Weekly v263 no49 p25-6 D 7 2016
Hooper, H. and Scanlon, L. G. Another way to climb a tree. 2017
Publishers Weekly v264 no25 p109 Je 19 2017
Hooper, K. Wait for dark. 2017
Publishers Weekly v264 no4 p56-7 Ja 23 2017
Hoopmann, K. All Birds Have Anxiety. 2017
Publishers Weekly v263 no52 p125 D 19 2016
Hoover, C. Without merit. 2017
Publishers Weekly v264 no34 p97 Ag 21 2017
Hope, A. The Ballroom. 2016
New York Times Book Review p19 O 2 2016 S. Ferguson
Hopgood, T. and Jenkins, M. Fabulous frogs. 2016
Natural History v125 no1 p44-7 D 2016/Ja 2017 D. Setton
Hopgood, T. and others. Walking in a Winter Wonderland. 2016
Publishers Weekly v263 no39 p92 S 26 2016
Hopkins, E. The you I've never known. 2017
Publishers Weekly v263 no43 p79 O 24 2016
Hopkins, J. N. The Genesis of roman architecture. 2016
  New York Review of Books v64 no7 p16-20 Ap 20 2017 I. D. Row-
  land
Hopkins, T. and Pépin, J. A grandfather's lessons. 2017
Publishers Weekly v264 no20 p51 My 15 2017
Hopkinson, D. A bandit's tale. 2016
Publishers Weekly v263 no49 p81-2 D 7 2016
Hopkinson, D. and Carpenter, N. A letter to my teacher. 2015
Publishers Weekly v264 no5 p201 Ja 30 2017
Hopkinson, D. and Husband, R. Steamboat school. 2016
Publishers Weekly v263 no49 p17 D 7 2016
Hopkinson, D. and Potter, G. Independence Cake. 2017
Publishers Weekly v264 no10 p59-61 Mr 6 2017
Horáček, P. and Davies, N. Song of the Wild. 2017
Publishers Weekly v264 no38 p70 S 18 2017
Horn, C. and others. Cook + Cork. 2016
Publishers Weekly v264 no34 p106 Ag 21 2017
Publishers Weekly v264 no35 p67 Ag 28 2017
Publishers Weekly v264 no35 p77d Ag 28 2017
Hornaday, A. Talking pictures. 2017
Publishers Weekly v264 no14 p66 Ap 3 2017
Hornfischer, J. D. The fleet at flood tide. 2016
Military History v33 no6 p74 Mr 2017 R. Guttman
Horowitz, A. Being a dog. 2016
  Harper's Magazine v334 no2000 p94-7 Ja 2017 G. Greenberg
  New York Times Book Review p10 N 13 2016 F. De Waal

O, The Oprah Magazine p145 D 2016 N. B.
Horowitz, A. Magpie murders. 2017
  O, The Oprah Magazine p76-89 Jl 2017 L. Schillinger
  Publishers Weekly v264 no36 p86 S 4 2017
  Time v189 no22 p51-2 Je 12 2017 S. Begley
Horowitz, D. and Glenn, M. Big agenda. 2017
Publishers Weekly v264 no7 p11 F 13 2017 C. Juris
Horowitz, D. Happier? 2018
Publishers Weekly v264 no26 p166 Je 26 2017
Horowitz, P. and Hayes, T. C. Learning the art of electronics. 2016
Physics Today v70 no5 p61-2 My 2017 P. J. H. Tjossem
Horowitz, R. and Gomez, B. Are we still friends? 2017
Publishers Weekly v263 no48 p65-7 N 28 2016
Horst, J. L. When it Grows Dark. 2017
Publishers Weekly v264 no27 p55 Jl 3 2017
Horta, P. L. Marvellous thieves. 2017
  Commonweal v144 no9 p34-5 My 19 2017 C. Wren
  Publishers Weekly v263 no46 p45 N 14 2016
Horton, L. K. and Mayer, K. Go big or go gnome! 2017
Publishers Weekly v264 no1 p54 Ja 2 2017
Hosansky, N. and others. The Abrahamic Encounter. 2016
Islamic Horizons v46 no4 p61 Jl/Ag 2017
Hosford, K. and Swiatkowska, G. How the queen found the
  perfect cup of tea. 2017
  Publishers Weekly v264 no3 p59 Ja 16 2017
Hoshino, T. and De Wolf, C. Me. 2017
Publishers Weekly v264 no17 p63 Ap 24 2017
Hosking, J. Three Years With the Rat. 2017
  New York Times Book Review p27 Ja 29 2017 J. Stuart
  Publishers Weekly v263 no44 p48 O 31 2016
Hoskyns, B. and Hoskyns, B. Joni. 2017
  Atlantic v320 no4 p36-8 N 2017 J. Hamilton
  Publishers Weekly v264 no21 p81-2 My 22 2017
Hossack, I. Everyday Delicious. 2017
Publishers Weekly v263 no52 p119 D 19 2016
Hossain, S. Z. Djinn City. 2017
Publishers Weekly v264 no36 p70 S 4 2017
Hosseini, A. The place of stones. 2017
Publishers Weekly v264 no29 p191 Jl 17 2017
Hostovský, E. and Long, F. The Hideout. 2017
Publishers Weekly v264 no19 p34 My 8 2017
Hotham, G. Stone's throw. 2016
Christianity Today v60 no9 p73 N 2016
Houarner, G. and Barnett, D. G. In the country of dreaming
  caravans. 2017
  Publishers Weekly v264 no32 p56 Ag 7 2017
Houellebecq, M. and Bowd, G. Unreconciled. 2017
  Esquire p50 S 2017 A. Westenfeld
  New York v50 no17 p137 Ag 21 2017 C. Lorentzen
Houghton, L. and others. 30-Second Ancient Rome. 2014
History Today v67 no2 p58 F 2017 D. Dunn
Houghton Mifflin Harcourt Publishing Co. Instant Pot Miracle.
  2017
  Publishers Weekly v264 no36 p84 S 4 2017
Hounam, D. A dangerous magic. 2017
Publishers Weekly v264 no29 p222 Jl 17 2017
Houser, S. and others. Girl code. 2017
Publishers Weekly v264 no4 p83 Ja 23 2017
Housewright, D. What the dead leave behind. 2017
Publishers Weekly v264 no15 p55 Ap 10 2017
Housman, A. E. A Shropshire lad. 1994
New Yorker v93 no18 p63-6 Je 26 2017 C. McGrath
Houston, C. Remembering Whitney. 2013
Publishers Weekly v264 no26 p81-8 Je 26 2017 M. Rotella
Houston, K. The Book. 2016
History Today v66 no10 p59 O 2016 J. Camplin
Houston, V. Dead spider. 2017
Publishers Weekly v264 no14 p56 Ap 3 2017
Houts, J. Literally me. 2017
Publishers Weekly v264 no36 p76-7 S 4 2017
Hovaguimian, V. Deep in the Woods. 2011
Publishers Weekly v264 no2 p65 Ja 9 2017
Howard, A. and Howard, A. Dinosaur Empire! 2017
Publishers Weekly v264 no23 p55 Je 5 2017
Howard, C. and others. Dreadnought And Shuttle. 2016
Publishers Weekly v264 no4 p62 Ja 23 2017

Publishers Weekly v264 no9 p66c F 27 2017

Howard, C. R. Distress Signals. 2016
Publishers Weekly v263 no51 p127 D 12 2016

Howard, D. and others. The architectural history of Venice. 2002
Time v188 no22-23 p108 N/D 2016 M. McCluskey

Howard, K. An unkindness of magicians. 2017
Publishers Weekly v264 no25 p96 Je 19 2017

Howard, P. H. Concentration and power in the food system. 2016
Washington Monthly p1 S/O 2016 L. Douglas

Howard, R. and Maupassant, G. D. Like death. 2017
Publishers Weekly v263 no45 p38 N 7 2016

Howard, V. Deep run roots. 2016
Publishers Weekly v263 no40 p114 O 3 2016

Howarth, J. and Howarth, J. The Abcs of Christmas. 2016
Publishers Weekly v263 no39 p87 S 26 2016

Howden, S. and others. Me tall, you small. 2017
Publishers Weekly v264 no4 p77 Ja 23 2017

Howden, S. and others. Moto and me. 2017
Publishers Weekly v264 no18 p61 My 1 2017

Howe, F. The needle's eye. 2016
America v217 no4 p46-9 Ag 21 2017 T. Donnellan
Commonweal v144 no7 p36-7 Ap 14 2017 A. Domestico
Publishers Weekly v263 no39 p80 S 26 2016

Howe, J. and Ito, J. Whiplash. 2016
New York Times Book Review p15 Ja 1 2017 K. Roose
Publishers Weekly v263 no42 p62 O 17 2016

Howe, K. J. The freedom broker. 2017
Publishers Weekly v263 no44 p52 O 31 2016
Time v189 no6 p53 F 20 2017

Howe, M. Magdalene. 2017
America v217 no4 p46-9 Ag 21 2017 T. Donnellan
Christian Century v134 no10 p57 My 10 2017 A. Frykholm

Howe, M. Nine Lessons I Learned from My Father. 2017
Publishers Weekly v264 no39 p101 S 25 2017

Howe, M. Preparing, adjusting, and loving the empty nest. 2017
Publishers Weekly v264 no24 p60-1 Je 12 2017

Howe, S. Debths. 2017
New Yorker v93 no23 p77-9 Ag 7 2017 D. Chiasson
New York Review of Books v64 no14 p31-3 S 28 2017 L. Hammer
Publishers Weekly v264 no20 p35 My 15 2017

Howell, H. The Scotsman who saved me. 2017
Publishers Weekly v264 no32 p57-8 Ag 7 2017

Howell, J. C. Worshipful. 2017
Christian Century v134 no17 p43 Ag 16 2017

Howells, D. Part of the Silence. 2017
Publishers Weekly v264 no21 p73 My 22 2017

Howes, K. and Hahn, R. Grandmother Thorn. 2017
Publishers Weekly v264 no24 p65 Je 12 2017

Howey, H. Machine learning. 2017
Publishers Weekly v264 no35 p110-1 Ag 28 2017

Howrey, M. The wanderers. 2017
Publishers Weekly v264 no4 p51 Ja 23 2017

Hoyos, D. Mastering the West. 2015
Weekly Standard v22 no7 p35-7 O 24 2016 J. E. Lendon

Hoyt, D. A. This book is not for you. 2017
Publishers Weekly v264 no39 p83 S 25 2017

Hsieh, W. W. and Murray, W. A savage war. 2016
Foreign Affairs v96 no1 p162 Ja/F 2017 L. D. Freedman
Military History v33 no5 p72 Ja 2017

Huang, Y. and Huang, Y. We wish you a Merry Christmas. 2017
Publishers Weekly v264 no36 p92 S 4 2017

Hubbard, C. A Mother's Love. 2017
Publishers Weekly v264 no3 p46 Ja 16 2017

Hubbard, C. A Simple Wish. 2017
Publishers Weekly v264 no33 p58 Ag 14 2017

Hubbard, C. Christmas at Promise Lodge. 2016
Publishers Weekly v263 no40 p21-90 O 3 2016

Hubbard, C. Weddings at Promise Lodge. 2017
Publishers Weekly v264 no21 p78-9 My 22 2017

Hubbard, J. Burgandy. 2017
Publishers Weekly v264 no30 p43 Jl 24 2017

Hubbard, L. R. Mission earth. 2017
Publishers Weekly v264 no14 p71 Ap 3, 2017

Hubbard, L. The talented Ribkins. 2017
Essence v48 no5 p66 S 2017 P. H. Bass
Publishers Weekly v264 no26 p150-1 Je 26 2017

Hubbell, V. P. Blood river rising. 2016
Missouri Life v44 no6 p21 S 2017 E. Beyers

Huber, A. I. This side of murder. 2017
Publishers Weekly v264 no32 p53-4 Ag 7 2017

Hubesch, N. and Valckx, C. Bruno. 2017
Publishers Weekly v264 no6 p68 F 6 2017

Huddy, D. and Sutton, E. The Christmas Eve tree. 2016
Publishers Weekly v263 no39 p93 S 26 2016

Hudson, G. Gork, the teenage dragon. 2017
New York Times Book Review p13 S 17 2017 E. Gilsdorf
Publishers Weekly v264 no16 p50 Ap 17 2017

Hudson, J. and Lovelock, J. James Lovelock Et Al. 2016
Discover v27 no10 p18 D 2016 G. Tarlach

Hudson, K. and Lewis, N. Where Jesus slept. 2016
Publishers Weekly v263 no39 p88 S 26 2016

Hudson, K. Too many carrots. 2016
Publishers Weekly v264 no13 p14 Mr 27 2017 C. Juris

Huett, C. Z. Top elf. 2017
Publishers Weekly v264 no36 p103 S 4 2017

Huffman, N. and others. Body horror. 2017
Publishers Weekly v264 no9 p89 F 27 2017

Huffman, N. and Taranto, T. Ars botanica. 2017
Publishers Weekly v264 no16 p56-7 Ap 17 2017

Hufford, L. Navigating the talent shift. 2016
People Management p55 O 2016

Hug, C. and Umland, A. Francis Picabia. 2016
New York Times Book Review p64 D 4 2016 A. Mobilio

Hughes, A. The coroner's daughter. 2017
New York Times Book Review p7 Je 11 2017 M. Stasio

Hughes, E. and Snyder, L. Charlie & Mouse. 2016
Publishers Weekly v264 no7 p76 F 13 2017

Hughes, E. and Taylor, S. A Brave Bear. 2016
Publishers Weekly v263 no49 p31 D 7 2016

Hughes, J. The Business of Excellence. 2016
People Management p56 N 2016

Hughes, K. L. and Butcher, J. Shadowed souls. 2016
Publishers Weekly v263 no39 p72 S 26 2016

Hughes, K. N. The Mapmaker's Daughter. 2017
New Yorker v93 no30 p71 O 2 2017
Publishers Weekly v264 no26 p165 Je 26 2017

Hughes, K. Victorians undone. 2017
History Today v67 no9 p96 S 2017 A. Lycett

Hughes, L. and Hughes, L. We're going on an egg hunt. 2017
Publishers Weekly v264 no3 p58 Ja 16 2017

Hughes, L. and Jones, P. Daddy's Sandwich. 2017
Publishers Weekly v264 no16 p68 Ap 17 2017

Hughes, L. and Miyares, D. That is my dream! 2017
Publishers Weekly v264 no34 p115 Ag 21 2017

Hughes, R. Cloud Farming in Wales. 2017
Publishers Weekly v264 no21 p77 My 22 2017

Hughes, R. The spectacle of skill. 2015
Claremont Review of Books v16 no4 p78-80 Fall 2016 B. Cole

Hughes, S. and Hasbun, R. Affections. 2017
Publishers Weekly v264 no30 p36 Jl 24 2017

Hughes, S. Whistling in the Dark. 2016
Publishers Weekly v264 no39 p108-10 S 25 2017

Hughes-Wilson, J. The Secret State. 2017
Publishers Weekly v263 no52 p117 D 19 2016

Hugues, P. and others. Hannah's dress. 2017
History Today v67 no7 p104-5 Jl 2017 A. Hájková

Huie, B. and Qiu Miaojin Notes of a crocodile. 2017
New York Times Book Review p25 My 7 2017 L. Core

Huie, W. Y. and Coy, J. Their great gift. 2016
Publishers Weekly v263 no49 p54 D 7 2016

Huillet, D. and others. Writings. 2016
Film Quarterly v70 no2 p103-6 Wint 2016 C. Tsui

Hujar, P. and Aletti, V. Lost Downtown. 2016
Art in America v105 no5 p57 My 2017

Hulbert, A. Off the charts. 2017
Publishers Weekly v264 no36 p78 S 4 2017

Hulbert, J. and Purvis, S. Guy Burgess. 2016
New York Review of Books v63 no20 p77-9 D 22 2016 I. Buruma

Hulin, R. Hey Harry, hey Matilda. 2017
Publishers Weekly v264 no42 p45 O 17 2016

Hulliung, M. Rousseau and the dilemmas of modernity. 2015
Society v54 no1 p83-5 F 2017 J. Marks

Humes, E. Door to door. 2016
  New York Times Book Review p24 Je 25 2017 J. Khatib
  Sierra v101 no5 p11 S/O 2016 K. Boelte
Humphreys, H. The Ghost Orchard. 2017
  Walrus v14 no7 p65 S 2017 S. Madwar
Humphries, J. Last Rites. 2017
  Publishers Weekly v263 no50 p53 D 5 2016
Huneven, M. Blame. 2009
  Publishers Weekly v264 no18 p37 My 1 2017
Hunsicker, H. The Devil's Country. 2017
  Publishers Weekly v264 no1 p39 Ja 2 2017
Hunsinger, G. The Beatitudes. 2015
  Christian Century v133 no24 p37-8 N 23 2016 G. Carey
Hunt, A. and others. 30-Second Ancient Rome. 2014
  History Today v67 no2 p58 F 2017 D. Dunn
Hunt, A. Heated Pursuit. 2016
  Publishers Weekly v263 no39 p73 S 26 2016
Hunt, E. S. and Williamson, B. The secret agent training manual.
  2017
  Publishers Weekly v264 no27 p76 Jl 3 2017
  Publishers Weekly v264 no31 p9-10 Jl 31 2017 C. Kirch
Hunt, H. L. And the spirit moved them. 2017
  Publishers Weekly v264 no12 p66 Mr 20 2017
Hunt, L. The evening road. 2017
  Indianapolis Monthly p23 F 2017 C. Fehrman
  New York Times Book Review p19 F 12 2017 K. Greenidge
  Publishers Weekly v263 no44 p48 O 31 2016
Hunt, M. and Nuchi, A. Bunk 9's Guide to Growing Up. 2017
  Publishers Weekly v264 no39 p109 S 25 2017
Hunt, N. and others. Walking on lava. 2017
  Publishers Weekly v264 no26 p172 Je 26 2017
Hunt, N. Where the wild winds are. 2017
  Publishers Weekly v264 no35 p46 Ag 28 2017 C. J.
Hunt, S. The dark dark. 2017
  New Yorker v93 no30 p71 O 2 2017
  Publishers Weekly v264 no20 p31 My 15 2017
Hunt, W. B. and others. The Origin Myth of Acoma Pueblo. 2015
  New York Review of Books v63 no16 p58-60 O 27 2016 I. Frazier
Hunter, A. and Julien, M. The only girl in the world. 2017
  Publishers Weekly v264 no41 p58 O 9 2017
Hunter, A. and Laurens, C. Who you think I am. 2017
  Publishers Weekly v264 no5 p173-4 Ja 30 2017
Hunter, A. and Muhlstein, A. The pen and the brush. 2017
  New York Review of Books v64 no1 p33-5 Ja 19 2017 A. Muhlstein
  New York Review of Books v64 no6 p25-7 Ap 6 2017 J. Barnes
Hunter, A. and Reza, P. The Gardens of Consolation. 2016
  New Yorker v92 no44 p69 Ja 9 2017
  Publishers Weekly v263 no40 p96 O 3 2016
Hunter, D. The place of stone. 2017
  Publishers Weekly v264 no32 p62 Ag 7 2017
Hunter, G. We were the lucky ones. 2017
  Publishers Weekly v263 no50 p43-4 D 5 2016
Hunter, J. M. The Trail drivers of Texas. 1985
  American Cowboy v23 no6 p23 Ap/My 2017
Hunter, L. Eat only when you're hungry. 2017
  New York v50 no16 p113 Ag 7 2017
  Publishers Weekly v264 no23 p26 Je 5 2017
Hunter, L. Human achievements. 2017
  Publishers Weekly v264 no16 p42 Ap 17 2017
Hunter, M. The end we start from. 2017
  Publishers Weekly v264 no36 p61 S 4 2017
Hunter, M. The Most Dangerous Duke in London. 2017
  Publishers Weekly v264 no16 p53 Ap 17 2017
Hunter, R. and Stevenson, R. L. The Land of Nod. 2017
  Publishers Weekly v263 no51 p146 D 12 2016
Hunter, S. G-man. 2017
  Publishers Weekly v264 no10 p39 Mr 6 2017
Hunter, S. I. A season of spells. 2016
  Publishers Weekly v263 no45 p45-6 N 7 2016
Hunter, T. W. To 'joy my freedom. 1997
  Nation v303 no25/26 p8 D 19 2016 E. A. Dunbar
Huntington, A. and Schaub, M. Fresh-picked poetry. 2017
  Publishers Weekly v264 no3 p61 Ja 16 2017
Huntley, S. The goddesses. 2017
  Publishers Weekly v264 no21 p67-8 My 22 2017
  Time v189 no22 p52 Je 12 2017 S. Begley

Hurd, B. Listening to the savage. 2016
  Orion Magazine v35 no6 p59 N/D 2016 N. Davis
Hurley, G. Aurore. 2017
  Publishers Weekly v264 no35 p105 Ag 28 2017
Hurley, K. The Stars Are Legion. 2017
  Publishers Weekly v263 no51 p128 D 12 2016
Hurme, S. B. Get the most out of retirement. 2017
  AARP: The Magazine v60 no2A p78 F/Mr 2017
Hurtado, L. W. Destroyer of the gods. 2016
  Publishers Weekly v263 no45 p27 N 7 2016
Hurtt, B. and others. The damned. 2017
  Publishers Weekly v264 no10 p48 Mr 6 2017
Hurwitz, G. The Nowhere Man. 2017
  Publishers Weekly v263 no46 p32 N 14 2016
  Publishers Weekly v264 no14 p71 Ap 3. 2017
Husband, A. and Newman, L. Hanukkah delight! 2016
  Publishers Weekly v263 no39 p87 S 26 2016
Husband, R. and Hopkinson, D. Steamboat school. 2016
  Publishers Weekly v263 no49 p17 D 7 2016
Huscroft, R. Tales from the long twelfth century. 2016
  History Today v67 no3 p58 Mr 2017 N. Vincent
Hussain, A. Muslims and the making of America. 2016
  Christian Century v134 no14 p43 Jl 5 2017
  Commonweal v144 no6 p29-30 Mr 24 2017 J. L. Fredericks
  Islamic Horizons v45 no6 p58 N/D 2016
Hussey, L. and Pace, A. M. Pigloo. 2016
  Publishers Weekly v263 no42 p69 O 17 2016
Hussey, M. and others. But What If There's No Chimney? 2016
  Publishers Weekly v263 no39 p86 S 26 2016
Hustvedt, S. A woman looking at men looking at women. 2016
  New York Times Book Review p16 D 18 2016 V. Gornick
  O, The Oprah Magazine p104 F 2017
  Publishers Weekly v263 no39 p82 S 26 2016
Hutchinson, I. House of lords and commons. 2016
  New Yorker v92 no38 p84-6 N 21 2016 D. Chiasson
  New York Times Book Review p18 N 27 2016 W. Logan
Hutchinson, S. and Dennis, S. Animal camouflage. 2017
  Publishers Weekly v264 no34 p113 Ag 21 2017
Hutchinson, S. D. We are the ants. 2016
  Publishers Weekly v263 no49 p105-6 D 7 2016
Hutchison, M. and Acosta, R. M. The Happiest Kids in the World.
  2017
  Publishers Weekly v264 no3 p55-6 Ja 16 2017
Hutchison, M. and others. Panther. 2016
  New York v49 no25 p122 D 12 2016 A. Riesman
Hutchisson, J. M. Ernest Hemingway. 2016
  New York Review of Books v64 no11 p34-6 Je 22 2017 F. O'Toole
  Phi Kappa Phi Forum v96 no4 p31 Wint 2016
Hutt, S. and others. Animals Are Delicious. 2016
  Publishers Weekly v263 no49 p56 D 7 2016
Huttenbach, L. L. Running With Raven. 2017
  Publishers Weekly v263 no48 p57 N 28 2016
Hutton, A. Running. 2012
  New York p131 Mr 6 2017
  New York Times Book Review p23 Mr 26 2017
  Publishers Weekly v263 no52 p91 D 19 2016
Hutton, K. Soldier boy. 2017
  Publishers Weekly v264 no18 p62 My 1 2017
Hwang, N. and Novelline, L. A. Piccadilly and the Waltzing Wind.
  2016
  Publishers Weekly v264 no4 p50g Ja 23 2017
Hyde, J. The Gut Makeover. 2017
  Publishers Weekly v264 no1 p53 Ja 2 2017
Hyewon Yum Puddle. 2016
  Publishers Weekly v263 no49 p16 D 7 2016
Hyewon Yum and Watts, J. A Piece of Home. 2016
  Publishers Weekly v263 no49 p35 D 7 2016
Hylen, S. E. A modest apostle. 2015
  Christian Century v133 no21 p22-3 O 12 2016
Hyman, L. J. and others. Let me tell you. 2015
  New York Review of Books v63 no16 p47-51 O 27 2016 J. C. Oates
Hyman, M. and Hyman, M. Shirley Jackson's "The Lottery" 2016
  New York Review of Books v63 no16 p47-51 O 27 2016 J. C. Oates
Hyman, M. The eat fat, get thin cookbook. 2016
  Publishers Weekly v263 no47 p103 N 21 2016
Hymowitz, K. S. The new Brooklyn. 2017

Publishers Weekly v263 no49 p46 D 7 2016

Ison, G. Hardcastle's Runaway. 2017
Publishers Weekly v264 no14 p54 Ap 3. 2017

Ispahani, F. Purifying the land of the pure. 2017
Foreign Affairs v96 no6 p171-2 N/D 2017 A. J. Nathan
Publishers Weekly v263 no51 p144 D 12 2016

Israel, J. The expanding blaze. 2017
Publishers Weekly v264 no30 p53-4 Jl 24 2017

Isserman, M. Continental divide. 2016
American History v52 no4 p71 O 2017 G. Long
Climbing no355 p17 Ag 2017

Ito, J. and Howe, J. Whiplash. 2016
New York Times Book Review p15 Ja 1 2017 K. Roose
Publishers Weekly v263 no42 p62 O 17 2016

Iturbe, A. and Thwaites, L. The librarian of Auschwitz. 2017
Publishers Weekly v264 no35 p131 Ag 28 2017

Ivanyi, R. and Berwald, J. Spineless. 2017
Publishers Weekly v264 no33 p62 Ag 14 2017

Ives, L. Impossible views of the world. 2017
New York Times Book Review p18 Ag 20 2017 S. Coll
Publishers Weekly v264 no24 p36-7 Je 12 2017

Ives, S. How to Impress a Marquess. 2016
Publishers Weekly v263 no39 p72-3 S 26 2016

Ivey, E. To the bright edge of the world. 2016
Publishers Weekly v263 no50 p69 D 5 2016

Ivy, A. Kill without shame. 2016
Publishers Weekly v263 no50 p57 D 5 2016

Ivy, A. Pretend You're Safe. 2017
Publishers Weekly v264 no29 p203 Jl 17 2017

Iwata, N. and Falksen, G. D. The transatlantic conspiracy. 2016
Publishers Weekly v263 no49 p113 D 7 2016

Izzard, E. and Zigman, L. Believe me. 2017
Publishers Weekly v264 no17 p79-80 Ap 24 2017
Publishers Weekly v264 no26 p12 Je 26 2017 C. Juris
Publishers Weekly v264 no31 p83 Jl 31 2017

J

Jaber, R. and Abu-Zeid, K. J. Confessions. 2016
New York Review of Books v64 no4 p29-32 Mr 9 2017 R. Creswell

Jackson, A. A surprised queenhood in the new black sun. 2017
Essence v48 no2 p63 Je 2017 P. H. Bass

Jackson, B. Forged in Desire. 2017
Publishers Weekly v263 no48 p53 N 28 2016

Jackson, E. and Barden, A. Picky Eaters. 2017
Publishers Weekly v263 no50 p72 D 5 2016

Jackson, J. Black Elk. 2016
Publishers Weekly v263 no39 p78 S 26 2016

Jackson, J. The almost sisters. 2017
Atlanta v57 no3 p34 Jl 2017 J. R. M.
Publishers Weekly v264 no18 p34 My 1 2017

Jackson, K. M. Insert Groom Here. 2016
Publishers Weekly v263 no48 p53-4 N 28 2016

Jackson, K. M. The betting vow. 2017
Publishers Weekly v264 no30 p46 Jl 24 2017

Jackson, K. M. To Me I Wed. 2017
Publishers Weekly v264 no12 p61 Mr 20 2017

Jackson, L. P. Chester B. Himes. 2017
Esquire p20 Ag 2017 A. Belth
Harper's Magazine no2007 p88-93 Ag 2017 T. Chatterton Williams
New Yorker v93 no31 p68 O 9 2017
New York Times Book Review p18 Ag 27 2017 M. P. Jeffries

Jackson, L. You will pay. 2017
Publishers Weekly v264 no17 p70 Ap 24 2017

Jackson, M. Don't I know you? 2017
Maclean's v129 no40 p77 O 10 2016 M. Doherty

Jackson, R. and Hawkes, K. Have a look, says book. 2016
Publishers Weekly v263 no49 p13 D 7 2016

Jackson, R. and Lee, S. This beautiful day. 2017
Publishers Weekly v264 no24 p63-5 Je 12 2017

Jackson, R. and Tillotson, K. All ears, all eyes. 2015
Publishers Weekly v264 no3 p57 Ja 16 2017

Jackson, S. and others. Bobby Flay fit. 2017
Publishers Weekly v264 no38 p65 S 18 2017

Jackson, S. and others. Let me tell you. 2015
New York Review of Books v63 no16 p47-51 O 27 2016 J. C. Oates

Jackson, T. and others. Engineering. 2017
Publishers Weekly v263 no51 p149 D 12 2016

Jackson, T. D. and Rosenthal, B. Allegedly. 2017
Publishers Weekly v263 no41 p47 O 10 2016
Publishers Weekly v263 no46 p59 N 14 2016
Publishers Weekly v264 no27 p36-40 Jl 3 2017 K. P. Goddu

Jackson, T. F. Selected Poems of Edna St. Vincent Millay. 2016
Christian Century v133 no24 p41-2 N 23 2016 J. W. Barbeau

Jackson, V. L. and others. The Wild Mammals of Missouri. 2016
Missouri Life v44 no2 p22 Ap 2017 M. W. Schwartz

Jackson, V. Perfect Gravity. 2017
Publishers Weekly v264 no38 p60-1 S 18 2017

Jackson, V. Wanted and Wired. 2017
Publishers Weekly v264 no7 p56 F 13 2017

Jackson-Opoku, S. and Lansana, Q. A. Revise the psalm. 2017
Chicago v66 no1 p47 Ja 2017 N. Rhee
Ebony v72 no3 p44 D 2016/Ja 2017 L. Cross
New York Times Book Review p19 Ag 6 2017 C. Rankine

Jacob, A. How to think. 2017
Publishers Weekly v264 no30 p51-2 Jl 24 2017

Jacob, C. Containment. 2017
Publishers Weekly v264 no36 p70 S 4 2017

Jacob, K. and Unerman, S. The Glass Wall. 2016
People Management p55 O 2016

Jacob-Freitag, S. and Lennartz, M. W. New architecture in wood. 2015
Architectural Record v204 no10 p46 O 2016 S. Hart

Jacobs, A. J. It's All Relative. 2017
Publishers Weekly v264 no39 p100 S 25 2017

Jacobs, D. L. Four Seasons in a Day. 2017
Publishers Weekly v264 no20 p50 My 15 2017
Publishers Weekly v264 no26 p146d Je 26 2017

Jacobs, J. Jane Jacobs. 2016
New Yorker v92 no30 p69-75 S 26 2016 A. Gopnik

Jacobs, J. M. Xinjiang and the modern Chinese state. 2016
Foreign Affairs v95 no6 p192 N/D 2016 A. J. Nathan

Jacobs, L. Beautiful money. 2017
Publishers Weekly v263 no48 p61 N 28 2016

Jacobsen, A. Phenomena. 2017
New Yorker v93 no9 p72 Ap 17 2017
New York Times Book Review p18 Ap 30 2017 D. Teresi
Publishers Weekly v264 no9 p88 F 27 2017

Jacobsen, A. The Pentagon's Brain. 2015
Bulletin of the Atomic Scientists v73 no3 p188-91 My 2017 B. Allenby

Jacobsen, T. W. The New Orleans Jazz Scene Today. 2016
Downbeat v84 no1 p81 Ja 2017 D. Kunian
New Orleans Magazine v51 no4 p50 F 2017 J. Debold

Jacobson, A. Carry This Book. 2016
Vanity Fair v58 no11 p96 N 2016 S. C.

Jacobson, A. The Darkness of Evil. 2017
Publishers Weekly v264 no4 p58 Ja 23 2017

Jacobson, H. Shylock is my name. 2016
Commonweal v143 no20 p26-7 D 16 2016 A. Sargeant
New Yorker v92 no33 p85-9 O 17 2016 A. Gopnik

Jacobson, S. and Colón, E. The torture report. 2017
New York Times Book Review p4 Ap 30 2017 J. Williams

Jacobson, S. The Torture Report. 2017
Publishers Weekly v264 no4 p67 Ja 23 2017

Jacoby, S. and Cotton, K. The road home. 2017
Publishers Weekly v264 no3 p57-9 Ja 16 2017

Jacques, D. Gardens of court and country. 2016
British Heritage Travel v38 no3 p75 My/Je 2017 S. Gutierrez

Jacques, J. Trans. 2015
New York Times Book Review p28 N 27 2016 J. Khatib

Jae Ho Chung Centrifugal empire. 2016
Foreign Affairs v96 no2 p186-7 Mr/Ap 2017 A. J. Nathan

Jaeggy, F. and Alhadeff, G. I am the brother of XX. 2017
New Yorker v93 no29 p98-100 S 25 2017 S. Heti

Jaeggy, F. and Proctor, M. Z. These Possible Lives. 2017
Publishers Weekly v264 no10 p49 Mr 6 2017

Jae-Jones, S. Wintersong. 2016
Publishers Weekly v263 no48 p68 N 28 2016

Jaff, S. Crown of stars. 2017

Publishers Weekly v264 no15 p57 Ap 10 2017

Jaffe, J. The Cooperstown casebook. 2017
Sports Illustrated v126 no18 p14 Je 26 2017 T. Keith

Jaffer, J. The drone memos. 2016
Nation v304 no12 p34-7 Ap 10 2017 K. J. Greenberg

Jahn, R. D. The breakout. 2017
Publishers Weekly v263 no47 p92 N 21 2016

Jahn, R. D. The dispatcher. 2011
Publishers Weekly v264 no8 p70 F 20 2017

Jahren, H. Lab girl. 2016
Entertainment Weekly no1444/1445 p108 D 16 2016 L. Greenblatt
Issues in Science & Technology v33 no1 p92-4 Fall 2016 E. T. Cloyd
Science News v190 no13 p40 D 24 2016
Science v354 no6317 p1228 D 9 2016 J. Fahrenkamp-Uppenbrink

Jakubowski, M. and Gustawsson, J. Block 46. 2017
Publishers Weekly v264 no32 p55 Ag 7 2017

Jalil, M. and others. The Abrahamic Encounter. 2016
Islamic Horizons v46 no4 p61 Jl/Ag 2017

James, A. Surfing with Sartre. 2017
New York Times Book Review p16 Ag 20 2017 J. Ryerson
Publishers Weekly v264 no26 p172 Je 26 2017

James, B. and James, R. M. The man from the train. 2017
Publishers Weekly v264 no21 p86 My 22 2017
Saturday Evening Post v289 no4 p24 Jl/Ag 2017

James, C. Play all. 2016
Harper's Magazine v333 no1998 p82-6 N 2016 W. Deresiewicz
New York Times Book Review p10 O 9 2016 J. Parker

James, D. and Kamin, D. Charlie Chaplin's Red letter days. 2017
Publishers Weekly v264 no6 p57 F 6 2017

James, E. Seven Minutes in Heaven. 2017
Publishers Weekly v263 no48 p54 N 28 2016

James, G. C. and Barnes, D. Crown. 2017
Publishers Weekly v264 no35 p125 Ag 28 2017

James, H. and others. The euro and the battle of ideas. 2016
Current History v116 no788 p116-9 Mr 2017 B. Eichengreen
Foreign Affairs v95 no6 p182-3 N/D 2016 A. Moravcsik
New York Review of Books v63 no19 p20-2 D 8 2016 R. Foroohar

James, H. F. and Brown, P. Mommy loves you! 2017
Publishers Weekly v264 no8 p83 F 20 2017

James, H. F. and Corke, E. Daddy's girl. 2017
Publishers Weekly v264 no16 p69 Ap 17 2017

James, H. Travels With Henry James. 2016
Publishers Weekly v263 no39 p80 S 26 2016

James, J. The glamour of strangeness. 2016
New Yorker v92 no43 p73 Ja 2 2017

James, L. and Ceulemans, E. Captain Pug. 2017
Publishers Weekly v264 no9 p102 F 27 2017

James, L. Empires in the Sun. 2017
Publishers Weekly v264 no16 p59 Ap 17 2017

James, M. J. Collecting evolution. 2017
New York Times Book Review p22-3 S 24 2017 D. Dobbs
Publishers Weekly v264 no8 p76 F 20 2017

James, P. D. Sleep no more. 2017
Publishers Weekly v264 no38 p56 S 18 2017

James, P. D. The Mistletoe Murder. 2016
Christianity Today v61 no1 p73 Ja/F 2017 J. Wilson
Publishers Weekly v263 no50 p67 D 5 2016

James, P. Need you dead. 2017
New York Times Book Review p8 Ag 13 2017 M. Stasio

James, P. The house on Cold Hill. 2016
Publishers Weekly v263 no43 p61 O 24 2016

James, R. M. and James, B. The man from the train. 2017
Publishers Weekly v264 no21 p86 My 22 2017
Saturday Evening Post v289 no4 p24 Jl/Ag 2017

James, R. Seven Suspects. 2017
Publishers Weekly v264 no32 p54 Ag 7 2017

Jameson, F. Raymond Chandler. 2016
New York Review of Books v63 no16 p38-9 O 27 2016 J. Banville

Jameson, K. Across a Dark Highland Shore. 2015
Publishers Weekly v264 no34 p98 Ag 21 2017

Jamieson, V. and Jamieson, V. All's faire in middle school. 2017
New York Times Book Review p25 Ag 27 2017 M. Ingall
Publishers Weekly v264 no29 p222 Jl 17 2017

Jamison, D. Strawberry Wine. 2017
Publishers Weekly v263 no51 p130-1 D 12 2016

Jamison, K. R. Robert Lowell, Setting the River on Fire. 2017
New Yorker v93 no5 p94-7 Mr 20 2017 D. Chiasson
New York Review of Books v64 no7 p4-8 Ap 20 2017 H. Vendler
New York Times Book Review p13 Mr 5 2017 P. Bosworth
Publishers Weekly v263 no48 p60-1 N 28 2016
Vanity Fair p100 Hollywood 2017 Supplement S. Crosley

Jamison, S. and others. The score takes care of itself. 2010
Forbes v198 no9 p34 D 30 2016 R. Karlgaard

Jamison, T. and Skinner, T. Log cabins past & present. 2008
Log Home Living v34 no3 p16 Ap 2017

Jance, J. A. Man overboard. 2017
Publishers Weekly v264 no5 p178-9 Ja 30 2017

Jane B. (Author) The Dead Silence. 2017
Publishers Weekly v264 no35 p72-9 Ag 28 2017

Janes, D. Stick or Twist. 2016
Publishers Weekly v263 no43 p60 O 24 2016

Janis-Norton, N. Calmer, Easier, Happier Screen Time. 2017
Publishers Weekly v264 no36 p85 S 4 2017

Jankelowitz, D. and Jankelowitz, M. Jack's Wife Freda. 2017
Publishers Weekly v263 no50 p64 D 5 2016
Publishers Weekly v264 no10 p26 Mr 6 2017 C. S.

Jankowski, J. and others. What a mess! 2017
Publishers Weekly v264 no35 p127 Ag 28 2017
Publishers Weekly v264 no39 p80e S 25 2017

Janowitz, T. Scream. 2016
Nation v303 no18 p33-6 O 31 2016 M. Dean

Jansen, G. Station to station. 2017
U.S. Catholic v82 no4 p41 Ap 2017 S. Johnson

Janssen, S. The world almanac and book of facts 2017. 2016
Weekly Standard v22 no24 p36-7 F 27 2017 J. Cost

Jaramillo, S. and Jaramillo, S. Los Pollitos / Little Chickies. 2016
Publishers Weekly v263 no49 p58 D 7 2016

Jaramillo, S. Little Mice / Ratoncitos. 2017
Publishers Weekly v264 no25 p110 Je 19 2017

Jaramillo, S. Little Skeletons / Esqueletitos. 2017
Publishers Weekly v264 no26 p178 Je 26 2017

Jarecki, A. The Highland Commander. 2017
Publishers Weekly v264 no21 p78 My 22 2017

Jarecki, A. The Highland Duke. 2017
Publishers Weekly v264 no6 p52 F 6 2017

Jarman, M. The heronry. 2017
Publishers Weekly v263 no52 p96 D 19 2016

Jarolim, E. Getting Naked for Money. 2016
Publishers Weekly v264 no16 p61 Ap 17 2017
Publishers Weekly v264 no17 p58d Ap 24 2017

Jarrett, M. Pressed for all time. 2016
Downbeat v84 no2 p95 F 2017 K. Micallef

Jarrow, G. Bubonic panic. 2016
Publishers Weekly v263 no49 p84 D 7 2016

Jarvis, P. and Toht, P. Pick a pine tree. 2017
Publishers Weekly v264 no36 p94 S 4 2017

Jarvis (Author) and Jarvis (Author) Alan's Big, Scary Teeth. 2016
Publishers Weekly v263 no49 p35 D 7 2016

Jarzab, A. Red Dirt. 2017
Publishers Weekly v264 no25 p115 Je 19 2017

Jasanoff, M. The Dawn Watch. 2017
Publishers Weekly v264 no26 p166 Je 26 2017

Jason, 1. On the Camino. 2017
Publishers Weekly v264 no18 p46 My 1 2017

Jaswal, B. K. Erotic Stories for Punjabi Widows. 2017
Publishers Weekly v264 no15 p49 Ap 10 2017

Jatkowska, A. and Hall, H. C. Star bright, Christmas night. 2017
Publishers Weekly v264 no36 p92 S 4 2017

Jay, A. and Rock, L. On that Christmas night. 2016
Publishers Weekly v263 no39 p94 S 26 2016

Jay, M. Supernormal. 2017
Publishers Weekly v264 no30 p50 Jl 24 2017

Jay, M. This way madness lies. 2016
New York Times Book Review p12 O 30 2016 P. McGrath

Jayde, F. and Melville, M. Midnight Omen. 2016
Publishers Weekly v264 no7 p54-5 F 13 2017
Publishers Weekly v264 no9 p66f F 27 2017

Jebber, M. and others. Amish brides. 2017
Publishers Weekly v264 no17 p75 Ap 24 2017

Jebelli, J. In Pursuit of Memory. 2017

Publishers Weekly v263 no52 p96 D 19 2016

Jones, B. J. George Lucas. 2016
New York Times Book Review p38-9 D 4 2016 T. Shone
Publishers Weekly v263 no41 p70 O 10 2016

Jones, C. and Walton, C. R. Ballplayer. 2017
Publishers Weekly v264 no4 p72 Ja 23 2017

Jones, C. The long dry. 2006
Publishers Weekly v264 no7 p44 F 13 2017

Jones, C. When We Rise. 2016
Publishers Weekly v263 no40 p112-3 O 3 2016
Publishers Weekly v263 no46 p22-3 N 14 2016 S. Maughan

Jones, D. and Beskow, K. 15 Minute Vegan. 2017
Publishers Weekly v264 no23 p47 Je 5 2017

Jones, D. David Bowie. 2017
Publishers Weekly v264 no30 p51 Jl 24 2017

Jones, D. Eleventh Grave in Moonlight. 2017
Publishers Weekly v263 no48 p50 N 28 2016

Jones, D. Fixing business. 2017
People Management p53 Je 2017

Jones, D. Leadership material. 2017
People Management p51 Jl 2017

Jones, D. The Templars. 2017
Military History v34 no5 p74 Ja 2018 W. J. Shepherd
Publishers Weekly v264 no28 p85 Jl 10 2017

Jones, G. L. Travels With Frank Lloyd Wright. 2017
Architectural Record v205 no7 p63 Jl 2017 S. Stephens

Jones, G. Proof of Concept. 2017
New York Times Book Review p35 My 21 2017 N. K. Jemisin
Publishers Weekly v264 no9 p83 F 27 2017

Jones, H. G. The salt line. 2017
Publishers Weekly v264 no30 p34-8 Jl 24 2017

Jones, H. K. and Homolka, G. Skinnytaste Fast and Slow. 2016
New York Times Book Review p76 D 4 2016
Publishers Weekly v263 no40 p115 O 3 2016

Jones, H. My Lai. 2017
MHQ: Quarterly Journal of Military History v30 no1 p94 Aut 2017
Military History v34 no2 p70-1 Jl 2017 D. T. Zabecki

Jones, J. L. and others. Brik. 2017
Publishers Weekly v264 no22 p71 My 29 2017

Jones, J. L. and others. Our cats are more famous than us. 2017
Publishers Weekly v264 no3 p47 Ja 16 2017

Jones, J. Limping but Blessed. 2017
Christian Century v134 no20 p42 S 27 2017 L. Binet

Jones, J. S. The Edit. 2016
Publishers Weekly v263 no41 p59 O 10 2016

Jones, K. and Jones, K. School of awake. 2017
Publishers Weekly v264 no30 p61 Jl 24 2017

Jones, K. and Smith, P. The year of needy girls. 2017
Publishers Weekly v263 no46 p30 N 14 2016

Jones, L. R. Bad deeds. 2017
Publishers Weekly v264 no25 p98 Je 19 2017

Jones, L. R. Damage Control. 2017
Publishers Weekly v263 no52 p104-5 D 19 2016

Jones, L. Y. and others. Saving Charlotte. 2017
New Yorker v93 no31 p68 O 9 2017

Jones, M. and McFadden, S. The Art of maintaining an empire. 2015
New York Review of Books v64 no7 p16-20 Ap 20 2017 I. D. Rowland

Jones, N. Z. and Boelts, M. A Bike Like Sergio's. 2016
Publishers Weekly v263 no49 p19 D 7 2016

Jones, P. and Hughes, L. Daddy's Sandwich. 2017
Publishers Weekly v264 no16 p68 Ap 17 2017

Jones, P. and Okstad, E. Squishy Mcfluff. 2014
Publishers Weekly v264 no17 p93 Ap 24 2017

Jones, R. and Bauer, M. D. Winter dance. 2017
Publishers Weekly v264 no40 p139 O 2 2017

Jones, R. P. The end of White Christian America. 2016
Commonweal v144 no10 p30-2 Je 2 2017 M. Peppard
Foreign Affairs v95 no6 p180 N/D 2016 W. Russell Mead

Jones, R. Violent borders. 2016
Current History v116 no786 p38-9 Ja 2017 N. Sigona

Jones, S. and Holland, L. A Birthday Party for Jesus. 2017
Publishers Weekly v264 no36 p97 S 4 2017

Jones, S. G. Mapping the Interior. 2017

Publishers Weekly v264 no15 p56-7 Ap 10 2017

Jones, S. G. Waging insurgent warfare. 2016
Military History v34 no2 p72 Jl 2017

Jones, S. In the Footsteps of Dracula. 2017
Publishers Weekly v264 no34 p96 Ag 21 2017

Jones, S. J. and Pedler, C. The Perfect Present. 2016
Publishers Weekly v263 no39 p88-90 S 26 2016

Jones, S. M. August Snow. 2017
Publishers Weekly v263 no47 p89-90 N 21 2016

Jones, S. Revolutionary Science. 2017
Publishers Weekly v263 no46 p47 N 14 2016

Jones, S. The Lovecraft Squad. 2017
Publishers Weekly v264 no33 p56 Ag 14 2017

Jones, T. Atlanta noir. 2017
Publishers Weekly v264 no23 p32 Je 5 2017

Jones, T. The Road to Akron. 2017
Publishers Weekly v264 no39 p66 S 25 2017
Publishers Weekly v264 no39 p80c-d S 25 2017

Jones, Z. K. and others. Clementine Loves Red. 2017
Publishers Weekly v264 no18 p57 My 1 2017

Jong, E. Fear of flying. 2003
Glamour v115 no7 p64-5 Jl 2017 A. Haglage

Jón Kalman Stefánsson, 1. and Roughton, P. Fish have no feet. 2016
Iceland Review v55 no1 p12 Ja/F 2017 V. Hafstad

Jonnes, J. Urban forests. 2016
Sierra v102 no1 p12 Ja/F 2017 J. B. Yoder

Jordan, J. This is not the end. 2016
Publishers Weekly v264 no24 p67 Je 12 2017

Jordan, M. D. Teaching bodies. 2017
Christian Century v134 no10 p36-7 My 10 2017 P. Christman

Jordan, R. H. Murder in the news. 2017
Publishers Weekly v264 no39 p101 S 25 2017

Jordan, S. and Greenberg, J. Meet Cindy Sherman. 2018
Publishers Weekly v264 no40 p141 O 2 2017

Jordan, S. While the duke was sleeping. 2016
Publishers Weekly v263 no40 p105-6 O 3 2016

Jorgensen, T. J. Strange glow. 2016
Physics Today v70 no1 p58-9 Ja 2017 M. Lavine

Joselit, J. W. Set in stone. 2017
Christianity Today v61 no5 p69 Je 2017

Joseph, L. So where are we? 2017
Publishers Weekly v264 no29 p195 Jl 17 2017

Joy, D. The weight of this world. 2017
Publishers Weekly v264 no3 p40 Ja 16 2017

Joy, M. and Foster, J. J. The schmuck in my office. 2017
Louisiana Life v37 no5 p14 My/Je 2017
Publishers Weekly v264 no3 p50 Ja 16 2017
Time v189 no14 p22 Ap 17 2017 S. Begley

Joyce, A. and Cave, N. The sick bag song. 2016
Publishers Weekly v263 no39 p80 S 26 2016

Joyce, S. and Seal, R. Lisbon. 2017
Publishers Weekly v264 no23 p47-8 Je 5 2017

Joyner, A. and Dubosarsky, U. One Little Goat. 2017
Publishers Weekly v264 no35 p125 Ag 28 2017

Joyner, A. and others. Bear Make Den. 2017
Publishers Weekly v264 no23 p50 Je 5 2017

Juan, A. and McGhee, A. Pablo & Birdy. 2017
Publishers Weekly v264 no22 p68 My 29 2017

Juanita, J. De Facto Feminism. 2016
Publishers Weekly v264 no40 p129 O 2 2017

Juarez, A. The Sitting Room. 2016
Publishers Weekly v264 no7 p57 F 13 2017
Publishers Weekly v264 no9 p66f-g F 27 2017

Jubber, N. The Timbuktu School for Nomads. 2016
New York Times Book Review p18-9 D 4 2016 L. Schillinger

Juby, S. The Fashion Committee. 2017
Publishers Weekly v264 no14 p77 Ap 3. 2017

Judah, T. In wartime. 2016
Commentary v143 no1 p53-5 Ja 2017 J. Kirchick
Foreign Affairs v95 no6 p186 N/D 2016 R. Legvold

Judd, D. and others. Donald Judd. 2016
New York Review of Books v64 no16 p30-3 O 26 2017 J. Perl

Jude, S. The May Queen murders. 2016
Publishers Weekly v263 no49 p116 D 7 2016

Judis, J. B. and Teixeira, R. The emerging Democratic majority.

Kang, A. and Weyant, C. I Am Not Scared. 2017
   Publishers Weekly v264 no8 p85 F 20 2017
Kang, A. N. and Kang, A. N. The very fluffy kitty, Papillon. 2016
   New York Times Book Review p31 N 13 2016 P. Brown
Kang, L. and Pedersen, N. Quackery. 2017
   Publishers Weekly v264 no29 p208 Jl 17 2017
Kangas, K. and Keithahn, M. N. Elfie. 2016
   South Dakota Magazine v32 no4 p65 N/D 2016
Kania, C. and Whittaker, A. Jazz. 2016
   Downbeat v83 no12 p92 D 2016 B. Reed
Kanigel, R. Eyes on the street. 2016
   America v215 no14 p32-4 N 7 2016 J. R. Kelly
   Architectural Record v204 no12 p34-5 D 2016 J. Merkel
   Atlantic v318 no4 p98-109 N 2016 N. Rich
   Claremont Review of Books v17 no3 p80-2 Summ 2017 B. C.
      Anderson
   Nation v304 no5 p27-31 F 20 2017 R. Tuhus-Dubrow
   New Yorker v92 no30 p69-75 S 26 2016 A. Gopnik
   New York Times Book Review p17 O 9 2016 G. Bellafante
   New York v49 no22 p110-3 O 31 2016 J. Davidson
Kann, V. and others. Peteriffic. 2017
   Publishers Weekly v264 no14 p75-6 Ap 3. 2017
Kanon, J. Defectors. 2017
   New York Times Book Review p26 Je 4 2017 P. Kerr
   Publishers Weekly v264 no14 p53 Ap 3. 2017
Kapic, K. M. Embodied hope. 2017
   Christianity Today v61 no7 p81 S 2017
Kaplan, A. Looking for The stranger. 2016
   Maclean's v129 no43 p62 O 31 2016 E. Donaldson
   New Yorker v92 no33 p99 O 17 2016
   New York Times Book Review p22-3 D 11 2016 J. Simon
   Weekly Standard v22 no17 p33-5 Ja 2 2017 W. H. Pritchard
Kaplan, A. There was always a place to crash. 2015
   Art in America v104 no10 p86 N 2016
Kaplan, D. The plan. 2017
   Weekly Standard v22 no41 p38-9 Jl 3 2017 M. Nelson
Kaplan, F. Dark territory. 2016
   Foreign Affairs v96 no3 p133-8 My/Je 2017 E. Parker
Kaplan, F. Lincoln and the Abolitionists. 2017
   New York Times Book Review p14 Je 25 2017 E. Foner
   Publishers Weekly v264 no17 p81 Ap 24 2017
Kaplan, J. Humans need not apply. 2015
   New Yorker v92 no42 p114-8 D 19 2016 E. Kolbert
Kaplan, R. D. Earning the Rockies. 2017
   Commonweal v144 no8 p42-4 My 5 2017 J. J. Sheehan
   Foreign Affairs v96 no3 p160 My/Je 2017 W. Russell Mead
   National Review v69 no7 p42 Ap 17 2017 P. Lettow
   New York Times Book Review p14 Ja 29 2017 J. Rauch
Kapur, R. The private life of Mrs Sharma. 2015
   New York Times Book Review p22 D 25 2016
   New York Times Book Review p9 D 18 2016 A. Sriram
   New York v49 no25 p144 D 12 2016 B. K.
Karabell, Z. Chester Alan Arthur. 2004
   New York Times Magazine p18-9 F 19 2017 A. Coe
Karaim, R. The winter in Anna. 2017
   Publishers Weekly v263 no41 p53 O 10 2016
Karapanou, M. and Emmerich, K. The sleepwalker. 2011
   Publishers Weekly v263 no46 p32-3 N 14 2016
   Saturday Evening Post v289 no1 p26 Ja/F 2017
Karas, G. B. and Edwards, M. A hat for Mrs. Goldman. 2016
   Good Housekeeping v263 no6 p87 D 2016
   New York Times Book Review p19 D 18 2016 M. Russo
   Publishers Weekly v263 no49 p23 D 7 2016
Karas, G. B. and Root, P. Anywhere Farm. 2017
   Publishers Weekly v263 no52 p123 D 19 2016
Karcher, C. L. A refugee from his race. 2016
   Weekly Standard v22 no7 p37-8 O 24 2016 E. M. Yoder Jr.
Karcz, L. The Gallery of Unfinished Girls. 2017
   Publishers Weekly v264 no21 p95 My 22 2017
Kareem, M. and others. Instructions Within. 2016
   Publishers Weekly v263 no42 p48 O 17 2016
Karl, G. and Sampson, C. Furious George. 2017
   Publishers Weekly v263 no43 p70 O 24 2016
Karosen, K. L. and Stiefel, C. Why Can't Grandma Remember My
      Name? 2016
   Time v188 no24 p66 D 12 2016 K. Salyer

Karp, C. and Karp, L. The ragtime traveler. 2017
   Publishers Weekly v264 no14 p54 Ap 3. 2017
Karp, M. Terminal. 2016
   Publishers Weekly v263 no41 p60-1 O 10 2016
   Publishers Weekly v263 no43 p50d O 24 2016
Karp, M. This vast southern empire. 2016
   Foreign Affairs v96 no1 p163-4 Ja/F 2017 W. R. Mead
   New York Review of Books v64 no11 p51-2 Je 22 2017 D. S. Reyn-
      olds
Karpowitz, D. College in prison. 2017
   Publishers Weekly v263 no45 p53 N 7 2016
Karst, L. A Measure of Murder. 2017
   Publishers Weekly v263 no50 p51 D 5 2016
Kasasian, M. R. The Secrets of Gaslight Lane. 2017
   Publishers Weekly v264 no8 p66 F 20 2017
Kaschock, K. Confessional Sci-Fi. 2017
   Publishers Weekly v264 no16 p40-1 Ap 17 2017
Kasius, J. and Federle, T. Life is like a musical. 2017
   Publishers Weekly v264 no33 p67 Ag 14 2017
Kasper, W. The Catholic Church. 2015
   America v215 p36-8 N 28 2016 L. Hansen
Kassabova, K. Border. 2017
   Christian Century v134 no18 p39-41 Ag 30 2017 A. Greenwald
   Publishers Weekly v264 no21 p84 My 22 2017
   Publishers Weekly v264 no35 p46 Ag 28 2017 C. J.
Katchur, K. The sisters of Blue Mountain. 2017
   Publishers Weekly v264 no9 p77 F 27 2017
Kateman, B. The reducetarian solution. 2017
   Publishers Weekly v264 no8 p80 F 20 2017
Kath, K. and Urban, L. Weekends with Max and his dad. 2016
   Publishers Weekly v263 no49 p66-7 D 7 2016
Katz, A. and Gilpin, S. That stinks! 2016
   Publishers Weekly v263 no49 p42 D 7 2016
Katz, G. C. Among the Red Stars. 2017
   Publishers Weekly v264 no35 p130-1 Ag 28 2017
Katz, J. Talking to animals. 2017
   Publishers Weekly v263 no52 p108 D 19 2016
Katz, K. and Katz, K. Baby's Big Busy Book. 2017
   Publishers Weekly v264 no6 p67 F 6 2017
Katz, Y. and Bohbot, A. The weapon wizards. 2017
   New York Times Book Review p21 F 5 2017 R. Brooks
Kauffman, L. A. Direct Action. 2017
   In These Times v41 no5 p34-5 My 2017 K. Aronoff
Kaufman, H. The story people. 2016
   Publishers Weekly v263 no39 p73-4 S 26 2016
Kaufman, S. and Jennings, P. Naughty Claudine's Christmas.
      2017
   Publishers Weekly v264 no36 p94 S 4 2017
Kaufman, S. and others. Confiscated! 2017
   Publishers Weekly v264 no23 p50 Je 5 2017
Kaufmann, M. Black Tudors. 2017
   Publishers Weekly v264 no35 p115-6 Ag 28 2017
Kaufmann, T. and others. A short life of Martin Luther. 2016
   Publishers Weekly v263 no45 p28 N 7 2016
Kaur, R. Milk and honey. 2015
   New York Times Book Review p24 D 25 2016
   Publishers Weekly v264 no3 p23-9 Ja 16 2017 D. Maryles
Kaurin, M. and Hedger, R. Almost autumn. 2017
   Publishers Weekly v263 no45 p62 N 7 2016
Kausikan, B. Dealing With an Ambiguous World. 2016
   Foreign Affairs v96 no2 p187-8 Mr/Ap 2017
Kaute, W. Murder in the city. 2017
   Publishers Weekly v264 no19 p52 My 8 2017
Kavanagh, T. Things we have in common. 2016
   New York Times Book Review p27 Ja 29 2017 J. Stuart
   Publishers Weekly v263 no44 p48-50 O 31 2016
Kaveny, C. A culture of engagement. 2016
   America v215 no19 p31-3 D 19 2016 E. M. Gaffney
   U.S. Catholic v82 no1 p41 Ja 2017 J. P. Nixon
Kaveny, C. Prophecy without contempt. 2016
   America v215 no19 p31-3 D 19 2016 E. M. Gaffney
   Christian Century v133 no21 p45-8 O 12 2016 D. O'Brien
Kawakami, H. and Powell, A. M. The Nakano thrift shop. 2016
   New York Times Book Review p26 Ag 13 2017 J. P. Nimura
   Publishers Weekly v264 no17 p62 Ap 24 2017
Kay, E. At Rope's End. 2017

2017
Washington Monthly v49 no6-8 p74-5 Je-Ag 2017 L. Drutman

Kindt, M. and Kindt, M. Dept. H. 2017
Publishers Weekly v264 no4 p67 Ja 23 2017

King, A. S. Me and Marvin Gardens. 2017
New York Times Book Review p17 Mr 12 2017 L. S. Park
Publishers Weekly v263 no43 p76-8 O 24 2016

King, A. S. Still life with tornado. 2016
Publishers Weekly v263 no49 p103 D 7 2016
Publishers Weekly v264 no5 p200 Ja 30 2017

King, B. and Preisle, J. Game face. 2017
Publishers Weekly v264 no39 p99 S 25 2017

King, B. Beryl Bainbridge. 2016
New York Review of Books v64 no3 p41-2 F 23 2017 D. Johnson
New York Times Book Review p27 D 11 2016 T. Mallon

King, B. Night sky with the naked eye. 2016
Sky & Telescope v133 no4 p57 Ap 2017 S. N. Johnson-Roehr

King, C. R. Redskins. 2016
Progressive p60-5 D 2016/Ja 2017 A. Maag

King, C. S. My Life, My Love, My Legacy. 2017
AARP: The Magazine v60 no1A p12 D 2016/Ja 2017
Essence v47 no10 p58 F 2017 P. H. Bass
New York Times Book Review p9 Ja 15 2017 P. J. Williams
Publishers Weekly v263 no48 p63 N 28 2016

King, D. The trial of Adolf Hitler. 2017
Publishers Weekly v264 no14 p66 Ap 3. 2017

King, G. and Wilson, P. Twilight of empire. 2017
Publishers Weekly v264 no39 p103 S 25 2017

King, J. and Faber, J. How to Talk So Little Kids Will Listen. 2017
Publishers Weekly v263 no45 p57 N 7 2016

King, J. C. Blood and Land. 2016
History Today v67 no4 p59 Ap 2017 J. Porter

King, J. Exonerated. 2014
U.S. Catholic v82 no9 p41 S 2017 E. Lefebvre

King, J. Michael Asher. 2016
Art in America v105 no5 p57 My 2017

King, L. and others. Survivance, Sovereignty, and Story. 2015
American Indian Quarterly v41 no2 p190-2 Spr 2017 M. N. Boyer-Kelly

King, L. R. Lockdown. 2017
Publishers Weekly v264 no17 p68-9 Ap 24 2017

King, M. A. The End of Alchemy. 2016
Weekly Standard v22 no9 p34-6 N 7 2016 J. Shelton

King, M. S. An Excess Male. 2017
Publishers Weekly v264 no28 p70 Jl 10 2017

King, R. A. Figures in stone. 2017
Publishers Weekly v264 no15 p66 Ap 10 2017

King, R. Mad enchantment. 2016
History Today v67 no1 p57 Ja 2017 T. Fowle
New York Times Book Review p68 D 4 2016 D. Solomon

King, R. S. Rock|salt|stone. 2017
Publishers Weekly v264 no8 p64 F 20 2017

King, S. and Chizmar, R. Gwendy's button box. 2017
Publishers Weekly v264 no16 p51 Ap 17 2017
Publishers Weekly v264 no26 p173 Je 26 2017

King, S. Carrie. 1999
Maclean's p60 Je 2017 P. S. Taylor

King, S. End of watch. 2016
AARP: The Magazine v59 no4A p14 Je/Jl 2016

King, S. Night Shift. 2012
Publishers Weekly v264 no30 p60 Jl 24 2017

King, S. Six Scary Stories. 2016
Publishers Weekly v263 no43 p61 O 24 2016

King, T. and Finch, D. Batman. 2017
Publishers Weekly v264 no5 p188 Ja 30 2017

Kingsbury, K. Dead and Breakfast. 2017
Publishers Weekly v263 no46 p35 N 14 2016

Kingsbury, K. Doom with a view. 2017
Publishers Weekly v264 no31 p65 Jl 31 2017

Kingsbury, K. Love story. 2017
Publishers Weekly v264 no15 p60 Ap 10 2017

Kingsford, E. Brain-powered weight loss. 2017
Publishers Weekly v264 no3 p55 Ja 16 2017

Kingsley, P. The new odyssey. 2017
Foreign Affairs v96 no2 p150-6 Mr/Ap 2017 E. Collett

New Yorker v93 no6 p71 Mr 27 2017
O, The Oprah Magazine p104 F 2017

Kingsnorth, P. and others. Walking on lava. 2017
Publishers Weekly v264 no26 p172 Je 26 2017

Kingsnorth, P. Beast. 2017
New York Times Book Review p18 S 17 2017 T. Koelb

Kingsnorth, P. Confessions of a recovering environmentalist and other essays. 2017
Publishers Weekly v264 no19 p46-8 My 8 2017
Sierra v102 no5 p11 St/O 2017 M. Berry

Kinnamon, M. The witness of religion in an age of fear. 2017
Christian Century v134 no12 p39-41 Je 7 2017 W. Willimon

Kinsella, S. and others. Home and away. 2017
New York Times Book Review p4 Ja 8 2017 J. Williams
Publishers Weekly v263 no50 p60 D 5 2016 S. Satterlee

Kinsella, S. My not so perfect life. 2017
Publishers Weekly v263 no47 p77 N 21 2016

Kinsella, W. Recipe for Hate. 2017
Publishers Weekly v264 no41 p69 O 9 2017

Kinsley, M. Old age. 2016
Claremont Review of Books v16 no4 p83-6 Fall 2016 D. Wiser Jr.

Kinzer, S. The true flag. 2016
America v216 no6 p45 Mr 20 2017 M. J. Davis
New Yorker v92 no48 p75 F 6 2017
New York Review of Books v64 no3 p37-40 F 23 2017 J. Lears
New York Times Book Review p19 Ja 29 2017 M. Lind
Publishers Weekly v263 no45 p50-1 N 7 2016
Washington Monthly p14-1 Ja/F 2017 J. Heilbrunn

Kipnis, L. Unwanted advances. 2017
Christian Century v134 no22 p28-32 O 25 2017 J. Dailey
Commentary v143 no6 p46-9 Je 2017 K. C. Johnson
New York Times Book Review p11 Ap 9 2017 J. Filipovic
O, The Oprah Magazine p112 My 2017 J. S. Bonner
Publishers Weekly v264 no7 p67 F 13 2017

Kippenberg, T. J. and others. Cavity Optomechanics. 2016
Physics Today v70 no2 p58-60 F 2017 P. Meystre

Kirby, M. J. A taste for monsters. 2016
Publishers Weekly v263 no49 p117-8 D 7 2016

Kirchick, J. The end of europe. 2017
Foreign Affairs v96 no3 p164 My/Je 2017 A. Moravcsik
National Review v69 no5 p40-1 Mr 20 2017 C. Berlinski
New York Review of Books v64 no15 p44-5 O 12 2017 A. Applebaum
Weekly Standard v22 no35 p34-5 My 22 2017 M. M. Rosen

Kirk, C. Be Mine in Good Hope. 2017
Publishers Weekly v263 no46 p38 N 14 2016

Kirk, D. and Kirk, D. Truckeroo school. 2017
Publishers Weekly v264 no20 p53 My 15 2017

Kirk, D. Rhino in the house. 2017
Publishers Weekly v264 no5 p26-168 Ja 30 2017

Kiros, T. and Chatzikonstantis, M. Provence to Pondicherry. 2017
Publishers Weekly v264 no10 p56-7 Mr 6 2017

Kirsanow, P. Target Omega. 2016
Publishers Weekly v264 no10 p40 Mr 6 2017

Kirsch, A. The global novel. 2017
New Republic v248 no5 p63-5 My 2017 S. Deb
New York Times Book Review p26 Je 25 2017 H. Scott Partington
Publishers Weekly v264 no13 p64a Mr 27 2017
Publishers Weekly v264 no7 p63 F 13 2017

Kirsch, A. The people and the books. 2016
New York Times Book Review p13 N 20 2016 R. Alter

Kirsch, D. R. and Ogas, O. The drug hunters. 2017
Publishers Weekly v263 no44 p65 O 31 2016

Kirsch, L. The Big Overnight. 2016
Publishers Weekly v264 no9 p81 F 27 2017

Kirsch, L. The Big Weekend. 2017
Publishers Weekly v264 no35 p109 Ag 28 2017
Publishers Weekly v264 no39 p80a S 25 2017

Kirschman, E. The Fifth Reflection. 2017
Publishers Weekly v264 no18 p39 My 1 2017

Kirschner, E. and Rather, D. What unites us. 2017
Publishers Weekly v264 no36 p82 S 4 2017

Kishtainy, N. A little history of economics. 2017
Foreign Affairs v96 no3 p157 My/Je 2017 R. N. Cooper

Kissileff, B. Reading Genesis. 2016
Christian Century v134 no10 p47-9 My 10 2017 A. L. Rosen

Knight, K. and others. Jake the fake keeps it real. 2017
  Publishers Weekly v263 no52 p124 D 19 2016
Knight, M. Eveningland. 2017
  New York Times Book Review p16 Ap 2 2017 R. Bass
  New York Times Book Review p22 Ap 9 2017
  Publishers Weekly v264 no4 p52 Ja 23 2017
Knight, T. and Quintero, I. Ugly Cat & Pablo. 2017
  Publishers Weekly v264 no17 p93 Ap 24 2017
Knisley, L. and Robbins, D. Margaret and the Moon. 2017
  Publishers Weekly v264 no19 p59 My 8 2017
Knock, T. J. The rise of a prairie statesman. 2016
  Nation v305 no5 p27-31 Ag 28 2017 R. Cooper
Knott, B. and Lux, T. I am flying into myself. 2017
  New Yorker v93 no7 p98-9 Ap 3 2017 D. Chiasson
  Publishers Weekly v264 no3 p38 Ja 16 2017 J. Stucky
Knowlton, C. Cattle kingdom. 2017
  American Cowboy v23 no6 p43 Ap/My 2017
  New York Times Book Review p22 Je 11 2017
  New York Times Book Review p37 Je 4 2017 E. Dolnick
  Publishers Weekly v264 no16 p58-9 Ap 17 2017
Knutson, A. C. and others. World War I and American art. 2016
  New York Review of Books v64 no9 p13-5 My 25 2017 J. Fenton
Ko, G. and Mullen, S. Real food heals. 2017
  Publishers Weekly v264 no25 p106 Je 19 2017
Ko, L. The leavers. 2017
  Entertainment Weekly no1451/1452 p111 F 3-10 2017 I. Bieden-
    harn
  Entertainment Weekly no1465 p63 My 12 2017
  Ms. v27 no1 p43 Spr 2017 R. Bacon
  New York Times Book Review p25 My 21 2017 Gish Jen
  Publishers Weekly v264 no31 p83 Jl 31 2017
  Publishers Weekly v264 no7 p46 F 13 2017
Kobek, J. The Future Won't Be Long. 2017
  Publishers Weekly v264 no26 p148 Je 26 2017
Kober, S. and Lehrhaupt, A. Chicken in school. 2017
  Publishers Weekly v264 no20 p54 My 15 2017
Kobliner, B. Make your kid a money genius (even if you're not)
    2017
  Publishers Weekly v264 no3 p56 Ja 16 2017
Koch, D. M. and Arenas, R. Before night falls. 1994
  Weekly Standard v22 no14 p12-3 D 12 2016 L. Smith
Koch, H. and Rydell, A. The Book Thieves. 2017
  Vanity Fair p100 Hollywood 2017 Supplement S. Crosley
Koch, J. Quench Your Own Thirst. 2016
  Weekly Standard v22 no12 p32-4 N 28 2016 M. M. Wooster
Kocher, A. and Wells, S. Eucharistic prayers. 2016
  Christian Century v133 no26 p43 D 21 2016
Koehler, C. and Sattin, S. Legend 1. 2016
  Publishers Weekly v263 no50 p58 D 5 2016
Koehler, F. and Esenwine, M. F. Flashlight night. 2017
  Publishers Weekly v264 no27 p74 Jl 3 2017
Koehn, N. Forged in crisis. 2017
  Fortune v176 no4 p32-3 S 15 2017 L. Entis
  Publishers Weekly v264 no29 p208 Jl 17 2017
Koenig, K. R. and O'Mahoney, P. Helping patients outsmart
    overeating. 2017
  Publishers Weekly v263 no47 p103 N 21 2016
Koerner, J. L. Bosch and Bruegel. 2016
  America v216 no9 p22-4 Ap 24 2017 K. S. Smith
  Commonweal v144 no7 p30-1 Ap 14 2017 F. Freeman
Koffsky, A. D. and Shipman, T. Judah Maccabee goes to the doc-
    tor. 2017
  Publishers Weekly v264 no36 p99 S 4 2017
Kohan, R. The Arena. 2017
  Publishers Weekly v264 no19 p52 My 8 2017
Kohler, A. and Eskin, M. Passing time. 2017
  Publishers Weekly v263 no46 p43 N 14 2016
Kohler, S. Once we were sisters. 2016
  Good Housekeeping v264 no2 p60 F 1 2017
  New York Times Book Review p9 Ja 29 2017 J. Van Der Leun
Kohn, S. C. and Ricard, M. A plea for the animals. 2016
  Tricycle: The Buddhist Review v26 no2 p90 Wint 2016 M. Scarles
Koike, M. and Boehm, D. B. The graveyard apartment. 2016
  New York Times Book Review p20-1 O 30 2016 T. Rafferty
Kokie, E. M. Radical. 2016
  Publishers Weekly v263 no49 p101 D 7 2016

Kolata, G. Mercies in disguise. 2017
  New York Review of Books v64 no17 p25-7 N 9 2017 A. Solomon
  New York Times Book Review p20 Ap 30 2017 M. Angrist
  Publishers Weekly v264 no4 p70 Ja 23 2017
Koldeweij, J. and Ilsink, M. Hieronymus Bosch. 2016
  New York Times Book Review p19 D 25 2016 N. Siegal
Koldeweij, J. and others. Hieronymus Bosch, painter and draught-
    sman. 2016
  New York Times Book Review p19 D 25 2016 N. Siegal
Kolenko, E. and others. Bread, toast, crumbs. 2017
  Publishers Weekly v264 no14 p69 Ap 3. 2017
Kolenko, E. and others. Nopalito. 2017
  Publishers Weekly v263 no50 p64 D 5 2016
Kolhatkar, S. Black edge. 2017
  Bloomberg Businessweek no4509 p62 Ja 30 2017 K. Burton
  New York Times Book Review p12 F 19 2017 A. R. Sorkin
Kolin, P. C. Benedict's Daughter. 2017
  Christian Century v134 no14 p42-3 Jl 5 2017 P. Mariani
  U.S. Catholic v82 no10 p41 O 2017
Koller, D. The Custer Conspiracy. 2016
  Publishers Weekly v264 no3 p44-5 Ja 16 2017
  Publishers Weekly v264 no9 p66b F 27 2017
Kolpak, D. and Finlay, K. Starfall. 2011
  Publishers Weekly v264 no4 p83 Ja 23 2017
Koltai, S. R. and Muspratt, M. Peace through entrepreneurship.
    2016
  Washington Monthly p5-1 Ja/F 2017 D. Stangler
Komisar, E. Being there. 2017
  Publishers Weekly v264 no10 p58 Mr 6 2017
Konadu, K. and Campbell, C. C. The Ghana Reader. 2016
  Foreign Affairs v95 no6 p195 N/D 2016 N. Van De Walle
Konar, A. Mischling. 2016
  Christian Century v133 no21 p37-9 O 12 2016 E. L. Brown
  Publishers Weekly v263 no50 p68 D 5 2016
Kondo, R. and others. The dam keeper. 2017
  Publishers Weekly v264 no30 p63 Jl 24 2017
Konig, C. and others. Owls. 1999
  New York Review of Books v64 no9 p20-1 My 25 2017 R. O. Pax-
    ton
Konigsberg, B. Honestly Ben. 2017
  Publishers Weekly v264 no1 p59 Ja 2 2017
Kono, Y. and others. Three balls of wool (can change the world)
    2017
  Publishers Weekly v264 no35 p125 Ag 28 2017
Koon, D. and Miscavige, R. Ruthless. 2016
  Weekly Standard v22 no8 p34-7 O 31 2016 C. Allen
Kooser, T. and Root, B. The Bell in the Bridge. 2016
  Publishers Weekly v263 no49 p19 D 7 2016
Kopelson, G. Reagan's 1968 dress rehearsal. 2016
  Weekly Standard v22 no5 p30-2 O 10 2016 F. Barnes
Kops, D. Alice Paul and the fight for women's rights. 2017
  Publishers Weekly v263 no51 p151 D 12 2016
Korbee, N. Egg Shop. 2017
  Publishers Weekly v264 no10 p55 Mr 6 2017
Korda, M. Alone. 2017
  British Heritage Travel v38 no5 p73 S/O 2017 J. Hogan
  Publishers Weekly v264 no20 p46 My 15 2017
Korelitz, J. H. The devil and Webster. 2017
  Publishers Weekly v264 no26 p174-5 Je 26 2017
  Publishers Weekly v264 no4 p54 Ja 23 2017
Koreto, R. J. Alice and the Assassin. 2017
  Publishers Weekly v264 no8 p68 F 20 2017
Koreto, R. J. Death at the Emerald. 2017
  Publishers Weekly v264 no38 p57 S 18 2017
Korkeakivi, A. Shining sea. 2017
  New York Times Book Review p26 Ja 1 2017 M. Peed
Korman, G. Restart. 2017
  Publishers Weekly v264 no14 p77 Ap 3. 2017
Kornberg, J. The pope's dilemma. 2015
  Commonweal v144 no4 p16-9 F 24 2017 J. Connelly
Kornblum, W. and Tonnelat, S. International express. 2017
  Publishers Weekly v264 no8 p78 F 20 2017
Kosann, M. R. A Possession Obsession. 2016
  Publishers Weekly v263 no40 p113 O 3 2016
Kosar, K. R. Moonshine. 2017
  Weekly Standard v22 no41 p29-30 Jl 3 2017 W. Groom

Koski, O. and others. The vacation guide to the solar system. 2017
Publishers Weekly v264 no14 p66-7 Ap 3. 2017
Kostakis, W. The Sidekicks. 2017
Publishers Weekly v264 no35 p131 Ag 28 2017
Koster, G. and Eastland, S. Little Red Ruthie. 2017
Publishers Weekly v264 no36 p99 S 4 2017
Kostova, E. The shadow land. 2017
New Yorker v93 no11 p69 My 1 2017
Publishers Weekly v264 no9 p68 F 27 2017
Kostyal, K. M. and others. Benjamin Franklin's wise words. 2017
Publishers Weekly v263 no46 p58 N 14 2016
Kotcheff, T. Director's Cut. 2017
Film Comment v53 no2 p79 Mr/Ap 2017 N. Pinkerton
Koter, D. Beyond ethnic politics in Africa. 2016
Foreign Affairs v96 no2 p189-90 Mr/Ap 2017 N. Van De Walle
Kotkin, S. Stalin. 2017
American Conservative v16 no5 p54-7 S/O 2017 J. Heilbrunn
Publishers Weekly v264 no39 p99 S 25 2017
Kotler, S. and Wheal, J. Stealing Fire. 2017
Publishers Weekly v264 no10 p12 Mr 6 2017 C. Juris
Koul, S. One day we'll all be dead and none of this will matter. 2017
Good Housekeeping v265 no1 p67 Jl 2017
New York Times Book Review p26 S 17 2017 H. Mlotek
Publishers Weekly v264 no11 p74 Mr 13 2017
Koutsakis, P. Athenian Blues. 2017
Publishers Weekly v264 no6 p48 F 6 2017
Kova, E. The alchemists of loom. 2017
Publishers Weekly v263 no42 p55 O 17 2016
Kova, E. The dragons of nova. 2017
Publishers Weekly v264 no21 p78 My 22 2017
Kovac, C. The cutaway. 2017
Publishers Weekly v264 no4 p57 Ja 23 2017
Kovalev, A. A. and Levine, S. I. Russia's dead end. 2017
Publishers Weekly v264 no23 p45 Je 5 2017
Kozlowski, B. and Wood, L. Cook Me a Rhyme. 2017
Publishers Weekly v264 no22 p69 My 29 2017
Kozubek, J. Modern Prometheus. 2016
Science v354 no6309 p189 O 14 2016 G. J. Annas
Kraak, S. Two Ways Home. 2016
Publishers Weekly v263 no51 p132 D 12 2016
Publishers Weekly v264 no4 p50e Ja 23 2017
Kraatz, J. The moon platoon. 2017
Publishers Weekly v264 no14 p77 Ap 3. 2017
Krabak, B. J. and others. The Long Distance Runner's Guide to Injury Prevention and Treatment. 2017
Publishers Weekly v264 no34 p107 Ag 21 2017
Kracht, C. and Bowles, D. Imperium. 2015
New York Times Book Review p32 N 20 2016 J. Khatib
Kraegel, K. and Kraegel, K. Green pants. 2017
New York Times Book Review p27 My 14 2017 M. Russo
New York Times Book Review p27 My 14 2017 R. Sepetys
Kragh, H. Simply Dirac. 2016
Publishers Weekly v264 no22 p60 My 29 2017
Publishers Weekly v264 no26 p136 Je 26 2017
Publishers Weekly v264 no26 p146e Je 26 2017
Krakauer, J. Missoula. 2015
Commentary v140 no2 p1-3 S 2015 J. Krakauer
Commentary v140 no2 p63-5 S 2015 K. C. Johnson
Krakoff, D. and others. Houses that we dreamt of. 2017
Architectural Digest v74 no10 p28 O 1 2017 A. Astley
Kramer, J. A. and Sassouni, M. The Green Umbrella. 2017
Publishers Weekly v263 no45 p60 N 7 2016
Kramer, K. Christmas at Two Love Lane. 2017
Publishers Weekly v264 no36 p75 S 4 2017
Kramer, L. S. Uncommon Voyage. 2017
Publishers Weekly v264 no16 p65 Ap 17 2017
Publishers Weekly v264 no17 p44 Ap 24 2017
Publishers Weekly v264 no17 p58e Ap 24 2017
Kramer, P. D. Ordinarily well. 2016
Issues in Science & Technology v33 no2 p92-4 Wint 2017 D. Healy
Krampien, C. and Keely, C. Here to there and me to you. 2017
Publishers Weekly v263 no48 p70 N 28 2016
Kranish, M. and Fisher, M. Trump revealed. 2016
Nation v303 no17 p32-6 O 24 2016 C. Lehmann

New York Review of Books v63 no20 p8-14 D 22 2016 M. Danner
Kranz, M. Building the internet of things. 2017
New York Times Book Review p20 D 18 2016
Krasikov, S. The patriots. 2017
New York Times Book Review p11 Ja 29 2017 N. Rich
Krasikov, S. The repatriates. 2017
Publishers Weekly v263 no47 p82 N 21 2016
Krasinski, N. and others. State Bird Provisions. 2017
Publishers Weekly v264 no36 p83 S 4 2017
Krasny, M. Let there be laughter. 2016
New York Times Book Review p49 D 4 2016 P. Keepnews
Krassner, P. and Groth, G. The realist cartoons. 2016
Reason v48 no8 p61 Ja 2017 J. Walker
Krastev, I. After Europe. 2017
Foreign Affairs v96 no6 p161 N/D 2017 A. Moravcsik
Krasznahorkai, L. and others. The world goes on. 2017
Publishers Weekly v264 no36 p62 S 4 2017
Kraus, C. After Kathy Acker. 2017
Publishers Weekly v264 no23 p43 Je 5 2017
Krauss, L. M. The Greatest Story Ever Told--So Far. 2017
Science v355 no6331 p1273 Mr 24 2017 M. Livio
Scientific American v316 no4 p76 Ap 2017 C. Moskowitz
Krauss, N. Forest dark. 2017
Martha Stewart Living p14 S 2017
Nation v305 no10 p32-4 O 23 2017 S. Halpern
New York Times Book Review p1-22 S 17 2017 P. Orner
New York Times Book Review p26 S 24 2017
New York v50 no17 p132-9 Ag 21 2017
Publishers Weekly v264 no18 p35 My 1 2017
Publishers Weekly v264 no26 p72-80 Je 26 2017 G. Habash
Publishers Weekly v264 no34 p78-9 Ag 21 2017 J. Buntin
Vanity Fair v59 no10 p128 O 2017 S. Crosley
Vogue v207 no9 p616 S 2017 C. Schama
Kravetz, L. D. Strange contagion. 2017
Discover v38 no6 p16 Jl/Ag 2017 G. Tarlach
New York Times Book Review p30 S 24 2017 C. Chabris
Publishers Weekly v264 no19 p51 My 8 2017
Krawcheck, S. Own It. 2017
Bloomberg Businessweek no4508 p59 Ja 23 2017 R. Greenfield
Krazy. 2016
Publishers Weekly v263 no42 p60 O 17 2016
Krebs, C. J. Why ecology matters. 2016
BioScience v67 no8 p769-70 Ag 2017 R. P. Keller
Krefft, V. The Man Who Made the Movies. 2017
Publishers Weekly v264 no36 p80 S 4 2017
Kreisler, J. and Ariely, D. Dollars and Sense. 2017
Publishers Weekly v264 no26 p28-33 Je 26 2017 J. Milliot
Publishers Weekly v264 no38 p62-3 S 18 2017
Kreiss, D. Prototype politics. 2016
New York Review of Books v64 no10 p59-61 Je 8 2017 S. Halpern
Krentz, J. A. Promise not to tell. 2018
Publishers Weekly v264 no40 p123 O 2 2017
Krentz, J. A. When all the girls have gone. 2016
Publishers Weekly v263 no45 p47 N 7 2016
Kreps, S. E. Drones. 2016
Foreign Affairs v95 no6 p153-8 N/D 2016 L. D. Freedman
Kress, N. Tomorrow's kin. 2017
Publishers Weekly v264 no23 p34 Je 5 2017
Kress, W. J. and Stine, J. K. Living in the anthropocene. 2017
Publishers Weekly v264 no27 p64 Jl 3 2017
Krey, P. D. and others. A short life of Martin Luther. 2016
Publishers Weekly v263 no45 p28 N 7 2016
Krieger, D. Giving Godhead. 2017
New York Times Book Review p10 Ag 6 2017 T. Simmons
New York Times Book Review p23 Ag 13 2017
Krieger, E. and Cocotos, T. N. Real or Fake? 2017
Publishers Weekly v264 no21 p94 My 22 2017
Krist, G. Empire of sin. 2014
New Orleans Magazine v51 no2 p40-1 D 2016 A. J. Johnson
Kristal, M. The new old house. 2017
Architectural Record v205 no5 p61 My 2017 W. Moonan
Kristeva, J. and others. Marriage as a fine art. 2016
New Republic v248 no1/2 p56-8 Ja/F 2017 V. Gornick
Kristian, G. Wings of the Storm. 2017
Publishers Weekly v264 no34 p95 Ag 21 2017
Kritzer, N. Cat Pictures Please and Other Stories. 2017

Publishers Weekly v264 no22 p50 My 29 2017

Krivak, A. The signal flame. 2017
  New York Times Book Review p17 Ja 29 2017 R. Robinson
  New York Times Book Review p24 O 1 2017 J. Khatib
  Publishers Weekly v263 no45 p36 N 7 2016

Kroese, R. The last iota. 2017
  Publishers Weekly v264 no14 p57 Ap 3. 2017

Kroll, B. The Hell of It All. 2017
  Publishers Weekly v264 no1 p40 Ja 2 2017

Krommes, B. and Sidman, J. Before morning. 2015
  New York Times Book Review p18 D 18 2016 L. S. Marcus
  New York Times Book Review p22 D 25 2016
  Publishers Weekly v263 no49 p30-1 D 7 2016

Kronberg, P. P. Cosmic magnetic fields. 2016
  Physics Today v70 no6 p66-7 Je 2017

Krosoczka, J. J. and Krosoczka, J. J. Naptastrophe! 2017
  Publishers Weekly v264 no13 p98 Mr 27 2017

Krueger, W. K. Sulfur Springs. 2017
  Publishers Weekly v264 no26 p158 Je 26 2017

Krukowski , D. The new analog. 2017
  New York Times Book Review p4 My 7 2017 J. Williams

Krupat, A. Companion to James Welch's The Heartsong of Charging Elk. 2015
  American Indian Quarterly v41 no2 p182-5 Spr 2017 L. R. Cooper

Kruschwitz, P. and others. 30-Second Ancient Rome. 2014
  History Today v67 no2 p58 F 2017 D. Dunn

Kryger, M. The Mystery of sleep. 2017
  Publishers Weekly v264 no8 p81 F 20 2017

Krynauw, T. and others. Faster higher smarter. 2016
  Science v354 no6317 p1224-5 D 9 2016 J. Mervis

Krynicki, R. and Cavanagh, C. Magnetic point. 2017
  Publishers Weekly v264 no38 p51 S 18 2017 C. Simic

Kryscynski, D. and others. Victory through organization. 2017
  People Management p52 Ap 2017

Krystal, A. This thing we call literature. 2016
  New York Review of Books v64 no14 p39-42 S 28 2017 E. Mendelson

Kuan, D. Lunch portraits. 2016
  Publishers Weekly v263 no47 p86-7 N 21 2016

Kubica, M. Every Last Lie. 2017
  Publishers Weekly v264 no14 p52 Ap 3. 2017

Kubicki, J. A Year of Daily Offerings. 2016
  U.S. Catholic v82 no1 p41 Ja 2017

Kudisch, E. Don't Feed the Trolls. 2017
  Publishers Weekly v264 no9 p84-5 F 27 2017

Kudlow, L. and Domitrovic, B. JFK and the Reagan revolution. 2016
  Forbes v198 no7 p32 N 29 2016
  National Review v69 no9 p37-8 My 15 2017 I. Brannon

Kuehn, S. When I am through with you. 2017
  Publishers Weekly v264 no22 p70 My 29 2017

Kugle, S. A. When sun meets moon. 2016
  Publishers Weekly v263 no45 p6 N 7 2016 M. Z. Nelson

Kuhlman, E. and Groenink, C. Hank's big day. 2016
  Publishers Weekly v263 no49 p12-3 D 7 2016

Kuhlmann, T. and others. Armstrong. 2016
  Publishers Weekly v263 no49 p11 D 7 2016

Kuhn, A. and others. ¡Cuba! 2016
  Chicago v65 no12 p62 D 2016 C. Boers

Kuhn, L. The selected letters of John Cage. 2016
  New York Review of Books v63 no16 p42-3 O 27 2016 T. Page

Kuhn, S. Heroine Worship. 2017
  Publishers Weekly v264 no23 p36 Je 5 2017

Kujawinski, P. and Halpern, J. Edgeland. 2017
  Publishers Weekly v264 no12 p73-4 Mr 20 2017

Kukafka, D. Girl in snow. 2017
  Publishers Weekly v264 no23 p26 Je 5 2017

Kukla, J. Patrick Henry. 2017
  Publishers Weekly v264 no22 p58-9 My 29 2017

Kukucha, C. J. and Chapnick, A. The Harper era in Canadian foreign policy. 2016
  Foreign Affairs v96 no1 p167-8 Ja/F 2017 R. Feinberg

Kulikov, B. and Bryant, J. Six dots. 2015
  Publishers Weekly v263 no49 p51 D 7 2016

Kulikowski, M. Imperial Triumph. 2016

History Today v67 no2 p56-7 F 2017 M. Leigh

Kumar, V. S. The Third squad. 2017
  Publishers Weekly v263 no47 p30 N 21 2016 J. F.
  Publishers Weekly v264 no5 p179 Ja 30 2017

Kunce, C. and Kunce, J. Hope's Melody. 2016
  Publishers Weekly v264 no13 p64f Mr 27 2017
  Publishers Weekly v264 no8 p84 F 20 2017

Kunzru, H. White tears. 2017
  New Yorker v93 no7 p91 Ap 3 2017
  New York Times Book Review p15 Ap 2 2017 S. Erickson
  New York Times Book Review p22 Ap 9 2017
  O, The Oprah Magazine p93 Ap 2017 E. Vanderhoof
  Publishers Weekly v263 no50 p47 D 5 2016
  Publishers Weekly v263 no51 p117-8 D 12 2016 J. W. McCormack
  Time v189 no11 p61 Mr 27 2017 C. Howorth

Kuo, M. Reading with Patrick. 2017
  New Yorker v93 no29 p97 S 25 2017
  Saturday Evening Post v289 no4 p24 Jl/Ag 2017

Kurbjuweit, D. Fear. 2017
  Publishers Weekly v264 no33 p48-9 Ag 14 2017

Kurilla, R. and Brendler, C. The Pickwicks' picnic. 2017
  Publishers Weekly v264 no30 p59 Jl 24 2017

Kurilla, R. and Calandrelli, E. Ada Lace, on the case. 2017
  Publishers Weekly v264 no29 p220 Jl 17 2017

Kurlander, E. Hitler's monsters. 2017
  National Review v69 no18 p36-8 O 2 2017 A. Stuttaford

Kurlansky, M. Havana. 2017
  New York Times Book Review p16-7 Je 4 2017 L. Schillinger
  Publishers Weekly v264 no2 p57 Ja 9 2017

Kurlansky, M. Paper. 2016
  New Yorker v92 no30 p75 S 26 2016

Kurlantzick, J. A great place to have a war. 2017
  New York Times Book Review p12 F 5 2017 S. Shane
  Publishers Weekly v263 no46 p43-4 N 14 2016
  Washington Monthly p6-1 Ja/F 2017 B. Dakin

Kurman, M. and Lipson, H. Driverless. 2016
  New York Review of Books v63 no18 p18-20 N 24 2016 S. Halpern

Kurtz, J. Planet Jupiter. 2017
  Publishers Weekly v264 no9 p100 F 27 2017

Kurtzman, H. and others. Trump. 2016
  Reason v49 no3 p64-5 Jl 2017 P. Bagge

Kurup, S. Understanding Louise Erdrich. 2016
  American Indian Quarterly v41 no3 p287-9 Summ 2017 D. Miller

Kushner, A. and Padura, L. Heretics. 2017
  Publishers Weekly v264 no5 p174 Ja 30 2017

Kushner, D. Alligator candy. 2016
  New York Times Book Review p36 My 14 2017 J. Khatib

Kushner, E. and others. Tremontaine. 2017
  Publishers Weekly v264 no15 p57-8 Ap 10 2017

Kushner, H. I. On the other hand. 2017
  Science v357 no6357 p1246 S 22 2017 D. Casasanto

Kuster, E. and others. Anne of green gables. 2017
  Publishers Weekly v264 no33 p83 Ag 14 2017

Kwak, J. Economism. 2016
  America v216 no7 p47 Ap 3 2017 C. R. Morris
  Publishers Weekly v263 no43 p69 O 24 2016

Kwan, J. and Kwan, J. How it feels to be a boat. 2017
  Publishers Weekly v264 no22 p67 My 29 2017

Kwan, K. Rich people problems. 2017
  Bloomberg Businessweek no4527 p90 Je 19 2017 T. Patterson
  New York Times Book Review p24 Je 11 2017 G. Cowles

Kyncl, R. and Peyvan, M. Streampunks. 2017
  New York Times Book Review p19 S 24 2017 A. Hess

L

A lowcountry heart. 2016
  New York Times Book Review p46 N 13 2016 G. Cowles

Laager, K. and Block, L. Resume Speed. 2016
  Publishers Weekly v263 no42 p54 O 17 2016

Laberis, S. and Shaffer, J. J. Prudence the part-time cow. 2017
  Publishers Weekly v264 no18 p56-7 My 1 2017

Labriola, A. and Faktorovich, A. The lonely barber. 2017
  Publishers Weekly v264 no9 p83-4 F 27 2017

Lee, F. Jade City. 2017
  Publishers Weekly v264 no41 p36 O 9 2017 J. B.
Lee, H. and Wharton, E. Four novels of the 1920s. 2015
  New York Review of Books v64 no9 p40-1 My 25 2017 M. Gorra
Lee, J. and Lee, J. Garbage Night. 2017
  Publishers Weekly v264 no18 p46 My 1 2017
Lee, J. and others. Burma Superstar. 2016
  Publishers Weekly v263 no47 p101 N 21 2016
Lee, J. God's Wolf. 2017
  Military History v34 no1 p71-2 My 2017 D. Saunders
Lee, J. High dive. 2016
  Commonweal v144 no2 p28-30 Ja 27 2017 A. Domestico
Lee, J. J. and others. Chef Roy Choi and the street food remix.
  2017
  Publishers Weekly v264 no23 p51 Je 5 2017
Lee, J. M. and Kim, C. The Boy Who Escaped Paradise. 2016
  Publishers Weekly v263 no39 p63-4 S 26 2016
Lee, J. Y. The Expatriates. 2016
  New York Times Book Review p80 D 4 2016 J. Khatib
Lee, K. and Kim, Y. I hear your voice. 2017
  Publishers Weekly v264 no23 p28-9 Je 5 2017
Lee, K. How I Became a North Korean. 2016
  New York Times Book Review p24 Ag 20 2017 J. Khatib
Lee, M. and Lee, M. Play with me! 2017
  Publishers Weekly v263 no44 p73 O 31 2016
Lee, M. J. Pachinko. 2017
  Ms. v27 no1 p46-7 Spr 2017
  New York Times Book Review p18 F 5 2017 K. Lee
  Publishers Weekly v263 no47 p77 N 21 2016
Lee, M. The gentleman's guide to vice and virtue. 2017
  Publishers Weekly v264 no17 p94 Ap 24 2017
Lee, M. Written out of history. 2017
  Publishers Weekly v264 no24 p12 Je 12 2017 C. Juris
Lee, R. A. A New Deal for South Dakota. 2016
  South Dakota Magazine v32 no6 p45 Mr/Ap 2017
Lee, R. The idea of you. 2017
  Essence v48 no3 p56 Jl 2017 P. H. Bass
Lee, S. and Barbo, M. The secret of a heart note. 2016
  Publishers Weekly v263 no41 p82 O 10 2016
Lee, S. and Jackson, R. This beautiful day. 2017
  Publishers Weekly v264 no24 p63-5 Je 12 2017
Lee, S. and Lee, S. Lines. 2017
  Publishers Weekly v264 no29 p215 Jl 17 2017
Lee, W. E. Waging War. 2016
  MHQ: Quarterly Journal of Military History v29 no4 p94 Summ
  2017 M. W. Robbins
Lee, Y. and others. The things you can see only when you slow
  down. 2017
  Publishers Weekly v263 no51 p143 D 12 2016
  Tricycle: The Buddhist Review v26 no3 p92-3 Spr 2017 M. Scarles
Lee-Barnewall, M. Neither complementarian nor egalitarian. 2016
  Christianity Today v61 no1 p53 Ja/F 2017 T. Schreiner
Leeds, P. Big shots. 2016
  Interview v47 no3 p26-7 Ap 2017
Leendertz, L. and Diacono, M. My Tiny Veg Plot. 2017
  Publishers Weekly v263 no47 p104 N 21 2016
Lee Shetterly, M. Hidden figures. 2016
  Ms. v26 no4 p41 Wint 2016 A. Dove-Viebahn
  New York Review of Books v64 no9 p38-9 My 25 2017 P. Nata-
  rajan
  New York Times Book Review p10-1 Ja 1 2017 J. Levin
  New York Times Book Review p26 Ja 8 2017
  New York Times Book Review p26 S 25 2016 G. Cowles
  Science v354 no6318 p1383 D 16 2016 C. Christian
  Virginia Living v15 no3 p31 Ap 2017 B. Glose
Leever, L. and Van Hooft, M. Mary has a baby. 2016
  Publishers Weekly v263 no39 p88 S 26 2016
Lefavour, C. Lights on, rats out. 2017
  New York Times Book Review p12 Jl 30 2017 D. Merkin
LeFlouria, T. L. Chained in silence. 2015
  Nation v303 no25/26 p8 D 19 2016 E. A. Dunbar
  Nation v33 no21 p11 N 21 2016 E. Hinton
Legenhausen, C. Fashion Jewelry. 2017
  Publishers Weekly v264 no23 p49 Je 5 2017
Legrand, C. and Zollars, J. Foxheart. 2016
  Publishers Weekly v263 no49 p78 D 7 2016

Legrand, C. Some kind of happiness. 2016
  Publishers Weekly v263 no49 p76-7 D 7 2016
Legrand, O. and others. The Baker Street Four. 2017
  Publishers Weekly v264 no20 p45 My 15 2017
Le Guin, U. K. and Attebery, B. The complete Orsinia. 2016
  Weekly Standard v22 no16 p36-7 D 26 2016 E. Mundahl
LeGuin, U. K. and Robbins, R. Wizard of Earthsea. 1968
  Esquire p48 S 2017 E. Sullivan
Le Guin, U. K. No time to spare. 2017
  Publishers Weekly v264 no33 p61 Ag 14 2017
Legutko, R. The demon in democracy. 2016
  Weekly Standard v22 no47 p38-41 Ag 21 2017 M. B. Crawford
Lehane, C. Murder in the manuscript room. 2017
  Publishers Weekly v264 no36 p68 S 4 2017
Lehane, D. Mystic river. 2001
  Entertainment Weekly no1465 p59 My 12 2017 I. Biedenharn
Lehane, D. Prayers for rain. 2013
  Entertainment Weekly no1465 p59 My 12 2017 I. Biedenharn
Lehane, D. Shutter Island. 2009
  Entertainment Weekly no1465 p59 My 12 2017 I. Biedenharn
Lehane, D. Since we fell. 2017
  AARP: The Magazine v60 no3A p18 Ap/My 2017 D. Donahue
  New York Times Book Review p24 Je 4 2017 N. Hawley
  New York v50 no9 p88 My 1 2017 D. L. Ulin
  Publishers Weekly v264 no13 p77-8 Mr 27 2017
  Publishers Weekly v264 no21 p14 My 22 2017 C. Juris
  Publishers Weekly v264 no36 p87 S 4 2017
  Saturday Evening Post v289 no3 p22 My/Je 2017
Lehmann-Haupt, R. and Nelson, M. In Her Own Sweet Time.
  2016
  USA Today Magazine v145 no2858 p81 N 2016
LeHoullier, C. Epic tomatoes. 2015
  Mother Earth News no280 p80-1 F/Mr 2017
Lehr, J. Parentspeak. 2017
  Publishers Weekly v263 no40 p115-6 O 3 2016
Lehrer, R. Being Fishkill. 2017
  Publishers Weekly v264 no38 p72-3 S 18 2017
Lehrhaupt, A. and Kober, S. Chicken in school. 2017
  Publishers Weekly v264 no20 p54 My 15 2017
Lehrke, A. and others. The water dragon's bride. 2017
  Publishers Weekly v264 no16 p55 Ap 17 2017
Lehrman, L. E. Churchill, Roosevelt & company. 2017
  National Review v69 no5 p41-3 Mr 20 2017 M. Knox Beran
Lehto, S. Preston Tucker and his battle to build the car of tomorrow.
  2016
  Weekly Standard v22 no27 p41-2 Mr 20 2017 W. Vatter
Le Huche, M. and Weinstone, D. All my friends are fast asleep.
  2017
  Publishers Weekly v264 no28 p86 Jl 10 2017
Leider, R. J. and Shapiro, D. A. Work reimagined. 2015
  AARP: The Magazine v59 no1A p60 D 2015/Ja 2016
Leigh, J. Avalanche. 2016
  New Yorker v92 no39 p91 N 28 2016
Leigh, M. Midnight Obsession. 2017
  Publishers Weekly v263 no45 p46 N 7 2016
Leigh, P. Southern Reconstruction. 2017
  Publishers Weekly v264 no17 p81 Ap 24 2017
Leigh, S. A Fading Sun. 2017
  Publishers Weekly v264 no22 p50 My 29 2017
Leijten, A. Lint Boy. 2017
  Publishers Weekly v264 no18 p63 My 1 2017
Leininger, R. Gumshoe for Two. 2017
  Publishers Weekly v264 no6 p49-50 F 6 2017
Leiris, A. You Will Not Have My Hate. 2016
  Weekly Standard v22 no15 p30-1 D 19 2016 S. Beck
Leithart, P. J. The end of Protestantism. 2016
  Christianity Today v60 no9 p69-71 N 2016 F. Sanders
Leland, J. Happiness is a choice you make. 2018
  Publishers Weekly v264 no39 p96 S 25 2017
Lelyveld, J. His final battle. 2016
  New York Times Book Review p11 S 25 2016 L. Olson
  New York Times Book Review p26 O 2 2016
Lemaître, P. and McGhee, H. M. Come with me. 2017
  New York Times Book Review p24 Ag 27 2017 R. J. Palacio
Lemaitre, P. and Wynne, F. Three days and a life. 2017
  Publishers Weekly v264 no38 p56 S 18 2017

Commonweal v143 no17 p29-32 O 21 2016 P. Steinfels
Foreign Affairs v95 no6 p178 N/D 2016 W. Russell Mead
Nation v303 no19 p27-32 N 7 2016 T. Shenk
Levine, A. and others. Who counts? 2017
Christian Century v134 no11 p43 My 24 2017
Publishers Weekly v264 no15 p74 Ap 10 2017
Levine, A. Mental Health Inc. 2017
Publishers Weekly v264 no12 p65 Mr 20 2017
Levine, D. D. Arabella and the Battle of Venus. 2017
Publishers Weekly v264 no21 p77 My 22 2017
Levine, G. C. and Brosnan, R. The lost kingdom of bamarre. 2017
Publishers Weekly v264 no9 p100 F 27 2017
Levine, L. B. Now I Know It's Not My Fault. 2016
Publishers Weekly v264 no17 p58f Ap 24 2017
Levine, L. Death of a bachelorette. 2017
Publishers Weekly v264 no19 p41 My 8 2017
Levine, P. My lost poets. 2016
New York Review of Books v64 no11 p42-3 Je 22 2017 C. Simic
Levine, P. The bread of time. 1994
New York Review of Books v64 no11 p42-3 Je 22 2017 C. Simic
Levine, P. The last shift. 2016
New York Review of Books v64 no11 p42-3 Je 22 2017 C. Simic
Publishers Weekly v263 no42 p47 O 17 2016
Levine, R. S. The lives of Frederick Douglass. 2015
Nation v304 no11 p27-31 Ap 3 2017 M. Karp
Levine, S. and Spookytooth, T. S. Tooth by tooth. 2016
Science v354 no6317 p1223 D 9 2016 C. Wolner
Levine, S. I. and Kovalev, A. A. Russia's dead end. 2017
Publishers Weekly v264 no23 p45 Je 5 2017
Levine, S. J. and others. A house in the country. 1984
New York Times Book Review p22 D 4 2016 A. Becker
Levingston, S. Kennedy and King. 2017
New York Times Book Review p9 Jl 2 2017 J. Goodman
Publishers Weekly v264 no14 p64 Ap 3. 2017
Levinson, C. and Brantley-Newton, V. The youngest marcher. 2015
Publishers Weekly v263 no51 p147 D 12 2016
Levinson, D. S. Tell Me How This Ends Well. 2017
Publishers Weekly v264 no8 p56 F 20 2017
Levinson, M. An extraordinary time. 2016
Claremont Review of Books v17 no1 p85-6 Wint 2016/2017 M. Barone
National Review v69 no2 p37-8 F 6 2017 J. Pethokoukis
Publishers Weekly v263 no39 p79 S 26 2016
Levis, C. and Rash, A. May I have a word? 2017
Publishers Weekly v264 no10 p61 Mr 6 2017
Levis, C. and Santoso, C. Ida, always. 2016
Publishers Weekly v263 no49 p32 D 7 2016
Levitan, D. Not a scientist. 2017
New York Times Book Review p4 Jl 16 2017 J. Williams
Publishers Weekly v263 no44 p65 O 31 2016
Science v356 no6334 p144-5 Ap 14 2017 S. Kirshenbaum
Scientific American v316 no4 p76 Ap 2017 C. Moskowitz
Skeptical Inquirer v41 no4 p60 Jl/Ag 2017
Levithan, D. and Cohn, R. The Twelve Days of Dash & Lily. 2016
Publishers Weekly v263 no39 p92 S 26 2016
Levitt, M. and Whidden, T. The Art and Science of Sails. 2016
Sail v48 no2 p24 F 2017 B. Hancock
Levy, A. and Scott-Clark, C. The exile. 2017
Foreign Affairs v96 no6 p155 N/D 2017 L. D. Freedman
Publishers Weekly v264 no13 p101 Mr 27 2017
Levy, A. The rules do not apply. 2017
Atlantic v319 no2 p46 Mr 2017 A. Hulbert
Entertainment Weekly no1457/1458 p105 Mr 17 2017 L. Greenblatt
Martha Stewart Living p10 Mr 2017
New York Times Book Review p10 Ap 9 2017 L. Jamison
O, The Oprah Magazine p91 Ap 2017 M. Filgate
Publishers Weekly v264 no1 p49 Ja 2 2017
Time v189 no11 p61 Mr 27 2017 E. Dockterman
Vanity Fair v59 no4 p116 Mr 2017 S. Crosley
Lévy, B. and Kennedy, S. B. The genius of Judaism. 2017
Commentary v143 no3 p40-4 Mr 2017
New Yorker v92 no47 p70 Ja 30 2017
New York Times Book Review p17 F 12 2017 D. Merkin
Publishers Weekly v263 no46 p50 N 14 2016

Levy, B. and others. No Barriers. 2017
Sierra v102 no3 p11 My/Je 2017 J. Hahn
Levy, D. and Baddeley, E. I dissent. 2016
American History v52 no3 p69 Ag 2017 G. Carrasco
Levy, D. and Ford, G. Soldier song. 2017
Publishers Weekly v263 no46 p59 N 14 2016
Levy, D. Hot Milk. 2016
Nation v305 no5 p32-4 Ag 28 2017 B. Rothfeld
New Yorker v92 no30 p75 S 26 2016
New York Times Book Review p24 Ag 6 2017 J. Khatib
Levy, D. Swimming home. 2012
Nation v305 no5 p32-4 Ag 28 2017 B. Rothfeld
Levy, D. The Early Novels. 2017
Nation v305 no5 p32-4 Ag 28 2017 B. Rothfeld
Levy, M. and Taylor, S. P.s. from Paris. 2017
Publishers Weekly v264 no29 p190-1 Jl 17 2017
Levy, N. Einstein and the Rabbi. 2017
Publishers Weekly v264 no28 p82 Jl 10 2017
Lewis, A. and Junker, P. Andrew Wyeth. 2017
Publishers Weekly v264 no18 p52 My 1 2017
Lewis, B. Learn to Sail Today! 2016
Sail v48 no1 p17 Ja 2017 A. Wisch
Lewis, B. The missing. 2009
Publishers Weekly v264 no34 p89 Ag 21 2017
Lewis, C. The enlightened Mr. Parkinson. 2017
Publishers Weekly v264 no22 p56 My 29 2017
Science News v192 no1 p27 Ag 5 2017
Lewis, C. Too fast to think. 2016
People Management p56 N 2016
Lewis, D. R. Footprints In The Dew. 2015
Publishers Weekly v263 no45 p54 N 7 2016
Publishers Weekly v263 no47 p76e N 21 2016
Lewis, E. B. and Asim, J. Preaching to the chickens. 2016
Publishers Weekly v263 no49 p50 D 7 2016
Lewis, E. Game of Shadows. 2017
Publishers Weekly v263 no44 p57 O 31 2016
Lewis, J. P. and others. Make the Earth your companion. 2017
Publishers Weekly v264 no3 p59 Ja 16 2017
Lewis, J. P. and Wright, J. Keep a pocket in your poem. 2017
Publishers Weekly v264 no3 p61 Ja 16 2017
Lewis, J. R. and others. March. 2015
New York Times Book Review p13 N 27 2016 J. Lucas
Lewis, M. The undoing project. 2016
Bloomberg Businessweek no4500 p80 N 21 2016 P. Coy
Bloomberg Businessweek no4503 p70 D 12 2016 P. Coy
Foreign Affairs v96 no3 p139-45 My/Je 2017 Y. Foong Khong
New York Review of Books v64 no7 p62-5 Ap 20 2017 T. Shaw
New York Times Book Review p1-15 D 18 2016 D. Leonhardt
New York Times Book Review p22 D 25 2016
New York Times Book Review p22 F 5 2017
Publishers Weekly v263 no52 p13 D 19 2016
Publishers Weekly v264 no14 p73-4 Ap 3. 2017
Washingtonian Magazine v52 no6 p45-6 Mr 2017 J. K. Glassman
Lewis, M. Who's Afraid? 2017
Publishers Weekly v264 no26 p160 Je 26 2017
Lewis, N. and Hudson, K. Where Jesus slept. 2016
Publishers Weekly v263 no39 p88 S 26 2016
Lewis, N. Gold. 2017
Forbes v200 no4 p11-2 O 24 2017
Lewis, P. and Fried, J. Charlemagne. 2016
Maclean's v129 no47 p62 N 28 2016 B. Bethune
Lewis, P. The Barrowfields. 2017
Louisiana Life v37 no5 p15 My/Je 2017
New York Times Book Review p18 Mr 26 2017 J. Silber
Publishers Weekly v264 no5 p170 Ja 30 2017
Lewis, R. Under surveillance. 2017
Publishers Weekly v264 no26 p166 Je 26 2017
Lewis, S. It can't happen here. 2005
New York Times Book Review p15 Ja 22 2017 B. Gage
Lewis, S. P. Dandy lion. 2017
New York p60-5 Mr 6 2017
Lewis, T. Gas Money. 2015
Publishers Weekly v264 no31 p44 Jl 31 2017
Lewis-Jones, H. and Herbert, K. Explorers' sketchbooks. 2017
Publishers Weekly v264 no8 p76 F 20 2017
Scientific American v316 no4 p76 Ap 2017 A. Gawrylewski

Mackenzie, V. The revolutionary life of Freda Bedi. 2017
Publishers Weekly v264 no7 p71 F 13 2017
Tricycle: The Buddhist Review v26 no3 p86-8 Spr 2017 J. D. Oliver

Mackey, J. and others. The whole foods diet. 2017
Texas Monthly v45 no7 p66-121 Jl 2017 T. Foster

Mackintosh, C. I see you. 2017
New York Times Book Review p7 Mr 5 2017 M. Stasio

Mackrell, J. Unfinished Palazzo. 2017
New York Times Book Review p21 O 15 2017 J. Martin

MacLachlan, P. and Boutavant, M. Barkus. 2017
Publishers Weekly v264 no16 p67 Ap 17 2017

MacLachlan, P. and dePaola, T. The moon's almost here! 2015
Publishers Weekly v263 no49 p44 D 7 2016

MacLachlan, P. and Sheban, C. Someone like me. 2017
Publishers Weekly v264 no21 p95 My 22 2017

MacLachlan, P. Just dance. 2017
Publishers Weekly v264 no26 p180 Je 26 2017

MacLachlan, P. The Poet's Dog. 2016
Publishers Weekly v263 no49 p66 D 7 2016

Maclagan, M. and Buckley, A. Talking Baby. 2016
Publishers Weekly v263 no42 p65 O 17 2016

Maclaren, S. Summer on Sunset Ridge. 2017
Publishers Weekly v263 no48 p56 N 28 2016

MacLaverty, B. Midwinter Break. 2017
Publishers Weekly v264 no26 p150 Je 26 2017

MacLean, D. and Fassler, J. Light the dark. 2017
Publishers Weekly v264 no26 p168 Je 26 2017

MacLean, N. Democracy in chains. 2017
Nation v305 no7 p27-31 S 25 2017 K. Phillips-Fein
New Republic v248 no10 p46-50 O 2017 A. Wolfe
New York Times Book Review p19 Ag 20 2017 H. Boushey
Publishers Weekly v264 no15 p63 Ap 10 2017
Reason v49 no5 p66-71 O 2017 B. Doherty

MacLean, S. The Day of the Duchess. 2017
Publishers Weekly v264 no21 p78 My 22 2017

Maclear, K. and Pak, K. The fog. 2017
Publishers Weekly v264 no14 p75 Ap 3. 2017

Maclear, K. and Shapiro, E. Yak and Dove. 2017
New York Times Book Review p24 S 10 2017 P. H. Reynolds
Publishers Weekly v264 no29 p218 Jl 17 2017

Maclear, K. and Turnham, C. The wish tree. 2016
New York Times Book Review p19 D 18 2016 M. Russo

Maclear, K. Birds Art Life. 2017
Publishers Weekly v263 no44 p65 O 31 2016

MacLeod, A. All the Beloved Ghosts. 2017
Publishers Weekly v264 no8 p58 F 20 2017

MacLeod, B. and Leonard, S. Come to dust. 2017
Publishers Weekly v264 no18 p42 My 1 2017

MacLeod, B. Thirteen Views of the Suicide Woods. 2017
New York Times Book Review p42-3 Je 4 2017 T. Rafferty
Publishers Weekly v264 no5 p185 Ja 30 2017

MacLeod, J. T. and Waisman, S. Yossi and the monkeys. 2017
Publishers Weekly v264 no4 p78 Ja 23 2017

Macleod, S. Phil Spector. 2017
Publishers Weekly v264 no33 p62 Ag 14 2017

Macmillan, G. Odd Child Out. 2017
Publishers Weekly v264 no35 p103-4 Ag 28 2017

MacNaughton, L. A kiss before doomsday. 2017
Publishers Weekly v264 no21 p77 My 22 2017

Macnaughton, W. and Nosrat, S. Salt, fat, acid, heat. 2017
Publishers Weekly v264 no10 p20-31 Mr 6 2017 C. Swanso
Publishers Weekly v264 no6 p64 F 6 2017

Macnaughton, W. and Paul, C. The gutsy girl. 2016
Sierra v101 no4 p11 Jl/Ag 2016 A. Andrews

MacNeal, D. and Kennedy, M. Bugged. 2017
Publishers Weekly v264 no20 p49 My 15 2017
Science v356 no6342 p1007 Je 9 2017 N. F. Quinn
Scientific American v317 no1 p72 Jl 2017 A. Gawrylewski

MacNeal, S. E. The Paris spy. 2017
Publishers Weekly v264 no23 p32 Je 5 2017

Macomber, D. Any dream will do. 2017
Publishers Weekly v264 no27 p62 Jl 3 2017

Macor, A. Rewrite man. 2017
Publishers Weekly v264 no4 p69-70 Ja 23 2017

Macpherson, C. The change catalyst. 2017

People Management p51 Jl 2017

Macrae, M. Plaid and Plagiarism. 2016
Publishers Weekly v264 no40 p99 O 3 2016

MacSweeney, C. and Luiselli, V. The story of my teeth. 2015
Entertainment Weekly no1449 p62 Ja 20 2017

MacSweeney, C. and Navarro, E. A working woman. 2017
Publishers Weekly v264 no33 p46 Ag 14 2017

MacSweeney, C. and Saldaña París, D. Among strange victims. 2016
New York Times Book Review p34 N 20 2016 L. Wright

MacVeagh, T. The Blue Marauders. 2016
Publishers Weekly v264 no26 p180-2 Je 26 2017
Publishers Weekly v264 no31 p58e Jl 31 2017

Macy, B. Truevine. 2016
New York Times Book Review p13 O 23 2016 E. E. Baptist

Macy, M. Bearly Departed. 2017
Publishers Weekly v264 no16 p48-9 Ap 17 2017

Macy, S. and Payne, C. F. Miss Mary Reporting. 2014
Publishers Weekly v263 no49 p50 D 7 2016

Macy, S. Motor girls. 2016
Publishers Weekly v263 no46 p58 N 14 2016

Mad Genius Tips. 2016
Publishers Weekly v263 no42 p63-4 O 17 2016

Madden, D. The World Beyond. 2017
Publishers Weekly v264 no38 p49-50 S 18 2017

Madden, T. F. Istanbul. 2016
National Review v68 no24 p38-40 D 31 2016 C. Berlinski
Publishers Weekly v263 no44 p66 O 31 2016

Maddox, B. Reading the Rocks. 2017
Publishers Weekly v264 no38 p63 S 18 2017

Maden, M. Tom Clancy point of contact. 2017
Publishers Weekly v264 no26 p12 Je 26 2017 C. Juris

Mader, C. R. and Mader, C. R. Stowaway in a sleigh. 2016
Publishers Weekly v263 no39 p88 S 26 2016

Madison, D. In my kitchen. 2017
Publishers Weekly v263 no47 p101-2 N 21 2016

Madley, B. An American Genocide. 2016
New York Review of Books v63 no18 p70-3 N 24 2016 P. Nabokov

Madrygin, R. The Solace of Trees. 2017
Publishers Weekly v264 no22 p43 My 29 2017

Madsbjerg, C. Sensemaking. 2017
Harvard Business Review v95 no4 p144-5 Jl/Ag 2017 J. Olejarz
Publishers Weekly v263 no52 p113 D 19 2016

Maes, I. and Dyson, K. Architects of the Euro. 2016
Foreign Affairs v95 no6 p182-3 N/D 2016 A. Moravcsik

Maese, F. and others. A midsummer night's dream. 2012
Publishers Weekly v264 no34 p14 Ag 21 2017 J. Milliot

Maffei, Y. My halal kitchen. 2016
Chicago v65 no12 p62 D 2016 C. Boers

Mafi, M. A little book of mystical secrets. 2017
Publishers Weekly v264 no7 p70 F 13 2017

Mafi, T. Furthermore. 2016
Publishers Weekly v263 no44 p72 O 31 2016
Publishers Weekly v263 no49 p78 D 7 2016

Magargle, N. A Time to Die, A Time to Live. 2017
Publishers Weekly v264 no33 p76 Ag 14 2017
Publishers Weekly v264 no35 p77d-e Ag 28 2017

Magariel, D. One of the boys. 2017
New Yorker v93 no8 p68 Ap 10 2017
New York Times Book Review p10 Ap 23 2017 A. Ruiz-Camacho
New York Times Book Review p23 Ap 30 2017
Publishers Weekly v264 no4 p54 Ja 23 2017

Magella, A. and others. Shadows on the lake. 2016
Publishers Weekly v263 no52 p100-1 D 19 2016

Maggor, N. Brahmin capitalism. 2017
Nation v304 no18 p24-8 Je 19 2017 E. Foner

Magli, G. Archaeoastronomy. 2015
Physics Today v69 no10 p58-61 O 2016

Magliaro, E. and Chien, C. Things to do. 2017
Publishers Weekly v263 no46 p54 N 14 2016

Magness, S. and Stulberg, B. Peak Performance. 2017
Publishers Weekly v264 no15 p64-5 Ap 10 2017

Magoon, S. and Bernstein, A. I have a balloon. 2017
Publishers Weekly v264 no27 p74 Jl 3 2017

Maguire, M. Three Days Breathing. 2016
Publishers Weekly v263 no43 p43-9 O 24 2016

New York v49 no22 p98-9 O 31 2016

Mangano, J. Inventing joy. 2017
Good Housekeeping v265 no5 p55-6 N 2017
Publishers Weekly v264 no39 p100 S 25 2017

Mangelsen, T. D. and Johnsgard, P. A. A chorus of cranes. 2015
Nebraska Life v21 no2 p77 Mr/Ap 2017 N. Buck

Mangina, J. L. Revelation. 2010
Publishers Weekly v263 no40 p100 O 3 2016

Manginis, G. Mount Sinai. 2016
History Today v66 no10 p64 O 2016 A. Cameron

Mangold, P. What the British Did. 2016
History Today v67 no3 p57 Mr 2017 R. Carver

Manguso, S. 300 arguments. 2017
Nation v304 no18 p42-4 Je 19 2017 C. Shane
New Republic v248 no3 p66-7 Mr 2017 R. Syme
Publishers Weekly v263 no50 p60-1 D 5 2016

Manion, M. Information for autocrats. 2015
Foreign Affairs v95 no6 p192-3 N/D 2016 A. J. Nathan

Mankell, H. and Thompson, L. Quicksand. 2016
Publishers Weekly v263 no46 p47-8 N 14 2016

Manley, C. and Berube, K. The summer Nick taught his cats to read. 2016
Publishers Weekly v263 no49 p41-2 D 7 2016
Publishers Weekly v263 no49 p41 D 7 2016

Mann, B. S. and Larabee, M. The pacific crest trail. 2016
Backpacker v45 no1 p84 Ja 2017

Mann, G. and others. Clockwork Cairo. 2017
Publishers Weekly v264 no18 p43 My 1 2017

Mann, J. K. and Mann, J. K. Sam and Jump. 2016
Publishers Weekly v263 no49 p24-5 D 7 2016

Mann, J. K. and McGhee, A. Percy, dog of destiny. 2017
Publishers Weekly v264 no4 p79 Ja 23 2017

Mann, M. E. and Toles, T. The madhouse effect. 2016
National Review v69 no3 p23-5 F 20 2017 I. Tuttle
Skeptical Inquirer v41 no2 p61 Mr/Ap 2017 B. Radford
Skeptical Inquirer v41 no5 p60-1 S/O 2017 R. Ladendorf

Mann, M. Yawn. 2017
Publishers Weekly v264 no7 p61-2 F 13 2017

Mann, S. and Mann, S. Remembered light. 2016
New York Times Book Review p62-3 D 4 2016 L. Sante

Mann, T. E. and others. One Nation After Trump. 2017
New York Times Book Review p22 O 1 2017 A. Berman

Mann, W. J. The wars of the Roosevelts. 2016
Foreign Affairs v96 no3 p161 My/Je 2017 W. Russell Mead
Publishers Weekly v263 no43 p73 O 24 2016

Manning, M. J. Laundry day. 2012
New York Times Book Review p16 Mr 12 2017 S. Hunt
Publishers Weekly v263 no50 p71 D 5 2016

Manning, M. One man's dark. 2016
Publishers Weekly v263 no42 p49 O 17 2016

Mansbach, A. and others. Jake the fake keeps it real. 2017
Publishers Weekly v263 no52 p124 D 19 2016

Manseau, P. Songs for the butcher's daughter. 2008
Publishers Weekly v264 no35 p96-7 Ag 28 2017 M. Dery

Manseau, P. The apparitionists. 2017
Harper's Magazine p83-5 O 2017 C. Smallwood
Publishers Weekly v264 no29 p206-8 Jl 17 2017
Publishers Weekly v264 no35 p96-7 Ag 28 2017 M. Dery

Manseau, P. Vows. 2005
Publishers Weekly v264 no35 p96-7 Ag 28 2017 M. Dery

Mansel, P. Aleppo. 2016
History Today v66 no10 p65 O 2016 R. Carver

Mansfield, A. and others. One lonely fish. 2017
Publishers Weekly v263 no48 p69 N 28 2016

Manson, M. The subtle art of not giving a fu*k. 2016
New York Times Book Review p31 N 6 2016 J. Newman
Publishers Weekly v264 no31 p34-5 Jl 31 2017 M. Burnett
Publishers Weekly v264 no31 p6 Jl 31 2017 J. Boog
Publishers Weekly v264 no33 p13 Ag 14 2017 C. Juris

Mantchev, L. and Yum, H. Someday, Narwhal. 2017
Publishers Weekly v264 no34 p108-9 Ag 21 2017

Manteith, J. and Shifman, M. Physics in a mad world. 2016
New York Review of Books v63 no19 p52-4 D 8 2016 J. Bernstein

Manton, E. and Bregman, R. Utopia for realists. 2017
Publishers Weekly v264 no5 p193 Ja 30 2017

Manuali, T. B. and others. Lidia's celebrate like an Italian. 2017

Publishers Weekly v264 no36 p83 S 4 2017

Manus, P. Fickle. 2017
Publishers Weekly v263 no45 p42 N 7 2016

Manyika, S. L. Like a Mule Bringing Ice Cream to the Sun. 2017
New Yorker v93 no10 p95 Ap 24 2017

Manzer, J. D. Willie Mae. 2016
Missouri Life v43 no7 p18 D 2016/Ja 2017

Manzetti, A. The Garden of Delight. 2017
Publishers Weekly v264 no6 p51 F 6 2017

Mapa, L. Duran Duran, Imelda Marcos, and Me. 2017
Publishers Weekly v264 no24 p49-50 Je 12 2017

Mapes, L. V. Witness tree. 2017
Natural History v125 no4 p47 Ap 2017 L. A. Marschall
Publishers Weekly v264 no9 p91 F 27 2017

Mara, N. and Vidal, A. So many feet. 2017
Publishers Weekly v264 no21 p90 My 22 2017
Publishers Weekly v264 no5 p26-168 Ja 30 2017

Marais, B. Hum if you don't know the words. 2017
O, The Oprah Magazine p91 S 2017 L. Haber
Publishers Weekly v264 no18 p33 My 1 2017

Maran, M. The new old me. 2017
O, The Oprah Magazine p93 Ap 2017 E. Vanderhoof
Publishers Weekly v263 no52 p112 D 19 2016

Marcal, K. and Vogel, S. Who cooked Adam Smith's dinner? 2016
New York Times Book Review p24 Je 18 2017 J. Khatib

Marchant, F. Said not said. 2017
Publishers Weekly v264 no16 p42-3 Ap 17 2017

Marchant, J. Cure. 2016
Entertainment Weekly no1454/1455 p100-1 F 24 2017 T. Jordan

Marche, S. and Fulford, S. The unmade bed. 2016
New York Times Book Review p10 Ap 2 2017 S. T. Loh

Marchetta, M. Tell the truth, shame the devil. 2016
New York Times Book Review p33 N 20 2016 M. Stasio

Marciniak, E. and Greg, W. Swallowing mercury. 2017
Publishers Weekly v264 no28 p60 Jl 10 2017

Marcoci, R. Louise Lawler. 2017
Art in America v105 no5 p57 My 2017

Marcum, A. Close to Om. 2018
Publishers Weekly v264 no38 p66 S 18 2017

Marcus, G. The old, weird America. 2011
U.S. Catholic v82 no2 p39 F 2017

Mares, D. R. and Trinkunas, H. A. Aspirational power. 2016
Foreign Affairs v95 no6 p185 N/D 2016 R. Feinberg

Maresca, M. R. An Import of Intrigue. 2016
Publishers Weekly v263 no40 p104-5 O 3 2016

Margalit, A. On betrayal. 2017
Christian Century v134 no10 p49-50 My 10 2017 D. O'Brien
New York Review of Books v64 no8 p52-4 My 11 2017 M. Walzer

Margolin, L. and others. Can I Wear My Kippah on Job Interviews? 2015
Publishers Weekly v263 no46 p52 N 14 2016
Publishers Weekly v263 no52 p90e D 19 2016

Margolis, S. Presidents' Day. 2017
Publishers Weekly v263 no51 p126-7 D 12 2016

Mari, C. and Brown, J. K. Ocean of Storms. 2016
Publishers Weekly v263 no43 p62 O 24 2016

Mariani, P. The whole harmonium. 2016
Christian Century v134 no9 p36-7 Ap 26 2017 J. Johnson

Marías, J. and Costa, M. J. Thus bad begins. 2016
New York Times Book Review p17 N 27 2016 K. Mahajan
New York Times Book Review p78 D 4 2016
New York v49 no24 p157 N 28 2016 B. K.
Publishers Weekly v264 no9 p97 F 27 2017
Time v188 no20 p55 N 14 2016 S. Begley

Marin, C. Cheech is not my real name. 2017
Publishers Weekly v263 no51 p135 D 12 2016
Publishers Weekly v263 no51 p17 D 12 2016 S. Maughan

Marino, G. Splotch. 2017
New York Times Book Review p14 Je 18 2017 T. Lichtenheld

Marion, I. The burning world. 2017
Publishers Weekly v263 no44 p57 O 31 2016

Mariotti, S. L. and Lane, J. H. A political companion to Marilynne Robinson. 2016
Christian Century v134 no19 p30-3 S 13 2017 B. J. Dueholm

Marissen, M. Bach & God. 2016
New Yorker v92 no43 p66-73 Ja 2 2017 A. Ross

McKay, J. J. Discovering the Mammoth. 2017
Publishers Weekly v264 no24 p55 Je 12 2017
McKean, D. and McKean, D. Black Dog. 2016
Publishers Weekly v263 no41 p65 O 10 2016
McKean, D. and others. The Weight of Words. 2017
Publishers Weekly v264 no34 p96 Ag 21 2017
McKee, A. How to be happy at work. 2017
People Management p46 Ag 2017
McKee, H. J. Introduction to Early American Masonry, Stone, Brick, Mortar, and Plaster. 1980
Old House Journal v45 no5 p8 Ag 2017
McKee, R. Dialogue. 2016
Publishers Weekly v263 no42 p23-30 O 17 2016 C. Teicher
McKelvey, K. and Lonergan, K. Dandelions. 2015
Publishers Weekly v264 no40 p113-4 O 2 2017
McKendrick, S. and Doyle, K. The art of the Bible. 2016
Christian Century v134 no2 p42 Ja 18 2017
McKenna, A. B. and Pérez, R. K. Jane. 2017
Publishers Weekly v264 no39 p94 S 25 2017
McKenna, J. Voices from the Easter Rising. 2017
Military History v34 no4 p72 N 2017
McKenna, L. and others. Christmas With My Cowboy. 2017
Publishers Weekly v264 no36 p74-5 S 4 2017
McKenna, L. Wind River Cowboy. 2017
Publishers Weekly v264 no9 p84 F 27 2017
McKenna, L. Wind River rancher. 2016
Publishers Weekly v263 no50 p55-6 D 5 2016
McKenna, L. Wrangler's challenge. 2017
Publishers Weekly v264 no39 p91-2 S 25 2017
McKenna, M. Big chicken. 2017
Science News v192 no5 p30 S 30 2017 C. Vanchieri
McKenzie-Jones, P. R. Clyde Warrior. 2015
American Indian Quarterly v41 no1 p93-5 Wint 2017 D. M. Cobb
McKeon, K. Jackie's girl. 2017
Publishers Weekly v264 no21 p14 My 22 2017 C. Juris
McKeown, J. C. A cabinet of ancient medical curiosities. 2017
Publishers Weekly v263 no43 p68 O 24 2016
McKevett, G. A. Every Body on Deck. 2017
Publishers Weekly v264 no11 p60-1 Mr 13 2017
McKibbens, R. blud. 2017
Publishers Weekly v264 no38 p50 S 18 2017
McKinlay, J. Death in the stacks. 2017
Publishers Weekly v264 no39 p87 S 25 2017
McKinley, M. and Avery, S. Ice Capades. 2017
Publishers Weekly v264 no39 p100 S 25 2017
McKinney, C. Do you know what a book publicist does? 2017
Publishers Weekly v264 no29 p212 Jl 17 2017
Publishers Weekly v264 no31 p58d Jl 31 2017
McKinty, A. Police at the station and they don't look friendly. 2017
Publishers Weekly v263 no47 p30 N 21 2016 J. F.
Publishers Weekly v264 no26 p174 Je 26 2017
McKissack, P. and Pinkney, J. B. Let's clap, jump, sing, and shout; dance, spin, and turn it out! 2017
Publishers Weekly v263 no46 p55 N 14 2016
McLaird, J. D. Hugh Glass. 2016
South Dakota Magazine v32 no4 p63 N/D 2016
McLane, M. N. Some say. 2017
Harper's Magazine v335 no2006 p81-3 Jl 2017 C. Smallwood
Publishers Weekly v264 no26 p153-4 Je 26 2017
McLaren, M. and McLaren, M. Pigeon P.I. 2017
Publishers Weekly v264 no32 p69 Ag 7 2017
McLaren, M. and McLaren, M. Rabbit magic. 2017
Publishers Weekly v263 no43 p74 O 24 2016
McLaughlin, C. and Kennedy-Moore, E. Growing friendships. 2017
Publishers Weekly v264 no20 p57 My 15 2017
McLaughlin, H. Grand slam. 2017
Publishers Weekly v264 no26 p163-4 Je 26 2017
McLaughlin, J. and Pla, S. J. The someday birds. 2017
Publishers Weekly v263 no45 p62 N 7 2016
McLaughlin, J. Dare to Lie. 2017
Publishers Weekly v264 no1 p43 Ja 2 2017
McLaughlin, L. and So, M. Wonderful You. 2017
Publishers Weekly v264 no6 p66 F 6 2017
McLayne, A. Highland Promise. 2017
Publishers Weekly v264 no34 p98 Ag 21 2017

McLean, A. and Vásquez, J. G. Lovers on All Saints' Day. 2015
New York Review of Books v63 no16 p68-9 O 27 2016 D. Gallagher
McLean, A. and Vásquez, J. G. Reputations. 2016
New Yorker v92 no32 p101 O 10 2016
New York Review of Books v63 no16 p68-9 O 27 2016 D. Gallagher
New York Times Book Review p11 O 9 2016 Yiyun Li
New York v49 no21 p120 O 17 2016 B. K.
McLean, P. E. The Soak. 2017
Publishers Weekly v264 no9 p74 F 27 2017
McLellan, E. Controlled Burn. 2017
Publishers Weekly v264 no26 p164 Je 26 2017
McLellan, G. B. and Zong, G. Mrs. McBee leaves room 3. 2017
Publishers Weekly v264 no7 p73 F 13 2017
McLelland, K. and Gifford, C. What's below? 2017
Publishers Weekly v263 no48 p69 N 28 2016
McLemore, A. When the moon was ours. 2016
New York Times Book Review p35 N 13 2016 J. Giles
McLemore, A. Wild beauty. 2017
Publishers Weekly v264 no36 p102 S 4 2017
McLemore, L. L. The Battle of New Orleans in history and memory. 2017
Louisiana Life v37 no3 p101 Ja/F 2017 J. Frois
McLeod, A. Astronomy in the ancient world. 2016
Physics Today v70 no9 p61-2 S 2017 G. Aldana
McMahon, J. R. Inish Clare. 2017
Publishers Weekly v264 no35 p111 Ag 28 2017
McMeekin, S. The Russian Revolution. 2017
Nation v305 no1 p40-3 Jl 3 2017 S. Pinkham
New York Times Book Review p14-5 Je 11 2017 G. Feifer
Publishers Weekly v264 no16 p59-60 Ap 17 2017
McMenamin, D. and Windhorst, B. Return of the king. 2017
Publishers Weekly v264 no17 p13 Ap 24 2017 C. Juris
McMichael, A. J. Climate change and the health of nations. 2017
Maclean's no1 p60-1 F 17 2017 B. Bethune
New Yorker v93 no13 p83 My 15 2017
Publishers Weekly v263 no46 p45 N 14 2016
Science v355 no6323 p355 Ja 27 2017 A. Makri
McMillan, C. The emancipation of Cecily McMillan. 2016
Progressive v81 no10 p39-41 N 2016 W. Meyer
McMillan, C. The necklace. 2017
Publishers Weekly v264 no19 p35 My 8 2017
McMillan, T. How Stella got her groove back. 1996
Time v190 no7 p53 Ag 21 2017 S. Begley
McMillan, T. I Almost Forgot About You. 2016
AARP: The Magazine v59 no4A p14 Je/Jl 2016 D. Donahue
McMorrow, T. E. and Ransome, J. Nutcracker in Harlem. 2016
Publishers Weekly v264 no36 p99 S 4 2017
McMullan, J. and others. I'm smart! 2017
Publishers Weekly v264 no22 p66 My 29 2017
McMullan, K. and Nyeu, T. Mama's kisses. 2017
Publishers Weekly v263 no52 p122 D 19 2016
McMullen, B. Mrs. Smith's Spy School for Girls. 2017
Publishers Weekly v264 no20 p56 My 15 2017
McNally, B. K. Wounded Warrior, Wounded Wife. 2016
Publishers Weekly v264 no5 p195 Ja 30 2017
Publishers Weekly v264 no9 p52 F 27 2017
Publishers Weekly v264 no9 p66k F 27 2017
McNally, J. and Pettit, K. Girls in the moon. 2016
Publishers Weekly v263 no40 p126-7 O 3 2016
McNamara, E. and Rankin, A. Toss your own salad. 2017
Publishers Weekly v264 no16 p61-2 Ap 17 2017
McNeal, L. The incident on the bridge. 2016
Publishers Weekly v263 no49 p114 D 7 2016
McNease, M. Last Room at the Cliff's Edge. 2016
Publishers Weekly v264 no13 p64a-b Mr 27 2017
Publishers Weekly v264 no8 p69-70 F 20 2017
McNeela, P. The Lost Son. 2016
Publishers Weekly v264 no35 p124 Ag 28 2017
Publishers Weekly v264 no39 p80c S 25 2017
McNeil, K. and Doerrfeld, C. Sleepy Toes. 2017
Publishers Weekly v263 no50 p72 D 5 2016
McNeil, R. and Machado de Assis Stories. 2014
Weekly Standard v22 no14 p30-3 D 12 2016 J. Epstein
McNicholl, D. The Moment of Truth. 2017

Menchin, S. and Phelan, M. What are you waiting for? 2017
Publishers Weekly v264 no14 p75 Ap 3. 2017
Mendelsohn, D. An odyssey. 2017
New York Review of Books v64 no16 p28-9 O 26 2017 P. Green
Publishers Weekly v264 no29 p211 Jl 17 2017
Mendelson, A. Chow chop suey. 2016
New York Times Book Review p19 Ja 8 2017 C. Kummer
Mendes, N. and others. Chiltern Firehouse. 2017
Publishers Weekly v264 no8 p79 F 20 2017
Menefee, C. and Arkush, M. Losing Isn't Everything. 2016
Publishers Weekly v263 no39 p79 S 26 2016
Sports Illustrated v125 no19 p28 D 12 2016 T. Keith
Meng Qingjin and Chiappe, L. M. Birds of stone. 2016
Science News v190 no11 p29 N 26 2016
Menkedick, S. Homing instincts. 2017
Publishers Weekly v264 no5 p189 Ja 30 2017
Menon, S. Choices. 2016
Foreign Affairs v96 no2 p187-8 Mr/Ap 2017
Menon, S. When Dimple met Rishi. 2017
Publishers Weekly v264 no13 p102 Mr 27 2017
Mensch, P. and others. The Age of Caesar. 2017
American Conservative v16 no2 p55-7 Mr/Ap 2017 S. Donoghue
Mentzel, C. Voice lessons. 2017
Publishers Weekly v264 no41 p22-3 O 9 2017 S. Maughan
Menzies, A. and Backman, F. And every morning the way home
  gets longer and longer. 2016
Publishers Weekly v263 no40 p95 O 3 2016
Menzies, A. and Lapidus, J. Stockholm delete. 2017
Publishers Weekly v264 no8 p68 F 20 2017
Menzies-Pike, C. The Long Run. 2017
Publishers Weekly v264 no4 p69 Ja 23 2017
Merali, Z. A big bang in a little room. 2017
Discover v38 no3 p20 Ap 2017 G. Tarlach
Science News v191 no8 p34 Ap 29 2017
Merbeth, K. S. Raid. 2017
Publishers Weekly v264 no24 p46 Je 12 2017
Mercer, J. Gay Pornography. 2017
Advocate no1093 p59-60 O/N 2017 J. Anderson-Minshall
Merchant, B. The one device. 2017
New York Times Book Review p1-22 Je 25 2017 L. Grossman
New York Times Book Review p22 Jl 2 2017
Time v189 no24 p18 Je 26 2017 S. Begley
Merchant, C. Spare the birds! 2016
Weekly Standard v22 no13 p30-2 D 5 2016 C. Irmscher
Merchant, N. The Power of Onlyness. 2017
Publishers Weekly v264 no22 p54 My 29 2017
Mercier, H. and Sperber, D. The enigma of reason. 2017
New Yorker v93 no2 p66-71 F 27 2017 E. Kolbert
Science v356 no6338 p589 My 12 2017 D. Frey
Merigeau, P. and Benderson, B. Jean Renoir. 2017
Film Comment v53 no1 p93 Ja/F 2017 M. Whittle
New York Review of Books v64 no14 p71-2 S 28 2017 L. Robson
Merkel, J. Colorful characters of St. Louis. 2016
Missouri Life v44 no6 p16 S 2017 E. Beyers
Merkin, D. This close to happy. 2017
America v216 no5 p42-3 Mr 6 2017 W. Massey
New Yorker v93 no4 p75 Mr 13 2017
New York Times Book Review p1-20 F 5 2017 A. Solomon
New York Times Book Review p23 F 12 2017
New York v50 no7 p84-5 Ap 3 2017
Publishers Weekly v263 no46 p44 N 14 2016
Mermin, N. D. Why quark rhymes with pork, and other scientific
  diversions. 2016
Physics Today v69 no11 p57-8 N 2016 S. Hossenfelder
Merridale, C. Lenin on the train. 2017
Foreign Affairs v96 no3 p168 My/Je 2017 R. Legvold
History Today v67 no3 p62 Mr 2017 P. Waldron
Nation v305 no1 p40-3 Jl 3 2017 S. Pinkham
New York Times Book Review p15 Je 11 2017 J. Rubenstein
Publishers Weekly v264 no3 p49 Ja 16 2017
Merrifield, A. The amateur. 2017
In These Times v41 no7 p38 Jl 2017
Merrill, A. and others. Everyday Africa. 2016
Vanity Fair v59 no1 p98 Holiday 2017 A. Tepper
Merrill, M. R. Redeeming Ruth. 2017
Christianity Today v61 no7 p81 S 2017

Merrill, R. Gertrude, Gumshoe. 2017
Publishers Weekly v264 no36 p69 S 4 2017
Publishers Weekly v264 no39 p80a S 25 2017
Merrill, R. Introducing Gertrude Gumshoe. 2016
Publishers Weekly v264 no7 p54 F 13 2017
Publishers Weekly v264 no9 p66e F 27 2017
Merrill, R. More Jesus Diet. 2016
Publishers Weekly v263 no41 p73 O 10 2016
Merritt, C. H. Healing spiritual wounds. 2017
America v217 no7 p28-33 O 2 2017 K. Oakes
Publishers Weekly v263 no51 p142 D 12 2016
Merritt, G. Slippery slope. 2017
New York Review of Books v64 no15 p44-5 O 12 2017 A. Apple-
  baum
Merrow, J. L. Wake Up Call. 2017
Publishers Weekly v264 no7 p56 F 13 2017
Merry, R. W. President McKinley. 2017
Publishers Weekly v264 no22 p54 My 29 2017
Merullo, R. The delight of being ordinary. 2017
Publishers Weekly v264 no7 p46-7 F 13 2017
Meschenmoser, S. and Meschenmoser, S. Pug Man's 3 Wishes.
  2016
Publishers Weekly v263 no49 p39-40 D 7 2016
Meschenmoser, S. Gordon and Tapir. 2016
Publishers Weekly v263 no49 p22 D 7 2016
Meshon, A. and Meshon, A. Delivery. 2016
Publishers Weekly v263 no45 p60 N 7 2016
Meshon, A. and Meshon, A. The best days are dog days. 2016
Publishers Weekly v263 no49 p31 D 7 2016
Mesrobian, C. and Maciel, A. Just a girl. 2017
Publishers Weekly v264 no1 p59 Ja 2 2017
Messer, C. and Messer, C. Grumpy pants. 2016
Publishers Weekly v263 no49 p22 D 7 2016
Messeri, L. Placing outer space. 2016
Physics Today v70 no3 p59-60 Mr 2017 M. Shindell
Messier, M. and Pratt, P. The branch. 2016
New York Times Book Review p29 N 13 2016
Messineo, T. The Fire by Night. 2017
Publishers Weekly v263 no39 p63 S 26 2016
Messner, K. and Neal, C. S. Over and under the pond. 2017
Publishers Weekly v264 no8 p85 F 20 2017
Messner, K. and Ross, H. Fergus and Zeke. 2017
Publishers Weekly v264 no23 p53 Je 5 2017
Messner, R. and others. Mountains. 2016
Natural History v125 no1 p40-3 D 2016/Ja 2017 L. A. Marschall
Messud, C. The burning girl. 2017
Glamour v115 no9 p40 S 2017 J. Harman
Maclean's v130 no8 p62-3 S 2017 E. Donaldson
New Yorker v93 no31 p68 O 9 2017
New York Review of Books v64 no14 p53-4 S 28 2017 M. Gorra
New York Times Book Review p12 S 10 2017 L. Lippman
O, The Oprah Magazine p97 O 2017 L. Schillinger
Publishers Weekly v264 no24 p36 Je 12 2017
Vanity Fair v59 no9 p138 S 2017 S. Crosley
Metaxas, E. Martin Luther. 2017
Publishers Weekly v264 no33 p74 Ag 14 2017
Metcalf, J. The museum at the end of the world. 2016
Maclean's v129 no41 p57-8 O 17 2016 M. Doherty
Metivier, G. and Van Wagoner, T. Cody and Grandpa's Christmas
  tradition. 2016
Publishers Weekly v263 no39 p93 S 26 2016
Metzger, N. and Scalzi, J. Miniatures. 2016
Publishers Weekly v263 no40 p103 O 3 2016
Meyer, D. and Seegers, K. L. Fever. 2017
Publishers Weekly v264 no28 p64 Jl 10 2017
Meyer, E. D. and others. Pierre Chareau. 2016
Publishers Weekly v263 no48 p57-64 N 28 2016
Meyer, G. J. The world remade. 2017
America v216 no9 p20-2 Ap 24 2017 J. Matteson
Publishers Weekly v264 no1 p50-1 Ja 2 2017
Meyer, M. Heartless. 2016
Entertainment Weekly no1440 p62 N 18 2016 J. Goodman
New York Times Book Review p23 D 25 2016
New York Times Book Review p23 Ja 1 2017
New York Times Book Review p35 D 11 2016
Publishers Weekly v263 no41 p20-1 O 10 2016

Meyer, M. The road to Sleeping Dragon. 2017
Publishers Weekly v264 no35 p46 Ag 28 2017 C. J.
Meyer, P. The Son. 2013
American Cowboy v23 no6 p23 Ap/My 2017
Meyer, S. The chemist. 2016
New York Times Book Review p78 D 4 2016
Publishers Weekly v264 no14 p72 Ap 3. 2017
Meyers, R. S. The widow of Wall Street. 2017
Publishers Weekly v264 no6 p42 F 6 2017
Meyers, W. and others. Man of peace. 2016
Publishers Weekly v264 no10 p48 Mr 6 2017
Tricycle: The Buddhist Review v27 no1 p94-6 Fall 2017 D. Zigmond
Mezrich, B. The 37th parallel. 2016
New York Times Book Review p30 N 27 2016 S. Kean
Mezrich, B. Woolly. 2017
Publishers Weekly v264 no20 p50 My 15 2017
Saturday Evening Post v289 no4 p24 Jl/Ag 2017
Scientific American v317 no2 p80 Ag 2017 A. Gawrylewski
Michel, K. and Van Schaik, C. The good book of human nature. 2016
Commonweal v144 no10 p34-7 Je 2 2017 L. T. Johnson
New York Review of Books v63 no16 p35-7 O 27 2016 G. W. Bowersock
Michele, M. Children of Hellions. 2016
Publishers Weekly v264 no7 p58 F 13 2017
Publishers Weekly v264 no9 p66b F 27 2017
Micheli, J. Cancer Is Funny. 2016
Christian Century v134 no10 p34-5 My 10 2017 D. A. Thompson
Michels, E. The Wicked Heir. 2017
Publishers Weekly v264 no19 p45 My 8 2017
Michelson, A. On the eve of the future. 2017
Film Comment v53 no3 p78 My/Je 2017 V. Lucca
Michelson, R. and Gudeon, K. The language of angels. 2015
Publishers Weekly v263 no48 p70-1 N 28 2016
Michna-Bales, J. Through darkness to light. 2017
Orion Magazine v36 no2 p62-3 Mr/Ap 2017 T. Brorby
Michnik, A. and others. Opposing Forces. 2016
Foreign Affairs v96 no1 p170-1 Ja/F 2017 R. Legvold
Michon, P. and others. Rimbaud the son. 2013
New York Review of Books v64 no14 p47-9 S 28 2017 W. Mason
Michon, P. and others. Small lives. 2008
New York Review of Books v64 no14 p47-9 S 28 2017 W. Mason
Michon, P. and others. The eleven. 2013
New York Review of Books v64 no14 p47-9 S 28 2017 W. Mason
Micklos, J. and McFarland, C. One leaf, two leaves, count with me. 2017
Publishers Weekly v264 no30 p58 Jl 24 2017
Middleton, D. and others. Trayaurus and the enchanted crystal. 2016
Publishers Weekly v263 no45 p14 N 7 2016 C. Juris
Midorikawa, E. and Sweeney, E. C. A secret sisterhood. 2017
Atlantic v320 no4 p49 N 2017 A. Hulbert
Publishers Weekly v264 no32 p63 Ag 7 2017
Miedoso, A. and Rivas, V. The haunted house next door. 2017
Publishers Weekly v264 no39 p106 S 25 2017
Miéville, C. October. 2017
Progressive v81 no6 p63-5 Ag/S 2017 N. Stockwell
Publishers Weekly v264 no10 p50 Mr 6 2017
Publishers Weekly v264 no14 p44-5 Ap 3. 2017 N. Zacek
Mignola, M. and others. Hellboy. 2017
Publishers Weekly v264 no16 p54 Ap 17 2017
Mignola, M. and Sniegoski, T. Grim Death and Bill the Electrocuted Criminal. 2017
Publishers Weekly v263 no50 p53 D 5 2016
Migoya, F. and Myhrvold, N. P. Modernist Bread. 2017
Publishers Weekly v264 no33 p22-41 Ag 14 2017 D. Lefferts
Miguéns, M. Á. and Keating, J. Shark lady. 2017
Publishers Weekly v264 no23 p51 Je 5 2017
Migunov, Y. and others. Monday starts on Saturday. 2017
Publishers Weekly v264 no35 p109-10 Ag 28 2017
Milanes, J. The Victoria in my head. 2017
Publishers Weekly v264 no26 p182 Je 26 2017
Milbank, J. and Pabst, A. The politics of virtue. 2016
Christian Century v134 no10 p45-6 My 10 2017 S. Wells
Milburn, G. J. and Bowen, W. P. Quantum optomechanics. 2016

Physics Today v70 no2 p58-60 F 2017 P. Meystre
Miles, A. The Gate to Everything. 2016
Publishers Weekly v263 no41 p63 O 10 2016
Publishers Weekly v263 no43 p50b O 24 2016
Miles, D. The Tale of the Axe. 2016
History Today v66 no10 p57-8 O 2016 A. Robinson
Miles, K. Quakeland. 2017
Publishers Weekly v264 no26 p170 Je 26 2017
Science v357 no6351 p555 Ag 11 2017 R. J. Murnane
Scientific American v317 no2 p80 Ag 2017 A. Marks
Time v190 no8 p58 Ag 28 2017 N. Hopper
Miles, M. and Clement, J. Screen schooled. 2017
Publishers Weekly v264 no34 p107 Ag 21 2017
Miles, M. R. The Long Goodbye. 2017
Christian Century v134 no9 p37 Ap 26 2017
Miles, T. The dawn of Detroit. 2017
Publishers Weekly v264 no32 p60 Ag 7 2017
Publishers Weekly v264 no35 p51 Ag 28 2017 J. Rosen
Miles, V. and Busquets, M. This too shall pass. 2016
New York Times Book Review p28 Mr 12 2017 J. Khatib
Miles, V. and Paz Soldán, E. Norte. 2016
New York Times Book Review p34 N 20 2016 L. Wright
Milevski, L. and others. MWD. 2017
Publishers Weekly v263 no47 p111 N 21 2016
Milevski, L. The evolution of modern grand strategic thought. 2016
Foreign Affairs v96 no1 p161-2 Ja/F 2017 L. D. Freedman
Miley, M. Murder in Disguise. 2017
Publishers Weekly v264 no25 p95-6 Je 19 2017
Miley, M. Renting Silence. 2016
Publishers Weekly v263 no42 p54 O 17 2016
Millard, C. Hero of the empire. 2016
Military History v33 no6 p72 Mr 2017 D. Saunders
New York Times Book Review p14 O 9 2016 A. Von Tunzelmann
New York Times Book Review p24 Je 11 2017 J. Khatib
New York Times Book Review p26 O 16 2016
Miller, A. The Crossing. 2015
New Yorker v93 no13 p83 My 15 2017
New York Times Book Review p16 Ja 29 2017 C. Messud
Miller, B. A Bustle in the Hedgerow. 2016
Publishers Weekly v264 no22 p48-9 My 29 2017
Publishers Weekly v264 no26 p146a Je 26 2017
Miller, B. The Aliens Are Coming! 2016
Science v354 no6311 p424 O 28 2016 M. Huerta
Miller, C. and Turner, K. But my family would never eat vegan! 2016
Publishers Weekly v263 no45 p56 N 7 2016
Miller, C. Up All Night. 2012
Commonweal v143 no19 p30-1 D 2 2016 G. Steinfels
Miller, D. A. Hidden Hitchcock. 2016
Film Quarterly v70 no4 p135-7 Summ 2017 B. Parker
Miller, D. AWOL on the Appalachian trail. 2011
Backpacker v45 no1 p16 Ja 2017
Miller, D. B. The girl in green. 2017
Publishers Weekly v263 no46 p29 N 14 2016
Miller, D. Strangers in our midst. 2016
New Yorker v92 no35 p84-9 O 31 2016 K. Sanneh
Miller, E. J. The news from the end of the world. 2017
Publishers Weekly v263 no51 p121 D 12 2016
Miller, F. and Darrow, G. Hard boiled. 2017
Publishers Weekly v264 no39 p94 S 25 2017
Miller, J. and Simmons, G. Bringing it home. 2017
Publishers Weekly v264 no34 p105 Ag 21 2017
Miller, J. The chapel car bride. 2017
Publishers Weekly v264 no9 p85 F 27 2017
Miller, K. and Saveri, L. The Newsstand. 2016
Art in America v105 no3 p63 Mr 2017
Miller, K. and Segel, J. Otherworld. 2017
Publishers Weekly v264 no38 p72 S 18 2017
Miller, K. Augustown. 2017
New Yorker v93 no14 p88-9 My 22 2017 L. Miller
New York Times Book Review p30 S 10 2017 V. V. Ganeshananthan
Publishers Weekly v264 no11 p55 Mr 13 2017
Miller, K. R. Beautiful bodies. 2017
New York Times Book Review p21 S 10 2017 M. Meltzer
Miller, L. and Stein, M. R. Blueprint for Counter Education. 2016

Earth Island Journal v32 no4 p54 Wint 2017 B. Buck

Moorcraft, P. Omar Al-Bashir and Africa's Longest War. 2016
Foreign Affairs v96 no1 p180 Ja/F 2017 N. Van De Walle

Moore, A. E. and others. Body horror. 2017
Publishers Weekly v264 no9 p89 F 27 2017

Moore, A. Jerusalem. 2016
National Review v69 no2 p45-6 F 6 2017 K. J. Torrance
New York Times Book Review p23 O 16 2016 D. Wolk
New York Times Book Review p30 O 23 2016

Moore, A. The Lighthouse. 2012
New York Times Book Review p19 S 10 2017 S. Wyndham

Moore, C. Margaret Thatcher. 2013
Claremont Review of Books v16 no4 p25-7 Fall 2016 F. Gray

Moore, D. B. The stars beneath our feet. 2017
Publishers Weekly v264 no28 p89 Jl 10 2017
Time v190 no12 p61 S 25 2017 S. Cooney

Moore, G. R. Cincinnati. 2007
Cincinnati Magazine v50 no5 p63 F 2017 A. Brandt

Moore, G. The last days of night. 2016
Publishers Weekly v263 no44 p70-1 O 31 2016

Moore, J. A. and others. Indigo. 2017
Publishers Weekly v264 no16 p48 Ap 17 2017

Moore, J. P. and Dalí, S. Les dîners de gala. 1973
Entertainment Weekly no1439 p62-3 N 11 2016 R. Kinane

Moore, J. W. and Patel, R. A history of the world in seven cheap things. 2017
Publishers Weekly v264 no35 p53 Ag 28 2017 J. Rosen

Moore, K. and Moore, K. The radium girls. 2017
Publishers Weekly v264 no12 p66 Mr 20 2017
Publishers Weekly v264 no16 p60 Ap 17 2017 K. Moore

Moore, L. The Unseen World. 2016
New York Times Book Review p24 Ag 6 2017 J. Khatib

Moore, M. The South's Best Butts. 2017
Publishers Weekly v264 no14 p69 Ap 3. 2017

Moore, N. Y. The South Side. 2016
U.S. Catholic v81 no12 p41 D 2016 R. McCarty

Moore, O. Shalom Sistas. 2017
Publishers Weekly v264 no33 p75 Ag 14 2017

Moore, R. The Bolt Supremacy. 2017
Publishers Weekly v264 no15 p65 My 10 2017

Moore, S. No fear! 2017
Publishers Weekly v264 no3 p60 Ja 16 2017

Moore, S. Strange Magic. 2017
Publishers Weekly v264 no17 p70 Ap 24 2017

Moore, T. Ageless Soul. 2017
AARP: The Magazine v30 no6A p15 O/N 2017 C. Ianzito

Moore, T. The Cyclist Who Went Out in the Cold. 2017
Publishers Weekly v263 no47 p100 N 21 2016

Moore, W. The Mesmerist. 2017
History Today v67 no9 p98-9 S 2017 J. Peakman

Moosewood (Company) The Moosewood Restaurant table. 2017
Publishers Weekly v264 no32 p66-7 Ag 7 2017

Mootoo, S. Moving forward sideways, like a crab. 2014
Advocate no1093 p32 O/N 2017 D. Guerrero

Moracho, C. A good idea. 2017
Publishers Weekly v263 no51 p150 D 12 2016

Morales, B. F. and Prichep, D. Kachka. 2017
Publishers Weekly v264 no34 p100-4 Ag 21 2017

Morales, Y. and Alexie, S. Thunder Boy Jr. 2016
Publishers Weekly v263 no49 p34 D 7 2016

Morales, Y. Rudas. 2016
Publishers Weekly v263 no43 p75 O 24 2016
Publishers Weekly v263 no49 p40 D 7 2016

Moralis, S. Breathe, mama, breathe. 2017
Publishers Weekly v263 no45 p57 N 7 2016

Moran, C. and others. The Econocracy. 2016
Weekly Standard v22 no29 p32-4 Ap 3 2017 I. M. Stelzer

Moran, C. How to be a woman. 2011
Entertainment Weekly no1454/1455 p30 F 24 2017 D. Coggan

Moran, C. How to Build a Girl. 2014
Commonweal v143 no19 p30-1 D 2 2016 G. Steinfels

Moran, C. Moranifesto. 2016
New York Times Book Review p15 D 11 2016 A. Zeisler

Moran, J. Trident. 2016
Publishers Weekly v264 no1 p40 Ja 2 2017
Publishers Weekly v264 no4 p50d Ja 23 2017

Mordden, E. When Broadway went to Hollywood. 2016
Film Quarterly v70 no2 p101-3 Wint 2016 C. Rickey

Morden, S. Down Station. 2017
Publishers Weekly v264 no9 p82 F 27 2017

Morden, S. The White City. 2017
Publishers Weekly v264 no9 p82 F 27 2017

Morduch, J. and Schneider, R. The financial diaries. 2017
New York Review of Books v64 no11 p49-50 Je 22 2017 J. Madrick
Publishers Weekly v264 no9 p90 F 27 2017

Moren, D. The Caledonian Gambit. 2017
Publishers Weekly v264 no16 p52 Ap 17 2017

Moreno-Garcia, S. Certain dark things. 2016
New York Times Book Review p83 D 4 2016 N. K. Jemisin

Moreno-Garcia, S. The beautiful ones. 2017
Publishers Weekly v264 no26 p122-7 Je 26 2017 R. Fox
Publishers Weekly v264 no34 p95 Ag 21 2017

Morfoot, P. Babazouk Blues. 2017
Publishers Weekly v264 no9 p79 F 27 2017

Morgan, A. and others. Spark. 2017
Publishers Weekly v263 no41 p68 O 10 2016

Morgan, B. and Ginsberg, A. The best minds of my generation. 2017
New York Times Book Review p18 Ag 6 2017 A. Douglas
Publishers Weekly v264 no2 p51 Ja 9 2017

Morgan, C. E. The sport of kings. 2016
Christian Century v134 no7 p41-2 Mr 29 2017 W. Bassett

Morgan, C. The Raven's Table. 2017
Publishers Weekly v264 no5 p185 Ja 30 2017

Morgan, I. Reagan. 2016
History Today v67 no2 p63 F 2017 A. Brown

Morgan, S. Holiday in the Hamptons. 2017
Publishers Weekly v264 no32 p58 Ag 7 2017

Morgan, T. Stealing Mr. Right. 2017
Publishers Weekly v264 no4 p64 Ja 23 2017

Morgensen, S. L. Spaces between us. 2011
American Indian Quarterly v41 no1 p96-9 Wint 2017 M. E. Cannella

Moriarty, L. Big little lies. 2014
New York Times Book Review p23 Ap 23 2017
New York Times Book Review p23 Ap 30 2017

Morieux, R. The Channel. 2016
History Today v67 no5 p100-1 My 2017 N. Aubert

Morimoto, M. Mastering the Art of Japanese Home Cooking. 2016
Publishers Weekly v263 no40 p113-4 O 3 2016

Morin, A. 13 Things Mentally Strong Parents Don't Do. 2017
Publishers Weekly v264 no25 p107 Je 19 2017

Morin, C. W. The Rebel's Wrath. 2016
Publishers Weekly v264 no21 p68 My 22 2017
Publishers Weekly v264 no26 p146b-c Je 26 2017

Morley, J. The ghost. 2017
Esquire p38 O 2017 A. Belth

Morowitz, H. J. and Smith, E. The origin and nature of life on Earth. 2016
Physics Today v70 no9 p58 S 2017 S. I. Walker

Morpurgo, M. An eagle in the snow. 2017
Publishers Weekly v263 no46 p57 N 14 2016

Morpurgo, M. Greatest animal stories. 2017
Publishers Weekly v264 no33 p82 Ag 14 2017

Morrill, S. The Lost Girl of Astor Street. 2017
Publishers Weekly v263 no47 p110 N 21 2016

Morris, A. and Noll, J. G. Atlantic Hotel. 2017
Publishers Weekly v264 no10 p38 Mr 6 2017

Morris, C. A. Marry Me Twice. 2014
Publishers Weekly v264 no6 p54 F 6 2017
Publishers Weekly v264 no9 p66e-f F 27 2017

Morris, C. and Brown, S. Mustaches for Maddie. 2017
Publishers Weekly v264 no34 p109 Ag 21 2017

Morris, C. R. A rabble of dead money. 2017
New York Times Book Review p14 Ap 23 2017 S. Mihm
New York Times Book Review p23 Ap 30 2017
Publishers Weekly v264 no4 p75 Ja 23 2017

Morris, D. Cats in Art. 2017
Publishers Weekly v264 no33 p65 Ag 14 2017

Morris, J. M. Eye on the Struggle. 2015
New York Times Book Review p20 Mr 5 2017 J. Khatib

Morris, J. M. The ambulance drivers. 2017

Publishers Weekly v264 no29 p197 Jl 17 2017
Nurkse, D. Love in the last days. 2017
  Publishers Weekly v264 no34 p86 Ag 21 2017
Nussbaum, M. C. Anger and forgiveness. 2016
  Nation v303 no25/26 p33-5 D 19 2016 A. Srinivasan
Nusseibeh, S. The story of reason in Islam. 2016
  Harper's Magazine v334 no2004 p82-7 My 2017 Y. Seale
  Humanist v77 no1 p44-5 Ja/F 2017 N. Kennedy
  Nation v305 no7 p32-5 S 25 2017 C. De Bellaigue
Nutting, A. Made for Love. 2017
  Entertainment Weekly no1474/1475 p119 Jl 21-28 2017 L. Green-
    blatt
  New York Times Book Review p17 S 3 2017 M. Tierce
  Publishers Weekly v264 no16 p34 Ap 17 2017
Nye, B. and others. At the bottom of the world. 2017
  Publishers Weekly v264 no16 p13 Ap 17 2017 C. Juris
  Publishers Weekly v264 no8 p84 F 20 2017
Nye, J. L. and Taylor, T. S. Moon beam. 2017
  Publishers Weekly v264 no22 p68-70 My 29 2017
Nyeu, T. and McMullan, K. Mama's kisses. 2017
  Publishers Weekly v263 no52 p122 D 19 2016

O

Oakley, C. Close enough to touch. 2017
  Publishers Weekly v263 no48 p40 N 28 2016
Oakley, J. L. The Jossing Affair. 2016
  Publishers Weekly v264 no32 p55-6 Ag 7 2017
  Publishers Weekly v264 no35 p77b Ag 28 2017
Oates, J. C. A Book of American Martyrs. 2017
  Entertainment Weekly no1451/1452 p109 F 3-10 2017 L. Green-
    blatt
  New Yorker v93 no4 p75 Mr 13 2017
  New York Review of Books v64 no5 p47-9 Mr 23 2017 R. Franklin
  New York Times Book Review p19 F 19 2017 A. Mathis
  O, The Oprah Magazine p105 Mr 2017
  Publishers Weekly v263 no51 p121-2 D 12 2016
Oates, J. C. Black water. 1992
  New York Times Book Review p13 O 9 2016 O. Steinhauer
  New York Times Book Review p24 S 17 2017 J. Khatib
  New York Times Book Review p26 O 16 2016
Oates, J. C. Dis mem ber. 2017
  Publishers Weekly v264 no16 p44-6 Ap 17 2017
Oates, J. C. Soul at the White Heat. 2016
  New York Times Book Review p82 D 4 2016 N. Dames
Obadare, E. Humor, silence, and civil society in Nigeria. 2016
  Foreign Affairs v96 no2 p190 Mr/Ap 2017 N. Van De Walle
Obadike, O. and Chestnut, M. The cut. 2017
  Publishers Weekly v264 no6 p64-5 F 6 2017
Obejas, A. and Hernandez, R. I. Papi. 2016
  Publishers Weekly v264 no22 p16-8 My 29 2017 C. Juris
Obejas, A. The tower of the Antilles. 2017
  Publishers Weekly v264 no18 p33-4 My 1 2017
Obermaier, F. and Obermayer, B. The Panama Papers. 2016
  New York Review of Books v63 no16 p33-5 O 27 2016 A. Rus-
    bridger
  New York Review of Books v63 no17 p47-8 N 10 2016 A. Rus-
    bridger
Obey, E. The Curse of the Braddock Brides. 2017
  Publishers Weekly v264 no10 p46 Mr 6 2017
Obioma, C. The fishermen. 2015
  Christian Century v133 no24 p32-4 N 23 2016 D. A. Hoekema
Oblivion, K. (. and Wilson, M. D. Supreme Villainy. 2017
  Publishers Weekly v264 no17 p73 Ap 24 2017
Obregon, N. Blue Light Yokohama. 2017
  Publishers Weekly v264 no4 p57 Ja 23 2017
O'Brien, A. S. In the shadow of the sun. 2017
  Publishers Weekly v264 no17 p92 Ap 24 2017
O'Brien, D. New Life. 2016
  Weekly Standard v22 no24 p37-9 F 27 2017 J. Matthew Wilson
O'Brien, E. The Little Red Chairs. 2016
  America v215 no11 p33 O 17 2016 D. Vellucci
O'Brien, J. and Castrovilla, S. Revolutionary rogues. 2017
  Publishers Weekly v264 no32 p71 Ag 7 2017
O'Brien, T. The things they carried. 1990

South Dakota Magazine p9 S/O 2017 Supplement
Ocejo, R. E. Masters of craft. 2017
  Publishers Weekly v264 no10 p52 Mr 6 2017
Ockwell-Smith, S. Gentle discipline. 2017
  New York Times Book Review p27 Ag 13 2017 J. Newman
  Publishers Weekly v264 no20 p52 My 15 2017
O'Connell, A. B. Our latest longest war. 2017
  Publishers Weekly v264 no7 p65-6 F 13 2017
O'Connell, M. and Dursteler, E. R. The Mediterranean world.
    2016
  New York Review of Books v63 no16 p35-7 O 27 2016 G. W. Bow-
    ersock
O'Connell, M. Dear Reader. 2017
  Publishers Weekly v264 no10 p62 Mr 6 2017
O'Connell, M. The Close Encounters Man. 2017
  Reason v49 no6 p77 N 2017 E. Boehm
O'Connell, M. To be a machine. 2017
  Harper's Magazine v334 no2001 p81-3 F 2017 C. Smallwood
  Humanist v77 no3 p42-3 My/Je 2017 M. Dunbar
  New Republic v248 no3 p68-71 Mr 2017 A. Wiener
  New York Times Book Review p17 Mr 19 2017 E. J. Emanuel
  Publishers Weekly v263 no45 p51 N 7 2016
  Science v355 no6329 p1029 Mr 10 2017 D. Greenbaum
O'Connor, M. K. and Budson, A. E. Seven steps to managing your
    memory. 2017
  Publishers Weekly v264 no18 p54-5 My 1 2017
O'Connor, M. R. Resurrection Science. 2015
  New York Review of Books v64 no7 p58-9 Ap 20 2017 T. Flannery
  Science v354 no6317 p1228-9 D 9 2016 C. Gramling
Odell, K. Day Drinking. 2017
  New Orleans Magazine v52 no1 p58 S 2017
Odhiambo, E. Auma's long run. 2017
  Publishers Weekly v264 no30 p60 Jl 24 2017
O'Donnell, A. A. Still pilgrim. 2017
  America v217 no4 p46-9 Ag 21 2017 T. Donnellan
  Christian Century v134 no17 p41-3 Ag 16 2017 C. Hughes
  U.S. Catholic v82 no11 p41 N 2017 N. Ripatrazone
Odumosu, T. and Narayanamurti, V. Cycles of invention and
    discovery. 2016
  Issues in Science & Technology v33 no4 p87-9 Summ 2017 G.
    P. Zachary
O'Farrell, M. This must be the place. 2016
  New York Times Book Review p56 Je 4 2017 J. Khatib
O'Ferrall, Z. M. and Prager, S. Queer, There, and Everywhere.
    2017
  Publishers Weekly v264 no20 p57 My 15 2017
Offe, C. Europe entrapped. 2014
  New York Review of Books v64 no1 p24-6 Ja 19 2017 T. G. Ash
Offer, A. and Söderberg, G. The Nobel factor. 2016
  Foreign Affairs v96 no2 p170 Mr/Ap 2017 R. N. Cooper
Offermann, A. and Anderson, M. T. Yvain. 2017
  New York Times Book Review p23 My 14 2017 M. Meloy
  Publishers Weekly v263 no51 p150-1 D 12 2016
Offit, P. A. Pandora's lab. 2016
  Publishers Weekly v264 no9 p93 F 27 2017
Offutt, J. and Hare, J. Ella Ewing. 2016
  Missouri Life v44 no2 p22 Ap 2017 M. W. Schwartz
Ogas, O. and Kirsch, D. R. The drug hunters. 2017
  Publishers Weekly v263 no44 p65 O 31 2016
Ogi, H. and Hirao, M. Electromagnetic acoustic transducers. 2016
  Physics Today v70 no6 p66-7 Je 2017
O'Guilin, P. The call. 2016
  Publishers Weekly v263 no49 p107 D 7 2016
Ogura, G. Startup. 2013
  Publishers Weekly v264 no8 p59-60 F 20 2017
Oh, E. and Day, A. Spirit hunters. 2017
  Publishers Weekly v264 no19 p61 My 8 2017
Oh, E. Flying lessons & other stories. 2017
  Publishers Weekly v263 no46 p56 N 14 2016
  Publishers Weekly v264 no17 p90 Ap 24 2017
  Time v188 no27-28 p112 D 26 2016 S. Begley
O'Hagan, A. The secret life. 2017
  Esquire p38 O 2017 A. Belth
  Publishers Weekly v264 no29 p208 Jl 17 2017
O'Hara, L. and O'Hara, N. Hortense and the shadow. 2017
  Publishers Weekly v264 no38 p69 S 18 2017

O'Harrow, R. The quartermaster. 2016
Military History v34 no2 p71 Jl 2017 A. Paletta
Ohi, D. R. and Reynolds, A. Sea Monkey & Bob. 2017
Publishers Weekly v264 no7 p73-6 F 13 2017
Ohler, N. and Whiteside, S. Drugs in the Third Reich. 2017
Esquire p40-2 Ap 2017 G. Pendle
New York Review of Books v64 no4 p14-5 Mr 9 2017 A. Beevor
New York Times Book Review p19 Ap 2 2017 D. Herzog
New York Times Book Review p22 Ap 9 2017
Publishers Weekly v263 no51 p51-5 D 12 2016 A. Coreno
Ohora, Z. and Dyckman, A. Horrible bear! 2016
Publishers Weekly v263 no49 p38 D 7 2016
Ohora, Z. and Rissi, A. M. The teacher's pet. 2017
New York Times Book Review p27 Ag 27 2017 M. Russo
Publishers Weekly v264 no20 p53 My 15 2017
Ohora, Z. and Vega, D. If your monster won't go to bed. 2017
Publishers Weekly v264 no1 p55 Ja 2 2017
Okawa, R. The Laws of Justice. 2016
Publishers Weekly v263 no39 p24 S 26 2016
Okeowo, A. A moonless, starless sky. 2017
Ms. v27 no3 p51 Fall 2017 E. A. Kaplan
Publishers Weekly v264 no27 p65 Jl 3 2017
O'Kif and Heos, B. Queen Dog. 2017
Publishers Weekly v263 no44 p73 O 31 2016
Oklap, E. and Pamuk, O. The red-haired woman. 2017
Publishers Weekly v264 no25 p87 Je 19 2017
Vogue v207 no9 p616 S 2017 C. Schama
Okorafor, N. and Amini, M. Chicken in the Kitchen. 2017
Publishers Weekly v264 no30 p57 Jl 24 2017
Okorafor, N. Binti. 2017
Publishers Weekly v263 no48 p52-3 N 28 2016
Oksanen, S. Norma. 2017
Publishers Weekly v264 no31 p68-9 Jl 31 2017
Okstad, E. and Grabill, R. Halloween good night. 2017
Publishers Weekly v264 no26 p179 Je 26 2017
Okstad, E. and Jones, P. Squishy Mcfluff. 2014
Publishers Weekly v264 no17 p93 Ap 24 2017
Okupe, R. and others. E.X.O. 2015
Publishers Weekly v263 no46 p59 N 14 2016
Publishers Weekly v263 no52 p90f D 19 2016
Okupe, R. and others. E.X.O. 2016
Publishers Weekly v264 no9 p66c F 27 2017
Okupe, R. and others. Malika. 2017
Publishers Weekly v264 no32 p75 Ag 7 2017
Publishers Weekly v264 no35 p77e Ag 28 2017
Older, D. J. Battle Hill Bolero. 2017
Publishers Weekly v263 no51 p129 D 12 2016
Older, M. Null states. 2017
Publishers Weekly v264 no29 p202-3 Jl 17 2017
Oldham, N. Bad Blood. 2017
Publishers Weekly v264 no4 p57 Ja 23 2017
Oldham, N. Headhunter. 2017
Publishers Weekly v264 no38 p58 S 18 2017
O'Leary, M. B. and Harris, M. Lessons for Nonprofit and Start-up Leaders. 2017
Publishers Weekly v264 no26 p168 Je 26 2017
O'Leary, S. and Morstad, J. When You Were Small. 2017
Walrus v14 no5 p56-7 Je 2017 K. Clare
O'Leary, S. and Qin Leng A family is a family is a family. 2016
Publishers Weekly v263 no49 p31 D 7 2016
Olendzki, A. Untangling self. 2016
Tricycle: The Buddhist Review v26 no2 p90 Wint 2016 M. Scarles
Olien, J. and others. Adrift. 2017
Publishers Weekly v263 no42 p66 O 17 2016
Olin, S. Reckless hearts. 2015
Publishers Weekly v264 no2 p48 Ja 9 2017
Oliver, C. Unleashing Demons. 2017
Foreign Affairs v96 no6 p122-6 N/D 2017 A. Menon
Oliver, L. and dePaola, T. Steppin' out. 2017
Publishers Weekly v264 no46 p55 N 14 2016
Oliver, M. Upstream. 2016
New York Times Book Review p26 D 18 2016 D. Kalotay
Olivera, R. and Olivera, R. ABCs on wheels. 2016
Publishers Weekly v263 no49 p19 D 7 2016
Oliveras, P. His Perfect Partner. 2017
Publishers Weekly v264 no35 p112 Ag 28 2017

Oller, J. The Swamp Fox. 2016
Military History v33 no6 p74 Mr 2017
Olmstead, R. Savage country. 2017
New York Times Book Review p18 O 15 2017 R. Bass
Publishers Weekly v264 no28 p60 Jl 10 2017
Oloixarac, P. and Kesey, R. Savage theories. 2017
New York Times Book Review p22 Mr 5 2017 J. Szalai
O, The Oprah Magazine p104 F 2017
Publishers Weekly v263 no44 p51 O 31 2016
O'Loughlin, E. Minds of winter. 2017
Publishers Weekly v264 no2 p38 Ja 9 2017
Olsen, H. The working class Republican. 2017
American Conservative v16 no5 p60-2 S/O 2017 M. Barone
Commentary v144 no2 p39-42 S 2017 K. Williamson
Weekly Standard v22 no44 p30-2 Jl 31 2017 J. Cost
Olsen, R. The girl before. 2016
AARP: The Magazine v60 no1A p12 D 2016/Ja 2017
Publishers Weekly v263 no43 p58 O 24 2016
Vanity Fair v59 no2 p38 F 2017 S. C.
Olshaker, M. and Osterholm, M. T. Deadliest enemy. 2017
Publishers Weekly v264 no5 p192 Ja 30 2017
Olshan, M. and Blackall, S. A voyage in the clouds. 2016
Publishers Weekly v263 no49 p18 D 7 2016
Olson, E. S. Zero-sum game. 2011
D: The Magazine of Dallas v43 no10 p58 O 2016 Z. Crain
Olson, K. E. Betrayed. 2017
Publishers Weekly v264 no5 p181-2 Ja 30 2017
Olson, L. Last Hope Island. 2016
Foreign Affairs v96 no2 p172 Mr/Ap 2017 L. D. Freedman
New York Times Book Review p20 My 7 2017 H. Evans
New York Times Book Review p34 My 14 2017
Olson, R. E. Essentials of Christian thought. 2016
Christianity Today p61 Mr 2017
Olson, S. Eruption. 2016
New York Times Book Review p30 S 25 2016 K. Tingley
Olstein, L. Late empire. 2017
Publishers Weekly v264 no38 p51-2 S 18 2017
Olyan, S. M. Friendship in the Hebrew Bible. 2017
America v216 no9 p28-37 Ap 24 2017 J. Racine
Publishers Weekly v263 no45 p25 N 7 2016
Olzmann, M. Contradictions in the design. 2016
Publishers Weekly v263 no42 p48 O 17 2016
O'Mahoney, P. and Koenig, K. R. Helping patients outsmart overeating. 2017
Publishers Weekly v263 no47 p103 N 21 2016
O'Mahony, S. The way we die now. 2017
Publishers Weekly v264 no19 p50 My 8 2017
O'Malley, J. W. The Jesuits and the popes. 2016
America v216 no10 p46-7 My 1 2017 R. E. Curran
O'Mara, J. and O'Mara, J. The Elephants of Art. 2016
Publishers Weekly v264 no13 p64f Mr 27 2017
Publishers Weekly v264 no9 p99 F 27 2017
O'Mara, T. Nasty Cutter. 2017
Publishers Weekly v263 no44 p54 O 31 2016
O'Meara, M. L. Let Go Heal Be Happy. 2016
Publishers Weekly v264 no7 p67-8 F 13 2017
Publishers Weekly v264 no9 p66i F 27 2017
Omotoso, Y. The Woman Next Door. 2016
O, The Oprah Magazine p105 Mr 2017
Publishers Weekly v263 no50 p43 D 5 2016
O'Murchu, D. Incarnation. 2017
U.S. Catholic v82 no8 p41 Ag 2017
One, M. and others. Chef Roy Choi and the street food remix. 2017
Publishers Weekly v264 no23 p51 Je 5 2017
O'Neil, C. Weapons of math destruction. 2016
Claremont Review of Books v17 no2 p61-3 Spr 2017 J. Derbyshire
New York Review of Books v63 no20 p32-4 D 22 2016 S. Halpern
New York Times Book Review p26 O 16 2016 J. Szalai
New York Times Book Review p34 O 9 2016 C. Shirky
O'Neil, K. Fever dogs. 2017
Publishers Weekly v264 no23 p28 Je 5 2017
O'Neill, D. The river wild. 2017
Publishers Weekly v264 no16 p49 Ap 17 2017
O'Neill, H. The Lonely Hearts Hotel. 2017
Publishers Weekly v264 no1 p36 Ja 2 2017

Ottolenghi, Y. and Tamimi, S. Jerusalem. 2012
  Progressive p60-3 D 2016/Ja 2017 A. Cusac
Oudolf, P. and Darke, R. Gardens of the High Line. 2017
  Architectural Record v205 no8 p51 Ag 2017 A. Shapiro
Ouriou, S. and Valdivia, P. And so it goes. 2017
  Publishers Weekly v264 no24 p63 Je 12 2017
Oust, G. Curried away. 2016
  Publishers Weekly v263 no44 p55-6 O 31 2016
Oust, G. Ginger snapped. 2017
  Publishers Weekly v264 no41 p45 O 9 2017
Ovchinnikov, A. and others. Humans, bow down. 2016
  Publishers Weekly v264 no10 p12 Mr 6 2017 C. Juris
Overbeck, L. M. and others. The Letters of Samuel Beckett. 2016
  New York Review of Books v63 no18 p37-41 N 24 2016 F. O'Toole
Overholt, C. A promise of ruin. 2017
  Publishers Weekly v264 no25 p94 Je 19 2017
Overton, H. The walls. 2017
  Publishers Weekly v264 no26 p158 Je 26 2017
Overton, T. and Berger, J. Landscapes. 2016
  Interview v46 no9 p44 N 2016 C. Wallace
Owen, A. Into the Gray Zone. 2017
  New York Times Book Review p13 Ag 27 2017 G. Johnson
  Publishers Weekly v264 no14 p63-4 Ap 3. 2017
  Scientific American v317 no1 p72 Jl 2017 A. Gawrylewski
  Walrus v14 no7 p65 S 2017 A. Tesar
Owen, D. Where the water goes. 2017
  New York Times Book Review p13 My 28 2017 D. Biello
  Publishers Weekly v264 no9 p94-5 F 27 2017
  Science v356 no6334 p146 Ap 14 2017 K. C. Rose
  Sierra v102 no4 p11 Jl/Ag 2017 L. Bliss
Owen, N. The Killing Files. 2017
  Publishers Weekly v264 no23 p34 Je 5 2017
Owens, R. Rick Owens interiors. 2017
  Esquire v34 My 2017 J. Roth
Owens, S. Jack of Hearts. 2017
  Publishers Weekly v264 no1 p43 Ja 2 2017
Owens, S. Knowledge, policy, and expertise. 2015
  Environment v59 no1 p39-40 2017 T. O'Riordan
Oxenbury, H. and Donaldson, J. The Giant Jumperee. 2017
  Publishers Weekly v264 no5 p201 Ja 30 2017
Oxenbury, H. and Knapman, T. Time Now to Dream. 2017
  Publishers Weekly v264 no3 p57 Ja 16 2017
Oxlade, C. and Haslam, J. A journey through transportation. 2017
  Publishers Weekly v264 no38 p73 S 18 2017
Oz, A. and De Lange, N. Judas. 2016
  America v216 no9 p52-4 Ap 24 2017 D. Vellucci
  Commonweal v144 no6 p25-6 Mr 24 2017 T. Novick
  Esquire v166 no4 p36 N 2016 J. Black
  New Yorker v92 no45 p79 Ja 16 2017
  New York Review of Books v64 no4 p35-6 Mr 9 2017 A. Margalit
  New York Times Book Review p26 D 11 2016 E. Barton
Oz, M. Food Can Fix It. 2017
  Good Housekeeping v265 no4 p91-2 O 2017 M. Oz
Ozawa, S. and others. Absolutely on music. 2016
  Opera News v81 no10 p62 Ap 2017 F. Cohn

P

Pabst, A. and Milbank, J. The politics of virtue. 2016
  Christian Century v134 no10 p45-6 My 10 2017 S. Wells
Pace, A. M. and Hussey, L. Pigloo. 2016
  Publishers Weekly v263 no42 p69 O 17 2016
Pace, F. J Class. 2014
  Sea Magazine v108 no12 p44 D 2016
Pacewicz, J. Partisans and partners. 2016
  Governing v30 no6 p17 Mr 2017 A. Greenblatt
Pachico, J. The lucky ones. 2017
  New York Times Book Review p22 Mr 19 2017 S. Paternostro
  Publishers Weekly v264 no3 p36 Ja 16 2017
  Vogue v207 no4 p186 Ap 2017 M. O'Grady
Padura, L. and Kushner, A. Heretics. 2017
  Publishers Weekly v264 no5 p174 Ja 30 2017
Paetro, M. and Patterson, J. Woman of God. 2016
  New York Times Book Review p26 O 16 2016
Page, J. and Westmore, M. Makeup man. 2017

Publishers Weekly v264 no4 p74 Ja 23 2017
Page, M. Why preservation matters. 2016
  Architectural Record v205 no2 p41 F 2017 J. Gauer
Page, R. and Jenkins, S. Flying frogs and walking fish. 2015
  Publishers Weekly v263 no49 p48 D 7 2016
Page, S. The Worthington Wife. 2016
  Publishers Weekly v263 no48 p54 N 28 2016
Page, T. and Page, T. Raised on Ritalin. 2016
  Publishers Weekly v264 no7 p59 F 13 2017
  Publishers Weekly v264 no9 p66j F 27 2017
Page, T. Music Chronicles 1940-1954. 2014
  New York Review of Books v64 no7 p38-40 Ap 20 2017 C. Carroll
Page, T. The state of music & other writings. 2016
  New York Review of Books v64 no7 p38-40 Ap 20 2017 C. Carroll
Paglia, C. Free Women, Free Men. 2017
  Publishers Weekly v264 no17 p90 Ap 24 2017
Paillole, P. and Key, C. The Spy in Hitler's Inner Circle. 2016
  Military History v33 no5 p73-4 Ja 2017 T. Zacharis
Paine, N. Building leadership development programmes. 2017
  People Management p51 D 2016/Ja 2017
Paintner, C. V. The wisdom of the body. 2017
  U.S. Catholic v82 no5 p41 My 2017
Paisley, E. Can your smartphone change the world? 2017
  Publishers Weekly v264 no30 p61 Jl 24 2017
Paisner, D. and John, D. The power of broke. 2016
  Black Enterprise v47 no5 p30 Ja/F 2017 L. D. Johnson
Pak, G. and others. Kingsway West. 2017
  D: The Magazine of Dallas v43 no10 p58 O 2016 Z. Crain
  Publishers Weekly v264 no24 p50 Je 12 2017
Pak, K. and Maclear, K. The fog. 2017
  Publishers Weekly v264 no14 p75 Ap 3. 2017
Pakenham, T. and Pakenham, T. Remarkable trees of the world. 2002
  Natural History v125 no1 p40-3 D 2016/Ja 2017 L. A. Marschall
Paknadel, A. and Trakhanov, A. Paknadel & Trakhanov's Turncoat. 2017
  Publishers Weekly v264 no29 p205 Jl 17 2017
Palacio, D. The mortifications. 2016
  New York Times Book Review p15 N 6 2016 D. Mengestu
Palacio, R. J. and Palacio, R. J. We're All Wonders. 2017
  Publishers Weekly v264 no4 p79 Ja 23 2017
Palacio, R. J. Wonder. 2012
  New York Times Book Review p23 Ja 1 2017
  New York Times Book Review p25 Ap 23 2017
  New York Times Book Review p25 Ap 30 2017
  New York Times Book Review p25 F 5 2017
  New York Times Book Review p25 Jl 30 2017
  New York Times Book Review p25 S 17 2017
  New York Times Book Review p27 O 16 2016
  Publishers Weekly v264 no34 p17 Ag 21 2017 C. Juris
Palacios, S. and others. Agnes and Clarabelle. 2016
  Publishers Weekly v263 no47 p109 N 21 2016
Palahniuk, C. Fight Club. 1996
  Entertainment Weekly no1468/1469 p107 Je 2-9 2017
Palast, G. and others. The best democracy money can buy. 2016
  Progressive p60-5 D 2016/Ja 2017 E. Rampell
Palazon, D. TIMOR RUNGURANGA. 2016
  Publishers Weekly v264 no4 p76 Ja 23 2017
  Publishers Weekly v264 no9 p66j F 27 2017
Palepu, H. How to pack. 2017
  Publishers Weekly v264 no4 p22-34 Ja 23 2017 S. J. Robbins
Palermo, S. G. and Song, C. Winter, winter, cold and snow. 2016
  Publishers Weekly v263 no42 p69 O 17 2016
Paley, G. and others. A Grace Paley reader. 2017
  Atlantic v319 no3 p38-40 Ap 2017 N. Dames
  Nation v305 no2 p27-31 Jl 17 2017 M. Doherty
  New York Review of Books v64 no15 p37-8 O 12 2017 D. Johnson
Pally, R. The reflective parent. 2017
  Publishers Weekly v264 no3 p56 Ja 16 2017
Palm, A. Riverine. 2016
  Orion Magazine v36 no1 p60-1 Ja/F 2017 J. Shipley
Palmatier, J. Reaping the Aurora. 2017
  Publishers Weekly v264 no26 p160 Je 26 2017
Palmer, A. A life well played. 2016
  New York Times Book Review p24 N 27 2016
  Publishers Weekly v263 no41 p20-1 O 10 2016

Pentecost, M. and Morton, B. Mission. 2017
People Management p52 Ap 2017

Penzler, O. and Sandford, J. The Best American Mystery Stories 2017. 2017
Publishers Weekly v264 no35 p105 Ag 28 2017

Penzler, O. Bibliomysteries. 2017
Publishers Weekly v264 no26 p156 Je 26 2017

Penzler, O. The Big Book of Rogues and Villains. 2017
Publishers Weekly v264 no35 p104 Ag 28 2017

Pépin, J. and Hopkins, T. A grandfather's lessons. 2017
Publishers Weekly v264 no20 p51 My 15 2017

Peppard, M. The World's Oldest Church. 2016
Commonweal v144 no10 p34-7 Je 2 2017 L. T. Johnson

Perabo, S. The fall of Lisa Bellow. 2017
Publishers Weekly v264 no2 p39 Ja 9 2017

Percy, B. The dark net. 2017
Publishers Weekly v264 no10 p43-4 Mr 6 2017

Percy, B. Thrill me. 2016
Commonweal v143 no19 p28-9 D 2 2016 D. Preziosi
Publishers Weekly v263 no42 p23-30 O 17 2016 C. Teicher

Perel, E. The state of affairs. 2017
Publishers Weekly v264 no29 p208-9 Jl 17 2017

Perelman, D. Smitten kitchen every day. 2017
Publishers Weekly v264 no32 p67 Ag 7 2017

Perennials. 2017
New York Times Book Review p13 Je 4 2017 J. C. Sullivan
Publishers Weekly v264 no15 p49 Ap 10 2017

Pérez, C. C. The first rule of punk. 2017
New York Times Book Review p29 Ag 27 2017 N. Beram

Perez, C. S. From unincorporated territory [guma'] 2014
Publishers Weekly v264 no34 p84 Ag 21 2017

Pérez, R. K. and McKenna, A. B. Jane. 2017
Publishers Weekly v264 no39 p94 S 25 2017

Perfit, M. and Brown, D. Older than dirt. 2017
Publishers Weekly v264 no29 p222-3 Jl 17 2017

Peri, A. The war within. 2017
Foreign Affairs v96 no2 p181-2 Mr/Ap 2017 R. Legvold

Perina, R. M. The Organization of American States As the Advocate and Guardian of Democracy. 2015
Foreign Affairs v95 no6 p183-4 N/D 2016 R. Feinberg

Perkins, J. M. and Gordon, W. Do all lives matter? 2017
U.S. Catholic v82 no8 p41 Ag 2017 J. M. Perkins

Perkins, J. M. Dream with me. 2017
Publishers Weekly v264 no4 p16-9 Ja 23 2017 L. Garrett
U.S. Catholic v82 no5 p41 My 2017

Perkins, K. The Haunting of Thores-Cross. 2016
Publishers Weekly v264 no19 p44 My 8 2017
Publishers Weekly v264 no21 p52 My 22 2017
Publishers Weekly v264 no21 p65a My 22 2017

Perkins, L. R. and Perkins, L. R. Frank and Lucky get schooled. 2016
Publishers Weekly v263 no49 p21-2 D 7 2016

Perkins, M. You bring the distant near. 2017
Publishers Weekly v264 no29 p221 Jl 17 2017

Perkins, S. Summer days and summer nights. 2016
Publishers Weekly v263 no49 p103-4 D 7 2016

Perkins, U. E. and Collier, B. Hey black child. 2017
Publishers Weekly v264 no39 p104-5 S 25 2017

Perl, J. Calder. 2017
New York Review of Books v64 no17 p20-2 N 9 2017 H. Spurling
Publishers Weekly v264 no23 p40 Je 5 2017
Publishers Weekly v264 no26 p21-7 Je 26 2017 A. Coreno

Perloff, M. Edge of irony. 2016
New York Review of Books v64 no11 p26-8 Je 22 2017 A. Kirsch

Perona, E. Murder at the male revue. 2017
Publishers Weekly v264 no21 p75-6 My 22 2017

Perrine, S. and Zinczenko, D. Zero sugar diet. 2016
New York Times Book Review p27 Ja 1 2017 J. Newman
Publishers Weekly v263 no47 p103-4 N 21 2016

Perrotta, T. Mrs. Fletcher. 2017
New Yorker v93 no23 p75-6 Ag 7 2017 L. Miller
New York Times Book Review p1-22 Ag 13 2017 C. Bachelder
New York Times Book Review p22 Ag 20 2017
New York Times Book Review p24 Ag 20 2017 G. Cowles
Publishers Weekly v264 no25 p89 Je 19 2017
Publishers Weekly v264 no33 p13 Ag 14 2017 C. Juris

Publishers Weekly v264 no40 p133 O 2 2017
Time v190 no7 p53 Ag 21 2017 D. D'Addario

Perry, A. A Christmas Return. 2017
Publishers Weekly v264 no39 p85 S 25 2017

Perry, A. Murder on the serpentine. 2017
Publishers Weekly v264 no3 p40 Ja 16 2017

Perry, C. and Perry, C. Scents and flavors. 2017
Islamic Horizons v46 no4 p61 Jl/Ag 2017

Perry, G. and Bar-el, D. It's great being a dad? 2017
Publishers Weekly v264 no16 p69 Ap 17 2017

Perry, S. After the eclipse. 2017
Entertainment Weekly no1480 p54-8 S 1 2017 I. Biedenharn
Entertainment Weekly no1485 p63 O 6 2017
Publishers Weekly v264 no30 p52 Jl 24 2017

Perry, S. The Essex Serpent. 2016
Entertainment Weekly no1471 p66 Je 23 2017
Publishers Weekly v264 no16 p34 Ap 17 2017

Perry, S. The Essex Serpent. 2017
New Yorker v93 no26 p87 S 4 2017

Perry, T. The Old Man. 2017
Publishers Weekly v263 no42 p51 O 17 2016
Publishers Weekly v264 no9 p96 F 27 2017

Perry-Mason, G. and Bridgforth, G. Girl, make your money grow! 2004
Black Enterprise v47 no5 p20 Ja/F 2017 D. D. Hughes

Persson, L. G. and Smith, N. The dying detective. 2017
New York Times Book Review p7 Je 11 2017 M. Stasio

Perur, S. and Shanbhag, V. Ghachar ghochar. 2017
New Yorker v93 no5 p97 Mr 20 2017
New York Times Book Review p27 Ap 9 2017 P. Sehgal
Publishers Weekly v263 no41 p54 O 10 2016

Pesta, A. and others. How dare the sun rise. 2017
Publishers Weekly v264 no12 p75 Mr 20 2017

Peter, C. and others. The Discipline 1. 2016
Publishers Weekly v263 no45 p49 N 7 2016

Peters, B. T. Called to be saints. 2016
Commonweal v144 no11 p31-2 Je 16 2017 P. Jordan

Peters, C. The king of inventors. 1993
New York Review of Books v64 no10 p25-8 Je 8 2017 R. Gottlieb

Peters, E. and Andersen, C. Indigenous in the city. 2013
American Indian Quarterly v40 no3 p283-5 Summ 2016 F. Delgado

Peters, E. and Hess, J. The painted queen. 2017
Publishers Weekly v264 no18 p38 My 1 2017

Peters, T. Sin boldly! 2015
Christian Century v134 no11 p36-7 My 24 2017 M. L. Riegel

Peters, V. Personal. 2016
Esquire p30 Ap 2017 J. Black

Peterson, E. H. As kingfishers catch fire. 2017
Christianity Today v61 no5 p71-4 Je 2017 E. H. Peterson

Peterson, E. The Dining Car. 2016
Publishers Weekly v264 no6 p44 F 6 2017
Publishers Weekly v264 no9 p52 F 27 2017
Publishers Weekly v264 no9 p66c F 27 2017

Peterson, J. and others. Eat Smart in Portugal. 2017
Publishers Weekly v264 no4 p22-34 Ja 23 2017 S. J. Robbins

Peterson, L. J. All day. 2017
Essence v48 no2 p62 Je 2017 P. H. Bass

Peterson, T. Beloved hope. 2017
Publishers Weekly v264 no19 p45 My 8 2017

Peterson, T. Treasured grace. 2017
Publishers Weekly v264 no4 p65-6 Ja 23 2017

Peterson, Z. L. Next Year, for Sure. 2017
Publishers Weekly v264 no3 p35 Ja 16 2017
Walrus v14 no6 p82 Jl/Ag 2017 D. Viola

Petit, Z. Treat Ideas Like Cats. 2016
Publishers Weekly v263 no42 p31-40 O 17 2016 J. McCartney

Petrarca, F. and Nichols, J. G. Canzoniere. 2000
American Scholar v86 no3 p5-9 Summ 2017 J. Tayler

Petričić, D. and Atwood, M. A Trio of Tolerable Tales. 2017
Publishers Weekly v264 no11 p84 Mr 13 2017

Petričić, D. and Stinson, K. The dance of the violin. 2017
Publishers Weekly v264 no8 p85 F 20 2017

Petriello, D. R. Bacteria and Bayonets. 2016
Military History v34 no1 p74 My 2017

Petroff, S. My new crush gave to me. 2017

Powers, A. Good booty. 2017
  New York Times Book Review p11 S 3 2017 F. Nicolay
  Publishers Weekly v264 no24 p56 Je 12 2017
Powers, C. and others. The Spree of 83. 2017
  Publishers Weekly v264 no19 p24 My 8 2017 S. Maughan
Powers, R. and Bradbury, D. Making house. 2017
  Better Homes & Gardens v95 no9 p70-5 S 2017 J. Lewis
Powers, R. No One Cares About Crazy People. 2017
  America v217 no6 p54 S 18 2017 E. Griffin
  New York Times Book Review p1-21 Ap 9 2017 R. Suskind
  Publishers Weekly v263 no44 p61 O 31 2016
Powers, Z. Gravity changes. 2017
  Publishers Weekly v264 no12 p50 Mr 20 2017
Poyer, D. Hunter killer. 2017
  Publishers Weekly v264 no33 p46 Ag 14 2017
Poyer, D. Onslaught. 2016
  Publishers Weekly v263 no40 p98 O 3 2016
Prager, S. and O'Ferrall, Z. M. Queer, There, and Everywhere. 2017
  Publishers Weekly v264 no20 p57 My 15 2017
Prahalad, C. K. The fortune at the bottom of the pyramid. 2006
  Monthly Labor Review p1-3 Mr 2017 H. O'Lawrence
Prakash, S. B. Imperial from the beginning. 2015
  Weekly Standard v22 no22 p33-4 F 13 2017 T. Helfman
Prange, B. and others. One north star. 2016
  Cabin Living p12 Ja/F 2017
Prasad, E. Gaining currency. 2017
  Foreign Affairs v96 no2 p157-63 Mr/Ap 2017 B. Eichengreen
Pratt, K. and others. France is a feast. 2016
  Publishers Weekly v264 no38 p62-4 S 18 2017
Pratt, P. and Messier, M. The branch. 2016
  New York Times Book Review p29 N 13 2016
Pratt, P. and Sage, J. Stop feedin' da boids! 2017
  Publishers Weekly v264 no7 p73 F 13 2017
Prebble, S. The bridge. 2017
  Publishers Weekly v264 no3 p41-2 Ja 16 2017
Preisle, J. and King, B. Game face. 2017
  Publishers Weekly v264 no39 p99 S 25 2017
Preller, J. Better off undead. 2017
  Publishers Weekly v264 no38 p71-2 S 18 2017
Prendergast, C. A history of modern French literature. 2016
  Publishers Weekly v264 no1 p48 Ja 2 2017
Prescott, D. Eat Delicious. 2017
  Publishers Weekly v264 no8 p79-80 F 20 2017
Presilla, M. E. Peppers of the Americas. 2017
  Publishers Weekly v264 no18 p53 My 1 2017
Pressler, D. and others. Back to school with Bigfoot. 2017
  Publishers Weekly v264 no20 p55 My 15 2017
Preston, D. The Lost City of the Monkey God. 2017
  Maclean's no1 p62 F 17 2017 B. Josef Grubisic
  National Review v69 no8 p42 My 1 2017 J. J. Miller
  New York Times Book Review p17 Ja 22 2017 B. I. Koerner
  New York Times Book Review p22 Ja 22 2017 G. Cowles
  New York Times Book Review p22 Ja 29 2017
  Publishers Weekly v264 no14 p73 Ap 3. 2017
  Publishers Weekly v264 no3 p14 Ja 16 2017 C. Juris
  Science News v191 no2 p28 F 4 2017 E. Wayman
  Virginia Living v15 no4 p29 Je 2017 B. Glose
Preston, J. A very English scandal. 2016
  Weekly Standard v22 no12 p30-2 N 28 2016 J. Bachrach
Preston, L. Goldilocks and the Water Bears. 2016
  Discover v27 no10 p18 D 2016 G. Tarlach
Preston, L. The Measure of the Moon. 2017
  Publishers Weekly v264 no9 p80 F 27 2017
Preston-Gannon, F. and others. Because of an acorn. 2016
  Natural History v125 no1 p44-7 D 2016/Ja 2017 D. Setton
  Science v354 no6317 p1224 D 9 2016 V. Thompson
Pretorius, F. and Gubser, S. S. The Little Book of Black Holes. 2017
  Publishers Weekly v264 no26 p115-20 Je 26 2017 A. Crowley
  Publishers Weekly v264 no27 p67 Jl 3 2017
Previn, S. and Previn, S. If snowflakes tasted like fruitcake. 2016
  Publishers Weekly v263 no42 p69 O 17 2016
Price, D. The song of the orphans. 2017
  Publishers Weekly v264 no22 p49-50 My 29 2017
Price, S. By Gaslight. 2016

Vanity Fair v58 no11 p96 N 2016 S. C.
Price, S. L. Playing Through the Whistle. 2016
  New York Times Book Review p58-60 D 4 2016 M. Tracy
Priceman, M. and Rusch, E. The music of life. 2017
  Publishers Weekly v264 no9 p103 F 27 2017
Prichep, D. and Morales, B. F. Kachka. 2017
  Publishers Weekly v264 no34 p100-4 Ag 21 2017
Priebe, G. and Duncan, D. The adventures of Henry Whiskers. 2017
  Publishers Weekly v263 no47 p109 N 21 2016
Priest, C. and others. Indigo. 2017
  Publishers Weekly v264 no16 p48 Ap 17 2017
Priest, C. Brimstone. 2017
  Publishers Weekly v264 no9 p81 F 27 2017
Prime, A. A. and Turtschaninoff, M. Maresi. 2017
  Publishers Weekly v263 no44 p77 O 31 2016
Prince, W. M. and others. One Week in the Library. 2016
  Publishers Weekly v263 no50 p58 D 5 2016
Princesse Camcam, I. and Berkner, L. Pillowland. 2017
  Publishers Weekly v264 no41 p66 O 9 2017
Prinstein, M. Popular. 2017
  Christian Century v134 no22 p43 O 25 2017
Pritchard, D. and others. A house in the country. 1984
  New York Times Book Review p22 D 4 2016 A. Becker
Pritts, N. Decoherence. 2017
  Publishers Weekly v264 no38 p50 S 18 2017
Probert, J. L. The Lovecraft Squad. 2017
  Publishers Weekly v263 no51 p128-9 D 12 2016
Probst, J. All or Nothing at All. 2017
  Publishers Weekly v264 no23 p38-9 Je 5 2017
Probst, J. Any time, any place. 2017
  Publishers Weekly v263 no50 p57 D 5 2016
Prochnik, G. Stranger in a strange land. 2016
  New York Times Book Review p23 My 7 2017 A. Newhouse
Proctor, M. Z. and Jaeggy, F. These Possible Lives. 2017
  Publishers Weekly v264 no10 p49 Mr 6 2017
Proctor, M. Z. Landslide. 2017
  Publishers Weekly v264 no22 p52-3 My 29 2017
Proctor, P. Containment and credibility. 2016
  Publishers Weekly v263 no40 p111 O 3 2016
Proenneke, R. and others. One man's wilderness. 1999
  National Parks v91 no2 p52-8 Spr 2017
Proffer Teasley, E. Brodsky among us. 2017
  Commentary v144 no1 p61-2 Jl/Ag 2017 M. Grinberg
Pronzini, B. and Muller, M. The Dangerous Ladies Affair. 2017
  Publishers Weekly v263 no47 p92-3 N 21 2016
Pronzini, B. Endgame. 2017
  Publishers Weekly v264 no17 p71 Ap 24 2017
Pronzini, B. The violated. 2016
  Publishers Weekly v264 no2 p41 Ja 9 2017
Prose, F. Mister monkey. 2016
  Maclean's v129 no45 p56-7 N 14 2016 B. Josef Grubisic
  New York Times Book Review p1-26 O 23 2016 C. Schine
  New York Times Book Review p26 O 30 2016
Prothero, D. R. and Callahan, T. D. UFOs, chemtrails, and aliens. 2017
  Publishers Weekly v264 no23 p46 Je 5 2017
Proulx, A. Barkskins. 2016
  AARP: The Magazine v59 no4A p14 Je/Jl 2016 D. Donahue
  New York Review of Books v64 no3 p22-3 F 23 2017 I. Frazier
  Orion Magazine v36 no1 p58 Ja/F 2017 D. Rothenberg
  Publishers Weekly v263 no50 p69 D 5 2016
Provost, S. H. Memortality. 2017
  Publishers Weekly v263 no47 p95 N 21 2016
Prowse, A. I Won't Be Home for Christmas. 2017
  Publishers Weekly v264 no18 p43-4 My 1 2017
Prud'homme, A. and others. France is a feast. 2016
  Publishers Weekly v264 no38 p62-4 S 18 2017
Prud'homme, A. The French chef in America. 2016
  Maclean's v129 no45 p57-8 N 14 2016 J. Latimer
  Weekly Standard v22 no4 p30-1 O 3 2016 A. Hender
Prudlo, D. S. Certain sainthood. 2015
  Commonweal v144 no10 p28-30 Je 2 2017 F. Oakley
Prueitt, E. and others. Tartine all day. 2017
  New York Times Book Review p38-9 Je 4 2017 J. Rosenstrach
  Publishers Weekly v264 no6 p64 F 6 2017

Christianity Today v60 no8 p84 O 2016

R

Raab, D. Writing for bliss. 2017
Publishers Weekly v264 no25 p102 Je 19 2017
Raab, L. Why don't we say what we mean? 2016
Publishers Weekly v263 no42 p62 O 17 2016
Rabin-Havt, A. Lies, Incorporated. 2016
Progressive p60-4 D 2016/Ja 2017 B. Lueders
Rabinovich, I. Yitzhak rabin. 2017
America v216 no12 p50-1 My 29 2017 K. P. Spicer
History Today v67 no9 p104-5 S 2017 C. Shindler
Rabinyan, D. and Cohen, J. All the Rivers. 2017
Publishers Weekly v264 no9 p71 F 27 2017
Weekly Standard v22 no39 p39-40 Je 19 2017 D. Scharper
Raboteau, A. J. American prophets. 2016
Christian Century v134 no16 p34-5 Ag 2 2017 D. Sack
Commonweal v143 no18 p43 N 11 2016 S. Haarman
Rachlin, B. Ghost of the innocent man. 2017
Publishers Weekly v264 no19 p46 My 8 2017
Publishers Weekly v264 no26 p54-62 Je 26 2017 A. Coreno
Rachman, G. Easternization. 2016
Foreign Affairs v96 no3 p172 My/Je 2017 A. J. Nathan
New York Review of Books v64 no8 p14-6 My 11 2017 J. T. Mathews
New York Times Book Review p31 My 14 2017 T. J. Christenson
Raczka, B. and Shin, S. Niko draws a feeling. 2017
Publishers Weekly v264 no5 p204 Ja 30 2017
Raczka, B. Wet cement. 2016
Publishers Weekly v263 no49 p55-6 D 7 2016
Raczka, L. Nothing. 2015
Publishers Weekly v264 no26 p183 Je 26 2017
Radel, T. Democrazy. 2017
Publishers Weekly v264 no6 p62 F 6 2017
Rademacher, K. H. and Turnbull, B. Following the red bird. 2017
Publishers Weekly v264 no15 p69 Ap 10 2017
Rader, D. Self-portrait as a Wikipedia entry. 2016
Publishers Weekly v264 no3 p37 Ja 16 2017
Radetzki, M. and Aguilera, R. F. The price of oil. 2016
Monthly Labor Review p1-3 Jl 2017 Y. Ivanchev
Radtke, K. Imagine wanting only this. 2017
New York Times Book Review p29 My 21 2017 A. Ulinich
Publishers Weekly v263 no52 p106 D 19 2016
Rae, K. Shattered. 2016
Publishers Weekly v264 no17 p58c Ap 24 2017
Raecke, R. and others. The Nutcracker & Mouseking. 2016
Publishers Weekly v263 no39 p93 S 26 2016
Ragan, T. R. Her Last Day. 2017
Publishers Weekly v264 no33 p52 Ag 14 2017
Ragsdale, L. and others. Alphabetter. 2017
Publishers Weekly v264 no14 p78 Ap 3. 2017
Rahe, P. A. Republics ancient and modern. 1992
Commentary v141 no9 p1-2 N 2016
Commentary v142 no4 p1-2 N 2016
Rahe, P. A. The Grand Strategy of Classical Sparta. 2015
Claremont Review of Books v16 no4 p61-3 Fall 2016 J. H. Maurer
Rahe, P. A. The Spartan regime. 2016
Commentary v142 no4 p53-4 N 2016 J. Howland
Rai, A. Wrong to need you. 2017
Publishers Weekly v264 no39 p91 S 25 2017
Raicovich, L. At the Lightning Field. 2017
Publishers Weekly v264 no7 p62 F 13 2017
Raine, K. The collected poems of Kathleen Raine. 2001
Commonweal v144 no4 p28-30 F 24 2017 A. Domestico
New York Times Book Review p22 O 23 2016 W. Logan
Rainer, T. Apprenticed to Venus. 2017
Publishers Weekly v264 no17 p78 Ap 24 2017
Rainey, B. and Rainey, D. The Art of Parenting. 2018
Publishers Weekly v264 no34 p23-8 Ag 21 2017 M. Z. Nelson
Raisin, R. A Natural. 2017
Publishers Weekly v264 no35 p100 Ag 28 2017
Rajendra, T. M. Migrants and citizens. 2017
Publishers Weekly v264 no24 p60 Je 12 2017
Rall, T. and others. The best democracy money can buy. 2016

Progressive p60-5 D 2016/Ja 2017 E. Rampell
Ramadan, A. D. The Clothesline Swing. 2017
Publishers Weekly v264 no15 p50 Ap 10 2017
Ramadan, E. and Garreta, A. Not one day. 2017
Publishers Weekly v264 no9 p72-3 F 27 2017
Ramadan, T. Introduction to Islam. 2017
Publishers Weekly v264 no33 p73 Ag 14 2017
Ramadier, C. and Bourgeau, V. Shhh! 2016
Publishers Weekly v263 no49 p59 D 7 2016
Ramadier, M. and Depommier, A. Sartre. 2017
Publishers Weekly v264 no38 p61 S 18 2017
Ramin, C. J. Crooked. 2017
Publishers Weekly v264 no16 p64 Ap 17 2017
Ramirez, B. R. Power from the margins. 2016
U.S. Catholic v82 no4 p41 Ap 2017
Ramirez, C. A. and Muñoz Molina, A. Like a fading shadow. 2017
Publishers Weekly v264 no22 p40 My 29 2017
Ramirez, M. and Ramirez, S. A. The Case for the Corporate Death Penalty. 2017
Publishers Weekly v263 no44 p63 O 31 2016
Ramos, F. and others. Sonia Delaunay. 2017
New York Times Book Review p29 Ag 27 2017 M. Russo
Ramsay, C. Standing Still. 2017
Publishers Weekly v264 no15 p56 Ap 10 2017
Ramsay, F. Copper kettle. 2017
Publishers Weekly v263 no43 p56 O 24 2016
Ramsay, H. A small-town bride. 2017
Publishers Weekly v264 no9 p84 F 27 2017
Ramsey, G. P. and others. The transformation of black music. 2017
Downbeat v84 no8 p83 Ag 2017 E. J. Holley
Randall, D. K. The King and Queen of Malibu. 2016
New York Times Book Review p24 Ap 2 2017 J. Khatib
Randall, E. The twelve days of Christmas. 2017
Publishers Weekly v264 no36 p94 S 4 2017
Randall, F. and Luzzatto, S. Primo Levi's resistance. 2016
Foreign Affairs v96 no1 p166 Ja/F 2017 A. Moravcsik
Randall, F. and Morselli, G. The communist. 2017
Publishers Weekly v264 no17 p60 Ap 24 2017
Randall, W. S. Unshackling America. 2017
Publishers Weekly v264 no18 p51-2 My 1 2017
Randolph, L. The Instant Pot Electric Pressure Cooker Cookbook. 2016
Publishers Weekly v264 no10 p20-31 Mr 6 2017 C. Swanso
Range, M. Horse and rider. 2010
Dressage Today v23 no9 p72 Je 2017 S. Von Dietze
Ranger, A. and others. Mutant bunny island. 2017
Publishers Weekly v264 no38 p69-71 S 18 2017
Ranger, A. and others. Opposite day. 2017
Publishers Weekly v263 no45 p59 N 7 2016
Rankin, A. and McNamara, E. Toss your own salad. 2017
Publishers Weekly v264 no16 p61-2 Ap 17 2017
Rankin, I. Rather Be the Devil. 2017
New York Times Book Review p15 F 5 2017 M. Stasio
Publishers Weekly v263 no47 p30 N 21 2016 J. F.
Publishers Weekly v263 no47 p92 N 21 2016
Rankin, J. and Hartmann, W. This is the chick. 2017
Publishers Weekly v264 no38 p68 S 18 2017
Ranney, K. The English Duke. 2017
Publishers Weekly v264 no5 p186 Ja 30 2017
Ransmeier, J. S. Sold people. 2017
Foreign Affairs v96 no6 p170 N/D 2017 A. J. Nathan
Ransom, C. and Grove, C. Amanda Panda quits kindergarten. 2017
Publishers Weekly v264 no20 p55 My 15 2017
Ransome, J. and Cline-Ransome, L. Germs. 2017
Publishers Weekly v263 no44 p79 O 31 2016
Ransome, J. and McMorrow, T. E. Nutcracker in Harlem. 2016
Publishers Weekly v264 no36 p99 S 4 2017
Ransome, J. E. and Cline-Ransome, L. Before she was Harriet. 2018
Publishers Weekly v264 no41 p65 O 9 2017
Ranucci, C. and Fliess, S. We Wish for a Monster Christmas. 207
Publishers Weekly v264 no36 p97 S 4 2017
Rao, J. C. and Rao, J. C. Luther and His Progeny. 2017
Nation v305 no3 p31-5 Jl 31 2017 E. Bruenig

Rao, S. Bollywood kitchen. 2017
Publishers Weekly v264 no34 p104 Ag 21 2017
Raphel, A. What Was It For. 2017
New York Times Book Review p26 Ag 6 2017 K. Rooney
Rapoport, R. and Lardner, R. The lost journalism of Ring
Lardner. 2017
Weekly Standard v22 no43 p30-2 Jl 24 2017
Rapoport, R. and Yoder, J. A. Math lab for kids. 2017
Publishers Weekly v264 no5 p206 Ja 30 2017
Rappaport, D. 42 Is Not Just a Number. 2017
Publishers Weekly v264 no28 p91 Jl 10 2017
Rappaport, E. A thirst for empire. 2017
Publishers Weekly v264 no23 p45-6 Je 5 2017
Rappaport, H. Caught in the revolution. 2017
New York Times Book Review p8 F 26 2017 O. Matthews
Publishers Weekly v263 no52 p108-10 D 19 2016
Rapport, M. The unruly city. 2017
New York Times Book Review p26 My 21 2017 R. Shorto
Publishers Weekly v264 no12 p67 Mr 20 2017
Raschka, C. and Fogliano, J. Old dog baby baby. 2016
New York Times Book Review p22 N 13 2016 M. Russo
Publishers Weekly v263 no49 p34 D 7 2016
Raschka, C. and Raschka, C. A song about myself. 2017
New York Times Book Review p15 Ap 9 2017 M. Russo
Publishers Weekly v264 no3 p63 Ja 16 2017
Rash, A. and Levis, C. May I have a word? 2017
Publishers Weekly v264 no10 p61 Mr 6 2017
Rashid, M. Out of the wild. 2016
Trail Rider v29 no1 p14 Ja/F 2017 C. Lamm
Raskin, E. Best intentions. 2017
Publishers Weekly v264 no25 p88-9 Je 19 2017
Rasmussen, E. and others. A midsummer night's dream. 2012
Publishers Weekly v264 no34 p14 Ag 21 2017 J. Milliot
Raspanti, J. J. and Taylor, D. Intimate warfare. 2017
Publishers Weekly v263 no42 p58-60 O 17 2016
Rathbone, E. Losing it. 2016
New York Times Book Review p28 Jl 23 2017 J. Khatib
Rathbun, R. The Great Wall of China and the Salton Sea. 2016
Christian Century v134 no19 p43 S 13 2017
Publishers Weekly v263 no41 p73 O 10 2016
Rather, D. and Kirschner, E. What unites us. 2017
Publishers Weekly v264 no36 p82 S 4 2017
Ratner, V. Music of the ghosts. 2017
Ms. v27 no1 p46-7 Spr 2017
New York Times Book Review p10 My 28 2017 G. Bahadur
New York Times Book Review p55 Je 4 2017
Publishers Weekly v264 no6 p42 F 6 2017
Ratterree, A. and Broach, E. The wolf keepers. 2016
Publishers Weekly v264 no49 p70 D 7 2016
Ratterree, A. and Slade, S. Dangerous Jane. 2017
Publishers Weekly v264 no32 p71 Ag 7 2017
Rausch, T. P. Systematic theology. 2016
America v215 p34-6 N 28 2016 T. W. Tilley
Rauser, R. and Schieber, J. An atheist and a Christian walk into a
bar... 2016
Publishers Weekly v263 no41 p74-5 O 10 2016
Rausing, S. Mayhem. 2017
Publishers Weekly v264 no33 p71 Ag 14 2017
Ravatn, A. and Hedger, R. The Bird Tribunal. 2017
Publishers Weekly v263 no48 p50 N 28 2016
Raverat, A. Lover. 2017
Publishers Weekly v264 no4 p51-2 Ja 23 2017
Rawlence, B. City of thorns. 2016
Phi Kappa Phi Forum v96 no4 p30 Wint 2016 B. Colvin
Rayborn, T. Beethoven's Skull. 2016
Publishers Weekly v263 no39 p77 S 26 2016
Raybourn, D. A perilous undertaking. 2017
Publishers Weekly v263 no46 p34 N 14 2016
Raymer, M. G. Quantum Physics. 2017
Skeptical Inquirer v41 no5 p60-1 S/O 2017 B. Radford
Raymond, E. and others. Humans, bow down. 2016
Publishers Weekly v264 no10 p12 Mr 6 2017 C. Juris
Raymond, J. Freebird. 2017
Publishers Weekly v264 no42 p44 O 17 2016
Raymond, M. D. and Engell, J. William Wordsworth. 1964
New York Review of Books v64 no3 p45-7 F 23 2017 H. Vendler

Raymundo, P. and Raymundo, P. Third grade mermaid. 2017
Publishers Weekly v263 no47 p109 N 21 2016
Rayn, A. B. Black-Winged Tuesday. 2016
Publishers Weekly v263 no47 p96 N 21 2016
Publishers Weekly v263 no52 p90a D 19 2016
Rayne, K. and others. Girl. 2017
Publishers Weekly v264 no20 p57 My 15 2017
Rayne, S. Death Notes. 2017
Publishers Weekly v263 no43 p58 O 24 2016
Rayner, R. P. and Collins, M. A. Road to Perdition. 2002
Publishers Weekly v263 no39 p68 S 26 2016
Read, P. The Art Teacher. 2017
Publishers Weekly v263 no46 p35 N 14 2016
Read, W. Ash Falls. 2017
Publishers Weekly v264 no16 p36 Ap 17 2017
Reagan, J. and Wildish, L. How to get a teacher ready. 2016
Publishers Weekly v264 no20 p54 My 15 2017
Reagan, J. and Wildish, L. How to raise a mom. 2017
Publishers Weekly v264 no8 p83 F 20 2017
Reardon, M. and Bennett, E. Noodles' & Albie's Birthday
Surprise. 2016
Publishers Weekly v264 no4 p50g Ja 23 2017
Reardon, S. The Prometheus man. 2017
Publishers Weekly v263 no43 p57 O 24 2016
Rebeck, T. I'm glad about you. 2016
New York Times Book Review p24 Mr 26 2017 J. Khatib
Reck, J. A short history of the girl next door. 2017
Publishers Weekly v264 no27 p77 Jl 3 2017
Record, A. and Paquette, A. Elf in the house. 2017
Publishers Weekly v264 no36 p94 S 4 2017
Rector, J. The Ridge. 2017
Publishers Weekly v264 no7 p54 F 13 2017
Redel, V. Before everything. 2017
Publishers Weekly v264 no16 p37 Ap 17 2017
Redford, K. A Very Cowboy Christmas. 2017
Publishers Weekly v264 no36 p75 S 4 2017
Redford, K. Blazing Hot Cowboy. 2017
Publishers Weekly v263 no46 p40 N 14 2016
Rediker, M. The fearless Benjamin Lay. 2017
Publishers Weekly v264 no26 p167-8 Je 26 2017
Redwood, J. Poison. 2013
Publishers Weekly v264 no38 p46 S 18 2017
Redzepi, N. L. Downtime. 2017
Publishers Weekly v264 no32 p66 Ag 7 2017
Reece, E. Utopia drive. 2016
New York Review of Books v64 no6 p18-20 Ap 6 2017 C. Benfey
Orion Magazine v36 no1 p59-60 Ja/F 2017 M. P. Branch
Reed, E. Ruined stones. 2017
Publishers Weekly v264 no18 p39 My 1 2017
Reed, J. Ten days that shook the world. 2007
In These Times v41 no10 p44 O 2017
Reed, J. The baker's appendix. 2017
Publishers Weekly v264 no10 p32 Mr 6 2017
Reed, K. Mormama. 2017
Publishers Weekly v264 no14 p58 Ap 3 2017
Reed, L. R. and Montijo, R. Benny Shark Goes to Friend School.
2017
Publishers Weekly v264 no20 p55 My 15 2017
Reed, L. W. Real heroes. 2016
Forbes v198 no7 p32 N 29 2016
Reed, M. No Rest for the Wicked. 2017
Publishers Weekly v264 no39 p80b S 25 2017
Reeder, L. Dust bowl girls. 2017
Publishers Weekly v264 no14 p73 Ap 3 2017
Reef, C. Florence Nightingale. 2017
Publishers Weekly v263 no40 p127 O 3 2016
Publishers Weekly v263 no49 p122 D 7 2016
Reep, D. C. Kiss'd. 2016
Publishers Weekly v264 no6 p70 F 6 2017
Publishers Weekly v264 no9 p66k F 27 2017
Rees, D. W. Mechanics of solids and structures. 2000
Physics Today v70 no5 p62 My 2017
Rees, M. The 7th Threat. 2017
Publishers Weekly v264 no19 p39 My 8 2017
Reese, B. and Charlesworth, L. Amazing Animals. 2017
Publishers Weekly v263 no50 p72 D 5 2016

Reese, B. Can you canoe? 2016
  Publishers Weekly v263 no49 p20 D 7 2016
Reese, B. Thousand Star Hotel. 2017
  New York Times Book Review p26 Ag 6 2017 K. Rooney
  Publishers Weekly v264 no26 p154 Je 26 2017
Reese, L. W. Trail sisters. 2013
  American Indian Quarterly v40 no3 p274-6 Summ 2016 A. L. Coleman
Reeve, P. and Baumard, N. The origins of fairness. 2016
  BioScience v67 no2 p180-2 F 2017 J. Witteveen
Reeve, P. Railhead. 2016
  Publishers Weekly v263 no49 p112-3 D 7 2016
Reeves, R. V. Dream hoarders. 2017
  National Review v69 no16 p42-4 Ag 28 2017 R. Verbruggen
Regan, P. Musical Christmas tree. 2017
  Publishers Weekly v264 no36 p92 S 4 2017
Regev, O. and others. Modern Fluid Dynamics for Physics and Astrophysics. 2016
  Physics Today v70 no5 p60 My 2017 G. Lodato
Regnerus, M. Cheap sex. 2017
  Christianity Today v61 no7 p81 S 2017
  Commentary v144 no2 p46-7 S 2017 N. S. Riley
Rehmeyer, J. Through the shadowlands. 2017
  Publishers Weekly v263 no52 p119-20 D 19 2016
  Scientific American v317 no2 p80 Ag 2017 C. Moskowitz
Reich, S. and Gustavson, A. Stand up and sing! 2017
  Publishers Weekly v264 no7 p75 F 13 2017
Reichs, K. Bones of the lost. 2013
  Publishers Weekly v264 no17 p73 Ap 24 2017
Reichs, K. Two nights. 2017
  Publishers Weekly v264 no18 p38 My 1 2017
  Publishers Weekly v264 no30 p11 Jl 24 2017 C. Juris
Reid, J. Sins of the younger sons. 2017
  Texas Monthly v45 no6 p64 Je 2017
Reid, K. and Maruk, D. Dennis Maruk. 2017
  Publishers Weekly v264 no35 p117 Ag 28 2017
Reid, M. DIY Mediation. 2016
  People Management p56 N 2016
Reid, N. Pretend we are lovely. 2017
  New York Times Book Review p21 Jl 30 2017 H. Pitlor
  Publishers Weekly v264 no20 p31 My 15 2017
Reid, R. L. Because it is so beautiful. 2017
  Earth Island Journal v32 no3 p55 Aut 2017 G. Wingenbach
Reid, T. R. A Fine Mess. 2017
  Foreign Affairs v96 no3 p157 My/Je 2017 R. N. Cooper
  New York Times Book Review p10 Je 25 2017 D. C. Johnston
  New York Times Book Review p22 Jl 2 2017
  Publishers Weekly v264 no2 p53 Ja 9 2017
Reilly, K. M. and Thompson, C. Fault Lines & Tectonic Plates. 2017
  Publishers Weekly v263 no51 p149 D 12 2016
Reilly, W. M. It takes one to tango. 2017
  New York Times Book Review p27 Ap 23 2017 J. Newman
Reinbold, C. and Monson, A. How we speak to one another. 2017
  Publishers Weekly v263 no42 p23-30 O 17 2016 C. Teicher
Reinhardt, D. M. Delectable Destinations. 2017
  Missouri Life v43 no7 p16 D 2016/Ja 2017 M. W. Schwartz
Reinhardt, D. Tell us something true. 2016
  Publishers Weekly v263 no49 p104 D 7 2016
Reinhardt, J. B. and Park, L. S. Yaks yak. 2016
  Publishers Weekly v263 no49 p27 D 7 2016
Reinhart, M. and Reinhart, M. Frozen. 2016
  Publishers Weekly v263 no41 p81 O 10 2016
Reinke, T. 12 ways your phone is changing you. 2017
  Christianity Today v61 no4 p64 My 2017 J. Haanen
Reisacher, E. A. Joyful witness in the Muslim world. 2016
  Christianity Today v61 no1 p55 Ja/F 2017 C. Horst
Reising, R. and others. What a mess! 2017
  Publishers Weekly v264 no35 p127 Ag 28 2017
  Publishers Weekly v264 no39 p80e S 25 2017
Reiss, A. The acid test. 2011
  Publishers Weekly v263 no45 p40 N 7 2016
Reiss, B. Wild nights. 2017
  Discover v38 no3 p20 Ap 2017 G. Tarlach
  Publishers Weekly v264 no5 p190 Ja 30 2017
  Time v189 no9 p20 Mr 13 2017 S. Begley

Weekly Standard v22 no35 p35-6 My 22 2017 K. Gulliver
Reiss, C. D. Bombshell. 2017
  Publishers Weekly v264 no11 p64 Mr 13 2017
Reitano, T. and Tinti, P. Migrant, Refugee, Smuggler, Savior. 2017
  Publishers Weekly v264 no7 p65 F 13 2017
Rekdal, P. The broken country. 2017
  Publishers Weekly v264 no29 p209 Jl 17 2017
Rekulak, J. The Impossible Fortress. 2017
  Publishers Weekly v264 no48 p40 N 28 2016
Rémond-Dalyac, E. and Dieterlé, N. Good night. 2017
  Publishers Weekly v264 no25 p110 Je 19 2017
Rendahl, E. Cover me in darkness. 2016
  Publishers Weekly v263 no43 p60 O 24 2016
Rendall, S. and Bruckner, P. The wisdom of money. 2017
  New York Times Book Review p15 My 14 2017 F. Salmon
Rendall, S. and others. Montaigne. 2017
  History Today v67 no7 p94-5 Jl 2017 N. Kenny
  National Review v69 no4 p39-44 Mr 6 2017 D. Green
  New Yorker v92 no45 p81-5 Ja 16 2017 A. Gopnik
Rendon, M. R. Murder on the red river. 2017
  Publishers Weekly v264 no5 p181 Ja 30 2017
Renfroe, R. and Robb, E. The Wonder of Christmas Devotions for the Season. 2016
  Publishers Weekly v263 no40 p84 O 3 2016 L. Garret
Renn, J. and Gutfreund, H. The formative years of general relativity. 2017
  New York Times Book Review p35 Ag 27 2017 J. Ryerson
  Science v357 no6353 p763 Ag 25 2017 A. Robinson
Renner, B. The big bad fox. 2017
  Publishers Weekly v264 no15 p75 Ap 10 2017
Reno, R. R. Resurrecting the Idea of a Christian Society. 2016
  America v215 no12 p36-7 O 24 2016 J. J. Conley
  National Review v68 no19 p48-9 O 24 2016 R. Lu
Rens, K. and Fawcett, H. Even the darkest stars. 2017
  Publishers Weekly v264 no30 p62 Jl 24 2017
Rens, K. and others. Samson. 2017
  Publishers Weekly v263 no47 p107 N 21 2016
Renzi, R. and others. Superman. 2016
  Publishers Weekly v263 no44 p60 O 31 2016
Repentance Ritual of the Emperor of Liang. 2016
  Tricycle: The Buddhist Review v26 no2 p90 Wint 2016 M. Scarles
Repino, R. D'arc. 2017
  Publishers Weekly v264 no10 p44-5 Mr 6 2017
Replogle, G. and others. Egoism. 2017
  Reason v49 no6 p77 N 2017 J. Walker
Rescek, S. and Burton, J. The Itsy Bitsy Duckling. 2017
  Publishers Weekly v263 no50 p72 D 5 2016
Rescek, S. and others. The Itsy Bitsy Dreidel. 2017
  Publishers Weekly v264 no36 p92 S 4 2017
Reséndez, A. The other slavery. 2016
  New York Review of Books v63 no18 p70-3 N 24 2016 P. Nabokov
Resnick, M. and Robyn, L. Soulmates. 2016
  Publishers Weekly v263 no41 p61 O 10 2016
Reston, J. A rift in the Earth. 2017
  New York Times Book Review p21 S 17 2017 M. J. Lewis
  Publishers Weekly v264 no31 p79 Jl 31 2017
Reve, G. and Garrett, S. The evenings. 2016
  Weekly Standard v22 no33 p42-3 My 8 2017 B. Bawer
Revel, S. Glenn Gould. 2016
  Publishers Weekly v263 no45 p49 N 7 2016
Revis, B. A World Without You. 2016
  Publishers Weekly v263 no49 p106 D 7 2016
Rex, A. and Campbell, S. XO, OX. 2017
  New York Times Book Review p18 Ja 15 2017 J. Livshin
  Publishers Weekly v263 no42 p66-8 O 17 2016
Rex, A. and Daywalt, D. The Legend of Rock Paper Scissors. 2017
  Publishers Weekly v264 no6 p68 F 6 2017
Rex, A. and Rex, A. Nothing rhymes with orange. 2017
  Publishers Weekly v264 no22 p68 My 29 2017
Rex, A. and Robinson, C. School's first day of school. 2016
  Publishers Weekly v263 no49 p25 D 7 2016
Reyes, E. and Alarcón, D. The book of Emma Reyes. 2017
  New Yorker v93 no28 p64 S 18 2017
Reyes, P. B. Nobody Cries When We Die. 2016
  Christian Century v134 no13 p39 Je 21 2017 R. Saler
Reyl, H. Kids like us. 2017

Ridgeway, J. and others. Hell is a very small place. 2016
New York Review of Books v63 no19 p24-6 D 8 2016 M. Garbus
Orion Magazine v35 no3 p56-9 My/Je 2016 K. Vandenberg
Ridings, S. P. The Chisholm trail. 1936
American Cowboy v23 no6 p23 Ap/My 2017
Ridland, J. Sir Gawain and the Green Knight. 2016
Weekly Standard v22 no45 p36-7 Ag 7 2017 J. M. Wilson
Ridler, J. Hex-rated. 2017
Publishers Weekly v264 no24 p47 Je 12 2017
Ridley, M. The evolution of everything. 2015
New York Times Book Review p24 D 18 2016 J. Khatib
Riebling, M. Church of spies. 2015
Commonweal v144 no4 p16-9 F 24 2017 J. Connelly
Rieff, D. In Praise of Forgetting. 2016
History Today v67 no3 p64 Mr 2017 D. Lowenthal
New York Times Book Review p28 My 7 2017 J. Khatib
Rieger, S. The Heirs. 2017
New York Times Book Review p18 Je 25 2017 C. Leavitt
Publishers Weekly v264 no11 p53 Mr 13 2017
Rifkin, M. Settler common sense. 2014
American Indian Quarterly v41 no2 p180-2 Spr 2017 G. D. Smithers
Rigaud, L. and Boisrobert, A. That's my hat! 2016
Publishers Weekly v263 no49 p60 D 7 2016
Riggle, N. On being awesome. 2017
Publishers Weekly v264 no29 p211 Jl 17 2017
Riggs, C. Trumpet of death. 2017
Publishers Weekly v264 no8 p67-8 F 20 2017
Riggs, K. and Dogi, F. Crowds of creatures. 2017
Publishers Weekly v264 no5 p203 Ja 30 2017
Riggs, N. The bright hour. 2017
Entertainment Weekly no1471 p66 Je 23 2017
Publishers Weekly v264 no17 p85 Ap 24 2017
Riggs, R. and Davidson, A. Tales of the Peculiar. 2016
New York Times Book Review p19 N 20 2016 B. D. Wong
Riggs, T. Real food, real simple. 2017
Publishers Weekly v263 no52 p119 D 19 2016
Rigolini, J. and others. Left behind. 2016
Foreign Affairs v96 no3 p167 My/Je 2017 R. Feinberg
Riley, D. Fly me. 2017
New Yorker v93 no25 p85 Ag 28 2017
New York Times Book Review p11 Je 25 2017 C. V. Watkins
Publishers Weekly v264 no17 p65 Ap 24 2017
Riley, G. First love. 2017
New York Times Book Review p11 My 21 2017 J. Lasdun
Riley, L. It happened on Love Street. 2017
Publishers Weekly v264 no14 p60 Ap 3. 2017
Riley, R. L. Inside the Clinton White House. 2016
Phi Kappa Phi Forum v97 no1 p31 Spr 2017
Time v188 no14 p60 O 10 2016 L. Rothman
Riley, V. and Walden, L. Bear Hugs. 2017
Publishers Weekly v264 no5 p202-3 Ja 30 2017
Riley-Webb, C. and Golio, G. Strange fruit. 2017
Publishers Weekly v264 no7 p75 F 13 2017
Rim, S. and Rim, S. Chee-Kee. 2017
Publishers Weekly v263 no47 p105-7 N 21 2016
Rimmington, N. and Barnhill, C. Rufus and the very special baby. 2016
Publishers Weekly v263 no39 p84 S 26 2016
Rimmington, N. and others. Clap, sing, dance! 2017
Publishers Weekly v264 no21 p90 My 22 2017
Rinaldi, T. The Red Bandanna. 2017
AARP: The Magazine v59 no5A p14 Ag/S 2016 D. D.
New York Times Book Review p30 O 30 2016 T. Vinciguerra
Ring, M. So High a Blood. 2017
Publishers Weekly v264 no7 p61 F 13 2017
Ringle, M. The Goblins of Bellwater. 2017
Publishers Weekly v264 no35 p111 Ag 28 2017
Rinker, S. D. and Lichtenheld, T. Goodnight, goodnight, construction site. 2011
Publishers Weekly v264 no31 p86 Jl 31 2017
Rinker, S. D. and Lichtenheld, T. Mighty, mighty construction site. 2017
New York Times Book Review p22-3 My 14 2017 J. Sturm
Publishers Weekly v263 no48 p65 N 28 2016
Rinker, S. D. and Parker, J. The 12 sleighs of Christmas. 2017

Publishers Weekly v264 no36 p91 S 4 2017
Rinker, S. D. and Rocco, J. Big machines. 2017
New York Times Book Review p29 Ag 27 2017 M. Russo
Publishers Weekly v264 no32 p70 Ag 7 2017
Rio, M. L. If We Were Villains. 2017
Publishers Weekly v264 no9 p71 F 27 2017
Riordan, R. For Magnus Chase: Hotel Valhalla guide to the Norse worlds. 2016
New York Times Book Review p19 N 20 2016 B. D. Wong
Riordan, R. The Hammer of Thor. 2016
New York Times Book Review p23 D 25 2016
New York Times Book Review p23 Ja 1 2017
New York Times Book Review p35 D 11 2016
New York Times Book Review p79 D 4 2016
Riordan, R. The hidden oracle. 2016
New York Times Book Review p35 D 11 2016
Rios, J. Shadowboxing. 2017
Publishers Weekly v264 no38 p53 S 18 2017
Rios, V. M. Punished. 2011
Nation v33 no21 p11 N 21 2016 E. Hinton
Ripani, M. and others. Energy from nuclear fission. 2016
Physics Today v70 no3 p61-2 Mr 2017 N. Corngold
Ripley, M. Mr. Campion's Abdication. 2017
Publishers Weekly v264 no36 p67-8 S 4 2017
Ripp, V. Hell's traces. 2017
Publishers Weekly v263 no51 p135-6 D 12 2016
Ripper, K. As La Vista Turns. 2017
Publishers Weekly v264 no4 p63-4 Ja 23 2017
Ripper, K. One Life to Lose. 2016
Publishers Weekly v263 no45 p47 N 7 2016
Ripper, K. The Queer and the Restless. 2016
Publishers Weekly v263 no40 p106-7 O 3 2016
Rips, N. Trying to float. 2016
New Yorker v92 no38 p88 N 21 2016
Ripsman, N. M. Peacemaking from above, peace from below. 2016
Foreign Affairs v95 no6 p172-3 N/D 2016 G. J. Ikenberry
Riss, S. and Sockwell, J. The optimist's guide to divorce. 2016
Publishers Weekly v264 no1 p47 Ja 2 2017
Rissi, A. M. and Ohora, Z. The teacher's pet. 2017
New York Times Book Review p27 Ag 27 2017 M. Russo
Publishers Weekly v264 no20 p53 My 15 2017
Ritvo, M. Four reincarnations. 2016
New York Times Book Review p19 F 5 2017 D. Orr
Rivadeneira, C. and Betz, K. Grit and grace. 2017
Publishers Weekly v264 no33 p82 Ag 14 2017
Rivas, V. and Miedoso, A. The haunted house next door. 2017
Publishers Weekly v264 no39 p106 S 25 2017
Rivera, K. A. The Tiger's Daughter. 2017
Publishers Weekly v264 no33 p54 Ag 14 2017
Rivera, L. The education of Margot Sanchez. 2017
New York Times Book Review p28 My 14 2017 I. Zoboi
Publishers Weekly v263 no47 p111 N 21 2016
Rivers, A. Best Laid Plans & Other Disasters. 2017
Publishers Weekly v264 no9 p53-66 F 27 2017
Rivers, K. Love, Ish. 2017
Publishers Weekly v264 no2 p68 Ja 9 2017
Rivers, M. The book of Joan. 2015
Publishers Weekly v264 no8 p60 F 20 2017
Rivers, S. The second Mrs. Hockaday. 2016
Publishers Weekly v264 no40 p96 O 3 2016
Rivkin-Fish, M. and others. Understanding health inequalities and justice. 2016
Science v354 no6315 p978 N 25 2016 D. Goldberg
Rix, L. and Szabó, M. Katalin Street. 2017
Publishers Weekly v264 no29 p193 Jl 17 2017
Rizvi, A. A. The atheist Muslim. 2016
Commentary v141 no9 p1-2 N 2016
Commentary v142 no4 p1-2 N 2016
Commentary v142 no4 p38-9 N 2016 O. Kessler
New York Times Book Review p10-1 Ja 15 2017 K. Abdul-Jabbar
Roach, M. Grunt. 2016
MHQ: Quarterly Journal of Military History v29 no2 p93-4 Wint 2017 R. Soodalter
Publishers Weekly v263 no40 p120 O 3 2016
Roads, A. Hunt the Dawn. 2016
Publishers Weekly v263 no44 p59 O 31 2016

Roscigno, V. J. and Danaher, W. F. The voice of southern labor. 2004
  Monthly Labor Review p1-2 My 2017 R. Weir
Rose, A. Men of war. 2015
  Military History v33 no6 p70-1 Mr 2017 S. L. Hoffman
Rose, A. The readymade thief. 2017
  O, The Oprah Magazine p91 S 2017 L. Schillinger
  Publishers Weekly v264 no26 p148 Je 26 2017
  Vanity Fair v59 no9 p138 S 2017 S. Crosley
Rose, D. L. and Veltkamp, J. Beauty and the Beak. 2017
  Publishers Weekly v264 no28 p87 Jl 10 2017
Rose, E. M. The murder of William of Norwich. 2015
  New York Review of Books v63 no16 p51-3 O 27 2016 E. Duffy
Rose, J. F. The well-tempered city. 2016
  Architectural Record v204 no11 p49 N 2016 J. Gauer
  Science v354 no6311 p423 O 28 2016 S. D. Campbell
Rose, K. Every Dark Corner. 2017
  Publishers Weekly v263 no52 p106 D 19 2016
Rose, L. A. America's sailors in the great war. 2017
  Military History v34 no2 p74 Jl 2017 R. Guttman
  Missouri Life v44 no2 p22 Ap 2017 M. W. Schwartz
Rose, M. J. The library of light and shadow. 2017
  Publishers Weekly v264 no21 p73 My 22 2017
Rosen, J. A torch kept lit. 2016
  American Conservative v16 no1 p48-51 Ja/F 2017 J. R. Coyne Jr.
  National Review v68 no19 p42-3 O 24 2016 M. K. Beran
  Weekly Standard v22 no10 p36 N 14 2016 A. S. Felzenberg
Rosen, J. L. Nine women, one dress. 2016
  New York Times Book Review p30 O 16 2016 S. Gilbert
Rosen, M. S. and others. Sergei M. Eisenstein. 2016
  Film Quarterly v70 no2 p111-3 Wint 2016 D. Polan
Rosen, M. The Disappearance of Emile Zola. 2017
  Publishers Weekly v264 no22 p52 My 29 2017
Rosen, R. A. and Mosnier, J. Julius Chambers. 2016
  Publishers Weekly v263 no43 p72 O 24 2016
Rosen, W. Miracle cure. 2017
  Publishers Weekly v264 no11 p74 Mr 13 2017
  Science News v191 no9 p29 My 13 2017
Rosenberg, A. and Xilonen, A. The Gringo Champion. 2017
  New York Times Book Review p26 F 19 2017 A. McCulloch
Rosenberg, M. and Shang, W. W. This is just a test. 2017
  New York Times Book Review p23 Ag 27 2017 S. Mosle
  Publishers Weekly v264 no16 p67 Ap 17 2017
Rosenberg, R. Jane Crow. 2017
  Advocate no1090 p59 Ap 2017
  Christian Century v134 no22 p40-1 O 25 2017 L. Schnabel
  Publishers Weekly v264 no3 p50 Ja 16 2017
Rosenblatt, D. Lost Boys. 2017
  Publishers Weekly v264 no23 p54 Je 5 2017
Rosenblatt, R. Thomas Murphy. 2016
  New York Times Book Review p24 Ja 15 2017 J. Khatib
Rosenblum, J. and Berg, J. Friction. 2017
  Fortune v175 no7 p18 Je 1 2017 A. Vandermey
Rosenblum, J. Beyond $15. 2017
  America v216 no11 p55 My 15 2017 T. Deignan
Rosenblum, N. L. Good neighbors. 2016
  New Yorker v92 no36 p72-5 N 7 2016 J. Rothman
Rosenblum, S. and Tipton, E. Beautiful Criminals. 2017
  Publishers Weekly v264 no26 p151 Je 26 2017
Rosenbluth, F. M. and Ferejohn, J. Forged through fire. 2017
  Foreign Affairs v96 no2 p167 Mr/Ap 2017 G. J. Ikenberry
Rosenbush, E. and Melucci, G. Know that what you eat you are. 2017
  Publishers Weekly v264 no39 p101 S 25 2017
Rosenfeld, D. The worlds we think we know. 2017
  Publishers Weekly v264 no11 p55-6 Mr 13 2017
Rosenfeld, G. D. What ifs of Jewish history. 2016
  History Today v67 no3 p60 Mr 2017 C. Shindler
Rosenfelt, D. Collared. 2017
  Publishers Weekly v264 no19 p39 My 8 2017
Rosengren, C. Velvet on a Tuesday afternoon. 2017
  Publishers Weekly v264 no38 p57-8 S 18 2017
Rosengren, J. The fight of their lives. 2014
  U.S. Catholic v82 no2 p33-5 F 2017 J. Rosengren
Rosenheim, J. L. Diane Arbus. 2016
  Art in America v104 no9 p68 O 2016

Rosenstiel, T. Shining City. 2017
  Publishers Weekly v263 no46 p31-2 N 14 2016
Rosenstock, B. and Grandpré, M. Vincent Can't Sleep. 2017
  Publishers Weekly v264 no41 p65 O 9 2017
Rosenthal, A. K. and Barrager, B. Uni the unicorn and the dream come true. 2017
  Publishers Weekly v264 no29 p219 Jl 17 2017
Rosenthal, A. K. and others. Dear girl. 2018
  Publishers Weekly v264 no41 p66 O 9 2017
Rosenthal, A. K. and White, T. That's me loving you. 2016
  Publishers Weekly v263 no44 p74-5 O 31 2016
Rosenthal, B. and Carman, P. Mr. Gedrick and me. 2017
  Publishers Weekly v264 no39 p108 S 25 2017
Rosenthal, B. and Jackson, T. D. Allegedly. 2017
  Publishers Weekly v263 no41 p47 O 10 2016
  Publishers Weekly v263 no46 p59 N 14 2016
  Publishers Weekly v264 no27 p36-40 Jl 3 2017 K. P. Goddu
Rosenthal, B. and Laskin, P. L. Ronit & Jamal. 2017
  Publishers Weekly v264 no48 p68-70 N 28 2016
Rosenthal, B. and McGinnis, M. The female of the species. 2016
  Publishers Weekly v263 no49 p114 D 7 2016
Rosenthal, B. and others. How dare the sun rise. 2017
  Publishers Weekly v264 no12 p75 Mr 20 2017
Rosenthal, B. and others. Muhammad Ali. 2017
  New York Times Book Review p15 F 12 2017 M. Russo
  Publishers Weekly v263 no51 p147 D 12 2016
Rosenthal, E. An American sickness. 2017
  America v217 no5 p44-7 S 4 2017 K. Sue Smith
  New York Review of Books v64 no12 p47-50 Jl 13 2017 P. Hartzband
  New York Times Book Review p1-20 Ap 9 2017 J. S. Hacker
  Publishers Weekly v264 no6 p56 F 6 2017
  Washington Monthly v49 no9/10 p122-5 S/O 2017 S. Brownlee
Rosenthal, G. G. Mate choice. 2017
  Science v357 no6356 p1103 S 15 2017 L. Sun
Rosenthal, M. and Verdick, E. Small Walt. 2017
  Publishers Weekly v264 no31 p88 Jl 31 2017
Rosenthal, P. and others. Dear girl. 2018
  Publishers Weekly v264 no41 p66 O 9 2017
Rosenzweig, J. and others. To build a free China. 2017
  Foreign Affairs v96 no3 p175 My/Je 2017 E. Pils
Rosenzweig, L. B. Hollywood's spies. 2017
  Publishers Weekly v264 no24 p54 Je 12 2017
Rosin, H. The end of men. 2012
  Publishers Weekly v264 no16 p40 Ap 17 2017
Rosner, E. Survivor Café. 2017
  Publishers Weekly v264 no26 p169 Je 26 2017
Rosoff, M. and Peet, M. Beck. 2016
  Publishers Weekly v264 no9 p101-3 F 27 2017
Ross, A. B. Miss Julia Weathers the Storm. 2017
  Publishers Weekly v264 no9 p77 F 27 2017
Ross, A. The industries of the future. 2016
  Foreign Affairs v96 no1 p159-60 Ja/F 2017 R. N. Cooper
Ross, C. The Lost Diaries of Susanna Moodie. 2017
  Maclean's v130 no4 p71 My 2017 B. Josef Grubisic
Ross, D. Doomed to succeed. 2015
  Foreign Affairs v95 no6 p132-8 N/D 2016 P. Gordon
Ross, H. and Messner, K. Fergus and Zeke. 2017
  Publishers Weekly v264 no23 p53 Je 5 2017
Ross, H. and Murray, D. Grimelda and the Spooktacular Pet Show. 2017
  Publishers Weekly v264 no26 p179 Je 26 2017
Ross, L. Death & the gravedigger's angel. 2017
  Publishers Weekly v263 no52 p102 D 19 2016
Ross, L. Reporting always. 2015
  New York Times Book Review p80 D 4 2016 J. Khatib
Ross, T. and others. Grandpa's great escape. 2017
  Publishers Weekly v263 no48 p67 N 28 2016
Rossen, J. Rossen to the Rescue. 2017
  Publishers Weekly v264 no25 p100 Je 19 2017
Rossi Gori, L. and others. Mincemeat. 2016
  Publishers Weekly v263 no46 p48 N 14 2016
Rossiter, C. and others. In focus. 2016
  Publishers Weekly v263 no41 p81 O 10 2016
Rosson, K. The mercy of the tide. 2017
  Publishers Weekly v264 no1 p41 Ja 2 2017

Rota, M. Taking Pascal's wager. 2016
Christianity Today v61 no1 p53 Ja/F 2017 C. Meister
Roth, C. and Kheiriyeh, R. Hold Your Temper, Tiger. 2017
Publishers Weekly v263 no52 p125 D 19 2016
Roth, K. B. Celine. 2014
Entertainment Weekly no1457/1458 p106 Mr 17 2017
Roth, P. Sabbath's theater. 1995
Esquire v167 no2 p108-13 Mr 2017
Roth, P. The plot against America. 2005
Foreign Policy no222 p72-3 Ja/F 2017 A. Kirsch
Roth, S. L. and others. Prairie dog song. 2016
Publishers Weekly v263 no49 p50 D 7 2016
Roth, V. Carve the mark. 2017
New York Times Book Review p25 F 5 2017
New York Times Book Review p27 Ja 29 2017 N. K. Jemisin
Seventeen v76 no2 p23 Mr 2017 J. Abidor
Roth, Z. The great suppression. 2016
New Republic v247 no11 p53-5 N 2016 A. Wolfe
New York Review of Books v63 no16 p26-8 O 27 2016 D. Cole
Rothberg, H. The perfect mix. 2017
Time v190 no2/3 p20 Jl 10-17 2017 S. Begley
Rothkopf, K. and Bishop, J. Matisse/Diebenkorn. 2016
New York Review of Books v64 no1 p12-4 Ja 19 2017 J. Perl
Rothmann, R. To die in spring. 2017
Publishers Weekly v264 no23 p1 Je 5 2017
Rothschild, H. The improbability of love. 2015
New York Times Book Review p24 Ja 1 2017 J. Khatib
Rothstein, R. The color of law. 2017
New York Times Book Review p15 Je 25 2017 D. Oshinsky
Publishers Weekly v264 no8 p75 F 20 2017
Vanity Fair v59 no6 p54 My 2017 S. C.
Washington Monthly v49 no6-8 p72-3 Je-Ag 2017 R. D. Kahlenberg
Rotner, S. and Rotner, S. Hello autumn! 2017
Publishers Weekly v264 no29 p216 Jl 17 2017
Rotner, S. Grow! Raise! Catch! 2016
Science v354 no6317 p1222-3 D 9 2016 C. Ash
Rouda, K. Best Day Ever. 2017
Publishers Weekly v264 no16 p34 Ap 17 2017
Roudinesco, É. and Porter, C. Freud. 2016
Maclean's v129 no50 p60-1 D 19 2016 B. Bethune
Nation v33 no21 p25-8 N 21 2016 S. Moyn
New York Review of Books v64 no3 p6-10 F 23 2017 F. Crews
Weekly Standard v22 no19 p30-3 Ja 23 2017 G. A. Hornstein
Roughton, P. and Halldor Laxness, P. Wayward heroes. 2016
Harper's Magazine v333 no1998 p87-93 N 2016 J. Taylor
Roughton, P. and Jón Kalman Stefánsson, Fish have no feet. 2016
Iceland Review v55 no1 p12 Ja/F 2017 V. Hafstad
Roughton, P. and Sigurðardóttir, S. The Good Lover. 2016
Iceland Review v55 no2 p8 Mr/Ap 2017 V. Hafstad
Rougle, C. and others. Red star. 1984
In These Times v41 no10 p45 O 2017
Rounding, V. The burning time. 2017
Publishers Weekly v264 no36 p80 S 4 2017
Rountree, S. and Desiato, A. Lifelong yoga. 2017
Publishers Weekly v264 no25 p107 Je 19 2017
Roussel, R. and Cuningham, R. C. Locus Solus. 1983
Publishers Weekly v263 no43 p54 O 24 2016 S. Satterlee
Roussey, C. and Roussey, C. My Lazy Cat. 2017
Publishers Weekly v264 no29 p33-188 Jl 17 2017
Publishers Weekly v264 no38 p68 S 18 2017
Roux, M. and Harwell, A. House of furies. 2017
Publishers Weekly v264 no11 p86-7 Mr 13 2017
Rovelli, C. and others. Reality is not what it seems. 2017
New York Times Book Review p15 Mr 5 2017 L. Randall
Publishers Weekly v263 no46 p44 N 14 2016
Rovelli, C. Seven Brief Lessons on Physics. 2016
Science v354 no6317 p1229 D 9 2016 S. Vignieri
Roveto, V. Bodys. 2016.
Publishers Weekly v263 no42 p48 O 17 2016
Rovin, J. and Shatner, W. Zero-G Green Space. 2017
Publishers Weekly v264 no29 p202 Jl 17 2017
Rowbotham, S. Rebel crossings. 2016
History Today v67 no7 p102-3 Jl 2017 P. Thane
Rowe, C. K. One True Life. 2016

Christian Century v134 no10 p26-7 My 10 2017 J. Tran
Rowe, C. Telling the map. 2017
Publishers Weekly v264 no22 p38-40 My 29 2017
Rowe, C. The spider and the fly. 2017
Publishers Weekly v263 no47 p100-1 N 21 2016
Rowe, J. A loving, faithful animal. 2017
New York Times Book Review p20 O 8 2017 S. Hunt
Publishers Weekly v264 no28 p60 Jl 10 2017
Rowe, M. Sin bravely. 2017
Christian Century v134 no9 p34-5 Ap 26 2017 T. Peters
Publishers Weekly v263 no46 p50 N 14 2016
Rowell, R. Carry on. 2015
Publishers Weekly v263 no49 p95 D 7 2016
Rowland, L. J. The Ripper's Shadow. 2017
Publishers Weekly v263 no43 p58-9 O 24 2016
Rowling, J. K. and Grandpré, M. Harry Potter and the Chamber of Secrets. 1999
New York Times Book Review p32-3 D 4 2016 J. Malouf
Rowling, J. K. and others. Harry Potter and the cursed child parts one and two. 2016
Publishers Weekly v264 no34 p8 Ag 21 2017
Rowling, J. K. Fantastic beasts and where to find them. 2001
Publishers Weekly v264 no13 p14 Mr 27 2017 C. Juris
Reason v48 no7 p48-55 D 2016 A. H. Sturgis
Rowson, P. Lethal Waves. 2017
Publishers Weekly v264 no15 p55 Ap 10 2017
Roxas, I. and Kelly, E. E. Hello universe. 2017
Publishers Weekly v263 no52 p124 D 19 2016
Roy, A. and others. Eat the sky, drink the ocean. 2014
Publishers Weekly v263 no52 p126-7 D 19 2016
Roy, A. Sleeping on Jupiter. 2015
New Yorker v92 no39 p91 N 28 2016
New York Times Book Review p9 S 25 2016 M. Suri
Roy, A. The ministry of utmost happiness. 2017
Atlantic v320 no1 p36-8 Jl/Ag 2017 P. Sehgal
Commonweal v114 no14 p35-6 S 8 2017 R. Boyagoda
New Yorker v93 no16 p98-101 Je 5 2017 J. Acocella
New York Review of Books v64 no12 p16-7 Jl 13 2017 F. Prose
New York Times Book Review p1-20 Je 11 2017 K. Mahajan
New York Times Book Review p23 Je 18 2017
New York Times Book Review p24 Je 25 2017 G. Cowles
Publishers Weekly v264 no15 p48 Ap 10 2017
Publishers Weekly v264 no25 p16 Je 19 2017 C. Juris
Publishers Weekly v264 no36 p87 S 4 2017
Saturday Evening Post v289 no3 p22 My/Je 2017
Time v189 no22 p50 Je 12 2017 S. Begley
Vanity Fair v59 no7 p50 Summ 2017 S. Crosley
Royal, P. The proud sinner. 2017
Publishers Weekly v263 no50 p51 D 5 2016
Royer, J. and others. Audubon. 2016
Earth Island Journal v32 no2 p54 Summ 2017 C. Ro
Publishers Weekly v264 no14 p61 Ap 3. 2017
Rozich, S. and others. Cook + Cork. 2016
Publishers Weekly v264 no34 p106 Ag 21 2017
Publishers Weekly v264 no35 p67 Ag 28 2017
Publishers Weekly v264 no35 p77d Ag 28 2017
Ru, M. and Evans, S. The Bee Who Sneezed. 2016
Missouri Life v43 no7 p18 D 2016/Ja 2017
Ruano, A. and Argueta, J. Somos Como Las Nubes / We Are Like the Clouds. 2016
Publishers Weekly v263 no43 p77 O 24 2016
Publishers Weekly v263 no49 p35 D 7 2016
Rubbino, S. and Almond, D. Harry Miller's run. 2017
Publishers Weekly v263 no51 p148 D 12 2016
Rubbino, S. and McCardie, A. Our very own dog. 2017
Publishers Weekly v263 no47 p106 N 21 2016
Rubenstein, J. The last days of Stalin. 2016
Foreign Affairs v96 no1 p170-1 Ja/F 2017 R. Legvold
Rubery, M. The untold story of the talking book. 2016
Publishers Weekly v264 no5 p198 Ja 30 2017
Rubin, A. and Salmieri, D. Dragons love tacos 2: the sequel. 2017
Publishers Weekly v264 no18 p58 My 1 2017
Rubin, A. and Salmieri, D. Dragons love tacos. 2012
New York Times Book Review p21 Jl 9 2017
Rubin, B. and Rubin, B. The Complete Jewish Study Bible. 2016
Publishers Weekly v263 no45 p12-6 N 7 2016 A. B. Westrick

Publishers Weekly v263 no47 p101 N 21 2016

Rydell, A. and Koch, H. The Book Thieves. 2017
Vanity Fair p100 Hollywood 2017 Supplement S. Crosley

Ryder, D. Deep into Trouble. 2017
Publishers Weekly v264 no4 p65 Ja 23 2017

Ryerson, R. A. John Adams's republic. 2016
Weekly Standard v22 no32 p37-9 My 1 2017 J. M. J. Banner

Ryherd, E. E. and others. Worship Space Acoustics. 2016
Physics Today v70 no1 p60-3 Ja 2017

Rylant, C. and Austin, M. Henny, Penny, Lenny, Denny, and Mike. 2017
Publishers Weekly v264 no28 p86-8 Jl 10 2017

Rylant, C. and Corace, J. The steadfast tin soldier. 2013
Publishers Weekly v263 no41 p79 O 10 2016
Publishers Weekly v263 no49 p30 D 7 2016

Rylant, C. and Davick, L. We love you, Rosie! 2017
Publishers Weekly v263 no48 p65 N 28 2016

Rylant, C. and Henry, S. Herbert's first Halloween. 2017
Publishers Weekly v264 no26 p177 Je 26 2017

Rylant, C. and Robinson, C. Little penguins. 2016
New York Times Book Review p18 D 18 2016 L. S. Marcus

Rylant, C. and Rylant, C. Nativity. 2017
Publishers Weekly v264 no36 p99 S 4 2017

Ryp, J. J. and others. Harbinger Renegade. 2017
Publishers Weekly v264 no14 p61 Ap 3. 2017

Ryrie, A. Protestants. 2017
National Review v69 no12 p35-8 Je 26 2017 R. Moore
Nation v305 no3 p31-5 Jl 31 2017 E. Bruenig
Publishers Weekly v264 no7 p70-1 F 13 2017
Time v189 no13 p54 Ap 10 2017 L. Rothman

S

Sabahattin Ali, C. 1. and others. Madonna in a Fur Coat. 2016
Publishers Weekly v264 no39 p82-3 S 25 2017

Sabella, J. L. An American conscience. 2017
America v216 no10 p49 My 1 2017 M. E. Marty

Sabuda, R. The Christmas story. 2016
Publishers Weekly v263 no39 p89 S 26 2016

Saburi, M. and Keller, J. Monster trucks. 2017
Publishers Weekly v264 no26 p179 Je 26 2017

Sachs, H. Toscanini. 2017
National Review v69 no15 p39-41 Ag 14 2017 J. Nordlinger
New York Review of Books v64 no17 p14-5 N 9 2017 T. Page
New York Times Book Review p1-20 Jl 2 2017 R. Gottlieb
New York Times Book Review p19 Jl 9 2017
Publishers Weekly v264 no4 p69 Ja 23 2017

Sachs, W. Fearless and free. 2017
O, The Oprah Magazine p105 Mr 2017 H. C.

Sachsman, D. B. and Bulla, D. W. Sensationalism. 2013
Skeptical Inquirer v41 no2 p62 Mr/Ap 2017 B. Radford

Sacks, J. Not in God's name. 2015
New York Times Book Review p24 F 26 2017 J. Khatib

Sacks, N. and others. May's wild walk. 2017
Publishers Weekly v264 no41 p70 O 9 2017

Sacks, O. The river of consciousness. 2017
Publishers Weekly v264 no26 p115-20 Je 26 2017 A. Crowley
Publishers Weekly v264 no39 p96 S 25 2017
Science News v192 no6 p28 O 14 2017 L. Sanders

Sadler, J. and Serdiville, R. Caesar's greatest victory. 2016
Military History v34 no2 p71-2 Jl 2017 D. Saunders

Sadler, J. Operation Agreement. 2016
Military History v33 no5 p72-3 Ja 2017 R. Guttman

Sáenz, B. A. The inexplicable logic of my life. 2017
Entertainment Weekly no1457/1458 p106 Mr 17 2017
New York Times Book Review p28 My 14 2017 I. Zoboi
Publishers Weekly v264 no1 p56 Ja 2 2017
Publishers Weekly v264 no22 p64 My 29 2017

Safirstein, J. Night and day. 2017
Publishers Weekly v264 no35 p126 Ag 28 2017

Safranski, R. and Dollenmayer, D. Goethe. 2017
New York Times Book Review p16 Je 18 2017 M. Hofmann
Publishers Weekly v264 no6 p55 F 6 2017

Sagalyn, L. B. Power at ground zero. 2016
Architectural Record v205 no9 p61 S 2017 A. Cohen

New York Review of Books v64 no4 p11-3 Mr 9 2017 M. Filler
New York Times Book Review p21 O 2 2016 E. L. Glaeser

Sage, J. and Pratt, P. Stop feedin' da boids! 2017
Publishers Weekly v264 no7 p73 F 13 2017

Sageer, J. A. and others. Julie Taboulie's Lebanese Kitchen. 2017
Publishers Weekly v264 no10 p55-6 Mr 6 2017

Sager, C. and Curtis, B. Living out loud. 2016
Sports Illustrated v125 no17 p22 N 21 2016 Double Issue T. Keith

Sager, C. B. They're playing our song. 2016
AARP: The Magazine v59 no6A p18 O/N 2016 D. Donahue

Sager, R. Final girls. 2017
Entertainment Weekly no1467 p58-63 My 26 2017 N. Serrao

Sager, R. K. The world's greatest chocolate-covered pork chops. 2017
Publishers Weekly v264 no15 p73 Ap 10 2017

Sagner, K. Women walking. 2017
Publishers Weekly v264 no32 p65-6 Ag 7 2017

Sagun, V. Big Gal Yoga. 2017
Publishers Weekly v263 no45 p19-28 N 7 2016 D. Lefferts

Sahni, H. and Theodoracopulos, M. In the Spirit of Gstaad. 2016
Vanity Fair v59 no1 p93 Holiday 2017

Saia, J. and Coulthurst, A. Of Fire and Stars. 2016
Publishers Weekly v263 no39 p95 S 26 2016
Publishers Weekly v263 no49 p110 D 7 2016

Saini, A. Inferior. 2017
Science News v192 no3 p27 S 2 2017 E. Engelhaupt
Scientific American v316 no6 p74 Je 2017

Saint, A. An Organic Architecture. 2017
Architectural Record v205 no7 p63 Jl 2017 S. Stephens

Saintcrow, L. Cormorant run. 2017
Publishers Weekly v264 no17 p72-3 Ap 24 2017

Saito, M. and Kaneko, Y. Into the Snow. 2016
Publishers Weekly v263 no49 p13-4 D 7 2016

Sakai, K. and Aman, K. The fox wish. 2017
Publishers Weekly v264 no4 p77 Ja 23 2017

Sakamoto, M. and Silva, S. Passover scavenger hunt. 2016
Publishers Weekly v264 no4 p78 Ja 23 2017

Sakey, M. Afterlife. 2017
Entertainment Weekly no1473 p62 Jl 7 2017 C. Collis
Publishers Weekly v264 no20 p40 My 15 2017

Saksen, Y. and others. Are You Brand Dead? 2017
Publishers Weekly v264 no35 p124 Ag 28 2017
Publishers Weekly v264 no39 p80c S 25 2017

Sakyong Mipham, R. The lost art of good conversation. 2017
Publishers Weekly v264 no33 p74 Ag 14 2017

Sala, R. The bloody cardinal. 2017
Publishers Weekly v264 no35 p113 Ag 28 2017

Sala, S. A Piece of My Heart. 2017
Publishers Weekly v264 no14 p60 Ap 3. 2017

Saldaña, C. and Loney, A. J. Bunnybear. 2016
Publishers Weekly v263 no45 p58-60 N 7 2016

Saldana, S. A country between. 2017
Publishers Weekly v263 no42 p58 O 17 2016

Saldaña París, D. and MacSweeney, C. Among strange victims. 2016
New York Times Book Review p34 N 20 2016 L. Wright

Sale, K. Human scale revisited. 2017
Reason v49 no1 p66-7 My 2017 J. McClaughry

Salerno, C. Sun & urn. 2017
Publishers Weekly v263 no52 p95 D 19 2016

Sales, J. and Bush, P. Uncertain glory. 2014
Publishers Weekly v264 no33 p45 Ag 14 2017

Sales, N. J. American girls. 2016
Christian Century v133 no22 p32-4 O 26 2016 C. L. Hearlson

Salk, S. and Bewkes, S. At home with dogs and their designers. 2017
House Beautiful v159 no8 p42 O 2017 H. Brown

Salle, D. How to see. 2016
New York Review of Books v64 no5 p20-2 Mr 23 2017 S. Schwartz
New York Times Book Review p57 D 4 2016 R. White

Salmieri, D. and Rubin, A. Dragons love tacos 2: the sequel. 2017
Publishers Weekly v264 no18 p58 My 1 2017

Salmieri, D. and Rubin, A. Dragons love tacos. 2012
New York Times Book Review p21 Jl 9 2017

Salvalaggio, K. Silent rain. 2017
Publishers Weekly v264 no11 p59 Mr 13 2017

Sartore, J. and Sartore, J. National Geographic, the photo ark. 2017
  Publishers Weekly v264 no3 p48-53 Ja 16 2017
Sasaki, F. and Share, D. Who reads poetry. 2017
  Publishers Weekly v264 no32 p64 Ag 7 2017
Sassa, M. and Mitchael, A. Copygirl. 2015
  Publishers Weekly v263 no46 p18-20 N 14 2016
Sasse, B. The vanishing American adult. 2017
  Commonweal v114 no14 p31-2 S 8 2017 S. Goldman
  National Review v69 no12 p38-9 Je 26 2017 K. S. Hymowitz
  New York Review of Books v64 no14 p34-6 S 28 2017 M. Tomasky
  New York Times Book Review p15 My 21 2017 J. Szalai
Sasso, S. E. and others. Who counts? 2017
  Christian Century v134 no11 p43 My 24 2017
  Publishers Weekly v264 no15 p74 Ap 10 2017
Sassouni, M. and Kramer, J. A. The Green Umbrella. 2017
  Publishers Weekly v263 no45 p60 N 7 2016
Satter, D. The Less You Know, the Better You Sleep. 2016
  America v216 no6 p44-5 Mr 20 2017 R. A. Schroth
  Commonweal v144 no1 p30-1 Ja 6 2017 J. Dill
Sattin, S. and Koehler, C. Legend 1. 2016
  Publishers Weekly v263 no50 p58 D 5 2016
Sattouf, R. and Taylor, S. The Arab of the future. 2015
  New York Review of Books v63 no16 p8-12 O 27 2016 S. Boxer
Sattouf, R. The Arab of the Future 2. 2016
  New York Times Book Review p13 F 12 2017 J. D. Giovanni
Satyal, R. No one can pronounce my name. 2017
  Entertainment Weekly no1466 p63 My 19 2017
  New York Times Book Review p30 My 14 2017 J. Sharma
  Publishers Weekly v264 no13 p69-70 Mr 27 2017
Sauer, T. and Cummings, T. Caring for Your Lion. 2017
  Publishers Weekly v264 no13 p98 Mr 27 2017
Saujani, R. Girls who code. 2017
  Publishers Weekly v264 no32 p72 Ag 7 2017
Saum, B. Black Elk Peak. 2017
  South Dakota Magazine v33 no3 p59 S/O 2017
Sauma, L. Flesh and Bone and Water. 2017
  New Yorker v93 no22 p73 Jl 31 2017
  Time v189 no22 p52 Je 12 2017 S. Begley
Saunders, C. and Warren, R. God's Great Love for You. 2017
  Publishers Weekly v264 no32 p72 Ag 7 2017
Saunders, G. Lincoln in the bardo. 2017
  America v216 no9 p54-8 Ap 24 2017 G. L. Buckley
  America v216 no9 p58-60 Ap 24 2017 J. Anderson
  Atlantic v319 no2 p36-8 Mr 2017 C. Crain
  Christian Century v134 no10 p37-8 My 10 2017 D. Crowe
  Entertainment Weekly no1453 p60 F 17 2017 L. Greenblatt
  Entertainment Weekly no1453 p61 F 17 2017 I. Biedenharn
  Entertainment Weekly no1454/1455 p102 F 24 2017
  Entertainment Weekly no1456 p70 Mr 10 2017
  Entertainment Weekly no1470 p60-1 Je 16 2017 L. Greenblatt
  Esquire v167 no2 p52 Mr 2017 A. Westenfeld
  Harper's Magazine v334 no2001 p81-3 F 2017 C. Smallwood
  In These Times v41 no3 p40-1 Mr 2017 C. Lehmann
  Maclean's v130 no2 p68 Mr 2017 E. Donaldson
  Nation v304 no16 p35-9 My 22 2017 J. Baskin
  New Yorker v92 no49 p89-92 F 13 2017 T. Mallon
  New York Review of Books v64 no7 p30-2 Ap 20 2017 C. Baxter
  New York Times Book Review p1-22 F 12 2017 C. Whitehead
  New York Times Book Review p20 Mr 5 2017 G. Cowles
  New York Times Book Review p22 F 19 2017
  New York Times Book Review p4 F 12 2017 J. Williams
  O, The Oprah Magazine p103 Mr 2017 H. Cain
  Publishers Weekly v264 no17 p89 Ap 24 2017
  Publishers Weekly v264 no40 p21-110 O 2 2017
  Time v189 no7/8 p101 F 27 2017 N. Hopper
  Tricycle: The Buddhist Review v26 no4 p88-90 Summ 2017 A. Barrodale
  Vanity Fair v59 no2 p38 F 2017 E. Schappell
Saunders, K. Five Children on the Western Front. 2014
  Publishers Weekly v263 no49 p68 D 7 2016
Savage, C. Power wars. 2015
  Foreign Affairs v96 no1 p148-55 Ja/F 2017 D. Johnsen
Savage, S. and Savage, S. Little Plane learns to write. 2017
  Publishers Weekly v264 no16 p66 Ap 17 2017
Savage, S. and Savage, S. The mixed-up truck. 2016

  Publishers Weekly v263 no49 p14-6 D 7 2016
Saveri, L. and Miller, K. The Newsstand. 2016
  Art in America v105 no3 p63 Mr 2017
Savery, A. Mexico. 2012
  Publishers Weekly v263 no42 p46 O 17 2016
Savile, S. Parallel Lines. 2017
  Publishers Weekly v264 no2 p45 Ja 9 2017
Savill, D. They Are Trying to Break Your Heart. 2016
  Publishers Weekly v263 no42 p45 O 17 2016
Savit, G. Anna and the Swallow Man. 2016
  Publishers Weekly v263 no49 p117 D 7 2016
Sax, D. The revenge of analog. 2016
  Maclean's v129 no50 p62 D 19 2016 M. Doherty
  New York Review of Books v64 no2 p4-6 F 9 2017 B. McKibben
  New York Times Book Review p21 D 11 2016 S. Timberg
Sayre, A. P. and Jenkins, S. Squirrels Leap, Squirrels sleep. 2016
  Publishers Weekly v263 no40 p127 O 3 2016
  Publishers Weekly v263 no49 p51 D 7 2016
Sayre, A. P. and Sayre, A. P. Best in snow. 2016
  Publishers Weekly v263 no42 p69 O 17 2016
  Publishers Weekly v263 no49 p45 D 7 2016
Scahill, J. The assassination complex. 2016
  Reason v48 no7 p60-1 D 2016 S. Shackford
Scaletta, K. Rooting for Rafael Rosales. 2017
  Publishers Weekly v264 no5 p205 Ja 30 2017
Scalise, M. The brand new catastrophe. 2017
  New York Times Book Review p38 My 14 2017 J. Walker
  Publishers Weekly v263 no41 p66 O 10 2016
Scalzi, J. and Metzger, N. Miniatures. 2016
  Publishers Weekly v263 no40 p103 O 3 2016
Scalzi, J. The Collapsing Empire. 2017
  Publishers Weekly v264 no5 p183 Ja 30 2017
  Wired v25 no3 p28 Mr 2017 K. M. McFarland
Scanlon, J. Until there is justice. 2016
  Christian Century v134 no4 p49-52 F 15 2017 S. Azaransky
Scanlon, L. G. and Hooper, H. Another way to climb a tree. 2017
  Publishers Weekly v264 no25 p109 Je 19 2017
Scanlon, L. G. and others. Bob, not Bob! 2017
  Publishers Weekly v263 no47 p105 N 21 2016
Scapellato, J. Big Lonesome. 2017
  New York Times Book Review p30 My 7 2017 M. Bojanowski
  Publishers Weekly v263 no51 p120-1 D 12 2016
Scaramucci, A. Hopping over the Rabbit Hole. 2016
  Forbes v198 no7 p32 N 29 2016
  Publishers Weekly v263 no46 p13 N 14 2016 J. Segura
Scarbrough, M. and others. All-time favorite sheet cakes & slab pies. 2017
  Publishers Weekly v264 no29 p212-3 Jl 17 2017
Scarlett, S. T. and Scarlett, S. T. Simple Rules. 2013
  Publishers Weekly v263 no52 p76 D 19 2016
Scarry, E. Naming thy name. 2016
  American Scholar v86 no1 p118-21 Wint 2017 A. Motion
  New Yorker v92 no46 p75 Ja 23 2017
Scego, I. and Richards, J. Adua. 2017
  Publishers Weekly v264 no16 p36 Ap 17 2017
Scelfo, J. and Heald, H. The women who made New York. 2016
  New York Times Book Review p44 D 4 2016 M. O'Connor
Schachner, J. and Schachner, J. Sarabella's thinking cap. 2017
  Publishers Weekly v264 no29 p218 Jl 17 2017
Schachter, A. W. No child left alone. 2016
  Commentary v142 no3 p46-7 O 2016 B. Mandel
Schadlow, N. War and the art of governance. 2017
  Weekly Standard v22 no34 p40-1 My 15 2017 M. T. Owens
Schaefer, A. and others. Because of an acorn. 2016
  Natural History v125 no1 p44-7 D 2016/Ja 2017 D. Setton
  Science v354 no6317 p1224 D 9 2016 V. Thompson
Schaefer, S. and Fischer, K. Zoo zen. 2017
  Publishers Weekly v264 no15 p74 Ap 10 2017
Schafer, G. and Piasecki, E. A place to call home. 2017
  Old House Journal v45 no7 p8 O 2017
Schafer, W. and others. The Weight of Words. 2017
  Publishers Weekly v264 no34 p96 Ag 21 2017
Schafer, W. and Schafer, W. The Best of Subterranean. 2017
  Publishers Weekly v264 no24 p46 Je 12 2017
Schaffir, J. What to believe when you're expecting. 2017
  Publishers Weekly v264 no38 p67 S 18 2017

Schama, S. The face of Britain. 2016
  Commentary v141 no10 p1-2 D 2016
  Commentary v142 no5 p1-2 D 2016
  Commentary v142 no5 p53-5 D 2016 W. Wheldon
  Foreign Affairs v96 no2 p178-9 Mr/Ap 2017 A. Moravcsik
  New York Review of Books v64 no3 p51-4 F 23 2017 A. Spawls
  New York Times Book Review p13 S 25 2016 C. Benfey
  Weekly Standard v22 no26 p37-8 Mr 13 2017 E. Short

Schapiro, M. and Morson, G. S. Cents and sensibility. 2017
  Harvard Business Review v95 no4 p144-5 Jl/Ag 2017 J. Olejarz
  Publishers Weekly v264 no14 p63 Ap 3. 2017

Schaub, E. O. Year of no clutter. 2017
  Publishers Weekly v264 no4 p76 Ja 23 2017

Schaub, M. and Huntington, A. Fresh-picked poetry. 2017
  Publishers Weekly v264 no3 p61 Ja 16 2017

Scheele, J. and Barker, M. Queer. 2016
  Publishers Weekly v263 no44 p60 O 31 2016

Schefer, J. L. and others. The ordinary man of cinema. 2016
  Film Comment v52 no6 p95 N/D 2016 P. Fileri
  Film Comment v52 no6 p96 N/D 2016 A. Curry

Scheffler, I. Cracking the cube. 2016
  Scientific American v315 no5 p76 N 2016 C. Moskowitz

Scheidel, W. The great leveler. 2016
  New Yorker v93 no8 p68 Ap 10 2017

Scheinerman, E. A Mathematician's anthology. 2017
  New York Times Book Review p31 My 7 2017 J. Ryerson

Schemel, P. Hit So Hard. 2017
  Publishers Weekly v264 no35 p118 Ag 28 2017

Schenck, B. W. Slaves of the Switchboard of Doom. 2017
  Publishers Weekly v264 no17 p73-4 Ap 24 2017

Schenone, L. The Dogs of Avalon. 2017
  Publishers Weekly v264 no25 p102 Je 19 2017

Scheve, K. and Stasavage, D. Taxing the ricj. 2016
  Foreign Affairs v95 no6 p175 N/D 2016 R. N. Cooper

Schewel, B. Seven ways of looking at religion. 2017
  Publishers Weekly v264 no24 p61 Je 12 2017

Schiavone, A. and Carden, J. Pontius Pilate. 2017
  Christian Century v134 no11 p43 My 24 2017
  Weekly Standard v22 no28 p35-6 Mr 27 2017 H. Andrews

Schieber, J. and Rauser, R. An atheist and a Christian walk into a bar... 2016
  Publishers Weekly v263 no41 p74-5 O 10 2016

Schieck, H. P. Key Nuclear Reaction Experiments. 2016
  Physics Today v69 no11 p58-9 N 2016 C. Bertulani

Schiff, S. The Witches. 2015
  New York Times Book Review p24 O 30 2016

Schillace, B. Clockwork Futures. 2017
  Science v357 no6355 p967 S 8 2017 D. M. Kahler

Schiller, S. Transfer Day. 2012
  Publishers Weekly v263 no51 p127 D 12 2016
  Publishers Weekly v264 no4 p50d Ja 23 2017

Schilling, G. Ripples in spacetime. 2017
  New York Times Book Review p35 Ag 27 2017 J. Ryerson

Schilling, H. and Gordon, R. J. Martin Luther. 2017
  Christianity Today v61 no1 p46-51 Ja/F 2017 B. Gordon
  Publishers Weekly v264 no19 p55 My 8 2017

Schine, C. They may not mean to, but they do. 2016
  New York Times Book Review p28 S 24 2017 J. Khatib

Schlicke, P. Simply Dickens. 2016
  Publishers Weekly v264 no23 p46 Je 5 2017
  Publishers Weekly v264 no26 p146e Je 26 2017

Schlink, B. and others. The woman on the stairs. 2017
  New Yorker v93 no11 p69 My 1 2017
  O, The Oprah Magazine p90 Ap 2017 H. Cain
  Publishers Weekly v264 no3 p42 Ja 16 2017

Schlitz, L. A. and Floca, B. Princess Cora and the Crocodile. 2017
  New York Times Book Review p17 Mr 12 2017 V. Brosgol
  Publishers Weekly v264 no3 p57 Ja 16 2017

Schloss, A. and Rochelle, C. Amazing (mostly) edible science. 2016
  Science v354 no6317 p1226-7 D 9 2016 K. Servick

Schlueter, N. W. and Wenzel, N. G. Selfish libertarians and socialist conservatives? 2017
  Claremont Review of Books v17 no3 p28-30 Summ 2017 D. Azerrad

Schmidt, A. and others. Christmas in a Cowboy's Arms. 2017

Publishers Weekly v264 no36 p76 S 4 2017

Schmidt, B. and others. The woman on the stairs. 2017
  O, The Oprah Magazine p90 Ap 2017 H. Cain
  Publishers Weekly v264 no3 p42 Ja 16 2017

Schmidt, B. T. and Maberry, J. Joe Ledger. 2017
  Publishers Weekly v264 no33 p50-2 Ag 14 2017

Schmidt, B. T. Infinite Stars. 2017
  Publishers Weekly v264 no36 p70 S 4 2017

Schmidt, L. E. Village atheists. 2016
  Humanist v77 no2 p40-1 Mr/Ap 2017 K. Ploetz

Schmidt, S. See what I have done. 2017
  Entertainment Weekly no1467 p58-63 My 26 2017 N. Serrao
  Entertainment Weekly no1477 p60-1 Ag 11 2017 L. Greenblatt
  Entertainment Weekly no1478 / 1479 p109 Ag 18-25 2017
  New York Times Book Review p12 Ag 27 2017 P. McGrath
  Publishers Weekly v264 no19 p33 My 8 2017
  Publishers Weekly v264 no35 p47 Ag 28 2017 J. Rosen
  Saturday Evening Post v289 no4 p24 Jl/Ag 2017

Schmitt, G. Shadow girl. 2017
  Publishers Weekly v264 no26 p159 Je 26 2017

Schneider, F. and Enste, D. H. The shadow economy. 2013
  Monthly Labor Review p1-4 Ap 2017 A. M. Koehn

Schneider, J. and Schneider, J. Kid Amazing vs. the Blob. 2017
  Publishers Weekly v264 no17 p91 Ap 24 2017

Schneider, M. K. School choice. 2016
  New York Review of Books v63 no19 p58-61 D 8 2016 D. Ravitch

Schneider, R. and Morduch, J. The financial diaries. 2017
  New York Review of Books v64 no11 p49-50 Je 22 2017 J. Madrick
  Publishers Weekly v264 no9 p90 F 27 2017

Schnur, S. and others. Potatoes at turtle rock. 2016
  Publishers Weekly v263 no39 p94 S 26 2016

Schoen, D. E. Putin's master plan. 2016
  National Review v68 no20 p44-5 N 7 2016 J. Fund

Schoen, D. E. The Nixon effect. 2016
  Claremont Review of Books v16 no4 p22-4 Fall 2016 J. J. Pitney Jr.

Schoenberger, N. Wayne and Ford. 2017
  Publishers Weekly v264 no18 p47 My 1 2017

Schoenbrod, D. and Fienberg, S. DC confidential. 2017
  Weekly Standard v22 no40 p32-4 Je 26 2017 S. Bangalore Prakash

Schofield, D. Killing pace. 2017
  Publishers Weekly v264 no36 p65 S 4 2017

Schoonebeek, D. and Prufer, K. Trebuchet. 2016
  Publishers Weekly v263 no42 p49-50 O 17 2016

Schoonmaker, T. and Lash, M. Southern accent. 2016
  Virginia Living v15 no6 p27 O 2017 B. Glose

Schor, E. Bridge of words. 2016
  New Yorker v92 no35 p90-5 O 31 2016 J. Acocella
  New York Times Book Review p37 N 13 2016 M. Wex

Schossow, P. and Schossow, P. Where Is Grandma? 2017
  Publishers Weekly v264 no23 p52 Je 5 2017

Schott, H. Love in a time of hate. 2017
  Publishers Weekly v264 no15 p70 Ap 10 2017

Schott, J. J. and Cimino-Isaacs, C. Trans-Pacific Partnership. 2016
  Foreign Affairs v95 no6 p174-5 N/D 2016 R. N. Cooper

Schrager, I. Studio 54. 2017
  Esquire p44 S 2017 B. Ratliff

Schrefer, E. Rescued. 2016
  Publishers Weekly v263 no49 p101-2 D 7 2016

Schroeder, C. C. and others. The undergraduate experience. 2016
  Change v49 no3 p45-51 My/Je 2017 M. T. Huber

Schroeder, L. and Ceccoli, N. The girl in the tower. 2016
  Publishers Weekly v264 no34 p93-4 Ag 21 2017

Schubert, L. and Colón, R. Listen: how Pete Seeger got America singing. 2017
  Publishers Weekly v264 no23 p51 Je 5 2017

Schuchts, B. Be transformed. 2017
  U.S. Catholic v82 no6 p41 Je 2017

Schuler, C. and others. Leo's gift. 2017
  Publishers Weekly v264 no36 p100 S 4 2017

Schulman, A. Waking the spirit. 2016
  New York Times Book Review p27 F 5 2017 M. Daum

Schultz, G. and others. Fairy tales for the disillusioned. 2016
  Maclean's v129 no47 p61 N 28 2016 B. Bethune

Schuman, R. Schadenfreude, a love story. 2017

Publishers Weekly v263 no43 p67 O 24 2016

Schumer, A. The Girl With the Lower Back Tattoo. 2016
New York Times Book Review p16 N 20 2016 A. Jacobs

Schuster, L. Dirty wars and polished silver. 2017
New York Times Book Review p27 S 17 2017 M. Daum

Schuth, K. Seminary formation. 2016
Commonweal v144 no3 p23-4 F 10 2017 T. Baker

Schutt, B. and Finch, J. R. The Himalayan codex. 2017
Publishers Weekly v264 no17 p68 Ap 24 2017

Schutt, B. Cannibalism. 2017
New Yorker v93 no23 p72 Ag 7 2017
New York Times Book Review p19 Mr 5 2017
New York Times Book Review p20 F 26 2017 S. Montgomery
Publishers Weekly v263 no43 p65 O 24 2016
Publishers Weekly v263 no51 p106-11 D 12 2016 A. Crowley
Publishers Weekly v264 no22 p63 My 29 2017
Science News v191 no3 p29 F 18 2017 S. Perkins
Scientific American v316 no2 p72 F 2017 R. F. Mandelbaum

Schuurman, D. J. and Cahalan, K. A. Calling in today's world. 2016
U.S. Catholic v81 no12 p41 D 2016

Schwab, K. The fourth industrial revolution. 2017
People Management p14 D 2016/Ja 2017

Schwab, V. E. A Conjuring of Light. 2017
New York Times Book Review p28 Mr 12 2017 G. Cowles

Schwab, V. This Savage Song. 2016
New York Times Book Review p28 Mr 12 2017 G. Cowles

Schwalbe, W. Books for Living. 2016
New York Times Book Review p17 D 25 2016 A. J. Jacobs
Publishers Weekly v263 no42 p60 O 17 2016

Schwandt, K. and Tabilio, M. Marco Polo. 2017
Publishers Weekly v264 no30 p63 Jl 24 2017

Schwartz, B. L. and Adelman, C. Midwestern native shrubs and trees. 2017
Missouri Life v44 no4 p20 Je 2017 L. A. Addington

Schwartz, C. W. and others. The Wild Mammals of Missouri. 2016
Missouri Life v44 no2 p22 Ap 2017 M. W. Schwartz

Schwartz, D. And we're off. 2017
Publishers Weekly v264 no14 p77 Ap 3. 2017
Publishers Weekly v264 no36 p90 S 4 2017
Seventeen v76 no4 p9 Jl/Ag 2017 R. Mosely

Schwartz, E. R. and others. The Wild Mammals of Missouri. 2016
Missouri Life v44 no2 p22 Ap 2017 M. W. Schwartz

Schwartz, G. Jheronimus Bosch. 2016
New York Times Book Review p19 D 25 2016 N. Siegal

Schwartz, J. and Smith, S. Town is by the Sea. 2017
New York Times Book Review p22 Je 11 2017
New York Times Book Review p41 Je 4 2017 M. Russo

Schwartz, J. D. Water in plain sight. 2016
Christian Century v134 no3 p32-3 F 2017 R. Sutterfield
New York Times Book Review p30 S 25 2016 K. Tingley

Schwartz, J. S. and Milligan, T. The ethics of space exploration. 2016
Physics Today v70 no5 p62 My 2017

Schwartz, M. J. Ties that bound. 2017
Christianity Today v61 no6 p89 Jl/Ag 2017 J. Wilson
New York Review of Books v64 no8 p55-7 My 11 2017 S. Dunn

Schwartz, R. The man who lit Lady Liberty. 2017
Publishers Weekly v264 no19 p53 My 8 2017
Publishers Weekly v264 no21 p65d My 22 2017

Schwartz, S. Y. and Goldstein, D. Unplug. 2017
Glamour v115 no3 p130 Mr 2017 S. G. Levy

Schwarz, A. ADHD nation. 2016
New York Times Book Review p24 O 15 2017 J. Khatib

Schwarz, V. and Schwarz, V. Counting with Tiny Cat. 2017
New York Times Book Review p28 Ag 27 2017 D. Yaccarino

Schwarzman, A. and others. Parallel Views. 2015
Art in America v104 no11 p65 D 2016

Schweblin, S. and McDowell, M. Fever dream. 2017
New York Times Book Review p22 Mr 5 2017 J. Szalai
O, The Oprah Magazine p104 F 2017
Publishers Weekly v263 no43 p52 O 24 2016
Virginia Living v15 no4 p29 Je 2017 B. Glose

Schwegel, T. The lies we tell. 2017
Publishers Weekly v264 no21 p71 My 22 2017

Schweig, S. V. Take nothing with you. 2016
Publishers Weekly v263 no42 p50 O 17 2016

Scillian, D. and Kelley, M. Missile toe. 2017
Publishers Weekly v264 no36 p98-9 S 4 2017

Sciolino, E. The Only Street in Paris. 2015
New York Times Book Review p28 N 6 2016 J. Khatib

Sciortino, F. and Bloom, N. Helloflo: the guide, period. 2017
Publishers Weekly v264 no39 p109 S 25 2017

Scofield, S. The Last Draft. 2017
Publishers Weekly v264 no21 p81 My 22 2017
Publishers Weekly v264 no26 p48-53 Je 26 2017 E. Jones

Scoles, S. Making contact. 2017
Publishers Weekly v264 no18 p49 My 1 2017
Science News v192 no1 p26 Ag 5 2017 E. Conover
Scientific American v317 no3 p88 S 2017 A. Gawrylewski

Scott, A. and Gratton, L. The 100 Year Life. 2016
People Management p14 D 2016/Ja 2017

Scott, A. O. Better Living Through Criticism. 2016
Film Quarterly v70 no2 p107-9 Wint 2016 J. Kirshner
Nation v303 no23/24 p27-31 D 5 2016 N. Dames
New York Review of Books v64 no14 p39-42 S 28 2017 E. Mendelson
New York Times Book Review p24 F 12 2017 J. Khatib

Scott, A. The Reluctant Highlander. 2017
Publishers Weekly v264 no17 p74-5 Ap 24 2017

Scott, E. and Agrawal, C. Vibrant India. 2017
Publishers Weekly v264 no10 p57 Mr 6 2017

Scott, E. and Nederlanden, E. D. Holiday cookies. 2017
Publishers Weekly v264 no29 p213 Jl 17 2017

Scott, E. R. Familiar strangers. 2016
Foreign Affairs v95 no6 p187 N/D 2016 R. Legvold

Scott, G. The Age of Olympus. 2017
Publishers Weekly v264 no9 p80 F 27 2017

Scott, J. and Cussler, C. The cutthroat. 2017
Publishers Weekly v264 no5 p176-7 Ja 30 2017

Scott, J. and others. Making good, an inspirational guide to being an artist craftsman. 2017
American Craft v77 no3 p20 Je/Jl 2017 M. Moses

Scott, J. C. Against the grain. 2017
Science News v192 no6 p28 O 14 2017 B. Bower
Science v357 no6350 p459 Ag 4 2017 S. Shablovsky

Scott, J. Careers for women. 2017
New York Times Book Review p15 S 10 2017 A. Gregory
New York Times Book Review p23 S 17 2017
Publishers Weekly v264 no18 p35 My 1 2017

Scott, K. and Willis, K. Botanicum. 2017
Publishers Weekly v264 no4 p81 Ja 23 2017

Scott, K. Radical candor. 2017
People Management p52 Mr 2017
Publishers Weekly v264 no1 p49 Ja 2 2017

Scott, L. The four-dimensional human. 2016
New York Times Book Review p14 Ja 1 2017 J. Silverman

Scott, M. Ancient worlds. 2016
New Yorker v93 no7 p91 Ap 3 2017

Scott, P. The Raj quartet. 2007
New York Times Book Review p13 S 10 2017 I. Chotiner

Scott, S. H. I, Eliza Hamilton. 2017
Publishers Weekly v264 no35 p99 Ag 28 2017

Scott, S. Unforgivable Love. 2017
Essence v48 no6 p76 O 2017 P. H. Bass

Scott, V. Titans. 2016
Publishers Weekly v263 no49 p113 D 7 2016

Scott-Clark, C. and Levy, A. The exile. 2017
Foreign Affairs v96 no6 p155 N/D 2017 L. D. Freedman
Publishers Weekly v264 no13 p101 Mr 27 2017

Scottoline, L. Damaged. 2016
Publishers Weekly v263 no40 p117 O 3 2016

Scottoline, L. One perfect lie. 2017
New York Times Book Review p28 My 7 2017
Publishers Weekly v264 no6 p46 F 6 2017

Scott-Railton, T. and Bourguignon, F. The globalization of inequality. 2015
Claremont Review of Books v16 no4 p55-6 Fall 2016 D. Lal

Scranton, R. and Bosch, T. What Future. 2017
Publishers Weekly v264 no38 p64 S 18 2017

Scritchfield, R. Body Kindness. 2016

Maclean's v129 no47 p61 N 28 2016 B. Bethune

Seiffert, R. A boy in winter. 2017
　New York Times Book Review p10 Ag 27 2017 L. Schillinger

Seigal, J. and Falière, A. Morris Wants More for Christmas. 2017
　Publishers Weekly v264 no36 p91-3 S 4 2017

Seignot, N. and Clutterbuck, D. Mentoring new parents at work. 2017
　People Management p52 F 2017

Seinfeld, J. Food swings. 2017
　Publishers Weekly v264 no10 p54 Mr 6 2017

Seiple, S. Death on the River of Doubt. 2017
　Publishers Weekly v263 no45 p63 N 7 2016

Seldon, A. The Cabinet Office, 1916-2016. 2016
　History Today v67 no4 p65 Ap 2017 R. Quinault

Selinger, J. V. Introduction to the Theory of Soft Matter. 2015
　Physics Today v69 no11 p60-1 N 2016 G. Grason

Selingo, J. J. There Is Life After College. 2016
　America v215 no13 p34-5 O 31 2016 J. Malesic
　Phi Kappa Phi Forum v97 no2 p28 Summ 2017 D. J. Silva

Selivanova, E. and Nellist, G. Twas the Evening of Christmas. 2017
　Publishers Weekly v264 no36 p98 S 4 2017

Sell, L. From Washington to Moscow. 2016
　New York Review of Books v63 no20 p97-100 D 22 2016 R. Cottrell

Sellani, S. and Sellani, S. The 40-year-old Vegan. 2017
　Publishers Weekly v264 no6 p63 F 6 2017

Sellers, L. J. Guilt Game. 2017
　Publishers Weekly v264 no16 p48 Ap 17 2017

Sellers, R. Peter O'Toole. 2016
　America v215 no18 p38-40 D 5 2016 R. A. Blake

Selzer, A. H. H. Holmes. 2017
　Publishers Weekly v264 no4 p70 Ja 23 2017

Semple, M. Today will be different. 2016
　Entertainment Weekly no1434 p59 O 7 2016 L. Greenblatt
　Ms. v26 no4 p42 Wint 2016
　New York Times Book Review p1-26 O 9 2016
　New York Times Book Review p26 O 16 2016
　Publishers Weekly v263 no42 p13 O 17 2016 C. Juris

Sem-Sandberg, S. and Paterson, A. The chosen ones. 2016
　New York Times Book Review p20 O 23 2016 S. R. Suleiman
　New York Times Book Review p24 Ag 20 2017 J. Khatib

Sendker, J. The Language of Solitude. 2017
　Publishers Weekly v264 no12 p55 Mr 20 2017

Senna, D. New People. 2017
　Entertainment Weekly no1478 / 1479 p109 Ag 18-25 2017
　Essence v48 no5 p68 S 2017 P. H. Bass
　Publishers Weekly v264 no25 p89 Je 19 2017

Sentenac, A. and Bec, C. Siberia 56. 2017
　Publishers Weekly v264 no8 p73 F 20 2017

Sentilles, S. Draw your weapons. 2017
　American Scholar v86 no3 p121-3 Summ 2017
　New York Times Book Review p6 S 24 2017 J. Williams
　O, The Oprah Magazine p83 Ag 2017 S. D'Erasmo
　Publishers Weekly v264 no19 p49 My 8 2017

Sepetys, R. Salt to the sea. 2016
　Publishers Weekly v263 no49 p119 D 7 2016

Serafim, L. From the devil's farm. 2017
　Publishers Weekly v263 no47 p91 N 21 2016

Serdiville, R. and Sadler, J. Caesar's greatest victory. 2016
　Military History v34 no2 p71-2 Jl 2017 D. Saunders

Serine, K. Concealed. 2017
　Publishers Weekly v264 no10 p46-7 Mr 6 2017

Sermak, K. Miss d and me. 2017
　Publishers Weekly v264 no23 p43 Je 5 2017

Serr, M. and Farnsworth, E. A Train Through Time. 2017
　Publishers Weekly v263 no50 p62 D 5 2016

Serrano, A. C. and Cross, E. Beyond the Sea. 2016
　Publishers Weekly v264 no16 p46-7 Ap 17 2017

Serrelli, E. and others. Evolutionary theory. 2016
　Science v353 no6307 p1505 S 30 2016 B. Autzen

Servon, L. The Unbanking of America. 2017
　Publishers Weekly v263 no42 p59 O 17 2016
　Reason v48 no10 p62-3 Mr 2017 J. D. Tuccille
　Washington Monthly v49 no3-5 p63-4 Mr-My 2017 L. Colarusso

Sesardic, N. When reason goes on holiday. 2016

National Review v69 no3 p52-3 F 20 2017 J. Postell

Settis, S. and Naffis-Sahely, A. If Venice dies. 2016
　Architectural Record v204 no10 p51 O 2016 P. Nobel
　Weekly Standard v22 no29 p34-6 Ap 3 2017 C. W. Westfall

Sevigny, M. L. Mythical river. 2016
　Orion Magazine v35 no4/5 p107-8 Jl-O 2016 A. C. Gottlieb

Sewell, M. A charm of goldfinches and other wild gatherings. 2017
　New York Times Book Review p6 S 24 2017 J. Williams

Sexsmith, R. Deer Life. 2017
　Publishers Weekly v264 no36 p70 S 4 2017

Sexton, J. Y. The people are going to rise like the waters upon your shore. 2017
　Indianapolis Monthly v41 no2 p25 S 2017 C. Fehrman
　Publishers Weekly v264 no20 p47-8 My 15 2017
　Publishers Weekly v264 no35 p48 Ag 28 2017 J. Rosen

Sexton, M. W. A kind of freedom. 2017
　Ebony v72 no11 p84 S 2017 S. E. Jamison
　New York Times Book Review p15 S 10 2017 J. McCarthy
　Publishers Weekly v264 no23 p27-8 Je 5 2017

Sexton, S. and Johnson, R. F. Plant kingdom of Charles Jones. 2016
　New York Times Book Review p62-3 D 4 2016 L. Sante

Seymour, G. No mortal thing. 2017
　Publishers Weekly v264 no24 p40-1 Je 12 2017

Seymour, R. Corbyn. 2016
　Foreign Affairs v96 no1 p166 Ja/F 2017 A. Moravcsik

Shaber, S. R. Louise's Lies. 2016
　Publishers Weekly v263 no41 p58-9 O 10 2016

Shachtman, T. How the French Saved America. 2017
　Publishers Weekly v264 no26 p168 Je 26 2017

Shafak, E. The Architect's Apprentice. 2015
　Weekly Standard v22 no6 p36 O 17 2016 A. Bakshian Jr.

Shafak, E. Three Daughters of Eve. 2017
　Publishers Weekly v264 no40 p114 O 2 2017

Shaffer, G. and Cumming, A. The adventures of Honey & Leon. 2017
　Publishers Weekly v264 no27 p72 Jl 3 2017

Shaffer, J. J. and Laberis, S. Prudence the part-time cow. 2017
　Publishers Weekly v264 no18 p56-7 My 1 2017

Shafto, S. and others. Writings. 2016
　Film Quarterly v70 no2 p103-6 Wint 2016 C. Tsui

Shakespeare, W. and Fischlin, D. Romeo & Juliet. 2014
　Publishers Weekly v263 no41 p79 O 10 2016

Shakespeare, W. and Gill, R. King Lear. 2013
　New York Review of Books v64 no3 p34-6 F 23 2017 S. Greenblatt

Shakespeare, W. and others. A midsummer night's dream. 2012
　Publishers Weekly v264 no34 p14 Ag 21 2017 J. Milliot

Shakespeare, W. and others. Hamlet. 2012
　Weekly Standard v22 no31 p43 Ap 17 2017 C. Atamian

Shakespeare, W. and others. The tragedy of King Lear. 2015
　New York Review of Books v64 no3 p34-6 F 23 2017 S. Greenblatt

Shalvis, J. Accidentally on Purpose. 2017
　Publishers Weekly v263 no50 p57 D 5 2016

Shalvis, J. Chasing Christmas Eve. 2017
　Entertainment Weekly no1486 p60-1 O 13 2017 M. L. Lenker
　Publishers Weekly v264 no36 p72 S 4 2017

Shames, S. L. Out of the Running. 2017
　Time v189 no6 p20 F 20 2017 S. Begley

Shames, T. An unsettling crime for Samuel Craddock. 2017
　Publishers Weekly v263 no44 p52 O 31 2016

Shamsie, K. Home fire. 2017
　New York Times Book Review p19 O 1 2017 P. Ho Davies
　O, The Oprah Magazine p92 S 2017 J. Milman
　Publishers Weekly v264 no26 p149 Je 26 2017

Shanahan, C. Into each room we enter without knowing. 2017
　O, The Oprah Magazine p92 Ap 2017

Shanbhag, V. and Perur, S. Ghachar ghochar. 2017
　New Yorker v93 no5 p97 Mr 20 2017
　New York Times Book Review p27 Ap 9 2017 P. Sehgal
　Publishers Weekly v263 no41 p54 O 10 2016

Shane, S. Objective Troy. 2015
　Foreign Affairs v95 no6 p153-8 N/D 2016 L. D. Freedman

Shanes, E. Young Mr Turner. 2016
　New York Review of Books v63 no18 p8-12 N 24 2016 J. Bell

Shang, W. W. and Rosenberg, M. This is just a test. 2017
　New York Times Book Review p23 Ag 27 2017 S. Mosle

Martha Stewart Living no271 p10 Ja/F 2017
Silvertown, J. Dinner with Darwin. 2017
  Science v357 no6355 p968-9 S 8 2017 M. V. Johnson
  Scientific American v317 no3 p88 S 2017 A. Gawrylewski
Silvestro, A. and Mai-Wyss, T. Bunny's book club. 2017
  Publishers Weekly v263 no46 p54 N 14 2016
Silvestro, A. and White, T. Mice skating. 2017
  Publishers Weekly v264 no40 p139 O 2 2017
Silvis, R. Two days gone. 2017
  New York Times Book Review p25 Ja 22 2017 M. Stasio
  Publishers Weekly v263 no43 p58 O 24 2016
Sima, J. and Sima, J. Not quite narwhal. 2017
  Publishers Weekly v263 no50 p71-3 D 5 2016
Simanek, E. and Arnold, R. Shots of knowledge. 2016
  D: The Magazine of Dallas v43 no10 p58 O 2016 Z. Crain
Simic, C. Scribbled in the dark. 2017
  Publishers Weekly v264 no16 p41 Ap 17 2017
Simmons, E. G. Talking Back to the Bible. 2016
  Publishers Weekly v264 no24 p62 Je 12 2017
  Publishers Weekly v264 no26 p146e-7f Je 26 2017
Simmons, G. and Miller, J. Bringing it home. 2017
  Publishers Weekly v264 no34 p105 Ag 21 2017
Simon, B. The Hamlet Fire. 2017
  Publishers Weekly v264 no31 p77 Jl 31 2017
Simon, C. As Dark As My Fur. 2017
  Publishers Weekly v264 no4 p59 Ja 23 2017
Simon, C. World Enough. 2017
  Publishers Weekly v264 no39 p87 S 25 2017
Simon, D. and others. The best democracy money can buy. 2016
  Progressive p60-5 D 2016/Ja 2017 E. Rampell
Simon, F. and Gill, O. L. The Monstrous Child. 2017
  Publishers Weekly v264 no17 p92 Ap 24 2017
Simon, H. Confessions of the Pricing Man. 2015
  Fortune v174 no8 p70 D 15 2016 V. Harnish
Simon, M. Real impact. 2017
  Publishers Weekly v264 no21 p82 My 22 2017
Simon, M. The wasp that brainwashed the caterpillar. 2016
  Science News v190 no8 p28 O 15 2016 C. Martin
Simon, S. N. and Allin, D. H. Our separate ways. 2016
  Foreign Affairs v95 no6 p132-8 N/D 2016 P. Gordon
Simon, W. E. Great Catholic parishes. 2016
  Commonweal v144 no3 p30-1 F 10 2017 E. Sauers
Simone, G. and others. Attack on Titan anthology. 2016
  Publishers Weekly v263 no44 p60 O 31 2016
Simone, G. and others. Leaving megalopolis. 2016
  Publishers Weekly v264 no3 p47 Ja 16 2017
Simons, D. M. Keep Her Safe. 2011
  Publishers Weekly v264 no30 p40 Jl 24 2017
Simpson, E. and Wiles, L. Thriving Abroad. 2017
  People Management p51 Jl 2017
Simpson, H. Cockfosters. 2015
  New York Times Book Review p22 Je 11 2017
  New York Times Book Review p25 Je 4 2017 E. Lipman
  Publishers Weekly v264 no17 p64-5 Ap 24 2017
Simpson, J. The word detective. 2016
  Christian Century v133 no26 p43 D 21 2016
  New York Times Book Review p17 N 6 2016 L. Truss
  New York Times Book Review p4 N 6 2016 J. Szalai
  Weekly Standard v22 no13 p40-2 D 5 2016 D. Skinner
Simpson, R. What the Dead Leave Behind. 2017
  Publishers Weekly v264 no13 p81 Mr 27 2017
Simpson, T. and others. Making good, an inspirational guide to
  being an artist craftsman. 2017
  American Craft v77 no3 p20 Je/Jl 2017 M. Moses
Sims, A. D. Lynched. 2017
  Publishers Weekly v263 no45 p24 N 7 2016 R. Farmer
Sims, G. The end of the web. 2017
  Publishers Weekly v264 no36 p68-9 S 4 2017
Sims, M. Arthur and Sherlock. 2017
  New York Times Book Review p22 F 5 2017
  New York Times Book Review p34-5 Je 4 2017 M. Stasio
  New York Times Book Review p8 Ja 29 2017 G. Moore
  Publishers Weekly v263 no48 p61 N 28 2016
Sims, N. and Neuzil, M. Canoes. 2016
  Cabin Living p12 Ja/F 2017
Sims, S. Bluefishing. 2017

Publishers Weekly v264 no33 p64 Ag 14 2017
Simsion, G. The Best of Adam Sharp. 2017
  Publishers Weekly v264 no10 p38-9 Mr 6 2017
Sin, R. H. Whiskey Words and a Shovel. 2017
  Ebony v72 no6 p31 Ap/My 2017 L. Cross
  Publishers Weekly v264 no16 p13 Ap 17 2017 C. Juris
Sincero, J. You Are a Badass at Making Money. 2017
  Publishers Weekly v264 no9 p95 F 27 2017
Sinclair, M. Never Kiss a Highlander. 2017
  Publishers Weekly v264 no24 p48 Je 12 2017
Sindu, S. J. Marriage of a thousand lies. 2017
  Publishers Weekly v264 no22 p32-4 My 29 2017
Sinek, S. and others. Find your why. 2017
  Publishers Weekly v264 no21 p35-42 My 22 2017 S. J. Robbins
Singer, M. and Masse, J. Echo echo. 2015
  Publishers Weekly v263 no49 p55 D 7 2016
Singer, M. and Valiant, K. Feel the beat. 2017
  Publishers Weekly v264 no3 p61 Ja 16 2017
Singer, M. Underground fugue. 2017
  New York Times Book Review p10 Ap 30 2017 L. Scholes
Singer, S. and Fairer, R. Alexander McQueen. 2016
  Vanity Fair v58 no12 p86 D 2016 J. Vitale
  Vogue v206 no12 p214 D 2016 M. O'Grady
Singh, A. The Second Anglo-Sikh War. 2016
  Military History v34 no4 p74-5 N 2017 D. Saunders
Singh, H. and others. Brik. 2017
  Publishers Weekly v264 no22 p71 My 29 2017
Singh, H. and others. Fortune makers. 2017
  Harvard Business Review v95 no2 p156-7 Mr/Ap 2017 A. Ignatius
Singh, L. and Frost, T. The Greatest Opposites Book on Earth.
  2017
  Publishers Weekly v264 no35 p126 Ag 28 2017
Singh, N. Silver silence. 2017
  Publishers Weekly v264 no17 p74 Ap 24 2017
Singh, V. Ambiguity machines. 2018
  Publishers Weekly v264 no34 p94 Ag 21 2017
Singleton, W. and others. The moonlight meeting. 2017
  Publishers Weekly v264 no39 p106 S 25 2017
Sinha, M. The Slave's cause. 2016
  New York Review of Books v63 no16 p63-5 O 27 2016 J. M.
  McPherson
Sinha, P. M. Crash. 2014
  Publishers Weekly v264 no10 p42-3 Mr 6 2017
Siniscalchi, V. and others. Confiscated! 2017
  Publishers Weekly v264 no23 p50 Je 5 2017
Siniscalchi, V. and others. Otter loves Easter. 2017
  Publishers Weekly v264 no3 p58 Ja 16 2017
Sinn, H. The Euro trap. 2014
  New York Review of Books v64 no1 p24-6 Ja 19 2017 T. G. Ash
Sipila, E. and Piprell, C. MOM. 2017
  Publishers Weekly v264 no8 p71 F 20 2017
Sirk, S. M. The Dead Husband Project. 2017
  Walrus v14 no9 p81 N 2017 D. Viola
Sirotich, E. and Sirotich, E. Found dogs. 2017
  Publishers Weekly v264 no24 p64 Je 12 2017
Sis, P. and Sis, P. Robinson. 2017
  Publishers Weekly v264 no28 p88 Jl 10 2017
Sisman, A. and Fermor, P. L. Patrick Leigh Fermor. 2017
  Publishers Weekly v264 no34 p100 Ag 21 2017
Sisman, A. John le Carré. 2015
  Nation v303 no17 p27-31 O 24 2016 I. Buruma
Sitaraman, G. The crisis of the middle class constitution. 2017
  Nation v305 no3 p27-31 Jl 31 2017 J. Purdy
  New Republic v248 no8/9 p74-9 Ag/S 2017 W. McCormack
  New York Times Book Review p1-10 Mr 26 2017 A. Deaton
  Washington Monthly v49 no9/10 p133-5 S/O 2017 K. Carty
Sittenfeld, C. American wife. 2008
  Time v189 no7/8 p101 F 27 2017 S. Begley
Six, S. and Nevin, J. C. What daddies like. 2017
  Publishers Weekly v264 no16 p69 Ap 17 2017
Siy, A. Voyager's greatest hits. 2017
  Publishers Weekly v264 no25 p114 Je 19 2017
Sjón, and Cribb, V. Moonstone. 2016
  Iceland Review v54 no5 p10 S-O 2016 V. Hafstad
  Nation v303 no22 p27-30 N 28 2016 C. Baxter
  New Yorker v92 no35 p89 O 31 2016

Time v189 no4 p49 Ja 23 2017 S. Begley

Smith, D. and Han, K. The vegetarian. 2015
  Christian Century v134 no8 p1 Ap 12 2017
  Entertainment Weekly no1444/1445 p104-5 D 16 2016 L. Greenblatt
  New York Times Book Review p12 D 11 2016
  New York Times Book Review p48 N 13 2016 Joumana Khatib

Smith, D. and Ibatoulline, B. The Hawk of the Castle. 2017
  Publishers Weekly v264 no6 p71 F 6 2017

Smith, D. Don't call us dead. 2017
  New Yorker v93 no30 p72-3 O 2 2017 D. Chiasson
  Publishers Weekly v264 no26 p97-102 Je 26 2017 A. Crowley
  Publishers Weekly v264 no29 p193 Jl 17 2017

Smith, D. E. African American lives in St. Louis, 1763-1865. 2017
  Missouri Life v44 no3 p20 My 2017 L. A. Addington

Smith, D. Rasputin. 2016
  Foreign Affairs v95 no6 p187-8 N/D 2016 R. Legvold
  Maclean's v129 no47 p60 N 28 2016 P. Treble
  New York Review of Books v63 no19 p40-1 D 8 2016 O. Figes
  Publishers Weekly v263 no39 p76 S 26 2016

Smith, D. The honeymoon. 2016
  New Yorker v92 no30 p75 S 26 2016

Smith, D. The last painting of Sara de Vos. 2016
  America v215 no13 p37-8 O 31 2016 J. Levasseur
  New York Times Book Review p24 Ap 9 2017 J. Khatib

Smith, E. and Morowitz, H. J. The origin and nature of life on Earth. 2016
  Physics Today v70 no9 p58 S 2017 S. I. Walker

Smith, E. E. The power of meaning. 2017
  Publishers Weekly v263 no45 p52 N 7 2016
  Walrus v14 no6 p82 Jl/Ag 2017 J. Johnson

Smith, E. Shakespeare's first folio. 2016
  Weekly Standard v22 no10 p37-8 N 14 2016 M. Mattix

Smith, E. The Making of Shakespeare's First Folio. 2016
  Weekly Standard v22 no10 p37-8 N 14 2016 M. Mattix

Smith, F. V. The Killing Fee. 2016
  Publishers Weekly v263 no41 p64 O 10 2016

Smith, G. T. Evangelical, sacramental, and Pentecostal. 2017
  Christianity Today p67-9 Ap 2017 M. Bird

Smith, H. A. and Smith, H. A. My daddy rules the world. 2017
  Ebony v72 no6 p31 Ap/My 2017 L. Cross
  Publishers Weekly v264 no16 p69 Ap 17 2017

Smith, H. The uncommon reader. 2017
  Publishers Weekly v264 no36 p79 S 4 2017

Smith, J. and Smith, J. It's Halloween, Chloe Zoe! 2017
  Publishers Weekly v264 no26 p177-9 Je 26 2017

Smith, J. E. Redeeming grace. 2017
  Publishers Weekly v263 no51 p132 D 12 2016

Smith, J. E. The philosopher. 2016
  Weekly Standard v22 no7 p33-4 O 24 2016 L. Klepp

Smith, J. E. Windfall. 2017
  Publishers Weekly v264 no31 p84 Jl 31 2017

Smith, J. F. Engineering Eden. 2016
  Sierra v102 no1 p12 Ja/F 2017 M. Engelhard

Smith, J. K. The Nine of Us. 2016
  New York Times Book Review p11 N 20 2016 M. Shnayerson

Smith, J. K. You are what you love. 2016
  Christianity Today v61 no1 p56 Ja/F 2017 A. Fadling
  Christianity Today v61 no1 p57 Ja/F 2017 R. Moore
  Publishers Weekly v263 no48 p20-4 N 28 2016 L. Garrett
  U.S. Catholic v82 no3 p41 Mr 2017

Smith, K. The x-files. 2017
  Publishers Weekly v264 no22 p67 My 29 2017

Smith, K. Wright on exhibit. 2017
  Architectural Record v205 no7 p59 Jl 2017 A. Paletta

Smith, L. and Harris, C. I'm just no good at rhyming and other noodlings for precocious children, typical youth, and weirdly immature grownups. 2017
  Publishers Weekly v264 no27 p79 Jl 3 2017

Smith, L. and John, J. Penguin problems. 2016
  New York Times Book Review p20 N 13 2016 M. Ian Black

Smith, L. and others. The Witch Who Came in from the Cold. 2017
  Publishers Weekly v264 no17 p73 Ap 24 2017

Smith, L. Dimestore. 2016
  Virginia Living v15 no1 p29 D 2016 B. Glose

Smith, L. E. Strange fruit. 1992
  Publishers Weekly v264 no18 p46 My 1 2017

Smith, L. L. The ice house. 2017
  Publishers Weekly v264 no39 p81 S 25 2017

Smith, L. Legally Charming. 2017
  Publishers Weekly v264 no39 p80b S 25 2017

Smith, L. The Rakehell's Seduction. 2017
  Publishers Weekly v264 no38 p61 S 18 2017

Smith, L. There is a tribe of kids. 2016
  Publishers Weekly v263 no49 p18 D 7 2016

Smith, L. Wolf's revenge. 2017
  Publishers Weekly v264 no32 p52 Ag 7 2017

Smith, M. A Spell in the Country. 2016
  Publishers Weekly v263 no46 p37-8 N 14 2016
  Publishers Weekly v263 no52 p73-4 D 19 2016
  Publishers Weekly v263 no52 p90c-d D 19 2016

Smith, M. A. Secular faith. 2015
  Washington Monthly p13 N/D 2016 S. Buntz

Smith, M. C. and Tavares, M. Lighter than air. 2017
  Publishers Weekly v264 no7 p74 F 13 2017

Smith, M. C. The girl from Venice. 2016
  New York Times Book Review p10-1 O 30 2016 C. Finch

Smith, M. Casting in Stone. 2016
  Publishers Weekly v263 no51 p130 D 12 2016
  Publishers Weekly v264 no4 p50a Ja 23 2017

Smith, M. F. Desperation Road. 2017
  Publishers Weekly v263 no46 p28 N 14 2016

Smith, M. G. and Flett, J. My heart fills with happiness. 2016
  Publishers Weekly v263 no49 p58 D 7 2016

Smith, M. The Road to Winter. 2017
  Publishers Weekly v264 no18 p60 My 1 2017

Smith, N. and Backman, F. Beartown. 2017
  Publishers Weekly v264 no19 p11 My 8 2017 C. Juris
  Publishers Weekly v264 no26 p173 Je 26 2017
  Publishers Weekly v264 no9 p72 F 27 2017

Smith, N. and Nesbø, J. The thirst. 2017
  Entertainment Weekly no1468/1469 p110 Je 2-9 2017
  New York Times Book Review p13 My 21 2017 M. Stasio
  Publishers Weekly v264 no21 p14 My 22 2017 C. Juris
  Publishers Weekly v264 no22 p61 My 29 2017

Smith, N. and Persson, L. G. The dying detective. 2017
  New York Times Book Review p7 Je 11 2017 M. Stasio

Smith, P. and Jones, K. The year of needy girls. 2017
  Publishers Weekly v263 no46 p30 N 14 2016

Smith, P. and others. The Golden shovel anthology. 2017
  New York Times Book Review p19 Ag 6 2017 C. Rankine

Smith, P. Devotion. 2017
  Publishers Weekly v264 no30 p53 Jl 24 2017
  Vanity Fair v59 no10 p128 O 2017 S. C.

Smith, P. Incendiary art. 2017
  Ebony v72 no4 p36 F 2017 L. Cross
  Publishers Weekly v263 no52 p96 D 19 2016

Smith, P. Just kids. 2010
  Commonweal v143 no19 p30-1 D 2 2016 G. Steinfels

Smith, R. and others. Romeo and Juliet. 2014
  Publishers Weekly v264 no41 p79 O 10 2016

Smith, R. B. and others. Walking in a Winter Wonderland. 2016
  Publishers Weekly v263 no39 p92 S 26 2016

Smith, R. Pokemon Go. 2016
  Publishers Weekly v264 no51 p9 D 12 2016

Smith, S. A. Russia in revolution. 2017
  Nation v305 no1 p40-3 Jl 3 2017 S. Pinkham
  Publishers Weekly v264 no3 p49 Ja 16 2017

Smith, S. and Bogart, J. E. The White Cat and the Monk. 2016
  Publishers Weekly v263 no49 p30 D 7 2016

Smith, S. and Cuevas, M. Smoot. 2017
  Publishers Weekly v264 no29 p217 Jl 17 2017

Smith, S. and Schwartz, J. Town is by the Sea. 2017
  New York Times Book Review p22 Je 11 2017
  New York Times Book Review p41 Je 4 2017 M. Russo

Smith, S. B. Modernity and its discontents. 2016
  Commonweal v143 no18 p38-9 N 11 2016 A. Wolfe

Smith, S. B. Prince Charles. 2017
  AARP: The Magazine v60 no3A p18 Ap/My 2017 D. Donahue
  New York Times Book Review p18 My 14 2017 W. Boyd

Smith, S. Follow Me Down. 2017

Publishers Weekly v264 no33 p53-5 Ag 14 2017

Solomon, S. Future humans. 2016
  Commonweal v144 no6 p30-3 Mr 24 2017 P. Lauritzen

Solovitch, S. and Haynes, B. D. Down the up staircase. 2017
  New York Times Book Review p30 My 14 2017 E. Dowling Taylor
  Publishers Weekly v264 no8 p77 F 20 2017

Soltes, E. Why they do it. 2016
  Harvard Business Review v94 no11 p110-1 N 2016 J. Olejarz

Soltvedt, B. and others. Eat Smart in Portugal. 2017
  Publishers Weekly v264 no4 p22-34 Ja 23 2017 S. J. Robbins

Solwitz, S. Once, in Lourdes. 2017
  Publishers Weekly v264 no11 p54-5 Mr 13 2017

Somà, M. and others. The call of the swamp. 2017
  New York Times Book Review p16 O 8 2017 B. Handy
  Publishers Weekly v264 no29 p218 Jl 17 2017

Somaini, A. and others. Sergei M. Eisenstein. 2016
  Film Quarterly v70 no2 p111-3 Wint 2016 D. Polan

Soman, D. and Davis, J. Ladybug Girl's day out with Grandpa. 2017
  Publishers Weekly v264 no18 p58 My 1 2017

Somers, N. and others. Hannah's dress. 2017
  History Today v67 no7 p104-5 Jl 2017 A. Hájková

Somerscales, G. and Dawkins, R. Science in the soul. 2017
  Publishers Weekly v264 no24 p56-7 Je 12 2017

Somerville, K. Ivory. 2017
  Publishers Weekly v263 no41 p67-8 O 10 2016

Sommer, C. and others. How we eat with our eyes and think with our stomach. 2017
  Publishers Weekly v264 no38 p66 S 18 2017

Sommer, J. and others. Jelly, garbage + toys. 2017
  Publishers Weekly v264 no40 p141 O 2 2017

Sonderegger, K. Systematic Theology. 2015
  Christian Century v134 no10 p27-8 My 10 2017 B. Myers

Song, C. and Palermo, S. G. Winter, winter, cold and snow. 2016
  Publishers Weekly v263 no42 p69 O 17 2016

Song, M. and Derby, S. A new school year. 2017
  Publishers Weekly v264 no20 p56 My 15 2017

Song, M. and Song, M. Tea With Oliver. 2017
  Publishers Weekly v264 no24 p63 Je 12 2017

Soni, J. and Goodman, R. A mind at play. 2017
  Fortune v176 no2 p17 Ag 1 2017 R. Hackett
  Publishers Weekly v264 no18 p50 My 1 2017
  Science News v192 no4 p32 S 16 2017

Sonnenblick, J. Falling over sideways. 2016
  Publishers Weekly v263 no49 p95 D 7 2016

Sontag, S. and Taylor, B. Debriefing. 2017
  Publishers Weekly v264 no38 p48 S 18 2017

Soo, L. and Nitanai, K. Kimono design. 2017
  Publishers Weekly v264 no14 p70 Ap 3. 2017

Soojung-Kim Pang, A. Rest. 2016
  New York Times Book Review p10 D 18 2016 A. Huffington
  Publishers Weekly v263 no39 p76 S 26 2016
  Time v188 no22-23 p18-7 N/D 2016 S. Begley

Sookocheff, C. and Fergus, M. Buddy and Earl and the great big baby. 2016
  Publishers Weekly v263 no49 p36 D 7 2016

Sookocheff, C. and Fergus, M. Buddy and Earl go to school. 2017
  Publishers Weekly v264 no20 p54 My 15 2017

Sookocheff, C. and Sookocheff, C. Wet. 2017
  Publishers Weekly v264 no15 p72-3 Ap 10 2017

Sorel, E. Mary Astor's Purple diary. 2016
  Film Comment v52 no6 p94-5 N/D 2016 D. Thomson
  New York Review of Books v64 no5 p39-42 Mr 23 2017 R. Gottlieb
  New York Times Book Review p1-17 Ja 1 2017 W. Allen
  New York Times Book Review p26 Ja 8 2017

Sorell, G. Mothers and other strangers. 2017
  Publishers Weekly v264 no13 p69 Mr 27 2017

Sotelino, K. and Nassar, R. Ancient Tillage. 2016
  Publishers Weekly v263 no45 p36 N 7 2016

Sotira, T. In Her Skin. 2016
  Publishers Weekly v263 no45 p63 N 7 2016
  Publishers Weekly v263 no47 p76f-g N 21 2016

Soufan, A. H. Anatomy of terror. 2017
  New York Times Book Review p19 Je 11 2017 C. Savage
  New York Times Book Review p23 Je 18 2017

Publishers Weekly v264 no10 p50 Mr 6 2017

Soule, M. Echoes of terror. 2017
  Publishers Weekly v264 no4 p59-60 Ja 23 2017

Southall, B. Sgt. Pepper's Lonely Hearts Club Band. 2017
  Publishers Weekly v264 no33 p21 Ag 14 2017 S. Maughan

Southard, S. Nagasaki. 2015
  Military History v33 no5 p75 Ja 2017

Sowell, T. Wealth, poverty and politics. 2016
  American Conservative v16 no4 p45-7 Jl/Ag 2017 A. Archie

Sowton, C. Dreamworking. 2017
  Publishers Weekly v263 no39 p26-30 S 26 2016 L. Garrett

Spaar, L. R. Orexia. 2017
  Publishers Weekly v264 no3 p37-8 Ja 16 2017

Spader, C. Feast of Raven. 2016
  Publishers Weekly v264 no3 p46 Ja 16 2017
  Publishers Weekly v264 no9 p66d F 27 2017

Spall, C. and others. Portmahomack on Tarbat Ness 2016. 2016
  History Today v67 no9 p92-3 S 2017 R. Hodges

Spampinato, F. and Wiedemann, J. Art Record Covers. 2017
  Vanity Fair v59 no4 p113 Mr 2017

Spann, S. Betrayal at Iga. 2017
  Publishers Weekly v264 no19 p39-40 My 8 2017

Sparks, C. Lotus Blue. 2017
  New York Times Book Review p35 My 21 2017 N. K. Jemisin
  Publishers Weekly v264 no5 p184 Ja 30 2017

Sparks, J. and Caldwell, S. Go west. 2017
  Publishers Weekly v263 no51 p144 D 12 2016

Sparwasser, N. and others. Mountains. 2016
  Natural History v125 no1 p40-3 D 2016/Ja 2017 L. A. Marschall

Speaking our truths. 2017
  Publishers Weekly v264 no34 p114 Ag 21 2017

Spear, T. Dreaming of a White Wolf Christmas. 2017
  Publishers Weekly v264 no36 p74 S 4 2017

Spence, C. Gastrophysics. 2017
  American Scholar v86 no3 p114-6 Summ 2017
  Science v356 no6343 p1129 Je 16 2017 J. Ubbink
  Time v190 no4 p54 Jl 24 2017 L. Feldman

Spenceley, A. and Piper, S. The Easter Story. 2017
  Publishers Weekly v264 no3 p58 Ja 16 2017

Spencer, H. Principles of Biology. 1989
  New York Times Book Review p16-7 F 26 2017 I. X. Kendi

Spencer, J. and Spencer, J. This land. 2017
  New York Times Book Review p32-3 Je 4 2017 D. Browning

Spencer, L. The Tipping Point of Oliver Bass. 2017
  Publishers Weekly v264 no24 p44-5 Je 12 2017
  Publishers Weekly v264 no26 p146c Je 26 2017

Spencer, M. W. and others. The Essential Louisiana Seafood Cookbook. 2016
  New Orleans Magazine v51 no2 p54 D 2016 J. Debold

Spencer, N. and Lieber, S. The Fix 1. 2016
  Publishers Weekly v263 no41 p65 O 10 2016

Spencer, R. C. The revolution has come. 2016
  New York Times Book Review p35 N 20 2016 J. Ryerson

Spencer, S. and Hilmes, O. Franz Liszt. 2016
  New York Review of Books v63 no17 p31-2 N 10 2016 L. Carey

Spencer, S. River Under the Road. 2017
  New York Times Book Review p21 Ag 20 2017 R. R. Cooper

Spencer, S. The Hidden. 2017
  Publishers Weekly v264 no18 p39 My 1 2017

Spencer, S. The Shivering Turn. 2017
  Publishers Weekly v263 no51 p126 D 12 2016

Spencer, W. B. The Unorthodox Dr. Draper and Other Stories. 2017
  Publishers Weekly v264 no20 p42 My 15 2017

Spengler, O. and Atkinson, C. F. Man and technics. 1976
  American Conservative v15 no6 p51-3 N/D 2016 B. R. Myers

Sperber, D. and Mercier, H. The enigma of reason. 2017
  New Yorker v93 no2 p66-71 F 27 2017 E. Kolbert
  Science v356 no6338 p589 My 12 2017 D. Frey

Sperber, J. Karl Marx. 2013
  New Yorker v92 no32 p90-7 O 10 2016 L. Menand

Spicer, A. and Cederström, C. Desperately Seeking Self-improvement. 2017
  Publishers Weekly v264 no35 p52 Ag 28 2017 J. Rosen

Spiegelman, N. I'm supposed to protect you from all this. 2016
  Publishers Weekly v263 no44 p71-2 O 31 2016

Spieker, D. The Way Magellan Must Have Felt. 2014

Stanley, D. and Stanley, D. Joplin, Wishing. 2017
  Publishers Weekly v264 no16 p67 Ap 17 2017
Stanley, J. Every Body Yoga. 2017
  Good Housekeeping v264 no5 p97-8 My 2017 K. Miller
  Publishers Weekly v263 no52 p120 D 19 2016
Stanley, M. Dying to live. 2017
  Publishers Weekly v264 no34 p91 Ag 21 2017
Stanley, T. J. and Danko, W. D. The millionaire next door. 1997
  Black Enterprise v47 no5 p20 Ja/F 2017 D. D. Hughes
Stansel, I. The last cowboys of San Geronimo. 2017
  Publishers Weekly v264 no22 p42 My 29 2017
Stanton, A. Waking in time. 2017
  Publishers Weekly v264 no4 p83 Ja 23 2017
Stanton, B. and others. Did you take the B from my _ook? 2017
  Publishers Weekly v264 no14 p78 Ap 3. 2017
Stapinski, H. Murder in Matera. 2017
  New Yorker v93 no32 p80 O 16 2017
  New York Times Book Review p18 Je 25 2017 M. Byrd
  Publishers Weekly v264 no10 p52 Mr 6 2017
Stapleton, L. C. The box project. 2016
  American Craft v77 no2 p16 Ap/My 2017 J. Shaykett
Star, N. Sisters One, Two, Three. 2017
  Publishers Weekly v263 no47 p82 N 21 2016
Stargardt, N. The German War. 2015
  Forbes v198 no7 p32 N 29 2016
  New York Times Book Review p24 Je 25 2017 J. Khatib
Starin, L. Splashdance. 2016
  Publishers Weekly v263 no49 p40-1 D 7 2016
Stark, A. The Consolations of mortality. 2016
  Commonweal v144 no4 p26-8 F 24 2017 D. Callahan
Stark, R. The triumph of faith. 2015
  Commonweal v144 no3 p35-6 F 10 2017 L. T. Johnson
Starkoff, V. and Springer, J. Along the river. 2017
  Publishers Weekly v264 no7 p76 F 13 2017
Starks, K. and others. Kill them all. 2017
  Publishers Weekly v264 no36 p77 S 4 2017
Starmer, A. Spontaneous. 2016
  Publishers Weekly v263 no44 p72 O 31 2016
Starnone, D. and Lahiri, J. Ties. 2017
  New York Times Book Review p10 Mr 26 2017 R. Donadio
  Publishers Weekly v264 no3 p35 Ja 16 2017
Starobin, P. Madness rules the hour. 2017
  MHQ: Quarterly Journal of Military History v30 no1 p93-4 Aut 2017 N. Tappan
  New York Times Book Review p22 Ap 23 2017 D. Goldfield
  Publishers Weekly v264 no9 p92 F 27 2017
Starr, K. Continental ambitions. 2016
  America v216 no9 p38-40 Ap 24 2017 T. J. Shelley
  Commonweal v144 no8 p38-40 My 5 2017 L. Tentler
Starritt, A. Late Fame. 2015
  Publishers Weekly v264 no24 p37 Je 12 2017
Stasavage, D. and Scheve, K. Taxing the ricj. 2016
  Foreign Affairs v95 no6 p175 N/D 2016 R. N. Cooper
Stathers, K. The bucket list. 2016
  Time v190 no2/3 p94-7 Jl 10-17 2017 L. Feldman
Statovci, P. and Hackston, D. My cat Yugoslavia. 2017
  Atlantic v319 no3 p40 Ap 2017 A. Hulbert
  New Yorker v93 no19 p69 Jl 3 2017
  New York Times Book Review p9 Ap 23 2017 T. Obreht
  Publishers Weekly v264 no7 p48 F 13 2017
Staub, J. and Büchert, E. S. The illustrated book of edible plants. 2017
  Log Home Living v34 no4 p20 My 2017
Staub, W. C. Dead of Winter. 2017
  Publishers Weekly v264 no38 p55-6 S 18 2017
Stauber, K. Spin the Sky. 2012
  Publishers Weekly v263 no39 p95 S 26 2016
St. Aubyn, E. Dunbar. 2017
  British Heritage Travel v38 no5 p72 S/O 2017
  Maclean's v130 no9 p77 O 2017 B. Bethune
  Publishers Weekly v264 no34 p83 Ag 21 2017
Stauffer, J. and Gates, H. L. The Portable Frederick Douglass. 2016
  Nation v304 no11 p27-31 Ap 3 2017 M. Karp
Stauth, C. and Dreeke, R. The Code of Trust. 2017
  Publishers Weekly v264 no26 p170 Je 26 2017

Staveley, B. Skullsworn. 2017
  Publishers Weekly v264 no9 p83 F 27 2017
Stavridis, J. Sea power. 2017
  Military History v34 no2 p74 Jl 2017
  Publishers Weekly v264 no15 p65 Ap 10 2017
St. Clair, K. The secret lives of color. 2017
  Publishers Weekly v264 no25 p100-1 Je 19 2017
Stead, E. E. and Cuevas, M. The uncorker of ocean bottles. 2016
  Publishers Weekly v263 no49 p18 D 7 2016
Stead, E. E. and Galing, E. Tony. 2017
  Publishers Weekly v263 no47 p105 N 21 2016
Stead, E. E. and Stead, P. The Purloining of Prince Oleomargarine. 2017
  Publishers Weekly v264 no28 p89 Jl 10 2017
Stead, P. and Stead, E. E. The Purloining of Prince Oleomargarine. 2017
  Publishers Weekly v264 no28 p89 Jl 10 2017
Stead, P. C. and Cordell, M. The only fish in the sea. 2017
  Publishers Weekly v264 no22 p65 My 29 2017
Stead, P. C. and Stead, P. C. Ideas are all around. 2016
  Publishers Weekly v263 no49 p22 D 7 2016
Stead, P. C. and Stead, P. C. Samson in the snow. 2016
  New York Times Book Review p18 D 18 2016 L. S. Marcus
  Publishers Weekly v264 no49 p17 D 7 2016
Stearns, R. E. Barbary Station. 2017
  Publishers Weekly v264 no39 p91 S 25 2017
Stedman, M. L. The light between oceans. 2012
  New York Times Book Review p24 O 16 2016
Stedman Jones, G. Karl Marx. 2016
  Nation v304 no6 p27-33 F 27 2017 B. Kunkel
  New Yorker v92 no32 p90-7 O 10 2016 L. Menand
  New York Times Book Review p24 O 23 2016 P. E. Gordon
Steel, D. The award. 2016
  Publishers Weekly v263 no46 p13 N 14 2016 J. Segura
Steel, D. The mistress. 2017
  Publishers Weekly v264 no3 p14 Ja 16 2017 C. Juris
Steel, D. The right time. 2017
  New York Times Book Review p23 S 17 2017
  New York Times Book Review p24 S 17 2017
Steele, A. Avengers of the Moon. 2017
  Publishers Weekly v263 no51 p127-8 D 12 2016
Steele, H. Pantheon. 2017
  Publishers Weekly v264 no28 p74 Jl 10 2017
Steele, M. Effortless entertaining cookbook. 2016
  Publishers Weekly v263 no42 p64 O 17 2016
Steele-Morgan, A. and others. Potatoes at turtle rock. 2016
  Publishers Weekly v263 no39 p94 S 26 2016
Steffens, R. So much things to say. 2017
  New York Times Book Review p10 Jl 30 2017 Touré
  Publishers Weekly v264 no19 p51 My 8 2017
Steig, W. and Steig, W. Amos & Boris. 2009
  U.S. Catholic v82 no2 p19 F 2017
Steiger, I. The empire's ghost. 2017
  Publishers Weekly v264 no13 p85 Mr 27 2017
Steigerwald, B. 30 days a black man. 2017
  Weekly Standard v22 no38 p38 Je 12 2017 J. Hill
Steiker, C. S. and Steiker, J. M. Courting death. 2016
  New York Review of Books v64 no10 p46-7 Je 8 2017 J. S. Rakoff
  Publishers Weekly v263 no39 p69 S 26 2016
Steimatsky, N. The face on film. 2016
  Film Comment v53 no1 p92-3 Ja/F 2017 M. J. Rowin
Stein, D. and others. Grow Your Own. 2017
  Publishers Weekly v264 no34 p106 Ag 21 2017
Stein, D. B. The Silver Baron's Wife. 2016
  Publishers Weekly v264 no21 p68 My 22 2017
  Publishers Weekly v264 no26 p146c Je 26 2017
Stein, D. E. and Stein, D. E. Ice boy. 2017
  Publishers Weekly v264 no5 p201 Ja 30 2017
Stein, J. E. and Vavouri, E. A Hanukkah with Mazel. 2016
  Publishers Weekly v263 no39 p86 S 26 2016
Stein, J. E. Eye of the sixties. 2016
  Art in America v104 no10 p83-6 N 2016 L. Wei
Stein, M. R. and Miller, L. Blueprint for Counter Education. 2016
  Art in America v105 no3 p63 Mr 2017
Stein, T. Brooklyn wars. 2017
  Publishers Weekly v264 no19 p36 My 8 2017

Stine, D. Hearing from God. 2017
Publishers Weekly v263 no46 p51 N 14 2016
Stine, J. K. and Kress, W. J. Living in the anthropocene. 2017
Publishers Weekly v264 no27 p64 Jl 3 2017
Stine, R. L. and Brown, M. T. Mary McScary. 2017
Publishers Weekly v264 no24 p63 Je 12 2017
Stine, R. L. Slappy Birthday to You. 2017
Publishers Weekly v263 no47 p108-10 N 21 2016
Stine, R. L. Young Scrooge. 2016
Publishers Weekly v263 no39 p92 S 26 2016
Stinson, K. and Petričić, D. The dance of the violin. 2017
Publishers Weekly v264 no8 p85 F 20 2017
Stirling, M. W. and others. The Origin Myth of Acoma Pueblo. 2015
New York Review of Books v63 no16 p58-60 O 27 2016 I. Frazier
Stirling, S. M. The sea peoples. 2017
Publishers Weekly v264 no33 p55 Ag 14 2017
Stites, R. and others. Red star. 1984
In These Times v41 no10 p45 O 2017
St. James, D. Asking for Truffle. 2017
Publishers Weekly v264 no31 p64-5 Jl 31 2017
Stock, C. and Sanchez, A. Karl, get out of the garden! 2016
Publishers Weekly v264 no7 p75 F 13 2017
Stockdale, S. and Stockdale, S. Fantastic flowers. 2017
Publishers Weekly v263 no52 p123 D 19 2016
Stockwell, R. and Gilroy, S. The Prize. 2013
New York Times Book Review p32 O 23 2016 J. Khatib
Stoecker, R. Liberating service learning and the rest of higher education civic engagement. 2016
Phi Kappa Phi Forum v96 no4 p31 Wint 2016
Stohl, M. Royce rolls. 2017
Publishers Weekly v264 no5 p205-7 Ja 30 2017
Stoker, B. and Luckhurst, R. Dracula. 2011
New York Times Book Review p4 F 5 2017 J. Williams
Stoker, S. Claiming Grace. 2017
Publishers Weekly v264 no4 p65 Ja 23 2017
Stokes, A. and Hansen, D. This house is mine. 2016
New York Times Book Review p50 D 4 2016 R. Marler
Stokes, J. W. Addison Cooke and the treasure of the Incas. 2016
Good Housekeeping v263 no6 p87 D 2016
Stoknes, P. E. What we think about when we try to think about global warming. 2015
BioScience v67 no3 p306-9 Mr 2017 R. D. Stevenson
Stoll, S. Ramp Hollow. 2017
Publishers Weekly v264 no36 p79 S 4 2017 S. Jones
Stone, B. and Yasuda, A. Explore Comets and Asteroids! 2017
Publishers Weekly v264 no25 p114 Je 19 2017
Stone, B. The upstarts. 2017
Harvard Business Review v95 no3 p160-1 My/Je 2017 W. Frick
New York Times Book Review p1-21 Je 25 2017 W. Isaacson
Publishers Weekly v264 no14 p73 Ap 3. 2017
Stone, D. The food explorer. 2018
Publishers Weekly v264 no35 p46 Ag 28 2017 C. J.
Stone, G. R. Sex and the constitution. 2017
Nation v304 no16 p39-41 My 22 2017 A. North
New York Times Book Review p21 Ap 2 2017 M. Kinsley
New York Times Book Review p22 Ap 9 2017
Publishers Weekly v264 no1 p49-50 Ja 2 2017
Stone, M. Border child. 2017
New Yorker v93 no31 p68 O 9 2017
Publishers Weekly v264 no8 p58 F 20 2017
Stone, R. and Dujardin, H. Add a Pinch cookbook. 2017
Publishers Weekly v263 no52 p118 D 19 2016
Stone, R. The making of the president 2016. 2017
Publishers Weekly v264 no7 p11 F 13 2017 C. Juris
Stone, T. and others. Not drunk enough. 2017
Publishers Weekly v264 no18 p46 My 1 2017
Stone, T. L. Girl rising. 2016
Publishers Weekly v264 no1 p58 Ja 2 2017
Stonger, S. Traditionally fermented foods. 2017
Publishers Weekly v264 no10 p24 Mr 6 2017 C. S.
Stoop, N. and Banks, K. Pup and bear. 2017
Publishers Weekly v264 no32 p69 Ag 7 2017
Stoop, N. and McDonnell, P. Shine! 2017
Publishers Weekly v264 no7 p76 F 13 2017
Storey, E. A Promise to Kill. 2017

Publishers Weekly v264 no22 p45 My 29 2017
Storey, E. Nothing short of dying. 2016
Publishers Weekly v263 no40 p117-8 O 3 2016
Stork, F. X. The memory of light. 2016
Publishers Weekly v263 no49 p99 D 7 2016
Storr, R. Intimate geometries. 2015
Art in America v105 no4 p61 Ap 2017
Storring, N. and Zipp, S. Vital little plans. 2016
Atlantic v318 no4 p98-109 N 2016 N. Rich
Nation v304 no5 p27-31 F 20 2017 R. Tuhus-Dubrow
New Republic v247 no12 p74-9 D 2016 M. Holleran
New Yorker v92 no30 p69-75 S 26 2016 A. Gopnik
New York Times Book Review p17 O 9 2016 G. Bellafante
New York v49 no22 p110-3 O 31 2016 J. Davidson
Reason v49 no4 p72-3 Ag/S 2017 S. R. Staley
Stothard, P. The Senecans. 2016
New Yorker v93 no23 p72 Ag 7 2017
Stott, R. In the days of rain. 2017
Publishers Weekly v264 no21 p87 My 22 2017
Stourton, J. Kenneth Clark. 2016
America v216 no8 p42-4 Ap 17 2017 R. Hosmer
History Today v67 no1 p61 Ja 2017 D. Seward
Weekly Standard v22 no21 p30-3 F 6 2017 T. Lee Simmons
Stout, H. S. American aristocrats. 2017
Publishers Weekly v264 no39 p97 S 25 2017
Stovell, S. Exquisite. 2017
Publishers Weekly v264 no35 p106 Ag 28 2017
Stradal, J. R. Kitchens of the Great Midwest. 2015
South Dakota Magazine p9 S/O 2017 Supplement
Strahs, K. The Lemonade Stand Cookbook. 2017
Publishers Weekly v264 no22 p69 My 29 2017
Publishers Weekly v264 no26 p146f-g Je 26 2017
Strand, G. The Brothers Vonnegut. 2015
Orion Magazine v35 no3 p54-5 My/Je 2016 C. Barnett
Strandberg, L. and others. West. 2011
Publishers Weekly v264 no9 p21-40 F 27 2017 R. Deahl
Strange, L. The secret of Nightingale Wood. 2016
Publishers Weekly v264 no34 p112 Ag 21 2017
Strangeway, R. J. and others. Space physics. 2016
Physics Today v70 no5 p62 My 2017
Stransky, O. and Francis, P. The name of God is mercy. 2016
Christian Century v133 no23 p37-9 N 9 2016 R. P. Carbine
Stratford, M. and others. Me tall, you small. 2017
Publishers Weekly v264 no4 p77 Ja 23 2017
Straub, E. Modern lovers. 2016
New York Times Book Review p24 Je 11 2017 J. Khatib
Straub, J. and others. Writings. 2016
Film Quarterly v70 no2 p103-6 Wint 2016 C. Tsui
Strauss, G. and Leonhard, H. The Hiding Game. 2017
Publishers Weekly v263 no48 p71 N 28 2016
Strauss, L. L. and Tugeau, J. A different kind of Passover. 2017
Publishers Weekly v264 no4 p78 Ja 23 2017
Strauss, M. A. and others. Welcome to the universe. 2016
New York Times Book Review p31 S 25 2016 J. Ryerson
Strauss, R. Worst. President. Ever. 2016
American History v52 no4 p66 O 2017 R. Winn
Strawn, B. A. The Old Testament is dying. 2017
America v216 no9 p28-37 Ap 24 2017 J. Racine
Christian Century v134 no10 p28-9 My 10 2017 J. E. Lapsley
Strawser, J. Almost Missed You. 2017
Publishers Weekly v264 no5 p174 Ja 30 2017
Straza, E. M. Comfort detox. 2017
Christianity Today p61 Mr 2017
Publishers Weekly v263 no51 p144 D 12 2016
Stribling, T. S. The store. 1985
New York Times Book Review p24 S 17 2017 G. Cowles
Strickland, S. and Powell, P. H. Loving vs. Virginia. 2017
Publishers Weekly v263 no46 p57 N 14 2016
Publishers Weekly v264 no14 p74 Ap 3. 2017
Strickland, T. and others. The Barefoot Book of Children. 2016
Publishers Weekly v263 no49 p45 D 7 2016
Stringer, L. and Going, K. L. The shape of the world. 2017
Publishers Weekly v264 no32 p71 Ag 7 2017
Strøksnes, M. and Nunnally, T. Shark drunk. 2017
Publishers Weekly v264 no15 p65 Ap 10 2017
Stroh, F. Beer Money. 2016

theory. 2017
Publishers Weekly v264 no35 p120 Ag 28 2017
Science News v192 no7 p28 O 28 2017 T. Siegfried
Sussman, E. and Hand, C. The afterlife of Holly Chase. 2017
Publishers Weekly v264 no36 p103 S 4 2017
Sussman, E. and others. Grandpa's great escape. 2017
Publishers Weekly v263 no48 p67 N 28 2016
Sutherland, J. Orwell's Nose. 2016
New Yorker v92 no37 p86 N 14 2016
Sutherland, K. A semi-definitive list of worst nightmares. 2017
Publishers Weekly v264 no29 p222 Jl 17 2017
Sutherland, K. and Anderson, J. L. The vanishing season. 2014
Publishers Weekly v264 no36 p64 S 4 2017
Sutherland, K. and Johnston, F. Teenage writings. 2017
British Heritage Travel v38 no3 p75 My/Je 2017 J. H.
Sutoris, P. Visions of Development. 2016
Film Quarterly v70 no4 p127-8 Summ 2017 N. Vachani
Sutphin, J. and others. Word of mouse. 2016
Publishers Weekly v263 no40 p123-4 O 3 2016
Suttie, I. The actual one. 2017
Publishers Weekly v263 no47 p100 N 21 2016
Sutton, E. and Davies, N. Many. 2017
Publishers Weekly v264 no41 p70-1 O 9 2017
Sutton, E. and Huddy, D. The Christmas Eve tree. 2016
Publishers Weekly v263 no39 p93 S 26 2016
Sutton, M. A. and Dochuk, D. Faith in the new millennium. 2016
Christian Century v133 no22 p41-2 O 26 2016 R. Balmer
Sutton, P. and Evanovich, J. Curious minds. 2016
Publishers Weekly v263 no40 p118 O 3 2016
Sutton, R. I. The Asshole Survival Guide. 2017
Publishers Weekly v264 no20 p46-7 My 15 2017
Sutton, R. K. Stark Mad Abolitionists. 2017
Publishers Weekly v264 no22 p57-8 My 29 2017
Sutton, S. E. When Ivory Towers Were Black. 2017
Publishers Weekly v263 no51 p136 D 12 2016
Suvada, E. This mortal coil. 2017
Publishers Weekly v264 no38 p74 S 18 2017
Suzman, J. Affluence Without Abundance. 2017
Science v356 no6345 p1340 Je 30 2017 A. Barnard
Swafford, J. Language of the spirit. 2017
Weekly Standard v22 no31 p34-7 Ap 17 2017 G. B. Stauffer
Swaim, B. The speechwriter. 2015
Weekly Standard v22 no8 p41-2 O 31 2016 B. Swaim
Swales, R. Big Hid. 2017
Publishers Weekly v264 no25 p108 Je 19 2017
Swan, R. and Summers, A. A Matter of Honor. 2016
Publishers Weekly v263 no39 p81 S 26 2016
Swank, D. G. Only You. 2016
Publishers Weekly v263 no39 p72 S 26 2016
Swann, M. and others. The compleat angler. 2014
Publishers Weekly v264 no24 p22 Je 12 2017 S. Maughan
Swanson, L. Summer Dance. 2011
Publishers Weekly v264 no16 p38-9 Ap 17 2017
Swanson, L. W. and others. The Beautiful Brain. 2017
Scientific American v316 no1 p68 Ja 2017 C. Moskowitz
Swanson, M. and Behr, R. Everywhere, wonder. 2017
Publishers Weekly v263 no51 p146 D 12 2016
Swanson, P. Her every fear. 2017
Good Housekeeping v264 no2 p60 F 1 2017
Publishers Weekly v263 no42 p52 O 17 2016
Swanwick, M. and others. The Witch Who Came in from the Cold. 2017
Publishers Weekly v264 no17 p73 Ap 24 2017
Swärd, A. and Bragan-Turner, D. Breathless. 2013
Ebony v72 no4 p36 F 2017 L. Cross
Publishers Weekly v263 no46 p39 N 14 2016
Sweazy, L. D. See also murder. 2015
Publishers Weekly v264 no5 p196-7 Ja 30 2017
Sweazy, L. D. Where I can see you. 2017
Publishers Weekly v263 no45 p42 N 7 2016
Sweeney, C. and Bothwick, F. Inclusive leadership. 2016
People Management p56 N 2016
Sweeney, C. D. The Nest. 2016
New York Times Book Review p24 Ap 23 2017 J. Khatib
Sweeney, E. C. and Midorikawa, E. A secret sisterhood. 2017
Atlantic v320 no4 p49 N 2017 A. Hulbert

Publishers Weekly v264 no32 p63 Ag 7 2017
Sweet, M. and Elliott, D. Baabwaa and Wooliam. 2017
New York Times Book Review p24 S 10 2017 P. H. Reynolds
Publishers Weekly v264 no29 p215-7 Jl 17 2017
Sweet, M. and Murray, C. Cricket in the thicket. 2017
Publishers Weekly v264 no9 p103 F 27 2017
Sweet, M. Some writer!: the story of E. B. White. 2016
New York Times Book Review p24 N 13 2016 A. Gopnik
Publishers Weekly v263 no49 p86 D 7 2016
Sweet, V. Slow medicine. 2017
Atlantic v320 no3 p37 O 2017 A. Hulbert
Good Housekeeping v265 no4 p67 O 2017
Swenson, O. and others. Seeking the shore. 2017
Publishers Weekly v264 no33 p58-9 Ag 14 2017
Swerts, A. and Van Lindenhuizen, E. Santa, Please Bring Me a Gnome. 2017
Publishers Weekly v264 no36 p100 S 4 2017
Swiatkowska, G. and Hosford, K. How the queen found the perfect cup of tea. 2017
Publishers Weekly v264 no3 p59 Ja 16 2017
Swidler, A. and Watkins, S. C. A fraught embrace. 2017
Foreign Affairs v96 no3 p176 My/Je 2017 N. Van De Walle
Swift, D. The Bughouse. 2017
Publishers Weekly v264 no21 p81 My 22 2017
Swift, G. Mothering Sunday. 2016
Weekly Standard v22 no4 p37-8 O 3 2016 S. Dahlie
Swinson, D. The second girl. 2016
New York Times Book Review p81 D 4 2016 M. Stasio
Swinton, J. Becoming friends of time. 2016
Christianity Today v61 no1 p56 Ja/F 2017 M. Barrett
Swong, S. and Wachtell, D. How do I explain this to my kids? 2017
New York Times Book Review p27 Ag 13 2017 J. Newman
Syed, M. Black box thinking. 2015
People Management p14 D 2016/Ja 2017
Sykes, C. J. How the right lost its mind. 2017
Commentary v144 no3 p46-8 O 2017 M. Lasswell
Progressive v81 no7 p63-5 O/N 2017 B. Lueders
Publishers Weekly v264 no26 p103-9 Je 26 2017 A. R. Albanese
Sykes, P. Party girls die in pearls. 2017
Publishers Weekly v264 no14 p50 Ap 3. 2017
Sykes, S. D. City of Masks. 2017
New York Times Book Review p15 Jl 23 2017 M. Stasio
Publishers Weekly v264 no18 p37 My 1 2017
Szabó, M. and Rix, L. Katalin Street. 2017
Publishers Weekly v264 no29 p193 Jl 17 2017
Szabó, M. and Szirtes, G. Iza's ballad. 2016
New York Times Book Review p39 N 13 2016 L. Groff
Szabó, M. The door. 2015
Publishers Weekly v263 no46 p22-3 N 14 2016 S. Maughan
Szalay, D. All that man is. 2016
New York Review of Books v64 no11 p47-8 Je 22 2017 M. Gorra
New York Times Book Review p16 O 9 2016 G. Greenwell
Szalay, D. London and the South-East. 2016
Publishers Weekly v264 no35 p98 Ag 28 2017
Szirtes, G. and others. The world goes on. 2017
Publishers Weekly v264 no36 p62 S 4 2017
Szirtes, G. and Szabó, M. Iza's ballad. 2016
New York Times Book Review p39 N 13 2016 L. Groff

T

Tabilio, M. and Schwandt, K. Marco Polo. 2017
Publishers Weekly v264 no30 p63 Jl 24 2017
Tabucchi, A. and Harris, E. For Isabel. 2017
Publishers Weekly v264 no31 p62-1 Jl 31 2017
Tackett, T. The coming of the terror in the French Revolution. 2015
New York Review of Books v64 no11 p38-40 Je 22 2017 C. Jones
Tadd, E. The infinite view. 2017
Publishers Weekly v264 no7 p69-70 F 13 2017
Tae Won Yu and Conigliaro, P. My First Baby Signs. 2017
Publishers Weekly v264 no6 p67 F 6 2017
Tagame, G. and others. My brother's husband. 2017
Publishers Weekly v264 no14 p61 Ap 3. 2017
Tahir, S. A Torch Against the Night. 2016

Publishers Weekly v263 no49 p112 D 7 2016

Tahmahkera, D. Tribal television. 2014
  American Indian Quarterly v41 no2 p193-5 Spr 2017 L. L. Beadling

Taibbi, M. and Juhasz, V. Insane clown president. 2016
  New York p133 Mr 6 2017
  New York Times Book Review p24 F 12 2017 G. ^Cowles
  New York Times Book Review p4 Ja 22 2017 J. Williams

Taibbi, M. I Can't Breathe. 2017
  Publishers Weekly v264 no26 p103-9 Je 26 2017 A. R. Albanese

Taira, K. and others. Naruto Chibi Sasukes Sharingan Legend 1. 2017
  Publishers Weekly v264 no39 p94 S 25 2017

Tait, A. and Chistyakov, I. The Day Will Pass Away. 2017
  Publishers Weekly v264 no19 p48 My 8 2017

Tait, K. Fake Plastic Love. 2017
  Publishers Weekly v264 no13 p68 Mr 27 2017

Takahashi, K. and Takahashi, K. Knock! Knock! 2016
  Publishers Weekly v263 no49 p60 D 7 2016

Takazawa, K. and Steinhoff, P. G. Destiny. 2017
  Publishers Weekly v264 no22 p56 My 29 2017

Takeda, S. Monstress 2. 2017
  New York Times Book Review p31 S 10 2017 N. K. Jemisin

Tal, A. The land is full. 2016
  Foreign Affairs v96 no1 p173 Ja/F 2017 J. Waterbury

Talese, G. High notes. 2017
  Nation v304 no11 p37-4 Ap 3 2017 M. Dean
  New York Times Book Review p15 Ja 29 2017 M. Gordon
  Publishers Weekly v263 no47 p100 N 21 2016

Talese, G. The Voyeur's Motel. 2016
  Nation v304 no11 p32-4 Ap 3 2017 M. Dean

Tallec, O. and Dunlap, C. This Book Will Not Be Fun. 2017
  Publishers Weekly v264 no16 p66 Ap 17 2017

Tallent, G. My absolute darling. 2017
  Glamour v115 no10 p144 O 2017 E. Egan
  O, The Oprah Magazine p99 O 2017 T. Lannamann
  Publishers Weekly v264 no26 p149-50 Je 26 2017
  Saturday Evening Post v289 no5 p24 S/O 2017

Talley, M. Footprints to Murder. 2016
  Publishers Weekly v263 no40 p100 O 3 2016

Tallis, N. Crown of Blood. 2016
  History Today v67 no3 p59 Mr 2017 W. Moore
  New York Times Book Review p26 D 25 2016 J. Zimmerman
  Publishers Weekly v263 no41 p69-70 O 10 2016

Tam, M. and Fong, H. Nom nom paleo. 2013
  Publishers Weekly v264 no33 p13 Ag 14 2017 C. Juris

Tam, M. and Fong, H. Ready or not! 2017
  Publishers Weekly v264 no33 p13 Ag 14 2017 C. Juris

Tamaki, J. and Beasley, K. Gertie's leap to greatness. 2016
  New York Times Book Review p20 O 9 2016 E. Egan

Tamaki, J. and Tamaki, J. Boundless. 2017
  Publishers Weekly v263 no51 p31-7 D 12 2016 H. Macdonald

Tamaki, M. Saving Montgomery Sole. 2016
  Publishers Weekly v263 no49 p102 D 7 2016

Tambakis, A. Swimming with Bridgeport girls. 2017
  Publishers Weekly v264 no20 p32 My 15 2017

Tamborski, M. N. and others. Positive discipline parenting tools. 2016
  Publishers Weekly v263 no40 p116 O 3 2016

Tamimi, S. and Ottolenghi, Y. Jerusalem. 2012
  Progressive p60-3 D 2016/Ja 2017 A. Cusac

Tamimi Arab, P. Amplifying Islam in the European soundscape. 2017
  Islamic Horizons v46 no4 p61 Jl/Ag 2017

Tamny, J. Who needs the Fed? 2016
  Claremont Review of Books v17 no1 p75-8 Wint 2016/2017 B. Domitrovic
  Forbes v198 no7 p32 N 29 2016

Tan, A. Where the past begins. 2017
  Publishers Weekly v264 no35 p123 Ag 28 2017
  Vanity Fair v59 no11 p70 N 2017 S. Crosley

Tan, C. Hard Rhythm. 2017
  Publishers Weekly v263 no52 p104 D 19 2016

Tan, D. and others. Burma Superstar. 2016
  Publishers Weekly v263 no47 p101 N 21 2016

Tan, S. and Tan, S. The singing bones. 2016

New York Times Book Review p36 N 13 2016 S. Harrison Smith
  Publishers Weekly v263 no49 p111 D 7 2016

Tanaka, Y. and Jenkins, E. Princessland. 2017
  Publishers Weekly v263 no46 p54 N 14 2016

Tanenbaum, R. K. Without fear or favor. 2017
  Publishers Weekly v264 no25 p93-4 Je 19 2017

Tanizaki, J. and Cronin, M. P. The maids. 2017
  Publishers Weekly v264 no9 p68 F 27 2017

Tanizaki, J. and Seidensticker, E. G. Some prefer nettles. 1995
  New York Review of Books v64 no10 p16-8 Je 8 2017 P. Iyer

Tanizaki, J. and Seidensticker, E. G. The Makioka sisters. 1995
  New York Review of Books v64 no10 p16-8 Je 8 2017 P. Iyer

Tanizaki, J. and Vincent, J. K. Devils in daylight. 2017.
  New York Review of Books v64 no10 p16-8 Je 8 2017 P. Iyer
  Publishers Weekly v264 no6 p40 F 6 2017

Tankard, B. The full tank life. 2016
  Essence v47 no8 p72 D 2016 P. H. Bass

Tanquary, K. The night parade. 2016
  Publishers Weekly v263 no49 p79-80 D 7 2016

Tapalansky, N. and Espinosa, A. Cast no shadow. 2017
  Publishers Weekly v264 no38 p74-5 S 18 2017

Taplin, J. Move fast and break things. 2017
  Publishers Weekly v264 no9 p93 F 27 2017

Tapp, P. G. How they decorated. 2017
  Harper's Magazine p91-3 Ap 2017 C. Smallwood
  House Beautiful v159 no4 p56-8 My 1 2017 K. O'Shea-Evans

Tapper, L. and Wilson, S. Hedgehugs. 2017
  Publishers Weekly v264 no34 p111 Ag 21 2017

Tara, S. The secret life of fat. 2016
  New Yorker v93 no7 p92-7 Ap 3 2017 J. Groopman
  New York Times Book Review p23 Ja 8 2017 R. M. Henig

Taranto, T. and Huffman, N. Ars botanica. 2017
  Publishers Weekly v264 no16 p56-7 Ap 17 2017

Tarkington, E. Only love can break your heart. 2016
  Virginia Living v15 no4 p29 Je 2017 B. Glose
  Virginia Living v15 no4 p29 Je 2017 B. Glose

Tarlo, E. Entanglement. 2016
  New York Times Book Review p14 D 4 2016 S. Lyall

Tarn, G. and Fine, T. The Modern Jewish Table. 2017
  Publishers Weekly v264 no10 p26 Mr 6 2017 C. S.

Tarn, N. Gondwana & other poems. 2017
  Publishers Weekly v264 no20 p35-6 My 15 2017

Tarpley, N. The Harlem Charade. 2017
  Publishers Weekly v263 no45 p61 N 7 2016

Tarquini, M. Hindsight. 2016
  Publishers Weekly v263 no39 p71 S 26 2016

Tarrant, S. The pornography industry. 2016
  New Yorker v92 no30 p64-8 S 26 2016 K. Forrester

Tarter, B. A saga of the New South. 2016
  American History v52 no2 p70 Je 2017 M. Oppenheim

Tash, S. The geek's guide to unrequited love. 2016
  Publishers Weekly v263 no49 p95-6 D 7 2016

Tashiro, T. Awkward. 2017
  New York Times Book Review p19 Je 25 2017 D. Menaker

Tasker, E. The Planet Factory. 2017
  Discover v38 no10 p18-9 D 2017 G. Tarlach
  Publishers Weekly v264 no34 p100-1 Ag 21 2017
  Sky & Telescope v134 no6 p39 D 2017 S. N. Johnson-Roehr

Tasso, M. and others. The pied piper of Hamelin. 2016
  Publishers Weekly v263 no49 p28 D 7 2016

Tata, A. J. Besieged. 2017
  Publishers Weekly v264 no3 p42 Ja 16 2017

Tatar, M. and Gates, H. L. The Annotated African American Folktales. 2017
  Publishers Weekly v264 no26 p48-53 Je 26 2017 E. Jones
  Publishers Weekly v264 no39 p97 S 25 2017

Tate, D. and Barton, C. Whoosh! 2016
  Publishers Weekly v263 no49 p54 D 7 2016

Tate, D. and Tate, D. Strong as Sandow. 2017
  Publishers Weekly v264 no27 p73 Jl 3 2017

Tate, G. Flyboy 2. 2016
  Publishers Weekly v263 no48 p28-34 N 28 2016 D. Patrick
  Rolling Stone no1272 p16 O 20 2016 W. Herme

Tate, J. Dome of the Hidden Pavilion. 2015
  New York Review of Books v64 no3 p26-30 F 23 2017 C. Simic

Taubes, G. The case against sugar. 2016

Atlantic v319 no1 p40-4 Ja/F 2017 D. Engber
New Yorker v93 no7 p92-7 Ap 3 2017 J. Groopman
New York Times Book Review p1-22 Ja 8 2017 D. Barber
New York Times Book Review p22 Ja 15 2017

Taubman, W. Gorbachev. 2017
National Review v69 no18 p35-6 O 2 2017 D. Pryce-Jones
New York Times Book Review p11 S 10 2017 P. Baker
Publishers Weekly v264 no31 p76 Jl 31 2017

Tavares, M. and Smith, M. C. Lighter than air. 2017
Publishers Weekly v264 no7 p74 F 13 2017

Tavares, M. and Tavares, M. Red and Lulu. 2017
Publishers Weekly v264 no36 p94-5 S 4 2017

Tavormina, P. and Ladner, M. The Del Posto cookbook. 2016
Publishers Weekly v263 no47 p102 N 21 2016

Tawada, Y. and Bernofsky, S. The memoirs of a polar bear. 2016
Harper's Magazine v333 no1998 p79-81 N 2016 C. Smallwood
New Yorker v93 no6 p71 Mr 27 2017
New York Times Book Review p11 N 27 2016 R. Ausubel
New York Times Book Review p78 D 4 2016

Taylor, A. American revolutions. 2016
Atlantic v318 no5 p36-8 D 2016 C. Fitz

Taylor, A. K. The shark club. 2017
Publishers Weekly v264 no17 p65 Ap 24 2017

Taylor, B. and Sontag, S. Debriefing. 2017
Publishers Weekly v264 no38 p48 S 18 2017

Taylor, B. Ring of Fire. 2017
Publishers Weekly v263 no48 p48 N 28 2016

Taylor, B. The hue and cry at our house. 2017
New York Times Book Review p16 Jl 9 2017 S. Harrigan
Publishers Weekly v264 no11 p73 Mr 13 2017
Texas Monthly v45 no6 p64 Je 2017

Taylor, B. Thieving weasels. 2016
Publishers Weekly v263 no44 p72 O 31 2016

Taylor, C. America 51. 2017
Publishers Weekly v264 no34 p17 Ag 21 2017 C. Juris

Taylor, C. Dying. 2017
Publishers Weekly v264 no7 p60 F 13 2017

Taylor, C. Opening Wednesday at a theater or drive-in near you. 2017
Publishers Weekly v264 no8 p74 F 20 2017

Taylor, D. and Kidd, C. Batman. 2012
New York Times Book Review p24 F 12 2017 G. ^Cowles

Taylor, D. and Raspanti, J. J. Intimate warfare. 2017
Publishers Weekly v263 no42 p58-60 O 17 2016

Taylor, D. H. Take Us to Your Chief. 2017
Publishers Weekly v264 no3 p33 Ja 16 2017

Taylor, E. D. The Original Black Elite. 2017
New Yorker v92 no47 p70 Ja 30 2017
New York Times Book Review p10 F 5 2017 L. O. Graham
New York Times Book Review p23 F 12 2017

Taylor, J. A map for wrecked girls. 2017
Publishers Weekly v264 no24 p67 Je 12 2017

Taylor, J. and others. In focus. 2016
Publishers Weekly v263 no41 p81 O 10 2016

Taylor, L. Strange the dreamer. 2017
Publishers Weekly v264 no22 p63-4 My 29 2017
Publishers Weekly v264 no3 p62 Ja 16 2017
Seventeen v76 no2 p22 Mr 2017 J. Abidor

Taylor, N. M. Driven toward madness. 2016
Publishers Weekly v263 no44 p66 O 31 2016

Taylor, S. and Binet, L. The seventh function of language. 2017
Christian Century v134 no20 p42 S 27 2017 L. Binet
Esquire p21 Ag 2017 A. Westenfeld
National Review v69 no18 p40-1 O 2 2017 E. Powers
New Republic v248 no10 p51-3 O 2017 S. Birkerts
New York Times Book Review p17 Ag 20 2017 N. Dames
New York v50 no16 p112 Ag 7 2017
Publishers Weekly v264 no25 p90 Je 19 2017

Taylor, S. and De Rosnay, T. Manderley forever. 2017
Louisiana Life v37 no5 p15 My/Je 2017

Taylor, S. and Echenoz, J. Special envoy. 2017
Publishers Weekly v264 no36 p65-6 S 4 2017

Taylor, S. and Hughes, E. A Brave Bear. 2016
Publishers Weekly v263 no49 p31 D 7 2016

Taylor, S. and Johnson, R. D. The campus rape frenzy. 2017
Commentary v143 no3 p54-6 Mr 2017

New York Times Book Review p11 Ap 9 2017 J. Filipovic
Weekly Standard v22 no26 p30-1 Mr 13 2017 A. B. Lloyd

Taylor, S. and Jullien, J. I Want to Be in a Scary Story. 2017
Publishers Weekly v264 no19 p58 My 8 2017

Taylor, S. and Kerangal, M. D. The heart. 2016
Time v189 no21 p27-8 Je 5 2017 B. Gates

Taylor, S. and Levy, M. P.s. from Paris. 2017
Publishers Weekly v264 no29 p190-1 Jl 17 2017

Taylor, S. and Sattouf, R. The Arab of the future. 2015
New York Review of Books v63 no16 p8-12 O 27 2016 S. Boxer

Taylor, S. Defiance. 2017
New York Times Book Review p10 O 1 2017 L. Elkin
New York Times Book Review p27 O 8 2017

Taylor, S. The Lauras. 2017
Entertainment Weekly no1478 / 1479 p109 Ag 18-25 2017
Publishers Weekly v264 no26 p150 Je 26 2017

Taylor, T. S. and Nye, J. L. Moon beam. 2017
Publishers Weekly v264 no22 p68-70 My 29 2017

Taylor, W. Definitions of indefinable things. 2017
Publishers Weekly v264 no7 p78 F 13 2017

Tazzyman, D. and Dougherty, J. Stinkbomb & Ketchup-Face and the badness of badgers. 2014
Publishers Weekly v263 no46 p56 N 14 2016

Tchaikovsky, A. The Bear and the Serpent. 2017
Publishers Weekly v264 no29 p201 Jl 17 2017

Tchaikovsky, A. The Tiger and the Wolf. 2017
Publishers Weekly v263 no47 p96 N 21 2016

Tea, M. Black wave. 2016
New Yorker v92 no40 p78 D 5 2016
New York Times Book Review p18 S 25 2016 L. Tanenbaum

Teague, M. and Teague, M. Jack and the beanstalk and the french fries. 2017
Publishers Weekly v264 no21 p89 My 22 2017

Teasdale, R. and others. The loyalist team. 2017
Publishers Weekly v264 no20 p47 My 15 2017

Tebbe, N. Religious freedom in an egalitarian age. 2017
Commonweal v144 no17 p26-30 O 20 2017 P. Horwitz

Tebow, T. Shaken. 2016
New York Times Book Review p24 N 27 2016
Publishers Weekly v263 no45 p14 N 7 2016 C. Juris

Tee, S. and Gutierrez, S. The Gross Cookbook. 2017
Publishers Weekly v264 no22 p69 My 29 2017

Tefre, M. and others. Seeds on Ice. 2016
Scientific American v315 no3 p86 S 2016 C. Moskowitz

Tegen, K. and Grant, M. Front Lines. 2016
Publishers Weekly v263 no49 p114 D 7 2016

Tegen, K. and others. How to be a bigger bunny. 2017
Publishers Weekly v263 no45 p60 N 7 2016

Tegmark, M. Life 3.0. 2017
New York Times Book Review p24 S 17 2017 G. Cowles
Publishers Weekly v264 no28 p78 Jl 10 2017
Publishers Weekly v264 no40 p135 O 2 2017
Science v357 no6350 p460 Ag 4 2017 H. Hirsh

Tehya, J. The wrong kind of Indian. 2017
Publishers Weekly v263 no48 p55 N 28 2016

Teicher, C. M. The trembling answers. 2017
Publishers Weekly v264 no8 p61-2 F 20 2017

Teig, K. and Ahearn, A. Full moon suppers at Salt Water Farm. 2017
Publishers Weekly v264 no8 p79 F 20 2017

Teixeira, R. and Judis, J. B. The emerging Democratic majority. 2002
Commentary v141 no10 p1-2 D 2016
Commentary v142 no5 p1-2 D 2016
Commentary v142 no5 p56-5 D 2016 M. Continetti

Tejaratchi, S. and Ridenour, A. The Krampus and the Old, Dark Christmas. 2016
Reason v48 no7 p58 D 2016 J. Walker

Teles, S. M. and Dagan, D. Prison break. 2016
Claremont Review of Books v17 no3 p15-9 Summ 2017 J. M. Bessette
Washington Monthly p1 S/O 2016 H. Schoenfeld

Telfer, T. and Darcy, D. Lady Killers. 2017
Publishers Weekly v264 no32 p61 Ag 7 2017

Telgemeier, R. and others. Ghosts. 2016
New York Times Book Review p24 O 30 2016

2017
Publishers Weekly v263 no51 p149 D 12 2016
Thompson, D. A. The virtual Body of Christ in a suffering world.
   2016
Christian Century v134 no6 p38-9 Mr 15 2017 A. Van Wyk
Christian Century v134 no6 p38 Mr 15 2017 A. Van Wyk
Thompson, D. Hit makers. 2017
Harvard Business Review v95 no1 p164-5 Ja/F 2017 T. Sullivan
Publishers Weekly v264 no14 p72 Ap 3. 2017
Thompson, D. The Orange Balloon Dog. 2017
Maclean's v130 no3 p68-9 Ap 2017 B. Bethune
Thompson, E. W. and others. But What If There's No Chimney?
   2016
Publishers Weekly v263 no39 p86 S 26 2016
Thompson, H. A. Blood in the water. 2016
Commentary v141 no9 p1-2 N 2016
Commentary v142 no4 p1-2 N 2016
Commentary v142 no4 p41-3 N 2016 B. McManus
Commonweal v144 no2 p25-7 Ja 27 2017 J. J. Sheehan
New York Times Book Review p32 Ag 27 2017 J. Khatib
Publishers Weekly v263 no44 p18-40 O 31 2016
Thompson, H. and Dunn, C. Marfa modern. 2016
Architectural Record v205 no6 p53 Je 2017 L. Raskin
Publishers Weekly v263 no39 p83 S 26 2016
Thompson, J. and Muller, E. Oakland noir. 2017
Publishers Weekly v264 no7 p53 F 13 2017
Thompson, J. and Thompson, J. K. Faraway fox. 2016
New York Times Book Review p33 N 13 2016 M. Russo
Thompson, J. L. and others. Cuisine Art Cocktails. 2016
Cincinnati Magazine v50 no2 p120 N 2016 A. Flango
Thompson, K. Santa's Countdown to Christmas. 2017
Publishers Weekly v264 no36 p97 S 4 2017
Thompson, L. A. and others. Two thruths and a lie. 2017
Publishers Weekly v264 no21 p94 My 22 2017
Thompson, L. and Mankell, H. Quicksand. 2016
Publishers Weekly v263 no46 p47-8 N 14 2016
Thompson, L. The goldfish boy. 2017
Publishers Weekly v263 no51 p148 D 12 2016
Thompson, L. The six. 2016
New York Times Book Review p28 O 8 2017 J. Khatib
Weekly Standard v22 no18 p34-5 Ja 16 2017 J. Bachrach
Thompson, M. A Space Traveler's Guide to the Solar System. 2016
New York Times Book Review p30 N 27 2016 S. Kean
Thompson, M. Golden. 2017
Publishers Weekly v264 no9 p91 F 27 2017
Thompson, N. Culture as weapon. 2017
Publishers Weekly v263 no48 p62 N 28 2016
Time v189 no3 p16 Ja 16 2017 S. Begley
Thompson, P. Outside the Law. 2017
Publishers Weekly v263 no45 p39-40 N 7 2016
Thompson, S. P. Bright line eating. 2017
Publishers Weekly v264 no14 p13 Ap 3. 2017 C. Juris
Thompson, T. Rosewater. 2016
Publishers Weekly v263 no40 p103 O 3 2016
Thompson, V. City of lies. 2017
Publishers Weekly v264 no38 p57 S 18 2017
Thompson, W. R. and Ganguly, S. Ascending India and its state
   capacity. 2016
Foreign Affairs v96 no3 p174 My/Je 2017 A. J. Nathan
Thoms, N. and Pintachan (Illustrator) Changing faces. 2017
Publishers Weekly v264 no36 p92 S 4 2017
Thomson, D. Television. 2016
Harper's Magazine v333 no1998 p82-6 N 2016 W. Deresiewicz
Thomson, D. Warner Bros. 2017
New York Times Book Review p12 S 3 2017 T. Shone
New York Times Book Review p26 S 10 2017
Publishers Weekly v264 no26 p172 Je 26 2017
Thomson, E. S. Dark Asylum. 2017
Publishers Weekly v264 no36 p66 S 4 2017
Thomson, L. The Dog Walker. 2017
Publishers Weekly v264 no20 p41 My 15 2017
Thor, B. Use of force. 2017
New York Times Book Review p24 Jl 30 2017
Publishers Weekly v264 no36 p86 S 4 2017
Thormaehlen, K. Aging gracefully. 2017
Publishers Weekly v264 no3 p50-1 Ja 16 2017

Thorn, M. and others. Otherworld Barbara. 2016
Publishers Weekly v264 no28 p56-7 Jl 10 2017 H. Macdonald
Thornburgh, B. Who's That Girl. 2017
Publishers Weekly v264 no19 p62 My 8 2017
Thorne, J. and others. Harry Potter and the cursed child parts one
   and two. 2016
Publishers Weekly v264 no34 p8 Ag 21 2017
Thorne, S. The hating game. 2016
New York Times Book Review p30 O 16 2016 S. Gilbert
Thorngren, J. T. Salvation on Death Row. 2018
Publishers Weekly v264 no29 p17-9 Jl 17 2017 L. Garrett
Thornton, M. Femme. 2016
Publishers Weekly v263 no52 p72-3 D 19 2016
Thorp, E. O. A man for all markets. 2016
Publishers Weekly v263 no44 p64 O 31 2016
Thorpe, H. The newcomers. 2017
Publishers Weekly v264 no40 p128-9 O 2 2017
Thorpe, L. The Book of Cheese. 2017
Publishers Weekly v264 no10 p32 Mr 6 2017
Thrall, N. The Only Language They Understand. 2017
New York Review of Books v64 no11 p44-7 Je 22 2017 D. Shulman
New York Times Book Review p14-5 My 28 2017 G. Beckerman
Time v189 no22 p53 Je 12 2017 K. Vick
Thubron, C. Night of fire. 2017
New York Times Book Review p16 F 12 2017 W. Lesser
Publishers Weekly v263 no43 p52 O 24 2016
Thubten Chodron, 1. and Tenzin Gyatso, D. L. Approaching the
   Buddhist path. 2017
Tricycle: The Buddhist Review v27 no1 p100-1 Fall 2017 M. Scar-
   les
Thubten Chodron, and Tenzin Gyatso, D. L. Approaching the
   Buddhist path. 2017
Publishers Weekly v264 no24 p59 Je 12 2017
Thuesen, P. J. and others. The Bible in American life. 2017
Christian Century v134 no19 p36-7 S 13 2017 Z. Hess
Thummler, B. and others. Anne of green gables. 2017
Publishers Weekly v264 no33 p83 Ag 14 2017
Thuras, D. and others. Atlas Obscura. 2016
New York Times Book Review p26 O 16 2016 J. Szalai
Virginia Living v15 no4 p29 Je 2017 B. Glose
Thurlo, D. Kill the heroes. 2017
Publishers Weekly v264 no24 p43 Je 12 2017
Thurman, R. A. and others. Man of peace. 2016
Publishers Weekly v264 no10 p48 Mr 6 2017
Tricycle: The Buddhist Review v27 no1 p94-6 Fall 2017 D. Zig-
   mond
Thwaites, L. and Iturbe, A. The librarian of Auschwitz. 2017
Publishers Weekly v264 no35 p131 Ag 28 2017
Thwaites, T. GoatMan. 2016
Harper's Magazine v334 no2000 p94-7 Ja 2017 G. Greenberg
Tiampo, M. and others. Parallel Views. 2015
Art in America v104 no11 p65 D 2016
Tiang, J. and Chan Ho-kei The Borrowed. 2017
New York Times Book Review p29 Ja 8 2017 M. Stasio
Publishers Weekly v263 no47 p91 N 21 2016
Tibi, M. and Lambert, F. Ö. The Bear Who Didn't Want to Miss
   Christmas. 2017
Publishers Weekly v264 no36 p91 S 4 2017
Tibon, A. and Rumley, G. The last Palestinian. 2017
Publishers Weekly v264 no22 p58 My 29 2017
Tickell, J. Kiss the ground. 2017
Publishers Weekly v264 no39 p100-1 S 25 2017
Tidbeck, K. Amatka. 2017
Publishers Weekly v264 no15 p46 Ap 10 2017
Tier, M. How to spot the next Starbucks, Whole Foods, Walmart, or
   McDonald's before its shares explode. 2017
Publishers Weekly v264 no23 p44 Je 5 2017
Tietz, C. and Barnett, V. J. Theologian of Resistance. 2016
Christian Century v134 no4 p58 F 15 2017
Tiffany, J. and others. Harry Potter and the cursed child parts one
   and two. 2016
Publishers Weekly v264 no34 p8 Ag 21 2017
Tiktin, C. Our marriage counselor. 2017
Publishers Weekly v263 no51 p122 D 12 2016
Tila, J. 101 asian dishes you need to cook before you die. 2017
Publishers Weekly v264 no20 p51 My 15 2017

Veyne, P. and Fagan, T. L. Palmyra. 2017
  History Today v67 no10 p96 O 2017 L. Gregoratti
Vicario, M. Your Holistically Hot Transformation. 2016
  Publishers Weekly v264 no13 p64e Mr 27 2017
  Publishers Weekly v264 no8 p81 F 20 2017
Vickers, B. The one King Lear. 2016
  New York Review of Books v64 no3 p34-6 F 23 2017 S. Greenblatt
Vickers, R. H. and others. Hello humpback! 2017
  Publishers Weekly v264 no25 p111 Je 19 2017
Victor Cunrui Xiong Heavenly Khan. 2014
  Publishers Weekly v264 no1 p36 Ja 2 2017
Vidal, A. and Mara, N. So many feet. 2017
  Publishers Weekly v264 no21 p90 My 22 2017
  Publishers Weekly v264 no5 p26-168 Ja 30 2017
Vidal, B. and others. Marti's song for freedom =. 2017
  Publishers Weekly v264 no19 p59 My 8 2017
Vidich, P. The good assassin. 2017
  Publishers Weekly v264 no5 p176 Ja 30 2017
Vieira, E. and others. Mutant bunny island. 2017
  Publishers Weekly v264 no38 p69-71 S 18 2017
Viertel, J. The secret life of the American musical. 2016
  America v215 no12 p34-6 O 24 2016 M. Tueth
Viets, E. Fire and Ashes. 2017
  Publishers Weekly v264 no21 p74 My 22 2017
Vieux-Chauvet, M. and Glover, K. L. Dance on the volcano. 2016
  New York Times Book Review p26 F 19 2017 A. McCulloch
  Publishers Weekly v263 no43 p55 O 24 2016
Vila-Matas, E. and Costa, M. J. Vampire in love. 2016
  New Yorker v92 no38 p88 N 21 2016
Viljoen, E. Ordinary goodness. 2017
  Publishers Weekly v263 no39 p26-30 S 26 2016 L. Garrett
  Publishers Weekly v263 no46 p49 N 14 2016
Villalobos, J. P. and Harvey, R. I'll sell you a dog. 2016
  New York Times Book Review p34 N 20 2016 L. Wright
Viloria, H. Born both. 2017
  New York Times Book Review p27 My 28 2017 M. Daum
  Publishers Weekly v263 no47 p99 N 21 2016
Vincent, I. Dinner with Edward. 2016
  New York Times Book Review p24 Je 18 2017 J. Khatib
Vincent, J. K. and Tanizaki, J. Devils in daylight. 2017
  New York Review of Books v64 no10 p16-8 Je 8 2017 P. Iyer
  Publishers Weekly v264 no6 p40 F 6 2017
Vinesse, C. Seven days of you. 2017
  Publishers Weekly v264 no1 p59 Ja 2 2017
Vingoe, M. Refuge. 2015
  Ms. v27 no2 p46-7 Summ 2017
  New York Times Book Review p30 S 10 2017 V. V. Ganeshananthan
  Publishers Weekly v264 no18 p35 My 1 2017
Viola, J. and others. Cyber World. 2016
  Publishers Weekly v263 no40 p103 O 3 2016
Virginia, K. and Khalsa, D. Essential kundalini yoga. 2017
  Publishers Weekly v263 no50 p65 D 5 2016
Virján, E. J. and others. What this story needs is a bang and a clang. 2017
  Publishers Weekly v263 no45 p59 N 7 2016
Visotzky, B. L. Aphrodite and the rabbis. 2016
  Commentary v141 no10 p1-4 D 2016
  Commentary v142 no5 p1-4 D 2016
  Commentary v142 no5 p47-50 D 2016 J. D. Levenson
Viva, F. and Viva, F. Sea change. 2016
  Publishers Weekly v264 no49 p90 D 7 2016
Vivian, S. The last boy and girl in the world. 2016
  Publishers Weekly v263 no49 p98 D 7 2016
Viviani, F. Fabio's 30-minute Italian. 2017
  Publishers Weekly v264 no18 p54 My 1 2017
Vizzone, R. Robin Vizzone's peculiar primitives. 2017
  Publishers Weekly v264 no14 p70 Ap 3 2017
Vladislavic, I. The exploded view. 2004
  Publishers Weekly v264 no45 p37 N 7 2016
  Publishers Weekly v264 no12 p45-6 Mr 20 2017 M. Seidel
Vlahos, L. Life in a fishbowl. 2017
  Publishers Weekly v263 no44 p77 O 31 2016
Voake, C. and Donaldson, J. The further adventures of owl and the pussy-cat. 2017
  Publishers Weekly v263 no45 p59 N 7 2016

Vogel, S. and Marcal, K. Who cooked Adam Smith's dinner? 2016
  New York Times Book Review p24 Je 18 2017 J. Khatib
Vogel, V. and others. Bob and Joss get lost. 2017
  Publishers Weekly v263 no50 p71 D 5 2016
Vogt, B. Why I am Catholic (and you should be too) 2017
  U.S. Catholic v82 no8 p41 Ag 2017
Voigt, C. and Zakimi, P. Teddy & Co. 2016
  Publishers Weekly v263 no39 p94 S 26 2016
Voiland, A. and Voiland, A. ABCs from space. 2017
  Publishers Weekly v264 no30 p59 Jl 24 2017
Volf, M. and McAnnally-Linz, R. Public faith in action. 2016
  U.S. Catholic v81 no11 p41 N 2016 E. Lefebvre
Volf, M. Flourishing. 2016
  Commonweal v144 no3 p37-8 F 10 2017 L. T. Johnson
Vollrath, D. E. Silverwood. 2015
  Publishers Weekly v263 no49 p80 D 7 2016
  Publishers Weekly v263 no52 p77 D 19 2016
Volodine, A. and Zuckerman, J. Radiant terminus. 2017
  Publishers Weekly v263 no51 p129 D 12 2016
Volokhonsky, L. and others. Novels, tales, journeys. 2016
  O, The Oprah Magazine p72 Ja 2017 L. Schillinger
Volokhonsky, L. and others. The unwomanly face of war. 2017
  New Yorker v93 no22 p73 Jl 31 2017
  New York Times Book Review p11 Ag 20 2017 R. Reich
  Publishers Weekly v264 no10 p49 Mr 6 2017
  Publishers Weekly v264 no30 p10 Jl 24 2017 R. Deahl
  Publishers Weekly v264 no36 p88 S 4 2017
  Vanity Fair v59 no8 p48 Ag 2017 S. Crosley
Volpentesta, L. Satan's Treasure. 2016
  Publishers Weekly v264 no15 p56 Ap 10 2017
  Publishers Weekly v264 no17 p58c Ap 24 2017
Von Dietze, S. and Hogg, C. Balance in movement. 2005
  Dressage Today v23 no9 p72 Je 2017 S. Von Dietze
Von Dietze, S. and others. Rider & horse, back to back. 2011
  Dressage Today v23 no9 p72 Je 2017 S. Von Dietze
Von Kitzing, C. and Lodding, L. R. The queen is coming to tea. 2017
  Publishers Weekly v263 no48 p67 N 28 2016
Von Kopp, D. and others. How we eat with our eyes and think with our stomach. 2017
  Publishers Weekly v264 no38 p66 S 18 2017
Von Moltke, J. The curious humanist. 2016
  Film Quarterly v70 no4 p131-3 Summ 2017 I. Lewit
Vonnegut, K. and Chermayeff, I. Sun, moon, star. 1980
  New York Times Book Review p19 D 18 2016 M. Russo
  Publishers Weekly v263 no39 p85 S 26 2016
Von Neumann-Cosel, I. and others. Rider & horse, back to back. 2011
  Dressage Today v23 no9 p72 Je 2017 S. Von Dietze
Von Tunzelmann, A. Blood and sand. 2016
  New Yorker v92 no35 p89 O 31 2016
  New York Times Book Review p17 O 16 2016 E. Thomas
Vrba, C. S. and Yerrill, G. The stable cat's Christmas. 2017
  Publishers Weekly v264 no36 p98 S 4 2017
Vrudny, K. Beauty's vineyard. 2016
  Christian Century v133 no22 p39-40 O 26 2016 A. M. Carpenter
Vu, T. Vietnam's communist revolution. 2017
  Foreign Affairs v96 no3 p173-4 My/Je 2017 A. J. Nathan
Vukovic, E. and DiTerlizzi, A. I wanna be a cowgirl. 2017
  Publishers Weekly v264 no38 p69 S 18 2017
Vukovic, E. and Florence, D. M. Jasmine Toguchi, mochi queen. 2017
  Publishers Weekly v264 no23 p53 Je 5 2017
Vyleta, D. Smoke. 2016
  Publishers Weekly v263 no40 p119 O 3 2016

W

The way of the strangers. 2016
  Foreign Affairs v96 no3 p170 My/Je 2017 J. Waterbury
Waal, F. B. Are We Smart Enough to Know How Smart Animals Are? 2016
  Sierra v101 no5 p11 S/O 2016 M. Berry
Wachtell, D. and Swong, S. How do I explain this to my kids? 2017

New York Times Book Review p27 Ag 13 2017 J. Newman

Wade, L. American Hookup. 2017
Commentary v143 no3 p56-7 Mr 2017 N. S. Riley
Publishers Weekly v263 no41 p66 O 10 2016

Wade, M. J. Adaptation in metapopulations. 2016
BioScience v67 no4 p393-4 Ap 2017 T. E. Farkas

Wadhams, P. A farewell to ice. 2017
Publishers Weekly v264 no26 p170 Je 26 2017
Wired v25 no9 p32 S 2017 A. Vlasits

Wadman, M. The vaccine race. 2016
Issues in Science & Technology v33 no4 p85-7 Summ 2017 K. B. Nelson
Publishers Weekly v263 no51 p139 D 12 2016
Science v355 no6324 p464 F 3 2017 E. C. Jonlin

Wagamese, R. Embers. 2016
Publishers Weekly v264 no6 p57-8 F 6 2017

Wagamese, R. Medicine walk. 2015
Orion Magazine v35 no4/5 p106-7 Jl-O 2016 A. Weldon

Wagers, K. B. Behind the throne. 2016
New York Times Book Review p35 O 9 2016 N. K. Jemisin

Wagner, D. The Politics of Murder. 2016
Progressive p60-5 D 2016/Ja 2017 E. Rampell

Wagner, E. Chief engineer. 2017
New York Times Book Review p9 Ag 13 2017 J. Alexiou
Publishers Weekly v264 no14 p63 Ap 3. 2017

Wagner, M. and others. Bear Make Den. 2017
Publishers Weekly v264 no23 p50 Je 5 2017

Wagner, M. E. America and the Great War. 2017
New York Review of Books v64 no14 p82-5 S 28 2017 A. Hochschild
Publishers Weekly v264 no11 p68 Mr 13 2017

Wagner, M. T. Finnigan the Circus Cat. 2016
Publishers Weekly v264 no1 p56 Ja 2 2017
Publishers Weekly v264 no4 p50g Ja 23 2017

Wagner, P. and Wieland, B. C. Sunvault. 2017
Publishers Weekly v264 no25 p96 Je 19 2017

Wagner, R. and Briggs, A. The penultimate curiosity. 2016
Issues in Science & Technology v33 no1 p94-5 Fall 2016 P. Kulkarni

Wagner-Peck, K. Not always happy. 2017
Publishers Weekly v264 no16 p64-5 Ap 17 2017

Waichler, I. Role Reversal. 2016
Publishers Weekly v264 no36 p85 S 4 2017
Publishers Weekly v264 no39 p80d S 25 2017

Wailes, N. and others. International and comparative employment relations. 2016
Monthly Labor Review p1-3 Je 2017 J. Wheeler

Waisman, S. and MacLeod, J. T. Yossi and the monkeys. 2017
Publishers Weekly v264 no4 p78 Ja 23 2017

Wait, R. The Followers. 2017
New York Times Book Review p23 S 10 2017 J. Scheeres

Waite, B. L. and others. The Long Distance Runner's Guide to Injury Prevention and Treatment. 2017
Publishers Weekly v264 no34 p107 Ag 21 2017

Waite, J. A beautiful, terrible thing. 2017
New York Times Book Review p31 Jl 23 2017 M. Daum
Publishers Weekly v264 no19 p52 My 8 2017

Waite, M. M. and others. Floret Farm's Cut Flower Garden. 2017
Martha Stewart Living p10 Mr 2017

Waites, J. C. and Waites, J. C. An artist's night before Christmas. 2017
Publishers Weekly v264 no36 p95 S 4 2017

Wajdowicz, J. Pride & joy. 2016
Publishers Weekly v264 no22 p26 My 29 2017

Wakefield, D. and Klinkowitz, J. Complete stories. 2017
National Review v69 no19 p52-3 O 16 2017 J. J. Miller
New York Times Book Review p12 O 15 2017 J. Walter

Wakeford, A. and Harman, T. Your baby's microbiome. 2017
Publishers Weekly v263 no52 p121 D 19 2016

Walcott, D. and Doig, P. Morning, Paramin. 2016
New York Review of Books v64 no6 p8-11 Ap 6 2017 J. Lucas

Walcott, D. and Maxwell, G. The Poetry of Derek Walcott 1948-2013. 2014
New York Review of Books v63 no17 p44-6 N 10 2016 M. Ford
New York Times Book Review p24 O 15 2017 J. Khatib

Walczak, R. and others. Particle physics in the LHC era. 2016

Physics Today v70 no6 p62 Je 2017 M. Cirelli

Walden, L. and others. In focus. 2016
Publishers Weekly v263 no41 p81 O 10 2016

Walden, L. and Riley, V. Bear Hugs. 2017
Publishers Weekly v264 no5 p202-3 Ja 30 2017

Walden, L. In Focus Cities. 2017
Publishers Weekly v264 no33 p81 Ag 14 2017

Walden, T. and Walden, T. Spinning. 2017
Publishers Weekly v264 no29 p223 Jl 17 2017

Waldman, A. A Really Good Day. 2017
Bloomberg Businessweek no4504 p60 D 19 2016 C. Battan
Harper's Bazaar no3650 p104 F 2017
New Republic v248 no1/2 p50-5 Ja/F 2017 C. Vaye Watkins
O, The Oprah Magazine p104 F 2017 L. Haber
Publishers Weekly v263 no39 p75 S 26 2016
Reason v49 no4 p77 Ag/S 2017 B. Doherty

Waldman, A. and Chabon, M. Kingdom of Olives and Ash. 2017
Christian Century v134 no12 p42 Je 7 2017
Commentary v144 no1 p50-2 Jl/Ag 2017 D. J. Greenbaum
Maclean's p58 Je 2017 B. Bethune
New York Review of Books v64 no11 p44-7 Je 22 2017 D. Shulman
New York Times Book Review p14-5 My 28 2017 G. Beckerman
Publishers Weekly v264 no7 p61 F 13 2017

Waldman, A. The Love Affairs of Nathaniel P. 2013
New York p69-74 F 9 2017

Waldman, M. The Second Amendment. 2014
New Orleans Magazine v51 no2 p40-1 D 2016 A. J. Johnson

Waldo, A. M. Brain training for riders. 2016
Trail Rider v29 no2 p12 Mr 2017 C. Lamm

Waldron, J. One another's equals. 2017
New York Times Book Review p16 Jl 23 2017 R. B. Reich

Waldstreicher, D. and Jefferson, T. Notes on the state of Virginia. 2002
New York Times Book Review p16-7 F 26 2017 I. X. Kendi

Waldstreicher, D. and Mason, M. John Quincy Adams and the politics of slavery. 2017
American History v52 no3 p66-7 Ag 2017 R. Culyer

Walker, A. J. The end of the world running club. 2017
Publishers Weekly v264 no31 p59 Jl 31 2017

Walker, B. and Anthony, B. Abe Lincoln On Acid. 2016
Publishers Weekly v263 no51 p130 D 12 2016
Publishers Weekly v264 no4 p44 Ja 23 2017
Publishers Weekly v264 no4 p46-50 Ja 23 2017
Publishers Weekly v264 no4 p50a Ja 23 2017

Walker, J. A. Wild Ride. 2017
Publishers Weekly v264 no7 p56 F 13 2017

Walker, J. L. and others. Egoism. 2017
Reason v49 no6 p77 N 2017 J. Walker

Walker, J. The world in flames. 2016
New York Times Book Review p39 D 11 2016 M. Daum

Walker, L. R. and Willig, M. R. Long-term ecological research. 2016
BioScience v67 no5 p477-8 My 2017 M. M. Fuller

Walker, M. and Klonsky, J. Let's pretend we never met. 2017
Publishers Weekly v264 no15 p73 Ap 10 2017

Walker, M. S. Quantum fuzz. 2017
Publishers Weekly v263 no46 p44 N 14 2016

Walker, M. The Templars' last secret. 2017
Publishers Weekly v264 no17 p67-8 Ap 24 2017

Walker, M. Why We Sleep. 2017
New York Times Book Review p16 O 15 2017 D. Kamp
Publishers Weekly v264 no34 p107 Ag 21 2017

Walker, R. L. and others. Understanding health inequalities and justice. 2016
Science v354 no6315 p978 N 25 2016 D. Goldberg

Walker, S. M. Sinking the Sultana. 2017
Publishers Weekly v264 no41 p71 O 9 2017

Walker, S. The captain class. 2017
Publishers Weekly v264 no15 p65-6 Ap 10 2017
Time v189 no18 p22 My 15 2017 S. Begley

Walker, S. The Long Hangover. 2018
Publishers Weekly v264 no39 p96 S 25 2017

Walker, S. The man in the tree. 2017
Publishers Weekly v264 no29 p201 Jl 17 2017

Walker, W. Emma in the night. 2017
Publishers Weekly v264 no23 p30 Je 5 2017

Walkley, L. and Adams, M. M. My first day of school. 2017
Publishers Weekly v264 no25 p111 Je 19 2017
Wall, M. Foo Fighters. 2017
Publishers Weekly v264 no25 p102-4 Je 19 2017
Wallace, A. and Bruner, G. Only you can save Christmas! 2017
Publishers Weekly v264 no36 p100 S 4 2017
Wallace, A. and Elkerton, A. How to catch an elf. 2016
Publishers Weekly v263 no39 p90 S 26 2016
Wallace, C. and others. Here, there, everywhere. 2017
Publishers Weekly v264 no41 p67-9 O 9 2017
Wallace, C. and Thomas, R. Long may she reign. 2017
Publishers Weekly v263 no50 p74 D 5 2016
Wallace, C. and White, S. Our broken pieces. 2017
Publishers Weekly v264 no23 p55 Je 5 2017
Wallace, D. Extraordinary adventures. 2017
New York Times Book Review p23 Je 4 2017 A. Leary
Publishers Weekly v264 no12 p52 Mr 20 2017
Wallace, D. Geoffrey Chaucer. 2017
Publishers Weekly v264 no23 p40 Je 5 2017
Wallace, M. Greater Gotham. 2018
American Scholar v86 no4 p116-8 Aut 2017 B. Kroeger
New York Times Book Review p17 O 15 2017 J. Berger
Wallace, M. Idle Ingredients. 2017
Publishers Weekly v263 no51 p129 D 12 2016
Wallace, R. and Melton, H. K. Spy sites of Washington, DC. 2017
Washingtonian Magazine v52 no6 p20 Mr 2017 R. Cartagena
Wallace, R. and Wallace, S. N. Bound by ice. 2017
Publishers Weekly v264 no29 p223 Jl 17 2017
Wallach, T. Thanks for the trouble. 2016
Publishers Weekly v263 no49 p105 D 7 2016
Waller, D. and Younger, R. The Reputation Game. 2017
Publishers Weekly v264 no34 p101 Ag 21 2017
Waller, S. B. The Forbidden Orchid. 2016
Publishers Weekly v263 no49 p119 D 7 2016
Walliams, D. and others. Grandpa's great escape. 2017
Publishers Weekly v263 no48 p67 N 28 2016
Wallis, M. The best land under heaven. 2017
New York Times Book Review p16 Jl 9 2017 D. Preston
Wallis, P. and others. What Does Consent Mean Again? 2017
Publishers Weekly v264 no39 p109 S 25 2017
Wallis, Q. and Brantley-Newton, V. A night out with Mama. 2017
Publishers Weekly v264 no35 p125-8 Ag 28 2017
Wallis, Q. and Miller, S. Shai & Emmie star in Break an egg! 2017
Publishers Weekly v264 no35 p128-30 Ag 28 2017
Wallis, T. and others. What Does Consent Mean Again? 2017
Publishers Weekly v264 no39 p109 S 25 2017
Wallmark, L. and Wu, K. Grace Hopper. 2017
Publishers Weekly v264 no19 p59 My 8 2017
Walls, J. The glass castle. 2005
New York Times Book Review p23 S 17 2017
New York Times Book Review p26-8 S 10 2017
Walls, L. D. Henry David Thoreau. 2017
National Review v69 no15 p38-9 Ag 14 2017 M. D. Aeschliman
Nation v304 no18 p29-32 Je 19 2017 J. Purdy
New Yorker v93 no26 p87 S 4 2017
New York Times Book Review p17 Jl 23 2017 F. Montaigne
New York Times Book Review p22 Jl 30 2017
Publishers Weekly v264 no16 p57 Ap 17 2017
Wallschlaeger, N. Crawlspace. 2017
Publishers Weekly v264 no16 p42 Ap 17 2017
Walravens, S. P. and Cabot, H. Geek girl rising. 2017
Good Housekeeping v264 no6 p60 Je 2017 R. Rothman
Walsh, B. and others. The score takes care of itself. 2010
Forbes v198 no9 p34 D 30 2016 R. Karlgaard
Walsh, C. and others. The score takes care of itself. 2010
Forbes v198 no9 p34 D 30 2016 R. Karlgaard
Walsh, C. Cowardice. 2014
New York Times Book Review p24 D 25 2016 J. Khatib
Walsh, C. Just look up. 2017
Publishers Weekly v264 no21 p79-80 My 22 2017
Walsh, S. and Parker, A. Tiny Blessings for a Merry Christmas. 2016
Publishers Weekly v263 no39 p87 S 26 2016
Walsh, S. K. and Emanuel, V. One more warbler. 2017
Texas Monthly v45 no5 p58 My 2017 K. Vine
Walter, J. My name is not Friday. 2016

Publishers Weekly v263 no49 p121 D 7 2016
Walther, P. New Deal Photography. 2016
Weekly Standard v22 no36 p37-8 My 29 2017 J. Weiser
Walton, C. Arms of Promise. 2016
Publishers Weekly v264 no5 p187-8 Ja 30 2017
Publishers Weekly v264 no9 p66a F 27 2017
Walton, C. R. and Jones, C. Ballplayer. 2017
Publishers Weekly v264 no4 p72 Ja 23 2017
Walton, I. and others. The compleat angler. 2014
Publishers Weekly v264 no24 p22 Je 12 2017 S. Maughan
Walton, J. Words on bathroom walls. 2017
Publishers Weekly v264 no20 p58 My 15 2017
Walton, N. and others. The Shakespeare Timeline Wallbook. 2017
Publishers Weekly v264 no4 p81 Ja 23 2017
Walton, R. The yearning life. 2016
Christian Century v133 no24 p42 N 23 2016
Walz, J. Walking Bridge. 2015
Nebraska Life v21 no4 p73 Jl/Ag 2017 E. Case
Wambach, A. Forward. 2016
Progressive p60-5 D 2016/Ja 2017 A. Maag
Wambaugh, J. The new centurions. 1970
Entertainment Weekly no1471 p65 Je 23 2017
Wan, J. and Gallion, S. L. Pug & Pig trick-or-treat. 2017
Publishers Weekly v264 no26 p177 Je 26 2017
Wan, J. and Gallion, S. L. Pug meets Pig. 2016
Publishers Weekly v263 no49 p40 D 7 2016
Wang, A. and Chau, A. The Nian monster. 2016
Publishers Weekly v263 no40 p122-3 O 3 2016
Publishers Weekly v263 no49 p64 D 7 2016
Wang, D. D. A new literary history of modern China. 2017
Commonweal v144 no15 p43 S 22 2017 N. Haggerty
Wang, D. The hidden light of Northern fires. 2017
Publishers Weekly v264 no27 p51-2 Jl 3 2017
Saturday Evening Post v289 no4 p24 Jl/Ag 2017
Wang, H. and others. Bronze and sunflower. 2017
New York Times Book Review p21 My 14 2017 L. See
Publishers Weekly v263 no52 p124-6 D 19 2016
Warburton, S. and Hart, C. The princess and the Christmas rescue. 2017
Publishers Weekly v264 no36 p94 S 4 2017
Ward, C. The girl from Rawblood. 2017
New York Times Book Review p30 Mr 12 2017 A. Meisel
Ward, E. Michael Bloomfield. 1983
Downbeat v83 no12 p80 D 2016 J. Johnson
Ward, F. E. The cowboy at work. 2013
American Cowboy v23 no5 p21 F/Mr 2017 B. Welch
Ward, G. C. and Burns, K. The Vietnam War. 2017
New York Times Book Review p16 S 17 2017 D. Greenberg
Ward, J. and Ghahremani, S. What will grow? 2017
Publishers Weekly v263 no52 p123 D 19 2016
Ward, J. Men We Reaped. 2013
New York v50 no17 p134-6 Ag 21 2017 B. Kachka
Ward, J. Salvage the bones. 2011
New York v50 no17 p134-6 Ag 21 2017 B. Kachka
Ward, J. Sing, unburied, sing. 2017
Esquire p50 S 2017 A. Westenfeld
Glamour v115 no9 p40 S 2017 J. Harman
Maclean's v130 no8 p63 S 2017 M. Doherty
Ms. v27 no3 p54-5 Fall 2017
New Yorker v93 no27 p69-71 S 11 2017 V. Cunningham
New York Times Book Review p1-24 S 24 2017 T. K. Smith
New York v50 no17 p134-6 Ag 21 2017 B. Kachka
O, The Oprah Magazine p98 O 2017 E. Danticat
Publishers Weekly v264 no27 p49 Jl 3 2017
Publishers Weekly v264 no38 p16 S 18 2017 C. Juris
Time v190 no9 p58-9 S 4 2017 S. Begley
Ward, J. The Fire This Time. 2016
New York Review of Books v64 no9 p22-3 My 25 2017 D. Pinckney
Publishers Weekly v263 no48 p28-34 N 28 2016 D. Patrick
Ward, L. Brobarians. 2017
Publishers Weekly v264 no1 p54 Ja 2 2017
Ward, M. H. The sea is quiet tonight. 2016
Publishers Weekly v263 no50 p63 D 5 2016
Publishers Weekly v264 no4 p44 Ja 23 2017
Publishers Weekly v264 no4 p50f Ja 23 2017

Ward, T. J. Out in the rural. 2016
Publishers Weekly v263 no42 p61 O 17 2016
Wardell, H. Holding Out for a Zero. 2016
Publishers Weekly v264 no36 p64 S 4 2017
Publishers Weekly v264 no39 p66 S 25 2017
Publishers Weekly v264 no39 p80b S 25 2017
Ward-Perkins, Z. and others. The Econocracy. 2016
Weekly Standard v22 no29 p32-4 Ap 3 2017 I. M. Stelzer
Ware, R. The lying game. 2017
Good Housekeeping v265 no2 p68 Ag 2017
New York Times Book Review p26 S 3 2017 R. Aikman
Publishers Weekly v264 no21 p73 My 22 2017
Saturday Evening Post v289 no4 p24 Jl/Ag 2017
Ware, R. The Woman in Cabin Ten. 2016
Publishers Weekly v264 no31 p12 Jl 31 2017 C. Juris
Publishers Weekly v264 no34 p17 Ag 21 2017 C. Juris
Warga, J. Here we are now. 2017
Publishers Weekly v264 no40 p141 O 2 2017
Warhol, A. The philosophy of Andy Warhol. 2007
Esquire p29 Je/Jl 2017 A. Carter
Warner, S. and Malone, S. Absolutely Alfie and the furry, purry secret. 2017
Publishers Weekly v264 no29 p220 Jl 17 2017
Warnes, T. and Corderoy, T. It's Christmas! 2017
Publishers Weekly v264 no36 p96 S 4 2017
Warr, M. and others. Of poetry & protest. 2016
Christian Century v134 no4 p58 F 15 2017
Warraich, H. Modern death. 2017
Discover v38 no3 p20 Ap 2017 G. Tarlach
Publishers Weekly v263 no50 p61-2 D 5 2016
Science v355 no6329 p1029 Mr 10 2017 D. Greenbaum
Scientific American v316 no2 p72 F 2017 C. Moskowitz
Warren, A. I Love It Though. 2017
Publishers Weekly v264 no8 p63 F 20 2017
Warren, E. This fight is our fight. 2017
New York Times Book Review p12 My 7 2017 P. Krugman
New York Times Book Review p27 My 7 2017
New York Times Book Review p34 My 14 2017
Publishers Weekly v264 no18 p13 My 1 2017 C. Juris
Warren, J. Remains. 2017
Publishers Weekly v264 no10 p44 Mr 6 2017
Warren, L. and others. David Bowie. 2016
Entertainment Weekly no1434 p56 O 7 2016 E. R. Brown
Warren, L. S. God's red son. 2017
Publishers Weekly v264 no7 p69 F 13 2017
Warren, R. and Saunders, C. God's Great Love for You. 2017
Publishers Weekly v264 no32 p72 Ag 7 2017
Warrick, J. Black flags. 2015
America v215 no14 p30-2 N 7 2016 J. Donnelly
Wars, K. Catalyst. 2016
Publishers Weekly v263 no40 p105 O 3 2016
Publishers Weekly v263 no43 p50a O 24 2016
Wartzman, R. The end of loyalty. 2017
Publishers Weekly v264 no12 p63 Mr 20 2017
Washburn, J. and others. Tartine all day. 2017
New York Times Book Review p38-9 Je 4 2017 J. Rosenstrach
Publishers Weekly v264 no6 p64 F 6 2017
Washington, J. and others. A history of violence. 2016
Current History v116 no787 p77-9 F 2017 S. Wolf
Wasilevich, M. Ugly Little Greens. 2017
Publishers Weekly v264 no18 p54 My 1 2017
Waskul, D. and Waskul, M. Ghostly encounters. 2016
Skeptical Inquirer v41 no2 p62-3 Mr/Ap 2017 B. Radford
Wasserstrom, J. N. The Oxford illustrated history of modern China. 2016
History Today v67 no5 p104-5 My 2017 J. Altehenger
Watchorn, M. William Faulkner. 2017
New York Review of Books v64 no7 p41-3 Ap 20 2017 T. Powers
Waters, A. Coming to my senses. 2017
Martha Stewart Living p14 S 2017
New York Times Book Review p15 S 24 2017 P. Wells
Publishers Weekly v264 no29 p209-10 Jl 17 2017
Waters, D. The saints of rattlesnake mountain. 2017
Publishers Weekly v264 no14 p50 Ap 3 2017
Waters, L. and Van Reybrouck, D. Against elections. 2016
Claremont Review of Books v17 no2 p14-6 Spr 2017 Y. Levin

Waters, L. The strength switch. 2017
Publishers Weekly v264 no16 p65 Ap 17 2017
Watkins, L. and Winnick, K. B. Good night, baby animals— you've had a busy day. 2017
Publishers Weekly v263 no45 p58 N 7 2016
Watkins, R. Pete with no pants. 2017
New York Times Book Review p27 My 14 2017 M. Russo
New York Times Book Review p27 My 14 2017 R. Sepetys
Publishers Weekly v264 no14 p75 Ap 3 2017
Watkins, S. C. and Swidler, A. A fraught embrace. 2017
Foreign Affairs v96 no3 p176 My/Je 2017 N. Van De Walle
Watkins, T. A Sick Life. 2017
Women's Health v14 no8 p38 O 2017
Watkinson, L. and others. Panther. 2016
New York v49 no25 p122 D 12 2016 A. Riesman
Watkinson, L. and others. The call of the swamp. 2017
New York Times Book Review p16 O 8 2017 B. Handy
Publishers Weekly v264 no29 p218 Jl 17 2017
Watson, B. Miss Jane. 2016
New York Times Book Review p20 Jl 16 2017 J. Khatib
Watson, J. Almost a Bride. 2017
Publishers Weekly v264 no1 p45 Ja 2 2017
Watson, J. D. and others. DNA. 2017
New York Times Book Review p4 Ag 20 2017 J. Williams
Watson, P. Convergence. 2017
New York Times Book Review p22 Mr 12 2017 J. L. Heilbron
Publishers Weekly v264 no1 p48 Ja 2 2017
Watson, P. Ice Ghosts. 2017
Discover v38 no3 p20 Ap 2017 G. Tarlach
New York Times Book Review p12 Ap 9 2017 I. McGuire
Publishers Weekly v264 no7 p63-4 F 13 2017
Weekly Standard v22 no43 p33-4 Jl 24 2017 A. Henderson
Watson, R. P. The ghost ship of Brooklyn. 2017
MHQ: Quarterly Journal of Military History v30 no1 p92-3 Aut 2017 K. M. Kostyal
Military History v34 no5 p73 Ja 2018 R. Guttman
Watson, R. Piecing me together. 2017
Ebony v72 no4 p36 F 2017 L. Cross
Publishers Weekly v263 no47 p110 N 21 2016
Watson, S. B. and others. My wounded island. 2017
Publishers Weekly v264 no24 p65 Je 12 2017
Watts, J. and Hyewon Yum A Piece of Home. 2016
Publishers Weekly v263 no49 p35 D 7 2016
Watts, K. Talk yourself happy. 2017
Publishers Weekly v263 no46 p52 N 14 2016
Watts, S. JFK and the masculine mystique. 2016
American History v52 no1 p70 Ap 2017 M. Dolan
New York Times Book Review p70 D 4 2016 A. Stanley
Watts, S. P. No One Is Coming to Save Us. 2017
New York Times Book Review p17 Ap 9 2017 J. Chang
O, The Oprah Magazine p109 My 2017 D. Akintoye
Publishers Weekly v264 no8 p54-6 F 20 2017
Vanity Fair v59 no5 p52 Ap 2017 S. Crosley
Watt Smith, T. The book of human emotions. 2016
New Yorker v92 no34 p81 O 24 2016
Waugh, E. The Complete Stories. 2012
New York Times Book Review p22 Je 11 2017
Wax, T. This Is Our Time. 2017
Christianity Today p73 Ap 2017
Waxman, D. Trouble in the tribe. 2016
Foreign Affairs v95 no6 p132-8 N/D 2016 P. Gordon
Way, M. and others. Christmas With My Cowboy. 2017
Publishers Weekly v264 no36 p74-5 S 4 2017
Wayne, T. Loner. 2016
New York Times Book Review p20 S 25 2016 L. Rosenfeld
We Told You So. 2016
Reason v48 no11 p69 Ap 2017 B. Doherty
Weatherall, J. O. Void. 2016
Physics Today v70 no9 p59-60 S 2017 T. Ryckman
Publishers Weekly v263 no42 p62 O 17 2016
Science News v190 no11 p28 N 26 2016 E. Conover
Weatherford, C. B. and Green, S. Dorothea Lange. 2017
Publishers Weekly v264 no7 p74 F 13 2017
Weatherford, C. B. and Pinkney, B. In your hands. 2017
Publishers Weekly v264 no29 p217 Jl 17 2017
Weatherford, C. B. and Velasquez, E. Schomburg. 2017

Weinstein, B. and others. All-time favorite sheet cakes & slab pies. 2017
Publishers Weekly v264 no29 p212-3 Jl 17 2017

Weinstone, D. and Le Huche, M. All my friends are fast asleep. 2017
Publishers Weekly v264 no28 p86 Jl 10 2017

Weir, A. Artemis. 2017
AARP: The Magazine v30 no6A p15 O/N 2017 C. Ianzito
Publishers Weekly v264 no26 p90-6 Je 26 2017 P. Cannon
Publishers Weekly v264 no38 p55 S 18 2017 A. Weir
Publishers Weekly v264 no41 p30-1 O 9 2017 J. B.

Weis, A. and Astor, L. Blackwell. 2017
New Orleans Magazine v51 no3 p48 Ja 2017 J. Debold

Weis, S. J. Go Go Yoga Kids. 2016
Publishers Weekly v264 no10 p57 Mr 6 2017
Publishers Weekly v264 no13 p64d Mr 27 2017

Weise, and Carrico, K. Tibet on fire. 2016
New York Review of Books v63 no20 p95-6 D 22 2016 J. Mirsky

Weisenfeld, J. New world a-coming. 2016
Publishers Weekly v263 no51 p143 D 12 2016

Weisman, J. and Beagle, P. S. The New Voices of Fantasy. 2017
Publishers Weekly v264 no24 p46 Je 12 2017

Weiss, J. S. Relationship Investing. 2017
Publishers Weekly v263 no44 p64-5 O 31 2016

Weiss, K. Pressed to death. 2017
Publishers Weekly v264 no4 p59 Ja 23 2017

Weiss-Wolf, J. Periods gone public. 2017
Ms. v27 no3 p53 Fall 2017 M. M. Ginty

Weitz, J. S. Quantitative viral ecology. 2015
Physics Today v70 no6 p65-6 Je 2017 M. C. Lagomarsino

Weitzman, S. and others. The FBI and religion. 2016
Reason v49 no3 p66-7 Jl 2017 A. Theoharis

Welborn, G. and Whitham, B. The Promise Bride. 2017
Publishers Weekly v264 no31 p69 Jl 31 2017

Welcome to my house. 2016
Publishers Weekly v264 no14 p78 Ap 3. 2017

Weldon, F. Before the War. 2017
New York Times Book Review p11 Mr 12 2017 S. Coll
Publishers Weekly v264 no4 p53 Ja 23 2017

Welky, D. A wretched and precarious situation. 2016
Discover v27 no10 p18 D 2016 G. Tarlach
New York Times Book Review p73 D 4 2016 S. Wheeler
Publishers Weekly v263 no44 p68 O 31 2016

Wellmon, C. Organizing Enlightenment. 2015
Change v48 no5 p64-70 S/O 2016 M. T. Huber

Wells, J. and others. Rider & horse, back to back. 2011
Dressage Today v23 no9 p72 Je 2017 S. Von Dietze

Wells, J. Reading Austen in America. 2017
Publishers Weekly v264 no29 p208 Jl 17 2017

Wells, K. The wellness mama cookbook. 2016
Publishers Weekly v263 no40 p113 O 3 2016

Wells, M. The harbors of the sun. 2017
Publishers Weekly v264 no23 p34-5 Je 5 2017

Wells, P. My Master Recipes. 2017
Publishers Weekly v264 no10 p20-31 Mr 6 2017 C. Swanso
Publishers Weekly v264 no3 p54 Ja 16 2017

Wells, R. and Wells, R. Fiona's little lie. 2016
Publishers Weekly v263 no49 p21 D 7 2016

Wells, R. Say hello, Sophie. 2017
Publishers Weekly v264 no8 p85 F 20 2017

Wells, S. and Kocher, A. Eucharistic prayers. 2016
Christian Century v133 no26 p43 D 21 2016

Welsh, J. The return of history. 2016
Foreign Affairs v96 no2 p168 Mr/Ap 2017 G. J. Ikenberry

Welsh, J. Weedgalized in Colorado. 2015
Publishers Weekly v264 no6 p63 F 6 2017
Publishers Weekly v264 no9 p66j-k F 27 2017

Welsh, K. The Wages of Sin. 2017
New York Times Book Review p9 Mr 19 2017 M. Stasio
Publishers Weekly v264 no1 p37 Ja 2 2017

Welsh-Huggins, A. The hunt. 2017
Publishers Weekly v264 no9 p80 F 27 2017

Welzen, J. I know numbers. 2017
Publishers Weekly v264 no30 p58 Jl 24 2017

Wen, L. and Fegan, B. C. Henry and the hidden treasure. 2017
Publishers Weekly v264 no31 p58e Jl 31 2017

Wendig, C. Star wars, aftermath. 2016
Publishers Weekly v264 no10 p12 Mr 6 2017 C. Juris

Wendig, C. Thunderbird. 2017
Publishers Weekly v264 no3 p45 Ja 16 2017

Wendler, J. W. and others. Siegelaub. 2015
Art in America v105 no3 p63 Mr 2017

Wenfang Tang Populist authoritarianism. 2016
Foreign Affairs v96 no3 p173 My/Je 2017 A. J. Nathan

Wenner, J. S. Rolling Stone. 2017
Rolling Stone no1289 p26 Je 15 2017

Wenning, M. and Sloterdijk, P. Rage and time. 2010
New York Review of Books v64 no15 p22-4 O 12 2017 J. Gray

Wenzel, B. and Bernstrom, D. One day in the eucalyptus, eucalyptus tree. 2016
Publishers Weekly v263 no49 p39 D 7 2016

Wenzel, B. and Wenzel, B. They all saw a cat. 2016
New York Times Book Review p34 D 4 2016
Publishers Weekly v263 no49 p26 D 7 2016

Wenzel, N. G. and Schlueter, N. W. Selfish libertarians and social-ist conservatives? 2017
Claremont Review of Books v17 no3 p28-30 Summ 2017 D. Az-errad

Werlin, N. And then there were four. 2017
Publishers Weekly v264 no18 p62 My 1 2017

Werline, R. A. and Flannery, F. The Bible in Political Debate. 2016
Publishers Weekly v263 no45 p17-8 N 7 2016 M. Z. Nelson

Werner, A. and Santos, A. Peru. 2015
Foreign Affairs v96 no1 p169 Ja/F 2017 R. Feinberg

Werstine, P. and others. Hamlet. 2012
Weekly Standard v22 no31 p43 Ap 17 2017 C. Atamian

Werstine, P. and others. The tragedy of King Lear. 2015
New York Review of Books v64 no3 p34-6 F 23 2017 S. Greenblatt

Wert, Y. and Li Jian The Magical Rooster. 2016
Publishers Weekly v263 no43 p77 O 24 2016

Wertheim, L. J. and Baleka, S. 4-minute fit. 2017
Publishers Weekly v264 no8 p80 F 20 2017
Sports Illustrated v126 no18 p14 Je 26 2017 T. Keith

Wertz, J. and Sher, E. The Emotionary. 2016
Publishers Weekly v263 no40 p125 O 3 2016

Wertz, J. Tenements, towers, & trash. 2017
Publishers Weekly v264 no25 p99 Je 19 2017

Weschler, L. Waves Passing in the Night. 2017
Publishers Weekly v263 no42 p59-60 O 17 2016

Wesolowski, M. Six Stories. 2017
Publishers Weekly v264 no15 p56 Ap 10 2017

Wessel, E. C. and Grebe, C. The ice beneath her. 2016
Publishers Weekly v263 no39 p70 S 26 2016

Wesselman, H. The re-enchantment. 2016
Publishers Weekly v263 no51 p144-5 D 12 2016

Wesson, R. Darwin's First Theory. 2017
Natural History v125 no5 p46 My 2017 L. A. Marschall
Publishers Weekly v264 no8 p76 F 20 2017

West, A. N. and Patterson, J. Z. Milena, or the most beautiful femur in the world. 2017
Publishers Weekly v264 no12 p59 Mr 20 2017

West, C. The memory of you. 2017
Publishers Weekly v264 no4 p65 Ja 23 2017

West, P. The United States of Soccer. 2016
New York Times Book Review p58-60 D 4 2016 M. Tracy
Publishers Weekly v263 no39 p80-1 S 26 2016

Westaby, S. Open heart. 2017
New York Times Book Review p26 Jl 2 2017 R. Pearson
Publishers Weekly v264 no17 p84 Ap 24 2017

Westacott, E. The wisdom of frugality. 2016
Weekly Standard v22 no22 p35-6 F 13 2017 L. Klepp

Westad, O. A. The cold war. 2017
New Republic v248 no11 p60-7 N 2017 P. Iber
Publishers Weekly v264 no31 p76 Jl 31 2017

Westerfeld, S. and Puvilland, A. The spill zone. 2017
New York Times Book Review p24 My 14 2017 C. Healy

Westermann, C. and Grubman, B. The Only Way I Can. 2017
Publishers Weekly v264 no10 p61 Mr 6 2017
Publishers Weekly v264 no20 p(Sp)46-54 My 15 2017

Westerson, J. Booke of the Hidden. 2017
Publishers Weekly v264 no35 p109 Ag 28 2017

Publishers Weekly v264 no38 p46 S 18 2017

Whitfield, K. S. and Finn, N. A. Spirituality for the sent. 2017
Christianity Today v61 no5 p69 Je 2017

Whitfield, S. Wives, fiancees, and side-chicks of hotlanta. 2017
Essence v47 no12 p70-2 Ap 2017 P. H. Bass

Whitham, B. and Welborn, G. The Promise Bride. 2017
Publishers Weekly v264 no31 p69 Jl 31 2017

Whiting, J. and others. Winterbay Abbey. 2016
Publishers Weekly v264 no26 p162 Je 26 2017
Publishers Weekly v264 no31 p58c-d Jl 31 2017

Whitley, Z. and Godfrey, M. Soul of a nation. 2017
Publishers Weekly v264 no26 p21-7 Je 26 2017 A. Coreno

Whitman, J. Q. Hitler's American model. 2017
Atlantic v320 no4 p42-4 N 2017 I. Katznelson
Reason v49 no1 p64-5 My 2017 M. Harwood

Whitman, W. Manly health and training. 2016
New York Times Book Review p21 S 3 2017 T. Genoways
Publishers Weekly v264 no1 p53 Ja 2 2017

Whitney, C. and Baier, B. Three days in January. 2017
Publishers Weekly v264 no4 p10 Ja 23 2017 C. Juris

Whitney, J. Finks. 2017
New Republic v248 no1/2 p68-70 Ja/F 2017 P. Iber
New York Times Book Review p4 F 12 2017 J. Williams

Whitney, Q. American luthier. 2016
Physics Today v70 no2 p60 F 2017 C. Waltham

Whitsitt, T. Fermentation on wheels. 2017
Publishers Weekly v264 no25 p106 Je 19 2017

Whittaker, A. and Kania, C. Jazz. 2016
Downbeat v83 no12 p92 D 2016 B. Reed

Whittaker, L. Isabella and the Tale of the Unanswered Question. 2013
Publishers Weekly v263 no52 p103-4 D 19 2016
Publishers Weekly v264 no4 p44 Ja 23 2017
Publishers Weekly v264 no4 p50c Ja 23 2017

Whittall, Z. The Best Kind of People. 2016
Publishers Weekly v264 no31 p60 Jl 31 2017

Whyte, C. Home Time 1. 2017
Publishers Weekly v264 no35 p54 Ag 28 2017 J. Rosen

Whyte, K. Hoover. 2017
New Yorker v93 no33 p93-7 O 23 2017 N. Lemann
Publishers Weekly v264 no32 p60-1 Ag 7 2017

Whyton, T. Beyond A love supreme. 2013
Downbeat v83 no12 p46-8 D 2016 J. Hale

Wicker, C. The simple faith of Franklin Delano Roosevelt. 2017
Publishers Weekly v264 no33 p75 Ag 14 2017

Wicker, M. Silencer. 2017
Publishers Weekly v264 no34 p87-8 Ag 21 2017

Wickham, C. Medieval Europe. 2016
Publishers Weekly v263 no41 p70 O 10 2016

Wickstrom, S. and Young, P. D. Mestizaje and globalization. 2014
American Indian Quarterly v40 no4 p379-82 Fall 2016 M. Milazzo

Wideman, J. E. Writing to save a life. 2016
Christian Century v134 no6 p39-40 Mr 15 2017 A. Frykholm
Nation v303 no25/26 p27-32 D 19 2016 J. McCarthy
New York Times Book Review p11 D 18 2016 G. L. Buckley
New York Times Magazine p15 Ap 30 2017 S. Anderson
New York Times Magazine p30-5 Ja 29 2017 T. C. Williams

Widener, T. and Winter, J. My name is James Madison Hemings. 2016
New York Times Book Review p28 N 13 2016 J. Asim
New York Times Book Review p34 D 4 2016

Widerstrom, J. Diet right for your personality type. 2017
New York Times Book Review p27 Ja 1 2017 J. Newman

Wiebe, J. R. The place of imagination. 2017
Christian Century v134 no18 p36-7 Ag 30 2017 K. B. Heidelberger

Wiebe, S. Invisible dead. 2017
Publishers Weekly v264 no13 p78 Mr 27 2017

Wiedemann, J. and Spampinato, F. Art Record Covers. 2017
Vanity Fair v59 no4 p113 Mr 2017

Wiedemann, J. National Geographic Infographics. 2016
Entertainment Weekly no1450 p62-3 Ja 27 2017 I. Biedenharn

Wiehl, L. and Stuart, S. The separatists. 2017
Publishers Weekly v264 no15 p55 Ap 10 2017

Wieland, B. C. and Wagner, P. Sunvault. 2017

Publishers Weekly v264 no25 p96 Je 19 2017

Wienand, V. and others. A Midsummer Night's Dream. 2014
Publishers Weekly v264 no34 p14 Ag 21 2017 J. Milliot

Wienand, V. and others. Hamlet. 2014
Weekly Standard v22 no31 p43 Ap 17 2017 C. Atamian

Wienand, V. and others. Romeo and Juliet. 2014
Publishers Weekly v263 no41 p79 O 10 2016

Wientge, K. Karma Khullar's mustache. 2017
Publishers Weekly v264 no23 p52-4 Je 5 2017

Wier, D. In the still of the night. 2017
Publishers Weekly v264 no38 p54 S 18 2017

Wiesner, D. and others. Fish Girl. 2017
New York Times Book Review p17 Mr 12 2017 V. Brosgol
Publishers Weekly v263 no52 p127 D 19 2016

Wigger, J. PTL. 2017
Publishers Weekly v264 no24 p61 Je 12 2017

Wight, E. and Bardhan-Quallen, S. The adventures of caveboy. 2017
Publishers Weekly v264 no29 p220 Jl 17 2017

Wiking, M. The little book of hygge. 2017
Entertainment Weekly no1459 p62-3 Mr 31 2017 T. Jordan
New York Times Book Review p20 Mr 5 2017 G. Cowles
New York Times Book Review p27 F 26 2017 J. Newman

Wilcox, H. 100 poems. 2016
Christian Century v133 no21 p55-6 O 12 2016 R. Lischer

Wilde, E. and Phillips, C. Dirty Sexy Saint. 2016
Publishers Weekly v263 no52 p72 D 19 2016

Wilde, L. and others. Happy is the bride. 2017
Publishers Weekly v264 no17 p75 Ap 24 2017

Wildish, L. and Reagan, J. How to get a teacher ready. 2016
Publishers Weekly v264 no20 p54 My 15 2017

Wildish, L. and Reagan, J. How to raise a mom. 2017
Publishers Weekly v264 no8 p83 F 20 2017

Wilentz, S. Bob Dylan in America. 2010
U.S. Catholic v82 no2 p39 F 2017

Wiles, L. and Simpson, E. Thriving Abroad. 2017
People Management p51 Jl 2017

Wiles, P. Secrets in the Sky. 2015
Publishers Weekly v263 no42 p47 O 17 2016
Publishers Weekly v263 no47 p76c N 21 2016

Wiley, S. and Cihon, C. The Fairytale Chicago of Francesca Finnegan. 2017
Publishers Weekly v264 no5 p185-6 Ja 30 2017
Publishers Weekly v264 no9 p66c-d F 27 2017

Wilke, C. and Dahlstrom, S. The green colt. 2016
American Cowboy v24 no1 p47 Je/Jl 2017

Wilkerson, I. The warmth of other suns. 2010
Humanities v37 no4 p1 Fall 2016 R. Early

Wilkes, J. D. The Vine That Ate the South. 2017
Publishers Weekly v263 no51 p128 D 12 2016

Wilkins, J. and others. What Does Consent Mean Again? 2017
Publishers Weekly v264 no39 p109 S 25 2017

Wilkins, R. L. Long road to hard truth. 2016
Publishers Weekly v264 no7 p68 F 13 2017
Publishers Weekly v264 no9 p66i F 27 2017

Wilkins, W. K. Nine days in May. 2017
Publishers Weekly v264 no15 p64 Ap 10 2017

Wilkinson, C. Peace out. 2015
Alternatives Journal (AJ) - Canada's Environmental Voice v42 no2 p78 2016 J. Gordon

Wilkinson, C. The birds of Opulence. 2016
Louisiana Life v37 no4 p14 Mr/Ap 2017

Wilkinson, J. H. All falling faiths. 2017
National Review v69 no6 p43-5 Ap 3 2017 J. Rosen
Weekly Standard v22 no28 p34-5 Mr 27 2017 T. Eastland

Wilkshire, N. Escape to Havana. 2016
Publishers Weekly v263 no43 p59 O 24 2016

Willems, M. and Willems, M. Sam, the most scaredy-cat kid in the whole world. 2017
Publishers Weekly v264 no34 p110 Ag 21 2017

Willems, M. and Willems, M. Welcome. 2017
New York Times Book Review p17 Jl 16 2017 M. Russo

Willett, E. The Cityborn. 2017
Publishers Weekly v264 no22 p49 My 29 2017

William, A. Medical medium life-changing foods. 2016
New York Times Book Review p76 D 4 2016

Williams, B. and Fox, M. The game don't change. 2016
  Publishers Weekly v263 no41 p60 O 10 2016
Williams, B. G. Counter jihad. 2017
  Publishers Weekly v263 no44 p67 O 31 2016
Williams, B. M. Proof. 2016
  Publishers Weekly v263 no42 p63 O 17 2016
Williams, C. K. Falling ill. 2017
  New Yorker v93 no9 p72 Ap 17 2017
  New York Review of Books v64 no10 p34-5 Je 8 2017 D. Chiasson
  Publishers Weekly v263 no47 p84 N 21 2016
Williams, C. K. Selected later poems. 2015
  New York Review of Books v64 no10 p34-5 Je 8 2017 D. Chiasson
Williams, D. K. Defenders of the unborn. 2016
  Christian Century v133 no23 p32-4 N 9 2016 D. Heim
Williams, D. When the English fall. 2017
  Christian Century v134 no16 p26-8 Ag 2 2017 V. Weaver-Zercher
  New York Times Book Review p16 S 3 2017 A. Deutsch
  New York Times Book Review p26 S 10 2017
  Publishers Weekly v264 no17 p72 Ap 24 2017
Williams, F. The nature fix. 2017
  Atlantic v319 no3 p41-3 Ap 2017 N. Rich
  Earth Island Journal v32 no2 p55 Summ 2017 G. Lida
  New York Times Book Review p14 Mr 5 2017 J. Mark
  Publishers Weekly v263 no42 p64 O 17 2016
  Sierra v102 no2 p9 Mr/Ap 2017 E. Osborn
Williams, G. The Guy, the Girl, the Artist and His Ex. 2017
  Publishers Weekly v264 no1 p59 Ja 2 2017
Williams, I. Water in May. 2017
  Publishers Weekly v264 no29 p33-188 Jl 17 2017
Williams, J. 99 stories of God. 2016
  Christian Century v133 no22 p38 O 26 2016 A. Frykholm
  Publishers Weekly v263 no44 p18-40 O 31 2016
Williams, J. C. White working class. 2017
  Commentary v144 no1 p48-50 Jl/Ag 2017 K. Hymowitz
  New York Times Book Review p4 Je 25 2017 J. Szalai
Williams, J. D. The atlas of forgotten places. 2017
  Publishers Weekly v264 no22 p42 My 29 2017
Williams, L. A selfie as big as the Ritz. 2017
  Publishers Weekly v264 no35 p102 Ag 28 2017
Williams, L. and Williams, L. If sharks disappeared. 2017
  Publishers Weekly v264 no17 p95 Ap 24 2017
Williams, M. and Cahan, R. Classic Chicago. 2016
  Chicago v66 no1 p39-41 Ja 2017 E. Fishman
Williams, M. and Cahan, R. Un-American. 2016
  Chicago v65 no11 p40 N 2016 J. Hardberger
Williams, M. and others. Remodelista. 2017
  Publishers Weekly v264 no38 p66-7 S 18 2017
Williams, M. Ireland's immortals. 2016
  New York Review of Books v64 no6 p39-41 Ap 6 2017 F. O'Toole
Williams, N. Trusting You & Other Lies. 2017
  Publishers Weekly v264 no17 p94 Ap 24 2017
Williams, P. The life of Bach. 2004
  Weekly Standard v22 no41 p36-8 Jl 3 2017 J. Check
Williams, R. and Carnovsky (Illustrator) Illuminature. 2016
  Publishers Weekly v264 no44 p78 O 31 2016
Williams, R. and others. Atlas of Animal Adventures. 2016
  Publishers Weekly v263 no44 p78 O 31 2016
Williams, R. S. An Odd Book. 2017
  Publishers Weekly v264 no24 p58 Je 12 2017
  Publishers Weekly v264 no26 p146d-e Je 26 2017
Williams, R. The sign and the sacrifice. 2017
  Christian Century v134 no5 p42 Mr 1 2017
Williams, S. Spies in the Congo. 2016
  Foreign Affairs v96 no1 p178 Ja/F 2017 N. Van De Walle
  Military History v33 no5 p74 Ja 2017
Williams, T. T. The hour of land. 2016
  New York Times Book Review p20 Jl 9 2017 J. Khatib
  Orion Magazine v35 no4/5 p106 Jl-O 2016 E. Kennedy
Williams, T. The second day of the renaissance. 2017
  Publishers Weekly v264 no10 p40 Mr 6 2017
Williams, T. The Witchwood Crown. 2017
  Publishers Weekly v264 no23 p36-7 Je 5 2017
Williams, W. Significant Zero. 2017
  Publishers Weekly v264 no32 p65 Ag 7 2017
Williams, Y. and Shih, B. The Black Panthers. 2016
  In These Times v41 no1 p38 Ja 2017

  New York Times Book Review p10 N 27 2016 R. Browne
Williams-Garcia, R. and others. Clayton Byrd goes underground. 2017
  New York Times Book Review p25 My 14 2017 M. Medina
  Publishers Weekly v264 no14 p76 Ap 3. 2017
Williamson, B. and Hunt, E. S. The secret agent training manual. 2017
  Publishers Weekly v264 no27 p76 Jl 3 2017
  Publishers Weekly v264 no31 p9-10 Jl 31 2017 C. Kirch
Williamson, J. Kahn at Penn. 2015
  New York Review of Books v64 no11 p14-7 Je 22 2017 M. Filler
Williamson, L. All About Mia. 2017
  Publishers Weekly v264 no26 p182 Je 26 2017
Willig, M. R. and Walker, L. R. Long-term ecological research. 2016
  BioScience v67 no5 p477-8 My 2017 M. M. Fuller
Willis, C. A lot like Christmas. 2017
  Publishers Weekly v264 no35 p110 Ag 28 2017
Willis, D. The dark and other love stories. 2017
  New York Times Book Review p26 Mr 19 2017 S. Ferguson
Willis, J. Ancient Gods. 2017
  Publishers Weekly v263 no51 p143 D 12 2016
Willis, J. The scientific search for alien life. 2016
  New York Times Book Review p31 S 25 2016 J. Ryerson
  Physics Today v70 no3 p59 Mr 2017 P. Smith
  Scientific American v315 no3 p86 S 2016 C. Moskowitz
Willis, K. and Scott, K. Botanicum. 2017
  Publishers Weekly v264 no4 p81 Ja 23 2017
Willis, L. C. Tell Me No Lies. 2017
  Publishers Weekly v263 no52 p103 D 19 2016
Willis, S. The struggle for sea power. 2017
  Military History v34 no4 p72-3 N 2017 A. Paletta
Willmetts, S. In secrecy's shadow. 2016
  Film Quarterly v70 no3 p103-4 Spr 2017 R. Prime
Willows, B. Fury's Bridge. 2017
  Publishers Weekly v264 no6 p53 F 6 2017
Wills, C. The illustrated encyclopedia of weaponry. 2012
  Military History v34 no2 p72 Jl 2017
Wills, G. What the Qur'an meant and why it matters. 2017
  Maclean's v130 no9 p77 O 2017 B. Bethune
  Publishers Weekly v264 no33 p76 Ag 14 2017
Willson-Broyles, R. and Avdic, A. The dying game. 2017
  Publishers Weekly v264 no23 p31-2 Je 5 2017
Willson-Broyles, R. and Vallgren, C. The tunnel. 2017
  Publishers Weekly v264 no15 p53-4 Ap 10 2017
Wilsdorf, A. and Miller, P. Z. Sophie's squash go to school. 2016
  Publishers Weekly v263 no49 p26 D 7 2016
Wilson, A. A talent for murder. 2017
  Publishers Weekly v264 no14 p52 Ap 3. 2017
Wilson, A. L. Here I walk. 2016
  Christianity Today v60 no10 p69 D 2016
Wilson, A. N. Charles Darwin. 2017
  Publishers Weekly v264 no41 p56 O 9 2017
Wilson, A. The lost frost girl. 2017
  Publishers Weekly v264 no40 p140 O 2 2017
Wilson, B. and Lee, A. First bite. 2015
  New York Times Book Review p36 D 11 2016 J. Khatib
Wilson, B. Heyday. 2016
  Claremont Review of Books v17 no2 p84-7 Spr 2017 M. Auslin
Wilson, B. I am Brian Wilson. 2016
  Maclean's v129 no42 p62 O 24 2016 C. Loudon
  New York Times Book Review p54-5 D 4 2016 A. Light
  Time v188 no14 p58-9 O 10 2016 I. Guzmán
Wilson, D. H. and others. Armstrong. 2016
  Publishers Weekly v263 no49 p11 D 7 2016
Wilson, E. A Very British Ending. 2016
  Publishers Weekly v263 no46 p36 N 14 2016
Wilson, E. Love game. 2016
  American Conservative v16 no1 p51-4 Ja/F 2017 F. Raphael
Wilson, E. O. and Macarthur, R. H. The theory of island biogeography. 2001
  Science v357 no6354 p885 S 1 2017 K. A. Triantis
Wilson, E. O. Half-earth. 2016
  Bulletin of the Atomic Scientists v73 no4 p284-7 Jl 2017 L. Heneghan
  New York Times Book Review p8-17 D 25 2016 M. Hong Kingston

Wilson, E. O. The Origins of Creativity. 2017
  Esquire p38 O 2017 A. Belth
  Publishers Weekly v264 no30 p52 Jl 24 2017
Wilson, F. Guilty thing. 2016
  New Yorker v92 no33 p100-3 O 17 2016 D. Chiasson
  New York Review of Books v63 no18 p24-6 N 24 2016 R. Holmes
  New York Times Book Review p22 O 30 2016 J. Sutherland
  New York Times Book Review p26 N 6 2016
  Publishers Weekly v263 no44 p18-40 O 31 2016
Wilson, G. Dead Reckoning. 2017
  Publishers Weekly v264 no18 p40 My 1 2017
Wilson, J. Chaos of empire. 2016
  Current History v116 no789 p157-9 Ap 2017 S. Ganguly
  New Yorker v93 no3 p79 Mr 6 2017
  Publishers Weekly v263 no39 p78 S 26 2016
Wilson, J. India conquered. 2016
  History Today v67 no4 p62 Ap 2017 Z. Masani
Wilson, J. M. The vision of the soul. 2017
  National Review v69 no16 p46 Ag 28 2017 J. E. J. Person
Wilson, K. and Chapman, J. Big bear, small mouse. 2016
  Publishers Weekly v263 no40 p121-2 O 3 2016
Wilson, K. and Liwska, R. Dormouse dreams. 2017
  Publishers Weekly v263 no48 p65 N 28 2016
Wilson, K. We eat our own. 2016
  New York Times Book Review p14 S 25 2016 J. Dee
Wilson, L. and Nour, D. Co-create. 2017
  People Management p53 Je 2017
Wilson, L. Louise Nevelson. 2016
  Art in America v105 no4 p59-61 Ap 2017 C. Rosenberger
Wilson, L. The riot. 2016
  Publishers Weekly v263 no39 p70 S 26 2016
Wilson, M. D. and Oblivion, K. (. Supreme Villainy. 2017
  Publishers Weekly v264 no17 p73 Ap 24 2017
Wilson, M. We now return to regular life. 2017
  Publishers Weekly v264 no23 p55 Je 5 2017
Wilson, N. D. The door before. 2016
  Christianity Today v61 no6 p89 Jl/Ag 2017 J. Wilson
Wilson, P. and King, G. Twilight of empire. 2017
  Publishers Weekly v264 no39 p103 S 25 2017
Wilson, R. C. Last year. 2016
  Publishers Weekly v263 no45 p45 N 7 2016
Wilson, R. R. and Cole-Dai, P. Poetry of presence. 2017
  South Dakota Magazine p10 S/O 2017 Supplement
Wilson, S. and Tapper, L. Hedgehugs. 2017
  Publishers Weekly v264 no34 p111 Ag 21 2017
Wilson, W. D. and Mouron, Q. Three Drops of Blood and a Cloud
    of Cocaine. 2017
  Publishers Weekly v264 no17 p69 Ap 24 2017
Wilson, W. G. Stormwater. 2016
  BioScience v67 no2 p179-80 F 2017 A. L. Mayer
Wimmer, M. and Keating, F. A. Abraham. 2015
  Publishers Weekly v263 no51 p147 D 12 2016
Winawer, M. The scribe of Siena. 2017
  Publishers Weekly v264 no11 p52 Mr 13 2017
Winchester, S. Pacific. 2015
  New York Times Book Review p28 Ja 8 2017 J. Khatib
Windhorst, B. and McMenamin, D. Return of the king. 2017
  Publishers Weekly v264 no17 p13 Ap 24 2017 C. Juris
Wine, M. Highland Vixen. 2017
  Publishers Weekly v263 no51 p131 D 12 2016
Winfrey, O. Food, health, and happiness. 2017
  New York Times Book Review p22 Ja 22 2017 G. Cowles
  O, The Oprah Magazine p144C F 2017 O. Winfrey
  Publishers Weekly v264 no3 p14 Ja 16 2017 C. Juris
Winfrey, O. The Wisdom of Sundays. 2017
  O, The Oprah Magazine p148 N 2017 O. Winfrey
Wingate, L. Before we were yours. 2017
  Publishers Weekly v264 no16 p34-6 Ap 17 2017
Winkless, L. Science and the City. 2016
  Science v354 no6310 p293 O 21 2016 S. Derrible
Winkowski, F. Trench Talk Trench Life. 2017
  Publishers Weekly v264 no14 p67 Ap 3. 2017
Winnick, K. B. and Watkins, L. Good night, baby animals—
    you've had a busy day. 2017
  Publishers Weekly v263 no45 p58 N 7 2016
Winograd, A. and others. Kerry James Marshall. 2016

New York Review of Books v64 no1 p40-2 Ja 19 2017 D. Pinckney
Winokur, J. and Reynolds, B. But Enough About Me. 2015
  AARP: The Magazine v59 no1A p10 D 2015/Ja 2016 A. O.
Winslow, D. The force. 2017
  Entertainment Weekly no1471 p64-5 Je 23 2017 A. Breznican
  New York Times Book Review p9 Je 25 2017 M. Stasio
  Publishers Weekly v264 no15 p54 Ap 10 2017
  Publishers Weekly v264 no27 p12 Jl 3 2017 C. Juris
Winspear, J. In This Grave Hour. 2017
  New York Times Book Review p9 Mr 19 2017 M. Stasio
  Publishers Weekly v264 no4 p56 Ja 23 2017
Winston, K. and Handke, P. The Moravian night. 2016
  New Yorker v92 no49 p95 F 13 2017
  New York Times Book Review p7 Ja 1 2017 J. Cohen
  Publishers Weekly v263 no41 p53 O 10 2016
Winston, S. The sweetest sound. 2017
  Publishers Weekly v263 no44 p76 O 31 2016
Winter, H. Sacrifice. 2017
  Publishers Weekly v264 no8 p69 F 20 2017
Winter, J. and Blitt, B. You never heard of Casey Stengel?! 2015
  Publishers Weekly v263 no49 p54 D 7 2016
Winter, J. and Innerst, S. Ruth Bader Ginsburg. 2018
  New York Times Book Review p29 Ag 27 2017 M. Russo
  Publishers Weekly v264 no27 p73 Jl 3 2017
Winter, J. and others. Mickey Mantle. 2017
  Publishers Weekly v264 no7 p74 F 13 2017
Winter, J. and Widener, T. My name is James Madison Hemings.
    2016
  New York Times Book Review p28 N 13 2016 J. Asim
  New York Times Book Review p34 D 4 2016
Winter, J. and Winter, J. Cowboy Charlie. 1995
  American Cowboy v23 no5 p50 F/Mr 2017 L. F.
Winter, J. and Winter, J. Nanuk the ice bear. 2016
  Natural History v125 no1 p44-7 D 2016/Ja 2017 D. Setton
Winter, J. and Winter, J. The secret project. 2017
  Publishers Weekly v263 no50 p75 D 5 2016
Winter, J. and Winter, J. The world is not a rectangle. 2017
  Publishers Weekly v264 no27 p73 Jl 3 2017
Winter, K. Lost in September. 2017
  Walrus v14 no8 p61-3 O 2017 M. Dean
Winter, M. Exes. 2017
  Publishers Weekly v263 no50 p43 D 5 2016
Winter, W. and others. David Bowie. 2016
  Entertainment Weekly no1434 p56 O 7 2016 E. R. Brown
Winter, W. C. The sleep solution. 2017
  Publishers Weekly v263 no52 p120 D 19 2016
Winterer, C. American enlightenments. 2016
  Claremont Review of Books v17 no2 p58-60 Spr 2017 R. Lerner
Winterson, J. Christmas Days. 2016
  New York Times Book Review p22 Ja 1 2017
  New York Times Book Review p7 D 25 2016 J. Rosenstrach
Winton, T. Island home. 2017
  New York Times Book Review p52 Je 4 2017 T. T. Williams
Winz, B. and Aughtmon, S. F. One dress, one year. 2016
  Publishers Weekly v264 no17 p20-6 Ap 24 2017 L. Garrett
Wirestone, M. The astonishing mistakes of Dahlia Moss. 2017
  Publishers Weekly v264 no3 p43-4 Ja 16 2017
Wirzba, N. Way of love. 2016
  Christian Century v133 no25 p38-9 D 7 2016 M. Z. Nelson
Wise, C. and Myers, M. The political economy of China-Latin
    American relations in the new millennium. 2016
  Foreign Affairs v96 no2 p179-80 Mr/Ap 2017 R. Feinberg
Wise, M. D. Producing predators. 2016
  American Indian Quarterly v41 no3 p289-91 Summ 2017 S. E.
    McFarland
Wiseman, D. and Hill, S. L. When Your Elephant Has the Sniffles.
    2017
  Publishers Weekly v264 no25 p110-1 Je 19 2017
Wiseman, E. M. The Life She Was Given. 2017
  Publishers Weekly v264 no24 p38 Je 12 2017
Wishart, D. J. Great Plains Indians. 2016
  South Dakota Magazine v32 no6 p43 Mr/Ap 2017
Wisnewski, A. and Wisnewski, A. Trio. 2017
  Publishers Weekly v264 no41 p64-6 O 9 2017
Wisniewski, M. Algren. 2017
  New York Times Book Review p15 N 13 2016 B. Bailey

Publishers Weekly v263 no40 p107 O 3 2016
Woodmansey, W. Spider from Mars. 2016
   Publishers Weekly v263 no46 p47 N 14 2016
Woodruff, B. and others. No Barriers. 2017
   Sierra v102 no3 p11 My/Je 2017 J. Hahn
Woods, S. and Hall, P. Barely legal. 2017
   Publishers Weekly v264 no25 p92 Je 19 2017
Woods, S. Fast & loose. 2017
   New York Times Book Review p27 My 7 2017
   Publishers Weekly v264 no9 p76 F 27 2017
Woods, S. Indecent exposure. 2017
   Publishers Weekly v264 no18 p40 My 1 2017
Woods, S. Quick & dirty. 2017
   Publishers Weekly v264 no32 p51 Ag 7 2017
Woods, T. The 1997 Masters. 2017
   New York Times Book Review p24 Ap 9 2017
   Publishers Weekly v264 no6 p61-2 F 6 2017
   Sports Illustrated v126 no9 p19-20 Mr 27 2017 T. Keith
Woodward, A. and Woodward, A. The Extra Special Baby. 2017
   Publishers Weekly v264 no36 p93 S 4 2017
Woodward, B. The Last of the President's Men. 2015
   America v215 no16 p33-5 N 21 2016 C. Herlinger
Woodward, K. L. Getting religion. 2016
   Christianity Today v61 no1 p55 Ja/F 2017 K. Du Mez
   Commonweal v144 no3 p28-9 F 10 2017 N. Dallavalle
   New York Times Book Review p13 O 16 2016 S. G. Freedman
   U.S. Catholic v81 no11 p41 N 2016
Woolfson, M. M. Colour. 2016
   Physics Today v70 no4 p56-8 Ap 2017 M. H. Brill
Woolsey, M. and Lee, A. Multiples Illuminated. 2016
   Publishers Weekly v263 no40 p116 O 3 2016
   Publishers Weekly v263 no43 p50f O 24 2016
Wooster, P. Ignite your spark. 2017
   Publishers Weekly v264 no1 p58 Ja 2 2017
Workman, H. and Eckwall, J. Almost a full moon. 2016
   Publishers Weekly v263 no42 p69 O 17 2016
   Publishers Weekly v263 no49 p30 D 7 2016
Worrall, B. L. What Doesn't Kill Us. 2014
   Publishers Weekly v263 no40 p115 O 3 2016
Worsley, L. Jane Austen at Home. 2017
   British Heritage Travel v38 no4 p72 Jl/Ag 2017 S. Gutierrez
   New York Review of Books v64 no14 p63-5 S 28 2017 R. B. Yeazell
   New York Times Book Review p9 Jl 16 2017 A. Bloom
   Publishers Weekly v264 no18 p50 My 1 2017
   Saturday Evening Post v289 no4 p24 Jl/Ag 2017
Worth, L. and Hansen, V. Rookie K-9 Unit Christmas. 2016
   Publishers Weekly v263 no43 p62 O 24 2016
Worth, R. F. A rage for order. 2016
   New York Times Book Review p24 Ap 23 2017 J. Khatib
Worthington, G. Children of the Fifth Sun. 2017
   Publishers Weekly v264 no21 p76 My 22 2017
Wragg, N. and Denise, A. Monster trucks. 2016
   Publishers Weekly v263 no49 p60-4 D 7 2016
Wray, J. The lost time accidents. 2016
   New York Times Book Review p24 F 19 2017 J. Khatib
Wright, C. Cake magic! 2016
   Publishers Weekly v264 no3 p23-9 Ja 16 2017 D. Maryles
Wright, C. F. and others. International and comparative employment relations. 2016
   Monthly Labor Review p1-3 Je 2017 J. Wheeler
Wright, C. J. Cultivating the fruit of the spirit. 2017
   Publishers Weekly v263 no51 p140 D 12 2016
Wright, C. J. How to preach and teach the Old Testament for all its worth. 2016
   Christianity Today v61 no1 p53-4 Ja/F 2017 Z. Eswine
Wright, C. J. The mission of God. 2006
   Christianity Today v61 no4 p65 My 2017 M. Farrelly
Wright, C. J. To the cross. 2017
   Christian Century v134 no5 p42 Mr 1 2017
Wright, I. T. Darling days. 2016
   Entertainment Weekly no1436/1437 p103 O 21 2016 I. Biedenharn
   New York Times Book Review p14 O 16 2016 A. Abbott
Wright, J. and Lewis, J. P. Keep a pocket in your poem. 2017
   Publishers Weekly v264 no3 p61 Ja 16 2017
Wright, J. and others. Instructions Within. 2016

Publishers Weekly v263 no42 p48 O 17 2016
Wright, J. Get well soon. 2017
   Publishers Weekly v263 no52 p115 D 19 2016
Wright, L. The First Mess Cookbook. 2017
   Publishers Weekly v264 no3 p54 Ja 16 2017
Wright, L. The terror years. 2016
   Commonweal v143 no18 p40-2 N 11 2016 J. Shepp
   New York Review of Books v63 no18 p51-3 N 24 2016 A. Rashid
Wright, R. The gold eaters. 2015
   New York Times Book Review p24 Ja 22 2017
Wright, R. Trudeaumania. 2016
   Maclean's v129 no40 p76 O 10 2016 A. Levine
Wright, R. Why Buddhism is true. 2017
   National Review v69 no17 p37-8 S 11 2017 M. B. Dougherty
   New York Times Book Review p17 Ag 13 2017 A. Damasio
   Publishers Weekly v264 no19 p53-4 My 8 2017
   Publishers Weekly v264 no34 p17 Ag 21 2017 C. Juris
Wright, S. J. and Fleming, M. I heart you. 2016
   Publishers Weekly v263 no44 p74 O 31 2016
   Publishers Weekly v263 no49 p32 D 7 2016
Wright, T. J. All measures short of war. 2017
   Weekly Standard v22 no44 p32-4 Jl 31 2017 J. C. Hirsch
Wu, A. and Valente, C. M. The refrigerator monologues. 2017
   Publishers Weekly v264 no16 p50 Ap 17 2017 G. Bond
Wu, C. and others. The Cherry bombe cookbook. 2017
   Publishers Weekly v264 no25 p106 Je 19 2017
Wu, K. and Clickard, C. Dumpling dreams. 2018
   Publishers Weekly v264 no32 p70 Ag 7 2017
Wu, K. and Wallmark, L. Grace Hopper. 2017
   Publishers Weekly v264 no19 p59 My 8 2017
Wu, T. The attention merchants. 2016
   Bloomberg Businessweek no4500 p80 N 21 2016 P. Coy
   Commentary v143 no2 p44-6 F 2017 N. S. Riley
   Maclean's v129 no43 p61-2 O 31 2016 M. Doherty
   New Republic v247 no11 p60-3 N 2016 T. Vanderbilt
   New York Review of Books v63 no16 p12-6 O 27 2016 J. Weisberg
   New York Times Book Review p13 N 13 2016 E. Bell
Wuertz, Y. G. Everything belongs to us. 2016
   New York Times Book Review p18 Mr 12 2017 C. Hyung-Oak Lee
   Publishers Weekly v263 no52 p94 D 19 2016
Wulf, A. The invention of nature. 2015
   New York Times Book Review p28 O 16 2016 J. Khatib
   Science News v190 no13 p40 D 24 2016
Wunsch, E. The movie version. 2016
   Publishers Weekly v263 no49 p100 D 7 2016
Wyatt, R. Can I Be Frank? 2011
   Publishers Weekly v264 no35 p72-9 Ag 28 2017
Wyatt, T. Chain Reaction. 2017
   Publishers Weekly v264 no1 p45 Ja 2 2017
Wynne, F. and Lemaitre, P. Three days and a life. 2017
   Publishers Weekly v264 no38 p56 S 18 2017
Wytsma, K. The myth of equality. 2017
   Publishers Weekly v264 no15 p70-1 Ap 10 2017

X

Xilonen, A. and Rosenberg, A. The Gringo Champion. 2017
   New York Times Book Review p26 F 19 2017 A. McCulloch
Xiong, V. C. Heavenly Khan. 2014
   Publishers Weekly v264 no4 p50b Ja 23 2017
Xu, R. and Pelham, C. Newsprints. 2017
   Publishers Weekly v263 no43 p79 O 24 2016
Xu Can and Wei Jie Home for Chinese New Year. 2017
   Publishers Weekly v264 no39 p105 S 25 2017
Xu Hongci and others. No Wall Too High. 2017
   Publishers Weekly v263 no46 p46 N 14 2016
Xu Bing, 1. and Stadtlander, B. Look! what do you see? 2017
   Publishers Weekly v264 no39 p111 S 25 2017
Xu Zhiyong, and others. To build a free China. 2017
   Foreign Affairs v96 no3 p175 My/Je 2017 E. Pils

Y

Yaccarino, D. and Bobowicz, P. Five little elves. 2015
   Publishers Weekly v263 no39 p87 S 26 2016

New York Times Book Review p21 Jl 9 2017
New York Times Book Review p34 N 13 2016 J. Doll
Publishers Weekly v263 no49 p104 D 7 2016
Publishers Weekly v263 no50 p67-70 D 5 2016
Seventeen v75 no11 p16 N 2016 J. Abidor
Time v188 no18 p46 O 31 2016 S. Begley

Yoon, S. and Yoon, S. Penguin's Christmas wish. 2016
Publishers Weekly v263 no39 p84 S 26 2016

Yoon Ha Lee Raven Stratagem. 2017
Publishers Weekly v264 no17 p72 Ap 24 2017

Yorinks, A. and others. Making scents. 2017
Publishers Weekly v264 no16 p71 Ap 17 2017

York, A. The Seventh Son. 2016
Publishers Weekly v264 no4 p65 Ja 23 2017
Publishers Weekly v264 no9 p66f F 27 2017

Yoshida, K. A. and others. Fall down 7 times get up 8. 2017
Publishers Weekly v264 no21 p87 My 22 2017

Yoshihara, M. and others. The fall of language in the age of English. 2015
Claremont Review of Books v16 no4 p76-7 Fall 2016 M. A. Heberle

Yoshimoto, B. and Yoneda, A. Moshi-moshi. 2016
O, The Oprah Magazine p72 Ja 2017 L. Haber
Vanity Fair v59 no1 p98 Holiday 2017 S. C.

Yoshimoto, M. Kuma Miko 1. 2016
Publishers Weekly v263 no39 p74 S 26 2016

Yoshitake, S. and Yoshitake, S. Still stuck. 2017
Publishers Weekly v264 no29 p215 Jl 17 2017

Yosses, B. and Kaminsky, P. The Sweet Spot. 2017
Publishers Weekly v264 no36 p83-4 S 4 2017

Youers, R. The forgotten girl. 2017
Publishers Weekly v264 no36 p86-7 S 4 2017

Young, A. and Young, A. A new friend for Sparkle. 2017
Publishers Weekly v264 no22 p66 My 29 2017

Young, D. Stasi child. 2017
Publishers Weekly v264 no24 p39-40 Je 12 2017

Young, E. and Young, E. The battles of Bridget Lee. 2016
Publishers Weekly v263 no39 p74 S 26 2016

Young, E. and Young, E. The cat from Hunger Mountain. 2016
Publishers Weekly v263 no40 p123 O 3 2016
Publishers Weekly v263 no49 p27 D 7 2016

Young, H. The shimmering road. 2017
Publishers Weekly v263 no51 p123-4 D 12 2016

Young, J. Faraway Green. 2016
Publishers Weekly v263 no52 p83-9 D 19 2016

Young, K. Bunk. 2017
Publishers Weekly v264 no33 p63 Ag 14 2017
Publishers Weekly v264 no40 p111-2 O 2 2017 D. Patrick

Young, M. and others. Cook + Cork. 2016
Publishers Weekly v264 no34 p106 Ag 21 2017
Publishers Weekly v264 no35 p67 Ag 28 2017
Publishers Weekly v264 no35 p77d Ag 28 2017

Young, M. Eat the apple. 2017
Publishers Weekly v264 no39 p95 S 25 2017

Young, M. S. Flood. 2017
Missouri Life v44 no6 p27 S 2017 L. Heck

Young, M. The Road to Ever After. 2016
Publishers Weekly v264 no38 p71 S 18 2017

Young, N. and Underwood, D. Super Saurus saves kindergarten. 2016
Publishers Weekly v264 no20 p53 My 15 2017

Young, P. D. and Wickstrom, S. Mestizaje and globalization. 2014
American Indian Quarterly v40 no4 p379-82 Fall 2016 M. Milazzo

Young, S. Double Talk. 2016
Publishers Weekly v263 no50 p53 D 5 2016
Publishers Weekly v264 no4 p50b Ja 23 2017

Young, S. Every little thing. 2017
Publishers Weekly v264 no4 p64 Ja 23 2017

Young Rewired State (Organization) Get coding! 2017
Publishers Weekly v264 no32 p72 Ag 7 2017

Younge, G. Another day in the death of America. 2016
America v216 no3 p46-7 F 6 2017 J. McDermott
Entertainment Weekly no1435 p59 O 14 2016 L. Greenblatt
Maclean's v129 no44 p112 N 7 2016 A. Domise
New York Times Book Review p30 O 30 2016 T. Vinciguerra

Younger, D. The Wrath of Con. 2016
Publishers Weekly v263 no52 p74 D 19 2016

Younger, R. and Waller, D. The Reputation Game. 2017
Publishers Weekly v264 no34 p101 Ag 21 2017

Youngquist, P. A pure solar world. 2016
Downbeat v83 no11 p64 N 2016 M. Longley

Yovanoff, B. Places no one knows. 2016
Publishers Weekly v263 no49 p110 D 7 2016

Yttrup, G. L. Home. 2017
Publishers Weekly v264 no7 p57-8 F 13 2017

Yuen Yuen Ang How China escaped the poverty trap. 2016
Foreign Affairs v96 no2 p186-7 Mr/Ap 2017 A. J. Nathan

Yu Hua and Barr, A. H. The seventh day. 2015
New York Review of Books v64 no11 p53-5 Je 22 2017 I. Johnson

Yukai Du and Gillespie, L. J. 100 Steps for Science. 2017
Publishers Weekly v264 no12 p72 Mr 20 2017

Yuknavitch, L. The Book of Joan. 2017
Entertainment Weekly no1463/1464 p112 Ap/My 2017
New York Times Book Review p1-22 Ap 30 2017 J. Vandermeer
Publishers Weekly v264 no8 p60 F 20 2017

Yuko Ota and Hirsh, A. Lucky Penny. 2016
Publishers Weekly v263 no49 p123 D 7 2016

Yuly, T. and Yuly, T. The Jelly Bean tree. 2017
Publishers Weekly v264 no19 p58 My 8 2017

Yum, H. and Mantchev, L. Someday, Narwhal. 2017
Publishers Weekly v264 no34 p108-9 Ag 21 2017

Z

Zabecki, D. T. and Gross, G. P. The myth and reality of German warfare. 2016
Military History v34 no1 p74 My 2017 R. Guttman

Zacchino, N. California comeback. 2016
Reason v48 no8 p58-9 Ja 2017 E. Grieder

Zachrison, C. and Nerjordet, A. Field guide to knitted birds. 2017
Publishers Weekly v264 no14 p70 Ap 3. 2017

Zagajewski, A. and Cavanagh, C. Slight exaggeration. 2017
Commonweal v144 no11 p37-8 Je 16 2017 A. Domestico
New Yorker v93 no16 p97 Je 5 2017
New York Times Book Review p25 Jl 23 2017 D. Fried
Publishers Weekly v263 no51 p134 D 12 2016

Zagarenski, P. and Zagarenski, P. Henry and Leo. 2016
Publishers Weekly v263 no49 p32 D 7 2016

Zahradnik, R. Lights out summer. 2017
Publishers Weekly v264 no32 p55 Ag 7 2017

Zak, D. Almighty. 2016
America v215 no19 p35-7 D 19 2016 C. Schaeffer-Duffy

Zakheim, D. S. Nehemia. 2016
Weekly Standard v22 no13 p29-30 D 5 2016 D. J. Wolpe

Zaki, M. and others. Instructions Within. 2016
Publishers Weekly v263 no42 p48 O 17 2016

Zakimi, P. and George, K. Secrets I know. 2017
Publishers Weekly v264 no11 p82 Mr 13 2017

Zakimi, P. and Voigt, C. Teddy & Co. 2016
Publishers Weekly v263 no39 p94 S 26 2016

Zamora, J. Unaccompanied. 2017
Publishers Weekly v264 no34 p88-9 Ag 21 2017

Zander, F. His Faithfulness Reaches to the Skies. 2015
Christianity Today v60 no9 p73 N 2016

Zander, T. Double Elephant 1973-74. 2016
Art in America v104 no9 p68 O 2016

Zandri, V. The Corruptions. 2017
Publishers Weekly v263 no46 p34 N 14 2016

Zappia, F. Eliza and her monsters. 2017
Publishers Weekly v264 no13 p102-3 Mr 27 2017

Zappia, N. A. Traders and raiders. 2014
American Indian Quarterly v40 no3 p280-2 Summ 2016 M. Hughes

Zapruder, A. Twenty-six seconds. 2016
New Yorker v92 no40 p78 D 5 2016
New York Times Book Review p70 D 4 2016 A. Stanley
Texas Monthly v45 no1 p68-80 Ja 2017 S. Harrigan

Zapruder, M. Why Poetry. 2017
New York Times Book Review p11 Ag 6 2017 S. White
New York Times Book Review p23 Ag 13 2017